The National Hockey League

Official Guide & Record Book 2000

THE NATIONAL HOCKEY LEAGUE
Official Guide & Record Book/2000

Copyright © 1999 by the National Hockey League.
Compiled by the NHL Public Relations Department and the 28 NHL Club Public Relations Directors.

Printed in Canada. All rights reserved under the Pan-American and International Copyright Conventions.

The book may not be reproduced in whole or in part in any form or by any means, electronic or mechanical, including photocopying, recording, or by any information storage and retrieval system now known or hereafter invented, without written permission from the publisher.

Published in Canada by:
Total Sports Canada, 194 Dovercourt Road, Toronto, Ontario M6J 3C8 Canada
   ISBN in Canada 0-920445-63-2

Published in the United States by:
Total Sports Publishing Inc., 100 Enterprise Drive, Kingston, NY 12401
   ISBN in USA 1-892129-11-6   ISSN 0828-6647

Staff

For the NHL: David McConnachie; Supervising Editor: Greg Inglis; Statistician: Benny Ercolani;
Editorial Staff: David Keon, Jackie Rinaldi, Kelley Rosset, Chris Tredree.

Managing Editor: Ralph Dinger   **Player Register Editor:** James Duplacey

Photo Editor: Eric Zweig   **Production Editors:** John Pasternak, Alex Dubiel

Assistant Editor: Paul Bontje   **European Statistical Consultant:** Patrick Houda

Contributors: Jim Anderson (IHL), Joe Bertagna, Michelle Bingley, Bob Borgen, Paul R. Carroll Jr., Steve Cherwonak (WPHL), Denis Demers (QMJHL), Bob Duff, Gene Dupras, Jeff Fanter (ECAC) Peter Fillman, Ernie Fitzsimmons, Mel Foster, Pierre Genest, Dan Gognavic, Lloyd Hamshaw (WHL), Lori Kessel (UHL), James Karkoski, Martin Kogler, Len Kotylo, Eric Lavigne, Eric Leblanc, Roger Leblond, Manon Gagnon Leroux (QMJHL); Douglas G. MacEachern, Roy W. Mackie, John MacKinnon (CHA), Al Mason, Penny McEwen, Herb Morrell (OHL), NHL Broadcasters' Association, NHL Central Registry, NHL Players' Association, Mark Paddock, John D. Painter (NCAA), Becky Pasternak, Brenda Pasternak, Stephanie Pasternak, John Paton, Kevin Patriquin, Jason Paul, Gary J. Pearce, Jean Pelland, Lisa Pepin (CHL), Valentina Riazanova, Jane Rodney, Jason Rothwell (ECHL), Ed Saunders (Hockey East), Sherry Skalko (CCHA), Ralph Slate, Doug Spencer (WCHA), Lane Startin, Bret Stothart (AHL), A.D. Suehsdorf, Tony Techko, Sammy Wallace (WCHL), William Wolper (UHL), Scott Woods (IHL).

Publisher: Dan Diamond

Data Management and Typesetting: Caledon Data Management, Hillsburgh, Ontario
Film Output and Scanning: Stafford Graphics, Toronto, Ontario
Printing: Moore Data Management Services, Scarborough, Ontario
Production Management: Dan Diamond and Associates, Inc., Toronto Ontario

Photo Credits

NHL Images: Andy McGowan, Anita Cechowski, Jill Oswskey.
Photographers: Graig Abel, Toronto; Marc Archambault, Montreal; Scott Audette, Tampa Bay; Steve Babineau; Bruce Bennett Studios; Andrew D. Bernstein/Andrew Bernstein Associates, Los Angeles; Mark Buckner, St. Louis; Scott Cunningham, Atlanta; Gregg Forwerck, Carolina; Barry Gossage, Phoenix; Jon Hayt, Tampa Bay; Mark A. Hicks/Action Image, Detroit; Hockey Hall of Fame Collections; Glenn James, Dallas; Robert Laberge, Montreal; Mitchell Layton, Washington; Silvia Pecota; Len Redkole, Philadelphia; Debora Robinson, Anaheim; John Russell, Nashville; Slapshot Photo, Chicago; Don Smith, San Jose; Diane Sobolewski; Teckles/McElligott Sports Focus Imaging, Ottawa; Sandra Tenuto, Phoenix; Gerry Thomas, Calgary and Edmonton; Jeff Vinnick, Vancouver; Bill Wippert, Buffalo.
Gretzky Career Retrospective: page 13, Hockey Hall of Fame (Gretzky collection); 14 (top), Andrew D. Bernstein; 14 (bottom) Bruce Bennett Studios; 17, CP Picture Archive (Charlie Palmer).

Distribution

Trade sales and distribution in Canada by:
North 49 Books, 35 Prince Andrew Drive, Toronto, Ontario M3C 2H2
416/449-4000; FAX 416/449-9924

Total Sports Canada, 194 Dovercourt Road, Toronto, Ontario M6J 3C8
416/531-6535; FAX 416/531-3939   e-mail: dda.nhl@sympatico.ca

Trade sales and distribution in the United States by:
Publishers Group West, 1700 Fourth Street, Berkeley, CA 94710

International representatives:
Barkers Worldwide Publications, Unit 6/7 The Elms Centre, Glaziers Lane, Normandy, Guildford, Surrey GU3 2DF England
Tel: 011/441/483/811-971 and FAX: 011/441/483/811-972 e-mail: sales@bwpu.demon.co.uk website: www.bwpu.demon.co.uk

Total Sports Canada books may be purchased for educational, business or sales promotional use.
For information please write to: Total Sports Canada, 194 Dovercourt Road, Toronto, Ontario M6J 3C8 Canada
e-mail: dda.nhl@sympatico.ca

Total Sports Canada™ is a trademark of Total Sports Inc. used under license.

Licensed by the National Hockey League.®

The National Hockey League
1251 Avenue of the Americas, 47th Floor, New York, New York 10020-1198
1800 McGill College Ave., Suite 2600, Montreal, Quebec H3A 3J6
50 Bay Street, 11th Floor, Toronto, Ontario M5J 2X8

Table of Contents

19 CLUBS   records, rosters, management

131 FINAL STATISTICS 1998-99

Table of Contents *continued*

Introduction

WELCOME TO *THE NHL OFFICIAL GUIDE & RECORD BOOK 2000.* This 68th edition has been substantially redesigned. An expanding National Hockey League combined with upgraded statistics tracking, e-mail and the internet have enabled us to provide more information on more players, resulting in the biggest changes in the *Guide & Record Book* since 1984, when it was first published in today's big-page format. These changes and the resulting growth—the book has jumped from 480 pages in 1998-99 to 608 today—enhance what was already the *Guide's* greatest strength: providing comprehensive statistical coverage of the National Hockey League, its players and top prospects in minor pro, European, junior or college leagues and conferences.

A special feature in this edition pays tribute to Wayne Gretzky. Number 99's retirement after 20 season of scoring pyrotechnics and ambassadorship on behalf of hockey has been acknowledged in many ways. His uniform number has been retired throughout the League and he has been inducted into the Hockey Hall of Fame, forgoing the customary three-year waiting period. The *Guide & Record Book's* "Gretzky Career Retrospective" begins on page 13. Many of the photos in this section and elsewhere in the *Guide* are excerpted from a new NHL book entitled *99: My Life In Pictures* by Wayne Gretzky with John Davidson. Details on this new book can be found on page 608.

The redesigned Player Register begins on page 263 with a new Prospect Register made up of active forwards and defensemen who have yet to play in the NHL. Players in the Prospect Register either have been recently drafted or signed as free agents by NHL clubs.

The NHL Player Register begins on page 313. It includes active forwards and defensemen who have appeared in an NHL regular-season or playoff game at any time. New for this year is the inclusion of the following statistical categories, listed from left to right as they appear in a player's panel: power-play goals (PP), shorthand goals (SH), game-winning goals (GW), shots on goal (S), percentage of shots that score (%), plus-minus rating (+/–), total faceoffs taken (TF*), faceoff winning percentage (F%*), hits (H*), shots blocked (SB*) and average time-on-ice per game played (Min*). Categories marked with an asterisk (*) are NHL Real-Time statistics gathered by teams of trained spotters who, working with IBM equipment and custom software, record hits, shots blocked, faceoff wins, etc. "on-the-fly" at each game. These statistics were kept officially for the first time in 1998-99, so no player in this year's *NHL Guide* has more than one year's worth of Real-Time statistics.

Another new feature is the addition of a photo of every player. Photos of forwards and defensemen with NHL experience accompany their data panels. Active goaltender photos are found on page 544.

The Goaltender and Retired Player registers are unchanged except for their order. Both Retired Registers are now grouped together. The order of the Registers is as follows: Prospect, NHL Player, Goaltender, Retired Player and Retired Goaltender.

A key to the abbreviations and symbols used in individual player and goaltender data panels is found on page 312. Late additions to the Registers plus a list of each NHL club's minor-pro affiliates is found on page 262.

This revamped Player Register, combined with the *Guide's* thorough coverage of last season in the NHL, enable it to act as an effective update to the *Total Hockey* encyclopedia that was published in 1998. The great success of *Total Hockey*—produced by the same editorial team as the *NHL Guide*—has facilitated improvements in the data base that drives both publications, enabling the Guide & Record Book to update the big encyclopedia. The second edition of *Total Hockey* will be published in October 2000. More information on *Total Hockey* is found on page 608.

For 1999-2000, the NHL welcomes the Atlanta Thrashers who will play in the Southeast Division of the Eastern Conference. Two additional franchises (Columbus Blue Jackets and Minnesota Wild) will begin play in 2000-2001. These new franchises are listed on page 129. With the addition of these clubs, the NHL will become a 30-team league, organized in two conferences, each of which will be made up of three five-team divisions. Divisional alignment and scheduling for 1999-2000 are described on the inside front cover.

As always, our thanks to readers, correspondents and members of the media who take the time to comment on the *Guide & Record Book*. Thanks as well to the people working in the communications departments of the NHL's member clubs and to their counterparts in the AHL, IHL, ECHL, Central, United, West Coast and Western Professional and junior leagues as well as in college athletic conferences and European hockey federations.

Best wishes for an enjoyable 1999-2000 NHL season.

ACCURACY REMAINS THE *GUIDE & RECORD BOOK*'S TOP PRIORITY.

We appreciate comments and clarification from our readers. Please direct these to:

- James Duplacey   Player Register Editor, 194 Dovercourt Road, Toronto, Ontario M6J 3C8. e-mail: jj.nhl@sympatico.ca.
- Greg Inglis   47th floor, 1251 Avenue of the Americas, New York, New York 10020-1198 . . . or . . .
- David Keon   50 Bay Street, 11th Floor, Toronto, Ontario, M5J 2X8

Your involvement makes a better book.

NATIONAL HOCKEY LEAGUE

Established November 22, 1917

New York, 1251 Avenue of the Americas, 47th Floor, New York, NY 10020-1198, 212/789-2000, Fax: 212/789-2020, PR Fax: 212/789-2080
Montréal, 1800 McGill College Avenue, Suite 2600, Montréal, Québec, H3A 3J6, 514/288-9220, Fax: 514/284-0300
Toronto, 50 Bay Street, 11th Floor, Toronto, Ontario, M5J 2X8, 416/981-2777, Fax: 416/981-2779
NHL Enterprises, L.P. — 1251 Avenue of the Americas, 47th Floor, New York, NY 10020-1198, (212) 789-2000, Fax: (212) 789-2020
NHL Enterprises Canada, L.P. — 50 Bay Street, 11th Floor, Toronto, Ontario, M5J 2X8, 416/981-2777, Fax: 416/981-2779
NHL Europe — Signaustrasse 1, 8008 Zurich — Switzerland
NHL Productions, 183 Oak Tree Road, Tappan, NY 10983-2809, 914/365-6701, Fax: 914/365-6010

Executive

Commissioner ... Gary B. Bettman
Executive Vice President, Chief Operating Officer ... Stephen J. Solomon
Executive Vice President and Chief Legal Officer ... William Daly
Executive Vice President and Director of Hockey Operations ... Colin Campbell
Executive Assistant to the Commissioner ... Debbie Jordan

Administration

Director of Administration ... Debbie Jordan
Director, Human Resources ... Janet Meyers

Broadcasting/NHL Productions

Group Vice President ... Glenn Adamo
Vice President, Broadcasting ... Adam Acone
Vice President, Scheduling and Operations ... Steve HatzePetros
Director, Broadcast Operations/NHLP ... Patti Fallick
Executive Producer ... Ken Rosen
Coordinating Producer ... Darryl Lepik
Manager, Broadcasting ... Phyllis Carangelo
Manager, Broadcasting ... Todd Goodman
Manager, Broadcasting ... Anthony Triano
Manager, Research ... Mark Erlichson
Manager, NHL Productions ... Peg Walsh

New Business Development

Vice President, Business Development ... Bryant S. McBride
Coordinator, Business Development ... Nirva Milord

Communications

Group Vice President, Communications ... Bernadette Mansur
Vice President, Media Relations ... Frank Brown
Vice President, Public Relations and Media Services (Toronto) ... Gary Meagher
Chief Statistician (Toronto) ... Benny Ercolani
Director, Public Relations ... Andrew McGowan
Manager, Media Services ... Susan Aglietti
Manager, Public Relations ... Amy Early
Manager, News Services ... Greg Inglis
Public Relations Coordinator (Toronto) ... David Keon
News Services Assistant ... Adam Schwartz
Public Relations Assistant ... Chris Tredree
Manager, Community Relations ... Adrienne Brautigan
Manager ... Sandra Carreon
Manager ... Tracey Warshaw
Publicist ... Joy Kalfus

Creative Services

Creative Director ... David Haney
Associate Director, Creative Services ... Kathy Drew

Finance

Group Vice President and Chief Financial Officer ... Craig Harnett
Vice President, Finance ... Joseph DeSousa
Controller, Broadcasting ... Megan O'Donnell
Controller and Office manager (Montreal) ... Olivia Pietrantonio

Hockey Operations

Executive VP and Director of Hockey Operations ... Colin Campbell
Senior VP Hockey Operations (Toronto) ... Jim Gregory
Vice President, Hockey Operations (Toronto) ... Mike Murphy
Hockey Operations Manager ... Claude Loiselle
Director, Central Registry (Montreal) ... Steve Pellegrini
Assistant Director, Central Registry (Montreal) ... Madeleine Supino
Director of Central Scouting (Toronto) ... Frank Bonello
Director of Officiating (Toronto) ... Bryan Lewis
Assistant Director of Officiating (Toronto) ... Charlie Banfield
Officiating Coordinator (Toronto) ... Rod Pasma
Consultant (Montreal) ... Brian F. O'Neill
Director of Alumni Relations ... Patrick Flatley
Video Director ... Damian Echevarrieta
Video Assistant ... Paul Kennedy
Video Coordinator (Toronto) ... Chris Edwards
Ice Technician ... Dan Craig

Information Technology

Director ... Peter DelGiacco
Assistant Director (Montreal) ... Luc Coulombe
Manager, Network Communication ... Patrick Powers
Senior Project Manager ... Lee Reichman
Manager, Technical Systems ... John Ho
Manager, Technical Support ... Dan O'Neill

Legal

Vice President and General Counsel ... David Zimmerman
Deputy General Counsel ... Julie Spas Grand

Pension

Director (Montreal) ... Yvon Chamberland
Controller, Pension (Montreal) ... Mary Skiadopoulos
Manager, Pension (Montreal) ... Lise de Jocas

Security

Vice President ... Dennis Cunningham
Director ... Joseph Caporicci

Special Events

Vice President ... Frank Supovitz
Director ... Anne I. Grotefeld
Director ... Ken Chin
Manager ... Kimberly Bodnar
Manager ... Danny Frank
Manager ... Michael Imbriani
Manager ... Bill Miller
Manager ... Sally Printz

Television and Business Affairs

Manager, Satellite Television ... Kenneth Gelman
Manager, NHL Video ... David Levy
Manager, International ... Susanna Mandel-Mantello

NHL ENTERPRISES, L.P.

Consumer Products/Retail Sales Marketing

Vice President, Consumer Products Marketing ... Brian Jennings
Vice President, NHLE, Canada ... Glenn Wakefield
Vice President, Consumer Products Marketing, Canada ... Barry Monahan
Group Director, Special Projects and Promotional Services ... Glenn Horine
Director, Center Ice Program and Sporting Goods ... Lloyd Haymes
Director, Consumer Products Marketing, Canada ... Karen Hanson
Director, Apparel and Headwear ... James Haskins
Director, Non-Apparel ... Judith Salsberg
Sales Manager, Eastern Region ... Adam Blinderman
Sales Manager, Midwest Region ... Cathy Groves
Manager, Youth Licensing ... Nelly Campana

Marketing

Group Vice President ... Ed Horne

Corporate Marketing

Director ... Tim Conway
Director ... Andrew Judelson
Director, Canada ... Laurie Kepron
Manager ... David Abrutyn

Club Marketing

Vice President ... Scott Carmichael
Director ... Susan Cohig

Youth Marketing

Vice President ... Dina Gilbertie
Director ... Elle Farrell

Printed Products Marketing

Director ... David McConnachie

Marketing Services and Special Projects

Group Director ... Glenn Horine
Director ... Mary Ellen Curran

Fan Development

Vice President ... Ken Yaffe
Director, Off-Ice Programs ... Brian Mullen
Director, Fan Development ... Alysse Soll
Director ... Kamini Sharma
Manager ... Michael Tusiani

International Marketing

Managing Director, NHL Europe ... Brad Kwong
Director, International Marketing, Asia/Pacific Rim ... Frank Nakano

Finance

Senior Controller, Consumer Products Marketing ... Mary McCarthy
Director, Accounting Operations ... Belinda Haeberlein
Finance Manager, Events ... Scott Weinfeld

Legal

Senior Vice President and General Counsel ... Richard Zahnd
Vice President and Associate General Counsel ... Mary Sotis
Senior Counsel – Legal and Business Affairs ... Leslie Gittess
Associate Counsel and Secretary ... Robert Hawkins
Associate Counsel – Intellectual Property ... Tom Prochonow
Staff Attorney ... Anita Andrade
Staff Attorney ... Yvette Quinson
Director, Licensing/Trademark Compliance ... Ruth Gruhin
Director of Contract Administration ... Heather Bell
Senior Intellectual Property Administrator ... Maria Liuzzo
Intellectual Property Administrator ... Samantha Payne

NHL Images

Manager ... Anita Cechowski
Coodinator ... Jill Oswskey

NHL Interactive CyberEnterprises (NHL ICE)

General Manager ... Tom Richardson
Director, Sales and Marketing ... Kenny Nova
Manager, Sales and Marketing ... Tom Leyden

BOARD OF GOVERNORS

Chairman of the Board – Harley N. Hotchkiss

Mighty Ducks of Anaheim

Tony Tavares	Governor
Michael D. Eisner	Alternate Governor
Pierre Gauthier	Alternate Governor
Rick Schlesinger	Alternate Governor

Atlanta Thrashers

Harvey W. Schiller	Governor
Dave Maggard	Alternate Governor

Boston Bruins

Jeremy M. Jacobs	Governor
Louis Jacobs	Alternate Governor
Harry J. Sinden	Alternate Governor

Buffalo Sabres

John Rigas	Governor
Seymour H. Knox, IV	Alternate Governor
Timothy J. Rigas	Alternate Governor
Michael J. Rigas	Alternate Governor
Robert O. Swados	Alternate Governor

Calgary Flames

Harley N. Hotchkiss	Governor
Byron J. Seaman	Alternate Governor
Al Coates	Alternate Governor
Ron Bremner	Alternate Governor
N. Murray Edwards	Alternate Governor
Grant Bartlett	Alternate Governor

Carolina Hurricanes

Peter Karmanos, Jr.	Governor
Jim Rutherford	Alternate Governor
Dean Jordan	Alternate Governor

Chicago Blackhawks

William W. Wirtz	Governor
Gene Gozdecki	Alternate Governor
Robert J. Pulford	Alternate Governor
W. Rockwell Wirtz	Alternate Governor

Colorado Avalanche

Charles M. Neinas	Governor
Pierre Lacroix	Alternate Governor

Dallas Stars

Tom Hicks	Governor
James R. Lites	Alternate Governor
Robert Gainey	Alternate Governor

Detroit Red Wings

Michael Ilitch	Governor
Jay A. Bielfield	Alternate Governor
Jim Devellano	Alternate Governor
Atanas Ilitch	Alternate Governor
Christopher Ilitch	Alternate Governor

Edmonton Oilers

James F. Hole	Governor
Glen Sather	Alternate Governor
Cal Nichols	Alternate Governor

Florida Panthers

William A. Torrey	Governor
H. Wayne Huizenga	Alternate Governor
Bryan Murray	Alternate Governor

Los Angeles Kings

Robert Sanderman	Governor
Philip F. Anschutz	Alternate Governor
Timothy J. Leiweke	Alternate Governor
Edward Roski, Jr.	Alternate Governor
David Taylor	Alternate Governor

Montréal Canadiens

Pierre Boivin	Governor
Fred Steer	Alternate Governor
Rejean Houle	Alternate Governor

Nashville Predators

Craig Leipold	Governor
David Poile	Alternate Governor
Jack Diller	Alternate Governor
Terry London	Alternate Governor

New Jersey Devils

Dr. John J. McMullen	Governor
Lou A. Lamoriello	Alternate Governor
Peter McMullen	Alternate Governor

New York Islanders

Steven Gluckstern	Governor
Edward Milstein	Alternate Governor
John Sanders	Alternate Governor
David Seldin	Alternate Governor
William Skehan	Alternate Governor

New York Rangers

David W. Checketts	Governor
Kenneth W. Munoz	Alternate Governor
Neil Smith	Alternate Governor

Ottawa Senators

Roderick M. Bryden	Governor
Roy Mlakar	Alternate Governor

Philadelphia Flyers

Edward M. Snider	Governor
Bob Clarke	Alternate Governor
Ronald K. Ryan	Alternate Governor
Philip I. Weinberg	Alternate Governor

Phoenix Coyotes

Richard T. Burke	Governor
Shawn Hunter	Alternate Governor
Robert D. Smith	Alternate Governor

Pittsburgh Penguins

Mario Lemieux	Governor
Craig Patrick	Alternate Governor

St. Louis Blues

Jerry E. Ritter	Governor
Mark Sauer	Alternate Governor
Larry Pleau	Alternate Governor

San Jose Sharks

George Gund III	Governor
Gordon Gund	Alternate Governor
Irvin A. Leonard	Alternate Governor
Greg Jamison	Alternate Governor
Dean Lombardi	Alternate Governor

Tampa Bay Lightning

Thomas S. Wilson	Governor
Ronald J. Campbell	Alternate Governor
Jay H. Feaster	Alternate Governor

Toronto Maple Leafs

Steve A. Stavro	Governor
Brian P. Bellmore	Alternate Governor
Ken Dryden	Alternate Governor
Richard A. Peddie	Alternate Governor

Vancouver Canucks

John E. McCaw, Jr.	Governor
Steve Bellringer	Alternate Governor
Stanley McCammon	Alternate Governor
Brian Burke	Alternate Governor

Washington Capitals

Richard M. Patrick	Governor
Ted Leonsis	Alternate Governor
Jon Ledecky	Alternate Governor

NHL Expansion Franchises

Columbus Blue Jackets

John H. McConnell	Governor
John P. McConnell	Alternate Governor
John S. Christie	Alternate Governor
Doug MacLean	Alternate Governor

Minnesota Wild

Robert O. Naegele, Jr.	Governor
Jac Sperling	Alternate Governor

Commissioner and League Presidents

Gary B. Bettman

Gary B. Bettman took office as the NHL's first Commissioner on February 1, 1993. Since the League was formed in 1917, there have been five League Presidents.

NHL President	Years in Office
Frank Calder	1917-1943
Mervyn "Red" Dutton	1943-1946
Clarence Campbell	1946-1977
John A. Ziegler, Jr.	1977-1992
Gil Stein	1992-1993

NHL Europe

Signaustrasse 1
8008 Zurich – Switzerland
Phone: 41(0)1 389-8080
Fax: 41(0)1 389-8090

Brad Kwong – Managing Director
J.D. Kershaw – Manager

Hockey Hall of Fame

BCE Place
30 Yonge Street
Toronto, Ontario M5E 1X8
Phone: 416/360-7735
Executive Fax: 416/360-1501
Resource Center/Retail Fax: 416/360-1316
www.hhof.com

William C. Hay – Chairman
Jeff Denomme – President
Bryan Black – Senior Vice President, Marketing
Craig Baines – Director, Business Development and Facilities
Jan Barrina – Manager, Special Events and Facility Sales
Craig Beckim – Associate Manager, Merchandising
Sandra Buffone – Controller and Office Manager
Craig Campbell – Manager, Resource Center
Ron Ellis – Director, Public Affairs
Barry Eversley – Manager, Building Services
Anthony Fusco – Manager, Information Systems
Kelly Massé – Executive Assistant, Marketing
Tim McWilliams – Manager, Attractions and Retail Services
Ray Paquet – Creative Director, Exhibits
Phil Pritchard – Director, Information and Acquisitions
Pearl Rajwanth – Executive Assistant

National Hockey League Players' Association

777 Bay Street, Suite 2400
Toronto, Ontario M5G 2C8
Phone: 416/408-4040
Fax: 416/408-3685
E-mail: www.nhlpa.com

Robert W. Goodenow – Executive Director and General Counsel
Jeff Citron, Chris DiFrancesco, – Associate Counsels
  Rick Olczyk, Ian Pulver
Ted Saskin – Senior Director, Business Affairs and Licensing
Jordan Banks, David Kleiman, – Associate Counsels, Licensing
  Mike Ouellet
Mike Gartner – Director of Business Relations
Ken Kim – Director, Marketing
Mike Castellarin – Manager, Club Marketing
Mathew Diamond – Manager, Corporate Marketing
Dave Tredgett – Executive Producer, Television
Chris Allard – Communications Co-ordinator
Barbara Larcina – Director of Business Operations
Kim Murdoch – Manager, Pensions and Benefits
Devin Smith – Manager, Media Relations at ext. 279 or
  e-mail: dsmith@nhlpa.com

NHL On-Ice Officials

Total NHL Games and 98-99 Games columns count regular-season games only.

Referees

#	Name	Birthplace	Birthdate	First NHL Game	Total NHL Games	98-99 Games
41	Stephane Auger	Montreal, Que.	12/9/70			
9	Blaine Angus	Shawville, Que.	9/25/61	10/17/92	111	36
30	Bernard DeGrace	Lameque, N.B.	5/1/67	10/15/91	*179	21
10	Paul Devorski	Guelph, Ont.	8/18/58	10/14/89	529	71
44	Harry Dumas	Philadelphia, PA	7/7/73			
51	Joe Ernst	Buffalo, NY	9/19/71			
11	Mark Faucette	Springfield, MA	6/9/58	12/23/87	624	57
2	Kerry Fraser	Sarnia, Ont.	5/30/52	4/6/75	1185	79
4	Terry Gregson	Erin, Ont.	11/7/53	12/19/81	1078	75
34	Conrad Haché	Sudbury, Ont.	5/15/72	2/27/95	*29	5
64	Shane Heyer	Summerland, B.C.	2/7/64	10/5/88	785	73
8	Dave Jackson	Montreal, Que.	11/28/64	12/23/90	387	72
33	Marc Joannette	Verdun, Que.	11/3/68			
18	Greg Kimmerly	Toronto, Ont.	12/8/64	11/30/96	27	21
12	Don Koharski	Halifax, N.S.	12/2/55	10/14/77	*1213	81
32	Tom Kowal	Vernon, B.C.	11/2/67			0
14	Dennis LaRue	Savannah, GA	7/14/59	3/26/91	217	71
49	Chris Lee	Saint John, N.B.	7/7/70			
28	Mike Leggo	North Bay, Ont.	10/7/64	3/3/98	14	12
27	Kevin Maguire	Toronto, Ont.	5/1/63	1/22/98	26	24
6	Dan Marouelli	Edmonton, Alta.	7/16/55	11/2/84	909	80
26	Rob Martell	Winnipeg, Man.	10/21/63	3/14/84	*20	14
7	Bill McCreary	Guelph, Ont.	11/17/55	11/3/84	936	73
19	Mick McGeough	Regina, Sask.	6/20/57	1/19/89	514	61
40	Brad Meier	Dayton, OH	4/11/67			0
93	Brian Murphy	Dover, NH	12/13/64	10/7/88	714	66
15	Dan O'Halloran	Essex, Ont.	3/25/64	10/14/95	85	43
37	Tim Peel	Toronto, Ont.	4/27/66			
52	Kevin Pollock	Kincardine, Ont.	7/2/70		0	0
20	Lance Roberts	Edmonton, Alta.	5/28/57	11/3/89	409	75
43	Chris Rooney	Boston, MA	5/26/74			
16	Rob Shick	Port Alberni, B.C.	12/4/57	4/6/86	710	64
22	Paul Stewart	Boston, MA	3/21/55	3/27/87	736	44
17	Richard Trottier	Laval, Que.	2/28/57	12/13/89	406	74
21	Don Van Massenhoven	London, Ont.	7/17/60	11/11/93	328	78
24	Stephen Walkom	North Bay, Ont.	8/8/63	10/18/92	327	79
53	Ian Walsh	Philadelphia, PA	5/9/72			
35	Dean Warren	Toronto, Ont.	7/22/63			
23	Brad Watson	Regina, Sask.	10/4/61	2/5/94	43	34
29	Scott Zelkin	Wilmette, IL	9/12/68	4/13/97	25	23

* Includes some games worked as a linesman.

Linesmen

#	Name	Birthplace	Birthdate	First NHL Game	Total NHL Games	98-99 Games
75	Derek Amell	Port Colborne, Ont.	9/16/68	10/13/97	83	60
94	Wayne Bonney	Ottawa, Ont.	5/27/53	10/10/79	1385	76
96	David Brisebois	Sudbury, Ont.	4/9/76			
55	Gord Broseker	Baltimore, MD	7/8/50	1/14/75	1722	63
74	Lonnie Cameron	Victoria, B.C.	7/15/64	10/5/96	199	65
67	Pierre Champoux	Ville St-Pierre, Que.	4/18/63	10/8/88	706	63
50	Kevin Collins	Springfield, MA	12/15/50	10/13/77	1685	71
88	Mike Cvik	Calgary, Alta.	7/6/62	10/8/87	780	64
45	Pat Dapuzzo	Hoboken, NJ	12/29/58	12/5/84	1072	71
54	Greg Devorski	Guelph, Ont.	8/3/69	10/9/93	368	60
68	Scott Driscoll	Seaforth, Ont.	5/2/68	10/10/92	434	70
70	Francois Gagnon	Montreal, Que.	3/16/70	10/17/98	33	33
63	Gerard Gauthier	Montreal, Que.	9/5/48	10/16/71	2075	66
66	Darren Gibbs	Edmonton, Alta.	9/30/66	10/1/97	96	62
91	Don Henderson	Calgary, Alta.	9/23/68	3/10/95	190	64
48	Swede Knox	Edmonton, Alta.	3/2/48	10/14/72	1983	66
71	Brad Kovachik	Woodstock, Ont.	3/7/71	10/10/96	161	68
86	Brad Lazarowich	Vancouver, B.C.	8/4/62	10/9/86	891	70
46	Dan McCourt	Falconbridge, Ont.	8/14/54	12/27/80	1278	63
90	Andy McElman	Chicago Heights, IL	8/4/61	10/7/93	365	69
39	Randy Mitton	Fredericton, N.B.	9/22/50	2/2/74	1766	65
41	Jean Morin	Sorel, Que.	8/10/63	10/5/91	495	69
40	Thor Nelson	Westminister, CA	1/6/68	2/16/95	152	47
77	Tim Nowak	Buffalo, NY	9/6/67	10/8/93	373	69
92	Dan O'Rourke	Calgary, Alta.	8/31/72			
79	Mark Paré	Windsor, Ont.	7/26/57	10/11/79	1468	70
87	Baron Parker	Vancouver, B.C.	3/5/67	1/25/95	307	70
72	Stephane Provost	Montreal, Que.	5/5/67	1/25/95	329	77
65	Pierre Racicot	Verdun, Que.	2/15/67	10/12/93	391	79
81	Troy Sartison	Swift Current, Sask.	2/25/70			
42	Ray Scapinello	Guelph, Ont.	11/5/46	10/17/71	2159	69
47	Dan Schachte	Madison, WI	7/13/58	10/6/82	1184	68
31	Lyle Seitz	Brooks, Alta.	1/22/69	10/6/92	*112	10
84	Anthony Sericolo	Troy, NY	7/17/68	10/21/98	29	29
57	Jay Sharrers	Jamaica, West Indies	7/3/67	10/6/90	579	72
56	Mark Wheler	North Battleford, Sask.	9/20/65	10/10/92	450	66

* Includes some games worked as a referee.

NHL History

1917 — National Hockey League organized November 22 in Montreal following suspension of operations by the National Hockey Association of Canada Limited (NHA). Montreal Canadiens, Montreal Wanderers, Ottawa Senators and Quebec Bulldogs attended founding meeting. Delegates decided to use NHA rules.

Toronto Arenas were later admitted as fifth team; Quebec decided not to operate during the first season. Quebec players allocated to remaining four teams.

Frank Calder elected president and secretary-treasurer.

First NHL games played December 19, with Toronto only arena with artificial ice. Clubs played 22-game split schedule.

1918 — Emergency meeting held January 3 due to destruction by fire of Montreal Arena which was home ice for both Canadiens and Wanderers.

Wanderers withdrew, reducing the NHL to three teams; Canadiens played remaining home games at 3,250-seat Jubilee rink.

Quebec franchise sold to P.J. Quinn of Toronto on October 18 on the condition that the team operate in Quebec City for 1918-19 season. Quinn did not attend the November League meeting and Quebec did not play in 1918-19.

1919-20 — NHL reactivated Quebec Bulldogs franchise. Former Quebec players returned to the club. New Mount Royal Arena became home of Canadiens. Toronto Arenas changed name to St. Patricks. Clubs played 24-game split schedule.

1920-21 — H.P. Thompson of Hamilton, Ontario made application for the purchase of an NHL franchise. Quebec franchise shifted to Hamilton with other NHL teams providing players to strengthen the club.

1921-22 — Split schedule abandoned. First and second place teams at the end of full schedule to play for championship.

1922-23 — Clubs agreed that players could not be sold or traded to clubs in any other league without first being offered to all other clubs in the NHL. In March, Foster Hewitt broadcasts radio's first hockey game.

1923-24 — Ottawa's new 10,000-seat arena opened. First U.S. franchise granted to Boston for following season.

Dr. Cecil Hart Trophy donated to NHL to be awarded to the player judged most useful to his team.

1924-25 — Canadian Arena Company of Montreal granted a franchise to operate Montreal Maroons. NHL now six team league with two clubs in Montreal. Inaugural game in new Montreal Forum played November 29, 1924 as Canadiens defeated Toronto 7-1. Forum was home rink for the Maroons, but no ice was available in the Canadiens arena November 29, resulting in shift to Forum.

Hamilton finished first in the standings, receiving a bye into the finals. But Hamilton players, demanding $200 each for additional games in the playoffs, went on strike. The NHL suspended all players, fining them $200 each. Stanley Cup finalist to be the winner of NHL semi-final between Toronto and Canadiens.

Prince of Wales and Lady Byng trophies donated to NHL.

Clubs played 30-game schedule.

1925-26 — Hamilton club dropped from NHL. Players signed by new New York Americans franchise. Franchise granted to Pittsburgh.

Clubs played 36-game schedule.

1926-27 — New York Rangers granted franchise May 15, 1926. Chicago Black Hawks and Detroit Cougars granted franchises September 25, 1926. NHL now ten-team league with an American and a Canadian Division.

Stanley Cup came under the control of NHL. In previous seasons, winners of the now-defunct Western or Pacific Coast leagues would play NHL champion in Cup finals.

Toronto franchise sold to a new company controlled by Hugh Aird and Conn Smythe. Name changed from St. Patricks to Maple Leafs.

Clubs played 44-game schedule.

The Montreal Canadiens donated the Vezina Trophy to be awarded to the team allowing the fewest goals-against in regular season play. The winning team would, in turn, present the trophy to the goaltender playing in the greatest number of games during the season.

1930-31 — Detroit franchise changed name from Cougars to Falcons. Pittsburgh transferred to Philadelphia for one season. Pirates changed name to Philadelphia Quakers. Trading deadline for teams set at February 15 of each year. NHL approved operation of farm teams by Rangers, Americans, Falcons and Bruins. Four-sided electric arena clock first demonstrated.

1931-32 — Philadelphia dropped out. Ottawa withdrew for one season. New Maple Leaf Gardens completed.

Clubs played 48-game schedule.

1932-33 — Detroit franchise changed name from Falcons to Red Wings. Franchise application received from St. Louis but refused because of additional travel costs. Ottawa team resumed play.

1933-34 — First All-Star Game played as a benefit for injured player Ace Bailey. Leafs defeated All-Stars 7-3 in Toronto.

1934-35 — Ottawa franchise transferred to St. Louis. Team called St. Louis Eagles and consisted largely of Ottawa's players.

1935-36 — Ottawa-St. Louis franchise terminated. Montreal Canadiens finished season with very poor record. To strengthen the club, NHL gave Canadiens first call on the services of all French-Canadian players for three seasons.

1937-38 — Second benefit all-star game staged November 2 in Montreal in aid of the family of the late Canadiens star Howie Morenz.

Montreal Maroons withdrew from the NHL on June 22, 1938, leaving seven clubs in the League.

1938-39 — Expenses for each club regulated at $5 per man per day for meals and $2.50 per man per day for accommodation.

1939-40 — Benefit All-Star Game played October 29, 1939 in Montreal for the children of the late Albert (Babe) Siebert.

1940-41 — Ross-Tyer puck adopted as the official puck of the NHL. Early in the season it was apparent that this puck was too soft. The Spalding puck was adopted in its place.

After the playoffs, Arthur Ross, NHL governor from Boston, donated a perpetual trophy to be awarded annually to the player voted outstanding in the league.

1941-42 — New York Americans changed name to Brooklyn Americans.

1942-43 — Brooklyn Americans withdrew from NHL, leaving six teams: Boston, Chicago, Detroit, Montreal, New York and Toronto. Playoff format saw first-place team play third-place team and second play fourth.

Clubs played 50-game schedule.

Frank Calder, president of the NHL since its inception, died in Montreal. Mervyn "Red" Dutton, former manager of the New York Americans, became president. The NHL commissioned the Calder Memorial Trophy to be awarded to the League's outstanding rookie each year.

1945-46 — Philadelphia, Los Angeles and San Francisco applied for NHL franchises.

The Philadelphia Arena Company of the American Hockey League applied for an injunction to prevent the possible operation of an NHL franchise in that city.

1946-47 — Mervyn Dutton retired as president of the NHL prior to the start of the season. He was succeeded by Clarence S. Campbell.

Individual trophy winners and all-star team members to receive $1,000 awards.

Playoff guarantees for players introduced.

Clubs played 60-game schedule.

1947-48 — The first annual All-Star Game for the benefit of the players' pension fund was played when the All-Stars defeated the Stanley Cup Champion Toronto Maple Leafs 4-3 in Toronto on October 13, 1947.

Ross Trophy, awarded to the NHL's outstanding player since 1941, to be awarded annually to the League's scoring leader.

Philadelphia and Los Angeles franchise applications refused.

National Hockey League Pension Society formed.

1949-50 — Clubs played 70-game schedule.

First intra-league draft held April 30, 1950. Clubs allowed to protect 30 players. Remaining players available for $25,000 each.

1951-52 — Referees included in the League's pension plan.

1952-53 — In May of 1952, City of Cleveland applied for NHL franchise. Application denied. In March of 1953, the Cleveland Barons of the AHL challenged the NHL champions for the Stanley Cup. The NHL governors did not accept this challenge.

1953-54 — The James Norris Memorial Trophy presented to the NHL for annual presentation to the League's best defenseman.

Intra-league draft rules amended to allow teams to protect 18 skaters and two goaltenders, claiming price reduced to $15,000.

1954-55 — Each arena to operate an "out-of-town" scoreboard. Referees and linesmen to wear shirts of black and white vertical stripes.

1956-57 — Standardized signals for referees and linesmen introduced.

1960-61 — Canadian National Exhibition, City of Toronto and NHL reach agreement for the construction of a Hockey Hall of Fame on the CNE grounds. Hall opens on August 26, 1961.

1963-64 — Player development league established with clubs operated by NHL franchises located in Minneapolis, St. Paul, Indianapolis, Omaha and, beginning in 1964-65, Tulsa. First universal amateur draft took place. All players of qualifying age (17) unaffected by sponsorship of junior teams available to be drafted.

1964-65 — Conn Smythe Trophy presented to the NHL to be awarded annually to the outstanding player in the Stanley Cup playoffs.

Minimum age of players subject to amateur draft changed to 18.

1965-66 — NHL announced expansion plans for a second six-team division to begin play in 1967-68.

1966-67 — Fourteen applications for NHL franchises received.

Lester Patrick Trophy presented to the NHL to be awarded annually for outstanding service to hockey in the United States.

NHL sponsorship of junior teams ceased, making all players of qualifying age not already on NHL-sponsored lists eligible for the amateur draft.

1967-68 — Six new teams added: California Seals, Los Angeles Kings, Minnesota North Stars, Philadelphia Flyers, Pittsburgh Penguins, St. Louis Blues. New teams to play in West Division. Remaining six teams to play in East Division.

Minimum age of players subject to amateur draft changed to 20.

Clubs played 74-game schedule.

Clarence S. Campbell Trophy awarded to team finishing the regular season in first place in West Division.

California Seals changed name to Oakland Seals on December 8, 1967.

1968-69 — Clubs played 76-game schedule.

Amateur draft expanded to cover any amateur player of qualifying age throughout the world.

1970-71 — Two new teams added: Buffalo Sabres and Vancouver Canucks. These teams joined East Division: Chicago switched to West Division.

Clubs played 78-game schedule.

1971-72 — Playoff format amended. In each division, first to play fourth; second to play third.

1972-73 — Soviet Nationals and Canadian NHL stars play eight-game pre-season series. Canadians win 4-3-1.

Two new teams added. Atlanta Flames join West Division; New York Islanders join East Division.

1974-75 — Two new teams added: Kansas City Scouts and Washington Capitals. Teams realigned into two nine-team conferences, the Prince of Wales made up of the Norris and Adams Divisions, and the Clarence Campbell made up of the Smythe and Patrick Divisions.

Clubs played 80-game schedule.

1976-77 — California franchise transferred to Cleveland. Team named Cleveland Barons. Kansas City franchise transferred to Denver. Team named Colorado Rockies.

1977-78 — Clarence S. Campbell retires as NHL president. Succeeded by John A. Ziegler, Jr.

1978-79 — Cleveland and Minnesota franchises merge, leaving NHL with 17 teams. Merged team placed in Adams Division, playing home games in Minnesota.

Minimum age of players subject to amateur draft changed to 19.

1979-80 — Four new teams added: Edmonton Oilers, Hartford Whalers, Quebec Nordiques and Winnipeg Jets.

Minimum age of players subject to entry draft changed to 18.

1980-81 — Atlanta franchise shifted to Calgary, retaining "Flames" name.

1981-82 — Teams realigned within existing divisions. New groupings based on geographical areas. Unbalanced schedule adopted.

1982-83 — Colorado Rockies franchise shifted to East Rutherford, New Jersey. Team named New Jersey Devils. Franchise moved to Patrick Division from Smythe; Winnipeg moved to Smythe Division from Norris.

NHL History — *continued*

1991-92 — San Jose Sharks added, making the NHL a 22-team league. NHL celebrates 75th Anniversary Season. The 1991-92 regular season suspended due to a strike by members of the NHL Players' Association on April 1, 1992. Play resumed April 12, 1992.

1992-93 — Gil Stein named NHL president (October, 1992). Gary Bettman named first NHL Commissioner (February, 1993). Ottawa Senators and Tampa Bay Lightning added, making the NHL a 24-team league. NHL celebrates Stanley Cup Centennial. Clubs played 84-game schedule.

1993-94 — Mighty Ducks of Anaheim and Florida Panthers added, making the NHL a 26-team league. Minnesota franchise shifted to Dallas, team named Dallas Stars. Prince of Wales and Clarence Campbell Conferences renamed Eastern and Western. Adams, Patrick, Norris and Smythe Divisions renamed Northeast, Atlantic, Central and Pacific. Winnipeg moved to Central Division from Pacific; Tampa Bay moved to Atlantic Division from Central; Pittsburgh moved to Northeast Division from Atlantic.

1994-95 — A labor disruption forced the cancellation of 468 games from October 1, 1994 to January 19, 1995. Clubs played a 48-game schedule that began January 20, 1995 and ended May 3, 1995. No inter-conference games were played.

1995-96 — Quebec franchise transferred to Denver. Team named Colorado Avalanche and placed in Pacific Division of Western Conference. Clubs to play 82-game schedule.

1996-97 — Winnipeg franchise transferred to Phoenix. Team named Phoenix Coyotes and placed in Central Division of Western Conference.

1997-98 — Hartford franchise transferred to Raleigh. Team named Carolina Hurricanes and remains in Northeast Division of Eastern Conference.

1998-99 — The addition of the Nashville Predators made the NHL a 27-team league and brought about the creation of two new divisions and a League-wide realignment in preparation for further expansion to 30 teams by 2000-2001. Nashville was added to the Central Division of the Western Conference, while Toronto moved into the Northeast Division of the Eastern Conference. Pittsburgh was shifted from the Northeast to the Atlantic, while Carolina left the Northeast for the newly created Southeast Division of the Eastern Conference. Florida, Tampa Bay and Washington also joined the Southeast. In the Western Conference, Calgary, Colorado, Edmonton and Vancouver make up the new Northwest Division. Dallas and Phoenix moved from the Central to the Pacific Division.

The NHL retired uniform number 99 in honor of all-time scoring leader Wayne Gretzky who retired at the end of the season.

1999-2000 — Atlanta Thrashers added, making the NHL a 28-team league.

Major Rule Changes

1910-11 — Game changed from two 30-minute periods to three 20-minute periods.

1911-12 — National Hockey Association (forerunner of the NHL) originated six-man hockey, replacing seven-man game.

1917-18 — Goalies permitted to fall to the ice to make saves. Previously a goaltender was penalized for dropping to the ice.

1918-19 — Penalty rules amended. For minor fouls, substitutes not allowed until penalized player had served three minutes. For major fouls, no substitutes for five minutes. For match fouls, no substitutes allowed for the remainder of the game.

With the addition of two lines painted on the ice twenty feet from center, three playing zones were created, producing a forty-foot neutral center ice area in which forward passing was permitted. Kicking the puck was permitted in this neutral zone.

Tabulation of assists began.

1921-22 — Goaltenders allowed to pass the puck forward up to their own blue line.

Overtime limited to twenty minutes.

Minor penalties changed from three minutes to two minutes.

1923-24 — Match foul defined as actions deliberately injuring or disabling an opponent. For such actions, a player was fined not less than $50 and ruled off the ice for the balance of the game. A player assessed a match penalty may be replaced by a substitute at the end of 20 minutes. Match penalty recipients must meet with the League president who can assess additional punishment.

1925-26 — Delayed penalty rules introduced. Each team must have a minimum of four players on the ice at all times.

Two rules were amended to encourage offense: No more than two defensemen permitted to remain inside a team's own blue line when the puck has left the defensive zone. A faceoff to be called for ragging the puck unless short-handed.

Team captains only players allowed to talk to referees

Goaltender's leg pads limited to 12-inch width.

Timekeeper's gong to mark end of periods rather than referee's whistle. Teams to dress a maximum of 12 players for each game from a roster of no more than 14 players.

1926-27 — Blue lines repositioned to sixty feet from each goal-line, thereby enlarging the neutral zone and standardizing distance from blueline to goal.

Uniform goal nets adopted throughout NHL with goal posts securely fastened to the ice.

1927-28 — To further encourage offense, forward passes allowed in defending and neutral zones and goaltender's pads reduced in width from 12 to 10 inches.

Game standardized at three twenty-minute periods of stop-time separated by ten-minute intermissions.

Teams to change ends after each period.

Ten minutes of sudden-death overtime to be played if the score is tied after regulation time.

Minor penalty to be assessed to any player other than a goaltender for deliberately picking up the puck while it is in play. Minor penalty to be assessed for deliberately shooting the puck out of play.

The Art Ross goal net adopted as the official net of the NHL.

Maximum length of hockey sticks limited to 53 inches measured from heel of blade to end of handle. No minimum length stipulated.

Home teams given choice of goals to defend at start of game.

1928-29 — Forward passing permitted in defensive and neutral zones and into attacking zone if pass receiver is in neutral zone when pass is made. No forward passing allowed inside attacking zone.

Minor penalty to be assessed to any player who delays the game by passing the puck back into his defensive zone.

Ten-minute overtime without sudden-death provision to be played in games tied after regulation time. Games tied after this overtime period declared a draw.

Exclusive of goaltenders, team to dress at least 8 and no more than 12 skaters.

NHL Attendance

| Season | Regular Season | | Playoffs | | Total |
	Games	Attendance	Games	Attendance	Attendance
1960-61	210	2,317,142	17	242,000	2,559,142
1961-62	210	2,435,424	18	277,000	2,712,424
1962-63	210	2,590,574	16	220,906	2,811,480
1963-64	210	2,732,642	21	309,149	3,041,791
1964-65	210	2,822,635	20	303,859	3,126,494
1965-66	210	2,941,164	16	249,000	3,190,184
1966-67	210	3,084,759	16	248,336	3,333,095
1967-68[1]	444	4,938,043	40	495,089	5,433,132
1968-69	456	5,550,613	33	431,739	5,982,352
1969-70	456	5,992,065	34	461,694	6,453,759
1970-71[2]	546	7,257,677	43	707,633	7,965,310
1971-72	546	7,609,368	36	582,666	8,192,034
1972-73[3]	624	8,575,651	38	624,637	9,200,288
1973-74	624	8,640,978	38	600,442	9,241,420
1974-75[4]	720	9,521,536	51	784,181	10,305,717
1975-76	720	9,103,761	48	726,279	9,830,040
1976-77	720	8,563,890	44	646,279	9,210,169
1977-78	720	8,526,564	45	686,634	9,213,198
1978-79	680	7,758,053	45	694,521	8,452,574
1979-80[5]	840	10,533,623	63	976,699	11,510,322
1980-81	840	10,726,198	68	966,390	11,692,588
1981-82	840	10,710,894	71	1,058,948	11,769,842
1982-83	840	11,020,610	66	1,088,222	12,028,832
1983-84	840	11,359,386	70	1,107,400	12,466,786
1984-85	840	11,633,730	70	1,107,500	12,741,230
1985-86	840	11,621,000	72	1,152,503	12,773,503
1986-87	840	11,855,880	87	1,383,967	13,239,847
1987-88	840	12,117,512	83	1,336,901	13,454,413
1988-89	840	12,417,969	83	1,327,214	13,745,183
1989-90	840	12,579,651	85	1,355,593	13,935,244
1990-91	840	12,343,897	92	1,442,203	13,786,100
1991-92[6]	880	12,769,676	86	1,327,920	14,097,596
1992-93[7]	1,008	14,158,177[8]	83	1,346,034	15,504,211
1993-94[9]	1,092	16,105,604[10]	90	1,440,095	17,545,699
1994-95	624[11]	9,233,884	81	1,329,130	10,563,014
1995-96	1,066	17,041,614	86	1,540,140	18,581,754
1996-97	1,066	17,640,529	82	1,494,878	19,135,407
1997-98	1,066	17,264,678	82	1,507,416	18,772,094
1998-99[12]	1,107	18,001,741	86	1,509,411	19,511,152

[1] First expansion: Los Angeles, Pittsburgh, California (Cleveland), Philadelphia, St. Louis and Minnesota (Dallas)
[2] Second expansion: Buffalo and Vancouver
[3] Third expansion: Atlanta (Calgary) and New York Islanders
[4] Fourth expansion: Kansas City (Colorado, New Jersey) and Washington
[5] Fifth expansion: Edmonton, Hartford, Quebec (Colorado) and Winnipeg
[6] Sixth expansion: San Jose
[7] Seventh expansion: Ottawa and Tampa Bay
[8] Includes 24 neutral site games
[9] Eighth expansion: Anaheim and Florida
[10] Includes 26 neutral site games
[11] Lockout resulted in the cancellation of 468 regular-season games.
[12] Ninth expansion: Nashville

Major Rule Changes — *continued*

1929-30 — Forward passing permitted inside all three zones but not permitted across either blue line.

Kicking the puck allowed, but a goal cannot be scored by kicking the puck in.

No more than three players including the goaltender may remain in their defensive zone when the puck has gone up ice. Minor penalties to be assessed for the first two violations of this rule in a game; major penalties thereafter.

Goaltenders forbidden to hold the puck. Pucks caught must be cleared immediately. For infringement of this rule, a faceoff to be taken ten feet in front of the goal with no player except the goaltender standing between the faceoff spot and the goal-line.

Highsticking penalties introduced.

Maximum number of players in uniform increased from 12 to 15.

December 21, 1929 — Forward passing rules instituted at the beginning of the 1929-30 season more than doubled number of goals scored. Partway through the season, these rules were further amended to read, "No attacking player allowed to precede the play when entering the opposing defensive zone." This is similar to modern offside rule.

1930-31 — A player without a complete stick ruled out of play and forbidden from taking part in further action until a new stick is obtained. A player who has broken his stick must obtain a replacement at his bench.

A further refinement of the offside rule stated that the puck must first be propelled into the attacking zone before any player of the attacking side can enter that zone; for infringement of this rule a faceoff to take place at the spot where the infraction took place.

1931-32 — Though there is no record of a team attempting to play with two goaltenders on the ice, a rule was instituted which stated that each team was allowed only one goaltender on the ice at one time.

Attacking players forbidden to impede the movement or obstruct the vision of opposing goaltenders.

Defending players with the exception of the goaltender forbidden from falling on the puck within 10 feet of the net.

1932-33 — Each team to have captain on the ice at all times.

If the goaltender is removed from the ice to serve a penalty, the manager of the club to appoint a substitute.

Match penalty with substitution after five minutes instituted for kicking another player.

1933-34 — Number of players permitted to stand in defensive zone restricted to three including goaltender.

Visible time clocks required in each rink.

Two referees replace one referee and one linesman.

1934-35 — Penalty shot awarded when a player is tripped and thus prevented from having a clear shot on goal, having no player to pass to other than the offending player. Shot taken from inside a 10-foot circle located 38 feet from the goal. The goaltender must not advance more than one foot from his goal-line when the shot is taken.

1937-38 — Rules introduced governing icing the puck.

Penalty shot awarded when a player other than a goaltender falls on the puck within 10 feet of the goal.

1938-39 — Penalty shot modified to allow puck carrier to skate in before shooting.

One referee and one linesman replace two referee system.

Blue line widened to 12 inches.

Maximum number of players in uniform increased from 14 to 15.

1939-40 — A substitute replacing a goaltender removed from ice to serve a penalty may use a goaltender's stick and gloves but no other goaltending equipment.

1940-41 — Flooding ice surface between periods made obligatory.

1941-42 — Penalty shots classified as minor and major. Minor shot to be taken from a line 28 feet from the goal. Major shot, awarded when a player is tripped with only the goaltender to beat, permits the player taking the penalty shot to skate right into the goalkeeper and shoot from point-blank range.

One referee and two linesmen employed to officiate games.

For playoffs, standby minor league goaltenders employed by NHL as emergency substitutes.

1942-43 — Because of wartime restrictions on train scheduling, regular-season overtime was discontinued on November 21, 1942.

Player limit reduced from 15 to 14. Minimum of 12 men in uniform abolished.

1943-44 — Red line at center ice introduced to speed up the game and reduce offside calls. This rule is considered to mark the beginning of the modern era in the NHL.

Delayed penalty rules introduced.

1945-46 — Goal indicator lights synchronized with official time clock required at all rinks.

1946-47 — System of signals by officials to indicate infractions introduced.

Linesmen from neutral cities employed for all games.

1947-48 — Goal awarded when a player with the puck has an open net to shoot at and a thrown stick prevents the shot on goal. Major penalty to any player who throws his stick in any zone other than defending zone. If a stick is thrown by a player in his defending zone but the thrown stick is not considered to have prevented a goal, a penalty shot is awarded.

All playoff games played until a winner determined, with 20-minute sudden-death overtime periods separated by 10-minute intermissions.

1949-50 — Ice surface painted white.

Clubs allowed to dress 17 players exclusive of goaltenders.

Major penalties incurred by goaltenders served by a member of the goaltender's team instead of resulting in a penalty shot.

1950-51 — Each team required to provide an emergency goaltender in attendance with full equipment at each game for use by either team in the event of illness or injury to a regular goaltender.

1951-52 — Home teams to wear basic white uniforms; visiting teams basic colored uniforms.

Goal crease enlarged from 3 × 7 feet to 4 × 8 feet.

Number of players in uniform reduced to 15 plus goaltenders.

Faceoff circles enlarged from 10-foot to 15-foot radius.

1952-53 — Teams permitted to dress 15 skaters on the road and 16 at home.

1953-54 — Number of players in uniform set at 16 plus goaltenders.

1954-55 — Number of players in uniform set at 18 plus goaltenders up to December 1 and 16 plus goaltenders thereafter. Teams agree to wear colored uniforms at home and white uniforms on the road.

1956-57 — Player serving a minor penalty allowed to return to ice when a goal is scored by opposing team.

1959-60 — Players prevented from leaving their benches to enter into an altercation. Substitutions permitted providing substitutes do not enter into altercation.

1960-61 — Number of players in uniform set at 16 plus goaltenders.

1961-62 — Penalty shots to be taken by the player against whom the foul was committed. In the event of a penalty shot called in a situation where a particular player hasn't been fouled, the penalty shot to be taken by any player on the ice when the foul was committed.

1964-65 — No bodily contact on faceoffs.

In playoff games, each team to have its substitute goaltender dressed in his regular uniform except for leg pads and body protector. All previous rules governing standby goaltenders terminated.

1965-66 — Teams required to dress two goaltenders for each regular-season game. Maximum stick length increased to 55 inches.

1966-67 — Substitution allowed on coincidental major penalties.

Between-periods intermissions fixed at 15 minutes.

1967-68 — If a penalty incurred by a goaltender is a co-incident major, the penalty to be served by a player of the goaltender's team on the ice at the time the penalty was called. Limit of curvature of hockey stick blade set at 1-1/2 inches.

1969-70 — Limit of curvature of hockey stick blade set at 1 inch.

1970-71 — Home teams to wear basic white uniforms; visiting teams basic colored uniforms.

Limit of curvature of hockey stick blade set at 1/2 inch.

Minor penalty for deliberately shooting the puck out of the playing area.

1971-72 — Number of players in uniform set at 17 plus 2 goaltenders.

Third man to enter an altercation assessed an automatic game misconduct penalty.

1972-73 — Minimum width of stick blade reduced to 2 inches from 2-1/2 inches.

1974-75 — Bench minor penalty imposed if a penalized player does not proceed directly and immediately to the penalty box.

1976-77 — Rule dealing with fighting amended to provide a major and game misconduct penalty for any player who is clearly the instigator of a fight.

1977-78 — Teams requesting a stick measurement to be assessed a minor penalty in the event that the measured stick does not violate the rules.

1979-80 — Wearing of helmets made mandatory for players entering the NHL.

1980-81 — Maximum stick length increased to 58 inches.

1981-82 — If both of a team's listed goaltenders are incapacitated, the team can dress and play any eligible goaltender who is available.

1982-83 — Number of players in uniform set at 18 plus 2 goaltenders.

1983-84 — Five-minute sudden-death overtime to be played in regular-season games that are tied at the end of regulation time.

1985-86 — Substitutions allowed in the event of co-incidental minor penalties. Maximum stick length increased to 60 inches.

1986-87 — Delayed off-side is no longer in effect once the players of the offending team have cleared the opponents' defensive zone.

1990-91 — The goal lines, blue lines, defensive zone face-off circles and markings all moved one foot out from the end boards, creating 11 feet of room behind the nets and shrinking the neutral zone from 60 to 58 feet.

1991-92 — Video replays employed to assist referees in goal/no goal situations. Size of goal crease increased. Crease changed to semi-circular configuration. Time clock to record tenths of a second in last minute of each period and overtime. Major and game misconduct penalty for checking from behind into boards. Penalties added for crease infringement and unnecessary contact with goaltender. Goal disallowed if puck enters net while a player of the attacking team is standing on the goal crease line, is in the goal crease or places his stick in the goal crease.

1992-93 — No substitutions allowed in the event of coincidental minor penalties called when both teams are at full strength. Wearing of helmets made optional for forwards and defensemen. Minor penalty for attempting to draw a penalty ("diving"). Major and game misconduct penalty for checking from behind into goal frame. Game misconduct penalty for instigating a fight. Highsticking redefined to include any use of the stick above waist-height. Previous rule stipulated shoulder-height.

1993-94 — High sticking redefined to allow goals scored with a high stick below the height of the crossbar of the goal frame.

1996-97 — Maximum stick length increased to 63 inches.

1998-99 — The league instituted a two-referee system with each team to play 20 regular-season games with two referees and a pair of linesmen. Also, the goal lines, blue lines, defensive zone face-off circles and markings all moved two feet closer to center, creating 13 feet of room behind the nets and cutting the neutral zone from 58 to 54 feet. The goal crease was altered so that it extends only one foot beyond each goal post (eight feet across in total) and has square sides for the first 4'6". Only the top of the crease remains rounded.

1999-2000 — Each team to play 25 home and 25 road games using the two-referee system. Crease rule revised to implement a "no harm, no foul, no video review" standard. An attacking player's position, whether inside or outside the crease, does not, in itself, determine whether a goal should be allowed or disallowed. The on-ice judgement of the referee(s) — instead of video review — will determine if a goal is "good" or not. Also, regular-season games tied at the end of three periods will result in each team being awarded one point in the standings. As before, there will be a five-minute sudden death overtime when the score is tied after three periods, but each team will play "four on four," with four skaters and a goalkeeper. In the event that penalties dictate that one team has a two-man advantage, the penalized team plays with three skaters while the team with the two-man advantage adds a fifth skater. A team scoring in overtime will receive one additional point in the standings.

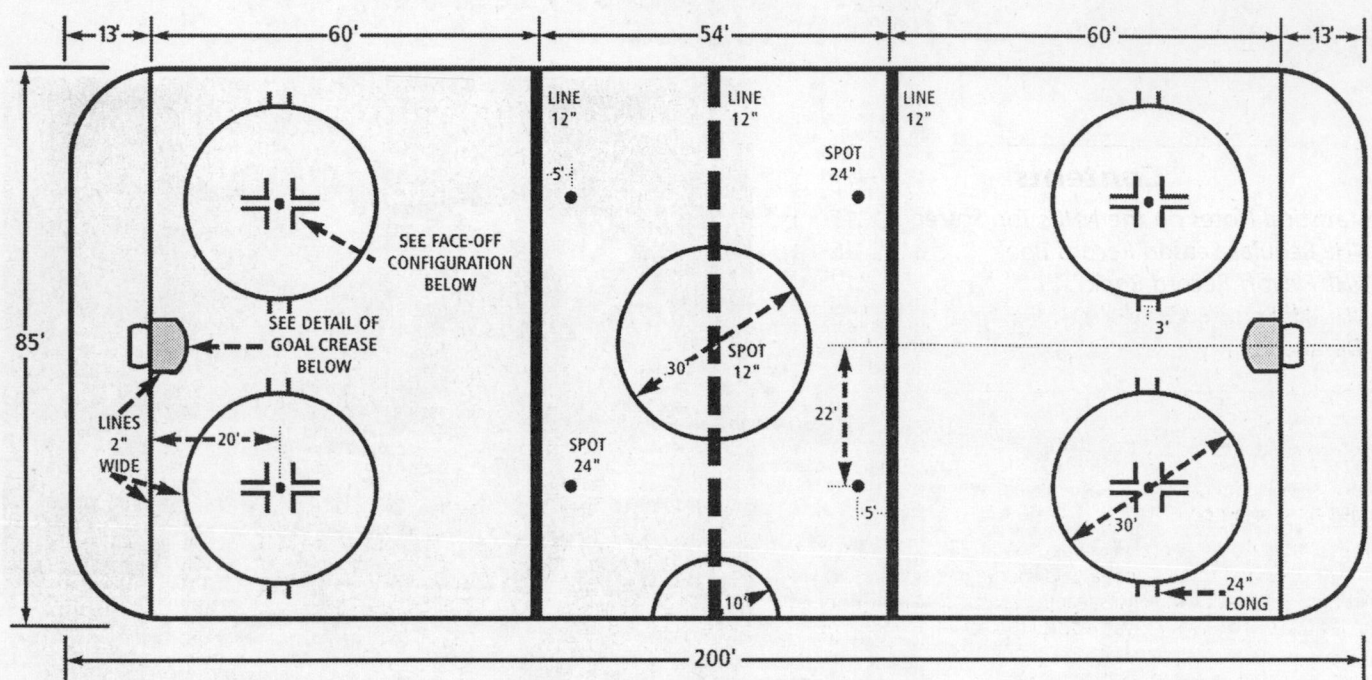

NHL RINK DIMENSIONS

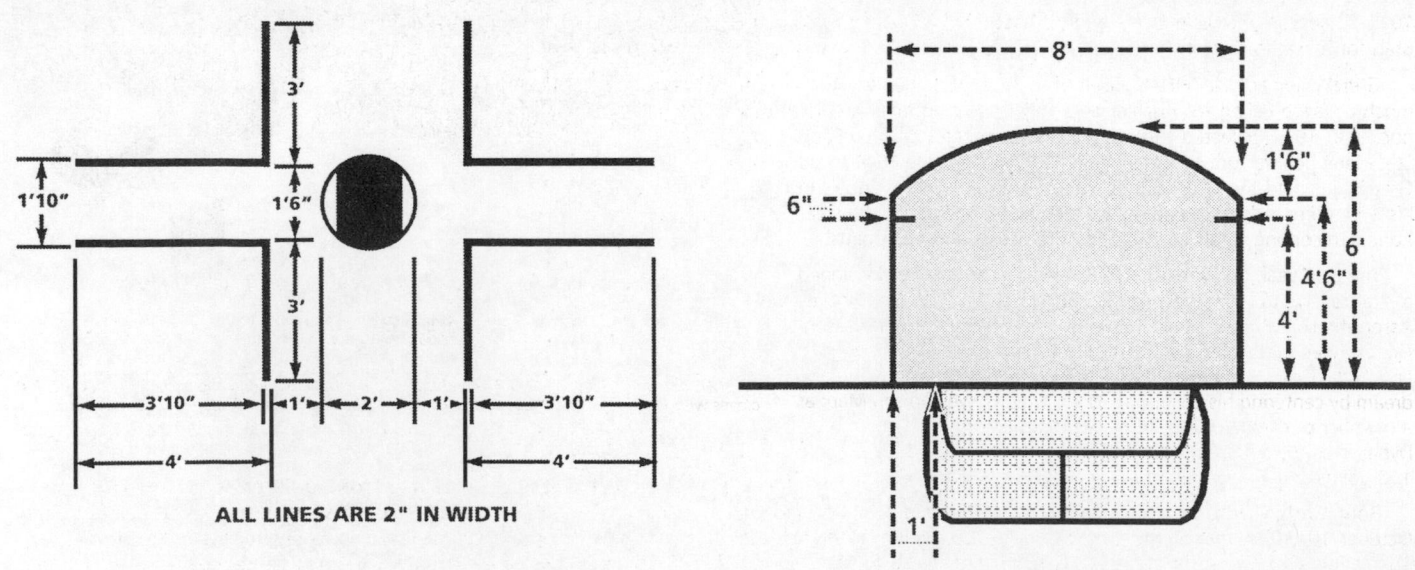

FACEOFF CONFIGURATION

CREASE DIMENSIONS

WAYNE GRETZKY
CAREER RETROSPECTIVE

Contents

WAYNE GRETZKY, "THE GREAT ONE," announced his retirement on April 16, 1999 after 20 seasons in which he dominated the National Hockey League unlike any other player in the League's 82-year history.

The 38-year-old Gretzky helped win four Stanley Cup Championships and three Canada Cup tournament titles. He owns 10 Art Ross Trophies as the NHL's leading scorer; nine Hart Trophies as the League's MVP; two Conn Smythe Trophies as playoff MVP. He has been awarded five Lady Byng Trophies as the NHL's most gentlemanly player. He's an eight-time First All-Star Team member and seven-time Second Team member. Gretzky holds virtually every offensive record in the National Hockey League and his tireless support of the game has contributed significantly to the popularity it enjoys today.

As a six-year-old, the Brantford, Ontario native was good enough to play on a 10-and-under team and even managed to score a goal. Four years later, a 11-year-old Gretzky finished the 1971-72 season with 378 goals and 120 assists in 85 games with Brantford's Nadrofsky Steelers.

Gretzky joined the OHA's Sault Ste. Marie Greyhounds with much advance billing for his first and only full year of major junior hockey in 1977. Selected third in the annual midget draft by Sault Ste. Marie behind Tom McCarthy and Paul Reinhart, the 16-year-old Gretzky justified the Greyhounds' faith in him, scoring six goals in his first game and proceeding to take OHA Rookie of the Year honors, recording totals of 70 goals, 112 assists and 182 points.

The next year, on June 13, 1978, the 17-year-old Gretzky signed a contract with the Indianapolis Racers of the World Hockey Association. On November 2, 1978, just eight games into the season, Gretzky was sold to the rival Edmonton Oilers along with Eddie Mio and Peter Driscoll. January 5, 1979, saw Gretzky realize a lifelong dream by centering his childhood idol Gordie Howe and son Mark as a member of the WHA All-Star Team that played a touring Moscow Dynamo club from the Soviet Union. He finished the 1978-79 season with 110 points and was named the league's Rookie of the Year.

Both Gretzky and the Oilers made their NHL debut in Chicago on October 10, 1979 against the Blackhawks. Although the Oilers lost, the 18-year-old Gretzky recorded his first NHL point, an assist on Kevin Lowe's goal at 9:49 of the first period. Four nights later, in Edmonton's third game of the season, Gretzky beat Vancouver Canucks goaltender Glen Hanlon to score his first NHL goal, on a power play at 18:51 of the third period. Gretzky finished the season with 137 points (51-86-137) and won the first of eight consecutive Hart Trophies as the most valuable player to his team.

Over the next eight seasons with the Oilers, from 1980-81 through

First NHL season, 1979-80: 137 points and the Hart Trophy. Taping only the heel of his stick and gloves without laces paid homage to one of Wayne's hockey heroes, Boston great Bobby Orr.

1987-88, Gretzky eclipsed even the lofty pace set in his rookie year, averaging nearly 192 points per season. Included are many record-shattering performances, such as: scoring 50 goals in his team's first 39 games in 1981-82; a consecutive point-scoring streak of 51 games to start the 1983-84 season; setting an all-time scoring record for the playoffs with 47 points in 1984-85 and setting the all-time regular-season mark with 215 points in 1985-86. The Oilers reached the Stanley Cup Finals five times, capturing the Cup four times. In addition, Gretzky was an integral part of the 1984 and 1987 Team Canada squads that won the Canada Cup.

On August 9, 1988, after helping Edmonton capture a fourth Stanley Cup and winning a second Conn Smythe Trophy as playoff MVP, Gretzky was traded to Los Angeles in one of the biggest sports deals in history. Gretzky and teammates Marty McSorley and Mike Krushelnyski were dealt to Los Angeles for center Jimmy Carson, left wing Martin Gelinas, three future first-round draft choices and cash.

That August day would change forever the NHL landscape in the United States. Gretzky joined a Kings team that had averaged just over 10,000 fans per game in its 21-year history. With Gretzky as the star attraction, hockey became one of the hottest tickets in pro sports in California. By 1991, the team would become the only franchise in Southern California to sell out every home game for an entire season. Hockey's success in a warm-weather environment paved the way for acceptance of the sport in America's Sun Belt. Gretzky's first season in a Kings uniform was an unqualified success, as the team finished with the most-improved record in the NHL (42-31-7) and placed second in the Smythe Division. Gretzky finished second in League scoring with 168 points (54-114-168) and won his ninth Hart Trophy.

On April 28, 1992, Gretzky's Kings were eliminated in a six-game opening-round playoff series by the Edmonton Oilers. It would be the Great One's last NHL game for more than eight months as a debilitating back injury, a herniated thoracic disk, would call into question whether Gretzky ever would be able to return. Experts said he would be out of hockey for at least a year, but by early December, Gretzky had resumed skating; on January 6, 1993, he was back in the Kings lineup for his 1,000th career game, assisting on two Kings goals in a 6-3 loss to the Tampa Bay Lightning.

Despite the eight-month layoff, Gretzky would rebound to register 65 points (16-49-65) in just 45 games and would lead the Kings to the Stanley Cup Finals for the only time in franchise history. Despite the loss in five games to the Montreal Canadiens, Gretzky proved he was back at the top of his game by registering 40 points in 24 post-season games.

Concluding the 1993-94 season, Gretzky captured his 10th and final Art Ross Trophy and added his fourth Lady Byng Trophy — marking his 10th multiple-award campaign. He also received the Lester Patrick Trophy recognizing his outstanding contribution to hockey in the United States. In 1994-95, Gretzky led the Kings in scoring for the sixth time in seven seasons before being traded to the St. Louis Blues. On Feb. 27, 1996, Gretzky went to the Blues in exchange for left wing Craig Johnson, center Roman Vopat, center Patrice Tardif and two draft choices. In his split season between the Kings and Blues, he recorded 102 points (23 goals, 79 assists), reaching the 100-point plateau for the 15th time in his career.

On July 12, 1996, Gretzky signed with the New York Rangers, joining his former Edmonton Oilers teammate Mark Messier. He made an immediate impact in New York, posting a 15-game scoring streak in his first month with the club. He recorded 97 points as the Rangers' top scorer and tallied a League leading 72 assists, tying the club's single season record for assists by a center.

Gretzky's trade to Los Angeles on August 9, 1988 was a defining event in the history of the National Hockey League. #99's arrival increased the profile of hockey in California and the rest of the United States, paving the way for further expansion in the 1990s.

In 1998 Gretzky realized a dream by competing for Canada at the Olympic Winter Games in Nagano, Japan. He concluded the year with his seventh selection to the NHL's Second All-Star Team and was named a finalist for the Lady Byng Trophy for sportsmanship. He led the League in assists once again with 67, including the 1,851st of his career, which made his assists total greater than any other player's career points total. The 1998-99 season saw Gretzky build his grand totals to 894 goals and 1,963 assists for 2,857 points in 1,487 career games. He won his final NHL individual award, the Lady Byng Trophy, and was inducted into the Hockey Hall of Fame without the customary three-year waiting period, capping a lifetime of thrills and achievement.

Gretzky's last NHL goal — March 29, 1999 vs. the New York Islanders — was a record setter. Combining regular-season and playoffs in the NHL and the World Hockey Association, this goal was Gretzky's 1,072nd, putting him one ahead of Gordie Howe.

CAREER REGULAR-SEASON RECORD VS. EACH CLUB

Opposition	GP	G	A	Pts.	PIM
Anaheim	23	5	25	30	12
Boston	53	25	48	73	18
Buffalo	55	27	56	83	6
Carolina/Hfd.	57	36	73	109	74
Calgary/Atl.	117	69	161	230	32
Chicago	60	25	77	102	24
Colorado	51	38	94	132	14
Dallas	58	44	72	116	23
Detroit	62	37	108	145	20
Edmonton	54	23	62	85	16
Florida	20	5	12	17	6
Los Angeles	69	60	119	179	38
Montreal	55	23	65	88	16
Nashville	2	1	7	8	0
New Jersey/Col.R.	67	32	91	123	14
NY Islanders	55	33	65	98	8
NY Rangers	46	34	47	81	10
Ottawa	17	3	25	28	12
Philadelphia	58	34	66	100	14
Phoenix/Wpg.	105	79	151	230	58
Pittsburgh	57	44	80	124	14
St. Louis	57	39	68	107	10
San Jose	32	12	39	51	2
Tampa Bay	20	5	19	24	2
Toronto	63	55	95	150	22
Vancouver	117	76	163	239	84
Washington	57	30	75	105	28
Total	**1487**	**894**	**1963**	**2857**	**577**

GRETZKY IN INTERNATIONAL HOCKEY

Year	Team	Event	GP	G	A	PTS	PIM
1978	Canada	World Junior	6	8	9	17	2
1981	Canada	Canada Cup	7	5	7	12	2
1982	Canada	World Champ.	10	6	8	14	0
1984	Canada	Canada Cup	8	5	7	12	2
1987	Canada	Canada Cup	9	3	18	21	2
1991	Canada	Canada Cup	7	4	8	12	2
1996	Canada	World Cup	8	3	4	7	2
1998	Canada	Olympics	6	0	4	4	2

99: My Life In Pictures

Gretzky's life in hockey
from #99's point of view.

350 photos, many rare
and unpublished.

Introduction, captions and
commentary by Wayne Gretzky.

Special essay by John Davidson.

Details on page 608.

GRETZKY AND ALL-TIME LEADERS FROM OTHER SPORTS

League		First Place	Second Place	Leader Ahead By
NBA	Career Points	Abdul-Jabbar (38,387)	Chamberlain (31,419)	22%
MLB	Career Home Runs	Aaron (755)	Ruth (714)	6%
	Career Hits	Rose (4,256)	Cobb (4,191)	2%
NFL	Career TD Passes	Marino (408)	Tarkenton (342)	19%
	Career Pass Yds.	Marino (58,913)	Elway (51,475)	14%
	Career Receiving Yds.	Rice (17,612)	Lofton (14,004)	26%
	Career Rushing Yds.	Payton (16,726)	Sanders (15,269)	9%
NHL	Career Goals	Gretzky (894)	Howe (801)	12%
	Career Assists	Gretzky (1,963)	Coffey (1,102)	78%
	Career Points	Gretzky (2,857)	Howe (1,850)	54%

SINGLE-GAME GOALS, ASSISTS AND POINTS BREAKDOWN

894 Goals

Games with	Goals
849	0
449	1
139	2
37	3
9	4
4	5

1,963 Assists

Games with	Assists
423	0
489	1
351	2
148	3
59	4
13	5
1	6
3	7

2,857 Points

Games with	Points
266	0
397	1
365	2
242	3
121	4
67	5
20	6
7	7

TEAMMATES

A total of 354 players have lined up alongside Wayne Gretzky as teammates in regular-season play between 1979-80 and 1998-99. These players have played more than 200 games with Gretzky:

Games	Player	Games	Player	Games	Player
858	Kurri, Jari	342	Gregg, Randy	241	Conacher, Pat
698	Messier, Mark	340	Fuhr, Grant	231	Moog, Andy
664	Huddy, Charlie	330	Granato, Tony	228	Leetch, Brian
661	Lowe, Kevin	327	Taylor, Dave	226	Duchesne, Steve
613	Hunter, Dave	316	McClelland, Kevin	226	MacTavish, Craig
591	Anderson, Glenn	314	Hrudey, Kelly	224	Graves, Adam
579	Fogolin, Lee	294	Hughes, Pat	221	Sundstrom, Niklas
556	McSorley, Marty	288	Beukeboom, Jeff	220	Tikkanen, Esa
546	Coffey, Paul	287	Watters, Tim	217	Tonelli, John
491	Robitaille, Luc	281	Blake, Rob	214	Miller, Jay
453	Semenko, Dave	262	Jackson, Don	213	Kudelski, Bob
420	Krushelnyski, Mike	257	Donnelly, Mike	205	Siltanen, Risto
379	Lumley, Dave	244	Sydor, Darryl	203	Samuelsson, Ulf.

HOME/ROAD BREAKDOWN, REGULAR SEASON

HOME

Season	Club	GP	G	A	PTS
1979-80	EDM	40	28	49	77
1980-81	EDM	40	29	62	91
1981-82	EDM	40	59	64	123
1982-83	EDM	40	31	63	94
1983-84	EDM	39	44	66	110
1984-85	EDM	40	34	70	104
1985-86	EDM	40	29	82	111
1986-87	EDM	40	36	71	107
1987-88	EDM	36	26	59	85
1988-89	L.A.	40	33	70	103
1989-90	L.A.	37	24	55	79
1990-91	L.A.	40	26	65	91
1991-92	L.A.	37	18	42	60
1992-93	L.A.	22	6	25	31
1993-94*	L.A.	39	17	53	70
1994-95	L.A.	24	9	19	28
1995-96	L.A.-STL	36	14	44	58
1996-97	NYR	41	15	42	57
1997-98	NYR	41	9	38	47
1998-99	NYR	32	5	25	30
Totals		**744**	**492**	**1064**	**1556**

ROAD

Season	Club	GP	G	A	PTS
1979-80	EDM	39	23	37	60
1980-81	EDM	40	26	47	73
1981-82	EDM	40	33	56	89
1982-83	EDM	40	40	62	102
1983-84	EDM	35	43	52	95
1984-85	EDM	40	39	65	104
1985-86	EDM	40	23	81	104
1986-87	EDM	39	26	50	76
1987-88	EDM	28	14	50	64
1988-89	L.A.	38	21	44	65
1989-90	L.A.	36	16	47	63
1990-91	L.A.	38	15	57	72
1991-92	L.A.	37	13	48	61
1992-93	L.A.	23	10	24	34
1993-94*	L.A.	40	20	34	54
1994-95	L.A.	24	2	18	20
1995-96	L.A.-STL	44	9	35	44
1996-97	NYR	41	10	30	40
1997-98	NYR	41	14	29	43
1998-99	NYR	38	4	28	32
Totals		**741**	**401**	**894**	**1295**

*Two neutral site games in 1993-94 not ncluded.

NHL RECORDS HELD OR SHARED BY WAYNE GRETZKY

Wayne Gretzky holds or shares 61 records listed in the *NHL Official Guide and Record Book*: 40 for the regular season, 15 for the Stanley Cup playoffs and six for the All-Star Game.

REGULAR-SEASON RECORDS (40)

GOALS (6)

MOST GOALS: 894 (1,487 games). Second: 801 — Gordie Howe, 26 seasons, 1,767 games

MOST GOALS, INCLUDING PLAYOFFS: 1,016 — 894 regular season and 122 playoff. Second: 869 – Gordie Howe, 801 regular season and 68 playoff

MOST GOALS, ONE SEASON: 92 – 1981-82, 80-game schedule. Second: 87 – Wayne Gretzky, 1983-84, 80-game schedule

MOST GOALS, ONE SEASON, INCLUDING PLAYOFFS: 100 – 1983-84, 87 goals in 74 regular season games and 13 goals in 19 playoff games. Second (tied): three players

MOST GOALS, 50 GAMES FROM START OF SEASON: 61 – 1981-82 (Oct. 7, 1981 to Jan. 22, 1982, 80-game schedule); 1983-84 (Oct. 5, 1983 to Jan. 25,1984, 80-game schedule. Next (third): 54 – Mario Lemieux, 1988-89 (Oct. 7, 1988 – Jan. 31, 1989, 80-game schedule)

MOST GOALS, ONE PERIOD: 4 – (Tied with 10 other players) Feb. 18, 1981, at Edmonton, third period (Edmonton 9, St. Louis 2)

ASSISTS (6)

MOST ASSISTS: 1,963 (1,487 games). Second: 1,102 – Paul Coffey, 19 seasons, 1,320 games

MOST ASSISTS, INCLUDING PLAYOFFS: 2,223 – 1,963 regular season and 260 playoff. Second: 1,226 – Paul Coffey, 1,090 regular season and 136 playoff

MOST ASSISTS, ONE SEASON: 163 – 1985-86, 80-game schedule. Next (eighth): 114 – Mario Lemieux and Wayne Gretzky tied, 1988-89, 80-game schedule

MOST ASSISTS, ONE SEASON, INCLUDING PLAYOFFS: 174 – 1985-86, 163 assists in 80 regular season games and 11 assists in 10 playoff games. Next (tied for 11th): 121 – Mario Lemieux 1988-89; 114 assists in 76 regular season games and seven assists in 11 playoff games

MOST ASSISTS, ONE GAME: 7 – (tied with Billy Taylor) done three times – Feb. 15, 1980 at Edmonton (Edmonton 8, Washington 2); Dec. 11, 1985 at Chicago (Edmonton 12, Chicago 9); Feb. 14, 1986 at Edmonton (Edmonton 8, Quebec 2). Second: 6 – 23 players

MOST ASSISTS, ONE ROAD GAME: 7 (tied with Billy Taylor) – Dec. 11, 1985 at Chicago (Edmonton 12, Chicago 9). Second: 6 – four players

POINTS (4)

MOST POINTS: 2,857 –1,487 games (894 goals, 1,963 assists). Second: 1,850 Gordie Howe, 1,767 games (801 goals, 1,049 assists)

MOST POINTS, INCLUDING PLAYOFFS: 3,239 – 2,857 regular season and 382 playoff. Second: 2,010 – Gordie Howe, 1,850 regular season and 160 playoff

MOST POINTS, ONE SEASON: 215 – 1985-86, 80-game schedule. Next (fifth): 199 – Mario Lemieux, 1988-89, 80-game schedule

MOST POINTS, ONE SEASON, INCLUDING PLAYOFFS: 255 – 1984-85; 208 points in 80 regular-season games and 47 points in 18 playoff games. Next (sixth): 218 – Mario Lemieux, 1988-89; 199 points in 76 regular-season games and 19 points in 11 playoff games

OVERTIME SCORING (1)

MOST OVERTIME ASSISTS, CAREER: 15. Second: 13 – Doug Gilmour, 16 seasons

SCORING BY A CENTER (6)

MOST GOALS BY A CENTER, CAREER: 894. Second: 731 – Marcel Dionne, 18 seasons

MOST GOALS BY A CENTER, ONE SEASON: 92 – 1981-82, 80-game schedule. Next (third): 85 – Mario Lemieux, 1988-89, 80-game schedule

MOST ASSISTS BY A CENTER, CAREER: 1,963. Second: 1,040 – Marcel Dionne, 18 seasons

MOST ASSISTS BY A CENTER, ONE SEASON: 163 – 1985-86, 80-game schedule. Second: Gretzky holds first through fifth positions

MOST POINTS BY A CENTER, CAREER: 2,857. Second: 1,771 – Marcel Dionne, 18 seasons

MOST POINTS BY A CENTER, ONE SEASON: 215 – 1985-86, 80-game schedule. Next (fifth): 199 – Mario Lemieux, 1988-89, 80-game schedule

SCORING BY A ROOKIE (1)

MOST ASSISTS, ONE GAME, BY A PLAYER IN HIS FIRST NHL SEASON: 7 – Feb. 15, 1980, at Edmonton (Edmonton 8, Washington 2). Second: 6 – Gary Suter, April 4, 1986 at Calgary (Calgary 9, Edmonton 3)

PER-GAME SCORING AVERAGES (4)

HIGHEST GOALS-PER-GAME AVERAGE, ONE SEASON: 1.18 – 1983-84, 87 goals in 74 games. Second (tied): 1.15 – Mario Lemieux (1992-93, 69 goals in 60 games) and Wayne Gretzky (1981-82, 92 goals in 80 games)

HIGHEST ASSISTS-PER-GAME AVERAGE, CAREER (300 MIN.): 1.321 – 1,963 assists in 1,487 games. Second: 1.183 – Mario Lemieux, 881 assists in 745 games

HIGHEST ASSISTS-PER-GAME AVERAGE, ONE SEASON: 2.04 – 1985-86, 163 assists in 80 games. Next (eighth): 1.52 – Mario Lemieux, 1992-93, 91 assists in 60 games

HIGHEST POINTS-PER-GAME AVERAGE, ONE SEASON (AMONG PLAYERS WITH 50-OR-MORE POINTS): 2.77 – 1983-84, 205 points in 74 games. Next (third): 2.67 – Mario Lemieux, 1992-93, 160 points in 60 games

SCORING PLATEAUS (12)

MOST 40-OR-MORE GOAL SEASONS: 12 in 20 seasons. Second: 10 – Marcel Dionne in 18 seasons

MOST CONSECUTIVE 40-OR-MORE GOAL SEASONS: 12 – 1979-80 to 1990-91. Second: 9 – Mike Bossy, 1977-78 to 1985-86

MOST 50-OR-MORE GOAL SEASONS: 9 (tied with Mike Bossy) – Gretzky in 20 seasons and Bossy in 10 seasons. Second: 6 – Guy Lafleur in 17 seasons

MOST 60-OR-MORE GOAL SEASONS: 5 (tied with Mike Bossy) – Gretzky in 20 seasons and Mike Bossy in 10 seasons. Second: 4 – Phil Esposito in 18 seasons

MOST CONSECUTIVE 60-OR-MORE GOAL SEASONS: 4 – 1981-82 to 1984-85. Second: 3 – Mike Bossy, 1980-81 to 1982-83

MOST 100-OR-MORE POINT SEASONS: 15. Second: 10 – Mario Lemieux in 12 seasons

MOST CONSECUTIVE 100-OR-MORE POINT SEASONS: 13 – 1979-80 to 1991-92. Second: 6 – six players

MOST THREE-OR-MORE GOAL GAMES, CAREER: 50 – 37 three-goal games; nine four-goal games; four five-goal games. Second: 39 – Mike Bossy in 10 seasons (30 three-goal games, nine four-goal games)

MOST THREE-GOAL GAMES, ONE SEASON: 10 (done twice) – 1981-82 (six three-goal games; three four-goal games; one five-goal game) and 1983-84 (six three-goal games, four four-goal games). Next (third): 9 – Mike Bossy (1980-81, six three-goal games, three four-goal games) and Mario Lemieux (seven three-goal games, one four-goal game, one five-goal game)

LONGEST CONSECUTIVE ASSIST-SCORING STREAK: 23 games – 1990-91, 48 assists. Second: 18 – Adam Oates, 1992-93, 28 assists

LONGEST CONSECUTIVE POINT-SCORING STREAK: 51 Games – 1983-84 (Oct. 5, 1983 to Jan. 28, 1984, 61 goals, 92 assists for 153 points). Second: 46 – Mario Lemieux, 1989-90 (39 goals, 64 assists)

LONGEST CONSECUTIVE POINT-SCORING STREAK FROM START OF SEASON: 51 – 1983-84; 61 goals, 92 assists for 153 points (Oct. 5, 1983 to Jan. 28, 1984)

PLAYOFF RECORDS (15)

PLAYOFF GOALS AND ASSISTS (7)

MOST PLAYOFF GOALS, CAREER: 122. Second: 109 – Mark Messier

MOST ASSISTS IN PLAYOFFS, CAREER: 260. Second: 186 – Mark Messier

MOST ASSISTS, ONE PLAYOFF YEAR: 31 – 1988 (19 games). Next (fourth): 28 – Mario Lemieux, 1991 (23 games)

MOST ASSISTS IN ONE SERIES (OTHER THAN FINAL): 14 – (tied with Rick Middleton) 1985 Conference Finals (six games vs. Chicago). Second: 13 – Doug Gilmour, 1994 Conference Semifinals (seven games vs. San Jose) and Wayne Gretzky, 1987 Division Semifinal (five games vs. Los Angeles)

MOST ASSISTS IN FINAL SERIES: 10 – 1988 (four games, plus suspended game vs. Boston). Second: 9 – three players

MOST ASSISTS, ONE PLAYOFF GAME: 6 – (tied with Mikko Leinonen) April 9, 1987 at Edmonton (Edmonton 13, Los Angeles 3). Second: 5 – 11 players

MOST ASSISTS, ONE PLAYOFF PERIOD: 3 — Three assists by one player in one period of a playoff game has been recorded on 70 occasions. Gretzky has had three assists in one period five times. (Ray Bourque, three times; Toe Blake, Jean Beliveau, Doug Harvey and Bobby Orr, twice)

PLAYOFF POINTS (4)

MOST POINTS, CARFFR: 382 – 122 goals and 260 assists. Second: 295 – Mark Messier, 109 goals and 186 assists

MOST POINTS, ONE PLAYOFF YEAR: 47 – 1985 (17 goals and 30 assists in 18 games). Second: 44 – Mario Lernieux, 1991 (16 goals, 28 assists in 23 games)

MOST POINTS IN FINAL SERIES: 13 – 1988 three goals and 10 assists (four games plus suspended game vs. Boston, three goals). Second: 12 – four players

MOST POINTS, ONE PLAYOFF PERIOD: 4 – (tied with nine other players) April 12, 1987 at Los Angeles, third period, one goal, three assists (Edmonton 6, Los Angeles 3)

PLAYOFF SHORTHANDED GOALS (2)

MOST SHORTHANDED GOALS, ONE PLAYOFF YEAR: 3 – (tied with five other players) 1983 (two vs. Winnipeg in Division Semifinals, won by Edmonton, 3-0; one vs. Calgary in Division Finals, won by Edmonton 4-1)

MOST SHORTHANDED GOALS, ONE PLAYOFF GAME: 2 – (tied with eight other players) April 6, 1983 at Edmonton (Edmonton 6, Winnipeg 3)

PLAYOFF GAME-WINNING GOALS (1)

MOST GAME-WINNING GOALS IN PLAYOFFS, CAREER: 24. Second: 19 – Claude Lemieux

PLAYOFF THREE-OR-MORE GOAL GAMES (1)

MOST THREE-OR-MORE GOAL GAMES: 10 (eight three-goal games, two four-goal games). Second (tied): 7 – Maurice Richard (four three-goal games, two four-goal games, one five-goal game) and Jari Kurri (six three-goal games, one four-goal game)

Wayne, Walter and Glenn Gretzky, May 19, 1984. Gretzky would win four Stanley Cup titles as an Edmonton Oiler in the 1980s. He was the NHL's top playoff scorer in each of the four championship seasons and won the Conn Smythe Trophy as playoff MVP in 1985 and 1988.

NHL ALL-STAR GAME RECORDS (6)

NHL ALL-STAR GAME GOALS (3)

MOST ALL-STAR GAME GOALS: 13 (in 17 games played). Second: 11 – Mario Lemieux (in eight games played)

MOST ALL-STAR GAME GOALS, ONE GAME: 4 (tied with three players) –1983 Campbell Conference

MOST ALL-STAR GAME GOALS, ONE PERIOD: 4 – 1983 Campbell Conference, third period

NHL ALL-STAR GAME ASSISTS (1)

MOST ALL-STAR GAME ASSISTS, CAREER: 12 – (tied with four players). Second: 10 – Paul Coffey (in 14 games played)

NHL ALL-STAR GAME POINTS (2)

MOST ALL-STAR GAME POINTS, CAREER: 25 – (13 goals, 12 assists in 17 games). Second: 22 – Mario Lemieux (11 goals, nine assists in eight games played)

MOST ALL-STAR GAME POINTS, ONE PERIOD: 4 – (tied with Mike Gartner and Adam Oates) 1983 Campbell Conference, third period (four goals)

WAYNE GRETZKY'S SEASON-BY-SEASON CAREER STATISTICS

WAYNE DOUGLAS "THE GREAT ONE" GRETZKY

(GREHTS-KEE)

Center. Shoots left. 6' 185 lbs. Born, Brantford, Ontario, January 26, 1961

Season	Club	League	GP	G	A	Pts	PIM	GP	G	A	PTS	PIM
1967-68	Brantford Nadrofsky Steelers	OMHA	....	1	....	....	....	....	....	....	....	....
1968-69	Brantford Nadrofsky Steelers	OMHA	....	27	....	....	....	....	....	....	....	....
1969-70	Brantford Nadrofsky Steelers	OMHA	62	104	63	167	....	....	....	....	....	....
1970-71	Brantford Nadrofsky Steelers	OMHA	76	196	120	316	....	....	....	....	....	....
1971-72	Brantford Nadrofsky Steelers	OMHA	85	378	139	517	....	....	....	....	....	....
1972-73	Brantford Turkstra Lumber	OMHA	....	105	....	....	....	....	....	....	....	....
1973-74	Brantford Turkstra Lumber	OMHA	....	192	....	....	....	....	....	....	....	....
1974-75	Brantford Charcon Chargers	OMHA	....	90	....	....	....	....	....	....	....	....
1975-76	Vaughan Nationals	OHA Jr. B	28	27	33	60	7	....	....	....	....	....
1976-77	Seneca Nationals	OHA Jr. B	32	36	36	72	35	23	40	35	75	....
	Peterborough Petes	OHA Jr. A	3	0	3	3	0	....	....	....	....	....
1977-78	Sault Ste. Marie Greyhounds	OHA Jr. A	64	70	112	182	14	13	6	20	26	0
	Team Canada	World-Jr.	8	8	9	17	2	....	....	....	....	....
1978-79	Indianapolis Racers	WHA	8	3	3	6	0	....	....	....	....	....
	Edmonton Oilers	WHA	72	43	61	104	19	13	*10	10	*20	2
1979-80	**Edmonton Oilers**	**NHL**	79	51	*86	*137	21	3	2	1	3	0
1980-81	**Edmonton Oilers**	**NHL**	80	55	*109	*164	28	9	7	14	21	4
1981-82	Team Canada	Can-Cup	7	5	7	12	2	....	....	....	....	....
	Edmonton Oilers	**NHL**	80	*92	*120	*212	26	5	5	7	12	8
	Team Canada	WEC-A	10	6	8	*14	0	....	....	....	....	....
1982-83	**Edmonton Oilers**	**NHL**	80	*71	*125	*196	59	16	12	*26	*38	4
1983-84	**Edmonton Oilers**	**NHL**	74	*87	*118	*205	39	19	13	*22	*35	12
1984-85	Team Canada	Can-Cup	8	5	7	12	2	....	....	....	....	....
	Edmonton Oilers	**NHL**	80	*73	*135	*208	52	18	17	*30	*47	4
1985-86	**Edmonton Oilers**	**NHL**	80	52	*163	*215	42	10	8	11	19	2
1986-87	**Edmonton Oilers**	**NHL**	79	*62	*121	*183	28	21	5	*29	*34	6
	NHL All-Stars	RV-87	2	0	4	4	0	....	....	....	....	....
1987-88	Team Canada	Can-Cup	9	3	*18	*21	2	....	....	....	....	....
	Edmonton Oilers	**NHL**	64	40	*109	149	24	19	12	*31	*43	16
1988-89	**Los Angeles Kings**	**NHL**	78	54	*114	168	26	11	5	17	22	0
1989-90	**Los Angeles Kings**	**NHL**	73	40	*102	*142	42	7	3	7	10	0
1990-91	**Los Angeles Kings**	**NHL**	78	41	*122	*163	16	12	4	11	15	2
1991-92	Team Canada	Can-Cup	7	4	8	12	2	....	....	....	....	....
	Los Angeles Kings	**NHL**	74	31	*90	121	34	6	2	5	7	2
1992-93	**Los Angeles Kings**	**NHL**	45	16	49	65	6	24	*15	*25	*40	4
1993-94	**Los Angeles Kings**	**NHL**	81	38	*92	*130	20	....	....	....	....	....
1994-95	**Los Angeles Kings**	**NHL**	48	11	37	48	6	....	....	....	....	....
1995-96	**Los Angeles Kings**	**NHL**	62	15	66	81	32	....	....	....	....	....
	St. Louis Blues	**NHL**	18	8	13	21	2	13	2	14	16	0
1996-97	Team Canada	W-Cup	6	3	4	7	2	....	....	....	....	....
	New York Rangers	**NHL**	82	25	*72	97	28	15	10	10	20	2
1997-98	**New York Rangers**	**NHL**	82	23	*67	90	28	....	....	....	....	....
	Team Canada	Olympics	6	0	4	4	2	....	....	....	....	....
1998-99	**New York Rangers**	**NHL**	70	9	53	62	14	....	....	....	....	....
NHL Totals	**20 seasons**	**NHL**	1487	*894	*1963	*2857	577	208	*122	*260	*382	66
WHA Totals	1 season	WHA	80	46	64	110	19	13	10	10	20	2
NHL/WHA Totals	**21 seasons**		1567	940	*2027	*2967	596	221	*132	*270	*402	68

* indicates League leader

HONOR ROLL

WJC All-Star Team (1978) • Best Forward WJC (1978) • OHA 2nd All-Star Team (1978) • WHA Second All-Star Team (1979) • Won Lou Kaplan Trophy (WHA Rookie-of-the-Year) (1979) • Won Hart Trophy (1980, 1981, 1982, 1983, 1984, 1985, 1986, 1987, 1989) • Won Lady Byng Trophy (1980, 1991, 1992, 1994, 1999) • NHL Second All-Star Team (1980, 1988, 1989, 1990, 1994, 1997, 1998) • NHL First All-Star Team (1981, 1982, 1983, 1984, 1985, 1986, 1987, 1991) • Won Art Ross Trophy (1981, 1982, 1983, 1984, 1985, 1986, 1987, 1990, 1991, 1994) • Won Lester B. Pearson Award (1982, 1983, 1984, 1985, 1987) • WEC-A All-Star Team (1982) • Canada Cup All-Star Team (1984, 1987, 1991) • Won Conn Smythe Trophy (1985, 1988) • NHL Plus/Minus Leader (1982, 1984, 1985, 1987) • Won Lester Patrick Award (1994).

TRANSACTIONS AND MILESTONES

Sault Ste. Marie Greyhounds (OHA Jr. A) 1st choice, 3rd overall, in 1977 OHA Jr. A Priority Draft. • Signed as an underage free agent by **Indianapolis Racers** (WHA), June 12, 1978. • Traded to **Edmonton Oilers** (WHA) by **Indianapolis Racers** (WHA) with Eddie Mio and Peter Driscoll for cash, November 2, 1978. • Claimed by **Edmonton Oilers** as a Priority Selection in 1979 Expansion Draft, June 9, 1979. • Recorded point #153 of season vs. Pittsburgh to become NHL's single season points leader, March 29, 1981. • Scored goal #50 of season vs. Philadelphia in only 39 games to establish new NHL record for fastest 50 goals, December 30, 1981. • Scored goal #77 of season vs. Buffalo to become NHL's all-time leading single-season scorer, February 24, 1982. • Traded to **Los Angeles Kings** by **Edmonton Oilers** with Mike Krushelnyski and Marty McSorley for Jimmy Carson, Martin Gelinas, Los Angeles Kings' 1st round choice in 1989 (later acquired by New Jersey, who selected Jason Miller), 1991 (Martin Rucinsky) and 1993 (Nick Stajduhar) Entry Drafts and cash, August 9, 1988. • Recorded career point #1851 vs. Edmonton to become NHL's all-time leading scorer, October 15, 1989. • Scored career goal #802 vs. Vancouver to become NHL's all-time leading goal scorer, March 23, 1994. • Traded to **St. Louis** by **Los Angeles Kings** for Craig Johnson, Patrice Tardif, Roman Vopat, St. Louis' 5th round choice (Peter Hogan) in 1996 Entry Draft and 1st round choice (Matt Zultek) in 1997 Entry Draft, February 27, 1996. • Signed as a free agent by **New York Rangers**, July 21, 1996. • Officially announced retirement, April 16, 1999. • Recorded point #2857 of career vs. Pittsburgh, April 18, 1999.

Mighty Ducks of Anaheim

1998-99 Results: 35w-34L-13T 83PTS. Third, Pacific Division

Year-by-Year Record

Season	GP	Home W	L	T	Road W	L	T	Overall W	L	T	GF	GA	Pts.	Finished	Playoff Result
1998-99	82	21	14	6	14	20	7	35	34	13	215	206	83	3rd, Pacific Div.	Lost Conf. Quarter-Final
1997-98	82	12	23	6	14	20	7	26	43	13	205	261	65	6th, Pacific Div.	Out of Playoffs
1996-97	82	23	12	6	13	21	7	36	33	13	245	233	85	2nd, Pacific Div.	Lost Conf. Semi-Final
1995-96	82	22	15	4	13	24	4	35	39	8	234	247	78	4th, Pacific Div.	Out of Playoffs
1994-95	48	11	9	4	5	18	1	16	27	5	125	164	37	6th, Pacific Div.	Out of Playoffs
1993-94	84	14	26	2	19	20	3	33	46	5	229	251	71	4th, Pacific Div.	Out of Playoffs

1999-2000 Schedule

Oct.	Sat.	2	at Dallas
	Tue.	5	at Phoenix
	Fri.	8	Dallas
	Mon.	11	San Jose*
	Wed.	13	at New Jersey
	Fri.	15	at Tampa Bay
	Sat.	16	at Florida
	Tue.	19	at Washington
	Thu.	21	at Chicago
	Sun.	24	Boston
	Wed.	27	Pittsburgh
	Fri.	29	Washington
	Sun.	31	Phoenix
Nov.	Wed.	3	Philadelphia
	Sun.	7	Edmonton
	Tue.	9	at Toronto
	Thu.	11	at Montreal
	Sat.	13	at Ottawa
	Mon.	15	at Detroit
	Wed.	17	Calgary
	Fri.	19	Chicago
	Mon.	22	Montreal
	Wed.	24	New Jersey
	Fri.	26	at Dallas*
	Sat.	27	at Nashville
Dec.	Wed.	1	Tampa Bay
	Fri.	3	Los Angeles
	Sat.	4	at Phoenix
	Wed.	8	Vancouver
	Fri.	10	Colorado
	Sun.	12	Atlanta
	Wed.	15	at Colorado
	Fri.	17	Chicago
	Sun.	19	Detroit
	Wed.	22	Phoenix
	Sun.	26	at San Jose*
	Mon.	27	at Edmonton
	Wed.	29	at Calgary
	Fri.	31	at Dallas
Jan.	Wed.	5	Florida
	Fri.	7	at Carolina

	Sat.	8	at Detroit
	Wed.	12	Ottawa
	Fri.	14	St. Louis
	Sat.	15	at Phoenix
	Mon.	17	Buffalo
	Wed.	19	Dallas
	Fri.	21	Colorado
	Sat.	22	at San Jose
	Wed.	26	NY Islanders
	Sat.	29	at Pittsburgh
	Mon.	31	at Boston
Feb.	Tue.	1	at Buffalo
	Thu.	3	at Philadelphia
	Tue.	8	at Los Angeles
	Wed.	9	Dallas
	Sat.	12	at St. Louis
	Mon.	14	at Chicago
	Wed.	16	Calgary
	Fri.	18	San Jose
	Mon.	21	St. Louis
	Wed.	23	Vancouver
	Sun.	27	Edmonton
	Tue.	29	at San Jose
Mar.	Thu.	2	at Vancouver
	Fri.	3	at Calgary
	Sun.	5	Nashville
	Wed.	8	NY Rangers
	Sat.	11	at St. Louis*
	Tue.	14	at Colorado
	Wed.	15	Los Angeles
	Fri.	17	San Jose
	Sun.	19	Detroit
	Tue.	21	at Los Angeles
	Wed.	22	at Edmonton
	Fri.	24	at Vancouver
	Sun.	26	Phoenix
Apr.	Sat.	1	at Los Angeles*
	Mon.	3	Nashville
	Wed.	5	at Chicago
	Fri.	7	at Nashville
	Sun.	9	Los Angeles*

* Denotes afternoon game.

Franchise date: June 15, 1993

PACIFIC DIVISION

7th NHL Season

Matt Cullen (left) and Marty McInnis celebrate a goal against the Vancouver Canucks. As a first-year player in 1997-98, Cullen's 27 points trailed only Paul Kariya among all-time Anaheim rookies.

1999-2000 Player Personnel

FORWARDS	HT	WT	S	Place of Birth	Date	1998-99 Club
AALTO, Antti	6-2	210	L	Lappeenranta, Finland	3/4/75	Anaheim
BALMOCHNYKH, Maxim	6-0	185	L	Lipetsk, USSR	3/7/79	Quebec (QMJHL)-Lada Togliatti
BANHAM, Frank	6-0	190	R	Calahoo, Alta.	4/14/75	Cincinnati (AHL)
CHOUINARD, Marc	6-5	200	R	Charlesbourg, Ont.	5/6/77	New Orleans-Cincinnati (AHL)
CULLEN, Matt	6-1	195	L	Virginia, MN	11/2/76	Anaheim-Cincinnati (AHL)
DAVIDSSON, Johan	6-1	190	R	Jonkoping, Sweden	1/6/76	Anaheim-Cincinnati (AHL)
DIROBERTO, Torrey	5-11	180	L	New York, NY	4/17/78	Seattle
DONATO, Ted	5-10	181	L	Boston, MA	4/28/69	Boston-NY Islanders-Ottawa
DRURY, Ted	6-0	208	L	Boston, MA	9/13/71	Anaheim
GRIMSON, Stu	6-5	227	L	Kamloops, B.C.	5/20/65	Anaheim
KARIYA, Paul	5-11	180	L	Vancouver, B.C.	10/16/74	Anaheim
LeBOUTILLIER, Peter	6-1	205	R	Minnedosa, Man.	1/11/75	Cincinnati (AHL)
LECLERC, Mike	6-1	205	L	Winnipeg, Man.	11/10/76	Anaheim-Cincinnati (AHL)
McINNIS, Marty	5-11	190	R	Weymouth, MA.	6/2/70	Calgary-Anaheim
McKENZIE, Jim	6-3	229	L	Gull Lake, Sask.	11/3/69	Anaheim
NIELSEN, Jeff	6-0	200	L	Grand Rapids, MN	9/20/71	Anaheim
RUCCHIN, Steve	6-3	215	L	Thunder Bay, Ont.	7/4/71	Anaheim
SELANNE, Teemu	6-0	200	R	Helsinki, Finland	7/3/70	Anaheim
STEVENSON, Jeremy	6-2	220	L	San Bernadino, CA	7/28/74	Cincinnati (AHL)
TUZZOLINO, Tony	6-2	208	R	Buffalo, NY	10/9/75	Cincinnati (AHL)-Cleveland
WREN, Bob	5-10	185	L	Preston, Ont.	9/16/74	Cincinnati (AHL)

DEFENSEMEN	HT	WT	S	Place of Birth	Date	1998-99 Club
FERGUSON, Scott	6-1	195	L	Camrose, Alta.	1/6/73	Anaheim-Cincinnati (AHL)
HALLER, Kevin	6-2	195	L	Trochu, Alta.	12/5/70	Anaheim
HAVELID, Niclas	5-11	200	L	Enkoping, Sweden	4/12/73	Malmo
MARSHALL, Jason	6-2	200	R	Cranbrook, B.C.	2/22/71	Anaheim
OLAUSSON, Fredrik	6-2	198	R	Dadesjo, Sweden	10/5/66	Anaheim
SALEI, Ruslan	6-2	205	L	Minsk, USSR	11/2/74	Anaheim
SHAW, Lloyd	6-3	220	L	Regina, Sask.	9/26/76	Cincinnati (AHL)-Huntington
TREBIL, Daniel	6-3	210	R	Bloomington, MN	4/10/74	Anaheim-Cincinnati (AHL)
TREPANIER, Pascal	6-0	205	R	Gaspe, Que.	9/4/73	Anaheim
TRNKA, Pavel	6-3	200	L	Plzen, Czech.	7/27/76	Anaheim
TVERDOVSKY, Oleg	6-0	195	L	Donetsk, USSR	5/18/76	Phoenix
VISHNEVSKI, Vitaly	6-1	190	L	Kharkov, USSR	3/18/80	Yaroslavl

GOALTENDERS	HT	WT	C	Place of Birth	Date	1998-99 Club
ASKEY, Tom	6-2	185	L	Kenmore, NY	10/4/74	Anaheim-Cincinnati (AHL)
HEBERT, Guy	5-11	185	L	Troy, NY	1/7/67	Anaheim
NAUMENKO, Gregg	6-0	195	L	Chicago, IL	3/30/77	Alaska-Anchorage
ROUSSEL, Dominic	6-1	191	L	Hull, Que.	2/22/70	Anaheim
RUSSELL, Blaine	5-11	180	L	Wetaskawin, Sask.	1/11/77	Huntington

1998-99 Scoring

*– rookie

Regular Season

Pos	#	Player	Team	GP	G	A	Pts	+/–	PIM	PP	SH	GW	GT	S	%
R	8	Teemu Selanne	ANA	75	47	60	107	18	30	25	0	7	1	281	16.7
L	9	Paul Kariya	ANA	82	39	62	101	17	40	11	2	4	0	429	9.1
C	20	Steve Rucchin	ANA	69	23	39	62	11	22	5	1	5	1	145	15.9
D	2	Fredrik Olausson	ANA	74	16	40	56	17	30	10	0	2	0	121	13.2
L	16	Marty McInnis	CGY	6	1	1	2	–1	6	0	0	0	7	14.3
			ANA	75	18	34	52	–14	36	11	1	5	0	139	12.9
			TOTAL	81	19	35	54	–15	42	11	1	5	0	146	13.0
R	17	Tomas Sandstrom	ANA	58	15	17	32	–5	42	7	0	2	0	107	14.0
C	39	Travis Green	ANA	79	13	17	30	–7	81	3	1	2	0	165	7.9
C	11	Matt Cullen	ANA	75	11	14	25	–12	47	5	1	1	1	112	9.8
D	24	Ruslan Salei	ANA	74	2	14	16	1	65	1	0	0	0	123	1.6
C	18	Ted Drury	ANA	75	5	6	11	2	83	0	0	0	0	79	6.3
L	33	Jim McKenzie	ANA	73	5	4	9	–18	99	1	0	1	0	59	8.5
R	19	Jeff Nielsen	ANA	80	5	4	9	–12	34	0	0	2	0	94	5.3
C	22	* Johan Davidsson	ANA	64	3	5	8	–9	14	1	0	1	0	48	6.3
C	14	* Antti Aalto	ANA	73	3	5	8	–12	24	2	0	0	0	61	4.9
D	23	Jason Marshall	ANA	72	1	7	8	–5	142	0	0	0	0	63	1.6
D	5	Kevin Haller	ANA	82	1	6	7	–1	122	0	0	0	0	64	1.6
D	27	* Pascal Trepanier	ANA	45	2	4	6	0	48	0	0	1	0	49	4.1
D	25	* Mike Crowley	ANA	20	2	3	5	–10	16	1	0	1	0	41	4.9
D	7	Pavel Trnka	ANA	63	0	4	4	–6	60	0	0	0	0	50	0.0
L	32	Stu Grimson	ANA	73	3	0	3	0	158	0	0	1	0	10	30.0
D	4	Jamie Pushor	ANA	70	1	2	3	–20	112	0	0	0	0	75	1.3
D	21	* Scott Ferguson	ANA	2	0	1	1	0	0	0	0	0	0	1	0.0
G	31	Guy Hebert	ANA	69	0	1	1	0	0	0	0	0	0	0	0.0
D	34	Daniel Trebil	ANA	6	0	0	0	–2	0	0	0	0	0	1	0.0
L	12	* Mike Leclerc	ANA	7	0	0	0	–2	4	0	0	0	0	1	0.0
G	30	Dominic Roussel	ANA	18	0	0	0	0	0	0	0	0	0	0	0.0

Goaltending

No.	Goaltender	GPI	Mins	Avg	W	L	T	EN	SO	GA	SA	S%
31	Guy Hebert	69	4083	2.42	31	29	9	3	6	165	2114	.922
30	Dominic Roussel	18	884	2.51	4	5	4	1	1	37	478	.923
	Totals	**82**	**4990**	**2.48**	**35**	**34**	**13**	**4**	**7**	**206**	**2596**	**.921**

Playoffs

Pos	#	Player	Team	GP	G	A	Pts	+/–	PIM	PP	SH	GW	OT	S	%
R	8	Teemu Selanne	ANA	4	2	2	4	–1	2	1	0	0	0	7	28.6
L	9	Paul Kariya	ANA	3	1	3	4	0	0	0	0	0	0	11	9.1
C	20	Steve Rucchin	ANA	4	0	3	3	0	0	0	0	0	0	10	0.0
L	16	Marty McInnis	ANA	4	2	0	2	–1	2	2	0	0	0	12	16.7
D	2	Fredrik Olausson	ANA	4	0	2	2	–4	4	0	0	0	0	6	0.0
D	23	Jason Marshall	ANA	4	1	0	1	–1	10	1	0	0	0	5	20.0
C	39	Travis Green	ANA	4	0	1	1	–4	4	0	0	0	0	12	0.0
D	7	Pavel Trnka	ANA	4	0	1	1	–3	2	0	0	0	0	2	0.0
D	34	Daniel Trebil	ANA	1	0	0	0	0	2	0	0	0	0	0	0.0
G	35	* Tom Askey	ANA	1	0	0	0	0	0	0	0	0	0	0	0.0
C	22	* Johan Davidsson	ANA	1	0	0	0	0	0	0	0	0	0	1	0.0
L	12	* Mike Leclerc	ANA	1	0	0	0	0	0	0	0	0	0	1	0.0
L	32	Stu Grimson	ANA	3	0	0	0	0	30	0	0	0	0	0	0.0
D	24	Ruslan Salei	ANA	3	0	0	0	–4	4	0	0	0	0	5	0.0
D	5	Kevin Haller	ANA	4	0	0	0	–1	2	0	0	0	0	7	0.0
G	31	Guy Hebert	ANA	4	0	0	0	0	0	0	0	0	0	0	0.0
L	33	Jim McKenzie	ANA	4	0	0	0	–2	4	0	0	0	0	5	0.0
R	17	Tomas Sandstrom	ANA	4	0	0	0	–2	4	0	0	0	0	9	0.0
C	18	Ted Drury	ANA	4	0	0	0	–6	0	0	0	0	0	4	0.0
R	19	Jeff Nielsen	ANA	4	0	0	0	–6	2	0	0	0	0	7	0.0
D	4	Jamie Pushor	ANA	4	0	0	0	–3	6	0	0	0	0	6	0.0
C	14	* Antti Aalto	ANA	4	0	0	0	0	2	0	0	0	0	6	0.0
C	11	Matt Cullen	ANA	4	0	0	0	–2	0	0	0	0	0	6	0.0

Goaltending

No.	Goaltender	GPI	Mins	Avg	W	L	EN	SO	GA	SA	S%
35	* Tom Askey	1	30	4.00	0	1	0	0	2	11	.818
31	Guy Hebert	4	208	4.33	0	3	0	0	15	124	.879
	Totals	**4**	**240**	**4.25**	**0**	**4**	**0**	**0**	**17**	**135**	**.874**

President and General Manager

GAUTHIER, PIERRE
President and General Manager, Mighty Ducks of Anaheim.
Born in Montreal, Que., May 28, 1953.

Following his resignation from the Ottawa Senators in June, Pierre Gauthier returned to the Mighty Ducks of Anaheim on July 16, 1998 when he was named club president. Three weeks later, on August 6, Gauthier succeeded Jack Ferreira as the second general manager in franchise history.

Gauthier returns to the Mighty Ducks after spending two-and-a-half seasons as general manager in Ottawa. The Senators qualified for the Stanley Cup Playoffs in each of Gauthier's two full seasons, reaching the postseason for the first time in 1997 and advancing to the second round in May of 1998. Gauthier served as assistant general manager of the Mighty Ducks from 1993 to 1995 before joining the Senators. He was a key part of management in starting up the Anaheim franchise in 1993.

Prior to his first stint with the Mighty Ducks, Gauthier had spent 12 seasons in the scouting department with the Quebec Nordiques. He had joined the club as a scout in 1983 and worked in that capacity for three seasons before being named assistant director of scouting in 1986. Gauthier was promoted to chief scout in 1988, serving at that capacity until he joined Anaheim in 1993.

Gauthier received a master's degree in sports administration in 1983 from the University of Minnesota, where he also served as a teaching associate in physical education. He is also a graduate of Syracuse University, where he earned a bachelor of science degree in physical education.

A native of Montreal, Gauthier and his wife, Manon Roberge, have a daughter, Catherine, and a son Vincent. The family resides in Irvine, California.

Club Records

Team

(Figures in brackets for season records are games played; records for fewest points, wins, ties, losses, goals, goals against are for 70 or more games)

Most Points 85   1996-97 (82)
Most Wins 36   1996-97 (82)
Most Ties 13   1996-97 (82); 1997-98 (82); 1998-99 (82)
Most Losses 46   1993-94 (84)
Most Goals 245   1996-97 (82)
Most Goals Against 261   1997-98 (82)
Fewest Points 65   1997-98 (82)
Fewest Wins 26   1997-98 (82)
Fewest Ties 5   1993-94 (84)
Fewest Losses 33   1996-97 (82)
Fewest Goals 205   1997-98 (82)
Fewest Goals Against 206   1998-99 (82)

Longest Winning Streak
Overall 7   Feb. 20-Mar. 7/99
Home 5   Twice
Away 4   Twice

Longest Undefeated Streak
Overall 12   Feb. 22-Mar. 19/97 (7 wins, 5 ties)
Home 14   Feb. 12-Apr. 9/97 (10 wins, 4 ties)
Away 5   Three times

Longest Losing Streak
Overall 8   Oct. 12-30/96
Home 6   Feb. 7-Mar. 11/98
Away 6   Four times

Longest Winless Streak
Overall 9   Twice
Home 6   Feb. 7-Mar. 11/98 (6 losses)
Away 10   Mar. 26-Oct. 11/95 (9 losses, 1 tie)

Most Shutouts, Season 7   1998-99 (82)
Most PIM, Season 1,843   1997-98 (82)
Most Goals, Game 8   Jan. 21/98 (Ana. 8, Fla. 3)

Individual

Most Seasons 6   Guy Hebert
Most Games 333   Joe Sacco
Most Goals, Career 168   Paul Kariya
Most Assists, Career 210   Paul Kariya
Most Points, Career 378   Paul Kariya (168G, 210A)
Most PIM, Career 788   Dave Karpa
Most Shutouts, Career 21   Guy Hebert

Longest Consecutive
Games Streak 159   Bobby Dollas (Oct. 9/95-Mar. 30/97)
Most Goals, Season 52   Teemu Selanne (1997-98)
Most Assists, Season 62   Paul Kariya (1998-99)

Most Points, Season 109   Teemu Selanne (1996-97; 51G, 58A)
Most PIM, Season 285   Todd Ewen (1995-96)

Most Points, Defenseman,
Season 56   Fredrik Olausson (1998-99; 16G, 40A)

Most Points, Center,
Season 67   Steve Rucchin (1996-97; 19G, 48A)

Most Points, Right Wing,
Season 109   Teemu Selanne (1996-97; 51G, 58A)

Most Points, Left Wing,
Season 108   Paul Kariya (1995-96; 50G, 58A)

Most Points, Rookie,
Season 39   Paul Kariya (1994-95; 18G, 21A)

Most Shutouts, Season 6   Guy Hebert (1998-99)

Most Goals, Game 3   Twelve times
Most Assists, Game 5   Dmitri Mironov (Dec. 12/97)

Most Points, Game 5   Five times

General Managers' History

Jack Ferreira, 1993-94 to 1997-98; Pierre Gauthier, 1998-99 to date.

Coaching History

Ron Wilson, 1993-94 to 1996-97; Pierre Page, 1997-98; Craig Hartsburg, 1998-99 to date.

Captains' History

Troy Loney, 1993-94; Randy Ladouceur, 1994-95, 1995-96; Paul Kariya, 1996-97; Paul Kariya and Teemu Selanne, 1997-98; Paul Kariya, 1998-99 to date.

All-time Record vs. Other Clubs

Regular Season

	At Home						On Road						Total					
	GP	W	L	T	GF	GA	PTS	GP	W	L	T	GF	GA	PTS	GP	W	L	T	GF	GA	PTS
Boston	5	2	1	9	12	5	5	2	3	0	14	16	4	10	4	5	1	23	28	9
Buffalo	5	2	3	0	12	13	4	5	2	1	14	12	5	10	4	5	1	26	25	9
Calgary	16	6	7	3	47	41	15	15	6	9	0	36	44	12	31	12	16	3	83	85	27
Carolina	5	3	2	0	21	17	6	5	1	4	0	8	14	2	10	4	6	0	29	31	8
Chicago	12	5	6	1	28	30	11	13	5	7	1	25	34	11	25	10	13	2	53	64	22
Colorado	11	4	5	2	28	26	10	11	3	6	2	33	42	8	22	7	11	4	61	68	18
Dallas	14	6	8	0	33	38	12	13	1	11	1	22	57	3	27	7	19	1	55	95	15
Detroit	12	3	7	2	26	42	8	12	1	8	3	30	47	5	24	4	15	5	56	89	13
Edmonton	16	10	5	1	50	44	21	15	8	7	0	35	28	16	31	18	12	1	85	72	37
Florida	5	2	3	0	18	17	4	4	1	2	1	11	10	4	9	3	4	2	29	27	8
Los Angeles	16	9	4	3	55	39	21	17	6	9	2	43	49	14	33	15	13	5	98	88	35
Montreal	4	1	3	0	15	17	2	5	2	2	1	15	17	5	9	3	5	1	30	34	7
Nashville	2	2	0	0	9	3	4	2	0	2	0	5	0	4	4	2	2	0	11	8	4
New Jersey	5	3	2	0	17	12	6	5	1	4	0	8	21	2	10	4	6	0	25	33	8
NY Islanders	5	1	2	2	11	14	4	5	2	1	1	15	12	5	10	3	3	4	26	26	9
NY Rangers	5	5	0	0	21	11	10	5	2	2	1	14	14	5	10	7	2	1	35	25	15
Ottawa	5	3	0	2	16	7	8	5	3	1	1	15	13	7	10	6	1	3	31	20	15
Philadelphia	5	2	1	2	18	17	5	5	1	2	2	9	14	4	10	3	4	3	27	31	9
Phoenix	13	9	3	1	42	28	19	13	6	6	1	44	45	13	26	15	9	2	86	73	32
Pittsburgh	5	2	3	0	18	21	4	5	0	3	2	13	21	2	10	2	6	2	31	42	6
St. Louis	12	3	8	1	30	38	7	12	5	5	2	38	40	12	24	8	13	3	68	78	19
San Jose	17	6	10	1	45	59	13	16	8	6	2	51	48	18	33	14	16	3	96	107	31
Tampa Bay	5	3	1	1	17	12	7	5	3	2	0	16	10	6	10	6	3	1	33	22	13
Toronto	10	4	5	1	29	27	9	11	1	6	4	23	36	6	21	5	11	5	52	63	15
Vancouver	15	4	7	4	38	48	12	16	6	10	0	42	56	12	31	10	17	4	80	104	24
Washington	5	3	1	1	16	15	7	5	2	3	0	8	9	4	10	5	4	1	24	24	11
Totals	**230**	**103**	**99**	**28**	**669**	**648**	**234**	**230**	**78**	**123**	**29**	**584**	**714**	**185**	**460**	**181**	**222**	**57**	**1253**	**1362**	**419**

Playoffs

	Series	W	L	GP	W	L	T	GF	GA	Last Mtg.	Round	Result
Detroit	2	0	2	8	0	8	0	14	30	1999	CQF	L 0-4
Phoenix	1	1	0	7	4	3	0	17	17	1997	CQF	W 4-3
Totals	3	1	2	15	4	11	0	31	47			

Carolina totals include Hartford, 1993-94 to 1996-97.
Colorado totals include Quebec, 1993-94 to 1994-95.
Phoenix totals include Winnipeg, 1993-94 to 1995-96.

Playoff Results 1999-95

Year	Round	Opponent	Result	GF	GA
1999	CQF	Detroit	L 0-4	6	17
1997	CSF	Detroit	L 0-4	8	13
	CQF	Phoenix	W 4-3	17	17

Abbreviations: Round: CSF – conference semi-final; CQF – conference quarter-final

1998-99 Results

Oct.	10	at	Washington	0-1		15		Dallas	1-3
	11	at	Philadelphia	1-4		18		Pittsburgh	5-3
	13	at	Montreal	0-1		20		New Jersey	3-4
	15	at	Chicago	5-3		21	at	Phoenix	3-3
	21		Boston	3-0		27		Colorado	3-4
	25		Phoenix	2-2		28	at	Colorado	2-6
	28		Tampa Bay	5-3		30	at	Edmonton	0-1
	30	at	Dallas	3-3	Feb.	3		Chicago	3-0
	31	at	St. Louis	2-2		5	at	Tampa Bay	5-3
Nov.	4		St. Louis	1-3		6	at	St. Louis	4-3
	6		San Jose	2-2		10		Philadelphia	5-4
	8		Detroit	2-3		12		Dallas	2-3
	11		Carolina	5-4		14	at	Phoenix	5-1
	13	at	Vancouver	2-5		15	at	Los Angeles	3-1
	14	at	Calgary	1-0		17		Edmonton	2-6
	16		Los Angeles	3-1		19	at	Calgary	3-6
	18		NY Rangers	3-1		20	at	Vancouver	5-1
	20		Edmonton	2-3		24	at	Edmonton	3-1
	22		Chicago	4-1		26		San Jose	3-1
	25	at	Detroit	2-5		27	at	San Jose	4-1
	27	at	Nashville	1-3	Mar.	3		Los Angeles	2-1
	29	at	Carolina	1-3		5		Nashville	3-2
Dec.	1	at	Pittsburgh	4-4		7		Detroit	3-1
	3	at	Chicago	1-4		10		Vancouver	4-4
	6	at	San Jose	2-1		12	at	Dallas	0-4
	9		Vancouver	4-4		13	at	Phoenix	0-1
	11		Washington	1-0		17		Ottawa	2-2
	13		Los Angeles	3-0		18	at	Los Angeles	4-2
	16		Nashville	6-1		21		Florida	2-5
	18		NY Islanders	2-2		26		Dallas	5-1
	21		Colorado	2-4		28		Calgary	5-1
	22	at	Colorado	1-0		31	at	New Jersey	1-7
	28	at	Ottawa	2-2	Apr.	2	at	NY Rangers	4-1
	30	at	Toronto	1-4		3	at	NY Islanders	2-2
Jan.	1	at	Buffalo	7-2		5	at	Detroit	2-3
	2	at	Boston	1-2		7	at	Dallas	1-5
	4	at	Nashville	1-2		9		San Jose	1-4
	6		Buffalo	2-3		11		Phoenix	3-0
	8		Phoenix	4-1		14		St. Louis	1-3
	10		Edmonton	6-4		15	at	Los Angeles	3-4
	13		Calgary	1-2		17	at	San Jose	3-3

Entry Draft
Selections 1999-93

1999 Pick		1997 Pick		1995 Pick		1993 Pick	
44	Jordan Leopold	18	Mikael Holmqvist	4	Chad Kilger	4	Paul Kariya
83	Niclas Havelid	45	Maxim Balmochnykh	29	Brian Wesenberg	30	Nikolai Tsulygin
105	Alexandr Chagodayev	72	Jay Legault	55	Mike Leclerc	56	Valeri Karpov
141	Maxim Rybin	125	Luc Vaillancourt	107	Igor Nikulin	82	Joel Gagnon
173	Jan Sandstrom	178	Tony Mohagen	133	Peter Leboutillier	108	Mikhail Shtalenkov
230	Petr Tenkrat	181	Mat Snesrud	159	Mike Laplante	134	Antti Aalto
258	Brian Gornick	209	Rene Stussi	185	Igor Karpenko	160	Matt Peterson
		235	Tommi Degerman			186	Tom Askey
1998 Pick						212	Vitaly Kozel
5	Vitaly Vishnevski	**1996** Pick		**1994** Pick		238	Anatoli Fedotov
32	Stephen Peat	9	Ruslan Salei	2	Oleg Tverdovsky	264	David Penney
112	Viktor Wallin	35	Matt Cullen	28	Johan Davidsson		
150	Trent Hunter	117	Brendan Buckley	67	Craig Reichert		
178	Jesse Fibiger	149	Blaine Russell	80	Byron Briske		
205	David Bernier	172	Timo Ahmaoja	106	Pavel Trnka		
233	Pelle Prestberg	198	Kevin Kellett	132	Jon Battaglia		
245	Andreas Andersson	224	Tobias Johansson	158	Mark (Rocky) Welsing		
				184	John Brad Englehart		
				236	Tommi Miettinen		
				262	Jeremy Stevenson		

Coach

HARTSBURG, CRAIG
Coach, Mighty Ducks of Anaheim. Born in Stratford, Ont., June 29, 1959.

On July 21, 1998, Craig Hartsburg signed a three-year contract to become the third head coach in the history of the Mighty Ducks of Anaheim. Hartsburg came to the Mighty Ducks after serving three seasons as head coach of the Chicago Blackhawks. During his tenure with Chicago, Hartsburg compiled a 104-102-40 record. He was the 30th head coach in Chicago Blackhawks history.

The Blackhawks posted a 40-28-14 record in Hartsburg's first season behind the bench in Chicago (1995-96), finishing second in the Central Division and third overall in the Western Conference. After a sweep of the Calgary Flames in the opening round of the playoffs, the Blackhawks fell to the eventual Stanley Cup champion Colorado Avalanche. Hartsburg led Chicago back to the Stanley Cup Playoffs in 1997, pushing the top-seeded Avalanche to six games in the first round before falling, four games to two. In 1997-98, Chicago stayed in contention for postseason play until the last week of the season, finishing just five points out of a playoff spot. Hartsburg's Blackhawks had the seventh-most rookie man-games played in the league (230) that year.

Before joining the Blackhawks, Hartsburg received his first head coaching job in 1994 with the Guelph Storm of the Ontario Hockey League. He was named OHL coach of the year after leading the Storm to a 47-14-5 record for a .750 winning percentage in 1994-95. Hartsburg also spent four years as an assistant coach with the Philadelphia Flyers from 1990 to 1994 and one season as an assistant coach with the Minnesota North Stars in 1989-90.

Hartsburg played his entire 10-year NHL career with Minnesota from 1979 to 1989. Known as an offensive defenseman, he was the North Stars' captain for six seasons until injuries forced him to retire from active play on January 13, 1989. Hartsburg was Minnesota's first round selection (sixth overall) in the 1979 NHL Entry Draft and immediately made an impact on the North Stars' blueline, scoring 44 points in 79 games during his rookie season. Hartsburg led all Minnesota defensemen in scoring each of his first four seasons. During the 1981 playoffs, he was a key player for the North Stars, scoring three goals and 12 assists to help lead the club to its first appearance in the Stanley Cup finals. Hartsburg also became the first North Stars defenseman to record a hat trick, netting three goals on November 1, 1986 vs. Chicago.

Hartsburg played in 570 games during his NHL career, scoring 98 goals and 315 assists for 413 points with 818 penalty minutes. He also appeared in 61 playoff games during his career, posting 15 goals and 27 assists for 42 points. Hartsburg holds or shares seven Stars' team records, including most assists (60) and most points (77) by a defenseman in one season. In February of 1992, he was voted to the North Stars' 25th Anniversary Dream Team by Minnesota fans.

A participant in three NHL All-Star Games (1980, 1982 and 1983), Hartsburg also competed in three World championship tournaments for Team Canada, including being chosen as best defenseman of the 1987 World Championships. He lists winning the Canada Cup championship in 1987 as his most memorable moment in hockey.

Hartsburg and his wife Peggy have two children, Christopher and Katie.

Coaching Record

Season	Team	Regular Season					Playoffs			
		Games	W	L	T	%	Games	W	L	%
1994-95	Guelph (OHL)	66	47	14	5	.750	14	10	4	.714
1995-96	Chicago (NHL)	82	40	28	14	.573	10	6	4	.600
1996-97	Chicago (NHL)	82	34	35	13	.494	6	2	4	.333
1997-98	Chicago (NHL)	82	30	39	13	.455	....	....	....	....
1998-99	Anaheim (NHL)	82	35	34	13	.506	4	0	4	.000
	NHL Totals	328	139	136	53	.505	20	8	12	.400

Club Directory

Anaheim Sports, Inc.
Arrowhead Pond of Anaheim
2695 Katella Ave.
Anaheim, CA 92806
Phone **714/940-2900**
FAX 714/940-2953
Ticket Information 714/704-2701
Website: www.mightyducks.com
Capacity: 17,174

Executive Management
Chairman and Governor	Tony Tavares
President and General Manager	Pierre Gauthier
Assistant General Manager	David McNab
Vice President, Finance/Administration	Andy Roundtree
Vice President, Sales & Marketing	Ron Minegar
Vice President, Advertising Sales and Broadcasting	Bob Wagner
Vice President, Communications	Tim Mead
Vice President, Business and Legal Affairs	Rick Schlesinger
Vice President, Hockey Operations	Jack Ferreira
Administrative Assistant, Chairman	Meta Maynard
Administrative Assistant, President and General Manager	Maureen Nyehott
Administrative Assistant, Finance/Administration	Monica Campanis
Administrative Assistant, Advertising Sales and Broadcasting	Sonia Salem
Administrative Assistant, Business Affairs	Tia Wood
Administrative Assistant, Communications	Lisa Parris

Coaching Staff
Head Coach	Craig Hartsburg
Assistant Coaches	Newell Brown, George Burnett
Goaltending Consultant	Francois Allaire

Hockey Club Operations
Chief Amateur Scout	Alain Chainey
Scouting Coordinator	Greg Carvel
Scouts	Richard Green, Mark Odnokon, Jan Danielson
Scouting Staff	Donald Marier, Mike McGraw, David McNamara, Konstantin Krylov, Ross Ainsworth
Pro Scout	Lucien DeBlois
Head Athletic Trainer	Chris Phillips
Equipment Manager	Mark O'Neill
Assistant Equipment Manager	John Allaway
Cincinnati Mighty Ducks (AHL) Head Coach	Moe Mantha
Team Physicians	Dr. Ronald Glousman, Dr. Craig Milhouse
Oral Surgeon	Dr. Jeff Pulver
Visiting Team Equipment Attendant	Chris Kincaid

Communications Department
Manager, Communications and Team Services	Rob Scichili
Manager, Publications	Doug Ward
Media Relations Representative	Alex Gilchrist
Community Relations Representative	Renee Zidan
Manager, Community Relations	Dennis Bickmeier
Team Photographer	V.J. Lovero (Lovero Group)

Finance and Administration Department
Director, Finance	John Rinehart
Sr. Financial Analyst	Amy Langdale
Business Development Analyst	Marc Kolin
Manager, Human Resources	Jenny Price
Manager, Information Services	Al Castro
Sr. Network Engineer	Neil Fariss
Sr. End User Analyst	Karen Turner
Assistant Controller	Melody Martin
Accountants	Jean Ouyang, Roseanna Sitzman
Accounting Assistants	Rob Dumlao, Trang Nguyen
Administrative Assistant, Human Resources	Cindy Williams
Human Resources Assistant	Alex Oftelie
Event Supervisor	John Drum
Administrative Assistant, Legal	Nadyne D'Antignac
Administrative Assistant, Operations	Leslie Flammini
General Manager, Disney ICE	Art Trottier
Receptionist	Sue Felix

Sales & Marketing Department
Director, Ticket Sales and Customer Service	Mike McCoy
Manager, Premium Ticket Services	Anne McNiff-Gaeta
Manager, Marketing and Promotions	Lisa Manning
Manager, Ticket Operations	Chad Canez
Ticketing Supervisor	Steph Olsen
Account Executives	Ron Campbell, Mike Gullo, Johnny O'Connor
Group Ticket Sales Executives	Kristen Atkinson, Ken Bamberg, Matt Cohen, Joe Furmanski
Administrative Assistants	Pat Navarro, Pat Lissy

Advertising Sales and Broadcasting Department
Director, Advertising Sales and Broadcasting	Lawrence Cohen
Director, Broadcasting	Mark Vittorio
Manager, Broadcasting	Dan Patin
Manager, Sponsorship Services	Sue O'Shea
Advertising Sales Managers	Richard McClemmy, Jennifer Flaa, Jamie Dyckes, Leanne Harvey, Brian Strohecker
Broadcast Advertising Sales Managers	John Davis, AnneMarie du LeBohn
Web Site Editor	Stuart Matthews
Sponsorship Services Representative	Jennifer Guran
Telecast Director	Aaron Teats
Production Assistant	Mike Levy
Television, KCAL (Ch. 9) & Fox Sports West 2 (Cable)	Chris Madsen, Brian Hayward
Radio, XTRA Sports (690 AM) & Mighty Ducks Radio Network	Steve Carroll, Darren Eliot
Administrative Assistant, Advertising	Janine Martin
Director, Entertainment	Rod Murray
Manager, Entertainment	Tim Beach
Practice Facilities	Disney ICE (300 W. Lincoln Ave.) and the Arrowhead Pond (2695 Katella Ave.)
Press Box Phone	714/704-2623
Press Room	714/704-2514 or 2517

Atlanta Thrashers

The Thrashers obtained the first player in franchise history when they acquired Damian Rhodes from Ottawa on June 18, 1999.

1999-2000 Schedule

Oct.	Sat.	2	New Jersey		Fri.	14	Philadelphia
	Thu.	7	Detroit		Sun.	16	at NY Rangers*
	Sat.	9	Buffalo		Mon.	17	at Boston*
	Thu.	14	at NY Islanders		Wed.	19	Boston
	Sat.	16	at Tampa Bay		Fri.	21	Florida
	Sun.	17	at NY Rangers		Mon.	24	NY Rangers
	Sat.	23	Colorado		Wed.	26	Phoenix
	Tue.	26	Calgary		Thu.	27	at Pittsburgh
	Wed.	27	at Toronto		Sat.	29	at Tampa Bay
	Sun.	31	Ottawa		Mon.	31	Pittsburgh
Nov.	Wed.	3	Tampa Bay	Feb.	Wed.	2	at Dallas
	Sat.	6	at Boston		Thu.	3	NY Rangers
	Wed.	10	at Florida		Wed.	9	at Pittsburgh
	Fri.	12	at New Jersey		Fri.	11	San Jose
	Sat.	13	at Montreal		Sat.	12	Chicago
	Wed.	17	Tampa Bay		Tue.	15	at St. Louis
	Fri.	19	Buffalo		Wed.	16	Montreal
	Sat.	20	at Buffalo		Sun.	20	at Phoenix
	Mon.	22	Vancouver		Tue.	22	at Colorado
	Thu.	25	Ottawa		Fri.	25	at Edmonton
	Sat.	27	at Florida		Sat.	26	at Calgary
	Sun.	28	Dallas		Tue.	29	Toronto
Dec.	Fri.	3	Florida	Mar.	Thu.	2	St. Louis
	Sat.	4	at NY Islanders		Sat.	4	at Ottawa
	Mon.	6	Nashville		Mon.	6	at Montreal
	Wed.	8	at Los Angeles		Fri.	10	New Jersey
	Fri.	10	at San Jose		Sun.	12	at Carolina*
	Sun.	12	at Anaheim		Mon.	13	Edmonton
	Wed.	15	Washington		Thu.	16	NY Islanders
	Fri.	17	Boston		Sat.	18	at Toronto
	Sat.	18	at Carolina		Tue.	21	at Ottawa
	Wed.	22	at Florida		Wed.	22	Montreal
	Thu.	23	at Philadelphia		Fri.	24	Pittsburgh
	Sun.	26	Tampa Bay		Sun.	26	Los Angeles
	Mon.	27	at Detroit		Tue.	28	at Washington
	Thu.	30	at Nashville		Fri.	31	at New Jersey
Jan.	Sat.	1	Carolina	Apr.	Sun.	2	NY Islanders*
	Tue.	4	at Buffalo		Tue.	4	Philadelphia
	Thu.	6	Washington		Thu.	6	at Philadelphia
	Sat.	8	at Washington		Sat.	8	Carolina*
	Wed.	12	Washington		Sun.	9	at Carolina*

* Denotes afternoon game.

Franchise date: June 25, 1997

EASTERN
NHL
CONFERENCE

1st
NHL
Season

SOUTHEAST
DIVISION

1999-2000 Player Personnel

FORWARDS	HT	WT	S	Place of Birth	Date	1998-99 Club
ADAMS, Bryan	6-0	185	L	Ft. St. James, B.C.	3/20/77	Michigan State
BOISVERT, Hugo	6-0	195	L	St-Eustache, Que.	5/22/75	Ohio State
BOTTERILL, Jason	6-4	220	L	Edmonton, Alta.	5/19/76	Dallas-Michigan
BRUNETTE, Andrew	6-0	212	L	Sudbury, Ont.	8/24/73	Nashville
BUCHBERGER, Kelly	6-2	210	L	Langenburg, Sask.	12/2/66	Edmonton
CLOUTIER, Sylvain	6-0	195	L	Mont-Laurier, Que.	2/13/74	Chicago-Indianapolis
EMERSON, Nelson	5-11	180	R	Hamilton, Ont.	8/17/67	Carolina-Chicago-Ottawa
FERRARO, Ray	5-9	193	L	Trail, B.C.	8/23/64	Los Angeles
GARPENLOV, Johan	5-11	185	L	Stockholm, Sweden	3/21/68	Florida
HULL, Jody	6-2	200	R	Petrolia, Ont.	2/2/69	Philadelphia
JOHNSON, Matt	6-5	232	L	Welland, Ont.	11/23/75	Los Angeles
KARLSSON, Andreas	6-3	193	L	Luvicka, Sweden	8/19/75	Leksands IF
LACHANCE, Bob	5-11	180	R	Northampton, MA	2/1/74	Indianapolis
LAMBERT, Denny	5-11	200	L	Wawa, Ont.	1/7/70	Nashville
LAW, Kirby	6-1	180	R	McCreary, Man.	3/11/77	Orlando-Adirondack
PROCHAZKA, Martin	5-11	180	R	Slany, Czech.	3/3/72	Petra Vsetin
SNYDER, Dan	6-0	185	L	Elmira, Ont.	2/23/78	Owen Sound
STAPLETON, Mike	5-10	183	R	Sarnia, Ont.	5/5/66	Phoenix
STEFAN, Patrik	6-1	205	L	Pribram, Czech.	9/16/80	Long Beach
SVARTVADET, Per	6-1	180	L	Solleftea, Sweden	5/17/75	MoDo Hockey
SYLVESTER, Dean	6-2	200	R	Weymouth, MA	12/30/72	Buffalo-Rochester
VASILJEVS, Herbert	5-11	170	R	Riga, USSR	5/27/76	Florida-Kentucky
VUJTEK, Vladimir	6-1	190	L	Ostrava, Czech.	2/17/72	HC Vitkovice
WARD, Ed	6-3	220	R	Edmonton, Alta.	11/10/69	Calgary
YAKE, Terry	5-11	190	R	New Westminster, B.C.	10/22/68	St. Louis-Worcester
YEGOROV, Alexei	5-11	185	L	St. Petersburg, USSR	5/21/75	Yaroslavl-St. Petersburg-Moscow D'amo

DEFENSEMEN						
BUZEK, Petr	6-0	205	L	Jihlava, Czech.	4/26/77	Dallas-Michigan
CLARK, Brett	6-1	182	L	Wapella, Sask.	12/23/76	Montreal-Fredericton
DEAN, Kevin	6-3	205	L	Madison, WI	4/1/69	New Jersey
GALANOV, Maxim	6-1	205	L	Krasnoyarsk, USSR	3/13/74	Pittsburgh
HARLOCK, David	6-2	205	L	Toronto, Ont.	3/16/71	NY Islanders
MURPHY, Gord	6-2	195	R	Willowdale, Ont.	3/23/67	Florida
SHANNON, Darryl	6-2	208	L	Barrie, Ont.	6/21/68	Buffalo
STAIOS, Steve	6-1	200	R	Hamilton, Ont.	7/28/73	Vancouver
TAMER, Chris	6-1	215	L	Dearborn, MI	11/17/70	Pittsburgh-NY Rangers
TREMBLAY, Yannick	6-2	185	R	Pointe-aux-Trembles, Que.	11/15/75	Toronto
VYSHEDKEVICH, Sergei	6-0	195	L	Dedovsk, USSR	1/3/75	Albany

GOALTENDERS	HT	WT	C	Place of Birth	Date	1998-99 Club
FANKHOUSER, Scott	6-2	195	L	Bismark, ND	7/1/75	U. Mass-Lowell
LANGKOW, Scott	5-11	190	L	Sherwood Park, Alta.	4/21/75	Phoenix-Las Vegas-Utah
MARACLE, Norm	5-8	195	L	Belleville, Ont.	10/2/74	Detroit-Adirondack
RHODES, Damian	6-0	190	L	St. Paul, MN	5/28/69	Ottawa
SCHWAB, Corey	6-0	180	L	North Battleford, Sask.	11/4/70	Tampa Bay-Cleveland

Entry Draft Selections 1999

General Managers' History
Don Waddell, 1999-2000.

1999
Pick
1	Patrik Stefan
30	Luke Sellars
68	Zdenek Blatny
98	David Kaczowka
99	Rob Zepp
128	Derek MacKenzie
159	Yuri Dobryshkin
188	Stephan Baby
217	Garnet Exelby
245	Tommi Santala
246	Ray Dilauro

Coaching History
Curt Fraser, 1999-2000.

Captains' History
TBD, 1999-2000.

General Manager

WADDELL, DON
General Manager, Atlanta Thrashers. Born in Detroit, MI, August 19, 1958.

Don Waddell was hired by the Thrashers as vice president and general manager on June 23, 1998 - almost a year to the day after the NHL granted a new franchise to Atlanta. He came to the club after having been the assistant general manager of the Stanley Cup champion Detroit Red Wings for the 1997-98 season. Prior to Detroit, he was vice president of RDV Sports, where he served on the Executive Committee which oversaw operations of the National Basketball Association's Orlando Magic, the International Hockey League's Orlando Solar Bears, Magic Fanattics (retail) and Magic Carpet Aviation. While at RDV Sports, Waddell was vice president and general manager of the IHL's Orlando Solar Bears from 1995 to 1997. Prior to the Solar Bears, he held the same role with the IHL's San Diego Gulls from 1990 to 1995. He also served as the club's head coach for the 1991-92 season, guiding the team to the franchise's first playoff berth. He spent two seasons with the IHL's Flint Spirits where he served as head coach and general manager in 1988-89, and general manager in 1989-90.

Waddell's playing experience includes being player/coach for the Flint Spirits from 1986 to 1988, and the Goaldiggers Hockey Club in Toledo, Ohio for the 1985-86 season. He was drafted by the NHL's Los Angeles Kings back in 1978, and spent three years with the organization from 1980 to 1983. He was a member of the 1983 U.S. National Team and had been a member of the 1980 gold medal Olympic hockey team, but was injured prior to play.

Waddell played Division I hockey at Northern Michigan University from 1976 to 1980, where he majored in business management. He was inducted into the Northern Michigan University Sports Hall of Fame in 1992.

Coach

FRASER, CURT
Coach, Atlanta Thrashers. Born in Cincinnati, OH, January 12, 1958.

Curt Fraser became the first head coach in the history of the Atlanta Thrashers on July 14, 1999. Fraser had spent the previous four seasons as the head coach of the IHL's Orlando Solar Bears, where he worked with Thrashers G.M. Don Waddell from 1995 to 1997.

In four seasons with the Solar Bears, Fraser's teams never won less than 42 games and topped 50 wins twice. Orlando reached the Turner Cup Final as a first-year expansion team under Fraser in 1995-96.

Fraser came to Orlando in 1995 after 12 years as a player in the NHL and five years as a coach in the professional ranks. He spent the 1994-95 season as an associate coach with the AHL's Syracuse Crunch, the top affiliate for the Vancouver Canucks. Before joining Syracuse, Fraser served first as an assistant coach and later head coach of the IHL's Milwaukee Admirals.

Prior to reaching the coaching ranks, Fraser was a highly respected left winger in the NHL with Vancouver, Chicago and Minnesota. In 704 career games, he scored 193 goals, notched 433 points and amassed 1,306 penalty minutes. Originally a second round pick of Vancouver in 1978, Fraser established himself as a hard working and fearless player, who combined toughness with the ability to score.

Fraser and his wife, Rhonda, have three sons, Casey, Jesse and Luke.

Coaching Record

Season	Team	Games	Regular Season W	L	T	%	Playoffs Games	W	L	%
1992-93	Milwaukee (IHL)	82	49	23	10	.659	6	2	4	.333
1993-94	Milwaukee (IHL)	81	40	24	17	.599	4	0	4	.000
1995-96	Orlando (IHL)	82	52	24	6	.671	23	11	12	.478
1996-97	Orlando (IHL)	82	53	24	5	.677	10	4	6	.400
1997-98	Orlando (IHL)	82	42	30	10	.573	17	9	8	.529
1998-99	Orlando (IHL)	82	45	33	4	.573	17	10	7	.588

Club Directory

Philips Arena

Atlanta Thrashers Hockey Club
One CNN Center, Box 105583
Atlanta, GA 30348-5583
Phone **404/827-5300**
FAX 404/827-5909
www.atlantathrashers.com
Capacity: 18,750

Executive Management
President and Governor	Dr. Harvey Schiller
Executive Vice President (Alternate Governor)	Dave Maggarci
Vice President and General Manager (Alternate Governor)	Don Waddell
Vice President of Sales and Marketing	Derek Schiller
Legal Council	David Payne
Vice President, Finance and Segment Controller	Matt Struer
Vice President and Television Executive Producer	Mike Pearl
Vice President of Public Relations	Greg Hughes
Assistant to the President	Michael Jackson

Hockey Operations
Assistant General Manager	Les Jackson
Director of Player Development and Evaluation	Bob Owen
Head Coach	Curt Fraser
Assistant Coaches	George Kingston, Jay Leach
Head Scout	Dan Marr
Director of Team Services	Michele Zarzaca
Manager of Hockey Operations	Jordy Bowman
Manager of Hockey Administration	Larry Simmons
Professional Scouts	Mark Dobson, Peter Mahovolich, Murray Oliver
Amateur Scouts	Bernd Freimuller, John Gill, John Perpich, Normand Poisson
Part-Time Scouts	Marcel Comeau, Pentti Katainen, Jan Lindegren
Coordinator of Scouting/Video	Jon Barkan
Strength and Conditioning Coach	Chris Reichart
Head Athletic Trainer	Scott Green
Assistant Athletic Trainer	Prentice Radford
Massage Therapist	Inar Treiguts
Head Equipment Manager	Bobby Stewart
Assistant Equipment Manager	Joe Guilmet
Team Physician	Dr. Scott Gillogly
Team Internist	Dr. William Whaley
Team Dentists	Dr. Gary Saban, Dr. Lawrence Slatzman, Dr. Brett Silverman
Assistant to Don Waddell	Carol Stidham
Produce Facility Manager	Shannon Grigsby

Administration
Assistants to Dr. Harvey Schiller	Katherine Daves, Farrah Downing
Assistant to Dave Maggard	Kim Kovacs
Assistant to Derek Schiller	Taelor Shackelford
Receptionist	Alycia Allgood

Corporate Sales (Philips Arena Sports Marketing)
Vice President of Broadcast and Corporate Sales	Tracy White
Director of Broadcast and Corporate Sales	Terri Scalcucci
Director of Sponsor Services	Linda Shepard
Senior Manager of Broadcast and Corporate Sales	Bill Abercrombie
Manager of Broadcast and Corporate Sales	Stewart Tanner
Manager of Broadcast and Corporate Sales	Arden Robbins
Manager of Broadcast Operations	Diana Corbin
Broadcast and Corporate Sales Assistant	Lisa C. Williams
Sponsor Services Assistants	Tijuanna Compton, Chris Carter
Executive Assistant	Catherine Mills

Finance/Accounting
Controller	David Kane
Senior Financial Analyst	Steve Adams
Manager of Accounting	Darius Nixon
Staff Accountant	Raiford Hodges

Human Resources
Director of Human Resources	Tim Goodly
Coordinator of Human Resources	Rhodes Scott
HRIS Coordinator	Deborah Owens

Legal
Senior Counsel	John Cooper
Paralegal	Anne Rollings
Assistants to David Payne	Eunah Majors, Shirlene Johnson

Marketing
Director of Marketing	Jim Pfeifer
Manager of Marketing	Rob Preiditsch
Manager of Fan Development	David Cole
Manager of Community Relations	Terry Hickman
Manager of Game Operations	Peter Sorckoff
Marketing Coordinator	Connie Zaleski
Fan Development Coordinator	Jon Mattson
Merchandise Coordinator	Elizabeth Dyhouse
Marketing Assistant	Ralph Humphlett
Mascot	Javier Presas

Media Relations
Director of Media Relations	Tom Hughes
Manager of Media Relations	Rob Koch
Multimedia Coordinator	John Heid
Junior Publicist	Susan Sanderman

MIS
Director of MIS	Cara Sherlock
Manager of MIS	Greg Ford
Information Technology Analyst	Eric Rising

Television/Radio Broadcasting
Coordinating Television Producer	Bill Kunz
Television Producer	Mark Stulberger
Television Director	Dan Reagan
Director of Radio Operations	Dan Kamal
Senior Director of Remote Television Operations	Tom Cox
Broadcasters	Matt McConnell, Darren Elliott, Scott Ferrall

Ticket Sales
Director of Ticket Sales	Dan Froehlich
Ticket Sales Manager	Keith Brennan
Ticket Operations Manager	Wendell Byrne
Account Executives	Chris Beaudin, Annette Dancausse, Evan Kellner, Travis Pelleymounter, Jenny Powers, Brandi Sutley
Ticket Operations Assistant	Scott Squillace

Boston Bruins

1998-99 Results: 39w-30L-13T 91PTS. Third, Northeast Division

Seen here wearing Boston's "third jersey," Byron Dafoe became the fourth goalie in Bruins history to reach double digits with 10 shutouts last season. Dafoe's 1.99 GAA was third best in the NHL.

1999-2000 Schedule

Oct.	Sat.	2	Carolina		Sat.	8	NY Islanders
	Mon.	4	at Toronto		Tue.	11	Toronto
	Thu.	7	at Ottawa		Thu.	13	Buffalo
	Sat.	9	Philadelphia		Sat.	15	at Montreal
	Mon.	11	Colorado*		Mon.	17	Atlanta*
	Wed.	13	at Colorado		Wed.	19	at Atlanta
	Fri.	15	at Dallas		Thu.	20	at Tampa Bay
	Sat.	16	at Phoenix		Sat.	22	at Florida
	Wed.	20	at Los Angeles		Mon.	24	Calgary
	Sat.	23	at San Jose		Thu.	27	Montreal
	Sun.	24	at Anaheim		Sat.	29	Buffalo
	Thu.	28	Tampa Bay		Mon.	31	Anaheim
	Sat.	30	Buffalo	Feb.	Tue.	1	at Ottawa
Nov.	Thu.	4	New Jersey		Thu.	3	Toronto
	Sat.	6	Atlanta		Tue.	8	Washington
	Wed.	10	at Buffalo		Fri.	11	at NY Rangers
	Thu.	11	Toronto		Sat.	12	Florida
	Sat.	13	at NY Rangers		Wed.	16	at Toronto
	Wed.	17	at New Jersey		Mon.	21	at Vancouver
	Thu.	18	NY Rangers		Wed.	23	at Edmonton
	Sat.	20	Washington		Fri.	25	at Washington
	Mon.	22	at Carolina		Sat.	26	at Pittsburgh
	Wed.	24	at Nashville		Tue.	29	Ottawa
	Fri.	26	Vancouver*	Mar.	Sat.	4	Philadelphia*
	Sun.	28	NY Islanders		Mon.	6	Ottawa
Dec.	Thu.	2	at Washington		Wed.	8	at Buffalo
	Sat.	4	Chicago		Fri.	10	at Carolina
	Thu.	9	Edmonton		Sat.	11	at Montreal
	Sat.	11	Detroit		Thu.	16	at Chicago
	Mon.	13	Phoenix		Sat.	18	Pittsburgh*
	Tue.	14	at Pittsburgh		Sun.	19	at Philadelphia*
	Fri.	17	at Atlanta		Tue.	21	Tampa Bay
	Sat.	18	at St. Louis		Thu.	23	Florida
	Tue.	21	Nashville		Sat.	25	Los Angeles*
	Thu.	23	Montreal		Wed.	29	at Montreal
	Mon.	27	at NY Islanders		Thu.	30	St. Louis
	Wed.	29	at New Jersey	Apr.	Sat.	1	NY Rangers*
	Thu.	30	at Ottawa		Tue.	4	at Tampa Bay
Jan.	Sat.	1	New Jersey		Wed.	5	at Florida
	Tue.	4	at NY Islanders		Sat.	8	at Philadelphia*
	Thu.	6	Carolina		Sun.	9	Pittsburgh

* Denotes afternoon game.

Franchise date: November 1, 1924

EASTERN
NHL CONFERENCE

NORTHEAST DIVISION

76th NHL Season

Year-by-Year Record

Season	GP	Home W	L	T	Road W	L	T	Overall W	L	T	GF	GA	Pts.	Finished		Playoff Result
1998-99	82	22	10	9	17	20	4	39	30	13	214	181	91	3rd,	Northeast Div.	Lost Conf. Semi-Final
1997-98	82	19	16	6	20	14	7	39	30	13	221	194	91	2nd,	Northeast Div.	Lost Conf. Quarter-Final
1996-97	82	14	20	7	12	27	2	26	47	9	234	300	61	6th,	Northeast Div.	Out of Playoffs
1995-96	82	22	14	5	18	17	6	40	31	11	282	269	91	2nd,	Northeast Div.	Lost Conf. Quarter-Final
1994-95	84	15	7	2	12	11	1	27	18	3	150	127	57	3rd,	Northeast Div.	Lost Conf. Quarter-Final
1993-94	84	20	14	8	22	15	5	42	29	13	289	252	97	1st,	Northeast Div.	Lost Conf. Semi-Final
1992-93	84	29	10	3	22	16	4	51	26	7	332	268	109	1st,	Adams Div.	Lost Div. Semi-Final
1991-92	80	23	11	6	13	21	6	36	32	12	270	275	84	2nd,	Adams Div.	Lost Conf. Championship
1990-91	80	26	9	5	18	15	7	44	24	12	299	264	100	1st,	Adams Div.	Lost Conf. Championship
1989-90	80	23	13	4	23	12	5	46	25	9	289	232	101	1st,	Adams Div.	Lost Div. Final
1988-89	80	17	15	8	20	14	6	37	29	14	289	256	88	2nd,	Adams Div.	Lost Div. Final
1987-88	80	24	13	3	20	17	3	44	30	6	300	251	94	2nd,	Adams Div.	Lost Final
1986-87	80	25	11	4	14	23	3	39	34	7	301	276	85	3rd,	Adams Div.	Lost Div. Semi-Final
1985-86	80	24	9	7	13	22	5	37	31	12	311	288	86	3rd,	Adams Div.	Lost Div. Semi-Final
1984-85	80	21	15	4	15	19	6	36	34	10	303	287	82	4th,	Adams Div.	Lost Div. Semi-Final
1983-84	80	25	12	3	24	13	3	49	25	6	336	261	104	1st,	Adams Div.	Lost Div. Semi-Final
1982-83	80	28	6	6	22	14	4	50	20	10	327	228	110	1st,	Adams Div.	Lost Conf. Championship
1981-82	80	24	12	4	19	15	6	43	27	10	323	285	96	2nd,	Adams Div.	Lost Div. Final
1980-81	80	26	10	4	11	20	9	37	30	13	316	272	87	2nd,	Adams Div.	Lost Prelim. Round
1979-80	80	27	9	4	19	12	9	46	21	13	310	234	105	2nd,	Adams Div.	Lost Quarter-Final
1978-79	80	25	10	5	18	13	9	43	23	14	316	270	100	1st,	Adams Div.	Lost Semi-Final
1977-78	80	29	6	5	22	12	6	51	18	11	333	218	113	1st,	Adams Div.	Lost Final
1976-77	80	27	7	6	22	16	2	49	23	8	312	240	106	1st,	Adams Div.	Lost Final
1975-76	80	27	5	8	21	10	9	48	15	17	313	237	113	1st,	Adams Div.	Lost Semi-Final
1974-75	80	29	5	6	11	21	8	40	26	14	345	245	94	2nd,	Adams Div.	Lost Prelim. Round
1973-74	78	33	4	2	19	13	7	52	17	9	349	221	113	1st,	East Div.	Lost Final
1972-73	78	27	10	2	24	12	3	51	22	5	330	235	107	2nd,	East Div.	Lost Quarter-Final
1971-72	**78**	**28**	**4**	**7**	**26**	**9**	**4**	**54**	**13**	**11**	**330**	**204**	**119**	**1st,**	**East Div.**	**Won Stanley Cup**
1970-71	78	33	4	2	24	10	5	57	14	7	399	207	121	1st,	East Div.	Lost Quarter-Final
1969-70	**76**	**27**	**3**	**8**	**13**	**14**	**11**	**40**	**17**	**19**	**277**	**216**	**99**	**2nd,**	**East Div.**	**Won Stanley Cup**
1968-69	76	29	3	6	13	15	10	42	18	16	303	221	100	2nd,	East Div.	Lost Semi-Final
1967-68	74	22	9	6	15	18	4	37	27	10	259	216	84	3rd,	East Div.	Lost Quarter-Final
1966-67	70	10	21	4	7	22	6	17	43	10	182	253	44	6th,		Out of Playoffs
1965-66	70	15	17	3	6	26	3	21	43	6	174	275	48	5th,		Out of Playoffs
1964-65	70	12	17	6	9	26	0	21	43	6	166	253	48	6th,		Out of Playoffs
1963-64	70	13	15	7	5	25	5	18	40	12	170	212	48	6th,		Out of Playoffs
1962-63	70	7	18	10	7	21	7	14	39	17	198	281	45	6th,		Out of Playoffs
1961-62	70	9	22	4	6	25	4	15	47	8	177	306	38	6th,		Out of Playoffs
1960-61	70	13	17	5	2	25	8	15	42	13	176	254	43	6th,		Out of Playoffs
1959-60	70	21	11	3	7	23	5	28	34	8	220	241	64	5th,		Out of Playoffs
1958-59	70	21	11	3	11	18	6	32	29	9	205	215	73	2nd,		Lost Semi-Final
1957-58	70	15	14	6	12	14	9	27	28	15	199	194	69	4th,		Lost Final
1956-57	70	20	9	6	14	15	6	34	24	12	195	174	80	3rd,		Lost Final
1955-56	70	14	14	7	9	20	6	23	34	13	147	185	59	5th,		Out of Playoffs
1954-55	70	16	10	9	7	16	12	23	26	21	169	188	67	4th,		Lost Semi-Final
1953-54	70	22	8	5	10	20	5	32	28	10	177	181	74	4th,		Lost Semi-Final
1952-53	70	19	10	6	9	19	7	28	29	13	152	172	69	3rd,		Lost Final
1951-52	70	15	12	8	10	17	8	25	29	16	162	176	66	4th,		Lost Semi-Final
1950-51	70	13	12	10	9	18	8	22	30	18	178	197	62	4th,		Lost Semi-Final
1949-50	70	15	12	8	7	20	8	22	32	16	198	228	60	5th,		Out of Playoffs
1948-49	60	18	10	2	11	13	6	29	23	8	178	163	66	2nd,		Lost Semi-Final
1947-48	60	12	8	10	11	16	3	23	24	13	167	168	59	3rd,		Lost Semi-Final
1946-47	60	18	7	5	8	16	6	26	23	11	190	175	63	3rd,		Lost Semi-Final
1945-46	50	11	5	4	13	13	4	24	18	8	167	156	56	2nd,		Lost Final
1944-45	50	11	12	2	5	18	2	16	30	4	179	219	36	4th,		Lost Semi-Final
1943-44	50	15	8	2	4	18	3	19	26	5	223	268	43	5th,		Out of Playoffs
1942-43	50	17	3	5	7	14	4	24	17	9	195	176	57	2nd,		Lost Final
1941-42	48	17	4	3	8	13	3	25	17	6	160	118	56	3rd,		Lost Semi-Final
1940-41	**48**	**15**	**4**	**5**	**12**	**4**	**8**	**27**	**8**	**13**	**168**	**102**	**67**	**1st,**		**Won Stanley Cup**
1939-40	48	20	3	1	11	9	4	31	12	5	170	98	67	1st,		
1938-39	**48**	**20**	**2**	**2**	**16**	**8**	**0**	**36**	**10**	**2**	**156**	**76**	**74**	**1st,**		**Won Stanley Cup**
1937-38	48	18	3	3	12	8	4	30	11	7	142	89	67	1st,	Amn. Div.	Lost Semi-Final
1936-37	48	9	11	4	14	7	3	23	18	7	120	110	53	2nd,	Amn. Div.	Lost Quarter-Final
1935-36	48	15	8	1	7	12	5	22	20	6	92	83	50	2nd,	Amn. Div.	Lost Quarter-Final
1934-35	48	17	7	0	9	9	6	26	16	6	129	112	58	1st,	Amn. Div.	Lost Semi-Final
1933-34	48	11	11	2	7	14	3	18	25	5	111	130	41	4th,	Amn. Div.	Out of Playoffs
1932-33	48	19	2	3	6	13	5	25	15	8	124	88	58	1st,	Amn. Div.	Lost Semi-Final
1931-32	48	11	10	3	4	11	9	15	21	12	122	117	42	4th,	Amn. Div.	Out of Playoffs
1930-31	44	16	1	5	12	9	1	28	10	6	143	90	62	1st,	Amn. Div.	Lost Semi-Final
1929-30	44	21	1	0	17	4	1	38	5	1	179	98	77	1st,	Amn. Div.	Lost Final
1928-29	**44**	**15**	**6**	**1**	**11**	**7**	**4**	**26**	**13**	**5**	**89**	**52**	**57**	**1st,**	**Amn. Div.**	**Won Stanley Cup**
1927-28	44	13	4	5	7	9	6	20	13	11	77	70	51	1st,	Amn. Div.	Lost Semi-Final
1926-27	44	15	7	0	6	13	3	21	20	3	97	89	45	2nd,	Amn. Div.	Lost Final
1925-26	36	10	7	1	7	8	3	17	15	4	92	85	38	4th,		Out of Playoffs
1924-25	30	3	12	0	3	12	0	6	24	0	49	119	12	6th,		Out of Playoffs

1999-2000 Player Personnel

FORWARDS	HT	WT	S	Place of Birth	Date	1998-99 Club
ALLISON, Jason	6-3	205	R	North York, Ont.	5/29/75	Boston
ANDREYCHUK, Dave	6-4	220	R	Hamilton, Ont.	9/29/63	New Jersey
AXELSSON, Per-Johan	6-1	174	L	Kungalv, Sweden	2/26/75	Boston
BATES, Shawn	5-11	205	R	Melrose, MA	4/3/75	Boston-Providence (AHL)
BELANGER, Ken	6-4	225	L	Sault Ste. Marie, Ont.	5/14/74	NY Islanders-Boston
CARTER, Anson	6-1	185	R	Toronto, Ont.	6/6/74	Boston-Utah
DiMAIO, Rob	5-10	190	R	Calgary, Alta.	2/19/68	Boston
DOWNEY, Aaron	6-0	210	R	Shelburne, Ont.	8/27/74	Providence (AHL)
ELORANTA, Mikko	6-0	185	L	Aura, Finland	8/24/72	TPS Turku
FERRARO, Peter	5-10	180	R	Port Jefferson, NY	1/24/73	Boston-Providence (AHL)
HEINZE, Steve	5-11	202	R	Lawrence, MA	1/30/70	Boston
HENDERSON, Jay	5-11	188	L	Edmonton, Alta.	9/17/78	Boston-Providence (AHL)
HULBIG, Joe	6-3	215	L	Norwood, MA	9/29/73	Edmonton-Hamilton
LAAKSONEN, Antti	6-0	180	L	Tammela, Finland	10/3/73	Boston-Providence (AHL)
MANN, Cameron	6-0	194	R	Thompson, Man.	4/20/77	Boston-Providence (AHL)
MATHIEU, Marquis	5-11	190	R	Hartford, CT	5/31/73	Boston-Providence (AHL)
MILANOVIC, Ryan	6-2	201	L	Toronto, Ont.	9/3/80	Kitchener
NICKULAS, Eric	5-11	190	R	Hyannis, MA	3/25/75	Boston-Providence (AHL)
NORDSTROM, Peter	6-1	200	L	Munkfors, Sweden	7/26/74	Farjestads BK-Bos-Prov (AHL)
PRONGER, Sean	6-2	205	L	Dryden, Ont.	11/30/72	Pit-Houston-NYR-L.A.
PRPIC, Joel	6-7	225	L	Sudbury, Ont.	9/25/74	Providence (AHL)
SAMSONOV, Sergei	5-8	184	R	Moscow, USSR	10/27/78	Boston
SAVAGE, Andre	6-0	195	R	Ottawa, Ont.	5/27/75	Boston-Providence (AHL)
THORNTON, Joe	6-4	225	L	London, Ont.	7/2/79	Boston
TROTTIER, Joel	6-0	190	R	Alexandria, Ont.	2/11/77	Providence (AHL)-Greenville
WILSON, Landon	6-2	216	R	St. Louis, MO	3/13/75	Boston-Providence (AHL)
ZEHR, Jeff	6-3	195	L	Woodstock, Ont.	12/10/78	Erie (OHL)-Sarnia
ZULTEK, Matt	6-4	222	L	Windsor, Ont.	3/12/79	Ottawa (OHL)
DEFENSEMEN						
ABRAHAMSSON, Elias	6-3	240	L	Uppsala, Sweden	6/15/77	Providence (AHL)
AITKEN, Johnathan	6-4	215	L	Edmonton, Alta.	5/24/78	Providence (AHL)
BOURQUE, Ray	5-11	219	L	Montreal, Que.	12/28/60	Boston
BOYNTON, Nicholas	6-2	210	R	Nobleton, Ont.	1/14/79	Ottawa (OHL)
CECH, Vratislav	6-3	196	L	Tabor, Czech.	1/28/79	Kitchener
GILL, Hal	6-7	240	L	Concord, MA	4/6/75	Boston
GIRARD, Jonathan	5-11	192	R	Joliette, Que.	5/27/80	Bathurst-Boston
McCAMBRIDGE, Keith	6-2	205	L	Thompson, Man.	2/1/74	Las Vegas-Long Beach
McLAREN, Kyle	6-4	219	L	Humboldt, Sask.	6/18/77	Boston
SMITH, Brandon	6-1	196	L	Hazelton, B.C.	2/25/73	Boston-Providence (AHL)
SWEENEY, Don	5-10	184	L	St. Stephen, N.B.	8/17/66	Boston
TIMANDER, Mattias	6-3	210	L	Solleftea, Sweden	4/16/74	Boston-Providence (AHL)
VAN ACKER, Eric	6-5	220	L	St-Jean, Que.	3/1/79	Baie-Comeau
VAN IMPE, Darren	6-1	205	L	Saskatoon, Sask.	5/18/73	Boston

GOALTENDERS	HT	WT	C	Place of Birth	Date	1998-99 Club
DAFOE, Byron	5-11	190	L	Sussex, England	2/25/71	Boston
GRAHAME, John	6-2	210	L	Denver, CO	8/31/75	Providence (AHL)
RAYCROFT, Andrew	6-0	150	L	Belleville, Ont.	5/4/80	Sudbury
TALLAS, Robbie	6-0	163	L	Edmonton, Alta.	3/20/73	Boston
WHITMORE, Kay	5-11	175	L	Sudbury, Ont.	4/10/67	Milwaukee-Hartford

Coach

BURNS, PAT

Coach, Boston Bruins. Born in St-Henri, Que., April 4, 1952.

Pat Burns has led the Bruins into the playoffs in both seasons behind the Bruins bench. The club's 30-point improvement in 1997-98 saw Burns honored with the Jack Adams Award, making him the first man to be named coach of the year on three occasions. The three victories have come with three different clubs.

Burns began his coaching career with the Hull Olympiques of the QMJHL. During his four seasons behind the Hull bench, he compiled a 138-136-6 record and a berth in the 1986 Memorial Cup finals. In 1987-88, he moved to the professional ranks, assuming the head coaching position with Montreal's AHL affiliate in Sherbrooke. After leading that team to a 42-34-4 record, he was named as the head coach in Montreal.

He was the NHL's winningest coach over his four-year tenure in Montreal, with a 174-104-42 record and .609 winning percentage from 1988-89 through 1991-92.

On May 29, 1992, Burns was named as the head coach for the Toronto Maple Leafs. In his first season with Toronto, he led the team to the highest single-season turnaround in club history with club records in regular season wins, points and home wins and playoff games and victories. Their 44-29-11 record in 1992-93 was a 32-point improvement from their 1991-92 campaign. His second season behind the Toronto bench earned the team consecutive 40-win seasons for the first time in club history.

Coaching Record

		Regular Season					Playoffs			
Season	Team	Games	W	L	T	%	Games	W	L	%
1983-84	Hull (QMJHL)	70	25	45	0	.357	....	....	....	....
1984-85	Hull (QMJHL)	68	33	34	1	.493	5	1	4	.200
1985-86	Hull (QMJHL)	72	54	18	0	.750	15	15	0	1.000
1986-87	Hull (QMJHL)	70	26	39	5	.407	8	4	4	.500
1987-88	Sherbrooke (AHL)	80	42	34	4	.550	6	2	4	.333
1988-89	**Montreal (NHL)**	**80**	**53**	**18**	**9**	**.719**	**21**	**14**	**7**	**.667**
1989-90	**Montreal (NHL)**	**80**	**41**	**28**	**11**	**.581**	**11**	**5**	**6**	**.455**
1990-91	**Montreal (NHL)**	**80**	**39**	**30**	**11**	**.556**	**13**	**7**	**6**	**.538**
1991-92	**Montreal (NHL)**	**80**	**41**	**28**	**11**	**.581**	**11**	**4**	**7**	**.364**
1992-93	**Toronto (NHL)**	**84**	**44**	**29**	**11**	**.589**	**21**	**11**	**10**	**.524**
1993-94	**Toronto (NHL)**	**84**	**43**	**29**	**12**	**.583**	**18**	**9**	**9**	**.500**
1994-95	**Toronto (NHL)**	**48**	**21**	**19**	**8**	**.521**	**7**	**3**	**4**	**.429**
1995-96	**Toronto (NHL)**	**65**	**25**	**30**	**10**	**.462**	....	....	....	....
1997-98	**Boston (NHL)**	**82**	**39**	**30**	**13**	**.555**	**6**	**2**	**4**	**.333**
1998-99	**Boston (NHL)**	**82**	**39**	**30**	**13**	**.555**	**12**	**6**	**6**	**.500**
	NHL Totals	**765**	**385**	**271**	**109**	**.575**	**120**	**61**	**59**	**.508**

1998-99 Scoring

* – rookie

Regular Season

Pos	#	Player	Team	GP	G	A	Pts	+/–	PIM	PP	SH	GW	GT	S	%
C	41	Jason Allison	BOS	82	23	53	76	5	68	5	1	3	0	158	14.6
R	12	Dmitri Khristich	BOS	79	29	42	71	11	48	13	1	6	1	144	20.1
D	77	Ray Bourque	BOS	81	10	47	57	–7	34	8	0	3	0	262	3.8
L	14	Sergei Samsonov	BOS	79	25	26	51	–6	18	6	0	8	1	160	15.6
C	6	Joe Thornton	BOS	81	16	25	41	3	69	7	0	1	0	128	12.5
L	33	Anson Carter	BOS	55	24	16	40	7	22	6	0	6	0	123	19.5
R	23	Steve Heinze	BOS	73	22	18	40	7	30	9	0	3	0	146	15.1
D	18	Kyle McLaren	BOS	52	6	18	24	1	48	3	0	0	0	97	6.2
L	19	Rob Dimaio	BOS	71	7	14	21	–14	95	1	0	0	0	121	5.8
D	20	Darren Van Impe	BOS	60	5	15	20	–5	66	4	0	0	0	92	5.4
R	11	P.J. Axelsson	BOS	77	7	10	17	–14	18	0	0	2	0	146	4.8
R	42	Peter Ferraro	BOS	46	6	8	14	10	44	1	0	1	0	61	9.8
D	36	Grant Ledyard	BOS	47	4	8	12	–8	33	1	0	2	0	47	8.5
D	32	Don Sweeney	BOS	81	2	10	12	14	64	0	0	0	0	79	2.5
C	26	Tim Taylor	BOS	49	4	7	11	–10	55	0	0	1	0	76	5.3
D	25	Hal Gill	BOS	80	3	7	10	–10	63	0	0	2	0	102	2.9
C	17 *	Shawn Bates	BOS	33	5	4	9	3	2	0	0	0	0	30	16.7
C	38	Chris Taylor	BOS	37	3	5	8	–3	12	0	1	0	0	60	5.0
R	10 *	Cameron Mann	BOS	33	5	2	7	0	17	1	0	1	1	42	11.9
L	16	Ken Belanger	NYI	9	1	1	2	1	30	0	0	0	0	3	33.3
			BOS	45	1	4	5	–2	152	0	0	0	0	16	6.3
			TOTAL	54	2	5	7	–1	182	0	0	0	0	19	10.5
R	27	Landon Wilson	BOS	22	3	3	6	0	17	0	0	0	0	32	9.4
D	37	Mattias Timander	BOS	22	0	6	6	4	10	0	0	0	0	22	0.0
D	44	Dave Ellett	BOS	54	0	6	6	11	25	0	0	0	0	45	0.0
L	22	Ken Baumgartner	BOS	69	1	3	4	–6	119	0	0	0	1	15	6.7
L	57 *	Antti Laaksonen	BOS	11	1	2	3	–1	2	0	0	0	0	8	12.5
C	21 *	Randy Robitaille	BOS	4	0	2	2	–1	0	0	0	0	0	5	0.0
G	34	Byron Dafoe	BOS	68	0	2	2	0	25	0	0	0	0	0	0.0
C	28 *	Andre Savage	BOS	6	1	0	1	2	0	0	0	0	0	8	12.5
C	72 *	Eric Nickulas	BOS	2	0	0	0	0	0	0	0	0	0	0	0.0
R	56 *	Peter Nordstrom	BOS	2	0	0	0	–1	0	0	0	0	0	0	0.0
D	29	Dennis Vaske	BOS	3	0	0	0	–3	6	0	0	0	0	0	0.0
D	55 *	Jonathan Girard	BOS	3	0	0	0	1	0	0	0	0	0	3	0.0
D	71	Terry Virtue	BOS	4	0	0	0	2	0	0	0	0	0	2	0.0
L	51 *	Jay Henderson	BOS	4	0	0	0	–1	2	0	0	0	0	4	0.0
D	53 *	Brandon Smith	BOS	5	0	0	0	2	0	0	0	0	0	2	0.0
C	61 *	Marquis Mathieu	BOS	9	0	0	0	–1	8	0	0	0	0	4	0.0
G	35	Robbie Tallas	BOS	17	0	0	0	0	0	0	0	0	0	0	0.0

Goaltending

No.	Goaltender	GPI	Mins	Avg	W	L	T	EN	SO	GA	SA	S%
34	Byron Dafoe	68	4001	1.99	32	23	11	3	10	133	1800	.926
35	Robbie Tallas	17	987	2.61	7	7	2	2	1	43	421	.898
	Totals	**82**	**5001**	**2.17**	**39**	**30**	**13**	**5**	**11**	**181**	**2226**	**.919**

Playoffs

Pos	#	Player	Team	GP	G	A	Pts	+/–	PIM	PP	SH	GW	OT	S	%
C	41	Jason Allison	BOS	12	2	9	11	1	6	1	0	0	0	28	7.1
D	77	Ray Bourque	BOS	12	1	9	10	1	14	0	0	0	0	44	2.3
C	6	Joe Thornton	BOS	11	3	6	9	1	4	2	0	2	0	15	20.0
R	23	Steve Heinze	BOS	12	4	3	7	–1	0	2	0	0	0	23	17.4
L	33	Anson Carter	BOS	12	4	3	7	–3	0	1	0	1	1	27	14.8
R	12	Dmitri Khristich	BOS	12	3	4	7	1	6	0	0	1	0	19	15.8
L	14	Sergei Samsonov	BOS	11	3	1	4	3	0	0	0	0	0	21	14.3
D	32	Don Sweeney	BOS	11	3	0	3	2	6	1	0	0	0	16	18.8
D	20	Darren Van Impe	BOS	11	1	2	3	–3	4	1	0	0	0	18	5.6
C	26	Tim Taylor	BOS	12	0	3	3	1	8	0	0	0	0	11	0.0
D	18	Kyle McLaren	BOS	12	0	3	3	4	10	0	0	0	0	21	0.0
L	19	Rob Dimaio	BOS	12	2	0	2	2	8	0	0	1	0	21	9.5
D	37	Mattias Timander	BOS	4	1	1	2	3	2	0	0	0	0	3	33.3
R	27	Landon Wilson	BOS	8	1	1	2	–2	8	1	0	1	0	14	7.1
R	11	P.J. Axelsson	BOS	12	1	1	2	–1	4	0	0	0	0	20	5.0
L	16	Ken Belanger	BOS	12	1	0	1	2	16	0	0	0	0	7	14.3
C	72 *	Eric Nickulas	BOS	1	0	0	0	0	2	0	0	0	0	0	0.0
R	10 *	Cameron Mann	BOS	1	0	0	0	0	0	0	0	0	0	0	0.0
C	21 *	Randy Robitaille	BOS	1	0	0	0	0	0	0	0	0	0	0	0.0
D	36	Grant Ledyard	BOS	2	0	0	0	–1	2	0	0	0	0	4	0.0
L	22	Ken Baumgartner	BOS	3	0	0	0	0	0	0	0	0	0	0	0.0
D	44	Dave Ellett	BOS	8	0	0	0	0	4	0	0	0	0	4	0.0
G	34	Byron Dafoe	BOS	12	0	0	0	0	2	0	0	0	0	0	0.0
C	17 *	Shawn Bates	BOS	12	0	0	0	–1	4	0	0	0	0	11	0.0
D	25	Hal Gill	BOS	12	0	0	0	–1	14	0	0	0	0	10	0.0

Goaltending

No.	Goaltender	GPI	Mins	Avg	W	L	EN	SO	GA	SA	S%
34	Byron Dafoe	12	768	2.03	6	6	1	2	26	330	.921
	Totals	**12**	**772**	**2.10**	**6**	**6**	**1**	**2**	**27**	**331**	**.918**

Coaching History

Art Ross, 1924-25 to 1927-28; Cy Denneny, 1928-29; Art Ross, 1929-30 to 1933-34; Frank Patrick, 1934-35, 1935-36; Art Ross, 1936-37 to 1938-39; Cooney Weiland, 1939-40, 1940-41; Art Ross, 1941-42 to 1944-45; Dit Clapper, 1945-46 to 1948-49; George Boucher, 1949-50; Lynn Patrick, 1950-51 to 1953-54; Lynn Patrick and Milt Schmidt, 1954-55; Milt Schmidt, 1955-56 to 1960-61; Phil Watson, 1961-62; Phil Watson and Milt Schmidt, 1962-63; Milt Schmidt, 1963-64 to 1965-66; Harry Sinden, 1966-67 to 1969-70; Tom Johnson, 1970-71, 1971-72; Tom Johnson and Bep Guidolin, 1972-73; Bep Guidolin, 1973-74; Don Cherry, 1974-75 to 1978-79; Fred Creighton and Harry Sinden, 1979-80; Gerry Cheevers, 1980-81 to 1983-84; Gerry Cheevers and Harry Sinden, 1984-85; Butch Goring, 1985-86; Butch Goring and Terry O'Reilly, 1986-87; Terry O'Reilly, 1987-88, 1988-89; Mike Milbury, 1989-90, 1990-91; Rick Bowness, 1991-92; Brian Sutter, 1992-93 to 1994-95; Steve Kasper, 1995-96, 1996-97; Pat Burns, 1997-98 to date.

Club Records

Team

(Figures in brackets for season records are games played; records for fewest points, wins, ties, losses, goals, goals against are for 70 or more games)

Most Points	**121**	1970-71 (78)
Most Wins	**57**	1970-71 (78)
Most Ties	**21**	1954-55 (70)
Most Losses	**47**	1961-62 (70), 1996-97 (82)
Most Goals	**399**	1970-71 (78)
Most Goals Against	**306**	1961-62 (70)
Fewest Points	**38**	1961-62 (70)
Fewest Wins	**14**	1962-63 (70)
Fewest Ties	**5**	1972-73 (78)
Fewest Losses	**13**	1971-72 (78)
Fewest Goals	**147**	1955-56 (70)
Fewest Goals Against	**172**	1952-53 (70)
Longest Winning Streak		
Overall	**14**	Dec. 3/29-Jan. 9/30
Home	***20**	Dec. 3/29-Mar. 18/30
Away	**8**	Feb. 17-Mar. 8/72, Mar. 15-Apr. 14/93
Longest Undefeated Streak		
Overall	**23**	Dec. 22/40-Feb. 23/41 (15 wins, 8 ties)
Home	**27**	Nov. 22/70-Mar. 20/71 (26 wins, 1 tie)
Away	**15**	Dec. 22/40-Mar. 16/41 (9 wins, 6 ties)
Longest Losing Streak		
Overall	**11**	Dec. 3/24-Jan. 5/25
Home	***11**	Dec. 8/24-Feb. 17/25
Away	**14**	Dec. 27/64-Feb. 21/65
Longest Winless Streak		
Overall	**20**	Jan. 28-Mar. 11/62 (16 losses, 4 ties)
Home	**11**	Dec. 8/24-Feb. 17/25 (11 losses)
Away	**14**	Three times
Most Shutouts, Season	**15**	1927-28 (44)
Most PIM, Season	**2,443**	1987-88 (80)
Most Goals, Game	**14**	Jan. 21/45 (NYR 3 at Bos. 14)

Individual

Most Seasons	**21**	John Bucyk
Most Games	**1,436**	John Bucyk
Most Goals, Career	**545**	John Bucyk
Most Assists, Career	**1,083**	Ray Bourque
Most Points, Career	**1,468**	Ray Bourque (385G, 1,083A)
Most PIM, Career	**2,095**	Terry O'Reilly
Most Shutouts, Career	**74**	Tiny Thompson
Longest Consecutive Games Streak	**418**	John Bucyk (Jan. 23/69-Mar. 2/75)
Most Goals, Season	**76**	Phil Esposito (1970-71)
Most Assists, Season	**102**	Bobby Orr (1970-71)
Most Points, Season	**152**	Phil Esposito (1970-71; 76G, 76A)
Most PIM, Season	**304**	Jay Miller (1987-88)
Most Points, Defenseman, Season	***139**	Bobby Orr (1970-71; 37G, 102A)
Most Points, Center, Season	**152**	Phil Esposito (1970-71; 76G, 76A)
Most Points, Right Wing, Season	**105**	Ken Hodge (1970-71; 43G, 62A), (1973-74; 50G, 55A), Rick Middleton (1983-84; 47G, 58A)
Most Points, Left Wing, Season	**116**	John Bucyk (1970-71; 51G, 65A)
Most Points, Rookie, Season	**102**	Joe Juneau (1992-93; 32G, 70A)
Most Shutouts, Season	**15**	Hal Winkler (1927-28)
Most Goals, Game	**4**	Nineteen times
Most Assists, Game	**6**	Ken Hodge (Feb. 9/71), Bobby Orr (Jan. 1/73)
Most Points, Game	**7**	Bobby Orr (Nov. 15/73; 3G, 4A), Phil Esposito (Dec. 19/74; 3G, 4A), Barry Pederson (Apr. 4/82; 3G, 4A), Cam Neely (Oct. 16/88; 3G, 4A)

* NHL Record.

Retired Numbers

2	Eddie Shore	1926-1940
3	Lionel Hitchman	1925-1934
4	Bobby Orr	1966-1976
5	Dit Clapper	1927-1947
7	Phil Esposito	1967-1975
9	John Bucyk	1957-1978
15	Milt Schmidt	1936-1955

All-time Record vs. Other Clubs

Regular Season

	At Home							On Road							Total						
	GP	W	L	T	GF	GA	PTS	GP	W	L	T	GF	GA	PTS	GP	W	L	T	GF	GA	PTS
Anaheim	5	3	2	0	16	14	6	5	2	2	1	12	9	5	10	5	4	1	28	23	11
Buffalo	94	53	29	12	365	286	118	95	32	48	15	287	352	79	189	85	77	27	652	638	197
Calgary	43	26	11	6	152	117	58	42	22	17	3	149	154	47	85	48	28	9	301	271	105
Carolina	68	44	17	7	257	176	95	66	30	29	7	230	226	67	134	74	46	14	487	402	162
Chicago	280	159	87	34	1012	791	352	282	94	144	44	754	908	232	562	253	231	78	1766	1699	584
Colorado	59	31	20	8	233	182	70	61	34	21	6	260	217	74	120	65	41	14	493	399	144
Dallas	57	40	8	9	249	136	89	57	29	16	12	211	166	70	114	69	24	21	460	302	159
Detroit	283	152	88	43	998	752	347	282	77	153	52	711	946	206	565	229	241	95	1709	1698	553
Edmonton	26	18	6	2	113	74	38	26	14	9	3	90	85	31	52	32	15	5	203	159	69
Florida	12	4	5	3	32	33	11	11	7	4	0	33	30	14	23	11	9	3	65	63	25
Los Angeles	58	43	11	4	274	161	90	57	31	20	6	214	197	68	115	74	31	10	488	358	158
Montreal	322	148	119	55	952	871	351	321	92	184	45	759	1089	229	643	240	303	100	1711	1960	580
Nashville	1	1	0	0	8	1	2	1	1	0	0	5	2	2	2	2	0	0	13	3	4
New Jersey	46	27	13	6	190	142	60	43	23	11	9	144	112	55	89	50	24	15	334	254	115
NY Islanders	49	27	12	10	191	140	64	51	24	21	6	168	171	54	100	51	33	16	359	311	118
NY Rangers	288	154	93	41	1042	808	349	292	111	126	55	824	888	277	580	265	219	96	1866	1696	626
Ottawa	20	14	4	2	85	53	30	18	14	2	2	63	32	30	38	28	6	4	148	85	60
Philadelphia	66	43	15	8	264	185	94	63	27	28	8	183	211	62	129	70	43	16	447	396	156
Phoenix	26	19	4	3	120	83	41	27	14	11	2	99	96	30	53	33	15	5	219	179	71
Pittsburgh	68	49	13	6	311	198	104	70	27	30	13	255	250	67	138	76	43	19	566	448	171
St. Louis	55	34	12	9	237	149	77	55	23	23	9	192	175	55	110	57	35	18	429	324	132
San Jose	7	5	0	2	26	17	12	7	4	1	2	29	18	10	14	9	1	4	55	35	22
Tampa Bay	13	9	1	3	45	29	21	13	6	5	2	35	33	14	26	15	6	5	80	62	35
Toronto	285	154	84	47	936	756	355	286	87	149	50	745	972	224	571	241	233	97	1681	1728	579
Vancouver	47	36	6	5	204	111	77	48	25	15	8	199	157	58	95	61	21	13	403	268	135
Washington	46	27	13	6	178	127	60	45	23	12	10	164	132	56	91	50	25	16	342	259	116
Defunct Clubs	164	112	39	13	525	306	237	164	79	67	18	496	440	176	328	191	106	31	1021	746	413
Totals	**2488**	**1432**	**712**	**344**	**9015**	**6698**	**3208**	**2488**	**952**	**1148**	**388**	**7311**	**8068**	**2292**	**4976**	**2384**	**1860**	**732**	**16326**	**14766**	**5500**

Playoffs

	Series	W	L	GP	W	L	T	GF	GA	Last Mtg.	Round	Result
Buffalo	7	5	2	39	21	18	0	146	130	1999	CSF	L 2-4
Carolina	3	3	0	19	12	7	0	63	48	1999	CQF	W 4-2
Chicago	6	5	1	22	16	5	1	97	63	1978	QF	W 4-0
Colorado	2	1	1	11	6	5	0	37	36	1983	DSF	W 3-1
Dallas	1	0	1	3	0	3	0	13	20	1981	PR	L 0-3
Detroit	7	4	3	33	19	14	0	96	98	1957	SF	W 4-1
Edmonton	2	0	2	9	1	8	0	20	41	1990	F	L 1-4
Florida	1	0	1	5	1	4	0	16	22	1996	CQF	L 1-4
Los Angeles	2	2	0	13	8	5	0	56	38	1977	QF	W 4-2
Montreal	28	7	21	139	52	87	0	339	430	1994	CQF	W 4-3
New Jersey	3	1	2	18	7	11	0	52	55	1995	CQF	L 1-4
NY Islanders	2	0	2	11	3	8	0	35	49	1983	CF	L 2-4
NY Rangers	9	6	3	42	22	18	2	114	104	1973	QF	L 1-4
Philadelphia	4	2	2	20	11	9	0	60	57	1978	SF	W 4-1
Pittsburgh	4	2	2	19	9	10	0	62	67	1992	CF	L 0-4
St. Louis	2	2	0	8	8	0	0	48	15	1972	SF	W 4-0
Toronto	13	5	8	62	30	31	1	153	150	1974	QF	W 4-0
Washington	2	1	1	10	6	4	0	28	21	1998	CQF	L 2-4
Defunct Clubs	3	1	2	11	4	5	2	20	20			
Totals	**101**	**47**	**54**	**494**	**236**	**252**	**6**	**1448**	**1464**			

Calgary totals include Atlanta Flames, 1972-73 to 1979-80.
Colorado totals include Quebec, 1979-80 to 1994-95.
New Jersey totals include Kansas City, 1974-75 to 1975-76, and Colorado Rockies, 1976-77 to 1981-82.
Phoenix totals include Winnipeg, 1979-80 to 1995-96.
Carolina totals include Hartford, 1979-80 to 1996-97.
Dallas totals include Minnesota, 1967-68 to 1992-93.

Playoff Results 1999-95

Year	Round	Opponent	Result	GF	GA
1999	CSF	Buffalo	L 2-4	14	17
	CQF	Carolina	W 4-2	16	10
1998	CQF	Washington	L 2-4	13	15
1996	CQF	Florida	L 1-4	16	22
1995	CQF	New Jersey	L 1-4	5	14

Abbreviations: Round: F – Final; **CF** – conference final; **CSF** – conference semi-final; **CQF** – conference quarter-final; **DSF** – division semi-final; **SF** – semi-final; **QF** – quarter-final; **PR** – preliminary round.

1998-99 Results

Oct.	10		St. Louis	3-3		18		Nashville	8-1
	12		NY Islanders	3-0		21		Ottawa	1-3
	14	at	Colorado	3-0		26	at	NY Islanders	1-4
	16	at	Los Angeles	1-2		28		New Jersey	0-2
	18	at	San Jose	3-0		30	at	Pittsburgh	2-5
	19	at	Phoenix	1-3		31		Carolina	0-0
	21	at	Anaheim	0-3	**Feb.**	2		Colorado	2-3
	24	at	New Jersey	1-3		4		NY Islanders	4-5
	28	at	Montreal	9-2		6	at	Philadelphia	2-2
	29		Montreal	1-1		7		NY Rangers	3-2
	31		Carolina	0-2		9	at	Edmonton	2-0
Nov.	3	at	Buffalo	2-4		12	at	Calgary	3-4
	5		Toronto	4-1		13	at	Vancouver	1-3
	7	at	Pittsburgh	0-0		18	at	Ottawa	0-2
	8	at	Carolina	5-2		21	at	Chicago	6-3
	13	at	NY Rangers	3-3		23		Ottawa	5-2
	14		Dallas	1-3		25		New Jersey	3-3
	19		Florida	5-5		27		Washington	4-3
	21		Washington	5-4	**Mar.**	2		Phoenix	3-2
	24	at	Tampa Bay	4-1		3	at	Carolina	1-2
	25	at	Florida	1-0		5	at	New Jersey	4-1
	27		Montreal	5-1		7		NY Rangers	1-3
Dec.	1		Vancouver	1-1		9		Florida	2-0
	5		Pittsburgh	2-1		12	at	NY Rangers	5-4
	10	at	Carolina	3-2		13	at	Buffalo	1-3
	12		Buffalo	1-4		17	at	Toronto	4-1
	16	at	Detroit	3-5		20		San Jose	2-2
	17		Ottawa	5-2		21	at	Washington	4-1
	19		Detroit	4-1		24	at	Ottawa	3-0
	21		Tampa Bay	3-2		25		Chicago	3-3
	23		Philadelphia	1-2		27	at	Toronto	2-2
	26	at	NY Islanders	2-4		30		Los Angeles	1-2
	28	at	Washington	1-5	**Apr.**	1	at	Montreal	3-2
	30	at	Nashville	5-2		3		Philadelphia	3-0
	31	at	Dallas	1-6		5		Montreal	3-0
Jan.	2		Anaheim	2-1		7	at	Florida	5-2
	4		Calgary	5-1		8	at	Tampa Bay	0-3
	7		Toronto	2-1		10		Tampa Bay	3-2
	9	at	Toronto	3-6		15		Pittsburgh	4-2
	15	at	Buffalo	1-2		17		Buffalo	2-1
	16		Tampa Bay	2-2		18	at	Philadelphia	1-3

Entry Draft
Selections 1999-85

1999
Pick
21 Nicholas Boynton
56 Matt Zultek
89 Kyle Wanvig
118 Jaakko Harikkala
147 Seamus Kotyk
179 Donald Choukalos
207 Greg Barber
236 John Cronin
247 Mikko Eloranta
264 Georgijs Pujacs

1998
Pick
48 Jonathon Girard
52 Bobby Allen
78 Peter Nordstrom
135 Andrew Raycroft
165 Ryan Milanovic

1997
Pick
1 Joe Thornton
8 Sergei Samsonov
27 Ben Clymer
54 Mattias Karlin
63 Lee Goren
81 Karol Bartanus
135 Denis Timofeev
162 Joel Trottier
180 Jim Baxter
191 Antti Laaksonen
218 Eric Van Acker
246 Jay Henderson

1996
Pick
8 Johnathan Aitken
45 Henry Kuster
53 Eric Naud
80 Jason Doyle
100 Trent Whitfield
132 Elias Abrahamsson
155 Chris Lane
182 Thomas Brown
208 Bob Prier
234 Anders Soderberg

1995
Pick
9 Kyle McLaren
21 Sean Brown
47 Paxton Schafer
73 Bill McCauley
99 Cameron Mann
151 Yevgeny Shaldybin
177 Per Johan Axelsson
203 Sergei Zhukov
229 Jonathan Murphy

1994
Pick
21 Evgeni Ryabchikov
47 Daniel Goneau
99 Eric Nickulas
125 Darren Wright
151 Andre Roy
177 Jeremy Schaefer
229 John Grahame
255 Neil Savary
281 Andrei Yakhanov

1993
Pick
25 Kevyn Adams
51 Matt Alvey
88 Charles Paquette
103 Shawn Bates
129 Andrei Sapozhnikov
155 Milt Mastad
181 Ryan Golden
207 Hal Gill
233 Joel Prpic
259 Joakim Persson

1992
Pick
16 Dmitri Kvartalnov
55 Sergei Zholtok
112 Scott Bailey
133 Jiri Dopita
136 Grigori Panteleev
184 Kurt Seher
208 Mattias Timander
232 Chris Crombie
256 Denis Chervyakov
257 Evgeny Pavlov

1991
Pick
18 Glen Murray
40 Jozef Stumpel
62 Marcel Cousineau
84 Brad Tiley
106 Mariusz Czerkawski
150 Gary Golczewski
172 John Moser
194 Daniel Hodge
216 Steve Norton
238 Stephen Lombardi
260 Torsten Kienass

1990
Pick
21 Bryan Smolinski
63 Cameron Stewart
84 Jerome Buckley
105 Mike Bales
126 Mark Woolf
147 Jim Mackey
168 John Gruden
189 Darren Wetherill
210 Dean Capuano
231 Andy Bezeau
252 Ted Miskolczi

1989
Pick
17 Shayne Stevenson
38 Mike Parson
57 Wes Walz
80 Jackson Penney
101 Mark Montanari
122 Stephen Foster
143 Otto Hascak
164 Rick Allain
185 James Lavish
206 Geoff Simpson
227 David Franzosa

1988
Pick
18 Robert Cimetta
60 Stephen Heinze
81 Joe Juneau
102 Daniel Murphy
123 Derek Geary
165 Mark Krys
186 Jon Rohloff
228 Eric Reisman
249 Doug Jones

1987
Pick
3 Glen Wesley
14 Stephane Quintal
56 Todd Lalonde
67 Darwin McPherson
77 Matt Delguidice
98 Ted Donato
119 Matt Glennon
140 Rob Cheevers
161 Chris Winnes
182 Paul Ohman
203 Casey Jones
224 Eric Lemarque
245 Sean Gorman

1986
Pick
13 Craig Janney
34 Pekka Tirkkonen
76 Dean Hall
97 Matt Pesklewis
118 Garth Premak
139 Paul Beraldo
160 Brian Ferreira
181 Jeff Flaherty
202 Greg Hawgood
223 Staffan Malmqvist
244 Joel Gardner

1985
Pick
31 Alain Cote
52 Bill Ranford
73 Jaime Kelly
94 Steve Moore
115 Gord Hynes
136 Per Martinelle
157 Randy Burridge
178 Gord Cruickshank
199 Dave Buda
210 Bob Beers
220 John Byce
241 Marc West

President and General Manager

SINDEN, HARRY
President and General Manager, Boston Bruins.
Born in Collins Bay, Ont., September 14, 1932.

Harry Sinden enters his eleventh season as the Bruins' president and his 28th season as the club's general manager.

Sinden's name has been synonymous with the Bruins organization for over 37 years. He has been instrumental in bringing a Stanley Cup, six Conference titles and ten Division championships to Boston. On October 17, 1995 with a 7-4 Boston win at St. Louis, he became the first general manager in the history of the NHL to record 1,000 victories as a g.m.

His many accomplishments, in addition to his knowledge and experience, led to his 1983 induction into the Hockey Hall of Fame in the Builder's category as he became the 23rd Bruin enshrined.

Sinden was a top amateur player in Canada as a defenseman who captained his Whitby Dunlops team to both the 1957 Allan Cup as Canada's Senior Amateur Champions and the 1958 World Championship title. He also competed in the 1960 Olympics in Squaw Valley, bringing a silver medal home to Canada.

He came to the Bruins organization in 1961 when he assumed the position of player-coach in Kingston, Ontario. After coaching Boston's minor league affiliate in Minneapolis, he became a player-coach in Oklahoma City and led that team to the 1966 CHL championship with eight consecutive playoff victories. He moved to Boston to assume the Bruins head coaching reins in 1966-67.

In 1972 he served as coach of Team Canada in the classic series between NHL players and the Soviet Union.

Sinden and his wife, Eleanor, reside in Winchester, MA. They have four daughters.

NHL Coaching Record

Season	Team	Games	Regular Season W	L	T	%	Playoffs Games	W	L	%
1966-67	Boston	70	17	43	10	.314				
1967-68	Boston	74	37	27	10	.568	4	0	4	.000
1968-69	Boston	76	42	18	16	.658	10	6	4	.600
1969-70	Boston	76	40	17	19	.651	14	12	2	.857*
1979-80	Boston	7	6	1	0	.857	10	4	6	.400
1984-85	Boston	24	11	10	3	.521	5	2	3	.400
	NHL Totals	327	153	116	58	.557	43	24	19	.558

* Stanley Cup win.

Club Directory

FleetCenter
One FleetCenter, Suite 250
Boston, Massachusetts 02114
Phone **617/624-1900**
FAX 617/523-7184
www.bostonbruins.com
Capacity: 17,565

Executive
Owner and Governor . . . . Jeremy M. Jacobs
Alternate Governor . . . . Louis Jacobs
President, General Manager and
Alternate Governor . . . . Harry Sinden
Vice President of Hockey Operations and
Assistant General Manager . . . . Mike O'Connell
Senior Assistant to the President . . . . Nate Greenberg
Assistant to the Vice President of
Hockey Operations . . . . Jeff Gorton
General Counsel . . . . Michael Wall
Director of Administration . . . . Dale Hamilton
Assistant to the President . . . . Joe Curnane
Team Travel Coordinator/Administrative Assistant . Carol Gould
Receptionist . . . . Karen Ondo

Coaching Staff
Coach . . . . Pat Burns
Assistant Coach . . . . Jacques Laperriere
Coach, Providence Bruins . . . . Peter Laviolette
Coach, Greenville Grrrowl . . . . John Marks

Scouting Staff
Director of Scouting . . . . Scott Bradley
Director of Development . . . . Bob Tindall
Scouting Staff . . . . Don Saatzer, Jean Ratelle, Daniel Dore,
David McNamara, Svenake Svensson, Yuri
Karmanov, Don Matheson, Ernie Gare, Gerry
Cheevers, Jim Morrison, Tim O'Connell, Tom
McVie, Nickolai Bobrov

Communications & Marketing Staff
Director of Media Relations . . . . Heidi Holland
Media Relations Assistant . . . . Mark Awdycki
Director of Marketing and Community Relations . . . Sue Byrne
Promotions Manager . . . . Susan Zemaitis
Community Relations Coordinator . . . . Heather Wright
Promotions Coordinator . . . . Tyrone Croom
Director of Alumni Community Relations . . . . John Bucyk
Administrative Assistant, Alumni Office . . . . . . Mal Viola

Medical and Training Staff
Athletic Trainer . . . . Don Del Negro
Physical Therapist . . . . Scott Waugh
Equipment Manager . . . . Peter Henderson
Assistant Equipment Manager . . . . Chris "Muggsy" Aldrich
Team Physicians . . . . Dr. Bertram Zarins, Dr. Ashby Moncure,
Dr. John J. Boyle
Team Dentists . . . . Dr. Edwin Riley, DMD, Dr. Bruce Donoff, DMD, MD,
Dr. Robert Amato, DMD
Team Opthalmic Consultant . . . . Dr. Bradford Shingleton
Team Psychologist . . . . Dr. Fred Neff

Ticketing and Finance Staff
Director of Ticket Operations . . . . Matt Brennan
Assistant Director of Ticket Operations . . . . . Jim Foley
Ticket Office Receptionist . . . . Jo-Ann Connolly-White
Controller . . . . Richard McGlinchey
Payroll Manager . . . . Barbara Johnson
Accounts Payable . . . . Linda Bartlett

Television and Radio
Broadcasters . . . . (UPN38 WSBK-TV) Dave Shea, Phil Esposito and
Gerry Cheevers
(NESN) Dale Arnold and Gord Kluzak
(Radio) Bob Neumeier and Bob Beers
TV Channels . . . . New England Sports Network (NESN) and
UPN38 WSBK-TV
Radio Station . . . . WBZ (1030 AM) and Bruins Radio Network

General Managers' History

Art Ross, 1924-25 to 1953-54; Lynn Patrick, 1954-55 to 1964-65; Hap Emms, 1965-66, 1966-67; Milt Schmidt, 1967-68 to 1971-72; Harry Sinden, 1972-73 to date.

Captains' History

No captain, 1924-25 to 1926-27; Lionel Hitchman, 1927-28 to 1930-31; George Owen, 1931-32; Dit Clapper, 1932-33 to 1937-38; Cooney Weiland, 1938-39; Dit Clapper, 1939-40 to 1945-46; Dit Clapper and John Crawford, 1946-47; John Crawford 1947-48 to 1949-50; Milt Schmidt, 1950-51 to 1953-54; Milt Schmidt, Ed Sanford, 1954-55; Fern Flaman, 1955-56 to 1960-61; Don McKenney, 1961-62, 1962-63; Leo Boivin, 1963-64 to 1965-66; John Bucyk, 1966-67; no captain, 1967-68 to 1972-73; John Bucyk, 1973-74 to 1976-77; Wayne Cashman, 1977-78 to 1982-83; Terry O'Reilly, 1983-84, 1984-85; Ray Bourque, Rick Middleton (co-captains) 1985-86 to 1987-88; Ray Bourque, 1988-89 to date.

Buffalo Sabres

1998-99 Results: 37W-28L-17T 91PTS. Fourth, Northeast Division

1999-2000 Schedule

Oct.	Sat.	2	at Detroit
	Fri.	8	Washington
	Sat.	9	at Atlanta
	Mon.	11	Phoenix
	Sat.	16	at Montreal
	Sun.	17	at Philadelphia
	Wed.	20	Nashville
	Fri.	22	Carolina
	Sat.	23	at Ottawa
	Wed.	27	Tampa Bay
	Fri.	29	Florida
	Sat.	30	at Boston
Nov.	Wed.	3	at Dallas
	Thu.	4	at Chicago
	Sat.	6	NY Islanders
	Wed.	10	Boston
	Fri.	12	at Tampa Bay
	Sat.	13	at Florida
	Tue.	16	at Pittsburgh
	Fri.	19	at Atlanta
	Sat.	20	Atlanta
	Wed.	24	Washington
	Fri.	26	St. Louis
	Sun.	28	at Tampa Bay
	Tue.	30	Pittsburgh
Dec.	Thu.	2	Philadelphia
	Sat.	4	NY Rangers
	Mon.	6	at Toronto
	Wed.	8	Ottawa
	Fri.	10	Chicago
	Tue.	14	Philadelphia
	Fri.	17	Florida
	Sat.	18	at NY Islanders
	Tue.	21	at NY Rangers
	Thu.	23	Colorado
	Mon.	27	at New Jersey
	Tue.	28	Detroit
Jan.	Sat.	1	Toronto
	Mon.	3	at Toronto
	Tue.	4	Atlanta
	Thu.	6	New Jersey

	Sat.	8	at Ottawa
	Thu.	13	at Boston
	Fri.	14	Montreal
	Mon.	17	at Anaheim
	Tue.	18	at Los Angeles
	Thu.	20	at Phoenix
	Sat.	22	at Carolina*
	Tue.	25	Tampa Bay
	Fri.	28	Ottawa
	Sat.	29	at Boston
Feb.	Tue.	1	Anaheim
	Thu.	3	Ottawa
	Tue.	8	at Colorado
	Thu.	10	at Nashville
	Sat.	12	at Philadelphia*
	Sun.	13	Edmonton*
	Wed.	16	at Pittsburgh
	Thu.	17	Vancouver
	Sat.	19	Los Angeles
	Mon.	21	New Jersey
	Fri.	25	NY Rangers
	Sat.	26	at Toronto
	Mon.	28	at Florida
Mar.	Wed.	1	at NY Rangers
	Sat.	4	at NY Islanders*
	Sun.	5	at Washington*
	Wed.	8	Boston
	Fri.	10	Montreal
	Sun.	12	NY Islanders*
	Wed.	15	at San Jose
	Thu.	16	at Vancouver
	Sat.	18	at Calgary
	Mon.	20	Montreal
	Thu.	23	Calgary
	Mon.	27	at Carolina
	Fri.	31	Carolina
Apr.	Sat.	1	at Montreal
	Mon.	3	Toronto
	Thu.	6	at New Jersey
	Fri.	7	Pittsburgh
	Sun.	9	at Washington*

* Denotes afternoon game.

Franchise date: May 22, 1970

NORTHEAST
DIVISION

**30th
NHL
Season**

Miroslav Satan reached the 40-goal plateau for the first time in 1998-99, leading the Sabres with 40 goals and 66 points. Injured throughout much of the playoffs, Satan still had eight points in 12 games as Buffalo reached the Stanley Cup Finals.

Year-by-Year Record

Season	GP	Home W	L	T	Road W	L	T	Overall W	L	T	GF	GA	Pts.	Finished		Playoff Result
1998-99	82	23	12	6	14	16	11	37	28	17	207	175	91	4th,	Northeast Div.	Lost Final
1997-98	82	20	13	8	16	16	9	36	29	17	211	187	89	3rd,	Northeast Div.	Lost Conf. Final
1996-97	82	24	11	6	16	19	6	40	30	12	237	208	92	1st,	Northeast Div.	Lost Conf. Semi-Final
1995-96	82	19	17	5	14	25	2	33	42	7	247	262	73	5th,	Northeast Div.	Out of Playoffs
1994-95	48	15	8	1	7	11	6	22	19	7	130	119	51	4th,	Northeast Div.	Lost Conf. Quarter-Final
1993-94	84	22	17	3	21	15	6	43	32	9	282	218	95	4th,	Northeast Div.	Lost Conf. Quarter-Final
1992-93	84	25	15	2	13	21	8	38	36	10	335	297	86	4th,	Adams Div.	Lost Div. Final
1991-92	80	22	13	5	9	24	7	31	37	12	289	299	74	3rd,	Adams Div.	Lost Div. Semi-Final
1990-91	80	15	13	12	16	17	7	31	30	19	292	278	81	3rd,	Adams Div.	Lost Div. Semi-Final
1989-90	80	27	11	2	18	16	6	45	27	8	286	248	98	2nd,	Adams Div.	Lost Div. Semi-Final
1988-89	80	25	12	3	13	23	4	38	35	7	291	299	83	3rd,	Adams Div.	Lost Div. Semi-Final
1987-88	80	19	14	7	18	18	4	37	32	11	283	305	85	3rd,	Adams Div.	Lost Div. Semi-Final
1986-87	80	18	18	4	10	26	4	28	44	8	280	308	64	5th,	Adams Div.	Out of Playoffs
1985-86	80	23	16	1	14	21	5	37	37	6	296	291	80	5th,	Adams Div.	Out of Playoffs
1984-85	80	23	10	7	15	18	7	38	28	14	290	237	90	3rd,	Adams Div.	Lost Div. Semi-Final
1983-84	80	25	9	6	23	16	1	48	25	7	315	257	103	2nd,	Adams Div.	Lost Div. Semi-Final
1982-83	80	25	7	8	13	22	5	38	29	13	318	285	89	3rd,	Adams Div.	Lost Div. Final
1981-82	80	23	8	9	16	18	6	39	26	15	307	273	93	3rd,	Adams Div.	Lost Div. Semi-Final
1980-81	80	21	7	12	18	13	9	39	20	21	327	250	99	1st,	Adams Div.	Lost Quarter-Final
1979-80	80	27	5	8	20	12	8	47	17	16	318	201	110	1st,	Adams Div.	Lost Semi-Final
1978-79	80	19	13	8	17	15	8	36	28	16	280	263	88	2nd,	Adams Div.	Lost Prelim. Round
1977-78	80	25	7	8	19	12	9	44	19	17	288	215	105	2nd,	Adams Div.	Lost Quarter-Final
1976-77	80	27	8	5	21	16	3	48	24	8	301	220	104	2nd,	Adams Div.	Lost Quarter-Final
1975-76	80	28	7	5	18	14	8	46	21	13	339	240	105	2nd,	Adams Div.	Lost Quarter-Final
1974-75	80	28	6	6	21	10	9	49	16	15	354	240	113	1st,	Adams Div.	Lost Final
1973-74	78	23	10	6	9	24	6	32	34	12	242	250	76	5th,	East Div.	Out of Playoffs
1972-73	78	30	6	3	7	21	11	37	27	14	257	219	88	4th,	East Div.	Lost Quarter-Final
1971-72	78	11	19	9	5	24	10	16	43	19	203	289	51	6th,	East Div.	Out of Playoffs
1970-71	78	16	13	10	8	26	5	24	39	15	217	291	63	5th,	East Div.	Out of Playoffs

1999-2000 Player Personnel

FORWARDS	HT	WT	S	Place of Birth	Date	1998-99 Club
AFINOGENOV, Maxim	5-11	176	L	Moscow, USSR	9/4/79	Moscow D'amo
BARNES, Stu	5-11	174	R	Spruce Grove, Alta.	12/25/70	Pittsburgh-Buffalo
BIENVENUE, Daniel	6-0	196	L	Val d'Or, Que.	6/10/77	Jacksonville-Baton Rouge
BROWN, Curtis	6-0	190	L	Unity, Sask.	2/12/76	Buffalo
BRUNEL, Craig	6-0	201	R	Winnipeg, Man.	11/12/79	Prince Albert
CUNNEYWORTH, Randy	6-0	198	L	Etobicoke, Ont.	5/10/61	Buffalo-Rochester
DAVIDSON, Matt	6-2	190	R	Flin Flon, Man.	8/9/77	Rochester
DUTIAUME, Mark	6-0	200	L	Winnipeg, Man.	1/31/77	Rochester-Binghamton
FISHER, Craig	6-3	180	L	Oshawa, Ont.	6/30/70	Rochester
GOLDADE, Aaron	6-0	180	L	Prince Albert, Sask.	7/30/80	Brandon
GROSEK, Michal	6-2	207	R	Vyskov, Czech.	6/1/75	Buffalo
HAMEL, Denis	6-2	200	L	Lachute, Que.	5/10/77	Rochester
HOLZINGER, Brian	5-11	190	R	Parma, OH	10/10/72	Buffalo
KOTALIK, Ales	6-1	198	R	Jindrichuv Hradec, Czech.	12/23/78	HC Budejovice
KRUSE, Paul	6-0	202	L	Merritt, B.C.	3/15/70	Buffalo
MARTIN, Jeff	6-1	177	L	Stratford, Ont.	4/26/79	Windsor
MILLEY, Norman	5-11	185	R	Toronto, Ont.	2/14/80	Sudbury
NICHOL, Scott	5-8	160	R	Edmonton, Alta.	12/31/74	Rochester
PANDOLFO, Mike	6-3	226	L	Winchester, MA	9/15/79	Boston University
PECA, Michael	5-11	181	R	Toronto, Ont.	3/26/74	Buffalo
PETERS, Andrew	6-4	195	L	St. Catharines, Ont.	5/5/80	Oshawa
PITTIS, Domenic	5-11	190	L	Calgary, Alta.	10/1/74	Buffalo-Rochester
PRESTON, Tim	6-0	193	L	Vancouver, B.C.	6/30/81	Seattle
PRIMEAU, Wayne	6-3	220	L	Scarborough, Ont.	6/4/76	Buffalo
RASMUSSEN, Erik	6-2	205	L	Minneapolis, MN	3/28/77	Buffalo-Rochester
RAY, Rob	6-0	203	L	Stirling, Ont.	6/8/68	Buffalo
SANDERSON, Geoff	6-0	190	L	Hay River, N.W.T.	2/1/72	Buffalo
SATAN, Miroslav	6-1	195	L	Topolcany, Czech.	10/22/74	Buffalo
VARADA, Vaclav	6-0	200	L	Vsetin, Czech.	4/26/76	Buffalo
WARD, Dixon	6-0	200	R	Leduc, Alta.	9/23/68	Buffalo
ZANUTTO, Mike	6-0	190	L	Burlington, Ont.	1/1/77	Team Canada
ZIGOMANIS, Michael	6-0	183	R	North York, Ont.	1/17/81	Kingston
DEFENSEMEN						
GRAND PIERRE, Jean-Luc	6-3	207	R	Montreal, Que.	2/2/77	Buffalo-Rochester
HOLLAND, Jason	6-2	193	R	Morinville, Alta.	4/30/76	Buffalo-Rochester
HOUDA, Doug	6-2	190	R	Blairmore, Alta.	6/3/66	Detroit-Adirondack
McKEE, Jay	6-3	195	L	Kingston, Ont.	9/8/77	Buffalo
PATRICK, James	6-2	198	R	Winnipeg, Man.	6/14/63	Buffalo
SARICH, Cory	6-3	175	R	Saskatoon, Sask.	8/16/78	Buffalo-Rochester
SMEHLIK, Richard	6-3	222	L	Ostrava, Czech.	1/23/70	Buffalo
WARRENER, Rhett	6-1	209	L	Shaunavon, Sask.	1/27/76	Florida-Buffalo
WOOLLEY, Jason	6-1	188	L	Toronto, Ont.	7/27/69	Buffalo
ZHITNIK, Alexei	5-11	204	L	Kiev, USSR	10/10/72	Buffalo

GOALTENDERS	HT	WT	C	Place of Birth	Date	1998-99 Club
BIRON, Martin	6-1	154	L	Lac St. Charles, Que.	8/15/77	Buffalo-Rochester
HASEK, Dominik	5-11	168	L	Pardubice, Czech.	1/29/65	Buffalo
ROLOSON, Dwayne	6-1	190	L	Simcoe, Ont.	10/12/69	Buffalo-Rochester

General Manager

REGIER, DARCY
General Manager, Buffalo Sabres. Born in Swift Current, Sask., Nov. 27, 1957.

Darcy Regier became the sixth general manager of the Buffalo Sabres on June 11, 1997 after a lengthy management apprenticeship in the New York Islanders organization. As a player, Regier played eight pro seasons, including part of the 1977-78 season with the Cleveland Barons and parts of the 1982-83 and 1983-84 campaigns with the New York Islanders.

He began his career as an administrator with the Islanders in 1984-85 and went on to serve in a variety of capacities including director of administration, assistant director of hockey operations, assistant coach and assistant general manager. He also served as an assistant coach with Hartford in 1991-92.

While with the Islanders, Regier benefitted from working with talented managers and coaches including Bill Torrey and Al Arbour. As a minor pro player with Indianapolis of the CHL he became associated with another important influence on his hockey career, current Detroit Red Wing executive Jim Devellano.

Regier and his wife Kathy have three sons, Jonathan, Justin and Jarrett.

Head Coach

RUFF, LINDY
Head Coach, Buffalo Sabres. Born in Warburg, Alta., February, 17, 1960.

A former captain of the Sabres, Lindy Ruff was appointed as the club's 15th head coach on July 21, 1997. In 1999, he led the Sabres to the Stanley Cup Finals for just the second time in club history. As a player, Ruff was drafted 32nd overall by the Sabres in the 1979 Entry Draft. He played both defense and left wing in an NHL career that spanned 12 seasons including 608 regular-season games with Buffalo. He became a playing assistant coach with Rochester of the AHL in 1991-92 and San Diego of the IHL in 1992-93. Ruff's San Diego club set a pro hockey record with 62 wins. In 1993-94 he became an NHL assistant coach with the Florida Panthers.

Ruff and his wife Gaye have four children.

Coaching Record

		Regular Season					Playoffs			
Season	**Team**	**Games**	**W**	**L**	**T**	**%**	**Games**	**W**	**L**	**%**
1997-98	Buffalo (NHL)	82	36	29	17	.543	15	10	5	.667
1998-99	Buffalo (NHL)	82	37	28	17	.555	21	14	7	.667
	NHL Totals	164	73	57	34	.549	36	24	12	.667

1998-99 Scoring

* – rookie

Regular Season

Pos	#	Player	Team	GP	G	A	Pts	+/–	PIM	PP	SH	GW	GT	S	%
R	81	Miroslav Satan	BUF	81	40	26	66	24	44	13	3	6	1	208	19.2
C	27	Michael Peca	BUF	82	27	29	56	7	81	10	0	8	1	199	13.6
L	18	Michal Grosek	BUF	76	20	30	50	21	102	4	0	3	1	140	14.3
C	37	Curtis Brown	BUF	78	16	31	47	23	56	5	1	3	3	128	12.5
R	15	Dixon Ward	BUF	78	20	24	44	10	44	2	1	4	1	101	19.8
C	90	Joe Juneau	WSH	63	14	27	41	–3	20	2	1	3	0	142	9.9
			BUF	9	1	1	2	–1	2	0	0	0	0	8	12.5
			TOTAL	72	15	28	43	–4	22	2	1	3	0	150	10.0
D	5	Jason Woolley	BUF	80	10	33	43	16	62	4	0	2	1	154	6.5
C	41	Stu Barnes	PIT	64	20	12	32	–12	20	13	0	3	0	155	12.9
			BUF	17	0	4	4	1	10	0	0	0	0	25	0.0
			TOTAL	81	20	16	36	–11	30	13	0	3	0	180	11.1
C	19	Brian Holzinger	BUF	81	17	17	34	2	45	5	0	2	0	143	11.9
D	44	Alexei Zhitnik	BUF	81	7	26	33	–6	96	3	1	2	0	185	3.8
R	25	Vaclav Varada	BUF	72	7	24	31	11	61	1	0	1	0	123	5.7
L	80	Geoff Sanderson	BUF	75	12	18	30	8	22	1	0	1	0	155	7.7
D	8	Darryl Shannon	BUF	71	3	12	15	28	52	1	0	0	1	80	3.8
D	42	Richard Smehlik	BUF	72	3	11	14	–9	44	0	0	0	0	61	4.9
C	22	Wayne Primeau	BUF	67	5	8	13	–6	38	0	0	0	1	55	9.1
C	9	* Erik Rasmussen	BUF	42	3	7	10	6	37	0	0	0	0	40	7.5
D	3	James Patrick	BUF	45	1	7	8	12	16	0	0	0	0	31	3.2
D	4	Rhett Warrener	FLA	48	0	7	7	–1	64	0	0	0	0	33	0.0
			BUF	13	1	0	1	3	20	0	0	0	0	11	9.1
			TOTAL	61	1	7	8	2	84	0	0	0	0	44	2.3
D	74	Jay McKee	BUF	72	0	6	6	20	75	0	0	0	0	57	0.0
L	17	Randy Cunneyworth	BUF	14	2	2	4	1	0	0	0	1	0	12	16.7
R	32	Rob Ray	BUF	76	0	4	4	–2	261	0	0	0	0	23	0.0
L	24	Paul Kruse	BUF	43	3	0	3	0	114	0	0	0	0	33	9.1
D	34	* J-Luc Grand-Pierre	BUF	16	0	1	1	0	17	0	0	0	0	11	0.0
D	21	Mike Hurlbut	BUF	1	0	0	0	2	0	0	0	0	0	2	0.0
R	46	* Dean Sylvester	BUF	1	0	0	0	–1	0	0	0	0	0	1	0.0
C	83	* Domenic Pittis	BUF	3	0	0	0	0	2	0	0	0	0	1	0.0
D	29	* Jason Holland	BUF	3	0	0	0	–1	8	0	0	0	0	2	0.0
D	6	* Cory Sarich	BUF	4	0	0	0	3	0	0	0	0	0	2	0.0
G	43	* Martin Biron	BUF	6	0	0	0	0	0	0	0	0	0	0	0.0
G	30	Dwayne Roloson	BUF	18	0	0	0	0	4	0	0	0	0	0	0.0
G	39	Dominik Hasek	BUF	64	0	0	0	0	14	0	0	0	0	0	0.0

Goaltending

No.	Goaltender	GPI	Mins	Avg	W	L	T	EN	SO	GA	SA	S%
39	Dominik Hasek	64	3817	1.87	30	18	14	2	9	119	1877	.937
43	* Martin Biron	6	281	2.14	1	2	1	1	0	10	120	.917
30	Dwayne Roloson	18	911	2.77	6	8	2	1	1	42	460	.909
	Totals	**82**	**5020**	**2.09**	**37**	**28**	**17**	**4**	**10**	**175**	**2461**	**.929**

Playoffs

Pos	#	Player	Team	GP	G	A	Pts	+/–	PIM	PP	SH	GW	OT	S	%
D	5	Jason Woolley	BUF	21	4	11	15	0	10	2	0	1	1	43	9.3
D	44	Alexei Zhitnik	BUF	21	4	11	15	–6	52	4	0	2	0	58	6.9
C	37	Curtis Brown	BUF	21	7	6	13	3	10	3	0	3	0	34	20.6
C	27	Michael Peca	BUF	21	5	8	13	1	18	2	1	0	0	37	13.5
R	15	Dixon Ward	BUF	21	7	5	12	6	32	0	2	3	0	38	18.4
C	90	Joe Juneau	BUF	20	3	8	11	–2	10	0	1	0	0	29	10.3
C	41	Stu Barnes	BUF	21	7	3	10	–1	6	4	0	1	0	30	23.3
L	80	Geoff Sanderson	BUF	19	4	6	10	5	14	0	0	1	0	53	7.5
R	25	Vaclav Varada	BUF	21	5	4	9	2	14	1	0	0	0	38	13.2
L	81	Miroslav Satan	BUF	12	3	5	8	3	2	1	0	1	1	25	12.0
C	19	Brian Holzinger	BUF	21	3	5	8	1	33	1	0	0	0	32	9.4
C	22	Wayne Primeau	BUF	19	3	4	7	0	6	1	0	0	0	22	13.6
C	9	* Erik Rasmussen	BUF	21	2	4	6	2	18	0	0	1	0	23	8.7
D	4	Rhett Warrener	BUF	20	1	3	4	12	32	0	0	0	0	21	4.8
L	18	Michal Grosek	BUF	13	0	4	4	1	28	0	0	0	0	20	0.0
D	42	Richard Smehlik	BUF	21	0	3	3	–4	10	0	0	0	0	20	0.0
D	74	Jay McKee	BUF	21	0	3	3	13	24	0	0	0	0	13	0.0
R	32	Rob Ray	BUF	5	1	0	1	1	0	0	0	1	0	1	100.0
G	39	Dominik Hasek	BUF	19	0	1	1	0	8	0	0	0	0	0	0.0
D	3	James Patrick	BUF	20	0	1	1	6	12	0	0	0	0	11	0.0
D	8	Darryl Shannon	BUF	2	0	0	0	–1	0	0	0	0	0	7	0.0
L	17	Randy Cunneyworth	BUF	3	0	0	0	–1	0	0	0	0	0	2	0.0
R	46	* Dean Sylvester	BUF	4	0	0	0	–1	2	0	0	0	0	2	0.0
G	30	Dwayne Roloson	BUF	4	0	0	0	0	0	0	0	0	0	0	0.0
L	24	Paul Kruse	BUF	10	0	0	0	0	4	0	0	0	0	0	0.0

Goaltending

No.	Goaltender	GPI	Mins	Avg	W	L	EN	SO	GA	SA	S%
39	Dominik Hasek	19	1217	1.77	13	6	2	2	36	587	.939
30	Dwayne Roloson	4	139	4.32	1	1	1	0	10	67	.851
	Totals	**21**	**1361**	**2.16**	**14**	**7**	**3**	**2**	**49**	**657**	**.925**

General Managers' History

Punch Imlach, 1970-71 to 1977-78; John Anderson, 1978-79; Scotty Bowman, 1979-80 to 1985-86; Scotty Bowman and Gerry Meehan, 1986-87; Gerry Meehan, 1987-88 to 1992-93; John Muckler, 1993-94 to 1996-97; Darcy Regier, 1997-98 to date.

Coaching History

Punch Imlach, 1970-71; Punch Imlach, Floyd Smith and Joe Crozier, 1971-72; Joe Crozier, 1972-73, 1973-74; Floyd Smith, 1974-75 to 1976-77; Marcel Pronovost, 1977-78; Marcel Pronovost and Billy Inglis, 1978-79; Scotty Bowman, 1979-80; Roger Neilson, 1980-81; Jim Roberts and Scotty Bowman, 1981-82; Scotty Bowman 1982-83 to 1984-85; Jim Schoenfeld and Scotty Bowman, 1985-86; Scotty Bowman, Craig Ramsay and Ted Sator, 1986-87; Ted Sator, 1987-88, 1988-89; Rick Dudley, 1989-90, 1990-91; Rick Dudley and John Muckler, 1991-92; John Muckler, 1992-93 to 1994-95; Ted Nolan, 1995-96, 1996-97; Lindy Ruff, 1997-98 to date.

Club Records

Team

(Figures in brackets for season records are games played; records for fewest points, wins, ties, losses, goals, goals against are for 70 or more games)

Most Points	**113**	1974-75 (80)
Most Wins	**49**	1974-75 (80)
Most Ties	**21**	1980-81 (80)
Most Losses	**44**	1986-87 (80)
Most Goals	**354**	1974-75 (80)
Most Goals Against	**308**	1986-87 (80)
Fewest Points	**51**	1971-72 (78)
Fewest Wins	**16**	1971-72 (78)
Fewest Ties	**6**	1985-86 (80)
Fewest Losses	**16**	1974-75 (80)
Fewest Goals	**203**	1971-72 (78)
Fewest Goals Against	**175**	1998-99 (82)
Longest Winning Streak		
Overall	**10**	Jan. 4-23/84
Home	**12**	Nov. 12/72-Jan. 7/73, Oct. 13-Dec. 10/89
Away	**10**	Dec. 10/83-Jan. 23/84
Longest Undefeated Streak		
Overall	**14**	Mar. 6-Apr. 6/80 (8 wins, 6 ties)
Home	**21**	Oct. 8/72-Jan. 7/73 (18 wins, 3 ties)
Away	**10**	Dec. 10/83-Jan. 23/84 (10 wins)
Longest Losing Streak		
Overall	**7**	Oct. 25-Nov. 8/70, Apr. 3-15/93, Oct. 9-22/93
Home	**6**	Oct. 10-Nov. 10/93, Mar. 3-Apr. 3/96
Away	**7**	Oct. 14-Nov. 7/70, Feb. 6-27/71, Jan. 10 Feb. 3/96
Longest Winless Streak		
Overall	**12**	Nov. 23-Dec. 20/91 (8 losses, 4 ties)
Home	**12**	Jan. 27-Mar. 10/91 (7 losses, 5 ties)
Away	**23**	Oct. 30/71-Feb. 19/72 (15 losses, 8 ties)
Most Shutouts, Season	**13**	1997-98 (82)
Most PIM, Season	**2,713**	1991-92 (80)
Most Goals, Game	**14**	Jan. 21/75 (Wsh. 2 at Buf. 14), Mar. 19/81 (Tor. 4 at Buf. 14)

Individual

Most Seasons	**17**	Gilbert Perreault
Most Games	**1,191**	Gilbert Perreault
Most Goals, Career	**512**	Gilbert Perreault
Most Assists, Career	**814**	Gilbert Perreault
Most Points, Career	**1,326**	Gilbert Perreault
Most PIM, Career	**2,529**	Rob Ray
Most Shutouts, Career	**41**	Dominik Hasek
Longest Consecutive Games Streak	**776**	Craig Ramsay (Mar. 27/73-Feb. 10/83)
Most Goals, Season	**76**	Alexander Mogilny (1992-93)
Most Assists, Season	**95**	Pat LaFontaine (1992-93)
Most Points, Season	**148**	Pat LaFontaine (1992-93; 53G, 95A)
Most PIM, Season	**354**	Rob Ray (1991-92)
Most Points, Defenseman, Season	**81**	Phil Housley (1989-90; 21G, 60A)
Most Points, Center, Season	**148**	Pat LaFontaine (1992-93; 53G, 95A)
Most Points, Right Wing, Season	**127**	Alexander Mogilny (1992-93; 76G, 51A)
Most Points, Left Wing, Season	**95**	Rick Martin (1974-75; 52G, 43A)
Most Points, Rookie, Season	**74**	Rick Martin (1971-72; 44G, 30A)
Most Shutouts, Season	**13**	Dominik Hasek (1997-98)
Most Goals, Game	**5**	Dave Andreychuk (Feb. 6/86)
Most Assists, Game	**5**	Gilbert Perreault (Feb. 1/76, Mar. 9/80, Jan. 4/84), Dale Hawerchuk (Jan. 15/92), Pat LaFontaine (Dec. 31/92, Feb. 10/93)
Most Points, Game	**7**	Gilbert Perreault (Feb. 1/76; 2G, 5A)

Retired Numbers

2	Tim Horton	1972-1974
7	Rick Martin	1971-1981
11	Gilbert Perreault	1970-1987
14	Rene Robert	1971-1979

Captains' History

Floyd Smith, 1970-71; Gerry Meehan, 1971-72 to 1973-74; Gerry Meehan and Jim Schoenfeld, 1974-75; Jim Schoenfeld, 1975-76, 1976-77; Danny Gare, 1977-78 to 1980-81; Danny Gare and Gilbert Perreault, 1981-82; Gilbert Perreault, 1982-83 to 1985-86; Gilbert Perreault and Lindy Ruff, 1986-87; Lindy Ruff, 1987-88; Lindy Ruff and Mike Foligno, 1988-89; Mike Foligno, 1989-90; Mike Foligno and Mike Ramsey, 1990-91; Mike Ramsey, 1991-92; Mike Ramsey and Pat LaFontaine, 1992-93; Pat LaFontaine and Alexander Mogilny, 1993-94; Pat LaFontaine, 1994-95 to 1996-97; Michael Peca and Donald Audette, 1997-98; Michael Peca, 1998-99 to date.

All-time Record vs. Other Clubs

Regular Season

	At Home							On Road							Total						
	GP	W	L	T	GF	GA	PTS	GP	W	L	T	GF	GA	PTS	GP	W	L	T	GF	GA	PTS
Anaheim	5	2	2	1	12	14	5	5	3	2	0	13	12	6	10	5	4	1	25	26	11
Boston	95	48	32	15	352	287	111	94	29	53	12	286	365	70	189	77	85	27	638	652	181
Calgary	42	24	13	5	177	125	53	42	16	15	11	138	145	43	84	40	28	16	315	270	96
Carolina	67	39	21	7	271	204	85	68	31	27	10	207	205	72	135	70	48	17	478	409	157
Chicago	49	30	13	6	187	128	66	47	15	26	6	128	154	36	96	45	39	12	315	282	102
Colorado	60	34	17	9	240	196	77	60	19	30	11	187	221	49	120	53	47	20	427	417	126
Dallas	49	26	13	10	177	131	62	50	20	24	6	149	161	46	99	46	37	16	326	292	108
Detroit	49	32	9	8	217	138	72	51	18	28	5	151	188	41	100	50	37	13	368	326	113
Edmonton	27	10	11	6	107	103	26	26	5	19	2	70	112	12	53	15	30	8	177	215	38
Florida	13	9	2	2	45	18	20	11	5	6	0	34	33	10	24	14	8	2	79	51	30
Los Angeles	49	25	15	9	199	146	59	50	22	19	9	175	172	53	99	47	34	18	374	318	112
Montreal	89	45	25	19	280	243	109	90	27	51	12	271	359	66	179	72	76	31	551	602	175
Nashville	1	0	1	0	2	4	0	1	1	0	0	3	1	2	2	1	1	0	5	5	2
New Jersey	44	27	12	5	186	140	59	44	23	12	9	157	131	55	88	50	24	14	343	271	114
NY Islanders	51	27	16	8	178	144	62	51	21	22	8	144	150	50	102	48	38	16	322	294	112
NY Rangers	58	35	16	7	249	182	77	56	18	24	14	149	185	50	114	53	40	21	398	367	127
Ottawa	18	12	5	1	66	27	25	20	10	4	6	59	40	26	38	22	9	7	125	67	51
Philadelphia	53	26	20	7	183	158	59	57	13	32	12	149	204	38	110	39	52	19	332	362	97
Phoenix	26	20	2	4	116	62	44	26	12	12	2	87	84	26	52	32	14	6	203	146	70
Pittsburgh	61	32	13	16	254	163	80	61	16	30	15	198	235	47	122	48	43	31	452	398	127
St. Louis	48	29	13	6	195	149	64	47	14	26	7	122	170	35	95	43	39	13	317	319	99
San Jose	8	8	0	0	41	23	16	7	1	3	3	25	26	5	15	9	3	3	66	49	21
Tampa Bay	13	6	6	1	33	41	13	13	10	2	1	45	25	21	26	16	8	2	78	66	34
Toronto	56	35	17	4	233	156	74	54	25	20	9	199	164	59	110	60	37	13	432	320	133
Vancouver	48	24	16	8	176	142	56	48	16	22	10	157	176	42	96	40	38	18	333	318	98
Washington	46	30	10	6	185	122	66	46	27	12	7	167	121	61	92	57	22	13	352	243	127
Defunct Clubs	23	13	5	5	94	63	31	23	12	8	3	97	76	27	46	25	13	8	191	139	58
Totals	**1148**	**648**	**325**	**175**	**4455**	**3309**	**1471**	**1148**	**429**	**529**	**190**	**3567**	**3915**	**1048**	**2296**	**1077**	**854**	**365**	**8022**	**7224**	**2519**

Playoffs

	Series	W	L	GP	W	L	T	GF	GA	Last Mtg.	Round	Result
Boston	7	2	5	39	18	21	0	130	146	1999	CSF	W 4-2
Chicago	2	2	0	9	8	1	0	36	17	1980	QF	W 4-0
Colorado	2	0	2	8	2	6	0	27	35	1985	DSF	L 2-3
Dallas	3	1	2	13	5	8	0	37	39	1999	F	L 2-4
Montreal	7	3	4	35	17	18	0	111	124	1998	CSF	W 4-0
New Jersey	1	0	1	7	3	4	0	14	14	1994	CQF	L 3-4
NY Islanders	3	0	3	16	4	12	0	45	59	1980	SF	L 2-4
NY Rangers	1	1	0	3	2	1	0	11	6	1978	PR	W 2-1
Ottawa	2	2	0	11	8	3	0	26	19	1999	CQF	W 4-0
Philadelphia	5	1	4	26	9	17	0	67	83	1998	CQF	W 4-1
Pittsburgh	1	0	1	3	1	2	0	9	9	1979	PR	L 1-2
St. Louis	1	1	0	3	2	1	0	7	8	1976	PR	W 2-1
Toronto	1	1	0	5	4	1	0	21	16	1999	CF	W 4-1
Vancouver	2	2	0	7	6	1	0	28	14	1981	PR	W 3-0
Washington	1	0	1	6	2	4	0	11	13	1998	CF	L 2-4
Totals	**39**	**16**	**23**	**191**	**91**	**100**	**0**	**580**	**595**			

Calgary totals include Atlanta Flames, 1972-73 to 1979-80. Carolina totals include Hartford, 1979-80 to 1996-97.
Colorado totals include Quebec, 1979-80 to 1994-95. Dallas totals include Minnesota, 1970-71 to 1992-93.
New Jersey totals include Kansas City, 1974-75 to 1975-76, and Colorado Rockies, 1976-77 to 1981-82.
Phoenix totals include Winnipeg, 1979-80 to 1995-96.

Playoff Results 1999-95

Year	Round	Opponent	Result	GF	GA
1999	F	Dallas	L 2-4	9	13
	CF	Toronto	W 4-1	21	16
	CSF	Boston	W 4-2	17	14
	CQF	Ottawa	W 4-0	12	6
1998	CF	Washington	L 2-4	11	13
	CSF	Montreal	W 4-0	17	10
	CQF	Philadelphia	W 4-1	18	9
1997	CSF	Philadelphia	L 1-4	13	21
	CQF	Ottawa	W 4-3	14	13
1995	CQF	Philadelphia	L 1-4	13	18

Abbreviations: Round: F – final; **CF** – conference final; **CSF** – conference semi-final; **CQF** – conference quarter-final; **DSF** – division semi-final; **SF** – semi-final; **QF** – quarter-final; **PR** – preliminary round.

1998-99 Results

Oct.	10	at	Dallas	1-4		18	at	Florida	4-0
	12	at	Colorado	3-0		19	at	Tampa Bay	1-2
	16		Florida	2-2		26		Phoenix	1-1
	17	at	Montreal	4-3		28		Nashville	2-4
	23		Washington	0-1		30		Los Angeles	4-1
	24	at	NY Islanders	4-5	**Feb.**	2	at	Pittsburgh	3-5
	27	at	NY Rangers	0-0		3		Colorado	3-5
	30		Toronto	4-1		6	at	Montreal	2-3
	31	at	Toronto	6-3		7	at	Washington	1-3
Nov.	3		Boston	4-2		9	at	Ottawa	1-1
	7	at	Philadelphia	2-2		11		Montreal	5-2
	10		Ottawa	2-2		13		NY Islanders	2-2
	12	at	Washington	2-0		15		Carolina	3-2
	14		Chicago	6-1		17		Toronto	2-3
	20		Toronto	4-1		19		San Jose	4-2
	21	at	Toronto	1-2		21		Detroit	4-4
	25		NY Rangers	4-2		24	at	Calgary	2-2
	28	at	Florida	2-6		26	at	Edmonton	3-6
	29	at	Tampa Bay	6-3		28	at	Vancouver	2-0
Dec.	2		Florida	2-1	**Mar.**	3		Edmonton	3-5
	4		Philadelphia	3-0		5		Dallas	2-1
	5	at	Nashville	3-1		7		Philadelphia	1-1
	8	at	St. Louis	2-2		8	at	Carolina	1-4
	11		NY Rangers	2-0		11		Tampa Bay	2-5
	12	at	Boston	4-1		13		Boston	3-1
	18		Montreal	4-2		15		NY Islanders	2-1
	19		Carolina	2-3		19	at	NY Rangers	3-2
	21	at	Carolina	4-1		23	at	New Jersey	1-1
	23		Tampa Bay	2-0		24	at	Detroit	1-2
	26	at	New Jersey	2-0		27	at	Pittsburgh	1-1
	28		New Jersey	4-7		28		Pittsburgh	4-3
	30		Ottawa	2-3		31	at	Chicago	1-2
Jan.	1		Anaheim	2-7	**Apr.**	3	at	Montreal	1-2
	2		Calgary	7-1		5		Pittsburgh	3-1
	6	at	Anaheim	3-2		6	at	NY Islanders	4-3
	7	at	Los Angeles	2-4		9		Florida	3-1
	9	at	San Jose	2-2		10	at	Ottawa	1-1
	11	at	Phoenix	0-1		13	at	Philadelphia	2-2
	13		St. Louis	2-4		14		New Jersey	1-2
	15		Boston	2-1		17	at	Boston	1-2
	16	at	Ottawa	1-1		18		Washington	3-0

Entry Draft Selections 1999-85

1999
Pick	
20	Barrett Heisten
35	Milan Bartovic
55	Doug Janik
64	Michael Zigomanis
73	Tim Preston
117	Karel Mosovsky
138	Ryan Miller
146	Matthew Kinch
178	Seneque Hyacinthe
206	Bret Dececco
235	Brad Self
263	Craig Brunel

1998
Pick	
18	Dimitri Kalinin
34	Andrew Peters
47	Norman Milley
50	Jaroslav Kristek
77	Mike Pandolfo
137	Aaron Goldade
164	Ales Kotalik
191	Brad Moran
218	David Moravec
249	Edo Terglav

1997
Pick	
21	Mika Noronen
48	Henrik Tallinder
69	Maxim Afinogenov
75	Jeff Martin
101	Luc Theoret
128	Torrey Diroberto
156	Brian Campbell
184	Jeremy Adduono
212	Kamil Piros
238	Dylan Kemp

1996
Pick	
7	Erik Rasmussen
27	Cory Sarich
33	Darren Van Oene
54	Francois Methot
87	Kurt Walsh
106	Mike Martone
115	Alexei Tezikov
142	Ryan Davis
161	Darren Mortier
222	Scott Buhler

1995
Pick	
14	Jay McKee
16	Martin Biron
42	Mark Dutiaume
68	Mathieu Sunderland
94	Matt Davidson
111	Marian Menhart
119	Kevin Popp
123	Daniel Bienvenue
172	Brian Scott
198	Mike Zanutto
224	Rob Skrlac

1994
Pick	
17	Wayne Primeau
43	Curtis Brown
69	Rumun Ndur
121	Sergei Klimentjev
147	Cal Benazic
168	Steve Plouffe
173	Shane Hnidy
176	Steve Webb
199	Bob Westerby
225	Craig Millar
251	Mark Polak
277	Shayne Wright

1993
Pick	
38	Denis Tsygurov
64	Ethan Philpott
116	Richard Safarik
142	Kevin Pozzo
168	Sergei Petrenko
194	Mike Barrie
220	Barrie Moore
246	Chris Davis
272	Scott Nichol

1992
Pick	
11	David Cooper
35	Jozef Cierny
59	Ondrej Steiner
80	Dean Melanson
83	Matthew Barnaby
107	Markus Ketterer
108	Yuri Khmylev
131	Paul Rushforth
179	Dean Tiltgen
203	Todd Simon
227	Rick Kowalsky
251	Chris Clancy

1991
Pick	
13	Philippe Boucher
35	Jason Dawe
57	Jason Young
72	Peter Ambroziak
101	Steve Shields
123	Sean O'Donnell
124	Brian Holzinger
145	Chris Snell
162	Jiri Kuntos
189	Tony Iob
211	Spencer Meany
233	Mikhail Volkov
255	Michael Smith

1990
Pick	
14	Brad May
82	Brian McCarthy
97	Richard Smehlik
100	Todd Bojcun
103	Brad Pascall
142	Viktor Gordiyuk
166	Milan Nedoma
187	Jason Winch
208	Sylvain Naud
229	Kenneth Martin
250	Brad Rubachuk

1989
Pick	
14	Kevin Haller
56	John (Scott) Thomas
77	Doug MacDonald
98	Ken Sutton
107	Bill Pye
119	Mike Barkley
161	Derek Plante
183	Donald Audette
194	Mark Astley
203	John Nelson
224	Todd Henderson
245	Michael Bavis

1988
Pick	
13	Joel Savage
55	Darcy Loewen
76	Keith E. Carney
89	Alexander Mogilny
97	Robert Ray
106	David Di Vita
118	Mike McLaughlin
139	Mike Griffith
160	Daniel Ruoho
181	Wade Flaherty
223	Thomas Nieman
244	Robert Wallwork

1987
Pick	
1	Pierre Turgeon
22	Brad Miller
53	Andrew MacVicar
84	John Bradley
85	David Pergola
106	Chris Marshall
127	Paul Flanagan
148	Sean Dooley
153	Tim Roberts
169	Grant Tkachuk
190	Ian Herbers
211	David Littman
232	Allan MacIsaac

1986
Pick	
5	Shawn Anderson
26	Greg Brown
47	Bob Corkum
56	Kevin Kerr
68	David Baseggio
89	Larry Rooney
110	Miguel Baldris
131	Mike Hartman
152	Francois Guay
173	Shawn Whitham
194	Kenton Rein
215	Troy Arndt

1985
Pick	
14	Calle Johansson
35	Benoit Hogue
56	Keith Gretzky
77	Dave Moylan
98	Ken Priestlay
119	Joe Reekie
140	Petri Matikainen
161	Trent Kaese
182	Jiri Sejba
203	Boyd Sutton
224	Guy Larose
245	Ken Baumgartner

Club Directory

Marine Midland Arena
One Seymour H. Knox III Plaza
Buffalo, NY 14203
Phone **716/855-4100**
Fax 716/855-4110
Ticket Office: 716/888-4000
Capacity: 18,595

Board of Niagara Frontier Hockey Management Corp. – General Partner

Chairman of the Board	John J. Rigas
Vice Chairman of the Board & Counsel	Robert O. Swados
Vice Chairman of the Board	Robert E. Rich, Jr.
Chief Executive Officer	Timothy J. Rigas
Director	Michael J. Rigas
Director	James P. Rigas
Director	George Strawbridge, Jr.
Director	Seymour H. Knox, IV

Partnership Board of Niagara Frontier Hockey L.P.
(includes above-listed Executives and Directors)
Edwin C. Andrews, Peter C. Andrews, William C. Cox, III, John B. Fisher, John E. Houghton, Howard T. Saperston, Jr., Paul A. Schoellkopf, William H. Weeks

Executive Department

Executive Vice President/Administration	Ron Bertovich
Executive Vice President/Finance & Business Development	Ed Hartman
Executive Vice President/Integrated Marketing	John Cimperman
Senior Vice President/Corporate Sales	Kerry Atkinson
Senior Vice President/Legal & Business Affairs	Kevin Billet
Senior Vice President/Marketing	Christye Peterson
Vice President/Communications	Michael Gilbert
Vice President/Corporate Relations	Seymour H. Knox, IV
Vice President/Ticket Sales & Operations	John Sinclair
Senior Director of Sports & Arena Planning	Chris Schoepflin
Special Consultant	Joe Crozier
Executive Assistants	Eleanore MacKenzie, Victoria Lehigh

Hockey Department

General Manager	Darcy Regier
Assistant to the General Manager	Larry Carriere
Director of Player Personnel	Don Luce
Professional Scouts	Kevin Devine, Frank Effinger, Terry Martin
Scouting Staff	Don Barrie, Jim Benning, Bo Berglund, Paul Merritt, Darryl Plandowski, Mike Racicot, Rudy Migay, David Volek
Head Coach	Lindy Ruff
Associate Coach	Don Lever
Assistant Coach	Mike Ramsey
Strength & Conditioning Coach	Doug McKenney
Assistant Strength Coach	Dennis Cole
Goaltender Coach	Jim Corsi
Administrative Assistant Coach	Jeff Holbrook
Head Trainer/Massage Therapist	Jim Pizzutelli
Head Equipment Manager	Rip Simonick
Assistant Equipment Manager	George Babcock
Administrative Assistant	Elaine Burzynski
On-Site Travel Coordinator	Kim Christiano

Medical

Club Doctor	John Marzo, M.D.
Club Doctor Emeritus	John L. Butsch, M.D.
Orthopedic	Les Bisson, M.D.
Doctors	Nicholas Aquino, M.D., William Hartrich, M.D.
Oral Surgeon	Steven Jensen, DDS
Club Dentist	Daniel Yustin, DDS, M.S.
Team Psychologist	Max Offenberger, Ph.D.
Physical Therapist	Joe Acquino

Administration

Human Resources Coordinator	Vanessa Barrons
Management Information Systems Manager	Ken Bass
Distribution Manager	Gerry Magill
Receptionists	Olive Anticola, Roza Barker

Broadcast Production

Director of Broadcast & Production Services	Joe Guarnieri
Broadcast Coordinator	Lisa Tzetzo
Editor/Technical Director	Eric Grossman
Producer	Lowell MacDonald
Director	Phil Mollica
Senior Commercial Producer/Editor	Joe Pinter

Broadcast Team: Rick Jeanneret (play-by-play), Jim Lorentz (color commentary), Danny Gare (reporter)

Radio Producer/Host	Mark Jeanneret
Flagship Stations:	
TV	Empire Sports Network
Radio	WHTT FM 104.1

Communications

Director of Media Relations	Gil Chorbajian
Communications Coordinator	Gregg Huller
Communications Graduate Assistant	Kevin Wiles
Director of Alumni Relations	Larry Playfair
Corporate & Community Relations Liaison	Gilbert Perreault
Team Photographer	Bill Wippert

Empire Sports Sales

Director of Corporate Sales	Dan Rozanski
National Sales Manager	Nick DiVico
Senior Account Managers	Steve Cuccia, Mark Kennedy
Vendor Programs Manager	Jim Harrington
Account Managers	Walter Bissett, Jr., Mike Jones, Melissa Lesh
Sales Support Account Executive	Len Synor
Traffic Coordinator	Corinne Moyer
Assistant Traffic Coordinator	Krista Argeros
Administrative Assistant/Empire Sports Sales	Hector Nieves

Finance

Controller	Matt Green
Accounting Managers (Buffalo Sabres)	Christine Ivansitz
Payroll Manager	Birgid Haensel
Finance Assistant	Sally Lippert

Marketing

Director of Canadian Marketing	Steve Katzman
Director of Promotions & Advertising	Tanya Isherwood
Director of Game Presentation & Special Events	Kathy Manley
Promotions & Advertising Coordinator	Tara Doster
Marketing Coordinator	Mark Mashiotta
Rochester Area Representative	Gary Sajdak
Graphic Artist	Vicki Sitek
Director of Community Relations	Ken Martin, Jr.
Community Relations Coordinator	Deidre Daniels
Administrative Assistant	Donna Webb-Smith

Ticket Sales & Operations

Season & Group Account Executives	Dan Carroll, Dave Forman, Jr., Don Fournier, Keri Francis, Grant Weber
Account Services Manager	Rose Thompson
Account Service Representatives	Roxanne Anderson, Andrea Giambra, Gretchen Huzinec, Elaine Fredo
Box Office Manager	Mike Tout
Assistant Box Office Manager	Christopher Makowski
Group Sales Coordinator	Paul Barker
Ticket Administrators	Lisa Wells, Marty Maloney, Cindi Reuther, Pete Riedy
Cash & Settlement Administrator	Jennifer Glowny
Database Manager	Marc Wittman

Merchandise

Director of Merchandise	Julie Regan
Merchandise Manager	Mike Kaminska
Store Manager	Tammy Preteroti
Inventory Control Manager	Glenn Barker
Administrative Assistant	Brenda Hawkins

Marine Midland Arena

Senior Director of Facilities Management	Stan Makowski
Director of Event Booking	Jennifer Stich
Asst. Dir. of Event Booking	Bridgette Cassidy
Event Managers	Matt Rabinowitz, John Faso
Administrative Assistant/ Operations	Tina Daniels
Communications Engineer	Al Weissman
Communications Technician	Mike Queeno
Chief Engineer	Barry Becker
Assistant Chief Engineer	Brian Drabek
Engineers	John Blake, Patrick Needham
Director of Suite Sales	Nick Turano
Suite Sales Associate	Todd Langdon
Coordinator of Suite Services	Michelle Mitchell
Director of Lacrosse & Amateur Athletics	Kurt Silcott

Calgary Flames

1998-99 Results: 30w-40L-12T 72PTS. Third, Northwest Division

1999-2000 Schedule

Oct.	Sat.	2	at San Jose		Sat.	8	Tampa Bay
	Wed.	6	St. Louis		Wed.	12	Dallas
	Fri.	8	Montreal		Sat.	15	Toronto
	Mon.	11	Carolina*		Tue.	18	Detroit
	Wed.	13	at Vancouver		Wed.	19	at Edmonton
	Fri.	15	Los Angeles		Fri.	21	Nashville
	Sat.	16	Vancouver		Mon.	24	at Boston
	Tue.	19	at St. Louis		Wed.	26	at Washington
	Fri.	22	at Florida		Fri.	28	at Detroit
	Sat.	23	at Tampa Bay		Sat.	29	at Nashville
	Tue.	26	at Atlanta	**Feb.**	Tue.	1	St. Louis
	Thu.	28	at Ottawa		Thu.	3	Chicago
	Sat.	30	at Toronto		Wed.	9	at Vancouver
Nov.	Wed.	3	Nashville		Thu.	10	at Colorado
	Sat.	6	Florida		Sat.	12	at Phoenix
	Wed.	10	San Jose		Mon.	14	at Los Angeles
	Sat.	13	Colorado		Wed.	16	at Anaheim
	Tue.	16	at Phoenix		Fri.	18	Edmonton
	Wed.	17	at Anaheim		Sat.	19	at Edmonton
	Fri.	19	Detroit		Wed.	23	Los Angeles
	Tue.	23	NY Islanders		Fri.	25	Phoenix
	Thu.	25	Chicago		Sat.	26	Atlanta
	Sat.	27	at Colorado	**Mar.**	Wed.	1	Pittsburgh
	Tue.	30	at Carolina		Fri.	3	Anaheim
Dec.	Thu.	2	at NY Islanders		Sun.	5	New Jersey
	Sat.	4	at New Jersey		Tue.	7	Colorado
	Mon.	6	at NY Rangers		Thu.	9	Toronto
	Tue.	7	at Montreal		Sat.	11	at Los Angeles
	Fri.	10	Vancouver		Mon.	13	at San Jose
	Sun.	12	at Chicago		Wed.	15	Ottawa
	Tue.	14	at St. Louis		Sat.	18	Buffalo
	Wed.	15	at Dallas		Sun.	19	at Edmonton
	Sat.	18	Ottawa		Wed.	22	at Detroit
	Tue.	21	Dallas		Thu.	23	at Buffalo
	Thu.	23	Edmonton		Sat.	25	at Nashville
	Sun.	26	at Vancouver		Fri.	31	Phoenix
	Mon.	27	Philadelphia	**Apr.**	Sat.	1	San Jose
	Wed.	29	Anaheim		Mon.	3	at Dallas
Jan.	Sun.	2	Vancouver*		Wed.	5	at St. Louis
	Wed.	5	at Colorado		Fri.	7	Colorado
	Thu.	6	at Chicago		Sat.	8	Edmonton

* Denotes afternoon game.

Franchise date: June 6, 1972
Transferred from Atlanta to Calgary,
June 24, 1980.

NORTHWEST DIVISION

28th NHL Season

Valeri Bure established career highs in goals (26), assists (27) and points (53) in 1998-99. Bure has set up at least 20 goals during each of his four full seasons in the NHL, and has twice topped 20 goals himself.

Year-by-Year Record

		Home			Road			Overall							
Season	GP	W	L	T	W	L	T	W	L	T	GF	GA	Pts.	Finished		Playoff Result
1998-99	82	15	20	6	15	20	6	30	40	12	211	234	72	3rd,	Northwest Div.	Out of Playoffs
1997-98	82	18	17	6	8	24	9	26	41	15	217	252	67	5th,	Pacific Div.	Out of Playoffs
1996-97	82	21	18	2	11	23	7	32	41	9	214	239	73	5th,	Pacific Div.	Out of Playoffs
1995-96	82	18	18	5	16	19	6	34	37	11	241	240	79	2nd,	Pacific Div.	Lost Conf. Quarter-Final
1994-95	48	15	7	2	9	10	5	24	17	7	163	135	55	1st,	Pacific Div.	Lost Conf. Quarter-Final
1993-94	84	25	12	5	17	17	8	42	29	13	302	256	97	1st,	Pacific Div.	Lost Conf. Quarter-Final
1992-93	84	23	14	5	20	16	6	43	30	11	322	282	97	2nd,	Smythe Div.	Lost Div. Semi-Final
1991-92	80	19	14	7	12	23	5	31	37	12	296	305	74	5th,	Smythe Div.	Out of Playoffs
1990-91	80	29	8	3	17	18	5	46	26	8	344	263	100	2nd,	Smythe Div.	Lost Div. Semi-Final
1989-90	80	28	7	5	14	16	10	42	23	15	348	265	99	1st,	Smythe Div.	Lost Div. Semi-Final
1988-89	**80**	**32**	**4**	**4**	**22**	**13**	**5**	**54**	**17**	**9**	**354**	**226**	**117**	**1st,**	**Smythe Div.**	**Won Stanley Cup**
1987-88	80	26	11	3	22	12	6	48	23	9	397	305	105	1st,	Smythe Div.	Lost Div. Final
1986-87	80	25	13	2	21	18	1	46	31	3	318	289	95	2nd,	Smythe Div.	Lost Div. Semi-Final
1985-86	80	23	11	6	17	20	3	40	31	9	354	315	89	2nd,	Smythe Div.	Lost Final
1984-85	80	23	11	6	18	16	6	41	27	12	363	302	94	3rd,	Smythe Div.	Lost Div. Semi-Final
1983-84	80	22	11	7	12	21	7	34	32	14	311	314	82	2nd,	Smythe Div.	Lost Div. Final
1982-83	80	21	12	7	11	22	7	32	34	14	321	317	78	2nd,	Smythe Div.	Lost Div. Final
1981-82	80	20	11	9	9	23	8	29	34	17	334	345	75	3rd,	Smythe Div.	Lost Div. Semi-Final
1980-81	80	25	5	10	14	22	4	39	27	14	329	298	92	3rd,	Patrick Div.	Lost Semi-Final
1979-80*	80	18	15	7	17	17	6	35	32	13	282	269	83	4th,	Patrick Div.	Lost Prelim. Round
1978-79*	80	25	11	4	16	20	4	41	31	8	327	280	90	4th,	Patrick Div.	Lost Prelim. Round
1977-78*	80	20	13	7	14	14	12	34	27	19	274	252	87	3rd,	Patrick Div.	Lost Prelim. Round
1976-77*	80	22	11	7	12	23	5	34	34	12	264	265	80	3rd,	Patrick Div.	Lost Prelim. Round
1975-76*	80	19	14	7	16	19	5	35	33	12	262	237	82	3rd,	Patrick Div.	Lost Prelim. Round
1974-75*	80	24	9	7	10	22	8	34	31	15	243	233	83	4th,	Patrick Div.	Out of Playoffs
1973-74*	78	17	15	7	13	19	7	30	34	14	214	238	74	4th,	West Div.	Lost Quarter-Final
1972-73*	78	16	16	7	9	22	8	25	38	15	191	239	65	7th,	West Div.	Out of Playoffs

* Atlanta Flames

1999-2000 Player Personnel

FORWARDS	HT	WT	S	Place of Birth	Date	1998-99 Club
BEGIN, Steve	5-11	185	L	Trois-Rivieres, Que.	6/14/78	Saint John
BETTS, Blair	6-1	183	L	Edmonton, Alta.	2/16/80	Prince George
BRIGLEY, Travis	6-1	195	L	Coronation, Alta.	6/16/77	Saint John
BURE, Valeri	5-10	180	R	Moscow, USSR	6/13/74	Calgary
CLARK, Chris	6-0	190	R	Manchester, CT	3/8/76	Saint John
CORBET, Rene	6-0	190	L	St-Hyacinthe, Que.	6/25/73	Colorado-Calgary
COWAN, Jeff	6-2	185	L	Scarborough, Ont.	9/27/76	Saint John
DOMAN, Matt	6-1	218	R	St. Cloud, MN	2/10/80	U. of Wisconsin
DOMENICHELLI, Hnat	6-0	190	L	Edmonton, Alta.	2/17/76	Calgary-Saint John
DUBINSKY, Steve	6-0	190	L	Montreal, Que.	7/9/70	Chicago-Calgary
EGELAND, Allan	6-0	175	L	Lethbridge, Alta.	1/31/73	Orlando-Saint John
FATA, Rico	5-11	202	L	Sault Ste. Marie, Ont.	2/12/80	London-Calgary
GRATTON, Benoit	5-10	182	L	Montreal, Que.	12/28/76	Washington-Portland (AHL)
IGINLA, Jarome	6-1	205	R	Edmonton, Alta.	7/1/77	Calgary
IRVING, Joel	6-3	210	R	Lumsden, Sask.	1/2/76	Saint John-Johnstown
McTAVISH, Dale	6-1	200	L	Eganville, Ont.	2/28/72	SaiPa-Canada
MURRAY, Marty	5-9	178	L	Deloraine, Man.	2/16/75	VSV Villach-Canada
NAZAROV, Andrei	6-5	230	R	Chelyabinsk, USSR	5/22/74	Tampa Bay-Calgary
ODUYA, Fredrik	6-3	220	L	Stockholm, Sweden	5/31/75	Orlando-Saint John
PETROVICKY, Ronald	5-11	185	R	Zilina, Czech.	2/15/77	Saint John
ROCHE, Dave	6-4	230	L	Lindsay, Ont.	6/13/75	Calgary-Saint John
ST. LOUIS, Martin	5-9	180	L	Laval, Que.	6/18/75	Calgary-Saint John
SAPRYKIN, Oleg	6-0	187	L	Moscow, USSR	2/12/81	Seattle
SAVARD, Marc	5-10	180	L	Ottawa, Ont.	7/17/77	NY Rangers-Hartford
SHANTZ, Jeff	6-0	195	R	Duchess, Alta.	10/10/73	Chicago-Calgary
STILLMAN, Cory	6-0	195	L	Peterborough, Ont.	12/20/73	Calgary
THOMPSON, Rocky	6-2	205	R	Calgary, Alta.	8/8/77	Calgary-Saint John
TKACZUK, Daniel	6-0	190	L	Toronto, Ont.	6/10/79	Barrie
TRIPP, John	6-2	207	R	Kingston, Ont.	5/4/77	Saint John-Johnstown
VARLAMOV, Sergei	5-11	190	L	Kiev, USSR	7/21/78	Saint John
WIEMER, Jason	6-1	225	L	Kimberley, B.C.	4/14/76	Calgary
WILM, Clarke	6-0	195	L	Central Butte, Sask.	10/24/76	Calgary
DEFENSEMEN						
ALBELIN, Tommy	6-1	195	L	Stockholm, Sweden	5/21/64	Calgary
BELAK, Wade	6-5	225	R	Saskatoon, Sask.	7/3/76	Col-Her-Cgy-Saint John
CHARRON, Eric	6-3	195	L	Verdun, Que.	1/14/70	Calgary-Saint John
DEMIDOV, Ilja	6-3	185	L	Moscow, USSR	4/14/79	Oshawa
GAUTHIER, Denis	6-2	205	L	Montreal, Que.	10/1/76	Calgary-Saint John
HOUSLEY, Phil	5-10	185	L	St. Paul, MN	3/9/64	Calgary
HULSE, Cale	6-3	215	R	Edmonton, Alta.	11/10/73	Calgary
MORRIS, Derek	6-0	200	R	Edmonton, Alta.	8/24/78	Calgary
REGEHR, Robyn	6-2	210	L	Recife, Brazil	4/19/80	Kamloops
SIMPSON, Todd	6-3	215	L	North Vancouver, B.C.	5/28/73	Calgary
SMITH, Steve	6-4	215	L	Glasgow, Scotland	4/30/63	Calgary
SOROCHAN, Lee	5-11	210	L	Edmonton, Alta.	9/9/75	Ft. Wayne-Hart-Cgy-Saint John
VELLINGA, Mike	6-1	218	R	Chatham, Ont.	8/19/78	Saint John-Orlando-Johnstown

GOALTENDERS	HT	WT	C	Place of Birth	Date	1998-99 Club
BRATHWAITE, Fred	5-7	170	L	Ottawa, Ont.	11/24/72	Canada-Calgary
FUHR, Grant	5-10	201	R	Spruce Grove, Alta.	9/28/62	St. Louis
GARNER, Tyrone	6-1	170	L	Stoney Creek, Ont.	7/27/78	Calgary-Oshawa
GIGUERE, Jean-Sebastien	6-0	175	L	Montreal, Que.	5/16/77	Calgary-Saint John
KARPENKO, Igor	5-8	175	L	Kiev, USSR	7/23/76	Johnstown-Saint John
MOSS, Tyler	6-0	184	R	Ottawa, Ont.	6/29/75	Calgary-Saint John-Orlando
TREFILOV, Andrei	6-0	190	L	Kirovo-Chepetsk, USSR	8/31/69	Kazan-Chi-Ind-Cgy-Det (IHL)

1998-99 Scoring

* – rookie

Regular Season

Pos	#	Player	Team	GP	G	A	Pts	+/–	PIM	PP	SH	GW	GT	S	%
L	16	Cory Stillman	CGY	76	27	30	57	7	38	9	3	5	1	175	15.4
D	6	Phil Housley	CGY	79	11	43	54	14	52	4	0	1	0	193	5.7
R	8	Valeri Bure	CGY	80	26	27	53	0	22	7	0	4	0	260	10.0
C	12	Jarome Iginla	CGY	82	28	23	51	1	58	7	0	4	1	211	13.3
C	21	Andrew Cassels	CGY	70	12	25	37	–12	18	4	1	3	0	97	12.4
D	53	Derek Morris	CGY	71	7	27	34	4	73	3	0	2	2	150	4.7
L	20	Rene Corbet	COL	53	8	14	22	3	58	2	0	1	0	82	9.8
			CGY	20	5	4	9	–2	10	1	0	0	0	45	11.1
			TOTAL	73	13	18	31	1	68	3	0	1	0	127	10.2
C	11	Jeff Shantz	CHI	7	1	0	1	–1	4	0	0	0	0	5	20.0
			CGY	69	12	17	29	15	40	1	1	3	0	77	15.6
			TOTAL	76	13	17	30	14	44	1	1	3	0	82	15.9
C	24	Jason Wiemer	CGY	78	8	13	21	–12	177	1	0	1	0	128	6.3
C	23	* Clarke Wilm	CGY	78	10	8	18	11	53	2	2	0	0	94	10.6
R	62	Andrei Nazarov	T.B.	26	2	0	2	–5	43	0	0	0	0	18	11.1
			CGY	36	5	9	14	1	30	0	0	2	1	53	9.4
			TOTAL	62	7	9	16	–4	73	0	0	2	1	71	9.9
D	55	Steve Smith	CGY	69	1	14	15	3	80	0	0	0	0	42	2.4
C	18	Steve Dubinsky	CHI	1	0	0	0	0	0	0	0	0	0	1	0.0
			CGY	61	4	10	14	–7	14	0	2	0	0	69	5.8
			TOTAL	62	4	10	14	–7	14	0	2	0	0	70	5.7
D	32	Cale Hulse	CGY	73	3	9	12	–8	117	0	0	0	0	83	3.6
C	17	Hnat Domenichelli	CGY	23	5	5	10	–4	11	3	0	0	0	45	11.1
D	27	Todd Simpson	CGY	73	2	8	10	18	151	0	0	0	0	52	3.8
R	42	Ed Ward	CGY	68	3	5	8	–4	67	0	0	0	0	56	5.4
D	3	* Denis Gauthier	CGY	55	3	4	7	3	68	0	0	0	0	40	7.5
L	25	Dave Roche	CGY	36	3	3	6	–1	44	1	0	2	0	30	10.0
D	5	Tommy Albelin	CGY	60	1	5	6	–11	8	0	0	0	0	54	1.9
L	28	Bob Bassen	CGY	41	1	2	3	–13	35	0	0	0	0	47	2.1
R	33	Greg Pankewicz	CGY	18	0	3	3	0	20	0	0	0	0	10	0.0
R	26	Tom Chorske	NYI	2	0	1	1	1	2	0	0	0	0	9	0.0
			WSH	17	0	2	2	–4	4	0	0	0	0	22	0.0
			CGY	7	0	0	0	–5	2	0	0	0	0	13	0.0
			TOTAL	26	0	3	3	–8	8	0	0	0	0	44	0.0
C	15	* Martin St. Louis	CGY	13	1	1	2	–2	10	0	0	0	0	14	7.1
G	40	Fred Brathwaite	CGY	28	0	2	2	0	2	0	0	0	0	0	0.0
C	26	* Eric Landry	CGY	3	0	1	1	1	0	0	0	0	0	1	0.0
D	19	Chris O'Sullivan	CGY	10	0	1	1	–1	2	0	0	0	0	10	0.0
G	30	* Tyler Moss	CGY	11	0	1	1	0	0	0	0	0	0	0	0.0
D	38	Eric Charron	CGY	12	0	1	1	–6	14	0	0	0	0	9	0.0
G	47	* J-S Giguere	CGY	15	0	1	1	0	4	0	0	0	0	0	0.0
R	44	* Rico Fata	CGY	20	0	1	1	0	4	0	0	0	0	13	0.0
G	31	Ken Wregget	CGY	27	0	1	1	0	8	0	0	0	0	0	0.0
D	29	* Wade Belak	COL	22	0	0	0	–2	71	0	0	0	0	5	0.0
			CGY	9	0	1	1	3	23	0	0	0	0	2	0.0
			TOTAL	31	0	1	1	1	94	0	0	0	0	7	0.0
D	33	* Lee Sorochan	CGY	2	0	0	0	–3	0	0	0	0	0	5	0.0
D	22	* Rocky Thompson	CGY	3	0	0	0	0	25	0	0	0	0	0	0.0
G	1	* Tyrone Garner	CGY	3	0	0	0	0	0	0	0	0	0	0	0.0
G	35	Andrei Trefilov	CHI	1	0	0	0	0	0	0	0	0	0	0	0.0
			CGY	4	0	0	0	0	0	0	0	0	0	0	0.0
			TOTAL	5	0	0	0	0	0	0	0	0	0	0	0.0

Goaltending

No.	Goaltender	GPI	Mins	Avg	W	L	T	EN	SO	GA	SA	S%
40	Fred Brathwaite	28	1663	2.45	11	9	7	3	1	68	796	.915
30	* Tyler Moss	11	550	2.51	3	7	0	0	0	23	295	.922
31	Ken Wregget	27	1590	2.53	10	12	4	2	1	67	712	.906
47	* J-S Giguere	15	860	3.21	6	7	1	2	0	46	447	.897
35	Andrei Trefilov	4	162	4.07	0	3	0	0	0	11	84	.869
1	* Tyrone Garner	3	139	5.18	0	2	0	0	0	12	74	.838
	Totals	**82**	**4990**	**2.81**	**30**	**40**	**12**	**7**	**2**	**234**	**2415**	**.903**

General Manager

COATES, AL
Executive Vice President/General Manager, Calgary Flames.
Born in Listowel, Ont., December 3, 1945.

Al Coates was named executive vice president of the Calgary Flames on June 22, 1995. On November 3, he was designated as the interim general manager, replacing Doug Risebrough. Coates' appointment as general manager became official on May 31, 1996. In this role, he is responsible for all aspects of hockey operations for the club.

Coates had been a member of the Flames senior management team since the club's arrival in Calgary in 1980. He has over 28 years of professional hockey experience, including 19 years of service with the Calgary Flames.

Following a playing career in Europe, Coates joined the Detroit Red Wings organization in 1971. He spent nine seasons with the Red Wings, working in various capacities. In the summer of 1980, he joined the Flames as the team's director of public relations. In August, 1982, Coates was named as the assistant to the president, working directly with then president and general manager Cliff Fletcher in a number of hockey administrative capacities. Later, on August 1, 1989, he was promoted to director of hockey administration. He continued his progression through the organization when, on September 8, 1991, he was named the team's assistant general manager, a position he held until his promotion to executive vice president and general manager.

Coates' work has involved player contracts, coordinating professional scouting, and working with the Flames development team in Saint John (AHL). Coates also now serves as the chairman of the executive committee of the American Hockey League. His progressive management and leadership style has helped shape the Flames franchise into a successful, respected organization both on and off the ice.

General Managers' History

Cliff Fletcher, 1972-73 to 1990-91; Doug Risebrough, 1991-92 to 1994-95; Doug Risebrough and Al Coates, 1995-96; Al Coates, 1996-97 to date.

Coaching History

Bernie Geoffrion, 1972-73, 1973-74; Bernie Geoffrion and Fred Creighton, 1974-75; Fred Creighton, 1975-76 to 1978-79; Al MacNeil, 1979-80 to 1981-82; Bob Johnson, 1982-83 to 1986-87; Terry Crisp, 1987-88 to 1989-90; Doug Risebrough, 1990-91; Doug Risebrough and Guy Charron, 1991-92; Dave King, 1992-93 to 1994-95; Pierre Page, 1995-96, 1996-97; Brian Sutter, 1997-98 to date.

Club Records

Team

(Figures in brackets for season records are games played; records for fewest points, wins, ties, losses, goals, goals against are for 70 or more games)

Most Points	117	1988-89 (80)
Most Wins	54	1988-89 (80)
Most Ties	19	1977-78 (80)
Most Losses	41	1996-97 (82),
		1997-98 (82)
Most Goals	397	1987-88 (80)
Most Goals Against	345	1981-82 (80)
Fewest Points	65	1972-73 (78)
Fewest Wins	25	1972-73 (78)
Fewest Ties	3	1986-87 (80)
Fewest Losses	17	1988-89 (80)
Fewest Goals	191	1972-73 (78)
Fewest Goals Against	226	1988-89 (80)

Longest Winning Streak
Overall ... 10 Oct. 14-Nov. 3/78
Home ... 9 Oct. 17-Nov. 15/78,
Jan. 3-Feb. 5/89,
Mar. 3-Apr. 1/90,
Feb. 21-Mar. 14/91
Away ... 7 Nov. 10-Dec. 4/88

Longest Undefeated Streak
Overall ... 13 Nov. 10-Dec. 8/88
(12 wins, 1 tie)
Home ... 18 Dec. 29/90-Mar. 14/91
(17 wins, 1 tie)
Away ... 9 Feb. 20-Mar. 21/88
(6 wins, 3 ties),
Nov. 11-Dec. 16/90
(6 wins, 3 ties)

Longest Losing Streak
Overall ... 11 Dec. 14/85-Jan. 7/86
Home ... 6 Dec. 5-31/98
Away ... 9 Dec. 1/85-Jan. 12/86

Longest Winless Streak
Overall ... 11 Dec. 14/85-Jan. 7/86
(11 losses),
Jan. 5-26/93
(9 losses, 2 ties)
Three times
Home ... 6
Away ... 13 Feb. 3-Mar. 29/73
(10 losses, 3 ties)
Most Shutouts, Season ... 8 1974-75 (80)
Most PIM, Season ... 2,655 1991-92 (80)
Most Goals, Game ... 13 Feb. 10/93
(S.J. 1 at Cgy. 13)

Individual

Most Seasons	13	Al MacInnis
Most Games	803	Al MacInnis
Most Goals, Career	364	Theoren Fleury
Most Assists, Career	609	Al MacInnis
Most Points, Career	830	Theoren Fleury
		(364G, 466A)
Most PIM, Career	2,405	Tim Hunter
Most Shutouts, Career	20	Dan Bouchard

Longest Consecutive
Games Streak ... 257 Brad Marsh
(Oct. 11/78-Nov. 10/81)
Most Goals, Season ... 66 Lanny McDonald
(1982-83)
Most Assists, Season ... 82 Kent Nilsson
(1980-81)
Most Points, Season ... 131 Kent Nilsson
(1980-81)
Most PIM, Season ... 375 Tim Hunter
(1988-89)

Most Points, Defenseman,
Season ... 103 Al MacInnis
(1990-91; 28G, 75A)
Most Points, Center,
Season ... 131 Kent Nilsson
(1980-81; 49G, 82A)
Most Points, Right Wing,
Season ... 110 Joe Mullen
(1988-89; 51G, 59A)
Most Points, Left Wing,
Season ... 90 Gary Roberts
(1991-92; 53G, 37A)
Most Points, Rookie,
Season ... 92 Joe Nieuwendyk
(1987-88; 51G, 41A)
Most Shutouts, Season ... 5 Dan Bouchard
(1973-74),
Phil Myre
(1974-75)
Most Goals, Game ... 5 Joe Nieuwendyk
(Jan. 11/89)
Most Assists, Game ... 6 Guy Chouinard
(Feb. 25/81),
Gary Suter
(Apr. 4/86)
Most Points, Game ... 7 Sergei Makarov
(Feb. 25/90; 2G, 5A)

Records include Atlanta Flames, 1972-73 through 1979-80.

Retired Numbers

9   Lanny McDonald   1981-1989

Captains' History

Keith McCreary, 1972-73 to 1974-75; Pat Quinn, 1975-76, 1976-77; Tom Lysiak, 1977-78, 1978-79; Jean Pronovost, 1979-80; Brad Marsh, 1980-81; Phil Russell, 1981-82, 1982-83; Lanny McDonald, Doug Risebrough (co-captains), 1983-84; Lanny McDonald, Doug Risebrough, Jim Peplinski (tri-captains), 1984-85 to 1986-87; Lanny McDonald, Jim Peplinski (co-captains), 1987-88; Lanny McDonald, Jim Peplinski, Tim Hunter (tri-captains), 1988-89; Brad McCrimmon, 1989-90; alternating captains, 1990-91; Joe Nieuwendyk, 1991-92 to 1994-95; Theoren Fleury, 1995-96, 1996-97; Todd Simpson, 1997-98 to date.

All-time Record vs. Other Clubs

Regular Season

	At Home							On Road							Total						
	GP	W	L	T	GF	GA	PTS	GP	W	L	T	GF	GA	PTS	GP	W	L	T	GF	GA	PTS
Anaheim	15	9	6	0	44	36	18	16	7	6	3	41	47	17	31	16	12	3	85	83	35
Boston	42	17	22	3	154	149	37	43	11	26	6	117	152	28	85	28	48	9	271	301	65
Buffalo	42	15	16	11	145	138	41	42	13	24	5	125	177	31	84	28	40	16	270	315	72
Carolina	25	19	5	1	126	83	39	26	13	9	4	97	84	30	51	32	14	5	223	167	69
Chicago	53	24	19	10	171	163	58	51	16	22	13	148	171	45	104	40	41	23	319	334	103
Colorado	34	19	9	6	137	101	44	33	12	12	9	118	129	33	67	31	21	15	255	230	77
Dallas	52	30	11	11	194	134	71	52	18	26	8	191	194	44	104	48	37	19	365	328	115
Detroit	50	28	16	6	201	157	62	49	15	25	9	152	185	39	99	43	41	15	353	342	101
Edmonton	67	37	24	6	296	242	80	68	22	36	10	237	275	54	135	59	60	16	533	517	134
Florida	5	2	2	1	11	11	5	5	3	2	0	13	10	6	10	5	4	1	24	21	11
Los Angeles	84	51	23	10	387	278	112	81	31	41	9	294	313	71	165	82	64	19	681	591	183
Montreal	42	13	24	5	128	147	31	42	11	24	7	103	151	29	84	24	48	12	231	298	60
Nashville	2	0	1	1	3	4	1	3	2	1	0	11	9	4	5	2	2	1	14	13	5
New Jersey	39	27	5	7	175	101	61	41	25	13	3	153	116	53	80	52	18	10	328	217	114
NY Islanders	47	23	13	11	168	140	57	46	17	25	4	124	185	33	93	35	38	20	292	325	90
NY Rangers	47	27	10	10	211	141	64	48	21	22	5	172	171	47	95	48	32	15	383	312	111
Ottawa	6	4	1	1	29	13	9	6	1	3	2	13	14	4	12	5	4	3	42	27	13
Philadelphia	49	24	16	9	200	161	57	48	13	32	3	128	190	29	97	37	48	12	328	351	86
Phoenix	61	36	18	7	276	200	79	60	21	28	11	209	236	53	121	57	46	18	485	436	132
Pittsburgh	42	25	10	7	185	130	57	42	10	22	10	130	159	30	84	35	32	17	315	289	87
St. Louis	52	26	22	4	181	156	56	53	21	24	8	169	187	50	105	47	46	12	350	343	106
San Jose	22	13	7	2	94	60	28	24	16	6	2	82	67	34	46	29	13	4	176	127	62
Tampa Bay	6	4	2	0	22	12	8	7	3	3	1	25	23	7	13	7	5	1	47	35	15
Toronto	52	30	17	5	216	168	65	49	17	25	7	179	188	41	101	47	42	12	395	356	106
Vancouver	85	54	19	12	364	246	120	85	37	31	17	290	298	91	170	91	50	29	654	544	211
Washington	36	24	6	6	152	85	54	37	14	18	5	131	141	33	73	38	24	11	283	226	87
Defunct Clubs	13	8	4	1	51	34	17	13	7	3	3	43	33	17	26	15	7	4	94	67	34
Totals	1070	589	328	153	4321	3290	1331	1070	392	509	169	3475	3905	953	2140	981	837	322	7796	7195	2284

Playoffs

	Series	W	L	GP	W	L	T	GF	GA	Last Mtg.	Round	Result
Chicago	3	2	1	12	7	5	0	37	33	1996	CQF	L 0-4
Dallas	1	0	1	6	2	4	0	18	25	1981	SF	L 2-4
Detroit	1	0	1	2	0	2	0	5	8	1978	PR	L 0-2
Edmonton	5	1	4	30	11	19	0	96	132	1991	DSF	L 3-4
Los Angeles	6	2	4	26	13	13	0	102	105	1993	DSF	L 2-4
Montreal	2	1	1	11	5	6	0	32	31	1989	F	W 4-2
NY Rangers	1	0	1	4	1	3	0	8	14	1980	PR	L 1-3
Philadelphia	2	1	1	11	4	7	0	28	43	1981	QF	W 4-3
St. Louis	1	1	0	7	4	3	0	28	22	1986	CF	W 4-3
San Jose	1	0	1	7	3	4	0	35	26	1995	CQF	L 3-4
Toronto	1	0	1	2	0	2	0	5	9	1979	PR	L 0-2
Vancouver	5	3	2	26	13	13	0	82	80	1994	CQF	L 3-4
Winnipeg	3	1	2	13	6	7	0	43	45	1987	DSF	L 2-4
Totals	32	12	20	156	87	69	0	529	590			

Carolina totals include Hartford, 1979-80 to 1996-97.
Colorado totals include Quebec, 1979-80 to 1994-95.   Dallas totals include Minnesota, 1972-73 to 1992-93.
New Jersey totals include Kansas City, 1974-75 to 1975-76, and Colorado Rockies, 1976-77 to 1981-82.
Phoenix totals include Winnipeg, 1979-80 to 1995-96.

Playoff Results 1999-95

Year	Round	Opponent	Result	GF	GA
1996	CQF	Chicago	L 0-4	7	16
1995	CQF	San Jose	L 3-4	35	26

Abbreviations: Round: F – Final;
CF – conference final; **CQF** – conference quarter-final;
DSF – division semi-final; **SF** – semi-final;
QF – quarter-final; **PR** – preliminary round.

1998-99 Results

Oct.	9		San Jose	3-3	13	at	Anaheim	2-1
	10	at	San Jose	5-3	14	at	Los Angeles	0-3
	16		Toronto	3-7	16	at	San Jose	3-3
	18	at	Detroit	0-2	19		Detroit	3-1
	20	at	Dallas	1-3	21	at	Colorado	2-4
	23	at	Nashville	4-3	28		Chicago	6-6
	24	at	St. Louis	3-4	30		St. Louis	4-3
	28		Pittsburgh	2-5	Feb. 1	at	Dallas	2-2
	30		Washington	0-0	2	at	Phoenix	2-2
Nov.	1	at	Chicago	4-1	4		Nashville	2-2
	3	at	Detroit	5-2	6		Ottawa	1-2
	6		Nashville	1-2	8		Edmonton	2-1
	8		Colorado	3-1	9	at	Colorado	2-1
	10		Los Angeles	5-4	12		Boston	4-3
	12		Vancouver	3-4	19		Anaheim	6-3
	14		Anaheim	0-1	20		Los Angeles	2-2
	16		Detroit	5-3	22		NY Rangers	6-2
	19	at	Montreal	3-4	24		Buffalo	2-2
	21	at	Ottawa	1-4	26		St. Louis	2-4
	23	at	Toronto	2-3	Mar. 1		San Jose	1-2
	25	at	Nashville	3-4	5	at	Vancouver	5-1
	27		Edmonton	2-3	6	at	Los Angeles	4-1
	28		Chicago	5-4	9	at	St. Louis	7-4
Dec.	3		Tampa Bay	4-1	12	at	Carolina	1-2
	5		Phoenix	2-3	13	at	Washington	5-4
	7		Dallas	2-3	16	at	Nashville	4-2
	11	at	Tampa Bay	2-1	17	at	Chicago	1-3
	12	at	Florida	4-2	21		NY Islanders	2-1
	14	at	NY Rangers	2-5	22	at	Edmonton	2-2
	17	at	Philadelphia	3-3	25		Montreal	2-1
	18	at	New Jersey	5-2	27	at	Phoenix	1-2
	22		Vancouver	3-5	28	at	Anaheim	1-5
	23	at	Vancouver	2-5	30	at	Colorado	3-3
	27		Colorado	1-2	Apr. 1		Phoenix	1-4
	29		Philadelphia	3-4	3		Toronto	1-5
	31		Montreal	1-2	7	at	Edmonton	2-4
Jan.	2	at	Buffalo	1-7	9		Edmonton	1-4
	4	at	Boston	1-5	12		Vancouver	0-2
	5	at	Pittsburgh	1-5	14	at	Vancouver	5-4
	8		Dallas	1-0	15		Colorado	5-1
	10		Florida	1-2	17	at	Edmonton	2-3

Entry Draft Selections 1999-85

1999
Pick
11 Oleg Saprykin
38 Dan Cavanaugh
77 Craig Andersson
106 Roman Rozakov
135 Matt Doman
153 Jesse Cook
166 Cory Pecker
170 Matt Underhill
190 Blair Stayzer
252 Dimitri Kirilenko

1998
Pick
6 Rico Fata
33 Blair Betts
62 Paul Manning
102 Shaun Sutter
108 Dany Sabourin
120 Brent Gauvreau
192 Radek Duda
206 Jonas Frogren
234 Kevin Mitchell

1997
Pick
6 Daniel Tkaczuk
32 Evan Lindsay
42 John Tripp
51 Dimitri Kokorev
60 Derek Schutz
70 Erik Andersson
92 Chris St. Croix
100 Ryan Ready
113 Martin Moise
140 Ilja Demidov
167 Jeremy Rondeau
223 Dustin Paul

1996
Pick
13 Derek Morris
39 Travis Brigley
40 Steve Begin
73 Dmitri Vlasenkov
89 Toni Lydman
94 Christian Lefebvre
122 Josef Straka
202 Ryan Wade
228 Ronald Petrovicky

1995
Pick
20 Denis Gauthier Jr.
46 Pavel Smirnov
72 Rocky Thompson
98 Jan Labraaten
150 Clarke Wilm
176 Ryan Gillis
233 Steve Shirreffs

1994
Pick
19 Chris Dingman
45 Dmitri Ryabykin
77 Chris Clark
91 Ryan Duthie
97 Johan Finnstrom
107 Nils Ekman
123 Frank Appel
149 Patrick Haltia
175 Ladislav Kohn
201 Keith McCambridge
227 Jorgen Jonsson
253 Mike Peluso
279 Pavel Torgayev

1993
Pick
18 Jesper Mattsson
44 Jamie Allison
70 Dan Tompkins
95 Jason Smith
96 Marty Murray
121 Darryl Lafrance
122 John Emmons
148 Andreas Karlsson
200 Derek Sylvester
252 German Titov
278 Burke Murphy

1992
Pick
6 Cory Stillman
30 Chris O'Sullivan
54 Mathias Johansson
78 Robert Svehla
102 Sami Helenius
126 Ravil Yakubov
129 Joel Bouchard
150 Pavel Rajnoha
174 Ryan Mulhern
198 Brandon Carper
222 Jonas Hoglund
246 Andrei Potaichuk

1991
Pick
19 Niklas Sundblad
41 Francois Groleau
52 Sandy McCarthy
63 Brian Caruso
85 Steven Magnusson
107 Jerome Butler
129 Bobby Marshall
140 Matt Hoffman
151 Kelly Harper
173 David St. Pierre
195 David Struch
217 Sergei Zolotov
239 Marko Jantunen
261 Andrei Trefilov

1990
Pick
11 Trevor Kidd
26 Nicolas P. Perreault
32 Vesa Viitakoski
41 Etienne Belzile
62 Glen Mears
83 Paul Kruse
125 Chris Tschupp
146 Dmitri Frolov
167 Shawn Murray
188 Mike Murray
209 Rob Sumner
230 invalid claim
251 Leo Gudas

1989
Pick
24 Kent Manderville
42 Ted Drury
50 Veli-Pekka Kautonen
63 Corey Lyons
70 Robert Reichel
84 Ryan O'Leary
105 F. (Toby) Kearney
147 Alex Nikolic
168 Kevin Wortman
189 Sergei Gomolyako
210 Dan Sawyer
231 Alexander Yudin
252 Kenneth Kennholt

1988
Pick
21 Jason Muzzatti
42 Todd Harkins
84 Gary Socha
85 Thomas Forslund
90 Scott Matusovich
126 Jonas Bergqvist
147 Stefan Nilsson
168 Troy Kennedy
189 Brett Peterson
210 Guy Darveau
231 Dave Tretowicz
252 Sergei Priakhan

1987
Pick
19 Bryan Deasley
25 Stephane Matteau
40 Kevin Grant
61 Scott Mahoney
70 Tim Harris
103 Tim Corkery
124 Joe Aloi
145 Peter Ciavaglia
166 Theoren Fleury
187 Mark Osiecki
208 William Sedergren
229 Peter Hasselblad
250 Magnus Svensson

1986
Pick
16 George Pelawa
37 Brian Glynn
79 Tom Quinlan
100 Scott Bloom
121 John Parker
142 Rick Lessard
163 Mark Olsen
184 Warren Sharples
205 Doug Pickell
226 Anders Lindstrom
247 Antonin Stavjana

1985
Pick
17 Chris Biotti
27 Joe Nieuwendyk
38 Jeff Wenaas
59 Lane MacDonald
80 Roger Johansson
101 Esa Keskinen
122 Tim Sweeney
143 Stu Grimson
164 Nate Smith
185 Darryl Olsen
206 Peter Romberg
227 Alexander Kozhevnikov
248 Bill Gregoire

Coach

SUTTER, BRIAN
Coach, Calgary Flames. Born in Viking, Alta., October 7, 1956.

Brian Sutter enters his third season as head coach of the Calgary Flames after recording a 30-40-12 record and a .439 winning percentage last year with a young rebuilding club. He is one of six Sutter brothers involved in hockey but the first to have either played or coached at the NHL level in their native province. Brian is the tenth head coach in Flames franchise history, and eighth in the 20 year history of the team in Calgary.

Following a 12 season playing career (1976-1988) with St. Louis, Sutter immediately joined the NHL coaching ranks as head coach of the team he captained for nine of his twelve seasons. He coached the Blues for four years (1988-92), before moving on to coach the Boston Bruins between 1992-95.

During his three seasons as head coach of the Boston Bruins, Sutter led the Bruins to the third best record in the NHL (120-73-23). During the 1992-93 season, Sutter coached his team to the second best overall record in the league (51-26-7, 109 points). The 1992-93 season marked the first time in ten years the Bruins posted a 50-win season and earned Sutter runner-up honors in the balloting for the Jack Adams Award as the league's top coach. In his second season behind the Bruins bench, Sutter coached one of the league's youngest rosters, including Bryan Smolinski and Joe Juneau, to 42 wins. Sutter's win percentage during his tenure with the Bruins was an impressive .609.

Sutter spent four seasons (1988-92) behind the bench of the St. Louis Blues where he exceeded Scotty Bowman's record to become the winningest coach in Blues history, posting a Blues' career record of 153-124-43 and .545 winning percentage. Sutter won coach-of-the-year honors in 1990-91 after leading his charges to a 47-22-11 record, second overall in the league.

Following his junior career with Lethbridge (WHL), Sutter was drafted by the St. Louis Blues as their second pick, 20th overall, in the 1976 Amateur Draft. Sutter played his entire twelve year NHL career with the Blues. His number 11 was retired by the Blues on December 30, 1988. Sutter ranks second all-time among Blues players in games played and third all-time in goals, assists and points.

Sutter and his wife, Judy, return to "Sutter Country" Alberta in the Sylvan Lake area during the off-season. They have one son, Shaun and one daughter, Abigail. Shaun was drafted by the Flames from the Lethbridge Hurricanes in the 1998 NHL Entry Draft.

Club Directory

Canadian Airlines Saddledome
P.O. Box 1540 Station M
Calgary, Alberta T2P 3B9
Phone **403/777-2177**
FAX 403/777-2195
Website: www.calgaryflames.com
Capacity: 17,139

Owners: Grant A. Bartlett (Alt. Governor), N. Murray Edwards (Alt. Governor), Harley N. Hotchkiss (Governor), Ronald V. Joyce, Alvin G. Libin, Allan P. Markin, J.R. (Bud) McCaig, Byron J. Seaman (Alt. Governor), Daryl K. Seaman

Management	
President & Chief Executive Officer – Alternate Governor	Ron Bremner
Executive Vice-President & General Manager – Alternate Governor	Al Coates
Vice President, Finance & Administration	Michael Holditch
Vice President, Corporate Development	Lanny McDonald
Vice President, Marketing & Sales	Garry McKenzie
Hockey Club Personnel	
Director, Player Personnel & GM S.J. Flames	Nick Polano
Director, Hockey Operations/Asst. Coach	Al MacNeil
Head Coach	Brian Sutter
Assistant Coach	Rich Preston
Assistant Coach	Jamie Hislop
Development Coach	Tom Watt
Director, Hockey Administration	Mike Burke
Video Coordinator	Gary Taylor
Pro Scout	Tod Button
Saint John Flames Head Coach	Rick Vaive
Goaltending Consultant	Glenn Hall
Scouts	Ian McKenzie, Guy Lapointe, Mike Polano
Scouting Staff	Glen Giovanucci, Tomas Jelinek, Larry Johnston, Nikolai Ladigan, Lars Norrman, Jarmo Torvanen
Exec. Asst. to President/CEO	Yvette Mutcheson
Exec. Asst. to GM and Hockey Operations	Brenda Koyich
Exec. Asst. to VP, Finance & Corporate Development	Terri Ludwig
Administration	
Controllers	Jackie Manwaring, Penny Payne
Assistant Controller	Karen Kingham
Communications	
Director, Communications	Peter Hanlon
Communications Assistant	Sean O'Brien
Admin. Assistant Communications	Bernie Hargrave
Exec. Dir. Flames Foundation/ Dir. Community Relations	Kathy Gieck
Community Relations Representative	Jim "Bearcat" Murray
Human Resources	
Director, Human Resources	Eleanor Culver
Marketing	
Director, Advertising and Promotions	John Vidalin
Retail Operations Manager	Dean Borle
Director, Advertising and Publishing	Pat Halls
Director, Executive Suites	Bob White
Business Development Manager	Al Molnar
Director, Game Presentation	TBA
Sales/Customer Service	
Director, Ticket Operations & Special Projects	Jack Maloney
Director, Ticket Sales	Richard Muschell
Medical/Training Staff	
Physiotherapist	Terry Kane
Athletic Therapist	Morris Boyer
Equipment Manager	Gus Thorson
Strength & Conditioning	Rich Hesketh
Head Physician - Sport Medicine	Dr. Willem Meeuwisse
Orthopedic Surgeon	Dr. Nicholas Mohtadi
Internal Medicine	Dr. Terry Groves
Team Dentist	Dr. Bill Blair
Sports Psychologist	Cal Botterill
Dressing Room Attendant	Les Jarvis
Dressing Room Attendant	Jules Carriere
Canadian Airlines Saddledome	
GM, Building Operations	Libby Raines
Operations Manager	George Greenwood
Food Services Asst. Manager	Art Hernandez
Concessions Manager	Sheila Parisien
Maintenance Superintendent	Ron Leopold
Security/Parking Superintendent	Bob Godun
Facility	
Location of Media Boxes	Print – north side TV & Radio – south side
Broadcast Stations	
Radio	66 CFR Radio (660 AM)
Television	Calgary 7 (Channels 2 & 7)

Coaching Record

		Regular Season					Playoffs			
Season	**Team**	**Games**	**W**	**L**	**T**	**%**	**Games**	**W**	**L**	**%**
1988-89	St. Louis (NHL)	80	33	35	12	.488	10	5	5	.500
1989-90	St. Louis (NHL)	80	37	34	9	.519	12	7	5	.583
1990-91	St. Louis (NHL)	80	47	22	11	.656	13	6	7	.462
1991-92	St. Louis (NHL)	80	36	33	11	.519	6	2	4	.333
1992-93	Boston (NHL)	84	51	26	7	.649	4	0	4	.000
1993-94	Boston (NHL)	84	42	29	13	.577	13	6	7	.462
1994-95	Boston (NHL)	48	27	18	3	.594	5	1	4	.200
1997-98	Calgary (NHL)	82	26	41	15	.409	....	....	....	....
1998-99	Calgary (NHL)	82	30	40	12	.439	....	....	....	....
	NHL Totals	**700**	**329**	**278**	**93**	**.536**	**63**	**27**	**36**	**.429**

Carolina Hurricanes

1998-99 Results: 34W-30L-18T 86PTS. First, Southeast Division

Year-by-Year Record

Season	GP	Home W	L	T	Road W	L	T	Overall W	L	T	GF	GA	Pts.	Finished		Playoff Result
1998-99	82	20	12	9	14	18	9	34	30	18	210	202	86	1st,	Southeast Div.	Lost Conf. Quarter-Final
1997-98	82	16	18	7	17	23	1	33	41	8	200	219	74	6th,	Northeast Div.	Out of Playoffs
1996-97*	82	23	15	3	9	24	8	32	39	11	226	256	75	5th,	Northeast Div.	Out of Playoffs
1995-96*	82	22	15	4	12	24	5	34	39	9	237	259	77	4th,	Northeast Div.	Out of Playoffs
1994-95*	48	12	10	2	7	14	3	19	24	5	127	141	43	5th,	Northeast Div.	Out of Playoffs
1993-94*	84	14	22	6	13	26	3	27	48	9	227	288	63	6th,	Northeast Div.	Out of Playoffs
1992-93*	84	12	25	5	14	27	1	26	52	6	284	369	58	5th,	Adams Div.	Out of Playoffs
1991-92*	80	13	17	10	13	24	3	26	41	13	247	283	65	4th,	Adams Div.	Lost Div. Semi-Final
1990-91*	80	18	16	6	13	22	5	31	38	11	238	276	73	4th,	Adams Div.	Lost Div. Semi-Final
1989-90*	80	17	18	5	21	15	4	38	33	9	275	268	85	4th,	Adams Div.	Lost Div. Semi-Final
1988-89*	80	21	17	2	16	21	3	37	38	5	299	290	79	4th,	Adams Div.	Lost Div. Semi-Final
1987-88*	80	21	14	5	14	24	2	35	38	7	249	267	77	4th,	Adams Div.	Lost Div. Semi-Final
1986-87*	80	26	9	5	17	21	2	43	30	7	287	270	93	1st,	Adams Div.	Lost Div. Semi-Final
1985-86*	80	21	17	2	19	19	2	40	36	4	332	302	84	4th,	Adams Div.	Lost Div. Final
1984-85*	80	17	18	5	13	23	4	30	41	9	268	318	69	5th,	Adams Div.	Out of Playoffs
1983-84*	80	19	16	5	9	26	5	28	42	10	288	320	66	5th,	Adams Div.	Out of Playoffs
1982-83*	80	13	22	5	6	32	2	19	54	7	261	403	45	5th,	Adams Div.	Out of Playoffs
1981-82*	80	13	17	10	8	24	8	21	41	18	264	351	60	5th,	Adams Div.	Out of Playoffs
1980-81*	80	14	17	9	7	24	9	21	41	18	292	372	60	4th,	Norris Div.	Out of Playoffs
1979 80*	80	22	12	6	5	22	13	27	34	19	303	312	73	4th,	Norris Div.	Lost Prelim. Round

* Hartford Whalers

1999-2000 Schedule

Oct.	Sat.	2	at Boston
	Thu.	7	at Philadelphia
	Fri.	8	at NY Rangers
	Mon.	11	at Calgary*
	Wed.	13	at Edmonton
	Fri.	15	at Vancouver
	Wed.	20	at Toronto
	Fri.	22	at Buffalo
	Sat.	23	at Pittsburgh
	Fri.	29	New Jersey
	Sat.	30	at NY Islanders
Nov.	Wed.	3	Toronto
	Fri.	5	at Detroit
	Sun.	7	Washington
	Wed.	10	NY Islanders
	Thu.	11	at Philadelphia
	Sat.	13	Tampa Bay
	Wed.	17	Ottawa
	Fri.	19	at Washington
	Sat.	20	Dallas
	Mon.	22	Boston
	Wed.	24	Vancouver
	Fri.	26	at Tampa Bay
	Sat.	27	Pittsburgh
	Tue.	30	Calgary
Dec.	Thu.	2	Toronto
	Sat.	4	at Colorado
	Tue.	7	at St. Louis
	Wed.	8	at Dallas
	Fri.	10	at Tampa Bay
	Wed.	15	Pittsburgh
	Sat.	18	Atlanta
	Mon.	20	Colorado
	Wed.	22	Detroit
	Thu.	23	at Ottawa
	Sun.	26	Florida
	Tue.	28	at Nashville
Jan.	Sat.	1	at Atlanta
	Tue.	4	Ottawa
	Thu.	6	at Boston
	Fri.	7	Anaheim

	Sun.	9	NY Rangers
	Tue.	11	Philadelphia
	Fri.	14	at Florida
	Mon.	17	at New Jersey
	Tue.	18	at NY Rangers
	Thu.	20	NY Rangers
	Sat.	22	Buffalo*
	Mon.	24	Montreal
	Tue.	25	Phoenix
	Fri.	28	New Jersey
	Sun.	30	at Montreal*
Feb.	Tue.	1	Florida
	Thu.	3	at Washington
	Tue.	8	at NY Islanders
	Sat.	12	at Tampa Bay
	Mon.	14	at Toronto
	Tue.	15	at Ottawa
	Thu.	17	Montreal
	Sat.	19	Tampa Bay
	Mon.	21	Washington*
	Thu.	24	Florida
	Sat.	26	at Florida
Mar.	Wed.	1	at Phoenix
	Thu.	2	at Los Angeles
	Sat.	4	at San Jose
	Wed.	8	Chicago
	Fri.	10	Boston
	Sun.	12	Atlanta*
	Wed.	15	Edmonton
	Fri.	17	at Washington
	Sat.	18	at Montreal
	Tue.	21	at New Jersey
	Wed.	22	St. Louis
	Sun.	26	NY Islanders*
	Mon.	27	Buffalo
	Wed.	29	Nashville
	Fri.	31	at Buffalo
Apr.	Sun.	2	Philadelphia*
	Mon.	3	at Pittsburgh
	Sat.	8	at Atlanta*
	Sun.	9	Atlanta*

* Denotes afternoon game.

The leading scorer in the history of the franchise, Ron Francis rejoined the team in Carolina in 1998-99. He contributed 21 goals and 31 assists as the Hurricanes made the playoffs for the first time since 1991-92 when the team was based in Hartford.

Franchise date: June 22, 1979
Transferred from Hartford to Carolina, June 25, 1997.

EASTERN NHL **CONFERENCE**

SOUTHEAST DIVISION

21st NHL Season

1999-2000 Player Personnel

FORWARDS	HT	WT	S	Place of Birth	Date	1998-99 Club
BATTAGLIA, Bates	6-2	185	L	Chicago, IL	12/13/75	Carolina
DANIELS, Jeff	6-1	200	L	Oshawa, Ont.	6/24/68	Nashville
DIONNE, Gilbert	6-1	195	L	Drummondville, Que.	9/19/70	Cincinnati
FRANCIS, Ron	6-3	200	L	Sault Ste. Marie, Ont.	3/1/63	Carolina
GELINAS, Martin	5-11	195	L	Shawinigan, Que.	6/5/70	Carolina
KAPANEN, Sami	5-10	170	L	Vantaa, Finland	6/14/73	Carolina
KOEHLER, Greg	6-2	195	L	Scarborough, Ont.	2/27/75	New Haven-Florida
KOVALENKO, Andrei	5-10	215	L	Balakovo, USSR	6/7/70	Edmonton-Philadelphia-Carolina
KRON, Robert	5-11	185	L	Brno, Czech.	2/27/67	Carolina
LYSAK, Brett	6-0	190	L	Edmonton, Alta.	12/30/80	Regina
MacDONALD, Craig	6-2	180	L	Antigonish, N.S.	4/7/77	Carolina-New Haven
MacNEIL, Ian	6-2	171	L	Halifax, N.S.	4/27/77	New Haven
MANDERVILLE, Kent	6-3	210	L	Edmonton, Alta.	4/12/71	Carolina
MORRONE, Mike	5-11	215	L	Windsor, Ont.	1/3/76	New Orleans
MURPHY, Ryan	6-1	192	L	Van Nuys, CA	3/21/79	Bowling Green
O'NEILL, Jeff	6-1	190	R	Richmond Hill, Ont.	2/23/76	Carolina
PETRUNIN, Andrei	5-9	169	L	Moscow, USSR	2/2/78	Muskegon
PRIMEAU, Keith	6-4	210	L	Toronto, Ont.	11/24/71	Carolina
RANHEIM, Paul	6-1	210	R	St. Louis, MO	1/25/66	Carolina
RITCHIE, Byron	5-10	180	L	Burnaby, B.C.	4/24/77	Carolina-New Haven
ROBERTS, Gary	6-1	190	L	North York, Ont.	5/23/66	Carolina
SIMON, Todd	5-10	190	R	Toronto, Ont.	4/21/72	Cincinnati
WESTLUND, Tommy	6-0	210	R	Fors, Sweden	12/29/74	New Haven
WILLIS, Shane	6-0	176	R	Edmonton, Alta.	6/13/77	Carolina-New Haven
DEFENSEMEN						
BANCROFT, Steve	6-1	214	L	Toronto, Ont.	10/6/70	Saint John-Providence (AHL)
BAXTER, Jim	6-2	186	R	Brantford, Ont.	8/24/79	Oshawa
COFFEY, Paul	6-0	190	L	Weston, Ont.	6/1/61	Chicago-Carolina
DANDENAULT, Eric	6-0	195	R	Sherbrooke, Que.	3/10/70	Cincinnati
FEDOTOV, Sergei	6-1	185	L	Moscow, USSR	1/24/77	New Haven-Florida
HALKO, Steven	6-1	195	R	Etobicoke, Ont.	3/8/74	Carolina-New Haven
HAMILTON, Hugh	6-1	175	L	Saskatoon, Sask.	2/11/77	New Haven-Florida
HILL, Sean	6-0	203	R	Duluth, MN	2/14/70	Carolina
KARPA, Dave	6-1	210	R	Regina, Sask.	5/7/71	Carolina
KUZNIK, Greg	6-0	182	L	Prince George, B.C.	6/12/78	New Haven-Florida
LESCHYSHYN, Curtis	6-1	205	L	Thompson, Man.	9/21/69	Carolina
McMAHON, Mark	6-1	179	L	Geralton, Ont.	2/10/78	Florida-Plymouth
PRATT, Nolan	6-2	195	L	Fort McMurray, Alta.	8/14/75	Carolina
TSELIOS, Nikos	6-4	187	L	Oak Park, IL	1/20/79	Plymouth
WESLEY, Glen	6-1	197	L	Red Deer, Alta.	10/2/68	Carolina

GOALTENDERS	HT	WT	C	Place of Birth	Date	1998-99 Club
FICHAUD, Eric	5-11	171	L	Anjou, Que.	11/4/75	Nashville-Milwaukee
FITZPATRICK, Mark	6-2	198	L	Toronto, Ont.	11/13/68	Chicago
IRBE, Arturs	5-8	175	L	Riga, Latvia	2/2/67	Carolina
MADDEN, Chris	6-0	177	L	Syracuse, NY	3/10/79	Guelph
PETRUK, Randy	5-9	178	R	Cranbrook, B.C.	4/23/78	Florida-New Haven

Coach

MAURICE, PAUL

Coach, Carolina Hurricanes. Born in Sault Ste. Marie, Ont., January 30, 1967.

Paul Maurice is entering his fifth year as the franchise's head coach and is the first head coach of the Carolina Hurricanes. Maurice became the tenth coach in the history of the franchise on November 6, 1995, just 12 games into the 1995-96 season. Maurice stepped in as the youngest coach in the National Hockey League and remains the youngest head coach in the NHL despite ranking in the top five in tenure among NHL head coaches. In franchise history, Maurice ranks second in all-time wins (128) and second in games coached (316). In the 1996-97 season, Maurice was chosen to coach in the 1997 NHL All-Star Game.

Maurice joined the Whalers in June of 1995 as an assistant coach after serving as the head coach of the Detroit Junior Red Wings for two seasons. The Junior Wings won the OHL Western Division regular season title and played for the 1995 Memorial Cup by winning the OHL playoffs. The Wings lost in the Cup finals to Kamloops. For his efforts, Maurice was the runner-up for OHL coach of the year honors in 1995. In the 1993-94 season, Maurice's squad won the OHL Hap Emms Division title and advanced to the finals of the OHL playoffs before losing in seven games to North Bay.

Maurice began his coaching career in 1986 as an assistant coach for the Detroit Junior Red Wings after an eye injury ended his junior playing career. He served six seasons in that capacity before taking over the head coaching responsibilities in the 1993-94 season.

Coaching Record

		Regular Season					Playoffs			
Season	Team	Games	W	L	T	%	Games	W	L	%
1993-94	Detroit (OHL)	66	42	20	4	.697	17	11	6	.647
1994-95	Detroit (OHL)	66	44	18	4	.727	21	16	5	.762
1995-96	**Hartford (NHL)**	**70**	**29**	**33**	**8**	**.471**	....	....	....	....
1996-97	**Hartford (NHL)**	**82**	**32**	**39**	**11**	**.457**	....	....	....	....
1997-98	**Carolina (NHL)**	**82**	**33**	**41**	**8**	**.451**	....	....	....	....
1998-99	**Carolina (NHL)**	**82**	**34**	**30**	**18**	**.524**	**6**	**2**	**4**	**.333**
	NHL Totals	**316**	**128**	**143**	**45**	**.476**	**6**	**2**	**4**	**.333**

1998-99 Scoring

* – rookie

Regular Season

Pos	#	Player	Team	GP	G	A	Pts	+/–	PIM	PP	SH	GW	GT	S	%
C	55	Keith Primeau	CAR	78	30	32	62	8	75	9	1	5	1	178	16.9
R	24	Sami Kapanen	CAR	81	24	35	59	–1	10	5	0	7	0	254	9.4
R	26	Ray Sheppard	CAR	74	25	33	58	4	16	5	0	4	1	188	13.3
C	21	Ron Francis	CAR	82	21	31	52	–2	34	8	0	2	1	133	15.8
L	10	Gary Roberts	CAR	77	14	28	42	2	178	1	1	4	0	138	10.1
L	51	Andrei Kovalenko	EDM	43	13	14	27	–4	30	2	0	3	1	75	17.3
			PHI	13	0	1	1	–5	2	0	0	0	0	8	0.0
			CAR	18	6	6	12	3	0	1	0	1	0	21	28.6
			TOTAL	74	19	21	40	–6	32	3	0	4	1	104	18.3
C	92	Jeff O'Neill	CAR	75	16	15	31	3	66	4	0	2	0	121	13.2
L	23	Martin Gelinas	CAR	76	13	15	28	3	67	0	0	2	2	111	11.7
R	18	Robert Kron	CAR	75	9	16	25	–13	10	3	1	2	0	134	6.7
D	2	Glen Wesley	CAR	74	7	17	24	14	44	0	0	2	1	112	6.3
L	28	Paul Ranheim	CAR	78	9	10	19	4	39	0	2	1	0	67	13.4
R	11	Kevin Dineen	CAR	67	8	10	18	5	97	0	0	1	0	86	9.3
L	13	Jon Battaglia	CAR	60	7	11	18	7	22	0	0	0	2	52	13.5
C	44	Kent Manderville	CAR	81	5	11	16	9	38	0	0	0	0	71	7.0
D	4	Nolan Pratt	CAR	61	1	14	15	15	95	0	0	1	0	46	2.2
D	77	Paul Coffey	CHI	10	0	4	4	–6	0	0	0	0	0	8	0.0
			CAR	44	2	8	10	–1	28	1	0	0	0	79	2.5
			TOTAL	54	2	12	14	–7	28	1	0	0	0	87	2.3
D	5	Marek Malik	CAR	52	2	9	11	–6	36	1	0	0	0	36	5.6
D	22	Sean Hill	CAR	54	0	10	10	9	48	0	0	0	0	44	0.0
D	7	Curtis Leschyshyn	CAR	65	2	7	9	–1	50	0	0	0	0	35	5.7
D	3	Steve Chiasson	CAR	28	1	8	9	7	16	1	0	0	0	74	1.4
D	14 *	Steven Halko	CAR	20	0	3	3	5	24	0	0	0	0	6	0.0
D	33	Dave Karpa	CAR	33	0	2	2	1	55	0	0	0	0	21	0.0
D	46 *	Mike Rucinski	CAR	15	0	1	1	1	8	0	0	0	0	8	0.0
C	15 *	Byron Ritchie	CAR	3	0	0	0	0	0	0	0	0	0	0	0.0
R	45 *	Shane Willis	CAR	7	0	0	0	–2	0	0	0	0	0	1	0.0
C	31 *	Craig MacDonald	CAR	11	0	0	0	0	0	0	0	0	0	5	0.0
G	37	Trevor Kidd	CAR	25	0	0	0	0	0	0	0	0	0	0	0.0
G	1	Arturs Irbe	CAR	62	0	0	0	0	10	0	0	0	0	0	0.0

Goaltending

No.	Goaltender	GPI	Mins	Avg	W	L	T	EN	SO	GA	SA	S%
1	Arturs Irbe	62	3643	2.22	27	20	12	3	6	135	1753	.923
37	Trevor Kidd	25	1358	2.70	7	10	6	3	2	61	640	.905
	Totals	**82**	**5022**	**2.41**	**34**	**30**	**18**	**6**	**8**	**202**	**2399**	**.916**

Playoffs

Pos	#	Player	Team	GP	G	A	Pts	+/–	PIM	PP	SH	GW	GT	S	%
R	26	Ray Sheppard	CAR	6	5	1	6	–2	2	1	0	1	1	23	21.7
D	3	Steve Chiasson	CAR	6	1	2	3	1	2	1	0	0	0	17	5.9
L	23	Martin Gelinas	CAR	6	0	3	3	–4	2	0	0	0	0	12	0.0
C	55	Keith Primeau	CAR	6	0	3	3	–3	6	0	0	0	0	9	0.0
L	13	Jon Battaglia	CAR	6	0	3	3	3	8	0	0	0	0	7	0.0
R	18	Robert Kron	CAR	5	2	0	2	2	0	0	0	1	0	10	20.0
R	24	Sami Kapanen	CAR	5	1	1	2	–2	0	0	0	0	0	8	12.5
L	10	Gary Roberts	CAR	6	1	1	2	–3	8	0	0	0	0	13	7.7
L	51	Andrei Kovalenko	CAR	4	0	2	2	1	2	0	0	0	0	3	0.0
C	21	Ron Francis	CAR	3	0	1	1	1	0	0	0	0	0	4	0.0
D	77	Paul Coffey	CAR	5	0	1	1	0	2	0	0	0	0	8	0.0
C	92	Jeff O'Neill	CAR	6	0	1	1	–5	0	0	0	0	0	11	0.0
C	31 *	Craig MacDonald	CAR	1	0	0	0	0	0	0	0	0	0	0	0.0
D	33	Dave Karpa	CAR	2	0	0	0	–2	2	0	0	0	0	0	0.0
D	4	Nolan Pratt	CAR	3	0	0	0	0	2	0	0	0	0	3	0.0
D	14 *	Steven Halko	CAR	4	0	0	0	–2	2	0	0	0	0	2	0.0
D	5	Marek Malik	CAR	4	0	0	0	–2	4	0	0	0	0	0	0.0
R	11	Kevin Dineen	CAR	6	0	0	0	0	8	0	0	0	0	4	0.0
D	7	Curtis Leschyshyn	CAR	6	0	0	0	–3	6	0	0	0	0	4	0.0
L	28	Paul Ranheim	CAR	6	0	0	0	0	2	0	0	0	0	5	0.0
D	2	Glen Wesley	CAR	6	0	0	0	0	2	0	0	0	0	15	0.0
G	1	Arturs Irbe	CAR	6	0	0	0	0	0	0	0	0	0	0	0.0
C	44	Kent Manderville	CAR	6	0	0	0	0	2	0	0	0	0	6	0.0

Goaltending

No.	Goaltender	GPI	Mins	Avg	W	L	EN	SO	GA	SA	S%
1	Arturs Irbe	6	408	2.21	2	4	1	0	15	181	.917
	Totals	**6**	**412**	**2.33**	**2**	**4**	**1**	**0**	**16**	**182**	**.912**

General Managers' History

Jack Kelly, 1979-80, 1980-81; Larry Pleau, 1981-82, 1982-83; Emile Francis, 1983-84 to 1988-89; Ed Johnston, 1989-90 to 1991-92; Brian Burke, 1992-93; Paul Holmgren, 1993-94; Jim Rutherford, 1994-95 to date.

Coaching History

Don Blackburn, 1979-80; Don Blackburn and Larry Pleau, 1980-81; Larry Pleau, 1981-82; Larry Kish, Larry Pleau and John Cuniff, 1982- 83; Jack Evans, 1983-84 to 1986-87; Jack Evans and Larry Pleau, 1987-88; Larry Pleau, 1988-89; Rick Ley, 1989-90, 1990-91; Jim Roberts, 1991-92; Paul Holmgren, 1992-93; Paul Holmgren and Pierre Maguire, 1993-94; Paul Holmgren, 1994-95; Paul Holmgren and Paul Maurice, 1995-96; Paul Maurice, 1996-97 to date.

Captains' History

Rick Ley, 1979-80; Rick Ley and Mike Rogers, 1980-81; Dave Keon, 1981-82; Russ Anderson, 1982-83; Mark Johnson, 1983-84; Mark Johnson and Ron Francis, 1984-85; Ron Francis, 1985-86 to 1990-91; Randy Ladouceur, 1991-92; Pat Verbeek, 1992-93 to 1994-95; Brendan Shanahan, 1995-96; Kevin Dineen, 1996-97, 1997-98; Keith Primeau, 1998-99 to date.

Club Records

Team

(Figures in brackets for season records are games played; records for fewest points, wins, ties, losses, goals, goals against are for 70 or more games)

Most Points	93	1986-87 (80)
Most Wins	43	1986-87 (80)
Most Ties	19	1979-80 (80)
Most Losses	54	1982-83 (80)
Most Goals	332	1985-86 (80)
Most Goals Against	403	1982-83 (80)
Fewest Points	45	1982-83 (80)
Fewest Wins	19	1982-83 (80)
Fewest Ties	4	1985-86 (80)
Fewest Losses	30	1986-87 (80); 1998-99 (82)
Fewest Goals	200	1997-98 (82)
Fewest Goals Against	202	1998-99 (82)

Longest Winning Streak
Overall	7	Mar. 16-29/85
Home	5	Mar. 17-29/85
Away	6	Nov. 10-Dec. 7/90

Longest Undefeated Streak
Overall	10	Jan. 20-Feb. 10/82
		(6 wins, 4 ties)
Home	7	Mar. 15-Apr. 5/86
		(5 wins, 2 ties)
Away	8	Nov. 11-Dec. 5/96
		(4 wins, 4 ties)

Longest Losing Streak
Overall	9	Feb. 19-Mar. 8/83
Home	6	Feb. 19-Mar. 12/83, Feb. 10-Mar. 3/85
Away	13	Dec. 18/82-Feb. 5/83

Longest Winless Streak
Overall	14	Jan. 4-Feb. 9/92 (8 losses, 6 ties)
Home	13	Jan. 15-Mar. 10/85 (11 losses, 2 ties)
Away	15	Nov. 11/79-Jan. 9/80 (11 losses, 4 ties)
Most Shutouts, Season	8	1998-99 (82)
Most PIM, Season	2,354	1992-93 (84)
Most Goals, Game	11	Feb. 12/84 (Edm. 0 at Hfd. 11), Oct. 19/85 (Mtl. 6 at Hfd. 11), Jan. 17/86 (Que. 6 at Hfd. 11), Mar. 15/86 (Chi. 4 at Hfd. 11)

Individual

Most Seasons	12	Kevin Dineen
Most Games	796	Ron Francis
Most Goals, Career	285	Ron Francis
Most Assists, Career	588	Ron Francis
Most Points, Career	873	Ron Francis (285G, 588A)
Most PIM, Career	1,368	Torrie Robertson
Most Shutouts, Career	13	Mike Liut
Longest Consecutive Games Streak	419	Dave Tippett (Mar. 3/84-Oct. 7/89)
Most Goals, Season	56	Blaine Stoughton (1979-80)
Most Assists, Season	69	Ron Francis (1989-90)
Most Points, Season	105	Mike Rogers (1979-80; 44G, 61A), (1980-81; 40G, 65A)
Most PIM, Season	358	Torrie Robertson (1985-86)
Most Points, Defenseman, Season	69	Dave Babych (1985-86; 14G, 55A)
Most Points, Center, Season	105	Mike Rogers (1979-80; 44G, 61A), (1980-81; 40G, 65A)
Most Points, Right Wing, Season	100	Blaine Stoughton (1979-80; 56G, 44A)
Most Points, Left Wing, Season	89	Geoff Sanderson (1992-93; 46G, 43A)
Most Points, Rookie, Season	72	Sylvain Turgeon (1983-84; 40G, 32A)
Most Shutouts, Season	6	Arturs Irbe (1998-99)
Most Goals, Game	4	Jordy Douglas (Feb. 3/80), Ron Francis (Feb. 12/84)
Most Assists, Game	6	Ron Francis (Mar. 5/87)
Most Points, Game	6	Paul Lawless (Jan. 4/87; 2G, 4A), Ron Francis (Mar. 5/87; 6A) (Oct. 8/89; 3G, 3A)

Records include Hartford Whalers, 1979-80 through 1996-97.

All-time Record vs. Other Clubs
Regular Season

		At Home							On Road							Total					
	GP	W	L	T	GF	GA	PTS	GP	W	L	T	GF	GA	PTS	GP	W	L	T	GF	GA	PTS
Anaheim	5	4	1	0	14	8	8	5	2	3	0	17	21	4	10	6	4	0	31	29	12
Boston	66	29	30	7	226	230	65	68	17	44	7	176	257	41	134	46	74	14	402	487	106
Buffalo	68	27	31	10	205	207	64	67	21	39	7	204	271	49	135	48	70	17	409	478	113
Calgary	26	9	13	4	84	97	22	25	5	19	1	83	126	11	51	14	32	5	167	223	33
Chicago	27	12	12	3	88	88	27	26	7	16	3	72	111	17	53	19	28	6	160	199	44
Colorado	59	24	24	11	197	205	59	61	17	35	9	185	258	43	120	41	59	20	382	463	102
Dallas	27	9	14	4	90	105	22	26	10	15	1	80	107	21	53	19	29	5	170	212	43
Detroit	26	16	9	1	94	69	33	27	7	14	6	74	104	20	53	23	23	7	168	173	53
Edmonton	26	11	10	5	107	92	27	27	5	18	4	81	111	14	53	16	28	9	188	203	41
Florida	12	5	6	1	36	35	11	13	3	5	5	27	37	11	25	8	11	6	63	72	22
Los Angeles	27	13	10	4	105	105	30	26	9	14	3	103	113	21	53	22	24	7	208	218	51
Montreal	68	27	32	9	209	243	63	65	15	43	7	189	278	37	133	42	75	16	398	521	100
Nashville	1	1	0	0	4	1	2	1	0	1	0	2	3	0	2	1	1	0	6	4	2
New Jersey	34	15	12	7	116	106	37	35	12	20	3	114	127	27	69	27	32	10	230	233	64
NY Islanders	35	17	13	5	128	122	39	34	13	17	4	97	117	30	69	30	30	9	225	239	69
NY Rangers	33	18	12	3	121	111	39	35	11	21	3	97	141	25	68	29	33	6	218	252	64
Ottawa	17	14	1	2	59	34	30	19	10	6	3	59	48	23	36	24	7	5	118	82	53
Philadelphia	34	10	17	7	118	136	27	33	8	22	3	87	129	19	67	18	39	10	205	265	46
Phoenix	25	12	7	6	97	78	30	28	14	12	2	103	98	30	53	26	19	8	200	176	60
Pittsburgh	38	17	18	3	147	146	37	36	11	20	5	139	168	27	74	28	38	8	286	314	64
St. Louis	27	11	14	2	85	86	24	27	8	17	2	84	109	18	54	19	31	4	169	195	42
San Jose	8	4	4	0	26	18	8	7	3	4	0	23	34	6	15	7	8	0	49	52	14
Tampa Bay	14	9	2	3	48	36	21	13	5	6	2	35	38	12	27	14	8	5	83	74	33
Toronto	27	16	7	4	123	90	36	27	14	9	4	104	95	32	54	30	16	8	227	185	68
Vancouver	26	12	10	4	86	89	28	27	9	12	6	75	95	24	53	21	22	10	161	184	52
Washington	36	12	18	6	99	118	30	34	11	21	2	92	115	24	70	23	39	8	191	233	54
Totals	792	354	327	111	2712	2655	819	792	247	453	92	2402	3111	586	1584	601	780	203	5114	5766	1405

Playoffs

	Series	W	L	GP	W	L	T	GF	GA	Last Mtg.	Round	Result
Boston	3	0	3	19	7	12	0	48	63	1999	CQF	L 2-4
Colorado	2	1	1	9	5	4	0	35	34	1987	DSF	L 2-4
Montreal	5	0	5	27	8	19	0	70	96	1992	DSF	L 3-4
Totals	10	1	9	55	20	35	0	157	194			

Playoff Results 1999-95

Year	Round	Opponent	Result	GF	GA
1999	CQF	Boston	L 2-4	14	17

Abbreviations: Round: CQF – conference quarter-final; **DSF** – division semi-final.

Calgary totals include Atlanta Flames, 1979-80.
Dallas totals include Minnesota, 1979-80 to 1992-93.
Phoenix totals include Winnipeg, 1979-80 to 1995-96.

Colorado totals include Quebec, 1979-80 to 1994-95.
New Jersey totals include Colorado Rockies, 1979-80 to 1981-82.

1998-99 Results

Oct.	10		Tampa Bay	4-4	14	Florida	3-2
	13	at	Nashville	2-3	16	Washington	2-3
	15		Dallas	2-2	18	Toronto	4-2
	17		Philadelphia	1-1	21 at	Detroit	1-4
	20		Vancouver	3-1	26 at	Pittsburgh	5-3
	24	at	Ottawa	3-1	28	NY Rangers	3-2
	25		Los Angeles	2-3	30 at	Montreal	3-1
	28		Chicago	2-0	31 at	Boston	0-0
	30		NY Rangers	0-1	Feb. 3	New Jersey	1-4
	31	at	Boston	2-0	5 at	Washington	1-4
Nov.	2		Colorado	2-3	6	Florida	3-3
	5	at	NY Islanders	6-3	10 at	Toronto	6-5
	6	at	Washington	3-2	12 at	NY Rangers	3-1
	8		Boston	2-5	13 at	New Jersey	4-6
	11	at	Anaheim	4-5	15 at	Buffalo	2-3
	12	at	San Jose	0-3	18	Washington	2-2
	14	at	Los Angeles	5-3	20 at	Tampa Bay	3-2
	17		Montreal	5-4	21	NY Islanders	4-1
	19	at	New Jersey	2-3	24 at	Toronto	2-2
	20		Philadelphia	1-3	26 at	Vancouver	0-1
	22		New Jersey	2-5	27 at	Edmonton	2-2
	25		San Jose	3-0	Mar. 3	Boston	2-1
	28	at	NY Islanders	3-1	6 at	Florida	2-2
	29		Anaheim	3-1	8	Buffalo	4-1
Dec.	2		Montreal	4-1	10	Pittsburgh	2-3
	4		Pittsburgh	3-3	12	Calgary	2-1
	5	at	Florida	3-3	15 at	Phoenix	5-5
	10		Boston	2-3	18 at	Colorado	2-3
	12		Detroit	3-0	21 at	Dallas	2-3
	15		Edmonton	3-0	22 at	St. Louis	2-5
	18	at	Ottawa	1-5	24	NY Islanders	2-1
	19	at	Buffalo	3-2	26	Toronto	2-7
	21		Buffalo	1-4	28	Tampa Bay	3-3
	23	at	NY Rangers	1-0	30 at	Philadelphia	3-3
	26		NY Rangers	3-6	Apr. 3 at	Chicago	1-2
	30		Tampa Bay	4-3	6	New Jersey	4-2
Jan.	1	at	Florida	3-3	7 at	Montreal	0-2
	2		Nashville	4-1	10 at	NY Islanders	6-1
	4		Ottawa	4-4	14	Washington	3-0
	7	at	Pittsburgh	2-4	16 at	Tampa Bay	2-2
	9	at	Philadelphia	0-2	17	Ottawa	1-1

Entry Draft
Selections 1999-85

1999
Pick
16	David Tanabe
49	Brett Lysak
84	Brad Fast
113	Ryan Murphy
174	Damian Surma
202	Jim Baxter
231	David Evans
237	Antti Jokela
259	Yauhenni Kurilin

1998
Pick
11	Jeff Heerema
70	Kevin Holdridge
71	Erik Cole
91	Josef Vasicek
93	Tommy Westlund
97	Chris Madden
184	Donald Smith
208	Jaroslav Svoboda
211	Mark Kosick
239	Brent McDonald

1997
Pick
22	Nikos Tselios
28	Brad Defauw
80	Francis Lessard
88	Shane Willis
142	Kyle Dafoe
169	Andrew Merrick
195	Niklas Nordgren
199	Randy Fitzgerald
225	Kent McDonell

1996
Pick
34	Trevor Wasyluk
61	Andrei Petrunin
88	Craig MacDonald
104	Steve Wasylko
116	Mark McMahon
143	Aaron Baker
171	Greg Kuznik
197	Kevin Marsh
223	Craig Adams
231	Askhat Rakhmatullin

1995
Pick
13	J-Sebastien Giguere
35	Sergei Fedotov
85	Ian MacNeil
87	Sami Kapanen
113	Hugh Hamilton
165	Byron Ritchie
191	Milan Kostolny
217	Mike Rucinski

1994
Pick
5	Jeff O'Neill
83	Hnat Domenichelli
109	Ryan Risidore
187	Tom Buckley
213	Ashlin Halfnight
230	Matt Ball
239	Brian Regan
265	Steve Nimigon

1993
Pick
2	Chris Pronger
72	Marek Malik
84	Trevor Roenick
115	Nolan Pratt
188	Emmanuel Legace
214	Dmitri Gorenko
240	Wes Swinson
266	Igor Chibirev

1992
Pick
9	Robert Petrovicky
47	Andrei Nikolishin
57	Jan Vopat
79	Kevin Smyth
81	Jason McBain
143	Jarret Reid
153	Ken Belanger
177	Konstantin Korotkov
201	Greg Zwakman
225	Steven Halko
249	Joacim Esbjors

1991
Pick
9	Patrick Poulin
31	Martin Hamrlik
53	Todd Hall
59	Mikael Nylander
75	Jim Storm
119	Mike Harding
141	Brian Mueller
163	Steve Yule
185	Chris Belanger
207	Jason Currie
229	Mike Santonelli
251	Rob Peters

1990
Pick
15	Mark Greig
36	Geoff Sanderson
57	Mike Lenarduzzi
78	Chris Bright
120	Cory Keenan
141	Jergus Baca
162	Martin D'Orsonnens
183	Corey Osmak
204	Espen Knutsen
225	Tommie Eriksen
246	Denis Chalifoux

1989
Pick
10	Robert Holik
52	Blair Atcheynum
73	Jim McKenzie
94	James Black
115	Jerome Bechard
136	Scott Daniels
157	Raymond Saumier
178	Michel Picard
199	Trevor Buchanan
220	John Battice
241	Peter Kasowski

1988
Pick
11	Chris Govedaris
32	Barry Richter
74	Dean Dyer
95	Scott Morrow
116	Corey Beaulieu
137	Kerry Russell
158	Jim Burke
179	Mark Hirth
200	Wayde Bucsis
221	Rob White
242	Dan Slatalla

1987
Pick
18	Jody Hull
39	Adam Burt
81	Terry Yake
102	Marc Rousseau
123	Jeff St. Cyr
144	Greg Wolf
165	John Moore
186	Joe Day
228	Kevin Sullivan
249	Steve Laurin

1986
Pick
11	Scott Young
32	Marc Laforge
74	Brian Chapman
95	Bill Horn
116	Joe Quinn
137	Steve Torrel
158	Ron Hoover
179	Robert Glasgow
200	Sean Evoy
221	Cal Brown
242	Brian Verbeek

1985
Pick
5	Dana Murzyn
26	Kay Whitmore
68	Gary Callaghan
110	Shane Churla
131	Chris Brant
152	Brian Puhalsky
173	Greg Dornbach
194	Paul Tory
215	Jerry Pawlowski
236	Bruce Hill

Club Directory

Entertainment and Sports Arena

Carolina Hurricanes
5000 Aerial Center Parkway
Suite 100
Morrisville, NC 27560
Phone **919/467-7825**
FAX 919/462-0123
Capacity: TBA

Executive Management
Chief Executive Officer/Governor	Peter Karmanos Jr.
General Partner	Thomas Thewes
President and Chief Operating Officer, Gale Force Holdings, LLP.	Dean Jordan
President and General Manager	Jim Rutherford

Hockey Operations
Assistant General Manager	Jason Karmanos
Vice President of Hockey Operations	Terry McDonnell
Head Coach	Paul Maurice
Assistant Coaches	Randy Ladouceur, Kevin McCarthy
Director of Amateur Scouting	Sheldon Ferguson
Amateur Scouts	Laurence Ferguson, Willy Langer, Willy Lindstrom, Bert Marshall, Tony MacDonald, Terry E. McDonnell
Pro Scout	Claude Larose
Goaltender Coach/Pro Scout	Steve Weeks
Head Athletic Therapist/Strength and Conditioning Coach	Peter Friesen
Assistant Athletic Therapist	Stu Lemke
Equipment Managers	Skip Cunningham, Wally Tatomir
Assistant Equipment Managers	Bob Gorman, Rick Szuber

Broadcasters
Television Play-by-Play	John Forslund
Television Analyst	Tripp Tracy
Radio Play-by-Play	Chuck Kaiton
TV	Hurricanes Television Network
Radio	Hurricanes Radio Network

Media Relations
Director of Media Relations	Chris Brown
Media Relations Manager	Jerry Peters
Media Relations Phone	(919) 467-7825, exts. 351, 354
Press Box Phone	TBD

President and General Manager

RUTHERFORD, JIM
President and General Manager, Carolina Hurricanes.
Born in Beeton, Ont., February 17, 1949.

Jim Rutherford, a former NHL goaltender, is the franchise's seventh general manager and the first general manager of the Carolina Hurricanes. Entering his sixth season, Rutherford has taken an aggressive approach towards improving the fortunes of the franchise through trades and the NHL draft.

A veteran of 13 NHL seasons, Rutherford began his professional goaltending career in 1969 as a first-round selection of the Detroit Red Wings. While playing for Detroit, Pittsburgh, Toronto and Los Angeles, Rutherford collected 14 career shutouts. For five seasons he also served as the Red Wings' player representative. Rutherford also played for Team Canada in the IIHF World Championships in Vienna in 1977 and Moscow in 1979.

After his playing days with the Red Wings, Rutherford joined Compuware to serve as the director of hockey operations for Compuware Sports Corporation. Rutherford gained a wealth of experience in youth hockey and junior programs. As a former player, coach, and general manager, his ability to develop players and produce winning programs is widely respected throughout the hockey community.

He started his management career by guiding Compuware Sports Corporation's purchase of the Windsor Spitfires of the Ontario Hockey League in April of 1984. During the next four years, Rutherford acted as general manager of the Spitfires. After the Spitfires advanced to the 1988 Memorial Cup finals, Rutherford led Compuware's efforts to bring the first American-based OHL franchise to Detroit on December 11, 1989. Rutherford was voted the 1987 executive of the year in both the OHL and the CHL and won the OHL executive of the year award again in 1988.

Sami Kapanen topped 20 goals and 30 assists for the second straight season in Carolina. His 59 points (24 goals, 35 assists) trailed only Keith Primeau among Hurricanes scorers.

Chicago Blackhawks

1998-99 Results: 29w-41l-12t 70pts. Third, Central Division

Tallying a career-high 44 goals in 1998-99, Tony Amonte was one of three players who tied for second in goals in the NHL. With his 75 points, Amonte led the Blackhawks in scoring for the third straight season.

1999-2000 Schedule

Oct.	Mon.	4	at San Jose	Sun.	9	Colorado
	Wed.	6	at Vancouver	Wed.	12	Vancouver
	Fri.	8	Phoenix	Thu.	13	at Detroit
	Sun.	10	Nashville	Sat.	15	at Colorado
	Fri.	15	Toronto	Mon.	17	San Jose*
	Sat.	16	at Pittsburgh	Wed.	19	at New Jersey
	Thu.	21	Anaheim	Fri.	21	St. Louis
	Sat.	23	Detroit	Sun.	23	Dallas
	Wed.	27	at Montreal	Thu.	27	Colorado
	Fri.	29	at Detroit	Sun.	30	at Vancouver
	Sat.	30	Los Angeles	Feb.	Wed. 2	at Edmonton
Nov.	Thu.	4	Buffalo	Thu.	3	at Calgary
	Fri.	5	at Nashville	Sat.	12	at Atlanta
	Sun.	7	NY Rangers	Mon.	14	Anaheim
	Wed.	10	Nashville	Wed.	16	Los Angeles
	Fri.	12	NY Islanders	Fri.	18	Washington
	Sun.	14	Edmonton	Sun.	20	Detroit*
	Tue.	16	at Los Angeles	Tue.	22	at Philadelphia
	Fri.	19	at Anaheim	Wed.	23	Nashville
	Sat.	20	at Phoenix	Fri.	25	at Dallas
	Wed.	24	at Edmonton	Sun.	27	at St. Louis*
	Thu.	25	at Calgary	Mar.	Wed. 1	Montreal
	Sat.	27	at St. Louis	Fri.	3	Tampa Bay
	Tue.	30	at Ottawa	Sun.	5	Phoenix*
Dec.	Fri.	3	Detroit	Tue.	7	at Nashville
	Sat.	4	at Boston	Wed.	8	at Carolina
	Mon.	6	Edmonton	Sat.	11	at Florida
	Thu.	9	New Jersey	Sun.	12	at Tampa Bay
	Fri.	10	at Buffalo	Wed.	15	at Toronto
	Sun.	12	Calgary	Thu.	16	Boston
	Tue.	14	at San Jose	Sat.	18	Dallas*
	Fri.	17	at Anaheim	Tue.	21	at Phoenix
	Sat.	18	at Los Angeles	Fri.	24	at Dallas
	Thu.	23	Dallas	Sun.	26	St. Louis*
	Sun.	26	Pittsburgh	Mon.	27	at Colorado
	Mon.	27	at Washington	Thu.	30	Toronto
	Thu.	30	Florida	Apr.	Sat. 1	at NY Islanders*
	Fri.	31	at Detroit	Sun.	2	Vancouver*
Jan.	Sun.	2	San Jose	Wed.	5	Anaheim
	Thu.	6	Calgary	Fri.	7	at St. Louis
	Sat.	8	at Nashville	Sun.	9	St. Louis*

* Denotes afternoon game.

Franchise date: September 25, 1926

WESTERN NHL CONFERENCE

CENTRAL DIVISION

74th NHL Season

Year-by-Year Record

Season	GP	Home W	Home L	Home T	Road W	Road L	Road T	Overall W	Overall L	Overall T	GF	GA	Pts.	Finished	Playoff Result
1998-99	82	20	17	4	9	24	8	29	41	12	202	248	70	3rd, Central Div.	Out of Playoffs
1997-98	82	14	19	8	16	20	5	30	39	13	192	199	73	5th, Central Div.	Out of Playoffs
1996-97	82	16	21	4	18	14	9	34	35	13	223	210	81	5th, Central Div.	Lost Conf. Quarter-Final
1995-96	82	22	13	6	18	15	8	40	28	14	273	220	94	2nd, Central Div.	Lost Conf. Semi-Final
1994-95	48	11	10	3	13	9	2	24	19	5	156	115	53	3rd, Central Div.	Lost Conf. Championship
1993-94	84	21	16	5	18	20	4	39	36	9	254	240	87	5th, Central Div.	Lost Conf. Quarter-Final
1992-93	84	25	11	6	22	14	6	47	25	12	279	230	106	1st, Norris Div.	Lost Div. Semi-Final
1991-92	80	23	9	8	13	20	7	36	29	15	257	236	87	2nd, Norris Div.	Lost Final
1990-91	80	28	8	4	21	15	4	49	23	8	284	211	106	1st, Norris Div.	Lost Div. Semi-Final
1989-90	80	25	13	2	16	20	4	41	33	6	316	294	88	1st, Norris Div.	Lost Conf. Championship
1988-89	80	16	14	10	11	27	2	27	41	12	297	335	66	4th, Norris Div.	Lost Conf. Championship
1987-88	80	21	17	2	9	24	7	30	41	9	284	328	69	3rd, Norris Div.	Lost Div. Semi-Final
1986-87	80	18	13	9	11	24	5	29	37	14	290	310	72	3rd, Norris Div.	Lost Div. Semi-Final
1985-86	80	23	12	5	16	21	3	39	33	8	351	349	86	1st, Norris Div.	Lost Div. Semi-Final
1984-85	80	22	16	2	16	19	5	38	35	7	309	299	83	2nd, Norris Div.	Lost Conf. Championship
1983-84	80	25	13	2	5	29	6	30	42	8	277	311	68	4th, Norris Div.	Lost Div. Semi-Final
1982-83	80	29	8	3	18	15	7	47	23	10	338	268	104	1st, Norris Div.	Lost Conf. Championship
1981-82	80	20	13	7	10	25	5	30	38	12	332	363	72	4th, Norris Div.	Lost Conf. Championship
1980-81	80	21	11	8	10	22	8	31	33	16	304	315	78	2nd, Smythe Div.	Lost Prelim. Round
1979-80	80	21	12	7	13	15	12	34	27	19	241	250	87	1st, Smythe Div.	Lost Quarter-Final
1978-79	80	18	12	10	11	24	5	29	36	15	244	277	73	1st, Smythe Div.	Lost Quarter-Final
1977-78	80	20	9	11	12	20	8	32	29	19	230	220	83	1st, Smythe Div.	Lost Quarter-Final
1976-77	80	19	16	5	7	27	6	26	43	11	240	298	63	3rd, Smythe Div.	Lost Prelim. Round
1975-76	80	17	15	8	15	15	10	32	30	18	254	261	82	1st, Smythe Div.	Lost Quarter-Final
1974-75	80	24	12	4	13	23	4	37	35	8	268	241	82	3rd, Smythe Div.	Lost Quarter-Final
1973-74	78	20	6	13	21	8	10	41	14	23	272	164	105	2nd, West Div.	Lost Semi-Final
1972-73	78	26	9	4	16	18	5	42	27	9	284	225	93	1st, West Div.	Lost Final
1971-72	78	28	3	8	18	14	7	46	17	15	256	166	107	1st, West Div.	Lost Semi-Final
1970-71	78	30	6	3	19	14	6	49	20	9	277	184	107	1st, West Div.	Lost Final
1969-70	76	26	7	5	19	15	4	45	22	9	250	170	99	1st, East Div.	Lost Semi-Final
1968-69	76	20	14	4	14	19	5	34	33	9	280	246	77	6th, East Div.	Out of Playoffs
1967-68	74	20	13	4	12	13	12	32	26	16	212	222	80	4th, East Div.	Lost Semi-Final
1966-67	70	24	5	6	17	12	6	41	17	12	264	170	94	1st,	Lost Semi-Final
1965-66	70	21	8	6	16	17	2	37	25	8	240	187	82	2nd,	Lost Semi-Final
1964-65	70	20	13	2	14	15	6	34	28	8	224	176	76	3rd,	Lost Final
1963-64	70	26	4	5	10	18	7	36	22	12	218	169	84	2nd,	Lost Semi-Final
1962-63	70	17	9	9	15	12	8	32	21	17	194	178	81	2nd,	Lost Semi-Final
1961-62	70	20	10	5	11	16	8	31	26	13	217	186	75	3rd,	Lost Final
1960-61	70	20	6	9	9	18	8	29	24	17	198	180	75	**3rd,**	**Won Stanley Cup**
1959-60	70	18	11	6	10	18	7	28	29	13	191	180	69	3rd,	Lost Semi-Final
1958-59	70	14	12	9	14	17	4	28	29	13	197	208	69	3rd,	Lost Semi-Final
1957-58	70	15	17	3	9	22	4	24	39	7	163	202	55	5th,	Out of Playoffs
1956-57	70	12	15	8	4	24	7	16	39	15	169	225	47	6th,	Out of Playoffs
1955-56	70	9	19	7	10	20	5	19	39	12	155	216	50	6th,	Out of Playoffs
1954-55	70	6	21	8	7	19	9	13	40	17	161	235	43	6th,	Out of Playoffs
1953-54	70	8	21	6	4	30	1	12	51	7	133	242	31	6th,	Out of Playoffs
1952-53	70	14	11	10	13	17	5	27	28	15	169	175	69	4th,	Lost Semi-Final
1951-52	70	9	19	7	8	25	2	17	44	9	158	241	43	6th,	Out of Playoffs
1950-51	70	8	22	5	5	25	5	13	47	10	171	280	36	6th,	Out of Playoffs
1949-50	70	13	18	4	9	20	6	22	38	10	203	244	54	6th,	Out of Playoffs
1948-49	60	13	12	5	8	19	3	21	31	8	173	211	50	5th,	Out of Playoffs
1947-48	60	10	17	3	10	17	3	20	34	6	195	225	46	6th,	Out of Playoffs
1946-47	60	10	17	3	9	20	1	19	37	4	193	274	42	6th,	Out of Playoffs
1945-46	50	15	5	5	8	15	2	23	20	7	200	178	53	3rd,	Lost Semi-Final
1944-45	50	9	14	2	4	16	5	13	30	7	141	194	33	5th,	Out of Playoffs
1943-44	50	15	6	4	7	17	1	22	23	5	178	187	49	4th,	Lost Final
1942-43	50	14	3	8	3	15	7	17	18	15	179	180	49	5th,	Out of Playoffs
1941-42	48	15	8	1	7	15	2	22	23	3	145	155	47	4th,	Lost Semi-Final
1940-41	48	11	10	3	5	15	4	16	25	7	112	139	39	5th,	Lost Semi-Final
1939-40	48	15	7	2	8	12	4	23	19	6	112	120	52	4th,	Lost Quarter-Final
1938-39	48	5	13	6	7	15	2	12	28	8	91	132	32	7th,	Out of Playoffs
1937-38	48	10	10	4	4	15	5	14	25	9	97	139	37	**3rd, Amn. Div.**	**Won Stanley Cup**
1936-37	48	8	13	3	6	14	4	14	27	7	99	131	35	4th, Amn. Div.	Out of Playoffs
1935-36	48	15	7	2	6	12	6	21	19	8	93	92	50	3rd, Amn. Div.	Lost Quarter-Final
1934-35	48	12	9	3	14	8	2	26	17	5	118	88	57	2nd, Amn. Div.	Lost Quarter-Final
1933-34	48	13	4	7	7	13	4	20	17	11	88	83	51	**2nd, Amn. Div.**	**Won Stanley Cup**
1932-33	48	12	7	5	4	13	7	16	20	12	88	101	44	4th, Amn. Div.	Out of Playoffs
1931-32	48	13	5	6	5	14	5	18	19	11	86	101	47	2nd, Amn. Div.	Lost Quarter-Final
1930-31	44	13	8	1	11	9	2	24	17	3	108	78	51	2nd, Amn. Div.	Lost Final
1929-30	44	12	9	1	9	9	4	21	18	5	117	111	47	2nd, Amn. Div.	Lost Quarter-Final
1928-29	44	4	13	6	4	16	2	7	29	8	33	85	22	5th, Amn. Div.	Out of Playoffs
1927-28	44	2	18	2	5	16	1	7	34	3	68	134	17	5th, Amn. Div.	Out of Playoffs
1926-27	44	12	8	2	7	14	1	19	22	3	115	116	41	3rd, Amn. Div.	Lost Quarter-Final

1999-2000 Player Personnel

FORWARDS	HT	WT	S	Place of Birth	Date	1998-99 Club
AMONTE, Tony	6-0	200	L	Hingham, MA	8/2/70	Chicago
CALDER, Kyle	5-11	180	L	Mannville, Alta.	1/5/79	Regina-Kamloops
CLARK, Wendel	5-11	194	L	Kelvington, Sask.	10/25/66	Tampa Bay-Detroit
DAZE, Eric	6-6	234	L	Montreal, Que.	7/2/75	Chicago
DUMONT, Jean-Pierre	6-2	200	L	Montreal, Que.	4/1/78	Chi-Port (AHL)-Chi (IHL)
GILMOUR, Doug	5-11	175	L	Kingston, Ont.	6/25/63	Chicago
HANKINSON, Casey	6-1	187	L	Edina, MN	5/8/76	Portland (AHL)
JANSSENS, Mark	6-3	212	L	Surrey, B.C.	5/19/68	Chicago
JONES, Ty	6-3	218	R	Richland, WA	2/22/79	Spokane-Kamloops-Chicago
LEROUX, Jean-Yves	6-2	211	L	Montreal, Que.	6/24/76	Chicago-Chicago (IHL)
MARHA, Josef	6-0	176	L	Havlickuv, Czech.	6/2/76	Ana-Cin (AHL)-Chi-Port (AHL)
McAMMOND, Dean	5-11	200	L	Grand Cache, Alta.	6/15/73	Edmonton-Chicago
MILLS, Craig	6-0	190	R	Toronto, Ont.	8/27/76	Chi-Chi (IHL)-Port (AHL)-Ind
MURRAY, Chris	6-2	209	R	Port Hardy, B.C.	10/25/74	Ottawa-Chicago
PROBERT, Bob	6-3	225	L	Windsor, Ont.	6/5/65	Chicago
SIMPSON, Reid	6-2	220	L	Flin Flon, Man.	5/21/69	Chicago
TARDIF, Steve	6-1	180	L	St-Agnes, Que.	3/29/77	Port (AHL)-Ind-Fla (ECHL)
VANDENBUSSCHE, Ryan	6-0	200	R	Simcoe, Ont.	2/28/73	Chi-Ind-Port (AHL)
WHITE, Todd	5-10	189	L	Kanata, Ont.	5/21/75	Chicago-Chicago (IHL)
ZHAMNOV, Alexei	6-1	200	L	Moscow, USSR	10/1/70	Chicago
DEFENSEMEN						
ALLISON, Jamie	6-1	195	L	Lindsay, Ont.	5/13/75	Saint John-Chi-Ind
BICANEK, Radim	6-1	195	L	Uherske Hradiste, Czech.	1/18/75	Ottawa-Grand Rapids-Chicago
BROWN, Brad	6-4	218	R	Baie Verte, Nfld.	12/27/75	Montreal-Chicago
ERIKSSON, Anders	6-3	218	L	Bollnas, Sweden	1/9/75	Detroit-Chicago
MANSON, Dave	6-2	219	L	Prince Albert, Sask.	1/27/67	Montreal-Chicago
McCABE, Bryan	6-1	210	L	St. Catharines, Ont.	6/8/75	Vancouver
MIRONOV, Boris	6-3	223	R	Moscow, USSR	3/21/72	Edmonton-Chicago
MUIR, Bryan	6-4	220	L	Winnipeg, Man.	6/8/73	N.J.-Alb-Chi-Port (AHL)
ROHLOFF, Todd	6-3	213	L	Grand Rapids, MN	1/16/74	Portland (AHL)-Indianapolis
ROYER, Remi	6-2	200	R	Donnacona, Que.	2/12/78	Chi-Ind-Port (AHL)
ZMOLEK, Doug	6-2	222	L	Rochester, MN	11/3/70	Chicago

GOALTENDERS	HT	WT	C	Place of Birth	Date	1998-99 Club
LAMOTHE, Marc	6-1	204	L	New Liskeard, Ont.	2/27/74	Indianapolis-Detroit (IHL)
LAROCQUE, Michel	5-11	200	L	Lahr, West Germany	10/3/76	Boston University
PASSMORE, Steve	5-9	165	L	Thunder Bay, Ont.	1/29/73	Edmonton-Hamilton
PELLETIER, Jonathan	5-11	165	L	Riviere-du-loup, Que.	4/15/80	Drummondville
THIBAULT, Jocelyn	5-11	170	L	Montreal, Que.	1/12/75	Montreal-Chicago

Coach

MOLLEKEN, LORNE
Coach, Chicago Blackhawks. Born in Regina, Sask., June 11, 1956.

The Chicago Blackhawks named Lorne Molleken as head coach on April 8, 1999. He had been serving as interim coach after replacing Dirk Graham on February 22. Molleken began the 1998-99 season as an assistant coach under Graham. He came to the Blackhawks from the Edmonton Oilers organization, where he had spent three seasons as head coach of the Oilers' minor-league affiliate teams in Hamilton and Cape Breton. Previously, Molleken guided Saskatoon to the Western Hockey League Finals in 1992 and 1994. He was named WHL Coach of the Year during the 1993-94 season and was a finalist for the award in 1991-92. Molleken began his coaching career in 1985 with the Swift Current Indians of the Saskatchewan Junior Hockey League.

Molleken played junior hockey in the WHL, and turned pro in 1976 with the Philadelphia Firebirds of the North American Hockey League. He went on to play seven years in the minors from 1977-78 to 1984-85, and was a goaltender on the Toledo Goaldiggers team that won 1982 and 1983 Turner Cup (IHL) championships. During his eight years of professional hockey, Molleken signed NHL contracts with Los Angeles, the New York Islanders and Minnesota, but did not see action at the NHL level.

He and his wife, Patsy, have two daughters, Tawna and Trisha, and one son, Jason.

Coaching Record

		Regular Season					Playoffs			
Season	Team	Games	W	L	T	%	Games	W	L	%
1989-90	Moose Jaw (WHL)	72	28	41	3	.410	....	....	....	....
1990-91	Moose Jaw (WHL)	72	31	39	2	.444	8	4	4	.500
1991-92	Saskatoon (WHL)	72	38	29	5	.563	22	14	8	.636
1992-93	Saskatoon (WHL)	72	42	27	3	.604	9	4	5	.444
1993-94	Saskatoon (WHL)	72	49	22	1	.688	16	11	5	.688
1994-95	Saskatoon (WHL)	72	41	23	8	.625	10	4	6	.400
1995-96	Cape Breton (AHL)	84	33	44	7	.435	....	....	....	....
1996-97	Hamilton (AHL)	80	28	39	13	.431	22	12	10	.545
1997-98	Hamilton (AHL)	80	36	22	22	.588	9	3	6	.333
1998-99	**Chicago (NHL)**	**23**	**13**	**6**	**4**	**.652**	**....**	**....**	**....**	**....**
	NHL Totals	**23**	**13**	**6**	**4**	**.652**	**....**	**....**	**....**	**....**

1998-99 Scoring

* – rookie

Regular Season

Pos	#	Player	Team	GP	G	A	Pts	+/–	PIM	PP	SH	GW	GT	S	%
R	10	Tony Amonte	CHI	82	44	31	75	0	60	14	3	8	0	256	17.2
C	36	Alexei Zhamnov	CHI	76	20	41	61	–10	50	8	1	2	1	200	10.0
C	93	Doug Gilmour	CHI	72	16	40	56	–16	56	7	1	4	0	110	14.5
D	3	Boris Mironov	EDM	63	11	29	40	6	104	5	0	4	1	138	8.0
			CHI	12	0	9	9	7	27	0	0	0	0	35	0.0
			TOTAL	75	11	38	49	13	131	5	0	4	1	173	6.4
L	55	Eric Daze	CHI	72	22	20	42	–13	22	8	0	2	3	189	11.6
L	34	Dean McAmmond	EDM	65	9	16	25	5	36	1	0	0	0	122	7.4
			CHI	12	1	4	5	3	2	0	0	1	0	16	6.3
			TOTAL	77	10	20	30	8	38	1	0	1	0	138	7.2
R	16	Ed Olczyk	CHI	61	10	15	25	–3	29	2	1	2	0	88	11.4
D	22	Dave Manson	MTL	11	0	2	2	–3	48	0	0	0	0	11	0.0
			CHI	64	6	15	21	4	107	2	0	0	0	134	4.5
			TOTAL	75	6	17	23	1	155	2	0	0	0	145	4.1
L	24	Bob Probert	CHI	78	7	14	21	–11	206	0	0	3	0	87	8.0
D	8	Anders Eriksson	DET	61	2	10	12	5	34	0	0	1	0	67	3.0
			CHI	11	0	8	8	6	0	0	0	0	0	12	0.0
			TOTAL	72	2	18	20	11	34	0	0	1	0	79	2.5
R	17	* Jean-Pierre Dumont	CHI	25	9	6	15	7	10	0	0	2	0	42	21.4
D	4	Doug Zmolek	CHI	62	0	14	14	1	102	0	0	0	0	33	0.0
C	26	* Todd White	CHI	35	5	8	13	–1	20	2	0	0	0	43	11.6
L	33	Reid Simpson	CHI	53	5	4	9	2	145	1	0	0	0	23	21.7
L	25	* Daniel Cleary	CHI	35	4	5	9	–1	24	0	0	0	0	49	8.2
L	23	Jean-Yves Leroux	CHI	40	3	5	8	–7	21	0	0	0	0	47	6.4
C	44	Josef Marha	ANA	10	0	1	1	–4	0	0	0	0	0	13	0.0
			CHI	22	2	5	7	5	4	1	0	1	0	32	6.3
			TOTAL	32	2	6	8	1	4	1	0	1	0	45	4.4
D	2	* Brad Brown	MTL	5	0	0	0	0	21	0	0	0	0	0	0.0
			CHI	61	1	7	8	–4	184	0	0	0	1	26	3.8
			TOTAL	66	1	7	8	–4	205	0	0	0	1	26	3.8
R	15	Chris Murray	OTT	38	1	6	7	–2	65	0	0	0	0	33	3.0
			CHI	4	0	0	0	0	14	0	0	0	0	4	0.0
			TOTAL	42	1	6	7	–2	79	0	0	0	0	37	2.7
D	37	* Bryan Muir	N.J.	1	0	0	0	0	0	0	0	0	0	4	0.0
			CHI	53	1	4	5	1	50	0	0	0	0	78	1.3
			TOTAL	54	1	4	5	1	50	0	0	0	0	82	1.2
D	38	Jamie Allison	CHI	39	2	2	4	0	62	0	0	0	0	24	8.3
C	20	Mark Janssens	CHI	60	1	0	1	–11	65	0	0	0	0	27	3.7
G	30	Mark Fitzpatrick	CHI	27	0	1	1	0	8	0	0	0	0	0	0.0
G	41	Jocelyn Thibault	MTL	10	0	0	0	0	0	0	0	0	0	0	0.0
			CHI	52	0	1	1	0	2	0	0	0	0	0	0.0
			TOTAL	62	0	1	1	0	2	0	0	0	0	0	0.0
R	19	Ryan Vandenbussche	CHI	6	0	0	0	0	17	0	0	0	0	3	0.0
C	14	* Sylvain Cloutier	CHI	7	0	0	0	–1	0	0	0	0	0	3	0.0
R	39	* Craig Mills	CHI	7	0	0	0	–2	2	0	0	0	0	1	0.0
R	27	* Ty Jones	CHI	8	0	0	0	–1	12	0	0	0	0	3	0.0
R	44	* Dennis Bonvie	CHI	11	0	0	0	–4	44	0	0	0	0	1	0.0
D	32	Radim Bicanek	OTT	7	0	0	0	–1	4	0	0	0	0	6	0.0
			CHI	7	0	0	0	–3	6	0	0	0	0	7	0.0
			TOTAL	14	0	0	0	–4	10	0	0	0	0	13	0.0
D	6	* Remi Royer	CHI	18	0	0	0	–10	67	0	0	0	0	24	0.0
D	5	Trent Yawney	CHI	20	0	0	0	–6	32	0	0	0	0	11	0.0

Goaltending

No.	Goaltender	GPI	Mins	Avg	W	L	T	EN	SO	GA	SA	S%
41	Jocelyn Thibault	52	3014	2.71	21	26	5	6	4	136	1435	.905
30	Mark Fitzpatrick	27	1403	2.74	6	8	6	2	0	64	682	.906
31	Jeff Hackett	10	524	3.78	2	6	1	3	0	33	256	.871
35	Andrei Trefilov	1	25	9.60	0	1	0	0	0	4	20	.800
	Totals	**82**	**4989**	**2.98**	**29**	**41**	**12**	**11**	**4**	**248**	**2404**	**.897**

Captains' History

Dick Irvin, 1926-27 to 1928-29; Duke Dukowski, 1929-30; Ty Arbour, 1930-31; Cy Wentworth, 1931-32; Helge Bostrom, 1932-33; Chuck Gardiner, 1933-34; no captain, 1934-35; Johnny Gottselig, 1935-36 to 1939-40; Earl Seibert, 1940-41, 1941-42; Doug Bentley, 1942-43, 1943-44; Clint Smith 1944-45; John Mariucci, 1945-46; Red Hamill, 1946-47; John Mariucci, 1947-48; Gaye Stewart, 1948-49; Doug Bentley, 1949-50; Jack Stewart, 1950-51, 1951-52; Bill Gadsby, 1952-53, 1953-54; Gus Mortson, 1954-55 to 1956-57; no captain, 1957-58; Ed Litzenberger, 1958-59 to 1960-61; Pierre Pilote, 1961-62 to 1967-68, no captain, 1968-69; Pat Stapleton, 1969-70; no captain, 1970-71 to 1974-75; Stan Mikita and Pit Martin, 1975-76; Stan Mikita, Pit Martin and Keith Magnuson, 1976-77; Keith Magnuson, 1977-78, 1978-79; Keith Magnuson and Terry Ruskowski, 1979-80; Terry Ruskowski, 1980-81, 1981-82; Darryl Sutter, 1982-83 to 1984-85; Darryl Sutter and Bob Murray, 1985-86; Darryl Sutter, 1986-87; no captain, 1987-88; Denis Savard and Dirk Graham, 1988-89; Dirk Graham, 1989-90 to 1994-95; Chris Chelios, 1995-96 to 1998-99.
Doug Gilmour, 1999-2000.

Club Records

Team

(Figures in brackets for season records are games played; records for fewest points, wins, ties, losses, goals, goals against are for 70 or more games)

Most Points 107 1970-71 (78), 1971-72 (78)
Most Wins 49 1970-71 (78), 1990-91 (80)
Most Ties 23 1973-74 (78)
Most Losses 51 1953-54 (70)
Most Goals 351 1985-86 (80)
Most Goals Against 363 1981-82 (80)
Fewest Points 31 1953-54 (70)
Fewest Wins 12 1953-54 (70)
Fewest Ties 6 1989-90 (80)
Fewest Losses 14 1973-74 (78)
Fewest Goals *133 1953-54 (70)
Fewest Goals Against 164 1973-74 (78)

Longest Winning Streak
Overall .... 8 Dec. 9-26/71, Jan. 4-21/81
Home .... 13 Nov. 11-Dec. 20/70
Away .... 7 Dec. 9-29/64

Longest Undefeated Streak
Overall .... 15 Jan. 14-Feb. 16/67 (12 wins, 3 ties)
Home .... 18 Oct. 11-Dec. 20/70 (16 wins, 2 ties)
Away .... 12 Nov. 2-Dec. 16/67 (6 wins, 6 ties)

Longest Losing Streak
Overall .... 13 Feb. 25-Oct. 11/51
Home .... 11 Feb. 8-Nov. 22/28
Away .... 17 Jan. 2-Oct. 7/54

Longest Winless Streak
Overall .... 21 Dec. 17/50-Jan. 28/51 (18 losses, 3 ties)
Home .... 15 Dec. 16/28-Feb. 28/29 (11 losses, 4 ties)
Away .... 23 Dec. 19/50-Oct. 11/51 (21 losses, 2 ties)

Most Shutouts, Season 15 1969-70 (76)
Most PIM, Season 2,663 1991-92 (80)
Most Goals, Game .... 12 Jan. 30/69 (Chi. 12 at Phi. 0)

Individual

Most Seasons .... 22 Stan Mikita
Most Games .... 1,394 Stan Mikita
Most Goals, Career .... 604 Bobby Hull
Most Assists, Career .... 926 Stan Mikita
Most Points, Career ..... 1,467 Stan Mikita (541g, 926a)
Most PIM, Career ...... 1,495 Chris Chelios
Most Shutouts, Career .... 74 Tony Esposito

Longest Consecutive
Games Streak .... 884 Steve Larmer (Oct. 6/82-Apr. 15/93)
Most Goals, Season .... 58 Bobby Hull (1968-69)
Most Assists, Season .... 87 Denis Savard (1981-82, 1987-88)
Most Points, Season .... 131 Denis Savard (1987-88; 44g, 87a)
Most PIM, Season .... 408 Mike Peluso (1991-92)

Most Points, Defenseman,
Season .... 85 Doug Wilson (1981-82; 39g, 46a)
Most Points, Center,
Season .... 131 Denis Savard (1987-88; 44g, 87a)
Most Points, Right Wing,
Season .... 101 Steve Larmer (1990-91; 44g, 57a)
Most Points, Left Wing,
Season .... 107 Bobby Hull (1968-69; 58g, 49a)
Most Points, Rookie,
Season .... 90 Steve Larmer (1982-83; 43g, 47a)
Most Shutouts, Season .... 15 Tony Esposito (1969-70)
Most Goals, Game .... 5 Grant Mulvey (Feb. 3/82)
Most Assists, Game .... 6 Pat Stapleton (Mar. 30/69)
Most Points, Game .... 7 Max Bentley (Jan. 28/43; 4g, 3a), Grant Mulvey (Feb. 3/82; 5g, 2a)

* NHL Record.

Retired Numbers

1	Glenn Hall	1957-1967
9	Bobby Hull	1957-1972
18	Denis Savard	1980-1990, 1995-1997
21	Stan Mikita	1958-1980
35	Tony Esposito	1969-1984

All-time Record vs. Other Clubs

Regular Season

	At Home						On Road						Total					
	GP	W	L	T	GF	GA	PTS	GP	W	L	T	GF	GA	PTS	GP	W	L	T	GF	GA	PTS
Anaheim	13	7	5	1	34	25	15	12	6	5	1	30	28	13	25	13	10	2	64	53	28
Boston	282	144	94	44	908	754	332	280	87	159	34	791	1012	208	562	231	253	78	1699	1766	540
Buffalo	47	26	15	6	154	128	58	49	13	30	6	128	187	32	96	39	45	12	282	315	90
Calgary	51	22	16	13	171	148	57	53	19	24	10	163	171	48	104	41	40	23	334	319	105
Carolina	26	16	7	3	111	72	35	27	12	12	3	88	88	27	53	28	19	6	199	160	62
Colorado	31	17	12	2	111	99	36	30	11	14	5	111	122	27	61	28	26	7	222	221	63
Dallas	99	62	25	12	396	257	136	102	42	45	15	318	342	99	201	104	70	27	714	599	235
Detroit	324	148	125	51	973	902	347	322	93	199	30	789	1106	216	646	241	324	81	1762	2008	563
Edmonton	34	18	11	5	137	122	41	35	16	15	4	129	132	36	69	34	26	9	266	254	77
Florida	5	1	3	1	16	22	3	5	3	2	0	20	14	6	10	4	5	1	36	36	9
Los Angeles	65	31	26	8	239	198	70	64	29	29	6	220	220	64	129	60	55	14	459	418	134
Montreal	271	93	123	55	728	754	241	271	52	171	48	638	1050	152	542	145	294	103	1366	1804	393
Nashville	3	3	0	0	14	8	6	3	1	1	1	8	9	3	6	4	1	1	22	17	9
New Jersey	43	24	10	9	173	118	57	42	16	15	11	132	125	43	85	40	25	20	305	243	100
NY Islanders	45	24	16	5	151	150	53	43	12	17	14	128	151	38	88	36	33	19	279	301	91
NY Rangers	282	127	113	42	860	782	296	283	112	116	55	801	834	279	565	239	229	97	1661	1616	575
Ottawa	6	3	1	2	15	13	8	6	2	0	4	20	17	8	12	7	3	2	35	30	16
Philadelphia	57	25	13	19	202	162	69	58	16	31	11	154	188	43	115	41	44	30	356	350	112
Phoenix	39	24	10	5	164	111	53	40	13	23	4	127	146	30	79	37	33	9	291	257	83
Pittsburgh	55	38	8	9	231	147	85	55	23	26	6	182	196	52	110	61	34	15	413	343	137
St. Louis	105	59	32	14	402	319	132	101	35	49	17	314	336	87	206	94	81	31	716	655	219
San Jose	15	8	5	2	51	42	18	16	8	8	0	46	39	16	31	16	13	2	97	81	34
Tampa Bay	9	4	3	2	25	24	10	8	2	4	2	19	21	6	17	6	7	4	44	45	16
Toronto	312	154	116	42	955	819	350	311	95	163	53	808	1061	243	623	249	279	95	1763	1880	593
Vancouver	61	41	14	6	232	138	88	62	19	28	15	180	186	53	123	60	42	21	412	324	141
Washington	36	21	10	5	142	108	47	37	13	20	4	117	135	30	73	34	30	9	259	243	77
Defunct Clubs	139	79	40	20	408	268	178	140	52	67	21	316	346	125	279	131	107	41	724	614	303
Totals	2455	1219	853	383	8003	6690	2821	2455	804	1275	376	6777	8262	1984	4910	2023	2128	759	14780	14952	4805

Playoffs

	Series	W	L	GP	W	L	T	GF	GA	Last Mtg.	Round	Result
Boston	6	1	5	22	5	16	1	63	97	1978	QF	L 0-4
Buffalo	2	0	2	9	1	8	0	17	36	1980	QF	L 0-4
Calgary	3	1	2	12	5	7	0	33	37	1996	CQF	W 4-0
Colorado	2	0	2	12	4	8	0	28	49	1997	CQF	L 2-4
Dallas	6	4	2	33	19	14	0	119	119	1991	DSF	L 2-4
Detroit	14	8	6	69	38	31	0	210	190	1995	CF	L 1-4
Edmonton	4	1	3	20	8	12	0	77	102	1992	CF	W 4-0
Los Angeles	1	1	0	5	4	1	0	10	7	1974	QF	W 4-1
Montreal	17	5	12	81	29	50	2	185	261	1976	QF	L 0-4
NY Islanders	2	0	2	6	0	6	0	6	21	1979	QF	L 0-4
NY Rangers	5	4	1	24	14	10	0	66	54	1973	SF	W 4-1
Philadelphia	1	1	0	4	4	0	0	20	8	1971	QF	W 4-0
Pittsburgh	2	1	1	8	4	4	0	24	23	1992	F	L 0-4
St. Louis	9	7	2	45	27	18	0	166	129	1993	DSF	L 0-4
Toronto	9	3	6	38	15	22	1	89	111	1995	CQF	W 4-3
Vancouver	2	1	1	9	5	4	0	24	24	1995	CSF	W 4-0
Defunct Clubs	4	2	2	9	6	3	0					
Totals	89	40	49	406	187	214	5	1153	1283			

Calgary totals include Atlanta Flames, 1972-73 to 1979-80.
Colorado totals include Quebec, 1979-80 to 1994-95.
New Jersey totals include Kansas City, 1974-75 to 1975-76, and Colorado Rockies, 1976-77 to 1981-82.
Phoenix totals include Winnipeg, 1979-80 to 1995-96.
Carolina totals include Hartford, 1979-80 to 1996-97.
Dallas totals include Minnesota, 1967-68 to 1992-93.

Playoff Results 1999-95

Year	Round	Opponent	Result	GF	GA
1997	CQF	Colorado	L 2-4	14	28
1996	CSF	Colorado	L 2-4	14	21
	CQF	Calgary	W 4-0	16	7
1995	CF	Detroit	L 1-4	12	13
	CSF	Vancouver	W 4-0	11	6
	CQF	Toronto	W 4-3	22	20

Abbreviations: Round: F – Final;
CF – conference final; **CSF** – conference semi-final;
CQF – conference quarter-final; **DSF** – division semi-final; **SF** – semi-final; **QF** – quarter-final.

1998-99 Results

Oct.	10		New Jersey	2-1		12	at	Colorado	1-4
	13	at	Dallas	1-3		15	at	NY Rangers	3-1
	15		Anaheim	3-5		17		Phoenix	1-1
	17		Dallas	4-3		21		Montreal	3-0
	19	at	Montreal	2-1		27	at	Edmonton	4-3
	22		San Jose	2-2		28	at	Calgary	6-6
	24		Nashville	5-4		30	at	Vancouver	2-3
	28	at	Carolina	0-2	Feb.	1	at	San Jose	1-5
	30		Florida	3-7		3	at	Anaheim	0-3
Nov.	1		Calgary	1-4		4	at	Los Angeles	2-3
	4	at	Florida	1-2		6	at	Phoenix	0-3
	6	at	Tampa Bay	2-2		10		San Jose	2-5
	8		Edmonton	2-3		12		Detroit	1-2
	10	at	St. Louis	2-5		13	at	Toronto	6-2
	12		Toronto	3-10		15	at	Ottawa	2-6
	14	at	Buffalo	1-6		17		Vancouver	4-0
	15		Ottawa	2-2		19	at	Dallas	1-5
	17	at	Nashville	2-1		21		Boston	3-6
	21	at	Los Angeles	0-5		24	at	St. Louis	3-1
	22	at	Anaheim	1-4		26		Los Angeles	1-2
	24	at	Phoenix	2-3		28		St. Louis	1-3
	28	at	Calgary	4-5	Mar.	6	at	San Jose	4-0
	29	at	Edmonton	3-2		7	at	Vancouver	2-2
Dec.	3		Anaheim	4-1		10		Nashville	5-2
	6		Tampa Bay	7-5		12	at	Nashville	3-5
	8	at	Detroit	2-3		14		St. Louis	2-5
	9		Edmonton	3-1		17		Calgary	3-1
	11		Toronto	2-3		20	at	Colorado	5-5
	13		Dallas	2-2		21		Colorado	4-3
	17		Washington	1-3		23	at	Pittsburgh	2-5
	19	at	Philadelphia	1-3		25	at	Boston	3-3
	20		Los Angeles	1-4		27	at	New Jersey	4-4
	23		Phoenix	4-3		28	at	St. Louis	3-1
	26		Philadelphia	2-3		31		Buffalo	2-1
	31		NY Islanders	1-0	Apr.	2	at	Detroit	3-5
Jan.	2	at	Detroit	2-5		3		Carolina	2-1
	3		Detroit	1-1		5		Vancouver	2-0
	5	at	NY Islanders	1-1		8		NY Rangers	6-2
	7	at	St. Louis	2-4		12	at	Washington	4-2
	9	at	Nashville	3-3		15		Nashville	4-2
	10		Colorado	2-3		17		Detroit	3-2

Entry Draft
Selections 1999-85

1999
Pick
23 Steve McCarthy
46 Dimitri Levinski
63 Stepan Mokhov
134 Michael Jacobsen
165 Michael Leighton
194 Mattias Wennerberg
195 Yorick Treille
223 Andrew Carver

1998
Pick
8 Mark Bell
94 Matthias Trattnig
156 Kent Huskins
158 Jari Viuhkola
166 Jonathan Pelletier
183 Tyler Arnason
210 Sean Griffin
238 Alexandre Couture
240 Andrei Yershov

1997
Pick
13 Daniel Cleary
16 Ty Jones
39 Jeremy Reich
67 Mike Souza
110 Benjamin Simon
120 Peter Gardiner
130 Kyle Calder
147 Heath Gordon
174 Jerad Smith
204 Sergei Shikhanov
230 Chris Feil

1996
Pick
31 Remi Royer
42 Jeff Paul
46 Geoff Peters
130 Andy Johnson
184 Mike Vellinga
210 Chris Twerdun
236 Alexei Kozyrev

1995
Pick
19 Dimitri Nabokov
45 Christian Laflamme
71 Kevin McKay
82 Chris Van Dyk
97 Pavel Kriz
146 Marc Magliarditi
149 Marty Wilford
175 Steve Tardif
201 Casey Hankinson
227 Mike Pittman

1994
Pick
14 Ethan Moreau
40 Jean-Yves Leroux
85 Steve McLaren
118 Marc Dupuis
144 Jim Enson
170 Tyler Prosofsky
196 Mike Josephson
222 Lubomir Jandera
248 Lars Weibel
263 Rob Mara

1993
Pick
24 Eric Lecompte
50 Eric Manlow
54 Bogdan Savenko
76 Ryan Huska
90 Eric Daze
102 Patrik Pysz
128 Jonni Vauhkonen
180 Tom White
206 Sergei Petrov
232 Mike Rusk
258 Mike McGhan
284 Tom Noble

1992
Pick
12 Sergei Krivokrasov
36 Jeff Shantz
41 Sergei Klimovich
89 Andy MacIntyre
113 Tim Hogan
137 Gerry Skrypec
161 Mike Prokopec
185 Layne Roland
209 David Hymovitz
233 Richard Raymond

1991
Pick
22 Dean McAmmond
39 Michael Pomichter
44 Jamie Matthews
66 Bobby House
71 Igor Kravchuk
88 Zac Boyer
110 Maco Balkovec
112 Kevin St. Jacques
132 Jacques Auger
154 Scott Kirton
176 Roch Belley
198 Scott MacDonald
220 A. Andriyevsky
242 Mike Larkin
264 Scott Dean

1990
Pick
16 Karl Dykhuis
37 Ivan Droppa
79 Chris Tucker
121 Brett Stickney
124 Derek Edgerly
163 Hugo Belanger
184 Owen Lessard
205 Erik Peterson
226 Steve Dubinsky
247 Dino Grossi

1989
Pick
6 Adam Bennett
27 Michael Speer
48 Bob Kellogg
111 Tommi Pullola
132 Tracy Egeland
153 Milan Tichy
174 Jason Greyerbiehl
195 Matt Saunders
216 Mike Kozak
237 Michael Doneghey

1988
Pick
8 Jeremy Roenick
50 Trevor Dam
71 Stefan Elvenas
92 Joe Cleary
113 Justin Lafayette
134 Craig Woodcroft
155 Jon Pojar
176 Mathew Hentges
197 Daniel Maurice
218 Dirk Tenzer
239 Andreas Lupzig

1987
Pick
8 Jimmy Waite
29 Ryan McGill
50 Cam Russell
60 Mike Dagenais
92 Ulf Sandstrom
113 Mike McCormick
134 Stephen Tepper
155 John Reilly
176 Lance Werness
197 Dale Marquette
218 Bill Lacouture
239 Mike Lappin

1986
Pick
14 Everett Sanipass
35 Mark Kurzawski
77 Frantisek Kucera
98 Lonnie Loach
119 Mario Doyon
140 Mike Hudson
161 Marty Nanne
182 Geoff Benic
203 Glen Lowes
224 Chris Thayer
245 Sean Williams

1985
Pick
11 Dave Manson
53 Andy Helmuth
74 Dan Vincellette
87 Rick Herbert
95 Brad Belland
116 Jonas Heed
137 Victor Posa
158 John Reid
179 Richard LaPlante
200 Brad Hamilton
221 Ian Pound
242 Rick Braccia

General Manager

MURRAY, BOB
General Manager, Chicago Blackhawks.
Born in Kingston, Ont., November 26, 1954.

Bob Murray was named as the sixth general manager in the history of the Chicago Blackhawks on July 3, 1997. Murray has been with the Blackhawk organization for more than 24 years, dating back to 1974 when he was drafted by the Blackhawks.

Murray spent his entire NHL playing career in Chicago, playing 1,008 games in a Blackhawk uniform. He became only the fourth player in team history to reach the 1,000-game plateau and during the 1990 Stanley Cup Playoffs, he became the first defenseman in team history to play over 100 playoff games.

He ranks first among all-time Blackhawk defensemen in games played and ranks second among all-time Blackhawk defensemen in career points with 514. During his 15-year Blackhawk career, Murray scored 132 goals (26th overall) and 382 assists (8th overall) totalling 514 points (12th overall). He played in two NHL All-Star Games (1981 and 1983) and recorded an assist.

Murray's playing career was marked by tremendous skill, endurance and determination. His great effort and preparation were well noted by the club, along with his organizational and management skills. All these traits convinced the Blackhawks to sign Murray as a pro scout in 1990. Within a year he was appointed director of player personnel, mastering the computerized system which keeps tabs on all players observed by the scouting staff.

Murray has directed the Blackhawks in the NHL Entry Draft since 1992, and his selections over the last six drafts have provided a solid foundation for the future of the organization. Murray's keen eye for talent has brought young NHL players like Eric Daze, Ethan Moreau and Jeff Shantz into the Blackhawks organization.

Prior to the 1995-96 season Murray was named as the club's assistant general manager.

Club Directory

United Center

Chicago Blackhawk Hockey Team, Inc.
1901 W. Madison Street
Chicago, IL 60612
Phone **312/455-7000**
FAX 312/455-7041
Internet Address
www.chicagoblackhawks.com
Capacity: 20,500

President . . . . William W. Wirtz
Senior Vice President . . . . Robert J. Pulford
Vice President . . . . Jack Davison
Vice President . . . . Peter R. Wirtz
General Manager . . . . Bob Murray
Director of Player Personnel . . . . Dale Tallon
Head Coach . . . . Lorne Molleken
Assistant Coach . . . . Denis Savard
Assistant Coach . . . . Trent Yawney
Goaltending Consultant . . . . Vladislav Tretiak
Pro Scout . . . . Dirk Graham
Chief Amateur Scout . . . . Michel Dumas
Amateur Scout . . . . Bruce Franklin
Amateur Scout . . . . Tim Higgins
Amateur Scout . . . . Steve Richmond
Amateur Scout . . . . Ron Anderson
European Scout . . . . Jan Blomgren
Executive Assistant . . . . Cindy Brueck
Assistant to the General Manager . . . . . . Steve Williams
Manager of Team Services. . . . . David Stensby

Medical Staff
Club Doctors . . . . Mark Bowen, Gordon Nuber
Team Dentist . . . . Dr. Daniel Mackey, Dr. Dean Sana
Oral Surgeon . . . . Dr. Eric Pulver
Eye Doctor . . . . Dr. Robert Stein
Head Trainer . . . . Michael Gapski
Equipment Manager . . . . Troy Parchman
Asst. Equipment Mgr. . . . . Lou Varga
Massage Therapist . . . . Pawel Prylinski

Public Relations/Marketing
Executive Director of Communications . . . . Jim DeMaria
Director of Community Relations/PR Assistant . . . . Barbara Davidson
Manager of Public Relations . . . . Tony Ommen
Executive Director of Marketing/Merchandising . . . Jim Sofranko
Dir. of Corporate Partnerships . . . . Elliot Bell
Manager, Client Services . . . . Kelly Bodnarchuk
Dir. of Projects & Development . . . . Carol Czaplicki
Manager, Special Events . . . . Matt Colleran
Manager, Game Operations . . . . Kellett McConville
Marketing Associate . . . . Alison Tragesser
Administrative Assistant. Angela Armbruster

Finance
Treasurer . . . . Robert Rinkus
Controller . . . . Tracy Hernandez
Accounting Manager. . . . . Deb Kulir
Accounting Clerk . . . . Rita Loretto

Ticketing
Director of Ticket Operations. . . . . James K. Bare
Ticket Sales Manager . . . . Doug Ryan
Senior Account Executive . . . . Danny Lucier
Account Executive . . . . Jamie Arbuckle
Sales Associate . . . . Brad Bober
Ticket Operations Manager . . . . Kathie Raimondi
Administrative Assistant . . . . Martha Webster

Miscellaneous Information
Team Photographers . . . . Ray Grabowski, Rob Grabowski
Organist . . . . Frank Pellico
Public Address Announcer. . . . . Harvey Wittenberg
Executive Offices/Home Ice . . . . United Center
Location of Press Box . . . . South Side of United Center
Ends of Rink . . . . Plexi-glass extends above boards all around rink
Club Colors . . . . Red, White & Black
Radio Station . . . . WMAQ (AM 670)
Television Station . . . . Fox Sports Chicago
Broadcasters . . . . Pat Foley, Bill Gardner, Jim Blaney

Coaching History

Pete Muldoon, 1926-27; Barney Stanley and Hugh Lehman, 1927-28; Herb Gardiner, 1928-29; Tom Shaughnessy and Bill Tobin, 1929-30; Dick Irvin, 1930-31; Bill Tobin, 1931-32; Emil Iverson, Godfrey Matheson and Tommy Gorman, 1932-33; Tommy Gorman, 1933-34; Clem Loughlin, 1934-35 to 1936-37; Bill Stewart, 1937-38; Bill Stewart and Paul Thompson, 1938-39; Paul Thompson, 1939-40 to 1943-44; Paul Thompson and Johnny Gottselig, 1944-45; Johnny Gottselig, 1945-46, 1946-47; Johnny Gottselig and Charlie Conacher, 1947-48; Charlie Conacher, 1948-49, 1949-50; Ebbie Goodfellow, 1950-51, 1951-52; Sid Abel, 1952-53, 1953-54; Frank Eddolls, 1954-55; Dick Irvin, 1955-56; Tommy Ivan, 1956-57; Tommy Ivan and Rudy Pilous, 1957-58; Rudy Pilous, 1958-59 to 1962-63; Billy Reay, 1963-64 to 1975-76; Billy Reay and Bill White, 1976-77; Bob Pulford, 1977-78, 1978-79; Eddie Johnston, 1979-80; Keith Magnuson, 1980-81; Keith Magnuson and Bob Pulford, 1981-82; Orval Tessier, 1982-83, 1983-84; Orval Tessier and Bob Pulford, 1984-85; Bob Pulford, 1985-86, 1986-87; Bob Murdoch, 1987-88; Mike Keenan, 1988-89 to 1991-92; Darryl Sutter, 1992-93 to 1994-95; Craig Hartsburg, 1995-96 to 1997-98; Dirk Graham and Lorne Molleken, 1998-99; Lorne Molleken, 1999-2000.

General Managers' History

Major Frederic McLaughlin, 1926-27 to 1941-42; Bill Tobin, 1942-43 to 1953-54; Tommy Ivan, 1954-55 to 1976-77; Bob Pulford, 1977-78 to 1989-90; Mike Keenan, 1990-91, 1991-92; Mike Keenan and Bob Pulford, 1992-93; Bob Pulford, 1993-94 to 1996-97; Bob Murray, 1997-98 to date.

Colorado Avalanche
1998-99 Results: 44W-28L-10T 98PTS. First, Northwest Division

1999-2000 Schedule

Oct.	Tue.	5	at Nashville
	Wed.	6	at Toronto
	Fri.	8	at Pittsburgh
	Sun.	10	at NY Islanders*
	Mon.	11	at Boston*
	Wed.	13	Boston
	Sat.	16	Ottawa
	Wed.	20	at Montreal
	Thu.	21	at Ottawa
	Sat.	23	at Atlanta
	Wed.	27	at Detroit
	Thu.	28	at Philadelphia
	Sat.	30	Phoenix*
Nov.	Wed.	3	St. Louis
	Fri.	5	NY Rangers
	Thu.	11	at Los Angeles
	Sat.	13	at Calgary
	Mon.	15	at Vancouver
	Wed.	17	Florida
	Fri.	19	NY Islanders
	Mon.	22	at Dallas
	Tue.	23	Los Angeles
	Fri.	26	at Phoenix
	Sat.	27	Calgary
	Tue.	30	at Vancouver
Dec.	Wed.	1	at Edmonton
	Sat.	4	Carolina
	Mon.	6	Vancouver
	Wed.	8	at San Jose
	Fri.	10	at Anaheim
	Sun.	12	at Vancouver
	Wed.	15	Anaheim
	Fri.	17	at Detroit
	Sat.	18	at Nashville
	Mon.	20	at Carolina
	Thu.	23	at Buffalo
	Mon.	27	St. Louis
	Wed.	29	Los Angeles
Jan.	Mon.	3	Edmonton
	Wed.	5	Calgary
	Fri.	7	Montreal

	Sun.	9	at Chicago
	Tue.	11	Nashville
	Thu.	13	Pittsburgh
	Sat.	15	Chicago
	Mon.	17	Phoenix
	Wed.	19	San Jose
	Fri.	21	at Anaheim
	Sun.	23	at Los Angeles*
	Tue.	25	at San Jose
	Thu.	27	at Chicago
	Sat.	29	at St. Louis
Feb.	Tue.	1	Vancouver
	Thu.	3	San Jose
	Tue.	8	Buffalo
	Thu.	10	Calgary
	Sun.	13	Detroit
	Tue.	15	at Washington
	Thu.	17	at New Jersey
	Fri.	10	at NY Rangers
	Sun.	20	Dallas*
	Tue.	22	Atlanta
	Fri.	25	at St. Louis
	Sun.	27	at Dallas
	Tue.	29	Edmonton
Mar.	Thu.	2	New Jersey
	Sat.	4	Tampa Bay
	Tue.	7	at Calgary
	Fri.	10	at Edmonton
	Sun.	12	Philadelphia
	Tue.	14	Anaheim
	Thu.	16	Nashville
	Sat.	18	Detroit*
	Mon.	20	Vancouver
	Thu.	23	at Phoenix
	Sun.	26	at Dallas*
	Mon.	27	Chicago
	Wed.	29	Edmonton
Apr.	Sun.	2	Dallas*
	Wed.	5	at Edmonton
	Fri.	7	at Calgary
	Sun.	9	Detroit*

* Denotes afternoon game.

Franchise date: June 22, 1979
Transferred from Quebec to Denver, June 21, 1995

WESTERN NHL CONFERENCE

NORTHWEST DIVISION

21st NHL Season

Milan Hejduk finished third in voting for the Calder Trophy last season, behind runner-up Marian Hossa and teammate Chris Drury. Hejduk's 34 assists and 48 points led all rookie scorers in 1998-99. He had two overtime goals among his six goals in 16 playoff games.

Year-by-Year Record

		Home			Road			Overall							
Season	GP	W	L	T	W	L	T	W	L	T	GF	GA	Pts.	Finished	Playoff Result
1998-99	82	21	14	6	23	14	4	44	28	10	239	205	98	1st, Northwest Div.	Lost Conf. Championship
1997-98	82	21	10	10	18	16	7	39	26	17	231	205	95	1st, Pacific Div.	Lost Conf. Quarter-Final
1996-97	82	26	10	5	23	14	4	49	24	9	277	205	107	1st, Pacific Div.	Lost Conf. Championship
1995-96*	**82**	**24**	**10**	**7**	**23**	**15**	**3**	**47**	**25**	**10**	**326**	**240**	**104**	**1st, Pacific Div.**	**Won Stanley Cup**
1994-95*	48	19	1	4	11	12	1	30	13	5	185	134	65	1st, Northeast Div.	Lost Conf. Quarter-Final
1993-94*	84	19	17	6	15	25	2	34	42	8	277	292	76	5th, Northeast Div.	Out of Playoffs
1992-93*	84	23	17	2	24	10	8	47	27	10	351	300	104	2nd, Adams Div.	Lost Div. Semi-Final
1991-92*	80	18	19	3	2	29	9	20	48	12	255	318	52	5th, Adams Div.	Out of Playoffs
1990-91*	80	9	23	8	7	27	6	16	50	14	236	354	46	5th, Adams Div.	Out of Playoffs
1989-90*	80	8	26	6	4	35	1	12	61	7	240	407	31	5th, Adams Div.	Out of Playoffs
1988-89*	80	16	20	4	11	26	3	27	46	7	269	342	61	5th, Adams Div.	Out of Playoffs
1987-88*	80	15	23	2	17	20	3	32	43	5	271	306	69	5th, Adams Div.	Out of Playoffs
1986-87*	80	20	13	7	11	26	3	31	39	10	267	276	72	4th, Adams Div.	Lost Div. Final
1985-86*	80	23	13	4	20	18	2	43	31	6	330	289	92	1st, Adams Div.	Lost Div. Semi-Final
1984-85*	80	24	12	4	17	18	5	41	30	9	323	275	91	2nd, Adams Div.	Lost Conf. Championship
1983-84*	80	24	11	5	18	17	5	42	28	10	360	278	94	3rd, Adams Div.	Lost Div. Final
1982-83*	80	23	10	7	11	24	5	34	34	12	343	336	80	4th, Adams Div.	Lost Div. Semi-Final
1981-82*	80	24	13	.3	9	18	13	33	31	16	356	345	82	4th, Adams Div.	Lost Conf. Championship
1980-81*	80	18	11	11	12	21	7	30	32	18	314	318	78	4th, Adams Div.	Lost Prelim. Round
1979-80*	80	17	16	7	8	28	4	25	44	11	248	313	61	5th, Adams Div.	Out of Playoffs

* Quebec Nordiques

1999-2000 Player Personnel

FORWARDS	HT	WT	S	Place of Birth	Date	1998-99 Club
ABID, Ramzi	6-2	195	L	Montreal, Que.	3/24/80	Chicoutimi-Bathurst
AUBIN, Serge	6-1	194	L	Val d'Or, Que.	2/15/75	Colorado-Hershey
BABENKO, Yuri	6-0	185	L	Penza, USSR	1/2/78	Hershey
BOOTLAND, Nick	6-0	210	L	Shelbourne, Ont.	7/31/78	Hershey
DEADMARSH, Adam	6-0	195	R	Trail, B.C.	5/10/75	Colorado
DINGMAN, Chris	6-4	245	L	Edmonton, Alta.	7/6/76	Cgy-Saint Jn-Col-Her
DONOVAN, Shean	6-3	210	R	Timmins, Ont.	1/22/75	Colorado
DRURY, Chris	5-10	180	R	Trumbull, CT	8/20/76	Colorado
FORSBERG, Peter	6-0	190	L	Ornskoldsvik, Sweden	7/20/73	Colorado
HEJDUK, Milan	5-11	165	R	Usti-nad-Labem, Czech.	2/14/76	Colorado
HINOTE, Dan	6-0	187	R	Leesburg, FL	1/30/77	Hershey
LARSEN, Brad	5-11	212	L	Nakusp, B.C.	1/28/77	Hershey
LAZAREV, Yevgeny	6-2	215	L	Kharkov, USSR	4/25/80	Hershey
LEMIEUX, Claude	6-1	215	R	Buckingham, Que.	7/16/65	Colorado
MATTE, Christian	5-11	170	R	Hull, Que.	1/20/75	Colorado-Hershey
NIEMINEN, Ville	5-11	205	L	Tampere, Finland	4/6/77	Hershey
ODGERS, Jeff	6-0	200	R	Spy Hill, Sask.	5/31/69	Colorado
PAHLSSON, Samual	5-11	190	L	Ornskoldsvik, Sweden	12/17/77	MoDo Hockey
PARKER, Scott	6-4	220	R	Hanford, CA	1/29/78	Colorado-Hershey
PODEIN, Shjon	6-2	200	L	Rochester, MN	3/5/68	Philadelphia-Colorado
SAKIC, Joe	5-11	185	L	Burnaby, B.C.	7/7/69	Colorado
SHEARER, Rob	5-10	190	R	Kitchener, Ont.	10/19/76	Hershey
TANGUAY, Alex	6-0	180	L	Ste-Justine, Que.	11/21/79	Hershey-Halifax
TIMMONS, K.C.	6-2	205	L	Victoria, B.C.	4/6/80	Tri-City
WILLSIE, Brian	6-0	190	R	London, Ont.	3/16/78	Hershey
YELLE, Stephane	6-1	190	L	Ottawa, Ont.	5/9/74	Colorado
DEFENSEMEN						
BERRY, Rick	6-1	192	L	Brandon, Man.	11/4/78	Hershey
BOWEN, Jason	6-4	220	L	Port Alice, B.C.	11/9/73	Hamilton
de VRIES, Greg	6-3	215	L	Sundridge, Ont.	1/4/73	Nashville-Colorado
FOOTE, Adam	6-1	205	R	Toronto, Ont.	7/10/71	Colorado
GAUL, Michael	6-1	200	R	Lachine, Que.	4/22/73	Lowell-Colorado-Hershey
HELENIUS, Sami	6-5	225	L	Helsinki, Finland	1/22/74	Cgy-Vegas-T.B.-Chi (IHL)-Her
KLEMM, Jon	6-3	200	R	Cranbrook, B.C.	1/8/70	Colorado
MESSIER, Eric	6-2	200	L	Drummondville, Que.	10/29/73	Colorado-Hershey
MILLER, Aaron	6-3	200	R	Buffalo, NY	8/11/71	Colorado
OZOLINSH, Sandis	6-3	205	L	Riga, Latvia	8/3/72	Colorado
RYAZANTSEV, Alexander	5-11	200	R	Moscow, USSR	3/15/80	Victoriaville
SCORSUNE, Matthew	6-3	190	R	Morristown, NJ	6/27/77	Harvard University
SKOULA, Martin	6-2	195	L	Litvinov, Czech.	10/28/79	Barrie-Hershey
SMITH, Dan	6-2	195	L	Fernie, B.C.	10/19/76	Colorado-Hershey
STOREY, Ben	6-2	180	L	Ottawa, Ont.	6/22/77	Harvard University-Hershey
WHITE, Brian	6-1	180	R	Winchester, MA	2/7/76	Colorado-Hershey

GOALTENDERS	HT	WT	C	Place of Birth	Date	1998-99 Club
AEBISCHER, David	6-1	185	L	Fribourg, Switz.	2/7/78	Hershey
CASSIVI, Frederic	6-4	205	L	Sorel, Que.	6/12/75	Cincinnati (IHL)
DENIS, Marc	6-0	190	L	Montreal, Que.	8/1/77	Colorado-Hershey
ROY, Patrick	6-0	192	L	Quebec City, Que.	10/5/65	Colorado
SAUVE, Phillipe	6-0	175	L	Buffalo, NY	2/27/80	Rimouski

Coaching History

Jacques Demers, 1979-80; Maurice Filion and Michel Bergeron, 1980-81; Michel Bergeron, 1981-82 to 1986-87; Andre Savard and Ron Lapointe, 1987-88; Ron Lapointe and Jean Perron, 1988-89; Michel Bergeron, 1989-90; Dave Chambers, 1990-91; Dave Chambers and Pierre Page, 1991-92; Pierre Page, 1992-93, 1993-94; Marc Crawford, 1994-95 to 1997-98; Bob Hartley, 1998-99 to date.

Coach

HARTLEY, BOB

Coach, Colorado Avalanche. Born in Hawkesbury, Ont., September 7, 1960.

Bob Hartley became the second coach of the Colorado Avalanche and the 11th coach in the club's overall history when he was named to the position on June 30, 1998. Hartley spent four years as a head coach with the organization's American Hockey League affiliates in Cornwall and Hershey compiling a record of 151-136-33 for a .523 winning percentage.

Hartley began his coaching career with the Hawksbury Hawks, where he won two Central Ontario Junior A championships in four seasons. In 1992 he became head coach of the Laval Titans of the Quebec Major Junior Hockey League, where he won another championship prior to becoming an assistant coach with the Cornwall Aces in 1993. He became head coach in Cornwall the following year and remained with the Avalanche affiliate after it relocated to Hershey for the 1996-97 season. Hartley coached Hershey to the Calder Cup championship that year. In addition to his on-ice success in Hershey, Hartley was known for his summer hockey camps and volunteer work within the community.

Hartley and his wife Micheline have two children, Kristin and Steve.

Coaching Record

		Regular Season					Playoffs			
Season	Team	Games	W	L	T	%	Games	W	L	%
1992-93	Laval (QMJHL)	70	43	25	2	.629	13	12	1	.923
1994-95	Cornwall (AHL)	80	38	33	9	.531	15	8	7	.533
1995-96	Cornwall (AHL)	80	34	39	7	.469	8	3	5	.375
1996-97	Hershey (AHL)	80	43	27	10	.600	23	15	8	.652
1997-98	Hershey (AHL)	80	36	37	7	.494	7	3	4	.429
1998-99	**Colorado (NHL)**	**82**	**44**	**28**	**10**	**.598**	**19**	**11**	**8**	**.579**
	NHL Totals	**82**	**44**	**28**	**10**	**.598**	**19**	**11**	**8**	**.579**

1998-99 Scoring

* – rookie

Regular Season

Pos	#	Player	Team	GP	G	A	Pts	+/–	PIM	PP	SH	GW	GT	S	%
C	21	Peter Forsberg	COL	78	30	67	97	27	108	9	2	7	0	217	13.8
C	19	Joe Sakic	COL	73	41	55	96	23	29	12	5	6	1	255	16.1
R	14	Theoren Fleury	CGY	60	30	39	69	18	68	7	3	3	1	250	12.0
			COL	15	10	14	24	8	18	1	0	2	1	51	19.6
			TOTAL	75	40	53	93	26	86	8	3	5	2	301	13.3
R	22	Claude Lemieux	COL	82	27	24	51	0	102	11	0	8	1	292	9.2
R	18	Adam Deadmarsh	COL	66	22	27	49	–2	99	10	0	3	1	152	14.5
R	23	* Milan Hejduk	COL	82	14	34	48	8	26	4	0	5	0	178	7.9
C	37	* Chris Drury	COL	79	20	24	44	9	62	6	0	3	1	138	14.5
L	13	Valeri Kamensky	COL	65	14	30	44	1	28	2	0	2	0	123	11.4
D	8	Sandis Ozolinsh	COL	39	7	25	32	10	22	4	0	3	0	81	8.6
D	52	Adam Foote	COL	64	5	16	21	20	92	3	0	0	0	83	6.0
D	2	Sylvain Lefebvre	COL	76	2	18	20	18	48	0	0	0	0	64	3.1
R	12	Shean Donovan	COL	68	7	12	19	4	37	1	0	1	0	81	8.6
D	3	Aaron Miller	COL	76	5	13	18	3	42	1	0	2	0	87	5.7
C	26	Stephane Yelle	COL	72	8	7	15	–8	40	1	0	0	0	99	8.1
D	5	Alexei Gusarov	COL	54	3	10	13	12	24	1	0	0	0	28	10.7
C	32	Dale Hunter	WSH	50	0	5	5	–7	102	0	0	0	0	18	0.0
			COL	12	2	4	6	0	17	0	0	0	0	6	33.3
			TOTAL	62	2	9	11	–7	119	0	0	0	0	24	8.3
L	25	Shjon Podein	PHI	14	1	0	1	–2	0	0	0	0	0	26	3.8
			COL	41	2	6	8	–3	24	0	0	0	0	49	4.1
			TOTAL	55	3	6	9	–5	24	0	0	0	0	75	4.0
D	29	Eric Messier	COL	31	4	2	6	0	14	1	0	1	0	30	13.3
R	36	Jeff Odgers	COL	75	2	3	5	–3	259	1	0	0	0	39	5.1
D	7	Greg De Vries	NSH	6	0	0	0	–4	4	0	0	0	0	1	0.0
			COL	67	1	3	4	–3	60	0	0	0	0	56	1.8
			TOTAL	73	1	3	4	–7	64	0	0	0	0	57	1.8
D	24	Jon Klemm	COL	39	1	2	3	4	31	0	0	0	0	28	3.6
D	4	Cam Russell	CHI	7	0	0	0	1	10	0	0	0	0	1	0.0
			COL	35	1	2	3	–5	84	0	0	0	0	14	7.1
			TOTAL	42	1	2	3	–4	94	0	0	0	0	15	6.7
R	17	* Christian Matte	COL	7	1	1	2	–2	0	0	0	0	0	9	11.1
L	16	Warren Rychel	COL	28	0	2	2	3	63	0	0	0	0	15	0.0
G	33	Patrick Roy	COL	61	0	2	2	0	28	0	0	0	0	0	0.0
D	15	* Michael Gaul	COL	1	0	0	0	0	0	0	0	0	0	1	0.0
C	44	* Serge Aubin	COL	1	0	0	0	0	0	0	0	0	0	1	0.0
D	59	* Brian White	COL	2	0	0	0	0	0	0	0	0	0	0	0.0
L	6	Chris Dingman	CGY	2	0	0	0	–2	17	0	0	0	0	1	0.0
			COL	1	0	0	0	0	7	0	0	0	0	0	0.0
			TOTAL	3	0	0	0	–2	24	0	0	0	0	1	0.0
G	30	* Marc Denis	COL	4	0	0	0	0	0	0	0	0	0	0	0.0
D	32	Jeff Buchanan	COL	6	0	0	0	1	6	0	0	0	0	1	0.0
D	43	* Dan Smith	COL	12	0	0	0	5	9	0	0	0	0	6	0.0
G	1	Craig Billington	COL	21	0	0	0	0	2	0	0	0	0	0	0.0
D	27	* Scott Parker	COL	27	0	0	0	–3	71	0	0	0	0	3	0.0

Goaltending

No.	Goaltender	GPI	Mins	Avg	W	L	T	EN	SO	GA	SA	S%
33	Patrick Roy	61	3648	2.29	32	19	8	4	5	139	1673	.917
30	* Marc Denis	4	217	2.49	1	1	1	0	0	9	110	.918
1	Craig Billington	21	1086	2.87	11	8	1	1	0	52	492	.894
	Totals	**82**	**4974**	**2.47**	**44**	**28**	**10**	**5**	**5**	**205**	**2280**	**.910**

Playoffs

Pos	#	Player	Team	GP	G	A	Pts	+/–	PIM	PP	SH	GW	OT	S	%
C	21	Peter Forsberg	COL	19	8	16	24	7	31	1	1	0	0	54	14.8
C	19	Joe Sakic	COL	19	6	13	19	–2	8	1	1	1	0	56	10.7
R	14	Theoren Fleury	COL	18	5	12	17	–2	20	2	0	0	0	56	8.9
R	22	Claude Lemieux	COL	19	3	11	14	5	26	1	0	0	0	69	4.3
R	18	Adam Deadmarsh	COL	19	8	4	12	2	20	3	0	0	0	44	18.2
R	23	* Milan Hejduk	COL	16	6	6	12	3	4	1	0	3	2	38	15.8
D	8	Sandis Ozolinsh	COL	19	4	8	12	–5	22	3	0	1	0	56	7.1
L	13	Valeri Kamensky	COL	10	4	5	9	5	4	1	0	1	0	18	22.2
C	37	* Chris Drury	COL	19	6	2	8	2	4	0	0	4	1	40	15.0
D	3	Aaron Miller	COL	19	1	5	6	8	10	0	0	0	0	22	4.5
D	52	Adam Foote	COL	19	2	3	5	3	24	1	0	0	0	28	7.1
C	32	Dale Hunter	COL	19	1	3	4	0	38	0	0	0	0	10	10.0
L	25	Shjon Podein	COL	19	1	1	2	–1	12	0	0	0	0	33	3.0
G	33	Patrick Roy	COL	19	0	2	2	0	4	0	0	0	0	1	0.0
D	7	Greg De Vries	COL	19	0	2	2	3	22	0	0	0	0	7	0.0
R	36	Jeff Odgers	COL	15	1	0	1	0	14	0	0	1	0	3	33.3
C	26	Stephane Yelle	COL	10	0	1	1	–1	6	0	0	0	0	18	0.0
L	16	Warren Rychel	COL	12	0	1	1	–1	14	0	0	0	0	6	0.0
D	2	Sylvain Lefebvre	COL	19	0	1	1	6	12	0	0	0	0	16	0.0
D	24	Jon Klemm	COL	19	0	1	1	1	10	0	0	0	0	11	0.0
G	1	Craig Billington	COL	1	0	0	0	0	0	0	0	0	0	0	0.0
D	29	Eric Messier	COL	3	0	0	0	–1	0	0	0	0	0	1	0.0
D	5	Alexei Gusarov	COL	5	0	0	0	1	2	0	0	0	0	2	0.0
R	12	Shean Donovan	COL	5	0	0	0	0	2	0	0	0	0	1	0.0

Goaltending

No.	Goaltender	GPI	Mins	Avg	W	L	EN	SO	GA	SA	S%
33	Patrick Roy	19	1173	2.66	11	8	1	1	52	650	.920
1	Craig Billington	1	9	6.67	0	0	0	0	1	6	.833
	Totals	**19**	**1185**	**2.73**	**11**	**8**	**1**	**1**	**54**	**657**	**.918**

Club Records

Team

(Figures in brackets for season records are games played; records for fewest points, wins, ties, losses, goals, goals against are for 70 or more games)

Most Points	107	1996-97 (82)
Most Wins	49	1996-97 (82)
Most Ties	18	1980-81 (80)
Most Losses	61	1989-90 (80)
Most Goals	360	1983-84 (80)
Most Goals Against	407	1989-90 (80)
Fewest Points	31	1989-90 (80)
Fewest Wins	12	1989-90 (80)
Fewest Ties	5	1987-88 (80)
Fewest Losses	24	1996-97 (82)
Fewest Goals	231	1997-98 (82)
Fewest Goals Against	205	1996-97 (82), 1997-98 (82), 1998-99 (82)

Longest Winning Streak
Overall	12	Jan. 10-Feb. 7/99
Home	10	Nov. 26/83-Jan. 10/84, Mar. 6-Apr. 16/95
Away	7	Jan. 10-Feb. 7/99

Longest Undefeated Streak
Overall	12	Dec. 23/96-Jan. 20/97 (9 wins, 3 ties), Jan. 10-Feb. 7/99 (12 wins)
Home	14	Nov. 19/83-Jan. 21/84 (11 wins, 3 ties)
Away	10	Jan. 10-Mar. 3/99 (8 wins, 2 ties)

Longest Losing Streak
Overall	14	Oct. 21-Nov. 19/90
Home	8	Oct. 21-Nov. 24/90
Away	18	Jan. 18-Apr. 1/90

Longest Winless Streak
Overall	17	Oct. 21-Nov. 25/90 (15 losses, 2 ties)
Home	11	Nov. 14-Dec. 26/89 (7 losses, 4 ties)
Away	33	Oct. 8/91-Feb. 27/92 (25 losses, 8 ties)
Most Shutouts, Season	8	1996-97 (82)
Most PIM, Season	2,104	1989-90 (80)
Most Goals, Game	12	Three times

Individual

Most Seasons	11	Michel Goulet
Most Games	813	Michel Goulet
Most Goals, Career	456	Michel Goulet
Most Assists, Career	668	Peter Stastny
Most Points, Career	1,048	Peter Stastny (380G, 668A)
Most PIM, Career	1,545	Dale Hunter
Most Shutouts, Career	17	Patrick Roy
Longest Consecutive Games Streak	312	Dale Hunter (Oct. 9/80-Mar. 13/84)
Most Goals, Season	57	Michel Goulet (1982-83)
Most Assists, Season	93	Peter Stastny (1981-82)
Most Points, Season	139	Peter Stastny (1981-82; 46G, 93A)
Most PIM, Season	301	Gord Donnelly (1987-88)
Most Points, Defenseman, Season	82	Steve Duchesne (1992-93; 20G, 62A)
Most Points, Center, Season	139	Peter Stastny (1981-82; 46G, 93A)

Most Points, Right Wing, Season	103	Jacques Richard (1980-81; 52G, 51A)
Most Points, Left Wing, Season	121	Michel Goulet (1983-84; 56G, 65A)
Most Points, Rookie, Season	109	Peter Stastny (1980-81; 39G, 70A)
Most Shutouts, Season	7	Patrick Roy (1996-97)
Most Goals, Game	5	Mats Sundin (Mar. 5/92), Mike Ricci (Feb. 17/94)
Most Assists, Game	5	Six times
Most Points, Game	8	Peter Stastny (Feb. 22/81; 4G, 4A), Anton Stastny (Feb. 22/81; 3G, 5A)

Records include Quebec Nordiques, 1979-80 through 1994-95.

Quebec Nordiques Retired Numbers

3	J.C. Tremblay	1972-1979
8	Marc Tardif	1979-1983
16	Michel Goulet	1979-1990

Captains' History

Marc Tardif, 1979-80, 1980-81; Robbie Ftorek and Andre Dupont, 1981-82; Mario Marois, 1982-83 to 1984-85; Mario Marois and Peter Stastny, 1985-86; Peter Stastny, 1986-87 to 1989-90; Joe Sakic and Steven Finn, 1990-91; Mike Hough, 1991-92; Joe Sakic, 1992-93 to date.

General Managers' History

Maurice Filion, 1979-80 to 1987-88; Martin Madden, 1988-89; Martin Madden and Maurice Filion, 1989-90; Pierre Page, 1990-91 to 1993-94; Pierre Lacroix, 1994-95 to date.

All-time Record vs. Other Clubs

Regular Season

	GP	W	L	T	GF	GA	PTS	GP	W	L	T	GF	GA	PTS	GP	W	L	T	GF	GA	PTS
			At Home							On Road							Total				
Anaheim	11	6	3	2	42	33	14	11	5	4	2	26	28	12	22	11	7	4	68	61	26
Boston	61	21	34	6	217	260	48	59	20	31	8	182	233	48	120	41	65	14	399	493	96
Buffalo	60	30	19	11	221	187	71	60	17	34	9	196	240	43	120	47	53	20	417	427	114
Calgary	33	12	12	9	129	118	33	34	9	19	6	101	137	24	67	21	31	15	230	255	57
Carolina	61	35	17	9	258	185	79	59	24	24	11	205	197	59	120	59	41	20	463	382	138
Chicago	30	14	11	5	122	111	33	31	12	17	2	99	111	26	61	26	28	7	221	222	59
Dallas	31	18	9	4	127	88	40	30	11	16	3	92	102	25	61	29	25	7	219	190	65
Detroit	31	17	10	4	120	106	38	30	12	17	1	95	111	25	61	29	27	5	215	217	63
Edmonton	33	15	16	2	139	138	32	33	12	19	2	105	151	26	66	27	35	4	244	289	58
Florida	7	2	2	3	19	19	7	8	7	1	0	35	22	14	15	9	3	3	54	41	21
Los Angeles	32	16	13	3	133	115	35	33	11	19	3	111	141	25	65	27	32	6	244	256	60
Montreal	61	30	26	5	205	215	65	60	14	37	9	190	253	37	121	44	63	14	395	468	102
Nashville	2	2	0	0	7	2	4	2	0	1	1	6	7	1	4	2	1	1	13	9	5
New Jersey	30	15	12	3	110	90	33	32	12	17	3	110	132	27	62	27	29	6	220	222	60
NY Islanders	30	18	10	2	115	92	38	29	13	15	1	102	116	27	59	31	25	3	217	208	65
NY Rangers	31	15	13	3	128	123	33	29	7	18	4	79	119	18	60	22	31	7	207	242	51
Ottawa	12	10	1	1	61	33	21	13	7	4	2	60	40	16	25	17	5	3	121	73	37
Philadelphia	30	10	9	11	112	109	31	31	8	21	2	83	115	18	61	18	30	13	195	224	49
Phoenix	31	14	13	4	116	115	32	30	13	11	6	115	112	32	61	27	24	10	231	227	64
Pittsburgh	29	14	13	2	131	116	30	32	13	15	4	131	135	30	61	27	28	6	262	251	60
St. Louis	31	16	11	4	107	91	36	30	8	19	3	95	126	19	61	24	30	7	202	217	55
San Jose	13	10	2	1	62	28	21	14	8	6	0	57	46	16	27	18	8	1	119	74	37
Tampa Bay	9	6	2	1	42	21	13	9	1	7	1	22	31	3	18	7	9	2	64	52	16
Toronto	29	17	7	5	111	87	39	30	14	13	3	121	102	31	59	31	20	8	232	189	70
Vancouver	34	15	12	7	114	99	37	33	16	12	5	135	119	37	67	31	24	12	249	218	74
Washington	30	14	12	4	98	107	32	30	10	16	4	99	124	24	60	24	28	8	197	231	56
Totals	**792**	**392**	**289**	**111**	**3046**	**2688**	**895**	**792**	**284**		**95**	**2652**	**3050**	**663**	**1584**	**676**	**702**	**206**	**5698**	**5738**	**1558**

Playoffs

	Series	W	L	GP	W	L	T	GF	GA	Last Mtg.	Round	Result
Boston	2	1	1	11	5	6	0	36	37	1983	DSF	L 1-3
Buffalo	2	2	0	8	6	2	0	35	27	1985	DSF	W 3-2
Chicago	2	2	0	12	8	4	0	49	28	1997	CQF	W 4-2
Dallas	1	0	1	7	3	4	0	16	23	1999	CF	L 3-4
Detroit	3	2	1	18	10	8	0	53	46	1999	CSF	W 4-2
Edmonton	2	1	1	12	7	5	0	35	30	1998	CQF	W 3-4
Florida	1	1	0	4	4	0	0	15	4	1996	F	W 4-0
Hartford	2	1	1	9	4	5	0	34	35	1987	DSF	W 4-2
Montreal	5	2	3	31	14	17	0	85	105	1993	DSF	L 2-4
NY Islanders	1	0	1	4	0	4	0	9	18	1982	CF	L 0-4
NY Rangers	1	0	1	6	2	4	0	19	25	1995	CQF	L 2-4
Philadelphia	2	0	2	11	4	7	0	29	39	1985	CF	L 2-4
San Jose	1	1	0	6	4	2	0	19	17	1999	CQF	W 4-2
Vancouver	1	1	0	6	4	2	0	24	17	1996	CQF	W 4-2
Totals	**26**	**14**	**12**	**145**	**75**	**70**	**0**	**458**	**451**			

Playoff Results 1999-95

Year	Round	Opponent	Result	GF	GA
1999	CF	Dallas	L 3-4	16	23
	CSF	Detroit	W 4-2	21	14
	CQF	San Jose	W 4-2	19	17
1998	CQF	Edmonton	L 3-4	16	19
1997	CF	Detroit	L 2-4	12	16
	CSF	Edmonton	W 4-1	19	11
	CQF	Chicago	W 4-2	28	14
1996	**F**	**Florida**	**W 4-0**	**15**	**4**
	CF	Detroit	W 4-2	20	16
	CSF	Chicago	W 4-2	21	14
	CQF	Vancouver	W 4-2	24	17
1995	CQF	NY Rangers	L 2-4	19	25

Abbreviations: Round: F – Final; **CF** – conference final; **CSF** – conference semi-final; **CQF** – conference quarter-final; **DSF** – division semi-final.

Calgary totals include Atlanta Flames, 1979-80.
Dallas totals include Minnesota, 1979-80 to 1992-93.
Phoenix totals include Winnipeg, 1979-80 to 1995-96.
Carolina totals include Hartford, 1979-80 to 1996-97.
New Jersey totals include Colorado Rockies, 1979-80 to 1981-82.

1998-99 Results

Oct.	10		Ottawa	3-4		12	Chicago	4-1
	12		Buffalo	0-3		16	St. Louis	2-0
	14		Boston	0-3		19	at Los Angeles	5-4
	15	at	Phoenix	2-5		21	Calgary	4-2
	18	al	Los Angeles	5-5		27	at Anaheim	4-3
	24		Edmonton	6-4		28	Anaheim	6-2
	26		Phoenix	1-5		30	San Jose	5-0
	29		San Jose	4-2	Feb.	2	at Boston	3-2
	31	at	Nashville	2-3		3	at Buffalo	5-3
Nov.	2	at	Carolina	3-2		5	at Detroit	3-1
	4	at	Toronto	0-3		7	at Dallas	3-0
	6	at	Edmonton	5-2		9	Calgary	1-2
	8	at	Calgary	1-3		13	Phoenix	1-4
	10	at	Phoenix	1-1		14	Philadelphia	4-4
	13		Tampa Bay	8-1		19	at Nashville	4-4
	15	at	Vancouver	2-1		21	at Dallas	1-1
	17		NY Islanders	5-2		23	Vancouver	4-4
	19		Vancouver	0-5		25	Pittsburgh	2-3
	21	at	Montreal	3-2		27	Nashville	3-1
	25	at	Edmonton	0-3	Mar.	1	Edmonton	3-4
	28		New Jersey	2-3		3	at Florida	7-5
Dec.	2		Detroit	4-2		4	at Tampa Bay	1-2
	4		St. Louis	2-0		7	at Pittsburgh	2-3
	5	at	St. Louis	3-1		9	at Washington	3-2
	8	at	NY Islanders	2-1		11	at Philadelphia	5-3
	9	at	NY Rangers	2-1		14	Detroit	1-3
	12		New Jersey	3-5		18	Carolina	3-2
	14		St. Louis	0-0		20	Chicago	5-5
	17	at	Vancouver	1-2		21	at Chicago	3-4
	19	at	San Jose	1-2		24	Vancouver	5-2
	21	at	Anaheim	4-2		26	Washington	3-1
	22		Anaheim	0-1		28	Los Angeles	7-2
	26		Dallas	2-4		30	Calgary	3-3
	27	at	Calgary	2-1		31	at San Jose	3-2
	29		Vancouver	4-2	Apr.	3	Edmonton	5-2
	31		NY Rangers	3-6		5	Los Angeles	4-1
Jan.	2	at	Los Angeles	2-4		7	Nashville	4-1
	4		Montreal	4-3		11	at St. Louis	0-3
	6		Florida	2-2		15	at Calgary	1-5
	9	at	Detroit	2-3		16	at Edmonton	1-5
	10	at	Chicago	3-2		18	Dallas	2-1

Entry Draft
Selections 1999-85

1999
Pick
25 Mihail Kuleshov
45 Martin Grenier
93 Branko Radivojevic
112 Sanny Lindstrom
122 Kristian Kovac
142 William Magnuson
152 Jordan Krestanovich
158 Anders Lovdahl
183 Riku Hahl
212 Radim Vrbata
240 Jeff Finger

1998
Pick
12 Alex Tanguay
17 Martin Skoula
19 Robyn Regeher
20 Scott Parker
28 Ramzi Abid
38 Philippe Sauve
53 Steve Moore
79 Yevgeny Lazarev
141 Kristinn Timmons
167 Alexander Ryazantsev

1997
Pick
26 Kevin Grimes
53 Graham Belak
55 Rick Berry
78 Ville Nieminen
87 Brad Larsen
133 Aaron Miskovich
161 David Aebischer
217 Doug Schmidt
243 Kyle Kidney
245 Stephen Lafleur

1996
Pick
25 Peter Ratchuk
51 Yuri Babenko
79 Mark Parrish
98 Ben Storey
107 Randy Petruk
134 Luke Curtin
146 Brian Willsie
160 Kai Fischer
167 Dan Hinote
176 Samuel Pahlsson
188 Roman Pylner
214 Matthew Scorsune
240 Justin Clark

1995
Pick
25 Marc Denis
51 Nic Beaudoin
77 John Tripp
81 Tomi Kallio
159 Brent Johnson
155 John Cirjak
181 Dan Smith
207 Tomi Hirvonen
228 Chris George

1994
Pick
12 Wade Belak
22 Jeffrey Kealty
35 Josef Marha
61 Sebastien Bety
72 Chris Drury
87 Milan Hejduk
113 Tony Tuzzolino
139 Nicholas Windsor
165 Calvin Elfring
191 Jay Bertsch
217 Tim Thomas
243 Chris Pittman
285 Steven Low

1993
Pick
10 Jocelyn Thibault
14 Adam Deadmarsh
49 Ashley Buckberger
75 Bill Pierce
101 Ryan Tocher
127 Anders Myrvold
137 Nicholas Checco
153 Christian Matte
179 David Ling
205 Petr Franek
231 Vincent Auger
257 Mark Pivetz
283 John Hillman

1992
Pick
4 Todd Warriner
28 Paul Brousseau
29 Tuomas Gronman
52 Emmanuel Fernandez
76 Ian McIntyre
100 Charlie Wasley
124 Paxton Schulte
148 Martin LePage
172 Mike Jickling
196 Steve Passmore
220 Anson Carter
244 Aaron Ellis

1991
Pick
1 Eric Lindros
24 Rene Corbet
46 Richard Brennan
68 Dave Karpa
90 Patrick Labrecque
103 Bill Lindsay
134 Mikael Johansson
156 Janne Laukkanen
157 Aaron Asp
178 Adam Bartell
188 Brent Brekke
200 Paul Koch
222 Doug Friedman
244 Eric Meloche

1990
Pick
1 Owen Nolan
22 Ryan Hughes
43 Bradley Zavisha
106 Jeff Parrott
127 Dwayne Norris
148 Andrei Kovalenko
158 Alexander Karpovtsev
169 Pat Mazzoli
190 Scott Davis
211 Mika Stromberg
232 Wade Klippenstein

1989
Pick
1 Mats Sundin
22 Adam Foote
43 Stephane Morin
54 John Tanner
68 Niklas Andersson
76 Eric Dubois
85 Kevin Kaiser
106 Dan Lambert
127 Sergei Mylnikov
148 Paul Krake
169 Viacheslav Bykov
190 Andrei Khomutov
211 Byron Witkowski
232 Noel Rahn

1988
Pick
3 Curtis Leschyshyn
5 Daniel Dore
24 Stephane Fiset
45 Petri Aaltonen
66 Darin Kimble
87 Stephane Venne
108 Ed Ward
129 Valeri Kamensky
150 Sakari Lindfors
171 Dan Wiebe
213 Alexei Gusarov
234 Claude Lapointe

1987
Pick
9 Bryan Fogarty
15 Joe Sakic
51 Jim Sprott
72 Kip Miller
93 Rob Mendel
114 Garth Snow
135 Tim Hanus
156 Jake Enebak
177 Jaroslav Sevcik
183 Ladislav Tresl
198 Darren Nauss
219 Mike Williams

1986
Pick
18 Ken McRae
39 Jean-Marc Routhier
41 Stephane Guerard
81 Ron Tugnutt
102 Gerald Bzdel
117 Scott White
123 Morgan Samuelsson
134 Mark Vermette
144 Jean-Francois Nault
165 Keith Miller
186 Pierre Millier
207 Chris Lappin
228 Martin Latreille
249 Sean Boudreault

1985
Pick
15 David Latta
36 Jason Lafreniere
57 Max Middendorf
65 Peter Massey
78 David Espe
99 Bruce Major
120 Andy Akervik
141 Mike Oliverio
162 Mario Brunetta
183 Brit Peer
204 Tom Sasso
225 Gary Murphy
246 Jean Bois

Club Directory

Pepsi Center

Pepsi Center
1000 Chopper Place
Denver, CO 80204
Phone **303/405-1100**
FAX 303/893-0614
Press Box 303/575-1926
www.coloradoavalanche.com
Capacity: 18,129

Owner & Governor	Donald L. Sturm
Alternate Governor, President & General Manager	Pierre Lacroix
Vice President & Assistant General Manager	Francois Giguere
Head Coach	Bob Hartley
Assistant Coach	Jacques Cloutier
Assistant Coach	Bryan Trottier
Video Coach	Paul Fixter
Vice President of Player Personnel	Michel Goulet
Director of Hockey Administration	Charlotte Grahame
Team Services Assistant	Heidi Roberson
Consultant to the President	Dave Draper
Chief Scout	Brian MacDonald
Pro Scout	Brad Smith
Scout	Yvon Gendron, Jim Hammett, Garth Joy, Steve Lyons, Don Paarup, Orval Tessier
European Scout	Jori Lehto
Computer Research Consultant	John Donohue
Strength & Conditioning Coach	Paul Goldberg
Head Athletic Trainer	Pat Karns
Kinesiologist	Matt Sokolowski
Massage Therapist	Gregorio Pradera
Equipment Manager	Wayne Flemming, Mark Miller
Assistant Equipment Manager	Eric Swartz

Communications Department

Vice President of Communications & Team Services	Jean Martineau
Assistant Director of Media Relations	Damen Zier
Director of Special Projects & New Media	Hayne Ellis

Miscellaneous

Team Colors	Burgundy, Silver, Blue, and Black
Press Box Location	Northeast Side – Level 6
Practice Facility	Family Sports Center
Minor League Affiliate	Hershey Bears (AHL)
Television Outlets	FOX Sports Rocky Mountain, KTVD UPN-20
Radio Flagship	KKFN AM-950

President and General Manager

LACROIX, PIERRE
President and General Manager, Colorado Avalanche.
Born in Montreal, Que., August 3, 1948.

Pierre Lacroix was appointed to the general manager's post on May 24, 1994 after 21 years as a respected player agent. In his first season as general manager, his leadership was instrumental in moving the team from 11th to second place in the NHL. Lacroix's second season began with the club's move to Denver. He set out to improve the team and did so through acquisitions that brought Claude Lemieux, Sandis Ozolinsh, Patrick Roy and Mike Keane to Colorado. The revamped Avs finished atop the Pacific Division and went on to win the Stanley Cup. He was named NHL executive of the year by *The Hockey News* and became president of the club's hockey operations in August, 1995.

Lacroix and his wife Colombe have two children. Martin is a player agent, Eric plays with the NY Rangers.

Patrick Roy won 32 games last season, including his 400th regular-season victory on February 5, 1999. Roy has a chance to become the winningest goalie of all time this season. He enters the 1999-2000 season just 35 wins behind Terry Sawchuk.

Dallas Stars

1998-99 Results: 51W-19L-12T 114PTS. First, Pacific Division

1999-2000 Schedule

Oct.	Fri.	1	Pittsburgh		Fri.	7	Vancouver
	Sat.	2	Anaheim		Tue.	11	at Edmonton
	Tue.	5	at Detroit		Wed.	12	at Calgary
	Fri.	8	at Anaheim		Sat.	15	at Vancouver
	Sat.	9	at San Jose		Wed.	19	at Anaheim
	Wed.	13	San Jose		Thu.	20	at Los Angeles
	Fri.	15	Boston		Sun.	23	at Chicago
	Sat.	16	at Nashville		Wed.	26	Los Angeles
	Wed.	20	Edmonton		Fri.	28	St. Louis
	Fri.	22	New Jersey		Mon.	31	Edmonton
	Mon.	25	at Toronto	Feb.	Wed.	2	Atlanta
	Sat.	30	Tampa Bay		Thu.	3	at Phoenix
Nov.	Wed.	3	Buffalo		Wed.	9	at Anaheim
	Fri.	5	at Phoenix		Fri.	11	at Los Angeles
	Sat.	6	at San Jose		Sun.	13	Washington
	Tue.	9	at St. Louis		Wed.	16	Nashville
	Wed.	10	Detroit		Fri.	18	Phoenix
	Wed.	17	at Washington		Sun.	20	at Colorado*
	Thu.	18	at Philadelphia		Mon.	21	at Nashville
	Sat.	20	at Carolina		Wed.	23	at Detroit
	Mon.	22	Colorado		Fri.	25	Chicago
	Wed.	24	Los Angeles		Sun.	27	Colorado
	Fri.	26	Anaheim*	Mar.	Wed.	1	Philadelphia
	Sun.	28	at Atlanta		Fri.	3	at Phoenix
	Tue.	30	at NY Islanders		Sun.	5	Detroit
Dec.	Wed.	1	at Montreal		Wed.	8	Vancouver
	Sat.	4	at Ottawa		Fri.	10	NY Islanders
	Mon.	6	Phoenix		Sun.	12	St. Louis*
	Wed.	8	Carolina		Mon.	13	at NY Rangers
	Fri.	10	Florida		Wed.	15	at New Jersey
	Sat.	11	at St. Louis		Sat.	18	at Chicago*
	Wed.	15	Calgary		Sun.	19	San Jose*
	Fri.	17	at Edmonton		Fri.	24	Chicago
	Sat.	18	at Vancouver		Sun.	26	Colorado*
	Tue.	21	at Calgary		Tue.	28	at Tampa Bay
	Thu.	23	at Chicago		Wed.	29	at Florida
	Mon.	27	San Jose	Apr.	Sun.	2	at Colorado*
	Wed.	29	NY Rangers		Mon.	3	Calgary
	Fri.	31	Anaheim		Wed.	5	at San Jose
Jan.	Mon.	3	Los Angeles		Fri.	7	at Los Angeles
	Wed.	5	Nashville		Sun.	9	Phoenix*

* Denotes afternoon game.

Franchise date: June 5, 1967
Transferred from Minnesota to Dallas,
June 9, 1993.

33rd NHL Season

PACIFIC DIVISION

Joe Nieuwendyk led all post-season scorers with 11 goals in 1999 and earned the Conn Smythe Trophy as playoff MVP. He had been ousted from the 1998 playoffs with a serious knee injury in the Stars' very first post-season game.

Year-by-Year Record

		Home			Road			Overall							
Season	GP	W	L	T	W	L	T	W	L	T	GF	GA	Pts.	Finished	Playoff Result
1998-99	**82**	**29**	**8**	**4**	**22**	**11**	**8**	**51**	**19**	**12**	**236**	**168**	**114**	**1st, Pacific Div.**	**Won Stanley Cup**
1997-98	82	26	8	7	23	14	4	49	22	11	242	167	109	1st, Central Div.	Lost Conf. Final
1996-97	82	25	13	3	23	13	5	48	26	8	252	198	104	1st, Central Div.	Lost Conf. Quarter-Final
1995-96	82	14	18	9	12	24	5	26	42	14	227	280	66	6th, Central Div.	Out of Playoffs
1994-95	48	9	10	5	8	13	3	17	23	8	136	135	42	5th, Central Div.	Lost Conf. Quarter-Final
1993-94	84	23	12	7	19	17	6	42	29	13	286	265	97	3rd, Central Div.	Lost Conf. Semi-Final
1992-93*	84	18	17	7	18	21	3	36	38	10	272	293	82	5th, Norris Div.	Out of Playoffs
1991-92*	80	20	16	4	12	26	2	32	42	6	246	278	70	4th, Norris Div.	Lost Div. Semi-Final
1990-91*	80	19	15	6	8	24	8	27	39	14	256	266	68	4th, Norris Div.	Lost Final
1989-90*	80	26	12	2	10	28	2	36	40	4	284	291	76	4th, Norris Div.	Lost Div. Semi-Final
1988-89*	80	17	15	8	10	22	8	27	37	16	258	278	70	3rd, Norris Div.	Lost Div. Semi-Final
1987-88*	80	10	24	6	9	24	7	19	48	13	242	349	51	5th, Norris Div.	Out of Playoffs
1986-87*	80	17	20	3	13	20	7	30	40	10	296	314	70	5th, Norris Div.	Out of Playoffs
1985-86*	80	21	15	4	17	18	5	38	33	9	327	305	85	2nd, Norris Div.	Lost Div. Semi-Final
1984-85*	80	14	19	7	11	24	5	25	43	12	268	321	62	4th, Norris Div.	Lost Div. Final
1983-84*	80	22	14	4	17	17	6	39	31	10	345	344	88	1st, Norris Div.	Lost Conf. Championship
1982-83*	80	23	6	11	17	18	5	40	24	16	321	290	96	2nd, Norris Div.	Lost Div. Final
1981-82*	80	21	7	12	16	16	8	37	23	20	346	288	94	1st, Norris Div.	Lost Div. Semi-Final
1980-81*	80	23	10	7	12	18	10	35	28	17	291	263	87	3rd, Adams Div.	Lost Final
1979-80*	80	25	8	7	11	20	9	36	28	16	311	253	88	3rd, Adams Div.	Lost Semi-Final
1978-79*	80	19	15	6	9	25	6	28	40	12	257	289	68	4th, Adams Div.	Out Of Playoffs
1977-78*	80	12	24	4	6	29	5	18	53	9	218	325	45	5th, Smythe Div.	Out of Playoffs
1976-77*	80	17	14	9	6	25	9	23	39	18	240	310	64	2nd, Smythe Div.	Lost Prelim. Round
1975-76*	80	15	22	3	5	31	4	20	53	7	195	303	47	4th, Smythe Div.	Out of Playoffs
1974-75*	80	17	20	3	6	30	4	23	50	7	221	341	53	4th, Smythe Div.	Out of Playoffs
1973-74*	78	18	15	6	5	23	11	23	38	17	235	275	63	7th, West Div.	Out of Playoffs
1972-73*	78	26	8	5	11	22	6	37	30	11	254	230	85	3rd, West Div.	Lost Quarter-Final
1971-72*	78	22	11	6	15	18	6	37	29	12	212	191	86	2nd, West Div.	Lost Quarter-Final
1970-71*	78	16	15	8	12	19	8	28	34	16	191	223	72	4th, West Div.	Lost Semi-Final
1969-70*	76	11	16	11	8	19	11	19	35	22	224	257	60	3rd, West Div.	Lost Quarter-Final
1968-69*	76	11	21	6	7	22	9	18	43	15	189	270	51	6th, West Div.	Out of Playoffs
1967-68*	74	17	12	8	10	20	7	27	32	15	191	226	69	4th, West Div.	Lost Semi-Final

* Minnesota North Stars

1999-2000 Player Personnel

FORWARDS	HT	WT	S	Place of Birth	Date	1998-99 Club
CARBONNEAU, Guy	5-11	186	R	Sept-Iles, Que.	3/18/60	Dallas
FAIRCHILD, Kelly	5-11	180	L	Hibbing, MN	4/9/73	Dallas-Michigan
GAVEY, Aaron	6-2	200	L	Sudbury, Ont.	2/22/74	Dallas-Michigan
HULL, Brett	5-10	201	R	Belleville, Ont.	8/9/64	Dallas
KEANE, Mike	6-0	185	R	Winnipeg, Man.	5/29/67	Dallas
LANGENBRUNNER, Jamie	6-1	208	R	Duluth, MN	7/24/75	Dallas
LEHTINEN, Jere	6-0	192	R	Espoo, Finland	6/24/73	Dallas
LIND, Juha	5-11	180	L	Helsinki, Finland	1/2/74	Jokerit
LUHNING, Warren	6-2	185	R	Edmonton, Alta.	7/3/75	NY Islanders-Lowell
MARSHALL, Grant	6-1	193	R	Mississauga, Ont.	6/9/73	Dallas
MODANO, Mike	6-3	200	L	Livonia, MI	6/7/70	Dallas
NIEUWENDYK, Joe	6-1	195	L	Oshawa, Ont.	9/10/66	Dallas
PATERA, Pavel	6-1	172	L	Kladno, Czech.	9/6/71	HC Vsetin
PLANTE, Derek	5-11	181	L	Cloquet, MN	1/17/71	Buffalo-Dallas
SIM, Jonathan	5-9	175	L	New Glasgow, N.S.	9/29/77	Dallas-Michigan
SKRUDLAND, Brian	6-0	195	L	Peace River, Alta.	7/31/63	Dallas
SLOAN, Blake	5-10	193	R	Park Ridge, IL	7/27/75	Dallas-Houston
WRIGHT, Jamie	6-0	185	L	Kitchener, Ont.	5/13/76	Dallas-Michigan
DEFENSEMEN						
CHAMBERS, Shawn	6-2	200	L	Sterling Heights, MI	10/11/66	Dallas
HATCHER, Derian	6-5	225	L	Sterling Heights, MI	6/4/72	Dallas
JACKMAN, Richard	6-2	180	R	Toronto, Ont.	6/28/78	Michigan
LETANG, Alan	6-1	205	R	Renfrew, Ont.	9/4/75	Canada-Michigan (IHL)
LUKOWICH, Brad	6-1	195	L	Cranbrook, B.C.	8/12/76	Dallas-Michigan
MATVICHUK, Richard	6-2	200	L	Edmonton, Alta.	2/5/73	Dallas
PUSHOR, Jamie	6-3	218	R	Lethbridge, Alta.	2/11/73	Anaheim
SYDOR, Darryl	6-0	195	L	Edmonton, Alta.	5/13/72	Dallas
WOTTON, Mark	6-0	190	L	Foxwarren, Man.	11/16/73	Syracuse
ZUBOV, Sergei	6-1	200	R	Moscow, USSR	7/22/70	Dallas
GOALTENDERS	**HT**	**WT**	**C**	**Place of Birth**	**Date**	**1998-99 Club**
BELFOUR, Ed	5-11	182	L	Carman, Man.	4/21/65	Dallas
FERNANDEZ, Manny	6-0	185	L	Etobicoke, Ont.	8/27/74	Dallas-Houston
TURCO, Marty	5-11	175	L	Sault Ste. Marie, Ont.	8/13/75	Michigan

Coaching History

Wren Blair, 1967-68; Wren Blair and John Muckler, 1968-69; Wren Blair and Charlie Burns, 1969-70; Jackie Gordon, 1970-71 to 1972-73; Jackie Gordon and Parker MacDonald, 1973-74; Jackie Gordon and Charlie Burns, 1974-75; Ted Harris, 1975-76, 1976-77; Ted Harris, André Beaulieu and Lou Nanne, 1977-78; Harry Howell and Glen Sonmor, 1978-79; Glen Sonmor, 1979-80 to 1981-82; Glen Sonmor and Murray Oliver, 1982-83; Bill Mahoney, 1983-84, 1984-85; Lorne Henning, 1985-86; Lorne Henning and Glen Sonmor, 1986-87; Herb Brooks, 1987-88; Pierre Page, 1988-89, 1989-90; Bob Gainey, 1990-91 to 1994-95; Bob Gainey and Ken Hitchcock, 1995-96; Ken Hitchcock, 1996-97 to date.

Coach

HITCHCOCK, KEN

Coach, Dallas Stars. Born in Edmonton, Alberta, December 17, 1951.

Ken Hitchcock coached the Dallas Stars to the first Stanley Cup championship in franchise history in 1999. That success culminated a season in which the Stars set franchise records with 51 victories (51-19-12) and 114 points, marking the third straight season in which Hitchcock's club established new highs in those categories.

Named to his current position on January 8, 1996, Hitchcock had previously enjoyed winning seasons in every year at every level at which he had coached. He posted an incredible 575-69 mark in 10 seasons of Canadian Triple A midget hockey with Sherwood Park in suburban Edmonton, and then went on to record-breaking success with a .693 winning percentage in six seasons with Kamloops of the Western Hockey League. Hitchcock was the WHL coach of the year in 1986-87 and again in 1989-90, when he also added honors as Canadian Major Junior coach of the year.

After a three-year stint (1990-93) as an assistant coach for the Philadelphia Flyers, Hitchcock returned to head coaching duties in the International Hockey League before earning his promotion to Dallas.

Coaching Record

		Regular Season					Playoffs			
Season	Team	Games	W	L	T	%	Games	W	L	%
1984-85	Kamloops (WHL)	71	52	17	2	.746	15	10	5	.667
1985-86	Kamloops (WHL)	72	49	19	4	.708	16	14	2	.875
1986-87	Kamloops (WHL)	72	55	14	3	.785	13	8	5	.615
1987-88	Kamloops (WHL)	72	45	26	1	.632	18	12	6	.667
1988-89	Kamloops (WHL)	72	34	33	5	.507	16	8	8	.500
1989-90	Kamloops (WHL)	72	56	16	0	.778	17	14	3	.824
1993-94	Kalamazoo (IHL)	81	48	26	7	.636	5	1	4	.200
1994-95	Kalamazoo (IHL)	81	43	24	14	.617	16	10	6	.625
1995-96	Michigan (IHL)	40	19	10	11	.613	....	....	....	....
	Dallas (NHL)	**43**	**15**	**23**	**5**	**.407**	....	....	....	....
1996-97	**Dallas (NHL)**	**82**	**48**	**26**	**8**	**.634**	**7**	**3**	**4**	**.429**
1997-98	**Dallas (NHL)**	**82**	**49**	**22**	**11**	**.665**	**17**	**10**	**7**	**.588**
1998-99	**Dallas (NHL)**	**82**	**51**	**19**	**12**	**.695**	**23**	**16**	**7**	**.696***
	NHL Totals	**289**	**163**	**90**	**36**	**.626**	**47**	**29**	**18**	**.617**

* Stanley Cup win.

1998-99 Scoring

* – rookie

Regular Season

Pos	#	Player	Team	GP	G	A	Pts	+/–	PIM	PP	SH	GW	GT	S	%
C	9	Mike Modano	DAL	77	34	47	81	29	44	6	4	7	1	224	15.2
L	22	Brett Hull	DAL	60	32	26	58	19	30	15	0	11	0	192	16.7
C	25	Joe Nieuwendyk	DAL	67	28	27	55	11	34	8	0	8	1	157	17.8
R	26	Jere Lehtinen	DAL	74	20	32	52	29	18	7	1	2	0	173	11.6
D	56	Sergei Zubov	DAL	81	10	41	51	9	20	5	0	3	0	155	6.5
D	5	Darryl Sydor	DAL	74	14	34	48	–1	50	9	0	2	1	163	8.6
L	15	Jamie Langenbrunner	DAL	75	12	33	45	10	62	4	0	1	0	145	8.3
R	16	Pat Verbeek	DAL	78	17	17	34	11	133	8	0	2	1	134	12.7
R	29	Grant Marshall	DAL	82	13	18	31	1	85	2	0	4	0	112	11.6
D	2	Derian Hatcher	DAL	80	9	21	30	21	102	3	0	2	0	125	7.2
C	33	Benoit Hogue	T.B.	62	11	14	25	–12	50	2	0	3	0	101	10.9
			DAL	12	1	3	4	2	4	0	0	0	0	20	5.0
			TOTAL	74	12	17	29	–10	54	2	0	3	0	121	9.9
R	12	Mike Keane	DAL	81	6	23	29	–2	62	1	1	1	0	106	5.7
C	41	Tony Hrkac	DAL	69	13	14	27	2	26	2	0	2	2	67	19.4
C	18	Derek Plante	BUF	41	4	11	15	3	12	0	0	0	0	66	6.1
			DAL	10	2	3	5	1	4	1	0	0	0	24	8.3
			TOTAL	51	6	14	20	4	16	1	0	0	0	90	6.7
L	14	Dave Reid	DAL	73	6	11	17	0	16	1	0	1	0	81	7.4
C	21	Guy Carbonneau	DAL	74	4	12	16	–3	31	0	0	2	0	60	6.7
D	24	Richard Matvichuk	DAL	64	3	9	12	23	51	1	0	0	0	54	5.6
D	27	Shawn Chambers	DAL	61	2	9	11	6	18	1	0	1	0	82	2.4
D	3	Craig Ludwig	DAL	80	2	6	8	5	87	0	0	0	0	39	5.1
C	10	Brian Skrudland	DAL	40	4	1	5	2	33	0	0	1	0	33	12.1
D	37 *	Brad Lukowich	DAL	14	1	2	3	3	19	0	0	0	0	8	12.5
L	17	Brent Severyn	DAL	30	1	2	3	–2	50	0	0	0	0	22	4.5
C	49 *	Jonathan Sim	DAL	7	1	0	1	1	12	0	0	0	0	8	12.5
C	39 *	Kelly Fairchild	DAL	1	0	0	0	0	0	0	0	0	0	4	0.0
G	30 *	Manny Fernandez	DAL	1	0	0	0	0	0	0	0	0	0	0	0.0
D	34 *	Petr Buzek	DAL	2	0	0	0	0	2	0	0	0	0	0	0.0
C	23	Aaron Gavey	DAL	7	0	0	0	–1	10	0	0	0	0	4	0.0
L	46 *	Jamie Wright	DAL	11	0	0	0	–3	0	0	0	0	0	10	0.0
R	11 *	Blake Sloan	DAL	14	0	0	0	–1	10	0	0	0	0	7	0.0
D	6	Doug Lidster	DAL	17	0	0	0	0	10	0	0	0	0	7	0.0
L	28 *	Jason Botterill	DAL	17	0	0	0	–2	23	0	0	0	0	8	0.0
G	1	Roman Turek	DAL	26	0	0	0	0	0	0	0	0	0	0	0.0
G	20	Ed Belfour	DAL	61	0	0	0	0	26	0	0	0	0	0	0.0

Goaltending

No.	Goaltender	GPI	Mins	Avg	W	L	T	EN	SO	GA	SA	S%
20	Ed Belfour	61	3536	1.99	35	15	9	0	5	117	1373	.915
30 *	Manny Fernandez	1	60	2.00	0	1	0	0	0	2	29	.931
1	Roman Turek	26	1382	2.08	16	3	3	1	1	48	562	.915
	Totals	**82**	**4986**	**2.02**	**51**	**19**	**12**	**1**	**6**	**168**	**1965**	**.915**

Playoffs

Pos	#	Player	Team	GP	G	A	Pts	+/–	PIM	PP	SH	GW	OT	S	%
C	9	Mike Modano	DAL	23	5	18	23	6	16	1	1	1	1	83	6.0
C	25	Joe Nieuwendyk	DAL	23	11	10	21	7	19	3	0	6	2	72	15.3
L	15	Jamie Langenbrunner	DAL	23	10	7	17	7	16	4	0	3	0	46	21.7
L	22	Brett Hull	DAL	22	8	7	15	3	4	3	0	2	1	86	9.3
R	26	Jere Lehtinen	DAL	23	10	3	13	8	2	1	1	0	0	55	18.2
D	56	Sergei Zubov	DAL	23	1	12	13	13	4	0	0	0	0	46	2.2
D	5	Darryl Sydor	DAL	23	3	9	12	8	16	1	0	1	0	49	6.1
L	14	Dave Reid	DAL	23	2	8	10	4	14	0	0	0	0	30	6.7
R	12	Mike Keane	DAL	23	5	2	7	–1	6	0	1	1	0	41	12.2
R	16	Pat Verbeek	DAL	18	3	4	7	4	14	0	0	1	0	33	9.1
D	2	Derian Hatcher	DAL	18	1	6	7	4	24	0	0	0	0	28	3.6
C	21	Guy Carbonneau	DAL	17	2	4	6	0	6	0	0	1	0	29	6.9
D	24	Richard Matvichuk	DAL	22	1	5	6	4	20	0	0	0	0	26	3.8
D	3	Craig Ludwig	DAL	23	1	4	5	2	20	0	0	0	0	6	16.7
R	29	Grant Marshall	DAL	14	0	3	3	1	20	0	0	0	0	23	0.0
C	41	Tony Hrkac	DAL	5	0	2	2	3	4	0	0	0	0	3	0.0
C	33	Benoit Hogue	DAL	14	0	2	2	–1	16	0	0	0	0	20	0.0
D	27	Shawn Chambers	DAL	17	0	2	2	–1	18	0	0	0	0	19	0.0
C	10	Brian Skrudland	DAL	19	0	2	2	0	16	0	0	0	0	10	0.0
R	11 *	Blake Sloan	DAL	19	0	2	2	–1	8	0	0	0	0	7	0.0
C	18	Derek Plante	DAL	6	1	0	1	0	4	0	0	0	0	8	12.5
D	37 *	Brad Lukowich	DAL	8	0	1	1	3	4	0	0	0	0	6	0.0
D	6	Doug Lidster	DAL	4	0	0	0	0	2	0	0	0	0	1	0.0
C	49 *	Jonathan Sim	DAL	4	0	0	0	–1	0	0	0	0	0	1	0.0
G	20	Ed Belfour	DAL	23	0	0	0	0	4	0	0	0	0	0	0.0

Goaltending

No.	Goaltender	GPI	Mins	Avg	W	L	EN	SO	GA	SA	S%
20	Ed Belfour	23	1544	1.67	16	7	1	3	43	617	.930
	Totals	**23**	**1547**	**1.71**	**16**	**7**	**1**	**3**	**44**	**618**	**.929**

Captains' History

Bob Woytowich, 1967-68; Elmer Vasko, 1968-69; Claude Larose, 1969-70; Ted Harris, 1970-71 to 1973-74; Bill Goldsworthy, 1974-75, 1975-76; Bill Hogaboam, 1976-77; Nick Beverley, 1977-78; J.P. Parise, 1978-79; Paul Shmyr, 1979-80, 1980-81; Tim Young, 1981-82; Craig Hartsburg, 1982-83; Craig Hartsburg and Brian Bellows, 1983-84; Craig Hartsburg, 1984-85 to 1987-88; Curt Fraser, Bob Rouse and Curt Giles, 1988-89; Curt Giles, 1989-90, 1990-91; Mark Tinordi, 1991-92 to 1993-94; Neal Broten and Derian Hatcher, 1994-95; Derian Hatcher, 1995-96 to date.

Club Records

Team

(Figures in brackets for season records are games played; records for fewest points, wins, ties, losses, goals, goals against are for 70 or more games)

Most Points 114 1998-99 (82)
Most Wins 51 1998-99 (82)
Most Ties 22 1969-70 (76)
Most Losses 53 1975-76, 1977-78 (80)
Most Goals 346 1981-82 (80)
Most Goals Against 349 1987-88 (80)
Fewest Points 45 1977-78 (80)
Fewest Wins 18 1968-69 (76), 1977-78 (80)
Fewest Ties 4 1989-90 (80)
Fewest Losses 19 1998-99 (82)
Fewest Goals 189 1968-69 (76)
Fewest Goals Against 167 1997-98 (82)
Longest Winning Streak
Overall .... 7 Mar. 16-28/80, Mar. 16-Apr. 2/97, Nov. 22-Dec. 5/97
Home .... 11 Nov. 4-Dec. 27/72
Away .... 7 Three times
Longest Undefeated Streak
Overall .... 15 Dec. 6/98-Jan. 6/99 (12 wins, 3 ties)
Home .... 13 Oct. 28-Dec. 27/72 (12 wins, 1 tie), Nov. 21/79-Jan. 9/80 (10 wins, 3 ties), Jan. 17-Mar. 17/91 (11 wins, 2 ties)
Away .... 10 Jan. 12-Mar. 4/99 (8 wins, 2 ties)
Longest Losing Streak
Overall .... 10 Feb. 1-20/76
Home .... 6 Jan. 17-Feb. 4/70
Away .... 8 Oct. 19-Nov. 13/75, Jan. 28-Mar. 3/88
Longest Winless Streak
Overall .... 20 Jan. 15-Feb. 28/70 (15 losses, 5 ties)
Home .... 12 Jan. 17-Feb. 25/70 (8 losses, 4 ties)
Away .... 23 Oct. 25/74-Jan. 28/75 (19 losses, 4 ties)
Most Shutouts, Season 10 1997-98 (82)
Most PIM, Season 2,313 1987-88 (80)
Most Goals, Game .... 15 Nov. 11/81 (Wpg. 2 at Min. 15)

Individual

Most Seasons .... 16 Neal Broten
Most Games .... 992 Neal Broten
Most Goals, Career .... 342 Brian Bellows
Most Assists, Career ...... 593 Neal Broten
Most Points, Career .... 867 Neal Broten (274G, 593A)
Most PIM, Career .... 1,883 Shane Churla
Most Shutouts, Career ..... 26 Cesare Maniago
Longest Consecutive Games Streak ... 442 Danny Grant (Dec. 4/68-Apr. 7/74)
Most Goals, Season .... 55 Dino Ciccarelli (1981-82), Brian Bellows (1989-90)
Most Assists, Season ...... 76 Neal Broten (1985-86)
Most Points, Season .... 114 Bobby Smith (1981-82; 43G, 71A)
Most PIM, Season .... 382 Basil McRae (1987-88)
Most Points, Defenseman, Season ... 77 Craig Hartsburg (1981-82; 17G, 60A)
Most Points, Center, Season ... 114 Bobby Smith (1981-82; 43G, 71A)
Most Points, Right Wing, Season ... 107 Dino Ciccarelli (1981-82; 55G, 52A)
Most Points, Left Wing, Season ... 99 Brian Bellows (1989-90; 55G, 44A)
Most Points, Rookie, Season ... 98 Neal Broten (1981-82; 38G, 60A)
Most Shutouts, Season ..... 9 Ed Belfour (1997-98)
Most Goals, Game .... 5 Tim Young (Jan. 15/79)
Most Assists, Game .... 5 Murray Oliver (Oct. 24/71), Larry Murphy (Oct. 17/89)
Most Points, Game .... 7 Bobby Smith (Nov. 11/81; 4G, 3A)

Records include Minnesota North Stars, 1967-68 through 1992-93.

General Managers' History

Wren Blair, 1967-68 to 1973-74; Jack Gordon, 1974-75 to 1976-77; Lou Nanne, 1977-78 to 1987-88; Jack Ferreira, 1988-89, 1989-90; Bob Clarke 1990-91, 1991-92; Bob Gainey, 1992-93 to date.

Dallas Stars Retired Numbers

7	Neal Broten	1980-1995, 1996-1997

Minnesota North Stars Retired Numbers

8	Bill Goldsworthy	1967-1976
19	Bill Masterton	1967-1968

All-time Record vs. Other Clubs

Regular Season

	At Home							On Road							Total						
	GP	W	L	T	GF	GA	PTS	GP	W	L	T	GF	GA	PTS	GP	W	L	T	GF	GA	PTS
Anaheim	13	11	1	1	57	22	23	14	8	6	0	38	33	16	27	19	7	1	95	55	39
Boston	57	16	29	12	166	211	44	57	8	40	9	136	249	25	114	24	69	21	302	460	69
Buffalo	50	24	20	6	161	149	54	49	13	26	10	131	177	36	99	37	46	16	292	326	90
Calgary	52	26	18	8	194	171	60	52	11	30	11	134	194	33	104	37	48	19	328	365	93
Carolina	26	15	10	1	107	80	31	27	14	9	4	105	90	32	53	29	19	5	212	170	63
Chicago	102	45	42	15	342	318	105	99	25	62	12	257	396	62	201	70	104	27	599	714	167
Colorado	30	16	11	3	102	92	35	31	9	18	4	88	127	22	61	25	29	7	190	219	57
Detroit	96	50	31	15	347	286	115	96	33	49	14	314	379	80	192	83	80	29	661	665	195
Edmonton	35	16	13	6	132	111	38	34	10	17	7	115	145	27	69	26	30	13	247	256	65
Florida	5	2	1	2	17	13	6	5	2	2	1	17	16	5	10	4	3	3	34	29	11
Los Angeles	70	42	16	12	284	190	96	69	24	27	18	209	236	66	139	66	43	30	493	426	162
Montreal	56	15	30	11	145	201	41	55	10	37	8	134	243	28	111	25	67	19	279	444	69
Nashville	2	1	1	0	2	2	2	2	2	0	0	7	3	4	4	3	1	0	9	5	6
New Jersey	41	24	11	6	159	109	54	40	18	19	3	125	135	39	81	42	30	9	284	244	93
NY Islanders	43	17	19	7	128	158	41	43	12	23	8	124	164	32	86	29	42	15	252	322	73
NY Rangers	57	17	30	10	170	212	44	58	13	34	11	157	202	37	115	30	64	21	327	414	81
Ottawa	7	4	3	0	26	15	8	6	4	2	0	18	15	8	13	8	5	0	44	30	16
Philadelphia	62	25	23	14	205	206	64	63	9	41	13	144	248	31	125	34	64	27	349	454	95
Phoenix	42	23	14	5	166	129	51	40	19	19	2	136	135	40	82	42	33	7	302	264	91
Pittsburgh	61	34	21	6	231	203	74	60	18	36	6	168	227	42	121	52	57	12	399	430	116
St. Louis	105	48	38	19	360	317	115	108	29	59	20	305	396	78	213	77	97	39	665	713	193
San Jose	16	8	6	2	49	41	18	16	10	6	0	48	37	20	32	18	12	2	97	78	38
Tampa Bay	8	6	1	1	31	19	13	9	6	1	2	26	14	14	17	12	2	3	57	33	27
Toronto	95	49	35	11	362	302	109	98	34	48	16	311	346	84	193	83	83	27	673	648	193
Vancouver	61	33	17	11	236	185	77	61	22	29	10	184	229	54	122	55	46	21	420	414	131
Washington	36	17	11	8	136	102	42	37	15	15	7	116	115	37	73	32	26	15	252	217	79
Defunct Clubs	33	19	8	6	123	86	44	32	10	16	6	84	105	26	65	29	24	12	207	191	70
Totals	**1261**	**603**	**460**	**198**	**4438**	**3930**	**1404**	**1261**	**388**	**671**	**202**	**3631**	**4656**	**978**	**2522**	**991**	**1131**	**400**	**8069**	**8586**	**2382**

Playoffs

	Series	W	L	GP	W	L	T	GF	GA	Last Mtg.	Round	Result
Boston	1	1	0	3	3	0	0	20	13	1981	PR	W 3-0
Buffalo	3	2	1	13	8	5	0	39	37	1999	F	W 4-2
Calgary	1	1	0	6	4	2	0	25	18	1981	SF	W 4-2
Chicago	6	2	4	33	14	19	0	119	119	1991	DSF	W 4-2
Colorado	1	1	0	7	4	3	0	23	16	1999	CF	W 4-3
Detroit	3	0	3	18	6	12	0	40	55	1998	CF	L 2-4
Edmonton	5	3	2	25	15	10	0	68	69	1999	CQF	W 4-0
Los Angeles	1	1	0	7	4	3	0	26	21	1968	QF	W 4-3
Montreal	2	1	1	13	6	7	0	37	48	1980	QF	W 4-3
NY Islanders	1	0	1	5	1	4	0	16	26	1981	F	L 1-4
Philadelphia	2	0	2	11	3	8	0	26	41	1980	SF	L 1-4
Pittsburgh	1	0	1	6	2	4	0	16	28	1991	F	L 2-4
St. Louis	11	6	5	62	34	28	0	191	174	1999	CSF	W 4-2
San Jose	1	1	0	6	4	2	0	16	12	1998	CQF	W 4-2
Toronto	2	2	0	7	6	1	0	35	26	1983	DSF	W 3-1
Vancouver	1	0	1	5	1	4	0	11	18	1994	CSF	L 1-4
Totals	**42**	**21**	**21**	**227**	**115**	**112**	**0**	**708**	**721**			

Calgary totals include Atlanta Flames, 1972-73 to 1979-80. Carolina totals include Hartford, 1979-80 to 1996-97.
Colorado totals include Quebec, 1979-80 to 1994-95.
New Jersey totals include Kansas City, 1974-75 to 1975-76, and Colorado Rockies, 1976-77 to 1981-82.
Phoenix totals include Winnipeg, 1979-80 to 1995-96.

Playoff Results 1999-95

Year	Round	Opponent	Result	GF	GA
1999	**F**	**Buffalo**	**W 4-2**	**13**	**9**
	CF	Colorado	W 4-3	23	16
	CSF	St. Louis	W 4-2	17	12
	CQF	Edmonton	W 4-0	11	7
1998	CF	Detroit	L 2-4	11	15
	CSF	Edmonton	W 4-1	9	5
	CQF	San Jose	W 4-2	16	12
1997	CQF	Edmonton	L 3-4	18	21
1995	CQF	Detroit	L 1-4	10	17

Abbreviations: Round: F – Final; **CF** – conference final; **CSF** – conference semi-final; **CQF** – conference quarter-final; **DSF** – division semi-final; **SF** – semi-final; **QF** – quarter-final; **PR** – preliminary round.

1998-99 Results

Oct.	10		Buffalo	4-1		18		Vancouver	3-5
	13		Chicago	3-1		20		Toronto	4-6
	15	at	Carolina	2-2		27		Los Angeles	3-2
	17	at	Chicago	3-4		29	at	Tampa Bay	4-1
	20		Calgary	3-1		30	at	Florida	5-2
	22		Phoenix	2-1	**Feb.**	1		Calgary	2-2
	24		San Jose	2-1		7		Colorado	0-3
	30		Anaheim	3-3		12	at	Anaheim	3-2
	31		Detroit	3-2		13	at	Los Angeles	3-2
Nov.	4	at	San Jose	0-4		15		Edmonton	4-1
	7	at	Los Angeles	4-3		17		Florida	2-1
	11		Phoenix	0-2		19		Chicago	5-1
	13	at	Detroit	5-1		21		Colorado	1-1
	14	at	Boston	3-1		23	at	Nashville	4-3
	20		NY Islanders	4-2		24		Nashville	1-2
	21	at	St. Louis	3-3		26		Pittsburgh	6-4
	23		San Jose	3-2		28		Los Angeles	1-0
	25		New Jersey	2-5	**Mar.**	2	at	NY Rangers	2-2
	27		Washington	4-0		4	at	NY Islanders	3-2
Dec.	2	at	San Jose	3-0		5	at	Buffalo	1-2
	4	at	Vancouver	1-4		7		St. Louis	4-3
	6	at	Edmonton	6-2		10		Edmonton	7-4
	7	at	Calgary	3-2		12		Anaheim	4-0
	9		San Jose	3-3		14	at	Philadelphia	1-1
	11		Montreal	3-2		16	at	Pittsburgh	2-2
	13	at	Chicago	2-2		17	at	Washington	1-2
	15		St. Louis	7-3		19		Ottawa	1-2
	18	at	Detroit	3-1		21		Carolina	3-2
	20	at	Ottawa	3-2		23	at	Phoenix	3-2
	21	at	Montreal	2-2		25	at	Los Angeles	2-1
	23	at	Toronto	5-1		26	at	Anaheim	1-5
	26	at	Colorado	4-2		28	at	Nashville	3-0
	28		Nashville	1-0		31		Tampa Bay	6-4
	31		Boston	6-1	**Apr.**	3	at	St. Louis	2-5
Jan.	1	at	Phoenix	2-1		4		Detroit	0-3
	6		Vancouver	6-4		7		Anaheim	5-1
	8	at	Calgary	0-1		9		NY Rangers	3-1
	10	at	Vancouver	0-2		11		Los Angeles	6-2
	12	at	Edmonton	2-2		14		Phoenix	4-2
	13	at	San Jose	2-1		17	at	Phoenix	0-2
	15	at	Anaheim	3-1		18	at	Colorado	1-2

Entry Draft
Selections 1999-85

1999
Pick
32	Michael Ryan
66	Dan Jancevski
96	Mathias Tjarnqvist
126	Jeff Bateman
156	Gregor Baumgartner
184	Justin Cox
186	Brett Draney
215	Jeff MacMillan
243	Brian Sullivan
265	Jamie Chamberlain
272	Mihail Donika

1998
Pick
39	John Erskine
57	Tyler Bouck
86	Gabriel Karlsson
153	Pavel Patera
173	Niko Kapanen
200	Scott Perry

1997
Pick
25	Brenden Morrow
52	Roman Lyashenko
77	Steve Gainey
105	Marc Kristoffersson
132	Teemu Elomo
160	Alexei Timkin
189	Jeff McKercher
216	Alexei Komarov
242	Brett McLean

1996
Pick
5	Richard Jackman
70	Jonathan Sim
90	Mike Hurley
112	Ryan Christie
113	Evgeny Tysbuk
166	Eoin McInerney
194	Joel Kwiatkowski
220	Nick Bootland

1995
Pick
11	Jarome Iginla
37	Patrick Cote
63	Petr Buzek
69	Sergey Gusev
115	Wade Strand
141	Dominic Marleau
173	Jeff Dewar
193	Anatoli Kovesnikov
202	Sergei Luchinkin
219	Stephen Lowe

1994
Pick
20	Jason Botterill
46	Lee Jinman
98	Jamie Wright
124	Marty Turco
150	Yevgeny Petrochinin
228	Marty Flichel
254	Jimmy Roy
280	Chris Szysky

1993
Pick
9	Todd Harvey
35	Jamie Langenbrunner
87	Chad Lang
136	Rick Mrozik
139	Per Svartvadet
165	Jeremy Stasiuk
191	Rob Lurtsema
243	Jordan Willis
249	Bill Lang
269	Cory Peterson

1992
Pick
34	Jarkko Varvio
58	Jeff Bes
88	Jere Lehtinen
130	Michael Johnson
154	Kyle Peterson
178	Juha Lind
202	Lars Edstrom
226	Jeff Romfo
250	Jeffrey Moen

1991
Pick
8	Richard Matvichuk
74	Mike Torchia
97	Mike Kennedy
118	Mark Lawrence
137	Geoff Finch
174	Michael Burkett
184	Derek Herlofsky
206	Tom Nemeth
228	Shayne Green
250	Jukka Suomalainen

1990
Pick
8	Derian Hatcher
50	Laurie Billeck
70	Cal McGowan
71	Frank Kovacs
92	Enrico Ciccone
113	Roman Turek
134	Jeff Levy
155	Doug Barrault
176	Joe Biondi
197	Troy Binnie
218	Ole-Eskild Dahlstrom
239	John McKersie

1989
Pick
7	Doug Zmolek
28	Mike Craig
60	Murray Garbutt
75	Jean-François Quintin
87	Pat MacLeod
91	Bryan Schoen
97	Rhys Hollyman
112	Scott Cashman
154	Jonathan Pratt
175	Kenneth Blum
196	Arturs Irbe
217	Tom Pederson
238	Helmut Balderis

1988
Pick
1	Mike Modano
40	Link Gaetz
43	Shaun Kane
64	Jeffrey Stop
148	Ken MacArthur
169	Travis Richards
190	Ari Matilainen
211	Grant Bischoff
232	Trent Andison

1987
Pick
6	David Archibald
35	Scott McCrady
48	Kevin Kaminski
73	John Weisbrod
88	Teppo Kivela
109	Darcy Norton
130	Timo Kulonen
151	Don Schmidt
172	Jarmo Myllys
193	Larry Olimb
214	Mark Felicio
235	Dave hields

1986
Pick
12	Warren Babe
30	Neil Wilkinson
33	Dean Kolstad
54	Eric Bennett
55	Rob Zettler
58	Brad Turner
75	Kirk Tomlinson
96	Jari Gronstrand
159	Scott Mathias
180	Lance Pitlick
201	Dan Keczmer
222	Garth Joy
243	Kurt Stahura

1985
Pick
51	Stephane Roy
69	Mike Berger
90	Dwight Mullins
111	Mike Mullowney
132	Mike Kelfer
153	Ross Johnson
174	Tim Helmer
195	Gordon Ernst
216	Ladislav Lubina
237	Tommy Sjodin

Club Directory

Reunion Arena

Dallas Stars Hockey Club, Inc.
Dr Pepper StarCenter
211 Cowboys Parkway
Irving, TX 75063
Phone **972/868-2890**
FAX 972/868-2860
Ticket Information 214/GO STARS
Capacity: 16,962

Chairman of the Board & Owner	Thomas O. Hicks
President/Alternate Governor	James R. Lites
V.P. of Hockey Operations	Bob Gainey
V.P. of Marketing and Broadcasting	Bill Strong
V.P. of Marketing and Promotion	Jeff Cogen
General Manager	Bob Gainey
Assistant General Manager	Doug Armstrong
Director of Player Personnel	Craig Button
Director of Hockey Administration	Dan Stuchal
Head Coach	Ken Hitchcock
Assistant Coaches	Doug Jarvis, Rick Wilson
Head Athletic Trainer	Dave Surprenant
Equipment Managers	Dave Smith, Rich Matthews
Strength and Conditioning Coach	J.J. McQueen
Director of Media Relations	Larry Kelly (972) 868-2807
Media Relations Manager	Kurt Daniels (972) 868-2818
P.R. Fax	(972) 868-2860
Radio Station	WBAP, 820 AM
TV Stations	KXTX, Ch. 39; Fox Sports Southwest
Web site	www.dallasstars.com

General Manager

GAINEY, BOB
Vice President of Hockey Operations/General Manager, Dallas Stars.
Born in Peterborough, Ont., December 13, 1953.

Bob Gainey enters his fourth season as the full-time general manager for the Dallas Stars after building the team into a Stanley Cup champion in 1999. Named general manager of the team on June 8, 1992, he held the dual role of coach and g.m. for over four seasons before relinquishing his head coaching duties on January 8, 1996. Having been appointed head coach of the Stars on June 19, 1990, Gainey's five-plus consecutive seasons behind the bench was the longest tenure of any head coach in franchise history. He is the Stars' sixth general manager and was the team's 16th head coach.

Under Gainey's tutelage, the Stars improved their regular-season record in each of Gainey's first four seasons as coach, going from 27 wins and 68 points in his first year to 42 wins and 97 points in 1993-94. In his first season, 1990-91, Gainey led the Stars through to the Stanley Cup finals, surprising Chicago and St. Louis and eliminating defending champion Edmonton before bowing in six games to Pittsburgh. He finished his reign behind the Stars bench with a 165-190-60 regular season record.

Elected to the Hockey Hall of Fame in 1992, Gainey was Montreal's first choice (eighth overall) in the 1973 Amateur Draft. During his 16-year career with the Canadiens, Gainey was a member of five Stanley Cup-winning teams and was named the Conn Smythe Trophy winner in 1979. He was a four-time recipient of the Frank Selke Trophy (1978-81), awarded to the League's top defensive forward, and participated in four NHL All-Star Games (1977, 1978, 1980 and 1981). He served as team captain for eight seasons (1981-89). During his career, he played in 1,160 regular-season games, registering 239 goals and 262 assists for 501 points. In addition, he tallied 73 points (25-48-73) in 182 post-season games.

Jere Lehtinen's defensive excellence was recognized once again as he won the Selke Trophy for the second straight time in 1998-99. A solid two-way player, Lehtinen also reached the 20-goal plateau for the second season in a row.

NHL Coaching Record

Season	Team	Regular Season					Playoffs			
		Games	W	L	T	%	Games	W	L	%
1990-91	Minnesota	80	27	39	14	.425	23	14	9	.643
1991-92	Minnesota	80	32	42	6	.438	7	3	4	.429
1992-93	Minnesota	84	36	38	10	.488	....	....	....	....
1993-94	Dallas	84	42	29	13	.577	9	5	4	.556
1994-95	Dallas	48	17	23	8	.438	5	1	4	.200
1995-96	Dallas	39	11	19	9	.397	....	....	....	....
	NHL Totals	**415**	**165**	**190**	**60**	**.470**	**44**	**23**	**21**	**.523**

Detroit Red Wings

1998-99 Results: 43W-32L-7T 93PTS. First, Central Division

With 34 wins last season, Chris Osgood improved to 166 wins for his career and moved past Harry Lumley for second all-time in Red Wings history. Detroit's winningest goaltender is Terry Sawchuk with 352 career victories.

1999-2000 Schedule

Oct.	Sat.	2	Buffalo		Sat.	8	Anaheim
	Tue.	5	Dallas		Tue.	11	at Montreal
	Thu.	7	at Atlanta		Thu.	13	Chicago
	Sat.	9	at Florida		Sun.	16	at Edmonton
	Wed.	13	St. Louis		Tue.	18	at Calgary
	Sat.	16	Philadelphia		Wed.	19	at Vancouver
	Wed.	20	San Jose		Sat.	22	at Ottawa
	Sat.	23	at Chicago		Wed.	26	Toronto
	Wed.	27	Colorado		Fri.	28	Calgary
	Fri.	29	Chicago		Sat.	29	New Jersey
	Sat.	30	at St. Louis		Mon.	31	at Phoenix
Nov.	Wed.	3	Los Angeles	Feb.	Thu.	3	at Los Angeles
	Fri.	5	Carolina		Tue.	8	St. Louis
	Sun.	7	at Tampa Bay		Thu.	10	at St. Louis
	Wed.	10	at Dallas		Sun.	13	at Colorado
	Fri.	12	Pittsburgh		Mon.	14	at Phoenix
	Sat.	13	at Toronto		Wed.	16	Vancouver
	Mon.	15	Anaheim		Fri.	18	Los Angeles
	Wed.	17	at Vancouver		Sun.	20	at Chicago*
	Fri.	19	at Calgary		Mon.	21	at NY Islanders*
	Sat.	20	at Edmonton		Wed.	23	Dallas
	Wed.	24	St. Louis		Fri.	25	NY Islanders
	Fri.	26	Edmonton		Sun.	27	Tampa Bay
	Sun.	28	Phoenix*	Mar.	Fri.	3	at Washington
Dec.	Wed.	1	San Jose		Sun.	5	at Dallas
	Fri.	3	at Chicago		Tue.	7	at Los Angeles
	Sat.	4	at Nashville		Wed.	8	at San Jose
	Wed.	8	Nashville		Fri.	10	at Nashville
	Fri.	10	Los Angeles		Tue.	14	Nashville
	Sat.	11	at Boston		Thu.	16	Toronto
	Wed.	15	Edmonton		Sat.	18	at Colorado*
	Fri.	17	Colorado		Sun.	19	at Anaheim
	Sun.	19	at Anaheim		Wed.	22	Calgary
	Mon.	20	at San Jose		Thu.	23	at Nashville
	Wed.	22	at Carolina		Sun.	26	NY Rangers*
	Mon.	27	Atlanta		Mon.	27	at NY Rangers
	Tue.	28	at Buffalo		Wed.	29	Vancouver
	Fri.	31	Chicago	Apr.	Sat.	1	at St. Louis*
Jan.	Sun.	2	at Pittsburgh		Sun.	2	Montreal
	Tue.	4	Phoenix		Fri.	7	Washington
	Thu.	6	Nashville		Sun.	9	at Colorado*

* Denotes afternoon game.

Franchise date: September 25, 1926

CENTRAL DIVISION

74th NHL Season

Year-by-Year Record

Season	GP	Home W	L	T	Road W	L	T	Overall W	L	T	GF	GA	Pts.	Finished		Playoff Result
1998-99	82	27	12	2	16	20	5	43	32	7	245	202	93	1st,	Central Div.	Lost Conf. Semi-Final
1997-98	82	25	8	8	19	15	7	44	23	15	250	196	103	2nd,	Central Div.	**Won Stanley Cup**
1996-97	82	20	12	9	18	14	9	38	26	18	253	197	94	2nd,	Central Div.	**Won Stanley Cup**
1995-96	82	36	3	2	26	10	5	62	13	7	325	181	131	1st,	Central Div.	Lost Conf. Championship
1994-95	48	17	4	3	16	7	1	33	11	4	180	117	70	1st,	Central Div.	Lost Final
1993-94	84	23	13	6	23	17	2	46	30	8	356	275	100	1st,	Central Div.	Lost Conf. Quarter-Final
1992-93	84	25	14	3	22	14	6	47	28	9	369	280	103	2nd,	Norris Div.	Lost Div. Semi-Final
1991-92	80	24	12	4	19	13	8	43	25	12	320	256	98	1st,	Norris Div.	Lost Div. Final
1990-91	80	26	14	0	8	24	8	34	38	8	273	298	76	3rd,	Norris Div.	Lost Div. Semi-Final
1989-90	80	20	14	6	8	24	8	28	38	14	288	323	70	5th,	Norris Div.	Out of Playoffs
1988-89	80	20	14	6	14	20	6	34	34	12	313	316	80	1st,	Norris Div.	Lost Div. Semi-Final
1987-88	80	24	10	6	17	18	5	41	28	11	322	269	93	1st,	Norris Div.	Lost Conf. Championship
1986-87	80	20	14	6	14	22	4	34	36	10	260	274	78	2nd,	Norris Div.	Lost Conf. Championship
1985-86	80	10	26	4	7	31	2	17	57	6	266	415	40	5th,	Norris Div.	Out of Playoffs
1984-85	80	19	14	7	8	27	5	27	41	12	313	357	66	3rd,	Norris Div.	Lost Div. Semi-Final
1983-84	80	18	20	2	13	22	5	31	42	7	298	323	69	3rd,	Norris Div.	Lost Div. Semi-Final
1982-83	80	14	19	7	7	25	8	21	44	15	263	344	57	5th,	Norris Div.	Out of Playoffs
1981-82	80	15	19	6	6	28	6	21	47	12	270	351	54	6th,	Norris Div.	Out of Playoffs
1980-81	80	16	15	9	3	28	9	19	43	18	252	339	56	5th,	Norris Div.	Out of Playoffs
1979-80	80	14	21	5	12	22	6	26	43	11	268	306	63	5th,	Norris Div.	Out of Playoffs
1978-79	80	15	17	8	8	24	8	23	41	16	252	295	62	5th,	Norris Div.	Out of Playoffs
1977-78	80	22	11	7	10	23	7	32	34	14	252	266	78	2nd,	Norris Div.	Lost Quarter-Final
1976-77	80	12	22	6	4	33	3	16	55	9	183	309	41	5th,	Norris Div.	Out of Playoffs
1975-76	80	17	15	8	9	29	2	26	44	10	226	300	62	4th,	Norris Div.	Out of Playoffs
1974-75	80	17	17	6	6	28	6	23	45	12	259	335	58	4th,	Norris Div.	Out of Playoffs
1973-74	78	21	12	6	8	27	4	29	39	10	255	319	68	6th,	East Div.	Out of Playoffs
1972-73	78	22	12	5	15	17	7	37	29	12	265	243	86	5th,	East Div.	Out of Playoffs
1971-72	78	25	11	3	8	24	7	33	35	10	261	262	76	5th,	East Div.	Out of Playoffs
1970-71	78	17	15	7	5	30	4	22	45	11	209	308	55	7th,	East Div.	Out of Playoffs
1969-70	76	20	11	7	20	10	8	40	21	15	246	199	95	3rd,	East Div.	Lost Quarter-Final
1968-69	76	23	8	7	10	23	5	33	31	12	239	221	78	5th,	East Div.	Out of Playoffs
1967-68	74	18	15	4	9	20	8	27	35	12	245	257	66	6th,	East Div.	Out of Playoffs
1966-67	70	21	11	3	6	28	1	27	39	4	212	241	58	5th,		Out of Playoffs
1965-66	70	20	8	7	11	19	5	31	27	12	221	194	74	4th,		Lost Final
1964-65	70	25	7	3	15	16	4	40	23	7	224	175	87	1st,		Lost Semi-Final
1963-64	70	23	9	3	7	20	8	30	29	11	191	204	71	4th,		Lost Final
1962-63	70	19	10	6	13	15	7	32	25	13	200	194	77	4th,		Lost Final
1961-62	70	17	11	7	6	22	7	23	33	14	184	219	60	5th,		Out of Playoffs
1960-61	70	15	13	7	10	16	9	25	29	16	195	215	66	4th,		Lost Final
1959-60	70	18	14	3	8	15	12	26	29	15	186	197	67	4th,		Lost Semi-Final
1958-59	70	13	17	5	12	20	3	25	37	8	167	218	58	6th,		Out of Playoffs
1957-58	70	16	11	8	13	18	4	29	29	12	176	207	70	3rd,		Lost Semi-Final
1956-57	70	23	7	5	15	13	7	38	20	12	198	157	88	1st,		Lost Semi-Final
1955-56	70	21	6	8	9	18	8	30	24	16	183	148	76	2nd,		Lost Final
1954-55	70	25	5	5	17	12	6	42	17	11	204	134	95	1st,		**Won Stanley Cup**
1953-54	70	24	4	7	13	15	7	37	19	14	191	132	88	1st,		**Won Stanley Cup**
1952-53	70	20	5	10	16	11	8	36	16	18	222	133	90	1st,		Lost Semi-Final
1951-52	70	24	7	4	20	7	8	44	14	12	215	133	100	1st,		**Won Stanley Cup**
1950-51	70	25	3	7	19	10	6	44	13	13	236	139	101	1st,		Lost Semi-Final
1949-50	70	19	9	7	18	10	7	37	19	14	229	164	88	1st,		**Won Stanley Cup**
1948-49	60	21	6	3	13	13	4	34	19	7	195	145	75	1st,		Lost Final
1947-48	60	16	9	5	14	9	7	30	18	12	187	148	72	2nd,		Lost Final
1946-47	60	14	10	6	8	17	5	22	27	11	190	193	55	4th,		Lost Semi-Final
1945-46	50	16	5	4	4	15	6	20	20	10	146	159	50	4th,		Lost Semi-Final
1944-45	50	19	5	1	12	9	4	31	14	5	218	161	67	2nd,		Lost Final
1943-44	50	18	5	2	8	13	4	26	18	6	214	177	58	2nd,		Lost Semi-Final
1942-43	50	16	4	5	9	10	6	25	14	11	169	124	61	1st,		**Won Stanley Cup**
1941-42	48	14	7	3	5	18	1	19	25	4	140	147	42	5th,		Lost Final
1940-41	48	14	5	5	7	11	6	21	16	11	112	102	53	3rd,		Lost Final
1939-40	48	11	10	3	5	16	3	16	26	6	90	126	38	5th,		Lost Semi-Final
1938-39	48	14	8	2	4	16	4	18	24	6	107	128	42	5th,		Lost Semi-Final
1937-38	48	8	10	6	4	15	5	12	25	11	99	133	35	4th,	Amn. Div.	Out of Playoffs
1936-37	48	14	5	5	11	9	4	25	14	9	128	102	59	1st,	Amn. Div.	**Won Stanley Cup**
1935-36	48	14	5	5	10	11	3	24	16	8	124	103	56	1st,	Amn. Div.	**Won Stanley Cup**
1934-35	48	11	8	5	8	14	2	19	22	7	127	114	45	4th,	Amn. Div.	Out of Playoffs
1933-34	48	15	5	4	9	9	6	24	14	10	113	98	58	1st,	Amn. Div.	Lost Final
1932-33*	48	17	6	1	8	9	7	25	15	8	111	93	58	2nd,	Amn. Div.	Lost Semi-Final
1931-32	48	15	3	6	3	17	4	18	20	10	95	108	46	3rd,	Amn. Div.	Lost Quarter-Final
1930-31**	44	10	7	5	6	14	2	16	21	7	102	105	39	4th,	Amn. Div.	Out of Playoffs
1929-30	44	9	10	3	5	14	3	14	24	6	117	133	34	4th,	Amn. Div.	Out of Playoffs
1928-29	44	11	6	5	8	10	4	19	16	9	72	63	47	3rd,	Amn. Div.	Lost Quarter-Final
1927-28	44	9	10	3	10	9	3	19	19	6	88	79	44	4th,	Amn. Div.	Out of Playoffs
1926-27***	44	5	16	0	7	12	4	12	28	4	76	105	28	5th,	Amn. Div.	Out of Playoffs

* Team name changed to Red Wings. ** Team name changed to Falcons. *** Team named Cougars.

1999-2000 Player Personnel

FORWARDS	HT	WT	S	Place of Birth	Date	1998-99 Club
AUDET, Philippe	6-2	175	L	Ottawa, Ont.	6/4/77	Detroit-Adirondack
BROWN, Doug	5-10	185	R	Southborough, MA	6/12/64	Detroit
DANDENAULT, Mathieu	6-0	174	R	Sherbrooke, Que.	2/3/76	Detroit
DRAPER, Kris	5-11	185	L	Toronto, Ont.	5/24/71	Detroit
FEDOROV, Sergei	6-1	200	L	Pskov, USSR	12/13/69	Detroit
GILCHRIST, Brent	5-11	180	L	Moose Jaw, Sask.	4/3/67	Detroit
HOLMSTROM, Tomas	6-0	200	L	Pitea, Sweden	1/23/73	Detroit
KOCUR, Joe	6-0	205	R	Calgary, Alta.	12/21/64	Detroit
KOZLOV, Vyacheslav	5-10	180	L	Voskresensk, USSR	5/3/72	Detroit
LAPLANTE, Darryl	6-1	185	L	Calgary, Alta.	3/28/77	Detroit-Adirondack
LAPOINTE, Martin	5-11	200	R	Ville Ste. Pierre, Que.	9/12/73	Detroit
LARIONOV, Igor	5-9	170	L	Voskresensk, USSR	12/3/60	Detroit
MALTBY, Kirk	6-0	180	R	Guelph, Ont.	12/22/72	Detroit
McCARTY, Darren	6-1	210	R	Burnaby, B.C.	4/1/72	Detroit
ROEST, Stacy	5-9	192	R	Lethbridge, Alta.	3/15/74	Detroit-Adirondack
SHANAHAN, Brendan	6-3	218	R	Mimico, Ont.	1/23/69	Detroit
YZERMAN, Steve	5-11	185	R	Cranbrook, B.C.	5/9/65	Detroit
DEFENSEMEN						
CHELIOS, Chris	6-1	190	R	Chicago, IL	1/25/62	Chicago-Detroit
FISCHER, Jiri	6-5	210	L	Horovice, Czech.	7/31/80	Hull
GOLUBOVSKY, Yan	6-3	183	R	Novosibirsk, USSR	3/9/76	Detroit-Adirondack
KRUPP, Uwe	6-6	235	R	Cologne, West Germany	6/24/65	Detroit
KUZNETSOV, Maxim	6-5	198	L	Pavlodar, USSR	3/24/77	Adirondack
LIDSTROM, Nicklas	6-2	185	L	Vasteras, Sweden	4/28/70	Detroit
WALLIN, Jesse	6-2	190	L	Saskatoon, Sask.	3/10/78	Adirondack
WARD, Aaron	6-2	200	R	Windsor, Ont.	1/17/73	Detroit

GOALTENDERS	HT	WT	C	Place of Birth	Date	1998-99 Club
LEGACE, Manny	5-9	162	L	Toronto, Ont.	2/4/73	Los Angeles-Long Beach
OSGOOD, Chris	5-10	160	L	Peace River, Alta.	11/26/72	Detroit
WREGGET, Ken	6-1	201	L	Brandon, Man.	3/25/64	Calgary

Director of Player Personnel/Coach

BOWMAN, WILLIAM SCOTT (SCOTTY)
Director of Player Personnel/Coach, Detroit Red Wings.
Born in Montreal, Que. September 18, 1933.

Scotty Bowman equalled Toe Blake's record for coaches in 1998 when he guided the Detroit Red Wings to a second consecutive Stanley Cup championship. The victory gave Bowman his eighth title as a coach and the ninth of his career including his victory as director of player development with the Pittsburgh Penguins in 1991. Bowman, who is also the all-time coaching leader in both regular-season and playoff victories, is the first coach to win the Stanley Cup with three different teams.

Bowman began his NHL coaching career with the St. Louis Blues and led the team to the Stanley Cup finals three years in a row from 1968 to 1970. He was then appointed head coach of the Montreal Canadiens and led the team to five Stanley Cup titles in eight years.

Following an eight-season term as the general manager of the Buffalo Sabres, and a brief stint as a commentator for CBC Television, Bowman joined the Pittsburgh Penguins as director of player development, but returned to coaching when head coach Bob Johnson became ill in September, 1991. Bowman was elected to the Hockey Hall of Fame as a builder in 1991.

NHL Coaching Record

		Regular Season					Playoffs			
Season	Team	Games	W	L	T	%	Games	W	L	%
1967-68	St. Louis	58	23	21	14	.517	18	8	10	.444
1968-69	St. Louis	76	37	25	14	.579	12	8	4	.667
1969-70	St. Louis	76	37	27	12	.566	16	8	8	.500
1970-71	St. Louis	28	13	10	5	.554	6	2	4	.333
1971-72	Montreal	78	46	16	16	.692	6	2	4	.333
1972-73	Montreal	78	52	10	16	.769	17	12	5	.706*
1973-74	Montreal	78	45	24	9	.635	6	2	4	.333
1974-75	Montreal	80	47	14	19	.706	11	6	5	.545
1975-76	Montreal	80	58	11	11	.794	13	12	1	.923*
1976-77	Montreal	80	60	8	12	.825	14	12	2	.857*
1977-78	Montreal	80	59	10	11	.806	15	12	3	.800*
1978-79	Montreal	80	52	17	11	.719	16	12	4	.750*
1979-80	Buffalo	80	47	17	16	.688	14	9	5	.643
1981-82	Buffalo	35	18	10	7	.614	4	1	3	.250
1982-83	Buffalo	80	38	29	13	.556	10	6	4	.600
1983-84	Buffalo	80	48	25	7	.644	3	0	3	.000
1984-85	Buffalo	80	38	28	14	.563	5	2	3	.400
1985-86	Buffalo	37	18	18	1	.500	....	....	....	....
1986-87	Buffalo	12	3	7	2	.333	....	....	....	....
1991-92	Pittsburgh	80	39	32	9	.544	21	16	5	.762*
1992-93	Pittsburgh	84	56	21	7	.708	12	7	5	.583
1993-94	Detroit	84	46	30	8	.595	7	3	4	.429
1994-95	Detroit	48	33	11	4	.729	18	12	6	.667
1995-96	Detroit	82	62	13	7	.799	19	10	9	.526
1996-97	Detroit	82	38	26	18	.573	20	16	4	.800*
1997-98	Detroit	82	44	23	15	.628	22	16	6	.727*
1998-99	Detroit	77	39	32	6	.545	10	6	4	.600
	NHL Totals	**1895**	**1096**	**515**	**284**	**.653**	**315**	**200**	**115**	**.635**

* Stanley Cup win.

1998-99 Scoring

* – rookie

Regular Season

Pos	#	Player	Team	GP	G	A	Pts	+/–	PIM	PP	SH	GW	GT	S	%
C	19	Steve Yzerman	DET	80	29	45	74	8	42	13	2	4	0	231	12.6
C	91	Sergei Fedorov	DET	77	26	37	63	9	66	6	2	3	0	224	11.6
C	8	Igor Larionov	DET	75	14	49	63	13	48	4	2	2	1	83	16.9
L	14	Brendan Shanahan	DET	81	31	27	58	2	123	5	0	5	0	288	10.8
L	13	Vyacheslav Kozlov	DET	79	29	29	58	10	45	6	1	4	2	209	13.9
D	5	Nicklas Lidstrom	DET	81	14	43	57	14	14	6	2	3	0	205	6.8
D	55	Larry Murphy	DET	80	10	42	52	21	42	5	1	2	0	168	6.0
L	71	Wendel Clark	T.B.	65	28	14	42	–25	35	11	0	2	1	171	16.4
			DET	12	4	2	6	1	2	0	0	1	0	44	9.1
			TOTAL	77	32	16	48	–24	37	11	0	3	1	215	14.9
R	25	Darren McCarty	DET	69	14	26	40	10	108	6	0	1	1	140	10.0
D	24	Chris Chelios	CHI	65	8	26	34	–4	89	2	1	0	1	172	4.7
			DET	10	1	1	2	5	4	1	0	1	0	15	6.7
			TOTAL	75	9	27	36	1	93	3	1	1	1	187	4.8
L	96	Tomas Holmstrom	DET	82	13	21	34	–11	69	5	0	4	0	100	13.0
R	20	Martin Lapointe	DET	77	16	13	29	7	141	7	1	4	0	153	10.5
R	17	Doug Brown	DET	80	9	19	28	5	42	3	1	1	0	180	5.0
C	33	Kris Draper	DET	80	4	14	18	2	79	0	1	1	0	78	5.1
L	18	Kirk Maltby	DET	53	8	6	14	–6	34	0	1	2	0	76	10.5
R	11	Mathieu Dandenault	DET	75	4	10	14	17	59	0	0	0	0	94	4.3
C	23 *	Stacy Roest	DET	59	4	8	12	–7	14	0	0	1	0	50	8.0
D	2	Ulf Samuelsson	NYR	67	4	8	12	6	93	0	0	0	0	37	10.8
			DET	4	0	0	0	–1	6	0	0	0	0	2	0.0
			TOTAL	71	4	8	12	5	99	0	0	0	0	39	10.3
D	27	Aaron Ward	DET	60	3	8	11	–5	52	0	0	0	0	46	6.5
D	34	Jamie Macoun	DET	69	1	10	11	–1	36	0	0	0	0	62	1.6
D	15	Todd Gill	STL	28	2	3	5	–6	16	1	0	0	1	36	5.6
			DET	23	2	2	4	–4	11	0	0	1	0	25	8.0
			TOTAL	51	4	5	9	–10	27	1	0	1	1	61	6.6
R	26	Joey Kocur	DET	39	2	5	7	0	87	0	0	0	0	20	10.0
D	4	Uwe Krupp	DET	22	3	2	5	0	6	0	0	0	0	32	9.4
G	30	Chris Osgood	DET	63	0	3	3	0	8	0	0	0	0	0	0.0
C	41	Brent Gilchrist	DET	5	1	0	1	–1	0	0	0	1	0	4	25.0
R	85	Petr Klima	DET	13	1	0	1	–3	4	0	0	1	0	12	8.3
D	3	Doug Houda	DET	3	0	1	1	–2	0	0	0	0	0	1	0.0
D	28 *	Yan Golubovsky	DET	17	0	1	1	4	16	0	0	0	0	10	0.0
C	21 *	Darryl Laplante	DET	3	0	0	0	0	0	0	0	0	0	0	0.0
L	22 *	Philippe Audet	DET	4	0	0	0	–2	0	0	0	0	0	3	0.0
G	38 *	Norm Maracle	DET	16	0	0	0	0	0	0	0	0	0	0	0.0
G	40	Bill Ranford	T.B.	32	0	0	0	0	2	0	0	0	0	0	0.0
			DET	4	0	0	0	0	0	0	0	0	0	0	0.0
			TOTAL	36	0	0	0	0	2	0	0	0	0	0	0.0

Goaltending

No.	Goaltender	GPI	Mins	Avg	W	L	T	EN	SO	GA	SA	S%
40	Bill Ranford	4	244	1.97	3	0	1	0	0	8	98	.918
38	* Norm Maracle	16	821	2.27	6	5	2	1	0	31	379	.918
30	Chris Osgood	63	3691	2.42	34	25	4	4	3	149	1654	.910
31	Kevin Hodson	4	175	3.09	0	2	0	0	0	9	79	.886
	Totals	**82**	**4962**	**2.44**	**43**	**32**	**7**	**5**	**3**	**202**	**2215**	**.909**

Playoffs

Pos	#	Player	Team	GP	G	A	Pts	+/–	PIM	PP	SH	GW	OT	S	%
C	19	Steve Yzerman	DET	10	9	4	13	2	0	4	0	2	0	41	22.0
D	5	Nicklas Lidstrom	DET	10	2	9	11	0	4	2	0	0	0	29	6.9
L	14	Brendan Shanahan	DET	10	3	7	10	2	6	1	0	1	0	31	9.7
C	91	Sergei Fedorov	DET	10	1	8	9	3	8	0	0	0	0	38	2.6
L	13	Vyacheslav Kozlov	DET	10	6	1	7	–3	4	3	0	0	0	28	21.4
L	96	Tomas Holmstrom	DET	10	4	3	7	2	4	2	0	1	0	26	15.4
L	71	Wendel Clark	DET	10	2	3	5	–1	10	1	0	0	0	29	6.9
R	17	Doug Brown	DET	10	2	2	4	0	4	1	0	1	0	15	13.3
D	24	Chris Chelios	DET	10	0	4	4	–6	14	0	0	0	0	21	0.0
D	2	Ulf Samuelsson	DET	9	0	3	3	1	10	0	0	0	0	6	0.0
R	25	Darren McCarty	DET	10	1	1	2	–1	23	0	0	0	0	15	6.7
C	8	Igor Larionov	DET	7	0	2	2	–1	0	0	0	0	0	3	0.0
D	55	Larry Murphy	DET	10	0	2	2	2	8	0	0	0	0	14	0.0
R	20	Martin Lapointe	DET	10	0	2	2	0	20	0	0	0	0	14	0.0
L	18	Kirk Maltby	DET	10	1	0	1	–2	8	0	0	1	1	13	7.7
D	15	Todd Gill	DET	2	0	1	1	0	0	0	0	0	0	3	0.0
D	27	Aaron Ward	DET	8	0	1	1	2	8	0	0	0	0	6	0.0
C	33	Kris Draper	DET	10	0	1	1	–1	6	0	0	0	0	9	0.0
R	11	Mathieu Dandenault	DET	10	0	1	1	0	0	0	0	0	0	15	0.0
D	34	Jamie Macoun	DET	1	0	0	0	–1	0	0	0	0	0	1	0.0
G	38 *	Norm Maracle	DET	2	0	0	0	0	0	0	0	0	0	0	0.0
C	41	Brent Gilchrist	DET	3	0	0	0	–2	0	0	0	0	0	2	0.0
G	40	Bill Ranford	DET	4	0	0	0	0	0	0	0	0	0	0	0.0
G	30	Chris Osgood	DET	6	0	0	0	0	0	0	0	0	0	0	0.0

Goaltending

No.	Goaltender	GPI	Mins	Avg	W	L	EN	SO	GA	SA	S%
30	Chris Osgood	6	358	2.35	4	2	0	1	14	172	.919
38	* Norm Maracle	2	58	3.10	0	0	0	0	3	22	.864
40	Bill Ranford	4	183	3.28	2	2	0	1	10	105	.905
	Totals	**10**	**604**	**2.68**	**6**	**4**	**0**	**2**	**27**	**299**	**.910**

Club Records

Team

(Figures in brackets for season records are games played; records for fewest points, wins, ties, losses, goals, goals against are for 70 or more games)

Record		
Most Points	**131**	1995-96 (82)
Most Wins	***62**	1995-96 (82)
Most Ties	**18**	1952-53 (70), 1980-81 (80), 1996-97 (82)
Most Losses	**57**	1985-86 (80)
Most Goals	**369**	1992-93 (84)
Most Goals Against	**415**	1985-86 (80)
Fewest Points	**40**	1985-86 (80)
Fewest Wins	**16**	1976-77 (80)
Fewest Ties	**4**	1966-67 (70)
Fewest Losses	**13**	1950-51 (70), 1995-96 (82)
Fewest Goals	**167**	1958-59 (70)
Fewest Goals Against	**132**	1953-54 (70)
Longest Winning Streak		
Overall	**9**	Mar. 3-21/51, Feb. 27-Mar. 20/55, Dec. 12-31/95, Mar. 3-22/96
Home	**14**	Jan. 21-Mar. 25/65
Away	**7**	Mar. 25-Apr. 14/95, Feb. 18-Mar. 20/96
Longest Undefeated Streak		
Overall	**15**	Nov. 27-Dec. 28/52 (8 wins, 7 ties)
Home	**18**	Nov. 19/31-Feb.28/32 (13 wins, 5 ties), Dec. 26/54-Mar. 20/55 (13 wins, 5 ties)
Away	**15**	Oct. 18-Dec. 20/51 (10 wins, 5 ties)
Longest Losing Streak		
Overall	**14**	Feb. 24-Mar. 25/82
Home	**7**	Feb. 20-Mar. 25/82
Away	**14**	Oct. 19-Dec. 21/66
Longest Winless Streak		
Overall	**19**	Feb. 26-Apr. 3/77 (18 losses, 1 tie)
Home	**10**	Dec. 11/85-Jan. 18/86 (9 losses, 1 tie)
Away	**26**	Dec. 15/76-Apr. 3/77 (23 losses, 3 ties)
Most Shutouts, Season	**13**	1953-54 (70)
Most. PIM, Season	**2,393**	1985-86 (80)
Most Goals, Game	**15**	Jan. 23/44 (NYR 0 at Det. 15)

Individual

Record		
Most Seasons	**25**	Gordie Howe
Most Games	**1,687**	Gordie Howe
Most Goals, Career	**786**	Gordie Howe
Most Assists, Career	**1,023**	Gordie Howe
Most Points, Career	**1,809**	Gordie Howe (786G, 1,023A)
Most PIM, Career	**2,090**	Bob Probert
Most Shutouts, Career	**85**	Terry Sawchuk
Longest Consecutive Games Streak	**548**	Alex Delvecchio (Dec. 13/56-Nov. 11/64)
Most Goals, Season	**65**	Steve Yzerman (1988-89)
Most Assists, Season	**90**	Steve Yzerman (1988-89)
Most Points, Season	**155**	Steve Yzerman (1988-89; 65G, 90A)
Most PIM, Season	**398**	Bob Probert (1987-88)
Most Points, Defenseman, Season	**77**	Paul Coffey (1993-94; 14G, 63A)
Most Points, Center, Season	**155**	Steve Yzerman (1988-89; 65G, 90A)
Most Points, Right Wing, Season	**103**	Gordie Howe (1968-69; 44G, 59A)
Most Points, Left Wing, Season	**105**	John Ogrodnick (1984-85; 55G, 50A)
Most Points, Rookie, Season	**87**	Steve Yzerman (1983-84; 39G, 48A)
Most Shutouts, Season	**12**	Terry Sawchuk (1951-52, 1953-54, 1954-55), Glenn Hall (1955-56)
Most Goals, Game	**6**	Syd Howe (Feb. 3/44)
Most Assists, Game	***7**	Billy Taylor (Mar. 16/47)
Most Points, Game	**7**	Carl Liscombe (Nov. 5/42; 3G, 4A), Don Grosso (Feb. 3/44; 1G, 6A), Billy Taylor (Mar. 16/47; 7A)

* NHL Record.

Retired Numbers

1	Terry Sawchuk	1949-55, 57-64, 68-69
6	Larry Aurie	1927-1939
7	Ted Lindsay	1944-57, 64-65
9	Gordie Howe	1946-1971
10	Alex Delvecchio	1951-1973
12	Sid Abel	1938-43, 45-52

All-time Record vs. Other Clubs

Regular Season

	At Home							On Road							Total						
	GP	W	L	T	GF	GA	PTS	GP	W	L	T	GF	GA	PTS	GP	W	L	T	GF	GA	PTS
Anaheim	12	8	1	3	47	30	19	12	7	3	2	42	26	16	24	15	4	5	89	56	35
Boston	282	153	77	52	946	711	358	283	88	152	43	752	998	219	565	241	229	95	1698	1709	577
Buffalo	51	28	18	5	188	151	61	49	9	32	8	138	217	26	100	37	50	13	326	368	87
Calgary	49	25	15	9	185	152	59	50	16	28	6	157	201	38	99	41	43	15	347	353	97
Carolina	27	14	7	6	104	74	34	26	9	16	1	69	91	19	53	23	23	7	173	168	53
Chicago	322	199	93	30	1106	780	428	324	125	148	51	902	973	301	646	324	241	81	2008	1762	729
Colorado	30	17	12	1	111	95	35	31	10	17	4	106	120	24	61	27	29	5	217	215	59
Dallas	96	49	33	14	379	314	112	96	31	50	15	286	347	77	192	80	83	29	665	661	189
Edmonton	34	17	14	3	129	123	37	34	13	16	5	137	147	31	68	30	30	8	266	270	68
Florida	5	3	1	1	21	15	7	5	3	1	1	17	11	7	10	6	2	2	38	26	14
Los Angeles	69	29	29	11	271	250	69	70	20	37	13	219	289	53	139	49	66	24	490	539	122
Montreal	278	129	96	53	797	709	311	278	65	170	43	628	985	173	556	194	266	96	1425	1694	484
Nashville	3	3	0	0	11	5	6	3	2	1	0	12	8	4	6	5	1	0	23	13	10
New Jersey	36	21	13	2	149	122	44	37	10	18	9	103	130	29	73	31	31	11	252	252	73
NY Islanders	41	22	17	2	147	130	46	42	16	23	3	124	155	35	83	38	40	5	271	285	81
NY Rangers	282	161	76	45	990	694	367	280	89	133	58	720	862	236	562	250	209	103	1710	1556	603
Ottawa	6	3	3	0	20	13	6	6	3	2	1	18	17	7	12	6	5	1	38	30	13
Philadelphia	55	27	18	10	195	175	64	56	13	32	11	166	226	37	111	40	50	21	361	401	101
Phoenix	41	21	15	5	168	143	47	39	13	15	11	125	125	37	80	34	30	16	293	268	84
Pittsburgh	62	38	12	12	240	169	88	61	15	42	4	180	270	34	123	53	54	16	420	439	122
St. Louis	96	41	38	17	350	303	99	97	27	54	16	267	348	70	193	68	92	33	617	651	169
San Jose	15	14	1	0	70	25	28	16	9	5	2	70	51	20	31	23	6	2	140	76	48
Tampa Bay	8	7	1	0	35	16	14	10	8	1	1	55	33	17	18	15	2	1	90	49	31
Toronto	315	164	105	46	942	773	374	312	104	163	45	838	1035	253	627	268	268	91	1780	1808	627
Vancouver	56	34	15	7	240	163	75	55	21	25	9	179	206	51	111	55	40	16	419	369	126
Washington	43	19	13	11	153	125	49	42	18	20	4	133	158	40	85	37	33	15	286	283	89
Defunct Clubs	141	76	40	25	430	307	177	141	49	63	29	364	375	127	282	125	103	54	794	682	304
Totals	**2455**	**1322**	**763**	**370**	**8424**	**6576**	**3014**	**2455**	**793**	**1267**	**395**	**6807**	**8407**	**1981**	**4910**	**2115**	**2030**	**765**	**15231**	**14983**	**4995**

Playoffs

	Series	W	L	GP	W	L	T	GF	GA	Last Mtg.	Round	Result
Anaheim	2	2	0	8	8	0	0	30	14	1999	CQF	W 4-0
Boston	7	3	4	33	14	19	0	98	96	1957	SF	L 1-4
Calgary	1	1	0	2	2	0	0	8	5	1978	PR	W 2-0
Chicago	14	6	8	69	31	38	0	190	210	1995	CF	W 4-1
Colorado	3	1	2	18	8	10	0	46	53	1999	CSF	L 2-4
Dallas	3	3	0	18	12	6	0	55	40	1998	CF	W 4-2
Edmonton	2	0	2	10	2	8	0	26	39	1988	CF	L 1-4
Montreal	12	7	5	62	29	33	0	149	161	1978	QF	L 1-4
New Jersey	1	0	1	4	0	4	0	7	16	1995	F	L 0-4
NY Rangers	5	4	1	23	13	10	0	57	49	1950	F	W 4-3
Philadelphia	1	1	0	4	4	0	0	16	6	1997	F	W 4-0
Phoenix	2	2	0	12	8	4	0	44	28	1998	CQF	W 4-2
St. Louis	6	4	2	35	20	15	0	111	92	1998	CSF	W 4-2
San Jose	2	1	1	11	7	4	0	51	27	1995	CSF	W 4-0
Toronto	23	11	12	117	59	58	0	321	311	1993	DSF	L 3-4
Washington	1	1	0	4	4	0	0	13	7	1998	F	W 4-0
Defunct Clubs	4	3	1	10	7	2	1	21	13			
Totals	**89**	**50**	**39**	**440**	**228**	**211**	**1**	**1243**	**1167**			

Playoff Results 1999-95

Year	Round	Opponent	Result	GF	GA
1999	CSF	Colorado	L 2-4	14	21
	CQF	Anaheim	W 4-0	17	6
1998	**F**	**Washington**	**W 4-0**	**13**	**7**
	CF	Dallas	W 4-2	15	11
	CSF	St. Louis	W 4-2	23	13
	CQF	Phoenix	W 4-2	24	18
1997	**F**	**Philadelphia**	**W 4-0**	**16**	**6**
	CF	Colorado	W 4-2	16	12
	CSF	Anaheim	W 4-0	13	8
	CQF	St. Louis	W 4-2	13	12
1996	CF	Colorado	L 2-4	16	20
	CSF	St. Louis	W 4-3	22	16
	CQF	Winnipeg	W 4-2	20	10
1995	F	New Jersey	L 0-4	7	16
	CF	Chicago	W 4-1	13	12
	CSF	San Jose	W 4-0	24	6
	CQF	Dallas	W 4-1	17	10

Abbreviations: Round: F – Final; **CF** – conference final; **CSF** – conference semi-final; **CQF** – conference quarter-final; **DSF** – division semi-final; **SF** – semi-final; **QF** – quarter-final; **PR** – preliminary round.

Calgary totals include Atlanta Flames, 1972-73 to 1979-80.
Carolina totals include Hartford, 1979-80 to 1996-97.
Colorado totals include Quebec, 1979-80 to 1994-95.
Dallas totals include Minnesota, 1967-68 to 1992-93.
New Jersey totals include Kansas City, 1974-75 to 1975-76, and Colorado Rockies, 1976-77 to 1981-82.
Phoenix totals include Winnipeg, 1979-80 to 1995-96.

1998-99 Results

Month	Day		Opponent	Score
Oct.	10	at	Toronto	1-2
	13	at	Washington	3-2
	16		St. Louis	4-1
	18		Calgary	2-0
	21		Nashville	5-2
	23		Toronto	3-5
	24	at	Montreal	3-0
	28	at	Florida	7-2
	29	at	St. Louis	1-3
	31	at	Dallas	2-3
Nov.	3		Calgary	2-5
	6	at	Phoenix	1-3
	8	at	Anaheim	3-2
	11		St. Louis	6-2
	13		Dallas	1-5
	16	at	Calgary	3-5
	18	at	Edmonton	6-2
	21	at	Vancouver	4-2
	25		Anaheim	5-2
	27		Vancouver	7-1
	29		San Jose	4-1
Dec.	2	at	Colorado	2-4
	4	at	San Jose	2-2
	5	at	Los Angeles	4-3
	8		Chicago	3-2
	11		Edmonton	3-2
	12	at	Carolina	0-3
	16		Boston	5-3
	18		Dallas	1-3
	19	at	Boston	1-4
	22		Phoenix	2-6
	23	at	Nashville	3-5
	26	at	St. Louis	3-4
	28		St. Louis	4-4
	31		Toronto	2-4
Jan.	2		Chicago	5-2
	3	at	Chicago	3-1
	6		Ottawa	0-2
	9		Colorado	3-2
	10	at	Ottawa	1-4
	12		Montreal	5-1
	14		Nashville	2-1
	16	at	Vancouver	2-2
	17	at	Edmonton	1-4
	19	at	Calgary	1-3
	21		Carolina	4-1
	26	at	Nashville	4-1
	30		NY Rangers	2-3
Feb.	1	at	New Jersey	2-2
	3		NY Islanders	5-1
	5		Colorado	1-3
	7	at	Pittsburgh	1-2
	9	at	Nashville	5-2
	11		Edmonton	4-2
	12	at	Chicago	2-1
	14	at	NY Rangers	4-2
	17		San Jose	3-1
	19		New Jersey	3-1
	21	at	Buffalo	4-4
	24		Los Angeles	2-3
	26		Florida	5-5
	27	at	NY Islanders	1-3
Mar.	5	at	Phoenix	7-2
	7	at	Anaheim	1-3
	9	at	Los Angeles	2-4
	12	at	San Jose	0-2
	14	at	Colorado	3-1
	17		Phoenix	3-4
	19	at	Tampa Bay	5-3
	21	at	Philadelphia	4-5
	24		Buffalo	2-1
	26		Tampa Bay	6-1
	28		Philadelphia	3-2
	31		Los Angeles	2-1
Apr.	2		Chicago	5-3
	4	at	Dallas	3-0
	5		Anaheim	3-2
	7		Vancouver	6-1
	9	at	St. Louis	1-1
	11		Pittsburgh	0-3
	14		Nashville	4-2
	17	at	Chicago	2-3

Entry Draft
Selections 1999-85

1999 Pick		**1994** Pick		**1990** Pick		**1987** Pick	
120	Jari Toulsa	23	Yan Golubovsky	3	Keith Primeau	11	Yves Racine
149	Andrei Maximenko	49	Mathieu Dandenault	45	Vyacheslav Kozlov	32	Gordon Kruppke
181	Kent McDonell	75	Sean Gillam	66	Stewart Malgunas	41	Bob Wilkie
210	Henrik Zetterberg	114	Frederic Deschenes	87	Tony Burns	52	Dennis Holland
238	Anton Borodkin	127	Doug Battaglia	108	Claude Barthe	74	Mark Reimer
266	Ken Davis	153	Pavel Agarkov	129	Jason York	95	Radomir Brazda
		205	Jason Elliot	150	Wes McCauley	116	Sean Clifford
1998 Pick		231	Jeff Mikesch	171	Anthony Gruba	137	Mike Gober
25	Jiri Fischer	257	Tomas Holmstrom	192	Travis Tucker	158	Kevin Scott
55	Ryan Barnes	283	Toivo Suursoo	213	Brett Larson	179	Mikko Haapakoski
56	Tomek Valtonen			234	John Hendry	200	Darin Bannister
84	Jake McCracken	**1993** Pick				221	Craig Quinlan
111	Brent Hobday	22	Anders Eriksson	**1989** Pick		242	Tomas Jansson
142	Calle Steen	48	Jonathan Coleman	11	Mike Sillinger		
151	Adam DeLeeuw	74	Kevin Hilton	32	Bob Boughner	**1986** Pick	
171	Pavel Datsyuk	97	John Jakopin	53	Nicklas Lidstrom	1	Joe Murphy
198	Jeremy Goetzinger	100	Benoit Larose	74	Sergei Fedorov	23	Adam Graves
226	David Petrasek	126	Norm Maracle	95	Shawn McCosh	43	Derek Mayer
256	Petja Pietilainen	152	Tim Spitzig	116	Dallas Drake	64	Tim Cheveldae
		178	Yuri Yeresko	137	Scott Zygulski	85	Johan Garpenlov
1997 Pick		204	Vitezslav Skuta	158	Andy Suhy	106	Jay Stark
49	Yuri Butsayev	230	Ryan Shanahan	179	Bob Jones	127	Per Djoos
76	Petr Sykora	256	James Kosecki	200	Greg Bignell	148	Dean Morton
102	Quintin Laing	282	Gordon Hunt	204	Rick Judson	169	Marc Potvin
129	John Wikstrom			221	Vladimir Konstantinov	190	Scott King
157	B.J. Young	**1992** Pick		242	Joseph Frederick	211	Tom Bissett
186	Mike Laceby	22	Curtis Bowen	246	Jason Glickman	232	Peter Ekroth
213	Steve Wilejto	46	Darren McCarty				
239	Greg Willers	70	Sylvain Cloutier	**1988** Pick		**1985** Pick	
		118	Mike Sullivan	17	Kory Kocur	8	Brent Fedyk
1996 Pick		142	Jason MacDonald	38	Serge Anglehart	29	Jeff Sharples
26	Jesse Wallin	166	Greg Scott	47	Guy Dupuis	50	Steve Chiasson
52	Aren Miller	183	Justin Krall	59	Petr Hrbek	71	Mark Gowans
108	Johan Forsander	189	C.J. Denomme	80	Sheldon Kennedy	92	Chris Luongo
135	Michal Podolka	214	Jeff Walker	143	Kelly Hurd	113	Randy McKay
144	Magnus Nilsson	238	Daniel McGillis	164	Brian McCormack	134	Thomas Bjur
162	Alexandre Jacques	262	Ryan Bach	185	Jody Praznik	155	Mike Luckraft
189	Colin Beardsmore			206	Glen Goodall	176	Rob Schenna
215	Craig Stahl	**1991** Pick		227	Darren Colbourne	197	Erik Hamalainen
241	Evgeniy Afanasiev	10	Martin Lapointe	248	Donald Stone	218	Bo Svanberg
		32	Jamie Pushor			239	Mikael Lindman
1995 Pick		54	Chris Osgood				
26	Maxim Kuznetsov	76	Michael Knuble				
52	Philippe Audet	98	Dmitri Motkov				
58	Darryl Laplante	142	Igor Malykhin				
104	Anatoly Ustugov	186	Jim Bermingham				
125	Chad Wilchynski	208	Jason Firth				
126	David Arsenault	230	Bart Turner				
156	Tyler Perry	252	Andrew Miller				
182	Per Eklund						
208	Andrei Samokvalov						
234	David Engblom						

General Manager

HOLLAND, KEN
General Manager, Detroit Red Wings. Born in Vernon, B.C., Nov. 10, 1955.

Entering his 16th year with the Detroit Red Wings, Ken Holland began his tenure as the club's general manager after serving as assistant general manager for the previous three seasons. Holland was elevated to his present position July 18, 1997.

In his new and expanded role, he oversees all aspects of hockey operations including all matters relating to player personnel, development, contract negotiations and player movements. Holland also continues to be Detroit's point person at the NHL Entry Draft, as he has for the past eight years. In that capacity, he was instrumental in selecting some of Detroit's best young talent, including Vyacheslav Kozlov, Darren McCarty, Chris Osgood and Martin Lapointe, along with several other top prospects.

Holland has deftly handled several different front-office duties for the club over the past 15 years. At the conclusion of his playing days as a goaltender, spending most of his pro career at the American Hockey League level, Holland began his off-ice career in 1985 as a western Canada scout followed by five years as amateur scouting director before promotions leading to his current position as general manager.

A native of Vernon, BC, Holland played in the junior ranks for Medicine Hat (WHL) in 1974-75. He was Toronto's 13th pick (188th overall) in the 1975 draft but never saw action with the Maple Leafs. Holland twice signed with NHL teams as a free agent — in 1980 with Hartford and 1983 with Detroit. He spent most of his pro career with AHL clubs in Binghamton and Springfield, along with Adirondack, but did appear in four NHL games, making his debut with Hartford in 1980-81 and playing three contests for Detroit in 1983-84.

Ken and wife Cindy have four children, Brad, Julie, Rachel and Greg, and reside in suburban Detroit.

Club Directory

Joe Louis Arena
600 Civic Center Drive
Detroit, Michigan 48226
Phone **313/396-7544**
FAX PR: 313/567-0296
www.detroitredwings.com
Capacity: 19,983

Owner	Mike Ilitch
Owner/Secretary-Treasurer	Marian Ilitch
Vice Presidents	Atanas Ilitch, Christopher Ilitch
Senior Vice-President	Jim Devellano
General Manager	Ken Holland
Assistant General Manager	Jim Nill
Head Coach	Scotty Bowman
Associate Coaches	Barry Smith, Dave Lewis
Goaltending Consultant	Jim Bedard
NHL Scout	Dan Belisle
Pro Scout/Minor League Player Development	Mark Howe
Eastern Scout	Joe McDonnell
Western Scout	Mark Leach
Director of European Scouting	Hakan Andersson
Czech, Slovak and Russian Scout	Vladimir Havluj
Scouts	Marty Stein, Bruce Southern
Executive Assistant	Nancy Beard
Administrative Assistant	Kristin Armstrong
Office Assistant	David Kolb
Director of Finance	Paul McDonald
Accounting Assistant	Cathy Witzke
Athletic Therapist	John Wharton
Assistant Athletic Therapist	Piet Van Zant
Equipment Manager	Paul Boyer
Assistant Equipment Manager	Tim Abbott
Assistant Equipment Manager	Rob Gagne
General Manger – Joe Louis Arena	Randy Lippe
Director of Operations	Tim Padgett
Senior Director of Merchandise	Denny Callahan
Senior Director of Box Office Operations	Bob Kerlin
Senior Director of Advertising Sales/ General Sales Manager	Bill Ley
Manager, Signage, Print and Promotions	Jeffrey Ajluni
Account Executives	Scott Miller, Andy Loughnane, Mary Greener
Broadcast Coordinator	Lori Mariles
Senior Director of Marketing and Communications	Ted Speers
Marketing Manager	Kevin Vaughn
Marketing Coordinator	Lori Shiels
Marketing Assistant	Erin Crawford
Season Ticket Sales Manager	Chuck Smith
Group Sales Coordinator	Lisa Maselli
Director of Public Relations	John Hahn
Community Relations Manager	Karen Davis
Public Relations Coordinator	Michael Kuta
Public Relations Assistant	Mark Kelly
Team Physicians	Dr. John Finley, D.O., Dr. David Collon, M.D.
Team Dentist	Dr. C.J. Regula, D.M.D.

General Managers' History

Art Duncan and Duke Keats, 1926-27; Jack Adams, 1927-28 to 1961-62; Sid Abel, 1962-63 to 1969-70; Sid Abel and Ned Harkness, 1970-71; Ned Harkness, 1971-72 to 1973-74; Alex Delvecchio, 1974-75, 1975-76; Alex Delvecchio and Ted Lindsay, 1976-77; Ted Lindsay, 1977-78 to 1979-80; Jimmy Skinner, 1980-81, 1981-82; Jim Devellano, 1982-83 to 1989-90; Bryan Murray, 1990-91 to 1993-94; Jim Devellano (Senior Vice President), 1994-95 to 1996-97; Ken Holland, 1997-98 to date.

Coaching History

Art Duncan, 1926-27; Jack Adams, 1927-28 to 1946-47; Tommy Ivan, 1947-48 to 1953-54; Jimmy Skinner, 1954-55 to 1956-57; Jimmy Skinner and Sid Abel, 1957-58; Sid Abel, 1958-59 to 1967-68; Bill Gadsby, 1968-69; Bill Gadsby and Sid Abel, 1969-70; Ned Harkness and Doug Barkley, 1970-71; Doug Barkley and John Wilson, 1971-72; John Wilson, 1972-73; Ted Garvin and Alex Delvecchio, 1973-74; Alex Delvecchio, 1974-75; Doug Barkley and Alex Delvecchio, 1975-76; Alex Delvecchio and Larry Wilson, 1976-77; Bobby Kromm, 1977-78, 1978-79; Bobby Kromm and Ted Lindsay, 1979-80; Ted Lindsay and Wayne Maxner, 1980-81; Wayne Maxner and Billy Dea, 1981-82; Nick Polano, 1982-83 to 1984-85; Harry Neale and Brad Park, 1985-86; Jacques Demers, 1986-87 to 1989-90; Bryan Murray, 1990-91 to 1992-93; Scotty Bowman, 1993-94 to 1997-98; Dave Lewis, Barry Smith (co-coaches) and Scotty Bowman, 1998-99; Scotty Bowman, 1999-2000.

Captains' History

Art Duncan, 1926-27; Reg Noble, 1927-28 to 1929-30; George Hay, 1930-31; Carson Cooper, 1931-32; Larry Aurie, 1932-33; Herbie Lewis, 1933-34; Ebbie Goodfellow, 1934-35; Doug Young, 1935-36 to 1937-38; Ebbie Goodfellow, 1938-39 to 1940-41; Ebbie Goodfellow and Syd Howe, 1941-42; Sid Abel, 1942-43; Mud Bruneteau, Bill Hollett (co-captains), 1943-44; Bill Hollett and Sid Abel, 1945-46; Sid Abel, 1946-47 to 1951-52; Ted Lindsay, 1952-53 to 1955-56; Red Kelly, 1956-57, 1957-58; Gordie Howe, 1958-59 to 1961-62; Alex Delvecchio, 1962-63 to 1972-73; Alex Delvecchio, Nick Libett, Red Berenson, Gary Bergman, Ted Harris, Mickey Redmond and Larry Johnston, 1973-74; Marcel Dionne, 1974-75; Danny Grant and Terry Harper, 1975-76; Danny Grant and Dennis Polonich, 1976-77; Dan Maloney and Dennis Hextall, 1977-78; Dennis Hextall, Nick Libett and Paul Woods, 1978-79; Dale McCourt, 1979-80; Errol Thompson and Reed Larson, 1980-81; Reed Larson, 1981-82; Danny Gare, 1982-83 to 1985-86; Steve Yzerman, 1986-87 to date.

Edmonton Oilers

1998-99 Results: 33W-37L-12T 78PTS. Second, Northwest Division

Year-by-Year Record

Season	GP	Home W	Home L	Home T	Road W	Road L	Road T	Overall W	Overall L	Overall T	GF	GA	Pts.	Finished		Playoff Result
1998-99	82	17	19	5	16	18	7	33	37	12	230	226	78	2nd,	Northwest Div.	Lost Conf. Quarter-Final
1997-98	82	20	16	5	15	21	5	35	37	10	215	224	80	3rd,	Pacific Div.	Lost Conf. Semi-Final
1996-97	82	21	16	4	15	21	5	36	37	9	252	247	81	3rd,	Pacific Div.	Lost Conf. Semi-Final
1995-96	82	15	21	5	15	23	3	30	44	8	240	304	68	5th,	Pacific Div.	Out of Playoffs
1994-95	48	11	12	1	6	15	3	17	27	4	136	183	38	5th,	Pacific Div.	Out of Playoffs
1993-94	84	17	22	3	8	23	11	25	45	14	261	305	64	6th,	Pacific Div.	Out of Playoffs
1992-93	84	16	21	5	10	29	3	26	50	8	242	337	60	5th,	Smythe Div.	Out of Playoffs
1991-92	80	22	13	5	14	21	5	36	34	10	295	297	82	3rd,	Smythe Div.	Lost Conf. Championship
1990-91	80	22	15	3	15	22	3	37	37	6	272	272	80	3rd,	Smythe Div.	Lost Conf. Championship
1989-90	**80**	**23**	**11**	**6**	**15**	**17**	**8**	**38**	**28**	**14**	**315**	**283**	**90**	**2nd,**	**Smythe Div.**	**Won Stanley Cup**
1988-89	80	21	16	3	17	18	5	38	34	8	325	306	84	3rd,	Smythe Div.	Lost Div. Semi-Final
1987-88	**80**	**28**	**8**	**4**	**16**	**17**	**7**	**44**	**25**	**11**	**363**	**288**	**99**	**2nd,**	**Smythe Div.**	**Won Stanley Cup**
1986-87	**80**	**29**	**6**	**5**	**21**	**18**	**1**	**50**	**24**	**6**	**372**	**284**	**106**	**1st,**	**Smythe Div.**	**Won Stanley Cup**
1985-86	80	32	6	2	24	11	5	56	17	7	426	310	119	1st,	Smythe Div.	Lost Div. Final
1984-85	**80**	**26**	**7**	**7**	**23**	**13**	**4**	**49**	**20**	**11**	**401**	**298**	**109**	**1st,**	**Smythe Div.**	**Won Stanley Cup**
1983-84	**80**	**31**	**5**	**4**	**26**	**13**	**1**	**57**	**18**	**5**	**446**	**314**	**119**	**1st,**	**Smythe Div.**	**Won Stanley Cup**
1982-83	80	25	9	6	22	12	6	47	21	12	424	315	106	1st,	Smythe Div.	Lost Final
1981-82	80	31	5	4	17	12	11	48	17	15	417	295	111	1st,	Smythe Div.	Lost Div. Semi-Final
1980-81	80	17	13	10	12	22	6	29	35	16	328	327	74	4th,	Smythe Div.	Lost Quarter-Final
1979-80	80	17	14	9	11	25	4	28	39	13	301	322	69	4th,	Smythe Div.	Lost Prelim. Round

1999-2000 Schedule

Oct.	Fri.	1	NY Rangers	Fri.	7	Tampa Bay
	Wed.	6	Montreal	Tue.	11	Dallas
	Thu.	7	at San Jose	Fri.	14	Toronto
	Sat.	9	St. Louis	Sun.	16	Detroit
	Wed.	13	Carolina	Wed.	19	Calgary
	Sat.	16	Los Angeles	Sat.	22	Vancouver
	Wed.	20	at Dallas	Mon.	24	Nashville
	Thu.	21	at St. Louis	Tue.	25	at Vancouver
	Sat.	23	at Nashville	Fri.	28	at Tampa Bay
	Tue.	26	Phoenix	Sat.	29	at Florida
	Sun.	31	Nashville	Mon.	31	at Dallas
Nov.	Wed.	3	Florida	Feb. Wed.	2	Chicago
	Fri.	5	St. Louis	Tue.	8	at Montreal
	Sun.	7	at Anaheim	Thu.	10	at Philadelphia
	Tue.	9	at Los Angeles	Fri.	11	at Pittsburgh
	Wed.	10	at Phoenix	Sun.	13	at Buffalo*
	Fri.	12	at St. Louis	Tue.	15	at Nashville
	Sun.	14	at Chicago	Fri.	18	at Calgary
	Sat.	20	Detroit	Sat.	19	Calgary
	Sun.	21	NY Islanders	Mon.	21	Los Angeles
	Wed.	24	Chicago	Wed.	23	Boston
	Fri.	26	at Detroit	Fri.	25	Atlanta
	Sat.	27	at Toronto	Sun.	27	at Anaheim
Dec.	Wed.	1	Colorado	Tue.	29	at Colorado
	Thu.	2	at Vancouver	Mar. Sat.	4	Pittsburgh
	Sat.	4	Vancouver	Tue.	7	Toronto
	Mon.	6	at Chicago	Fri.	10	Colorado
	Wed.	8	at NY Rangers	Sun.	12	at Nashville*
	Thu.	9	at Boston	Mon.	13	at Atlanta
	Sat.	11	at New Jersey*	Wed.	15	at Carolina
	Tue.	14	at NY Islanders	Fri.	17	Ottawa
	Wed.	15	at Detroit	Sun.	19	Calgary
	Fri.	17	Dallas	Wed.	22	Anaheim
	Sun.	19	Ottawa	Sat.	25	Vancouver
	Tue.	21	Washington	Mon.	27	at San Jose
	Thu.	23	at Calgary	Wed.	29	at Colorado
	Mon.	27	Anaheim	Apr. Sat.	1	Phoenix
	Thu.	30	at Los Angeles	Mon.	3	San Jose
Jan.	Sat.	1	at Phoenix	Wed.	5	Colorado
	Mon.	3	at Colorado	Fri.	7	at Vancouver
	Wed.	5	San Jose	Sat.	8	at Calgary

* Denotes afternoon game.

Franchise date: June 22, 1979

NORTHWEST DIVISION

21st NHL Season

Combining toughness and scoring talent, Bill Guerin topped the Oilers with 30 goals, 34 assists and 64 points, while his 133 penalty minutes trailed only Sean Brown's 188. Guerin established new career highs in each of those categories.

1999-2000 Player Personnel

FORWARDS	HT	WT	S	Place of Birth	Date	1998-99 Club
BERANEK, Josef	6-2	195	L	Litvinov, Czech.	10/25/69	Edmonton
CHIMERA, Jason	6-0	180	L	Edmonton, Alta.	5/2/79	Medicine Hat-Brandon
CLEARY, Daniel	6-0	203	L	Carbonear, Nfld.	12/18/78	Chi-Port (AHL)-Hamilton
COMRIE, Paul	5-11	192	L	Edmonton, Alta.	2/7/77	U. of Denver-Hamilton
COPELAND, Adam	6-1	215	R	St. Catharines, Ont.	6/5/76	Hamilton-New Orleans
DEVEREAUX, Boyd	6-2	195	L	Seaforth, Ont.	4/16/78	Edmonton-Hamilton
DOWD, Jim	6-1	190	R	Brick, NJ	12/25/68	Edmonton-Hamilton
FALLOON, Pat	5-11	190	R	Foxwarren, Man.	9/22/72	Edmonton
GRIER, Michael	6-1	227	R	Detroit, MI	1/5/75	Edmonton
GUERIN, Bill	6-2	210	R	Wilbraham, MA	11/9/70	Edmonton
HENRICH, Michael	6-2	206	R	Thornhill, Ont.	3/3/80	Barrie
HINZ, Chad	5-10	190	R	Saskatoon, Sask.	3/21/79	Moose Jaw-Hamilton
HOUDE, Eric	5-11	191	L	Montreal, Que.	12/19/76	Montreal-Fredericton
KILGER, Chad	6-3	215	L	Cornwall, Ont.	11/27/76	Chicago-Edmonton
LaCOUTURE, Dan	6-3	210	L	Hyannis, MA	4/18/77	Edmonton-Hamilton
LARAQUE, Georges	6-3	230	R	Montreal, Que.	12/7/76	Edmonton-Hamilton
LINDQUIST, Fredrik	6-0	190	L	Sodertalje, Sweden	6/21/73	Edmonton-Hamilton
MARCHANT, Todd	5-10	178	L	Buffalo, NY	8/12/73	Edmonton
MOREAU, Ethan	6-2	211	L	Huntsville, Ont.	9/22/75	Chicago-Edmonton
MURRAY, Rem	6-2	195	L	Stratford, Ont.	10/9/72	Edmonton
RIESEN, Michel	6-2	190	R	Oberbalm, Switzerland	4/11/79	Hamilton
SARNO, Peter	5-11	185	L	Toronto, Ont.	7/26/79	Sarnia
SELIVANOV, Alex	6-0	208	L	Moscow, USSR	3/23/71	Tampa Bay-Cleveland-Edmonton
SMYTH, Ryan	6-1	195	L	Banff, Alta.	2/21/76	Edmonton
SPIRIDONOV, Maxim	5-10	185	L	Moscow, USSR	4/7/78	Grand Rapids-Springfield
TARVAINEN, Jussi	6-3	215	R	Lahti, Finland	5/31/76	JyP Jyvaskyla
WEIGHT, Doug	5-11	200	L	Warren, MI	1/21/71	Edmonton
DEFENSEMEN						
BOLIBRUCK, Kevin	6-1	200	L	Peterborough, Ont.	2/8/77	Hamilton
BROWN, Sean	6-3	205	L	Oshawa, Ont.	11/5/76	Edmonton
DESCOTEAUX, Matthieu	6-3	220	L	Pierreville, Que.	9/23/77	Hamilton
HAJT, Chris	6-3	206	L	Saskatoon, Sask.	7/5/78	Hamilton
HAMRLIK, Roman	6-2	215	L	Gottwaldov, Czech.	4/12/74	Edmonton
HAUER, Brett	6-2	200	R	Richfield, MN	7/11/71	Manitoba
HENRY, Alex	6-5	220	L	Elliot Lake, Ont.	10/18/79	London
LAFLAMME, Christian	6-1	210	R	St. Charles, Que.	11/24/76	Chi-Port (AHL)-Edm
MILLAR, Craig	6-2	205	L	Winnipeg, Man.	7/12/76	Edmonton-Hamilton
MUSIL, Frank	6-3	215	L	Pardubice, Czech.	12/17/64	Edmonton
NIINIMAA, Janne	6-1	220	L	Raahe, Finland	5/22/75	Edmonton
NORTON, Brad	6-4	225	L	Cambridge, MA	2/13/75	Hamilton
POTI, Tom	6-3	215	L	Worcester, MA	3/22/77	Edmonton
SMITH, Jason	6-3	210	R	Calgary, Alta.	11/2/73	Toronto-Edmonton
YERKOVICH, Sergei	6-3	210	L	Minsk, USSR	9/3/74	Hamilton

GOALTENDERS	HT	WT	C	Place of Birth	Date	1998-99 Club
ANTILA, Kristian	6-3	207	L	Vammala, Finland	1/10/80	Ilves Tampere
HAUSER, Adam	6-2	192	L	Bovey, MN	5/27/80	U. of Minnesota
HEFFLER, Eric	6-3	190	L	Williamsville, NY	2/29/76	St. Lawrence-Hamilton
MINARD, Mike	6-3	205	L	Owen Sound, Ont.	11/1/76	Dayton-Hamilton-Milwaukee
RANFORD, Bill	5-11	185	L	Brandon, Man.	12/14/66	Tampa Bay-Detroit
SALO, Tommy	5-11	173	L	Surahammar, Sweden	2/1/71	NY Islanders-Edmonton

Coach

LOWE, KEVIN
Coach, Edmonton Oilers. Born in Lachute, Que., April 15, 1959.

After a brilliant 19-year playing career with the Edmonton Oilers and New York Rangers, Kevin Lowe announced his retirement on July 30, 1998 and joined the Edmonton Oilers coaching staff. He replaced Ron Low as head coach on June 18, 1999.

Lowe was the Oilers' first-ever draft pick when he was selected 21st overall in the 1979 NHL Amateur Draft. He went on to play in 1,254 regular season games and 214 playoff games, winning six Stanley Cup championships; the first five with Edmonton (1984, 1985, 1987, 1988, 1990) followed by a sixth title with the Rangers in 1994.

Besides being the first draft choice in Oilers' history, Lowe also scored the first goal in team history on October 10, 1979. He holds the Oilers' record for most games played in both the regular season (1,037) and playoffs (172), and became the fifth captain in Oilers' history in 1990-91. He was no less a leader off the ice, becoming the only player to win the King Clancy Memorial Trophy and the Budweiser/NHL Man of the Year Award in the same season (1989-90). Both awards are presented for leadership qualities and humanitarian contributions. His work with the Edmonton Christmas Bureau has set the standard for the Oilers' commitment to community involvement.

Lowe and his wife Karen, a two-time Olympic bronze medalist for Canada at the 1988 Winter Olympics in Calgary, have four children.

1998-99 Scoring

* – rookie

Regular Season

Pos	#	Player	Team	GP	G	A	Pts	+/–	PIM	PP	SH	GW	GT	S	%
R	9	Bill Guerin	EDM	80	30	34	64	7	133	13	0	2	1	261	11.5
L	20	Josef Beranek	EDM	66	19	30	49	6	23	7	0	2	0	160	11.9
R	25	Mike Grier	EDM	82	20	24	44	5	54	3	2	1	0	143	14.0
R	10	Pat Falloon	EDM	82	17	23	40	–4	20	8	0	2	0	152	11.2
L	17	Rem Murray	EDM	78	21	18	39	4	20	4	1	4	1	116	18.1
C	39	Doug Weight	EDM	43	6	31	37	–8	12	1	0	0	1	79	7.6
L	26	Todd Marchant	EDM	82	14	22	36	3	65	3	1	2	0	183	7.7
R	28	Alexander Selivanov	T.B.	43	6	13	19	–8	18	1	0	0	0	120	5.0
			EDM	29	8	6	14	0	24	1	0	1	0	57	14.0
			TOTAL	72	14	19	33	–8	42	2	0	1	0	177	7.9
D	22	Roman Hamrlik	EDM	75	8	24	32	9	70	3	0	0	0	172	4.7
L	94	Ryan Smyth	EDM	71	13	18	31	0	62	6	0	2	2	161	8.1
D	44	Janne Niinimaa	EDM	81	4	24	28	7	88	2	0	1	0	142	2.8
C	15	Chad Kilger	CHI	64	14	11	25	–1	30	2	1	1	1	68	20.6
			EDM	13	1	1	2	–3	4	0	0	0	0	13	7.7
			TOTAL	77	15	12	27	–4	34	2	1	1	1	81	18.5
L	18	Ethan Moreau	CHI	66	9	6	15	–5	84	0	0	1	0	80	11.3
			EDM	14	1	5	6	2	8	0	0	1	0	16	6.3
			TOTAL	80	10	11	21	–3	92	0	0	2	0	96	10.4
D	5 *	Tom Poti	EDM	73	5	16	21	10	42	2	0	3	0	94	5.3
D	21	Jason Smith	TOR	60	2	11	13	–9	40	0	0	0	0	53	3.8
			EDM	12	1	1	2	0	11	0	0	0	0	15	6.7
			TOTAL	72	3	12	15	–9	51	0	0	0	0	68	4.4
C	19	Boyd Devereaux	EDM	61	6	8	14	2	23	0	1	4	1	39	15.4
D	24	Christian Laflamme	CHI	62	2	11	13	0	70	0	0	0	0	53	3.8
			EDM	11	0	1	1	–3	0	0	0	0	0	15	0.0
			TOTAL	73	2	12	14	–3	70	0	0	0	0	68	2.9
R	16	Kelly Buchberger	EDM	52	4	4	8	–6	68	0	2	1	0	29	13.8
D	23 *	Sean Brown	EDM	51	0	7	7	1	188	0	0	0	0	27	0.0
R	42	Kevin Brown	EDM	12	4	2	6	–2	0	2	0	0	0	13	30.8
R	27 *	Georges Laraque	EDM	39	3	2	5	–1	57	0	0	0	0	17	17.6
D	46	Todd Reirden	EDM	17	2	3	5	–1	20	0	0	0	0	26	7.7
D	33	Marty McSorley	EDM	46	2	3	5	–5	101	0	0	0	0	29	6.9
D	8	Frank Musil	EDM	39	0	3	3	0	34	0	0	0	0	9	0.0
R	34	Vladimir Vorobiev	EDM	2	2	0	2	1	2	0	0	0	0	5	40.0
D	32 *	Craig Millar	EDM	24	0	2	2	–6	19	0	0	0	0	18	0.0
R	38	Chris Ferraro	EDM	2	1	0	1	1	0	0	0	0	0	1	100.0
G	29 *	Steve Passmore	EDM	6	0	1	1	0	2	0	0	0	0	0	0.0
G	30	Bob Essensa	EDM	39	0	1	1	0	0	0	0	0	0	0	0.0
C	34	Jim Dowd	EDM	1	0	0	0	0	0	0	0	0	0	1	0.0
L	12	Joe Hulbig	EDM	1	0	0	0	1	2	0	0	0	0	2	0.0
L	28	Bill Huard	EDM	3	0	0	0	0	0	0	0	0	0	2	0.0
L	15 *	Dan Lacouture	EDM	3	0	0	0	1	0	0	0	0	0	0	0.0
C	21	Daniel Lacroix	EDM	4	0	0	0	0	13	0	0	0	0	5	0.0
R	7 *	Fredrik Lindquist	EDM	8	0	0	0	–2	2	0	0	0	0	6	0.0
G	35	Tommy Salo	NYI	51	0	0	0	0	12	0	0	0	0	0	0.0
			EDM	13	0	0	0	0	0	0	0	0	0	0	0.0
			TOTAL	64	0	0	0	0	12	0	0	0	0	0	0.0

Goaltending

No.	Goaltender	GPI	Mins	Avg	W	L	T	EN	SO	GA	SA	S%
35	Tommy Salo	13	700	2.31	8	2	2	0	0	27	279	.903
30	Mikhail Shtalenkov	34	1819	2.67	12	17	3	2	3	81	782	.896
30	Bob Essensa	39	2091	2.75	12	14	6	2	0	96	974	.901
29	* Steve Passmore	6	362	2.82	1	4	1	1	0	17	183	.907
	Totals	**82**	**4997**	**2.71**	**33**	**37**	**12**	**5**	**3**	**226**	**2223**	**.898**

Playoffs

Pos	#	Player	Team	GP	G	A	Pts	+/–	PIM	PP	SH	GW	OT	S	%
L	94	Ryan Smyth	EDM	3	3	0	3	–1	0	2	0	0	0	7	42.9
L	18	Ethan Moreau	EDM	4	0	3	3	3	6	0	0	0	0	6	0.0
C	39	Doug Weight	EDM	4	1	1	2	–3	15	0	0	0	0	4	25.0
L	17	Rem Murray	EDM	4	1	1	2	–1	2	0	0	0	0	6	16.7
L	26	Todd Marchant	EDM	4	1	1	2	2	12	0	0	0	0	10	10.0
R	25	Mike Grier	EDM	4	1	1	2	3	6	0	0	0	0	9	11.1
R	9	Bill Guerin	EDM	3	0	2	2	–4	2	0	0	0	0	8	0.0
R	28	Alexander Selivanov	EDM	2	0	1	1	0	2	0	0	0	0	3	0.0
R	10	Pat Falloon	EDM	4	0	1	1	0	4	0	0	0	0	6	0.0
D	21	Jason Smith	EDM	4	0	1	1	0	4	0	0	0	0	1	0.0
D	24	Christian Laflamme	EDM	4	0	1	1	–4	2	0	0	0	0	5	0.0
D	5 *	Tom Poti	EDM	4	0	1	1	–3	2	0	0	0	0	9	0.0
D	8	Frank Musil	EDM	1	0	0	0	–1	2	0	0	0	0	2	0.0
R	34	Vladimir Vorobiev	EDM	1	0	0	0	–1	0	0	0	0	0	1	0.0
D	23 *	Sean Brown	EDM	1	0	0	0	0	10	0	0	0	0	0	0.0
C	19	Boyd Devereaux	EDM	1	0	0	0	0	0	0	0	0	0	3	0.0
L	20	Josef Beranek	EDM	2	0	0	0	–1	4	0	0	0	0	0	0.0
D	33	Marty McSorley	EDM	3	0	0	0	1	2	0	0	0	0	3	0.0
D	22	Roman Hamrlik	EDM	3	0	0	0	1	2	0	0	0	0	1	0.0
R	16	Kelly Buchberger	EDM	4	0	0	0	–4	0	0	0	0	0	2	0.0
D	44	Janne Niinimaa	EDM	4	0	0	0	–2	2	0	0	0	0	5	0.0
G	35	Tommy Salo	EDM	4	0	0	0	0	0	0	0	0	0	0	0.0
C	15	Chad Kilger	EDM	4	0	0	0	–2	4	0	0	0	0	1	0.0
R	27 *	Georges Laraque	EDM	4	0	0	0	–2	2	0	0	0	0	1	0.0

Goaltending

No.	Goaltender	GPI	Mins	Avg	W	L	EN	SO	GA	SA	S%
35	Tommy Salo	4	296	2.23	0	4	0	0	11	149	.926
	Totals	**4**	**298**	**2.21**	**0**	**4**	**0**	**0**	**11**	**149**	**.926**

General Managers' History

Larry Gordon, 1979-80; Glen Sather, 1980-81 to date.

Club Records

Team

(Figures in brackets for season records are games played; records for fewest points, wins, ties, losses, goals, goals against are for 70 or more games)

Most Points	119	1983-84 (80), 1985-86 (80)
Most Wins	57	1983-84 (80)
Most Ties	16	1980-81 (80)
Most Losses	50	1992-93 (84)
Most Goals	*446	1983-84 (80)
Most Goals Against	327	1980-81 (80)
Fewest Points	60	1992-93 (84)
Fewest Wins	25	1993-94 (84)
Fewest Ties	5	1983-84 (80)
Fewest Losses	17	1981-82 (80), 1985-86 (80)
Fewest Goals	215	1997-98 (82)
Fewest Goals Against	224	1997-98 (82)
Longest Winning Streak		
Overall	8	Five times
Home	8	Jan. 19-Feb. 22/85, Feb. 24-Apr. 2/86
Away	8	Dec. 9/86-Jan. 17/87
Longest Undefeated Streak		
Overall	15	Oct. 11-Nov. 9/84 (12 wins, 3 ties)
Home	14	Nov. 15/89-Jan. 6/90 (11 wins, 3 ties)
Away	9	Jan. 17-Mar. 2/82 (6 wins, 3 ties), Nov. 23/82-Jan. 18/83 (7 wins, 2 ties)
Longest Losing Streak		
Overall	11	Oct. 16-Nov. 7/93
Home	9	Oct. 16-Nov. 24/93
Away	9	Nov. 25-Dec. 30/80
Longest Winless Streak		
Overall	14	Oct. 11-Nov. 7/93 (13 losses, 1 tie)
Home	9	Oct. 16-Nov. 24/93 (9 losses)
Away	9	Three times
Most Shutouts, Season	8	1997-98 (82)
Most PIM, Season	2,173	1987-88 (80)
Most Goals, Game	13	Nov. 19/83 (N.J. 4 at Edm. 13), Nov. 8/85 (Van. 0 at Edm. 13)

Individual

Most Seasons	15	Kevin Lowe
Most Games	1,037	Kevin Lowe
Most Goals, Career	583	Wayne Gretzky
Most Assists, Career	1,086	Wayne Gretzky
Most Points, Career	1,669	Wayne Gretzky (583G, 1,086A)
Most PIM, Career	1,747	Kelly Buchberger
Most Shutouts, Career	14	Curtis Joseph
Longest Consecutive Games Streak	521	Craig MacTavish (Oct. 11/86-Jan. 2/93)
Most Goals, Season	*92	Wayne Gretzky (1981-82)
Most Assists, Season	*163	Wayne Gretzky (1985-86)
Most Points, Season	*215	Wayne Gretzky (1985-86; 52G, 163A)
Most PIM, Season	286	Steve Smith (1987-88)
Most Points, Defenseman, Season	138	Paul Coffey (1985-86; 48G, 90A)
Most Points, Center, Season	*215	Wayne Gretzky (1985-86; 52G, 163A)
Most Points, Right Wing, Season	135	Jari Kurri (1984-85; 71G, 64A)
Most Points, Left Wing, Season	106	Mark Messier (1982-83; 48G, 58A)
Most Points, Rookie, Season	75	Jari Kurri (1980-81; 32G, 43A)
Most Shutouts, Season	8	Curtis Joseph (1997-98)
Most Goals, Game	5	Wayne Gretzky (Feb. 18/81, Dec. 30/81, Dec. 15/84, Dec. 6/87), Jari Kurri (Nov. 19/83), Pat Hughes (Feb. 3/84)
Most Assists, Game	*7	Wayne Gretzky (Feb. 15/80, Dec. 11/85, Feb. 14/86)
Most Points, Game	8	Wayne Gretzky (Nov. 19/83; 3G, 5A), (Jan. 4/84; 4G, 4A), Paul Coffey (Mar. 14/86; 2G, 6A)

* NHL Record.

Captains' History

Ron Chipperfield, 1979-80; Blair MacDonald and Lee Fogolin, 1980-81; Lee Fogolin, 1981-82, 1982-83; Wayne Gretzky, 1983-84 to 1987-88; Mark Messier, 1988-89 to 1990-91; Kevin Lowe, 1991-92; Craig MacTavish, 1992-93, 1993-94; Shayne Corson, 1994-95; Kelly Buchberger, 1995-96 to 1998-99.

Retired Numbers

3	Al Hamilton	1972-1980
99	Wayne Gretzky	1979-1988

Coaching History

Glen Sather, 1979-80; Bryan Watson and Glen Sather, 1980-81; Glen Sather, 1981-82 to 1988-89; John Muckler, 1989-90, 1990-91; Ted Green, 1991-92, 1992-93; Ted Green and Glen Sather, 1993-94; George Burnett and Ron Low, 1994-95; Ron Low, 1995-96 to 1998-99; Kevin Lowe, 1999-2000.

All-time Record vs. Other Clubs

Regular Season

	At Home							On Road							Total						
	GP	W	L	T	GF	GA	PTS	GP	W	L	T	GF	GA	PTS	GP	W	L	T	GF	GA	PTS
Anaheim	15	7	8	0	28	35	14	16	5	10	1	44	50	11	31	12	18	1	72	85	25
Boston	26	9	14	3	85	90	21	26	6	18	2	74	113	14	52	15	32	5	159	203	35
Buffalo	26	19	5	2	112	70	40	27	11	10	6	103	107	28	53	30	15	8	215	177	68
Calgary	68	36	22	10	275	237	82	67	24	37	6	242	296	54	135	60	59	16	517	533	136
Carolina	27	18	5	4	111	81	40	26	10	11	5	92	107	25	53	28	16	9	203	188	65
Chicago	35	15	16	4	132	129	34	34	11	18	5	122	137	27	69	26	34	9	254	266	61
Colorado	33	19	12	2	151	105	40	33	16	15	2	138	139	34	66	35	27	4	289	244	74
Dallas	34	17	10	7	145	115	41	35	13	16	6	111	132	32	69	30	26	13	256	247	73
Detroit	34	16	13	5	147	137	37	34	14	17	3	123	129	31	68	30	30	8	270	266	68
Florida	4	2	2	0	12	10	4	5	1	3	1	13	15	3	9	3	5	1	25	25	7
Los Angeles	67	34	19	14	316	249	82	67	28	25	14	285	271	70	134	62	44	28	601	520	152
Montreal	28	13	15	0	92	92	26	26	8	14	4	82	91	20	54	21	29	4	174	183	46
Nashville	2	2	0	0	7	4	4	2	0	1	1	4	6	1	4	2	1	1	11	10	5
New Jersey	29	14	9	6	130	106	34	29	14	13	2	98	101	30	58	28	22	8	228	207	64
NY Islanders	26	16	6	4	99	74	36	27	6	12	9	101	115	21	53	22	18	13	200	189	57
NY Rangers	26	11	13	2	96	92	24	26	13	7	6	102	97	32	52	24	20	8	198	189	56
Ottawa	6	4	1	1	25	16	9	6	3	2	1	14	10	7	12	7	3	2	39	26	16
Philadelphia	26	14	7	5	94	77	33	27	6	19	2	76	122	14	53	20	26	7	170	199	47
Phoenix	62	39	19	4	279	210	82	61	33	24	4	277	247	70	123	72	43	8	556	457	152
Pittsburgh	27	21	5	1	142	91	43	27	12	13	2	120	106	26	54	33	18	3	262	197	69
St. Louis	34	18	13	3	132	123	39	34	16	14	4	136	126	36	68	34	27	7	268	249	75
San Jose	23	16	4	3	91	52	35	22	9	11	2	71	78	20	45	25	15	5	162	130	55
Tampa Bay	7	5	2	0	17	16	10	7	3	2	2	18	19	8	14	8	4	2	35	35	18
Toronto	34	19	9	6	158	117	44	33	14	17	2	143	137	30	67	33	26	8	301	254	74
Vancouver	67	45	16	6	318	208	96	69	33	27	9	282	256	75	136	78	43	15	600	464	171
Washington	26	12	10	4	105	85	28	26	9	15	2	91	109	20	52	21	25	6	196	194	48
Totals	**792**	**441**	**255**	**96**	**3299**	**2621**	**978**	**792**	**318**	**371**	**103**	**2962**	**3116**	**739**	**1584**	**759**	**626**	**199**	**6261**	**5737**	**1717**

Playoffs

	Series	W	L	GP	W	L	T	GF	GA	Last Mtg.	Round	Result
Boston	2	2	0	9	8	1	0	41	20	1990	F	W 4-1
Calgary	5	4	1	30	19	11	0	132	96	1991	DSF	W 4-3
Chicago	4	3	1	20	12	8	0	102	77	1992	CF	L 0-4
Colorado	2	1	1	12	5	7	0	30	35	1998	CQF	W 4-3
Dallas	5	2	3	25	10	15	0	69	68	1999	CQF	L 0-4
Detroit	2	2	0	10	8	2	0	39	26	1988	CF	W 4-1
Los Angeles	7	5	2	36	24	12	0	154	127	1992	DSF	W 4-2
Montreal	1	1	0	3	3	0	0	15	6	1981	PR	W 3-0
NY Islanders	3	1	2	15	6	9	0	47	58	1984	F	W 4-1
Philadelphia	3	2	1	15	8	7	0	49	44	1987	F	W 4-3
Vancouver	2	2	0	9	7	2	0	35	20	1992	DF	W 4-2
Winnipeg	6	6	0	26	22	4	0	120	75	1990	DSF	W 4-3
Totals	**42**	**31**	**11**	**210**	**132**	**78**	**0**	**833**	**652**			

Calgary totals include Atlanta Flames, 1979-80.
Colorado totals include Quebec, 1979-80 to 1994-95.
New Jersey totals include Colorado Rockies, 1979-80 to 1981-82.

Playoff Results 1999-95

Year	Round	Opponent	Result	GF	GA
1999	CQF	Dallas	L 0-4	7	11
1998	CSF	Dallas	L 1-4	5	9
	CQF	Colorado	W 4-3	19	16
1997	CSF	Colorado	L 1-4	11	19
	CQF	Dallas	W 4-3	21	18

Abbreviations: Round: F – Final; **CF** – conference final; **CSF** – conference semi-final; **CQF** – conference quarter-final; **DF** – division final; **DSF** – division semi-final; **PR** – preliminary round.

Carolina totals include Hartford, 1979-80 to 1996-97.
Dallas totals include Minnesota, 1979-80 to 1992-93.
Phoenix totals include Winnipeg, 1979-80 to 1995-96.

1998-99 Results

Oct.	10		Los Angeles	1-2		14	at	Vancouver	3-1
	13		Toronto	2-3		17		Detroit	4-1
	14	at	Vancouver	4-1		21	at	San Jose	3-3
	17	at	New Jersey	4-2		27		Chicago	3-4
	20	at	NY Rangers	2-3		30		Anaheim	1-0
	21	at	NY Islanders	4-2	**Feb.**	1		St. Louis	3-4
	24	at	Colorado	4-6		3		Ottawa	2-2
	28		Washington	8-2		5		Nashville	4-2
	31		Pittsburgh	4-1		8	at	Calgary	1-2
Nov.	2		Vancouver	5-3		9		Boston	0-2
	4		Nashville	3-2		11	at	Detroit	2-4
	6		Colorado	2-5		13	at	St. Louis	3-2
	8	at	Chicago	3-2		15	at	Dallas	1-4
	11	at	Toronto	2-3		17	at	Anaheim	6-2
	12	at	Ottawa	1-1		18	at	Los Angeles	2-3
	14	at	Montreal	4-1		21		NY Rangers	1-2
	18		Detroit	2-6		24		Anaheim	1-2
	20	at	Anaheim	3-2		26		Buffalo	6-3
	21	at	Phoenix	2-3		27		Carolina	2-2
	25		Colorado	3-0	**Mar.**	1	at	Colorado	4-3
	27	at	Calgary	3-2		3	at	Buffalo	5-3
	29		Chicago	2-3		5	at	Pittsburgh	2-2
Dec.	2		Phoenix	4-3		6	at	Washington	3-4
	4		Tampa Bay	1-2		10	at	Dallas	4-7
	6		Dallas	2-6		13	at	St. Louis	4-6
	8	at	Nashville	3-3		14	at	Nashville	1-3
	9	at	Chicago	1-3		17		New Jersey	1-4
	11	at	Detroit	2-3		20		Vancouver	4-3
	13	at	Philadelphia	2-2		22		Calgary	2-2
	15	at	Carolina	0-3		24		Montreal	0-2
	18	at	Tampa Bay	4-1		26		St. Louis	2-1
	19	at	Florida	1-3		28		San Jose	5-2
	23		San Jose	3-5		30		Phoenix	4-7
	27		Vancouver	3-0	**Apr.**	1		Toronto	1-5
	29		Montreal	2-5		3	at	Colorado	2-5
Jan.	3		Philadelphia	3-3		7		Calgary	4-2
	5		Los Angeles	3-4		9	at	Calgary	4-1
	7	at	Phoenix	7-1		10	at	Vancouver	1-1
	9	at	Los Angeles	1-1		12	at	San Jose	5-4
	10	at	Anaheim	4-6		16		Colorado	5-1
	12		Dallas	2-2		17		Calgary	3-2

Entry Draft
Selections 1999-85

1999
Pick
13 Jani Rita
36 Alexei Semenov
41 Tony Salmelainen
81 Adam Hauser
91 Mike Comrie
139 Jonathan Fauteux
171 Chris Legg
199 Christian Chartier
256 Tomas Groschl

1998
Pick
13 Michael Henrich
67 Alex Henry
99 Shawn Horcoff
113 Kristian Antila
128 Paul Elliott
144 Oleg Smirnov
159 Trevor Ettinger
186 Michael Morrison
213 Christian Lefebvre
241 Maxim Spiridonov

1997
Pick
14 Michel Riesen
41 Patrick Dovigi
68 Sergei Yerkovich
94 Jonas Elofsson
121 Jason Chimera
141 Peter Sarno
176 Kevin Bolibruck
187 Chad Hinz
205 Chris Kerr
231 Alexandre Fomitchev

1996
Pick
6 Boyd Devereaux
19 Matthieu Descoteaux
32 Chris Hajt
59 Tom Poti
114 Brian Urick
141 Bryan Randall
168 David Bernier
170 Brandon Lafrance
195 Fernando Pisani
221 John Hultberg

1995
Pick
6 Steve Kelly
31 Georges Laraque
57 Lukas Zib
83 Mike Minard
109 Jan Snopek
161 Martin Cerven
187 Stephen Douglas
213 Jiri Antonin

1994
Pick
4 Jason Bonsignore
6 Ryan Smyth
32 Mike Watt
53 Corey Neilson
60 Brad Symes
79 Adam Copeland
95 Jussi Tarvainen
110 Jon Gaskins
136 Terry Marchant
160 Curtis Sheptak
162 Dmitri Shulga
179 Chris Wickenheiser
185 Rob Guinn
188 Jason Reid
214 Jeremy Jablonski
266 Ladislav Benysek

1993
Pick
7 Jason Arnott
16 Nick Stajduhar
33 David Vyborny
59 Kevin Paden
60 Alexander Kerch
111 Miroslav Satan
163 Alexander Zhurik
189 Martin Bakula
215 Brad Norton
241 Oleg Maltsev
267 Ilja Byakin

1992
Pick
13 Joe Hulbig
37 Martin Reichel
61 Simon Roy
65 Kirk Maltby
96 Ralph Intranuovo
109 Joaquin Gage
157 Steve Gibson
181 Kyuin Shim
190 Colin Schmidt
205 Marko Tuomainen
253 Bryan Rasmussen

1991
Pick
12 Tyler Wright
20 Martin Rucinsky
34 Andrew Verner
56 George Breen
78 Mario Nobili
93 Ryan Haggerty
144 David Oliver
166 Gary Kitching
210 Vegar Barlie
232 Evgeny Belosheikin
254 Juha Riihijarvi

1990
Pick
17 Scott Allison
38 Alexandre Legault
59 Joe Crowley
67 Joel Blain
101 Greg Louder
122 Keijo Sailynoja
143 Mike Power
164 Roman Mejzlik
185 Richard Zemlicka
206 Petr Korinek
227 invalid claim
248 Sami Nuutinen

1989
Pick
15 Jason Soules
36 Richard Borgo
78 Josef Beranek
92 Peter White
120 Anatoli Semenov
140 Davis Payne
141 Sergei Yashin
162 Darcy Martini
225 Roman Bozek

1988
Pick
19 Francois Leroux
39 Petro Koivunen
53 Trevor Sim
61 Collin Bauer
82 Cam Brauer
103 Don Martin
124 Len Barrie
145 Mike Glover
166 Shjon Podein
187 Tom Cole
208 Vladimir Zubkov
229 Darin MacDonald
250 Tim Tisdale

1987
Pick
21 Peter Soberlak
42 Brad Werenka
63 Geoff Smith
64 Peter Eriksson
105 Shaun Van Allen
126 Radek Toupal
147 Tomas Srsen
168 Age Ellingsen
189 Gavin Armstrong
210 Mike Tinkham
231 Jeff Pauletti
241 Jesper Duus
252 Igor Vyazmikin

1986
Pick
21 Kim Issel
42 Jamie Nichols
63 Ron Shudra
84 Dan Currie
105 David Haas
126 Jim Ennis
147 Ivan Matulik
168 Nicolas Beaulieu
189 Mike Greenlay
210 Matt Lanza
231 Mojmir Bozik
252 Tony Hand

1985
Pick
20 Scott Metcalfe
41 Todd Carnelley
62 Mike Ware
104 Tomas Kapusta
125 Brian Tessier
146 Shawn Tyers
167 Tony Fairfield
188 Kelly Buchberger
209 Mario Barbe
230 Peter Headon
251 John Haley

Club Directory

Skyreach Centre

Edmonton Oilers
11230 – 110 Street
Edmonton, Alberta T5G 3H7
Phone **780/414-4000**
Ticketing 780/414-4400
FAX 780/414-4659
Capacity: 17,100

Owner	Edmonton Investors Group Ltd.
Governor	Jim Hole
President/General Manager	Glen Sather
Executive Vice-President/ Assistant General Manager	Bruce MacGregor
Vice-President, Hockey Operations	TBD
Head Coach	Kevin Lowe
Assistant Coaches	Ted Green, Craig MacTavish
Chief Scout	Barry Fraser
Director of Hockey Personnel/Hockey Operations	Kevin Prendergast
Director of Hockey Administration	Peter Stephan
Director of Research, Analysis and Software Development	Sean Draper
Video Coordinator	Brian Ross
Scouting Staff	Ed Chadwick, Brad Davis, Lorne Davis, Harry Howell, Gilles Leger, Chris McCarthy, Kent Nilsson, Dave Semenko, Tom Thompson
Executive Assistant to the President	Sara Adamson
Executive Assistant to the Vice-President	Yvonne Ewaskow
Receptionist/Secretary	Cheryl Zaruk

Medical and Training Staff

Athletic Trainer/Therapist	Ken Lowe
Equipment Manager	Barrie Stafford
Assistant Equipment Manager	Lyle Kulchisky
Massage Therapist	Stewart Poirier
Team Medical Chief of Staff/ Director of Glen Sather Sports Medicine Clinic	Dr. David C. Reid
Team Physician	Dr. Boris Boyko
Team Dermatologist	Dr. Don Groot
Team Dentists	Dr. Tony Sneazwell, Dr. Brian Nord
Fitness Consultant	Dr. Art Quinney
Physical Therapy Consultant	Dr. Dave Magee
Team Optometrist	Dr. Brent Saik
Fitness Consultant	Daryl Duke

Finance

Vice-President, Finance	Doug Thomson
Director of Finance	Darryl Boessenkool
Manager Payroll & Benefits	Pat Stanic
Financial Analyst	Colleen Stewart
Systems Administrators	Terry Rhoades, Rod Pruden
Finance Staff	Donna Chizen, Lynn Schmidl, Michelle Schwendeman

Public Relations

Vice President, Public Relations	Bill Tuele
Information Coordinator	Steve Knowles
Public Relations Manager	Bryn Griffiths
Public & Community Relations Coordinator	Fiona Liew
Public Relations & Special Events Assistant	Warren Suitor

Business Operations

Executive Vice-President, Business Operations	Doug Piper
Vice-President, Sponsorships, Sales & Services	Allan Watt
Vice-President, Corporate Communications & Marketing	Trish Kerr
Manager, Corporate Sponsorships	Brad MacGregor
Manager, Corporate Sponsorships	Greg McDannold
Manager, Corporate Sponsorships	Sean Price
Coordinator, Sponsorships, Sales & Services	Nicole Wiens
Communications & Marketing Coordinator	Melanie Harysh
Manager, Marketing Programs	Natalie Minckler
Executive Assistant, Business Operations	Trena Jackson
Director of Broadcast	Don Metz
Game Night Operations	Glenn Wiun
Publications Coordinator	Steve Sandor
New Media Coordinator	Andreas Schwabe

Properties

Director of Properties	Darrell Holowaychuk
Product Manager	Brent Gibbs
Properties Manager	Linda Malito
Administration/Staffing Coordinator	Heather Allen
Warehouse Manager	Doug Wadlow
Systems Coordinator	Lena Gilje

Ticket Operations

Director of Ticket Operations	John Yeomans
Box Office Manager	Bob Haromy
Ticket Client Services	Sheila McCaskill, Sandy Langley, Sherry Smith
Suite Manager	Lori-Ann Blonke

Ticket Sales

Director of Ticket Sales	Michael Lake
Group Sales Representatives	Greg Hope, Emiliano Diaz-Page
Corporate Sales Representatives	Damon Bunting, Darren Simmons, Robbin Tylor

Skyreach Centre

Location of Press Box	East Side at top (Radio/TV) West Side at top (Media)
Ends of Rink	Herculite extends above boards around rink

Team Information

Training Camp Site	Skyreach Centre; Edmonton, Alberta
Television Outlets	A-Channel (Local) CBXT TV & CTV SportsNet (Regional & National)
Radio Flagship Station	630 CHED (AM); Rod Phillips (Play-by-play) & Morley Scott (colour)

President and General Manager

SATHER, GLEN CAMERON
President and General Manager, Edmonton Oilers.
Born in High River, Alta., Sept. 2, 1943.

The architect of the Edmonton Oilers' five Stanley Cup championships, Glen Sather is one of the most respected administrators in the NHL. The 1999-2000 season is his 19th as general manager of the NHL Oilers and his 24th with Edmonton since joining the organization in August of 1976.

Named coach and vice president of hockey operation for the Oilers when the franchise joined the NHL in June of 1979, Sather became coach, general manager and club president in May of 1980. He coached through the 1988-89 season and also returned for 60 games behind the bench in 1993-94. His .616 winning percentage in 842 regular-season games ranks seventh on the NHL's all-time coaching list. His playoff winning percentage of .706 ranks first.

Sather-coached teams won the Stanley Cup four times in the 1980s. As general manager, Sather was instrumental in the Oilers' fifth Cup triumph in 1990.

He has extensive international hockey experience, most recently as g.m. and coach of Team Canada at the 1996 World Cup of Hockey. He has also coached or managed tournament-winning teams at the Canada Cup and the IIHF World Championships.

Sather played for six different teams during a ten-year NHL career. He scored 80 goals in 658 games.

NHL Coaching Record

Season	Team	Games	Regular Season W	L	T	%	Playoffs Games	W	L	%
1979-80	Edmonton	80	28	39	13	.431	3	0	3	.000
1980-81	Edmonton	62	25	26	11	.492	9	5	4	.555
1981-82	Edmonton	80	48	17	15	.694	5	2	3	.400
1982-83	Edmonton	80	47	21	12	.663	16	11	5	.687
1983-84	Edmonton	80	57	18	5	.744	19	15	4	.789*
1984-85	Edmonton	80	49	20	11	.681	18	15	3	.833*
1985-86	Edmonton	80	56	17	7	.744	10	6	4	.600
1986-87	Edmonton	80	50	24	6	.663	21	16	5	.762*
1987-88	Edmonton	80	44	25	11	.619	18	16	2	.889*
1988-89	Edmonton	80	38	34	8	.538	7	3	4	.429
1993-94	Edmonton	60	22	27	11	.458	....	....	....	....
NHL Totals		**842**	**464**	**268**	**110**	**.616**	**126**	**89**	**37**	**.706**

* Stanley Cup win.

Florida Panthers

1998-99 Results: 30w-34L-18T 78PTS. Second, Southeast Division

Year-by-Year Record

Season	GP	Home			Road			Overall						Finished	Playoff Result
		W	L	T	W	L	T	W	L	T	GF	GA	Pts.		
1998-99	82	17	17	7	13	17	11	30	34	18	210	228	78	2nd, Southeast Div.	Out of Playoffs
1997-98	82	11	24	6	13	19	9	24	43	15	203	256	63	6th, Atlantic Div.	Out of Playoffs
1996-97	82	21	12	8	14	16	11	35	28	19	221	201	89	3rd, Atlantic Div.	Lost Conf. Quarter-Final
1995-96	82	25	12	4	16	19	6	41	31	10	254	234	92	3rd, Atlantic Div.	Lost Final
1994-95	48	9	12	3	11	10	3	20	22	6	115	127	46	5th, Atlantic Div.	Out of Playoffs
1993-94	84	15	18	9	18	16	8	33	34	17	233	233	83	5th, Atlantic Div.	Out of Playoffs

1999-2000 Schedule

Oct.	Sat.	2	Washington	Fri.	14	Carolina
	Wed.	6	Los Angeles	Sat.	15	at Tampa Bay
	Sat.	9	Detroit	Mon.	17	Philadelphia*
	Tue.	12	at Montreal	Wed.	19	Washington
	Wed.	13	at Toronto	Fri.	21	at Atlanta
	Sat.	16	Anaheim	Sat.	22	Boston
	Wed.	20	Vancouver	Wed.	26	New Jersey
	Fri.	22	Calgary	Thu.	27	at Philadelphia
	Sun.	24	at Philadelphia	Sat.	29	Edmonton
	Wed.	27	NY Islanders	**Feb.** Tue.	1	at Carolina
	Fri.	29	at Buffalo	Wed.	2	Montreal
	Sat.	30	at Ottawa	Wed.	9	San Jose
Nov.	Wed.	3	at Edmonton	Fri.	11	at Ottawa
	Fri.	5	at Vancouver	Sat.	12	at Boston
	Sat.	6	at Calgary	Mon.	14	at Montreal
	Wed.	10	Atlanta	Wed.	16	NY Rangers
	Sat.	13	Buffalo	Sat.	19	Pittsburgh
	Wed.	17	at Colorado	Mon.	21	Ottawa*
	Thu.	18	at St. Louis	Wed.	23	at Washington
	Sat.	20	Pittsburgh	Thu.	24	at Carolina
	Wed.	24	Philadelphia	Sat.	26	Carolina
	Fri.	26	NY Rangers	Mon.	28	Buffalo
	Sat.	27	Atlanta	**Mar.** Wed.	1	Toronto
Dec.	Fri.	3	at Atlanta	Fri.	3	at NY Rangers
	Sat.	4	Washington	Sat.	4	St. Louis
	Wed.	8	at Phoenix	Tue.	7	at Washington
	Fri.	10	at Dallas	Fri.	10	at Tampa Bay
	Sat.	11	at Nashville	Sat.	11	Chicago
	Wed.	15	Nashville	Thu.	16	at Pittsburgh
	Fri.	17	at Buffalo	Sat.	18	at NY Islanders
	Sat.	18	at Pittsburgh	Sun.	19	at New Jersey
	Mon.	20	Toronto	Tue.	21	at NY Rangers
	Wed.	22	Atlanta	Thu.	23	at Boston
	Sun.	26	at Carolina	Sat.	25	Montreal
	Mon.	27	at Tampa Bay	Wed.	29	Dallas
	Thu.	30	at Chicago	Fri.	31	Ottawa
Jan.	Sat.	1	Tampa Bay*	**Apr.** Sat.	1	Tampa Bay
	Wed.	5	at Anaheim	Mon.	3	New Jersey
	Thu.	6	at Los Angeles	Wed.	5	Boston
	Sat.	8	at San Jose	Sat.	8	at New Jersey*
	Wed.	12	NY Islanders	Sun.	9	at NY Islanders*

* Denotes afternoon game.

Rob Niedermayer, facing off against Nashville's Greg Johnson, rebounded from an injury-plagued 1997-98 campaign to collect 18 goals and 33 assists for Florida in 82 games last season. Only Ray Whitney had more points for the Panthers.

Franchise date: June 14, 1993

7th NHL Season

SOUTHEAST DIVISION

1999-2000 Player Personnel

FORWARDS

	HT	WT	S	Place of Birth	Date	1998-99 Club
BOGUNIECKI, Eric	5-8	192	R	New Haven, CT	5/6/75	Fort Wayne
BURE, Pavel	5-10	189	L	Moscow, USSR	3/31/71	Florida
CABANA, Chad	6-1	205	L	Bonnyville, Alta.	10/1/74	New Haven
DUERDEN, Dave	6-2	201	L	Oshawa, Ont.	4/11/77	Miami-Kentucky
DVORAK, Radek	6-1	194	R	Tabor, Czech.	3/9/77	Florida
FERGUSON, Craig	5-11	190	L	Castro Valley, CA	4/8/70	New Haven
HARVEY, Paul	6-4	196	R	South Boston, MA	8/8/78	Erie (OHL)
HAY, Dwayne	6-0	219	L	London, Ont.	2/11/77	Florida-New Haven
HICKS, Alex	6-0	190	L	Calgary, Alta.	9/4/69	San Jose-Florida
JOHNSON, Ryan	6-1	200	L	Thunder Bay, Ont.	6/14/76	Florida-New Haven
KOZLOV, Viktor	6-5	232	R	Togliatti, USSR	2/14/75	Florida
KVASHA, Oleg	6-5	216	R	Moscow, USSR	7/26/78	Florida
LINDSAY, Bill	6-0	195	L	Big Fork, MT	5/17/71	Florida
LONG, Andrew	6-2	181	R	Toronto, Ont.	8/10/78	New Haven-Miami
MELLANBY, Scott	6-1	205	R	Montreal, Que.	6/11/66	Florida
NIEDERMAYER, Rob	6-2	204	L	Cassiar, B.C.	12/28/74	Florida
NILSON, Marcus	6-2	193	R	Balsta, Sweden	3/1/78	Florida-Topeka-New Haven
NOVOSELTSEV, Ivan	6-1	183	L	Golitsino, USSR	1/23/79	Sarnia
PARRISH, Mark	5-11	191	R	Edina, MN	2/2/77	Florida-New Haven
REICHERT, Craig	6-1	200	R	Winnipeg, Man.	5/11/74	Cincinnati (AHL)
SHVIDKI, Denis	6-0	195	L	Kharkov, USSR	11/21/80	Barrie
SMITH, Nick	6-2	180	L	Hamilton, Ont.	3/23/79	Barrie
STEWART, Cam	5-11	196	L	Kitchener, Ont.	9/18/71	Houston
WELLS, Chris	6-6	223	L	Calgary, Alta.	11/12/75	Florida-New Haven
WHITNEY, Ray	5-10	175	R	Fort Saskatchewan, Alta.	5/8/72	Florida
WORRELL, Peter	6-6	235	L	Pierrefonds, Que.	8/18/77	Florida-New Haven

DEFENSEMEN

	HT	WT	S	Place of Birth	Date	1998-99 Club
ALLEN, Chris	6-2	187	R	Chatham, Ont.	5/8/78	Florida-New Haven
BOYLE, Dan	5-11	190	R	Ottawa, Ont.	7/12/76	Florida-Kentucky
DOELL, Curtis	5-11	209	R	Saskatoon, Sask.	10/3/76	Kentucky
FERENCE, Brad	6-3	196	R	Calgary, Alta.	4/2/79	Spokane-Tri-City
HEDICAN, Bret	6-2	205	L	St. Paul, MN	8/10/70	Vancouver-Florida
JAKOPIN, John	6-5	239	R	Toronto, Ont.	5/16/75	Florida-New Haven
KUBA, Filip	6-3	202	L	Ostrava, Czech.	12/29/76	Florida-Kentucky
LAUS, Paul	6-1	212	R	Beamsville, Ont.	9/26/70	Florida
PITLICK, Lance	6-0	205	R	Minneapolis, MN	11/5/67	Ottawa
RATCHUK, Peter	6-1	185	L	Buffalo, NY	9/10/77	Florida-New Haven
SPACEK, Jaroslav	5-11	198	L	Rokycany, Czech.	2/11/74	Florida-New Haven
SVEHLA, Robert	6-1	210	R	Martin, Czech.	1/2/69	Florida
TETARENKO, Joey	6-2	212	R	Prince Albert, Sask.	3/3/78	New Haven
THOMPSON, Brent	6-2	205	L	Calgary, Alta.	1/9/71	Hartford
WARD, Lance	6-3	215	L	Lloydminster, Alta.	6/2/78	Miami-Fort Wayne-New Haven
WARE, Jeff	6-4	220	L	Toronto, Ont.	5/19/77	St. John's-Florida-New Haven
WILSON, Mike	6-6	212	L	Brampton, Ont.	2/26/75	Buffalo-Florida-Las Vegas

GOALTENDERS

	HT	WT	C	Place of Birth	Date	1998-99 Club
BACH, Ryan	6-1	185	L	Sherwood Park, Alta.	10/21/73	Utah-Los Angeles-Long Beach
BURKE, Sean	6-4	210	L	Windsor, Ont.	1/29/67	Florida
KIDD, Trevor	6-2	190	L	Dugald, Man.	3/29/72	Carolina
SHULMISTRA, Richard	6-2	185	R	Sudbury, Ont.	4/1/71	Manitoba-Albany

1998-99 Scoring

* – rookie

Regular Season

Pos	#	Player	Team	GP	G	A	Pts	+/–	PIM	PP	SH	GW	GT	S	%
C	14	Ray Whitney	FLA	81	26	38	64	–3	18	7	0	6	1	193	13.5
C	44	Rob Niedermayer	FLA	82	18	33	51	–13	50	6	1	3	2	142	12.7
C	25	Viktor Kozlov	FLA	65	16	35	51	13	24	5	1	1	0	209	7.7
R	27	Scott Mellanby	FLA	67	18	27	45	5	85	4	0	3	3	136	13.2
R	19	Radek Dvorak	FLA	82	19	24	43	7	29	0	4	0	0	182	10.4
R	21	* Mark Parrish	FLA	73	24	13	37	–6	25	5	0	5	1	129	18.6
D	24	Robert Svehla	FLA	80	8	29	37	–13	83	4	0	0	1	157	5.1
L	11	Bill Lindsay	FLA	75	12	15	27	–1	92	0	1	2	0	135	8.9
L	16	* Oleg Kvasha	FLA	68	12	13	25	5	45	4	0	2	1	138	8.7
D	4	Bret Hedican	VAN	42	2	11	13	7	34	0	2	0	1	52	3.8
			FLA	25	3	7	10	–2	17	0	0	1	0	38	7.9
			TOTAL	67	5	18	23	5	51	0	2	1	1	90	5.6
L	29	Johan Garpenlov	FLA	64	8	9	17	–9	42	0	1	0	1	71	11.3
R	10	Pavel Bure	FLA	11	13	3	16	3	4	5	1	0	1	44	29.5
C	9	Kirk Muller	FLA	82	4	11	15	–11	49	0	0	1	0	107	3.7
D	8	* Jaroslav Spacek	FLA	63	3	12	15	15	28	2	1	0	0	92	3.3
D	2	Terry Carkner	FLA	62	2	9	11	0	54	0	0	0	0	25	8.0
D	3	Paul Laus	FLA	75	1	9	10	–1	218	0	0	0	0	54	1.9
L	28	Peter Worrell	FLA	62	4	5	9	0	258	0	0	2	0	50	8.0
D	26	* Dan Boyle	FLA	22	3	5	8	0	6	1	0	1	0	31	9.7
R	22	Dino Ciccarelli	FLA	14	6	1	7	–1	27	5	0	1	0	23	26.1
D	5	Gord Murphy	FLA	51	0	7	7	4	16	0	0	0	0	56	0.0
L	18	Alex Hicks	S.J.	4	0	1	1	–1	4	0	0	0	0	4	0.0
			FLA	51	0	6	6	–4	58	0	0	0	0	47	0.0
			TOTAL	55	0	7	7	–5	62	0	0	0	0	51	0.0
G	31	Sean Burke	FLA	59	0	4	4	0	27	0	0	0	0	0	0.0
D	7	Mike Wilson	BUF	30	1	2	3	10	47	0	0	1	0	40	2.5
			FLA	4	0	0	0	2	0	0	0	0	0	8	0.0
			TOTAL	34	1	2	3	12	47	0	0	1	0	48	2.1
L	12	* Marcus Nilson	FLA	8	1	1	2	2	5	0	0	1	0	7	14.3
D	6	* Peter Ratchuk	FLA	24	1	1	2	–1	10	0	0	0	0	34	2.9
C	23	Chris Wells	FLA	20	0	2	2	–4	31	0	0	0	0	28	0.0
C	17	* Ryan Johnson	FLA	1	0	1	1	0	0	0	0	0	0	1	100.0
D	26	David Nemirovsky	FLA	2	0	1	1	1	0	0	0	0	0	2	0.0
D	33	* Filip Kuba	FLA	5	0	1	1	2	0	0	0	0	0	5	0.0
D	15	* Jeff Ware	FLA	6	0	1	1	–6	6	0	0	0	0	1	0.0
D	12	* Chris Allen	FLA	1	0	0	0	0	0	0	0	0	0	0	0.0
D	15	* John Jakopin	FLA	3	0	0	0	–1	0	0	0	0	0	2	0.0
R	37	* Herbert Vasiljevs	FLA	5	0	0	0	–1	2	0	0	0	0	6	0.0
L	12	* Dwayne Hay	FLA	9	0	0	0	–1	0	0	0	0	0	3	0.0
G	1	Kirk McLean	FLA	30	0	0	0	0	2	0	0	0	0	0	0.0

Goaltending

No.	Goaltender	GPI	Mins	Avg	W	L	T	EN	SO	GA	SA	S%
31	Sean Burke	59	3402	2.66	21	24	14	3	3	151	1624	.907
1	Kirk McLean	30	1597	2.74	9	10	4	1	2	73	727	.900
	Totals	**82**	**5017**	**2.73**	**30**	**34**	**18**	**4**	**5**	**228**	**2355**	**.903**

Pavel Bure had 13 goals in just 11 games after his trade to the Panthers on January 17, 1999 but a knee injury brought an early end to his season.

General Manager

MURRAY, BRYAN CLARENCE
Vice President and General Manager, Florida Panthers.
Born in Shawville, Que., December 5, 1942.

Bryan Murray is entering his sixth season as vice president and general manager of the Panthers.

Before joining the Panthers, he served as coach and general manager of the Detroit Red Wings from 1990-93 and as general manager during the 1993-94 campaign. In 328 games under Murray's control, the Wings won a total of 170 games, while losing 121 and tying 37, an average of 43 wins and 94 points a season. Bryan left his mark in the NHL record book as a coach with a career record of 484-368-123 (.559 winning pct.) in 975 regular-season games, placing him seventh on the all-time victory list.

Murray broke into the NHL coaching ranks with the Washington Capitals on November 11, 1981. He spent the next 8½ seasons with the Caps and earned the Jack Adams Award as the NHL's coach of the year in 1983-84. In 1988-89, he led the Capitals to the Patrick Division title, the only first-place finish in team history. On January 15, 1990, Bryan was replaced by his brother, Terry.

Born in Shawville, Quebec on Dec. 5, 1942, Bryan is a graduate of McGill University in Montreal. He spent four years as athletic director and hockey coach at the school before leaving to coach the Regina Pats to a WHL title in 1979-80. Bryan moved up to the Hershey Bears (AHL) the following season and was named *The Hockey News'* minor league coach of the year after guiding that team to its best record in 40 years.

Bryan and his wife, Geri, have two daughters, Heide and Brittany.

Captains' History

Brian Skrudland, 1993-94 to 1996-97; Scott Mellanby, 1997-98 to date.

General Managers' History

Bob Clarke, 1993-94; Bryan Murray, 1994-95 to date.

NHL Coaching Record

Season	Team	Regular Season				Playoffs			
		Games	W	L	T	%	Games	W	L	%
1981-82	Washington	76	25	28	13	.477	....	....	....	....
1982-83	Washington	80	39	25	16	.588	4	1	3	.250
1983-84	Washington	80	48	27	5	.631	8	4	4	.500
1984-85	Washington	80	46	25	9	.631	5	2	3	.400
1985-86	Washington	80	50	23	7	.669	9	5	4	.556
1986-87	Washington	80	38	32	10	.538	7	3	4	.429
1987-88	Washington	80	38	33	9	.531	14	7	7	.500
1988-89	Washington	80	41	29	10	.575	6	2	4	.333
1989-90	Washington	46	18	24	4	.435	....	....	....	....
1990-91	Detroit	80	34	38	8	.475	7	3	4	.429
1991-92	Detroit	80	43	25	12	.613	11	4	7	.364
1992-93	Detroit	84	47	28	9	.613	7	3	4	.429
1997-98	Florida	59	17	31	11	.381	....	....	....	....
	NHL Totals	**975**	**484**	**368**	**123**	**.559**	**78**	**34**	**44**	**.436**

Club Records

Team

(Figures in brackets for season records are games played; records for fewest points, wins, ties, losses, goals, goals against are for 70 or more games)

Most Points	92	1995-96 (82)
Most Wins	41	1995-96 (82)
Most Ties	19	1996-97 (82)
Most Losses	43	1997-98 (82)
Most Goals	254	1995-96 (82)
Most Goals Against	256	1997-98 (82)
Fewest Points	63	1997-98 (82)
Fewest Wins	24	1997-98 (82)
Fewest Ties	10	1995-96 (82)
Fewest Losses	28	1996-97 (82)
Fewest Goals	203	1997-98 (82)
Fewest Goals Against	201	1996-97 (82)

Longest Winning Streak

Overall	7	Nov. 2-14/95
Home	5	Nov. 5-14/95
Away	4	Dec. 2-12/95, Nov. 13-Dec 1/96, Oct. 25-Nov. 22/97

Longest Undefeated Streak

Overall	12	Oct. 5-30/96 (8 wins, 4 ties)
Home	8	Nov. 5-26/95 (7 wins, 1 tie)
Away	7	Twice

Longest Losing Streak

Overall	13	Feb. 7-Mar. 23/98
Home	6	Feb. 25-Mar. 23/98
Away	7	Feb. 7-Mar. 21/98

Longest Winless Streak

Overall	15	Feb. 1-Mar. 23/98 (14 losses, 1 tie)
Home	8	Feb. 1-Mar. 23/98 (7 losses, 1 tie)
Away	16	Jan. 2-Mar. 21/98 (12 losses, 4 ties)

Most Shutouts, Season	6	1994-95 (48)
Most PIM, Season	1,676	1997-98 (82)
Most Goals, Game	10	Nov. 26/97 (Bos. 5 at Fla. 10)

Individual

Most Seasons	6	Several Players
Most Games	443	Bill Lindsay
Most Goals, Career	135	Scott Mellanby
Most Assists, Career	160	Scott Mellanby
Most Points, Career	295	Scott Mellanby (135G, 160A)
Most PIM, Career	1,307	Paul Laus
Most Shutouts, Career	13	John Vanbiesbrouck

Longest Consecutive

Games Streak	221	Robert Svehla (Oct. 13/95-Mar. 4/98)
Most Goals, Season	32	Scott Mellanby (1995-96); Ray Whitney (1997-98)
Most Assists, Season	49	Robert Svehla (1995-96)
Most Points, Season	70	Scott Mellanby (1995-96; 32G, 38A)
Most PIM, Season	313	Paul Laus (1996-97)
Most Shutouts, Season	4	John Vanbiesbrouck (1994-95, 1997-98)

Most Points, Defenseman, Season	57	Robert Svehla (1995-96; 8G, 49A)
Most Points, Center, Season	61	Rob Niedermayer (1995-96; 26G, 35A)
Most Points, Right Wing, Season	70	Scott Mellanby (1995-96; 32G, 38A)
Most Points, Left Wing, Season	64	Ray Whitney (1998-99; 26G, 38A)
Most Points, Rookie, Season	50	Jesse Belanger (1993-94; 17G, 33A)
Most Goals, Game	3	Seven times
Most Assists, Game	4	Scott Mellanby (Nov. 26/97)
Most Points, Game	4	Jesse Belanger (Jan. 19/94; 2G, 2A); Scott Mellanby (Jan. 4/97; 1G, 3A); (Nov. 26/97; 4A); Ray Whitney (Nov. 26/97; 2G, 2A)

All-time Record vs. Other Clubs

Regular Season

			At Home							On Road							Total			
	GP	W	L	T	GF	GA	PTS	GP	W	L	T	GF	GA	PTS	GP	W	L	T	GF	GA	PTS
Anaheim	4	1	1	2	10	11	4	5	3	2	0	17	18	6	9	4	3	2	27	29	10
Boston	11	4	7	0	30	33	8	12	5	4	3	33	32	13	23	9	11	3	63	65	21
Buffalo	11	6	5	0	33	34	12	13	2	9	2	18	45	6	24	8	14	2	51	79	18
Calgary	5	2	3	0	10	13	4	5	2	1	2	11	11	5	10	4	5	1	21	24	9
Carolina	13	5	3	5	37	27	15	12	6	5	1	35	36	13	25	11	8	6	72	63	28
Chicago	5	2	3	0	14	20	4	5	3	1	1	22	16	7	10	5	4	1	36	36	11
Colorado	8	1	7	0	22	35	2	7	2	2	3	19	19	7	15	3	9	3	41	54	9
Dallas	5	2	2	1	16	17	5	5	1	2	2	13	17	4	10	3	4	3	29	34	9
Detroit	5	1	3	1	11	17	3	5	1	3	1	15	21	3	10	2	6	2	26	38	6
Edmonton	5	3	1	1	15	13	7	4	2	2	0	10	12	4	9	5	3	1	25	25	11
Los Angeles	5	2	0	3	14	7	7	5	2	3	0	17	15	4	10	4	3	3	31	22	11
Montreal	12	6	4	2	41	33	14	11	5	5	1	27	34	11	23	11	9	3	68	67	25
Nashville	1	1	0	0	4	1	2	1	1	0	0	1	0	2	2	2	0	0	5	1	4
New Jersey	15	6	5	4	36	34	16	14	4	7	3	27	38	11	29	10	12	7	63	72	27
NY Islanders	15	8	4	3	46	38	19	15	8	5	2	39	36	18	30	16	9	5	85	74	37
NY Rangers	15	6	8	1	37	44	13	14	5	5	4	36	38	14	29	11	13	5	73	82	27
Ottawa	12	7	4	1	44	36	15	12	7	3	2	38	26	16	24	14	7	3	82	62	31
Philadelphia	14	4	6	0	38	48	8	15	6	5	4	37	33	16	29	10	15	4	75	81	24
Phoenix	5	2	3	0	17	13	4	6	2	2	2	16	15	6	11	4	5	2	33	28	10
Pittsburgh	12	6	6	0	33	30	12	13	2	9	2	33	50	6	25	8	15	2	66	80	18
St. Louis	5	1	3	1	12	15	3	5	1	3	1	9	13	3	10	2	6	2	21	28	6
San Jose	5	1	0	4	13	10	6	5	1	2	2	12	12	4	10	2	2	6	25	22	10
Tampa Bay	15	11	2	2	43	21	24	15	7	4	4	39	31	18	30	18	6	6	82	52	42
Toronto	7	2	2	3	21	18	7	6	1	5	0	14	26	2	13	3	7	3	35	44	9
Vancouver	5	2	2	1	11	16	5	5	1	3	1	11	15	5	10	3	3	4	22	31	10
Washington	15	6	7	2	40	43	14	15	6	4	5	39	43	14	30	11	13	6	79	86	28
Totals	**230**	**98**	**95**	**37**	**648**	**627**	**233**	**230**	**85**		**97**	**48**	**588**	**652**	**218**	**460**	**183**	**192**	**85**	**1236**	**1279**	**451**

Playoffs

	Series	W	L	GP	W	L	T	GF	GA	Last Mtg.	Round	Result
Boston	1	1	0	5	4	1	0	22	16	1996	CQF	W 4-1
Colorado	1	0	1	4	0	4	0	4	15	1996	F	L 0-4
NY Rangers	1	0	1	5	1	4	0	10	13	1997	CQF	L 1-4
Philadelphia	1	1	0	6	4	2	0	15	11	1996	CSF	W 4-2
Pittsburgh	1	1	0	7	4	3	0	20	15	1996	CF	W 4-3
Totals	**5**	**3**	**2**	**27**	**13**	**14**	**0**	**71**	**70**			

Playoff Results 1999-95

Year	Round	Opponent	Result	GF	GA
1997	CQF	NY Rangers	L 1-4	10	13
1996	F	Colorado	L 0-4	4	15
	CF	Pittsburgh	W 4-3	20	15
	CSF	Philadelphia	W 4-2	15	11
	CQF	Boston	W 4-1	22	16

Abbreviations: Round: F – Final;
CF – conference final; **CSF** – conference semi-final;
CQF – conference quarter-final.

Colorado totals include Quebec, 1993-94 to 1994-95.
Phoenix totals include Winnipeg, 1993-94 to 1995-96.

Carolina totals include Hartford, 1993-94 to 1996-97.

1998-99 Results

Oct.	9		Tampa Bay	4-1	18		Buffalo	0-4
	10	at	Nashville	1-0	20	at	NY Islanders	5-2
	16	at	Buffalo	2-2	21	at	NY Rangers	2-1
	21		Los Angeles	1-1	26	at	Philadelphia	3-3
	23		Vancouver	0-5	27		Montreal	2-1
	24	at	Washington	2-2	30		Dallas	2-5
	28		Detroit	2-7	Feb. 3		Toronto	5-2
	30	at	Chicago	7-3	5	at	Pittsburgh	0-3
	31	at	New Jersey	1-3	6	at	Carolina	3-3
Nov.	2	at	NY Islanders	2-6	8		St. Louis	4-5
	4		Chicago	2-1	11	at	Ottawa	3-1
	7		New Jersey	3-4	13	at	Montreal	0-4
	11		NY Rangers	4-1	15		San Jose	2-2
	12	at	Philadelphia	2-1	17	at	Dallas	1-2
	14	at	Pittsburgh	0-4	18	at	St. Louis	0-0
	19	at	Boston	5-5	20		Phoenix	7-1
	21	at	New Jersey	3-3	24		Philadelphia	5-3
	22		Philadelphia	1-2	26	at	Detroit	5-5
	25		Boston	0-1	27	at	Toronto	1-4
	27	at	Tampa Bay	2-1	Mar. 3		Colorado	5-7
	28		Buffalo	6-2	6		Carolina	2-2
Dec.	1	at	NY Rangers	4-5	8	at	Montreal	5-2
	2	at	Buffalo	1-2	9	at	Boston	0-2
	5		Carolina	3-3	11	at	Washington	2-1
	9		Ottawa	6-5	13		Tampa Bay	1-0
	12		Calgary	2-4	17	at	San Jose	2-4
	16		Pittsburgh	4-1	20	at	Los Angeles	3-4
	19		Edmonton	3-1	21	at	Anaheim	5-2
	23		Washington	0-4	24		NY Rangers	1-2
	26	at	Tampa Bay	3-1	26		Nashville	4-1
	28		NY Islanders	5-1	28		New Jersey	2-2
	30	at	Pittsburgh	4-7	31		NY Islanders	3-5
Jan.	1		Carolina	3-3	Apr. 1	at	Washington	3-5
	2		Pittsburgh	2-4	3		Ottawa	4-6
	5	at	Phoenix	2-2	5		Washington	0-3
	6	at	Colorado	2-2	7		Boston	2-5
	8	at	Vancouver	1-1	9	at	Buffalo	1-3
	10	at	Calgary	2-1	10	at	Toronto	1-9
	13		Toronto	3-3	12	at	Ottawa	2-0
	14	at	Carolina	2-3	14		Montreal	3-2
	16		NY Islanders	1-0	17		Tampa Bay	6-2

Entry Draft Selections 1999-93

1999
Pick
12	Denis Shvidki
40	Alexander Auld
70	Niklas Hagman
80	Jean-Francois Laniel
103	Morgan McCormick
109	Rod Sarich
169	Brad Woods
198	Travis Eagles
227	Jonathan Charron

1998
Pick
30	Kyle Rossiter
61	Joe DiPenta
63	Lance Ward
89	Ryan Jardine
117	Jaroslav Spacek
148	Chris Ovington
176	B.J. Ketcheson
203	Ian Jacobs
231	Adrian Wischer

1997
Pick
20	Mike Brown
47	Kristian Huselius
56	Vratislav Cech
74	Nick Smith
95	Ivan Novoseltsev
127	Pat Parthenais
155	Keith Delaney
183	Tyler Palmer
211	Doug Schueller
237	Benoit Cote

1996
Pick
20	Marcus Nilson
60	Chris Allen
65	Oleg Kvasha
82	Joey Tetarenko
129	Andrew Long
156	Gaetan Poirier
183	Alexandre Couture
209	Denis Khloptonov
235	Russell Smith

1995
Pick
10	Radek Dvorak
36	Aaron MacDonald
62	Mike O'Grady
80	Dave Duerden
88	Daniel Tjarnqvist
114	Francois Cloutier
166	Peter Worrell
192	Filip Kuba
218	David Lemanowicz

1994
Pick
1	Ed Jovanovski
27	Rhett Warrener
31	Jason Podollan
36	Ryan Johnson
84	David Nemirovsky
105	Dave Geris
157	Matt O'Dette
183	Jasson Boudrias
235	Tero Lehtera
261	Per Gustafsson

1993
Pick
5	Rob Niedermayer
41	Kevin Weekes
57	Chris Armstrong
67	Mikael Tjallden
78	Steve Washburn
83	Bill McCauley
109	Todd MacDonald
135	Alain Nasreddine
161	Trevor Doyle
187	Briane Thompson
213	Chad Cabana
239	John Demarco
265	Eric Montreuil

Coaching History

Roger Neilson, 1993-94, 1994-95; Doug MacLean, 1995-96. 1996-97; Doug MacLean and Bryan Murray, 1997-98; Terry Murray 1998-99 to date.

Coach

MURRAY, TERRY RODNEY
Coach, Florida Panthers. Born in Shawville, Que., July 20, 1950.

Florida vice president and general manager Bryan Murray appointed his brother Terry Murray to the Panthers coaching position on June 21, 1998. Terry becomes the fourth coach in franchise history, taking over from his brother who served on an interim basis after taking over from Doug MacLean during the 1997-98 season. Terry previously took over the coaching reigns from Bryan when he replaced him as bench boss with the Washington Capitals during the 1989-90 campaign.

Terry Murray has spent nine seasons as an NHL head coach and has a career coaching record of 311-232-76 for a .564 winning percentage. He has posted winning records in seven of his nine NHL seasons.

Murray was named head coach of the Philadelphia Flyers on June 23, 1994 and coached the team for three seasons. He compiled a record of 118-64-30 and won two Atlantic Division titles. Murray was a finalist for the Jack Adams Award as coach of the year following the 1994-95 season and guided the Flyers to the Stanley Cup finals in 1997. His playoff winning percentage of .609 in Philadelphia is better than Fred Shero (.578), Pat Quinn (.564) or Mike Keenan (.561).

Terry replaced Bryan as coach of the Capitals back on January 15, 1990. In his first full season behind the bench in 1990-91, he led Washington to the Wales Conference finals for the first time in club history. During his tenure with the Capitals, Murray had a record of 163-134-28. In between his coaching stints in Washington and Philadelphia, he served briefly as coach of the Panthers' International Hockey League affiliate in Cincinnati. Murray had a record of 17-7-4 in 28 games with the Cyclones to close out the 1993-94 season and guide them to a second-place finish in the IHL's Central Division.

Over a 12-year professional playing career, Terry Murray appeared in 302 NHL regular-season games with the California Golden Seals, Philadelphia Flyers, Detroit Red Wings and Washington Capitals. He had four goals and 76 assists for 80 points and had 199 penalty minutes. Terry and his wife Linda have two daughters, Megan and Lindsey.

Coaching Record

Season	Team	Games	Regular Season W	L	T	%	Playoffs Games	W	L	%
1988-89	Baltimore (AHL)	80	30	46	4	.400	....	....	....	....
1989-90	Baltimore (AHL)	44	26	17	1	.603	....	....	....	....
1989-90	**Washington (NHL)**	34	18	14	2	.559	15	8	7	.533
1990-91	**Washington (NHL)**	80	37	36	7	.506	11	5	6	.455
1991-92	**Washington (NHL)**	80	45	27	8	.613	7	3	4	.429
1992-93	**Washington (NHL)**	84	43	34	7	.554	6	2	4	.333
1993-94	**Washington (NHL)**	47	20	23	4	.468	....	....	....	....
	Cincinnati (IHL)	28	17	7	4	.679	11	6	5	.545
1994-95	**Philadelphia (NHL)**	48	28	16	4	.625	15	10	5	.667
1995-96	**Philadelphia (NHL)**	82	45	24	13	.628	12	6	6	.500
1996-97	**Philadelphia (NHL)**	82	45	24	13	.628	19	12	7	.632
1998-99	**Florida (NHL)**	82	30	34	18	.476	....	....	....	....
	NHL Totals	619	311	232	76	.564	85	46	39	.541

Club Directory

National Car Rental Center
One Panthers Parkway
Sunrise, FL 33323
Phone **954/835-7000**
FAX 954/835-7600
Website: www.flpanthers.com
Capacity: 19,200

Florida Panthers Holdings
Chairman	H. Wayne Huizenga
Vice Chairman & President	Richard C. Rochon
Vice President	Alex Muxo

Executive
President & Governor	William A. Torrey
Senior Vice President	Steve Dangerfield
Vice President and General Manager	Bryan Murray
Vice President of Corporate Sales & Client Services	Kimberly Terranova
Executive Assistants to Presidents	Deanna Cocozzelli, Cathy Stevenson
Executive Assistant to Senior Vice President	Janine Shea
Executive Assistant to Vice President & General Manager	Vanessa Rey
Administrative Assistant to Vice President of Corporate Sales & Client Services	Susan Ferro

Hockey Operations
Assistant General Manager	Chuck Fletcher
Head Coach	Terry Murray
Assistant Coaches	Slavomir Lener, Bill Smith
Director of Professional Player Evaluation	Michael Abbamont
Pro Scout	Duane Sutter
Director of Amateur Scouting	Tim Murray
Amateur Scouts	Billy Dea, Ron Harris, Wayne Meier, Todd Hearty, Sean O'Brien
Chief European Scout	Pavel Routa
Scouting & Video Coordinator	Brent Flahr
Head Medical Trainer	Stan Wong
Strength & Conditioning Coach	Ian Pyka
Head Equipment Manager	Mark Brennan
Equipment Manager	Scott Tinkler
Team Services Coordinator	Marni Share
Equipment Staff	Jonas Kalkstein
Internist	Charles Posternack, M.D.
Orthopedic Surgeon	Jeffrey Minkoff, M.D.
Assistant Physicians	Stephen R. Southworth, M.D., James Guerra, M.D.
Team Cardiologist	Howard Bush, M.D.
Plastic Surgeon	Harry K. Moon
Team Dentist	Martin Robins, D.D.S.

Communications Department
Director of Communications	Mike Hanson
Community Development Manager	Hillary Reynolds
Youth & Amateur Hockey Manager	TBA
Publications Coordinator	Michael Citro
Media Relations Coordinator	Chris Kelleher
Communications Coordinator	Mary Lou Veroline
Administrative Assistant to Director of Communications	Giselle Seoane

Corporate Sales & Client Services Department
Director of Client Services	Brette Sadler
Corporate Sales Manager	Scott Baynes
Corporate Account Manager	Jason Camp
Corporate Sales Account Executive	Craig Petrus
Corporate Account Coordinator	Marcie Maggio
Client Services Coordinator	Michelle Marchand

Finance & Administration
Director of Information Technology	Kelly Connor
Director of Finance/Controller	Evelyn Lopez
Office Manager	Laura Barrera
Accounting Manager	Michele Gilbert
Manager of Human Resources/Payroll	Mary Santimaw
Staff Accountants	Ana Carrasquilla, Tammy Gasiorek
Systems Analysts	Mark Littell, Robert Azopardi
Payroll Coordinator	Gloria Julienne
Office Services Administrator	Lee Bancroft
Human Resources Administrator	Cheryl Udrich
Administrative Assistant to Director of Finance/Controller	Cathy Cuffe

Game Presentation/Promotions Department
Director of Game Presentation	Scott Cunningham
Director of Promotions	Ed Krajewski
Game Presentation Producer	Marc Bick
Promotions Coordinator	Keith Martin
Promotions Coordinator	Anthony Van Daley
Mascot Coordinator	Phil Crowhurst

Merchandise Department
Director of Merchandising	Ron Dennis
Retail Manager	Maria Cocozzelli
Buyer	Jennifer Borell

Ticket Operations and Sales Department
Director of Group & Season Ticket Sales	Chris Trinceri
Director of Ticket & Game-Day Operations	Scott Wampold
Director of Suite & Club Level Services	Steve Woznick
Manager of Ticket Operations	Matt Coyne
Manager of Suite & Club Level Services	Susan McKenzie
Account Executives	Valerie Stephens, Yosvani Barreiro, Richard Powers
Guest Services/Ticket Coordinator	Jon Lakamp
Suite & Club Level Services Representative	Kathy Stock

General Information
Press Box Phone	(954) 835-7801
Television	SportsChannel Florida
Television Announcers	Jeff Rimer, Denis Potvin
Radio Flagship	WQAM 560 AM
Radio Announcers	Jiggs McDonald, Randy Moller

Los Angeles Kings

1998-99 Results: 32w-45l-5t 69pts. Fifth, Pacific Division

1999-2000 Schedule

Oct.	Sat.	2	at Nashville
	Mon.	4	at St. Louis
	Wed.	6	at Florida
	Thu.	7	at Tampa Bay
	Sat.	9	at Washington
	Fri.	15	at Calgary
	Sat.	16	at Edmonton
	Wed.	20	Boston
	Fri.	22	Phoenix
	Sun.	24	San Jose
	Tue.	26	Washington
	Thu.	28	Pittsburgh
	Sat.	30	at Chicago
Nov.	Tue.	2	at Pittsburgh
	Wed.	3	at Detroit
	Sat.	6	Philadelphia
	Tue.	9	Edmonton
	Thu.	11	Colorado
	Sun.	14	at Phoenix
	Tue.	16	Chicago
	Thu.	18	Phoenix
	Sat.	20	Montreal
	Tue.	23	at Colorado
	Wed.	24	at Dallas
	Sat.	27	San Jose*
Dec.	Fri.	3	at Anaheim
	Sat.	4	Tampa Bay
	Wed.	8	Atlanta
	Fri.	10	at Detroit
	Sat.	11	at Montreal
	Tue.	14	at New Jersey
	Wed.	15	at NY Rangers
	Sat.	18	Chicago
	Wed.	22	at San Jose
	Sun.	26	Phoenix
	Wed.	29	at Colorado
	Thu.	30	Edmonton
Jan.	Mon.	3	at Dallas
	Tue.	4	at St. Louis
	Thu.	6	Florida
	Tue.	11	Ottawa

	Thu.	13	St. Louis
	Sat.	15	at San Jose
	Tue.	18	Buffalo
	Thu.	20	Dallas
	Sun.	23	Colorado*
	Wed.	26	at Dallas
	Thu.	27	at Nashville
	Sat.	29	at Toronto
	Mon.	31	NY Islanders
Feb.	Thu.	3	Detroit
	Tue.	8	Anaheim
	Wed.	9	at Phoenix
	Fri.	11	Dallas
	Mon.	14	Calgary
	Wed.	16	at Chicago
	Fri.	18	at Detroit
	Sat.	19	at Buffalo
	Mon.	21	at Edmonton
	Wed.	23	at Calgary
	Fri.	25	at Vancouver
	Sat.	26	at San Jose
	Tue.	29	Vancouver
Mar.	Thu.	2	Carolina
	Sat.	4	Nashville
	Tue.	7	Detroit
	Thu.	9	NY Rangers
	Sat.	11	Calgary
	Mon.	13	Vancouver
	Wed.	15	at Anaheim
	Fri.	17	St. Louis
	Sun.	19	Nashville
	Tue.	21	Anaheim
	Thu.	23	at Philadelphia
	Sat.	25	at Boston*
	Sun.	26	at Atlanta
	Wed.	29	San Jose
Apr.	Sat.	1	Anaheim*
	Mon.	3	at Phoenix
	Wed.	5	at Vancouver
	Fri.	7	Dallas
	Sun.	9	at Anaheim*

* Denotes afternoon game.

Franchise date: June 5, 1967

PACIFIC DIVISION

33rd NHL Season

After nine seasons with the Buffalo Sabres, Donald Audette came to Los Angeles in 1998-99. His 18 goals, and six on the power play, were the Kings' second-best totals last season. Audette's plus/minus rating of +7 was the team's best.

Year-by-Year Record

Season	GP	Home W	L	T	Road W	L	T	Overall W	L	T	GF	GA	Pts.	Finished		Playoff Result
1998-99	82	18	20	3	14	25	2	32	45	5	189	222	69	5th,	Pacific Div.	Out of Playoffs
1997-98	82	22	16	3	16	17	8	38	33	11	227	225	87	2nd,	Pacific Div.	Lost Conf. Quater-Final
1996-97	82	18	16	7	10	27	4	28	43	11	214	268	67	6th,	Pacific Div.	Out of Playoffs
1995-96	82	16	16	9	8	24	9	24	40	18	256	302	66	6th,	Pacific Div.	Out of Playoffs
1994-95	48	7	11	6	9	12	3	16	23	9	142	174	41	4th,	Pacific Div.	Out of Playoffs
1993-94	84	18	19	5	9	26	7	27	45	12	294	322	66	5th,	Pacific Div.	Out of Playoffs
1992-93	84	22	15	5	17	20	5	39	35	10	338	340	88	3rd,	Smythe Div.	Lost Final
1991-92	80	20	11	9	15	20	5	35	31	14	287	296	84	2nd,	Smythe Div.	Lost Div. Semi-Final
1990-91	80	26	9	5	20	15	5	46	24	10	340	254	102	1st,	Smythe Div.	Lost Div. Final
1989-90	80	21	16	3	13	23	4	34	39	7	338	337	75	4th,	Smythe Div.	Lost Div. Final
1988-89	80	25	12	3	17	19	4	42	31	7	376	335	91	2nd,	Smythe Div.	Lost Div. Final
1987-88	80	19	18	3	11	24	5	30	42	8	318	359	68	4th,	Smythe Div.	Lost Div. Semi-Final
1986-87	80	20	17	3	11	24	5	31	41	8	318	341	70	4th,	Smythe Div.	Lost Div. Semi-Final
1985-86	80	9	27	4	14	22	4	23	49	8	284	389	54	5th,	Smythe Div.	Out of Playoffs
1984-85	80	20	14	6	14	18	8	34	32	14	339	326	82	4th,	Smythe Div.	Lost Div. Semi-Final
1983-84	80	13	19	8	10	25	5	23	44	13	309	376	59	5th,	Smythe Div.	Out of Playoffs
1982-83	80	20	13	7	7	28	5	27	41	12	308	365	66	5th,	Smythe Div.	Out of Playoffs
1981-82	80	19	15	6	5	26	9	24	41	15	314	369	63	4th,	Smythe Div.	Lost Div. Final
1980-81	80	22	11	7	21	13	6	43	24	13	337	290	99	2nd,	Norris Div.	Lost Prelim. Round
1979-80	80	18	13	9	12	23	5	30	36	14	290	313	74	2nd,	Norris Div.	Lost Prelim. Round
1978-79	80	20	13	7	14	21	5	34	34	12	292	286	80	3rd,	Norris Div.	Lost Prelim. Round
1977-78	80	18	16	6	13	18	9	31	34	15	243	245	77	3rd,	Norris Div.	Lost Prelim. Round
1976-77	80	20	13	7	14	18	8	34	31	15	271	241	83	2nd,	Norris Div.	Lost Quarter-Final
1975-76	80	22	13	5	16	20	4	38	33	9	263	265	85	2nd,	Norris Div.	Lost Quarter-Final
1974-75	80	22	7	11	20	10	10	42	17	21	269	185	105	2nd,	Norris Div.	Lost Prelim. Round
1973-74	78	22	13	4	11	20	8	33	33	12	233	231	78	3rd,	West Div.	Lost Quarter-Final
1972-73	78	21	11	7	10	25	4	31	36	11	232	245	73	6th,	West Div.	Out of Playoffs
1971-72	78	14	23	2	6	26	7	20	49	9	206	305	49	7th,	West Div.	Out of Playoffs
1970-71	78	17	14	8	8	26	5	25	40	13	239	303	63	5th,	West Div.	Out of Playoffs
1969-70	76	12	22	4	2	30	6	14	52	10	168	290	38	6th,	West Div.	Out of Playoffs
1968-69	76	19	14	5	5	28	5	24	42	10	185	260	58	4th,	West Div.	Lost Semi-Final
1967-68	74	20	13	4	11	20	6	31	33	10	200	224	72	2nd,	West Div.	Lost Quarter-Final

1999-2000 Player Personnel

FORWARDS	HT	WT	S	Place of Birth	Date	1998-99 Club
AUDETTE, Donald	5-8	184	R	Laval, Que.	9/23/69	Los Angeles
BARNEY, Scott	6-4	198	R	Oshawa, Ont.	3/27/79	Peterborough-Springfield
BARRIE, Len	6-0	200	L	Kimberley, B.C.	6/4/69	Frankfurt
BLAKE, Jason	5-10	180	L	Moorhead, MN	9/2/73	North Dakota-LA Kings-Orlando
BRENNAN, Kip	6-4	196	L	Kingston, Ont.	8/27/80	Sudbury
CHARTRAND, Brad	5-11	185	L	Winnipeg, Man.	12/14/74	St. John's
HUARD, Bill	6-1	215	L	Welland, Ont.	6/24/67	Edmonton-Houston
JOHNSON, Craig	6-2	197	L	St. Paul, MN	3/8/72	Los Angeles
LaFAYETTE, Nathan	6-1	200	R	New Westminster, B.C.	2/17/73	Los Angeles-Long Beach
LAPERRIERE, Ian	6-1	197	R	Montreal, Que.	1/19/74	Los Angeles
MacLEAN, Donald	6-2	199	L	Sydney, N.S.	1/14/77	Springfield-Grand Rapids
McKENNA, Steve	6-8	247	L	Toronto, Ont.	8/21/73	Los Angeles
MURRAY, Glen	6-3	222	R	Halifax, N.S.	11/1/72	Los Angeles
PALFFY, Zigmund	5-10	183	L	Skalica, Czech.	5/5/72	HK 36 Skalica-NY Islanders
PODOLLAN, Jason	6-1	198	R	Vernon, B.C.	2/18/76	Tor-St.J's-L.A.-Long Beach
ROBITAILLE, Luc	6-1	205	L	Montreal, Que.	2/17/66	Los Angeles
ROSA, Pavel	6-0	195	R	Most, Czech.	6/7/77	Los Angeles-Long Beach
SMOLINSKI, Bryan	6-1	202	R	Toledo, OH	12/27/71	NY Islanders
STUMPEL, Jozef	6-3	216	R	Nitra, Czech.	7/20/72	Los Angeles
THOMAS, Scott	6-2	195	R	Buffalo, NY	1/18/70	Manitoba
TSYPLAKOV, Vladimir	6-1	197	L	Moscow, USSR	4/18/69	Los Angeles
TUOMAINEN, Marko	6-3	203	R	Kuopio, Finland	4/25/72	HIFK Helsinki

DEFENSEMEN	HT	WT	S	Place of Birth	Date	1998-99 Club
BERG, Aki-Petteri	6-3	203	L	Turku, Finland	2/28/77	TPS Turku
BLAKE, Rob	6-4	220	R	Simcoe, Ont.	12/10/69	Los Angeles
BOUCHER, Philippe	6-2	214	R	St. Apollinaire, Que.	3/24/73	Los Angeles
GALLEY, Garry	6-0	207	L	Montreal, Que.	4/16/63	Los Angeles
KABERLE, Frantisek	6-0	185	L	Kladno, Czech.	11/8/73	MoDo Hockey
KARALAHTI, Jere	6-2	210	R	Helsinki, Finland	3/25/75	HIFK Helsinki
MacISAAC, Dave	6-2	225	L	Arlington, MA	4/23/72	Philadelphia (AHL)
MODRY, Jaroslav	6-2	219	L	Ceske-Budejovice, Czech.	2/27/71	Los Angeles-Long Beach
NEMECEK, Jan	6-1	215	R	Pisek, Czech.	2/14/76	Los Angeles-Long Beach
NORSTROM, Mattias	6-2	201	L	Stockholm, Sweden	1/2/72	Los Angeles
O'DONNELL, Sean	6-3	230	L	Ottawa, Ont.	10/13/71	Los Angeles

GOALTENDERS	HT	WT	C	Place of Birth	Date	1998-99 Club
COUSINEAU, Marcel	5-9	180	L	Delson, Que.	4/30/73	NY Islanders-Lowell
FISET, Stephane	6-1	198	L	Montreal, Que.	6/17/70	Los Angeles
STORR, Jamie	6-2	198	L	Brampton, Ont.	12/28/75	Los Angeles
VOLKOV, Alexey	6-1	185	L	Sverdlovsk, USSR	3/15/80	Halifax

1998-99 Scoring

*– rookie

Regular Season

Pos	#	Player	Team	GP	G	A	Pts	+/–	PIM	PP	SH	GW	GT	S	%
L	20	Luc Robitaille	L.A.	82	39	35	74	-1	54	11	0	7	0	292	13.4
R	10	Donald Audette	L.A.	49	18	18	36	7	51	6	0	2	0	152	11.8
D	4	Rob Blake	L.A.	62	12	23	35	-7	128	5	1	2	0	216	5.6
C	15	Jozef Stumpel	L.A.	64	13	21	34	-18	10	1	0	1	0	131	9.9
R	27	Glen Murray	L.A.	61	16	15	31	-14	36	3	3	3	0	173	9.2
C	26	Ray Ferraro	L.A.	65	13	18	31	0	59	4	0	4	0	84	15.5
L	9	Vladimir Tsyplakov	L.A.	69	11	12	23	-7	32	0	2	2	0	111	9.9
C	12	* Olli Jokinen	L.A.	66	9	12	21	-10	44	3	1	1	0	87	10.3
C	23	Craig Johnson	L.A.	69	7	12	19	-12	32	2	0	2	0	94	7.4
R	19	Russ Courtnall	L.A.	57	6	13	19	-9	19	0	1	1	0	77	7.8
R	55	* Pavel Rosa	L.A.	29	4	12	16	0	6	0	0	0	0	61	6.6
D	3	Garry Galley	L.A.	60	4	12	16	-9	30	3	0	0	0	77	5.2
D	8	Doug Bodger	L.A.	65	3	11	14	1	34	0	0	0	0	67	4.5
D	6	Sean O'Donnell	L.A.	80	1	13	14	1	186	0	0	0	0	64	1.6
C	22	Ian Laperriere	L.A.	72	3	10	13	-5	138	0	0	1	0	62	4.8
C	11	Brandon Convery	VAN	12	2	7	9	5	8	0	0	1	0	12	16.7
			L.A.	3	0	0	0	-1	4	0	0	0	0	2	0.0
			TOTAL	15	2	7	9	4	12	0	0	1	0	14	14.3
D	44	Dave Babych	PHI	33	2	4	6	0	20	2	0	0	0	44	4.5
			L.A.	8	0	2	2	-2	2	0	0	0	0	5	0.0
			TOTAL	41	2	6	8	-2	22	2	0	0	0	49	4.1
D	43	Philippe Boucher	L.A.	45	2	6	8	-12	32	1	0	0	0	87	2.3
D	14	Mattias Norstrom	L.A.	78	2	5	7	-10	36	0	1	0	0	61	3.3
R	45	Sandy Moger	L.A.	42	3	2	5	-9	26	0	0	2	0	28	10.7
C	24	* Nathan Lafayette	L.A.	33	2	2	4	0	35	0	1	1	0	42	4.8
L	21	* Josh Green	L.A.	27	1	3	4	-5	8	1	0	0	0	35	2.9
D	48	* Mark Visheau	L.A.	28	1	3	4	-7	107	0	0	0	0	10	10.0
C	29	Sean Pronger	PIT	2	0	0	0	0	0	0	0	0	0	3	0.0
			NYR	14	0	3	3	-3	4	0	0	0	0	3	0.0
			L.A.	13	0	1	1	2	4	0	0	0	0	8	0.0
			TOTAL	29	0	4	4	-1	8	0	0	0	0	14	0.0
L	17	Matt Johnson	L.A.	49	2	1	3	-5	131	0	0	0	0	14	14.3
C	11	* Jason Blake	L.A.	1	1	0	1	1	0	0	0	0	0	5	20.0
D	54	* Jan Nemecek	L.A.	6	1	0	1	-1	4	0	0	1	0	8	12.5
L	7	Steve McKenna	L.A.	20	1	0	1	-3	36	0	0	1	0	12	8.3
D	33	Jaroslav Modry	L.A.	5	0	1	1	0	0	0	0	0	0	11	0.0
G	32	* Manny Legace	L.A.	17	0	1	1	0	0	0	0	0	0	0	0.0
G	1	* Jamie Storr	L.A.	28	0	1	1	0	6	0	0	0	0	0	0.0
G	31	* Ryan Bach	L.A.	3	0	0	0	0	0	0	0	0	0	0	0.0
L	42	Dan Bylsma	L.A.	8	0	0	0	-1	2	0	0	0	0	3	0.0
C	28	Jason Podollan	TOR	4	0	0	0	0	0	0	0	0	0	2	0.0
			L.A.	6	0	0	0	-3	0	0	0	0	0	7	0.0
			TOTAL	10	0	0	0	-3	0	0	0	0	0	9	0.0
G	35	Stephane Fiset	L.A.	42	0	0	0	0	2	0	0	0	0	0	0.0

Goaltending

No.	Goaltender	GPI	Mins	Avg	W	L	T	EN	SO	GA	SA	S%
1	* Jamie Storr	28	1525	2.40	12	12	3	4	61	724	.916
32	* Manny Legace	17	899	2.60	2	9	2	0	39	439	.911
35	Stephane Fiset	42	2403	2.60	18	21	1	2	3	104	1217	.915
31	* Ryan Bach	3	108	4.44	0	3	0	0	0	8	66	.879
	Totals	82	4960	2.69	32	45	5	10	8	222	2456	.910

General Managers' History

Larry Regan, 1967-68 to 1972-73; Larry Regan and Jake Milford, 1973-74; Jake Milford, 1974-75 to 1976-77; George Maguire, 1977-78 to 1982-83; George Maguire and Rogie Vachon, 1983-84; Rogie Vachon, 1984-85 to 1991-92; Nick Beverley, 1992-93, 1993-94; Sam McMaster, 1994-95 to 1996-97; Dave Taylor, 1997-98 to date.

General Manager

TAYLOR, DAVE

General Manager, Los Angeles Kings. Born in Levack, Ont., December 4, 1955.

No player in the history of the Kings ever wore the uniform with more distinction and class than Dave Taylor. For 17 seasons, Taylor gave his all, both on and off the ice, receiving All-Star status for his outstanding play.

Fittingly, after finishing his illustrious career during the 1993-94 season, Taylor remains a key part of the Kings organization, now serving as vice president and general manager for the NHL club. Taylor assumed his current responsibilities on April 22, 1997, becoming the seventh GM in team history. He joined the Kings front office four years ago as an assistant to his predecessor, Sam McMaster.

An All-American hockey player while at Clarkson College, Taylor was relatively unknown when the Kings' picked him in the 15th round of the 1975 draft. His grit and work ethic kept him around long enough to hook up with a center named Marcel Dionne, who virtually ignited Taylor's career. As a member of the renowned Triple Crown line with Dionne and left winger Charlie Simmer, Taylor became a prolific scorer and a fearsome checker. Taylor's NHL career stats include a Kings-record 1,111 games, 431 goals, 638 assists and 1,069 points.

A five-time NHL All-Star Game selection, Taylor served as the Kings captain for four seasons (1985-89). After posting career highs in goals (47) and points (112) during the 1980-81 season, Taylor earned a spot on the NHL Second All-Star Team. On April 3, 1995, Taylor's jersey No. 18 was retired, joining Rogie Vachon (No. 30) and Marcel Dionne (No. 16) on the wall of the Great Western Forum. For all his individual accomplishments in hockey, his crowing glory was reaching the Stanley Cup Finals with the 1992-93 Kings.

Away from the ice, Taylor has worked tirelessly for numerous charities throughout the years. Each year he hosts the Dave Taylor Golf Classic benefiting the Cystic Fibrosis Foundation, which annually raises more than $125,000. In 1991, the NHL honored Taylor's contributions to hockey and the community by awarding him both the Bill Masterton and King Clancy trophies.

Dave and his wife, Beth, live in Tarzana, CA with their daughters Jamie and Katie.

Coaching History

Red Kelly, 1967-68, 1968-69; Hal Laycoe and John Wilson, 1969-70; Larry Regan, 1970-71; Larry Regan and Fred Glover, 1971-72; Bob Pulford, 1972-73 to 1976-77; Ron Stewart, 1977-78; Bob Berry, 1978-79 to 1980-81; Parker MacDonald and Don Perry, 1981-82; Don Perry, 1982-83; Don Perry, Rogie Vachon and Roger Neilson, 1983-84; Pat Quinn, 1984-85, 1985-86; Pat Quinn and Mike Murphy 1986-87; Mike Murphy, Rogie Vachon and Robbie Ftorek, 1987-88; Robbie Ftorek, 1988-89; Tom Webster, 1989-90 to 1991-92; Barry Melrose, 1992-93, 1993-94; Barry Melrose and Rogie Vachon, 1994-95; Larry Robinson, 1995-96 to 1998-99; Andy Murray, 1999-2000.

Captains' History

Bob Wall, 1967-68, 1968-69; Larry Cahan, 1969-70, 1970-71; Bob Pulford, 1971-72, 1972-73; Terry Harper, 1973-74, 1974-75; Mike Murphy, 1975-76 to 1980-81; Dave Lewis, 1981-82, 1982-83; Terry Ruskowski, 1983-84, 1984-85; Dave Taylor, 1985-86 to 1988-89; Wayne Gretzky, 1989-90 to 1991-92; Wayne Gretzky and Luc Robitaille, 1992-93; Wayne Gretzky, 1993-94, 1994-95; Wayne Gretzky and Rob Blake, 1995-96; Rob Blake, 1996-97 to date.

Club Records

Team

(Figures in brackets for season records are games played; records for fewest points, wins, ties, losses, goals, goals against are for 70 or more games)

Most Points	105	1974-75 (80)
Most Wins	46	1990-91 (80)
Most Ties	21	1974-75 (80)
Most Losses	52	1969-70 (76)
Most Goals	376	1988-89 (80)
Most Goals Against	389	1985-86 (80)
Fewest Points	38	1969-70 (76)
Fewest Wins	14	1969-70 (76)
Fewest Ties	5	1998-99 (82)
Fewest Losses	17	1974-75 (80)
Fewest Goals	168	1969-70 (76)
Fewest Goals Against	185	1974-75 (80)

Longest Winning Streak

Overall	8	Oct. 21-Nov. 7/72
Home	12	Oct. 10-Dec. 5/92
Away	8	Dec. 18/74-Jan. 16/75

Longest Undefeated Streak

Overall	11	Feb. 28-Mar. 24/74 (9 wins, 2 ties)
Home	13	Oct. 10-Dec. 8/92 (12 wins, 1 tie)
Away	11	Oct. 10-Dec. 11/74 (6 wins, 5 ties)

Longest Losing Streak

Overall	10	Feb. 22-Mar. 9/84
Home	9	Feb. 8-Mar. 12/86
Away	12	Jan. 11-Feb. 15/70

Longest Winless Streak

Overall	17	Jan. 29-Mar. 5/70 (13 losses, 4 ties)
Home	9	Jan. 29-Mar. 5/70 (8 losses, 1 tie), Feb. 8-Mar. 12/86 (9 losses)
Away	21	Jan. 11-Apr. 3/70 (17 losses, 4 ties)

Most Shutouts, Season	9	1974-75 (80)
Most PIM, Season	2,228	1990-91 (80)
Most Goals, Game	12	Nov. 28/84 (Van. 1 at L.A. 12)

Individual

Most Seasons	17	Dave Taylor
Most Games	1,111	Dave Taylor
Most Goals, Career	550	Marcel Dionne
Most Assists, Career	757	Marcel Dionne
Most Points, Career	1,307	Marcel Dionne
Most PIM, Career	1,846	Marty McSorley
Most Shutouts, Career	32	Rogie Vachon

Longest Consecutive

Games Streak	324	Marcel Dionne (Jan. 7/78-Jan. 9/82)
Most Goals, Season	70	Bernie Nicholls (1988-89)
Most Assists, Season	122	Wayne Gretzky (1990-91)
Most Points, Season	168	Wayne Gretzky (1988-89; 54G, 114A)
Most PIM, Season	399	Marty McSorley (1992-93)

Most Points, Defenseman, Season	76	Larry Murphy (1980-81; 16G, 60A)
Most Points, Center, Season	168	Wayne Gretzky (1988-89; 54G, 114A)
Most Points, Right Wing, Season	112	Dave Taylor (1980-81; 47G, 65A)
Most Points, Left Wing, Season	*125	Luc Robitaille (1992-93; 63G, 62A)
Most Points, Rookie, Season	84	Luc Robitaille (1986-87; 45G, 39A)
Most Shutouts, Season	8	Rogie Vachon (1976-77)
Most Goals, Game	4	Sixteen times
Most Assists, Game	6	Bernie Nicholls (Dec. 1/88), Tomas Sandstrom (Oct. 9/93)
Most Points, Game	8	Bernie Nicholls (Dec. 1/88; 2G, 6A)

* NHL Record.

Retired Numbers

16	Marcel Dionne	1975-1987
18	Dave Taylor	1977-1994
30	Rogie Vachon	1971-1978

All-time Record vs. Other Clubs

Regular Season

			At Home							On Road							Total					
	GP	W	L	T	GF	GA	PTS	GP	W	L	T	GF	GA	PTS	GP	W	L	T	GF	GA	PTS
Anaheim	17	9	6	2	49	43	20	16	4	9	3	39	55	11	33	13	15	5	88	98	31
Boston	57	20	31	6	197	214	46	58	11	43	4	161	274	26	115	31	74	10	358	488	72
Buffalo	50	19	22	9	172	175	47	49	15	25	9	146	199	39	99	34	47	18	318	374	86
Calgary	81	41	31	9	313	294	91	84	23	51	10	278	387	56	165	64	82	19	591	681	147
Carolina	26	14	9	3	113	103	31	27	10	13	4	105	105	24	53	24	22	7	218	208	55
Chicago	64	29	29	6	220	220	64	65	26	31	8	198	239	60	129	55	60	14	418	459	124
Colorado	33	19	11	3	141	111	41	32	13	16	3	115	133	29	65	32	27	6	256	244	70
Dallas	69	27	24	18	236	209	72	70	16	42	12	190	284	44	139	43	66	30	426	493	116
Detroit	70	37	20	13	289	219	87	69	29	29	11	250	271	69	139	66	49	24	539	490	156
Edmonton	67	25	28	14	271	285	64	67	19	34	14	249	316	52	134	44	62	28	520	601	116
Florida	5	3	2	0	15	17	6	5	0	2	3	7	14	3	10	3	4	3	22	31	9
Montreal	61	17	35	9	188	243	43	61	7	43	11	154	282	25	122	24	78	20	342	525	68
Nashville	2	0	2	0	4	7	0	2	1	1	0	6	6	2	4	1	3	0	10	13	2
New Jersey	39	27	6	6	198	119	60	39	17	17	5	140	129	39	78	44	23	11	338	248	99
NY Islanders	41	19	15	7	149	134	45	41	13	24	4	115	154	30	82	32	39	11	264	288	75
NY Rangers	56	22	25	9	185	202	53	54	15	33	6	153	216	36	110	37	58	15	338	418	89
Ottawa	6	6	0	0	35	13	12	6	1	4	1	14	20	3	12	7	4	1	49	33	15
Philadelphia	62	20	34	8	184	211	48	60	15	38	7	153	234	37	122	35	72	15	337	445	85
Phoenix	60	22	28	10	243	245	54	63	23	31	9	219	262	55	123	45	59	19	462	507	109
Pittsburgh	66	41	17	8	253	175	90	68	21	38	9	213	252	51	134	62	55	17	466	427	141
St. Louis	68	33	25	10	240	199	76	68	15	44	9	174	259	39	136	48	69	19	414	458	115
San Jose	23	16	6	1	86	61	33	24	9	12	3	76	86	21	47	25	18	4	162	147	54
Tampa Bay	7	1	6	0	16	26	2	6	3	3	0	14	14	6	13	4	9	0	30	40	8
Toronto	64	34	21	9	230	187	77	64	20	33	11	213	257	51	128	54	54	20	443	444	128
Vancouver	89	47	29	13	369	286	107	87	28	45	14	280	341	70	176	75	74	27	649	627	177
Washington	43	25	12	6	170	132	56	42	18	18	6	159	179	42	85	43	30	12	329	311	98
Defunct Clubs	35	27	6	2	141	76	56	34	11	14	9	91	109	31	69	38	20	11	232	185	87
Totals	**1261**	**600**	**480**	**181**	**4707**	**4206**	**1381**	**1261**	**383**	**693**	**185**	**3912**	**5077**	**951**	**2522**	**983**	**1173**	**366**	**8619**	**9283**	**2332**

Playoffs

	Series	W	L	GP	W	L	T	GF	GA	Last Mtg.	Round	Result
Boston	2	0	2	13	5	8	0	38	56	1977	QF	L 2-4
Calgary	6	4	2	26	13	13	0	105	112	1993	DSF	W 4-2
Chicago	1	0	1	5	1	4	0	7	10	1974	QF	L 1-4
Dallas	1	0	1	7	3	4	0	21	26	1968	QF	L 3-4
Edmonton	7	2	5	36	12	24	0	127	154	1992	DSF	L 2-4
Montreal	1	0	1	6	1	5	0	12	15	1993	F	L 1-4
NY Islanders	1	0	1	4	1	3	0	10	21	1980	PR	L 1-3
NY Rangers	2	0	2	6	1	5	0	14	32	1981	PR	L 1-3
St. Louis	2	0	2	8	0	8	0	13	32	1998	CQF	L 0-4
Toronto	3	1	2	12	5	7	0	31	41	1993	CF	W 4-3
Vancouver	3	2	1	17	9	8	0	66	60	1993	DF	W 4-2
Defunct Clubs	1	1	0	4	3	0	23	25			
Totals	**30**	**10**	**20**	**146**	**55**	**91**	**0**	**467**	**584**			

Calgary totals include Atlanta Flames, 1972-73 to 1979-80.
Colorado totals include Quebec, 1979-80 to 1994-95.
New Jersey totals include Kansas City, 1974-75 to 1975-76, and Colorado Rockies, 1976-77 to 1981-82.
Phoenix totals include Winnipeg, 1979-80 to 1995-96.
Carolina totals include Hartford, 1979-80 to 1996-97.
Dallas totals include Minnesota, 1967-68 to 1992-93.

Playoff Results 1999-95

Year	Round	Opponent	Result	GF	GA
1998	CQF	St. Louis	L 0-4	8	16

Abbreviations: Round: F – Final;
CF – conference final; **CQF** – conference quarter-final;
DF – division final; **DSF** – division semi-final;
QF – quarter-final; **PR** – preliminary round.

1998-99 Results

Oct.	10	at Edmonton	2-1		14	Calgary	3-0
	12	at Vancouver	2-4		16	Pittsburgh	1-5
	16	Boston	2-1		19	Colorado	4-5
	18	Colorado	5-5		21	New Jersey	2-3
	21	at Florida	1-1		27	at Dallas	2-3
	23	at Tampa Bay	2-3		29	at Washington	6-3
	25	at Carolina	3-2		30	at Buffalo	1-4
	27	at NY Islanders	0-1	Feb.	1	at Philadelphia	2-4
	28	at New Jersey	4-0		4	Chicago	3-2
	30	Tampa Bay	0-3		6	San Jose	2-0
Nov.	1	Phoenix	0-3		10	at Phoenix	0-3
	5	St. Louis	2-2		11	Philadelphia	4-3
	7	Dallas	3-4		13	Dallas	2-3
	9	at Vancouver	4-3		15	Anaheim	1-3
	10	at Calgary	4-5		18	Edmonton	3-2
	12	Nashville	1-3		20	at Calgary	2-2
	14	Carolina	3-5		22	at St. Louis	1-5
	16	at Anaheim	1-3		24	at Detroit	3-2
	18	at San Jose	4-5		26	at Chicago	2-1
	19	NY Rangers	1-5		28	at Dallas	0-1
	21	Chicago	5-0	Mar.	3	at Anaheim	1-2
	28	Phoenix	0-4		4	Nashville	3-4
	30	at Montreal	1-3		6	Calgary	1-4
Dec.	2	at Toronto	1-3		8	Detroit	4-2
	3	at Ottawa	1-3		13	Vancouver	3-1
	5	Detroit	3-4		15	Ottawa	4-0
	9	Washington	2-1		18	Anaheim	2-4
	12	Vancouver	3-0		20	Florida	4-3
	13	at Anaheim	0-3		21	at Phoenix	1-4
	17	NY Islanders	4-5		25	Dallas	1-2
	19	at St. Louis	2-5		28	at Colorado	2-7
	20	at Chicago	4-1		30	at Boston	2-1
	22	at Pittsburgh	3-0		31	at Detroit	1-2
	26	Phoenix	1-2	Apr.	3	at Nashville	2-3
	28	at Phoenix	4-2		5	at Colorado	1-4
	30	San Jose	5-1		8	at San Jose	3-2
Jan.	2	Colorado	4-2		11	at Dallas	2-6
	5	at Edmonton	4-3		12	at Nashville	4-3
	7	Buffalo	4-2		15	Anaheim	4-3
	9	Edmonton	1-1		16	at San Jose	2-0
	11	at San Jose	0-4		18	St. Louis	2-3

Entry Draft
Selections 1999-85

1999
Pick
43	Andrei Shefer
74	Jason Crain
76	Frantisek Kaberle
92	Cory Campbell
104	Brian McGrattan
125	Daniel Johansson
133	Jean-Francois Nogues
193	Kevin Baker
222	George Parros
250	Noah Clarke

1998
Pick
21	Mathieu Biron
46	Justin Papineau
76	Alexei Volkov
103	Kip Brennan
133	Joe Rullier
163	Tomas Zizka
190	Tommi Hannus
217	Jim Henkel
248	Matthew Yeats

1997
Pick
3	Olli Jokinen
15	Matt Zultek
29	Scott Barney
83	Joseph Corvo
99	Sean Blanchard
137	Richard Seeley
150	Jeff Katcher
193	Jay Kopischke
220	Konrad Brand

1996
Pick
30	Josh Green
37	Marian Cisar
57	Greg Phillips
84	Mikael Simons
96	Eric Belanger
120	Jesse Black
123	Peter Hogan
190	Stephen Valiquette
193	Kai Nurminen
219	Sebastien Simard

1995
Pick
3	Aki-Petteri Berg
33	Donald MacLean
50	Pavel Rosa
59	Vladimir Tsyplakov
118	Jason Morgan
137	Igor Melyakov
157	Benoit Larose
163	Juha Vuorivirta
215	Brian Stewart

1994
Pick
7	Jamie Storr
33	Matt Johnson
59	Vitali Yachmenev
111	Chris Schmidt
163	Luc Gagne
189	Andrew Dale
215	Jan Nemecek
241	Sergei Shalomai

1993
Pick
42	Shayne Toporowski
68	Jeffrey Mitchell
94	Bob Wren
105	Frederick Beaubien
117	Jason Saal
120	Tomas Vlasak
146	Jere Karalahti
172	Justin Martin
198	John-Tra Dillabough
224	Martin Strbak
250	Kimmo Timonen
276	Patrick Howald

1992
Pick
39	Justin Hocking
63	Sandy Allan
87	Kevin Brown
111	Jeff Shevalier
135	Raymond Murray
207	Magnus Wernblom
231	Ryan Pisiak
255	Jukka Tiilikainen

1991
Pick
42	Guy Leveque
79	Keith Redmond
81	Alexei Zhitnik
108	Pauli Jaks
130	Brett Seguin
152	Kelly Fairchild
196	Craig Brown
218	Mattias Olsson
240	Andre Bouliane
262	Michael Gaul

1990
Pick
7	Darryl Sydor
28	Brandy Semchuk
49	Bob Berg
91	David Goverde
112	Erik Andersson
133	Robert Lang
154	Dean Hulett
175	Denis LeBlanc
196	Patrik Ross
217	K.J. (Kevin) White
238	Troy Mohns

1989
Pick
39	Brent Thompson
81	Jim Maher
102	Eric Ricard
103	Thomas Newman
123	Daniel Rydmark
144	Ted Kramer
165	Sean Whyte
182	Jim Giacin
186	Martin Maskarinec
207	Jim Hiller
228	Steve Jaques
249	Kevin Sneddon

1988
Pick
7	Martin Gelinas
28	Paul Holden
49	John Van Kessel
70	Rob Blake
91	Jeff Robison
109	Micah Aivazoff
112	Robert Larsson
133	Jeff Kruesel
154	Timo Peltomaa
175	Jim Larkin
196	Brad Hyatt
217	Doug Laprade
238	Joe Flanagan

1987
Pick
4	Wayne McBean
27	Mark Fitzpatrick
43	Ross Wilson
90	Mike Vukonich
111	Greg Batters
132	Kyosti Karjalainen
174	Jeff Gawlicki
195	John Preston
216	Rostislav Vlach
237	Mikael Lindholm

1986
Pick
2	Jimmy Carson
44	Denis Larocque
65	Sylvain Couturier
86	Dave Guden
107	Robb Stauber
128	Sean Krakiwsky
149	Rene Chapdelaine
170	Trevor Pochipinski
191	Paul Kelly
212	Russ Mann
233	Brian Hayton

1985
Pick
9	Craig Duncanson
10	Dan Gratton
30	Par Edlund
72	Perry Florio
93	Petr Prajsler
135	Tim Flannigan
156	John Hyduke
177	Steve Horner
219	Trent Ciprick
240	Marian Horwath

Coach

MURRAY, ANDY
Coach, Los Angeles Kings. Born in Gladstone, Man., March 3, 1951.

Andy Murray became the 19th head coach in Kings history on June 14, 1999. His coaching experience dates back to 1974 and includes seven seasons as an NHL assistant or associate coach with the Winnipeg Jets (1993 to 1995), Minnesota North Stars (1990 to 1992) and Philadelphia Flyers (1988 to 1990). As an assistant coach in Minnesota, Murray reached the Stanley Cup Finals in 1991.

In addition to his NHL service, Murray brings to the Kings a tremendous amount of international coaching experience. As head coach of the Canadian National Team, he guided his team to a 77-29-14 record and the Gold Medal in the 1997 World Hockey Championships with a team that featured Kings captain Rob Blake.

From 1976 to 1978, Murray served his first head coaching position with the Brandon Travelers of the Manitoba Junior Hockey League. He moved on to become head coach for Brandon University from 1978 to 1981, leading the Bobcats to the #1 ranking in Canadian University hockey during his final year. In 1981-82, Murray moved to Switzerland, where for the next seven years he coached several Swiss-A Division teams.

Murray returned to North America as an assistant coach for the Hershey Bears of the American Hockey League in 1987 and helped guide the Bears to the 1988 Calder Cup Championship. In 1992, Murray returned to Europe to coach Lugano in Switzerland and then Eisbaren Berlin in Germany a year later. Most recently, Murray served as the head coach for Shattuck-St. Mary's in Faribault, Minnesota, where he led the prep school to a 70-9-2 record and the Midget Triple A USA Hockey national championship in 1998-99.

Murray and his wife, Ruth, have three children, sons Braden and Jordan, and daughter, Sarah.

Club Directory

Staples Center

STAPLES Center
111 South Figueroa Street
Los Angeles, CA 90015
Phone **213/742-7100**
GM FAX 310/535-4504
PR FAX 310/535-4540
Website: www.lakings.com
Capacity: 18,500

Executive
Owner	Philip F. Anschutz
Owner	Edward P. Roski
Governor	Robert Sanderman
President/Alternate Governor	Timothy J. Leiweke
Executive Vice President, General Counsel	Ted Fikre
Special Assistant to the President	Rogie Vachon
Executive Assistant to the President	Lisa Tran
Assistant To Executive Vice President, General Counsel	Tiffany Collins

Hockey Operations
Senior Vice President/General Manager	Dave Taylor
Assistant General Manager	Kevin Gilmore
Director, Player Personnel	Bill O'Flaherty
Assistant to the General Manager	John Wolf
Executive Assistant to the General Manager	Marcia Galloway
Head Coach	Andy Murray
Assistant Coaches	Dave Tippett, Mark Hardy, Ray Bennett
Director, Amateur Scouting	Al Murray
Director, Pro Scouting	Ace Bailey
Scouting Staff	Serge Aubry, Greg Dreschel, Rob Laird, Vaclav Nedomansky, John Stanton, Ari Vuori
Video Coordinator	Bill Gurney

Medical
Trainer	Peter Demers
Massage Therapist/Assistant Athletic Trainer	Rick Burrill
Rehabilitation Coach	Robert Zolg
Strength Coach	Joe Horrigan
Fitness Consultant	Guy Lemasurier
Team Physician	Dr. Ronald Kvitne

Jobe Orthopaedic Clinic
Internist	Dr. Michael Mellman
Dentist	Dr. Jeffrey Hoy
Opthamologist	Dr. Howard Lazerson

Equipment Staff
Equipment Manager	Peter Millar
Assistant Equipment Manager	Rick Garcia
Equipment Coordinator	Grady Clark

Media Relations/Team Services
Director, Media Relations/Team Services	Mike Altieri
Manager, Media Relations/Media Relations	Jeff Moeller
Media Relations Assistant	Jason Pommier
Team Photography	Andrew D. Bernstein, Robert Mora

Finance/Accounting/Ticket Operations
Executive Vice President, Chief Financial Officer	Dan Beckerman
Director, Finance	Peter Mazur
Director, Ticket Operations	Jeremy Brollier
Payroll Manager	Tom Barganski
Accounts Payable	Emma Harris
Accounts Receivable	Heather O'Connor
Ticket Coordinator	Bobby Anderson
Ticket Coordinator	Nell Nicolas
Assistant to Executive Vice President, Chief Financial Officer	Kely Lyon

Sales and Marketing
Executive Vice President, Sales and Marketing	John Rizzardini
Director, Group and Inside Sales	Bill Chapin
Director, Marketing and Promotions	Kurt Schwartzkopf
Assistant to Executive Vice President, Sales and Marketing	Jackie C. Howard

Client Services
Vice President, Client Services	Sheila Gonzaga
Account Executive	Susan Long
Account Executive	Kevin Donovan
Manager, Client Services	Amy Banachowski
Account Coordinator	Jason Bednar
Account Coordinator	Jennifer Cordova
Account Coordinator	Cortney Soroka
Executive Assistant/Account Coordinator	Courtney Coffland

Community/Fan Development
Director, Community Development	Kelly Davis
Director, Fan Development	Steve Bogoyevac
Community Relations Coordinator	Kris Nakamura
Fan Development Assistant	Annie Camins

Merchandise
Director, Merchandise	Doreen Imperial
Pro Shop	Scott Nady

Entertainment and Events
Director, Entertainment and Events	Marianne Herman
Public Address Announcer	David Courtney
Supervisor, Off-Ice Officials	Bill Meuris

Broadcasting
Play-by-Play Announcer, Television	Bob Miller
Play-by-Play Announcer, Radio	Nick Nickson
Color Commentator, Television	Jim Fox
Color Commentator, Radio	Daryl Evans
Television Network	Fox Sports Net West
Flagship Radio Station	KRLA (1110 AM)
Team Colors	Purple, White, Black and Silver
Training Center	Kings Training Center
Location of Bob Miller Press Box	Upper concourse, west side

Montreal Canadiens

1998-99 Results: 32W-39L-11T 75PTS. Fifth, Northeast Division

With 44 points in 1998-99, Saku Koivu was the first European player to lead the Canadiens in scoring since Mats Naslund topped the team in 1988-89.

Franchise date: November 22, 1917

EASTERN NHL CONFERENCE

NORTHEAST DIVISION

83rd NHL Season

Year-by-Year Record

Season	GP	Home W	L	T	Road W	L	T	Overall W	L	T	GF	GA	Pts.	Finished	Playoff Result
1998-99	82	21	15	5	11	24	6	32	39	11	184	209	75	5th, Northeast Div.	Out of Playoffs
1997-98	82	15	17	9	22	15	4	37	32	13	235	208	87	4th, Northeast Div.	Lost Conf. Semi-Final
1996-97	82	17	17	7	14	19	8	31	36	15	249	276	77	4th, Northeast Div.	Lost Conf. Quarter-Final
1995-96	82	23	12	6	17	20	4	40	32	10	265	248	90	3rd, Northeast Div.	Lost Conf. Quarter-Final
1994-95	48	15	5	4	3	18	3	18	23	7	125	148	43	6th, Northeast Div.	Out of Playoffs
1993-94	84	26	12	4	15	17	10	41	29	14	283	248	96	3rd, Northeast Div.	Lost Conf. Quarter-Final
1992-93	**84**	**27**	**13**	**2**	**21**	**17**	**4**	**48**	**30**	**6**	**326**	**280**	**102**	**3rd, Adams Div.**	**Won Stanley Cup**
1991-92	80	27	8	5	14	20	6	41	28	11	267	207	93	1st, Adams Div.	Lost Div. Final
1990-91	80	23	12	5	16	18	6	39	30	11	273	249	89	2nd, Adams Div.	Lost Div. Final
1989-90	80	26	8	6	15	20	5	41	28	11	288	234	93	3rd, Adams Div.	Lost Div. Final
1988-89	80	30	6	4	23	12	5	53	18	9	315	218	115	1st, Adams Div.	Lost Final
1987-88	80	26	8	6	19	14	7	45	22	13	298	238	103	1st, Adams Div.	Lost Div. Final
1986-87	80	27	9	4	14	20	6	41	29	10	277	241	92	2nd, Adams Div.	Lost Conf. Championship
1985-86	**80**	**25**	**11**	**4**	**15**	**22**	**3**	**40**	**33**	**7**	**330**	**280**	**87**	**2nd, Adams Div.**	**Won Stanley Cup**
1984-85	80	24	10	6	17	17	6	41	27	12	309	262	94	1st, Adams Div.	Lost Div. Final
1983-84	80	19	19	2	16	21	3	35	40	5	286	295	75	4th, Adams Div.	Lost Conf. Championship
1982-83	80	25	6	9	17	18	5	42	24	14	350	286	98	2nd, Adams Div.	Lost Div. Semi-Final
1981-82	80	25	6	9	21	11	8	46	17	17	360	223	109	1st, Adams Div.	Lost Div. Semi-Final
1980-81	80	31	7	2	14	15	11	45	22	13	332	232	103	1st, Norris Div.	Lost Prelim. Round
1979-80	80	30	7	3	17	13	10	47	20	13	328	240	107	1st, Norris Div.	Lost Quarter-Final
1978-79	**80**	**29**	**6**	**5**	**23**	**11**	**6**	**52**	**17**	**11**	**337**	**204**	**115**	**1st, Norris Div.**	**Won Stanley Cup**
1977-78	**80**	**32**	**4**	**4**	**27**	**6**	**7**	**59**	**10**	**11**	**359**	**183**	**129**	**1st, Norris Div.**	**Won Stanley Cup**
1976-77	**80**	**33**	**1**	**6**	**27**	**7**	**6**	**60**	**8**	**12**	**387**	**171**	**132**	**1st, Norris Div.**	**Won Stanley Cup**
1975-76	**80**	**32**	**3**	**5**	**26**	**8**	**6**	**58**	**11**	**11**	**337**	**174**	**127**	**1st, Norris Div.**	**Won Stanley Cup**
1974-75	80	27	8	5	20	6	14	47	14	19	374	225	113	1st, Norris Div.	Lost Semi-Final
1973-74	78	24	12	3	21	12	6	45	24	9	293	240	99	2nd, East Div.	Lost Quarter-inal
1972-73	**78**	**29**	**4**	**6**	**23**	**6**	**10**	**52**	**10**	**16**	**329**	**184**	**120**	**1st, East Div.**	**Won Stanley Cup**
1971-72	78	29	3	7	17	13	9	46	16	16	307	205	108	3rd, East Div.	Lost Quarter-Final
1970-71	**78**	**29**	**7**	**3**	**13**	**16**	**10**	**42**	**23**	**13**	**291**	**216**	**97**	**3rd, East Div.**	**Won Stanley Cup**
1969-70	76	21	9	8	17	13	8	38	22	16	244	201	92	5th, East Div.	Out of Playoffs
1968-69	**76**	**26**	**7**	**5**	**20**	**12**	**6**	**46**	**19**	**11**	**271**	**202**	**103**	**1st, East Div.**	**Won Stanley Cup**
1967-68	**74**	**26**	**5**	**6**	**16**	**17**	**4**	**42**	**22**	**10**	**236**	**167**	**94**	**1st, East Div.**	**Won Stanley Cup**
1966-67	70	19	9	7	13	16	6	32	25	13	202	188	77	2nd,	Lost Final
1965-66	**70**	**23**	**11**	**1**	**18**	**10**	**7**	**41**	**21**	**8**	**239**	**173**	**90**	**1st,**	**Won Stanley Cup**
1964-65	**70**	**20**	**8**	**7**	**16**	**15**	**4**	**36**	**23**	**11**	**211**	**185**	**83**	**2nd,**	**Won Stanley Cup**
1963-64	70	22	7	6	14	14	7	36	21	13	209	167	85	1st,	Lost Semi-Final
1962-63	70	15	10	10	13	9	13	28	19	23	225	183	79	3rd,	Lost Semi-Final
1961-62	70	26	2	7	16	12	7	42	14	14	259	166	98	1st,	Lost Semi-Final
1960-61	70	24	6	5	17	13	5	41	19	10	254	188	92	1st,	Lost Semi-Final
1959-60	**70**	**23**	**4**	**8**	**17**	**14**	**4**	**40**	**18**	**12**	**255**	**178**	**92**	**1st,**	**Won Stanley Cup**
1958-59	**70**	**21**	**8**	**6**	**18**	**10**	**7**	**39**	**18**	**13**	**258**	**158**	**91**	**1st,**	**Won Stanley Cup**
1957-58	**70**	**23**	**6**	**6**	**20**	**9**	**6**	**43**	**17**	**10**	**250**	**158**	**96**	**1st,**	**Won Stanley Cup**
1956-57	**70**	**23**	**6**	**6**	**12**	**17**	**6**	**35**	**23**	**12**	**210**	**155**	**82**	**2nd,**	**Won Stanley Cup**
1955-56	**70**	**29**	**5**	**1**	**16**	**10**	**9**	**45**	**15**	**10**	**222**	**131**	**100**	**1st,**	**Won Stanley Cup**
1954-55	70	26	5	4	15	13	7	41	18	11	228	157	93	2nd,	Lost Final
1953-54	70	27	5	3	8	19	8	35	24	11	195	141	81	2nd,	Lost Final
1952-53	**70**	**18**	**12**	**5**	**10**	**11**	**14**	**28**	**23**	**19**	**155**	**148**	**75**	**2nd,**	**Won Stanley Cup**
1951-52	70	22	8	5	12	18	5	34	26	10	195	164	78	2nd,	Lost Final
1950-51	70	17	10	8	8	20	7	25	30	15	173	184	65	3rd,	Lost Final
1949-50	70	17	8	10	12	14	9	29	22	19	172	150	77	2nd,	Lost Semi-Final
1948-49	60	19	13	4	9	15	6	28	23	9	152	126	65	3rd,	Lost Semi-Final
1947-48	60	13	13	4	7	16	7	20	29	11	147	169	51	5th,	Out of Playoffs
1946-47	60	19	6	5	15	10	5	34	16	10	189	138	78	1st,	Lost Final
1945-46	**50**	**16**	**6**	**3**	**12**	**11**	**2**	**28**	**17**	**5**	**172**	**134**	**61**	**1st,**	**Won Stanley Cup**
1944-45	50	21	2	2	17	6	2	38	8	4	228	121	80	1st,	Lost Semi-Final
1943-44	**50**	**22**	**0**	**3**	**16**	**5**	**4**	**38**	**5**	**7**	**234**	**109**	**83**	**1st,**	**Won Stanley Cup**
1942-43	50	14	4	7	5	15	5	19	19	12	181	191	50	4th,	Lost Semi-Final
1941-42	48	12	10	2	6	17	1	18	27	3	134	173	39	6th,	Lost Quarter-Final
1940-41	48	11	9	4	5	17	2	16	26	6	121	147	38	6th,	Lost Quarter-Final
1939-40	48	5	14	5	5	19	0	10	33	5	90	167	25	7th,	Out of Playoffs
1938-39	48	8	11	5	7	13	4	15	24	9	115	146	39	6th,	Lost Quarter-Final
1937-38	48	13	4	7	5	13	6	18	17	13	123	128	49	3rd, Cdn. Div.	Lost Semi-Final
1936-37	48	16	8	0	8	10	6	24	18	6	115	111	54	1st, Cdn. Div.	Lost Semi-Final
1935-36	48	5	11	8	6	15	3	11	26	11	82	123	33	4th, Cdn. Div.	Out of Playoffs
1934-35	48	11	11	2	8	12	4	19	23	6	110	145	44	3rd, Cdn. Div.	Lost Quarter-Final
1933-34	48	11	6	2	6	14	4	22	20	6	99	101	50	2nd, Cdn. Div.	Lost Quarter-Final
1932-33	48	15	5	4	3	20	1	18	25	5	92	115	41	3rd, Cdn. Div.	Lost Quarter-Final
1931-32	48	18	3	3	7	13	4	25	16	7	128	111	57	1st, Cdn. Div.	Lost Semi-Final
1930-31	**44**	**15**	**3**	**4**	**11**	**7**	**4**	**26**	**10**	**8**	**129**	**89**	**60**	**1st, Cdn. Div.**	**Won Stanley Cup**
1929-30	**44**	**13**	**5**	**4**	**8**	**9**	**5**	**21**	**14**	**9**	**142**	**114**	**51**	**2nd, Cdn. Div.**	**Won Stanley Cup**
1928-29	44	12	4	6	10	3	9	22	7	15	71	43	59	1st, Cdn. Div.	Lost Semi-Final
1927-28	44	12	7	3	14	4	4	26	11	7	116	48	59	1st, Cdn. Div.	Lost Semi-Final
1926-27	44	15	5	2	13	9	0	28	14	2	99	67	58	2nd, Cdn. Div.	Lost Semi-Final
1925-26	36	5	12	1	6	12	0	11	24	1	79	108	23	7th,	Out of Playoffs
1924-25	30	10	5	0	7	6	2	17	11	2	93	56	36	3rd,	Lost Final
1923-24	**24**	**10**	**2**	**0**	**3**	**9**	**0**	**13**	**11**	**0**	**59**	**48**	**26**	**2nd,**	**Won Stanley Cup**
1922-23	24	10	2	0	3	7	2	13	9	2	73	61	28	2nd,	Lost NHL Final
1921-22	24	8	3	1	4	8	0	12	11	1	88	94	25	3rd,	Out of Playoffs
1920-21	24	9	3	0	4	8	0	13	11	0	112	99	26	3rd and 2nd*	Out of Playoffs
1919-20	24	9	4	0	4	8	0	13	11	0	129	113	26	2nd and 3rd*	Out of Playoffs
1918-19	18	7	2	0	3	6	0	10	8	0	88	78	20	1st and 2nd*	Cup Final but no Decision
1917-18	22	8	3	0	5	6	0	13	10	0	115	84	26	1st and 3rd*	Lost NHL Final

* Season played in two halves with no combined standing at end.
From 1917-18 through 1925-26, NHL champions played against PCHA/WCHL champions for Stanley Cup.

1999-2000 Player Personnel

FORWARDS	HT	WT	S	Place of Birth	Date	1998-99 Club
ASHAM, Arron	5-11	194	R	Portage La Prairie, Man.	4/13/78	Montreal-Fredericton
BASHKIROV, Andrei	6-0	198	L	Shelekhov, USSR	6/22/70	Mtl-Fred-Fort Wayne
BELANGER, Jesse	6-1	190	R	St. Georges de Beauce, Que.	6/15/69	Cleveland
BRUNET, Benoit	6-0	198	L	Ste-Anne-de-Bellevue, Que.	8/24/68	Montreal
CHOUINARD, Eric	6-3	198	L	Atlanta, GA	7/8/80	Quebec (QMJHL)-Fredericton
CORSON, Shayne	6-1	202	L	Barrie, Ont.	8/13/66	Montreal
CUMMINS, Jim	6-2	219	R	Dearborn, MI	5/17/70	Phoenix
DARBY, Craig	6-3	200	R	Oneida, NY	9/26/72	Milwaukee
DELISLE, Jonathan	5-10	180	R	Ste-Anne-des-Plaines, Que.	6/30/77	Montreal-Fredericton
DWYER, Gordie	6-2	216	L	Dalhousie, NB	1/25/78	Fredericton-New Orleans
HARRIS, Darcy	6-1	194	R	O'Leary, P.E.I.	12/22/78	Fredericton
HIGGINS, Matt	6-2	188	L	Calgary, Alta.	10/29/77	Montreal-Fredericton
KOIVU, Saku	5-10	183	L	Turku, Finland	11/23/74	Montreal
LINDEN, Trevor	6-4	220	R	Medicine Hat, Alta.	4/11/70	NY Islanders
McCLEARY, Trent	6-0	180	R	Swift Current, Sask.	9/8/72	Montreal
MORIN, Olivier	6-0	177	R	Montreal, Que.	4/2/78	New Orleans
MORISSETTE, Dave	6-1	224	L	Baie Comeau, Que.	12/24/71	Montreal-Fredericton
OLSON, Boyd	6-1	188	L	Edmonton, Alta.	4/4/76	Fredericton
PETROV, Oleg	5-8	175	L	Moscow, USSR	4/18/71	Ambri-Piotta
POULIN, Patrick	6-1	218	L	Vanier, Que.	4/23/73	Montreal
RUCINSKY, Martin	6-1	205	L	Most, Czech.	3/11/71	CHZ Litvinov-Montreal
RYAN, Terry	6-1	202	L	St. John's, Nfld.	1/14/77	Montreal-Fredericton
SAVAGE, Brian	6-2	192	L	Sudbury, Ont.	2/24/71	Montreal
STEVENSON, Turner	6-3	226	R	Prince George, B.C.	5/18/72	Montreal
THORNTON, Scott	6-3	216	L	London, Ont.	1/9/71	Montreal
WARD, Jason	6-2	192	R	Chapleau, Ont.	1/16/79	Windsor-Plymouth-Fredericton
ZHOLTOK, Sergei	6-0	187	R	Riga, Latvia	2/12/72	Montreal-Fredericton
ZUBRUS, Dainius	6-3	220	L	Elektrenai, USSR	6/16/78	Philadelphia-Montreal
DEFENSEMEN						
BOUILLON, Francis	5-8	186	L	New York, NY	10/17/75	Fredericton
BRISEBOIS, Patrice	6-2	204	R	Montreal, Que.	1/27/71	Montreal
BRISKE, Byron	6-3	200	R	Humboldt, Sask.	1/23/76	Cincinnati (AHL)
GUREN, Miloslav	6-2	209	L	Uherske Hradiste, Czech.	9/24/76	Montreal-Fredericton
LACHANCE, Scott	6-1	209	L	Charlottesville, VA	10/22/72	NY Islanders-Montreal
MALAKHOV, Vladimir	6-4	227	L	Ekaterinburg, USSR	8/30/68	Montreal
NASREDDINE, Alain	6-1	201	L	Montreal, Que.	7/10/75	Chi-Port (AHL)-Mtl-Fred
RAZIN, Gennady	6-4	201	L	Kharkov, USSR	2/3/78	Fredericton
RICHTER, Barry	6-2	200	L	Madison, WI	9/11/70	NY Islanders
RIVET, Craig	6-2	197	R	North Bay, Ont.	9/13/74	Montreal
ROBIDAS, Stephane	5-10	180	R	Sherbrooke, Que.	3/3/77	Fredericton
SIDULOV, Konstantin	6-1	176	R	Chelyabinsk, USSR	1/1/77	Fredericton-Miami
ULANOV, Igor	6-3	211	L	Krasnokamsk, USSR	10/1/69	Montreal
WEINRICH, Eric	6-1	215	L	Roanoke, VA	12/19/66	Chicago-Montreal

GOALTENDERS	HT	WT	C	Place of Birth	Date	1998-99 Club
CHABOT, Frederic	5-11	187	L	Hebertville-Station, Que.	2/12/68	Montreal-Houston
GARON, Mathieu	6-2	187	R	Chandler, Que.	1/9/78	Fredericton
HACKETT, Jeff	6-1	195	L	London, Ont.	6/1/68	Chicago-Montreal
THEODORE, Jose	5-10	182	R	Laval, Que.	9/13/76	Montreal-Fredericton

Coaching History

Jack Laviolette, 1909-10; Adolphe Lecours, 1910-11; Napoleon Dorval, 1911-12, 1912-13; Jimmy Gardner, 1913-14, 1914-15; Newsy Lalonde, 1915-16 to 1920-21; Newsy Lalonde and Léo Dandurand, 1921-22; Léo Dandurand, 1922-23 to 1925-26; Cecil Hart, 1926-27 to 1931-32; Newsy Lalonde, 1932-33, 1933-34; Newsy Lalonde and Léo Dandurand, 1934-35; Sylvio Mantha, 1935-36; Cecil Hart, 1936-37, 1937-38; Cecil Hart and Jules Dugal, 1938-39; Babe Siebert, 1939*; Pit Lepine, 1939-40; Dick Irvin 1940-41 to 1954-55; Toe Blake, 1955-56 to 1967-68; Claude Ruel, 1968-69, 1969-70; Claude Ruel and Al MacNeil, 1970-71; Scotty Bowman, 1971-72 to 1978-79; Bernie Geoffrion and Claude Ruel, 1979-80; Claude Ruel, 1980-81; Bob Berry, 1981-82, 1982-83; Bob Berry and Jacques Lemaire, 1983-84; Jacques Lemaire, 1984-85; Jean Perron, 1985-86 to 1987-88; Pat Burns, 1988-89 to 1991-92; Jacques Demers, 1992-93 to 1994-95; Jacques Demers and Mario Tremblay, 1995-96; Mario Tremblay, 1996-97; Alain Vigneault, 1997-98 to date.

* Named coach in summer but died before 1939-40 season began.

Coach

VIGNEAULT, ALAIN

Coach, Montreal Canadiens. Born in Quebec, Que., May 14, 1961.

Alain Vigneault was named the 24th head coach in the history of the Montreal Canadiens on May 26, 1997, becoming the second youngest coach in team history.

Vigneault, who guided the Canadiens to the Eastern Conference semi-finals during his first season, possesses more than eleven years of coaching experience. He coached the QMJHL Beauport Harfangs for two seasons (1995-96 and 1996-97), following more than three years as an assistant coach with the NHL Ottawa Senators.

Vigneault was the head coach of the Hull Olympiques for five seasons (1987 to 1992), leading his team to the Memorial Cup Tournament in his first season. His coaching career began in 1986-87 with the Trois-Rivières Draveurs of the QMJHL. As head coach at the junior hockey level, Vigneault had a record of 257 victories, 213 losses and 35 ties. In 580 games (season and playoffs), he posted a .541 winning percentage.

Vigneault was assistant coach on Canada's National Junior Team in 1989 and 1991, winning the gold medal at the 1991 World Junior Championships in Saskatoon. He was honored once as CHL coach of the year (1987-88), and twice as head coach of the QMJHL Second All-Star Team.

Alain Vigneault played a total of 42 games in the NHL from 1981 to 1983 with the St. Louis Blues. He resides in Montreal with his spouse, Josée Doucet, and their two daughters, Andréanne and Janie.

1998-99 Scoring

* – rookie

Regular Season

Pos	#	Player	Team	GP	G	A	Pts	+/–	PIM	PP	SH	GW	GT	S	%
C	11	Saku Koivu	MTL	65	14	30	44	–7	38	4	2	0	0	145	9.7
L	26	Martin Rucinsky	MTL	73	17	17	34	–25	50	5	0	1	0	180	9.4
D	38	Vladimir Malakhov	MTL	62	13	21	34	–7	77	8	0	3	0	143	9.1
L	27	Shayne Corson	MTL	63	12	20	32	–10	147	7	0	4	0	142	8.5
L	17	Benoit Brunet	MTL	60	14	17	31	–1	31	4	2	0	0	115	12.2
R	23	Turner Stevenson	MTL	69	10	17	27	6	88	0	0	2	1	102	9.8
D	5	Stephane Quintal	MTL	82	8	19	27	–23	84	1	1	4	0	159	5.0
L	49	Brian Savage	MTL	54	16	10	26	–14	20	5	0	4	1	124	12.9
C	37	Patrick Poulin	MTL	81	8	17	25	6	21	0	1	1	0	87	9.2
C	34	Sergei Zholtok	MTL	70	7	15	22	–12	6	2	0	3	0	102	6.9
D	22	Eric Weinrich	CHI	14	1	3	4	–13	12	0	0	0	0	24	4.2
			MTL	66	6	12	18	–12	77	4	0	1	1	95	6.3
			TOTAL	80	7	15	22	–25	89	4	0	1	1	119	5.9
R	44	Jonas Hoglund	MTL	74	8	10	18	–5	16	1	0	0	1	122	6.6
R	28	Dainius Zubrus	PHI	63	3	5	8	–5	25	0	1	0	0	49	6.1
			MTL	17	3	5	8	–3	4	0	0	1	0	31	9.7
			TOTAL	80	6	10	16	–8	29	0	1	1	0	80	7.5
R	21	Jason Dawe	NYI	22	2	3	5	0	8	0	0	0	0	29	6.9
			MTL	37	4	5	9	0	14	1	0	1	0	52	7.7
			TOTAL	59	6	8	14	0	22	1	0	1	0	81	7.4
D	43	Patrice Brisebois	MTL	54	3	9	12	–8	28	1	0	1	0	90	3.3
D	55	Igor Ulanov	MTL	76	3	9	12	–3	109	0	0	0	0	55	5.5
C	24	Scott Thornton	MTL	47	7	4	11	–2	87	1	0	1	1	56	12.5
D	20	Scott Lachance	NYI	59	1	8	9	–19	30	1	0	0	0	37	2.7
			MTL	17	1	1	2	–2	11	0	0	0	0	22	4.5
			TOTAL	76	2	9	11	–21	41	1	0	0	0	59	3.4
D	52	Craig Rivet	MTL	66	2	8	10	–3	66	0	0	0	0	39	5.1
D	29	Brett Clark	MTL	61	2	2	4	–3	16	0	0	0	0	36	5.6
C	15	Eric Houde	MTL	8	1	1	2	–2	2	0	0	1	0	4	25.0
C	46	* Matt Higgins	MTL	25	1	0	1	–2	0	0	0	0	0	12	8.3
D	48	* Miloslav Guren	MTL	12	0	1	1	–1	4	0	0	0	0	11	0.0
G	31	Jeff Hackett	CHI	10	0	0	0	0	6	0	0	0	0	0	0.0
			MTL	53	0	1	1	0	6	0	0	0	0	0	0.0
			TOTAL	63	0	1	1	0	12	0	0	0	0	0	0.0
L	14	* Terry Ryan	MTL	1	0	0	0	0	5	0	0	0	0	0	0.0
R	42	* Jonathan Delisle	MTL	1	0	0	0	0	0	0	0	0	0	0	0.0
D	53	* Sylvain Blouin	MTL	5	0	0	0	0	19	0	0	0	0	1	0.0
R	30	Jean-Francois Jomphe	PHX	1	0	0	0	0	2	0	0	0	0	0	0.0
			MTL	6	0	0	0	0	0	0	0	0	0	4	0.0
			TOTAL	7	0	0	0	0	2	0	0	0	0	4	0.0
C	45	* Arron Asham	MTL	7	0	0	0	–4	0	0	0	0	0	5	0.0
L	36	Dave Morissette	MTL	10	0	0	0	1	52	0	0	0	0	2	0.0
L	35	Andrei Bashkirov	MTL	10	0	0	0	–3	0	0	0	0	0	4	0.0
G	39	Frederic Chabot	MTL	11	0	0	0	0	2	0	0	0	0	0	0.0
D	56	* Alain Nasreddine	CHI	7	0	0	0	–2	19	0	0	0	0	2	0.0
			MTL	8	0	0	0	1	33	0	0	0	0	1	0.0
			TOTAL	15	0	0	0	–1	52	0	0	0	0	3	0.0
G	60	* Jose Theodore	MTL	18	0	0	0	0	0	0	0	0	0	0	0.0
C	6	Trent McCleary	MTL	46	0	0	0	–1	29	0	0	0	0	18	0.0

Goaltending

No.	Goaltender	GPI	Mins	Avg	W	L	T	EN	SO	GA	SA	S%
39	Frederic Chabot	11	430	2.23	1	3	0	0	0	16	188	.915
31	Jeff Hackett	53	3091	2.27	24	20	9	2	5	117	1360	.914
41	Jocelyn Thibault	10	529	2.61	3	4	2	0	1	23	250	.908
60	* Jose Theodore	18	913	3.29	4	12	0	1	1	50	406	.877
	Totals	**82**	**4988**	**2.51**	**32**	**39**	**11**	**3**	**7**	**209**	**2207**	**.905**

Captains' History

Jack Laviolette, 1909-10; Newsy Lalonde, 1910-11; Jack Laviolette, 1911-12; Newsy Lalonde, 1912-13; Jimmy Gardner, 1913-14, 1914-15; Howard McNamara, 1915-16; Newsy Lalonde, 1916-17 to 1921-22; Sprague Cleghorn, 1922-23 to 1924-25; Bill Coutu, 1925-26; Sylvio Mantha, 1926-27 to 1931-32; George Hainsworth, 1932-33; Sylvio Mantha, 1933-34 to 1935-36; Babe Siebert, 1936-37 to 1938-39; Walter Buswell, 1939-40; Toe Blake, 1940-41 to 1946-47; Toe Blake and Bill Durnan, 1947-48; Emile Bouchard, 1948-49 to 1955-56; Maurice Richard, 1956-57 to 1959-60; Doug Harvey, 1960-61; Jean Béliveau, 1961-62 to 1970-71; Henri Richard, 1971-72 to 1974-75; Yvan Cournoyer, 1975-76 to 1978-79; Serge Savard, 1979-80, 1980-81; Bob Gainey, 1981-82 to 1988-89; Guy Carbonneau and Chris Chelios (co-captains), 1989-90; Guy Carbonneau, 1990-91 to 1993-94; Kirk Muller and Mike Keane, 1994-95; Mike Keane and Pierre Turgeon, 1995-96; Pierre Turgeon and Vincent Damphousse, 1996-97; Vincent Damphousse, 1997-98, 1998-99.

Coaching Record

		Regular Season					Playoffs			
Season	Team	Games	W	L	T	%	Games	W	L	%
1986-87	Trois-Rivières (QMJHL)	65	26	37	2	.415	....	....	....	....
1987-88	Hull (QMJHL)	70	43	23	4	.643	19	12	7	.632
1988-89	Hull (QMJHL)	66	36	25	5	.583	9	5	4	.556
1989-90	Hull (QMJHL)	70	36	29	5	.550	11	4	7	.364
1990-91	Hull (QMJHL)	65	33	25	7	.562	6	2	4	.333
1991-92	Hull (QMJHL)	68	40	23	5	.625	6	2	4	.333
1995-96	Beauport (QMJHL)	31	19	7	5	.694	20	13	7	.650
1996-97	Beauport (QMJHL)	70	24	44	2	.357	4	1	3	.250
1997-98	**Montreal (NHL)**	**82**	**37**	**32**	**13**	**.530**	**10**	**4**	**6**	**.400**
1998-99	**Montreal (NHL)**	**82**	**32**	**39**	**11**	**.457**	**....**	**....**	**....**	**....**
	NHL Totals	**164**	**69**	**71**	**24**	**.494**	**10**	**4**	**6**	**.400**

Club Records

Team

(Figures in brackets for season records are games played; records for fewest points, wins, ties, losses, goals, goals against are for 70 or more games)

Most Points	*132	1976-77 (80)
Most Wins	60	1976-77 (80)
Most Ties	23	1962-63 (70)
Most Losses	40	1983-84 (80)
Most Goals	387	1976-77 (80)
Most Goals Against	295	1983-84 (80)
Fewest Points	65	1950-51 (70)
Fewest Wins	25	1950-51 (70)
Fewest Ties	5	1983-84 (80)
Fewest Losses	*8	1976-77 (80)
Fewest Goals	155	1952-53 (70)
Fewest Goals Against	*131	1955-56 (70)
Longest Winning Streak		
Overall	12	Jan. 6-Feb. 3/68
Home	13	Nov. 2/43-Jan. 8/44, Jan. 30-Mar. 26/77
Away	8	Dec. 18/77-Jan. 18/78, Jan. 21-Feb. 21/82
Longest Undefeated Streak		
Overall	28	Dec. 18/77-Feb. 23/78 (23 wins, 5 ties)
Home	*34	Nov. 1/76-Apr. 2/77 (28 wins, 6 ties)
Away	*23	Nov. 27/74-Mar. 12/75 (14 wins, 9 ties)
Longest Losing Streak		
Overall	12	Feb. 13-Mar. 13/26
Home	7	Dec. 16/39-Jan. 18/40
Away	10	Jan. 16-Mar. 13/26
Longest Winless Streak		
Overall	12	Feb. 13-Mar. 13/26 (12 losses), Nov. 28-Dec. 29/35 (8 losses, 4 ties)
Home	15	Dec. 16/39-Mar. 7/40 (12 losses, 3 ties)
Away	12	Nov. 26/33-Jan. 28/34 (8 losses, 4 ties), Oct. 20/50-Dec. 13/51 (8 losses, 4 ties)
Most Shutouts, Season	*22	1928-29 (44)
Most PIM, Season	1,847	1995-96 (82)
Most Goals, Game	*16	Mar. 3/20 (Mtl. 16 at Que. 3)

Individual

Most Seasons	20	Henri Richard, Jean Béliveau
Most Games	1,256	Henri Richard
Most Goals, Career	544	Maurice Richard
Most Assists, Career	728	Guy Lafleur
Most Points, Career	1,246	Guy Lafleur (518G, 728A)
Most PIM, Career	2,248	Chris Nilan
Most Shutouts, Career	75	George Hainsworth
Longest Consecutive Games Streak	560	Doug Jarvis (Oct. 8/75-Apr. 4/82)
Most Goals, Season	60	Steve Shutt (1976-77), Guy Lafleur (1977-78)
Most Assists, Season	82	Peter Mahovlich (1974-75)
Most Points, Season	136	Guy Lafleur (1976-77; 56G, 80A)
Most PIM, Season	358	Chris Nilan (1984-85)
Most Points, Defenseman, Season	85	Larry Robinson (1976-77; 19G, 66A)
Most Points, Center, Season	117	Peter Mahovlich (1974-75; 35G, 82A)
Most Points, Right Wing, Season	136	Guy Lafleur (1976-77; 56G, 80A)
Most Points, Left Wing, Season	110	Mats Naslund (1985-86; 43G, 67A)
Most Points, Rookie, Season	71	Mats Naslund (1982-83; 26G, 45A), Kjell Dahlin (1985-86; 32G, 39A)
Most Shutouts, Season	*22	George Hainsworth (1928-29)
Most Goals, Game	6	Newsy Lalonde (Jan. 10/20)
Most Assists, Game	6	Elmer Lach (Feb. 6/43)
Most Points, Game	8	Maurice Richard (Dec. 28/44; 5G, 3A), Bert Olmstead (Jan. 9/54; 4G, 4A)

* NHL Record.

Retired Numbers

1	Jacques Plante	1952-1963
2	Doug Harvey	1947-1961
4	Jean Béliveau	1950-1971
7	Howie Morenz	1923-1937
9	Maurice Richard	1942-1960
10	Guy Lafleur	1971-1984
16	Henri Richard	1955-1975

All-time Record vs. Other Clubs

Regular Season

	At Home							On Road							Total						
	GP	W	L	T	GF	GA	PTS	GP	W	L	T	GF	GA	PTS	GP	W	L	T	GF	GA	PTS
Anaheim	5	2	2	1	17	15	5	4	3	1	0	17	15	6	9	5	3	1	34	30	11
Boston	321	184	92	45	1089	759	413	322	119	148	55	871	952	293	643	303	240	100	1960	1711	706
Buffalo	90	51	27	12	359	271	114	89	25	45	19	243	280	69	179	76	72	31	602	551	183
Calgary	42	24	11	7	151	103	55	42	24	13	5	147	128	53	84	48	24	12	298	231	108
Carolina	65	43	15	7	278	109	93	68	32	27	9	243	209	73	133	75	42	16	521	398	166
Chicago	271	171	52	48	1050	638	390	271	123	93	55	754	728	301	542	294	145	103	1804	1366	691
Colorado	60	37	14	9	253	190	83	61	26	30	5	215	205	57	121	63	44	14	468	395	140
Dallas	55	37	10	8	243	134	82	56	30	15	11	201	145	71	111	67	25	19	444	279	153
Detroit	278	170	65	43	985	628	383	278	96	129	53	709	797	245	556	266	194	96	1694	1425	628
Edmonton	26	14	8	4	91	82	32	28	15	13	0	92	92	30	54	29	21	4	183	174	62
Florida	11	5	5	1	34	27	11	12	4	6	2	33	41	10	23	9	11	3	67	68	21
Los Angeles	61	43	7	11	282	154	97	61	35	17	9	243	188	79	122	78	24	20	525	342	176
Nashville	1	1	0	0	3	2	2	1	0	0	1	2	2	1	2	1	0	1	5	4	3
New Jersey	44	28	10	6	166	116	62	44	24	17	3	176	128	51	88	52	27	9	342	244	113
NY Islanders	50	29	12	9	188	150	67	50	22	23	5	148	160	49	100	51	35	14	336	310	116
NY Rangers	280	188	56	36	1104	640	412	280	113	113	54	820	816	280	560	301	169	90	1924	1456	692
Ottawa	20	12	5	3	64	53	27	18	11	7	0	56	50	22	38	23	12	3	120	103	49
Philadelphia	64	32	19	13	235	198	77	63	23	26	14	190	194	60	127	55	45	27	425	392	137
Phoenix	26	22	3	1	133	61	45	26	11	9	6	101	86	28	52	33	12	7	234	147	73
Pittsburgh	72	54	10	8	347	184	116	72	34	25	13	255	218	81	144	88	35	21	602	402	197
St. Louis	56	40	9	7	246	149	87	55	28	12	15	192	140	71	111	68	21	22	438	289	158
San Jose	8	6	0	2	31	12	14	7	3	2	2	19	20	8	15	9	2	4	50	32	22
Tampa Bay	12	7	4	1	36	30	15	13	4	6	3	30	33	11	25	11	10	4	66	63	26
Toronto	320	195	85	40	1137	789	430	320	114	162	44	836	966	272	640	309	247	84	1973	1755	702
Vancouver	49	37	8	4	238	126	78	48	32	8	8	187	119	72	97	69	16	12	425	245	150
Washington	50	30	13	7	202	105	67	49	20	20	9	155	133	49	99	50	33	16	357	238	116
Defunct Clubs	231	148	58	25	779	469	321	230	98	97	35	586	606	231	461	246	155	60	1365	1075	552
Totals	**2568**	**1610**	**600**	**358**	**9741**	**6274**	**3578**	**2568**	**1069**	**1064**	**435**	**7521**	**7451**	**2573**	**5136**	**2679**	**1664**	**793**	**17262**	**13725**	**6151**

Playoffs

	Series	W	L	GP	W	L	T	GF	GA	Last Mtg.	Round	Result
Boston	28	21	7	139	87	52	0	430	339	1994	CQF	L 3-4
Buffalo	7	4	3	35	18	17	0	124	111	1998	CSF	L 0-4
Calgary	2	1	1	11	6	5	0	31	32	1989	F	L 2-4
Chicago	17	12	5	81	50	29	2	261	185	1976	QF	W 4-0
Colorado	5	3	2	31	17	14	0	105	85	1993	DSF	W 4-2
Dallas	2	1	1	13	7	6	0	48	37	1980	QF	L 3-4
Detroit	12	5	7	62	33	29	0	161	149	1978	QF	W 4-1
Edmonton	1	0	1	3	0	3	0	6	15	1981	PR	L 0-3
Hartford	5	5	0	27	19	8	0	96	70	1992	DSF	W 4-3
Los Angeles	1	1	0	5	4	1	0	15	12	1993	F	W 4-1
NY Islanders	4	3	1	22	14	8	0	64	55	1993	CF	W 4-1
NY Rangers	14	7	7	61	34	25	2	188	158	1996	CQF	L 2-4
New Jersey	1	0	1	5	1	4	0	11	22	1997	CQF	L 1-4
Philadelphia	4	3	1	21	14	7	0	72	52	1989	CF	W 4-2
Pittsburgh	1	1	0	6	4	2	0	18	15	1998	CQF	W 4-2
St. Louis	3	3	0	12	12	0	0	42	14	1977	QF	W 4-0
Toronto	15	8	7	71	42	29	0	215	160	1979	QF	W 4-0
Vancouver	1	1	0	5	4	1	0	20	9	1975	QF	W 4-1
Defunct Clubs	11*	6	4	28	15	9	4	70	71			
Totals	**134***	**85**	**48**	**638**	**381**	**249**	**8**	**1977**	**1591**			

* 1919 Final incomplete due to influenza epidemic.

Calgary totals include Atlanta Flames, 1972-73 to 1979-80. Carolina totals include Hartford, 1979-80 to 1996-97.
Colorado totals include Quebec, 1979-80 to 1994-95. Dallas totals include Minnesota, 1967-68 to 1992-93.
New Jersey totals include Kansas City, 1974-75 to 1975-76, and Colorado Rockies, 1976-77 to 1981-82.
Phoenix totals include Winnipeg, 1979-80 to 1995-96.

Playoff Results 1999-95

Year	Round	Opponent	Result	GF	GA
1998	CSF	Buffalo	L 0-4	10	17
	CQF	Pittsburgh	W 4-2	18	15
1997	CQF	New Jersey	L 1-4	11	22
1996	CQF	NY Rangers	L 2-4	17	19

Abbreviations: Round: F – Final; **CF** – conference final; **CSF** – conference semi-final; **CQF** – conference quarter-final; **DSF** – division semi-final; **QF** – quarter-final; **PR** – preliminary round.

1998-99 Results

Oct.	10		NY Rangers	7-1		12	at	Detroit	1-5
	13		Anaheim	1-0		15	at	Washington	3-0
	16	at	Washington	2-2		16		NY Rangers	3-0
	17		Buffalo	3-4		18		Washington	4-4
	19		Chicago	1-2		21	at	Chicago	0-3
	21		Ottawa	3-2		26	at	Tampa Bay	2-1
	24		Detroit	0-3		27	at	Florida	1-2
	28		Boston	2-9		30		Carolina	1-3
	29	at	Boston	1-1		31		Pittsburgh	3-5
	31	at	Ottawa	1-5	**Feb.**	3		Vancouver	2-1
Nov.	4	at	NY Rangers	4-1		4	at	Philadelphia	2-5
	7		NY Islanders	4-2		6		Buffalo	3-2
	9		Philadelphia	5-1		9	at	Pittsburgh	2-3
	11	at	New Jersey	0-3		11	at	Buffalo	2-5
	12	at	NY Islanders	0-4		13		Florida	4-0
	14		Edmonton	1-4		17	at	NY Rangers	6-3
	17	at	Carolina	4-5		18	at	Philadelphia	3-1
	19		Calgary	4-3		20	at	Toronto	2-3
	21		Colorado	2-3		25	at	Ottawa	1-3
	27	at	Boston	1-5		27		Ottawa	4-1
	28		Pittsburgh	3-4	**Mar.**	2		Philadelphia	4-1
	30		Los Angeles	3-1		3	at	Pittsburgh	4-4
Dec.	2	at	Carolina	1-4		6		Tampa Bay	1-6
	4	at	New Jersey	1-1		8		Florida	2-5
	5		Toronto	3-4		11	at	St. Louis	3-0
	9	at	Phoenix	2-4		13		Toronto	2-1
	11	at	Dallas	2-3		18		Nashville	3-2
	12	at	Nashville	2-2		20		Washington	0-1
	14		Phoenix	2-2		22		San Jose	1-1
	18	at	Buffalo	2-4		24	at	Edmonton	2-0
	19		New Jersey	1-1		25	at	Calgary	1-2
	21		Dallas	2-2		27	at	Vancouver	1-5
	23	at	Ottawa	1-3	**Apr.**	1		Boston	2-3
	26	at	Toronto	2-1		3		Buffalo	2-1
	29	at	Edmonton	5-2		5	at	Boston	0-3
	31	at	Calgary	2-1		7		Carolina	2-0
Jan.	2	at	Vancouver	2-1		8	at	NY Islanders	1-3
	4	at	Colorado	3-4		10		New Jersey	2-6
	7		Tampa Bay	4-1		13	at	Tampa Bay	2-2
	9		NY Islanders	3-2		14	at	Florida	2-3
	11		St. Louis	3-1		17		Toronto	3-2

Entry Draft
Selections 1999-85

1999
Pick
39	Alexander Buturlin
58	Matt Carkner
97	Chris Dyment
107	Evan Lindsay
136	Dustin Jamieson
145	Marc-Andre Thinel
150	Matt Shasby
167	Sean Dixon
196	Vadim Tarasov
225	Mikko Hyytia
253	Jerome Marois

1998
Pick
16	Eric Chouinard
45	Mike Ribeiro
75	Francois Beauchemin
132	Andrei Bashkirov
152	Gordie Dwyer
162	Andrei Markov
189	Andrei Kruchinin
201	Craig Murray
216	Michael Ryder
247	Darcy Harris

1997
Pick
11	Jason Ward
37	Gregor Baumgartner
65	Ilkka Mikkola
91	Daniel Tetrault
118	Konstantin Sidulov
122	Gennady Razin
145	Jonathan Desroches
172	Ben Guite
197	Petr Kubos
202	Andrei Sidyakin
228	Jarl-Espen Ygranes

1996
Pick
18	Matt Higgins
44	Mathieu Garon
71	Arron Asham
92	Kim Staal
99	Etienne Drapeau
127	Daniel Archambault
154	Brett Clark
181	Timo Vertala
207	Mattia Baldi
233	Michel Tremblay

1995
Pick
8	Terry Ryan
60	Miroslav Guren
74	Martin Hohenberger
86	Jonathan Delisle
112	Niklas Anger
138	Boyd Olson
164	Stephane Robidas
190	Greg Hart
216	Eric Houde

1994
Pick
18	Brad Brown
44	Jose Theodore
54	Chris Murray
70	Marko Kiprusoff
74	Martin Belanger
96	Arto Kuki
122	Jimmy Drolet
148	Joel Irving
174	Jessie Rezansoff
200	Peter Strom
226	Tomas Vokoun
252	Chris Aldous
278	Ross Parsons

1993
Pick
21	Saku Koivu
47	Rory Fitzpatrick
73	Sebastien Bordeleau
85	Adam Wiesel
99	Jean-Francois Houle
113	Jeff Lank
125	Dion Darling
151	Darcy Tucker
177	David Ruhly
203	Alan Letang
229	Alexandre Duchesne
255	Brian Larochelle
281	Russell Guzior

1992
Pick
20	David Wilkie
33	Valeri Bure
44	Keli Corpse
68	Craig Rivet
82	Louis Bernard
92	Marc Lamothe
116	Don Chase
140	Martin Sychra
164	Christian Proulx
188	Michael Burman
212	Earl Cronan
236	Trent Cavicchi
260	Hiroyuki Miura

1991
Pick
17	Brent Bilodeau
28	Jim Campbll
43	Craig Darby
61	Yves Sarault
73	Vladimir Vujtek
83	Sylvain Lapointe
100	Brad Layzell
105	Tony Prpic
127	Oleg Petrov
149	Brady Kramer
171	Brian Savage
193	Scott Fraser
215	Greg MacEachern
237	Paul Lepler
259	Dale Hooper

1990
Pick
12	Turner Stevenson
39	Ryan Kuwabara
58	Charles Poulin
60	Robert Guillet
81	Gilbert Dionne
102	Paul DiPietro
123	Craig Conroy
144	Stephen Rohr
165	Brent Fleetwood
186	Derek Maguire
207	Mark Kettelhut
228	John Uniac
249	Sergei Martynyuk

1989
Pick
13	Lindsay Vallis
30	Patrice Brisebois
41	Steve Larouche
51	Pierre Sevigny
83	Andre Racicot
104	Marc Deschamps
146	Craig Ferguson
167	Patrick Lebeu
188	Roy Mitchell
209	Ed Henrich
230	Justin Duberman
251	Steve Cadieux

1988
Pick
20	Eric Charron
34	Martin St. Amour
46	Neil Carnes
83	Patrik Kjellberg
93	Peter Popovic
104	Jean-Claude Bergeron
125	Patrik Carnback
146	Tim Chase
167	Sean Hill
188	Harijs Vitolinsh
209	Yuri Krivokhizha
230	Kevin Dahl
251	Dave Kunda

1987
Pick
17	Andrew Cassels
33	John LeClair
38	Eric Desjardins
44	Mathieu Schneider
58	Francois Gravel
80	Kris Miller
101	Steve McCool
122	Les Kuntar
143	Rob Kelley
164	Will Geist
185	Eric Tremblay
206	Barry McKinlay
227	Ed Ronan
248	Bryan Herring

1986
Pick
15	Mark Pederson
27	Benoit Brunet
57	Jyrki Lumme
78	Brent Bobyck
94	Eric Aubertin
99	Mario Milani
120	Steve Bisson
141	Lyle Odelein
162	Rick Hayward
183	Antonin Routa
204	Eric Bohemier
225	Charlie Moore
246	Karel Svoboda

1985
Pick
12	Jose Charbonneau
16	Tom Chorske
33	Todd Richards
47	Rocky Dundas
75	Martin Desjardins
79	Brent Gilchrist
96	Tom Sagissor
117	Donald Dufresne
142	Ed Cristofoli
163	Mike Claringbull
184	Roger Beedon
198	Maurice Mansi
205	Chad Arthur
226	Mike Bishop
247	John Ferguson Jr.

General Managers' History

Jack Laviolette and Joseph Cattarinich, 1909-1910; George Kennedy, 1910-11 to 1920-21; Leo Dandurand, 1921-22 to 1934-35; Ernest Savard, 1935-36; Cecil Hart, 1936-37 to 1938-39; Jules Dugal, 1939-40; Tom P. Gorman, 1940-41 to 1945-46; Frank J. Selke, 1946-47 to 1963-64; Sam Pollock, 1964-65 to 1977-78; Irving Grundman, 1978-79 to 1982-83; Serge Savard, 1983-84 to 1994-95; Serge Savard and Réjean Houle, 1995-96; Réjean Houle, 1996-97 to date.

General Manager

HOULE, RÉJEAN
Vice President, Hockey and General Manager, Montreal Canadiens.
Born in Rouyn-Noranda, Que., October 25, 1949.

Réjean Houle was appointed general manager of the Montreal Canadiens on October 21, 1995. His appointment represents the high point of a career that began at age 16 with the Montreal Junior Canadiens.

Houle was a member of five Stanley Cup Championship teams during his playing career with the Canadiens. From 1969 to 1983, he played for 11 seasons with the Canadiens, with the exception of a 3-year stint with the Quebec Nordiques of the World Hockey Association (1973 to 1976). Houle played in 635 NHL regular season games, posting totals of 161 goals and 247 assists (408 points). He also participated in the NHL playoffs on ten occasions (90 games).

Prior to becoming general manager of the Canadiens, and following his playing career, Houle was an executive with Molson Breweries.

Club Directory

Centre Molson
1260 de La Gauchetière St. W.
Montréal, QC H3B 5E8
Phone **514/932-2582**
FAX (Hockey) 514/932-8736
Team Services 514/989-2717
P.R. 514/932-9296
Media 514/932-8285
Web site: www.canadiens.com
Capacity: 21,273

Owner: Molson Inc.
President and Governor	Pierre Boivin
Vice-President Hockey, General Manager and Alternate Governor	Réjean Houle
Vice-President, Finance and Administration and Alternate Governor	Fred Steer
Vice-President and General Manager, Molson Centre	Aldo Giampaolo
Vice-President, Communications and Marketing Services	Bernard Brisset
Administrative Assistant to the General Manager	Phil Scheuer
Consultant to the General Manager	Jacques Lemaire
Head Coach	Alain Vigneault
Assistant Coaches	Clément Jodoin, Roland Melanson
Chief Scout	Pierre Dorion
Director of Player Development and Scout	Claude Ruel
Pro Scouts	Pierre Mondou, Mario Tremblay
Director of European Pro-Scouting	Dave King
Director of Team Services	Michèle Lapointe
Scouting Staff	Neil Armstrong, Fred E. Bandel, Elmer Benning, Frédérick Corey, Hannu Laine, Mats Naslund, Gerry O'Flaherty, Doug Robinson, Antonin Routa, Richard Scammell, Nikolai Vakourov

AHL Affiliation
Les Citadelles de Québec
Colisée de Québec – 250, Wilfrid Laurier Blvd. – Québec, QC G1L 5A7 – Tel.: (418) 525-5333

Governor	Phil Scheuer
President	Maurice Tanguay
General Manager	Raymond Bolduc
Head Coach	Michel Therrien
Assistant Coach	Gerry Fleming, Éric Lavigne
Managing Assistant – Communications and Hockey Operations	Nicole Bouchard

Medical and Training Staff
Club Physician and Chief Surgeon	Dr. David Mulder
Senior Medical Consultant	Dr. D.G. Kinnear
Orthopaedist	Dr. Eric Lenczner
Ophthalmologist	Dr. John Little
Dentist	Dr. Pierre Desautels
General Physician	Dr. Vincent Lacroix
Athletic Trainer	Gaétan Lefebvre
Assistant to the Athletic Trainer	Graham Rynbend
Strength & Conditioning Coach	Stéphane Dubé
Supervisor of Purchasing, Hockey	Eddy Palchak
Equipment Manager	Pierre Gervais
Assistants to the Equipment Manager	Robert Boulanger, Pierre Ouellette
Video Supervisor	Mario Leblanc

Advertising and Sponsorship
EFFIX Inc.	François-Xavier Seigneur

Communications
Director of Communications	Donald Beauchamp
Assistant to the Director of Communications	Dominick Saillant
Broadcast and Production Supervisor	Frédérique Cardinal
Administrative-Assistant, Communications Department	Sylvie Lambert
Coordinator - Photos and Archives	Claude Rompré
Supervisor-Production Room (Jumbotron)	Paul Shubin
Game Presentation Supervisor	Michel Quidoz
Web	Michel Poulin

Finance
Executive Director of Finance	Jacques Aubé
Controller	Dennis McKinley
Administrative Supervisor	Dave Poulton
Controller - Financial Reporting	Françoise Brault
Supervisor - Accounting, Centre Molson Operations	Linda Guertin
Accounting Supervisors	Paule Jolicoeur, Pascale Pépin
M.I.S. Director	Sylvain Roy

Centre Molson
Executive Director, Building Operations	Alain Gauthier
Executive Director, Sales and Marketing	Richard Primeau
Executive Director, Events	Louise Laliberté
Director, Souvenir Boutiques	Yves Renaud
Director, Ticket Office	Cathy D'Ascoli

Executive Assistants
President, Lise Beaudry; General Manager, Donna Stuart; V.P. Communications, Normande Herget; V.P. Finance, Susan Cryans; V.P. and General Manager (Centre Molson) Vicki Mercuri; Hockey, Claudine Crépin

Location of Press Box	Suspended above ice – East Side
Location of Radio and TV booth	Suspended above ice – West side
Club colours	Red, white and blue
Club trains at	Centre Molson
Play-by-play – Radio/TV	Claude Quenneville, Pierre Houde, André Côté, Pierre Rinfret (French), Dino Sisto (English), Paul Romanuk (English)
TV Channels	CBFT (2), TQS (35) (French)
Cable TV	RDS (33) (French), TSN (28) (English)
Radio Stations	CKAC (730) (French), CJAD (800) (English)

Nashville Predators

1998-99 Results: 28W-47L-7T 63PTS. Fourth, Central Division

Year-by-Year Record

		Home			Road			Overall							
Season	GP	W	L	T	W	L	T	W	L	T	GF	GA	Pts.	Finished	Playoff Result
1998-99	82	15	22	4	13	25	3	28	47	7	190	261	63	4th, Central Div.	Out of Playoffs

1999-2000 Schedule

Oct.	Sat.	2	Los Angeles		Sat.	8	Chicago
	Tue.	5	Colorado		Tue.	11	at Colorado
	Sun.	10	at Chicago		Thu.	13	Vancouver
	Mon.	11	at Toronto		Sat.	15	Pittsburgh
	Thu.	14	San Jose		Tue.	18	Phoenix
	Sat.	16	Dallas		Fri.	21	at Calgary
	Wed.	20	at Buffalo		Sun.	23	at Vancouver
	Sat.	23	Edmonton		Mon.	24	at Edmonton
	Thu.	28	at San Jose		Thu.	27	Los Angeles
	Sat.	30	at Vancouver		Sat.	29	Calgary
	Sun.	31	at Edmonton		Mon.	31	at NY Rangers
Nov.	Wed.	3	at Calgary	**Feb.**	Wed.	2	at NY Islanders
	Fri.	5	Chicago		Thu.	3	at New Jersey
	Wed.	10	at Chicago		Thu.	10	Buffalo
	Thu.	11	at Ottawa		Sat.	12	Washington
	Sat.	13	at Pittsburgh		Tue.	15	Edmonton
	Thu.	18	Montreal		Wed.	16	at Dallas
	Sat.	20	Vancouver		Fri.	18	St. Louis
	Mon.	22	at St. Louis		Mon.	21	Dallas
	Wed.	24	Boston		Wed.	23	at Chicago
	Fri.	26	at Washington		Sat.	26	Tampa Bay
	Sat.	27	Anaheim		Tue.	29	New Jersey
	Tue.	30	Phoenix	**Mar.**	Thu.	2	at San Jose
Dec.	Thu.	2	at St. Louis		Sat.	4	at Los Angeles
	Sat.	4	Detroit		Sun.	5	at Anaheim
	Mon.	6	at Atlanta		Tue.	7	Chicago
	Wed.	8	at Detroit		Fri.	10	Detroit
	Fri.	10	St. Louis		Sun.	12	Edmonton*
	Sat.	11	Florida		Tue.	14	at Detroit
	Tue.	14	at Tampa Bay		Thu.	16	at Colorado
	Wed.	15	at Florida		Fri.	17	at Phoenix
	Sat.	18	Colorado		Sun.	19	at Los Angeles
	Sun.	19	at Philadelphia		Tue.	21	Philadelphia
	Tue.	21	at Boston		Thu.	23	Detroit
	Thu.	23	St. Louis		Sat.	25	Calgary
	Sun.	26	at St. Louis		Tue.	28	NY Islanders
	Tue.	28	Carolina		Wed.	29	at Carolina
	Thu.	30	Atlanta		Fri.	31	Vancouver
Jan.	Sat.	1	San Jose*	**Apr.**	Mon.	3	at Anaheim
	Wed.	5	at Dallas		Wed.	5	at Phoenix
	Thu.	6	at Detroit		Fri.	7	Anaheim

* Denotes afternoon game.

Tom Fitzgerald became the first captain of the Nashville Predators when he signed with the team as a free agent on July 6, 1998. Back in 1993, Fitzgerald was the first forward selected by the Florida Panthers in that year's Expansion Draft.

Franchise date: June 25, 1997

2nd NHL Season

CENTRAL DIVISION

1999-2000 Player Personnel

FORWARDS	HT	WT	S	Place of Birth	Date	1998-99 Club
ARKHIPOV, Denis	6-3	196	L	Kazan, USSR	5/19/79	Ak Bars Kazan
BORDELEAU, Sebastien	5-11	187	R	Vancouver, B.C.	2/15/75	Nashville
CISAR, Marian	6-0	176	R	Bratislava, Czech.	2/25/78	Milwaukee
COTE, Patrick	6-3	199	L	Lasalle, Que.	1/24/75	Nashville
CROWE, Philip	6-2	215	L	Nanton, Alta.	4/14/70	Ott-Cin (IHL)-Det (IHL)-Vegas
DANIELS, Jeff	6-1	200	L	Oshawa, Ont.	6/24/68	Nashville-Milwaukee
GOSSELIN, David	6-0	175	R	Levis, Que.	6/22/77	Milwaukee
HALL, Adam	6-3	200	R	Kalamazoo, MI	8/14/80	Michigan State
HENDERSON, Matt	6-1	200	L	White Bear Lake, MN	6/22/74	Nashville-Milwaukee
JOHNSON, Greg	5-10	185	L	Thunder Bay, Ont.	3/16/71	Nashville
KJELLBERG, Patrik	6-2	196	L	Falun, Sweden	6/17/69	Nashville
KOCH, Geoff	6-1	190	L	Exeter, NH	6/27/79	U. of Michigan
KRIVOKRASOV, Sergei	5-11	185	L	Angarsk, USSR	4/15/74	Nashville
LEGWAND, David	6-1	175	L	Detroit, MI	8/17/80	Nashville-Plymouth
MOWERS, Mark	5-11	188	R	Whitesboro, NY	1/6/74	Nashville-Milwaukee
PELTONEN, Ville	5-11	180	L	Vantaa, Finland	5/24/73	Nashville
PETERSON, Brent	6-3	200	L	Calgary, Alta.	7/20/72	T.B.-Clev-Grand Rap
RIVA, Danny	6-0	190	R	Framingham, MA	9/17/75	RPI Engineers
ROBITAILLE, Randy	5-11	190	L	Ottawa, Ont.	10/12/75	Boston-Providence (AHL)
RONNING, Cliff	5-8	167	L	Burnaby, B.C.	10/1/65	Phoenix-Nashville
SYKORA, Petr	6-2	180	R	Pardubice, Czech.	12/21/78	Nashville-Milwaukee
TURCOTTE, Darren	6-0	178	L	Boston, MA	3/2/68	Nashville
VALICEVIC, Robert	6-2	197	R	Detroit, MI	1/6/71	Nashville-Houston
WALKER, Scott	5-10	189	R	Montreal, Que.	7/19/73	Nashville
WASHBURN, Steve	6-2	198	L	Ottawa, Ont.	4/10/75	Fla-New Haven-Van-Syr
YACHMENEV, Vitali	5-9	180	L	Chelyabinsk, USSR	1/8/75	Nashville-Milwaukee

DEFENSEMEN	HT	WT	S	Place of Birth	Date	1998-99 Club
BEAUCHESNE, Martin	6-0	200	L	Cap-de-la-madaleine, Que.	7/8/80	Sherbrooke
BOIKOV, Alexander	6-0	195	L	Chelyabinsk, USSR	2/7/75	Kentucky-Rochester
BOUCHARD, Joel	6-0	190	L	Montreal, Que.	1/23/74	Nashville
BOUGHNER, Bob	6-0	206	R	Windsor, Ont.	3/8/71	Nashville
HILL, Ed	6-3	215	L	Newburyport, MA	10/24/80	Barrie
HUTCHINSON, Andrew	6-2	186	R	Evaston, IL	3/24/80	Michigan State
KECZMER, Dan	6-1	190	L	Mt. Clemens, MI	5/25/68	Dallas-Michigan-Nashville
KLIMENTIEV, Sergei	5-11	200	L	Kiev, USSR	4/5/75	Philadelphia (AHL)-Milwaukee
LINTNER, Richard	6-3	194	R	Trencin, Czech.	11/15/77	Springfield-Milwaukee
MORE, Jayson	6-1	210	R	Souris, Man.	1/12/69	Nashville
MORO, Marc	6-1	225	L	Toronto, Ont.	7/17/77	Milwaukee
SAUER, Kent	6-2	226	R	St. Cloud, MN	5/10/79	U. of Minn-Duluth
TIMONEN, Kimmo	5-9	180	L	Kuopio, Finland	3/18/75	Nashville-Milwaukee
VOPAT, Jan	6-0	205	L	Most, Czech.	3/22/73	Nashville

GOALTENDERS	HT	WT	C	Place of Birth	Date	1998-99 Club
DUNHAM, Mike	6-3	200	L	Johnson City, NY	6/1/72	Nashville
FINLEY, Brian	6-2	180	R	Sault Ste. Marie, Ont.	7/3/81	Barrie
HIRSCH, Corey	5-10	175	L	Medicine Hat, Alta.	7/1/72	Vancouver-Syracuse
MASON, Chris	6-0	200	L	Red Deer, Alta.	4/20/76	Nashville-Milwaukee
VOKOUN, Tomas	5-11	208	R	Karlovy Vary, Czech.	7/2/76	Nashville-Milwaukee

1998-99 Scoring

* – rookie

Regular Season

Pos	#	Player	Team	GP	G	A	Pts	+/–	PIM	PP	SH	GW	GT	S	%
C	7	Cliff Ronning	PHX	7	2	5	7	3	2	2	0	1	0	18	11.1
			NSH	72	18	35	53	–6	40	8	0	3	0	239	7.5
			TOTAL	79	20	40	60	–3	42	10	0	4	0	257	7.8
C	22	Greg Johnson	NSH	68	16	34	50	–8	24	2	3	0	0	120	13.3
R	25	Sergei Krivokrasov	NSH	70	25	23	48	–5	42	10	0	6	1	208	12.0
C	71	Sebastien Bordeleau	NSH	72	16	24	40	–14	26	1	2	3	0	168	9.5
R	24	Scott Walker	NSH	71	15	25	40	0	103	0	1	2	0	96	15.6
R	21	Tom Fitzgerald	NSH	80	13	19	32	–18	48	0	0	1	0	180	7.2
R	10	Patric Kjellberg	NSH	71	11	20	31	–13	24	2	0	2	0	103	10.7
L	19	Andrew Brunette	NSH	77	11	20	31	–10	26	7	0	1	0	65	16.9
R	20	Jamie Heward	NSH	63	6	12	18	–24	44	4	0	1	0	124	4.8
R	43	Vitali Yachmenev	NSH	55	7	10	17	–10	10	0	1	2	0	83	8.4
D	15	Drake Berehowsky	NSH	74	2	15	17	–9	140	0	0	0	0	79	2.5
L	28	Denny Lambert	NSH	76	5	11	16	–3	218	1	0	0	0	66	7.6
D	42	Joel Bouchard	NSH	64	4	11	15	–10	60	0	0	0	0	78	5.1
D	27	John Slaney	NSH	46	2	12	14	–12	14	0	0	1	0	84	2.4
D	6	Bob Boughner	NSH	79	3	10	13	–6	137	0	0	1	0	59	5.1
D	44 *	Kimmo Timonen	NSH	50	4	8	12	–4	30	1	0	0	0	75	5.3
D	5	Jan Vopat	NSH	55	5	6	11	0	28	0	0	0	0	46	10.9
L	16	Ville Peltonen	NSH	14	5	5	10	1	2	1	0	0	0	31	16.1
C	9	Darren Turcotte	NSH	40	4	5	9	–11	16	0	0	1	0	73	5.5
C	12	Robert Valicevic	NSH	19	4	2	6	4	2	0	0	2	0	23	17.4
R	18 *	Mark Mowers	NSH	30	0	6	6	–4	4	0	0	0	0	24	0.0
L	32	Jeff Daniels	NSH	9	1	3	4	–1	2	0	0	0	0	8	12.5
C	7	Jeff Nelson	NSH	9	2	1	3	–1	2	0	0	0	0	8	25.0
L	17 *	Patrick Cote	NSH	70	1	2	3	–7	242	0	0	0	0	21	4.8
D	4	Jay More	NSH	18	0	2	2	2	18	0	0	0	0	24	0.0
L	8	Doug Friedman	NSH	2	0	1	1	0	14	0	0	0	0	3	0.0
D	40 *	Karlis Skrastins	NSH	2	0	1	1	0	0	0	0	0	0	0	0.0
G	29 *	Tomas Vokoun	NSH	37	0	1	1	0	6	0	0	0	0	1	0.0
D	2	Dan Keczmer	DAL	22	0	1	1	–2	22	0	0	0	0	12	0.0
			NSH	16	0	0	0	–3	12	0	0	0	0	12	0.0
			TOTAL	38	0	1	1	–5	34	0	0	0	0	24	0.0
C	11 *	David Legwand	NSH	1	0	0	0	0	0	0	0	0	0	2	0.0
D	2	Rob Zettler	NSH	2	0	0	0	–2	2	0	0	0	0	0	0.0
C	50 *	Petr Sykora	NSH	2	0	0	0	–1	0	0	0	0	0	2	0.0
L	47 *	Matt Henderson	NSH	2	0	0	0	–1	2	0	0	0	0	0	0.0
R	12	Brad Smyth	NSH	3	0	0	0	–1	6	0	0	0	0	5	0.0
G	30 *	Chris Mason	NSH	3	0	0	0	0	0	0	0	0	0	0	0.0
G	35	Eric Fichaud	NSH	9	0	0	0	0	0	0	0	0	0	0	0.0
G	1	Mike Dunham	NSH	44	0	0	0	0	4	0	0	0	0	0	0.0

Goaltending

No.	Goaltender	GPI	Mins	Avg	W	L	T	EN	SO	GA	SA	S%
29	* Tomas Vokoun	37	1954	2.95	12	18	4	4	1	96	1041	.908
1	Mike Dunham	44	2472	3.08	16	23	3	3	1	127	1387	.908
35	Eric Fichaud	9	447	3.22	0	6	0	1	0	24	229	.895
30	* Chris Mason	3	69	5.22	0	0	0	0	0	6	44	.864
	Totals	**82**	**4964**	**3.15**	**28**	**47**	**7**	**8**	**2**	**261**	**2709**	**.904**

General Manager

POILE, DAVID
General Manager, Nashville Predators.
Born in Toronto, Ont., February 14, 1949.

The first-year success of the Nashville Predators further solidified General Manager David Poile's already impressive reputation in the NHL.

Known for his patience, loyalty, determination and thoroughness, Poile exhausted every conceivable option to launch and build the Predators.

Since joining the Predators on July 9, 1997, Poile made a commitment to building for the future, surrounding himself with one of the youngest and most talented staffs in the National Hockey League. Along with head coach Barry Trotz and assistant coaches Paul Gardner and Brent Peterson, Poile has also brought assistant general manager Ray Shero to Nashville as well as Chief Amateur Scout Craig Channell and Director of Player Personnel Paul Fenton. Through Poile and his staff's efforts, the Predators compiled a 28-47-7 first-year record, one of the best expansion marks in NHL history. He has secured Cliff Ronning, Scott Walker, Darren Turcotte, Ville Peltonen, Vitali Yachmenev, Kimmo Timonen and Tomas Vokoun by signing them to contract extensions. Through various transactions over the past year, the Predators had seven of the first 72 picks in the 1999 NHL entry draft and a league-high 15 picks overall. Poile also has stockpiled the Predators IHL affiliate, the Milwaukee Admirals, with an assortment of young talent, including the International Hockey League's American-born Rookie of the Year Mark Mowers, Karlis Skrastins, Matt Henderson, Petr Sykora, Richard Lintner and Marc Moro. In the last week of the 1998-99 season, Poile signed the Predators first-ever draft selection, David Legwand.

Prior to joining Nashville, Poile spent 15 seasons as vice president/general manager of the Washington Capitals. During his tenure in Washington, the Capitals made fourteen post-season appearances, winning their first Patrick Division title in 1989 and advancing to the Conference Finals in 1990. During Poile's fifteen years in Washington, the Capitals compiled a record of 594-454-132, finished first or second in the Atlantic Division eight seasons and recorded 90-or-more points seven different seasons. Poile's Capitals were ranked in the NHL's top five in winning percentage during his fifteen years with a .559 mark.

Poile started his professional hockey career as an administrative assistant for the Atlanta Flames in 1972, shortly after graduating from Northeastern University in Boston. At Northeastern, he was hockey team captain, leading scorer and most valuable player for two years.

In 1977, he was named assistant general manager of the Atlanta Flames (moved to Calgary in 1980), serving as the manager and coordinator of the Calgary farm club.

Poile is a member of the NHL's general managers committee and was instrumental in the NHL's adoption of the instant replay rule in 1991. He was awarded Inside Hockey's Man of the Year for his leadership on the issue. He was also twice honored as The Sporting News NHL Executive of the Year following the 1982-83 and 1983-84 seasons. Poile served as general manager of the 1998 and 1999 U.S. National Team for the International Ice Hockey Federation World Championships.

Poile was introduced to hockey by watching his father, Norman "Bud" Poile, play seven seasons in the NHL. Bud later became general manager for the Vancouver Canucks and the Philadelphia Flyers, both NHL expansion franchises at the time. In 1989, Bud was a co-winner of the Lester Patrick Award (an annual award for outstanding service to hockey in the United States), and was inducted into the Hockey Hall of Fame a year later.

David and his wife, Elizabeth, reside in Nashville and have two children, Brian and Lauren, who are currently enrolled at Boston College.

Club Records

Team

(Figures in brackets for season records are games played; records for fewest points, wins, ties, losses, goals, goals against are for 70 or more games)

Most Points	63	1998-99 (82)
Most Wins	28	1998-99 (82)
Most Ties	7	1998-99 (82)
Most Losses	47	1998-99 (82)
Most Goals	190	1998-99 (82)
Most Goals Against	261	1998-99 (82)
Fewest Points	63	1998-99 (82)
Fewest Wins	28	1998-99 (82)
Fewest Ties	7	1998-99 (82)
Fewest Losses	47	1998-99 (82)
Fewest Goals	190	1998-99 (82)
Fewest Goals Against	261	1998-99 (82)

Longest Winning Streak

Overall	3	Dec. 19-26/98
Home	2	Five times
Away	3	Feb. 12-24/99

Longest Undefeated Streak

Overall	3	Twice
Home	5	Dec. 8-26/98
Away	3	Twice

Longest Losing Streak

Overall	4	Twice
Home	5	Jan. 21-Feb. 15/99
Away	5	Twice

Longest Winless Streak

Overall	5	Oct. 17-24/98
Home	9	Jan. 21-Mar. 2/99
Away	5	Three times
Most Shutouts, Season	2	1998-99 (82)
Most PIM, Season	1,420	1998-99 (82)
Most Goals, Game	6	Dec. 19/98 (Nsh. 6 at Van. 4)

Individual

Most Seasons	1	Many players
Most Games	80	Tom Fitzgerald
Most Goals, Career	25	Sergei Krivokrasov
Most Assists, Career	35	Cliff Ronning
Most Points, Career	53	Cliff Ronning (18G, 35A)
Most PIM, Career	218	Denny Lambert
Most Shutouts, Career	1	Mike Dunham, Thomas Vokoun

Longest Consecutive Games Streak	49	Tom Fitzgerald (Dec. 30/98-date)
Most Goals, Season	25	Sergei Krivokrasov (1998-99)
Most Assists, Season	35	Cliff Ronning (1998-99)
Most Points, Season	53	Cliff Ronning (1998-99; 18G, 35A)
Most PIM, Season	218	Denny Lambert (1998-99)

Most Points, Defenseman, Season	18	Jamie Heward (1998-99; 6G, 12A)
Most Points, Center, Season	53	Cliff Ronning (1998-99; 18G, 35A)
Most Points, Right Wing, Season	48	Sergei Krivokrasov (1998-99; 25G, 23A)
Most Points, Left Wing, Season	31	Patrick Kjellberg (1998-99; 11G, 20A)
Most Points, Rookie, Season	12	Kimmo Timonen (1998-99; 4G, 8A)
Most Shutouts, Season	1	Mike Dunham (1998-99), Thomas Vokoun (1998-99)
Most Goals, Game	2	Twelve times
Most Assists, Game	3	Sebastien Bordeleau (Mar. 7/99)
Most Points, Game	4	Sebastien Bordeleau (Dec. 19/98; 2G, 2A), Sergei Krivokrasov (Dec. 19/98; 2G, 2A)

General Managers' History

David Poile, 1998-99 to date.

Coaching History

Barry Trotz, 1998-99 to date.

Captains' History

Tom Fitzgerald, 1998-99 to date.

The Predators acquired Cliff Ronning in a trade with Phoenix on October 31, 1998. His 35 assists and 53 points in 72 games with Nashville were tops on the team. In total, Ronning had 20 goals and 40 assists in 79 games last season.

All-time Record vs. Other Clubs

Regular Season

	At Home							On Road							Total						
	GP	W	L	T	GF	GA	PTS	GP	W	L	T	GF	GA	PTS	GP	W	L	T	GF	GA	PTS
Anaheim	2	2	0	0	5	2	4	2	0	2	0	3	9	0	4	2	0	0	8	11	4
Boston	1	0	1	0	2	5	0	1	1	0	0	8	0	2	2	1	1	0	10	5	2
Buffalo	1	0	1	0	1	3	0	1	1	0	0	4	2	2	2	1	1	0	5	5	2
Calgary	3	1	2	0	9	11	2	2	1	0	1	4	3	3	5	2	2	1	13	14	5
Carolina	1	1	0	0	3	2	2	1	0	1	0	1	4	0	2	1	1	0	4	6	2
Chicago	3	1	1	0	9	8	3	3	0	3	0	8	14	0	6	1	4	1	17	22	3
Colorado	2	1	0	1	7	6	3	2	0	2	0	2	7	0	4	1	2	1	9	13	3
Dallas	2	0	2	0	3	7	0	2	1	1	0	2	2	2	4	1	3	0	5	9	2
Detroit	3	1	2	0	8	12	2	3	0	3	0	5	11	0	6	1	5	0	13	23	2
Edmonton	2	1	1	0	6	4	3	2	0	2	0	4	7	0	4	1	3	0	10	11	3
Florida	1	0	1	0	0	1	0	1	1	0	0	4	0	2	2	1	1	0	4	1	2
Los Angeles	2	1	1	0	6	6	2	2	2	0	0	7	4	4	4	3	1	0	13	10	6
Montreal	1	0	0	1	2	2	1	1	0	1	0	2	3	0	2	0	1	1	4	5	1
New Jersey	1	0	1	0	1	4	0	1	1	0	0	3	2	2	2	1	1	0	4	6	2
NY Islanders	1	0	1	0	3	6	0	1	1	0	0	2	1	2	2	1	1	0	5	7	2
NY Rangers	1	0	1	0	4	7	0	1	0	1	0	1	5	0	2	0	2	0	5	12	0
Ottawa	1	0	1	0	1	3	0	1	0	1	0	0	3	0	2	0	2	0	1	6	0
Philadelphia	1	0	1	0	1	2	0	1	0	1	0	0	8	0	2	0	2	0	1	10	0
Phoenix	2	1	1	0	3	5	2	2	1	1	0	7	7	2	4	2	2	0	10	12	4
Pittsburgh	1	0	1	0	2	3	0	1	0	1	1	1	1	1	2	0	1	1	3	4	1
St. Louis	3	1	2	0	9	13	2	3	1	2	0	5	12	2	6	2	4	0	14	25	4
San Jose	2	1	1	0	5	5	2	2	1	1	0	5	5	2	4	2	2	0	10	10	4
Tampa Bay	1	0	1	0	2	3	0	1	1	0	0	3	0	2	2	1	1	0	5	3	2
Toronto	0	0	0	0	0	0	0	1	0	0	1	2	2	1	1	0	0	1	2	2	1
Vancouver	2	2	0	0	9	5	4	2	1	0	1	9	9	3	4	3	0	1	18	14	6
Washington	1	1	0	0	3	1	2	1	0	1	0	3	2	2	2	1	0	0	6	3	4
Totals	41	15	22	4	104	126	34	41	13	25	3	86	135	29	82	28	47	7	190	261	63

1998-99 Results

Date	Opp	Score	Date	Opp	Score
Oct. 10	Florida	0-1	15	Phoenix	2-0
13	Carolina	3-2	18	at Boston	1-8
17	at Ottawa	1-3	19	at Vancouver	4-1
19	at Toronto	2-2	21	Tampa Bay	2-3
21	at Detroit	2-5	26	Detroit	1-4
23	Calgary	3-4	28	at Buffalo	4-2
24	at Chicago	4-5	30	at New Jersey	3-2
27	Vancouver	5-4	31	Phoenix	1-5
31	Colorado	3-2	Feb. 4	at Calgary	2-2
Nov. 4	at Edmonton	2-3	5	at Edmonton	2-4
6	at Calgary	2-1	9	Detroit	2-5
7	at Vancouver	3-5	12	at NY Islanders	2-1
10	at San Jose	4-2	13	Pittsburgh	2-3
12	at Los Angeles	3-1	15	NY Rangers	4-7
14	at St. Louis	1-5	19	Colorado	4-4
17	Chicago	1-2	20	at St. Louis	4-3
19	St. Louis	3-2	23	Dallas	3-4
21	NY Islanders	3-6	24	at Dallas	2-1
24	at St. Louis	0-4	27	at Colorado	1-3
25	Calgary	4-3	Mar. 2	St. Louis	1-5
27	Anaheim	3-1	4	at Los Angeles	4-3
29	at NY Rangers	1-5	5	at Anaheim	2-3
Dec. 1	Ottawa	1-3	7	at Phoenix	3-4
5	Buffalo	1-3	10	at Chicago	2-5
8	Edmonton	3-3	12	Chicago	5-3
10	San Jose	2-1	14	Edmonton	3-1
12	Montreal	2-2	16	Calgary	2-4
16	at Anaheim	1-6	18	at Montreal	2-3
17	at San Jose	1-3	20	at Pittsburgh	1-1
19	at Vancouver	6-4	24	Tampa Bay	3-0
23	Detroit	5-3	26	at Florida	1-4
26	Washington	3-1	28	Dallas	0-3
28	at Dallas	0-1	30	at Washington	3-2
30	Boston	2-5	Apr. 1	Philadelphia	1-2
Jan. 1	St. Louis	5-6	3	Los Angeles	3-2
2	at Carolina	1-4	7	at Colorado	1-4
4	Anaheim	2-1	9	at Phoenix	4-3
7	San Jose	3-4	12	Los Angeles	3-4
9	Chicago	3-3	14	at Detroit	2-4
11	at Philadelphia	0-8	15	at Chicago	2-4
14	at Detroit	1-2	17	New Jersey	1-4

Entry Draft
Selections 1999-98

1999
Pick

6	Brian Finley
33	Jonas Andersson
52	Adam Hall
54	Andrew Hutchinson
61	Ed Hill
65	Jan Lasak
72	Brett Angel
121	Yevgeny Pavlov
124	Alexandr Krevsun
131	Konstantin Panov
162	Timo Helbling
191	Martin Erat
205	Kyle Kettles
220	Miroslav Durak
248	Darren Haydar

1998
Pick

2	David Legwand
60	Denis Arkhipov
85	Geoff Koch
88	Kent Sauer
138	Martin Beauchesne
147	Craig Brunel
202	Martin Bartek
230	Karlis Skrastins

Coach

TROTZ, BARRY
Coach, Nashville Predators. Born in Winnipeg, Man., July 15, 1962.

No NHL coach, let alone a first-year NHL coach, faced a greater challenge than Barry Trotz entering the 1998-99 season.

Trotz and his staff entered training camp with no nucleus from the previous season and with few players who had ever played together. The coaching staff had four weeks to assess the team's talent pool, select the best players and prepare for a rigorous 82-game inaugural season. All Trotz did was then lead the expansion Predators to a successful 28-47-7 record. The 28 victories ranks third in expansion history and Trotz and his coaching staff overcame the loss of 398 man games due to injury and the use of 40 different players to record the 28 victories. He saw seven different players make their NHL debut over the course of the season and 17 different players posted career years. Trotz recorded his first NHL victory in a 3-2 decision on October 13, 1998 vs. Carolina and notched wins over the two-time defending Stanley Cup Champion Detroit Red Wings, the 1999 Stanley Cup Champion Dallas Stars, the Phoenix Coyotes, the Colorado Avalanche, the Buffalo Sabres and the New Jersey Devils.

Trotz realized his dream of becoming an NHL Head Coach on August 6, 1997, after serving five seasons as head coach and director of hockey operations for the American Hockey League's Portland Pirates. He and assistant Paul Gardner spent the 1997-98 season scouting in preparation for the inaugural season.

Trotz began his coaching career in 1984 as assistant coach with the University of Manitoba for one season, before serving two seasons as the head coach and general manager of the Dauphin Kings Junior Hockey Club from 1985-87. He became head coach of the University of Manitoba during the 1987 season and also served as a scout for the Spokane Chiefs of the Western Hockey League that season. Trotz joined the Washington Capitals organization as their chief western scout during the 1988 season. The Winnipeg, Manitoba native was appointed an assistant coach of the Capitals' American Hockey League affiliate in Baltimore prior to the 1991 season before being named head coach prior to the 1992 season. When the franchise relocated to Portland, he guided the Pirates to two AHL Calder Cup Final appearances in the club's first four seasons. He led the Pirates to a league-best 43-27-10 record, captured the Calder Cup Championship and was named the American Hockey League Coach of the Year following the 1994-95 season.

In 1995, Trotz guided Portland to a new North American professional hockey league record 17-game unbeaten streak (14-0-3). He was named head coach for the U.S. Team at the American Hockey League All-Star Game in 1996.

Prior to his coaching career, Trotz played junior hockey for the Western Hockey League's Regina Pats from 1979-83. During that time, he recorded 39 goals, 121 assists for 160 points, along with 490 penalty minutes in 204 games.

Barry and his wife, Kim reside in Brentwood along with their three children Shalan, Tyson and Tiana.

Coaching Record

Season	Team	Games	Regular Season W	L	T	%	Games	Playoffs W	L	%
1992-93	Baltimore (AHL)	80	28	40	12	.425	7	3	4	.429
1993-94	Portland (AHL)	80	43	27	10	.600	8	6	2	.750
1994-95	Portland (AHL)	80	46	22	12	.650	7	3	4	.429
1995-96	Portland (AHL)	80	32	38	10	.463	24	14	10	.583
1996-97	Portland (AHL)	80	37	33	10	.525	5	2	3	.400
1998-99	**Nashville (NHL)**	**82**	**28**	**47**	**7**	**.384**	....	....	....	....
	NHL Totals	82	28	47	7	.384	....	....	....	....

Club Directory

Gaylord Entertainment Center
501 Broadway
Nashville, TN 37203
Phone **615/770-2300**
FAX 615/770-2309
Ticket Information 615/770-PUCK
www.nashvillepredators.com
Capacity: 17,298

Owner, Chairman and Governor	Craig Leipold
General Partner	Nashville Predators, LLC
Limited Partner	Gaylord Entertainment
Alternate Governor	Terry London
President, COO and Alternate Governor	Jack Diller
Executive Vice President/General Manager and Alternate Governor	David Poile
Executive Vice President/Business Operations	Tom Ward
Vice President/Chief Financial Officer	Ed Lang
Vice President/Communications & Development	Gerry Helper

Hockey Operations

Assistant General Manager	Ray Shero
Head Coach	Barry Trotz
Assistant Coaches	Paul Gardner, Brent Peterson
Strength and Conditioning Coach	Mark Nemish
Goaltending Coach	Mitch Korn
Director of Player Personnel	Paul Fenton
Chief Amateur Scout	Craig Channell
Scouting Coordinator	Stu Judge
Professional Scout	Fred Devereaux
European Scout	Alexei Dementiev
Quebec Scout	Luc Gauthier
Eastern Canada Scout	Alan Hepple
Western Canada Scout	Rick Knickle
Ontario Scout	Greg Royce
Maritimes Scout	Darrell Young
Saskatchewan Scout	Glen Zacharias
Minnesota Scout	Jim Johanson
Amateur Scout	Lucas Bergman
Head Athletic Trainer	Dan Redmond
Equipment Manager	Pete Rogers
Assistant Equipment Manager	Chris Scoppetto
Massage Therapist	Anthony Garrett
Nutritionist	Donna Gurchiek
Video Coordinator	Robert Bouchard
Manager of Team Services/Media Relations	Frank Buonomo
Hockey Operations Assistant	Mike Corbett
Executive Assistant	Kalli Quinn

Team Doctors

Team Physician	Dr. Michael J. Pagnani, MD
Team Dentist	Dr. James W. McPherson Jr., DDS
Team Ophthalmologist	Dr. Daniel Weikert, MD
Team Plastic Surgeon	Dr. Bryan D. Oslin, MD, Dr. Donald Griffin, MD
Team Neuropsychologist	Dr. Gary S. Solomon, Ph. D.
Team Neurosurgeon	Dr. Carl Hampf, MD
Team Internist	Dr. Richard W. Garman MD

Comunications/Development

Communications Coordinator	Judd Hancock
Publications/Internet Coordinator	Ken Anderson
Communications Assistant	Greg Harvey
Graphics Artist, Communications and Development	Maggie Bizwell
Director of Community Relations/ Executive Director of Predators Foundation	Jenny Hannon
Community Relations Coordinator	Alexis Herbster
Amateur Hockey Coordinator	Marc Spigel
Team Photographer	John Russell

Business/Marketing/Corporate Sales

Director of Premium Seating/Sponsor Services	Susie Masotti
Director of Marketing	Randy Campbell
Premium Seating Managers	Britt Kincheloe, Evelyn Finch
Managing Director, Corporate Sponsorship	TBA
National Sales Manager	Bill McKay
Local Sales Manager, Corporate Sponsorship	David Nivison, Kennon Dennis
Account Executives	Tommy Lynch
Marketing Manager/Special Events	Polly Pearce
Manager Promotions	Jim Hennessey
Manager Game Operations	TBA
Promotions Assistant	Bryan Shaffer
Promotions/Entertainment Coordinator	Chris Pappas
Entertainment Coordinator	Brett Rhinehardt
Graphic Artist, Marketing	Mike Towsen
Sponsor Service Account Managers	Holly Conner, Jennie Wise
Administrative Assistants	Linda Adams, Kelly Preuett

Finance/Human Resources

Director of Finance	Julie Gillen
Director of Human Resources	Kim Marrone

Television/Radio Broadcast Department

Director of Broadcasting	John Guagliano
Manager of Technical Services	Jimmy Corn
Feature Producer	Erik Barnhart
Broadcasters	Pete Weber, Terry Crisp

Ticket Operations

Director of Ticket Sales	Scott Loft
Club/Suite Sales Executive	Tom Phillips
Group Sales Manager	Allison Gay
Account Executives	Sid Chambless, Geoff Dunnuck, Slayton Gorman, Jonathan Tuschl, Bill Walker
Fan Relations Manager	Lisa Hays
Fan Relations Account Service Representatives	Gene Connelly, Josh Gravot, Nat Harden
Ticket Sales Administrative Assistant	Annie Snelgrove
Radio Flagship	WTN-FM (99.7 FM)
TV Flagship	WNAB-TV & FOX Sports Net South

New Jersey Devils

1998-99 Results: 47w-24L-11T 105PTS. First, Atlantic Division

Year-by-Year Record

Season	GP	Home			Road			Overall			GF	GA	Pts.	Finished		Playoff Result
		W	L	T	W	L	T	W	L	T						
1998-99	82	19	14	8	28	10	3	47	24	11	248	196	105	1st,	Atlantic Div.	Lost Conf. Quarter-Final
1997-98	82	29	10	2	19	13	9	48	23	11	225	166	107	1st,	Atlantic Div.	Lost Conf. Quarter-Final
1996-97	82	23	9	9	22	14	5	45	23	14	231	182	104	1st,	Atlantic Div.	Lost Conf. Semi-Final
1995-96	82	22	17	2	15	16	10	37	33	12	215	202	86	6th,	Atlantic Div.	Out of Playoffs
1994-95	**48**	**14**	**4**	**6**	**8**	**14**	**2**	**22**	**18**	**8**	**136**	**121**	**52**	**2nd,**	**Atlantic Div.**	**Won Stanley Cup**
1993-94	84	29	11	2	18	14	10	47	25	12	306	220	106	2nd,	Atlantic Div.	Lost Conf. Championship
1992-93	84	24	14	4	16	23	3	40	37	7	308	299	87	4th,	Patrick Div.	Lost Div. Semi-Final
1991-92	80	24	12	4	14	19	3	38	31	11	289	259	87	4th,	Patrick Div.	Lost Div. Semi-Final
1990-91	80	23	10	7	9	23	8	32	33	15	272	264	79	4th,	Patrick Div.	Lost Div. Semi-Final
1989-90	80	22	15	3	15	19	6	37	34	9	295	288	83	2nd,	Patrick Div.	Lost Div. Semi-Final
1988-89	80	17	18	5	10	23	7	27	41	12	281	325	66	5th,	Patrick Div.	Out of Playoffs
1987-88	80	23	16	1	15	20	5	38	36	6	295	296	82	4th,	Patrick Div.	Lost Conf. Championship
1986-87	80	20	17	3	9	28	3	29	45	6	293	368	64	6th,	Patrick Div.	Out of Playoffs
1985-86	80	17	21	2	11	28	1	28	49	3	300	374	59	6th,	Patrick Div.	Out of Playoffs
1984-85	80	13	21	6	9	27	4	22	48	10	264	346	54	5th,	Patrick Div.	Out of Playoffs
1983-84	80	10	28	2	7	28	5	17	56	7	231	350	41	5th,	Patrick Div.	Out of Playoffs
1982-83	80	11	20	9	6	29	5	17	49	14	230	338	48	5th,	Patrick Div.	Out of Playoffs
1981-82**	80	14	21	5	4	28	8	18	49	13	241	362	49	5th,	Smythe Div.	Out of Playoffs
1980-81**	80	15	16	9	7	29	4	22	45	13	258	344	57	5th,	Smythe Div.	Out of Playoffs
1979-80**	80	12	20	8	7	28	5	19	48	13	234	308	51	6th,	Smythe Div.	Out of Playoffs
1978-79**	80	8	24	8	7	29	4	15	53	12	210	331	42	4th,	Smythe Div.	Out of Playoffs
1977-78**	80	17	14	9	2	26	12	19	40	21	257	305	59	2nd,	Smythe Div.	Lost Prelim. Round
1976-77**	80	12	20	8	8	26	6	20	46	14	226	307	54	5th,	Smythe Div.	Out of Playoffs
1975-76*	80	8	24	8	4	32	4	12	56	12	190	351	36	5th,	Smythe Div.	Out of Playoffs
1974-75*	80	12	20	8	3	34	3	15	54	11	184	328	41	5th,	Smythe Div.	Out of Playoffs

* Kansas City Scouts. ** Colorado Rockies.

1999-2000 Schedule

Oct.	Sat.	2	at Atlanta
	Thu.	7	Pittsburgh
	Sat.	9	Tampa Bay
	Mon.	11	at Ottawa*
	Wed.	13	Anaheim
	Sat.	16	NY Islanders
	Fri.	22	at Dallas
	Sat.	23	at St. Louis
	Wed.	27	St. Louis
	Fri.	29	at Carolina
	Sat.	30	at Philadelphia
Nov.	Wed.	3	Montreal
	Thu.	4	at Boston
	Sat.	6	Toronto
	Tue.	9	Philadelphia
	Fri.	12	Atlanta
	Sat.	13	at Washington
	Wed.	17	Boston
	Sat.	20	Ottawa*
	Wed.	24	at Anaheim
	Thu.	25	at Phoenix
	Sun.	28	at San Jose
Dec.	Wed.	1	NY Rangers
	Fri.	3	Ottawa
	Sat.	4	Calgary
	Tue.	7	Pittsburgh
	Thu.	9	at Chicago
	Sat.	11	Edmonton*
	Tue.	14	Los Angeles
	Thu.	16	at Montreal
	Sat.	18	Washington
	Sun.	19	at NY Islanders
	Wed.	22	Philadelphia
	Thu.	23	at Toronto
	Sun.	26	at NY Rangers*
	Mon.	27	Buffalo
	Wed.	29	Boston
Jan.	Sat.	1	at Boston
	Mon.	3	at Ottawa*
	Wed.	5	at Pittsburgh
	Thu.	6	at Buffalo

	Sat.	8	Phoenix
	Tue.	11	at Tampa Bay
	Fri.	14	Washington
	Sat.	15	at Philadelphia
	Mon.	17	Carolina
	Wed.	19	Chicago
	Fri.	21	NY Islanders
	Wed.	26	at Florida
	Fri.	28	at Carolina
	Sat.	29	at Detroit
Feb.	Wed.	2	at NY Rangers
	Thu.	3	Nashville
	Tue.	8	at NY Rangers
	Wed.	9	NY Rangers
	Sun.	13	San Jose*
	Tue.	15	Philadelphia
	Thu.	17	Colorado
	Sat.	19	NY Islanders*
	Mon.	21	at Buffalo
	Thu.	24	at Montreal
	Fri.	25	Toronto
	Sun.	27	Montreal
	Tue.	29	at Nashville
Mar.	Thu.	2	at Colorado
	Sat.	4	at Vancouver
	Sun.	5	at Calgary
	Fri.	10	at Atlanta
	Sat.	11	at Washington
	Mon.	13	at Pittsburgh
	Wed.	15	Dallas
	Fri.	17	Tampa Bay
	Sun.	19	Florida
	Tue.	21	Carolina
	Fri.	24	at NY Islanders
	Sat.	25	at Toronto
	Tue.	28	at Pittsburgh
	Fri.	31	Atlanta
Apr.	Sun.	2	at Tampa Bay
	Mon.	3	at Florida
	Thu.	6	Buffalo
	Sat.	8	Florida*

* Denotes afternoon game.

Franchise date: June 11, 1974
Transferred from Denver to New Jersey, June 30, 1982.
Previously transferred from Kansas City to Denver.

ATLANTIC DIVISION

26th NHL Season

A candidate for the Calder Trophy in 1997-98, Patrik Elias collected 50 points on 17 goals and 33 assists as a second-year player in 1998-99. He led all Devils forwards with a plus/minus rating of +19.

1999-2000 Player Personnel

FORWARDS	HT	WT	S	Place of Birth	Date	1998-99 Club
ARNOTT, Jason	6-4	220	R	Collingwood, Ont.	10/11/74	New Jersey
BERTRAND, Eric	6-1	205	L	St. Ephrem, Que.	4/16/75	Albany
BICEK, Jiri	5-10	195	L	Kosice, Czech.	12/3/78	Albany
BRULE, Steve	6-0	200	R	Montreal, Que.	1/15/75	Albany
BRYLIN, Sergei	5-10	190	L	Moscow, USSR	1/13/74	New Jersey
DAGENAIS, Pierre	6-4	215	L	Blainville, Que.	3/4/78	Albany
DUCE, Bryan	6-0	200	R	Thunder Bay, Ont.	1/15/78	Albany-Augusta
ELIAS, Patrik	6-1	200	L	Trebic, Czech.	4/13/76	New Jersey
GOMEZ, Scott	5-11	200	L	Anchorage, Alaska	12/23/79	Tri-City
GRON, Stanislav	6-2	210	L	Bratislava, Czech.	10/28/78	Kootenay-Utah
HELD, Ryan	6-2	175	L	London, Ont.	1/30/80	Kitchener
HOLIK, Bobby	6-4	230	R	Jihlava, Czech.	1/1/71	New Jersey
LAKOVIC, Sasha	6-0	210	L	Vancouver, B.C.	9/7/71	New Jersey-Albany
MADDEN, John	5-11	195	L	Barrie, Ont.	5/4/75	New Jersey-Albany
McKAY, Randy	6-2	210	R	Montreal, Que.	1/25/67	New Jersey
MORRISON, Brendan	5-11	190	L	Pitt Meadows, B.C.	8/15/75	New Jersey
NEMCHINOV, Sergei	6-0	200	L	Moscow, USSR	1/14/64	NY Islanders-New Jersey
OLIWA, Krzysztof	6-5	235	L	Tychy, Poland	4/12/73	New Jersey
PANDOLFO, Jay	6-1	200	L	Winchester, MA	12/27/74	New Jersey
PEDERSON, Denis	6-2	205	R	Prince Albert, Sask.	9/10/75	New Jersey
ROCHEFORT, Richard	5-10	195	R	North Bay, Ont.	1/7/77	Albany
ROLSTON, Brian	6-2	200	L	Flint, MI	2/21/73	New Jersey
SHARIFIJANOV, Vadim	6-0	205	L	Ufa, USSR	12/23/75	New Jersey-Albany
SKRLAC, Rob	6-5	240	L	Campbell, B.C.	6/10/76	Albany
SYKORA, Petr	5-11	190	L	Plzen, Czech.	11/19/76	New Jersey
THOMPSON, Chris	6-1	210	L	Prince Albert, Sask.	4/10/78	Albany-Augusta
WILLIAMS, Jeff	6-1	200	L	Pointe-Claire, Que.	2/11/76	Albany

DEFENSEMEN	HT	WT	S	Place of Birth	Date	1998-99 Club
BOMBARDIR, Brad	6-1	205	L	Powell River, B.C.	5/5/72	New Jersey
DANEYKO, Ken	6-1	215	L	Windsor, Ont.	4/17/64	New Jersey
DEWOLF, Josh	6-2	200	L	Bloomington, MN	7/25/77	Albany
GOC, Sascha	6-1	225	R	Calw, Germany	4/17/79	Albany
JOHNSTONE, Alex	6-1	205	L	Halifax, N.S.	12/28/79	Halifax
KESA, Teemu	6-1	189	R	Helsinki, Finland	6/7/81	Ilves Tampere
KROUPA, Vlastimil	6-3	215	L	Most, Czech.	4/27/75	Kansas City-Albany
LAKOS, Andre	6-6	210	R	Toronto, Ont.	7/29/79	Barrie
MITCHELL, Willie	6-3	210	L	Ft. McNeill, B.C.	4/23/77	Clarkson-Albany
NEHRLING, Lucas	6-5	225	R	Peterborough, Ont.	8/14/79	Kingston-Guelph
NIEDERMAYER, Scott	6-0	205	L	Edmonton, Alta.	8/31/73	New Jersey-Utah
ODELEIN, Lyle	5-11	210	R	Quill Lake, Sask.	7/21/68	New Jersey
RAFALSKI, Brian	5-11	200	R	Dearborn, MI	9/28/73	HIFK Helsinki
SOURAY, Sheldon	6-4	230	L	Elk Point, Alta.	7/13/76	New Jersey
STEVENS, Scott	6-1	215	L	Kitchener, Ont.	4/1/64	New Jersey
SUTTON, Ken	6-1	205	L	Edmonton, Alta.	11/5/69	New Jersey-Albany
WHITE, Colin	6-3	215	L	New Glasgow, N.S.	12/12/77	Albany

GOALTENDERS	HT	WT	C	Place of Birth	Date	1998-99 Club
BRODEUR, Martin	6-2	205	L	Montreal, Que.	5/6/72	New Jersey
BUZAK, Mike	6-3	220	L	Edson, Alta.	2/10/73	Albany
DAMPHOUSSE, J-F	6-0	175	L	St-Alexis-des-Monts, Que.	7/21/79	Moncton-Albany
HENRY, Frederic	5-11	180	L	Cap-Rouge, Que.	8/9/77	Albany
TERRERI, Chris	5-9	170	L	Providence, RI	11/15/64	New Jersey

1998-99 Scoring

* – rookie

Regular Season

Pos	#	Player	Team	GP	G	A	Pts	+/–	PIM	PP	SH	GW	GT	S	%
C	17	Petr Sykora	N.J.	80	29	43	72	16	22	15	0	7	0	222	13.1
C	16	Bobby Holik	N.J.	78	27	37	64	16	119	5	0	8	0	253	10.7
L	14	Brian Rolston	N.J.	82	24	33	57	11	14	5	5	3	0	210	11.4
R	25	Jason Arnott	N.J.	74	27	27	54	10	79	8	0	3	1	200	13.5
L	26	Patrik Elias	N.J.	74	17	33	50	19	34	3	0	2	0	157	10.8
C	9 *	Brendan Morrison	N.J.	76	13	33	46	–4	18	5	0	2	0	111	11.7
D	27	Scott Niedermayer	N.J.	72	11	35	46	16	26	1	1	3	0	161	6.8
R	21	Randy McKay	N.J.	70	17	20	37	10	143	3	0	5	0	136	12.5
D	24	Lyle Odelein	N.J.	70	5	26	31	6	114	1	0	0	1	101	5.0
L	23	Dave Andreychuk	N.J.	52	15	13	28	1	20	4	0	3	1	110	13.6
L	20	Jay Pandolfo	N.J.	70	14	13	27	3	10	1	1	4	0	100	14.0
R	8 *	Vadim Sharifijanov	N.J.	53	11	16	27	11	28	1	0	2	0	71	15.5
D	4	Scott Stevens	N.J.	75	5	22	27	29	64	0	0	1	0	111	4.5
C	10	Denis Pederson	N.J.	76	11	12	23	–10	66	3	0	1	0	145	7.6
C	12	Sergei Nemchinov	NYI	67	8	8	16	–17	22	1	0	0	0	61	13.1
			N.J.	10	4	0	4	4	6	1	0	1	0	13	30.8
			TOTAL	77	12	8	20	–13	28	2	0	1	0	74	16.2
C	18	Sergei Brylin	N.J.	47	5	10	15	8	28	3	0	1	0	51	9.8
L	29	Krzysztof Oliwa	N.J.	64	5	7	12	4	240	0	0	1	0	59	8.5
D	3	Ken Daneyko	N.J.	82	2	9	11	27	63	0	0	0	0	63	3.2
D	28	Kevin Dean	N.J.	62	1	10	11	4	22	1	0	0	0	51	2.0
C	19	Bob Carpenter	N.J.	56	2	8	10	–3	36	0	0	0	0	69	2.9
D	6	Brad Bombardir	N.J.	56	1	7	8	–4	16	0	0	0	0	47	2.1
D	2	Sheldon Souray	N.J.	70	1	7	8	5	110	0	0	0	0	101	1.0
G	30	Martin Brodeur	N.J.	70	0	4	4	0	4	0	0	0	0	0	0.0
L	32	Sasha Lakovic	N.J.	16	0	3	3	0	59	0	0	0	0	10	0.0
D	7	Ken Sutton	N.J.	5	1	0	1	1	0	0	0	0	0	5	20.0
L	11 *	John Madden	N.J.	4	0	1	1	–2	0	0	0	0	0	4	0.0
G	31	Chris Terreri	N.J.	12	0	1	1	0	0	0	0	0	0	0	0.0
L	22	Scott Daniels	N.J.	1	0	0	0	0	0	0	0	0	0	0	0.0

Goaltending

No.	Goaltender	GPI	Mins	Avg	W	L	T	EN	SO	GA	SA	S%
30	Martin Brodeur	70	4239	2.29	39	21	10	4	4	162	1728	.906
31	Chris Terreri	12	726	2.48	8	3	1	0	1	30	294	.898
	Totals	**82**	**4986**	**2.36**	**47**	**24**	**11**	**4**	**5**	**196**	**2026**	**.903**

Playoffs

Pos	#	Player	Team	GP	G	A	Pts	+/–	PIM	PP	SH	GW	OT	S	%
C	16	Bobby Holik	N.J.	7	0	7	7	–1	6	0	0	0	0	21	0.0
C	17	Petr Sykora	N.J.	7	3	3	6	–3	4	0	0	1	0	12	25.0
R	21	Randy McKay	N.J.	7	3	2	5	1	2	0	0	1	0	16	18.8
L	26	Patrik Elias	N.J.	7	0	5	5	0	6	0	0	0	0	14	0.0
C	18	Sergei Brylin	N.J.	5	3	1	4	2	4	1	0	1	0	12	25.0
R	25	Jason Arnott	N.J.	7	2	2	4	–3	4	1	0	0	0	12	16.7
D	27	Scott Niedermayer	N.J.	7	1	3	4	–5	18	1	0	0	0	13	7.7
D	4	Scott Stevens	N.J.	7	2	1	3	–2	10	2	0	0	0	14	14.3
D	24	Lyle Odelein	N.J.	7	0	3	3	–1	10	0	0	0	0	12	0.0
L	23	Dave Andreychuk	N.J.	4	2	0	2	0	4	0	0	0	0	7	28.6
G	30	Martin Brodeur	N.J.	7	0	2	2	0	2	0	0	0	0	0	0.0
C	9 *	Brendan Morrison	N.J.	7	0	2	2	–1	0	0	0	0	0	10	0.0
L	14	Brian Rolston	N.J.	7	1	0	1	–1	2	0	1	0	0	15	6.7
L	20	Jay Pandolfo	N.J.	7	1	0	1	–5	0	0	0	0	0	10	10.0
D	2	Sheldon Souray	N.J.	2	0	1	1	1	0	0	0	0	0	0	0.0
C	10	Denis Pederson	N.J.	3	0	1	1	0	0	0	0	0	0	3	0.0
L	29	Krzysztof Oliwa	N.J.	1	0	0	0	0	2	0	0	0	0	0	0.0
C	12	Sergei Nemchinov	N.J.	4	0	0	0	–2	0	0	0	0	0	2	0.0
R	8 *	Vadim Sharifijanov	N.J.	4	0	0	0	0	0	0	0	0	0	3	0.0
D	6	Brad Bombardir	N.J.	5	0	0	0	0	0	0	0	0	0	2	0.0
C	19	Bob Carpenter	N.J.	7	0	0	0	–1	2	0	0	0	0	7	0.0
D	3	Ken Daneyko	N.J.	7	0	0	0	3	8	0	0	0	0	5	0.0
D	28	Kevin Dean	N.J.	7	0	0	0	–4	0	0	0	0	0	7	0.0

Goaltending

No.	Goaltender	GPI	Mins	Avg	W	L	EN	SO	GA	SA	S%
30	Martin Brodeur	7	425	2.82	3	4	1	0	20	139	.856
	Totals	**7**	**429**	**2.94**	**3**	**4**	**1**	**0**	**21**	**140**	**.850**

General Managers' History

Sid Abel, 1974-75, 1975-76; Ray Miron, 1976-77 to 1980-81; Billy MacMillan, 1981-82, 1982-83; Billy MacMillan and Max McNab, 1983-84; Max McNab 1984-85 to 1986-87; Lou Lamoriello, 1987-88 to date.

General Manager

LAMORIELLO, LOU
President and General Manager, New Jersey Devils.
Born in Providence, RI, October 21, 1942.

Lou Lamoriello's life-long dedication to the game of hockey was rewarded in 1992 when he was named a recipient of the Lester Patrick Trophy for outstanding service to hockey in the United States. Lamoriello is entering his 13th season as president and general manager of the Devils following more than 20 years with Providence College as a player, coach and administrator. His trades, signings and draft choices helped lead the Devils to their first Stanley Cup championship in 1995. A member of the varsity hockey Friars during his undergraduate days, he became an assistant coach with the college club after graduating in 1963. Lamoriello was later named head coach and in the ensuing 15 years, led his teams to a 248-179-13 record, a .578 winning percentage and appearances in 10 post-season tournaments, including the 1983 NCAA Final Four. Lamoriello also served a five-year term as athletic director at Providence and was a co-founder of Hockey East, one of the strongest collegiate hockey conferences in the U.S. He remained as athletic director until he was hired as president of the Devils on April 30, 1987. He assumed the dual responsibility of general manager on September 10, 1987. He was g.m. of Team USA for the first World Cup of Hockey in 1996 as the U.S. captured the championship. He was also the g.m. for the 1998 U.S. Olympic Team.

Coaching History

Bep Guidolin, 1974-75; Bep Guidolin, Sid Abel and Eddie Bush, 1975-76; John Wilson, 1976-77; Pat Kelly, 1977-78; Pat Kelly and Aldo Guidolin, 1978-79; Don Cherry, 1979-80; Bill MacMillan, 1980-81; Bert Marshall and Marshall Johnston, 1981-82; Bill MacMillan, 1982-83; Bill MacMillan and Tom McVie, 1983-84; Doug Carpenter, 1984-85 to 1986-87; Doug Carpenter and Jim Schoenfeld, 1987-88; Jim Schoenfeld, 1988-89; Jim Schoenfeld and John Cunniff, 1989-90; John Cunniff and Tom McVie, 1990-91; Tom McVie, 1991-92; Herb Brooks, 1992-93; Jacques Lemaire, 1993-94 to 1997-98; Robbie Ftorek, 1998-99 to date.

Captains' History

Simon Nolet, 1974-75 to 1976-77; Wilf Paiement, 1977-78; Gary Croteau, 1978-79; Mike Christie, Rene Robert and Lanny McDonald, 1979-80; Lanny McDonald, 1980-81; Lanny McDonald and Rob Ramage, 1981-82; Don Lever, 1982-83; Don Lever and Mel Bridgman, 1983-84; Mel Bridgman, 1984-85 to 1986-87; Kirk Muller, 1987-88 to 1990-91; Bruce Driver, 1991-92; Scott Stevens, 1992-93 to date.

Club Records

Team

(Figures in brackets for season records are games played; records for fewest points, wins, ties, losses, goals, goals against are for 70 or more games)

Most Points	107	1997-98 (82)
Most Wins	48	1997-98 (82)
Most Ties	21	1977-78 (80)
Most Losses	56	1983-84 (80), 1975-76 (80)
Most Goals	308	1992-93 (84)
Most Goals Against	374	1985-86 (80)
Fewest Points	*36	1975-76 (80)
	41	1983-84 (80)
Fewest Wins	*12	1975-76 (80)
	17	1982-83 (80), 1983-84 (80)
Fewest Ties	3	1985-86 (80)
Fewest Losses	23	1996-97 (82); 1997-98 (82)
Fewest Goals	*184	1974-75 (80)
	225	1997-98 (82)
Fewest Goals Against	166	1997-98 (82)

Longest Winning Streak

Overall	8	Oct. 27-Nov. 15/97
Home	8	Oct. 9-Nov. 7/87
Away	5	Four times

Longest Undefeated Streak

Overall	13	Jan. 24-Feb. 20/97 (6 wins, 7 ties), Jan. 31-Mar. 12/98 (9 wins, 4 ties)
Home	15	Jan. 8-Mar. 15/97 (9 wins, 6 tie)
Away	8	Nov. 5-Dec. 2/93 (5 wins, 3 ties), Jan. 31-Mar. 12/98 (5 wins, 3 ties)

Longest Losing Streak

Overall	*14	Dec. 30/75-Jan. 29/76
	10	Oct. 14-Nov. 4/83
Home	9	Dec. 22/85-Feb. 6/86
Away	12	Oct. 19-Dec. 1/83

Longest Winless Streak

Overall	*27	Feb. 12-Apr. 4/76 (21 losses, 6 ties)
	18	Oct. 20-Nov. 26/82 (14 losses 4 ties)
Home	*14	Feb. 12-Mar. 30/76 (10 losses, 4 ties), Feb. 4-Mar. 31/79 (12 losses, 2 ties)
	9	Dec. 22/85-Feb. 6/86 (9 losses)
Away	*32	Nov. 12/77-Mar. 15/78 (22 losses, 10 ties)
	14	Dec. 26/82-Mar. 5/83 (13 losses, 1 tie)

Most Shutouts, Season	13	1996-97 (82)
Most PIM, Season	2,494	1988-89 (80)
Most Goals, Game	9	Seven times

Individual

Most Seasons	16	Ken Daneyko
Most Games	992	Ken Daneyko
Most Goals, Career	347	John MacLean
Most Assists, Career	354	John MacLean
Most Points, Career	701	John MacLean (347G, 354A)
Most PIM, Career	2,241	Ken Daneyko
Most Shutouts, Career	36	Martin Brodeur
Longest Consecutive Games Streak	388	Ken Daneyko (Nov. 4/89-Mar. 29/94)

Most Goals, Season	46	Pat Verbeek (1987-88)
Most Assists, Season	60	Scott Stevens (1993-94)
Most Points, Season	94	Kirk Muller (1987-88)
Most PIM, Season	295	Krzysztof Oliwa (1997-98)
Most Points, Defenseman, Season	78	Scott Stevens (1993-94; 18G, 60A)
Most Points, Center, Season	94	Kirk Muller (1987-88; 37G, 57A)
Most Points, Right Wing, Season	*87	Wilf Paiement (1977-78; 31G, 56A)
	87	John MacLean (1988-89; 42G, 45A)
Most Points, Left Wing, Season	86	Kirk Muller (1989-90; 30G, 56A)
Most Points, Rookie, Season	63	Kevin Todd (1991-92; 21G, 42A)
Most Shutouts, Season	10	Martin Brodeur (1996-97, 1997-98)
Most Goals, Game	4	Bob MacMillan (Jan. 8/82), Pat Verbeek (Feb. 28/88)
Most Assists, Game	5	Greg Adams (Oct. 10/85), Kirk Muller (Mar. 25/87), Tom Kurvers (Feb. 13/89)
Most Points, Game	6	Kirk Muller (Nov. 29/86; 3G, 3A)

* Records include Kansas City Scouts and Colorado Rockies, 1974-75 through 1981-82.

All-time Record vs. Other Clubs

Regular Season

	At Home							On Road							Total					
	GP	W	L	T	GF	GA	PTS	GP	W	L	T	GF	GA	PTS	GP	W	L	T	GF	GA	PTS
Anaheim	5	4	1	0	21	8	8	5	2	3	0	12	17	4	10	6	4	0	33	25	12
Boston	43	11	23	9	112	144	31	46	13	27	6	142	190	32	89	24	50	15	254	334	63
Buffalo	44	12	23	9	131	157	33	44	12	27	5	140	186	29	88	24	50	14	271	343	62
Calgary	41	13	25	3	116	153	29	39	5	27	7	101	175	17	80	18	52	10	217	328	46
Carolina	35	20	12	3	127	114	43	34	12	15	7	106	116	31	69	32	27	10	233	230	74
Chicago	42	15	16	11	125	132	41	43	10	24	9	118	173	29	85	25	40	20	243	305	70
Colorado	32	17	12	3	132	110	37	30	12	15	3	90	110	27	62	29	27	6	222	220	64
Dallas	40	19	18	3	135	125	41	41	11	24	6	109	159	28	81	30	42	9	244	284	69
Detroit	37	18	10	9	130	103	45	36	13	21	2	122	149	28	73	31	31	11	252	252	73
Edmonton	29	13	14	2	101	98	28	29	9	14	6	106	130	24	58	22	28	8	207	228	52
Florida	14	7	4	3	38	27	17	15	5	6	4	34	36	14	29	12	10	7	72	63	31
Los Angeles	39	17	17	5	129	140	39	39	6	27	6	119	198	18	78	23	44	11	248	338	57
Montreal	44	17	24	3	128	176	37	44	10	28	6	116	166	26	88	27	52	9	244	342	63
Nashville	1	0	1	0	2	3	0	1	1	0	0	4	1	2	2	1	1	0	6	4	2
NY Islanders	71	27	34	10	239	266	64	72	13	50	9	204	323	35	143	40	84	19	443	589	99
NY Rangers	73	36	32	5	252	255	77	71	19	39	13	215	292	51	144	55	71	18	467	547	128
Ottawa	13	8	3	2	43	28	18	14	9	4	1	37	28	19	27	17	7	3	80	56	37
Philadelphia	70	36	29	5	256	261	77	72	18	46	8	181	293	44	142	54	75	13	437	554	121
Phoenix	25	9	10	6	80	78	24	27	5	19	3	72	104	13	52	14	29	9	152	182	37
Pittsburgh	68	33	23	12	258	232	78	66	25	37	4	228	263	54	134	58	60	16	486	495	132
St. Louis	43	19	17	7	140	126	45	42	10	25	7	130	180	27	85	29	42	14	270	306	72
San Jose	8	4	3	1	30	17	9	7	4	2	1	21	14	9	15	8	5	2	51	31	18
Tampa Bay	16	14	1	1	64	22	29	15	8	4	3	43	36	19	31	22	5	4	107	58	48
Toronto	37	14	12	11	133	116	39	38	9	25	4	123	160	22	75	23	37	15	256	276	61
Vancouver	45	19	20	6	143	149	44	45	9	25	11	126	167	29	90	28	45	17	269	316	73
Washington	69	32	30	7	214	207	71	69	21	43	5	197	273	47	138	53	73	12	411	480	118
Defunct Clubs	8	4	2	2	25	19	10	8	2	3	3	19	27	7	16	6	5	5	44	46	17
Totals	**992**	**438**	**416**	**138**	**3304**	**3266**	**1014**	**992**	**273**	**580**	**139**	**2915**	**3966**	**685**	**1984**	**711**	**996**	**277**	**6219**	**7232**	**1699**

Playoffs

	Series	W	L	GP	W	L	T	GF	GA	Last Mtg.	Round	Result
Boston	3	2	1	18	11	7	0	55	52	1995	CQF	W 4-1
Buffalo	1	1	0	7	4	3	0	14	14	1994	CQF	W 4-3
Detroit	1	1	0	4	4	0	0	16	7	1995	F	W 4-0
Montreal	1	1	0	6	4	2	0	22	11	1997	CQF	W 4-1
NY Islanders	1	1	0	6	4	2	0	23	18	1988	DSF	W 4-2
NY Rangers	3	0	3	19	7	12	0	46	56	1997	CSF	L 1-4
Ottawa	1	0	1	6	2	4	0	12	13	1998	CQF	L 2-4
Philadelphia	2	1	1	8	4	4	0	23	20	1995	CF	W 4-2
Pittsburgh	4	1	3	24	11	13	0	65	77	1999	CQF	L 3-4
Washington	2	1	1	13	6	7	0	43	44	1990	DSF	L 2-4
Totals	**19**	**9**	**10**	**110**	**57**	**43**	**0**	**319**	**312**			

Playoff Results 1999-95

Year	Round	Opponent	Result	GF	GA
1999	CQF	Pittsburgh	L 3-4	18	21
1998	CQF	Ottawa	L 2-4	12	13
1997	CSF	NY Rangers	L 1-4	5	10
	CQF	Montreal	W 4-1	22	11
1995	**F**	**Detroit**	**W 4-0**	**16**	**7**
	CF	Philadelphia	W 4-2	20	14
	CSF	Pittsburgh	W 4-1	17	8
	CQF	Boston	W 4-1	14	5

Abbreviations: Round: F – Final; **CF** – conference final; **CSF** – conference semi-final; **CQF** – conference quarter-final; **DSF** – division semi-final.

Calgary totals include Atlanta Flames, 1974-75 to 1979-80.
Colorado totals include Quebec, 1979-80 to 1994-95.
Phoenix totals include Winnipeg, 1979-80 to 1995-96.
Carolina totals include Hartford, 1979-80 to 1996-97.
Dallas totals include Minnesota, 1974-75 to 1992-93.

1998-99 Results

Date		Opponent	Result		Date		Opponent	Result
Oct. 10	at	Chicago	1-2		18	at	San Jose	1-3
14		Pittsburgh	1-3		20	at	Anaheim	4-3
16	at	NY Rangers	2-1		21	at	Los Angeles	3-2
17		Edmonton	2-4		26		Ottawa	4-1
22	at	Philadelphia	3-2		28	at	Boston	2-0
24		Boston	3-1		30		Nashville	2-3
28		Los Angeles	0-4	Feb. 1		Detroit	2-2
29	at	NY Islanders	2-1		3	at	Carolina	4-1
31		Florida	3-1		4	at	St. Louis	2-0
Nov. 3		NY Rangers	3-1		6		Toronto	2-3
7	at	Florida	4-3		9		Vancouver	3-4
8	at	Tampa Bay	1-3		12		Washington	2-3
11		Montreal	3-0		13		Carolina	6-4
13		Pittsburgh	4-3		15		Toronto	3-3
14	at	Philadelphia	1-6		17		Tampa Bay	7-1
19		Carolina	3-2		19	at	Detroit	1-3
21		Florida	3-3		20		NY Islanders	2-3
22	at	Carolina	5-2		22	at	Tampa Bay	3-2
25	at	Dallas	5-2		25	at	Boston	3-3
26	at	Phoenix	2-3		28		Phoenix	4-1
28	at	Colorado	3-2	Mar. 3	at	Toronto	5-2
Dec. 1	at	Washington	4-0		5		Boston	1-4
4		Montreal	1-1		7	at	NY Islanders	3-2
5	at	NY Islanders	7-5		9	at	Pittsburgh	3-2
8		Philadelphia	5-5		15	at	Vancouver	2-1
10	at	Philadelphia	5-4		17	at	Edmonton	4-1
12		Colorado	5-3		20	at	Toronto	1-3
16		NY Rangers	6-3		23		Buffalo	1-1
18		Calgary	2-5		25		Pittsburgh	5-3
19	at	Montreal	1-1		27		Chicago	4-4
23		St. Louis	4-2		28	at	Florida	2-2
26		Buffalo	0-2		31		Anaheim	7-1
28	at	Buffalo	7-4	Apr. 3	at	Pittsburgh	4-2
30	at	Washington	3-2		4		NY Rangers	4-1
Jan. 2	at	Ottawa	0-6		6	at	Carolina	2-4
5		San Jose	3-3		8		Washington	1-0
6	at	NY Rangers	2-3		10	at	Montreal	6-2
9		Washington	2-3		12		NY Islanders	2-4
11		Ottawa	2-4		14	at	Buffalo	2-1
14	at	Ottawa	2-3		16		Philadelphia	3-2
15		Tampa Bay	3-1		17	at	Nashville	4-1

Entry Draft Selections 1999-85

1999
Pick
- 27 Ari Ahonen
- 42 Mike Commodore
- 50 Brett Clouthier
- 95 Andre Lakos
- 100 Teemu Kesa
- 185 Scott Cameron
- 214 Chris Hartsburg
- 242 Justin Dziama

1998
Pick
- 26 Mike Van Ryn
- 27 Scott Gomez
- 37 Christian Berglund
- 82 Brian Gionta
- 96 Mikko Jokela
- 105 Pierre Dagenais
- 119 Anton But
- 143 Ryan Flinn
- 172 Jacques Lariviere
- 199 Erik Jensen
- 227 Marko Ahosilta
- 257 Ryan Held

1997
Pick
- 24 J-F Damphousse
- 38 Stanislav Gron
- 104 Lucas Nehrling
- 131 Jiri Bicek
- 159 Sascha Goc
- 188 Mathieu Benoit
- 215 Scott Clemmensen
- 241 Jan Sorinko

1996
Pick
- 10 Lance Ward
- 38 Wesley Mason
- 41 Joshua Dewolf
- 47 Pierre Dagenais
- 49 Colin White
- 63 Scott Parker
- 91 Josef Boumedienne
- 101 Josh MacNevin
- 118 Glenn Crawford
- 145 Sean Ritchlin
- 173 Daryl Andrews
- 199 Willie Mitchell
- 205 Jay Bertsch
- 225 Pasi Petrilainen

1995
Pick
- 18 Petr Sykora
- 44 Nathan Perrott
- 70 Sergei Vyshedkevich
- 78 David Gosselin
- 79 Alyn McCauley
- 96 Henrik Rehnberg
- 122 Chris Mason
- 148 Adam Young
- 174 Richard Rochefort
- 200 Frederic Henry
- 226 Colin O'Hara

1994
Pick
- 25 Vadim Sharifijanov
- 51 Patrik Elias
- 71 Sheldon Souray
- 103 Zdenek Skorepa
- 129 Christian Gosselin
- 134 Ryan Smart
- 155 Luciano Caravaggio
- 181 Jeff Williams
- 207 Eric Bertrand
- 233 Steve Sullivan
- 259 Scott Swanjord
- 269 Mike Hanson

1993
Pick
- 13 Denis Pederson
- 32 Jay Pandolfo
- 39 Brendan Morrison
- 65 Krzysztof Oliwa
- 110 John Guirestante
- 143 Steve Brule
- 169 Nikolai Zavarukhin
- 195 Thomas Cullen
- 221 Judd Lambert
- 247 Jimmy Provencher
- 273 Michael Legg

1992
Pick
- 18 Jason Smith
- 42 Sergei Brylin
- 66 Cale Hulse
- 90 Vitali Tomilin
- 94 Scott McCabe
- 114 Ryan Black
- 138 Daniel Trebil
- 162 Geordie Kinnear
- 186 Stephane Yelle
- 210 Jeff Toms
- 234 Heath Weenk
- 258 Vladislav Yakovenko

1991
Pick
- 3 Scott Niedermayer
- 11 Brian Rolston
- 33 Donevan Hextall
- 55 Fredrik Lindqvist
- 77 Bradley Willner
- 121 Curt Regnier
- 143 David Craievich
- 165 Paul Wolanski
- 187 Daniel Reimann
- 231 Kevin Riehl
- 253 Jason Hehr

1990
Pick
- 20 Martin Brodeur
- 24 David Harlock
- 29 Chris Gotziaman
- 53 Michael Dunham
- 56 Brad Bombardir
- 64 Mike Bodnarchuk
- 95 Dean Malkoc
- 104 Petr Kuchyna
- 116 Lubomir Kolnik
- 137 Chris McAlpine
- 179 Jaroslav Modry
- 200 Corey Schwab
- 221 Valeri Zelepukin
- 242 Todd Reirden

1989
Pick
- 5 Bill Guerin
- 18 Jason Miller
- 26 Jarrod Skalde
- 47 Scott Pellerin
- 89 Mike Heinke
- 110 David Emma
- 152 Sergei Starikov
- 173 Andre Faust
- 215 Jason Simon
- 236 Peter Larsson

1988
Pick
- 12 Corey Foster
- 23 Jeff Christian
- 54 Zdeno Ciger
- 65 Matt Ruchty
- 75 Scott Luik
- 96 Chris Nelson
- 117 Chad Johnson
- 138 Chad Erickson
- 159 Bryan Lafort
- 180 Sergei Svetlov
- 201 Bob Woods
- 207 Alexander Semak
- 222 Charles Hughes
- 243 Michael Pohl

1987
Pick
- 2 Brendan Shanahan
- 23 Rickard Persson
- 65 Brian Sullivan
- 86 Kevin Dean
- 107 Ben Hankinson
- 128 Tom Neziol
- 149 Jim Dowd
- 170 John Blessman
- 191 Peter Fry
- 212 Alain Charland

1986
Pick
- 3 Neil Brady
- 24 Todd Copeland
- 45 Janne Ojanen
- 62 Marc Laniel
- 66 Anders Carlsson
- 108 Troy Crowder
- 129 Kevin Todd
- 150 Ryan Pardoski
- 171 Scott McCormack
- 192 Frederic Chabot
- 213 John Andersen
- 236 Doug Kirton

1985
Pick
- 3 Craig Wolanin
- 24 Sean Burke
- 32 Eric Weinrich
- 45 Myles O'Connor
- 66 Gregg Polak
- 108 Bill McMillan
- 129 Kevin Schrader
- 150 Ed Krayer
- 171 Jamie Huscroft
- 192 Terry Shold
- 213 Jamie McKinley
- 234 David Williams

Coach

FTOREK, ROBBIE
Coach, New Jersey Devils. Born in Needham, MA, January 2, 1952.

The New Jersey Devils promoted Robbie Ftorek to the position of head coach on May 21, 1998. Ftorek will be entering his ninth season with the organization, having joined the Devils on July 9, 1991. He spent two seasons as an assistant coach, having also served the organization in that capacity during the 1991-92 season. Ftorek was head coach of the Devils' top minor-league development club for four seasons, 1992-93 through 1995-96, and led the Albany River Rats to the 1995 American Hockey League's Calder Cup championship.

Prior to joining the Devils, Ftorek spent two seasons in the Quebec Nordiques organization. He was named head coach of the Halifax Citadels (AHL) prior to 1989-90 and assumed the post as Nordiques' assistant coach during that season. Ftorek began his coaching career upon his retirement as a player when he was named to guide the New Haven Nighthawks (AHL) in 1985. On December 9, 1987, Ftorek was named head coach of the Los Angeles Kings, where he guided the team to a 65-56-11 (.534) mark over one and a half seasons.

Coaching Record

Season	Team		Regular Season					Playoffs			
		Games	W	L	T	%		Games	W	L	%
1985-86	New Haven (AHL)	80	36	37	7	.494		5	1	4	.200
1986-87	New Haven (AHL)	80	44	25	11	.619		7	3	4	.429
1987-88	New Haven (AHL)	27	16	8	3	.667		...	...	...	...
	Los Angeles (NHL)	52	23	25	4	**.481**		5	1	4	**.200**
1988-89	**Los Angeles (NHL)**	80	42	31	7	**.569**		11	4	7	**.364**
1989-90	Halifax (AHL)	48	25	19	4	.563		...	...	...	...
1992-93	Utica (AHL)	80	33	36	11	.481		5	1	4	.200
1993-94	Albany (AHL)	80	38	34	8	.525		5	1	4	.200
1994-95	Albany (AHL)	80	46	17	17	.681		14	12	2	.857
1995-96	Albany (AHL)	80	54	19	17	.719		4	1	3	.250
1998-99	**New Jersey (NHL)**	82	47	24	11	**.640**		7	3	4	**.429**
	NHL Totals	214	112	80	22	**.575**		23	8	15	**.348**

Club Directory

Continental Airlines Arena
50 Route 120 North
P.O. Box 504
East Rutherford, NJ 07073
Phone **201/935-6050**
FAX 201/935-2127
Website:
www.newjerseydevils.com
Capacity: 19,040

Chairman	Dr. John J. McMullen
President/General Manager	Louis A. Lamoriello
Executive Vice President	Peter S. McMullen
Executive Vice President	Chris Modrzynski
Vice President, General Counsel	Joseph C. Benedetti
Vice President, Ticket Operations	Terry Farmer
Vice President, Corporate Partnerships	Kenneth F. Ferriter
Vice President, Communications/Broadcasting	Rick Minch
Vice President, Finance	Scott Struble

Hockey Club Personnel

Head Coach	Robbie Ftorek
Assistant Coaches	Viacheslav Fetisov, Larry Robinson
Goaltending Coach	Jacques Caron
Director of Scouting	David Conte
Assistant Director of Scouting	Claude Carrier
Scouting Staff	Glen Dirk, Milt Fisher, Ferny Flaman, Dan Labraaten, Chris Lamoriello, Joe Mahoney, Larry Perris, Marcel Pronovost, Lou Reycroft, Vaclav Slansky, Jr., Geoff Stevens, Ed Thomlinson, Les Widdifield
Pro Scouting Staff	Andre Boudrias, Bob Hoffmeyer, Jan Ludvig
Hockey Operations Video Coordinator	Taran Singleton
Scouting Staff Assistant	Callie A. Smith
Medical Trainer	Bill Murray
Strength/Conditioning Coordinator	Michael Vasalani
Equipment Manager	Dana McGuane
Assistant Equipment Managers	Harry Bricker, Lou Centanni
Massage Therapist	Juergen Merz
Team Cardiologist	Dr. Joseph Niznik
Team Dentist	Dr. H. Hugh Gardy
Team Optometrist	Dr. Paul Berman
Team Orthopedists	Dr. Barry Fisher, Dr. Len Jaffe
Exercise Physiologist	Dr. Garret Caffrey
Physical Therapist	David M. Feniger
Video Consultant	Mitch Kaufman
Head Coach, Albany	John Cunniff
Assistant Coaches, Albany	Bob Carpenter, Dennis Gendron
Athletic Trainer, Albany	Chris Scarlata
Equipment Manager, Albany	Jason McGrath
Assistant Equipment Manager, Albany	Damion Parmelee

Administration Department

Hockey Operations Executive Assistant to the President/General Manager	Marie Carnevale
Corporate Executive Assistant to the President/General Manager	Mary K. Morrison
Receptionists	Jelsa Belotta, Pat Maione
Administrative Assistant to the Executive Vice Presidents	Sharon Calandra
Corporate Staff Assistant	Mary Montemurro
Operations Staff Assistant	Adam Manger

Ticket Department

Director, Ticket Operations	Tom Bates
Director, Customer Service/Gold Circle	TBA
Director, Customer Service/Season Ticket Accounts	Dave Beck
Customer Service Representative	Andrea Marchesani
Director, Group Sales	Neil Desormeaux
Group Account Manager	Rich Davis

Marketing Department

Director, Season Ticket Sales	Mike Yencik
Account Managers	Chris Brehm, Carmine D'Urso, Todd Hyland, Joe Lawrence, Nick Mike-Mayer, Vincent Occhipinti, Mauricio Ramirez, Derek Smith, Keith Veltre
Account Managers, Corporate Partnerships	Michael DeMartino, Mike Kozak
Coordinator, Corporate Partner Services	Kelly A. Klunk
Assistant Director, Community Development	Paul Viola
Community Development Assistant	Brad Preston
Coordinator, Game Entertainment	William Ackerman
Sales Receptionist	Christie Zdanowicz

Communications Department

Director, Public Relations	Kevin Dessart
Director, Information/Publications	Mike Levine
Coordinator,Communications	Jana Spaulding
Communications Assistant	Jeff Altstadter

Finance Department

Assistant Controller	Craig Wolman
Staff Accountants	Suzanne Folkerts, Patrick Kennedy, Michael Merolla
Administrative Assistant	Eileen Musikant

Merchandising Department

Director, Merchandising	Stan Brajer
Merchandising Manager	David Perricone
Customer Service Representative	Tracey Lundquist

Computer Operations

Director, Programming/Computer Operations	Jack Skelley
Systems Administrator	Mike Tukes
Director, Internet Operations	Alan Kudlac

Television/Radio

Television Outlet	FOX Sports Net New York
Broadcasters	Mike Emrick (Play-by-Play), Glenn Resch (Color)
Radio Outlet	WABC 77AM
Broadcasters	Mike Miller (Play-by-Play), Randy Velischek (Color)

New York Islanders

1998-99 Results: 24W-48L-10T 58PTS. Fifth, Atlantic Division

Islanders defenseman Zdeno Chara mixes it up with Lubos Bartecko against the boards at the St. Louis blueline. At 6'9" and 255 pounds, Chara is the biggest player in the history of the NHL—though only an inch taller than Steve McKenna of the L.A. Kings.

Franchise date: June 6, 1972

ATLANTIC DIVISION

28th NHL Season

Year-by-Year Record

		Home			Road			Overall							
Season	GP	W	L	T	W	L	T	W	L	T	GF	GA	Pts.	Finished	Playoff Result
1998-99	82	11	23	7	13	25	3	24	48	10	194	244	58	5th, Atlantic Div.	Out of Playoffs
1997-98	82	17	20	4	13	21	7	30	41	11	212	225	71	4th, Atlantic Div.	Out of Playoffs
1996-97	82	19	18	4	10	23	8	29	41	12	240	250	70	7th, Atlantic Div.	Out of Playoffs
1995-96	82	14	21	6	8	29	4	22	50	10	229	315	54	7th, Atlantic Div.	Out of Playoffs
1994-95	48	10	11	3	5	17	2	15	28	5	126	158	35	7th, Atlantic Div.	Out of Playoffs
1993-94	84	23	15	4	13	21	8	36	36	12	282	264	84	4th, Atlantic Div.	Lost Conf. Quarter-Final
1992-93	84	20	19	3	20	18	4	40	37	7	335	297	87	3rd, Patrick Div.	Lost Conf. Championship
1991-92	80	20	15	5	14	20	6	34	35	11	291	299	79	5th, Patrick Div.	Out of Playoffs
1990-91	80	15	19	6	10	26	4	25	45	10	223	290	60	6th, Patrick Div.	Out of Playoffs
1989-90	80	15	17	8	16	21	3	31	38	11	281	288	73	4th, Patrick Div.	Lost Div. Semi-Final
1988-89	80	19	18	3	9	29	2	28	47	5	265	325	61	6th, Patrick Div.	Out of Playoffs
1987-88	80	24	10	6	15	21	4	39	31	10	308	267	88	1st, Patrick Div.	Lost Div. Semi-Final
1986-87	80	20	15	5	15	18	7	35	33	12	279	281	82	3rd, Patrick Div.	Lost Div. Final
1985-86	80	22	11	7	17	18	5	39	29	12	327	284	90	3rd, Patrick Div.	Lost Div. Semi-Final
1984-85	80	26	11	3	14	23	3	40	34	6	345	312	86	3rd, Patrick Div.	Lost Div. Final
1983-84	80	28	11	1	22	15	3	50	26	4	357	269	104	1st, Patrick Div.	Lost Final
1982-83	**80**	**26**	**11**	**3**	**16**	**15**	**9**	**42**	**26**	**12**	**302**	**226**	**96**	**2nd, Patrick Div.**	**Won Stanley Cup**
1981-82	**80**	**33**	**3**	**4**	**21**	**13**	**6**	**54**	**16**	**10**	**385**	**250**	**118**	**1st, Patrick Div.**	**Won Stanley Cup**
1980-81	**80**	**23**	**6**	**11**	**25**	**12**	**3**	**48**	**18**	**14**	**355**	**260**	**110**	**1st, Patrick Div.**	**Won Stanley Cup**
1979-80	**80**	**26**	**9**	**5**	**13**	**19**	**8**	**39**	**28**	**13**	**281**	**247**	**91**	**2nd, Patrick Div.**	**Won Stanley Cup**
1978-79	80	31	3	6	20	12	8	51	15	14	358	214	116	1st, Patrick Div.	Lost Semi-Final
1977-78	80	29	3	8	19	14	7	48	17	15	334	210	111	1st, Patrick Div.	Lost Quarter-Final
1976-77	80	24	11	5	23	10	7	47	21	12	288	193	106	2nd, Patrick Div.	Lost Semi-Final
1975-76	80	24	8	8	18	13	9	42	21	17	297	190	101	2nd, Patrick Div.	Lost Semi-Final
1974-75	80	22	6	12	11	19	10	33	25	22	264	221	88	3rd, Patrick Div.	Lost Semi-Final
1973-74	78	13	17	9	6	24	9	19	41	18	182	247	56	8th, East Div.	Out of Playoffs
1972-73	78	10	25	4	2	35	2	12	60	6	170	347	30	8th, East Div.	Out of Playoffs

1999-2000 Player Personnel

FORWARDS	HT	WT	S	Place of Birth	Date	1998-99 Club
ANDERSSON, Niklas	5-9	175	L	Kungalv, Sweden	5/20/71	Chicago (IHL)
CZERKAWSKI, Mariusz	6-0	195	L	Radomsko, Poland	4/13/72	NY Islanders
FERRARO, Chris	5-10	180	R	Port Jefferson, NY	1/24/73	Edmonton-Hamilton
GREEN, Josh	6-4	212	L	Camrose, Alta.	11/16/77	Los Angeles-Springfield
HAGGERTY, Sean	6-1	186	L	Rye, NY	2/11/76	Lowell
HRKAC, Tony	5-11	170	L	Thunder Bay, Ont.	7/7/66	Dallas
ISBISTER, Brad	6-3	222	R	Edmonton, Alta.	5/7/77	Phoenix-Springfield-Las Vegas
JOKINEN, Olli	6-3	208	L	Kuopio, Finland	12/5/78	Los Angeles-Springfield
JONSSON, Jorgen	6-0	185	L	Angelholm, Sweden	9/29/72	Farjestads BK
KROG, Jason	5-11	191	R	Fernie, B.C.	10/9/75	New Hampshire
LACROIX, Daniel	6-2	205	L	Montreal, Que.	3/11/69	Edmonton-Hamilton
LAPOINTE, Claude	5-9	181	L	Lachine, Que.	10/11/68	NY Islanders
LAWRENCE, Mark	6-4	215	R	Burlington, Ont.	1/27/72	NY Islanders-Lowell
MAPLETOFT, Justin	6-1	180	L	Lloydminster, Sask.	1/11/81	Red Deer
NABOKOV, Dmitri	6-2	209	R	Novosibirsk, USSR	1/4/77	NY Islanders-Lowell
ODJICK, Gino	6-3	210	L	Maniwaki, Que.	9/7/70	NY Islanders
ORSZAGH, Vladimir	5-11	173	L	Banska Bystrica, Czech.	5/24/77	Lowell
PEARSON, Scott	6-1	205	L	Cornwall, Ont.	12/19/69	Chicago (IHL)
RUPP, Michael	6-5	218	L	Cleveland, OH	1/13/80	Erie (OHL)
WATT, Mike	6-2	212	L	Seaforth, Ont.	3/31/76	NY Islanders
WEBB, Steve	6-0	195	R	Peterborough, Ont.	4/20/75	NY Islanders-Lowell
DEFENSEMEN						
BIRON, Mathieu	6-6	212	R	Lac St-Charles, Que.	4/29/80	Shawinigan
BREWER, Eric	6-3	195	L	Vernon, B.C.	4/17/79	NY Islanders
BRIMANIS, Aris	6-3	210	R	Cleveland, OH	3/14/72	Grand Rapids-Fredericton
CAIRNS, Eric	6-6	230	L	Oakville, Ont.	6/27/74	Hartford-NY Islanders-Lowell
CHARA, Zdeno	6-9	255	L	Trencin, Czech.	3/18/77	NY Islanders-Lowell
CHEBATURKIN, Vladimir	6-2	213	L	Tyumen, USSR	4/23/75	NY Islanders-Lowell
EAKINS, Dallas	6-2	195	L	Dade City, FL	2/27/67	Tor-Chi (IHL)-St.J's
GIROUX, Ray	6-0	180	L	North Bay, Ont.	7/20/76	Lowell
HEWARD, Jamie	6-2	207	R	Regina, Sask.	3/30/71	Nashville
JONSSON, Kenny	6-3	195	L	Angelholm, Sweden	10/6/74	NY Islanders
KUDROC, Kristian	6-6	229	R	Michalovce, Czech.	5/21/81	HK Michalovce
MALKOC, Dean	6-3	215	L	Vancouver, B.C.	1/26/70	NY Islanders-Lowell
MEZEI, Branislav	6-4	221	L	Nitra, Czech.	10/8/80	Belleville
PILON, Richard	6-0	205	L	Saskatoon, Sask.	4/30/68	NY Islanders
SCHULTZ, Ray	6-2	200	L	Red Deer, Alta.	11/14/76	NY Islanders-Lowell
GOALTENDERS	**HT**	**WT**	**C**	**Place of Birth**	**Date**	**1998-99 Club**
FLAHERTY, Wade	6-0	170	L	Terrace, B.C.	1/11/68	NY Islanders-Lowell
LUONGO, Roberto	6-3	175	L	Montreal, Que.	4/4/79	ValD'Or-Bathurst
POTVIN, Felix	6-1	190	L	Anjou, Que.	6/23/71	Toronto-NY Islanders
VALIQUETTE, Stephen	6-5	190	L	Etobicoke, Ont.	8/20/77	Hampton Rds.-Lowell

Coach

GORING, BUTCH
Coach, New York Islanders. Born in St. Boniface, Man., October 22, 1949.

Former New York Islanders star Butch Goring re-joined the team as its head coach on April 30, 1999 and has been entrusted with the task of trying to restore a little bit of the Islanders tradition to a franchise that last made the playoffs during the 1993-1994 season.

Goring played 16 seasons in the NHL with three different teams - the Los Angeles Kings, New York Islanders, and Boston Bruins - but it was his stay on Long Island that defined his career. Goring was the last piece of the puzzle that included the likes of Mike Bossy, Billy Smith, Denis Potvin, Bryan Trottier, and Bob Nystrom, and he helped the Isles win four consecutive Stanley Cup titles from 1980 to 1983. Perhaps Goring's greatest individual accomplishment as a player came in the 1981 playoffs when he had 10 goals and 10 assists in 18 games to earn the Conn Smythe Trophy as the most valuable player of the post-season.

Along with an impressive resume as a player, Goring's coaching background also has plenty of peaks, including back-to-back Turner Cup titles with the International Hockey League's Denver/Utah Grizzlies in 1995 and 1996. Goring began his head coaching career with the Boston Bruins in 1985-86. In a little over a season in Boston, Goring had a winning 42-38-13 record. Goring was an Islanders assistant under Al Arbour in 1989-90. He has also had head coaching stints in the Western Hockey League (WHL) and the American Hockey League (AHL).

Goring and his wife, Cathy, have two daughters, Shannon and Kellie.

Coaching Record

		Regular Season					Playoffs			
Season	Team	Games	W	L	T	%	Games	W	L	%
1985-86	**Boston (NHL)**	**80**	**37**	**31**	**12**	**.538**	**3**	**0**	**3**	**.000**
1986-87	**Boston (NHL)**	**13**	**5**	**7**	**1**	**.423**	....	....	....	....
1987-88	Spokane (WHL)	72	37	32	3	.535	15	7	8	.467
1988-89	Spokane (WHL)	11	2	9	0	.182	....	....	....	....
1990-91	Capital Dist. (AHL)	80	28	43	9	.406	....	....	....	....
1991-92	Capital Dist. (AHL)	80	32	37	11	.469	7	3	4	.429
1992-93	Capital Dist. (AHL)	80	34	34	12	.500	4	0	4	.000
1993-94	Las Vegas (IHL)	81	52	18	11	.710	5	1	4	.200
1994-95	Denver (IHL)	81	57	18	6	.741	17	15	2	.882
1995-96	Utah (IHL)	82	49	29	4	.622	22	15	7	.682
1996-97	Utah (IHL)	82	43	33	6	.561	7	3	4	.429
1997-98	Utah (IHL)	82	47	27	8	.622	4	1	3	.250
1998-99	Utah (IHL)	82	39	34	9	.530	....	....	....	....
	NHL Totals	**93**	**42**	**38**	**13**	**.522**	**3**	**0**	**3**	**.000**

Coaching History

Phil Goyette and Earl Ingarfield, 1972-73; Al Arbour, 1973-74 to 1985-86; Terry Simpson, 1986-87, 1987-88; Terry Simpson and Al Arbour, 1988-89; Al Arbour, 1989-90 to 1993-94; Lorne Henning, 1994-95; Mike Milbury, 1995-96; Mike Milbury and Rick Bowness, 1996-97; Rick Bowness and Mike Milbury, 1997-98; Mike Milbury and Bill Stewart, 1998-99; Butch Goring, 1999-2000.

1998-99 Scoring

* – rookie

Regular Season

Pos	#	Player	Team	GP	G	A	Pts	+/–	PIM	PP	SH	GW	GT	S	%
R	16	Zigmund Palffy	NYI	50	22	28	50	–6	34	5	2	1	0	168	13.1
C	32	Trevor Linden	NYI	82	18	29	47	–14	32	8	1	1	0	167	10.8
C	20	Bryan Smolinski	NYI	82	16	24	40	–7	49	7	0	3	0	223	7.2
R	25	Mariusz Czerkawski	NYI	78	21	17	38	–10	14	4	0	1	2	205	10.2
C	13	Claude Lapointe	NYI	82	14	23	37	–19	62	2	2	1	0	134	10.4
R	44	Mark Lawrence	NYI	60	14	16	30	–8	38	4	0	2	1	88	15.9
C	11	Craig Janney	T.B.	38	4	18	22	–13	10	2	0	0	1	36	11.1
			NYI	18	1	4	5	–2	4	0	0	0	0	9	11.1
			TOTAL	56	5	22	27	–15	14	2	0	0	1	45	11.1
D	29	Kenny Jonsson	NYI	63	8	18	26	–18	34	6	0	0	0	91	8.8
C	10	Mats Lindgren	EDM	48	5	12	17	4	22	0	1	0	0	53	9.4
			NYI	12	5	3	8	2	2	3	0	1	0	30	16.7
			TOTAL	60	10	15	25	6	24	3	1	1	0	83	12.0
L	12	* Mike Watt	NYI	75	8	17	25	–2	12	0	0	4	0	75	10.7
D	38	Barry Richter	NYI	72	6	18	24	–4	34	0	0	2	0	111	5.4
D	4	* Eric Brewer	NYI	63	5	6	11	–14	32	2	0	0	0	63	7.9
D	3	* Zdeno Chara	NYI	59	2	6	8	–8	83	0	1	0	0	56	3.6
D	6	David Harlock	NYI	70	2	6	8	–16	68	0	0	0	0	35	5.7
L	24	Gino Odjick	NYI	23	4	3	7	–2	133	1	0	2	0	28	14.3
C	11	Kevin Miller	NYI	33	1	5	6	–5	13	0	0	0	0	37	2.7
D	2	Richard Pilon	NYI	52	0	4	4	–8	88	0	0	0	0	27	0.0
L	14	Joe Sacco	NYI	73	3	0	3	–24	45	0	1	2	0	84	3.6
D	36	Ted Crowley	COL	7	0	1	1	–1	2	0	0	0	0	10	0.0
			NYI	6	1	1	2	0	0	1	0	0	0	10	10.0
			TOTAL	13	1	2	3	–1	2	1	0	0	0	20	5.0
D	33	Eric Cairns	NYI	9	0	3	3	1	23	0	0	0	0	2	0.0
C	37	* Dmitri Nabokov	NYI	4	0	2	2	4	2	0	0	0	0	4	0.0
R	49	* Vladimir Orsagh	NYI	12	1	0	1	2	6	0	0	0	0	5	20.0
D	39	Dean Malkoc	NYI	2	0	1	1	3	7	0	0	0	0	1	0.0
C	67	Mike Kennedy	NYI	1	0	0	0	0	2	0	0	0	0	0	0.0
D	36	* Ray Schultz	NYI	4	0	0	0	–2	7	0	0	0	0	2	0.0
G	1	* Marcel Cousineau	NYI	6	0	0	0	0	0	0	0	0	0	0	0.0
D	55	* Vlad Chebaturkin	NYI	8	0	0	0	6	12	0	0	0	0	4	0.0
L	18	Mike Hough	NYI	11	0	0	0	–2	2	0	0	0	0	4	0.0
R	48	* Warren Luhning	NYI	11	0	0	0	–4	8	0	0	0	0	11	0.0
G	28	Felix Potvin	TOR	5	0	0	0	0	0	0	0	0	0	0	0.0
			NYI	11	0	0	0	0	0	0	0	0	0	0	0.0
			TOTAL	16	0	0	0	0	0	0	0	0	0	0	0.0
G	30	Wade Flaherty	NYI	20	0	0	0	0	4	0	0	0	0	0	0.0
R	8	Steve Webb	NYI	45	0	0	0	–10	32	0	0	0	0	18	0.0

Goaltending

No.	Goaltender	GPI	Mins	Avg	W	L	T	EN	SO	GA	SA	S%
35	Tommy Salo	51	3018	2.62	17	26	7	5	5	132	1368	.904
1	* Marcel Cousineau	6	293	2.87	0	4	0	0	0	14	119	.882
30	Wade Flaherty	20	1048	3.03	5	11	2	3	0	53	491	.892
28	Felix Potvin	11	606	3.66	2	7	1	0	0	37	345	.893
	Totals	**82**	**4990**	**2.93**	**24**	**48**	**10**	**8**	**5**	**244**	**2331**	**.895**

General Manager

MILBURY, MIKE
General Manager, New York Islanders. Born in Walpole, MA, June 17, 1952.

Milbury came to the Islanders with 20 years of professional hockey experience with the Boston Bruins — as a player, assistant coach, assistant general manager, general manager and coach on both the NHL and AHL levels. Milbury took over as general manager from Don Maloney on December 12, 1995.

Milbury joined the Boston organization after graduating from Colgate University with a degree in urban sociology and enjoyed a ten-year playing career with the team. He retired May 6, 1985 and took over as assistant coach. He returned to the ice late in the 1985-86 season when injuries decimated the Bruins defense.

Milbury's playing career concluded after the 1986-87 season and on July 16, 1987 he took over as coach of the Maine Mariners, Boston's top AHL affiliate. In his first year with the team he guided the Mariners to the AHL's Northern Division title and was named both AHL coach of the year and *The Hockey News* minor league coach of the year.

He was named the assistant general manager and coach of the Boston Bruins May 16, 1989. He guided the Bruins to consecutive 100-point seasons and Adams Division titles, the 1990 Presidents' Trophy and Wales Conference championship, and an appearance in the Stanley Cup finals in 1990. He earned coach of the year honors from both *The Hockey News* and *The Sporting News* for this effort.

Milbury and his wife, Debbie, have two sons, Owen and Luke, and two daughters, Alison and Caitlin.

NHL Coaching Record

		Regular Season					Playoffs			
Season	Team	Games	W	L	T	%	Games	W	L	%
1989-90	Boston	80	46	25	9	.631	21	13	8	.619
1990-91	Boston	80	44	24	12	.606	19	10	9	.526
1995-96	NY Islanders	82	22	50	10	.329	....	....	....	....
1996-97	NY Islanders	45	13	23	9	.389	....	....	....	....
1997-98	NY Islanders	19	8	9	2	.474	....	....	....	....
	NHL Totals	**306**	**133**	**131**	**42**	**.503**	**40**	**23**	**17**	**.575**

General Managers' History

Bill Torrey, 1972-73 to 1991-92; Don Maloney, 1992-93 to 1994-95; Don Maloney and Mike Milbury, 1995-96; Mike Milbury, 1996-97 to date.

Club Records

Team

(Figures in brackets for season records are games played; records for fewest points, wins, ties, losses, goals, goals against are for 70 or more games)

Most Points	**118**	1981-82 (80)
Most Wins	**54**	1981-82 (80)
Most Ties	**22**	1974-75 (80)
Most Losses	**60**	1972-73 (78)
Most Goals	**385**	1981-82 (80)
Most Goals Against	**347**	1972-73 (78)
Fewest Points	**30**	1972-73 (78)
Fewest Wins	**12**	1972-73 (78)
Fewest Ties	**4**	1983-84 (80)
Fewest Losses	**15**	1978-79 (80)
Fewest Goals	**170**	1972-73 (78)
Fewest Goals Against	**190**	1975-76 (80)
Longest Winning Streak		
Overall	**15**	Jan. 21-Feb. 20/82
Home	**14**	Jan. 2-Feb. 27/82
Away	**8**	Feb. 27-Mar. 31/81
Longest Undefeated Streak		
Overall	**15**	Jan. 21-Feb. 20/82 (15 wins), Nov. 4-Dec. 4/80 (13 wins, 2 ties)
Home	**23**	Oct. 17/78-Jan. 27/79 (19 wins, 4 ties), Jan. 2-Apr. 3/82 (21 wins, 2 ties)
Away	**8**	Four times
Longest Losing Streak		
Overall	**12**	Dec. 27/72-Jan. 16/73, Nov. 22-Dec. 15/88
Home	**5**	Five times
Away	**15**	Jan. 20-Mar. 31/73
Longest Winless Streak		
Overall	**15**	Nov. 22-Dec. 21/72 (12 losses, 3 ties)
Home	**9**	Mar. 2-Apr. 6/99 (7 losses, 2 ties)
Away	**20**	Nov. 3/72-Jan. 13/73 (19 losses, 1 tie)
Most Shutouts, Season	**10**	1975-76 (80)
Most PIM, Season	**1,857**	1986-87 (80)
Most Goals, Game	**11**	Dec. 20/83 (Pit. 3 at NYI 11), Mar. 3/84 (NYI 11 at Tor. 6)

Individual

Most Seasons	**17**	Billy Smith
Most Games	**1,123**	Bryan Trottier
Most Goals, Career	**573**	Mike Bossy
Most Assists, Career	**853**	Bryan Trottier
Most Points, Career	**1,353**	Bryan Trottier (500G, 853A)
Most PIM, Career	**1,879**	Mick Vukota
Most Shutouts, Career	**25**	Glenn Resch
Longest Consecutive Games Streak	**576**	Bill Harris (Oct. 7/72-Nov. 30/79)
Most Goals, Season	**69**	Mike Bossy (1978-79)
Most Assists, Season	**87**	Bryan Trottier (1978-79)
Most Points, Season	**147**	Mike Bossy (1981-82; 64G, 83A)
Most PIM, Season	**356**	Brian Curran (1986-87)
Most Points, Defenseman, Season	**101**	Denis Potvin (1978-79; 31G, 70A)
Most Points, Center, Season	**134**	Bryan Trottier (1978-79; 47G, 87A)
Most Points, Right Wing, Season	**147**	Mike Bossy (1981-82; 64G, 83A)
Most Points, Left Wing, Season	**100**	John Tonelli (1984-85; 42G, 58A)
Most Points, Rookie, Season	**95**	Bryan Trottier (1975-76; 32G, 63A)
Most Shutouts, Season	**7**	Glenn Resch (1975-76)
Most Goals, Game	**5**	Bryan Trottier (Dec. 23/78, Feb. 13/82), John Tonelli (Jan. 6/81)
Most Assists, Game	**6**	Mike Bossy (Jan. 6/81)
Most Points, Game	**8**	Bryan Trottier (Dec. 23/78; 5G, 3A)

Captains' History

Ed Westfall, 1972-73 to 1975-76; Ed Westfall and Clark Gillies, 1976-77; Clark Gillies, 1977-78, 1978-79; Denis Potvin, 1979-80 to 1986-87; Brent Sutter, 1987-88 to 1990-91; Brent Sutter and Pat Flatley, 1991-92; Pat Flatley, 1992-93 to 1995-96; no captain, 1996-97; Bryan McCabe and Trevor Linden, 1997-98; Trevor Linden, 1998-99.

Retired Numbers

5	Denis Potvin	1973-1988
9	Clark Gillies	1974-1986
22	Mike Bossy	1977-1987
23	Bob Nystrom	1972-1986
31	Billy Smith	1972-1989

All-time Record vs. Other Clubs

Regular Season

	At Home							On Road							Total						
	GP	W	L	T	GF	GA	PTS	GP	W	L	T	GF	GA	PTS	GP	W	L	T	GF	GA	PTS
Anaheim	5	2	2	1	12	15	5	5	2	1	2	14	11	6	10	4	3	3	26	26	11
Boston	51	21	24	6	171	168	48	49	12	27	10	140	191	34	100	33	51	16	311	359	82
Buffalo	51	22	21	8	150	144	52	51	16	27	8	144	178	40	102	38	48	16	294	322	92
Calgary	46	25	12	9	185	124	59	47	13	23	11	140	168	37	93	38	35	20	325	292	96
Carolina	34	17	13	4	117	97	38	35	13	17	5	122	128	31	69	30	30	9	239	225	69
Chicago	43	17	12	14	151	128	48	45	16	24	5	150	151	37	88	33	36	19	301	279	85
Colorado	29	15	13	1	116	102	31	30	10	18	2	92	115	22	59	25	31	3	208	217	53
Dallas	43	23	12	8	164	124	54	43	19	17	7	158	128	45	86	42	29	15	322	252	99
Detroit	42	23	16	3	155	124	49	41	17	22	2	130	147	36	83	40	38	5	285	271	85
Edmonton	27	12	6	9	115	101	33	26	6	16	4	74	99	16	53	18	22	13	189	200	49
Florida	15	5	8	2	36	39	12	15	4	8	3	38	46	11	30	9	16	5	74	85	23
Los Angeles	41	24	13	4	154	115	52	41	15	19	7	134	149	37	82	39	32	11	288	264	89
Montreal	50	23	22	5	160	148	51	50	12	29	9	150	188	33	100	35	51	14	310	336	84
Nashville	1	0	1	0	1	2	0	1	1	0	0	6	3	2	2	1	1	0	7	5	2
New Jersey	72	50	13	9	323	204	109	71	34	27	10	266	239	78	143	84	40	19	589	443	187
NY Rangers	83	52	24	7	337	252	111	83	24	50	9	249	324	57	166	76	74	16	586	576	168
Ottawa	14	3	8	3	46	55	9	13	3	7	3	42	47	9	27	6	15	6	88	102	18
Philadelphia	85	47	24	14	331	243	108	82	23	50	9	241	313	55	167	70	74	23	572	556	163
Phoenix	27	13	7	7	108	84	33	26	14	9	3	97	81	31	53	27	16	10	205	165	64
Pittsburgh	73	38	27	8	297	242	84	75	29	35	11	265	283	69	148	67	62	19	562	525	153
St. Louis	45	24	10	11	173	113	59	44	18	17	9	144	158	45	89	42	27	20	317	271	104
San Jose	8	5	2	1	37	25	11	7	4	2	1	25	15	9	15	9	4	2	62	40	20
Tampa Bay	15	5	9	1	40	46	11	16	8	7	1	49	39	17	31	13	16	2	89	85	28
Toronto	43	24	16	3	178	131	51	45	21	21	3	160	152	45	88	45	37	6	338	283	96
Vancouver	43	23	11	9	162	120	55	45	21	21	3	148	148	45	88	44	32	12	310	268	100
Washington	71	40	30	1	274	222	81	71	29	32	10	229	230	68	142	69	62	11	503	452	149
Defunct Clubs	13	11	0	2	75	33	24	13	4	5	4	35	41	12	26	15	5	6	110	74	36
Totals	**1070**	**564**	**356**	**150**	**4068**	**3201**	**1278**	**1070**	**388**	**531**	**151**	**3442**	**3772**	**927**	**2140**	**952**	**887**	**301**	**7510**	**6973**	**2205**

Playoffs

	Series	W	L	GP	W	L	T	GF	GA	Last Mtg.	Round	Result
Boston	2	2	0	11	8	3	0	49	35	1983	CF	W 4-2
Buffalo	3	3	0	16	12	4	0	59	45	1980	SF	W 4-2
Chicago	2	2	0	6	6	0	0	21	6	1979	QF	W 4-0
Colorado	1	1	0	4	4	0	0	18	9	1982	CF	W 4-0
Dallas	1	1	0	5	4	1	0	26	16	1981	F	W 4-1
Edmonton	3	2	1	15	9	6	0	58	47	1984	F	L 1-4
Los Angeles	1	1	0	4	3	1	0	21	10	1980	PR	W 3-1
Montreal	4	1	3	22	8	14	0	55	64	1993	CF	L 1-4
New Jersey	1	0	1	6	2	4	0	18	23	1988	DSF	L 2-4
NY Rangers	8	5	3	39	20	19	0	129	132	1994	CQF	L 0-4
Philadelphia	4	1	3	25	11	14	0	69	83	1987	DF	L 3-4
Pittsburgh	3	3	0	19	11	8	0	67	58	1993	DF	W 4-3
Toronto	2	1	1	10	6	4	0	33	20	1981	PR	W 3-0
Vancouver	2	2	0	6	6	0	0	26	14	1982	F	W 4-0
Washington	6	5	1	30	18	12	0	99	88	1993	DSF	W 4-2
Totals	**43**	**30**	**13**	**218**	**128**	**90**	**0**	**748**	**650**			

Calgary totals include Atlanta Flames, 1972-73 to 1979-80. Carolina totals include Hartford, 1979-80 to 1996-97.
Colorado totals include Quebec, 1979-80 to 1994-95. Dallas totals include Minnesota, 1972-73 to 1992-93.
New Jersey totals include Kansas City, 1974-75 to 1975-76, and Colorado Rockies, 1976-77 to 1981-82.
Phoenix totals include Winnipeg, 1979-80 to 1995-96.

Playoff Results 1999-95

Year	Round	Opponent	Result	GF	GA

(Last playoff appearance: 1994)

Abbreviations: Round: F – Final;
CF – conference final; **CQF** – conference quarter-final;
DF – division final; **DSF** – division semi-final;
SF – semi-final; **QF** – quarter-final;
PR – preliminary round.

1998-99 Results

Oct.	10		Pittsburgh	3-4		11	at	Washington	3-4
	12	at	Boston	0-3		13	at	NY Rangers	3-4
	14	at	Tampa Bay	2-0		16	at	Florida	0-1
	17	at	St. Louis	1-0		20		Florida	2-5
	21		Edmonton	2-4		21	at	Pittsburgh	5-2
	22	at	NY Rangers	2-3		26		Boston	4-1
	24		Buffalo	5-4		29		Phoenix	4-4
	27		Los Angeles	1-0		30	at	Ottawa	2-9
	29		New Jersey	1-2	**Feb.**	3	at	Detroit	1-5
	31		Philadelphia	3-2		4	at	Boston	5-4
Nov.	2		Florida	6-2		7		Vancouver	3-3
	5		Carolina	3-6		9		Washington	1-2
	7	at	Montreal	2-4		12		Nashville	1-2
	9	at	Toronto	3-1		13	at	Buffalo	2-2
	10	at	Pittsburgh	2-3		15		Tampa Bay	3-3
	12		Montreal	4-0		17		Pittsburgh	3-1
	14		Washington	3-5		20	at	New Jersey	3-2
	17	at	Colorado	2-5		21	at	Carolina	1-4
	20	at	Dallas	2-4		25		Toronto	1-4
	21	at	Nashville	6-3		27		Detroit	3-1
	25		Philadelphia	4-2	**Mar.**	2		Ottawa	2-4
	26	at	Ottawa	1-4		4		Dallas	2-3
	28		Carolina	1-3		6	at	Philadelphia	3-3
Dec.	2		NY Rangers	2-3		7		New Jersey	2-4
	4	at	Washington	1-5		9		Philadelphia	2-2
	5		New Jersey	5-7		11		Toronto	1-2
	8		Colorado	1-2		14		NY Rangers	2-3
	12		Tampa Bay	1-2		15	at	Buffalo	1-2
	15	at	San Jose	1-0		19	at	Vancouver	3-1
	17	at	Los Angeles	5-4		21	at	Calgary	1-2
	18	at	Anaheim	2-2		24	at	Carolina	1-2
	20	at	Phoenix	2-4		27		Ottawa	3-7
	22		St. Louis	3-3		29	at	NY Rangers	1-3
	26		Boston	4-2		31	at	Florida	5-3
	28	at	Florida	1-5	**Apr.**	3		Anaheim	2-2
	29	at	Tampa Bay	0-3		6		Buffalo	3-4
	31	at	Chicago	0-1		8		Montreal	3-1
Jan.	2		San Jose	3-4		10		Carolina	1-6
	5		Chicago	1-1		12	at	New Jersey	4-2
	7	at	Philadelphia	0-5		14	at	Toronto	2-3
	9	at	Montreal	2-3		17	at	Pittsburgh	7-2

Entry Draft
Selections 1999-85

1999
Pick
5	Tim Connolly
8	Taylor Pyatt
10	Branislav Mezei
28	Kristian Kudroc
78	Mattias Weinhandl
87	Brian Collins
101	Juraj Kolnik
102	Johan Halvardsson
130	Justin Mapletoft
140	Adam Johnson
163	Bjorn Melin
228	Radek Martinek
255	Brett Henning
268	Tyler Scott

1998
Pick
9	Michael Rupp
36	Chris Neilson
95	Andy Burnham
123	Jiri Dopita
155	Kevin Clauson
182	Evgeny Korolev
209	Frederik Brindamour
237	Ben Blais
242	Jason Doyle
250	Radek Matejovsky

1997
Pick
4	Roberto Luongo
5	Eric Brewer
31	Jeff Zehr
59	Jarrett Smith
79	Robert Schnabel
85	Petr Mika
115	Adam Edinger
139	Bobby Leavins
166	Kris Knoblauch
196	Jeremy Symington
222	Ryan Clark

1996
Pick
3	Jean-Pierre Dumont
29	Dan Lacouture
56	Zdeno Chara
83	Tyrone Garner
109	Andy Berenzweig
128	Petr Sachl
138	Todd Miller
165	Joe Prestifilippo
192	Evgeny Korolev
218	Mike Muzechka

1995
Pick
2	Wade Redden
28	Jan Hlavac
41	Denis Smith
106	Vladimir Orszagh
158	Andrew Taylor
210	David MacDonald
211	Mike Broda

1994
Pick
9	Brett Lindros
38	Jason Holland
63	Jason Strudwick
90	Brad Lukowich
112	Mark McArthur
116	Albert O'Connell
142	Jason Stewart
194	Mike Loach
203	Peter Hogardh
220	Gord Walsh
246	Kirk Dewaele
272	Dick Tarnstrom

1993
Pick
23	Todd Bertuzzi
40	Bryan McCabe
66	Vladim Chebaturkin
92	Warren Luhning
118	Tommy Salo
144	Peter Leboutillier
170	Darren Van Impe
196	Rod Hinks
222	Daniel Johansson
248	Stephane Larocque
274	Carl Charland

1992
Pick
5	Darius Kasparaitis
56	Jarrett Deuling
104	Tomas Klimt
105	Ryan Duthie
128	Derek Armstrong
152	Vladimir Grachev
159	Steve O'Rourke
176	Jason Widmer
200	Daniel Paradis
224	David Wainwright
248	Andrei Vasiljev

1991
Pick
4	Scott Lachance
26	Zigmund Palffy
48	Jamie McLennan
70	Milan Hnilicka
92	Steve Junker
114	Robert Valicevic
136	Andreas Johansson
158	Todd Sparks
180	John Johnson
202	Robert Canavan
224	Marcus Thuresson
246	Marty Schriner

1990
Pick
6	Scott Scissons
27	Chris Taylor
48	Dan Plante
90	Chris Marinucci
111	Joni Lehto
132	Michael Guilbert
153	Sylvain Fleury
174	John Joyce
195	Richard Enga
216	Martin Lacroix
237	Andy Shirr

1989
Pick
2	Dave Chyzowski
23	Travis Green
44	Jason Zent
65	Brent Grieve
86	Jace Reed
99	Steve Young
99	Kevin O'Sullivan
128	Jon Larson
133	Brett Harkins
149	Phil Huber
170	Matthew Robbins
191	Vladimir Malakhov
212	Kelly Ens
233	Iain Fraser

1988
Pick
16	Kevin Cheveldayoff
29	Wayne Doucet
37	Sean LeBrun
58	Danny Lorenz
79	Andre Brassard
100	Paul Rutherford
111	Pavel Gross
121	Jason Rathbone
142	Yves Gaucher
163	Marty McInnis
184	Jeff Blumer
205	Jeff Kampersal
226	Phillip Neururer
247	Joe Capprini

1987
Pick
13	Dean Chynoweth
34	Jeff Hackett
55	Dean Ewen
76	George Maneluk
97	Petr Vlk
118	Rob DiMaio
139	Knut Walbye
160	Jeff Saterdalen
181	Shawn Howard
202	John Herlihy
223	Michael Erickson
244	Will Averill

1986
Pick
17	Tom Fitzgerald
38	Dennis Vaske
59	Bill Berg
80	Shawn Byram
101	Dean Sexsmith
104	Todd McLellan
122	Tony Schmalzbauer
138	Will Anderson
143	Richard Pilon
164	Peter Harris
185	Jeff Jablonski
206	Kerry Clark
227	Dan Beaudette
248	Paul Thompson

1985
Pick
6	Brad Dalgarno
13	Derek King
34	Brad Lauer
55	Jeff Finley
76	Kevin Herom
89	Tommy Hedlund
97	Jeff Sveen
118	Rod Dallman
139	Kurt Lackten
160	Hank Lammens
181	Rich Wiest
202	Real Arsenault
223	Mike Volpe
244	Tony Grenier

With the trade of Zigmund Palffy to Los Angeles, Polish-born Mariusz Czerkawski will be counted on to provide even more offense for the Islanders. His 21 goals in 1998-99 marked the second-highest total of his career.

Club Directory

Nassau Veterans'
Memorial Coliseum
Uniondale, NY 11553
Phone **516/832-4200**
FAX 516/542-9348
www.newyorkislanders.com
Capacity: 16,297

New York Islanders Executive Office
Co-Chairman & Governor	Steven M. Gluckstern
Co-Chairman & Alternate Governor	Edward Milstein
President	John Sanders
Alternate Governor	William M. Skehan
Senior Vice President/CFO	Arthur McCarthy

Hockey Operations
General Manager	Mike Milbury
Asst. General Manager and Director of Player Personnel	Gordie Clark
Head Coach	Butch Goring
Asst. to the G.M./Manager, Player Contracts	Mike Santos
Manager, Hockey Administration	Joanne Holewa
Administrative Assistant	Pam Genzardi
Associate Coach	Lorne Henning
Assistant Coach	Greg Cronin
Scout and Organizational Coach	Gilles Gilbert
Strength and Conditioning Coach	Scott Livingston
Head Amateur Scout	Tony Feltrin
Western Scout	Earl Ingarfield
Director of European Scouting	Anders Kallur
Director of Pro Scouting	Ken Morrow
Assistant Director of Pro Scouting	Kevin Maxwell
Scouting Staff	Jim Madigan, Jim McMahon, Mario Saraceno, Karel Pavlik
Video Coordinator	Bob Smith

Medical Staff
Director of Medical Services	Dr. Elliot Pellman
Internist	Dr. Clifford Cooper
Team Orthopedists	Dr. Elliott Hershman, Dr. Kenneth Montgomery, Dr. Stephen Nicholas
Team Dentists	Dr. Bruce Michnick, Dr. Jan Sherman

Training/Equipment Staff
Head Trainer	Rich Campbell
Assistant Trainer	Sean Donellan
Head Equipment Manager	Joe McMahon
Assistant Equipment Managers	Rick Harper, Eric Miklich
Lockerroom Attendants	Charles E. Nass, Matt Brager, Mike Ross

Administration and Sales
Senior Vice President of Operations	Bob Brennfleck
Vice President of Administration	Janet L. Kask
Vice President of Communications	Chris Botta
Vice President of Hockey Operations	Daren L. Anderson
Director of Corporate Sales	Bill Kain
Director of Corporate Relations	Bob Nystrom
Director of Community Relations	Tom Bigliani
Director of Production and Creative Services	Greg Bedard
Director of Box Office Operations	Vincent DiOrio
Director of Ticket Sales and Operations	Kyle Draper
Director of Merchandise	Chris DiPierri
Director of Facilities Operations	Sam Buonagura
Controller	Ralph Sellitti
Assistant Controller	Ginna Cotton
Suite Manager	Joann DiStefano
Manager of Information Systems	David Harel
Manager of Ticket Operations	Katherine Pauletti
Team Store Managers	Danny DiPierri, Maryanne Steves, Tim Steves
Payroll Manager	Christine Bowler
Manager, Office Services	Margaret Barrett
Corporate Advertising Account Executive	Ted Van Zelst
Group Sales Manager	Andrew Smith
Corporate Ticket Sales	Erik Scheibe, Anthony Mercogliano, Ryan Gano
Customer Service Manager	Kerry Cornils
Customer Service Representative	Ken Keane
Sales Representatives	Larry Fitzpatrick, Mike Clough, Patrick Duffy
Game Operations & Promotions Coordinator	Ryan Halkett
Sponsor Services Coordinator	Alice Vanderveldt
Sponsor Services Assistant	Erica Blauberg
Media Relations Assistant	Jason Lagnese
Publications Assistant	Kerry Gwydir
Executive Suite Assistant	Linda Statkevicus
Staff Accountant	Heather Jabick
Accounts Payable Bookkeeper	Maria Corvino
Promotional Coordinator	Randy Risorto
Special Events Coordinator	Eric Levy
Creative Services Coordinator	Mauricio Acosta
Executive Assistant	Cathy Malzone
Receptionists	Chere O'Neill, Giovanni Giovanniello
Office Attendant	Todd Aronovitch

Team Information
Colors	Orange, Blue, White
Television Coverage	FOX Sports New York
Announcers	Howie Rose, Joe Micheletti
Radio	ONE-ON-ONE SPORTS AM 620
Radio Announcers	Jim Cerny, Chris King

New York Rangers

1998-99 Results: 33W-38L-11T 77PTS. Fourth, Atlantic Division

Only Martin Brodeur and Guy Hebert played more games in goal than the 68 Mike Richter saw action in for the Rangers last season. The Rangers have added defensive help for this season with the signings of Stephane Quintal, Sylvain Lefebvre, and back-up goalie Kirk McLean.

1999-2000 Schedule

Oct.	Fri.	1	at Edmonton
	Sat.	2	at Vancouver
	Tue.	5	Ottawa
	Fri.	8	Carolina
	Sun.	10	Phoenix*
	Mon.	11	at NY Islanders
	Thu.	14	Pittsburgh
	Sun.	17	Atlanta
	Tue.	19	San Jose
	Wed.	20	at Philadelphia
	Fri.	22	Philadelphia
	Sun.	24	Vancouver
	Sat.	30	at Montreal
Nov.	Wed.	3	NY Islanders
	Fri.	5	at Colorado
	Sun.	7	at Chicago
	Wed.	10	Ottawa
	Thu.	11	at Washington
	Sat.	13	Boston
	Thu.	18	at Boston
	Sat.	20	at Toronto
	Wed.	24	at Tampa Bay
	Fri.	26	at Florida
Dec.	Wed.	1	at New Jersey
	Fri.	3	Montreal
	Sat.	4	at Buffalo
	Mon.	6	Calgary
	Wed.	8	Edmonton
	Wed.	15	Los Angeles
	Fri.	17	Washington
	Sun.	19	Tampa Bay
	Tue.	21	Buffalo
	Thu.	23	at NY Islanders
	Sun.	26	New Jersey*
	Tue.	28	at Phoenix
	Wed.	29	at Dallas
Jan.	Sun.	2	at Montreal
	Mon.	3	St. Louis
	Wed.	5	Toronto
	Sat.	8	at Toronto
	Sun.	9	at Carolina

	Sat.	15	at NY Islanders*
	Sun.	16	Atlanta*
	Tue.	18	Carolina
	Thu.	20	at Carolina
	Sat.	22	at St. Louis
	Mon.	24	at Atlanta
	Tue.	25	at Pittsburgh
	Thu.	27	Toronto
	Sat.	29	at Ottawa
	Mon.	31	Nashville
Feb.	Wed.	2	New Jersey
	Thu.	3	at Atlanta
	Tue.	8	New Jersey
	Wed.	9	at New Jersey
	Fri.	11	Boston
	Sun.	13	NY Islanders
	Tue.	15	at Tampa Bay
	Wed.	16	at Florida
	Fri.	18	Colorado
	Sun.	20	Philadelphia
	Tue.	22	Pittsburgh
	Fri.	25	at Buffalo
	Sat.	26	at Ottawa
Mar.	Wed.	1	Buffalo
	Fri.	3	Florida
	Mon.	6	at San Jose
	Wed.	8	at Anaheim
	Thu.	9	at Los Angeles
	Sat.	11	at Pittsburgh
	Mon.	13	Dallas
	Wed.	15	Tampa Bay
	Sat.	18	at Philadelphia*
	Sun.	19	at Pittsburgh
	Tue.	21	Florida
	Thu.	23	Washington
	Sun.	26	at Detroit*
	Mon.	27	Detroit
Apr.	Sat.	1	at Boston*
	Mon.	3	at Washington
	Wed.	5	Montreal
	Sun.	9	Philadelphia*

* Denotes afternoon game.

Franchise date: May 15, 1926

ATLANTIC DIVISION

74th NHL Season

Year-by-Year Record

Season	GP	Home W	Home L	Home T	Road W	Road L	Road T	Overall W	Overall L	Overall T	GF	GA	Pts.	Finished		Playoff Result
1998-99	82	17	19	5	16	19	6	33	38	11	217	227	77	4th,	Atlantic Div.	Out of Playoffs
1997-98	82	14	18	9	11	21	9	25	39	18	197	231	68	5th,	Atlantic Div.	Out of Playoffs
1996-97	82	21	14	6	17	20	4	38	34	10	258	231	86	4th,	Atlantic Div.	Lost Conf. Final
1995-96	82	22	10	9	19	17	5	41	27	14	272	237	96	2nd,	Atlantic Div.	Lost Conf. Semi-Final
1994-95	48	11	10	3	11	13	0	22	23	3	139	134	47	4th,	Atlantic Div.	Lost Conf. Semi-Final
1993-94	84	28	8	6	24	16	2	52	24	8	299	231	112	1st,	Atlantic Div.	Won Stanley Cup
1992-93	84	20	17	5	14	22	6	34	39	11	304	308	79	6th,	Patrick Div.	Out of Playoffs
1991-92	80	28	8	4	22	17	1	50	25	5	321	246	105	1st,	Patrick Div.	Lost Div. Final
1990-91	80	22	11	7	14	20	6	36	31	13	297	265	85	2nd,	Patrick Div.	Lost Div. Semi-Final
1989-90	80	20	11	9	16	20	4	36	31	13	279	267	85	1st,	Patrick Div.	Lost Div. Final
1988-89	80	21	17	2	16	18	6	37	35	8	310	307	82	3rd,	Patrick Div.	Lost Div. Semi-Final
1987-88	80	22	13	5	14	21	5	36	34	10	300	283	82	5th,	Patrick Div.	Out of Playoffs
1986-87	80	18	18	4	16	20	4	34	38	8	307	323	76	4th,	Patrick Div.	Lost Div. Semi-Final
1985-86	80	20	18	2	16	20	4	36	38	6	280	276	78	4th,	Patick Div.	Lost Conf. Championship
1984-85	80	16	18	6	10	26	4	26	44	10	295	345	62	4th,	Patrick Div.	Lost Div. Semi-Final
1983-84	80	27	12	1	15	17	8	42	29	9	314	304	93	4th,	Patrick Div.	Lost Div. Semi-Final
1982-83	80	24	13	3	11	22	7	35	35	10	306	287	80	4th,	Patrick Div.	Lost Div. Final
1981-82	80	19	15	6	20	12	8	39	27	14	316	306	92	2nd,	Patrick Div.	Lost Div. Final
1980-81	80	17	13	10	13	23	4	30	36	14	312	317	74	4th,	Patrick Div.	Lost Semi-Final
1979-80	80	22	10	8	16	22	2	38	32	10	308	284	86	3rd,	Patrick Div.	Lost Quarter-Final
1978-79	80	19	13	8	21	16	3	40	29	11	316	292	91	3rd,	Patrick Div.	Lost Final
1977-78	80	18	15	7	12	22	6	30	37	13	279	280	73	4th,	Patrick Div.	Lost Prelim. Round
1976-77	80	17	18	5	12	19	9	29	37	14	272	310	72	4th,	Patrick Div.	Out of Playoffs
1975-76	80	16	16	8	13	26	1	29	42	9	262	333	67	4th,	Patrick Div.	Out of Playoffs
1974-75	80	21	11	8	16	18	6	37	29	14	319	276	88	2nd,	Patrick Div.	Lost Prelim. Round
1973-74	78	26	7	6	14	17	8	40	24	14	300	251	94	3rd,	East Div.	Lost Semi-Final
1972-73	78	26	8	5	21	15	3	47	23	8	297	208	102	3rd,	East Div.	Lost Semi-Final
1971-72	78	26	6	7	22	11	6	48	17	13	317	192	109	2nd,	East Div.	Lost Final
1970-71	78	30	2	7	19	16	4	49	18	11	259	177	109	2nd,	East Div.	Lost Semi-Final
1969-70	76	22	8	8	16	14	8	38	22	16	246	189	92	4th,	East Div.	Lost Quarter-Final
1968-69	76	27	7	4	14	19	5	41	26	9	231	196	91	3rd,	East Div.	Lost Quarter-Final
1967-68	74	22	8	7	17	15	5	39	23	12	226	183	90	2nd,	East Div.	Lost Quarter-Final
1966-67	70	18	12	5	12	16	7	30	28	12	188	189	72	4th,		Lost Semi-Final
1965-66	70	12	16	7	6	25	4	18	41	11	195	261	47	6th,		Out of Playoffs
1964-65	70	8	19	8	12	19	4	20	38	12	179	246	52	5th,		Out of Playoffs
1963-64	70	14	13	8	8	25	2	22	38	10	186	242	54	5th,		Out of Playoffs
1962-63	70	12	17	6	10	19	6	22	36	12	211	233	56	5th,		Out of Playoffs
1961-62	70	16	11	8	10	21	4	26	32	12	195	207	64	4th,		Lost Semi-Final
1960-61	70	15	15	5	7	23	5	22	38	10	204	248	54	5th,		Out of Playoffs
1959-60	70	10	15	10	7	23	5	17	38	15	187	247	49	6th,		Out of Playoffs
1958-59	70	14	16	5	12	16	7	26	32	12	201	217	64	5th,		Out of Playoffs
1957-58	70	14	15	6	18	10	7	32	25	13	195	188	77	2nd,		Lost Semi-Final
1956-57	70	15	12	8	11	18	6	26	30	14	184	227	66	4th,		Lost Semi-Final
1955-56	70	20	7	8	12	21	2	32	28	10	204	203	74	3rd,		Lost Semi-Final
1954-55	70	10	12	13	7	23	5	17	35	18	150	210	52	5th,		Out of Playoffs
1953-54	70	18	12	5	11	19	5	29	31	10	161	182	68	5th,		Out of Playoffs
1952-53	70	11	14	10	6	23	6	17	37	16	152	211	50	6th,		Out of Playoffs
1951-52	70	16	13	6	7	21	7	23	34	13	192	219	59	5th,		Out of Playoffs
1950-51	70	14	11	10	6	18	11	20	29	21	169	201	61	5th,		Out of Playoffs
1949-50	70	19	12	4	9	19	7	28	31	11	170	189	67	4th,		Lost Final
1948-49	60	13	12	5	5	19	6	18	31	11	133	172	47	6th,		Out of Playoffs
1947-48	60	11	12	7	10	14	6	21	26	13	176	201	55	4th,		Lost Semi-Final
1946-47	60	11	14	5	11	18	1	22	32	6	167	186	50	5th,		Out of Playoffs
1945-46	50	8	12	5	5	16	4	13	28	9	144	191	35	6th,		Out of Playoffs
1944-45	50	7	11	7	4	18	3	11	29	10	154	247	32	6th,		Out of Playoffs
1943-44	50	4	17	4	2	22	1	6	39	5	162	310	17	6th,		Out of Playoffs
1942-43	50	7	13	5	4	18	3	11	31	8	161	253	30	6th,		Out of Playoffs
1941-42	48	15	8	1	14	9	1	29	17	2	177	143	60	1st,		Lost Semi-Final
1940-41	48	13	7	4	8	12	4	21	19	8	143	125	50	4th,		Lost Quarter-Final
1939-40	48	17	4	3	10	7	7	27	11	10	136	77	64	2nd,		Won Stanley Cup
1938-39	48	13	8	3	13	8	3	26	16	6	149	105	58	2nd,		Lost Semi-Final
1937-38	48	15	5	4	12	10	2	27	15	6	149	96	60	2nd,	Amn. Div.	Lost Quarter-Final
1936-37	48	9	7	8	10	13	1	19	20	9	117	106	47	3rd,	Amn. Div.	Lost Final
1935-36	48	11	6	7	8	11	5	19	17	12	91	96	50	4th,	Amn. Div.	Out of Playoffs
1934-35	48	11	8	5	11	12	1	22	20	6	137	139	50	3rd,	Amn. Div.	Lost Semi-Final
1933-34	48	11	7	6	10	12	2	21	19	8	120	113	50	3rd,	Amn. Div.	Lost Quarter-Final
1932-33	48	12	7	5	11	10	3	23	17	8	135	107	54	3rd,	Amn. Div.	Won Stanley Cup
1931-32	48	13	7	4	10	10	4	23	17	8	134	112	54	1st,	Amn. Div.	Lost Final
1930-31	44	11	5	6	8	12	2	19	16	9	106	87	47	3rd,	Amn. Div.	Lost Semi-Final
1929-30	44	11	5	6	6	12	4	17	17	10	136	143	44	3rd,	Amn. Div.	Lost Semi-Final
1928-29	44	12	6	4	9	7	6	21	13	10	72	65	52	2nd,	Amn. Div.	Lost Final
1927-28	44	10	8	4	9	8	5	19	16	9	94	79	47	2nd,	Amn. Div.	Won Stanley Cup
1926-27	44	13	5	4	12	8	2	25	13	6	95	72	56	1st,	Amn. Div.	Lost Quarter-Final

1999-2000 Player Personnel

FORWARDS	HT	WT	S	Place of Birth	Date	1998-99 Club
ARMSTRONG, Derek	5-11	188	R	Ottawa, Ont.	4/23/73	NY Rangers-Hartford
BRENDL, Pavel	6-0	204	R	Opocno, Czech.	3/23/81	Calgary (WHL)
CHERNESKI, Stefan	6-0	200	L	Winnipeg, Man.	9/19/78	Hartford
FLEURY, Theoren	5-6	180	R	Oxbow, Sask.	6/29/68	Calgary-Colorado
FORTIER, Francois	5-11	190	L	Beauport, Que.	6/13/79	Sherbrooke-Hartford
GERNANDER, Ken	5-10	180	L	Coleraine, MN	6/30/69	Hartford
GONEAU, Daniel	6-0	194	L	Montreal, Que.	1/16/76	Hartford
GRAVES, Adam	6-0	205	L	Toronto, Ont.	4/12/68	NY Rangers
HALL, Todd	6-1	212	L	Hamden, CT	1/22/73	Hartford
HARDER, Mike	6-0	180	R	Winnipeg, Man.	2/8/73	Rochester
HARVEY, Todd	6-0	200	R	Hamilton, Ont.	2/17/75	NY Rangers
HLAVAC, Jan	6-0	183	L	Prague, Czech.	9/20/76	Sparta Praha
KAMENSKY, Valeri	6-2	198	R	Voskresensk, USSR	4/18/66	Colorado
KANE, Boyd	6-1	207	L	Swift Current, Sask.	4/18/78	Hartford-Charlotte
KENADY, Chris	6-2	195	R	Mound, MN	4/10/73	Utah-Long Beach-Hartford
KNUBLE, Mike	6-3	208	R	Toronto, Ont.	7/4/72	NY Rangers
LACROIX, Eric	6-2	210	L	Montreal, Que.	7/15/71	Col-L.A.-NYR
LANGDON, Darren	6-1	200	L	Deer Lake, Nfld.	1/8/71	NY Rangers
LUNDMARK, Jamie	6-0	174	R	Edmonton, Alta.	1/16/81	Moose Jaw
MacLEAN, John	6-0	200	R	Oshawa, Ont.	11/20/64	NY Rangers
MALHOTRA, Manny	6-2	210	L	Mississauga, Ont.	5/18/80	NY Rangers
NEDVED, Petr	6-3	195	L	Liberec, Czech.	12/9/71	Las Vegas-NY Rangers
SMYTH, Brad	6-0	200	R	Ottawa, Ont.	3/13/73	Nashville-Milwaukee-Hartford
STEVENS, Kevin	6-3	230	L	Brockton, MA	4/15/65	NY Rangers
STOCK, P.J.	5-10	190	L	Victoriaville, Que.	5/26/75	NY Rangers-Hartford
TAYLOR, Tim	6-1	185	L	Stratford, Ont.	2/6/69	Boston
WITEHALL, Johan	6-1	198	L	Kungsbacka, Sweden	1/7/72	NY Rangers-Hartford
YORK, Michael	5-9	179	R	Pontiac, MI	1/3/78	Michigan State-Hartford

DEFENSEMEN						
BROWN, Jeff	6-1	217	R	Mississauga, Ont.	4/24/78	Hartford-Charlotte
CARPENTIER, Benjamin	6-2	195	L	Grand-Mere, Que.	6/13/78	Charlotte-Hartford
DOIG, Jason	6-3	220	R	Montreal, Que.	1/29/77	Phoenix-Springfield-Hartford
HENRY, Burke	6-2	190	L	Ste. Rose, Man.	1/21/79	Brandon
JARVIS, Wes	6-4	203	L	Toronto, Ont.	4/16/79	Kitchener-Canada
JOHNSSON, Kim	6-1	175	L	Malmo, Sweden	3/16/76	Malmo IF
KLOUCEK, Tomas	6-2	205	L	Prague, Czech.	3/7/80	Cape Breton
LEETCH, Brian	6-1	190	L	Corpus Christi, TX	3/3/68	NY Rangers
LEFEBVRE, Sylvain	6-2	205	L	Richmond, Que.	10/14/67	Colorado
NAMESTNIKOV, John	5-11	190	R	Arzamis-Ig, USSR	10/9/71	Lowell
NDUR, Rumun	6-2	200	L	Zaria, Nigeria	7/7/75	Buffalo-NY Rangers-Hartford
POPOVIC, Peter	6-6	235	L	Koping, Sweden	2/10/68	NY Rangers
PURINTON, Dale	6-2	190	L	Fort Wayne, IN	10/11/76	Hartford
QUINTAL, Stephane	6-3	230	R	Boucherville, Que.	10/22/68	Montreal
SCHNEIDER, Mathieu	5-10	192	L	New York, NY	6/12/69	NY Rangers
VASILIEV, Alexei	6-1	190	L	Yaroslavl, USSR	9/1/77	Hartford
VIRTUE, Terry	6-0	200	R	Scarborough, Ont.	8/12/70	Boston-Providence (AHL)

GOALTENDERS	HT	WT	C	Place of Birth	Date	1998-99 Club
HEIL, Jeff	6-1	190	L	Bloomington, MN	9/17/75	Hartford-Charlotte
HNILICKA, Milan	6-0	180	L	Litomerice, Czech.	6/25/73	Sparta Praha
LABBE, Jean-Francois	5-9	170	L	Sherbrooke, Que.	6/15/72	Hartford
McLEAN, Kirk	6-0	180	L	Willowdale, Ont.	6/26/66	Florida
RICHTER, Mike	5-11	187	L	Abington, PA	9/22/66	NY Rangers

1998-99 Scoring
* – rookie

Regular Season

Pos	#	Player	Team	GP	G	A	Pts	+/-	PIM	PP	SH	GW	GT	S	%
C	99	Wayne Gretzky	NYR	70	9	53	62	-23	14	3	0	3	1	132	6.8
R	15	John MacLean	NYR	82	28	27	55	5	46	11	1	2	0	231	12.1
D	2	Brian Leetch	NYR	82	13	42	55	-7	42	4	0	1	0	184	7.1
L	9	Adam Graves	NYR	82	38	15	53	-12	47	14	2	7	0	239	15.9
C	93	Petr Nedved	NYR	56	20	27	47	-6	50	9	1	3	0	153	13.1
C	33	Marc Savard	NYR	70	9	36	45	-7	38	4	0	1	0	116	7.8
L	17	Kevin Stevens	NYR	81	23	20	43	-10	64	8	0	3	0	136	16.9
R	24	Niklas Sundstrom	NYR	81	13	30	43	-2	20	1	2	3	0	89	14.6
R	22	Mike Knuble	NYR	82	15	20	35	-7	26	3	0	1	0	113	13.3
D	25	Mathieu Schneider	NYR	75	10	24	34	-19	71	5	0	2	0	159	6.3
R	20	Todd Harvey	NYR	37	11	17	28	-1	72	6	0	2	1	58	19.0
C	6 *	Manny Malhotra	NYR	73	8	8	16	-2	13	1	0	2	0	61	13.1
R	26 *	Mike Maneluk	PHI	13	2	6	8	4	8	0	0	0	0	23	8.7
			CHI	28	4	3	7	2	8	1	0	1	0	29	13.8
			NYR	4	0	0	0	-1	4	0	0	0	0	3	0.0
			TOTAL	45	6	9	15	5	20	1	0	1	0	55	10.9
L	37	Brent Fedyk	NYR	67	4	6	10	-11	30	0	1	0	0	47	8.5
D	23	Jeff Beukeboom	NYR	45	0	9	9	-2	60	0	0	0	0	8	0.0
C	21	Scott Fraser	NYR	28	2	4	6	-12	14	1	0	0	0	35	5.7
D	4	Chris Tamer	PIT	11	0	0	0	-2	32	0	0	0	0	2	0.0
			NYR	52	1	5	6	-12	92	0	0	1	0	46	2.2
			TOTAL	63	1	5	6	-14	124	0	0	1	0	48	2.1
D	34	Peter Popovic	NYR	68	1	4	5	-12	40	0	0	0	0	64	1.6
L	28	Eric Lacroix	COL	7	0	0	0	-2	0	0	0	0	0	4	0.0
			L.A.	27	0	1	1	-5	12	0	0	0	0	17	0.0
			NYR	30	2	1	3	-5	4	0	0	1	0	17	11.8
			TOTAL	64	2	2	4	-12	18	0	0	1	0	38	5.3
D	12 *	Richard Brennan	NYR	24	1	3	4	-4	23	0	0	0	0	36	2.8
D	36 *	Rumun Ndur	BUF	8	0	0	0	1	16	0	0	0	0	1	0.0
			NYR	31	1	3	4	-2	46	0	0	0	0	21	4.8
			TOTAL	39	1	3	4	-1	62	0	0	0	0	22	4.5
L	10	Esa Tikkanen	NYR	32	0	3	3	-5	38	0	0	0	0	25	0.0
D	8	Jan Mertzig	NYR	23	0	2	2	-5	8	0	0	0	0	10	0.0
C	18	Derek Armstrong	NYR	3	0	0	0	0	0	0	0	0	0	1	0.0
D	14	Geoff Smith	NYR	4	0	0	0	-5	2	0	0	0	0	2	0.0
L	14	Johan Witehall	NYR	4	0	0	0	0	0	0	0	0	0	1	0.0
C	28	P.J. Stock	NYR	5	0	0	0	-1	6	0	0	0	0	0	0.0
C	14	Christian Dube	NYR	6	0	0	0	0	0	0	0	0	0	0	0.0
G	39 *	Dan Cloutier	NYR	22	0	0	0	0	0	0	0	0	0	0	0.0
L	19	Darren Langdon	NYR	44	0	0	0	-3	80	0	0	0	0	8	0.0
G	35	Mike Richter	NYR	68	0	0	0	0	0	0	0	0	0	0	0.0

Goaltending

No.	Goaltender	GPI	Mins	Avg	W	L	T	EN	SO	GA	SA	S%
35	Mike Richter	68	3878	2.63	27	30	8	6	4	170	1898	.910
39	* Dan Cloutier	22	1097	2.68	6	8	3	2	0	49	570	.914
	Totals	82	4996	2.73	33	38	11	8	4	227	2476	.908

Captains' History

Bill Cook, 1926-27 to 1936-37; Art Coulter, 1937-38 to 1941-42; Ott Heller, 1942-43 to 1944-45; Neil Colville 1945-46 to 1948-49; Buddy O'Connor, 1949-50; Frank Eddolls, 1950-51; Frank Eddolls and Allan Stanley, 1951-52; Allan Stanley, 1952-53; Allan Stanley and Don Raleigh, 1953-54; Don Raleigh, 1954-55; Harry Howell, 1955-56, 1956-57; Red Sullivan, 1957-58 to 1960-61; Andy Bathgate, 1961-62, 1962-63; Andy Bathgate and Camille Henry, 1963-64; Camille Henry and Bob Nevin, 1964-65; Bob Nevin 1965-66 to 1970-71; Vic Hadfield, 1971-72 to 1973-74; Brad Park, 1974-75; Brad Park and Phil Esposito, 1975-76; Phil Esposito, 1976-77, 1977-78; Dave Maloney, 1978-79, 1979-80; Dave Maloney, Walt Tkaczuk and Barry Beck, 1980-81; Barry Beck, 1981-82 to 1985-86; Ron Greschner, 1986-87; Ron Greschner and Kelly Kisio, 1987-88; Kelly Kisio, 1988-89 to 1990-91; Mark Messier, 1991-92 to 1996-97; Brian Leetch, 1997-98 to date.

General Manager

SMITH, NEIL
General Manager, New York Rangers. Born in Toronto, Ont., January 9, 1954.

As he enters his eleventh season with the club, Neil Smith joins the legendary Lester Patrick and Emile Francis among the longest-serving leaders in club history. Since taking over the reigns as general manager on July 17, 1989, Smith has seen the team win three division titles, two Presidents' Trophy honors and a Stanley Cup championship. The championship in 1993-94 was the culmination of a season in which the Rangers set club records with 52 wins and 112 points and ended a 54-year run of Stanley Cup frustration. Following the season, Neil was rewarded as *The Hockey News* executive of the year.

In his first three seasons as Rangers general manager, the club finished in first place twice and enjoyed the best three consecutive finishes in team history. After the 1991-92 season, Smith was named NHL executive of the year by the *Sporting News*.

On June 19, 1992, he was promoted to the position of president and general manager, becoming the ninth president in Rangers' history and the first president to also hold the title of general manager.

A native of Toronto, Ontario, Smith played junior hockey at Brockville, Ontario, before entering Western Michigan University where he became an All-American defenseman as a freshman and team captain in his second year.

After being selected by the New York Islanders in the NHL Amateur Draft and playing two seasons in the International Hockey League, Neil joined the Islanders scouting department during the 1980-81 season. Following two seasons in that capacity, he joined the Detroit Red Wings in 1982 as director of professional scouting and soon after became director of their farm system.

Smith was then named director of scouting, and general manager/governor of the Adirondack Red Wings of the AHL, where he won two Calder Cup championships.

General Managers' History

Lester Patrick, 1927-28 to 1945-46; Frank Boucher, 1946-47 to 1954-55; Muzz Patrick, 1955-56 to 1963-64; Emile Francis, 1964-65 to 1974-75; Emile Francis and John Ferguson, 1975-76; John Ferguson, 1976-77, 1977-78; John Ferguson and Fred Shero, 1978-79, Fred Shero, 1979-80; Fred Shero and Craig Patrick, 1980-81; Craig Patrick, 1981-82 to 1985-86; Phil Esposito, 1986-87 to 1988-89; Neil Smith, 1989-90 to date.

Club Records

Team

(Figures in brackets for season records are games played; records for fewest points, wins, ties, losses, goals, goals against are for 70 or more games)

Most Points	**112**	1993-94 (84)
Most Wins	**52**	1993-94 (84)
Most Ties	**21**	1950-51 (70)
Most Losses	**44**	1984-85 (80)
Most Goals	**371**	1991-92 (80)
Most Goals Against	**345**	1984-85 (80)
Fewest Points	**47**	1965-66 (70)
Fewest Wins	**17**	1952-53 (70), 1954-55 (70), 1959-60 (70)
Fewest Ties	**5**	1991-92 (80)
Fewest Losses	**17**	1971-72 (78)
Fewest Goals	**150**	1954-55 (70)
Fewest Goals Against	**177**	1970-71 (78)
Longest Winning Streak		
Overall	**10**	Dec. 19/39-Jan. 13/40, Jan. 19-Feb. 10/73
Home	**14**	Dec. 19/39-Feb. 25/40
Away	**7**	Jan. 12-Feb. 12/35, Oct. 28-Nov. 29/78
Longest Undefeated Streak		
Overall	**19**	Nov. 23/39-Jan. 13/40 (14 wins, 5 ties)
Home	**26**	Mar. 29/70-Jan. 31/71 (19 wins, 7 ties)
Away	**11**	Nov. 5/39-Jan. 13/40 (6 wins, 5 ties)
Longest Losing Streak		
Overall	**11**	Oct. 30-Nov. 27/43
Home	**7**	Oct. 20-Nov. 14/76, Mar. 24-Apr. 14/93
Away	**10**	Oct. 30-Dec. 23/43
Longest Winless Streak		
Overall	**21**	Jan. 23-Mar. 19/44 (17 losses, 4 ties)
Home	**10**	Jan. 30-Mar. 19/44 (7 losses, 3 ties)
Away	**16**	Oct. 9-Dec. 20/52 (12 losses, 4 ties)
Most Shutouts, Season	**13**	1928-29 (44)
Most PIM, Season	**2,018**	1989-90 (80)
Most Goals, Game	**12**	Nov. 21/71 (Cal. 1 at NYR 12)

Individual

Most Seasons	**17**	Harry Howell
Most Games	**1,160**	Harry Howell
Most Goals, Career	**406**	Rod Gilbert
Most Assists, Career	**615**	Rod Gilbert
Most Points, Career	**1,021**	Rod Gilbert (406G, 615A)
Most PIM, Career	**1,226**	Ron Greschner
Most Shutouts, Career	**49**	Ed Giacomin
Longest Consecutive Games Streak	**560**	Andy Hebenton (Oct. 7/55-Mar. 24/63)
Most Goals, Season	**52**	Adam Graves (1993-94)
Most Assists, Season	**80**	Brian Leetch (1991-92)
Most Points, Season	**109**	Jean Ratelle (1971-72; 46G, 63A)
Most PIM, Season	**305**	Troy Mallette (1989-90)
Most Points, Defenseman, Season	**102**	Brian Leetch (1991-92; 22G, 80A)
Most Points, Center, Season	**109**	Jean Ratelle (1971-72; 46G, 63A)
Most Points, Right Wing, Season	**97**	Rod Gilbert (1971-72; 43G, 54A), (1974-75; 36G, 61A)
Most Points, Left Wing, Season	**106**	Vic Hadfield (1971-72; 50G, 56A)
Most Points, Rookie, Season	**76**	Mark Pavelich (1981-82; 33G, 43A)
Most Shutouts, Season	**13**	John Ross Roach (1928-29)
Most Goals, Game	**5**	Don Murdoch (Oct. 12/76), Mark Pavelich (Feb. 23/83)
Most Assists, Game	**5**	Walt Tkaczuk (Feb. 12/72), Rod Gilbert (Mar. 2/75, Mar. 30/75, Oct. 8/76), Don Maloney (Jan. 3/87), Brian Leetch (Apr. 18/95), Wayne Gretzky (Feb. 15/99)
Most Points, Game	**7**	Steve Vickers (Feb. 18/76; 3G, 4A)

Retired Numbers

1	Ed Giacomin	1965-1976
7	Rod Gilbert	1960-1978

All-time Record vs. Other Clubs

Regular Season

	At Home							On Road							Total						
	GP	W	L	T	GF	GA	PTS	GP	W	L	T	GF	GA	PTS	GP	W	L	T	GF	GA	PTS
Anaheim	5	2	2	1	14	14	5	5	0	5	0	11	21	0	10	2	7	1	25	35	5
Boston	292	126	111	55	888	824	307	288	93	154	41	808	1042	227	580	219	205	96	1696	1866	534
Buffalo	56	24	18	14	185	149	62	58	16	35	7	182	249	39	114	40	53	21	367	398	101
Calgary	48	22	21	5	171	172	49	47	10	27	10	141	211	30	95	32	48	15	312	383	79
Carolina	35	21	11	3	141	97	45	33	12	18	3	111	121	27	68	33	29	6	252	218	72
Chicago	283	116	112	55	834	801	287	282	113	127	42	782	860	268	565	229	239	97	1616	1661	555
Colorado	29	18	7	4	119	79	40	31	13	15	3	123	128	29	60	31	22	7	242	207	69
Dallas	58	34	13	11	202	157	79	57	30	17	10	212	170	70	115	64	30	21	414	327	149
Detroit	280	133	89	58	862	720	324	282	76	161	45	694	990	197	562	209	250	103	1556	1710	521
Edmonton	26	7	13	6	97	102	20	26	13	11	2	92	96	28	52	20	24	8	189	198	48
Florida	14	5	5	4	38	36	14	15	8	6	1	44	37	17	29	13	11	5	82	73	31
Los Angeles	54	33	15	6	216	153	72	56	25	22	9	202	185	59	110	58	37	15	418	338	131
Montreal	280	113	113	54	816	820	280	280	56	188	36	640	1104	148	560	169	301	90	1456	1924	428
Nashville	1	1	0	0	5	1	2	1	1	0	0	7	4	2	2	2	0	0	12	5	4
New Jersey	71	39	19	13	292	215	91	73	32	36	5	255	252	69	144	71	55	18	547	467	160
NY Islanders	83	50	24	9	324	249	109	83	24	52	7	252	337	55	166	74	76	16	576	586	164
Ottawa	13	8	5	0	50	38	16	13	9	2	2	40	32	20	26	17	7	2	90	70	36
Philadelphia	97	43	31	23	319	280	109	96	36	46	14	279	319	86	193	79	77	37	598	599	195
Phoenix	26	16	8	2	121	96	34	27	13	11	3	95	95	29	53	29	19	5	216	191	63
Pittsburgh	88	46	34	8	356	296	100	87	39	34	14	329	313	92	175	85	68	22	685	609	192
St. Louis	57	44	7	6	238	129	94	59	27	23	9	189	173	63	116	71	30	15	427	302	157
San Jose	7	6	0	1	36	21	13	8	7	0	1	34	17	15	15	13	0	2	70	38	28
Tampa Bay	17	9	7	1	60	59	19	15	6	7	2	51	52	14	32	15	14	3	111	111	33
Toronto	273	116	101	56	842	798	288	272	81	152	39	713	935	201	545	197	253	95	1555	1733	489
Vancouver	51	37	9	5	232	130	79	48	33	12	3	199	154	69	99	70	21	8	431	284	148
Washington	72	34	30	8	277	253	76	74	29	36	9	245	274	67	146	63	66	17	522	527	143
Defunct Clubs	139	87	30	22	460	290	196	139	82	34	23	441	291	187	278	169	64	45	901	581	383
Totals	**2455**	**1190**	**835**	**430**	**8195**	**6979**	**2810**	**2455**	**884**	**1231**	**340**	**7171**	**8462**	**2108**	**4910**	**2074**	**2066**	**770**	**15366**	**15441**	**4918**

Playoffs

	Series	W	L	GP	W	L	T	GF	GA	Last Mtg.	Round	Result
Boston	9	3	6	42	18	22	2	104	114	1973	QF	W 4-1
Buffalo	1	0	1	3	1	2	0	6	11	1978	PR	L 1-2
Calgary	1	1	0	4	3	1	0	14	8	1980	PR	W 3-1
Chicago	5	1	4	24	10	14	0	54	66	1973	SF	L 1-4
Colorado	1	1	0	6	4	2	0	25	19	1995	CQF	W 4-2
Detroit	5	1	4	23	10	13	0	49	57	1950	F	L 3-4
Florida	1	1	0	5	4	1	0	13	10	1997	CQF	W 4-1
Los Angeles	2	2	0	6	5	1	0	32	14	1981	PR	W 3-1
Montreal	14	7	7	61	25	34	2	158	188	1996	CQF	W 4-2
New Jersey	3	3	0	19	12	7	0	56	46	1997	CSF	W 4-1
NY Islanders	8	3	5	39	19	20	0	132	129	1994	CQF	W 4-0
Philadelphia	10	4	6	47	20	27	0	153	157	1997	CF	L 1-4
Pittsburgh	3	0	3	15	3	12	0	45	65	1996	CSF	L 1-4
St. Louis	1	1	0	6	4	2	0	29	22	1981	QF	W 4-2
Toronto	8	5	3	35	19	16	0	86	86	1971	QF	W 4-2
Vancouver	1	1	0	7	4	3	0	21	19	1994	F	W 4-3
Washington	4	2	2	22	11	11	0	71	75	1994	CSF	W 4-1
Defunct	9	6	3	22	11	7	4	43	29			
Totals	**86**	**42**	**44**	**386**	**183**	**195**	**8**	**1091**	**1114**			

Calgary totals include Atlanta Flames, 1972-73 to 1979-80.
Carolina totals include Hartford, 1979-80 to 1996-97.
Colorado totals include Quebec, 1979-80 to 1994-95.
Dallas totals include Minnesota, 1967-68 to 1992-93.
New Jersey totals include Kansas City, 1974-75 to 1975-76, and Colorado Rockies, 1976-77 to 1981-82.
Phoenix totals include Winnipeg, 1979-80 to 1995-96.

Playoff Results 1999-95

Year	Round	Opponent	Result	GF	GA
1997	CF	Philadelphia	L 1-4	13	20
	CSF	New Jersey	W 4-1	10	5
	CQF	Florida	W 4-1	13	10
1996	CSF	Pittsburgh	L 1-4	15	21
	CQF	Montreal	W 4-2	19	17
1995	CSF	Philadelphia	L 0-4	10	18
	CQF	Quebec	W 4-2	25	19

Abbreviations: Round: F – Final; **CF** – conference final; **CSF** – conference semi-final; **CQF** – conference quarter-final; **SF** – semi-final; **QF** – quarter-final; **PR** – preliminary round

1998-99 Results

Oct.	9		Philadelphia	0-1		15		Chicago	1-3
	10	at	Montreal	1-7		16	at	Montreal	0-3
	12		St. Louis	2-4		19		Ottawa	1-2
	16		New Jersey	1-2		21		Florida	1-2
	17	at	Pittsburgh	3-3		26	at	Washington	4-1
	20		Edmonton	3-2		28	at	Carolina	2-3
	22		NY Islanders	3-2		30	at	Detroit	3-2
	24	at	Philadelphia	2-2	**Feb.**	1		Washington	1-3
	27		Buffalo	0-0		4		Vancouver	8-4
	30		Carolina	1-0		7	at	Boston	2-3
Nov.	3	at	New Jersey	1-3		12		Carolina	1-3
	4		Montreal	1-4		14		Detroit	2-4
	7	at	Toronto	6-6		15	at	Nashville	7-4
	10	at	Tampa Bay	10-2		17		Montreal	3-6
	11	at	Florida	1-4		19		Pittsburgh	6-1
	13		Boston	3-3		21	at	Edmonton	2-1
	18	at	Anaheim	1-3		22	at	Calgary	2-6
	19	at	Los Angeles	5-1		26		Phoenix	3-0
	21	at	San Jose	2-2		28		Philadelphia	6-5
	25	at	Buffalo	2-4	**Mar.**	2		Dallas	2-2
	27	at	Pittsburgh	2-2		4	at	Washington	4-2
	29		Nashville	5-1		7	at	Boston	3-1
Dec.	1		Florida	5-4		8		Toronto	3-2
	2	at	NY Islanders	3-2		10		Ottawa	0-3
	5	at	Ottawa	2-1		12		Boston	4-5
	7		Toronto	6-2		14	at	NY Islanders	3-2
	9		Colorado	1-2		15		Washington	1-1
	11	at	Buffalo	0-2		19		Buffalo	2-3
	14		Calgary	5-2		21		Pittsburgh	2-2
	16	at	New Jersey	3-6		22	at	Tampa Bay	3-6
	19	at	Toronto	4-7		24	at	Florida	2-1
	23		Carolina	0-1		27	at	Philadelphia	1-3
	26	at	Carolina	6-3		29		NY Islanders	3-1
	30	at	Phoenix	1-3	**Apr.**	2		Anaheim	1-4
	31	at	Colorado	6-3		4	at	New Jersey	1-4
Jan.	2	at	St. Louis	1-0		5	at	Philadelphia	5-1
	4		San Jose	4-3		8	at	Chicago	2-6
	6		New Jersey	2-5		9	at	Dallas	1-3
	7	at	Washington	1-5		12		Tampa Bay	2-1
	10		Tampa Bay	5-2		15	at	Ottawa	2-2
	13		NY Islanders	4-3		18		Pittsburgh	1-2

Entry Draft
Selections 1999-85

1999
Pick
4	Pavel Brendl
9	Jamie Lundmark
59	David Inman
79	Johan Asplund
90	Patrick Aufiero
137	Garett Bembridge
177	Jay Dardis
197	Arto Laatikainen
226	Evgeny Gusakov
251	Peter Henning
254	Alexei Bulatov

1998
Pick
7	Manny Malhotra
40	Randy Copley
66	Jason Labarbera
114	Boyd Kane
122	Patrick Leahy
131	Tomas Kloucek
180	Stefan Lundqvist
207	Johan Witehall
235	Jan Mertzig

1997
Pick
19	Stefan Cherneski
46	Wes Jarvis
73	Burke Henry
93	Tomi Kallarsson
126	Jason McLean
134	Johan Lindbom
136	Michael York
154	Shawn Degagne
175	Johan Holmqvist
182	Mike Mottau
210	Andrew Proskurnicki
236	Richard Miller

1996
Pick
22	Jeff Brown
48	Daniel Goneau
76	Dmitri Subbotin
131	Colin Pepperall
158	Ola Sandberg
185	Jeff Dessner
211	Ryan McKie
237	Ronnie Sundin

1995
Pick
39	Christian Dube
65	Mike Martin
91	Marc Savard
110	Alexei Vasiliev
117	Dale Purinton
143	Peter Slamiar
169	Jeff Heil
195	Ilja Gorohov
221	Bob Maudie

1994
Pick
26	Dan Cloutier
52	Rudolf Vercik
78	Adam Smith
100	Alexander Korobolin
104	Sylvain Blouin
130	Martin Ethier
135	Yuri Litvinov
156	David Brosseau
182	Alexei Lazarenko
208	Craig Anderson
209	Vitali Yeremeyev
234	Eric Boulton
260	Radoslav Kropac
267	Jamie Butt
286	Kim Johnsson

1993
Pick
8	Niklas Sundstrom
34	Lee Sorochan
61	Maxim Galanov
86	Sergei Olimpiyev
112	Gary Roach
138	Dave Trofimenkoff
162	Sergei Kondrashkin
164	Todd Marchant
190	Eddy Campbell
216	Ken Shepard
242	Andrei Kudinov
261	Pavel Komarov
268	Maxim Smelnitsky

1992
Pick
24	Peter Ferraro
48	Mattias Norstrom
72	Eric Cairns
85	Chris Ferraro
120	Dmitri Starostenko
144	David Dal Grande
168	Matt Oates
192	Mickey Elick
216	Dan Brierley
240	Vladimir Vorobjev

1991
Pick
15	Alexei Kovalev
37	Darcy Werenka
96	Corey Machanic
125	Fredrik Jax
128	Barry Young
147	John Rushin
169	Corey Hirsch
191	Viacheslav Uvayev
213	Jamie Ram
235	Vitali Chinakhov
257	Brian Wiseman

1990
Pick
13	Michael Stewart
34	Doug Weight
55	John Vary
69	Jeff Nielsen
76	Rick Willis
85	Sergei Zubov
99	Lubos Rob
118	Jason Weinrich
139	Bryan Lonsinger
160	Todd Hedlund
181	Andrew Silverman
202	Jon Hillebrandt
223	Brett Lievers
244	Sergei Nemchinov

1989
Pick
20	Steven Rice
40	Jason Prosofsky
45	Rob Zamuner
49	Louie DeBrusk
67	Jim Cummins
88	Aaron Miller
118	Joby Messier
139	Greg Leahy
160	Greg Spenrath
181	Mark Bavis
202	Roman Oksyuta
223	Steve Locke
244	Ken MacDermid

1988
Pick
22	Troy Mallette
26	Murray Duval
68	Tony Amonte
99	Martin Bergeron
110	Dennis Vial
131	Mike Rosati
152	Eric Couvrette
173	Shorty Forrest
194	Paul Cain
202	Eric Fenton
215	Peter Fiorentino
236	Keith Slifstien

1987
Pick
10	Jayson More
31	Daniel Lacroix
46	Simon Gagne
69	Michael Sullivan
94	Eric O'Borsky
115	Ludek Cajka
136	Clint Thomas
157	Charles Wiegand
178	Eric Burrill
199	David Porter
205	Brett Barnett
220	Lance Marciano

1986
Pick
9	Brian Leetch
51	Bret Walter
53	Shawn Clouston
72	Mark Janssens
93	Jeff Bloemberg
114	Darren Turcotte
135	Robb Graham
156	Barry Chyzowski
177	Pat Scanlon
198	Joe Ranger
219	Russell Parent
240	Soren True

1985
Pick
7	Ulf Dahlen
28	Mike Richter
49	Sam Lindstahl
70	Pat Janostin
91	Brad Stephan
112	Brian McReynolds
133	Neil Pilon
154	Larry Bernard
175	Stephane Brochu
196	Steve Nemeth
217	Robert Burakowsky
238	Rudy Poeschek

Coach

MUCKLER, JOHN
Coach, New York Rangers. Born in Midland, Ont., April 3, 1934.

John Muckler begins his second full season behind the New York Rangers bench in 1999-2000, having taken over as coach of the club on February 19, 1998. Muckler is the 28th head coach in the history of the Rangers and has been involved with professional hockey since the 1959-60 season. He has served in various capacities in the National Hockey League, including nine years as a head coach.

Muckler spent the 1966-67 season as the director of player personnel for the Rangers before joining the Minnesota North Stars organization for the following six seasons. He coached the team briefly during the 1968-69 campaign. Muckler rejoined the Rangers organization in 1973 and spent four seasons as head coach of their minor-league affiliate in Providence.

Muckler's head coaching experience includes serving with the Buffalo Sabres from 1991-92 to 1994-95, posting a 125-109-34 record and ranking second on the team's all-time list for games coached with 268. Prior to joining Buffalo, he was head coach of the Edmonton Oilers from 1989-90 to 1990-91, posting a 75-65-20 record. Muckler guided the Oilers to a Stanley Cup title in 1990 and was an associate coach with Edmonton's four Stanley Cup championship teams of the 1980s.

NHL Coaching Record

			Regular Season				Playoffs			
Season	Team	Games	W	L	T	%	Games	W	L	%
1968-69	Minnesota	35	6	23	6	.257	....	....	....	....
1989-90	Edmonton	80	38	28	14	.563	22	16	6	.727*
1990-91	Edmonton	80	37	37	6	.500	18	9	9	.500
1991-92	Buffalo	52	22	22	8	.500	7	3	4	.429
1992-93	Buffalo	84	38	36	10	.512	8	4	4	.500
1993-94	Buffalo	84	43	32	9	.565	7	3	4	.429
1994-95	Buffalo	48	22	19	7	.531	5	1	4	.200
1997-98	NY Rangers	25	8	15	2	.360	....	....	....	....
1998-99	NY Rangers	82	33	38	11	.470	....	....	....	....
	NHL Totals	**570**	**247**	**250**	**73**	**.497**	**67**	**36**	**31**	**.537**

* Won Stanley Cup.

Club Directory

Madison Square Garden
14th Floor
2 Pennsylvania Plaza
New York, New York 10121
Phone **212/465-6000**
PR FAX 212/465-6494
www.newyorkrangers.com
Capacity: 18,200

Executive Management
Chief Executive Officer/Governor	David W. Checketts
President and General Manager/Alternate Governor	Neil Smith
Executive Vice President and General Counsel	Kenneth W. Munoz
Senior Vice President, MSG Sports	Francis P. Murphy
Vice President, Legal and Business Affairs	Marc Schoenfeld
Vice President, Controller	John Cudmore
Alternate Governor	Kenneth W. Munoz

Hockey Club Personnel
Assistant General Manager	Don Maloney
Head Coach	John Muckler
Assistant Coaches	Keith Acton, Charlie Huddy, John Tortorella
Development Coach	John Paddock
Assistant Development Coach	Mike Busniuk
Goaltending Analyst	Sam St. Laurent
Director of Scouting	Martin Madden
Amateur Scouting Staff	Darwin Bennett, Ray Clearwater, Herb Hammond, Martin Madden Jr., Christer Rockstom, Dick Todd
Professional Scouting Staff	Dave Brown, Kevin McDonald, E.J. McGuire
Scouting Manager	Bill Short
Video Assistant	Jerry Dineen

Operations Department
Vice President of Operations	Mark Piazza
Director of Business Operations	Barbara Dand
Director of Team Operations	Darren Blake
Executive Administrative Assistant	Anne Marie Gilmartin
Operations Assistant	Victor Saljanen

Public Relations Department
Vice President of Public Relations	John Rosasco
Manager of Public Relations	Jason Vogel
Public Relations Assistant	Jeff Schwartzenberg
Community Relations Assistant	Jennifer Schoenfeld

Marketing Department
Vice President of Marketing	Jeanie Baumgartner
Director of New Business	Rob Capill
Director of Marketing Partnerships	Rob Scolaro
Community Relations Representative and Director of Special Projects	Rod Gilbert
Manager of Game Presentation	Sammy Chol
Community and Fan Development Coordinator	Janet Duch
Marketing Assistant	John Commiskey
Marketing Assistant	Michele Gisler

Medical\Training Staff
Team Physician and Orthopedic Surgeon	Dr. Barton Nisonson
Assistant Team Physician	Dr. Anthony Maddalo
Medical Consultants	Drs. Howard Chester, Frank Gardner, Ronald Weissman
Team Dentists	Drs. Irwin Miller and Don Soloman
Sports Physiologist	Howie Wenger
Medical Trainer	Jim Ramsay
Equipment Manager	Mike Folga
Assistant Equipment Manager	Acacio Marques
Massage Therapist	Bruce Lifrieri
Coaching Staff Assistant	Pat Boller

Additional Information
Executive Offices	Madison Square Garden
Home Ice	Madison Square Garden
Largest Crowd	18,200
Press Facilities	33rd Street
Television Facilities	31st Street
Radio Facilities	33rd Street
Rink Dimensions	200 feet by 85 feet
Ends and Sides of Rink	Plexiglass (8 feet)
Club Colors	Blue, Red, White
Uniforms	Home- Base color white, trimmed with blue and red Road- Base color blue, trimmed with red and white Third- Base color navy blue, trimmed with silver, red and white
Practice Facility	Rye, New York

Coaching History

Lester Patrick, 1926-27 to 1938-39; Frank Boucher, 1939-40 to 1947-48; Frank Boucher and Lynn Patrick, 1948-49; Lynn Patrick, 1949-50; Neil Colville, 1950-51; Neil Colville and Bill Cook, 1951-52; Bill Cook, 1952-53; Frank Boucher and Muzz Patrick, 1953-54; Muzz Patrick, 1954-55; Phil Watson, 1955-56 to 1958-59; Phil Watson and Alf Pike, 1959-60; Alf Pike, 1960-61; Doug Harvey, 1961-62; Muzz Patrick and Red Sullivan, 1962-63; Red Sullivan, 1963-64, 1964-65; Red Sullivan and Emile Francis, 1965-66; Emile Francis, 1966-67, 1967-68; Bernie Geoffrion and Emile Francis, 1968-69; Emile Francis, 1969-70 to 1972-73; Larry Popein and Emile Francis, 1973-74; Emile Francis, 1974-75; Ron Stewart and John Ferguson, 1975-76; John Ferguson, 1976-77; Jean-Guy Talbot, 1977-78; Fred Shero, 1978-79, 1979-80; Fred Shero and Craig Patrick, 1980-81; Herb Brooks, 1981-82 to 1983-84; Herb Brooks and Craig Patrick, 1984-85; Ted Sator, 1985-86; Ted Sator, Tom Webster and Phil Esposito, 1986-87; Michel Bergeron, 1987-88; Michel Bergeron and Phil Esposito, 1988-89; Roger Neilson, 1989-90 to 1991-92; Roger Neilson and Ron Smith, 1992-93; Mike Keenan, 1993-94; Colin Campbell, 1994-95 to 1996-97; Colin Campbell and John Muckler, 1997-98; John Muckler, 1998-99 to date.

Ottawa Senators

1998-99 Results: 44w-23L-15T 103PTS. First, Northeast Division

Year-by-Year Record

		Home			Road			Overall						
Season	GP	W	L	T	W	L	T	W	L	T	GF	GA	Pts.	Finished	Playoff Result
1998-99	82	22	11	8	22	12	7	44	23	15	239	179	103	1st,	Northeast Div.	Lost Conf. Quarter-Final
1997-98	82	18	16	7	16	17	8	34	33	15	193	200	83	5th,	Northeast Div.	Lost Conf. Semi-Final
1996-97	82	16	17	8	15	19	7	31	36	15	226	234	77	3rd,	Northeast Div.	Lost Conf. Quarter-Final
1995-96	82	8	28	5	10	31	0	18	59	5	191	291	41	6th,	Northeast Div.	Out of Playoffs
1994-95	48	5	16	3	4	18	2	9	34	5	117	174	23	7th,	Northeast Div.	Out of Playoffs
1993-94	84	8	30	4	6	31	5	14	61	9	201	397	37	7th,	Northeast Div.	Out of Playoffs
1992-93	84	9	29	4	1	41	0	10	70	4	202	395	24	6th,	Adams Div.	Out of Playoffs

1999-2000 Schedule

Oct.	Sat.	2	at Philadelphia
	Tue.	5	at NY Rangers
	Thu.	7	Boston
	Sat.	9	Toronto
	Mon.	11	New Jersey*
	Thu.	14	at Phoenix
	Sat.	16	at Colorado
	Thu.	21	Colorado
	Sat.	23	Buffalo
	Thu.	28	Calgary
	Sat.	30	Florida
	Sun.	31	at Atlanta
Nov.	Wed.	3	at Washington
	Thu.	4	Pittsburgh
	Sat.	6	Montreal
	Wed.	10	at NY Rangers
	Thu.	11	Nashville
	Sat.	13	Anaheim
	Wed.	17	at Carolina
	Thu.	18	San Jose
	Sat.	20	at New Jersey*
	Thu.	25	at Atlanta
	Fri.	26	at Pittsburgh
	Sun.	28	Philadelphia*
	Tue.	30	Chicago
Dec.	Fri.	3	at New Jersey
	Sat.	4	Dallas
	Wed.	8	at Buffalo
	Sat.	11	NY Islanders*
	Mon.	13	at Toronto
	Thu.	16	at Vancouver
	Sat.	18	at Calgary
	Sun.	19	at Edmonton
	Thu.	23	Carolina
	Mon.	27	Montreal
	Wed.	29	at Montreal
	Thu.	30	Boston
Jan.	Mon.	3	New Jersey*
	Tue.	4	at Carolina
	Thu.	6	Phoenix
	Sat.	8	Buffalo
	Tue.	11	at Los Angeles
	Wed.	12	at Anaheim
	Sun.	16	at Washington*
	Mon.	17	at NY Islanders*
	Thu.	20	at Philadelphia
	Sat.	22	Detroit
	Mon.	24	at Toronto
	Wed.	26	St. Louis
	Fri.	28	at Buffalo
	Sat.	29	NY Rangers
Feb.	Tue.	1	Boston
	Thu.	3	at Buffalo
	Fri.	11	Florida
	Sat.	12	at Montreal
	Tue.	15	Carolina
	Thu.	17	Tampa Bay
	Sat.	19	Vancouver*
	Mon.	21	at Florida*
	Thu.	24	at Tampa Bay
	Sat.	26	NY Rangers
	Mon.	28	at Pittsburgh
	Tue.	29	at Boston
Mar.	Thu.	2	at NY Islanders
	Sat.	4	Atlanta
	Mon.	6	at Boston
	Thu.	9	Pittsburgh
	Sat.	11	Toronto
	Wed.	15	at Calgary
	Fri.	17	at Edmonton
	Sat.	18	at Vancouver
	Tue.	21	Atlanta
	Thu.	23	Toronto
	Sat.	25	Washington
	Tue.	28	Philadelphia
	Thu.	30	at Tampa Bay
	Fri.	31	at Florida
Apr.	Sun.	2	at St. Louis*
	Tue.	4	Washington
	Thu.	6	NY Islanders
	Sat.	8	at Montreal
	Sun.	9	Tampa Bay

* Denotes afternoon game.

Franchise date: December 16, 1991

EASTERN NHL CONFERENCE

NORTHEAST DIVISION

8th NHL Season

Ron Tugnutt's 1.79 goals-against average in 1998-99 was the lowest mark in the NHL since Tony Esposito's 1.77 in 1971-72. Tugnutt and Damien Rhodes split Ottawa's netminding duties last season but with Rhodes now in Atlanta, Tugnutt should see more action this year.

1999-2000 Player Personnel

FORWARDS	HT	WT	S	Place of Birth	Date	1998-99 Club
ALFREDSSON, Daniel	5-11	194	R	Goteborg, Sweden	12/11/72	Ottawa
ARVEDSON, Magnus	6-2	198	L	Karlstad, Swe.	11/25/71	Ottawa
BONK, Radek	6-3	210	L	Krnov, Czech.	1/9/76	Ottawa
BUTSAYEV, Viacheslav	6-2	200	L	Togliatti, USSR	6/13/70	Florida-Fort Wayne-Ottawa
CIERNIK, Ivan	6-1	198	L	Levice, Czech.	10/30/77	Adirondack-Cincinnati (AHL)
DACKELL, Andreas	5-11	191	R	Gavle, Sweden	12/29/72	Ottawa
DINEEN, Kevin	5-11	190	R	Quebec City, Que.	10/28/63	Carolina
EMMONS, John	6-2	205	L	San Jose, CA	8/17/74	Detroit (IHL)
GARDINER, Bruce	6-1	193	R	Barrie, Ont.	2/11/72	Ottawa
GOROVOKOV, Konstantin	5-11	176	L	Novosibirsk, USSR	8/31/77	SKA St. Petersburg
HOSSA, Marian	6-1	194	L	Stara Lubovna, Czech.	1/12/79	Ottawa
MARTINS, Steve	5-9	175	L	Gatineau, Que.	4/13/72	Ottawa-Detroit (IHL)
McEACHERN, Shawn	5-11	195	L	Waltham, MA	2/28/69	Ottawa
MILLER, Kevin	5-11	190	R	Lansing, MI	9/2/65	NY Islanders-Chicago (IHL)
NEIL, Christopher	6-0	210	R	Markdale, Ont.	6/18/79	North Bay
PAVLIKOVSKY, Rastisla	5-10	195	L	Dubnica, Czech.	9/8/79	Cin (IHL)-Cin (AHL)
PRIER, Bob	6-1	210	R	Pembroke, Ont.	8/5/76	St. Lawrence
PROSPAL, Vaclav	6-2	185	L	Ceske-Budejovice, Czech.	2/17/75	Ottawa
ROY, Andre	6-3	202	L	Port Chester, NY	2/8/75	Fort Wayne
SARAULT, Yves	6-1	185	L	Valleyfield, Que.	12/23/72	Ottawa-Detroit (IHL)
SCHASTLIVY, Petr	6-0	191	L	Angarsk, USSR	4/18/79	Yaroslavl
SZYSKY, Chris	5-11	205	R	White City, Sask.	6/8/76	Canada-Grand Rapids
VAN ALLEN, Shaun	6-1	200	L	Calgary, Alta.	8/29/67	Ottawa
WALLACE, Buddy	6-1	195	L	Palantine, IL	12/18/75	Lowell (AHL)
YASHIN, Alexei	6-3	225	R	Sverdlovsk, USSR	11/5/73	Ottawa
ZAMUNER, Rob	6-2	206	L	Oakville, Ont.	9/17/69	Tampa Bay

DEFENSEMEN						
GRIMES, Kevin	6-2	205	L	Ottawa, Ont.	8/19/79	Kingston
GRUDEN, John	6-0	190	L	Virginia, MN	6/4/70	Ottawa-Detroit (IHL)
JOSEPH, Chris	6-2	212	R	Burnaby, B.C.	9/10/69	Phi-Cin (IHL)-Phi (AHL)
KRAVCHUK, Igor	6-1	200	L	Ufa, USSR	9/13/66	Ottawa
LAUKKANEN, Janne	6-0	180	L	Lahti, Finland	3/19/70	Ottawa
PHILLIPS, Chris	6-2	200	L	Fort McMurray, Alta.	3/9/78	Ottawa
RACHUNEK, Karel	6-0	183	R	Gottwaldov, Czech.	8/27/79	ZPS Zlin
REDDEN, Wade	6-2	193	L	Lloydminster, Sask.	6/12/77	Ottawa
SALO, Sami	6-3	190	R	Turku, Finland	9/2/74	Ottawa-Detroit (IHL)
TRAVERSE, Patrick	6-3	190	L	Montreal, Que.	3/14/74	Ottawa
YORK, Jason	6-2	198	R	Nepean, Ont.	5/20/70	Ottawa

GOALTENDERS	HT	WT	C	Place of Birth	Date	1998-99 Club
FOUNTAIN, Mike	6-1	176	L	North York, Ont.	1/26/72	New Haven
HURME, Jani	6-0	187	L	Turku, Finland	1/7/75	Detroit (IHL)-Cincinnati (IHL)
LALIME, Patrick	6-2	170	L	St. Bonaventure, Que.	7/7/74	Kansas City
TUGNUTT, Ron	5-11	155	L	Scarborough, Ont.	10/22/67	Ottawa

General Managers' History

Mel Bridgman, 1992-93; Randy Sexton, 1993-94, 1994-95; Randy Sexton and Pierre Gauthier, 1995-96; Pierre Gauthier, 1996-97, 1997-98; Rick Dudley, 1998-99; Marshall Johnston, 1999-2000.

General Manager

JOHNSTON, MARSHALL
General Manager, Ottawa Senators. Born in Birch Hills, Sask., June 6, 1941.

Marshall Johnston was named general manager of the Ottawa Senators on June 8, 1999, replacing Rick Dudley. Johnson joined the Senators in July 1996 as director of player personnel. He worked through his first season in 1996-97 with the Senators' pro and amateur scouts and guided the staff during the 1997 NHL Entry Draft that saw the club pick Marian Hossa of Slovakia as its first selection, twelfth overall.

After a successful seven-year NHL career on the ice (1967 to 1974), Johnston coached the California Golden Seals during parts of the 1973-74 and 1974-75 seasons. He then became head coach of Denver University, his alma mater, for four seasons, leading the Pioneers to the WCHA title and being named the Conference Coach of the Year in 1976-77.

Johnston joined the Colorado Rockies as assistant general manager and assistant coach on May 4, 1981 and served as head coach for the final 56 games of the 1981-82 season. Following the season, Johnston was named head coach of Canada's entry at the World Championships. After the Colorado franchise moved to New Jersey, he remained with the club as an assistant coach until being promoted to director of player personnel. He spent 10 years in New Jersey (1983 to 1993) as director of player personnel for the Devils, the 1995 Stanley Cup champions. While heading New Jersey's scouting department, the Devils drafted, among others, Scott Niedermayer, Brian Rolston, Martin Brodeur, Bill Guerin, Zdeno Ciger, Brendan Shanahan, Craig Wolanin, Sean Burke, Kirk Muller and Kirk McLean.

Johnston spent two years as executive director of CIPRO, a hockey scouting group jointly owned and operated by the Dallas Stars, Hartford Whalers, Philadelphia Flyers and Winnipeg Jets, prior to joining the New York Islanders' scouting staff in 1995-96.

Marshall and his wife Barbara have two daughters, Jill and Amy.

1998-99 Scoring

* – rookie

Regular Season

Pos	#	Player	Team	GP	G	A	Pts	+/–	PIM	PP	SH	GW	GT	S	%
C	19	Alexei Yashin	OTT	82	44	50	94	16	54	19	0	5	1	337	13.1
L	15	Shawn McEachern	OTT	77	31	25	56	8	46	7	0	4	1	223	13.9
R	10	Andreas Dackell	OTT	77	15	35	50	9	30	6	0	3	0	107	14.0
L	20	Magnus Arvedson	OTT	80	21	26	47	33	50	0	4	6	0	136	15.4
L	21	Andreas Johansson	OTT	69	21	16	37	1	34	7	0	6	0	144	14.6
R	7	Nelson Emerson	CAR	35	8	13	21	1	36	3	0	0	1	84	9.5
			CHI	27	4	10	14	8	13	0	0	1	1	94	4.3
			OTT	3	1	1	2	–1	2	0	0	0	0	10	10.0
			TOTAL	65	13	24	37	8	51	3	0	1	2	188	6.9
C	13	Vaclav Prospal	OTT	79	10	26	36	8	58	2	0	3	0	114	8.8
D	33	Jason York	OTT	79	4	31	35	17	48	2	0	0	1	177	2.3
R	11	Daniel Alfredsson	OTT	58	11	22	33	8	14	3	0	5	0	163	6.7
C	14	Radek Bonk	OTT	81	16	16	32	15	48	0	1	6	0	110	14.5
R	18 *	Marian Hossa	OTT	60	15	15	30	18	37	1	0	2	2	124	12.1
D	6	Wade Redden	OTT	72	8	21	29	7	54	3	0	1	1	127	6.3
L	28	Ted Donato	BOS	14	1	3	4	0	4	0	0	0	0	22	4.5
			NYI	55	7	11	18	–10	27	2	0	0	0	68	10.3
			OTT	13	3	2	5	2	10	1	0	0	0	16	18.8
			TOTAL	82	11	16	27	–8	41	3	0	0	0	106	10.4
D	29	Igor Kravchuk	OTT	79	4	21	25	14	32	3	0	0	0	171	2.3
D	5 *	Sami Salo	OTT	61	7	12	19	20	24	2	0	1	0	106	6.6
C	22	Shaun Van Allen	OTT	79	6	11	17	3	30	0	1	0	0	47	12.8
C	25	Bruce Gardiner	OTT	59	4	8	12	6	43	0	0	1	0	70	5.7
D	27	Janne Laukkanen	OTT	50	1	11	12	18	40	0	0	0	0	46	2.2
D	3 *	Patrick Traverse	OTT	46	1	9	10	12	22	0	0	0	0	35	2.9
D	2	Lance Pitlick	OTT	50	3	6	9	7	33	0	0	0	0	34	8.8
C	16	Steve Martins	OTT	36	4	3	7	4	10	1	0	1	0	27	14.8
R	12	David Oliver	OTT	17	2	5	7	1	4	0	0	0	0	18	11.1
D	4	Chris Phillips	OTT	34	3	3	6	–5	32	2	0	0	0	51	5.9
L	9	Bill Berg	OTT	44	2	2	4	4	28	0	0	0	1	40	5.0
G	1	Damian Rhodes	OTT	45	1	1	2	0	4	0	0	0	0	1	100.0
C	7	Viacheslav Butsayev	FLA	1	0	0	0	–1	2	0	0	0	0	0	0.0
			OTT	2	0	1	1	0	2	0	0	0	0	5	0.0
			TOTAL	3	0	1	1	–1	4	0	0	0	0	5	0.0
R	26	Philip Crowe	OTT	8	0	1	1	1	4	0	0	0	0	2	0.0
L	37	Yves Sarault	OTT	11	0	1	1	1	4	0	0	0	0	7	0.0
D	24	John Gruden	OTT	13	0	1	1	0	8	0	0	0	0	10	0.0
G	31	Ron Tugnutt	OTT	43	0	0	0	0	0	0	0	0	0	0	0.0

Goaltending

No.	Goaltender	GPI	Mins	Avg	W	L	T	EN	SO	GA	SA	S%
31	Ron Tugnutt	43	2508	1.79	22	10	8	2	3	75	1005	.925
1	Damian Rhodes	45	2480	2.44	22	13	7	1	3	101	1060	.905
	Totals	**82**	**4999**	**2.15**	**44**	**23**	**15**	**3**	**6**	**179**	**2068**	**.913**

Playoffs

Pos	#	Player	Team	GP	G	A	Pts	+/–	PIM	PP	SH	GW	OT	S	%
R	7	Nelson Emerson	OTT	4	1	3	4	0	0	0	0	0	0	12	8.3
R	11	Daniel Alfredsson	OTT	4	1	2	3	–1	4	1	0	0	0	13	7.7
D	6	Wade Redden	OTT	4	1	2	3	–1	2	1	0	0	0	11	9.1
L	15	Shawn McEachern	OTT	4	2	0	2	1	6	1	0	0	0	11	18.2
D	33	Jason York	OTT	4	1	1	2	–1	4	0	0	0	0	12	8.3
R	18 *	Marian Hossa	OTT	4	0	2	2	1	4	0	0	0	0	11	0.0
L	20	Magnus Arvedson	OTT	3	0	1	1	–1	2	0	0	0	0	8	0.0
R	10	Andreas Dackell	OTT	4	0	1	1	–3	0	0	0	0	0	3	0.0
L	28	Ted Donato	OTT	1	0	0	0	0	0	0	0	0	0	0	0.0
L	9	Bill Berg	OTT	2	0	0	0	0	0	0	0	0	0	0	0.0
G	31	Ron Tugnutt	OTT	2	0	0	0	0	0	0	0	0	0	0	0.0
D	2	Lance Pitlick	OTT	2	0	0	0	–1	0	0	0	0	0	2	0.0
G	1	Damian Rhodes	OTT	2	0	0	0	0	0	0	0	0	0	0	0.0
L	21	Andreas Johansson	OTT	2	0	0	0	–3	0	0	0	0	0	4	0.0
C	25	Bruce Gardiner	OTT	3	0	0	0	0	4	0	0	0	0	4	0.0
D	4	Chris Phillips	OTT	3	0	0	0	–1	0	0	0	0	0	1	0.0
C	22	Shaun Van Allen	OTT	4	0	0	0	–1	0	0	0	0	0	2	0.0
D	29	Igor Kravchuk	OTT	4	0	0	0	–5	0	0	0	0	0	12	0.0
D	27	Janne Laukkanen	OTT	4	0	0	0	1	4	0	0	0	0	8	0.0
C	19	Alexei Yashin	OTT	4	0	0	0	–4	10	0	0	0	0	24	0.0
C	13	Vaclav Prospal	OTT	4	0	0	0	–2	0	0	0	0	0	6	0.0
C	14	Radek Bonk	OTT	4	0	0	0	–1	6	0	0	0	0	8	0.0
D	5 *	Sami Salo	OTT	4	0	0	0	–3	0	0	0	0	0	10	0.0

Goaltending

No.	Goaltender	GPI	Mins	Avg	W	L	EN	SO	GA	SA	S%
1	Damian Rhodes	2	150	2.40	0	2	0	0	6	65	.908
31	Ron Tugnutt	2	118	3.05	0	2	0	0	6	41	.854
	Totals	**4**	**271**	**2.66**	**0**	**4**	**0**	**0**	**12**	**106**	**.887**

Club Records

Team

(Figures in brackets for season records are games played; records for fewest points, wins, ties, losses, goals, goals against are for 70 or more games)

Most Points	103	1998-99 (82)
Most Wins	44	1998-99 (82)
Most Ties	15	1996-97 (82), 1997-98 (82), 1998-99 (82)
Most Losses	70	1992-93 (84)
Most Goals	239	1998-99 (82)
Most Goals Against	397	1993-94 (84)
Fewest Points	24	1992-93 (84)
Fewest Wins	10	1992-93 (84)
Fewest Ties	4	1992-93 (84)
Fewest Losses	36	1996-97 (82)
Fewest Goals	191	1995-96 (82)
Fewest Goals Against	179	1998-99 (82)

Longest Winning Streak

Overall	4	Three times
Home	4	Three times
Away	5	Apr. 3-19/98

Longest Undefeated Streak

Overall	5	Oct. 15-23/97 (4 wins, 1 tie)
Home	8	Feb. 5-Mar. 20/98 (5 wins, 3 ties)
Away	6	Mar. 29-Apr. 19/98 (5 wins, 1 tie)

** NHL records do not include neutral site games

Longest Losing Streak

Overall	14	Mar. 2-Apr. 7/93
Home	*11	Oct. 27-Dec. 8/93
Away	*38	Oct. 10/92-Apr. 3/93**

Longest Winless Streak

Overall	21	Oct. 10-Nov. 23/92 (20 losses, 1 tie)
Home	*17	Oct. 28/95-Jan. 27/96 (15 losses, 2 ties)
Away	*38	Oct. 10/92-Apr. 3/93 (38 losses)
Most Shutouts, Season	8	1997-98 (82)
Most PIM, Season	1,716	1992-93 (84)
Most Goals, Game	7	Four times

Individual

Most Seasons	6	Alexei Yashin
Most Games, Career	422	Alexei Yashin
Most Goals, Career	178	Alexei Yashin
Most Assists, Career	225	Alexei Yashin
Most Points, Career	403	Alexei Yashin (178G, 225A)
Most PIM, Career	600	Dennis Vial
Most Shutouts, Career	11	Damian Rhodes

Longest Consecutive Games Streak 210 Alexei Yashin (Feb. 23/95-date)

Most Goals, Season	44	Alexei Yashin (1998-99)
Most Assists, Season	50	Alexei Yashin (1998-99)
Most Points, Season	94	Alexei Yashin (1998-99; 44G, 50A)
Most PIM, Season	318	Mike Peluso (1992-93)
Most Points, Defenseman, Season	63	Norm Maciver (1992-93; 17G, 46A)
Most Points, Center, Season	94	Alexei Yashin (1998-99; 44G, 50A)
Most Points, Right Wing, Season	71	Daniel Alfredsson (1996-97; 24G, 47A)
Most Points, Left Wing, Season	56	Shawn McEachern (1998-99; 31G, 25A)
Most Points, Rookie, Season	79	Alexei Yashin (1993-94; 30G, 49A)
Most Shutouts, Season	5	Damian Rhodes (1997-98)
Most Goals, Game	3	Thirteen times
Most Assists, Game	4	Alexei Yashin (Nov. 5/93)
Most Points, Game	6	Dan Quinn (Oct. 15/95; 3G, 3A)

* NHL Record.

Coaching History

Rick Bowness, 1992-93 to 1994-95; Rick Bowness, Dave Allison and Jacques Martin, 1995-96; Jacques Martin, 1996-97 to date.

Captains' History

Laurie Boschman, 1992-93; Brad Shaw, Mark Lamb and Gord Dineen, 1993-94; Randy Cunneyworth, 1994-95 to 1997-98; Alexei Yashin, 1998-99.

All-time Record vs. Other Clubs

Regular Season

			At Home						On Road						Total					
	GP	W	L	T	GF	GA	PTS	GP	W	L	T	GF	GA	PTS	GP	W	L	T	GF	GA	PTS
Anaheim	5	1	3	1	13	15	3	5	0	3	2	7	16	2	10	1	6	3	20	31	5
Boston	18	2	14	2	32	63	6	20	4	14	2	53	85	10	38	6	28	4	85	148	16
Buffalo	20	4	10	6	40	59	14	18	5	12	1	27	66	11	38	9	22	7	67	125	25
Calgary	6	3	1	2	14	13	8	6	1	4	1	13	29	3	12	4	5	3	27	42	11
Carolina	19	6	10	3	48	59	15	17	1	14	2	34	59	4	36	7	24	5	82	118	19
Chicago	6	2	4	0	17	20	4	6	1	3	2	13	15	4	12	3	7	2	30	35	8
Colorado	13	4	7	2	40	60	10	12	1	10	1	33	61	3	25	5	17	3	73	121	13
Dallas	6	2	4	0	15	18	4	7	3	4	0	15	26	6	13	5	8	0	30	44	10
Detroit	6	2	3	1	17	18	5	6	3	0	3	13	20	6	12	5	6	1	30	38	11
Edmonton	6	2	3	1	10	14	5	6	1	4	1	16	25	3	12	3	7	2	26	39	8
Florida	12	3	7	2	26	38	8	12	4	7	1	36	44	9	24	7	14	3	62	82	17
Los Angeles	6	4	1	1	20	14	9	6	0	6	0	13	35	0	12	4	7	1	33	49	9
Montreal	18	7	11	0	50	56	14	20	5	12	3	53	64	13	38	12	23	3	103	120	27
Nashville	1	1	0	0	3	1	2	1	0	0	1	3	1	2	2	0	0	1	6	2	4
New Jersey	14	4	9	1	28	37	9	13	3	8	2	28	43	8	27	7	17	3	56	80	17
NY Islanders	13	7	3	3	47	42	17	14	8	3	3	55	46	19	27	15	6	6	102	88	36
NY Rangers	13	2	9	2	32	40	6	13	5	8	0	38	50	10	26	7	17	2	70	90	16
Philadelphia	14	4	9	1	36	50	9	13	3	10	0	32	55	6	27	7	19	1	68	105	15
Phoenix	8	1	6	1	16	31	3	6	3	2	1	24	24	7	14	4	8	2	40	55	10
Pittsburgh	17	3	11	3	37	61	9	17	1	13	3	35	71	5	34	4	24	6	72	132	14
St. Louis	6	1	5	0	12	29	2	6	3	2	1	20	17	7	12	4	7	1	32	46	9
San Jose	6	2	0	4	18	15	8	6	2	4	0	8	11	4	12	4	4	4	26	26	12
Tampa Bay	13	6	7	0	42	34	12	13	7	5	1	39	38	15	26	13	12	1	81	72	27
Toronto	7	4	2	1	19	15	9	9	2	7	0	21	32	4	16	6	9	1	40	47	13
Vancouver	6	3	2	1	15	18	7	6	2	3	1	12	18	5	12	5	5	2	27	36	12
Washington	13	6	6	1	48	45	13	14	5	8	1	33	54	11	27	11	14	2	81	99	24
Totals	**272**	**86**	**147**	**39**	**695**	**865**	**211**	**272**	**74**	**169**	**29**	**674**	**1005**	**177**	**544**	**160**	**316**	**68**	**1369**	**1870**	**388**

Playoffs

	Series	W	L	GP	W	L	T	GF	GA	Last Mtg.	Round	Result
Buffalo	2	0	2	11	3	8	0	19	26	1999	CQF	L 0-4
New Jersey	1	1	0	6	4	2	0	13	12	1998	CQF	W 4-2
Washington	1	0	1	5	1	4	0	7	18	1998	CSF	L 1-4
Totals	**4**	**1**	**3**	**22**	**8**	**14**	**0**	**39**	**56**			

Playoff Results 1999-95

Year	Round	Opponent	Result	GF	GA
1999	CQF	Buffalo	L 0-4	6	12
1998	CSF	Washington	L 1-4	7	18
	CQF	New Jersey	W 4-2	13	12
1997	CQF	Buffalo	L 3-4	13	14

Abbreviations: Round: CSF – conference semi-final; **CQF** – conference quarter-final.

Colorado totals include Quebec, 1992-93 to 1994-95.
Dallas totals include Minnesota, 1992-93.

Carolina totals include Hartford, 1992-93 to 1996-97.
Phoenix totals include Winnipeg, 1992-93 to 1995-96.

Retired Numbers

8   Frank Finnigan   1924-1934

1998-99 Results

Oct.	10	at	Colorado	4-3		16	Buffalo	1-1
	11	at	Phoenix	4-1		18	Philadelphia	0-5
	17		Nashville	3-1		19	at NY Rangers	2-1
	21	at	Montreal	2-3		21	at Boston	3-1
	22		St. Louis	3-5		26	at New Jersey	1-4
	24		Carolina	1-3		30	NY Islanders	9-2
	29		Philadelphia	3-1	Feb.	1	at Vancouver	1-0
	31		Montreal	5-1		3	at Edmonton	2-2
Nov.	1	at	Philadelphia	5-4		6	at Calgary	1-1
	5		Pittsburgh	2-4		9	Buffalo	1-1
	7		Washington	5-8		11	Florida	1-3
	10	at	Buffalo	2-2		13	Washington	2-1
	12		Edmonton	1-1		15	Chicago	6-2
	14	at	Toronto	1-2		18	Boston	2-0
	15	at	Chicago	2-2		20	Philadelphia	4-1
	20	at	Washington	4-1		23	at Boston	2-5
	21		Calgary	4-1		25	Montreal	3-1
	23		Vancouver	4-3		27	at Montreal	1-4
	26		NY Islanders	4-1	Mar.	2	at NY Islanders	4-2
Dec.	1	at	Toronto	2-3		4	at Philadelphia	5-0
	3		Nashville	3-1		6	Toronto	3-1
	3		Los Angeles	3-1		8	Tampa Bay	9-3
	5		NY Rangers	1-2		10	at NY Rangers	3-0
	8	at	Tampa Bay	3-4		13	at San Jose	2-3
	9	at	Florida	5-6		15	at Los Angeles	0-4
	12		Phoenix	0-2		17	at Anaheim	2-2
	17	at	Boston	2-5		19	at Dallas	2-1
	18		Carolina	2-5		20	at St. Louis	2-1
	20		Dallas	2-3		24	Boston	0-3
	23		Montreal	3-1		26	San Jose	1-1
	26	at	Pittsburgh	1-2		27	at NY Islanders	7-3
	28		Anaheim	2-3		30	at Pittsburgh	6-4
	30	at	Buffalo	3-2	Apr.	1	Pittsburgh	3-3
Jan.	1	at	Washington	4-3		3	at Florida	6-4
	2		New Jersey	6-0		5	at Tampa Bay	4-4
	4	at	Carolina	4-4		7	at Toronto	2-4
	6	at	Detroit	2-0		8	Toronto	3-1
	8		Tampa Bay	5-1		10	Buffalo	1-1
	10		Detroit	4-1		12	Florida	0-2
	11	at	New Jersey	4-2		15	NY Rangers	2-2
	14		New Jersey	3-2		17	at Carolina	1-1

Entry Draft
Selections 1999-92

1999
Pick
26	Martin Havlat
48	Simon Lajeunesse
62	Teemu Sainomaa
94	Chris Kelly
154	Andrew Ianiero
164	Martin Prusek
201	Mikko Ruutu
209	Layne Ulmer
213	Alexandre Giroux
269	Konstantin Gorovikov

1998
Pick
15	Mathieu Chouinard
44	Mike Fisher
58	Chris Bala
74	Julien Vauclair
101	Petr Schastlivy
130	Gavin McLeod
161	Christopher Neil
188	Michael Periard
223	Sergei Verenikin
246	Rastisla Pavlikovsky

1997
Pick
12	Marian Hossa
58	Jani Hurme
66	Josh Langfeld
119	Magnus Arvedsson
146	Jeff Sullivan
173	Robin Bacul
203	Nick Gillis
229	Karel Rachunek

1996
Pick
1	Chris Phillips
81	Antti-Jussi Niemi
136	Andreas Dackell
163	Francois Hardy
212	Erich Goldmann
216	Ivan Ciernik
239	Sami Salo

1995
Pick
1	Bryan Berard
27	Marc Moro
53	Brad Larsen
89	Kevin Bolibruck
103	Kevin Boyd
131	David Hruska
183	Kaj Linna
184	Ray Schultz
231	Erik Kaminski

1994
Pick
3	Radek Bonk
29	Stanislav Neckar
81	Bryan Masotta
131	Mike Gaffney
133	Daniel Alfredsson
159	Doug Sproule
210	Frederic Cassivi
211	Danny Dupont
237	Stephen MacKinnon
274	Antti Tormanen

1993
Pick
1	Alexandre Daigle
27	Radim Bicanek
53	Patrick Charbonneau
91	Cosmo Dupaul
131	Rick Bodkin
157	Sergei Poleschuk
183	Jason Disher
209	Toby Kvalevog
227	Pavol Demitra
235	Rick Schuwerk

1992
Pick
2	Alexei Yashin
25	Chad Penney
50	Patrick Traverse
73	Radek Hamr
98	Daniel Guerard
121	Al Sinclair
146	Jaroslav Miklenda
169	Jay Kenney
194	Claude Savoie
217	Jake Grimes
242	Tomas Jelinek
264	Petter Ronnqvist

Club Directory

Corel Centre

Corel Centre
1000 Palladium Drive
Kanata, Ontario
K2V 1A5
Phone **613/599-0250**
FAX 613/599-5562
Website:
www.ottawasenators.com
Capacity: 18,500

Chairman and Governor	Rod Bryden
President and CEO	Roy Mlakar
General Manager	Marshall Johnston
Director, Hockey Operations	Trevor Timmins
Director, Player Personnel	Jarmo Kekalainen
Head Coach	Jacques Martin
Assistant Coaches	Perry Pearn, Andre Savard
Strength & Conditioning & Video Coach	Randy Lee
Chief Scout (Amateur)	Frank Jay
VP, Communications	Phil Legault
Director, Media Relations	Morgan Quarry
Manager, Media Relations	Steve Keogh
Assistant, Hockey Operations & Media Relations	Jennifer Eves
Head Athletic Trainer	Kevin Wagner
Head Equipment Manager	Ed Georgica
Assistant Equipment Manager	John Gervais
Massage Therapist	Brad Joyal
Arena (Capacity)	Corel Centre (18,500)
General Office Phone	(613) 599-0250
Media Relations Phone	(613) 599-0327 / 599-0306 / 599-0326
Press Box Phone	(613) 599-4801
Media Relations Fax	(613) 599-5562
Team Colors	Red, Gold & Black
Radio	OSR 1200 (English), CJRC (French)
Commercial TV	CJOH TV
Cable TV	CTV SportsNet

Coach

MARTIN, JACQUES
Coach, Ottawa Senators. Born in St. Pascal, Ont., October 1, 1952.

Jacques Martin led the Ottawa Senators to their best season in team history in 1998-99, breaking team records for wins (44) and points (103) the club had established the year before. He was rewarded with the Jack Adams Award as coach of the year.

When appointed the Senators' third head coach on January 24, 1996, Martin brought ten years of NHL coaching experience, including five with the Quebec Nordiques, an organization often compared with the Senators, in that both teams were built around young, talented players requiring patience and teaching.

Martin's coaching career began at the collegiate level in 1976. He was appointed head coach of the Guelph Platers (now Storm) in 1985, winning the OHL title, the Memorial Cup and being named the OHL coach of the year. That summer, Martin became head coach of the St. Louis Blues. In his NHL rookie year, he lead the Blues to the Norris Division championship and, in two seasons with the Blues, posted a 66-71-23 record. He then spent two seasons as an assistant to Chicago's head coach Mike Keenan, before joining the Nordiques in 1990. With Quebec, he worked four years as assistant coach and one year (1993-94) as both head coach and general manager of the AHL Cornwall Aces.

Coaching Record

Season	Team	Games	Regular Season W	L	T	%	Playoffs Games	W	L	%
1983-84	Peterborough (OHL)	70	43	23	4	.643	....	....	....	....
1984-85	Peterborough (OHL)	66	42	20	4	.667	....	....	....	....
1985-86	Guelph (OHL)	66	41	23	2	.636	....	....	....	....
1986-87	**St. Louis (NHL)**	**80**	**32**	**33**	**15**	**.494**	**6**	**2**	**4**	**.333**
1987-88	**St. Louis (NHL)**	**80**	**34**	**38**	**8**	**.475**	**10**	**5**	**5**	**.500**
1993-94	Cornwall (AHL)	80	33	36	11	.481	13	8	5	.615
1995-96	**Ottawa (NHL)**	**38**	**10**	**24**	**4**	**.316**	....	....	....	....
1996-97	**Ottawa (NHL)**	**82**	**31**	**36**	**15**	**.470**	**7**	**3**	**4**	**.429**
1997-98	**Ottawa (NHL)**	**82**	**34**	**33**	**15**	**.506**	**11**	**5**	**6**	**.455**
1998-99	**Ottawa (NHL)**	**82**	**44**	**23**	**15**	**.628**	**4**	**0**	**4**	**.000**
	NHL Totals	**444**	**185**	**187**	**72**	**.498**	**38**	**15**	**23**	**.395**

The two-way talents of Magnus Arvedson were a big reason for Ottawa's success last season. Arvedson was tied for third on the team with 21 goals and was the runner-up behind Jere Lehtinen for the Selke Trophy.

Philadelphia Flyers

1998-99 Results: 37w-26l-19t 93pts. Second, Atlantic Division

One of the best defensemen in the NHL, Eric Desjardins recorded career highs with 15 goals and 51 points last season. Only Al MacInnis, Nicklas Lidstrom, Ray Bourque and Chris Pronger received more votes for the Norris Trophy.

1999-2000 Schedule

Oct.	Sat.	2	Ottawa	Tue.	11	at Carolina	
	Thu.	7	Carolina	Fri.	14	at Atlanta	
	Sat.	9	at Boston	Sat.	15	New Jersey	
	Tue.	12	at Washington	Mon.	17	at Florida*	
	Thu.	14	Montreal	Thu.	20	Ottawa	
	Sat.	16	at Detroit	Sun.	23	at Pittsburgh	
	Sun.	17	Buffalo	Thu.	27	Florida	
	Wed.	20	NY Rangers	Sat.	29	at Montreal*	
	Fri.	22	at NY Rangers	Sun.	30	at Washington*	
	Sun.	24	Florida	Feb. Thu.	3	Anaheim	
	Tue.	26	Vancouver	Wed.	9	at Toronto	
	Thu.	28	Colorado	Thu.	10	Edmonton	
	Sat.	30	New Jersey	Sat.	12	Buffalo*	
Nov.	Wed.	3	at Anaheim	Tue.	15	at New Jersey	
	Fri.	5	at San Jose	Thu.	17	NY Islanders	
	Sat.	6	at Los Angeles	Sat.	19	Washington	
	Tue.	9	at New Jersey	Sun.	20	at NY Rangers	
	Thu.	11	Carolina	Tue.	22	Chicago	
	Sat.	13	San Jose*	Thu.	24	Pittsburgh	
	Thu.	18	Dallas	Sat.	26	at NY Islanders	
	Sat.	20	Tampa Bay	Tue.	29	at St. Louis	
	Mon.	22	at Tampa Bay	Mar. Wed.	1	at Dallas	
	Wed.	24	at Florida	Sat.	4	at Boston*	
	Fri.	26	Toronto*	Sun.	5	NY Islanders	
	Sun.	28	at Ottawa*	Wed.	8	at Tampa Bay	
Dec.	Thu.	2	at Buffalo	Thu.	9	Washington	
	Sat.	4	at Montreal	Sun.	12	at Colorado	
	Sun.	5	St. Louis	Mon.	13	at Phoenix	
	Thu.	9	Toronto	Thu.	16	Montreal	
	Sat.	11	at Toronto	Sat.	18	NY Rangers*	
	Tue.	14	at Buffalo	Sun.	19	Boston*	
	Thu.	16	Phoenix	Tue.	21	at Nashville	
	Sat.	18	Tampa Bay	Thu.	23	Los Angeles	
	Sun.	19	Nashville	Sun.	26	at Pittsburgh*	
	Wed.	22	at New Jersey	Tue.	28	at Ottawa	
	Thu.	23	Atlanta	Apr. Sat.	1	at Pittsburgh*	
	Mon.	27	at Calgary	Sun.	2	at Carolina*	
	Wed.	29	at Vancouver	Tue.	4	at Atlanta	
Jan.	Sun.	2	at NY Islanders*	Thu.	6	Atlanta	
	Thu.	6	NY Islanders	Sat.	8	Boston*	
	Sat.	8	Pittsburgh	Sun.	9	at NY Rangers*	

* Denotes afternoon game.

Franchise date: June 5, 1967

ATLANTIC DIVISION

33rd NHL Season

Year-by-Year Record

Season	GP	Home W	L	T	Road W	L	T	Overall W	L	T	GF	GA	Pts.	Finished	Playoff Result
1998-99	82	21	9	11	16	17	8	37	26	19	231	196	93	2nd, Atlantic Div.	Lost Conf. Quarter-Final
1997-98	82	24	11	6	18	18	5	42	29	11	242	193	95	2nd, Atlantic Div.	Lost Conf. Quarter-Final
1996-97	82	23	12	6	22	12	7	45	24	13	274	217	103	2nd, Atlantic Div.	Lost Final
1995-96	82	27	9	5	18	15	8	45	24	13	282	208	103	1st, Atlantic Div.	Lost Conf. Semi-Final
1994-95	48	16	7	1	12	9	3	28	16	4	150	132	60	1st, Atlantic Div.	Lost Conf. Championship
1993-94	84	19	20	3	16	19	7	35	39	10	294	314	80	6th, Atlantic Div.	Out of Playoffs
1992-93	84	23	14	5	13	23	6	36	37	11	319	319	83	5th, Patrick Div.	Out of Playoffs
1991-92	80	22	11	7	10	26	4	32	37	11	252	273	75	6th, Patrick Div.	Out of Playoffs
1990-91	80	18	16	6	15	21	4	33	37	10	252	267	76	5th, Patrick Div.	Out of Playoffs
1989-90	80	17	19	4	13	20	7	30	39	11	290	297	71	6th, Patrick Div.	Out of Playoffs
1988-89	80	22	15	3	14	21	5	36	36	8	307	285	80	4th, Patrick Div.	Lost Conf. Championship
1987-88	80	20	14	6	18	19	3	38	33	9	292	292	85	3rd, Patrick Div.	Lost Div. Semi-Final
1986-87	80	29	9	2	17	17	6	46	26	8	310	245	100	1st, Patrick Div.	Lost Final
1985-86	80	33	6	1	20	17	3	53	23	4	335	241	110	1st, Patrick Div.	Lost Div. Semi-Final
1984-85	80	32	4	4	21	16	3	53	20	7	348	241	113	1st, Patrick Div.	Lost Final
1983-84	80	25	10	5	19	16	5	44	26	10	350	290	98	3rd, Patrick Div.	Lost Div. Semi-Final
1982-83	80	29	8	3	20	15	5	49	23	8	326	240	106	1st, Patrick Div.	Lost Div. Semi-Final
1981-82	80	25	10	5	13	21	6	38	31	11	325	313	87	3rd, Patrick Div.	Lost Div. Semi-Final
1980-81	80	23	9	8	18	15	7	41	24	15	313	249	97	2nd, Patrick Div.	Lost Quarter-Final
1979-80	80	27	5	8	21	7	12	48	12	20	327	254	116	1st, Patrick Div.	Lost Final
1978-79	80	26	10	4	14	15	11	40	25	15	281	248	95	2nd, Patrick Div.	Lost Quarter-Final
1977-78	80	29	6	5	16	14	10	45	20	15	296	200	105	2nd, Patrick Div.	Lost Semi-Final
1976-77	80	33	6	1	15	10	15	48	16	16	323	213	112	1st, Patrick Div.	Lost Semi-Final
1975-76	80	36	2	2	15	11	14	51	13	16	348	209	118	1st, Patrick Div.	Lost Final
1974-75	**80**	**32**	**6**	**2**	**19**	**12**	**9**	**51**	**18**	**11**	**293**	**181**	**113**	**1st, Patrick Div.**	**Won Stanley Cup**
1973-74	**78**	**28**	**6**	**5**	**22**	**10**	**7**	**50**	**16**	**12**	**273**	**164**	**112**	**1st, West Div.**	**Won Stanley Cup**
1972-73	78	27	8	4	10	22	7	37	30	11	296	256	85	2nd, West Div.	Lost Semi-Final
1971-72	78	19	13	7	7	25	7	26	38	14	200	236	66	5th, West Div.	Out of Playoffs
1970-71	78	20	10	9	8	23	8	28	33	17	207	225	73	3rd, West Div.	Lost Quarter-Final
1969-70	76	11	14	13	6	21	11	17	35	24	197	225	58	5th, West Div.	Out of Playoffs
1968-69	76	14	16	8	6	19	13	20	35	21	174	225	61	3rd, West Div.	Lost Quarter-Final
1967-68	74	17	13	7	14	19	4	31	32	11	173	179	73	1st, West Div.	Lost Quarter-Final

1999-2000 Player Personnel

FORWARDS	HT	WT	S	Place of Birth	Date	1998-99 Club
ALBERT, Chris	5-11	195	R	Ottawa, Ont.	10/12/72	Cin (AHL)-Mich-Phi (AHL)
ANDERSSON, Mikael	5-11	181	L	Malmo, Sweden	5/10/66	Tampa Bay-Philadelphia
BELANGER, Francis	6-2	216	L	Bellefeuille, Que.	1/15/78	Philadelphia (AHL)
BOULERICE, Jesse	6-1	214	R	Plattsburgh, NY	8/10/78	Philadelphia (AHL)-New Orleans
BRIND'AMOUR, Rod	6-1	202	L	Ottawa, Ont.	8/9/70	Philadelphia
BUREAU, Marc	6-1	198	R	Trois-Rivières, Que.	5/19/66	Philadelphia
CERVEN, Martin	6-4	200	L	Trencin, Czech.	3/7/77	Phi (AHL)-Mohawk Valley
FEDORUK, Todd	6-1	205	L	Redwater, Alta.	2/13/79	Regina-Prince Albert
FEDOTENKO, Ruslan	6-1	191	L	Kiev, USSR	1/18/79	Sioux CIty
GAGNE, Simon	6-0	175	L	Ste. Foy, Que.	2/29/80	Quebec (QMJHL)
GREIG, Mark	5-11	190	R	High River, Alta.	1/25/70	Phi-Phi (AHL)
HEALEY, Paul	6-2	196	R	Edmonton, Alta.	3/20/75	Philadelphia (AHL)
JONES, Keith	6-2	200	L	Brantford, Ont.	11/8/68	Colorado-Philadelphia
LANGKOW, Daymond	5-11	175	L	Edmonton, Alta	9/27/76	T.B.-Clev-Phi
LeCLAIR, John	6-3	226	L	St. Albans, VT	7/5/69	Philadelphia
LINDROS, Eric	6-4	236	R	London, Ont.	2/28/73	Philadelphia
MANELUK, Mike	5-11	188	R	Winnipeg, Man.	10/1/73	Phi-Chi-NYR
McCARTHY, Sandy	6-3	225	R	Toronto, Ont.	6/15/72	Tampa Bay-Philadelphia
McLAREN, Steve	6-0	194	L	Owen Sound, Ont.	2/3/75	Philadelphia (AHL)
MONTGOMERY, Jim	5-10	185	R	Montreal, Que.	6/30/69	Philadelphia (AHL)
O'BRIEN, Sean	6-1	200	L	Belmont, MA	2/9/72	Syracuse-Philadelphia (AHL)
RECCHI, Mark	5-10	185	L	Kamloops, B.C.	2/1/68	Montreal-Philadelphia
RENBERG, Mikael	6-2	218	L	Pitea, Sweden	5/5/72	Tampa Bay-Philadelphia
VOPAT, Roman	6-3	223	L	Litvinov, Czech.	4/21/76	L.A.-Chi-Phi
WESENBERG, Brian	6-3	187	R	Peterborough, Ont.	5/9/77	Phi-Phi (AHL)
WHITE, Peter	5-11	200	L	Montreal, Que.	3/15/69	Phi-Phi (AHL)
ZELEPUKIN, Valeri	6-1	200	L	Voskresensk, USSR	9/17/68	Philadelphia
ZENT, Jason	5-11	204	L	Buffalo, NY	4/15/71	Phi-Phi (AHL)
DEFENSEMEN						
BAST, Ryan	6-2	190	L	Spruce Grove, Alta.	8/27/75	Saint Jn-Phi-Phi (AHL)
BURT, Adam	6-2	207	L	Detroit, MI	1/15/69	Carolina-Philadelphia
CHERNOV, Mikhail	6-2	196	R	Prokopjevsk, USSR	11/11/78	Philadelphia (AHL)
DELMORE, Andy	6-1	192	R	LaSalle, Ont.	12/26/76	Phi-Phi (AHL)
DESJARDINS, Eric	6-1	200	R	Rouyn, Que.	6/14/69	Philadelphia
DYKHUIS, Karl	6-3	214	L	Sept-Iles, Que.	7/8/72	Tampa Bay-Philadelphia
EATON, Mark	6-3	195	L	Wilmington, DE	5/6/77	Philadelphia (AHL)
LANK, Jeff	6-3	205	L	Indian Head, Sask.	3/1/75	Philadelphia (AHL)
McGILLIS, Daniel	6-2	225	L	Hawkesbury, Ont.	7/1/72	Philadelphia
MELANSON, Dean	5-11	211	R	Antigonish, N.S.	11/19/73	Rochester
RICHARDSON, Luke	6-4	210	L	Ottawa, Ont.	3/26/69	Philadelphia
SKROBOT, Sergei	6-3	191	R	Moscow, USSR	3/19/80	Tverskoi HC
THERIEN, Chris	6-5	230	L	Ottawa, Ont.	12/14/71	Philadelphia
TORY, Jeff	5-11	190	R	Burnaby, B.C.	5/9/73	Houston

GOALTENDERS	HT	WT	C	Place of Birth	Date	1998-99 Club
AMIDOVSKI, Bujar	5-11	173	L	Toronto, Ont.	2/19/77	L'siana-Phi (AHL)-Saint Jn
BOUCHER, Brian	6-1	190	L	Woonsocket, RI	1/2/77	Philadelphia (AHL)
LITTLE, Neil	6-1	193	L	Medicine Hat, Alta.	12/18/71	Grand Rapids
PELLETIER, Jean-Marc	6-3	200	L	Atlanta, GA	3/4/78	Phi-Phi (AHL)
VANBIESBROUCK, John	5-8	176	L	Detroit, MI	9/4/63	Philadelphia

President and General Manager

CLARKE, ROBERT EARLE (BOB)
President/General Manager, Philadelphia Flyers.
Born in Flin Flon, Man., August 13, 1949.

Bob Clarke was named president and general manager of the Philadelphia Flyers on June 15, 1994. Clarke's appointment marks the second time he has served as the Flyers' general manager. The Flin Flon native was the Flyers' vice president and general manager from 1984-90. During his eleven years as the team's general manager, the Flyers have won five divisional titles, three conference championships, reached the Stanley Cup semifinals five times and the Finals three times.

Prior to re-joining the Flyers' family in 1994, Clarke served as vice president and general manager of the Florida Panthers. In 1993-94, their first season in the NHL, the Panthers established NHL records for wins (33) and points (83) by an expansion franchise. Clarke also served as the vice president and general manager of the Minnesota North Stars from 1990-92, guiding the team to the Stanley Cup Finals in 1991.

As a player, the former Philadelphia captain led his club to Stanley Cup championships in 1974 and 1975 and captured numerous individual awards, including the Hart Trophy as the League's most valuable player in 1973, 1975 and 1976. The four-time All-Star also received the Bill Masterton Memorial Trophy (perseverance and dedication) in 1972 and the Frank J. Selke Trophy (top defensive forward) in 1983. He appeared in eight All-Star Games and was elected to the Hockey Hall of Fame in 1987. He was awarded the Lester Patrick Trophy in 1979-80 in recognition of his contribution to hockey in the United States. Clarke appeared in 1,144 regular season games, recording 358 goals and 852 assists for 1,210 points. He also added 119 points in 136 playoff games.

General Managers' History

Bud Poile, 1967-68, 1968-69, Bud Poile and Keith Allen, 1969-70; Keith Allen, 1970-71 to 1982-83; Bob McCammon, 1983-84; Bob Clarke, 1984-85 to 1989-90; Russ Farwell, 1990-91 to 1993-94; Bob Clarke, 1994-95 to date.

1998-99 Scoring

* – rookie

Regular Season

Pos	#	Player	Team	GP	G	A	Pts	+/–	PIM	PP	SH	GW	GT	S	%
C	88	Eric Lindros	PHI	71	40	53	93	35	120	10	1	2	3	242	16.5
L	10	John LeClair	PHI	76	43	47	90	36	30	16	0	7	3	246	17.5
C	17	Rod Brind'Amour	PHI	82	24	50	74	3	47	10	0	3	2	191	12.6
R	20	Keith Jones	COL	12	2	2	4	–6	20	1	0	0	0	11	18.2
			PHI	66	18	31	49	29	78	2	0	3	0	124	14.5
			TOTAL	78	20	33	53	23	98	3	0	3	0	135	14.8
R	11	Mark Recchi	MTL	61	12	35	47	–4	28	3	0	2	0	152	7.9
			PHI	10	4	2	6	–3	6	0	0	0	0	19	21.1
			TOTAL	71	16	37	53	–7	34	3	0	2	0	171	9.4
D	37	Eric Desjardins	PHI	68	15	36	51	18	38	6	0	2	0	190	7.9
D	3	Daniel McGillis	PHI	78	8	37	45	16	61	6	0	4	0	164	4.9
R	19	Mikael Renberg	T.B.	20	4	8	12	–2	4	2	0	0	0	42	9.5
			PHI	46	11	15	26	7	14	4	0	2	0	112	9.8
			TOTAL	66	15	23	38	5	18	6	0	2	0	154	9.7
C	18	Daymond Langkow	T.B.	22	4	6	10	0	15	1	0	1	0	40	10.0
			PHI	56	10	13	23	–8	24	3	1	1	0	109	9.2
			TOTAL	78	14	19	33	–8	39	4	1	2	0	149	9.4
D	25	Steve Duchesne	L.A.	60	4	19	23	–6	22	1	0	1	0	99	4.0
			PHI	11	2	5	7	0	2	1	0	1	0	19	10.5
			TOTAL	71	6	24	30	–6	24	2	0	2	0	118	5.1
L	26	Valeri Zelepukin	PHI	74	16	9	25	0	48	0	0	5	0	129	12.4
D	6	Chris Therien	PHI	74	3	15	18	16	48	1	0	0	0	115	2.6
R	8	Jody Hull	PHI	72	3	11	14	–2	12	0	0	1	1	73	4.1
L	21	Sandy McCarthy	T.B.	67	5	7	12	–22	135	1	0	0	0	89	5.6
			PHI	13	0	1	1	–2	25	0	0	0	0	18	0.0
			TOTAL	80	5	8	13	–24	160	1	0	0	0	107	4.7
C	28	Marc Bureau	PHI	71	4	6	10	–2	10	0	0	0	0	52	7.7
D	5	* Dmitri Tertyshny	PHI	62	2	8	10	–1	30	1	0	0	0	68	2.9
L	32	Craig Berube	WSH	66	5	4	9	–7	166	0	0	0	0	45	11.1
			PHI	11	0	0	0	–3	28	0	0	0	0	7	0.0
			TOTAL	77	5	4	9	–10	194	0	0	0	0	52	9.6
D	24	Karl Dykhuis	T.B.	33	2	1	3	–21	18	0	0	0	0	27	7.4
			PHI	45	2	4	6	–2	32	1	0	0	0	61	3.3
			TOTAL	78	4	5	9	–23	50	1	0	0	0	88	4.5
L	14	Mikael Andersson	T.B.	40	2	3	5	–8	4	0	0	0	0	40	5.0
			PHI	7	0	1	1	1	0	0	0	0	0	11	0.0
			TOTAL	47	2	4	6	–7	4	0	0	0	0	51	3.9
D	22	Luke Richardson	PHI	78	0	6	6	–3	106	0	0	0	0	49	0.0
R	9	Mark Greig	PHI	7	1	3	4	1	2	0	0	0	0	9	11.1
D	2	Adam Burt	CAR	51	0	3	3	3	46	0	0	0	0	37	0.0
			PHI	17	0	1	1	1	14	0	0	0	0	24	0.0
			TOTAL	68	0	4	4	4	60	0	0	0	0	61	0.0
L	29	Roman Vopat	L.A.	3	0	0	0	0	6	0	0	0	0	2	0.0
			CHI	3	0	0	0	–4	4	0	0	0	0	0	0.0
			PHI	48	0	3	3	–3	80	0	0	0	0	25	0.0
			TOTAL	54	0	3	3	–7	90	0	0	0	0	27	0.0
G	27	Ron Hextall	PHI	23	0	2	2	0	2	0	0	0	0	0	0.0
D	43	* Andy Delmore	PHI	2	0	1	1	–1	0	0	0	0	0	2	0.0
D	32	* Ryan Bast	PHI	2	0	1	1	0	0	0	0	0	0	1	0.0
G	34	John Vanbiesbrouck	PHI	62	0	1	1	0	12	0	0	0	0	0	0.0
R	54	* Brian Wesenberg	PHI	1	0	0	0	1	5	0	0	0	0	0	0.0
G	49	* Jean-Marc Pelletier	PHI	1	0	0	0	0	0	0	0	0	0	0	0.0
D	25	Chris Joseph	PHI	2	0	0	0	0	2	0	0	0	0	1	0.0
L	21	Dan Kordic	PHI	2	0	0	0	–1	2	0	0	0	0	0	0.0
L	40	Jason Zent	PHI	2	0	0	0	0	0	0	0	0	0	1	0.0
C	14	Peter White	PHI	3	0	0	0	0	0	0	0	0	0	0	0.0
C	15	Richard Park	PHI	7	0	0	0	–1	0	0	0	0	0	5	0.0

Goaltending

No.	Goaltender	GPI	Mins	Avg	W	L	T	EN	SO	GA	SA	S%
34	John Vanbiesbrouck	62	3712	2.18	27	18	15	4	6	135	1380	.902
27	Ron Hextall	23	1235	2.53	10	7	4	0	0	52	464	.888
49	* Jean-Marc Pelletier	1	60	5.00	0	1	0	0	0	5	29	.828
	Totals	**82**	**5025**	**2.34**	**37**	**26**	**19**	**4**	**7**	**196**	**1877**	**.896**

Playoffs

Pos	#	Player	Team	GP	G	A	Pts	+/–	PIM	PP	SH	GW	OT	S	%
D	37	Eric Desjardins	PHI	6	2	2	4	1	4	1	0	1	0	21	9.5
C	17	Rod Brind'Amour	PHI	6	1	3	4	1	0	0	0	0	0	19	5.3
L	10	John LeClair	PHI	6	3	0	3	0	12	2	0	0	0	15	20.0
R	20	Keith Jones	PHI	6	2	1	3	4	14	0	0	0	0	11	18.2
C	28	Marc Bureau	PHI	6	0	2	2	2	2	0	0	0	0	3	0.0
D	25	Steve Duchesne	PHI	6	0	2	2	2	2	0	0	0	0	10	0.0
C	18	Daymond Langkow	PHI	6	0	2	2	3	2	0	0	0	0	4	0.0
R	26	Valeri Zelepukin	PHI	4	1	0	1	1	4	0	0	1	0	5	20.0
D	24	Karl Dykhuis	PHI	5	1	0	1	1	4	0	0	0	0	12	8.3
L	32	Craig Berube	PHI	6	1	0	1	1	4	0	0	0	0	7	14.3
R	9	Mark Greig	PHI	2	0	1	1	1	0	0	0	0	0	3	0.0
L	14	Mikael Andersson	PHI	6	0	1	1	1	2	0	0	0	0	7	0.0
R	11	Mark Recchi	PHI	6	0	1	1	–1	2	0	0	0	0	18	0.0
R	19	Mikael Renberg	PHI	6	0	1	1	–1	0	0	0	0	0	18	0.0
L	21	Sandy McCarthy	PHI	6	0	1	1	1	0	0	0	0	0	7	0.0
D	3	Daniel McGillis	PHI	6	0	1	1	2	12	0	0	0	0	15	0.0
D	5	* Dmitri Tertyshny	PHI	1	0	0	0	0	2	0	0	0	0	1	0.0
D	2	Adam Burt	PHI	6	0	0	0	1	4	0	0	0	0	3	0.0
R	8	Jody Hull	PHI	6	0	0	0	–1	4	0	0	0	0	6	0.0
G	34	John Vanbiesbrouck	PHI	6	0	0	0	0	2	0	0	0	0	0	0.0
D	6	Chris Therien	PHI	6	0	0	0	1	6	0	0	0	0	6	0.0

Goaltending

No.	Goaltender	GPI	Mins	Avg	W	L	EN	SO	GA	SA	S%
34	John Vanbiesbrouck	6	369	1.46	2	4	0	1	9	146	.938
	Totals	**6**	**372**	**1.45**	**2**	**4**	**0**	**1**	**9**	**146**	**.938**

Club Records

Team

(Figures in brackets for season records are games played; records for fewest points, wins, ties, losses, goals, goals against are for 70 or more games)

Most Points	118	1975-76 (80)
Most Wins	53	1984-85 (80), 1985-86 (80)
Most Ties	*24	1969-70 (76)
Most Losses	39	1993-94 (84)
Most Goals	350	1983-84 (80)
Most Goals Against	319	1992-93 (84)
Fewest Points	58	1969-70 (76)
Fewest Wins	17	1969-70 (76)
Fewest Ties	4	1985-86 (80)
Fewest Losses	12	1979-80 (80)
Fewest Goals	173	1967-68 (74)
Fewest Goals Against	164	1973-74 (78)
Longest Winning Streak		
Overall	13	Oct. 19-Nov. 17/85
Home	*20	Jan. 4-Apr. 3/76
Away	8	Dec. 22/82-Jan. 16/83
Longest Undefeated Streak		
Overall	*35	Oct. 14/79-Jan. 6/80 (25 wins, 10 ties)
Home	26	Oct. 11/79-Feb. 3/80 (19 wins, 7 ties)
Away	16	Oct. 20/79-Jan. 6/80 (11 wins, 5 ties)
Longest Losing Streak		
Overall	6	Mar. 25-Apr. 4/70, Dec. 5-Dec. 17/92, Jan. 25-Feb. 5/94
Home	5	Jan. 30-Feb. 15/69
Away	8	Oct. 25-Nov. 26/72
Longest Winless Streak		
Overall	12	Feb. 24-Mar. 16/99 (8 losses, 4 ties)
Home	8	Dec. 19/68-Jan. 18/69 (4 losses, 4 ties)
Away	19	Oct. 23/71-Jan. 27/72 (15 losses, 4 ties)
Most Shutouts, Season	13	1974-75 (80)
Most PIM, Season	2,621	1980-81 (80)
Most Goals, Game	13	Mar. 22/84 (Pit. 4 at Phi. 13), Oct. 18/84 (Van. 2 at Phi. 13)

Individual

Most Seasons	15	Bobby Clarke
Most Games	1,144	Bobby Clarke
Most Goals, Career	420	Bill Barber
Most Assists, Career	852	Bobby Clarke
Most Points, Career	1,210	Bobby Clarke (358G, 852A)
Most PIM, Career	1,683	Rick Tocchet
Most Shutouts, Career	50	Bernie Parent
Longest Consecutive Game Streak	484	Rod Brind'Amour (Feb. 24/93-date)
Most Goals, Season	61	Reggie Leach (1975-76)
Most Assists, Season	89	Bobby Clarke (1974-75, 1975-76)
Most Points, Season	123	Mark Recchi (1992-93; 53G, 70A)
Most PIM, Season	*472	Dave Schultz (1974-75)
Most Points, Defenseman, Season	82	Mark Howe (1985-86; 24G, 58A)
Most Points, Center, Season	119	Bobby Clarke (1975-76; 30G, 89A)
Most Points, Right Wing, Season	123	Mark Recchi (1992-93; 53G, 70A)
Most Points, Left Wing, Season	112	Bill Barber (1975-76; 50G, 62A)
Most Points, Rookie, Season	82	Mikael Renberg (1993-94; 38G, 44A)
Most Shutouts, Season	12	Bernie Parent (1973-74, 1974-75)
Most Goals, Game	4	Fourteen times
Most Assists, Game	6	Eric Lindros (Feb. 26/97)
Most Points, Game	8	Tom Bladon (Dec. 11/77; 4G, 4A)

* NHL Record.

Retired Numbers

1	Bernie Parent	1967-1971, 1973-1979
4	Barry Ashbee	1970-1974
7	Bill Barber	1972-1985
16	Bobby Clarke	1969-1984

Captains' History

Lou Angotti, 1967-68; Ed Van Impe, 1968-69 to 1971-72; Ed Van Impe and Bobby Clarke, 1972-73; Bobby Clarke, 1973-74 to 1978-79; Mel Bridgman, 1979-80, 1980-81; Bill Barber, 1981-82; Bill Barber and Bobby Clarke, 1982-83; Bobby Clarke, 1983-84; Dave Poulin, 1984-85 to 1988-89; Dave Poulin and Ron Sutter, 1989-90; Ron Sutter, 1990-91; Rick Tocchet, 1991-92; no captain, 1992-93; Kevin Dineen, 1993-94; Eric Lindros, 1994-95 to date.

All-time Record vs. Other Clubs

Regular Season

	At Home							On Road							Total						
	GP	W	L	T	GF	GA	PTS	GP	W	L	T	GF	GA	PTS	GP	W	L	T	GF	GA	PTS
Anaheim	5	2	1	2	14	9	6	5	2	2	1	17	18	5	10	4	3	3	31	27	11
Boston	63	28	27	8	211	183	64	66	15	43	8	185	264	38	129	43	70	16	396	447	102
Buffalo	57	32	13	12	204	149	76	53	20	26	7	158	183	47	110	52	39	19	362	332	123
Calgary	48	32	13	3	190	120	67	49	16	24	9	161	200	41	97	48	37	12	351	328	108
Carolina	33	22	8	3	129	87	47	34	17	10	7	136	118	41	67	39	18	10	265	205	88
Chicago	58	31	16	11	188	154	73	57	13	25	19	162	202	45	115	44	41	30	350	356	118
Colorado	31	21	8	2	115	83	44	30	9	10	11	109	112	29	61	30	18	13	224	195	73
Dallas	63	41	9	13	248	144	95	62	23	25	14	206	205	60	125	64	34	27	454	349	155
Detroit	56	32	13	11	226	166	75	55	18	27	10	175	195	46	111	50	40	21	401	361	121
Edmonton	27	19	6	2	122	76	40	26	7	14	5	77	94	19	53	26	20	7	199	170	59
Florida	15	5	6	4	33	37	14	14	10	4	0	48	38	20	29	15	10	4	81	75	34
Los Angeles	60	38	15	7	234	153	83	62	34	20	8	211	184	76	122	72	35	15	445	337	159
Montreal	63	26	23	14	194	190	66	64	19	32	13	198	235	51	127	45	55	27	392	425	117
Nashville	1	1	0	0	8	0	2	1	1	0	0	2	1	2	2	2	0	0	10	1	4
New Jersey	72	46	18	8	293	181	100	70	29	36	5	261	256	63	142	75	54	13	554	437	163
NY Islanders	82	50	23	9	313	241	109	85	24	47	14	243	331	62	167	74	70	23	556	572	171
NY Rangers	96	46	36	14	319	279	106	97	31	43	23	280	319	85	193	77	79	37	599	598	191
Ottawa	13	10	3	0	55	32	20	14	9	4	1	50	36	19	27	19	7	1	105	68	39
Phoenix	27	20	7	0	119	74	40	26	14	10	2	92	80	30	53	34	17	2	211	154	70
Pittsburgh	93	71	15	7	404	235	149	93	33	42	18	301	327	84	186	104	57	25	705	562	233
St. Louis	63	42	11	10	249	143	94	63	31	25	7	199	185	69	126	73	36	17	448	328	163
San Jose	7	4	2	1	25	15	9	8	6	1	1	25	14	13	15	10	3	2	50	29	22
Tampa Bay	15	9	1	5	52	27	23	16	10	5	1	52	44	21	31	19	6	6	104	71	44
Toronto	57	37	12	8	228	134	82	57	24	20	13	194	187	61	114	61	32	21	422	321	143
Vancouver	49	34	14	1	218	144	69	49	27	10	12	198	141	66	98	61	24	13	416	285	135
Washington	73	44	24	5	274	204	93	70	31	26	13	236	234	75	143	75	50	18	510	438	168
Defunct Clubs	34	24	4	6	137	67	54	35	13	14	8	102	89	34	69	37	18	14	239	156	88
Totals	**1261**	**767**	**328**	**166**	**4802**	**3335**	**1700**	**1261**	**486**	**545**	**230**	**4078**	**4292**	**1202**	**2522**	**1253**	**873**	**396**	**8880**	**7627**	**2902**

Playoffs

	Series	W	L	GP	W	L	T	GF	GA	Last Mtg.	Round	Result
Boston	4	2	2	20	9	11	0	57	60	1978	QF	L 1-4
Buffalo	5	4	1	26	17	9	0	83	67	1998	CQF	W 1-4
Calgary	2	1	1	11	7	4	0	43	28	1981	QF	L 3-4
Chicago	1	0	1	4	0	4	0	8	20	1971	QF	L 0-4
Colorado	2	2	0	11	7	4	0	39	29	1985	CF	W 4-2
Dallas	2	2	0	11	8	3	0	41	26	1980	SF	W 4-1
Detroit	1	0	1	4	0	4	0	6	16	1997	F	L 0-4
Edmonton	3	1	2	15	7	8	0	44	49	1987	F	L 3-4
Florida	1	0	1	6	2	4	0	11	15	1996	CSF	L 2-4
Montreal	4	1	3	21	6	15	0	52	72	1989	CF	L 2-4
New Jersey	2	1	1	8	4	4	0	20	23	1995	CF	L 2-4
NY Islanders	4	3	1	25	14	11	0	83	69	1987	DF	W 4-3
NY Rangers	10	6	4	47	27	20	0	157	153	1997	CF	W 4-1
Pittsburgh	2	2	0	12	8	4	0	51	37	1997	CQF	W 4-1
St. Louis	2	0	2	11	3	8	0	20	34	1969	QF	L 0-4
Tampa Bay	1	1	0	6	4	2	0	26	13	1996	CQF	W 4-2
Toronto	4	3	1	23	14	9	0	78	56	1999	CQF	L 2-4
Vancouver	1	1	0	3	2	1	0	15	9	1979	PR	W 2-1
Washington	3	1	2	16	7	9	0	55	65	1989	DSF	W 4-2
Totals	**54**	**31**	**23**	**280**	**147**	**133**	**0**	**889**	**841**			

Calgary totals include Atlanta Flames, 1972-73 to 1979-80. Carolina totals include Hartford, 1979-80 to 1996-97.
Colorado totals include Quebec, 1979-80 to 1994-95. Dallas totals include Minnesota, 1967-68 to 1992-93.
New Jersey totals include Kansas City, 1974-75 to 1975-76, and Colorado Rockies, 1976-77 to 1981-82.
Phoenix totals include Winnipeg, 1979-80 to 1995-96.

Playoff Results 1999-95

Year	Round	Opponent	Result	GF	GA
1999	CQF	Toronto	L 2-4	11	9
1998	CQF	Buffalo	L 1-4	9	18
1997	F	Detroit	L 0-4	6	16
	CF	NY Rangers	W 4-1	20	13
	CSF	Buffalo	W 4-1	21	13
	CQF	Pittsburgh	W 4-1	20	13
1996	CSF	Florida	L 2-4	11	15
	CQF	Tampa Bay	W 4-2	26	13
1995	CF	New Jersey	L 2-4	14	20
	CSF	NY Rangers	W 4-0	18	10
	CQF	Buffalo	W 4-1	18	13

Abbreviations: Round: F – Final; **CF** – conference final; **CSF** – conference semi-final; **CQF** – conference quarter-final; **DF** – division final; **DSF** – division semi-final; **SF** – semi-final; **QF** – quarter-final; **PR** – preliminary round.

1998-99 Results

Oct.	9	at	NY Rangers	1-0		16		Toronto	3-4
	11		Anaheim	4-1		18	at	Ottawa	5-0
	16	at	Tampa Bay	5-2		21		Washington	4-1
	17	at	Carolina	1-1		26		Florida	3-3
	20		San Jose	3-1		28		Phoenix	4-2
	22		New Jersey	2-3		30		Tampa Bay	6-2
	24		NY Rangers	2-2	**Feb.**	1		Los Angeles	4-2
	27		St. Louis	2-1		4		Montreal	5-2
	29	at	Ottawa	1-3		6		Boston	2-2
	31	at	NY Islanders	2-3		10	at	Anaheim	4-5
Nov.	1		Ottawa	4-5		11	at	Los Angeles	3-4
	3	at	Pittsburgh	4-4		14	at	Colorado	4-4
	7		Buffalo	2-2		16	at	Phoenix	4-1
	9	at	Montreal	1-5		18		Montreal	1-3
	12		Florida	1-2		20	at	Ottawa	1-4
	14		New Jersey	6-1		21		Pittsburgh	2-1
	17	at	Pittsburgh	4-1		24	at	Florida	3-5
	20	at	Carolina	3-1		26	at	Tampa Bay	1-4
	22	at	Florida	2-1		28	at	NY Rangers	5-6
	25	at	NY Islanders	2-4	**Mar.**	2	at	Montreal	1-4
	27		Toronto	4-3		4		Ottawa	0-5
	29		Vancouver	6-2		6		NY Islanders	3-3
Dec.	4	at	Buffalo	0-3		7	at	Buffalo	1-1
	5		Washington	2-1		9	at	NY Islanders	2-2
	8	at	New Jersey	5-5		11		Colorado	3-5
	10		New Jersey	4-5		13	at	Pittsburgh	0-4
	12	at	Toronto	3-0		14		Dallas	1-1
	13		Edmonton	2-2		16	at	St. Louis	2-5
	17		Calgary	3-3		21		Detroit	5-4
	19		Chicago	3-1		22	at	Toronto	3-1
	20		Tampa Bay	2-2		27		NY Rangers	3-1
	23	at	Boston	2-1		28	at	Detroit	2-3
	26	at	Chicago	3-2		30		Carolina	3-3
	28	at	San Jose	1-1	**Apr.**	1	at	Nashville	2-1
	29	at	Calgary	4-3		3	at	Boston	0-3
	31	at	Vancouver	6-2		5		NY Rangers	1-5
Jan.	3	at	Edmonton	3-3		8		Pittsburgh	3-1
	7		NY Islanders	5-0		10	at	Washington	2-1
	9		Carolina	2-0		13		Buffalo	2-2
	11		Nashville	8-0		16	at	New Jersey	2-3
	13	at	Washington	3-0		18		Boston	3-1

Entry Draft
Selections 1999-85

1999
Pick
22	Maxime Ouellet
119	Jeff Feniak
160	Konstantin Rudenko
200	Pavel Kasparik
208	Vaclav Pletka
224	David Nystrom

1998
Pick
22	Simon Gagne
42	Jason Beckett
51	Ian Forbes
109	Jean-Philippe Morin
124	Francis Belanger
139	Garrett Prosofsky
168	Antero Niittymaki
175	Cam Ondrik
195	Tomas Divisek
222	Lubomir Pistek
243	Petr Hubacek
253	Bruno St. Jacques
258	Sergei Skrobat

1997
Pick
30	Jean-Marc Pelletier
50	Pat Kavanagh
62	Kris Mallette
103	Mihail Chernov
158	Jordon Flodell
164	Todd Fedoruk
214	Marko Kauppinen
240	Par Styf

1996
Pick
15	Dainius Zubrus
64	Chester Gallant
124	Per-Ragna Bergqvist
133	Jesse Boulerice
187	Roman Malov
213	Jeff Milleker

1995
Pick
22	Brian Boucher
48	Shane Kenny
100	Radovan Somik
132	Dimitri Tertyshny
135	Jamie Sokolsky
152	Martin Spanhel
178	Martin Streit
204	Ruslan Shafikov
230	Jeff Lank

1994
Pick
62	Artem Anisimov
88	Adam Magarrell
101	Sebastien Vallee
140	Alexander Selivanov
166	Colin Forbes
192	Derek Diener
202	Raymond Giroux
218	Johan Hedberg
244	Andre Payette
270	Jan Lipiansky

1993
Pick
36	Janne Niinimaa
71	Vaclav Prospal
77	Milos Holan
114	Vladimir Krechin
140	Mike Crowley
166	Aaron Israel
192	Paul Healey
218	Tripp Tracy
226	E.J. Bradley
244	Jeffrey Staples
270	Kenneth Hemmenway

1992
Pick
7	Ryan Sittler
15	Jason Bowen
31	Denis Metlyuk
103	Vladislav Buljin
127	Roman Zolotov
151	Kirk Daubenspeck
175	Claude Jutras Jr.
199	Jonas Hakansson
223	Chris Herperger
247	Patrice Paquin

1991
Pick
6	Peter Forsberg
50	Yanick Dupre
86	Aris Brimanis
94	Yanick Degrace
116	Clayton Norris
122	Dmitri Yushkevich
138	Andrei Lomakin
182	James Bode
204	Josh Bartell
226	Neil Little
248	John Porco

1990
Pick
4	Mike Ricci
25	Chris Simon
40	Mikael Renberg
42	Terran Sandwith
44	Kimbi Daniels
46	Bill Armstrong
47	Chris Therien
52	Al Kinisky
88	Dan Kordic
109	Viacheslav Butsayev
151	Patrik Englund
172	Toni Porkka
193	Greg Hanson
214	Tommy Soderstrom
235	William Lund

1989
Pick
33	Greg Johnson
34	Patrik Juhlin
72	Reid Simpson
117	Niklas Eriksson
138	John Callahan Jr.
159	Sverre Sears
180	Glen Wisser
201	Al Kummu
222	Matt Brait
243	James Pollio

1988
Pick
14	Claude Boivin
35	Pat Murray
56	Craig Fisher
63	Dominic Roussel
77	Scott Lagrand
98	Edward O'Brien
119	Gordie Frantti
140	Jamie Cooke
161	Johan Salle
182	Brian Arthur
203	Jeff Dandreta
224	Scott Billey
245	Drahomir Kadlec

1987
Pick
20	Darren Rumble
30	Jeff Harding
62	Martin Hostak
83	Tomaz Eriksson
104	Bill Gall
125	Tony Link
146	Mark Strapon
167	Darryl Ingham
188	Bruce McDonald
209	Steve Morrow
230	Darius Rusnak
251	Dale Roehl

1986
Pick
20	Kerry Huffman
23	Jukka Seppo
28	Kent Hawley
83	Mark Bar
125	Steve Scheifele
146	Sami Wahlsten
167	Murray Baron
188	Blaine Rude
209	Shawn Sabol
230	Brett Lawrence
251	Daniel Stephano

1985
Pick
21	Glen Seabrooke
42	Bruce Rendall
48	Darryl Gilmour
63	Shane Whelan
84	Paul Marshall
105	Daril Holmes
126	Ken Alexander
147	Tony Horacek
168	Mike Cusack
189	Gordon Murphy
231	Rod Williams
252	Paul Maurice

Coaching History

Keith Allen, 1967-68, 1968-69; Vic Stasiuk, 1969-70, 1970-71; Fred Shero, 1971-72 to 1977-78; Bob McCammon and Pat Quinn, 1978-79; Pat Quinn, 1979-80, 1980-81; Pat Quinn and Bob McCammon, 1981-82; Bob McCammon, 1982-83, 1983-84; Mike Keenan, 1984-85 to 1987-88; Paul Holmgren, 1988-89 to 1990-91; Paul Holmgren and Bill Dineen, 1991-92; Bill Dineen, 1992-93; Terry Simpson, 1993-94; Terry Murray, 1994-95 to 1996-97; Wayne Cashman and Roger Neilson, 1997-98; Roger Neilson, 1998-99 to date.

Coach

NEILSON, ROGER PAUL
Coach, Philadelphia Flyers. Born in Toronto, Ont., June 16, 1934.

On March 9, 1998, Roger Neilson took over from Wayne Cashman behind the Flyers bench. The Philadelphia job is Neilson's seventh head coaching assignment in the NHL. He had been serving as an assistant coach in St. Louis until he was hired by the Flyers. Neilson guided Philadelphia to a 10-9-2 record over the final 21 games of the 1997-98 season and spent his first full season behind the Flyers' bench in 1998-99.

His previous NHL head coaching jobs have been with the Toronto Maple Leafs, Buffalo Sabres, Vancouver Canucks, Los Angeles Kings, New York Rangers and Florida Panthers. Neilson's Rangers posted the NHL's best record in 1991-92.

Neilson began his coaching career in 1966-67 and spent 10 seasons with the Peterborough Petes.

NHL Coaching Record

Season	Team	Regular Season					Playoffs			
		Games	W	L	T	%	Games	W	L	%
1977-78	Toronto	80	41	29	10	.575	13	6	7	.462
1978-79	Toronto	80	34	33	13	.506	6	2	4	.333
1980-81	Buffalo	80	39	20	21	.619	8	4	4	.500
1981-82	Vancouver	5	4	0	1	.900	17	11	6	.647
1982-83	Vancouver	80	30	35	15	.469	4	1	3	.250
1983-84	Vancouver	48	17	26	5	.406	....	....	....	....
1983-84	Los Angeles	28	8	17	3	.339	....	....	....	....
1989-90	NY Rangers	80	36	31	13	.531	10	5	5	.500
1990-91	NY Rangers	80	36	31	13	.531	6	2	4	.333
1991-92	NY Rangers	80	50	25	5	.656	13	6	7	.462
1992-93	NY Rangers	40	19	17	4	.525	....	....	....	....
1993-94	Florida	84	33	34	17	.494	....	....	....	....
1994-95	Florida	48	20	22	6	.479	....	....	....	....
1997-98	Philadelphia	21	10	9	2	.524	5	1	4	.200
1998-99	Philadelphia	82	37	26	19	.567	6	2	4	.333
	NHL Totals	**916**	**414**	**355**	**147**	**.532**	**88**	**40**	**48**	**.455**

Club Directory

First Union Center
3601 South Broad Street
Philadelphia, PA 19148
Phone 215/465-4500
PR FAX 215/389-9403
www.philadelphiaflyers.com
Capacity: 19,519

Executive Management
Chairman	Ed Snider
Limited Partners	Pat Croce, Jay Snider, Sylvan and Fran Tobin
President and General Manager	Bob Clarke
Chairman of the Board, Emeritus	Joe Scott
Chief Operating Officer	Ron Ryan
Executive Vice President	Keith Allen
Governor	Ed Snider
Alternate Governors	Bob Clarke, Ron Ryan, Phil Weinberg
Executive Assistant	Kathy Nasevich
Receptionist	Carol Poole

Hockey Club Personnel
Head Coach	Roger Neilson
Assistant General Manager	Paul Holmgren
Assistant Coaches	Wayne Cashman, Craig Ramsay
Goaltending Coach	Rejean Lemelin
Skating Coach	David Roy
Video Coach	Rob Cookson
Chief Scout	Dennis Patterson
Scouting Staff	Serge Boudreault, John Chapman, Inge Hammarstrom, Simon Nolet, Chris Pryor, Blair Reid, Vaclav Slansky, Evgeny Zimin
Pro Scout	Al Hill
Assistant to the President	Barry Hanrahan
Computer Analyst	David Gelberg
Executive Assistant	Dianna Taylor
Receptionist	Judy DiCinti

Medical/Training Staff
Team Physicians	Arthur Bartolozzi, M.D., Jeff Hartzell, M.D., Gary Dorshimer, M.D., Mike Weinik, M.D., Guy Lanzi, D.M.D.
Athletic Trainer	John Worley
Strength and Conditioning Instructor	Jim McCrossin
Head Equipment Manager	Jim Evers
Equipment Managers	Rusty Pearl, Anthony Oratorio
Training Center Maintenance	Tim Tocci

Public Relations Department
Director of Public Relations	Zack Hill
Director of Publications	Joe Klueg
Director of Community Relations	Linda Panasci
Director of Youth Hockey and Fan Development	Eric Turner
Director of Fan Services	Joe Kadlec
Assistant Director of Publications	Linda Held
Assistant Director of Youth Hockey and Fan Development	Melissa Wilson
Coordinator, Fan Development	Brian Parks
Public Relations Assistants	Lisa Hanrahan, Jill Lipson
Archivist	Kerrianne Farrelly
Interactive Media Coordinator	Steve Majewski

Sales/Marketing Department
Vice President, Sales	Jack Betson
Vice President, Sales and Marketing	Kathi Gillin
Ticket Manager	Cecilia Baker
Manager, Sales and Services	Nicole Allison
Assistant Manager, Sales and Services	Elyse Moreno
Administration	Debbie Brown
Assistant Ticket Manager	Chelsie Snyder
Ticket Office Assistants	Pat Piazza, Lisa Albertson, Linda DiTommaso

Finance Department
Director of Finance	Dave Jablonski
Controller	Lisa Cataldo
Payroll Accountant	Susann Schaffer
Accounts Payable Manager	Marilyn Trout

Advertising Sales Department
Vice President, Sales	Joe Croce
Executive Assistant	Donna Schroeder
Director, Advertising Sales	Jeffrey Kirk
General Sales Manager	John McGuinness
National Sales Manager	Bill Drolet
Manager, Advertising Services	Joanne Meyers
Senior Account Executive	Joe Watson
Account Executives	Mike Garrity, Robert Kasilowski, Bo Koelle, Ray Lyons, Tom McCarthy, Steve Rex
Sales Associate	Lyndsey Igiel
Manager of Client Services	Megan Bossuyt
Senior Account Coordinator	Thea Crum
Account Coordinators	Kathleen Conway, Rita Kradzinski, Colleen Molloy, Kevin Morley
Sponsorship Manager	Maura Hood

Broadcast Department
TV Play-by-Play, Analyst, Color Commentary	Jim Jackson, Gary Dornhoefer, Steve Coates
Radio Play-by-Play, Color Commentary	Tim Saunders, Brian Propp
Executive Producer/Director of Broadcasting	Bryan Cooper
Associate Producer	Jennifer Culp
Director, Flyers Game Operations	Brian Mantai
Public Address Announcer	Lou Nolan
TV Rightsholders	Comcast SportsNet, UPN-57 WPSG-TV
Radio Rightsholder	SportsRadio 610 WIP (610 AM)

Flyers Wives Charities
Executive Director	Fran Tobin
Director	Rita Johanson
Assistant Director	Diane Smith
Event Coordinators	Laurie Mellon, Susan Wechsler

Phoenix Coyotes

1998-99 Results: 39w-31L-12T 90PTS. Second, Pacific Division

1999-2000 Schedule

Oct.	Sat.	2	at St. Louis	Mon.	10	at NY Islanders
	Tue.	5	Anaheim	Wed.	12	Pittsburgh
	Fri.	8	at Chicago	Sat.	15	Anaheim
	Sun.	10	at NY Rangers*	Mon.	17	at Colorado
	Mon.	11	at Buffalo	Tue.	18	at Nashville
	Thu.	14	Ottawa	Thu.	20	Buffalo
	Sat.	16	Boston	Sun.	23	San Jose
	Fri.	22	at Los Angeles	Tue.	25	at Carolina
	Sat.	23	Washington	Wed.	26	at Atlanta
	Tue.	26	at Edmonton	Fri.	28	at Washington
	Thu.	28	at Vancouver	Mon.	31	Detroit
	Sat.	30	at Colorado*	Feb. Tue.	1	at San Jose
	Sun.	31	at Anaheim	Thu.	3	Dallas
Nov.	Wed.	3	at San Jose	Wed.	9	Los Angeles
	Fri.	5	Dallas	Sat.	12	Calgary
	Wed.	10	Edmonton	Mon.	14	Detroit
	Fri.	12	Vancouver	Fri.	18	at Dallas
	Sun.	14	Los Angeles	Sun.	20	Atlanta
	Tue.	16	Calgary	Tue.	22	at Montreal
	Thu.	18	at Los Angeles	Wed.	23	at Toronto
	Sat.	20	Chicago	Fri.	25	at Calgary
	Thu.	25	New Jersey	Sun.	27	at Vancouver
	Fri.	26	Colorado	Mar. Wed.	1	Carolina
	Sun.	28	at Detroit*	Fri.	3	Dallas
	Tue.	30	at Nashville	Sun.	5	at Chicago*
Dec.	Thu.	2	Tampa Bay	Tue.	7	at St. Louis
	Sat.	4	Anaheim	Thu.	9	NY Islanders
	Mon.	6	at Dallas	Sat.	11	Vancouver
	Wed.	8	Florida	Mon.	13	Philadelphia
	Sat.	11	at Pittsburgh	Wed.	15	St. Louis
	Mon.	13	at Boston	Fri.	17	Nashville
	Thu.	16	at Philadelphia	Tue.	21	Chicago
	Sun.	19	San Jose*	Thu.	23	Colorado
	Tue.	21	St. Louis	Fri.	24	at San Jose
	Wed.	22	at Anaheim	Sun.	26	at Anaheim
	Sun.	26	at Los Angeles	Fri.	31	at Calgary
	Tue.	28	NY Rangers	Apr. Sat.	1	at Edmonton
Jan.	Sat.	1	Edmonton	Mon.	3	Los Angeles
	Tue.	4	at Detroit	Wed.	5	Nashville
	Thu.	6	at Ottawa	Fri.	7	San Jose
	Sat.	8	at New Jersey	Sun.	9	at Dallas*

* Denotes afternoon game.

Franchise date: June 22, 1979
Transferred from Winnipeg to Phoenix,
July 1, 1996

21st NHL Season

PACIFIC DIVISION

Jeremy Roenick's team-leading 72 points last season represented his highest total since three straight 100-point seasons with Chicago between 1991 and 1994. With 90 points in 1998-99, the Coyotes enjoyed the second best regular season in franchise history.

Year-by-Year Record

		Home			Road			Overall						
Season	GP	W	L	T	W	L	T	W	L	T	GF	GA	Pts.	Finished	Playoff Result
1998-99	82	23	13	5	16	18	7	39	31	12	205	197	90	2nd, Pacific Div.	Lost Conf. Quarter-Final
1997-98	82	19	16	6	16	19	6	35	35	12	224	227	82	4th, Central Div.	Lost Conf. Quarter-Final
1996-97	82	15	19	7	23	18	0	38	37	7	240	243	83	3rd, Central Div.	Lost Conf. Quarter-Final
1995-96*	82	22	16	3	14	24	3	36	40	6	275	291	78	5th, Central Div.	Lost Conf. Quarter-Final
1994-95*	48	10	10	4	6	15	3	16	25	7	157	177	39	6th, Central Div.	Out of Playoffs
1993-94*	84	15	23	4	9	28	5	24	51	9	245	344	57	6th, Central Div.	Out of Playoffs
1992-93*	84	23	16	3	17	21	4	40	37	7	322	320	87	4th, Smythe Div.	Lost Div. Semi-Final
1991-92*	80	20	14	6	13	18	9	33	32	15	251	244	81	4th, Smythe Div.	Lost Div. Semi-Final
1990-91*	80	17	18	5	9	25	6	26	43	11	260	288	63	5th, Smythe Div.	Out of Playoffs
1989-90*	80	22	13	5	15	19	6	37	32	11	298	290	85	3rd, Smythe Div.	Lost Div. Semi-Final
1988-89*	80	17	18	5	9	24	7	26	42	12	300	355	64	5th, Smythe Div.	Out of Playoffs
1987-88*	80	20	14	6	13	22	5	33	36	11	292	310	77	3rd, Smythe Div.	Lost Div. Semi-Final
1986-87*	80	25	12	3	15	20	5	40	32	8	279	271	88	3rd, Smythe Div.	Lost Div. Final
1985-86*	80	18	19	3	8	28	4	26	47	7	295	372	59	3rd, Smythe Div.	Lost Div. Semi-Final
1984-85*	80	21	13	6	22	14	4	43	27	10	358	332	96	2nd, Smythe Div.	Lost Div. Final
1983-84*	80	17	15	8	14	23	3	31	38	11	340	374	73	4th, Smythe Div.	Lost Div. Semi-Final
1982-83*	80	22	16	2	11	23	6	33	39	8	311	333	74	4th, Smythe Div.	Lost Div. Semi-Final
1981-82*	80	18	13	9	15	20	5	33	33	14	319	332	80	2nd, Norris Div.	Lost Div. Semi-Final
1980-81*	80	7	25	8	2	32	6	9	57	14	246	400	32	6th, Smythe Div.	Out of Playoffs
1979-80*	80	13	19	8	7	30	3	20	49	11	214	314	51	5th, Smythe Div.	Out of Playoffs

* Winnipeg Jets

1999-2000 Player Personnel

FORWARDS	HT	WT	S	Place of Birth	Date	1998-99 Club
ADAMS, Greg	6-3	195	L	Nelson, B.C.	8/15/63	Phoenix
ALATALO, Mika	6-0	190	L	Oulu, Finland	5/11/71	TPS Turku
BRIERE, Daniel	5-9	185	L	Gatineau, Que.	10/6/77	Phoenix-Las Vegas-Springfield
DeBRUSK, Louie	6-2	230	L	Cambridge, Ont.	3/19/71	Phx-Vegas-Sprfld-Long Beach
DOAN, Shane	6-2	217	R	Halkirk, Alta.	10/10/76	Phoenix
DRAKE, Dallas	6-1	185	L	Trail, B.C.	2/4/69	Phoenix
FRANCZ, Robert	6-1	194	L	Bad Muskau, East Germany	3/30/78	Peterborough-Springfield
GREEN, Travis	6-2	196	R	Castlegar, B.C.	12/20/70	Anaheim
HANSEN, Tavis	6-2	204	R	Prince Albert, Sask.	6/17/75	Phoenix-Springfield
HEALEY, Eric	6-0	195	L	Hull, MA	1/20/75	St. John's-Orlando
KING, Steven	6-0	195	R	Greenwich, RI	7/22/69	Providence (AHL)
LETOWSKI, Trevor	5-10	173	R	Thunder Bay, Ont.	4/5/77	Phoenix-Springfield
MURRAY, Rob	6-1	180	R	Toronto, Ont.	4/4/67	Phoenix-Springfield
OLIVER, David	6-0	190	R	Sechelt, B.C.	4/17/71	Ottawa-Houston
REICHEL, Robert	5-10	185	L	Litvinov, Czech.	6/25/71	NY Islanders-Phoenix
ROENICK, Jeremy	6-0	192	R	Boston, MA	1/17/70	Phoenix
SMITH, Wyatt	5-11	198	L	Thief River Falls, MN	2/13/77	U. of Minnesota
SULLIVAN, Mike	6-2	190	L	Marshfield, MA	2/27/68	Phoenix
TKACHUK, Keith	6-2	220	L	Melrose, MA	3/28/72	Phoenix
TOCCHET, Rick	6-0	210	R	Scarborough, Ont.	4/9/64	Phoenix
TOPOROWSKI, Shayne	6-2	216	R	Paddockwood, Sask.	8/6/75	Worcester
TRUDEL, Jean-Guy	6-0	200	L	Sudbury, Ont.	10/18/75	Kansas City
WANSBOROUGH, Shawn	6-0	200	L	Deseronto, Ont.	6/3/74	Orlando-Long Beach-Las Vegas
YLONEN, Juha	6-1	185	L	Helsinki, Finland	2/13/72	Phoenix
DEFENSEMEN						
ANDREYEV, Alexander	6-4	220	L	Riga, Latvia	9/14/79	Moose Jaw
CARNEY, Keith	6-2	205	L	Providence, RI	2/3/70	Phoenix
CULL, Trent	6-3	210	L	Brampton, Ont.	9/27/73	Houston
CULLEN, David	6-2	209	R	St. Catharines, Ont.	12/30/76	U. of Maine
DAIGNEAULT, J.J.	5-10	192	L	Montreal, Que.	10/12/65	Nashville-Phoenix
FOCHT, Dan	6-6	240	L	Regina, Sask.	12/31/77	Mississippi-Springfield
GAGNON, Sean	6-2	219	L	Sault Ste. Marie, Ont.	9/11/73	Phoenix-Springfield
GILL, Todd	6-0	185	L	Cardinal, Ont.	11/9/65	St. Louis-Detroit
LEROUX, Francois	6-6	235	L	Ste.-Adele, Que.	4/18/70	Grand Rapids
LUMME, Jyrki	6-1	205	L	Tampere, Finland	7/16/66	Phoenix
MARTONE, Mike	6-2	200	R	Sault Ste. Marie, Ont.	9/26/77	Springfield-Mississippi
McCANN, Sean	6-0	193	R	North York, Ont.	9/18/71	Orlando-Springfield
NECKAR, Stanislav	6-1	212	L	Ceske Budejovice, Czech.	12/22/75	Ottawa-NY Rangers-Phoenix
NUMMINEN, Teppo	6-1	195	R	Tampere, Finland	7/3/68	Phoenix
QUINT, Deron	6-2	219	L	Durham, NH	3/12/76	Phoenix
SAFRONOV, Kirill	6-2	196	L	Leningrad, USSR	2/26/81	St. Petersburg
SCHNABEL, Robert	6-6	216	L	Prague, Czech.	11/10/78	Springfield
SUCHY, Radoslav	6-1	185	L	Poprad, Czech.	4/7/76	Springfield
TILEY, Brad	6-1	204	L	Markdale, Ont.	7/5/71	Phoenix-Springfield

GOALTENDERS	HT	WT	C	Place of Birth	Date	1998-99 Club
DAIGLE, Sylvain	5-8	185	R	St-Hyacinthe, Que.	10/20/76	Springfield
ESCHE, Robert	6-1	204	L	Utica, NY	1/22/78	Springfield-Phoenix
KHABIBULIN, Nikolai	6-1	196	L	Sverdlovsk, USSR	1/13/73	Phoenix
SHTALENKOV, Mikhail	6-2	185	L	Moscow, USSR	10/20/65	Edmonton-Phoenix

Coach

FRANCIS, BOB

Coach, Phoenix Coyotes. Born in North Battleford, Sask., December 5, 1958.

The Phoenix Coyotes named Bob Francis as the team's new Head Coach on June 16, 1999. Francis became the 14th Head Coach in franchise history and the third since moving to Phoenix in 1996.

Francis joined the Coyotes after two successful seasons as an assistant coach with the Boston Bruins. The son of former NHL great Emile Francis joined the Bruins as an assistant on June 27, 1997. He had previously spent two seasons in the Boston organization as head coach of the Bruins' AHL affiliate in Providence. Francis led the baby Bruins to a 65-80-15 record in that span.

Francis began his coaching career with the Calgary Flames organization in the 1986-87 season, first as a player/assistant coach with Calgary's IHL affiliate in Salt Lake City. Francis helped guide the Golden Eagles to the IHL championship, winning the Turner Cup that season and successfully defending its title the following year with Francis serving as a full-time assistant coach. In 1989-90, Francis became the Golden Eagles' head coach and held that position for four seasons. The highlight of his coaching career at Salt Lake City was a 50-win season during the 1990-91 campaign. When Calgary moved their development team to Saint John (AHL) in 1993-94, Francis moved as well and served as their head coach before joining Providence.

Before his move to the coaching ranks, Francis played four years of college hockey at the University of New Hampshire (ECAC). He signed as a free agent with Calgary on October 27, 1980 and was traded to the Detroit Red Wings on December 2, 1982. Francis spent most of his professional career at the minor-league level playing in 14 NHL games with Detroit during the 1982-83 season. In his final three seasons with Salt Lake City (IHL), Francis scored 85 goals and added 129 assists for 214 points in 217 games.

Bob and his wife Deborah have two daughters, Kelley and Kristine, and one son, Ryan.

Coaching Record

		Regular Season					Playoffs			
Season	Team	Games	W	L	T	%	Games	W	L	%
1989-90	Salt Lake (IHL)	82	37	36	9	.506	10	5	5	.500
1990-91	Salt Lake (IHL)	83	50	28	5	.633	4	0	4	.000
1991-92	Salt Lake (IHL)	82	33	40	9	.457	5	1	4	.200
1992-93	Salt Lake (IHL)	82	38	39	5	.494	....		....	....
1993-94	Saint John (AHL)	80	37	33	10	.512	7	3	4	.429
1994-95	Saint John (AHL)	80	27	40	13	.419	5	1	4	.200
1995-96	Providence (AHL)	80	30	40	10	.438	4	1	3	.250
1996-97	Providence (AHL)	80	35	40	5	.469	10	4	6	.400

1998-99 Scoring

* – rookie

Regular Season

Pos	#	Player	Team	GP	G	A	Pts	+/–	PIM	PP	SH	GW	GT	S	%
C	97	Jeremy Roenick	PHX	78	24	48	72	7	130	4	0	3	0	203	11.8
C	16	Robert Reichel	NYI	70	19	37	56	–15	50	5	1	1	1	186	10.2
			PHX	13	7	6	13	2	4	3	0	3	0	50	14.0
			TOTAL	83	26	43	69	–13	54	8	1	4	1	236	11.0
L	7	Keith Tkachuk	PHX	68	36	32	68	22	151	11	2	7	1	258	14.0
R	22	Rick Tocchet	PHX	81	26	30	56	5	147	6	1	5	0	178	14.6
L	17	Greg Adams	PHX	75	19	24	43	–1	26	5	0	3	0	176	10.8
D	27	Teppo Numminen	PHX	82	10	30	40	3	30	1	0	0	2	156	6.4
R	11	Dallas Drake	PHX	53	9	22	31	17	65	0	0	3	0	105	8.6
D	20	Jyrki Lumme	PHX	60	7	21	28	5	34	1	0	4	0	121	5.8
D	10	Oleg Tverdovsky	PHX	82	7	18	25	11	32	2	0	2	0	117	6.0
C	36	Juha Ylonen	PHX	59	6	17	23	18	20	2	0	1	0	66	9.1
C	8 *	Daniel Briere	PHX	64	8	14	22	–3	30	2	0	2	0	90	8.9
R	19	Shane Doan	PHX	79	6	16	22	–5	54	0	0	0	0	156	3.8
C	21	Bob Corkum	PHX	77	9	10	19	–9	17	0	0	0	0	146	6.2
C	14	Mike Stapleton	PHX	76	9	9	18	–6	34	0	2	2	0	106	8.5
D	3	Keith Carney	PHX	82	2	14	16	15	62	0	2	0	0	62	3.2
D	5	Deron Quint	PHX	60	5	8	13	–10	20	2	0	0	0	94	5.3
D	33	J.J. Daigneault	NSH	35	2	2	4	–4	38	1	0	1	0	38	5.3
			PHX	35	0	7	7	–8	32	0	0	0	0	27	0.0
			TOTAL	70	2	9	11	–12	70	1	0	1	0	65	3.1
R	16	Brad Isbister	PHX	32	4	4	8	1	46	0	0	2	0	48	8.3
R	15	Jim Cummins	PHX	55	1	7	8	3	190	0	0	0	0	26	3.8
L	26	Mike Sullivan	PHX	63	2	4	6	–11	24	0	1	1	0	66	3.0
C	50 *	Trevor Letowski	PHX	14	2	2	4	1	2	0	0	0	0	8	25.0
R	23	Stephen Leach	OTT	9	0	2	2	–1	6	0	0	0	0	4	0.0
			PHX	22	1	1	2	–6	37	0	0	0	0	23	4.3
			TOTAL	31	1	3	4	–7	43	0	0	0	0	27	3.7
C	47 *	Tavis Hansen	PHX	20	2	1	3	–4	12	0	0	0	0	14	14.3
C	12	Rob Murray	PHX	13	1	2	3	2	4	0	0	0	0	11	9.1
D	24	Stan Neckar	OTT	3	0	2	2	–1	0	0	0	0	0	2	0.0
			NYR	18	0	0	0	–1	8	0	0	0	0	8	0.0
			PHX	11	0	1	1	3	10	0	0	0	0	6	0.0
			TOTAL	32	0	3	3	1	18	0	0	0	0	16	0.0
D	6	Jamie Huscroft	VAN	26	0	1	1	–3	63	0	0	0	0	20	0.0
			PHX	11	0	1	1	–1	27	0	0	0	0	7	0.0
			TOTAL	37	0	2	2	–4	90	0	0	0	0	27	0.0
D	4	Gerald Diduck	PHX	44	0	2	2	9	72	0	0	0	0	39	0.0
D	55 *	Jason Doig	PHX	9	0	1	1	2	10	0	0	0	0	0	0.0
L	44	Andrei Vasilyev	PHX	1	0	0	0	–2	0	0	0	0	0	0	0.0
G	31 *	Scott Langkow	PHX	1	0	0	0	0	0	0	0	0	0	0	0.0
L	49	Joe Dziedzic	PHX	2	0	0	0	–2	0	0	0	0	0	1	0.0
D	48 *	Sean Gagnon	PHX	2	0	0	0	–2	7	0	0	0	0	1	0.0
G	42 *	Robert Esche	PHX	3	0	0	0	0	0	0	0	0	0	0	0.0
R	18	Brian Noonan	PHX	7	0	0	0	–3	0	0	0	0	0	1	0.0
D	39	Brad Tiley	PHX	8	0	0	0	–1	0	0	0	0	0	1	0.0
L	29	Louie Debrusk	PHX	15	0	0	0	–2	34	0	0	0	0	6	0.0
G	28	Jim Waite	PHX	16	0	0	0	0	2	0	0	0	0	0	0.0
G	30	Mikhail Shtalenkov	EDM	34	0	0	0	0	2	0	0	0	0	0	0.0
			PHX	4	0	0	0	0	0	0	0	0	0	0	0.0
			TOTAL	38	0	0	0	0	2	0	0	0	0	0	0.0
G	35	Nikolai Khabibulin	PHX	63	0	0	0	0	8	0	0	0	0	0	0.0

Goaltending

No.	Goaltender	GPI	Mins	Avg	W	L	T	EN	SO	GA	SA	S%
35	Nikolai Khabibulin	63	3657	2.13	32	23	7	6	8	130	1681	.923
30	Mikhail Shtalenkov	4	243	2.22	1	2	1	1	0	9	104	.913
28	Jim Waite	16	898	2.74	6	5	4	0	1	41	390	.895
42	* Robert Esche	3	130	3.23	0	1	0	0	0	7	50	.860
31	* Scott Langkow	1	35	5.14	0	0	0	0	0	3	17	.824
	Totals	**82**	**4985**	**2.37**	**39**	**31**	**12**	**7**	**9**	**197**	**2249**	**.912**

Playoffs

Pos	#	Player	Team	GP	G	A	Pts	+/–	PIM	PP	SH	GW	OT	S	%
R	11	Dallas Drake	PHX	7	4	3	7	3	4	2	0	1	0	18	22.2
R	19	Shane Doan	PHX	7	2	2	4	4	6	0	0	2	1	17	11.8
C	16	Robert Reichel	PHX	7	1	3	4	–2	2	0	0	0	0	16	6.3
L	7	Keith Tkachuk	PHX	7	1	3	4	–4	13	1	0	0	0	22	4.5
D	27	Teppo Numminen	PHX	7	2	1	3	–5	4	2	0	0	0	18	11.1
D	3	Keith Carney	PHX	7	1	2	3	5	10	0	0	0	0	5	20.0
R	22	Rick Tocchet	PHX	7	0	3	3	–3	8	0	0	0	0	14	0.0
L	29	Louie Debrusk	PHX	6	2	0	2	–1	6	0	0	0	0	5	40.0
R	23	Stephen Leach	PHX	7	1	1	2	0	2	0	0	0	0	4	25.0
C	36	Juha Ylonen	PHX	2	0	2	2	2	2	0	0	0	0	2	0.0
R	18	Brian Noonan	PHX	5	0	2	2	2	4	0	0	0	0	10	0.0
D	10	Oleg Tverdovsky	PHX	6	0	2	2	3	6	0	0	0	0	6	0.0
L	17	Greg Adams	PHX	3	1	0	1	1	0	0	0	0	0	9	11.1
C	14	Mike Stapleton	PHX	7	1	0	1	–1	0	0	0	0	0	3	33.3
R	15	Jim Cummins	PHX	3	0	1	1	1	0	0	0	0	0	0	0.0
D	24	Stan Neckar	PHX	6	0	1	1	3	4	0	0	0	0	0	0.0
C	21	Bob Corkum	PHX	7	0	1	1	1	4	0	0	0	0	6	0.0
D	20	Jyrki Lumme	PHX	7	0	1	1	–2	6	0	0	0	0	8	0.0
C	97	Jeremy Roenick	PHX	1	0	0	0	–1	0	0	0	0	0	2	0.0
D	39	Brad Tiley	PHX	1	0	0	0	0	0	0	0	0	0	0	0.0
C	47 *	Tavis Hansen	PHX	2	0	0	0	1	0	0	0	0	0	1	0.0
D	4	Gerald Diduck	PHX	3	0	0	0	–1	2	0	0	0	0	4	0.0
L	26	Mike Sullivan	PHX	5	0	0	0	0	2	0	0	0	0	2	0.0
D	33	J.J. Daigneault	PHX	6	0	0	0	–1	8	0	0	0	0	4	0.0
G	35	Nikolai Khabibulin	PHX	7	0	0	0	0	2	0	0	0	0	0	0.0

Goaltending

No.	Goaltender	GPI	Mins	Avg	W	L	EN	SO	GA	SA	S%
35	Nikolai Khabibulin	7	449	2.41	3	4	1	0	18	236	.924
	Totals	**7**	**453**	**2.52**	**3**	**4**	**1**	**0**	**19**	**237**	**.920**

Club Records

Team

(Figures in brackets for season records are games played; records for fewest points, wins, ties, losses, goals, goals against are for 70 or more games)

Most Points 96   1984-85 (80)
Most Wins 43   1984-85 (80)
Most Ties 15   1991-92 (80)
Most Losses 57   1980-81 (80)
Most Goals................. 358   1984-85 (80)
Most Goals Against....... 400   1984-85 (80)
Fewest Points.............. 32   1980-81 (80)
Fewest Wins............... 9   1980-81 (80)
Fewest Ties.............. 6   1995-96 (82)
Fewest Losses............ 27   1984-85 (80)
Fewest Goals............. 205   1998-99 (82)
Fewest Goals Against....... 197   1998-99 (82)

Longest Winning Streak
Overall.................... 9   Mar. 8-27/85
Home.................. 9   Dec. 27/92-Jan. 23/93
Away 8   Feb. 25-Apr. 6/85

Longest Undefeated Streak
Overall.................... 14   Oct. 25-Nov. 28/98
  (12 wins, 2 ties)
Home.................. 11   Dec. 23/83-Feb. 5/84
  (6 wins, 5 ties),
  Oct. 15-Dec. 20/98
  (10 wins, 1 tie)
Away 9   Feb. 25-Apr. 7/85
  (8 wins, 1 tie)

Longest Losing Streak
Overall 10   Nov. 30-Dec. 20/80,
  Feb. 6-25/94
Home.................... 5   Oct. 29-Nov. 13/93
Away.................... 13   Jan. 26-Apr. 14/94

Longest Winless Streak
Overall .... *30   Oct. 19-Dec. 20/80
  (23 losses, 7 ties)
Home.................... 14   Oct. 19-Dec. 14/80
  (9 losses, 5 ties)
Away.................... 18   Oct. 10-Dec. 20/80
  (16 losses, 2 ties)

Most Shutouts, Season 9   1998-99 (82)
Most PIM, Season........ 2,278   1987-88 (80)
Most Goals, Game 12   Feb. 25/85
  (Wpg. 12 at NYR 5)

Individual

Most Seasons 14   Thomas Steen
Most Games 950   Thomas Steen
Most Goals, Career 379   Dale Hawerchuk
Most Assists, Career........ 553   Thomas Steen
Most Points, Career 929   Dale Hawerchuk
  (379G, 550A)
Most PIM, Career 1,338   Laurie Boschman
Most Shutouts, Career....... 21   Nikolai Khabibulin

Longest Consecutive
Games Streak............. 475   Dale Hawerchuk
  (Dec. 19/82-Dec. 10/88)
Most Goals, Season 76   Teemu Selanne
  (1992-93)
Most Assists, Season 79   Phil Housley
  (1992-93)
Most Points, Season......... 132   Teemu Selanne
  (1992-93; 76G, 56A)
Most PIM, Season........... 347   Tie Domi
  (1993-94)

Most Points, Defenseman,
Season 97   Phil Housley
  (1992-93; 18G, 79A)

Most Points, Center,
Season 130   Dale Hawerchuk
  (1984-85; 53G, 77A)

Most Points, Right Wing,
Season 132   Teemu Selanne
  (1992-93; 76G, 56A)

Most Points, Left Wing,
Season 98   Keith Tkachuk
  (1995-96; 50G, 48A)

Most Points, Rookie,
Season .... *132   Teemu Selanne
  (1992-93; 76G, 56A)

Most Shutouts, Season........ 8   Nikolai Khabibulin
  (1998-99)

Most Goals, Game 5   Willy Lindstrom
  (Mar. 2/82),
  Alexei Zhamnov
  (Apr. 1/95)

Most Assists, Game 5   Dale Hawerchuk
  (Mar. 6/84, Mar. 18/89,
  Mar. 4/90),
  Phil Housley
  (Jan. 18/93)

Most Points, Game 6   Willy Lindstrom
  (Mar. 2/82; 5G, 1A),
  Dale Hawerchuk
  (Dec. 14/83; 3G, 3A,
  Mar. 5/88; 2G, 4A,
  Mar. 18/89; 1G, 5A),
  Thomas Steen
  (Oct. 24/84; 2G, 4A),
  Ed Olczyk
  (Dec. 21/91; 2G, 4A)

* NHL Record.

Coaching History

Tom McVie and Bill Sutherland, 1979-80; Tom McVie, Bill Sutherland and Mike Smith, 1980-81; Tom Watt, 1981-82, 1982-83; Tom Watt and Barry Long, 1983-84; Barry Long, 1984-85; Barry Long and John Ferguson, 1985-86; Dan Maloney, 1986-87, 1987-88; Dan Maloney and Rick Bowness, 1988-89; Bob Murdoch, 1989-90, 1990-91; John Paddock, 1991-92 to 1993-94; John Paddock and Terry Simpson, 1994-95; Terry Simpson, 1995-96; Don Hay, 1996-97; Jim Schoenfeld, 1997-98, 1998-99; Bob Francis, 1999-2000.

Captains' History

Lars-Erik Sjoberg, 1979-80; Morris Lukowich, 1980-81; Dave Christian, 1981-82; Dave Christian and Lucien DeBlois, 1982-83; Lucien DeBlois, 1983-84; Dale Hawerchuk, 1984-85 to 1988-89; Randy Carlyle, Dale Hawerchuk and Thomas Steen (tri-captains), 1989-90; Randy Carlyle and Thomas Steen (co-captains), 1990-91; Troy Murray, 1991-92; Troy Murray and Dean Kennedy, 1992-93; Dean Kennedy and Keith Tkachuk, 1993-94; Keith Tkachuk, 1994-95; Kris King, 1995-96; Keith Tkachuk, 1996-97 to date.

Winnipeg Jets Retired Numbers

9	Bobby Hull	1972-1980
25	Thomas Steen	1981-1995

All-time Record vs. Other Clubs

Regular Season

	GP	W	L	T	GF	GA	PTS	GP	W	L	T	GF	GA	PTS	GP	W	L	T	GF	GA	PTS
			At Home							On Road							Total				
Anaheim	13	6	6	1	45	44	13	13	3	9	1	28	42	7	26	9	15	2	73	86	20
Boston	27	11	14	2	96	99	24	26	4	19	3	83	120	11	53	15	33	5	179	219	35
Buffalo	26	12	12	2	84	87	26	26	2	20	4	62	116	8	52	14	32	6	146	203	34
Calgary	60	28	21	11	236	209	67	61	18	36	7	200	276	43	121	46	57	18	436	485	110
Carolina	28	12	14	2	98	103	26	25	7	12	6	78	97	20	53	19	26	8	176	200	46
Chicago	40	23	13	4	146	127	50	39	10	24	5	111	164	25	79	33	37	9	257	291	75
Colorado	30	11	13	6	112	115	28	31	13	14	4	115	116	30	61	24	27	10	227	231	58
Dallas	40	19	19	2	135	136	40	42	14	23	5	129	166	33	82	33	42	7	264	302	73
Detroit	39	15	13	11	125	125	41	41	15	21	5	143	168	35	80	30	34	16	268	293	76
Edmonton	61	24	33	4	247	277	52	62	19	39	4	210	279	42	123	43	72	8	457	556	94
Florida	6	2	2	2	15	16	6	5	3	2	0	13	17	6	11	5	4	2	28	33	12
Los Angeles	63	31	23	9	262	219	71	60	28	22	10	245	243	66	123	59	45	19	507	462	137
Montreal	26	9	11	6	86	101	24	26	3	22	1	61	133	7	52	12	33	7	147	234	31
Nashville	2	1	1	0	7	7	2	2	1	1	0	5	3	2	4	2	2	0	12	10	4
New Jersey	27	19	5	3	104	72	41	25	10	9	6	78	80	26	52	29	14	9	182	152	67
NY Islanders	26	9	14	3	81	97	21	27	7	13	7	84	108	21	53	16	27	10	165	205	42
NY Rangers	27	11	13	3	95	95	25	26	8	16	2	96	121	18	53	19	29	5	191	216	43
Ottawa	6	2	3	1	24	24	5	8	6	1	1	31	16	13	14	8	4	2	55	40	18
Philadelphia	26	10	14	2	80	92	22	27	7	20	0	74	119	14	53	17	34	2	154	211	36
Pittsburgh	26	10	13	3	95	94	23	27	8	19	0	77	114	16	53	18	32	3	172	208	39
St. Louis	41	20	15	6	137	128	46	40	11	19	10	117	147	32	81	31	34	16	254	275	78
San Jose	21	12	6	3	71	56	27	19	9	8	2	72	67	20	40	21	14	5	143	123	47
Tampa Bay	7	4	3	0	22	16	8	7	4	3	0	25	22	8	14	8	6	0	47	38	16
Toronto	38	20	12	6	157	137	46	39	21	16	2	150	138	44	77	41	28	8	307	275	90
Vancouver	59	29	22	8	227	220	66	62	17	36	9	181	238	43	121	46	58	17	408	458	109
Washington	27	14	7	6	102	97	34	26	6	17	3	74	111	15	53	20	24	9	176	208	49
Totals	**792**	**364**	**322**	**106**	**2889**	**2793**	**834**	**792**	**254**	**441**	**97**	**2542**	**3221**	**605**	**1584**	**618**	**763**	**203**	**5431**	**6014**	**1439**

Playoffs

	Series	W	L	GP	W	L	T	GF	GA	Last Mtg.	Round	Result
Anaheim	1	0	1	7	3	4	0	17	17	1997	CQF	L 3-4
Calgary	3	2	1	13	7	6	0	45	43	1987	DSF	W 4-2
Detroit	2	0	2	12	4	8	0	28	44	1998	CQF	L 2-4
Edmonton	6	0	6	26	4	22	0	75	120	1990	DSF	L 3-4
St. Louis	2	0	2	11	4	7	0	29	39	1999	CQF	L 3-4
Vancouver	2	0	2	13	5	8	0	34	50	1993	DSF	L 2-4
Totals	**16**	**2**	**14**	**82**	**27**	**55**	**0**	**228**	**313**			

Playoff Results 1999-95

Year	Round	Opponent	Result	GF	GA
1999	CQF	St. Louis	L 3-4	16	19
1998	CQF	Detroit	L 2-4	18	24
1997	CQF	Anaheim	L 3-4	17	17
1996	CQF	Detroit	L 2-4	10	20

Abbreviations: Round: CQF – conference quarter-final; **DSF** – division semi-final.

Calgary totals include Atlanta Flames, 1979-80.
Colorado totals include Quebec, 1979-80 to 1994-95.
New Jersey totals include Colorado Rockies, 1979-80 to 1981-82.
Carolina totals include Hartford, 1979-80 to 1996-97.
Dallas totals include Minnesota, 1979-80 to 1992-93.

1998-99 Results

Oct.	11	Ottawa	1-4	21	Anaheim	3-3
	15	Colorado	5-2	26	at Buffalo	1-1
	19	Boston	3-1	28	at Philadelphia	2-4
	22	at Dallas	1-2	29	at NY Islanders	4-4
	25	at Anaheim	2-2	31	at Nashville	5-1
	26	at Colorado	5-1	Feb. 2	Calgary	2-2
	28	at San Jose	4-2	4	San Jose	3-1
Nov.	1	at Los Angeles	3-0	6	Chicago	3-0
	6	Detroit	3-1	8	San Jose	0-3
	10	Colorado	1-1	10	Los Angeles	3-0
	11	at Dallas	2-0	13	at Colorado	4-1
	14	Tampa Bay	4-1	14	Anaheim	1-5
	18	Vancouver	4-2	16	Philadelphia	1-4
	20	San Jose	2-1	19	at Tampa Bay	2-4
	21	Edmonton	3-2	20	at Florida	1-7
	24	Chicago	3-2	22	at Pittsburgh	1-4
	26	New Jersey	3-2	24	at Washington	2-1
	28	at Los Angeles	4-0	26	at NY Rangers	0-3
Dec.	2	at Edmonton	3-4	28	at New Jersey	1-4
	5	at Calgary	3-2	Mar. 2	at Boston	2-3
	6	at Vancouver	3-3	5	Detroit	2-7
	9	Montreal	4-2	7	Nashville	4-3
	12	at Ottawa	2-0	9	at San Jose	2-4
	14	at Montreal	2-2	11	Vancouver	0-3
	16	at Toronto	2-5	13	Anaheim	1-0
	17	at St. Louis	2-3	15	Carolina	5-5
	20	NY Islanders	4-2	17	at Detroit	4-3
	22	at Detroit	6-2	18	at St. Louis	4-2
	23	at Chicago	3-4	21	Los Angeles	4-1
	26	at Los Angeles	2-1	23	Dallas	2-3
	28	Los Angeles	2-4	25	Washington	4-2
	30	NY Rangers	3-1	27	Calgary	2-1
Jan.	1	Dallas	1-2	29	at Vancouver	0-1
	5	Florida	2-2	30	at Edmonton	7-4
	7	Edmonton	1-7	Apr. 1	at Calgary	4-1
	8	at Anaheim	1-4	6	San Jose	0-1
	11	Buffalo	1-0	9	Nashville	3-4
	13	Pittsburgh	5-3	11	at Anaheim	0-3
	15	at Nashville	0-2	14	at Dallas	2-4
	17	at Chicago	1-1	15	St. Louis	4-6
	19	St. Louis	4-2	17	at Dallas	2-0

Entry Draft Selections 1999-85

1999
Pick
15	Scott Kelman
19	Kirill Safronov
53	Brad Ralph
71	Jason Jaspers
116	Ryan Lauzon
123	Preston Mizzi
168	Erik Leverstrom
234	Goran Bezina
262	Alexei Litvinenko

1998
Pick
14	Patrick DesRochers
43	Ossi Vaananen
73	Pat O'Leary
100	Ryan Vanbuskirk
115	Jay Leach
116	Josh Blackburn
129	Robert Schnabel
160	Rickard Wallin
187	Erik Westrum
214	Justin Hanson

1997
Pick
43	Juha Gustafsson
96	Scott McCallum
123	Curtis Suter
151	Robert Francz
207	Alex Andreyev
233	Wyatt Smith

1996
Pick
11	Dan Focht
24	Daniel Briere
62	Per-Anton Lundstrom
119	Richard Lintner
139	Robert Esche
174	Trevor Letowski
200	Nicholas Lent
226	Marc-Etienne Hubert

1995
Pick
7	Shane Doan
32	Marc Chouinard
34	Jason Doig
67	Brad Isbister
84	Justin Kurtz
121	Brian Elder
136	Sylvain Daigle
162	Paul Traynor
188	Jaroslav Obsut
189	Frederik Loven
214	Rob Deciantis

1994
Pick
30	Deron Quint
56	Dorian Anneck
58	Tavis Hansen
82	Steve Cheredaryk
108	Craig Mills
143	Steve Vezina
146	Chris Kibermanis
186	Ramil Saifullin
212	Henrik Smangs
238	Mike Mader
264	Jason Issel

1993
Pick
15	Mats Lindgren
31	Scott Langkow
43	Alexei Budayev
79	Ruslan Batyrshin
93	Ravil Gusmanov
119	Larry Courville
145	Michal Grosek
171	Martin Woods
197	Adrian Murray
217	Vladimir Potapov
223	Ilja Stashenkov
228	Harijs Vitolinsh
285	Russell Hewson

1992
Pick
17	Sergei Bautin
27	Boris Mironov
60	Jeremy Stevenson
84	Mark Visheau
132	Alexander Alexeyev
155	Artur Oktyabrev
156	Andrei Raisky
204	Nikolai Khaibulin
228	Yevgeny Garanin
229	Teemu Numminen
252	Andrei Karpovtsev
254	Ivan Vologzhaninov

1991
Pick
5	Aaron Ward
49	Dmitri Filimonov
91	Juha Ylonen
99	Yan Kaminsky
115	Jeff Sebastian
159	Jeff Ricciardi
181	Sean Gauthier
203	Igor Ulanov
225	Jason Jennings
247	Sergei Sorokin

1990
Pick
19	Keith Tkachuk
35	Mike Muller
74	Roman Meluzin
75	Scott Levins
77	Alexei Zhamnov
98	Craig Martin
119	Daniel Jardemyr
140	John Lilley
161	Henrik Andersson
182	Rauli Raitanen
203	Mika Alatalo
224	Sergei Selyanin
245	Keith Morris

1989
Pick
4	Stu Barnes
25	Dan Ratushny
46	Jason Cirone
62	Kris Draper
64	Mark Brownschidle
69	Alain Roy
109	Dan Bylsma
130	Pekka Peltola
131	Doug Evans
151	Jim Solly
172	Stephane Gauvin
193	Joe Larson
214	Bradley Podiak
235	Evgeny Davydov
240	Sergei Kharin

1988
Pick
10	Teemu Selanne
31	Russell Romaniuk
52	Stephane Beauregard
73	Brian Hunt
94	Anthony Joseph
101	Benoit Lebeau
115	Ronald Jones
127	Markus Akerblom
136	Jukka Marttila
157	Mark Smith
178	Mike Helber
199	Pavel Kostichkin
220	Kevin Heise
241	Kyle Galloway

1987
Pick
16	Bryan Marchment
37	Patrik Erickson
79	Don McLennan
96	Ken Gernander
100	Darrin Amundson
121	Joe Harwell
142	Tod Hartje
163	Markku Kyllonen
184	Jim Fernholz
226	Roger Rougelot
247	Hans Goran Elo

1986
Pick
8	Pat Elynuik
29	Teppo Numminen
50	Esa Palosaari
71	Hannu Jarvenpaa
92	Craig Endean
113	Robertson Bateman
155	Frank Furlan
176	Mark Green
197	John Blue
218	Matt Cote
239	Arto Blomsten

1985
Pick
18	Ryan Stewart
39	Roger Ohman
60	Daniel Berthiaume
81	Fredrik Olausson
102	John Borrell
123	Danton Cole
144	Brent Mowery
165	Tom Draper
186	Nevin Kardum
207	Dave Quigley
228	Chris Norton
249	Anssi Melametsa

General Managers' History

John Ferguson, 1979-80 to 1987-88; John Ferguson and Mike Smith, 1988-89; Mike Smith, 1989-90 to 1992-93; Mike Smith and John Paddock, 1993-94; John Paddock, 1994-95, 1995-96; John Paddock and Bobby Smith, 1996-97; Bobby Smith, 1997-98 to date.

General Manager

SMITH, BOBBY
General Manager, Phoenix Coyotes.
Born in North Sydney, N.S., February 12, 1958.

After 15 outstanding seasons as a National Hockey League player including eight years as the vice president of the NHL Players' Association, Bobby Smith became the Phoenix Coyotes first executive vice president of hockey operations on May 21, 1996.

A product of Ottawa's minor hockey system, in 1978 Smith was named Canadian Major Junior player of the year and was drafted by the Minnesota North Stars first overall in the NHL Entry Draft. A year later, he was named the Calder Trophy winner as the NHL's top rookie after scoring 30 goals and 74 points in his first season. Smith went on to have a remarkable NHL career with Minnesota and Montreal. Smith played in 1,077 games with the North Stars and Canadiens recording (357-679) 1,036 points. He led the North Stars in scoring three of his first four years with the club. His finest season with Minnesota came during the 1981-82 campaign when Smith achieved career highs in games played (80), goals (43), assists (71) and points (114). He was one of three players who played on both of Minnesota's Stanley Cup Finalist teams in 1981 and 1991. Following a trade to Montreal in 1983, Smith played seven seasons with the Canadiens, recording 70-plus points in five of those years. In 1986, he helped guide the Canadiens to a Stanley Cup victory over the Calgary Flames. Smith scored the Stanley Cup game-winning goal in a 4-3 win over Calgary. After 13 playoff seasons and 184 games with Minnesota and Montreal, Smith retired with 64 goals and 96 assists for 160 points, ranking him 12th on the NHL all-time playoff point leaders list. Smith also played in four NHL All-Star Games (1981, 1982, 1989, 1991) during his career.

After retiring from hockey, Smith focused his energy on education and completed two degrees at the Curt Carlson School of Management at the University of Minnesota; a Bachelor of Science (in business) and a Masters of Business Administration.

Bobby and his wife Elizabeth along with their three children Ryan, Megan and Daniel reside in Scottsdale, AZ.

Club Directory

America West Arena
9375 E. Bell Road
Scottsdale, AZ 85260
Phone **480/473-5600**
FAX 480/473-5699
Website:
www.phoenixcoyotes.com
Capacity: 16,210

CEO & Governor	Richard Burke
President & Alternate Governor	Shawn Hunter
General Manager & Alternate Governor	Bobby Smith
President, Coyotes Ice, LLC	Mike O'Hearn
Executive Assistant to the President	Lisa Mardeusz
Executive Assistant, Hockey Operations	Lesa Guth

Hockey Operations
Assistant General Manager	Taylor Burke
Director of Hockey Operations	Laurence Gilman
Director of Player Personnel	Sean Coady
Director of Player Development	Gordie Roberts
Director of Amateur Scouting	Bill Lesuk
Assistant Director of Amateur Scouting	Vaughn Karpan
Professional Scout	Tom Kurvers
Director of Information, Hockey Operations	Igor Kuperman
Head Coach	Bob Francis
Assistant Coaches	Rick Bowness, Wayne Fleming
Goaltending Coach	Benoit Allaire
Strength & Conditioning Coach	Stieg Theander
Amateur Scouts	Terry Doran, Connie Broden, Blair Mackasey, Glen Sonmor, Paul Coady, Pelle Eklund, Evzen Slansky, Boris Yemeljanov
Athletic Therapist	Gord Hart
Equipment Managers	Stan Wilson, Tony DaCosta
Massage Therapist	Jukka Nieminen
Assistant Equipment Manager	Tony Silva
Video Coordinator	Steve Peters
Team Physician	Matt Maddox, D.O.
Team Dentists	Dr. Rick Lawson, Dr. Lawrence Emmott
Springfield Falcons (AHL) Head Coach	Dave Farrish
Springfield Falcons (AHL) Assistant Coach	Ron Wilson

Communications
Vice President of Media & Player Relations	Richard Nairn
Manager of Media Relations	Rick Braunstein
Manager of Publications/Media Relations Coordinator	Merit Tully
Media Relations Interns	Andy Rich, Tobin Ernst

Broadcasting
Vice President of Broadcasting	Mark Hulsey
Broadcasting Manager	Craig Amazeen
TV Play-by-Play	Doug McLeod
TV Color Commentator	Charlie Simmer
Radio Play-by-Play	Curt Keilback
Radio Color Commentator	Jim Johnson

Business Development
Vice President of Business Operations	Joe Levy
Director of Suite Sales	Renee Tauer
Suite Sales Coordinator	Lisa Gonzalez
Website Coordinator	John Mellor

Community Relations
Director of Community Relations/Exec. Dir – Phx. Coyotes Goals For Kids Foundation	Lori Summers
Administrative Assistant	Marcy Fileccia

Corporate Sales & Service
Vice President of Corporate Sales	Tim Weil
Director of Corporate Sales	Matt Stys
Senior Corporate Account Executive	Kelly Staley
Corporate Account Executives	Tara Pisciotta, Jeff Pilcher

Finance & Administration
Chief Financial Officer/VP Administration	Mark Peterson
Controller	Joe Leibfried
Director of Information Technology	Ken Oates
Assistant Controller	Larry Silver
Payroll Administrator	Cheri Sedor

Marketing
Director of Marketing	Tim McBride
Director of Corporate Communications	Jeffrey Hecht
Game Operations Coordinator	Brett Rogers

Ticket Sales & Service
Director of Ticket Operations	Bruce Bielenberg
Group Sales Manager	Brian Tollefson
Season Sales Manager	Jim Willits
Account Executives	John Allen, Kristin Joch, Adam Link, Ann Marie Montaldi, Scott Newhouse, Amy Sun, Brian Wilkinson
Customer Service Representatives	Scott Epp, Skye Bickar
Receptionist	Maryjane DeBiasio
Summer Sales Associates	Matt Cunningham, E.A. McDonough, Jeremy Packer, Amy Robertson, Karen Sabo, Andrew Spence

America West Arena
Executive Director	Justin Maloof
Director of Administration	Mica Berroteran
Director of Facility Operations	Don Moffatt
Coordinator of Facility Operations	Scott Gruber
Director of Amateur Hockey	Keith Blase
Assistant Director of Amateur Hockey	Tim Sanche
Program Administrator	Fred Frank
Director of Programming/Skating	Julie Patterson
Assistant Skating Director	Amanda Gagnon
Manager, Coyotes Ice Sports	Paul Warriner

Team Information
Training Camp	Scottsdale, Arizona
Cable Television Station	FOX SPORTS NET Arizona
Broadcast Television Stations	KTVK (Ch. 3), KASW (WB-61)
Radio Stations	KDKB 93.3 FM, KDUS 1060 AM

Pittsburgh Penguins

1998-99 Results: 38W-30L-14T 90PTS. Third, Atlantic Division

1999-2000 Schedule

Oct.	Fri.	1	at Dallas		Thu.	13	at Colorado
	Thu.	7	at New Jersey		Sat.	15	at Nashville
	Fri.	8	Colorado		Wed.	19	St. Louis
	Thu.	14	at NY Rangers		Sat.	22	at Montreal
	Sat.	16	Chicago		Sun.	23	Philadelphia
	Sat.	23	Carolina		Tue.	25	NY Rangers
	Wed.	27	at Anaheim		Thu.	27	Atlanta
	Thu.	28	at Los Angeles		Sat.	29	Anaheim
	Sat.	30	at San Jose		Mon.	31	at Atlanta
Nov.	Tue.	2	Los Angeles	Feb.	Tue.	1	Washington
	Thu.	4	at Ottawa		Thu.	3	NY Islanders
	Sat.	6	Tampa Bay		Wed.	9	Atlanta
	Wed.	10	Montreal		Fri.	11	Edmonton
	Fri.	12	at Detroit		Sat.	12	at NY Islanders
	Sat.	13	Nashville		Mon.	14	Vancouver
	Tue.	16	Buffalo		Wed.	16	Buffalo
	Thu.	18	at Tampa Bay		Sat.	19	at Florida
	Sat.	20	at Florida		Mon.	21	at Tampa Bay
	Tue.	23	Toronto		Tue.	22	at NY Rangers
	Fri.	26	Ottawa		Thu.	24	at Philadelphia
	Sat.	27	at Carolina		Sat.	26	Boston
	Tue.	30	at Buffalo		Mon.	28	Ottawa
Dec.	Thu.	2	San Jose	Mar.	Wed.	1	at Calgary
	Sat.	4	at Toronto		Sat.	4	at Edmonton
	Tue.	7	at New Jersey		Wed.	8	Montreal
	Thu.	9	Washington		Thu.	9	at Ottawa
	Sat.	11	Phoenix		Sat.	11	NY Rangers
	Tue.	14	Boston		Mon.	13	New Jersey
	Wed.	15	at Carolina		Thu.	16	Florida
	Sat.	18	Florida		Sat.	18	at Boston*
	Mon.	20	at Montreal		Sun.	19	NY Rangers
	Tue.	21	at NY Islanders		Tue.	21	at NY Islanders
	Thu.	23	Tampa Bay		Fri.	24	at Atlanta
	Sun.	26	at Chicago		Sun.	26	at Philadelphia*
	Wed.	29	at Washington		Tue.	28	New Jersey
	Thu.	30	NY Islanders		Thu.	30	at Washington
Jan.	Sun.	2	Detroit	Apr.	Sat.	1	Philadelphia*
	Wed.	5	New Jersey		Mon.	3	Carolina
	Fri.	7	Toronto		Wed.	5	at Toronto
	Sat.	8	at Philadelphia		Fri.	7	at Buffalo
	Wed.	12	at Phoenix		Sun.	9	at Boston

* Denotes afternoon game.

Year-by-Year Record

		Home			Road			Overall						
Season	GP	W	L	T	W	L	T	W	L	T	GF	GA	Pts.	Finished	Playoff Result
1998-99	82	21	10	10	17	20	4	38	30	14	242	225	90	3rd, Atlantic Div.	Lost Conf. Semi-Final
1997-98	82	21	10	10	19	14	8	40	24	18	228	188	98	1st, Northeast Div.	Lost Conf. Quarter-Final
1996-97	82	25	11	5	13	25	3	38	36	8	285	280	84	2nd, Northeast Div.	Lost Conf. Quarter-Final
1995-96	82	32	9	0	17	20	4	49	29	4	362	284	102	1st, Northeast Div.	Lost Conf. Championship
1994-95	48	18	5	1	11	11	2	29	16	3	181	158	61	2nd, Northeast Div.	Lost Conf. Semi-Final
1993-94	84	25	9	8	19	18	5	44	27	13	299	285	101	1st, Northeast Div.	Lost Conf. Quarter-Final
1992-93	84	32	6	4	24	15	3	56	21	7	367	268	119	1st, Patrick Div.	Lost Div. Final
1991-92	**80**	**21**	**13**	**6**	**18**	**19**	**3**	**39**	**32**	**9**	**343**	**308**	**87**	**3rd, Patrick Div.**	**Won Stanley Cup**
1990-91	**80**	**25**	**12**	**3**	**16**	**21**	**3**	**41**	**33**	**6**	**342**	**305**	**88**	**1st, Patrick Div.**	**Won Stanley Cup**
1989-90	80	22	15	3	10	25	5	32	40	8	318	359	72	5th, Patrick Div.	Out of Playoffs
1988-89	80	24	13	3	16	20	4	40	33	7	347	349	87	2nd, Patrick Div.	Lost Div. Final
1987-88	80	22	12	6	14	23	3	36	35	9	319	316	81	6th, Patrick Div.	Out of Playoffs
1986-87	80	19	15	6	11	23	6	30	38	12	297	290	72	5th, Patrick Div.	Out of Playoffs
1985-86	80	20	15	5	14	23	3	34	38	8	313	305	76	5th, Patrick Div.	Out of Playoffs
1984-85	80	17	20	3	7	31	2	24	51	5	276	385	53	6th, Patrick Div.	Out of Playoffs
1983-84	80	7	29	4	9	29	2	16	58	6	254	390	38	6th, Patrick Div.	Out of Playoffs
1982-83	80	14	22	4	4	31	5	18	53	9	257	394	45	6th, Patrick Div.	Out of Playoffs
1981-82	80	21	11	8	10	25	5	31	36	13	310	337	75	4th, Patrick Div.	Lost Div. Semi-Final
1980-81	80	21	16	3	9	21	10	30	37	13	302	345	73	3rd, Norris Div.	Lost Prelim. Round
1979-80	80	20	13	7	10	24	6	30	37	13	251	303	73	3rd, Norris Div.	Lost Prelim. Round
1978-79	80	23	12	5	13	19	8	36	31	13	281	279	85	2nd, Norris Div.	Lost Quarter-Final
1977-78	80	16	15	9	9	22	9	25	37	18	254	321	68	4th, Norris Div.	Out of Playoffs
1976-77	80	22	12	6	12	21	7	34	33	13	240	252	81	3rd, Norris Div.	Lost Prelim. Round
1975-76	80	23	11	6	12	22	6	35	33	12	339	303	82	3rd, Norris Div.	Lost Prelim. Round
1974-75	80	25	5	10	12	23	5	37	28	15	326	289	89	3rd, Norris Div.	Lost Quarter-Final
1973-74	78	15	18	6	13	23	3	28	41	9	242	273	65	5th, West Div.	Out of Playoffs
1972-73	78	24	11	4	8	26	5	32	37	9	257	265	73	5th, West Div.	Out of Playoffs
1971-72	78	18	15	6	8	23	8	26	38	14	220	258	66	4th, West Div.	Lost Quarter-Final
1970-71	78	18	12	9	3	25	11	21	37	20	221	240	62	6th, West Div.	Out of Playoffs
1969-70	76	17	13	8	9	25	4	26	38	12	182	238	64	2nd, West Div.	Lost Semi-Final
1968-69	76	12	20	6	8	25	5	20	45	11	189	252	51	5th, West Div.	Out of Playoffs
1967-68	74	15	12	10	12	22	3	27	34	13	195	216	67	5th, West Div.	Out of Playoffs

Franchise date: June 5, 1967

EASTERN NHL CONFERENCE

ATLANTIC DIVISION

33rd NHL Season

With 35 goals and 48 assists, Martin Straka trailed only NHL leader Jaromir Jagr among Penguins scorers. Straka scored his 35 goals on just 177 shots, giving him a shooting percentage of 19.8, second in the league behind Dmitri Khristich (20.1%).

1999-2000 Player Personnel

FORWARDS	HT	WT	S	Place of Birth	Date	1998-99 Club
BARNABY, Matthew	6-0	188	L	Ottawa, Ont.	5/4/73	Buffalo-Pittsburgh
BROWN, Rob	5-10	177	L	Kingston, Ont.	4/10/68	Pittsburgh
CROZIER, Greg	6-4	200	L	Calgary, Alta.	7/6/76	U. of Michigan
DOME, Robert	6-0	215	L	Skalica, Czech.	1/29/79	Syracuse-Houston
HRDINA, Jan	6-0	197	R	Hradec Kralove, Czech.	2/5/76	Pittsburgh
JAGR, Jaromir	6-2	230	L	Kladno, Czech.	2/15/72	Pittsburgh
KOLKUNOV, Alexei	6-0	201	R	Belgorod, USSR	2/3/77	Syracuse
KOVALEV, Alexei	6-2	215	L	Togliatti, USSR	2/24/73	NY Rangers-Pittsburgh
LANG, Robert	6-2	216	L	Teplice, Czech.	12/19/70	Pittsburgh
MATHIEU, Alexandre	6-2	176	L	Repentigny, Que.	2/12/79	Halifax
MILLER, Kip	5-10	190	L	Lansing, MI	6/11/69	Pittsburgh
MORAN, Ian	6-0	206	R	Cleveland, OH	8/24/72	Pittsburgh
MOROZOV, Aleksey	6-1	198	L	Moscow, USSR	2/16/77	Pittsburgh
MOROZOV, Valentin	5-11	196	L	Moscow, USSR	6/1/75	Syracuse
PROTSENKO, Boris	5-11	197	R	Kiev, USSR	8/21/78	Syracuse
SONNENBERG, Martin	6-0	184	L	Wetaskiwin, Alta.	1/23/78	Pittsburgh-Syracuse
STRAKA, Martin	5-10	175	L	Plzen, Czech.	9/3/72	Pittsburgh
TITOV, German	6-1	201	L	Moscow, USSR	10/16/65	Pittsburgh

DEFENSEMEN						
BUTENSCHON, Sven	6-4	215	L	Itzehoe, West Germany	3/22/76	Pittsburgh-Houston
FERENCE, Andrew	5-10	190	L	Edmonton, Alta.	3/17/79	Portland (WHL)-Kansas City
HATCHER, Kevin	6-3	230	R	Detroit, MI	9/9/66	Pittsburgh
JONSSON, Hans	6-1	183	L	Jarved, Sweden	8/2/73	MoDo Hockey
KASPARAITIS, Darius	5-11	212	L	Elektrenai, USSR	10/16/72	Pittsburgh
KELLEHER, Chris	6-1	210	L	Cambridge, MA	3/23/75	Syracuse
MELICHAR, Josef	6-2	204	L	Budejovice, Czech.	1/20/79	Tri-City
O'CONNOR, Tom	6-2	190	L	Springfield, MA	1/9/76	Syracuse-Wheeling
ROZSIVAL, Michal	6-1	200	R	Vlasim, Czech.	9/3/78	Syracuse
SKRBEK, Pavel	6-3	212	L	Kladno, Czech.	8/9/78	Pittsburgh-Syracuse
SLEGR, Jiri	6-0	207	L	Jihlava, Czech.	5/30/71	Pittsburgh
WERENKA, Brad	6-1	224	L	Two Hills, Alta.	2/12/69	Pittsburgh

GOALTENDERS	HT	WT	C	Place of Birth	Date	1998-99 Club
AUBIN, Jean-Sebastien	5-11	183	R	Montreal, Que.	7/19/77	Pittsburgh-Kansas City
BARRASSO, Tom	6-3	211	R	Boston, MA	3/31/65	Pittsburgh
HILLIER, Craig	6-1	184	L	Cole Harbour, N.S.	2/28/78	Syracuse
SKUDRA, Peter	6-1	185	L	Riga, USSR	4/24/73	Pittsburgh

Coach

CONSTANTINE, KEVIN
Head Coach, Pittsburgh Penguins.
Born in International Falls, MN, December 27, 1958.

Recognized as one of the bright young coaches in the game, Kevin Constantine was named head coach of the Penguins on June 12, 1997.

The former college goaltender now has four-plus seasons of NHL coaching experience on his resume, including 157 games as head coach of the San Jose Sharks from 1993-95. Constantine led the young Sharks to two playoff appearances during his tenure, and oversaw a much-publicized playoff upset of Detroit in 1994.

Constantine played three seasons as a goaltender at Rensselaer Polytechnic Institute (RPI) from 1978-80 and was a ninth-round draft choice of the Montreal Canadiens in 1978. He had a brief tryout with the Canadiens in 1980.

He began to attract notice as a young coach when he led Rochester to the USHL title in 1987-88. He landed his first professional head coaching job at age 32 in 1991-92 and rewarded his bosses by leading Kansas City to the International Hockey League championship. In two seasons with the Blades, Constantine compiled a record of 102-48-14, prompting a promotion to the NHL and San Jose in 1993-94. He was 55-78-24 in two-plus seasons with the Sharks.

Coaching Record

Season	Team	Games	Regular Season W	L	T	%	Games	Playoffs W	L	%
1985-86	North Iowa (USHL)	48	17	31	0	.354	....	....	....	....
1987-88	Rochester (USHL)	48	39	7	2	.833	15	9	4	.692*
1991-92	Kansas City (IHL)	82	56	22	4	.707	15	12	3	.800
1992-93	Kansas City (IHL)	82	46	26	10	.622	12	6	6	.500
1993-94	San Jose (NHL)	84	33	35	16	.488	14	7	7	.500
1994-95	San Jose (NHL)	48	19	25	4	.438	11	4	7	.364
1995-96	San Jose (NHL)	25	3	18	4	.250	....	....	....	....
1997-98	Pittsburgh (NHL)	82	40	24	18	.598	6	2	4	.333
1998-99	Pittsburgh (NHL)	82	38	30	14	.549	13	6	7	.462
	NHL Totals	321	133	132	56	.502	44	19	25	.432

* includes 2 ties.

1998-99 Scoring
* – rookie

Regular Season

Pos	#	Player	Team	GP	G	A	Pts	+/-	PIM	PP	SH	GW	GT	S	%
R	68	Jaromir Jagr	PIT	81	44	83	127	17	66	10	1	7	2	343	12.8
C	82	Martin Straka	PIT	80	35	48	83	12	26	5	4	4	1	177	19.8
L	9	German Titov	PIT	72	11	45	56	18	34	3	1	3	1	113	9.7
R	27	Alexei Kovalev	NYR	14	3	4	7	-6	12	1	0	1	0	35	8.6
			PIT	63	20	26	46	8	37	5	1	4	0	156	12.8
			TOTAL	77	23	30	53	2	49	6	1	5	0	191	12.0
C	20	Robert Lang	PIT	72	21	23	44	-10	24	7	0	3	3	137	15.3
C	37	Kip Miller	PIT	77	19	23	42	1	22	1	0	4	0	125	15.2
C	38 *	Jan Hrdina	PIT	82	13	29	42	-2	40	3	0	2	0	94	13.8
D	4	Kevin Hatcher	PIT	66	11	27	38	11	24	4	2	3	0	131	8.4
R	44	Rob Brown	PIT	58	13	11	24	-15	16	9	0	1	0	78	16.7
D	5	Brad Werenka	PIT	81	6	18	24	17	93	1	0	4	0	77	7.8
D	71	Jiri Slegr	PIT	63	3	21	24	13	86	1	0	0	0	91	3.3
R	36	Matthew Barnaby	BUF	44	4	14	18	-2	143	0	0	0	0	52	7.7
			PIT	18	2	2	4	-10	34	1	0	0	0	27	7.4
			TOTAL	62	6	16	22	-12	177	1	0	3	0	79	7.6
R	95	Alexei Morozov	PIT	67	9	10	19	5	14	0	0	0	0	75	12.0
R	25	Dan Kesa	PIT	67	2	8	10	-9	27	0	0	1	0	33	6.1
D	8	Bobby Dollas	PIT	70	2	8	10	-3	60	0	0	0	0	34	5.9
D	24	Ian Moran	PIT	62	4	5	9	1	37	0	1	0	0	65	6.2
D	47 *	Maxim Galanov	PIT	51	4	3	7	-8	14	2	1	0	0	44	9.1
D	16	Jeff Serowik	PIT	26	0	6	6	-4	16	0	0	0	0	26	0.0
D	11	Darius Kasparaitis	PIT	48	1	4	5	12	70	0	0	0	0	32	3.1
G	35	Tom Barrasso	PIT	43	0	3	3	0	20	0	0	0	0	0	0.0
L	12 *	Martin Sonnenberg	PIT	44	1	1	2	-2	19	0	0	0	0	12	8.3
L	18	Patrick Lebeau	PIT	8	1	1	2	-1	0	1	0	0	0	4	25.0
D	49	Greg Andrusak	PIT	7	0	1	1	4	4	0	0	0	0	2	0.0
D	46	Victor Ignatjev	PIT	11	0	1	1	-3	6	0	0	0	0	5	0.0
C	18 *	Ryan Savoia	PIT	3	0	0	0	-1	0	0	0	0	0	5	0.0
D	46 *	Pavel Skrbek	PIT	4	0	0	0	2	2	0	0	0	0	1	0.0
C	17 *	Brian Bonin	PIT	5	0	0	0	-3	0	0	0	0	0	5	0.0
D	22 *	Sven Butenschon	PIT	17	0	0	0	-7	6	0	0	0	0	8	0.0
G	30 *	J-Sebastien Aubin	PIT	17	0	0	0	0	0	0	0	0	0	0	0.0
D	6	Neil Wilkinson	PIT	24	0	0	0	-2	22	0	0	0	0	11	0.0
G	1 *	Peter Skudra	PIT	37	0	0	0	0	2	0	0	0	0	0	0.0
C	29	Tyler Wright	PIT	61	0	0	0	-2	90	0	0	0	0	16	0.0

Goaltending

No.	Goaltender	GPI	Mins	Avg	W	L	T	EN	SO	GA	SA	S%
30 *	J-Sebastien Aubin	17	756	2.22	4	3	6	0	2	28	304	.908
35	Tom Barrasso	43	2306	2.55	19	16	3	4	4	98	993	.901
1 *	Peter Skudra	37	1914	2.79	15	11	5	6	3	89	822	.892
	Totals	**82**	**5011**	**2.69**	**38**	**30**	**14**	**10**	**9**	**225**	**2129**	**.894**

Playoffs

Pos	#	Player	Team	GP	G	A	Pts	+/-	PIM	PP	SH	GW	OT	S	%
C	82	Martin Straka	PIT	13	6	9	15	0	6	1	0	0	0	27	22.2
R	68	Jaromir Jagr	PIT	9	5	7	12	1	16	1	0	1	1	32	15.6
R	27	Alexei Kovalev	PIT	10	5	7	12	0	14	0	0	1	0	24	20.8
C	37	Kip Miller	PIT	13	2	7	9	-1	19	1	0	0	0	18	11.1
L	9	German Titov	PIT	11	3	5	8	4	4	0	0	0	0	15	20.0
R	44	Rob Brown	PIT	13	2	5	7	-2	8	2	0	0	0	14	14.3
C	38 *	Jan Hrdina	PIT	13	4	1	5	-1	12	1	0	1	0	14	28.6
D	4	Kevin Hatcher	PIT	13	2	3	5	1	4	1	0	0	0	22	9.1
D	71	Jiri Slegr	PIT	13	1	3	4	-1	12	0	0	1	0	17	5.9
R	95	Alexei Morozov	PIT	10	1	1	2	1	0	0	0	0	0	13	7.7
D	5	Brad Werenka	PIT	13	1	1	2	0	6	0	0	0	0	10	10.0
C	20	Robert Lang	PIT	12	0	2	2	-3	0	0	0	0	0	9	0.0
D	24	Ian Moran	PIT	13	0	2	2	-3	6	0	0	0	0	12	0.0
D	49	Greg Andrusak	PIT	13	0	2	2	1	9	0	0	0	0	9	11.1
D	8	Bobby Dollas	PIT	13	0	1	1	-4	6	0	0	0	0	6	16.7
R	25	Dan Kesa	PIT	13	0	1	1	-2	0	0	0	0	0	5	20.0
D	23	Victor Ignatjev	PIT	1	0	0	0	0	0	0	0	0	0	0	0.0
D	47 *	Maxim Galanov	PIT	1	0	0	0	0	0	0	0	0	0	0	0.0
L	28	Todd Hlushko	PIT	2	0	0	0	1	2	0	0	0	0	1	0.0
C	17 *	Brian Bonin	PIT	3	0	0	0	-1	0	0	0	0	0	4	0.0
L	12 *	Martin Sonnenberg	PIT	7	0	0	0	-2	0	0	0	0	0	5	0.0
G	35	Tom Barrasso	PIT	13	0	0	0	0	4	0	0	0	0	0	0.0
C	29	Tyler Wright	PIT	13	0	0	0	0	2	0	0	0	0	3	0.0
R	36	Matthew Barnaby	PIT	13	0	0	0	-2	35	0	0	0	0	10	0.0

Goaltending

No.	Goaltender	GPI	Mins	Avg	W	L	EN	SO	GA	SA	S%
35	Tom Barrasso	13	787	2.67	6	7	1	1	35	350	.900
	Totals	**13**	**793**	**2.72**	**6**	**7**	**1**	**1**	**36**	**351**	**.897**

Club Records

Team

(Figures in brackets for season records are games played; records for fewest points, wins, ties, losses, goals, goals against are for 70 or more games)

Most Points	119	1992-93 (84)
Most Wins	56	1992-93 (84)
Most Ties	20	1970-71 (78)
Most Losses	58	1983-84 (80)
Most Goals	367	1992-93 (84)
Most Goals Against	394	1982-83 (80)
Fewest Points	38	1983-84 (80)
Fewest Wins	16	1983-84 (80)
Fewest Ties	4	1995-96 (82)
Fewest Losses	21	1992-93 (84)
Fewest Goals	182	1969-70 (76)
Fewest Goals Against	188	1997-98 (82)
Longest Winning Streak		
Overall	*17	Mar. 9-Apr. 10/93
Home	11	Jan. 5-Mar. 7/91
Away	7	Mar. 14-Apr. 9/93
Longest Undefeated Streak		
Overall	18	Mar. 9-Apr. 14/93 (17 wins, 1 tie)
Home	20	Nov. 30/74-Feb. 22/75 (12 wins, 8 ties)
Away	8	Mar. 14-Apr. 14/93 (7 wins, 1 tie)
Longest Losing Streak		
Overall	11	Jan. 22-Feb. 10/83
Home	7	Oct. 8-29/83
Away	18	Dec. 23/82-Mar. 4/83
Longest Winless Streak		
Overall	18	Jan. 2-Feb. 10/83 (17 losses, 1 tie)
Home	11	Oct. 8-Nov. 19/83 (9 losses, 2 ties)
Away	18	Oct. 25/70-Jan. 14/71 (11 losses, 7 ties), Dec. 23/82-Mar. 4/83 (18 losses)
Most Shutouts, Season	9	1998-99 (82)
Most PIM, Season	*2,670	1988-89 (80)
Most Goals, Game	12	Mar. 15/75 (Wsh. 1 at Pit. 12), Dec. 26/91 (Tor. 1 at Pit. 12)

Individual

Most Seasons	12	Mario Lemieux
Most Games	753	Jean Pronovost
Most Goals, Career	613	Mario Lemieux
Most Assists, Career	881	Mario Lemieux
Most Points, Career	1,494	Mario Lemieux (613G, 881A)
Most PIM, Career	980	Troy Loney
Most Shutouts, Career	21	Tom Barrasso
Longest Consecutive Games Streak	320	Ron Schock (Oct. 24/73-Apr. 3/77)
Most Goals, Season	85	Mario Lemieux (1988-89)
Most Assists, Season	114	Mario Lemieux (1988-89)
Most Points, Season	199	Mario Lemieux (1988-89; 85G, 114A)
Most PIM, Season	409	Paul Baxter (1981-82)
Most Points, Defenseman, Season	113	Paul Coffey (1988-89; 30G, 83A)
Most Points, Center, Season	199	Mario Lemieux (1988-89; 85G, 114A)
Most Points, Right Wing, Season	*149	Jaromir Jagr (1995-96; 62G, 87A)
Most Points, Left Wing, Season	123	Kevin Stevens (1991-92; 54G, 69A)
Most Points, Rookie, Season	100	Mario Lemieux (1984-85; 43G, 57A)
Most Shutouts, Season	7	Tom Barrasso (1997-98)
Most Goals, Game	5	Mario Lemieux (Three times)
Most Assists, Game	6	Ron Stackhouse (Mar. 8/75), Greg Malone (Nov. 28/79), Mario Lemieux (Three times)
Most Points, Game	8	Mario Lemieux (Oct. 15/88; 3G, 5A, Dec. 31/88; 5G, 3A)

* NHL Record.

Retired Numbers

21	Michel Brière	1969-1970
66	Mario Lemieux	1984-1997

Coaching History

Red Sullivan, 1967-68, 1968-69; Red Kelly, 1969-70 to 1971-72; Red Kelly and Ken Schinkel, 1972-73; Ken Schinkel and Marc Boileau, 1973-74; Marc Boileau, 1974-75; Marc Boileau and Ken Schinkel, 1975-76; Ken Schinkel, 1976-77; John Wilson, 1977-78 to 1979-80; Eddie Johnston, 1980-81 to 1982-83; Lou Angotti, 1983-84; Bob Berry, 1984-85 to 1986-87; Pierre Creamer, 1987-88; Gene Ubriaco, 1988-89; Gene Ubriaco and Craig Patrick, 1989-90; Bob Johnson, 1990-91, 1991-92; Scotty Bowman, 1991-92, 1992-93; Eddie Johnston, 1993-94 to 1995-96; Eddie Johnston and Craig Patrick, 1996-97; Kevin Constantine, 1997-98 to date.

Captains' History

Ab McDonald, 1967-68; no captain, 1968-69 to 1972-73; Ron Schock, 1973-74 to 1976-77; Jean Pronovost, 1977-78; Orest Kindrachuk, 1978-79 to 1980-81; Randy Carlyle, 1981-82 to 1983-84; Mike Bullard, 1984-85, 1985-86; Mike Bullard and Terry Ruskowski, 1986-87; Dan Frawley and Mario Lemieux, 1987-88; Mario Lemieux, 1988-89 to 1993-94; Ron Francis, 1994-95; Mario Lemieux, 1995-96, 1996-97; Ron Francis, 1997-98; Jaromir Jagr, 1998-99 to date.

All-time Record vs. Other Clubs

Regular Season

	At Home							On Road							Total						
	GP	W	L	T	GF	GA	PTS	GP	W	L	T	GF	GA	PTS	GP	W	L	T	GF	GA	PTS
Anaheim	5	3	0	2	21	13	8	5	3	2	0	21	18	6	10	6	2	2	42	31	14
Boston	70	30	27	13	250	255	73	68	13	49	6	198	311	32	138	43	76	19	448	566	105
Buffalo	61	30	16	15	235	198	75	61	13	32	16	163	254	42	122	43	48	31	398	452	117
Calgary	42	22	10	10	159	130	54	42	10	25	7	130	185	27	84	32	35	17	289	315	81
Carolina	36	20	11	5	168	139	45	38	18	17	3	146	147	39	74	38	28	8	314	286	84
Chicago	55	26	23	6	196	182	58	55	8	38	9	147	231	25	110	34	61	15	343	413	83
Colorado	32	15	13	4	135	131	34	29	13	14	2	116	131	28	61	28	27	6	251	262	62
Dallas	60	36	18	6	227	168	78	61	21	34	6	203	231	48	121	57	52	12	430	399	126
Detroit	61	42	15	4	270	180	88	62	12	38	12	169	240	36	123	54	53	16	439	420	124
Edmonton	27	13	12	2	106	120	28	27	5	21	1	91	142	11	54	18	33	3	197	262	39
Florida	13	9	2	2	50	33	20	12	6	6	0	30	33	12	25	15	8	2	80	66	32
Los Angeles	68	38	21	9	252	213	85	66	17	41	8	175	253	42	134	55	62	17	427	466	127
Montreal	72	25	34	13	218	255	63	72	10	54	8	184	347	28	144	35	88	21	402	602	91
Nashville	1	0	0	1	1	1	1	1	1	0	0	3	2	2	2	1	0	1	4	3	3
New Jersey	66	37	25	4	263	228	78	68	23	33	12	232	258	58	134	60	58	16	495	486	136
NY Islanders	75	35	29	11	283	265	81	73	27	38	8	242	297	62	148	62	67	19	525	562	143
NY Rangers	87	34	39	14	313	329	82	88	34	46	8	296	356	76	175	68	85	22	609	685	158
Ottawa	17	13	1	3	71	35	29	17	11	3	3	61	37	25	34	24	4	6	132	72	54
Philadelphia	93	42	33	18	327	301	102	93	15	71	7	235	404	37	186	57	104	25	562	705	139
Phoenix	27	19	8	0	114	77	38	26	13	10	3	94	95	29	53	32	18	3	208	172	67
St. Louis	60	29	19	12	227	181	70	61	15	40	6	165	238	36	121	44	59	18	392	419	106
San Jose	6	3	2	1	32	20	7	8	6	1	1	47	16	13	14	9	3	2	79	36	20
Tampa Bay	13	9	2	2	57	28	20	13	8	4	1	47	38	17	26	17	6	3	104	66	37
Toronto	59	32	21	6	250	189	70	58	20	27	11	193	236	51	117	52	48	17	443	425	121
Vancouver	47	32	8	7	221	164	71	47	22	21	4	178	169	48	94	54	29	11	399	333	119
Washington	73	39	27	7	288	238	85	76	30	39	7	283	324	67	149	69	66	14	571	562	152
Defunct Clubs	35	22	6	7	148	93	51	34	13	10	11	108	101	37	69	35	16	18	256	194	88
Totals	**1261**	**655**	**422**	**184**	**4882**	**4166**	**1494**	**1261**	**387**	**714**	**160**	**3957**	**5094**	**934**	**2522**	**1042**	**1136**	**344**	**8839**	**9260**	**2428**

Playoffs

	Series	W	L	GP	W	L	T	GF	GA	Last Mtg.	Round	Result
Boston	4	2	2	19	10	9	0	67	62	1992	CF	W 4-0
Buffalo	1	1	0	3	2	1	0	9	9	1979	PR	W 2-1
Chicago	2	1	1	8	4	4	0	23	24	1992	F	W 4-0
Dallas	1	1	0	6	4	2	0	28	16	1991	F	W 4-2
Florida	1	0	1	7	3	4	0	15	20	1996	CF	L 3-4
Montreal	1	0	1	6	2	4	0	15	18	1998	CQF	L 2-4
New Jersey	4	3	1	24	13	11	0	77	65	1999	CQF	W 4-3
NY Islanders	3	0	3	19	8	11	0	58	67	1993	DF	L 3-4
NY Rangers	3	3	0	15	12	3	0	65	45	1996	CSF	W 4-1
Philadelphia	2	0	2	12	4	8	0	37	51	1997	CQF	L 1-4
St. Louis	3	1	2	13	6	7	0	40	45	1981	PR	L 2-3
Toronto	3	0	3	12	4	8	0	27	39	1999	CSF	L 2-4
Washington	5	4	1	31	18	13	0	106	103	1996	CQF	W 4-2
Defunct Clubs	1	1	0	4	4	0	0	13	6			
Totals	**34**	**17**	**17**	**179**	**94**	**85**	**0**	**579**	**570**			

Playoff Results 1999-95

Year	Round	Opponent	Result	GF	GA
1999	CSF	Toronto	L 2-4	14	18
	CQF	New Jersey	W 4-3	21	18
1998	CQF	Montreal	L 2-4	15	18
1997	CQF	Philadelphia	L 1-4	13	20
1996	CF	Florida	L 3-4	15	20
	CSF	NY Rangers	W 4-1	21	15
	CQF	Washington	W 4-2	21	17
1995	CSF	New Jersey	L 1-4	8	17
	CQF	Washington	W 4-3	29	26

Abbreviations: Round: F – Final; **CF** – conference final; **CSF** – conference semi-final; **CQF** – conference quarter-final; **DF** – division final; **PR** – preliminary round.

Calgary totals include Atlanta Flames, 1972-73 to 1979-80. Carolina totals include Hartford, 1979-80 to 1996-97.
Colorado totals include Quebec, 1979-80 to 1994-95. Dallas totals include Minnesota, 1967-68 to 1992-93.
New Jersey totals include Kansas City, 1974-75 to 1975-76, and Colorado Rockies, 1976-77 to 1981-82.
Phoenix totals include Winnipeg, 1979-80 to 1995-96.

1998-99 Results

Oct.	10	at	NY Islanders	4-3		26		Carolina	3-5
	14	at	New Jersey	3-1		28		Toronto	6-0
	17		NY Rangers	3-3		30		Boston	5-2
	21	at	Tampa Bay	0-5		31	at	Montreal	5-3
	24		Toronto	4-6	**Feb.**	2		Buffalo	5-3
	26	at	Toronto	2-0		5		Florida	3-0
	28	at	Calgary	5-2		7		Detroit	2-1
	30	at	Vancouver	2-2		9		Montreal	3-2
	31	at	Edmonton	1-4		11		Vancouver	6-5
Nov.	3		Philadelphia	4-4		13	at	Nashville	3-2
	5	at	Ottawa	4-2		15		Washington	7-3
	7		Boston	0-0		17	at	NY Islanders	1-3
	10		NY Islanders	3-2		19	at	NY Rangers	1-6
	13	at	New Jersey	3-4		21	at	Philadelphia	1-2
	14		Florida	4-0		22		Phoenix	4-1
	17		Philadelphia	1-4		25	at	Colorado	3-2
	19	at	Tampa Bay	5-1		26	at	Dallas	4-6
	21		Tampa Bay	5-2		28	at	Washington	3-4
	25	at	Washington	4-5	**Mar.**	3		Montreal	4-4
	27		NY Rangers	2-2		5		Edmonton	2-2
	28	at	Montreal	4-3		7		Colorado	1-3
Dec.	1		Anaheim	4-4		9		New Jersey	2-3
	4	at	Carolina	3-3		10	at	Carolina	3-2
	5	at	Boston	1-2		13		Philadelphia	4-0
	12	at	St. Louis	4-3		16		Dallas	2-2
	15		Tampa Bay	3-2		17	at	Tampa Bay	2-0
	16	at	Florida	1-4		20		Nashville	1-1
	19		Washington	3-0		21	at	NY Rangers	2-2
	21	at	Toronto	1-7		23		Chicago	5-2
	22		Los Angeles	0-3		25	at	New Jersey	3-5
	26		Ottawa	2-1		27		Buffalo	1-1
	30		Florida	7-4		28	at	Buffalo	3-4
Jan.	2	at	Florida	4-2		30		Ottawa	4-6
	5		Calgary	5-1	**Apr.**	1	at	Ottawa	3-3
	7		Carolina	4-2		3		New Jersey	2-4
	9		St. Louis	2-1		5	at	Buffalo	1-3
	13	at	Phoenix	3-5		8	at	Philadelphia	1-3
	15	at	San Jose	2-3		11	at	Detroit	3-0
	16	at	Los Angeles	5-1		15	at	Boston	2-4
	18	at	Anaheim	3-5		17		NY Islanders	2-7
	21		NY Islanders	2-5		18	at	NY Rangers	2-1

Entry Draft
Selections 1999-85

1999
Pick
18	Konstantin Koltsov
51	Matt Murley
57	Jeremy Van Hoof
86	Sebastien Caron
115	Ryan Malone
144	Tomas Skvaridlo
157	Vladimir Malenkykh
176	Doug Meyer
204	Tom Kostopoulos
233	Darcy Robinson
261	Andrew McPherson

1998
Pick
23	Milan Kraft
54	Alexander Zevakhin
80	David Cameron
110	Scott Myers
134	Robert Scuderi
169	Jan Fadmy
196	Joel Scherban
224	Mika Lehto
244	Toby Peterson
254	Matt Hussey

1997
Pick
17	Robert Dome
44	Brian Gaffaney
71	Josef Melichar
97	Alexandre Mathieu
124	Harlan Pratt
152	Petr Havelka
179	Mark Moore
208	Andrew Ference
234	Eric Lind

1996
Pick
23	Craig Hillier
28	Pavel Skrbek
72	Boyd Kane
77	Boris Protsenko
105	Michal Rozsival
150	Peter Bergman
186	Eric Meloche
238	Timo Seikkula

1995
Pick
24	Alexei Morozov
76	J-Sebastien Aubin
102	Oleg Belov
128	Jan Hrdina
154	Alexei Kolkunov
180	Derrick Pyke
206	Sergei Voronov
232	Frank Ivankovic

1994
Pick
24	Chris Wells
50	Richard Park
57	Sven Butenschon
73	Greg Crozier
76	Alexei Krivchenkov
102	Thomas O'Connor
128	Clint Johnson
154	Valentin Morozov
161	Serge Aubin
180	Drew Palmer
206	Boris Zelenko
232	Jason Godbout
258	Mikhail Kazakevich
284	Brian Leitza

1993
Pick
26	Stefan Bergkvist
52	Domenic Pittis
62	Dave Roche
104	Jonas Andersson-Junkka
130	Chris Kelleher
156	Patrick Lalime
182	Sean Selmser
208	Larry McMorran
234	Timothy Harberts
260	Leonid Toropchenko
286	Hans Jonsson

1992
Pick
19	Martin Straka
43	Marc Hussey
67	Travis Thiessen
91	Todd Klassen
115	Philipp De Rouville
139	Artem Kopot
163	Jan Alinc
187	Fran Bussey
211	Brian Bonin
235	Brian Callahan

1991
Pick
16	Markus Naslund
38	Rusty Fitzgerald
60	Shane Peacock
82	Joe Tamminen
104	Robert Melanson
126	Brian Clifford
148	Ed Patterson
170	Peter McLaughlin
192	Jeff Lembke
214	Chris Tok
236	Paul Dyck
258	Pasi Huura

1990
Pick
5	Jaromir Jagr
61	Joe Dziedzic
68	Chris Tamer
89	Brian Farrell
107	Ian Moran
110	Denis Casey
130	Mika Valila
131	Ken Plaquin
145	Pat Neaton
152	Petteri Koskimaki
173	Ladislav Karabin
194	Timothy Fingerhut
215	Michael Thompson
236	Brian Bruininks

1989
Pick
16	Jamie Heward
37	Paul Laus
58	John Brill
79	Todd Nelson
100	Tom Nevers
121	Mike Markovich
126	Mike Needham
142	Patrick Schafhauser
163	Dave Shute
184	Andrew Wolf
205	Greg Hagen
226	Scott Farrell
247	Jason Smart

1988
Pick
4	Darrin Shannon
25	Mark Major
62	Daniel Gauthier
67	Mark Recchi
88	Greg Andrusak
130	Troy Mick
151	Jeff Blaeser
172	Rob Gaudreau
193	Donald Pancoe
214	Cory Laylin
235	Darren Stolk

1987
Pick
5	Chris Joseph
26	Richard Tabaracci
47	Jamie Leach
68	Risto Kurkinen
89	Jeff Waver
110	Shawn McEachern
131	Jim Bodden
152	Jiri Kucera
173	Jack MacDougall
194	Daryn McBride
215	Mark Carlson
236	Ake Lilljebjorn

1986
Pick
4	Zarley Zalapski
25	Dave Capuano
46	Brad Aitken
67	Rob Brown
88	Sandy Smith
109	Jeff Daniels
130	Doug Hobson
151	Steve Rohlik
172	Dave McLlwain
193	Kelly Cain
214	Stan Drulia
235	Rob Wilson

1985
Pick
2	Craig Simpson
23	Lee Giffin
58	Bruce Racine
86	Steve Gotaas
107	Kevin Clemens
114	Stuart Marston
128	Steve Titus
149	Paul Stanton
170	Jim Paek
191	Steve Shaunessy
212	Doug Greschuk
233	Gregory Choules

General Manager

PATRICK, CRAIG
General Manager, Pittsburgh Penguins. Born in Detroit, MI, May 20, 1946.

Known for his calm and patient management style, Patrick has led the Penguins to two Stanley Cup championships, one Presidents' Trophy title and five division championships since taking over as g.m. on Dec. 5, 1989.

Patrick also has served two stints as interim coach of the Penguins, most recently over the final 20 games of the 1996-97 season.

A member of one of hockey's most famous families — including grandfather Lester, father Lynn and uncle Muzz — Patrick played collegiate hockey at the University of Denver and captained the Pioneers to the NCAA championship in 1969. He played eight NHL seasons with four different teams, registering 72 goals and 163 points in 401 games before retiring in 1979. He made the transition to management and coaching when he landed the dual role of assistant coach and assistant g.m. of the 1980 U.S. Olympic Team that won the gold medal at Lake Placid.

Patrick joined the New York Rangers organization as director of operations in 1980 and became the youngest general manager in club history one year later. He served in that capacity through the 1985-86 season, leading his team to the playoffs every year.

Prior to joining the Penguins, Patrick spent two years as director of athletics and recreation at the University of Denver.

NHL Coaching Record

			Regular Season					Playoffs			
Season	Team	Games	W	L	T	%	Games	W	L	%
1980-81	NY Rangers	60	26	23	11	.525	14	7	7	.500
1984-85	NY Rangers	35	11	22	2	.343	3	0	3	.000
1989-90	Pittsburgh	54	22	26	6	.463	....	....	....	....
1996-97	Pittsburgh	20	7	10	3	.425	5	1	4	.200
	NHL Totals	**169**	**66**	**81**	**22**	**.456**	**22**	**8**	**14**	**.364**

Club Directory

Civic Arena
66 Mario Lemieux Place
Pittsburgh, PA 15219
Phone **412/642-1300**
FAX 412/642-1859
Media Relations FAX
412/642-1322
Capacity: 16,958

Administration
Owner and Chairman of the Board	Mario Lemieux
President, CEO and General Manager	Craig Patrick
Executive Vice President and COO	David Andrews
Vice President, General Counsel	Greg Cribbs
Executive Assistant	Elaine Heufelder
Receptionist	Kelly Hart

Hockey Operations
Assistant General Manager	Ed Johnston
Head Coach	Kevin Constantine
Assistant Coaches	Mike Eaves, Don Jackson, Troy Ward
Goaltending Coach and Scout	Gilles Meloche
Head Scout	Greg Malone
Pro Scout	Rick Kehoe
Scouts	Herb Brooks, Charlie Hodge, Mark Kelley
Strength and Conditioning Coach	John Welday
Equipment Manager	Steve Latin
Trainers	Mark Mortland, Scott Johnson
Team Physician	Dr. Charles Burke
Executive Assistant	Tracey Botsford
Assistant Equipment Manager	Paul Flati
Head Coach, Wilkes-Barre/Scranton	Glenn Patrick

Communications
Vice President, Communications	Tom McMillan
Director of Media Relations	Steve Bovino
Assistant Director, Media Relations	Brian Coe
Director of Public Relations	Cindy Himes
Director of Entertainment	Paul Barto
Assistant Director, Entertainment	Mike Wurman
Manager, Community Relations	Renee Petrichevich
Alumni and Community Relations Associate	Joe Mullen
Creative Director	Barb Pilarski
Youth Hockey Coordinator	Mark Shuttleworth

Finance
Vice President, Finance and Administration	Bob Vogel
Controller	Kevin Hart
Accounting Staff	Tawni Love, Troy Ussack, Andrea Winschel

Ticketing
Vice President, Ticketing	Mark Anderson
Director, Premium Seating	Terri Smith
Manager, Premium Services	Michelle Follen
Assistant Manager, Premium Services	Sherry Huggins
Group Sales	Mike Guiffre, Ted Miller, Chuck Pukansky
Box Office Manager	Carol Coulson
Manager, Ticket Operations	Laura Bryer
Senior Ticket Sales Manager	James Santilli
Manager, Inside Ticket Sales	Chad Slencak
Box Office Staff	Kelly Gabany, Daneen Napolitano
Account Executives	Pete Bakarat, Bonnie Golinski, Mike McLaughlin, Joe Traynor, Craig Wheeler
Customer Service Representatives	Kristen Abbott, Lynda Gladding, Jill Weisbrod

Corporate Sales
Vice President, Corporate Sales	David Soltesz
Managers, Corporate Sponsorships	Kimberley Bogesdorfer, Mimi York
Manager, Sales Service	Marie Mays
Assistant Managers, Sales Service	Amy Gillespie, Beth McQuiston

General Information
TV Station	Fox Sports Net Pittsburgh
TV Announcers	Mike Lange, TBA
Flagship Radio Station	TBA
Radio Announcers	TBA
Minor League Affiliates	Wilkes-Barre/Scranton (AHL) Wheeling (ECHL)

General Managers' History

Jack Riley, 1967-68 to 1969-70; Red Kelly, 1970-71; Red Kelly and Jack Riley, 1971-72; Jack Riley, 1972-73; Jack Riley and Jack Button, 1973-74; Jack Button, 1974-75; Wren Blair, 1975-76; Wren Blair and Baz Bastien, 1976-77; Baz Bastien, 1977-78 to 1982-83; Ed Johnston, 1983-84 to 1987-88; Tony Esposito, 1988-89; Tony Esposito and Craig Patrick, 1989-90; Craig Patrick, 1990-91 to date.

St. Louis Blues

1998-99 Results: 37w-32L-13T 87PTS. Second, Central Division

1999-2000 Schedule

Oct.	Sat.	2	Phoenix		Sat.	8	Vancouver
	Mon.	4	Los Angeles		Tue.	11	at San Jose
	Wed.	6	at Calgary		Thu.	13	at Los Angeles
	Sat.	9	at Edmonton		Fri.	14	at Anaheim
	Wed.	13	at Detroit		Wed.	19	at Pittsburgh
	Sat.	16	Toronto		Fri.	21	at Chicago
	Tue.	19	Calgary		Sat.	22	NY Rangers
	Thu.	21	Edmonton		Wed.	26	at Ottawa
	Sat.	23	New Jersey		Fri.	28	at Dallas
	Wed.	27	at New Jersey		Sat.	29	Colorado
	Sat.	30	Detroit	Feb.	Tue.	1	at Calgary
Nov.	Wed.	3	at Colorado		Thu.	3	at Vancouver
	Fri.	5	at Edmonton		Tue.	8	at Detroit
	Sun.	7	at Vancouver		Thu.	10	Detroit
	Tue.	9	Dallas		Sat.	12	Anaheim
	Fri.	12	Edmonton		Tue.	15	Atlanta
	Sat.	13	at NY Islanders		Fri.	18	at Nashville
	Wed.	17	at Toronto		Mon.	21	at Anaheim
	Thu.	18	Florida		Wed.	23	at San Jose
	Sat.	20	San Jose		Fri.	25	Colorado
	Mon.	22	Nashville		Sun.	27	Chicago*
	Wed.	24	at Detroit		Tue.	29	Philadelphia
	Fri.	26	at Buffalo	Mar.	Thu.	2	at Atlanta
	Sat.	27	Chicago		Sat.	4	at Florida
Dec.	Thu.	2	Nashville		Tue.	7	Phoenix
	Sat.	4	San Jose		Thu.	9	Vancouver
	Sun.	5	at Philadelphia		Sat.	11	Anaheim*
	Tue.	7	Carolina		Sun.	12	at Dallas*
	Fri.	10	at Nashville		Wed.	15	at Phoenix
	Sat.	11	Dallas		Fri.	17	at Los Angeles
	Tue.	14	Calgary		Mon.	20	Washington
	Sat.	18	Boston		Wed.	22	at Carolina
	Tue.	21	at Phoenix		Fri.	24	at Tampa Bay
	Thu.	23	at Nashville		Sun.	26	at Chicago*
	Sun.	26	Nashville		Wed.	29	Toronto
	Mon.	27	at Colorado		Thu.	30	at Boston
	Thu.	30	San Jose	Apr.	Sat.	1	Detroit*
Jan.	Sat.	1	at Washington		Sun.	2	Ottawa*
	Mon.	3	at NY Rangers		Wed.	5	Calgary
	Tue.	4	Los Angeles		Fri.	7	Chicago
	Thu.	6	Montreal		Sun.	9	at Chicago*

* Denotes afternoon game.

Year-by-Year Record

Season	GP	Home W	L	T	Road W	L	T	Overall W	L	T	GF	GA	Pts.	Finished		Playoff Result
1998-99	82	18	17	6	19	15	7	37	32	13	237	209	87	2nd,	Central Div.	Lost Conf. Semi-Final
1997-98	82	26	10	5	19	19	3	45	29	8	256	204	98	3rd,	Central Div.	Lost Conf. Semi-Final
1996-97	82	17	20	4	19	15	7	36	35	11	236	239	83	4th,	Central Div.	Lost Conf. Quarter-Final
1995-96	82	15	17	9	17	17	7	32	34	16	219	248	80	4th,	Central Div.	Lost Conf. Semi-Final
1994-95	48	16	6	2	12	9	3	28	15	5	178	135	61	2nd,	Central Div.	Lost Conf. Quarter-Final
1993-94	84	23	11	8	17	22	3	40	33	11	270	283	91	4th,	Central Div.	Lost Conf. Quarter-Final
1992-93	84	22	13	7	15	23	4	37	36	11	282	278	85	4th,	Norris Div.	Lost Div. Final
1991-92	80	25	12	3	11	21	8	36	33	11	279	266	83	3rd,	Norris Div.	Lost Div. Semi-Final
1990-91	80	24	9	7	23	13	4	47	22	11	310	250	105	2nd,	Norris Div.	Lost Div. Final
1989-90	80	20	15	5	17	19	4	37	34	9	295	279	83	2nd,	Norris Div.	Lost Div. Final
1988-89	80	22	11	7	11	24	5	33	35	12	275	285	78	2nd,	Norris Div.	Lost Div. Final
1987-88	80	18	17	5	16	21	3	34	38	8	278	294	76	2nd,	Norris Div.	Lost Div. Final
1986-87	80	21	12	7	11	21	8	32	33	15	281	293	79	1st,	Norris Div.	Lost Div. Semi-Final
1985-86	80	23	11	6	14	23	3	37	34	9	302	291	83	3rd,	Norris Div.	Lost Conf. Championship
1984-85	80	21	12	7	16	19	5	37	31	12	299	288	86	1st,	Norris Div.	Lost Div. Semi-Final
1983-84	80	23	14	3	9	27	4	32	41	7	293	316	71	2nd,	Norris Div.	Lost Div. Final
1982-83	80	16	16	8	9	24	7	25	40	15	285	316	65	4th,	Norris Div.	Lost Div. Semi-Final
1981-82	80	22	14	4	10	26	4	32	40	8	315	349	72	3rd	Norris Div.	Lost Div. Final
1980-81	80	29	7	4	16	11	13	45	18	17	352	281	107	1st,	Smythe Div.	Lost Quarter-Final
1979-80	80	20	13	7	14	21	5	34	34	12	266	278	80	2nd,	Smythe Div.	Lost Prelim. Round
1978-79	80	14	20	6	4	30	6	18	50	12	249	348	48	3rd,	Smythe Div.	Out of Playoffs
1977-78	80	12	20	8	8	27	5	20	47	13	195	304	53	4th,	Smythe Div.	Out of Playoffs
1976-77	80	22	13	5	10	26	4	32	39	9	239	276	73	1st,	Smythe Div.	Lost Quarter-Final
1975-76	80	20	12	8	9	25	6	29	37	14	249	290	72	3rd,	Smythe Div.	Lost Prelim. Round
1974-75	80	23	13	4	12	18	10	35	31	14	269	267	84	2nd,	Smythe Div.	Lost Prelim. Round
1973-74	78	16	16	7	10	24	5	26	40	12	206	248	64	6th,	West Div.	Out of Playoffs
1972-73	78	21	11	7	11	23	5	32	34	12	233	251	76	4th,	West Div.	Lost Quarter-Final
1971-72	78	17	17	5	11	22	6	28	39	11	208	247	67	3rd,	West Div.	Lost Semi-Final
1970-71	78	23	7	9	11	18	10	34	25	19	223	208	87	2nd,	West Div.	Lost Quarter-Final
1969-70	76	24	9	5	13	18	7	37	27	12	224	179	86	1st,	West Div.	Lost Final
1968-69	76	21	8	9	16	17	5	37	25	14	204	157	88	1st,	West Div.	Lost Final
1967-68	74	18	12	7	9	19	9	27	31	16	177	191	70	3rd,	West Div.	Lost Final

Franchise date: June 5, 1967

WESTERN
NHL
CONFERENCE

**CENTRAL
DIVISION**

**33rd
NHL
Season**

Not only did Pavol Demitra lead the Blues in most offensive categories in 1998-99, his 89 points saw him crack the top 10 in the NHL in scoring. His 37 goals ranked 14th overall.

1999-2000 Player Personnel

FORWARDS	HT	WT	S	Place of Birth	Date	1998-99 Club
BARTECKO, Lubos	6-1	200	L	Kezmarok, Czech.	7/14/76	SKP Poprad-St. Louis-Worcester
BLOUIN, Sylvain	6-2	207	L	Montreal, Que.	5/21/74	Montreal-Fredericton
CAMPBELL, Jim	6-2	205	R	Worcester, MA	4/3/73	St. Louis
CHASE, Kelly	5-11	201	R	Porcupine Plain, Sask.	10/25/67	St. Louis
CONROY, Craig	6-2	198	R	Potsdam, NY	9/4/71	St. Louis
CORSO, Daniel	5-10	183	L	Montreal, Que.	4/3/78	Worcester
COURTNALL, Geoff	6-1	204	L	Duncan, B.C.	8/18/62	St. Louis
DEMITRA, Pavol	6-0	196	L	Dubnica, Czech.	11/29/74	St. Louis
EASTWOOD, Mike	6-3	209	R	Ottawa, Ont.	7/1/67	St. Louis
HANDZUS, Michal	6-5	210	L	Banska Bystrica, Czech.	3/11/77	St. Louis
HECHT, Jochen	6-3	196	L	Mannheim, West Germany	6/21/77	St. Louis-Worcester
LOW, Reed	6-5	220	R	Moose Jaw, Sask.	6/21/76	Worcester
MAYERS, Jamal	6-1	212	R	Toronto, Ont.	10/24/74	St. Louis-Worcester
NAGY, Ladislav	5-11	183	L	Saca, Czech.	6/1/79	Halifax-Worcester
NASH, Tyson	6-0	185	L	Edmonton, Alta.	3/11/75	St. Louis-Worcester
PELLERIN, Scott	5-11	189	L	Shediac, N.B.	1/9/70	St. Louis
POESCHEK, Rudy	6-2	218	R	Kamloops, B.C.	9/29/66	St. Louis
REASONER, Marty	6-1	203	L	Rochester, NY	2/26/77	St. Louis-Worcester
RHEAUME, Pascal	6-1	209	L	Quebec, Que.	6/21/73	St. Louis
ROY, Stephane	5-11	191	L	Ste-Martine, Que.	1/26/76	Worcester
TURGEON, Pierre	6-1	195	L	Rouyn, Que.	8/28/69	St. Louis
YOUNG, Scott	6-1	200	R	Clinton, MA	10/1/67	St. Louis
DEFENSEMEN						
BERGEVIN, Marc	6-1	214	L	Montreal, Que.	8/11/65	St. Louis
DIENER, Derek	6-5	200	L	Burnaby, B.C.	7/13/76	Worcester
FINLEY, Jeff	6-2	205	L	Edmonton, Alta.	4/14/67	NY Rangers-Hartford-St. Louis
FITZPATRICK, Rory	6-2	208	R	Rochester, NY	1/11/75	St. Louis-Worcester
HARLTON, Tyler	6-2	212	L	Pense, Sask.	1/11/76	Worcester-Peoria
HELMER, Bryan	6-1	200	R	Sault Ste. Marie, Ont.	7/15/72	Phx-Vegas-StL-Wor
HORACEK, Jan	6-4	206	R	Benesov, Czech.	5/22/79	Slavia Praha-Worcester
MacINNIS, Al	6-2	209	R	Inverness, N.S.	7/11/63	St. Louis
McALPINE, Chris	6-0	210	R	Roseville, MN	12/1/71	St. Louis
PERSSON, Ricard	6-2	205	L	Ostersund, Sweden	8/24/69	St. Louis-Worcester
PROCHAZKA, Libor	6-0	185	R	Vlasim, Czech.	4/25/74	HC Trinec
PRONGER, Chris	6-6	220	L	Dryden, Ont.	10/10/74	St. Louis
RIVERS, Jamie	6-0	190	L	Ottawa, Ont.	3/16/75	St. Louis
SALVADOR, Bryce	6-2	194	L	Brandon, Man.	2/11/76	Worcester
SMITH, Matt	6-6	215	R	Kent, England	12/23/76	Peoria-Worcester

GOALTENDERS	HT	WT	C	Place of Birth	Date	1998-99 Club
JOHNSON, Brent	6-2	200	L	Farmington, MI	3/12/77	St. Louis-Worcester
McLENNAN, Jamie	6-0	190	L	Edmonton, Alta.	6/30/71	St. Louis
PARENT, Rich	6-3	195	L	Montreal, Que.	1/12/73	St. Louis-Worcester
RUDKOWSKY, Cody	6-1	200	L	Willingdon, Alta.	7/21/78	Seattle
TUREK, Roman	6-3	190	R	Pisek, Czech.	5/21/70	Dallas

Coaching History

Lynn Patrick and Scotty Bowman, 1967-68; Scotty Bowman, 1968-69, 1969-70; Al Arbour and Scotty Bowman, 1970-71; Sid Abel, Bill McCreary and Al Arbour, 1971-72; Al Arbour and Jean-Guy Talbot, 1972-73; Jean-Guy Talbot and Lou Angotti, 1973-74; Lou Angotti, Lynn Patrick and Garry Young, 1974-75; Garry Young, Lynn Patrick and Leo Boivin, 1975-76; Emile Francis, 1976-77; Leo Boivin and Barclay Plager, 1977-78; Barclay Plager, 1978-79; Barclay Plager and Red Berenson, 1979-80; Red Berenson, 1980-81; Red Berenson and Emile Francis, 1981-82; Emile Francis and Barclay Plager, 1982-83; Jacques Demers, 1983-84 to 1985-86; Jacques Martin, 1986-87, 1987-88; Brian Sutter, 1988-89 to 1991-92; Bob Plager and Bob Berry, 1992-93; Bob Berry, 1993-94; Mike Keenan, 1994-95, 1995-96; Mike Keenan, Jim Roberts and Joel Quenneville, 1996-97; Joel Quenneville, 1997-98 to date.

Coach

QUENNEVILLE, JOEL
Head Coach, St. Louis Blues.
Born in Windsor, Ont., September 15, 1958.

Joel Quenneville was named head coach on January 6, 1997, becoming the 19th head coach in Blues history. His first game in St. Louis was on January 7, 1997. In his first full season behind the bench in 1997-98, coach "Q" guided the Blues to the league's fourth-best record (45-29-8) and to the second round of the Stanley Cup Playoffs.

Prior to joining the Blues the former NHL defenseman spent three seasons with the Colorado Avalanche organization as an assistant coach. He was instrumental in the Avalanche's drive for their first Stanley Cup championship during the 1995-96 season.

Prior to joining the Avalanche he was head coach for the Springfield Indians of the American Hockey League during the 1993-94 season. He retired from hockey after the 1991-92 season after serving the St. John's Maple Leafs (AHL) as a player/coach. Quenneville played 13 NHL seasons and finished with 803 career games played, 54 goals, 136 assists and 705 penalty minutes. His best years on the ice were spent with Hartford where he earned most valuable defenseman honors in 1985 and 1986. He played an integral part in helping Hartford win a divisional championship in 1986-87.

Quenneville and his wife Elizabeth have three children: Dylan, Lily and Anna.

Coaching Record

		Regular Season					Playoffs			
Season	Team	Games	W	L	T	%	Games	W	L	%
1993-94	Springfield (AHL)	80	29	38	13	.443	6	2	4	.333
1996-97	**St. Louis (NHL)**	**40**	**18**	**15**	**7**	**.538**	**6**	**2**	**4**	**.333**
1997-98	**St. Louis (NHL)**	**82**	**45**	**29**	**8**	**.598**	**10**	**6**	**4**	**.600**
1998-99	**St. Louis (NHL)**	**82**	**37**	**32**	**13**	**.530**	**13**	**6**	**7**	**.462**
	NHL Totals	**204**	**100**	**76**	**28**	**.559**	**29**	**14**	**15**	**.483**

1998-99 Scoring

* – rookie

Regular Season

Pos	#	Player	Team	GP	G	A	Pts	+/–	PIM	PP	SH	GW	GT	S	%
R	38	Pavol Demitra	STL	82	37	52	89	13	16	14	0	10	1	259	14.3
C	77	Pierre Turgeon	STL	67	31	34	65	4	36	10	0	5	2	193	16.1
D	2	Al MacInnis	STL	82	20	42	62	33	70	11	1	2	2	314	6.4
R	48	Scott Young	STL	75	24	28	52	8	27	8	0	4	0	205	11.7
D	44	Chris Pronger	STL	67	13	33	46	3	113	8	0	0	0	172	7.6
L	33	Scott Pellerin	STL	80	20	21	41	1	42	0	5	4	0	138	14.5
C	22	Craig Conroy	STL	69	14	25	39	14	38	0	1	1	0	134	10.4
C	32	Mike Eastwood	STL	82	9	21	30	6	36	0	0	0	0	76	11.8
R	27	Terry Yake	STL	60	9	18	27	–9	34	3	0	4	0	59	15.3
C	25	Pascal Rheaume	STL	60	9	18	27	10	24	2	0	0	0	85	10.6
R	10	Jim Campbell	STL	55	4	21	25	–8	41	1	0	0	0	99	4.0
L	34	Michel Picard	STL	45	11	11	22	5	16	0	0	2	0	69	15.9
R	23	Blair Atcheynum	NSH	53	8	6	14	–10	16	2	0	1	0	70	11.4
			STL	12	2	2	4	2	2	0	0	1	0	23	8.7
			TOTAL	65	10	8	18	–8	18	2	0	2	0	93	10.8
R	56	* Lubos Bartecko	STL	32	5	11	16	4	6	0	0	1	0	37	13.5
C	26	* Michal Handzus	STL	66	4	12	16	–9	30	0	0	0	0	78	5.1
D	7	Ricard Persson	STL	54	1	12	13	4	94	0	0	0	0	52	1.9
L	14	Geoff Courtnall	STL	24	5	7	12	2	28	1	0	2	0	60	8.3
C	15	* Marty Reasoner	STL	22	3	7	10	2	8	1	0	0	0	33	9.1
R	39	Kelly Chase	STL	45	3	7	10	2	143	0	0	1	0	25	12.0
C	21	* Jamal Mayers	STL	34	4	5	9	–3	40	0	0	0	0	48	8.3
L	18	Tony Twist	STL	63	2	6	8	0	149	0	0	0	0	23	8.7
D	6	Jamie Rivers	STL	76	2	5	7	–3	47	1	0	0	0	78	2.6
D	36	Bryan Helmer	PHX	11	0	0	0	2	23	0	0	0	0	11	0.0
			STL	29	0	4	4	3	19	0	0	0	0	38	0.0
			TOTAL	40	0	4	4	5	42	0	0	0	0	49	0.0
D	37	Jeff Finley	NYR	2	0	0	0	–1	0	0	0	0	0	0	0.0
			STL	30	1	2	3	12	20	0	0	0	0	16	6.3
			TOTAL	32	1	2	3	11	20	0	0	0	0	16	6.3
D	19	Chris McAlpine	STL	51	1	1	2	–10	50	0	0	0	0	56	1.8
D	4	Marc Bergevin	STL	52	1	1	2	–14	99	0	0	0	0	40	2.5
D	42	Rory Fitzpatrick	STL	1	0	0	0	–3	2	0	0	0	0	0	0.0
L	9	* Tyson Nash	STL	2	0	0	0	–1	5	0	0	0	0	1	0.0
C	55	* Jochen Hecht	STL	3	0	0	0	–2	0	0	0	0	0	4	0.0
G	35	Jim Carey	STL	4	0	0	0	0	0	0	0	0	0	0	0.0
G	1	* Brent Johnson	STL	6	0	0	0	0	0	0	0	0	0	0	0.0
G	30	* Rich Parent	STL	10	0	0	0	0	2	0	0	0	0	0	0.0
D	20	Rudy Poeschek	STL	16	0	0	0	0	33	0	0	0	0	8	0.0
D	28	Brad Shaw	WSH	4	0	0	0	0	4	0	0	0	0	5	0.0
			STL	12	0	0	0	0	4	0	0	0	0	10	0.0
			TOTAL	16	0	0	0	0	8	0	0	0	0	15	0.0
G	29	Jamie McLennan	STL	33	0	0	0	0	0	0	0	0	0	0	0.0
G	31	Grant Fuhr	STL	39	0	0	0	0	12	0	0	0	0	0	0.0

Goaltending

No.	Goaltender	GPI	Mins	Avg	W	L	T	EN	SO	GA	SA	S%
1	* Brent Johnson	6	286	2.10	3	2	0	0	0	10	127	.921
29	Jamie McLennan	33	1763	2.38	13	14	4	3	3	70	640	.891
31	Grant Fuhr	39	2193	2.44	16	11	8	1	2	89	827	.892
30	* Rich Parent	10	519	2.54	4	3	1	1	1	22	193	.886
35	Jim Carey	4	202	3.86	1	2	0	0	0	13	76	.829
	Totals	**82**	**4989**	**2.51**	**37**	**32**	**13**	**5**	**6**	**209**	**1868**	**.888**

Playoffs

Pos	#	Player	Team	GP	G	A	Pts	+/–	PIM	PP	SH	GW	OT	S	%
C	77	Pierre Turgeon	STL	13	4	9	13	3	6	0	0	2	2	42	9.5
D	2	Al MacInnis	STL	13	4	8	12	–2	20	2	0	0	0	66	6.1
R	48	Scott Young	STL	13	4	7	11	2	10	1	0	1	1	40	10.0
R	38	Pavol Demitra	STL	13	5	4	9	–5	4	3	0	1	1	31	16.1
L	14	Geoff Courtnall	STL	13	2	4	6	–4	10	2	0	0	0	18	11.1
D	44	Chris Pronger	STL	13	1	4	5	–2	28	1	0	0	0	43	2.3
R	23	Blair Atcheynum	STL	13	1	3	4	2	6	0	0	0	0	19	5.3
C	22	Craig Conroy	STL	13	2	1	3	–3	6	0	0	0	0	20	10.0
D	37	Jeff Finley	STL	13	1	2	3	–4	8	0	0	1	0	5	20.0
R	27	Terry Yake	STL	13	1	2	3	–3	14	1	0	0	0	13	7.7
D	7	Ricard Persson	STL	13	0	3	3	–1	17	0	0	0	0	12	0.0
C	55	* Jochen Hecht	STL	5	2	0	2	4	0	0	0	0	0	20	10.0
D	6	Jamie Rivers	STL	9	1	1	2	–2	2	1	0	1	0	4	25.0
C	32	Mike Eastwood	STL	13	1	1	2	2	6	0	0	0	0	8	12.5
C	26	* Michal Handzus	STL	11	0	2	2	0	8	0	0	0	0	16	0.0
C	25	Pascal Rheaume	STL	5	1	0	1	1	4	0	0	0	0	10	10.0
L	33	Scott Pellerin	STL	8	1	0	1	–2	4	0	0	0	0	11	9.1
C	21	* Jamal Mayers	STL	11	0	1	1	–2	8	0	0	0	0	9	0.0
G	31	Grant Fuhr	STL	13	0	1	1	0	2	0	0	0	0	0	0.0
L	18	Tony Twist	STL	1	0	0	0	–1	0	0	0	0	0	0	0.0
G	29	Jamie McLennan	STL	1	0	0	0	0	6	0	0	0	0	0	0.0
L	9	* Tyson Nash	STL	1	0	0	0	–3	2	0	0	0	0	0	0.0
D	28	Brad Shaw	STL	4	0	0	0	2	0	0	0	0	0	3	0.0
L	34	Michel Picard	STL	5	0	0	0	–3	2	0	0	0	0	7	0.0
R	56	* Lubos Bartecko	STL	5	0	0	0	–3	2	0	0	0	0	8	0.0
D	19	Chris McAlpine	STL	13	0	0	0	0	2	0	0	0	0	7	0.0

Goaltending

No.	Goaltender	GPI	Mins	Avg	W	L	EN	SO	GA	SA	S%
29	Jamie McLennan	1	37	0.00	0	1	1	0	0	7	1.000
31	Grant Fuhr	13	790	2.35	6	6	1	1	31	305	.898
	Totals	**13**	**832**	**2.38**	**6**	**7**	**2**	**1**	**33**	**314**	**.895**

Club Records

Team

(Figures in brackets for season records are games played; records for fewest points, wins, ties, losses, goals, goals against are for 70 or more games)

Most Points	107	1980-81 (80)
Most Wins	47	1990-91 (80)
Most Ties	19	1970-71 (78)
Most Losses	50	1978-79 (80)
Most Goals	352	1980-81 (80)
Most Goals Against	349	1981-82 (80)
Fewest Points	48	1978-79 (80)
Fewest Wins	18	1978-79 (80)
Fewest Ties	7	1983-84 (80)
Fewest Losses	18	1980-81 (80)
Fewest Goals	177	1967-68 (74)
Fewest Goals Against	157	1968-69 (76)

Longest Winning Streak
Overall .... 7 — Jan. 21-Feb. 3/88, Mar. 19-31/91, Oct. 3-18/97
Home .... 9 — Jan. 26-Feb. 26/91
Away .... 6 — Feb. 1-Mar. 2/99

Longest Undefeated Streak
Overall .... 12 — Nov. 10-Dec. 8/68 (5 wins, 7 ties)
Home .... 11 — Three times
Away .... 7 — Three times

Longest Losing Streak
Overall .... 7 — Nov. 12-26/67, Feb. 12-25/89
Home .... 5 — Nov. 19-Dec. 6/77, Jan. 21-Feb. 13/99
Away .... 10 — Jan. 20-Mar. 8/82

Longest Winless Streak
Overall .... 12 — Jan. 17-Feb. 15/78 (10 losses, 2 ties)
Home .... 7 — Dec. 28/82-Jan. 25/83 (5 losses, 2 ties)
Away .... 17 — Jan. 23-Oct. 9/74 (13 losses, 4 ties)

Most Shutouts, Season .... 13 — 1968-69 (76)
Most PIM, Season .... 2,041 — 1990-91 (80)
Most Goals, Game .... 11 — Feb. 26/94 (St.L. 11 at Ott. 1)

Individual

Most Seasons	13	Bernie Federko
Most Games	927	Bernie Federko
Most Goals, Career	527	Brett Hull
Most Assists, Career	721	Bernie Federko
Most Points, Career	1,073	Bernie Federko (352G, 721A)
Most PIM, Career	1,786	Brian Sutter
Most Shutouts, Career	16	Glenn Hall

Longest Consecutive Games Streak .... 662 — Garry Unger (Feb. 7/71-Apr. 8/79)
Most Goals, Season .... 86 — Brett Hull (1990-91)
Most Assists, Season .... 90 — Adam Oates (1990-91)
Most Points, Season .... 131 — Brett Hull (1990-91) (86G, 45A)
Most PIM, Season .... 306 — Bob Gassoff (1975-76)

Most Points, Defenseman, Season .... 78 — Jeff Brown (1992-93; 25G, 53A)
Most Points, Center, Season .... 115 — Adam Oates (1990-91; 25G, 90A)
Most Points, Right Wing, Season .... 131 — Brett Hull (1990-91; 86G, 45A)
Most Points, Left Wing, Season .... 102 — Brendan Shanahan (1993-94; 52G, 50A)
Most Points, Rookie, Season .... 73 — Jorgen Pettersson (1980-81; 37G, 36A)
Most Shutouts, Season .... 8 — Glenn Hall (1968-69)
Most Goals, Game .... 6 — Red Berenson (Nov. 7/68)
Most Assists, Game .... 5 — Brian Sutter (Nov. 22/88), Bernie Federko (Feb. 27/88), Adam Oates (Jan. 26/91)
Most Points, Game .... 7 — Red Berenson (Nov. 7/68; 6G, 1A), Garry Unger (Mar. 13/71; 3G, 4A)

Captains' History

Al Arbour, 1967-68 to 1969-70; Red Berenson and Barclay Plager, 1970-71; Barclay Plager, 1971-72 to 1975-76; no captain, 1976-77; Red Berenson, 1977-78; Barry Gibbs, 1978-79; Brian Sutter, 1979-80 to 1987-88; Bernie Federko, 1988-89; Rick Meagher, 1989-90; Scott Stevens, 1990-91; Garth Butcher, 1991-92; Brett Hull, 1992-93 to 1994-95; Brett Hull, Shayne Corson and Wayne Gretzky, 1995-96; no captain, 1996-97; Chris Pronger, 1997-98 to date.

Retired Numbers

3	Bob Gassoff	1973-1977
8	Barclay Plager	1967-1977
11	Brian Sutter	1976-1988
24	Bernie Federko	1976-1989

All-time Record vs. Other Clubs

Regular Season

		At Home						On Road							Total					
	GP	W	L	T	GF	GA	PTS	GP	W	L	T	GF	GA	PTS	GP	W	L	T	GF	GA	PTS
Anaheim	12	5	5	2	40	38	12	12	8	3	1	38	30	17	24	13	8	3	78	68	29
Boston	55	23	23	9	175	192	55	55	12	34	9	149	237	33	110	35	57	18	324	429	88
Buffalo	47	26	14	7	170	122	59	48	13	29	6	149	195	32	95	39	43	13	319	317	91
Calgary	53	24	21	8	187	169	56	52	22	26	4	156	181	48	105	46	47	12	343	350	104
Carolina	27	17	8	2	109	84	36	27	14	11	2	86	85	30	54	31	19	4	195	169	66
Chicago	101	49	35	17	336	314	115	105	32	59	14	319	402	78	206	81	94	31	655	716	193
Colorado	30	19	8	3	126	95	41	31	11	16	4	91	107	26	61	30	24	7	217	202	67
Dallas	108	59	29	20	396	305	138	105	38	48	19	317	360	95	213	97	77	39	713	665	233
Detroit	97	54	27	16	348	267	124	96	38	41	17	303	350	93	193	92	68	33	651	617	217
Edmonton	34	14	16	4	126	136	32	34	13	18	3	123	132	29	68	27	34	7	249	268	61
Florida	5	3	1	1	13	9	7	5	3	1	1	15	12	7	10	6	2	2	28	21	14
Los Angeles	68	44	15	9	259	174	97	68	25	33	10	199	240	60	136	69	48	19	458	414	157
Montreal	55	12	28	15	140	192	39	56	9	40	7	149	246	25	111	21	68	22	289	438	64
Nashville	3	2	1	0	12	5	4	3	2	1	0	13	9	4	6	4	2	0	25	14	8
New Jersey	42	25	10	7	180	130	57	43	17	19	7	126	140	41	85	42	29	14	306	270	98
NY Islanders	44	17	18	9	158	144	43	45	10	24	11	113	173	31	89	27	42	20	271	317	74
NY Rangers	59	23	27	9	173	189	55	57	7	44	6	129	238	20	116	30	71	15	302	427	75
Ottawa	6	2	3	1	17	20	5	6	5	1	0	29	12	10	12	7	4	1	46	32	15
Philadelphia	63	25	31	7	185	199	57	63	11	42	10	143	249	32	126	36	73	17	328	448	89
Phoenix	40	19	11	10	147	117	48	41	15	20	6	128	137	36	81	34	31	16	275	254	84
Pittsburgh	61	40	15	6	238	165	86	60	19	29	12	181	227	50	121	59	44	18	419	392	136
San Jose	17	12	5	0	61	40	24	14	11	2	1	49	32	23	31	23	7	1	110	72	47
Tampa Bay	8	7	1	0	31	19	14	9	4	3	2	30	28	10	17	11	4	2	61	47	24
Toronto	96	55	28	13	331	270	123	95	26	58	11	275	358	63	191	81	86	24	606	628	186
Vancouver	61	35	18	8	232	178	78	62	30	25	7	198	185	67	123	65	43	15	430	363	145
Washington	37	16	13	8	153	124	40	36	13	20	3	107	131	29	73	29	33	11	260	255	69
Defunct Clubs	32	25	4	3	131	55	53	33	11	10	12	95	100	34	65	36	14	15	226	155	87
Totals	1261	652	415	194	4474	3752	1498	1261	419	657	185	3710	4596	1023	2522	1071	1072	379	8184	8348	2521

Playoffs

	Series	W	L	GP	W	L	T	GF	GA	Last Mtg.	Round	Result
Boston	2	0	2	8	0	8	0	15	48	1972	SF	L 0-4
Buffalo	1	0	1	3	1	2	0	8	7	1976	PR	L 1-2
Calgary	1	0	1	7	3	4	0	22	28	1986	CF	L 3-4
Chicago	9	2	7	45	18	27	0	129	166	1993	DSF	W 4-0
Dallas	11	5	6	62	28	34	0	174	191	1999	CSF	L 2-4
Detroit	6	2	4	35	15	20	0	92	111	1998	CQF	L 2-4
Los Angeles	2	2	0	8	8	0	0	32	13	1998	CSF	W 4-0
Montreal	3	0	3	12	0	12	0	14	42	1977	QF	L 0-4
NY Rangers	1	0	1	6	2	4	0	22	29	1981	QF	L 2-4
Philadelphia	2	2	0	11	8	3	0	34	20	1969	QF	W 4-0
Phoenix	2	2	0	11	7	4	0	39	29	1999	CQF	W 4-3
Pittsburgh	3	2	1	13	7	6	0	45	40	1981	PR	W 3-2
Toronto	5	3	2	31	17	14	0	88	90	1996	CQF	W 4-2
Vancouver	1	0	1	7	3	4	0	27	27	1995	CQF	L 3-4
Totals	49	20	29	259	117	142	0	741	841			

Calgary totals include Atlanta Flames, 1972-73 to 1979-80.
Colorado totals include Quebec, 1979-80 to 1994-95.
New Jersey totals include Kansas City, 1974-75 to 1975-76.
Phoenix totals include Winnipeg, 1979-80 to 1995-96.
Carolina totals include Hartford, 1979-80 to 1996-97.
Dallas totals include Minnesota, 1967-68 to 1992-93.
New Jersey totals include Kansas City, 1974-75 to 1975-76, and Colorado Rockies, 1976-77 to 1981-82.

Playoff Results 1999-95

Year	Round	Opponent	Result	GF	GA
1999	CSF	Dallas	L 2-4	12	17
	CQF	Phoenix	W 4-3	19	16
1998	CSF	Detroit	L 2-4	13	23
	CQF	Los Angeles	W 4-0	16	8
1997	CQF	Detroit	L 2-4	12	13
1996	CSF	Detroit	L 3-4	16	22
	CQF	Toronto	W 4-2	21	15
1995	CQF	Vancouver	L 3-4	27	27

Abbreviations: Round: CF – conference final; CSF – conference semi-final; CQF – conference quarter-final; DSF – division semi-final; SF – semi-final; QF – quarter-final; PR – preliminary round.

1998-99 Results

Oct.	10	at	Boston	3-3	21		Toronto	2-4
	12	at	NY Rangers	4-2	26	at	San Jose	3-0
	16	at	Detroit	1-4	28	at	Vancouver	4-2
	17		NY Islanders	0-1	30	at	Calgary	3-4
	22	at	Ottawa	5-3	Feb. 1	at	Edmonton	4-3
	24		Calgary	4-3	4		New Jersey	0-2
	27	at	Philadelphia	1-2	6		Anaheim	3-4
	29		Detroit	3-1	8	at	Florida	5-4
	31		Anaheim	2-2	10	at	Tampa Bay	5-4
Nov.	4	at	Anaheim	3-1	11		San Jose	1-5
	5	at	Los Angeles	2-2	13		Edmonton	2-3
	7	at	San Jose	2-2	15		Vancouver	8-1
	10		Chicago	5-2	18		Florida	0-0
	11	at	Detroit	2-6	20		Nashville	3-4
	14		Nashville	5-1	22		Los Angeles	5-1
	19	at	Nashville	2-3	24		Chicago	1-3
	21		Dallas	3-3	26	at	Calgary	4-2
	24		Nashville	4-0	28	at	Chicago	3-1
	27		San Jose	2-4	Mar. 2	at	Nashville	5-1
	28		Washington	4-2	4		Toronto	0-4
Dec.	4	at	Colorado	0-2	7	at	Dallas	3-4
	5		Colorado	1-3	9		Calgary	4-7
	8		Buffalo	2-2	11		Montreal	0-3
	12		Pittsburgh	3-4	13		Edmonton	6-4
	14	at	Colorado	0-0	14	at	Chicago	5-2
	15	at	Dallas	3-7	16		Philadelphia	5-2
	17		Phoenix	3-2	18		Phoenix	2-2
	19		Los Angeles	5-2	20		Ottawa	2-3
	22	at	NY Islanders	3-3	22		Carolina	5-2
	23	at	New Jersey	2-4	25	at	Vancouver	4-1
	26		Detroit	4-3	26	at	Edmonton	1-2
	28	at	Detroit	4-4	28	at	Chicago	1-3
Jan.	1	at	Nashville	6-5	Apr. 1		Tampa Bay	3-0
	2		NY Rangers	0-1	3		Dallas	5-2
	4		Vancouver	4-0	5	at	Toronto	2-2
	7		Chicago	4-2	7	at	Washington	4-2
	9	at	Pittsburgh	1-2	9		Detroit	1-1
	11	at	Montreal	1-3	11		Colorado	2-4
	13	at	Buffalo	4-2	14	at	Anaheim	3-1
	16	at	Colorado	0-2	15	at	Phoenix	6-4
	19	at	Phoenix	2-4	18	at	Los Angeles	3-2

Entry Draft
Selections 1999-85

1999
Pick
17	Barret Jackman
85	Peter Smrek
114	Chad Starling
143	Trevor Byrne
180	Tore Vikingstad
203	Phil Osaer
221	Colin Hemingway
232	Alexander Khavanov
260	Brian McMeekin
270	James Desmarais

1998
Pick
24	Christian Backman
41	Maxim Linnik
83	Matt Walker
157	Brad Voth
170	Andrei Trochinsky
197	Brad Twordik
225	Vevgeny Pastukh
255	John Pohl

1997
Pick
40	Tyler Rennette
86	Didier Tremblay
98	Jan Horacek
106	Jame Pollock
149	Nicholas Bilotto
177	Ladislav Nagy
206	Bobby Haglund
232	Dmitri Plekhanov
244	Marek Ivan

1996
Pick
14	Marty Reasoner
67	Gordie Dwyer
95	Jonathan Zukiwsky
97	Andrei Petrakov
159	Stephen Wagner
169	Daniel Corso
177	Reed Low
196	Andrei Podkonicky
203	Anthony Hutchins
229	Konstantin Shafranov

1995
Pick
49	Jochen Hecht
75	Scott Roche
101	Michal Handzus
127	Jeff Ambrosio
153	Denis Hamel
179	J-Luc Grand-Pierre
205	Derek Bekar
209	Libor Zabransky

1994
Pick
68	Stephane Roy
94	Tyler Harlton
120	Edvin Frylen
172	Roman Vopat
198	Steve Noble
224	Marc Stephan
250	Kevin Harper
276	Scott Fankhouser

1993
Pick
37	Maxim Bets
63	Jamie Rivers
89	Jamal Mayers
141	Todd Kelman
167	Mike Buzak
193	Eric Boguniecki
219	Michael Grier
245	Libor Prochazka
271	Alexander Vasilevsky
275	Christer Olsson

1992
Pick
38	Igor Korolev
62	Vitali Karamnov
64	Vitali Prokhorov
86	Lee J. Leslie
134	Bob Lachance
158	Ian LaPerriere
160	Lance Burns
180	Igor Boldin
182	Nicholas Naumenko
206	Todd Harris
230	Yuri Gunko
259	Wade Salzman

1991
Pick
27	Steve Staios
64	Kyle Reeves
65	Nathan Lafayette
87	Grayden Reid
109	Jeff Callinan
131	Bruce Gardiner
153	Terry Hollinger
175	Christopher Kenady
197	Jed Fiebelkorn
219	Chris MacKenzie
241	Kevin Rappana
263	Mike Veisor

1990
Pick
33	Craig Johnson
54	Patrice Tardif
96	Jason Ruff
117	Kurtis Miller
138	Wayne Conlan
180	Parris Duffus
201	Steve Widmeyer
222	Joe Hawley
243	Joe Fleming

1989
Pick
9	Jason Marshall
31	Rick Corriveau
55	Denny Felsner
93	Daniel Laperriere
114	David Roberts
124	Derek Frenette
135	Jeff Batters
156	Kevin Plager
177	John Roderick
198	John Valo
219	Brian Lukowski

1988
Pick
9	Rod Brind' Amour
30	Adrien Plavsic
51	Rob Fournier
72	Jaan Luik
105	Dave Lacouture
114	Dan Fowler
135	Matt Hayes
156	John McCoy
177	Tony Twist
198	Bret Hedican
219	Heath DeBoer
240	Michael Francis

1987
Pick
12	Keith Osborne
54	Kevin Miehm
59	Robert Nordmark
75	Darin Smith
82	Andy Rymsha
117	Rob Robinson
138	Todd Crabtree
159	Guy Hebert
180	Robert Dumas
201	David Marvin
207	Andy Cesarski
222	Dan Rolfe
243	Ray Savard

1986
Pick
10	Jocelyn Lemieux
31	Mike Posma
52	Tony Hejna
73	Glen Featherstone
87	Michael Wolak
115	Mike O'Toole
136	Andy May
157	Randy Skarda
178	Martyn Ball
199	Rod Thacker
220	Terry MacLean
234	Bill Butler
241	David O'Brien

1985
Pick
37	Herb Raglan
44	Nelson Emerson
54	Ned Desmond
100	Dan Brooks
121	Rich Burchill
138	Pat Jablonski
159	Scott Brickey
180	Jeff Urban
201	Vince Guidotti
222	Ron Saatzer
243	Dave Jecha

General Manager

PLEAU, LARRY
General Manager, St. Louis Blues. Born in Lynn, MA, June 29, 1947.

Larry Pleau was named general manager on June 9, 1997, becoming the tenth person to hold that position in team history.

Pleau joined the Blues after spending eight seasons with the New York Rangers organization, most recently as vice president of player personnel. He joined the Rangers in 1989 as assistant general manager of player development. During Pleau's tenure in New York, the Rangers drafted NHL stars Sergei Zubov, Doug Weight, Alexei Kovalev, Niklas Sundstrom, Todd Marchant and Sergei Nemchinov, along with Corey Hirsch, Daniel Goneau and Mattias Norstrom. Prior to joining the Rangers, Pleau spent 17 seasons with the Hartford Whalers organization as a player, assistant coach, head coach, general manager and minor league general manager and head coach. He was also instrumental in drafting Ray Ferraro, Ron Francis, Kevin Dineen and Ulf Samuelsson while a member of the Whalers organization.

Pleau played three seasons with the Montreal Canadiens (1969-1972) in the National Hockey League before being the first player signed by the Hartford Whalers of the World Hockey Association. He was a center/left wing for the Whalers from 1972 until his retirement in 1979. He played in 468 regular season games for Hartford, accumulating 157 goals and 215 assists for 372 points. He also played for the 1968 United States Olympic Team, the 1969 U.S. National Team and for Team USA in the 1976 Canada Cup tournament.

Pleau and his wife, Wendy, have a son, Steve, and a daughter, Shannon.

NHL Coaching Record

Season	Team	Regular Season					Playoffs			
		Games	W	L	T	%	Games	W	L	%
1980-81	Hartford	20	6	12	2	.350	....	....	....	....
1981-82	Hartford	80	21	41	18	.375	....	....	....	....
1982-83	Hartford	18	4	13	1	.250	....	....	....	....
1987-88	Hartford	26	13	13	0	.500	6	2	4	.333
1988-89	Hartford	80	37	38	5	.494	4	0	4	.000
	NHL Totals	**224**	**81**	**117**	**26**	**.420**	**10**	**2**	**8**	**.200**

Club Directory

Kiel Center
1401 Clark Avenue
St. Louis, MO 63103-2709
Phone **314/622-2500**
FAX 314/622-2582
Website: www.stlouisblues.com
Capacity: 19,260

Owner	Clark Enterprises
Chairman of the Board	Jerry Ritter
President & CEO	Mark Sauer
Senior Vice President & General Manager	Larry Pleau
Senior Vice President, Marketing & Communications	Jim Woodcock
Senior Vice President, Kiel Center	Roger Dixon
Vice President, Sales	Bruce Affleck
Vice President, Operations	Fred Corsi
Vice President, Human Resources	David Coverstone
Vice President, Food & Merchandise	Dennis Petrullo
Vice President, Finance & Hockey Administration	Jarry Jasiek
Vice President, Marketing	JoAnn Miles
Advisor to the President	Ron Caron

Hockey Operations
General Manager	Larry Pleau
Assistant General Manager	John Ferguson Jr.
Head Coach	Joel Quenneville
Assistant Coaches	Mike Kitchen, Jim Roberts
Golatending Coach	Keith Allain
Director of Pro Scouting	Bob Plager
Pro Scout	Bill Dineen
Director of Amateur Scouting	Teddy Hampson
Special Assignment	Jack Evans, Peter Stastny
Amateur Scouts	Anders Steen, Bill Terry, Rick Meagher
Part-time Scouts	Jim Bzdel, Dick Cherry, Wayne Mundey, Miroslav Termer, Georgi Zhuravlev, Paul Guay
Director of Team Services	Michael Caruso
Video Coordinator	Jamie Kompon
Executive Assistant to the General Manager	Donna Lembke
Head Coach, Worcester IceCats	Greg Gilbert
Associate Coach, Worcester IceCats	Steve Pleau

Medical Staff
Athletic Trainer	Ray Barile
Massage Therapist	Jeff Wright
Strength & Conditioning Coordinator	Aaron Komarek
Equipment Manager	Bert Godin
Assistant Equipment Manager	Eric Bechtol
Equipment Assistant	Greg Cable
Orthopedic Surgeon	Dr. Jerome Gilden, Dr. Rick Wright, Dr. Matt Matava
Internist	Dr. Aaron Birenbaum, Dr. William Birenbaum
General Surgery	Dr. Michael Brunt
Dentist	Dr. Glenn Edwards
Optometrist	Dr. N. Rex Ghormley

Communications/Marketing
Director of Communications	Jeff Trammel
Assistant Director of Communications	Joe Campbell
Communications Manager	Stanley Richardson
Manager of Publications	Renee St. John
Director of Corporate Sponsorships	Chris Arger
Manager of Corporate Sales & Promotions	Rob Rixford
Manager of Community Relations/ Fan Development	Maureen Cierpot
Manager of Amateur Hockey & Community Programs	Dan Kelly
Marketing/Public Relations Assistant	Donna Quirk
Receptionists	Marian Brooks, Jeffrey Sevier

Finance/Sales
Director of Finance	Jeff Horstmann
Sales Representatives	Jill Mann, Jennifer Foppe, Kourtney Hacker, Katie Kelley, Ashley Zurawski, Kris Francis, Paula Barnes, Jill Serve, Kari Palmer, Jennifer Gruner
Accounting Staff	Jim Bergman, Craig Bryant, Phil Siddle, Pam Pflasterer, Crystal Strasburg, Michelle Daily, Traci Hinterser, Mindy Wallace
Radio Stations	KMOX 1120 am
TV Stations	Fox Sports Midwest, KPLR-TV, WBII

General Managers' History

Lynn Patrick, 1967-68; Scotty Bowman, 1968-69 to 1970-71; Lynn Patrick, 1971-72; Sid Abel, 1972-73; Charles Catto, 1973-74; Gerry Ehman, 1974-75; Dennis Ball, 1975-76; Emile Francis, 1976-77 to 1982-83; Ron Caron, 1983-84 to 1993-94; Mike Keenan, 1994-95, 1995-96; Mike Keenan and Ron Caron, 1996-97; Larry Pleau, 1997-98 to date.

San Jose Sharks

1998-99 Results: 31W-33L-18T 80PTS. Fourth, Pacific Division

Year-by-Year Record

Season	GP	Home W	L	T	Road W	L	T	Overall W	L	T	GF	GA	Pts.	Finished	Playoff Result
1998-99	82	17	15	9	14	18	9	31	33	18	196	191	80	4th, Pacific Div.	Lost Conf. Quarter-Final
1997-98	82	17	19	5	17	19	5	34	38	10	210	216	78	4th, Pacific Div.	Lost Conf. Quarter-Final
1996-97	82	14	23	4	13	24	4	27	47	8	211	278	62	7th, Pacific Div.	Out of Playoffs
1995-96	82	12	26	3	8	29	4	20	55	7	252	357	47	7th, Pacific Div.	Out of Playoffs
1994-95	48	10	13	1	9	12	3	19	25	4	129	161	42	3rd, Pacific Div.	Lost Conf. Semi-Final
1993-94	84	19	13	10	14	22	6	33	35	16	252	265	82	3rd, Pacific Div.	Lost Conf. Semi-Final
1992-93	84	8	33	1	3	38	1	11	71	2	218	414	24	6th, Smythe Div.	Out of Playoffs
1991-92	80	14	23	3	3	35	2	17	58	5	219	359	39	6th, Smythe Div.	Out of Playoffs

1999-2000 Schedule

Oct.				Jan.			
Sat.	2		Calgary	Sat.	1	at Nashville*
Mon.	4		Chicago	Sun.	2	at Chicago
Thu.	7		Edmonton	Wed.	5	at Edmonton
Sat.	9		Dallas	Sat.	8	Florida
Mon.	11		at Anaheim*	Tue.	11	St. Louis
Wed.	13		at Dallas	Sat.	15	Los Angeles
Thu.	14		at Nashville	Mon.	17	at Chicago*
Sat.	16		at Washington	Wed.	19	at Colorado
Tue.	19		at NY Rangers	Sat.	22	Anaheim
Wed.	20		at Detroit	Sun.	23	at Phoenix
Sat.	23		Boston	Tue.	25	Colorado
Sun.	24		at Los Angeles	Fri.	28	at Vancouver
Thu.	28		Nashville	Sat.	29	NY Islanders
Sat.	30		Pittsburgh	**Feb.** Tue.	1	Phoenix
Sun.	31		Washington	Thu.	3	at Colorado
Nov. Wed.	3		Phoenix	Tue.	8	at Tampa Bay
Fri.	5		Philadelphia	Wed.	9	at Florida
Sat.	6		Dallas	Fri.	11	at Atlanta
Tue.	9		at Vancouver	Sun.	13	at New Jersey*
Wed.	10		at Calgary	Tue.	15	at NY Islanders
Sat.	13		at Philadelphia*	Fri.	18	at Anaheim
Mon.	15		at Toronto	Wed.	23	St. Louis
Tue.	16		at Montreal	Sat.	26	Los Angeles
Thu.	18		at Ottawa	Tue.	29	Anaheim
Sat.	20		at St. Louis	**Mar.** Thu.	2	Nashville
Tue.	23		Montreal	Sat.	4	Carolina
Sat.	27		at Los Angeles*	Mon.	6	NY Rangers
Sun.	28		New Jersey	Wed.	8	Detroit
Dec. Wed.	1		at Detroit	Mon.	13	Calgary
Thu.	2		at Pittsburgh	Wed.	15	Buffalo
Sat.	4		at St. Louis	Fri.	17	at Anaheim
Mon.	6		Tampa Bay	Sun.	19	at Dallas*
Wed.	8		Colorado	Wed.	22	Vancouver
Fri.	10		Atlanta	Fri.	24	Phoenix
Tue.	14		Chicago	Mon.	27	Edmonton
Sun.	19		at Phoenix*	Wed.	29	at Los Angeles
Mon.	20		Detroit	**Apr.** Sat.	1	at Calgary
Wed.	22		Los Angeles	Mon.	3	at Edmonton
Sun.	26		Anaheim*	Wed.	5	Dallas
Mon.	27		at Dallas	Fri.	7	at Phoenix
Thu.	30		at St. Louis	Sun.	9	Vancouver

* Denotes afternoon game.

Franchise date: May 9, 1990

WESTERN CONFERENCE

PACIFIC DIVISION

9th NHL Season

Vincent Damphousse had seven goals and six assists for 13 points in just 12 games with San Jose after being dealt from Montreal at the trade deadline. His seventh game in a Sharks jersey was the 1,000th of his NHL career.

1999-2000 Player Personnel

FORWARDS	HT	WT	S	Place of Birth	Date	1998-99 Club
BRADLEY, Matt	6-2	195	R	Stittsville, Ont.	6/13/78	Kentucky
BURNETT, Garrett	6-3	225	L	Coquitlam, B.C.	9/23/75	Kentucky
CRAVEN, Murray	6-3	190	L	Medicine Hat, Alta.	7/20/64	San Jose
DAMPHOUSSE, Vincent	6-1	191	L	Montreal, Que.	12/17/67	Montreal-San Jose
DEULING, Jarrett	6-0	200	L	Vernon, B.C.	3/4/74	Kentucky
FRIESEN, Jeff	6-1	200	L	Meadow Lake, Sask.	8/5/76	San Jose
GRANATO, Tony	5-10	185	R	Downers Grove, IL	7/25/64	San Jose
KOROLYUK, Alexander	5-9	190	L	Moscow, USSR	1/15/76	San Jose-Kentucky
LANDRY, Eric	5-11	190	L	Gatineau, Que.	1/20/75	Calgary-Saint John
LUNDBOHM, Andy	6-4	225	L	Roseau, MN	3/24/77	Army
MARLEAU, Patrick	6-2	205	L	Swift Current, Sask.	9/15/79	San Jose
MATTEAU, Stephane	6-4	220	L	Rouyn-Noranda, Que.	9/2/69	San Jose
MYHRES, Brantt	6-4	220	R	Edmonton, Alta.	3/18/74	San Jose-Kentucky
NITTEL, Adam	6-2	220	R	Kitchener, Ont.	7/17/78	Mississauga-S.S. Marie
NOLAN, Owen	6-1	215	R	Belfast, Ireland	2/12/72	San Jose
RICCI, Mike	6-0	190	L	Scarborough, Ont.	10/27/71	San Jose
ROED, Peter	5-11	190	L	St. Paul, MN	11/15/76	Richmond
SMITH, Mark	5-10	190	L	Edmonton, Alta.	10/24/77	Kentucky
STERN, Ron	6-0	200	R	Ste. Agathe, Que.	1/11/67	San Jose
STURM, Marco	6-0	195	L	Dingolfing, West Germany	9/8/78	San Jose
SUNDSTROM, Niklas	6-0	185	L	Ornskoldsvik, Sweden	6/6/75	NY Rangers
SUTTER, Ron	6-0	180	R	Viking, Alta.	12/2/63	San Jose
DEFENSEMEN						
GOSSELIN, Christian	6-5	235	R	Laval, Que.	8/21/76	Kentucky
HANNAN, Scott	6-2	215	L	Richmond, B.C.	1/23/79	Kelowna-San Jose-Kentucky
HEINS, Shawn	6-4	220	L	Eganville, Ont.	12/24/73	Canada-San Jose-Kentucky
JILLSON, Jeff	6-3	219	R	Providence, RI	7/24/80	U. of Michigan
MARCHMENT, Bryan	6-1	200	L	Scarborough, Ont.	5/1/69	San Jose
NORTON, Jeff	6-2	200	L	Acton, MA	11/25/65	Florida-San Jose
PIETROPAULO, Didier	6-1	200	L	Laval, Que.	2/9/79	Rouyn-Noranda
RAGNARSSON, Marcus	6-1	215	L	Ostervala, Sweden	8/13/71	San Jose
RATHJE, Mike	6-5	230	L	Mannville, Alta.	5/11/74	San Jose
ROUSE, Bob	6-2	215	R	Surrey, B.C.	6/18/64	San Jose
STUART, Brad	6-2	210	L	Rocky Mountain House, Alta.	11/6/79	Regina-Calgary (WHL)
SUTER, Gary	6-0	205	L	Madison, WI	6/24/64	San Jose
SUTTON, Andy	6-6	245	L	Edmonton, Alta.	3/10/75	San Jose-Kentucky

GOALTENDERS	HT	WT	C	Place of Birth	Date	1998-99 Club
FRIESEN, Terry	5-11	190	L	Winkler, Man.	10/29/77	Richmond-Kentucky
HEDBERG, Johan	5-11	180	L	Leksand, Sweden	5/5/73	Leksands IF
KIPRUSOFF, Miikka	6-0	180	L	Turku, Finland	10/26/76	TPS Turku
NABOKOV, John	6-0	195	L	Ust-Kamenogorsk, USSR	7/25/75	Kentucky
SHIELDS, Steve	6-3	215	L	Toronto, Ont.	7/19/72	San Jose
VERNON, Mike	5-9	180	L	Calgary, Alta.	2/24/63	San Jose

Coach

SUTTER, DARRYL JOHN
Coach, San Jose Sharks. Born in Viking, Alta., August 19, 1958.

Darryl Sutter became the Sharks' fifth head coach on June 9, 1997. Sutter played eight NHL seasons, all with the Chicago Blackhawks (1979-87). He began his coaching career as an assistant in Chicago in 1987-88 before taking over as head coach of the Blackhawks' IHL affiliate that played in Saginaw (1988-89) and in Indianapolis (1989-90). His club won an IHL Turner Cup championship in 1990 and Sutter was named coach of the year.

He later served as an associate coach under Mike Keenan in Chicago in 1990-91 and 1991-92 and began a three-year tenure as head coach of the Blackhawks in 1992-93. As coach of Chicago, Sutter's teams reached the playoffs in all three seasons. His career winning percentage of .569 ranks second among Chicago coaches. He resigned as head coach following the 1994-95 season to spend more time with his family and worked as a consultant to the Blackhawks for special assignments in 1995-96 and 1996-97.

In 17 years of hockey as a player and coach, Sutter has never failed to qualify for post-season play. During his eight-year playing career, he scored 161 goals and added 118 assists in 406 regular-season games. He added 24 goals and 19 assists in 51 playoff games. Drafted 179th overall by Chicago in the 1978 NHL Entry Draft, he scored a remarkable 40 goals during his rookie season. The left winger served as team captain from 1982-83 until injuries forced his retirement after the 1986-87 season.

He is one of six brothers to play in the NHL. The others are Brian, Brent, Duane, Rich and Ron. All are involved in the Sutter Foundation which raises raises money for non-profit organizations in their home province of Alberta.

Coaching Record

		Regular Season					Playoffs			
Season	Team	Games	W	L	T	%	Games	W	L	%
1988-89	Saginaw (IHL)	82	46	26	10	.560	6	2	4	.333
1989-90	Indianapolis (IHL)	82	53	21	8	.646	14	12	2	.857
1992-93	**Chicago (NHL)**	**84**	**47**	**25**	**12**	**.631**	**4**	**0**	**4**	**.000**
1993-94	**Chicago (NHL)**	**84**	**39**	**36**	**9**	**.518**	**6**	**2**	**4**	**.333**
1994-95	**Chicago (NHL)**	**48**	**24**	**19**	**5**	**.552**	**16**	**9**	**7**	**.563**
1997-98	**San Jose (NHL)**	**82**	**34**	**38**	**10**	**.476**	**6**	**2**	**4**	**.333**
1998-99	**San Jose (NHL)**	**82**	**31**	**33**	**18**	**.488**	**6**	**2**	**4**	**.333**
	NHL Totals	**380**	**175**	**151**	**54**	**.532**	**38**	**15**	**23**	**.395**

1998-99 Scoring

* – rookie

Regular Season

Pos	#	Player	Team	GP	G	A	Pts	+/–	PIM	PP	SH	GW	GT	S	%
L	39	Jeff Friesen	S.J.	78	22	35	57	3	42	10	1	3	1	215	10.2
C	25	Vincent Damphousse	MTL	65	12	24	36	–7	46	3	2	2	0	147	8.2
			S.J.	12	7	6	13	3	4	3	0	1	0	43	16.3
			TOTAL	77	19	30	49	–4	50	6	2	3	0	190	10.0
R	17	Joe Murphy	S.J.	76	25	23	48	10	73	7	0	2	1	176	14.2
C	14	Patrick Marleau	S.J.	81	21	24	45	10	24	4	0	4	1	134	15.7
R	11	Owen Nolan	S.J.	78	19	26	45	16	129	6	2	3	1	207	9.2
C	18	Mike Ricci	S.J.	82	13	26	39	1	68	2	1	2	1	98	13.3
C	19	Marco Sturm	S.J.	78	16	22	38	7	52	3	2	3	2	140	11.4
D	2	Bill Houlder	S.J.	76	9	23	32	8	40	7	0	5	0	115	7.8
R	15 *	Alexander Korolyuk	S.J.	55	12	18	30	3	26	2	0	0	1	96	12.5
R	37	Stephane Matteau	S.J.	68	8	15	23	2	73	0	0	0	0	72	11.1
D	5	Jeff Norton	FLA	3	0	0	0	0	2	0	0	0	0	2	0.0
			S.J.	69	4	18	22	2	42	2	0	1	0	68	5.9
			TOTAL	72	4	18	22	2	44	2	0	1	0	70	5.7
R	22	Ronnie Stern	S.J.	78	7	9	16	–3	158	1	0	2	0	94	7.4
L	26	Dave Lowry	S.J.	61	6	9	15	–5	24	2	0	0	1	58	10.3
D	40	Mike Rathje	S.J.	82	5	9	14	15	36	2	0	1	0	67	7.5
L	32	Murray Craven	S.J.	43	4	10	14	–3	18	0	1	1	0	55	7.3
D	10	Marcus Ragnarsson	S.J.	74	0	13	13	7	66	0	0	0	0	87	0.0
L	21	Tony Granato	S.J.	35	6	6	12	4	54	0	1	1	1	65	9.2
D	3	Bob Rouse	S.J.	70	0	11	11	0	44	0	0	0	0	75	0.0
C	12	Ron Sutter	S.J.	59	3	6	9	–8	40	0	0	1	0	67	4.5
D	27	Bryan Marchment	S.J.	59	2	6	8	–7	101	0	0	0	0	49	4.1
D	4	Andrei Zyuzin	S.J.	25	3	1	4	5	38	2	0	0	0	44	6.8
L	36	Stephen Guolla	S.J.	14	2	2	4	3	6	0	0	1	0	22	9.1
D	42 *	Andy Sutton	S.J.	31	0	3	3	–4	65	0	0	0	0	24	0.0
C	8	Jarrod Skalde	S.J.	17	1	1	2	–6	4	0	0	0	1	17	5.9
D	6 *	Scott Hannan	S.J.	5	0	2	2	0	6	0	0	0	0	4	0.0
C	9	Bernie Nicholls	S.J.	10	0	2	2	–4	4	0	0	0	0	11	0.0
R	33	Brantt Myhres	S.J.	30	1	0	1	–2	116	0	0	0	0	7	14.3
C	13	Jamie Baker	S.J.	1	0	1	1	1	0	0	0	0	0	1	0.0
L	7	Shawn Burr	S.J.	18	0	1	1	–3	29	0	0	0	0	22	0.0
G	31	Steve Shields	S.J.	37	0	1	1	0	6	0	0	0	0	0	0.0
R	25	Mike Craig	S.J.	1	0	0	0	–1	0	0	0	0	0	1	0.0
D	20	Gary Suter	S.J.	1	0	0	0	0	0	0	0	0	0	1	0.0
G	30	Sean Gauthier	S.J.	1	0	0	0	0	0	0	0	0	0	0	0.0
D	23 *	Shawn Heins	S.J.	5	0	0	0	0	13	0	0	0	0	4	0.0
G	29	Mike Vernon	S.J.	49	0	0	0	0	8	0	0	0	0	0	0.0

Goaltending

No.	Goaltender	GPI	Mins	Avg	W	L	T	EN	SO	GA	SA	S%
30	Sean Gauthier	1	3	0.00	0	0	0	0	0	0	2	1.000
31	Steve Shields	37	2162	2.22	15	11	8	1	4	80	1011	.921
29	Mike Vernon	49	2831	2.27	16	22	10	3	4	107	1200	.911
	Totals	**82**	**5016**	**2.28**	**31**	**33**	**18**	**4**	**8**	**191**	**2217**	**.914**

Playoffs

Pos	#	Player	Team	GP	G	A	Pts	+/–	PIM	PP	SH	GW	OT	S	%
D	5	Jeff Norton	S.J.	6	0	7	7	5	10	0	0	0	0	3	0.0
C	25	Vincent Damphousse	S.J.	6	3	2	5	1	6	0	2	0	0	22	13.6
C	18	Mike Ricci	S.J.	6	2	3	5	1	10	1	0	0	0	9	22.2
L	39	Jeff Friesen	S.J.	6	2	2	4	–1	14	1	0	0	0	20	10.0
C	19	Marco Sturm	S.J.	6	2	2	4	1	4	0	0	1	0	15	13.3
R	15 *	Alexander Korolyuk	S.J.	6	1	3	4	–3	2	0	0	1	0	7	14.3
D	2	Bill Houlder	S.J.	6	3	0	3	2	4	3	0	0	0	8	37.5
C	14	Patrick Marleau	S.J.	6	2	1	3	–1	4	2	0	0	0	7	28.6
R	17	Joe Murphy	S.J.	6	0	3	3	0	4	0	0	0	0	21	0.0
L	21	Tony Granato	S.J.	6	1	1	2	–1	2	0	0	0	0	5	20.0
R	11	Owen Nolan	S.J.	6	1	1	2	0	6	0	0	0	0	26	3.8
G	29	Mike Vernon	S.J.	5	0	1	1	0	0	0	0	0	0	0	0.0
D	10	Marcus Ragnarsson	S.J.	6	0	1	1	–4	6	0	0	0	0	9	0.0
L	26	Dave Lowry	S.J.	1	0	0	0	0	0	0	0	0	0	0	0.0
G	31	Steve Shields	S.J.	1	0	0	0	0	0	0	0	0	0	0	0.0
L	37	Stephane Matteau	S.J.	5	0	0	0	–3	6	0	0	0	0	4	0.0
D	27	Bryan Marchment	S.J.	6	0	0	0	0	4	0	0	0	0	7	0.0
D	3	Bob Rouse	S.J.	6	0	0	0	–1	6	0	0	0	0	4	0.0
R	22	Ronnie Stern	S.J.	6	0	0	0	–1	6	0	0	0	0	10	0.0
C	12	Ron Sutter	S.J.	6	0	0	0	–1	4	0	0	0	0	10	0.0
D	40	Mike Rathje	S.J.	6	0	0	0	–6	4	0	0	0	0	4	0.0

Goaltending

No.	Goaltender	GPI	Mins	Avg	W	L	EN	SO	GA	SA	S%
29	Mike Vernon	5	321	2.43	2	3	0	0	13	172	.924
31	Steve Shields	1	60	6.00	0	1	0	0	6	36	.833
	Totals	**6**	**381**	**2.99**	**2**	**4**	**0**	**0**	**19**	**208**	**.909**

Captains' History

Doug Wilson, 1991-92, 1992-93; Bob Errey, 1993-94; Bob Errey and Jeff Odgers, 1994-95; Jeff Odgers, 1995-96; Todd Gill, 1996-97, 1997-98; Owen Nolan, 1998-99 to date.

Coaching History

George Kingston, 1991-92, 1992-93; Kevin Constantine, 1993-94, 1994-95; Kevin Constantine and Jim Wiley, 1995-96; Al Sims, 1996-97; Darryl Sutter, 1997-98 to date.

Club Records

Team

(Figures in brackets for season records are games played; records for fewest points, wins, ties, losses, goals, goals against are for 70 or more games)

Most Points	82	1993-94 (84)
Most Wins	34	1997-98 (82)
Most Ties	18	1998-99 (82)
Most Losses	*71	1992-93 (84)
Most Goals	252	1993-94 (84), 1995-96 (82)
Most Goals Against	414	1992-93 (84)
Fewest Points	24	1992-93 (84)
Fewest Wins	11	1992-93 (84)
Fewest Ties	*2	1992-93 (84)
Fewest Losses	33	1998-99 (82)
Fewest Goals	196	1998-99 (82)
Fewest Goals Against	191	1998-99 (82)

Longest Winning Streak

Overall	7	Mar. 24-Apr. 5/94
Home	5	Jan. 21-Feb. 15/95
Away	4	Four times

Longest Undefeated Streak

Overall	9	Mar. 20-Apr. 5/94 (7 wins, 2 ties)
Home	6	Three times
Away	6	Twice

Longest Losing Streak

Overall	*17	Jan. 4-Feb. 12/93
Home	9	Nov. 19-Dec. 19/92
Away	19	Nov. 27/92-Feb. 12/93

Longest Winless Streak

Overall	20	Dec. 29/92-Feb. 12/93 (19 losses, 1 tie)
Home	9	Nov. 19-Dec. 19/92 (9 losses)
Away	19	Nov. 27/92-Feb. 12/93 (19 losses)

Most Shutouts, Season	8	1998-99 (82)
Most PIM, Season	2134	1992-93 (84)
Most Goals, Game	10	Jan. 13/96 (S.J. 10 at Pit. 8)

Individual

Most Seasons	6	Mike Rathje, Ray Whitney
Most Games, Career	366	Jeff Friesen
Most Goals, Career	111	Jeff Friesen
Most Assists, Career	142	Jeff Friesen
Most Points, Career	253	Jeff Friesen (111G, 142A)
Most PIM, Career	1,001	Jeff Odgers
Most Shutouts, Career	9	Mike Vernon

Longest Consecutive Games Streak	141	Mike Ricci (Nov. 22/97-date)
Most Goals, Season	31	Owen Nolan (1996-97); Jeff Friesen (1997-98)

Most Assists, Season	52	Kelly Kisio (1992-93)
Most Points, Season	78	Kelly Kisio (1992-93; 26G, 52A)
Most PIM, Season	326	Link Gaetz (1991-92)
Most Shutouts, Season	5	Mike Vernon (1997-98)
Most Points, Defenseman, Season	64	Sandis Ozolinsh (1993-94; 26G, 38A)
Most Points, Center, Season	78	Kelly Kisio (1992-93; 26G, 52A)
Most Points, Right Wing, Season	68	Sergei Makarov (1993-94; 30G, 38A)
Most Points, Left Wing, Season	66	Johan Garpenlov (1992-93; 22G, 44A)
Most Points, Rookie, Season	59	Pat Falloon (1991-92; 25G, 34A)
Most Goals, Game	4	Owen Nolan (Dec. 19/95)
Most Assists, Game	4	Three times
Most Points, Game	5	Owen Nolan (Dec. 19/95; 4G, 1A), Marco Sturm (Dec. 23/98; 3G, 2A)

* NHL Record.

General Manager

LOMBARDI, DEAN
Executive Vice President and General Manager, San Jose Sharks.
Born in Holyoke, MA, March 5, 1958.

Dean Lombardi is the architect who built the San Jose hockey club. A charter member of the Sharks' management team, Lombardi joined the club in 1990 as assistant general manager after having served in a similar capacity with the Minnesota North Stars. He was named San Jose's director of hockey operations on June 26, 1992 and became the club's general manager on March 6, 1996. As the team's top hockey executive, he oversees player personnel decisions, negotiates player contracts and coordinates the efforts of the Sharks' scouting and player evaluation departments.

Lombardi has spent considerable effort in building a professional scouting staff, reorganizing the amateur scouting department, and establishing a system to evaluate pro players at all levels. He has stood firm in building the Sharks through the draft. San Jose draft picks making important contributions to the club include forwards Jeff Friesen, Patrick Marleau and Marco Sturm, along with defensemen Marcus Ragnarsson and Mike Rathje.

After the 1993-94 season that saw the Sharks post an NHL record single season improvement of 58 points, Lombardi finished third in *The Hockey News* award voting for executive of the year.

General Managers' History

Jack Ferreira, 1991-92; Chuck Grillo (V.P. Director of Player Personnel), 1992-93 to 1995-96; Dean Lombardi, 1996-97 to date.

All-time Record vs. Other Clubs

Regular Season

	GP	W	L	T	GF	GA	PTS	GP	W	L	T	GF	GA	PTS	GP	W	L	T	GF	GA	PTS
			At Home							On Road							Total				
Anaheim	16	6	8	2	48	51	14	17	10	4	3	59	45	21	33	16	14	3	107	96	35
Boston	7	1	4	2	18	29	4	7	0	5	2	17	26	2	14	1	9	4	35	55	6
Buffalo	7	3	1	3	26	25	9	8	0	8	0	23	41	0	15	3	9	3	49	66	9
Calgary	24	6	16	2	67	82	14	22	7	13	2	60	94	16	46	13	29	4	127	176	30
Carolina	7	4	3	0	34	23	8	8	4	4	0	18	26	8	15	8	7	0	52	49	16
Chicago	16	8	8	0	39	46	16	15	5	8	2	42	51	12	31	13	16	2	81	97	28
Colorado	14	6	8	0	46	57	12	13	2	10	1	28	62	5	27	8	18	1	74	119	17
Dallas	16	6	10	0	37	48	12	16	6	8	2	41	49	14	32	12	18	2	78	97	26
Detroit	16	5	9	2	51	70	12	15	1	14	0	25	70	2	31	6	23	2	76	140	14
Edmonton	22	11	9	2	78	71	24	23	4	16	3	52	91	11	45	15	25	5	130	162	35
Florida	5	2	1	2	12	12	6	5	0	1	4	10	13	4	10	2	2	6	22	25	10
Los Angeles	24	12	9	3	86	76	27	23	6	16	1	61	86	13	47	18	25	4	147	162	40
Montreal	7	2	3	2	20	19	6	6	0	6	2	12	31	2	15	2	9	4	32	50	8
Nashville	2	1	1	0	5	5	2	2	1	1	0	5	5	2	4	2	2	0	10	10	4
New Jersey	7	2	4	1	14	21	5	8	3	4	1	17	30	7	15	5	8	2	31	51	12
NY Islanders	7	2	4	1	15	25	5	8	2	5	1	25	37	5	15	4	9	2	40	62	10
NY Rangers	8	0	7	1	17	34	1	7	0	6	1	21	36	1	15	0	13	2	38	70	2
Ottawa	6	4	2	0	11	8	8	6	0	2	4	15	18	4	12	4	4	4	26	26	12
Philadelphia	8	1	6	1	14	25	3	7	2	4	1	15	25	5	15	3	10	2	29	50	8
Phoenix	19	8	9	2	67	72	18	21	6	12	3	56	71	15	40	14	21	5	123	143	33
Pittsburgh	8	1	6	1	16	47	3	6	2	3	1	20	32	5	14	3	9	2	36	79	8
St. Louis	14	2	11	1	32	49	5	17	5	12	0	40	61	10	31	7	23	1	72	110	15
Tampa Bay	7	2	5	0	24	26	4	7	3	4	0	16	20	6	14	5	9	0	40	46	10
Toronto	14	5	7	2	30	38	12	14	4	9	1	38	56	9	28	9	16	3	68	94	21
Vancouver	24	8	11	5	72	75	21	22	6	15	1	55	87	13	46	14	26	6	127	162	34
Washington	7	3	3	1	20	21	7	7	2	5	0	17	23	4	14	5	8	1	37	44	11
Totals	**312**	**111**	**165**	**36**	**899**	**1055**	**258**	**312**	**81**	**197**	**34**	**788**	**1186**	**196**	**624**	**192**	**362**	**70**	**1687**	**2241**	**454**

Playoffs

	Series	W	L	GP	W	L	T	GF	GA	Last Mtg.	Round	Result
Calgary	1	1	0	7	4	3	0	26	35	1995	CQF	W 4-3
Colorado	1	0	1	6	2	4	0	19	19	1999	CQF	L 2-4
Dallas	1	0	1	6	2	4	0	12	16	1998	CQF	W 2-4
Detroit	2	1	1	11	4	7	0	27	51	1995	CSF	L 0-4
Toronto	1	0	1	7	3	4	0	21	26	1994	CSF	L 3-4
Totals	**6**	**2**	**4**	**37**	**15**	**22**	**0**	**103**	**147**			

Playoff Results 1999-95

Year	Round	Opponent	Result	GF	GA
1999	CQF	Colorado	L 2-4	17	19
1998	CQF	Dallas	L 2-4	12	16
1995	CSF	Detroit	L 0-4	6	24
	CQF	Calgary	W 4-3	26	35

Abbreviations: Round: CSF – conference semi-final; **CQF** – conference quarter-final.

Carolina totals include Hartford, 1991-92 to 1996-97.
Dallas totals include Minnesota, 1991-92 to 1992-93.
Colorado totals include Quebec, 1991-92 to 1994-95.
Phoenix totals include Winnipeg, 1991-92 to 1995-96.

1998-99 Results

Oct.	9	at Calgary	3-3		15	Pittsburgh	3-2
	10	at Calgary	3-5		16	Calgary	3-3
	18	Boston	0-3		18	New Jersey	3-1
	20	at Philadelphia	1-3		21	Edmonton	3-3
	22	at Chicago	2-2		26	St. Louis	0-3
	24	at Dallas	1-2		30	at Colorado	0-5
	28	Phoenix	2-4	Feb.	1	Chicago	5-1
	29	at Colorado	2-4		4	at Phoenix	1-3
	31	Tampa Bay	6-1		6	at Los Angeles	0-2
Nov.	4	Dallas	4-0		8	at Phoenix	3-0
	6	at Anaheim	2-2		10	at Chicago	5-2
	7	St. Louis	2-2		11	at St. Louis	5-1
	10	Nashville	2-4		13	at Tampa Bay	3-0
	12	Carolina	3-0		15	at Florida	2-2
	18	Los Angeles	5-4		17	at Detroit	1-3
	20	Phoenix	1-2		19	at Buffalo	2-4
	21	NY Rangers	2-2		20	at Washington	1-3
	23	at Dallas	2-3		24	Vancouver	1-1
	25	at Carolina	0-3		26	at Anaheim	1-3
	27	at St. Louis	4-2		27	Anaheim	1-4
	29	at Detroit	1-4	Mar.	1	at Calgary	2-1
Dec.	2	Dallas	0-3		3	at Vancouver	4-3
	4	Detroit	2-2		6	Chicago	0-4
	6	Anaheim	1-2		9	Phoenix	4-2
	9	at Dallas	3-3		12	Detroit	2-0
	10	at Nashville	1-2		13	Ottawa	3-2
	12	Washington	2-1		17	Florida	4-2
	15	NY Islanders	0-1		20	at Boston	2-2
	17	Nashville	3-1		22	at Montreal	1-1
	19	Colorado	2-1		24	at Toronto	8-5
	23	at Edmonton	5-3		26	at Ottawa	1-1
	26	Vancouver	2-0		28	at Edmonton	2-5
	28	Philadelphia	1-1		31	Colorado	2-3
	30	at Los Angeles	1-5	Apr.	2	at Vancouver	7-0
Jan.	2	at NY Islanders	4-3		3	Vancouver	5-2
	4	at NY Rangers	3-4		6	at Phoenix	1-0
	5	at New Jersey	3-3		8	at Los Angeles	4-1
	7	at Nashville	4-3		9	at Anaheim	4-1
	9	Buffalo	2-2		12	Edmonton	4-5
	11	Los Angeles	4-0		16	Los Angeles	0-2
	13	Dallas	1-2		17	Anaheim	3-3

Entry Draft Selections 1999-91

1999

Pick	
14	Jeff Jillson
82	Mark Concannon
111	Willie Levesque
155	Nicholas Dimitrakos
229	Eric Betournay
241	Doug Murray
257	Hannes Hyvonen

1998

Pick	
3	Brad Stuart
29	Jonathon Cheechoo
65	Eric LaPlante
98	Rob Davison
104	Miroslav Zalesak
127	Brandon Coalter
145	Mikael Samuelsson
185	Robert Mulick
212	Jim Fahey

1997

Pick	
2	Patrick Marleau
23	Scott Hannan
82	Adam Colagiacomo
107	Adam Nittel
163	Joe Dusbabek
192	Cam Severson
219	Mark Smith

1996

Pick	
2	Andrei Zyuzin
21	Marco Sturm
55	Terry Friesen
102	Matt Bradley
137	Michel Larocque
164	Jake Deadmarsh
191	Cory Cyrenne
217	David Thibeault

1995

Pick	
12	Teemu Riihijarvi
38	Peter Roed
64	Marko Makinen
90	Vesa Toskala
116	Miikka Kiprusoff
130	Michal Bros
140	Timo Hakanen
142	Jaroslav Kudrna
167	Brad Mehalko
168	Robert Jindrich
194	Ryan Kraft
220	Miiko Markkanen

1994

Pick	
11	Jeff Friesen
37	Angel Nikolov
66	Alexei Yegorov
89	Vaclav Varada
115	Brian Swanson
141	Alexander Korolyuk
167	Sergei Gorbachev
193	Eric Landry
219	Yevgeny Nabokov
240	Tomas Pisa
245	Aniket Dhadphale
271	David Beauregard

1993

Pick	
6	Viktor Kozlov
28	Shean Donovan
45	Vlastimil Kroupa
58	Ville Peltonen
80	Alexander Osadchy
106	Andrei Buschan
132	Petri Varis
154	Fredrik Oduya
158	Anatoli Filatov
184	Todd Holt
210	Jonas Forsberg
236	Jeff Salajko
262	Jamie Matthews

1992

Pick	
3	Mike Rathje
10	Andrei Nazarov
51	Alexander Cherbajev
75	Jan Caloun
99	Marcus Ragnarsson
123	Michal Sykora
147	Eric Bellerose
171	Ryan Smith
195	Chris Burns
219	A. Kholomeyev
243	Victor Ignatjev

1991

Pick	
2	Pat Falloon
23	Ray Whitney
30	Sandis Ozolinsh
45	Dody Wood
67	Kerry Toporowski
89	Dan Ryder
111	Fredrik Nilsson
133	Jaroslav Otevrel
155	Dean Grillo
177	Corwin Saurdiff
199	Dale Craigwell
221	Aaron Kriss
243	Mikhail Kravets

Club Directory

San Jose Arena
525 West Santa Clara Street
San Jose, CA 95113
Phone **408/287-7070**
FAX 408/999-5797
Internet http://www.sj-sharks.com
Capacity: 17,483

Executive Staff

Owner & Chairman	George Gund III
Co-Owner	Gordon Gund
President & Chief Executive Officer	Greg Jamison
Senior Executive Vice President & Chief Operating Officer	Frank Jirik
Executive Vice President of Business Operations	Malcolm Bordelon
Executive Vice President & General Manager (San Jose Arena)	Jim Goddard
Executive Vice President & General Counsel	Don Gralnek
Executive Vice President of Ventures	Matt Levine
Executive Vice President & General Manager	Dean Lombardi
Executive Vice President & Chief Financial Officer	Gregg Olson
Vice Chairman	Tom McEnery
Vice President of Corporate Partnerships	Greg Elliott
Vice President of Building Operations	Rich Sotelo
Vice President of Sales & Marketing	Kent Russell
Executive Assistant	Michelle Simmons

Hockey

Assistant General Manager	Wayne Thomas
Head Coach	Darryl Sutter
Assistant Coach	Paul Baxter
Assistant Coach	Bob Berry
Director of Pro Development	Doug Wilson
Senior Professional Scout	John Ferguson
Professional Scout	Barry Long
Professional Scout	Cap Raeder
Director of Amateur Scouting	Tim Burke
Chief Scout	Ray Payne
Assistant to the General Manager	Joe Will
Scouts	Pat Funk, Rob Grillo, Brian Gross, Karel Masopust
Executive Assistant	Brenda Will
Video Scouting Coordinator	Bob Friedlander
Goaltender Consultant	Warren Strelow
Head Athletic Trainer	Ray Tufts, ATC
Athletic Trainer	Tom Woodcock
Strength & Conditioning Coordinator	Mac Read
Massage Therapist	Wes Howard
Equipment Manager	Mike Aldrich
Assistant Equipment Manager	Kurt Harvey
Equipment Assistant & Equipment Transportation	Jason Rudee
Team Services Coordinator	Aaron Abrams
Director of Hockey Operations, Kentucky Thoroughblades	Jim Wiley
Head Coach, Kentucky Thoroughblades	Roy Sommer
Assistant Coach, Kentucky Thoroughblades	Nick Fotiu
Head Trainer, Kentucky Thoroughblades	Jerry Iannarelli
Team Physician	Arthur J. Ting, M.D.
Team Dentist	Robert Bonahoom, D.D.S.
Team Vision Specialist	Vincent S. Zuccaro, O.D., F.A.A.O.
Medical Staff	Warren King, M.D., Mark Sontag, M.D., Will Straw, M.D.

Business Operations

Director of Broadcasting	Frank Albin
Director of Media Relations	Ken Arnold
Director of Sponsorship	Mark Foxton
Director of Event Presentation	Jason Minsky
Director of Community Development	Eric Stanion
Director of Internet Services	TBA
Sponsorship Services Manager	TBA
Sponsorship Sales Manager	Jennifer Birmingham, Bryan Deierling, Chris Parker
Internet Services Manager	Kimberly Brown
The Sharks Foundation Manager	Jackie Fuce
Mascot Operations Manager	Tim Patnode
Media Relations Manager	Roger Ross
Corporate Sales Account Manager	Dave Severson
Sponsorship Promotions/Broadcast Manager	Anna Traggio
Community Development & Education Manager	Julie Vennewitz
Community Development Coordinator	Chris Bradford
Media Relations Coordinator	Scott Emmert
Community Development Coordinator	Kimberly McIntyre
Event Presentation Coordinator	Steve Maroni
Executive Assistant	Mary Grace Miller

Marketing

Director of Advertising & Publicity	Beth Brigino
Director of Suite Hospitality	Jay O'Sullivan
Director of Ticket Operations	Mary Enriquez
Tennis Tournament Manager, Sybase Open	Kristi Breisch
Account Sales Managers	Jeff Goda, Mike Hollywood, Andy Fiske
Sybase Open Director of Sales/ Assistant Tournament Director	Bill Rapp
Suite Hospitality Manager	TBA
Account Service Manager	Sharon Holman, Kristin Lyon, Kathy Payne
Marketing Manager	Jim Sparaco
Ticket Operations Coordinator	John Castro
Marketing Coordinator	Steward Diner
Administrative Assistant	Christine Guerrero

Finance

Director of Finance	Ken Caveney
Finance Manager	Steve Calamia
Human Resources Manager	Carol Ross
Information Systems Manager	James Struckle
Staff Accountant	Jim Boyle, Tina Park
Payroll Accounting Associate	Sue Feachen
Accounts Payable Accounting Associate	Catherine Layman
Accounts Receivable Accounting Associate	Diane Rubino
System Support Specialist	Josh Schlieff, Frank Frasula
Executive Assistant	Tricia Nordquist

Building Operations

Director of Ticket Operations	Daniel DeBoer
Director of Booking & Events	Steve Kirsner
Director of Booking & Events	TBA
Director of Guest Services	Ken Sweezey
Facilities Technical Director	Greg Carrolan
Chief Engineer	Jay Farr
Telephone Systems Manager	Bob Davis
Building Services Manager	Bruce Tharaldson, Monte Chavez
Assistant Building Services Manager	Frank Peinado
Security Manager	Geoff Pepe
Ticket Operations Manager	Judy Jones
Ushering & Emergency Medical Manager	TBA
Parking and Carousel Manager	Kimberley Gutierrez
Recruiting and Training Manager	Jason Parker
Building Services Coordinator	George Gund IV, Greg Gund, Rose Juarez, Peggy Roland
Mailroom Coordinator	Richard Perez
Guest Services Coordinator	Julie Radford, Vikki Klass, Andrea Teed
Executive Assistant	Christine de la Cruz, Beth Ganeff
Administrative Assistant	Maureen Miller
Engineers	Michael Garcia, James Engle, Jeff Cassidy, Robert Dougherty, Eric Gold, Diane Kirkpatrick, Mike Murphy
Engineering Administrative Assistant	Melanie Mathis
Cleaning Supervisor	Ray Romero
Conversion Supervisor	Carlos Munoz
Parking Coordinator	Patrick Doherty

ARAMARK Sports & Entertainment

Human Resources Director	Adrian Flores
General Manager	Dale Haynes
Concessions Manager	David Casarez
Assistant Concessions Manager	Gretchen La Due
Food and Beverage Warehouse Manager	Jerry Watson
Restaurant Manager	TBA
Suite Catering Manager	Jeff Dal Bon
Merchandise Manager	Eric Pearson
Merchandise Warehouse Manager	Steve Alt
F & B Director	TBA
Executive Sous Chef	Victor Lopez
Executive Chef	Dennis Glafkides
Suite Supervisor	Bruce Ross
Catering Supervisor	Susan Friedlander
Buyer/Inventory Control	Kris Fasoli
Financial Controller	Linda Wilczewski

Miscellaneous

Team Colors	Deep Pacific Teal, Shimmering Gray, Burnt Orange & Black
Television Station	Fox Sports Net Bay Area
Radio Network Flagship	KARA (105.7 FM)/KLIV (1590 AM)
Television Play-By-Play Broadcaster	Randy Hahn
Television Color Analyst	Steve Konroyd
Radio Play-By-Play Broadcaster	Dan Rusanowsky
Radio Color Analyst	Drew Remenda
Team Photographers	Don Smith, Rocky Widner
P.A. Announcer	Joe Ike
Organist	Jim Sealy
Mascot	S.J. Sharkie

Tampa Bay Lightning

1998-99 Results: 19w-54l-9t 47pts. Fourth, Southeast Division

Year-by-Year Record

Season	GP	Home W	L	T	Road W	L	T	Overall W	L	T	GF	GA	Pts.	Finished		Playoff Result
1998-99	82	12	25	4	7	29	5	19	54	9	179	292	47	4th,	Southeast Div.	Out of Playoffs
1997-98	82	11	23	7	6	32	3	17	55	10	151	269	44	7th,	Atlantic Div.	Out of Playoffs
1996-97	82	15	18	8	17	22	2	32	40	10	217	247	74	6th,	Atlantic Div.	Out of Playoffs
1995-96	82	22	14	5	16	18	7	38	32	12	238	248	88	5th,	Atlantic Div.	Lost Conf. Quarter-Final
1994-95	48	10	14	0	7	14	3	17	28	3	120	144	37	6th,	Atlantic Div.	Out of Playoffs
1993-94	84	14	22	6	16	21	5	30	43	11	224	251	71	7th,	Atlantic Div.	Out of Playoffs
1992-93	84	12	27	3	11	27	4	23	54	7	245	332	53	6th,	Norris Div.	Out of Playoffs

1999-2000 Schedule

Oct.	Sat.	2	NY Islanders	Sat.	15	Florida	
	Thu.	7	Los Angeles	Mon.	17	Washington*	
	Sat.	9	at New Jersey	Thu.	20	Boston	
	Fri.	15	Anaheim	Sat.	22	at NY Islanders	
	Sat.	16	Atlanta	Mon.	24	at Washington	
	Tue.	19	Vancouver	Tue.	25	at Buffalo	
	Sat.	23	Calgary	Fri.	28	Edmonton	
	Wed.	27	at Buffalo	Sat.	29	Atlanta	
	Thu.	28	at Boston	**Feb.**	Tue.	1	Toronto
	Sat.	30	at Dallas		Thu.	3	Montreal
Nov.	Wed.	3	at Atlanta		Tue.	8	San Jose
	Sat.	6	at Pittsburgh		Thu.	10	at NY Islanders
	Sun.	7	Detroit		Sat.	12	Carolina
	Tue.	9	at Washington		Tue.	15	NY Rangers
	Fri.	12	Buffalo		Thu.	17	at Ottawa
	Sat.	13	at Carolina		Sat.	19	at Carolina
	Wed.	17	at Atlanta		Mon.	21	Pittsburgh
	Thu.	18	Pittsburgh		Thu.	24	Ottawa
	Sat.	20	at Philadelphia		Sat.	26	at Nashville
	Mon.	22	Philadelphia		Sun.	27	at Detroit
	Wed.	24	NY Rangers	**Mar.**	Wed.	1	Washington
	Fri.	26	Carolina		Fri.	3	at Chicago
	Sun.	28	Buffalo		Sat.	4	at Colorado
Dec.	Wed.	1	at Anaheim		Wed.	8	Philadelphia
	Thu.	2	at Phoenix		Fri.	10	Florida
	Sat.	4	at Los Angeles		Sun.	12	Chicago
	Mon.	6	at San Jose		Tue.	14	at Montreal
	Fri.	10	Carolina		Wed.	15	at NY Rangers
	Tue.	14	Nashville		Fri.	17	at New Jersey
	Sat.	18	at Philadelphia		Sun.	19	at Washington*
	Sun.	19	at NY Rangers		Tue.	21	at Boston
	Tue.	21	Toronto		Fri.	24	St. Louis
	Thu.	23	at Pittsburgh		Sun.	26	Montreal
	Sun.	26	at Atlanta		Tue.	28	Dallas
	Mon.	27	Florida		Thu.	30	Ottawa
Jan.	Sat.	1	at Florida*	**Apr.**	Sat.	1	at Florida
	Wed.	5	at Vancouver		Sun.	2	New Jersey
	Fri.	7	at Edmonton		Tue.	4	Boston
	Sat.	8	at Calgary		Thu.	6	at Montreal
	Tue.	11	New Jersey		Sat.	8	at Toronto
	Thu.	13	NY Islanders		Sun.	9	at Ottawa

* Denotes afternoon game.

First-overall draft choice Vincent Lecavalier showed great improvement as the 1998-99 season progressed. Though Tampa Bay was the NHL's lowest-scoring team, Lecavalier finished among the top rookie scorers with 13 goals, 15 assists and 28 points.

Sergey Gusev was obtained in a trade with Dallas on March 21, 1999. He was named top defenseman with the Stars' Michigan K-Wings farm club in 1996-97 and scored his first NHL goal during the 1998-99 season.

Franchise date: December 16, 1991

EASTERN CONFERENCE
SOUTHEAST DIVISION

8th NHL Season

1999-2000 Player Personnel

FORWARDS

	HT	WT	S	Place of Birth	Date	1998-99 Club
BURR, Shawn	6-1	205	L	Sarnia, Ont.	7/1/66	San Jose-Kentucky
CARDARELLI, Joe	6-0	203	L	Vancouver, B.C.	6/13/77	Chesapeake-Cleveland
DAIGLE, Alexandre	6-0	195	L	Montreal, Que.	2/7/75	Philadelphia-Tampa Bay
DELISLE, Xavier	5-11	182	R	Quebec City, Que.	5/24/77	Tampa Bay-Cleveland
ELICH, Matt	6-3	187	R	Detroit, MI	9/22/79	Kingston
FORBES, Colin	6-3	205	L	New Westminster, B.C.	2/16/76	Philadelphia-Tampa Bay
FREADRICH, Kyle	6-6	225	L	Edmonton, Alta.	12/28/78	Regina-Syracuse-Louisiana
GRATTON, Chris	6-4	218	L	Brantford, Ont.	7/5/75	Philadelphia-Tampa Bay
GUOLLA, Stephen	6-0	190	L	Scarborough, Ont.	3/15/73	San Jose-Kentucky
JOHANSSON, Andreas	6-0	205	L	Hofors, Sweden	5/19/73	Ottawa
KELLY, Steve	6-1	190	L	Vancouver, B.C.	10/26/76	Tampa Bay-Cleveland
LECAVALIER, Vincent	6-4	180	L	Ile Bizard, Que.	4/21/80	Tampa Bay
NYLANDER, Michael	5-11	195	L	Stockholm, Sweden	10/3/72	Calgary-Tampa Bay
PERSHIN, Eduard	6-0	191	L	Nizhnekamsk, USSR	9/1/77	Chesapeake-Cleveland
PETROVICKY, Robert	5-11	172	L	Kosice, Czech.	10/26/73	Grand Rapids-Tampa Bay
RICHER, Stephane	6-2	215	R	Ripon, Que.	6/7/66	Tampa Bay
ROMINSKI, Dale	6-2	200	R	Farmington Hills, MI	10/1/75	U. of Michigan
ST. PIERRE, Samuel	6-1	170	L	Laurierville, Que.	6/28/79	Drummondville-Cleveland
SHEVALIER, Jeff	5-11	180	L	Mississauga, Ont.	3/14/74	Cincinnati (IHL)
SILLINGER, Mike	5-10	190	R	Regina, Sask.	6/29/71	Philadelphia-Tampa Bay
SPRING, Corey	6-4	214	L	Cranbrook, B.C.	5/31/71	Tampa Bay-Cleveland
TUCKER, Darcy	5-10	179	L	Castor, Alta.	3/15/75	Tampa Bay

DEFENSEMEN

	HT	WT	S	Place of Birth	Date	1998-99 Club
ASTASHENKO, Kaspars	6-2	183	L	Riga, Latvia	2/17/75	Cincinnati (IHL)-Dayton
BANNISTER, Drew	6-2	200	R	Belleville, Ont.	9/4/74	Tampa Bay-Las Vegas
BETIK, Karel	6-2	208	L	Karvina, Czech.	10/28/78	Tampa Bay-Cleveland
CROSS, Cory	6-5	219	L	Lloydminster, Alta.	1/3/71	Tampa Bay
CULLIMORE, Jassen	6-5	225	L	Simcoe, Ont.	12/4/72	Tampa Bay
GUSEV, Sergey	6-1	195	L	Nizhny Tagil, USSR	7/31/75	Dallas-Michigan-Tampa Bay
HOULDER, Bill	6-2	210	L	Thunder Bay, Ont.	3/11/67	San Jose
KOS, Kyle	6-3	184	L	Hope, B.C.	5/25/79	Red Deer-Kamloops
KUBINA, Pavel	6-3	213	R	Celadna, Czech.	4/15/77	Tampa Bay-Cleveland
KUPARINEN, Mikko	6-2	213	L	Kerava, Finland	3/29/77	HPK-Ahmat-G. Rapids
LAROCQUE, Mario	6-2	182	L	Montreal, Que.	4/24/78	Tampa Bay-Plymouth
MARA, Paul	6-4	202	L	Ridgewood, NJ	9/7/79	Tampa Bay-Plymouth
McBAIN, Mike	6-2	195	L	Kimberley, B.C.	1/12/77	Tampa Bay-Cleveland
ROBINSON, Jason	6-2	190	L	Goderich, Ont.	8/22/78	Chesapeake-Cleveland
SKOPINTSEV, Andrei	6-0	185	R	Elekrostal, USSR	9/28/71	Tampa Bay-Cleveland
SVOBODA, Petr	6-1	180	L	Most, Czech.	2/14/66	Philadelphia-Tampa Bay
VON STEFENELLI, Phil	6-1	200	L	Vancouver, B.C.	4/10/69	Frankfurt-Frankfurt
ZYUZIN, Andrei	6-1	195	L	Ufa, USSR	1/21/78	San Jose-Kentucky

GOALTENDERS

	HT	WT	C	Place of Birth	Date	1998-99 Club
BIERK, Zac	6-4	186	L	Peterborough, Ont.	9/17/76	Tampa Bay-Cleveland
BRADETTE, Martin	6-0	185	L	Lavalle, Que.	1/20/77	Clev-Wins-Sal-Chesapeake-Bir
CLOUTIER, Dan	6-1	182	L	Mont-Laurier, Que.	4/22/76	NY Rangers
HODSON, Kevin	6-0	182	L	Winnipeg, Man.	3/27/72	Detroit-Adirondack-Tampa Bay
PUPPA, Daren	6-4	205	R	Kirkland Lake, Ont.	3/23/65	Tampa Bay

Coach

LUDZIK, STEVE
Coach, Tampa Bay Lightning. Born in Toronto, Ont., April 3, 1962.

Steve Ludzik was named as the Lightning head coach on July 14, 1999, rejoining friend, and once-again boss, Rick Dudley. Ludzik became the fourth head coach in franchise history, and the first under the new ownership of Palace Sports and Entertainment, following a successful three-year run with the Detroit Vipers in which he racked up a regular-season record of 154-58-34 behind the bench. Also during his time in Detroit, Ludzik took the IHL franchise to the Turner Cup Finals two years in a row, winning it on the first trip in 1997. The Vipers' 122 points in 1996-97 marked the third-highest point total in IHL history. His .695 winning percentage is tops all-time in the IHL.

The position in Tampa Bay marks Ludzik's first as a head coach in the NHL. In addition to his coaching time in Detroit, Ludzik also had a successful tenure as bench boss for the Muskegon Fury of then Colonial Hockey League (now UHL). With Ludzik behind the bench the Fury posted a 77-51-10 record in his two seasons and reached the League finals in 1994-95. Ludzik became an associate coach under Rick Dudley in Detroit the following season.

During his playing career, Ludzik spent nine seasons in the NHL with the Chicago Blackhawks and Buffalo Sabres, playing 424 games, scoring 46 goals with 93 assists. Ludzik also spent time with the International Hockey League's Saginaw Hawks (1988-89), and American Hockey League's Rochester Americans (1989 to 1992).

Coaching Record

			Regular Season				Playoffs			
Season	Team	Games	W	L	T	%	Games	W	L	%
1993-94	Muskegon (CoHL)	64	35	24	5	.586	3	0	3	.000
1994-95	Muskegon (CoHL)	74	42	27	5	.601	17	10	7	.588
1996-97	Detroit (IHL)	82	57	17	8	.744	17	12	5	.706
1997-98	Detroit (IHL)	82	47	20	15	.665	23	14	9	.609
1998-99	Detroit (IHL)	82	50	21	11	.677	11	6	5	.545

1998-99 Scoring

* – rookie

Regular Season

Pos	#	Player	Team	GP	G	A	Pts	+/–	PIM	PP	SH	GW	GT	S	%
C	16	Darcy Tucker	T.B.	82	21	22	43	–34	176	8	2	3	0	178	11.8
C	77	Chris Gratton	PHI	26	1	7	8	–8	41	0	0	0	0	54	1.9
			T.B.	52	7	19	26	–20	102	1	0	1	1	127	5.5
			TOTAL	78	8	26	34	–28	143	1	0	1	1	181	4.4
R	44	Stephane Richer	T.B.	64	12	21	33	–10	22	3	2	1	0	139	8.6
C	8	* Vincent Lecavalier	T.B.	82	13	15	28	–19	23	2	0	2	1	125	10.4
D	23	Petr Svoboda	PHI	25	4	2	6	5	28	1	1	1	0	37	10.8
			T.B.	34	1	16	17	–4	53	0	0	0	0	46	2.2
			TOTAL	59	5	18	23	1	81	1	1	1	0	83	6.0
D	13	* Pavel Kubina	T.B.	68	9	12	21	–33	80	3	1	1	1	119	7.6
L	27	Colin Forbes	PHI	66	9	7	16	0	51	0	0	4	0	92	9.8
			T.B.	14	3	1	4	–5	10	0	1	0	0	25	12.0
			TOTAL	80	12	8	20	–5	61	0	1	4	0	117	10.3
L	7	Rob Zamuner	T.B.	58	8	11	19	–15	24	1	1	2	0	89	9.0
D	4	Cory Cross	T.B.	67	2	16	18	–25	92	0	0	0	0	96	2.1
R	21	Alexandre Daigle	PHI	31	3	2	5	–1	2	1	0	1	0	26	11.5
			T.B.	32	6	6	12	–12	2	3	0	2	0	56	10.7
			TOTAL	63	9	8	17	–13	4	4	0	1	2	82	11.0
D	5	Jassen Cullimore	T.B.	78	5	12	17	–22	81	1	0	0	0	73	6.8
C	9	Michael Nylander	CGY	9	2	3	5	1	2	1	0	0	0	7	28.6
			T.B.	24	2	7	9	–10	6	0	0	0	0	26	7.7
			TOTAL	33	4	10	14	–9	8	1	0	0	0	33	12.1
C	26	Mike Sillinger	PHI	25	0	3	3	–9	8	0	0	0	0	23	0.0
			T.B.	54	8	2	10	–20	28	0	2	0	0	69	11.6
			TOTAL	79	8	5	13	–29	36	0	2	0	0	92	8.7
D	3	* Sergey Gusev	DAL	22	1	4	5	5	6	0	0	0	0	30	3.3
			T.B.	14	0	3	3	–8	10	0	0	0	0	16	0.0
			TOTAL	36	1	7	8	–3	16	0	0	0	0	46	2.2
D	49	David Wilkie	T.B.	46	1	7	8	–19	69	0	0	0	0	35	2.9
C	14	Robert Petrovicky	T.B.	28	3	4	7	–8	6	0	0	0	0	32	9.4
D	2	Mike McBain	T.B.	37	0	6	6	–11	14	0	0	0	0	22	0.0
D	28	Kjell Samuelsson	T.B.	46	1	4	5	–6	38	0	0	0	0	22	4.5
C	11	Steve Kelly	T.B.	34	1	3	4	–15	27	0	0	1	0	15	6.7
G	32	Corey Schwab	T.B.	40	0	4	4	0	4	0	0	0	0	0	0.0
L	27	Brent Peterson	T.B.	20	2	1	3	–2	0	0	0	0	0	16	12.5
D	23	Michal Sykora	T.B.	10	1	2	3	–7	0	0	0	1	0	24	4.2
C	64	Jason Bonsignore	T.B.	23	0	3	3	–4	8	0	0	0	0	12	0.0
D	22	* Paul Mara	T.B.	1	1	2	3	–3	0	1	0	0	0	1	100.0
D	46	Andrei Skopintsev	T.B.	19	1	1	2	1	10	0	0	0	0	17	5.9
D	6	* Karel Betik	T.B.	3	0	2	2	–3	2	0	0	0	0	2	0.0
D	3	* Sami Helenius	CGY	4	0	0	0	–1	8	0	0	0	0	0	0.0
			T.B.	4	1	0	1	–3	15	0	1	0	0	3	33.3
			TOTAL	8	1	0	1	–5	23	0	1	0	0	4	25.0
C	20	Corey Spring	T.B.	8	0	1	1	1	0	0	0	0	0	6	0.0
L	15	Paul Ysebaert	T.B.	10	0	1	1	–5	2	0	0	0	0	10	0.0
G	93	Daren Puppa	T.B.	13	0	1	1	0	0	0	0	0	0	0	0.0
G	1	* Zac Bierk	T.B.	1	0	0	0	0	0	0	0	0	0	0	0.0
C	43	* Xavier Delisle	T.B.	2	0	0	0	0	0	0	0	0	0	1	0.0
C	12	John Cullen	T.B.	4	0	0	0	–2	2	0	0	0	0	3	0.0
G	35	* Derek Wilkinson	T.B.	5	0	0	0	0	0	0	0	0	0	0	0.0
D	71	* Mario Larocque	T.B.	5	0	0	0	–4	16	0	0	0	0	3	0.0
G	31	Kevin Hodson	DET	5	0	0	0	0	0	0	0	0	0	0	0.0
			T.B.	5	0	0	0	0	0	0	0	0	0	0	0.0
			TOTAL	9	0	0	0	0	0	0	0	0	0	0	0.0

Goaltending

No.	Goaltender	GPI	Mins	Avg	W	L	T	EN	SO	GA	SA	S%
1	* Zac Bierk	1	59	2.03	0	1	0	0	0	2	21	.905
31	Kevin Hodson	5	238	2.77	2	1	1	0	0	11	118	.907
93	Daren Puppa	13	691	2.87	5	6	1	1	2	33	350	.906
35	* Derek Wilkinson	5	253	3.08	1	3	1	0	0	13	128	.898
32	Corey Schwab	40	2146	3.52	8	25	3	2	0	126	1153	.891
40	Bill Ranford	32	1568	3.90	3	18	3	2	1	102	858	.881
	Totals	**82**	**4974**	**3.52**	**19**	**54**	**9**	**5**	**4**	**292**	**2633**	**.889**

Coaching History

Terry Crisp, 1992-93 to 1996-97; Terry Crisp, Rick Paterson and Jacques Demers, 1997-98; Jacques Demers, 1998-99; Steve Ludzik, 1999-2000.

Club Records

Team

(Figures in brackets for season records are games played; records for fewest points, wins, ties, losses, goals, goals against are for 70 or more games)

Most Points	88	1995-96 (82)
Most Wins	38	1995-96 (82)
Most Ties	12	1995-96 (82)
Most Losses	55	1997-98 (82)
Most Goals	245	1992-93 (84)
Most Goals Against	332	1992-93 (84)
Fewest Points	44	1997-98 (82)
Fewest Wins	17	1997-98 (82)
Fewest Ties	7	1992-93 (84)
Fewest Losses	32	1995-96 (82)
Fewest Goals	151	1997-98 (82)
Fewest Goals Against	247	1996-97 (82)

Longest Winning Streak

Overall	5	Twice
Home	6	Feb. 15-Mar. 10/96
Away	4	Jan. 6-13/97

Longest Undefeated Streak

Overall	7	Feb. 28-Mar. 13/96 (5 wins, 2 ties)
Home	8	Twice
Away	6	Dec. 28/93-Jan. 12/94 (5 wins, 1 tie)

Longest Losing Streak

Overall	13	Jan. 3-Feb. 2/98
Home	10	Jan. 3-Feb. 26/98
Away	11	Oct. 24-Dec. 10/98

Longest Winless Streak

Overall	16	Twice
Home	11	Jan. 2-Feb. 26/98 (10 losses, 1 tie)
Away	16	Oct. 10-Dec. 10/97 (15 losses, 1 ties)
Most Shutouts, Season	6	1996-97 (82)
Most PIM, Season	1,823	1997-98 (82)
Most Goals, Game	7	Five times

Individual

Most Seasons	7	Mikael Andersson, Rob Zamuner
Most Games, Career	475	Rob Zamuner
Most Goals, Career	111	Brian Bradley
Most Assists, Career	189	Brian Bradley
Most Points, Career	300	Brian Bradley (111G, 189A)
Most PIM, Career	620	Chris Gratton
Most Shutouts, Career	12	Daren Puppa
Longest Consecutive Games Streak	226	Rob Zamuner (Nov. 1/95-Mar. 30/98)
Most Goals, Season	42	Brian Bradley (1992-93)
Most Assists, Season	56	Brian Bradley (1995-96)

Most Points, Season	86	Brian Bradley (1992-93; 42G, 44A)
Most PIM, Season	258	Enrico Ciccone (1995-96)
Most Shutouts, Season	5	Daren Puppa (1995-96)
Most Points, Defenseman, Season	65	Roman Hamrlik (1995-96; 16G, 49A)
Most Points, Center, Season	86	Brian Bradley (1992-93; 42G, 44A)
Most Points, Right Wing, Season	60	Dino Ciccarelli (1996-97; 35G, 25A)
Most Points, Left Wing, Season	51	Chris Kontos (1992-93; 27G, 24A)
Most Points, Rookie, Season	43	Rob Zamuner (1992-93; 15G, 28A)
Most Goals, Game	4	Chris Kontos (Oct. 7/92)
Most Assists, Game	4	Joe Reekie (Oct. 7/92), Marc Bureau (Feb. 1/93)
Most Points, Game	6	Doug Crossman (Nov. 7/92; 3G, 3A)

Captains' History

No captain, 1992-93 to 1994-95; Paul Ysebaert, 1995-96, 1996-97; Paul Ysebaert and Mikael Renberg, 1997-98; Rob Zamuner, 1998-99.

All-time Record vs. Other Clubs

Regular Season

		At Home							On Road							Total					
	GP	W	L	T	GF	GA	PTS	GP	W	L	T	GF	GA	PTS	GP	W	L	T	GF	GA	PTS
Anaheim	5	2	3	0	10	16	4	5	1	3	1	12	17	3	10	3	6	1	22	33	7
Boston	13	5	6	2	33	35	12	13	1	9	3	29	45	5	26	6	15	5	62	80	17
Buffalo	13	2	10	1	25	45	5	13	6	6	1	41	33	13	26	8	16	2	66	78	18
Calgary	7	3	3	1	23	25	7	6	2	4	0	12	22	4	13	5	7	1	35	47	11
Carolina	13	6	5	2	38	35	14	14	2	9	3	36	48	7	27	8	14	5	74	83	21
Chicago	8	4	2	2	21	19	10	9	3	4	2	24	25	8	17	7	6	4	45	44	18
Colorado	9	7	1	1	31	22	15	9	2	6	1	21	42	5	18	9	7	2	52	64	20
Dallas	9	1	6	2	14	26	4	8	1	6	1	19	31	3	17	2	12	3	33	57	7
Detroit	10	1	8	1	33	55	3	8	1	7	0	16	35	2	18	2	15	1	49	90	5
Edmonton	7	2	3	2	19	18	6	7	2	5	0	16	17	4	14	4	8	2	35	35	10
Florida	15	4	7	4	31	39	12	15	2	11	2	21	43	6	30	6	18	6	52	82	18
Los Angeles	6	3	3	0	14	14	6	7	6	1	0	26	16	12	13	9	4	0	40	30	18
Montreal	13	6	4	3	33	30	15	12	4	7	1	30	36	9	25	10	11	4	63	66	24
Nashville	1	1	0	0	3	0	2	1	0	1	0	0	3	0	2	1	1	0	3	3	2
New Jersey	15	4	8	3	36	43	11	16	1	14	1	22	64	3	31	5	22	4	58	107	14
NY Islanders	16	7	8	1	39	49	15	15	9	5	1	46	40	19	31	16	13	2	85	89	34
NY Rangers	15	7	6	2	52	51	16	16	7	7	1	59	60	15	32	14	13	3	111	111	31
Ottawa	13	5	7	1	38	39	11	13	7	6	0	34	42	14	26	12	13	1	72	81	25
Philadelphia	16	5	10	1	44	52	11	15	1	9	5	27	52	7	31	6	19	6	71	104	18
Phoenix	7	3	4	0	22	25	6	7	3	4	0	16	22	6	14	6	8	0	38	47	12
Pittsburgh	13	4	8	1	38	47	9	13	2	9	2	28	57	6	26	6	17	3	66	104	15
St. Louis	9	3	4	2	28	30	8	8	1	7	0	19	31	2	17	4	11	2	47	61	10
San Jose	7	4	3	0	20	16	8	7	5	2	0	26	24	10	14	9	5	0	46	40	18
Toronto	10	1	9	0	18	38	2	12	5	7	0	31	46	10	22	6	16	0	49	84	12
Vancouver	6	3	3	0	19	21	6	6	0	6	0	9	31	0	12	3	9	0	28	52	6
Washington	16	4	11	1	32	52	9	16	5	7	4	40	57	14	32	9	18	5	72	109	23
Totals	**272**	**96**	**143**	**33**	**711**	**845**	**225**	**272**	**80**	**163**	**29**	**663**	**938**	**189**	**544**	**176**	**306**	**62**	**1374**	**1783**	**414**

Playoffs

	Series	W	L	GP	W	L	T	GF	GA	Last Mtg.	Round	Result
Philadelphia	1	0	1	6	2	4	0	13	26	1996	CQF	L 2-4
Totals	**1**	**0**	**1**	**6**	**2**	**4**	**0**	**13**	**26**			

Playoff Results 1999-95

Year	Round	Opponent	Result	GF	GA
1996	CQF	Philadelphia	L 2-4	13	26

Abbreviations: Round: CQF – conference quarter-final.

Carolina totals include Hartford, 1992-93 to 1996-97.
Dallas totals include Minnesota, 1992-93.

Colorado totals include Quebec, 1992-93 to 1994-95.
Phoenix totals include Winnipeg, 1992-93 to 1995-96.

1998-99 Results

Oct.	9	at	Florida	1-4	15	at	New Jersey	1-3
	10	at	Carolina	4-4	16	at	Boston	2-2
	14		NY Islanders	0-2	19		Buffalo	2-1
	16		Philadelphia	2-5	21	at	Nashville	3-2
	18		Washington	1-4	26		Montreal	1-2
	21		Pittsburgh	5-0	29		Dallas	1-4
	23		Los Angeles	3-2	30	at	Philadelphia	2-6
	25		Vancouver	3-2	**Feb.** 2		Toronto	0-3
	28	at	Anaheim	3-5	3	at	Washington	1-10
	30	at	Los Angeles	3-0	5		Anaheim	3-5
	31	at	San Jose	1-6	10		St. Louis	4-5
Nov.	4	at	Washington	5-2	13		San Jose	1-3
	6		Chicago	2-2	15	at	NY Islanders	3-3
	8		New Jersey	3-1	17	at	New Jersey	1-7
	10		NY Rangers	2-10	19		Phoenix	4-2
	13	at	Colorado	1-8	20		Carolina	2-3
	14	at	Phoenix	1-4	22		New Jersey	2-3
	19		Pittsburgh	1-5	26		Philadelphia	4-1
	21	at	Pittsburgh	2-5	**Mar.** 2		Washington	2-8
	24		Boston	1-4	4		Colorado	2-1
	27		Florida	1-2	6	at	Montreal	6-1
	29		Buffalo	3-6	8	at	Ottawa	3-9
Dec.	3	at	Calgary	1-4	9	at	Toronto	1-6
	4	at	Edmonton	2-1	11	at	Buffalo	5-2
	6	at	Chicago	5-7	13	at	Florida	0-1
	8		Ottawa	2-4	17		Pittsburgh	0-2
	11		Calgary	1-2	19		Detroit	3-5
	12	at	NY Islanders	2-1	22		NY Rangers	6-3
	15	at	Pittsburgh	2-3	24		Nashville	0-3
	18		Edmonton	1-4	26	at	Detroit	1-6
	20	at	Philadelphia	2-2	28	at	Carolina	3-3
	21	at	Boston	2-3	31	at	Dallas	4-6
	23	at	Buffalo	0-2	**Apr.** 1	at	St. Louis	0-3
	26		Florida	1-3	3		Washington	4-3
	29		NY Islanders	3-0	5		Ottawa	4-4
	30	at	Carolina	3-4	8		Boston	3-0
Jan.	4	at	Toronto	4-5	10	at	Boston	2-2
	7	at	Montreal	1-4	12	at	NY Rangers	1-2
	8	at	Ottawa	1-5	13		Montreal	2-2
	10	at	NY Rangers	2-5	16		Carolina	2-2
	12		Toronto	3-4	17	at	Florida	2-6

Entry Draft
Selections 1999-92

1999 Pick		1997 Pick		1995 Pick		1993 Pick	
47	Sheldon Keefe	7	Paul Mara	5	Daymond Langkow	3	Chris Gratton
67	Evegeny Konstantinov	33	Kyle Kos	30	Mike McBain	29	Tyler Moss
75	Brett Scheffelmaier	61	Matt Elich	56	Shane Willis	55	Allan Egeland
88	Jimmie Olvestad	108	Mark Thompson	108	Konsta Golokhvastov	81	Marian Kacir
127	Kaspars Astashenko	109	Jan Sulc	134	Eduard Pershin	107	Ryan Brown
148	Michal Lanicek	112	Karel Betik	160	Cory Murphy	133	Kiley Hill
182	Fedor Fedorov	153	Andrei Skopintsev	186	Joe Cardarelli	159	Mathieu Raby
187	Ivan Rachunek	168	Justin Jack	212	Zac Bierk	185	Ryan Nauss
216	Erkki Rajamaki	170	Eero Somervuori			211	Alexandre Laporte
244	Mikko Kuparinen	185	Samuel St-Pierre	**1994 Pick**		237	Brett Duncan
		198	Shawn Skolney	8	Jason Wiemer	263	Mark Szoke
1998 Pick		224	Paul Comrie	34	Colin Cloutier		
1	Vincent Lecavalier			55	Vadim Epachintsev	**1992 Pick**	
64	Brad Richards	**1996 Pick**		86	Dmitri Klevakin	1	Roman Hamrlik
72	Dimitry Afanasenkov	16	Mario Larocque	137	Daniel Juden	26	Drew Bannister
92	Eric Beaudoin	69	Curtis Tipler	138	Bryce Salvador	49	Brent Gretzky
121	Curtis Rich	125	Jason Robinson	164	Chris Maillet	74	Aaron Gavey
146	Sergei Kuznetsov	152	Nikolai Ignatov	190	Alexei Baranov	97	Brantt Myhres
174	Brett Allan	157	Xavier Delisle	216	Yuri Smirnov	122	Martin Tanguay
194	Oak Hewer	179	Pavel Kubina	242	Shawn Gervais	145	Derek Wilkinson
221	Daniel Hulak			268	Brian White	170	Dennis Maxwell
229	Chris Lyness					193	Andrew Kemper
252	Martin Cibak					218	Marc Tardif
						241	Tom MacDonald

General Managers' History

Phil Esposito, 1992-93 to 1997-98; Jacques Demers, 1998-99; Rick Dudley, 1999-2000.

General Manager

DUDLEY, RICK
General Manager, Tampa Bay Lightning.
Born in Toronto, Ont., January 31, 1949.

Rick Dudley was named Vice President of Hockey Operations for Palace Sports and Entertainment (PS&E) on June 8, 1999 and took on the job of overseeing all aspects of Tampa Bay Lightning hockey operations when PS&E consummated its acquisition of the hockey club. On July 14, 1999, Dudley was officially named the club's General Manager.

The hiring of Dudley in Tampa Bay was made possible after the Ottawa Senators reached a compensation agreement with Palace Sports and Entertainment. The move returned Dudley to his former employer (PS&E) after one season as the General Manager in Ottawa. In his one season there, the Senators finished with 103 points, an increase of 20 points from the previous campaign. Ottawa finished with the third best overall record in the NHL during the 1998-99 season.

Before joining Ottawa, Dudley was the General Manager of PS&E's Detroit Vipers in the International Hockey League. In Detroit, he served as general manager and head coach during the team's first two years of existence before handing over the coaching duties to Steve Ludzik and concentrating solely on his front office work for the next two seasons.

Dudley is credited with finding the likes of Detroit's first two players in Petr Sykora and Miroslav Satan as well as bringing over 17-year-old phenom Sergei Samsonov. Samsonov helped lead the Vipers to the 1996 Turner Cup Championship and became the NHL's Rookie of the Year the following season.

A lifetime hockey man, Dudley was the head coach of the IHL's Phoenix Roadrunners in 1993-94. He took over the reigns of a last-place club and led them to the league's best record over the rest of the season. His other head coaching jobs came with the IHL's San Diego Gulls (1992-93), NHL's Buffalo Sabres (1989 to 1992), AHL's New Haven Nighthawks (1988-89), IHL's Flint Spirits (1986 to 1988), and ECHL's Carolina Thunderbirds (1981 to 1986). Dudley amassed a 476-196-51 lifetime record as a head coach.

His professional playing career spanned 13 seasons where he spent time in the AHL (Cleveland, Cincinnati, Fredericton), IHL (Flint), WHA (Cincinnati) and National Hockey League (Buffalo and Winnipeg).

NHL Coaching Record

			Regular Season				Playoffs			
Season	Team	Games	W	L	T	%	Games	W	L	%
1989-90	Buffalo	80	45	27	8	.613	6	2	4	.333
1990-91	Buffalo	80	31	30	9	.506	6	2	4	.333
1991-92	Buffalo	28	9	15	4	.393	....	....	....	....
	NHL Totals	**188**	**85**	**72**	**31**	**.535**	**12**	**4**	**8**	**.333**

Club Directory

Ice Palace

Ice Palace
401 Channelside Drive
Tampa, FL 33602
Admin. Office **813/301-6500**
FAX 813/229-3350
Ticket Info. 813/301-6600
www.tampabaylightning.com
Capacity: 19,758

Executive Staff
Owners: Palace Sports & Entertainment, Bill Davidson, David Hermelin, Robert Sosnick
President of Palace Sports & Entertainment/Governor. . Tom Wilson
President of Tampa Bay Lightning/
   Alternate Governor. . . . . Ron Campbell
Senior Vice President of Finance . . . . Pete Hess
Senior Vice President of Arena Management . . . . . Hugh Lombardi
Senior Vice President of Sales and Marketing . . . . . Michael Yormark
Executive Assistant . . . . Kris Harrell

Hockey Operations
Vice President of Hockey Operations/
   General Manager. . . . . Rick Dudley
Assistant General Manager/Alternate Governor . . . Jay H. Feaster
Senior Advisor to the General Manager . . . . Cliff Fletcher
Head Coach. . . . . Steve Ludzik
Assistant Coaches . . . . John Cullen, John Torchetti
Special Skills Coach . . . . Paul Vincent
Goaltending Consultant . . . . Jeff Reese
Scouting Coordinator . . . . Jake Goertzen
Scouting Staff: Stephen Baker, Randy Hansch, Dave Heitz, Karri Kettunen, Scott Luce,
          Scott MacPherson, Dennis McIvor, Craig Muni, Rick Patterson, Miroslav Prihoda,
          Vladimir Repnev, Richard Rose, Buck Steele, Luke Williams
Director of Team Services . . . . Phil Thibodeau
Head Medical Trainer . . . . Dave Boyer
Strength & Conditioning Trainer . . . . Brian Peterson
Assistant Strength & Conditioning Trainer. . . . . . . John Shipman
Equipment Manager . . . . Jocko Cayer
Assistant Equipment Managers . . . . Jim Pickard, Ray Thill
Hockey Operations Assistant . . . . Kathy Skelton
Video Coordinator. . . . . Nigel Kirwan
Team Physician . . . . Dr. David Leffers
General Manager Detroit Vipers . . . . Grant Sonier
Head Coach Detroit Vipers . . . . Paulin Bordeleau

Community Relations
Director of Community Development . . . . Donna Ferris
Community Youth Development Manager . . . . David Walkowiak
Community Development Manager . . . . Stephanie Hanchey
Community Development Coordinator . . . . Stacey Segal
Mascot Coordinator . . . . Jason Franke

Executive Suites & Premium Seating
Director of Suite Service . . . . Marie Wenger
Suite Sales Manager . . . . Pamela B. Goniwiecha
Suite Service Managers . . . . Theresa Huffman
Premium Seating Coordinator . . . . Ken Kacsur

Finance
Senior Vice President of Finance . . . . Pete Hess
Director of Finance . . . . Brad Whalen
Controller . . . . Robin Hughes
Accounting Manager. . . . . Foster Atteberry
Accounts Payable . . . . Tim Winans
Accounts Receivable . . . . Alina Simonds
Staff Accountants . . . . Kelly Papas, Doug Riefler
Administrative Assistant. . . . . Evie Williams

Box Office
Box Office Manager. . . . . Maryruth Hughey
Assistant Box Office Managers . . . . Marilyn Brace, Aaron Corso, Jim Mannino
Box Office Supervisors . . . . Adam Burr, Tierney Moore, Michele Spadavecchia

Ticket Operations
Vice President of Ticket Sales. . . . . Steve DeLay
Director of Group Events . . . . Lynn Wittenburg
Marketing Manager. . . . . Damion Chatmon
Corporate Account Managers . . . . Joe Andrade, Chris Gargani, Chris Hibbs,
          Heather Johnson, Bryan Maki, Mike Ondrejko,
          Martin Quessenberry, Dave Smith
Group Event Coordinators. . . . . Kristy Bauer, John Fisher, Brent Stehlik,
          Rebecca Rogers
Account Executives . . . . Heather Bllom, Stacey Borsik, Stephen Kirby,
          Chris Kremer, Tony LaForgia, Ashlie Rolley
Sales Coordinator . . . . Patsy Vold

Marketing
Vice President of Integrated Sales . . . . Pedro Goncalves
Vice President of Corporate Sales/Client Services. . . Kevin Klein
Director of Client Services/Special Events . . . . April Melquist
Director of Gane Operations/Creative Services . . . . Killeen Mullen
Client Services Managers . . . . Katherine Lesinski, Sonya Michael, Lisa Testa
Corporate Marketing Sales Executive . . . . Tom DeCaprio
Corporate Marketing Managers . . . . Michelle Chesebro, Gerry Zimmerman
Promotions Director. . . . . Jason Gulledge
Promotions Coordinator . . . . Travis Flee
Broadcasting Production Manager. . . . . Jim Ciotoli
Marketing Services Manager . . . . Bina Kumar

Public Relations
Vice President of Public Relations . . . . Bill Wickett
Director of Public Relations . . . . Jay Preble
Public Relations Manager . . . . Brian Potter

Broadcast Information
Television. . . . . Sunshine Network, WTTA 38
Television Broadcasters . . . . Rick Peckham, Bobby Taylor
Radio . . . . WDAE 1250 AM
Radio Broadcaster . . . . John Ahlers

Toronto Maple Leafs

1998-99 Results: 45W-30L-7T 97PTS. Second, Northeast Division

TORONTO MAPLE LEAFS ®

With 83 points (31 goals, 52 assists) Mats Sundin led the Maple Leafs in scoring for the fifth consecutive season. Sundin also led the team with 16 points in the playoffs as the Leafs reached the Eastern Conference finals.

1999-2000 Schedule

Oct.	Sat.	2	at Montreal		Fri.	7	at Pittsburgh
	Mon.	4	Boston		Sat.	8	NY Rangers
	Wed.	6	Colorado		Tue.	11	at Boston
	Sat.	9	at Ottawa		Fri.	14	at Edmonton
	Mon.	11	Nashville		Sat.	15	at Calgary
	Wed.	13	Florida		Mon.	17	at Vancouver
	Fri.	15	at Chicago		Sat.	22	Washington
	Sat.	16	at St. Louis		Mon.	24	Ottawa
	Wed.	20	Carolina		Wed.	26	at Detroit
	Sat.	23	Montreal		Thu.	27	at NY Rangers
	Mon.	25	Dallas		Sat.	29	Los Angeles
	Wed.	27	Atlanta	**Feb.**	Tue.	1	at Tampa Bay
	Sat.	30	Calgary		Thu.	3	at Boston
Nov.	Wed.	3	at Carolina		Wed.	9	Philadelphia
	Fri.	5	at Washington		Sat.	12	Vancouver
	Sat.	6	at New Jersey		Mon.	14	Carolina
	Tue.	9	Anaheim		Wed.	16	Boston
	Thu.	11	at Boston		Sat.	19	at Montreal
	Sat.	13	Detroit		Wed.	23	Phoenix
	Mon.	15	San Jose		Fri.	25	at New Jersey
	Wed.	17	St. Louis		Sat.	26	Buffalo
	Sat.	20	NY Rangers		Tue.	29	at Atlanta
	Tue.	23	at Pittsburgh	**Mar.**	Wed.	1	at Florida
	Fri.	26	at Philadelphia*		Sat.	4	Montreal
	Sat.	27	Edmonton		Mon.	6	at Vancouver
	Mon.	29	Washington		Tue.	7	at Edmonton
Dec.	Thu.	2	at Carolina		Thu.	9	at Calgary
	Sat.	4	Pittsburgh		Sat.	11	at Ottawa
	Mon.	6	Buffalo		Wed.	15	Chicago
	Thu.	9	at Philadelphia		Thu.	16	at Detroit
	Sat.	11	Philadelphia		Sat.	18	Atlanta
	Mon.	13	Ottawa		Wed.	22	NY Islanders
	Wed.	15	NY Islanders		Thu.	23	at Ottawa
	Sat.	18	Montreal		Sat.	25	New Jersey
	Mon.	20	at Florida		Wed.	29	at St. Louis
	Tue.	21	at Tampa Bay		Thu.	30	at Chicago
	Thu.	23	New Jersey	**Apr.**	Sat.	1	at Washington
	Wed.	29	at NY Islanders		Mon.	3	at Buffalo
Jan.	Sat.	1	at Buffalo		Wed.	5	Pittsburgh
	Mon.	3	Buffalo		Fri.	7	at NY Islanders
	Wed.	5	at NY Rangers		Sat.	8	Tampa Bay

* Denotes afternoon game.

Franchise date: November 22, 1917

NORTHEAST DIVISION

83rd NHL Season

Year-by-Year Record

		Home			Road			Overall							
Season	**GP**	**W**	**L**	**T**	**W**	**L**	**T**	**W**	**L**	**T**	**GF**	**GA**	**Pts.**	**Finished**	**Playoff Result**
1998-99	82	23	13	5	22	17	2	45	30	7	268	231	97	2nd, Northeast Div.	Lost Conf. Championship
1997-98	82	16	20	5	14	23	4	30	43	9	194	237	69	6th, Central Div.	Out of Playoffs
1996-97	82	18	20	3	12	24	5	30	44	8	230	273	68	6th, Central Div.	Out of Playoffs
1995-96	82	19	15	7	15	21	5	34	36	12	247	252	80	3rd, Central Div.	Lost Conf. Quarter-Final
1994-95	48	15	7	2	6	12	6	21	19	8	135	146	50	4th, Central Div.	Lost Conf. Quarter-Final
1993-94	84	23	15	4	20	14	8	43	29	12	280	243	98	2nd, Central Div.	Lost Conf. Championship
1992-93	84	25	11	6	19	18	5	44	29	11	288	241	99	3rd, Norris Div.	Lost Conf. Championship
1991-92	80	21	16	3	9	27	4	30	43	7	234	294	67	5th, Norris Div.	Out of Playoffs
1990-91	80	15	21	4	8	25	7	23	46	11	241	318	57	5th, Norris Div.	Out of Playoffs
1989-90	80	24	14	2	14	24	2	38	38	4	337	358	80	3rd, Norris Div.	Lost Div. Semi-Final
1988-89	80	15	20	5	13	26	1	28	46	6	259	342	62	5th, Norris Div.	Out of Playoffs
1987-88	80	14	20	6	7	29	4	21	49	10	273	345	52	4th, Norris Div.	Lost Div. Semi-Final
1986-87	80	22	14	4	10	28	2	32	42	6	286	319	70	4th, Norris Div.	Lost Div. Final
1985-86	80	16	21	3	9	27	4	25	48	7	311	386	57	4th, Norris Div.	Lost Div. Final
1984-85	80	10	28	2	10	24	6	20	52	8	253	358	48	5th, Norris Div.	Out of Playoffs
1983-84	80	17	16	7	9	29	2	26	45	9	303	387	61	5th, Norris Div.	Out of Playoffs
1982-83	80	20	15	5	8	25	7	28	40	12	293	330	68	3rd, Norris Div.	Lost Div. Semi-Final
1981-82	80	12	20	8	8	24	8	20	44	16	298	380	56	5th, Norris Div.	Out of Playoffs
1980-81	80	14	21	5	14	16	10	28	37	15	322	367	71	5th, Adams Div.	Lost Prelim. Round
1979-80	80	17	19	4	18	21	1	35	40	5	304	327	75	4th, Adams Div.	Lost Prelim. Round
1978-79	80	20	12	8	14	21	5	34	33	13	267	252	81	3rd, Adams Div.	Lost Quarter-Final
1977-78	80	21	13	6	20	16	4	41	29	10	271	237	92	3rd, Adams Div.	Lost Semi-Final
1976-77	80	18	13	9	15	19	6	33	32	15	301	285	81	3rd, Adams Div.	Lost Quarter-Final
1975-76	80	23	12	5	11	19	10	34	31	15	294	276	83	3rd, Adams Div.	Lost Quarter-Final
1974-75	80	19	12	9	12	21	7	31	33	16	280	309	78	3rd, Adams Div.	Lost Quarter-Final
1973-74	78	21	11	7	14	16	9	35	27	16	274	230	86	4th, East Div.	Lost Quarter-Final
1972-73	78	20	12	7	7	29	3	27	41	10	247	279	64	6th, East Div.	Out of Playoffs
1971-72	78	21	11	7	12	20	7	33	31	14	209	208	80	4th, East Div.	Lost Quarter-Final
1970-71	78	24	9	6	13	24	2	37	33	8	248	211	82	4th, East Div.	Lost Quarter-Final
1969-70	76	18	13	7	11	21	6	29	34	13	222	242	71	6th, East Div.	Out of Playoffs
1968-69	76	20	8	10	15	18	5	35	26	15	234	217	85	4th, East Div.	Lost Quarter-Final
1967-68	74	24	9	4	9	22	6	33	31	10	209	176	76	5th, East Div.	Out of Playoffs
1966-67	**70**	**21**	**8**	**6**	**11**	**19**	**5**	**32**	**27**	**11**	**204**	**211**	**75**	**3rd,**	**Won Stanley Cup**
1965-66	70	22	9	4	12	16	7	34	25	11	208	187	79	3rd,	Lost Semi-Final
1964-65	70	17	15	3	13	11	11	30	26	14	204	173	74	4th,	Lost Semi-Final
1963-64	**70**	**22**	**7**	**6**	**11**	**18**	**6**	**33**	**25**	**12**	**192**	**172**	**78**	**3rd,**	**Won Stanley Cup**
1962-63	**70**	**21**	**8**	**6**	**14**	**15**	**6**	**35**	**23**	**12**	**221**	**180**	**82**	**1st,**	**Won Stanley Cup**
1961-62	**70**	**25**	**5**	**5**	**12**	**17**	**6**	**37**	**22**	**11**	**232**	**180**	**85**	**2nd,**	**Won Stanley Cup**
1960-61	70	21	6	8	18	13	4	39	19	12	234	176	90	2nd,	Lost Semi-Final
1959-60	70	20	9	6	15	17	3	35	26	9	199	195	79	2nd,	Lost Final
1958-59	70	17	13	5	10	19	6	27	32	11	189	201	65	4th,	Lost Final
1957-58	70	12	16	7	9	22	4	21	38	11	192	226	53	6th,	Out of Playoffs
1956-57	70	12	16	7	9	18	8	21	34	15	174	192	57	5th,	Out of Playoffs
1955-56	70	19	10	6	5	23	7	24	33	13	153	181	61	4th,	Lost Semi-Final
1954-55	70	14	10	11	10	14	11	24	24	22	147	135	70	3rd,	Lost Semi-Final
1953-54	70	22	6	7	10	18	7	32	24	14	152	131	78	3rd,	Lost Semi-Final
1952-53	70	17	12	6	10	18	7	27	30	13	156	167	67	5th,	Out of Playoffs
1951-52	70	17	10	8	12	15	8	29	25	16	168	157	74	3rd,	Lost Semi-Final
1950-51	**70**	**22**	**8**	**5**	**19**	**8**	**8**	**41**	**16**	**13**	**212**	**138**	**95**	**2nd,**	**Won Stanley Cup**
1949-50	70	18	9	8	13	18	4	31	27	12	176	173	74	3rd,	Lost Semi-Final
1948-49	**60**	**12**	**8**	**10**	**10**	**17**	**3**	**22**	**25**	**13**	**147**	**161**	**57**	**4th,**	**Won Stanley Cup**
1947-48	**60**	**22**	**3**	**5**	**10**	**12**	**8**	**32**	**15**	**13**	**182**	**143**	**77**	**1st,**	**Won Stanley Cup**
1946-47	**60**	**20**	**8**	**2**	**11**	**11**	**8**	**31**	**19**	**10**	**209**	**172**	**72**	**2nd,**	**Won Stanley Cup**
1945-46	50	10	13	2	9	11	5	19	24	7	174	185	45	5th,	Out of Playoffs
1944-45	**50**	**13**	**9**	**3**	**11**	**13**	**1**	**24**	**22**	**4**	**183**	**161**	**52**	**3rd,**	**Won Stanley Cup**
1943-44	50	13	11	1	10	12	3	23	23	4	214	174	50	3rd,	Lost Semi-Final
1942-43	50	17	6	2	5	13	7	22	19	9	198	159	53	3rd,	Lost Semi-Final
1941-42	**48**	**18**	**6**	**0**	**9**	**12**	**3**	**27**	**18**	**3**	**158**	**136**	**57**	**2nd,**	**Won Stanley Cup**
1940-41	48	16	5	3	12	9	3	28	14	6	145	99	62	2nd,	Lost Semi-Final
1939-40	48	15	3	6	10	14	0	25	17	6	134	110	56	3rd,	Lost Final
1938-39	48	13	8	3	6	12	6	19	20	9	114	107	47	3rd,	Lost Final
1937-38	48	13	6	5	11	9	4	24	15	9	151	127	57	1st, Cdn. Div.	Lost Final
1936-37	48	14	9	1	8	12	4	22	21	5	119	115	49	3rd, Cdn. Div.	Lost Quarter-Final
1935-36	48	15	4	5	8	15	1	23	19	6	126	106	52	2nd, Cdn. Div.	Lost Final
1934-35	48	16	6	2	14	8	2	30	14	4	157	111	64	1st, Cdn. Div.	Lost Final
1933-34	48	19	2	3	7	11	6	26	13	9	174	119	61	1st, Cdn. Div.	Lost Semi-Final
1932-33	48	16	4	4	8	14	2	24	18	6	119	111	54	1st, Cdn. Div.	Lost Final
1931-32	**48**	**17**	**4**	**3**	**6**	**14**	**4**	**23**	**18**	**7**	**155**	**127**	**53**	**2nd, Cdn. Div.**	**Won Stanley Cup**
1930-31	44	15	4	3	7	9	6	22	13	9	118	99	53	2nd, Cdn. Div.	Lost Quarter-Final
1929-30	44	10	8	4	7	13	2	17	21	6	116	124	40	4th, Cdn. Div.	Out of Playoffs
1928-29	44	15	5	2	6	13	3	21	18	5	85	69	47	3rd, Cdn. Div.	Lost Semi-Final
1927-28	44	9	8	5	9	10	3	18	18	8	89	88	44	4th, Cdn. Div.	Out of Playoffs
1926-27*	44	10	10	2	5	14	3	15	24	5	79	94	35	5th, Cdn. Div.	Out of Playoffs
1925-26	36	11	5	2	1	16	1	12	21	3	92	114	27	6th,	Out of Playoffs
1924-25	30	10	5	0	9	6	0	19	11	0	90	84	38	2nd,	Lost NHL S-Final
1923-24	24	7	5	0	3	9	0	10	14	0	59	85	20	3rd,	Out of Playoffs
1922-23	24	10	1	1	3	9	0	13	10	1	82	88	27	3rd,	Out of Playoffs
1921-22	**24**	**8**	**4**	**0**	**5**	**6**	**1**	**13**	**10**	**1**	**98**	**97**	**27**	**2nd,**	**Won Stanley Cup**
1920-21	24	9	3	0	6	6	0	15	9	0	105	100	30	2nd and 1st***	Lost NHL Final
1919-20**	24	8	4	0	4	8	0	12	12	0	119	106	24	3rd and 2nd***	Out of Playoffs
1918-19	18	5	4	0	0	9	0	5	13	0	64	92	10	3rd and 3rd***	Out of Playoffs
1917-18	**22**	**10**	**1**	**0**	**3**	**8**	**0**	**13**	**9**	**0**	**108**	**109**	**26**	**2nd and 1st*** **	**Won Stanley Cup**

* Name changed from St. Patricks to Maple Leafs. ** Name changed from Arenas to St. Patricks.
*** Season played in two halves with no combined standing at end.
From 1917-18 through 1925-26, NHL champions played against PCHA/WCHL champions for Stanley Cup.

1999-2000 Player Personnel

FORWARDS	HT	WT	S	Place of Birth	Date	1998-99 Club
ADAMS, Kevyn	6-1	195	R	Washington, D.C.	10/8/74	Toronto-St. John's
BEREZIN, Sergei	5-10	200	R	Voskresensk, USSR	11/5/71	Toronto
BOHONOS, Lonny	5-11	190	R	Winnipeg, Man.	5/20/73	Toronto-St. John's
BONSIGNORE, Jason	6-4	220	R	Rochester, NY	4/15/76	Tampa Bay-Cleveland
CHARRON, Craig	5-10	175	R	North Easton, MA	11/15/67	Lowell
DOMI, Tie	5-10	200	R	Windsor, Ont.	11/1/69	Toronto
HOGLUND, Jonas	6-3	215	R	Hammaro, Swe.	8/29/72	Montreal
HOUSE, Bobby	6-1	205	R	Whitehorse, Yukon	1/7/73	Augusta-Albany-Springfield
JOHNSON, Mike	6-2	197	R	Scarborough, Ont.	10/3/74	Toronto
KING, Derek	6-0	212	L	Hamilton, Ont.	2/11/67	Toronto
KING, Kris	5-11	208	L	Bracebridge, Ont.	2/18/66	Toronto
KOHN, Ladislav	5-11	194	L	Uherske Hradiste, Czech.	3/4/75	Toronto-St. John's
KOROLEV, Igor	6-1	195	L	Moscow, USSR	9/6/70	Toronto
MAIR, Adam	6-1	195	R	Hamilton, Ont.	2/15/79	Owen Sound-Toronto-St. John's
McCAULEY, Alyn	5-11	200	L	Brockville, Ont.	5/29/77	Toronto
MODIN, Fredrik	6-4	220	L	Sundsvall, Sweden	10/8/74	Toronto
NEMIROVSKY, David	6-1	192	R	Toronto, Ont.	8/1/76	Florida-Fort Wayne-St. John's
PERREAULT, Yanic	5-11	188	L	Sherbrooke, Que.	4/4/71	Los Angeles-Toronto
SHANNON, Darrin	6-2	210	L	Barrie, Ont.	12/8/69	Grand Rapids
SULLIVAN, Steve	5-9	155	R	Timmins, Ont.	7/6/74	Toronto
SUNDIN, Mats	6-4	228	R	Bromma, Sweden	2/13/71	Toronto
THOMAS, Steve	5-11	185	L	Stockport, England	7/15/63	Toronto
VALK, Garry	6-1	205	L	Edmonton, Alta.	11/27/67	Toronto
WARRINER, Todd	6-1	200	L	Blenheim, Ont.	1/3/74	Toronto
WISEMAN, Brian	5-8	175	L	Chatham, Ont.	7/13/71	Houston
DEFENSEMEN						
ANDRUSAK, Greg	6-1	190	R	Cranbrook, B.C.	11/14/69	EHC Berlin-Houston-Pit
BERARD, Bryan	6-1	190	L	Woonsocket, RI	3/5/77	NY Islanders-Toronto
COTE, Sylvain	6-0	190	R	Quebec City, Que.	1/19/66	Toronto
KABERLÉ, Tomas	6-2	200	L	Rakovnik, Czech.	3/2/78	Toronto
KARPOVTSEV, Alexander	6-1	205	R	Moscow, USSR	4/7/70	NY Rangers-Toronto
MARKOV, Daniil	6-1	196	L	Moscow, USSR	7/11/76	Toronto
McALLISTER, Chris	6-7	235	L	Saskatoon, Sask.	6/16/75	Vancouver-Syracuse-Toronto
SANDWITH, Terran	6-4	210	L	Edmonton, Alta.	4/17/72	Cincinnati (AHL)
YUSHKEVICH, Dimitri	6-0	208	R	Yaroslavl, USSR	11/19/71	Toronto

GOALTENDERS	HT	WT	C	Place of Birth	Date	1998-99 Club
HEALY, Glenn	5-9	192	L	Pickering, Ont.	8/23/62	Toronto-Chicago (IHL)
JOSEPH, Curtis	5-11	190	L	Keswick, Ont.	4/29/67	Toronto
WAITE, Jimmy	6-1	180	L	Sherbrooke, Que.	4/15/69	Phoenix-Springfield-Utah

General Managers' History

Conn Smythe, 1927-28 to 1956-57; Hap Day, 1957-58; Punch Imlach, 1958-59 to 1968-69; Jim Gregory, 1969-70 to 1978-79; Punch Imlach, 1979-80, 1980-81; Punch Imlach and Gerry McNamara, 1981-82; Gerry McNamara, 1982-83 to 1987-88; Gord Stellick, 1988-89; Floyd Smith, 1989-90, 1990-91; Cliff Fletcher, 1991-92 to 1996-97; Ken Dryden, 1997-98, 1998-99; Pat Quinn, 1999-2000.

Coach and General Manager

QUINN, PAT
Coach and General Manager, Toronto Maple Leafs.
Born in Hamilton, Ont., January 29, 1943.

Pat Quinn became the 25th head coach of the Toronto Maple Leafs on June 26, 1998 and quickly turned the club's fortunes around. He earned a nomination for the Jack Adams Award as coach of the year in his first year behind the bench in Toronto after guiding the Leafs to a club record 45 victories. After the season, Quinn was named General Manager on July 14, 1999. He becomes the first man since Punch Imlach in the 1960s to serve the dual role in Toronto. Quinn served as both coach and general manager during much of his time with the Vancouver Canucks.

Quinn joined the Canucks as president and general manager in 1987 and took over the coaching reigns on January 31, 1991. He guided the Canucks to single-season records for wins (46) and points (101) in 1992-93, and led the team to the Stanley Cup Finals in 1994. Quinn had previously guided Philadelphia to the Stanley Cup Finals in 1980. He won the Jack Adams Award with the Flyers in 1979-80 and in Vancouver in 1992-93. He also coached in Los Angeles from 1984 to 1987.

Quinn spent the 1968-69 and 1969-70 seasons in a Maple Leafs uniform. He played 99 games for Toronto and later played for Vancouver and the Atlanta Flames. He holds a law degree from Widener University, Delaware School of Law.

NHL Coaching Record

		Regular Season					Playoffs			
Season	Team	Games	W	L	T	%	Games	W	L	%
1978-79	Philadelphia	30	18	8	4	.667	8	3	5	.375
1979-80	Philadelphia	80	48	12	20	.725	19	13	6	.684
1980-81	Philadelphia	80	41	24	15	.606	12	6	6	.500
1981-82	Philadelphia	72	34	29	9	.535	....	....	....	....
1984-85	Los Angeles	80	34	32	14	.513	3	0	3	.000
1985-86	Los Angeles	80	23	49	8	.338	....	....	....	....
1986-87	Los Angeles	42	18	20	4	.476	....	....	....	....
1990-91	Vancouver	26	9	13	4	.423	6	2	4	.333
1991-92	Vancouver	80	42	26	12	.600	13	6	7	.462
1992-93	Vancouver	84	46	29	9	.601	12	6	6	.500
1993-94	Vancouver	84	41	40	3	.506	24	15	9	.625
1995-96	Vancouver	6	3	3	0	.500	6	2	4	.333
1998-99	Toronto	82	45	30	7	.591	17	9	8	.529
	Totals	**826**	**402**	**315**	**109**	**.553**	**120**	**62**	**58**	**.517**

1998-99 Scoring

* – rookie

Regular Season

Pos	#	Player	Team	GP	G	A	Pts	+/–	PIM	PP	SH	GW	GT	S	%
C	13	Mats Sundin	TOR	82	31	52	83	22	58	4	0	6	0	209	14.8
L	32	Steve Thomas	TOR	78	28	45	73	26	33	11	0	7	0	209	13.4
L	94	Sergei Berezin	TOR	76	37	22	59	16	12	9	1	4	0	263	14.1
L	7	Derek King	TOR	81	24	28	52	15	20	8	0	4	0	150	16.0
C	22	Igor Korolev	TOR	66	13	34	47	11	46	1	0	2	0	99	13.1
R	20	Mike Johnson	TOR	79	20	24	44	13	35	5	3	2	0	149	13.4
C	44	Yanic Perreault	L.A.	64	10	17	27	–3	30	2	2	1	0	113	8.8
			TOR	12	7	8	15	10	12	2	1	2	0	28	25.0
			TOTAL	76	17	25	42	7	42	4	3	3	0	141	12.1
C	11	Steve Sullivan	TOR	63	20	20	40	12	28	4	0	5	0	110	18.2
D	34	Bryan Berard	NYI	31	4	11	15	–6	26	2	0	3	0	72	5.6
			TOR	38	5	14	19	7	22	2	0	2	1	63	7.9
			TOTAL	69	9	25	34	1	48	4	0	5	1	135	6.7
L	19	Fredrik Modin	TOR	67	16	15	31	14	35	1	0	3	1	108	14.8
R	10	Garry Valk	TOR	77	8	21	29	8	53	1	0	0	1	93	8.6
D	3	Sylvain Cote	TOR	79	5	24	29	22	28	0	0	1	0	119	4.2
D	36	Dimitri Yushkevich	TOR	78	6	22	28	25	88	2	1	0	0	95	6.3
D	52	Alexander Karpovtsev	NYR	2	1	0	1	1	0	0	0	0	0	4	25.0
			TOR	56	2	25	27	38	52	1	0	1	0	61	3.3
			TOTAL	58	3	25	28	39	52	1	0	1	0	65	4.6
C	18	Alyn McCauley	TOR	39	9	15	24	7	2	1	0	1	1	76	11.8
R	28	Tie Domi	TOR	72	8	14	22	5	198	0	0	1	0	65	12.3
D	15	* Tomas Kaberle	TOR	57	4	18	22	3	12	0	0	2	0	71	5.6
L	8	Todd Warriner	TOR	53	9	10	19	–6	28	1	0	1	0	96	9.4
D	55	* Daniil Markov	TOR	57	4	8	12	5	47	0	0	0	1	34	11.8
D	38	Yannick Tremblay	TOR	35	2	7	9	0	16	0	0	0	0	37	5.4
G	31	Curtis Joseph	TOR	67	0	5	5	0	6	0	0	0	0	0	0.0
L	12	Kris King	TOR	67	2	2	4	–16	105	0	1	1	0	34	5.9
R	39	* Ladislav Kohn	TOR	16	1	3	4	1	4	0	0	0	0	23	4.3
D	33	Chris McAllister	VAN	28	1	1	2	–7	63	0	0	0	1	6	16.7
			TOR	20	0	2	2	4	39	0	0	0	0	12	0.0
			TOTAL	48	1	3	4	–3	102	0	0	0	1	18	5.6
R	16	Lonny Bohonos	TOR	7	3	0	3	3	4	0	0	0	0	13	23.1
D	2	Dallas Eakins	TOR	18	0	2	2	3	24	0	0	0	0	11	0.0
C	42	* Kevyn Adams	TOR	1	0	0	0	0	0	0	0	0	0	1	0.0
G	35	Jeff Reese	TOR	2	0	0	0	0	0	0	0	0	0	0	0.0
D	4	Kevin Dahl	TOR	3	0	0	0	0	2	0	0	0	0	0	0.0
G	30	Glenn Healy	TOR	9	0	0	0	0	0	0	0	0	0	0	0.0

Goaltending

No.	Goaltender	GPI	Mins	Avg	W	L	T	EN	SO	GA	SA	S%
31	Curtis Joseph	67	4001	2.56	35	24	7	4	3	171	1903	.910
30	Glenn Healy	9	546	2.97	6	3	0	1	0	27	257	.895
28	Felix Potvin	5	299	3.81	3	2	0	1	0	19	142	.866
35	Jeff Reese	2	106	4.53	1	1	0	0	0	8	51	.843
	Totals	**82**	**4972**	**2.79**	**45**	**30**	**7**	**6**	**3**	**231**	**2359**	**.902**

Playoffs

Pos	#	Player	Team	GP	G	A	Pts	+/–	PIM	PP	SH	GW	OT	S	%
C	13	Mats Sundin	TOR	17	8	8	16	2	16	3	0	2	0	44	18.2
L	94	Sergei Berezin	TOR	17	6	6	12	0	4	2	0	2	1	65	9.2
L	32	Steve Thomas	TOR	17	6	3	9	–1	12	2	0	1	0	41	14.6
R	16	Lonny Bohonos	TOR	9	3	6	9	3	2	0	0	0	0	26	11.5
C	44	Yanic Perreault	TOR	17	3	6	9	–6	6	0	0	2	1	15	20.0
D	34	Bryan Berard	TOR	17	1	8	9	–10	8	1	0	0	0	29	3.4
R	10	Garry Valk	TOR	17	3	4	7	–1	22	0	0	1	1	14	21.4
C	11	Steve Sullivan	TOR	13	3	3	6	–3	14	2	0	0	0	21	14.3
D	36	Dimitri Yushkevich	TOR	17	1	5	6	7	22	1	0	0	0	17	5.9
D	55	* Daniil Markov	TOR	17	0	6	6	9	18	0	0	0	0	11	0.0
R	20	Mike Johnson	TOR	17	3	2	5	–1	4	0	0	1	0	26	11.5
D	52	Alexander Karpovtsev	TOR	14	1	3	4	–7	12	1	0	0	0	13	7.7
L	7	Derek King	TOR	16	1	3	4	0	4	0	0	0	0	26	3.8
D	3	Sylvain Cote	TOR	17	2	1	3	–3	10	0	0	0	0	19	10.5
D	15	* Tomas Kaberle	TOR	14	0	3	3	0	2	0	0	0	0	14	0.0
L	12	Kris King	TOR	17	1	1	2	–1	25	0	0	0	0	15	6.7
C	42	* Kevyn Adams	TOR	7	0	2	2	–2	14	0	0	0	0	9	0.0
R	28	Tie Domi	TOR	14	0	2	2	–1	24	0	0	0	0	7	0.0
C	21	* Adam Mair	TOR	5	1	0	1	–1	14	0	0	0	0	3	33.3
D	33	Chris McAllister	TOR	6	0	1	1	–1	4	0	0	0	0	2	0.0
G	30	Glenn Healy	TOR	1	0	0	0	0	0	0	0	0	0	0	0.0
D	2	Dallas Eakins	TOR	1	0	0	0	0	0	0	0	0	0	0	0.0
C	22	Igor Korolev	TOR	1	0	0	0	0	0	0	0	0	0	0	0.0
R	39	* Ladislav Kohn	TOR	2	0	0	0	0	5	0	0	0	0	0	0.0
L	19	Fredrik Modin	TOR	8	0	0	0	–2	6	0	0	0	0	11	0.0
L	8	Todd Warriner	TOR	9	0	0	0	0	2	0	0	0	0	12	0.0
G	31	Curtis Joseph	TOR	17	0	0	0	0	2	0	0	0	0	1	0.0

Goaltending

No.	Goaltender	GPI	Mins	Avg	W	L	EN	SO	GA	SA	S%
30	Glenn Healy	1	20	0.00	0	0	0	0	0	5	1.000
31	Curtis Joseph	17	1011	2.43	9	8	5	1	41	440	.907
	Totals	**17**	**1036**	**2.66**	**9**	**8**	**5**	**1**	**46**	**450**	**.898**

Captains' History

Hap Day, 1927-28 to 1936-37; Charlie Conacher, 1937-38; Red Horner, 1938-39, 1939-40; Syl Apps, 1940-41 to 1942-43; Bob Davidson, 1943-44, 1944-45; Syl Apps, 1945-46 to 1947-48; Ted Kennedy, 1948-49 to 1954-55; Sid Smith, 1955-56; Jim Thomson, Ted Kennedy, 1956-57; George Armstrong, 1957-58 to 1968-69; Dave Keon, 1969-70 to 1974-75; Darryl Sittler, 1975-76 to 1980-81; Rick Vaive, 1981-82 to 1985-86; no captain, 1986-87 to 1988-89; Rob Ramage, 1989-90, 1990-91; Wendel Clark, 1991-92 to 1993-94; Doug Gilmour, 1994-95 to 1996-97; Mats Sundin, 1997-98 to date.

Club Records

Team

(Figures in brackets for season records are games played; records for fewest points, wins, ties, losses, goals, goals against are for 70 or more games)

Most Points	**99**	1992-93 (84)
Most Wins	**45**	1998-99 (82)
Most Ties	**22**	1954-55 (70)
Most Losses	**52**	1984-85 (80)
Most Goals	**337**	1989-90 (80)
Most Goals Against	**387**	1983-84 (80)
Fewest Points	**48**	1984-85 (80)
Fewest Wins	**20**	1981-82 (80), 1984-85 (80)
Fewest Ties	**4**	1989-90 (80)
Fewest Losses	**16**	1950-51 (70)
Fewest Goals	**147**	1954-55 (70)
Fewest Goals Against	***131**	1953-54 (70)
Longest Winning Streak		
Overall	**10**	Oct. 7-28/93
Home	**9**	Nov. 11-Dec. 26/53
Away	**7**	Nov. 14-Dec. 15/40, Dec. 4/60-Jan. 5/61
Longest Undefeated Streak		
Overall	**11**	Oct. 15-Nov. 8/50 (8 wins, 3 ties), Jan. 6-Feb. 1/94 (7 wins, 4 ties)
Home	**18**	Nov. 28/33-Mar. 10/34 (15 wins, 3 ties), Oct. 31/53-Jan. 23/54 (16 wins, 2 ties)
Away	**9**	Nov. 30/47-Jan. 11/48 (4 wins, 5 ties)
Longest Losing Streak		
Overall	**10**	Jan. 15-Feb. 8/67
Home	**7**	Nov. 11-Dec. 5/84
Away	**11**	Feb. 20-Apr. 1/88
Longest Winless Streak		
Overall	**15**	Dec. 26/87-Jan. 25/88 (11 losses, 4 ties)
Home	**11**	Dec. 19/87-Jan. 25/88 (7 losses, 4 ties)
Away	**18**	Oct. 6/82-Jan. 5/83 (13 losses, 5 ties)
Most Shutouts, Season	**13**	1953-54 (70)
Most PIM, Season	**2,419**	1989-90 (80)
Most Goals, Game	**14**	Mar. 16/57 (NYR 1 at Tor. 14)

Individual

Most Seasons	**21**	George Armstrong
Most Games	**1,187**	George Armstrong
Most Goals, Career	**389**	Darryl Sittler
Most Assists, Career	**620**	Borje Salming
Most Points, Career	**916**	Darryl Sittler (389G, 527A)
Most PIM, Career	**1,670**	Dave Williams
Most Shutouts, Career	**62**	Turk Broda
Longest Consecutive Games Streak	**486**	Tim Horton (Feb. 11/61-Feb. 4/68)
Most Goals, Season	**54**	Rick Vaive (1981-82)
Most Assists, Season	**95**	Doug Gilmour (1992-93)
Most Points, Season	**127**	Doug Gilmour (1992-93; 32G, 95A)
Most PIM, Season	**365**	Tie Domi (1997-98)
Most Points, Defenseman, Season	**79**	Ian Turnbull (1976-77; 22G, 57A)
Most Points, Center, Season	**127**	Doug Gilmour (1992-93; 32G, 95A)
Most Points, Right Wing, Season	**97**	Wilf Paiement (1980-81; 40G, 57A)
Most Points, Left Wing, Season	**99**	Dave Andreychuk (1993-94; 53G, 46A)
Most Points, Rookie, Season	**66**	Peter Ihnacak (1982-83; 28G, 38A)
Most Shutouts, Season	**13**	Harry Lumley (1953-54)
Most Goals, Game	**6**	Corb Denneny (Jan. 26/21), Darryl Sittler (Feb. 7/76)
Most Assists, Game	**6**	Babe Pratt (Jan. 8/44), Doug Gilmour (Feb. 13/93)
Most Points, Game	***10**	Darryl Sittler (Feb. 7/76; 6G, 4A)

* NHL Record.

Retired Numbers

5	Bill Barilko	1946-1951
6	Ace Bailey	1926-1934

Honored Numbers

1	Turk Broda	1936-43, 45-52
	Johnny Bower	1958-1970
7	King Clancy	1930-1937
	Tim Horton	1949-50, 51-70
9	Charlie Conacher	1929-1938
	Ted Kennedy	1942-55, 56-57
10	Syl Apps	1936-43, 45-48
	George Armstrong	1949-50, 51-71

All-time Record vs. Other Clubs

Regular Season

	At Home							On Road							Total						
	GP	W	L	T	GF	GA	PTS	GP	W	L	T	GF	GA	PTS	GP	W	L	T	GF	GA	PTS
Anaheim	11	6	1	4	36	23	16	10	5	4	1	27	29	11	21	11	5	5	63	52	27
Boston	286	149	87	50	972	745	348	285	84	154	47	756	936	215	571	233	241	97	1728	1681	563
Buffalo	54	20	25	9	164	199	49	56	17	35	4	156	233	38	110	37	60	13	320	432	87
Calgary	49	25	17	7	188	179	57	52	17	30	5	168	216	39	101	42	47	12	356	395	96
Carolina	27	9	14	4	95	104	22	27	7	16	4	90	123	18	54	16	30	8	185	227	40
Chicago	311	163	95	53	1061	808	379	312	116	154	42	819	955	274	623	279	249	95	1880	1763	653
Colorado	30	13	14	3	102	121	29	29	7	17	5	87	111	19	59	20	31	8	189	232	48
Dallas	98	48	34	16	346	311	112	95	35	49	11	302	362	81	193	83	83	27	648	673	193
Detroit	312	163	104	45	1035	838	371	315	105	164	46	773	942	256	627	268	268	91	1808	1780	627
Edmonton	33	17	14	2	137	143	36	34	9	19	6	117	158	24	67	26	33	8	254	301	60
Florida	6	5	1	0	26	14	10	7	2	2	3	18	21	7	13	7	3	3	44	35	17
Los Angeles	64	33	20	11	257	213	77	64	21	34	9	187	230	51	128	54	54	20	444	443	128
Montreal	320	162	114	44	966	836	368	320	85	195	40	789	1137	210	640	247	309	84	1755	1973	578
Nashville	1	0	0	1	2	2	1	0	0	0	0	0	0	0	1	0	0	1	2	2	1
New Jersey	38	25	9	4	160	123	54	37	12	14	11	116	133	35	75	37	23	15	276	256	89
NY Islanders	45	21	21	3	152	160	45	43	16	24	3	131	178	35	88	37	45	6	283	338	80
NY Rangers	272	152	81	39	935	713	343	273	101	116	56	798	842	258	545	253	197	95	1733	1555	601
Ottawa	9	7	2	0	32	21	14	7	2	4	1	15	19	5	16	9	6	1	47	40	19
Philadelphia	57	20	24	13	187	194	53	57	12	37	8	134	228	32	114	32	61	21	321	422	85
Phoenix	39	16	21	2	138	150	34	38	12	20	6	137	157	30	77	28	41	8	275	307	64
Pittsburgh	58	27	20	11	236	193	65	59	21	32	6	189	250	48	117	48	52	17	425	443	113
St. Louis	95	58	26	11	358	275	127	96	28	55	13	270	331	69	191	86	81	24	628	606	196
San Jose	14	9	4	1	56	38	19	14	7	5	2	38	30	16	28	16	9	3	94	68	35
Tampa Bay	12	7	5	0	46	31	14	10	9	1	0	38	18	18	22	16	6	0	84	49	32
Vancouver	56	26	20	10	209	186	62	55	18	27	10	182	191	46	111	44	47	20	391	377	108
Washington	39	21	14	4	179	138	46	40	12	26	2	109	155	26	79	33	40	6	288	293	72
Defunct Clubs	232	158	53	21	860	515	337	233	84	120	29	607	745	197	465	242	173	50	1467	1260	534
Totals	**2568**	**1360**	**840**	**368**	**8935**	**7273**	**3088**	**2568**	**844**	**1354**	**370**	**7053**	**8730**	**2058**	**5136**	**2204**	**2194**	**738**	**15988**	**16003**	**5146**

Playoffs

	Series	W	L	GP	W	L	T	GF	GA	Last Mtg.	Round	Result
Boston	13	8	5	62	31	30	1	150	153	1974	QF	L 0-4
Buffalo	1	0	1	5	1	4	0	16	21	1999	CF	L 1-4
Calgary	1	1	0	2	2	0	0	9	5	1979	PR	W 2-0
Chicago	9	6	3	38	22	15	1	111	89	1995	CQF	L 3-4
Dallas	2	0	2	7	1	6	0	26	35	1983	DSF	L 1-3
Detroit	23	12	11	117	58	59	0	311	321	1993	DSF	W 4-3
Los Angeles	3	2	1	12	7	5	0	41	31	1993	CF	L 3-4
Montreal	15	7	8	71	29	42	0	160	215	1979	QF	L 0-4
NY Islanders	2	1	1	10	4	6	0	20	33	1981	PR	L 0-3
NY Rangers	8	3	5	35	16	19	0	86	86	1971	QF	L 2-4
Philadelphia	4	1	3	23	9	14	0	56	78	1999	CQF	W 4-2
Pittsburgh	3	3	0	12	8	4	0	39	27	1999	CSF	W 4-2
St. Louis	5	2	3	31	14	17	0	90	88	1996	CQF	L 2-4
San Jose	1	1	0	7	4	3	0	26	21	1994	CSF	W 4-3
Vancouver	1	0	1	5	1	4	0	9	16	1994	CF	L 1-4
Defunct	8	6	2	24	12	10	2	59	57			
Totals	**99**	**53**	**46**	**461**	**219**	**238**	**4**	**1209**	**1292**			

Calgary totals include Atlanta Flames, 1972-73 to 1979-80.
Colorado totals include Quebec, 1979-80 to 1994-95.
Carolina totals include Hartford, 1979-80 to 1996-97.
Dallas totals include Minnesota, 1967-68 to 1992-93.
New Jersey totals include Kansas City, 1974-75 to 1975-76, and Colorado Rockies, 1976-77 to 1981-82.
Phoenix totals include Winnipeg, 1979-80 to 1995-96.

Playoff Results 1999-95

Year	Round	Opponent	Result	GF	GA
1999	CF	Buffalo	L 1-4	16	21
	CSF	Pittsburgh	W 4-2	18	14
	CQF	Philadelphia	W 4-2	9	11
1996	CQF	St. Louis	L 2-4	15	21
1995	CQF	Chicago	L 3-4	20	22

Abbreviations: Round: CF – conference final; **CSF** – conference semi-final; **CQF** – conference quarter-final; **DSF** – division semi-final; **QF** – quarter-final; **PR** – preliminary round.

1998-99 Results

Oct.	10		Detroit	2-1		13	at	Florida	3-3
	13	at	Edmonton	3-2		16	at	Philadelphia	4-3
	16	at	Calgary	7-3		18	at	Carolina	2-4
	17	at	Vancouver	1-4		20	at	Dallas	6-4
	19		Nashville	2-2		21	at	St. Louis	4-2
	23	at	Detroit	5-3		28	at	Pittsburgh	0-6
	24	at	Pittsburgh	6-4		30		Washington	5-3
	26		Pittsburgh	0-2	**Feb.**	2	at	Tampa Bay	3-0
	30	at	Buffalo	1-4		3	at	Florida	2-5
	31		Buffalo	3-6		6	at	New Jersey	3-2
Nov.	4		Colorado	3-0		10		Carolina	5-6
	5	at	Boston	1-4		13		Chicago	2-6
	7		NY Rangers	6-6		15	at	New Jersey	3-3
	9		NY Islanders	1-3		17	at	Buffalo	3-2
	11		Edmonton	3-2		20		Montreal	3-2
	12	at	Chicago	10-3		22	at	Washington	3-4
	14		Ottawa	2-1		24		Carolina	2-2
	18	at	Washington	1-4		25	at	NY Islanders	4-1
	20	at	Buffalo	1-4		27		Florida	4-1
	21		Buffalo	2-1	**Mar.**	3		New Jersey	2-5
	23		Calgary	3-2		4	at	St. Louis	4-0
	25		Vancouver	5-1		6	at	Ottawa	1-3
	27	at	Philadelphia	3-4		8	at	NY Rangers	2-3
	28		Ottawa	3-2		9		Tampa Bay	6-1
Dec.	2		Los Angeles	3-1		11	at	NY Islanders	2-1
	5	at	Montreal	4-3		13	at	Montreal	1-2
	7	at	NY Rangers	2-6		17		Boston	1-4
	11	at	Chicago	3-2		20		New Jersey	3-1
	12		Philadelphia	0-3		22		Philadelphia	1-3
	16		Phoenix	5-2		24		San Jose	5-8
	19		NY Rangers	7-4		26	at	Carolina	7-2
	21		Pittsburgh	7-1		27		Boston	2-2
	23		Dallas	1-5		31	at	Vancouver	6-5
	26		Montreal	1-2	**Apr.**	1	at	Edmonton	5-1
	30		Anaheim	4-1		3	at	Calgary	5-1
	31	at	Detroit	4-2		5		St. Louis	2-2
Jan.	2		Washington	2-5		7		Ottawa	4-2
	4		Tampa Bay	5-4		8	at	Ottawa	1-3
	7	at	Boston	1-2		10		Florida	9-1
	9		Boston	6-3		14		NY Islanders	3-2
	12	at	Tampa Bay	4-3		17	at	Montreal	2-3

Entry Draft
Selections 1999-85

1999
Pick
24	Luca Cereda
60	Peter Reynolds
108	Mirko Murovic
110	Jonathan Zion
151	Vaclav Zavoral
161	Jan Sochor
211	Vladimir Kulkov
239	Pierre Hedin
267	Peter Metcalf

1998
Pick
10	Nikolai Antropov
35	Petr Svoboda
69	Jamie Hodson
87	Alexei Ponikarovsky
126	Morgan Warren
154	Allan Rourke
181	Jonathan Gagnon
215	Dwight Wolfe
228	Mihail Travnicek
236	Sergei Rostov

1997
Pick
57	Jeff Farkas
84	Adam Mair
111	Frantisek Mrazek
138	Eric Gooldy
165	Hugo Marchand
190	Shawn Thornton
194	Russ Bartlett
221	Jonathan Hedstrom

1996
Pick
36	Marek Posmyk
50	Francis Larivee
66	Mike Lankshear
68	Konstantin Kalmikov
86	Jason Sessa
103	Vladimir Antipov
110	Peter Cava
111	Brandon Sugden
140	Dmitriy Yakushin
148	Chris Bogas
151	Lucio DeMartinis
178	Reggie Berg
204	Tomas Kaberle
230	Jared Hope

1995
Pick
15	Jeff Ware
54	Ryan Pepperall
139	Doug Bonner
145	Yannick Tremblay
171	Marek Melenovsky
197	Mark Murphy
223	Daniil Markov

1994
Pick
16	Eric Fichaud
48	Sean Haggerty
64	Fredrik Modin
126	Mark Deyell
152	Kam White
178	Tommi Rajamaki
204	Rob Butler
256	Sergei Berezin
282	Doug Nolan

1993
Pick
12	Kenny Jonsson
19	Landon Wilson
123	Zdenek Nedved
149	Paul Vincent
175	Jeff Andrews
201	David Brumby
253	Kyle Ferguson
279	Mikhail Lapin

1992
Pick
8	Brandon Convery
23	Grant Marshall
77	Nikolai Borschevsky
95	Mark Raiter
101	Janne Gronvall
106	Chris Deruiter
125	Mikael Hakansson
149	Patrik Augusta
173	Ryan Vandenbussche
197	Wayne Clarke
221	Sergei Simonov
245	Nathan Dempsey

1991
Pick
47	Yanic Perreault
69	Terry Chitaroni
102	Alexei Kudashov
113	Jeff Perry
120	Alexander Kuzminsky
135	Martin Prochazka
160	Dmitri Mironov
164	Robb McIntyre
167	Tomas Kucharcik
179	Guy Lehoux
201	Gary Miller
223	Jonathan Kelley
245	Chris O'Rourke

1990
Pick
10	Drake Berehowsky
31	Felix Potvin
73	Darby Hendrickson
80	Greg Walters
115	Alexander Godynyuk
136	Eric Lacroix
157	Dan Stiver
178	Robert Horyna
199	Rob Chebator
220	Scott Malone
241	Nick Vachon

1989
Pick
3	Scott Thornton
12	Rob Pearson
21	Steve Bancroft
66	Matt Martin
96	Keith Carney
108	David Burke
125	Michael Doers
129	Keith Merkler
150	Derek Langille
171	Jeffrey St. Laurent
192	Justin Tomberlin
213	Mike Jackson
234	Steve Chartrand

1988
Pick
6	Scott Pearson
27	Tie Domi
48	Peter Ing
69	Ted Crowley
88	Leonard Esau
132	Matt Mallgrave
153	Roger Elvenas
174	Mike Delay
195	David Sacco
216	Mike Gregorio
237	Peter DeBoer

1987
Pick
7	Luke Richardson
28	Daniel Marois
49	John McIntyre
71	Joe Sacco
91	Mike Eastwood
112	Damian Rhodes
133	Trevor Jobe
154	Chris Jensen
175	Brian Blad
196	Ron Bernacci
217	Ken Alexander
238	Alex Weinrich

1986
Pick
6	Vincent Damphousse
36	Darryl Shannon
48	Sean Boland
69	Kent Hulst
90	Scott Taylor
111	Stephane Giguere
132	Danny Hie
153	Stephen Brennan
174	Brian Bellefeuille
195	Sean Davidson
216	Mark Holick
237	Brian Hoard

1985
Pick
1	Wendel Clark
22	Ken Spangler
43	Dave Thomlinson
64	Greg Vey
85	Jeff Serowik
106	Jiri Latal
127	Tim Bean
148	Andy Donahue
169	Todd Whittemore
190	Bob Reynolds
211	Tim Armstrong
232	Mitch Murphy

Coaching History

Conn Smythe, 1927-28 to 1929-30; Conn Smythe and Art Duncan, 1930-31; Art Duncan and Dick Irvin, 1931-32; Dick Irvin, 1932-33 to 1939-40; Hap Day, 1940-41 to 1949-50; Joe Primeau, 1950-51 to 1952-53; King Clancy, 1953-54 to 1955-56; Howie Meeker, 1956-57; Billy Reay, 1957-58; Billy Reay and Punch Imlach, 1958-59; Punch Imlach, 1959-60 to 1968-69; John McLellan, 1969-70, 1970-71; John McLellan and King Clancy, 1971-72; John McLellan, 1972-73; Red Kelly, 1973-74 to 1976-77; Roger Neilson, 1977-78, 1978-79; Floyd Smith, Dick Duff and Punch Imlach, 1979-80; Punch Imlach, Joe Crozier and Mike Nykoluk, 1980-81; Mike Nykoluk, 1981-82 to 1983-84; Dan Maloney, 1984-85, 1985-86; John Brophy, 1986-87, 1987-88; John Brophy and George Armstrong, 1988-89; Doug Carpenter, 1989-90; Doug Carpenter and Tom Watt, 1990-91; Tom Watt, 1991-92; Pat Burns, 1992-93 to 1994-95; Pat Burns and Nick Beverley, 1995-96; Mike Murphy, 1996-97, 1997-98; Pat Quinn, 1998-99 to date.

Club Directory

Air Canada Centre

Air Canada Centre
40 Bay St., Suite 400
Toronto, Ontario M5J 2X2
Phone **416/815-5700**
FAX 416/359-9331
Website:
www.torontomapleleafs.com
Capacity: 18,819

Board of Directors
Steve A. Stavro (Chairman of the Board and N.H.L. Governor), Brian P. Bellmore (Alternate N.H.L. Governor), Larry Tanenbaum , Robert G. Bertram, John MacIntyre, Dean Metcalf

Advisory Board
J. Donald Crump, Chris Dundas, Terence V. Kelly, Ted Nikolaou, W. Ron Pringle, George E. Whyte

Maple Leaf Sports & Entertainment Ltd.
Chairman of the Board and N.H.L. Governor	Steve A. Stavro
Alternate N.H.L. Governor	Brian P. Bellmore
President and Chief Executive Officer	Richard Peddie
Executive Vice-President	Ken Dryden
Sr. Vice-President and General Manager, Air Canada Centre and Maple Leaf Gardens	Bob Hunter
Sr. Vice-President, Business	Tom Anselmi
Sr. Vice-President, Finance and Administration	Ian Clarke
Vice-President, Sports Communications and Community Development	John Lashway
Vice-President, People	Mardi Walker
Vice-President, General Counsel	Robin Brudner
Vice-President, Marketing	Derek Chalmers
Vice-President, Sales and Service	Chris Overholt
Corporate Secretary	Paul Perantinos

Maple Leafs Management
President and Alternate N.H.L. Governor	Ken Dryden
General Manager and Head Coach	Pat Quinn
Director, Player Personnel	Nick Beverley
Assistant to the President	Bill Watters
Director, Player Evaluation	Joe Yannetti
Assistant Coaches	Rick Ley, Alpo Suhonen
Developmental Coach	Paul Dennis
Strength and Conditioning Coach	Phil Walker
Community Representative	Darryl Sittler
Scouts	George Armstrong, Jack Gardiner, Mark Hillier, Larry Hornung, Bob Johnson, Peter Johnson, Floyd Smith
European Scouts	Leonid Vaysfeld, Jan Kovac, Thommie Bergman
Manager, Hockey Operations	Casey Vanden Heuvel
Travel Coordinator	Mary Speck
Scout Coordinator	Christine Buchanan
Executive Assistant to President	Ann Clark
Executive Assistant to General Manager	Maria Tomasevic

Maple Leafs Communications and Community Development
Vice-President, Sports Communications and Community Development	John Lashway
Manager, Media Relations	Pat Park
Coordinator, Media Relations	Anthony Alfred
Coordinator, Media Relations	Dave Griffiths
Manager, Community Relations	Kristy Fletcher
Manager, Community Development	Angela McManus
Coordinator, Community Relations	Cora Mattholie
Coordinators, Game Operations and Promotions	Mike Ferriman, Nancy Gilks
Assistant, Game Operations and Promotions	Greg Schell
Alumni Relations	Jennifer Woods
Executive Assistant, Communications	Laura Leite

Maple Leafs Medical and Training Staff
Head Athletic Therapist	Chris Broadhurst
Athletic Therapist	Brent Smith
Equipment Manager	Brian Papineau
Assistant Equipment Manager	Dave Aleo
Trainer	Scott McKay
Team Doctors	Dr. Michael Clarfield, Dr. Darrell Ogilvie-Harris, Dr. Leith Douglas, Dr. Rob Devenyi, Dr. Simon McGrail
Team Dentist	Dr. Ernie Lewis
Team Psychologist	Robert Offenberger, Ph. D.

St. John's Maple Leafs (American Hockey League Affiliate)
Head Coach	Al MacAdam
Player/Assistant Coach	Greg Smyth
Athletic Therapist	Nick Addey-Jibb
Equipment Manager	Don Alcock
Director of Operations	Glen Stanford
Media/Team Services Coordinator	Chris Schwartz

Air Canada Centre/Maple Leaf Gardens
Director, Building Operations	Diego Roccasalva
Director, Event Operations and Production	Jim Roe
Director, Event Personnel and Guest Services	Kim Bedier
Director, Programming and Event Marketing	Patti-Anne Tarlton
Sr. Manager, Ticket Operations	Donna Henderson
Sr. Manager, Communications and Public Relations	Karen Petcoff
Manager, Building Operations	Steve Bodolay
Manager, MLG Building Operations	Bernie Fournier
Manager, Video and Sound Production	Curtis Emerson
Director, Marketing Services	Joyce Van Zeumeren
Director, Executive Suites Services	Nancy Read
Director, Food and Beverage Operations	Garth Essery
Director, Consumer Products	Jeff Newman

Broadcast Information
Radio Play-By-Play	Joe Bowen, Dennis Beyak
Radio Analyst	Jim Ralph
Television Play-By-Play	Bob Cole, Joe Bowen
Television Analyst	Harry Neale

Vancouver Canucks

1998-99 Results: 23w-47L-12T 58PTS. Fourth, Northwest Division

Year-by-Year Record

Season	GP	Home W	L	T	Road W	L	T	Overall W	L	T	GF	GA	Pts.	Finished		Playoff Result
1998-99	82	14	21	6	9	26	6	23	47	12	192	258	58	4th,	Northwest Div.	Out of Playoffs
1997-98	82	15	22	4	10	21	10	25	43	14	224	273	64	7th,	Pacific Div.	Out of Playoffs
1996-97	82	20	17	4	15	23	3	35	40	7	257	273	77	4th,	Pacific Div.	Out of Playoffs
1995-96	82	15	19	7	17	16	8	32	35	15	278	278	79	3rd,	Pacific Div.	Lost Conf. Quarter-Final
1994-95	48	10	8	6	8	10	6	18	18	12	153	148	48	2nd,	Pacific Div.	Lost Conf. Semi-Final
1993-94	84	20	19	3	21	21	0	41	40	3	279	276	85	2nd,	Pacific Div.	Lost Final
1992-93	84	27	11	4	19	18	5	46	29	9	346	278	101	1st,	Smythe Div.	Lost Div. Final
1991-92	80	23	10	7	19	16	5	42	26	12	285	250	96	1st,	Smythe Div.	Lost Div. Final
1990-91	80	18	17	5	10	26	4	28	43	9	243	315	65	4th,	Smythe Div.	Lost Div. Semi-Final
1989-90	80	13	16	11	12	25	3	25	41	14	245	306	64	5th,	Smythe Div.	Out of Playoffs
1988-89	80	19	15	6	14	24	2	33	39	8	251	253	74	4th,	Smythe Div.	Lost Div. Semi-Final
1987-88	80	15	20	5	10	26	4	25	46	9	272	320	59	5th,	Smythe Div.	Out of Playoffs
1986-87	80	17	19	4	12	24	4	29	43	8	282	314	66	5th,	Smythe Div.	Out of Playoffs
1985-86	80	17	18	5	6	26	8	23	44	13	282	333	59	4th,	Smythe Div.	Lost Div. Semi-Final
1984-85	80	15	21	4	10	25	5	25	46	9	284	401	59	5th,	Smythe Div.	Out of Playoffs
1983-84	80	20	16	4	12	23	5	32	39	9	306	328	73	3rd,	Smythe Div.	Lost Div. Semi-Final
1982-83	80	20	12	8	10	23	7	30	35	15	303	309	75	3rd,	Smythe Div.	Lost Div. Semi-Final
1981-82	80	20	8	12	10	25	5	30	33	17	290	286	77	2nd,	Smythe Div.	Lost Final
1980-81	80	17	12	11	11	20	9	28	32	20	289	301	76	3rd,	Smythe Div.	Lost Prelim. Round
1979-80	80	14	17	9	13	20	7	27	37	16	256	281	70	3rd,	Smythe Div.	Lost Prelim. Round
1978-79	80	15	18	7	10	24	6	25	42	13	217	291	63	2nd,	Smythe Div.	Lost Prelim. Round
1977-78	80	13	15	12	7	28	5	20	43	17	239	320	57	3rd,	Smythe Div.	Out of Playoffs
1976-77	80	13	21	6	12	21	7	25	42	13	235	294	63	4th,	Smythe Div.	Out of Playoffs
1975-76	80	22	11	7	11	21	8	33	32	15	271	272	81	2nd,	Smythe Div.	Lost Prelim. Round
1974-75	80	23	12	5	15	20	5	38	32	10	271	254	86	1st,	Smythe Div.	Lost Quarter-Final
1973-74	78	14	18	7	10	25	4	24	43	11	224	296	59	7th,	East Div.	Out of Playoffs
1972-73	78	17	18	4	5	29	5	22	47	9	233	339	53	7th,	East Div.	Out of Playoffs
1971-72	78	14	20	5	6	30	3	20	50	8	203	297	48	7th,	East Div.	Out of Playoffs
1970-71	78	17	18	4	7	28	4	24	46	8	229	296	56	6th,	East Div.	Out of Playoffs

1999-2000 Schedule

Oct.	Sat.	2	NY Rangers		Thu.	13	at Nashville
	Wed.	6	Chicago		Sat.	15	Dallas
	Sat.	9	Montreal*		Mon.	17	Toronto
	Wed.	13	Calgary		Wed.	19	Detroit
	Fri.	15	Carolina		Sat.	22	at Edmonton
	Sat.	16	at Calgary		Sun.	23	Nashville
	Tue.	19	at Tampa Bay		Tue.	25	Edmonton
	Wed.	20	at Florida		Fri.	28	San Jose
	Sat.	23	at NY Islanders		Sun.	30	Chicago
	Sun.	24	at NY Rangers	Feb.	Tue.	1	at Colorado
	Tue.	26	at Philadelphia		Thu.	3	St. Louis
	Thu.	28	Phoenix		Wed.	9	Calgary
	Sat.	30	Nashville		Sat.	12	at Toronto
Nov.	Fri.	5	Florida		Mon.	14	at Pittsburgh
	Sun.	7	St. Louis		Wed.	16	at Detroit
	Tue.	9	San Jose		Thu.	17	at Buffalo
	Fri.	12	at Phoenix		Sat.	19	at Ottawa*
	Mon.	15	Colorado		Mon	21	Boston
	Wed.	17	Detroit		Wed.	23	at Anaheim
	Sat.	20	at Nashville		Fri.	25	Los Angeles
	Mon.	22	at Atlanta		Sun.	27	Phoenix
	Wed.	24	at Carolina		Tue.	29	at Los Angeles
	Fri.	26	at Boston*	Mar.	Thu.	2	Anaheim
	Sat.	27	at Montreal		Sat.	4	New Jersey
	Tue.	30	Colorado		Mon.	6	Toronto
Dec.	Thu.	2	Edmonton		Wed.	8	at Dallas
	Sat.	4	at Edmonton		Thu.	9	at St. Louis
	Mon.	6	at Colorado		Sat.	11	at Phoenix
	Wed.	8	at Anaheim		Mon.	13	at Los Angeles
	Fri.	10	at Calgary		Thu.	16	Buffalo
	Sun.	12	Colorado		Sat.	18	Ottawa
	Thu.	16	Ottawa		Mon.	20	at Colorado
	Sat.	18	Dallas		Wed.	22	at San Jose
	Wed.	22	Washington		Fri.	24	Anaheim
	Sun.	26	Calgary		Sat.	25	at Edmonton
	Wed.	29	Philadelphia		Wed.	29	at Detroit
Jan.	Sun.	2	at Calgary*		Fri.	31	at Nashville
	Wed.	5	Tampa Bay	Apr.	Sun.	2	at Chicago*
	Fri.	7	at Dallas		Wed.	5	Los Angeles
	Sat.	8	at St. Louis		Fri.	7	Edmonton
	Wed.	12	at Chicago		Sun.	9	at San Jose

Denotes afternoon game.

Franchise date: May 22, 1970

WESTERN CONFERENCE

NORTHWEST DIVISION

30th NHL Season

Adrian Aucoin led all NHL defensemen with 23 goals in 1998-99, nearly doubling his previous career total of 13 goals in 155 games. Aucoin's 18 power-play goals trailed only Teemu Selanne (25) and Alexei Yashin (19).

1999-2000 Player Personnel

FORWARDS	HT	WT	S	Place of Birth	Date	1998-99 Club
BERTUZZI, Todd	6-3	224	L	Sudbury, Ont.	2/2/75	Vancouver
BRASHEAR, Donald	6-2	225	L	Bedford, IN	1/7/72	Vancouver
BROWN, Mike	6-5	185	L	Surrey, B.C.	4/27/79	Kamloops
CASSELS, Andrew	6-1	185	L	Bramalea, Ont.	7/23/69	Calgary
COOKE, Matt	5-11	200	L	Belleville, Ont.	9/7/78	Vancouver-Syracuse
DRUKEN, Harold	6-0	205	L	St. John's, Nfld.	1/26/79	Plymouth
GENDRON, Martin	5-9	190	R	Valleyfield, Que.	2/15/74	Fredericton
HENDRICKSON, Darby	6-0	195	L	Richfield, MN	8/28/72	Toronto-Vancouver
HOLDEN, Josh	6-0	190	L	Calgary, Alta.	1/18/78	Vancouver-Syracuse
KARIYA, Steve	5-9	165	R	North Vancouver, B.C.	12/22/77	U. of Maine
KAVANAGH, Pat	6-3	192	R	Ottawa, Ont.	3/14/79	Peterborough
KLATT, Trent	6-1	205	R	Robbinsdale, MN	1/30/71	Philadelphia-Vancouver
MARTYNYUK, Denis	6-3	190	L	Kapfenberg, Austria	7/26/79	SKA Spartak
MAY, Brad	6-1	210	L	Toronto, Ont.	11/29/71	Vancouver
MESSIER, Mark	6-1	205	L	Edmonton, Alta.	1/18/61	Vancouver
MOGILNY, Alexander	5-11	200	L	Khabarovsk, USSR	2/18/69	Vancouver
MORRISON, Justin	6-3	205	R	Los Angeles, CA	9/10/79	Colorado College
NASLUND, Markus	5-11	195	L	Ornskoldsvik, Sweden	7/30/73	Vancouver
RUUTU, Jarkko	6-2	194	L	Vantaa, Finland	8/23/75	HIFK Helsinki
SCHAEFER, Peter	5-11	195	L	Yellow Grass, Sask.	7/12/77	Vancouver-Syracuse
SEDIN, Daniel	6-1	194	L	Ornskoldsvik, Sweden	9/26/80	MoDo Hockey
SEDIN, Henrik	6-2	196	L	Ornskoldsvik, Sweden	9/26/80	MoDo Hockey

DEFENSEMEN						
ALLEN, Bryan	6-4	210	L	Kingston, Ont.	8/21/80	Oshawa
AUCOIN, Adrian	6-2	210	R	Ottawa, Ont.	7/3/73	Vancouver
BARON, Murray	6-3	215	L	Prince George, B.C.	6/1/67	Vancouver
BODGER, Doug	6-2	210	L	Chemainus, B.C.	6/18/66	Los Angeles
JOVANOVSKI, Ed	6-2	210	L	Windsor, Ont.	6/26/76	Florida-Vancouver
KOMARNISKI, Zenith	6-0	200	L	Edmonton, Alta.	8/13/78	Syracuse
OHLUND, Mattias	6-2	220	L	Pitea, Sweden	9/9/76	Vancouver
O'SULLIVAN, Chris	6-2	205	L	Dorchester, MA	5/15/74	Calgary-Saint John-Hartford
SOPEL, Brent	6-1	205	R	Calgary, Alta.	1/7/77	Vancouver-Syracuse

GOALTENDERS	HT	WT	C	Place of Birth	Date	1998-99 Club
KEYES, Tim	5-11	185	L	Gananoque, Ont.	5/28/76	Augusta-Syracuse-Charlotte
SNOW, Garth	6-3	200	L	Wrentham, MA	7/28/69	Vancouver
WEEKES, Kevin	6-0	195	L	Toronto, Ont.	4/4/75	Vancouver-Detroit (IHL)

1998-99 Scoring

* – rookie

Regular Season

Pos	#	Player	Team	GP	G	A	Pts	+/−	PIM	PP	SH	GW	GT	S	%
L	19	Markus Naslund	VAN	80	36	30	66	−13	74	15	2	3	1	205	17.6
C	11	Mark Messier	VAN	59	13	35	48	−12	33	4	2	0	0	97	13.4
R	89	Alexander Mogilny	VAN	59	14	31	45	0	58	3	2	1	1	110	12.7
R	17	* Bill Muckalt	VAN	73	16	20	36	−9	98	4	2	1	0	119	13.4
D	2	Mattias Ohlund	VAN	74	9	26	35	−19	83	2	1	1	0	129	7.0
D	6	Adrian Aucoin	VAN	82	23	11	34	−14	77	18	2	3	1	174	13.2
C	15	Dave Gagner	FLA	36	4	10	14	−7	39	2	0	0	1	50	8.0
			VAN	33	2	12	14	−9	24	0	0	1	0	50	4.0
			TOTAL	69	6	22	28	−16	63	2	0	1	1	100	6.0
D	55	Ed Jovanovski	FLA	41	3	13	16	−4	82	1	0	1	0	68	4.4
			VAN	31	2	9	11	−5	44	0	0	0	0	41	4.9
			TOTAL	72	5	22	27	−9	126	1	0	1	0	109	4.6
C	20	Dave Scatchard	VAN	82	13	13	26	−12	140	0	2	2	0	130	10.0
D	4	Bryan McCabe	VAN	69	7	14	21	−11	120	1	2	0	0	98	7.1
L	8	Donald Brashear	VAN	82	8	10	18	−25	209	2	0	1	0	112	7.1
L	9	Brad May	VAN	66	6	11	17	−14	102	1	0	1	0	91	6.6
L	44	Todd Bertuzzi	VAN	32	8	8	16	−6	44	1	0	3	0	72	11.1
C	27	Harry York	NYR	5	0	0	0	−1	4	0	0	0	0	5	0.0
			PIT	2	0	0	0	0	0	0	0	0	0	0	0.0
			VAN	49	7	9	16	−2	20	1	0	0	1	55	12.7
			TOTAL	56	7	9	16	−3	24	1	0	0	1	60	11.7
C	22	Peter Zezel	VAN	41	6	8	14	5	16	1	0	2	0	45	13.3
R	26	Trent Klatt	PHI	2	0	0	0	0	0	0	0	0	0	2	0.0
			VAN	73	4	10	14	−3	12	0	0	0	0	58	6.9
			TOTAL	75	4	10	14	−3	12	0	0	0	0	60	6.7
C	14	Darby Hendrickson	TOR	35	2	3	5	−4	30	0	0	0	0	34	5.9
			VAN	27	2	2	4	−15	22	1	0	0	0	36	5.6
			TOTAL	62	4	5	9	−19	52	1	0	0	0	70	5.7
L	29	* Peter Schaefer	VAN	25	4	4	8	−1	8	1	0	1	0	24	16.7
D	23	Murray Baron	VAN	81	2	6	8	−23	115	0	0	0	0	53	3.8
D	21	* Josh Holden	VAN	30	2	4	6	−10	10	1	0	0	0	44	4.5
D	18	Bert Robertsson	VAN	39	2	2	4	−7	13	0	0	0	0	13	15.4
D	34	Jason Strudwick	VAN	65	0	3	3	−19	114	0	0	0	0	25	0.0
D	5	Dana Murzyn	VAN	12	0	2	2	1	21	0	0	0	0	7	0.0
C	24	* Matt Cooke	VAN	30	0	2	2	−12	27	0	0	0	0	22	0.0
R	25	Steve Staios	VAN	57	0	2	2	−12	54	0	0	0	0	33	0.0
D	3	* Brent Sopel	VAN	5	1	0	1	−1	4	1	0	0	0	5	20.0
G	30	Garth Snow	VAN	65	0	1	1	0	34	0	0	0	0	0	0.0
C	7	* Robb Gordon	VAN	4	0	0	0	0	2	0	0	0	0	1	0.0
G	35	* Kevin Weekes	VAN	11	0	0	0	0	0	0	0	0	0	0	0.0
C	28	Steve Washburn	FLA	4	0	0	0	−1	4	0	0	0	0	0	0.0
			VAN	8	0	0	0	0	2	0	0	0	0	6	0.0
			TOTAL	12	0	0	0	−1	6	0	0	0	0	6	0.0
G	31	Corey Hirsch	VAN	20	0	0	0	0	0	0	0	0	0	0	0.0

Goaltending

No.	Goaltender	GPI	Mins	Avg	W	L	T	EN	SO	GA	SA	S%
30	Garth Snow	65	3501	2.93	20	31	8	5	6	171	1715	.900
31	Corey Hirsch	20	919	3.13	3	8	0	1	0	48	435	.890
35	* Kevin Weekes	11	532	3.83	0	8	1	0	0	34	257	.868
	Totals	**82**	**4981**	**3.11**	**23**	**47**	**12**	**5**	**7**	**258**	**2412**	**.893**

Coach

CRAWFORD, MARC
Coach, Vancouver Canucks. Born in Belleville, Ont., February 13, 1961.

Marc Crawford became the 15th Head Coach in Canucks history on January 24, 1999. Crawford began his NHL coaching career with the Quebec Nordiques in 1994 and won a Stanley Cup in 1996 when the team moved to Denver to become the Colorado Avalanche. With the win, Crawford became the third-youngest coach in NHL history to win a Stanley Cup. Crawford coached the Avalanche for two seasons after winning the Cup before leaving following the 1997-98 season. He began the 1998-99 season as a colour commentator for CBC's Hockey Night in Canada before joining the Canucks.

Crawford was the Head Coach for Team Canada at the 1998 Olympic Winter Games in Nagano, Japan and he was an assistant coach with Canada's silver medal-winning team in the 1996 World Cup of Hockey. He began his coaching career when he was hired by Brian Burke as a playing assistant with Fredericton (AHL) for the 1987-88 season. At the end of the year he moved to Milwaukee where he served as an assistant coach for the Canucks' IHL minor league affiliate for the 1988-89 campaign. He then moved to Cornwall where he served as the Royals' General Manager and Head Coach in 1989-90.

After two seasons with Cornwall, Crawford went on to coach the St. John's Maple Leafs of the AHL before joining the Nordiques in 1994. He was awarded the 1995 Jack Adams Trophy as the NHL Coach of the Year, becoming the first rookie coach to win the award since it was inaugurated in 1974.

Crawford played every game of his six-year NHL career with the Vancouver Canucks, recording 19 goals and 31 assists in 176 games. He was a rookie on the Canucks team that made a run to the Stanley Cup finals to face the NY Islanders in 1982.

Coaching History

Hal Laycoe, 1970-71, 1971-72; Vic Stasiuk, 1972-73; Bill McCreary and Phil Maloney, 1973-74; Phil Maloney, 1974-75, 1975-76; Phil Maloney and Orland Kurtenbach, 1976-77; Orland Kurtenbach, 1977-78; Harry Neale, 1978-79 to 1980-81; Harry Neale and Roger Neilson, 1981-82; Roger Neilson, 1982-83; Roger Neilson and Harry Neale, 1983-84; Harry Neale and Bill Laforge, 1984-85; Tom Watt, 1985-86, 1986-87; Bob McCammon, 1987-88 to 1989-90; Bob McCammon and Pat Quinn, 1990-91; Pat Quinn, 1991-92 to 1993-94; Rick Ley, 1994-95; Rick Ley and Pat Quinn, 1995-96; Tom Renney, 1996-97; Tom Renney and Mike Keenan, 1997-98; Mike Keenan and Marc Crawford, 1998-99; Marc Crawford, 1999-2000.

Coaching Record

Season	Team	Regular Season					Playoffs			
		Games	W	L	T	%	Games	W	L	%
1989-90	Cornwall (OHL)	66	24	38	4	.394	6	2	4	.333
1990-91	Cornwall (OHL)	66	23	42	1	.356	....	....	....	....
1991-92	St. John's (AHL)	80	39	29	12	.562	16	11	5	.688
1992-93	St. John's (AHL)	80	41	26	13	.594	9	4	5	.444
1993-94	St. John's (AHL)	80	45	23	12	.638	11	6	5	.545
1994-95	**Quebec (NHL)**	**48**	**30**	**13**	**5**	**.677**	**6**	**2**	**4**	**.333**
1995-96	**Colorado (NHL)**	**82**	**47**	**25**	**10**	**.634**	**22**	**16**	**6**	**.727***
1996-97	**Colorado (NHL)**	**82**	**49**	**24**	**9**	**.652**	**17**	**10**	**7**	**.588**
1997-98	**Colorado (NHL)**	**82**	**39**	**26**	**17**	**.579**	**7**	**3**	**4**	**.429**
1998-99	**Vancouver (NHL)**	**37**	**8**	**23**	**6**	**.297**	**....**	**....**	**....**	**....**
	NHL Totals	**331**	**173**	**111**	**47**	**.594**	**52**	**31**	**21**	**.596**

* Stanley Cup win.

Club Records

Team

(Figures in brackets for season records are games played; records for fewest points, wins, ties, losses, goals, goals against are for 70 or more games)

Most Points	101	1992-93 (84)
Most Wins	46	1992-93 (84)
Most Ties	20	1980-81 (80)
Most Losses	50	1971-72 (78)
Most Goals	346	1992-93 (84)
Most Goals Against	401	1984-85 (80)
Fewest Points	48	1971-72 (78)
Fewest Wins	20	1971-72 (78), 1977-78 (80)
Fewest Ties	3	1993-94 (84)
Fewest Losses	26	1991-92 (80)
Fewest Goals	192	1998-99 (82)
Fewest Goals Against	250	1991-92 (80)

Longest Winning Streak

Overall	7	Feb. 10-23/89
Home	9	Nov. 6-Dec. 9/92
Away	5	Jan. 14-25/92, Oct. 6-Nov. 2/93

Longest Undefeated Streak

Overall	10	Mar. 5-25/77 (5 wins, 5 ties)
Home	18	Nov. 4/92-Jan. 16/93 (16 wins, 2 ties)
Away	5	Six times

Longest Losing Streak

Overall	10	Oct. 23-Nov. 11/97
Home	6	Dec. 18/70-Jan. 20/71
Away	12	Nov. 28/81-Feb. 6/82

Longest Winless Streak

Overall	13	Nov. 9-Dec. 7/73 (10 losses, 3 ties)
Home	11	Dec. 18/70-Feb. 6/71 (10 losses, 1 tie)
Away	20	Jan. 2-Apr. 2/86 (14 losses, 6 ties)

Most Shutouts, Season	8	1974-75 (80)
Most PIM, Season	2,326	1992-93 (84)
Most Goals, Game	11	Mar. 28/71 (Cal. 5 at Van. 11), Nov. 25/86 (L.A. 5 at Van. 11), Mar. 1/92 (Cgy. 0 at Van. 11)

Individual

Most Seasons	13	Stan Smyl
Most Games	896	Stan Smyl
Most Goals, Career	262	Stan Smyl
Most Assists, Career	411	Stan Smyl
Most Points, Career	673	Stan Smyl (262G, 411A)
Most PIM, Career	2,127	Gino Odjick
Most Shutouts, Career	20	Kirk McLean
Longest Consecutive Games Streak	482	Trevor Linden (Oct. 4/90-Dec. 1/96)
Most Goals, Season	60	Pavel Bure (1992-93, 1993-94)
Most Assists, Season	62	André Boudrias (1974-75)
Most Points, Season	110	Pavel Bure (1992-93; 60G, 50A)
Most PIM, Season	372	Donald Brashear (1997-98)

Most Points, Defenseman, Season	63	Doug Lidster (1986-87; 12G, 51A)
Most Points, Center, Season	91	Patrik Sundstrom (1983-84; 38G, 53A)
Most Points, Right Wing, Season	110	Pavel Bure (1992-93; 60G, 50A)
Most Points, Left Wing, Season	81	Darcy Rota (1982-83; 42G, 39A)
Most Points, Rookie, Season	60	Ivan Hlinka (1981-82; 23G, 37A), Pavel Bure (1991-92; 34G, 26A)
Most Shutouts, Season	6	Gary Smith (1974-75), Garth Snow (1998-99)
Most Goals, Game	4	Several times
Most Assists, Game	6	Patrik Sundstrom (Feb. 29/84)
Most Points, Game	7	Patrik Sundstrom (Feb. 29/84; 1G, 6A)

Retired Numbers

12	Stan Smyl	1978-1991

Captains' History

Orland Kurtenbach, 1970-71 to 1973-74; no captain, 1974-75; Andre Boudrias, 1975-76; Chris Oddleifson, 1976-77; Don Lever, 1977-78; Don Lever and Kevin McCarthy, 1978-79; Kevin McCarthy, 1979-80 to 1981-82; Stan Smyl, 1982-83 to 1989-90; Dan Quinn, Doug Lidster and Trevor Linden, 1990-91; Trevor Linden, 1991-92 to 1996-97; Mark Messier, 1997-98 to date.

General Managers' History

Bud Poile, 1970-71 to 1972-73; Hal Laycoe, 1973-74; Phil Maloney, 1974-75 to 1976-77; Jake Milford, 1977-78 to 1981-82; Harry Neale, 1982-83 to 1984-85; Jack Gordon, 1985-86, 1986-87; Pat Quinn, 1987-88 to 1997-98; Brian Burke, 1998-99 to date.

All-time Record vs. Other Clubs

Regular Season

	GP	W	L	T	GF	GA	PTS	GP	W	L	T	GF	GA	PTS	GP	W	L	T	GF	GA	PTS
			At Home							On Road							Total				
Anaheim	16	10	6	0	56	42	20	15	7	4	4	48	38	18	31	17	10	4	104	80	38
Boston	48	15	25	8	157	199	38	47	6	36	5	111	204	17	95	21	61	13	268	403	55
Buffalo	48	22	16	10	176	157	54	48	16	24	8	142	176	40	96	38	40	18	318	333	94
Calgary	85	31	37	17	298	290	79	85	19	54	12	246	364	50	170	50	91	29	544	654	129
Carolina	27	12	9	6	95	75	30	26	10	12	4	89	86	24	53	22	21	10	184	161	54
Chicago	62	28	19	15	186	180	71	61	14	41	6	138	232	34	123	42	60	21	324	412	105
Colorado	33	12	16	5	119	135	29	34	12	15	7	99	114	31	67	24	31	12	218	249	60
Dallas	61	29	22	10	229	184	68	61	17	33	11	185	236	45	122	46	55	21	414	420	113
Detroit	55	25	21	9	206	199	59	56	15	34	7	163	240	37	111	40	55	16	369	419	96
Edmonton	69	27	33	9	256	282	63	67	16	45	6	208	318	38	136	43	78	15	464	600	101
Florida	5	1	1	3	15	11	5	5	2	1	2	16	11	5	10	3	3	4	31	22	10
Los Angeles	87	45	28	14	341	280	104	89	29	47	13	286	369	71	176	74	75	27	627	649	175
Montreal	48	8	32	8	119	187	24	49	8	37	4	126	238	20	97	16	69	12	245	425	44
Nashville	2	1	1	0	9	9	2	2	0	2	0	5	9	0	4	1	3	0	14	18	2
New Jersey	45	25	9	11	167	126	61	45	20	19	6	149	143	46	90	45	28	17	316	269	107
NY Islanders	45	21	21	3	148	148	45	43	11	23	9	120	162	31	88	32	44	12	268	310	76
NY Rangers	48	12	33	3	154	199	27	51	9	37	5	130	232	23	99	21	70	8	284	431	50
Ottawa	6	3	2	1	18	12	7	6	2	3	1	18	15	5	12	5	5	2	36	27	12
Philadelphia	49	10	27	12	141	198	32	49	14	34	1	144	218	29	98	24	61	13	285	416	61
Phoenix	62	36	17	9	238	181	81	59	22	29	8	220	227	52	121	58	46	17	458	408	133
Pittsburgh	47	21	22	4	169	178	46	47	8	32	7	164	221	23	94	29	54	11	333	399	69
St. Louis	62	25	30	7	185	198	57	61	18	35	8	178	232	44	123	43	65	15	363	430	101
San Jose	22	15	6	1	87	55	31	24	11	8	5	75	72	27	46	26	14	6	162	127	58
Tampa Bay	6	6	0	0	31	9	12	6	3	3	0	21	19	6	12	9	3	0	52	28	18
Toronto	55	27	18	10	191	182	64	56	20	26	10	186	209	50	111	47	44	20	377	391	114
Washington	36	16	15	5	121	116	37	37	12	21	4	107	127	28	73	28	36	9	228	243	65
Defunct Clubs	19	14	3	2	82	48	30	19	10	8	1	71	68	21	38	24	11	3	153	116	51
Totals	**1148**	**497**	**469**	**182**	**3994**	**3860**	**1176**	**1148**	**331**	**664**	**153**	**3445**	**4580**	**815**	**2296**	**828**	**1133**	**335**	**7439**	**8440**	**1991**

Playoffs

	Series	W	L	GP	W	L	T	GF	GA	Last Mtg.	Round	Result
Buffalo	2	0	2	7	1	6	0	14	28	1981	PR	L 0-3
Calgary	5	2	3	25	12	13	0	80	82	1994	CQF	W 4-3
Chicago	2	1	1	9	4	5	0	24	24	1995	CSF	L 0-4
Colorado	1	0	1	6	2	4	0	17	24	1996	CQF	L 2-4
Dallas	1	1	0	5	4	1	0	18	11	1994	CSF	W 4-1
Edmonton	2	0	2	9	2	7	0	20	35	1992	DF	L 2-4
Los Angeles	3	1	2	17	8	9	0	60	66	1993	DF	L 2-4
Montreal	1	0	1	5	1	4	0	9	20	1975	QF	L 1-4
NY Islanders	2	0	2	6	0	6	0	14	26	1982	F	L 0-4
NY Rangers	1	0	1	7	3	4	0	19	21	1994	F	L 3-4
Philadelphia	1	0	1	3	1	2	0	9	15	1979	PR	L 1-2
St. Louis	1	1	0	7	4	3	0	27	27	1995	CQF	W 4-3
Toronto	1	1	0	5	4	1	0	16	9	1994	CF	W 4-1
Winnipeg	2	2	0	13	8	5	0	50	34	1993	DSF	W 4-2
Totals	**25**	**9**	**16**	**124**	**54**	**70**	**0**	**377**	**422**			

Playoff Results 1999-95

Year	Round	Opponent	Result	GF	GA
1996	CQF	Colorado	L 2-4	17	24
1995	CSF	Chicago	L 0-4	6	11
	CQF	St. Louis	W 4-3	27	27

Abbreviations: Round: F – Final;
CF – conference final; **CSF** – conference semi-final;
CQF – conference quarter-final; **DF** – division final;
DSF – division semi-final; **QF** – quarter-final;
PR – preliminary round.

Calgary totals include Atlanta Flames, 1972-73 to 1979-80.
Colorado totals include Quebec, 1979-80 to 1994-95.
New Jersey totals include Kansas City, 1974-75 to 1975-76, and Colorado Rockies, 1976-77 to 1981-82.
Phoenix totals include Winnipeg, 1979-80 to 1995-96.
Carolina totals include Hartford, 1979-80 to 1996-97.
Dallas totals include Minnesota, 1970-71 to 1992-93.

1998-99 Results

Oct.	12		Los Angeles	4-2	14		Edmonton	1-3
	14		Edmonton	1-4	16		Detroit	2-2
	17		Toronto	4-1	18	at	Dallas	5-3
	20	at	Carolina	1-3	19	at	Nashville	1-4
	21	at	Washington	2-1	28		St. Louis	2-5
	23	at	Florida	5-0	30		Chicago	3-2
	25	at	Tampa Bay	2-3	Feb. 1		Ottawa	0-1
	27	at	Nashville	4-5	3	at	Montreal	1-2
	30		Pittsburgh	2-2	4	at	NY Rangers	4-8
Nov.	1		Washington	4-1	7	at	NY Islanders	3-3
	2	at	Edmonton	3-5	9		New Jersey	4-3
	7		Nashville	5-3	11	at	Pittsburgh	5-6
	9		Los Angeles	3-4	13		Boston	3-1
	12	at	Calgary	4-3	15	at	St. Louis	1-8
	13		Anaheim	5-2	17	at	Chicago	0-4
	15		Colorado	1-2	20		Anaheim	1-5
	18	at	Phoenix	2-4	23	at	Colorado	4-4
	19	at	Colorado	5-0	24	at	San Jose	1-1
	21		Detroit	2-4	26		Carolina	1-0
	23	at	Ottawa	3-4	28		Buffalo	0-2
	25	at	Toronto	1-5	Mar. 3		San Jose	3-4
	27	at	Detroit	1-7	5		Calgary	1-5
	29	at	Philadelphia	2-6	7		Chicago	2-2
Dec.	1	at	Boston	1-1	10	at	Anaheim	4-4
	4		Dallas	4-1	11	at	Phoenix	3-0
	6		Phoenix	3-3	13	at	Los Angeles	1-3
	9	at	Anaheim	4-4	15		New Jersey	1-2
	12	at	Los Angeles	0-3	19		NY Islanders	1-3
	17		Colorado	2-1	20	at	Edmonton	3-4
	19		Nashville	4-6	24	at	Colorado	2-5
	22	at	Calgary	5-3	25		St. Louis	1-4
	23		Calgary	5-2	27		Montreal	5-1
	26	at	San Jose	0-2	29		Phoenix	1-0
	27	at	Edmonton	0-3	31		Toronto	5-6
	29		Colorado	2-4	Apr. 2		San Jose	0-7
	31		Philadelphia	2-6	3	at	San Jose	2-5
Jan.	2		Montreal	1-2	5	at	Chicago	1-2
	4	at	St. Louis	0-4	7	at	Detroit	1-6
	6	at	Dallas	4-6	10		Edmonton	1-1
	8		Florida	1-1	12	at	Calgary	2-0
	10		Dallas	2-0	14	at	Calgary	4-5

Entry Draft Selections 1999-85

1999
Pick
2	Daniel Sedin
3	Henrik Sedin
69	Rene Vydareny
129	Ryan Thorpe
172	Josh Reed
189	Kevin Swanson
218	Markus Kankaanpera
271	Darrell Hay

1998
Pick
4	Bryan Allen
31	Artem Chubarov
68	Jarkko Ruutu
81	Justin Morrison
90	Regan Darby
136	David Jonsson
140	Rick Bertran
149	Paul Cabana
177	Vincent Malts
204	Graig Mischler
219	Curtis Valentine
232	Jason Metcalfe

1997
Pick
10	Brad Ference
34	Ryan Bonni
36	Harold Druken
64	Kyle Freadrich
90	Chris Stanley
114	David Darguzas
117	Matt Cockell
144	Matt Cooke
148	Larry Shapley
171	Rod Leroux
201	Denis Martynyuk
227	Peter Brady

1996
Pick
12	Josh Holden
75	Zenith Komarniski
93	Jonas Soling
121	Tyler Prosofsky
147	Nolan McDonald
175	Clint Cabana
201	Jeff Scissons
227	Lubomir Vaic

1995
Pick
40	Chris McAllister
61	Larry Courville
66	Peter Schaefer
92	Lloyd Shaw
120	Todd Norman
144	Brent Sopel
170	Stewart Bodtker
196	Tyler Willis
222	Jason Cugnet

1994
Pick
13	Mattias Ohlund
39	Robb Gordon
42	Dave Scatchard
65	Chad Allan
92	Mike Dubinsky
117	Yanick Dube
169	Yuri Kuznetsov
195	Rob Trumbley
221	Bill Muckalt
247	Tyson Nash
273	Robert Longpre

1993
Pick
20	Mike Wilson
46	Rick Girard
98	Dieter Kochan
124	Scott Walker
150	Troy Creurer
176	Yevgeny Babariko
202	Sean Tallaire
254	Bert Robertsson
280	Sergei Tkachenko

1992
Pick
21	Libor Polasek
40	Mike Peca
45	Michael Fountain
69	Jeff Connolly
93	Brent Tully
110	Brian Loney
117	Adrian Aucoin
141	Jason Clark
165	Scott Hollis
213	Sonny Mignacca
237	Mark Wotton
261	Aaron Boh

1991
Pick
7	Alex Stojanov
29	Jassen Cullimore
51	Sean Pronger
95	Danny Kesa
117	Evgeny Namestnikov
139	Brent Thurston
161	Eric Johnson
183	David Neilson
205	Brad Barton
227	Jason Fitzsimmons
249	Xavier Majic

1990
Pick
2	Petr Nedved
18	Shawn Antoski
23	Jiri Slegr
65	Darin Bader
86	Gino Odjick
128	Daryl Filipek
149	Paul O'Hagan
170	Mark Cipriano
191	Troy Neumier
212	Tyler Ertel
233	Karri Kivi

1989
Pick
8	Jason Herter
29	Robert Woodward
71	Brett Hauer
113	Pavel Bure
134	James Revenberg
155	Rob Sangster
176	Sandy Moger
197	Gus Morschauser
218	Hayden O'Rear
239	Darcy Cahill
248	Jan Bergman

1988
Pick
2	Trevor Linden
33	Leif Rohlin
44	Dane Jackson
107	Corrie D'Alessio
122	Phil Von Stefenelli
128	Dixon Ward
149	Greg Geldart
170	Roger Akerstrom
191	Paul Constantin
212	Chris Wolanin
233	Stefan Nilsson

1987
Pick
24	Rob Murphy
45	Steve Veilleux
66	Doug Torrel
87	Sean Fabian
108	Garry Valk
129	Todd Fanning
150	Viktor Tumenev
171	Craig Daly
192	John Fletcher
213	Roger Hansson
233	Neil Eisenhut
234	Matt Evo

1986
Pick
7	Dan Woodley
49	Don Gibson
70	Ronnie Stern
91	Eric Murano
112	Steve Herniman
133	Jon Helgeson
154	Jeff Noble
175	Matt Merton
196	Marc Lyons
217	Todd Hawkins
238	Vladimir Krutov

1985
Pick
4	Jim Sandlak
25	Troy Gamble
46	Shane Doyle
67	Randy Siska
88	Robert Kron
109	Martin Hrstka
130	Brian McFarlane
151	Hakan Ahlund
172	Curtis Hunt
193	Carl Valimont
214	Igor Larionov
235	Darren Taylor

Club Directory

General Motors Place
800 Griffiths Way
Vancouver, B.C. V6B 6G1
Phone **604/899-4600**
FAX 604/899-4640
Website: www.canucks.com
Capacity: 18,422

Orca Bay Sports & Entertainment Executive Directory
Chairman, OBSE; Governor, NBA and NHL	John E. McCaw, Jr.
Deputy Chairman, OBSE; Alternate Governor, NBA and NHL	Stanley B. McCammon
President and Chief Executive Officer, Alternate Governor, NBA and NHL	Stephen T. Bellringer
President & General Manager, Vancouver Canucks, Alternate Governor, NHL	Brian P. Burke
Executive Vice President, Business	David Cobb
Vice President, Finance & Chief Financial Officer	Victor de Bonis
Vice President, Communications & Community Investment	Kevin Gass
Vice President & General Manager, Operations	Harvey Jones

Hockey Operations
President & General Manager	Brian P. Burke
Senior Vice-President, Director Hockey Operations	David M. Nonis
Vice President, Player Personnel	Steve Tambellini
Vice President, Amateur Scouting	Mike Penny
Executive Assistant to Mr. Burke & Mr. Nonis	Patti Timms
Scouting Information Coordinator	Jonathan Wall
Senior Editor, Alumni Liaison	Norm Jewison
Manager, Media Relations	Chris Brumwell
Assistant, Media Relations	Reid Mitchell
Manager, Community Relations	Veronica Varhaug
Coordinator, Education Programs & Community Relations	Lisa Ryan
Assistant, Community Relations & Hockey Development	Cheryl Reardon
Administrative Assistant, Media & Community Relations	Karen Girardi
Head Coach	Mark Crawford
Assistant Coaches	Jack McIlhargey, Mike Johnston
Head Coach, Syracuse Crunch	Stan Smyl
Assistant Coach, Syracuse Crunch	Barry Smith
Strength & Conditioning Coach	Peter Twist
Goaltending Consultant	Andy Moog
Video Coordinator	Eric Crawford
Medical Trainer	Mike Burnstein
Massage Therapist	Dave Schima
Assistant Medical Trainer	Jon Sanderson
Equipment Manager	Pat O'Neill
Assistant Equipment Manager	Darren Granger
Dressing Room Attendant	Tim Gross
Team Doctors	Dr. Ross Davidson, Dr. Simon Horlick, Dr. Rui Avelar
Team Dentist	Dr. David Lawson
Team Chiropractor	Dr. Sid Sheard
Team Optometrist	Dr. Alan R. Boyco
Medical Trainer, Syracuse Crunch	Ralph Krugler
Equipment Trainer, Syracuse Crunch	Rodney Blachford
Professional Scout	Shawn Dineen
European Scout	Thomas Gradin
Russian Scout	Sergei Chibisov
Amateur Scouts	Ken Slater, Ron Delorme, Jack McCartan, Barry Dean, Dave Morrison, Daryl Stanley, Jim Eagle, Mike McHugh, Tim Lenardon

Team Travel Department
Travel Manager	Cathie Moroney
Team Services Coordinator	Chantal Hassard

Communications & Community Investment
Vice President, Communications & Community Investment	Kevin Gass
Executive Asst. to the Vice President Communications/Community Investment	Lisa McFadden
Director, Corporate Communications	Nancy McHarg

Broadcasting & Game Presentation
Vice President, Broadcasting	Chris Hebb
Executive Assistant & Promotions Coordinator	Shannon Baker
Manager and Director of In-house Productions	Paul Brettell
Producer, Canucks	Mike Hall
Associate Producer	Al Klein

Business Development
Vice President, Business Development	Leila Bell-Irving
Director, Business Development	Dave Doroghy
Director, Business Development	David Altman
Director, Business Development	Ric Thomsen

Customer Sales and Service
Vice President, Customer Sales and Service	John Rocha
Executive Assistant	Annabelle Kroes
Director, Customer Sales and Service	Caley Denton
Director, Customer Sales	Roger Lemire
Administrative Assistant	Mary Nagy
Director, Executive Suite Service and Operations	Valerie Lewis
Director, Executive Suite Sales and Marketing	Chris Bradley

Finance, Administration and People Development
Vice President, Finance	Victor de Bonis
Director of Finance	Chris Samis
Vice President, People Development & Administration	Susanne Haine
Executive Asst. to the Vice President, People Development & Administration	Catherine Anderson

Authentic Fan Apparel and Collectibles
Director of Retail Operations	Alan Fey

President and General Manager

BURKE, BRIAN
President and General Manager, Vancouver Canucks.
Born in Providence, RI, June 30, 1955.

The Vancouver Canucks announced the appointment of Brian Burke to the position of president and general manager on June 22, 1998. Burke became the eighth general manager in Canucks history after serving as the National Hockey League's senior vice president and director of hockey operations for the past five years.

Burke joins the Canucks with experience in every area of the hockey business. He is a strong negotiator with valuable time spent as a general manager, an NHL senior vice president and player agent. He has a keen eye for hockey talent and has an appreciation for the challenges of operating an NHL franchise in Canada.

In five years as NHL senior vice president, Burke was most visible in his role as the league's chief disciplinarian. He spent much of his time overseeing the league's on-ice officials and was responsible for many disciplinary decisions handed down by the NHL based on his interpretation of league rules. Brian worked closely with NHL commissioner Gary Bettman on the direction of the league and was a key member of the group that introduced NHL excitement to Japan last October when the Vancouver Canucks and Mighty Ducks of Anaheim opened the 1997-98 regular season in Tokyo.

Brian Burke was appointed general manager of the Hartford Whalers on May 26, 1992. In his only season in Hartford, Brian made a number of player moves, changed the team's uniform and completed a major draft-day trade in 1993. After acquiring a second overall selection from San Jose, Burke selected Chris Pronger who has developed into one of the NHL's premier defencemen as is evidenced by his nomination for the 1998 Norris Trophy.

Burke's prior experience with the Canucks began when he was named vice president and director of hockey operations on June 2, 1987. Burke worked with former Canucks president and general manager Pat Quinn for five seasons and assisted in rebuilding Vancouver's team through his contract negotiation skills and his overseeing of the club's scouting systems and its minor league affiliates. Burke helped reshape the Canucks from a 59 point team in 1987 88, to a 96 point team in his final season of 1991-92. It was the first time since the 1974-75 regular season that the Canucks finished first in the Smythe Division.

Brian has four children who reside in the Boston area.

Washington Capitals
1998-99 Results: 31w-45l-6t 68pts. Third, Southeast Division

With 21 goals, Sergei Gonchar trailed only Adrian Aucoin among NHL defensemen and was second on the Capitals behind sniper Peter Bondra (31 goals). Gonchar was one of five Washington players with a positive plus/minus rating.

1999-2000 Schedule

Oct.	Sat.	2	at Florida
	Fri.	8	at Buffalo
	Sat.	9	Los Angeles
	Tue.	12	Philadelphia
	Sat.	16	San Jose
	Tue.	19	Anaheim
	Sat.	23	at Phoenix
	Tue.	26	at Los Angeles
	Fri.	29	at Anaheim
	Sun.	31	at San Jose
Nov.	Wed.	3	Ottawa
	Fri.	5	Toronto
	Sun.	7	at Carolina
	Tue.	9	Tampa Bay
	Thu.	11	NY Rangers
	Sat.	13	New Jersey
	Wed.	17	Dallas
	Fri.	19	Carolina
	Sat.	20	at Boston
	Wed.	24	at Buffalo
	Fri.	26	Nashville
	Sat.	27	at NY Islanders
	Mon.	29	at Toronto
Dec.	Thu.	2	Boston
	Sat.	4	at Florida
	Tue.	7	NY Islanders
	Thu.	9	at Pittsburgh
	Mon.	13	Montreal
	Wed.	15	at Atlanta
	Fri.	17	at NY Rangers
	Sat.	18	at New Jersey
	Tue.	21	at Edmonton
	Wed.	22	at Vancouver
	Mon.	27	Chicago
	Wed.	29	Pittsburgh
Jan.	Sat.	1	St. Louis
	Tue.	4	Montreal
	Thu.	6	at Atlanta
	Sat.	8	Atlanta
	Wed.	12	at Atlanta
	Fri.	14	at New Jersey
	Sun.	16	Ottawa*
	Mon.	17	at Tampa Bay*
	Wed.	19	at Florida
	Sat.	22	at Toronto
	Mon.	24	Tampa Bay
	Wed.	26	Calgary
	Fri.	28	Phoenix
	Sun.	30	Philadelphia*
Feb.	Tue.	1	at Pittsburgh
	Thu.	3	Carolina
	Tue.	8	at Boston
	Thu.	10	at Montreal
	Sat.	12	at Nashville
	Sun.	13	at Dallas
	Tue.	15	Colorado
	Fri.	18	at Chicago
	Sat.	19	at Philadelphia
	Mon.	21	at Carolina*
	Wed.	23	Florida
	Fri.	25	Boston
	Sat.	26	at Montreal
	Mon.	28	at NY Islanders
Mar.	Wed.	1	at Tampa Bay
	Fri.	3	Detroit
	Sun.	5	Buffalo*
	Tue.	7	Florida
	Thu.	9	at Philadelphia
	Sat.	11	New Jersey
	Wed.	15	NY Islanders
	Fri.	17	Carolina
	Sun.	19	Tampa Bay*
	Mon.	20	at St. Louis
	Thu.	23	at NY Rangers
	Sat.	25	at Ottawa
	Tue.	28	Atlanta
	Thu.	30	Pittsburgh
Apr.	Sat.	1	Toronto
	Mon.	3	NY Rangers
	Tue.	4	at Ottawa
	Fri.	7	at Detroit
	Sun.	9	Buffalo*

* Denotes afternoon game.

Franchise date: June 11, 1974

EASTERN NHL **CONFERENCE**

SOUTHEAST DIVISION

26th NHL Season

Year-by-Year Record

Season	GP	Home W	L	T	Road W	L	T	Overall W	L	T	GF	GA	Pts.	Finished		Playoff Result
1998-99	82	16	23	2	15	22	4	31	45	6	200	218	68	3rd,	Southeast Div.	Out of Playoffs
1997-98	82	23	12	6	17	18	6	40	30	12	219	202	92	3rd,	Atlantic Div.	Lost Final
1996-97	82	19	17	5	14	23	4	33	40	9	214	231	75	5th,	Atlantic Div.	Out of Playoffs
1995-96	82	21	15	5	18	17	6	39	32	11	234	204	89	4th,	Atlantic Div.	Lost Conf. Quarter-Final
1994-95	48	15	6	3	7	12	5	22	18	8	136	120	52	3rd,	Atlantic Div.	Lost Conf. Quarter-Final
1993-94	84	17	16	9	22	19	1	39	35	10	277	263	88	3rd,	Atlantic Div.	Lost Conf. Semi-Final
1992-93	84	21	15	6	22	19	1	43	34	7	325	286	93	2nd,	Patrick Div.	Lost Div. Semi-Final
1991-92	80	25	12	3	20	15	5	45	27	8	330	275	98	2nd,	Patrick Div.	Lost Div. Semi-Final
1990-91	80	21	14	5	16	22	2	37	36	7	258	258	81	3rd,	Patrick Div.	Lost Div. Final
1989-90	80	19	18	3	17	20	3	36	38	6	284	275	78	3rd,	Patrick Div.	Lost Conf. Championship
1988-89	80	25	12	3	16	17	7	41	29	10	305	259	92	1st,	Patrick Div.	Lost Div. Semi-Final
1987-88	80	22	14	4	16	19	5	38	33	9	281	249	85	2nd,	Patrick Div.	Lost Div. Final
1986-87	80	22	15	3	16	17	7	38	32	10	285	278	86	2nd,	Patrick Div.	Lost Div. Semi-Final
1985-86	80	30	8	2	20	15	5	50	23	7	315	272	107	2nd,	Patrick Div.	Lost Div. Final
1984-85	80	27	11	2	19	14	7	46	25	9	322	240	101	2nd,	Patrick Div.	Lost Div. Final
1983-84	80	26	11	3	22	16	2	48	27	5	308	226	101	2nd,	Patrick Div.	Lost Div. Final
1982-83	80	22	12	6	17	13	10	39	25	16	306	283	94	3rd,	Patrick Div.	Lost Div. Semi-Final
1981-82	80	16	16	8	10	25	5	26	41	13	319	338	65	5th,	Patrick Div.	Out of Playoffs
1980-81	80	16	17	7	10	19	11	26	36	18	286	317	70	5th,	Patrick Div.	Out of Playoffs
1979-80	80	20	14	6	7	26	7	27	40	13	261	293	67	5th,	Patrick Div.	Out of Playoffs
1978-79	80	15	19	6	9	22	9	24	41	15	273	338	63	4th,	Norris Div.	Out of Playoffs
1977-78	80	10	23	7	7	26	7	17	49	14	195	321	48	5th,	Norris Div.	Out of Playoffs
1976-77	80	17	15	8	7	27	6	24	42	14	221	307	62	4th,	Norris Div.	Out of Playoffs
1975-76	80	6	26	8	5	33	2	11	59	10	224	394	32	5th,	Norris Div.	Out of Playoffs
1974-75	80	7	28	5	1	39	0	8	67	5	181	446	21	5th,	Norris Div.	Out of Playoffs

1999-2000 Player Personnel

FORWARDS

	HT	WT	S	Place of Birth	Date	1998-99 Club
BLACK, James	6-0	202	L	Regina, Sask.	8/15/69	Chicago (IHL)-Washington
BONDRA, Peter	6-1	200	L	Luck, USSR	2/7/68	Washington
BULIS, Jan	6-0	208	L	Pardubice, Czech.	3/18/78	Washington-Cincinnati (IHL)
DAHLEN, Ulf	6-2	195	L	Ostersund, Sweden	1/12/67	HV Jonkoping
EAGLES, Mike	5-10	190	L	Sussex, N.B.	3/7/63	Washington
HALPERN, Jeff	6-0	195	R	Potomac, MD	5/3/76	Princeton-Portland (AHL)
HALVERSON, Trevor	6-0	194	L	White River, Ont.	4/6/71	Washington-Portland (AHL)
HERR, Matt	6-2	204	L	Hackensack, NJ	5/26/76	Washington-Portland (AHL)
KLEE, Ken	6-1	212	R	Indianapolis, IN	4/24/71	Washington
KONOWALCHUK, Steve	6-2	207	L	Salt Lake City, UT	11/11/72	Washington
METROPOLIT, Glen	6-0	185	R	Toronto, Ont.	6/25/74	Grand Rapids
NELSON, Jeff	6-0	190	L	Prince Albert, Sask.	12/18/72	Nashville-Milwaukee
NIKOLISHIN, Andrei	5-11	200	L	Vorkuta, USSR	3/25/73	Moscow D'amo-Washington
OATES, Adam	5-11	185	R	Weston, Ont.	8/27/62	Washington
PELUSO, Mike	6-1	195	R	Bismark, ND	9/2/74	Portland (AHL)
SACCO, Joe	6-1	195	L	Medford, MA	2/4/69	NY Islanders
SHMYR, Jason	6-4	220	L	Fairview, Alta.	7/27/75	Long Beach-San Diego-Man
SIMON, Chris	6-4	235	L	Wawa, Ont.	1/30/72	Washington
SVEJKOVSKY, Jaroslav	6-1	185	R	Plzen, Czech.	10/1/76	Washington
TOMS, Jeff	6-5	200	L	Swift Current, Sask.	6/4/74	Washington-Portland (AHL)
VOLCHKOV, Alexander	6-2	204	L	Moscow, USSR	9/25/77	Port (AHL)-Cin (IHL)
WHITFIELD, Trent	5-11	190	L	Estevan, Sask.	6/17/77	Portland (AHL)-Hampton Roads
ZEDNIK, Richard	6-0	199	L	Bystrica, Czech.	1/6/76	Washington

DEFENSEMEN

	HT	WT	S	Place of Birth	Date	1998-99 Club
BAUMGARTNER, Nolan	6-1	200	R	Calgary, Alta.	3/23/76	Washington-Portland (AHL)
BOILEAU, Patrick	6-0	190	R	Montreal, Que.	2/22/75	Wsh-Port (AHL)-Ind
GONCHAR, Sergei	6-2	212	L	Chelyabinsk, USSR	4/13/74	Washington
HUSCROFT, Jamie	6-2	210	R	Creston, B.C.	1/9/67	Vancouver-Phoenix
JOHANSSON, Calle	5-11	200	L	Goteborg, Sweden	2/14/67	Washington
MIRONOV, Dmitri	6-3	224	R	Moscow, USSR	12/25/65	Washington
POAPST, Steve	6-0	200	L	Cornwall, Ont.	1/3/69	Washington-Portland (AHL)
SHIRREFFS, Steve	6-3	220	R	Norwich, VT	2/18/76	Princeton
STORK, Dean	6-3	205	L	Edmonton, Alta.	10/2/75	U. Mass-Amherst-Portland (AHL)
TEZIKOV, Alexei	6-1	198	L	Togliatti, USSR	6/22/78	Moncton-Roch-Wsh-Cin (IHL)
WITT, Brendan	6-1	226	L	Humbolt, Sask.	2/20/75	Washington

GOALTENDERS

	HT	WT	C	Place of Birth	Date	1998-99 Club
BILLINGTON, Craig	5-10	170	L	London, Ont.	9/11/66	Colorado
BROCHU, Martin	5-11	204	L	Anjou, Que.	3/10/73	Washington-Portland (AHL)-Utah
KOLZIG, Olaf	6-3	225	L	Johannesburg, South Africa	4/9/70	Washington

1998-99 Scoring

*– rookie

Regular Season

Pos	#	Player	Team	GP	G	A	Pts	+/-	PIM	PP	SH	GW	GT	S	%
R	12	Peter Bondra	WSH	66	31	24	55	-1	56	6	3	5	1	284	10.9
C	77	Adam Oates	WSH	59	12	42	54	-1	22	3	0	0	0	79	15.2
L	23	Brian Bellows	WSH	76	17	19	36	-12	26	8	0	3	0	166	10.2
C	13	Andrei Nikolishin	WSH	73	8	27	35	0	28	0	1	1	0	121	6.6
D	55	Sergei Gonchar	WSH	53	21	10	31	1	57	13	1	3	0	180	11.7
C	28	James Black	WSH	75	16	14	30	5	14	1	1	3	0	135	11.9
D	6	Calle Johansson	WSH	67	8	21	29	10	22	2	0	2	1	145	5.5
C	22	Steve Konowalchuk	WSH	45	12	12	24	0	26	4	1	2	0	98	12.2
C	8	Jan Bulis	WSH	38	7	16	23	3	6	3	0	3	0	57	12.3
D	2	Ken Klee	WSH	78	7	13	20	-9	80	0	0	1	0	132	5.3
L	44	Richard Zednik	WSH	49	9	8	17	-6	50	1	0	2	0	115	7.8
D	15	Dmitri Mironov	WSH	46	2	14	16	-5	80	2	0	0	0	86	2.3
L	34	Jaroslav Svejkovsky	WSH	25	6	8	14	-2	12	4	0	2	0	50	12.0
C	20	Michal Pivonka	WSH	36	5	6	11	-6	12	2	0	0	0	30	16.7
L	17	Chris Simon	WSH	23	3	7	10	-4	48	0	0	0	0	29	10.3
C	9	Joe Reekie	WSH	73	0	10	10	11	68	0	0	0	0	81	0.0
C	48	* Benoit Gratton	WSH	16	4	3	7	-1	16	0	0	0	0	24	16.7
D	19	Brendan Witt	WSH	54	2	5	7	-6	87	0	0	0	0	51	3.9
L	10	Kelly Miller	WSH	62	2	5	7	-5	29	0	0	1	0	49	4.1
D	36	Mike Eagles	WSH	52	4	2	6	-5	50	0	0	0	0	41	9.8
L	21	Jeff Toms	WSH	21	1	5	6	0	2	0	0	0	0	30	3.3
D	24	Mark Tinordi	WSH	48	0	6	6	-8	108	0	0	0	0	32	0.0
D	39	Enrico Ciccone	T.B.	16	1	1	2	-1	24	0	0	0	0	9	11.1
			WSH	43	2	0	2	-6	103	0	0	0	1	43	4.7
			TOTAL	59	3	1	4	-7	127	0	0	0	1	52	5.8
C	26	* Matthew Herr	WSH	30	2	2	4	-7	8	1	0	0	0	40	5.0
R	18	Trevor Halverson	WSH	17	0	4	4	-5	28	0	0	0	0	16	0.0
G	37	Olaf Kolzig	WSH	64	0	2	2	0	19	0	0	0	0	0	0.0
D	41	Patrick Boileau	WSH	4	0	1	1	-4	2	0	0	0	0	7	0.0
G	40	Mike Rosati	WSH	1	0	0	0	0	0	0	0	0	0	0	0.0
C	14	Patrick Augusta	WSH	2	0	0	0	0	0	0	0	0	0	4	0.0
G	1	* Martin Brochu	WSH	2	0	0	0	0	0	0	0	0	0	0	0.0
R	14	Patrice Lefebvre	WSH	4	0	0	0	-2	2	0	0	0	0	4	0.0
D	38	* Nolan Baumgartner	WSH	5	0	0	0	-3	0	0	0	0	0	1	0.0
D	4	* Alexei Tezikov	WSH	5	0	0	0	-1	0	0	0	0	0	4	0.0
D	3	Stewart Malgunas	WSH	10	0	0	0	-5	6	0	0	0	0	2	0.0
D	33	Steve Poapst	WSH	22	0	0	0	-8	8	0	0	0	0	11	0.0
G	31	Rick Tabaracci	WSH	23	0	0	0	0	2	0	0	0	0	0	0.0

Goaltending

No.	Goaltender	GPI	Mins	Avg	W	L	T	EN	SO	GA	SA	S%
40	Mike Rosati	1	28	0.00	1	0	0	0	0	0	12	1.000
31	Rick Tabaracci	23	1193	2.51	4	12	3	3	2	50	530	.906
37	Olaf Kolzig	64	3586	2.58	26	31	3	5	4	154	1538	.900
1	* Martin Brochu	2	120	3.00	0	2	0	0	0	6	55	.891
	Totals	82	4959	2.64	31	45	6	8	6	218	2143	.898

Coach

WILSON, RON
Coach, Washington Capitals. Born in Windsor, Ont., May 28, 1955.

In his first season as head coach of the Washington Capitals, Wilson's team came within reach of the Cup when, after posting a 40-30-12 regular season record, the Caps advanced to the Stanley Cup finals for the first time in the franchise's 24-year history.

Prior to joining the Capitals, Wilson served as head coach of the Mighty Ducks of Anaheim for four years. In his last season with the Ducks (1996-97) he led the team to its first playoff appearance. Wilson posted a 120-145-31 (.458) overall record in Anaheim. He also spent three years in Vancouver as an assistant coach to Pat Quinn from 1990-93.

Wilson, 44, also served as the head coach for Team USA at the 1996 World Cup of Hockey. Team USA won the championship series, two games to one, over Canada.

Wilson has significant playing experience in professional, amateur and international hockey. He played four years at Providence College where he was a two-time All-American and two-time ECAC First Team All-Star. Wilson was ECAC player of the year in 1975 when he led the nation in scoring with 26-61-87 points in 27 games. He remains Providence's all-time leading scorer and ranks as the NCAA all-time leading scorer among defensemen with 250 points. Wilson received a Bachelor of Arts degree in economics from Providence College.

Drafted by the Toronto Maple Leafs (132nd overall) in 1975, Wilson began his professional hockey career in 1976-77 with the Dallas Blackhawks in the Central Hockey League. He joined the Toronto Maple Leafs in 1977-78, playing in 64 NHL contests over three seasons. Wilson then moved to Switzerland in 1980 and competed for the Swiss teams Kloten and Davos for six seasons. The former defenseman/winger signed with the Minnesota North Stars as a free agent in 1985 where he played through 1988. Ron enjoyed his finest offensive season in 1986-87 when he recorded 12 goals and 29 assists in 65 games with the North Stars.

Although born in Canada, Wilson was raised in the United States and remains a U.S. citizen. He was a four-time player for U.S. National Teams (1975, 1981, 1983, 1987) and coached the 1994 squad at the World Championships in Italy, leading Team USA to a 4-4-0 record with a fourth-place finish. Wilson also coached the 1996 squad, earning a bronze medal for Team USA.

Coaching Record

			Regular Season				Playoffs			
Season	Team	Games	W	L	T	%	Games	W	L	%
1993-94	Anaheim (NHL)	84	33	46	5	.423	....	....	....	....
1994-95	Anaheim (NHL)	48	16	27	5	.385	....	....	....	....
1995-96	Anaheim (NHL)	82	35	39	8	.476	....	....	....	....
1996-97	Anaheim (NHL)	82	36	33	13	.518	11	4	7	.364
1997-98	Washington (NHL)	82	40	30	12	.561	21	12	9	.571
1998-99	Washington (NHL)	82	31	45	6	.415	....	....	....	....
	NHL Totals	460	191	220	49	.468	32	16	16	.500

Adam Oates collected at least 40 assists for the 12th consecutive season in 1998-99, setting up a team-leading 42 goals for the Capitals. While he has been best known for his picture-perfect passing during his 13 NHL seasons, Oates needs only 12 more goals to reach the 300-goal plateau.

Coaching History

Jim Anderson, Red Sullivan and Milt Schmidt, 1974-75; Milt Schmidt and Tom McVie, 1975-76; Tom McVie, 1976-77, 1977-78; Danny Belisle, 1978-79; Danny Belisle and Gary Green, 1979-80; Gary Green, 1980-81; Gary Green, Roger Crozier and Bryan Murray, 1981-82; Bryan Murray, 1982-83 to 1988-89; Bryan Murray and Terry Murray, 1989-90; Terry Murray, 1990-91 to 1992-93; Terry Murray and Jim Schoenfeld, 1993-94; Jim Schoenfeld, 1994-95 to 1996-97; Ron Wilson, 1997-98 to date.

Club Records

Team

(Figures in brackets for season records are games played; records for fewest points, wins, ties, losses, goals, goals against are for 70 or more games)

Most Points	107	1985-86 (80)
Most Wins	50	1985-86 (80)
Most Ties	18	1980-81 (80)
Most Losses	67	1974-75 (80)
Most Goals	330	1991-92 (80)
Most Goals Against	*446	1974-75 (80)
Fewest Points	*21	1974-75 (80)
Fewest Wins	*8	1974-75 (80)
Fewest Ties	5	1974-75 (80), 1983-84 (80)
Fewest Losses	23	1985-86 (80)
Fewest Goals	181	1974-75 (80)
Fewest Goals Against	202	1997-98 (82)

Longest Winning Streak

Overall	10	Jan. 27-Feb. 18/84
Home	9	Mar. 3-Oct. 6/89
Away	6	Feb. 26-Apr. 1/84

Longest Undefeated Streak

Overall	14	Nov. 24-Dec. 23/82 (9 wins, 5 ties), Jan. 17-Feb. 18/84 (13 wins, 1 tie)
Home	13	Nov. 25/92-Jan. 31/93 (9 wins, 4 ties)
Away	10	Nov. 24/82-Jan. 8/83 (6 wins, 4 ties)

Longest Losing Streak

Overall	*17	Feb. 18-Mar. 26/75
Home	*11	Feb. 18-Mar. 30/75
Away	37	Oct. 9/74-Mar. 26/75

Longest Winless Streak

Overall	25	Nov. 29/75-Jan. 21/76 (22 losses, 3 ties)
Home	14	Dec. 3/75-Jan. 21/76 (11 losses, 3 ties)
Away	37	Oct. 9/74-Mar. 26/75 (37 losses)

Most Shutouts, Season	9	1995-96 (82)
Most PIM, Season	2,204	1989-90 (80)
Most Goals, Game	12	Feb. 6/90 (Que. 2 at Wsh. 12)

Individual

Most Seasons	13	Michal Pivonka, Kelly Miller
Most Games	940	Kelly Miller
Most Goals, Career	397	Mike Gartner
Most Assists, Career	418	Michal Pivonka
Most Points, Career	789	Mike Gartner (397G, 392A)
Most PIM, Career	2,003	Dale Hunter
Most Shutouts, Career	14	Jim Carey
Longest Consecutive Games Streak	422	Bob Carpenter (Oct. 7/81-Nov. 22/86)
Most Goals, Season	60	Dennis Maruk (1981-82)
Most Assists, Season	76	Dennis Maruk (1981-82)
Most Points, Season	136	Dennis Maruk (1981-82; 60G, 76A)
Most PIM, Season	339	Alan May (1989-90)
Most Points, Defenseman, Season	81	Larry Murphy (1986-87; 23G, 58A)
Most Points, Center, Season	136	Dennis Maruk (1981-82; 60G, 76A)
Most Points, Right Wing, Season	102	Mike Gartner (1984-85; 50G, 52A)
Most Points, Left Wing, Season	87	Ryan Walter (1981-82; 38G, 49A)
Most Points, Rookie, Season	67	Bobby Carpenter (1981-82; 32G, 35A), Chris Valentine (1981-82; 30G, 37A)
Most Shutouts, Season	9	Jim Carey (1995-96)
Most Goals, Game	5	Bengt Gustafsson (Jan. 8/84), Peter Bondra (Feb. 5/94)
Most Assists, Game	6	Mike Ridley (Jan. 7/89)
Most Points, Game	7	Dino Ciccarelli (Mar. 18/89; 4G, 3A)

* NHL Record.

Retired Numbers

5	Rod Langway	1982-1993
7	Yvon Labre	1974-1981

Captains' History

Doug Mohns, 1974-75; Bill Clement and Yvon Labre, 1975-76; Yvon Labre, 1976-77, 1977-78; Guy Charron, 1978-79; Ryan Walter, 1979-80 to 1981-82; Rod Langway, 1982-83 to 1991-92; Rod Langway and Kevin Hatcher, 1992-93; Kevin Hatcher, 1993-94; Dale Hunter, 1994-95 to 1998-99; Adam Oates, 1999-2000.

All-time Record vs. Other Clubs

Regular Season

		At Home							On Road							Total					
	GP	W	L	T	GF	GA	PTS	GP	W	L	T	GF	GA	PTS	GP	W	L	T	GF	GA	PTS
Anaheim	5	3	2	0	9	8	6	5	1	3	1	15	16	3	10	4	5	1	24	24	9
Boston	45	12	23	10	132	164	34	46	13	27	6	127	178	32	91	25	50	16	259	342	66
Buffalo	46	12	27	7	121	167	31	46	10	30	6	122	185	26	92	22	57	13	243	352	57
Calgary	37	18	14	5	141	131	41	36	6	24	6	85	152	18	73	24	38	11	226	283	59
Carolina	34	21	11	2	115	92	44	36	18	12	6	118	99	42	70	39	23	8	233	191	86
Chicago	37	20	13	4	135	117	44	36	10	21	5	108	142	25	73	30	34	9	243	259	69
Colorado	30	16	10	4	124	99	36	30	12	14	4	107	98	28	60	28	24	8	231	197	64
Dallas	37	15	15	7	115	116	37	36	11	17	8	102	136	30	73	26	32	15	217	252	67
Detroit	42	20	18	4	158	133	44	43	13	19	11	125	153	37	85	33	37	15	283	286	81
Edmonton	26	15	9	2	109	91	32	26	10	12	4	85	105	24	52	25	21	6	194	196	56
Florida	15	6	5	4	43	39	16	15	7	6	2	43	40	16	30	13	11	6	86	79	32
Los Angeles	42	18	18	6	179	159	42	43	12	25	6	132	170	30	85	30	43	12	311	329	72
Montreal	49	20	20	9	133	155	49	50	13	30	7	105	202	33	99	33	50	16	238	357	82
Nashville	1	0	1	0	2	3	0	1	0	1	0	1	3	0	2	0	2	0	3	6	0
New Jersey	69	43	21	5	273	197	91	69	30	32	7	207	214	67	138	73	53	12	480	411	158
NY Islanders	71	32	29	10	230	229	74	71	30	40	1	222	274	61	142	62	69	11	452	503	135
NY Rangers	74	36	29	9	274	245	81	72	30	34	8	253	277	68	146	66	63	17	527	522	149
Ottawa	14	8	5	1	54	33	17	13	6	6	1	45	48	13	27	14	11	2	99	81	30
Philadelphia	70	26	31	13	234	236	65	73	24	44	5	204	274	53	143	50	75	18	438	510	118
Phoenix	26	17	6	3	111	74	37	27	7	14	6	97	102	20	53	24	20	9	208	176	57
Pittsburgh	76	39	30	7	324	283	85	73	27	39	7	238	288	61	149	66	69	14	562	571	146
St. Louis	36	20	13	3	131	107	43	37	13	16	8	124	153	34	73	33	29	11	255	260	77
San Jose	7	5	2	0	23	17	10	7	3	3	1	21	20	7	14	8	5	1	44	37	17
Tampa Bay	16	7	5	4	57	40	18	16	11	4	1	52	32	23	32	18	9	5	109	72	41
Toronto	40	26	12	2	155	109	54	39	14	21	4	138	179	32	79	40	33	6	293	288	86
Vancouver	37	21	12	4	127	107	46	36	15	16	5	116	121	35	73	36	28	9	243	228	81
Defunct Clubs	10	2	8	0	28	42	4	10	4	5	1	30	39	9	20	6	13	1	58	81	13
Totals	**992**	**478**	**389**	**125**	**3537**	**3193**	**1081**	**992**	**350**	**515**	**127**	**3022**	**3700**	**827**	**1984**	**828**	**904**	**252**	**6559**	**6893**	**1908**

Playoffs

	Series	W	L	GP	W	L	T	GF	GA	Last Mtg.	Round	Result
Boston	2	1	1	10	4	6	0	15	13	1998	CQF	W 4-2
Buffalo	1	1	0	6	4	2	0	13	11	1998	CF	W 4-2
Detroit	1	0	1	4	0	4	0	7	13	1998	F	L 0-4
New Jersey	2	1	1	13	7	6	0	44	43	1990	DSF	W 4-2
NY Islanders	6	1	5	30	12	18	0	88	89	1993	DSF	L 2-4
NY Rangers	4	2	2	22	11	11	0	75	71	1994	CSF	L 1-4
Ottawa	1	1	0	5	4	1	0	18	7	1998	CSF	W 4-1
Philadelphia	3	2	1	16	9	7	0	65	55	1989	DSF	L 2-4
Pittsburgh	5	1	4	31	13	18	0	103	106	1996	CQF	L 2-4
Totals	**25**	**10**	**15**	**137**	**64**	**73**	**0**	**434**	**433**			

Playoff Results 1999-95

Year	Round	Opponent	Result	GF	GA
1998	F	Detroit	L 0-4	7	13
	CF	Buffalo	W 4-2	13	11
	CSF	Ottawa	W 4-1	18	7
	CQF	Boston	W 4-2	15	13
1996	CQF	Pittsburgh	L 2-4	17	21
1995	CQF	Pittsburgh	L 3-4	26	29

Abbreviations: Round: F – Final; **CF** – conference final; **CSF** – conference semi-final; **CQF** – conference quarter-final; **DSF** – division semi-final.

Calgary totals include Atlanta Flames, 1974-75 to 1979-80.
Colorado totals include Quebec, 1979-80 to 1994-95.
New Jersey totals include Kansas City, 1974-75 to 1975-76, and Colorado Rockies, 1976-77 to 1981-82.
Phoenix totals include Winnipeg, 1979-80, 1995-96.
Carolina totals include Hartford, 1979-80 to 1996-97.
Dallas totals include Minnesota, 1974-75 to 1992-93.

1998-99 Results

Oct.	10		Anaheim	1-0		18	at Montreal	4-4
	13		Detroit	2-3		21	at Philadelphia	1-4
	16		Montreal	2-2		26	NY Rangers	1-4
	18	at	Tampa Bay	4-1		29	Los Angeles	3-6
	21		Vancouver	1-2		30	at Toronto	3-5
	23	at	Buffalo	1-0	Feb.	1	at NY Rangers	3-1
	24		Florida	2-2		3	Tampa Bay	10-1
	28	at	Edmonton	2-8		5	Carolina	4-1
	30	at	Calgary	0-0		7	Buffalo	3-1
Nov.	1		Vancouver	1-4		9	at NY Islanders	2-1
	4		Tampa Bay	2-5		12	at New Jersey	3-2
	6		Carolina	2-3		13	at Ottawa	1-2
	7	at	Ottawa	8-5		15	at Pittsburgh	3-7
	12		Buffalo	3-2		18	at Carolina	2-2
	14	at	NY Islanders	5-3		20	San Jose	3-1
	18		Toronto	4-1		22	Toronto	4-3
	20		Ottawa	1-4		24	Phoenix	1-2
	21	at	Boston	4-5		27	at Boston	3-4
	25		Pittsburgh	5-4		28	Pittsburgh	4-3
	27	at	Dallas	0-4	Mar.	2	at Tampa Bay	8-2
	28	at	St. Louis	2-4		4	NY Rangers	2-4
Dec.	1		New Jersey	2-3		6	Edmonton	4-3
	4		NY Islanders	5-1		9	Colorado	2-3
	5	at	Philadelphia	1-2		11	Florida	1-2
	9	at	Los Angeles	1-2		13	Calgary	4-5
	11	at	Anaheim	0-1		15	at NY Rangers	1-1
	12	at	San Jose	1-2		17	Dallas	2-1
	17	at	Chicago	3-1		20	at Montreal	1-0
	19	at	Pittsburgh	0-3		21	Boston	1-4
	23	at	Florida	4-0		25	at Phoenix	1-4
	26	at	Nashville	1-3		26	at Colorado	1-3
	28		Boston	5-1		30	Nashville	2-3
	30		New Jersey	2-3	Apr.	1	Florida	5-3
Jan.	1		Ottawa	3-4		3	at Tampa Bay	3-4
	2	at	Toronto	5-2		5	at Florida	3-0
	7		NY Rangers	5-1		7	St. Louis	2-4
	9	at	New Jersey	3-1		8	at New Jersey	0-1
	11	at	NY Islanders	4-3		10	Philadelphia	1-2
	13		Philadelphia	0-3		12	Chicago	2-4
	15		Montreal	0-3		14	at Carolina	0-3
	16	at	Carolina	3-2		18	at Buffalo	0-3

Entry Draft
Selections 1999-85

1999
Pick
7	Kris Beech
29	Michal Sivek
31	Charlie Stephens
34	Ross Lupaschuk
37	Nolan Yonkman
132	Roman Tvrdon
175	Kyle Clark
192	David Johansson
219	Maxim Orlov
249	Igor Shadilov

1998
Pick
49	Jomar Cruz
59	Todd Hornung
106	Krys Barch
107	Chris Corrinet
118	Mike Siklenka
125	Erik Wendell
179	Nathan Forster
193	Ratislav Stana
220	Michael Farrell
251	Blake Evans

1997
Pick
9	Nicholas Boynton
35	J-F Fortin
89	Curtis Cruickshank
116	Kevin Caulfield
143	Henrik Petre
200	Pierre-Luc Therrien
226	Matt Oikawa

1996
Pick
4	Alexander Volchkov
17	Jaroslav Svejkovsky
43	Jan Bulis
58	Sergei Zimakov
74	Dave Weninger
78	Shawn McNeil
85	Justin Davis
126	Matthew Lahey
153	Andrew Van Bruggen
180	Michael Anderson
206	Oleg Orekhovsky
232	Chad Cavanagh

1995
Pick
17	Brad Church
23	Miikka Elomo
43	Dwayne Hay
93	Sebasti Charpentier
95	Joel Theriault
105	Benoit Gratton
124	Joel Cort
147	Frederick Jobin
199	Vasili Turkovsky
225	Scott Swanson

1994
Pick
10	Nolan Baumgartner
15	Alexander Kharlamov
41	Scott Cherrey
93	Matthew Herr
119	Yanick Jean
145	Dmitri Mekeshkin
171	Daniel Reja
197	Chris Patrick
223	John Tuohy
249	Richard Zednik
275	Sergei Tertyshny

1993
Pick
11	Brendan Witt
17	Jason Allison
69	Patrick Boileau
147	Frank Banham
173	Daniel Hendrickson
174	Andrew Brunette
199	Joel Poirier
225	Jason Gladney
251	Mark Seliger
277	Dany Bousquet

1992
Pick
14	Sergei Gonchar
32	Jim Carey
53	Stefan Ustorf
71	Martin Gendron
119	John Varga
167	Mark Matier
191	Mike Mathers
215	Brian Stagg
239	Gregory Callahan
263	Billy Jo MacPherson

1991
Pick
14	Pat Peake
21	Trevor Halverson
25	Eric Lavigne
36	Jeff Nelson
58	Steve Konowalchuk
80	Justin Morrison
146	Dave Morissette
168	Rick Corriveau
190	Trevor Duhaime
209	Rob Leask
212	Carl LeBlanc
234	Rob Puchniak
256	Bill Kovacs

1990
Pick
9	John Slaney
30	Rod Pasma
51	Chris Longo
72	Randy Pearce
93	Brian Sakic
94	Mark Ouimet
114	Andrei Kovalev
135	Roman Kontsek
156	Peter Bondra
159	Steve Martell
177	Ken Klee
198	Michael Boback
219	Alan Brown
240	Todd Hlushko

1989
Pick
19	Olaf Kolzig
35	Byron Dafoe
59	Jim Mathieson
61	Jason Woolley
82	Trent Klatt
145	Dave Lorentz
166	Dean Holoien
187	Victor Gervais
208	Jiri Vykoukal
229	Andrei Sidorov
250	Ken House

1988
Pick
15	Reginald Savage
36	Tim Taylor
41	Wade Bartley
57	Duane Derksen
78	Rob Krauss
120	Dmitri Khristich
141	Keith Jones
144	Brad Schlegel
162	Todd Hilditch
183	Petr Pavlas
192	Mark Sorensen
204	Claudio Scremin
225	Chris Venkus
246	Ron Pascucci

1987
Pick
36	Jeff Ballantyne
57	Steve Maltais
78	Tyler Larter
99	Pat Beauchesne
120	Rich Defreitas
141	Devon Oleniuk
162	Thomas Sjogren
204	Chris Clarke
225	Milos Vanik
240	Dan Brettschneider
246	Ryan Kummu

1986
Pick
19	Jeff Greenlaw
40	Steve Seftel
60	Shawn Simpson
61	Jimmy Hrivnak
82	Erin Ginnell
103	John Purves
124	Stefan Nilsson
145	Peter Choma
166	Lee Davidson
187	Tero Toivola
208	Bobby Bobcock
229	John Schratz
250	Scott McCrory

1985
Pick
19	Yvon Corriveau
40	John Druce
61	Rob Murray
82	Bill Houlder
83	Larry Shaw
103	Claude Dumas
124	Doug Stromback
145	Jamie Nadjiwan
166	Mark Haarmann
187	Steve Hollett
208	Dallas Eakins
229	Steve Hrynewich
250	Frank DiMuzio

Club Directory

MCI Center

MCI Center
601 F Street, NW
Washington, DC 20004
Phone **202/661-5000**
PR FAX 202/661-5113
www.washingtoncaps.com
Capacity: 19,740

Capitals Team Management

Owner	Ted Leonsis
Owner	Jonathan Ledecky
President and Governor	Dick Patrick
Sr. VP of Business Operations	Declan J. Bolger
Vice President/General Manager	George McPhee
Director of Hockey Operations	Shawn Simpson
Assistant to the GM	Frank Provenzano
Dir. Of Amateur Scouting	Ross Mahoney
Head Coach	Ron Wilson
Assistant Coaches	Tim Army, Tim Hunter
Goaltender Consultant	Dave Prior
Strength & Conditioning Coach	Frank Costello
Player Development Instructor	Dale Hunter
Team Physician	Dr. Ben Shaffer
Trainer	Greg Smith
Equipment Manager	Doug Shearer
Asst. Equipment Manager	Craig Leydig
Equipment Assistant	Brian Metzger
Massage Therapist	Curt Millar

Communications Staff

Director, PR	Doug Hicks
Asst. Director, PR	Jesse Price
Press Room Phone	202-628-3200 x7500
Press Room Fax	202-661-5011
Press Box Phone	202-628-3200 x7639, 7641
Press Entrance	202-628-3200 x7599

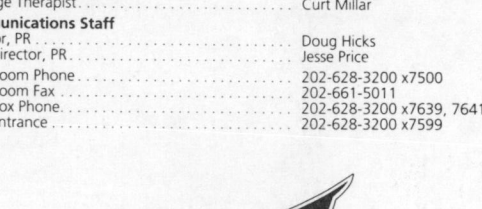

General Managers' History

Milt Schmidt, 1974-75; Milt Schmidt and Max McNab, 1975-76; Max McNab, 1976-77 to 1980-81; Max McNab and Roger Crozier, 1981-82; David Poile, 1982-83 to 1996-97; George McPhee, 1997-98 to date.

General Manager

McPHEE, GEORGE
General Manager, Washington Capitals. Born in Guelph, Ont., July 2, 1958.
On June 9, 1997, George McPhee became the fifth General Manager of the Washington Capitals. In his first year on the job, McPhee led the Caps to the Stanley Cup Finals for the first time in franchise history. His astute late-season deals in 1997-98 added key contributors like Esa Tikkanen and Brian Bellows to Washington's Stanley Cup run. McPhee provides the Capitals with the leadership and knowledge to bring the Stanley Cup Finals back to Washington in the years to come.

A back injury forced McPhee to retire as an active player at the conclusion of the 1988-89 season, after a seven year playing career with the New York Rangers and New Jersey Devils. McPhee originally signed as a free agent with the Rangers in July, 1982, after graduating from Bowling Green State University with a business degree. McPhee did not waste any time in college, tallying 40 goals and 48 assists in his freshman season and easily winning CCHA rookie of the year honors. His outstanding collegiate hockey career was capped off when he was named the recipient of the Hobey Baker Award as the top U.S. collegiate player in his senior season. McPhee also earned All-America honors as a senior and finished his career at Bowling Green as the CCHA's all-time leading scorer with 114-153-267. He was the first player in CCHA history to make the Conference's all-academic team three straight seasons.

Despite playing only 66 games last season, Peter Bondra was the Capitals' leading goal scorer for the fourth year in a row. With 31 goals and 24 assists, Bondra was the team's top point-getter for the second straight season.

NHL Expansion Franchises

Two ADDITIONAL FRANCHISES will join the National Hockey League in 2000-2001. The addition of the Columbus Blue Jackets and Minnesota Wild will result in a 30-team NHL made up of two 15-team conferences, each of which is comprised of three five-team divisions. Divisional alignment and scheduling are described on the inside front cover of this book.

Columbus Blue Jackets

First NHL season 2000-2001

Central Division, Western Conference

150 East Wilson Bridge Road
Suite 235
Worthington, OH 43085
Tel: 614/540 GOAL (4625)
Fax: 614/540-1189

www.columbusbluejackets.com

CLUB OFFICERS AND EXECUTIVES

Chairman of the Board and Owner	John H. McConnell
President and General Manager	Doug MacLean
Assistant General Manager	Jim Clark
Vice President of Business Development and Broadcasting	Michael Humes
General Counsel	Greg Kirstein

MEDIA INFORMATION

Vice President of Marketing	David Paitson
Manager of Multimedia and Publications	Gary Kohn

Minnesota Wild

First NHL season 2000-2001

Northwest Division, Western Conference

Piper Jaffrey Plaza
444 Cedar Street, Suite 900
St. Paul, MN 55101
Tel: 651/222-WILD (9453)
Fax: 651/222-1065

www.wild.com

CLUB OFFICERS AND EXECUTIVES

Chairman	Bob Neagele, Jr.
Chief Executive Officer	Jac K. Sperling
Chief Financial Officer	Martha Larson
New Saint Paul Arena Project Director	Ray Chandler
General Manager of New Saint Paul Arena	Chris Hanson
Vice President of Coporate Marketing	Carin Anderson
Director of Retail Operations and Fan Developement	Matt Majka
Director of Suite Sales	Tim Wegscheid

COMMUNICATIONS AND INFORMATION

Vice President of Comminucations	Bill Robertson
Communications Assistant	Brian Hutchinson
Communications Staff	Aaron Sickman

NHL League and Team Websites

National Hockey League   **www.nhl.com**

Anaheim . . . . .www.mightyducks.com
Atlanta . . . . .www.atlantathrashers.com
Boston . . . . .www.bostonbruins.com
Buffalo . . . . .www.sabres.com
Calgary . . . . .www.calgaryflames.com
Carolina . . . . .www.caneshockey.com
Chicago . . . . .www.chicagoblackhawks.com
Colorado . . . . .www.coloradoavalanche.com
Columbus . . . . .www.columbusbluejackets.com
Dallas . . . . .www.dallasstars.com
Detroit . . . . .www.detroitredwings.com
Edmonton . . . . .www.edmontonoilers.com
Florida . . . . .www.flpanthers.com
Los Angeles . . . . .www.lakings.com
Minnesota . . . . .www.wild.com
Montreal . . . . .www.canadiens.com
Nashville . . . . .www.nashvillepredators.com
New Jersey . . . . .www.newjerseydevils.com
NY Islanders . . . . .www.newyorkislanders.com
NY Rangers . . . . .www.newyorkrangers.com
Ottawa . . . . .www.ottawasenators.com
Philadelphia . . . . .www.philadelphiaflyers.com
Phoenix . . . . .www.phoenixcoyotes.com
Pittsburgh . . . . .www.nhlpenguins.com
St. Louis . . . . .www.stlouisblues.com
San Jose . . . . .www.sj-sharks.com
Tampa Bay . . . . .www.tampabaylightning.com
Toronto . . . . .www.torontomapleleafs.com
Vancouver . . . . .www.vancouvercanucks.com
Washington . . . . .www.washingtoncaps.com

1998-99 Final Statistics

Standings

Abbreviations: GA–goals against; **GF**–goals for; **GP**–games played; **L**–losses; **PTS**–points; **T** – ties; **W**–wins; **%**–percentage of games won.

EASTERN CONFERENCE

Northeast Division

	GP	W	L	T	GF	GA	PTS	%
Ottawa	82	44	23	15	239	179	103	.628
Toronto	82	45	30	7	268	231	97	.591
Boston	82	39	30	13	214	181	91	.555
Buffalo	82	37	28	17	207	175	91	.555
Montreal	82	32	39	11	184	209	75	.457

Atlantic Division

	GP	W	L	T	GF	GA	PTS	%
New Jersey	82	47	24	11	248	196	105	.640
Philadelphia	82	37	26	19	231	196	93	.567
Pittsburgh	82	38	30	14	242	225	90	.549
NY Rangers	82	33	38	11	217	227	77	.470
NY Islanders	82	24	48	10	194	244	58	.354

Southeast Division

	GP	W	L	T	GF	GA	PTS	%
Carolina	82	34	30	18	210	202	86	.524
Florida	82	30	34	18	210	228	78	.476
Washington	82	31	45	6	200	218	68	.415
Tampa Bay	82	19	54	9	179	292	47	.287

WESTERN CONFERENCE

Central Division

	GP	W	L	T	GF	GA	PTS	%
Detroit	82	43	32	7	245	202	93	.567
St. Louis	82	37	32	13	237	209	87	.530
Chicago	82	29	41	12	202	248	70	.427
Nashville	82	28	47	7	190	261	63	.384

Pacific Division

	GP	W	L	T	GF	GA	PTS	%
Dallas	82	51	19	12	236	168	114	.695
Phoenix	82	39	31	12	205	197	90	.549
Anaheim	82	35	34	13	215	206	83	.506
San Jose	82	31	33	18	196	191	80	.488
Los Angeles	82	32	45	5	189	222	69	.421

Northwest Division

	GP	W	L	T	GF	GA	PTS	%
Colorado	82	44	28	10	239	205	98	.598
Edmonton	82	33	37	12	230	226	78	.476
Calgary	82	30	40	12	211	234	72	.439
Vancouver	82	23	47	12	192	258	58	.354

Brett Hull led the NHL with 11 game-winning goals during the 1998-99 regular season, one more than former Blues teammate Pavol Demitra. Hull added two more game-winners in the playoffs, including the Stanley Cup winner in triple overtime.

INDIVIDUAL LEADERS

Goal Scoring

Player	Team	GP	G
Teemu Selanne	Anaheim	75	47
Jaromir Jagr	Pittsburgh	81	44
Tony Amonte	Chicago	82	44
Alexei Yashin	Ottawa	82	44
John LeClair	Philadelphia	76	43
Joe Sakic	Colorado	73	41
Eric Lindros	Philadelphia	71	40
Theoren Fleury	Cgy., Col.	75	40
Miroslav Satan	Buffalo	81	40
Luc Robitaille	Los Angeles	82	39
Paul Kariya	Anaheim	82	39

Assists

Player	Team	GP	A
Jaromir Jagr	Pittsburgh	81	83
Peter Forsberg	Colorado	78	67
Paul Kariya	Anaheim	82	62
Teemu Selanne	Anaheim	75	60
Joe Sakic	Colorado	73	55
Wayne Gretzky	NY Rangers	70	53
Eric Lindros	Philadelphia	71	53
Theoren Fleury	Cgy., Col.	75	53
Jason Allison	Boston	82	53
Mats Sundin	Toronto	82	52
Pavol Demitra	St. Louis	82	52

Power-play Goals

Player	Team	GP	PP
Teemu Selanne	Anaheim	75	25
Alexei Yashin	Ottawa	82	19
Adrian Aucoin	Vancouver	82	18
John LeClair	Philadelphia	76	16

Short-handed Goals

Player	Team	GP	SH
Joe Sakic	Colorado	73	5
Scott Pellerin	St. Louis	80	5
Brian Rolston	New Jersey	82	5

Game-winning Goals

Player	Team	GP	GW
Brett Hull	Dallas	60	11
Pavol Demitra	St. Louis	82	10
Joe Nieuwendyk	Dallas	67	8
Bobby Holik	New Jersey	78	8
Sergei Samsonov	Boston	79	8
Claude Lemieux	Colorado	82	8
Tony Amonte	Chicago	82	8
Michael Peca	Buffalo	82	8

Game-tying Goals

Player	Team	GP	GT
Scott Mellanby	Florida	67	3
Eric Lindros	Philadelphia	71	3
Robert Lang	Pittsburgh	72	3
Eric Daze	Chicago	72	3
John LeClair	Philadelphia	76	3
Curtis Brown	Buffalo	78	3

Shots

Player	Team	GP	S
Paul Kariya	Anaheim	82	429
Jaromir Jagr	Pittsburgh	81	343
Alexei Yashin	Ottawa	82	337
Al MacInnis	St. Louis	82	314
Theoren Fleury	Cgy., Col.	75	301

Shooting Percentage
(minimum 82 shots)

Player	Team	GP	G	S	%
Dmitri Khristich	Boston	79	29	144	20.1
Martin Straka	Pittsburgh	80	35	177	19.8
Dixon Ward	Buffalo	78	20	101	19.8
Anson Carter	Boston	55	24	123	19.5
Miroslav Satan	Buffalo	81	40	208	19.2

Penalty Minutes

Player	Team	GP	PIM
Rob Ray	Buffalo	76	261
Jeff Odgers	Colorado	75	259
Peter Worrell	Florida	62	258
Patrick Cote	Nashville	70	242
Krzysztof Oliwa	New Jersey	64	240

Plus/Minus

Player	Team	GP	+/–
Alexander Karpovtsev	NYR., Tor	58	39
John LeClair	Philadelphia	76	36
Eric Lindros	Philadelphia	71	35
Magnus Arvedson	Ottawa	80	33
Al MacInnis	St. Louis	82	33

Individual Leaders

Abbreviations: * – rookie eligible for Calder Trophy; **A** – assists; **G** – goals; **GP** – games played; **GT** – game-tying goals; **GW** – game-winning goals; **PIM** – penalties in minutes; **PP** – power play goals; **Pts** – points; **S** – shots on goal; **SH** – short-handed goals; **%** – percentage of shots on goal resulting in goals; **+/–** – difference between Goals For (**GF**) scored when a player is on the ice with his team at even strength or short-handed and Goals Against (**GA**) scored when the same player is on the ice with his team at even strength or on a power play.

Individual Scoring Leaders for Art Ross Trophy

Player	Team	GP	G	A	Pts	+/–	PIM	PP	SH	GW	GT	S	%
Jaromir Jagr	Pittsburgh	81	44	83	127	17	66	10	1	7	2	343	12.8
Teemu Selanne	Anaheim	75	47	60	107	18	30	25	0	7	1	281	16.7
Paul Kariya	Anaheim	82	39	62	101	17	40	11	2	4	0	429	9.1
Peter Forsberg	Colorado	78	30	67	97	27	108	9	2	7	0	217	13.8
Joe Sakic	Colorado	73	41	55	96	23	29	12	5	6	1	255	16.1
Alexei Yashin	Ottawa	82	44	50	94	16	54	19	0	5	1	337	13.1
Eric Lindros	Philadelphia	71	40	53	93	35	120	10	1	2	3	242	16.5
Theoren Fleury	Cgy., Col.	75	40	53	93	26	86	8	3	5	2	301	13.3
John LeClair	Philadelphia	76	43	47	90	36	30	16	0	7	3	246	17.5
Pavol Demitra	St. Louis	82	37	52	89	13	16	14	0	10	1	259	14.3
Martin Straka	Pittsburgh	80	35	48	83	12	26	5	4	4	1	177	19.8
Mats Sundin	Toronto	82	31	52	83	22	58	4	0	6	0	209	14.8
Mike Modano	Dallas	77	34	47	81	29	44	6	4	7	1	224	15.2
Jason Allison	Boston	82	23	53	76	5	68	5	1	3	0	158	14.6
Tony Amonte	Chicago	82	44	31	75	0	60	14	3	8	0	256	17.2
Luc Robitaille	Los Angeles	82	39	35	74	–1	54	11	0	7	0	292	13.4
Steve Yzerman	Detroit	80	29	45	74	8	42	13	2	4	0	231	12.6
Rod Brind'amour	Philadelphia	82	24	50	74	3	47	10	0	3	2	191	12.6
Steve Thomas	Toronto	78	28	45	73	26	33	11	0	7	0	209	13.4
Petr Sykora	New Jersey	80	29	43	72	16	22	15	0	7	0	222	13.1
Jeremy Roenick	Phoenix	78	24	48	72	7	130	4	0	3	0	203	11.8
Dmitri Khristich	Boston	79	29	42	71	11	48	13	1	6	1	144	20.1
Robert Reichel	NYI, Phx.	83	26	43	69	–13	54	8	1	4	1	236	11.0
Keith Tkachuk	Phoenix	68	36	32	68	22	151	11	2	7	1	258	14.0
Miroslav Satan	Buffalo	81	40	26	66	24	44	13	3	6	1	208	19.2
Markus Naslund	Vancouver	80	36	30	66	–13	74	15	2	3	1	205	17.6

Defensemen Scoring Leaders

Player	Team	GP	G	A	Pts	+/–	PIM	PP	SH	GW	GT	S	%
Al MacInnis	St. Louis	82	20	42	62	33	70	11	1	2	2	314	6.4
Nicklas Lidstrom	Detroit	81	14	43	57	14	14	6	1	3	0	205	6.8
Ray Bourque	Boston	81	10	47	57	–7	34	8	0	3	0	262	3.8
Fredrik Olausson	Anaheim	74	16	40	56	17	30	10	0	2	0	121	13.2
Brian Leetch	NY Rangers	82	13	42	55	–7	42	4	0	1	0	184	7.1
Phil Housley	Calgary	79	11	43	54	14	52	4	0	1	0	193	5.7
Larry Murphy	Detroit	80	10	42	52	21	42	5	1	2	0	168	6.0
Eric Desjardins	Philadelphia	68	15	36	51	18	38	6	0	2	0	190	7.9
Sergei Zubov	Dallas	81	10	41	51	9	20	5	0	3	0	155	6.5
Boris Mironov	Edm., Chi.	75	11	38	49	13	131	4	0	4	1	173	6.4

18-year veteran Al MacInnis won the Norris Trophy for the first time in his career in 1998-99. He led all defensemen with 62 points and 314 shots on goal. Equally effective in his own end, MacInnis ranked among the NHL leaders with a +33 rating.

CONSECUTIVE SCORING STREAKS

Goals

Games	Player	Team	G
8	Miroslav Satan	Buffalo	11
8	Teemu Selanne	Anaheim	10
7	Eric Lindros	Philadelphia	7
6	Bobby Holik	New Jersey	7
6	Ray Sheppard	Carolina	7
6	Tony Amonte	Chicago	7
6	Rob Brown	Pittsburgh	6
6	Kip Miller	Pittsburgh	6
6	Miroslav Satan	Buffalo	6
5	Alexei Yashin	Ottawa	9
5	Brendan Shanahan	Detroit	7
5	Bill Guerin	Edmonton	7
5	Pavol Demitra	St. Louis	7
5	Robert Lang	Pittsburgh	6
5	Eric Lindros	Philadelphia	6
5	Eric Lindros	Philadelphia	6
5	Sergei Krivokrasov	Nashville	6
5	Brett Hull	Dallas	5
5	Fredrik Olausson	Anaheim	5
5	Greg Johnson	Nashville	5
5	Alexei Yashin	Ottawa	5
5	Adam Deadmarsh	Colorado	5

Assists

Games	Player	Team	A
9	John LeClair	Philadelphia	11
8	Jaromir Jagr	Pittsburgh	11
7	Eric Lindros	Philadelphia	15
7	Peter Forsberg	Colorado	11
7	Paul Kariya	Anaheim	11
7	Teemu Selanne	Anaheim	9
7	Alexei Yashin	Ottawa	9
7	Peter Forsberg	Colorado	8
7	Rod Brind'Amour	Philadelphia	7
7	Andrei Kovalenko	Edmonton	7
6	Jaromir Jagr	Pittsburgh	9
6	Petr Sykora	New Jersey	9
6	Kyle Mclaren	Boston	9
6	Wayne Gretzky	NY Rangers	8
6	Jaromir Jagr	Pittsburgh	8
6	Mats Sundin	Toronto	8
6	Steve Thomas	Toronto	8
6	Michal Grosek	Buffalo	8
6	Petr Sykora	New Jersey	8
6	Theoren Fleury	Cgy., Col.	7
6	Jiri Slegr	Pittsburgh	7
6	Steve Rucchin	Anaheim	7
6	Chris Chelios	Chicago	6
6	Bobby Holik	New Jersey	6

Points

Games	Player	Team	G	A	PTS
18	Eric Lindros	Philadelphia	14	21	35
17	Teemu Selanne	Anaheim	15	14	29
13	Jaromir Jagr	Pittsburgh	8	17	25
11	Sergei Fedorov	Detroit	7	10	17
11	Alexei Yashin	Ottawa	7	9	16
11	Paul Kariya	Anaheim	7	9	16
10	Kip Miller	Pittsburgh	9	8	17
10	Keith Tkachuk	Phoenix	9	6	15
10	Peter Forsberg	Colorado	3	11	14
10	Steve Thomas	Toronto	3	10	13
10	Alexei Kovalev	NYR., Pit.	6	6	12
9	Teemu Selanne	Anaheim	8	10	18
9	Jaromir Jagr	Pittsburgh	5	11	16
9	John LeClair	Philadelphia	5	11	16
9	Peter Forsberg	Colorado	8	7	15
9	Miroslav Satan	Buffalo	11	4	15
9	Theoren Fleury	Cgy., Col.	7	7	14
9	John MacLean	NY Rangers	3	11	14
9	Darren McCarty	Detroit	4	10	14
9	Mike Modano	Dallas	4	8	12
9	Brian Rolston	New Jersey	5	6	11

Chris Drury of the Colorado Avalanche won the Calder Trophy as rookie of the year in 1998-99. He and Florida's Mark Parrish were the only rookies to reach the 20-goal plateau last season. Drury added six playoff goals, including four game-winners. He and teammate Milan Hejduk were the only rookies to score post-season overtime goals.

Individual Rookie Scoring Leaders

Rookie	Team	GP	G	A	Pts	+/-	PIM	PP	SH	GW	GT	S	%
Milan Hejduk	Colorado	82	14	34	48	8	26	4	0	5	0	178	7.9
Brendan Morrison	New Jersey	76	13	33	46	−4	18	5	0	2	0	111	11.7
Chris Drury	Colorado	79	20	24	44	9	62	6	0	3	1	138	14.5
Jan Hrdina	Pittsburgh	82	13	29	42	−2	40	3	0	2	0	94	13.8
Mark Parrish	Florida	73	24	13	37	−6	25	5	0	5	1	129	18.6
Bill Muckalt	Vancouver	73	16	20	36	−9	98	4	2	1	0	119	13.4
Marian Hossa	Ottawa	60	15	15	30	18	37	1	0	2	2	124	12.1
Alexander Korolyuk	San Jose	55	12	18	30	3	26	2	0	0	1	96	12.5
Vincent Lecavalier	Tampa Bay	82	13	15	28	−19	23	2	0	2	1	125	10.4
Vadim Sharifijanov	New Jersey	53	11	16	27	11	28	1	0	2	0	71	15.5

Goal Scoring

Name	Team	GP	G
Mark Parrish	Florida	73	24
Chris Drury	Colorado	79	20
Bill Muckalt	Vancouver	73	16
Marian Hossa	Ottawa	60	15
Milan Hejduk	Colorado	82	14
Brendan Morrison	New Jersey	76	13
Jan Hrdina	Pittsburgh	82	13
Vincent Lecavalier	Tampa Bay	82	13
Alexander Korolyuk	San Jose	55	12
Oleg Kvasha	Florida	68	12
Vadim Sharifijanov	New Jersey	53	11
Clarke Wilm	Calgary	78	10
Jean-Pierre Dumont	Chicago	25	9
Olli Jokinen	Los Angeles	66	9
Pavel Kubina	Tampa Bay	68	9

Assists

Name	Team	GP	A
Milan Hejduk	Colorado	82	34
Brendan Morrison	New Jersey	76	33
Jan Hrdina	Pittsburgh	82	29
Chris Drury	Colorado	79	24
Bill Muckalt	Vancouver	73	20
Alexander Korolyuk	San Jose	55	18
Tomas Kaberle	Toronto	57	18
Mike Watt	NY Islanders	75	17
Vadim Sharifijanov	New Jersey	53	16
Tom Poti	Edmonton	73	16
Marian Hossa	Ottawa	60	15
Vincent Lecavalier	Tampa Bay	82	15
Daniel Briere	Phoenix	64	14
Oleg Kvasha	Florida	68	13
Mark Parrish	Florida	73	13

Power-play Goals

Name	Team	GP	PP
Chris Drury	Colorado	79	6
Mark Parrish	Florida	73	5
Brendan Morrison	New Jersey	76	5
Oleg Kvasha	Florida	68	4
Bill Muckalt	Vancouver	73	4
Milan Hejduk	Colorado	82	4
Pavel Kubina	Tampa Bay	68	1

Short-handed Goals

Name	Team	GP	SH
Bill Muckalt	Vancouver	73	2
Clarke Wilm	Calgary	78	2
Sami Helenius	Cgy., T.B.	8	1
Zdeno Chara	NY Islanders	59	1
Jaroslav Spacek	Florida	63	1
Olli Jokinen	Los Angeles	66	1
Pavel Kubina	Tampa Bay	68	1

Game-winning Goals

Name	Team	GP	GW
Mark Parrish	Florida	73	5
Milan Hejduk	Colorado	82	5
Mike Watt	NY Islanders	75	4
Tom Poti	Edmonton	73	3
Chris Drury	Colorado	79	3

Game-tying Goals

Name	Team	GP	GT
Marian Hossa	Ottawa	60	2
Cameron Mann	Boston	33	1
Maxim Galanov	Pittsburgh	51	1
Alexander Korolyuk	San Jose	55	1
Daniil Markov	Toronto	57	1
Brad Brown	Mtl., Chi.	66	1
Oleg Kvasha	Florida	68	1
Pavel Kubina	Tampa Bay	68	1
Mark Parrish	Florida	73	1
Chris Drury	Colorado	79	1
Vincent Lecavalier	Tampa Bay	82	1

Shots

Name	Team	GP	S
Milan Hejduk	Colorado	82	178
Oleg Kvasha	Florida	68	138
Chris Drury	Colorado	79	138
Mark Parrish	Florida	73	129
Vincent Lecavalier	Tampa Bay	82	125

Shooting Percentage
(minimum 82 shots)

Name	Team	GP	G	S	%
Mark Parrish	Florida	73	24	129	18.6
Chris Drury	Colorado	79	20	138	14.5
Jan Hrdina	Pittsburgh	82	13	94	13.8
Bill Muckalt	Vancouver	73	16	119	13.4
Alexander Korolyuk	San Jose	55	12	96	12.5

Penalty Minutes

Name	Team	GP	PIM
Peter Worrell	Florida	62	258
Patrick Cote	Nashville	70	242
Brad Brown	Mtl., Chi.	66	205
Sean Brown	Edmonton	51	188
Mark Visheau	Los Angeles	28	107

Plus/Minus

Name	Team	GP	+/-
Sami Salo	Ottawa	61	20
Marian Hossa	Ottawa	60	18
Jaroslav Spacek	Florida	63	15
Patrick Traverse	Ottawa	46	12
Vadim Sharifijanov	New Jersey	53	11
Clarke Wilm	Calgary	78	11

Three-or-More-Goal Games

Player	Team	Date	Final Score				G
Jason Allison	Boston	Feb. 04	NYI	5	Bos.	4	3
Tony Amonte	Chicago	Nov. 28	Chi.	4	Cgy.	5	3
Tony Amonte	Chicago	Mar. 28	St.L.	1	Chi.	3	3
Magnus Arvedson	Ottawa	Mar. 08	T.B.	3	Ott.	9	3
Stu Barnes	Pittsburgh	Nov. 25	Pit.	4	Wsh.	5	3
Sergei Berezin	Toronto	Feb. 10	Car.	6	Tor.	5	3
Sergei Berezin	Toronto	Apr. 01	Tor.	5	Edm.	1	3
Peter Bondra	Washington	Nov. 07	Wsh.	8	Ott.	5	3
Peter Bondra	Washington	Feb. 03	T.B.	1	Wsh.	10	4
Peter Bondra	Washington	Feb. 05	Car.	1	Wsh.	4	3
Pavel Bure	Florida	Jan. 26	Fla.	3	Phi.	3	3
Pavel Bure	Florida	Mar. 03	Col.	7	Fla.	5	3
Anson Carter	Boston	Apr. 07	Bos.	5	Fla.	2	3
Wendel Clark	Tampa Bay	Dec. 30	T.B.	3	Car.	4	3
Wendel Clark	Tampa Bay	Mar. 06	T.B.	6	Mtl.	1	3
Wendel Clark	Tampa Bay	Mar. 19	Det.	5	T.B.	3	3
Craig Conroy	St. Louis	Feb. 26	St.L.	4	Cgy.	2	3
Vincent Damphousse	San Jose	Apr. 03	Van.	2	S.J.	5	3
*Jean-Pierre Dumont	Chicago	Apr. 08	NYR	2	Chi.	6	3
Theoren Fleury	Calgary	Oct. 10	Cgy.	5	S.J.	3	3
Theoren Fleury	Calgary	Nov. 01	Cgy.	4	Chi.	1	3
Theoren Fleury	Colorado	Mar. 28	L.A.	2	Col.	7	3
Peter Forsberg	Colorado	Mar. 03	Col.	7	Fla.	5	3
Mike Grier	Edmonton	Mar. 20	Van.	3	Edm.	4	3
Bobby Holik	New Jersey	Dec. 23	St.L.	2	N.J.	3	3
Valeri Kamensky	Colorado	Nov. 06	Col.	5	Edm.	2	3
Dmitri Khristich	Boston	Feb. 21	Bos.	6	Chi.	3	3
Vyacheslav Kozlov	Detroit	Feb. 21	Det.	4	Buf.	4	3
John LeClair	Philadelphia	Oct. 16	Phi.	5	T.B.	2	3
John LeClair	Philadelphia	Nov. 29	Van.	2	Phi.	6	4

Player	Team	Date	Final Score				G
Al MacInnis	St. Louis	Oct. 12	St.L.	4	NYR	2	3
Mike Modano	Dallas	Dec. 23	Dal.	5	Tor.	1	3
Mike Modano	Dallas	Feb. 19	Chi.	1	Dal.	5	3
Mike Modano	Dallas	Feb. 23	Dal.	4	Nsh.	3	3
Markus Naslund	Vancouver	Dec. 04	Dal.	1	Van.	4	3
Petr Nedved	NY Rangers	Feb. 28	Phi.	5	NYR	6	3
Zigmund Palffy	NY Islanders	Apr. 17	NYI	7	Pit.	2	3
*Mark Parrish	Florida	Oct. 30	Fla.	7	Chi.	3	4
Yanic Perreault	Toronto	Apr. 07	Ott.	2	Tor.	4	3
Luc Robitaille	Los Angeles	Apr. 12	L.A.	4	Nsh.	3	3
Joe Sakic	Colorado	Feb. 19	Col.	4	Nsh.	4	3
*Sami Salo	Ottawa	Mar. 30	Ott.	6	Pit.	4	3
Geoff Sanderson	Buffalo	Oct. 31	Buf.	6	Tor.	3	3
Teemu Selanne	Anaheim	Jan. 01	Ana.	7	Buf.	2	3
Alexander Selivano	Edmonton	Feb. 17	Edm.	6	Ana.	2	3
Brendan Shanahan	Detroit	Oct. 16	St.L.	1	Det.	4	3
Brendan Shanahan	Detroit	Mar. 05	Det.	7	Phx.	2	3
Kevin Stevens	NY Rangers	Nov. 10	NYR	10	T.B.	2	3
Martin Straka	Pittsburgh	Nov. 28	Pit.	4	Mtl.	3	3
Marco Sturm	San Jose	Dec. 23	S.J.	5	Edm.	3	3
Steve Sullivan	Toronto	Apr. 10	Fla.	1	Tor.	9	4
Mats Sundin	Toronto	Nov. 12	Tor.	10	Chi.	3	3
Keith Tkachuk	Phoenix	Mar. 07	Nsh.	3	Phx.	4	3
Pierre Turgeon	St. Louis	Nov. 10	Chi.	2	St.L.	5	3
Dixon Ward	Buffalo	Nov. 25	NYR	2	Buf.	4	3
Alexei Yashin	Ottawa	Mar. 04	Ott.	5	Phi.	0	3

NOTE: 56 Three-or-more-goal games
recorded in 1998-99.

John LeClair (above) enjoyed two hat tricks during a 43-goal campaign that saw him finish fifth in the NHL. Curtis Joseph (right) set a Maple Leafs record with 35 wins in 1998-99. "Cujo" finished as the runner-up to Dominik Hasek in Vezina Trophy voting.

Goaltending Leaders

Minimum 26 games

Goals Against Average

Goaltender	Team	GPI	Mins	GA	Avg
Ron Tugnutt	Ottawa	43	2508	75	1.79
Dominik Hasek	Buffalo	64	3817	119	1.87
Byron Dafoe	Boston	68	4001	133	1.99
Ed Belfour	Dallas	61	3536	117	1.99
Roman Turek	Dallas	26	1382	48	2.08

Save Percentage

Goaltender	Team	GPI	MINS	GA	SA	S%	W	L	T
Dominik Hasek	Buffalo	64	3817	119	1877	.937	30	18	14
Byron Dafoe	Boston	68	4001	133	1800	.926	32	23	11
Ron Tugnutt	Ottawa	43	2508	75	1005	.925	22	10	8
Nikolai Khabibulin	Phoenix	63	3657	130	1681	.923	32	23	7
Arturs Irbe	Carolina	62	3643	135	1753	.923	27	20	12

Wins

Goaltender	Team	GPI	MINS	W	L	T
Martin Brodeur	New Jersey	70	4239	39	21	10
Ed Belfour	Dallas	61	3536	35	15	9
Curtis Joseph	Toronto	67	4001	35	24	7
Chris Osgood	Detroit	63	3691	34	25	4
Patrick Roy	Colorado	61	3648	32	19	8
Nikolai Khabibulin	Phoenix	63	3657	32	23	7
Byron Dafoe	Boston	68	4001	32	23	11

Shutouts

Goaltender	Team	GPI	MINS	SO	W	L	T
Byron Dafoe	Boston	68	4001	10	32	23	11
Dominik Hasek	Buffalo	64	3817	9	30	18	14
Nikolai Khabibulin	Phoenix	63	3657	8	32	23	7
Garth Snow	Vancouver	65	3501	6	20	31	8
Arturs Irbe	Carolina	62	3643	6	27	20	12
John Vanbiesbrouck	Philadelphia	62	3712	6	27	18	15
Guy Hebert	Anaheim	69	4083	6	31	29	9

Team-by-Team Point Totals

1994-95 to 1998-99

(Ranked by five-year winning %)

	98-99	97-98	96-97	95-96	94-95	W%
Detroit	93	103	94	131	70	.653
Col./Que.	98	95	107	104	65	.623
New Jersey	105	107	104	86	52	.604
Philadelphia	93	95	103	103	60	.604
Dallas	114	109	104	66	42	.578
Pittsburgh	90	98	84	102	61	.578
St. Louis	87	98	83	80	61	.544
Buffalo	91	89	92	73	51	.525
Boston	91	91	61	91	57	.520
Washington	68	92	75	89	52	.500
NY Rangers	77	68	86	96	47	.497
Phx./Wpg.	90	82	83	78	39	.495
Montreal	75	87	77	90	43	.495
Chicago	70	73	81	94	53	.493
Florida	78	63	89	92	46	.489
Toronto	97	69	68	80	50	.484
Car./Hfd.	86	74	75	77	43	.472
Anaheim	83	65	85	78	37	.463
Calgary	72	67	73	79	55	.460
Edmonton	78	80	81	68	38	.459
Los Angeles	69	87	67	66	41	.439
Ottawa	103	83	77	41	23	.435
Vancouver	58	64	77	79	48	.433
San Jose	80	78	62	47	42	.411
Tampa Bay	47	44	74	88	37	.387
Nashville	63	---	---	---	---	.384
NY Islanders	58	71	70	54	35	.383

Team Record When Scoring First Goal of a Game

Team	GP	FG	W	L	T
Dallas	82	54	40	7	7
New Jersey	82	49	36	7	6
Ottawa	82	48	33	6	9
Detroit	82	49	34	10	5
Philadelphia	82	47	27	7	13
Buffalo	82	39	31	4	4
Toronto	82	47	31	12	4
San Jose	82	47	28	9	10
St. Louis	82	44	29	9	6
Carolina	82	46	29	11	6
Anaheim	82	42	27	6	9
Boston	82	39	28	5	6
Colorado	82	41	28	8	5
Phoenix	82	41	27	7	7
Pittsburgh	82	42	27	10	5
Montreal	82	43	27	11	5
Edmonton	82	37	27	9	1
Los Angeles	82	38	25	9	4
Florida	82	38	23	8	7
Calgary	82	36	22	10	4
Chicago	82	36	22	11	3
NY Islanders	82	38	21	12	5
Washington	82	33	22	9	2
NY Rangers	82	30	18	5	7
Vancouver	82	35	16	13	6
Nashville	82	26	16	7	3
Tampa Bay	82	36	14	15	7

Team Plus/Minus Differential

Team	GF	PPGF	Net GF	GA	PPGA	Net GA	Goal Differential
Toronto	268	53	**215**	231	64	**167**	+ 48
Ottawa	239	59	**180**	179	44	**135**	+ 45
New Jersey	248	60	**188**	196	47	**149**	+ 39
Buffalo	207	49	**158**	175	55	**120**	+ 38
Dallas	236	74	**162**	168	43	**125**	+ 37
Colorado	239	71	**168**	205	63	**142**	+ 26
Philadelphia	231	65	**166**	196	53	**143**	+ 23
Detroit	245	67	**178**	202	45	**157**	+ 21
Carolina	210	42	**168**	202	51	**151**	+ 17
St. Louis	237	61	**176**	209	47	**162**	+ 14
San Jose	196	53	**143**	191	61	**130**	+ 13
Phoenix	205	41	**164**	197	45	**152**	+ 12
Pittsburgh	242	65	**177**	225	56	**169**	+ 8
Edmonton	230	63	**167**	226	67	**159**	+ 8
Calgary	211	51	**160**	234	78	**156**	+ 4
Boston	214	65	**149**	181	33	**140**	+ 1
Florida	210	51	**159**	228	67	**161**	− 2
Anaheim	215	83	**132**	206	60	**146**	− 14
Washington	200	52	**148**	218	55	**163**	− 15
Chicago	202	50	**152**	248	80	**168**	− 16
Los Angeles	189	43	**146**	222	47	**175**	− 29
Montreal	184	50	**134**	209	44	**165**	− 31
NY Rangers	217	71	**146**	227	48	**179**	− 33
Nashville	190	40	**150**	261	75	**186**	− 36
NY Islanders	194	54	**140**	244	60	**184**	− 44
Vancouver	192	57	**135**	258	77	**181**	− 46
Tampa Bay	179	43	**136**	292	68	**224**	− 88

Team Record when Leading, Trailing, Tied

	Leading after						Trailing after						Tied after					
	1 period			2 periods			1 period			2 periods			1 period			2 periods		
Team	W	L	T	W	L	T	W	L	T	W	L	T	W	L	T	W	L	T
Anaheim	21	4	9	28	3	7	3	17	3	2	21	4	11	13	1	5	10	2
Boston	20	2	6	27	1	3	9	18	4	3	20	2	10	10	3	9	9	8
Buffalo	21	2	2	28	1	3	2	17	6	5	21	5	14	9	9	4	6	9
Calgary	15	5	3	21	5	2	5	19	4	2	23	5	10	16	5	7	12	5
Carolina	17	5	5	25	2	6	3	9	6	3	22	6	14	16	7	6	6	6
Chicago	13	6	2	20	2	2	4	23	5	3	33	5	12	12	5	6	6	5
Colorado	21	3	2	27	2	1	10	14	6	5	21	2	13	11	2	12	5	7
Dallas	27	1	5	38	2	5	10	6	2	1	14	2	14	12	5	12	3	5
Detroit	26	4	5	34	3	2	5	13	0	2	23	2	12	15	2	7	6	3
Edmonton	15	5	1	24	4	2	3	19	4	2	29	5	15	13	7	7	4	5
Florida	15	4	3	23	3	2	1	16	9	2	27	8	14	14	6	5	4	8
Los Angeles	21	6	4	23	4	1	3	27	0	3	30	0	8	12	1	6	11	4
Montreal	15	5	1	25	4	5	2	17	2	1	23	2	15	17	8	6	12	4
Nashville	12	5	2	17	2	5	6	28	2	5	39	0	10	14	3	6	6	2
New Jersey	25	6	1	37	3	4	8	11	2	3	15	2	14	7	8	7	6	5
NY Islanders	9	5	2	19	3	4	5	23	2	2	35	2	10	20	6	3	10	4
NY Rangers	16	3	6	21	2	5	5	21	2	7	27	1	12	14	3	5	9	5
Ottawa	25	2	4	32	2	2	7	16	4	1	18	3	12	5	7	11	3	10
Philadelphia	18	5	8	29	2	8	3	12	2	3	19	5	11	9	9	5	6	5
Phoenix	17	5	5	28	2	8	5	16	3	3	21	3	17	10	4	8	8	1
Pittsburgh	19	8	2	27	5	3	3	15	7	6	23	7	16	7	5	5	2	4
San Jose	20	4	6	23	3	3	2	16	7	1	25	6	9	13	5	7	6	9
St. Louis	24	6	4	26	3	6	5	16	3	5	26	2	8	10	6	6	3	5
Tampa Bay	10	13	2	12	8	1	0	30	2	1	41	4	9	11	5	6	5	4
Toronto	19	8	2	37	1	2	10	12	3	4	23	3	16	10	2	4	6	2
Vancouver	10	7	3	17	5	0	4	27	4	2	38	6	9	13	5	4	4	6
Washington	16	4	2	23	1	2	5	29	3	1	34	2	12	1	7	10	2	X

Team Statistics

TEAMS' HOME-AND-ROAD RECORD

Eastern Conference

	Home								Road							
	GP	W	L	T	GF	GA	PTS	%	GP	W	L	T	GF	GA	PTS	%
N.J	41	19	14	8	123	102	46	.561	41	28	10	3	125	94	59	.720
OTT	41	22	11	8	120	79	52	.634	41	22	12	7	119	100	51	.622
TOR	41	23	13	5	135	111	51	.622	41	22	17	2	133	120	46	.561
PHI	41	21	9	11	128	90	53	.646	41	16	17	8	103	106	40	.488
BOS	41	22	10	9	112	79	53	.646	41	17	20	4	102	102	38	.463A
BUF	41	23	12	6	117	88	52	.634	41	14	16	11	90	87	39	.476
PIT	41	21	10	10	132	103	52	.634	41	17	20	4	110	122	38	.463
CAR	41	20	12	9	110	96	49	.598	41	14	18	9	100	106	37	.451
FLA	41	17	17	7	115	114	41	.500	41	13	17	11	95	114	37	.451
NYR	41	17	19	5	105	102	39	.476	41	16	19	6	112	125	38	.463
MTL	41	21	15	5	105	97	47	.573	41	11	24	6	79	112	28	.341
WSH	41	16	23	2	107	111	34	.415	41	15	22	4	93	107	34	.415
NYI	41	11	23	7	104	122	29	.354	41	13	25	3	90	122	29	.354
T.B.	41	12	25	4	90	127	28	.341	41	7	29	5	89	165	19	.232
Total	**574**	**265**	**213**	**96**	**1603**	**1421**	**626**	**.545**	**574**	**225**	**266**	**83**	**1440**	**1582**	**533**	**.464**

Western Conference

	GP	W	L	T	GF	GA	PTS	%	GP	W	L	T	GF	GA	PTS	%
DAL	41	29	8	4	134	86	62	.756	41	22	11	8	102	82	52	.634
COL	41	21	14	6	127	100	48	.585	41	23	14	4	112	105	50	.610
DET	41	27	12	2	137	96	56	.683	41	16	20	5	108	106	37	.451
PHX	41	23	13	5	106	97	51	.622	41	16	18	7	99	100	39	.476
ST.L.	41	18	17	6	118	99	42	.512	41	19	15	7	119	110	45	.549
ANA	41	21	14	6	121	96	48	.585	41	14	20	7	94	110	35	.427
S.J.	41	17	15	9	96	86	43	.524	41	14	18	9	100	105	37	.451
EDM	41	17	19	5	113	112	39	.476	41	16	18	7	117	114	39	.476
CGY	41	15	20	6	103	110	36	.439	41	15	20	6	108	124	36	.439
CHI	41	20	17	4	109	112	44	.537	41	9	24	8	93	136	26	.317
L.A.	41	18	20	3	105	107	39	.476	41	14	25	2	84	115	30	.366
NSH	41	15	22	4	104	126	34	.415	41	13	25	3	86	135	29	.354
VAN	41	14	21	6	95	111	34	.415	41	9	26	6	97	147	24	.293
Total	**533**	**255**	**212**	**66**	**1468**	**1338**	**576**	**.540**	**533**	**200**	**254**	**79**	**1319**	**1489**	**479**	**.449**
	1107	**520**	**425**	**162**	**3071**	**2759**	**1202**	**.543**	**1107**	**425**	**520**	**162**	**2759**	**3071**	**1012**	**.457**

TEAMS' DIVISIONAL RECORD

Northeast Division

	Against Own Division								Against Other Division							
	GP	W	L	T	GF	GA	PTS	%	GP	W	L	T	GF	GA	PTS	%
OTT	20	8	8	4	42	42	20	.500	62	36	15	11	197	137	83	.669
TOR	20	8	11	1	43	55	17	.425	62	37	19	6	225	176	80	.645
BOS	20	11	7	2	57	40	24	.600	62	28	23	11	157	141	67	.540
BUF	20	10	6	4	54	37	24	.600	62	27	22	13	153	138	67	.540
MTL	20	7	12	1	40	62	15	.375	62	25	27	10	144	147	60	.484
Total	**100**	**44**	**44**	**12**	**236**	**236**	**100**	**.500**	**310**	**153**	**106**	**51**	**876**	**739**	**357**	**.576**

Atlantic Division

	GP	W	L	T	GF	GA	PTS	%	GP	W	L	T	GF	GA	PTS	%
N.J.	20	15	4	1	71	55	31	.775	62	32	20	10	177	141	74	.597
PHI	20	7	8	5	58	54	19	.475	62	30	18	14	173	142	74	.597
PIT	20	5	11	4	46	64	14	.350	62	33	19	10	196	161	76	.613
NYR	20	8	8	4	52	52	20	.500	62	25	30	7	165	175	57	.460
NYI	20	7	11	2	57	59	16	.400	62	17	37	8	137	185	42	.339
Total	**100**	**42**	**42**	**16**	**284**	**284**	**100**	**.500**	**310**	**137**	**124**	**49**	**848**	**804**	**323**	**.521**

Southeast Division

	GP	W	L	T	GF	GA	PTS	%	GP	W	L	T	GF	GA	PTS	%
CAR	15	5	2	8	41	38	18	.600	67	29	28	10	169	164	68	.507
FLA	15	6	4	5	36	34	17	.567	67	24	30	13	174	194	61	.455
WSH	15	8	5	2	53	31	18	.600	67	23	40	4	147	187	50	.373
T.B.	15	2	10	3	32	59	7	.233	67	17	44	6	147	233	40	.299
Total	**60**	**21**	**21**	**18**	**162**	**162**	**60**	**.500**	**268**	**93**	**142**	**33**	**637**	**778**	**219**	**.409**

Central Division

	GP	W	L	T	GF	GA	PTS	%	GP	W	L	T	GF	GA	PTS	%
DET	18	12	4	2	62	40	26	.722	64	31	28	5	183	162	67	.523
ST.L.	18	10	6	2	59	46	22	.611	64	27	26	11	178	163	65	.508
CHI	18	7	10	1	47	56	15	.417	64	22	31	11	155	192	55	.430
NSH	18	4	13	1	44	70	9	.250	64	24	34	6	146	191	54	.422
Total	**72**	**33**	**33**	**6**	**212**	**212**	**72**	**.500**	**256**	**104**	**119**	**33**	**662**	**708**	**241**	**.471**

Pacific Division

	GP	W	L	T	GF	GA	PTS	%	GP	W	L	T	GF	GA	PTS	%
DAL	24	18	4	2	62	43	38	.792	58	33	15	10	174	125	76	.655
PHX	24	11	11	2	47	46	24	.500	58	28	20	10	158	151	66	.569
ANA	24	12	7	5	62	48	29	.604	58	23	27	8	153	158	54	.466
S.J.	24	7	14	3	47	55	17	.354	58	24	19	15	149	136	63	.543
L.A.	24	6	18	0	41	67	12	.250	58	26	27	5	148	155	57	.491
Total	**120**	**54**	**54**	**12**	**259**	**259**	**120**	**.500**	**290**	**134**	**108**	**48**	**782**	**725**	**316**	**.545**

Northwest Division

	GP	W	L	T	GF	GA	PTS	%	GP	W	L	T	GF	GA	PTS	%
COL	18	8	8	2	48	52	18	.500	64	36	20	8	191	153	80	.625
EDM	18	12	4	2	57	40	26	.722	64	21	33	10	173	186	52	.406
CGY	18	6	10	2	45	50	14	.389	64	24	30	10	166	184	58	.453
VAN	18	6	10	2	46	54	14	.389	64	17	37	10	146	204	44	.344
Total	**72**	**32**	**32**	**8**	**196**	**196**	**72**	**.500**	**256**	**98**	**120**	**38**	**676**	**727**	**234**	**.457**

TEAM STREAKS

Consecutive Wins

Games	Team	From	To
12	Colorado	Jan. 10	Feb. 7
10	Pittsburgh	Jan. 28	Feb. 15
8	Phoenix	Nov. 11	Nov. 28
8	Detroit	Mar. 24	Apr. 7
7	Anaheim	Feb. 20	Mar. 7
6	Dallas	Dec. 23	Jan. 6
6	Pittsburgh	Dec. 26	Jan. 9
6	Washington	Feb. 1	Feb. 12
6	Detroit	Feb. 9	Feb. 19
6	Chicago	Apr. 3	Apr. 17

Consecutive Home Wins

Games	Team	From	To
9	Pittsburgh	Jan. 28	Feb. 22
9	Chicago	Mar. 17	Apr. 17
7	Toronto	Nov. 11	Dec. 2
7	Buffalo	Nov. 14	Dec. 18
7	Phoenix	Nov. 14	Dec. 20
7	Ottawa	Feb. 13	Mar. 8
7	Detroit	Mar. 24	Apr.7
6	Detroit	Nov. 25	Dec. 16
5	Dallas	Oct. 10	Oct. 24
5	New Jersey	Oct. 31	Nov. 19
5	Dallas	Dec. 11	Jan. 6
5	Pittsburgh	Dec. 26	Jan. 9
5	Colorado	Jan. 12	Jan. 30
5	Montreal	Feb. 3	Mar. 2
5	Washington	Feb. 3	Feb. 22
5	Dallas	Feb. 26	Mar. 12
5	Buffalo	Mar. 13	Apr. 9
5	Boston	Apr. 3	Apr. 17

Consecutive Road Wins

Games	Team	From	To
7	Colorado	Jan. 10	Feb. 7
7	Dallas	Jan. 13	Feb. 23
6	Phoenix	Oct. 26	Nov. 28
6	St. Louis	Feb. 1	Mar. 2
5	New Jersey	Jan. 20	Feb. 4
5	New Jersey	Mar. 3	Mar. 17
5	Ottawa	Mar. 19	Apr. 3
4	New Jersey	Oct. 16	Nov. 7
4	New Jersey	Nov. 28	Dec. 10
4	Buffalo	Dec. 12	Jan. 6
4	Los Angeles	Dec. 20	Jan. 5
4	Montreal	Dec. 26	Jan. 2
4	Ottawa	Jan. 6	Jan. 21
4	Anaheim	Feb. 5	Feb. 15
4	San Jose	Feb. 8	Feb. 13
4	Calgary	Feb. 9	Mar. 9
4	Toronto	Mar. 26	Apr. 3
4	St. Louis	Apr. 7	Apr. 18

Consecutive Undefeated

Games	Team	W	T	From	To
15	Dallas	12	3	Dec. 6	Jan. 6
15	Philadelphia	10	5	Dec. 12	Jan. 13
14	Phoenix	12	2	Oct. 25	Nov. 28
12	Colorado	12	0	Jan. 10	Feb. 7
11	Ottawa	8	3	Dec. 28	Jan. 16
10	Pittsburgh	10	0	Jan. 28	Feb. 15
	Buffalo	6	3	Oct. 27	Nov. 20
9	Colorado	8	1	Mar. 24	Apr. 11
9	Detroit	8	1	Mar. 24	Apr. 9
8	Boston	6	2	Nov. 19	Dec. 10
8	New Jersey	6	2	Nov. 28	Dec. 16
8	Buffalo	7	1	Nov. 29	Dec. 18
8	Philadelphia	6	2	Jan. 18	Feb. 6
8	Anaheim	7	1	Feb. 20	Mar. 10
8	San Jose	5	3	Mar. 9	Mar. 26
7	Calgary	5	2	Feb. 8	Feb. 24
7	Detroit	6	1	Feb. 9	Feb. 21
7	Dallas	6	1	Feb. 12	Feb. 23
7	Pittsburgh	4	3	Mar. 10	Mar. 23
7	New Jersey	4	3	Mar. 23	Apr. 4
7	Toronto	5	2	Mar. 26	Apr. 7

Consecutive Home Undefeated

Games	Team	W	T	From	To
11	Phoenix	10	1	Oct. 15	Dec. 20
11	Pittsburgh	9	2	Jan. 28	Mar. 5
10	Buffalo	9	1	Oct. 30	Dec. 18
10	New Jersey	7	3	Oct. 31	Dec. 16
10	Colorado	8	2	Mar. 18	Apr. 18
9	Chicago	9	0	Mar. 17	Apr. 17
8	Montreal	4	4	Dec. 14	Jan. 18
7	Dallas	6	1	Oct. 10	Oct. 31
7	St. Louis	5	2	Oct. 24	Nov. 24
7	Toronto	7	0	Nov. 11	Dec. 2
7	Dallas	6	1	Nov. 27	Jan. 6
7	Philadelphia	4	3	Dec. 13	Jan. 11
7	Ottawa	5	2	Dec. 23	Jan. 16
7	Colorado	6	1	Jan. 4	Jan. 30
7	Phoenix	5	2	Jan. 11	Feb. 6
7	Philadelphia	5	2	Jan. 21	Feb. 6
7	Ottawa	7	0	Feb. 13	Mar. 8
7	Detroit	7	0	Mar. 24	Apr. 7

Consecutive Road Undefeated

Games	Team	W	T	From	To
10	Philadelphia	7	3	Dec. 8	Jan. 18
10	Colorado	8	2	Jan. 10	Mar. 3
10	Dallas	8	2	Jan. 12	Mar. 4
9	Dallas	7	2	Dec. 6	Jan. 1
7	Phoenix	6	1	Oct. 25	Nov. 28
7	New Jersey	6	1	Nov. 28	Dec. 30
7	Buffalo	6	1	Nov. 29	Jan. 6
7	Ottawa	6	1	Dec. 30	Jan. 21
7	New Jersey	6	1	Feb. 22	Mar. 17
7	Ottawa	5	2	Mar. 17	Apr. 5
6	Boston	4	2	Nov. 7	Dec. 10
6	Calgary	4	2	Feb. 1	Mar. 9
6	St. Louis	6	0	Feb. 1	Mar. 2
6	San Jose	3	3	Mar. 1	Mar. 26
6	Boston	5	1	Mar. 17	Apr. 7
5	Dallas	4	1	Nov. 7	Dec. 2
5	New Jersey	5	0	Jan. 20	Feb. 4
5	San Jose	4	1	Feb. 8	Feb. 15
5	St. Louis	4	1	Apr. 5	Apr. 18

TEAM PENALTIES

Abbreviations: GP – games played; **PEN** – total penalty minutes including bench minutes; **BMI** – total bench minor minutes; **AVG** – average penalty minutes/game calculated by dividing total penalty minutes by games played

Team	GP	PEN	BMI	AVG
OTT	82	892	12	10.9
PIT	82	977	12	11.9
PHI	82	1075	12	13.1
NYR	82	1087	14	13.3
TOR	82	1095	16	13.4
DAL	82	1108	8	13.5
NYI	82	1111	22	13.5
CAR	82	1158	10	14.1
BOS	82	1182	6	14.4
DET	82	1202	10	14.7
WSH	82	1281	6	15.6
MTL	82	1299	14	15.8
STL	82	1308	6	16.0
T.B	82	1316	10	16.0
ANA	82	1323	14	16.1
N.J	82	1355	14	16.5
EDM	82	1373	12	16.7
CGY	82	1389	8	16.9
L.A	82	1383	14	16.9
PHX	82	1412	12	17.2
NSH	82	1420	14	17.3
S.J	82	1423	10	17.4
FLA	82	1522	18	18.6
BUF	82	1561	16	19.0
COL	82	1619	14	19.7
VAN	82	1764	16	21.5
CHI	82	1807	8	22.0
Total	**1107**	**35442**	**328**	**32.0**

Teemu Selanne topped the NHL with 25 power-play goals amongst his league-leading 47 tallies in 1998-99. With Selanne leading the way, the Mighty Ducks were the NHL's most dangerous team with the man advantage.

TEAMS' POWER-PLAY RECORD

Abbreviations: ADV – total advantages; **PPGF** – power-play goals for; **%** – calculated by dividing number of power-play goals by total advantages.

Home

	Team	GP	ADV	PPGF	%
1	ANA	41	192	49	25.5
2	DAL	41	213	47	22.1
3	COL	41	207	44	21.3
4	STL	41	155	33	21.3
5	N.J	41	152	32	21.1
6	PHI	41	189	39	20.6
7	MTL	41	175	34	19.4
8	NYI	41	176	34	19.3
9	NYR	41	195	36	18.5
10	DET	41	211	38	18.0
11	BOS	41	181	31	17.1
12	WSH	41	151	24	15.9
13	FLA	41	185	29	15.7
14	VAN	41	183	28	15.3
15	PIT	41	189	29	15.3
16	OTT	41	223	34	15.2
17	EDM	41	207	31	15.0
18	T.B	41	160	24	15.0
19	L.A	41	177	26	14.7
20	TOR	41	174	25	14.4
21	CHI	41	188	27	14.4
22	BUF	41	181	24	13.3
23	NSH	41	183	24	13.1
24	CGY	41	169	21	12.4
25	S.J	41	199	23	11.6
26	PHX	41	177	20	11.3
27	CAR	41	190	21	11.1
TOTAL		**1107**	**4982**	**827**	**16.6**

Road

Team	GP	ADV	PPGF	%
NYR	41	153	35	22.9
PIT	41	174	36	20.7
STL	41	146	28	19.2
WSH	41	150	28	18.7
N.J	41	152	28	18.4
ANA	41	186	34	18.3
BOS	41	187	34	18.2
VAN	41	175	29	16.6
COL	41	168	27	16.1
CGY	41	188	30	16.0
CHI	41	147	23	15.6
S.J	41	200	30	15.0
DAL	41	180	27	15.0
TOR	41	193	28	14.5
OTT	41	174	25	14.4
DET	41	204	29	14.2
EDM	41	231	32	13.9
BUF	41	182	25	13.7
PHI	41	197	26	13.2
T.B	41	150	19	12.7
PHX	41	165	21	12.7
NYI	41	165	20	12.1
FLA	41	195	22	11.3
L.A	41	150	17	11.3
NSH	41	141	16	11.3
CAR	41	192	21	10.9
MTL	41	169	16	9.5
TOTAL	**1107**	**4714**	**706**	**15.0**

Overall

Team	GP	ADV	PPGF	%
ANA	82	378	83	22.0
NYR	82	348	71	20.4
STL	82	301	61	20.3
N.J	82	304	60	19.7
COL	82	375	71	18.9
DAL	82	393	74	18.8
PIT	82	363	65	17.9
BOS	82	368	65	17.7
WSH	82	301	52	17.3
PHI	82	386	65	16.8
DET	82	415	67	16.1
VAN	82	358	57	15.9
NYI	82	341	54	15.8
CHI	82	335	50	14.9
OTT	82	397	59	14.9
MTL	82	344	50	14.5
TOR	82	367	53	14.4
EDM	82	438	63	14.4
CGY	82	357	51	14.3
T.B	82	310	43	13.9
BUF	82	363	49	13.5
FLA	82	380	51	13.4
S.J	82	399	53	13.3
L.A	82	327	43	13.1
NSH	82	324	40	12.3
PHX	82	342	41	12.0
CAR	82	382	42	11.0
TOTAL	**1107**	**9696**	**1533**	**15.8**

SHORT-HANDED GOALS FOR

Home

	Team	GP	SHGF
1	EDM	41	7
2	PIT	41	7
3	VAN	41	6
4	L.A	41	6
5	FLA	41	5
6	TOR	41	5
7	MTL	41	5
8	CHI	41	5
9	DET	41	5
10	NSH	41	4
11	COL	41	4
12	S.J	41	4
13	PHX	41	4
14	T.B	41	4
15	BUF	41	4
16	ST.L	41	4
17	NYR	41	3
18	CGY	41	3
19	BOS	41	3
20	NYI	41	3
21	WSH	41	3
22	DAL	41	3
23	N.J	41	3
24	OTT	41	3
25	ANA	41	2
26	CAR	41	2
27	PHI	41	1
TOTAL		**1107**	**109**

Road

Team	GP	SHGF
VAN	41	11
DET	41	9
CGY	41	9
T.B	41	7
L.A	41	6
FLA	41	5
NYI	41	4
WSH	41	4
S.J	41	4
NYR	41	4
N.J	41	4
PHX	41	4
PHI	41	3
ST.L	41	3
PIT	41	3
ANA	41	3
OTT	41	3
CAR	41	3
CHI	41	3
DAL	41	3
COL	41	3
MTL	41	3
NSH	41	3
BUF	41	2
TOR	41	1
EDM	41	1
BOS	41	0
TOTAL	**1107**	**111**

Overall

Team	GP	SHGF
VAN	82	17
DET	82	14
CGY	82	12
T.B	82	12
FLA	82	11
L.A	82	10
PIT	82	10
S.J	82	8
MTL	82	8
NYI	82	8
WSH	82	8
CHI	82	8
EDM	82	8
PHX	82	8
NYR	82	7
STL	82	7
TOR	82	7
N.J	82	7
NSH	82	7
COL	82	7
ANA	82	7
OTT	82	6
DAL	82	6
BUF	82	6
CAR	82	5
PHI	82	4
BOS	82	3
TOTAL	**1107**	**220**

TEAMS' PENALTY KILLING RECORD

Abbreviations: TSH – total times short-handed; **PPGA** – power-play goals against; **%** – calculated by dividing times short minus power-play goals against by times short.

Home

	Team	GP	TSH	PPGA	%
1	BOS	41	145	11	92.4
2	NYR	41	180	19	89.4
3	OTT	41	166	20	88.0
4	PHX	41	174	21	87.9
5	DET	41	170	21	87.6
6	STL	41	194	24	87.6
7	S.J	41	215	27	87.4
8	DAL	41	166	22	86.7
9	CAR	41	156	21	86.5
10	MTL	41	175	24	86.3
11	ANA	41	194	27	86.1
12	WSH	41	163	23	85.9
13	VAN	41	210	30	85.7
14	L.A	41	175	25	85.7
15	BUF	41	195	28	85.6
16	N.J	41	152	22	85.5
17	PIT	41	149	22	85.2
18	NYI	41	168	25	85.1
19	PHI	41	148	22	85.1
20	T.B	41	183	29	84.2
21	NSH	41	175	31	82.3
22	COL	41	197	36	81.7
23	CHI	41	191	37	80.6
24	FLA	41	168	33	80.4
25	EDM	41	172	35	79.7
26	CGY	41	175	37	78.9
27	TOR	41	158	34	78.5
TOTAL		**1107**	**4714**	**706**	**85.0**

Road

Team	GP	TSH	PPGA	%
MTL	41	169	20	88.2
STL	41	193	23	88.1
DET	41	185	24	87.0
BUF	41	204	27	86.8
BOS	41	160	22	86.3
DAL	41	153	21	86.3
PHX	41	174	24	86.2
L.A	41	155	22	85.8
COL	41	189	27	85.7
N.J	41	173	25	85.5
CAR	41	190	30	84.2
EDM	41	202	32	84.2
OTT	41	151	24	84.1
PHI	41	185	31	83.2
FLA	41	202	34	83.2
WSH	41	190	32	83.2
ANA	41	193	33	82.9
S.J	41	192	34	82.3
NYI	41	195	35	82.1
TOR	41	167	30	82.0
NYR	41	156	29	81.4
T.B	41	204	39	80.9
CGY	41	211	41	80.6
VAN	41	240	47	80.4
CHI	41	214	43	79.9
PIT	41	153	34	77.8
NSH	41	182	44	75.8
TOTAL	**1107**	**4982**	**827**	**83.4**

Overall

Team	GP	TSH	PPGA	%
BOS	82	305	33	89.2
STL	82	387	47	87.9
DET	82	355	45	87.3
MTL	82	344	44	87.2
PHX	82	348	45	87.1
DAL	82	319	43	86.5
BUF	82	399	55	86.2
OTT	82	317	44	86.1
L.A	82	330	47	85.8
NYR	82	336	48	85.7
N.J	82	325	47	85.5
CAR	82	346	51	85.3
S.J	82	407	61	85.0
ANA	82	387	60	84.5
WSH	82	353	56	84.4
PHI	82	333	53	84.1
COL	82	386	63	83.7
NYI	82	363	60	83.5
VAN	82	450	77	82.9
T.B	82	387	68	82.4
EDM	82	374	67	82.1
FLA	82	370	67	81.9
PIT	82	302	56	81.5
TOR	82	325	64	80.3
CHI	82	405	80	80.2
CGY	82	386	78	79.8
NSH	82	357	75	79.0
TOTAL	**1107**	**9696**	**1533**	**84.2**

SHORT-HANDED GOALS AGAINST

Home

	Team	GP	SHGA
1	CAR	41	1
2	PHX	41	1
3	N.J	41	1
4	DET	41	1
5	S.J	41	2
6	ANA	41	2
7	BOS	41	3
8	TOR	41	3
9	NYI	41	3
10	WSH	41	3
11	DAL	41	3
12	ST.L	41	3
13	CGY	41	3
14	MTL	41	4
15	NSH	41	4
16	BUF	41	4
17	NYR	41	4
18	FLA	41	5
19	EDM	41	5
20	VAN	41	5
21	T.B	41	6
22	L.A	41	6
23	OTT	41	6
24	CHI	41	7
25	PHI	41	7
26	COL	41	7
27	PIT	41	9
TOTAL		**1107**	**111**

Road

Team	GP	SHGA
PHI	41	0
ST.L	41	1
DAL	41	1
S.J	41	2
CGY	41	2
BUF	41	3
TOR	41	3
CHI	41	4
T.B	41	4
NYR	41	4
N.J	41	4
NYI	41	4
COL	41	4
WSH	41	4
VAN	41	4
PHX	41	4
PIT	41	5
ANA	41	5
L.A	41	5
CAR	41	5
EDM	41	5
DET	41	6
FLA	41	6
BOS	41	6
MTL	41	6
NSH	41	7
OTT	41	7
TOTAL	**1107**	**109**

Overall

Team	GP	SHGA
S.J	82	4
ST.L	82	4
DAL	82	4
N.J	82	5
PHX	82	5
CGY	82	6
TOR	82	6
CAR	82	6
PHI	82	7
DET	82	7
NYI	82	7
WSH	82	7
ANA	82	7
BUF	82	7
NYR	82	9
BOS	82	9
VAN	82	9
T.B	82	10
MTL	82	10
CHI	82	10
NSH	82	10
EDM	82	10
FLA	82	11
L.A	82	11
COL	82	12
OTT	82	13
PIT	82	14
TOTAL	**1107**	**220**

Overtime Results

1989-90 to 1998-99

Team	1998-99 GP	W	L	T	1997-98 GP	W	L	T	1996-97 GP	W	L	T	1995-96 GP	W	L	T	1994-95 GP	W	L	T	1993-94 GP	W	L	T	1992-93 GP	W	L	T	1991-92 GP	W	L	T	1990-91 GP	W	L	T	1989-90 GP	W	L	T
ANA	17	1	3	13	20	3	4	13	16	3	0	13	16	6	2	8	7	2	0	5	12	2	5	5																
BOS	17	2	2	13	17	3	1	13	15	3	3	9	19	2	6	11	8	2	3	3	17	2	2	13	15	5	3	7	20	6	2	12	17	5	0	12	14	3	2	9
BUF	23	3	3	17	21	3	1	17	21	5	4	12	15	2	6	7	9	1	1	7	13	0	4	9	18	4	4	10	16	2	2	12	24	3	2	19	15	4	3	8
CGY	16	3	1	12	22	4	3	15	16	3	4	9	16	2	3	11	9	1	1	7	18	3	2	13	19	4	4	11	19	2	5	12	15	3	4	8	21	3	3	15
HFD/CAR	24	1	5	18	12	2	2	8	18	3	4	11	14	2	3	9	9	1	1	7	14	4	1	9	18	3	9	6	18	2	3	13	9	1	1	7	9	0	0	9
CHI	15	1	2	12	18	1	4	13	19	1	5	13	19	1	4	14	7	2	0	5	16	2	5	9	16	1	3	12	19	2	2	15	12	3	1	8	10	2	2	6
QUE/COL	12	2	0	10	22	2	3	17	15	2	3	10	6	1	0	5	8	0	0	8	15	3	3	9	15	4	1	10	17	0	5	12	18	1	3	14	8	0	1	7
MIN/DAL	16	3	1	12	17	5	1	11	15	4	3	8	15	1	0	14	9	0	1	8	22	6	3	13	10	0	0	10	8	0	2	6	17	0	3	14	11	3	4	4
DET	10	2	1	7	15	0	0	15	27	7	2	18	11	3	1	7	4	0	0	4	15	5	2	8	11	2	0	9	16	3	1	12	14	2	4	8	17	2	1	14
EDM	20	3	5	12	15	3	2	10	16	1	6	9	14	4	2	8	7	1	2	4	21	1	6	14	17	5	4	8	12	0	2	10	15	4	5	6	20	5	1	14
FLA	21	1	2	18	20	3	2	15	26	3	4	19	13	0	3	10	9	0	3	6	24	2	5	17																
L.A.	12	5	2	5	16	3	2	11	14	0	3	11	23	3	2	18	9	0	0	9	18	3	3	12	13	2	1	10	16	1	1	14	16	4	2	10	12	3	2	7
MTL	15	0	4	11	20	3	4	13	21	2	4	15	15	2	3	10	10	1	2	7	19	3	2	14	14	5	3	6	20	6	3	11	17	3	3	11	17	4	2	11
N.J.	15	3	1	11	16	2	3	11	17	1	2	14	19	7	0	12	11	1	2	8	14	1	1	12	11	4	0	7	17	2	4	11	17	1	1	15	16	3	4	9
NSH	10	1	2	7																																				
NYI	17	1	6	10	13	0	2	11	17	3	2	12	17	2	5	10	7	1	1	5	19	5	2	12	13	3	3	7	16	3	2	11	15	2	3	10	16	3	2	11
NYR	19	5	3	11	24	2	4	18	13	3	0	10	17	2	1	14	3	0	0	3	12	3	1	8	17	2	4	11	11	5	1	5	16	1	2	13	17	2	2	13
OTT	18	1	2	15	17	2	0	15	17	0	2	15	8	0	3	5	7	1	1	5	17	4	4	9	10	0	6	4												
PHI	24	2	3	19	15	3	1	11	18	3	2	13	20	4	3	13	8	3	1	4	18	3	5	10	17	4	2	11	17	2	4	11	11	1	0	10	18	2	5	11
WPG/PHX	15	2	1	12	14	0	2	12	16	5	4	7	8	2	0	6	9	0	2	7	15	1	5	9	11	2	2	7	20	1	4	15	14	1	2	11	19	4	4	11
PIT	22	7	1	14	23	2	3	18	13	1	4	8	9	3	2	4	5	1	1	3	19	4	2	13	10	3	0	7	12	2	1	9	12	4	2	6	14	3	3	8
ST.L.	15	1	1	13	12	2	2	8	13	1	1	11	18	1	1	16	7	1	1	5	17	4	2	11	17	2	4	11	15	2	2	11	18	3	4	11	15	2	4	9
S.J.	21	1	2	18	12	0	2	10	12	3	1	8	9	1	1	7	5	1	0	4	19	2	1	16	10	3	5	2	9	1	3	5								
T.B.	12	1	2	9	13	0	3	10	16	4	2	10	18	3	3	12	7	2	2	3	18	3	4	11	14	3	4	7												
TOR	14	6	1	7	10	1	0	9	10	1	1	8	18	4	2	12	8	0	0	8	17	4	1	12	13	1	1	11	11	4	0	7	17	4	2	11	11	3	4	4
VAN	13	0	1	12	17	0	3	14	14	5	2	7	20	1	4	15	13	0	1	12	12	5	4	3	10	1	0	9	17	4	1	12	15	3	3	9	21	2	5	14
WSH	11	2	3	6	17	4	1	12	13	2	2	9	16	4	1	11	9	0	1	8	14	2	2	10	11	2	2	7	12	2	2	8	14	4	3	7	9	2	1	6
Totals	222	60		162	219	54		165	214	70		144	201	64		137	101	26		75	214	74		140	165	65		100	169	52		117	166	54		112	155	55		100

1998-99

Home Team Wins: 28
Visiting Team Wins: 32

1998-99 Penalty shots

Scored

Geoff Courtnall (St. Louis) scored against Chris Osgood (Detroit), October 29. Final score: Detroit 1 at St. Louis 3.

Scott Niedermayer (New Jersey) scored against Jose Theodore (Montreal), November 11. Final score: Montreal 0 at New Jersey 3.

Adam Oates (Washington) scored against Curtis Joseph (Toronto), November 18. Final score: Toronto 1 at Washington 4.

Markus Naslund (Vancouver) scored against Mike Dunham (Nashville), December 19. Final score: Nashville 6 at Vancouver 4.

John MacLean (NY Rangers) scored against Bill Ranford (Tampa Bay), January 10. Final score: Tampa Bay 2 at New York 5.

Peter Bondra (Washington) scored against Stephane Fiset (Los Angeles), January 29. Final score: Los Angeles 6 at Washington 3.

Tomas Sandstrom (Anaheim) scored against Stephane Fiset (Los Angeles), February 15. Final score: Anaheim 3 at Los Angeles 1.

Paul Kariya (Anaheim) scored against Corey Hirsch (Vancouver), February 20. Final score: Anaheim 5 at Vancouver 1.

Pavel Bure (Florida) scored against Chris Osgood (Detroit), February 26. Final score: Florida 5 at Detroit 5.

Ray Whitney (Florida) scored against Guy Hebert (Anaheim), March 21. Final score: Florida 5 at Anaheim 2.

Jason Allison (Boston) scored against Ron Tugnutt (Ottawa), March 23. Final score: Boston 3 at Ottawa 0.

Stopped

Mike Richter (NY Rangers) stopped Claude Lapointe (NY Islanders), October 22. Final score: NY Islanders 2 at NY Rangers 3.

Robbie Tallas (Boston) stopped Daymond Langkow (Tampa Bay), November 24. Final score: Boston 4 at Tampa Bay 1.

Eric Fichaud (Nashville) stopped Shaun Van Allen (Ottawa), December 1, Final score: Ottawa 3 at Nashville 1.

Rick Tabaracci (Washington) stopped Mariusz Czerkawski (NY Islanders), December 4. Final score: NY Islanders 1 at Washington 5.

Tyler Moss (Calgary) stopped Mike Modano (Dallas), December 7. Final score: Dallas 3 at Calgary 2.

Garth Snow (Vancouver) stopped Owen Nolan (San Jose), December 26. Final score: Vancouver 0 at San Jose 2.

Rick Tabaracci (Washington) stopped Jay Pandolfo (New Jersey), December 30. Final score: New Jersey 3 at Washington 2.

Corey Hirsch (Vancouver) stopped Martin Rucinsky (Montreal), January 2. Final score: Montreal 2 at Vancouver 1.

Tom Barrasso (Pittsburgh) stopped Sami Kapanen (Carolina), January 7. Final score: Carolina 2 at Pittsburgh 4.

Steve Shields (San Jose) stopped Terry Yake (St. Louis), January 26. Final score: St. Louis 3 at San Jose 0.

Jamie Storr (Los Angeles) stopped Todd White (Chicago), February 26. Final score: Los Angeles 2 at Chicago 1.

Ron Tugnutt (Ottawa) stopped Steve Sullivan (Toronto), March 6. Final score: Toronto 1 at Ottawa 3.

Curtis Joseph (Toronto) stopped Landon Wilson (Boston), March 17. Final score: Boston 4 at Toronto 1.

Stephane Fiset (Los Angeles) stopped Paul Kariya (Anaheim), March 18. Final score: Anaheim 4 at Los Angeles 2.

Rick Tabaracci (Washington) stopped Robert Reichel (Phoenix), March 25. Final score: Washington 2 at Phoenix 4.

Kirk McLean (Florida) stopped Ted Donato (Ottawa), April 12. Final score: Florida 2 at Ottawa 0.

Summary

27 penalty shots resulted in 11 goals

NHL Record Book

Year-By-Year Final Standings & Leading Scorers

*Stanley Cup winner

1917-18

First Half

Team	GP	W	L	T	GF	GA	PTS
Montreal	14	10	4	0	81	47	20
Toronto	14	8	6	0	71	75	16
Ottawa	14	5	9	0	67	79	10
**Mtl. Wanderers	6	1	5	0	17	35	2

**Montreal Arena burned down and Wanderers forced to withdraw from League. Montreal Canadiens and Toronto each counted a win for defaulted games with Wanderers.

Second Half

Team	GP	W	L	T	GF	GA	PTS
*Toronto	8	5	3	0	37	34	10
Ottawa	8	4	4	0	35	35	8
Montreal	8	3	5	0	34	37	6

Leading Scorers

Player	Club	GP	G	A	PTS	PIM
Malone, Joe	Montreal	20	44	4	48	30
Denneny, Cy	Ottawa	20	36	10	46	80
Noble, Reg	Toronto	20	30	10	40	35
Lalonde, Newsy	Montreal	14	23	7	30	31
Denneny, Corb	Toronto	21	20	9	29	14
Cameron, Harry	Toronto	21	17	10	27	28
Pitre, Didier	Montreal	20	17	6	23	29
Gerard, Eddie	Ottawa	20	13	7	20	26
Darragh, Jack	Ottawa	18	14	5	19	26
Nighbor, Frank	Ottawa	10	11	8	19	6
Meeking, Harry	Toronto	21	10	9	19	28

1918-19

First Half

Team	GP	W	L	T	GF	GA	PTS
**Montreal	10	7	3	0	57	50	14
Ottawa	10	5	5	0	39	39	10
Toronto	10	3	7	0	42	49	6

Second Half

Team	GP	W	L	T	GF	GA	PTS
Ottawa	8	7	1	0	32	14	14
Montreal	8	3	5	0	31	28	6
Toronto	8	2	6	0	22	43	4

**NHL Champion (No Stanley Cup Champion due to Influenza Epidemic.)

Leading Scorers

Player	Club	GP	G	A	PTS	PIM
Lalonde, Newsy	Montreal	17	23	10	33	42
Cleghorn, Odie	Montreal	18	21	6	27	33
Nighbor, Frank	Ottawa	18	18	9	27	27
Denneny, Cy	Ottawa	18	18	6	24	55
Pitre, Didier	Montreal	17	14	4	18	15
Skinner, Alf	Toronto	16	12	5	17	26
Cleghorn, Sprague	Ottawa	18	7	9	16	27
Cameron, Harry	Tor., Ott.	14	11	4	15	35
Darragh, Jack	Ottawa	14	11	4	15	30
Randall, Ken	Toronto	15	9	6	15	26

1919-20

First Half

Team	GP	W	L	T	GF	GA	PTS
Ottawa	12	9	3	0	59	23	18
Montreal	12	8	4	0	62	51	16
Toronto	12	5	7	0	52	62	10
Quebec	12	2	10	0	44	81	4

Second Half

Team	GP	W	L	T	GF	GA	PTS
*Ottawa	12	10	2	0	62	41	20
Montreal	12	5	7	0	67	62	10
Toronto	12	7	5	0	67	44	14
Quebec	12	2	10	0	47	96	4

Leading Scorers

Player	Club	GP	G	A	PTS	PIM
Malone, Joe	Quebec	24	39	10	49	12
Lalonde, Newsy	Montreal	23	37	9	46	34
Nighbor, Frank	Ottawa	23	26	15	41	18
Denneny, Corb	Toronto	24	24	12	36	20
Darragh, Jack	Ottawa	23	22	14	36	22
Noble, Reg	Toronto	24	24	9	33	51
Arbour, Amos	Montreal	22	21	5	26	13
Wilson, Cully	Toronto	23	20	6	26	86
Pitre, Didier	Montreal	22	14	12	26	6
Broadbent, Punch	Ottawa	21	19	6	25	40

1920-21

First Half

Team	GP	W	L	T	GF	GA	PTS
*Ottawa	10	8	2	0	49	23	16
Toronto	10	5	5	0	39	47	10
Montreal	10	4	6	0	37	51	8
Hamilton	10	3	7	0	34	38	6

Second Half

Team	GP	W	L	T	GF	GA	PTS
Toronto	14	10	4	0	66	53	20
Montreal	14	9	5	0	75	48	18
Ottawa	14	6	8	0	48	52	12
Hamilton	14	3	11	0	58	94	6

Leading Scorers

Player	Club	GP	G	A	PTS	PIM
Lalonde, Newsy	Montreal	24	32	11	43	36
Dye, Babe	Ham., Tor.	24	35	5	40	32
Denneny, Cy	Ottawa	24	34	5	39	10
Malone, Joe	Hamilton	20	28	9	37	6
Nighbor, Frank	Ottawa	24	19	10	29	10
Noble, Reg	Toronto	24	19	8	27	54
Cameron, Harry	Toronto	24	18	9	27	35
Prodgers, Goldie	Hamilton	24	18	9	27	8
Denneny, Corb	Toronto	20	19	7	26	29
Darragh, Jack	Ottawa	24	11	15	26	20

All-Time Standings of NHL Teams

(ranked by percentage)

Active Clubs

Team	Games	Wins	Losses	Ties	Goals For	Goals Against	Points	%	First Season
Montreal	5136	2679	1664	793	17262	13725	6151	.599	1917-18
Philadelphia	2522	1253	873	396	8880	7627	2902	.575	1967-68
Boston	4976	2384	1860	732	16326	14766	5500	.553	1924-25
Buffalo	2296	1077	854	365	8022	7224	2519	.549	1970-71
Edmonton	1584	759	626	199	6261	5737	1717	.542	1979-80
Calgary	2140	981	837	322	7796	7195	2284	.534	1972-73
NY Islanders	2140	952	887	301	7510	6973	2205	.515	1972-73
Detroit	4910	2115	2030	765	15231	14983	4995	.509	1926-27
Toronto	5136	2204	2194	738	15988	16003	5146	.501	1917-18
NY Rangers	4910	2074	2066	770	15366	15441	4918	.501	1926-27
St. Louis	2522	1071	1072	379	8184	8348	2521	.500	1967-68
Colorado	1584	676	702	206	5698	5738	1558	.492	1979-80
Florida	460	183	192	85	1236	1279	451	.490	1993-94
Chicago	4910	2023	2128	759	14780	14952	4805	.489	1926-27
Pittsburgh	2522	1042	1136	344	8839	9260	2428	.481	1967-68
Washington	1984	828	904	252	6559	6893	1908	.481	1974-75
Dallas	2522	991	1131	400	8069	8586	2382	.472	1967-68
Los Angeles	2522	983	1173	366	8619	9283	2332	.462	1967-68
Anaheim	460	181	222	57	1253	1362	419	.455	1993-94
Phoenix	1584	618	763	203	5431	6014	1439	.454	1979-80
Carolina	1584	601	780	203	5114	5766	1405	.443	1979-80
Vancouver	2296	828	1133	335	7439	8440	1991	.434	1970-71
New Jersey	1984	711	996	277	6219	7232	1699	.428	1974-75
Nashville	82	28	47	7	190	261	63	.384	1998-99
Tampa Bay	544	176	306	62	1374	1783	414	.381	1992-93
San Jose	624	192	362	70	1687	2241	454	.364	1991-92
Ottawa	544	160	316	68	1369	1870	388	.357	1992-93

Defunct Clubs

Team	Games	Wins	Losses	Ties	Goals For	Goals Against	Points	%	First Season	Last Season
Ottawa Senators	542	258	221	63	1458	1333	579	.534	1917-18	1933-34
Montreal Maroons	622	271	260	91	1474	1405	633	.509	1924-25	1937-38
NY/Brooklyn Americans	784	255	402	127	1643	2182	637	.406	1925-26	1941-42
Hamilton Tigers	126	47	78	1	414	475	95	.377	1920-21	1924-25
Cleveland Barons	160	47	87	26	470	617	120	.375	1976-77	1977-78
Pittsburgh Pirates	212	67	122	23	376	519	157	.370	1925-26	1929-30
Calif./Oakland Seals	698	182	401	115	1826	2580	479	.343	1967-68	1975-76
St. Louis Eagles	48	11	31	6	86	144	28	.292	1934-35	1934-35
Quebec Bulldogs	24	4	20	0	91	177	8	.167	1919-20	1919-20
Montreal Wanderers	6	1	5	0	17	35	2	.167	1917-18	1917-18
Philadelphia Quakers	44	4	36	4	76	184	12	.136	1930-31	1930-31

Calgary totals include Atlanta, 1972-73 to 1979-80.
Carolina totals include Hartford, 1979-80 to 1996-97.
Colorado totals include Quebec, 1979-80 to 1994-95.
Dallas totals include Minnesota, 1967-68 to 1992-93.
Detroit totals include Cougars, 1926-27 to 1929-30, and Falcons, 1930-31 to 1931-32.
New Jersey totals include Kansas City, 1974-75 to 1975-76, and Colorado Rockies, 1976-77 to 1981-82.
Phoenix totals include Winnipeg, 1979-80 to 1995-96.
Toronto totals include Arenas, 1917-18 to 1918-19, and St. Patricks, 1919-20 to 1925-26.

1921-22

Team	GP	W	L	T	GF	GA	PTS
Ottawa	24	14	8	2	106	84	30
*Toronto	24	13	10	1	98	97	27
Montreal	24	12	11	1	88	94	25
Hamilton	24	7	17	0	88	105	14

Leading Scorers

Player	Club	GP	G	A	PTS	PIM
Broadbent, Punch	Ottawa	24	32	14	46	24
Denneny, Cy	Ottawa	22	27	12	39	18
Dye, Babe	Toronto	24	30	7	37	18
Malone, Joe	Hamilton	24	25	7	32	4
Cameron, Harry	Toronto	24	19	8	27	18
Denneny, Corb	Toronto	24	19	7	26	28
Noble, Reg	Toronto	24	17	8	25	10
Cleghorn, Odie	Montreal	23	21	3	24	26
Cleghorn, Sprague	Montreal	24	17	7	24	63
Reise Sr., Leo	Hamilton	24	9	14	23	8

1922-23

Team	GP	W	L	T	GF	GA	PTS
*Ottawa	24	14	9	1	77	54	29
Montreal	24	13	9	2	73	61	28
Toronto	24	13	10	1	82	88	27
Hamilton	24	6	18	0	81	110	12

Leading Scorers

Player	Club	GP	G	A	PTS	PIM
Dye, Babe	Toronto	22	26	11	37	19
Denneny, Cy	Ottawa	24	21	10	31	20
Adams, Jack	Toronto	23	19	9	28	42
Boucher, Billy	Montreal	24	23	4	27	52
Cleghorn, Odie	Montreal	24	19	7	26	14
Roach, Mickey	Hamilton	23	17	8	25	8
Boucher, George	Ottawa	23	15	9	24	44
Joliat, Aurel	Montreal	24	13	9	22	31
Noble, Reg	Toronto	24	12	10	22	41
Wilson, Cully	Hamilton	23	16	3	19	46

1923-24

Team	GP	W	L	T	GF	GA	PTS
Ottawa	24	16	8	0	74	54	32
*Montreal	24	13	11	0	59	48	26
Toronto	24	10	14	0	59	85	20
Hamilton	24	9	15	0	63	68	18

Leading Scorers

Player	Club	GP	G	A	PTS	PIM
Denneny, Cy	Ottawa	21	22	1	23	10
Boucher, Billy	Montreal	23	16	6	22	33
Joliat, Aurel	Montreal	24	15	5	20	19
Dye, Babe	Toronto	19	17	2	19	23
Boucher, George	Ottawa	21	14	5	19	28
Burch, Billy	Hamilton	24	16	2	18	4
Clancy, King	Ottawa	24	9	8	17	18
Adams, Jack	Toronto	22	13	3	16	49
Morenz, Howie	Montreal	24	13	3	16	20
Noble, Reg	Toronto	23	12	3	15	23

1924-25

Team	GP	W	L	T	GF	GA	PTS
Hamilton	30	19	10	1	90	60	39
Toronto	30	19	11	0	90	84	38
**Montreal	30	17	11	2	93	56	36
Ottawa	30	17	12	1	83	66	35
Mtl. Maroons	30	9	19	2	45	65	20
Boston	30	6	24	0	49	119	12

**NHL Champion (Stanley Cup won by Victoria Cougars, WCHL)

Leading Scorers

Player	Club	GP	G	A	PTS	PIM
Dye, Babe	Toronto	29	38	6	44	41
Denneny, Cy	Ottawa	28	27	15	42	16
Joliat, Aurel	Montreal	24	29	11	40	85
Morenz, Howie	Montreal	30	27	7	34	31
Boucher, Billy	Montreal	30	18	13	31	92
Adams, Jack	Toronto	27	21	8	29	66
Burch, Billy	Hamilton	27	20	4	24	10
Green, Red	Hamilton	30	19	4	23	63
Herberts, Jimmy	Boston	30	17	5	22	50
Day, Hap	Toronto	26	10	12	22	27

1925-26

Team	GP	W	L	T	GF	GA	PTS
Ottawa	36	24	8	4	77	42	52
*Mtl. Maroons	36	20	11	5	91	73	45
Pittsburgh	36	19	16	1	82	70	39
Boston	36	17	15	4	92	85	38
NY Americans	36	12	20	4	68	89	28
Toronto	36	12	21	3	92	114	27
Montreal	36	11	24	1	79	108	23

Leading Scorers

Player	Club	GP	G	A	PTS	PIM
Stewart, Nels	Mtl. Maroons	36	34	8	42	119
Denneny, Cy	Ottawa	36	24	12	36	18
Cooper, Carson	Boston	36	28	3	31	10
Herberts, Jimmy	Boston	36	26	5	31	47
Morenz, Howie	Montreal	31	23	3	26	39
Adams, Jack	Toronto	36	21	5	26	52
Joliat, Aurel	Montreal	35	17	9	26	52
Burch, Billy	NY Americans	36	22	3	25	33
Smith, Hooley	Ottawa	28	16	9	25	53
Nighbor, Frank	Ottawa	35	12	13	25	40

1926-27

Canadian Division

Team	GP	W	L	T	GF	GA	PTS
*Ottawa	44	30	10	4	86	69	64
Montreal	44	28	14	2	99	67	58
Mtl. Maroons	44	20	20	4	71	68	44
NY Americans	44	17	25	2	82	91	36
Toronto	44	15	24	5	79	94	35

American Division

Team	GP	W	L	T	GF	GA	PTS
New York	44	25	13	6	95	72	56
Boston	44	21	20	3	97	89	45
Chicago	44	19	22	3	115	116	41
Pittsburgh	44	15	26	3	79	108	33
Detroit	44	12	28	4	76	105	28

Leading Scorers

Player	Club	GP	G	A	PTS	PIM
Cook, Bill	New York	44	33	4	37	58
Irvin, Dick	Chicago	43	18	18	36	34
Morenz, Howie	Montreal	44	25	7	32	49
Fredrickson, Frank	Det., Bos.	41	18	13	31	46
Dye, Babe	Chicago	41	25	5	30	14
Bailey, Ace	Toronto	42	15	13	28	82
Boucher, Frank	New York	44	13	15	28	17
Burch, Billy	NY Americans	43	19	8	27	40
Oliver, Harry	Boston	42	18	6	24	17
Keats, Duke	Bos., Det.	42	16	8	24	52

1927-28

Canadian Division

Team	GP	W	L	T	GF	GA	PTS
Montreal	44	26	11	7	116	48	59
Mtl. Maroons	44	24	14	6	96	77	54
Ottawa	44	20	14	10	78	57	50
Toronto	44	18	18	8	89	88	44
NY Americans	44	11	27	6	63	128	28

American Division

Team	GP	W	L	T	GF	GA	PTS
Boston	44	20	13	11	77	70	51
*New York	44	19	16	9	94	79	47
Pittsburgh	44	19	17	8	67	76	46
Detroit	44	19	19	6	88	79	44
Chicago	44	7	34	3	68	134	17

Leading Scorers

Player	Club	GP	G	A	PTS	PIM
Morenz, Howie	Montreal	43	33	18	51	66
Joliat, Aurel	Montreal	44	28	11	39	105
Boucher, Frank	New York	44	23	12	35	15
Hay, George	Detroit	42	22	13	35	20
Stewart, Nels	Mtl. Maroons	41	27	7	34	104
Gagne, Art	Montreal	44	20	10	30	75
Cook, Bun	New York	44	14	14	28	45
Carson, Bill	Toronto	32	20	6	26	36
Finnigan, Frank	Ottawa	38	20	5	25	34
Cook, Bill	New York	43	18	6	24	42
Keats, Duke	Det., Chi.	38	14	10	24	60

1928-29

Canadian Division

Team	GP	W	L	T	GF	GA	PTS
Montreal	44	22	7	15	71	43	59
NY Americans	44	19	13	12	53	53	50
Toronto	44	21	18	5	85	69	47
Ottawa	44	14	17	13	54	67	41
Mtl. Maroons	44	15	20	9	67	65	39

American Division

Team	GP	W	L	T	GF	GA	PTS
*Boston	44	26	13	5	89	52	57
New York	44	21	13	10	72	65	52
Detroit	44	19	16	9	72	63	47
Pittsburgh	44	9	27	8	46	80	26
Chicago	44	7	29	8	33	85	22

Leading Scorers

Player	Club	GP	G	A	PTS	PIM
Bailey, Ace	Toronto	44	22	10	32	78
Stewart, Nels	Mtl. Maroons	44	21	8	29	74
Cooper, Carson	Detroit	43	18	9	27	14
Morenz, Howie	Montreal	42	17	10	27	47
Blair, Andy	Toronto	44	12	15	27	41
Boucher, Frank	New York	44	10	16	26	8
Oliver, Harry	Boston	43	17	6	23	24
Cook, Bill	New York	43	15	8	23	41
Ward, Jimmy	Mtl. Maroons	43	14	8	22	46

Seven players tied with 19 points

1929-30

Canadian Division

Team	GP	W	L	T	GF	GA	PTS
Mtl. Maroons	44	23	16	5	141	114	51
*Montreal	44	21	14	9	142	114	51
Ottawa	44	21	15	8	138	118	50
Toronto	44	17	21	6	116	124	40
NY Americans	44	14	25	5	113	161	33

American Division

Team	GP	W	L	T	GF	GA	PTS
Boston	44	38	5	1	179	98	77
Chicago	44	21	18	5	117	111	47
New York	44	17	17	10	136	143	44
Detroit	44	14	24	6	117	133	34
Pittsburgh	44	5	36	3	102	185	13

Leading Scorers

Player	Club	GP	G	A	PTS	PIM
Weiland, Cooney	Boston	44	43	30	73	27
Boucher, Frank	New York	42	26	36	62	16
Clapper, Dit	Boston	44	41	20	61	48
Cook, Bill	New York	44	29	30	59	56
Kilrea, Hec	Ottawa	44	36	22	58	72
Stewart, Nels	Mtl. Maroons	44	39	16	55	81
Morenz, Howie	Montreal	44	40	10	50	72
Himes, Normie	NY Americans	44	28	22	50	15
Lamb, Joe	Ottawa	44	29	20	49	119
Gainor, Norm	Boston	42	18	31	49	39

1930-31

Canadian Division

Team	GP	W	L	T	GF	GA	PTS
*Montreal	44	26	10	8	129	89	60
Toronto	44	22	13	9	118	99	53
Mtl. Maroons	44	20	18	6	105	106	46
NY Americans	44	18	16	10	76	74	46
Ottawa	44	10	30	4	91	142	24

American Division

Team	GP	W	L	T	GF	GA	PTS
Boston	44	28	10	6	143	90	62
Chicago	44	24	17	3	108	78	51
New York	44	19	16	9	106	87	47
Detroit	44	16	21	7	102	105	39
Philadelphia	44	4	36	4	76	184	12

Leading Scorers

Player	Club	GP	G	A	PTS	PIM
Morenz, Howie	Montreal	39	28	23	51	49
Goodfellow, Ebbie	Detroit	44	25	23	48	32
Conacher, Charlie	Toronto	37	31	12	43	78
Cook, Bill	New York	43	30	12	42	39
Bailey, Ace	Toronto	40	23	19	42	46
Primeau, Joe	Toronto	38	9	32	41	18
Stewart, Nels	Mtl. Maroons	42	25	14	39	75
Boucher, Frank	New York	44	12	27	39	20
Weiland, Cooney	Boston	44	25	13	38	14
Cook, Bun	New York	44	18	17	35	72
Joliat, Aurel	Montreal	43	13	22	35	73

1931-32

Canadian Division

Team	GP	W	L	T	GF	GA	PTS
Montreal	48	25	16	7	128	111	57
*Toronto	48	23	18	7	155	127	53
Mtl. Maroons	48	19	22	7	142	139	45
NY Americans	48	16	24	8	95	142	40

American Division

Team	GP	W	L	T	GF	GA	PTS
New York	48	23	17	8	134	112	54
Chicago	48	18	19	11	86	101	47
Detroit	48	18	20	10	95	108	46
Boston	48	15	21	12	122	117	42

Leading Scorers

Player	Club	GP	G	A	PTS	PIM
Jackson, Harvey	Toronto	48	28	25	53	63
Primeau, Joe	Toronto	46	13	37	50	25
Morenz, Howie	Montreal	48	24	25	49	46
Conacher, Charlie	Toronto	44	34	14	48	66
Cook, Bill	New York	48	34	14	48	33
Trottier, Dave	Mtl. Maroons	48	26	18	44	94
Smith, Reg	Mtl. Maroons	43	11	33	44	49
Siebert, Babe	Mtl. Maroons	48	21	18	39	64
Clapper, Dit	Boston	48	17	22	39	21
Joliat, Aurel	Montreal	48	15	24	39	46

1932-33

Canadian Division

Team	GP	W	L	T	GF	GA	PTS
Toronto	48	24	18	6	119	111	54
Mtl. Maroons	48	22	20	6	135	119	50
Montreal	48	18	25	5	92	115	41
NY Americans	48	15	22	11	91	118	41
Ottawa	48	11	27	10	88	131	32

American Division

Team	GP	W	L	T	GF	GA	PTS
Boston	48	25	15	8	124	88	58
Detroit	48	25	15	8	111	93	58
*New York	48	23	17	8	135	107	54
Chicago	48	16	20	12	88	101	44

Leading Scorers

Player	Club	GP	G	A	PTS	PIM
Cook, Bill	New York	48	28	22	50	51
Jackson, Harvey	Toronto	48	27	17	44	43
Northcott, Baldy	Mtl. Maroons	48	22	21	43	30
Smith, Reg	Mtl. Maroons	48	20	21	41	66
Haynes, Paul	Mtl. Maroons	48	16	25	41	18
Joliat, Aurel	Montreal	48	18	21	39	53
Barry, Marty	Boston	48	24	13	37	40
Cook, Bun	New York	48	22	15	37	35
Stewart, Nels	Boston	47	18	18	36	62
Morenz, Howie	Montreal	46	14	21	35	32
Gagnon, Johnny	Montreal	48	12	23	35	64
Shore, Eddie	Boston	48	8	27	35	102
Boucher, Frank	New York	47	7	28	35	4

1933-34

Canadian Division

Team	GP	W	L	T	GF	GA	PTS
Toronto	48	26	13	9	174	119	61
Montreal	48	22	20	6	99	101	50
Mtl. Maroons	48	19	18	11	117	122	49
NY Americans	48	15	23	10	104	132	40
Ottawa	48	13	29	6	115	143	32

American Division

Team	GP	W	L	T	GF	GA	PTS
Detroit	48	24	14	10	113	98	58
*Chicago	48	20	17	11	88	83	51
New York	48	21	19	8	120	113	50
Boston	48	18	25	5	111	130	41

Leading Scorers

Player	Club	GP	G	A	PTS	PIM
Conacher, Charlie	Toronto	42	32	20	52	38
Primeau, Joe	Toronto	45	14	32	46	8
Boucher, Frank	New York	48	14	30	44	4
Barry, Marty	Boston	48	27	12	39	12
Dillon, Cecil	New York	48	13	26	39	10
Stewart, Nels	Boston	48	21	17	38	68
Jackson, Harvey	Toronto	38	20	18	38	38
Joliat, Aurel	Montreal	48	22	15	37	27
Smith, Reg	Mtl. Maroons	47	18	19	37	58
Thompson, Paul	Chicago	48	20	16	36	17

1934-35

Canadian Division

Team	GP	W	L	T	GF	GA	PTS
Toronto	48	30	14	4	157	111	64
*Mtl. Maroons	48	24	19	5	123	92	53
Montreal	48	19	23	6	110	145	44
NY Americans	48	12	27	9	100	142	33
St. Louis	48	11	31	6	86	144	28

American Division

Team	GP	W	L	T	GF	GA	PTS
Boston	48	26	16	6	129	112	58
Chicago	48	26	17	5	118	88	57
New York	48	22	20	6	137	139	50
Detroit	48	19	22	7	127	114	45

Leading Scorers

Player	Club	GP	G	A	PTS	PIM
Conacher, Charlie	Toronto	47	36	21	57	24
Howe, Syd	St.L., Det.	50	22	25	47	34
Aurie, Larry	Detroit	48	17	29	46	24
Boucher, Frank	New York	48	13	32	45	2
Jackson, Harvey	Toronto	42	22	22	44	27
Lewis, Herb	Detroit	47	16	27	43	26
Chapman, Art	NY Americans	47	9	34	43	4
Barry, Marty	Boston	48	20	20	40	33
Schriner, Sweeney	NY Americans	48	18	22	40	6
Stewart, Nels	Boston	47	21	18	39	45
Thompson, Paul	Chicago	48	16	23	39	20

1935-36

Canadian Division

Team	GP	W	L	T	GF	GA	PTS
Mtl. Maroons	48	22	16	10	114	106	54
Toronto	48	23	19	6	126	106	52
NY Americans	48	16	25	7	109	122	39
Montreal	48	11	26	11	82	123	33

American Division

Team	GP	W	L	T	GF	GA	PTS
*Detroit	48	24	16	8	124	103	56
Boston	48	22	20	6	92	83	50
Chicago	48	21	19	8	93	92	50
New York	48	19	17	12	91	96	50

Leading Scorers

Player	Club	GP	G	A	PTS	PIM
Schriner, Sweeney	NY Americans	48	19	26	45	8
Barry, Marty	Detroit	48	21	19	40	16
Thompson, Paul	Chicago	45	17	23	40	19
Thoms, Bill	Toronto	48	23	15	38	29
Conacher, Charlie	Toronto	44	23	15	38	74
Smith, Reg	Mtl. Maroons	47	19	19	38	75
Romnes, Doc	Chicago	48	13	25	38	6
Chapman, Art	NY Americans	47	10	28	38	14
Lewis, Herb	Detroit	45	14	23	37	25
Northcott, Baldy	Mtl. Maroons	48	15	21	36	41

1936-37

Canadian Division

Team	GP	W	L	T	GF	GA	PTS
Montreal	48	24	18	6	115	111	54
Mtl. Maroons	48	22	17	9	126	110	53
Toronto	48	22	21	5	119	115	49
NY Americans	48	15	29	4	122	161	34

American Division

Team	GP	W	L	T	GF	GA	PTS
*Detroit	48	25	14	9	128	102	59
Boston	48	23	18	7	120	110	53
New York	48	19	20	9	117	106	47
Chicago	48	14	27	7	99	131	35

Leading Scorers

Player	Club	GP	G	A	PTS	PIM
Schriner, Sweeney	NY Americans	48	21	25	46	17
Apps Sr., Syl	Toronto	48	16	29	45	10
Barry, Marty	Detroit	48	17	27	44	6
Aurie, Larry	Detroit	45	23	20	43	20
Jackson, Harvey	Toronto	46	21	19	40	12
Gagnon, Johnny	Montreal	48	20	16	36	38
Gracie, Bob	Mtl. Maroons	47	11	25	36	18
Stewart, Nels	Bos., NYA	43	23	12	35	37
Thompson, Paul	Chicago	47	17	18	35	28
Cowley, Bill	Boston	46	13	22	35	4

1937-38

Canadian Division

Team	GP	W	L	T	GF	GA	PTS
Toronto	48	24	15	9	151	127	57
NY Americans	48	19	18	11	110	111	49
Montreal	48	18	17	13	123	128	49
Mtl. Maroons	48	12	30	6	101	149	30

American Division

Team	GP	W	L	T	GF	GA	PTS
Boston	48	30	11	7	142	89	67
New York	48	27	15	6	149	96	60
*Chicago	48	14	25	9	97	139	37
Detroit	48	12	25	11	99	133	35

Leading Scorers

Player	Club	GP	G	A	PTS	PIM
Drillon, Gordie	Toronto	48	26	26	52	4
Apps Sr., Syl	Toronto	47	21	29	50	9
Thompson, Paul	Chicago	48	22	22	44	14
Mantha, Georges	Montreal	47	23	19	42	12
Dillon, Cecil	New York	48	21	18	39	6
Cowley, Bill	Boston	48	17	22	39	8
Schriner, Sweeney	NY Americans	49	21	17	38	22
Thoms, Bill	Toronto	48	14	24	38	14
Smith, Clint	New York	48	14	23	37	0
Stewart, Nels	NY Americans	48	19	17	36	29
Colville, Neil	New York	45	17	19	36	11

1938-39

Team	GP	W	L	T	GF	GA	PTS
*Boston	48	36	10	2	156	76	74
New York	48	26	16	6	149	105	58
Toronto	48	19	20	9	114	107	47
NY Americans	48	17	21	10	119	157	44
Detroit	48	18	24	6	107	128	42
Montreal	48	15	24	9	115	146	39
Chicago	48	12	28	8	91	132	32

Leading Scorers

Player	Club	GP	G	A	PTS	PIM
Blake, Toe	Montreal	48	24	23	47	10
Schriner, Sweeney	NY Americans	48	13	31	44	20
Cowley, Bill	Boston	34	8	34	42	2
Smith, Clint	New York	48	21	20	41	2
Barry, Marty	Detroit	48	13	28	41	4
Apps Sr., Syl	Toronto	44	15	25	40	4
Anderson, Tom	NY Americans	48	13	27	40	10
Gottselig, Johnny	Chicago	48	16	23	39	15
Haynes, Paul	Montreal	47	5	33	38	27
Conacher, Roy	Boston	47	26	11	37	12
Carr, Lorne	NY Americans	46	19	18	37	16
Colville, Neil	New York	48	18	19	37	12
Watson, Phil	New York	48	15	22	37	42

1939-40

Team	GP	W	L	T	GF	GA	PTS
Boston	48	31	12	5	170	98	67
*New York	48	27	11	10	136	77	64
Toronto	48	25	17	6	134	110	56
Chicago	48	23	19	6	112	120	52
Detroit	48	16	26	6	90	126	38
NY Americans	48	15	29	4	106	140	34
Montreal	48	10	33	5	90	167	25

Leading Scorers

Player	Club	GP	G	A	PTS	PIM
Schmidt, Milt	Boston	48	22	30	52	37
Dumart, Woody	Boston	48	22	21	43	16
Bauer, Bobby	Boston	48	17	26	43	2
Drillon, Gordie	Toronto	43	21	19	40	13
Cowley, Bill	Boston	48	13	27	40	24
Hextall Sr., Bryan	New York	48	24	15	39	52
Colville, Neil	New York	48	19	19	38	22
Howe, Syd	Detroit	46	14	23	37	17
Blake, Toe	Montreal	48	17	19	36	48
Armstrong, Murray	NY Americans	48	16	20	36	12

Kraut Line center Milt Schmidt topped the NHL scoring list in 1939-40, followed by wingers Woody Dumart and Bobby Bauer. Seen here with Bill Quackenbush, Schmidt served as Bruins captain from 1950 to 1954 when he became coach.

Though less famous than older brothers Charlie and Lionel, Roy Conacher was a scoring sensation with the Boston Bruins and Chicago Black Hawks during the late '30s and 1940s. He joined his siblings in the Hockey Hall of Fame in 1998.

1942-43

Team	GP	W	L	T	GF	GA	PTS
*Detroit	50	25	14	11	169	124	61
Boston	50	24	17	9	195	176	57
Toronto	50	22	19	9	198	159	53
Montreal	50	19	19	12	181	191	50
Chicago	50	17	18	15	179	180	49
New York	50	11	31	8	161	253	30

Leading Scorers

Player	Club	GP	G	A	PTS	PIM
Bentley, Doug	Chicago	50	33	40	73	18
Cowley, Bill	Boston	48	27	45	72	10
Bentley, Max	Chicago	47	26	44	70	2
Patrick, Lynn	New York	50	22	39	61	28
Carr, Lorne	Toronto	50	27	33	60	15
Taylor, Billy	Toronto	50	18	42	60	2
Hextall Sr., Bryan	New York	50	27	32	59	28
Blake, Toe	Montreal	48	23	36	59	28
Lach, Elmer	Montreal	45	18	40	58	14
O'Connor, Buddy	Montreal	50	15	43	58	2

1943-44

Team	GP	W	L	T	GF	GA	PTS
*Montreal	50	38	5	7	234	109	83
Detroit	50	26	18	6	214	177	58
Toronto	50	23	23	4	214	174	50
Chicago	50	22	23	5	178	187	49
Boston	50	19	26	5	223	268	43
New York	50	6	39	5	162	310	17

Leading Scorers

Player	Club	GP	G	A	PTS	PIM
Cain, Herb	Boston	48	36	46	82	4
Bentley, Doug	Chicago	50	38	39	77	22
Carr, Lorne	Toronto	50	36	38	74	9
Liscombe, Carl	Detroit	50	36	37	73	17
Lach, Elmer	Montreal	48	24	48	72	23
Smith, Clint	Chicago	50	23	49	72	4
Cowley, Bill	Boston	36	30	41	71	12
Mosienko, Bill	Chicago	50	32	38	70	10
Jackson, Art	Boston	49	28	41	69	8
Bodnar, Gus	Toronto	50	22	40	62	18

1944-45

Team	GP	W	L	T	GF	GA	PTS
Montreal	50	38	8	4	228	121	80
Detroit	50	31	14	5	218	161	67
*Toronto	50	24	22	4	183	161	52
Boston	50	16	30	4	179	219	36
Chicago	50	13	30	7	141	194	33
New York	50	11	29	10	154	247	32

Leading Scorers

Player	Club	GP	G	A	PTS	PIM
Lach, Elmer	Montreal	50	26	54	80	37
Richard, Maurice	Montreal	50	50	23	73	36
Blake, Toe	Montreal	49	29	38	67	15
Cowley, Bill	Boston	49	25	40	65	2
Kennedy, Ted	Toronto	49	29	25	54	14
Mosienko, Bill	Chicago	50	28	26	54	0
Carveth, Joe	Detroit	50	26	28	54	6
DeMarco Sr., Ab	New York	50	24	30	54	10
Smith, Clint	Chicago	50	23	31	54	0
Howe, Syd	Detroit	46	17	36	53	6

1945-46

Team	GP	W	L	T	GF	GA	PTS
*Montreal	50	28	17	5	172	134	61
Boston	50	24	18	8	167	156	56
Chicago	50	23	20	7	200	178	53
Detroit	50	20	20	10	146	159	50
Toronto	50	19	24	7	174	185	45
New York	50	13	28	9	144	191	35

Leading Scorers

Player	Club	GP	G	A	PTS	PIM
Bentley, Max	Chicago	47	31	30	61	6
Stewart, Gaye	Toronto	50	37	15	52	8
Blake, Toe	Montreal	50	29	21	50	2
Smith, Clint	Chicago	50	26	24	50	2
Richard, Maurice	Montreal	50	27	21	48	50
Mosienko, Bill	Chicago	40	18	30	48	12
DeMarco Sr., Ab	New York	50	20	27	47	20
Lach, Elmer	Montreal	50	13	34	47	34
Kaleta, Alex	Chicago	49	19	27	46	17
Taylor, Billy	Toronto	48	23	18	41	14
Horeck, Pete	Chicago	50	20	21	41	34

1946-47

Team	GP	W	L	T	GF	GA	PTS
Montreal	60	34	16	10	189	138	78
*Toronto	60	31	19	10	209	172	72
Boston	60	26	23	11	190	175	63
Detroit	60	22	27	11	190	193	55
New York	60	22	32	6	167	186	50
Chicago	60	19	37	4	193	274	42

Leading Scorers

Player	Club	GP	G	A	PTS	PIM
Bentley, Max	Chicago	60	29	43	72	12
Richard, Maurice	Montreal	60	45	26	71	69
Taylor, Billy	Detroit	60	17	46	63	35
Schmidt, Milt	Boston	59	27	35	62	40
Kennedy, Ted	Toronto	60	28	32	60	27
Bentley, Doug	Chicago	52	21	34	55	18
Bauer, Bobby	Boston	58	30	24	54	4
Conacher, Roy	Detroit	60	30	24	54	6
Mosienko, Bill	Chicago	59	25	27	52	2
Dumart, Woody	Boston	60	24	28	52	12

1947-48

Team	GP	W	L	T	GF	GA	PTS
*Toronto	60	32	15	13	182	143	77
Detroit	60	30	18	12	187	148	72
Boston	60	23	24	13	167	168	59
New York	60	21	26	13	176	201	55
Montreal	60	20	29	11	147	169	51
Chicago	60	20	34	6	195	225	46

Leading Scorers

Player	Club	GP	G	A	PTS	PIM
Lach, Elmer	Montreal	60	30	31	61	72
O'Connor, Buddy	New York	60	24	36	60	8
Bentley, Doug	Chicago	60	20	37	57	16
Stewart, Gaye	Tor., Chi.	61	27	29	56	83
Bentley, Max	Chi., Tor.	59	26	28	54	14
Poile, Bud	Tor., Chi.	58	25	29	54	17
Richard, Maurice	Montreal	53	28	25	53	89
Apps Sr., Syl	Toronto	55	26	27	53	12
Lindsay, Ted	Detroit	60	33	19	52	95
Conacher, Roy	Chicago	52	22	27	49	4

1948-49

Team	GP	W	L	T	GF	GA	PTS
Detroit	60	34	19	7	195	145	75
Boston	60	29	23	8	178	163	66
Montreal	60	28	23	9	152	126	65
*Toronto	60	22	25	13	147	161	57
Chicago	60	21	31	8	173	211	50
New York	60	18	31	11	133	172	47

Leading Scorers

Player	Club	GP	G	A	PTS	PIM
Conacher, Roy	Chicago	60	26	42	68	8
Bentley, Doug	Chicago	58	23	43	66	38
Abel, Sid	Detroit	60	28	26	54	49
Lindsay, Ted	Detroit	50	26	28	54	97
Conacher, Jim	Det., Chi.	59	26	23	49	43
Ronty, Paul	Boston	60	20	29	49	11
Watson, Harry	Toronto	60	26	19	45	0
Reay, Billy	Montreal	60	22	23	45	33
Bodnar, Gus	Chicago	59	19	26	45	14
Peirson, Johnny	Boston	59	22	21	43	45

1949-50

Team	GP	W	L	T	GF	GA	PTS
*Detroit	70	37	19	14	229	164	88
Montreal	70	29	22	19	172	150	77
Toronto	70	31	27	12	176	173	74
New York	70	28	31	11	170	189	67
Boston	70	22	32	16	198	228	60
Chicago	70	22	38	10	203	244	54

Leading Scorers

Player	Club	GP	G	A	PTS	PIM
Lindsay, Ted	Detroit	69	23	55	78	141
Abel, Sid	Detroit	69	34	35	69	46
Howe, Gordie	Detroit	70	35	33	68	69
Richard, Maurice	Montreal	70	43	22	65	114
Ronty, Paul	Boston	70	23	36	59	8
Conacher, Roy	Chicago	70	25	31	56	16
Bentley, Doug	Chicago	64	20	33	53	28
Peirson, Johnny	Boston	57	27	25	52	49
Prystai, Metro	Chicago	65	29	22	51	31
Guidolin, Bep	Chicago	70	17	34	51	42

1940-41

Team	GP	W	L	T	GF	GA	PTS
*Boston	48	27	8	13	168	102	67
Toronto	48	28	14	6	145	99	62
Detroit	48	21	16	11	112	102	53
New York	48	21	19	8	143	125	50
Chicago	48	16	25	7	112	139	39
Montreal	48	16	26	6	121	147	38
NY Americans	48	8	29	11	99	186	27

Leading Scorers

Player	Club	GP	G	A	PTS	PIM
Cowley, Bill	Boston	46	17	45	62	16
Hextall Sr., Bryan	New York	48	26	18	44	16
Drillon, Gordie	Toronto	42	23	21	44	2
Apps Sr., Syl	Toronto	41	20	24	44	6
Patrick, Lynn	New York	48	20	24	44	12
Howe, Syd	Detroit	48	20	24	44	8
Colville, Neil	New York	48	14	28	42	28
Wiseman, Eddie	Boston	48	16	24	40	10
Bauer, Bobby	Boston	48	17	22	39	2
Schriner, Sweeney	Toronto	48	24	14	38	6
Conacher, Roy	Boston	40	24	14	38	7
Schmidt, Milt	Boston	44	13	25	38	23

1941-42

Team	GP	W	L	T	GF	GA	PTS
New York	48	29	17	2	177	143	60
*Toronto	48	27	18	3	158	136	57
Boston	48	25	17	6	160	118	56
Chicago	48	22	23	3	145	155	47
Detroit	48	19	25	4	140	147	42
Montreal	48	18	27	3	134	173	39
Brooklyn	48	16	29	3	133	175	35

Leading Scorers

Player	Club	GP	G	A	PTS	PIM
Hextall Sr., Bryan	New York	48	24	32	56	30
Patrick, Lynn	New York	47	32	22	54	18
Grosso, Don	Detroit	48	23	30	53	13
Watson, Phil	New York	48	15	37	52	48
Abel, Sid	Detroit	48	18	31	49	45
Blake, Toe	Montreal	47	17	28	45	19
Thoms, Bill	Chicago	47	15	30	45	8
Drillon, Gordie	Toronto	48	23	18	41	6
Apps Sr., Syl	Toronto	38	18	23	41	0
Anderson, Tom	Brooklyn	48	12	29	41	54

Ted Lindsay watches as a shot taken by Gordie Howe eludes Canadiens goalie Gerry McNeil. Linemates Lindsay, Sid Abel and Howe finished 1-2-3 in NHL scoring in 1949-50. Howe and Lindsay finished back-to-back atop the scoring list in 1951-52 and 1952-53.

1950-51

Team	GP	W	L	T	GF	GA	PTS
Detroit	70	44	13	13	236	139	101
*Toronto	70	41	16	13	212	138	95
Montreal	70	25	30	15	173	184	65
Boston	70	22	30	18	178	197	62
New York	70	20	29	21	169	201	61
Chicago	70	13	47	10	171	280	36

Leading Scorers

Player	Club	GP	G	A	PTS	PIM
Howe, Gordie	Detroit	70	43	43	86	74
Richard, Maurice	Montreal	65	42	24	66	97
Bentley, Max	Toronto	67	21	41	62	34
Abel, Sid	Detroit	69	23	38	61	30
Schmidt, Milt	Boston	62	22	39	61	33
Kennedy, Ted	Toronto	63	18	43	61	32
Lindsay, Ted	Detroit	67	24	35	59	110
Sloan, Tod	Toronto	70	31	25	56	105
Kelly, Red	Detroit	70	17	37	54	24
Smith, Sid	Toronto	70	30	21	51	10
Gardner, Cal	Toronto	66	23	28	51	42

1951-52

Team	GP	W	L	T	GF	GA	PTS
*Detroit	70	44	14	12	215	133	100
Montreal	70	34	26	10	195	164	78
Toronto	70	29	25	16	168	157	74
Boston	70	25	29	16	162	176	66
New York	70	23	34	13	192	219	59
Chicago	70	17	44	9	158	241	43

Leading Scorers

Player	Club	GP	G	A	PTS	PIM
Howe, Gordie	Detroit	70	47	39	86	78
Lindsay, Ted	Detroit	70	30	39	69	123
Lach, Elmer	Montreal	70	15	50	65	36
Raleigh, Don	New York	70	19	42	61	14
Smith, Sid	Toronto	70	27	30	57	6
Geoffrion, Bernie	Montreal	67	30	24	54	66
Mosienko, Bill	Chicago	70	31	22	53	10
Abel, Sid	Detroit	62	17	36	53	32
Kennedy, Ted	Toronto	70	19	33	52	33
Schmidt, Milt	Boston	69	21	29	50	57
Peirson, Johnny	Boston	68	20	30	50	30

1952-53

Team	GP	W	L	T	GF	GA	PTS
Detroit	70	36	16	18	222	133	90
*Montreal	70	28	23	19	155	148	75
Boston	70	28	29	13	152	172	69
Chicago	70	27	28	15	169	175	69
Toronto	70	27	30	13	156	167	67
New York	70	17	37	16	152	211	50

Leading Scorers

Player	Club	GP	G	A	PTS	PIM
Howe, Gordie	Detroit	70	49	46	95	57
Lindsay, Ted	Detroit	70	32	39	71	111
Richard, Maurice	Montreal	70	28	33	61	112
Hergesheimer, Wally	New York	70	30	29	59	10
Delvecchio, Alex	Detroit	70	16	43	59	28
Ronty, Paul	New York	70	16	38	54	20
Prystai, Metro	Detroit	70	16	34	50	12
Kelly, Red	Detroit	70	19	27	46	8
Olmstead, Bert	Montreal	69	17	28	45	83
Mackell, Fleming	Boston	65	27	17	44	63
McFadden, Jim	Chicago	70	23	21	44	29

1953-54

Team	GP	W	L	T	GF	GA	PTS
*Detroit	70	37	19	14	191	132	88
Montreal	70	35	24	11	195	141	81
Toronto	70	32	24	14	152	131	78
Boston	70	32	28	10	177	181	74
New York	70	29	31	10	161	182	68
Chicago	70	12	51	7	133	242	31

Leading Scorers

Player	Club	GP	G	A	PTS	PIM
Howe, Gordie	Detroit	70	33	48	81	109
Richard, Maurice	Montreal	70	37	30	67	112
Lindsay, Ted	Detroit	70	26	36	62	110
Geoffrion, Bernie	Montreal	54	29	25	54	87
Olmstead, Bert	Montreal	70	15	37	52	85
Kelly, Red	Detroit	62	16	33	49	18
Reibel, Earl	Detroit	69	15	33	48	18
Sandford, Ed	Boston	70	16	31	47	42
Mackell, Fleming	Boston	67	15	32	47	60
Mosdell, Kenny	Montreal	67	22	24	46	64
Ronty, Paul	New York	70	13	33	46	18

1954-55

Team	GP	W	L	T	GF	GA	PTS
*Detroit	70	42	17	11	204	134	95
Montreal	70	41	18	11	228	157	93
Toronto	70	24	24	22	147	135	70
Boston	70	23	26	21	169	188	67
New York	70	17	35	18	150	210	52
Chicago	70	13	40	17	161	235	43

Leading Scorers

Player	Club	GP	G	A	PTS	PIM
Geoffrion, Bernie	Montreal	70	38	37	75	57
Richard, Maurice	Montreal	67	38	36	74	125
Béliveau, Jean	Montreal	70	37	36	73	58
Reibel, Earl	Detroit	70	25	41	66	15
Howe, Gordie	Detroit	64	29	33	62	68
Sullivan, Red	Chicago	69	19	42	61	51
Olmstead, Bert	Montreal	70	10	48	58	103
Smith, Sid	Toronto	70	33	21	54	14
Mosdell, Kenny	Montreal	70	22	32	54	82
Lewicki, Danny	New York	70	29	24	53	8

1955-56

Team	GP	W	L	T	GF	GA	PTS
*Montreal	70	45	15	10	222	131	100
Detroit	70	30	24	16	183	148	76
New York	70	32	28	10	204	203	74
Toronto	70	24	33	13	153	181	61
Boston	70	23	34	13	147	185	59
Chicago	70	19	39	12	155	216	50

Leading Scorers

Player	Club	GP	G	A	PTS	PIM
Béliveau, Jean	Montreal	70	47	41	88	143
Howe, Gordie	Detroit	70	38	41	79	100
Richard, Maurice	Montreal	70	38	33	71	89
Olmstead, Bert	Montreal	70	14	56	70	94
Sloan, Tod	Toronto	70	37	29	66	100
Bathgate, Andy	New York	70	19	47	66	59
Geoffrion, Bernie	Montreal	59	29	33	62	66
Reibel, Earl	Detroit	68	17	39	56	10
Delvecchio, Alex	Detroit	70	25	26	51	24
Creighton, Dave	New York	70	20	31	51	43
Gadsby, Bill	New York	70	9	42	51	84

1956-57

Team	GP	W	L	T	GF	GA	PTS
Detroit	70	38	20	12	198	157	88
*Montreal	70	35	23	12	210	155	82
Boston	70	34	24	12	195	174	80
New York	70	26	30	14	184	227	66
Toronto	70	21	34	15	174	192	57
Chicago	70	16	39	15	169	225	47

Leading Scorers

Player	Club	GP	G	A	PTS	PIM
Howe, Gordie	Detroit	70	44	45	89	72
Lindsay, Ted	Detroit	70	30	55	85	103
Béliveau, Jean	Montreal	69	33	51	84	105
Bathgate, Andy	New York	70	27	50	77	60
Litzenberger, Ed	Chicago	70	32	32	64	48
Richard, Maurice	Montreal	63	33	29	62	74
McKenney, Don	Boston	69	21	39	60	31
Moore, Dickie	Montreal	70	29	29	58	56
Richard, Henri	Montreal	63	18	36	54	71
Ullman, Norm	Detroit	64	16	36	52	47

1957-58

Team	GP	W	L	T	GF	GA	PTS
*Montreal	70	43	17	10	250	158	96
New York	70	32	25	13	195	188	77
Detroit	70	29	29	12	176	207	70
Boston	70	27	28	15	199	194	69
Chicago	70	24	39	7	163	202	55
Toronto	70	21	38	11	192	226	53

Leading Scorers

Player	Club	GP	G	A	PTS	PIM
Moore, Dickie	Montreal	70	36	48	84	65
Richard, Henri	Montreal	67	28	52	80	56
Bathgate, Andy	New York	65	30	48	78	42
Howe, Gordie	Detroit	64	33	44	77	40
Horvath, Bronco	Boston	67	30	36	66	71
Litzenberger, Ed	Chicago	70	32	30	62	63
Mackell, Fleming	Boston	70	20	40	60	72
Béliveau, Jean	Montreal	55	27	32	59	93
Delvecchio, Alex	Detroit	70	21	38	59	22
McKenney, Don	Boston	70	28	30	58	22

1958-59

Team	GP	W	L	T	GF	GA	PTS
*Montreal	70	39	18	13	258	158	91
Boston	70	32	29	9	205	215	73
Chicago	70	28	29	13	197	208	69
Toronto	70	27	32	11	189	201	65
New York	70	26	32	12	201	217	64
Detroit	70	25	37	8	167	218	58

Leading Scorers

Player	Club	GP	G	A	PTS	PIM
Moore, Dickie	Montreal	70	41	55	96	61
Béliveau, Jean	Montreal	64	45	46	91	67
Bathgate, Andy	New York	70	40	48	88	48
Howe, Gordie	Detroit	70	32	46	78	57
Litzenberger, Ed	Chicago	70	33	44	77	37
Geoffrion, Bernie	Montreal	59	22	44	66	30
Sullivan, Red	New York	70	21	42	63	56
Hebenton, Andy	New York	70	33	29	62	8
McKenney, Don	Boston	70	32	30	62	20
Sloan, Tod	Chicago	59	27	35	62	79

1959-60

Team	GP	W	L	T	GF	GA	PTS
*Montreal	70	40	18	12	255	178	92
Toronto	70	35	26	9	199	195	79
Chicago	70	28	29	13	191	180	69
Detroit	70	26	29	15	186	197	67
Boston	70	28	34	8	220	241	64
New York	70	17	38	15	187	247	49

Leading Scorers

Player	Club	GP	G	A	PTS	PIM
Hull, Bobby	Chicago	70	39	42	81	68
Horvath, Bronco	Boston	68	39	41	80	60
Béliveau, Jean	Montreal	60	34	40	74	57
Bathgate, Andy	New York	70	26	48	74	28
Richard, Henri	Montreal	70	30	43	73	66
Howe, Gordie	Detroit	70	28	45	73	46
Geoffrion, Bernie	Montreal	59	30	41	71	36
McKenney, Don	Boston	70	20	49	69	28
Stasiuk, Vic	Boston	69	29	39	68	121
Prentice, Dean	New York	70	32	34	66	43

1960-61

Team	GP	W	L	T	GF	GA	PTS
Montreal	70	41	19	10	254	188	92
Toronto	70	39	19	12	234	176	90
*Chicago	70	29	24	17	198	180	75
Detroit	70	25	29	16	195	215	66
New York	70	22	38	10	204	248	54
Boston	70	15	42	13	176	254	43

Leading Scorers

Player	Club	GP	G	A	PTS	PIM
Geoffrion, Bernie	Montreal	64	50	45	95	29
Béliveau, Jean	Montreal	69	32	58	90	57
Mahovlich, Frank	Toronto	70	48	36	84	131
Bathgate, Andy	New York	70	29	48	77	22
Howe, Gordie	Detroit	64	23	49	72	30
Ullman, Norm	Detroit	70	28	42	70	34
Kelly, Red	Toronto	64	20	50	70	12
Moore, Dickie	Montreal	57	35	34	69	62
Richard, Henri	Montreal	70	24	44	68	91
Delvecchio, Alex	Detroit	70	27	35	62	26

1961-62

Team	GP	W	L	T	GF	GA	PTS
Montreal	70	42	14	14	259	166	98
*Toronto	70	37	22	11	232	180	85
Chicago	70	31	26	13	217	186	75
New York	70	26	32	12	195	207	64
Detroit	70	23	33	14	184	219	60
Boston	70	15	47	8	177	306	38

Leading Scorers

Player	Club	GP	G	A	PTS	PIM
Hull, Bobby	Chicago	70	50	34	84	35
Bathgate, Andy	New York	70	28	56	84	44
Howe, Gordie	Detroit	70	33	44	77	54
Mikita, Stan	Chicago	70	25	52	77	97
Mahovlich, Frank	Toronto	70	33	38	71	87
Delvecchio, Alex	Detroit	70	26	43	69	18
Backstrom, Ralph	Montreal	66	27	38	65	29
Ullman, Norm	Detroit	70	26	38	64	54
Hay, Bill	Chicago	60	11	52	63	34
Provost, Claude	Montreal	70	33	29	62	22

While players like Dickie Moore (left) were topping the scoring list, men like Doug Harvey and Jacques Plante (below) were responsible for keeping the puck out of the Montreal net. Harvey won the Norris Trophy four times in five years when the Canadiens monopolized the Stanley Cup from 1956 to 1960. Plante won the Vezina Trophy five years in a row.

1962-63

Team	GP	W	L	T	GF	GA	PTS
*Toronto	70	35	23	12	221	180	82
Chicago	70	32	21	17	194	178	81
Montreal	70	28	19	23	225	183	79
Detroit	70	32	25	13	200	194	77
New York	70	22	36	12	211	233	56
Boston	70	14	39	17	198	281	45

Leading Scorers

Player	Club	GP	G	A	PTS	PIM
Howe, Gordie	Detroit	70	38	48	86	100
Bathgate, Andy	New York	70	35	46	81	54
Mikita, Stan	Chicago	65	31	45	76	69
Mahovlich, Frank	Toronto	67	36	37	73	56
Richard, Henri	Montreal	67	23	50	73	57
Béliveau, Jean	Montreal	69	18	49	67	68
Bucyk, John	Boston	69	27	39	66	36
Delvecchio, Alex	Detroit	70	20	44	64	8
Hull, Bobby	Chicago	65	31	31	62	27
Oliver, Murray	Boston	65	22	40	62	38

1963-64

Team	GP	W	L	T	GF	GA	PTS
Montreal	70	36	21	13	209	167	85
Chicago	70	36	22	12	218	169	84
*Toronto	70	33	25	12	192	172	78
Detroit	70	30	29	11	191	204	71
New York	70	22	38	10	186	242	54
Boston	70	18	40	12	170	212	48

Leading Scorers

Player	Club	GP	G	A	PTS	PIM
Mikita, Stan	Chicago	70	39	50	89	146
Hull, Bobby	Chicago	70	43	44	87	50
Béliveau, Jean	Montreal	68	28	50	78	42
Bathgate, Andy	NYR, Tor.	71	19	58	77	34
Howe, Gordie	Detroit	69	26	47	73	70
Wharram, Kenny	Chicago	70	39	32	71	18
Oliver, Murray	Boston	70	24	44	68	41
Goyette, Phil	New York	67	24	41	65	15
Gilbert, Rod	New York	70	24	40	64	62
Keon, Dave	Toronto	70	23	37	60	6

1964-65

Team	GP	W	L	T	GF	GA	PTS
Detroit	70	40	23	7	224	175	87
*Montreal	70	36	23	11	211	185	83
Chicago	70	34	28	8	224	176	76
Toronto	70	30	26	14	204	173	74
New York	70	20	38	12	179	246	52
Boston	70	21	43	6	166	253	48

Leading Scorers

Player	Club	GP	G	A	PTS	PIM
Mikita, Stan	Chicago	70	28	59	87	154
Ullman, Norm	Detroit	70	42	41	83	70
Howe, Gordie	Detroit	70	29	47	76	104
Hull, Bobby	Chicago	61	39	32	71	32
Delvecchio, Alex	Detroit	68	25	42	67	16
Provost, Claude	Montreal	70	27	37	64	28
Gilbert, Rod	New York	70	25	36	61	52
Pilote, Pierre	Chicago	68	14	45	59	162
Bucyk, John	Boston	68	26	29	55	24
Backstrom, Ralph	Montreal	70	25	30	55	41
Esposito, Phil	Chicago	70	23	32	55	44

1965-66

Team	GP	W	L	T	GF	GA	PTS
*Montreal	70	41	21	8	239	173	90
Chicago	70	37	25	8	240	187	82
Toronto	70	34	25	11	208	187	79
Detroit	70	31	27	12	221	194	74
Boston	70	21	43	6	174	275	48
New York	70	18	41	11	195	261	47

Leading Scorers

Player	Club	GP	G	A	PTS	PIM
Hull, Bobby	Chicago	65	54	43	97	70
Mikita, Stan	Chicago	68	30	48	78	58
Rousseau, Bobby	Montreal	70	30	48	78	20
Béliveau, Jean	Montreal	67	29	48	77	50
Howe, Gordie	Detroit	70	29	46	75	83
Ullman, Norm	Detroit	70	31	41	72	35
Delvecchio, Alex	Detroit	70	31	38	69	16
Nevin, Bob	New York	69	29	33	62	10
Richard, Henri	Montreal	62	22	39	61	47
Oliver, Murray	Boston	70	18	42	60	30

1966-67

Team	GP	W	L	T	GF	GA	PTS
Chicago	70	41	17	12	264	170	94
Montreal	70	32	25	13	202	188	77
*Toronto	70	32	27	11	204	211	75
New York	70	30	28	12	188	189	72
Detroit	70	27	39	4	212	241	58
Boston	70	17	43	10	182	253	44

Leading Scorers

Player	Club	GP	G	A	PTS	PIM
Mikita, Stan	Chicago	70	35	62	97	12
Hull, Bobby	Chicago	66	52	28	80	52
Ullman, Norm	Detroit	68	26	44	70	26
Wharram, Kenny	Chicago	70	31	34	65	21
Howe, Gordie	Detroit	69	25	40	65	53
Rousseau, Bobby	Montreal	68	19	44	63	58
Esposito, Phil	Chicago	69	21	40	61	40
Goyette, Phil	New York	70	12	49	61	6
Mohns, Doug	Chicago	61	25	35	60	58
Richard, Henri	Montreal	65	21	34	55	28
Delvecchio, Alex	Detroit	70	17	38	55	10

Stan Mikita is alone in front of Roger Crozier, while Bill Gadsby and teammate Doug Mohns watch from the corner. Mikita was the last player to lead the NHL in scoring during the "Original Six" era. His 97 points in 1966-67 tied Bobby Hull's pre-expansion record.

1967-68

East Division

Team	GP	W	L	T	GF	GA	PTS
*Montreal	74	42	22	10	236	167	94
New York	74	39	23	12	226	183	90
Boston	74	37	27	10	259	216	84
Chicago	74	32	26	16	212	222	80
Toronto	74	33	31	10	209	176	76
Detroit	74	27	35	12	245	257	66

West Division

Team	GP	W	L	T	GF	GA	PTS
Philadelphia	74	31	32	11	173	179	73
Los Angeles	74	31	33	10	200	224	72
St. Louis	74	27	31	16	177	191	70
Minnesota	74	27	32	15	191	226	69
Pittsburgh	74	27	34	13	195	216	67
Oakland	74	15	42	17	153	219	47

Leading Scorers

Player	Club	GP	G	A	PTS	PIM
Mikita, Stan	Chicago	72	40	47	87	14
Esposito, Phil	Boston	74	35	49	84	21
Howe, Gordie	Detroit	74	39	43	82	53
Ratelle, Jean	New York	74	32	46	78	18
Gilbert, Rod	New York	73	29	48	77	12
Hull, Bobby	Chicago	71	44	31	75	39
Ullman, Norm	Det., Tor.	71	35	37	72	28
Delvecchio, Alex	Detroit	74	22	48	70	14
Bucyk, John	Boston	72	30	39	69	8
Wharram, Kenny	Chicago	74	27	42	69	18

1968-69

East Division

Team	GP	W	L	T	GF	GA	PTS
*Montreal	76	46	19	11	271	202	103
Boston	76	42	18	16	303	221	100
New York	76	41	26	9	231	196	91
Toronto	76	35	26	15	234	217	85
Detroit	76	33	31	12	239	221	78
Chicago	76	34	33	9	280	246	77

West Division

Team	GP	W	L	T	GF	GA	PTS
St. Louis	76	37	25	14	204	157	88
Oakland	76	29	36	11	219	251	69
Philadelphia	76	20	35	21	174	225	61
Los Angeles	76	24	42	10	185	260	58
Pittsburgh	76	20	45	11	189	252	51
Minnesota	76	18	43	5	189	270	51

Leading Scorers

Player	Club	GP	G	A	PTS	PIM
Esposito, Phil	Boston	74	49	77	126	79
Hull, Bobby	Chicago	74	58	49	107	48
Howe, Gordie	Detroit	76	44	59	103	58
Mikita, Stan	Chicago	74	30	67	97	52
Hodge, Ken	Boston	75	45	45	90	75
Cournoyer, Yvan	Montreal	76	43	44	87	31
Delvecchio, Alex	Detroit	72	25	58	83	8
Berenson, Red	St. Louis	76	35	47	82	43
Béliveau, Jean	Montreal	69	33	49	82	55
Mahovlich, Frank	Detroit	76	49	29	78	38
Ratelle, Jean	New York	75	32	46	78	26

1969-70

East Division

Team	GP	W	L	T	GF	GA	PTS
Chicago	76	45	22	9	250	170	99
*Boston	76	40	17	19	277	216	99
Detroit	76	40	21	15	246	199	95
New York	76	38	22	16	246	189	92
Montreal	76	38	22	16	244	201	92
Toronto	76	29	34	13	222	242	71

West Division

Team	GP	W	L	T	GF	GA	PTS
St. Louis	76	37	27	12	224	179	86
Pittsburgh	76	26	38	12	182	238	64
Minnesota	76	19	35	22	224	257	60
Oakland	76	22	40	14	169	243	58
Philadelphia	76	17	35	24	197	225	58
Los Angeles	76	14	52	10	168	290	38

Leading Scorers

Player	Club	GP	G	A	PTS	PIM
Orr, Bobby	Boston	76	33	87	120	125
Esposito, Phil	Boston	76	43	56	99	50
Mikita, Stan	Chicago	76	39	47	86	50
Goyette, Phil	St. Louis	72	29	49	78	16
Tkaczuk, Walt	New York	76	27	50	77	38
Ratelle, Jean	New York	75	32	42	74	28
Berenson, Red	St. Louis	67	33	39	72	38
Parise, Jean-Paul	Minnesota	74	24	48	72	72
Howe, Gordie	Detroit	76	31	40	71	58
Mahovlich, Frank	Detroit	74	38	32	70	59
Balon, Dave	New York	76	33	37	70	100
McKenzie, John	Boston	72	29	41	70	114

1970-71

East Division

Team	GP	W	L	T	GF	GA	PTS
Boston	78	57	14	7	399	207	121
New York	78	49	18	11	259	177	109
*Montreal	78	42	23	13	291	216	97
Toronto	78	37	33	8	248	211	82
Buffalo	78	24	39	15	217	291	63
Vancouver	78	24	46	8	229	296	56
Detroit	78	22	45	11	209	308	55

West Division

Team	GP	W	L	T	GF	GA	PTS
Chicago	78	49	20	9	277	184	107
St. Louis	78	34	25	19	223	208	87
Philadelphia	78	28	33	17	207	225	73
Minnesota	78	28	34	16	191	223	72
Los Angeles	78	25	40	13	239	303	63
Pittsburgh	78	21	37	20	221	240	62
California	78	20	53	5	199	320	45

Leading Scorers

Player	Club	GP	G	A	PTS	PIM
Esposito, Phil	Boston	78	76	76	152	71
Orr, Bobby	Boston	78	37	102	139	91
Bucyk, John	Boston	78	51	65	116	8
Hodge, Ken	Boston	78	43	62	105	113
Hull, Bobby	Chicago	78	44	52	96	32
Ullman, Norm	Toronto	73	34	51	85	24
Cashman, Wayne	Boston	77	21	58	79	100
McKenzie, John	Boston	65	31	46	77	120
Keon, Dave	Toronto	76	38	38	76	4
Béliveau, Jean	Montreal	70	25	51	76	40
Stanfield, Fred	Boston	75	24	52	76	12

1971-72

East Division

Team	GP	W	L	T	GF	GA	PTS
*Boston	78	54	13	11	330	204	119
New York	78	48	17	13	317	192	109
Montreal	78	46	16	16	307	205	108
Toronto	78	33	31	14	209	208	80
Detroit	78	33	35	10	261	262	76
Buffalo	78	16	43	19	203	289	51
Vancouver	78	20	50	8	203	297	48

West Division

Team	GP	W	L	T	GF	GA	PTS
Chicago	78	46	17	15	256	166	107
Minnesota	78	37	29	12	212	191	86
St. Louis	78	28	39	11	208	247	67
Pittsburgh	78	26	38	14	220	258	66
Philadelphia	78	26	38	14	200	236	66
California	78	21	39	18	216	288	60
Los Angeles	78	20	49	9	206	305	49

Leading Scorers

Player	Club	GP	G	A	PTS	PIM
Esposito, Phil	Boston	76	66	67	133	76
Orr, Bobby	Boston	76	37	80	117	106
Ratelle, Jean	New York	63	46	63	109	4
Hadfield, Vic	New York	78	50	56	106	142
Gilbert, Rod	New York	73	43	54	97	64
Mahovlich, Frank	Montreal	76	43	53	96	36
Hull, Bobby	Chicago	78	50	43	93	24
Cournoyer, Yvan	Montreal	73	47	36	83	15
Bucyk, John	Boston	78	32	51	83	4
Clarke, Bobby	Philadelphia	78	35	46	81	87
Lemaire, Jacques	Montreal	77	32	49	81	26

1972-73

East Division

Team	GP	W	L	T	GF	GA	PTS
*Montreal	78	52	10	16	329	184	120
Boston	78	51	22	5	330	235	107
NY Rangers	78	47	23	8	297	208	102
Buffalo	78	37	27	14	257	219	88
Detroit	78	37	29	12	265	243	86
Toronto	78	27	41	10	247	279	64
Vancouver	78	22	47	9	233	339	53
NY Islanders	78	12	60	6	170	347	30

West Division

Team	GP	W	L	T	GF	GA	PTS
Chicago	78	42	27	9	284	225	93
Philadelphia	78	37	30	11	296	256	85
Minnesota	78	37	30	11	254	230	85
St. Louis	78	32	34	12	233	251	76
Pittsburgh	78	32	37	9	257	265	73
Los Angeles	78	31	36	11	232	245	73
Atlanta	78	25	38	15	191	239	65
California	78	16	46	16	213	323	48

Leading Scorers

Player	Club	GP	G	A	PTS	PIM
Esposito, Phil	Boston	78	55	75	130	87
Clarke, Bobby	Philadelphia	78	37	67	104	80
Orr, Bobby	Boston	63	29	72	101	99
MacLeish, Rick	Philadelphia	78	50	50	100	69
Lemaire, Jacques	Montreal	77	44	51	95	16
Ratelle, Jean	NY Rangers	78	41	53	94	12
Redmond, Mickey	Detroit	76	52	41	93	24
Bucyk, John	Boston	78	40	53	93	12
Mahovlich, Frank	Montreal	78	38	55	93	51
Pappin, Jim	Chicago	76	41	51	92	82

1973-74

East Division

Team	GP	W	L	T	GF	GA	PTS
Boston	78	52	17	9	349	221	113
Montreal	78	45	24	9	293	240	99
NY Rangers	78	40	24	14	300	251	94
Toronto	78	35	27	16	274	230	86
Buffalo	78	32	34	12	242	250	76
Detroit	78	29	39	10	255	319	68
Vancouver	78	24	43	11	224	296	59
NY Islanders	78	19	41	18	182	247	56

West Division

Team	GP	W	L	T	GF	GA	PTS
*Philadelphia	78	50	16	12	273	164	112
Chicago	78	41	14	23	272	164	105
Los Angeles	78	33	33	12	233	231	78
Atlanta	78	30	34	14	214	238	74
Pittsburgh	78	28	41	9	242	273	65
St. Louis	78	26	40	12	206	248	64
Minnesota	78	23	38	17	235	275	63
California	78	13	55	10	195	342	36

Leading Scorers

Player	Club	GP	G	A	PTS	PIM
Esposito, Phil	Boston	78	68	77	145	58
Orr, Bobby	Boston	74	32	90	122	82
Hodge, Ken	Boston	76	50	55	105	43
Cashman, Wayne	Boston	78	30	59	89	111
Clarke, Bobby	Philadelphia	77	35	52	87	113
Martin, Rick	Buffalo	78	52	34	86	38
Apps Jr., Syl	Pittsburgh	75	24	61	85	37
Sittler, Darryl	Toronto	78	38	46	84	55
MacDonald, Lowell	Pittsburgh	78	43	39	82	14
Park, Brad	NY Rangers	78	25	57	82	148
Hextall, Dennis	Minnesota	78	20	62	82	138

Formerly a member of the Montreal Canadiens, Red Berenson became the first player from a 1967 expansion team to crack the top 10 in NHL scoring. Berenson finished eighth in the league with 82 points for St. Louis in 1968-69.

1974-75
PRINCE OF WALES CONFERENCE
Norris Division

Team	GP	W	L	T	GF	GA	PTS
Montreal	80	47	14	19	374	225	113
Los Angeles	80	42	17	21	269	185	105
Pittsburgh	80	37	28	15	326	289	89
Detroit	80	23	45	12	259	335	58
Washington	80	8	67	5	181	446	21

Adams Division

Team	GP	W	L	T	GF	GA	PTS
Buffalo	80	49	16	15	354	240	113
Boston	80	40	26	14	345	245	94
Toronto	80	31	33	16	280	309	78
California	80	19	48	13	212	316	51

CLARENCE CAMPBELL CONFERENCE
Patrick Division

Team	GP	W	L	T	GF	GA	PTS
*Philadelphia	80	51	18	11	293	181	113
NY Rangers	80	37	29	14	319	276	88
NY Islanders	80	33	25	22	264	221	88
Atlanta	80	34	31	15	243	233	83

Smythe Division

Team	GP	W	L	T	GF	GA	PTS
Vancouver	80	38	32	10	271	254	86
St. Louis	80	35	31	14	269	267	84
Chicago	80	37	35	8	268	241	82
Minnesota	80	23	50	7	221	341	53
Kansas City	80	15	54	11	184	328	41

Leading Scorers

Player	Club	GP	G	A	PTS	PIM
Orr, Bobby	Boston	80	46	89	135	101
Esposito, Phil	Boston	79	61	66	127	62
Dionne, Marcel	Detroit	80	47	74	121	14
Lafleur, Guy	Montreal	70	53	66	119	37
Mahovlich, Pete	Montreal	80	35	82	117	64
Clarke, Bobby	Philadelphia	80	27	89	116	125
Robert, Rene	Buffalo	74	40	60	100	75
Gilbert, Rod	NY Rangers	76	36	61	97	22
Perreault, Gilbert	Buffalo	68	39	57	96	36
Martin, Rick	Buffalo	68	52	43	95	72

1975-76
PRINCE OF WALES CONFERENCE
Norris Division

Team	GP	W	L	T	GF	GA	PTS
*Montreal	80	58	11	11	337	174	127
Los Angeles	80	38	33	9	263	265	85
Pittsburgh	80	35	33	12	339	303	82
Detroit	80	26	44	10	226	300	62
Washington	80	11	59	10	224	394	32

Adams Division

Team	GP	W	L	T	GF	GA	PTS
Boston	80	48	15	17	313	237	113
Buffalo	80	46	21	13	339	240	105
Toronto	80	34	31	15	294	276	83
California	80	27	42	11	250	278	65

CLARENCE CAMPBELL CONFERENCE
Patrick Division

Team	GP	W	L	T	GF	GA	PTS
Philadelphia	80	51	13	16	348	209	118
NY Islanders	80	42	21	17	297	190	101
Atlanta	80	35	33	12	262	237	82
NY Rangers	80	29	42	9	262	333	67

Smythe Division

Team	GP	W	L	T	GF	GA	PTS
Chicago	80	32	30	18	254	261	82
Vancouver	80	33	32	15	271	272	81
St. Louis	80	29	37	14	249	290	72
Minnesota	80	20	53	7	195	303	47
Kansas City	80	12	56	12	190	351	36

Leading Scorers

Player	Club	GP	G	A	PTS	PIM
Lafleur, Guy	Montreal	80	56	69	125	36
Clarke, Bobby	Philadelphia	76	30	89	119	13
Perreault, Gilbert	Buffalo	80	44	69	113	36
Barber, Bill	Philadelphia	80	50	62	112	104
Larouche, Pierre	Pittsburgh	76	53	58	111	33
Ratelle, Jean	Bos., NYR	80	36	69	105	18
Mahovlich, Pete	Montreal	80	34	71	105	76
Pronovost, Jean	Pittsburgh	80	52	52	104	24
Sittler, Darryl	Toronto	79	41	59	100	90
Apps Jr., Syl	Pittsburgh	80	32	67	99	24

1976-77
PRINCE OF WALES CONFERENCE
Norris Division

Team	GP	W	L	T	GF	GA	PTS
*Montreal	80	60	8	12	387	171	132
Los Angeles	80	34	31	15	271	241	83
Pittsburgh	80	34	33	13	240	252	81
Washington	80	24	42	14	221	307	62
Detroit	80	16	55	9	183	309	41

Adams Division

Team	GP	W	L	T	GF	GA	PTS
Boston	80	49	23	8	312	240	106
Buffalo	80	48	24	8	301	220	104
Toronto	80	33	32	15	301	285	81
Cleveland	80	25	42	13	240	292	63

CLARENCE CAMPBELL CONFERENCE
Patrick Division

Team	GP	W	L	T	GF	GA	PTS
Philadelphia	80	48	16	16	323	213	112
NY Islanders	80	47	21	12	288	193	106
Atlanta	80	34	34	12	264	265	80
NY Rangers	80	29	37	14	272	310	72

Smythe Division

Team	GP	W	L	T	GF	GA	PTS
St. Louis	80	32	39	9	239	276	73
Minnesota	80	23	39	18	240	310	64
Chicago	80	26	43	11	240	298	63
Vancouver	80	25	42	13	235	294	63
Colorado	80	20	46	14	226	307	54

Leading Scorers

Player	Club	GP	G	A	PTS	PIM
Lafleur, Guy	Montreal	80	56	80	136	20
Dionne, Marcel	Los Angeles	80	53	69	122	12
Shutt, Steve	Montreal	80	60	45	105	28
MacLeish, Rick	Philadelphia	79	49	48	97	42
Perreault, Gilbert	Buffalo	80	39	56	95	30
Young, Tim	Minnesota	80	29	66	95	58
Ratelle, Jean	Boston	78	33	61	94	22
McDonald, Lanny	Toronto	80	46	44	90	77
Sittler, Darryl	Toronto	73	38	52	90	89
Clarke, Bobby	Philadelphia	80	27	63	90	71

1977-78
PRINCE OF WALES CONFERENCE
Norris Division

Team	GP	W	L	T	GF	GA	PTS
*Montreal	80	59	10	11	359	183	129
Detroit	80	32	34	14	252	266	78
Los Angeles	80	31	34	15	243	245	77
Pittsburgh	80	25	37	18	254	321	68
Washington	80	17	49	14	195	321	48

Adams Division

Team	GP	W	L	T	GF	GA	PTS
Boston	80	51	18	11	333	218	113
Buffalo	80	44	19	17	288	215	105
Toronto	80	41	29	10	271	237	92
Cleveland	80	22	45	13	230	325	57

CLARENCE CAMPBELL CONFERENCE
Patrick Division

Team	GP	W	L	T	GF	GA	PTS
NY Islanders	80	48	17	15	334	210	111
Philadelphia	80	45	20	15	296	200	105
Atlanta	80	34	27	19	274	252	87
NY Rangers	80	30	37	13	279	280	73

Smythe Division

Team	GP	W	L	T	GF	GA	PTS
Chicago	80	32	29	19	230	220	83
Colorado	80	19	40	21	257	305	59
Vancouver	80	20	43	17	239	320	57
St. Louis	80	20	47	13	195	304	53
Minnesota	80	18	53	9	218	325	45

Leading Scorers

Player	Club	GP	G	A	PTS	PIM
Lafleur, Guy	Montreal	79	60	72	132	26
Trottier, Bryan	NY Islanders	77	46	77	123	46
Sittler, Darryl	Toronto	80	45	72	117	100
Lemaire, Jacques	Montreal	76	36	61	97	14
Potvin, Denis	NY Islanders	80	30	64	94	81
Bossy, Mike	NY Islanders	73	53	38	91	6
O'Reilly, Terry	Boston	77	29	61	90	211
Perreault, Gilbert	Buffalo	79	41	48	89	20
Clarke, Bobby	Philadelphia	71	21	68	89	83
McDonald, Lanny	Toronto	74	47	40	87	54
Paiement, Wilf	Colorado	80	31	56	87	114

1978-79
PRINCE OF WALES CONFERENCE
Norris Division

Team	GP	W	L	T	GF	GA	PTS
*Montreal	80	52	17	11	337	204	115
Pittsburgh	80	36	31	13	281	279	85
Los Angeles	80	34	34	12	292	286	80
Washington	80	24	41	15	273	338	63
Detroit	80	23	41	16	252	295	62

Adams Division

Team	GP	W	L	T	GF	GA	PTS
Boston	80	43	23	14	316	270	100
Buffalo	80	36	28	16	280	263	88
Toronto	80	34	33	13	267	252	81
Minnesota	80	28	40	12	257	289	68

CLARENCE CAMPBELL CONFERENCE
Patrick Division

Team	GP	W	L	T	GF	GA	PTS
NY Islanders	80	51	15	14	358	214	116
Philadelphia	80	40	25	15	281	248	95
NY Rangers	80	40	29	11	316	292	91
Atlanta	80	41	31	8	327	280	90

Smythe Division

Team	GP	W	L	T	GF	GA	PTS
Chicago	80	29	36	15	244	277	73
Vancouver	80	25	42	13	217	291	63
St. Louis	80	18	50	12	249	348	48
Colorado	80	15	53	12	210	331	42

Leading Scorers

Player	Club	GP	G	A	PTS	PIM
Trottier, Bryan	NY Islanders	76	47	87	134	50
Dionne, Marcel	Los Angeles	80	59	71	130	30
Lafleur, Guy	Montreal	80	52	77	129	28
Bossy, Mike	NY Islanders	80	69	57	126	25
MacMillan, Bob	Atlanta	79	37	71	108	14
Chouinard, Guy	Atlanta	80	50	57	107	14
Potvin, Denis	NY Islanders	73	31	70	101	58
Federko, Bernie	St. Louis	74	31	64	95	14
Taylor, Dave	Los Angeles	78	43	48	91	124
Gillies, Clark	NY Islanders	75	35	56	91	68

1979-80
PRINCE OF WALES CONFERENCE
Norris Division

Team	GP	W	L	T	GF	GA	PTS
Montreal	80	47	20	13	328	240	107
Los Angeles	80	30	36	14	290	313	74
Pittsburgh	80	30	37	13	251	303	73
Hartford	80	27	34	19	303	312	73
Detroit	80	26	43	11	268	306	63

Adams Division

Team	GP	W	L	T	GF	GA	PTS
Buffalo	80	47	17	16	318	201	110
Boston	80	46	21	13	310	234	105
Minnesota	80	36	28	16	311	253	88
Toronto	80	35	40	5	304	327	75
Quebec	80	25	44	11	248	313	61

CLARENCE CAMPBELL CONFERENCE
Patrick Division

Team	GP	W	L	T	GF	GA	PTS
Philadelphia	80	48	12	20	327	254	116
*NY Islanders	80	39	28	13	281	247	91
NY Rangers	80	38	32	10	308	284	86
Atlanta	80	35	32	13	282	269	83
Washington	80	27	40	13	261	293	67

Smythe Division

Team	GP	W	L	T	GF	GA	PTS
Chicago	80	34	27	19	241	250	87
St. Louis	80	34	34	12	266	278	80
Vancouver	80	27	37	16	256	281	70
Edmonton	80	28	39	13	301	322	69
Winnipeg	80	20	49	11	214	314	51
Colorado	80	19	48	13	234	308	51

Leading Scorers

Player	Club	GP	G	A	PTS	PIM
Dionne, Marcel	Los Angeles	80	53	84	137	32
Gretzky, Wayne	Edmonton	79	51	86	137	21
Lafleur, Guy	Montreal	74	50	75	125	12
Perreault, Gilbert	Buffalo	80	40	66	106	57
Rogers, Mike	Hartford	80	44	61	105	10
Trottier, Bryan	NY Islanders	78	42	62	104	68
Simmer, Charlie	Los Angeles	64	56	45	101	65
Stoughton, Blaine	Hartford	80	56	44	100	16
Sittler, Darryl	Toronto	73	40	57	97	62
MacDonald, Blair	Edmonton	80	46	48	94	6
Federko, Bernie	St. Louis	79	38	56	94	24

1980-81

PRINCE OF WALES CONFERENCE
Norris Division

Team	GP	W	L	T	GF	GA	PTS
Montreal	80	45	22	13	332	232	103
Los Angeles	80	43	24	13	337	290	99
Pittsburgh	80	30	37	13	302	345	73
Hartford	80	21	41	18	292	372	60
Detroit	80	19	43	18	252	339	56

Adams Division

Team	GP	W	L	T	GF	GA	PTS
Buffalo	80	39	20	21	327	250	99
Boston	80	37	30	13	316	272	87
Minnesota	80	35	28	17	291	263	87
Quebec	80	30	32	18	314	318	78
Toronto	80	28	37	15	322	367	71

CLARENCE CAMPBELL CONFERENCE
Patrick Division

Team	GP	W	L	T	GF	GA	PTS
*NY Islanders	80	48	18	14	355	260	110
Philadelphia	80	41	24	15	313	249	97
Calgary	80	39	27	14	329	298	92
NY Rangers	80	30	36	14	312	317	74
Washington	80	26	36	18	286	317	70

Smythe Division

Team	GP	W	L	T	GF	GA	PTS
St. Louis	80	45	18	17	352	281	107
Chicago	80	31	33	16	304	315	78
Vancouver	80	28	32	20	289	301	76
Edmonton	80	29	35	16	328	327	74
Colorado	80	22	45	13	258	344	57
Winnipeg	80	9	57	14	246	400	32

Leading Scorers

Player	Club	GP	G	A	PTS	PIM
Gretzky, Wayne	Edmonton	80	55	109	164	28
Dionne, Marcel	Los Angeles	80	58	77	135	70
Nilsson, Kent	Calgary	80	49	82	131	26
Bossy, Mike	NY Islanders	79	68	51	119	32
Taylor, Dave	Los Angeles	72	47	65	112	130
Stastny, Peter	Quebec	77	39	70	109	37
Simmer, Charlie	Los Angeles	65	56	49	105	62
Rogers, Mike	Hartford	80	40	65	105	32
Federko, Bernie	St. Louis	78	31	73	104	47
Richard, Jacques	Quebec	78	52	51	103	39
Middleton, Rick	Boston	80	44	59	103	16
Trottier, Bryan	NY Islanders	73	31	72	103	74

1981-82

CLARENCE CAMPBELL CONFERENCE
Norris Division

Team	GP	W	L	T	GF	GA	PTS
Minnesota	80	37	23	20	346	288	94
Winnipeg	80	33	33	14	319	332	80
St. Louis	80	32	40	8	315	349	72
Chicago	80	30	38	12	332	363	72
Toronto	80	20	44	16	298	380	56
Detroit	80	21	47	12	270	351	54

Smythe Division

Team	GP	W	L	T	GF	GA	PTS
Edmonton	80	48	17	15	417	295	111
Vancouver	80	30	33	17	290	286	77
Calgary	80	29	34	17	334	345	75
Los Angeles	80	24	41	15	314	369	63
Colorado	80	18	49	13	241	362	49

PRINCE OF WALES CONFERENCE
Adams Division

Team	GP	W	L	T	GF	GA	PTS
Montreal	80	46	17	17	360	223	109
Boston	80	43	27	10	323	285	96
Buffalo	80	39	26	15	307	273	93
Quebec	80	33	31	16	356	345	82
Hartford	80	21	41	18	264	351	60

Patrick Division

Team	GP	W	L	T	GF	GA	PTS
*NY Islanders	80	54	16	10	385	250	118
NY Rangers	80	39	27	14	316	306	92
Philadelphia	80	38	31	11	325	313	87
Pittsburgh	80	31	36	13	310	337	75
Washington	80	26	41	13	319	338	65

Leading Scorers

Player	Club	GP	G	A	PTS	PIM
Gretzky, Wayne	Edmonton	80	92	120	212	26
Bossy, Mike	NY Islanders	80	64	83	147	22
Stastny, Peter	Quebec	80	46	93	139	91
Maruk, Dennis	Washington	80	60	76	136	128
Trottier, Bryan	NY Islanders	80	50	79	129	88
Savard, Denis	Chicago	80	32	87	119	82
Dionne, Marcel	Los Angeles	78	50	67	117	50
Smith, Bobby	Minnesota	80	43	71	114	82
Ciccarelli, Dino	Minnesota	76	55	51	106	138
Taylor, Dave	Los Angeles	78	39	67	106	130

1982-83

CLARENCE CAMPBELL CONFERENCE
Norris Division

Team	GP	W	L	T	GF	GA	PTS
Chicago	80	47	23	10	338	268	104
Minnesota	80	40	24	16	321	290	96
Toronto	80	28	40	12	293	330	68
St. Louis	80	25	40	15	285	316	65
Detroit	80	21	44	15	263	344	57

Smythe Division

Team	GP	W	L	T	GF	GA	PTS
Edmonton	80	47	21	12	424	315	106
Calgary	80	32	34	14	321	317	78
Vancouver	80	30	35	15	303	309	75
Winnipeg	80	33	39	8	311	333	74
Los Angeles	80	27	41	12	308	365	66

PRINCE OF WALES CONFERENCE
Adams Division

Team	GP	W	L	T	GF	GA	PTS
Boston	80	50	20	10	327	228	110
Montreal	80	42	24	14	350	286	98
Buffalo	80	38	29	13	318	285	89
Quebec	80	34	34	12	343	336	80
Hartford	80	19	54	7	261	403	45

Patrick Division

Team	GP	W	L	T	GF	GA	PTS
Philadelphia	80	49	23	8	326	240	106
*NY Islanders	80	42	26	12	302	226	96
Washington	80	39	25	16	306	283	94
NY Rangers	80	35	35	10	306	287	80
New Jersey	80	17	49	14	230	338	48
Pittsburgh	80	18	53	9	257	394	45

Leading Scorers

Player	Club	GP	G	A	PTS	PIM
Gretzky, Wayne	Edmonton	80	71	125	196	59
Stastny, Peter	Quebec	75	47	77	124	78
Savard, Denis	Chicago	78	35	86	121	99
Bossy, Mike	NY Islanders	79	60	58	118	20
Dionne, Marcel	Los Angeles	80	56	51	107	22
Pederson, Barry	Boston	77	46	61	107	47
Messier, Mark	Edmonton	77	48	58	106	72
Goulet, Michel	Quebec	80	57	48	105	51
Anderson, Glenn	Edmonton	72	48	56	104	70
Nilsson, Kent	Calgary	80	46	58	104	10
Kurri, Jari	Edmonton	80	45	59	104	22

1983-84

CLARENCE CAMPBELL CONFERENCE
Norris Division

Team	GP	W	L	T	GF	GA	PTS
Minnesota	80	39	31	10	345	344	88
St. Louis	80	32	41	7	293	316	71
Detroit	80	31	42	7	298	323	69
Chicago	80	30	42	8	277	311	68
Toronto	80	26	45	9	303	387	61

Smythe Division

Team	GP	W	L	T	GF	GA	PTS
*Edmonton	80	57	18	5	446	314	119
Calgary	80	34	32	14	311	314	82
Vancouver	80	32	39	9	306	328	73
Winnipeg	80	31	38	11	340	374	73
Los Angeles	80	23	44	13	309	376	59

PRINCE OF WALES CONFERENCE
Adams Division

Team	GP	W	L	T	GF	GA	PTS
Boston	80	49	25	6	336	261	104
Buffalo	80	48	25	7	315	257	103
Quebec	80	42	28	10	360	278	94
Montreal	80	35	40	5	286	295	75
Hartford	80	28	42	10	288	320	66

Patrick Division

Team	GP	W	L	T	GF	GA	PTS
NY Islanders	80	50	26	4	357	269	104
Washington	80	48	27	5	308	226	101
Philadelphia	80	44	26	10	350	290	98
NY Rangers	80	42	29	9	314	304	93
New Jersey	80	17	56	7	231	350	41
Pittsburgh	80	16	58	6	254	390	38

Leading Scorers

Player	Club	GP	G	A	PTS	PIM
Gretzky, Wayne	Edmonton	74	87	118	205	39
Coffey, Paul	Edmonton	80	40	86	126	104
Goulet, Michel	Quebec	75	56	65	121	76
Stastny, Peter	Quebec	80	46	73	119	73
Bossy, Mike	NY Islanders	67	51	67	118	8
Pederson, Barry	Boston	80	39	77	116	64
Kurri, Jari	Edmonton	64	52	61	113	14
Trottier, Bryan	NY Islanders	68	40	71	111	59
Federko, Bernie	St. Louis	79	41	66	107	43
Middleton, Rick	Boston	80	47	58	105	14

1984-85

CLARENCE CAMPBELL CONFERENCE
Norris Division

Team	GP	W	L	T	GF	GA	PTS
St. Louis	80	37	31	12	299	288	86
Chicago	80	38	35	7	309	299	83
Detroit	80	27	41	12	313	357	66
Minnesota	80	25	43	12	268	321	62
Toronto	80	20	52	8	253	358	48

Smythe Division

Team	GP	W	L	T	GF	GA	PTS
*Edmonton	80	49	20	11	401	298	109
Winnipeg	80	43	27	10	358	332	96
Calgary	80	41	27	12	363	302	94
Los Angeles	80	34	32	14	339	326	82
Vancouver	80	25	46	9	284	401	59

PRINCE OF WALES CONFERENCE
Adams Division

Team	GP	W	L	T	GF	GA	PTS
Montreal	80	41	27	12	309	262	94
Quebec	80	41	30	9	323	275	91
Buffalo	80	38	28	14	290	237	90
Boston	80	36	34	10	303	287	82
Hartford	80	30	41	9	268	318	69

Patrick Division

Team	GP	W	L	T	GF	GA	PTS
Philadelphia	80	53	20	7	348	241	113
Washington	80	46	25	9	322	240	101
NY Islanders	80	40	34	6	345	312	86
NY Rangers	80	26	44	10	295	345	62
New Jersey	80	22	48	10	264	346	54
Pittsburgh	80	24	51	5	276	385	53

Leading Scorers

Player	Club	GP	G	A	PTS	PIM
Gretzky, Wayne	Edmonton	80	73	135	208	52
Kurri, Jari	Edmonton	73	71	64	135	30
Hawerchuk, Dale	Winnipeg	80	53	77	130	74
Dionne, Marcel	Los Angeles	80	46	80	126	46
Coffey, Paul	Edmonton	80	37	84	121	97
Bossy, Mike	NY Islanders	76	58	59	117	38
Ogrodnick, John	Detroit	79	55	50	105	30
Savard, Denis	Chicago	79	38	67	105	56
Federko, Bernie	St. Louis	76	30	73	103	27
Gartner, Mike	Washington	80	50	52	102	71

1985-86

CLARENCE CAMPBELL CONFERENCE
Norris Division

Team	GP	W	L	T	GF	GA	PTS
Chicago	80	39	33	8	351	349	86
Minnesota	80	38	33	9	327	305	85
St. Louis	80	37	34	9	302	291	83
Toronto	80	25	48	7	311	386	57
Detroit	80	17	57	6	266	415	40

Smythe Division

Team	GP	W	L	T	GF	GA	PTS
Edmonton	80	56	17	7	426	310	119
Calgary	80	40	31	9	354	315	89
Winnipeg	80	26	47	7	295	372	59
Vancouver	80	23	44	13	282	333	59
Los Angeles	80	23	49	8	284	389	54

PRINCE OF WALES CONFERENCE
Adams Division

Team	GP	W	L	T	GF	GA	PTS
Quebec	80	43	31	6	330	289	92
*Montreal	80	40	33	7	330	280	87
Boston	80	37	31	12	311	288	86
Hartford	80	40	36	4	332	302	84
Buffalo	80	37	37	6	296	291	80

Patrick Division

Team	GP	W	L	T	GF	GA	PTS
Philadelphia	80	53	23	4	335	241	110
Washington	80	50	23	7	315	272	107
NY Islanders	80	39	29	12	327	284	90
NY Rangers	80	36	38	6	280	276	78
Pittsburgh	80	34	38	8	313	305	76
New Jersey	80	28	49	3	300	374	59

Leading Scorers

Player	Club	GP	G	A	PTS	PIM
Gretzky, Wayne	Edmonton	80	52	163	215	52
Lemieux, Mario	Pittsburgh	79	48	93	141	43
Coffey, Paul	Edmonton	79	48	90	138	120
Kurri, Jari	Edmonton	78	68	63	131	22
Bossy, Mike	NY Islanders	80	61	62	123	14
Stastny, Peter	Quebec	76	41	81	122	60
Savard, Denis	Chicago	80	47	69	116	111
Naslund, Mats	Montreal	80	43	67	110	16
Hawerchuk, Dale	Winnipeg	80	46	59	105	44
Broten, Neal	Minnesota	80	29	76	105	47

1986-87
CLARENCE CAMPBELL CONFERENCE
Norris Division

Team	GP	W	L	T	GF	GA	PTS
St. Louis	80	32	33	15	281	293	79
Detroit	80	34	36	10	260	274	78
Chicago	80	29	37	14	290	310	72
Toronto	80	32	42	6	286	319	70
Minnesota	80	30	40	10	296	314	70

Smythe Division

Team	GP	W	L	T	GF	GA	PTS
*Edmonton	80	50	24	6	372	284	106
Calgary	80	46	31	3	318	289	95
Winnipeg	80	40	32	8	279	271	88
Los Angeles	80	31	41	8	318	341	70
Vancouver	80	29	43	8	282	314	66

PRINCE OF WALES CONFERENCE
Adams Division

Team	GP	W	L	T	GF	GA	PTS
Hartford	80	43	30	7	287	270	93
Montreal	80	41	29	10	277	241	92
Boston	80	39	34	7	301	276	85
Quebec	80	31	39	10	267	276	72
Buffalo	80	28	44	8	280	308	64

Patrick Division

Team	GP	W	L	T	GF	GA	PTS
Philadelphia	80	46	26	8	310	245	100
Washington	80	38	32	10	285	278	86
NY Islanders	80	35	33	12	279	281	82
NY Rangers	80	34	38	8	307	323	76
Pittsburgh	80	30	38	12	297	290	72
New Jersey	80	29	45	6	293	368	64

Leading Scorers

Player	Club	GP	G	A	PTS	PIM
Gretzky, Wayne	Edmonton	79	62	121	183	28
Kurri, Jari	Edmonton	79	54	54	108	41
Lemieux, Mario	Pittsburgh	63	54	53	107	57
Messier, Mark	Edmonton	77	37	70	107	73
Gilmour, Doug	St. Louis	80	42	63	105	58
Ciccarelli, Dino	Minnesota	80	52	51	103	92
Hawerchuk, Dale	Winnipeg	80	47	53	100	54
Goulet, Michel	Quebec	75	49	47	96	61
Kerr, Tim	Philadelphia	75	58	37	95	57
Bourque, Ray	Boston	78	23	72	95	36

1987-88
CLARENCE CAMPBELL CONFERENCE
Norris Division

Team	GP	W	L	T	GF	GA	PTS
Detroit	80	41	28	11	322	269	93
St. Louis	80	34	38	8	278	294	76
Chicago	80	30	41	9	284	328	69
Toronto	80	21	49	10	273	345	52
Minnesota	80	19	48	13	242	349	51

Smythe Division

Team	GP	W	L	T	GF	GA	PTS
Calgary	80	48	23	9	397	305	105
*Edmonton	80	44	25	11	363	288	99
Winnipeg	80	33	36	11	292	310	77
Los Angeles	80	30	42	8	318	359	68
Vancouver	80	25	46	9	272	320	59

PRINCE OF WALES CONFERENCE
Adams Division

Team	GP	W	L	T	GF	GA	PTS
Montreal	80	45	22	13	298	238	103
Boston	80	44	30	6	300	251	94
Buffalo	80	37	32	11	283	305	85
Hartford	80	35	38	7	249	267	77
Quebec	80	32	43	5	271	306	69

Patrick Division

Team	GP	W	L	T	GF	GA	PTS
NY Islanders	80	39	31	10	308	267	88
Washington	80	38	33	9	281	249	85
Philadelphia	80	38	33	9	292	292	85
New Jersey	80	38	36	6	295	296	82
NY Rangers	80	36	34	10	300	283	82
Pittsburgh	80	36	35	9	319	316	81

Leading Scorers

Player	Club	GP	G	A	PTS	PIM
Lemieux, Mario	Pittsburgh	76	70	98	168	92
Gretzky, Wayne	Edmonton	64	40	109	149	24
Savard, Denis	Chicago	80	44	87	131	95
Hawerchuk, Dale	Winnipeg	80	44	77	121	59
Robitaille, Luc	Los Angeles	80	53	58	111	82
Stastny, Peter	Quebec	76	46	65	111	69
Messier, Mark	Edmonton	77	37	74	111	103
Carson, Jimmy	Los Angeles	80	55	52	107	45
Loob, Hakan	Calgary	80	50	56	106	47
Goulet, Michel	Quebec	80	48	58	106	56

1988-89
CLARENCE CAMPBELL CONFERENCE
Norris Division

Team	GP	W	L	T	GF	GA	PTS
Detroit	80	34	34	12	313	316	80
St. Louis	80	33	35	12	275	285	78
Minnesota	80	27	37	16	258	278	70
Chicago	80	27	41	12	297	335	66
Toronto	80	28	46	6	259	342	62

Smythe Division

Team	GP	W	L	T	GF	GA	PTS
*Calgary	80	54	17	9	354	226	117
Los Angeles	80	42	31	7	376	335	91
Edmonton	80	38	34	8	325	306	84
Vancouver	80	33	39	8	251	253	74
Winnipeg	80	26	42	12	300	355	64

PRINCE OF WALES CONFERENCE
Adams Division

Team	GP	W	L	T	GF	GA	PTS
Montreal	80	53	18	9	315	218	115
Boston	80	37	29	14	289	256	88
Buffalo	80	38	35	7	291	299	83
Hartford	80	37	38	5	299	290	79
Quebec	80	27	46	7	269	342	61

Patrick Division

Team	GP	W	L	T	GF	GA	PTS
Washington	80	41	29	10	305	259	92
Pittsburgh	80	40	33	7	347	349	87
NY Rangers	80	37	35	8	310	307	82
Philadelphia	80	36	36	8	307	285	80
New Jersey	80	27	41	12	281	325	66
NY Islanders	80	28	47	5	265	325	61

Leading Scorers

Player	Club	GP	G	A	PTS	PIM
Lemieux, Mario	Pittsburgh	76	85	114	199	100
Gretzky, Wayne	Los Angeles	78	54	114	168	26
Yzerman, Steve	Detroit	80	65	90	155	61
Nicholls, Bernie	Los Angeles	79	70	80	150	96
Brown, Rob	Pittsburgh	68	49	66	115	118
Coffey, Paul	Pittsburgh	75	30	83	113	193
Mullen, Joe	Calgary	79	51	59	110	16
Kurri, Jari	Edmonton	76	44	58	102	69
Carson, Jimmy	Edmonton	80	49	51	100	36
Robitaille, Luc	Los Angeles	78	46	52	98	65

1989-90
CLARENCE CAMPBELL CONFERENCE
Norris Division

Team	GP	W	L	T	GF	GA	PTS
Chicago	80	41	33	6	316	294	88
St. Louis	80	37	34	9	295	279	83
Toronto	80	38	38	4	337	358	80
Minnesota	80	36	40	4	284	291	76
Detroit	80	28	38	14	288	323	70

Smythe Division

Team	GP	W	L	T	GF	GA	PTS
Calgary	80	42	23	15	348	265	99
*Edmonton	80	38	28	14	315	283	90
Winnipeg	80	37	32	11	298	290	85
Los Angeles	80	34	39	7	338	337	75
Vancouver	80	25	41	14	245	306	64

PRINCE OF WALES CONFERENCE
Adams Division

Team	GP	W	L	T	GF	GA	PTS
Boston	80	46	25	9	289	232	101
Buffalo	80	45	27	8	286	248	98
Montreal	80	41	28	11	288	234	93
Hartford	80	38	33	9	275	268	85
Quebec	80	12	61	7	240	407	31

Patrick Division

Team	GP	W	L	T	GF	GA	PTS
NY Rangers	80	36	31	13	279	267	85
New Jersey	80	37	34	9	295	288	83
Washington	80	36	38	6	284	275	78
NY Islanders	80	31	38	11	281	288	73
Pittsburgh	80	32	40	8	318	359	72
Philadelphia	80	30	39	11	290	297	71

Leading Scorers

Player	Club	GP	G	A	PTS	PIM
Gretzky, Wayne	Los Angeles	73	40	102	142	42
Messier, Mark	Edmonton	79	45	84	129	79
Yzerman, Steve	Detroit	79	62	65	127	79
Lemieux, Mario	Pittsburgh	59	45	78	123	78
Hull, Brett	St. Louis	80	72	41	113	24
Nicholls, Bernie	L.A., NYR	79	39	73	112	86
Turgeon, Pierre	Buffalo	80	40	66	106	29
LaFontaine, Pat	NY Islanders	74	54	51	105	38
Coffey, Paul	Pittsburgh	80	29	74	103	95
Sakic, Joe	Quebec	80	39	63	102	27
Oates, Adam	St. Louis	80	23	79	102	30

1990-91
CLARENCE CAMPBELL CONFERENCE
Norris Division

Team	GP	W	L	T	GF	GA	PTS
Chicago	80	49	23	8	284	211	106
St. Louis	80	47	22	11	310	250	105
Detroit	80	34	38	8	273	298	76
Minnesota	80	27	39	14	256	266	68
Toronto	80	23	46	11	241	318	57

Smythe Division

Team	GP	W	L	T	GF	GA	PTS
Los Angeles	80	46	24	10	340	254	102
Calgary	80	46	26	8	344	263	100
Edmonton	80	37	37	6	272	272	80
Vancouver	80	28	43	9	243	315	65
Winnipeg	80	26	43	11	260	288	63

PRINCE OF WALES CONFERENCE
Adams Division

Team	GP	W	L	T	GF	GA	PTS
Boston	80	44	24	12	299	264	100
Montreal	80	39	30	11	273	249	89
Buffalo	80	31	30	19	292	278	81
Hartford	80	31	38	11	238	276	73
Quebec	80	16	50	14	236	354	46

Patrick Division

Team	GP	W	L	T	GF	GA	PTS
*Pittsburgh	80	41	33	6	342	305	88
NY Rangers	80	36	31	13	297	265	85
Washington	80	37	36	7	258	258	81
New Jersey	80	32	33	15	272	264	79
Philadelphia	80	33	37	10	252	267	76
NY Islanders	80	25	45	10	223	290	60

Leading Scorers

Player	Club	GP	G	A	PTS	PIM
Gretzky, Wayne	Los Angeles	78	41	122	163	16
Hull, Brett	St. Louis	78	86	45	131	22
Oates, Adam	St. Louis	61	25	90	115	29
Recchi, Mark	Pittsburgh	78	40	73	113	48
Cullen, John	Pit., Hfd.	78	39	71	110	101
Sakic, Joe	Quebec	80	48	61	109	24
Yzerman, Steve	Detroit	80	51	57	108	34
Fleury, Theoren	Calgary	79	51	53	104	136
MacInnis, Al	Calgary	78	28	75	103	90
Larmer, Steve	Chicago	80	44	57	101	79

1991-92
CLARENCE CAMPBELL CONFERENCE
Norris Division

Team	GP	W	L	T	GF	GA	PTS
Detroit	80	43	25	12	320	256	98
Chicago	80	36	29	15	257	236	87
St. Louis	80	36	33	11	279	266	83
Minnesota	80	32	42	6	246	278	70
Toronto	80	30	43	7	234	294	67

Smythe Division

Team	GP	W	L	T	GF	GA	PTS
Vancouver	80	42	26	12	285	250	96
Los Angeles	80	35	31	14	287	296	84
Edmonton	80	36	34	10	295	297	82
Winnipeg	80	33	32	15	251	244	81
Calgary	80	31	37	12	296	305	74
San Jose	80	17	58	5	219	359	39

PRINCE OF WALES CONFERENCE
Adams Division

Team	GP	W	L	T	GF	GA	PTS
Montreal	80	41	28	11	267	207	93
Boston	80	36	32	12	270	275	84
Buffalo	80	31	37	12	289	299	74
Hartford	80	26	41	13	247	283	65
Quebec	80	20	48	12	255	318	52

Patrick Division

Team	GP	W	L	T	GF	GA	PTS
NY Rangers	80	50	25	5	321	246	105
Washington	80	45	27	8	330	275	98
*Pittsburgh	80	39	32	9	343	308	87
New Jersey	80	38	31	11	289	259	87
NY Islanders	80	34	35	11	291	299	79
Philadelphia	80	32	37	11	252	273	75

Leading Scorers

Player	Club	GP	G	A	PTS	PIM
Lemieux, Mario	Pittsburgh	64	44	87	131	94
Stevens, Kevin	Pittsburgh	80	54	69	123	254
Gretzky, Wayne	Los Angeles	74	31	90	121	34
Hull, Brett	St. Louis	73	70	39	109	48
Robitaille, Luc	Los Angeles	80	44	63	107	95
Messier, Mark	NY Rangers	79	35	72	107	76
Roenick, Jeremy	Chicago	80	53	50	103	23
Yzerman, Steve	Detroit	79	45	58	103	64
Leetch, Brian	NY Rangers	80	22	80	102	26
Oates, Adam	St. L., Bos.	80	20	79	99	22

1992-93
CLARENCE CAMPBELL CONFERENCE
Norris Division

Team	GP	W	L	T	GF	GA	PTS
Chicago	84	47	25	12	279	230	106
Detroit	84	47	28	9	369	280	103
Toronto	84	44	29	11	288	241	99
St. Louis	84	37	36	11	282	278	85
Minnesota	84	36	38	10	272	293	82
Tampa Bay	84	23	54	7	245	332	53

Smythe Division

Vancouver	84	46	29	9	346	278	101
Calgary	84	43	30	11	322	282	97
Los Angeles	84	39	35	10	338	340	88
Winnipeg	84	40	37	7	322	320	87
Edmonton	84	26	50	8	242	337	60
San Jose	84	11	71	2	218	414	24

PRINCE OF WALES CONFERENCE
Adams Division

Boston	84	51	26	7	332	268	109
Quebec	84	47	27	10	351	300	104
*Montreal	84	48	30	6	326	280	102
Buffalo	84	38	36	10	335	297	86
Hartford	84	26	52	6	284	369	58
Ottawa	84	10	70	4	202	395	24

Patrick Division

Pittsburgh	84	56	21	7	367	268	119
Washington	84	43	34	7	325	286	93
NY Islanders	84	40	37	7	335	297	87
New Jersey	84	40	37	7	308	299	87
Philadelphia	84	36	37	11	319	319	83
NY Rangers	84	34	39	11	304	308	79

Leading Scorers

Player	Club	GP	G	A	PTS	PIM
Lemieux, Mario	Pittsburgh	60	69	91	160	38
LaFontaine, Pat	Buffalo	84	53	95	148	63
Oates, Adam	Boston	84	45	97	142	32
Yzerman, Steve	Detroit	84	58	79	137	44
Selanne, Teemu	Winnipeg	84	76	56	132	45
Turgeon, Pierre	NY Islanders	83	58	74	132	26
Mogilny, Alexander	Buffalo	77	76	51	127	40
Gilmour, Doug	Toronto	83	32	95	127	100
Robitaille, Luc	Los Angeles	84	63	62	125	100
Recchi, Mark	Philadelphia	84	53	70	123	95

1993-94
EASTERN CONFERENCE
Northeast Division

Team	GP	W	L	T	GF	GA	PTS
Pittsburgh	84	44	27	13	299	285	101
Boston	84	42	29	13	289	252	97
Montreal	84	41	29	14	283	248	96
Buffalo	84	43	32	9	282	218	95
Quebec	84	34	42	8	277	292	76
Hartford	84	27	48	9	227	288	63
Ottawa	84	14	61	9	201	397	37

Atlantic Division

*NY Rangers	84	52	24	8	299	231	112
New Jersey	84	47	25	12	306	220	106
Washington	84	39	35	10	277	263	88
NY Islanders	84	36	36	12	282	264	84
Florida	84	33	34	17	233	233	83
Philadelphia	84	35	39	10	294	314	80
Tampa Bay	84	30	43	11	224	251	71

WESTERN CONFERENCE
Central Division

Detroit	84	46	30	8	356	275	100
Toronto	84	43	29	12	280	243	98
Dallas	84	42	29	13	286	265	97
St. Louis	84	40	33	11	270	283	91
Chicago	84	39	36	9	254	240	87
Winnipeg	84	24	51	9	245	344	57

Pacific Division

Calgary	84	42	29	13	302	256	97
Vancouver	84	41	40	3	279	276	85
San Jose	84	33	35	16	252	265	82
Anaheim	84	33	46	5	229	251	71
Los Angeles	84	27	45	12	294	322	66
Edmonton	84	25	45	14	261	305	64

Leading Scorers

Player	Club	GP	G	A	PTS	PIM
Gretzky, Wayne	Los Angeles	81	38	92	130	20
Fedorov, Sergei	Detroit	82	56	64	120	34
Oates, Adam	Boston	77	32	80	112	45
Gilmour, Doug	Toronto	83	27	84	111	105
Bure, Pavel	Vancouver	76	60	47	107	86
Roenick, Jeremy	Chicago	84	46	61	107	125
Recchi, Mark	Philadelphia	84	40	67	107	46
Shanahan, Brendan	St. Louis	81	52	50	102	211
Andreychuk, Dave	Toronto	83	53	46	99	98
Jagr, Jaromir	Pittsburgh	80	32	67	99	61

1994-95
EASTERN CONFERENCE
Northeast Division

Team	GP	W	L	T	GF	GA	PTS
Quebec	48	30	13	5	185	134	65
Pittsburgh	48	29	16	3	181	158	61
Boston	48	27	18	3	150	127	57
Buffalo	48	22	19	7	130	119	51
Hartford	48	19	24	5	127	141	43
Montreal	48	18	23	7	125	148	43
Ottawa	48	9	34	5	117	174	23

Atlantic Division

Philadelphia	48	28	16	4	150	132	60
*New Jersey	48	22	18	8	136	121	52
Washington	48	22	18	8	136	120	52
NY Rangers	48	22	23	3	139	134	47
Florida	48	20	22	6	115	127	46
Tampa Bay	48	17	28	3	120	144	37
NY Islanders	48	15	28	5	126	158	35

WESTERN CONFERENCE
Central Division

Detroit	48	33	11	4	180	117	70
St. Louis	48	28	15	5	178	135	61
Chicago	48	24	19	5	156	115	53
Toronto	48	21	19	8	135	146	50
Dallas	48	17	23	8	136	135	42
Winnipeg	48	16	25	7	157	177	39

Pacific Division

Calgary	48	24	17	7	163	135	55
Vancouver	48	18	18	12	153	148	48
San Jose	48	19	25	4	129	161	42
Los Angeles	48	16	23	9	142	174	41
Edmonton	48	17	27	4	136	183	38
Anaheim	48	16	27	5	125	164	37

Leading Scorers

Player	Club	GP	G	A	PTS	PIM
Jagr, Jaromir	Pittsburgh	48	32	38	70	37
Lindros, Eric	Philadelphia	46	29	41	70	60
Zhamnov, Alexei	Winnipeg	48	30	35	65	20
Sakic, Joe	Quebec	47	19	43	62	30
Francis, Ron	Pittsburgh	44	11	48	59	18
Fleury, Theoren	Calgary	47	29	29	58	112
Coffey, Paul	Detroit	45	14	44	58	72
Renberg, Mikael	Philadelphia	47	26	31	57	20
LeClair, John	Mtl., Phi.	46	26	28	54	30
Messier, Mark	NY Rangers	46	14	39	53	40
Oates, Adam	Boston	48	12	41	53	8

1995-96
EASTERN CONFERENCE
Northeast Division

Team	GP	W	L	T	GF	GA	PTS
Pittsburgh	82	49	29	4	362	284	102
Boston	82	40	31	11	282	269	91
Montreal	82	40	32	10	265	248	90
Hartford	82	34	39	9	237	259	77
Buffalo	82	33	42	7	247	262	73
Ottawa	82	18	59	5	191	291	41

Atlantic Division

Philadelphia	82	45	24	13	282	208	103
NY Rangers	82	41	27	14	272	237	96
Florida	82	41	31	10	254	234	92
Washington	82	39	32	11	234	204	89
Tampa Bay	82	38	32	12	238	248	88
New Jersey	82	37	33	12	215	202	86
NY Islanders	82	22	50	10	229	315	54

WESTERN CONFERENCE
Central Division

Detroit	82	62	13	7	325	181	131
Chicago	82	40	28	14	273	220	94
Toronto	82	34	36	12	247	252	80
St. Louis	82	32	34	16	219	248	80
Winnipeg	82	36	40	6	275	291	78
Dallas	82	26	42	14	227	280	66

Pacific Division

*Colorado	82	47	25	10	326	240	104
Calgary	82	34	37	11	241	240	79
Vancouver	82	32	35	15	278	278	79
Anaheim	82	35	39	8	234	247	78
Edmonton	82	30	44	8	240	304	68
Los Angeles	82	24	40	18	256	302	66
San Jose	82	20	55	7	252	357	47

Leading Scorers

Player	Club	GP	G	A	PTS	PIM
Lemieux, Mario	Pittsburgh	70	69	92	161	54
Jagr, Jaromir	Pittsburgh	82	62	87	149	96
Sakic, Joe	Colorado	82	51	69	120	44
Francis, Ron	Pittsburgh	77	27	92	119	56
Forsberg, Peter	Colorado	82	30	86	116	47
Lindros, Eric	Philadelphia	73	47	68	115	163
Kariya, Paul	Anaheim	82	50	58	108	20
Selanne, Teemu	Wpg., Ana.	79	40	68	108	22
Mogilny, Alexander	Vancouver	79	55	52	107	16
Fedorov, Sergei	Detroit	78	39	68	107	48

Between them, Wayne Gretzky and Mario Lemieux won every NHL scoring title from 1980-81 to 1993-94. Gretzky won the Art Ross Trophy a record 10 times during that span, while Lemieux won it four times. Mario won again in 1995-96 and 1996-97.

1996-97

EASTERN CONFERENCE
Northeast Division

Team	GP	W	L	T	GF	GA	PTS
Buffalo	82	40	30	12	237	208	92
Pittsburgh	82	38	36	8	285	280	84
Ottawa	82	31	36	15	226	234	77
Montreal	82	31	36	15	249	276	77
Hartford	82	32	39	11	226	256	75
Boston	82	26	47	9	234	300	61

Atlantic Division

Team	GP	W	L	T	GF	GA	PTS
New Jersey	82	45	23	14	231	182	104
Philadelphia	82	45	24	13	274	217	103
Florida	82	35	28	19	221	201	89
NY Rangers	82	38	34	10	258	231	86
Washington	82	33	40	9	214	231	75
Tampa Bay	82	32	40	10	217	247	74
NY Islanders	82	29	41	12	240	250	70

WESTERN CONFERENCE
Central Division

Team	GP	W	L	T	GF	GA	PTS
Dallas	82	48	26	8	252	198	104
*Detroit	82	38	26	18	253	197	94
Phoenix	82	38	37	7	240	243	83
St. Louis	82	36	35	11	236	239	83
Chicago	82	34	35	13	223	210	81
Toronto	82	30	44	8	230	273	68

Pacific Division

Team	GP	W	L	T	GF	GA	PTS
Colorado	82	49	24	9	277	205	107
Anaheim	82	36	33	13	245	233	85
Edmonton	82	36	37	9	252	247	81
Vancouver	82	35	40	7	257	273	77
Calgary	82	32	41	9	214	239	73
Los Angeles	82	28	43	11	214	268	67
San Jose	82	27	47	8	211	278	62

Leading Scorers

Player	Club	GP	G	A	PTS	PIM
Lemieux, Mario	Pittsburgh	76	50	72	122	65
Selanne, Teemu	Anaheim	78	51	58	109	34
Kariya, Paul	Anaheim	69	44	55	99	6
LeClair, John	Philadelphia	82	50	47	97	58
Gretzky, Wayne	NY Rangers	82	25	72	97	28
Jagr, Jaromir	Pittsburgh	63	47	48	95	40
Sundin, Mats	Toronto	82	41	53	94	59
Palffy, Zigmund	NY Islanders	80	48	42	90	43
Francis, Ron	Pittsburgh	81	27	63	90	20
Shanahan, Brendan	Hfd., Det.	81	47	41	88	131

1997-98

EASTERN CONFERENCE
Northeast Division

Team	GP	W	L	T	GF	GA	PTS
Pittsburgh	82	40	24	18	228	188	98
Boston	82	39	30	13	221	194	91
Buffalo	82	36	29	17	211	187	89
Montreal	82	37	32	13	235	208	87
Ottawa	82	34	33	15	193	200	83
Carolina	82	33	41	8	200	219	74

Atlantic Division

Team	GP	W	L	T	GF	GA	PTS
New Jersey	82	48	23	11	225	166	107
Philadelphia	82	42	29	11	242	193	95
Washington	82	40	30	12	219	202	92
NY Islanders	82	30	41	11	212	225	71
NY Rangers	82	25	39	18	197	231	68
Florida	82	24	43	15	203	256	63
Tampa Bay	82	17	55	10	151	269	44

WESTERN CONFERENCE
Central Division

Team	GP	W	L	T	GF	GA	PTS
Dallas	82	49	22	11	242	167	109
*Detroit	82	44	23	15	250	196	103
St. Louis	82	45	29	8	256	204	98
Phoenix	82	35	35	12	224	227	82
Chicago	82	30	39	13	192	199	73
Toronto	82	30	43	9	194	237	69

Pacific Division

Team	GP	W	L	T	GF	GA	PTS
Colorado	82	39	26	17	231	205	95
Los Angeles	82	38	33	11	227	225	87
Edmonton	82	35	37	10	215	224	80
San Jose	82	34	38	10	210	216	78
Calgary	82	26	41	15	217	252	67
Anaheim	82	26	43	13	205	261	65
Vancouver	82	25	43	14	224	273	64

Leading Scorers

Player	Club	GP	G	A	PTS	PIM
Jagr, Jaromir	Pittsburgh	77	35	67	102	64
Forsberg, Peter	Colorado	72	25	66	91	94
Bure, Pavel	Vancouver	82	51	39	90	48
Gretzky, Wayne	NY Rangers	82	23	67	90	28
LeClair, John	Philadelphia	82	51	36	87	32
Palffy, Zigmund	NY Islanders	82	45	42	87	34
Francis, Ron	Pittsburgh	81	25	62	87	20
Selanne, Teemu	Anaheim	73	52	34	86	30
Allison, Jason	Boston	81	33	50	83	60
Stumpel, Jozef	Los Angeles	77	21	58	79	53

1998-99

EASTERN CONFERENCE
Northeast Division

Team	GP	W	L	T	GF	GA	PTS
Ottawa	82	44	23	15	239	179	103
Toronto	82	45	30	7	268	231	97
Boston	82	39	30	13	214	181	91
Buffalo	82	37	28	17	207	175	91
Montreal	82	32	39	11	184	209	75

Atlantic Division

Team	GP	W	L	T	GF	GA	PTS
New Jersey	82	47	24	11	248	196	105
Philadelphia	82	37	26	19	231	196	93
Pittsburgh	82	38	30	14	242	225	90
Ny Rangers	82	33	38	11	217	227	77
Ny Islanders	82	24	48	10	194	244	58

Southeast Division

Team	GP	W	L	T	GF	GA	PTS
Carolina	82	34	30	18	210	202	86
Florida	82	30	34	18	210	228	78
Washington	82	31	45	6	200	218	68
Tampa Bay	82	19	54	9	179	292	47

WESTERN CONFERENCE
Central Division

Team	GP	W	L	T	GF	GA	PTS
Detroit	82	43	32	7	245	202	93
St Louis	82	37	32	13	237	209	87
Chicago	82	29	41	12	202	248	70
Nashville	82	28	47	7	190	261	63

Pacific Division

Team	GP	W	L	T	GF	GA	PTS
*Dallas	82	51	19	12	236	168	114
Phoenix	82	39	31	12	205	197	90
Anaheim	82	35	34	13	215	206	83
San Jose	82	31	33	18	196	191	80
Los Angeles	82	32	45	5	189	222	69

Northwest Division

Team	GP	W	L	T	GF	GA	PTS
Colorado	82	44	28	10	239	205	98
Edmonton	82	33	37	12	230	226	78
Calgary	82	30	40	12	211	234	72
Vancouver	82	23	47	12	192	258	58

Leading Scorers

Player	Club	GP	G	A	PTS	PIM
Jagr, Jaromir	Pittsburgh	81	44	83	127	66
Selanne, Teemu	Anaheim	75	47	60	107	30
Kariya, Paul	Anaheim	82	39	62	101	40
Forsberg, Peter	Colorado	78	30	67	97	108
Sakic, Joe	Colorado	73	41	55	96	29
Yashin, Alexei	Ottawa	82	44	50	94	54
Lindros, Eric	Philadelphia	71	40	53	93	120
Fleury, Theoren	Cgy., Col.	75	40	53	93	86
Leclair, John	Philadelphia	76	43	47	90	30
Demitra, Pavol	St Louis	82	37	52	89	16

Note: Detailed statistics for 1998-99 are listed in the Final Statistics, 1998-99 section of the *NHL Official Guide & Record Book.* **See page 131.**

Jaromir Jagr became the first player trained in Europe to win the Art Ross Trophy in 1994-95. He has established himself as the best offensive player in the NHL today by winning the scoring title again in 1997-98 and 1998-99.

Team Records
Regular Season
FINAL STANDINGS

MOST POINTS, ONE SEASON:
- **132 —Montreal Canadiens,** 1976-77. 60w-8L-12T. 80GP
- 131 —Detroit Red Wings, 1995-96. 62w-13L-7T. 82GP
- 129 —Montreal Canadiens, 1977-78. 59w-10L-11T. 80GP

BEST WINNING PERCENTAGE, ONE SEASON:
- **.875 —Boston Bruins,** 1929-30. 38w-5L-1T. 77PTS in 44GP
- .830 —Montreal Canadiens, 1943-44. 38w-5L-7T. 83PTS in 50GP
- .825 —Montreal Canadiens, 1976-77. 60w-8L-12T. 132PTS in 80GP
- .806 —Montreal Canadiens, 1977-78. 59w-10L-11T. 129PTS in 80GP
- .800 —Montreal Canadiens, 1944-45. 38w-8L-4T. 80PTS in 50GP

FEWEST POINTS, ONE SEASON:
- **8 —Quebec Bulldogs,** 1919-20. 4w-20L-0T. 24GP
- 10 —Toronto Arenas, 1918-19. 5w-13L-0T. 18GP
- 12 —Hamilton Tigers, 1920-21. 6w-18L-0T. 24GP
- —Hamilton Tigers, 1922-23. 6w-18L-0T. 24GP
- —Boston Bruins, 1924-25. 6w-24L-0T. 30GP
- —Philadelphia Quakers, 1930-31. 4w-36L-4T. 44GP

FEWEST POINTS, ONE SEASON (MINIMUM 70-GAME SCHEDULE):
- **21 —Washington Capitals,** 1974-75. 8w-67L-5T. 80GP
- 24 —Ottawa Senators, 1992-93. 10w-70L-4T. 84GP
- —San Jose Sharks, 1992-93. 11w-71L-2T. 84GP
- 30 —NY Islanders, 1972-73. 12w-60L-6T. 78GP

WORST WINNING PERCENTAGE, ONE SEASON:
- **.131 —Washington Capitals,** 1974-75. 8w-67L-5T. 21PTS in 80GP
- .136 —Philadelphia Quakers, 1930-31. 4w-36L-4T. 12PTS in 44GP
- .143 —Ottawa Senators, 1992-93. 10w-70L-4T. 24PTS in 84GP
- .143 —San Jose Sharks, 1992-93. 11w-71L-2T. 24PTS in 84GP
- .148 —Pittsburgh Pirates, 1929-30. 5w-36L-3T. 13PTS in 44GP

TEAM WINS

Most Wins

MOST WINS, ONE SEASON:
- **62 —Detroit Red Wings,** 1995-96. 82GP
- 60 —Montreal Canadiens, 1976-77. 80GP
- 59 —Montreal Canadiens, 1977-78. 80GP

MOST HOME WINS, ONE SEASON:
- **36 —Philadelphia Flyers,** 1975-76. 40GP
- —**Detroit Red Wings,** 1995-96. 41GP
- 33 —Boston Bruins, 1970-71. 39GP
- —Boston Bruins, 1973-74. 39GP
- —Montreal Canadiens, 1976-77. 40GP
- —Philadelphia Flyers, 1976-77. 40GP
- —NY Islanders, 1981-82. 40GP
- —Philadelphia Flyers, 1985-86. 40GP

MOST ROAD WINS, ONE SEASON
- **28 —New Jersey Devils,** 1998-99. 41GP.
- 27 —Montreal Canadiens, 1976-77. 40GP
- —Montreal Canadiens, 1977-78. 40GP
- 26 —Boston Bruins, 1971-72. 39GP
- —Montreal Canadiens, 1975-76. 40GP
- —Edmonton Oilers, 1983-84. 40GP
- —Detroit Red Wings, 1995-96. 41GP

Fewest Wins

FEWEST WINS, ONE SEASON:
- **4 —Quebec Bulldogs,** 1919-20. 24GP
- —**Philadelphia Quakers,** 1930-31. 44GP
- 5 —Toronto Arenas, 1918-19. 18GP
- —Pittsburgh Pirates, 1929-30. 44GP

FEWEST WINS, ONE SEASON (MINIMUM 70-GAME SCHEDULE):
- **8 —Washington Capitals,** 1974-75. 80GP
- 9 —Winnipeg Jets, 1980-81. 80GP
- 10 —Ottawa Senators, 1992-93. 84GP

FEWEST HOME WINS, ONE SEASON:
- **2 —Chicago Blackhawks,** 1927-28. 22GP
- 3 —Boston Bruins, 1924-25. 15GP
- —Chicago Blackhawks, 1928-29. 22GP
- —Philadelphia Quakers, 1930-31. 22GP

FEWEST HOME WINS, ONE SEASON (MINIMUM 70-GAME SCHEDULE):
- **6 —Chicago Blackhawks,** 1954-55. 35GP
- —**Washington Capitals,** 1975-76. 40GP
- 7 —Boston Bruins, 1962-63. 35GP
- —Washington Capitals, 1974-75. 40GP
- —Winnipeg Jets, 1980-81. 40GP
- —Pittsburgh Penguins, 1983-84. 40GP

FEWEST ROAD WINS, ONE SEASON:
- **0 —Toronto Arenas,** 1918-19. 9GP
- —**Quebec Bulldogs,** 1919-20. 12GP
- —**Pittsburgh Pirates,** 1929-30. 22GP
- 1 —Hamilton Tigers, 1921-22. 12GP
- —Toronto St. Patricks, 1925-26. 18GP
- —Philadelphia Quakers, 1930-31. 22GP
- —NY Americans, 1940-41. 24GP
- * —Ottawa Senators, 1992-93. 41GP

FEWEST ROAD WINS, ONE SEASON (MINIMUM 70-GAME SCHEDULE):
- **1 —Washington Capitals,** 1974-75. 40GP
- * —**Ottawa Senators,** 1992-93. 41GP
- 2 —Boston Bruins, 1960-61. 35GP
- —Los Angeles Kings, 1969-70. 38GP
- —NY Islanders, 1972-73. 39GP
- —California Seals, 1973-74. 39GP
- —Colorado Rockies, 1977-78. 40GP
- —Winnipeg Jets, 1980-81. 40GP
- —Quebec Nordiques, 1991-92. 40GP

TEAM LOSSES

Fewest Losses

FEWEST LOSSES, ONE SEASON:
- **5 —Ottawa Senators,** 1919-20. 24GP
- —**Boston Bruins,** 1929-30. 44GP
- —**Montreal Canadiens,** 1943-44. 50GP

FEWEST HOME LOSSES, ONE SEASON:
- **0 —Ottawa Senators,** 1922-23. 12GP
- —**Montreal Canadiens,** 1943-44. 25GP
- 1 —Toronto Arenas, 1917-18. 11GP
- —Ottawa Senators, 1918-19. 9GP
- —Ottawa Senators, 1919-20. 12GP
- —Toronto St. Patricks, 1922-23. 12GP
- —Boston Bruins, 1929-30. 22GP
- —Boston Bruins, 1930-31. 22GP
- —Montreal Canadiens, 1976-77. 40GP
- —Quebec Nordiques, 1994-95. 24GP

FEWEST ROAD LOSSES, ONE SEASON:
- **3 —Montreal Canadiens,** 1928-29. 22GP
- 4 —Ottawa Senators, 1919-20. 12GP
- —Montreal Canadiens, 1927-28. 22GP
- —Boston Bruins, 1929-30. 20GP
- —Boston Bruins, 1940-41. 24GP

FEWEST LOSSES, ONE SEASON (MINIMUM 70-GAME SCHEDULE):
- **8 —Montreal Canadiens,** 1976-77. 80GP
- 10 —Montreal Canadiens, 1972-73. 78GP
- —Montreal Canadiens, 1977-78. 80GP
- 11 —Montreal Canadiens, 1975-76. 80GP

FEWEST HOME LOSSES, ONE SEASON (MINIMUM 70-GAME SCHEDULE):
- **1 —Montreal Canadiens,** 1976-77. 40GP
- 2 —Montreal Canadiens, 1961-62. 35GP
- —NY Rangers, 1970-71. 39GP
- —Philadelphia Flyers, 1975-76. 40GP

FEWEST ROAD LOSSES, ONE SEASON (MINIMUM 70-GAME SCHEDULE):
- **6 —Montreal Canadiens,** 1972-73. 39GP
- —**Montreal Canadiens,** 1974-75. 40GP
- —**Montreal Canadiens,** 1977-78. 40GP
- 7 —Detroit Red Wings, 1951-52. 35GP
- —Montreal Canadiens, 1976-77. 40GP
- —Philadelphia Flyers, 1979-80. 40GP

Most Losses

MOST LOSSES, ONE SEASON:
- **71 —San Jose Sharks,** 1992-93. 84GP
- 70 —Ottawa Senators, 1992-93. 84GP
- 67 —Washington Capitals, 1974-75. 80GP
- 61 —Quebec Nordiques, 1989-90. 80GP
- —Ottawa Senators, 1993-94. 84GP

MOST HOME LOSSES, ONE SEASON:
- ***32 —San Jose Sharks,** 1992-93. 41GP
- 29 —Pittsburgh Penguins, 1983-84. 40GP
- * —Ottawa Senators, 1993-94. 41GP

MOST ROAD LOSSES, ONE SEASON:
- ***40 —Ottawa Senators,** 1992-93. 41GP
- 39 —Washington Capitals, 1974-75. 40GP
- 37 —California Seals, 1973-74. 39GP
- * —San Jose Sharks, 1992-93. 41GP

---

* – Does not include neutral site games.

TEAM TIES

Most Ties

MOST TIES, ONE SEASON:
24 —Philadelphia Flyers, 1969-70. 76GP
23 —Montreal Canadiens, 1962-63. 70GP
—Chicago Blackhawks, 1973-74. 78GP

MOST HOME TIES, ONE SEASON:
13 —NY Rangers, 1954-55. 35GP
—Philadelphia Flyers, 1969-70. 38GP
—California Seals, 1971-72. 39GP
—California Seals, 1972-73. 39GP
—Chicago Blackhawks, 1973-74. 39GP

MOST ROAD TIES, ONE SEASON:
15 —Philadelphia Flyers, 1976-77. 40GP
14 —Montreal Canadiens, 1952-53. 35GP
—Montreal Canadiens, 1974-75. 40GP
—Philadelphia Flyers, 1975-76. 40GP

Fewest Ties

FEWEST TIES, ONE SEASON (Since 1926-27):
1 —Boston Bruins, 1929-30. 44GP
2 —Montreal Canadians, 1926-27. 44GP
—NY Americans, 1926-27. 44GP
—Boston Bruins, 1938-39. 48GP
—NY Rangers, 1941-42. 48GP
—San Jose Sharks, 1992-93. 84GP

FEWEST TIES, ONE SEASON (MINIMUM 70-GAME SCHEDULE):
2 —San Jose Sharks, 1992-93. 84GP
3 —New Jersey Devils, 1985-86. 80GP
—Calgary Flames, 1986-87. 80GP
—Vancouver Canucks, 1993-94. 84GP

WINNING STREAKS

LONGEST WINNING STREAK, ONE SEASON:
17 Games —Pittsburgh Penguins, Mar. 9 - Apr. 10, 1993.
15 Games —NY Islanders, Jan. 21 - Feb. 20, 1982.
14 Games —Boston Bruins, Dec. 3, 1929 - Jan. 9, 1930.

LONGEST HOME WINNING STREAK, ONE SEASON:
20 Games —Boston Bruins, Dec. 3, 1929 - Mar. 18, 1930.
—Philadelphia Flyers, Jan. 4 - Apr. 3, 1976.

LONGEST ROAD WINNING STREAK, ONE SEASON:
10 Games —Buffalo Sabres, Dec. 10, 1983 - Jan. 23, 1984.
8 Games —Boston Bruins, Feb. 17 - Mar. 8, 1972.
—Los Angeles Kings, Dec. 18, 1974 - Jan. 16, 1975.
—Montreal Canadiens, Dec. 18, 1977 - Jan. 18, 1978.
—NY Islanders, Feb. 27 - Mar. 29, 1981.
—Montreal Canadiens, Jan. 21 - Feb. 21, 1982.
—Philadelphia Flyers, Dec. 22, 1982 - Jan. 16, 1983.
—Winnipeg Jets, Feb. 25 - Apr. 6, 1985.
—Edmonton Oilers, Dec. 9, 1986 - Jan. 17, 1987.
—Boston Bruins, Mar. 15 - Apr. 14, 1993.

LONGEST WINNING STREAK FROM START OF SEASON:
10 Games —Toronto Maple Leafs, 1993-94.
8 Games —Toronto Maple Leafs, 1934-35.
—Buffalo Sabres, 1975-76.
7 Games —Edmonton Oilers, 1983-84.
—Quebec Nordiques, 1985-86.
—Pittsburgh Penguins, 1986-87.
—Pittsburgh Penguins, 1994-95.

LONGEST HOME WINNING STREAK FROM START OF SEASON:
11 Games —Chicago Blackhawks, 1963-64.
10 Games —Ottawa Senators, 1925-26.
9 Games —Montreal Canadiens, 1953-54.
—Chicago Blackhawks, 1971-72.

LONGEST ROAD WINNING STREAK FROM START OF SEASON:
7 Games —Toronto Maple Leafs, Nov. 14 - Dec. 15, 1940.

LONGEST WINNING STREAK, INCLUDING PLAYOFFS:
15 Games —Detroit Red Wings, Feb. 27 - Apr. 5, 1955. Nine regular-season games, six playoff games.

LONGEST HOME WINNING STREAK, INCLUDING PLAYOFFS:
24 Games —Philadelphia Flyers, Jan. 4 - Apr. 25, 1976. Twenty regular-season games, four playoff games.

LONGEST ROAD WINNING STREAK, INCLUDING PLAYOFFS:
8 Games —NY Islanders, Apr. 4 - May 1, 1980. One regular season game, seven playoff games.

UNDEFEATED STREAKS

LONGEST UNDEFEATED STREAK, ONE SEASON:
35 Games —Philadelphia Flyers, Oct. 14, 1979 - Jan. 6, 1980. 25w-10T.
28 Games —Montreal Canadiens, Dec. 18, 1977 - Feb. 23, 1978. 23w-5T.
23 Games —Boston Bruins, Dec. 22, 1940 - Feb. 23, 1941. 15w-8T.
—Philadelphia Flyers, Jan. 29 - Mar. 18, 1976. 17w-6T.

LONGEST HOME UNDEFEATED STREAK, ONE SEASON:
34 Games —Montreal Canadiens, Nov. 1, 1976 - Apr. 2, 1977. 28w-6T.
27 Games —Boston Bruins, Nov. 22, 1970 - Mar. 20, 1971. 26w-1T.

LONGEST ROAD UNDEFEATED STREAK, ONE SEASON:
23 Games —Montreal Canadiens, Nov. 27, 1974 - Mar. 12, 1975. 14w-9T.
17 Games —Montreal Canadiens, Dec. 18, 1977 - Mar. 1, 1978. 14w-3T.
16 Games —Philadelphia Flyers, Oct. 20, 1979 - Jan. 6, 1980. 11w-5T.

LONGEST UNDEFEATED STREAK FROM START OF SEASON:
15 Games —Edmonton Oilers, 1984-85. 12w-3T.
14 Games —Montreal Canadiens, 1943-44. 11w-3T.
13 Games —Montreal Canadiens, 1972-73. 9w-4T.
—Pittsburgh Penguins, 1994-95. 12w-1T.

LONGEST HOME UNDEFEATED STREAK FROM START OF SEASON:
25 Games —Montreal Canadiens, Oct. 30, 1943 - Mar. 18, 1944. 22w-3T.

LONGEST ROAD UNDEFEATED STREAK FROM START OF SEASON:
15 Games —Detroit Red Wings, Oct. 18 - Dec. 20, 1951. 10w-5T.

LONGEST UNDEFEATED STREAK, INCLUDING PLAYOFFS:
21 Games —Pittsburgh Penguins, Mar. 9 - Apr. 22, 1993. 17w-1T in regular season and 3w in playoffs.

LONGEST HOME UNDEFEATED STREAK, INCLUDING PLAYOFFS:
38 Games —Montreal Canadiens, Nov. 1, 1976 - Apr. 26, 1977. 28w-6T in regular season and 4w in playoff.

LONGEST ROAD UNDEFEATED STREAK, INCLUDING PLAYOFFS:
13 Games —Montreal Canadiens, Feb. 26 - Apr. 20, 1980. 6w-4T in regular season and 3w in playoffs.
—NY Islanders, Mar. 16 - May 1, 1980. 3w-3T in regular season and 7w in playoffs.

LOSING STREAKS

LONGEST LOSING STREAK, ONE SEASON:
17 Games —Washington Capitals, Feb. 18 - Mar. 26, 1975.
—San Jose Sharks, Jan. 4 - Feb. 12, 1993.
15 Games —Philadelphia Quakers, Nov. 29, 1930 - Jan. 8, 1931.

LONGEST HOME LOSING STREAK, ONE SEASON:
11 Games —Boston Bruins, Dec. 8, 1924 - Feb. 17, 1925.
—Washington Capitals, Feb. 18 - Mar. 30, 1975.
—Ottawa Senators, Oct. 27 - Dec. 8, 1993.

LONGEST ROAD LOSING STREAK, ONE SEASON:
*38 Games —Ottawa Senators, Oct. 10, 1992 - Apr. 3, 1993.
37 Games —Washington Capitals, Oct. 9, 1974 - Mar. 26, 1975.

LONGEST LOSING STREAK FROM START OF SEASON:
11 Games —NY Rangers, 1943-44.
7 Games —Montreal Canadiens, 1938-39.
—Chicago Blackhawks, 1947-48.
—Washington Capitals, 1983-84.
—Chicago Blackhawks, 1997-98.

LONGEST HOME LOSING STREAK FROM START OF SEASON:
8 Games —Los Angeles Kings, Oct. 13 - Nov. 6, 1971.

LONGEST ROAD LOSING STREAK FROM START OF SEASON:
*38 Games —Ottawa Senators, Oct. 10, 1992 - Apr. 3, 1993.

WINLESS STREAKS

LONGEST WINLESS STREAK, ONE SEASON:
30 Games —Winnipeg Jets, Oct. 19 - Dec. 20, 1980. 23L-7T.
27 Games —Kansas City Scouts, Feb. 12 - Apr. 4, 1976. 21L-6T.
25 Games —Washington Capitals, Nov. 29, 1975 - Jan. 21, 1976. 22L-3T.

LONGEST HOME WINLESS STREAK, ONE SEASON:
17 Games —Ottawa Senators, Oct. 28, 1995 - Jan. 27, 1996. 15L-2T.
15 Games —Chicago Blackhawks, Dec. 16, 1928 - Feb. 28, 1929. 11L-4T.
—Montreal Canadiens, Dec. 16, 1939 - Mar. 7, 1940. 12L-3T.

LONGEST ROAD WINLESS STREAK, ONE SEASON:
*38 Games —Ottawa Senators, Oct. 10, 1992 - Apr. 3, 1993. 38L-0T.
37 Games —Washington Capitals, Oct. 9, 1974 - Mar. 26, 1975. 37L-0T.

LONGEST WINLESS STREAK FROM START OF SEASON:
15 Games —NY Rangers, 1943-44. 14L-1T.
11 Games —Pittsburgh Pirates, 1927-28. 8L-3T.
—Minnesota North Stars, 1973-74. 5L-6T.
—San Jose Sharks, 1995-96. 7L-4T.

LONGEST HOME WINLESS STREAK FROM START OF SEASON:
11 Games —Pittsburgh Penguins, Oct. 8 - Nov. 19, 1983. 9L-2T.

LONGEST ROAD WINLESS STREAK FROM START OF SEASON:
*38 Games —Ottawa Senators, Oct. 10, 1992 - Apr. 3, 1993. 38L-0T.

* – Does not include neutral site games.

NON-SHUTOUT STREAKS

LONGEST NON-SHUTOUT STREAK:
264 Games — Calgary Flames, Nov. 12, 1981 - Jan. 9, 1985.
262 Games — Los Angeles Kings, Mar. 15, 1986 - Oct. 25, 1989.
244 Games — Washington Capitals, Oct. 31, 1989 - Nov. 11, 1993.
230 Games — Quebec Nordiques, Feb. 10, 1980 - Jan. 13, 1983.
229 Games — Edmonton Oilers, Mar. 15, 1981 - Feb. 11, 1984.

LONGEST NON-SHUTOUT STREAK INCLUDING PLAYOFFS:
264 Games — Los Angeles Kings, Mar. 15, 1986 - Apr. 6, 1989.
(5 playoff games in 1987; 5 in 1988; 2 in 1989).
262 Games — Chicago Blackhawks, Mar. 14, 1970 - Feb. 21, 1973. (8 playoff games in 1970; 18 in 1971; 8 in 1972).
251 Games — Quebec Nordiques, Feb. 10, 1980 - Jan. 13, 1983. (5 playoff games in 1981; 16 in 1982).
245 Games — Pittsburgh Penguins, Jan. 7, 1989 - Oct. 26, 1991. (11 playoff games in 1989; 23 in 1991).

TEAM GOALS

Most Goals

MOST GOALS, ONE SEASON:
446 — Edmonton Oilers, 1983-84. 80GP
426 — Edmonton Oilers, 1985-86. 80GP
424 — Edmonton Oilers, 1982-83. 80GP
417 — Edmonton Oilers, 1981-82. 80GP
401 — Edmonton Oilers, 1984-85. 80GP

MOST GOALS, ONE TEAM, ONE GAME:
16 — Montreal Canadiens, Mar. 3, 1920, at Quebec. Defeated Que. Bulldogs 16-3.

MOST GOALS, BOTH TEAMS, ONE GAME:
21 — Montreal Canadiens, Toronto St. Patricks, at Montreal, Jan. 10, 1920. Montreal won 14-7.
— **Edmonton Oilers, Chicago Blackhawks,** at Chicago, Dec. 11, 1985. Edmonton won 12-9.
20 — Edmonton Oilers, Minnesota North Stars, at Edmonton, Jan. 4, 1984. Edmonton won 12-8.
— Toronto Maple Leafs, Edmonton Oilers, at Toronto, Jan. 8, 1986. Toronto won 11-9.
19 — Montreal Wanderers, Toronto Arenas, at Montreal, Dec. 19, 1917. Montreal won 10-9.
— Montreal Canadiens, Quebec Bulldogs, at Quebec, Mar. 3, 1920. Montreal won 16-3.
— Montreal Canadiens, Hamilton Tigers, at Montreal, Feb. 26, 1921. Montreal won 13-6.
— Boston Bruins, NY Rangers, at Boston, Mar. 4, 1944. Boston won 10-9.
— Boston Bruins, Detroit Red Wings, at Detroit, Mar. 16, 1944. Detroit won 10-9.
— Vancouver Canucks, Minnesota North Stars, at Vancouver, Oct. 7, 1983. Vancouver won 10-9.

MOST GOALS, ONE TEAM, ONE PERIOD:
9 — Buffalo Sabres, Mar. 19, 1981, at Buffalo, second period during 14-4 win over Toronto.
8 — Detroit Red Wings, Jan. 23, 1944, at Detroit, third period during 15-0 win over NY Rangers.
— Boston Bruins, Mar. 16, 1969, at Boston, second period during 11-3 win over Toronto.
— NY Rangers, Nov. 21, 1971, at New York, third period during 12-1 win over California.
— Philadelphia Flyers, Mar. 31, 1973, at Philadelphia, second period during 10-2 win over NY Islanders.
— Buffalo Sabres, Dec. 21, 1975, at Buffalo, third period during 14-2 win over Washington.
— Minnesota North Stars, Nov. 11, 1981, at Minnesota, second period during 15-2 win over Winnipeg.
— Pittsburgh Penguins, Dec. 17, 1991, at Pittsburgh, second period during 10-2 win over San Jose.
— Washington Capitals, Feb. 3, 1999, at Washington, second period during 10-1 win over Tampa Bay.

MOST GOALS, BOTH TEAMS, ONE PERIOD:
12 — Buffalo Sabres, Toronto Maple Leafs, at Buffalo, March 19, 1981, second period. Buffalo scored 9 goals, Toronto 3. Buffalo won 14-4.
— **Edmonton Oilers, Chicago Blackhawks,** at Chicago, Dec. 11, 1985, second period. Edmonton scored 6 goals, Chicago 6. Edmonton won 12-9.
10 — NY Rangers, NY Americans, at NY Americans, March 16, 1939, third period. NY Rangers scored 7 goals, NY Americans 3. NY Rangers won 11-5.
— Toronto Maple Leafs, Detroit Red Wings, at Detroit, March 17, 1946, third period. Toronto scored 6 goals, Detroit 4. Toronto won 11-7.
— Vancouver Canucks, Buffalo Sabres, at Buffalo, Jan. 8, 1976, third period. Buffalo scored 6 goals, Vancouver 4. Buffalo won 8-5.
— Buffalo Sabres, Montreal Canadiens, at Montreal, Oct. 26, 1982, first period. Montreal scored 5 goals, Buffalo 5. 7-7 tie.
— Boston Bruins, Quebec Nordiques, at Quebec, Dec. 7, 1982, second period. Quebec scored 6 goals, Boston 4. Quebec won 10-5.
— Calgary Flames, Vancouver Canucks, at Vancouver, Jan. 16, 1987, first period. Vancouver scored 6 goals, Calgary 4. Vancouver won 9-5.
— Winnipeg Jets, Detroit Red Wings, at Detroit, Nov. 25, 1987, third period. Detroit scored 7 goals, Winnipeg 3. Detroit won 10-8.
— Chicago Blackhawks, St. Louis Blues, at St. Louis, March 15, 1988, third period. Chicago scored 5 goals, St. Louis 5. 7-7 tie.

MOST CONSECUTIVE GOALS, ONE TEAM, ONE GAME:
15 — Detroit Red Wings, Jan. 23, 1944, at Detroit. Defeated NY Rangers 15-0.

Fewest Goals

FEWEST GOALS, ONE SEASON:
33 — Chicago Blackhawks, 1928-29. 44GP
45 — Montreal Maroons, 1924-25. 30GP
46 — Pittsburgh Pirates, 1928-29. 44GP

FEWEST GOALS, ONE SEASON (MINIMUM 70-GAME SCHEDULE):
133 — Chicago Blackhawks, 1953-54. 70GP
147 — Toronto Maple Leafs, 1954-55. 70GP
— Boston Bruins, 1955-56. 70GP
150 — NY Rangers, 1954-55. 70GP

TEAM POWER-PLAY GOALS

MOST POWER-PLAY GOALS, ONE SEASON:
119 — Pittsburgh Penguins, 1988-89. 80GP
113 — Detroit Red Wings, 1992-93. 84GP
111 — NY Rangers, 1987-88. 80GP
110 — Pittsburgh Penguins, 1987-88. 80GP
— Winnipeg Jets, 1987-88, 80GP

TEAM SHORTHAND GOALS

MOST SHORTHAND GOALS, ONE SEASON:
36 — Edmonton Oilers, 1983-84. 80GP
28 — Edmonton Oilers, 1986-87. 80GP
27 — Edmonton Oilers, 1985-86. 80GP
— Edmonton Oilers, 1988-89. 80GP

TEAM GOALS-PER-GAME

HIGHEST GOALS-PER-GAME AVERAGE, ONE SEASON:
5.58 — Edmonton Oilers, 1983-84. 446G in 80GP
5.38 — Montreal Canadiens, 1919-20. 129G in 24GP
5.33 — Edmonton Oilers, 1985-86. 426G in 80GP
5.30 — Edmonton Oilers, 1982-83. 424G in 80GP
5.23 — Montreal Canadiens, 1917-18. 115G in 22GP

LOWEST GOALS-PER-GAME AVERAGE, ONE SEASON:
.75 — Chicago Blackhawks, 1928-29, 33G in 44GP
1.05 — Pittsburgh Pirates, 1928-29. 46G in 44GP
1.20 — NY Americans, 1928-29. 53G in 44GP

TEAM ASSISTS

MOST ASSISTS, ONE SEASON:
737 — Edmonton Oilers, 1985-86. 80GP
736 — Edmonton Oilers, 1983-84. 80GP
706 — Edmonton Oilers, 1981-82. 80GP

FEWEST ASSISTS, ONE SEASON:
45 — NY Rangers, 1926-27. 44GP

FEWEST ASSISTS, ONE SEASON (MINIMUM 70-GAME SCHEDULE):
206 — Chicago Blackhawks, 1953-54. 70GP

TEAM TOTAL POINTS

MOST SCORING POINTS, ONE SEASON:
1,182 — Edmonton Oilers, 1983-84. 80GP
1,163 — Edmonton Oilers, 1985-86. 80GP
1,123 — Edmonton Oilers, 1981-82. 80GP

MOST SCORING POINTS, ONE TEAM, ONE GAME:
40 — Buffalo Sabres, Dec. 21, 1975, at Buffalo. Buffalo defeated Washington 14-2, receiving 26A.
39 — Minnesota North Stars, Nov. 11, 1981, at Minnesota. Minnesota defeated Winnipeg 15-2, receiving 24A.
37 — Detroit Red Wings, Jan. 23, 1944, at Detroit. Detroit defeated NY Rangers 15-0, receiving 22A.
— Toronto Maple Leafs, Mar. 16, 1957, at Toronto. Toronto defeated NY Rangers 14-1, receiving 23A.
— Buffalo Sabres, Feb. 25, 1978, at Cleveland. Buffalo defeated Cleveland 13-3, receiving 24A.
— Calgary Flames, Feb. 10, 1993, at Calgary. Calgary defeated San Jose 13-1, receiving 24A.

MOST SCORING POINTS, BOTH TEAMS, ONE GAME:
62 — Edmonton Oilers, Chicago Blackhawks, at Chicago, Dec. 11, 1985. Edmonton won 12-9. Edmonton had 24A, Chicago, 17.
53 — Quebec Nordiques, Washington Capitals, at Washington, Feb. 22, 1981. Quebec won 11-7. Quebec had 22A, Washington, 13.
— Edmonton Oilers, Minnesota North Stars, at Edmonton, Jan. 4, 1984. Edmonton won 12-8. Edmonton had 20A, Minnesota 13.
— Minnesota North Stars, St. Louis Blues, at St. Louis, Jan. 27, 1984. Minnesota won 10-8. Minnesota had 19A, St. Louis 16.
— Toronto Maple Leafs, Edmonton Oilers, at Toronto, Jan. 8, 1986. Toronto won 11-9. Toronto had 17A, Edmonton 16.
52 — Mtl. Maroons, NY Americans, at New York, Feb. 18, 1936. 8-8 tie. New York had 20A, Montreal 16. (3A allowed for each goal.)
— Vancouver Canucks, Minnesota North Stars, at Vancouver, Oct. 7, 1983. Vancouver won 10-9. Vancouver had 16A, Minnesota 17.

MOST SCORING POINTS, ONE TEAM, ONE PERIOD:
23 —**NY Rangers,** Nov. 21, 1971, at New York, third period during 12-1 win over California. NY Rangers scored 8G and 15A.
—**Buffalo Sabres,** Dec. 21, 1975, at Buffalo, third period during 14-2 win over Washington. Buffalo scored 8G and 15A.
—**Buffalo Sabres,** March 19, 1981, at Buffalo, second period during 14-4 win over Toronto. Buffalo scored 9G and 14A.
22 —Detroit Red Wings, Jan. 23, 1944, at Detroit, third period during 15-0 win over NY Rangers. Detroit scored 8G and 14A.
—Boston Bruins, March 16, 1969, at Boston, second period during 11-3 win over Toronto Maple Leafs. Boston scored 8G and 14A.
—Minnesota North Stars, Nov. 11, 1981, at Minnesota, second period during 15-2 win over Winnipeg. Minnesota scored 8G and 14A.
—Pittsburgh Penguins, Dec. 17, 1991, at Pittsburgh, second period during 10-2 win over San Jose. Pittsburgh scored 8G and 14A.
—Washington Capitals, Feb. 3, 1999, at Washington, second period during 10-1 win over Tampa Bay. Washington scored 8G and 14A.

MOST SCORING POINTS, BOTH TEAMS, ONE PERIOD:
35 —**Edmonton, Oilers, Chicago Blackhawks,** at Chicago, Dec. 11, 1985, second period. Edmonton had 6G, 12A; Chicago, 6G, 11A. Edmonton won 12-9.
31 —Buffalo Sabres, Toronto Maple Leafs, at Buffalo, March 19, 1981, second period. Buffalo had 9G, 14A; Toronto, 3G, 5A. Buffalo won 14-4.
29 —Winnipeg Jets, Detroit Red Wings, at Detroit, Nov. 25, 1987, third period. Detroit had 7G, 13A; Winnipeg had 3G, 6A. Detroit won 10-8.
—Chicago Blackhawks, St. Louis Blues, at St. Louis, March 15, 1988, third period. St. Louis had 5G, 10A; Chicago had 5G, 9A. 7-7 tie.

FASTEST GOALS

FASTEST SIX GOALS, BOTH TEAMS
3 Minutes, 15 Seconds — Montreal Canadiens, Toronto Maple Leafs, at Montreal, Jan. 4, 1944, first period. Montreal scored 4G, Toronto 2. Montreal won 6-3.

FASTEST FIVE GOALS, BOTH TEAMS:
1 Minute, 24 Seconds — **Chicago Blackhawks, Toronto Maple Leafs,** at Toronto, Oct. 15, 1983, second period. Scorers: Gaston Gingras, Toronto, 16:49; Denis Savard, Chicago, 17:12; Steve Larmer, Chicago, 17:27; Savard, 17:42; John Anderson, Toronto, 18:13. Toronto won 10-8.
1 Minute, 39 Seconds — Detroit Red Wings, Toronto Maple Leafs, at Toronto, Nov. 15, 1944, third period. Scorers: Ted Kennedy, Toronto, 10:36 and 10:55; Hal Jackson, Detroit, 11:48; Steve Wochy, Detroit, 12:02; Don Grosso, Detroit, 12:15. Detroit won 8-4.

FASTEST FIVE GOALS, ONE TEAM:
2 Minutes, 7 Seconds — **Pittsburgh Penguins,** at Pittsburgh, Nov. 22, 1972, third period. Scorers: Bryan Hextall, 12:00; Jean Pronovost, 12:18; Al McDonough, 13:40; Ken Schinkel, 13:49; Ron Schock, 14:07. Pittsburgh defeated St. Louis 10-4.
2 Minutes, 37 Seconds — NY Islanders, at New York, Jan. 26, 1982, first period. Scorers: Duane Sutter, 1:31; John Tonelli, 2:30; Bryan Trottier, 2:46; Bryan Trottier, 3:31; Duane Sutter, 4:08. NY Islanders defeated Pittsburgh 9-2.
2 Minutes, 55 Seconds — Boston Bruins, at Boston, Dec. 19, 1974. Scorers: Bobby Schmautz, 19:13 (first period); Ken Hodge, 0:18; Phil Esposito, 0:43; Don Marcotte, 0:58; John Bucyk, 2:08 (second period). Boston defeated NY Rangers 11-3.

FASTEST FOUR GOALS, BOTH TEAMS:
53 Seconds — **Chicago Blackhawks, Toronto Maple Leafs,** at Toronto, Oct. 15, 1983, second period. Scorers: Gaston Gingras, Toronto, 16:49; Denis Savard, Chicago, 17:12; Steve Larmer, Chicago, 17:27; and Savard, 17:42. Toronto won 10-8.
57 Seconds — Quebec Nordiques, Detroit Red Wings, at Quebec, Jan. 27, 1990, first period. Scorers: Paul Gillis, Quebec, 18:01; Claude Loiselle, Quebec, 18:12; Joe Sakic, Quebec, 18:27; and Jimmy Carson, Detroit, 18:58. Detroit won 8-6.
1 Minute, 1 Second — Colorado Rockies, NY Rangers, at New York, Jan. 15, 1980, first period. Scorers: Doug Sulliman, NY Rangers, 7:52; Ed Johnstone, NY Rangers, 7:57; Warren Miller, NY Rangers, 8:20; Rob Ramage, Colorado, 8:53. 6-6 tie.
— Chicago Blackhawks, Toronto Maple Leafs, at Toronto, Oct. 15, 1983, second period. Scorers: Denis Savard, Chicago, 17:12; Steve Larmer, Chicago, 17:27; Savard, 17:42; John Anderson, Toronto, 18:13. Toronto won 10-8.

FASTEST FOUR GOALS, ONE TEAM:
1 Minute, 20 Seconds — **Boston Bruins,** at Boston, Jan. 21, 1945, second period. Scorers: Bill Thoms, 6:34; Frank Mario, 7:08 and 7:27; and Ken Smith, 7:54. Boston defeated NY Rangers 14-3.

FASTEST THREE GOALS, BOTH TEAMS:
15 Seconds — **Minnesota North Stars, NY Rangers,** at Minnesota, Feb. 10, 1983, second period. Scorers: Mark Pavelich, NY Rangers, 19:18; Ron Greschner, NY Rangers, 19:27; Willi Plett, Minnesota, 19:33. Minnesota won 7-5.
18 Seconds — Montreal Canadiens, NY Rangers, at Montreal, Dec. 12, 1963, first period. Scorers: Dave Balon, Montreal, 0:58; Gilles Tremblay, Montreal, 1:04; Camille Henry, NY Rangers, 1:16. Montreal won 6-4.
— California Golden Seals, Buffalo Sabres, at California, Feb. 1, 1976, third period. Scorers: Jim Moxey, California, 19:38; Wayne Merrick, California, 19:45; Danny Gare, Buffalo, 19:56. Buffalo won 9-5.

FASTEST THREE GOALS, ONE TEAM:
20 Seconds — **Boston Bruins,** at Boston, Feb. 25, 1971, third period. Scorers: John Bucyk, 4:50; Ed Westfall, 5:02; Ted Green, 5:10. Boston defeated Vancouver 8-3.
21 Seconds — Chicago Blackhawks, at New York, Mar. 23, 1952, third period. Bill Mosienko scored all three goals, at 6:09, 6:20 and 6:30. Chicago defeated NY Rangers 7-6.
— Washington Capitals, at Washington, Nov. 23, 1990, first period. Scorers: Michal Pivonka, 16:18; Stephen Leach, 16:29 and 16:39. Washington defeated Pittsburgh 7-3.

FASTEST THREE GOALS FROM START OF PERIOD, BOTH TEAMS:
1 Minute, 5 Seconds — **Hartford Whalers, Montreal Canadiens,** at Montreal, March 11, 1989, second period. Scorers: Kevin Dineen, Hartford, 0:11; Guy Carbonneau, Montreal, 0:36; Petr Svoboda, Montreal, 1:05. Montreal won 5-3.

FASTEST THREE GOALS FROM START OF PERIOD, ONE TEAM:
53 Seconds — **Calgary Flames,** at Calgary, Feb. 10, 1993, third period. Scorers: Gary Suter, 0:17; Chris Lindbergh, 0:40; Ron Stern, 0:53. Calgary defeated San Jose 13-1.

FASTEST TWO GOALS, BOTH TEAMS:
2 Seconds — **St. Louis Blues, Boston Bruins,** at Boston, Dec. 19, 1987, third period. Scorers: Ken Linseman, Boston, 19:50; Doug Gilmour, St. Louis, 19:52. St. Louis won 7-5.
3 Seconds — Chicago Blackhawks, Minnesota North Stars, at Minnesota, Nov. 5, 1988, third period. Scorers: Steve Thomas, Chicago, 6:03; Dave Gagner, Minnesota, 6:06. 5-5 tie.

FASTEST TWO GOALS, ONE TEAM:
4 Seconds — **Montreal Maroons,** at Montreal, Jan. 3, 1931, third period. Nels Stewart scored both goals, at 8:24 and 8:28. Mtl. Maroons defeated Boston 5-3.
—**Buffalo Sabres,** at Buffalo, Oct. 17, 1974, third period. Scorers: Lee Fogolin, 14:55; Don Luce, 14:59. Buffalo defeated California 6-1.
—**Toronto Maple Leafs,** at Quebec, Dec. 29, 1988, third period. Scorers: Ed Olczyk, 5:24; Gary Leeman, 5:28. Toronto defeated Quebec 6-5.
—**Calgary Flames,** at Quebec, Oct. 17, 1989, third period. Scorers: Doug Gilmour, 19:45; Paul Ranheim, 19:49. Calgary and Quebec tied 8-8.
—**Winnipeg Jets,** at Winnipeg, Dec. 15, 1995, second period. Deron Quint scored both goals, at 7:51 and 7:55. Winnipeg defeated Edmonton 9-4.

FASTEST TWO GOALS FROM START OF GAME, ONE TEAM:
24 Seconds — **Edmonton Oilers,** Mar. 28, 1982, at Los Angeles. Scorers: Mark Messier, 0:14; Dave Lumley, 0:24. Edmonton defeated Los Angeles 6-2.
29 Seconds — Pittsburgh Penguins, Dec. 6, 1980, at Pittsburgh. Scorers: George Ferguson, 0:17; Greg Malone, 0:29. Pittsburgh defeated Chicago 6-4.
32 Seconds — Calgary Flames, Mar. 11, 1987, at Hartford. Scorers: Doug Risebrough, 0:09; Colin Patterson, 0:32. Calgary defeated Hartford 6-1.

FASTEST TWO GOALS FROM START OF PERIOD, BOTH TEAMS:
14 Seconds — **NY Rangers, Quebec Nordiques,** at Quebec, Nov. 5, 1983, third period. Scorers: Andre Savard, Quebec, 0:08; Pierre Larouche, NY Rangers, 0:14. 4-4 tie.
26 Seconds — Buffalo Sabres, St. Louis Blues, at Buffalo, Jan. 3, 1993, third period. Scorers: Alexander Mogilny, Buffalo, 0:08; Phillippe Bozon, St. Louis, 0:26. Buffalo won 6-5.
28 Seconds — Boston Bruins, Montreal Canadiens, at Montreal, Oct. 11, 1989, third period. Scorers: Jim Wiemer, Boston 0:10; Tom Chorske, Montreal 0:28. Montreal won 4-2.

FASTEST TWO GOALS FROM START OF PERIOD, ONE TEAM:
21 Seconds — **Chicago Blackhawks,** Nov. 5, 1983, at Minnesota, second period. Scorers: Ken Yaremchuk, 0:12; Darryl Sutter, 0:21. Minnesota defeated Chicago 10-5.
30 Seconds — Washington Capitals, Jan. 27, 1980, at Washington, second period. Scorers: Mike Gartner, 0:08; Bengt Gustafsson, 0:30. Washington defeated NY Islanders 7-1.
31 Seconds —Buffalo Sabres, Jan. 10, 1974, at Buffalo, third period. Scorers: Rene Robert, 0:21; Rick Martin, 0:31. Buffalo defeated NY Rangers 7-2.
— NY Islanders, Feb. 22, 1986, at New York, third period. Scorers: Roger Kortko, 0:10; Bob Bourne, 0:31. NY Islanders defeated Detroit 5-2.

It was a real shootout at the Chicago Stadium when the Oilers met the Blackhawks on December 11, 1985. Several combined team records were set during the Oilers' 12-9 victory. Jari Kurri scored a hat trick that night. Wayne Gretzky had seven assists.

50, 40, 30, 20-GOAL SCORERS

MOST 50-OR-MORE-GOAL SCORERS, ONE SEASON:

3 — **Edmonton Oilers,** 1983-84. Wayne Gretzky, 87; Glenn Anderson, 54; Jari Kurri, 52. 80GP
— **Edmonton Oilers,** 1985-86. Jari Kurri, 68; Glenn Anderson, 54; Wayne Gretzky, 52. 80GP
2 — Boston Bruins, 1970-71. Phil Esposito, 76; John Bucyk, 51. 78GP
— Boston Bruins, 1973-74. Phil Esposito, 68; Ken Hodge, 50. 78GP
— Philadelphia Flyers, 1975-76. Reggie Leach, 61; Bill Barber, 50. 80GP
— Pittsburgh Penguins, 1975-76. Pierre Larouche, 53; Jean Pronovost, 52. 80GP
— Montreal Canadiens, 1976-77. Steve Shutt, 60; Guy Lafleur, 56. 80GP
— Los Angeles Kings, 1979-80. Charlie Simmer, 56; Marcel Dionne, 53. 80GP
— Montreal Canadiens, 1979-80. Pierre Larouche, 50; Guy Lafleur, 50. 80GP
— Los Angeles Kings, 1980-81. Marcel Dionne, 58; Charlie Simmer, 56. 80GP
— Edmonton Oilers, 1981-82. Wayne Gretzky, 92; Mark Messier, 50. 80GP
— NY Islanders, 1981-82. Mike Bossy, 64; Bryan Trottier, 50. 80GP
— Edmonton Oilers, 1984-85. Wayne Gretzky, 73; Jari Kurri, 71. 80GP
— Washington Capitals, 1984-85. Bob Carpenter, 53; Mike Gartner, 50. 80GP
— Edmonton Oilers, 1986-87. Wayne Gretzky, 62; Jari Kurri, 54. 80GP
— Calgary Flames, 1987-88. Joe Nieuwendyk, 51; Hakan Loob, 50. 80GP
— Los Angeles Kings, 1987-88. Jimmy Carson, 55; Luc Robitaille, 53. 80GP
— Los Angeles Kings, 1988-89. Bernie Nicholls, 70; Wayne Gretzky, 54. 80GP
— Calgary Flames, 1988-89. Joe Nieuwendyk, 51; Joe Mullen, 51. 80GP
— Buffalo Sabres, 1992-93. Alexander Mogilny, 76; Pat LaFontaine, 53. 84GP
— Pittsburgh Penguins, 1992-93. Mario Lemieux, 69; Kevin Stevens, 55. 84GP
— St. Louis Blues, 1992-93. Brett Hull, 54; Brendan Shanahan, 51. 84GP
— St. Louis Blues, 1993-94. Brett Hull, 57; Brendan Shanahan, 52. 84GP
— Detroit Red Wings, 1993-94. Sergei Fedorov, 56; Ray Sheppard, 52. 84GP
— Pittsburgh Penguins, 1995-96. Mario Lemieux, 69; Jaromir Jagr, 62. 82GP

MOST 40-OR-MORE-GOAL SCORERS, ONE SEASON:

4 — **Edmonton Oilers,** 1982-83. Wayne Gretzky, 71; Glenn Anderson, 48; Mark Messier, 48; Jari Kurri, 45. 80GP
— **Edmonton Oilers,** 1983-84. Wayne Gretzky, 87; Glenn Anderson, 54; Jari Kurri, 52; Paul Coffey, 40. 80GP
— **Edmonton Oilers,** 1984-85. Wayne Gretzky, 73; Jari Kurri, 71; Mike Krushelnyski, 43; Glenn Anderson, 42. 80GP
— **Edmonton Oilers,** 1985-86. Jari Kurri, 68; Glenn Anderson, 54; Wayne Gretzky, 52; Paul Coffey, 48. 80GP
— **Calgary Flames,** 1987-88. Joe Nieuwendyk, 51; Hakan Loob, 50; Mike Bullard, 48; Joe Mullen, 40. 80GP
3 — Boston Bruins, 1970-71. Phil Esposito, 76; John Bucyk, 51; Ken Hodge, 43. 78GP
— NY Rangers, 1971-72. Vic Hadfield, 50; Jean Ratelle, 46; Rod Gilbert, 43. 78GP
— Buffalo Sabres, 1975-76. Danny Gare, 50; Rick Martin, 49; Gilbert Perreault, 44. 80GP
— Montreal Canadiens, 1979-80. Guy Lafleur, 50; Pierre Larouche, 50; Steve Shutt, 47. 80GP
— Buffalo Sabres, 1979-80. Danny Gare, 56; Rick Martin, 45; Gilbert Perreault, 40. 80GP
— Los Angeles Kings, 1980-81. Marcel Dionne, 58; Charlie Simmer, 56; Dave Taylor, 47. 80GP
— Los Angeles Kings, 1984-85. Marcel Dionne, 46; Bernie Nicholls, 46; Dave Taylor, 41. 80GP
— NY Islanders, 1984-85. Mike Bossy, 58; Brent Sutter, 42; John Tonelli; 42. 80GP
— Chicago Blackhawks, 1985-86. Denis Savard, 47; Troy Murray, 45; Al Secord, 40. 80GP
— Chicago Blackhawks, 1987-88. Denis Savard, 44; Rick Vaive, 43; Steve Larmer, 41. 80GP
— Edmonton Oilers, 1987-88. Craig Simpson, 43; Jari Kurri, 43; Wayne Gretzky, 40. 80GP
— Los Angeles Kings, 1988-89. Bernie Nicholls, 70; Wayne Gretzky, 54; Luc Robitaille, 46. 80GP
— Los Angeles Kings, 1990-91. Luc Robitaille, 45; Tomas Sandstrom, 45; Wayne Gretzky 41. 80GP
— Pittsburgh Penguins, 1991-92. Kevin Stevens, 54; Mario Lemieux, 44; Joe Mullen, 42. 80GP
— Pittsburgh Penguins, 1992-93. Mario Lemieux, 69; Kevin Stevens, 55; Rick Tocchet, 48. 84GP
— Calgary Flames, 1993-94. Gary Roberts, 41; Robert Reichel, 40; Theoren Fleury, 40. 84GP
— Pittsburgh Penguins, 1995-96. Mario Lemieux, 69; Jaromir Jagr, 62; Petr Nedved, 45. 82GP

MOST 30-OR-MORE GOAL SCORERS, ONE SEASON:

6 — **Buffalo Sabres,** 1974-75. Rick Martin, 52; Rene Robert, 40; Gilbert Perreault, 39; Don Luce, 33; Rick Dudley, Danny Gare, 31 each. 80GP
— **NY Islanders,** 1977-78. Mike Bossy, 53; Bryan Trottier, 46; Clark Gillies, 35; Denis Potvin, Bob Nystrom, Bob Bourne, 30 each. 80GP
— **Winnipeg Jets,** 1984-85. Dale Hawerchuk, 53; Paul MacLean, 41; Laurie Boschman, Brian Mullen, 32 each; Doug Smail, 31; Thomas Steen, 30. 80GP
5 — Chicago Blackhawks, 1968-69. 76GP
— Boston Bruins, 1970-71. 78GP
— Montreal Canadiens, 1971-72. 78GP
— Philadelphia Flyers, 1972-73. 78GP
— Boston Bruins, 1973-74. 78GP
— Montreal Canadiens, 1974-75. 80GP
— Montreal Canadiens, 1975-76. 80GP
— Pittsburgh Penguins, 1975-76. 80GP
— NY Islanders, 1978-79. 80GP
— Detroit Red Wings, 1979-80. 80GP
— Philadelphia Flyers, 1979-80. 80GP
— NY Islanders, 1980-81. 80GP
— St. Louis Blues, 1980-81. 80GP
— Chicago Blackhawks, 1981-82. 80GP
— Edmonton Oilers, 1981-82. 80GP
— Montreal Canadiens, 1981-82. 80GP
— Quebec Nordiques, 1981-82. 80GP
— Washington Capitals, 1981-82. 80GP
— Edmonton Oilers, 1982-83. 80GP
— Edmonton Oilers, 1983-84. 80GP
— Edmonton Oilers, 1984-85. 80GP
— Los Angeles Kings, 1984-85. 80GP
— Edmonton Oilers, 1985-86. 80GP
— Edmonton Oilers, 1986-87. 80GP
— Edmonton Oilers, 1987-88. 80GP
— Edmonton Oilers, 1988-89. 80GP
— Detroit Red Wings, 1991-92. 80GP
— NY Rangers, 1991-92. 80GP
— Pittsburgh Penguins, 1991-92. 80GP
— Detroit Red Wings, 1992-93. 84GP
— Pittsburgh Penguins, 1992-93. 84GP

MOST 20-OR-MORE GOAL SCORERS, ONE SEASON:

11 — **Boston Bruins,** 1977-78; Peter McNab, 41; Terry O'Reilly, 29; Bobby Schmautz, Stan Jonathan, 27 each; Jean Ratelle, Rick Middleton, 25 each; Wayne Cashman, 24; Gregg Sheppard, 23; Brad Park, 22; Don Marcotte, Bob Miller, 20 each. 80GP
10 — Boston Bruins, 1970-71. 78GP
— Montreal Canadiens, 1974-75. 80GP
— St. Louis Blues, 1980-81. 80GP

The 1968-69 Chicago Blackhawks were the first team in NHL history to have five players score 30 goals or more. Stan Mikita, Ken Wharram, Eric Nesterenko and Dennis Hull each scored exactly 30 that year, while Bobby Hull (right) set a new NHL record with 58 goals. Despite their offensive prowess, the Black Hawks finished last in the six-team East Division and missed the playoffs, though their 77 points in 76 games would have seen them finish ahead of five of the six teams in the West Division.

100-POINT SCORERS

MOST 100 OR-MORE-POINT SCORERS, ONE SEASON:
4 —**Boston Bruins,** 1970-71, Phil Esposito, 76G-76A-152PTS; Bobby Orr, 37G-102A-139PTS; John Bucyk, 51G-65A-116PTS; Ken Hodge, 43G-62A-105PTS. 78GP
—**Edmonton Oilers,** 1982-83, Wayne Gretzky, 71G-125A-196PTS; Mark Messier, 48G-58A-106PTS; Glenn Anderson, 48G-56A-104PTS; Jari Kurri, 45G-59A-104PTS. 80GP
—**Edmonton Oilers,** 1983-84, Wayne Gretzky, 87G-118A-205PTS; Paul Coffey, 40G-86A-126PTS; Jari Kurri, 52G-61A-113PTS; Mark Messier, 37G-64A-101PTS. 80GP
—**Edmonton Oilers,** 1985-86, Wayne Gretzky, 52G-163A-215PTS; Paul Coffey, 48G-90A-138PTS; Jari Kurri, 68G-63A-131PTS; Glenn Anderson, 54G-48A-102PTS. 80GP
—**Pittsburgh Penguins,** 1992-93, Mario Lemieux, 69G-91A-160PTS; Kevin Stevens, 55G-56A-111PTS; Rick Tocchet, 48G-61A-109PTS; Ron Francis, 24G-76A-100PTS. 84GP
3 —**Boston Bruins,** 1973-74, Phil Esposito, 68G-77A-145PTS; Bobby Orr, 32G-90A-122PTS; Ken Hodge, 50G-55A-105PTS. 78GP
—**NY Islanders,** 1978-79, Bryan Trottier, 47G-87A-134PTS; Mike Bossy, 69G-57A-126PTS; Denis Potvin, 31G-70A-101PTS. 80GP
—**Los Angeles Kings,** 1980-81, Marcel Dionne, 58G-77A-135PTS; Dave Taylor, 47 G-65A-112PTS; Charlie Simmer, 56G-49A-105PTS. 80GP
—**Edmonton Oilers,** 1984-85, Wayne Gretzky, 73G-135A-208PTS; Jari Kurri, 71G-64A-135PTS; Paul Coffey, 37G-84A-121PTS. 80GP
—**NY Islanders,** 1984-85, Mike Bossy, 58G-59A-117PTS; Brent Sutter, 42G-60A-102PTS; John Tonelli, 42G-58A-100PTS. 80GP
—**Edmonton Oilers,** 1986-87, Wayne Gretzky, 62G-121A-183PTS; Jari Kurri, 54G-54A-108PTS; Mark Messier, 37G-70A-107PTS. 80GP
—**Pittsburgh Penguins,** 1988-89, Mario Lemieux, 85G-114A-199PTS; Rob Brown, 49G-66A-115PTS; Paul Coffey, 30G-83A-113PTS. 80GP
—**Pittsburgh Penguins,** 1995-96, Mario Lemieux, 69G-92A-161PTS; Jaromir Jagr, 62G-87A-149PTS; Ron Francis, 27G-92A-119PTS. 82GP

SHOTS ON GOAL

MOST SHOTS, BOTH TEAMS, ONE GAME:
141 —**NY Americans, Pittsburgh Pirates,** Dec. 26, 1925, at New York. NY Americans, who won game 3-1, had 73 shots; Pit. Pirates, 68 shots.

MOST SHOTS, ONE TEAM, ONE GAME:
83 —**Boston Bruins,** March 4, 1941, at Boston. Boston defeated Chicago 3-2.
73 —NY Americans, Dec. 26, 1925, at New York. NY Americans defeated Pit. Pirates 3-1.
—Boston Bruins, March 21, 1991, at Boston. Boston tied Quebec 3-3.
72 —Boston Bruins, Dec. 10, 1970, at Boston. Boston defeated Buffalo 8-2.

MOST SHOTS, ONE TEAM, ONE PERIOD:
33 —**Boston Bruins,** March 4, 1941, at Boston, second period. Boston defeated Chicago 3-2.

TEAM GOALS-AGAINST

Fewest Goals-Against

FEWEST GOALS AGAINST, ONE SEASON:
42 —**Ottawa Senators,** 1925-26. 36GP
43 —Montreal Canadiens, 1928-29. 44GP
48 —Montreal Canadiens, 1923-24. 24GP
—Montreal Canadiens, 1927-28. 44GP

FEWEST GOALS AGAINST, ONE SEASON (MINIMUM 70-GAME SCHEDULE):
131 —**Toronto Maple Leafs,** 1953-54. 70GP
—**Montreal Canadiens,** 1955-56. 70GP
132 —Detroit Red Wings, 1953-54. 70GP
133 —Detroit Red Wings, 1951-52. 70GP
—Detroit Red Wings, 1952-53. 70GP

LOWEST GOALS-AGAINST-PER-GAME AVERAGE, ONE SEASON:
.98 —**Montreal Canadiens,** 1928-29. 43GA in 44GP.
1.09 —Montreal Canadiens, 1927-28. 48GA in 44GP.
1.17 —Ottawa Senators, 1925-26. 42GA in 36GP.

Most Goals-Against

MOST GOALS AGAINST, ONE SEASON:
446 —**Washington Capitals,** 1974-75. 80GP
415 —Detroit Red Wings, 1985-86. 80GP
414 —San Jose Sharks, 1992-93. 84GP
407 —Quebec Nordiques, 1989-90. 80GP
403 —Hartford Whalers, 1982-83. 80GP

HIGHEST GOALS-AGAINST-PER-GAME AVERAGE, ONE SEASON:
7.38 —**Quebec Bulldogs,** 1919-20, 177GA in 24GP.
6.20 —NY Rangers, 1943-44, 310GA in 50GP.
5.58 —Washington Capitals, 1974-75, 446GA in 80GP.

MOST POWER-PLAY GOALS AGAINST, ONE SEASON:
122 —**Chicago Blackhawks,** 1988-89. 80GP
120 —Pittsburgh Penguins, 1987-88. 80GP
115 —New Jersey Devils, 1988-89. 80GP
—Ottawa Senators, 1992-93. 84GP
114 —Los Angeles Kings, 1992-93. 84GP

MOST SHORTHAND GOALS AGAINST, ONE SEASON:
22 —**Pittsburgh Penguins,** 1984-85. 80GP
—**Minnesota North Stars,** 1991-92. 80GP
—**Colorado Avalanche,** 1995-96. 82GP
21 —Calgary Flames, 1984-85. 80GP
—Pittsburgh Penguins, 1989-90. 80GP

SHUTOUTS

MOST SHUTOUTS, ONE SEASON:
22 —**Montreal Canadiens,** 1928-29. All by George Hainsworth. 44GP
16 —NY Americans, 1928-29. Roy Worters had 13; Flat Walsh 3. 44GP
15 —Ottawa Senators, 1925-26. All by Alex Connell. 36GP
—Ottawa Senators, 1927-28. All by Alex Connell. 44GP
—Boston Bruins, 1927-28. All by Hal Winkler. 44GP
—Chicago Blackhawks, 1969-70. All by Tony Esposito. 76GP

MOST CONSECUTIVE SHUTOUTS, ONE SEASON:
6 —**Ottawa Senators,** Jan. 31 - Feb. 18, 1928.

MOST CONSECUTIVE SHUTOUTS TO START SEASON:
5 —**Toronto Maple Leafs,** Nov. 13 - 22, 1930.

MOST GAMES SHUTOUT, ONE SEASON:
20 —**Chicago Blackhawks,** 1928-29. 44GP

MOST CONSECUTIVE GAMES SHUTOUT:
8 —**Chicago Blackhawks,** Feb. 7 - 28, 1929.

MOST CONSECUTIVE GAMES SHUTOUT TO START SEASON:
3 —**Montreal Maroons,** Nov. 11 - 18, 1930.

TEAM PENALTIES

MOST PENALTY MINUTES, ONE SEASON:
2,713 —**Buffalo Sabres,** 1991-92. 80GP
2,670 —Pittsburgh Penguins, 1988-89. 80GP
2,663 —Chicago Blackhawks, 1991-92. 80GP
2,643 —Calgary Flames, 1991-92. 80GP
2,621 —Philadelphia Flyers, 1980-81. 80GP

MOST PENALTIES, BOTH TEAMS, ONE GAME:
85 Penalties — Edmonton Oilers (44), Los Angeles Kings (41) at Los Angeles, Feb. 28, 1990. Edmonton received 26 minors, 7 majors, 6 10-minute misconducts, 4 game misconducts and 1 match penalty; Los Angeles received 26 minors, 9 majors, 3 10-minute misconducts and 3 game misconducts.

MOST PENALTY MINUTES, BOTH TEAMS, ONE GAME:
406 Minutes — Minnesota North Stars, Boston Bruins at Boston, Feb. 26, 1981. Minnesota received 18 minors, 13 majors, 4 10-minute misconducts and 7 game misconducts, a total of 211PIM. Boston received 20 minors, 13 majors, 3 10-minute misconducts and six game misconducts; a total of 195PIM.

MOST PENALTIES, ONE TEAM, ONE GAME:
44 —**Edmonton Oilers,** Feb. 28, 1990, at Los Angeles. Edmonton received 26 minors, 7 majors, 6 10-minute misconducts, 4 game misconducts and 1 match penalty.
42 —Minnesota North Stars, Feb. 26, 1981, at Boston. Minnesota received 18 minors, 13 majors, 4 10-minute misconducts and 7 game misconducts.
—Boston Bruins, Feb. 26, 1981, at Boston vs. Minnesota. Boston received 20 minors, 13 majors, 3 10-minute misconducts and 6 game misconducts.

MOST PENALTY MINUTES, ONE TEAM, ONE GAME:
211 —**Minnesota North Stars,** Feb. 26, 1981, at Boston. Minnesota received 18 minors, 13 majors, 4 10-minute misconducts and 7 game misconducts.

MOST PENALTIES, BOTH TEAMS, ONE PERIOD:
67 —**Minnesota North Stars, Boston Bruins,** at Boston, Feb. 26, 1981, first period. Minnesota received 15 minors, 8 majors, 4 10-minute misconducts and 7 game misconducts, a total of 34 penalties. Boston had 16 minors, 8 majors, 3 10-minute misconducts and 6 game misconducts, a total of 33 penalties.

MOST PENALTY MINUTES, BOTH TEAMS, ONE PERIOD:
372 —**Los Angeles Kings, Philadelphia Flyers** at Philadelphia, March 11, 1979, first period. Philadelphia received 4 minors, 8 majors, 6 10-minute misconducts and 8 game misconducts for 188 minutes. Los Angeles received 2 minors, 8 majors, 6 10-minute misconducts and 8 game misconducts for 184 minutes.

MOST PENALTIES, ONE TEAM, ONE PERIOD:
34 —**Minnesota North Stars,** Feb. 26, 1981, at Boston, first period. 15 minors, 8 majors, 4 10-minute misconducts, 7 game misconducts.

MOST PENALTY MINUTES, ONE TEAM, ONE PERIOD:
188 —**Philadelphia Flyers,** March 11, 1979, at Philadelphia vs. Los Angeles, first period. Flyers received 4 minors, 8 majors, 6 10-minute misconducts and 8 game misconducts.

NHL Individual Scoring Records – History

Six INDIVIDUAL SCORING RECORDS stand as benchmarks in the history of the game: most goals, single-season and career; most assists, single-season and career; and most points, single-season and career. The evolution of these six records is traced here, beginning with 1917-18, the NHL's first season. New research has resulted in changes to scoring records in the NHL's first four seasons.

MOST GOALS, ONE SEASON

44 – Joe Malone, Montreal, 1917-18.
Scored goal #44 against Toronto's Harry Holmes on March 2, 1918 and finished season with 44 goals.
50 – Maurice Richard, Montreal, 1944-45.
Scored goal #45 against Toronto's Frank McCool on February 25, 1945 and finished the season with 50 goals.
50 – Bernie Geoffrion, Montreal, 1960-61.
Scored goal #50 against Toronto's Cesare Maniago on March 16, 1961 and finished the season with 50 goals.
50 – Bobby Hull, Chicago, 1961-62.
Scored goal #50 against NY Rangers' Gump Worsley on March 25, 1962 and finished the season with 50 goals.
54 – Bobby Hull, Chicago, 1965-66.
Scored goal #51 against NY Rangers' Cesare Maniago on March 12, 1966 and finished the season with 54 goals.
58 – Bobby Hull, Chicago, 1968-69.
Scored goal #55 against Boston's Gerry Cheevers on March 20, 1969 and finished the season with 58 goals.
76 – Phil Esposito, Boston, 1970-71.
Scored goal #59 against Los Angeles' Denis DeJordy on March 11, 1971 and finished the season with 76 goals.
92 – Wayne Gretzky, Edmonton, 1981-82.
Scored goal #77 against Buffalo's Don Edwards on February 24, 1982 and finished the season with 92 goals.

MOST ASSISTS, ONE SEASON

10 – Cy Denneny, Ottawa, 1917-18.
   – Reg Noble, Toronto, 1917-18.
   – Harry Cameron, Toronto, 1917-18.
15 – Frank Nighbor, Ottawa, 1919-20.
18 – Dick Irvin, Chicago, 1926-27.
18 – Howie Morenz, Montreal, 1927-28.
36 – Frank Boucher, NY Rangers, 1929-30.
37 – Joe Primeau, Toronto, 1931-32.
45 – Bill Cowley, Boston, 1940-41.
45 – Bill Cowley, Boston, 1942-43.
49 – Clint Smith, Chicago, 1943-44.
54 – Elmer Lach, Montreal, 1944-45.
55 – Ted Lindsay, Detroit, 1949-50.
56 – Bert Olmstead, Montreal, 1955-56.
58 – Jean Beliveau, Montreal, 1960-61.
58 – Andy Bathgate, NY Rangers/Toronto, 1963-64.
59 – Stan Mikita, Chicago, 1964-65.
62 – Stan Mikita, Chicago, 1966-67.
77 – Phil Esposito, Boston, 1968-69.
87 – Bobby Orr, Boston, 1969-70.
102 – Bobby Orr, Boston, 1970-71.
109 – Wayne Gretzky, Edmonton, 1980-81.
120 – Wayne Gretzky, Edmonton, 1981-82.
125 – Wayne Gretzky, Edmonton, 1982-83.
135 – Wayne Gretzky, Edmonton, 1984-85.
163 – Wayne Gretzky, Edmonton, 1985-86.

MOST POINTS, ONE SEASON

48 – Joe Malone, Montreal, 1917-18.
49 – Joe Malone, Montreal, 1919-20.
51 – Howie Morenz, Montreal, 1927-28.
73 – Cooney Weiland, Boston, 1929-30.
73 – Doug Bentley, Chicago, 1942-43.
82 – Herb Cain, Boston, 1943-44.
86 – Gordie Howe, Detroit, 1950-51.
95 – Gordie Howe, Detroit, 1952-53.
96 – Dickie Moore, Montreal, 1958-59.
97 – Bobby Hull, Chicago, 1965-66.
97 – Stan Mikita, Chicago, 1966-67.
126 – Phil Esposito, Boston, 1968-69.
152 – Phil Esposito, Boston, 1970-71.
164 – Wayne Gretzky, Edmonton, 1980-81.
212 – Wayne Gretzky, Edmonton, 1981-82.
215 – Wayne Gretzky, Edmonton, 1985-86.

MOST REGULAR-SEASON GOALS, CAREER

44 – Joe Malone, 1917-18, Montreal.
Malone led the NHL in goals in the league's first season and finished with 44 goals in 22 games in 1917-18.
54 – Cy Denneny, 1918-19, Ottawa.
Denneny passed Malone during the 1918-19 season, finishing the year with a two-year total of 54 goals. He held the career goal-scoring mark until 1919-20.
143 – Joe Malone, Montreal, Quebec Bulldogs, Hamilton.
Malone passed Denneny in 1919-20 and remained the NHL's career goal-scoring leader until his retirement. He finished with a career total of 143 goals.
246 – Cy Denneny, Ottawa, Boston.
Denneny passed Malone with goal #144 in 1922-23 and remained the NHL's career goal-scoring leader until his retirement. He finished with a career total of 246 goals.
270 – Howie Morenz, Montreal, NY Rangers, Chicago.
Morenz passed Denneny with goal #247 in 1933-34 and finished his career with 270 goals.
324 – Nels Stewart, Montreal Maroons, Boston, NY Americans.
Stewart passed Morenz with goal #271 in 1936-37 and remained the NHL's career goal-scoring leader until his retirement. He finished his career with 324 goals.
544 – Maurice Richard, Montreal.
Richard passed Nels Stewart with goal #325 on Nov. 8, 1952 and remained the NHL's career goal-scoring leader until his retirement. He finished his career with 544 goals.
801 – Gordie Howe, Detroit, Hartford.
Howe passed Richard with goal #545 on Nov. 10, 1963 and remained the NHL's career goal-scoring leader until his retirement. He finished his career with 801 goals.
894 – Wayne Gretzky, Edmonton, Los Angeles, St. Louis, NY Rangers.
Gretzky passed Gordie Howe with goal #802 on March 23, 1994. He retired as the NHL's current goal-scoring leader with 894.

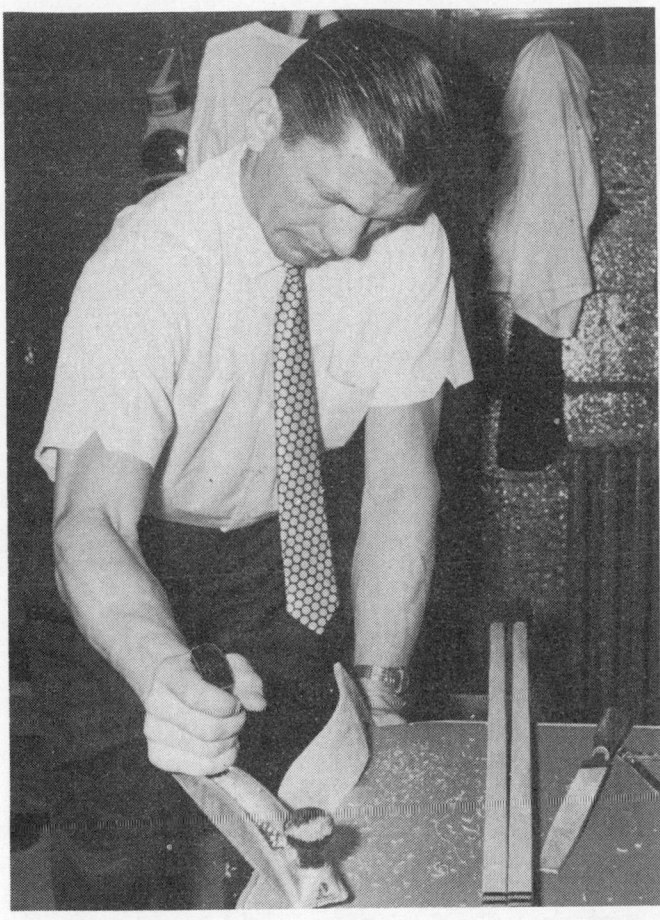

Detroit's Gordie Howe (opposite) became the NHL's all-time leading scorer on January 16, 1960 when he registered the 947th point of his career. Early in the third period of the Red Wings' 3-1 win over the Black Hawks, Howe took a pass from Warren Godfrey and whipped a wrist shot past Chicago's Glenn Hall to set the new mark. Stan Mikita (left) does some fine tuning on his instrument of choice, a hockey stick with a decided banana-blade curve. Mikita set a new NHL standard for single-season assists in 1964-65 with 59 helpers. Two years later, he broke his own mark with 62 assists in 1966-67.

MOST REGULAR-SEASON POINTS, CAREER (minimum 100 points)

100 – Joe Malone, Montreal, Quebec Bulldogs, Hamilton.
In 1919-20, Malone became the first player in NHL history to record 100 points.

200 – Cy Denneny, Ottawa.
In 1923-24, Denneny became the first player in NHL history to record 200 points.

300 – Cy Denneny, Ottawa.
In 1926-27, Denneny became the first player in NHL history to record 300 points.

315 – Cy Denneny, Ottawa, Boston.
Denneny retired as the NHL's career point-scoring leader in 1929 with 315 points.

467 – Howie Morenz, Montreal, Chicago, NY Rangers.
Morenz passed Cy Denneny with point #316 in 1931-32. At the time his career ended in 1937, he was the NHL's career point-scoring leader with 467 points.

515 – Nels Stewart, Montreal Maroons, Boston, NY Americans.
Stewart passed Morenz with point #468 in 1938-39. He retired as the NHL's career point-scoring leader in 1940 with 515 points.

528 – Syd Howe, Ottawa, Philadelphia Quakers, Toronto, St. Louis Eagles, Detroit.
Howe passed Nels Stewart with point #516 on March 8, 1945. He retired as the NHL's career point-scoring leader in 1946 with 528 points.

548 – Bill Cowley, St. Louis Eagles, Boston.
Cowley passed Syd Howe with point #529 on Feb. 12, 1947. He retired as the NHL's career point-scoring leader in 1947 with 548 points.

610 – Elmer Lach, Montreal.
Lach passed Bill Cowley with point #549 on Feb. 23, 1952. He remained the NHL's career point-scoring leader until he was overtaken by Maurice Richard in 1953-54. He finished his career with 623 points.

946 – Maurice Richard, Montreal.
Richard passed teammate Elmer Lach with point #611 on Dec. 12, 1953. He remained the NHL's career point-scoring leader until he was overtaken by Gordie Howe in 1959-60. He finished his career with 965 points.

1,850 – Gordie Howe, Detroit, Hartford.
Howe passed Richard with point #947 on Jan. 16, 1960. He retired as the NHL's career point-scoring leader in 1980 with 1,850 points.

2,857 – Wayne Gretzky, Edmonton, Los Angeles, St. Louis, NY Rangers.
Gretzky passed Howe with point #1,851 on Oct. 15, 1989. He retired as the NHL's current career points leader with 2,857.

MOST REGULAR-SEASON ASSISTS, CAREER
(minimum 100 assists)

100 – Frank Boucher, Ottawa, NY Rangers.
In 1930-31, Boucher became the first NHL player to reach the 100-assist milestone.

262 – Frank Boucher, Ottawa, NY Rangers.
Boucher retired as the NHL's career assist leader in 1938 with 252. He returned to the NHL in 1943-44 and remained the NHL's career assist leader until he was overtaken by Bill Cowley in 1943-44. He finished his career with 262 assists.

353 – Bill Cowley, St. Louis Eagles, Boston.
Cowley passed Boucher with assist #263 in 1943-44. He retired as the NHL's career assist leader in 1947 with 353.

408 – Elmer Lach, Montreal.
Lach passed Cowley with assist #354 in 1951-52. He retired as the NHL's career assist leader in 1954 with 408.

1,049 – Gordie Howe, Detroit, Hartford.
Howe passed Lach with assist #409 in 1957-58. He retired as the NHL's career assist leader in 1980 with 1,049.

1,963 – Wayne Gretzky, Edmonton, Los Angeles, St. Louis, NY Rangers. Gretzky passed Howe with assist #1,050 in 1988-89. He retired as the NHL's current career assist leader with 1,963.

Individual Records
Regular Season

SEASONS

MOST SEASONS:
26 —Gordie Howe, Detroit, 1946-47 – 1970-71; Hartford, 1979-80.
24 —Alex Delvecchio, Detroit, 1950-51 – 1973-74.
—Tim Horton, Toronto, NY Rangers, Pittsburgh, Buffalo, 1949-50, 1951-52 – 1973-74.
23 —John Bucyk, Detroit, Boston, 1955-56 – 1977-78.
22 —Dean Prentice, NY Rangers, Boston, Detroit, Pittsburgh, Minnesota, 1952-53 – 1973-74.
—Doug Mohns, Boston, Chicago, Minnesota, Atlanta, Washington, 1953-54 – 1974-75.
—Stan Mikita, Chicago, 1958-59 – 1979-80.

GAMES

MOST GAMES:
1,767 —Gordie Howe, Detroit, 1946-47 – 1970-71; Hartford, 1979-80.
1,549 —Alex Delvecchio, Detroit, 1950-51 – 1973-74.
1,540 —John Bucyk, Detroit, Boston, 1955-56 – 1977-78.

MOST GAMES, INCLUDING PLAYOFFS:
1,924 —Gordie Howe, Detroit, Hartford, 1,767 regular-season and 157 playoff games.
1,670 —Alex Delvecchio, Detroit, 1,549 regular-season and 121 playoff games.
1,664 —John Bucyk, Detroit, Boston, 1,540 regular-season and 124 playoff games.

MOST CONSECUTIVE GAMES:
964 —Doug Jarvis, Montreal, Washington, Hartford, from Oct. 8, 1975 – Oct. 10, 1987.
914 —Garry Unger, Toronto, Detroit, St. Louis, Atlanta, from Feb. 24, 1968 – Dec. 21, 1979.
884 —Steve Larmer, Chicago, from Oct. 6, 1982 – Apr. 16, 1993.
776 —Craig Ramsay, Buffalo, from Mar. 27, 1973 – Feb. 10, 1983.
630 —Andy Hebenton, NY Rangers, Boston, from Oct. 6, 1956 – Mar. 22, 1964.

GOALS

MOST GOALS:
894 —Wayne Gretzky, Edmonton, Los Angeles, St. Louis, NY Rangers, in 20 seasons, 1,487GP.
801 —Gordie Howe, Detroit, Hartford, in 26 seasons, 1,767GP.
731 —Marcel Dionne, Detroit, Los Angeles, NY Rangers, in 18 seasons, 1,348GP.
717 —Phil Esposito, Chicago, Boston, NY Rangers, in 18 seasons, 1,282GP.
708 —Mike Gartner, Washington, Minnesota, NY Rangers, Toronto, Phoenix, in 19 seasons, 1,432GP.

MOST GOALS, INCLUDING PLAYOFFS:
1,016 —Wayne Gretzky, Edmonton, Los Angeles, St. Louis, NY Rangers, 894 regular-season and 122 playoff goals.
869 —Gordie Howe, Detroit, Hartford, 801 regular-season and 68 playoff goals.
778 —Phil Esposito, Chicago, Boston, NY Rangers, 717 regular-season and 61 playoff goals.
752 —Marcel Dionne, Detroit, Los Angeles, NY Rangers, 731 regular-season and 21 playoff goals.

MOST GOALS, ONE SEASON:
92 —Wayne Gretzky, Edmonton, 1981-82. 80 game schedule.
87 —Wayne Gretzky, Edmonton, 1983-84. 80 game schedule.
86 —Brett Hull, St. Louis, 1990-91. 80 game schedule.
85 —Mario Lemieux, Pittsburgh, 1988-89. 80 game schedule.
76 —Phil Esposito, Boston, 1970-71. 78 game schedule.
—Alexander Mogilny, Buffalo, 1992-93. 84 game schedule.
—Teemu Selanne, Winnipeg, 1992-93. 84 game schedule.
73 —Wayne Gretzky, Edmonton, 1984-85. 80 game schedule.
72 —Brett Hull, St. Louis, 1989-90. 80 game schedule.
71 —Wayne Gretzky, Edmonton, 1982-83. 80 game schedule.
—Jari Kurri, Edmonton, 1984-85. 80 game schedule.
70 —Mario Lemieux, Pittsburgh, 1987-1988. 80 game schedule.
—Bernie Nicholls, Los Angeles, 1988-89. 80 game schedule.
—Brett Hull, St. Louis, 1991-92. 80 game schedule.

MOST GOALS, ONE SEASON, INCLUDING PLAYOFFS:
100 —Wayne Gretzky, Edmonton, 1983-84, 87G in 74 regular-season games and 13G in 19 playoff games.
97 —Wayne Gretzky, Edmonton, 1981-82, 92G in 80 regular-season games and 5G in 5 playoff games.
—Mario Lemieux, Pittsburgh, 1988-89, 85G in 76 regular-season games and 12G in 11 playoff games.
—Brett Hull, St. Louis, 1990-91, 86G in 78 regular-season games and 11G in 13 playoff games.
90 —Wayne Gretzky, Edmonton, 1984-85, 73G in 80 regular-season games and 17G in 18 playoff games.
—Jari Kurri, Edmonton, 1984-85, 71G in 80 regular-season games and 19G in 18 playoff games.
85 —Mike Bossy, NY Islanders, 1980-81, 68G in 79 regular-season games and 17G in 18 playoff games.
—Brett Hull, St. Louis, 1989-90, 72G in 80 regular-season games and 13G in 12 playoff games.
83 —Wayne Gretzky, Edmonton, 1982-83, 71G in 73 regular-season games and 12G in 16 playoff games.
—Alexander Mogilny, Buffalo, 1992-93, 76G in 77 regular-season games and 7G in 7 playoff games.

MOST GOALS, 50 GAMES FROM START OF SEASON:
61 —Wayne Gretzky, Edmonton, 1981-82. Oct. 7, 1981 - Jan. 22, 1982. (80-game schedule)
—Wayne Gretzky, Edmonton, 1983-84. Oct. 5, 1983 - Jan. 25, 1984. (80-game schedule)
54 —Mario Lemieux, Pittsburgh, 1988-89. Oct. 7, 1988 - Jan. 31, 1989. (80-game schedule)
53 —Wayne Gretzky, Edmonton, 1984-85. Oct. 11, 1984 - Jan. 28, 1985. (80-game schedule).
52 —Brett Hull, St. Louis, 1990-91. Oct. 4, 1990 - Jan. 26, 1991. (80-game schedule).
50 —Maurice Richard, Montreal, 1944-45. Oct. 28, 1944 - March 18, 1945. (50-game schedule)
—Mike Bossy, NY Islanders, 1980-81. Oct. 11, 1980 - Jan. 24, 1981. (80-game schedule)
—Brett Hull, St. Louis, 1991-92. Oct. 5, 1991 – Jan 28, 1992. (80 game schedule)

MOST GOALS, ONE GAME:
7 —Joe Malone, Que. Bulldogs, Jan. 31, 1920, at Quebec. Quebec 10, Toronto 6.
6 —Newsy Lalonde, Montreal, Jan. 10, 1920, at Montreal. Montreal 14, Toronto 7.
—Joe Malone, Que. Bulldogs, March 10, 1920, at Quebec. Quebec 10, Ottawa 4.
—Corb Denneny, Toronto, Jan. 26, 1921, at Toronto. Toronto 10, Hamilton 3.
—Cy Denneny, Ottawa, Mar. 7, 1921, at Ottawa. Ottawa 12, Hamilton 5.
—Syd Howe, Detroit, Feb. 3, 1944, at Detroit. Detroit 12, NY Rangers 2.
—Red Berenson, St. Louis, Nov. 7, 1968, at Philadelphia. St. Louis 8, Philadelphia 0.
—Darryl Sittler, Toronto, Feb. 7, 1976, at Toronto. Toronto 11, Boston 4.

Bernie Nicholls (being chased by Charlie Huddy) is one of only eight players in NHL history to score 70 goals or more in a single season. Nicholls retired early in the 1998-99 season with 469 career goals.

Only former Oilers teammate Wayne Gretzky has more career assists than Paul Coffey when the regular season and playoffs are combined. Coffey is now a member of the Carolina Hurricanes.

MOST GOALS, ONE ROAD GAME:
6—**Red Berenson,** St. Louis, Nov. 7, 1968, at Philadelphia. St. Louis 8, Philadelphia 0.
5 —Joe Malone, Montreal, Dec. 19, 1917, at Ottawa. Montreal 9, Ottawa 4.
  —Red Green, Hamilton, Dec. 5, 1924, at Toronto. Hamilton 10, Toronto 3.
  —Babe Dye, Toronto, Dec. 22, 1924, at Boston. Toronto 10, Boston 2.
  —Harry Broadbent, Mtl. Maroons, Jan. 7, 1925, at Hamilton. Mtl. Maroons 6, Hamilton 2.
  —Don Murdoch, NY Rangers, Oct. 12, 1976, at Minnesota. NY Rangers 10, Minnesota 4.
  —Tim Young, Minnesota, Jan. 15, 1979, at NY Rangers. Minnesota 8, NY Rangers 1.
  —Willy Lindstrom, Winnipeg, Mar. 2, 1982, at Philadelphia. Winnipeg 7, Philadelphia 6.
  —Bengt Gustafsson, Washington, Jan. 8, 1984, at Philadelphia. Washington 7, Philadelphia 1.
  —Wayne Gretzky, Edmonton, Dec. 15, 1984, at St. Louis. Edmonton 8, St. Louis 2.
  —Dave Andreychuk, Buffalo, Feb. 6, 1986, at Boston. Buffalo 8, Boston 6.
  —Mats Sundin, Quebec, Mar. 5, 1992, at Hartford. Quebec 10, Hartford 4.
  —Mario Lemieux, Pittsburgh, Apr. 9, 1993, at New York. Pittsburgh 10, NY Rangers 4.
  —Mike Ricci, Quebec, Feb. 17, 1994, at San Jose. Quebec 8, San Jose 2.
  —Alexei Zhamnov, Winnipeg, Apr. 1, 1995, at Los Angeles. Winnipeg 7, Los Angeles 7.

MOST GOALS, ONE PERIOD:
4—**Harvey Jackson,** Toronto, Nov. 20, 1934, at St. Louis, third period. Toronto 5, St. Louis Eagles 2.
  —**Max Bentley,** Chicago, Jan. 28, 1943, at Chicago, third period. Chicago 10, NY Rangers 1.
  —**Clint Smith,** Chicago, Mar. 4, 1945, at Chicago, third period. Chicago 6, Montreal 4.
  —**Red Berenson,** St. Louis, Nov. 7, 1968, at Philadelphia, second period. St. Louis 8, Philadelphia 0.
  —**Wayne Gretzky,** Edmonton, Feb. 18, 1981, at Edmonton, third period. Edmonton 9, St. Louis 2.
  —**Grant Mulvey,** Chicago, Feb. 3, 1982, at Chicago, first period. Chicago 9, St. Louis 5.
  —**Bryan Trottier,** NY Islanders, Feb. 13, 1982, at New York, second period. NY Islanders 8, Philadelphia 2.
  —**Al Secord,** Chicago, Jan. 7, 1987, at Chicago, second period. Chicago 6, Toronto 4.
  —**Joe Nieuwendyk,** Calgary, Jan. 11, 1989, at Calgary, second period. Calgary 8, Winnipeg 3.
  —**Peter Bondra,** Washington, Feb. 5, 1994, at Washington, first period. Washington 6, Tampa Bay 3.
  —**Mario Lemieux,** Pittsburgh, Jan. 26, 1997, at Montreal, third period. Pittsburgh 5, Montreal 2.

ASSISTS

MOST ASSISTS:
1,963—**Wayne Gretzky,** Edmonton, Los Angeles, St. Louis, NY Rangers, in 20 seasons, 1,487GP.
1,102 —Paul Coffey, Edmonton, Pittsburgh, Los Angeles, Detroit, Hartford, Philadelphia, Chicago, Carolina, in 19 seasons, 1,322GP.
1,083 —Ray Bourque, Boston, in 20 seasons, 1,453GP.
1,050 —Mark Messier, Edmonton, NY Rangers, Vancouver, in 20 seasons, 1,413GP
1,049 —Gordie Howe, Detroit, Hartford in 26 seasons, 1,767GP.

MOST ASSISTS, INCLUDING PLAYOFFS:
2,223—**Wayne Gretzky,** Edmonton, Los Angeles, St. Louis, NY Rangers, 1,963 regular-season and 260 playoff assists.
1,239 —Paul Coffey, Edmonton, Pittsburgh, Los Angeles, Detroit, Hartford, Philadelphia, Chicago, Carolina, 1,102 regular-season and 137 playoff assists.
1,236 —Mark Messier, Edmonton, NY Rangers, Vancouver, 1,050 regular-season and 186 playoff assists.
1,208 —Ray Bourque, Boston, 1,083 regular season and 125 playoff assists.
1,141 —Gordie Howe, Detroit, Hartford, 1,049 regular-season and 92 playoff assists.

MOST ASSISTS, ONE SEASON:
163—**Wayne Gretzky,** Edmonton, 1985-86. 80 game schedule.
135 —Wayne Gretzky, Edmonton, 1984-85. 80 game schedule.
125 —Wayne Gretzky, Edmonton, 1982-83. 80 game schedule.
122 —Wayne Gretzky, Los Angeles, 1990-91. 80 game schedule.
121 —Wayne Gretzky, Edmonton, 1986-87. 80 game schedule.
120 —Wayne Gretzky, Edmonton, 1981-82. 80 game schedule.
118 —Wayne Gretzky, Edmonton, 1983-84. 80 game schedule.
114 —Wayne Gretzky, Los Angeles, 1988-89. 80 game schedule.
  —Mario Lemieux, Pittsburgh, 1988-89. 80 game schedule.
109 —Wayne Gretzky, Edmonton, 1980-81. 80 game schedule.
  —Wayne Gretzky, Edmonton, 1987-88. 80 game schedule.
102 —Bobby Orr, Boston, 1970-71. 78 game schedule.
  —Wayne Gretzky, Los Angeles, 1989-90. 80 game schedule.

MOST ASSISTS, ONE SEASON, INCLUDING PLAYOFFS:

174 —**Wayne Gretzky,** Edmonton, 1985-86, 163A in 80 regular-season games and 11A in 10 playoff games.
165 —Wayne Gretzky, Edmonton, 1984-85, 135A in 80 regular-season games and 30A in 18 playoff games.
151 —Wayne Gretzky, Edmonton, 1982-83, 125A in 80 regular-season games and 26A in 16 playoff games.
150 —Wayne Gretzky, Edmonton, 1986-87, 121A in 79 regular-season games and 29A in 21 playoff games.
140 —Wayne Gretzky, Edmonton, 1983-84, 118A in 74 regular-season games and 22A in 19 playoff games.
    —Wayne Gretzky, Edmonton, 1987-88, 109A in 64 regular-season games and 31A in 19 playoff games.
133 —Wayne Gretzky, Los Angeles, 1990-91, 122A in 78 regular-season games and 11A in 12 playoff games.
131 —Wayne Gretzky, Los Angeles, 1988-89, 114A in 78 regular-season games and 17A in 11 playoff games.
127 —Wayne Gretzky, Edmonton, 1981-82, 120A in 80 regular-season games and 7A in 5 playoff games.
123 —Wayne Gretzky, Edmonton, 1980-81, 109A in 80 regular-season games and 14A in 9 playoff games.
121 —Mario Lemieux, Pittsburgh, 1988-89, 114A in 76 regular-season games and 7A in 11 playoff games.

MOST ASSISTS, ONE GAME:

7 —**Billy Taylor,** Detroit, Mar. 16, 1947, at Chicago. Detroit 10, Chicago 6.
  —**Wayne Gretzky,** Edmonton, Feb. 15, 1980, at Edmonton. Edmonton 8, Washington 2.
  —**Wayne Gretzky,** Edmonton, Dec. 11, 1985, at Chicago. Edmonton 12, Chicago 9.
  —**Wayne Gretzky,** Edmonton, Feb. 14, 1986, at Edmonton. Edmonton 8, Quebec 2.
6 —Elmer Lach, Montreal, Feb. 6, 1943.
  —Babe Pratt, Toronto, Jan. 8, 1944.
  —Don Grosso, Detroit, Feb. 3, 1944.
  —Pat Stapleton, Chicago, Mar. 30, 1969.
  —Ken Hodge, Boston, Feb. 9, 1971.
  —Bobby Orr, Boston, Jan. 1, 1973.
  —Ron Stackhouse, Pittsburgh, Mar. 8, 1975.
  —Greg Malone, Pittsburgh, Nov. 28, 1979.
  —Mike Bossy, NY Islanders, Jan. 6, 1981.
  —Guy Chouinard, Calgary, Feb. 25, 1981.
  —Mark Messier, Edmonton, Jan. 4, 1984.
  —Patrik Sundstrom, Vancouver, Feb 29, 1984.
  —Wayne Gretzky, Edmonton, Dec. 20, 1985.
  —Paul Coffey, Edmonton, Mar. 14, 1986.
  —Gary Suter, Calgary, Apr. 4, 1986.
  —Ron Francis, Hartford, Mar. 5, 1987.
  —Mario Lemieux, Pittsburgh, Oct. 15, 1988.
  —Bernie Nicholls, Los Angeles, Dec. 1, 1988.
  —Mario Lemieux, Pittsburgh, Dec. 31, 1988.
  —Mario Lemieux, Pittsburgh, Dec. 5, 1992.
  —Doug Gilmour, Toronto, Feb. 13, 1993.
  —Tomas Sandstrom, Los Angeles, Oct. 9, 1993.
  —Eric Lindros, Philadelphia, Feb. 26, 1997.

MOST ASSISTS, ONE ROAD GAME:

7 —**Billy Taylor,** Detroit, Mar. 16, 1947, at Chicago. Detroit 10, Chicago 6.
  —**Wayne Gretzky,** Edmonton, Dec. 11, 1985, at Chicago. Edmonton 12, Chicago 9.
6 —Bobby Orr, Boston, Jan. 1, 1973, at Vancouver. Boston 8, Vancouver 2.
  —Patrik Sundstrom, Vancouver, Feb. 29, 1984, at Pittsburgh. Vancouver 9, Pittsburgh 5.
  —Mario Lemieux, Pittsburgh, Dec. 5, 1992, at San Jose. Pittsburgh 9, San Jose 4.
  —Eric Lindros, Philadelphia, Feb. 26, 1997, at Ottawa. Philadelphia 8, Ottawa 5.

MOST ASSISTS, ONE PERIOD:

5 —**Dale Hawerchuk,** Winnipeg, Mar. 6, 1984, at Los Angeles, second period. Winnipeg 7, Los Angeles 3.
4 —Four assists have been recorded in one period on 53 occasions since Buddy O'Connor of Montreal first accomplished the feat vs. NY Rangers on Nov. 8, 1942. Most recent player, Paul Kariya of Anaheim, (Dec. 16, 1998 vs Nashville).

POINTS

MOST POINTS:

2,857 —**Wayne Gretzky,** Edmonton, Los Angeles, St. Louis, NY Rangers, in 20 seasons, 1,487GP (894G-1963A).
1,850 —Gordie Howe, Detroit, Hartford, in 26 seasons, 1,767GP (801G-1049A).
1,771 —Marcel Dionne, Detroit, Los Angeles, NY Rangers, in 18 seasons, 1,348GP (731G-1,040A).
1,660 —Mark Messier, Edmonton, NY Rangers, Vancouver, in 20 seasons, 1,413GP (610G-1,050A).
1,590 —Phil Esposito, Chicago, Boston, NY Rangers in 18 seasons, 1,282GP (717G-873A).

MOST POINTS, INCLUDING PLAYOFFS:

3,239 —**Wayne Gretzky,** Edmonton, Los Angeles, St. Louis, NY Rangers, 2,857 regular-season and 382 playoff points.
2,010 —Gordie Howe, Detroit, Hartford, 1,850 regular-season and 160 playoff points.
1,955 —Mark Messier, Edmonton, NY Rangers, Vancouver, 1,660 regular-season and 295 playoff points.
1,816 —Marcel Dionne, Detroit, Los Angeles, NY Rangers, 1,771 regular-season and 45 playoff points.
1,727 —Phil Esposito, Chicago, Boston, NY Rangers, 1,590 regular-season and 137 playoff points.

MOST POINTS, ONE SEASON:

215 —**Wayne Gretzky,** Edmonton, 1985-86. 80 game schedule.
212 —Wayne Gretzky, Edmonton, 1981-82. 80 game schedule.
208 —Wayne Gretzky, Edmonton, 1984-85. 80 game schedule.
205 —Wayne Gretzky, Edmonton, 1983-84. 80 game schedule.
199 —Mario Lemieux, Pittsburgh, 1988-89. 80 game schedule.
196 —Wayne Gretzky, Edmonton, 1982-83. 80 game schedule.
183 —Wayne Gretzky, Edmonton, 1986-87. 80 game schedule.
168 —Mario Lemieux, Pittsburgh, 1987-88, 80 game schedule.
    —Wayne Gretzky, Los Angeles, 1988-89. 80 game schedule.
164 —Wayne Gretzky, Edmonton, 1980-81. 80 game schedule.
163 —Wayne Gretzky, Los Angeles, 1990-91. 80 game schedule.
161 —Mario Lemieux, Pittsburgh, 1995-96. 82 game schedule.
160 —Mario Lemieux, Pittsburgh, 1992-93. 84 game schedule.

MOST POINTS, ONE SEASON, INCLUDING PLAYOFFS:

255 —**Wayne Gretzky,** Edmonton, 1984-85, 208PTS in 80 regular-season games and 47PTS in 18 playoff games.
240 —Wayne Gretzky, Edmonton, 1983-84, 205PTS in 74 regular-season games and 35PTS in 19 playoff games.
234 —Wayne Gretzky, Edmonton, 1982-83, 196PTS in 80 regular-season games and 38PTS in 16 playoff games.
    —Wayne Gretzky, Edmonton, 1985-86, 215PTS in 80 regular-season games and 19PTS in 10 playoff games.
224 —Wayne Gretzky, Edmonton, 1981-82, 212PTS in 80 regular-season games and 12PTS in 5 playoff games.
218 —Mario Lemieux, Pittsburgh, 1988-89, 199PTS in 76 regular-season games and 19PTS in 11 playoff games.
217 —Wayne Gretzky, Edmonton, 1986-87, 183PTS in 79 regular-season games and 34PTS in 21 playoff games.
192 —Wayne Gretzky, Edmonton, 1987-88, 149PTS in 64 regular-season games and 43PTS in 19 playoff games.
190 —Wayne Gretzky, Los Angeles, 1988-89, 168PTS in 78 regular-season games and 22PTS in 11 playoff games.
188 —Mario Lemieux, Pittsburgh, 1995-96, 161PTS in 70 regular-season games and 27PTS in 18 playoff games.
185 —Wayne Gretzky, Edmonton, 1980-81, 164PTS in 80 regular-season games and 21PTS in 9 playoff games.

Mark Messier stands fourth all-time in NHL scoring and needs just 40 points this season to reach 1,700 in his career. Messier became the 10th player in NHL history to score 600 goals on October 23, 1998.

MOST POINTS, ONE GAME:

10 —Darryl Sittler, Toronto, Feb. 7, 1976, at Toronto, 6G-4A. Toronto 11, Boston 4.
8 —Maurice Richard, Montreal, Dec. 28, 1944, at Montreal, 5G-3A. Montreal 9, Detroit 1.
—Bert Olmstead, Montreal, Jan. 9, 1954, at Montreal, 4G-4A. Montreal 12, Chicago 1.
—Tom Bladon, Philadelphia, Dec. 11, 1977, at Philadelphia, 4G-4A. Philadelphia 11, Cleveland 1.
—Bryan Trottier, NY Islanders, Dec. 23, 1978, at NY Islanders, 5G-3A. NY Islanders 9, NY Rangers 4.
—Peter Stastny, Quebec, Feb. 22, 1981, at Washington, 4G-4A. Quebec 11, Washington 7.
—Anton Stastny, Quebec, Feb. 22, 1981, at Washington, 3G-5A. Quebec 11, Washington 7.
—Wayne Gretzky, Edmonton, Nov. 19, 1983, at Edmonton, 3G-5A. Edmonton 13, New Jersey 4.
—Wayne Gretzky, Edmonton, Jan. 4, 1984, at Edmonton, 4G-4A. Edmonton 12, Minnesota 8.
—Paul Coffey, Edmonton, Mar. 14, 1986, at Edmonton, 2G-6A. Edmonton 12, Detroit 3.
—Mario Lemieux, Pittsburgh, Oct. 15, 1988, at Pittsburgh, 2G-6A. Pittsburgh 9, St. Louis 2.
—Bernie Nicholls, Los Angeles, Dec. 1, 1988, at Los Angeles, 2G-6A. Los Angeles 9, Toronto 3.
—Mario Lemieux, Pittsburgh, Dec. 31, 1988, at Pittsburgh, 5G-3A. Pittsburgh 8, New Jersey 6.

MOST POINTS, ONE ROAD GAME:

8 —Peter Stastny, Quebec, Feb. 22, 1981, at Washington, 4G-4A. Quebec 11, Washington 7.
—**Anton Stastny,** Quebec, Feb. 22, 1981, at Washington, 3G-5A. Quebec 11, Washington 7.
7 —Billy Taylor, Detroit, Mar. 16, 1947, at Chicago, 7A. Detroit 10, Chicago 6.
—Red Berenson, St. Louis, Nov. 7, 1968, at Philadelphia, 6G-1A. St. Louis 8, Philadelphia 0.
—Gilbert Perreault, Buffalo, Feb. 1, 1976, at California, 2G-5A. Buffalo 9, California 5.
—Peter Stastny, Quebec, Apr. 1, 1982, at Boston, 3G-4A. Quebec 8, Boston 5.
—Wayne Gretzky, Edmonton, Nov. 6, 1983, at Winnipeg, 4G-3A. Edmonton 8, Winnipeg 5.
—Patrik Sundstrom, Vancouver, Feb. 29, 1984, at Pittsburgh, 1G-6A. Vancouver 9, Pittsburgh 5.
—Wayne Gretzky, Edmonton, Dec. 11, 1985, at Chicago. 7A, Edmonton 12, Chicago 9.
—Cam Neely, Boston, Oct. 16, 1988, at Chicago, 3G-4A. Boston 10, Chicago 3.
—Mario Lemieux, Pittsburgh, Jan. 21, 1989, at Edmonton, 2G-5A. Pittsburgh 7, Edmonton 4.
—Dino Ciccarelli, Washington, Mar. 18, 1989, at Hartford, 4G-3A. Washington 8, Hartford 2.
—Mats Sundin, Quebec, Mar. 5, 1992, at Hartford, 5G-2A. Quebec 10, Hartford 4.
—Mario Lemieux, Pittsburgh, Dec. 5, 1992, at San Jose, 1G-6A. Pittsburgh 9, San Jose 4.
—Eric Lindros, Philadelphia, Feb. 26, 1997, at Ottawa, 1G-6A. Philadelphia 8, Ottawa 5.

MOST POINTS, ONE PERIOD:

6 —Bryan Trottier, NY Islanders, Dec. 23, 1978, at NY Islanders, second period. 3G-3A. NY Islanders 9, NY Rangers 4.
5 —Les Cunningham, Chicago, Jan. 28, 1940, at Chicago, third period. 2G- 3A. Chicago 8, Montreal 1.
—Max Bentley, Chicago, Jan. 28, 1943, at Chicago, third period. 4G-1A, Chicago 10, NY Rangers 1.
—Leo Labine, Boston, Nov. 28, 1954, at Boston, second period, 3G-2A. Boston 6, Detroit 2.
—Darryl Sittler, Toronto, Feb. 7, 1976, at Toronto, second period. 3G-2A. Toronto 11, Boston 4.
—Grant Mulvey, Chicago, Feb. 3, 1982, at Chicago, first period. 4G-1A. Chicago 9, St. Louis 5.
—Dale Hawerchuk, Winnipeg, Mar. 6, 1984, at Los Angeles, second period. 5A. Winnipeg 7, Los Angeles 3.
—Jari Kurri, Edmonton, Oct. 26, 1984, at Edmonton, second period. 2G-3A. Edmonton 8, Los Angeles 2.
—Pat Elynuik, Winnipeg, Jan. 20, 1989, at Winnipeg, second period. 2G- 3A. Winnipeg 7, Pittsburgh 3.
—Ray Ferraro, Hartford, Dec. 9, 1989, at Hartford, first period. 3G-2A. Hartford 7, New Jersey 3.
—Stephane Richer, Montreal, Feb. 14, 1990, at Montreal, first period. 2G- 3A. Montreal 11, Vancouver 1.
—Cliff Ronning, Vancouver, Apr. 15, 1993, at Los Angeles, third period. 3G- 2A. Vancouver 8, Los Angeles 6.
—Peter Forsberg, Colorado, Mar. 3, 1999, at Florida, third period. 2G- 3A. Colorado 7, Florida 5.

POWER-PLAY and SHORTHAND GOALS

MOST POWER-PLAY GOALS, ONE SEASON:

34 —Tim Kerr, Philadelphia, 1985-86. 80 game schedule.
32 —Dave Andreychuk, Buffalo, Toronto, 1992-93. 84 game schedule.
31 —Joe Nieuwendyk, Calgary, 1987-88. 80 game schedule.
—Mario Lemieux, Pittsburgh, 1988-89. 80 game schedule.
—Mario Lemieux, Pittsburgh, 1995-96. 82 game schedule.
29 —Michel Goulet, Quebec, 1987-88. 80 game schedule.
—Brett Hull, St. Louis, 1990-91. 80 game schedule.
—Brett Hull, St. Louis, 1992-93. 84 game schedule.

MOST SHORTHAND GOALS, ONE SEASON:

13 —Mario Lemieux, Pittsburgh, 1988-89. 80 game schedule.
12 —Wayne Gretzky, Edmonton, 1983-84. 80 game schedule.
11 —Wayne Gretzky, Edmonton, 1984-85. 80 game schedule.
10 —Marcel Dionne, Detroit, 1974-75. 80 game schedule.
—Mario Lemieux, Pittsburgh, 1987-88. 80 game schedule.
—Dirk Graham, Chicago, 1988-89. 80 game schedule.

MOST SHORTHAND GOALS, ONE GAME:

3 —Theoren Fleury, Calgary, Mar. 9, 1991, at St. Louis. Calgary 8, St. Louis 4.

OVERTIME SCORING

MOST OVERTIME GOALS, CAREER:

9 —Mario Lemieux, Pittsburgh.
—**Steve Thomas,** Toronto, Chicago, NY Islanders, New Jersey.
8 —Bob Sweeney, Boston, Buffalo, Calgary.
—Tomas Sandstrom, NY Rangers, Los Angeles, Pittsburgh, Detroit, Anaheim.
—Jaromir Jagr, Pittsburgh.
7 —Geoff Courtnall, Boston, Edmonton, Washington, Vancouver, St. Louis.
—Jari Kurri, Edmonton, Los Angeles, NY Rangers, Anaheim, Colorado.
—Stephane Richer, Montreal, New Jersey, Tampa Bay.
—Mike Gartner, Washington, Minnesota, NY Rangers, Toronto, Phoenix.
—Wendel Clark, Toronto, Quebec, NY Islanders, Tampa Bay, Detroit.
—Brian Bellows, Minnesota, Montreal, Tampa Bay, Anaheim, Washington.
—Pierre Turgeon, Buffalo, NY Islanders, Montreal, St. Louis.

MOST OVERTIME ASSISTS, CAREER:

15 —Wayne Gretzky, Edmonton, Los Angeles, St. Louis, NY Rangers.
13 —Doug Gilmour, St. Louis, Calgary, Toronto, New Jersey, Chicago.
12 —Adam Oates, Detroit, St. Louis, Boston, Washington.
11 —Mark Messier, Edmonton, NY Rangers, Vancouver.
—Paul Coffey, Edmonton, Pittsburgh, Los Angeles, Detroit, Hartford, Philadelphia, Carolina.
10 —Mario Lemieux, Pittsburgh.
—Scott Stevens, Washington, St. Louis, New Jersey.

MOST OVERTIME POINTS, CAREER:

19 —Mario Lemieux, Pittsburgh. 9G-10A.
17 —Mark Messier, Edmonton, NY Rangers, Vancouver. 6G-11A.
—Wayne Gretzky, Edmonton, Los Angeles, St. Louis, NY Rangers. 2G-15A.
16 —Steve Thomas, Toronto, Chicago, NY Islanders, New Jersey. 9G-7A.
14 —Tomas Sandstrom, NY Rangers, Los Angeles, Pittsburgh, Detroit, Anaheim. 8G-6A.
—Ray Bourque, Boston. 5G-9A.
—Doug Gilmour, St. Louis, Calgary, Toronto, New Jersey. 1G-13A.
—Adam Oates, Detroit, St. Louis, Boston, Washington. 2G-12A.

SCORING BY A CENTER

MOST GOALS BY A CENTER, CAREER

894 —Wayne Gretzky, Edmonton, Los Angeles, St. Louis, NY Rangers, in 20 seasons.
731 —Marcel Dionne, Detroit, Los Angeles, NY Rangers, in 18 seasons.
717 —Phil Esposito, Chicago, Boston, NY Rangers, in 18 seasons.
613 —Mario Lemieux, Pittsburgh, in 12 seasons.
610 —Mark Messier, Edmonton, NY Rangers, Vancouver, in 20 seasons.

MOST GOALS BY A CENTER, ONE SEASON:

92 —Wayne Gretzky, Edmonton, 1981-82. 80 game schedule.
87 —Wayne Gretzky, Edmonton, 1983-84. 80 game schedule.
85 —Mario Lemieux, Pittsburgh, 1988-89. 80 game schedule.
76 —Phil Esposito, Boston, 1970-71. 78 game schedule.
73 —Wayne Gretzky, Edmonton, 1984-85. 80 game schedule.

It's now been more than 23 years since Darryl Sittler set an NHL record with 10 points against the Boston Bruins. Sittler's six goals that night included a hat trick in the second and third periods.

MOST ASSISTS BY A CENTER, CAREER:
 1,963 — **Wayne Gretzky,** Edmonton, Los Angeles, St. Louis, NY Rangers, in 20 seasons.
 1,050 — Mark Messier, Edmonton, NY Rangers, Vancouver, in 20 seasons.
 1,040 — Marcel Dionne, Detroit, Los Angeles, NY Rangers, in 18 seasons.
 1,037 — Ron Francis, Hartford, Pittsburgh, Carolina, in 18 seasons.
   926 — Stan Mikita, Chicago, in 22 seasons.

MOST ASSISTS BY A CENTER, ONE SEASON:
 163 — **Wayne Gretzky,** Edmonton, 1985-86. 80 game schedule.
 135 — Wayne Gretzky, Edmonton, 1984-85. 80 game schedule.
 125 — Wayne Gretzky, Edmonton, 1982-83. 80 game schedule.
 122 — Wayne Gretzky, Los Angeles, 1990-91. 80 game schedule.
 121 — Wayne Gretzky, Edmonton, 1986-87. 80 game schedule.

MOST POINTS BY A CENTER, CAREER:
 2,857 — **Wayne Gretzky,** Edmonton, Los Angeles, St. Louis, NY Rangers, in 20 seasons.
 1,771 — Marcel Dionne, Detroit, Los Angeles, NY Rangers, in 18 seasons.
 1,660 — Mark Messier, Edmonton, NY Rangers, Vancouver, in 20 seasons.
 1,590 — Phil Esposito, Chicago, Boston, NY Rangers, in 18 seasons.
 1,486 — Ron Francis, Hartford, Pittsburgh, Carolina, in 18 seasons.

MOST POINTS BY A CENTER, ONE SEASON:
 215 — **Wayne Gretzky,** Edmonton, 1985-86. 80 game schedule.
 212 — Wayne Gretzky, Edmonton, 1981-82. 80 game schedule.
 208 — Wayne Gretzky, Edmonton, 1984-85. 80 game schedule.
 205 — Wayne Gretzky, Edmonton, 1983-84. 80 game schedule.
 199 — Mario Lemieux, Pittsburgh, 1988-89. 80 game schedule.

SCORING BY A LEFT WING

MOST GOALS BY A LEFT WING, CAREER:
 610 — **Bobby Hull,** Chicago, Winnipeg, Hartford, in 16 seasons.
 556 — John Bucyk, Detroit, Boston, in 23 seasons.
 548 — Michel Goulet, Quebec, Chicago, in 15 seasons.
 533 — Frank Mahovlich, Toronto, Detroit, Montreal, in 18 seasons.
 532 — Dave Andreychuk, Buffalo, Toronto, New Jersey, in 17 seasons.

MOST GOALS BY A LEFT WING, ONE SEASON:
 63 — **Luc Robitaille,** Los Angeles, 1992-93. 84 game schedule.
 60 — Steve Shutt, Montreal, 1976-77. 80 game schedule.
 58 — Bobby Hull, Chicago, 1968-69. 76 game schedule.
 57 — Michel Goulet, Quebec, 1982-83. 80 game schedule.
 56 — Charlie Simmer, Los Angeles, 1979-80. 80 game schedule.
   — Charlie Simmer, Los Angeles, 1980-81. 80 game schedule.
   — Michel Goulet, Quebec, 1983-84. 80 game schedule.

MOST ASSISTS BY A LEFT WING, CAREER:
 813 — **John Bucyk,** Detroit, Boston, in 23 seasons.
 608 — Dave Andreychuk, Buffalo, Toronto, New Jersey, in 17 seasons.
 604 — Michel Goulet, Quebec, Chicago, in 15 seasons.
 579 — Brian Propp, Philadelphia, Boston, Minnesota, Hartford, in 15 seasons.
 570 — Frank Mahovlich, Toronto, Detroit, Montreal, in 18 seasons.

MOST ASSISTS BY A LEFT WING, ONE SEASON:
 70 — **Joe Juneau,** Boston, 1992-93. 84 game schedule.
 69 — Kevin Stevens, Pittsburgh, 1991-92. 80 game schedule.
 67 — Mats Naslund, Montreal, 1985-86. 80 game schedule.
 65 — John Bucyk, Boston, 1970-71. 78 game schedule.
   — Michel Goulet, Quebec, 1983-84. 80 game schedule.
 64 — Mark Messier, Edmonton, 1983-84. 80 game schedule.

MOST POINTS BY A LEFT WING, CAREER:
 1,369 — **John Bucyk,** Detroit, Boston, in 23 seasons.
 1,170 — Bobby Hull, Chicago, Winnipeg, Hartford, in 16 seasons.
 1,152 — Michel Goulet, Quebec, Chicago, in 15 seasons.
 1,140 — Dave Andreychuk, Buffalo, Toronto, New Jersey, in 17 seasons.
 1,103 — Frank Mahovlich, Toronto, Detroit, Montreal, in 18 seasons.

MOST POINTS BY A LEFT WING, ONE SEASON:
 125 — **Luc Robitaille,** Los Angeles, 1992-93. 84 game schedule.
 123 — Kevin Stevens, Pittsburgh, 1991-92. 80 game schedule.
 121 — Michel Goulet, Quebec, 1983-84. 80 game schedule.
 116 — John Bucyk, Boston, 1970-71. 78 game schedule.
 112 — Bill Barber, Philadelphia, 1975-76. 80 game schedule.

SCORING BY A RIGHT WING

MOST GOALS BY A RIGHT WING, CAREER:
 801 — **Gordie Howe,** Detroit, Hartford, in 26 seasons.
 708 — Mike Gartner, Washington, Minnesota, NY Rangers, Toronto, Phoenix, in 19 seasons.
 608 — Dino Ciccarelli, Minnesota, Washington, Detroit, Tampa Bay, Florida, in 19 seasons.
 601 — Jari Kurri, Edmonton, Los Angeles, NY Rangers, Anaheim, Colorado, in 17 seasons.
 573 — Mike Bossy, NY Islanders, in 10 seasons.

MOST GOALS BY A RIGHT WING, ONE SEASON:
 86 — **Brett Hull,** St. Louis, 1990-91. 80 game schedule.
 76 — Alexander Mogilny, Buffalo, 1992-93. 84 game schedule.
   — Teemu Selanne, Winnipeg, 1992-93. 84 game schedule.
 72 — Brett Hull, St. Louis, 1989-90. 80 game schedule.
 71 — Jari Kurri, Edmonton, 1984-85. 80 game schedule.
 70 — Brett Hull, St. Louis, 1991-92. 80 game schedule.

MOST ASSISTS BY A RIGHT WING, CAREER:
 1,049 — **Gordie Howe,** Detroit, Hartford, in 26 seasons.
 797 — Jari Kurri, Edmonton, Los Angeles, NY Rangers, Anaheim, Colorado, in 17 seasons.
 793 — Guy Lafleur, Montreal, NY Rangers, Quebec, in 17 seasons.
 638 — Dave Taylor, Los Angeles, in 17 seasons.
 627 — Mike Gartner, Washington, Minnesota, NY Rangers, Toronto, Phoenix, in 19 seasons.

MOST ASSISTS BY A RIGHT WING, ONE SEASON:
 87 — **Jaromir Jagr,** Pittsburgh, 1995-96. 82 game schedule.
 83 — Mike Bossy, NY Islanders, 1981-82. 80 game schedule.
   — Jaromir Jagr, Pittsburgh, 1998-99. 82 game schedule.
 80 — Guy Lafleur, Montreal, 1976-77. 80 game schedule.
 77 — Guy Lafleur, Montreal, 1978-79. 80 game schedule.

Luc Robitaille scored his 500th career goal on January 7, 1999. The NHL's single-season leader for goals and points by a left winger, Robitaille ranked among the league's top scorers with 39 goals last season.

MOST POINTS BY A RIGHT WING, CAREER:
1,850—**Gordie Howe,** Detroit, Hartford, in 26 seasons.
1,398—Jari Kurri, Edmonton, Los Angeles, NY Rangers, Anaheim, Colorado, in 17 seasons.
1,353—Guy Lafleur, Montreal, NY Rangers, Quebec, in 17 seasons.
1,335—Mike Gartner, Washington, Minnesota, NY Rangers, Toronto, Phoenix, in 19 seasons.

MOST POINTS BY A RIGHT WING, ONE SEASON:
149—**Jaromir Jagr,** Pittsburgh, 1995-96. 82 game schedule.
147—Mike Bossy, NY Islanders, 1981-82. 80 game schedule.
136—Guy Lafleur, Montreal, 1976-77. 80 game schedule.
135—Jari Kurri, Edmonton, 1984-85. 80 game schedule.
132—Guy Lafleur, Montreal, 1977-78. 80 game schedule.
—Teemu Selanne, Winnipeg, 1992-93. 84 game schedule.

SCORING BY A DEFENSEMAN

MOST GOALS BY A DEFENSEMAN, CAREER:
385—**Paul Coffey,** Edmonton, Pittsburgh, Los Angeles, Detroit, Hartford, Philadelphia, Chicago, Carolina, in 19 seasons.
—**Ray Bourque,** Boston, in 20 seasons.
310—Denis Potvin, NY Islanders, in 15 seasons.
302—Phil Housley, Buffalo, Winnipeg, St. Louis, Calgary, New Jersey, Washington, in 17 seasons.
290—Al MacInnis, Calgary, St. Louis, in 18 seasons.

MOST GOALS BY A DEFENSEMAN, ONE SEASON:
48—**Paul Coffey,** Edmonton, 1985-86. 80 game schedule.
46—Bobby Orr, Boston, 1974-75. 80 game schedule.
40—Paul Coffey, Edmonton, 1983-84. 80 game schedule.
39—Doug Wilson, Chicago, 1981-82. 80 game schedule.
37—Bobby Orr, Boston, 1970-71. 78 game schedule.
—Bobby Orr, Boston, 1971-72. 78 game schedule.
—Paul Coffey, Edmonton, 1984-85. 80 game schedule.

MOST GOALS BY A DEFENSEMAN, ONE GAME:
5—**Ian Turnbull,** Toronto, Feb. 2, 1977, at Toronto. Toronto 9, Detroit 1.
4—Harry Cameron, Toronto, Dec. 26, 1917, at Toronto. Toronto 7, Montreal 5.
—Harry Cameron, Montreal, Mar. 3, 1920, at Quebec City. Montreal 16, Que. Bulldogs 3.
—Sprague Cleghorn, Montreal, Jan. 14, 1922, at Montreal. Montreal 10, Hamilton 6.
—Johnny McKinnon, Pit. Pirates, Nov. 19, 1929, at Pittsburgh. Pit. Pirates 10, Toronto 5.
—Hap Day, Toronto, Nov. 19, 1929, at Pittsburgh. Pit. Pirates 10, Toronto 5.
—Tom Bladon, Philadelphia, Dec. 11, 1977, at Philadelphia. Philadelphia 11, Cleveland 1.
—Ian Turnbull, Los Angeles, Dec. 12, 1981, at Los Angeles. Los Angeles 7, Vancouver 5.
—Paul Coffey, Edmonton, Oct. 26, 1984, at Calgary. Edmonton 6, Calgary 5.

MOST ASSISTS BY A DEFENSEMAN, CAREER:
1,102—**Paul Coffey,** Edmonton, Pittsburgh, Los Angeles, Detroit, Hartford, Philadelphia, Chicago, Carolina, in 19 seasons.
1,083—Ray Bourque, Boston, in 20 seasons.
880—Larry Murphy, Los Angeles, Washington, Minnesota, Pittsburgh, Toronto, Detroit, in 19 seasons.
775—Al MacInnis, Calgary, St. Louis, in 18 seasons.
773—Phil Housley, Buffalo, Winnipeg, St. Louis, Calgary, New Jersey, Washington, in 17 seasons.

MOST ASSISTS BY A DEFENSEMAN, ONE SEASON:
102—**Bobby Orr,** Boston, 1970-71. 78 game schedule.
90—Paul Coffey, Edmonton, 1985-86. 80 game schedule.
90—Bobby Orr, Boston, 1973-74. 78 game schedule.
89—Bobby Orr, Boston, 1974-75. 80 game schedule.

MOST ASSISTS BY A DEFENSEMAN, ONE GAME:
6—**Babe Pratt,** Toronto, Jan. 8, 1944, at Toronto. Toronto 12, Boston 3.
—**Pat Stapleton,** Chicago, Mar. 30, 1969, at Chicago. Chicago 9, Detroit 5.
—**Bobby Orr,** Boston, Jan. 1, 1973, at Vancouver. Boston 8, Vancouver 2.
—**Ron Stackhouse,** Pittsburgh, Mar. 8, 1975, at Pittsburgh. Pittsburgh 8, Philadelphia 2.
—**Paul Coffey,** Edmonton, Mar. 14, 1986, at Edmonton. Edmonton 12, Detroit 3.
—**Gary Suter,** Calgary, Apr. 4, 1986, at Calgary. Calgary 9, Edmonton 3.

MOST POINTS BY A DEFENSEMAN, CAREER:
1,487—**Paul Coffey,** Edmonton, Pittsburgh, Los Angeles, Detroit, Hartford, Philadelphia, Chicago, Carolina, in 18 seasons.
1,468—Ray Bourque, Boston, in 20 seasons.
1,155—Larry Murphy, Los Angeles, Washington, Minnesota, Pittsburgh, Toronto, Detroit, in 19 seasons.
1,075—Phil Housley, Buffalo, Winnipeg, St. Louis, Calgary, New Jersey, Washington, in 17 seasons.
1,065—Al MacInnis, Calgary, St. Louis, in 18 seasons.

MOST POINTS BY A DEFENSEMAN, ONE SEASON:
139—**Bobby Orr,** Boston, 1970-71. 78 game schedule.
138—Paul Coffey, Edmonton, 1985-86. 80 game schedule.
135—Bobby Orr, Boston, 1974-75. 80 game schedule.
126—Paul Coffey, Edmonton, 1983-84. 80 game schedule.
122—Bobby Orr, Boston, 1973-74. 78 game schedule.

MOST POINTS BY A DEFENSEMAN, ONE GAME:
8—**Tom Bladon,** Philadelphia, Dec. 11, 1977, at Philadelphia. 4G-4A. Philadelphia 11, Cleveland 1.
—**Paul Coffey,** Edmonton, Mar. 14, 1986, at Edmonton. 2G-6A. Edmonton 12, Detroit 3.
7—Bobby Orr, Boston, Nov. 15, 1973, at Boston. 3G-4A. Boston 10, NY Rangers 2.

SCORING BY A GOALTENDER

MOST POINTS BY A GOALTENDER, CAREER:
48—**Tom Barrasso,** Buffalo, Pittsburgh, in 16 seasons. (48A)
46—Grant Fuhr, Edmonton, Toronto, Buffalo, Los Angeles, St. Louis, in 18 seasons. (46A)

MOST POINTS BY A GOALTENDER, ONE SEASON:
14—**Grant Fuhr,** Edmonton, 1983-84. (14A)
9—Curtis Joseph, St. Louis, 1991-92. (9A)
8—Mike Palmateer, Washington, 1980-81. (8A)
—Grant Fuhr, Edmonton, 1987-88. (8A)
—Ron Hextall, Philadelphia, 1988-89. (8A)
—Tom Barrasso, Pittsburgh, 1992-93. (8A)
7—Ron Hextall, Philadelphia, 1987-88. (1G-6A)
—Mike Vernon, Calgary, 1987-88. (7A)

MOST POINTS BY A GOALTENDER, ONE GAME:
3—**Jeff Reese,** Calgary, Feb. 10, 1993, at Calgary. Calgary 13, San Jose 1. (3A)

With three assists last season Tom Barrasso now has 48 in his career, moving him past Grant Fuhr for the most career points by a goaltender.

SCORING BY A ROOKIE

MOST GOALS BY A ROOKIE, ONE SEASON:
76 —**Teemu Selanne,** Winnipeg, 1992-93. 84 game schedule.
53 —Mike Bossy, NY Islanders, 1977-78. 80 game schedule.
51 —Joe Nieuwendyk, Calgary, 1987-88. 80 game schedule.
45 —Dale Hawerchuk, Winnipeg, 1981-82. 80 game schedule.
  —Luc Robitaille, Los Angeles, 1986-87. 80 game schedule.

MOST GOALS BY A PLAYER IN HIS FIRST NHL SEASON, ONE GAME:
5 —**Howie Meeker,** Toronto, Jan. 8, 1947, at Toronto. Toronto 10, Chicago 4.
  —**Don Murdoch,** NY Rangers, Oct. 12, 1976, at Minnesota. NY Rangers 10, Minnesota 4.

MOST GOALS BY A PLAYER IN HIS FIRST NHL GAME:
3 —**Alex Smart,** Montreal, Jan. 14, 1943, at Montreal. Montreal 5, Chicago 1.
  —**Real Cloutier,** Quebec, Oct. 10, 1979, at Quebec. Atlanta 5, Quebec 3.

MOST ASSISTS BY A ROOKIE, ONE SEASON:
70 —**Peter Stastny,** Quebec, 1980-81. 80 game schedule.
  —**Joe Juneau,** Boston, 1992-93. 84 game schedule.
63 —Bryan Trottier, NY Islanders, 1975-76. 80 game schedule.
62 —Sergei Makarov, Calgary, 1989-90. 80 game schedule.
60 —Larry Murphy, Los Angeles, 1980-81. 80 game schedule.

MOST ASSISTS BY A PLAYER IN HIS FIRST NHL SEASON, ONE GAME:
7 —**Wayne Gretzky,** Edmonton, Feb. 15, 1980, at Edmonton. Edmonton 8, Washington 2.
6 —Gary Suter, Calgary, Apr. 4, 1986, at Calgary. Calgary 9, Edmonton 3.

MOST ASSISTS BY A PLAYER IN HIS FIRST NHL GAME:
4 —**Earl Reibel,** Detroit, Oct. 8, 1953, at Detroit. Detroit 4, NY Rangers 1.
  —**Roland Eriksson,** Minnesota, Oct. 6, 1976, at New York. NY Rangers 6, Minnesota 5.
3 —Al Hill, Philadelphia, Feb. 14, 1977, at Philadelphia. Philadelphia 6, St. Louis 4.

MOST POINTS BY A ROOKIE, ONE SEASON:
132 —**Teemu Selanne,** Winnipeg, 1992-93. 84 game schedule.
109 —Peter Stastny, Quebec, 1980-81. 80 game schedule.
103 —Dale Hawerchuk, Winnipeg, 1981-82. 80 game schedule.
102 —Joe Juneau, Boston, 1992-93. 84 game schedule.
100 —Mario Lemieux, Pittsburgh, 1984-85. 80 game schedule.

MOST POINTS BY A PLAYER IN HIS FIRST NHL SEASON, ONE GAME:
8 —**Peter Stastny,** Quebec, Feb. 22, 1981, at Washington. 4G-4A. Quebec 11, Washington 7.
  —**Anton Stastny,** Quebec, Feb. 22, 1981, at Washington. 3G-5A. Quebec 11, Washington 7.
7 —Wayne Gretzky, Edmonton, Feb. 15, 1980, at Edmonton. 7A. Edmonton 8, Washington 2.
  —Sergei Makarov, Calgary, Feb. 25, 1990, at Calgary. 2G-5A. Calgary 10, Edmonton 4.
6 —Wayne Gretzky, Edmonton, Mar. 29, 1980, at Toronto. 2G-4A. Edmonton 8, Toronto 5.
  —Gary Suter, Calgary, Apr. 4, 1986, at Calgary. 6A. Calgary 9, Edmonton 3.

MOST POINTS BY A PLAYER IN HIS FIRST NHL GAME:
5 —**Al Hill,** Philadelphia, Feb. 14, 1977, at Philadelphia. 2G-3A. Philadelphia 6, St. Louis 4.
4 —Alex Smart, Montreal, Jan. 14, 1943, at Montreal. 3G-1A. Montreal 5, Chicago 1.
  —Earl Reibel, Detroit, Oct. 8, 1953, at Detroit. 4A. Detroit 4, NY Rangers 1.
  —Roland Eriksson, Minnesota, Oct. 6, 1976 at New York. 4A. NY Rangers 6, Minnesota 5.

SCORING BY A ROOKIE DEFENSEMAN

MOST GOALS BY A ROOKIE DEFENSEMAN, ONE SEASON:
23 —**Brian Leetch,** NY Rangers, 1988-89. 80 game schedule.
22 —Barry Beck, Col. Rockies, 1977-78. 80 game schedule.
19 —Reed Larson, Detroit, 1977-78. 80 game schedule.
  —Phil Housley, Buffalo, 1982-83. 80 game schedule.

MOST ASSISTS BY A ROOKIE DEFENSEMAN, ONE SEASON:
60 —**Larry Murphy,** Los Angeles, 1980-81. 80 game schedule.
55 —Chris Chelios, Montreal, 1984-85. 80 game schedule.
50 —Stefan Persson, NY Islanders, 1977-78. 80 game schedule.
  —Gary Suter, Calgary, 1985-86. 80 game schedule.
49 —Nicklas Lidstrom, Detroit, 1991-92. 80 game schedule.

MOST POINTS BY A ROOKIE DEFENSEMAN, ONE SEASON:
76 —**Larry Murphy,** Los Angeles, 1980-81. 80 game schedule.
71 —Brian Leetch, NY Rangers, 1988-89. 80 game schedule.
68 —Gary Suter, Calgary, 1985-86. 80 game schedule.
66 —Phil Housley, Buffalo, 1982-83. 80 game schedule.
65 —Ray Bourque, Boston, 1979-80. 80 game schedule.

Howie Meeker posed for a picture with coach Hap Day after scoring five goals in a game on January 8, 1947. Meeker's 27 goals that season stood as a Maple Leafs rookie record for 36 years.

PER-GAME SCORING AVERAGES

HIGHEST GOALS-PER-GAME AVERAGE, CAREER
(AMONG PLAYERS WITH 200 OR MORE GOALS):
.823 —**Mario Lemieux,** Pittsburgh, 613G, 745GP, from 1984-85 – 1996-97.
.762 —Mike Bossy, NY Islanders, 573G, 752GP, from 1977-78 – 1986-87.
.754 —Cy Denneny, Ottawa, Boston, 246G, 326GP, from 1917-18 – 1928-29.
.681 —Brett Hull, Calgary, St. Louis, Dallas, 586G, 861GP, from 1986-87 – 1998-99.
.645 —Teemu Selanne, Winnipeg, Anaheim, 313G, 485GP, from 1992-93 – 1998-99.
.610 —Eric Lindros, Philadelphia, 263G, 431GP, from 1992-93 – 1998-99.

HIGHEST GOALS-PER-GAME AVERAGE, ONE SEASON
(AMONG PLAYERS WITH 20-OR-MORE GOALS):
2.20 —**Joe Malone,** Montreal, 1917-18, with 44G in 20GP.
1.80 —Cy Denneny, Ottawa, 1917-18, with 36G in 20GP.
1.64 —Newsy Lalonde, Montreal, 1917-18, with 23G in 14GP.
1.63 —Joe Malone, Quebec, 1919-20, with 39G in 24GP.
1.61 —Newsy Lalonde, Montreal, 1919-20, with 37G in 23GP.

HIGHEST GOALS-PER-GAME AVERAGE, ONE SEASON
(AMONG PLAYERS WITH 50-OR-MORE GOALS):
1.18 —**Wayne Gretzky,** Edmonton, 1983-84, with 87G in 74GP.
1.15 —Wayne Gretzky, Edmonton, 1981-82, with 92G in 80GP.
—Mario Lemieux, Pittsburgh, 1992-93, with 69G in 60GP.
1.12 —Mario Lemieux, Pittsburgh, 1988-89, with 85G in 76GP.
1.10 —Brett Hull, St. Louis, 1990-91, with 86G in 78GP.
1.02 —Cam Neely, Boston, 1993-94, with 50G in 49GP.
1.00 —Maurice Richard, Montreal, 1944-45, with 50G in 50GP.

HIGHEST ASSISTS-PER-GAME AVERAGE, CAREER
(AMONG PLAYERS WITH 300 OR MORE ASSISTS):
1.320 —**Wayne Gretzky,** Edmonton, Los Angeles, St. Louis, NY Rangers, 1,963A, 1,487GP from 1979-80 – 1998-99.
1.183 —Mario Lemieux, Pittsburgh, 881A, 745GP from 1984-85 – 1996-97.
.982 —Bobby Orr, Boston, Chicago, 645A, 657GP from 1966-67 – 1978-79.
.907 —Peter Forsberg, Quebec, Colorado, 312A, 344GP from 1994-95 – 1998-99.
.867 —Adam Oates, Detroit, St. Louis, Boston, Washington, 838A, 967GP from 1984-85 – 1998-99.

HIGHEST ASSISTS-PER-GAME AVERAGE, ONE SEASON
(AMONG PLAYERS WITH 35-OR-MORE ASSISTS):
2.04 —**Wayne Gretzky,** Edmonton, 1985-86, with 163A in 80GP.
1.70 —Wayne Gretzky, Edmonton, 1987-88, with 109A in 64GP.
1.69 —Wayne Gretzky, Edmonton, 1984-85, with 135A in 80GP.
1.59 —Wayne Gretzky, Edmonton, 1983-84, with 118A in 74GP.
1.56 —Wayne Gretzky, Edmonton, 1982-83, with 125A in 80GP.
1.56 —Wayne Gretzky, Los Angeles, 1990-91, with 122A in 78GP.
1.53 —Wayne Gretzky, Edmonton, 1986-87, with 121A in 79GP.
1.52 —Mario Lemieux, Pittsburgh, 1992-93, with 91A in 60GP.
1.50 —Wayne Gretzky, Edmonton, 1981-82, with 120A in 80GP.
1.50 —Mario Lemieux, Pittsburgh, 1988-89, with 114A in 76GP.

HIGHEST POINTS-PER-GAME AVERAGE, CAREER:
(AMONG PLAYERS WITH 500 OR MORE POINTS):
2.005 —**Mario Lemieux,** Pittsburgh, 1,494PTS (613G-881A), 745GP from 1984-85 – 1996-97.
1.921 —Wayne Gretzky, Edmonton, Los Angeles, St. Louis, NY Rangers, 2,857PTS (894G-1,963A), 1,487GP from 1979-80 – 1998-99.
1.497 —Mike Bossy, NY Islanders, 1,126PTS (573G-553A), 752GP from 1977-78 – 1986 87.
1.393 —Bobby Orr, Boston, Chicago, 915PTS (270G-645A), 657GP from 1966-67 – 1978-79.
1.392 —Eric Lindros, Philadelphia, 600PTS (263G-337A), 431GP from 1992-93 – 1998-99.

HIGHEST POINTS-PER-GAME AVERAGE, ONE SEASON
(AMONG PLAYERS WITH 50-OR-MORE POINTS):
2.77 —**Wayne Gretzky,** Edmonton, 1983-84, with 205PTS in 74GP.
2.69 —Wayne Gretzky, Edmonton, 1985-86, with 215PTS in 80GP.
2.67 —Mario Lemieux, Pittsburgh, 1992-93, with 160PTS in 60GP.
2.65 —Wayne Gretzky, Edmonton, 1981-82, with 212PTS in 80GP.
2.62 —Mario Lemieux, Pittsburgh, 1988-89, with 199PTS in 78GP.
2.60 —Wayne Gretzky, Edmonton, 1984-85, with 208PTS in 80GP.
2.45 —Wayne Gretzky, Edmonton, 1982-83, with 196PTS in 80GP.
2.33 —Wayne Gretzky, Edmonton, 1987-88, with 149PTS in 64GP.
2.32 —Wayne Gretzky, Edmonton, 1986-87, with 183PTS in 79GP.
2.30 —Mario Lemieux, Pittsburgh, 1995-96 with 161PTS in 70GP.
2.18 —Mario Lemieux, Pittsburgh, 1987-88 with 168PTS in 77GP.
2.15 —Wayne Gretzky, Los Angeles, 1988-89, with 168PTS in 78GP.
2.09 —Wayne Gretzky, Los Angeles, 1990-91, with 163 PTS in 78GP.
2.08 —Mario Lemieux, Pittsburgh, 1989-90, with 123 PTS in 59GP.
2.05 —Wayne Gretzky, Edmonton, 1980-81, with 164PTS in 80GP.

SCORING PLATEAUS

MOST 20-OR-MORE GOAL SEASONS:
22 —**Gordie Howe,** Detroit, Hartford, in 26 seasons.
17 —Marcel Dionne, Detroit, Los Angeles, NY Rangers, in 18 seasons.
—Mike Gartner, Washington, Minnesota, NY Rangers, Toronto, Phoenix, in 19 seasons.
—Wayne Gretzky, Edmonton, Los Angeles, St. Louis, NY Rangers, in 20 seasons.
—Ron Francis, Hartford, Pittsburgh, Carolina, in 18 seasons.
16 —Phil Esposito, Chicago, Boston, NY Rangers, in 18 seasons.
—Norm Ullman, Detroit, Toronto, in 20 seasons.
—John Bucyk, Detroit, Boston, in 23 seasons.
—Mark Messier, Edmonton, NY Rangers, Vancouver, in 20 seasons.

MOST CONSECUTIVE 20-OR-MORE GOAL SEASONS:
22 —**Gordie Howe,** Detroit, 1949-50 – 1970-71.
17 —Marcel Dionne, Detroit, Los Angeles, NY Rangers, 1971-72 – 1987-88.
16 —Phil Esposito, Chicago, Boston, NY Rangers, 1964-65 – 1979-80.
15 —Mike Gartner, Washington, Minnesota, NY Rangers, Toronto, 1979-80 – 1993-94.
14 —Maurice Richard, Montreal, 1943-44 – 1956-57.
—Stan Mikita, Chicago, 1961-62 – 1974-75.
—Michel Goulet, Quebec, Chicago, 1979-80 – 1992-93.

MOST 30-OR-MORE GOAL SEASONS:
17 —**Mike Gartner,** Washington, Minnesota, NY Rangers, Toronto, Phoenix, in 19 seasons.
14 —Gordie Howe, Detroit, Hartford, in 26 seasons.
—Marcel Dionne, Detroit, Los Angeles, NY Rangers, in 18 seasons.
—Wayne Gretzky, Edmonton, Los Angeles, St. Louis, NY Rangers, in 20 seasons.
13 —Bobby Hull, Chicago, Winnipeg, Hartford, in 16 seasons.
—Phil Esposito, Chicago, Boston, NY Rangers, in 18 seasons.

Gordie Howe's mark of 22 seasons with 20-or-more goals is a testament to his durability and longevity.

MOST CONSECUTIVE 30-OR-MORE GOAL SEASONS:
15 —**Mike Gartner,** Washington, Minnesota, NY Rangers, Toronto, 1979-80 –
1993-94.
13 —Bobby Hull, Chicago, 1959-60 – 1971-72.
— Phil Esposito, Boston, NY Rangers, 1967-68 – 1979-80.
— Wayne Gretzky, Edmonton, Los Angeles, 1979-80 – 1991-92.
12 —Marcel Dionne, Detroit, Los Angeles, 1974-75 – 1985-86.
10 —Darryl Sittler, Toronto, Philadelphia, 1973-74 – 1982-83.
— Mike Bossy, NY Islanders, 1977-78 – 1986-87.
— Jari Kurri, Edmonton, 1980-81 – 1989-90.

MOST 40-OR-MORE GOAL SEASONS:
12 —**Wayne Gretzky,** Edmonton, Los Angeles, St. Louis, NY Rangers,
in 20 seasons.
10 —Marcel Dionne, Detroit, Los Angeles, NY Rangers, in 18 seasons.
— Mario Lemieux, Pittsburgh, in 12 seasons.
9 —Mike Bossy, NY Islanders, in 10 seasons.
— Mike Gartner, Washington, Minnesota, NY Rangers, Toronto, Phoenix,
in 19 seasons.

MOST CONSECUTIVE 40-OR-MORE GOAL SEASONS:
12 —**Wayne Gretzky,** Edmonton, Los Angeles, 1979-80 – 1990-91.
9 —Mike Bossy, NY Islanders, 1977-78 – 1985-86.
8 —Luc Robitaille, Los Angeles, 1986-87 – 1993-94.
7 —Phil Esposito, Boston, 1968-69 – 1974-75.
— Michel Goulet, Quebec, 1981-82 – 1987-88.
— Jari Kurri, Edmonton, 1982-83 – 1988-89.

MOST 50-OR-MORE GOAL SEASONS:
9 —**Mike Bossy,** NY Islanders, in 10 seasons.
—**Wayne Gretzky,** Edmonton, Los Angeles, St. Louis, NY Rangers,
in 20 seasons.
6 —Guy Lafleur, Montreal, NY Rangers, Quebec, in 17 seasons.
— Marcel Dionne, Detroit, Los Angeles, NY Rangers, in 18 seasons.
— Mario Lemieux, Pittsburgh, in 12 seasons.
5 —Bobby Hull, Chicago, Winnipeg, Hartford, in 16 seasons.
— Phil Esposito, Chicago, Boston, NY Rangers, in 18 seasons.
— Brett Hull, Calgary, St. Louis, Dallas, in 13 seasons.
— Steve Yzerman, Detroit, in 16 seasons.

MOST CONSECUTIVE 50-OR-MORE GOAL SEASONS:
9 —**Mike Bossy,** NY Islanders, 1977-78 – 1985-86.
8 —Wayne Gretzky, Edmonton, 1979-80 – 1986-87.
6 —Guy Lafleur, Montreal, 1974-75 – 1979-80.
5 —Phil Esposito, Boston, 1970-71 – 1974-75.
— Marcel Dionne, Los Angeles, 1978-79 – 1982-83.
— Brett Hull, St. Louis, 1989-90 – 1993-94.

MOST 60-OR-MORE GOAL SEASONS:
5 —**Mike Bossy,** NY Islanders, in 10 seasons.
—**Wayne Gretzky,** Edmonton, Los Angeles, St. Louis, NY Rangers,
in 20 seasons.
4 —Phil Esposito, Chicago, Boston, NY Rangers, in 18 seasons.
— Mario Lemieux, Pittsburgh, in 12 seasons.

MOST CONSECUTIVE 60-OR-MORE GOAL SEASONS:
4 —**Wayne Gretzky,** Edmonton, 1981-82 – 1984-85.
3 —Mike Bossy, NY Islanders, 1980-81 – 1982-83.
— Brett Hull, St. Louis, 1989-90 – 1991-92.
2 —Phil Esposito, Boston, 1970-71 – 1971-72, 1973-74 – 1974-75.
— Jari Kurri, Edmonton, 1984-85 – 1985-86.
— Mario Lemieux, Pittsburgh, 1987-88 – 1988-89.
— Steve Yzerman, Detroit, 1988-89 – 1989-90.
— Pavel Bure, Vancouver, 1992-93 – 1993-94.

MOST 100-OR-MORE POINT SEASONS:
15 —**Wayne Gretzky,** Edmonton, Los Angeles, St. Louis, NY Rangers,
in 20 seasons.
10 —Mario Lemieux, Pittsburgh, in 12 seasons.
8 —Marcel Dionne, Detroit, Los Angeles, NY Rangers, in 18 seasons.
7 —Mike Bossy, NY Islanders, in 10 seasons.
— Peter Stastny, Quebec, New Jersey, St. Louis, in 15 seasons.

MOST CONSECUTIVE 100-OR-MORE POINT SEASONS:
13 —**Wayne Gretzky,** Edmonton, Los Angeles, 1979-80 – 1991-92.
6 —Bobby Orr, Boston, 1969-70 – 1974-75.
— Guy Lafleur, Montreal, 1974-75 – 1979-80.
— Mike Bossy, NY Islanders, 1980-81 – 1985-86.
— Peter Stastny, Quebec, 1980-81 – 1985-86.
— Mario Lemieux, Pittsburgh, 1984-85 – 1989-90.
— Steve Yzerman, Detroit, 1987-88 – 1992-93.

THREE-OR-MORE-GOAL GAMES

MOST THREE-OR-MORE GOAL GAMES, CAREER:
50 —**Wayne Gretzky,** Edmonton, Los Angeles, St. Louis, NY Rangers, in 20
seasons, 37 three-goal games, 9 four-goal games, 4 five-goal games.
39 —Mike Bossy, NY Islanders, in 10 seasons, 30 three-goal games,
9 four-goal games.
— Mario Lemieux, Pittsburgh, in 12 seasons, 26 three-goal games, 10 four-goal
games and 3 five-goal games.
32 —Phil Esposito, Chicago, Boston, NY Rangers, in 18 seasons, 27 three-goal
games, 5 four-goal games.
28 —Bobby Hull, Chicago, Winnipeg, Hartford, in 16 seasons, 24 three-goal
games, 4 four-goal games.
— Marcel Dionne, Detroit, Los Angeles, NY Rangers, in 18 seasons,
25 three-goal games, 3 four-goal games.
— Brett Hull, Calgary, St. Louis, Dallas, in 13 seasons, 26 three-goal games, 2
four-goal games.
26 —Cy Denneny, Ottawa in 12 seasons. 20 three-goal games,
5 four-goal games, 1 six-goal game.
— Maurice Richard, Montreal, in 18 seasons, 23 three-goal games,
2 four-goal games, 1 five-goal game.

MOST THREE-OR-MORE GOAL GAMES, ONE SEASON:
10 —**Wayne Gretzky,** Edmonton, 1981-82. 6 three-goal games, 3 four-goal
games, 1 five-goal game.
—**Wayne Gretzky,** Edmonton, 1983-84. 6 three-goal games, 4 four-goal
games.
9 —Mike Bossy, NY Islanders, 1980-81. 6 three-goal games, 3 four-goal games.
— Mario Lemieux, Pittsburgh, 1988-89. 7 three-goal games, 1 four-goal game,
1 five-goal game.
8 —Brett Hull, St. Louis, 1991-92. 8 three-goal games.
7 —Joe Malone, Montreal, 1917-18. 2 three-goal games, 2 four-goal games,
3 five-goal games.
— Phil Esposito, Boston, 1970-71. 7 three-goal games.
— Rick Martin, Buffalo, 1975-76. 6 three-goal games, 1 four-goal game.
— Alexander Mogilny, Buffalo, 1992-93. 5 three-goal games, 2 four-goal games.

*An early era NHL star with the Ottawa Senators and
Montreal Maroons, Punch Broadbent's 16-game
goal-scoring streak in 1921-22 remains a
record to this day. Broadbent scored
27 goals during the streak.*

SCORING STREAKS

LONGEST CONSECUTIVE GOAL-SCORING STREAK:
16 Games —Harry Broadbent, Ottawa, 1921-22. 27 goals during streak.
14 Games —Joe Malone, Montreal, 1917-18. 35 goals during streak.
13 Games —Newsy Lalonde, Montreal, 1920-21. 24 goals during streak.
— Charlie Simmer, Los Angeles, 1979-80. 17 goals during streak.
12 Games —Cy Denneny, Ottawa, 1917-18. 23 goals during streak.
— Dave Lumley, Edmonton, 1981-82. 15 goals during streak.
— Mario Lemieux, Pittsburgh, 1992-93. 18 goals during streak.

LONGEST CONSECUTIVE ASSIST-SCORING STREAK:
23 Games —Wayne Gretzky, Los Angeles, 1990-91. 48A during streak.
18 Games —Adam Oates, Boston, 1992-93. 28A during streak.
17 Games —Wayne Gretzky, Edmonton, 1983-84. 38A during streak.
— Paul Coffey, Edmonton, 1985-86. 27A during streak.
— Wayne Gretzky, Los Angeles, 1989-90. 35A during streak.
15 Games —Jari Kurri, Edmonton, 1983-84. 21A during streak.
— Brian Leetch, NY Rangers, 1991-92. 23A during streak.

LONGEST CONSECUTIVE POINT SCORING STREAK:
51 Games —Wayne Gretzky, Edmonton, 1983-84. 61G-92A-153PTS during streak.
46 Games —Mario Lemieux, Pittsburgh, 1989-90. 39G-64A-103PTS during streak.
39 Games —Wayne Gretzky, Edmonton, 1985-86. 33G-75A-108PTS during streak.
30 Games —Wayne Gretzky, Edmonton, 1982-83. 24G-52A-76PTS during streak.
— Mats Sundin, Quebec, 1992-93. 21G-25A-46PTS during streak.
28 Games —Guy Lafleur, Montreal, 1976-77. 19G-42A-61PTS during streak.
— Wayne Gretzky, Edmonton, 1984-85. 20G-43A-63PTS during streak.
— Mario Lemieux, Pittsburgh, 1985-86. 21G-38A-59PTS during streak.
— Paul Coffey, Edmonton, 1985-86. 16G-39A-55PTS during streak.
— Steve Yzerman, Detroit, 1988-89. 29G-36A-65PTS during streak.

LONGEST CONSECUTIVE POINT-SCORING STREAK
FROM START OF SEASON:
51 Games —Wayne Gretzky, Edmonton, 1983-84. 61G-92A-153PTS during streak which was stopped by goaltender Markus Mattsson and Los Angeles on Jan. 28, 1984.

LONGEST CONSECUTIVE POINT-SCORING STREAK BY A DEFENSEMAN:
28 Games —Paul Coffey, Edmonton, 1985-86. 16G-39A-55PTS during streak.
19 Games —Ray Bourque, Boston, 1987-88. 6G-21A-27PTS during streak.
17 Games —Ray Bourque, Boston, 1984-85. 4G-24A-28PTS during streak.
— Brian Leetch, NY Rangers, 1991-92. 5G-24A-29PTS during streak.
16 Games —Gary Suter, Calgary, 1987-88. 8G-17A-25PTS during streak.
15 Games —Bobby Orr, Boston, 1970-71. 10G-23A-33PTS during streak.
— Bobby Orr, Boston, 1973-74. 8G-15A-23PTS during streak.
— Steve Duchesne, Quebec, 1992-93. 4G-17A-21PTS during streak.
— Chris Chelios, Chicago, 1995-96. 4G-16A-20PTS during streak.

FASTEST GOALS AND ASSISTS

FASTEST GOAL FROM START OF A GAME:
5 Seconds — Doug Small, Winnipeg, Dec. 20, 1981, at Winnipeg. Winnipeg 5, St. Louis 4.
— **Bryan Trottier,** NY Islanders, Mar. 22, 1984, at Boston. NY Islanders 3, Boston 3.
— **Alexander Mogilny,** Buffalo, Dec. 21, 1991, at Toronto. Buffalo 4, Toronto 1.
6 Seconds — Henry Boucha, Detroit, Jan. 28, 1973, at Montreal. Detroit 4, Montreal 2.
— Jean Pronovost, Pittsburgh, Mar. 25, 1976, at St. Louis. St. Louis 5, Pittsburgh 2.
7 Seconds — Charlie Conacher, Toronto, Feb. 6, 1932, at Toronto. Toronto 6, Boston 0.
— Danny Gare, Buffalo, Dec. 17, 1978, at Buffalo. Buffalo 6, Vancouver 3.
— Dave Williams, Los Angeles, Feb. 14, 1987 at Los Angeles. Los Angeles 5, Harford 2.
8 Seconds — Ron Martin, NY Americans, Dec. 4, 1932, at New York. NY Americans 4, Montreal 2.
— Chuck Arnason, Col. Rockies, Jan. 28, 1977, at Atlanta. Col. Rockies 3, Atlanta 3.
— Wayne Gretzky, Edmonton, Dec. 14, 1983, at New York. Edmonton 9, NY Rangers 4.
— Gaetan Duchesne, Washington, Mar. 14, 1987, at St. Louis. Washington 3, St. Louis 3.
— Tim Kerr, Philadelphia, Mar. 7, 1989, at Philadelphia. Philadelphia 4, Edmonton 4.
— Grant Ledyard, Buffalo, Dec. 4, 1991, at Winnipeg. Buffalo 4, Winnipeg 4.
— Brent Sutter, Chicago, Feb. 5, 1995, at Vancouver. Chicago 9, Vancouver 4.
— Paul Kariya, Anaheim, Mar. 9, 1997, at Colorado. Anaheim 2, Colorado 2.
— Tony Hrkac, Dallas, Nov. 7, 1998, at Los Angeles. Dallas 4, Los Angeles 3.
— Sergei Fedorov, Detroit, Nov. 21, 1998, at Vancouver. Detroit 4, Vancouver 2.

FASTEST GOAL FROM START OF A PERIOD:
4 Seconds — Claude Provost, Montreal, Nov. 9, 1957, at Montreal, second period. Montreal 4, Boston 2.
— **Denis Savard,** Chicago, Jan. 12, 1986, at Chicago, third period. Chicago 4, Hartford 2.

FASTEST GOAL BY A PLAYER IN HIS FIRST NHL GAME:
15 Seconds — Gus Bodnar, Toronto, Oct. 30, 1943. Toronto 5, NY Rangers 2.
18 Seconds — Danny Gare, Buffalo, Oct. 10, 1974. Buffalo 9, Boston 5.
20 Seconds — Alexander Mogilny, Buffalo, Oct. 5, 1989. Buffalo 4, Quebec 3.

FASTEST TWO GOALS:
4 Seconds — Nels Stewart, Mtl. Maroons, Jan. 3, 1931, at Montreal at 8:24 and 8:28, third period. Mtl. Maroons 5, Boston 3.
— **Deron Quint,** Winnipeg, Dec. 15, 1995, at Winnipeg at 7:51 and 7:55, second period. Winnipeg 9, Edmonton 4.
5 Seconds — Pete Mahovlich, Montreal, Feb. 20, 1971, at Montreal at 12:16 and 12:21, third period. Montreal 7, Chicago 1.
6 Seconds — Jim Pappin, Chicago, Feb. 16, 1972, at Chicago at 2:57 and 3:03, third period. Chicago 3, Philadelphia 3.
— Ralph Backstrom, Los Angeles, Nov. 2, 1972, at Los Angeles at 8:30 and 8:36, third period. Los Angeles 5, Boston 2.
— Lanny McDonald, Calgary, Mar. 22, 1984, at Calgary at 16:23 and 16:29, first period. Detroit 6, Calgary 4.
— Sylvain Turgeon, Hartford, Mar. 28, 1987, at Hartford at 13:59 and 14:05, second period. Hartford 5, Pittsburgh 4.

FASTEST THREE GOALS:
21 Seconds — Bill Mosienko, Chicago, Mar. 23, 1952, at New York, against goaltender Lorne Anderson. Mosienko scored at 6:09, 6:20 and 6:30 of third period, all with both teams at full strength. Chicago 7, NY Rangers 6.
44 Seconds — Jean Béliveau, Montreal, Nov. 5, 1955, at Montreal, against goaltender Terry Sawchuk. Béliveau scored at :42, 1:08 and 1:26 of second period, all with Montreal holding a 6-4 man advantage. Montreal 4, Boston 2.

FASTEST THREE ASSISTS:
21 Seconds — Gus Bodnar, Chicago, Mar. 23, 1952, at New York, Bodnar assisted on Bill Mosienko's three goals at 6:09, 6:20 and 6:30 of third period. Chicago 7, NY Rangers 6.
44 Seconds — Bert Olmstead, Montreal, Nov. 5, 1955, at Montreal, Olmstead assisted on Jean Béliveau's three goals at :42, 1:08 and 1:26 of second period. Montreal 4, Boston 2.

SHOTS ON GOAL

MOST SHOTS ON GOAL, ONE SEASON:
550 —Phil Esposito, Boston, 1970-71. 78 game schedule.
429 —Paul Kariya, Anaheim, 1998-99. 82 game schedule.
426 —Phil Esposito, Boston, 1971-72. 78 game schedule.
414 —Bobby Hull, Chicago, 1968-69. 76 game schedule.

PENALTIES

MOST PENALTY MINUTES, CAREER:
3,966 —Dave Williams, Toronto, Vancouver, Detroit, Los Angeles, Hartford, in 14 seasons, 962GP.
3,565 —Dale Hunter, Quebec, Washington, Colorado, in 19 seasons, 1,407GP.
3,319 —Marty McSorley, Pittsburgh, Edmonton, Los Angeles, NY Rangers, San Jose, in 16 seasons, 934GP.
3,146 —Tim Hunter, Calgary, Quebec, Vancouver, San Jose, in 16 seasons, 815GP.
3,043 —Chris Nilan, Montreal, NY Rangers, Boston, in 13 seasons, 688GP.

MOST PENALTY MINUTES, CAREER, INCLUDING PLAYOFFS:
4,421 —Dave Williams, Toronto, Vancouver, Detroit, Los Angeles, Hartford, 3,966 in regular-season; 455 in playoffs.
4,294 —Dale Hunter, Quebec, Washington, Colorado, 3,565 in regular-season; 729 in playoffs.
3,693 —Marty McSorley, Pittsburgh, Edmonton, Los Angeles, NY Rangers, San Jose, 3,319 in regular-season; 374 in playoffs.
3,584 —Chris Nilan, Montreal, NY Rangers, Boston, 3,043 in regular-season; 541 in playoffs.

MOST PENALTY MINUTES, ONE SEASON:
472 —Dave Schultz, Philadelphia, 1974-75.
409 —Paul Baxter, Pittsburgh, 1981-82.
408 —Mike Peluso, Chicago, 1991-92.
405 —Dave Schultz, Los Angeles, Pittsburgh, 1977-78.

MOST PENALTIES, ONE GAME:
10 — Chris Nilan, Boston, Mar. 31, 1991, at Boston against Hartford.
6 minors, 2 majors, 1 10-minute misconduct, 1 game misconduct.
9 — Jim Dorey, Toronto, Oct. 16, 1968, at Toronto against Pittsburgh. 4 minors, 2 majors, 2 10-minute misconducts, 1 game misconduct.
— Dave Schultz, Pittsburgh, Apr. 6, 1978, at Detroit. 5 minors, 2 majors, 2 10-minute misconducts.
— Randy Holt, Los Angeles, Mar. 11, 1979, at Philadelphia. 1 minor, 3 majors, 2 10-minute misconducts, 3 game misconducts.
— Russ Anderson, Pittsburgh, Jan. 19, 1980, at Pittsburgh. 3 minors, 3 majors, 3 game misconducts.
— Kim Clackson, Quebec, Mar. 8, 1981, at Quebec. 4 minors, 3 majors, 2 game misconducts.
— Terry O'Reilly, Boston, Dec. 19, 1984 at Hartford. 5 minors, 3 majors, 1 game misconduct.
— Larry Playfair, Los Angeles, Dec. 9, 1986, at NY Islanders. 6 minors, 2 majors, 1 10-minute misconduct.
— Marty McSorley, Los Angeles, Apr. 14, 1992, at Vancouver. 5 minors, 2 majors, 1 10-minute misconduct, 1 game misconduct.

MOST PENALTY MINUTES, ONE GAME:
67 — Randy Holt, Los Angeles, Mar. 11, 1979, at Philadelphia. 1 minor, 3 majors, 2 10-minute misconducts, 3 game misconducts.
55 — Frank Bathe, Philadelphia, Mar. 11, 1979, at Philadelphia. 3 majors, 2 10-minute misconducts, 2 game misconducts.
51 — Russ Anderson, Pittsburgh, Jan. 19, 1980, at Pittsburgh. 3 minors, 3 majors, 3 game misconducts.

MOST PENALTIES, ONE PERIOD:
9 — Randy Holt, Los Angeles, Mar. 11, 1979, at Philadelphia, first period. 1 minor, 3 majors, 2 10-minute misconducts, 3 game misconducts.

MOST PENALTY MINUTES, ONE PERIOD:
67 — Randy Holt, Los Angeles, Mar. 11, 1979, at Philadelphia, first period. 1 minor, 3 majors, 2 10-minute misconducts, 3 game misconducts.

GOALTENDING

MOST GAMES APPEARED IN BY A GOALTENDER, CAREER:
971 — Terry Sawchuk, Detroit, Boston, Toronto, Los Angeles, NY Rangers from 1949-50 – 1969-70.
906 — Glenn Hall, Detroit, Chicago, St. Louis from 1952-53 – 1970-71.
886 — Tony Esposito, Montreal, Chicago from 1968-69 – 1983-84.
861 — Gump Worsley, NY Rangers, Montreal, Minnesota from 1952-53 – 1973-74.

MOST CONSECUTIVE COMPLETE GAMES BY A GOALTENDER:
502 — Glenn Hall, Detroit, Chicago. Played 502 games from beginning of 1955-56 season - first 12 games of 1962-63. In his 503rd straight game, Nov. 7, 1962, at Chicago, Hall was removed from the game against Boston with a back injury in the first period.

MOST GAMES APPEARED IN BY A GOALTENDER, ONE SEASON:
79 — Grant Fuhr, St. Louis, 1995-96.
77 — Martin Brodeur, New Jersey, 1995-96.
75 — Grant Fuhr, Edmonton, 1987-88.
74 — Ed Belfour, Chicago, 1990-91.
— Arturs Irbe, San Jose, 1993-94.
— Felix Potvin, Toronto, 1996-97.

MOST MINUTES PLAYED BY A GOALTENDER, CAREER:
57,228 — Terry Sawchuk, Detroit, Boston, Toronto, Los Angeles, NY Rangers, from 1949-50 – 1969-70.

MOST MINUTES PLAYED BY A GOALTENDER, ONE SEASON:
4,433 — Martin Brodeur, New Jersey, 1995-96.

MOST SHUTOUTS, CAREER:
103 — Terry Sawchuk, Detroit, Boston, Toronto, Los Angeles, NY Rangers in 21 seasons.
94 — George Hainsworth, Montreal, Toronto in 10 seasons.
84 — Glenn Hall, Detroit, Chicago, St. Louis in 16 seasons.

MOST SHUTOUTS, ONE SEASON:
22 — George Hainsworth, Montreal, 1928-29. 44GP
15 — Alex Connell, Ottawa, 1925-26. 36GP
— Alex Connell, Ottawa, 1927-28. 44GP
— Hal Winkler, Boston, 1927-28. 44GP
— Tony Esposito, Chicago, 1969-70. 63GP
14 — George Hainsworth, Montreal, 1926-27. 44GP

LONGEST SHUTOUT SEQUENCE BY A GOALTENDER:
461 Minutes, 29 Seconds — Alex Connell, Ottawa, 1927-28, six consecutive shutouts. (Forward passing not permitted in attacking zones in 1927-1928.)
343 Minutes, 5 Seconds — George Hainsworth, Montreal, 1928-29, four consecutive shutouts.
324 Minutes, 40 Seconds — Roy Worters, NY Americans, 1930-31, four consecutive shutouts.
309 Minutes, 21 Seconds — Bill Durnan, Montreal, 1948-49, four consecutive shutouts.

MOST WINS BY A GOALTENDER, CAREER:
447 — Terry Sawchuk, Detroit, Boston, Toronto, Los Angeles, NY Rangaers, in 21 seasons. 971GP
434 — Jacques Plante, Montreal, NY Rangers, St. Louis, Toronto, Boston, in 18 seasons. 837GP
423 — Tony Esposito, Montreal, Chicago, in 16 seasons. 886GP

MOST WINS BY A GOALTENDER, ONE SEASON:
47 — Bernie Parent, Philadelphia, 1973-74. 73GP
44 — Bernie Parent, Philadelphia, 1974-75. 68GP
— Terry Sawchuk, Detroit, 1950-51. 70GP
— Terry Sawchuk, Detroit, 1951-52. 70GP

LONGEST WINNING STREAK BY A GOALTENDER, ONE SEASON:
17 — Gilles Gilbert, Boston, 1975-76.
14 — Tiny Thompson, Boston, 1929-30.
— Ross Brooks, Boston, 1973-74.
— Don Beaupre, Minnesota, 1985-86.
— Tom Barrasso, Pittsburgh, 1992-93.

LONGEST UNDEFEATED STREAK BY A GOALTENDER, ONE SEASON:
32 Games — Gerry Cheevers, Boston, 1971-72. 24w-8t
31 Games — Pete Peeters, Boston, 1982-83. 26w-5t
27 Games — Pete Peeters, Philadelphia, 1979-80. 22w-5t
23 Games — Frank Brimsek, Boston, 1940-41. 15w-8t
— Glenn Resch, NY Islanders, 1978-79. 15w-8t
— Grant Fuhr, Edmonton, 1981-82. 15w-8t

LONGEST UNDEFEATED STREAK BY A GOALTENDER IN HIS FIRST NHL SEASON:
23 Games — Grant Fuhr, 1981-82. 15w-8t.

LONGEST UNDEFEATED STREAK BY A GOALTENDER FROM START OF CAREER:
16 Games — Patrick Lalime, Pittsburgh, 1996-97. 14w-2t.

MOST 40-OR-MORE WIN SEASONS BY A GOALTENDER:
3 — Terry Sawchuk, Detroit, Boston, Toronto, Los Angeles, NY Rangers, in 21 seasons.
— Jacques Plante, Montreal, NY Rangers, St. Louis, Toronto, Boston, in 18 seasons.
2 — Bernie Parent, Boston, Philadelphia, Toronto, in 13 seasons.
— Ken Dryden, Montreal, in 8 seasons.
— Ed Belfour, Chicago, San Jose, Dallas, in 9 seasons.

MOST CONSECUTIVE 40-OR-MORE WIN SEASONS BY A GOALTENDER:
2 — Terry Sawchuk, Detroit, 1950-51 – 1951-52.
— Bernie Parent, Philadelphia, 1973-74 – 1974-75.
— Ken Dryden, Montreal, 1975-76 – 1976-77.

MOST 30-OR-MORE WIN SEASONS BY A GOALTENDER:
9 — Patrick Roy, Montreal, Colorado in 15 seasons.
8 — Tony Esposito, Montreal, Chicago in 16 seasons.
7 — Jacques Plante, Montreal, NY Rangers, St. Louis, Toronto, Boston in 18 seasons.
— Ken Dryden, Montreal, in 8 seasons.
6 — Glenn Hall, Detroit, Chicago, St. Louis in 18 seasons.

MOST CONSECUTIVE 30-OR-MORE WIN SEASONS BY A GOALTENDER:
7 — Tony Esposito, Chicago, 1969-70 – 1975-76.
6 — Jacques Plante, Montreal, 1954-55 – 1959-60.
5 — Terry Sawchuk, Detroit, 1950-51 – 1954-55.
— Ken Dryden, Montreal, 1974-75 – 1978-79.
4 — Ed Giacomin, NY Rangers, 1966-67 – 1969-70.

MOST LOSSES BY A GOALTENDER, CAREER:
352 — Gump Worsley, NY Rangers, Montreal, Minnesota, in 21 seasons. 861GP
351 — Gilles Meloche, Chicago, California, Cleveland, Minnesota, Pittsburgh, in 18 seasons. 788GP
330 — Terry Sawchuk, Detroit, Boston, Toronto, Los Angeles, NY Rangers, in 21 seasons. 971GP

MOST LOSSES BY A GOALTENDER, ONE SEASON:
48 — Gary Smith, California, 1970-71.
47 — Al Rollins, Chicago, 1953-54.

Good as NHL goalies are today, no one is likely to match George Hainsworth's record of 22 shutouts in 1928-29. Hainsworth allowed just 43 goals in 44 games that year. Of course, NHL rules prohibited forward passing in the offensive zone back then.

Active NHL Players' Three-or-More-Goal Games

Regular Season

Teams named are the ones the players were with at the time of their multiple-scoring games. Players listed alphabetically.

Mike Ricci's only NHL hat trick came against his current team, the Sharks. Ricci had five goals against the Sharks at San Jose on February 17, 1994. At the time, he was a member of the Quebec Nordiques.

Player	Team	3-Goals	4-Goals	5-Goals
Adams, Greg	Vancouver	1	1	—
Alfredsson, Daniel	Ottawa	1	—	—
Allison, Jason	Boston	3	—	—
Amonte, Tony	NYR, Chi	6	—	—
Andersson, Mikael	Tampa Bay	1	—	—
Andersson, Niklas	NY Islanders	1	—	—
Andreychuk, Dave	Buf., Tor.	7	2	1
Arnott, Jason	Edmonton	2	—	—
Arvedson, Magnus	Ottawa	1	—	—
Audette, Donald	Buffalo	2	—	—
Babych, Dave	Vancouver	1	—	—
Barnes, Stu	Wpg., Pit.	3	—	—
Bellows, Brian	Min., Mtl., T.B.	6	3	—
Beranek, Josef	Philadelphia	1	—	—
Berezin, Sergei	Toronto	2	—	—
Bondra, Peter	Washington	8	4	1
Bourque, Ray	Boston	1	—	—
Brind'Amour, Rod	Philadelphia	1	—	—
Brown, Doug	Detroit	1	—	—
Brown, Rob	Pittsburgh	7	—	—
Buchberger, Kelly	Edmonton	1	—	—
Bure, Pavel	Van., Fla.	10	1	—
Bure, Valeri	Calgary	1	—	—
Burr, Shawn	Detroit	3	—	—
Burridge, Randy	Bos., Wsh.	4	—	—
Butsayev, Viacheslav	Philadelphia	1	—	—
Carbonneau, Guy	Montreal	2	—	—
Carter, Anson	Boston	1	—	—
Clark, Wendel	Tor., Que., T.B.	10	2	—
Coffey, Paul	Edmonton	4	1	—
Conroy, Craig	St. Louis	1	—	—
Corson, Shayne	Mtl., Edm.	3	—	—
Courtnall, Geoff	Bos., Wsh., St.L.	4	—	—
Courtnall, Russ	Tor., Mtl., Min., Van.	5	—	—
Craven, Murray	Philadelphia	3	—	—
Cunneyworth, R.	Pittsburgh	1	1	—
Czerkawski, Mariusz	Edmonton	2	—	—
Dahlen, Ulf	NYR, Min., S.J.	4	—	—
Daigle, Alexandre	Ott., Phi.	2	—	—
Damphousse, V.	Tor., Edm., Mtl., S.J.	11	1	—
Dawe, Jason	Buffalo	2	—	—
Daze, Eric	Chicago	1	1	—
Dineen, Kevin	Hfd., Phi.	9	1	—
Dionne, Gilbert	Montreal	1	—	—
Druce, John	Wsh., L.A.	2	—	—
Duchesne, Steve	L.A., Phi., St.L.	3	—	—
Dumont, Jean-Pierre	Chicago	1	—	—
Emerson, Nelson	Winnipeg	1	—	—
Errey, Bob	Pittsburgh	1	—	—
Fedorov, Sergei	Detroit	1	1	1
Ferraro, Ray	Hfd., NYI, NYR	7	1	—
Fleury, Theoren	Cgy., Col.	14	—	—
Forsberg, Peter	Colorado	4	—	—
Francis, Ron	Hfd., Pit.	10	1	—
Friesen, Jeff	San Jose	1	—	—
Gagner, Dave	Min., Dal., Fla.	4	1	—
Garpenlov, Johan	Det., S.J., Fla.	2	1	—
Gelinas, Martin	Edm., Van.	2	1	—
Gilchrist, Brent	Montreal	1	—	—
Gilmour, Doug	St.L., Tor.	3	—	—
Granato, Tony	NYR, L.A., S.J.	6	1	—
Gratton, Chris	Tampa Bay	1	—	—
Graves, Adam	Edm., NYR	6	—	—
Green, Travis	NY Islanders	1	—	—
Grier, Mike	Edmonton	1	—	—
Grosek, Michal	Buffalo	1	—	—
Guerin, Bill	New Jersey	1	—	—
Harvey, Todd	Dallas	1	—	—
Hatcher, Kevin	Wsh., Dal.	2	—	—
Heinze, Steve	Boston	4	—	—
Hogue, Benoit	NY Islanders	1	—	—
Holik, Bobby	New Jersey	3	—	—
Housley, Phil	Buffalo	2	—	—
Hull, Brett	Cgy., St.L.	26	2	—
Hull, Jody	Hartford	1	—	—
Jagr, Jaromir	Pittsburgh	4	—	—
Janney, Craig	Bos., St.L.	3	—	—
Juneau, Joe	Bos., Wsh.	2	—	—
Kamensky, Valeri	Colorado	5	—	—
Kapanen, Sami	Carolina	2	—	—
Kariya, Paul	Anaheim	3	—	—
Khristich, Dimitri	Was., Bos.	3	—	—
King, Derek	NYI, Tor.	6	1	—
Klatt, Trent	Philadelphia	1	—	—
Klima, Petr	Det., Edm.	6	—	—
Konowalchuk, Steve	Washington	2	—	—
Korolev, Igor	Winnipeg	1	—	—
Kovalenko, Andrei	Quebec	1	—	—
Kovalev, Alexei	NY Rangers	2	—	—
Kozlov, Vyacheslav	Detroit	2	1	—
Krupp, Uwe	Quebec	1	—	—
Krygier, Todd	Washington	1	—	—
Lacroix, Eric	Colorado	1	—	—
Larionov, Igor	Van., S.J.	4	—	—
Larouche, Steve	Ottawa	1	—	—
LeClair, John	Philadelphia	7	2	—
Lemieux, Claude	Mtl., N.J., Col.	7	—	—
Lemieux, Jocelyn	Chicago	2	—	—
Linden, Trevor	Vancouver	4	—	—
Lindros, Eric	Philadelphia	9	1	—
MacInnis, Al	Cgy., St. L.	3	—	—
MacLean, John	New Jersey	6	—	—
Malakhov, Vladimir	Montreal	1	—	—
Maltby, Kirk	Detroit	1	—	—
Manderville, Kent	Hartford	1	—	—
McEachern, Shawn	Ottawa	1	—	—
McInnis, Marty	Calgary	1	—	—
McKay, Randy	New Jersey	1	—	—
McKenzie, Jim	Phoenix	1	—	—
Messier, Mark	Edm., NYR	15	4	—
Miller, Kevin	Det., St.L., S.J.	4	—	—
Modano, Mike	Min., Dal.	6	1	—
Mogilny, Alexander	Buf., Van.	12	2	—
Muller, Kirk	N.J., Mtl., Tor.	7	—	—
Murray, Glen	Los Angeles	1	—	—
Murray, Rem	Edmonton	1	—	—
Murzyn, Dana	Calgary	1	—	—
Naslund, Markus	Pit., Van.	3	—	—
Nedved, Petr	Pit., NYR	1	1	—
Nemchinov, Sergei	NY Rangers	1	—	—
Nieuwendyk, Joe	Cgy., Dal.	8	3	1
Nolan, Owen	Que., S.J.	8	1	—
Noonan, Brian	Chi., NYR	3	1	—
Nylander, Michael	Hartford	1	—	—
Oates, Adam	Bos., Wsh.	6	1	—
Odelein, Lyle	Montreal	1	—	—
Olczyk, Ed	Tor., NYR, Wpg., L.A.	5	—	—
Oliver, David	Edmonton	1	—	—
O'Neill, Jeff	Hartford	1	—	—
Palffy, Zigmund	NY Islanders	6	—	—
Parrish, Mark	Florida	—	1	—
Perreault, Yanic	L.A., Tor.	2	1	—
Pivonka, Michal	Washington	1	—	—
Plante, Derek	Buffalo	1	—	—
Probert, Bob	Detroit	1	—	—
Ranheim, Paul	Calgary	1	—	—
Recchi, Mark	Pit., Mtl.	3	—	—
Reichel, Robert	Cgy., NYI	5	—	—
Reid, Dave	Bos., Dal.	2	—	—
Renberg, Mikael	Phi., T.B.	2	—	—
Ricci, Mike	Quebec	—	—	1
Richer, Stephane	Mtl., N.J.	8	1	—
Roberts, Gary	Cgy., Car.	10	1	—
Robitaille, Luc	L.A., Pit.	10	3	—
Roenick, Jeremy	Chicago	4	2	—
Rolston, Brian	New Jersey	1	—	—
Ronning, Cliff	St.L., Van.	3	—	—
Rucinsky, Martin	Montreal	2	—	—
Sakic, Joe	Que., Col.	6	1	—
Salo, Sami	Ottawa	1	—	—
Samsonov, Sergei	Boston	1	—	—
Sanderson, Geoff	Har., Buf.	6	—	—
Sandstrom, Tomas	NYR, L.A.	7	1	—
Satan, Miroslav	Buffalo	2	—	—
Savage, Brian	Montreal	2	1	—
Selanne, Teemu	Wpg., Ana.	13	2	—
Selivanov, Alexander	Edmonton	1	—	—
Semak, Alexander	New Jersey	1	—	—
Shanahan, Brendan	N.J., St.L., Hfd., Det	12	—	—
Sheppard, Ray	Buf., Det., S.J, Fla.	12	—	—
Smolinski, Bryan	Boston	1	—	—
Smyth, Ryan	Edmonton	1	—	—
Stern, Ronnie	Calgary	3	—	—
Stevens, Kevin	Pit., NYR	9	2	—
Stillman, Cory	Calgary	1	—	—
Straka, Martin	Pittsburgh	3	—	—
Stumpel, Jozef	Bos., L.A.	2	—	—
Sturm, Marco	San Jose	1	—	—
Sullivan, Steve	Toronto	—	1	—
Sundin, Mats	Que., Tor.	5	1	1
Svejkovsky, Jaroslav	Washington	1	—	—
Sydor, Darryl	Dallas	1	—	—
Thomas, Steve	Chi., NYI	4	2	—
Titov, German	Calgary	2	—	—
Tkachuk, Keith	Phoenix	6	2	—
Tocchet, Rick	Phi., Pit., L.A., Bos.	12	2	—
Turcotte, Darren	NY Rangers	4	—	—
Turgeon, Pierre	Buf., NYI, Mtl., St.L.	13	—	—
Valk, Garry	Anaheim	1	—	—
Verbeek, Pat	N.J., Hfd, NYR, Dal.	11	1	—
Vukota, Mick	NY Islanders	1	—	—
Ward, Dixon	Buffalo	1	—	—
Weight, Doug	Edmonton	1	—	—
Wesley, Glen	Boston	1	—	—
Wiemer, Jason	Tampa Bay	1	—	—
Yachmenev, Vitali	Los Angeles	1	—	—
Yake, Terry	Anaheim	1	—	—
Yashin, Alexei	Ottawa	5	—	—
Yegorov, Alexei	San Jose	1	—	—
Young, Scott	Que., Col.	4	—	—
Yzerman, Steve	Detroit	17	1	—
Ysebaert, Paul	Detroit	1	—	—
Zamuner, Rob	Tampa Bay	1	—	—
Zezel, Peter	Philadelphia	1	—	—
Zhamnov, Alexei	Wpg., Chi	5	—	1

Top 100 All-Time Goal-Scoring Leaders

*active player

Player	Seasons	Games	Goals	Goals per game
1. Wayne Gretzky, Edm., L.A., St.L., NYR .	20	1487	894	.601
2. Gordie Howe, Det., Hfd.	26	1767	801	.453
3. Marcel Dionne, Det., L.A., NYR	18	1348	731	.542
4. Phil Esposito, Chi., Bos., NYR	18	1282	717	.559
5. Mike Gartner, Wsh., Min., NYR, Tor., Phx.	19	1432	708	.494
6. Mario Lemieux, Pit.	12	745	613	.823
7. Bobby Hull, Chi., Wpg., Hfd.	16	1063	610	.574
* 8. Mark Messier, Edm., NYR, Van.	20	1413	610	.432
9. Dino Ciccarelli, Min., Wsh., Det., T.B., Fla.	19	1232	608	.494
10. Jari Kurri, Edm., L.A., NYR, Ana., Col.	17	1251	601	.480
* 11. Steve Yzerman, Det.	16	1178	592	.503
* 12. Brett Hull, Cgy., St.L., Dal.	14	861	586	.681
13. Mike Bossy, NYI	10	752	573	.762
14. Guy Lafleur, Mtl., NYR, Que.	17	1126	560	.497
15. John Bucyk, Det., Bos.	23	1540	556	.361
16. Michel Goulet, Que., Chi.	15	1089	548	.503
17. Maurice Richard, Mtl.	18	978	544	.556
18. Stan Mikita, Chi.	22	1394	541	.388
19. Frank Mahovlich, Tor., Det., Mtl.	18	1181	533	.451
* 20. Dave Andreychuk, Buf., Tor., N.J.	17	1210	532	.440
21. Bryan Trottier, NYI, Pit.	18	1279	524	.410
22. Dale Hawerchuk, Wpg., Buf., St.L., Phi.	16	1188	518	.436
* 23. Luc Robitaille, L.A., Pit., NYR	13	971	517	.532
24. Gilbert Perreault, Buf.	17	1191	512	.430
25. Jean Beliveau, Mtl.	20	1125	507	.451
26. Joe Mullen, St.L., Cgy., Pit., Bos.	17	1062	502	.473
27. Lanny McDonald, Tor., Col., Cgy.	16	1111	500	.450
28. Glenn Anderson, Edm., Tor., NYR, St.L.	16	1129	498	.441
29. Jean Ratelle, NYR, Bos.	21	1281	491	.383
30. Norm Ullman, Det., Tor.	20	1410	490	.348
* 31. Brian Bellows, Min., Mtl., T.B., Ana., Wsh.	17	1188	485	.408
32. Darryl Sittler, Tor., Phi., Det.	15	1096	484	.442
* 33. Pat Verbeek, N.J., Hfd., NYR, Dal.	17	1225	478	.390
34. Bernie Nicholls, L.A., NYR, Edm., N.J., Chi., S.J.	18	1127	475	.421
35. Denis Savard, Chi., Mtl., T.B.	17	1196	473	.395
36. Pat LaFontaine, NYI, Buf., NYR	15	865	468	.541
37. Alex Delvecchio, Det.	24	1549	456	.294
38. Peter Stastny, Que., N.J., St.L.	15	977	450	.461
* 39. Ron Francis, Hfd., Pit., Car.	18	1329	449	.338
40. Rick Middleton, NYR, Bos.	14	1005	448	.446
41. Rick Vaive, Van., Tor., Chi., Buf.	13	876	441	.503
42. Steve Larmer, Chi., NYR	15	1006	441	.438
43. Dave Taylor, L.A.	17	1111	431	.388
44. Yvan Cournoyer, Mtl.	16	968	428	.442
* 45. Joe Nieuwendyk, Cgy., Dal.	13	835	425	.509
46. Brian Propp, Phi., Bos., Min., Hfd.	15	1016	425	.418
47. Steve Shutt, Mtl., L.A.	13	930	424	.456
48. Bill Barber, Phi.	12	903	420	.465
49. Garry Unger, Tor., Det., St.L., Atl., L.A., Edm.	16	1105	413	.374
* 50. Rick Tocchet, Phi., Pit., L.A., Bos., Wsh., Phx.	15	990	411	.415
51. Rod Gilbert, NYR	18	1065	406	.381
52. John Ogrodnick, Det., Que., NYR	14	928	402	.433
* 53. Pierre Turgeon, Buf., NYI, Mtl., St.L.	12	877	397	.453
* 54. Doug Gilmour, St.L., Cgy., Tor., N.J., Chi.	16	1197	397	.332
55. Dave Keon, Tor., Hfd.	18	1296	396	.306
56. Cam Neely, Van., Bos.	13	726	395	.544
57. Pierre Larouche, Pit., Mtl., Hfd., NYR.	14	812	395	.486
* 58. Brendan Shanahan, N.J., St.L., Hfd., Det.	12	869	394	.453
* 59. Tomas Sandstrom, NYR, L.A., Pit., Det., Ana.	15	983	394	.401
60. Bernie Geoffrion, Mtl., NYR	16	883	393	.445
* 61. Stephane Richer, Mtl., N.J., T.B.	15	930	392	.422
62. Dean Prentice, NYR, Bos., Det., Pit., Min.	22	1378	391	.284
63. Jean Pronovost, Pit., Atl., Wsh.	14	998	391	.392
* 64. John MacLean, N.J., S.J., NYR	15	1067	388	.364
* 65. Paul Coffey, Edm., Pit., L.A., Det., Hfd., Phi., Chi., Car.	19	1322	385	.291
* 66. Ray Bourque, Bos.	20	1453	385	.265
67. Rick Martin, Buf., L.A.	11	685	384	.561
68. Reggie Leach, Bos., Cal., Phi., Det.	13	934	381	.408
69. Ted Lindsay, Det., Chi.	17	1068	379	.355
* 70. Joe Sakic, Que., Col.	11	792	375	.473
71. Butch Goring, L.A., NYI, Bos.	16	1107	375	.339
* 72. Theoren Fleury, Cgy., Col.	11	806	374	.464
73. Rick Kehoe, Tor., Pit.	14	906	371	.409
74. Tim Kerr, Phi., NYR, Hfd.	13	655	370	.565
75. Bernie Federko, St.L., Det.	14	1000	369	.369
76. Jacques Lemaire, Mtl.	12	853	366	.429

Glenn Anderson fell just short of the 500-goal milestone, ending his career with 498. Anderson's 417 goals as an Oiler trails only Wayne Gretzky (583) and Jari Kurri (474).

Player	Seasons	Games	Goals	Goals per game
* 77. Geoff Courtnall, Bos., Edm., Wsh., St.L., Van.	16	1042	365	.350
78. Brent Sutter, NYI, Chi.	18	1111	363	.327
79. Peter McNab, Buf., Bos., Van., N.J.	14	954	363	.381
80. Ivan Boldirev, Bos., Cal., Chi., Atl., Van., Det.	15	1052	361	.343
81. Henri Richard, Mtl.	20	1256	358	.285
82. Bobby Clarke, Phi.	15	1144	358	.313
83. Bobby Smith, Min., Mtl.	15	1077	357	.331
84. Dennis Maruk, Cal., Cle., Min., Wsh.	14	888	356	.401
85. Wilf Paiement, K.C., Col., Tor., Que., NYR, Buf., Pit.	14	946	356	.376
86. Mike Foligno, Det., Buf., Tor., Fla.	15	1018	355	.349
87. Danny Gare, Buf., Det., Edm.	13	827	354	.428
* 88. Steve Thomas, Tor., Chi., NYI, N.J.	15	938	352	.375
89. Andy Bathgate, NYR, Tor., Det., Pit.	17	1069	349	.326
90. Rick MacLeish, Phi., Hfd., Pit., Det	14	846	349	.413
* 91. Vincent Damphousse, Tor., Edm., Mtl., S.J.	13	1005	347	.345
* 92. Ray Sheppard, Buf., NYR, Det., S.J., Fla., Car.	12	770	347	.451
* 93. Ray Ferraro, Hfd., NYI, NYR, L.A	15	1020	346	.339
* 94. Jaromir Jagr, Pit.	9	662	345	.521
* 95. Jeremy Roenick, Chi., Phx.	11	753	344	.457
96. Charlie Simmer, Cal., Cle., L.A., Bos., Pit.	14	712	342	.480
* 97. Ed Olczyk, Chi., Tor., Wpg., NYR, L.A., Pit.	15	998	340	.341
98. Dave Christian, Wpg., Wsh., Bos., St L., Chi.	15	1009	340	.337
* 99. Kirk Muller, N.J., Mtl., NYI, Tor., Fla.	15	1114	338	.303
* 100. Kevin Dineen, Hfd., Phi., Car.	15	992	338	.341

Top 100 Active Goal-Scoring Leaders

* active player

	Player	Seasons	Games	Goals	Goals per game
1.	Mark Messier, Edm., NYR, Van.	20	1413	610	.432
2.	Steve Yzerman, Det.	16	1178	592	.503
3.	Brett Hull, Cgy., St.L., Dal.	14	861	586	.681
4.	Dave Andreychuk, Buf., Tor., N.J.	17	1210	532	.440
5.	Luc Robitaille, L.A., Pit., NYR	13	971	517	.532
6.	Brian Bellows, Min., Mtl., T.B., Ana., Wsh.	17	1188	485	.408
7.	Pat Verbeek, N.J., Hfd., NYR, Dal.	17	1225	478	.390
8.	Ron Francis, Hfd., Pit., Car.	18	1329	449	.338
9.	Joe Nieuwendyk, Cgy., Dal.	13	835	425	.509
10.	Rick Tocchet, Phi., Pit., L.A., Bos., Wsh., Phx.	15	990	411	.415
11.	Doug Gilmour, St.L., Cgy., Tor., N.J., Chi.	16	1197	397	.332
12.	Pierre Turgeon, Buf., NYI, Mtl., St.L.	12	877	397	.453
13.	Tomas Sandstrom, NYR, L.A., Pit., Det., Ana.	15	983	394	.401
14.	Brendan Shanahan, N.J., St.L., Hfd., Det.	12	869	394	.453
15.	Stephane Richer, Mtl., N.J., T.B.	15	930	392	.422
16.	John MacLean, N.J., S.J., NYR	15	1067	388	.364
17.	Paul Coffey, Edm., Pit., L.A., Det., Hfd., Phi., Chi., Car.	19	1322	385	.291
18.	Ray Bourque, Bos.	20	1453	385	.265
19.	Joe Sakic, Que., Col.	11	792	375	.473
20.	Theoren Fleury, Cgy., Col.	11	806	374	.464
21.	Geoff Courtnall, Bos., Edm., Wsh., St.L., Van.	16	1042	365	.350
22.	Steve Thomas, Tor., Chi., NYI, N.J.	15	938	352	.375
23.	Ray Sheppard, Buf., NYR, Det., S.J., Fla., Car.	12	770	347	.451
24.	Vincent Damphousse, Tor., Edm., Mtl., S.J.	13	1005	347	.345
25.	Ray Ferraro, Hfd., NYI, NYR, L.A.	15	1020	346	.339
26.	Jaromir Jagr, Pit.	9	662	345	.521
27.	Jeremy Roenick, Chi., Phx.	11	753	344	.457
28.	Ed Olczyk, Chi., Tor., Wpg., NYR, L.A., Pit.	15	998	340	.341
29.	Kevin Dineen, Hfd., Phi., Car.	15	992	338	.341
30.	Kirk Muller, N.J., Mtl., NYI, Tor., Fla.	15	1114	338	.303
31.	Mark Recchi, Pit., Phi., Mtl.	11	781	333	.426
32.	Alexander Mogilny, Buf., Van.	10	646	329	.509
33.	Wendel Clark, Tor., Que., NYI, T.B., Det.	14	760	326	.429
34.	Greg Adams, N.J., Van., Dal., Phx.	15	927	325	.351
35.	Claude Lemieux, Mtl., N.J., Col.	16	918	325	.354
36.	Dave Gagner, NYR, Min., Dal., Tor., Cgy., Fla., Van.	15	946	318	.336
37.	Peter Bondra, Wsh.	9	610	316	.518
38.	Kevin Stevens, Pit., Bos., L.A., NYR	12	749	315	.421
39.	Teemu Selanne, Wpg., Ana.	7	485	313	.645
40.	Petr Klima, Det., Edm., T.B., L.A., Pit.	13	786	313	.398
41.	Mike Modano, Min., Dal.	11	710	311	.438
42.	Phil Housley, Buf., Wpg., St.L., Cgy., N.J., Wsh.	17	1210	302	.250
43.	Russ Courtnall, Tor., Mtl., Min., Dal., Van., NYR, L.A.	16	1029	297	.289
44.	Mats Sundin, Que., Tor.	9	693	296	.427
45.	Gary Roberts, Cgy., Car.	12	723	291	.402
46.	Al MacInnis, Cgy., St.L.	18	1142	290	.254
47.	Adam Oates, Det., St.L., Bos., Wsh.	14	967	288	.298
48.	Trevor Linden, Van., NYI	11	809	275	.340
49.	Larry Murphy, L.A., Wsh., Min., Pit., Tor., Det.	19	1477	275	.186
50.	Sergei Fedorov, Det.	9	604	274	.454
51.	Rod Brind'Amour, St.L., Phi.	11	778	273	.351
52.	Keith Tkachuk, Wpg., Phx.	8	526	272	.517
53.	Adam Graves, Det., Edm., NYR	12	830	270	.325
54.	John LeClair, Mtl., Phi.	9	583	269	.461
55.	Pavel Bure, Van., Fla.	8	439	267	.608
56.	Murray Craven, Det., Phi., Hfd., Van., Chi., S.J.	17	1052	266	.253
57.	Eric Lindros, Phi.	7	431	263	.610
58.	Derek King, NYI, Hfd., Tor.	13	808	259	.321
59.	Scott Mellanby, Phi., Edm., Fla.	14	939	256	.273
60.	Guy Carbonneau, Mtl., St.L., Dal.	18	1249	250	.200
61.	Tony Amonte, NYR, Chi.	9	615	247	.402
62.	Tony Granato, NYR, L.A., S.J.	11	665	238	.358
63.	Shayne Corson, Mtl., Edm., St.L.	14	872	233	.267
64.	Ulf Dahlen, NYR, Min., Dal., S.J., Chi.	10	686	231	.337
65.	Dmitri Khristich, Wsh., L.A., Bos.	9	627	225	.359
66.	Joe Murphy, Det., Edm., Chi., St.L., S.J.	13	710	220	.310
67.	Peter Zezel, Phi., St.L., Wsh., Tor., Dal., N.J., Van.	15	873	219	.251
68.	Kevin Hatcher, Wsh., Dal., Pit.	15	1026	219	.213
69.	Cliff Ronning, St.L., Van., Phx., Nsh.	13	774	216	.279
70.	Geoff Sanderson, Hfd., Car., Van., Buf.	9	589	212	.360

Doug Gilmour enters the 1999-2000 season just three short of the 400-goal plateau. Gilmour had 16 goals for Chicago during an injury-plagued 1998-99 campaign.

	Player	Games	Goals	Goals per game
71.	Scott Young, Hfd., Pit., Que., Col., Ana., St.L.	11	747	210	.281
72.	Owen Nolan, Que., Col., S.J.	9	565	210	.372
73.	Robert Reichel, Cgy., NYI, Phx.	8	602	209	.347
74.	Benoit Hogue, Buf., NYI, Tor., Dal., T.B.	12	744	209	.281
75.	Steve Duchesne, L.A., Phi., Que., St.L., Ott.	13	916	208	.227
76.	Ron Sutter, Phi., St.L., Que., NYI, Bos., S.J.	17	994	199	.200
77.	Darren Turcotte, NYR, Hfd., Wpg., S.J., St.L., Nsh.	11	626	195	.312
78.	Randy Cunneyworth, Buf., Pit., Wpg., Hfd., Chi., Ott.	16	866	189	.218
79.	Craig Janney, Bos., St.L., S.J., Wpg., Phx., T.B., NYI	12	760	188	.247
80.	Donald Audette, Buf., L.A.	10	458	182	.397
81.	Shawn Burr, Det., T.B., S.J.	15	874	181	.207
82.	Gary Suter, Cgy., Chi., S.J.	14	919	181	.197
83.	Martin Gelinas, Edm., Que., Van., Car.	11	663	181	.273
84.	Michal Pivonka, Wsh.	13	825	181	.219
85.	Kelly Miller, NYR, Wsh.	15	1057	181	.171
86.	Rob Brown, Pit., Hfd., Chi., Dal., L.A.	10	493	180	.365
87.	Keith Primeau, Det., Hfd., Car.	9	597	179	.300
88.	Petr Nedved, Van., St.L., NYR, Pit.	8	497	178	.358
89.	Alexei Yashin, Ott.	6	422	178	.422
90.	Brian Leetch, NYR	12	807	177	.219
91.	Bobby Holik, Hfd., N.J.	9	638	177	.277
92.	Scott Stevens, Wsh., St.L., N.J.	17	1275	171	.134
93.	Bob Errey, Pit., Buf., S.J., Det., Dal., NYR	15	895	170	.190
94.	Paul Kariya, Ana.	5	302	168	.556
95.	Zigmund Palffy, NYI	6	331	168	.508
96.	Valeri Kamensky, Que., Col.	8	460	166	.361
97.	Chris Chelios, Mtl., Chi., Det.	16	1076	165	.153
98.	Alexei Zhamnov, Wpg., Chi.	7	455	164	.360
99.	Nelson Emerson, St.L., Wpg., Hfd., Car., Chi., Ott.	9	589	164	.278
100.	Vyacheslav Kozlov, Det.	8	463	164	.354

Top 100 All-Time Assist Leaders

* active player

	Player	Seasons	Games	Assists	Assists per game
1.	Wayne Gretzky, Edm., L.A., St.L., NYR .	20	1487	**1963**	1.320
* 2.	Paul Coffey, Edm., Pit., L.A., Det., Hfd., Phi., Chi., Car..........	19	1322	**1102**	.834
* 3.	Ray Bourque, Bos.........	20	1453	**1083**	.745
* 4.	Mark Messier, Edm., NYR, Van......	20	1413	**1050**	.743
5.	Gordie Howe, Det., Hfd...........	26	1767	**1049**	.594
6.	Marcel Dionne, Det., L.A., NYR	18	1348	**1040**	.772
* 7.	Ron Francis, Hfd., Pit., Car........	18	1329	**1037**	.780
8.	Stan Mikita, Chi...............	22	1394	**926**	.664
9.	Bryan Trottier, NYI, Pit..........	18	1279	**901**	.704
* 10.	Steve Yzerman, Det.............	16	1178	**891**	.756
11.	Dale Hawerchuk, Wpg., Buf., St.L., Phi.	16	1188	**891**	.750
12.	Mario Lemieux, Pit.............	12	745	**881**	1.183
* 13.	Larry Murphy, L.A., Wsh., Min., Pit., Tor., Det.........	19	1477	**880**	.596
14.	Phil Esposito, Chi., Bos., NYR	18	1282	**873**	.681
15.	Denis Savard, Chi., Mtl., T.B.......	17	1196	**865**	.723
16.	Bobby Clarke, Phi.............	15	1144	**852**	.745
* 17.	Adam Oates, Det., St.L., Bos., Wsh.....	14	967	**838**	.867
* 18.	Doug Gilmour, St.L., Cgy., Tor., N.J., Chi.........	16	1197	**835**	.698
19.	Alex Delvecchio, Det...........	24	1549	**825**	.533
20.	Gilbert Perreault, Buf..........	17	1191	**814**	.683
21.	John Bucyk, Det., Bos..........	23	1540	**813**	.528
22.	Jari Kurri, Edm., L.A., NYR, Ana., Col. ..	17	1251	**797**	.637
23.	Guy Lafleur, Mtl., NYR, Que........	17	1126	**793**	.704
24.	Peter Stastny, Que., N.J., St.L.......	15	977	**789**	.808
25.	Jean Ratelle, NYR, Bos..........	21	1281	**776**	.606
* 26.	Al MacInnis, Cgy., St.L..........	18	1142	**775**	.679
* 27.	Phil Housley, Buf., Wpg., St.L., Cgy., N.J., Wsh............	17	1210	**773**	.639
28.	Bernie Federko, St.L., Det.........	14	1000	**761**	.761
29.	Larry Robinson, Mtl., L.A........	20	1384	**750**	.542
30.	Denis Potvin, NYI.............	15	1060	**742**	.700
31.	Norm Ullman, Det., Tor..........	20	1410	**739**	.524
32.	Bernie Nicholls, L.A., NYR, Edm., N.J., Chi., S.J.............	18	1127	**734**	.651
33.	Jean Beliveau, Mtl.............	20	1125	**712**	.633
* 34.	Dale Hunter, Que., Wsh., Col.......	19	1407	**697**	.495
35.	Henri Richard, Mtl.............	20	1256	**688**	.548
36.	Brad Park, NYR, Bos., Det.........	17	1113	**683**	.614
37.	Bobby Smith, Min., Mtl..........	15	1077	**679**	.630
38.	Bobby Orr, Bos., Chi............	12	657	**645**	.982
39.	Dave Taylor, L.A.............	17	1111	**638**	.574
40.	Darryl Sittler, Tor., Phi., Det.......	15	1096	**637**	.581
41.	Borje Salming, Tor., Det.........	17	1148	**637**	.555
42.	Neal Broten, Min., Dal., N.J., L.A.....	17	1099	**634**	.577
* 43.	Chris Chelios, Mtl., Chi., Det.......	16	1076	**633**	.588
* 44.	Scott Stevens, Wsh., St.L., N.J.	17	1275	**628**	.493
45.	Mike Gartner, Wsh., Min., NYR, Tor., Phx.............	19	1432	**627**	.438
46.	Andy Bathgate, NYR, Tor., Det., Pit.	17	1069	**624**	.584
47.	Rod Gilbert, NYR	18	1065	**615**	.577
* 48.	Dave Andreychuk, Buf., Tor., N.J.	17	1210	**608**	.502
49.	Michel Goulet, Que., Chi..........	15	1089	**604**	.555
* 50.	Joe Sakic, Que., Col............	11	792	**604**	.763
51.	Glenn Anderson, Edm., Tor., NYR, St.L.	16	1129	**601**	.532
* 52.	Pierre Turgeon, Buf., NYI, Mtl., St.L.	12	877	**600**	.684
53.	Dino Ciccarelli, Min., Wsh., Det., T.B., Fla.............	19	1232	**592**	.481
54.	Dave Keon, Tor., Hfd.	18	1296	**590**	.455
55.	Doug Wilson, Chi., S.J...........	16	1024	**590**	.576
* 56.	Vincent Damphousse, Tor., Edm., Mtl., S.J..............	13	1005	**582**	.579
* 57.	Dave Babych, Wpg., Hfd., Van., Phi., L.A...........	19	1195	**581**	.486
58.	Brian Propp, Phi., Bos., Min., Hfd.	15	1016	**579**	.570
* 59.	Brian Leetch, NYR	12	807	**578**	.716
60.	Steve Larmer, Chi., NYR	15	1006	**571**	.568
61.	Frank Mahovlich, Tor., Det., Mtl.	18	1181	**570**	.483
* 62.	Gary Suter, Cgy., Chi., S.J.........	14	919	**563**	.613
* 63.	Craig Janney, Bos., St.L., S.J., Wpg., Phx., T.B., NYI	12	760	**563**	.741
64.	Joe Mullen, St.L., Cgy., Pit., Bos.	17	1062	**561**	.528
65.	Bobby Hull, Chi., Wpg., Hfd.	16	1063	**560**	.527
* 66.	Luc Robitaille, L.A., Pit., NYR	13	971	**559**	.576
67.	Mike Bossy, NYI..............	10	752	**553**	.735
68.	Thomas Steen, Wpg............	14	950	**553**	.582
* 69.	Kirk Muller, N.J., Mtl., NYI, Tor., Fla.	15	1114	**553**	.496
70.	Ken Linseman, Phi., Edm., Bos., Tor.	14	860	**551**	.641
71.	Tom Lysiak, Atl., Chi...........	13	919	**551**	.600
72.	Mark Howe, Hfd., Phi., Det........	16	929	**545**	.587
73.	Pat LaFontaine, NYI, Buf., NYR	15	865	**545**	.630
74.	Red Kelly, Det., Tor., L.A.........	21	1316	**542**	.412
75.	Rick Middleton, NYR, Bos.........	14	1005	**540**	.537
* 76.	Brian Bellows, Min., Mtl., T.B., Ana., Wsh..........	17	1188	**537**	.452

Guy Lafleur only led the NHL in assists once (with 80 for the Montreal Canadiens in 1976-77), but by the time he ended his career as a member of the New York Rangers in 1990-91, his 793 career assists ranked him 11th all-time.

	Player	Seasons	Games	Assists	Assist per game
77.	Dennis Maruk, Cal., Cle., Min., Wsh. ...	14	888	**522**	.588
* 78.	Jaromir Jagr, Pit..............	9	662	**517**	.781
79.	Wayne Cashman, Bos............	17	1027	**516**	.502
80.	Butch Goring, L.A., NYI, Bos.	17	1107	**513**	.463
81.	John Tonelli, NYI, Cgy., L.A., Chi., Que. ..	14	1028	**511**	.497
* 82.	Mark Recchi, Pit., Phi., Mtl........	11	781	**509**	.652
83.	Lanny McDonald, Tor., Col., Cgy.	16	1111	**506**	.455
84.	Ivan Boldirev, Bos., Cal., Chi., Atl., Van., Det..............	15	1052	**505**	.480
85.	Randy Carlyle, Tor., Pit., Wpg........	17	1055	**499**	.473
* 86.	Murray Craven, Det., Phi., Hfd., Van., Chi., S.J.............	17	1052	**491**	.467
* 87.	Pat Verbeek, N.J., Hfd., NYR, Dal.....	17	1225	**487**	.398
88.	Pit Martin, Det., Bos., Chi., Van.	17	1101	**485**	.441
89.	Pete Mahovlich, Det., Mtl., Pit.	16	884	**485**	.549
* 90.	Theoren Fleury, Cgy., Col.	11	806	**480**	.596
91.	Ken Hodge, Chi., Bos., NYR	14	881	**472**	.536
92.	Ted Lindsay, Det., Chi...........	17	1068	**472**	.442
93.	Jacques Lemaire, Mtl............	12	853	**469**	.550
94.	Dean Prentice, NYR, Bos., Det., Pit., Min..............	22	1378	**469**	.340
95.	Phil Goyette, Mtl., NYR, St.L., Buf.	16	941	**467**	.496
96.	Mike Ridley, NYR, Wsh., Tor., Van.	12	866	**466**	.538
97.	Brent Sutter, NYI, Chi...........	18	1111	**466**	.419
* 98.	Rick Tocchet, Phi., Pit., L.A., Bos., Wsh., Phx..............	15	990	**466**	.471
99.	Bill Barber, Phi..............	12	903	**463**	.513
100.	Reed Larson, Det., Bos., Edm., NYI, Min., Buf..............	14	904	**463**	.512

Top 100 Active Assist Leaders

* active player

Player	Seasons	Games	Assists	Assists per game
1. **Paul Coffey**, Edm., Pit., L.A., Det., Hfd., Phi., Chi., Car.	19	1322	**1102**	.834
2. **Ray Bourque**, Bos.	20	1453	**1083**	.745
3. **Mark Messier**, Edm., NYR, Van.	20	1413	**1050**	.743
4. **Ron Francis**, Hfd., Pit., Car.	18	1329	**1037**	.780
5. **Steve Yzerman**, Det.	16	1178	**891**	.756
6. **Larry Murphy**, L.A., Wsh., Min., Pit., Tor., Det.	19	1477	**880**	.596
7. **Adam Oates**, Det., St.L., Bos., Wsh.	14	967	**838**	.867
8. **Doug Gilmour**, St.L., Cgy., Tor., N.J., Chi.	16	1197	**835**	.698
9. **Al MacInnis**, Cgy., St.L.	18	1142	**775**	.679
10. **Phil Housley**, Buf., Wpg., St.L., Cgy., N.J., Wsh.	17	1210	**773**	.639
11. **Chris Chelios**, Mtl., Chi., Det.	16	1076	**633**	.588
12. **Scott Stevens**, Wsh., St.L., N.J.	17	1275	**628**	.493
13. **Dave Andreychuk**, Buf., Tor., N.J.	17	1210	**608**	.502
14. **Joe Sakic**, Que., Col.	11	792	**604**	.763
15. **Pierre Turgeon**, Buf., NYI, Mtl., St.L.	12	877	**600**	.684
16. **Vincent Damphousse**, Tor., Edm., Mtl., S.J.	13	1005	**582**	.579
17. **Dave Babych**, Wpg., Hfd., Van., Phi., L.A.	19	1195	**581**	.486
18. **Brian Leetch**, NYR	12	807	**578**	.716
19. **Gary Suter**, Cgy., Chi., S.J.	14	919	**563**	.613
20. **Craig Janney**, Bos., St.L., S.J., Wpg., Phx., T.B., NYI	12	760	**563**	.741
21. **Luc Robitaille**, L.A., Pit., NYR	13	971	**559**	.576
22. **Kirk Muller**, N.J., Mtl., NYI, Tor., Fla.	15	1114	**553**	.496
23. **Brian Bellows**, Min., Mtl., T.B., Ana., Wsh.	17	1188	**537**	.452
24. **Jaromir Jagr**, Pit.	9	662	**517**	.781
25. **Mark Recchi**, Pit., Phi., Mtl.	11	781	**509**	.652
26. **Murray Craven**, Det., Phi., Hfd., Van., Chi., S.J.	17	1052	**491**	.467
27. **Pat Verbeek**, N.J., Hfd., NYR, Dal.	17	1225	**487**	.398
28. **Theoren Fleury**, Cgy., Col.	11	806	**480**	.596
29. **Rick Tocchet**, Phi., Pit., L.A., Bos., Wsh., Phx.	15	990	**466**	.471
30. **Tomas Sandstrom**, NYR, L.A., Pit., Det., Ana.	15	983	**462**	.470
31. **Steve Duchesne**, L.A., Phi., Que., St.L., Ott.	13	916	**460**	.502
32. **Brett Hull**, Cgy., St.L., Dal.	14	861	**459**	.533
33. **Ed Olczyk**, Chi., Tor., Wpg., NYR, L.A., Pit.	15	998	**450**	.451
34. **Jeremy Roenick**, Chi., Phx.	11	753	**449**	.596
35. **Russ Courtnall**, Tor., Mtl., Min., Dal., Van., NYR, L.A.	16	1029	**447**	.434
36. **James Patrick**, NYR, Hfd., Cgy., Buf.	16	980	**446**	.455
37. **Garry Galley**, L.A., Wsh., Bos., Phi., Buf.	15	1023	**440**	.430
38. **Rod Brind'Amour**, St.L., Phi.	11	778	**430**	.553
39. **Geoff Courtnall**, Bos., Edm., Wsh., St.L., Van.	16	1042	**430**	.413
40. **Mike Modano**, Min., Dal.	11	710	**424**	.597
41. **Doug Bodger**, Pit., Buf., S.J., N.J., L.A.	15	1058	**421**	.398
42. **Mats Sundin**, Que., Tor.	9	693	**419**	.605
43. **Michal Pivonka**, Wsh.	13	825	**418**	.507
44. **Steve Thomas**, Tor., Chi., NYI, N.J.	15	938	**417**	.445
45. **Kevin Hatcher**, Wsh., Dal., Pit.	15	1026	**417**	.406
46. **Dave Ellett**, Wpg., Tor., N.J., Bos.	15	1077	**407**	.378
47. **Brendan Shanahan**, N.J., St.L., Hfd., Det.	12	869	**407**	.468
48. **Cliff Ronning**, St.L., Van., Phx., Nsh.	13	774	**403**	.521
49. **Dave Gagner**, NYR, Min., Dal., Tor., Cgy., Fla., Van.	15	946	**401**	.424
50. **John MacLean**, N.J., S.J., NYR	15	1067	**400**	.375
51. **Sergei Fedorov**, Det.	9	604	**398**	.659
52. **Joe Nieuwendyk**, Cgy., Dal.	13	835	**398**	.477
53. **Guy Carbonneau**, Mtl., St.L., Dal.	18	1249	**397**	.318
54. **Fredrik Olausson**, Wpg., Edm., Ana., Pit.	13	861	**396**	.460
55. **Ray Ferraro**, Hfd., NYI, NYR, L.A.	15	1020	**395**	.387
56. **Peter Zezel**, Phi., St.L., Wsh., Tor., Dal., N.J., Van.	15	873	**389**	.446
57. **Alexander Mogilny**, Buf., Van.	10	646	**385**	.596
58. **Kevin Dineen**, Hfd., Phi., Car.	15	992	**382**	.385
59. **Kevin Stevens**, Pit., Bos., L.A., NYR	12	749	**366**	.489
60. **Stephane Richer**, Mtl., N.J., T.B.	15	930	**362**	.389
61. **Trevor Linden**, Van., NYI	11	809	**358**	.443
62. **Doug Weight**, NYR, Edm.	9	547	**351**	.642
63. **Greg Adams**, N.J., Van., Dal., Phx.	15	927	**349**	.376
64. **Shayne Corson**, Mtl., Edm., St.L.	14	872	**348**	.399

A runner-up for the Norris Trophy two years in a row, Nicklas Lidstrom decided not to return to his native Sweden and re-signed with the Red Wings for the 1999-2000 season. Lidstrom's 43 assists last season trailed only Raymond Bourque among NHL defensemen and gave him 322 in his career.

Player	Games	Assists	Assists per game
65. **Derek King**, NYI, Hfd., Tor.	13	808	**344**	.426
66. **Calle Johansson**, Buf., Wsh.	12	850	**344**	.405
67. **Eric Lindros**, Phi.	7	431	**337**	.782
68. **Igor Larionov**, Van., S.J., Det.	9	584	**331**	.567
69. **Teemu Selanne**, Wpg., Ana.	7	485	**331**	.682
70. **Claude Lemieux**, Mtl., N.J., Col.	16	918	**326**	.355
71. **Andrew Cassels**, Mtl., Hfd., Cgy.	10	649	**324**	.499
72. **Glen Wesley**, Bos., Hfd., Car.	12	877	**322**	.367
73. **Nicklas Lidstrom**, Det.	8	612	**322**	.526
74. **Ron Sutter**, Phi., St.L., Que., NYI, Bos., S.J.	17	994	**320**	.322
75. **Scott Mellanby**, Phi., Edm., Fla.	14	939	**318**	.339
76. **Petr Svoboda**, Mtl., Buf., Phi., T.B.	15	939	**315**	.335
77. **Joe Juneau**, Bos., Wsh., Buf.	8	482	**315**	.654
78. **Peter Forsberg**, Que., Col.	5	344	**312**	.907
79. **Teppo Numminen**, Wpg., Phx.	11	793	**307**	.387
80. **Gary Roberts**, Cgy., Car.	12	723	**305**	.422
81. **Sergei Zubov**, NYR, Pit., Dal.	7	461	**299**	.649
82. **Robert Reichel**, Cgy., NYI, Phx.	8	602	**298**	.495
83. **Steve Smith**, Edm., Chi., Cgy.	15	771	**297**	.385
84. **Jeff Norton**, NYI, S.J., St.L., Edm., T.B., Fla.	12	663	**296**	.446
85. **Benoit Hogue**, Buf., NYI, Tor., Dal., T.B.	12	744	**296**	.398
86. **Eric Desjardins**, Mtl., Phi.	11	746	**291**	.390
87. **Ray Sheppard**, Buf., NYR, Det., S.J., Fla., Car.	12	770	**290**	.377
88. **Scott Young**, Hfd., Pit., Que., Col., Ana., St.L.	11	747	**287**	.384
89. **Zarley Zalapski**, Pit., Hfd., Cgy., Mtl.	11	625	**283**	.453
90. **Kelly Miller**, NYR, Wsh.	15	1057	**282**	.267
91. **Dmitri Khristich**, Wsh., L.A., Bos.	9	627	**282**	.450
92. **Jamie Macoun**, Cgy., Tor., Det.	17	1128	**282**	.250
93. **Jyrki Lumme**, Mtl., Van., Phx.	11	714	**281**	.394
94. **Joe Murphy**, Det., Edm., Chi., St.L., S.J.	13	710	**275**	.387
95. **Alexei Zhamnov**, Wpg., Chi.	7	455	**275**	.604
96. **Ulf Samuelsson**, Hfd., Pit., NYR, Det.	15	1031	**273**	.265
97. **Dave Manson**, Chi., Edm., Wpg., Phx., Mtl.	13	919	**270**	.294
98. **John LeClair**, Mtl., Phi.	9	583	**269**	.461
99. **Doug Lidster**, Van., NYR, St.L., Dal.	16	897	**268**	.299
100. **Grant Ledyard**, NYR, L.A., Wsh., Buf., Dal., Van., Bos.	15	913	**266**	.291

Top 100 All-Time Point Leaders

* active player

A feisty forward who was known as "the Rat" during his career with the Philadelphia Flyers, Edmonton Oilers, Boston Bruins and Toronto Maple Leafs, Ken Linseman's 807 career points rank him among the top 100 scorers of all time.

	Player	Seasons	Games	Goals	Assists	Points	Points per game
1.	Wayne Gretzky, Edm., L.A., St.L., NYR	20	1487	894	1963	**2857**	1.921
2.	Gordie Howe, Det., Hfd.	26	1767	801	1049	**1850**	1.047
3.	Marcel Dionne, Det., L.A., NYR	18	1348	731	1040	**1771**	1.314
* 4.	Mark Messier, Edm., NYR, Van.	20	1413	610	1050	**1660**	1.175
5.	Phil Esposito, Chi., Bos., NYR	18	1282	717	873	**1590**	1.240
6.	Mario Lemieux, Pit.	12	745	613	881	**1494**	2.005
* 7.	Paul Coffey, Edm., Pit., L.A., Det., Hfd., Phi., Chi., Car.	19	1322	385	1102	**1487**	1.125
* 8.	Ron Francis, Hfd., Pit., Car.	18	1329	449	1037	**1486**	1.118
* 9.	Steve Yzerman, Det.	16	1178	592	891	**1483**	1.259
* 10.	Ray Bourque, Bos.	20	1453	385	1083	**1468**	1.010
11.	Stan Mikita, Chi.	22	1394	541	926	**1467**	1.052
12.	Bryan Trottier, NYI, Pit.	18	1279	524	901	**1425**	1.114
13.	Dale Hawerchuk, Wpg., Buf., St.L., Phi.	16	1188	518	891	**1409**	1.186
14.	Jari Kurri, Edm., L.A., NYR, Ana., Col.	17	1251	601	797	**1398**	1.118
15.	John Bucyk, Det., Bos.	23	1540	556	813	**1369**	.889
16.	Guy Lafleur, Mtl., NYR, Que.	17	1126	560	793	**1353**	1.202
17.	Denis Savard, Chi., Mtl., T.B.	17	1196	473	865	**1338**	1.119
18.	Mike Gartner, Wsh., Min., NYR, Tor., Phx.	19	1432	708	627	**1335**	.932
19.	Gilbert Perreault, Buf.	17	1191	512	814	**1326**	1.113
20.	Alex Delvecchio, Det.	24	1549	456	825	**1281**	.827
21.	Jean Ratelle, NYR, Bos.	21	1281	491	776	**1267**	.989
22.	Peter Stastny, Que., N.J., St.L.	15	977	450	789	**1239**	1.268
* 23.	Doug Gilmour, St.L., Cgy., Tor., N.J., Chi.	16	1197	397	835	**1232**	1.029
24.	Norm Ullman, Det., Tor.	20	1410	490	739	**1229**	.872
25.	Jean Beliveau, Mtl.	20	1125	507	712	**1219**	1.084
26.	Bobby Clarke, Phi.	15	1144	358	852	**1210**	1.058
27.	Bernie Nicholls, L.A., NYR, Edm., N.J., Chi., S.J.	18	1127	475	734	**1209**	1.073
28.	Dino Ciccarelli, Min., Wsh., Det., T.B., Fla.	19	1232	608	592	**1200**	.974
29.	Bobby Hull, Chi., Wpg., Hfd.	16	1063	610	560	**1170**	1.101
* 30.	Larry Murphy, L.A., Wsh., Min., Pit., Tor., Det.	19	1477	275	880	**1155**	.782
31.	Michel Goulet, Que., Chi.	15	1089	548	604	**1152**	1.058
* 32.	Dave Andreychuk, Buf., Tor., N.J.	17	1210	532	608	**1140**	.942
33.	Bernie Federko, St.L., Det.	14	1000	369	761	**1130**	1.130
34.	Mike Bossy, NYI	10	752	573	553	**1126**	1.497
* 35.	Adam Oates, Det., St.L., Bos., Wsh.	14	967	288	838	**1126**	1.164
36.	Darryl Sittler, Tor., Phi., Det.	15	1096	484	637	**1121**	1.023
37.	Frank Mahovlich, Tor., Det., Mtl.	18	1181	533	570	**1103**	.934
38.	Glenn Anderson, Edm., Tor., NYR, St.L.	16	1129	498	601	**1099**	.973
* 39.	Luc Robitaille, L.A., Pit., NYR	13	971	517	559	**1076**	1.108
* 40.	Phil Housley, Buf., Wpg., St.L., Cgy., N.J., Wsh.	17	1210	302	773	**1075**	.888
41.	Dave Taylor, L.A.	17	1111	431	638	**1069**	.962
* 42.	Al MacInnis, Cgy., St.L.	18	1142	290	775	**1065**	.933
43.	Joe Mullen, St.L., Cgy., Pit., Bos.	17	1062	502	561	**1063**	1.001
44.	Denis Potvin, NYI	15	1060	310	742	**1052**	.992
45.	Henri Richard, Mtl.	20	1256	358	688	**1046**	.833
* 46.	Brett Hull, Cgy., St.L., Dal.	14	861	586	459	**1045**	1.214
47.	Bobby Smith, Min., Mtl.	15	1077	357	679	**1036**	.962
* 48.	Brian Bellows, Min., Mtl., T.B., Ana., Wsh.	17	1188	485	537	**1022**	.860
49.	Rod Gilbert, NYR	18	1065	406	615	**1021**	.959
50.	Dale Hunter, Que., Wsh., Col.	19	1407	323	697	**1020**	.725
51.	Pat LaFontaine, NYI, Buf., NYR	15	865	468	545	**1013**	1.171
52.	Steve Larmer, Chi., NYR	15	1006	441	571	**1012**	1.006
53.	Lanny McDonald, Tor., Col., Cgy.	16	1111	500	506	**1006**	.905
54.	Brian Propp, Phi., Bos., Min., Hfd.	15	1016	425	579	**1004**	.988
* 55.	Pierre Turgeon, Buf., NYI, Mtl., St.L.	12	877	397	600	**997**	1.137
56.	Rick Middleton, NYR, Bos.	14	1005	448	540	**988**	.983
57.	Dave Keon, Tor., Hfd.	18	1296	396	590	**986**	.761
* 58.	Joe Sakic, Que., Col.	11	792	375	604	**979**	1.236
59.	Andy Bathgate, NYR, Tor., Det., Pit.	17	1069	349	624	**973**	.910
* 60.	Pat Verbeek, N.J., Hfd., NYR, Dal.	17	1225	478	487	**965**	.788
61.	Maurice Richard, Mtl.	18	978	544	421	**965**	.987
62.	Larry Robinson, Mtl., L.A.	20	1384	208	750	**958**	.692

	Player	Seasons	Games	Goals	Assists	Points	Points per game
* 63.	Vincent Damphousse, Tor., Edm., Mtl., S.J.	13	1005	347	582	**929**	.924
64.	Neal Broten, Min., Dal., N.J., L.A.	17	1099	289	634	**923**	.840
65.	Bobby Orr, Bos., Chi.	12	657	270	645	**915**	1.393
66.	Brad Park, NYR, Bos., Det.	17	1113	213	683	**896**	.805
* 67.	Kirk Muller, N.J., Mtl., NYI, Tor., Fla.	15	1114	338	553	**891**	.800
68.	Butch Goring, L.A., NYI, Bos.	17	1107	375	513	**888**	.802
69.	Bill Barber, Phi.	12	903	420	463	**883**	.978
70.	Dennis Maruk, Cal., Cle., Min., Wsh.	14	888	356	522	**878**	.989
* 71.	Rick Tocchet, Phi., Pit., L.A., Bos., Wsh., Phx.	15	990	411	466	**877**	.886
72.	Ivan Boldirev, Bos., Cal., Chi., Atl., Van., Det.	15	1052	361	505	**866**	.823
73.	Yvan Cournoyer, Mtl.	16	968	428	435	**863**	.892
* 74.	Jaromir Jagr, Pit.	9	662	345	517	**862**	1.302
75.	Dean Prentice, NYR, Bos., Det., Pit., Min.	22	1378	391	469	**860**	.624
* 76.	Tomas Sandstrom, NYR, L.A., Pit., Det., Ana.	15	983	394	462	**856**	.871
* 77.	Theoren Fleury, Cgy., Col.	11	806	374	480	**854**	1.060
78.	Ted Lindsay, Det., Chi.	17	1068	379	472	**851**	.797
79.	Tom Lysiak, Atl., Chi.	13	919	292	551	**843**	.917
* 80.	Mark Recchi, Pit., Phi., Mtl.	11	781	333	509	**842**	1.078
81.	John Tonelli, NYI, Cgy., L.A., Chi., Que.	14	1028	325	511	**836**	.813
82.	Jacques Lemaire, Mtl.	12	853	366	469	**835**	.979
83.	Brent Sutter, NYI, Chi.	18	1111	363	466	**829**	.746
84.	John Ogrodnick, Det., Que., NYR	14	928	402	425	**827**	.891
85.	Doug Wilson, Chi., S.J.	16	1024	237	590	**827**	.808
* 86.	Joe Nieuwendyk, Cgy., Dal.	13	835	425	398	**823**	.986
87.	Red Kelly, Det., Tor., L.A.	21	1316	281	542	**823**	.625
88.	Pierre Larouche, Pit., Mtl., Hfd., NYR	14	812	395	427	**822**	1.012
89.	Bernie Geoffrion, Mtl., NYR	16	883	393	429	**822**	.931
90.	Steve Shutt, Mtl., L.A.	13	930	424	393	**817**	.878
91.	Thomas Steen, Wpg.	14	950	264	553	**817**	.860
92.	Wilf Paiement, K.C., Col., Tor., Que., NYR, Buf., Pit.	14	946	356	458	**814**	.860
93.	Peter McNab, Buf., Bos., Van., N.J.	14	954	363	450	**813**	.852
94.	Pit Martin, Det., Bos., Chi., Van.	17	1101	324	485	**809**	.735
95.	Ken Linseman, Phi., Edm., Bos., Tor.	14	860	256	551	**807**	.938
96.	Garry Unger, Tor., Det., St.L., Atl., L.A., Edm.	16	1105	413	391	**804**	.728
* 97.	Brendan Shanahan, N.J., St.L., Hfd., Det.	12	869	394	407	**801**	.922
98.	Ken Hodge, Chi., Bos., NYR	14	881	328	472	**800**	.908
* 99.	Scott Stevens, Wsh., St.L., N.J.	17	1275	171	628	**799**	.627
* 100.	Chris Chelios, Mtl., Chi., Det.	16	1076	165	633	**798**	.742

Top 100 Active Points Leaders

* active player

Mark Recchi was traded from Montreal back to Philadelphia for Danius Zubrus and draft picks on March 10, 1999. With 53 points last season, Recchi topped 800 for his career. He needs 58 points this season to reach 900

	Player	Seasons	Games	Goals	Assists	Points	Points per game
1.	Mark Messier, Edm., NYR, Van.	20	1413	610	1050	**1660**	1.175
2.	Paul Coffey, Edm., Pit., L.A., Det., Hfd., Phi., Chi., Car.	19	1322	385	1102	**1487**	1.125
3.	Ron Francis, Hfd., Pit., Car.	18	1329	449	1037	**1486**	1.118
4.	Steve Yzerman, Det.	16	1178	592	891	**1483**	1.259
5.	Ray Bourque, Bos.	20	1453	385	1083	**1468**	1.010
6.	Doug Gilmour, St.L., Cgy., Tor., N.J., Chi.	16	1197	397	835	**1232**	1.029
7.	Larry Murphy, L.A., Wsh., Min., Pit., Tor., Det.	19	1477	275	880	**1155**	.782
8.	Dave Andreychuk, Buf., Tor., N.J.	17	1210	532	608	**1140**	.942
9.	Adam Oates, Det., St.L., Bos., Wsh.	14	967	288	838	**1126**	1.164
10.	Luc Robitaille, L.A., Pit., NYR	13	971	517	559	**1076**	1.108
11.	Phil Housley, Buf., Wpg., St.L., Cgy., N.J., Wsh.	17	1210	302	773	**1075**	.888
12.	Al MacInnis, Cgy., St.L.	18	1142	290	775	**1065**	.933
13.	Brett Hull, Cgy., St.L., Dal.	14	861	586	459	**1045**	1.214
14.	Brian Bellows, Min., Mtl., T.B., Ana., Wsh.	17	1188	485	537	**1022**	.860
15.	Pierre Turgeon, Buf., NYI, Mtl., St.L.	12	877	397	600	**997**	1.137
16.	Joe Sakic, Que., Col.	11	792	375	604	**979**	1.236
17.	Pat Verbeek, N.J., Hfd., NYR, Dal.	17	1225	478	487	**965**	.788
18.	Vincent Damphousse, Tor., Edm., Mtl., S.J.	13	1005	347	582	**929**	.924
19.	Kirk Muller, N.J., Mtl., NYI, Tor., Fla.	15	1114	338	553	**891**	.800
20.	Rick Tocchet, Phi., Pit., L.A., Bos., Wsh., Phx.	15	990	411	466	**877**	.886
21.	Jaromir Jagr, Pit.	9	662	345	517	**862**	1.302
22.	Tomas Sandstrom, NYR, L.A., Pit., Det., Ana.	15	983	394	462	**856**	.871
23.	Theoren Fleury, Cgy., Col.	11	806	374	480	**854**	1.060
24.	Mark Recchi, Pit., Phi., Mtl.	11	781	333	509	**842**	1.078
25.	Joe Nieuwendyk, Cgy., Dal.	13	835	425	398	**823**	.986
26.	Brendan Shanahan, N.J., St.L., Hfd., Det.	12	869	394	407	**801**	.922
27.	Scott Stevens, Wsh., St.L., N.J.	17	1275	171	628	**799**	.627
28.	Chris Chelios, Mtl., Chi., Det.	16	1076	165	633	**798**	.742
29.	Geoff Courtnall, Bos., Edm., Wsh., St.L., Van.	16	1042	365	430	**795**	.763
30.	Jeremy Roenick, Chi., Phx.	11	753	344	449	**793**	1.053
31.	Ed Olczyk, Chi., Tor., Wpg., NYR, L.A., Pit.	15	998	340	450	**790**	.792
32.	John MacLean, N.J., S.J., NYR	15	1067	388	400	**788**	.739
33.	Steve Thomas, Tor., Chi., NYI, N.J.	15	938	352	417	**769**	.820
34.	Murray Craven, Det., Phi., Hfd., Van., Chi., S.J.	17	1052	266	491	**757**	.720
35.	Brian Leetch, NYR	12	807	177	578	**755**	.936
36.	Stephane Richer, Mtl., N.J., T.B.	15	930	392	362	**754**	.811
37.	Craig Janney, Bos., St.L., S.J., Wpg., Phx., T.B., NYI	12	760	188	563	**751**	.988
38.	Gary Suter, Cgy., Chi., S.J.	14	919	181	563	**744**	.810
39.	Russ Courtnall, Tor., Mtl., Min., Dal., Van., NYR, L.A.	16	1029	297	447	**744**	.723
40.	Ray Ferraro, Hfd., NYI, NYR, L.A.	15	1020	346	395	**741**	.726
41.	Mike Modano, Min., Dal.	11	710	311	424	**735**	1.035
42.	Dave Babych, Wpg., Hfd., Van., Phi., L.A.	19	1195	142	581	**723**	.605
43.	Kevin Dineen, Hfd., Phi., Car.	15	992	338	382	**720**	.726
44.	Dave Gagner, NYR, Min., Dal., Tor., Cgy., Fla., Van.	15	946	318	401	**719**	.760
45.	Mats Sundin, Que., Tor.	9	693	296	419	**715**	1.032
46.	Alexander Mogilny, Buf., Van.	10	646	329	385	**714**	1.105
47.	Rod Brind'Amour, St.L., Phi.	11	778	273	430	**703**	.904
48.	Kevin Stevens, Pit., Bos., L.A., NYR	12	749	315	366	**681**	.909
49.	Greg Adams, N.J., Van., Dal., Phx.	15	927	325	349	**674**	.727
50.	Sergei Fedorov, Det.	9	604	274	398	**672**	1.113
51.	Steve Duchesne, L.A., Phi., Que., St.L., Ott.	13	916	208	460	**668**	.729
52.	Claude Lemieux, Mtl., N.J., Col.	16	918	325	326	**651**	.709
53.	Guy Carbonneau, Mtl., St.L., Dal.	18	1249	250	397	**647**	.518
54.	Teemu Selanne, Wpg., Ana.	7	485	313	331	**644**	1.328
55.	Ray Sheppard, Buf., NYR, Det., S.J., Fla., Car.	12	770	347	290	**637**	.827
56.	Kevin Hatcher, Wsh., Dal., Pit.	15	1026	219	417	**636**	.620
57.	Trevor Linden, Van., NYI	11	809	275	358	**633**	.782
58.	Cliff Ronning, St.L., Van., Phx., Nsh.	13	774	216	403	**619**	.800
59.	Peter Zezel, Phi., St.l., Wsh., Tor., Dal., N.J., Van.	15	873	219	389	**608**	.696
60.	Derek King, NYI, Hfd., Tor.	13	808	259	344	**603**	.746
61.	Eric Lindros, Phi.	7	431	263	337	**600**	1.392
62.	Michal Pivonka, Wsh.	13	825	181	418	**599**	.726
63.	Gary Roberts, Cgy., Car.	12	723	291	305	**596**	.824
64.	Shayne Corson, Mtl., Edm., St.L.	14	872	233	348	**581**	.666
65.	Scott Mellanby, Phi., Edm., Fla.	14	939	256	318	**574**	.611
66.	James Patrick, NYR, Hfd., Cgy., Buf.	16	980	127	446	**573**	.585
67.	Petr Klima, Det., Edm., T.B., L.A., Pit.	13	786	313	260	**573**	.729
68.	Dave Ellett, Wpg., Tor., N.J., Bos.	15	1077	151	407	**558**	.518
69.	Wendel Clark, Tor., Que., NYI, T.B., Det.	14	760	326	232	**558**	.734
70.	Garry Galley, L.A., Wsh., Bos., Phi., Buf.	15	1023	110	440	**550**	.538
71.	Peter Bondra, Wsh.	9	610	316	229	**545**	.893
72.	John LeClair, Mtl., Phi.	9	583	269	269	**538**	.923
73.	Doug Bodger, Pit., Buf., S.J., N.J., L.A.	15	1058	106	421	**527**	.498
74.	Fredrik Olausson, Wpg., Edm., Ana., Pit.	13	861	128	396	**524**	.609
75.	Ron Sutter, Phi., St.L., Que., NYI, Bos., S.J.	17	994	199	320	**519**	.522
76.	Tony Amonte, NYR, Chi.	9	615	247	263	**510**	.829
77.	Keith Tkachuk, Wpg., Phx.	8	526	272	237	**509**	.968
78.	Dmitri Khristich, Wsh., L.A., Bos.	9	627	225	282	**507**	.809
79.	Robert Reichel, Cgy., NYI, Phx.	8	602	209	298	**507**	.842
80.	Benoit Hogue, Buf., NYI, Tor., Dal., T.B.	12	744	209	296	**505**	.679
81.	Adam Graves, Det., Edm., NYR	12	830	270	231	**501**	.604
82.	Scott Young, Hfd., Pit., Que., Col., Ana., St.L.	11	747	210	287	**497**	.665
83.	Joe Murphy, Det., Edm., Chi., St.L., S.J.	13	710	220	275	**495**	.697
84.	Pavel Bure, Van., Fla.	8	439	267	227	**494**	1.125
85.	Doug Weight, NYR, Edm.	9	547	134	351	**485**	.887
86.	Ulf Dahlen, NYR, Min., Dal., S.J., Chi.	10	686	231	249	**480**	.700
87.	Tony Granato, NYR, L.A., S.J.	11	665	238	232	**470**	.707
88.	Kelly Miller, NYR, Wsh.	15	1057	181	282	**463**	.438
89.	Igor Larionov, Van., S.J., Det.	9	584	129	331	**460**	.788
90.	Andrew Cassels, Mtl., Hfd., Cgy.	10	649	134	324	**458**	.706
91.	Randy Burridge, Bos., Wsh., L.A., Buf.	13	706	199	251	**450**	.637
92.	Calle Johansson, Buf., Wsh.	12	850	100	344	**444**	.522
93.	Peter Forsberg, Que., Col.	5	344	128	312	**440**	1.279
94.	Alexei Zhamnov, Wpg., Chi.	7	455	164	275	**439**	.965
95.	Shawn Burr, Det., T.B., S.J.	15	874	181	257	**438**	.501
96.	Owen Nolan, Que., Col., S.J.	9	565	210	224	**434**	.768
97.	Joe Juneau, Bos., Wsh., Buf.	8	482	114	315	**429**	.890
98.	Glen Wesley, Bos., Hfd., Car.	12	877	106	322	**428**	.488
99.	Nelson Emerson, St.L., Wpg., Hfd., Car., Chi., Ott.	9	589	164	260	**424**	.720
100.	Nicklas Lidstrom, Det.	8	612	101	322	**423**	.691

All-Time Games Played Leaders

Regular Season

active player

Rank	Player	Team	Seasons	GP
1.	Gordie Howe	Detroit	25	1,687
		Hartford	1	80
		Total	**26**	**1,767**
2.	Alex Delvecchio	**Detroit**	**24**	**1,549**
3.	John Bucyk	Detroit	2	104
		Boston	21	1,436
		Total	**23**	**1,540**
4.	Wayne Gretzky	Edmonton	9	696
		Los Angeles	7¾	539
		St. Louis	¼	18
		NY Rangers	3	234
		Total	**20**	**1,487**
*5.	Larry Murphy	Los Angeles	3¼	242
		Washington	5½	453
		Minnesota	1¾	121
		Pittsburgh	4½	336
		Toronto	1¾	151
		Detroit	2¼	174
		Total	**19**	**1,477**
*6.	Ray Bourque	**Boston**	**20**	**1,453**
7.	Tim Horton	Toronto	19¾	1,185
		NY Rangers	1¼	93
		Pittsburgh	1	44
		Buffalo	2	124
		Total	**24**	**1,446**
8.	Mike Gartner	Washington	9¾	758
		Minnesota	1	80
		NY Rangers	4	322
		Toronto	2¼	130
		Phoenix	2	142
		Total	**19**	**1,432**
*9.	Mark Messier	Edmonton	12	851
		NY Rangers	6	421
		Vancouver	2	141
		Total	**20**	**1,413**
10.	Harry Howell	NY Rangers	17	1,160
		California	1½	83
		Los Angeles	2½	168
		Total	**21**	**1,411**
11.	Norm Ullman	Detroit	12½	875
		Toronto	7½	535
		Total	**20**	**1,410**
12.	Dale Hunter	Quebec	7	523
		Washington	11¾	872
		Colorado	¼	12
		Total	**19**	**1,407**
13.	Stan Mikita	**Chicago**	**22**	**1,394**
14.	Doug Mohns	Boston	11	710
		Chicago	6½	415
		Minnesota	2½	162
		Atlanta	1	28
		Washington	1	75
		Total	**22**	**1,390**
15.	Larry Robinson	Montreal	17	1,202
		Los Angeles	3	182
		Total	**20**	**1,384**
16.	Dean Prentice	NY Rangers	10½	666
		Boston	3	170
		Detroit	3½	230
		Pittsburgh	2	144
		Minnesota	3	168
		Total	**22**	**1,378**
17.	Ron Stewart	Toronto	13	838
		Boston	2	126
		St. Louis	½	19
		NY Rangers	4	306
		Vancouver	1	42
		NY Islanders	½	22
		Total	**21**	**1,353**
18.	Marcel Dionne	Detroit	4	309
		Los Angeles	11¾	921
		NY Rangers	2¼	118
		Total	**18**	**1,348**
*19.	Ron Francis	Hartford	9¾	714
		Pittsburgh	7¼	533
		Carolina	1	82
		Total	**18**	**1,329**
*20.	Paul Coffey	Edmonton	7	532
		Pittsburgh	4¾	331
		Los Angeles	¾	60
		Detroit	3½	231
		Hartford	¼	20
		Philadelphia	1¾	94
		Chicago	¼	10
		Carolina	¾	44
		Total	**19**	**1,322**
21.	Red Kelly	Detroit	12½	846
		Toronto	7½	470
		Total	**20**	**1,316**
22.	Dave Keon	Toronto	15	1,062
		Hartford	3	234
		Total	**18**	**1,296**
23.	Phil Esposito	Chicago	4	235
		Boston	8¼	625
		NY Rangers	5¾	422
		Total	**18**	**1,282**
24.	Jean Ratelle	NY Rangers	15¼	862
		Boston	5¾	419
		Total	**21**	**1,281**
25.	Bryan Trottier	NY Islanders	15	1,123
		Pittsburgh	3	156
		Total	**18**	**1,279**
*26.	Scott Stevens	Washington	8	601
		St. Louis	1	78
		New Jersey	8	596
		Total	**17**	**1,275**
27.	Craig Ludwig	Montreal	8	597
		NY Islanders	1	75
		Minnesota	2	151
		Dallas	6	433
		Total	**17**	**1,256**
28.	Henri Richard	**Montreal**	**20**	**1,256**
29.	Kevin Lowe	Edmonton	15	1,037
		NY Rangers	4	217
		Total	**19**	**1,254**
30.	Jari Kurri	Edmonton	10	754
		Los Angeles	4¾	331
		NY Rangers	¼	14
		Anaheim	1	82
		Colorado	1	70
		Total	**17**	**1,251**
*31.	Guy Carbonneau	Montreal	13	912
		St. Louis	1	42
		Dallas	4	295
		Total	**18**	**1,249**
32.	Bill Gadsby	Chicago	8½	468
		NY Rangers	6½	457
		Detroit	5	323
		Total	**20**	**1,248**
33.	Allan Stanley	NY Rangers	6¼	307
		Chicago	1¾	111
		Boston	2	129
		Toronto	10	633
		Philadelphia	1	64
		Total	**21**	**1,244**
34.	Dino Ciccarelli	Minnesota	8¾	602
		Washington	3¼	223
		Detroit	4	254
		Tampa Bay	1½	111
		Florida	1½	42
		Total	**19**	**1,232**
35.	Eddie Westfall	Boston	11	734
		NY Islanders	7	493
		Total	**18**	**1,227**
*36.	Pat Verbeek	New Jersey	7	463
		Hartford	5¾	433
		NY Rangers	1¼	88
		Dallas	3	241
		Total	**17**	**1,225**
37.	Brad McCrimmon	Boston	3	228
		Philadelphia	5	367
		Calgary	3	231
		Detroit	3	203
		Hartford	3	156
		Phoenix	1	37
		Total	**18**	**1,222**
38.	Eric Nesterenko	Toronto	5	206
		Chicago	16	1,013
		Total	**21**	**1,219**
*39.	Phil Housley	Buffalo	8	608
		Winnipeg	3	232
		St. Louis	1	26
		Calgary	2¾	181
		New Jersey	¼	22
		Washington	2	141
		Total	**17**	**1,210**
*40.	Dave Andreychuk	Buffalo	10½	763
		Toronto	3¼	223
		New Jersey	3¼	224
		Total	**17**	**1,210**
41.	Marcel Pronovost	Detroit	16	983
		Toronto	5	223
		Total	**21**	**1,206**
*42.	Doug Gilmour	St. Louis	5	384
		Calgary	3½	266
		Toronto	5¼	392
		New Jersey	1¼	83
		Chicago	1	72
		Total	**16**	**1,197**
43.	Denis Savard	Chicago	12¼	881
		Montreal	3	210
		Tampa Bay	1¾	105
		Total	**17**	**1,196**
*44.	Dave Babych	Winnipeg	5¼	390
		Hartford	5¾	349
		Vancouver	6¾	409
		Philadelphia	1	39
		Los Angeles	¼	8
		Total	**19**	**1,195**
45.	Gilbert Perreault	**Buffalo**	**17**	**1,191**
46.	Dale Hawerchuk	Winnipeg	9	713
		Buffalo	5	342
		St. Louis	¾	66
		Philadelphia	1¼	67
		Total	**16**	**1,188**
*47.	Brian Bellows	Minnesota	10	753
		Montreal	3	200
		Tampa Bay	1¼	86
		Anaheim	¾	62
		Washington	2	87
		Total	**17**	**1,188**
48.	George Armstrong	**Toronto**	**21**	**1,187**
49.	Frank Mahovlich	Toronto	11¾	720
		Detroit	2¾	198
		Montreal	3½	263
		Total	**18**	**1,181**
*50.	Steve Yzerman	**Detroit**	**16**	**1,178**
51.	Bob Carpenter	Washington	6¼	490
		NY Rangers	½	28
		Los Angeles	1¾	120
		Boston	3½	187
		New Jersey	6	353
		Total	**18**	**1,178**
52.	Don Marshall	Montreal	10	585
		NY Rangers	7	479
		Buffalo	1	62
		Toronto	1	50
		Total	**19**	**1,176**
53.	Bob Gainey	**Montreal**	**16**	**1,160**
54.	Leo Boivin	Toronto	3¼	137
		Boston	11½	717
		Detroit	1¼	85
		Pittsburgh	1½	114
		Minnesota	1½	97
		Total	**19**	**1,150**
55.	Borje Salming	Toronto	16	1,099
		Detroit	1	49
		Total	**17**	**1,148**
56.	Bobby Clarke	**Philadelphia**	**15**	**1,144**
*57.	Al MacInnis	Calgary	13	803
		St. Louis	5	339
		Total	**18**	**1,142**
58.	Glenn Anderson	Edmonton	11½	845
		Toronto	2¾	221
		NY Rangers	¼	12
		St. Louis	1½	51
		Total	**16**	**1,129**
*59.	Jamie Macoun	Calgary	8½	586
		Toronto	6¼	466
		Detroit	1¼	76
		Total	**16**	**1,128**
60.	Bob Nevin	Toronto	5¾	250
		NY Rangers	7¼	505
		Minnesota	2	138
		Los Angeles	3	235
		Total	**18**	**1,128**
61.	Murray Oliver	Detroit	2½	101
		Boston	6½	429
		Toronto	3	226
		Minnesota	5	371
		Total	**17**	**1,127**
62.	Bernie Nicholls	Los Angeles	8½	602
		NY Rangers	1¾	104
		Edmonton	1¼	95
		New Jersey	1½	84
		Chicago	2	107
		San Jose	3	135
		Total	**18**	**1,127**
63.	Guy Lafleur	Montreal	14	961
		NY Rangers	1	67
		Quebec	2	98
		Total	**17**	**1,126**
64.	Jean Beliveau	**Montreal**	**20**	**1,125**
*65.	Kirk Muller	New Jersey	7	556
		Montreal	3¾	267
		NY Islanders	¾	27
		Toronto	1¼	102
		Florida	2¼	162
		Total	**15**	**1,114**

	Player	Team	Seasons	GP
66.	**Brad Park**	NY Rangers	7½	465
		Boston	7½	501
		Detroit	2	147
		Total	**17**	**1,113**
67.	**Doug Harvey**	Montreal	14	890
		NY Rangers	3	151
		Detroit	1	2
		St. Louis	1	70
		Total	**19**	**1,113**
68.	**Lanny McDonald**	Toronto	6½	477
		Colorado	1¾	142
		Calgary	7¾	492
		Total	**16**	**1,111**
69.	**Dave Taylor**	**Los Angeles**	**17**	**1,111**
70.	**Brent Sutter**	NY Islanders	11¼	694
		Chicago	6¾	417
		Total	**18**	**1,111**
71.	**Butch Goring**	Los Angeles	10¾	736
		NY Islanders	4¾	332
		Boston	½	39
		Total	**16**	**1,107**
72.	**Garry Unger**	Toronto	½	15
		Detroit	3	216
		St. Louis	8½	662
		Atlanta	1	79
		Los Angeles	¾	58
		Edmonton	2¼	75
		Total	**16**	**1,105**
73.	**Pit Martin**	Detroit	3¼	119
		Boston	1¾	111
		Chicago	10¼	740
		Vancouver	1¾	131
		Total	**17**	**1,101**
74.	**Neal Broten**	Minnesota	13	876
		Dallas	2	116
		New Jersey	1¾	88
		Los Angeles	¼	19
		Total	**17**	**1,099**
75.	**Jay Wells**	Los Angeles	9	604
		Philadelphia	1¾	126
		Buffalo	2	85
		NY Rangers	3¼	186
		St. Louis	1	76
		Tampa Bay	1	21
		Total	**18**	**1,098**
76.	**Gordie Roberts**	Hartford	1½	107
		Minnesota	7	555
		Philadelphia	¼	11
		St. Louis	2½	166
		Pittsburgh	1¾	134
		Boston	2	124
		Total	**15**	**1,097**
77.	**Darryl Sittler**	Toronto	11½	844
		Philadelphia	2½	191
		Detroit	1	61
		Total	**15**	**1,096**
78.	**Craig MacTavish**	Boston	5	217
		Edmonton	8¾	701
		NY Rangers	¼	12
		Philadelphia	1¾	100
		St. Louis	1¼	63
		Total	**17**	**1,093**
79.	**Michel Goulet**	Quebec	10¾	813
		Chicago	4¼	276
		Total	**15**	**1,089**
80.	**Carol Vadnais**	Montreal	2	42
		Oakland	2	152
		California	1¾	94
		Boston	3½	263
		NY Rangers	6¾	485
		New Jersey	1	51
		Total	**17**	**1,087**
81.	**Brad Marsh**	Atlanta	2	160
		Calgary	1¼	97
		Philadelphia	6¾	514
		Toronto	2¾	181
		Detroit	1¼	75
		Ottawa	1	59
		Total	**15**	**1,086**
82.	**Bob Pulford**	Toronto	14	947
		Los Angeles	2	132
		Total	**16**	**1,079**
* 83.	**Dave Ellett**	Winnipeg	6¼	475
		Toronto	6½	446
		New Jersey	¼	20
		Boston	2	136
		Total	**15**	**1,077**
84.	**Bobby Smith**	Minnesota	8¼	572
		Montreal	6¾	505
		Total	**15**	**1,077**
* 85.	**Chris Chelios**	Montreal	7	402
		Chicago	8¼	65
		Detroit	¼	10
		Total	**16**	**1,076**
86.	**Craig Ramsay**	**Buffalo**	**14**	**1,070**
87.	**Mike Ramsey**	Buffalo	13¾	911
		Pittsburgh	1¼	77
		Detroit	3	82
		Total	**18**	**1,070**
88.	**Andy Bathgate**	NY Rangers	11¾	719
		Toronto	1¼	70
		Detroit	2	130
		Pittsburgh	2	150
		Total	**17**	**1,069**
89.	**Ted Lindsay**	Detroit	14	862
		Chicago	3	206
		Total	**17**	**1,068**
* 90.	**John MacLean**	New Jersey	13¼	934
		San Jose	¾	51
		NY Rangers	1	82
		Total	**15**	**1,067**
91.	**Terry Harper**	Montreal	10	554
		Los Angeles	3	234
		Detroit	4	252
		St. Louis	1	11
		Colorado	1	15
		Total	**19**	**1,066**
92.	**Rod Gilbert**	**NY Rangers**	**18**	**1,065**
93.	**Bobby Hull**	Chicago	15	1,036
		Winnipeg	⅔	18
		Hartford	⅓	9
		Total	**16**	**1,063**
94.	**Joe Mullen**	St. Louis	4½	301
		Calgary	4½	345
		Pittsburgh	6	379
		Boston	1	37
		Total	**16**	**1,062**
95.	**Denis Potvin**	**NY Islanders**	**15**	**1,060**
* 96.	**Doug Bodger**	Pittsburgh	4¼	299
		Buffalo	7	479
		San Jose	2¼	166
		New Jersey	½	49
		Los Angeles	1	65
		Total	**15**	**1,058**
* 97.	**Kelly Miller**	NY Rangers	2½	117
		Washington	12½	940
		Total	**15**	**1,057**
98.	**Jean Guy Talbot**	Montreal	13	791
		Minnesota	¼	4
		Detroit	½	32
		St. Louis	2½	172
		Buffalo	¾	57
		Total	**17**	**1,056**
99.	**Randy Carlyle**	Toronto	2	94
		Pittsburgh	5¾	397
		Winnipeg	9¼	564
		Total	**17**	**1,055**
100.	**Ivan Boldirev**	Boston	1¼	13
		California	2¾	191
		Chicago	4¾	384
		Atlanta	1	65
		Vancouver	2¾	216
		Detroit	2½	183
		Total	**15**	**1,052**
* 101.	**Murray Craven**	Detroit	2	46
		Philadelphia	7¼	523
		Hartford	1½	128
		Vancouver	1¼	88
		Chicago	3	157
		San Jose	2	110
		Total	**17**	**1,052**
102.	**Eddie Shack**	NY Rangers	2¼	141
		Toronto	8¾	504
		Boston	2	120
		Los Angeles	1¼	84
		Buffalo	1½	111
		Pittsburgh	1¼	87
		Total	**17**	**1,047**
103.	**Rob Ramage**	Colorado	3	234
		St. Louis	5¾	441
		Calgary	1¼	80
		Toronto	2	160
		Minnesota	1	34
		Tampa Bay	¾	66
		Montreal	½	14
		Philadelphia	¾	15
		Total	**15**	**1,044**
* 104.	**Geoff Courtnall**	Boston	4¾	259
		Edmonton	¼	12
		Washington	2	159
		St. Louis	4¾	320
		Vancouver	4¼	292
		Total	**16**	**1,042**
105.	**Serge Savard**	Montreal	15	917
		Winnipeg	2	123
		Total	**17**	**1,040**
* 106.	**Bob Rouse**	Minnesota	5¾	351
		Washington	2	130
		Toronto	3¼	237
		Detroit	4	247
		San Jose	1	70
		Total	**16**	**1,035**
107.	**Ron Ellis**	**Toronto**	**16**	**1,034**
108.	**Harold Snepsts**	Vancouver	11¾	781
		Minnesota	1	71
		Detroit	3	120
		St. Louis	1¼	61
		Total	**17**	**1,033**
109.	**Ralph Backstrom**	Montreal	14½	844
		Los Angeles	2¼	172
		Chicago	¼	16
		Total	**17**	**1,032**
* 110.	**Ulf Samuelsson**	Hartford	6¾	463
		Pittsburgh	4¼	277
		NY Rangers	3¾	287
		Detroit	¼	4
		Total	**15**	**1,031**
111.	**Dick Duff**	Toronto	9¾	582
		NY Rangers	¾	43
		Montreal	5	305
		Los Angeles	¾	39
		Buffalo	1¾	61
		Total	**18**	**1,030**
* 112.	**Russ Courtnall**	Toronto	5¼	309
		Montreal	3¾	250
		Minnesota	1	84
		Dallas	1½	116
		Vancouver	2¼	141
		NY Rangers	¼	14
		Los Angeles	2	115
		Total	**16**	**1,029**
113.	**John Tonelli**	NY Islanders	7¾	584
		Calgary	2¼	161
		Los Angeles	3	231
		Chicago	¾	33
		Quebec	¼	19
		Total	**14**	**1,028**
114.	**Gaetan Duchesne**	Washington	6	451
		Quebec	2	150
		Minnesota	4	297
		San Jose	1¾	117
		Florida	¼	13
		Total	**14**	**1,028**
115.	**Wayne Cashman**	**Boston**	**17**	**1,027**
* 116.	**Kevin Hatcher**	Washington	10	685
		Dallas	2	121
		Pittsburgh	3	220
		Total	**15**	**1,026**
117.	**Doug Wilson**	Chicago	14	938
		San Jose	2	86
		Total	**16**	**1,024**
118.	**Keith Acton**	Montreal	4¼	228
		Minnesota	4¼	343
		Edmonton	1	72
		Philadelphia	4½	303
		Washington	¼	6
		NY Islanders	¾	71
		Total	**15**	**1,023**
* 119.	**Gary Galley**	Los Angeles	4½	291
		Washington	1½	76
		Boston	3½	257
		Philadelphia	3¼	236
		Buffalo	2¼	163
		Total	**15**	**1,023**
120.	**Jim Neilson**	NY Rangers	12	810
		California	2	98
		Cleveland	2	115
		Total	**16**	**1,023**
* 121.	**Ray Ferraro**	Hartford	6¼	442
		NY Islanders	4¾	316
		NY Rangers	¾	65
		Los Angeles	3¼	197
		Total	**15**	**1,020**
122.	**Don Lever**	Vancouver	7⅔	593
		Atlanta	⅓	28
		Calgary	1¼	85
		Colorado	¾	59
		New Jersey	3	216
		Buffalo	2	39
		Total	**15**	**1,020**
123.	**Mike Foligno**	Detroit	2½	186
		Buffalo	9	664
		Toronto	2¾	129
		Florida	¾	39
		Total	**15**	**1,018**
124.	**Charlie Huddy**	Edmonton	11	694
		Los Angeles	3¼	226
		Buffalo	2½	85
		St. Louis	¼	12
		Total	**17**	**1,017**
125.	**Phil Russell**	Chicago	6¾	504
		Atlanta	1¼	93
		Calgary	3	229
		New Jersey	2¾	172
		Buffalo	1¼	18
		Total	**15**	**1,016**
126.	**Brian Propp**	Philadelphia	10¾	790
		Boston	¼	14
		Minnesota	3	147
		Hartford	1	65
		Total	**15**	**1,016**

	Player	Team	Seasons	GP
127.	Laurie Boschman	Toronto	2¾	187
		Edmonton	1	73
		Winnipeg	7¼	526
		New Jersey	2	153
		Ottawa	1	70
		Total	**14**	**1,009**
128.	Dave Christian	Winnipeg	4	230
		Washington	6½	504
		Boston	1½	128
		St. Louis	1	78
		Chicago	2	69
		Total	**15**	**1,009**
129.	Dave Lewis	NY Islanders	6¾	514
		Los Angeles	3¼	221
		New Jersey	3	209
		Detroit	2	64
		Total	**15**	**1,008**
130.	Bob Murray	Chicago	15	1,008
131.	Jim Roberts	Montreal	9⅔	611
		St. Louis	5⅓	395
		Total	**15**	**1,006**

	Player	Team	Seasons	GP
132.	Steve Larmer	Chicago	13	891
		NY Rangers	2	115
		Total	**15**	**1,006**
* 133.	Vincent Danphousse	Toronto	5	394
		Edmonton	1	80
		Montreal	6¾	519
		San Jose	¼	12
		Total	**13**	**1,005**
134.	Rick Middleton	NY Rangers	2	124
		Boston	12	881
		Total	**14**	**1,005**
135.	Claude Provost	Montreal	15	1,005
136.	Ryan Walter	Washington	4	307
		Montreal	9	604
		Vancouver	2	92
		Total	**15**	**1,003**
137.	Vic Hadfield	NY Rangers	13	839
		Pittsburgh	3	163
		Total	**16**	**1,002**
138.	Bernie Federko	St. Louis	14	927
		Detroit	1	73
		Total	**15**	**1,000**

Bernie Federko played exactly 1,000 games in his NHL career. He is the Blues' all-time leader in seasons (13), games (927), assists (721) and points (1,073).

All-Time Penalty-Minute Leaders

* active player

(Regular season. Minimum 2,000 minutes)

	Player	Seasons	Games	Penalty Minutes	Mins. per game
1.	Dave Williams, Tor., Van., Det., L.A., Hfd..	14	962	**3966**	4.12
2.	Dale Hunter, Que., Wsh., Col.	19	1407	**3565**	2.53
* 3.	Marty McSorley, Pit., Edm., L.A., NYR, S.J.	16	934	**3319**	3.55
4.	Tim Hunter, Cgy., Que., Van., S.J.	16	815	**3146**	3.86
5.	Chris Nilan, Mtl., NYR, Bos.	13	688	**3043**	4.42
* 6.	Bob Probert, Det., Chi.	13	726	**2907**	4.00
* 7.	Rick Tocchet, Phi., Pit., L.A., Bos., Wsh., Phx.	15	990	**2773**	2.80
* 8.	Pat Verbeek, N.J., Hfd., NYR, Dal.	17	1225	**2665**	2.18
* 9.	Craig Berube, Phi., Tor., Cgy., Wsh.	13	796	**2651**	3.33
* 10.	Dave Manson, Chi., Edm., Wpg., Phx., Mtl.	13	919	**2604**	2.83
11.	Willi Plett, Atl., Cgy., Min., Bos.	13	834	**2572**	3.08
* 12.	Rob Ray, Buf.	10	645	**2529**	3.92
* 13.	Joe Kocur, Det., NYR, Van.	15	820	**2519**	3.07
* 14.	Scott Stevens, Wsh., St.L., N.J.	17	1275	**2504**	1.96
* 15.	Tie Domi, Tor., NYR, Wpg.	10	558	**2458**	4.41
16.	Basil McRae, Que., Tor., Det., Min., T.B., St.L., Chi.	16	576	**2457**	4.27
* 17.	Ulf Samuelsson, Hfd., Pit., NYR, Det.	15	1031	**2395**	2.32
18.	Jay Wells, L.A., Phi., Buf., NYR, St.L., T.B.	18	1098	**2359**	2.15
19.	Garth Butcher, Van., St.L., Que., Tor.	14	897	**2302**	2.57
20.	Shane Churla, Hfd., Cgy., Min., Dal., L.A., NYR	11	488	**2301**	4.72
21.	Dave Schultz, Phi., L.A., Pit., Buf.	9	535	**2294**	4.29
* 22.	Gino Odjick, Van., NYI	9	480	**2291**	4.77
* 23.	Chris Chelios, Mtl., Chi., Det.	16	1076	**2282**	2.12
24.	Laurie Boschman, Tor., Edm., Wpg., N.J., Ott.	14	1009	**2265**	2.24
* 25.	Ken Baumgartner, L.A., NYI, Tor., Ana., Bos.	12	696	**2244**	3.22
* 26.	Ken Daneyko, N.J.	16	992	**2241**	2.26
27.	Rob Ramage, Col., St.L., Cgy., Tor., Min., T.B., Mtl., Phi.	15	1044	**2226**	2.13
28.	Bryan Watson, Mtl., Det., Oak., Pit., St.L., Wsh.	16	878	**2212**	2.52
29.	Terry O'Reilly, Bos.	14	891	**2095**	2.35
30.	Al Secord, Bos., Chi., Tor., Phi.	12	766	**2093**	2.73
* 31.	Steve Smith, Edm., Chi., Cgy.	15	771	**2080**	2.70
* 32.	Mick Vukota, NYI, T.B., Mtl.	11	574	**2071**	3.61
33.	Gord Donnelly, Que., Wpg., Buf., Dal.	12	554	**2069**	3.73
34.	Mike Foligno, Det., Buf., Tor., Fla.	15	1018	**2049**	2.01
35.	Phil Russell, Chi., Atl., Cgy., N.J., Buf.	15	1016	**2038**	2.01
* 36.	Gary Roberts, Cgy., Car.	12	723	**2017**	2.79
37.	Harold Snepsts, Van., Min., Det., St.L.	17	1033	**2009**	1.94

Dale Hunter, jostling for position with defenseman Jeff Brown in front of the Quebec net, retired after the 1998-99 season. He was just 401 penalty minutes behind all-time leader Dave "Tiger" Williams.

Goaltending Records

All-Time Shutout Leaders

Goaltender	Team	Seasons	Games	Shutouts
Terry Sawchuk	Detroit	14	734	85
(1949-1970)	Boston	2	102	11
	Toronto	3	91	4
	Los Angeles	1	36	2
	NY Rangers	1	8	1
	Total	21	971	**103**
George Hainsworth	Montreal	7½	318	75
(1926-1937)	Toronto	3½	147	19
	Total	11	465	**94**
Glenn Hall	Detroit	4	148	17
(1952-1971)	Chicago	10	618	51
	St. Louis	4	140	16
	Total	18	906	**84**
Jacques Plante	Montreal	11	556	58
(1952-1973)	NY Rangers	2	98	5
	St. Louis	2	69	10
	Toronto	2¾	106	7
	Boston	¼	8	2
	Total	18	837	**82**
Tiny Thompson	Boston	10¼	468	74
(1928-1940)	Detroit	1¾	85	7
	Total	12	553	**81**
Alex Connell	Ottawa	8	293	64
(1924-1937)	Detroit	1	48	6
	NY Americans	1	1	0
	Mtl. Maroons	2	75	11
	Total	12	417	**81**
Tony Esposito	Montreal	1	13	2
(1968-1984)	Chicago	15	873	74
	Total	16	886	**76**
Lorne Chabot	NY Rangers	2	80	21
(1926-1937)	Toronto	5	214	33
	Montreal	1	47	8
	Chicago	1	48	8
	Mtl. Maroons	1	16	2
	NY Americans	1	6	1
	Total	11	411	**73**
Harry Lumley	Detroit	6½	324	26
(1943-1960)	NY Rangers	½	1	0
	Chicago	2	134	5
	Toronto	4	267	34
	Boston	3	78	6
	Total	16	804	**71**
Roy Worters	Pittsburgh Pirates	3	123	21
(1925-1937)	NY Americans	9	360	45
	*Montreal		1	0
	Total	12	484	**66**
Turk Broda	Toronto	14	629	**62**
(1936-1952)				
John Ross Roach	Toronto	7	222	13
(1921-1935)	NY Rangers	4	89	30
	Detroit	3	180	15
	Total	14	491	**58**
Clint Benedict	Ottawa	7	158	19
(1917-1930)	Mtl. Maroons	6	204	38
	Total	13	362	**57**

Goaltender	Team	Seasons	Games	Shutouts
Bernie Parent	Boston	2	57	1
(1965-1979)	Philadelphia	9½	486	50
	Toronto	1½	65	3
	Total	13	608	**54**
Ed Giacomin	NY Rangers	10¼	539	49
(1965-1978)	Detroit	2¾	71	5
	Total	13	610	**54**
David Kerr	Mtl. Maroons	3	101	11
(1930-1941)	NY Americans	1	1	0
	NY Rangers	7	324	40
	Total	11	426	**51**
Rogie Vachon	Montreal	5¼	206	13
(1966-1982)	Los Angeles	6¾	389	32
	Detroit	2	109	4
	Boston	2	91	2
	Total	16	795	**51**
Ken Dryden	Montreal	8	397	**46**
(1970-1979)				
Patrick Roy	Montreal	11½	551	29
(1984-1999)	Colorado	3½	227	17
	Total	15	778	**46**
Ed Belfour	Chicago	7⅔	415	30
(1988-1999)	San Jose	⅓	13	1
	Dallas	2	122	14
	Total	10	550	**45**
Gump Worsley	NY Rangers	10	582	24
(1952-1974)	Montreal	6½	172	16
	Minnesota	4½	107	3
	Total	21	861	**43**
Charlie Gardiner	Chicago	7	316	**42**
(1927-1934)				
Dominik Hasek	Chicago	2	25	1
(1990-1999)	Buffalo	7	389	41
	Total	9	414	**42**
Frank Brimsek	Boston	9	444	35
(1938-1950)	Chicago	1	70	5
	Total	10	514	**40**
Johnny Bower	NY Rangers	3	77	5
(1953-1970)	Toronto	12	475	32
	Total	15	552	**37**
Martin Brodeur	New Jersey	7	375	**36**
(1991-1999)				
John Vanbiesbrouck	NY Rangers	11	449	16
(1981-1999)	Florida	5	268	13
	Philadelphia	1	62	6
	Total	17	779	**35**
Bill Durnan	Montreal	7	383	**34**
(1943-1950)				
Tom Barrasso	Buffalo	5¼	226	13
(1983-1999)	Pittsburgh	10¾	442	21
	Total	16	708	**34**
Eddie Johnston	Boston	11	444	27
(1962-1978)	Toronto	1	26	1
	St. Louis	3⅔	118	4
	Chicago	⅓	4	0
	Total	16	592	**32**

*Played 1 game for Canadiens in 1929-30.

Ten or More Shutouts, One Season

Number of Shutouts	Goaltender	Team	Season	Length of Schedule
22	George Hainsworth	Montreal	1928-29	44
15	Alex Connell	Ottawa	1925-26	36
	Alex Connell	Ottawa	1927-28	44
	Hal Winkler	Boston	1927-28	44
	Tony Esposito	Chicago	1969-70	76
14	George Hainsworth	Montreal	1926-27	44
13	Clint Benedict	Mtl. Maroons	1926-27	44
	Alex Connell	Ottawa	1926-27	44
	George Hainsworth	Montreal	1927-28	44
	John Ross Roach	NY Rangers	1928-29	44
	Roy Worters	NY Americans	1928-29	44
	Harry Lumley	Toronto	1953-54	70
	Dominik Hasek	Buffalo	1997-98	82
12	Tiny Thompson	Boston	1928-29	44
	Lorne Chabot	Toronto	1928-29	44
	Chuck Gardiner	Chicago	1930-31	44
	Terry Sawchuk	Detroit	1951-52	70
	Terry Sawchuk	Detroit	1953-54	70
	Terry Sawchuk	Detroit	1954-55	70
	Glenn Hall	Detroit	1955-56	70
	Bernie Parent	Philadelphia	1973-74	78
	Bernie Parent	Philadelphia	1974-75	80

Number of Shutouts	Goaltender	Team	Season	Length of Schedule
11	Lorne Chabot	NY Rangers	1927-28	44
	Harry Holmes	Detroit	1927-28	44
	Clint Benedict	Mtl. Maroons	1928-29	44
	Joe Miller	Pittsburgh Pirates	1928-29	44
	Tiny Thompson	Boston	1932-33	48
	Terry Sawchuk	Detroit	1950-51	70
10	Lorne Chabot	NY Rangers	1926-27	44
	Roy Worters	Pittsburgh Pirates	1927-28	44
	Clarence Dolson	Detroit	1928-29	44
	John Ross Roach	Detroit	1932-33	48
	Chuck Gardiner	Chicago	1933-34	48
	Tiny Thompson	Boston	1935-36	48
	Frank Brimsek	Boston	1938-39	48
	Bill Durnan	Montreal	1948-49	60
	Gerry McNeil	Montreal	1952-53	70
	Harry Lumley	Toronto	1952-53	70
	Tony Esposito	Chicago	1973-74	78
	Ken Dryden	Montreal	1976-77	80
	Martin Brodeur	New Jersey	1996-97	82
	Martin Brodeur	New Jersey	1997-98	82
	Byron Dafoe	**Boston**	**1998-99**	**82**

All-Time Win Leaders

(Minimum 200 Wins)

Wins		Goaltender	GP	Dec.	Losses	Ties	%
447		Terry Sawchuk	971	949	330	172	.562
434		Jacques Plante	837	826	246	146	.614
423		Tony Esposito	886	881	306	152	.566
412	*	Patrick Roy	778	750	243	95	.613
407		Glenn Hall	906	896	326	163	.545
398	*	Grant Fuhr	845	792	282	112	.573
372		Andy Moog	713	669	209	88	.622
355		Rogie Vachon	795	773	291	127	.541
347	*	Mike Vernon	673	653	223	83	.595
345	*	Tom Barrasso	708	672	248	79	.572
335		Gump Worsley	861	837	352	150	.490
333	*	John Vanbiesbrouck	779	741	303	105	.520
330		Harry Lumley	804	802	329	143	.501
305		Billy Smith	680	643	233	105	.556
302		Turk Broda	629	627	224	101	.562
296	*	Ron Hextall	608	579	214	69	.571
294		Mike Liut	663	639	271	74	.518
289		Ed Giacomin	610	594	208	97	.568
286		Dan Bouchard	655	631	232	113	.543
284		Tiny Thompson	553	553	194	75	.581
276	*	Ed Belfour	550	525	174	75	.597
271		Bernie Parent	608	590	198	121	.562
271		Kelly Hrudey	677	624	265	88	.505
270		Gilles Meloche	788	752	351	131	.446
268		Don Beaupre	667	620	277	75	.493
258		Ken Dryden	397	389	57	74	.758
252		Frank Brimsek	514	514	182	80	.568
250		Johnny Bower	552	535	195	90	.551
248	*	Curtis Joseph	524	505	196	61	.551
246		George Hainsworth	465	465	145	74	.609
246		Pete Peeters	489	452	155	51	.601
236		Reggie Lemelin	507	461	162	63	.580
236	*	Bill Ranford	631	582	273	73	.468
234		Eddie Johnston	592	572	257	81	.480
231		Glenn Resch	571	537	224	82	.507
230		Gerry Cheevers	418	406	102	74	.658
230	*	Mike Richter	492	461	174	57	.561
230	*	Kirk McLean	567	541	244	67	.487
219		John Ross Roach	492	491	204	68	.515
215		Greg Millen	604	588	284	89	.441
211	*	Ken Wregget	546	500	238	51	.473
208		Bill Durnan	383	382	112	62	.626
208		Don Edwards	459	437	155	74	.561
206		Roger Crozier	518	473	197	70	.510
204		Rick Wamsley	407	381	131	46	.596
203		Dave Kerr	427	426	148	75	.565
201	*	Martin Brodeur	375	363	105	57	.632
201		Lorne Chabot	411	411	148	62	.564

* active player

Active Shutout Leaders

(Minimum 19 Shutouts)

Goaltender	Teams	Seasons	Games	Shutouts
Patrick Roy	Montreal, Colorado	15	778	46
Ed Belfour	Chi., S.J., Dal.	9	550	45
Dominik Hasek	Chicago, Buffalo	9	414	42
Martin Brodeur	New Jersey	7	375	36
John Vanbiesbrouck	NYR, Fla., Phi.	17	779	35
Tom Barrasso	Buffalo, Pittsburgh	16	708	34
Grant Fuhr	Edm., Tor., Buf., L.A., St.L.	18	845	25
Chris Osgood	Detroit	6	284	23
Ron Hextall	Phi., Que., NYI	13	608	23
Guy Hebert	St. Louis, Anaheim	8	369	22
Mike Richter	NY Rangers	10	492	22
Curtis Joseph	St.L., Edm., Tor.	10	524	22
Kirk McLean	N.J., Van., Car., Fla.	14	567	22
Mike Vernon	Cgy., Det., S.J.	16	673	22
Nikolai Khabibulin	Winnipeg, Phoenix	5	284	21
Arturs Irbe	S.J., Dal., Van., Car.	8	321	19
Jeff Hackett	NYI, S.J., Chi., Mtl.	10	347	19
Daren Puppa	Buf., Tor., T.B.	14	424	19
Sean Burke	N.J., Hfd., Car., Van., Phi., Fla.	11	529	19

Active Goaltending Leaders

(Ranked by winning percentage; minimum 250 games played)

Goaltender	Teams	Seasons	GP	Decisions	W	L	T	Winning %
Chris Osgood	Detroit	6	284	277	166	77	34	.661
Martin Brodeur	New Jersey	7	375	363	201	105	57	.632
Patrick Roy	Montreal, Colorado	15	778	750	412	243	95	.613
Ed Belfour	Chi., S.J., Dal.	10	550	525	276	174	75	.597
Mike Vernon	Cgy., Det., S.J.	16	673	653	347	223	83	.595
Grant Fuhr	Edm., Tor., Buf., L.A., St.L.	18	845	792	398	282	112	.573
Tom Barrasso	Buffalo, Pittsburgh	16	708	672	345	248	79	.572
Ron Hextall	Phi., Que., NYI	13	608	579	296	214	69	.571
Dominik Hasek	Chicago, Buffalo	9	414	396	195	139	62	.571
Mike Richter	NY Rangers	10	492	461	230	174	57	.561
Curtis Joseph	St. L., Edm., Tor.	10	524	505	248	196	61	.551
Daren Puppa	Buf., Tor., T.B.	14	424	391	178	159	54	.524
Nikolai Khabibulin	Winnipeg, Phoenix	6	284	269	126	113	30	.524
John Vanbiesbrouck	NYR, Fla., Phi.	17	779	741	333	303	105	.520
Jocelyn Thibault	Que., Col., Mtl., Chi.	6	267	248	111	101	36	.520
Felix Potvin	Toronto, NY Islanders	8	380	368	162	156	50	.508
Stephane Fiset	Que., Col., L.A.	10	334	314	141	137	36	.506
Trevor Kidd	Calgary, Carolina	7	250	232	100	97	35	.506

Goals Against Average Leaders

(minimum 13 games played, 1994-95; minimum 27 games played, 1992-93 to 1993-94, 1995-96 to date; 25 games played, 1926-27 to 1991-92; 15 games played, 1917-18 to 1925-26.)

Season	Goaltender and Club	GP	Mins.	GA	SO	AVG.	Season	Goaltender and Club	GP	Mins.	GA	SO	AVG.
1998-99	Ron Tugnutt, Ottawa	43	2,508	75	3	1.79	1957-58	Jacques Plante, Montreal	57	3,386	119	9	2.11
1997-98	Ed Belfour, Dallas	61	3,581	112	9	1.88	1956-57	Jacques Plante, Montreal	61	3,660	123	9	2.02
1996-97	Martin Brodeur, New Jersey	67	3,838	120	10	1.88	1955-56	Jacques Plante, Montreal	64	3,840	119	7	1.86
1995-96	Ron Hextall, Philadelphia	53	3,102	112	4	2.17	1954-55	Terry Sawchuk, Detroit	68	4,080	132	12	1.94
1994-95	Dominik Hasek, Buffalo	41	2,416	85	5	2.11	1953-54	Harry Lumley, Toronto	69	4,140	128	13	1.86
1993-94	Dominik Hasek, Buffalo	58	3,358	109	7	1.95	1952-53	Terry Sawchuk, Detroit	63	3,780	120	9	1.90
1992-93	Felix Potvin, Toronto	48	2,781	116	2	2.50	1951-52	Terry Sawchuk, Detroit	70	4,200	133	12	1.90
1991-92	Patrick Roy, Montreal	67	3,935	155	5	2.36	1950-51	Al Rollins, Toronto	40	2,367	70	5	1.77
1990-91	Ed Belfour, Chicago	74	4,127	170	4	2.47	1949-50	Bill Durnan, Montreal	64	3,840	141	8	2.20
1989-90	Mike Liut, Hartford, Washington	37	2,161	91	4	2.53	1948-49	Bill Durnan, Montreal	60	3,600	126	10	2.10
1988-89	Patrick Roy, Montreal	48	2,744	113	4	2.47	1947-48	Turk Broda, Toronto	60	3,600	143	5	2.38
1987-88	Pete Peeters, Washington	35	1,896	88	2	2.78	1946-47	Bill Durnan, Montreal	60	3,600	138	4	2.30
1986-87	Brian Hayward, Montreal	37	2,178	102	1	2.81	1945-46	Bill Durnan, Montreal	40	2,400	104	4	2.60
1985-86	Bob Froese, Philadelphia	51	2,728	116	5	2.55	1944-45	Bill Durnan, Montreal	50	3,000	121	1	2.42
1984-85	Tom Barrasso, Buffalo	54	3,248	144	5	2.66	1943-44	Bill Durnan, Montreal	50	3,000	109	2	2.18
1983-84	Pat Riggin, Washington	41	2,299	102	4	2.66	1942-43	Johnny Mowers, Detroit	50	3,010	124	6	2.47
1982-83	Pete Peeters, Boston	62	3,611	142	8	2.36	1941-42	Frank Brimsek, Boston	47	2,930	115	3	2.35
1981-82	Denis Herron, Montreal	27	1,547	68	3	2.64	1940-41	Turk Broda, Toronto	48	2,970	99	5	2.00
1980-81	Richard Sevigny, Montreal	33	1,777	71	2	2.40	1939-40	Dave Kerr, NY Rangers	48	3,000	77	8	1.54
1979-80	Bob Sauve, Buffalo	32	1,880	74	4	2.36	1938-39	Frank Brimsek, Boston	43	2,610	68	10	1.56
1978-79	Ken Dryden, Montreal	47	2,814	108	5	2.30	1937-38	Tiny Thompson, Boston	48	2,970	89	7	1.80
1977-78	Ken Dryden, Montreal	52	3,071	105	5	2.05	1936-37	Norman Smith, Detroit	48	2,980	102	6	2.05
1976-77	Michel Larocque, Montreal	26	1,525	53	4	2.09	1935-36	Tiny Thompson, Boston	48	2,930	82	10	1.68
1975-76	Ken Dryden, Montreal	62	3,580	121	8	2.03	1934-35	Lorne Chabot, Chicago	48	2,940	88	8	1.80
1974-75	Bernie Parent, Philadelphia	68	4,041	137	12	2.03	1933-34	Wilf Cude, Detroit, Montreal	30	1,920	47	5	1.47
1973-74	Bernie Parent, Philadelphia	73	4,314	136	12	1.89	1932-33	Tiny Thompson, Boston	48	3,000	88	11	1.76
1972-73	Ken Dryden, Montreal	54	3,165	119	6	2.26	1931-32	Chuck Gardiner, Chicago	48	2,989	92	4	1.85
1971-72	Tony Esposito, Chicago	48	2,780	82	9	1.77	1930-31	Roy Worters, NY Americans	44	2,760	74	8	1.61
1970-71	Jacques Plante, Toronto	40	2,329	73	4	1.88	1929-30	Tiny Thompson, Boston	44	2,680	98	3	2.19
1969-70	Ernie Wakely, St. Louis	30	1,651	58	4	2.11	1928-29	George Hainsworth, Montreal	44	2,800	43	22	0.92
1968-69	Jacques Plante, St. Louis	37	2,139	70	5	1.96	1927-28	George Hainsworth, Montreal	44	2,730	48	13	1.05
1967-68	Gump Worsley, Montreal	40	2,213	73	6	1.98	1926-27	Clint Benedict, Mtl. Maroons	43	2,748	65	13	1.42
1966-67	Glenn Hall, Chicago	32	1,664	66	2	2.38	1925-26	Alex Connell, Ottawa	36	2,251	42	15	1.12
1965-66	Johnny Bower, Toronto	35	1,998	75	3	2.25	1924-25	Georges Vezina, Montreal	30	1,860	56	5	1.81
1964-65	Johnny Bower, Toronto	34	2,040	81	3	2.38	1923-24	Georges Vezina, Montreal	24	1,459	48	3	1.97
1963-64	Johnny Bower, Toronto	51	3,009	106	5	2.11	1922-23	Clint Benedict, Ottawa	24	1,478	54	4	2.18
1962-63	Jacques Plante, Montreal	56	3,320	138	5	2.49	1921-22	Clint Benedict, Ottawa	24	1,508	84	2	3.34
1961-62	Jacques Plante, Montreal	70	4,200	166	4	2.37	1920-21	Clint Benedict, Ottawa	24	1,457	75	2	3.09
1960-61	Johnny Bower, Toronto	58	3,480	145	2	2.50	1919-20	Clint Benedict, Ottawa	24	1,444	64	5	2.66
1959-60	Jacques Plante, Montreal	69	4,140	175	3	2.54	1918-19	Clint Benedict, Ottawa	18	1,113	53	2	2.86
1958-59	Jacques Plante, Montreal	67	4,000	144	9	2.16	1917-18	Georges Vezina, Montreal	21	1,282	84	1	3.93

All-Time Regular Season NHL Coaching Register

Regular Season, 1917-99

Coach	Team	Games Coached	Wins	Losses	Ties	%Wins	Years	Cup Wins	Career
Abel, Sid	Chicago	140	39	79	22	.357	2		
	Detroit	811	340	339	132	.501	12		
	St. Louis	10	3	6	1	.350	1		
	Kansas City	3	0	3	0	.000	1		
	Total	964	382	427	155	.477	16		1952-76
Adams, Jack	Toronto	18	10	7	1	.583	1		
	Detroit	964	413	390	161	.512	20	3	
	Total	982	423	397	162	.513	21	3	1922-47
Allen, Keith	Philadelphia	150	51	67	32	.447	2		1967-69
Allison, Dave	Ottawa	25	2	22	1	.100	1		1995-96
Anderson, Jim	Washington	54	4	45	5	.120	1		1974-75
Angotti, Lou	St. Louis	32	6	20	6	.281	2		
	Pittsburgh	80	16	58	6	.238	1		
	Total	112	22	78	12	.250	3		1973-84
Arbour, Al	St. Louis	107	42	40	25	.509	3		
	NY Islanders	1499	739	537	223	.567	19	4	
	Total	1606	781	577	248	.564	22	4	1970-94
Armstrong, George	Toronto	47	17	26	4	.404	1		1988-89
Barkley, Doug	Detroit	77	20	46	11	.331	3		1970-76
Beaulieu, Andre	Minnesota	32	6	23	3	.234	1		1977-78
Belisle, Danny	Washington	96	28	51	17	.380	2		1978-80
Berenson, Red	St. Louis	204	100	72	32	.569	3		1979-82
Bergeron, Michel	Quebec	634	265	283	86	.486	8		
	NY Rangers	158	73	67	18	.519	2		
	Total	792	338	350	104	.492	10		1980-90
Berry, Bob	Los Angeles	240	107	94	39	.527	3		
	Montreal	223	116	71	36	.601	3		
	Pittsburgh	240	88	127	25	.419	3		
	St. Louis	157	73	63	21	.532	2		
	Total	860	384	355	121	.517	11		1978-94
Beverley, Nick	Toronto	17	9	6	2	.588	1		1995-96
Blackburn, Don	Hartford	140	42	63	35	.425	2		1979-81
Blair, Wren	Minnesota	147	48	65	34	.442	3		1967-70
Blake, Toe	Montreal	914	500	255	159	.634	13	8	1955-68
Boileau, Marc	Pittsburgh	151	66	61	24	.517	3		1973-76
Boivin, Leo	St. Louis	97	28	53	16	.371	2		1975-78
Boucher, Frank	NY Rangers	527	181	263	83	.422	11	1	1939-54
Boucher, George	Mtl. Maroons	12	6	5	1	.542	1		
	Ottawa	48	13	29	6	.333	1		
	St. Louis	35	9	20	6	.343	1		
	Boston	70	22	32	16	.429	1		
	Total	165	50	86	29	.391	4		1930-50
Bowman, Scotty	St. Louis	238	110	83	45	.557	4		
	Montreal	634	419	110	105	.744	8	5	
	Buffalo	404	210	134	60	.594	7		
	Pittsburgh	164	95	53	16	.628	2	1	
	Detroit	455	262	135	58	.640	6	2	
	Total	1895	1096	515	284	.653	27	8	1967-99
Bowness, Rick	Winnipeg	28	8	17	3	.339	1		
	Boston	80	36	32	12	.525	1		
	Ottawa	235	39	178	18	.204	4		
	NY Islanders	100	38	50	12	.440	2		
	Total	443	121	277	45	.324	8		1988-98
Brooks, Herb	NY Rangers	285	131	113	41	.532	4		
	Minnesota	80	19	48	13	.319	1		
	New Jersey	84	40	37	7	.518	1		
	Total	449	190	198	61	.491	6		1981-93
Brophy, John	Toronto	193	64	111	18	.378	3		1986-89
Burnett, George	Edmonton	35	12	20	3	.386	1		1994-95
Burns, Charlie	Minnesota	86	22	50	14	.337	2		1969-75
Burns, Pat	Montreal	320	174	104	42	.609	4		
	Toronto	281	133	107	41	.546	4		
	Boston	164	78	60	26	.555	2		
	Total	765	385	271	109	.575	10		1988-99
Bush, Eddie	Kansas City	32	1	23	8	.156	1		1975-76
Campbell, Colin	NY Rangers	269	118	108	43	.519	4		1994-98
Caroll, Dick	Toronto	64	33	31	0	.516	3	1	1917-21
Carpenter, Doug	New Jersey	290	100	166	24	.386	4		
	Toronto	91	39	47	5	.456	2		
	Total	381	139	213	29	.403	6		1984-91
Cashman, Wayne	Philadelphia	61	32	20	9	.598	1		1997-98
Chambers, Dave	Quebec	98	19	64	15	.270	2		1990-92
Charron, Guy	Calgary	16	6	7	3	.469	1		1991-92
Cheevers, Gerry	Boston	376	204	126	46	.604	5		1980-85
Cherry, Don	Boston	400	231	105	64	.658	5		
	Colorado	80	19	48	13	.319	1		
	Total	480	250	153	77	.601	6		1974-80
Clancy, King	Mtl. Maroons	18	6	11	1	.361	1		
	Toronto	225	89	84	52	.511	4		
	Total	243	95	95	53	.500	5		1937-72
Clapper, Dit	Boston	230	102	88	40	.530	4		1945-49
Cleghorn, Odie	Pittsburgh	168	62	86	20	.429	4		1925-29
Cleghorn, Sprague	Mtl. Maroons	48	19	22	7	.469	1		1931-32
Colville, Neil	NY Rangers	93	26	41	26	.419	2		1950-52
Conacher, Charlie	Chicago	162	56	84	22	.414	3		1947-50
Conacher, Lionel	NY Americans	44	14	25	5	.375	1		1929-30
Constantine, Kevin	San Jose	157	55	78	24	.427	3		
	Pittsburgh	164	78	54	32	.573	2		
	Total	321	133	132	56	.502	5		1993-99
Cook, Bill	NY Rangers	117	34	59	24	.393	2		1951-53
Crawford, Marc	Quebec	48	30	13	5	.677	1		
	Colorado	246	135	75	36	.622	3	1	
	Vancouver	37	8	23	6	.297	1		
	Total	331	173	111	47	.594	5	1	1994-99
Creamer, Pierre	Pittsburgh	80	36	35	9	.506	1		1987-88
Creighton, Fred	Atlanta	348	156	136	56	.529	5		
	Boston	73	40	20	13	.637	1		
	Total	421	196	156	69	.548	6		1974-80
Crisp, Terry	Calgary	240	144	63	33	.669	3	1	
	Tampa Bay	391	142	204	45	.421	6		
	Total	631	286	267	78	.515	9	1	1987-98
Crozier, Joe	Buffalo	192	77	80	35	.492	3		
	Toronto	40	13	22	5	.388	1		
	Total	232	90	102	40	.474	4		1971-81
Crozier, Roger	Washington	1	0	1	0	.000	1		1981-82
Cunniff, John	Hartford	13	3	9	1	.269	1		
	New Jersey	133	59	56	18	.511	2		
	Total	146	62	65	19	.490	3		1982-91
Dandurand, Leo	Montreal	163	78	76	9	.506	6	1	1921-35
Day, Hap	Toronto	546	259	206	81	.549	10	5	1940-60
Dea, Billy	Detroit	11	3	8	0	.273	1		1981-82
Delvecchio, Alex	Detroit	245	82	131	32	.400	4		1973-77
Demers, Jacques	Quebec	80	25	44	11	.381	2		
	St. Louis	240	106	106	28	.500	3		
	Detroit	320	137	136	47	.502	4		
	Montreal	221	107	87	27	.545	4	1	
	Tampa Bay	145	34	94	17	.293	2		
	Total	1006	409	467	130	.471	14	1	1979-99
Denneny, Cy	Boston	44	26	13	5	.648	1	1	
	Ottawa	48	11	27	10	.333	1		
	Total	92	37	40	15	.484	2	1	1928-33
Dineen, Bill	Philadelphia	140	60	60	20	.500	2		1991-93
Dudley, Rick	Buffalo	188	85	72	31	.535	3		1989-92
Duff, Dick	Toronto	2	0	2	0	.000	1		1979-80
Dugal, Jules	Montreal	18	9	6	3	.583	1		1938-39
Duncan, Art	Detroit	33	10	21	2	.333	1		
	Toronto	47	21	16	10	.553	2	1	
	Total	80	31	37	12	.463	3	1	1926-32
Dutton, Red	NY Americans	288	90	151	47	.394	6		
	Brooklyn	48	16	29	3	.365	1		
	Total	336	106	180	50	.390	7		1935-42
Eddolls, Frank	Chicago	70	13	40	17	.307	1		1954-55
Esposito, Phil	NY Rangers	45	24	21	0	.533	2		1986-89
Evans, Jack	California	80	27	42	11	.406	1		
	Cleveland	160	47	87	26	.375	2		
	Hartford	374	163	174	37	.485	5		
	Total	614	237	303	74	.446	8		1975-88
Fashoway, Gordie	Oakland	10	4	5	1	.450	1		1967-68
Ferguson, John	NY Rangers	121	43	59	19	.434	2		
	Winnipeg	14	7	6	1	.536	1		
	Total	135	50	65	20	.444	3		1975-86
Filion, Maurice	Quebec	6	1	3	2	.333	1		1980-81
Francis, Emile	NY Rangers	654	342	209	103	.602	10		
	St. Louis	124	46	64	14	.427	3		
	Total	778	388	273	117	.574	13		1965-83

Butch Goring spent 11 of the last 12 years coaching in the minors before returning to the NHL as coach of the New York Islanders this season. Goring had a record of 42-38-13 in 93 games as coach of the Boston Bruins in 1985-86 and 1986-87.

Coach	Team	Games Coached	Wins	Losses	Ties	%Wins	Years	Cup Wins	Career
Fredrickson, Frank	Pittsburgh	44	5	36	3	.148	1		1929-30
Ftorek, Robbie	Los Angeles	132	65	56	11	.534	2		
	New Jersey	82	47	24	11	.640	1		
	Total	214	112	80	22	.575	3		1987-99
Gadsby, Bill	Detroit	78	35	31	12	.526	2		1968-70
Gainey, Bob	Minnesota	244	95	119	30	.451	3		
	Dallas	171	70	71	30	.497	3		
	Total	415	165	190	60	.470	6		1990-96
Gardiner, Herb	Chicago	44	7	29	8	.250	1		1928-29
Gardner, Jimmy	Hamilton	30	19	10	1	.650	1		1924-25
Garvin, Ted	Detroit	11	2	8	1	.227	1		1973-74
Geoffrion, Bernie	NY Rangers	43	22	18	3	.547	1		
	Atlanta	208	77	92	39	.464	3		
	Montreal	30	15	9	6	.600	1		
	Total	281	114	119	48	.491	5		1968-80
Gerard, Eddie	Ottawa	22	9	13	0	.409	1		
	Mtl. Maroons	294	129	122	43	.512	7	1	
	NY Americans	92	34	40	18	.467	2		
	St. Louis	13	2	11	0	.154	1		
	Total	421	174	186	61	.486	11	1	1917-35
Gill, David	Ottawa	132	64	41	27	.587	3	1	1926-29
Glover, Fred	Oakland	152	51	76	25	.418	2		
	California	204	45	131	28	.289	4		
	Los Angeles	68	18	42	8	.324	1		
	Total	424	114	249	61	.341	7		1968-74
Goodfellow, Ebbie	Chicago	140	30	91	19	.282	2		1950-52
Gordon, Jackie	Minnesota	289	116	123	50	.488	5		1970-75
Goring, Butch	Boston	93	42	38	13	.522	2		1985-87
Gorman, Tommy	NY Americans	80	31	33	16	.488	2		
	Chicago	73	28	28	17	.500	2	1	
	Mtl. Maroons	174	74	71	29	.509	4	1	
	Total	327	133	132	62	.502	8	2	1925-38
Gottselig, Johnny	Chicago	187	62	105	20	.385	4		1944-48
Goyette, Phil	NY Islanders	48	6	38	4	.167	1		1972-73
Graham, Dirk	Chicago	59	16	35	8	.339	1		1998-99
Green, Gary	Washington	157	50	78	29	.411	3		1979-82
Green, Pete	Ottawa	186	118	60	8	.656	7	3	1919-26
Green, Shorty	NY Americans	44	11	27	6	.318	1		1927-28
Green, Ted	Edmonton	188	65	102	21	.402	3		1991-94
Guidolin, Aldo	Colorado	59	12	39	8	.271	1		1978-79
Guidolin, Bep	Boston	104	72	23	9	.736	2		
	Kansas City	125	26	84	15	.268	2		
	Total	229	98	107	24	.480	4		1972-76
Harkness, Ned	Detroit	38	12	22	4	.368	1		1970-71
Harris, Ted	Minnesota	179	48	104	27	.344	3		1975-78
Hart, Cecil	Montreal	394	196	125	73	.590	9	2	1926-39
Hartley, Bob	Colorado	82	44	28	10	.598	1		1998-99
Hartsburg, Craig	Chicago	246	104	102	40	.504	3		
	Anaheim	82	35	34	13	.506	1		
	Total	328	139	136	53	.505	4		1995-99
Harvey, Doug	NY Rangers	70	26	32	12	.457	1		1961-62
Hay, Don	Phoenix	82	38	37	7	.506	1		1996-97
Heffernan, Frank	Toronto	12	5	7	0	.417	1		1919-20
Henning, Lorne	Minnesota	158	68	72	18	.487	2		
	NY Islanders	48	15	28	5	.365	1		
	Total	206	83	100	23	.459	3		1985-95
Hitchcock, Ken	Dallas	289	163	90	36	.626	1		1995-99
Holmgren, Paul	Philadelphia	264	107	126	31	.464	4		
	Hartford	161	54	93	14	.379	4		
	Total	425	161	219	45	.432	8		1988-96
Howell, Harry	Minnesota	11	3	6	2	.364	1		1978-79
Imlach, Punch	Toronto	770	370	275	125	.562	12	4	
	Buffalo	119	32	62	25	.374	2		
	Total	889	402	337	150	.537	14	4	1958-80
Ingarfield, Earl	NY Islanders	30	6	22	2	.233	1		1972-73
Inglis, Bill	Buffalo	56	28	18	10	.589	1		1978-79
Irvin, Dick	Chicago	114	43	56	15	.443	2		
	Toronto	427	216	152	59	.575	9	1	
	Montreal	896	431	313	152	.566	15	3	
	Total	1437	690	521	226	.559	26	4	1930-56
Ivan, Tommy	Detroit	470	262	118	90	.653	7	3	
	Chicago	103	26	56	21	.354	2		
	Total	573	288	174	111	.599	9	3	1947-58
Iverson, Emil	Chicago	21	8	7	6	.524	1		1932-33
Johnson, Bob	Calgary	400	193	155	52	.548	5		
	Pittsburgh	80	41	33	6	.550	1	1	
	Total	480	234	188	58	.548	6	1	1982-91
Johnson, Marshall	Colorado	56	15	32	9	.348	1		1981-82
Johnson, Tom	Boston	208	142	43	23	.738	3	1	1970-73
Johnston, Eddie	Chicago	80	34	27	19	.544	1		
	Pittsburgh	516	232	224	60	.508	7		
	Total	596	266	251	79	.513	8		1979-97
Johnston, Marshall	California	69	13	45	11	.268	2		1973-75
Kasper, Steve	Boston	164	66	78	20	.463	2		1995-97
Keats, Duke	Detroit	11	2	7	2	.273	1		1926-27
Keenan, Mike	Philadelphia	320	190	102	28	.638	4		
	Chicago	320	153	126	41	.542	4		
	NY Rangers	84	52	24	8	.667	1	1	
	St. Louis	163	75	66	22	.528	3		
	Vancouver	108	36	54	18	.417	2		
	Total	995	506	372	117	.567	14	1	1984-99
Kelly, Pat	Colorado	101	22	54	25	.342	2		1977-79
Kelly, Red	Los Angeles	150	55	75	20	.433	2		
	Pittsburgh	274	90	132	52	.423	4		
	Toronto	318	133	123	62	.516	4		
	Total	742	278	330	134	.465	10		1967-77

Coach	Team	Games Coached	Wins	Losses	Ties	%Wins	Years	Cup Wins	Career
King, Dave	Calgary	216	109	76	31	.576	3		1992-95
Kingston, George	San Jose	164	28	129	7	.192	2		1991-93
Kish, Larry	Hartford	49	12	32	5	.296	1		1982-83
Kromm, Bobby	Detroit	231	79	111	41	.431	3		1977-80
Kurtenbach, Orland	Vancouver	125	36	62	27	.396	2		1976-78
LaForge, Bill	Vancouver	20	4	14	2	.250	1		1984-85
Lalonde, Newsy	Montreal	207	96	97	14	.498	8		
	NY Americans	44	17	25	2	.409	1		
	Ottawa	88	31	45	12	.420	2		
	Total	339	144	167	28	.466	11		1917-35
Lapointe, Ron	Quebec	89	33	50	6	.404	2		1987-89
Laycoe, Hal	Los Angeles	24	5	18	1	.229	1		
	Vancouver	156	44	96	16	.333	2		
	Total	180	49	114	17	.319	3		1969-72
Lehman, Hugh	Chicago	21	3	17	1	.167	1		1927-28
Lemaire, Jacques	Montreal	97	48	37	12	.557	2		
	New Jersey	378	199	122	57	.602	5	1	
	Total	475	247	159	69	.593	7	1	1983-98
Lepine, Pit	Montreal	48	10	33	5	.260	1		1939-40
LeSueur, Percy	Hamilton	10	3	7	0	.300	1		1923-24
Lewis, Dave*	Detroit	5	4	0	1	.900	1		1998-99
	*Results shared with co-coach Barry Smith								
Ley, Rick	Hartford	160	69	71	20	.494	2		
	Vancouver	124	47	50	27	.488	2		
	Total	284	116	121	47	.491	4		1989-96
Lindsay, Ted	Detroit	29	5	21	3	.224	2		1979-81
Long, Barry	Winnipeg	205	87	93	25	.485	3		1983-86
Loughlin, Clem	Chicago	144	61	63	20	.493	3		1934-37
Low, Ron	Edmonton	341	139	162	40	.466	5		1994-99
MacDonald, Parker	Minnesota	61	20	30	11	.418	1		
	Los Angeles	42	13	24	5	.369	1		
	Total	103	33	54	16	.398	2		1973-82
MacLean, Doug	Florida	187	83	71	33	.532	3		1995-98
MacMillan, Bill	Colorado	80	22	45	13	.356	1		
	New Jersey	100	19	67	14	.260	2		
	Total	180	41	112	27	.303	3		1980-84
MacNeil, Al	Montreal	55	31	15	9	.645	1	1	
	Atlanta	80	35	32	13	.519	1		
	Calgary	160	68	61	31	.522	2		
	Total	295	134	108	53	.544	4	1	1970-82
Magnuson, Keith	Chicago	132	49	57	26	.470	2		1980-82
Maguire, Pierre	Hartford	67	23	37	7	.396	1		1993-94
Mahoney, Bill	Minnesota	93	42	39	12	.516	2		1983-85
Maloney, Dan	Toronto	160	45	100	15	.328	2		
	Winnipeg	212	91	93	28	.495	3		
	Total	372	136	193	43	.423	5		1984-89
Maloney, Phil	Vancouver	232	95	105	32	.478	4		1973-77
Mantha, Sylvio	Montreal	48	11	26	11	.344	1		1935-36
Marshall, Bert	Colorado	24	3	17	4	.208	1		1981-82
Martin, Jacques	St. Louis	160	66	71	23	.484	2		
	Ottawa	284	119	116	49	.505	4		
	Total	444	185	187	72	.498	6		1986-99
Matheson, Godfrey	Chicago	2	0	2	0	.000	1		1932-33
Maurice, Paul	Hartford	152	61	72	19	.464	2		
	Carolina	164	67	71	26	.488	2		
	Total	316	128	143	45	.476	4		1995-99
Maxner, Wayne	Detroit	129	34	68	27	.368	2		1980-82
McCammon, Bob	Philadelphia	218	119	68	31	.617	4		
	Vancouver	294	102	156	36	.408	4		
	Total	512	221	224	67	.497	8		1978-91
McCreary, Bill	St. Louis	24	6	14	4	.333	1		
	Vancouver	41	9	25	7	.305	1		
	California	32	8	20	4	.313	1		
	Total	97	23	59	15	.314	3		1971-75
McLellan, John	Toronto	295	117	136	42	.468	4		1969-73
McVie, Tom	Washington	204	49	122	33	.321	3		
	Winnipeg	105	20	67	18	.276	2		
	New Jersey	153	57	74	22	.444	3		
	Total	462	126	263	73	.352	8		1975-92
Meeker, Howie	Toronto	70	21	34	15	.407	1		1956-57
Melrose, Barry	Los Angeles	209	79	101	29	.447	3		1992-95
Milbury, Mike	Boston	160	90	49	21	.628	2		
	NY Islanders	191	56	111	24	.356	4		
	Total	351	146	160	45	.480	6		1989-99
Molleken, Lorne	Chicago	23	13	6	4	.652	1		1998-99
Muckler, John	Minnesota	35	6	23	6	.257	1		
	Edmonton	160	75	65	20	.531	2	1	
	Buffalo	268	125	109	34	.530	4		
	NY Rangers	107	41	53	13	.444	2		
	Total	570	247	250	73	.497	9	1	1968-90
Muldoon, Pete	Chicago	44	19	22	3	.466	1		1926-27
Munro, Dunc	Mtl. Maroons	76	37	29	10	.553	2		1929-31
Murdoch, Bob	Winnipeg	160	63	75	22	.463	2		1989-91
Murphy, Mike	Los Angeles	65	20	37	8	.369	2		
	Toronto	164	60	87	17	.418	2		
	Total	229	80	124	25	.404	4		1986-98
Murray, Bryan	Washington	672	343	246	83	.572	9		
	Detroit	244	124	91	29	.568	3		
	Florida	59	17	31	11	.381	1		
	Total	975	484	368	123	.559	13		1981-98
Murray, Terry	Washington	325	163	134	28	.545	5		
	Philadelphia	212	118	64	30	.627	3		
	Florida	82	30	34	18	.476	1		
	Total	619	311	232	76	.564	9		1989-99
Nanne, Lou	Minnesota	29	7	18	4	.310	1		1977-78
Neale, Harry	Vancouver	407	142	189	76	.442	6		

Coach	Team	Games Coached	Wins	Losses	Ties	%Wins	Years	Cup Wins	Career
	Detroit	35	8	23	4	.286	1		
	Total	442	150	212	80	.430	7		1978-86
Neilson, Roger	Toronto	160	75	62	23	.541	2		
	Buffalo	80	39	20	21	.619	1		
	Vancouver	133	51	61	21	.462	3		
	Los Angeles	28	8	17	3	.339	1		
	NY Rangers	280	141	104	35	.566	4		
	Florida	132	53	56	23	.489	2		
	Philadelphia	103	47	35	21	.558	2		
	Total	916	414	355	147	.532	15		1977-99
Nolan, Ted	Buffalo	164	73	72	19	.503	2		1995-97
Nykoluk, Mike	Toronto	280	89	144	47	.402	4		1980-84
O'Donohue, George	Toronto	24	13	10	1	.563	1	1	1921-22
O'Reilly, Terry	Boston	227	115	86	26	.564	3		1986-89
Oliver, Murray	Minnesota	41	21	12	8	.610	2		1981-83
Olmstead, Bert	Oakland	64	11	37	16	.297	1		1967-68
Paddock, John	Winnipeg	281	106	138	37	.443	4		1991-95
Page, Pierre	Minnesota	160	63	77	20	.456	2		
	Quebec	230	98	103	29	.489	3		
	Calgary	164	66	78	20	.463	2		
	Anaheim	82	26	43	13	.396	1		
	Total	636	253	301	82	.462	8		1988-98
Park, Brad	Detroit	45	9	34	2	.222	1		1985-86
Paterson, Rick	Tampa Bay	8	0	8	0	.000	1		1997-98
Patrick, Craig	NY Rangers	95	37	45	13	.458	2		
	Pittsburgh	74	29	36	9	.453	2		
	Total	169	66	81	22	.456	4		1980-97
Patrick, Frank	Boston	96	48	36	12	.563	2		1934-36
Patrick, Lester	NY Rangers	604	281	216	107	.554	13	2	1926-39
Patrick, Lynn	NY Rangers	107	40	51	16	.449	2		
	Boston	310	117	130	63	.479	5		
	St. Louis	26	8	15	3	.365	3		
	Total	443	165	196	82	.465	10		1948-76
Patrick, Muzz	NY Rangers	136	43	66	27	.415	4		1953-63
Perron, Jean	Montreal	240	126	84	30	.588	3	1	
	Quebec	47	16	26	5	.394	1		
	Total	287	142	110	35	.556	4	1	1985-89
Perry, Don	Los Angeles	168	52	85	31	.402	3		1981-84
Pike, Alf	NY Rangers	123	36	66	21	.378	2		1959-61
Pilous, Rudy	Chicago	387	162	151	74	.514	6	1	1957-63
Plager, Barclay	St. Louis	178	49	96	33	.368	4		1977-83
Plager, Bob	St. Louis	11	4	6	1	.409	1		1992-93
Pleau, Larry	Hartford	224	81	117	26	.420	5		1980-89
Polano, Nick	Detroit	240	79	127	34	.400	3		1982-85
Popein, Larry	NY Rangers	41	18	14	9	.549	1		1973-74
Powers, Eddie	Toronto	90	41	46	3	.472	3		1923-26
Primeau, Joe	Toronto	210	97	71	42	.562	3	1	1950-53
Pronovost, Marcel	Buffalo	104	52	29	23	.611	2		1977-79
Pulford, Bob	Los Angeles	396	178	150	68	.535	5		
	Chicago	455	187	197	71	.489	7		
	Total	851	365	347	139	.511	12		1972-88
Quenneville, Joel	St. Louis	204	100	76	28	.559	3		1996-99
Querrie, Charles	Toronto	6	3	3	0	.500	1		1922-23
Quinn, Mike	Quebec	24	4	20	0	.167	1		1919-20
Quinn, Pat	Philadelphia	262	141	73	48	.630	4		
	Los Angeles	202	75	101	26	.436	3		
	Vancouver	280	141	111	28	.554	5		
	Toronto	82	45	30	7	.591	1		
	Total	826	402	315	109	.553	13		1978-99
Ramsay, Craig	Buffalo	21	4	15	2	.238	1		1986-87
Randall, Ken	Hamilton	14	6	8	0	.429	1		1923-24
Reay, Billy	Toronto	90	26	50	14	.367	2		
	Chicago	1012	516	335	161	.589	14		
	Total	1102	542	385	175	.571	16		1957-77
Regan, Larry	Los Angeles	88	27	47	14	.386	2		1970-72
Renney, Tom	Vancouver	101	39	53	9	.431	2		1996-98
Risebrough, Doug	Calgary	144	71	56	17	.552	2		1990-92
Roberts, Jim	Buffalo	45	21	16	8	.556	1		
	Hartford	80	26	41	13	.406	1		
	St. Louis	9	3	3	3	.500	1		
	Total	134	50	60	24	.463	3		1981-97
Robinson, Larry	Los Angeles	328	122	161	45	.441	4		1995-99
Rodden, Mike	Toronto	30	8	18	4	.333	1		1926-27
Romeril, Alex	Toronto	14	7	6	1	.536	1		1926-27
Ross, Art	Mtl. Wanderers	6	1	5	0	.167	1		
	Hamilton	24	6	18	0	.250	1		
	Boston	728	361	277	90	.558	16	1	
	Total	758	368	300	90	.545	18	1	1917-45
Ruel, Claude	Montreal	305	172	82	51	.648	5	2	1968-81
Ruff, Lindy	Buffalo	164	83	57	24	.579	2		1997-99
Sather, Glen	Edmonton	842	464	268	110	.616	11	4	1979-94
Sator, Ted	NY Rangers	99	41	48	10	.465	2		
	Buffalo	207	96	89	22	.517	3		
	Total	306	137	137	32	.500	5		1985-89
Savard, Andre	Quebec	24	10	13	1	.438	1		1987-88
Schinkel, Ken	Pittsburgh	203	83	92	28	.478	4		1972-77
Schmidt, Milt	Boston	726	245	360	121	.421	11		
	Washington	44	5	34	5	.170	2		
	Total	770	250	394	126	.406	13		1954-76
Schoenfeld, Jim	Buffalo	43	19	19	5	.500	1		
	New Jersey	124	50	59	15	.464	3		
	Washington	249	113	102	34	.522	4		
	Phoenix	164	74	66	24	.524	2		
	Total	580	256	248	78	.509	10		1985-99
Shaughnessy, Tom	Chicago	21	10	8	3	.548	1		1929-30
Shero, Fred	Philadelphia	554	308	151	95	.642	7	2	
	NY Rangers	180	82	74	24	.522	3		
	Total	734	390	225	119	.612	10	2	1971-81
Simpson, Joe	NY Americans	144	42	72	30	.396	3		1932-35
Simpson, Terry	NY Islanders	187	81	82	24	.497	3		
	Philadelphia	84	35	39	10	.476	1		
	Winnipeg	97	43	47	7	.479	2		
	Total	368	159	168	41	.488	6		1986-96
Sims, Al	San Jose	82	27	47	8	.378	1		1996-97
Sinden, Harry	Boston	327	153	116	58	.557	6	1	1966-85
Skinner, Jimmy	Detroit	247	123	78	46	.591	4	1	1954-58
Smeaton, Cooper	Philadelphia	44	4	36	4	.136	1		1930-31
Smith, Alf	Ottawa	18	12	6	0	.667	1		1918-19
Smith, Barry*	Detroit	5	4	0	1	.900	1		1998-99
*Results shared with co-coach Dave Lewis									
Smith, Floyd	Buffalo	241	143	62	36	.668	4		
	Toronto	68	30	33	5	.478	1		
	Total	309	173	95	41	.626	5		1971-80
Smith, Mike	Winnipeg	23	2	17	4	.174	1		1980-81
Smith, Ron	NY Rangers	44	15	22	7	.420	1		1992-93
Smythe, Conn	Toronto	134	57	57	20	.500	4		1927-31
Sonmor, Glen	Minnesota	417	174	161	82	.516	7		1978-87
Sproule, Harry	Toronto	12	7	5	0	.583	1		1919-20
Stanley, Barney	Chicago	23	4	17	2	.217	1		1927-28
Stasiuk, Vic	Philadelphia	154	45	68	41	.425	2		
	California	75	21	38	16	.387	1		
	Vancouver	78	22	47	9	.340	1		
	Total	307	88	153	66	.394	4		1969-73
Stewart, Bill	Chicago	69	22	35	12	.406	1	1	1937-39
Stewart, Bill	NY Islanders	37	11	19	7	.329	1		1998-99
Stewart, Ron	NY Rangers	39	15	20	4	.436	1		
	Los Angeles	80	31	34	15	.481	1		
	Total	119	46	54	19	.466	2		1975-78
Sullivan, Red	NY Rangers	196	58	103	35	.385	4		
	Pittsburgh	150	47	79	24	.393	2		
	Washington	18	2	16	0	.111	1		
	Total	364	107	198	59	.375	7		1962-75
Sutherland, Bill	Winnipeg	32	7	22	3	.266	2		1979-81
Sutter, Brian	St. Louis	320	153	124	43	.545	4		
	Boston	216	120	73	23	.609	3		
	Calgary	164	56	81	27	.424	2		
	Total	700	329	278	93	.536	9		1988-99
Sutter, Darryl	Chicago	216	110	80	26	.569	3		
	San Jose	164	65	71	28	.482	2		
	Total	380	175	151	54	.532	5		1992-99
Talbot, Jean-Guy	St. Louis	120	52	53	15	.496	2		
	NY Rangers	80	30	37	13	.456	1		
	Total	200	82	90	28	.480	3		1972-78
Tessier, Orval	Chicago	213	99	93	21	.514	3		1982-85
Thompson, Paul	Chicago	272	104	127	41	.458	7		1938-45
Thompson, Percy	Hamilton	48	13	35	0	.271	2		1920-22
Tobin, Bill	Chicago	71	29	29	13	.500	2		1929-32
Tremblay, Mario	Montreal	159	71	63	25	.525	2		1995-97
Trotz, Barry	Nashville	82	28	47	7	.384	1		1998-99
Ubriaco, Gene	Pittsburgh	106	50	47	9	.514	2		1988-90
Vachon, Rogie	Los Angeles	10	4	3	3	.550	2		1983-95
Vigneault, Alain	Montreal	164	69	71	24	.494	2		1997-99
Watson, Bryan	Edmonton	18	4	9	5	.361	1		1980-81
Watson, Phil	NY Rangers	295	119	124	52	.492	5		
	Boston	84	16	55	13	.268	2		
	Total	379	135	179	65	.442	7		1955-63
Watt, Tom	Winnipeg	181	72	85	24	.464	3		
	Vancouver	160	52	87	21	.391	2		
	Toronto	149	52	80	17	.406	2		
	Total	490	176	252	62	.422	7		1981-92
Webster, Tom	NY Rangers	18	5	9	4	.389	1		
	Los Angeles	240	115	94	31	.544	3		
	Total	258	120	103	35	.533	4		1986-92
Weiland, Cooney	Boston	96	58	20	18	.698	2	1	1939-41
White, Bill	Chicago	46	16	24	6	.413	1		1976-77
Wiley, Jim	San Jose	57	17	37	3	.325	1		1995-96
Wilson, Johnny	Los Angeles	52	9	34	9	.260	1		
	Detroit	145	67	56	22	.538	2		
	Colorado	80	20	46	14	.338	1		
	Pittsburgh	240	91	105	44	.471	3		
	Total	517	187	241	89	.448	7		1969-80
Wilson, Larry	Detroit	36	3	29	4	.139	1		1976-77
Wilson, Ron	Anaheim	296	120	145	31	.458	4		
	Washington	164	71	75	18	.488	2		
	Total	460	191	220	49	.468	6		1993-99
Young, Garry	California	12	2	7	3	.292	1		
	St. Louis	98	41	41	16	.500	2		
	Total	110	43	48	19	.477	3		1972-76

Year-by-Year Individual Regular-Season Leaders

Season	Goals		Assists		Points		Penalty Minutes	
1917-18	Joe Malone	44	Cy Denney / Reg Noble / Harry Cameron	10 / 10 / 10	Joe Malone	48	Joe Hall	100
1918-19	Newsy Lalonde	23	Newsy Lalonde / Eddie Gerard	10 / 10	Newsy Lalonde	33	Joe Hall	135
1919-20	Joe Malone	39	Frank Nighbor	15	Joe Malone	49	Cully Wilson	86
1920-21	Babe Dye	35	Jack Darragh	15	Newsy Lalonde	43	Bert Corbeau	86
1921-22	Punch Broadbent	32	Punch Broadbent / Leo Reise	14 / 14	Punch Broadbent	46	Sprague Cleghorn	63
1922-23	Babe Dye	26	Edmond Bouchard	12	Babe Dye	37	Billy Boucher	52
1923-24	Cy Denneny	22	King Clancy	8	Cy Denneny	23	Bert Corbeau	55
1924-25	Babe Dye	38	Cy Denneny	15	Babe Dye	44	Billy Boucher	92
1925-26	Nels Stewart	34	Frank Nighbor	13	Nels Stewart	42	Bert Corbeau	121
1926-27	Bill Cook	33	Dick Irvin	18	Bill Cook	37	Nels Stewart	133
1927-28	Howie Morenz	33	Howie Morenz	18	Howie Morenz	51	Eddie Shore	165
1928-29	Ace Bailey	22	Frank Boucher	16	Ace Bailey	32	Red Dutton	139
1929-30	Cooney Weiland	43	Frank Boucher	36	Cooney Weiland	73	Joe Lamb	119
1930-31	Charlie Conacher	31	Joe Primeau	32	Howie Morenz	51	Harvey Rockburn	118
1931-32	Charlie Conacher / Bill Cook	34 / 34	Joe Primeau	37	Harvey Jackson	53	Red Dutton	107
1932-33	Bill Cook	28	Frank Boucher	28	Bill Cook	50	Red Horner	144
1933-34	Charlie Conacher	32	Joe Primeau	32	Charlie Conacher	52	Red Horner	126 *
1934-35	Charlie Conacher	36	Art Chapman	34	Charlie Conacher	57	Red Horner	125
1935-36	Charlie Conacher / Bill Thoms	23 / 23	Art Chapman	28	Sweeney Schriner	45	Red Horner	167
1936-37	Larry Aurie / Nels Stewart	23 / 23	Syl Apps Sr.	29	Sweeney Schriner	46	Red Horner	124
1937-38	Gordie Drillon	26	Syl Apps Sr.	29	Gordie Drillon	52	Red Horner	82 *
1938-39	Roy Conacher	26	Bill Cowley	34	Toe Blake	47	Red Horner	85
1939-40	Bryan Hextall	24	Milt Schmidt	30	Milt Schmidt	52	Red Horner	87
1940-41	Bryan Hextall	26	Bill Cowley	45	Bill Cowley	62	Jimmy Orlando	99
1941-42	Lynn Patrick	32	Phil Watson	37	Bryan Hextall Sr.	56	Jimmy Orlando	81 **
1942-43	Doug Bentley	33	Bill Cowley	45	Doug Bentley	73	Jimmy Orlando	89 *
1943-44	Doug Bentley	38	Clint Smith	49	Herb Cain	82	Mike McMahon Sr.	98
1944-45	Maurice Richard	50	Elmer Lach	54	Elmer Lach	80	Pat Egan	86
1945-46	Gaye Stewart	37	Elmer Lach	34	Max Bentley	61	Jack Stewart	73
1946-47	Maurice Richard	45	Billy Taylor	46	Max Bentley	72	Gus Mortson	133
1947-48	Ted Lindsay	33	Doug Bentley	37	Elmer Lach	61	Bill Barilko	147
1948-49	Sid Abel	28	Doug Bentley	43	Roy Conacher	68	Bill Ezinicki	145
1949-50	Maurice Richard	43	Ted Lindsay	55	Ted Lindsay	78	Bill Ezinicki	144
1950-51	Gordie Howe	43	Gordie Howe	43	Gordie Howe	86	Gus Mortson	142
1951-52	Gordie Howe	47	Elmer Lach	50	Gordie Howe	86	Gus Kyle	127
1952-53	Gordie Howe	49	Gordie Howe	46	Gordie Howe	95	Maurice Richard	112
1953-54	Maurice Richard	37	Gordie Howe	48	Gordie Howe	81	Gus Mortson	132
1954-55	Maurice Richard / Bernie Geoffrion	38 / 38	Bert Olmstead	48	Bernie Geoffrion	75	Fernie Flaman	150
1955-56	Jean Beliveau	47	Bert Olmstead	56	Jean Beliveau	88	Lou Fontinato	202
1956-57	Gordie Howe	44	Ted Lindsay	55	Gordie Howe	89	Gus Mortson	147
1957-58	Dickie Moore	36	Henri Richard	52	Dickie Moore	84	Lou Fontinato	152
1958-59	Jean Beliveau	45	Dickie Moore	55	Dickie Moore	96	Ted Lindsay	184
1959-60	Bobby Hull	39	Don McKenney	49	Bobby Hull	81	Carl Brewer	150
1960-61	Bernie Geoffrion	50	Jean Beliveau	58	Bernie Geoffrion	95	Pierre Pilote	165
1961-62	Bobby Hull	50	Andy Bathgate	56	Bobby Hull / Andy Bathgate	84 / 84	Lou Fontinato	167
1962-63	Gordie Howe	38	Henri Richard	50	Gordie Howe	86	Howie Young	273
1963-64	Bobby Hull	43	Andy Bathgate	58	Stan Mikita	89	Vic Hadfield	151
1964-65	Norm Ullman	42	Stan Mikita	59	Stan Mikita	87	Carl Brewer	177
1965-66	Bobby Hull	54	Stan Mikita / Bobby Rousseau / Jean Beliveau	48 / 48 / 48	Bobby Hull	97	Reggie Fleming	166
1966-67	Bobby Hull	52	Stan Mikita	62	Stan Mikita	97	John Ferguson	177
1967-68	Bobby Hull	44	Phil Esposito	49	Stan Mikita	87	Barclay Plager	153
1968-69	Bobby Hull	58	Phil Esposito	77	Phil Esposito	126	Forbes Kennedy	219
1969-70	Phil Esposito	43	Bobby Orr	87	Bobby Orr	120	Keith Magnuson	213
1970-71	Phil Esposito	76	Bobby Orr	102	Phil Esposito	152	Keith Magnuson	291
1971-72	Phil Esposito	66	Bobby Orr	80	Phil Esposito	133	Bryan Watson	212
1972-73	Phil Esposito	55	Phil Esposito	75	Phil Esposito	130	Dave Schultz	259
1973-74	Phil Esposito	68	Bobby Orr	90	Phil Esposito	145	Dave Schultz	348
1974-75	Phil Esposito	61	Bobby Orr / Bobby Clarke	89 / 89	Bobby Orr	135	Dave Schultz	472
1975-76	Reggie Leach	61	Bobby Clarke	89	Guy Lafleur	125	Steve Durbano	370
1976-77	Steve Shutt	60	Guy Lafleur	80	Guy Lafleur	136	Dave Williams	338
1977-78	Guy Lafleur	60	Bryan Trottier	77	Guy Lafleur	132	Dave Schultz	405
1978-79	Mike Bossy	69	Bryan Trottier	87	Bryan Trottier	134	Dave Williams	298
1979-80	Charlie Simmer / Danny Gare / Blaine Stoughton	56 / 56 / 56	Wayne Gretzky	86	Marcel Dionne / Wayne Gretzky	137 / 137	Jimmy Mann	287
1980-81	Mike Bossy	68	Wayne Gretzky	109	Wayne Gretzky	164	Dave Williams	343
1981-82	Wayne Gretzky	92	Wayne Gretzky	120	Wayne Gretzky	212	Paul Baxter	409
1982-83	Wayne Gretzky	71	Wayne Gretzky	125	Wayne Gretzky	196	Randy Holt	275
1983-84	Wayne Gretzky	87	Wayne Gretzky	118	Wayne Gretzky	205	Chris Nilan	338
1984-85	Wayne Gretzky	73	Wayne Gretzky	135	Wayne Gretzky	208	Chris Nilan	358
1985-86	Jari Kurri	68	Wayne Gretzky	163	Wayne Gretzky	215	Joey Kocur	377
1986-87	Wayne Gretzky	62	Wayne Gretzky	121	Wayne Gretzky	183	Tim Hunter	361
1987-88	Mario Lemieux	70	Wayne Gretzky	109	Mario Lemieux	168	Bob Probert	398
1988-89	Mario Lemieux	85	Mario Lemieux / Wayne Gretzky	114 / 114	Mario Lemieux	199	Tim Hunter	375
1989-90	Brett Hull	72	Wayne Gretzky	102	Wayne Gretzky	142	Basil McRae	351
1990-91	Brett Hull	86	Wayne Gretzky	122	Wayne Gretzky	163	Rob Ray	350
1991-92	Brett Hull	70	Wayne Gretzky	90	Mario Lemieux	131	Mike Peluso	408
1992-93	Teemu Selanne / Alexander Mogilny	76 / 76	Adam Oates	97	Mario Lemieux	160	Marty McSorley	399
1993-94	Pavel Bure	60	Wayne Gretzky	92	Mario Lemieux	130	Tie Domi	347
1994-95	Peter Bondra	34	Ron Francis	48	Jaromir Jagr / Eric Lindros	70 / 70	Enrico Ciccone	225
1995-96	Mario Lemieux	69	Mario Lemieux / Ron Francis	92 / 92	Mario Lemieux	161	Matthew Barnaby	335
1996-97	Keith Tkachuk	52	Mario Lemieux / Wayne Gretzky	72 / 72	Mario Lemieux	122	Gino Odjick	371
1997-98	Teemu Selanne / Peter Bondra	52 / 52	Jaromir Jagr / Wayne Gretzky	67 / 67	Jaromir Jagr	102	Donald Brashear	372
1998-99	Teemu Selanne	47	Jaromir Jagr	83	Jaromir Jagr	127	Rob Ray	261

* Match Misconduct penalty not included in total penalty minutes. ** Three Match Misconduct penalties not included in total penalty minutes.
1946-47 was the first season that a Match penalty was automatically written into the player's total penalty minutes as 20 minutes.
Beginning in 1947-48 all penalties, Match, Game Misconduct, and Misconduct, are written as 10 minutes.

One Season Scoring Records

Goals-Per-Game Leaders, One Season

(Among players with 20 goals or more in one season)

Player	Team	Season	Games	Goals	Average
Joe Malone	Montreal	1917-18	20	44	2.20
Cy Denneny	Ottawa	1917-18	20	36	1.80
Newsy Lalonde	Montreal	1917-18	14	23	1.64
Joe Malone	Quebec	1919-20	24	39	1.63
Newsy Lalonde	Montreal	1919-20	23	37	1.61
Reg Noble	Toronto	1917-18	20	30	1.50
Babe Dye	Ham., Tor.	1920-21	24	35	1.46
Cy Denneny	Ottawa	1920-21	24	34	1.42
Joe Malone	Hamilton	1920-21	20	28	1.40
Newsy Lalonde	Montreal	1918-19	17	23	1.35
Newsy Lalonde	Montreal	1920-21	24	32	1.33
Punch Broadbent	Ottawa	1921-22	24	32	1.33
Babe Dye	Toronto	1924-25	29	38	1.31
Babe Dye	Toronto	1921-22	24	30	1.25
Cy Denneny	Ottawa	1921-22	22	27	1.23
Aurel Joliat	Montreal	1924-25	24	29	1.21
Wayne Gretzky	Edmonton	1983-84	74	87	1.18
Babe Dye	Toronto	1922-23	22	26	1.18
Odie Cleghorn	Montreal	1918-19	18	21	1.17
Wayne Gretzky	Edmonton	1981-82	80	92	1.15
Mario Lemieux	Pittsburgh	1992-93	60	69	1.15
Frank Nighbor	Ottawa	1919-20	23	26	1.13
Mario Lemieux	Pittsburgh	1988-89	76	85	1.12
Brett Hull	St. Louis	1990-91	78	86	1.10
Cy Denneny	Ottawa	1923-24	21	22	1.05
Joe Malone	Hamilton	1921-22	24	25	1.04
Billy Boucher	Montreal	1922-23	24	25	1.04
Cam Neely	Boston	1993-94	49	50	1.02
Maurice Richard	Montreal	1944-45	50	50	1.00
Howie Morenz	Montreal	1924-25	30	30	1.00
Reg Noble	Toronto	1919-20	24	24	1.00
Corb Denneny	Toronto	1919-20	24	24	1.00
Alexander Mogilny	Buffalo	1992-93	77	76	0.99
Mario Lemieux	Pittsburgh	1995-96	70	69	0.99
Cooney Weiland	Boston	1929-30	44	43	0.98
Phil Esposito	Boston	1970-71	78	76	0.97
Jari Kurri	Edmonton	1984-85	73	71	0.97

Only five players in NHL history have averaged more than a goal per game since Rocket Richard scored 50 goals in 50 games in 1944-45. The last to do so was Cam Neely, who scored 50 goals in 49 games during an injury-plagued 1993-94 campaign.

Assists-Per-Game Leaders, One Season

(Among players with 35 assists or more in one season)

Player	Team	Season	Games	Assists	Average
Wayne Gretzky	Edmonton	1985-86	80	163	2.04
Wayne Gretzky	Edmonton	1987-88	64	109	1.70
Wayne Gretzky	Edmonton	1984-85	80	135	1.69
Wayne Gretzky	Edmonton	1983-84	74	118	1.59
Wayne Gretzky	Edmonton	1982-83	80	125	1.56
Wayne Gretzky	Los Angeles	1990-91	78	122	1.56
Wayne Gretzky	Edmonton	1986-87	79	121	1.53
Mario Lemieux	Pittsburgh	1992-93	60	91	1.52
Wayne Gretzky	Edmonton	1981-82	80	120	1.50
Mario Lemieux	Pittsburgh	1988-89	76	114	1.50
Adam Oates	St. Louis	1990-91	61	90	1.48
Wayne Gretzky	Los Angeles	1988-89	78	114	1.46
Wayne Gretzky	Los Angeles	1989-90	73	102	1.40
Wayne Gretzky	Edmonton	1980-81	80	109	1.36
Mario Lemieux	Pittsburgh	1991-92	64	87	1.36
Mario Lemieux	Pittsburgh	1989-90	59	78	1.32
Bobby Orr	Boston	1970-71	78	102	1.31
Mario Lemieux	Pittsburgh	1995-96	70	92	1.31
Mario Lemieux	Pittsburgh	1987-88	77	98	1.27
Bobby Orr	Boston	1973-74	74	90	1.22
Wayne Gretzky	Los Angeles	1991-92	74	90	1.22
Ron Francis	Pittsburgh	1995-96	77	92	1.19
Mario Lemieux	Pittsburgh	1985-86	79	93	1.18
Bobby Clarke	Philadelphia	1975-76	76	89	1.17
Peter Stastny	Quebec	1981-82	80	93	1.16
Adam Oates	Boston	1992-93	84	97	1.15
Doug Gilmour	Toronto	1992-93	83	95	1.14
Wayne Gretzky	Los Angeles	1993-94	81	92	1.14
Paul Coffey	Edmonton	1985-86	79	90	1.14
Bobby Orr	Boston	1969-70	76	87	1.14
Bryan Trottier	NY Islanders	1978-79	76	87	1.14
Bobby Orr	Boston	1972-73	63	72	1.14
Bill Cowley	Boston	1943-44	36	41	1.14
Pat LaFontaine	Buffalo	1992-93	84	95	1.13
Steve Yzerman	Detroit	1988-89	80	90	1.13
Paul Coffey	Pittsburgh	1987-88	46	52	1.13
Bobby Orr	Boston	1974-75	80	89	1.11
Bobby Clarke	Philadelphia	1974-75	80	89	1.11
Paul Coffey	Pittsburgh	1988-89	75	83	1.11
Wayne Gretzky	Los Angeles	1992-93	45	49	1.11
Denis Savard	Chicago	1982-83	78	86	1.10
Ron Francis	Pittsburgh	1994-95	44	48	1.09
Denis Savard	Chicago	1981-82	80	87	1.09
Denis Savard	Chicago	1987-88	80	87	1.09
Wayne Gretzky	Edmonton	1979-80	79	86	1.09
Paul Coffey	Edmonton	1983-84	80	86	1.08
Elmer Lach	Montreal	1944-45	50	54	1.08
Peter Stastny	Quebec	1985-86	76	81	1.07
Jaromir Jagr	Pittsburgh	1995-96	82	87	1.06
Mark Messier	Edmonton	1989-90	79	84	1.06
Peter Forsberg	Colorado	1995-96	82	86	1.05
Paul Coffey	Edmonton	1984-85	80	84	1.05
Marcel Dionne	Los Angeles	1979-80	80	84	1.05
Bobby Orr	Boston	1971-72	76	80	1.05
Mike Bossy	NY Islanders	1981-82	80	83	1.04
Adam Oates	Boston	1993-94	77	80	1.04
Phil Esposito	Boston	1968-69	74	77	1.04
Bryan Trottier	NY Islanders	1983-84	68	71	1.04
Pete Mahovlich	Montreal	1974-75	80	82	1.03
Kent Nilsson	Calgary	1980-81	80	82	1.03
Peter Stastny	Quebec	1982-83	75	77	1.03
Jaromir Jagr	**Pittsburgh**	**1998-99**	**81**	**83**	**1.02**
Doug Gilmour	Toronto	1993-94	83	84	1.01
Bernie Nicholls	Los Angeles	1988-89	79	80	1.01
Guy Lafleur	Montreal	1979-80	74	75	1.01
Guy Lafleur	Montreal	1976-77	80	80	1.00
Marcel Dionne	Los Angeles	1984-85	80	80	1.00
Brian Leetch	NY Rangers	1991-92	80	80	1.00
Bryan Trottier	NY Islanders	1977-78	77	77	1.00
Mike Bossy	NY Islanders	1983-84	67	67	1.00
Jean Ratelle	NY Rangers	1971-72	63	63	1.00
Steve Yzerman	Detroit	1993-94	58	58	1.00
Ron Francis	Hartford	1985-86	53	53	1.00
Guy Chouinard	Calgary	1980-81	52	52	1.00
Elmer Lach	Montreal	1943-44	48	48	1.00

Points-Per-Game Leaders, One Season

(Among players with 50 points or more in one season)

Player	Team	Season	Games	Points	Average	Player	Team	Season	Games	Points	Average
Wayne Gretzky	Edmonton	1983-84	74	205	2.77	Peter Stastny	Quebec	1982-83	75	124	1.65
Wayne Gretzky	Edmonton	1985-86	80	215	2.69	Bobby Orr	Boston	1973-74	74	122	1.65
Mario Lemieux	Pittsburgh	1992-93	60	160	2.67	Kent Nilsson	Calgary	1980-81	80	131	1.64
Wayne Gretzky	Edmonton	1981-82	80	212	2.65	Wayne Gretzky	Los Angeles	1991-92	74	121	1.64
Mario Lemieux	Pittsburgh	1988-89	76	199	2.62	Denis Savard	Chicago	1987-88	80	131	1.64
Wayne Gretzky	Edmonton	1984-85	80	208	2.60	Steve Yzerman	Detroit	1992-93	84	137	1.63
Wayne Gretzky	Edmonton	1982-83	80	196	2.45	Marcel Dionne	Los Angeles	1978-79	80	130	1.63
Wayne Gretzky	Edmonton	1987-88	64	149	2.33	Dale Hawerchuk	Winnipeg	1984-85	80	130	1.63
Wayne Gretzky	Edmonton	1986-87	79	183	2.32	Mark Messier	Edmonton	1989-90	79	129	1.63
Mario Lemieux	Pittsburgh	1995-96	70	161	2.30	Bryan Trottier	NY Islanders	1983-84	68	111	1.63
Mario Lemieux	Pittsburgh	1987-88	77	168	2.18	Pat LaFontaine	Buffalo	1991-92	57	93	1.63
Wayne Gretzky	Los Angeles	1988-89	78	168	2.15	Charlie Simmer	Los Angeles	1980-81	65	105	1.62
Wayne Gretzky	Los Angeles	1990-91	78	163	2.09	Guy Lafleur	Montreal	1978-79	80	129	1.61
Mario Lemieux	Pittsburgh	1989-90	59	123	2.08	Bryan Trottier	NY Islanders	1981-82	80	129	1.61
Wayne Gretzky	Edmonton	1980-81	80	164	2.05	Phil Esposito	Boston	1974-75	79	127	1.61
Mario Lemieux	Pittsburgh	1991-92	64	131	2.05	Steve Yzerman	Detroit	1989-90	79	127	1.61
Bill Cowley	Boston	1943-44	36	71	1.97	Peter Stastny	Quebec	1985-86	76	122	1.61
Phil Esposito	Boston	1970-71	78	152	1.95	Mario Lemieux	Pittsburgh	1996-97	76	122	1.61
Wayne Gretzky	Los Angeles	1989-90	73	142	1.95	Michel Goulet	Quebec	1983-84	75	121	1.61
Steve Yzerman	Detroit	1988-89	80	155	1.94	Wayne Gretzky	Los Angeles	1993-94	81	130	1.60
Bernie Nicholls	Los Angeles	1988-89	79	150	1.90	Bryan Trottier	NY Islanders	1977-78	77	123	1.60
Adam Oates	St. Louis	1990-91	61	115	1.89	Bobby Orr	Boston	1972-73	63	101	1.60
Phil Esposito	Boston	1973-74	78	145	1.86	Guy Chouinard	Calgary	1980-81	52	83	1.60
Jari Kurri	Edmonton	1984-85	73	135	1.85	Elmer Lach	Montreal	1944-45	50	80	1.60
Mike Bossy	NY Islanders	1981-82	80	147	1.84	Pierre Turgeon	NY Islanders	1992-93	83	132	1.59
Jaromir Jagr	Pittsburgh	1995-96	82	149	1.82	Steve Yzerman	Detroit	1987-88	64	102	1.59
Mario Lemieux	Pittsburgh	1985-86	79	141	1.78	Mike Bossy	NY Islanders	1978-79	80	126	1.58
Bobby Orr	Boston	1970-71	78	139	1.78	Paul Coffey	Edmonton	1983-84	80	126	1.58
Jari Kurri	Edmonton	1983-84	64	113	1.77	Marcel Dionne	Los Angeles	1984-85	80	126	1.58
Pat LaFontaine	Buffalo	1992-93	84	148	1.76	Bobby Orr	Boston	1969-70	76	120	1.58
Bryan Trottier	NY Islanders	1978-79	76	134	1.76	Eric Lindros	Philadelphia	1995-96	73	115	1.58
Mike Bossy	NY Islanders	1983-84	67	118	1.76	Charlie Simmer	Los Angeles	1979-80	64	101	1.58
Paul Coffey	Edmonton	1985-86	79	138	1.75	Teemu Selanne	Winnipeg	1992-93	84	132	1.57
Phil Esposito	Boston	1971-72	76	133	1.75	**Jaromir Jagr**	**Pittsburgh**	**1998-99**	**81**	**127**	**1.57**
Peter Stastny	Quebec	1981-82	80	139	1.74	Bobby Clarke	Philadelphia	1975-76	76	119	1.57
Wayne Gretzky	Edmonton	1979-80	79	137	1.73	Guy Lafleur	Montreal	1975-76	80	125	1.56
Jean Ratelle	NY Rangers	1971-72	63	109	1.73	Dave Taylor	Los Angeles	1980-81	72	112	1.56
Marcel Dionne	Los Angeles	1979-80	80	137	1.71	Denis Savard	Chicago	1982-83	78	121	1.55
Herb Cain	Boston	1943-44	48	82	1.71	Ron Francis	Pittsburgh	1995-96	77	119	1.55
Guy Lafleur	Montreal	1976-77	80	136	1.70	Mike Bossy	NY Islanders	1985-86	80	123	1.54
Dennis Maruk	Washington	1981-82	80	136	1.70	Bobby Orr	Boston	1971-72	76	117	1.54
Phil Esposito	Boston	1968-69	74	126	1.70	Kevin Stevens	Pittsburgh	1991-92	80	123	1.54
Guy Lafleur	Montreal	1974-75	70	119	1.70	Mike Bossy	NY Islanders	1984-85	76	117	1.54
Mario Lemieux	Pittsburgh	1986-87	63	107	1.70	Kevin Stevens	Pittsburgh	1992-93	72	111	1.54
Adam Oates	Boston	1992-93	84	142	1.69	Doug Bentley	Chicago	1943-44	50	77	1.54
Bobby Orr	Boston	1974-75	80	135	1.69	Doug Gilmour	Toronto	1992-93	83	127	1.53
Marcel Dionne	Los Angeles	1980-81	80	135	1.69	Marcel Dionne	Los Angeles	1976-77	80	122	1.53
Guy Lafleur	Montreal	1977-78	78	132	1.69	Eric Lindros	Philadelphia	1996-97	52	79	1.52
Guy Lafleur	Montreal	1979-80	74	125	1.69	Eric Lindros	Philadelphia	1994-95	46	70	1.52
Rob Brown	Pittsburgh	1988-89	68	115	1.69	Marcel Dionne	Detroit	1974-75	80	121	1.51
Jari Kurri	Edmonton	1985-86	78	131	1.68	Dale Hawerchuk	Winnipeg	1987-88	80	121	1.51
Brett Hull	St. Louis	1990-91	78	131	1.68	Paul Coffey	Pittsburgh	1988-89	75	113	1.51
Phil Esposito	Boston	1972-73	78	130	1.67	Jaromir Jagr	Pittsburgh	1996-97	63	95	1.51
Cooney Weiland	Boston	1929-30	44	73	1.66	Cam Neely	Boston	1993-94	49	74	1.51
Alexander Mogilny	Buffalo	1992-93	77	127	1.65						

Wayne Gretzky and Mario Lemieux are the only players in modern hockey to average more than two points per game. Bill Cowley (#10, with teammate Dit Clapper) was almost the first to achieve this feat when he had 71 points in just 36 games in 1943-44.

Eric Vail (left) of the Atlanta Flames and Pittsburgh's Pierre Larouche (below) were rookie sensations in 1974-75. At the time, Vail's 39 goals were second all-time among rookie scorers behind the 44 goals scored by Rick Martin in 1971-72. Larouche had 31 goals and 37 assists in 1974-75. Vail scored 16 goals in his sophomore season, while Larouche scored 53.

Rookie Scoring Records

All-Time Top 50 Goal-Scoring Rookies

	Rookie	Team	Position	Season	GP	G	A	PTS
1.	* Teemu Selanne	Winnipeg	Right wing	1992-93	84	**76**	56	132
2.	* Mike Bossy	NY Islanders	Right wing	1977-78	73	**53**	38	91
3.	* Joe Nieuwendyk	Calgary	Center	1987-88	75	**51**	41	92
4.	* Dale Hawerchuk	Winnipeg	Center	1981-82	80	**45**	58	103
	* Luc Robitaille	Los Angeles	Left wing	1986-87	79	**45**	39	84
6.	Rick Martin	Buffalo	Left wing	1971-72	73	**44**	30	74
	Barry Pederson	Boston	Center	1981-82	80	**44**	48	92
8.	Steve Larmer	Chicago	Right wing	1982-83	80	**43**	47	90
	* Mario Lemieux	Pittsburgh	Center	1984-85	73	**43**	57	100
10.	Eric Lindros	Philadelphia	Center	1992-93	61	**41**	34	75
11.	Darryl Sutter	Chicago	Left wing	1980-81	76	**40**	22	62
	Sylvain Turgeon	Hartford	Left wing	1983-84	76	**40**	32	72
	Warren Young	Pittsburgh	Left wing	1984-85	80	**40**	32	72
14.	* Eric Vail	Atlanta	Left wing	1974-75	72	**39**	21	60
	Anton Stastny	Quebec	Left wing	1980-81	80	**39**	46	85
	* Peter Stastny	Quebec	Center	1980-81	77	**39**	70	109
	Steve Yzerman	Detroit	Center	1983-84	80	**39**	48	87
18.	* Gilbert Perreault	Buffalo	Center	1970-71	78	**38**	34	72
	Neal Broten	Minnesota	Center	1981-82	73	**38**	60	98
	Ray Sheppard	Buffalo	Right wing	1987-88	74	**38**	27	65
	Mikael Renberg	Philadelphia	Left wing	1993-94	83	**38**	44	82
22.	Jorgen Pettersson	St. Louis	Left wing	1980-81	62	**37**	36	73
	Jimmy Carson	Los Angeles	Centre	1986-87	80	**37**	42	79
24.	Mike Foligno	Detroit	Right wing	1979-80	80	**36**	35	71
	Mike Bullard	Pittsburgh	Center	1981-82	75	**36**	27	63
	Paul MacLean	Winnipeg	Right wing	1981-82	74	**36**	25	61
	Tony Granato	NY Rangers	Right wing	1988-89	78	**36**	27	63
28.	Marian Stastny	Quebec	Right wing	1981-82	74	**35**	54	89
	Brian Bellows	Minnesota	Right wing	1982-83	78	**35**	30	65
	Tony Amonte	NY Rangers	Right wing	1991-92	79	**35**	34	69
31.	Nels Stewart	Mtl. Maroons	Center	1925-26	36	**34**	8	42
	* Danny Grant	Minnesota	Left wing	1968-69	75	**34**	31	65
	Norm Ferguson	Oakland	Right wing	1968-69	76	**34**	20	54
	Brian Propp	Philadelphia	Left wing	1979-80	80	**34**	41	75
	Wendel Clark	Toronto	Left wing	1985-86	66	**34**	11	45
	* Pavel Bure	Vancouver	Right wing	1991-92	65	**34**	26	60
37.	* Willi Plett	Atlanta	Right wing	1976-77	64	**33**	23	56
	Dale McCourt	Detroit	Center	1977-78	76	**33**	39	72
	Mark Pavelich	NY Rangers	Center	1981-82	79	**33**	43	76
	Ron Flockhart	Philadelphia	Center	1981-82	72	**33**	39	72
	Steve Bozek	Los Angeles	Center	1981-82	71	**33**	23	56
	Jason Arnott	Edmonton	Center	1993-94	78	**33**	35	68
43.	Bill Mosienko	Chicago	Right wing	1943-44	50	**32**	38	70
	Michel Bergeron	Detroit	Right wing	1975-76	72	**32**	27	59
	* Bryan Trottier	NY Islanders	Center	1975-76	80	**32**	63	95
	Don Murdoch	NY Rangers	Right wing	1976-77	59	**32**	24	56
	Jari Kurri	Edmonton	Left wing	1980-81	75	**32**	43	75
	Bobby Carpenter	Washington	Center	1981-82	80	**32**	35	67
	Kjell Dahlin	Montreal	Right wing	1985-86	77	**32**	39	71
	Petr Klima	Detroit	Left wing	1985-86	74	**32**	24	56
	Darren Turcotte	NY Rangers	Right wing	1989-90	76	**32**	34	66
	Joe Juneau	Boston	Center	1992-93	84	**32**	70	102

* Calder Trophy Winner

All-Time Top 50 Point-Scoring Rookies

	Rookie	Team	Position	Season	GP	G	A	PTS
1.	* Teemu Selanne	Winnipeg	Right wing	1992-93	84	76	56	**132**
2.	* Peter Stastny	Quebec	Center	1980-81	77	39	70	**109**
3.	* Dale Hawerchuk	Winnipeg	Center	1981-82	80	45	58	**103**
4.	Joe Juneau	Boston	Center	1992-93	84	32	70	**102**
5.	* Mario Lemieux	Pittsburgh	Center	1984-85	73	43	57	**100**
6.	Neal Broten	Minnesota	Center	1981-82	73	38	60	**98**
7.	* Bryan Trottier	NY Islanders	Center	1975-76	80	32	63	**95**
8.	Barry Pederson	Boston	Center	1981-82	80	44	48	**92**
	* Joe Nieuwendyk	Calgary	Center	1987-88	75	51	41	**92**
10.	* Mike Bossy	NY Islanders	Right wing	1977-78	73	53	38	**91**
11.	* Steve Larmer	Chicago	Right wing	1982-83	80	43	47	**90**
12.	Marian Stastny	Quebec	Right wing	1981-82	74	35	54	**89**
13.	Steve Yzerman	Detroit	Center	1983-84	80	39	48	**87**
14.	* Sergei Makarov	Calgary	Right wing	1989-90	80	24	62	**86**
15.	Anton Stastny	Quebec	Left wing	1980-81	80	39	46	**85**
16.	* Luc Robitaille	Los Angeles	Left wing	1986-87	79	45	39	**84**
17.	Mikael Renberg	Philadelphia	Left wing	1993-94	83	38	44	**82**
18.	Jimmy Carson	Los Angeles	Center	1986-87	80	37	42	**79**
	Sergei Fedorov	Detroit	Center	1990-91	77	31	48	**79**
	Alexei Yashin	Ottawa	Center	1993-94	83	30	49	**79**
21.	Marcel Dionne	Detroit	Center	1971-72	78	28	49	**77**
22.	Larry Murphy	Los Angeles	Defense	1980-81	80	16	60	**76**
	Mark Pavelich	NY Rangers	Center	1981-82	79	33	43	**76**
	Dave Poulin	Philadelphia	Center	1983-84	73	31	45	**76**
25.	Brian Propp	Philadelphia	Left wing	1979-80	80	34	41	**75**
	Jari Kurri	Edmonton	Left wing	1980-81	75	32	43	**75**
	Denis Savard	Chicago	Center	1980-81	76	28	47	**75**
	Mike Modano	Minnesota	Center	1989-90	80	29	46	**75**
	Eric Lindros	Philadelphia	Center	1992-93	61	41	34	**75**
30.	Rick Martin	Buffalo	Left wing	1971-72	73	44	30	**74**
	* Bobby Smith	Minnesota	Center	1978-79	80	30	44	**74**
32.	Jorgen Pettersson	St. Louis	Left wing	1980-81	62	37	36	**73**
33.	* Gilbert Perreault	Buffalo	Center	1970-71	78	38	34	**72**
	Dale McCourt	Detroit	Center	1977-78	76	33	39	**72**
	Ron Flockhart	Philadelphia	Center	1981-82	72	33	39	**72**
	Sylvain Turgeon	Hartford	Left wing	1983-84	76	40	32	**72**
	Warren Young	Pittsburgh	Left wing	1984-85	80	40	32	**72**
	Carey Wilson	Calgary	Center	1984-85	74	24	48	**72**
	Alexei Zhamnov	Winnipeg	Center	1992-93	68	25	47	**72**
40.	Mike Foligno	Detroit	Right wing	1979-80	80	36	35	**71**
	Dave Christian	Winnipeg	Center	1980-81	80	28	43	**71**
	Mats Naslund	Montreal	Left wing	1982-83	74	26	45	**71**
	Kjell Dahlin	Montreal	Right wing	1985-86	77	32	39	**71**
	* Brian Leetch	NY Rangers	Defense	1988-89	68	23	48	**71**
45.	Bill Mosienko	Chicago	Right wing	1943-44	50	32	38	**70**
46.	Roland Eriksson	Minnesota	Center	1976-77	80	25	44	**69**
	Tony Amonte	NY Rangers	Right wing	1991-92	79	35	34	**69**
48.	Jude Drouin	Minnesota	Center	1970-71	75	16	52	**68**
	Pierre Larouche	Pittsburgh	Center	1974-75	79	31	37	**68**
	Ron Francis	Hartford	Center	1981-82	59	25	43	**68**
	* Gary Suter	Calgary	Defense	1985-86	80	18	50	**68**
	Jason Arnott	Edmonton	Center	1993-94	84	33	35	**68**

* Calder Trophy Winner

Ken Hodge

Mark Messier

Rick Vaive

50-Goal Seasons

Player	Team	Date of 50th Goal	Score	Goaltender	Player's Game No.	Team Game No.	Total Goals	Total Games	Age When First 50th Scored (Yrs. & Mos.)
Maurice Richard	Mtl.	18-3-45	Mtl. 4 at Bos. 2	Harvey Bennett	50	50	50	50	23.7
Bernie Geoffrion	Mtl.	16-3-61	Tor. 2 at Mtl. 5	Cesare Maniago	62	68	50	64	30.1
Bobby Hull	Chi.	25-3-62	Chi. 1 at NYR 4	Gump Worsley	70	70	50	70	23.2
Bobby Hull	Chi.	2-3-66	Det. 4 at Chi. 5	Hank Bassen	52	57	54	65	
Bobby Hull	Chi.	18-3-67	Chi. 5 at Tor. 9	Bruce Gamble	63	66	52	66	
Bobby Hull	Chi.	5-3-69	NYR 4 at Chi. 4	Ed Giacomin	64	66	58	74	
Phil Esposito	Bos.	20-2-71	Bos. 4 at L.A. 5	Denis DeJordy	58	58	76	78	29.0
John Bucyk	Bos.	16-3-71	Bos. 11 at Det. 4	Roy Edwards	69	69	51	78	35.10
Phil Esposito	Bos.	20-2-72	Bos. 3 at Chi. 1	Tony Esposito	60	60	66	76	
Bobby Hull	Chi.	2-4-72	Det. 1 at Chi. 6	Andy Brown	78	78	50	78	
Vic Hadfield	NYR	2-4-72	Mtl. 6 at NYR 5	Denis DeJordy	78	78	50	78	31.6
Phil Esposito	Bos.	25-3-73	Buf. 1 at Bos. 6	Roger Crozier	75	75	55	78	
Mickey Redmond	Det.	27-3-73	Det. 8 at Tor. 1	Ron Low	73	75	52	76	25.3
Rick MacLeish	Phi.	1-4-73	Phi. 4 at Pit. 5	Cam Newton	78	78	50	78	23.2
Phil Esposito	Bos.	20-2-74	Bos. 5 at Min. 5	Cesare Maniago	56	56	68	78	
Mickey Redmond	Det.	23-3-74	NYR 3 at Det 5	Ed Giacomin	69	71	51	76	
Ken Hodge	Bos.	6-4-74	Bos. 2 at Mtl. 6	Michel Larocque	75	77	50	76	29.10
Rick Martin	Buf.	7-4-74	St. L. 2 at Buf. 5	Wayne Stephenson	78	78	52	78	22.9
Phil Esposito	Bos.	8-2-75	Bos. 8 at Det. 5	Jim Rutherford	54	54	61	79	
Guy Lafleur	Mtl.	29-3-75	K.C. 1 at Mtl. 4	Denis Herron	66	76	53	70	23.6
Danny Grant	Det.	2-4-75	Wsh. 3 at Det. 8	John Adams	78	78	50	80	29.2
Rick Martin	Buf.	3-4-75	Bos. 2 at Buf. 4	Ken Broderick	67	79	52	68	
Reggie Leach	Phi.	14-3-76	Atl. 1 at Phi. 6	Dan Bouchard	69	69	61	80	25.11
Jean Pronovost	Pit.	24-3-76	Bos. 5 at Pit. 5	Gilles Gilbert	74	74	52	80	30.3
Guy Lafleur	Mtl.	27-3-76	K.C. 2 at Mtl. 8	Denis Herron	76	76	56	80	
Bill Barber	Phi.	3-4-76	Buf. 2 at Phi. 5	Al Smith	79	79	50	80	23.9
Pierre Larouche	Pit.	3-4-76	Wsh. 5 at Pit. 4	Ron Low	75	79	53	76	20.5
Danny Gare	Buf.	4-4-76	Tor. 2 at Buf. 5	Gord McRae	79	80	50	79	21.11
Steve Shutt	Mtl.	1-3-77	Mtl. 5 at NYI 4	Glenn Resch	65	65	60	80	24.8
Guy Lafleur	Mtl.	6-3-77	Mtl. 1 at Buf. 4	Don Edwards	68	68	56	80	
Marcel Dionne	L.A.	2-4-77	Min. 2 at L.A. 7	Pete LoPresti	79	79	53	80	25.8
Guy Lafleur	Mtl.	8-3-78	Wsh. 3 at Mtl. 4	Jim Bedard	63	65	60	78	
Mike Bossy	NYI	1-4-78	Wsh. 2 at NYI 3	Bernie Wolfe	69	76	53	73	21.2
Mike Bossy	NYI	24-2-79	Det. 1 at NYI 3	Rogie Vachon	58	58	69	80	
Marcel Dionne	L.A.	11-3-79	L.A. 3 at Phi. 6	Wayne Stephenson	68	68	59	80	
Guy Lafleur	Mtl.	31-3-79	Pit. 3 at Mtl. 5	Denis Herron	76	76	52	80	
Guy Chouinard	Atl.	6-4-79	NYR 2 at Atl. 9	John Davidson	79	79	50	80	22.5
Marcel Dionne	L.A.	12-3-80	L.A. 2 at Pit. 4	Nick Ricci	70	70	53	80	
Mike Bossy	NYI	16-3-80	NYI 6 at Chi. 1	Tony Esposito	68	71	51	75	
Charlie Simmer	L.A.	19-3-80	Det. 3 at L.A. 4	Jim Rutherford	57	73	56	64	26.0
Pierre Larouche	Mtl.	25-3-80	Chi. 4 at Mtl. 8	Tony Esposito	72	75	50	73	
Danny Gare	Buf.	27-3-80	Det. 1 at Buf. 10	Jim Rutherford	71	75	56	76	
Blaine Stoughton	Hfd.	28-3-80	Hfd. 4 at Van. 4	Glen Hanlon	75	75	56	80	27.0
Guy Lafleur	Mtl.	2-4-80	Mtl. 7 at Det. 2	Rogie Vachon	72	78	50	74	
Wayne Gretzky	Edm.	2-4-80	Min. 1 at Edm. 1	Gary Edwards	78	79	51	79	19.2
Reggie Leach	Phi.	3-4-80	Wsh. 2 at Phi. 4	empty net	75	79	50	76	
Mike Bossy	NYI	24-1-81	Que. 3 at NYI 7	Ron Grahame	50	50	68	79	
Charlie Simmer	L.A.	26-1-81	L.A. 7 at Que. 5	Michel Dion	51	51	56	65	
Marcel Dionne	L.A.	8-3-81	L.A. 4 at Wpg. 1	Markus Mattsson	68	68	58	80	
Wayne Babych	St. L.	12-3-81	St. L. 3 at Mtl. 4	Richard Sevigny	70	68	54	78	22.9
Wayne Gretzky	Edm.	15-3-81	Edm. 3 at Cgy. 3	Pat Riggin	69	69	55	80	
Rick Kehoe	Pit.	16-3-81	Pit. 7 at Edm. 6	Eddie Mio	70	70	55	80	29.7
Jacques Richard	Que.	29-3-81	Mtl. 0 at Que. 4	Richard Sevigny	76	75	52	78	28.6
Dennis Maruk	Wsh.	5-4-81	Det. 2 at Wsh. 7	Larry Lozinski	80	80	50	80	25.3
Wayne Gretzky	Edm.	30-12-81	Phi. 5 at Edm. 7	empty net	39	39	92	80	
Dennis Maruk	Wsh.	21-2-82	Wpg. 3 at Wsh. 6	Doug Soetaert	61	61	60	80	
Mike Bossy	NYI	4-3-82	Tor. 1 at NYI 10	Michel Larocque	66	66	64	80	
Dino Ciccarelli	Min.	8-3-82	St. L. 1 at Min. 8	Mike Liut	67	68	55	76	21.7
Rick Vaive	Tor.	24-3-82	St. L. 3 at Tor. 4	Mike Liut	72	75	54	77	22.10
Blaine Stoughton	Hfd.	28-3-82	Min. 5 at Hfd. 2	Gilles Meloche	76	76	52	80	
Rick Middleton	Bos.	28-3-82	Bos. 5 at Buf. 9	Paul Harrison	72	77	51	75	28.11
Marcel Dionne	L.A.	30-3-82	Cgy. 7 at L.A. 5	Pat Riggin	75	77	50	78	
Mark Messier	Edm.	31-3-82	L.A. 3 at Edm. 7	Mario Lessard	78	79	50	78	21.3
Bryan Trottier	NYI	3-4-82	Phi. 3 at NYI 6	Pete Peeters	79	79	50	80	25.9
Lanny McDonald	Cgy.	18-2-83	Cgy. 1 at Buf. 5	Bob Sauve	60	60	66	80	30.0
Wayne Gretzky	Edm.	19-2-83	Edm. 10 at Pit. 7	Nick Ricci	60	60	71	80	
Michel Goulet	Que.	5-3-83	Hfd. 3 at Que. 10	Mike Veisor	67	67	57	80	22.11
Mike Bossy	NYI	12-3-83	Wsh. 2 at NYI 6	Al Jensen	70	71	60	79	
Marcel Dionne	L.A.	17-3-83	Que. 3 at L.A. 4	Dan Bouchard	71	71	56	80	
Al Secord	Chi.	20-3-83	Tor. 3 at Chi. 7	Mike Palmateer	73	73	54	80	25.0
Rick Vaive	Tor.	30-3-83	Tor. 4 at Det. 2	Gilles Gilbert	76	78	51	78	
Wayne Gretzky	Edm.	7-1-84	Hfd. 3 at Edm. 5	Greg Millen	42	42	87	74	
Michel Goulet	Que.	8-3-84	Que. 8 at Pit. 6	Denis Herron	63	69	56	75	
Rick Vaive	Tor.	14-3-84	Min. 3 at Tor. 3	Gilles Meloche	69	72	52	76	
Mike Bullard	Pit.	14-3-84	Pit. 6 at L.A. 7	Markus Mattsson	71	72	51	76	23.0
Jari Kurri	Edm.	15-3-84	Edm. 2 at Mtl. 3	Rick Wamsley	57	73	52	64	23.10
Glenn Anderson	Edm.	21-3-84	Hfd. 3 at Edm. 5	Greg Millen	76	76	54	80	23.6
Tim Kerr	Phi.	22-3-84	Pit. 4 at Phi. 13	Denis Herron	74	75	54	79	24.3
Mike Bossy	NYI	31-3-84	NYI 3 at Wsh. 1	Pat Riggin	67	79	51	67	

Player	Team	Date of 50th Goal	Score		Goaltender	Player's Game No.	Team Game No.	Total Goals	Total Games	Age When First 50th Scored (Yrs. & Mos.)
Wayne Gretzky	Edm.	26-1-85	Pit. 3	at Edm. 6	Denis Herron	49	49	73	80	
Jari Kurri	Edm.	3-2-85	Hfd. 3	at Edm. 6	Greg Millen	50	53	71	73	
Mike Bossy	NYI	5-3-85	Phi. 5	at NYI 4	Bob Froese	61	65	58	76	
Michel Goulet	Que.	6-3-85	Buf. 3	at Que. 4	Tom Barrasso	62	73	55	69	
Tim Kerr	Phi.	7-3-85	Wsh. 6	at Phi. 9	Pat Riggin	63	65	54	74	
John Ogrodnick	Det.	13-3-85	Det. 6	at Edm. 7	Grant Fuhr	69	69	55	79	25.9
Bob Carpenter	Wsh.	21-3-85	Wsh. 2	at Mtl. 3	Steve Penney	72	72	53	80	21.9
Dale Hawerchuk	Wpg.	29-3-85	Chi. 5	at Wpg. 5	W. Skorodenski	77	77	53	80	21.11
Mike Gartner	Wsh.	7-4-85	Pit. 3	at Wsh. 7	Brian Ford	80	80	50	80	25.5
Jari Kurri	Edm.	4-3-86	Edm. 6	at Van. 4	Richard Brodeur	63	65	68	78	
Mike Bossy	NYI	11-3-86	Cgy. 4	at NYI 8	Rejean Lemelin	67	67	61	80	
Glenn Anderson	Edm.	14-3-86	Det. 3	at Edm. 12	Greg Stefan	63	71	54	72	
Michel Goulet	Que.	17-3-86	Que. 8	at Mtl. 6	Patrick Roy	67	72	53	75	
Wayne Gretzky	Edm.	18-3-86	Wpg. 2	at Edm. 6	Brian Hayward	72	72	52	80	
Tim Kerr	Phi.	20-3-86	Pit. 1	at Phi. 5	Roberto Romano	68	72	58	76	
Wayne Gretzky	Edm.	4-2-87	Edm. 6	at Min. 5	Don Beaupre	55	55	62	79	
Dino Ciccarelli	Min.	7-3-87	Pit. 7	at Min. 3	Gilles Meloche	66	66	52	80	
Mario Lemieux	Pit.	12-3-87	Que. 3	at Pit. 6	Mario Gosselin	53	70	54	63	21.5
Tim Kerr	Phi.	17-3-87	NYR 1	at Phi. 4	J. Vanbiesbrouck	67	71	58	75	
Jari Kurri	Edm.	17-3-87	N.J. 4	at Edm. 7	Craig Billington	69	70	54	79	
Mario Lemieux	Pit.	2-2-88	Wsh. 2	at Pit. 3	Pete Peeters	51	54	70	77	
Steve Yzerman	Det.	1-3-88	Buf. 0	at Det. 4	Tom Barrasso	64	64	50	64	22.10
Joe Nieuwendyk	Cgy.	12-3-88	Buf. 4	at Cgy. 10	Tom Barrasso	66	70	51	75	21.5
Craig Simpson	Edm.	15-3-88	Buf. 4	at Edm. 6	Jacques Cloutier	71	71	56	80	21.1
Jimmy Carson	L.A.	26-3-88	Chi. 5	at L.A. 9	Darren Pang	77	77	55	88	19.8
Luc Robitaille	L.A.	1-4-88	L.A. 6	at Cgy. 3	Mike Vernon	79	79	53	80	21.10
Hakan Loob	Cgy.	3-4-88	Min. 1	at Cgy. 4	Don Beaupre	80	80	50	80	27.9
Stephane Richer	Mtl.	3-4-88	Mtl. 4	at Buf. 4	Tom Barrasso	72	80	50	72	21.10
Mario Lemieux	Pit.	20-1-89	Pit. 3	at Wpg. 7	Pokey Reddick	44	46	85	76	
Bernie Nicholls	L.A.	28-1-89	Edm. 7	at L.A. 6	Grant Fuhr	51	51	70	79	27.7
Steve Yzerman	Det.	5-2-89	Det. 6	at Wpg. 2	Pokey Reddick	55	55	65	80	
Wayne Gretzky	L.A.	4-3-89	Phi. 2	at L.A. 6	Ron Hextall	66	67	54	78	
Joe Nieuwendyk	Cgy.	21-3-89	NYI 1	at Cgy. 4	Mark Fitzpatrick	72	74	51	77	
Joe Mullen	Cgy.	31-3-89	Wpg. 1	at Cgy. 4	Bob Essensa	78	79	51	79	32.1
Brett Hull	St. L.	6-2-90	Tor. 4	at St. L 6	Jeff Reese	54	54	72	80	25.6
Steve Yzerman	Det.	24-2-90	Det. 3	at NYI 3	Glenn Healy	63	63	62	79	
Cam Neely	Bos.	10-3-90	Bos. 3	at NYI 3	Mark Fitzpatrick	69	71	55	76	24.9
Luc Robitaille	L.A.	21-3-90	L.A. 3	at Van. 4	Kirk McLean	79	79	52	80	
Brian Bellows	Min.	22-3-90	Min. 5	at Det. 1	Tim Cheveldae	75	75	55	80	25.6
Pat LaFontaine	NYI	24-3-90	NYI 5	at Edm. 5	Bill Ranford	71	77	54	74	25.1
Stephane Richer	Mtl.	24-3-90	Mtl. 4	at Hfd. 7	Peter Sidorkiewicz	75	77	51	75	
Gary Leeman	Tor.	28-3-90	NYI 6	at Tor. 3	Mark Fitzpatrick	78	78	51	80	26.1
Brett Hull	St. L.	25-1-91	St. L. 9	at Det. 4	David Gagnon	49	49	86	78	
Cam Neely	Bos.	26-3-91	Bos. 7	at Que. 4	empty net	67	78	51	69	
Theoren Fleury	Cgy.	26-3-91	Van. 2	at Cgy. 7	Bob Mason	77	77	51	79	22.9
Steve Yzerman	Det.	30-3-91	NYR 5	at Det. 6	Mike Richter	79	79	51	80	
Brett Hull	St. L.	28-1-92	St. L. 3	at L.A. 3	Kelly Hrudey	50	50	70	73	
Jeremy Roenick	Chi.	7-3-92	Chi. 2	at Bos. 1	Daniel Berthiaume	67	67	53	80	22.2
Kevin Stevens	Pit.	24-3-92	Pit. 3	at Det. 4	Tim Cheveldae	74	74	54	80	26.11
Gary Roberts	Cgy.	31-3-92	Edm. 2	at Cgy. 5	Bill Ranford	73	77	53	76	25.10
Alexander Mogilny	Buf.	3-2-93	Hfd. 2	at Buf. 3	Sean Burke	46	53	76	77	23.11
Teemu Selanne	Wpg.	28-2-93	Min. 6	at Wpg. 7	Darcy Wakaluk	63	63	76	84	22.6
Pavel Bure	Van.	1-3-93	Van. 5	at Buf. 2*	Grant Fuhr	63	63	60	83	21.11
Steve Yzerman	Det.	10-3-93	Det. 6	at Edm. 3	Bill Ranford	70	70	58	84	
Luc Robitaille	L.A.	15-3-93	L.A. 4	at Buf. 2	Grant Fuhr	69	69	63	84	
Brett Hull	St. L.	20-3-93	St. L. 2	at L.A. 3	Robb Stauber	73	73	54	80	
Mario Lemieux	Pit.	21-3-93	Pit. 6	at Edm. 4**	Ron Tugnutt	48	72	69	60	
Kevin Stevens	Pit.	21-3-93	Pit. 6	at Edm. 4**	Ron Tugnutt	62	72	55	72	
Dave Andreychuk	Tor.	23-3-93	Tor. 5	at Wpg. 4	Bob Essensa	72	73	54	83	29.6
Pat LaFontaine	Buf.	28-3-93	Ott. 1	at Buf. 3	Peter Sidorkiewicz	75	75	53	84	
Pierre Turgeon	NYI	2-4-93	NYI 3	at NYR 2	Mike Richter	75	76	58	83	23.8
Mark Recchi	Phi.	3-4-93	T.B. 2	at Phi. 6	J-C Bergeron	77	77	53	84	25.2
Jeremy Roenick	Chi.	15-4-93	Tor. 2	at Chi. 3	Felix Potvin	84	84	50	84	
Brendan Shanahan	St. L.	15-4-93	T.B. 5	at St. L 6	Pat Jablonski	71	84	51	71	24.3
Cam Neely	Bos.	7-3-94	Wsh. 3	at Bos. 6	Don Beaupre	44	66	50	49	
Sergei Fedorov	Det.	15-3-94	Van. 2	at Det. 5	Kirk McLean	67	69	56	82	24.3
Pavel Bure	Van.	23-3-94	Van. 6	at L.A. 3	empty net	65	73	60	76	
Adam Graves	NYR	23-3-94	NYR 5	at Edm. 3	Bill Ranford	74	74	51	84	25.11
Dave Andreychuk	Tor	24-3-94	S.J. 2	at Tor. 1	Arturs Irbe	73	74	53	83	
Brett Hull	St. L.	25-3-94	Dal. 3	at St. L 5	Andy Moog	71	74	52	81	
Ray Sheppard	Det.	29-3-94	Hfd. 2	at Det. 6	Sean Burke	74	76	52	82	27.10
Brendan Shanahan	St. L	12-4-94	St. L 5	at Dal. 9	Andy Moog	80	83	52	81	
Mike Modano	Dal.	12-4-94	St. L 5	at Dal. 9	Curtis Joseph	75	83	50	76	23.11
Mario Lemieux	Pit.	23-2-96	Hfd. 4	at Pit. 5	Sean Burke	50	59	69	70	
Jaromir Jagr	Pit.	23-2-96	Hfd. 4	at Pit. 5	Sean Burke	59	59	62	82	24.0
Alexander Mogilny	Van.	29-2-96	St. L. 2	at Van. 2	Grant Fuhr	60	63	55	79	
Peter Bondra	Wsh.	3-4-96	Wsh. 5	at Buf. 1	Andrei Trefilov	62	77	52	67	28.1
Joe Sakic	Col.	7-4-96	Col. 4	at Dal. 1	empty net	79	79	51	82	26.7
John LeClair	Phi.	10-4-96	Phi. 5	at N.J. 1	Corey Schwab	80	80	51	82	26.7
Keith Tkachuk	Wpg.	12-4-96	L.A. 3	at Wpg. 5	empty net	75	81	50	76	24.0
Paul Kariya	Ana.	14-4-96	Wpg. 2	at Ana. 5	N. Khabibulin	82	82	50	82	21.5
Keith Tkachuk	Phx.	6-4-97	Phx. 1	at Col. 2	Patrick Roy	78	79	52	81	
Teemu Selanne	Ana.	9-4-97	L.A. 1	at Ana. 4	empty net	77	81	51	78	
Mario Lemieux	Pit.	11-4-97	Pit. 2	at Fla. 4	J. Vanbiesbrouck	75	81	50	76	
John LeClair	Phi.	13-4-97	N.J. 4	at Phi. 5	Mike Dunham	82	82	50	82	
Teemu Selanne	Ana.	25-3-98	Ana. 3	at Chi. 2	Jeff Hackett	66	71	52	73	
John LeClair	Phi.	13-4-98	Phi. 1	at Buf. 2	Dominik Hasek	79	79	51	82	
Pavel Bure	Van.	17-4-98	Cgy. 4	at Van. 2	Dwayne Roloson	81	81	51	82	
Peter Bondra	Wsh.	18-4-98	Wsh. 4	at Car. 3	Mike Fountain	75	80	52	76	

* neutral site game played at Hamilton; ** neutral site game played at Cleveland

Cam Neely

Jeremy Roenick

Pavel Bure

100-Point Seasons

Bobby Orr

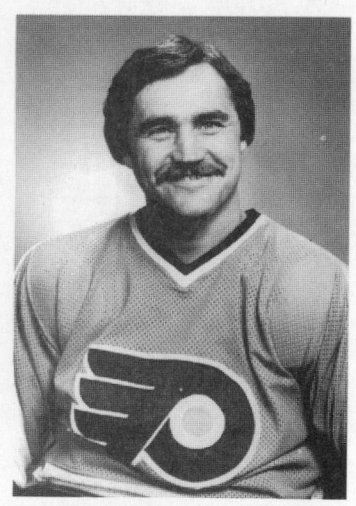

Rick MacLeish

Denis Potvin

Player	Team	Date of 100th Point	G or A	Score		Player's Game No.	Team Game No.	Points G - A PTS	Total Games	Age when first 100th point scored (Yrs. & Mos.)
Phil Esposito	Bos.	2-3-69	(G)	Pit. 0	at Bos. 4	60	62	49-77 — 126	74	27.1
Bobby Hull	Chi.	20-3-69	(G)	Chi. 5	at Bos. 5	71	71	58-49 — 107	76	30.2
Gordie Howe	Det.	30-3-69	(G)	Det. 5	at Chi. 9	76	76	44-59 — 103	76	41.0
Bobby Orr	Bos.	15-3-70	(G)	Det. 5	at Bos. 5	67	67	33-87 — 120	76	22.11
Phil Esposito	Bos.	6-2-71	(A)	Buf. 3	at Bos. 4	51	51	76-76 — 152	78	
Bobby Orr	Bos.	22-2-71	(A)	Bos. 4	at L.A. 5	58	58	37-102 — 139	78	
John Bucyk	Bos.	13-3-71	(G)	Bos. 6	at Van. 3	68	68	51-65 — 116	78	35.10
Ken Hodge	Bos.	21-3-71	(A)	Buf. 7	at Bos. 5	72	72	43-62 — 105	78	26.9
Jean Ratelle	NYR	18-2-72	(A)	NYR 2	at Cal. 2	58	58	46-63 — 109	63	31.4
Phil Esposito	Bos.	19-2-72	(A)	Bos. 6	at Min. 4	59	59	66-67 — 133	76	
Bobby Orr	Bos.	2-3-72	(A)	Van. 3	at Mtl. 3	64	64	37-80 — 117	76	
Vic Hadfield	NYR	25-3-72	(A)	NYR 3	at Mtl. 3	74	74	50-56 — 106	78	31.5
Phil Esposito	Bos.	3-3-73	(A)	Bos. 1	at Mtl. 5	64	64	55-75 — 130	78	
Bobby Clarke	Phi.	29-3-73	(G)	Atl. 2	at Phi. 4	76	76	37-67 — 104	78	23.7
Bobby Orr	Bos.	31-3-73	(G)	Bos. 3	at Tor. 7	62	77	29-72 — 101	63	
Rick MacLeish	Phi.	1-4-73	(G)	Phi. 4	at Pit. 5	78	78	50-50 — 100	78	23.3
Phil Esposito	Bos.	13-2-74	(A)	Bos. 9	at Cal. 6	53	53	68-77 — 145	78	
Bobby Orr	Bos.	12-3-74	(A)	Buf. 0	at Bos. 4	62	66	32-90 — 122	74	
Ken Hodge	Bos.	24-3-74	(A)	Mtl. 3	at Bos. 6	72	72	50-55 — 105	76	
Phil Esposito	Bos.	8-2-75	(A)	Bos. 8	at Det. 5	54	54	61-66 — 127	79	
Bobby Orr	Bos.	13-2-75	(A)	Bos. 1	at Buf. 3	57	57	46-89 — 135	80	
Guy Lafleur	Mtl.	7-3-75	(A)	Wsh. 4	at Mtl. 8	56	66	53-66 — 119	70	24.6
Pete Mahovlich	Mtl.	9-3-75	(G)	Mtl. 5	at NYR 3	67	67	35-82 — 117	80	29.5
Marcel Dionne	Det.	9-3-75	(A)	Det. 5	at Phi. 8	67	67	47-74 — 121	80	23.7
Bobby Clarke	Phi.	22-3-75	(A)	Min. 0	at Phi. 8	72	72	27-89 — 116	80	
Rene Robert	Buf.	5-4-75	(A)	Buf. 4	at Tor. 2	74	80	40-60 — 100	74	26.4
Guy Lafleur	Mtl.	10-3-76	(G)	Mtl. 5	at Chi. 1	69	69	56-69 — 125	80	
Bobby Clarke	Phi.	11-3-76	(A)	Buf. 1	at Phi. 6	64	68	30-89 — 119	76	
Bill Barber	Phi.	18-3-76	(A)	Van. 2	at Phi. 3	71	71	50-62 — 112	80	23.8
Gilbert Perreault	Buf.	21-3-76	(A)	K.C. 1	at Buf. 3	73	73	44-69 — 113	80	25.4
Pierre Larouche	Pit.	24-3-76	(G)	Bos. 5	at Pit. 5	70	74	53-58 — 111	76	20.4
Pete Mahovlich	Mtl.	28-3-76	(A)	Mtl. 2	at Bos. 2	77	77	34-71 — 105	80	
Jean Ratelle	Bos.	30-3-76	(G)	Buf. 4	at Bos. 4	77	77	36-69 — 105	80	
Jean Pronovost	Pit.	3-4-76	(A)	Wsh. 5	at Pit. 4	79	79	52-52 — 104	80	30.4
Darryl Sittler	Tor.	3-4-76	(A)	Bos. 4	at Tor. 2	78	79	41-59 — 100	79	26.7
Guy Lafleur	Mtl.	26-2-77	(A)	Clev. 3	at Mtl. 5	63	63	56-80 — 136	80	
Marcel Dionne	L.A.	5-3-77	(G)	Pit. 3	at L.A. 3	67	67	53-69 — 122	80	
Steve Shutt	Mtl.	27-3-77	(A)	Mtl. 6	at Det. 0	77	77	60-45 — 105	80	24.9
Bryan Trottier	NYI	25-2-78	(A)	Chi. 1	at NYI 7	59	60	46-77 — 123	77	21.7
Guy Lafleur	Mtl.	28-2-78	(A)	Det. 3	at Mtl. 9	69	61	60-72 — 132	78	
Darryl Sittler	Tor.	12-3-78	(A)	Tor. 7	at Pit. 1	67	67	45-72 — 117	80	
Guy Lafleur	Mtl.	27-2-79	(A)	Mtl. 3	at NYI 7	61	61	52-77 — 129	80	
Bryan Trottier	NYI	6-3-79	(A)	Buf. 3	at NYI 2	59	63	47-87 — 134	76	
Marcel Dionne	L.A.	8-3-79	(A)	L.A. 4	at Buf. 6	66	66	59-71 — 130	80	
Mike Bossy	NYI	11-3-79	(G)	NYI 4	at Bos. 4	66	66	69-57 — 126	80	22.2
Bob MacMillan	Atl.	15-3-79	(A)	Atl. 4	at Phi. 5	68	69	37-71 — 108	79	26.6
Guy Chouinard	Atl.	30-3-79	(A)	L.A. 3	at Atl. 5	75	75	50-57 — 107	80	22.5
Denis Potvin	NYI	8-4-79	(A)	NYI 5	at NYR 2	73	80	31-70 — 101	73	25.5
Marcel Dionne	L.A.	6-2-80	(A)	L.A. 3	at Hfd. 7	53	53	53-84 — 137	80	
Guy Lafleur	Mtl.	10-2-80	(A)	Mtl. 3	at Bos. 2	55	55	50-75 — 125	74	
Wayne Gretzky	Edm.	24-2-80	(A)	Bos. 4	at Edm. 2	61	62	51-86 — 137	79	19.2
Bryan Trottier	NYI	30-3-80	(A)	NYI 9	at Que. 6	75	77	42-62 — 104	78	
Gilbert Perreault	Buf.	1-4-80	(A)	Buf. 5	at Atl. 2	77	77	40-66 — 106	80	
Mike Rogers	Hfd.	4-4-80	(A)	Que. 2	at Hfd. 9	79	79	44-61 — 105	80	25.5
Charlie Simmer	L.A.	5-4-80	(G)	Van. 5	at L.A. 3	64	80	56-45 — 101	64	26.0
Blaine Stoughton	Hfd.	6-4-80	(A)	Det. 3	at Hfd. 5	80	80	56-44 — 100	80	27.0
Wayne Gretzky	Edm.	6-2-81	(G)	Wpg. 4	at Edm. 10	53	53	55-109 — 164	80	
Marcel Dionne	L.A.	12-2-81	(A)	L.A. 5	at Chi. 5	58	58	58-77 — 135	80	
Charlie Simmer	L.A.	14-2-81	(A)	Bos. 5	at L.A. 4	59	59	56-49 — 105	65	
Kent Nilsson	Cgy.	27-2-81	(A)	Hfd. 1	at Cgy. 5	64	64	49-82 — 131	80	24.6
Mike Bossy	NYI	3-3-81	(G)	Edm. 8	at NYI 8	65	66	68-51 — 119	79	
Dave Taylor	L.A.	14-3-81	(G)	Min. 4	at L.A. 10	63	70	47-65 — 112	72	25.3
Mike Rogers	Hfd.	22-3-81	(A)	Tor. 3	at Hfd. 3	74	74	40-65 — 105	80	
Bernie Federko	St. L.	28-3-81	(A)	Buf. 4	at St. L. 7	74	76	31-73 — 104	78	24.10
Rick Middleton	Bos.	28-3-81	(A)	Chi. 2	at Bos. 5	76	76	44-59 — 103	80	27.4
Jacques Richard	Que.	29-3-81	(A)	Mtl. 0	at Que. 4	75	76	52-51 — 103	78	28.6
Bryan Trottier	NYI	29-3-81	(G)	NYI 5	at Wsh. 4	69	76	31-72 — 103	73	
Peter Stastny	Que.	29-3-81	(A)	Mtl. 0	at Que. 4	73	76	39-70 — 109	77	24.6
Wayne Gretzky	Edm.	27-12-81	(G)	L.A. 3	at Edm. 10	38	38	92-120 — 212	80	
Mike Bossy	NYI	13-2-82	(G)	Phi. 2	at NYI 8	55	55	64-83 — 147	80	
Peter Stastny	Que.	16-2-82	(A)	Wpg. 3	at Que. 7	60	60	46-93 — 139	80	
Dennis Maruk	Wsh.	20-2-82	(G)	Wsh. 3	at Min. 7	60	60	60-76 — 136	80	26.3
Bryan Trottier	NYI	23-2-82	(A)	Chi. 1	at NYI 5	61	61	50-79 — 129	80	
Denis Savard	Chi.	27-2-82	(A)	Chi. 5	at L.A. 3	64	64	32-87 — 119	80	21.1
Bobby Smith	Min.	3-3-82	(A)	Det. 4	at Min. 6	66	66	43-71 — 114	80	24.1
Marcel Dionne	L.A.	6-3-82	(A)	L.A. 6	at Hfd. 7	64	66	50-67 — 117	78	
Dave Taylor	L.A.	20-3-82	(A)	Pit. 5	at L.A. 7	71	72	39-67 — 106	78	
Dale Hawerchuk	Wpg.	24-3-82	(G)	L.A. 3	at Wpg.	74	74	45-58 — 103	80	18.11
Dino Ciccarelli	Min.	27-3-82	(A)	Min. 6	at Bos. 5	72	76	55-52 — 107	76	21.8
Glenn Anderson	Edm.	28-3-82	(G)	Edm. 6	at L.A. 2	78	78	38-67 — 105	80	21.7
Mike Rogers	NYR	2-4-82	(G)	Pit. 7	at NYR 5	79	79	38-65 — 103	80	

Player	Team	Date of 100th Point	G or A	Score		Player's Game No.	Team Game No.	Points G - A PTS	Total Games	Age when first 100th point scored (Yrs. & Mos.)
Wayne Gretzky	Edm.	5-1-83	(A)	Edm. 8	at Wpg. 3	42	42	71-125 — 196	80	
Mike Bossy	NYI	3-3-83	(A)	Tor. 1	at NYI. 5	66	67	60-58 — 118	79	
Peter Stastny	Que.	5-3-83	(A)	Hfd. 3	at Que. 10	62	67	47-77 — 124	75	
Denis Savard	Chi.	6-3-83	(A)	Mtl. 4	at Chi. 5	65	67	35-86 — 121	78	
Mark Messier	Edm.	23-3-83	(G)	Edm. 4	at Wpg. 7	73	76	48-58 — 106	77	22.2
Barry Pederson	Bos.	26-3-83	(A)	Hfd. 4	at Bos. 7	73	76	46-61 — 107	77	22.0
Marcel Dionne	L.A.	26-3-83	(A)	Edm. 9	at L.A. 3	75	75	56-51 — 107	80	
Michel Goulet	Que.	27-3-83	(A)	Que. 6	at Buf. 6	77	77	57-48 — 105	80	22.11
Glenn Anderson	Edm.	29-3-83	(A)	Edm. 7	at Van. 4	70	78	48-56 — 104	72	
Jari Kurri	Edm.	29-3-83	(A)	Edm. 7	at Van. 4	78	78	45-59 — 104	80	22.10
Kent Nilsson	Cgy.	29-3-83	(G)	L.A. 3	at Cgy. 5	78	78	46-58 — 104	80	
Wayne Gretzky	Edm.	18-12-83	(G)	Edm. 7	at Wpg. 5	34	34	87-118 — 205	74	
Paul Coffey	Edm.	4-3-84	(A)	Mtl. 1	at Edm. 6	68	68	40-86 — 126	80	22.9
Michel Goulet	Que.	4-3-84	(A)	Que. 1	at Buf. 1	62	67	56-65 — 121	75	
Jari Kurri	Edm.	7-3-84	(G)	Chi. 4	at Edm. 7	53	69	52-61 — 113	64	
Peter Stastny	Que.	8-3-84	(A)	Que. 8	at Pit. 6	69	69	46-73 — 119	80	
Mike Bossy	NYI	8-3-84	(A)	Tor. 5	at NYI 9	56	68	51-67 — 118	67	
Barry Pederson	Bos.	14-3-84	(A)	Bos. 4	at Det. 2	71	71	39-77 — 116	80	
Bryan Trottier	NYI	18-3-84	(G)	NYI 4	at Hfd. 5	62	73	40-71 — 111	68	
Bernie Federko	St. L.	20-3-84	(A)	Wpg. 3	at St. L. 9	75	76	41-66 — 107	79	
Rick Middleton	Bos.	27-3-84	(A)	Bos. 6	at Que. 4	77	77	47-58 — 105	80	
Dale Hawerchuk	Wpg.	27-3-84	(G)	Wpg. 3	at L.A. 3	77	77	37-65 — 102	80	
Mark Messier	Edm.	27-3-84	(G)	Edm. 9	at Cgy. 2	72	79	37-64 — 101	73	
Wayne Gretzky	Edm.	29-12-84	(A)	Det. 3	at Edm. 6	35	35	73-135 — 208	80	
Jari Kurri	Edm.	29-1-85	(A)	Edm. 4	at Cgy. 2	48	51	71-64 — 135	73	
Mike Bossy	NYI	23-2-85	(G)	Bos. 1	at NYI 7	56	60	58-59 — 117	76	
Dale Hawerchuk	Wpg.	25-2-85	(A)	Wpg. 12	at NYR 5	64	64	53-77 — 130	80	
Marcel Dionne	L.A.	5-3-85	(A)	Pit. 0	at L.A. 6	66	66	46-80 — 126	80	
Brent Sutter	NYI	12-3-85	(A)	NYI 6	at St. L. 5	68	68	42-60 — 102	72	22.10
John Ogrodnick	Det.	22-3-85	(A)	NYR 3	at Det. 5	73	73	55-50 — 105	79	25.9
Paul Coffey	Edm.	26-3-85	(G)	Edm. 7	at NYI 5	74	74	37-84 — 121	80	
Denis Savard	Chi.	29-3-85	(A)	Chi. 5	at Wpg. 5	75	76	38-67 — 105	79	
Peter Stastny	Que.	2-4-85	(A)	Bos. 4	at Que. 6	74	77	32-68 — 100	75	
Bernie Federko	St. L.	4-4-85	(A)	NYR 4	at St. L. 9	74	78	30-73 — 103	76	
John Tonelli	NYI	6-4-85	(G)	NJ 5	at NYI 5	80	80	42-58 — 100	80	28.1
Paul MacLean	Wpg.	6-4-85	(A)	Wpg. 6	at Edm. 5	78	79	41-60 — 101	79	27.1
Bernie Nicholls	L.A.	6-4-85	(A)	Van. 4	at L.A. 4	80	80	46-54 — 100	80	22.9
Mike Gartner	Wsh.	7-4-85	(G)	Pit. 3	at Wsh. 7	80	80	50-52 — 102	80	25.6
Mario Lemieux	Pit.	7-4-85	(G)	Pit. 3	at Wsh. 7	73	80	43-57 — 100	73	19.6
Wayne Gretzky	Edm.	4-1-86	(A)	Hfd. 3	at Edm. 4	39	39	52-163 — 215	80	
Mario Lemieux	Pit.	15-2-86	(G)	Van. 4	at Pit. 9	55	56	48-93 — 141	79	
Paul Coffey	Edm.	19-2-86	(A)	Tor. 5	at Edm. 9	59	60	48-90 — 138	79	
Peter Stastny	Que.	1-3-86	(A)	Buf. 8	at Que. 4	66	68	41-81 — 122	76	
Jari Kurri	Edm.	2-3-86	(G)	Phi. 1	at Edm. 2	62	64	68-63 — 131	78	
Mike Bossy	NYI	8-3-86	(A)	Wsh. 6	at NYI 2	65	65	61-62 — 123	80	
Denis Savard	Chi.	12-3-86	(A)	Buf. 7	at Chi. 6	69	69	47-69 — 116	80	
Mats Naslund	Mtl.	13-3-86	(A)	Mtl. 2	at Bos. 3	70	70	43-67 — 110	80	26.4
Michel Goulet	Que.	24-3-86	(A)	Que. 1	at Min. 0	70	75	53-50 — 103	75	
Glenn Anderson	Edm.	25-3-86	(G)	Edm. 7	at Det. 2	66	74	54-48 — 102	72	
Neal Broten	Min.	26-3-86	(A)	Min. 6	at Tor. 1	76	76	29-76 — 105	80	26.4
Dale Hawerchuk	Wpg.	31-3-86	(A)	Wpg. 5	at L.A. 2	78	78	46-59 — 105	80	
Bernie Federko	St. L.	5-4-86	(G)	Chi. 5	at St. L. 7	79	79	34-68 — 102	80	
Wayne Gretzky	Edm.	11-1-87	(A)	Cgy. 3	at Edm. 5	42	42	62-121 — 183	79	
Jari Kurri	Edm.	14-3-87	(A)	Buf. 3	at Edm. 5	67	68	54-54 — 108	79	
Mario Lemieux	Pit.	18-3-87	(A)	St. L. 4	at Pit. 5	55	72	54-53 — 107	63	
Mark Messier	Edm.	19-3-87	(A)	Edm. 4	at Cgy. 5	71	71	37-70 — 107	77	
Dino Ciccarelli	Min.	30-3-87	(A)	NYR 6	at Min. 5	78	78	52-51 — 103	80	
Doug Gilmour	St. L.	2-4-87	(A)	Buf. 3	at St. L. 5	78	78	42-63 — 105	80	23.10
Dale Hawerchuk	Wpg.	5-4-87	(A)	Wpg. 3	at Cgy. 1	80	80	47-53 — 100	80	
Mario Lemieux	Pit.	20-1-88	(G)	Pit. 8	at Chi. 3	45	48	70-98 — 168	77	
Wayne Gretzky	Edm.	11-2-88	(A)	Edm. 7	at Van. 2	43	56	40-109 — 149	64	
Denis Savard	Chi.	12-2-88	(A)	St. L. 3	at Chi. 4	57	57	44-87 — 131	80	
Dale Hawerchuk	Wpg.	23-2-88	(A)	Wpg. 4	at Pit. 3	61	61	44-77 — 121	80	
Steve Yzerman	Det.	27-2-88	(A)	Det. 4	at Que. 5	63	63	50-52 — 102	64	22.10
Peter Stastny	Que.	8-3-88	(A)	Hfd. 4	at Que. 6	63	67	46-65 — 111	76	
Mark Messier	Edm.	15-3-88	(A)	Buf. 4	at Edm. 6	68	71	37-74 — 111	77	
Jimmy Carson	L.A.	26-3-88	(A)	Chi. 5	at L.A. 9	77	77	55-52 — 107	80	19.8
Hakan Loob	Cgy.	26-3-88	(A)	Van. 1	at Cgy. 6	76	76	50-56 — 106	80	27.9
Mike Bullard	Cgy.	26-3-88	(A)	Van. 1	at Cgy. 6	76	76	48-55 — 103	79	27.1
Michel Goulet	Que.	27-3-88	(A)	Pit. 6	at Que. 3	76	76	48-58 — 106	80	
Luc Robitaille	L.A.	30-3-88	(G)	Cgy. 7	at L.A. 9	78	78	53-58 — 111	80	22.1
Mario Lemieux	Pit.	31-12-88	(A)	N.J. 6	at Pit. 8	36	38	85-114 — 199	76	
Wayne Gretzky	L.A.	21-1-89	(A)	L.A. 4	at Hfd. 5	47	48	54-114 — 168	78	
Bernie Nicholls	L.A.	21-1-89	(A)	L.A. 4	at Hfd. 5	48	48	70-80 — 150	79	
Steve Yzerman	Det.	27-1-89	(G)	Tor. 1	at Det. 8	50	50	65-90 — 155	80	
Rob Brown	Pit.	16-3-89	(A)	Pit. 2	at N.J. 1	60	72	49-66 — 115	68	20.11
Paul Coffey	Pit.	20-3-89	(A)	Pit. 2	at Min. 7	69	74	30-83 — 113	75	
Joe Mullen	Cgy.	23-3-89	(A)	L.A. 2	at Cgy. 4	74	75	51-59 — 110	79	32.1
Jari Kurri	Edm.	29-3-89	(A)	Edm. 5	at Van. 2	75	79	44-58 — 102	76	
Jimmy Carson	Edm.	2-4-89	(A)	Edm. 2	at Cgy. 4	80	80	49-51 — 100	80	
Mario Lemieux	Pit.	28-1-90	(G)	Pit. 2	at Buf. 7	50	50	45-78 — 123	59	
Wayne Gretzky	L.A.	30-1-90	(A)	N.J. 2	at L.A. 5	51	51	40-102 — 142	73	
Steve Yzerman	Det.	19-2-90	(A)	Mtl. 5	at Det. 5	61	61	62-65 — 127	79	
Mark Messier	Edm.	20-2-90	(A)	Edm. 4	at Van. 2	62	62	45-84 — 129	79	
Brett Hull	St. L.	3-3-90	(A)	NYI 4	at St. L. 5	67	67	72-41 — 113	80	25.7
Bernie Nicholls	NYR	12-3-90	(A)	NYI 4	at NYR 2	70	71	39-73 — 112	79	
Pierre Turgeon	Buf.	25-3-90	(G)	N.J. 4	at Buf. 3	76	76	40-66 — 106	80	20.7
Paul Coffey	Pit.	25-3-90	(A)	Pit. 2	at Hfd. 4	77	77	29-74 — 103	80	
Pat LaFontaine	NYI	27-3-90	(G)	Cgy. 4	at NYI 2	72	78	54-51 — 105	74	25.1

Dale Hawerchuk

Denis Savard

Dave Taylor

John Cullen

Al MacInnis

Doug Weight

Player	Team	Date of 100th Point	G or A	Score		Player's Game No.	Team Game No.	Points G - A PTS	Total Games	Age when first 100th point scored (Yrs. & Mos.)
Adam Oates	St. L.	29-3-90	(G)	Pit 4	at St. L. 5	79	79	23-79 — 102	80	27.7
Joe Sakic	Que.	31-3-90	(G)	Hfd. 3	at Que. 2	79	79	39-63 — 102	80	20.8
Ron Francis	Hfd.	31-3-90	(G)	Hfd. 3	at Que. 2	79	79	32-69 — 101	80	27.0
Luc Robitaille	L.A.	1-4-90	(A)	L.A. 4	at Cgy. 8	80	80	52-49 — 101	80	
Wayne Gretzky	L.A.	30-1-91	(A)	N.J. 4	at L.A. 2	50	51	41-122 — 163	78	
Brett Hull	St. L.	23-2-91	(G)	Bos. 2	at St. L. 9	60	62	86-45 — 131	78	
Mark Recchi	Pit.	5-3-91	(G)	Van. 1	at Pit. 4	66	67	40-73 — 113	78	23.1
Steve Yzerman	Det.	10-3-91	(G)	Det. 4	at St. L. 1	72	72	51-57 — 108	80	
John Cullen	Hfd.	16-3-91	(G)	N.J. 2	at Hfd. 6	71	71	39-71 — 110	78	26.7
Adam Oates	St. L.	17-3-91	(A)	St. L. 4	at Chi. 6	54	73	25-90 — 115	61	
Joe Sakic	Que.	19-3-91	(G)	Edm. 7	at Que. 6	74	74	48-61 — 109	80	
Steve Larmer	Chi.	24-3-91	(A)	Min. 4	at Chi. 5	76	76	44-57 — 101	80	29.9
Theoren Fleury	Cgy.	26-3-91	(A)	Van. 2	at Cgy. 7	77	77	51-53 — 104	79	22.9
Al MacInnis	Cgy.	28-3-91	(A)	Edm. 4	at Cgy. 4	78	78	28-75 — 103	78	27.8
Brett Hull	St. L.	2-3-92	(G)	St. L. 5	at Van. 3	66	66	70-39 — 109	73	
Wayne Gretzky	L.A.	3-3-92	(A)	Phi. 1	at L.A. 4	60	66	31-90 — 121	74	
Kevin Stevens	Pit.	7-3-92	(A)	Pit. 3	at L.A. 5	66	66	54-69 — 123	80	26.11
Mario Lemieux	Pit.	10-3-92	(G)	Cgy. 2	at Pit. 5	53	67	44-87 — 131	64	
Luc Robitaille	L.A.	17-3-92	(G)	Wpg. 4	at L.A. 5	73	73	44-63 — 107	80	
Mark Messier	NYR	22-3-92	(A)	N.J. 3	at NYR 6	74	75	35-72 — 107	79	
Jeremy Roenick	Chi.	29-3-92	(A)	Tor. 1	at Chi. 5	77	77	53-50 — 103	80	22.2
Steve Yzerman	Det.	14-4-92	(G)	Det. 7	at Min. 4	79	80	45-58 — 103	79	
Brian Leetch	NYR	16-4-92	(G)	Pit. 1	at NYR 7	80	80	22-80 — 102	80	24.1
Mario Lemieux	Pit.	31-12-92	(G)	Tor. 3	at Pit. 3	38	39	69-91 — 160	60	
Pat LaFontaine	Buf.	10-2-93	(A)	Buf. 6	at Wpg. 2	55	55	53-95 — 148	84	
Adam Oates	Bos.	14-2-93	(A)	Bos. 3	at T.B. 3	58	58	45-97 — 142	84	
Steve Yzerman	Det.	24-2-93	(G)	Det. 7	at Buf. 10	64	64	58-79 — 137	84	
Pierre Turgeon	NYI	28-2-93	(G)	NYI 7	at Hfd. 6	62	63	58-74 — 132	83	
Doug Gilmour	Tor.	3-3-93	(A)	Min. 4	at Tor. 3	64	64	32-95 — 127	83	
Alexander Mogilny	Buf.	5-3-93	(A)	Hfd. 4	at Buf. 2	58	65	76-51 — 127	77	24.1
Mark Recchi	Phi.	7-3-93	(G)	Phi. 3	at N.J. 7	66	66	53-70 — 123	84	
Teemu Selanne	Wpg.	9-3-93	(A)	Wpg. 4	at T.B. 3	68	68	76-56 — 132	84	22.7
Luc Robitaille	L.A.	15-3-93	(A)	L.A. 4	at Buf. 2	69	69	63-62 — 125	84	
Kevin Stevens	Pit.	23-3-93	(A)	S.J. 2	at Pit. 7	63	73	55-56 — 111	72	
Mats Sundin	Que.	27-3-93	(G)	Phi. 3	at Que. 8	71	75	47-67 — 114	80	22.1
Pavel Bure	Van.	1-4-93	(G)	Van. 5	at T.B. 3	77	77	60-50 — 110	83	22.0
Jeremy Roenick	Chi.	4-4-93	(G)	St. L. 4	at Chi. 5	79	79	50-57 — 107	84	
Craig Janney	St. L.	4-4-93	(G)	St. L. 4	at Chi. 5	79	79	24-82 — 106	84	25.7
Rick Tocchet	Pit.	7-4-93	(G)	Mtl. 3	at Pit. 4	77	81	48-61 — 109	80	28.11
Joe Sakic	Que.	8-4-93	(A)	Que. 2	at Bos. 6	75	81	48-57 — 105	78	
Ron Francis	Pit.	9-4-93	(A)	Pit. 10	at NYR 4	82	82	24-76 — 100	84	
Brett Hull	St. L.	11-4-93	(G)	Min. 1	at St. L. 5	78	82	54-47 — 101	80	
Theoren Fleury	Cgy.	11-4-93	(G)	Cgy. 3	at Van. 6	82	82	34-66 — 100	83	
Joe Juneau	Bos.	14-4-93	(A)	Bos. 4	at Ott. 2	84	84	32-70 — 102	84	25.3
Wayne Gretzky	L.A.	14-2-94	(A)	Bos. 3	at L.A. 2	56	56	38-92 — 130	81	
Sergei Fedorov	Det.	1-3-94	(A)	Cgy. 2	at Det. 5	63	63	56-64 — 120	82	24.2
Doug Gilmour	Tor.	23-3-94	(A)	Tor. 1	at Fla. 1	74	74	27-84 — 111	83	
Adam Oates	Bos.	26-3-94	(A)	Mtl. 3	at Bos. 6	68	75	32-80 — 112	77	
Mark Recchi	Phi.	27-3-94	(A)	Ana. 3	at Phi. 2	76	76	40-67 — 107	84	
Pavel Bure	Van.	28-3-94	(A)	Tor. 2	at Van. 3	68	76	60-47 — 107	76	
Jeremy Roenick	Chi.	31-3-94	(G)	Chi. 3	at Wsh. 6	78	78	46-61 — 107	84	
Brendan Shanahan	St. L.	12-4-94	(G)	St. L. 5	at Dal. 9	80	83	52-50 — 102	81	25.2
Mario Lemieux	Pit.	16-1-96	(G)	Col. 5	at Pit. 2	38	44	69-92 — 161	70	
Jaromir Jagr	Pit.	6-2-96	(G)	Bos. 5	at Pit. 6	52	52	62-87 — 149	82	23.12
Ron Francis	Pit.	9-3-96	(A)	N.J. 4	at Pit. 3	61	66	27-92 — 119	77	
Peter Forsberg	Col.	9-3-96	(A)	Col. 7	at Van. 5	68	68	30-86 — 116	82	22.7
Joe Sakic	Col.	17-3-96	(A)	Edm. 1	at Col. 8	70	70	51-69 — 120	82	
Teemu Selanne	Ana.	25-3-96	(A)	Ana. 1	at Det. 5	70	73	40-68 — 108	79	
Alexander Mogilny	Van.	25-3-96	(A)	L.A. 1	at Van. 4	72	75	55-52 — 107	79	
Eric Lindros	Phi.	25-3-96	(A)	Hfd. 0	at Phi. 3	65	73	47-68 — 115	73	23.0
Wayne Gretzky	St. L.	28-3-96	(A)	N.J. 4	at St. L. 4	76	75	23-79 — 102	80	
Doug Weight	Edm.	30-3-96	(G)	Tor. 4	at Edm. 3	76	76	25-79 — 104	82	25.3
Sergei Fedorov	Det.	2-4-96	(A)	Det. 3	at S.J. 6	72	76	39-68 — 107	78	
Paul Kariya	Ana.	7-4-96	(G)	Ana. 5	at S.J. 3	78	78	50-58 — 108	82	21.5
Mario Lemieux	Pit.	8-3-97	(A)	Phi. 2	at Pit. 3	61	65	50-72 — 122	76	
Teemu Selanne	Ana.	1-4-97	(A)	Chi. 3	at Ana. 3	74	78	51-58 — 109	78	
Jaromir Jagr	Pit.	15-4-98	(G)	T.B. 1	at Pit. 5	76	80	35-67 — 102	77	
Jaromire Jagr	Pit.	13-3-99	(G)	Phi. 0	at Pit. 4	65	65	44-83 — 127	81	
Teemu Selanne	Ana.	5-4-99	(A)	Ana. 2	at Det. 3	69	76	47-60 — 107	75	
Paul Kariya	Ana.	17-4-99	(G)	Ana. 3	at S.J. 3	82	82	39-62 — 101	82	

Wayne Gretzky scored five goals in a game four times in his career. The first time was on February 18, 1981 when he put three pucks past Mike Liut and two past Ed Staniowski in Edmonton's 9-2 win over the St. Louis Blues.

Five-or-more-Goal Games

Player	Team	Date	Score		Opposing Goaltender
SEVEN GOALS					
Joe Malone	Quebec Bulldogs	Jan. 31/20	Tor. 6	at Que. 10	Ivan Mitchell
SIX GOALS					
Newsy Lalonde	Montreal	Jan. 10/20	Tor. 7	at Mtl. 14	Ivan Mitchell
Joe Malone	Quebec Bulldogs	Mar. 10/20	Ott. 4	at Que. 10	Clint Benedict
Corb Denneny	Toronto St. Pats	Jan. 26/21	Ham. 3	at Tor. 10	Howard Lockhart
Cy Denneny	Ottawa Senators	Mar. 7/21	Ham. 5	at Ott. 12	Howard Lockhart
Syd Howe	Detroit	Feb. 3/44	NYR 2	at Det. 12	Ken McAuley
Red Berenson	St. Louis	Nov. 7/68	St. L. 8	at Phil 0	Doug Favell
Darryl Sittler	Toronto	Feb. 7/76	Bos. 4	at Tor. 11	Dave Reece
FIVE GOALS					
Joe Malone	Montreal	Dec. 19/17	Mtl. 7	at Ott. 4	Clint Benedict
Harry Hyland	Mtl. Wanderers	Dec. 19/17	Tor. 9	at Mtl. W. 10	Arthur Brooks
Joe Malone	Montreal	Jan. 12/18	Ott. 4	at Mtl. 9	Clint Benedict
Joe Malone	Montreal	Feb. 2/18	Tor. 2	at Mtl. 11	Harry Holmes
Mickey Roach	Toronto St. Pats	Mar. 6/20	Que. 2	at Tor. 11	Frank Brophy
Newsy Lalonde	Montreal	Feb. 16/21	Ham. 5	at Mtl. 10	Howard Lockhart
Babe Dye	Toronto St. Pats	Dec. 16/22	Mtl. 2	at Tor. 7	Georges Vezina
Red Green	Hamilton Tigers	Dec. 5/24	Ham. 10	at Tor. 3	John Ross Roach
Babe Dye	Toronto St. Pats	Dec. 22/24	Tor. 10	at Bos. 1	Charles Stewart
Harry Broadbent	Mtl. Maroons	Jan. 7/25	Mtl. 6	at Ham. 2	Jake Forbes
Pit Lepine	Montreal	Dec. 14/29	Ott. 4	at Mtl. 6	Alex Connell
Howie Morenz	Montreal	Mar. 18/30	NYA 3	at Mtl. 8	Roy Worters
Charlie Conacher	Toronto	Jan. 19/32	NYA 3	at Tor. 11	Roy Worters
Ray Getliffe	Montreal	Feb. 6/43	Bos. 3	at Mtl. 8	Frank Brimsek
Maurice Richard	Montreal	Dec. 28/44	Det. 1	at Mtl. 9	Harry Lumley
Howie Meeker	Toronto	Jan. 8/47	Chi. 4	at Tor. 10	Paul Bibeault
Bernie Geoffrion	Montreal	Feb. 19/55	NYR 2	at Mtl. 10	Gump Worsley
Bobby Rousseau	Montreal	Feb. 1/64	Det. 3	at Mtl. 9	Roger Crozier
Yvan Cournoyer	Montreal	Feb. 15/75	Chi. 3	at Mtl. 12	Mike Veisor
Don Murdoch	NY Rangers	Oct. 12/76	NYR 10	at Min. 4	Gary Smith
Ian Turnbull	Toronto	Feb. 2/77	Det. 1	at Tor. 9	Ed Giacomin (2) Jim Rutherford (3)
Bryan Trottier	NY Islanders	Dec. 23/78	NYR 4	at NYI 9	Wayne Thomas (4) John Davidson (1)
Tim Young	Minnesota	Jan. 15/79	Min. 8	at NYR 1	Doug Soetaert (3) Wayne Thomas (2)
John Tonelli	NY Islanders	Jan. 6/81	Tor. 3	at NYI 6	Jiri Crha (4) empty net (1)
Wayne Gretzky	Edmonton	Feb. 18/81	St L. 2	at Edm. 9	Mike Liut (3) Ed Staniowski (2)
Wayne Gretzky	Edmonton	Dec. 30/81	Phi. 5	at Edm. 7	Pete Peeters (4) empty net (1)
Grant Mulvey	Chicago	Feb. 3/82	St L. 5	at Chi. 9	Mike Liut (4) Gary Edwards (1)
Bryan Trottier	NY Islanders	Feb. 13/82	Phi. 2	at NYI 8	Pete Peeters
Willy Lindstrom	Winnipeg	Mar. 2/82	Wpg. 7	at Phi. 6	Pete Peeters
Mark Pavelich	NY Rangers	Feb. 23/83	Hfd. 3	at NYR 11	Greg Millen
Jari Kurri	Edmonton	Nov. 19/83	N.J. 4	at Edm. 13	Glenn Resch (3) Ron Low (2)
Bengt Gustafsson	Washington	Jan. 8/84	Wsh 7	at Phi. 1	Pelle Lindbergh
Pat Hughes	Edmonton	Feb. 3/84	Cgy. 5	at Edm. 10	Don Edwards (3) Rejean Lemelin (2)
Wayne Gretzky	Edmonton	Dec. 15/84	Edm 8	at St. L. 2	Rick Wamsley (4) Mike Liut(1)
Dave Andreychuk	Buffalo	Feb. 6/86	Buf. 8	at Bos. 6	Pat Riggin (1) Doug Keans (4)
Wayne Gretzky	Edmonton	Dec. 6/87	Min. 4	at Edm. 10	Don Beaupre (4) Kari Takko (1)
Mario Lemieux	Pittsburgh	Dec. 31/88	N.J. 6	at Pit. 8	Bob Sauve (3) Chris Terreri (2)
Joe Nieuwendyk	Calgary	Jan. 11/89	Wpg. 3	at Cgy. 8	Daniel Berthiaume
Mats Sundin	Quebec	Mar. 5/92	Que. 10	at Hfd. 4	Peter Sidorkiewicz (3) Kay Whitmore (2)
Mario Lemieux	Pittsburgh	Apr. 9/93	Pit 10	at NYR 4	Corey Hirsch (3) Mike Richter (2)
Peter Bondra	Washington	Feb. 5/94	T.B. 3	at Wsh. 6	Darren Puppa (4) Pat Jablonski (1)
Mike Ricci	Quebec	Feb. 17/94	Que. 8	at S.J. 2	Arturs Irbe (3) Jimmy Waite (2)
Alexei Zhamnov	Winnipeg	Apr. 1/95	Wpg. 7	at L.A. 7	Kelly Hrudey (3) Grant Fuhr (2)
Mario Lemieux	Pittsburgh	Mar. 26/96	St L. 4	at Pit. 8	Grant Fuhr (1) Jon Casey (4)
Sergei Fedorov	Detroit	Dec. 26/96	Wsh. 4	at Det. 5	Jim Carey

Players' 500th Goals
Regular Season

Player	Team	Date	Game No.		Score	Opposing Goaltender	Total Goals	Total Games
Maurice Richard	Montreal	Oct. 19/57	863	Chi. 1	at Mtl. 3	Glenn Hall	544	978
Gordie Howe	Detroit	Mar. 14/62	1,045	Det. 2	at NYR 3	Gump Worsley	801	1,767
Bobby Hull	Chicago	Feb. 21/70	861	NYR. 2	at Chi. 4	Ed Giacomin	610	1,063
Jean Béliveau	Montreal	Feb. 11/71	1,101	Min. 2	at Mtl. 6	Gilles Gilbert	507	1,125
Frank Mahovlich	Montreal	Mar. 21/73	1,105	Van. 2	at Mtl. 3	Dunc Wilson	533	1,181
Phil Esposito	Boston	Dec. 22/74	803	Det. 4	at Bos. 5	Jim Rutherford	717	1,282
John Bucyk	Boston	Oct. 30/75	1,370	St. L. 2	at Bos. 3	Yves Bélanger	556	1,540
Stan Mikita	Chicago	Feb. 27/77	1,221	Van. 4	at Chi. 3	Cesare Maniago	541	1,394
Marcel Dionne	Los Angeles	Dec. 14/82	887	L.A. 2	at Wsh. 7	Al Jensen	731	1,348
Guy Lafleur	Montreal	Dec. 20/83	918	Mtl. 6	at N.J. 0	Glenn Resch	560	1,126
Mike Bossy	NY Islanders	Jan. 2/86	647	Bos. 5	at NYI 7	empty net	573	752
Gilbert Perreault	Buffalo	Mar. 9/86	1,159	NJ 3	at Buf. 4	Alain Chevrier	512	1,191
Wayne Gretzky	Edmonton	Nov. 22/86	575	Van. 2	at Edm. 5	empty net	894	1,487
Lanny McDonald	Calgary	Mar. 21/89	1,107	NYI 1	at Cgy. 4	Mark Fitzpatrick	500	1,111
Bryan Trottier	NY Islanders	Feb. 13/90	1,104	Cgy. 4	at NYI 2	Rick Wamsley	524	1,279
Mike Gartner	NY Rangers	Oct. 14/91	936	Wsh. 5	at NYR 3	Mike Liut	708	1,432
Michel Goulet	Chicago	Feb. 16/92	951	Cgy. 5	at Chi. 5	Jeff Reese	548	1,089
Jari Kurri	Los Angeles	Oct. 17/92	833	Bos. 6	at L.A. 8	empty net	601	1,251
Dino Ciccarelli	Detroit	Jan. 8/94	946	Det. 6	at L.A. 3	Kelly Hrudey	608	1,232
Mario Lemieux	Pittsburgh	Oct. 26/95	605	Pit. 7	at NYI 5	Tommy Soderstrom	613	745
*Mark Messier	NY Rangers	Nov. 6/95	1,141	Cgy. 2	at NYR 4	Rick Tabaracci	610	1,413
*Steve Yzerman	Detroit	Jan. 17/96	906	Col. 2	at Det. 3	Patrick Roy	592	1,178
Dale Hawerchuk	St. Louis	Jan. 31/96	1,103	St. L. 4	at Tor. 0	Felix Potvin	518	1,188
*Brett Hull	St. Louis	Dec. 22/96	693	L.A. 4	at St. L. 7	Stephane Fiset	586	861
Joe Mullen	Pittsburgh	Mar. 14/97	1,052	Pit. 3	at Col. 6	Patrick Roy	502	1,062
*Dave Andreychuk	New Jersey	Mar. 15/97	1,070	Wsh. 2	at N.J. 3	Bill Ranford	532	1,210
*Luc Robitaille	Los Angeles	Jan. 7/99	928	Buf. 2	at L.A. 4	Dwayne Roloson	517	971

*Active

With Wayne Gretzky's retirement, Mark Messier is now the NHL's active scoring leader. Messier topped the 500-goal plateau on November 6, 1995. He enters the 1999-2000 season with 610 goals. His next one will move him past Bobby Hull on the all-time list.

Players' 1,000th Points
Regular Season

Player	Team	Date	Game No.	G or A		Score	Total Points G	A	PTS	Total Games
Gordie Howe	Detroit	Nov. 27/60	938	(A)	Tor. 0	at Det. 2	801-1,049		1,850	1,767
Jean Béliveau	Montreal	Mar. 3/68	911	(G)	Mtl. 2	at Det. 5	507-712		1,219	1,125
Alex Delvecchio	Detroit	Feb. 16/69	1,143	(A)	LA 3	at Det. 6	456-825		1,281	1,549
Bobby Hull	Chicago	Dec. 12/70	909	(A)	Minn. 3	at Chi. 5	610-560		1,170	1,063
Norm Ullman	Toronto	Oct. 16/71	1,113	(A)	NYR 5	at Tor. 3	490-739		1,229	1,410
Stan Mikita	Chicago	Oct. 15/72	924	(A)	St.L. 3	at Chi. 1	541-926		1,467	1,394
John Bucyk	Boston	Nov. 9/72	1,144	(G)	Det. 3	at Bos. 8	556-813		1,369	1,540
Frank Mahovlich	Montreal	Feb. 17/73	1,090	(A)	Phi. 7	at Mtl. 6	533-570		1,103	1,181
Henri Richard	Montreal	Dec. 20/73	1,194	(A)	Mtl. 2	at Buf. 2	358-688		1,046	1,256
Phil Esposito	Boston	Feb. 15/74	745	(A)	Bos. 4	at Van. 2	717-873		1,590	1,282
Rod Gilbert	NY Rangers	Feb. 19/77	1,027	(G)	NYR 2	at NYI 5	406-615		1,021	1,065
Jean Ratelle	Boston	Apr. 3/77	1,007	(A)	Tor. 4	at Bos. 7	491-776		1,267	1,281
Marcel Dionne	Los Angeles	Jan. 7/81	740	(G)	L.A. 5	at Hfd. 3	731-1,040		1,771	1,348
Guy Lafleur	Montreal	Mar. 4/81	720	(A)	Mtl. 9	at Wpg. 3	560-793		1,353	1,126
Bobby Clarke	Philadelphia	Mar. 19/81	922	(G)	Bos. 3	at Phi. 5	358-852		1,210	1,144
Gilbert Perreault	Buffalo	Apr. 3/82	871	(A)	Buf. 5	at Mtl.4	512-814		1,326	1,191
Darryl Sittler	Philadelphia	Jan. 20/83	927	(A)	Cgy 2	at Phi. 5	484-637		1,121	1,096
Wayne Gretzky	Edmonton	Dec. 19/84	424	(A)	L.A. 3	at Edm. 7	894-1,963		2,857	1,487
Bryan Trottier	NY Islanders	Jan. 29/85	726	(A)	Min. 4	at NYI 4	524-901		1,425	1,279
Mike Bossy	NY Islanders	Jan. 24/86	656	(A)	NYI 7	at Wsh. 5	573-553		1,126	752
Denis Potvin	NY Islanders	Apr. 4/87	987	(G)	Buf. 6	at NYI 6	310-742		1,052	1,060
Bernie Federko	St. Louis	Mar 19/88	855	(A)	Hfd. 5	at St.L. 3	369-761		1,130	1,000
Lanny McDonald	Calgary	Mar. 7/89	1,101	(G)	Wpg. 5	at Cgy. 9	500-506		1,006	1,111
Peter Stastny	Quebec	Oct. 19/89	682	(G)	Que. 5	at Chi. 3	450-789		1,239	977
Jari Kurri	Edmonton	Jan. 2/90	716	(A)	Edm. 6	at St.L. 4	601-797		1,398	1,251
Denis Savard	Chicago	Mar. 11/90	727	(A)	St.L. 6	at Chi. 4	473-865		1,338	1,196
*Paul Coffey	Pittsburgh	Dec. 22/90	770	(A)	Pit. 4	at NYI 3	385-1,102		1,487	1,322
*Mark Messier	Edmonton	Jan. 13/91	822	(A)	Edm. 5	at Phi. 3	610-1,050		1,660	1,413
Dave Taylor	Los Angeles	Feb. 5/91	930	(A)	L.A. 3	at Phi. 2	431-638		1,069	1,111
Michel Goulet	Chicago	Feb. 23/91	878	(G)	Chi. 3	at Min. 3	548-604		1,152	1,089
Dale Hawerchuk	Buffalo	Mar. 8/91	781	(A)	Chi. 5	at Buf. 3	518-891		1,409	1,188
Bobby Smith	Minnesota	Nov. 30/91	986	(A)	Min. 4	at Tor. 3	357-679		1,036	1,077
Mike Gartner	NY Rangers	Jan. 4/92	971	(G)	NYR 4	at N.J. 6	708-627		1,335	1,432
*Ray Bourque	Boston	Feb. 29/92	933	(A)	Wsh. 5	at Bos. 5	385-1,083		1,468	1,453
Mario Lemieux	Pittsburgh	Mar. 24/92	513	(A)	Pit. 3	at Det. 4	613-881		1,494	745
Glenn Anderson	Toronto	Feb. 22/93	954	(G)	Tor. 8	at Van. 1	498-601		1,099	1,129
*Steve Yzerman	Detroit	Feb. 24/93	737	(A)	Det. 7	at Buf. 10	592-891		1,483	1,178
*Ron Francis	Pittsburgh	Oct. 28/93	893	(G)	Que. 7	at Pit. 3	449-1,037		1,486	1,329
Bernie Nicholls	New Jersey	Feb. 13/94	858	(A)	N.J. 3	at T.B. 3	475-734		1,209	1,127
Dino Ciccarelli	Detroit	Mar. 9/94	957	(A)	Det. 5	at Cgy. 1	608-592		1,200	1,232
Brian Propp	Hartford	Mar. 19/94	1,008	(G)	Hfd. 5	at Phi. 3	425-579		1,004	1,016
Joe Mullen	Pittsburgh	Feb. 7/95	935	(A)	Fla. 3	at Pit. 7	502-561		1,063	1,062
Steve Larmer	NY Rangers	Mar. 8/95	983	(A)	N.J. 4	at NYR 6	441-571		1,012	1,006
*Doug Gilmour	Toronto	Dec. 23/95	935	(A)	Edm. 1	at Tor. 6	397-835		1,232	1,197
*Larry Murphy	Toronto	Mar. 27/96	1,228	(G)	Tor. 6	at Van. 2	275-880		1,155	1,477
*Dave Andreychuk	New Jersey	Apr. 7/96	998	(G)	NYR 2	at N.J. 4	532-608		1,140	1,210
*Adam Oates	Washington	Oct. 8/97	830	(G)	Wsh. 6	at NYI 3	288-838		1,126	967
*Phil Housley	Washington	Nov. 8/97	1,081	(A)	Edm. 1	at Wsh. 2	302-773		1,075	1,210
Dale Hunter	Washington	Jan. 9/98	1,308	(A)	Phi. 1	at Wsh. 4	323-697		1,020	1,407
Pat Lafontaine	NY Rangers	Jan. 22/98	847	(G)	Phi. 4	at NYR 3	468-545		1,013	865
*Luc Robitaille	Los Angeles	Jan. 29/98	882	(A)	Cgy. 3	at L.A. 5	517-559		1,076	971
*Al MacInnis	St. Louis	Apr. 7/98	1,056	(A)	St. L. 3	at Det. 5	290-775		1,065	1,142
*Brett Hull	Dallas	Nov. 14/98	815	(A)	Dal. 3	at Bos. 1	586-459		1,045	861
*Brian Bellows	Washington	Jan. 2/99	1,147	(A)	Tor. 2	at Wsh. 5	485-537		1,022	1,188

*Active

Jari Kurri hit the 1,000-point plateau on January 2, 1990. Wayne Gretzky and Mark Messier are the only other Edmonton players to reach the milestone. Kurri retired as the top European scorer in NHL history, recording 1,398 points on 601 goals and 797 assists.

Individual Awards

Hart Memorial Trophy

Art Ross Trophy

Calder Memorial Trophy

James Norris Memorial Trophy

HART MEMORIAL TROPHY

An annual award **"to the player adjudged to be the most valuable to his team."** Winner selected in a poll by the Professional Hockey Writers' Association in the 27 NHL cities (28 in 1999-2000) at the end of the regular schedule. The winner receives $10,000 and the runners-up $6,000 and $4,000.

History: The Hart Memorial Trophy was presented by the National Hockey League in 1960 after the original Hart Trophy was retired to the Hockey Hall of Fame. The original Hart Trophy was donated to the NHL in 1923 by Dr. David A. Hart, father of Cecil Hart, former manager-coach of the Montreal Canadiens.

1998-99 Winner: Jaromir Jagr, Pittsburgh Penguins
      Runners-up: Alexei Yashin, Ottawa Senators
                       Dominik Hasek, Buffalo Sabres

Right winger Jaromir Jagr of the Pittsburgh Penguins captured the Hart Memorial Trophy for the first time in his career, having finished second in the voting in 1995 and 1998. Jagr was the top selection on 51 of 56 ballots en route to 543 points, followed by Alexei Yashin of Ottawa (226 points) and the two-time reigning Hart Trophy winner Dominik Hasek of Buffalo (172).

Jagr recorded the second highest point total of his career in 1998-99, leading the NHL with 127 points (44 goals, 83 assists) in 81 games. Jagr's efforts helped the Penguins finish third in the Atlantic Division with a 38-30-14 record for 90 points.

CALDER MEMORIAL TROPHY

An annual award **"to the player selected as the most proficient in his first year of competition in the National Hockey League."** Winner selected in a poll by the Professional Hockey Writers' Association at the end of the regular schedule. The winner receives $10,000 and the runners-up $6,000 and $4,000.

History: From 1936-37 until his death in 1943, Frank Calder, NHL President, bought a trophy each year to be given permanently to the outstanding rookie. After Calder's death, the NHL presented the Calder Memorial Trophy in his memory and the trophy is to be kept in perpetuity. To be eligible for the award, a player cannot have played more than 25 games in any single preceding season nor in six or more games in each of any two preceding seasons in any major professional league. Beginning in 1990-91, to be eligible for this award a player must not have attained his twenty-sixth birthday by September 15th of the season in which he is eligible.

1998-99 Winner: Chris Drury, Colorado Avalanche
      Runners-up: Marian Hossa, Ottawa Senators
                       Milan Hejduk, Colorado Avalanche

Center Chris Drury of the Colorado Avalanche was selected as the winner of the Calder Memorial Trophy. Drury received 32 first-place votes and was named on 54 of 56 ballots for 448 points, ahead of Ottawa Senators winger Marian Hossa (269 points) and Avalanche teammate Milan Hejduk (184).

After a four-year career at Boston University that included an NCAA championship and three All-America selections, Chris Drury earned a regular spot on one of the League's most talented rosters. He finished third among rookies in scoring with 44 points (20 goals, 24 assists) in 79 games and led all rookies with six power-play goals. Drury was Colorado's fifth choice, 72nd overall, in the 1994 Entry Draft.

ART ROSS TROPHY

An annual award **"to the player who leads the league in scoring points at the end of the regular season."** The winner receives $10,000 and the runners-up $6,000 and $4,000.

History: Arthur Howie Ross, former manager-coach of the Boston Bruins, presented the trophy to the National Hockey League in 1947. If two players finish the schedule with the same number of points, the trophy is awarded in the following manner: 1. Player with most goals. 2. Player with fewer games played. 3. Player scoring first goal of the season.

1998-99 Winner: Jaromir Jagr, Pittsburgh Penguins
      Runners-up: Teemu Selanne, Mighty Ducks of Anaheim
                       Paul Kariya, Mighty Ducks of Anaheim

Right winger Jaromir Jagr of the Pittsburgh Penguins received his second consecutive, and third career, Art Ross Trophy after leading the League with 127 points (44 goals, 83 assists) in 81 games. The total represented the second-best mark in Jagr's nine-year NHL career. The Kladno, Czech Republic native made history in winning his first career Art Ross Trophy title in 1995 by becoming the first European-trained player to capture the Award.

Jagr joins a group of seven scoring greats to have won three or more Art Ross Trophy titles: Wayne Gretzky (10), Gordie Howe (six), Mario Lemieux (six), Phil Esposito (five), Stan Mikita (four), Bobby Hull (three) and Guy Lafleur (three).

JAMES NORRIS MEMORIAL TROPHY

An annual award **"to the defense player who demonstrates throughout the season the greatest all-round ability in the position."** Winner selected in a poll by the Professional Hockey Writers' Association at the end of the regular schedule. The winner receives $10,000 and the runners-up $6,000 and $4,000.

History: The James Norris Memorial Trophy was presented in 1953 by the four children of the late James Norris in memory of the former owner-president of the Detroit Red Wings.

1998-99 Winner: Al MacInnis, St. Louis Blues
      Runners-up: Nicklas Lidstrom, Detroit Red Wings
                       Ray Bourque, Boston Bruins

Al MacInnis of the St. Louis Blues won the Norris Trophy for the first time in his career. It was his fifth appearance as a Norris Trophy finalist. He had finished second to Ray Bourque in 1990 and 1991, and third in the voting in 1989 and 1994, all as a member of the Calgary Flames. This year, MacInnis received first-place votes on 54 of 56 ballots in accumulating 548 points, a runaway victory over Detroit's Nicklas Lidstrom (234 points) and Boston's Ray Bourque (157).

MacInnis led all defensemen in scoring this season with 62 points (20 goals, 42 assists) and shots on goal (314), was second in plus-minus (+33) and fourth in ice time (29.1 minutes per game). He is the first Blues defenseman in franchise history to win the Norris Trophy.

Vezina Trophy

Lady Byng Memorial Trophy

Frank J. Selke Trophy

Conn Smythe Trophy

VEZINA TROPHY

An annual award "to the goalkeeper adjudged to be the best at his position" as voted by the general managers of each of the 27 clubs (28 in 1999-2000). Over-all winner receives $10,000, runners-up $6,000 and $4,000.

History: Leo Dandurand, Louis Letourneau and Joe Cattarinich, former owners of the Montreal Canadiens, presented the trophy to the National Hockey League in 1926-27 in memory of Georges Vezina, outstanding goalkeeper of the Canadiens who collapsed during an NHL game on November 28, 1925, and died of tuberculosis a few months later. Until the 1981-82 season, the goalkeeper(s) of the team allowing the fewest number of goals during the regular season were awarded the Vezina Trophy.

1998-99 Winner: Dominik Hasek, Buffalo Sabres
Runners-up: Curtis Joseph, Toronto Maple Leafs
Byron Dafoe, Boston Bruins

Dominik Hasek of the Buffalo Sabres captured the Vezina Trophy for the fifth time in the last six seasons. Hasek emerged as the winner of a tight, three-way contest, named on 21 of 27 ballots and receiving eight first-place votes to edge Curtis Joseph of the Toronto Maple Leafs. Joseph earned votes on 16 of 27 ballots, including 10 first-place votes, for 64 points, six ahead of third-place Byron Dafoe of the Boston Bruins.

Hasek led NHL goaltenders in save percentage for the sixth consecutive season, stopping 93.7% of the shots he faced, and finished second in goals-against average (1.87) and shutouts (nine). He also reached the 30-win plateau for the fourth time in his career (30-18-14).

CONN SMYTHE TROPHY

An annual award "to the most valuable player for his team in the playoffs." Winner selected by the Professional Hockey Writers' Association at the conclusion of the final game in the Stanley Cup Finals. The winner receives $10,000.

History: Presented by Maple Leaf Gardens Limited in 1964 to honor Conn Smythe, the former coach, manager, president and owner-governor of the Toronto Maple Leafs.

1998-99 Winner: Joe Nieuwendyk, Dallas Stars

Joe Nieuwendyk was presented with the Conn Smythe Trophy following the first Stanley Cup victory in the history of the Dallas Stars franchise. Nieuwendyk led all playoff scorers with 11 goals, tying Joe Sakic's record with six game-winners. His 21 points trailed only Colorado's Peter Forsberg and teammate Mike Modano.

LADY BYNG MEMORIAL TROPHY

An annual award "to the player adjudged to have exhibited the best type of sportsmanship and gentlemanly conduct combined with a high standard of playing ability." Winner selected in a poll by the Professional Hockey Writers' Association at the end of the regular schedule. The winner receives $10,000 and the runners-up $6,000 and $4,000.

History: Lady Byng, wife of Canada's Governor-General at the time, presented the Lady Byng Trophy in 1925. After Frank Boucher of the New York Rangers won the award seven times in eight seasons, he was given the trophy to keep and Lady Byng donated another trophy in 1936. After Lady Byng's death in 1949, the National Hockey League presented a new trophy, changing the name to Lady Byng Memorial Trophy.

1998-99 Winner: Wayne Gretzky, New York Rangers
Runners-up: Nicklas Lidstrom, Detroit Red Wings
Teemu Selanne, Mighty Ducks of Anaheim

Center Wayne Gretzky of the New York Rangers earned the fifth and final Lady Byng Memorial Trophy victory of his brilliant career. Gretzky was named on 34 of 56 ballots and received 268 points to edge Detroit defenseman Nicklas Lidstrom, (233 points) whose second-place finish was the highest by a defenseman since Detroit's Red Kelly in 1954. Gretzky concluded his incomparable career by leading the Rangers in scoring for the third consecutive season with 62 points (9 goals, 53 assists), tying for sixth in the League in assists. He received just 14 penalty minutes.

FRANK J. SELKE TROPHY

An annual award "to the forward who best excels in the defensive aspects of the game." Winner selected in a poll by the Professional Hockey Writers' Association at the end of the regular schedule. The winner receives $10,000 and the runners-up $6,000 and $4,000.

History: Presented to the National Hockey League in 1977 by the Board of Governors of the NHL in honor of Frank J. Selke, one of the great architects of NHL championship teams.

1998-99 Winner: Jere Lehtinen, Dallas Stars
Runners-up: Magnus Arvedson, Ottawa Senators
Michael Peca, Buffalo Sabres

Right winger Jere Lehtinen of the Dallas Stars captured his second consecutive Frank J. Selke Trophy, becoming the first repeat winner since Dallas teammate Guy Carbonneau captured the award in 1988 and 1989 as a member of the Montreal Canadiens.

Lehtinen received votes on 52 of 56 ballots for 393 points, edging first-time nominee Magnus Arvedson of the Ottawa Senators (311 points) and 1997 Selke Trophy winner Michael Peca of the Buffalo Sabres (286).

Lehtinen tied for the club lead in plus-minus (+29), helping the Stars allow the fewest goals of any club in the regular season (168). Lehtinen is one of four Selke winners among Stars' personnel, joining Carbonneau, General Manager Bob Gainey and assistant coach Doug Jarvis.

WILLIAM M. JENNINGS TROPHY

An annual award "to the goalkeeper(s) having played a minimum of 25 games for the team with the fewest goals scored against it." Winners selected on regular-season play. Overall winner receives $10,000, runners-up $6,000 and $4,000.

History: The Jennings Trophy was presented in 1981-82 by the National Hockey League's Board of Governors to honor the late William M. Jennings, longtime governor and president of the New York Rangers and one of the great builders of hockey in the United States.

1998-99 Winner: Ed Belfour and Roman Turek, Dallas Stars
Runners-up: Dominik Hasek, Buffalo Sabres
Ron Tugnutt and Damian Rhodes, Ottawa Senators

Goaltenders Ed Belfour and Roman Turek of the Dallas Stars were the winners of the William M. Jennings Trophy after posting the League's stingiest defensive record, allowing just 168 goals in 82 games. Belfour appeared in 61 games, registering a 35-15-9 record, 1.99 goals-against average and five shutouts. Turek's performance in a backup role was equally impressive, notching a 16-3-3 record, a 2.08 goals-against average and one shutout in 26 games. Belfour captured the Jennings Trophy for the fourth time in his career, having previously won as a member of the Chicago Blackhawks in 1991, 1993 and 1995. Turek, acquired from Dallas by St. Louis on June 20, 1999, won his first career NHL Trophy.

LESTER B. PEARSON AWARD

An annual award presented to the NHL's outstanding player as selected by the members of the National Hockey League Players' Association. The winner receives $10,000.

History: The award was presented in 1970-71 by the NHLPA in honor of the late Lester B. Pearson, former Prime Minister of Canada.

1998-99 Winner: Jaromir Jagr, Pittsburgh Penguins

Right winger Jaromir Jagr captured the Lester B. Pearson Award for the first time in his career. Jagr designated an orphanage in the Czech Republic as the recipient of the $10,000 prize that accompanies the Award. The four other finalists for the 1999 Lester B. Pearson Award were Dominik Hasek of the Buffalo Sabres, Curtis Joseph of the Toronto Maple Leafs, Teemu Selanne of the Anaheim Mighty Ducks and Alexei Yashin of the Ottawa Senators.

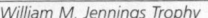

William M. Jennings Trophy

Jack Adams Award

Bill Masterton Trophy

Lester Patrick Trophy

Lester B. Pearson Award

JACK ADAMS AWARD

An annual award presented by the National Hockey League Broadcasters' Association to "the NHL coach adjudged to have contributed the most to his team's success." Winner selected by a poll among members of the NHL Broadcasters' Association at the end of the regular season. The winner receives $1,000 from the NHLBA.

History: The award was presented by the NHL Broadcasters' Association in 1974 to commemorate the late Jack Adams, coach and general manager of the Detroit Red Wings, whose lifetime dedication to hockey serves as an inspiration to all who aspire to further the game.

1998-99 Winner: **Jacques Martin, Ottawa Senators**
    Runners-up: Pat Quinn, Toronto Maple Leafs
                 Ken Hitchcock, Dallas Stars

Ottawa Senators head coach Jacques Martin captured the Jack Adams Award for the first time in his career. He had previously been a finalist in 1996-97, finishing third after leading Ottawa to its first playoff berth. Martin polled 43 of a possible 75 first-place votes in 1998-99 for a total of 270 points, ahead of Toronto Maple Leafs coach Pat Quinn, who finished second with 176 points, including 18 first-place votes. Ken Hitchcock of Dallas, a finalist for the third straight year, finished with a total of 108 points, including seven first-place votes.

In Martin's third full season behind the Ottawa bench, the Senators enjoyed their most successful regular season since they joined the NHL in 1992-93. Ottawa finished first in the Northeast Division and third in the NHL overall with a 44-23-15 record for 103 points, a 20-point gain over 1997-98.

BILL MASTERTON MEMORIAL TROPHY

An annual award under the trusteeship of the Professional Hockey Writers' Association to "the National Hockey League player who best exemplifies the qualities of perseverance, sportsmanship and dedication to hockey." Winner selected by a poll among the 27 chapters of the PHWA at the end of the regular season (28 in 1999-2000). A $2,500 grant from the PHWA is awarded annually to the Bill Masterton Scholarship Fund, based in Bloomington, MN, in the name of the Masterton Trophy winner.

History: The trophy was presented by the NHL Writers' Association in 1968 to commemorate the late Bill Masterton, a player of the Minnesota North Stars, who exhibited to a high degree the qualities of perseverance, sportsmanship and dedication to hockey, and who died January 15, 1968.

1998-99 Winner: **John Cullen, Tampa Bay Lightning**
    Runners-up: Paul Kariya, Mighty Ducks of Anaheim
                 Raymond Bourque, Boston Bruins

On March 28, 1997, John Cullen was diagnosed with non-Hodgkin's lymphoma when a baseball-sized mass was discovered in his chest. When chemotherapy and radiation treatments failed to eradicate the cancer, he underwent a bone-marrow transplant. On April 27, 1998 doctors declared his cancer was in remission. Cullen beat the odds and overcame the doubts and returned to play professional hockey again. On October 14, 1998, John took the opening face-off in the Lightning's regular-season home opener against the New York Islanders. He is believed to be the first professional athlete to play competitively after a bone-marrow transplant. After a successful 11-year career, Cullen officially hung up his No. 12 jersey on November 27, 1998 and became an assistant coach with the Lightning.

As hard as John worked to beat cancer and play hockey again, he has worked even harder to educate people and raise money to fight this deadly disease through his involvement with programs such as Hockey Fights Cancer and the Tampa Bay Lightning Cancer Research Fund.

LESTER PATRICK TROPHY

An annual award "for outstanding service to hockey in the United States." Eligible recipients are players, officials, coaches, executives and referees. Winners are selected by an award committee consisting of the president of the NHL, an NHL governor, a representative of the New York Rangers, a member of the Hockey Hall of Fame builder's section, a member of the Hockey Hall of Fame player's section, a member of the U.S. Hockey Hall of Fame, a member of the NHL Broadcasters' Association and a member of the Professional Hockey Writers' Association. Each except the League President is rotated annually. The winner receives a miniature of the trophy.

History: Presented by the New York Rangers in 1966 to honor the late Lester Patrick, longtime general manager and coach of the New York Rangers, whose teams finished out of the playoffs only once in his first 16 years with the club.

1998-99 Winners: **Harry Sinden**
                     U.S. Olympic Women's Hockey Team

Boston Bruins President and General Manager Harry Sinden has been an integral part of the Bruins organization for more than 30 seasons, starting as a player-coach at the minor league level before advancing to head coaching duties and the front office. Having served his 10th season as president of the Bruins and in his 27th season as the team's general manager, Sinden is the longest-serving GM in the NHL.

As head coach, Sinden led the Bruins to the 1970 Stanley Cup championship, and has been a part of six conference championships, 10 division championships and 28 winning seasons. He also is the first general manager in NHL history to record more than 1,000 victories.

In addition to his work with the Bruins, Sinden has long been a member of several NHL committees which have forwarded rules recommendations to the League's Board of Governors. He also has served on the USA Hockey International Council that oversees international teams and programs for USA Hockey. Sinden received hockey's top honor, election to the Hockey Hall of Fame, in 1983, and was one of the 30 inaugural inductees into the International Ice Hockey Federation Hall of Fame in 1997.

The 1998 U.S. Olympic Women's Ice Hockey Team becomes only the second team to be named in the 33-year history of the Lester Patrick Award. The first squad selected was the 1980 U.S. Olympic Men's Ice Hockey Team. The 1998 USA team made history and captured the world's attention by earning the first Olympic women's ice hockey gold medal on February 7, 1998, in Nagano, Japan.

Coached by Ben Smith (Gloucester, Mass.), the U.S. contingent posted a perfect 6-0-0 Olympic record, including a 3-1 victory over defending world champion Canada in the gold medal game. During the squad's 32-game pre-Olympic tour, the U.S. women amassed a 24-7-1 overall record that included top honors at the 1997 Three Nations Cup, the only international tournament held in the six months prior to the Winter Games. Team USA earned a 3-0 victory against Canada in the championship game, marking the first time Canada was held scoreless in international competition. Cammi Granato (Downers Grove, Ill.) served as team captain while Karyn Bye (River Falls, Wis.) served as assistant captain

King Clancy Memorial Trophy

Bud Light Plus-Minus Award

KING CLANCY MEMORIAL TROPHY

An annual award "to the player who best exemplifies leadership qualities on and off the ice and has made a noteworthy humanitarian contribution in his community."

History: The King Clancy Memorial Trophy was presented to the National Hockey League by the Board of Governors in 1988 to honor the late Frank "King" Clancy.

1998-99 Winner: Rob Ray, Buffalo Sabres
          Runner-up: Curtis Joseph, Toronto Maple Leafs

Buffalo Sabres right winger Rob Ray was the 1998-99 recipient of the King Clancy Memorial Trophy for his enthusiastic commitment to numerous charities in Western New York. His personal involvement with those less fortunate has made the 10-year Sabres veteran one of the team's most popular players. Ray has long-term associations with the Roswell Park Cancer Institute, Children's Hospital, March of Dimes Birth Defects Foundation and the Make-A-Wish Foundation of Western New York. In addition, he awards an $8,000 annual scholarship to a local college student, makes more than 75 hospital visits a year and has developed the "Rob Ray's Christmas Program", which provides clothing, toys and food to families during the holiday season.

Last February Ray was recognized as the recipient of the NHL Foundation Player Award honoring the NHL player who applies the core values of hockey - commitment, perseverance and teamwork - to enrich the lives of people in his community.

BUD LIGHT PLUS-MINUS AWARD

An annual award "to the player, having played a minimum of 60 games, who leads the League in plus/minus statistics" at the end of the regular season. Bud Light will contribute $5,000 on behalf of the winner to the charity of his choice.

History: This award was first presented to the NHL in 1996-97 by Anheuser-Busch Inc. to recognize the League leader in plus-minus statistics. Plus-minus statistics are calculated by giving a player a "plus" when on-ice for an even-strength or shorthand goal scored by his team. He receives a "minus" when on-ice for an even-strength or shorthand goal scored by the opposing team. A plus-minus award has been presented since the 1982-83 season.

1998-99 Winner: John LeClair, Philadelphia Flyers

John LeClair won his second +/- award in three years, posting a +36 rating in 76 games to edge teammate Eric Lindros (+35), St. Louis Blues defenseman Al MacInnis (+33) and Ottawa Senators rookie Magnus Arvedson (+33). LeClair entered the final game of the season tied with Lindros, but posted a +1 in Philadelphia's 3-1 victory over the Boston Bruins to win the award outright.

Team Award

PRESIDENTS' TROPHY

An annual award to the club finishing the regular-season with the best overall record. The winner receives $350,000, to be split between the team and its players.

History: Presented to the National Hockey League in 1985-86 by the NHL Board of Governors to recognize the team compiling the top regular-season record.

1998-99 Winner: Dallas Stars
          Runners-up: New Jersey Devils
                         Ottawa Senators

The Dallas Stars won the Presidents' Trophy for the second straight season, establishing new team records with 51 victories (51-19-12) and 114 points. The New Jersey Devils were runners-up for the second straight season and third time overall, posting a record of 47-24-11 for 105 points. The Ottawa Senators enjoyed their best season, ending the year with 103 points after posting a record of 44-23-15.

PRESIDENTS' TROPHY

	Winner	Runner-up
1999	Dallas Stars	New Jersey Devils
1998	Dallas Stars	New Jersey Devils
1997	Colorado Avalanche	Dallas Stars
1996	Detroit Red Wings	Colorado Avalanche
1995	Detroit Red Wings	Quebec Nordiques
1994	New York Rangers	New Jersey Devils
1993	Pittsburgh Penguins	Boston Bruins
1992	New York Rangers	Washington Capitals
1991	Chicago Blackhawks	St. Louis Blues
1990	Boston Bruins	Calgary Flames
1989	Calgary Flames	Montreal Canadiens
1988	Calgary Flames	Montreal Canadiens
1987	Edmonton Oilers	Philadelphia Flyers
1986	Edmonton Oilers	Philadelphia Flyers

Presidents' Trophy

Teemu Selanne

Rocket Richard (above) led the NHL in goals five times in his career. Teemu Selanne has led (or shared the lead) three times, including a 76-goal season in 1992–93. He is the first winner of the Maurice Richard Trophy (left). Jaromir Jagr's 44 goals last year marked the third-best total of his career, while 44 established new highs for Tony Amonte and Alexei Yashin.

Jaromir Jagr

Tony Amonte

Alexei Yashin

MAURICE "ROCKET" RICHARD TROPHY

An annual award "presented to the player finishing the regular season as the League's goal-scoring leader.

History: A gift to the NHL from the Montreal Canadiens in 1999, the Maurice "Rocket" Richard Trophy honors one of the game's greatest stars. During his 18-year career with the Canadiens from 1942-43 through 1959-60, Richard was the first player in NHL history to score 50 goals in a season and 500 in his career. He played on eight Stanley Cup champions and led the League in goal scoring five times.

1998-99 Winner: Teemu Selanne, Mighty Ducks of Anaheim
Runners-up: Jaromir Jagr, Pittsburgh Penguins (tie)
Tony Amonte, Chicago Blackhawks (tie)
Alexei Yashin, Ottawa Senators (tie)

Right winger Teemu Selanne of the Mighty Ducks of Anaheim became the first recipient of the Maurice "Rocket" Richard Trophy when he led the NHL with 47 goals in 1998-99. Selanne, who in two previous seasons had tied for the NHL's goal-scoring lead, was alone at the top this time, edging Pittsburgh's Jaromir Jagr, Chicago's Tony Amonte and Ottawa's Alexei Yashin, who all scored 44 times. The Mighty Ducks posted a record of 20-10-5 in the 35 games in which Selanne scored a goal. His eight-game goal-scoring streak from February 17 through March 5 tied Buffalo's Miroslav Satan for the longest streak of any player in the NHL in 1998-99.

NHL AWARD MONEY BREAKDOWN — 1998-99
(Players on each club determine how team award money is divided. All award monies are in U.S. funds.)

TEAM AWARDS

Stanley Cup Playoffs	Number of Clubs	Share Per Club	Total
Conference Quarter-Final Losers	8	$ 237,500	$1,900,000
Conference Semi-Final Losers	4	412,500	1,650,000
Conference Championship Losers	2	737,500	1,475,000
Stanley Cup Loser	1	1,137,500	1,137,500
Stanley Cup Winners	1	1,812,500	1,812,500
TOTAL PLAYOFF AWARD MONEY			$7,975,000

Final Standings, Regular Season	Number of Clubs	Share Per Club	Total
Presidents' Trophy			
Club's Share	1	$ 100,000	$ 100,000
Players' Share	1	250,000	250,000
Division Winners	4	425,000	1,700,000
Division Second Place	4	200,000	800,000
TOTAL REGULAR-SEASON AWARD MONEY			$2,850,000

INDIVIDUAL AWARDS	Winner	First Runner-up	Second Runner-up
Hart, Calder, Norris, Ross, Vezina, Byng, Selke, Jennings, Masterton Trophies	$10,000	$6,000	$4,000
King Clancy Trophy	$ 3,000	$1,000	
Conn Smythe Trophy	$10,000		
TOTAL INDIVIDUAL AWARD MONEY			$194,000

ALL-STARS	Number of winners	Per Player	Total
First Team All-Stars	6	$10,000	$ 60,000
Second Team All-Stars	6	5,000	$ 30,000
All-Star Game Winners			$250,000
TOTAL ALL-STAR AWARD MONEY			$340,000
TOTAL ALL AWARDS			**$11,359,000**

NATIONAL HOCKEY LEAGUE INDIVIDUAL AWARD WINNERS

ART ROSS TROPHY

	Winner	Runner-up
1999	Jaromir Jagr, Pit.	Teemu Selanne, Ana.
1998	Jaromir Jagr, Pit.	Peter Forsberg, Col.
1997	Mario Lemieux, Pit.	Teemu Selanne, Ana.
1996	Mario Lemieux, Pit.	Jaromir Jagr, Pit.
1995	Jaromir Jagr, Pit.	Eric Lindros, Phi.
1994	Wayne Gretzky, L.A.	Sergei Fedorov, Det.
1993	Mario Lemieux, Pit.	Pat LaFontaine, Buf.
1992	Mario Lemieux, Pit.	Kevin Stevens, Pit.
1991	Wayne Gretzky, L.A.	Brett Hull, St.L.
1990	Wayne Gretzky, L.A.	Mark Messier, Edm.
1989	Mario Lemieux, Pit.	Wayne Gretzky, L.A.
1988	Mario Lemieux, Pit.	Wayne Gretzky, Edm.
1987	Wayne Gretzky, Edm.	Jari Kurri, Edm.
1986	Wayne Gretzky, Edm.	Mario Lemieux, Pit.
1985	Wayne Gretzky, Edm.	Jari Kurri, Edm.
1984	Wayne Gretzky, Edm.	Paul Coffey, Edm.
1983	Wayne Gretzky, Edm.	Peter Stastny, Que.
1982	Wayne Gretzky, Edm.	Mike Bossy, NYI
1981	Wayne Gretzky, Edm.	Marcel Dionne, L.A.
1980	Marcel Dionne, L.A.	Wayne Gretzky, Edm.
1979	Bryan Trottier, NYI	Marcel Dionne, L.A.
1978	Guy Lafleur, Mtl.	Bryan Trottier, NYI
1977	Guy Lafleur, Mtl.	Marcel Dionne, L.A.
1976	Guy Lafleur, Mtl.	Bobby Clarke, Phi.
1975	Bobby Orr, Bos.	Phil Esposito, Bos.
1974	Phil Esposito, Bos.	Bobby Orr, Bos.
1973	Phil Esposito, Bos.	Bobby Clarke, Phi.
1972	Phil Esposito, Bos.	Bobby Orr, Bos.
1971	Phil Esposito, Bos.	Bobby Orr, Bos.
1970	Bobby Orr, Bos.	Phil Esposito, Bos.
1969	Phil Esposito, Bos.	Bobby Hull, Chi.
1968	Stan Mikita, Chi.	Phil Esposito, Bos.
1967	Stan Mikita, Chi.	Bobby Hull, Chi.
1966	Bobby Hull, Chi.	Stan Mikita, Chi.
1965	Stan Mikita, Chi.	Norm Ullman, Det.
1964	Stan Mikita, Chi.	Bobby Hull, Chi.
1963	Gordie Howe, Det.	Andy Bathgate, NYR
1962	Bobby Hull, Chi.	Andy Bathgate, NYR
1961	Bernie Geoffrion, Mtl.	Jean Beliveau, Mtl.
1960	Bobby Hull, Chi.	Bronco Horvath, Bos.
1959	Dickie Moore, Mtl.	Jean Beliveau, Mtl.
1958	Dickie Moore, Mtl.	Henri Richard, Mtl.
1957	Gordie Howe, Det.	Ted Lindsay, Det.
1956	Jean Beliveau, Mtl.	Gordie Howe, Det.
1955	Bernie Geoffrion, Mtl.	Maurice Richard, Mtl.
1954	Gordie Howe, Det.	Maurice Richard, Mtl.
1953	Gordie Howe, Det.	Ted Lindsay, Det.
1952	Gordie Howe, Det.	Ted Lindsay, Det.
1951	Gordie Howe, Det.	Maurice Richard, Mtl.
1950	Ted Lindsay, Det.	Sid Abel, Det.
1949	Roy Conacher, Chi.	Doug Bentley, Chi.
1948*	Elmer Lach, Mtl.	Buddy O'Connor, NYR
1947	Max Bentley, Chi.	Maurice Richard, Mtl.
1946	Max Bentley, Chi.	Gaye Stewart, Tor.
1945	Elmer Lach, Mtl.	Maurice Richard, Mtl.
1944	Herb Cain, Bos.	Doug Bentley, Chi.
1943	Doug Bentley, Chi.	Bill Cowley, Bos.
1942	Bryan Hextall Sr., NYR	Lynn Patrick, NYR
1941	Bill Cowley, Bos.	Bryan Hextall Sr., NYR
1940	Milt Schmidt, Bos.	Woody Dumart, Bos.
1939	Toe Blake, Mtl.	Sweeney Schriner, NYA
1938	Gordie Drillon, Tor.	Syl Apps Sr., Tor.
1937	Sweeney Schriner, NYA	Syl Apps Sr., Tor.
1936	Sweeney Schriner, NYA	Marty Barry, Det.
1935	Charlie Conacher, Tor.	Syd Howe, St.L-Det.
1934	Charlie Conacher, Tor.	Joe Primeau, Tor
1933	Bill Cook, NYR	Harvey Jackson, Tor.
1932	Harvey Jackson, Tor.	Joe Primeau, Tor.
1931	Howie Morenz, Mtl.	Ebbie Goodfellow, Det.
1930	Cooney Weiland, Bos.	Frank Boucher, NYR
1929	Ace Bailey, Tor.	Nels Stewart, Mtl.M
1928	Howie Morenz, Mtl.	Aurel Joliat, Mtl.
1927	Bill Cook, NYR	Dick Irvin, Chi.
1926	Nels Stewart, Mtl.M.	Cy Denneny, Ott.
1925	Babe Dye, Tor.	Cy Denneny, Ott.
1924	Cy Denneny, Ott.	Billy Boucher, Mtl.
1923	Babe Dye, Tor.	Cy Denneny, Ott.
1922	Punch Broadbent, Ott.	Cy Denneny, Ott.
1921	Newsy Lalonde, Mtl.	Babe Dye, Ham., Tor.
1920	Joe Malone, Que.	Newsy Lalonde, Mtl.
1919	Newsy Lalonde, Mtl.	Odie Cleghorn, Mtl.
1918	Joe Malone, Mtl.	Cy Denneny, Ott.

* Trophy first awarded in 1948.
Scoring leaders listed from 1918 to 1947.

HART TROPHY

	Winner	Runner-up
1999	Jaromir Jagr, Pit.	Alexei Yashin, Ott.
1998	Dominik Hasek, Buf.	Jaromir Jagr, Pit.
1997	Dominik Hasek, Buf.	Paul Kariya, Ana.
1996	Mario Lemieux, Pit.	Mark Messier, NYR
1995	Eric Lindros, Phi.	Jaromir Jagr, Pit.
1994	Sergei Fedorov, Det.	Dominik Hasek, Buf.
1993	Mario Lemieux, Pit.	Doug Gilmour, Tor.
1992	Mark Messier, NYR	Patrick Roy, Mtl.
1991	Brett Hull, St.L.	Wayne Gretzky, L.A.
1990	Mark Messier, Edm.	Ray Bourque, Bos.
1989	Wayne Gretzky, L.A.	Mario Lemieux, Pit.
1988	Mario Lemieux, Pit.	Grant Fuhr, Edm.
1987	Wayne Gretzky, Edm.	Ray Bourque, Bos.
1986	Wayne Gretzky, Edm.	Mario Lemieux, Pit.
1985	Wayne Gretzky, Edm.	Dale Hawerchuk, Wpg.
1984	Wayne Gretzky, Edm.	Rod Langway, Wsh.
1983	Wayne Gretzky, Edm.	Pete Peeters, Bos.
1982	Wayne Gretzky, Edm.	Bryan Trottier, NYI
1981	Wayne Gretzky, Edm.	Mike Liut, St.L.
1980	Wayne Gretzky, Edm.	Marcel Dionne, L.A.
1979	Bryan Trottier, NYI	Guy Lafleur, Mtl
1978	Guy Lafleur, Mtl.	Bryan Trottier, NYI
1977	Guy Lafleur, Mtl.	Bobby Clarke, Phi.
1976	Bobby Clarke, Phi.	Denis Potvin, NYI
1975	Bobby Clarke, Phi.	Rogie Vachon, L.A.
1974	Phil Esposito, Bos.	Bernie Parent, Phi.
1973	Bobby Clarke, Phi.	Phil Esposito, Bos.
1972	Bobby Orr, Bos.	Ken Dryden, Mtl.
1971	Bobby Orr, Bos.	Phil Esposito, Bos.
1970	Bobby Orr, Bos.	Tony Esposito, Chi.
1969	Phil Esposito, Bos.	Jean Beliveau, Mtl.
1968	Stan Mikita, Chi.	Jean Beliveau, Mtl.
1967	Stan Mikita, Chi.	Ed Giacomin, NYR
1966	Bobby Hull, Chi.	Jean Beliveau, Mtl.
1965	Bobby Hull, Chi.	Norm Ullman, Det.
1964	Jean Beliveau, Mtl.	Bobby Hull, Chi.
1963	Gordie Howe, Det.	Stan Mikita, Chi.
1962	Jacques Plante, Mtl.	Doug Harvey, NYR
1961	Bernie Geoffrion, Mtl.	Johnny Bower, Tor.
1960	Gordie Howe, Det.	Bobby Hull, Chi.
1959	Andy Bathgate, NYR	Gordie Howe, Det.
1958	Gordie Howe, Det.	Andy Bathgate, NYR
1957	Gordie Howe, Det.	Jean Beliveau, Mtl.
1956	Jean Beliveau, Mtl.	Tod Sloan, Tor.
1955	Ted Kennedy, Tor.	Harry Lumley, Tor.
1954	Al Rollins, Chi.	Red Kelly, Det.
1953	Gordie Howe, Det.	Al Rollins, Chi.
1952	Gordie Howe, Det.	Elmer Lach, Mtl.
1951	Milt Schmidt, Bos.	Maurice Richard, Mtl.
1950	Chuck Rayner, NYR	Ted Kennedy, Tor.
1949	Sid Abel, Det.	Bill Durnan, Mtl.
1948	Buddy O'Connor, NYR	Frank Brimsek, Bos.
1947	Maurice Richard, Mtl.	Milt Schmidt, Bos.
1946	Max Bentley, Chi.	Gaye Stewart, Tor.
1945	Elmer Lach, Mtl.	Maurice Richard, Mtl.
1944	Babe Pratt, Tor.	Bill Cowley, Bos.
1943	Bill Cowley, Bos.	Doug Bentley, Chi.
1942	Tom Anderson, Bro.	Syl Apps Sr., Tor.
1941	Bill Cowley, Bos.	Dit Clapper, Bos.
1940	Ebbie Goodfellow, Det.	Syl Apps Sr., Tor.
1939	Toe Blake, Mtl.	Syl Apps Sr., Tor.
1938	Eddie Shore, Bos.	Paul Thompson, Chi.
1937	Babe Siebert, Mtl.	Lionel Conacher, Mtl.M
1936	Eddie Shore, Bos.	Hooley Smith, Mtl.M
1935	Eddie Shore, Bos.	Charlie Conacher, Tor.
1934	Aurel Joliat, Mtl.	Lionel Conacher, Chi.
1933	Eddie Shore, Bos.	Bill Cook, NYR
1932	Howie Morenz, Mtl.	Ching Johnson, NYR
1931	Howie Morenz, Mtl.	Eddie Shore, Bos.
1930	Nels Stewart, Mtl.M.	Lionel Hitchman, Bos.
1929	Roy Worters, NYA	Ace Bailey, Tor.
1928	Howie Morenz, Mtl.	Roy Worters, Pit.
1927	Herb Gardiner, Mtl.	Bill Cook, NYR
1926	Nels Stewart, Mtl.M.	Sprague Cleghorn, Bos.
1925	Billy Burch, Ham.	Howie Morenz, Mtl.
1924	Frank Nighbor, Ott.	Sprague Cleghorn, Mtl.

1998-99 NHL Player of the Week Award Winners

Player of the Week

Week	Player	Team
Oct. 12-18	Brendan Shanahan	Detroit
Oct. 19-25	Mats Sundin	Toronto
Oct. 26-Nov. 1	Arturs Irbe	Carolina
Nov. 2-8	Mark Recchi	Montreal
Nov. 9-15	Jimmy Waite	Phoenix
Nov. 16-22	Paul Kariya	Anaheim
Nov. 23-29	John LeClair	Philadelphia
Nov. 30-Dec. 6	Dominik Hasek	Buffalo
Dec. 7-13	Dominik Hasek	Buffalo
Dec. 14-20	Ray Bourque	Boston
Dec. 21-27	Mike Modano	Dallas
Dec. 28-Jan. 3	Jeff Hackett	Montreal
Jan. 4-10	Ron Tugnutt	Ottawa
Jan. 11-17	Eric Lindros	Philadelphia
Jan. 18-24	Joe Sakic	Colorado
Jan. 25-31	Jaromir Jagr	Pittsburgh
Feb. 1-7	Peter Bondra	Washington
Feb. 8-14	Mike Vernon	San Jose
Feb. 15-21	Miroslav Satan	Buffalo
Feb. 22-28	Teemu Selanne	Anaheim
Mar. 1-7	Peter Forsberg	Colorado
Mar. 8-14	Steve Shields	San Jose
Mar. 15-21	Miroslav Satan	Buffalo
Mar. 22-28	Patrick Roy	Colorado
Mar. 29-Apr. 4	Sergei Berezin	Toronto
Apr. 5-11	Dominik Hasek	Buffalo
Apr. 12-18	Wayne Gretzky	New York

1998-99 Player of the Month

Month	Player	Team
October	Artus Irbe	Carolina
November	Eric Lindros	Philadelphia
December	Dominik Hasek	Buffalo
January	Patrik Roy	Colorado
February	Teemu Selanne	Anaheim
March	Jaromir Jagr	Pittsburgh
April	Bryon Dafoe	Boston

1998-99 Rookie of the Month

Month	Player	Team
October	Mark Parrish	Florida
November	Ollie Jokinen	Los Angelas
December	Vadim Sharifijanov	New Jersey
January	Jan Hrdina	Pittsburgh
February	Vincent Lecavalier	Tampa Bay
March	Marian Hossa	Ottawa
April	Jean-Pierre Dumont	Chicago

LADY BYNG TROPHY

	Winner	Runner-up
1999	Wayne Gretzky, NYR.	Nicklas Lidstrom, Det.
1998	Ron Francis, Pit.	Teemu Selanne, Ana.
1997	Paul Kariya, Ana.	Teemu Selanne, Ana.
1996	Paul Kariya, Ana.	Adam Oates, Bos.
1995	Ron Francis, Pit.	Adam Oates, Bos.
1994	Wayne Gretzky, L.A.	Adam Oates, Bos.
1993	Pierre Turgeon, NYI	Adam Oates, Bos.
1992	Wayne Gretzky, L.A.	Joe Sakic, Que.
1991	Wayne Gretzky, L.A.	Brett Hull, St.L.
1990	Brett Hull, St.L.	Wayne Gretzky, L.A.
1989	Joe Mullen, Cgy.	Wayne Gretzky, L.A.
1988	Mats Naslund, Mtl.	Wayne Gretzky, Edm.
1987	Joe Mullen, Cgy.	Wayne Gretzky, Edm.
1986	Mike Bossy, NYI	Jari Kurri, Edm.
1985	Jari Kurri, Edm.	Joe Mullen, St.L.
1984	Mike Bossy, NYI	Rick Middleton, Bos.
1983	Mike Bossy, NYI	Rick Middleton, Bos.
1982	Rick Middleton, Bos.	Mike Bossy, NYI
1981	Rick Kehoe, Pit.	Wayne Gretzky, Edm.
1980	Wayne Gretzky, Edm.	Marcel Dionne, L.A.
1979	Bob MacMillan, Atl.	Marcel Dionne, L.A.
1978	Butch Goring, L.A.	Peter McNab, Bos.
1977	Marcel Dionne, L.A.	Jean Ratelle, Bos.
1976	Jean Ratelle, NYR-Bos.	Jean Pronovost, Pit.
1975	Marcel Dionne, Det.	John Bucyk, Bos.
1974	John Bucyk, Bos.	Lowell MacDonald, Pit.
1973	Gilbert Perreault, Buf.	Jean Ratelle, NYR
1972	Jean Ratelle, NYR	John Bucyk, Bos.
1971	John Bucyk, Bos.	Dave Keon, Tor.
1970	Phil Goyette, St.L.	John Bucyk, Bos.
1969	Alex Delvecchio, Det.	Ted Hampson, Oak.
1968	Stan Mikita, Chi.	John Bucyk, Bos.
1967	Stan Mikita, Chi.	Dave Keon, Tor.
1966	Alex Delvecchio, Det.	Bobby Rousseau, Mtl.
1965	Bobby Hull, Chi.	Alex Delvecchio, Det.
1964	Ken Wharram, Chi.	Dave Keon, Tor.
1963	Dave Keon, Tor.	Camille Henry, NYR
1962	Dave Keon, Tor.	Claude Provost, Mtl.
1961	Red Kelly, Tor.	Norm Ullman, Det.
1960	Don McKenney, Bos.	Andy Hebenton, NYR
1959	Alex Delvecchio, Det.	Andy Hebenton, NYR
1958	Camille Henry, NYR	Don Marshall, Mtl.
1957	Andy Hebenton, NYR	Earl Reibel, Det.
1956	Earl Reibel, Det.	Floyd Curry, Mtl.
1955	Sid Smith, Tor.	Danny Lewicki, NYR
1954	Red Kelly, Det.	Don Raleigh, NYR
1953	Red Kelly, Det.	Wally Hergesheimer, NYR
1952	Sid Smith, Tor.	Red Kelly, Det.
1951	Red Kelly, Det.	Woody Dumart, Bos.
1950	Edgar Laprade, NYR	Red Kelly, Det.
1949	Bill Quackenbush, Det.	Harry Watson, Tor.
1948	Buddy O'Connor, NYR	Syl Apps Sr., Tor
1947	Bobby Bauer, Bos.	Syl Apps Sr., Tor.
1946	Toe Blake, Mtl.	Clint Smith, Chi.
1945	Bill Mosienko, Chi.	Syd Howe, Det.
1944	Clint Smith, Chi.	Herb Cain, Bos.
1943	Max Bentley, Chi.	Buddy O'Connor, Mtl.
1942	Syl Apps Sr., Tor.	Gordie Drillon, Tor.
1941	Bobby Bauer, Bos.	Gordie Drillon, Tor
1940	Bobby Bauer, Bos.	Clint Smith, NYR
1939	Clint Smith, NYR	Marty Barry, Det.
1938	Gordie Drillon, Tor.	Clint Smith, NYR
1937	Marty Barry, Det.	Gordie Drillon, Tor.
1936	Doc Romnes, Chi.	Sweeney Schriner, NYA
1935	Frank Boucher, NYR	Russ Blinco, Mtl.M
1934	Frank Boucher, NYR	Joe Primeau, Tor.
1933	Frank Boucher, NYR	Joe Primeau, Tor.
1932	Joe Primeau, Tor.	Frank Boucher, NYR
1931	Frank Boucher, NYR	Normie Himes, NYA
1930	Frank Boucher, NYR	Normie Himes, NYA
1929	Frank Boucher, NYR	Harry Darragh, Pit.
1928	Frank Boucher, NYR	George Hay, Det.
1927	Billy Burch, NYA	Dick Irvin, Chi.
1926	Frank Nighbor, Ott.	Billy Burch, NYA
1925	Frank Nighbor, Ott.	none

FRANK J. SELKE TROPHY WINNERS

	Winner	Runner-up
1999	Jere Lehtinen, Dal.	Magnus Arvedson, Ott.
1998	Jere Lehtinen, Dal.	Michael Peca, Buf.
1997	Michael Peca, Buf.	Peter Forsberg, Col.
1996	Sergei Fedorov, Det.	Ron Francis, Pit.
1995	Ron Francis, Pit.	Esa Tikkanen, St.L.
1994	Sergei Fedorov, Det.	Doug Gilmour, Tor.
1993	Doug Gilmour, Tor.	Dave Poulin, Bos.
1992	Guy Carbonneau, Mtl.	Sergei Fedorov, Det.
1991	Dirk Graham, Chi.	Esa Tikkanen, Edm.
1990	Rick Meagher, St.L.	Guy Carbonneau, Mtl.
1989	Guy Carbonneau, Mtl.	Esa Tikkanen, Edm.
1988	Guy Carbonneau, Mtl.	Steve Kasper, Bos.
1987	Dave Poulin, Phi.	Guy Carbonneau, Mtl.
1986	Troy Murray, Chi.	Ron Sutter, Phi.
1985	Craig Ramsay, Buf.	Doug Jarvis, Wsh.
1984	Doug Jarvis, Wsh.	Bryan Trottier, NYI
1983	Bobby Clarke, Phi.	Jari Kurri, Edm.
1982	Steve Kasper, Bos.	Bob Gainey, Mtl.
1981	Bob Gainey, Mtl.	Craig Ramsay, Buf.
1980	Bob Gainey, Mtl.	Craig Ramsay, Buf.
1979	Bob Gainey, Mtl.	Don Marcotte, Bos.
1978	Bob Gainey, Mtl.	Craig Ramsay, Buf.

VEZINA TROPHY

	Winner	Runner-up
1999	Dominik Hasek, Buf.	Curtis Joseph, Tor.
1998	Dominik Hasek, Buf.	Martin Brodeur, N.J.
1997	Dominik Hasek, Buf.	Martin Brodeur, N.J.
1996	Jim Carey, Wsh.	Chris Osgood, Det.
1995	Dominik Hasek, Buf.	Ed Belfour, Chi.
1994	Dominik Hasek, Buf.	John Vanbiesbrouck, Fla.
1993	Ed Belfour, Chi.	Tom Barrasso, Pit.
1992	Patrick Roy, Mtl.	Kirk McLean, Van.
1991	Ed Belfour, Chi.	Patrick Roy, Mtl.
1990	Patrick Roy, Mtl.	Daren Puppa, Buf.
1989	Patrick Roy, Mtl.	Mike Vernon, Cgy.
1988	Grant Fuhr, Edm.	Tom Barrasso, Buf.
1987	Ron Hextall, Phi.	Mike Liut, Hfd.
1986	John Vanbiesbrouck, NYR	Bob Froese, Phi.
1985	Pelle Lindbergh, Phi.	Tom Barrasso, Buf.
1984	Tom Barrasso, Buf.	Rejean Lemelin, Cgy.
1983	Pete Peeters, Bos.	Roland Melanson, NYI
1982	Billy Smith, NYI	Grant Fuhr, Edm.
1981	Richard Sevigny, Mtl.	Pete Peeters, Phi.
	Denis Herron, Mtl.	Rick St. Croix, Phi.
	Michel Larocque, Mtl.	
1980	Bob Sauve, Buf.	Gerry Cheevers, Bos.
	Don Edwards, Buf.	Gilles Gilbert, Bos.
1979	Ken Dryden, Mtl.	Glenn Resch, NYI
	Michel Larocque, Mtl.	Billy Smith, NYI
1978	Ken Dryden, Mtl.	Bernie Parent, Phi.
	Michel Larocque	Wayne Stephenson, Phi.
1977	Ken Dryden, Mtl.	Glenn Resch, NYI
	Michel Larocque, Mtl.	Billy Smith, NYI
1976	Ken Dryden, Mtl.	Glenn Resch, NYI
		Billy Smith, NYI
1975	Bernie Parent, Phi.	Rogie Vachon, L.A.
		Gary Edwards, L.A.
1974	Bernie Parent, Phi. (tie)	Gilles Gilbert, Bos.
	Tony Esposito, Chi. (tie)	
1973	Ken Dryden, Mtl.	Ed Giacomin, NYR
		Gilles Villemure, NYR
1972	Tony Esposito, Chi.	Cesare Maniago, Min.
	Gary Smith, Chi.	Gump Worsley, Min.
1971	Ed Giacomin, NYR	Tony Esposito, Chi.
	Gilles Villemure, NYR	
1970	Tony Esposito, Chi.	Jacques Plante, St.L.
		Ernie Wakely, St.L.
1969	Jacques Plante, St.L.	Ed Giacomin, NYR
	Glenn Hall, St.L.	
1968	Gump Worsley, Mtl.	Johnny Bower, Tor.
	Rogie Vachon, Mtl.	Bruce Gamble, Tor.
1967	Glenn Hall, Chi.	Charlie Hodge, Mtl.
	Denis Dejordy, Chi.	
1966	Gump Worsley, Mtl.	Glenn Hall, Chi.
	Charlie Hodge, Mtl	
1965	Terry Sawchuk, Tor.	Roger Crozier, Det.
	Johnny Bower, Tor.	
1964	Charlie Hodge, Mtl.	Glenn Hall, Chi.
1963	Glenn Hall, Chi.	Johnny Bower, Tor.
		Don Simmons, Tor.
1962	Jacques Plante, Mtl.	Johnny Bower, Tor.
1961	Johnny Bower, Tor	Glenn Hall, Chi.
1960	Jacques Plante, Mtl.	Glenn Hall, Chi.
1959	Jacques Plante, Mtl.	Johnny Bower, Tor.
		Ed Chadwick, Tor.
1958	Jacques Plante, Mtl.	Gump Worsley, NYR
		Marcel Paille, NYR
1957	Jacques Plante, Mtl.	Glenn Hall, Det.
1956	Jacques Plante, Mtl.	Glenn Hall, Det.
1955	Terry Sawchuk, Det.	Harry Lumley, Tor.
1954	Harry Lumley, Tor.	Terry Sawchuk, Det.
1953	Terry Sawchuk, Det.	Gerry McNeil, Mtl.
1952	Terry Sawchuk, Det.	Al Rollins, Tor.
1951	Al Rollins, Tor.	Terry Sawchuk, Det.
1950	Bill Durnan, Mtl.	Harry Lumley, Det.
1949	Bill Durnan, Mtl.	Harry Lumley, Det.
1948	Turk Broda, Tor.	Harry Lumley, Det.
1947	Bill Durnan, Mtl.	Turk Broda, Tor.
1946	Bill Durnan, Mtl.	Frank Brimsek, Bos.
1945	Bill Durnan, Mtl.	Frank McCool, Tor. (tie)
		Harry Lumley, Det. (tie)
1944	Bill Durnan, Mtl.	Paul Bibeault, Tor.
1943	Johnny Mowers, Det.	Turk Broda, Tor.
1942	Frank Brimsek, Bos.	Turk Broda, Tor.
1941	Turk Broda, Tor.	Frank Brimsek, Bos. (tie)
		Johnny Mowers, Det. (tie)
1940	Dave Kerr, NYR	Frank Brimsek, Bos.
1939	Frank Brimsek, Bos.	Dave Kerr, NYR
1938	Tiny Thompson, Bos.	Dave Kerr, NYR
1937	Norman Smith, Det.	Dave Kerr, NYR
1936	Tiny Thompson, Bos.	Mike Karakas, Chi.
1935	Lorne Chabot, Chi.	Alex Connell, Mtl.M
1934	Charlie Gardiner, Chi.	Wilf Cude, Det.
1933	Tiny Thompson, Bos.	John Ross Roach, Det.
1932	Charlie Gardiner, Chi.	Alex Connell, Det.
1931	Roy Worters, NYA	Charlie Gardiner, Chi.
1930	Tiny Thompson, Bos.	Charlie Gardiner, Chi.
1929	George Hainsworth, Mtl.	Tiny Thompson, Bos.
1928	George Hainsworth, Mtl.	Alex Connell, Ott.
1927	George Hainsworth, Mtl.	Clint Benedict, Mtl.M

BILL MASTERTON TROPHY WINNERS

1999	John Cullen	Tampa Bay
1998	Jamie McLennan	St. Louis
1997	Tony Granato	San Jose
1996	Gary Roberts	Calgary
1995	Pat LaFontaine	Buffalo
1994	Cam Neely	Boston
1993	Mario Lemieux	Pittsburgh
1992	Mark Fitzpatrick	NY Islanders
1991	Dave Taylor	Los Angeles
1990	Gord Kluzak	Boston
1989	Tim Kerr	Philadelphia
1988	Bob Bourne	Los Angeles
1987	Doug Jarvis	Hartford
1986	Charlie Simmer	Boston
1985	Anders Hedberg	NY Rangers
1984	Brad Park	Detroit
1983	Lanny McDonald	Calgary
1982	Glenn Resch	Colorado
1981	Blake Dunlop	St. Louis
1980	Al MacAdam	Minnesota
1979	Serge Savard	Montreal
1978	Butch Goring	Los Angeles
1977	Ed Westfall	NY Islanders
1976	Rod Gilbert	NY Rangers
1975	Don Luce	Buffalo
1974	Henri Richard	Montreal
1973	Lowell MacDonald	Pittsburgh
1972	Bobby Clarke	Philadelphia
1971	Jean Ratelle	NY Rangers
1970	Pit Martin	Chicago
1969	Ted Hampson	Oakland

CALDER MEMORIAL TROPHY WINNERS

	Winner	Runner-up
1999	Chris Drury, Col.	Marian Hossa, Ott.
1998	Sergei Samsonov, Bos.	Mattias Ohlund, Van.
1997	Bryan Berard, NYI	Jarome Iginla, Cgy.
1996	Daniel Alfredsson, Ott.	Eric Daze, Chi.
1995	Peter Forsberg, Que.	Jim Carey, Wsh.
1994	Martin Brodeur, N.J.	Jason Arnott, Edm.
1993	Teemu Selanne, Wpg.	Joe Juneau, Bos.
1992	Pavel Bure, Van.	Nicklas Lidstrom, Det
1991	Ed Belfour, Chi.	Sergei Fedorov, Det.
1990	Sergei Makarov, Cgy.	Mike Modano, Min.
1989	Brian Leetch, NYR	Trevor Linden, Van.
1988	Joe Nieuwendyk, Cgy.	Ray Sheppard, Buf.
1987	Luc Robitaille, L.A.	Ron Hextall, Phi.
1986	Gary Suter, Cgy.	Wendel Clark, Tor.
1985	Mario Lemieux, Pit.	Chris Chelios, Mtl.
1984	Tom Barrasso, Buf.	Steve Yzerman, Det.
1983	Steve Larmer, Chi	Phil Housley, Buf.
1982	Dale Hawerchuk, Wpg.	Barry Pederson, Bos.
1981	Peter Stastny, Que.	Larry Murphy, L.A.
1980	Ray Bourque, Bos.	Mike Foligno, Det.
1979	Bobby Smith, Min	Ryan Walter, Wsh.
1978	Mike Bossy, NYI	Barry Beck, Col.
1977	Willi Plett, Atl.	Don Murdoch, NYR
1976	Bryan Trottier, NYI	Glenn Resch, NYI
1975	Eric Vail, Atl.	Pierre Larouche, Pit.
1974	Denis Potvin, NYI	Tom Lysiak, Atl.
1973	Steve Vickers, NYR	Bill Barber, Phi.
1972	Ken Dryden, Mtl.	Rick Martin, Buf.
1971	Gilbert Perreault, Buf.	Jude Drouin, Min.
1970	Tony Esposito, Chi.	Bill Fairbairn, NYR
1969	Danny Grant, Min.	Norm Ferguson, Oak.
1968	Derek Sanderson, Bos.	Jacques Lemaire, Mtl.
1967	Bobby Orr, Bos.	Ed Van Impe, Chi.
1966	Brit Selby, Tor.	Bert Marshall, Det.
1965	Roger Crozier, Det.	Ron Ellis, Tor.
1964	Jacques Laperriere, Mtl.	John Ferguson, Mtl.
1963	Kent Douglas, Tor.	Doug Barkley, Det.
1962	Bobby Rousseau, Mtl.	Cliff Pennington, Bos.
1961	Dave Keon, Tor.	Bob Nevin, Tor.
1960	Bill Hay, Chi.	Murray Oliver, Det.
1959	Ralph Backstrom, Mtl.	Carl Brewer, Tor.
1958	Frank Mahovlich, Tor.	Bobby Hull, Chi.
1957	Larry Regan, Bos.	Ed Chadwick, Tor.
1956	Glenn Hall, Det.	Andy Hebenton, NYR
1955	Ed Litzenberger, Chi.	Don McKenney, Bos.
1954	Camille Henry, NYR	Earl Reibel, Det.
1953	Gump Worsley, NYR	Gord Hannigan, Tor.
1952	Bernie Geoffrion, Mtl.	Hy Buller, NYR
1951	Terry Sawchuk, Det.	Al Rollins, Tor.
1950	Jack Gelineau, Bos.	Phil Maloney, Bos.
1949	Pentti Lund, NYR	Allan Stanley, NYR
1948	Jim McFadden, Det.	Pete Babando, Bos.
1947	Howie Meeker, Tor.	Jimmy Conacher, Det.
1946	Edgar Laprade, NYR	George Gee, Chi.
1945	Frank McCool, Tor.	Ken Smith, Bos.
1944	Gus Bodnar, Tor.	Bill Durnan, Mtl.
1943	Gaye Stewart, Tor.	Glen Harmon, Mtl.
1942	Grant Warwick, NYR	Buddy O'Connor, Mtl.
1941	Johnny Quilty, Mtl.	Johnny Mowers, Det.
1940	Kilby MacDonald, NYR	Wally Stanowski, Tor.
1939	Frank Brimsek, Bos.	Roy Conacher, Bos.
1938	Cully Dahlstrom, Chi.	Murph Chamberlain, Tor.
1937	Syl Apps Sr., Tor.	Gordie Drillon, Tor.
1936	Mike Karakas, Chi.	Bucko McDonald, Det.
1935	Sweeney Schriner, NYA	Bert Connolly, NYR
1934	Russ Blinko, Mtl.M.	
1933	Carl Voss, Det.	

CONN SMYTHE TROPHY WINNERS

1999	Joe Nieuwendyk	Dallas
1998	Steve Yzerman	Detroit
1997	Mike Vernon	Detroit
1996	Joe Sakic	Colorado
1995	Claude Lemieux	New Jersey
1994	Brian Leetch	NY Rangers
1993	Patrick Roy	Montreal
1992	Mario Lemieux	Pittsburgh
1991	Mario Lemieux	Pittsburgh
1990	Bill Ranford	Edmonton
1989	Al MacInnis	Calgary
1988	Wayne Gretzky	Edmonton
1987	Ron Hextall	Philadelphia
1986	Patrick Roy	Montreal
1985	Wayne Gretzky	Edmonton
1984	Mark Messier	Edmonton
1983	Billy Smith	NY Islanders
1982	Mike Bossy	NY Islanders
1981	Butch Goring	NY Islanders
1980	Bryan Trottier	NY Islanders
1979	Bob Gainey	Montreal
1978	Larry Robinson	Montreal
1977	Guy Lafleur	Montreal
1976	Reggie Leach	Philadelphia
1975	Bernie Parent	Philadelphia
1974	Bernie Parent	Philadelphia
1973	Yvan Cournoyer	Montreal
1972	Bobby Orr	Boston
1971	Ken Dryden	Montreal
1970	Bobby Orr	Boston
1969	Serge Savard	Montreal
1968	Glenn Hall	St. Louis
1967	Dave Keon	Toronto
1966	Roger Crozier	Detroit
1965	Jean Béliveau	Montreal

JAMES NORRIS TROPHY WINNERS

	Winner	Runner-up
1999	Al MacInnis, St.L.	Nicklas Lidstrom, Det.
1998	Rob Blake, L.A.	Nicklas Lidstrom, Det.
1997	Brian Leetch, NYR	V. Konstantinov, Det.
1996	Chris Chelios, Chi.	Ray Bourque, Bos.
1995	Paul Coffey, Det.	Chris Chelios, Chi.
1994	Ray Bourque, Bos.	Scott Stevens, N.J.
1993	Chris Chelios, Chi.	Ray Bourque, Bos.
1992	Brian Leetch, NYR	Ray Bourque, Bos.
1991	Ray Bourque, Bos.	Al MacInnis, Cgy.
1990	Ray Bourque, Bos.	Al MacInnis, Cgy.
1989	Chris Chelios, Mtl	Paul Coffey, Pit.
1988	Ray Bourque, Bos.	Scott Stevens, Wsh.
1987	Ray Bourque, Bos.	Mark Howe, Phi.
1986	Paul Coffey, Edm.	Mark Howe, Phi.
1985	Paul Coffey, Edm.	Ray Bourque, Bos.
1984	Rod Langway, Wsh.	Paul Coffey, Edm.
1983	Rod Langway, Wsh.	Mark Howe, Phi.
1982	Doug Wilson, Chi.	Ray Bourque, Bos.
1981	Randy Carlyle, Pit.	Denis Potvin, NYI
1980	Larry Robinson, Mtl	Borje Salming, Tor.
1979	Denis Potvin, NYI	Larry Robinson, Mtl.
1978	Denis Potvin, NYI	Brad Park, Bos.
1977	Larry Robinson, Mtl.	Borje Salming, Tor.
1976	Denis Potvin, NYI	Brad Park, NYR-Bos.
1975	Bobby Orr, Bos.	Denis Potvin, NYI
1974	Bobby Orr, Bos.	Brad Park, NYR
1973	Bobby Orr, Bos.	Guy Lapointe, Mtl.
1972	Bobby Orr, Bos.	Brad Park, NYR
1971	Bobby Orr, Bos.	Brad Park, NYR
1970	Bobby Orr, Bos.	Brad Park, NYR
1969	Bobby Orr, Bos.	Tim Horton, Tor.
1968	Bobby Orr, Bos.	J.C. Tremblay, Mtl
1967	Harry Howell, NYR	Pierre Pilote, Chi.
1966	Jacques Laperriere, Mtl.	Pierre Pilote, Chi.
1965	Pierre Pilote, Chi.	Jacques Laperriere, Mtl.
1964	Pierre Pilote, Chi.	Tim Horton, Tor.
1963	Pierre Pilote, Chi.	Carl Brewer, Tor.
1962	Doug Harvey, NYR	Pierre Pilote, Chi.
1961	Doug Harvey, Mtl.	Marcel Pronovost, Det.
1960	Doug Harvey, Mtl.	Allan Stanley, Tor.
1959	Tom Johnson, Mtl.	Bill Gadsby, NYR
1958	Doug Harvey, Mtl.	Bill Gadsby, NYR
1957	Doug Harvey, Mtl.	Red Kelly, Det.
1956	Doug Harvey, Mtl.	Bill Gadsby, NYR
1955	Doug Harvey, Mtl.	Red Kelly, Det.
1954	Red Kelly, Det.	Doug Harvey, Mtl.

KING CLANCY MEMORIAL TROPHY WINNERS

1999	Rob Ray	Buffalo
1998	Kelly Chase	St. Louis
1997	Trevor Linden	Vancouver
1996	Kris King	Winnipeg
1995	Joe Nieuwendyk	Calgary
1994	Adam Graves	NY Rangers
1993	Dave Poulin	Boston
1992	Ray Bourque	Boston
1991	Dave Taylor	Los Angeles
1990	Kevin Lowe	Edmonton
1989	Bryan Trottier	NY Islanders
1988	Lanny McDonald	Calgary

LESTER PATRICK TROPHY WINNERS

1999	Harry Sinden	
	1998 U.S. Olympic Women's Hockey Team	
1998	Peter Karmanos	
	Neal Broten	
	John Mayasich	
	Max McNab	
1997	Seymour H. Knox III	
	Bill Cleary	
	Pat LaFontaine	
1996	George Gund	
	Ken Morrow	
	Milt Schmidt	
1995	Joe Mullen	
	Brian Mullen	
	Bob Fleming	
1994	Wayne Gretzky	
	Robert Ridder	
1993	*Frank Boucher	
	*Mervyn (Red) Dutton	
	Bruce McNall	
	Gil Stein	
1992	Al Arbour	
	Art Berglund	
	Lou Lamoriello	
1991	Rod Gilbert	
	Mike Ilitch	
1990	Len Ceglarski	
1989	Dan Kelly	
	Lou Nanne	
	*Lynn Patrick	
	Bud Poile	
1988	Keith Allen	
	Fred Cusick	
	Bob Johnson	
1987	*Hobey Baker	
	Frank Mathers	
1986	John MacInnes	
	Jack Riley	
1985	Jack Butterfield	
	Arthur M. Wirtz	
1984	John A. Ziegler Jr.	
	*Arthur Howie Ross	
1983	Bill Torrey	
1982	Emile P. Francis	
1981	Charles M. Schulz	
1980	Bobby Clarke	
	Edward M. Snider	
	Frederick A. Shero	
	1980 U.S. Olympic Hockey Team	
1979	Bobby Orr	
1978	Phil Esposito	
	Tom Fitzgerald	
	William T. Tutt	
	William W. Wirtz	
1977	John P. Bucyk	
	Murray A. Armstrong	
	John Mariucci	
1976	Stanley Mikita	
	George A. Leader	
	Bruce A. Norris	
1975	Donald M. Clark	
	William L. Chadwick	
	Thomas N. Ivan	
1974	Alex Delvecchio	
	Murray Murdoch	
	*Weston W. Adams, Sr.	
	*Charles L. Crovat	
1973	Walter L. Bush, Jr.	
1972	Clarence S. Campbell	
	John A. "Snooks" Kelly	
	Ralph "Cooney" Weiland	
	*James D. Norris	
1971	William M. Jennings	
	*John B. Sollenberger	
	*Terrance G. Sawchuk	
1970	Edward W. Shore	
	*James C. V. Hendy	
1969	Robert M. Hull	
	*Edward J. Jeremiah	
1968	Thomas F. Lockhart	
	*Walter A. Brown	
	*Gen. John R. Kilpatrick	
1967	Gordon Howe	
	*Charles F. Adams	
	*James Norris, Sr.	
1966	J.J. "Jack" Adams	
	* awarded posthumously	

MAURICE "ROCKET" RICHARD TROPHY WINNER

1999	Teemu Selanne	Anaheim

BUD LIGHT PLUS-MINUS AWARD WINNERS

1999	John LeClair	Philadelphia
1998	Chris Pronger	St. Louis
1997	John LeClair	Philadelphia

WILLIAM M. JENNINGS TROPHY WINNERS

	Winner	Runner-up
1999	Ed Belfour, Dal.	Dominik Hasek, Buf.
	Roman Turek	
1998	Martin Brodeur, N.J.	Ed Belfour, Dal.
1997	Martin Brodeur, N.J.	Chris Osgood, Det.
	Mike Dunham	Mike Vernon
1996	Chris Osgood, Det.	Martin Brodeur, N.J.
	Mike Vernon	
1995	Ed Belfour, Chi.	Mike Vernon, Det.
		Chris Osgood
1994	Dominik Hasek, Buf.	Martin Brodeur, N.J.
	Grant Fuhr	Chris Terreri
1993	Ed Belfour, Chi.	Felix Potvin, Tor.
		Grant Fuhr
1992	Patrick Roy, Mtl.	Ed Belfour, Chi.
1991	Ed Belfour, Chi.	Patrick Roy, Mtl.
1990	Andy Moog, Bos.	Patrick Roy, Mtl.
	Rejean Lemelin	Brian Hayward
1989	Patrick Roy, Mtl.	Mike Vernon, Cgy.
	Brian Hayward	Rick Wamsley
1988	Patrick Roy, Mtl.	Clint Malarchuk, Wsh.
	Brian Hayward	Pete Peeters
1987	Patrick Roy, Mtl.	Ron Hextall, Phi.
	Brian Hayward	
1986	Bob Froese, Phi.	Al Jensen, Wsh.
	Darren Jensen	Pete Peeters
1985	Tom Barrasso, Buf.	Pat Riggin, Wsh.
	Bob Sauve	
1984	Al Jensen, Wsh.	Tom Barrasso, Buf.
	Pat Riggin	Bob Sauve
1983	Rollie Melanson, NYI	Pete Peeters, Bos.
	Billy Smith	
1982	Rick Wamsley, Mtl.	Billy Smith, NYI
	Denis Herron	Rollie Melanson

LESTER B. PEARSON AWARD WINNERS

1999	Jaromir Jagr	Pittsburgh
1998	Dominik Hasek	Buffalo
1997	Dominik Hasek	Buffalo
1996	Mario Lemieux	Pittsburgh
1995	Eric Lindros	Philadelphia
1994	Sergei Fedorov	Detroit
1993	Mario Lemieux	Pittsburgh
1992	Mark Messier	NY Rangers
1991	Brett Hull	St. Louis
1990	Mark Messier	Edmonton
1989	Steve Yzerman	Detroit
1988	Mario Lemieux	Pittsburgh
1987	Wayne Gretzky	Edmonton
1986	Mario Lemieux	Pittsburgh
1985	Wayne Gretzky	Edmonton
1984	Wayne Gretzky	Edmonton
1983	Wayne Gretzky	Edmonton
1982	Wayne Gretzky	Edmonton
1981	Mike Liut	St. Louis
1980	Marcel Dionne	Los Angeles
1979	Marcel Dionne	Los Angeles
1978	Guy Lafleur	Montreal
1977	Guy Lafleur	Montreal
1976	Guy Lafleur	Montreal
1975	Bobby Orr	Boston
1974	Phil Esposito	Boston
1973	Bobby Clarke	Philadelphia
1972	Jean Ratelle	NY Rangers
1971	Phil Esposito	Boston

JACK ADAMS AWARD WINNERS

	Winner	Runner-up
1999	Jacques Martin, Ott.	Pat Quinn, Van.
1998	Pat Burns, Bos.	Larry Robinson, L.A.
1997	Ted Nolan, Buf.	Ken Hitchcock, Dal.
1996	Scotty Bowman, Det.	Doug MacLean, Fla.
1995	Marc Crawford, Que.	Scotty Bowman, Det.
1994	Jacques Lemaire, N.J.	Kevin Constantine, S.J.
1993	Pat Burns, Tor.	Brian Sutter, Bos.
1992	Pat Quinn, Van.	Roger Neilson, NYR
1991	Brian Sutter, St.L.	Tom Webster, L.A.
1990	Bob Murdoch, Wpg.	Mike Milbury, Bos.
1989	Pat Burns, Mtl.	Bob McCammon, Van.
1988	Jacques Demers, Det.	Terry Crisp, Cgy.
1987	Jacques Demers, Det.	Jack Evans, Hfd.
1986	Glen Sather, Edm.	Jacques Demers, St.L.
1985	Mike Keenan, Phi.	Barry Long, Wpg.
1984	Bryan Murray, Wsh.	Scotty Bowman, Buf.
1983	Orval Tessier, Chi.	
1982	Tom Watt, Wpg.	
1981	Red Berenson, St.L.	Bob Berry, L.A.
1980	Pat Quinn, Phi.	
1979	Al Arbour, NYI	Fred Shero, NYR
1978	Bobby Kromm, Det.	Don Cherry, Bos.
1977	Scotty Bowman, Mtl.	Tom McVie, Wsh.
1976	Don Cherry, Bos.	
1975	Bob Pulford, L.A.	
1974	Fred Shero, Phi.	

NHL Amateur and Entry Draft

A busy session of wheeling and dealing on draft day saw the expansion Atlanta Thrashers wind up with the top pick. They selected Patrik Stefan, who had spent the previous two seasons with the Long Beach Ice Dogs of the IHL. Stefan was seen as the most physically mature of the top players available in 1999

History

Year	Site	Date	Total Players Drafted
1963	Queen Elizabeth Hotel	June 5	21
1964	Queen Elizabeth Hotel	June 11	24
1965	Queen Elizabeth Hotel	April 27	11
1966	Mount Royal Hotel	April 25	24
1967	Queen Elizabeth Hotel	June 7	18
1968	Queen Elizabeth Hotel	June 13	24
1969	Queen Elizabeth Hotel	June 12	84
1970	Queen Elizabeth Hotel	June 11	115
1971	Queen Elizabeth Hotel	June 10	117
1972	Queen Elizabeth Hotel	June 8	152
1973	Mount Royal Hotel	May 15	168
1974	NHL Montreal Office	May 28	247
1975	NHL Montreal Office	June 3	217
1976	NHL Montreal Office	June 1	135
1977	NHL Montreal Office	June 14	185
1978	Queen Elizabeth Hotel	June 15	234
1979	Queen Elizabeth Hotel	August 9	126
1980	Montreal Forum	June 11	210
1981	Montreal Forum	June 10	211
1982	Montreal Forum	June 9	252
1983	Montreal Forum	June 8	242
1984	Montreal Forum	June 9	250
1985	Toronto Convention Centre	June 15	252
1986	Montreal Forum	June 21	252
1987	Joe Louis Sports Arena	June 13	252
1988	Montreal Forum	June 11	252
1989	Metropolitan Sports Center	June 17	252
1990	B. C. Place	June 16	250
1991	Memorial Auditorium	June 9	264
1992	Montreal Forum	June 20	264
1993	Colisée de Québec	June 26	286
1994	Hartford Civic Center	June 28-29	286
1995	Edmonton Coliseum	July 8	234
1996	Kiel Center	June 22	241
1997	Civic Arena	June 21	246
1998	Marine Midland Arena	June 27	258
1999	Fleet Center	June 26	272

* The NHL Amateur Draft became the NHL Entry Draft in 1979

First Selections

Year	Player	Pos	Drafted By	Drafted From	Age
1969	Rejean Houle	LW	Montreal	Montreal Jr. Canadiens	19.8
1970	Gilbert Perreault	C	Buffalo	Montreal Jr. Canadiens	19.7
1971	Guy Lafleur	RW	Montreal	Quebec Remparts	19.9
1972	Billy Harris	RW	NY Islanders	Toronto Marlboros	20.4
1973	Denis Potvin	D	NY Islanders	Ottawa 67's	19.7
1974	Greg Joly	D	Washington	Regina Pats	20.0
1975	Mel Bridgman	C	Philadelphia	Victoria Cougars	20.1
1976	Rick Green	D	Washington	London Knights	20.3
1977	Dale McCourt	C	Detroit	St. Catharines Fincups	20.4
1978	Bobby Smith	C	Minnesota	Ottawa 67's	20.4
1979	Rob Ramage	D	Colorado	London Knights	20.5
1980	Doug Wickenheiser	C	Montreal	Regina Pats	19.2
1981	Dale Hawerchuk	C	Winnipeg	Cornwall Royals	18.2
1982	Gord Kluzak	D	Boston	Nanaimo Islanders	18.3
1983	Brian Lawton	C	Minnesota	Mount St. Charles HS	18.11
1984	Mario Lemieux	C	Pittsburgh	Laval Voisins	18.8
1985	Wendel Clark	LW/D	Toronto	Saskatoon Blades	18.7
1986	Joe Murphy	C	Detroit	Michigan State	18.8
1987	Pierre Turgeon	C	Buffalo	Granby Bisons	17.10
1988	Mike Modano	C	Minnesota	Prince Albert Raiders	18.0
1989	Mats Sundin	RW	Quebec	Nacka (Sweden)	18.4
1990	Owen Nolan	RW	Quebec	Cornwall Royals	18.4
1991	Eric Lindros	C	Quebec	Oshawa Generals	18.3
1992	Roman Hamrlik	D	Tampa Bay	ZPS Zlin (Czech.)	18.2
1993	Alexandre Daigle	C	Ottawa	Victoriaville Tigres	18.5
1994	Ed Jovanovski	D	Florida	Windsor Spitfires	18.0
1995	Bryan Berard	D	Ottawa	Detroit Jr. Red Wings	18.4
1996	Chris Phillips	D	Ottawa	Prince Albert Raiders	18.3
1997	Joe Thornton	C	Boston	Sault Ste. Marie	17.11
1998	Vincent Lecavalier	C	Tampa Bay	Rimouski Oceanic	18.2
1999	Patrik Stefan	C	Atlanta	Long Beach Ice Dogs	18.9

Draft Summary

Following is a summary of the number of players drafted from the Ontario Hockey League (OHL), Western Hockey League (WHL), Quebec Major Junior Hockey League (QMJHL), United States Colleges, United States High Schools, European Leagues and other Leagues throughout North America since 1969:

	OHL	WHL	QMJHL	US Colleges	US HS	International	Other
1969	36	20	11	7	0	1	9
1970	51	22	13	16	0	0	13
1971	41	28	13	22	0	0	13
1972	46	44	30	21	0	0	11
1973	56	49	24	25	0	0	14
1974	69	66	40	41	0	6	25
1975	55	57	28	59	0	6	12
1976	47	33	18	26	0	8	3
1977	42	44	40	49	0	5	5
1978	59	48	22	73	0	16	16
1979	48	37	19	15	0	6	1
1980	73	41	24	42	7	13	10
1981	59	37	28	21	17	32	17
1982	60	55	17	20	47	35	18
1983	57	41	24	14	35	34	37
1984	55	38	16	22	44	40	36
1985	59	47	15	20	48	31	31
1986	66	32	22	22	40	28	42
1987	32	36	17	40	69	38	20
1988	32	30	22	48	56	39	25
1989	39	44	16	48	47	38	20
1990	39	33	14	38	57	53	16
1991	43	40	25	43	37	55	21
1992	57	45	22	9	25	84	22
1993	60	44	23	17	33	78	31
1994	45	66	28	6	28	80	33
1995	54	55	35	5	2	69	14
1996	51	54	31	25	6	58	16
1997	52	63	19	26	4	63	19
1998	50	44	41	27	7	75	14
1999	52	40	20	36	9	94	21
Total	1585	1333	717	883	618	1085	585

Total Drafted, 1969-1999:   6,806

Ontario Hockey League

Club	'69	'70	'71	'72	'73	'74	'75	'76	'77	'78	'79	'80	'81	'82	'83	'84	'85	'86	'87	'88	'89	'90	'91	'92	'93	'94	'95	'96	'97	'98	'99	Total
Peterborough	5	5	4	5	9	4	8	1	4	6	9	10	3	5	7	3	9	2	5	2	2	4	3	4	2	5	4	5	1	4		144
Oshawa	5	4	3	5	5	7	6	6	1	3	3	2	9	5	5	6	6	6	3	2	4	2	4	4	4	1	10	1	3	4	3	132
Kitchener	1	6	2	8	4	13	3	1	3	4	4	4	5	5	8	4	6	3	2	1	7	5	3	1	4	2	4	2	3	5	-	123
London	4	9	1	5	6	6	3	5	4	3	6	2	5	5	3	7	1	3	2	6	3	3	1	3	4	1	1	4	1	8	4	119
Ottawa	2	4	3	4	6	5	6	5	5	5	3	8	4	9	2	2	3	3	2	1	-	5	5	6	4	1	1	2	5	2	6	119
Sudbury	-	-	-	6	6	4	5	4	4	3	7	2	4	-	2	5	3	1	-	1	2	8	2	10	2	2	1	3	5	5		97
S.S. Marie	-	-	-	4	5	2	5	1	5	3	3	8	1	6	4	5	7	1	2	3	1	2	7	3	4	3	4	1	4	1		95
Kingston	-	-	-	-	4	4	6	4	9	2	8	5	2	1	3	3	4	1	1	-	2	2	3	5	2	3	4	4	1	4		87
Niagara Falls	4	2	1	4	-	-	-	2	3	5	8	6	6	-	-	-	-	4	4	4	4	3	2	6	-	-	9					72
Windsor	-	-	-	-	-	2	1	4	2	3	5	3	2	2	3	7	-	5	2	1	-	3	-	3	4	1	5	1	2			61
Guelph	-	-	-	-	-	-	-	-	1	5	3	8	2	-	4	-	-	2	2	7	5	6	1	5	3							54
North Bay	-	-	-	-	-	-	-	-	-	4	4	3	3	3	1	4	2	5	2	7	2	1	1	2	2							49
Belleville	-	-	-	-	-	-	-	-	3	4	4	5	2	-	4	2	1	4	-	3	3	-	5	2	5							47
Det./Plymouth	-	-	-	-	-	-	-	-	-	-	-	-	2	2	7	2	6	3	4	2	2											30
Owen Sound	-	-	-	-	-	-	-	-	-	-	-	1	1	2	4	3	2	3	2	1	-											19
Barrie	-	-	-	-	-	-	-	-	-	-	-	-	-	-	-	2	4	3	6													15
Sarnia	-	-	-	-	-	-	-	-	-	-	-	-	-	-	1	7	2	3	1													14
Erie	-	-	-	-	-	-	-	-	-	-	-	-	-	-	-	-	-	3	1	2	6											6
Brampton	-	-	-	-	-	-	-	-	-	-	-	-	-	-	-	-	-	-	-	2												2

Teams no longer operating

Club	'69	'70	'71	'72	'73	'74	'75	'76	'77	'78	'79	'80	'81	'82	'83	'84	'85	'86	'87	'88	'89	'90	'91	Total
Toronto	3	7	6	5	6	8	4	4	7	5	4	10	2	6	4	4	3	4	1	2	2	-	-	97
Hamilton	2	3	5	4	6	4	7	3	-	8	1	-	-	-	-	3	6	4	4	-	-	2	-	62
St. Catharines	5	5	8	5	4	7	8	4	6	-	-	-	-	-	-	-	-	-	-	-	-	-	-	52
Cornwall	-	-	-	-	-	-	-	-	-	-	7	4	3	2	2	3	3	2	3	3	5	-	-	37
Brantford	-	-	-	-	-	-	-	-	3	8	5	2	7	2	-	-	-	-	-	-	-	-	-	27
Montreal	5	6	8	1	-	-	-	-	-	-	-	-	-	-	-	-	-	-	-	-	-	-	-	20
Newmarket	-	-	-	-	-	-	-	-	-	-	-	-	-	-	-	-	-	3	2	-	-	-	-	5

Year	Total Ontario Drafted	Total Players Drafted	Ontario %
1969	36	84	42.9
1970	51	115	44.3
1971	41	117	35.0
1972	46	152	30.3
1973	56	168	33.3
1974	69	247	27.9
1975	55	217	25.3
1976	47	135	34.8
1977	42	185	22.7
1978	59	234	25.2
1979	48	126	38.1
1980	73	210	34.8
1981	59	211	28.0
1982	60	252	23.8
1983	57	242	23.6
1984	55	250	22.0
1985	59	252	23.4
1986	66	252	26.2
1987	32	252	12.7
1988	32	252	12.7
1989	39	252	15.5
1990	39	250	15.6
1991	43	264	16.3
1992	57	264	21.6
1993	60	286	21.0
1994	45	286	15.7
1995	54	234	23.1
1996	51	241	21.1
1997	52	246	21.1
1998	50	258	19.4
1999	52	272	19.1
Total	**1585**	**6806**	**23.3**

Western Hockey League

Club	'69	'70	'71	'72	'73	'74	'75	'76	'77	'78	'79	'80	'81	'82	'83	'84	'85	'86	'87	'88	'89	'90	'91	'92	'93	'94	'95	'96	'97	'98	'99	Total
Regina	-	-	5	5	1	8	5	3	1	4	1	3	5	6	8	4	4	3	2	-	5	1	-	4	-	3	2	4	3	2	4	96
Saskatoon	1	-	1	3	8	4	5	3	4	1	2	2	3	5	5	3	1	5	4	4	3	2	2	3	2	4	2	2	2	2	4	92
Portland	-	-	-	-	-	-	-	4	8	7	8	6	7	7	5	2	4	3	1	4	1	1	4	4	3	2	1	3	3	1		89
Medicine Hat	-	-	-	4	6	4	5	3	5	4	-	4	2	1	2	1	6	2	5	1	4	1	3	3	1	6	2	7	2	3	1	88
Brandon	-	3	1	5	2	7	4	-	3	1	10	5	2	2	1	3	2	1	3	3	-	1	1	1	2	5	6	2	5	4	-	85
Kamloops	-	-	-	-	4	4	4	4	-	-	2	4	4	4	4	3	1	5	4	6	3	2	9	5	4	3	1	4				84
Lethbridge	-	-	-	3	2	3	5	4	1	4	7	2	1	5	1	-	3	3	4	7	3	4	3	3	1	5	1	-				75
Seattle	-	-	-	-	-	-	-	4	2	3	-	6	-	1	3	1	2	4	2	6	3	2	4	5	5	1	8	2	6			70
Prince Albert	-	-	-	-	-	-	-	-	-	4	2	2	6	6	1	3	3	4	6	2	5	3	4	3	5	3	3	3				65
Spokane	-	-	-	-	-	-	-	-	1	-	-	-	1	3	2	1	5	7	4	4	4	5	4	1	1							43
Swift Current	1	-	1	-	3	6	-	-	-	-	-	-	5	2	2	2	1	1	5	4	1	2	2	1								43
Moose Jaw	-	-	-	-	-	-	-	-	-	-	4	1	3	-	3	1	2	3	2	3	4	4	4	2	1							37
Tri-City	-	-	-	-	-	-	-	-	-	-	-	-	-	4	3	3	5	2	2	6	6	1	4	1								37
Red Deer	-	-	-	-	-	-	-	-	-	-	-	-	-	-	3	5	2	4	3	5	1											23
Kelowna	-	-	-	-	-	-	-	-	-	-	-	-	-	-	-	-	4	7	2	2												15
Prince George	-	-	-	-	-	-	-	-	-	-	-	-	-	-	2	2	2	4	2													12
Calgary	-	-	-	-	-	-	-	-	-	-	-	-	-	-	3	-	3	6														12
Edmonton	-	-	-	-	-	-	-	-	-	-	-	-	-	-	-	4	-	-														4
Kootenay	-	-	-	-	-	-	-	-	-	-	-	-	-	-	-	-	-	2														2

Teams no longer operating

Club	'69	'70	'71	'72	'73	'74	'75	'76	'77	'78	'79	'80	'81	'82	'83	'84	'85	'86	'87	'88	'89	'90	'91	'92	'93	Total
Victoria	-	-	-	2	2	5	7	4	3	3	1	8	6	2	3	4	2	1	2	4	4	2	-	1	2	70
Calgary	3	5	2	7	4	8	4	4	4	3	-	2	5	4	3	3	3	2	-	-	-	-	-	-	-	66
New Westm'r	-	-	-	6	8	7	9	5	8	6	5	1	-	-	2	1	1	2	1	-	-	-	-	-	-	62
Flin Flon	4	4	5	2	4	7	4	3	1	5	-	-	-	-	-	-	-	-	-	-	-	-	-	-	-	39
Winnipeg	3	2	4	2	5	4	4	-	4	-	-	1	4	1	-	-	-	-	-	-	-	-	-	-	-	34
Edmonton	4	4	5	6	6	2	3	2	-	2	-	-	-	-	-	-	-	-	-	-	-	-	-	-	-	34
Billings	-	-	-	-	-	-	-	-	4	3	4	2	-	-	-	-	-	-	-	-	-	-	-	-	-	13
Estevan	4	4	4	-	-	-	-	-	-	-	-	-	-	-	-	-	-	-	-	-	-	-	-	-	-	12
Tacoma	-	-	-	-	-	-	-	-	-	-	-	-	-	-	-	-	-	-	-	3	2	5	2	-	-	12
Kelowna	-	-	-	-	-	-	-	-	-	-	-	2	4	5	-	-	-	-	-	-	-	-	-	-	-	11
Nanaimo	-	-	-	-	-	-	-	-	5	1	-	-	-	-	-	-	-	-	-	-	-	-	-	-	-	6
Vancouver	-	-	-	2	-	-	-	-	-	-	-	-	-	-	-	-	-	-	-	-	-	-	-	-	-	2

Year	Total Western Drafted	Total Players Drafted	Western %
1969	20	84	23.8
1970	22	115	19.1
1971	28	117	23.9
1972	44	152	28.9
1973	49	168	29.2
1974	66	247	26.7
1975	57	217	26.3
1976	33	135	24.4
1977	44	185	23.8
1978	48	234	20.5
1979	37	126	29.4
1980	41	210	19.5
1981	37	211	17.5
1982	55	252	21.8
1983	41	242	16.9
1984	37	250	14.8
1985	48	252	19.0
1986	32	252	12.7
1987	36	252	14.3
1988	30	252	11.9
1989	44	252	17.5
1990	33	250	13.2
1991	40	264	15.2
1992	45	264	17.0
1993	44	286	15.4
1994	66	286	23.0
1995	55	234	23.5
1996	54	241	22.4
1997	63	246	25.6
1998	44	258	17.0
1999	40	272	14.7
Total	**1333**	**6806**	**19.6**

Only the Peterborough Petes have sent more players on to the NHL since 1969 than the Oshawa Generals, who provided the #1 pick in Eric Lindros back in 1991. Lindros led the Flyers with 93 points last year. He's led the team in scoring three times in the last five seasons.

Quebec Major Junior Hockey League

Club	'69	'70	'71	'72	'73	'74	'75	'76	'77	'78	'79	'80	'81	'82	'83	'84	'85	'86	'87	'88	'89	'90	'91	'92	'93	'94	'95	'96	'97	'98	'99	Total
Shawinigan	3	2	1	6	1	5	3	–	3	–	–	2	2	5	5	2	–	2	1	–	2	–	2	3	1	1	2	4	1	3	1	63
Sherbrooke	–	–	2	2	4	3	7	5	6	3	4	1	5	2	–	–	–	–	–	3	2	4	–	1	5	–	59
Hull	–	–	–	–	3	2	2	3	–	3	1	–	3	1	–	4	3	2	2	3	3	3	1	3	3	–	3	4	55
Drummondville	2	4	1	4	2	1	–	–	–	–	–	1	2	2	2	4	1	–	4	2	2	1	4	3	2	2	–	46
Chicoutimi	–	–	–	–	1	–	5	1	1	3	6	1	3	–	3	1	2	1	1	–	1	1	3	2	–	2	1	–	41
Granby	–	–	–	–	–	–	2	1	3	2	2	4	–	2	–	2	–	1	5	2	3	1	–	30
Victoriaville	–	–	–	–	–	–	–	–	–	–	4	–	1	–	2	6	1	1	3	2	1	2	23
Beauport	–	–	–	–	–	–	–	–	–	–	–	1	3	1	3	7	3	3	–	–	21
St. Hyacinthe	–	–	–	–	–	–	–	–	–	–	3	1	2	1	4	–	4	–	–	–	15
Val D'Or	–	–	–	–	–	–	–	–	–	–	–	1	2	4	2	–	3	12
Halifax	–	–	–	–	–	–	–	–	–	–	–	3	1	3	3	–	10
Rimouski	–	–	–	–	–	–	–	–	–	–	–	–	5	2	7
Quebec	–	–	–	–	–	–	–	–	–	–	–	–	4	3	7
Moncton	–	–	–	–	–	–	–	–	–	1	1	2	2	6
Rouyn-Noranda	–	–	–	–	–	–	–	–	–	–	3	1	4
Cape Breton	–	–	–	–	–	–	–	–	–	–	3	–	3
Baie-Comeau	–	–	–	–	–	–	–	–	–	–	3	–	3
Acadie-Bathurst	–	–	–	–	–	–	–	–	–	–	–	2	2

Teams no longer operating

Club																																Total
Laval	–	–	–	1	–	2	1	1	4	2	1	–	–	2	1	2	–	5	3	1	3	3	4	1	2	5	4	2	1	3	–	54
Quebec	1	1	2	4	6	6	1	3	7	1	3	2	2	1	2	2	3	–	47
Trois Rivieres	–	1	2	2	2	3	2	6	3	2	2	2	1	3	–	3	–	1	3	3	1	2	1	–	47
Cornwall	2	1	2	6	4	8	1	3	1	6	1	5	5	–	–	–	–	–	–	–	45
Montreal	–	–	–	4	4	8	1	3	2	4	3	–	3	–	32
Sorel	2	3	1	3	1	8	1	1	3	–	5	–	–	–	28
Verdun	–	1	1	2	–	1	3	3	–	3	3	–	3	0	3	1	–	3	–	27
St. Jean	–	–	–	–	–	–	–	–	2	–	1	1	0	3	1	–	3	1	2	1	1	–	16
Longueuil	–	–	–	–	–	–	–	–	–	1	2	1	2	1	–	2	3	–	12
St. Jerome	1	–	1	–	–	–	–	–	–	–	–	–	–	2

Year	Total Quebec Drafted	Total Players Drafted	Quebec %
1969	11	84	13.1
1970	13	115	11.3
1971	13	117	11.1
1972	30	152	19.7
1973	24	168	14.3
1974	40	247	16.2
1975	28	217	12.9
1976	18	135	13.3
1977	40	185	21.6
1978	22	234	9.4
1979	19	126	15.1
1980	24	210	11.4
1981	28	211	13.3
1982	17	252	6.7
1983	24	242	9.9
1984	16	250	6.4
1985	15	252	5.9
1986	22	252	8.7
1987	17	252	6.7
1988	22	252	8.7
1989	16	252	6.3
1990	14	250	5.6
1991	25	264	9.5
1992	22	264	8.3
1993	23	286	8.0
1994	28	286	9.7
1995	35	234	14.9
1996	31	241	12.8
1997	19	246	7.7
1998	41	258	15.9
1999	20	272	7.3
Total	**717**	**6806**	**10.5**

United States Colleges

Club	'69	'70	'71	'72	'73	'74	'75	'76	'77	'78	'79	'80	'81	'82	'83	'84	'85	'86	'87	'88	'89	'90	'91	'92	'93	'94	'95	'96	'97	'98	'99	Total
Minnesota	1	3	2	–	–	9	4	4	5	5	2	3	1	1	–	2	1	1	1	–	–	–	2	3	2	1	3	57
Michigan	1	–	–	–	2	2	3	3	1	6	–	4	–	–	1	1	–	1	2	3	5	4	2	1	1	–	3	1	3	2	52
Michigan Tech	–	3	1	2	5	4	4	1	2	1	4	–	2	2	2	1	1	2	1	2	–	1	2	–	1	–	45
Boston U.	–	4	–	1	1	1	4	5	1	–	1	–	1	1	2	2	3	1	2	2	1	1	–	1	1	2	3	43
Denver	1	3	2	4	2	3	1	2	2	2	1	–	1	–	1	2	4	1	1	–	–	–	3	–	1	39
Wisconsin	–	1	2	4	5	4	4	2	3	–	1	–	3	2	–	1	1	–	1	–	1	–	1	–	2	38
Michigan State	–	1	–	1	1	1	1	–	2	–	2	–	2	–	1	1	4	4	5	4	1	1	1	1	1	2	38
North Dakota	2	3	3	1	4	2	1	–	1	2	3	3	1	–	1	–	–	–	2	1	1	–	–	2	–	1	34
Clarkson	–	2	2	1	–	2	–	2	2	1	1	1	1	–	1	1	–	1	3	2	1	1	–	3	1	31
Providence	–	–	–	–	3	2	3	4	–	5	4	1	2	–	1	1	–	–	1	–	–	–	1	2	–	30
New Hampshire	–	–	1	1	3	6	–	4	1	1	2	1	1	2	–	–	–	1	–	–	1	–	1	27
Harvard	–	–	2	–	–	2	–	2	2	–	–	1	1	–	2	–	1	1	2	–	–	2	–	1	26
Cornell	–	–	–	2	1	1	–	1	1	1	–	1	1	1	–	1	2	–	1	2	5	2	–	–	1	–	2	26
Boston College	–	1	–	–	–	1	1	–	5	–	2	1	1	–	–	1	2	–	2	–	–	–	2	3	3	–	25
Colorado	2	1	–	–	1	3	1	2	2	–	1	–	3	–	1	–	1	–	2	–	–	–	3	1	25
Bowling Green	–	–	–	–	1	3	2	1	1	1	1	–	1	–	–	3	2	1	3	1	–	1	1	1	24
Notre Dame	–	2	3	–	7	2	–	3	1	1	–	–	1	–	–	–	–	–	1	2	–	2	24
Lake Superior	–	–	–	1	1	1	–	3	–	–	–	1	–	3	2	3	1	–	1	1	1	1	23
W. Michigan	–	–	–	–	–	2	–	2	–	2	2	2	1	1	1	1	4	–	2	–	1	1	–	22
St. Lawrence	–	–	–	–	1	4	–	–	3	–	1	1	1	1	1	1	2	–	1	1	1	1	22
RPI	–	–	–	–	1	3	–	1	2	1	1	–	2	2	–	3	1	–	–	1	–	2	22
Northern Mich.	–	–	–	–	–	4	–	1	2	1	–	4	1	1	–	1	–	–	1	–	17
Vermont	–	–	–	–	4	–	1	1	–	1	1	2	–	1	–	1	–	1	–	17
Maine	–	–	–	–	–	–	–	–	–	1	–	3	2	1	–	–	1	1	1	4	17
Ohio State	–	–	–	–	–	–	2	1	–	–	2	2	–	1	1	1	1	–	1	–	1	15
Miami of Ohio	–	–	–	–	–	–	–	1	–	2	4	2	–	1	1	1	1	–	14
Minn.-Duluth	–	2	1	–	–	1	1	–	–	–	2	1	2	1	–	–	1	–	13
Brown	–	–	–	1	2	1	3	2	–	1	–	1	–	–	11
Colgate	–	–	–	–	1	–	2	1	–	–	–	1	1	2	2	–	10
Yale	–	–	1	–	1	–	2	–	1	–	1	2	1	–	1	–	10
Northeastern	–	–	–	–	–	–	–	–	–	–	–	–	–	1	1	10

Colleges with fewer than 10 players drafted:

9 - Princeton; **8** - Ferris State; **6** - Illinois-Chicago, St. Louis; **5** - Dartmouth, Merrimack, Pennsylvania, Lowell; **4** - Alaska-Anchorage, Union College; **3** - Babson College, St. Cloud State; **2** - Alaska-Fairbanks; **1** - American International College, Army, Bemidji State, Greenway, Hamilton, St. Anselen College, St. Thomas, Salem State, San Diego U., Wisconsin-River Falls, Air Force

Year	Total College Drafted	Total Players Drafted	College %
1969	7	84	8.3
1970	16	115	13.9
1971	22	117	18.8
1972	21	152	13.8
1973	25	168	14.9
1974	41	247	16.6
1975	59	217	26.7
1976	26	135	19.3
1977	49	185	26.5
1978	73	234	31.2
1979	15	126	11.9
1980	42	210	20.0
1981	21	211	10.0
1982	20	252	7.9
1983	14	242	5.8
1984	22	250	8.8
1985	20	252	7.9
1986	22	252	8.7
1987	40	252	15.9
1988	48	252	19.0
1989	48	252	19.0
1990	38	250	15.2
1991	43	264	16.3
1992	9	264	3.4
1993	17	286	5.9
1994	6	286	2.1
1995	5	234	2.1
1996	25	241	10.4
1997	26	246	10.5
1998	27	258	10.4
1999	36	272	13.2
Total	**883**	**6806**	**13.2**

United States High Schools (10 or more players drafted)

Club	'80	'81	'82	'83	'84	'85	'86	'87	'88	'89	'90	'91	'92	'93	'94	'95	'96	'97	'98	'99	Total
Northwood Prep (NY)	–	–	2	1	–	2	2	4	1	3	1	–	1	1	–	–	–	–	–	19
Belmont Hill (MA)	–	–	1	–	2	1	2	1	3	2	1	–	1	–	–	–	–	16
Cushing Acad. (MA)	–	–	–	1	–	–	3	2	3	1	–	2	2	–	1	1	–	–	16
Edina (MN)	–	1	4	2	2	–	1	2	2	1	–	1	–	–	–	–	16
Hill-Murray (MN)	–	–	3	–	3	3	–	2	3	–	–	1	–	–	15
Mount St. Charles (RI)	–	1	–	3	1	–	2	1	2	1	1	–	–	12
Culver Mil. Acad. (IN)	–	–	–	–	2	1	2	1	2	2	–	–	12
Catholic Memorial (MA)	–	–	–	–	2	–	1	1	2	–	2	1	2	–	–	1	–	12
Canterbury (CT)	–	–	–	–	–	2	–	3	–	2	–	2	1	–	–	10
Matignon (MA)	1	1	1	–	3	–	3	–	1	–	–	–	10
Roseau (MN)	1	–	1	1	1	–	1	3	1	–	–	10

Year	Total USHS Drafted	Total Players Drafted	USHS %
1980	7	210	3.3
1981	17	211	8.1
1982	47	252	18.6
1983	35	242	14.5
1984	44	250	17.6
1985	48	252	19.1
1986	40	252	15.9
1987	69	252	27.4
1988	56	252	22.2
1989	47	252	18.7
1990	57	250	22.8
1991	37	264	14.0
1992	25	264	9.5
1993	33	286	11.5
1994	28	286	9.7
1995	2	234	0.9
1996	6	241	2.4
1997	4	246	1.6
1998	7	258	2.7
1999	9	272	3.3
Total	**618**	**6806**	**9.1**

International

Country	'69	'70	'71	'72	'73	'74	'75	'76	'77	'78	'79	'80	'81	'82	'83	'84	'85	'86	'87	'88	'89	'90	'91	'92	'93	'94	'95	'96	'97	'98	'99	Total
USSR/CIS	–	–	–	–	1	–	2	–	–	–	3	5	1	2	11	18	14	25	45	31	35	27	17	16	22	29						307
Sweden	–	–	–	–	5	2	5	2	8	5	9	14	14	10	14	16	9	15	14	9	7	11	11	18	17	8	16	14	19	24		296
Czech Republic and Slovakia	–	–	–	–	–	–	–	–	2	1	–	4	13	8	6	11	5	8	21	9	17	15	18	21	14	17	20	20				252
Finland	1	–	–	–	1	3	2	3	2	–	4	12	5	9	10	4	10	6	7	3	9	6	8	12	7	11	12	17				181
Germany	–	–	–	–	–	–	2	–	2	–	1	2	1	–	1	2	–	1	1	3	1	1	3	1	–							23
Switzerland	–	–	–	–	1	–	–	–	–	–	–	–	–	–	1	2	1	–	1	3	2	3										14
Norway	–	–	–	–	–	–	–	–	–	–	–	–	–	2	–	2	1	–	–	1	–											6
Denmark	–	–	–	–	–	–	–	–	–	–	1	1	–	–	–	–	–	–	–	–	–	–	–									2
Scotland	–	–	–	–	–	–	–	–	–	–	–	1	–	–	–	–	–	–	–	–	–	–										1
Poland	–	–	–	–	–	–	–	–	–	–	–	–	–	–	–	–	–	–	1	–	–	–										1
Japan	–	–	–	–	–	–	–	–	–	–	–	–	–	–	–	–	–	–	–	1	–											1
Hungary	–	–	–	–	–	–	–	–	–	–	–	–	–	–	–	–	–	–	–	–	–	–	–						1			1

Czech Republic and Slovakia

Club	'69	'70	'71	'72	'73	'74	'75	'76	'77	'78	'79	'80	'81	'82	'83	'84	'85	'86	'87	'88	'89	'90	'91	'92	'93	'94	'95	'96	'97	'98	'99	Total
Chemopetrol Litvinov[1]	–	–	–	–	–	–	–	–	–	–	–	–	3	1	2	–	–	–	2	2	1	3	2	4	2	2	2	1	1			28
Dukla Jihlava	–	–	–	–	–	–	–	–	–	–	–	2	4	3	1	–	3	1	1	3	2	1	1	1	2	2	–	–				27
HC Ceske Budejovice[6]	–	–	–	–	–	–	–	–	–	–	–	2	1	1	–	1	–	1	2	–	1	2	3	1	2	1	1					19
Sparta Praha	–	–	–	–	–	–	–	–	–	–	–	1	–	2	1	1	1	2	1	2	–	1	1	–	1	–	1	1	–			16
Slovan Bratislava	–	–	–	–	–	1	1	–	–	–	2	–	1	1	1	–	–	3	–	1	1	1	3	2								16
ZPS Zlin[2]	–	–	–	–	–	–	–	–	–	1	–	1	1	1	–	–	2	2	1	–	2	–	1	2	2							16
HC Kladno[7]	–	–	–	–	–	–	–	–	2	1	–	1	–	–	1	2	–	1	2	–	2	–	2	–	2							15
Dukla Trencin	–	–	–	–	–	–	–	–	–	–	1	–	–	–	–	1	–	2	2	–	1	2	1									15
Slavia Praha	–	–	–	–	–	–	–	–	–	–	1	–	–	–	–	–	–	1	–	4	5	2										13
HC Vitkovice[8]	–	–	–	–	–	1	–	1	–	1	–	–	–	–	1	1	3	1	1	1	–	1	1									12
HC Kosice[2]	–	–	–	–	–	–	–	1	2	–	2	–	1	–	1	–	–	–	–	–	–	1	1	1								12
HC Pardubice[4]	–	–	–	–	–	–	–	–	2	–	2	–	1	–	–	2	1	1	–													9
Interconex Plzen[9]	–	–	–	–	–	–	–	–	–	–	1	–	1	3	–	1	1	–	1													9
Zetor Brno	–	–	–	–	–	–	–	–	–	1	3	–	2	–	1	1																8
HC Olomouc[5]	–	–	–	–	–	–	–	–	–	–	–	–	2	–	1	2	–	1														7
AC Nitra	–	–	–	–	–	–	–	–	–	2	1	–	1	1																		5
ZTK Zvolen	–	–	–	–	–	–	–	–	1	–	1	1	–	2																		5
ZTS Martin	–	–	–	–	–	–	–	–	–	1	–	2																				3
Petra Vsetin	–	–	–	–	–	–	–	–	–	–	–	–	2	1																		3
IS Banska Bystrica	–	–	–	–	–	–	–	–	–	–	1	1																				2
ZPA Presov	–	–	–	–	–	–	–	–	1	–	1																					2
Partizan Liptovsky Mikulas	–	–	–	–	–	1	–	–																								2
Zelezarny Trinec	–	–	–	–	–	–	–	–	–	2																						2
VTJ Pisek	–	–	–	–	–	1	–	1																								2
Michalovce	–	–	–	–	–	–	–	–	–	2																						2
Ingstav Brno	–	–	–	–	1																											1
Banik Sokolov	–	–	–	–	–	–	1																									1
Havlickuv Brod	–	–	–	–	–	–	–	1																								1

Former club names: [1]–CHZ Litvinov, [2]–TJ Gottwaldov, TJ Zlin, [3]–VSZ Kosice, [4]–Tesla Pardubice, [5]–DS Olomouc, [6]–Motor Ceske Budejovice, [7]–Poldi Kladno, [8]–TJ Vitkovice, [9]–Skoda Plzen

Finland

Club	'69	'70	'71	'72	'73	'74	'75	'76	'77	'78	'79	'80	'81	'82	'83	'84	'85	'86	'87	'88	'89	'90	'91	'92	'93	'94	'95	'96	'97	'98	'99	Total
TPS Turku	–	–	–	–	–	–	–	–	1	6	–	–	1	1	–	–	–	–	3	2	3	1	3	3	1							25
HIFK Helsinki	1	–	–	–	1	–	1	–	–	1	1	2	2	1	–	2	1	–	–	2	–	1	–	1	2	4						23
Ilves Tampere	–	–	–	–	1	2	–	2	–	2	2	–	1	–	1	–	1	1	–	–	2	–	1	1								18
Jokerit Helsinki	–	–	–	–	–	–	2	1	–	–	1	–	1	1	–	2	–	3	–	1	–	1	1	1	3							18
Tappara Tampere	–	–	–	–	–	1	–	–	–	2	–	4	1	–	1	–	1	–	1	1	2	–										13
Assat Pori	–	–	–	2	–	–	1	–	2	2	–	1	–	1	–	1	1	1	–	1	1											13
Karpat Oulu	–	–	–	–	1	–	1	–	1	2	2	–	1	–	1	–	1	1														11
Lukko Rauma	–	–	–	2	1	–	–	2	–	1	–	1	–	1	–	1	–	–	2													11
Kiekko-Espoo	–	–	–	–	–	–	–	–	–	1	1	2	1	2	1	–	2															11
Reipas Lahti	–	–	–	–	1	1	1	–	2	–	1	1																				7
JyP HT Jyvaskyla	–	–	–	–	–	–	–	–	–	–	–	2	1	3																		7
HPK Hameenlinna	–	–	–	–	–	–	–	–	–	–	–	1	1	1																		6
KalPa Kuopio	–	–	–	–	–	–	–	1	2	–	1	1																				5
Kiekoo-67 Turku	–	–	–	–	–	–	–	–	–	3																						3
SaiPa Lappeenranta	–	–	–	–	1	–	1																									2
Sapko Savonlinna	–	–	–	–	–	1	1																									2
Sport Vaasa	–	–	–	–	–	1	–	1																								2
GrIFK Kauniainen	–	–	–	–	–	–	–	1																								1
Koo Koo Kouvola	–	–	–	–	–	1																										1
S-Kiekko Seinajoki	–	–	–	–	1																											1
Junkkarit Kalajoki	–	–	–	–	–	–	–	–	1																							1

Eight years and a trade have gone by since the Pittsburgh Penguins selected Sweden's Markus Naslund with their first choice (16th overall) in 1991. Naslund was the Canucks' best offensive player in 1998-99, leading the team with 36 goals and 66 points. His 15 power-play goals were tied for fifth in the NHL.

Russia/C.I.S.

Club	'74	'75	'76	'77	'78	'79	'80	'81	'82	'83	'84	'85	'86	'87	'88	'89	'90	'91	'92	'93	'94	'95	'96	'97	'98	'99	Total
CSKA Moscow	–	–	–	1	–	–	1	4	–	1	1	1	5	8	3	4	7	3	5	2	3	–	1	–	–	3	53
Dynamo Moscow	–	–	–	–	–	–	–	–	2	3	4	7	10	2	1	7	1	1	1	–	–	–	1	1	–	–	41
Krylja Sovetov Moscow	–	–	–	–	–	–	–	–	–	1	1	2	4	3	1	5	3	2	1	1	–	–	–	–	–	2	26
Spartak Moscow	–	–	–	–	–	–	–	–	–	–	1	4	–	6	1	–	–	–	1	4	–	6	1	–	–	1	16
Traktor Chelyabinsk	–	–	–	–	–	–	–	–	–	–	2	–	2	7	1	1	–	1	1	–	1	1	–	–	–	1	15
Torpedo Yaroslavl	–	–	–	–	–	–	–	–	1	2	–	1	–	5	1	1	3	1	3	1	–	–	–	–	–	1	15
Sokol Kiev	–	–	–	–	1	–	–	1	–	1	2	3	1	–	2	–	–	–	–	–	–	–	–	–	–	–	11
Khimik Voskresensk	–	–	–	–	1	–	–	1	3	1	2	–	1	–	–	–	–	–	2	–	–	–	–	–	–	–	11
Dynamo-2 Moscow	–	–	–	–	–	–	–	–	–	–	2	1	2	–	3	3	–	–	–	–	–	–	–	–	–	–	11
Pardaugava Riga[1]	–	1	–	–	–	–	–	–	1	2	–	1	4	1	–	–	–	–	–	–	–	–	–	–	–	–	10
Lada Togliatti	–	–	–	–	–	–	–	–	–	–	1	2	–	–	–	1	3	1	2	–	–	–	–	–	–	–	10
Torpedo-2 Yaroslavl	–	–	–	–	–	–	–	–	–	–	–	–	–	–	1	2	2	4	–	–	–	–	–	–	–	–	9
Severstal Cherepovets[5]	–	–	–	–	–	–	–	–	1	1	–	–	–	1	–	1	–	–	–	–	5	–	–	–	–	–	9
Torpedo Ust Kamenogorsk	–	–	–	–	–	–	–	–	–	–	1	1	2	1	–	–	2	1	–	–	–	–	–	–	–	–	8
SKA St. Peterburg[2]	–	–	1	–	–	–	–	–	2	1	–	1	–	–	–	–	–	–	–	–	2	–	–	–	–	–	8
Salavat Yulayev Ufa	–	–	–	–	–	–	–	–	–	–	–	2	2	1	1	–	1	–	–	–	–	–	–	–	–	–	7
CSKA-2 Moscow	–	–	–	–	–	–	–	–	–	–	–	–	1	–	2	2	–	–	–	–	–	–	–	–	–	–	5
Tivali Minsk[3]	–	–	–	–	–	–	–	–	–	–	–	–	–	2	1	–	–	–	–	–	–	–	–	–	–	–	4
Avangard Omsk	–	–	–	–	–	–	–	–	–	–	–	–	–	–	–	3	–	1	–	–	–	–	–	–	–	–	4
Kristall Elektrostal	–	–	–	–	–	–	–	–	–	–	3	–	–	1	–	–	–	–	–	–	–	–	–	–	–	–	4
Torpedo Nizhny Novgorod[4]	–	–	–	–	–	–	–	–	–	–	–	1	2	–	–	–	–	–	–	–	–	–	–	–	–	–	3
Avtomobilist Yekaterinburg	–	–	–	–	–	–	–	–	–	–	–	–	–	–	–	–	–	1	–	–	1	1	–	–	–	–	3
Molot Perm	–	–	–	–	–	–	–	–	–	–	–	–	–	–	–	–	1	1	–	–	–	–	–	–	–	–	2
Itil Kazan	–	–	–	–	–	–	–	–	–	–	–	–	–	–	–	–	–	1	–	–	1	–	–	–	–	–	2
CSK VVS Samara	–	–	–	–	–	–	–	–	–	–	–	–	–	–	–	–	1	–	–	–	–	–	1	–	–	–	2
HC CSKA Moscow	–	–	–	–	–	–	–	–	–	–	–	–	–	–	–	–	–	–	–	–	–	–	–	–	2	–	2
Metallurg Novokuznetsk	–	–	–	–	–	–	–	–	–	–	–	–	–	–	–	–	–	–	–	–	–	–	–	–	2	–	2
Argus Moscow	–	–	–	–	–	–	–	–	–	–	–	–	–	–	1	–	–	–	–	–	–	–	–	–	–	–	1
Dizelist Penza	–	–	–	–	–	–	–	–	–	–	–	–	–	–	–	–	1	–	–	–	–	–	–	–	–	–	1
Dynamo Kharkov	–	–	–	–	–	–	–	–	1	–	–	–	–	–	–	–	–	–	–	–	–	–	–	–	–	–	1
Izhorets St. Peterburg	–	–	–	–	–	–	–	–	–	–	–	–	–	–	1	–	–	–	–	–	–	–	–	–	–	–	1
Khimik Novopolotsk	–	–	–	–	–	–	–	–	–	–	–	–	–	–	–	–	1	–	–	–	–	–	–	–	–	–	1
Kristall Saratov	–	–	–	–	–	–	–	–	–	–	–	–	–	–	–	–	1	–	–	–	–	–	–	–	–	–	1
Krylja Sovetov-2 Moscow	–	–	–	–	–	–	–	–	–	–	–	–	–	–	–	–	1	–	–	–	–	–	–	–	–	–	1
Mechel Chelyabinsk	–	–	–	–	–	–	–	–	–	–	–	–	–	–	–	–	1	–	–	–	–	–	–	–	–	–	1
Salavat Novoil Ufa	–	–	–	–	–	–	–	–	–	–	–	–	–	–	–	–	–	1	–	–	–	–	–	–	–	–	1
Neftekhimik Nizhnekamsk	–	–	–	–	–	–	–	–	–	–	–	–	–	–	–	–	–	–	–	–	–	1	–	–	–	–	1
Severstal-2 Cherepovets	–	–	–	–	–	–	–	–	–	–	–	–	–	–	–	–	–	–	–	–	–	–	–	–	1	–	1
AK Bars-2 Kazan	–	–	–	–	–	–	–	–	–	–	–	–	–	–	–	–	–	–	–	–	–	–	–	–	–	1	1
Lada-2 Togliatti	–	–	–	–	–	–	–	–	–	–	–	–	–	–	–	–	–	–	–	–	–	–	–	–	–	1	1
Dynamo 81 Riga	–	–	–	–	–	–	–	–	–	–	–	–	–	–	–	–	–	–	–	–	–	–	–	–	–	1	1

Former club names: [1]–Dynamo Riga, HC Riga, [2]–SKA Leningrad, [3]–Dynamo Minsk, [4]–Torpedo Gorky, [5]–Metallurg Cherepovets

Sweden

Club	'74	'75	'76	'77	'78	'79	'80	'81	'82	'83	'84	'85	'86	'87	'88	'89	'90	'91	'92	'93	'94	'95	'96	'97	'98	'99	Total
Farjestad Karlstad	–	–	2	2	–	1	2	1	1	2	–	–	1	–	1	2	1	–	2	–	3	6	1				29
MoDo Hockey Ornskoldsvik	–	1	–	1	–	1	2	–	1	–	2	2	5	–	3	3	–	7									28
Djurgarden Stockholm	1	1	–	2	–	2	1	–	2	1	–	2	1	1	2	1	1	–	3	2	2	–	1				27
AIK Solna	–	1	–	1	1	–	2	3	1	–	4	–	–	1	1	1	–	1	–	–	1	1	3				22
Leksand	1	–	–	1	–	1	–	2	2	1	1	2	1	–	2	–	2	2	–	1	–	2	–				21
Vastra Frolunda Goteborg	–	–	–	–	–	–	2	1	–	1	1	–	1	–	3	1	1	–	1	2							15
Brynas Gavle	1	–	–	1	1	1	–	4	–	–	1	1	1	–	1	1	2	1									18
Sodertalje	–	–	–	1	1	2	1	2	–	2	–	1	–	2	–	–	–	1	1								14
HV 71 Jonkoping	–	–	–	–	–	–	–	1	1	–	1	–	–	2	–	2	1	4	3								16
Skelleftea	–	1	1	–	–	1	1	–	1	–	–	–	–	–	1	–	1	–									10
Rogle Angelholm	–	–	–	–	–	–	–	1	2	–	–	2	2	1	–	–	1										9
Vasteras	–	–	–	–	–	–	–	–	2	2	1	1	1	–													8
Lulea	–	–	–	–	1	1	–	1	1	1	–	–	–	–	1	1											8
Sundsvall Timra[1]	–	–	–	–	1	2	–	1	1	–	–	–	–	1													7
Malmo	–	–	–	–	–	–	–	–	1	–	1	1	1	–	2	–	1										7
Bjorkloven Umea	–	–	–	2	1	–	1	–	1	–	–																5
Orebro	–	–	1	–	1	–	1	–	1	–	–	–	–	–													5
Hammarby Stockholm	–	–	–	1	1	–	–	1	–	–	1	–	1														5
Nacka	–	–	–	–	1	–	–	1	–	1	–	2															4
Mora	–	–	–	–	–	–	–	–	–	–	1	1	1														4
Huddinge	–	–	–	–	–	–	–	1	–	1	–	2	–	1													4
Falun	–	–	–	–	1	–	–	1	–	1																	3
Team Kiruna	–	–	1	–	1	–	1																				3
Boden	1	–	–	–	–	1	–	1																			3
Pitea	–	–	–	1	–	–	1	1																			3
Troja	–	–	–	–	1	1	1																				3
Ostersund	–	–	–	–	1	1																					2
Grums	–	–	–	–	1	–	1																				2
Almtuna	–	–	–	–	1																						1
Danderyd Hockey	–	–	–	1																							1
Fagersta	–	–	–	–	1																						1
Karskoga	1	–	–																								1
Stocksund	–	–	–	1																							1
S/G Hockey 83 Gavle	–	–	–	1																							1
Talje	–	–	–	–	1																						1
Tunabro	1																										1
Uppsala	–	–	–	1																							1
Vallentuna	–	–	–	1																							1
Vita Hasten	–	–	–	–	1																						1

Former club names: [1]–Timra

Year	Total International Drafted	Total Players Drafted	International %
1969	1	84	1.2
1970	0	115	0
1971	0	117	0
1972	0	152	0
1973	0	168	0
1974	6	247	2.4
1975	6	217	2.8
1976	8	135	5.9
1977	5	185	2.7
1978	16	234	6.8
1979	6	126	4.8
1980	13	210	6.2
1981	32	211	15.2
1982	35	252	13.9
1983	34	242	14.0
1984	40	250	17.6
1985	31	252	12.3
1986	28	252	11.1
1987	38	252	15.1
1988	39	252	15.5
1989	38	252	15.1
1990	53	250	21.2
1991	55	264	20.8
1992	84	264	31.4
1993	78	286	27.3
1994	80	286	27.9
1995	69	234	29.5
1996	58	241	24.0
1997	63	246	25.6
1998	75	258	29.0
1999	94	272	34.5
Total	**1085**	**6806**	**15.9**

Note: Players drafted in the international category played outside North America in their draft year. European-born players drafted from the OHL, QMJHL, WHL or U.S. Colleges are not counted as International players. See Country of Origin, below.

1999 Entry Draft Analysis

Country of Origin

Country	Players Drafted
Canada	107
USA	50
Russia	27
Sweden	22
Czech Republic	18
Finland	18
Slovakia	12
Kazakhstan	5
Switzerland	2
Latvia	2
Austria	2
Belarus	2
Ukraine	1
France	1
Hungary	1
Norway	1
Croatia	1

Position

Position	Players Drafted
Defense	87
Center	56
Right Wing	55
Left Wing	44
Goaltender	30

Birth Year

Year	Players Drafted
1981	124
1980	88
1979	42
1978	5
1977	3
1976	2
1975	4
1973	2
1972	2

First Round Draft Selections, 1999

1. ATLANTA • **PATRIK STEFAN** • C • The most physically mature player available in the 1999 Draft, Patrik Stefan is a tall and upright skater with a good change of pace that can alter the look of an offensive rush. He has size and strength, scoring ability, a physical presence and good hockey sense. Stefan is very strong on face-offs and is an excellent passer. He played two seasons with Long Beach in the IHL and was named to the Western Conference All-Star Team in 1999.

2. VANCOUVER • **DANIEL SEDIN** • LW • Playing against men in the Swedish Elite League, Daniel Sedin led his team in scoring and ranked 13th in the league as MoDo finished in first place. He is a high scoring, highly skilled finesse player, but does not neglect his defensive duties. With his fine hockey sense, Sedin is able to see plays develop and has great anticipation. He is a great passer and has outstanding playmaking skills. Sedin plays with confidence and has the maturity to handle the pressure off the ice.

3. VANCOUVER • **HENRIK SEDIN** • C • A little bigger and grittier than his more offensively oriented twin brother, Henrik Sedin ranked third on his team, and 28th in the league in scoring as MoDo finished in first place. A highly skilled finesse forward, Sedin also contributes defensively. He is fast and strong on his skates and his excellent vision and fine hockey sense make him an excellent passer He has been a consistent producer at every level and is comfortable with the pressure of off-ice stardom.

4. NY RANGERS • **PAVEL BRENDL** • RW • A powerful skater with deceptive speed, Pavel Brendl led the WHL with 73 goals and 134 points in 1998-99. He added 21 goals and 25 assists in 20 playoff games as Calgary reached the Memorial Cup tourney. He also showed improved defensive play in the postseason. Brendl is extremely accurate with both his passes and his shot and exhibits exceptional strength and balance when fending off checking opponents. Though not overly physical, he will take a check to complete the play.

5. NY ISLANDERS • **TIM CONNOLLY** • C • The top-rated American player in the draft, Tim Connolly is a good, quick and agile skater with speed. Though his season was cut short by a broken leg, Connolly was still named the Erie Otters' most outstanding player. A feisty, competitive player, Connolly also excels at the finesse game and is a tremendous deker with excellent finish on his backhand. He has a hard, accurate shot with a quick release.

6. NASHVILLE • **BRIAN FINLEY** • G • Considered to be by far the best goalie available in the draft, Brian Finley set Barrie Colts records for average and save percentage as a rookie in 1997-98, then surpassed those totals in 1998-99. A butterfly-style goaltender, Finley stays square to the shot and has smooth controlled movement. He has quick reflexes and fast feet. His hands are good, but he has a tendency to juggle the puck. Finley is rarely caught out of position.

7. WASHINGTON • **KRIS BEECH** • C • An explosive skater with a quick first step and fluid stride, Kris Beech is a playmaking center with tremendous puck-handling skills. He set a record in the puck control event (16.671 seconds) at the 1999 Top Prospects skills evaluation. Beech is a player who relies on his overall talent more than physical play, though he is a gritty player who is getting stronger.

8. NY ISLANDERS • **TAYLOR PYATT** • C • Taylor Pyatt is a power forward with a good wrist shot and slap shot. At 6'3½" and 220 pounds, he can be a physical presence on the ice. He's also a powerful skater who won the Fastest Skater event at the 1999 Top Prospects Game. Pyatt is a very good player on the powerplay and is extremely strong in front of the net. He has the ability to score the big goals.

9. NY RANGERS • **JAMIE LUNDMARK** • C • A good skater with quick acceleration, Jamie Lundmark set records in the 60' sprint and 150' sprint at the 1999 Top Prospects Game. He was named to the WHL All-Rookie team in 1998-99. Lundmark has great vision and uses his teammates very well. He also has an accurate wrist shot and is a threat to score from anywhere in the offensive zone. He is not an overly physical player, but works hard through adversity.

10. NY ISLANDERS • **BRANISLAV MEZEI** • D • Branislav Mezei was a member of the Slovak team that won a bronze medal at the 1999 World Junior Championships. He also anchored the defense for the OHL champion Belleville Bulls. At 6'4½" and 221 pounds, Mezei likes to take out his man with authority. He's also a well-balanced skater who is capable of making end-to-end rushes. Mezei is an intense competitor with impressive strength.

11. CALGARY • **OLEG SAPRYKIN** • C-LW • A finalist for WHL Rookie of the Year honors, Oleg Saprykin goes to the net well and has good quickness around the goal. He handles the puck extremely well when in motion and has a hard accurate shot off the wing. An aggressive forechecker, Saprykin is an abrasive player who can irritate opponents He competes hard and is an excellent two-way player. Saprykin's father played for Moscow's Central Red Army team.

12. FLORIDA • **DENIS SHVIDKI** • RW • His first season in North America was considered something of a disappointment, though Denis Shvidki still accumulated 94 points in 61 games with the Barrie Colts. Shvidki is an excellent skater with effortless acceleration and good balance. He has excellent touch with the puck and can pinpoint passes for his teammates. He is very alert around the net and has very good hockey instincts. Shvidki is primarily an offensive player, but is aware of his defensive responsibilities.

13. EDMONTON • **JANI RITA** • F • Seen as an Esa Tikkanen type, Finland's Jani Rita is a strong defensive forward. He has an excellent attitude towards the game and is eager to learn and improve. A decent passer and playmaker, Rita has a hard shot and can score in many different ways. He is a fast skater with good acceleration, balance and speed. Rita is a hard-working team player who is more of a power forward than a finesse player.

14. SAN JOSE • **JEFF JILLSON** • D • At 6'3" and 219 pounds, Jeff Jillson is a defenseman who uses his ample size and strength to advantage. He is also a very good skater with a strong stride. Jillson passes the puck well and carries it quickly and efficiently from his own zone. He has a good shot from the point and uses his backhand well in both shooting and passing situations. Jillson plays the body well and can keep the front of his net clear.

15. PHOENIX • **SCOTT KELMAN** • C • A strong skater with long, smooth strides, Scott Kelman is seen as a character player who is a better playmaker than scorer. He exhibits very good on-ice awareness and anticipation of the developing play. He positions himself well in the offensive zone. Kelman is also a talented baseball player who pitched a no-hitter for Team Manitoba in the Canada Blue Jays Cup.

16. CAROLINA • **DAVID TANABE** • D • An excellent skater with agility and strong balance, David Tanabe was named All-State at Hill Murray High School before entering the University of Wisconsin in 1998-99. Tanabe likes to rush the puck and has a hard shot from the point. He is used on the powerplay and to kill penalties and likes to get involved in the physical aspects of the game. Tanabe played for the U.S. team at the 1999 World Junior Championships.

17. ST. LOUIS • **BARRET JACKMAN** • D • The captain of the Regina Pats, Barret Jackman is a punishing player in the defensive end and a good open-ice hitter. He is also a powerful skater who can change directions quickly and lead the offensive rush. Jackman reads the play well and excels at the transition game. He has a hard, accurate slap shot from the blueline and is used on the opposite point for the powerplay. Jackman is looked upon as a team leader.

18. PITTSBURGH • **KONSTANTIN KOLTSOV** • F • A strong and tireless skater, Konstantin Koltsov is a dynamic offensive forward. He has a good selection of shots and can score many different ways. He is a finesse player, but can perform in a physical game. Koltsov represented Belarus at both the World Junior Championships and the World Championships in 1999. He led his team in scoring at the World Junior Championships and at the B-Pool Under-18 World Tournament.

19. PHOENIX • **KIRIL SAFRONOV** • D • Primarily a defensive defenseman, 6'2", 196-pound Kiril Safronov has the size and strength to play a physical game. He was the youngest member of the Russian team that won the 1999 World Junior Championships. Safronov has good mobility and pivots well to either side. He's an intelligent player with a good understanding of the game and very reliable in the defensive zone.

20. BUFFALO • **BARRETT HEISTEN** • LW • Barrett Heisten is a physical forward with outstanding overall speed and quickness. He can handle the puck in tight situations and is a strong playmaker from the corners. Heisten also has a good shot with a quick release and uses his backhand effectively. He is a hard-working player with grit and character.

21. BOSTON • **NICK BOYNTON** • D • Originally selected ninth overall by Washington in 1997, Nick Boynton re-entered the draft in 1999 after helping the Ottawa 67s win the Memorial Cup. A strong skater with great vision of the ice, Boynton passes the puck well and has a hard, accurate shot from the point. He possesses great stamina and is a good physical presence on the ice. He plays with poise and confidence and is used in all aspects of the game.

22. PHILADELPHIA • **MAXIME OUELLET** • G • He's not rated as high as Brian Finley, but many scouts believe Maxime Ouellet will eventually be the better NHL goalie. He relies on the butterfly, but is also a very stable standup goaltender. Ouellet likes to come out to challenge the shooter. He has very good quickness and reaction time. His glove hand is excellent and he uses his blocker well. Ouellet is effective at using his stick to prevent passes out front or deflect shots into the corner.

23. CHICAGO • **STEVE McCARTHY** • D • A strong skater who can reach top speed quickly, Steve McCarthy is an offensive defenseman who can read and react to the developing play extremely well. A crisp, accurate passer, he is very adept at making the outlet pass and jumping into the offensive play. McCarthy is used in all game situations and is a steady, reliable player.

24. TORONTO • **LUCA CEREDA** • C • Hoping to become the first Swiss-born player to reach the NHL, Luca Cereda played with former NHLers Oleg Petrov and Paul DiPietro with top Swiss club Ambri-Piotta in 1998-99. Cereda is a strong puckhandler with excellent passing skills and has a good physical presence on the ice. He likes to lead the play and is very dangerous in the offensive zone.

25. COLORADO • **MIKHAIL KULESHOV** • LW • A player with size and skating ability, Mikhail Kuleshov is a crafty puckhandler with good speed. He has a strong hockey sense and fine passing ability. He has a good overall skill level and likes to rush the puck. Kuleshov is capable of going from end to end. He is used in all situations and is a good team player.

26. OTTAWA • **MARTIN HAVLAT** • F • Only the Sedin twins were higher ranked European prospects than Martin Havlat of the Czech Republic, but most scouts feel he must get much stronger to play in the NHL. Havlat has excellent speed and good balance and is an offensive player who drives the net. He is an offensive catalyst who can make things happen and can get aggressive when he needs to.

27. NEW JERSEY • **ARI AHONEN** • G • Although rated second among European goaltenders, Finland's Ari Ahonen was selected ahead of Russia's Evgeny Konstantinov. Ahonen has good size and quickness with fast reflexes. He has a good glove hand and makes good use of his stick. Ahonen reads the play well and is a strong competitor. He led Finland to a gold medal in the 1999 Under-18 World Tournament.

28. NY ISLANDERS • **KRISTIAN KUDROC** • D • At 6'6" and 229 pounds, Kristian Kudroc is a good checker who moves very well for his size. He works well in the defensive zone, but also has solid puck-handling and passing skills and is able to join in the offensive rush. Kudroc has a good shot from the point and is very eager to learn and improve. He plays for a lower profile team in Slovakia, but has been playing in the men's league for two years and had a strong showing at the 1999 European Junior Championships.

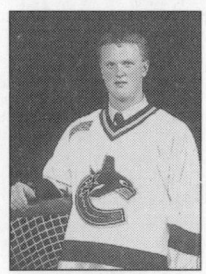

NHL IMAGES PHOTOS

Players selected first through tenth in the 1999 NHL Entry Draft: (All rows left to right)
Top row: 1. Patrik Stefan, C, Atlanta; 2. Daniel Sedin, LW, Vancouver
Second row: 3. Henrik Sedin, C, Vancouver; 4. Pavel Brendl, RW, NY Rangers
Third row: 5. Tim Connolly, C, NY Islanders; 6. Brian Finley, G, Nashville
Fourth row: 7. Kris Beech, C, Washington; 8. Taylor Pyatt, C, NY Islanders
Fifth row: 9. Jamie Lundmark, C, NY Rangers; 10. Branislav Mezei, NY Islanders.

1999 Entry Draft

Transferred draft choice notation:

Example: Col.-Ana. represents a draft choice transferred from Colorado to Anaheim.

Pick	Player	Claimed By	Amateur Club	Position
ROUND #1				
1	STEFAN, Patrik	T.B.-Van.-Atl	Long Beach	C
2	SEDIN, Daniel	Atl.-Van.	MoDo	LW
3	SEDIN, Henrik	Van.	MoDo	C
4	BRENDL, Pavel	Chi.-Van.-T.B.-NYR	Calgary	RW
5	CONNOLLY, Tim	NYI	Erie	C
6	FINLEY, Brian	Nsh.	Barrie	G
7	BEECH, Kris	Wsh.	Calgary	C
8	PYATT, Taylor	L.A.-NYI	Sudbury	LW
9	LUNDMARK, Jamie	Cgy.-NYR	Moose Jaw	C
10	MEZEI, Branislav	Mtl.-NYI	Belleville	D
11	SAPRYKIN, Oleg	NYR-Cgy	Seattle	C
12	SHVIDKY, Denis	Fla.	Barrie	RW
13	RITA, Jani	Edm.	Jokerit Helsinki	RW
14	JILLSON, Jeff	S.J.	U. of Michigan	D
15	KELMAN, Scott	Ana.-Phx.	Seattle	C
16	TANABE, David	Car.	U. of Wisconsin	D
17	JACKMAN, Barret	St.L.	Regina	D
18	KOLTSOV, Konstantin	Pit.	Cherepovets	LW
19	SAFRONOV, Kirill	Phx.	St. Petersburg	D
20	HEISTEN, Barrett	Buf.	U. of Maine	LW
21	BOYNTON, Nicholas	Bos.	Ottawa	D
22	OUELLET, Maxime	Phi.	Quebec	G
23	MCCARTHY, Steve	Det.-Chi.	Kootenay	D
24	CEREDA, Luca	Tor.	Ambri	C
25	KULESHOV, Mikhail	Col.	Cherepovets	LW
26	HAVLAT, Martin	Ott.	Trinec	C
27	AHONEN, Ari	N.J.	JyP HT Jr.	G
28	KUDROC, Kristian	Dal.-NYI	Michalovce	D
ROUND #2				
29	SIVEK, Michal	T.B.-Wsh.	HC Kladno Jr.	C
30	SELLARS, Luke	Atl.	Ottawa	D
31	STEPHENS, Charlie	Van.-Col.-Wsh	Guelph	F
32	RYAN, Michael	NYI-Dal.	Boston College H.S.	C
33	ANDERSSON, Jonas	Nsh.	AIK Solna Jr.	RW
34	LUPASCHUK, Ross	Wsh.	Prince Albert	D
35	BARTOVIC, Milan	L.A.-Buf.	Dukla Trencin Jrs.	RW
36	SEMENOV, Alexei	Edm.	Sudbury	D
37	YONKMAN, Nolan	Wsh.	Kelowna	D
38	CAVANAUGH, Dan	Cgy.	Boston University	F
39	BUTURLIN, Alexander	Mtl.	CSKA Moscow Jr.	LW
40	AULD, Alexander	St.L.-Fla.	North Bay	G
41	SALMELAINEN, Tony	Edm.	HIFK Helsinki	LW
42	COMMODORE, Mike	N.J.	U. of North Dakota	D
43	SHEFER, Andrei	L.A.	Cherepovets	LW
44	LEOPOLD, Jordan	NYR-Ott.-Ana.	U. of Minnesota	D
45	GRENIER, Martin	Fla.-Nsh.-Col.	Quebec	D
46	LEVINSKY, Dmitri	Chi.	Cherepovets	RW
47	KEEFE, Sheldon	S.J.-Det.-T.B.	Barrie	RW
48	LAJEUNESSE, Simon	Ana.-Ott.	Moncton	G
49	LYSAK, Brett	Car.	Regina	C
50	CLOUTHIER, Brett	St.L.-N.J.	Kingston	LW
51	MURLEY, Matt	Pit.	R.P.I.	LW
52	HALL, Adam	Nsh.	Michigan State	RW
53	RALPH, Brad	Phx.	Oshawa	LW
54	HUTCHINSON, Andrew	Col.-Nsh.	Michigan State	D
55	JANIK, Doug	Buf.	U. of Maine	D
56	ZULTEK, Matt	Bos.	Ottawa	LW
57	VAN HOOF, Jeremy	Pit.	Ottawa	D
58	CARKNER, Matt	Phi.-Mtl.	Peterborough	D
59	INMAN, David	Det.-NYR	U. of Notre Dame	C
60	REYNOLDS, Peter	Tor.	London	D
61	HILL, Ed	Col.-Nsh.	Barrie	D
62	SAINOMAA, Teemu	Ott.	Jokerit Helsinki Jr.	LW
63	MOKHOV, Stepan	N.J.-Chi.	Cherepovets	D
64	ZIGOMANIS, Michael	Dal.-Buf.	Kingston	C
65	LASAK, Jan	Nsh.	ZTK Zvolen Jr.	G
66	JANCEVSKI, Dan	St.L.-Dal.	London	D
ROUND #3				
67	KONSTANTINOV, Yevgeny	T.B.	Ak-Bars Kazan-2	G
68	BLATNY, Zdenek	Atl.	Seattle	C
69	VYDARENY, Rene	Van.	Bratislava Jr.	D
70	HAGMAN, Niklas	Fla.	HIFK Helsinki Jr.	LW
71	JASPERS, Jason	NYI-Phx.	Sudbury	F
72	ANGEL, Brett	Nsh.	North Bay	D
73	PRESTON, Tim	Wsh.-Buf.	Seattle	LW
74	CRAIN, Jason	L.A.	Ohio State	D
75	SCHEFFELMAIER, Brett	Van.-T.B.	Medicine Hat	D
76	KABERLE, Frantisek	Chi.-L.A.	MoDo	D
77	ANDERSSON, Craig	Cgy.	Guelph	G
78	WEINHANDL, Mattias	Mtl.-NYI	Troja-Ljungby	RW
79	ASPLUND, Johan	NYR	Brynas Gavle	G
80	LANIEL, Jean-Francois	Fla.	Shawinigan	G
81	HAUSER, Adam	Edm.	U. of Minnesota	G
82	CONCANNON, Mark	S.J.	Winchendon	LW
83	HAVELID, Niklas	Ana.	Malmo	D
84	FAST, Brad	Car.	Prince George	D
85	SMREK, Peter	St.L.	Des Moines	D
86	CARON, Sebastien	Pit.	Rimouski	G
87	COLLINS, Brian	Phx.-NYI	St. John's	C
88	OLVESTAD, Jimmie	Buf.-Van.-T.B.	Djurgarden Jr.	LW
89	WANVIG, Kyle	Bos.	Kootenay	RW
90	AUFIERO, Patrick	Phi.-Cgy.-NYR	Boston University	D
91	COMRIE, Mike	Det.-Nsh.-Edm.	U. of Michigan	C
92	CAMPBELL, Cory	Tor.-L.A.	Belleville	G
93	RADIVOJEVIC, Branko	Col.	Belleville	RW
94	KELLY, Chris	Ott.	London	F
95	LAKOS, Andre	N.J.	Barrie	D
96	TJARNQVIST, Mathias	Dal.	Rogle Angelholm	C

ROUND #4

#	Name	Team	Club	Pos
97	DYMENT, Chris	T.B.-Chi.-Mtl.	Boston University	D
98	KACZOWKA, David	Atl.	Seattle	LW
99	ZEPP, Rob	Van.-Atl.	Plymouth	G
100	KESA, Teemu	N.J.	Ilves Jr.	D
101	KOLNIK, Juraj	NYI	Rimouski	RW
102	HALVARDSSON, Johan	Nsh.-NYI	HV 71 Jonkoping	D
103	MCCORMICK, Morgan	Wsh.-Fla.	Kingston	RW
104	MCGRATTAN, Brian	L.A.	Sudbury	RW
105	CHAGODAYEV, Alexander	Chi.-Ana.	CSKA Moscow	C
106	ROZAKOV, Rail	Cgy.	Lada Togliatti-2	D
107	LINDSAY, Evan	Mtl.	Prince Albert	G
108	MUROVIC, Mirko	NYR-Tor.	Moncton	LW
109	SARICH, Rod	Fla.	Calgary	D
110	ZION, Jonathan	Edm.-Tor.	Ottawa	D
111	LEVESQUE, Willie	S.J.	Northeastern	RW
112	LINDSTROM, Sanny	Ana.-Col.	Huddinge	D
113	MURPHY, Ryan	Car.	Bowling Green	LW
114	STARLING, Chad	St.L.	Kamloops	D
115	MALONE, Ryan	Pit.	Omaha	LW
116	LAUZON, Ryan	Phx.	Hull	C
117	MOSOVSKY, Karel	Buf.	Regina	LW
118	HARIKKALA, Jaakko	Bos.	Lukko Rauma	D
119	FENIAK, Jeff	Phi.	Calgary	D
120	TOLSA, Jari	Det.	Vastra Frolunda Jr.	C
121	PAVLOV, Yevgeny	Tor.-Car.-Nsh.	Lada Togliatti	LW
122	KOVAC, Kristian	Col.	Kosice Jr.	RW
123	MIZZI, Preston	Ott.-NYI-Phx.	Peterborough	C
124	KREVSUN, Alexander	Det.-Nsh.	Samara	RW
125	JOHANSSON, Daniel	N.J.-NYI-L.A.	MoDo Jr.	C
126	BATEMAN, Jeff	Dal.	Brampton	C

ROUND #5

#	Name	Team	Club	Pos
127	ASTASHENKO, Kaspars	T.B.	Cincinnati	D
128	MACKENZIE, Derek	Atl.	Sudbury	C
129	THORPE, Ryan	Van.	Spokane	LW
130	MAPLETOFT, Justin	NYI	Red Deer	C
131	PANOV, Konstantin	Nsh.	Kamloops	RW
132	TVRDON, Roman	Wsh.	Dukla Trencin Jr.	C
133	NOGUES, Jean-Francois	L.A.	Victoriaville	G
134	JACOBSEN, Michael	Chi.	Belleville	D
135	DOMAN, Matt	Cgy.	U. of Wisconsin	RW
136	JAMIESON, Dustin	Mtl.	Sarnia	LW
137	BEMBRIDGE, Garett	NYR	Saskatoon	RW
138	MILLER, Ryan	Fla.-Buf.	Soo	G
139	FAUTEUX, Jonathon	Edm.	Val D'Or	D
140	JOHNSON, Adam	S.J.-Fla.-NYI	Greenway	D
141	RYBIN, Maxim	Ana.	Spartak Moscow	RW
142	MAGNUSON, William	Car.-Col.	Lake Superior St.	D
143	BYRNE, Trevor	St.L.	Deerfield Academy	D
144	SKVARIDLO, Tomas	Pit.	ZTK Zvolen Jr.	LW
145	THINEL, Marc-Andre	Phx.-S.J.-Mtl.	Victoriaville	RW
146	KINCH, Matthew	Buf.	Calgary	D
147	KOTYK, Seamus	Bos.	Ottawa	G
148	LANICEK, Michal	Phi.-T.B.	Slavia Praha Jr.	G
149	MAXIMENKO, Andrei	Det.-S.J.-Det.	Soviet Wings	LW
150	SHASBY, Matt	Mtl.	Des Moines	D
151	ZAVORAL, Vaclav	Tor.	Litvinov Jr.	LW
152	KRESTANOVICH, Jordan	Col.	Calgary	LW
153	COOK, Jesse	Cgy.	U. of Denver	D
154	IANIERO, Andrew	Ott.	Kingston	LW
155	DIMITRAKOS, Nicholas	N.J.-S.J.	U. of Maine	RW
156	BAUMGARTNER, Gregor	Dal.	Acadie-Bathurst	C
157	MALENKIKH, Vladimir	Pit.	Lada Togliatti	D

ROUND #6

#	Name	Team	Club	Pos
158	LOVDAHL, Anders	T.B.-Col.	HV 71 Jr.	C
159	DOBRYSHKIN, Yuri	Atl.	Soviet Wings	LW
160	RUDENKO, Konstantin	Van.-Phi.	Cherepovets-2	LW
161	SOCHOR, Jan	NYI-Tor.	Slavia Praha	RW
162	HELBLING, Timo	Nsh.	Davos	D
163	MELIN, Bjorn	Wsh.-NYI	HV 71 Jr.	RW
164	PRUSEK, Martin	L.A.-Col.-Chi.-Ott.	HC Vitkovice	G
165	LEIGHTON, Michael	Chi.	Windsor	G
166	PECKER, Cory	Cgy.	Sault Ste. Marie	C
167	DIXON, Sean	Mtl.	Erie	D
168	LEVERSTROM, Erik	NYR-Mtl.-Phx.	Grums	D
169	WOODS, Brad	Fla.	Brampton	D
170	UNDERHILL, Matt	Cgy.	Cornell	G
171	LEGG, Chris	Edm.	London Jr. B	C
172	REED, Josh	S.J.-Van.	Vernon	D
173	SANDSTROM, Jan	Ana.	AIK Solna	D
174	SURMA, Damian	Car.	Plymouth	LW
175	CLARK, Kyle	St.L.-Wsh.	Harvard	RW
176	MEYER, Doug	Pit.	U. of Minnesota	LW
177	DARDIS, Jay	Phx.-NYR	Proctor	C
178	HYACINTHE, Seneque	Buf.	Val D'Or	LW
179	CHOUKALOS, Donald	Bos.	Regina	G
180	VIKINGSTAD, Tore	Phi.-St.L.	Farjestads	W
181	MCDONELL, Kent	Det.	Guelph	RW
182	FEDOROV, Fedor	Tor.-NYI-T.B.	Port Huron	C
183	HAHL, Riku	Col.	Hameenlinna	C
184	COX, Justin	Ott.-Fla.-Atl.-Dal.	Prince George	RW
185	CAMERON, Scott	N.J.	Barrie	C
186	DRANEY, Brett	Dal.	Kamloops	LW

ROUND #7

#	Name	Team	Club	Pos
187	RACHUNEK, Ivan	T.B.	ZPS Zlin Jr.	LW
188	BABY, Stephan	Atl.	Green Bay	RW
189	SWANSON, Kevin	Van.	Kelowna	G
190	STAYZER, Blair	NYI-Cgy.	Windsor	LW
191	ERAT, Martin	Nsh.	ZPS Zlin Jr.	LW
192	JOHANSSON, David	Wsh.	AIK Solna Jr.	D
193	BAKER, Kevin	L.A.	Belleville	RW
194	WENNERBERG, Mattias	Chi.	MoDo Jr.	C
195	TREILLE, Yorick	Cgy.-Chi.	U. of Mass-Lowell	RW
196	TARASOV, Vadim	Mtl.	Novokuznetsk	G
197	LAATIKAINEN, Arto	NYR	Kiekko-Espoo	D
198	EAGLES, Travis	Fla.	Prince George	RW
199	CHARTIER, Christian	Edm.	Saskatoon	D
200	KASPARIK, Pavel	S.J.-Phi.	IHC Pisek	C
201	RUUTU, Mikko	Ana.-Ott.	HIFK Helsinki	W
202	BAXTER, Jim	Car.	Oshawa	D
203	OSAER, Phil	St.L.	Ferris State	G
204	KOSTOPOULOS, Tom	Pit.	London	RW
205	KETTLES, Kyle	Phx.-Nsh.	Selkirk/Neepawa	G
206	DECECCO, Bret	Buf.	Seattle	RW
207	BARBER, Greg	Bos.	Victoria	RW
208	PLETKA, Vaclav	Phi.	Trinec	LW
209	ULMER, Layne	Ott.	Swift Current	C
210	ZETTERBERG, Henrik	Det.	Sundsvall Timra	LW
211	KULKOV, Vladimir	Tor.	CSKA Moscow Jr	D
212	VRBATA, Radim	Col.	Hull	RW
213	GIROUX, Alexandre	Ott.	Hull	F
214	HARTSBURG, Chris	N.J.	Colorado College	F
215	MACMILLAN, Jeff	Dal.	Oshawa	D

ROUND #8

#	Name	Team	Club	Pos
216	RAJAMAKI, Erkki	T.B.	HIFK Helsinki	W
217	EXELBY, Garnet	Atl.	Saskatoon	D
218	KANKAANPERA, Markus	Van.	JyP HT Jyvaskyla	D
219	ORLOV, Maxim	NYI-Wsh.	CSKA Moscow Jr.	C
220	DURAK, Miroslav	Nsh.	Slovan Bratislava	D
221	HEMINGWAY, Colin	Wsh.-St.L.	Surrey	W
222	PARROS, George	L.A.	Chicago	RW
223	CARVER, Andrew	Chi.	Hull	D
224	NYSTROM, David	Cgy.-Phi.	Vastra Frolunda	W
225	HYYTIA, Mikko	Mtl.	JyP HT Jyvaskyla	C
226	GUSAKOV, Evgeny	NYR	Lada Togliatti	LW
227	CHARRON, Jonathan	Fla.	Val D'Or	G
228	MARTINEK, Radek	Edm.-NYI	Ceske Budejovice	W
229	BETOURNAY, Eric	S.J.	Acadie-Bathurst	C
230	TENKRAT, Petr	Ana.	Kladno	W
231	EVANS, David	Car.	Clarkson	RW
232	KHAVANOV, Alexander	St.L.	Moscow Dynamo	D
233	ROBINSON, Darcy	Pit.	Saskatoon	D
234	BEZINA, Goran	Phx.	Fribourg Jr.	D
235	SELF, Brad	Buf.	Peterborough	C
236	CRONIN, John	Bos.	Nobles Prep.	D
237	JOKELA, Antti	Phi.-Car.	Lukko Rauma Jr.	G
238	BORODKIN, Anton	Det.	Kamloops	LW
239	HEDIN, Pierre	Tor.	MoDo	D
240	FINGER, Jeff	Col.	Green Bay	D
241	MURRAY, Doug	Ott.-S.J.	Apple Core	D
242	DZIAMA, Justin	N.J.	Nobles Prep.	RW
243	SULLIVAN, Brian	Dal.	Thayer Academy	D

ROUND #9

#	Name	Team	Club	Pos
244	KUPARINEN, Mikko	T.B.	Grand Rapids	D
245	SANTALA, Tommy	Atl.	Jokerit Helsinki	F
246	DILAURO, Ray	Van.-Atl.	St. Lawrence	D
247	ELORANTA, Mikko	NYI-Bos.	Jokerit Helsinki	W
248	HAYDAR, Darren	Nsh.	U. of New Hampshire	RW
249	SHADILOV, Igor	Wsh.-Chi.-Wsh.	Moscow Dynamo	D
250	CLARKE, Noah	L.A.	Des Moines	LW
251	HENNING, Peter	Chi.-NYR	MoDo	C
252	KIRILENKO, Dimitri	Cgy.	CSKA Moscow	C
253	MAROIS, Jerome	Mtl.	Quebec	LW
254	BULATOV, Alexei	NYR	Yekaterinburg	LW
255	HENNING, Brett	Fla.-NYI	U. of Notre Dame	C
256	GROSCHL, Tomas	Edm.	Leksands IF	W
257	HYVONEN, Hannes	S.J.	Kiekko-Espoo	D
258	GORNICK, Brian	Ana.	Air Force Academy	C
259	KURILIN, Yauhenni	Car.	Anchorage	C
260	MCMEEKIN, Brian	St.L.	Cornell	D
261	MCPHERSON, Andrew	Pit.	R.P.I.	LW
262	LITVINENKO, Alexei	Phx.	Kamenogorsk	D
263	BRUNEL, Craig	Buf.	Prince Albert	RW
264	PUJJACS, Georgijs	Bos.	Dynamo Riga	D
265	CHAMBERLAIN, Jamie	Phi.-Dal.	Peterborough	RW
266	DAVIS, Ken	Det.	Portland	RW
267	METCALF, Peter	Tor.	U. of Maine	D
268	SCOTT, Tyler	Col.-NYI	Upper Canada College	D
269	GOROVIKOV, Konstantin	Ott.	SKA St. Peterburg	F
270	DESMARAIS, James	N.J.-St.L.	Rouyn Noranda	C
271	HAY, Darrell	Van.	Tri-City	D
272	DONIKA, Mihail	Dal.	Torpedo Yaroslavl	D

Draft Choices, 1998-69

1998

FIRST ROUND

Selection	Claimed By	Amateur Club	
1 LECAVALIER, Vincent	Fla -S.J -T.B.	Rimouski	C
2 LEGWAND, David	T.B -S.J.-Nsh.	Plymouth	C
3 STUART, Brad	Nsh.-S.J.	Regina	D
4 ALLEN, Bryan	Van.	Oshawa	D
5 VISHNEVSKY, Vitaly	Ana.	Torpedo-2 Yaroslavl	D
6 FATA, Rico	Cgy.	London	C
7 MALHOTRA, Manny	NYR	Guelph	C
8 BELL, Mark	Tor -Chi.	Ottawa	LW
9 RUPP, Michael	NYI	Erie	LW
10 ANTROPOV, Nikolai	Chi -Tor.	Torpedo Ust-Kamenogorsk	C
11 HEEREMA, Jeff	Car.	Sarnia	RW
12 TANGUAY, Alex	S.J.-Col.	Halifax	C
13 HENRICH, Michael	Edm.	Barrie	RW
14 DESROCHERS, Patrick	Phx.	Sarnia	G
15 CHOUINARD, Mathieu	Ott.	Shawinigan	C
16 CHOUINARD, Eric	Mtl.	Quebec	C
17 SKOULA, Martin	L.A -Col.	Barrie	D
18 KALININ, Dimitri	Buf.	Traktor Chelyabinsk	D
19 REGEHER, Robyn	Bos.-Col.	Kamloops	D
20 PARKER, Scott	Wsh.-Col.	Kelowna	D
21 BIRON, Mathieu	Col -L.A.	Shawinigan	D
22 GAGNE, Simon	Phi -T.B -Phi.	Quebec	C
23 KRAFT, Milan	T.B.	Keramika Plzen Jr.	C
24 BACKMAN, Christian	St.L.	Vastra Frolunda Jr.	D
25 FISCHER, Jiri	Det.	Hull	D
26 VAN RYN, Mike	N.J.	U. of Michigan	D
27 GOMEZ, Scott	Dal -N.J.	Tri-City	C

SECOND ROUND

28 ABID, Ramzi	T.B.-Col.	Chicoutimi	LW
29 CHEECHOO, Jonathan	Nsh -S.J.	Belleville	RW
30 ROSSITER, Kyle	Fla.	Spokane	D
31 CHUBAROV, Artem	Van.	Dynamo Moscow	C
32 PEAT, Stephen	Ana.	Red Deer	D
33 BETTS, Blair	Cgy.	Prince George	C
34 PETERS, Andrew	NYR-Buf.	Oshawa	LW
35 SVOBODA, Petr	Tor.	Havlickuv Brod	C
36 NEILSON, Chris	NYI	Calgary	C
37 BERGLUND, Christian	N.J.	Farjestad Karlstad Jr.	C
38 SAUVE, Philippe	Chi-Col.	Rimouski	G
39 ERSKINE, John	Car -N.J -Dal	London	D
40 COPLEY, Randy	NYR	Cape Breton	RW
41 LINNIK, Maxim	S.J -Det.-St.L.	St. Thomas Jr. B	D
42 BECKETT, Jason	Edm -Phi.	Seattle	D
43 VAANANEN, Ossi	Phx.	Jokerit Helsinki Jr.	D
44 FISHER, Mike	Ott.	Sudbury	C
45 RIBEIRO, Mike	Mtl.	Rouyn-Noranda	C
46 PAPINEAU, Justin	L.A.	Belleville	C
47 MILLEY, Norman	Buf.	Sudbury	RW
48 GIRARD, Jonathan	Bos.	Laval	D
49 CRUZ, Jomar	Wsh	Brandon	G
50 KRISTEK, Jaroslav	Col -S.J -Buf.	ZPS Zlin	RW
51 FORBES, Ian	Phi.	Guelph	D
52 ALLEN, Bobby	Bos.	Boston College	D
53 MOORE, Steve	Col.	Harvard	C
54 ZEVAKHIN, Alexander	Pit.	CSKA Moscow	RW
55 BARNES, Ryan	St.L-Det.	Sudbury	LW
56 VALTONEN, Tomek	Det.	Ilves Tampere Jr.	LW
57 BOUCK, Tyler	N.J.-Dal.	Prince George	RW
58 BALA, Chris	Dal.-Phi -Ott.	Harvard	LW

1997

FIRST ROUND

Selection	Claimed By	Amateur Club	
1 THORNTON, Joe	Bos.	Sault Ste. Marie	C
2 MARLEAU, Patrick	S.J.	Seattle	C
3 JOKINEN, Olli	L.A.	HIFK Helsinki	C
4 LUONGO, Roberto	Tor.-NYI	Val D'Or	G
5 BREWER, Eric	NYI	Prince George	D
6 TKACZUK, Daniel	Cgy.	Barrie	C
7 MARA, Paul	T.B.	Sudbury	D
8 SAMSONOV, Sergei	Car.-Bos.	Detroit	LW
9 BOYNTON, Nicholas	Wsh.	Ottawa	D
10 FERENCE, Brad	Van.	Spokane	D
11 WARD, Jason	Mtl.	Erie	D
12 HOSSA, Marian	Ott.	Dukla Trencin	RW
13 CLEARY, Daniel	Chi.	Belleville	LW
14 RIESEN, Michel	Edm.	Biel-Bienne	LW
15 ZULTEK, Matt	St.L-Edm.- St.L.-L.A.	Ottawa	LW
16 JONES, Ty	Pho.-Chi.	Spokane	RW
17 DOME, Robert	Pit.	Long Beach/ Las Vegas	RW
18 HOLMQVIST, Mikael	Ana.	Djurgarden	C
19 CHERNESKI, Stefan	NYR	Brandon	RW
20 BROWN, Mike	Fla.	Red Deer	C
21 NORONEN, Mika	Buf.	Tappara Tampere	G
22 TSELIOS, Nikos	Det.-Car.	Belleville	D
23 HANNAN, Scott	Phi.-Car.-S.J.	Kelowna	D
24 DAMPHOUSSE, J-F	N.J.	Moncton	G
25 MORROW, Brenden	Dal.	Portland	LW
26 GRIMES, Kevin	Col.	Kingston	D

SECOND ROUND

27 CLYMER, Ben	Bos.	U. of Minnesota	D
28 DEFAUW, Brad	S.J.-Car.	U. of North Dakota	LW
29 BARNEY, Scott	L.A.	Peterborough	C
30 PELLETIER, Jean-Marc	Tor.-Phi.	Cornell U.	G
31 ZEHR, Jeff	NYI	Windsor	LW
32 LINDSAY, Evan	Cgy.	Prince Albert	G
33 KOS, Kyle	T.B.	Red Deer	D
34 BONNI, Ryan	Car.-Van.	Saskatoon	D
35 FORTIN, J-F	Wsh.	Sherbrooke	D
36 DRUKEN, Harold	Van.	Detroit	LW
37 BAUMGARTNER, Gregor	Mtl.	Laval	C
38 GRON, Stanislav	Ott.-N.J.	Slovan Bratislava Jr.	C
39 REICH, Jeremy	Chi.	Seattle	C
40 RENNETTE, Tyler	St.L.	North Bay	C
41 DOVIGI, Patrick	Edm.	Erie	G
42 TRIPP, John	St.L.-Cgy.	Oshawa	RW
43 GUSTAFSSON, Juha	Pho.	Kiekko-Espoo Jr.	D
44 GAFFANEY, Brian	Pit.	North Iowa Jr. A	D
45 BALMOCHNYKH, Maxim	Ana.	Lada Togliatti	LW
46 JARVIS, Wes	NYR	Kitchener	D
47 HUSELIUS, Kristian	Fla.	Farjestad Karlstad	LW
48 TALLINDER, Henrik	Buf.	AIK Solna	D
49 BUTSAYEV, Yuri	Det.	Lada Togliatti	C
50 KAVANAGH, Pat	Phi.	Peterborough	RW
51 KOKOREV, Dmitri	N.J.-Car.-Cgy.	Dynamo-2 Moscow	D
52 LYASHENKO, Roman	Dal.	Torpedo Yaroslavl	C
53 BELAK, Graham	Col.	Edmonton	D

1996

FIRST ROUND

Selection	Claimed By	Amateur Club	
1 PHILLIPS, Chris	Ott.	Prince Albert	D
2 ZYUZIN, Andrei	S.J.	Salavat Yulayev Ufa	D
3 DUMONT, Jean-Pierre	NYI	Val d'Or	RW
4 VOLCHKOV, Alexander	L.A.-Wsh.	Barrie	C
5 JACKMAN, Richard	Dal.	Sault Ste. Marie	D
6 DEVEREAUX, Boyd	Edm.	Kitchener	C
7 RASMUSSEN, Erik	Buf.	U. of Minnesota	C
8 AITKEN, Johnathan	Hfd.-Bos.	Medicine Hat	D
9 SALEI, Ruslan	Ana.	Las Vegas	D
10 WARD, Lance	N.J.	Red Deer	D
11 FOCHT, Dan	Pho.	Tri-City	D
12 HOLDEN, Josh	Van.	Regina	C
13 MORRIS, Derek	Cgy.	Regina	D
14 REASONER, Marty	St.L.-Edm.-St.L.	Boston College	C
15 ZUBRUS, Dainius	Tor.-Phi.	Pembroke	RW
16 LAROCQUE, Mario	T.B.	Hull	D
17 SVEJKOVSKY, Jaroslav	Wsh.	Tri-City	RW
18 HIGGINS, Matt	Mtl.	Moose Jaw	C
19 DESCOTEAUX, Matthieu	Bos -Edm.	Shawinigan	D
20 NILSON, Marcus	Fla.	Djurgarden Stockholm	C
21 STURM, Marco	Chi.-S.J.	Landshut	C
22 BROWN, Jeff	NYR	Sarnia	D
23 HILLIER, Craig	Pit.	Ottawa	G
24 BRIERE, Daniel	Phi.-Pho.	Drummondville	C
25 RATCHUK, Peter	Col.	Shattuck St. Mary's	D
26 WALLIN, Jesse	Det.	Red Deer	D

SECOND ROUND

27 SARICH, Cory	Ott.-St.L.-Buf.	Saskatoon	D
28 SKRBEK, Pavel	S.J.-N.J.-Pit.	HC Kladno	D
29 LACOUTURE, Dan	NYI	Jr. Whalers	LW
30 GREEN, Josh	L.A.	Medicine Hat	LW
31 ROYER, Remi	Dal.-Pho.- S.J.-Chi.	St-Hyacinthe	D
32 HAJT, Chris	Edm.	Guelph	D
33 VAN OENE, Darren	Buf.	Brandon	LW
34 WASYLUK, Trevor	Hfd.	Medicine Hat	LW
35 CULLEN, Matt	Ana.	St. Cloud State	C
36 POSMYK, Marek	N.J.-Tor.	Dukla Jihlava	D
37 CISAR, Marian	Pho.-L.A.	Slovan Bratislava	W
38 MASON, Wesley	Van.-N.J.	Sarnia	LW
39 BRIGLEY, Travis	Cgy.	Lethbridge	LW
40 BEGIN, Steve	St.L.-Cgy.	Val d'Or	C
41 DEWOLF, Joshua	Tor.-Pit.-N.J.	Twin Cities	D
42 PAUL, Jeff	T.B.-Col.	Niagara Falls	D
43 BULIS, Jan	Wsh.	Barrie	C
44 GARON, Mathieu	Mtl.	Victoriaville	G
45 KUSTER, Henry	Bos.	Medicine Hat	RW
46 PETERS, Geoff	Fla.-S.J.-Chi.	Niagara Falls	C
47 DAGENAIS, Pierre	Chi.-T.B -N.J.	Moncton	LW
48 GONEAU, Daniel	NYR	Granby	LW
49 WHITE, Colin	Pit.-N.J.	Hull	D
50 LARIVEE, Francis	Phi.-Tor.	Laval	G
51 BABENKO, Yuri	Col.	Krylja Sovetov	C
52 MILLER, Aren	Det.	Spokane	G

1995

FIRST ROUND

Selection	Claimed By	Amateur Club	
1. BERARD, Bryan	Ott.	Detroit	D
2. REDDEN, Wade	NYI	Brandon	D
3. BERG, Aki-Petteri	L.A.	Kiekko-67 Turku	D
4. KILGER, Chad	Ana.	Kingston	C
5. LANGKOW, Daymond	T.B.	Tri-City	C
6. KELLY, Steve	Edm.	Prince Albert	C
7. DOAN, Shane	Wpg.	Kamloops	RW
8. RYAN, Terry	Mtl.	Tri-City	LW
9. McLAREN, Kyle	Hfd.-Bos.	Tacoma	D
10. DVORAK, Radek	Fla.	HC Ceske Budejovice	W
11. IGINLA, Jarome	Dal.	Kamloops	C
12. RIIHIJARVI, Teemu	S.J.	Kiekko-Espoo Jr.	LW
13. GIGUERE, J-Sebastien	NYR-Hfd.	Halifax	G
14. McKEE, Jay	Van.-Buf.	Niagara Falls	D
15. WARE, Jeff	Tor.	Oshawa	D
16. BIRON, Martin	Buf.	Beauport	G
17. CHURCH, Brad	Wsh.	Prince Albert	LW
18. SYKORA, Petr	N.J.	Detroit	C
19. NABOKOV, Dmitri	Chi.	Krylja Sovetov	C
20. GAUTHIER, Denis Jr	Cgy.	Drummondville	D
21. BROWN, Sean	Bos.	Belleville	D
22. BOUCHER, Brian	Phi.	Tri-City	G
23. ELOMO, Miika	St.L.-Wsh.	Kiekko-67 Turku	LW
24. MOROZOV, Alexei	Pit.	Krylja Sovetov	RW
25. DENIS, Marc	Col.	Chicoutimi	G
26. KUZNETSOV, Maxim	Det.	Dynamo Moscow	D

SECOND ROUND

27. MORO, Marc	Ott.	Kingston	D
28. HLAVAC, Jan	NYI	Sparta Praha	LW
29. WESENBERG, Brian	Ana.	Guelph	RW
30. McBAIN, Mike	T.B.	Red Deer	D
31. LARAQUE, Georges	Edm.	St-Jean	RW
32. CHOUINARD, Marc	Wpg.	Beauport	C
33. MacLEAN, Donald	L.A.	Beauport	C
34. DOIG, Jason	Mtl.-Wpg.	Laval	D
35. FEDOTOV, Sergei	Hfd.	Dynamo Moscow	D
36. MacDONALD, Aaron	Fla.	Swift Current	G
37. COTE, Patrick	Dal.	Beauport	LW
38. ROED, Peter	S.J.	White Bear Lake	C
39. DUBE, Christian	NYR	Sherbrooke	C
40. McALLISTER, Chris	Van.	Saskatoon	D
41. SMITH, Denis (D.J.)	Tor.-NYI	Windsor	D
42. DUTIAUME, Mark	Buf.	Brandon	LW
43. HAY, Dwayne	Wsh.	Guelph	LW
44. PERROTT, Nathan	N.J.	Oshawa	RW
45. LAFLAMME, Christian	Chi.	Beauport	D
46. SMIRNOV, Pavel	Cgy.	Molot Perm	RW/C
47. SCHAFER, Paxton	Bos.	Medicine Hat	G
48. KENNY, Shane	Phi.	Owen Sound	C
49. HECHT, Jochen	St.L.	Mannheim	C
50. ROSA, Pavel	Pit.-L.A.	Litvinov Jr.	RW
51. BEAUDOIN, Nic	Col.	Detroit	LW
52. AUDET, Philippe	Det.	Granby	LW

A Stanley Cup champion in 1999, Derian Hatcher has been a member of the Stars organization since Minnesota selected him eighth overall in the 1990 Entry Draft. Big brother Kevin Hatcher had been Washington's first round draft choice (17th overall) back in 1984.

1994

FIRST ROUND

Selection	Claimed By	Amateur Club	
1. JOVANOVSKI, Ed	Fla.	Windsor	D
2. TVERDOVSKY, Oleg	Ana.	Soviet Wings	D
3. BONK, Radek	Ott.	Las Vegas	C
4. BONSIGNORE, Jason	Wpg.-Edm.	Niagara Falls	C
5. O'NEILL, Jeff	Hfd.	Guelph	C
6. SMYTH, Ryan	Edm.	Moose Jaw	LW
7. STORR, Jamie	L.A.	Owen Sound	G
8. WIEMER, Jason	T.B.	Portland	LW
9. LINDROS, Brett	Que.-NYI	Kingston	RW
10. BAUMGARTNER, Nolan	Phi.-Que.-Tor.-Wsh.	Kamloops	D
11. FRIESEN, Jeff	S.J.	Regina	LW
12. BELAK, Wade	NYI-Que.	Saskatoon	D
13. OHLUND, Mattias	Van.	Pitea	D
14. MOREAU, Ethan	Chi.	Niagara Falls	LW
15. KHARLAMOV, Alexander	Wsh.	CSKA Moscow	C
16. FICHAUD, Eric	St.L.-Wsh.-Tor.	Chicoutimi	G
17. PRIMEAU, Wayne	Buf.	Owen Sound	C
18. BROWN, Brad	Mtl.	North Bay	D
19. DINGMAN, Chris	Cgy.	Brandon	LW
20. BOTTERILL, Jason	Dal.	U. of Michigan	LW
21. RYABCHIKOV, Evgeni	Bos.	Molot Perm	G
22. KEALTY, Jeffrey	Tor.-Que.	Catholic Memorial	D
23. GOLUBOVSKY, Yan	Det.	CSKA Jr. Moscow	D
24. WELLS, Chris	Pit.	Seattle	G
25. SHARIFIJANOV, Vadim	N.J.	Salavat Yulayev ufa	RW
26. CLOUTIER, Dan	NYR	Sault Ste. Marie	G

SECOND ROUND

Selection	Claimed By	Amateur Club	
27. WARRENER, Rhett	Fla.	Saskatoon	D
28. DAVIDSSON, Johan	Ana.	HV 71	C
29. NECKAR, Stanislav	Ott.	Ceske Budejovice	D
30. QUINT, Deron	Wpg.	Seattle	D
31. PODOLLAN, Jason	Hfd.-Fla.	Spokane	C
32. WATT, Mike	Edm.	Stratford Jr. B	LW
33. JOHNSON, Matt	L.A.	Peterborough	LW
34. CLOUTIER, Colin	T.B.	Brandon	C
35. MARHA, Josef	Que.	Dukla Jihlava	C
36. JOHNSON, Ryan	Phi.-Fla.	Thunder Bay Jr. A	C
37. NIKOLOV, Angel	S.J.	Litvinov	D
38. HOLLAND, Jason	NYI	Kamloops	D
39. GORDON, Robb	Van.	Powell River Jr. A	C
40. LEROUX, Jean-Yves	Chi.	Beauport	LW
41. CHERREY, Scott	Wsh.	North Bay	LW
42. SCATCHARD, Dave	St.L.-Van.	Portland	C
43. BROWN, Curtis	Buf.	Moose Jaw	C
44. THEODORE, Jose	Mtl.	St-Jean	G
45. RYABYKIN, Dmitri	Cgy.	Dynamo-2	D
46. JINMAN, Lee	Dal.	North Bay	C
47. GONEAU, Daniel	Bos.	Laval	LW
48. HAGGERTY, Sean	Tor.	Detroit	LW
49. DANDENAULT, Mathieu	Det.	Sherbrooke	RW
50. PARK, Richard	Pit.	Belleville	C
51. ELIAS, Patrik	N.J.	Kladno	LW
52. VERCIK, Rudolf	NYR	Slovan Bratislava	LW

1993

FIRST ROUND

Selection	Claimed By	Amateur Club	
1. DAIGLE, Alexandre	Ott.	Victoriaville	C
2. PRONGER, Chris	S.J.-Hfd.	Peterborough	D
3. GRATTON, Chris	T.B.	Kingston	C
4. KARIYA, Paul	Ana.	University of Maine	LW
5. NIEDERMAYER, Rob	Fla.	Medicine Hat	C
6. KOZLOV, Viktor	Hfd.-S.J.	Dynamo Moscow	LW
7. ARNOTT, Jason	Edm.	Oshawa	C
8. SUNDSTROM, Niklas	NYR	MoDo	LW
9. HARVEY, Todd	Dal.	Detroit	C
10. THIBAULT, Jocelyn	Phi.-Que.	Sherbrooke	G
11. WITT, Brendan	St. L.-Wsh.	Seattle	D
12. JONSSON, Kenny	Buf.-Tor.	Rogle Angelholm	D
13. PEDERSON, Denis	N.J.	Prince Albert	C
14. DEADMARSH, Adam	NYI-Que.	Portland	C
15. LINDGREN, Mats	Wpg.	Skelleftea	C
16. STAJDUHAR, Nick	L.A.-Edm.	London	D
17. ALLISON, Jason	Wsh.	London	C
18. MATTSSON, Jesper	Cgy.	Malmo	C
19. WILSON, Landon	Tor.	Dubuque Jr. A	RW
20. WILSON, Mike	Van.	Sudbury	D
21. KOIVU, Saku	Mtl.	TPS Turku	C
22. ERIKSSON, Anders	Det.	MoDo	D
23. BERTUZZI, Todd	Que.-NYI	Guelph	C
24. LECOMPTE, Eric	Chi.	Hull	LW
25. ADAMS, Kevyn	Bos.	Miami-Ohio	C
26. BERGQVIST, Stefan	Pit.	Leksand	D

SECOND ROUND

Selection	Claimed By	Amateur Club	
27. BICANEK, Radim	Ott.	Dukla Jihlava	D
28. DONOVAN, Shean	S.J.	Ottawa	RW
29. MOSS, Tyler	T.B.	Kingston	G
30. TSULYGIN, Nikolai	Ana.	Salavat Yulalev Ufa	D
31. LANGKOW, Scott	Fla.-Wpg.	Portland	G
32. PANDOLFO, Jay	Hfd.-N.J.	Boston University	LW
33. VYBORNY, David	Edm.	Sparta Praha	C
34. SOROCHAN, Lee	NYR	Lethbridge	D
35. LANGENBRUNNER, Jamie	Dal.	Cloquet	C
36. NIINIMAA, Janne	Phi.	Karpat Oulu	D
37. BETS, Maxim	St. L.	Spokane	LW
38. TSYGUROV, Denis	Buf.	Lada Togliatti	D
39. MORRISON, Brendan	N.J.	Penticton T-II Jr. A	C
40. McCABE, Bryan	NYI	Spokane	D
41. WEEKES, Kevin	Wpg.-Fla.	Owen Sound	G
42. TOPOROWSKI, Shayne	L.A.	Prince Albert	RW
43. BUDAYEV, Alexei	Wsh.-Wpg.	Kristall Elektrostal	C
44. ALLISON, Jamie	Cgy.	Detroit	D
45. KROUPA, Vlastimil	Tor.-Hfd.-S.J.	Chemopetrol Litvinov	D
46. GIRARD, Rick	Van.	Swift Current	C
47. FITZPATRICK, Rory	Mtl.	Sudbury	D
48. COLEMAN, Jonathan	Det.	Andover Academy	D
49. BUCKBERGER, Ashley	Que.	Swift Current	RW
50. MANLOW, Eric	Chi.	Kitchener	C
51. ALVEY, Matt	Bos.	Springfield Jr. B	RW
52. PITTIS, Domenic	Pit.	Lethbridge	C

1992

FIRST ROUND

Selection	Claimed By	Amateur Club	
1. HAMRLIK, Roman	T.B.	ZPS Zlin (Czech.)	D
2. YASHIN, Alexei	Ott.	Dynamo Moscow (CIS)	C
3 RATHJE, Mike	S.J.	Medicine Hat	D
4. WARRINER, Todd	Que.	Windsor	LW
5. KASPARAITIS, Darius	Tor.-NYI	Dynamo Moscow (CIS)	D
6. STILLMAN, Cory	Cgy.	Windsor	C
7. SITTLER, Ryan	Phi.	Nichols	LW
8. CONVERY, Brandon	NYI-Tor.	Sudbury	C
9. PETROVICKY, Robert	Hfd.	Dukla Trencin (Czech.)	C
10. NAZAROV, Andrei	Min.-S.J.	Dynamo Moscow	LW
11. COOPER, David	Buf.	Medicine Hat	D
12. KRIVOKRASOV, Sergei	Wpg.-Chi.	CSKA Moscow (CIS)	RW
13. HULBIG, Joe	Edm.	St. Sebastian's	LW
14. GONCHAR, Sergei	St.L.-Wsh.	Chelybinsk (CIS)	D
15. BOWEN, Jason	L.A.-Pit.-Phi.	Tri-City	LW
16. KVARTALNOV, Dmitri	Bos.	San Diego	LW
17. BAUTIN, Sergei	Chi.-Wpg.	Dynamo Moscow (CIS)	D
18. SMITH, Jason	N.J.	Regina	D
19. STRAKA, Martin	Pit.	Skoda Plzen (Czech.)	C
20. WILKIE, David	Mtl.	Kamloops	D
21. POLASEK, Libor	Van.	TJ Vitkovice (Czech.)	C
22. BOWEN, Curtis	Det.	Ottawa	LW
23. MARSHALL, Grant	Wsh.-Tor.	Ottawa	RW
24. FERRARO, Peter	NYR	Waterloo Jr. A	C

SECOND ROUND

Selection	Claimed By	Amateur Club	
25. PENNEY, Chad	Ott.	North Bay	LW
26. BANNISTER, Drew	T.B.	Sault-Ste-Marie	D
27. MIRONOV, Boris	S.J.-Chi.-Wpg.	CSKA Moscow (CIS)	D
28. BROUSSEAU, Paul	Que.	Hull	RW
29. GRONMAN, Toumas	Tor.-Que.	Tacoma	D
30. O'SULLIVAN, Chris	Cgy.	Catholic Memorial	D
31. METLYUK, Denis	Phi.	Lada Togliatti (CIS)	C
32. CAREY, Jim	NYI-Tor.-Wsh.	Catholic Memorial	G
33. BURE, Valeri	Hfd.-Mtl.	Spokane	LW
34. VARVIO, Jarkko	Min.	HPK (Finland)	RW
35. CIERNY, Jozef	Buf.	ZTK Zvolen (Czech.)	LW
36. SHANTZ, Jeff	Wpg.-Chi.	Regina	C
37. REICHEL, Martin	Edm.	Freiburg (Germany)	RW
38. KOROLEV, Igor	St.L.	Dynamo Moscow	RW
39. HOCKING, Justin	L.A.	Spokane	D
40. PECA, Mike	Bos.-Van.	Ottawa	C
41. KLIMOVICH, Sergei	Chi.	Dynamo Moscow	C
42. BRYLIN, Sergei	N.J.	CSKA Moscow (CIS)	C
43. HUSSEY, Marc	Pit.	Moose Jaw	D
44. CORPSE, Keli	Mtl.	Kingston	C
45. FOUNTAIN, Michael	Van.	Oshawa	G
46. McCARTY, Darren	Det.	Belleville	RW
47. NIKOLISHIN, Andrei	Wsh.-Hfd.	Dynamo Moscow	LW
48. NORSTROM, Mattias	NYR	AIK (Sweden)	D

1991

FIRST ROUND

Selection	Claimed By	Amateur Club	
1. LINDROS, Eric	Que.	Oshawa	C
2. FALLOON, Pat	S.J.	Spokane	RW
3. NIEDERMAYER, Scott	Tor.-N.J.	Kamloops	D
4. LACHANCE, Scott	NYI	Boston University	D
5. WARD, Aaron	Wpg.	U. of Michigan	D
6. FORSBERG, Peter	Phi.	MoDo (Sweden)	C
7. STOJANOV, Alex	Van.	Hamilton	RW
8. MATVICHUK, Richard	Min.	Saskatoon	D
9. POULIN, Patrick	Hfd.	St.-Hyacinthe	LW
10. LAPOINTE, Martin	Det.	Laval	RW
11. ROLSTON, Brian	N.J.	Detroit Comp. Jr. A	C
12. WRIGHT, Tyler	Edm.	Swift Current	C
13. BOUCHER, Phillipe	Buf.	Granby	D
14. PEAKE, Pat	Wsh.	Detroit	C
15. KOVALEV, Alexei	NYR	D'amo Moscow	RW
16. NASLUND, Markus	Pit.	MoDo	RW
17. BILODEAU, Brent	Mtl.	Seattle	D
18. MURRAY, Glen	Bos.	Sudbury	RW
19. SUNDBLAD, Niklas	Cgy.	AIK (Sweden)	RW
20. RUCINSKY, Martin	L.A.-Edm.	CHZ Litvinov (Czech.)	LW
21. HALVERSON, Trevor	St.L.-Wsh.	North Bay	LW
22. McAMMOND, Dean	Chi.	Prince Albert	C

SECOND ROUND

Selection	Claimed By	Amateur Club	
23. WHITNEY, Ray	S.J.	Spokane	C
24. CORBET, Rene	Que.	Drummondville	LW
25. LAVIGNE, Eric	Tor.-Que.-Wsh.	Hull	D
26. PALFFY, Zigmund	NYI	AC Nitra (Czech.)	LW
27. STAIOS, Steve	Wpg.-St.L.	Niagara Falls	D
28. CAMPBELL, Jim	Phi.-Mtl.	Northwood Prep	C
29. CULLIMORE, Jassen	Van.	Peterborough	D
30. OZOLINSH, Sandis	Min.-S.J.	Dynamo Riga (USSR)	D
31. HAMRLIK, Martin	Hfd.	TJ Zin (Czech.)	D
32. PUSHOR, Jamie	Det.	Lethbridge	D
33. HEXTALL, Donevan	N.J.	Prince Albert	LW
34. VERNER, Andrew	Edm.	Peterborough	G
35. DAWE, Jason	Buf.	Peterborough	LW
36. NELSON, Jeff	Wsh.	Prince Albert	C
37. WERENKA, Darcy	NYR	Lethbridge	D
38. FITZGERALD, Rusty	Pit.	Duluth East HS	C
39. POMICHTER, Michael	Mtl.-Chi.	Springfield Jr. B	C
40. STUMPEL, Jozef	Bos.	AC Nitra (Czech.)	RW
41. GROLEAU, Francois	Cgy.	Shawinigan	D
42. LEVEQUE, Guy	L.A.	Cornwall	C
43. DARBY, Craig	St.L.-Mtl.	Albany Academy	C
44. MATTHEWS, Jamie	Chi.	Sudbury	C

1990

FIRST ROUND

Selection	Claimed By	Amateur Club	
1. NOLAN, Owen	Que.	Cornwall	RW
2. NEDVED, Petr	Van.	Seattle	C
3. PRIMEAU, Keith	Det.	Niagara Falls	C
4. RICCI, Mike	Phi.	Peterborough	C
5. JAGR, Jaromir	Pit.	Poldi Kladno (Czech.)	LW
6. SCISSONS, Scott	NYI	Saskatoon	C
7. SYDOR, Darryl	L.A.	Kamloops	D
8. HATCHER, Derian	Min.	North Bay	D
9. SLANEY, John	Wsh.	Cornwall	D
10. BEREHOWSKY, Drake	Tor.	Kingston	D
11. KIDD, Trevor	N.J.-Cgy.	Brandon	G
12. STEVENSON, Turner	St.L.-Mtl.	Seattle	RW
13. STEWART, Michael	NYR	Michigan State	D
14. MAY, Brad	Wpg.-Buf.	Niagara Falls	LW
15. GREIG, Mark	Hfd.	Lethbridge	RW
16. DYKHUIS, Karl	Chi.	Hull	D
17. ALLISON, Scott	Edm.	Prince Albert	C
18. ANTOSKI, Shawn	Mtl.-St.L.-Van.	North Bay	LW
19. TKACHUK, Keith	Buf.-Wpg.	Malden Catholic	LW
20. BRODEUR, Martin	Cgy.-N.J.	St. Hyacinthe	G
21. SMOLINSKI, Bryan	Bos.	Michigan State	C

SECOND ROUND

Selection	Claimed By	Amateur Club	
22. HUGHES, Ryan	Que.	Cornell	C
23. SLEGR, Jiri	Van.	CHZ Litvinov (Czech.)	D
24. HARLOCK, David	Det.-Cgy.-N.J.	U. of Michigan	D
25. SIMON, Chris	Phi.	Ottawa	LW
26. PERREAULT, Nicolas P.	Pit.-Cgy.	Hawkesbury Jr. A	D
27. TAYLOR, Chris	NYI	London	C
28. SEMCHUK, Brandy	L.A.	Canadian National	RW
29. GOTZIAMAN, Chris	Min.-Cgy.-N.J.	Roseau	RW
30. PASMA, Rod	Wsh.	Cornwall	D
31. POTVIN, Felix	Tor.	Chicoutimi	G
32. VIITAKOSKI, Vesa	N.J.-Cgy.	SaiPa (Finland)	LW
33. JOHNSON, Craig	St.L.	Hill-Murray HS	C
34. WEIGHT, Doug	NYR	Lake Superior	C
35. MULLER, Mike	Wpg.	Wayzata	D
36. SANDERSON, Geoff	Hfd.	Swift Current	C
37. DROPPA, Ivan	Chi.	Partizan (Czech.)	D
38. LEGAULT, Alexandre	Edm.	Boston University	RW
39. KUWABARA, Ryan	Mtl.	Ottawa	RW
40. RENBERG, Mikael	Buf.-Phi.	Pitea (Sweden)	LW
41. BELZILE, Etienne	Cgy.	Cornell	D
42. SANDWITH, Terran	Bos.-Phi.	Tri-Cities	D

1989

FIRST ROUND

Selection	Claimed By	Amateur Club	
1. SUNDIN, Mats	Que.	Nacka (Sweden)	RW
2. CHYZOWSKI, Dave	NYI	Kamloops	LW
3. THORNTON, Scott	Tor.	Belleville	C
4. BARNES, Stu	Wpg.	Tri-Cities	C
5. GUERIN, Bill	N.J.	Springfield Jr. B	RW
6. BENNETT, Adam	Chi.	Sudbury	D
7. ZMOLEK, Doug	Min.	John Marshall	D
8. HERTER, Jason	Van.	U. of North Dakota	D
9. MARSHALL, Jason	St.L.	Vernon Jr. A	D
10. HOLIK, Robert	Hfd.	Dukla Jihlava (Czech.)	C
11. SILLINGER, Mike	Det.	Regina	C
12. PEARSON, Rob	Phi.-Tor.	Belleville	RW
13. VALLIS, Lindsay	NYR-Mtl.	Seattle	RW
14. HALLER, Kevin	Buf.	Regina	D
15. SOULES, Jason	Edm.	Niagara Falls	D
16. HEWARD, Jamie	Pit.	Regina	RW
17. STEVENSON, Shayne	Bos.	Kitchener	RW
18. MILLER, Jason	L.A.-Edm.-N.J.	Medicine Hat	C
19. KOLZIG, Olaf	Wsh.	Tri-Cities	G
20. RICE, Steven	Mtl.-NYR	Kitchener	RW
21. BANCROFT, Steve	Cgy.-Tor.	Belleville	D

SECOND ROUND

Selection	Claimed By	Amateur Club	
22. FOOTE, Adam	Que.	Sault Ste. Marie	D
23. GREEN, Travis	NYI	Spokane	C
24. MANDERVILLE, Kent	Tor.-Cgy.	Notre Dame Jr. A	LW
25. RATUSHNY, Dan	Wpg.	Cornell	D
26. SKALDE, Jarrod	N.J.	Oshawa	C
27. SPEER, Michael	Chi.	Guelph	D
28. CRAIG, Mike	Min.	Oshawa	RW
29. WOODWARD, Robert	Van.	Deerfield	LW
30. BRISEBOIS, Patrice	St.L.-Mtl.	Laval	D
31. CORRIVEAU, Rick	Hfd.-St.L.	London	D
32. BOUGHNER, Bob	Det.	Sault-Ste. Marie	D
33. JOHNSON, Greg	Phi.	Thunder Bay Jr. A	C
34. JUHLIN, Patrik	NYR-Phi.	Vasteras (Sweden)	LW
35. DAFOE, Byron	Buf.-Wsh.	Portland	D
36. BORGO, Richard	Edm.	Kitchener	G
37. LAUS, Paul	Pit.	Niagara Falls	D
38. PARSON, Mike	Bos.	Guelph	G
39. THOMPSON, Brent	L.A.	Medicine Hat	D
40. PROSOFSKY, Jason	Wsh.-NYR	Medicine Hat	RW
41. LAROUCHE, Steve	Mtl.	Trois-Rivieres	C
42. DRURY, Ted	Cgy.	Fairfield Prep	C

1988

FIRST ROUND

Selection	Claimed By	Amateur Club	
1. MODANO, Mike	Min.	Prince Albert	C
2. LINDEN, Trevor	Van.	Medicine Hat	RW
3. LESCHYSHYN, Curtis	Que.	Saskatoon	D
4. SHANNON, Darrin	Pit.	Windsor	LW
5. DORE, Daniel	NYR-Que.	Drummondville	RW
6. PEARSON, Scott	Tor.	Kingston	LW
7. GELINAS, Martin	L.A.	Hull	LW
8. ROENICK, Jeremy	Chi.	Thayer Academy	C
9. BRIND'AMOUR, Rod	St.L.	Notre Dame Jr. A	C
10. SELANNE, Teemu	Wpg.	Jokerit (Finland)	RW
11. GOVEDARIS, Chris	Hfd.	Toronto	LW
12. FOSTER, Corey	N.J.	Peterborough	D
13. SAVAGE, Joel	Buf.	Victoria	RW
14. BOIVIN, Claude	Phi.	Drummondville	LW
15. SAVAGE, Reginald	Wsh.	Victoriaville	C
16. CHEVELDAYOFF, Kevin	NYI	Brandon	D
17. KOCUR, Kory	Det.	Saskatoon	RW
18. CIMETTA, Robert	Bos	Toronto	LW
19. LEROUX, Francois	Edm.	St. Jean	D
20. CHARRON, Eric	Mtl.	Trois-Rivieres	D
21. MUZZATTI, Jason	Cgy.	Michigan State	G

SECOND ROUND

Selection	Claimed By	Amateur Club	
22. MALLETTE, Troy	Min.-NYR	Sault Ste. Marie	C
23. CHRISTIAN, Jeff	Van.-N.J.	London	LW
24. FISET, Stephane	Que.	Victoriaville	G
25. MAJOR, Mark	Pit.	North Bay	D
26. DUVAL, Murray	NYR	Spokane	RW
27. DOMI, Tie	Tor.	Peterborough	RW
28. HOLDEN, Paul	L.A.	London	D
29. DOUCET, Wayne	Chi.-NYI	Hamilton	LW
30. PLAVSIC, Adrien	St.L.	U. of New Hampshire	D
31. ROMANIUK, Russell	Wpg.	St. Boniface Jr. A	LW
32. RICHTER, Barry	Hfd.	Culver Academy	D
33. ROHLIN, Leif	N.J.-Van.	Vasteras (Sweden)	D
34. ST. AMOUR, Martin	Buf.-Mtl.	Verdun	LW
35. MURRAY, Pat	Phi.	Michigan State	LW
36. TAYLOR, Tim	Wsh.	London	C
37. LEBRUN, Sean	NYI	New Westminster	LW
38. ANGLEHART, Serge	Det.	Drummondville	D
39. KOIVUNEN, Petro	Bos.-Edm.	Espoo (Finland)	C
40. GAETZ, Link	Edm.-Min.	Spokane	D
41. BARTLEY, Wade	Mtl.-St L.-Wsh.	Dauphin Jr. A	D
42. HARKINS, Todd	Cgy.	Miami-Ohio	RW

1987

FIRST ROUND

Selection	Claimed By	Amateur Club	
1. TURGEON, Pierre	Buf.	Granby	C
2. SHANAHAN, Brendan	N.J.	London	C
3. WESLEY, Glen	Van.-Bos.	Portland	D
4. McBEAN, Wayne	Min.-L.A.	Medicine Hat	D
5. JOSEPH, Chris	Pit.	Seattle	D
6. ARCHIBALD, David	L.A.-Min.	Portland	C/LW
7. RICHARDSON, Luke	Tor.	Peterborough	D
8. WAITE, Jimmy	Chi.	Chicoutimi	G
9. FOGARTY, Bryan	Que.	Kingston	D
10. MORE, Jayson	NYR	New Westminster	D
11. RACINE, Yves	Det.	Longueuil	D
12. OSBORNE, Keith	St.L.	North Bay	RW
13. CHYNOWETH, Dean	NYI	Medicine Hat	D
14. QUINTAL, Stephane	Bos.	Granby	D
15. SAKIC, Joe	Wsh.-Que.	Swift Current	C
16. MARCHMENT, Bryan	Wpg.	Belleville	D
17. CASSELS, Andrew	Mtl.	Ottawa	C
18. HULL, Jody	Hfd.	Peterborough	RW
19. DEASLEY, Bryan	Cgy.	U. of Michigan	LW
20. RUMBLE, Darren	Phi.	Kitchener	D
21. SOBERLAK, Peter	Edm.	Swift Current	LW

SECOND ROUND

Selection	Claimed By	Amateur Club	
22. MILLER, Brad	Buf.	Regina	D
23. PERSSON, Rickard	N.J.	Ostersund (Sweden)	D
24. MURPHY, Rob	Van.	Laval	C
25. MATTEAU, Stephane	Min.-Cgy.	Hull	LW
26. TABARACCI, Richard	Pit.	Cornwall	G
27. FITZPATRICK, Mark	L.A.	Medicine Hat	G
28. MAROIS, Daniel	Tor.	Chicoutimi	RW
29. McGILL, Ryan	Chi.	Swift Current	D
30. HARDING, Jeff	Que.-Phi.	St. Michael's Jr. B	LW
31. LACROIX, Daniel	NYR	Granby	LW
32. KRUPPKE, Gordon	Det.	Prince Albert	D
33. LECLAIR, John	St.L.-Mtl.	Bellows Academy	LW
34. HACKETT, Jeff	NYI	Oshawa	G
35. McCRADY, Scott	Bos.-Min.	Medicine Hat	D
36. BALLANTYNE, Jeff	Wsh.	Ottawa	D
37. ERICKSSON, Patrik	Wpg.	Brynas (Sweden)	C
38. DESJARDINS, Eric	Mtl.	Granby	D
39. BURT, Adam	Hfd.	North Bay	D
40. GRANT, Kevin	Cgy.	Kitchener	D
41. WILKIE, Bob	Phi.-Det.	Swift Current	D
42. WERENKA, Brad	Edm.	N. Michigan	D

1986

FIRST ROUND

Selection	Claimed By	Amateur Club	
1 MURPHY, Joe	Det.	Michigan State	C
2. CARSON, Jimmy	L.A.	Verdun	C
3. BRADY, Neil	N.J.	Medicine Hat	C
4. ZALAPSKI, Zarley	Pit.	Canadian National	D
5. ANDERSON, Shawn	Buf.	Canadian National	D
6 DAMPHOUSSE, Vincent	Tor.	Laval	LW
7. WOODLEY, Dan	Van.	Portland	C
8. ELYNUIK, Pat	Wpg.	Prince Albert	RW
9. LEETCH, Brian	NYR	Avon Old Farms HS	D
10. LEMIEUX, Jocelyn	St.L.	Laval	RW
11 YOUNG, Scott	Hfd.	Boston University	RW
12. BABE, Warren	Min.	Lethbridge	LW
13. JANNEY, Craig	Bos.	Boston College	C
14. SANIPASS, Everett	Chi.	Verdun	LW
15 PEDERSON, Mark	Mtl.	Medicine Hat	LW
16. PELAWA, George	Cgy.	Bemidji HS	RW
17 FITZGERALD, Tom	NYI	Austin Prep	C
18. McRAE, Ken	Que.	Sudbury	C
19. GREENLAW, Jeff	Wsh.	Canadian National	LW
20. HUFFMAN, Kerry	Phi.	Guelph	D
21. ISSEL, Kim	Edm.	Prince Albert	RW

SECOND ROUND

Selection	Claimed By	Amateur Club	
22. GRAVES, Adam	Det.	Windsor	C
23. SEPPO, Jukka	L.A.-Phi.	Sport (Finland)	LW
24 COPELAND, Todd	N.J.	Belmont Hill HS	D
25. CAPUANO, Dave	Pit.	Mt. St. Charles HS	C
26 BROWN, Greg	Buf.	St. Mark's	D
27. BRUNET, Benoit	Tor.-Mtl.	Hull	LW
28. HAWLEY, Kent	Van.-Phi.	Ottawa	C
29. NUMMINEN, Teppo	Wpg.	Tappara (Finland)	D
30. WILKINSON, Neil	NYR-Min.	Selkirk	D
31. POSMA, Mike	St.L.	Buffalo Jr. A	D
32. LaFORGE, Marc	Hfd.	Kingston	D
33. KOLSTAD, Dean	Min.	Prince Albert	D
34. TIRKKONEN, Pekka	Bos.	SaPKo (Finland)	C
35. KURZAWSKI, Mark	Chi.	Windsor	D
36. SHANNON, Darryl	Mtl.-Tor.	Windsor	D
37. GLYNN, Brian	Cgy.	Saskatoon	D
38. VASKE, Dennis	NYI	Armstrong HS	D
39. ROUTHIER, Jean-Marc	Que.	Hull	RW
40 SEFTEL, Steve	Wsh.	Kingston	LW
41. GUERARD, Stephane	Phi.-Que.	Shawinigan	D
42. NICHOLS, Jamie	Edm.	Portland	LW

1985

FIRST ROUND

Selection	Claimed By	Amateur Club	
1. CLARK, Wendel	Tor.	Saskatoon	D
2. SIMPSON, Craig	Pit.	Michigan State	C
3. WOLANIN, Craig	N.J.	Kitchener	D
4. SANDLAK, Jim	Van.	London	RW
5. MURZYN, Dana	Hfd.	Calgary	D
6 DALGARNO, Brad	Min.-NYI	Hamilton	RW
7. DAHLEN, Ulf	NYR	Ostersund (Sweden)	C
8. FEDYK, Brent	Det.	Regina	RW
9. DUNCANSON, Craig	L.A.	Sudbury	LW
10. GRATTON, Dan	Bos.-L.A.	Oshawa	C
11. MANSON, David	Chi.	Prince Albert	D
12. CHARBONNEAU, Jose	St.L.-Mtl.	Drummondville	RW
13. KING, Derek	NYI	Sault Ste. Marie	LW
14. JOHANSSON, Calle	Buf.	V. Frolunda (Sweden)	D
15. LATTA, Dave	Que.	Kitchener	LW
16. CHORSKE, Tom	Mtl.	Minneapolis SW HS	LW
17. BIOTTI, Chris	Cgy.	Belmont Hill HS	D
18. STEWART, Ryan	Wpg.	Kamloops	C
19. CORRIVEAU, Yvon	Wsh.	Toronto	LW
20. METCALFE, Scott	Edm.	Kingston	LW
21. SEABROOKE, Glen	Phi.	Peterborough	C

SECOND ROUND

Selection	Claimed By	Amateur Club	
22. SPANGLER, Ken	Tor.	Calgary	D
23. GIFFIN, Lee	Pit.	Oshawa	RW
24. BURKE, Sean	N.J.	Toronto	G
25. GAMBLE, Troy	Van.	Medicine Hat	G
26. WHITMORE, Kay	Hfd.	Peterborough	G
27. NIEUWENDYK, Joe	Min.-Cgy.	Cornell	C
28. RICHTER, Mike	NYR	Northwood Prep.	G
29. SHARPLES, Jeff	Det.	Kelowna	D
30. EDLUND, Par	L.A.	Bjorkloven (Sweden)	RW
31. COTE, Alain	Bos.	Quebec	D
32. WEINRICH, Eric	Chi.-N.J.	North Yarmouth	D
33. RICHARD, Todd	Mtl.	Armstrong HS	D
34. LAUER, Brad	NYI	Regina	RW
35. HOGUE, Benoit	Buf.	St-Jean	C
36. LAFRENIERE, Jason	Que.	Hamilton	C
37. RAGLAN, Herb	Mtl.-St.L.	Kingston	RW
38. WENAAS, Jeff	Cgy.	Medicine Hat	C
39. OHMAN, Roger	Wpg.	Leksand (Sweden)	D
40. DRUCE, John	Wsh.	Peterborough	RW
41. CARNELLEY, Todd	Edm.	Kamloops	D
42. RENDALL, Bruce	Phi.	Chatham	LW

1984

FIRST ROUND

Selection	Claimed By	Amateur Club	
1. LEMIEUX, Mario	Pit.	Laval	C
2. MULLER, Kirk	N.J.	Cdn-Nat.-Guelph	C
3. OLCZYK, Ed	L.A.-Chi.	U.S. National	RW
4. IAFRATE, Al	Tor.	U.S. National-Belleville	D
5. SVOBODA, Petr	Hfd.-Mtl.	CHZ (Czech.)	D
6. REDMOND, Craig	Chi.-L.A.	Canadian National	D
7. BURR, Shawn	Det.	Kitchener	C
8. CORSON, Shayne	St.L.-Mtl.	Brantford	C
9. BODGER, Doug	Wpg.-Pit.	Kamloops Jr. A	D
10. DAIGNEAULT, J.J.	Van.	Cdn. Nat.-Longueuil	D
11. COTE, Sylvain	Mtl.-Hfd.	Quebec	D
12. ROBERTS, Gary	Cgy.	Ottawa	LW
13. QUINN, David	Min.	Kent HS	D
14. CARKNER, Terry	NYR	Peterborough	D
15. STIENBURG, Trevor	Que.	Guelph	C
16. BELANGER, Roger	Phi.-Pit.	Kingston	D
17. HATCHER, Kevin	Wsh.	North Bay	D
18. ANDERSSON, Mikael	Buf.	V. Frolunda (Sweden)	C
19. PASIN, Dave	Bos.	Prince Albert	RW
20. MacPHERSON, Duncan	NYI	Saskatoon	D
21. ODELEIN, Selmar	Edm.	Regina	D

SECOND ROUND

Selection	Claimed By	Amateur Club	
22. SMYTH, Greg	Phi.	London	D
23. BILLINGTON, Craig	N.J.	Belleville	G
24. WILKS, Brian	L.A.	Kitchener	C
25. GILL, Todd	Tor.	Windsor	D
26. BENNING, Brian	Hfd.-St.L.	Portland	D
27. MELLANBY, Scott	Chi.-Phi.	Henry Carr Jr. B	RW
28. HOUDA, Doug	Det.	Calgary	D
29. RICHER, Stephane	St.L.-Mtl.	Granby	C
30. DOURIS, Peter	Wpg.	U. of New Hampshire	C
31. ROHLICEK, Jeff	Van.	Portland	LW
32. HRKAC, Anthony	Mtl.-St.L.	Orillia Jr. A	C
33. SABOURIN, Ken	Cgy.	Sault Ste. Marie	D
34. LEACH, Stephen	Min.-Wsh.	Matignon HS	RW
35. HELMINEN, Raimo	NYR	Ilves (Finland)	C
36. BROWN, Jeff	Que.	Sudbury	D
37. CHYCHRUN, Jeff	Phi.	Kingston	D
38. RANHEIM, Paul	Wsh.-Cgy.	Edina Hornets HS	C
39. TRAPP, Doug	Buf.	Regina	LW
40. PODLOSKI, Ray	Bos.	Portland	C
41. MELANSON, Bruce	NYI	Oshawa	RW
42. REAUGH, Daryl	Edm.	Kamloops Jr. A	G

1983

FIRST ROUND

Selection	Claimed By	Amateur Club	
1. LAWTON, Brian	Pit.-Min.	Mount St. Charles HS	C
2. TURGEON, Sylvain	Hfd.	Hull	C
3. LaFONTAINE, Pat	N.J.-NYI	Verdun	C
4. YZERMAN, Steve	Det.	Peterborough	C
5. BARRASSO, Tom	St.L.-L.A.-Buf.	Acton-Boxboro HS	G
6. MacLEAN, John	L.A.-N.J.	Oshawa	RW
7. COURTNALL, Russ	Tor.	Victoria	C
8. McBAIN, Andrew	Wpg.	North Bay	RW
9. NEELY, Cam	Van.	Portland	RW
10. LACOMBE, Normand	Cgy.-Buf.	U. of New Hampshire	RW
11. CREIGHTON, Adam	Que.-Buf.	Ottawa	C
12. GAGNER, Dave	NYR	Brantford	C
13. QUINN, Dan	Buf.-Cgy.	Belleville	C
14. DOLLAS, Bobby	Wsh.-Wpg.	Laval	D
15. ERREY, Bob	Min.-Pit.	Peterborough	LW
16. DIDUCK, Gerald	NYI	Lethbridge	D
17. TURCOTTE, Alfie	Mtl.	Portland	C
18. CASSIDY, Bruce	Chi.	Ottawa	D
19. BEUKEBOOM, Jeff	Edm.	Sault Ste. Marie	D
20. JENSEN, David	Phi.-Hfd.	Lawrence	C
21. MARKWART, Nevin	Bos.	Regina	LW

SECOND ROUND

Selection	Claimed By	Amateur Club	
22. CHARLESWORTH, Todd	Pit.	Oshawa	D
23. SIREN, Ville	Hfd.	Ilves (Finland)	D
24. EVANS, Shawn	N.J.	Peterborough	D
25. LAMBERT, Lane	Det.	Saskatoon	RW
26. LEMIEUX, Claude	St.L.-Mtl.	Trois-Rivières	RW
27. MOMESSO, Sergio	L.A.-Mtl.	Shawinigan	C
28. JACKSON, Jeff	Tor.	Brantford	LW
29. BERRY, Brad	Wpg.	St. Albert	D
30. BRUCE, Dave	Van.	Kitchener	RW
31. TUCKER, John	Cgy.-Buf.	Kitchener	C
32. HEROUX, Yves	Que.	Chicoutimi	RW
33. HEATH, Randy	NYR	Portland	LW
34. HAJDU, Richard	Wsh.-Buf.	Kamloops Jr. A	LW
35. FRANCIS, Todd	Mtl.	Brantford	RW
36. PARKS, Malcolm	Min.	St. Albert	C
37. McKECHNEY, Garnet	NYI	Kitchener	RW
38. MUSIL, Frantisek	Mtl.-Min.	Tesla (Czech.)	D
39. PRESLEY, Wayne	Chi.	Kitchener	RW
40. GOLDEN, Mike	Edm.	Reading HS	C
41. ZEZEL, Peter	Phi.	Toronto	C
42. JOHNSTON, Greg	Bos.	Toronto	RW

1982

FIRST ROUND

Selection	Claimed By	Amateur Club	
1. KLUZAK, Gord	Col.-Bos.	Nanaimo	D
2. BELLOWS, Brian	Det.-Min.	Kitchener	RW
3. NYLUND, Gary	Tor.	Portland	D
4. SUTTER, Ron	Hfd.-Phi.	Lethbridge	C
5. STEVENS, Scott	L.A.-Wsh.	Kitchener	D
6. HOUSLEY, Phil	Wsh.-Buf.	S. St. Paul HS	D
7. YAREMCHUK, Ken	Chi.	Portland	C
8. TROTTIER, Rocky	St.L.-N.J.	Nanaimo	RW
9. CYR, Paul	Cgy.-Buf.	Victoria	LW
10. SUTTER, Rich	Pit.	Lethbridge	RW
11. PETIT, Michel	Van.	Sherbrooke	D
12. KYTE, Jim	Wpg.	Cornwall	D
13. SHAW, David	Que.	Kitchener	D
14. LAWLESS, Paul	Phi.-Hfd.	Windsor	LW
15. KONTOS, Chris	NYR	Toronto	C
16. ANDREYCHUK, Dave	Buf.	Oshawa	LW
17. CRAVEN, Murray	Min.-Det.	Medicine Hat	C
18. DANEYKO, Ken	Bos.-N.J.	Seattle	D
19. HEROUX, Alain	Mtl.	Chicoutimi	LW
20. PLAYFAIR, Jim	Edm.	Portland	D
21. FLATLEY, Pat	NYI	U. of Wisconsin	RW

SECOND ROUND

Selection	Claimed By	Amateur Club	
22. CURRAN, Brian	Col.-Bos.	Portland	D
23. COURTEAU, Yves	Det.	Laval	RW
24. LEEMAN, Gary	Tor.	Regina	D
25. IHNACAK, Peter	Hfd.-Tor.	Sparta (Czech.)	C
26. ANDERSON, Mike	L.A.-Buf.	N. St. Paul HS	C
27. HEIDT, Mike	Wsh.-L.A.	Calgary	D
28. BADEAU, Rene	St.L.-Chi.	Quebec	D
29. REIERSON, Dave	Cgy.	Prince Albert	D
30. JOHANSSON, Jens	Buf.	Pitea (Sweden)	D
31. GAUVREAU, Jocelyn	Pit.-Mtl.	Granby	D
32. CARLSON, Kent	Van.-Mtl.	St. Lawrence University	D
33. MALEY, David	Wpg.-Mtl.	Edina HS	C
34. GILLIS, Paul	Que.	Niagara Falls	C
35. PATERSON, Mark	Phi.-Hfd.	Ottawa	D
36. SANDSTROM, Tomas	NYR	Farjestads (Sweden)	RW
37. KROMM, Richard	Buf.-Cgy.	Portland	LW
38. HRYNEWICH, Tim	Min.-Pit.	Sudbury	LW
39. BYERS, Lyndon	Bos.	Regina	RW
40. SANDELIN, Scott	Mtl.	Hibbing HS	D
41. GRAVES, Steve	Edm.	Sault Ste. Marie	C
42. SMITH, Vern	NYI	Lethbridge	D

1981

FIRST ROUND

Selection	Claimed By	Amateur Club	
1. HAWERCHUK, Dale	Wpg.	Cornwall	C
2. SMITH, Doug	Det.-L.A.	Ottawa	C
3. CARPENTER, Bobby	Col.-Wsh.	St. John's HS	C
4. FRANCIS, Ron	Hfd.	Sault Ste. Marie	C
5. CIRELLA, Joe	Wsh.-Col.	Oshawa	D
6. BENNING, Jim	Tor.	Portland	D
7. HUNTER, Mark	Pit.-Mtl.	Brantford	RW
8. FUHR, Grant	Edm.	Victoria	G
9. PATRICK, James	NYR	Prince Albert	D
10. BUTCHER, Garth	Van.	Regina	D
11. MOLLER, Randy	Que.	Lethbridge	D
12. TANTI, Tony	Chi.	Oshawa	RW
13. MEIGHAN, Ron	Min.	Niagara Falls	D
14. LEVEILLE, Normand	Bos.	Chicoutimi	LW
15. MacINNIS, Allan	Cgy.	Kitchener	D
16. SMITH, Steve	Phi.	Sault Ste. Marie	D
17. DUDACEK, Jiri	Buf.	Poldi Kladno (Czech.)	RW
18. DELORME, Gilbert	L.A.-Mtl.	Chicoutimi	D
19. INGMAN, Jan	Mtl.	Farjestad (Sweden)	LW
20. RUFF, Marty	St.L.	Lethbridge	D
21. BOUTILIER, Paul	NYI	Sherbrooke	D

SECOND ROUND

Selection	Claimed By	Amateur Club	
22. ARNIEL, Scott	Wpg.	Cornwall	LW
23. LOISELLE, Claude	Det.	Windsor	C
24. YAREMCHUK, Gary	Col.-Tor.	Portland	C
25. GRIFFIN, Kevin	Hfd.-Chi.	Portland	LW
26. CHERNOMAZ, Rich	Wsh.-Col.	Victoria	C
27. DONNELLY, Dave	Tor.-Min.	St. Albert	C
28. GATZOS, Steve	Pit.	Sault Ste. Marie	RW
29. STRUEBY, Todd	Edm.	Regina	LW
30. ERIXON, Jan	NYR	Skelleftea (Sweden)	RW
31. SANDS, Mike	Van.-Min.	Sudbury	G
32. ERIKSSON, Lars	Que.-Mtl.	Brynas (Sweden)	G
33. HIRSCH, Tom	Chi.-Min.	Patrick Henry HS	D
34. PREUSS, Dave	Min.	St. Thomas Academy	RW
35. DUFOUR, Luc	Bos.	Chicoutimi	RW
36. NORDIN, Hakan	Cgy.-St.L.	Farjestad (Sweden)	D
37. COSTELLO, Rich	Phi.	Natick HS	C
38. VIRTA, Hannu	Buf.	TPS (Finland)	D
39. KENNEDY, Dean	L.A.	Brandon	D
40. CHELIOS, Chris	Mtl.	Moose Jaw	D
41. WAHLSTEN, Jali	St.L.-Min.	TPS (Finland)	C
42. DINEEN, Gord	NYI	Sault Ste. Marie	D

1980

FIRST ROUND

Selection	Claimed By	Amateur Club	
1. WICKENHEISER, Doug	Col.-Mtl.	Regina	C
2. BABYCH, Dave	Wpg.	Portland	D
3. SAVARD, Denis	Que.-Chi.	Montreal	C
4. MURPHY, Larry	Det.-L.A.	Peterborough	D
5. VEITCH, Darren	Wsh.	Regina	D
6. COFFEY, Paul	Edm.	Kitchener	D
7. LANZ, Rick	Van.	Oshawa	D
8. ARTHUR, Fred	Hfd.	Cornwall	D
9. BULLARD, Mike	Pit.	Brantford	C
10. FOX, Jimmy	L.A.	Ottawa	RW
11. BLAISDELL, Mike	Tor.-Det.	Regina	RW
12. WILSON, Rik	St.L.	Kingston	D
13. CYR, Denis	Cgy.	Montreal	RW
14. MALONE, Jim	NYR	Toronto	C
15. DUPONT, Jerome	Chi.	Toronto	D
16. PALMER, Brad	Min.	Victoria	LW
17. SUTTER, Brent	NYI	Red Deer	C
18. PEDERSON, Barry	Bos.	Victoria	C
19 GAGNE, Paul	Mtl.-Col.	Windsor	LW
20. PATRICK, Steve	Buf.	Brandon	RW
21. STOTHERS, Mike	Phi.	Kingston	D

SECOND ROUND

Selection	Claimed By	Amateur Club	
22. WARD, Joe	Col.	Seattle	C
23. MANTHA, Moe	Wpg.	Toronto	D
24. ROCHEFORT, Normand	Que.	Quebec	D
25. MUNI, Craig	Det.-Tor.	Kingston	D
26. McGILL, Bob	Wsh.-Tor.	Victoria	D
27. NATTRESS, Ric	Edm.-Mtl.	Brantford	D
28. LUDZIK, Steve	Van.-Chi.	Niagara Falls	C
29. GALARNEAU, Michel	Hfd.	Hull	C
30. SOLHEIM, Ken	Pit.-Chi.	Medicine Hat	LW
31. CURTALE, Tony	L.A.-Cgy.	Brantford	D
32. LaVALLEE, Kevin	Tor.-Cgy.	Brantford	LW
33. TERRION, Greg	St.L.-L.A.	Brantford	LW
34. MORRISON, Dave	Cgy.-L.A.	Peterborough	RW
35. ALLISON, Mike	NYR	Sudbury	LW
36. DAWES, Len	Chi.	Victoria	D
37. BEAUPRE, Don	Min.	Sudbury	G
38. HRUDEY, Kelly	NYI	Medicine Hat	G
39. KONROYD, Steve	Cgy.	Oshawa	D
40. CHABOT, John	Mtl.	Hull	C
41. MOLLER, Mike	Buf.	Lethbridge	RW
42. FRASER, Jay	Phi.	Ottawa	LW

1979

FIRST ROUND

Selection	Claimed By	Amateur Club	
1. RAMAGE, Rob	Col.	London	D
2. TURNBULL, Perry	St.L.	Portland	C
3. FOLIGNO, Mike	Det.	Sudbury	RW
4. GARTNER, Mike	Wsh.	Niagara Falls	RW
5. VAIVE, Rick	Van.	Sherbrooke	RW
6. HARTSBURG, Craig	Min.	Sault St. Marie	D
7. BROWN, Keith	Chi.	Portland	D
8. BOURQUE, Raymond	L.A.-Bos.	Verdun	D
9. BOSCHMAN, Laurie	Tor.	Brandon	C
10. McCARTHY, Tom	Wsh.-Min.	Oshawa	LW
11. RAMSEY, Mike	Buf.	U. of Minnesota	D
12. REINHART, Paul	Atl.	Kitchener	D
13. SULLIMAN, Doug	NYR	Kitchener	RW
14. PROPP, Brian	Phi.	Brandon	LW
15. McCRIMMON, Brad	Bos.	Brandon	D
16. WELLS, Jay	Mtl.-L.A.	Kingston	D
17. SUTTER, Duane	NYI	Lethbridge	RW
18. ALLISON, Ray	Hfd.	Brandon	RW
19. MANN, Jimmy	Wpg.	Sherbrooke	RW
20. GOULET, Michel	Que.	Quebec	LW
21. LOWE, Kevin	Edm.	Quebec	D

SECOND ROUND

Selection	Claimed By	Amateur Club	
22. WESLEY, Blake	Col.-Phi.	Portland	D
23. PEROVICH, Mike	St.L.-Atl.	Brandon	D
24. RAUSSE, Errol	Det.-Wsh.	Seattle	LW
25. JONSSON, Tomas	Wsh.-NYI	MoDo AIK (Sweden)	D
26. ASHTON, Brent	Van.	Saskatoon	LW
27. GINGRAS, Gaston	Min.-Mtl.	Hamilton	D
28. TRIMPER, Tim	Chi.	Peterborough	LW
29. HOPKINS, Dean	L.A.	London	RW
30. HARDY, Mark	Tor.-L.A.	Montreal	D
31. MARSHALL, Paul	Wsh.-Pit.	Brantford	LW
32. RUFF, Lindy	Buf.	Lethbridge	D
33. RIGGIN, Pat	Atl.	London	G
34. HOSPODAR, Ed	NYR	Ottawa	D
35. LINDBERGH, Pelle	Phi.	AIK Solna (Sweden)	G
36. MORRISON, Doug	Bos.	Lethbridge	RW
37. NASLUND, Mats	Mtl.	Brynas IFK (Sweden)	LW
38. CARROLL, Billy	NYI	London	C
39. SMITH, Stuart	Hfd.	Peterborough	D
40. CHRISTIAN, Dave	Wpg.	U. of North Dakota	C
41. HUNTER, Dale	Que.	Sudbury	C
42. BROTEN, Neal	Min.	U. of Minnesota	C

1978

FIRST ROUND

Selection	Claimed By	Amateur Club	
1. SMITH, Bobby	Min.	Ottawa	C
2. WALTER, Ryan	Wsh.	Seattle	LW
3. BABYCH, Wayne	St.L.	Portland	RW
4. DERLAGO, Bill	Van.	Brandon	C
5. GILLIS, Mike	Col.	Kingston	LW
6. WILSON, Behn	Pit.-Phi.	Kingston	D
7. LINSEMAN, Ken	NYR-Phi.	Kingston	C
8. GEOFFRION, Danny	L.A.-Mtl.	Cornwall	RW
9. HUBER, Willie	Det.	Hamilton	D
10. HIGGINS, Tim	Chi.	Ottawa	RW
11. MARSH, Brad	Atl.	London	D
12. PETERSON, Brent	Tor.-Det.	Portland	C
13. PLAYFAIR, Larry	Buf.	Portland	D
14. LUCAS, Danny	Phi.	Sault Ste. Marie	RW
15. TAMBELLINI, Steve	NYI	Lethbridge	C
16. SECORD, Al	Bos.	Hamilton	LW
17. HUNTER, Dave	Mtl.	Sudbury	LW
18. COULIS, Tim	Wsh.	Hamilton	LW

SECOND ROUND

Selection	Claimed By	Amateur Club	
19. PAYNE, Steve	Min.	Ottawa	LW
20. MULVEY, Paul	Wsh.	Portland	RW
21. QUENNEVILLE, Joel	Tor.	Windsor	D
22. FRASER, Curt	Van.	Victoria	LW
23. MacKINNON, Paul	Wsh.	Peterborough	D
24. CHRISTOFF, Steve	Min.	U. of Minnesota	C
25. MEEKER, Mike	Pit.	Peterborough	RW
26. MALONEY, Don	NYR	Kitchener	LW
27. MALINOWSKI, Merlin	Col.	Medicine Hat	C
28. HICKS, Glenn	Det.	Flin Flon	LW
29. LECUYER, Doug	Chi.	Portland	LW
30. YAKIWCHUK, Dale	Mtl.	Portland	C
31. JENSEN, Al	Det.	Hamilton	G
32. McKEGNEY, Tony	Buf.	Kingston	LW
33. SIMURDA, Mike	Phi.	Kingston	RW
34. JOHNSTON, Randy	NYI	Peterborough	D
35. NICOLSON, Graeme	Bos.	Cornwall	D
36. CARTER, Ron	Mtl.	Sherbrooke	RW

1977

FIRST ROUND

Selection	Claimed By	Amateur Club	
1. McCOURT, Dale	Det.	St. Catharines	C
2. BECK, Barry	Col.	New Westminster	D
3. PICARD, Robert	Wsh.	Montreal	D
4. GILLIS, Jere	Van.	Sherbrooke	LW
5. CROMBEEN, Mike	Cle.	Kingston	RW
6. WILSON, Doug	Chi.	Ottawa	D
7. MAXWELL, Brad	Min.	New Westminster	D
8 DEBLOIS, Lucien	NYR	Sorel	C
9. CAMPBELL, Scott	St.L.	London	D
10. NAPIER, Mark	Atl.-Mtl.	Toronto	RW
11. ANDERSON, John	Tor.	Toronto	RW
12. JOHANSEN, Trevor	Pit.-Tor.	Toronto	D
13. DUGUAY, Ron	L.A.-NYR	Sudbury	C
14. SEILING, Ric	Buf.	St. Catharines	RW
15. BOSSY, Mike	NYI	Laval	RW
16. FOSTER, Dwight	Bos.	Kitchener	C/RW
17. McCARTHY, Kevin	Phi.	Winnipeg	D
18. DUPONT, Norm	Mtl.	Montreal	C

SECOND ROUND

Selection	Claimed By	Amateur Club	
19. SAVARD, Jean	Det.-Chi.	Quebec	C
20. ZAHARKO, Miles	Col.-Atl.	New Westminster	D
21. LOFTHOUSE, Mark	Wsh.	New Westminster	RW
22. BANDURA, Jeff	Van.	Portland	D
23. CHICOINE, Daniel	Cle.	Sherbrooke	RW
24. GLADNEY, Bob	Chi.-Tor.	Oshawa	D
25. SEMENKO, Dave	Min.	Brandon	LW
26. KEATING, Mike	NYR	St. Catharines	LW
27. LABATTE, Neil	St.L.	Toronto	D
28. LAURENCE, Don	Atl.	Kitchener	C
29. SAGANIUK, Rocky	Tor.	Lethbridge	RW
30. HAMILTON, Jim	Pit.	London	RW
31. HILL, Brian	L.A.-Atl.	Medicine Hat	RW
32. ARESHENKOFF, Ron	Buf.	Medicine Hat	C
33. TONELLI, John	NYI	Toronto	LW
34. PARRO, Dave	Bos.	Saskatoon	G
35. GORENCE, Tom	Phi.	U. of Minnesota	RW
36. LANGWAY, Rod	Mtl.	U. of New Hampshire	D

1976

FIRST ROUND

Selection	Claimed By	Amateur Club	
1. GREEN, Rick	K.C.-Wsh.	London	D
2. CHAPMAN, Blair	Pit.	Saskatoon	RW
3. SHARPLEY, Glen	Min.	Hull	C
4. WILLIAMS, Fred	Det.	Saskatoon	C
5. JOHANSSON, Bjorn	Cal.	Sweden	D
6. MURDOCH, Don	NYR	Medicine Hat	RW
7. FEDERKO, Bernie	St.L.	Saskatoon	C
8. SHAND, Dave	Van.-Atl.	Peterborough	D
9. CLOUTIER, Real	Chi.	Quebec	RW
10. PHILLIPOFF, Harold	Atl.	New Westminster	LW
11. GARDNER, Paul	Pit.-K.C.	Oshawa	C
12. LEE, Peter	Tor.-Mtl.	Ottawa	RW
13. SCHUTT, Rod	L.A.-Mtl.	Sudbury	LW
14. McKENDRY, Alex	NYI	Sudbury	LW
15. CARROLL, Greg	Buf.-Wsh.	Medicine Hat	C
16. PACHAL, Clayton	Bos.	New Westminster	C
17. SUZOR, Mark	Phi.	Kingston	D
18. BAKER, Bruce	Mtl.	Ottawa	RW

SECOND ROUND

Selection	Claimed By	Amateur Club	
19. MALONE, Greg	Wsh.-Pit.	Oshawa	C
20. SUTTER, Brian	K.C.-St.L.	Lethbridge	LW
21. CLIPPINGDALE, Steve	Min.-L.A.	New Westminster	LW
22. LARSON, Reed	Det.	U. of Minnesota	D
23. STENLUND, Vern	Cal.	London	C
24. FARRISH, Dave	NYR	Sudbury	D
25. SMRKE, John	St.L.	Toronto	LW
26. MANNO, Bob	Van.	St. Catharines	D
27. McDILL, Jeff	Chi.	Victoria	RW
28. SIMPSON, Bobby	Atl.	Sherbrooke	LW
29. MARSH, Peter	Pit.	Sherbrooke	RW
30. CARLYLE, Randy	Tor.	Sudbury	D
31. ROBERTS, Jim	L.A.-Min.	Ottawa	LW
32. KASZYCKI, Mike	NYI	Sault Ste. Marie	C
33. KOWAL, Joe	Buf.	Hamilton	LW
34. GLOECKNER, Larry	Bos.	Victoria	D
35. CALLANDER, Drew	Phi.	Regina	C
36. MELROSE, Barry	Mtl.	Kamloops	D

1975

FIRST ROUND

Selection	Claimed By	Amateur Club	
1. BRIDGMAN, Mel	Wsh.-Phi.	Victoria	C
2. DEAN, Barry	K.C.	Medicine Hat	LW
3. KLASSEN, Ralph	Cal.	Saskatoon	C
4. MAXWELL, Brian	Min.	Medicine Hat	D
5. LAPOINTE, Rick	Det.	Victoria	D
6. ASHBY, Don	Tor.	Calgary	C
7. VAYDIK, Greg	Chi.	Medicine Hat	C
8. MULHERN, Richard	Atl.	Sherbrooke	D
9. SADLER, Robin	St.L.-Mtl.	Edmonton	D
10. BLIGHT, Rick	Van.	Brandon	RW
11. PRICE, Pat	NYI	Saskatoon	D
12. DILLON, Wayne	NYR	Toronto	C
13. LAXTON, Gord	Pit.	New Westminster	G
14. HALWARD, Doug	Bos.	Peterborough	D
15. MONDOU, Pierre	L.A.-Mtl.	Montreal	C
16. YOUNG, Tim	Mtl.-L.A.	Ottawa	C
17. SAUVE, Bob	Buf.	Laval	G
18. FORSYTH, Alex	Phi.-Wsh.	Kingston	C

SECOND ROUND

Selection	Claimed By	Amateur Club	
19. SCAMURRA, Peter	Wsh.	Peterborough	D
20. CAIRNS, Don	K.C.	Victoria	LW
21. MARUK, Dennis	Cal.	London	C
22. ENGBLOM, Brian	Min.-Mtl.	U. of Wisconsin	D
23. ROLLINS, Jerry	Det.	Winnipeg	D
24. JARVIS, Doug	Tor.	Peterborough	C
25. ARNDT, Daniel	Chi.	Saskatoon	LW
26. BOWNESS, Rick	Atl.	Montreal	RW
27. STANIOWSKI, Ed	St.L.	Regina	G
28. GASSOFF, Brad	Van.	Kamloops	D
29. SALVIAN, David	NYI	St. Catharines	RW
30. SOETAERT, Doug	NYR	Edmonton	G
31. ANDERSON, Russ	Pit.	U. of Minnesota	D
32. SMITH, Barry	Bos.	New Westminster	C
33. BUCYK, Terry	L.A.	Lethbridge	RW
34. GREENBANK, Kelvin	Mtl.	Winnipeg	RW
35. BREITENBACH, Ken	Buf.	St. Catharines	D
36. MASTERS, Jamie	Phi.-St.L.	Ottawa	D

1974

FIRST ROUND

Selection	Claimed By	Amateur Club	
1. JOLY, Greg	Wsh.	Regina	D
2. PAIEMENT, Wilfred	K.C.	St. Catharines	RW
3. HAMPTON, Rick	Cal.	St. Catharines	D
4. GILLIES, Clark	NYI	Regina	LW
5. CONNOR, Cam	Van.-Mtl.	Flin Flon	RW
6. HICKS, Doug	Min.	Flin Flon	D
7. RISEBROUGH, Doug	St.L.-Mtl.	Kitchener	C
8. LAROUCHE, Pierre	Pit.	Sorel	C
9. LOCHEAD, Bill	Det.	Oshawa	LW
10. CHARTRAW, Rick	Atl.-Mtl.	Kitchener	D
11. FOGOLIN, Lee	Buf.	Oshawa	D
12. TREMBLAY, Mario	L.A.-Mtl.	Montreal	RW
13. VALIQUETTE, Jack	Tor.	Sault Ste. Marie	C
14. MALONEY, Dave	NYR	Kitchener	D
15. McTAVISH, Gord	Mtl.	Sudbury	C
16. MULVEY, Grant	Chi.	Calgary	RW
17. CHIPPERFIELD, Ron	Phi.-Cal.	Brandon	C
18. LARWAY, Don	Bos.	Swift Current	RW

SECOND ROUND

Selection	Claimed By	Amateur Club	
19. MARSON, Mike	Wsh.	Sudbury	LW
20. BURDON, Glen	K.C.	Regina	C
21. AFFLECK, Bruce	Cal.	U. of Denver	D
22. TROTTIER, Bryan	NYI	Swift Current	C
23. SEDLBAUER, Ron	Van.	Kitchener	LW
24. NANTAIS, Rick	Min.	Quebec	LW
25. HOWE, Mark	St.L.-Bos.	Toronto	D
26. HESS, Bob	Pit.-St.L.	New Westminster	D
27. COSSETTE, Jacques	Det.-Pit.	Sorel	RW
28. CHOUINARD, Guy	Atl.	Quebec	C
29. GARE, Danny	Buf.	Calgary	RW
30. MacGREGOR, Gary	L.A.-Mtl.	Cornwall	C
31. WILLIAMS, Dave	Tor.	Swift Current	LW
32. GRESCHNER, Ron	NYR	New Westminster	D
33. LUPIEN, Gilles	Mtl.	Montreal	D
34. DAIGLE, Alain	Chi.	Trois-Rivières	RW
35. McLEAN, Don	Phi.	Sudbury	D
36. STURGEON, Peter	Bos.	Kitchener	LW

1973

FIRST ROUND

Selection	Claimed By	Amateur Club	
1. POTVIN, Denis	NYI	Ottawa	D
2. LYSIAK, Tom	Cal.-Mtl.-Atl.	Medicine Hat	C
3. VERVERGAERT, Dennis	Van.	London	RW
4. McDONALD, Lanny	Tor.	Medicine Hat	RW
5. DAVIDSON, John	Atl.-Mtl.-St.L.	Calgary	G
6. SAVARD, Andre	L.A.-Bos.	Quebec	C
7. STOUGHTON, Blaine	Pit.	Flin Flon	RW
8. GAINEY, Bob	St.L.-Mtl.	Peterborough	LW
9. DAILEY, Bob	Min.-Mtl.-Van.	Toronto	D
10. NEELY, Bob	Phi.-Tor.	Peterborough	LW
11. RICHARDSON, Terry	Det.	New Westminster	G
12. TITANIC, Morris	Buf.	Sudbury	LW
13. ROTA, Darcy	Chi.	Edmonton	LW
14. MIDDLETON, Rick	NYR	Oshawa	RW
15. TURNBULL, Ian	Bos.-Tor.	Ottawa	D
16. MERCREDI, Vic	Mtl.-Atl.	New Westminster	C

SECOND ROUND

Selection	Claimed By	Amateur Club	
17. GOLDUP, Glen	NYI-Mtl.	Toronto	RW
18. DUNLOP, Blake	Cal.-Min.	Ottawa	C
19. BORDELEAU, Paulin	Van.	Toronto	RW
20. GOODENOUGH, Larry	Tor.-Phi.	London	D
21. VAIL, Eric	Atl.	Sudbury	LW
22. MARRIN, Peter	L.A.-Mtl.	Toronto	C
23. BIANCHIN, Wayne	Pit.	Flin Flon	LW
24. PESUT, George	St.L.	Saskatoon	D
25. ROGERS, John	Min.	Edmonton	RW
26. LEVINS, Brent	Phi.	Swift Current	LW
27. CAMPBELL, Colin	Det.-Pit.	Peterborough	D
28. LANDRY, Jean	Buf.	Quebec	D
29. THOMAS, Reg	Chi.	London	LW
30. HICKEY, Pat	NYR	Hamilton	LW
31. JONES, Jim	Bos.	Peterborough	RW
32. ANDRUFF, Ron	Mtl.	Flin Flon	C

1972

FIRST ROUND

Selection	Claimed By	Amateur Club	
1. HARRIS, Billy	NYI	Toronto	RW
2. RICHARD, Jacques	Atl.	Quebec	LW
3. LEVER, Don	Van.	Niagara Falls	C
4. SHUTT, Steve	L.A.-Mtl.	Toronto	LW
5. SCHOENFELD, Jim	Buf.	Niagara Falls	D
6. LAROCQUE, Michel	Cal.-Mtl.	Ottawa	G
7. BARBER, Bill	Phi.	Kitchener	LW
8. GARDNER, Dave	Pit.-Min.-Mtl.	Toronto	C
9. MERRICK, Wayne	St.L.	Ottawa	C
10. BLANCHARD, Albert	Det.-NYR	Kitchener	LW
11. FERGUSON, George	Tor.	Toronto	C
12. BYERS, Jerry	Min.	Kitchener	LW
13. RUSSELL, Phil	Chi.	Edmonton	D
14. VAN BOXMEER, John	Mtl.	Guelph	D
15. MacMILLAN, Bobby	NYR	St. Catharines	RW
16. BLOOM, Mike	Bos.	St. Catharines	LW

SECOND ROUND

Selection	Claimed By	Amateur Club	
17. HENNING Lorne	NYI	New Westminster	C
18. BIALOWAS, Dwight	Atl.	Regina	D
19. McSHEFFREY, Brian	Van.	Ottawa	RW
20. KOZAK, Don	L.A.	Edmonton	RW
21. SACHARUK, Larry	Buf.-NYR	Saskatoon	D
22. CASSIDY, Tom	Cal.	Kitchener	C
23. BLADON, Tom	Phi.	Edmonton	D
24. LYNCH, Jack	Pit.	Oshawa	D
25. CARRIERE, Larry	St.L.-Buf.	Loyola College	D
26. GUITE, Pierre	Det.	St. Catharines	LW
27. OSBURN, Randy	Tor.	London	LW
28. WEIR, Stan	Min.-Cal.	Medicine Hat	C
29. OGILVIE, Brian	Chi.	Edmonton	C
30. LUKOWICH, Bernie	Mtl.-Pit.	New Westminster	RW
31. VILLEMURE, Rene	NYR	Shawinigan	LW
32. ELDER, Wayne	Bos.	London	D

1971

FIRST ROUND

Selection	Claimed By	Amateur Club	
1. LAFLEUR, Guy	Cal.-Mtl.	Quebec	RW
2. DIONNE, Marcel	Det.	St. Catharines	C
3. GUEVREMONT, Jocelyn	Van.	Montreal	D
4. CARR, Gene	Pit.-St.L.	Flin Flon	C
5. MARTIN, Rick	Buf.	Montreal	LW
6. JONES, Ron	L.A.-Bos.	Edmonton	D
7. ARNASON, Chuck	Min.-Mtl.	Flin Flon	RW
8. WRIGHT, Larry	Phi.	Regina	C
9. PLANTE, Pierre	Tor.-Phi.	Drummondville	RW
10. VICKERS, Steve	St.L.-NYR	Toronto	LW
11. WILSON, Murray	Mtl.	Ottawa	LW
12. SPRING, Dan	Chi.	Edmonton	C
13. DURBANO, Steve	NYR	Toronto	D
14. O'REILLY, Terry	Bos.	Oshawa	RW

SECOND ROUND

Selection	Claimed By	Amateur Club	
15. BAIRD, Ken	Cal.	Flin Flon	D
16. BOUCHA, Henry	Det.	U.S. Nationals	C
17. LALONDE, Bobby	Van.	Montreal	C
18. McKENZIE, Brian	Pit.	St. Catharines	LW
19. RAMSAY, Craig	Buf.	Peterborough	LW
20. ROBINSON, Larry	L.A.-Mtl.	Kitchener	D
21. NORRISH, Rod	Min.	Regina	LW
22. KEHOE, Rick	Phi.-Tor.	Hamilton	RW
23. FORTIER, Dave	Tor.	St. Catharines	D
24. DEGUISE, Michel	St.L.-Mtl.	Sorel	G
25. FRENCH, Terry	Mtl.	Ottawa	C
26. KRYSKOW, Dave	Chi.	Edmonton	LW
27. WILLIAMS, Tom	NYR	Hamilton	LW
28. RIDLEY, Curt	Bos.	Portage	G

1970

FIRST ROUND

Selection	Claimed By	Amateur Club	
1. PERREAULT, Gilbert	Buf.	Montreal	C
2. TALLON, Dale	Van.	Toronto	D
3. LEACH, Reg	L.A.-Bos.	Flin Flon	LW
4. MacLEISH, Rick	Phi.-Bos.	Peterborough	C
5. MARTINIUK, Ray	Oak.-Mtl.	Flin Flon	G
6. LEFLEY, Chuck	Min.-Mtl.	Canadian Nationals	C
7. POLIS, Greg	Pit.	Estevan	LW
8. SITTLER, Darryl	Tor.	London	C
9. PLUMB, Ron	Bos.	Peterborough	D
10. ODDLEIFSON, Chris	St.L.-Oak.	Winnipeg	C
11. GRATTON, Norm	Mtl.-NYR	Montreal	LW
12. LAJEUNESSE, Serge	Det.	Montreal	RW
13. STEWART, Bob	Bos.	Oshawa	D
14. MALONEY, Dan	Chi.	London	LW

SECOND ROUND

Selection	Claimed By	Amateur Club	
15. DEADMARSH, Butch	Buf.	Brandon	LW
16. HARGREAVES, Jim	Van.	Winnipeg	D
17. HARVEY, Fred	L.A.-Min.	Hamilton	RW
18. CLEMENT, Bill	Phi.	Ottawa	C
19. LAFRAMBOISE, Pete	Oak.	Ottawa	C
20. BARRETT, Fred	Min.	Toronto	D
21. STEWART, John	Pit.	Flin Flon	LW
22. THOMPSON, Errol	Tor.	Charlottetown	LW
23. KEOGAN, Murray	St.L.	U. of Minnesota	C
24. McDONOUGH, Al	Mtl.-L.A.	St. Catharines	RW
25. MURPHY, Mike	NYR	Toronto	RW
26. GUINDON, Bobby	Det.	Montreal	LW
27. BOUCHARD, Dan	Bos.	London	G
28. ARCHAMBAULT, Mike	Chi.	Drummondville	LW

1969

FIRST ROUND

Selection	Claimed By	Amateur Club	
1. HOULE, Rejean	Mtl.	Montreal	LW
2. TARDIF, Marc	Mtl.	Montreal	LW
3. TANNAHILL, Don	Min.-Bos.	Niagara Falls	LW
4. SPRING, Frank	Pit.-Bos.	Edmonton	RW
5. REDMOND, Dick	L.A.-Mtl.-Min.	St. Catharines	D
6. CURRIER, Bob	Phi.	Cornwall	C
7. FEATHERSTONE, Tony	Oak.	Peterborough	RW
8. DUPONT, André	St.L.-NYR	Montreal	D
9. MOSER, Ernie	Det.-Tor.	Estevan	RW
10. RUTHERFORD, Jim	Det.	Hamilton	G
11. BOLDIREV, Ivan	Bos.	Oshawa	C
12. JARRY, Pierre	NYR	Ottawa	LW
13. BORDELEAU, J.-P.	Chi.	Montreal	RW
14. O'BRIEN, Dennis	Min.	St. Catharines	D

SECOND ROUND

Selection	Claimed By	Amateur Club	
15. KESSELL, Rick	Pit.	Oshawa	C
16. HOGANSON, Dale	L.A.	Estevan	D
17. CLARKE, Bobby	Phi.	Flin Flon	C
18. STACKHOUSE, Ron	Oak.	Peterborough	D
19. LOWE, Mike	St.L.	Loyola College	
20. BRINDLEY, Doug	Tor.	Niagara Falls	C
21. GARWASIUK, Ron	Det.	Regina	LW
22. QUOQUOCHI, Art	Bos.	Montreal	
23. WILSON, Bert	NYR	London	LW
24. ROMANCHYCH, Larry	Chi.	Flin Flon	RW
25. GILBERT, Gilles	Min.	London	G
26. BRIERE, Michel	Pit.	Shawinigan Falls	C
27. BODDY, Greg	L.A.	Edmonton	D
28. BROSSART, Bill	Phi.	Estevan	D

The Boston Bruins picked Reg Leach third overall in the 1970 draft. They used the fourth pick to claim Rick MacLeish. Both players went on to stardom with the Philadelphia Flyers. Leach had 61 goals in 1975-76 and added a record 19 more in the playoffs.

NHL All-Stars

Active Players' All-Star Selection Records

GOALTENDERS

Player	First Team Selections	Second Team Selections	Total
Dominik Hasek	(5) 1993-94; 1994-95; 1996-97; 1997-98; 1998-99.	(0)	5
Patrick Roy	(3) 1988-89; 1989-90; 1991-92.	(2) 1987-88; 1990-91.	5
Ed Belfour	(2) 1990-91; 1992-93.	(1) 1994-95.	3
Tom Barrasso	(1) 1983-84.	(2) 1984-85; 1992-93.	3
Grant Fuhr	(1) 1987-88.	(1) 1981-82.	2
J.Vanbiesbrouck	(1) 1985-86.	(1) 1993-94.	2
Martin Brodeur	(0)	(2) 1996-97; 1997-98.	2
Ron Hextall	(1) 1986-87.	(0)	1
Jim Carey	(1) 1995-96.	(0)	1
Mike Vernon	(0)	(1) 1988-89.	1
Daren Puppa	(0)	(1) 1989-90.	1
Kirk McLean	(0)	(1) 1991-92.	1
Chris Osgood	(0)	(1) 1995-96.	1
Byron Dafoe	(0)	(1) 1998-99.	1

DEFENSEMEN

Player	First Team Selections	Second Team Selections	Total
Ray Bourque	(12) 1979-80; 1981-82; 1983-84; 1984-85; 1986-87; 1987-88; 1989-90; 1990-91; 1991-92; 1992-93; 1993-94; 1995-96.	(6) 1980-81; 1982-83; 1985-86; 1988-89; 1994-95; 1998-99.	18
Paul Coffey	(4) 1984-85; 1985-86; 1988-89; 1994-95.	(4) 1981-82; 1982-83; 1983-84; 1989-90.	8
Chris Chelios	(4) 1988-89; 1992-93; 1994-95; 1995-96.	(2) 1990-91; 1996-97.	6
Al MacInnis	(3) 1989-90; 1990-91; 1998-99.	(3) 1986-87; 1988-89; 1993-94.	6
Brian Leetch	(2) 1991-92; 1996-97.	(3) 1990-91; 1993-94; 1995-96.	5
Scott Stevens	(2) 1987-88; 1993-94.	(2) 1991-92; 1996-97.	4
Larry Murphy	(0)	(3) 1986-87; 1992-93; 1994-95.	3
Nicklas Lidstrom	(2) 1997-98; 1998-99.	(0)	2
Sandis Ozolinsh	(1) 1996-97.	(0)	1
Rob Blake	(1) 1997-98.	(0)	1
Gary Suter	(0)	(1) 1987-88.	1
Phil Housley	(0)	(1) 1991-92.	1
Chris Pronger	(0)	(1) 1997-98.	1
Scott Niedermayer	(0)	(1) 1998-99.	1
Eric Desjardins	(0)	(1) 1998-99.	1

CENTERS

Player	First Team Selections	Second Team Selections	Total
Mark Messier	(2) 1989-90; 1991-92.	(0)	2
Peter Forsberg	(2) 1997-98; 1998-99.	(0)	2
Eric Lindros	(1) 1994-95.	(1) 1995-96.	2
Sergei Fedorov	(1) 1993-94.	(0)	1
Adam Oates	(0)	(1) 1990-91.	1
Alexei Zhamnov	(0)	(1) 1994-95.	1
Alexei Yashin	(0)	(1) 1998-99.	1

RIGHT WINGERS

Player	First Team Selections	Second Team Selections	Total
Jaromir Jagr	(4) 1994-95; 1995-96; 1997-98; 1998-99.	(1) 1996-97.	5
Teemu Selanne	(2) 1992-93; 1996-97.	(2) 1997-98; 1998-99.	4
Brett Hull	(3) 1989-90; 1990-91; 1991-92.	(0)	3
Alexander Mogilny	(0)	(2) 1992-93; 1995-96.	2
Pavel Bure	(1) 1993-94.	(0)	1
Mark Recchi	(0)	(1) 1991-92.	1
Theoren Fleury	(0)	(1) 1994-95.	1

LEFT WINGERS

Player	First Team Selections	Second Team Selections	Total
Luc Robitaille	(5) 1987-88; 1988-89; 1989-90; 1990-91; 1992-93.	(2) 1986-87; 1991-92.	7
John LeClair	(2) 1994-95; 1997-98.	(3) 1995-96; 1996-97; 1998-99.	5
Paul Kariya	(3) 1995-96; 1996-97; 1998-99.	(0)	3
Mark Messier	(2) 1981-82; 1982-83.	(1) 1983-84.	3
Kevin Stevens	(1) 1991-92.	(2) 1990-91; 1992-93.	3
Keith Tkachuk	(0)	(2) 1994-95; 1997-98.	2
Brendan Shanahan	(1) 1993-94.	(0)	1
Brian Bellows	(0)	(1) 1989-90.	1
Adam Graves	(0)	(1) 1993-94.	1

Leading NHL All-Stars 1930-99

Player	Pos	Team	NHL Seasons	First Team Selections	Second Team Selections	Total Selections
Howe, Gordie	RW	Detroit	26	12	9	21
* Bourque, Ray	D	Boston	20	12	6	18
Gretzky, Wayne	C	Edm., L.A.	20	8	7	15
Richard, Maurice	RW	Montreal	18	8	6	14
Hull, Bobby	LW	Chicago	16	10	2	12
Harvey, Doug	D	Mtl., NYR	19	10	1	11
Hall, Glenn	G	Det., Chi., St.L.	18	7	4	11
Beliveau, Jean	C	Montreal	20	6	4	10
Seibert, Earl	D	NYR, Chi	15	4	6	10
Orr, Bobby	D	Boston	12	8	1	9
Lindsay, Ted	LW	Detroit	17	8	1	9
Mahovlich, Frank	LW	Tor., Det., Mtl.	18	3	6	9
Shore, Eddie	D	Boston	14	7	1	8
Mikita, Stan	C	Chicago	22	6	2	8
Kelly, Red	D	Detroit	20	6	2	8
Esposito, Phil	C	Boston	18	6	2	8
Pilote, Pierre	D	Chicago	14	5	3	8
Lemieux, Mario	C	Pittsburgh	12	5	3	8
* Coffey, Paul	D	Edm., Pit., Det.	19	4	4	8
Brimsek, Frank	G	Boston	10	2	6	8
Bossy, Mike	RW	NY Islanders	10	5	3	8
* Robitaille, Luc	LW	Los Angeles	13	5	2	7
Potvin, Denis	D	NY Islanders	15	5	2	7
Park, Brad	D	NYR, Bos.	17	5	2	7
Plante, Jacques	G	Mtl., Tor.	18	3	4	7
Gadsby, Bill	D	Chi., NYR, Det.	20	3	4	7
Sawchuk, Terry	G	Detroit	21	3	4	7
Durnan, Bill	G	Montreal	7	6	0	6
Lafleur, Guy	RW	Montreal	16	6	0	6
Dryden, Ken	G	Montreal	8	5	1	6
* Chelios, Chris	D	Mtl., Chi.	16	4	2	6
* MacInnis, Al	D	Cgy., St.L.	18	3	3	6
Clapper, Dit	RW/D	Boston	20	3	3	6
Robinson, Larry	D	Montreal	20	3	3	6
Horton, Tim	D	Toronto	24	3	3	6
Salming, Borje	D	Toronto	17	1	5	6
* Hasek, Dominik	G	Buffalo	9	5	0	5
Cowley, Bill	C	Boston	13	4	1	5
* Messier, Mark	LW/C	Edm., NYR	20	4	1	5
Jackson, Harvey	LW	Toronto	15	4	1	5
* Jagr, Jaromir	RW	Pittsburgh	9	4	1	5
Goulet, Michel	LW	Quebec	15	3	2	5
Conacher, Charlie	RW	Toronto	12	3	2	5
Stewart, Jack	D	Detroit	12	3	2	5
Lach, Elmer	C	Montreal	14	3	2	5
Quackenbush, Bill	D	Det., Bos.	14	3	2	5
Blake, Toe	LW	Montreal	15	3	2	5
Esposito, Tony	G	Chicago	16	3	2	5
* Roy, Patrick	G	Montreal	15	2	3	5
Reardon, Ken	D	Montreal	7	2	3	5
Kurri, Jari	RW	Edmonton	16	2	3	5
Apps Sr., Syl	C	Toronto	10	2	3	5
Giacomin, Ed	G	NY Rangers	13	2	3	5
* Leetch, Brian	D	NY Rangers	10	2	3	5
* LeClair, John	LW	Mtl., Phi.	9	2	3	5

*   Active

Position Leaders in All-Star Selections

Position	Player	First Team	Second Team	Total
GOAL	Glenn Hall	7	4	11
	Frank Brimsek	2	6	8
	Jacques Plante	3	4	7
	Terry Sawchuk	3	4	7
	Bill Durnan	6	0	6
	Ken Dryden	5	1	6
DEFENSE	* Ray Bourque	12	6	18
	Doug Harvey	10	1	11
	Earl Seibert	4	6	10
	Bobby Orr	8	1	9
	Eddie Shore	7	1	8
	Red Kelly	6	2	8
	Pierre Pilote	5	3	8
	* Paul Coffey	4	4	8

Position	Player	First Team	Second Team	Total
LEFT WING	Bobby Hull	10	2	12
	Ted Lindsay	8	1	9
	Frank Mahovlich	3	6	9
	* Luc Robitaille	5	2	7
	Harvey Jackson	4	1	5
	Michel Goulet	3	2	5
	Toe Blake	3	2	5
RIGHT WING	Gordie Howe	12	9	21
	Maurice Richard	8	6	14
	Mike Bossy	5	3	8
	Guy Lafleur	6	0	6
	Charlie Conacher	3	2	5
	Jari Kurri	2	3	5
CENTER	Wayne Gretzky	8	7	15
	Jean Beliveau	6	4	10
	Stan Mikita	6	2	8
	Phil Esposito	6	2	8
	Mario Lemieux	5	3	8

* active player

All-Star Teams
1930-99

Voting for the NHL All-Star Team is conducted among the representatives of the Professional Hockey Writers' Association at the end of the season.

Following is a list of the First and Second All-Star Teams since their inception in 1930-31.

First Team		Second Team
1998-99		
Hasek, Dominik, Buf.	G	Dafoe, Byron, Bos.
MacInnis, Al, St. L.	D	Bourque, Ray, Bos.
Lindstrom, Nicklas, Det.	D	Desjardins, Eric, Phi.
Forsberg, Peter, Col.	C	Yashin, Alexei, Ott.
Jagr, Jaromir, Pit.	RW	Selanne, Teemu, Ana.
Kariya, Paul, Ana.	LW	LeClair, John, Phi.
1997-98		
Hasek, Dominik, Buf.	G	Brodeur, Martin, N.J.
Lidstrom, Nicklas, Det.	D	Pronger, Chris, St.L.
Blake, Rob, L.A.	D	Niedermayer, Scott, N.J.
Forsberg, Peter, Col.	C	Gretzky, Wayne, NYR
Jagr, Jaromir, Pit.	RW	Selanne, Teemu, Ana.
LeClair, John, Phi.	LW	Tkachuk, Keith, Phx.
1996-97		
Hasek, Dominik, Buf.	G	Brodeur, Martin, N.J.
Leetch, Brian, NYR	D	Chelios, Chris, Chi.
Ozolinsh, Sandis, Col.	D	Stevens, Scott, N.J.
Lemieux, Mario, Pit.	C	Gretzky, Wayne, NYR
Selanne, Teemu, Ana.	RW	Jagr, Jaromir, Pit.
Kariya, Paul, Ana.	LW	LeClair, John, Phi.
1995-96		
Carey, Jim, Wsh.	G	Osgood, Chris, Det.
Chelios, Chris, Chi.	D	Konstantinov, V., Det.
Bourque, Ray, Bos.	D	Leetch, Brian, NYR.
Lemieux, Mario, Pit.	C	Lindros, Eric, Phi.
Jagr, Jaromir, Pit.	RW	Mogilny, Alexander, Van.
Kariya, Paul, Ana.	LW	LeClair, John, Phi.
1994-95		
Hasek, Dominik, Buf.	G	Belfour, Ed, Chi.
Coffey, Paul, Det.	D	Bourque, Ray, Bos.
Chelios, Chris, Chi.	D	Murphy, Larry, Pit.
Lindros, Eric, Phi.	C	Zhamnov, Alexei, Wpg.
Jagr, Jaromir, Pit.	RW	Fleury, Theoren, Cgy.
LeClair, John, Mtl., Phi.	LW	Tkachuk, Keith, Wpg.
1993-94		
Hasek, Dominik, Buf.	G	Vanbiesbrouck, John, Fla.
Bourque, Ray, Bos.	D	MacInnis, Al, Cgy.
Stevens, Scott, N.J.	D	Leetch, Brian, NYR
Fedorov, Sergei, Det.	C	Gretzky, Wayne, L.A.
Bure, Pavel, Van.	RW	Neely, Cam, Bos.
Shanahan, Brendan, St. L.	LW	Graves, Adam, NYR
1992-93		
Belfour, Ed, Chi.	G	Barrasso, Tom, Pit.
Chelios, Chris, Chi.	D	Murphy, Larry, Pit.
Bourque, Ray, Bos.	D	Iafrate, Al, Wsh.
Lemieux, Mario, Pit.	C	LaFontaine, Pat, Buf.
Selanne, Teemu, Wpg.	RW	Mogilny, Alexander, Buf.
Robitaille, Luc, L.A.	LW	Stevens, Kevin, Pit.
1991-92		
Roy, Patrick, Mtl.	G	McLean, Kirk, Van.
Leetch, Brian, NYR	D	Housley, Phil, Wpg.
Bourque, Ray, Bos.	D	Stevens, Scott, N.J.
Messier, Mark, NYR	C	Lemieux, Mario, Pit.
Hull, Brett, St. L.	RW	Recchi, Mark, Pit., Phi.
Stevens, Kevin, Pit.	LW	Robitaille, Luc, L.A.

First Team		Second Team
1990-91		
Belfour, Ed, Chi.	G	Roy, Patrick, Mtl.
Bourque, Ray, Bos.	D	Chelios, Chris, Chi.
MacInnis, Al, Cgy.	D	Leetch, Brian, NYR
Gretzky, Wayne, L.A.	C	Oates, Adam, St. L.
Hull, Brett, St. L.	RW	Neely, Cam, Bos.
Robitaille, Luc, L.A.	LW	Stevens, Kevin, Pit.
1989-90		
Roy, Patrick, Mtl.	G	Puppa, Daren, Buf.
Bourque, Ray, Bos.	D	Coffey, Paul, Pit.
MacInnis, Al, Cgy.	D	Wilson, Doug, Chi.
Messier, Mark, Edm.	C	Gretzky, Wayne, L.A.
Hull, Brett, St. L.	RW	Neely, Cam, Bos.
Robitaille, Luc, L.A.	LW	Bellows, Brian, Min.
1988-89		
Roy, Patrick, Mtl.	G	Vernon, Mike, Cgy.
Chelios, Chris, Mtl.	D	MacInnis, Al, Cgy.
Coffey, Paul, Pit.	D	Bourque, Ray, Bos.
Lemieux, Mario, Pit.	C	Gretzky, Wayne, L.A.
Mullen, Joe, Cgy.	RW	Kurri, Jari, Edm.
Robitaille, Luc, L.A.	LW	Gallant, Gerard, Det.

First Team		Second Team
1987-88		
Fuhr, Grant, Edm.	G	Roy, Patrick, Mtl.
Bourque, Ray, Bos.	D	Suter, Gary, Cgy.
Stevens, Scott, Wsh.	D	McCrimmon, Brad, Cgy.
Lemieux, Mario, Pit.	C	Gretzky, Wayne, Edm.
Loob, Hakan, Cgy.	RW	Neely, Cam, Bos.
Robitaille, Luc, L.A.	LW	Goulet, Michel, Que.
1986-87		
Hextall, Ron, Phi.	G	Liut, Mike, Hfd.
Bourque, Ray, Bos.	D	Murphy, Larry, Wsh.
Howe, Mark, Phi.	D	MacInnis, Al, Cgy.
Gretzky, Wayne, Edm.	C	Lemieux, Mario, Pit.
Kurri, Jari, Edm.	RW	Kerr, Tim, Phi.
Goulet, Michel, Que.	LW	Robitaille, Luc, L.A.
1985-86		
Vanbiesbrouck, John, NYR	G	Froese, Bob, Phi.
Coffey, Paul, Edm.	D	Robinson, Larry, Mtl.
Howe, Mark, Phi.	D	Bourque, Ray, Bos.
Gretzky, Wayne, Edm.	C	Lemieux, Mario, Pit.
Bossy, Mike, NYI	RW	Kurri, Jari, Edm.
Goulet, Michel, Que.	LW	Naslund, Mats, Mtl.

Raymond Bourque regained his All-Star status in 1998-99, being named to the Second Team for the sixth time in his career. With his 12 selections to the First Team, Bourque has gained more All-Star honors (18) than any player other than Gordie Howe.

First Team		Second Team

1984-85

First Team	Pos	Second Team
Lindbergh, Pelle, Phi.	G	Barrasso, Tom, Buf.
Coffey, Paul, Edm.	D	Langway, Rod, Wsh.
Bourque, Ray, Bos.	D	Wilson, Doug, Chi.
Gretzky, Wayne, Edm.	C	Hawerchuk, Dale, Wpg.
Kurri, Jari, Edm.	RW	Bossy, Mike, NYI
Ogrodnick, John, Det.	LW	Tonelli, John, NYI

1983-84

First Team	Pos	Second Team
Barrasso, Tom, Buf.	G	Riggin, Pat, Wsh.
Langway, Rod, Wsh.	D	Coffey, Paul, Edm.
Bourque, Ray, Bos.	D	Potvin, Denis, NYI
Gretzky, Wayne, Edm.	C	Trottier, Bryan, NYI
Bossy, Mike, NYI	RW	Kurri, Jari, Edm.
Goulet, Michel, Que.	LW	Messier, Mark, Edm.

1982-83

First Team	Pos	Second Team
Peeters, Pete, Bos.	G	Melanson, Rollie, NYI
Howe, Mark, Phi.	D	Bourque, Ray, Bos.
Langway, Rod, Wsh.	D	Coffey, Paul, Edm.
Gretzky, Wayne, Edm.	C	Savard, Denis, Chi.
Bossy, Mike, NYI	RW	McDonald, Lanny, Cgy.
Messier, Mark, Edm.	LW	Goulet, Michel, Que.

1981-82

First Team	Pos	Second Team
Smith, Billy, NYI	G	Fuhr, Grant, Edm.
Wilson, Doug, Chi.	D	Coffey, Paul, Edm.
Bourque, Ray, Bos.	D	Engblom, Brian, Mtl.
Gretzky, Wayne, Edm.	C	Trottier, Bryan, NYI
Bossy, Mike, NYI	RW	Middleton, Rick, Bos.
Messier, Mark, Edm.	LW	Tonelli, John, NYI

1980-81

First Team	Pos	Second Team
Liut, Mike, St.L.	G	Lessard, Mario, L.A.
Potvin, Denis, NYI	D	Robinson, Larry, Mtl.
Carlyle, Randy, Pit.	D	Bourque, Ray, Bos.
Gretzky, Wayne, Edm.	C	Dionne, Marcel, L.A.
Bossy, Mike, NYI	RW	Taylor, Dave, L.A.
Simmer, Charlie, L.A.	LW	Barber, Bill, Phi.

1979-80

First Team	Pos	Second Team
Esposito, Tony, Chi.	G	Edwards, Don, Buf.
Robinson, Larry, Mtl.	D	Salming, Borje, Tor.
Bourque, Ray, Bos.	D	Schoenfeld, Jim, Buf.
Dionne, Marcel, L.A.	C	Gretzky, Wayne, Edm.
Lafleur, Guy, Mtl	RW	Gare, Danny, Buf.
Simmer, Charlie, L.A.	LW	Shutt, Steve, Mtl.

1978-79

First Team	Pos	Second Team
Dryden, Ken, Mtl.	G	Resch, Glenn, NYI
Potvin, Denis, NYI	D	Salming, Borje, Tor.
Robinson, Larry, Mtl.	D	Savard, Serge, Mtl.
Trottier, Bryan, NYI	C	Dionne, Marcel, L.A.
Lafleur, Guy, Mtl.	RW	Bossy, Mike, NYI
Gillies, Clark, NYI	LW	Barber, Bill, Phi.

1977-78

First Team	Pos	Second Team
Dryden, Ken, Mtl.	G	Edwards, Don, Buf.
Potvin, Denis, NYI	D	Robinson, Larry, Mtl.
Park, Brad, Bos.	D	Salming, Borje, Tor.
Trottier, Bryan, NYI	C	Sittler, Darryl, Tor.
Lafleur, Guy, Mtl.	RW	Bossy, Mike, NYI
Gillies, Clark, NYI	LW	Shutt, Steve, Mtl.

1976-77

First Team	Pos	Second Team
Dryden, Ken, Mtl.	G	Vachon, Rogie, L.A.
Robinson, Larry, Mtl.	D	Potvin, Denis, NYI
Salming, Borje, Tor.	D	Lapointe, Guy, Mtl.
Dionne, Marcel, L.A.	C	Perreault, Gilbert, Buf.
Lafleur, Guy, Mtl.	RW	McDonald, Lanny, Tor.
Shutt, Steve, Mtl.	LW	Martin, Rick, Buf.

1975-76

First Team	Pos	Second Team
Dryden, Ken, Mtl.	G	Resch, Glenn, NYI
Potvin, Denis, NYI	D	Salming, Borje, Tor.
Park, Brad, Bos.	D	Lapointe, Guy, Mtl.
Clarke, Bobby, Phi.	C	Perreault, Gilbert, Buf.
Lafleur, Guy, Mtl.	RW	Leach, Reggie, Phi.
Barber, Bill, Phi.	LW	Martin, Rick, Buf.

1974-75

First Team	Pos	Second Team
Parent, Bernie, Phi.	G	Vachon, Rogie, L.A.
Orr, Bobby, Bos.	D	Lapointe, Guy, Mtl.
Potvin, Denis, NYI	D	Salming, Borje, Tor.
Clarke, Bobby, Phi.	C	Esposito, Phil, Bos.
Lafleur, Guy, Mtl.	RW	Robert, René, Buf.
Martin, Rick, Buf.	LW	Vickers, Steve, NYR

1973-74

First Team	Pos	Second Team
Parent, Bernie, Phi.	G	Esposito, Tony, Chi.
Orr, Bobby, Bos.	D	White, Bill, Chi.
Park, Brad, NYR	D	Ashbee, Barry, Phi.
Esposito, Phil, Bos.	C	Clarke, Bobby, Phi.
Hodge, Ken, Bos.	RW	Redmond, Mickey, Det.
Martin, Rick, Buf.	LW	Cashman, Wayne, Bos.

1972-73

First Team	Pos	Second Team
Dryden, Ken, Mtl.	G	Esposito, Tony, Chi.
Orr, Bobby, Bos.	D	Park, Brad, NYR
Lapointe, Guy, Mtl.	D	White, Bill, Chi.
Esposito, Phil, Bos.	C	Clarke, Bobby, Phi.
Redmond, Mickey, Det.	RW	Cournoyer, Yvan, Mtl.
Mahovlich, Frank, Mtl.	LW	Hull, Dennis, Chi.

1971-72

First Team	Pos	Second Team
Esposito, Tony, Chi.	G	Dryden, Ken, Mtl.
Orr, Bobby, Bos.	D	White, Bill, Chi.
Park, Brad, NYR	D	Stapleton, Pat, Chi.
Esposito, Phil, Bos.	C	Ratelle, Jean, NYR
Gilbert, Rod, NYR	RW	Cournoyer, Yvan, Mtl.
Hull, Bobby, Chi.	LW	Hadfield, Vic, NYR

1970-71

First Team	Pos	Second Team
Giacomin, Ed, NYR	G	Plante, Jacques, Tor.
Orr, Bobby, Bos.	D	Park, Brad, NYR
Tremblay, J.C., Mtl.	D	Stapleton, Pat, Chi.
Esposito, Phil, Bos.	C	Keon, Dave, Tor.
Hodge, Ken, Bos.	RW	Cournoyer, Yvan, Mtl.
Bucyk, John, Bos.	LW	Hull, Bobby, Chi.

1969-70

First Team	Pos	Second Team
Esposito, Tony, Chi.	G	Giacomin, Ed, NYR
Orr, Bobby, Bos.	D	Brewer, Carl, Det.
Park, Brad, NYR	D	Laperriere, Jacques, Mtl.
Esposito, Phil, Bos.	C	Mikita, Stan, Chi.
Howe, Gordie, Det.	RW	McKenzie, John, Bos.
Hull, Bobby, Chi.	LW	Mahovlich, Frank, Det.

1968-69

First Team	Pos	Second Team
Hall, Glenn, St.L.	G	Giacomin, Ed, NYR
Orr, Bobby, Bos.	D	Green, Ted, Bos.
Horton, Tim, Tor.	D	Harris, Ted, Mtl.
Esposito, Phil, Bos.	C	Béliveau, Jean, Mtl.
Howe, Gordie, Det.	RW	Cournoyer, Yvan, Mtl.
Hull, Bobby, Chi.	LW	Mahovlich, Frank, Det.

1967-68

First Team	Pos	Second Team
Worsley, Gump, Mtl.	G	Giacomin, Ed, NYR
Orr, Bobby, Bos.	D	Tremblay, J.C., Mtl.
Horton, Tim, Tor.	D	Neilson, Jim, NYR
Mikita, Stan, Chi.	C	Esposito, Phil, Bos.
Howe, Gordie, Det.	RW	Gilbert, Rod, NYR
Hull, Bobby, Chi.	LW	Bucyk, John, Bos.

1966-67

First Team	Pos	Second Team
Giacomin, Ed, NYR	G	Hall, Glenn, Chi.
Pilote, Pierre, Chi.	D	Horton, Tim, Tor.
Howell, Harry, NYR	D	Orr, Bobby, Bos.
Mikita, Stan, Chi.	C	Ullman, Norm, Det.
Wharram, Kenny, Chi.	RW	Howe, Gordie, Det.
Hull, Bobby, Chi.	LW	Marshall, Don, NYR

1965-66

First Team	Pos	Second Team
Hall, Glenn, Chi.	G	Worsley, Gump, Mtl.
Laperriere, Jacques, Mtl.	D	Stanley, Allan, Tor.
Pilote, Pierre, Chi.	D	Stapleton, Pat, Chi.
Mikita, Stan, Chi.	C	Béliveau, Jean, Mtl.
Howe, Gordie, Det.	RW	Rousseau, Bobby, Mtl.
Hull, Bobby, Chi.	LW	Mahovlich, Frank, Tor.

1964-65

First Team	Pos	Second Team
Crozier, Roger, Det.	G	Hodge, Charlie, Mtl.
Pilote, Pierre, Chi.	D	Gadsby, Bill, Det.
Laperriere, Jacques, Mtl.	D	Brewer, Carl, Tor.
Ullman, Norm, Det.	C	Mikita, Stan, Chi.
Provost, Claude, Mtl.	RW	Howe, Gordie, Det.
Hull, Bobby, Chi.	LW	Mahovlich, Frank, Tor.

1963-64

First Team	Pos	Second Team
Hall, Glenn, Chi.	G	Hodge, Charlie, Mtl.
Pilote, Pierre, Chi.	D	Vasko, Elmer, Chi.
Horton, Tim, Tor.	D	Laperriere, Jacques, Mtl.
Mikita, Stan, Chi.	C	Béliveau, Jean, Mtl.
Wharram, Kenny, Chi.	RW	Howe, Gordie, Det.
Hull, Bobby, Chi.	LW	Mahovlich, Frank, Tor.

1962-63

First Team	Pos	Second Team
Hall, Glenn, Chi.	G	Sawchuk, Terry, Det.
Pilote, Pierre, Chi.	D	Horton, Tim, Tor.
Brewer, Carl, Tor.	D	Vasko, Elmer, Chi.
Mikita, Stan, Chi.	C	Richard, Henri, Mtl.
Howe, Gordie, Det.	RW	Bathgate, Andy, NYR
Mahovlich, Frank, Tor.	LW	Hull, Bobby, Chi.

1961-62

First Team	Pos	Second Team
Plante, Jacques, Mtl.	G	Hall, Glenn, Chi.
Harvey, Doug, NYR	D	Brewer, Carl, Tor.
Talbot, Jean-Guy, Mtl.	D	Pilote, Pierre, Chi.
Mikita, Stan, Chi.	C	Keon, Dave, Tor.
Bathgate, Andy, NYR	RW	Howe, Gordie, Det.
Hull, Bobby, Chi.	LW	Mahovlich, Frank, Tor.

1960-61

First Team	Pos	Second Team
Bower, Johnny, Tor.	G	Hall, Glenn, Chi.
Harvey, Doug, Mtl.	D	Stanley, Allan, Tor.
Pronovost, Marcel, Det.	D	Pilote, Pierre, Chi.
Béliveau, Jean, Mtl.	C	Richard, Henri, Mtl.
Geoffrion, Bernie, Mtl.	RW	Howe, Gordie, Det.
Mahovlich, Frank, Tor.	LW	Moore, Dickie, Mtl.

1959-60

First Team	Pos	Second Team
Hall, Glenn, Chi.	G	Plante, Jacques, Mtl.
Harvey, Doug, Mtl.	D	Stanley, Allan, Tor.
Pronovost, Marcel, Det.	D	Pilote, Pierre, Chi.
Béliveau, Jean, Mtl.	C	Horvath, Bronco, Bos.
Howe, Gordie, Det.	RW	Geoffrion, Bernie, Mtl.
Hull, Bobby, Chi.	LW	Prentice, Dean, NYR

1958-59

First Team	Pos	Second Team
Plante, Jacques, Mtl.	G	Sawchuk, Terry, Det.
Johnson, Tom, Mtl.	D	Pronovost, Marcel, Det
Gadsby, Bill, NYR	D	Harvey, Doug, Mtl.
Béliveau, Jean, Mtl.	C	Richard, Henri, Mtl.
Bathgate, Andy, NYR	RW	Howe, Gordie, Det.
Moore, Dickie, Mtl.	LW	Delvecchio, Alex, Det

1957-58

First Team		Second Team
Hall, Glenn, Chi.	G	Plante, Jacques, Mtl.
Harvey, Doug, Mtl.	D	Flaman, Fern, Bos.
Gadsby, Bill, NYR	D	Pronovost, Marcel, Det.
Richard, Henri, Mtl.	C	Béliveau, Jean, Mtl.
Howe, Gordie, Det.	RW	Bathgate, Andy, NYR
Moore, Dickie, Mtl.	LW	Henry, Camille, NYR

1956-57

First Team		Second Team
Hall, Glenn, Det.	G	Plante, Jacques, Mtl.
Harvey, Doug, Mtl.	D	Flaman, Fern, Bos.
Kelly, Red, Det.	D	Gadsby, Bill, NYR
Béliveau, Jean, Mtl.	C	Litzenberger, Ed, Chi.
Howe, Gordie, Det.	RW	Richard, Maurice, Mtl.
Lindsay, Ted, Det.	LW	Chevrefils, Real, Bos.

1955-56

First Team		Second Team
Plante, Jacques, Mtl.	G	Hall, Glenn, Det.
Harvey, Doug, Mtl.	D	Kelly, Red, Det.
Gadsby, Bill, NYR	D	Johnson, Tom, Mtl.
Béliveau, Jean, Mtl.	C	Sloan, Tod, Tor.
Richard, Maurice, Mtl.	RW	Howe, Gordie, Det.
Lindsay, Ted, Det.	LW	Olmstead, Bert, Mtl.

1954-55

First Team		Second Team
Lumley, Harry, Tor.	G	Sawchuk, Terry, Det.
Harvey, Doug, Mtl.	D	Goldham, Bob, Det.
Kelly, Red, Det.	D	Flaman, Fern, Bos.
Béliveau, Jean, Mtl.	C	Mosdell, Ken, Mtl.
Richard, Maurice, Mtl.	RW	Geoffrion, Bernie, Mtl.
Smith, Sid, Tor.	LW	Lewicki, Danny, NYR

1953-54

First Team		Second Team
Lumley, Harry, Tor.	G	Sawchuk, Terry, Det.
Kelly, Red, Det.	D	Gadsby, Bill, Chi.
Harvey, Doug, Mtl.	D	Horton, Tim, Tor.
Mosdell, Kenny, Mtl.	C	Kennedy, Ted, Tor.
Howe, Gordie, Det.	RW	Richard, Maurice, Mtl.
Lindsay, Ted, Det.	LW	Sandford, Ed, Bos.

1952-53

First Team		Second Team
Sawchuk, Terry, Det.	G	McNeil, Gerry, Mtl.
Kelly, Red, Det.	D	Quackenbush, Bill, Bos.
Harvey, Doug, Mtl.	D	Gadsby, Bill, Chi.
Mackell, Fleming, Bos.	C	Delvecchio, Alex, Det.
Howe, Gordie, Det.	RW	Richard, Maurice, Mtl.
Lindsay, Ted, Det.	LW	Olmstead, Bert, Mtl.

1951-52

First Team		Second Team
Sawchuk, Terry, Det.	G	Henry, Jim, Bos.
Kelly, Red, Det.	D	Buller, Hy, NYR
Harvey, Doug, Mtl.	D	Thomson, Jimmy, Tor.
Lach, Elmer, Mtl.	C	Schmidt, Milt, Bos.
Howe, Gordie, Det.	RW	Richard, Maurice, Mtl.
Lindsay, Ted, Det.	LW	Smith, Sid, Tor.

1950-51

First Team		Second Team
Sawchuk, Terry, Det.	G	Rayner, Chuck, NYR
Kelly, Red, Det.	D	Thomson, Jim, Tor.
Quackenbush, Bill, Bos.	D	Reise Jr., Leo, Det.
Schmidt, Milt, Bos.	C	Abel, Sid, Det.
	(tied)	Kennedy, Ted, Tor.
Howe, Gordie, Det.	RW	Richard, Maurice, Mtl.
Lindsay, Ted, Det.	LW	Smith, Sid, Tor.

1949-50

First Team		Second Team
Durnan, Bill, Mtl.	G	Rayner, Chuck, NYR
Mortson, Gus, Tor.	D	Reise Jr., Leo, Det.
Reardon, Ken, Mtl.	D	Kelly, Red, Det.
Abel, Sid, Det.	C	Kennedy, Ted, Tor.
Richard, Maurice, Mtl.	RW	Howe, Gordie, Det.
Lindsay, Ted, Det.	LW	Leswick, Tony, NYR

1948-49

First Team		Second Team
Durnan, Bill, Mtl.	G	Rayner, Chuck, NYR
Quackenbush, Bill, Det.	D	Harmon, Glen, Mtl.
Stewart, Jack, Det.	D	Reardon, Ken, Mtl.
Abel, Sid, Det.	C	Bentley, Doug, Chi.
Richard, Maurice, Mtl.	RW	Howe, Gordie, Det.
Conacher, Roy, Chi.	LW	Lindsay, Ted, Det.

1947-48

First Team		Second Team
Broda, Turk, Tor.	G	Brimsek, Frank, Bos.
Quackenbush, Bill, Det.	D	Reardon, Ken, Mtl.
Stewart, Jack, Det.	D	Colville, Neil, NYR
Lach, Elmer, Mtl.	C	O'Connor, Buddy, NYR
Richard, Maurice, Mtl.	RW	Poile, Bud, Chi.
Lindsay, Ted, Det.	LW	Stewart, Gaye, Chi.

1946-47

First Team		Second Team
Durnan, Bill, Mtl.	G	Brimsek, Frank, Bos.
Reardon, Ken, Mtl.	D	Stewart, Jack, Det.
Bouchard, Butch, Mtl.	D	Quackenbush, Bill, Det.
Schmidt, Milt, Bos.	C	Bentley, Max, Chi.
Richard, Maurice, Mtl.	RW	Bauer, Bobby, Bos.
Bentley, Doug, Chi.	LW	Dumart, Woody, Bos.

1945-46

First Team		Second Team
Durnan, Bill, Mtl.	G	Brimsek, Frank, Bos.
Crawford, Jack, Bos.	D	Reardon, Ken, Mtl.
Bouchard, Butch, Mtl.	D	Stewart, Jack, Det.
Bentley, Max, Chi.	C	Lach, Elmer, Mtl.
Richard, Maurice, Mtl.	RW	Mosienko, Bill, Chi.
Stewart, Gaye, Tor.	LW	Blake, Toe, Mtl.
Irvin, Dick, Mtl.	Coach	Gottselig, Johnny, Chi.

1944-45

First Team		Second Team
Durnan, Bill, Mtl.	G	Karakas, Mike, Chi.
Bouchard, Butch, Mtl.	D	Harmon, Glen, Mtl.
Hollett, Flash, Det.	D	Pratt, Babe, Tor.
Lach, Elmer, Mtl.	C	Cowley, Bill, Bos.
Richard, Maurice, Mtl.	RW	Mosienko, Bill, Chi.
Blake, Toe, Mtl.	LW	Howe, Syd, Det.
Irvin, Dick, Mtl.	Coach	Adams, Jack, Det.

1943-44

First Team		Second Team
Durnan, Bill, Mtl.	G	Bibeault, Paul, Tor.
Seibert, Earl, Chi.	D	Bouchard, Butch, Mtl.
Pratt, Babe, Tor.	D	Clapper, Dit, Bos.
Cowley, Bill, Bos.	C	Lach, Elmer, Mtl.
Carr, Lorne, Tor.	RW	Richard, Maurice, Mtl.
Bentley, Doug, Chi.	LW	Cain, Herb, Bos.
Irvin, Dick, Mtl.	Coach	Day, Hap, Tor.

1942-43

First Team		Second Team
Mowers, Johnny, Det.	G	Brimsek, Frank, Bos.
Seibert, Earl, Chi.	D	Crawford, Jack, Bos.
Stewart, Jack, Det.	D	Hollett, Flash, Bos.
Cowley, Bill, Bos.	C	Apps Sr., Syl, Tor.
Carr, Lorne, Tor.	RW	Hextall Sr., Bryan, NYR
Bentley, Doug, Chi.	LW	Patrick, Lynn, NYR
Adams, Jack, Det.	Coach	Ross, Art, Bos.

1941-42

First Team		Second Team
Brimsek, Frank, Bos.	G	Broda, Turk, Tor.
Seibert, Earl, Chi.	D	Egan, Pat, Bro.
Anderson, Tom, Bro.	D	McDonald, Bucko, Tor.
Apps Sr., Syl, Tor.	C	Watson, Phil, NYR
Hextall Sr., Bryan, NYR	RW	Drillon, Gordie, Tor.
Patrick, Lynn, NYR	LW	Abel, Sid, Det.
Boucher, Frank, NYR	Coach	Thompson, Paul, Chi.

1940-41

First Team		Second Team
Broda, Turk, Tor.	G	Brimsek, Frank, Bos.
Clapper, Dit, Bos.	D	Seibert, Earl, Chi.
Stanowski, Wally, Tor.	D	Heller, Ott, NYR
Cowley, Bill, Bos.	C	Apps Sr., Syl, Tor.
Hextall Sr., Bryan, NYR	RW	Bauer, Bobby, Bos.
Schriner, Sweeney, Tor.	LW	Dumart, Woody, Bos.
Weiland, Cooney, Bos.	Coach	Irvin, Dick, Mtl.

1939-40

First Team		Second Team
Kerr, Dave, NYR	G	Brimsek, Frank, Bos.
Clapper, Dit, Bos.	D	Coulter, Art, NYR
Goodfellow, Ebbie, Det.	D	Seibert, Earl, Chi.
Schmidt, Milt, Bos.	C	Colville, Neil, NYR
Hextall Sr., Bryan, NYR	RW	Bauer, Bobby, Bos.
Blake, Toe, Mtl.	LW	Dumart, Woody, Bos.
Thompson, Paul, Chi.	Coach	Boucher, Frank, NYR

1938-39

First Team		Second Team
Brimsek, Frank, Bos.	G	Robertson, Earl, NYA
Shore, Eddie, Bos.	D	Seibert, Earl, Chi.
Clapper, Dit, Bos.	D	Coulter, Art, NYR
Apps Sr., Syl, Tor.	C	Colville, Neil, NYR
Drillon, Gordie, Tor.	RW	Bauer, Bobby, Bos.
Blake, Toe, Mtl.	LW	Gottselig, Johnny, Chi.
Ross, Art, Bos.	Coach	Dutton, Red, NYA

1937-38

First Team		Second Team
Thompson, Tiny, Bos.	G	Kerr, Dave, NYR
Shore, Eddie, Bos.	D	Coulter, Art, NYR
Siebert, Babe, Mtl.	D	Seibert, Earl, Chi.
Cowley, Bill, Bos.	C	Apps Sr., Syl, Tor.
Dillon, Cecil, NYR	RW	
Drillon, Gordie, Tor.	(tied)	
Thompson, Paul, Chi.	LW	Blake, Toe, Mtl.
Patrick, Lester, NYR	Coach	Ross, Art, Bos.

1936-37

First Team		Second Team
Smith, Norman, Det.	G	Cude, Wilf, Mtl.
Siebert, Babe, Mtl.	D	Seibert, Earl, Chi.
Goodfellow, Ebbie, Det.	D	Conacher, Lionel, Mtl. M.
Barry, Marty, Det.	C	Chapman, Art, NYA
Aurie, Larry, Det.	RW	Dillon, Cecil, NYR
Jackson, Harvey, Tor.	LW	Schriner, Sweeney, NYA
Adams, Jack, Det.	Coach	Hart, Cecil, Mtl.

1935-36

First Team		Second Team
Thompson, Tiny, Bos.	G	Cude, Wilf, Mtl.
Shore, Eddie, Bos.	D	Seibert, Earl, Chi.
Siebert, Babe, Bos.	D	Goodfellow, Ebbie, Det.
Smith, Hooley, Mtl. M.	C	Thoms, Bill, Tor.
Conacher, Charlie, Tor.	RW	Dillon, Cecil, NYR
Schriner, Sweeney, NYA	LW	Thompson, Paul, Chi.
Patrick, Lester, NYR	Coach	Gorman, Tommy, Mtl. M.

1934-35

First Team		Second Team
Chabot, Lorne, Chi.	G	Thompson, Tiny, Bos.
Shore, Eddie, Bos.	D	Wentworth, Cy, Mtl. M.
Seibert, Earl, NYR	D	Coulter, Art, Chi.
Boucher, Frank, NYR	C	Weiland, Cooney, Det.
Conacher, Charlie, Tor.	RW	Clapper, Dit, Bos.
Jackson, Harvey, Tor.	LW	Joliat, Aurel, Mtl.
Patrick, Lester, NYR	Coach	Irvin, Dick, Tor.

1933-34

First Team		Second Team
Gardiner, Chuck, Chi.	G	Worters, Roy, NYA
Clancy, King, Tor.	D	Shore, Eddie, Bos.
Conacher, Lionel, Chi.	D	Johnson, Ching, NYR
Boucher, Frank, NYR	C	Primeau, Joe, Tor.
Conacher, Charlie, Tor.	RW	Cook, Bill, NYR
Jackson, Harvey, Tor.	LW	Joliat, Aurel, Mtl.
Patrick, Lester, NYR	Coach	Irvin, Dick, Tor.

1932-33

First Team		Second Team
Roach, John Ross, Det.	G	Gardiner, Chuck, Chi.
Shore, Eddie, Bos.	D	Clancy, King, Tor.
Johnson, Ching, NYR	D	Conacher, Lionel, Mtl. M.
Boucher, Frank, NYR	C	Morenz, Howie, Mtl.
Cook, Bill, NYR	RW	Conacher, Charlie, Tor.
Northcott, Baldy, Mtl M	LW	Jackson, Harvey, Tor.
Patrick, Lester, NYR	Coach	Irvin, Dick, Tor.

1931-32

First Team		Second Team
Gardiner, Chuck, Chi.	G	Worters, Roy, NYA
Shore, Eddie, Bos.	D	Mantha, Sylvio, Mtl.
Johnson, Ching, NYR	D	Clancy, King, Tor.
Morenz, Howie, Mtl.	C	Smith, Hooley, Mtl. M.
Cook, Bill, NYR	RW	Conacher, Charlie, Tor.
Jackson, Harvey, Tor.	LW	Joliat, Aurel, Mtl.
Patrick, Lester, NYR	Coach	Irvin, Dick, Tor.

1930-31

First Team		Second Team
Gardiner, Chuck, Chi.	G	Thompson, Tiny, Bos.
Shore, Eddie, Bos.	D	Mantha, Sylvio, Mtl.
Clancy, King, Tor.	D	Johnson, Ching, NYR
Morenz, Howie, Mtl.	C	Boucher, Frank, NYR
Cook, Bill, NYR	RW	Clapper, Dit, Bos.
Joliat, Aurel, Mtl.	LW	Cook, Bun, NYR
Patrick, Lester, NYR	Coach	Irvin, Dick, Chi.

All-Star Game Results

Year	Venue	Score	Coaches	Attendance
1999	Tampa Bay	North America 8, World 6	Lindy Ruff, Ken Hitchcock	19,758
1998	Vancouver	North America 8, World 7	Jacques Lemaire, Ken Hitchcock	18,422
1997	San Jose	Eastern 11, Western 7	Doug MacLean, Ken Hitchcock	17,422
1996	Boston	Eastern 5, Western 4	Doug MacLean, Scotty Bowman	17,565
1994	NY Rangers	Eastern 9, Western 8	Jacques Demers, Barry Melrose	18,200
1993	Montreal	Wales 16, Campbell 6	Scotty Bowman, Mike Keenan	17,137
1992	Philadelphia	Campbell 10, Wales 6	Bob Gainey, Scotty Bowman	17,380
1991	Chicago	Campbell 11, Wales 5	John Muckler, Mike Milbury	18,472
1990	Pittsburgh	Wales 12, Campbell 7	Pat Burns, Terry Crisp	16,236
1989	Edmonton	Campbell 9, Wales 5	Glen Sather, Terry O'Reilly	17,503
1988	St. Louis	Wales 6, Campbell 5 OT	Mike Keenan, Glen Sather	17,878
1986	Hartford	Wales 4, Campbell 3 OT	Mike Keenan, Glen Sather	15,100
1985	Calgary	Wales 6, Campbell 4	Al Arbour, Glen Sather	16,825
1984	New Jersey	Wales 7, Campbell 6	Al Arbour, Glen Sather	18,939
1983	NY Islanders	Campbell 9, Wales 3	Roger Neilson, Al Arbour	15,230
1982	Washington	Wales 4, Campbell 2	Al Arbour, Glen Sonmor	18,130
1981	Los Angeles	Campbell 4, Wales 1	Pat Quinn, Scotty Bowman	15,761
1980	Detroit	Wales 6, Campbell 3	Scotty Bowman, Al Arbour	21,002
1978	Buffalo	Wales 3, Campbell 2 OT	Scotty Bowman, Fred Shero	16,433
1977	Vancouver	Wales 4, Campbell 3	Scotty Bowman, Fred Shero	15,607
1976	Philadelphia	Wales 7, Campbell 5	Floyd Smith, Fred Shero	16,436
1975	Montreal	Wales 7, Campbell 1	Bep Guidolin, Fred Shero	16,080
1974	Chicago	West 6, East 4	Billy Reay, Scotty Bowman	16,426
1973	New York	East 5, West 4	Tom Johnson, Billy Reay	16,986
1972	Minnesota	East 3, West 2	Al MacNeil, Billy Reay	15,423
1971	Boston	West 2, East 1	Scotty Bowman, Harry Sinden	14,790
1970	St. Louis	East 4, West 1	Claude Ruel, Scotty Bowman	16,587
1969	Montreal	East 3, West 3	Toe Blake, Scotty Bowman	16,260
1968	Toronto	Toronto 4, All-Stars 3	Punch Imlach, Toe Blake	15,753
1967	Montreal	Montreal 3, All-Stars 0	Toe Blake, Sid Abel	14,284
1965	Montreal	All-Stars 5, Montreal 2	Billy Reay, Toe Blake	13,529
1964	Toronto	All-Stars 3, Toronto 2	Sid Abel, Punch Imlach	14,232
1963	Toronto	All-Stars 3, Toronto 3	Sid Abel, Punch Imlach	14,034
1962	Toronto	Toronto 4, All-Stars 1	Punch Imlach, Rudy Pilous	14,236
1961	Chicago	All-Stars 3, Chicago 1	Sid Abel, Rudy Pilous	14,534
1960	Montreal	All-Stars 2, Montreal 1	Punch Imlach, Toe Blake	13,949
1959	Montreal	Montreal 6, All-Stars 1	Toe Blake, Punch Imlach	13,818
1958	Montreal	Montreal 6, All-Stars 3	Toe Blake, Milt Schmidt	13,989
1957	Montreal	All-Stars 5, Montreal 3	Milt Schmidt, Toe Blake	13,003
1956	Montreal	All-Stars 1, Montreal 1	Jim Skinner, Toe Blake	13,095
1955	Detroit	Detroit 3, All-Stars 1	Jim Skinner, Dick Irvin	10,111
1954	Detroit	All-Stars 2, Detroit 2	King Clancy, Jim Skinner	10,689
1953	Montreal	All-Stars 3, Montreal 1	Lynn Patrick, Dick Irvin	14,153
1952	Detroit	1st team 1, 2nd team 1	Tommy Ivan, Dick Irvin	10,680
1951	Toronto	1st team 2, 2nd team 2	Joe Primeau, Hap Day	11,469
1950	Detroit	Detroit 7, All-Stars 1	Tommy Ivan, Lynn Patrick	9,166
1949	Toronto	All-Stars 3, Toronto 1	Tommy Ivan, Hap Day	13,541
1948	Chicago	All-Stars 3, Toronto 1	Tommy Ivan, Hap Day	12,794
1947	Toronto	All-Stars 4, Toronto 3	Dick Irvin, Hap Day	14,169

There was no All-Star contest during the calendar year of 1966 because the game was moved from the start of season to mid-season. In 1979, the Challenge Cup series between the Soviet Union and Team NHL replaced the All-Star Game. In 1987, Rendez-Vous '87, two games between the Soviet Union and Team NHL replaced the All-Star Game. Rendez-Vous '87 scores: game one, NHL All-Stars 4, Soviet Union 3; game two, Soviet Union 5, NHL All-Stars 3. There was no All-Star Game in 1995 due to a labor disruption.

NHL ALL-ROOKIE TEAM

Voting for the NHL All-Rookie Team is conducted among the representatives of the Professional Hockey Writers' Association at the end of the season. The rookie all-star team was first selected for the 1982-83 season.

1998-99
Jamie Storr, Los Angeles	Goal
Tom Poti, Edmonton	Defense
Sami Salo, Ottawa	Defense
Chris Drury, Colorado	Forward
Milan Hejduk, Colorado	Forward
Marian Hossa, Ottawa	Forward

1997-98
Jamie Storr, Los Angeles	Goal
Mattias Ohlund, Vancouver	Defense
Derek Morris, Calgary	Defense
Sergei Samsonov, Boston	Forward
Patrik Elias, New Jersey	Forward
Mike Johnson, Toronto	Forward

1995-96
Corey Hirsch, Vancouver	Goal
Ed Jovanovski, Florida	Defense
Kyle McLaren, Boston	Defense
Daniel Alfredsson, Ottawa	Forward
Eric Daze, Chicago	Forward
Petr Sykora, New Jersey	Forward

1993-94
Martin Brodeur, New Jersey	Goal
Chris Pronger, Hartford	Defense
Boris Mironov, Wpg., Edm.	Defense
Jason Arnott, Edmonton	Center
Mikael Renberg, Philadelphia	Wing
Oleg Petrov, Montreal	Wing

1991-92
Dominik Hasek, Chicago	Goal
Nicklas Lidstrom, Detroit	Defense
Vladimir Konstantinov, Detroit	Defense
Kevin Todd, New Jersey	Center
Tony Amonte, NY Rangers	Right Wing
Gilbert Dionne, Montreal	Left Wing

1996-97
Patrick Lalime, Pittsburgh	
Bryan Berard, NY Islanders	
Janne Niinimaa, Philadelphia	
Jarome Iginla, Calgary	
Jim Campbell, St. Louis	
Sergei Berezin, Toronto	

1994-95
Jim Carey, Washington	
Chris Therien, Philadelphia	
Kenny Jonsson, Toronto	
Peter Forsberg, Quebec	
Jeff Friesen, San Jose	
Paul Kariya, Anaheim	

1992-93
Felix Potvin, Toronto	
Vladimir Malakhov, NY Islanders	
Scott Niedermayer, New Jersey	
Eric Lindros, Philadelphia	
Teemu Selanne, Winnipeg	
Joe Juneau, Boston	

1990-91
Ed Belfour, Chicago	
Eric Weinrich, New Jersey	
Rob Blake, Los Angeles	
Sergei Fedorov, Detroit	
Ken Hodge, Boston	
Jaromir Jagr, Pittsburgh	

1989-90
Bob Essensa, Winnipeg	Goal
Brad Shaw, Hartford	Defense
Geoff Smith, Edmonton	Defense
Mike Modano, Minnesota	Center
Sergei Makarov, Calgary	Right Wing
Rod Brind'Amour, St. Louis	Left Wing

1987-88
Darren Pang, Chicago	Goal
Glen Wesley, Boston	Defense
Calle Johansson, Buffalo	Defense
Joe Nieuwendyk, Calgary	Center
Ray Sheppard, Buffalo	Right Wing
Iain Duncan, Winnipeg	Left Wing

1985-86
Patrick Roy, Montreal	Goal
Gary Suter, Calgary	Defense
Dana Murzyn, Hartford	Defense
Mike Ridley, NY Rangers	Center
Kjell Dahlin, Montreal	Right Wing
Wendel Clark, Toronto	Left Wing

1983-84
Tom Barrasso, Buffalo	Goal
Thomas Eriksson, Philadelphia	Defense
Jamie Macoun, Calgary	Defense
Steve Yzerman, Detroit	Center
Hakan Loob, Calgary	Right Wing
Sylvain Turgeon, Hartford	Left Wing

1988-89
Peter Sidorkiewicz, Hartford	Goal
Brian Leetch, NY Rangers	Defense
Zarley Zalapski, Pittsburgh	Defense
Trevor Linden, Vancouver	Center
Tony Granato, NY Rangers	Right Wing
David Volek, NY Islanders	Left Wing

1986-87
Ron Hextall, Philadelphia	
Steve Duchesne, Los Angeles	
Brian Benning, St. Louis	
Jimmy Carson, Los Angeles	
Jim Sandlak, Vancouver	
Luc Robitaille, Los Angeles	

1984-85
Steve Penney, Montreal	
Chris Chelios, Montreal	
Bruce Bell, Quebec	
Mario Lemieux, Pittsburgh	
Tomas Sandstrom, NY Rangers	
Warren Young, Pittsburgh	

1982-83
Pelle Lindbergh, Philadelphia	
Scott Stevens, Washington	
Phil Housley, Buffalo	
Dan Daoust, Montreal/Toronto	
Steve Larmer, Chicago	
Mats Naslund, Montreal	

1998-99 All-Star Game Summary

January 24, 1999 at Tampa Bay   North America 8, World 6

PLAYERS ON ICE: **North America** — Brodeur, Belfour, Tugnutt, MacInnis, Blake, Pronger, L. Murphy, S. Stevens, Sydor, Bourque, Kariya, Recchi, Modano, LeClair, Amonte, Shanahan, W. Clark, Tkachuk, Robitaille, Fleury, K. Primeau, Lindros, Roenick, Gretzky.

The World — Hasek, Irbe, Khabibulin, Lidstrom, Hamrlik, Norstrom, Numminen, Ohlund, Zhitnik, Zubov, Forsberg, Holik, Yashin, Selanne, Bondra, Sundin, Sturm, Naslund, Straka, Demitra, Khristich, Krivokrasov, Jagr.

SUMMARY
First Period
1. North America	Modano (1)	(Robitaille, Pronger)	4:09
2. World	Sturm (1)	(Forsberg, Sundin)	9:42
3. North America	Robitaille (1)	(Roenick, Clark)	10:06
4. North America	Kariya (1)	(Modano, Amonte)	16:45
5. North America	Recchi (1)	(Gretzky, Fleury)	17:18

PENALTIES: None

Second Period
6. North America	Bourque (1)	(Modano)	0:17
7. North America	Gretzky (1)	(Fleury, Pronger)	1:14
8. World	Selanne (1)	(Yashin, Irbe)	2:02
9. World	Demitra (1)	(Zhinik, Sundin)	8:59
10. North America	Blake (1)	(Gretzky, Recchi)	14:23
11. World	Ohlund (1)	(Naslund, Sundin)	15:08

PENALTIES: None

Third Period
12. World	Sundin (1)	(Ohlund, Jagr)	2:57
13. North America	Sydor (1)	(Modano, Amonte)	4:03
14. World	Zubov (1)	(Khristich, Holik)	4:20

Penalties: MacInnis North America (tripping)

SHOTS ON GOAL BY:
North America	19	15	15	**49**
World	9	15	12	**36**

	Goaltenders:	Time	SA	GA	ENG	Dec
N. America	Brodeur	20:00	9	1	0	
N. America	Tugnutt	20:00	15	3	0	W
N. America	Belfour	20:00	12	2	0	
World	Hasek	20:00	19	4	0	
World	Irbe	20:00	15	3	0	L
World	Khabibulin	20:00	15	1	0	

PP Conversions: North America 0/0; World 0/1.

Referee: Paul Devorski   Linesmen: Pierre Champoux, Brian Murphy
Attendance: 19,758.

2TORONTO

All-Star Game Records 1947 through 1999

TEAM RECORDS

MOST GOALS, BOTH TEAMS, ONE GAME:
22 — Wales 16, Campbell 6, 1993 at Montreal
19 — Wales 12, Campbell 7, 1990 at Pittsburgh
18 — East 11, West 7, 1997 at San Jose
17 — East 9, West 8, 1994 at NY Rangers
16 — Campbell 11, Wales 5, 1991 at Chicago
— Campbell 10, Wales 6, 1992 at Philadelphia
15 — North America 8, World 7, 1998 at Vancouver
14 — Campbell 9, Wales 5, 1989 at Edmonton
— North America 8, World 6, 1999 at Tampa Bay

FEWEST GOALS, BOTH TEAMS, ONE GAME:
2 — NHL All-Stars 1, Montreal Canadiens 1, 1956 at Montreal
— First Team All-Stars 1, Second Team All-Stars 1, 1952 at Detroit
3 — West 2, East 1, 1971 at Boston
— Montreal Canadiens 3, NHL All-Stars 0, 1967 at Montreal
— NHL All-Stars 2, Montreal Canadiens 1, 1960 at Montreal

MOST GOALS, ONE TEAM, ONE GAME:
16 — Wales 16, Campbell 6, 1993 at Montreal
12 — Wales 12, Campbell 7, 1990 at Pittsburgh
11 — Campbell 11, Wales 5, 1991 at Chicago
— East 11, West 7, 1997 at San Jose
10 — Campbell 10, Wales 6, 1992 at Philadelphia

FEWEST GOALS, ONE TEAM, ONE GAME:
0 — NHL All-Stars 0, Montreal Canadiens 3, 1967 at Montreal
1 — 17 times (1981, 1975, 1971, 1970, 1962, 1961, 1960, 1959, both teams 1956, 1955, 1953, both teams 1952, 1950, 1949, 1948)

MOST SHOTS, BOTH TEAMS, ONE GAME (SINCE 1955):
102 — 1994 at NY Rangers — East 9 (56 shots), West 8 (46 shots)
90 — 1993 at Montreal — Wales 16 (49 shots), Campbell 6 (41 shots)
87 — 1990 at Pittsburgh — Wales 12 (45 shots), Campbell 7 (42 shots)
— 1997 at San Jose — East 11 (41 shots), West 7 (46 shots)
85 — 1999 at Tampa Bay — North America 8 (49 shots), World 6 (36 shots)

FEWEST SHOTS, BOTH TEAMS, ONE GAME (SINCE 1955):
52 — 1978 at Buffalo — Campbell 3 (12 shots), Wales 3 (40 shots)
53 — 1960 at Montreal — NHL All-Stars 2 (27 shots) Montreal Canadiens 1 (26 shots)
55 — 1956 at Montreal — NHL All-Stars 1 (28 shots) Montreal Canadiens 1 (27 shots)
— 1971 at Boston — West 2 (28 shots) East 1 (27 shots)

MOST SHOTS, ONE TEAM, ONE GAME (SINCE 1955):
56 — 1994 at NY Rangers — East (9-8 vs. West)
49 — 1993 at Montreal — Wales (16-6 vs. Campbell)
— 1999 at Tampa Bay — North America (8-6 vs. World)
46 — 1994 at NY Rangers — West (8-9 vs. East)
— 1997 at San Jose — West (7-11 vs. East)

FEWEST SHOTS, ONE TEAM, ONE GAME (SINCE 1955):
12 — 1978 at Buffalo — Campbell (2-3 vs. Wales)
17 — 1970 at St. Louis — West (1-4 vs. East)
23 — 1961 at Chicago — Chicago Black Hawks (1-3 vs. NHL All-Stars)
24 — 1976 at Philadelphia — Campbell (5-7 vs. Wales)

MOST POWER-PLAY GOALS, BOTH TEAMS, ONE GAME (SINCE 1950):
3 — 1953 at Montreal — NHL All-Stars 3 (2 power-play goals), Montreal Canadiens 1 (1 power-play goal)
— 1954 at Detroit — NHL All-Stars 2 (1 power-play goal) Detroit Red Wings 2 (2 power-play goals)
— 1958 at Montreal — NHL All-Stars 3 (1 power-play goal) Montreal Canadiens 6 (2 power-play goals)

FEWEST POWER-PLAY GOALS, BOTH TEAMS, ONE GAME (SINCE 1950):
0 — 17 times (1952, 1959, 1960, 1967, 1968, 1969, 1972, 1973, 1976, 1980, 1981, 1984, 1985, 1992, 1994, 1996, 1999)

FASTEST TWO GOALS, BOTH TEAMS, FROM START OF GAME:
37 seconds — 1970 at St. Louis — Jacques Laperriere of East scored at 20 seconds and Dean Prentice of West scored at 37 seconds. Final score: East 4, West 1.
2:15 — 1998 at Vancouver — Teemu Selanee scored at 0:53 and Jaromir Jagr scored at 2:15 for World. Final score: North America 8, World 7.
3:37 — 1993 at Montreal — Mike Gartner scored at 3:15 and at 3:37 for Wales. Final score: Wales 16, Campbell 6.

FASTEST TWO GOALS, BOTH TEAMS:
8 seconds — 1997 at San Jose — Owen Nolan scored at 18:54 and 19:02 of second period for West. Final Score: East 11, West 7.
10 seconds — 1976 at Philadelphia — Dennis Ververgaert scored at 4:33 and at 4:43 of third period for Campbell. Final score: Wales 7, Campbell 5.
13 seconds — 1998 at Vancouver — Teemu Selanne scored at 4:00 of first period for World and John LeClair scored at 4:13 for North America. Final score: North America 8, World 7.

FASTEST THREE GOALS, BOTH TEAMS:
1:08 — 1993 at Montreal — all by Wales — Mike Gartner scored at 3:15 and at 3:37 of first period; Peter Bondra scored at 4:23. Final score: Wales 16, Campbell 6.
1:14 — 1994 at NY Rangers — Bob Kudelski scored at 9:46 of first period for East; Sergei Fedorov scored at 10:20 for West; Eric Lindros scored at 11:00 for East. Final score: East 9, West 8.
1:23 — 1999 at Tampa Bay — Mats Sundin scored at 2:57 of third period for World; Darryl Sydor scored at 4:02 for North America; Sergei Zubov scored at 4:20 for World. Final score: North America 8, World 6.

FASTEST FOUR GOALS, BOTH TEAMS:
2:24 — 1997 at San Jose — Brendan Shanahan scored at 16:38 of second period for West; Dale Hawerchuk scored at 17:28 for East; Owen Nolan scored at 18:54 and 19:02 for West. Final score: East 11, West 7.
3:04 — 1997 at San Jose — Mark Recchi scored at 15:32 of first period for East; Dale Hawerchuk scored at 16:19 for East; Pavel Bure scored at 17:36 for West; Paul Kariya scored at 18:36 for West. Final score: East 11, West 7.
3:29 — 1994 at NY Rangers — Jeremy Roenick scored at 7:31 of first period for West; Bob Kudelski scored at 9:46 for East; Sergei Fedorov scored at 10:20 for West; Eric Lindros scored at 11:00 for East. Final score: East 9, West 8.

FASTEST TWO GOALS, ONE TEAM, FROM START OF GAME:
2:15 — 1998 at Vancouver — World — Teemu Selanee scored at 0:53 and Jaromir Jagr scored at 2:15. Final score: North America 8, World 7.
3:37 — 1993 at Montreal — Wales — Mike Gartner scored at 3:15 and at 3:37. Final score: Wales 16, Campbell 6.
4:19 — 1980 at Detroit — Wales — Larry Robinson scored at 3:58 and Steve Payne scored at 4:19. Final score: Wales 6, Campbell 3.

FASTEST TWO GOALS, ONE TEAM:
8 seconds — 1997 at San Jose — West — Owen Nolan scored at 18:54 and at 19:02 of second period. Final score: East 11, West 7.
10 seconds — 1976 at Philadelphia — Campbell — Dennis Ververgaert scored at 4:33 and at 4:43 of third period. Final score: Wales 7, Campbell 5.
14 seconds — 1989 at Edmonton — Campbell — Steve Yzerman and Gary Leeman scored at 17:21 and 17:35 of second period. Final score: Campbell 9, Wales 5.

FASTEST THREE GOALS, ONE TEAM:
1:08 — 1993 at Montreal — Wales — Mike Gartner scored at 3:15 and 3:37 of first period; Peter Bondra scored at 4:23. Final score: Wales 16, Campbell 6.
1:32 — 1980 at Detroit — Wales — Ron Stackhouse scored at 11:40 of third period; Craig Hartsburg scored at 12:40; Reed Larson scored at 13:12. Final score: Wales 6, Campbell 3.
1:42 — 1993 at Montreal — Wales — Alexander Mogilny scored at 11:40 of first period; Pierre Turgeon scored at 13:05; Mike Gartner scored at 13:22. Final score: Wales 16, Campbell 6.

FASTEST FOUR GOALS, ONE TEAM:
4:19 — 1992 at Philadelphia — Campbell — Brian Bellows scored at 7:40 of second period; Jeremy Roenick scored at 8:13; Theoren Fleury scored at 11:06, Brett Hull scored at 11:59. Final score: Campbell 10, Wales 6.
4:26 — 1980 at Detroit — Wales — Ron Stackhouse scored at 11:40 of third period; Craig Hartsburg scored at 12:40; Reed Larson scored at 13:12; Real Cloutier scored at 16:06. Final score: Wales 6, Campbell 3.
4:29 — 1999 at Tampa Bay — North America — Paul Kariya scored at 16:45 of first period; Mark Recchi scored at 17:18; Ray Bourque scored at 0:17 of second period; Wayne Gretzky scored at 1:14. Final score: North America 8, World 6.

MOST GOALS, BOTH TEAMS, ONE PERIOD:
10 — 1997 at San Jose — Second period — East (6), West (4). Final score: East 11, West 7.
9 — 1990 at Pittsburgh — First period — Wales (7), Campbell (2). Final score: Wales 12, Campbell 7.
8 — 1992 at Philadelphia — Second period — Campbell (6), Wales (2). Final Score: Campbell 10, Wales 6.
— 1993 at Montreal — Second period — Wales (6), Campbell (2). Final score: Wales 16, Campbell 6.
— 1993 at Montreal — Third period — Wales (4), Campbell (4). Final score: Wales 16, Campbell 6.

MOST GOALS, ONE TEAM, ONE PERIOD:
7 — 1990 at Pittsburgh — First period — Wales. Final score: Wales 12, Campbell 7.
6 — 1983 at NY Islanders — Third period — Campbell.
Final score: Campbell 9, Wales 3.
— 1992 at Philadelphia — Second Period — Campbell.
Final score: Campbell 10, Wales 6.
— 1993 at Montreal — First period — Wales.
Final score: Wales 16, Campbell 6.
— 1993 at Montreal — Second period — Wales.
Final score: Wales 16, Campbell 6.
— 1997 at San Jose — Second period — East.
Final score: East 11, West 7.

MOST SHOTS, BOTH TEAMS, ONE PERIOD:
39 — 1994 at NY Rangers — Second period — West (21) East (18).
Final score: East 9, West 8.
36 — 1990 at Pittsburgh — Third period — Campbell (22), Wales (14).
Final score: Wales 12, Campbell 7.
— 1994 at NY Rangers — First period — East (19), West (17).
Final score: East 9, West 8.

MOST SHOTS, ONE TEAM, ONE PERIOD:
22 — 1990 at Pittsburgh — Third period — Campbell.
Final score: Wales 12, Campbell 7.
— 1991 at Chicago — Third Period — Wales.
Final score: Campbell 11, Wales 5.
— 1993 at Montreal — First period — Wales.
Final score: Wales 16, Campbell 6.

FEWEST SHOTS, BOTH TEAMS, ONE PERIOD:
9 — 1971 at Boston — Third period — East (2), West (7).
Final score: West 2, East 1.
— 1980 at Detroit — Second period — Campbell (4), Wales (5).
Final score: Wales 6, Campbell 3.
13 — 1982 at Washington — Third period — Campbell (6), Wales (7).
Final score: Wales 4, Campbell 2.
14 — 1978 at Buffalo — First period — Campbell (7), Wales (7).
Final score: Wales 3, Campbell 2.
— 1986 at Hartford — First period — Campbell (6), Wales (8).
Final score: Wales 4, Campbell 3.

FEWEST SHOTS, ONE TEAM, ONE PERIOD:
2 — 1971 at Boston — Third period — East.
Final score: West 2, East 1.
— 1978 at Buffalo — Second period — Campbell.
Final score: Wales 3, Campbell 2.
3 — 1978 at Buffalo — Third period — Campbell.
Final score: Wales 3, Campbell 2.
4 — 1955 at Detroit — First period — NHL All-Stars.
Final score: Detroit Red Wings 3, NHL All-Stars 1.
4 — 1980 at Detroit — Second period — Campbell.
Final score: Wales 6, Campbell 3.

INDIVIDUAL RECORDS

Games

MOST GAMES PLAYED:
23 — **Gordie Howe** from 1948 through 1980
17 — Wayne Gretzky from 1980 through 1999
— Ray Bourque from 1981 through 1999
15 — Frank Mahovlich from 1959 through 1974
14 — Paul Coffey from 1982 through 1997

Goals

MOST GOALS (CAREER):
13 — **Wayne Gretzky** in 17GP
11 — Mario Lemieux in 8GP
10 — Gordie Howe in 23GP
8 — Frank Mahovlich in 15GP
7 — Maurice Richard in 13GP

MOST GOALS, ONE GAME:
4 — **Wayne Gretzky,** Campbell, 1983
— **Mario Lemieux,** Wales, 1990
— **Vince Damphousse,** Campbell, 1991
— **Mike Gartner,** Wales, 1993
3 — Ted Lindsay, Detroit Red Wings, 1950
— Mario Lemieux, Wales, 1988
— Pierre Turgeon, Wales, 1993
— Mark Recchi, East, 1997
— Owen Nolan, West, 1997
— Teemu Selanne, World, 1998

MOST GOALS, ONE PERIOD:
4 — **Wayne Gretzky,** Campbell, Third period, 1983
3 — Mario Lemieux, Wales, First period, 1990
— Vince Damphousse, Campbell, Third period, 1991
— Mike Gartner, Wales, First period, 1993
2 — Ted Lindsay, Detroit, First period, 1950
— Wally Hergesheimer, NHL All-Stars, First period, 1953
— Andy Bathgate, NHL All-Stars, Third period, 1958
— Frank Mahovlich, Toronto, First period, 1963
— Dennis Ververgaert, Campbell, Third period, 1976
— Richard Martin, Wales, Third period, 1977
— Pierre Turgeon, Wales, First period, 1990
— Luc Robitaille, Campbell, Third period, 1990
— Theoren Fleury, Campbell, Second period, 1992
— Brett Hull, Campbell, Second period, 1992
— Rick Tocchet, Wales, Second period, 1993
— Pavel Bure, Campbell, Third period, 1993
— Mark Recchi, East, Second period, 1997
— Owen Nolan, West, Second period, 1997
— Teemu Selanne, World, First period, 1998

Assists

MOST ASSISTS (CAREER):
12 — **Adam Oates** in 5GP
— Mark Messier in 13GP
— Joe Sakic in 7GP
— Ray Bourque in 17GP
— Wayne Gretzky in 17GP
10 — Paul Coffey in 14GP

MOST ASSISTS, ONE GAME:
5 — **Mats Naslund,** Wales, 1988
4 — Ray Bourque, Wales, 1985
— Adam Oates, Campbell, 1991
— Adam Oates, Wales, 1993
— Mark Recchi, Wales, 1993
— Pierre Turgeon, East All-Stars, 1994

MOST ASSISTS, ONE PERIOD:
4 — **Adam Oates,** Wales, First period, 1993
3 — Mark Messier, Campbell, Third period, 1983

No one has collected more points against his fellow All-Stars than Wayne Gretzky, whose 13 goals and 25 points are both NHL records. Gretzky earned his third and final All-Star MVP award at the Game in Tampa Bay in 1999.

Points

MOST POINTS, CAREER:
25 — **Wayne Gretzky** (13G-12A in 17GP)
20 — Mario Lemieux (11G-9A in 8GP)
19 — Gordie Howe (10G-9A in 23GP)
17 — Mark Messier (5G-12A in 13GP)
16 — Ray Bourque (4G-12A in 17GP)

MOST POINTS, ONE GAME:
6 — **Mario Lemieux,** Wales, 1988 (3G-3A)
5 — Mats Naslund, Wales, 1988 (5A)
— Adam Oates, Campbell, 1991 (1G-4A)
— Mike Gartner, Wales, 1993 (4G-1A)
— Mark Recchi, Wales, 1993 (1G-4A)
— Pierre Turgeon, Wales, 1993 (3G-2A)

MOST POINTS, ONE PERIOD:
4 — **Wayne Gretzky,** Campbell, Third period, 1983 (4G)
— **Mike Gartner,** Wales, First period, 1993 (3G-1A)
— **Adam Oates,** Wales, First period, 1993 (4A)
3 — Gordie Howe, NHL All-Stars, Second period, 1965 (1G-2A)
— Pete Mahovlich, Wales, First period, 1976 (1G-2A)
— Mark Messier, Campbell, Third period, 1983 (3A)
— Mario Lemieux, Wales, Second period, 1988 (1G-2A)
— Mario Lemieux, Wales, First period, 1990 (3G)
— Vince Damphousse, Campbell, Third period, 1991 (3G)
— Mark Recchi, Wales, Second period, 1993 (1G-2A)

Power-Play Goals

MOST POWER-PLAY GOALS, CAREER:
6 — **Gordie Howe** in 23GP
3 — Bobby Hull in 12GP
2 — Maurice Richard in 13GP

Fastest Goals

FASTEST GOAL FROM START OF GAME:
19 seconds — **Ted Lindsay,** Detroit, 1950
20 seconds — Jacques Laperriere, East All-Stars, 1970
21 seconds — Mario Lemieux, Wales, 1990
36 seconds — Chico Maki, West All-Stars, 1971
37 seconds — Dean Prentice, West All-Stars, 1970

FASTEST GOAL FROM START OF A PERIOD:
17 seconds — **Ray Bourque,** North America, 1999 (second period)
19 seconds — Ted Lindsay, Detroit, 1950 (first period)
— Rick Tocchet, Wales, 1993 (second period)
20 seconds — Jacques Laperriere, East, 1970 (first period)
21 seconds — Mario Lemieux, Wales, 1990 (first period)
26 seconds — Wayne Gretzky, Campbell, 1982 (second period)

FASTEST TWO GOALS (ONE PLAYER) FROM START OF GAME:
3:37 — **Mike Gartner,** Wales, 1993, at 3:15 and 3:37.
4:00 — Teemu Selanne, World, 1998, at 0:53 and 4:00
5:25 — Wally Hergesheimer, NHL All-Stars, 1953, at 4:06 and 5:25.

FASTEST TWO GOALS (ONE PLAYER) FROM START OF A PERIOD:
3:37 — **Mike Gartner,** Wales, 1993, at 3:15 and 3:37 of first period.
4:00 — Teemu Selanne, World, 1998, at 0:53 and 4:00
4:43 — Dennis Ververgaert, Campbell, 1976, at 4:33 and 4:43 of third period.

FASTEST TWO GOALS (ONE PLAYER):
8 seconds — **Owen Nolan,** West, 1997. Scored at 18:54 and 19:02 of second period.
10 seconds — Dennis Ververgaert, Campbell, 1976. Scored at 4:33 and 4:43 of third period.
22 seconds — Mike Gartner, Wales, 1993. Scored at 3:15 and 3:37 of first period.

Penalties

MOST PENALTY MINUTES:
27 — **Gordie Howe** in 23GP
21 — Gus Mortson in 9GP
16 — Harry Howell in 7GP

Goaltenders

MOST GAMES PLAYED:
13 — **Glenn Hall** from 1955-1969
11 — Terry Sawchuk from 1950-1968
8 — Jacques Plante from 1956-1970
— Patrick Roy from 1988-1998
6 — Tony Esposito from 1970-1980
— Ed Giacomin from 1967-1973
— Grant Fuhr from 1982-1989

MOST MINUTES PLAYED:
467 — **Terry Sawchuk** in 11GP
421 — Glenn Hall in 13GP
370 — Jacques Plante in 8GP
209 — Turk Broda in 4GP
190 — Patrick Roy in 8GP
182 — Ed Giacomin in 6GP
177 — Grant Fuhr in 6GP

MOST GOALS AGAINST:
24 — **Patrick Roy** in 8GP
22 — Glenn Hall in 13GP
21 — Mike Vernon in 5GP
19 — Terry Sawchuk in 11GP
18 — Jacques Plante in 8GP
— Andy Moog in 4GP

BEST GOALS-AGAINST-AVERAGE AMONG THOSE WITH AT LEAST TWO GAMES PLAYED:
0.68 — **Gilles Villemure** in 3GP
1.02 — Frank Brimsek in 2GP
1.59 — Johnny Bower in 4GP
1.64 — Gump Worsley in 4GP
1.98 — Gerry McNeil in 3GP
2.03 — Don Edwards in 2GP
2.44 — Terry Sawchuk in 11GP

From Left to right: Tommy Ivan, Ken Reardon, Elmer Lach, Bill Quackenbush,
Turk Broda, Clarence Campbell, Rocket Richard, Ted Lindsay. Lindsay's goal
19 seconds into the 1950 All-Star Game set a record that has yet to be equalled.

Hockey Hall of Fame

(Year of induction is listed after each Honoured Members name)

By waiving the mandatory three-year waiting period, the Hockey Hall of Fame allowed #99 to be inducted in 1999. Wayne Gretzky is the tenth player to receive early enshrinement. He will be the last one to be accorded this special honor.

Location: BCE Place, at the corner of Front and Yonge Streets in the heart of downtown Toronto. Easy access from all major highways running into Toronto. Close to TTC and Union Station.

Telephone: administration (416) 360-7735; information (416) 360-7765.

Summer and Christmas/March break hours: Monday to Saturday 9:30 a.m. to 6 p.m.; Sunday 10:00 a.m. to 6 p.m.

Fall/Winter/Spring hours (except Christmas/March break): Monday to Friday 10 a.m. to 5 p.m.; Saturday 9:30 a.m. to 6 p.m.; Sunday 10:30 a.m. to 5 p.m.

The Hockey Hall of Fame can be booked for private functions after hours.

Website address: www.hhof.com

History: The Hockey Hall of Fame was established in 1943. Members were first honoured in 1945. On August 26, 1961, the Hockey Hall of Fame opened its doors to the public in a building located on the grounds of the Canadian National Exhibition in Toronto. The Hockey Hall of Fame relocated to its new site at BCE Place and welcomed the hockey world on June 18, 1993.

Honour Roll: There are 316 Honoured Members in the Hockey Hall of Fame. 216 have been inducted as players, 86 as builders and 14 as Referees/Linesmen. In addition, there are 62 media honourees.

Sponsors: Special thanks to Blockbuster Video, Bell Canada, Coca-Cola Canada, Household Finance, Ford of Canada, IBM Canada, Imperial Oil, International Ice Hockey Federation, Kodak Canada, Molson Breweries, National Hockey League, London Life, TSN/RDS and The Toronto Sun.

PLAYERS

Abel, Sidney Gerald 1969
* Adams, John James "Jack" 1959
* Apps, Charles Joseph Sylvanus "Syl" 1961
  Armstrong, George Edward 1975
* Bailey, Irvine Wallace "Ace" 1975
* Bain, Donald H. "Dan" 1945
* Baker, Hobart "Hobey" 1945
  Barber, William Charles "Bill" 1990
* Barry, Martin J. "Marty" 1965
  Bathgate, Andrew James "Andy" 1978
* Bauer, Robert Theodore "Bobby" 1996
  Béliveau, Jean Arthur 1972
* Benedict, Clinton S. 1965
* Bentley, Douglas Wagner 1964
* Bentley, Maxwell H. L. 1966
* Blake, Hector Toe 1966
  Boivin, Leo Joseph 1986
* Boon, Richard R. "Dickie" 1952
  Bossy, Michael 1991
  Bouchard, Butch Joseph "Butch" 1966
* Boucher, Frank 1958
* Boucher, George "Buck" 1960
  Bower, John William 1976
* Bowie, Russell 1945
* Brimsek, Francis Charles 1966
* Broadbent, Harry L. "Punch" 1962
* Broda, Walter Edward "Turk" 1967
  Bucyk, John Paul 1981
* Burch, Billy 1974
* Cameron, Harold Hugh "Harry" 1962
  Cheevers, Gerald Michael "Gerry" 1985
* Clancy, Francis Michael "King" 1958
* Clapper, Aubrey "Dit" 1947
  Clarke, Robert "Bobby" 1987
* Cleghorn, Sprague 1958
* Colville, Neil MacNeil 1967
* Conacher, Charles W. 1961
* Conacher, Lionel Pretoria 1994
* Conacher, Roy Gordon 1998
* Connell, Alex 1958
* Cook, Fred "Bun" 1995
* Cook, William Osser 1952
  Coulter, Arthur Edmund 1974
  Cournoyer, Yvan Serge 1982
* Cowley, William Mailes 1968
* Crawford, Samuel Russell "Rusty" 1962
* Darragh, John Proctor "Jack" 1962
* Davidson, Allan M. "Scotty" 1950
* Day, Clarence Henry Hap 1961
  Delvecchio, Alex 1977
* Denneny, Cyril "Cy" 1959
  Dionne, Marcel 1992
* Drillon, Gordon Arthur 1975

* Drinkwater, Charles Graham 1950
  Dryden, Kenneth Wayne 1983
  Dumart, Woodrow "Woody" 1992
* Dunderdale, Thomas 1974
* Durnan, William Ronald 1964
* Dutton, Mervyn A. "Red" 1958
* Dye, Cecil Henry "Babe" 1970
  Esposito, Anthony James "Tony" 1988
  Esposito, Philip Anthony 1984
* Farrell, Arthur F. 1965
  Flaman, Ferdinand Charles "Fern" 1990
* Foyston, Frank 1958
* Fredrickson, Frank 1958
  Gadsby, William Alexander 1970
  Gainey, Bob 1992
* Gardiner, Charles Robert "Chuck" 1945
* Gardiner, Herbert Martin "Herb" 1958
* Gardner, James Henry "Jimmy" 1962
  Geoffrion, Jos. A. Bernard "Boom Boom" 1972
* Gerard, Eddie 1945
  Giacomin, Edward "Eddie" 1987
  Gilbert, Rodrigue Gabriel "Rod" 1982
* Gilmour, Hamilton Livingstone "Billy" 1962
* Goheen, Frank Xavier "Moose" 1952
* Goodfellow, Ebenezer R. "Ebbie" 1963
  Goulet, Michel 1998
* Grant, Michael "Mike" 1950
* Green, Wilfred "Shorty" 1962
  Gretzky, Wayne Douglas 1999
* Griffis, Silas Seth "Si" 1950
* Hainsworth, George 1961
  Hall, Glenn Henry 1975
* Hall, Joseph Henry 1961
* Harvey, Douglas Norman 1973
* Hay, George 1958
* Hern, William Milton "Riley" 1962
* Hextall, Bryan Aldwyn 1969
* Holmes, Harry Hap 1972
* Hooper, Charles Thomas "Tom" 1962
  Horner, George Reginald "Red" 1965
* Horton, Miles Gilbert "Tim" 1977
  Howe, Gordon 1972
* Howe, Sydney Harris 1965
  Howell, Henry Vernon "Harry" 1979
  Hull, Robert Marvin 1983
* Hutton, John Bower "Bouse" 1962
* Hyland, Harry M. 1962
  Irvin, James Dickenson "Dick" 1958
  Jackson, Harvey "Busher" 1971
* Johnson, Ernest "Moose" 1952
* Johnson, Ivan "Ching" 1958
  Johnson, Thomas Christian 1970
* Joliat, Aurel 1947

* Keats, Gordon "Duke" 1958
  Kelly, Leonard Patrick "Red" 1969
  Kennedy, Theodore Samuel "Teeder" 1966
  Keon, David Michael 1986
  Lach, Elmer James 1966
  Lafleur, Guy Damien 1988
* Lalonde, Edouard Charles "Newsy" 1950
  Laperriere, Jacques 1987
  Lapointe, Guy 1993
  Laprade, Edgar 1993
* Laviolette, Jean Baptiste "Jack" 1962
* Lehman, Hugh 1958
  Lemaire, Jacques Gerard 1984
  Lemieux, Mario 1997
* LeSueur, Percy 1961
* Lewis, Herbert A. 1989
  Lindsay, Robert Blake Theodore "Ted" 1966
* Lumley, Harry 1980
* MacKay, Duncan "Mickey" 1952
  Mahovlich, Frank William 1981
* Malone, Joseph "Joe" 1950
* Mantha, Sylvio 1960
* Marshall, John "Jack" 1965
* Maxwell, Fred G. "Steamer" 1962
  McDonald, Lanny 1992
* McGee, Frank 1945
* McGimsie, William George "Billy" 1962
* McNamara, George 1958
  Mikita, Stanley 1983
  Moore, Richard Winston 1974
* Moran, Patrick Joseph "Paddy" 1958
* Morenz, Howie 1945
* Mosienko, William "Billy" 1965
* Nighbor, Frank 1947
* Noble, Edward Reginald "Reg" 1962
* O'Connor, Herbert William "Buddy" 1988
* Oliver, Harry 1967
  Olmstead, Murray Bert "Bert" 1985
  Orr, Robert Gordon 1979
  Parent, Bernard Marcel 1984
  Park, Douglas Bradford "Brad" 1988
* Patrick, Joseph Lynn 1980
* Patrick, Lester 1947
  Perreault, Gilbert 1990
  Phillips, Tommy 1945
  Pilote, Joseph Albert Pierre Paul 1975
* Pitre, Didier "Pit" 1962
  Plante, Joseph Jacques Omer 1978
  Potvin, Denis 1991
* Pratt, Walter "Babe" 1966
* Primeau, A. Joseph 1963
  Pronovost, Joseph René Marcel 1978
  Pulford, Bob 1991

* Pulford, Harvey 1945
  Quackenbush, Hubert George "Bill" 1976
* Rankin, Frank 1961
  Ratelle, Joseph Gilbert Yvan Jean "Jean" 1985
  Rayner, Claude Earl "Chuck" 1973
  Reardon, Kenneth Joseph 1966
  Richard, Joseph Henri 1979
  Richard, Joseph Henri Maurice "Rocket" 1961
* Richardson, George Taylor 1950
* Roberts, Gordon 1971
  Robinson, Larry 1995
* Ross, Arthur Howie 1945
* Russel, Blair 1965
* Russell, Ernest 1965
* Ruttan, J.D. "Jack" 1962
  Salming, Borje Anders 1996
  Savard, Serge A. 1986
* Sawchuk, Terrance Gordon "Terry" 1971
* Scanlan, Fred 1965
  Schmidt, Milton Conrad "Milt" 1961
* Schriner, David "Sweeney" 1962
* Seibert, Earl Walter 1963
* Seibert, Oliver Levi 1961
* Shore, Edward W. "Eddie" 1947
  Shutt, Stephen 1993
* Siebert, Albert C. "Babe" 1964
* Simpson, Harold Edward "Bullet Joe" 1962
  Sittler, Darryl Glen 1989
* Smith, Alfred E. 1962
  Smith, Clint 1991
* Smith, Reginald "Hooley" 1972
* Smith, Thomas James 1973
  Smith, William John "Billy" 1993
  Stanley, Allan Herbert 1981
* Stanley, Russell "Barney" 1962
  Stastny, Peter 1998
* Stewart, John Sherratt "Black Jack" 1964
* Stewart, Nelson "Nels" 1962
* Stuart, Bruce 1961
* Stuart, Hod 1945
* Taylor, Frederic "Cyclone" (O.B.E.) 1947
* Thompson, Cecil R. "Tiny" 1959
  Tretiak, Vladislav 1989
* Trihey, Col. Harry J. 1950
  Trottier, Bryan 1997
  Ullman, Norman V. Alexander "Norm" 1982
* Vezina, Georges 1945
* Walker, John Phillip "Jack" 1960
* Walsh, Martin "Marty" 1962
* Watson, Harry E. 1962
  Watson, Harry 1994
* Weiland, Ralph "Cooney" 1971
* Westwick, Harry 1962
* Whitcroft, Fred 1962
* Wilson, Gordon Allan "Phat" 1962
  Worsley, Lorne John "Gump" 1980
* Worters, Roy 1969

BUILDERS

  Adams, Charles 1960
* Adams, Weston W. 1972
* Ahearn, Thomas Franklin "Frank" 1962
* Ahearne, John Francis "Bunny" 1977
* Allan, Sir Montagu (C.V.O.) 1945
  Allen, Keith 1992
  Arbour, Alger Joseph "Al" 1996
* Ballard, Harold Edwin 1977
  Bauer, Father David 1989
* Bickell, John Paris 1978
  Bowman, Scott 1991
* Brown, George V. 1961
* Brown, Walter A. 1962
* Buckland, Frank 1975
  Butterfield, Jack Arlington 1980
* Calder, Frank 1947
* Campbell, Angus D. 1964
* Campbell, Clarence Sutherland 1966
* Cattarinich, Joseph 1977
* Dandurand, Joseph Viateur "Leo" 1963
* Dilio, Francis Paul 1964
* Dudley, George S. 1958
* Dunn, James A. 1968
  Francis, Emile 1982
* Gibson, Dr. John L. "Jack" 1976
* Gorman, Thomas Patrick "Tommy" 1963
* Griffiths, Frank A. 1993
* Hanley, William 1986
* Hay, Charles 1974

* Hendy, James C. 1968
* Hewitt, Foster 1965
* Hewitt, William Abraham 1947
* Hume, Fred J. 1962
* Imlach, George "Punch" 1984
* Ivan, Thomas N. 1974
* Jennings, William M. 1975
* Johnson, Bob 1992
* Juckes, Gordon W. 1979
* Kilpatrick, Gen. John Reed 1960
* Knox, Seymour H. III 1993
* Leader, George Alfred 1969
  LeBel, Robert 1970
* Lockhart, Thomas F. 1965
* Loicq, Paul 1961
* Mariucci, John 1985
  Mathers, Frank 1992
* McLaughlin, Major Frederic 1963
* Milford, John "Jake" 1984
  Molson, Hon. Hartland de Montarville 1973
  Morrison, Ian "Scotty" 1999
* Murray, Monsinger Athol 1998
* Nelson, Francis 1947
* Norris, Bruce A. 1969
* Norris, Sr., James 1958
* Norris, James Dougan 1962
* Northey, William M. 1947
* O'Brien, John Ambrose 1962
  O'Neill, Brian 1994
* Page, Fred 1993
* Patrick, Frank 1958
* Pickard, Allan W. 1958
* Pilous, Rudy 1985
  Poile, Norman "Bud" 1990
  Pollock, Samuel Patterson Smyth 1978
* Raymond, Sen. Donat 1958
* Robertson, John Ross 1947
* Robinson, Claude C. 1947
* Ross, Philip D. 1976
  Sabetzki, Dr. Gunther 1995
  Sather, Glen 1997
* Selke, Frank J. 1960
  Sinden, Harry James 1983
* Smith, Frank D. 1962
* Smythe, Conn 1958
  Snider, Edward M. 1988
* Stanley of Preston, Lord (G.C.B.) 1945
* Sutherland, Cap. James T. 1947
* Tarasov, Anatoli V. 1974
  Torrey, Bill 1995
* Turner, Lloyd 1958
* Tutt, William Thayer 1978
* Voss, Carl Potter 1974
* Waghorn, Fred C. 1961
* Wirtz, Arthur Michael 1971
  Wirtz, William W. "Bill" 1976
  Ziegler, John A. Jr. 1987

REFEREES/LINESMEN

  Armstrong, Neil 1991
  Ashley, John George 1981
  Chadwick, William L. 1964
  D'Amico, John 1993
* Elliott, Chaucer 1961
* Hayes, George William 1988
* Hewitson, Robert W. 1963
* Ion, Fred J. "Mickey" 1961
  Pavelich, Matt 1987
* Rodden, Michael J. "Mike" 1962
* Smeaton, J. Cooper 1961
  Storey, Roy Alvin "Red" 1967
  Udvari, Frank Joseph 1973
  van Hellemond, Andy 1999

Hockey Hall of Fame Game
*Saturday November 20, 1999
New York Rangers vs. Toronto
Maple Leafs at the Air Canada
Centre in Toronto.*

Elmer Ferguson Memorial Award Winners

In recognition of distinguished members of the newspaper profession whose words have brought honor to journalism and to hockey. Selected by the Professional Hockey Writers' Association.

* Barton, Charlie, Buffalo-Courier Express 1985
* Beauchamp, Jacques, Montreal Matin/Journal de Montréal 1984
* Brennan, Bill, Detroit News 1987
* Burchard, Jim, New York World Telegram 1984
* Burnett, Red, Toronto Star 1984
* Carroll, Dink, Montreal Gazette 1984
  Coleman, Jim, Southam Newspapers 1984
  Conway, Russ, Eagle-Tribune 1999
* Damata, Ted, Chicago Tribune 1984
  Delano, Hugh, New York Post 1991
  Desjardins, Marcel, Montréal La Presse 1984
* Dulmage, Jack, Windsor Star 1984
  Dunnell, Milt, Toronto Star 1984
* Ferguson, Elmer, Montreal Herald/Star 1984
  Fisher, Red, Montreal Star/Gazette 1985
* Fitzgerald, Tom, Boston Globe 1984
  Frayne, Trent, Toronto Telegram/Globe and Mail/Sun 1984
  Gatecliff, Jack, St. Catherines Standard 1995
  Gross, George, Toronto Telegram/Sun 1985
  Johnston, Dick, Buffalo News 1986
* Laney, Al, New York Herald-Tribune 1984
  Larochelle, Claude, Le Soleil 1989
  L'Esperance, Zotique, Journal de Montréal/le Petit Journal 1985
* Mayer, Charles, le Journal de Montréal/la Patrie 1985
  MacLeod, Rex, Toronto Globe and Mail/Star 1987
  McKenzie, Ken, The Hockey News 1997
  Monahan, Leo, Boston Daily Record/Record-American/Herald American 1986
  Moriarty, Tim, UPI/Newsday 1986
* Nichols, Joe, New York Times 1984
* O'Brien, Andy, Weekend Magazine 1985
  Orr, Frank, Toronto Star 1989
  Olan, Ben, New York Associated Press 1987
* O'Meara, Basil, Montreal Star 1984
  Pedneault, Yvon, La Presse/Le Journale de Montreal 1998
  Proudfoot, Jim, Toronto Star 1988
  Raymond, Bertrand, le Journal de Montréal 1990
  Rosa, Fran, Boston Globe 1987
  Strachan, Al, Globe and Mail/Toronto Sun 1993
* Vipond, Jim, Toronto Globe and Mail 1984
  Walter, Lewis, Detroit Times 1984
  Young, Scott, Toronto Globe and Mail/Telegram 1988

Foster Hewitt Memorial Award Winners

In recognition of members of the radio and television industry who made outstanding contributions to their profession and the game during their career in hockey broadcasting. Selected by the NHL Broadcasters' Association.

  Cole, Bob, Hockey Night in Canada 1996
  Cusick, Fred, Boston 1984
* Darling, Ted, Buffalo 1994
* Gallivan, Danny, Montreal 1984
  Garneau, Richard, Montreal 1999
* Hart, Gene, Philadelphia 1997
* Hewitt, Foster, Toronto 1984
  Irvin, Dick, Montreal 1988
* Kelly, Dan, St. Louis 1989
  Lecavelier, René, Montreal 1984
  Lynch, Budd, Detroit 1985
  Martyn, Bruce, Detroit 1991
  McDonald, Jiggs, Los Angeles, Atlanta, NY Islanders 1990
  McFarlane, Brian, Hockey Night in Canada 1995
* McKnight, Wes, Toronto 1986
  Meeker, Howie, Hockey Night in Canada 1998
  Pettit, Lloyd, Chicago 1986
  Robson, Jim, Vancouver 1987
  Shaver, Al, Minnesota 1993
* Smith, Doug, Montreal 1985
  Wilson, Bob, Boston 1987

* Deceased

United States Hockey Hall of Fame

The United States Hockey Hall of Fame is located in Eveleth, Minnesota, 60 miles north of Duluth, on Highway 53. The facility is open Monday to Saturday 9 a.m. to 5 p.m. and Sundays 10 a.m to 3 p.m.; Individual Admission is $3.50 for adults, $3.00 for juniors (13-17), and $2.75 for children (6-12). Call for any further information: 1-800-443-7825 or 218-744-5167. Website address: www.ushockeyhall.com

The Hall was dedicated and opened on June 21, 1973, largely as the result of the work of D. Kelly Campbell, Chairman of the Eveleth Civic Association's Project H Committee. There are now 100 enshrinees consisting of 60 players, 22 coaches, 16 administrators, one player/administrator and one referee. New members are inducted annually in October and must have made a significant contribution toward hockey in the United States during the course of their careers. Support for the Hall comes from sponsorship and membership programs, grants from the hockey community, and government agencies.

PLAYERS

* Abel, Clarence "Taffy" 1973
* Baker, Hobart "Hobey" 1973
  Bartholome, Earl 1977
* Bessone, Peter 1978
  Blake, Robert 1985
  Boucha, Henry 1995
  Brimsek, Frank 1973
  Cavanagh, Joe 1994
* Chaisson, Ray 1974
* Chase, John P. 1973
  Christian, Roger 1989
  Christian, William "Bill" 1984
  Cleary, Robert 1981
  Cleary, William 1976
* Conroy, Anthony 1975
  Curran, Mike 1998
  Dahlstrom, Carl "Cully" 1973
* Desjardins, Victor 1974
  Desmond, Richard 1988
* Dill, Robert 1979
  Everett, Doug 1974
  Ftorek, Robbie 1991
* Garrison, John B. 1973
  Garrity, Jack 1986
* Goheen, Frank "Moose" 1973
  Grant, Wally 1994
* Harding, Austin "Austie" 1975
* Iglehart, Stewart 1975
* Johnson, Virgil 1974
* Karakas, Mike 1973
  Kirrane, Jack 1987
* Lane, Myles J. 1973
  Langevin, David R. 1993
  Larson, Reed 1996
* Linder, Joseph 1975
* LoPresti, Sam L. 1973
* Mariucci, John 1973
  Matchefts, John 1991
  Mather, Bruce 1998
  Mayasich, John 1976
  McCartan, Jack 1983
  Moe, William 1974
  Morrow, Ken 1995
* Moseley, Fred 1975
  Mullen, Joe 1998
* Murray, Sr.Hugh "Muzz" 1987
* Nelson, Hubert "Hub" 1978
* Nyrop, William D. 1997
  Olson , Eddie 1977
* Owen, Jr., George 1973
* Palmer, Winthrop 1973
  Paradise, Robert 1989
  Purpur, Clifford "Fido" 1974
  Riley, William 1977
* Romnes, Elwin "Doc" 1973
  Rondeau, Richard 1985
  Sheehy, Timothy K. 1997

* Williams, Thomas 1981
* Winters, Frank "Coddy" 1973
* Yackel, Ken 1986

COACHES

* Almquist, Oscar 1983
  Bessone, Amo 1992
  Brooks, Herbert 1990
  Ceglarski, Len 1992
* Fullerton, James 1992
  Gambucci, Sergio 1996
* Gordon, Malcolm K. 1973
  Harkness, Nevin D. "Ned" 1994
  Heyliger, Victor 1974
  Holt, Jr. Charles E. 1997
  Ikola, Willard 1990
* Jeremiah, Edward J. 1973
* Johnson, Bob 1991
* Kelley, John "Snooks" 1974
  Kelley, John H. "Jack" 1993
  Patrick, Craig 1996
  Pleban, Jon "Connie" 1990
  Riley, Jack 1979
* Ross, Larry 1988
* Thompson, Clifford, R. 1973
* Stewart, William 1982
* Winsor, Alfred "Ralph" 1973

ADMINISTRATORS

* Brown, George V. 1973
* Brown, Walter A. 1973
  Bush, Walter 1980
  Clark, Donald 1978
  Claypool, James 1995
* Gibson, J.C. "Doc" 1973
* Jennings, William M. 1981
* Kahler, Nick 1980
* Lockhart, Thomas F. 1973
  Marvin, Cal 1982
  Ridder, Robert 1976
  Schulz, Charles M. 1993
  Trumble, Harold 1985
* Tutt, William Thayer 1973
  Wirtz, William W. "Bill" 1984
* Wright, Lyle Z.1973

PLAYER/ADMINISTRATOR

Nanne, Lou 1998

REFEREE

Chadwick, William 1974

*Deceased

Joe Mullen was the first American to record 1,000 points in the NHL when he reached that milestone on February 7, 1995. He is still the only U.S.-born player to score 500 goals, retiring after the 1996-97 season with 502. A graduate of Boston College, Mullen played for the St. Louis Blues, Calgary Flames, Pittsburgh Penguins and Boston Bruins. He won back-to-back Stanley Cup titles with Pittsburgh in 1991 and 1992.

Results

1999 Stanley Cup Playoffs

CONFERENCE QUARTER-FINALS
(Best-of-seven series)

Eastern Conference

Series 'A'

Thu. Apr. 22	Pittsburgh 1	At	New Jersey 3
Sat. Apr. 24	Pittsburgh 4	At	New Jersey 1
Sun. Apr. 25	New Jersey 3	At	Pittsburgh 4
Tue. Apr. 27	New Jersey 4	At	Pittsburgh 2
Fri. Apr. 30	Pittsburgh 3	At	New Jersey 4
Sun. May 2	New Jersey 2	At	Pittsburgh 3 ot
Tue. May 4	Pittsburgh 4	At	New Jersey 2

(Pittsburgh Won Series 4-3)

Series 'B'

Wed. Apr. 21	Buffalo 2	At	Ottawa 1
Fri. Apr. 23	Buffalo 3	At	Ottawa 2 ot
Sun. Apr. 25	Ottawa 0	At	Buffalo 3
Tue. Apr. 27	Ottawa 3	At	Buffalo 4

(Buffalo Won Series 4-0)

Series 'C'

Thu. Apr. 22	Boston 2	At	Carolina 0
Sat. Apr. 24	Boston 2	At	Carolina 3 ot
Mon. Apr. 26	Carolina 3	At	Boston 2
Wed. Apr. 28	Carolina 1	At	Boston 4
Fri. Apr. 30	Boston 4	At	Carolina 3 ot
Sun. May 2	Carolina 0	At	Boston 3

(Boston Won Series 4-2)

Series 'D'

Thu. Apr. 22	Philadelphia 3	At	Toronto 0
Sat. Apr. 24	Philadelphia 1	At	Toronto 2
Mon. Apr. 26	Toronto 2	At	Philadelphia 1
Wed. Apr. 28	Toronto 2	At	Philadelphia 5
Fri. Apr. 30	Philadelphia 1	At	Toronto 2 ot
Sun. May 2	Toronto 1	At	Philadelphia 0

(Toronto Won Series 4-2)

Western Conference

Series 'E'

Wed. Apr. 21	Edmonton 1	At	Dallas 2
Fri. Apr. 23	Edmonton 2	At	Dallas 3
Sun. Apr. 25	Dallas 3	At	Edmonton 2
Tue. Apr. 27	Dallas 3	At	Edmonton 2 ot

(Dallas Won Series 4-0)

Series 'F'

Sat. Apr. 24	Colorado 3	At	San Jose 1
Mon. Apr. 26	Colorado 2	At	San Jose 1 ot
Wed. Apr. 28	San Jose 4	At	Colorado 2
Fri. Apr. 30	San Jose 7	At	Colorado 3
Sat. May 1	San Jose 1	At	Colorado 6
Mon. May 3	Colorado 3	At	San Jose 2 ot

(Colorado Won Series 4-2)

Series 'G'

Wed. Apr. 21	Anaheim 3	At	Detroit 5
Fri. Apr. 23	Anaheim 1	At	Detroit 5
Sun. Apr. 25	Detroit 4	At	Anaheim 2
Tue. Apr. 27	Detroit 3	At	Aanaheim 0

(Detroit Won Series 4-0)

Series 'H'

Thu. Apr. 22	St Louis 3	At	Phoenix 1
Sat. Apr. 24	St Louis 3	At	Phoenix 4 ot
Sun. Apr. 25	Phoenix 5	At	St Louis 4
Tue. Apr. 27	Phoenix 2	At	St Louis 1
Fri. Apr. 30	St Louis 2	At	Phoenix 1 ot
Sun. May 2	Phoenix 3	At	St Louis 5
Tue. May 4	St Louis 1	At	Phoenix 0 ot

(St Louis Won Series 4-3)

CONFERENCE SEMI-FINALS
(Best-of-seven series)

Eastern Conference

Series 'I'

Fri. May 7	Pittsburgh 2	At	Toronto 0
Sun. May 9	Pittsburgh 2	At	Toronto 4
Tue. May 11	Toronto 3	At	Pittsburgh 4
Thu. May 13	Toronto 3	At	Pittsburgh 2 ot
Sat. May 15	Pittsburgh 1	At	Toronto 4
Mon. May 17	Toronto 4	At	Pittsburgh 3 ot

(Toronto Won Series 4-2)

Series 'J'

Thu. May 6	Buffalo 2	At	Boston 4
Sun. May 9	Buffalo 3	At	Boston 1
Wed. May 12	Boston 2	At	Buffalo 3
Fri. May 14	Boston 0	At	Buffalo 3
Sun. May 16	Buffalo 3	At	Boston 5
Tue. May 18	Boston 2	At	Buffalo 3

(Buffalo Won Series 4-2)

Western Conference

Series 'K'

Thu. May 6	St Louis 0	At	Dallas 3
Sat. May 8	St Louis 4	At	Dallas 5 ot
Mon. May 10	Dallas 2	At	St Louis 3 ot
Wed. May 12	Dallas 2	At	St Louis 3 ot
Sat. May 15	St Louis 1	At	Dallas 3
Mon. May 17	Dallas 2	At	St Louis 1 ot

(Dallas Won Series 4-2)

Series 'L'

Fri. May 7	Detroit 3	At	Colorado 2 ot
Sun. May 9	Detroit 4	At	Colorado 0
Tue. May 11	Colorado 5	At	Detroit 3
Thu. May 13	Colorado 6	At	Detroit 2
Sun. May 16	Detroit 0	At	Colorado 3
Tue. May 18	Colorado 5	At	Ddetroit 2

(Colorado Won Series 4-2)

CONFERENCE FINALS
(Best-of-seven series)

Eastern Conference

Series 'M'

Sun. May 23	Buffalo 5	At	Toronto 4
Tue. May 25	Buffalo 3	At	Toronto 6
Thu. May 27	Toronto 2	At	Buffalo 4
Sat. May 29	Toronto 2	At	Buffalo 5
Mon. May 31	Buffalo 4	At	Toronto 2

(Buffalo Won Series 4-1)

Western Conference

Series 'N'

Sat. May 22	Colorado 2	At	Dallas 1
Mon. May 24	Colorado 2	At	Dallas 4
Wed. May 26	Dallas 3	At	Colorado 0
Fri. May 28	Dallas 2	At	Colorado 3 ot
Sun. May 30	Colorado 7	At	Dallas 5
Tue. Jun. 1	Dallas 4	At	Colorado 1
Fri. Jun. 4	Colorado 1	At	Dallas 4

(Dallas Won Series 4-3)

STANLEY CUP CHAMPIONSHIP
(Best-of-seven series)

Series 'O'

Tue. Jun. 8	Buffalo 3	At	Dallas 2 ot
Thu. Jun. 10	Buffalo 2	At	Dallas 4
Sat. Jun. 12	Dallas 2	At	Buffalo 1
Tue. Jun. 15	Dallas 1	At	Buffalo 2
Thu. Jun. 17	Buffalo 0	At	Dallas 2
Sat. Jun. 19	Dallas 2	At	Buffalo 1 ot

(Dallas Won Series 4-2)

Team Playoff Records

	GP	W	L	GF	GA	%
Dallas	23	16	7	64	44	.696
Buffalo	21	14	7	59	49	.667
Colorado	19	11	8	56	54	.579
Toronto	17	9	8	43	46	.529
Detroit	10	6	4	31	27	.600
Boston	12	6	6	30	27	.500
Pittsburgh	13	6	7	35	36	.462
St. Louis	13	6	7	31	33	.462
New Jersey	7	3	4	18	21	.429
Phoenix	7	3	4	16	19	.429
Philadelphia	6	2	4	11	9	.333
San Jose	6	2	4	17	19	.333
Carolina	6	2	4	10	16	.333
Edmonton	4	0	4	7	11	.000
Ottawa	4	0	4	6	12	.000
Anaheim	4	0	4	6	17	.000

Individual Leaders

Abbreviations: *– rookie eligible for Calder Trophy; **A** – assists; **G** – goals; **GP** – Games Played; **OT** – overtime goals; **GW** – game-winning goals; **PIM** – penalties in minutes; **PP** – power play goals; **Pts** – points; **S** – shots on goal; **SH** – short-handed goals; **%** – percentage shots resulting in goals; **+/–** – difference between Goals For (**GF**) scored when a player is on the ice with his team at even strength or short-handed and Goals Against (**GA**) scored when the same player is on the ice with his team at even strength or on a power play.

Playoff Scoring Leaders

Player	Team	GP	G	A	PTS	+/–	PIM	PP	SH	GW	OT	S	%
Peter Forsberg	Colorado	19	8	16	24	7	31	1	1	0	0	54	14.8
Mike Modano	Dallas	23	5	18	23	6	16	1	1	1	1	83	6.0
Joe Nieuwendyk	Dallas	23	11	10	21	7	19	3	0	6	2	72	15.3
Joe Sakic	Colorado	19	6	13	19	2-	8	1	1	1	0	56	10.7
Jamie Langenbrunner	Dallas	23	10	7	17	7	16	4	0	3	0	46	21.7
Theoren Fleury	Colorado	18	5	12	17	2-	20	2	0	0	0	56	8.9
Mats Sundin	Toronto	17	8	8	16	2	16	3	0	2	0	44	18.2
Brett Hull	Dallas	22	8	7	15	3	4	3	0	2	1	86	9.3
Martin Straka	Pittsburgh	13	6	9	15	0	6	1	0	0	0	27	22.2
Jason Woolley	Buffalo	21	4	11	15	0	10	2	0	1	1	43	9.3
Alexei Zhitnik	Buffalo	21	4	11	15	6-	52	4	0	2	0	58	6.9
Claude Lemieux	Colorado	19	3	11	14	5	26	1	0	0	0	69	4.3
Jere Lehtinen	Dallas	23	10	3	13	8	2	1	1	0	0	55	18.2
Steve Yzerman	Detroit	10	9	4	13	2	0	4	0	2	0	41	22.0
Curtis Brown	Buffalo	21	7	6	13	3	10	3	0	3	0	34	20.6
Michael Peca	Buffalo	21	5	8	13	1	18	2	1	0	0	37	13.5
Pierre Turgeon	St. Louis	13	4	9	13	3	6	0	0	0	2	42	9.5
Sergei Zubov	Dallas	23	1	12	13	13	4	0	0	0	0	46	2.2

Playoff Defensemen Scoring Leaders

Player	Team	GP	G	A	Pts	+/–	PIM	PP:	SH	GW	OT	S	%
Jason Woolley	Buffalo	21	4	11	15	0	10	2	0	1	1	43	9.3
Alexei Zhitnik	Buffalo	21	4	11	15	6-	52	4	0	2	0	58	6.9
Sergei Zubov	Dallas	23	1	12	13	13	4	0	0	0	0	46	2.2
Al MacInnis	St. Louis	13	4	8	12	2-	20	2	0	0	0	66	6.1
Sandis Ozolinsh	Colorado	19	4	8	12	5-	22	3	0	1	0	56	7.1
Darryl Sydor	Dallas	23	3	9	12	8	16	1	0	1	0	49	6.1
Nicklas Lidstrom	Detroit	10	2	9	11	0	4	2	0	0	0	29	6.9
Ray Bourque	Boston	12	1	9	10	1	14	0	0	0	0	44	2.3
Bryan Berard	Toronto	17	1	8	9	10-	8	1	0	0	0	29	3.4
Derian Hatcher	Dallas	18	1	6	7	4	24	0	0	0	0	28	3.6
Jeff Norton	San Jose	6	0	7	7	5	10	0	0	0	0	3	.0

GOALTENDING LEADERS

Goals Against Average

Goaltender	Team	GPI	Mins	GA	Avg.
Ed Belfour	Dallas	23	1544	43	1.67
Dominik Hasek	Buffalo	19	1217	36	1.77
Byron Dafoe	Boston	12	768	26	2.03
Grant Fuhr	St. Louis	13	790	31	2.35
Curtis Joseph	Toronto	17	1011	41	2.43

Wins

Goaltender	Team	GPI	Mins	W	L
Ed Belfour	Dallas	23	1544	16	7
Dominik Hasek	Buffalo	19	1217	13	6
Patrick Roy	Colorado	19	1173	11	8
Curtis Joseph	Toronto	17	1011	9	8
Byron Dafoe	Boston	12	768	6	6
Tom Barrasso	Pittsburgh	13	787	6	7
Grant Fuhr	St. Louis	13	790	6	6

Save Percentage

Goaltender	Team	GPI	Mins	GA	SA	S%	W	L
Dominik Hasek	Buffalo	19	1217	36	587	.939	13	6
Ed Belfour	Dallas	23	1544	43	617	.930	16	7
Byron Dafoe	Boston	12	768	26	330	.921	6	6
Patrick Roy	Colorado	19	1173	52	650	.920	11	8
Curtis Joseph	Toronto	17	1011	41	440	.907	9	8

Shutouts

Goaltender	Team	GPI	Mins	SO
Ed Belfour	Dallas	23	1544	3
Byron Dafoe	Boston	12	768	2
Dominik Hasek	Buffalo	19	1217	2
Bill Ranford	Detroit	4	183	1
Chris Osgood	Detroit	6	358	1
John Vanbiesbrouck	Philadelphia	6	369	1
Tom Barrasso	Pittsburgh	13	787	1
Grant Fuhr	St. Louis	13	790	1
Curtis Joseph	Toronto	17	1011	1
Patrick Roy	Colorado	19	1173	1

Goal Scoring

Name	Team	GP	G
Joe Nieuwendyk	Dallas	23	11
Jere Lehtinen	Dallas	23	10
Jamie Langenbrunner	Dallas	23	10
Steve Yzerman	Detroit	10	9
Mats Sundin	Toronto	17	8
Peter Forsberg	Colorado	19	8
Adam Deadmarsh	Colorado	19	8
Brett Hull	Dallas	22	8
Stu Barnes	Buffalo	21	7
Dixon Ward	Buffalo	21	7
Curtis Brown	Buffalo	21	7

Assists

Name	Team	GP	A
Mike Modano	Dallas	23	18
Peter Forsberg	Colorado	19	16
Joe Sakic	Colorado	19	13
Theoren Fleury	Colorado	18	12
Sergei Zubov	Dallas	23	12
Claude Lemieux	Colorado	19	11
Jason Woolley	Buffalo	21	11
Alexei Zhitnik	Buffalo	21	11
Joe Nieuwendyk	Dallas	23	10

Power-play Goals

Name	Team	GP	PP
Steve Yzerman	Detroit	10	4
Stu Barnes	Buffalo	21	4
Alexei Zhitnik	Buffalo	21	4
Jamie Langenbrunner	Dallas	23	4
Bill Houlder	San Jose	6	3
Vyacheslav Kozlov	Detroit	10	3
Pavol Demitra	St. Louis	13	3
Mats Sundin	Toronto	17	3
Sandis Ozolinsh	Colorado	19	3
Adam Deadmarsh	Colorado	19	3
Curtis Brown	Buffalo	21	3
Brett Hull	Dallas	22	3
Joe Nieuwendyk	Dallas	23	3

Game-winning Goals

Name	Team	GP	GW
Joe Nieuwendyk	Dallas	23	6
*Chris Drury	Colorado	19	4
*Milan Hejduk	Colorado	16	3
Dixon Ward	Buffalo	21	3
Curtis Brown	Buffalo	21	3
Jamie Langenbrunner	Dallas	23	3

Short-handed Goals

Name	Team	GP	SH
Vincent Damphousse	San Jose	6	2
Dixon Ward	Buffalo	21	2
Brian Rolston	New Jersey	7	1
Joe Sakic	Colorado	19	1
Peter Forsberg	Colorado	19	1
Joe Juneau	Buffalo	20	1
Michael Peca	Buffalo	21	1
Mike Keane	Dallas	23	1
Mike Modano	Dallas	23	1
Jere Lehtinen	Dallas	23	1

Overtime Goals

Name	Team	GP	OT
Pierre Turgeon	St. Louis	13	2
*Milan Hejduk	Colorado	16	2
Joe Nieuwendyk	Dallas	23	2

Shots

Name	Team	GP	S
Brett Hull	Dallas	22	86
Mike Modano	Dallas	23	83
Joe Nieuwendyk	Dallas	23	72
Claude Lemieux	Colorado	19	69
Al MacInnis	St. Louis	13	66

Plus/Minus

Name	Team	GP	+/-
Jay Mckee	Buffalo	21	13
Sergei Zubov	Dallas	23	13
Rhett Warrener	Buffalo	20	12
*Daniil Markov	Toronto	17	9
Aaron Miller	Colorado	19	8
Darryl Sydor	Dallas	23	8
Jere Lehtinen	Dallas	23	8

TEAMS' PLAYOFF HOME/ROAD RECORD

	HOME						ROAD					
	GP	W	L	GF	GA	%	GP	W	L	GF	GA	%
DAL	12	9	3	38	25	.750	11	7	4	26	19	.636
BUF	10	8	2	29	16	.800	11	6	5	30	33	.545
COL	9	3	6	20	29	.333	10	8	2	36	25	.800
TOR	9	5	4	24	22	.556	8	4	4	19	24	.500
DET	5	2	3	17	20	.400	5	4	1	14	7	.800
BOS	6	4	2	18	12	.667	6	2	4	12	15	.333
PIT	6	3	3	18	18	.500	7	3	4	17	18	.429
ST.L.	6	3	3	17	16	.500	7	3	4	14	17	.429
N.J.	4	2	2	10	12	.500	3	1	2	8	9	.333
PHX	4	1	3	6	9	.250	3	2	1	10	10	.667
PHI	3	1	2	6	5	.333	3	1	2	5	4	.333
S.J.	3	0	3	4	8	.000	3	2	1	13	11	.667
CAR	3	1	2	6	8	.333	3	1	2	4	8	.333
EDM	2	0	2	4	6	.000	2	0	2	3	5	.000
OTT	2	0	2	3	5	.000	2	0	2	3	7	.000
ANA	2	0	2	2	7	.000	2	0	2	4	10	.000
Total	86	42	44	222	218	.488	86	44	42	218	222	.512

TEAM PENALTIES

Abbreviations: GP – games played; **PEN** – total penalty minutes, including bench penalties; **BMI** – total bench penalty minutes; **AVG** – average penalty minutes per game.

Team	GP	PEN	BMI	AVG
CAR	6	62	0	10.3
BOS	12	126	2	10.5
OTT	4	46	0	11.5
DAL	23	279	2	12.1
N.J.	7	86	2	12.3
PHX	7	95	0	13.6
DET	10	137	0	13.7
PHI	6	82	0	13.7
ST.L.	13	179	2	13.8
PIT	13	183	2	14.1
TOR	17	252	0	14.8
COL	19	309	0	16.3
BUF	21	349	4	16.6
S.J.	6	102	0	17.0
ANA	4	80	0	20.0
EDM	4	85	0	21.3
TOT	86	2452	14	28.5

TEAMS' POWER-PLAY RECORD

Abbreviations: Adv-total advantages; **PPGF**-power play goals for; **%** arrived by dividing number of power-play goals by total advantages.

	HOME					ROAD					OVERALL				
	TEAM	GP	ADV	PPGF	PCTG	TEAM	GP	ADV	PPGF	PCTG	TEAM	GP	ADV	PPGF	PCTG
1	PIT	6	22	6	27.3	N.J.	3	12	4	33.3	DET	10	59	14	23.7
2	DET	5	30	7	23.3	BUF	11	46	13	28.3	ANA	4	20	4	20.0
3	ANA	2	10	2	20.0	DET	5	29	7	24.1	BUF	21	95	19	20.0
4	BOS	6	32	6	18.8	S.J.	3	23	5	21.7	N.J.	7	27	5	18.5
5	ST.L.	6	32	6	18.8	COL	10	43	9	20.9	ST.L.	13	61	11	18.0
6	OTT	2	18	3	16.7	ANA	2	10	2	20.0	PIT	13	45	8	17.8
7	EDM	2	12	2	16.7	ST.L.	7	29	5	17.2	S.J.	6	41	7	17.1
8	PHI	3	16	2	12.5	TOR	8	37	6	16.2	BOS	12	59	9	15.3
9	BUF	10	49	6	12.2	PHX	3	19	3	15.8	COL	19	96	14	14.6
10	TOR	9	50	6	12.0	DAL	11	45	6	13.3	TOR	17	87	12	13.8
11	DAL	12	62	7	11.3	BOS	6	27	3	11.1	PHX	7	41	5	12.2
12	S.J.	3	18	2	11.1	CAR	3	11	1	9.1	DAL	23	107	13	12.1
13	CAR	3	10	1	10.0	PHI	3	11	1	9.1	EDM	4	17	2	11.8
14	COL	9	53	5	9.4	PIT	7	23	2	8.7	OTT	4	27	3	11.1
15	PHX	4	22	2	9.1	OTT	2	9	0	.0	PHI	6	27	3	11.1
16	N.J.	4	15	1	6.7	EDM	2	5	0	.0	CAR	6	21	2	9.5
Total		86	451	64	14.2		86	379	67	17.7		86	830	131	15.8

TEAMS' PENALTY KILLING RECORD

Abbreviations: TSH – Total times short-handed; **PPGA** – power-play goals against; **%** arrived by dividing times short minus power-play goals against by times short.

	HOME					ROAD					OVERALL				
	Team	GP	TSH	PPGA	%	Team	GP	TSH	PPGA	%	Team	GP	TSH	PPGA	%
1	N.J.	4	13	1	92.3	EDM	2	10	0	100.0	EDM	4	22	2	90.9
2	CAR	3	11	1	90.9	DAL	11	54	3	94.4	DAL	23	95	9	90.5
3	ST.L.	6	33	4	87.9	PHI	3	17	1	94.1	ST.L.	13	71	8	88.7
4	BUF	10	41	5	87.8	PIT	7	27	2	92.6	PIT	13	50	6	88.0
5	DAL	12	41	6	85.4	ST.L.	7	38	4	89.5	BUF	21	118	17	85.6
6	EDM	2	12	2	83.3	S.J.	3	24	3	87.5	PHI	6	34	5	85.3
7	PIT	6	23	4	82.6	DET	5	28	4	85.7	N.J.	7	26	4	84.6
8	BOS	6	23	4	82.6	BUF	11	77	12	84.4	CAR	6	24	4	83.3
9	COL	9	56	11	80.4	COL	10	50	8	84.0	S.J.	6	42	7	83.3
10	OTT	2	10	2	80.0	TOR	8	37	6	83.8	BOS	12	47	8	83.0
11	TOR	9	34	7	79.4	BOS	6	24	4	83.3	COL	19	106	19	82.1
12	S.J.	3	18	4	77.8	N.J.	3	13	3	76.9	DET	10	50	9	82.0
13	DET	5	22	5	77.3	CAR	3	13	3	76.9	TOR	17	71	13	81.7
14	PHI	3	17	4	76.5	OTT	2	8	2	75.0	OTT	4	18	4	77.8
15	PHX	4	17	4	76.5	ANA	2	15	4	73.3	PHX	7	33	9	72.7
16	ANA	2	8	3	62.5	PHX	3	16	5	68.8	ANA	4	23	7	69.6
Total		86	379	67	82.3		86	451	64	85.8		86	830	131	84.2

SHORT HAND GOALS FOR

	For			Against	
Team	Games	Goals	Team	Games	Goals
BUF	21	4	DAL	23	0
DAL	23	3	BUF	21	0
S.J.	6	2	N.J.	7	0
COL	19	2	PHX	7	0
N.J.	7	1	CAR	6	0
OTT	4	0	PHI	6	0
EDM	4	0	OTT	4	0
ANA	4	0	EDM	4	0
CAR	6	0	ANA	4	0
PHI	6	0	PIT	13	1
PHX	7	0	BOS	12	1
DET	10	0	DET	10	1
BOS	12	0	S.J.	6	1
PIT	13	0	ST.L.	13	2
ST.L.	13	0	COL	19	3
TOR	17	0	TOR	17	3
Total	86	12	**Total**	86	12

Ed Belfour silenced his critics with his outstanding performance during the 1999 Stanley Cup playoffs. Belfour led all goalies with 16 wins, three shutouts and a 1.67 goals-against average as Dallas won the Stanley Cup for the first time in franchise history.

Stanley Cup Record Book

History: The Stanley Cup, the oldest trophy competed for by professional athletes in North America, was donated by Frederick Arthur, Lord Stanley of Preston and son of the Earl of Derby, in 1893. Lord Stanley purchased the trophy for 10 guineas ($50 at that time) for presentation to the amateur hockey champions of Canada. Since 1910, when the National Hockey Association took possession of the Stanley Cup, the trophy has been the symbol of professional hockey supremacy. It has been competed for only by NHL teams since 1926 and has been under the exclusive control of the NHL since 1946.

Stanley Cup Standings

1918-99

(ranked by Cup wins)

Teams	Cup Wins	Yrs.	Series	Wins	Losses	Games Wins	Losses	Ties	Goals For	Goals Against	Winning %
Montreal	23[1]	72	134[2]	85	48	638 381	249	8	1977	1591	.603
Toronto	13	59	99	53	46	461 219	238	4	1209	1292	.479
Detroit	9	48	89	50	39	440 228	211	1	1243	1167	.519
Boston	5	59	101	47	54	494 236	252	6	1448	1464	.484
Edmonton	5	16	42	31	11	210 132	78	0	833	652	.629
NY Rangers	4	48	86	42	44	386 183	195	8	1091	1114	.484
NY Islanders	4	17	43	30	13	218 128	90	0	748	650	.587
Chicago	3	52	89	40	49	406 187	214	5	1171	1298	.467
Philadelphia	2	25	54	31	23	280 147	133	0	889	841	.525
Pittsburgh	2	19	34	17	17	179 94	85	0	579	570	.525
Dallas[3]	1	22	42	21	21	227 115	112	0	708	721	.507
Calgary[4]	1	21	32	12	20	156 69	87	0	529	573	.442
Colorado[5]	1	13	26	14	12	145 75	70	0	458	451	.517
New Jersey[6]	1	11	19	9	10	110 57	43	0	319	312	.518
St. Louis	0	29	49	20	29	259 117	142	0	741	841	.452
Buffalo	0	23	39	16	23	191 91	100	0	580	595	.476
Los Angeles	0	20	30	10	20	146 55	91	0	467	584	.377
Vancouver	0	16	25	9	16	124 54	70	0	377	422	.435
Washington	0	15	25	10	15	137 64	73	0	434	433	.467
Phoenix[7]	0	14	16	2	14	82 27	55	0	228	313	.329
Carolina[8]	0	9	10	1	9	55 20	35	0	157	194	.364
San Jose	0	4	6	2	4	37 15	22	0	103	147	.405
Ottawa	0	3	4	1	3	22 8	14	0	39	56	.364
Florida	0	2	5	3	2	27 13	14	0	71	70	.481
Anaheim	0	2	3	1	2	15 4	11	0	31	47	.267
Tampa Bay	0	1	1	0	1	6 2	4	0	13	26	.333

[1] Montreal also won the Stanley Cup in 1916.
[2] 1919 final incomplete due to influenza epidemic.
[3] Includes totals of Minnesota 1967-93.
[4] Includes totals of Atlanta Flames 1972-80.
[5] Includes totals of Quebec 1979-95.
[6] Includes totals of Colorado Rockies 1976-82.
[7] Includes totals of Winnipeg 1979-96.
[8] Includes totals of Hartford 1979-97.

Stanley Cup Winners Prior to Formation of NHL in 1917

Season	Champions	Manager	Coach
1916-17	Seattle Metropolitans	Pete Muldoon	Pete Muldoon
1915-16	Montreal Canadiens	George Kennedy	George Kennedy
1914-15	Vancouver Millionaires	Frank Patrick	Frank Patrick
1913-14	Toronto Blueshirts	Jack Marshall	Scotty Davidson*
1912-13**	Quebec Bulldogs	M.J. Quinn	Joe Malone*
1911-12	Quebec Bulldogs	M.J. Quinn	C. Nolan
1910-11	Ottawa Senators		Bruce Stuart*
1909-10	Montreal Wanderers	R. R. Boon	Pud Glass*
1908-09	Ottawa Senators		Bruce Stuart*
1907-08	Montreal Wanderers	R. R. Boon	Cecil Blachford
1906-07	Montreal Wanderers (Mar., 1907)	R. R. Boon	Cecil Blachford
1906-07	Kenora Thistles (Jan., 1907)	F.A. Hudson	Tommy Phillips*
1905-06	Montreal Wanderers (Mar., 1906)	Cecil Blachford*	
1905-06	Ottawa Silver Seven (Feb., 1906)		A. T. Smith
1904-05	Ottawa Silver Seven		A. T. Smith
1903-04	Ottawa Silver Seven		A. T. Smith
1902-03	Ottawa Silver Seven (Mar. 1903)		A. T. Smith
1902-03	Montreal A.A.A. (Feb., 1903)		C. McKerrow
1901-02	Montreal A.A.A. (Mar., 1902)		C. McKerrow
1901-02	Winnipeg Victorias (Jan., 1902)		
1900-01	Winnipeg Victorias		D. H. Bain*
1899-1900	Montreal Shamrocks		H.J. Trihey*
1898-99	Montreal Shamrocks (Mar., 1899)		H.J. Trihey*
1898-99	Montreal Victorias (Feb., 1899)		Mike Grant*
1897-98	Montreal Victorias		F. Richardson
1896-97	Montreal Victorias		Mike Grant*
1895-96	Montreal Victorias (Dec., 1896)		Mike Grant*
1895-96	Winnipeg Victorias (Feb., 1896)		J.C. G. Armytage
1894-95	Montreal Victorias		Mike Grant*
1893-94	Montreal A.A.A.		
1892-93	Montreal A.A.A.		

* In the early years the teams were frequently run by the Captain. *Indicates Captain
** Victoria defeated Quebec in challenge series. No official recognition.

Stanley Cup Winners

Year	W&L in Finals	Winner	Coach	Finalist	Coach
1999	4-2	Dallas	Ken Hitchcock	Buffalo	Lindy Ruff
1998	4-0	Detroit	Scotty Bowman	Washington	Ron Wilson
1997	4-0	Detroit	Scotty Bowman	Philadelphia	Terry Murray
1996	4-0	Colorado	Marc Crawford	Florida	Doug MacLean
1995	4-0	New Jersey	Jacques Lemaire	Detroit	Scotty Bowman
1994	4-3	NY Rangers	Mike Keenan	Vancouver	Pat Quinn
1993	4-1	Montreal	Jacques Demers	Los Angeles	Barry Melrose
1992	4-0	Pittsburgh	Scotty Bowman	Chicago	Mike Keenan
1991	4-2	Pittsburgh	Bob Johnson	Minnesota	Bob Gainey
1990	4-1	Edmonton	John Muckler	Boston	Mike Milbury
1989	4-2	Calgary	Terry Crisp	Montreal	Pat Burns
1988	4-0	Edmonton	Glen Sather	Boston	Terry O'Reilly
1987	4-3	Edmonton	Glen Sather	Philadelphia	Mike Keenan
1986	4-1	Montreal	Jean Perron	Calgary	Bob Johnson
1985	4-1	Edmonton	Glen Sather	Philadelphia	Mike Keenan
1984	4-1	Edmonton	Glen Sather	NY Islanders	Al Arbour
1983	4-0	NY Islanders	Al Arbour	Edmonton	Glen Sather
1982	4-0	NY Islanders	Al Arbour	Vancouver	Roger Neilson
1981	4-1	NY Islanders	Al Arbour	Minnesota	Glen Sonmor
1980	4-2	NY Islanders	Al Arbour	Philadelphia	Pat Quinn
1979	4-1	Montreal	Scotty Bowman	NY Rangers	Fred Shero
1978	4-2	Montreal	Scotty Bowman	Boston	Don Cherry
1977	4-0	Montreal	Scotty Bowman	Boston	Don Cherry
1976	4-0	Montreal	Scotty Bowman	Philadelphia	Fred Shero
1975	4-2	Philadelphia	Fred Shero	Buffalo	Floyd Smith
1974	4-2	Philadelphia	Fred Shero	Boston	Bep Guidolin
1973	4-2	Montreal	Scotty Bowman	Chicago	Billy Reay
1972	4-2	Boston	Tom Johnson	NY Rangers	Emile Francis
1971	4-3	Montreal	Al MacNeil	Chicago	Billy Reay
1970	4-0	Boston	Harry Sinden	St. Louis	Scotty Bowman
1969	4-0	Montreal	Claude Ruel	St. Louis	Scotty Bowman
1968	4-0	Montreal	Toe Blake	St. Louis	Scotty Bowman
1967	4-2	Toronto	Punch Imlach	Montreal	Toe Blake
1966	4-2	Montreal	Toe Blake	Detroit	Sid Abel
1965	4-3	Montreal	Toe Blake	Chicago	Billy Reay
1964	4-3	Toronto	Punch Imlach	Detroit	Sid Abel
1963	4-1	Toronto	Punch Imlach	Detroit	Sid Abel
1962	4-2	Toronto	Punch Imlach	Chicago	Rudy Pilous
1961	4-2	Chicago	Rudy Pilous	Detroit	Sid Abel
1960	4-0	Montreal	Toe Blake	Toronto	Punch Imlach
1959	4-1	Montreal	Toe Blake	Toronto	Punch Imlach
1958	4-2	Montreal	Toe Blake	Boston	Milt Schmidt
1957	4-1	Montreal	Toe Blake	Boston	Milt Schmidt
1956	4-1	Montreal	Toe Blake	Detroit	Jimmy Skinner
1955	4-3	Detroit	Jimmy Skinner	Montreal	Dick Irvin
1954	4-3	Detroit	Tommy Ivan	Montreal	Dick Irvin
1953	4-1	Montreal	Dick Irvin	Boston	Lynn Patrick
1952	4-0	Detroit	Tommy Ivan	Montreal	Dick Irvin
1951	4-1	Toronto	Joe Primeau	Montreal	Dick Irvin
1950	4-3	Detroit	Tommy Ivan	NY Rangers	Lynn Patrick
1949	4-0	Toronto	Hap Day	Detroit	Tommy Ivan
1948	4-0	Toronto	Hap Day	Detroit	Tommy Ivan
1947	4-2	Toronto	Hap Day	Montreal	Dick Irvin
1946	4-1	Montreal	Dick Irvin	Boston	Dit Clapper
1945	4-3	Toronto	Hap Day	Detroit	Jack Adams
1944	4-0	Montreal	Dick Irvin	Chicago	Paul Thompson
1943	4-0	Detroit	Jack Adams	Boston	Art Ross
1942	4-3	Toronto	Hap Day	Detroit	Jack Adams
1941	4-0	Boston	Cooney Weiland	Detroit	Ebbie Goodfellow
1940	4-2	NY Rangers	Frank Boucher	Toronto	Dick Irvin
1939	4-1	Boston	Art Ross	Toronto	Dick Irvin
1938	3-1	Chicago	Bill Stewart	Toronto	Dick Irvin
1937	3-2	Detroit	Jack Adams	NY Rangers	Lester Patrick
1936	3-1	Detroit	Jack Adams	Toronto	Dick Irvin
1935	3-0	Mtl. Maroons	Tommy Gorman	Toronto	Dick Irvin
1934	3-1	Chicago	Tommy Gorman	Detroit	Herbie Lewis
1933	3-1	NY Rangers	Lester Patrick	Toronto	Dick Irvin
1932	3-0	Toronto	Dick Irvin	NY Rangers	Lester Patrick
1931	3-2	Montreal	Cecil Hart	Chicago	Dick Irvin
1930	2-0	Montreal	Cecil Hart	Boston	Art Ross
1929	2-0	Boston	Cy Denneny	NY Rangers	Lester Patrick
1928	3-2	NY Rangers	Lester Patrick	Mtl. Maroons	Eddie Gerard
1927	2-0-2	Ottawa	Dave Gill	Boston	Art Ross

The National Hockey League assumed control of Stanley Cup competition after 1926

Year	W&L in Finals	Winner	Coach	Finalist	Coach
1926	3-1	Mtl. Maroons	Eddie Gerard	Victoria	Lester Patrick
1925	3-1	Victoria	Lester Patrick	Montreal	Leo Dandurand
1924	2-0	Montreal	Leo Dandurand	Cgy. Tigers	—
	2-0			Van. Maroons	—
1923	2-0	Ottawa	Pete Green	Edm. Eskimos	—
	3-1			Van. Maroons	—
1922	3-2	Tor. St. Pats	George O'Donohue	Van. Millionaires	Frank Patrick
1921	3-2	Ottawa	Pete Green	Van. Millionaires	Frank Patrick
1920	3-2	Ottawa	Pete Green	Seattle	—
1919	2-2-1	No decision - series between Montreal and Seattle cancelled due to influenza epidemic			
1918	3-2	Tor. Arenas	Dick Carroll	Van. Millionaires	Frank Patrick

Championship Trophies

PRINCE OF WALES TROPHY

Beginning with the 1993-94 season, the club which advances to the Stanley Cup Finals as the winner of the Eastern Conference Championship is presented with the Prince of Wales Trophy.

History: His Royal Highness, the Prince of Wales, donated the trophy to the National Hockey League in 1924. From 1927-28 through 1937-38, the award was presented to the team finishing first in the American Division of the NHL. From 1938-39, when the NHL reverted to one section, to 1966-67, it was presented to the team winning the NHL regular season championship. With expansion in 1967-68, it again became a divisional trophy, awarded to the regular season champions of the East Division through to the end of the 1973-74 season. Beginning in 1974-75, it was awarded to the regular-season winner of the conference bearing the name of the trophy. From 1981-82 to 1992-93 the trophy was presented to the playoff champion in the Wales Conference. Since 1993-94, the trophy has been presented to the playoff champion in the Eastern Conference.

1998-99 Winner: Buffalo Sabres

The Buffalo Sabres won their first Prince of Wales Trophy since 1980 on May 31, 1999 after defeating the Toronto Maple Leafs 4-2 in game five of the Eastern Conference Championship series. Before defeating the Leafs, the Sabres had series wins over the Ottawa Senators and Boston Bruins.

PRINCE OF WALES TROPHY WINNERS

1998-99	**Buffalo Sabres**	1960-61	Montreal Canadiens
1997-98	Washington Capitals	1959-60	Montreal Canadiens
1996-97	Philadelphia Flyers	1958-59	Montreal Canadiens
1995-96	Florida Panthers	1957-58	Montreal Canadiens
1994-95	New Jersey Devils	1956-57	Detroit Red Wings
1993-94	New York Rangers	1955-56	Detroit Red Wings
1992-93	Montreal Canadiens	1954-55	Detroit Red Wings
1991-92	Pittsburgh Penguins	1953-54	Detroit Red Wings
1990-91	Pittsburgh Penguins	1952-53	Detroit Red Wings
1989-90	Boston Bruins	1951-52	Detroit Red Wings
1988-89	Montreal Canadiens	1950-51	Detroit Red Wings
1987-88	Boston Bruins	1949-50	Detroit Red Wings
1986-87	Philadelphia Flyers	1948-49	Detroit Red Wings
1985-86	Montreal Canadiens	1947-48	Toronto Maple Leafs
1984-85	Philadelphia Flyers	1946-47	Montreal Canadiens
1983-84	New York Islanders	1945-46	Montreal Canadiens
1982-83	New York Islanders	1944-45	Montreal Canadiens
1981-82	New York Islanders	1943-44	Montreal Canadiens
1980-81	Montreal Canadiens	1942-43	Detroit Red Wings
1979-80	Buffalo Sabres	1941-42	New York Rangers
1978-79	Montreal Canadiens	1940-41	Boston Bruins
1977-78	Montreal Canadiens	1939-40	Boston Bruins
1976-77	Montreal Canadiens	1938-39	Boston Bruins
1975-76	Montreal Canadiens	1937-38	Boston Bruins
1974-75	Buffalo Sabres	1936-37	Detroit Red Wings
1973-74	Boston Bruins	1935-36	Detroit Red Wings
1972-73	Montreal Canadiens	1934-35	Boston Bruins
1971-72	Boston Bruins	1933-34	Detroit Red Wings
1970-71	Boston Bruins	1932-33	Boston Bruins
1969-70	Chicago Blackhawks	1931-32	New York Rangers
1968-69	Montreal Canadiens	1930-31	Boston Bruins
1967-68	Montreal Canadiens	1929-30	Boston Bruins
1966-67	Chicago Blackhawks	1928-29	Boston Bruins
1965-66	Montreal Canadiens	1927-28	Boston Bruins
1964-65	Detroit Red Wings	1926-27	Ottawa Senators
1963-64	Montreal Canadiens	1925-26	Montreal Maroons
1962-63	Toronto Maple Leafs	1924-25	Montreal Canadiens
1961-62	Montreal Canadiens	1923-24	Montreal Canadiens

CLARENCE S. CAMPBELL BOWL

Beginning with the 1993-94 season, the club which advances to the Stanley Cup Finals as the winner of the Western Conference Championship is presented with the Clarence S. Campbell Bowl.

History: Presented by the member clubs in 1968 for perpetual competition by the National Hockey League in recognition of the services of Clarence S. Campbell, President of the NHL from 1946 to 1977. From 1967-68 through 1973-74, the trophy was awarded to the regular season champions of the West Division. Beginning in 1974-75, it was awarded to the regular-season winner of the conference bearing the name of the trophy. From 1981-82 to 1992-93 the trophy was presented to the playoff champion in the Campbell Conference. Since 1993-94, the trophy has been presented to the playoff champion in the Western Conference. The trophy itself is a hallmark piece made of sterling silver and was crafted by a British silversmith in 1878.

1998-99 Winner: Dallas Stars

The Dallas Stars won their first Clarence Campbell Bowl since moving to Texas from Minnesota in 1993 by defeating the Colorado Avalanche 4-1 in game seven of the Western Conference Championship series. Before defeating the Avalanche, the Stars had series wins over the Edmonton Oilers and St. Louis Blues.

CLARENCE S. CAMPBELL BOWL WINNERS

1998-99	**Dallas Stars**	1982-83	Edmonton Oilers
1997-98	Detroit Red Wings	1981-82	Vancouver Canucks
1996-97	Detroit Red Wings	1980-81	New York Islanders
1995-96	Colorado Avalanche	1979-80	Philadelphia Flyers
1994-95	Detroit Red Wings	1978-79	New York Islanders
1993-94	Vancouver Canucks	1977-78	New York Islanders
1992-93	Los Angeles Kings	1976-77	Philadelphia Flyers
1991-92	Chicago Blackhawks	1975-76	Philadelphia Flyers
1990-91	Minnesota North Stars	1974-75	Philadelphia Flyers
1989-90	Edmonton Oilers	1973-74	Philadelphia Flyers
1988-89	Calgary Flames	1972-73	Chicago Blackhawks
1987-88	Edmonton Oilers	1971-72	Chicago Blackhawks
1986-87	Edmonton Oilers	1970-71	Chicago Blackhawks
1985-86	Calgary Flames	1969-70	St. Louis Blues
1984-85	Edmonton Oilers	1968-69	St. Louis Blues
1983-84	Edmonton Oilers	1967-68	Philadelphia Flyers

Prince of Wales Trophy

Clarence S. Campbell Bowl

Stanley Cup

Stanley Cup Winners

Rosters and Final Series Scores

1998-99 — Dallas Stars — Derian Hatcher (Captain), Ed Belfour, Guy Carbonneau, Shawn Chambers, Benoit Hogue, Tony Hrkac, Brett Hull, Mike Keane, Jamie Langenbrunner, Jere Lehtinen, Craig Ludwig, Grant Marshall, Richard Matvichuk, Mike Modano, Joe Nieuwendyk, Derek Plante, Dave Reid, Jon Sim, Brian Skrudland, Blake Sloan, Darryl Sydor, Roman Turek, Pat Verbeek, Sergei Zubov, Thomas Hicks (Chairman of the Board and Owner), Jim Lites (President), Bob Gainey (Vice President, Hockey Operations and General Manager), Doug Armstrong (Assistant General Manager), Craig Button (Director of Player Personnel), Ken Hitchcock (Head Coach), Doug Jarvis (Assistant Coach), Rick Wilson (Assistant Coach), Rick McLaughlin (Vice President and Chief Financial Officer), Jeff Cogen (Vice President, Marketing and Promotion), Bill Strong (Vice President, Marketing and Broadcasting), Tim Bernhardt (Director of Amateur Scouting), Doug Overton (Director of Pro Scouting), Bob Gernander (Chief Scout), Stu MacGregor (Western Scout), Dave Suprenant (Medical Trainer), Dave Smith (Equipment Manager), Rich Matthews (Equipment Manager), J.J. McQueen (Strength and Conditioning Coach), Rick St. Croix (Goaltending Consultant), Dan Stuchal (Director of Team Services), Larry Kelly (Director of Public Relations).

Scores: June 8, at Dallas - Buffalo 3, Dallas 2; June 10, at Dallas - Dallas 4, Buffalo 2; June 12, at Buffalo - Dallas 2, Buffalo 1; June 15, at Buffalo - Buffalo 2, Dallas 1; June 17, at Dallas - Dallas 2, Buffalo 0; June 19, at Buffalo - Dallas 2, Buffalo 1.

1997-98 — Detroit Red Wings — Steve Yzerman (Captain), Doug Brown, Mathieu Dandenault, Kris Draper, Anders Eriksson, Sergei Fedorov, Viacheslav Fetisov, Brent Gilchrist, Kevin Hodson, Tomas Holmstrom, Michael Knuble, Joey Kocur, Vladimir Konstantinov, Vyacheslav Kozlov, Martin Lapointe, Igor Larionov, Nicklas Lidstrom, Jamie Macoun, Kirk Maltby, Darren McCarty, Dmitri Mironov, Larry Murphy, Chris Osgood, Bob Rouse, Brendan Shanahan, Aaron Ward, Mike Ilitch, (Owner/Chairman), Marian Ilitch (Owner), Atanas Ilitch (Vice President), Christopher Ilitch (Vice President), Denise Ilitch, Ronald Ilitch, Michael Ilitch Jr., Lisa Ilitch Murray, Carole Ilitch Trepeck, Jim Devellano (Senior Vice President), Scotty Bowman (Head Coach), Ken Holland (General Manager), Don Waddell (Assistant General Manager), Barry Smith (Associate Coach), Dave Lewis (Associate Coach), Jim Bedard (Goaltending Consultant), Jim Nill (Director of Player Development), Dan Belisle (Pro Scout), Mark Howe (Pro Scout), Hakan Andersson (Director of European Scouting), Mark Leach (USA Scout), Moe McDonnell (Eastern Scout), Bruce Haralson (Western Scout), John Wharton (Athletic Trainer), Paul Boyer (Equipment Manager) Tim Abbott (Assistant Equipment Manager), Bob Huddleston (Masseur), Sergei Mnatsakanov (Masseur), Wally Crossman (Dressing Room Assistant).

Scores: June 9, at Detroit — Detroit 2, Washington 1; June 11, at Detroit — Detroit 5, Washington 4; June 13, at Washington — Detroit 2, Washington 1; June 16, at Washington — Detroit 4, Washington 1.

1996-97 — Detroit Red Wings — Steve Yzerman (Captain), Doug Brown, Mathieu Dandenault, Kris Draper, Sergei Fedorov, Viacheslav Fetisov, Kevin Hodson, Tomas Holmstrom, Joe Kocur, Vladimir Konstantinov, Vyacheslav Kozlov, Martin Lapointe, Igor Larionov, Nicklas Lidstrom, Kirk Maltby, Darren McCarty, Larry Murphy, Chris Osgood, Jamie Pushor, Bob Rouse, Tomas Sandstrom, Brendan Shanahan, Tim Taylor, Mike Vernon, Aaron Ward, Mike Ilitch (Owner/Chairman), Marian Ilitch (Owner), Atanas Ilitch (Vice President), Christopher Ilitch (Vice President), Denise Ilitch Lites, Ronald Ilitch, Michael Ilitch, Jr., Lisa Ilitch Murray, Carole Ilitch Trepeck, Jim Devellano (Senior Vice President), Scotty Bowman (Head Coach/Director of Player Personnel), Ken Holland (Assistant General Manager), Barry Smith (Associate Coach), Dave Lewis (Associate Coach), Mike Krushelnyski (Assistant Coach). Jim Nill (Director of Player Development), Dan Belisle (Pro Scout), Mark Howe (Pro Scout), Hakan Andersson (Director of European Scouting), John Wharton (Athletic Trainer), Paul Boyer (Equipment Manager) Tim Abbott (Assistant Equipment Manager), Sergei Mnatsakanov (Masseur).
Scores: May 31, at Philadelphia — Detroit 4, Philadelphia 2; June 3, at Philadelphia — Detroit 4, Philadelphia 2; June 5, at Detroit — Detroit 6, Philadelphia 1; June 7, at Detroit — Detroit 2, Philadelphia 1.

1995-96 — Colorado Avalanche — Joe Sakic (Captain), Rene Corbet, Adam Deadmarsh, Stephane Fiset, Adam Foote, Peter Forsberg, Alexei Gusarov, Dave Hannan, Valeri Kamensky, Mike Keane, Jon Klemm, Uwe Krupp, Sylvain Lefebvre, Claude Lemieux, Curtis Leschyshyn, Troy Murray, Sandis Ozolinsh, Mike Ricci, Patrick Roy, Warren Rychel, Chris Simon, Craig Wolanin, Stephane Yelle, Scott Young, Charlie Lyons (Chairman, CEO), Pierre Lacroix (Exec. V.P., G.M.), Marc Crawford (Head Coach), Joel Quenneville (Assistant Coach), Jacques Cloutier (Assistant Coach), Francois Giguere (Assistant General Manager), Michel Goulet (Director of Player Personnel), Dave Draper (Chief Scout), Jean Martineau (Director of Public Relations), Pat Karns (Trainer), Matthew Sokolowski (Assistant Trainer), Rob McLean (Equipment Manager), Mike Kramer (Assistant Equipment Manager), Brock Gibbins (Assistant Equipment Manager), Skip Allen (Strength and Conditioning Coach), Paul Fixter (Video Coordinator), Leo Vyssokov (Massage Therapist).
Scores: June 4, at Colorado — Colorado 3, Florida 1; June 6, at Colorado — Colorado 8, Florida 1; June 8, at Florida — Colorado 3, Florida 2; June 10, at Florida — Colorado 1, Florida 0.

1994-95 — New Jersey Devils — Scott Stevens (Captain), Tommy Albelin, Martin Brodeur, Neil Broten, Sergei Brylin, Bob Carpenter, Shawn Chambers, Tom Chorske, Danton Cole, Ken Daneyko, Kevin Dean, Jim Dowd, Bruce Driver (Alternate Captain), Bill Guerin, Bobby Holik, Claude Lemieux, John MacLean (Alternate Captain), Chris McAlpine, Randy McKay, Scott Niedermayer, Mike Peluso, Stephane J.J. Richer, Brian Rolston, Chris Terreri, Valeri Zelepukin, Dr. John J. McMullen (Owner/Chairman), Peter S. McMullen (Owner), Lou Lamoriello (President/General Manager), Jacques Lemaire (Head Coach), Jacques Caron (Goaltender Coach), Dennis Gendron (Assistant Coach), Larry Robinson (Assistant Coach), Robbie Ftorek (AHL Coach), Alex Abasto (Assistant Equipment Manager), Bob Huddleston (Massage Therapist), David Nichols (Equipment Manager), Ted Schuch (Medical Trainer), Mike Vasalani (Strength Coach), David Conte (Director of Scouting) Claude Carrier (Scout), Milt Fisher (Scout), Dan Labraaten (Scout), Marcel Pronovost (Scout).
Scores: June 17, at Detroit — New Jersey 2, Detroit 1; June 20, at Detroit — New Jersey 4, Detroit 2; June 22, at New Jersey — New Jersey 5, Detroit 2; June 24, at New Jersey — New Jersey 5, Detroit 2.

1993-94 — New York Rangers — Mark Messier (Captain), Brian Leetch, Kevin Lowe, Adam Graves, Steve Larmer, Glenn Anderson, Jeff Beukeboom, Greg Gilbert, Mike Hartman, Glenn Healy, Mike Hudson, Alexander Karpovtsev, Joe Kocur, Alexei Kovalev, Nick Kypreos, Doug Lidster, Stephane Matteau, Craig MacTavish, Sergei Nemchinov, Brian Noonan, Ed Olczyk, Mike Richter, Esa Tikkanen, Jay Wells, Sergei Zubov, Neil Smith (President, General Manager and Governor), Robert Gutkowski, Stanley Jaffe, Kenneth Munoz (Governors), Larry Pleau (Assistant General Manager), Mike Keenan (Head Coach), Colin Campbell (Associate Coach), Dick Todd (Assistant Coach), Matthew Loughren (Manager, Team Operations), Barry Watkins (Director, Communications), Christer Rockstrom, Tony Feltrin, Martin Madden, Herb Hammond, Darwin Bennett (Scouts), Dave Smith, Joe Murphy, Mike Folga, Bruce Lifrieri (Trainers).
Scores: May 31, at New York — Vancouver 3, NY Rangers 2; June 2, at New York — NY Rangers 3, Vancouver 1; June 4, at Vancouver — NY Rangers 5, Vancouver 1; June 7, at Vancouver — NY Rangers 4, Vancouver 2; June 9, at New York — Vancouver 6, at NY Rangers 3; June 11, at Vancouver — Vancouver 4, NY Rangers 1; June 14, at New York — NY Rangers 3, Vancouver 2.

1992-93 — Montreal Canadiens — Guy Carbonneau (Captain), Patrick Roy, Mike Keane, Eric Desjardins, Stephan Lebeau, Mathieu Schneider, Jean-Jacques Daigneault, Denis Savard, Lyle Odelein, Todd Ewen, Kirk Muller, John LeClair, Gilbert Dionne, Benoit Brunet, Patrice Brisebois, Paul Di Pietro, Andre Racicot, Donald Dufresne, Mario Roberge, Sean Hill, Ed Ronan, Kevin Haller, Vincent Damphousse, Brian Bellows, Gary Leeman, Rob Ramage, Ronald Corey (President), Serge Savard (Managing Director & Vice-President Hockey), Jacques Demers (Head Coach), Jacques Laperriere (Assistant Coach), Charles Thiffault (Assistant Coach), Francois Allaire (Goaltending Instructor), Jean Béliveau (Senior Vice-President, Corporate Affairs), Fred Steer (Vice-President, Finance & Adminstration), Aldo Giampaolo (Vice-President, Operations), Bernard Brisset (Vice-President, Marketing & Communications), André Boudrias (Assistant to the Managing Director & Director of Scouting), Jacques Lemaire (Assistant to the Managing Director), Gaeten Lefebvre (Athletic Trainer), John Shipman (Assistant to the Athletic Trainer), Eddy Palchak (Equipment Manager), Pierre Gervais (Assistant to the Equipment Manager), Robert Boulanger (Assistant to the Equipment Manager), Pierre Ouellete (Assistant to the Equipment Manager).
Scores: June 1, at Montreal — Los Angeles 4, Montreal 1; June 2, at Montreal — Montreal 3, Los Angeles 2; June 5, at Los Angeles — Montreal 4, Los Angeles 3; June 7, at Los Angeles — Montreal 3, Los Angeles 2; June 9, at Montreal — Montreal 4, Los Angeles 1.

Mark Messier celebrated Stanley Cup championships with Wayne Gretzky in 1984, 1985, 1987 and 1988. After Gretzky was traded to Los Angeles, Messier captained the Oilers to a fifth Stanley Cup title in 1990.

1991-92 — Pittsburgh Penguins — Mario Lemieux (Captain), Ron Francis, Bryan Trottier, Kevin Stevens, Bob Errey, Phil Bourque, Troy Loney, Rick Tocchet, Joe Mullen, Jaromir Jagr, Jiri Hrdina, Shawn McEachern, Ulf Samuelsson, Kjell Samuelsson, Larry Murphy, Gord Roberts, Jim Paek, Paul Stanton, Tom Barrasso, Ken Wregget, Jay Caufield, Jamie Leach, Wendell Young, Grant Jennings, Peter Taglianetti, Jock Callander, Dave Michayluk, Mike Needham, Jeff Chychrun, Ken Priestlay, Jeff Daniels, Howard Baldwin (Owner and President), Morris Belzberg (Owner), Thomas Ruta (Owner), Donn Patton (Executive Vice President and Chief Financial Officer), Paul Martha (Executive Vice President and General Counsel), Craig Patrick (Executive Vice President and General Manager), Bob Johnson (Coach), Scotty Bowman (Director of Player Development and Coach), Barry Smith, Rick Kehoe, Pierre McGuire, Gilles Meloche, Rick Paterson (Assistant Coaches), Steve Latin (Equipment Manager), Skip Thayer (Trainer), John Welday (Strength and Conditioning Coach), Greg Malone, Les Binkley, Charlie Hodge, John Gill, Ralph Cox (Scouts).
Scores: May 26, at Pittsburgh — Pittsburgh 5, Chicago 4; May 28, at Pittsburgh — Pittsburgh 3, Chicago 1; May 30, at Chicago — Pittsburgh 1, Chicago 0; June 1, at Chicago — Pittsburgh 6, Chicago 5.

1990-91 — Pittsburgh Penguins — Mario Lemieux (Captain), Paul Coffey, Randy Hillier, Bob Errey, Tom Barrasso, Phil Bourque, Jay Caufield, Ron Francis, Randy Gilhen, Jiri Hrdina, Jaromir Jagr, Grant Jennings, Troy Loney, Joe Mullen, Larry Murphy, Jim Paek, Frank Pietrangelo, Barry Pederson, Mark Recchi, Gordie Roberts, Ulf Samuelsson, Paul Stanton, Kevin Stevens, Peter Taglianetti, Bryan Trottier, Scott Young, Wendell Young, Edward J. DeBartolo, Sr. (Owner), Marie D. DeBartolo York (President), Paul Martha (Vice-President & General Counsel), Craig Patrick (General Manager), Scotty Bowman (Director of Player Development & Recruitment), Bob Johnson (Coach), Rick Kehoe (Assistant Coach), Gilles Meloche (Goaltending Coach & Scout), Rick Paterson (Assistant Coach), Barry Smith (Assistant Coach), Steve Latin (Equipment Manager), Skip Thayer (Trainer), John Welday (Strength & Conditioning Coach), Greg Malone (Scout).
Scores: May 15, at Pittsburgh — Minnesota 5, Pittsburgh 4; May 17, at Pittsburgh — Pittsburgh 4, Minnesota 1; May 19, at Minnesota — Minnesota 3, Pittsburgh 1; May 21, at Minnesota — Pittsburgh 5, Minnesota 3; May 23, at Pittsburgh — Pittsburgh 6, Minnesota 4; May 25, at Minnesota — Pittsburgh 8, Minnesota 0.

1989-90 — Edmonton Oilers — Kevin Lowe, Steve Smith, Jeff Beukeboom, Mark Lamb, Joe Murphy, Glenn Anderson, Mark Messier, Adam Graves, Craig MacTavish, Kelly Buchberger, Jari Kurri, Craig Simpson, Martin Gelinas, Randy Gregg, Charlie Huddy, Geoff Smith, Reijo Ruotsalainen, Craig Muni, Bill Ranford, Dave Brown, Pokey Reddick, Petr Klima, Esa Tikkanen, Grant Fuhr, Peter Pocklington (Owner), Glen Sather (President/General Manager), John Muckler (Coach), Ted Green (Co-Coach), Ron Low (Ass't Coach), Bruce MacGregor (Ass't General Manager), Barry Fraser (Director of Player Personnel), John Blackwell (Director of Operations, AHL), Ace Bailey, Ed Chadwick, Lorne Davis, Harry Howell, Matti Vaisanen and Albert Reeves (Scouts), Bill Tuele (Director of Public Relations), Werner Baum (Controller), Dr. Gordon Cameron (Medical Chief of Staff), Dr. David Reid (Team Physician), Barrie Stafford (Athletic Trainer), Ken Lowe (Athletic Therapist), Stuart Poirier (Massage Therapist), Lyle Kulchisky (Ass't Trainer).
Scores: May 15, at Boston — Edmonton 3, Boston 2; May 18, at Boston — Edmonton 7, Boston 2; May 20, at Edmonton — Boston 2, Edmonton 1; May 22, at Edmonton — Edmonton 5, Boston 1; May 24, at Boston — Edmonton 4, Boston 1.

1988-89 — Calgary Flames — Mike Vernon, Rick Wamsley, Al MacInnis, Brad McCrimmon, Dana Murzyn, Ric Nattress, Joe Mullen, Lanny McDonald (Co-captain), Gary Roberts, Colin Patterson, Hakan Loob, Theoren Fleury, Jiri Hrdina, Tim Hunter (Ass't. captain), Gary Suter, Mark Hunter, Jim Peplinski (Co-captain), Joe Nieuwendyk, Brian MacLellan, Joel Otto, Jamie Macoun, Doug Gilmour, Rob Ramage. Norman Green, Harley Hotchkiss, Norman Kwong, Sonia Scurfield, B.J. Seaman, D.K. Seaman (Owners), Cliff Fletcher (President and General Manager), Al MacNeil (Ass't General Manager), Al Coates (Ass't to the President), Terry Crisp (Head Coach), Doug Risebrough, Tom Watt (Ass't Coaches), Glenn Hall (Goaltending Consultant), Jim Murray (Trainer), Bob Stewart (Equipment Manager), Al Murray (Ass't Trainer).
Scores: May 14, at Calgary — Calgary 3, Montreal 2; May 17, at Calgary— Montreal 4, Calgary 2; May 19, at Montreal — Montreal 4, Calgary 3; May 21, at Montreal — Calgary 4, Montreal 2; May 23, at Calgary — Calgary 3, Montreal 2; May 25, at Montreal — Calgary 4, Montreal 2.

1987-88 — Edmonton Oilers — Keith Acton, Glenn Anderson, Jeff Beukeboom, Geoff Courtnall, Grant Fuhr, Randy Gregg, Wayne Gretzky, Dave Hannan, Charlie Huddy, Mike Krushelnyski, Jari Kurri, Normand Lacombe, Kevin Lowe, Craig MacTavish, Kevin McClelland, Marty McSorley, Mark Messier, Craig Muni, Bill Ranford, Craig Simpson, Steve Smith, Esa Tikkanen, Peter Pocklington (Owner), Glen Sather (General Manager/Coach), John Muckler (Co-Coach), Ted Green (Ass't Coach), Bruce MacGregor (Ass't General Manager), Barry Fraser (Director of Player Personnel), Bill Tuele (Director of Public Relations), Dr. Gordon Cameron (Team Physician), Peter Millar (Athletic Therapist), Barrie Stafford (Trainer), Juergen Mers (Massage Therapist), Lyle Kulchisky (Ass't Trainer).
Scores: May 18, at Edmonton — Edmonton 2, Boston 1; May 20, at Edmonton — Edmonton 4, Boston 2; May 22, at Boston — Edmonton 6, Boston 3; May 24, at Boston — Boston 3, Edmonton 3 (suspended due to power failure); May 26, at Edmonton — Edmonton 6, Boston 3.

1986-87 — Edmonton Oilers — Glenn Anderson, Jeff Beukeboom, Kelly Buchberger, Paul Coffey, Grant Fuhr, Randy Gregg, Wayne Gretzky, Charlie Huddy, Dave Hunter, Mike Krushelnyski, Jari Kurri, Moe Lemay, Kevin Lowe, Craig MacTavish, Kevin McClelland, Marty McSorley, Mark Messier, Andy Moog, Craig Muni, Kent Nilsson, Jaroslav Pouzar, Reijo Ruotsalainen, Steve Smith, Esa Tikkanen, Peter Pocklington (Owner), Glen Sather (General Manager/Coach), John Muckler (Co-Coach), Ted Green (Ass't. Coach), Ron Low (Ass't. Coach), Bruce MacGregor (Ass't. General Manager), Barry Fraser (Director of Player Personnel), Peter Millar (Athletic Therapist), Barrie Stafford (Trainer), Lyle Kulchisky (Ass't Trainer).
Scores: May 17, at Edmonton — Edmonton 4, Philadelphia 2; May 20, at Edmonton — Edmonton 3, Philadelphia 2; May 22, at Philadelphia — Philadelphia 5, Edmonton 3; May 24, at Philadelphia — Edmonton 4, Philadelphia 1; May 26, at Edmonton — Philadelphia 4, Edmonton 3; May 28, at Philadelphia — Philadelphia 3, Edmonton 2; May 31, at Edmonton — Edmonton 3, Philadelphia 1.

1985-86 — Montreal Canadiens — Bob Gainey, Doug Soetaert, Patrick Roy, Rick Green, David Maley, Ryan Walter, Serge Boisvert, Mario Tremblay, Bobby Smith, Craig Ludwig, Tom Kurvers, Kjell Dahlin, Larry Robinson, Guy Carbonneau, Chris Chelios, Petr Svoboda, Mats Naslund, Lucien DeBlois, Steve Rooney, Gaston Gingras, Mike Lalor, Chris Nilan, John Kordic, Claude Lemieux, Mike McPhee, Brian Skrudland, Stephane Richer, Ronald Corey (President), Serge Savard (General Manager), Jean Perron (Coach), Jacques Laperrière (Ass't. Coach), Jean Béliveau (Vice President), Francois-Xavier Seigneur (Vice President), Fred Steer (Vice President), Jacques Lemaire (Ass't. General Manager), André Boudrias (Ass't. General Manager), Claude Ruel, Yves Belanger (Athletic Therapist), Gaetan Lefebvre (Ass't. Athletic Therapist), Eddy Palchek (Trainer), Sylvain Toupin (Ass't. Trainer).
Scores: May 16, at Calgary — Calgary 5, Montreal 2; May 18, at Calgary — Montreal 3, Calgary 2; May 20, at Montreal — Montreal 5, Calgary 3; May 22, at Montreal — Montreal 1, Calgary 0; May 24, at Calgary — Montreal 4, Calgary 3.

1984-85 — Edmonton Oilers — Glenn Anderson, Bill Carroll, Paul Coffey, Lee Fogolin, Grant Fuhr, Randy Gregg, Wayne Gretzky, Charlie Huddy, Pat Hughes, Dave Hunter, Don Jackson, Mike Krushelnyski, Jari Kurri, Willy Lindstrom, Kevin Lowe, Dave Lumley, Kevin McClelland, Larry Melnyk, Mark Messier, Andy Moog, Mark Napier, Jaroslav Pouzar, Dave Semenko, Esa Tikkanen, Peter Pocklington (Owner), Glen Sather (General Manager/Coach), John Muckler (Ass't. Coach), Ted Green (Ass't. Coach), Bruce MacGregor (Ass't. General Manager), Barry Fraser (Director of Player Personnel/Chief Scout), Peter Millar (Athletic Therapist), Barrie Stafford, Lyle Kulchisky (Trainers)
Scores: May 21, at Philadelphia — Philadelphia 4, Edmonton 1; May 23, at Philadelphia — Edmonton 3, Philadelphia 1; May 25, at Edmonton — Edmonton 4, Philadelphia 3; May 28, at Edmonton — Edmonton 5, Philadelphia 3; May 30, at Edmonton — Edmonton 8, Philadelphia 3.

1983-84 — Edmonton Oilers — Glenn Anderson, Paul Coffey, Pat Conacher, Lee Fogolin, Grant Fuhr, Randy Gregg, Wayne Gretzky, Charlie Huddy, Pat Hughes, Dave Hunter, Don Jackson, Jari Kurri, Willy Lindstrom, Ken Linseman, Kevin Lowe, Dave Lumley, Kevin McClelland, Mark Messier, Andy Moog, Jaroslav Pouzar, Dave Semenko, Peter Pocklington (Owner), Glen Sather (General Manager/Coach), John Muckler (Ass't. Coach), Ted Green (Ass't. Coach), Bruce MacGregor (Ass't. General Manager), Barry Fraser (Director of Player Personnel/Chief Scout), Peter Millar (Athletic Therapist), Barrie Stafford (Trainer)
Scores: May 10, at New York — Edmonton 1, NY Islanders 0; May 12, at New York — NY Islanders 6, Edmonton 1; May 15, at Edmonton — Edmonton 7, NY Islanders 2; May 17, at Edmonton — Edmonton 7, NY Islanders 2; May 19, at Edmonton — Edmonton 5, NY Islanders 2.

1982-83 — New York Islanders — Mike Bossy, Bob Bourne, Paul Boutilier, Billy Carroll, Greg Gilbert, Clark Gillies, Butch Goring, Mats Hallin, Tomas Jonsson, Anders Kallur, Gord Lane, Dave Langevin, Mike McEwen, Rollie Melanson, Wayne Merrick, Ken Morrow, Bob Nystrom, Stefan Persson, Denis Potvin, Billy Smith, Brent Sutter, Duane Sutter, John Tonelli, Bryan Trottier, Al Arbour (coach), Lorne Henning (ass't coach), Bill Torrey (general manager), Ron Waske, Jim Pickard (trainers)
Scores: May 10, at Edmonton — NY Islanders 2, Edmonton 0; May 12, at Edmonton — NY Islanders 6, Edmonton 3; May 14, at New York — NY Islanders 5, Edmonton 1; May 17, at New York — NY Islanders 4, Edmonton 2

1981-82 — New York Islanders — Mike Bossy, Bob Bourne, Billy Carroll, Butch Goring, Greg Gilbert, Clark Gillies, Tomas Jonsson, Anders Kallur, Gord Lane, Dave Langevin, Hector Marini, Mike McEwen, Rollie Melanson, Wayne Merrick, Ken Morrow, Bob Nystrom, Stefan Persson, Denis Potvin, Billy Smith, Brent Sutter, Duane Sutter, John Tonelli, Bryan Trottier, Al Arbour (coach), Lorne Henning (ass't coach), Bill Torrey (general manager), Jim Devellano (ass't. general manager/dir. of scouting), Ron Waske, Jim Pickard (trainers)
Scores: May 8, at New York — NY Islanders 6, Vancouver 5; May 11, at New York — NY Islanders 6, Vancouver 4; May 13, at Vancouver — NY Islanders 3, Vancouver 0; May 16, at Vancouver — NY Islanders 3, Vancouver 1

1980-81 — New York Islanders — Denis Potvin, Mike McEwen, Ken Morrow, Gord Lane, Bob Lorimer, Stefan Persson, Dave Langevin, Mike Bossy, Bryan Trottier, Butch Goring, Wayne Merrick, Clark Gillies, John Tonelli, Bob Nystrom, Bill Carroll, Bob Bourne, Hector Marini, Anders Kallur, Duane Sutter, Garry Howatt, Lorne Henning, Billy Smith, Rollie Melanson, Al Arbour (coach), Bill Torrey (general manager), Jim Devellano (chief scout), Ron Waske, Jim Pickard (trainers).
Scores: May 12, at New York — NY Islanders 6, Minnesota 3; May 14, at New York — NY Islanders 6, Minnesota 3; May 17, at Minnesota — NY Islanders 7, Minnesota 5; May 19, at Minnesota— Minnesota 4, NY Islanders 2; May 21, at New York — NY Islanders 5, Minnesota 1.

1979-80 — New York Islanders — Gord Lane, Jean Potvin, Bob Lorimer, Denis Potvin, Stefan Persson, Ken Morrow, Dave Langevin, Duane Sutter, Garry Howatt, Clark Gillies, Lorne Henning, Wayne Merrick, Bob Bourne, Steve Tambellini, Bryan Trottier, Mike Bossy, Bob Nystrom, John Tonelli, Anders Kallur, Butch Goring, Alex McKendry, Glenn Resch, Billy Smith, Al Arbour (coach), Bill Torrey (general manager), Jim Devellano (chief scout), Ron Waske, Jim Pickard (trainers).
Scores: May 13, at Philadelphia — NY Islanders 4, Philadelphia 3; May 15, at Philadelphia — Philadelphia 8, NY Islanders 3; May 17, at New York — NY Islanders 6, Philadelphia 2; May 19, at New York — NY Islanders 5, Philadelphia 2; May 22 at Philadelphia — Philadelphia 6, NY Islanders 3; May 24, at New York — NY Islanders 5, Philadelphia 4.

1978-79 — Montreal Canadiens — Ken Dryden, Larry Robinson, Serge Savard, Guy Lapointe, Brian Engblom, Gilles Lupien, Rick Chartraw, Guy Lafleur, Steve Shutt, Jacques Lemaire, Yvan Cournoyer, Réjean Houle, Pierre Mondou, Bob Gainey, Doug Jarvis, Yvon Lambert, Doug Risebrough, Pierre Larouche, Mario Tremblay, Cam Connor, Pat Hughes, Rod Langway, Mark Napier, Michel Larocque, Richard Sévigny, Scotty Bowman (coach), Irving Grundman (managing director), Eddy Palchak, Pierre Meilleur (trainers).
Scores: May 13, at Montreal — NY Rangers 4, Montreal 1; May 15, at Montreal — Montreal 6, NY Rangers 2; May 17, at New York — Montreal 4, NY Rangers 1; May 19, at New York — Montreal 4, NY Rangers 3; May 21, at Montreal — Montreal 4, NY Rangers 1.

1977-78 — Montreal Canadiens — Ken Dryden, Larry Robinson, Serge Savard, Guy Lapointe, Bill Nyrop, Pierre Bouchard, Brian Engblom, Gilles Lupien, Rick Chartraw, Guy Lafleur, Steve Shutt, Jacques Lemaire, Yvan Cournoyer, Réjean Houle, Pierre Mondou, Bob Gainey, Doug Jarvis, Yvon Lambert, Doug Risebrough, Pierre Larouche, Mario Tremblay, Michel Larocque, Murray Wilson, Scotty Bowman (coach), Sam Pollock (general manager), Eddy Palchak, Pierre Meilleur (trainers).
Scores: May 13, at Montreal — Montreal 4, Boston 1; May 16, at Montreal — Montreal 3, Boston 2; May 18, at Boston — Boston 4, Montreal 0; May 21, at Boston — Boston 4, Montreal 3; May 23, at Montreal — Montreal 4, Boston 1; May 25, at Boston — Montreal 4, Boston 1.

1976-77 — Montreal Canadiens — Ken Dryden, Guy Lapointe, Larry Robinson, Serge Savard, Jimmy Roberts, Rick Chartraw, Bill Nyrop, Pierre Bouchard, Brian Engblom, Yvan Cournoyer, Guy Lafleur, Jacques Lemaire, Steve Shutt, Pete Mahovlich, Murray Wilson, Doug Jarvis, Yvon Lambert, Bob Gainey, Doug Risebrough, Mario Tremblay, Rejean Houle, Pierre Mondou, Mike Polich, Michel Larocque, Scotty Bowman (coach), Sam Pollock (general manager), Eddy Palchak, Pierre Meilleur (trainers).
Scores: May 7, at Montreal — Montreal 7, Boston 3; May 10, at Montreal — Montreal 3, Boston 0; May 12, at Boston — Montreal 4, Boston 2; May 14, at Boston — Montreal 2, Boston 1.

1975-76 — Montreal Canadiens — Ken Dryden, Serge Savard, Guy Lapointe, Larry Robinson, Bill Nyrop, Pierre Bouchard, Jimmy Roberts, Guy Lafleur, Steve Shutt, Pete Mahovlich, Yvan Cournoyer, Jacques Lemaire, Yvon Lambert, Bob Gainey, Doug Jarvis, Doug Risebrough, Murray Wilson, Mario Tremblay, Rick Chartraw, Michel Larocque, Scotty Bowman (coach), Sam Pollock (general manager), Eddy Palchak, Pierre Meilleur (trainers).
Scores: May 9, at Montreal — Montreal 4, Philadelphia 3; May 11, at Montreal — Montreal 2, Philadelphia 1; May 13, at Philadelphia — Montreal 3, Philadelphia 2; May 16, at Philadelphia — Montreal 5, Philadelphia 3.

1974-75 — Philadelphia Flyers — Bernie Parent, Wayne Stephenson, Ed Van Impe, Tom Bladon, André Dupont, Joe Watson, Jimmy Watson, Ted Harris, Larry Goodenough, Rick MacLeish, Bobby Clarke, Bill Barber, Reggie Leach, Gary Dornhoefer, Ross Lonsberry, Bob Kelly, Terry Crisp, Don Saleski, Dave Schultz, Orest Kindrachuk, Bill Clement, Fred Shero (coach), Keith Allen (general manager), Frank Lewis, Jim McKenzie (trainers).
Scores: May 15, at Philadelphia — Philadelphia 4, Buffalo 1; May 18, at Philadelphia — Philadelphia 2, Buffalo 1; May 20, at Buffalo — Buffalo 5, Philadelphia 4; May 22, at Buffalo — Buffalo 4, Philadelphia 2; May 25, at Philadelphia — Philadelphia 5, Buffalo 1; May 27, at Buffalo — Philadelphia 2, Buffalo 0.

1973-74 — Philadelphia Flyers — Bernie Parent, Ed Van Impe, Tom Bladon, André Dupont, Joe Watson, Jimmy Watson, Barry Ashbee, Bill Barber, Dave Schultz, Don Saleski, Gary Dornhoefer, Terry Crisp, Bobby Clarke, Simon Nolet, Ross Lonsberry, Rick MacLeish, Bill Flett, Orest Kindrachuk, Bill Clement, Bob Kelly, Bruce Cowick, Al MacAdam, Bobby Taylor, Fred Shero (coach), Keith Allen (general manager), Frank Lewis, Jim McKenzie (trainers).
Scores: May 7, at Boston — Boston 3, Philadelphia 2; May 9, at Boston — Philadelphia 3, Boston 2; May 12, at Philadelphia — Philadelphia 4, Boston 1; May 14, at Philadelphia — Philadelphia 4, Boston 2; May 16, at Boston — Boston 5, Philadelphia 1; May 19, at Philadelphia — Philadelphia 1, Boston 0.

1972-73 — Montreal Canadiens — Ken Dryden, Guy Lapointe, Serge Savard, Larry Robinson, Jacques Laperrière, Bob Murdoch, Pierre Bouchard, Jimmy Roberts, Yvan Cournoyer, Frank Mahovlich, Jacques Lemaire, Pete Mahovlich, Marc Tardif, Henri Richard, Réjean Houle, Guy Lafleur, Chuck Lefley, Claude Larose, Murray Wilson, Steve Shutt, Michel Plasse, Scotty Bowman (coach), Sam Pollock (general manager), Ed Palchak, Bob Williams (trainers).
Scores: April 29, at Montreal — Montreal 8, Chicago 3; May 1, at Montreal — Montreal 4, Chicago 1; May 3, at Chicago — Chicago 7, Montreal 4; May 6, at Chicago — Montreal 4, Chicago 0; May 8, at Montreal — Chicago 8, Montreal 7; May 10, at Chicago — Montreal 6, Chicago 4.

1971-72 — Boston Bruins — Gerry Cheevers, Eddie Johnston, Bobby Orr, Ted Green, Carol Vadnais, Dallas Smith, Don Awrey, Phil Esposito, Ken Hodge, John Bucyk, Mike Walton, Wayne Cashman, Garnet Bailey, Derek Sanderson, Fred Stanfield, Ed Westfall, John McKenzie, Don Marcotte, Garry Peters, Chris Hayes, Tom Johnson (coach), Milt Schmidt (general manager), Dan Canney, John Forristall (trainers).
Scores: April 30, at Boston — Boston 6, NY Rangers 5; May 2, at Boston — Boston 2, NY Rangers 1; May 4, at New York — NY Rangers 5, Boston 2; May 7, at New York — Boston 3, NY Rangers 2; May 9, at Boston — NY Rangers 3, Boston 2; May 11, at New York — Boston 3, NY Rangers 0.

1970-71 — Montreal Canadiens — Ken Dryden, Rogie Vachon, Jacques Laperrière, J.C. Tremblay, Guy Lapointe, Terry Harper, Pierre Bouchard, Jean Béliveau, Marc Tardif, Yvan Cournoyer, Réjean Houle, Claude Larose, Henri Richard, Phil Roberto, Pete Mahovlich, Leon Rochefort, John Ferguson, Bobby Sheehan, Jacques Lemaire, Frank Mahovlich, Bob Murdoch, Chuck Lefley, Al MacNeil (coach), Sam Pollock (general manager), Yvon Belanger, Ed Palchak (trainers).
Scores: May 4, at Chicago — Chicago 7, Montreal 1; May 6, at Chicago — Chicago 5, Montreal 3; May 9, at Montreal — Montreal 4, Chicago 2; May 11, at Montreal — Montreal 5, Chicago 2; May 13, at Chicago — Chicago 2, Montreal 0; May 16, at Montreal — Montreal 4, Chicago 3; May 18, at Chicago — Montreal 3, Chicago 2.

1969-70 — Boston Bruins — Gerry Cheevers, Eddie Johnston, Bobby Orr, Rick Smith, Dallas Smith, Bill Speer, Gary Doak, Don Awrey, Phil Esposito, Ken Hodge, John Bucyk, Wayne Carleton, Wayne Cashman, Derek Sanderson, Fred Stanfield, Ed Westfall, John McKenzie, Jim Lorentz, Don Marcotte, Bill Lesuk, Dan Schock, Harry Sinden (coach), Milt Schmidt (general manager), Dan Canney, John Forristall (trainers).
Scores: May 3, at St. Louis — Boston 6, St. Louis 1; May 5, at St. Louis — Boston 6, St. Louis 2; May 7, at Boston — Boston 4, St. Louis 1; May 10, at Boston — Boston 4, St. Louis 3.

1968-69 — Montreal Canadiens — Gump Worsley, Rogie Vachon, Jacques Laperrière, J.C. Tremblay, Ted Harris, Serge Savard, Terry Harper, Larry Hillman, Jean Béliveau, Ralph Backstrom, Dick Duff, Yvan Cournoyer, Claude Provost, Bobby Rousseau, Henri Richard, John Ferguson, Christian Bordeleau, Mickey Redmond, Jacques Lemaire, Lucien Grenier, Tony Esposito, Claude Ruel (coach), Sam Pollock (general manager), Larry Aubut, Eddy Palchak (trainers).
Scores: April 27, at Montreal — Montreal 3, St. Louis 1; April 29, at Montreal — Montreal 3, St. Louis 1; May 1 at St. Louis — Montreal 4, St. Louis 0; May 4, at St. Louis — Montreal 2, St. Louis 1.

1967-68 — Montreal Canadiens — Gump Worsley, Rogie Vachon, Jacques Laperrière, J.C. Tremblay, Ted Harris, Serge Savard, Terry Harper, Carol Vadnais, Jean Béliveau, Gilles Tremblay, Ralph Backstrom, Dick Duff, Claude Larose, Yvan Cournoyer, Claude Provost, Bobby Rousseau, Henri Richard, John Ferguson, Danny Grant, Jacques Lemaire, Mickey Redmond, Toe Blake (coach), Sam Pollock (general manager), Larry Aubut, Eddy Palchak (trainers).
Scores: May 5, at Montreal — Montreal 3, St. Louis 2; May 7, at St. Louis — Montreal 1, St. Louis 0; May 9, at Montreal — Montreal 4, St. Louis 3; May 11, at Montreal — Montreal 3, St. Louis 2.

1966-67 — Toronto Maple Leafs — Johnny Bower, Terry Sawchuk, Larry Hillman, Marcel Pronovost, Tim Horton, Bob Baun, Aut Erickson, Allan Stanley, Red Kelly, Ron Ellis, George Armstrong, Pete Stemkowski, Dave Keon, Mike Walton, Jim Pappin, Bob Pulford, Brian Conacher, Eddie Shack, Frank Mahovlich, Milan Marcetta, Larry Jeffrey, Bruce Gamble, Punch Imlach (manager-coach), Bob Haggart (trainer).
Scores: April 20, at Montreal — Toronto 2, Montreal 6; April 22, at Montreal — Toronto 3, Montreal 0; April 25, at Toronto — Toronto 3, Montreal 2; April 27, at Toronto — Toronto 2, Montreal 6; April 29 at Montreal — Toronto 4, Montreal 1; May 2, at Toronto — Toronto 3, Montreal 1.

1965-66 — Montreal Canadiens — Gump Worsley, Charlie Hodge, Jean-Claude Tremblay, Ted Harris, Jean-Guy Talbot, Terry Harper, Jacques Laperrière, Noel Price, Jean Béliveau, Ralph Backstrom, Dick Duff, Gilles Tremblay, Claude Larose, Yvan Cournoyer, Claude Provost, Bobby Rousseau, Henri Richard, Dave Balon, John Ferguson, Leon Rochefort, Jim Roberts, Toe Blake (coach), Sam Pollock (general manager), Larry Aubut, Andy Galley (trainers).
Scores: April 24, at Montreal — Detroit 3, Montreal 2; April 26, at Montreal — Detroit 5, Montreal 2; April 28, at Detroit — Montreal 4, Detroit 2; May 1, at Detroit — Montreal 2, Detroit 1; May 3, at Montreal — Montreal 5, Detroit 1; May 5, at Detroit — Montreal 3, Detroit 2.

1964-65 — Montreal Canadiens — Gump Worsley, Charlie Hodge, Jean-Claude Tremblay, Ted Harris, Jean-Guy Talbot, Terry Harper, Jacques Laperrière, Jean Gauthier, Noel Picard, Jean Béliveau, Ralph Backstrom, Dick Duff, Claude Larose, Yvan Cournoyer, Claude Provost, Bobby Rousseau, Henri Richard, Dave Balon, John Ferguson, Red Berenson, Jim Roberts, Toe Blake (coach), Sam Pollock (general manager), Larry Aubut, Andy Galley (trainers).
Scores: April 17, at Montreal — Montreal 3, Chicago 2; April 20, at Montreal — Montreal 2, Chicago 0; April 22, at Chicago — Montreal 1, Chicago 3; April 25, at Chicago — Montreal 1, Chicago 5; April 7, at Montreal — Montreal 6, Chicago 0; April 29, at Chicago — Montreal 1, Chicago 2; May 1, at Montreal — Montreal 4, Chicago 0.

1963-64 — Toronto Maple Leafs — Johnny Bower, Carl Brewer, Tim Horton, Bob Baun, Allan Stanley, Larry Hillman, Al Arbour, Red Kelly, Gerry Ehman, Andy Bathgate, George Armstrong, Ron Stewart, Dave Keon, Billy Harris, Don McKenney, Jim Pappin, Bob Pulford, Eddie Shack, Frank Mahovlich, Ed Litzenberger, Punch Imlach (manager-coach), Bob Haggert (trainer).
Scores April 11, at Toronto — Toronto 3, Detroit 2; April 14, at Toronto — Toronto 3, Detroit 4; April 16, at Detroit — Toronto 3, Detroit 4; April 18, at Detroit — Toronto 4, Detroit 2; April 21, at Toronto — Toronto 1, Detroit 2; April 23, at Detroit — Toronto 4, Detroit 3; April 25, at Toronto — Toronto 4, Detroit 0.

1962-63 — Toronto Maple Leafs — Johnny Bower, Don Simmons, Carl Brewer, Tim Horton, Kent Douglas, Allan Stanley, Bob Baun, Larry Hillman, Red Kelly, Dick Duff, George Armstrong, Bob Nevin, Ron Stewart, Dave Keon, Billy Harris, Bob Pulford, Eddie Shack, Ed Litzenberger, Frank Mahovlich, John MacMillan, Punch Imlach (manager-coach), Bob Haggert (trainer).
Scores: April 9, at Toronto — Toronto 4, Detroit 2; April 11, at Toronto — Toronto 4, Detroit 2; April 14, at Detroit — Toronto 2, Detroit 3; April 16, at Detroit — Toronto 4, Detroit 2; April 18, at Toronto — Toronto 3, Detroit 1.

1961-62 — Toronto Maple Leafs — Johnny Bower, Don Simmons, Carl Brewer, Tim Horton, Bob Baun, Allan Stanley, Al Arbour, Larry Hillman, Red Kelly, Dick Duff, George Armstrong, Frank Mahovlich, Bob Nevin, Ron Stewart, Billy Harris, Bert Olmstead, Bob Pulford, Eddie Shack, Dave Keon, Ed Litzenberger, John MacMillan, Punch Imlach (manager-coach), Bob Haggert (trainer).
Scores: April 10, at Toronto — Toronto 4, Chicago 1; April 12, at Toronto — Toronto 3, Chicago 2; April 15, at Chicago — Toronto 0, Chicago 3; April 17, at Chicago — Toronto 1, Chicago 4; April 19, at Toronto — Toronto 8, Chicago 4; April 22, at Chicago — Toronto 2, Chicago 1.

1960-61 — Chicago Black Hawks — Glenn Hall, Al Arbour, Pierre Pilote, Elmer Vasko, Jack Evans, Dollard St. Laurent, Reggie Fleming, Tod Sloan, Ron Murphy, Ed Litzenberger, Bill Hay, Bobby Hull, Ab McDonald, Eric Nesterenko, Kenny Wharram, Earl Balfour, Stan Mikita, Murray Balfour, Chico Maki, Wayne Hicks, Tommy Ivan (manager), Rudy Pilous (coach), Nick Garen (trainer).
Scores: April 6, at Chicago — Chicago 3, Detroit 2; April 8, at Detroit — Detroit 3, Chicago 1; April 10, at Chicago — Chicago 3, Detroit 1; April 12, at Detroit — Detroit 2, Chicago 1; April 14, at Chicago — Chicago 6, Detroit 3; April 16, at Detroit — Chicago 5, Detroit 1.

1959-60 — Montreal Canadiens — Jacques Plante, Charlie Hodge, Doug Harvey, Tom Johnson, Bob Turner, Jean-Guy Talbot, Albert Langlois, Ralph Backstrom, Jean Béliveau, Marcel Bonin, Bernie Geoffrion, Phil Goyette, Bill Hicke, Don Marshall, Ab McDonald, Dickie Moore, André Pronovost, Claude Provost, Henri Richard, Maurice Richard, Frank Selke (manager), Toe Blake (coach), Hector Dubois, Larry Aubut (trainers)
Scores: April 7, at Montreal — Montreal 4, Toronto 2; April 9, at Montreal — Montreal 2, Toronto 1; April 12, at Toronto — Montreal 5, Toronto 2; April 14, at Toronto — Montreal 4, Toronto 0.

1958-59 — Montreal Canadiens — Jacques Plante, Charlie Hodge, Doug Harvey, Tom Johnson, Bob Turner, Jean-Guy Talbot, Albert Langlois, Bernie Geoffrion, Ralph Backstrom, Bill Hicke, Maurice Richard, Claude Moore, Ab McDonald, Henri Richard, Marcel Bonin, Phil Goyette, Don Marshall, André Pronovost, Jean Béliveau, Frank Selke (manager), Toe Blake (coach), Hector Dubois, Larry Aubut (trainers).
Scores: April 9, at Montreal — Montreal 5, Toronto 3; April 11, at Montreal — Montreal 3, Toronto 1; April 14, at Toronto — Toronto 3, Montreal 2; April 16, at Toronto — Montreal 3, Toronto 2; April 18, at Montreal — Montreal 5, Toronto 3.

1957-58 — Montreal Canadiens — Jacques Plante, Gerry McNeil, Doug Harvey, Tom Johnson, Bob Turner, Dollard St-Laurent, Jean-Guy Talbot, Albert Langlois, Jean Béliveau, Bernie Geoffrion, Maurice Richard, Dickie Moore, Bert Olmstead, Henri Richard, Marcel Bonin, Phil Goyette, Don Marshall, André Pronovost, Connie Broden, Frank Selke (manager), Toe Blake (coach), Hector Dubois, Larry Aubut (trainers).
Scores: April 8, at Montreal — Montreal 2, Boston 1; April 10, at Montreal — Boston 5, Montreal 2; April 13, at Boston — Montreal 3, Boston 0; April 15, at Boston — Boston 3, Montreal 1; April 17, at Montreal — Montreal 3, Boston 2; April 20, at Boston — Montreal 5, Boston 3.

The Montreal Canadiens capped their run of five straight Stanley Cup titles in 1960, then won the Cup again in 1965, 1966, 1968 and 1969. Jean Beliveau (wearing the C) and Henri Richard (A in the second row from the top) were both members of all nine of those championship teams.

1956-57 — **Montreal Canadiens** — Jacques Plante, Gerry McNeil, Doug Harvey, Tom Johnson, Bob Turner, Dollard St. Laurent, Jean-Guy Talbot, Jean Béliveau, Bernie Geoffrion, Floyd Curry, Dickie Moore, Maurice Richard, Claude Provost, Bert Olmstead, Henri Richard, Phil Goyette, Don Marshall, André Pronovost, Connie Broden, Frank Selke (manager), Toe Blake (coach), Hector Dubois, Larry Aubut (trainers).
Scores: April 6, at Montreal — Montreal 5, Boston 1; April 9, at Montreal — Montreal 1, Boston 0; April 11, at Boston — Montreal 4, Boston 2; April 14, at Boston — Boston 2, Montreal 0; April 16, at Montreal — Montreal 5, Boston 1.

1955-56 — **Montreal Canadiens** — Jacques Plante, Doug Harvey, Butch Bouchard, Bob Turner, Tom Johnson, Jean-Guy Talbot, Dollard St. Laurent, Jean Béliveau, Bernie Geoffrion, Bert Olmstead, Floyd Curry, Jackie Leclair, Maurice Richard, Dickie Moore, Henri Richard, Kenny Mosdell, Don Marshall, Claude Provost, Frank Selke (manager), Toe Blake (coach), Hector Dubois (trainer).
Scores: March 31, at Montreal — Montreal 6, Detroit 4; April 3, at Montreal — Montreal 5, Detroit 1; April 5, at Detroit — Detroit 3, Montreal 1; April 8, at Detroit — Montreal 3, Detroit 0; April 10, at Montreal — Montreal 3, Detroit 1.

1954-55 — **Detroit Red Wings** — Terry Sawchuk, Red Kelly, Bob Goldham, Marcel Pronovost, Benny Woit, Jim Hay, Larry Hillman, Ted Lindsay, Tony Leswick, Gordie Howe, Alex Delvecchio, Marty Pavelich, Glen Skov, John Wilson, Bill Dineen, Vic Stasiuk, Marcel Bonin, Jack Adams (manager), Jimmy Skinner (coach), Carl Mattson (trainer).
Scores: April 3, at Detroit — Detroit 4, Montreal 2; April 5, at Detroit — Detroit 7, Montreal 1, April 7, at Montreal — Montreal 4, Detroit 2; April 9, at Montreal — Montreal 5, Detroit 3; April 10, at Detroit — Detroit 5, Montreal 1; April 12, at Montreal — Montreal 6, Detroit 3; April 14, at Detroit — Detroit 3, Montreal 1

1953-54 — **Detroit Red Wings** — Terry Sawchuk, Red Kelly, Bob Goldham, Benny Woit, Marcel Pronovost, Al Arbour, Keith Allen, Ted Lindsay, Tony Leswick, Gordie Howe, Marty Pavelich, Alex Delvecchio, Metro Prystai, Glen Skov, Bill Dineen, Jimmy Peters Sr., Earl Reibel, Vic Stasiuk, Jack Adams (manager), Tommy Ivan (coach), Carl Mattson (trainer).
Scores: April 4, at Detroit — Detroit 3, Montreal 1; April 6, at Detroit — Montreal 3, Detroit 1; April 8, at Montreal — Detroit 5, Montreal 2; April 10, at Montreal — Detroit 2, Montreal 0; April 11, at Detroit — Montreal 1, Detroit 0; April 13, at Montreal — Montreal 4, Detroit 1; April 16, at Detroit — Detroit 2, Montreal 1

1952-53 — **Montreal Canadiens** — Gerry McNeil, Jacques Plante, Doug Harvey, Butch Bouchard, Tom Johnson, Dollard St. Laurent, Bud MacPherson, Maurice Richard, Elmer Lach, Bert Olmstead, Bernie Geoffrion, Floyd Curry, Paul Masnick, Billy Reay, Dickie Moore, Kenny Mosdell, Dick Gamble, Johnny McCormack, Lorne Davis, Calum MacKay, Eddie Mazur, Frank Selke (manager), Dick Irvin (coach), Hector Dubois (trainer).
Scores: April 9, at Montreal — Montreal 4, Boston 2; April 11, at Montreal — Boston 4, Montreal 1; April 12, at Boston — Montreal 3, Boston 0; April 14, at Boston — Montreal 7, Boston 3; April 16, at Montreal — Montreal 1, Boston 0.

1951-52 — **Detroit Red Wings** — Terry Sawchuk, Bob Goldham, Benny Woit, Red Kelly, Leo Reise Jr., Marcel Pronovost, Ted Lindsay, Tony Leswick, Gordie Howe, Metro Prystai, Marty Pavelich, Sid Abel, Glen Skov, Alex Delvecchio, John Wilson, Vic Stasiuk, Larry Zeidel, Jack Adams (manager) Tommy Ivan (coach), Carl Mattson (trainer).
Scores: April 10, at Montreal — Detroit 3, Montreal 1; April 12, at Montreal — Detroit 2, Montreal 1; April 13, at Detroit — Detroit 3, Montreal 0; April 15, at Detroit — Detroit 3, Montreal 0.

1950-51 — **Toronto Maple Leafs** — Turk Broda, Al Rollins, Jim Thomson, Gus Mortson, Bill Barilko, Bill Juzda, Fern Flaman, Hugh Bolton, Ted Kennedy, Sid Smith, Tod Sloan, Cal Gardner, Howie Meeker, Harry Watson, Max Bentley, Joe Klukay, Danny Lewicki, Ray Timgren, Fleming Mackell, Johnny McCormack, Bob Hassard, Conn Smythe (manager), Tim Daly (trainer).
Scores: April 11, at Toronto — Toronto 3, Montreal 2; April 14, at Toronto — Montreal 3, Toronto 2; April 17, at Montreal — Toronto 2, Montreal 1; April 19, at Montreal — Toronto 3, Montreal 2; April 21, at Toronto — Toronto 3, Montreal 2.

1949-50 — **Detroit Red Wings** — Harry Lumley, Jack Stewart, Leo Reise Jr., Clare Martin, Al Dewsbury, Lee Fogolin, Marcel Pronovost, Red Kelly, Ted Lindsay, Sid Abel, Gordie Howe, George Gee, Jimmy Peters Sr., Marty Pavelich, Jim McFadden, Pete Babando, Max McNab, Gerry Couture, Joe Carveth, Steve Black, Larry Wilson, Jack Adams (manager), Tommy Ivan (coach), Carl Mattson (trainer).
Scores: April 11, at Detroit — Detroit 4, NY Rangers 1; April 13, at Toronto* — NY Rangers 3, Detroit 1, April 15, at Toronto — Detroit 4, NY Rangers 0; April 18, at Detroit — NY Rangers 4, Detroit 3; April 20, at Detroit — NY Rangers 2, Detroit 1; April 22, at Detroit — Detroit 5, NY Rangers 4; April 23, at Detroit — Detroit 4, NY Rangers 3.

* Ice was unavailable in Madison Square Garden and Rangers elected to play second and third games on Toronto ice.

1948-49 — **Toronto Maple Leafs** — Turk Broda, Jim Thomson, Gus Mortson, Bill Barilko, Garth Boesch, Bill Juzda, Ted Kennedy, Howie Meeker, Vic Lynn, Harry Watson, Bill Ezinicki, Cal Gardner, Max Bentley, Joe Klukay, Sid Smith, Don Metz, Ray Timgren, Fleming Mackell, Harry Taylor, Bob Dawes, Tod Sloan, Conn Smythe (manager), Hap Day (coach), Tim Daly (trainer).
Scores: April 8, at Detroit — Toronto 3, Detroit 2; April 10, at Detroit — Toronto 3, Detroit 1; April 13, at Toronto — Toronto 3, Detroit 1; April 16, at Toronto — Toronto 3, Detroit 1.

1947-48 — **Toronto Maple Leafs** — Turk Broda, Jim Thomson, Wally Stanowski, Garth Boesch, Bill Barilko, Gus Mortson, Phil Samis, Syl Apps Sr., Bill Ezinicki, Harry Watson, Ted Kennedy, Howie Meeker, Vic Lynn, Nick Metz, Max Bentley, Joe Klukay, Les Costello, Don Metz, Sid Smith, Conn Smythe (manager), Hap Day (coach), Tim Daly (trainer).
Scores: April 7, at Toronto — Toronto 5, Detroit 3; April 10, at Toronto — Toronto 4, Detroit 2; April 11, at Detroit — Toronto 2, Detroit 0; April 14, at Detroit — Toronto 7, Detroit 2.

When Punch Imlach coached the Leafs to the Stanley Cup in 1962 it marked the team's first championship since Bill Barilko's overtime goal in 1951. Toronto won championships again under Imlach in 1963, 1964 and 1967.

1946-47 — Toronto Maple Leafs — Turk Broda, Garth Boesch, Gus Mortson, Jim Thomson, Wally Stanowski, Bill Barilko, Harry Watson, Bud Poile, Ted Kennedy, Syl Apps Sr., Don Metz, Nick Metz, Bill Ezinicki, Vic Lynn, Howie Meeker, Gaye Stewart, Joe Klukay, Gus Bodnar, Bob Goldham, Conn Smythe (manager), Hap Day (coach), Tim Daly (trainer).
Scores: April 8, at Montreal — Montreal 6, Toronto 0; April 10, at Montreal — Toronto 4, Montreal 0; April 12, at Toronto — Toronto 4, Montreal 2; April 15, at Toronto — Toronto 2, Montreal 1; April 17, at Montreal — Montreal 3, Toronto 1; April 19, at Toronto — Toronto 2, Montreal 1.

1945-46 — Montreal Canadiens — Elmer Lach, Toe Blake, Maurice Richard, Bob Fillion, Dutch Hiller, Murph Chamberlain, Ken Mosdell, Buddy O'Connor, Glen Harmon, Jimmy Peters Sr., Butch Bouchard, Billy Reay, Ken Reardon, Leo Lamoureux, Frank Eddolls, Gerry Plamondon, Bill Durnan, Tommy Gorman (manager), Dick Irvin (coach), Ernie Cook (trainer).
Scores: March 30, at Montreal — Montreal 4, Boston 3; April 2, at Montreal — Montreal 3, Boston 2; April 4, at Boston — Montreal 4, Boston 2; April 7, at Boston — Boston 3, Montreal 2; April 9, at Montreal — Montreal 6, Boston 3.

1944-45 — Toronto Maple Leafs — Don Metz, Frank McCool, Wally Stanowski, Reg Hamilton, Elwyn Morris, Johnny McCreedy, Tommy O'Neill, Ted Kennedy, Babe Pratt, Gus Bodnar, Art Jackson, Jack McLean, Mel Hill, Nick Metz, Bob Davidson, Sweeney Schriner, Lorne Carr, Conn Smythe (manager), Frank Selke (business manager), Hap Day (coach), Tim Daly (trainer).
Scores: April 6, at Detroit — Toronto 1, Detroit 0; April 8, at Detroit — Toronto 2, Detroit 0; April 12, at Toronto — Toronto 1, Detroit 0; April 14, at Toronto — Detroit 5, Toronto 3; April 19, at Detroit — Detroit 2, Toronto 0; April 21, at Toronto — Detroit 1, Toronto 0; April 22, at Detroit — Toronto 2, Detroit 1.

1943-44 — Montreal Canadiens — Toe Blake, Maurice Richard, Elmer Lach, Ray Getliffe, Murph Chamberlain, Phil Watson, Butch Bouchard, Glen Harmon, Buddy O'Connor, Jerry Heffernan, Mike McMahon Sr., Leo Lamoureux, Fernand Majeau, Bob Fillion, Bill Durnan, Tommy Gorman (manager), Dick Irvin (coach), Ernie Cook (trainer).
Scores: April 4, at Montreal — Montreal 5, Chicago 1; April 6, at Chicago — Montreal 3, Chicago 1; April 9, at Chicago — Montreal 3, Chicago 2; April 13, at Montreal — Montreal 5, Chicago 4.

1942-43 — Detroit Red Wings — Jack Stewart, Jimmy Orlando, Sid Abel, Alex Motter, Harry Watson, Joe Carveth, Mud Bruneteau, Eddie Wares, Johnny Mowers, Cully Simon, Don Grosso, Carl Liscombe, Connie Brown, Syd Howe, Les Douglas, Hal Jackson, Joe Fisher, Jack Adams (manager), Ebbie Goodfellow (playing-coach), Honey Walker (trainer).
Scores: April 1, at Detroit — Detroit 6, Boston 2; April 4, at Detroit — Detroit 4, Boston 3; April 7, at Boston — Detroit 4, Boston 0; April 8, at Boston — Detroit 2, Boston 0.

1941-42 — Toronto Maple Leafs — Wally Stanowski, Syl Apps Sr., Bob Goldham, Gordie Drillon, Hank Goldup, Ernie Dickens, Sweeney Schriner, Bucko McDonald, Bob Davidson, Nick Metz, Bingo Kampman, Don Metz, Gaye Stewart, Turk Broda, Johnny McCreedy, Lorne Carr, Pete Langelle, Billy Taylor, Conn Smythe (manager), Hap Day (coach), Frank Selke (business manager), Tim Daly (trainer).
Scores: April 4, at Toronto — Detroit 3, Toronto 2; April 7, at Toronto — Detroit 4, Toronto 2; April 9, at Detroit — Detroit 5, Toronto 2; April 12, at Detroit — Toronto 4, Detroit 3; April 14, at Toronto — Toronto 9, Detroit 3; April 16, at Detroit — Toronto 3, Detroit 0; April 18, at Toronto — Toronto 3, Detroit 1.

1940-41 — Boston Bruins — Bill Cowley, Des Smith, Dit Clapper, Frank Brimsek, Flash Hollett, John Crawford, Bobby Bauer, Pat McReavy, Herb Cain, Mel Hill, Milt Schmidt, Woody Dumart, Roy Conacher, Terry Reardon, Art Jackson, Eddie Wiseman, Art Ross (manager), Cooney Weiland (coach), Win Green (trainer).
Scores: April 6, at Boston — Detroit 2, Boston 3; April 8, at Boston — Detroit 1, Boston 2; April 10, at Detroit — Boston 4, Detroit 2; April 12, at Detroit — Boston 3, Detroit 1.

1939-40 — New York Rangers — Dave Kerr, Art Coulter, Ott Heller, Alex Shibicky, Mac Colville, Neil Colville, Phil Watson, Lynn Patrick, Clint Smith, Muzz Patrick, Babe Pratt, Bryan Hextall Sr., Kilby Macdonald, Dutch Hiller, Alf Pike, Sanford Smith, Lester Patrick (manager), Frank Boucher (coach), Harry Westerby (trainer).
Scores: April 2, at New York — NY Rangers 2, Toronto 1; April 3, at New York — NY Rangers 6, Toronto 2; April 6, at Toronto — NY Rangers 1, Toronto 2; April 9, at Toronto — NY Rangers 0, Toronto 3; April 11, at Toronto — NY Rangers 2, Toronto 1; April 13, at Toronto — NY Rangers 3, Toronto 2.

1938-39 — Boston Bruins — Bobby Bauer, Mel Hill, Flash Hollett, Roy Conacher, Gord Pettinger, Milt Schmidt, Woody Dumart, Jack Crawford, Ray Getliffe, Frank Brimsek, Eddie Shore, Dit Clapper, Bill Cowley, Jack Portland, Red Hamill, Cooney Weiland, Art Ross (manager-coach), Win Green (trainer).
Scores: April 6, at Boston — Toronto 1, Boston 2; April 9, at Boston — Toronto 3, Boston 2; April 11, at Toronto — Toronto 1, Boston 3; April 13, at Toronto — Toronto 0, Boston 2; April 16, at Boston — Toronto 1, Boston 3.

1937-38 — Chicago Black Hawks — Art Wiebe, Carl Voss, Hal Jackson, Mike Karakas, Mush March, Jack Shill, Earl Seibert, Cully Dahlstrom, Alex Levinsky, Johnny Gottselig, Lou Trudel, Pete Palangio, Bill MacKenzie, Doc Romnes, Paul Thompson, Roger Jenkins, Alf Moore, Bert Connolly, Virgil Johnson, Paul Goodman, Bill Stewart (manager-coach), Eddie Froelich (trainer).
Scores: April 5, at Toronto — Chicago 3, Toronto 1; April 7, at Toronto — Chicago 1, Toronto 5; April 10, at Chicago — Chicago 2, Toronto 1; April 12, at Chicago — Chicago 4, Toronto 1.

1936-37 — Detroit Red Wings — Norman Smith, Pete Kelly, Larry Aurie, Herbie Lewis, Hec Kilrea, Mud Bruneteau, Syd Howe, Wally Kilrea, Jimmy Franks, Bucko McDonald, Gord Pettinger, Ebbie Goodfellow, John Gallagher, Ralph Bowman, John Sorrell, Marty Barry, Earl Robertson, John Sherf, Howard Mackie, Jack Adams (manager-coach), Honey Walker (trainer).
Scores: April 6, at New York — Detroit 1, NY Rangers 5; April 8, at Detroit — Detroit 4, NY Rangers 2; April 11, at Detroit — Detroit 0, NY Rangers 1; April 13, at Detroit — Detroit 1, NY Rangers 0; April 15, at Detroit — Detroit 3, NY Rangers 0.

1935-36 — Detroit Red Wings — John Sorrell, Syd Howe, Marty Barry, Herbie Lewis, Mud Bruneteau, Wally Kilrea, Hec Kilrea, Gord Pettinger, Bucko McDonald, Ralph Bowman, Pete Kelly, Doug Young, Ebbie Goodfellow, Norman Smith, Jack Adams (manager-coach), Honey Walker (trainer).
Scores: April 5, at Detroit — Detroit 3, Toronto 1; April 7, at Detroit — Detroit 9, Toronto 4; April 9, at Toronto — Detroit 3, Toronto 4; April 11, at Toronto — Detroit 3, Toronto 2.

1934-35 — Montreal Maroons — Lionel Conacher, Cy Wentworth, Alex Connell, Toe Blake, Stewart Evans, Earl Robinson, Bill Miller, Dave Trottier, Jimmy Ward, Larry Northcott, Hooley Smith, Russ Blinco, Allan Shields, Sammy McManus, Gus Marker, Bob Gracie, Herb Cain, Tommy Gorman (manager-coach), Bill O'Brien (trainer).
Scores: April 4, at Toronto — Mtl. Maroons 3, Toronto 2; April 6, at Toronto — Mtl. Maroons 3, Toronto 1; April 9, at Montreal — Mtl. Maroons 4, Toronto 1.

1933-34 — Chicago Black Hawks — Clarence Abel, Rosie Couture, Lou Trudel, Lionel Conacher, Paul Thompson, Leroy Goldsworthy, Art Coulter, Roger Jenkins, Don McFayden, Tom Cook, Doc Romnes, Johnny Gottselig, Mush March, Johnny Sheppard, Chuck Gardiner (captain), Bill Kendall, Tommy Gorman (manager-coach), Eddie Froelich (trainer).
Scores: April 3, at Detroit — Chicago 2, Detroit 1; April 5, at Detroit — Chicago 4, Detroit 1; April 8, at Chicago — Detroit 5, Chicago 2; April 10, at Chicago — Chicago 1, Detroit 0.

1932-33 — New York Rangers — Ching Johnson, Butch Keeling, Frank Boucher, Art Somers, Babe Siebert, Bun Cook, Andy Aikenhead, Ott Heller, Oscar Asmundson, Gord Pettinger, Doug Brennan, Cecil Dillon, Bill Cook (captain), Murray Murdoch, Earl Seibert, Lester Patrick (manager-coach), Harry Westerby (trainer).
Scores: April 4, at New York — NY Rangers 5, Toronto 1; April 8, at Toronto — NY Rangers 3, Toronto 1; April 11, at Toronto — Toronto 3, NY Rangers 2; April 13, at Toronto — NY Rangers 1, Toronto 0.

1931-32 — Toronto Maple Leafs — Charlie Conacher, Harvey Jackson, King Clancy, Andy Blair, Red Horner, Lorne Chabot, Alex Levinsky, Joe Primeau, Hal Darragh, Hal Cotton, Frank Finnigan, Hap Day, Ace Bailey, Bob Gracie, Fred Robertson, Earl Miller, Conn Smythe (manager), Dick Irvin (coach), Tim Daly (trainer).
Scores: April 5, at New York — Toronto 6, NY Rangers 4; April 7, at Boston* — Toronto 6, NY Rangers 2; April 9, at Toronto — Toronto 6, NY Rangers 4.
* Ice was unavailable in Madison Square Garden and Rangers elected to play the second game on neutral ice.

1930-31 — Montreal Canadiens — George Hainsworth, Wildor Larochelle, Marty Burke, Sylvio Mantha, Howie Morenz, Johnny Gagnon, Aurel Joliat, Armand Mondou, Pit Lepine, Albert Leduc, Georges Mantha, Art Lesieur, Nick Wasnie, Bert McCaffrey, Gus Rivers, Jean Pusie, Léo Dandurand (manager), Cecil Hart (coach), Ed Dufour (trainer).
Scores: April 3, at Chicago — Montreal 2, Chicago 1; April 5, at Chicago — Chicago 2, Montreal 1; April 9, at Montreal — Chicago 3, Montreal 2; April 11, at Montreal — Montreal 4, Chicago 2; April 14, at Montreal — Montreal 2, Chicago 0.

1929-30 — Montreal Canadiens — George Hainsworth, Marty Burke, Sylvio Mantha, Howie Morenz, Bert McCaffrey, Aurel Joliat, Albert Leduc, Pit Lepine, Wildor Larochelle, Nick Wasnie, Gerald Carson, Armand Mondou, Georges Mantha, Gus Rivers, Léo Dandurand (manager), Cecil Hart (coach), Ed Dufour (trainer).
Scores: April 1, at Boston — Montreal 3, Boston 0; April 3, at Montreal — Montreal 4, Boston 3.

1928-29 — Boston Bruins — Tiny Thompson, Eddie Shore, Lionel Hitchman, Perk Galbraith, Eric Pettinger, Frank Fredrickson, Mickey Mackay, Red Green, Dutch Gainor, Harry Oliver, Eddie Rodden, Dit Clapper, Cooney Weiland, Lloyd Klein, Cy Denneny, Bill Carson, George Owen, Myles Lane, Art Ross (manager-coach), Win Green (trainer).
Scores: March 28, at Boston — Boston 2, NY Rangers 0; March 29, at New York — Boston 2, NY Rangers 1.

1927-28 — New York Rangers — Lorne Chabot, Clarence Abel, Leon Bourgault, Ching Johnson, Bill Cook, Bun Cook, Frank Boucher, Bill Boyd, Murray Murdoch, Paul Thompson, Alex Gray, Joe Miller, Patsy Callighen, Lester Patrick (manager-coach), Harry Westerby (trainer).
Scores: April 5, at Montreal — Mtl. Maroons 2, NY Rangers 0; April 7, at Montreal — NY Rangers 2, Mtl. Maroons 1; April 10, at Montreal — Mtl. Maroons 2, NY Rangers 0; April 12, at Montreal — NY Rangers 1, Mtl. Maroons 0; April 14, at Montreal — NY Rangers 2, Mtl. Maroons 1.

1926-27 — Ottawa Senators — Alex Connell, King Clancy, George Boucher, Ed Gorman, Frank Finnigan, Alex Smith, Hec Kilrea, Hooley Smith, Cy Denneny, Frank Nighbor, Jack Adams, Milt Halliday, Dave Gill (manager-coach).
Scores: April 7, at Boston — Ottawa 0, Boston 0; April 9, at Boston — Ottawa 3, Boston 1; April 11, at Ottawa — Boston 1, Ottawa 1; April 13, at Ottawa — Ottawa 3, Boston 1.

1925-26 — Montreal Maroons — Clint Benedict, Reg Noble, Frank Carson, Dunc Munro, Nels Stewart, Harry Broadbent, Babe Siebert, Chuck Dinsmore, Bill Phillips, Hobie Kitchen, Sam Rothschield, Albert Holway, George Horne, Bernie Brophy, Eddie Gerard (manager-coach), Bill O'Brien (trainer).
Scores: March 30, at Montreal — Mtl. Maroons 3, Victoria 0; April 1, at Montreal — Mtl. Maroons 3, Victoria 0; April 3, at Montreal — Victoria 3, Mtl. Maroons 2; April 6, at Montreal — Mtl. Maroons 2, Victoria 0.

The series in the spring of 1926 ended the annual playoffs between the champions of the East and the champions of the West. Since 1926-27 the annual playoffs in the National Hockey League have decided the Stanley Cup champions.

1924-25 — Victoria Cougars — Harry Holmes, Clem Loughlin, Gord Fraser, Frank Fredrickson, Jack Walker, Wilf Hart, Harold Halderson, Frank Foyston, Wally Elmer, Harry Meeking, Jocko Anderson, Lester Patrick (manager-coach).
Scores: March 21, at Victoria — Victoria 5, Montreal 2; March 23, at Vancouver — Victoria 3, Montreal 1; March 27, at Victoria — Montreal 4, Victoria 2; March 30, at Victoria — Victoria 6, Montreal 1.

1923-24 — Montreal Canadiens — Georges Vezina, Sprague Cleghorn, Billy Couture, Howie Morenz, Aurel Joliat, Billy Boucher, Odie Cleghorn, Sylvio Mantha, Bobby Boucher, Billy Bell, Billy Cameron, Joe Malone, Charles Fortier, Leo Dandurand (manager-coach).
Scores: March 18, at Montreal — Montreal 3, Van. Maroons 2; March 20, at Montreal — Montreal 2, Van. Maroons 1. March 22, at Montreal — Montreal 6, Cgy. Tigers 1; March 25, at Ottawa* — Montreal 3, Cgy. Tigers 0.
* Game transferred to Ottawa to benefit from artificial ice surface.

1922-23 — Ottawa Senators — George Boucher, Lionel Hitchman, Frank Nighbor, King Clancy, Harry Helman, Clint Benedict, Jack Darragh, Eddie Gerard, Cy Denneny, Harry Broadbent, Tommy Gorman (manager), Pete Green (coach), F. Dolan (trainer).
Scores: March 16, at Vancouver — Ottawa 1, Van. Maroons 0; March 19, at Vancouver — Van. Maroons 4, Ottawa 1; March 23, at Vancouver — Ottawa 3, Van. Maroons 2; March 26, at Vancouver — Ottawa 5, Van. Maroons 1; March 29, at Vancouver — Ottawa 2, Edm. Eskimos 1; March 31, at Vancouver — Ottawa 1, Edm. Eskimos 0.

Lester Patrick (middle row, fourth from the left) was a Stanley Cup champion as a member of the Montreal Wanderers in 1906 and 1907.
His brother Frank won with the Vancouver Millionaires in 1915. Lester's sons Muzz and Lynn were members of the 1940 New York Rangers.
Grandson Craig Patrick built Pittsburgh's 1991 and 1992 Stanley Cup champions.

1921-22 — Toronto St. Pats — Ted Stackhouse, Corb Denneny, Rod Smylie, Lloyd Andrews, John Ross Roach, Harry Cameron, Billy Stuart, Babe Dye, Ken Randall, Reg Noble, Eddie Gerard (borrowed for one game from Ottawa), Stan Jackson, Nolan Mitchell, Charlie Querrie (manager), George O'Donohue (coach).
Scores: March 17, at Toronto — Van. Millionaires 4, Toronto 3; March 20, at Toronto — Toronto 2, Van. Millionaires 1; March 23, at Toronto — Van. Millionaires 3, Toronto 0; March 25, at Toronto — Toronto 6, Van. Millionaires 0; March 28, at Toronto — Toronto 5, Van. Millionaires 1.

1920-21 — Ottawa Senators — Jack McKell, Jack Darragh, Morley Bruce, George Boucher, Eddie Gerard, Clint Benedict, Sprague Cleghorn, Frank Nighbor, Harry Broadbent, Cy Denneny, Leth Graham, Tommy Gorman (manager), Pete Green (coach), F. Dolan (trainer).
Scores: March 21, at Vancouver — Van. Millionaires 2, Ottawa 1; March 24, at Vancouver — Ottawa 4, Van. Millionaires 3; March 28, at Vancouver — Ottawa 3, Van. Millionaires 2; March 31, at Vancouver — Van. Millionaires 3, Ottawa 2; April 4, at Vancouver — Ottawa 2, Van. Millionaires 1.

1919-20 — Ottawa Senators — Jack McKell, Jack Darragh, Morley Bruce, Horrace Merrill, George Boucher, Eddie Gerard, Clint Benedict, Sprague Cleghorn, Frank Nighbor, Harry Broadbent, Cy Denneny, Price, Tommy Gorman (manager), Pete Green (coach).
Scores: March 22, at Ottawa — Ottawa 3, Seattle 2; March 24, at Ottawa — Ottawa 3, Seattle 0; March 27, at Ottawa — Seattle 3, Ottawa 1; March 30, at Toronto* — Seattle 5, Ottawa 2; April 1, at Toronto* — Ottawa 6, Seattle 1.
* Games transferred to Toronto to benefit from artificial ice surface.

1918-19 — No decision, Series halted by Spanish influenza epidemic, illness of several players and death of Joe Hall of Montreal Canadiens from flu. Five games had been played when the series was halted, each team having won two and tied one. The results are shown:
Scores: March 19, at Seattle — Seattle 7, Montreal 0; March 22, at Seattle — Montreal 4, Seattle 2; March 24, at Seattle — Seattle 7, Montreal 2; March 26, at Seattle — Montreal 0, Seattle 0; March 30, at Seattle — Montreal 4, Seattle 3.

1917-18 — Toronto Arenas — Rusty Crawford, Harry Meeking, Ken Randall, Corb Denneny, Harry Cameron, Jack Adams, Alf Skinner, Harry Mummery, Harry Holmes, Reg Noble, Sammy Hebert, Jack Marks, Jack Coughlin, Charlie Querrie (manager), Dick Carroll (coach), Frank Carroll (trainer).
Scores: March 20, at Toronto — Toronto 5, Van. Millionaires 3; March 23, at Toronto — Van. Millionaires 6, Toronto 4; March 26, at Toronto — Toronto 6, Van. Millionaires 3; March 28, at Toronto — Van. Millionaires 8, Toronto 1; March 30, at Toronto — Toronto 2, Van. Millionaires 1.

1916-17 — Seattle Metropolitans — Harry Holmes, Ed Carpenter, Cully Wilson, Jack Walker, Bernie Morris, Frank Foyston, Roy Rickey, Jim Riley, Bobby Rowe (captain), Peter Muldoon (manager).
Scores: March 17, at Seattle — Montreal 8, Seattle 4; March 20, at Seattle — Seattle 6, Montreal 1; March 23, at Seattle — Seattle 4, Montreal 1; March 25, at Seattle — Seattle 9, Montreal 1.

1915-16 — Montreal Canadiens — Georges Vezina, Bert Corbeau, Jack Laviolette, Newsy Lalonde, Louis Berlinguette, Goldie Prodgers, Howard McNamara, Didier Pitre, Skene Ronan, Amos Arbour, Georges Poulin, Jacques Fournier, George Kennedy (manager).
Scores: March 20, at Montreal — Portland 2, Montreal 0; March 22, at Montreal — Montreal 2, Portland 1; March 25, at Montreal — Montreal 6, Portland 3; March 28, at Montreal — Portland 6, Montreal 5; March 30, at Montreal — Montreal 2, Portland 1.

1914-15 — Vancouver Millionaires — Kenny Mallen, Frank Nighbor, Fred (Cyclone) Taylor, Hughie Lehman, Lloyd Cook, Mickey MacKay, Barney Stanley, Jim Seaborn, Si Griffis (captain), Jean Matz, Frank Patrick (playing manager).
Scores: March 22, at Vancouver — Van. Millionaires 6, Ottawa 2; March 24, at Vancouver — Van. Millionaires 8, Ottawa 3; March 26, at Vancouver — Van. Millionaires 12, Ottawa 3.

1913-14 — Toronto Blueshirts — Con Corbeau, F. Roy McGiffen, Jack Walker, George McNamara, Cully Wilson, Frank Foyston, Harry Cameron, Harry Holmes, Alan M. Davidson (captain), Harriston, Jack Marshall (playing-manager), Frank and Dick Carroll (trainers).
Scores: March 14, at Toronto — Toronto 5, Victoria 2; March 17, at Toronto — Toronto 6, Victoria 5; March 19, at Toronto — Toronto 2, Victoria 1.

1912-13 — Quebec Bulldogs — Joe Malone, Joe Hall, Paddy Moran, Harry Mummery, Tommy Smith, Jack Marks, Russell Crawford, Billy Creighton, Jeff Malone, Rocket Power, M.J. Quinn (manager), D. Beland (trainer).
Scores: March 8, at Quebec — Que. Bulldogs 14, Sydney 3; March 10, at Quebec — Que. Bulldogs 6, Sydney 2.
Victoria challenged Quebec but the Bulldogs refused to put the Stanley Cup in competition so the two teams played an exhibition series with Victoria winning two games to one by scores of 7-5, 3-6, 6-1. It was the first meeting between the Eastern champions and the Western champions. The following year, and until the Western Hockey League disbanded after the 1926 playoffs, the Cup went to the winner of the series between East and West.

1911-12 — Quebec Bulldogs — Goldie Prodgers, Joe Hall, Walter Rooney, Paddy Moran, Jack Marks, Jack McDonald, Eddie Oatman, George Leonard, Joe Malone (captain), C. Nolan (coach), M.J. Quinn (manager), D. Beland (trainer).
Scores: March 11, at Quebec — Que. Bulldogs 9, Moncton 3; March 13, at Quebec — Que. Bulldogs 8, Moncton 0.
Prior to 1912, teams could challenge the Stanley Cup champions for the title, thus there was more than one Championship Series played in most of the seasons between 1894 and 1911.

1910-11 — Ottawa Senators — Hamby Shore, Percy LeSueur, Jack Darragh, Bruce Stuart, Marty Walsh, Bruce Ridpath, Fred Lake, Albert (Dubby) Kerr, Alex Currie, Horace Gaul.
Scores: March 13, at Ottawa — Ottawa 7, Galt 4; March 16, at Ottawa — Ottawa 13, Port Arthur 4.

1909-10 — Montreal Wanderers — Cecil W. Blachford, Ernie (Moose) Johnson, Ernie Russell, Riley Hern, Harry Hyland, Jack Marshall, Frank (Pud) Glass (captain), Jimmy Gardner, R. R. Boon (manager).
Scores: March 12, at Montreal — Mtl. Wanderers 7, Berlin (Kitchener) 3.

1908-09 — Ottawa Senators — Fred Lake, Percy LeSueur, Fred (Cyclone) Taylor, H.L. (Billy) Gilmour, Albert Kerr, Edgar Dey, Marty Walsh, Bruce Stuart (captain).
Scores: Ottawa, as champions of the Eastern Canada Hockey Association took over the Stanley Cup in 1909 and, although a challenge was accepted by the Cup trustees from Winnipeg Shamrocks, games could not be arranged because of the lateness of the season. No other challenges were made in 1909. The following season — 1909-10 — however, the Senators accepted two challenges as defending Cup Champions. The first was against Galt in a two-game, total-goals series, and the second against Edmonton, also a two-game, total-goals series. Results: January 5, at Ottawa —Ottawa 12, Galt 3; January 7, at Ottawa — Ottawa 3, Galt 1. January 18, at Ottawa — Ottawa 8, Edm. Eskimos 4; January 20, at Ottawa — Ottawa 13, Edm. Eskimos 7.

1907-08 — Montreal Wanderers — Riley Hern, Art Ross, Walter Smaill, Frank (Pud) Glass, Bruce Stuart, Ernie Russell, Ernie (Moose) Johnson, Cecil Blachford (captain), Tom Hooper, Larry Gilmour, Ernie Liffiton, R.R. Boon (manager).
Scores: Wanderers accepted four challenges for the Cup: January 9, at Montreal — Mtl. Wanderers 9, Ott. Victorias 3; January 13, at Montreal — Mtl. Wanderers 13, Ott. Victorias 1; March 10, at Montreal — Mtl. Wanderers 11, Wpg. Maple Leafs 5; March 12, at Montreal — Mtl. Wanderers 9, Wpg. Maple Leafs 3; March 14, at Montreal — Mtl. Wanderers 6, Toronto (OPHL) 4. At start of following season, 1908-09, Wanderers were challenged by Edmonton. Results: December 28, at Montreal — Mtl. Wanderers 7, Edm. Eskimos 3; December 30, at Montreal — Edm. Eskimos 7, Mtl. Wanderers 6. Total goals: Mtl. Wanderers 13, Edm. Eskimos 10.

1906-07 — (March) — Montreal Wanderers — W. S. (Billy) Strachan, Riley Hern, Lester Patrick, Hod Stuart, Frank (Pud) Glass, Ernie Russell, Cecil Blachford (captain), Ernie (Moose) Johnson, Rod Kennedy, Jack Marshall, R.R. Boon (manager).
Scores: March 23, at Winnipeg — Mtl. Wanderers 7, Kenora 2; March 25, at Winnipeg — Kenora 6, Mtl. Wanderers 5. Total goals: Mtl. Wanderers 12, Kenora 8.

1906-07 — (January) — Kenora Thistles — Eddie Geroux, Art Ross, Si Griffis, Tom Hooper, Billy McGimsie, Roxy Beaudro, Tom Phillips.
Scores: January 17, at Montreal — Kenora 4, Mtl. Wanderers 2; Jan. 21, at Montreal — Kenora 8, Mtl. Wanderers 6.

1905-06 — (March) — Montreal Wanderers — Henri Menard, Billy Strachan, Rod Kennedy, Lester Patrick, Frank (Pud) Glass, Ernie Russell, Ernie (Moose) Johnson, Cecil Blachford (captain), Josh Arnold, R.R. Boon (manager).
Scores: March 14, at Montreal — Mtl. Wanderers 9, Ottawa 1; March 17, at Ottawa — Ottawa 9, Mtl. Wanderers 3. Total goals: Mtl. Wanderers 12, Ottawa 10. Wanderers accepted a challenge from New Glasgow, N.S., prior to the start of the 1906-07 season. Results: December 27, at Montreal — Mtl. Wanderers 10, New Glasgow 3; December 29, at Montreal — Mtl. Wanderers 7, New Glasgow 2.

1905-06 — (February) — Ottawa Silver Seven — Harvey Pulford (captain), Arthur Moore, Harry Westwick, Frank McGee, Alf Smith (playing coach), Billy Gilmour, Billy Hague, Percy LeSueur, Harry Smith, Tommy Smith, Dion, Ebbs.
Scores: February 27, at Ottawa — Ottawa 16, Queen's University 7; February 28, at Ottawa — Ottawa 12, Queen's University 7; March 6, at Ottawa — Ottawa 6, Smiths Falls 5; March 8, at Ottawa — Ottawa 8, Smiths Falls 2.

1904-05 — Ottawa Silver Seven — Dave Finnie, Harvey Pulford (captain), Arthur Moore, Harry Westwick, Frank McGee, Alf Smith (playing coach), Billy Gilmour, Frank White, Horace Gaul, Hamby Shore, Bones Allen.
Scores: January 13, at Ottawa — Ottawa 9, Dawson City 2; January 16, at Ottawa — Ottawa 23, Dawson City 2; March 7, at Ottawa — Rat Portage 9, Ottawa 3; March 9, at Ottawa — Ottawa 4, Rat Portage 2; March 11, at Ottawa — Ottawa 5, Rat Portage 4.

1903-04 — Ottawa Silver Seven — S.C. (Suddy) Gilmour, Arthur Moore, Frank McGee, J.B. (Bouse) Hutton, H.L. (Billy) Gilmour, Jim McGee, Harry Westwick, E. H. (Harvey) Pulford (captain), Scott, Alf Smith (playing coach).
Scores: December 30, at Ottawa — Ottawa 9, Wpg. Rowing Club 1; January 1, at Ottawa — Wpg. Rowing Club 6, Ottawa 2; January 4, at Ottawa — Ottawa 2, Wpg. Rowing Club 0. February 23, at Ottawa — Ottawa 6, Tor. Marlboros 3; February 25, at Ottawa — Ottawa 11, Tor. Marlboros 2; March 2, at Montreal — Ottawa 5, Mtl. Wanderers 5. Following the tie game, a new two-game series was ordered to be played in Ottawa but the Wanderers refused unless the tie game was replayed in Montreal. When no settlement could be reached, the series was abandoned and Ottawa retained the Cup and accepted a two-game challenge from Brandon. Results: (both games at Ottawa), March 9, Ottawa 6, Brandon 3; March 11, Ottawa 9, Brandon 3.

1902-03 — (March) — Ottawa Silver Seven — S.C. (Suddy) Gilmour, P.T. (Percy) Sims, J.B. (Bouse) Hutton, D.J. (Dave) Gilmour, H.L. (Billy) Gilmour, Harry Westwick, Frank McGee, F.H. Wood, A.A. Fraser, Charles D. Spittal, E.H. (Harvey) Pulford (captain), Arthur Moore, Alf Smith (coach.)
Scores: March 7, at Montreal — Ottawa 1, Mtl. Victorias 1; March 10, at Ottawa — Ottawa 8, Mtl. Victorias 0. Total goals: Ottawa 9, Mtl. Victorias 1. March 12, at Ottawa — Ottawa 6, Rat Portage 2; March 14, at Ottawa — Ottawa 4, Rat Portage 2.

1902-03 — (February) — Montreal AAA — Tom Hodge, R.R. (Dickie) Boon, W.C. (Billy) Nicholson, Tom Phillips, Art Hooper, W.J. (Billy) Bellingham, Charles A. Liffiton, Jack Marshall, Jim Gardner, Cecil Blachford, George Smith.
Scores: January 29, at Montreal — Mtl. AAA 8, Wpg. Victorias 1; January 31, at Montreal — Wpg. Victorias 2, Mtl. AAA 2; February 2, at Montreal — Wpg. Victorias 4, Mtl. AAA 2; February 4, at Montreal — Mtl. AAA 5, Wpg. Victorias 1.

1901-02 — (March) — Montreal AAA — Tom Hodge, R.R. (Dickie) Boon, William C. (Billy) Nicholson, Archie Hooper, W.J. (Billy) Bellingham, Charles A. Liffiton, Jack Marshall, Roland Elliott, Jim Gardner.
Scores: March 13, at Winnipeg — Wpg. Victorias 1, Mtl. AAA 0; March 15, at Winnipeg — Mtl. AAA 5, Wpg. Victorias 0; March 17, at Winnipeg — Mtl. AAA 2, Wpg. Victorias 1.

1901-02 — (January) — Winnipeg Victorias — Burke Wood, A.B. (Tony) Gingras, Charles W. Johnstone, R.M. (Rod) Flett, Magnus L. Flett, Dan Bain (captain), Fred Scanlon, F. Cadham, G. Brown.
Scores: January 21, at Winnipeg — Wpg. Victorias 5, Tor Wellingtons 3; January 23, at Winnipeg — Wpg. Victorias 5, Tor. Wellingtons 3.

1900-01 — Winnipeg Victorias — Burke Wood, Jack Marshall, A.B. (Tony) Gingras, Charles W. Johnstone, R.M. (Rod) Flett, Magnus L. Flett, Dan Bain (captain), G. Brown.
Scores: January 29, at Montreal — Wpg. Victorias 4, Mtl. Shamrocks 3; January 31, at Montreal — Wpg. Victorias 2, Mtl. Shamrocks 1.

1899-1900 — Montreal Shamrocks — Joe McKenna, Frank Tansey, Frank Wall, Art Farrell, Fred Scanlon, Harry Trihey (captain), Jack Brannen.
Scores: February 12, at Montreal — Mtl. Shamrocks 4, Wpg. Victorias 3; February 14, at Montreal — Wpg. Victorias 3, Mtl. Shamrocks 2; February 16, at Montreal — Mtl Shamrocks 5, Wpg. Victorias 4; March 5, at Montreal — Mtl. Shamrocks 10, Halifax 2; March 7, at Montreal — Mtl. Shamrocks 11, Halifax 0.

1898-99 — (March) — Montreal Shamrocks — Jim McKenna, Frank Tansey, Frank Wall, Harry Trihey (captain), Art Farrell, Fred Scanlon, Jack Brannen, John Dobby, Charles Hoerner.
Scores: March 14, at Montreal — Mtl. Shamrocks 6, Queen's University 2.

1898-99 — (February) — Montreal Victorias — Gordon Lewis, Mike Grant, Graham Drinkwater, Cam Davidson, Bob McDougall, Ernie McLea, Frank Richardson, Jack Ewing, Russell Bowie, Douglas Acer, Fred McRobie.
Scores: February 15, at Montreal — Mtl. Victorias 2, Wpg. Victorias 1; February 18, at Montreal — Mtl. Victorias 3, Wpg. Victorias 2.

1897-98 — Montreal Victorias — Gordon Lewis, Hartland McDougall, Mike Grant, Graham Drinkwater, Cam Davidson, Bob McDougall, Ernie McLea, Frank Richardson (captain), Jack Ewing. The Victorias as champions of the Amateur Hockey Association, retained the Cup and were not called upon to defend it.

1896-97 — Montreal Victorias — Gordon Lewis, Harold Henderson, Mike Grant (captain), Cam Davidson, Graham Drinkwater, Robert McDougall, Ernie McLea, Shirley Davidson, Hartland McDougall, Jack Ewing, Percy Molson, David Gillilan, McLellan.
Scores: December 27, at Montreal — Mtl. Victorias 15, Ott. Capitals 2.

1895-96 — (December) — Montreal Victorias — Harold Henderson, Mike Grant (captain), Robert McDougall, Graham Drinkwater, Shirley Davidson, Ernie McLea, Robert Jones, Cam Davidson, David Gillilan, Stanley Willett.
Scores: December 30, at Winnipeg — Mtl. Victorias 6, Wpg. Victorias 5.

1895-96 — (February) — Winnipeg Victorias — G.H. Merritt, Rod Flett, Fred Higginbotham, Jack Armitage (captain), C.J. (Tote) Campbell, Dan Bain, Charles Johnstone, H. Howard.
Scores: February 14, at Montreal — Wpg. Victorias 2, Mtl. Victorias 0.

1894-95 — Montreal Victorias — Robert Jones, Harold Henderson, Mike Grant (captain), Shirley Davidson, Bob McDougall, Norman Rankin, Graham Drinkwater, Roland Elliot, William Pullan, Hartland McDougall, Jim Fenwick, A. McDougall. Montreal Victorias, as champions of the Amateur Hockey Association, were prepared to defend the Stanley Cup. However, the Stanley Cup trustees had already accepted a challenge match between the 1894 champion Montreal AAA and Queen's University. It was declared that if Montreal AAA defeated Queen's University, Montreal Victorias would be declared Stanley Cup champions. If Queen's University won, the Cup would go to the university club. In a game played March 9, 1895, Montreal AAA defeated Queen's University 5-1. As a result, Montreal Victorias were awarded the Stanley Cup.

1893-94 — Montreal AAA — Herbert Collins, Allan Cameron, George James, Billy Barlow, Clare Mussen, Archie Hodgson, Haviland Routh, Alex Irving, James Stewart, A.C. (Toad) Wand, A. Kingan.
Scores: March 17, at Mtl. Victorias — Mtl. AAA 3, Mtl. Victorias 2; March 22, at Montreal — Mtl. AAA 3, Ott. Capitals 1.

1892-93 — Montreal AAA — Tom Paton, James Stewart, Allan Cameron, Haviland Routh, Archie Hodgson, Billy Barlow, A.B. Kingan, G.S. Lowe.
In accordance with the terms governing the presentation of the Stanley Cup, it was awarded for the first time to the Montreal AAA as champions of the Amateur Hockey Association in 1893. Once Montreal AAA had been declared holders of the Stanley Cup, any Canadian hockey team could challenge for the trophy.

All-Time NHL Playoff Formats

1917-18 — The regular-season was split into two halves. The winners of both halves faced each other in a two-game, total-goals series for the NHL championship and the right to meet the PCHA champion in the best-of-five Stanley Cup Finals.

1918-19 — Same as 1917-18, except that the Stanley Cup Finals was extended to a best-of-seven series.

1919-20 — Same as 1917-1918, except that Ottawa won both halves of the split regular-season schedule to earn an automatic berth into the best-of-five Stanley Cup Finals against the PCHA champions.

1921-22 — The top two teams at the conclusion of the regular-season faced each other in a two-game, total-goals series for the NHL championship. The NHL champion then moved on to play the winner of the PCHA-WCHL playoff series in the best-of-five Stanley Cup Finals.

1922-23 — The top two teams at the conclusion of the regular-season faced each other in a two-game, total-goals series for the NHL championship. The NHL champion then moved on to play the PCHA champion in the best-of-three Stanley Cup Semi-Finals, and the winner of the Semi-Finals played the WCHL champion, which had been given a bye, in the best-of-three Stanley Cup Finals.

1923-24 — The top two teams at the conclusion of the regular-season faced each other in a two-game, total-goals series for the NHL championship. The NHL champion then moved to play the loser of the PCHA-WCHL playoff (the winner of the PCHA-WCHL playoff earned a bye into the Stanley Cup Finals) in the best-of-three Stanley Cup Semi-Finals. The winner of this series met the PCHA-WCHL playoff winner in the best-of-three Stanley Cup Finals.

1924-25 — The first place team (Hamilton) at the conclusion of the regular-season was supposed to play the winner of a two-game, total goals series between the second (Toronto) and third (Montreal) place clubs. However, Hamilton refused to abide by this new format, demanding greater compensation than offered by the League. Thus, Toronto and Montreal played their two-game, total-goals series, and the winner (Montreal) earned the NHL title and then played the WCHL champion (Victoria) in the best-of-five Stanley Cup Finals.

1925-26 — The format which was intended for 1924-25 went into effect. The winner of the two-game, total-goals series between the second and third place teams squared off against the first place team in the two-game, total-goals NHL championship series. The NHL champion then moved on to play the WHL champion in the best-of-five Stanley Cup Finals.

After the 1925-26 season, the NHL was the only major professional hockey league still in existence and consequently took over sole control of the Stanley Cup competition.

1926-27 — The 10-team league was divided into two divisions — Canadian and American — of five teams apiece. In each division, the winner of the two-game, total-goals series between the second and third place teams faced the first place team in a two-game, total-goals series for the division title. The two division title winners then met in the best-of-five Stanley Cup Finals.

1928-29 — Both first place teams in the two divisions played each other in a best-of-five series. Both second place teams in the two divisions played each other in a two-game, total-goals series as did the two third place teams. The winners of these latter two series then played each other in a best-of-three series for the right to meet the winner of the series between the two first place clubs. This Stanley Cup Final was a best-of-three.

> Series A: First in Canadian Division versus first in American (best-of-five)
> Series B: Second in Canadian Division versus second in American (two-game, total-goals)
> Series C: Third in Canadian Division versus third in American (two-game, total-goals)
> Series D: Winner of Series B versus winner of Series C (best-of-three)
> Series E: Winner of Series A versus winner of Series D (best of three) for Stanley Cup

1931-32 — Same as 1928-29, except that Series D was changed to a two-game, total-goals format and Series E was changed to best of five.

1936-37 — Same as 1931-32, except that Series B, C, and D were each best-of-three.

1938-39 — With the NHL reduced to seven teams, the two-division system was replaced by one seven-team league. Based on final regular-season standings, the following playoff format was adopted:

> Series A: First versus Second (best-of-seven)
> Series B: Third versus Fourth (best-of-three)
> Series C: Fifth versus Sixth (best-of-three)
> Series D: Winner of Series B versus winner of Series C (best-of-three)
> Series E: Winner of Series A versus winner of Series D (best-of-seven)

1942-43 — With the NHL reduced to six teams (the "original six"), only the top four finishers qualified for playoff action. The best-of-seven Semi-Finals pitted Team #1 vs Team #3 and Team #2 vs Team #4. The winners of each Semi-Final series met in the best-of-seven Stanley Cup Finals.

1967-68 — When it doubled in size from 6 to 12 teams, the NHL once again was divided into two divisions — East and West — of six teams apiece. The top four clubs in each division qualified for the playoffs (all series were best-of-seven):

> Series A; Team #1 (East) vs Team #3 (East)
> Series B: Team #2 (East) vs Team #4 (East)
> Series C: Team #1 (West) vs Team #3 (West)
> Series D: Team #2 (West) vs Team #4 (West)
> Series E: Winner of Series A vs winner of Series B
> Series F: Winner of Series C vs winner of Series D
> Series G: Winner of Series E vs Winner of Series F

1970-71 — Same as 1967-68 except that Series E matched the winners of Series A and D; and Series F matched the winners of Series B and C.

1971-72 — Same as 1970-71, except that Series A and C matched Team #1 vs Team #4, and Series B and D matched Team #2 vs Team #3.

1974-75 — With the League now expanded to 18 teams in four divisions, a completely new playoff format was introduced. First, the #2 and #3 teams in each of the four divisions were pooled together in the Preliminary round. These eight (#2 and #3) clubs were ranked #1 to #8 based on regular-season record:

> Series A: Team #1 vs Team #8 (best-of-three)
> Series B: Team #2 vs Team #7 (best-of-three)
> Series C: Team #3 vs Team #6 (best-of-three)
> Series D: Team #4 vs Team #5 (best-of-three)
> The winners of this Preliminary round then pooled together with the four division winners, which had received byes into this Quarter-Final round. These eight teams were again ranked #1 to #8 based on regular-season record:
> Series E: Team #1 vs Team #8 (best-of-seven)
> Series F: Team #2 vs Team #7 (best-of-seven)
> Series G: Team #3 vs Team #6 (best-of-seven)
> Series H: Team #4 vs Team #5 (best-of-seven)
> The four Quarter-Finals winners, which moved on to the Semi-Finals, were then ranked #1 to #4 based on regular season record:
> Series I: Team #1 vs Team #4 (best-of-seven)
> Series J: Team #2 vs Team #3 (best-of-seven)
> Series K: Winner of Series I vs winner of Series J (best-of-seven)

1977-78 — Same as 1974-75, except that the Preliminary round consisted of the #2 teams in the four divisions and the next four teams based on regular-season record (not their standings within their divisions).

1979-80 — With the addition of four WHA franchises, the League expanded its playoff structure to include 16 of its 21 teams. The four first place teams in the four divisions automatically earned playoff berths. Among the 17 other clubs, the top 12, according to regular-season record, also earned berths. All 16 teams were then pooled together and ranked #1 to #16 based on regular-season record:

> Series A: Team #1 vs Team #16 (best-of-five)
> Series B: Team #2 vs Team #15 (best-of-five)
> Series C: Team #3 vs Team #14 (best-of-five)
> Series D: Team #4 vs Team #13 (best-of-five)
> Series E: Team #5 vs Team #12 (best-of-five)
> Series F: Team #6 vs Team #11 (best-of-five)
> Series G: Team #7 vs Team #10 (best-of-five)
> Series H: Team #8 vs Team # 9 (best-of-five)
> The eight Preliminary round winners, ranked #1 to #8 based on regular-season record, moved on to the Quarter-Finals:
> Series I: Team #1 vs Team #8 (best-of-seven)
> Series J: Team #2 vs Team #7 (best-of-seven)
> Series K: Team #3 vs Team #6 (best-of-seven)
> Series L: Team #4 vs Team #5 (best-of-seven)
> The eight Quarter-Finals winners, ranked #1 to #4 based on regular-season record, moved on to the semi-finals:
> Series M: Team #1 vs Team #4 (best-of-seven)
> Series N: Team #2 vs Team #3 (best-of-seven)
> Series O: Winner of Series M vs winner of Series N (best-of-seven)

1981-82 — The first four teams in each division earned playoff berths. In each division, the first-place team opposed the fourth-place team and the second-place team opposed the third-place team in a best-of-five Division Semi-Final series (DSF). In each division, the two winners of the DSF met in a best-of-seven Division Final series (DF). The two winners in each conference met in a best-of-seven Conference Final series (CF). In the Prince of Wales Conference, the Adams Division winner opposed the Patrick Division winner; in the Clarence Campbell Conference, the Smythe Division winner opposed the Norris Division winner. The two CF winners met in a best-of-seven Stanley Cup Final (F) series.

1986-87 — Division Semi-Final series changed from best-of-five to best-of-seven.

1993-94 — The NHL's playoff draw conference-based rather than division-based. At the conclusion of the regular season, the top eight teams in each of the Eastern and Western Conferences qualify for the playoffs. The teams that finish in first place in each of the League's divisions are seeded first and second in each conference's playoff draw and are assured of home ice advantage in the first two playoff rounds. The remaining teams are seeded based on their regular-season point totals. In each conference, the team seeded #1 plays #8; #2 vs. #7; #3 vs. #6; and #4 vs. #5. All series are best-of-seven with home ice rotating on a 2-2-1-1-1 basis, with the exception of matchups between Central and Pacific Division teams. These matchups will be played on a 2-3-2 basis to reduce travel. In a 2-3-2 series, the team with the most points will have its choice to start the series at home or on the road. The Eastern Conference champion will face the Western Conference champion in the Stanley Cup Final.

1994-95 — Same as 1993-94, except that in first, second or third-round playoff series involving Central and Pacific Division teams, the team with the better record has the choice of using either a 2-3-2 or a 2-2-1-1-1 format. When a 2-3-2 format is selected, the higher-ranked team also has the choice of playing games 1, 2, 6 and 7 at home or playing games 3, 4 and 5 at home. The format for the Stanley Cup Final remains 2-2-1-1-1.

1998-99 — The NHL's clubs are re-aligned into two conferences each consisting of three divisions. The number of teams qualifying for the 1999 Stanley Cup Playoffs remains unchanged at 16.

First-round playoff berths will be awarded to the first-place team in each division as well as to the next five best teams based on regular-season point totals in each conference. The three division winners in each conference will be seeded first through third for the playoffs and the next five best teams, in order of points, will be seeded fourth through eighth. In each conference, the team seeded #1 will play #8; #2 vs. #7; #3 vs. #6; and #4 vs. #5 in the quarterfinal round. Home-ice in the Conference Quarterfinals is granted to those teams seeded first through fourth in each conference.

In the Conference Semifinals and Conference Finals, teams will be re-seeded according to the same criteria as the Conference Quarterfinals. Higher seeded teams will have home ice advantage.

The 1994-95 New Jersey Devils were real road warriors, winning a record 10 games away from home en route to the Stanley Cup. After opening the Finals with two wins in Detroit, the Devils returned home to claim the franchise's first championship on June 24, 1995.

Team Records

1918-1999

GAMES PLAYED

MOST GAMES PLAYED BY ALL TEAMS, ONE PLAYOFF YEAR:
92 — 1991. There were 51 DSF, 24 DF, 11 CF and 6 F games.
90 — 1994. There were 48 CQF, 23 CSF, 12 CF and 7 F games.
87 — 1987. There were 44 DSF, 25 DF, 11 CF and 7 F games.

MOST GAMES PLAYED, ONE TEAM, ONE PLAYOFF YEAR:
26 — Philadelphia Flyers, 1987. Won DSF 4-2 against NY Rangers, DF 4-3 against NY Islanders, CF 4-2 against Montreal, and lost F 4-3 against Edmonton.
24 — Pittsburgh Penguins,1991. Won DSF 4-3 against New Jersey, DF 4-1 against Washington, CF 4-2 against Boston, and F 4-2 against Minnesota.
— Los Angeles Kings, 1993. Won DSF 4-2 against Calgary, DF 4-2 against Vancouver, CF 4-3 against Toronto, and lost F 4-1 against Montreal.
— Vancouver Canucks, 1994. Won CQF 4-3 against Calgary, CSF 4-1 against Dallas, CF 4-1 against Toronto, and lost F 4-3 against NY Rangers.

PLAYOFF APPEARANCES

MOST STANLEY CUP CHAMPIONSHIPS:
23 — Montreal Canadiens 1924-30-31-44-46-53-56-57-58-59-60-65-66-68-69-71-73-76-77-78-79-86-93
13 — Toronto Maple Leafs 1918-22-32-42-45-47-48-49-51-62-63-64-67
9 — Detroit Red Wings 1936-37-43-50-52-54-55-97-98

MOST CONSECUTIVE STANLEY CUP CHAMPIONSHIPS:
5 — Montreal Canadiens (1956-57-58-59-60)
4 — Montreal Canadiens (1976-77-78-79)
— NY Islanders (1980-81-82-83)

MOST FINAL SERIES APPEARANCES:
32 — Montreal Canadiens in 82-year history.
21 — Toronto Maple Leafs in 82-year history.
— Detroit Red Wings in 72-year history.

MOST CONSECUTIVE FINAL SERIES APPEARANCES:
10 — Montreal Canadiens, (1951-60, inclusive)
5 — Montreal Canadiens, (1965-69, inclusive)
— NY Islanders, (1980-84, inclusive)

MOST YEARS IN PLAYOFFS:
72 — Montreal Canadiens in 82-year history.
59 — Toronto Maple Leafs in 82-year history.
— Boston Bruins in 75-year history.

MOST CONSECUTIVE PLAYOFF APPEARANCES:
29 — Boston Bruins (1968-96, inclusive)
28 — Chicago Blackhawks (1970-97, inclusive)
24 — Montreal Canadiens (1971-94, inclusive)
21 — Montreal Canadiens (1949-69, inclusive)
20 — Detroit Red Wings (1939-58, inclusive)
— St. Louis Blues (1980-99, inclusive)

TEAM WINS

MOST HOME WINS, ONE TEAM, ONE PLAYOFF YEAR:
11 — Edmonton Oilers, 1988 in 11 home-ice games.
10 — Edmonton Oilers, 1985 in 10 home-ice games.
— Montreal Canadiens, 1986 in 11 home-ice games.
— Montreal Canadiens, 1993 in 11 home-ice games.

MOST ROAD WINS, ONE TEAM, ONE PLAYOFF YEAR:
10 — New Jersey Devils, 1995. Won three at Boston in CQF; two at Pittsburgh in CSF; three at Philadelphia in CF; and two at Detroit in F series.
8 — NY Islanders, 1980. Won two at Los Angeles in PR; three at Boston in QF; two at Buffalo in SF; and one at Philadelphia in F series.
— Philadelphia Flyers, 1987. Won two at NY Rangers in DSF; two at NY Islanders in DF; three at Montreal in CF; and one at Edmonton in F series.
— Edmonton Oilers, 1990. Won one at Winnipeg in DSF; two at Los Angeles in DF; two at Chicago in CF and three at Boston in F series.
— Pittsburgh Penguins, 1992. Won two at Washington in DSF; two at NY Rangers in DF; two at Boston in CF; and two at Chicago in F series.
— Vancouver Canucks, 1994. Won three at Calgary in CQF; two at Dallas in CSF; one at Toronto in CF; and two at NY Rangers in F series.
— Colorado Avalanche, 1996. Won two at Vancouver in CQF; two at Chicago in CSF; two at Detroit in CF; and two at Florida in F series.
— Detroit Red Wings, 1998. Won two at Phoenix in CQF; three at St. Louis in CSF; one at Dallas in CF; and two at Washington in F series.
— Colorado Avalanche, 1999. Won three at San Jose in CQF; won three at Detroit in CSF; and won two at Dallas in CF.

MOST ROAD WINS, ALL TEAMS, ONE PLAYOFF YEAR:
46 — 1987. Of 87 games played, road teams won 46 (22 DSF, 14 DF, 8 CF and 2 in Stanley Cup final).

MOST OVERTIME WINS, ONE TEAM, ONE PLAYOFF YEAR:
10 — Montreal Canadiens, 1993. Two against Quebec in DSF; three against Buffalo in DF; two against NY Islanders in CF; and three against Los Angeles in F. Montreal played 20 games.
6 — NY Islanders, 1980. One against Los Angeles in PR; two against Boston in QF; one against Buffalo in SF; and two against Philadelphia in F. Islanders played 21 games.
— Vancouver Canucks, 1994. Three against Calgary in CQF; one against Dallas in CSF; one against Toronto in CF; and one against NY Rangers in F. Vancouver played 24 games.

MOST OVERTIME WINS AT HOME, ONE TEAM, ONE PLAYOFF YEAR:
4 — St. Louis Blues, 1968. Won one vs. Philadelphia in QF and three vs. Minnesota in SF.
— Montreal Canadiens, 1993. Won one vs. Quebec in DSF, one vs. Buffalo in DF, one vs. NY Islanders in CF and one vs. Los Angeles in F series.

MOST OVERTIME WINS ON THE ROAD, ONE TEAM, ONE PLAYOFF YEAR:
6 — Montreal Canadiens, 1993. Won one vs. Quebec in DSF, two vs. Buffalo in DF, one vs. NY Islanders in CF and two vs. Los Angeles in F series.

TEAM LOSSES

MOST LOSSES, ONE TEAM, ONE PLAYOFF YEAR:
 11 — Philadelphia Flyers, 1987. Lost two vs. NY Rangers in DSF; three vs. NY Islanders in DF; two vs. Montreal in CF; and four vs. Edmonton in F series.

MOST HOME LOSSES, ONE TEAM, ONE PLAYOFF YEAR:
 6 — Philadelphia Flyers, 1987. Lost one vs. NY Rangers in DSF; two vs. NY Islanders in DF; two vs. Montreal in CF; and one vs. Edmonton in F series.
   — Washington Capitals, 1998. Lost two vs. Boston in CQF; two vs. Buffalo in CF; and two vs. Detroit in F series.
   — Colorado Avalanche, 1999. Lost two vs. San Jose in CQF; two in Detroit in CSF; and two vs. Dallas in CF series.

MOST ROAD LOSSES, ONE TEAM, ONE PLAYOFF YEAR:
 6 — St. Louis Blues, 1968. Lost two at Philadelphia in QF; two at Minnesota in SF; and two at Montreal in F series.
   — St. Louis Blues, 1970. Lost two at Minnesota in QF; two at Pittsburgh in SF; and two at Boston in F series.
   — NY Islanders, 1984. Lost one at NY Rangers in DSF; two at Montreal in CF; and three at Edmonton in F series.
   — Los Angeles Kings, 1993. Lost one at Calgary in DSF; one at Vancouver in DF; two at Toronto in CF; and two at Montreal in F series.

MOST OVERTIME LOSSES, ONE TEAM, ONE PLAYOFF YEAR:
 4 — Montreal Canadiens, 1951. Lost four vs. Toronto in F series.
   — St. Louis Blues, 1968. Lost one vs. Philadelphia in QF; one vs. Minnesota in SF; and two vs. Montreal in F series.
   — Los Angeles Kings, 1991. Lost one vs. Vancouver in DSF; and three vs. Edmonton in DF series.
   — Los Angeles Kings, 1993. Lost one vs. Toronto in CF; and three vs. Montreal in F series.
   — Philadelphia Flyers, 1996. Lost two vs. Tampa Bay in CQF; and two vs. Florida in CSF series.

MOST OVERTIME LOSSES AT HOME, ONE TEAM, ONE PLAYOFF YEAR:
 2 — Two overtime losses at home by one team in one playoff year has occurred 39 times. The Pittsburgh Penguins are the most recent team to equal this mark when they lost twice in overtime at home to the Toronto Maple Leafs in the 1999 Stanley Cup CSF series.

MOST OVERTIME LOSSES ON THE ROAD, ONE TEAM, ONE PLAYOFF YEAR:
 3 — Los Angeles Kings, 1991. Lost one at Vancouver in DSF; and two at Edmonton in DF series.
   — St. Louis Blues, 1996. Lost two at Toronto in CQF; and one at Detroit in CSF series.
   — Dallas Stars, 1999. Lost two at St. Louis in CSF; and one at Colorado in CF series.

PLAYOFF WINNING STREAKS

LONGEST PLAYOFF WINNING STREAK:
 14 — Pittsburgh Penguins. Streak started May 9, 1992, at Pittsburgh with a 5-4 win in fourth game of DF series against NY Rangers, won by Pittsburgh 4-2. Continued with a four-game win over Boston in 1992 CF and a four-game sweep of Chicago in 1992 F. Pittsburgh then won the first three games of 1993 DSF versus New Jersey. New Jersey ended the streak April 25, 1993, at New Jersey with a 4-1 win.
 12 — Edmonton Oilers. Streak started May 15, 1984, at Edmonton with a 7-2 win in third game of F series against NY Islanders won by Edmonton 4-1. Continued with a three-game sweep of Winnipeg in 1985 DF, Edmonton then won the first two games of 1985 CF versus Chicago. Chicago ended the streak May 9, 1985, at Chicago with a 5-2 win.

MOST CONSECUTIVE WINS, ONE TEAM, ONE PLAYOFF YEAR:
 11 — Chicago Blackhawks in 1992. Chicago won last three games of DSF against St. Louis to win series 4-2 and then defeated Detroit 4-0 in DF and Edmonton 4-0 in CF.
   — Pittsburgh Penguins in 1992. Pittsburgh won last three games of DF against NY Rangers to win series 4-2 and then defeated Boston 4-0 in CF and Chicago 4-0 in F.
   — Montreal Canadiens in 1993. Montreal won last four games of DSF against Quebec to win series 4-2, defeated Buffalo 4-0 in DF and won first three games of CF against NY Islanders.

PLAYOFF LOSING STREAKS

LONGEST PLAYOFF LOSING STREAK:
 16 Games — Chicago Blackhawks. Streak started in 1975 QF against Buffalo when Chicago lost last two games. Then Chicago lost four games to Montreal in 1976 QF; two games to NY Islanders in 1977 PR; four games to Boston in 1978 QF and four games to NY Islanders in 1979 QF. Streak ended on April 8, 1980 when Chicago defeated St. Louis 3-2 in the opening game of their 1980 PR series.
 12 Games — Toronto Maple Leafs. Streak started on April 16, 1979 as Toronto lost four straight games in a QF series against Montreal. Continued with three-game PR defeats versus Philadelphia and NY Islanders in 1980 and 1981 respectively. Toronto failed to qualify for the 1982 playoffs and lost the first two games of a 1983 DSF against Minnesota. Toronto ended the streak with a 6-3 win against the North Stars on April 9, 1983.

After winning their first Stanley Cup title in 1991, Mario Lemieux and the Pittsburgh Penguins went on a record tear to ensure back-to-back championships. The Penguins won 11 games in a row to wrap up the 1992 playoffs, then stretched their post-season winning streak to 14 with three wins in 1993.

MOST GOALS IN A SERIES, ONE TEAM

MOST GOALS, ONE TEAM, ONE PLAYOFF SERIES:
44 — **Edmonton Oilers** in 1985 CF. Edmonton won best-of-seven series 4-2, outscoring Chicago 44-25.
35 — Edmonton Oilers in 1983 DF. Edmonton won best-of-seven series 4-1, outscoring Calgary 35-13.
— Calgary Flames in 1995 CQF. Calgary lost best-of-seven series 3-4, outscoring San Jose 35-26.

MOST GOALS, ONE TEAM, TWO-GAME SERIES:
11 — **Buffalo Sabres** in 1977 PR. Buffalo won best-of-three series 2-0, outscoring Minnesota 11-3.
— **Toronto Maple Leafs** in 1978 PR. Toronto won best-of-three series 2-0, outscoring Los Angeles 11-3.
10 — Boston Bruins in 1927 QF. Boston won two-game total goal series 10-5.

MOST GOALS, ONE TEAM, THREE-GAME SERIES:
23 — **Chicago Blackhawks** in 1985 DSF. Chicago won best-of-five series 3-0, outscoring Detroit 23-8.
20 — Minnesota North Stars in 1981 PR. Minnesota won best-of-five series 3-0, outscoring Boston 20-13.
— NY Islanders in 1981 PR. New York won best-of-five series 3-0, outscoring Toronto 20-4.

MOST GOALS, ONE TEAM, FOUR-GAME SERIES:
28 — **Boston Bruins** in 1972 SF. Boston won best-of-seven series 4-0, outscoring St. Louis 28-8.

MOST GOALS, ONE TEAM, FIVE-GAME SERIES:
35 — **Edmonton Oilers** in 1983 DF. Edmonton won best-of-seven series 4-1, outscoring Calgary 35-13.
32 — Edmonton Oilers in 1987 DSF. Edmonton won best-of-seven series 4-1, outscoring Los Angeles 32-20.
28 — NY Rangers in 1979 QF. NY Rangers won best-of-seven series 4-1, outscoring Philadelphia 28-8.
27 — Philadelphia Flyers in 1980 SF. Philadelphia won best-of-seven series 4-1, outscoring Minnesota 27-14.
— Los Angeles Kings, in 1982 DSF. Los Angeles won best-of-five series 3-2, outscoring Edmonton 27-23.

MOST GOALS, ONE TEAM, SIX-GAME SERIES:
44 — **Edmonton Oilers** in 1985 CF. Edmonton won best-of-seven series 4-2, outscoring Chicago 44-25.
33 — Chicago Blackhawks in 1985 DF. Chicago won best-of-seven series 4-2, outscoring Minnesota 33-29.
— Montreal Canadiens in 1973 F. Montreal won best-of-seven series 4-2, outscoring Chicago 33-23.
— Los Angeles Kings in 1993 DSF. Los Angeles won best-of-seven series 4-2, outscoring Calgary 33-28.

MOST GOALS, ONE TEAM, SEVEN-GAME SERIES:
35 — **Calgary Flames** in 1995 CQF. Calgary lost best-of-seven series 3-4, outscoring San Jose 35-26.
33 — Philadelphia Flyers in 1976 QF. Philadelphia won best-of-seven series 4-3, outscoring Toronto 33-23.
— Boston Bruins in 1983 DF. Boston won best-of-seven series 4-3, outscoring Buffalo 33-23.
— Edmonton Oilers in 1984 DF. Edmonton won best-of-seven series 4-3, outscoring Calgary 33-27.

FEWEST GOALS IN A SERIES, ONE TEAM

FEWEST GOALS, ONE TEAM, TWO-GAME SERIES:
0 — **NY Americans** in 1929 SF. Lost two-game total-goal series 1-0 against NY Rangers.
— **Chicago Blackhawks** in 1935 SF. Lost two-game total-goal series 1-0 against Mtl. Maroons.
— **Mtl. Maroons** in 1937 SF. Lost best-of-three series 2-0 to NY Rangers while being outscored 5-0.
— **NY Americans** in 1939 QF. Lost best-of-three series 2-0 to Toronto while being outscored 6-0.

FEWEST GOALS, ONE TEAM, THREE-GAME SERIES:
1 — **Mtl. Maroons** in 1936 SF. Lost best-of-five series 3-0 to Detroit and were outscored 6-1.

FEWEST GOALS, ONE TEAM, FOUR-GAME SERIES:
2 — **Boston Bruins** in 1935 SF. Toronto won best-of-five series 3-1, outscoring Boston 7-2.
— **Montreal Canadiens** in 1952 F. Detroit won best-of-seven series 4-0, outscoring Montreal 11-2.

FEWEST GOALS, ONE TEAM, FIVE-GAME SERIES:
5 — **NY Rangers** in 1928 F. NY Rangers won best-of-five series 3-2, while being outscored by Mtl. Maroons 6-5.
— **Boston Bruins** in 1995 CQF. New Jersey won best-of-seven series 4-1, while outscoring Boston 14-5.
— **New Jersey Devils** in 1997 CSF. NY Rangers won best-of-seven series 4-1, while outscoring New Jersey 10-5.

FEWEST GOALS, ONE TEAM, SIX-GAME SERIES:
5 — **Boston Bruins** in 1951 SF. Toronto won best-of-seven series 4-1 with 1 tie, outscoring Boston 17-5.

FEWEST GOALS, ONE TEAM, SEVEN-GAME SERIES:
9 — **Toronto Maple Leafs**, in 1945 F. Toronto won best-of- seven series 4-3; teams tied in scoring 9-9.
— **Detroit Red Wings**, in 1945 F. Toronto won best-of-seven series 4-3; teams tied in scoring 9-9.

Having beaten the Blues with a Stanley Cup sweep in 1970, Bobby Orr and the big, bad Bruins ran roughshod over St. Louis again in 1972. Boston scored 28 goals during a sweep of their semifinal series, the most goals ever scored in a four-game series.

MOST GOALS IN A SERIES, BOTH TEAMS

MOST GOALS, BOTH TEAMS, ONE PLAYOFF SERIES:
69 — **Edmonton Oilers, Chicago Blackhawks** in 1985 CF. Edmonton won best-of-seven series 4-2, outscoring Chicago 44-25.
62 — Chicago Blackhawks, Minnesota North Stars in 1985 DF. Chicago won best-of-seven series 4-2, outscoring Minnesota 33-29.
61 — Los Angeles Kings, Calgary Flames in 1993 DSF. Los Angeles won best-of-seven series 4-2, outscoring Calgary 33-28.
— San Jose Sharks, Calgary Flames in 1995 CQF. San Jose won best-of-seven series 4-3, while being outscored 35-26.

MOST GOALS, BOTH TEAMS, TWO-GAME SERIES:
17 — **Toronto St. Patricks, Montreal Canadiens** in 1918 NHL F. Toronto won two-game total goal series 10-7.
15 — Boston Bruins, Chicago Blackhawks in 1927 QF. Boston won two-game total goal series 10-5.
— Pittsburgh Penguins, St. Louis Blues in 1975 PR. Pittsburgh won best-of-three series 2-0, outscoring St. Louis 9-6.

MOST GOALS, BOTH TEAMS, THREE-GAME SERIES:
33 — **Minnesota North Stars, Boston Bruins** in 1981 PR. Minnesota won best-of-five series 3-0, outscoring Boston 20-13.
31 — Chicago Blackhawks, Detroit Red Wings in 1985 DSF. Chicago won best-of-five series 3-0, outscoring Detroit 23-8.
28 — Toronto Maple Leafs, NY Rangers in 1932 F. Toronto won best-of-five series 3-0, outscoring New York 18-10.

MOST GOALS, BOTH TEAMS, FOUR-GAME SERIES:
36 — **Boston Bruins, St. Louis Blues** in 1972 SF. Boston won best-of-seven series 4-0, outscoring St. Louis 28-8.
— **Minnesota North Stars, Toronto Maple Leafs** in 1983 DSF. Minnesota won best-of-five series 3-1; teams tied in scoring 18-18.
— **Edmonton Oilers, Chicago Blackhawks** in 1983 CF. Edmonton won best-of-seven series 4-0, outscoring Chicago 25-11.
35 — NY Rangers, Los Angeles Kings in 1981 PR. NY Rangers won best-of-five series 3-1, outscoring Los Angeles 23-12.

MOST GOALS, BOTH TEAMS, FIVE-GAME SERIES:
52 — **Edmonton Oilers, Los Angeles Kings** in 1987 DSF. Edmonton won best-of-seven series 4-1, outscoring Los Angeles 32-20.
50 — Los Angeles Kings, Edmonton Oilers in 1982 DSF. Los Angeles won best-of-five series 3-2, outscoring Edmonton 27-23.
48 — Edmonton Oilers, Calgary Flames in 1983 DF. Edmonton won best-of-seven series 4-1, outscoring Calgary 35-13.
— Calgary Flames, Los Angeles Kings in 1988 DSF. Calgary won best-of-seven series 4-1, outscoring Los Angeles 30-18.

MOST GOALS, BOTH TEAMS, SIX-GAME SERIES:
69 — **Edmonton Oilers, Chicago Blackhawks** in 1985 CF. Edmonton won best-of-seven series 4-2, outscoring Chicago 44-25.
62 — Chicago Blackhawks, Minnesota North Stars in 1985 DF. Chicago won best-of-seven series 4-2, outscoring Minnesota 33-29.
61 — Los Angeles Kings, Calgary Flames in 1993 DSF. Los Angeles won best-of-seven series 4-2, outscoring Calgary 33-28.

MOST GOALS, BOTH TEAMS, SEVEN-GAME SERIES:
61 — **San Jose Sharks, Calgary Flames** in 1995 CQF. San Jose won best-of-seven series 4-3, while being outscored 35-26.
60 — Edmonton Oilers, Calgary Flames in 1984 DF. Edmonton won best-of-seven series 4-3, outscoring Calgary 33-27.

FEWEST GOALS IN A SERIES, BOTH TEAMS

FEWEST GOALS, BOTH TEAMS, TWO-GAME SERIES:
1 — **NY Rangers, NY Americans,** in 1929 SF. NY Rangers defeated NY Americans 1-0 in two-game, total-goal series.
— Mtl. Maroons, Chicago Blackhawks in 1935 SF. Mtl. Maroons defeated Chicago 1-0 in two-game, total-goal series.

FEWEST GOALS, BOTH TEAMS, THREE-GAME SERIES:
7 — **Boston Bruins, Montreal Canadiens** in 1929 SF. Boston won best-of-five series 3-0, outscoring Montreal 5-2.
— Detroit Red Wings, Mtl. Maroons in 1936 SF. Detroit won best-of-five series 3-0, outscoring Mtl. Maroons 6-1.

FEWEST GOALS, BOTH TEAMS, FOUR-GAME SERIES:
9 — **Toronto Maple Leafs, Boston Bruins** in 1935 SF. Toronto won best-of-five series 3-1, outscoring Boston 7-2.

FEWEST GOALS, BOTH TEAMS, FIVE-GAME SERIES:
11 — **NY Rangers, Mtl. Maroons** in 1928 F. NY Rangers won best-of-five series 3-2, while being outscored by Mtl. Maroons 6-5.

FEWEST GOALS, BOTH TEAMS, SIX-GAME SERIES:
20 — **Toronto Maple Leafs, Philadelphia Flyers** in 1999 CQF. Toronto won best-of-seven series 4-2, being outscored by Philadelphia 11-9.

FEWEST GOALS, BOTH TEAMS, SEVEN-GAME SERIES:
18 — **Toronto Maple Leafs, Detroit Red Wings** in 1945 F. Toronto won best-of-seven series 4-3; teams tied in scoring 9-9.

MOST GOALS IN A GAME OR PERIOD

MOST GOALS, ONE TEAM, ONE GAME:
13 — **Edmonton Oilers** at Edmonton, April 9, 1987. Edmonton 13, Los Angeles 3. Edmonton won best-of-seven DSF 4-1.
12 — Los Angeles Kings at Los Angeles, April 10, 1990. Los Angeles 12, Calgary 4. Los Angeles won best-of-seven DSF 4-2.
11 — Montreal Canadiens at Montreal, March 30, 1944. Montreal 11, Toronto 0. Canadiens won best-of-seven SF 4-1.
— Edmonton Oilers at Edmonton, May 4, 1985. Edmonton 11, Chicago 2. Edmonton won best-of-seven CF 4-2.

Philadelphia's John Vanbiesbrouck held Toronto to just nine goals in the first round of last year's playoffs, but the Maple Leafs still won the series. The combined total of 20 goals scored was the fewest ever in a six-game series.

MOST GOALS, ONE TEAM, ONE PERIOD:
7 — **Montreal Canadiens,** March 30, 1944, at Montreal in third period, during 11-0 win against Toronto.

MOST GOALS, BOTH TEAMS, ONE GAME:
18 — **Los Angeles Kings, Edmonton Oilers** at Edmonton, April 7, 1982. Los Angeles 10, Edmonton 8. Los Angeles won best-of-five DSF 3-2.
17 — Pittsburgh Penguins, Philadelphia Flyers at Pittsburgh, April 25, 1989. Pittsburgh 10, Philadelphia 7. Philadelphia won best-of-seven DF 4-3.
16 — Edmonton Oilers, Los Angeles Kings at Edmonton, April 9, 1987. Edmonton 13, Los Angeles 3. Edmonton won best-of-seven DSF 4-1.
— Los Angeles Kings, Calgary Flames at Los Angeles, April 10, 1990. Los Angeles 12, Calgary 4. Los Angeles won best-of-seven DF 4-2.

MOST GOALS, BOTH TEAMS, ONE PERIOD:
9 — **NY Rangers, Philadelphia Flyers,** April 24, 1979, at Philadelphia, third period. NY Rangers won 8-3, scoring six of nine third-period goals.
— **Los Angeles Kings, Calgary Flames,** at Los Angeles, April 10, 1990, second period. Los Angeles won 12-4, scoring five of nine second-period goals.
8 — Chicago Blackhawks, Montreal Canadiens, at Montreal, May 8, 1973, second period. Chicago won 8-7, scoring five of eight second-period goals.
— Chicago Blackhawks, Edmonton Oilers, at Chicago, May 12, 1985, first period. Chicago won 8-6, scoring five of eight first-period goals.
— Edmonton Oilers, Winnipeg Jets, at Edmonton, April 6, 1988, third period. Edmonton won 7-4, scoring six of eight third period goals.
— Hartford Whalers, Montreal Canadiens, at Hartford, April 10, 1988, third period. Hartford won 7-5, scoring five of eight third period goals.
— Vancouver Canucks, NY Rangers, at New York, June 9, 1994, third period. Vancouver won 6-3, scoring five of eight third period goals.

TEAM POWER-PLAY GOALS

MOST POWER-PLAY GOALS BY ALL TEAMS, ONE PLAYOFF YEAR:
199 — **1988** in 83 games.

MOST POWER-PLAY GOALS, ONE TEAM, ONE PLAYOFF YEAR:
35 — **Minnesota North Stars,** 1991 in 23 games.
32 — Edmonton Oilers, 1988 in 18 games.
31 — NY Islanders, 1981, in 18 games.

MOST POWER-PLAY GOALS, ONE TEAM, ONE SERIES:
15 — **NY Islanders** in 1980 F against Philadelphia. NY Islanders won series 4-2.
— **Minnesota North Stars** in 1991 DSF against Chicago. Minnesota won series 4-2.
13 — NY Islanders in 1981 QF against Edmonton. NY Islanders won series 4-2.
— Calgary Flames in 1986 CF against St. Louis. Calgary won series 4-3.
12 — Toronto Maple Leafs in 1976 QF series won by Philadelphia 4-3.

MOST POWER-PLAY GOALS, BOTH TEAMS, ONE SERIES:
21 — **NY Islanders, Philadelphia Flyers** in 1980 F, won by NY Islanders 4-2. NY Islanders had 15 and Flyers 6.
— **NY Islanders, Edmonton Oilers** in 1981 QF, won by NY Islanders 4-2. NY Islanders had 13 and Edmonton 8.
— **Philadelphia Flyers, Pittsburgh Penguins** in 1989 DF, won by Philadelphia 4-3. Philadelphia had 11 and Pittsburgh 10.
— **Minnesota North Stars, Chicago Blackhawks** in 1991 DSF, won by Minnesota 4-2. Minnesota had 15 and Chicago 6.
20 — Toronto Maple Leafs, Philadelphia Flyers in 1976 QF series won by Philadelphia 4-3. Toronto had 12 and Philadelphia 8.

MOST POWER-PLAY GOALS, ONE TEAM, ONE GAME:
6 — **Boston Bruins,** April 2, 1969, at Boston against Toronto. Boston won 10-0.

MOST POWER-PLAY GOALS, BOTH TEAMS, ONE GAME:
8 — **Minnesota North Stars, St. Louis Blues,** April 24, 1991 at Minnesota. Minnesota had 4, St. Louis 4. Minnesota won 8-4.
7 — Minnesota North Stars, Edmonton Oilers, April 28, 1984 at Minnesota. Minnesota had 4, Edmonton 3. Edmonton won 8-5.
— Philadelphia Flyers, NY Rangers, April 13, 1985 at New York. Philadelphia had 4, NY Rangers 3. Philadelphia won 6-5.
— Edmonton Oilers, Chicago Blackhawks, May 14, 1985 at Edmonton. Chicago had 5, Edmonton 2. Edmonton won 10-5.
— Edmonton Oilers, Los Angeles Kings, April 9, 1987 at Edmonton. Edmonton had 5, Los Angeles 2. Edmonton won 13-3.
— Vancouver Canucks, Calgary Flames, April 9, 1989 at Vancouver. Vancouver had 4, Calgary 3. Vancouver won 5-3.

MOST POWER-PLAY GOALS, ONE TEAM, ONE PERIOD:
4 — **Toronto Maple Leafs,** March 26, 1936, second period against Boston at Toronto. Toronto won 8-3.
— **Minnesota North Stars,** April 28, 1984, second period against Edmonton at Minnesota. Edmonton won 8-5.
— **Boston Bruins,** April 11, 1991, third period against Hartford at Boston. Boston won 6-1.
— **Minnesota North Stars,** April 24, 1991, second period against St. Louis at Minnesota. Minnesota won 8-4.
— **St. Louis Blues,** April 27, 1998, third period at Los Angeles. St. Louis won 4-3.

MOST POWER-PLAY GOALS, BOTH TEAMS, ONE PERIOD:
5 — **Minnesota North Stars, Edmonton Oilers,** April 28, 1984, second period, at Minnesota. Minnesota had 4 and Edmonton 1. Edmonton won 8-5.
— **Vancouver Canucks, Calgary Flames,** April 9, 1989, third period at Vancouver. Vancouver had 3 and Calgary 2. Vancouver won 5-3.
— **Minnesota North Stars, St. Louis Blues,** April 24, 1991, second period, at Minnesota. Minnesota had 4 and St. Louis 1. Minnesota won 8-4.

TEAM SHORTHAND GOALS

MOST SHORTHAND GOALS BY ALL TEAMS, ONE PLAYOFF YEAR:
33 — **1988,** in 83 games.

MOST SHORTHAND GOALS, ONE TEAM, ONE PLAYOFF YEAR:
10 — Edmonton Oilers, 1983, in 16 games.
  9 — NY Islanders, 1981, in 19 games.
  8 — Philadelphia Flyers, 1989, in 19 games.

MOST SHORTHAND GOALS, ONE TEAM, ONE SERIES:
6 — Calgary Flames in 1995 against San Jose in best-of-seven CQF won by San Jose 4-3.
  — **Vancouver Canucks** in 1995 against St. Louis in best-of-seven CQF won by Vancouver 4-3.
  5 — Edmonton Oilers in 1983 against Calgary in best-of-seven DF won by Edmonton 4-1.
  — NY Rangers in 1979 against Philadelphia in best-of-seven QF, won by NY Rangers 4-1.

MOST SHORTHAND GOALS, BOTH TEAMS, ONE SERIES:
7 — Boston Bruins (4), NY Rangers (3), in 1958 SF won by Boston 4-2.
  — **Edmonton Oilers (5), Calgary Flames (2),** in 1983 DF won by Edmonton 4-1.
  — **Vancouver Canucks (6), St. Louis Blues (1),** in 1995 CQF won by Vancouver 4-3.

MOST SHORTHAND GOALS, ONE TEAM, ONE GAME:
3 — Boston Bruins, April 11, 1981, at Minnesota. Minnesota won 6-3.
  — **NY Islanders,** April 17, 1983, at NY Rangers. NY Rangers won 7-6.
  — **Toronto Maple Leafs,** May 8, 1994, at San Jose. Toronto won 8-3.

MOST SHORTHAND GOALS, BOTH TEAMS, ONE GAME:
4 — NY Islanders, NY Rangers, April 17, 1983, at NY Rangers. NY Islanders had 3 shorthand goals, NY Rangers 1. NY Rangers won 7-6.
  — **Boston Bruins, Minnesota North Stars,** April 11, 1981, at Minnesota. Boston had 3 shorthand goals, Minnesota 1. Minnesota won 6-3.
  — **San Jose Sharks, Toronto Maple Leafs,** May 8, 1994, at San Jose. Toronto had 3 shorthand goals, San Jose 1. Toronto won 8-3.
  3 — Toronto Maple Leafs, Detroit Red Wings, April 5, 1947, at Toronto. Toronto had 2 shorthand goals, Detroit 1. Toronto won 6-1.
  — NY Rangers, Boston Bruins, April 1, 1958, at Boston. NY Rangers had 2 shorthand goals, Boston 1. NY Rangers won 5-2.
  — Minnesota North Stars, Philadelphia Flyers, May 4, 1980, at Minnesota. Minnesota had 2 shorthand goals, Philadelphia 1. Philadelphia won 5-3.
  — Edmonton Oilers, Winnipeg Jets, April 9, 1988, at Winnipeg. Winnipeg had 2 shorthand goals, Edmonton 1. Winnipeg won 6-4.
  — New Jersey Devils, NY Islanders, April 14, 1988, at New Jersey. New Jersey had 2 shorthand goals, New Jersey 1. New Jersey won 6-5.
  — Montreal Canadiens, New Jersey Devils, April 17, 1997, at New Jersey. Montreal had 2 shorthand goals, New Jersey 1. New Jersey won 5-2

MOST SHORTHAND GOALS, ONE TEAM, ONE PERIOD:
2 — Toronto Maple Leafs, April 5, 1947, at Toronto against Detroit, first period. Toronto won 6-1.
  — **Toronto Maple Leafs,** April 13, 1965, at Toronto against Montreal, first period. Montreal won 4-3.
  — **Boston Bruins,** April 20, 1969, at Boston against Montreal, first period. Boston won 3-2.
  — **Boston Bruins,** April 8, 1970, at Boston against NY Rangers, second period. Boston won 8-2.
  — **Boston Bruins,** April 30, 1972, at Boston against NY Rangers, first period. Boston won 6-5.
  — **Chicago Blackhawks,** May 3, 1973, at Chicago against Montreal, first period. Chicago won 7-4.
  — **Montreal Canadiens,** April 23, 1978, at Detroit, first period. Montreal won 8-0.
  — **NY Islanders,** April 8, 1980, at New York against Los Angeles, second period. NY Islanders won 8-1.
  — **Los Angeles Kings,** April 9, 1980, at NY Islanders, first period. Los Angeles won 6-3.
  — **Boston Bruins,** April 13, 1980, at Pittsburgh, second period. Boston won 8-3.
  — **Minnesota North Stars,** May 4, 1980, at Minnesota against Philadelphia, second period. Philadelphia won 5-3.
  — **Boston Bruins,** April 11, 1981, at Minnesota, third period. Minnesota won 6-3.
  — **NY Islanders,** May 12, 1981, at New York against Minnesota, first period. NY Islanders won 6-3.
  — **Montreal Canadiens,** April 7, 1982, at Montreal against Quebec, third period. Montreal won 5-1.
  — **Edmonton Oilers,** April 24, 1983, at Edmonton against Chicago, third period. Edmonton won 8-4.
  — **Winnipeg Jets,** April 14, 1985, at Calgary, second period. Winnipeg won 5-3.
  — **Boston Bruins,** April 6, 1988, at Boston against Buffalo, first period. Boston won 7-3.
  — **NY Islanders,** April 14, 1988, at New Jersey, third period. New Jersey won 6-5.
  — **Detroit Red Wings,** April 29, 1993, at Toronto, second period. Detroit won 7-3.
  — **Toronto Maple Leafs,** May 8, 1994, at San Jose, third period. Toronto won 8-3.
  — **Calgary Flames,** May 11, 1995, at San Jose, first period. Calgary won 9-2.
  — **Vancouver Canucks,** May 15, 1995, at St. Louis, second period. Vancouver won 6-5.
  — **Montreal Canadiens,** April 17, 1997, at New Jersey, second period. New Jersey won 5-2.
  — **Philadelphia Flyers,** April 26, 1997, at Philadelphia against Pittsburgh, first period. Philadelphia won 6-3.
  — **Phoenix Coyotes,** April 24, 1998, at Detroit, second period. Phoenix won 7-4.
  — **Buffalo Sabres,** April 27, 1998, at Buffalo against Philadelphia, second period. Buffalo won 6-1.
  — **San Jose Sharks,** April 30, 1999, at Colorado, third period. San Jose won 7-3.

MOST SHORTHAND GOALS, BOTH TEAMS, ONE PERIOD:
3 — Toronto Maple Leafs, Detroit Red Wings, April 5, 1947, at Toronto, first period. Toronto had 2 shorthand goals, Detroit 1. Toronto won 6-1.
  — **Toronto Maple Leafs, San Jose Sharks,** May 8, 1994, at San Jose, third period. Toronto had 2 shorthand goals, San Jose 1. Toronto won 8-3.

FASTEST GOALS

FASTEST FIVE GOALS, BOTH TEAMS:
3 Minutes, 6 Seconds — Chicago Blackhawks, Minnesota North Stars, at Chicago April 21, 1985. Keith Brown scored for Chicago at 1:12, second period; Ken Yaremchuk, Chicago, 1:27; Dino Ciccarelli, Minnesota, 2:48; Tony McKegney, Minnesota, 4:07; and Curt Fraser, Chicago, 4:18. Chicago won 6-2 and best-of-seven DF 4-2.
3 Minutes, 20 Seconds — Minnesota North Stars, Philadelphia Flyers, at Philadelphia, April 29, 1980. Paul Shmyr scored for Minnesota at 13:20, first period; Steve Christoff, Minnesota, 13:59; Ken Linseman, Philadelphia, 14:54; Tom Gorence, Philadelphia, 15:36; and Linseman, 16:40. Minnesota won 6-5. Philadelphia won best-of-seven SF 4-1.
4 Minutes, 19 Seconds — Toronto Maple Leafs, NY Rangers at Toronto, April 9, 1932. Ace Bailey scored for Toronto at 15:07, third period; Fred Cook, NY Rangers, 16:32; Bob Gracie, Toronto, 17:36; Frank Boucher, NY Rangers, 18:26 and 19:26. Toronto won 6-4 and best-of-five F 3-0.

FASTEST FIVE GOALS, ONE TEAM:
3 Minutes, 36 Seconds — Montreal Canadiens at Montreal, March 30, 1944, against Toronto. Toe Blake scored at 7:58 of third period and again at 8:37; Maurice Richard, 9:17; Ray Getliffe, 10:33; and Buddy O'Connor, 11:34. Canadiens won 11-0 and best-of-seven SF 4-1.

FASTEST FOUR GOALS, BOTH TEAMS:
1 Minute, 33 Seconds — Philadelphia Flyers, Toronto Maple Leafs at Philadelphia, April 20, 1976. Don Saleski of Philadelphia scored at 10:04 of second period; Bob Neely, Toronto, 10:42; Gary Dornhoefer, Philadelphia, 11:24; and Don Saleski, 11:37. Philadelphia won 7-1 and best-of-seven QF series 4-3.
1 minute, 34 seconds — Montreal Canadiens, Calgary Flames at Montreal, May 20, 1986. Joel Otto of Calgary scored at 17:59 of first period; Bobby Smith, Montreal, 18:25; Mats Naslund, Montreal, 19:17; and Bob Gainey, Montreal, 19:33. Montreal won 5-3 and best-of-seven F series 4-1.
1 Minute, 38 Seconds — Boston Bruins, Philadelphia Flyers at Philadelphia, April 26, 1977. Gregg Sheppard of Boston scored at 14:01 of second period; Mike Milbury, Boston, 15:01; Gary Dornhoefer, Philadelphia, 15:16; and Jean Ratelle, Boston, 15:39. Boston won 5-4 and best-of-seven SF series 4-0.

FASTEST FOUR GOALS, ONE TEAM:
2 Minutes, 35 Seconds — Montreal Canadiens at Montreal, March 30, 1944, against Toronto. Toe Blake scored at 7:58 and 8:37 of third period; Maurice Richard, 9:17; Ray Getliffe, 10:33. Montreal won 11-0 and best-of-seven SF 4-1.

FASTEST THREE GOALS, BOTH TEAMS:
21 Seconds — Edmonton Oilers, Chicago Blackhawks at Edmonton, May 7, 1985. Behn Wilson scored for Chicago at 19:22 of third period, Jari Kurri at 19:36 and Glenn Anderson at 19:43 for Edmonton. Edmonton won 7-3 and best-of-seven CF 4-2.
27 Seconds — Phoenix Coyotes, Detroit Red Wings at Detroit, April 24, 1998. Jeremy Roenick scored for Phoenix at 13:24 of the second period. Mathieu Dandenault scored for Detroit at 13:32, and Keith Tkachuk scored for Phoenix at 13:51. Phoenix won 7-4, Detroit won the best-of-seven CQF 4-2.
30 Seconds — Chicago Blackhawks, Pittsburgh Penguins at Chicago, June 1, 1992. Dirk Graham scored for Chicago at 6:21 of first period, Kevin Stevens for Pittsburgh at 6:33 and Dirk Graham at 6:51. Pittsburgh won 6-5 and best-of-seven F 4-0.

FASTEST THREE GOALS, ONE TEAM:
23 Seconds — Toronto Maple Leafs at Toronto, April 12, 1979, against Atlanta. Darryl Sittler scored at 4:04 in first period and again at 4:16 and Ron Ellis at 4:27. Leafs won 7-4 and best-of-three PR 2-0.
38 Seconds — NY Rangers at New York, April 12, 1986 against Philadelphia. Jim Wiemer scored at 12:29 of third period, Bob Brooke at 12:43 and Ron Greschner at 13:07. NY Rangers won 5-2 and best-of-five DSF 3-2.
56 Seconds — Montreal Canadiens at Detroit, April 6, 1954. Dickie Moore scored at 15:03 of first period, Maurice Richard at 15:28 and again at 15:59. Montreal won 3-1. Detroit won best-of-seven F 4-3.

FASTEST TWO GOALS, BOTH TEAMS:
5 Seconds — Pittsburgh Penguins, Buffalo Sabres at Buffalo, April 14, 1979. Gilbert Perreault scored for Buffalo at 12:59 and Jim Hamilton for Pittsburgh at 13:04 of first period. Pittsburgh won 4-3 and best-of-three PR 2-1.
8 Seconds — Minnesota North Stars, St. Louis Blues at Minnesota, April 9, 1989. Bernie Federko scored for St. Louis at 2:28 of third period and Perry Berezan at 2:36 for Minnesota. Minnesota won 5-4. St. Louis won best-of-seven DSF 4-1.
  — Phoenix Coyotes, Detroit Red Wings, at Detroit, April 24, 1998. Jeremy Roenick scored for Phoenix at 13:24 of the second period and Mathieu Dandenault scored for Detroit at 13:32. Phoenix won 7-4, Detroit won the best-of-seven CQF 4-2.
9 Seconds — NY Islanders, Washington Capitals at Washington, April 10, 1986. Bryan Trottier scored for New York at 18:26 of second period and Scott Stevens at 18:35 for Washington. Washington won 5-2, and best-of-five DSF 3-0.
  — Buffalo Sabres, Toronto Maple Leafs at Toronto, May 23, 1999. Vaclav Varada scored at 4:23 of first period for Buffalo and Mats Sundin scored at 4:32 for Toronto. Buffalo won 5-4, and best of seven CF 4-1.

FASTEST TWO GOALS, ONE TEAM:
5 Seconds — Detroit Red Wings at Detroit, April 11, 1965, against Chicago. Norm Ullman scored at 17:35 and 17:40, second period. Detroit won 4-2. Chicago won best-of-seven SF 4-3.

Mud Bruneteau's overtime goal in 1936 came more than a full game's worth of time after Brett Hull's triple overtime winner in 1999. Bruneteau's goal at 16:30 of the sixth overtime period gave the Detroit Red Wings a 1-0 victory over the Montreal Maroons.

OVERTIME

SHORTEST OVERTIME:
   9 Seconds — Montreal Canadiens, Calgary Flames, at Calgary, May 18, 1986. Montreal won 3-2 on Brian Skrudland's goal and captured the best-of-seven F 4-1.
   11 Seconds — NY Islanders, NY Rangers, at NY Rangers, April 11, 1975. NY Islanders won 4-3 on Jean-Paul Parise's goal and captured the best-of-three PR 2-1.

LONGEST OVERTIME:
116 Minutes, 30 Seconds — Detroit Red Wings, Mtl. Maroons at Montreal, March 24, 25, 1936. Detroit 1, Mtl. Maroons 0. Mud Bruneteau scored, assisted by Hec Kilrea, at 16:30 of sixth overtime period, or after 176 minutes, 30 seconds from start of game, which ended at 2:25 a.m. Detroit won best-of-five SF 3-0.

MOST OVERTIME GAMES, ONE PLAYOFF YEAR:
   28 — 1993. Of 85 games played, 28 went into overtime.
   21 — 1999. Of 86 games played, 21 went into overtime.
   19 — 1996. Of 86 games played, 19 went into overtime.
      — 1998. Of 82 games played, 19 went into overtime.
   18 — 1994. Of 90 games played, 18 went into overtime.
      — 1995. Of 81 games played, 18 went into overtime.

FEWEST OVERTIME GAMES, ONE PLAYOFF YEAR:
   0 — 1963. None of the 16 games went into overtime, the only year since 1926 that no overtime was required in any playoff series.

MOST OVERTIME GAMES, ONE SERIES:
   5 — Toronto Maple Leafs, Montreal Canadiens in 1951. Toronto won best-of-seven F 4-1.
   4 — Toronto Maple Leafs, Boston Bruins in 1933. Toronto won best-of-five SF 3-2.
      — Boston Bruins, NY Rangers in 1939. Boston won best-of-seven SF 4-3.
      — St. Louis Blues, Minnesota North Stars in 1968. St. Louis won best-of-seven SF 4-3.
      — Dallas Stars, St. Louis Blues in 1999. Dallas won best-of-seven CSF 4-2.

THREE-OR-MORE GOAL GAMES

MOST THREE-OR-MORE GOAL GAMES BY ALL TEAMS, ONE PLAYOFF YEAR:
   12 — 1983 in 66 games.
      — **1988** in 83 games.
   11 — 1985 in 70 games.
      — 1992 in 86 games.

MOST THREE-OR-MORE GOAL GAMES, ONE TEAM, ONE PLAYOFF YEAR:
   6 — **Edmonton Oilers** in 16 games, 1983.
      — **Edmonton Oilers** in 18 games, 1985.

SHUTOUTS

MOST SHUTOUTS, ONE PLAYOFF YEAR, ALL TEAMS:
   18 — 1997. Of 82 games played, Colorado and NY Rangers had 3 each, Edmonton, New Jersey, and St. Louis had 2 each, while Anaheim, Buffalo, Detroit, Florida, Ottawa and Phoenix had 1 each.
   16 — 1994. Of 90 games played, NY Rangers and Vancouver had 4 each, Toronto had 3, Buffalo had 2, while Washington, Detroit and New Jersey had 1 each.

FEWEST SHUTOUTS, ONE PLAYOFF YEAR, ALL TEAMS:
   0 — 1959. 18 games played.

MOST SHUTOUTS, BOTH TEAMS, ONE SERIES:
   5 — 1945 F, Toronto Maple Leafs, Detroit Red Wings. Toronto had 3 shutouts, Detroit 2. Toronto won best-of-seven series 4-3.
      — **1950 SF, Toronto Maple Leafs, Detroit Red Wings.** Toronto had 3 shutouts, Detroit 2. Detroit won best-of-seven series 4-3.

TEAM PENALTIES

FEWEST PENALTIES, BOTH TEAMS, BEST-OF-SEVEN SERIES:
   19 — Detroit Red Wings, Toronto Maple Leafs in 1945 F, won by Toronto 4-3. Detroit received 10 minors, Toronto had 9 minors.

FEWEST PENALTIES, ONE TEAM, BEST-OF-SEVEN SERIES:
   9 — Toronto Maple Leafs in 1945 F, won by Toronto 4-3 against Detroit.

MOST PENALTIES, BOTH TEAMS, ONE SERIES:
 219 — New Jersey Devils, Washington Capitals in 1988 DF won by New Jersey 4-3. New Jersey received 98 minors, 11 majors, 9 misconducts and 1 match penalty. Washington received 80 minors, 11 majors, 8 misconducts and 1 match penalty.

MOST PENALTY MINUTES, BOTH TEAMS, ONE SERIES:
 656 — New Jersey Devils, Washington Capitals in 1988 DF won by New Jersey 4-3. New Jersey had 351 minutes; Washington 305.

MOST PENALTIES, ONE TEAM, ONE SERIES:
 119 — New Jersey Devils in 1988 DF versus Washington. New Jersey received 98 minors, 11 majors, 9 misconducts and 1 match penalty.

MOST PENALTY MINUTES, ONE TEAM, ONE SERIES:
 351 — New Jersey Devils in 1988 DF versus Washington. Series won by New Jersey 4-3.

MOST PENALTIES, BOTH TEAMS, ONE GAME:
   66 — Detroit Red Wings, St. Louis Blues, at St. Louis, April 12, 1991. Detroit received 33 penalties; St. Louis 33. St. Louis won 6-1.
   62 — New Jersey Devils, Washington Capitals, at New Jersey, April 22, 1988. New Jersey received 32 penalties; Washington 30. New Jersey won 10-4.

MOST PENALTY MINUTES, BOTH TEAMS, ONE GAME:
 298 Minutes — Detroit Red Wings, St. Louis Blues, at St. Louis, April 12, 1991. Detroit received 33 penalties for 152 minutes; St. Louis 33 penalties for 146 minutes. St. Louis won 6-1.
 267 Minutes — NY Rangers, Los Angeles Kings, at Los Angeles, April 9, 1981. NY Rangers received 31 penalties for 142 minutes; Los Angeles 28 penalties for 125 minutes. Los Angeles won 5-4.

MOST PENALTIES, ONE TEAM, ONE GAME:
   33 — Detroit Red Wings, at St. Louis, April 12,1991. St. Louis won 6-1.
      — **St. Louis Blues,** at St. Louis, April 12, 1991. St. Louis won 6-1.
   32 — New Jersey Devils, at Washington, April 22,1988. New Jersey won 10-4.
   31 — NY Rangers, at Los Angeles, April 9, 1981. Los Angeles won 5-4.
   30 — Philadelphia Flyers, at Toronto, April 15, 1976. Toronto won 5-4.

MOST PENALTY MINUTES, ONE TEAM, ONE GAME:
 152 — Detroit Red Wings, at St. Louis, April 12, 1991. St. Louis won 6-1.
 146 — St. Louis Blues, at St. Louis, April 12, 1991. St. Louis won 6-1.
 142 — NY Rangers, at Los Angeles, April 9, 1981. Los Angeles won 5-4.

MOST PENALTIES, BOTH TEAMS, ONE PERIOD:
   43 — NY Rangers, Los Angeles Kings, at Los Angeles, April 9, 1981, first period. NY Rangers had 24 penalties; Los Angeles 19. Los Angeles won 5-4.

MOST PENALTY MINUTES, BOTH TEAMS, ONE PERIOD:
 248 — NY Islanders, Boston Bruins, at Boston, April 17, 1980, first period. Each team received 124 minutes. Islanders won 5-4.

MOST PENALTIES, ONE TEAM, ONE PERIOD:
   24 — NY Rangers, at Los Angeles, April 9, 1981, first period. Los Angeles won 5-4.

MOST PENALTY MINUTES, ONE TEAM, ONE PERIOD:
 125 — NY Rangers, at Los Angeles, April 9, 1981, first period. Los Angeles won 5-4.

Individual Records

GAMES PLAYED

MOST YEARS IN PLAYOFFS:
20 — **Gordie Howe, Detroit, Hartford** (1947-58 incl.; 60-61; 63-66 incl.; 70 & 80)
— **Larry Robinson, Montreal, Los Angeles** (1973-92 incl.)
19 — Red Kelly, Detroit, Toronto
— Ray Bourque, Boston

MOST CONSECUTIVE YEARS IN PLAYOFFS:
20 — **Larry Robinson, Montreal, Los Angeles** (1973-1992, inclusive).
17 — Brad Park, NY Rangers, Boston, Detroit (1969-1985, inclusive).
— Ray Bourque, Boston (1980-96, inclusive).
16 — Jean Beliveau, Montreal (1954-69, inclusive).
— Bob Gainey, Montreal (1974-89, inclusive).
— Dale Hunter, Quebec, Washington (1981-96, inclusive)

MOST PLAYOFF GAMES:
236 — **Mark Messier, Edmonton, NY Rangers**
227 — Larry Robinson, Montreal, Los Angeles
225 — Glenn Anderson, Edmonton, Toronto, NY Rangers, St. Louis
221 — Bryan Trottier, NY Islanders, Pittsburgh
214 — Kevin Lowe, Edmonton, NY Rangers

GOALS

MOST GOALS IN PLAYOFFS (CAREER):
122 — **Wayne Gretzky, Edmonton, Los Angeles, St. Louis, NY Rangers**
109 — Mark Messier, Edmonton, NY Rangers
106 — Jari Kurri, Edmonton, Los Angeles, NY Rangers, Anaheim
93 — Glenn Anderson, Edmonton, Toronto, NY Rangers, St. Louis
85 — Mike Bossy, NY Islanders

MOST GOALS, ONE PLAYOFF YEAR:
19 — **Reggie Leach, Philadelphia,** 1976. 16 games.
— **Jari Kurri, Edmonton,** 1985. 18 games.
18 — Joe Sakic, Colorado, 1996. 22 games.
17 — Newsy Lalonde, Montreal, 1919. 10 games.
— Mike Bossy, NY Islanders, 1981. 18 games.
— Steve Payne, Minnesota, 1981. 19 games.
— Mike Bossy, NY Islanders, 1982. 19 games.
— Mike Bossy, NY Islanders, 1983. 19 games
— Wayne Gretzky, Edmonton, 1985. 18 games.
— Kevin Stevens, Pittsburgh, 1991. 24 games.

MOST GOALS IN ONE SERIES (OTHER THAN FINAL):
12 — **Jari Kurri, Edmonton,** in 1985 CF, 6 games vs. Chicago.
11 — Newsy Lalonde, Montreal, in 1919 NHL F, 5 games vs. Ottawa.
10 — Tim Kerr, Philadelphia, in 1989 DF, 7 games vs. Pittsburgh.
9 — Reggie Leach, Philadelphia, in 1976 SF, 5 games vs. Boston.
— Bill Barber, Philadelphia, in 1980 SF, 5 games vs. Minnesota.
— Mike Bossy, NY Islanders, in 1983 CF, 6 games vs. Boston.
— Mario Lemieux, Pittsburgh, in 1989 DF, 7 games vs. Philadelphia.

MOST GOALS IN FINAL SERIES:
9 — **Babe Dye, Toronto,** in 1922, 5 games vs. Van. Millionaires.
8 — Alf Skinner, Toronto, in 1918, 5 games vs. Van. Millionaires.
7 — Jean Beliveau, Montreal, in 1956, 5 games vs. Detroit.
— Mike Bossy, NY Islanders, in 1982, 4 games vs. Vancouver.
— Wayne Gretzky, Edmonton, in 1985, 5 games vs. Philadelphia.

MOST GOALS, ONE GAME:
5 — **Newsy Lalonde, Montreal,** March 1, 1919, at Montreal. Final score: Montreal 6, Ottawa 3.
— **Maurice Richard, Montreal,** March 23, 1944, at Montreal. Final score: Montreal 5, Toronto 1.
— **Darryl Sittler, Toronto,** April 22, 1976, at Toronto. Final score: Toronto 8, Philadelphia 5.
— **Reggie Leach, Philadelphia,** May 6, 1976, at Philadelphia. Final score: Philadelphia 6, Boston 3.
— **Mario Lemieux, Pittsburgh,** April 25, 1989, at Pittsburgh. Final score: Pittsburgh 10, Philadelphia 7.

MOST GOALS, ONE PERIOD:
4 — **Tim Kerr, Philadelphia,** April 13, 1985, at New York vs. NY Rangers, second period. Final score: Philadelphia 6, NY Rangers 5.
— **Mario Lemieux, Pittsburgh,** April 25, 1989, at Pittsburgh vs. Philadelphia, first period. Final score: Pittsburgh 10, Philadelphia 7.

ASSISTS

MOST ASSISTS IN PLAYOFFS (CAREER):
260 — **Wayne Gretzky, Edmonton, Los Angeles, St. Louis, NY Rangers**
186 — Mark Messier, Edmonton, NY Rangers
137 — Paul Coffey, Edmonton, Pittsburgh, Los Angeles, Detroit, Philadelphia, Carolina
127 — Jari Kurri, Edmonton, Los Angeles, NY Rangers, Anaheim
125 — Ray Bourque, Boston

MOST ASSISTS, ONE PLAYOFF YEAR:
31 — **Wayne Gretzky, Edmonton,** 1988. 19 games.
30 — Wayne Gretzky, Edmonton, 1985. 18 games.
29 — Wayne Gretzky, Edmonton, 1987. 21 games.
28 — Mario Lemieux, Pittsburgh, 1991. 23 games.
26 — Wayne Gretzky, Edmonton, 1983. 16 games.

MOST ASSISTS IN ONE SERIES (OTHER THAN FINAL):
14 — **Rick Middleton, Boston,** in 1983 DF, 7 games vs. Buffalo.
— **Wayne Gretzky, Edmonton,** in 1985 CF, 6 games vs. Chicago.
13 — Wayne Gretzky, Edmonton, in 1987 DSF, 5 games vs. Los Angeles.
— Doug Gilmour, Toronto, in 1994 CSF, 7 games vs. San Jose.
11 — Mark Messier, Edmonton, in 1989 DSF, 7 games vs. Los Angeles.
— Al MacInnis, Calgary, in 1984 DF, 7 games vs. Edmonton.
— Mike Ridley, Washington, in 1992 DSF, 7 games vs. Pittsburgh.
— Ron Francis, Pittsburgh, in 1995 CQF, 7 games vs. Washington.
10 — Fleming Mackell, Boston, in 1958 SF, 6 games vs. NY Rangers.
— Stan Mikita, Chicago, in 1962 SF, 6 games vs. Montreal.
— Bob Bourne, NY Islanders, in 1983 DF, 6 games vs. NY Rangers.
— Wayne Gretzky, Edmonton, in 1988 DSF, 5 games vs. Winnipeg.
— Mario Lemieux, Pittsburgh, in 1992 DSF, 6 games vs. Washington.

MOST ASSISTS IN FINAL SERIES:
10 — **Wayne Gretzky, Edmonton,** in 1988, 4 games plus suspended game vs. Boston.
9 — Jacques Lemaire, Montreal, in 1973, 6 games vs. Chicago.
— Wayne Gretzky, Edmonton, in 1987, 7 games vs. Philadelphia.
— Larry Murphy, Pittsburgh, in 1991, 6 games vs. Minnesota.

MOST ASSISTS, ONE GAME:
6 — **Mikko Leinonen, NY Rangers,** April 8, 1982, at New York. Final score: NY Rangers 7, Philadelphia 3.
— **Wayne Gretzky, Edmonton,** April 9, 1987, at Edmonton. Final score: Edmonton 13, Los Angeles 3.
5 — Toe Blake, Montreal, March 23, 1944, at Montreal. Final score: Montreal 5, Toronto 1.
— Maurice Richard, Montreal, March 27, 1956, at Montreal. Final score: Montreal 7, NY Rangers 0.
— Bert Olmstead, Montreal, March 30, 1957, at Montreal. Final score: Montreal 8, NY Rangers 3.
— Don McKenney, Boston, April 5, 1958, at Boston. Final score: Boston 8, NY Rangers 2.
— Stan Mikita, Chicago, April 4, 1973, at Chicago. Final score: Chicago 7, St. Louis 1.
— Wayne Gretzky, Edmonton, April 8, 1981, at Montreal. Final score: Edmonton 6, Montreal 3.
— Paul Coffey, Edmonton, May 14, 1985, at Edmonton. Final score: Edmonton 6, Chicago 5.
— Doug Gilmour, St. Louis, April 15, 1986, at Minnesota. Final score: St. Louis 6, Minnesota 3.
— Risto Siltanen, Quebec, April 14, 1987, at Hartford. Final score: Quebec 7, Hartford 5.
— Patrik Sundstrom, New Jersey, April 22, 1988, at New Jersey. Final score: New Jersey 10, Washington 4.
— Geoff Courtnall, St. Louis Blues, April 23, 1998, at St. Louis. Final score: St. Louis 8, Los Angeles 3.

MOST ASSISTS, ONE PERIOD:
3 — Three assists by one player in one period of a playoff game has been recorded on 71 occasions. Mike Ricci of the San Jose Sharks is the most recent to equal this mark with 3 assists in the third period at Colorado, April 28, 1999. Final score: San Jose 4, Colorado 2.
— Wayne Gretzky has had 3 assists in one period 5 times; Ray Bourque, 3 times. Toe Blake, Jean Beliveau, Doug Harvey and Bobby Orr, twice. Nick Metz of Toronto was the first player to be credited with 3 assists in one period of a playoff game Mar. 21, 1941 at Toronto vs. Boston.

POINTS

MOST POINTS IN PLAYOFFS (CAREER):
382 — **Wayne Gretzky, Edmonton, Los Angeles, St. Louis, NY Rangers,** 122G, 260A
295 — Mark Messier, Edmonton, NY Rangers, 109G, 186A
233 — Jari Kurri, Edmonton, Los Angeles, NY Rangers, Anaheim, 106G, 127A
214 — Glenn Anderson, Edmonton, Toronto, NY Rangers, St. Louis, 93G, 121A
196 — Paul Coffey, Edmonton, Pittsburgh, Los Angeles, Detroit, Philadelphia, Carolina, 59G, 137A

MOST POINTS, ONE PLAYOFF YEAR:
47 — **Wayne Gretzky, Edmonton,** in 1985. 17 goals, 30 assists in 18 games.
44 — Mario Lemieux, Pittsburgh, in 1991. 16 goals, 28 assists in 23 games.
43 — Wayne Gretzky, Edmonton, in 1988. 12 goals, 31 assists in 19 games.
40 — Wayne Gretzky, Los Angeles, in 1993. 15 goals, 25 assists in 24 games.
38 — Wayne Gretzky, Edmonton, in 1983. 12 goals, 26 assists in 16 games.

MOST POINTS IN ONE SERIES (OTHER THAN FINAL):
19 — Rick Middleton, Boston, in 1983 DF, 7 games vs. Buffalo. 5 goals, 14 assists.
18 — Wayne Gretzky, Edmonton, in 1985 CF, 6 games vs. Chicago. 4 goals, 14 assists.
17 — Mario Lemieux, Pittsburgh, in 1992 DSF, 6 games vs. Washington. 7 goals, 10 assists.
16 — Barry Pederson, Boston, in 1983 DF, 7 games vs. Buffalo. 7 goals, 9 assists.
  — Doug Gilmour, Toronto, in 1994 CSF, 7 games vs. San Jose. 3 goals, 13 assists.
15 — Jari Kurri, Edmonton, in 1985 CF, 6 games vs. Chicago. 12 goals, 3 assists.
  — Wayne Gretzky, Edmonton, in 1987 DSF, 5 games vs. Los Angeles. 2 goals, 13 assists.
  — Tim Kerr, Philadelphia, in 1989 DF, 7 games vs. Pittsburgh. 10 goals, 5 assists.
  — Mario Lemieux, Pittsburgh, in 1991 CF, 6 games vs. Boston. 6 goals, 9 assists.

MOST POINTS IN FINAL SERIES:
13 — Wayne Gretzky, Edmonton, in 1988, 4 games plus suspended game vs. Boston. 3 goals, 10 assists.
12 — Gordie Howe, Detroit, in 1955, 7 games vs. Montreal. 5 goals, 7 assists.
  — Yvan Cournoyer, Montreal, in 1973, 6 games vs. Chicago. 6 goals, 6 assists.
  — Jacques Lemaire, Montreal, in 1973, 6 games vs. Chicago. 3 goals, 9 assists.
  — Mario Lemieux, Pittsburgh, in 1991, 5 games vs. Minnesota. 5 goals, 7 assists.

MOST POINTS, ONE GAME:
8 — Patrik Sundstrom, New Jersey, April 22, 1988 at New Jersey during 10-4 win over Washington. Sundstrom had 3 goals, 5 assists.
  — **Mario Lemieux, Pittsburgh,** April 25, 1989 at Pittsburgh during 10-7 win over Philadelphia. Lemieux had 5 goals, 3 assists.
7 — Wayne Gretzky, Edmonton, April 17, 1983 at Calgary during 10-2 win. Gretzky had 4 goals, 3 assists.
  — Wayne Gretzky, Edmonton, April 25,1985 at Winnipeg during 8-3 win. Gretzky had 3 goals, 4 assists.
  — Wayne Gretzky, Edmonton, April 9, 1987, at Edmonton during 13-3 win over Los Angeles. Gretzky had 1 goal, 6 assists.
6 — Dickie Moore, Montreal, March 25, 1954, at Montreal during 8-1 win over Boston. Moore had 2 goals, 4 assists.
  — Phil Esposito, Boston, April 2, 1969, at Boston during 10-0 win over Toronto. Esposito had 4 goals, 2 assists.
  — Darryl Sittler, Toronto, April 22, 1976, at Toronto during 8-5 win over Philadelphia. Sittler had 5 goals, 1 assist.
  — Guy Lafleur, Montreal, April 11, 1977, at Montreal during 7-2 win over St. Louis. Lafleur had 3 goals, 3 assists.
  — Mikko Leinonen, NY Rangers, April 8, 1982, at New York during 7-3 win over Philadelphia. Leinonen had 6 assists.
  — Paul Coffey, Edmonton, May 14, 1985 at Edmonton during 10-5 win over Chicago. Coffey had 1 goal, 5 assists.
  — John Anderson, Hartford, April 12, 1986 at Hartford during 9-4 win over Quebec. Anderson had 2 goals, 4 assists.
  — Mario Lemieux, Pittsburgh, April 23, 1992 at Pittsburgh during 6-4 win over Washington. Lemieux had 3 goals, 3 assists.
  — Geoff Courtnall, St. Louis Blues, April 23, 1998 at St. Louis during 8-3 win over Los Angeles. Courtnall had 1 goal, 5 assists.

MOST POINTS, ONE PERIOD:
4 — Maurice Richard, Montreal, March 29, 1945, at Montreal vs. Toronto. Third period, 3 goals, 1 assist. Final score: Montreal 10, Toronto 3.
  — **Dickie Moore, Montreal,** March 25, 1954, at Montreal vs. Boston. First period, 2 goals, 2 assists. Final score: Montreal 8, Boston 1.
  — **Barry Pederson, Boston,** April 8, 1982, at Boston vs. Buffalo. Second period, 3 goals, 1 assist. Final score: Boston 7, Buffalo 3.
  — **Peter McNab, Boston,** April 11, 1982, at Buffalo. Second period, 1 goal, 3 assists. Final score: Boston 5, Buffalo 2.
  — **Tim Kerr, Philadelphia,** April 13, 1985 at New York. Second period, 4 goals. Final score: Philadelphia 6, Rangers 5.
  — **Ken Linseman, Boston,** April 14, 1985 at Boston vs. Montreal. Second period, 2 goals, 2 assists. Final score: Boston 7, Montreal 6.
  — **Wayne Gretzky, Edmonton,** April 12, 1987, at Los Angeles. Third period, 1 goal, 3 assists. Final score: Edmonton 6, Los Angeles 3.
  — **Glenn Anderson, Edmonton,** April 6, 1988, at Edmonton vs. Winnipeg. Third period, 3 goals, 1 assist. Final score: Edmonton 7, Winnipeg 4.
  — **Mario Lemieux, Pittsburgh,** April 25, 1989, at Pittsburgh vs. Philadelphia. First period, 4 goals. Final score: Pittsburgh 10, Philadelphia 7.
  — **Dave Gagner, Minnesota,** April 8, 1991, at Minnesota vs. Chicago. First period, 2 goals, 2 assists. Final score: Chicago 6, Minnesota 5.
  — **Mario Lemieux, Pittsburgh,** April 23, 1992, at Pittsburgh vs. Washington. Second period, 2 goals, 2 assists. Final score: Pittsburgh 6, Washington 4.

POWER-PLAY GOALS

MOST POWER-PLAY GOALS IN PLAYOFFS (CAREER):
35 — Mike Bossy, NY Islanders
34 — Dino Ciccarelli, Minnesota, Washington, Detroit
  — Wayne Gretzky, Edmonton, Los Angeles, St. Louis, NY Rangers
28 — Mario Lemieux, Pittsburgh
27 — Denis Potvin, NY Islanders

MOST POWER-PLAY GOALS, ONE PLAYOFF YEAR:
9 — Mike Bossy, NY Islanders, 1981. 18 games against Toronto, Edmonton, NY Rangers and Minnesota.
  — **Cam Neely, Boston,** 1991. 19 games against Hartford, Montreal, Pittsburgh.
8 — Tim Kerr, Philadelphia, 1989. 19 games.
  — John Druce, Washington, 1990. 15 games.
  — Brian Propp, Minnesota, 1991. 23 games.
  — Mario Lemieux, Pittsburgh, 1992. 15 games.

MOST POWER-PLAY GOALS, ONE PLAYOFF SERIES:
6 — Chris Kontos, Los Angeles, 1989, DSF vs. Edmonton, won by Los Angeles 4-3.
5 — Andy Bathgate, Detroit, 1966, SF vs. Chicago, won by Detroit 4-2.
  — Denis Potvin, NY Islanders, 1981, QF vs. Edmonton, won by NY Islanders 4-2.
  — Ken Houston, Calgary, 1981, QF vs. Philadelphia, won by Calgary 4-0.
  — Rick Vaive, Chicago, 1988, DSF vs. St. Louis, won by St. Louis 4-1.
  — Tim Kerr, Philadelphia, 1989, DF vs. Pittsburgh, won by Philadelphia 4-3.
  — Mario Lemieux, Pittsburgh, 1989, DF vs. Philadelphia won by Philadelphia 4-3.
  — John Druce, Washington, 1990, DF vs. NY Rangers won by Washington 4-1.
  — Pat LaFontaine, Buffalo, 1992, DSF vs. Boston won by Boston 4-3.
  — Adam Graves, NY Rangers, 1996, CQF vs Montreal, won by NY Rangers 4-2.

MOST POWER-PLAY GOALS, ONE GAME:
3 — Syd Howe, Detroit, March 23, 1939, at Detroit vs. Montreal. Detroit won 7-3.
  — **Sid Smith, Toronto,** April 10, 1949, at Detroit. Toronto won 3-1.
  — **Phil Esposito, Boston,** April 2, 1969, at Boston vs. Toronto. Boston won 10-0.
  — **John Bucyk, Boston,** April 21, 1974, at Boston vs. Chicago. Boston won 8-6.
  — **Denis Potvin, NY Islanders,** April 17, 1981, at New York vs. Edmonton. NY Islanders won 6-3.
  — **Tim Kerr, Philadelphia,** April 13, 1985, at NY Rangers. Philadelphia won 6-5.
  — **Jari Kurri, Edmonton,** April 9, 1987, at Edmonton vs. Los Angeles. Edmonton won 13-3.
  — **Mark Johnson, New Jersey,** April 22, 1988, at New Jersey vs. Washington. New Jersey won 10-4.
  — **Dino Ciccarelli, Detroit,** April 29, 1993, at Toronto. Detroit won 7-3.
  — **Dino Ciccarelli, Detroit,** May 11, 1995, at Dallas. Detroit won 5-1.
  — **Valeri Kamensky, Colorado,** April 24, 1997, at Colorado vs. Chicago. Colorado won 7-0.

MOST POWER-PLAY GOALS, ONE PERIOD:
3 — Tim Kerr, Philadelphia, April 13, 1985 at New York, second period in 6-5 win vs. NY Rangers.
2 — Two power-play goals have been scored by one player in one period on 53 occasions. Charlie Conacher of Toronto was the first to score two power-play goals in one period, setting the mark on March 26, 1936. Brendan Shanahan of the Detroit Red Wings is the most recent to equal this mark with two power-play goals in the first period at Phoenix, May 3, 1998. Final score: Detroit 5, Phoenix 2.

SHORTHAND GOALS

MOST SHORTHAND GOALS IN PLAYOFFS (CAREER):
14 — Mark Messier, Edmonton, NY Rangers
11 — Wayne Gretzky, Edmonton, Los Angeles, St. Louis
10 — Jari Kurri, Edmonton, Los Angeles, NY Rangers
8 — Ed Westfall, Boston, NY Islanders
  — Hakan Loob, Calgary

MOST SHORTHAND GOALS, ONE PLAYOFF YEAR:
3 — Derek Sanderson, Boston, 1969. 1 against Toronto in QF, won by Boston 4-0; 2 against Montreal in SF, won by Montreal, 4-2.
  — **Bill Barber, Philadelphia,** 1980. All against Minnesota in SF, won by Philadelphia 4-1.
  — **Lorne Henning, NY Islanders,** 1980. 1 against Boston in QF won by NY Islanders 4-1; 1 against Buffalo in SF, won by NY Islanders 4-2, 1 against Philadelphia in F, won by NY Islanders 4-2.
  — **Wayne Gretzky, Edmonton,** 1983. 2 against Winnipeg in DSF won by Edmonton 3-0; 1 against Calgary in DF, won by Edmonton 4-1.
  — **Wayne Presley, Chicago,** 1989. All against Detroit in DSF won by Chicago 4-2.
  — **Todd Marchant, Edmonton,** 1997. 1 against Dallas in CQF won by Edmonton 4-3; 2 against Colorado in CSF won by Colorado 4-1.

MOST SHORTHAND GOALS, ONE PLAYOFF SERIES:
3 — Bill Barber, Philadelphia, 1980, SF vs. Minnesota, won by Philadelphia 4-1.
  — **Wayne Presley, Chicago,** 1989, DSF vs. Detroit, won by Chicago 4-2.
2 — Mac Colville, NY Rangers, 1940, SF vs. Boston, won by NY Rangers 4-2.
  — Jerry Toppazzini, Boston, 1958, SF vs. NY Rangers, won by Boston 4-2.
  — Dave Keon, Toronto, 1963, F vs. Detroit, won by Toronto 4-1.
  — Bob Pulford, Toronto, 1964, F vs. Detroit, won by Toronto 4-3.
  — Serge Savard, Montreal, 1968, F vs. St. Louis, won by Montreal 4-0.
  — Derek Sanderson, Boston, 1969, SF vs. Montreal, won by Montreal 4-2.
  — Bryan Trottier, NY Islanders, 1980, PR vs. Los Angeles, won by NY Islanders 3-1.
  — Bobby Lalonde, Boston, 1981, PR vs. Minnesota, won by Minnesota 3-0.
  — Butch Goring, NY Islanders, 1981, SF vs. NY Rangers, won by NY Islanders 4-0.
  — Wayne Gretzky, Edmonton, 1983, DSF vs. Winnipeg, won by Edmonton 3-0.
  — Mark Messier, Edmonton, 1983, DF vs. Calgary, won by Edmonton 4-1.
  — Jari Kurri, Edmonton, 1983, CF vs. Chicago, won by Edmonton 4-0.
  — Wayne Gretzky, Edmonton, 1985, DF vs. Winnipeg, won by Edmonton 4-0.
  — Kevin Lowe, Edmonton, 1987, F vs. Philadelphia, won by Edmonton 4-3.
  — Bob Gould, Washington, 1988, DSF vs. Philadelphia, won by Washington 4-3.
  — Dave Poulin, Philadelphia, 1989, DF vs. Pittsburgh, won by Philadelphia 4-3.
  — Russ Courtnall, Montreal, 1991, DF vs. Boston, won by Boston 4-3.
  — Sergei Fedorov, Detroit, 1992 DSF vs. Minnesota, won by Detroit 4-3.
  — Mark Messier, NY Rangers, 1992, DSF vs. New Jersey, won by NY Rangers 4-3.
  — Tom Fitzgerald, NY Islanders, 1993, DF vs. Pittsburgh, won by NY Islanders 4-3.
  — Mark Osborne, Toronto, 1994, CSF vs. San Jose, won by Toronto 4-3.
  — Tony Amonte, Chicago, 1997, CQF vs. Colorado, won by Colorado 4-2.
  — Brian Rolston, New Jersey, 1997, CQF vs. Montreal, won by New Jersey 4-1.
  — Rod Brind'Amour, Philadelphia, 1997, CQF vs. Pittsburgh, won by Philadelphia 4-1.
  — Todd Marchant, Edmonton, 1997, CSF vs. Colorado, won by Colorado 4-1.
  — Jeremy Roenick, Phoenix, 1998, CQF vs. Detroit, won by Detroit 4-2.
  — Vincent Damphousse, San Jose, 1999, CQF vs. Colorado, won by Colorado 4-2.
  — Dixon Ward, Buffalo, 1999, CF vs. Toronto, won by Buffalo 4-1.

MOST SHORTHAND GOALS, ONE GAME:
2 — **Dave Keon, Toronto,** April 18, 1963, at Toronto, in 3-1 win vs. Detroit.
— **Bryan Trottier, NY Islanders,** April 8, 1980 at New York, in 8-1 win vs. Los Angeles.
— **Bobby Lalonde, Boston,** April 11, 1981 at Minnesota, in 6-3 win by Minnesota.
— **Wayne Gretzky, Edmonton,** April 6, 1983 at Edmonton, in 6-3 win vs. Winnipeg.
— **Jari Kurri, Edmonton,** April 24, 1983, at Edmonton, in 8-3 win vs. Chicago.
— **Mark Messier, NY Rangers,** April 21, 1992, at New York, in 7-3 loss vs. New Jersey.
— **Tom Fitzgerald, NY Islanders,** May 8, 1993, at New York, in 6-5 win vs. Pittsburgh.
— **Rod Brind'Amour, Philadelphia,** April 26, 1997, at Philadelphia, in 6-3 win vs. Pittsburgh.
— **Jeremy Roenick, Phoenix,** April 24, 1998, at Detroit, in 7-4 win by Phoenix.
— **Vincent Damphousse, San Jose,** April 30, 1999, at Colorado, in 7-3 win by San Jose.

MOST SHORTHAND GOALS, ONE PERIOD:
2 — **Bryan Trottier, NY Islanders,** April 8, 1980, second period at New York in 8-1 win vs. Los Angeles.
— **Bobby Lalonde, Boston,** April 11, 1981, third period at Minnesota in 6-3 win by Minnesota.
— **Jari Kurri, Edmonton,** April 24, 1983, third period at Edmonton in 8-4 win vs. Chicago.
— **Rod Brind'Amour, Philadelphia,** April 26, 1997, first period at Philadelphia in 6-3 win vs. Pittsburgh.
— **Jeremy Roenick, Phoenix,** April 24, 1998, second period at Detroit in 7-4 win by Phoenix.
— **Vincent Damphousse, San Jose,** April 30, 1999, third period at Colorado, in 7-3 win by San Jose.

GAME-WINNING GOALS

MOST GAME-WINNING GOALS IN PLAYOFFS (CAREER):
24 — **Wayne Gretzky,** Edmonton, Los Angeles, St. Louis, NY Rangers
19 — **Claude Lemieux,** Montreal, New Jersey, Colorado
18 — **Maurice Richard,** Montreal
17 — **Mike Bossy,** NY Islanders
— **Glenn Anderson,** Edmonton, Toronto, NY Rangers, St. Louis

MOST GAME-WINNING GOALS, ONE PLAYOFF YEAR:
6 — **Joe Sakic, Colorado,** 1996. 22 games.
— **Joe Nieuwendyk, Dallas,** 1999. 23 games.
5 — **Mike Bossy, NY Islanders,** 1983. 19 games.
— **Jari Kurri, Edmonton,** 1987. 21 games.
— **Bobby Smith, Minnesota,** 1991. 23 games.
— **Mario Lemieux, Pittsburgh,** 1992. 15 games.

MOST GAME-WINNING GOALS, ONE PLAYOFF SERIES:
4 — **Mike Bossy, NY Islanders,** 1983, CF vs. Boston, won by NY Islanders 4-2.

OVERTIME GOALS

MOST OVERTIME GOALS IN PLAYOFFS (CAREER):
6 — **Maurice Richard, Montreal** (1 in 1946; 3 in 1951; 1 in 1957; 1 in 1958.)
5 — **Glenn Anderson,** Edmonton, Toronto, NY Rangers, St. Louis
4 — **Bob Nystrom,** NY Islanders
— **Dale Hunter,** Quebec, Washington
— **Wayne Gretzky,** Edmonton, Los Angeles
— **Stephane Richer,** Montreal, New Jersey
— **Joe Murphy,** Edmonton, Chicago
— **Esa Tikkanen,** Edmonton, NY Rangers
3 — **Mel Hill,** Boston
— **Rene Robert,** Buffalo
— **Danny Gare,** Buffalo
— **Jacques Lemaire,** Montreal
— **Bobby Clarke,** Philadelphia
— **Terry O'Reilly,** Boston
— **Mike Bossy,** NY Islanders
— **Steve Payne,** Minnesota
— **Ken Morrow,** NY Islanders
— **Lanny McDonald,** Toronto, Calgary
— **Peter Stastny,** Quebec
— **Dino Ciccarelli,** Minnesota, Washington
— **Russ Courtnall,** Montreal
— **Kirk Muller,** Montreal
— **Doug Gilmour,** St. Louis, Calgary, Toronto
— **Greg Adams,** Vancouver
— **Claude Lemieux,** Montreal, Colorado
— **Mike Gartner,** Washington, Toronto
— **Jeremy Roenick,** Chicago, Phoenix

MOST OVERTIME GOALS, ONE PLAYOFF YEAR:
3 — **Mel Hill, Boston,** 1939. All against NY Rangers in best-of-seven SF, won by Boston 4-3.
— **Maurice Richard, Montreal,** 1951. 2 against Detroit in best-of-seven SF, won by Montreal 4-2; 1 against Toronto best-of-seven F, won by Toronto 4-1.

MOST OVERTIME GOALS, ONE PLAYOFF SERIES:
3 — **Mel Hill, Boston,** 1939, SF vs. NY Rangers, won by Boston 4-3. Hill scored at 59:25 of overtime March 21 for a 2-1 win; at 8:24, March 23 for a 3-2 win; and at 48:00, April 2 for a 2-1 win.

One of the greatest two-way talents in NHL history, Dave Keon was the first player to score two shorthand goals in one playoff game. Keon helped the Maple Leafs win the Stanley Cup in 1962, 1963, 1964 and 1967. He is the only Toronto player to win the Conn Smythe Trophy.

SCORING BY A DEFENSEMAN

MOST GOALS BY A DEFENSEMAN, ONE PLAYOFF YEAR:
12 — Paul Coffey, Edmonton, 1985. 18 games.
11 — Brian Leetch, NY Rangers, 1994. 23 games.
 9 — Bobby Orr, Boston, 1970. 14 games.
  — Brad Park, Boston, 1978. 15 games.
 8 — Denis Potvin, NY Islanders, 1981. 18 games.
  — Ray Bourque, Boston, 1983. 17 games.
  — Denis Potvin, NY Islanders, 1983. 20 games.
  — Paul Coffey, Edmonton, 1984. 19 games.

MOST GOALS BY A DEFENSEMAN, ONE GAME:
 3 — Bobby Orr, Boston, April 11, 1971 at Montreal. Final score:
  Boston 5, Montreal 2.
  — **Dick Redmond, Chicago,** April 4, 1973 at Chicago. Final score:
  Chicago 7, St. Louis 1.
  — **Denis Potvin, NY Islanders,** April 17, 1981 at New York. Final score:
  NY Islanders 6, Edmonton 3.
  — **Paul Reinhart, Calgary,** April 14, 1983 at Edmonton. Final score:
  Edmonton 6, Calgary 3.
  — **Doug Halward, Vancouver,** April 7, 1984 at Vancouver. Final score:
  Vancouver 7, Calgary 0.
  — **Paul Reinhart, Calgary,** April 8, 1984 at Vancouver. Final score:
  Calgary 5, Vancouver 1.
  — **Al Iafrate, Washington,** April 26, 1993 at Washington. Final score:
  Washington 6, NY Islanders 4.
  — **Eric Desjardins, Montreal,** June 3, 1993 at Montreal. Final score:
  Montreal 3, Los Angeles 2.
  — **Gary Suter, Chicago,** April 24, 1994, at Chicago. Final score:
  Chicago 4, Toronto 3.
  — **Brian Leetch, NY Rangers,** May 22, 1995 at Philadelphia. Final score:
  Philadelphia 4, NY Rangers 3.

MOST ASSISTS BY A DEFENSEMAN, ONE PLAYOFF YEAR:
25 — Paul Coffey, Edmonton, 1985. 18 games.
24 — Al MacInnis, Calgary, 1989. 22 games.
23 — Brian Leetch, NY Rangers, 1994. 23 games.
19 — Bobby Orr, Boston, 1972. 15 games.
18 — Ray Bourque, Boston, 1988. 23 games.
  — Ray Bourque, Boston, 1991. 19 games.
  — Larry Murphy, Pittsburgh, 1991. 23 games.

MOST ASSISTS BY A DEFENSEMAN, ONE GAME:
 5 — Paul Coffey, Edmonton, May 14, 1985 at Edmonton vs. Chicago. Edmonton
  won 10-5.
  — Risto Siltanen, Quebec, April 14, 1987 at Hartford. Quebec won 7-5.

MOST POINTS BY A DEFENSEMAN, ONE PLAYOFF YEAR:
37 — Paul Coffey, Edmonton, in 1985. 12 goals, 25 assists in 18 games.
34 — Brian Leetch, NY Rangers, in 1994. 11 goals, 23 assists in 23 games.
31 — Al MacInnis, Calgary, in 1989. 7 goals, 24 assists in 22 games.
25 — Denis Potvin, NY Islanders, in 1981. 8 goals, 17 assists in 18 games.
  — Ray Bourque, Boston, in 1991. 7 goals, 18 assists in 19 games.

MOST POINTS BY A DEFENSEMAN, ONE GAME:
 6 — Paul Coffey, Edmonton, May 14, 1985 at Edmonton vs. Chicago. 1 goal,
  5 assists. Edmonton won 10-5.
 5 — Eddie Bush, Detroit, April 9, 1942, at Detroit vs. Toronto. 1 goal, 4 assists.
  Detroit won 5-2.
  — Bob Dailey, Philadelphia, May 1, 1980, at Philadelphia vs. Minnesota. 1 goal,
  4 assists. Philadelphia won 7-0.
  — Denis Potvin, NY Islanders, April 17, 1981, at New York vs. Edmonton. 3 goals,
  2 assists. NY Islanders won 6-3.
  — Risto Siltanen, Quebec, April 14, 1987, at Hartford. 5 assists. Quebec won 7-5.

SCORING BY A ROOKIE

MOST GOALS BY A ROOKIE, ONE PLAYOFF YEAR:
14 — Dino Ciccarelli, Minnesota, 1981. 19 games.
11 — Jeremy Roenick, Chicago, 1990. 20 games.
10 — Claude Lemieux, Montreal, 1986. 20 games.
 9 — Pat Flatley, NY Islanders, 1984. 21 games
 8 — Steve Christoff, Minnesota, 1980. 14 games.
  — Brad Palmer, Minnesota, 1981. 19 games.
  — Mike Krushelnyski, Boston, 1983. 17 games.
  — Bob Joyce, Boston, 1988. 23 games.

MOST POINTS BY A ROOKIE, ONE PLAYOFF YEAR:
21 — Dino Ciccarelli, Minnesota, in 1981. 14 goals, 7 assists in 19 games.
20 — Don Maloney, NY Rangers, in 1979. 7 goals, 13 assists in 18 games.

THREE-OR-MORE-GOAL GAMES

MOST THREE-OR-MORE-GOAL GAMES IN PLAYOFFS (CAREER):
10 — Wayne Gretzky, Edmonton, Los Angeles, St. Louis, NY Rangers. Eight
  three-goal games; two four-goal games.
 7 — Maurice Richard, Montreal. Four three-goal games; two four-goal games; one
  five-goal game.
  — Jari Kurri, Edmonton, Los Angeles, NY Rangers. Six three-goal games; one
  four-goal game.
 6 — Dino Ciccarelli, Minnesota, Washington, Detroit. Five three-goal games; one
  four-goal game.
 5 — Mike Bossy, NY Islanders. Four three-goal games; one four-goal game.

MOST THREE-OR-MORE-GOAL GAMES, ONE PLAYOFF YEAR:
 4 — Jari Kurri, Edmonton, 1985. 1 four-goal game, 3 three-goal games.
 3 — Mark Messier, Edmonton, 1983. 3 three-goal games.
  — Mike Bossy, NY Islanders, 1983. 1 four-goal game, 2 three-goal games
 2 — Newsy Lalonde, Montreal, 1919. 1 five-goal game, 1 four-goal game.
  — Maurice Richard, Montreal, 1944. 1 five-goal game; 1 three-goal game.
  — Doug Bentley, Chicago, 1944. 2 three-goal games.
  — Norm Ullman, Detroit, 1964. 2 three-goal games.
  — Phil Esposito, Boston, 1970. 2 three-goal games.
  — Pit Martin, Chicago, 1973. 2 three-goal games.
  — Rick MacLeish, Philadelphia, 1975. 2 three-goal games.
  — Lanny McDonald, Toronto, 1977. 1 three-goal game; 1 four-goal game.
  — Wayne Gretzky, Edmonton, 1981. 2 three-goal games.
  — Wayne Gretzky, Edmonton, 1983. 2 four-goal games.
  — Wayne Gretzky, Edmonton, 1985. 2 three-goal games.
  — Petr Klima, Detroit, 1988. 2 three-goal games.
  — Cam Neely, Boston, 1991. 2 three-goal games.
  — Wayne Gretzky, NY Rangers, 1997. 2 three-goal games.
  — Daniel Alfredsson, Ottawa, 1998. 2 three-goal games.

MOST THREE-OR-MORE-GOAL GAMES, ONE PLAYOFF SERIES:
 3 — Jari Kurri, Edmonton 1985, CF vs. Chicago won by Edmonton 4-2. Kurri
  scored 3 G May 7 at Edmonton in 7-3 win, 3 G May 14 at Edmonton in 10-5
  win and 4 G May 16 at Chicago in 8-2 win.
 2 — Doug Bentley, Chicago, 1944, SF vs. Detroit, won by Chicago 4-1. Bentley
  scored 3 G Mar. 28 at Chicago in 7-1 win and 3 G Mar. 30 at Detroit in 5-2 win.
  — Norm Ullman, Detroit, 1964, SF vs. Chicago, won by Detroit 4-3. Ullman scored
  3 G Mar. 29 at Chicago in 7-1 win and 3 G April 7 at Detroit in 7-2 win.
  — Mark Messier, Edmonton, 1983, DF vs. Calgary won by Edmonton 4-1. Messier
  scored 4 G April 14 at Edmonton in 6-3 win and 3 G April 17 at Calgary in 10-2
  win.
  — Mike Bossy, NY Islanders, 1983, CF vs. Boston won by NY Islanders 4-2. Bossy
  scored 3 G May 3 at New York in 8-3 win and 4 G May 7 at New York in 8-4
  win.

SCORING STREAKS

LONGEST CONSECUTIVE GOAL-SCORING STREAK, ONE PLAYOFF YEAR:
10 Games — Reggie Leach, Philadelphia, 1976. Streak started April 17 at Toronto and
  ended May 9 at Montreal. He scored one goal in each of eight games;
  two in one game; and five in another; a total of 15 goals.

LONGEST CONSECUTIVE POINT-SCORING STREAK, ONE PLAYOFF YEAR:
18 games — Bryan Trottier, NY Islanders, 1981. 11 goals, 18 assists, 29 points.
17 games — Wayne Gretzky, Edmonton, 1988. 12 goals, 29 assists, 41 points.
  — Al MacInnis, Calgary, 1989. 7 goals, 19 assists, 26 points.

LONGEST CONSECUTIVE POINT-SCORING STREAK,
MORE THAN ONE PLAYOFF YEAR:
27 games — Bryan Trottier, NY Islanders, 1980, 1981 and 1982. 7 games in 1980
  (3 G, 5 A, 8 PTS), 18 games in 1981 (11 G, 18 A, 29 PTS), and two games
  in 1982 (2 G, 3 A, 5 PTS). Total points, 42.
19 games — Wayne Gretzky, Edmonton, Los Angeles, 1988 and 1989. 17 games in
  1988 (12 G, 29 A, 41 PTS with Edmonton), 2 games in 1989 (1 G, 2 A,
  3 PTS with Los Angeles). Total points, 44.

FASTEST GOALS

FASTEST GOAL FROM START OF GAME:
6 Seconds — Don Kozak, Los Angeles, April 17, 1977, at Los Angeles vs. Boston
  and goaltender Gerry Cheevers. Los Angeles won 7-4.
7 Seconds — Bob Gainey, Montreal, May 5, 1977, at New York vs. NY Islanders and
  goaltender Glenn Resch. Montreal won 2-1.
  — Terry Murray, Philadelphia, April 12, 1981, at Quebec vs. goaltender Dan
  Bouchard. Quebec won 4-3 in overtime.
8 Seconds — Stan Smyl, Vancouver, April 7, 1982, at Vancouver vs. Calgary and
  goaltender Pat Riggin. Vancouver won 5-3.

FASTEST GOAL FROM START OF PERIOD (OTHER THAN FIRST):
6 Seconds — Pelle Eklund, Philadelphia, April 25, 1989, at Pittsburgh vs. goaltender
  Tom Barrasso, second period. Pittsburgh won 10-7.
9 Seconds — Bill Collins, Minnesota, April 9, 1968, at Minnesota vs. Los Angeles and
  goaltender Wayne Rutledge, third period. Minnesota won 7-5.
  — Dave Balon, Minnesota, April 25, 1968, at St. Louis vs. goaltender Glenn Hall,
  third period. Minnesota won 5-1.
  — Murray Oliver, Minnesota, April 8, 1971, at St. Louis vs. goaltender Ernie
  Wakely, third period. St. Louis won 4-2.
  — Clark Gillies, NY Islanders, April 15, 1977, at Buffalo vs. goaltender Don
  Edwards, third period. NY Islanders won 4-3.
  — Eric Vail, Atlanta, April 11, 1978, at Atlanta vs. Detroit and goaltender Ron
  Low, third period. Detroit won 5-3.
  — Stan Smyl, Vancouver, April 10, 1979, at Philadelphia vs. goaltender Wayne
  Stephenson, third period. Vancouver won 3-2.
  — Wayne Gretzky, Edmonton, April 6, 1983, at Edmonton vs. Winnipeg and
  goaltender Brian Hayward, second period. Edmonton won 6-3.
  — Mark Messier, Edmonton, April 16, 1984, at Calgary vs. goaltender Don
  Edwards, third period. Edmonton won 5-3.
  — Brian Skrudland, Montreal, May 18, 1986 at Calgary vs. goaltender Mike
  Vernon, overtime. Montreal won 3-2.

FASTEST TWO GOALS:
5 Seconds — Norm Ullman, Detroit, at Detroit, April 11, 1965, vs. Chicago and
  goaltender Glenn Hall. Ullman scored at 17:35 and 17:40 of second period.
  Detroit won 4-2.

FASTEST TWO GOALS FROM START OF A GAME:
1 Minute, 8 Seconds — Dick Duff, Toronto, April 9, 1963 at Toronto vs. Detroit and
  goaltender Terry Sawchuk. Duff scored at 49 seconds and 1:08. Final score:
  Toronto 4, Detroit 2.

FASTEST TWO GOALS FROM START OF A PERIOD:
35 Seconds — **Pat LaFontaine, NY Islanders,** May 19, 1984 at Edmonton vs. goaltender Andy Moog. LaFontaine scored at 13 and 35 seconds of third period. Final score: Edmonton 5, NY Islanders 2.

PENALTIES

MOST PENALTY MINUTES IN PLAYOFFS (CAREER):
729 — Dale Hunter, Quebec, Washington, Colorado
541 — Chris Nilan, Montreal, NY Rangers, Boston
489 — Claude Lemieux, Montreal, New Jersey, Colorado
466 — Willi Plett, Atlanta, Calgary, Minnesota, Boston
455 — Dave Williams, Toronto, Vancouver, Los Angeles

MOST PENALTIES, ONE GAME:
8 — **Forbes Kennedy, Toronto,** April 2, 1969, at Boston. Four minors, 2 majors, 1 10-minute misconduct. Final score: Boston 10, Toronto 0.
— **Kim Clackson, Pittsburgh,** April 14, 1980, at Boston. Five minors, 2 majors, 1 10-minute misconduct. Final score: Boston 6, Pittsburgh 2

MOST PENALTY MINUTES, ONE GAME:
42 — **Dave Schultz, Philadelphia,** April 22, 1976, at Toronto. One minor, 2 majors, 1 10-minute misconduct and 2 game-misconducts. Final score: Toronto 8, Philadelphia 5.

MOST PENALTIES, ONE PERIOD AND MOST PENALTY MINUTES, ONE PERIOD:
6 Penalties; 39 Minutes — **Ed Hospodar, NY Rangers,** April 9, 1981, at Los Angeles, first period. Two minors, 1 major, 1 10-minute misconduct, 2 game misconducts. Final score: Los Angeles 5, NY Rangers 4.

GOALTENDING

MOST PLAYOFF GAMES APPEARED IN BY A GOALTENDER (CAREER):
179 — Patrick Roy, Montreal, Colorado
150 — Grant Fuhr, Edmonton, Toronto, Buffalo, Los Angeles, St. Louis
134 — Mike Vernon, Calgary, Detroit, San Jose
132 — Bill Smith, Los Angeles, NY Islanders
— Andy Moog, Edmonton, Boston, Dallas, Montreal

MOST MINUTES PLAYED BY A GOALTENDER (CAREER):
11,055 — Patrick Roy, Montreal, Colorado
8,834 — Grant Fuhr, Edmonton, Toronto, Buffalo, Los Angeles, St. Louis
7,977 — Mike Vernon, Calgary, Detroit, San Jose
7,645 — Bill Smith, Los Angeles, NY Islanders
7,452 — Andy Moog, Edmonton, Boston, Dallas, Montreal

MOST MINUTES PLAYED BY A GOALTENDER, ONE PLAYOFF YEAR:
1,544 — Kirk McLean, Vancouver, 1994. 24 games.
— Ed Belfour, Dallas, 1999. 23 games.
1,540 — Ron Hextall, Philadelphia, 1987. 26 games.
1,477 — Mike Richter, NY Rangers, 1994. 23 games.
1,454 — Patrick Roy, Colorado, 1996. 22 games.

MOST SHUTOUTS IN PLAYOFFS (CAREER):
15 — Clint Benedict, Ottawa, Mtl. Maroons
14 — Jacques Plante, Montreal, St. Louis
13 — Turk Broda, Toronto
12 — Terry Sawchuk, Detroit, Toronto, Los Angeles
— Patrick Roy, Montreal, Colorado

MOST SHUTOUTS, ONE PLAYOFF YEAR:
4 — Clint Benedict, Mtl. Maroons, 1926. 8 games.
— Clint Benedict, Mtl. Maroons, 1928. 9 games.
— Dave Kerr, NY Rangers, 1937. 9 games.
— Frank McCool, Toronto, 1945. 13 games.
— Terry Sawchuk, Detroit, 1952. 8 games.
— Bernie Parent, Philadelphia, 1975. 17 games.
— Ken Dryden, Montreal, 1977. 14 games.
— Mike Richter, NY Rangers, 1994. 23 games.
— Kirk McLean, Vancouver, 1994. 24 games.
— Olaf Kolzig, Washington, 1998. 21 games.

MOST SHUTOUTS, ONE PLAYOFF SERIES:
3 — Dave Kerr, NY Rangers, in 1940 SF, 6 games vs. Boston.
— Frank McCool, Toronto, in 1945 F, 7 games vs. Detroit.
— Turk Broda, Toronto, in 1950 SF, 7 games vs. Detroit.
— Felix Potvin, Toronto, in 1994 CQF, 6 games vs. Chicago.
— Martin Brodeur, New Jersey, in 1995 CQF, 5 games vs. Boston.

MOST WINS BY A GOALTENDER, (CAREER):
110 — Patrick Roy, Montreal, Colorado
92 — Grant Fuhr, Edmonton, Buffalo, St. Louis
88 — Bill Smith, Los Angeles, NY Islanders
80 — Ken Dryden, Montreal

MOST WINS BY A GOALTENDER, ONE PLAYOFF YEAR:
16 — Grant Fuhr, Edmonton, 1988. 19 games.
— Mike Vernon, Calgary, 1989. 22 games.
— Bill Ranford, Edmonton, 1990. 22 games.
— Tom Barrasso, Pittsburgh, 1992. 21 games.
— Patrick Roy, Montreal, 1993. 20 games.
— Mike Richter, NY Rangers, 1994. 23 games.
— Martin Brodeur, New Jersey, 1995. 20 games.
— Patrick Roy, Colorado, 1996. 22 games.
— Mike Vernon, Detroit, 1997. 20 games.
— Chris Osgood, Detroit, 1998. 22 games.
— Ed Belfour, Dallas, 1999. 23 games.

MOST CONSECUTIVE WINS BY A GOALTENDER, MORE THAN ONE PLAYOFF YEAR:
14 — **Tom Barrasso, Pittsburgh,** 1992, 1993; 3 wins against NY Rangers in 1992 DF, won by Pittsburgh 4-2; 4 wins against Boston in 1992 CF, won by Pittsburgh 4-0; 4 wins against Chicago in 1992 F, won by Pittsburgh 4-0; 3 wins against New Jersey in 1993 DSF, won by Pittsburgh 4-1.

MOST CONSECUTIVE WINS BY A GOALTENDER, ONE PLAYOFF YEAR:
11 — **Ed Belfour, Chicago,** 1992. 3 wins against St. Louis in DSF, won by Chicago 4-2; 4 wins against Detroit in DF, won by Chicago 4-0; and 4 wins against Edmonton in CF, won by Chicago 4-0.
— **Tom Barrasso, Pittsburgh,** 1992. 3 wins against NY Rangers in DF, won by Pittsburgh 4-2; 4 wins against Boston in CF, won by Pittsburgh 4-0; and 4 wins against Chicago in F, won by Pittsburgh 4-0.
— **Patrick Roy, Montreal,** 1993. 4 wins against Quebec in DSF, won by Montreal 4-2; 4 wins against Buffalo in DF, won by Montreal 4-0; and 3 wins against NY Islanders in CF, won by Montreal 4-1.

LONGEST SHUTOUT SEQUENCE:
248 Minutes, 32 Seconds — **Norm Smith, Detroit,** 1936. In best-of-five SF, Smith shut out Mtl. Maroons 1-0, March 24, in 116:30 overtime; shut out Maroons 3-0 in second game, March 26; and was scored against at 12:02 of first period, March 29, by Gus Marker. Detroit won SF 3-0.

MOST CONSECUTIVE SHUTOUTS:
3 — **Clint Benedict, Mtl. Maroons,** 1926. Benedict shut out Ottawa 1-0, Mar. 27; he then shut out Victoria twice, 3-0, Mar. 30; 3-0, Apr. 1. Mtl. Maroons won NHL F vs. Ottawa 2 goals to 1 and won the best-of-five F vs. Victoria 3-1.
— **John Roach, NY Rangers,** 1929. Roach shut out NY Americans twice, 0-0, Mar. 19; 1-0, Mar. 21; he then shut out Toronto 1-0, Mar. 24. NY Rangers won QF vs. NY Americans 1 goal to 0 and won the best-of-three SF vs. Toronto 2-0.
— **Frank McCool, Toronto,** 1945. McCool shut out Detroit 1-0, April 6; 2-0, April 8; 1-0, April 12. Toronto won the best-of-seven F 4-3.

Early Playoff Records

1893-1918
Team Records

MOST GOALS, BOTH TEAMS, ONE GAME:
25 — **Ottawa Silver Seven, Dawson City** at Ottawa, Jan. 16, 1905. Ottawa 23, Dawson City 2. Ottawa won best-of-three series 2-0.

MOST GOALS, ONE TEAM, ONE GAME:
23 — **Ottawa Silver Seven** at Ottawa, Jan. 16, 1905. Ottawa defeated Dawson City 23-2.

MOST GOALS, BOTH TEAMS, BEST-OF-THREE SERIES:
42 — **Ottawa Silver Seven, Queen's University** at Ottawa, 1906. Ottawa defeated Queen's 16-7, Feb. 27, and 12-7, Feb. 28.

MOST GOALS, ONE TEAM, BEST-OF-THREE SERIES:
32 — **Ottawa Silver Seven** in 1905 at Ottawa. Defeated Dawson City 9-2, Jan. 13, and 23-2, Jan. 16.

MOST GOALS, BOTH TEAMS, BEST-OF-FIVE SERIES:
39 — **Toronto Arenas, Vancouver Millionaires** at Toronto, 1918. Toronto won 5-3, Mar. 20; 6-3, Mar. 26; 2-1, Mar. 30. Vancouver won 6-4, Mar. 23, and 8-1, Mar. 28. Toronto scored 18 goals; Vancouver 21.

MOST GOALS, ONE TEAM, BEST-OF-FIVE SERIES:
26 — **Vancouver Millionaires** in 1915 at Vancouver. Defeated Ottawa Senators 6-2, Mar. 22; 8-3, Mar. 24; and 12-3 Mar. 26.

Individual Records

MOST GOALS IN PLAYOFFS:
63 — **Frank McGee, Ottawa Silver Seven,** in 22 playoff games. Seven goals in four games, 1903; 21 goals in eight games, 1904; 18 goals in four games, 1905; 17 goals in six games, 1906.

MOST GOALS, ONE PLAYOFF SERIES:
15 — **Frank McGee, Ottawa Silver Seven,** in two games in 1905 at Ottawa. Scored one goal, Jan. 13, in 9-2 victory over Dawson City and 14 goals, Jan. 16, in 23-2 victory.

MOST GOALS, ONE PLAYOFF GAME:
14 — **Frank McGee, Ottawa Silver Seven,** Jan. 16, 1905 at Ottawa in 23-2 victory over Dawson City.

FASTEST THREE GOALS:
40 Seconds — **Marty Walsh, Ottawa Senators,** at Ottawa, March 16, 1911, at 3:00, 3:10, and 3:40 of third period. Ottawa defeated Port Arthur 13-4.

All-Time Playoff Goal Leaders since 1918
(40 or more goals)

Player	Teams	Yrs.	GP	G
Wayne Gretzky	Edm., L.A., St.L., NYR	16	208	122
* Mark Messier	Edm., NYR	17	236	109
Jari Kurri	Edm., L.A., NYR, Ana., Col.	14	200	106
Glenn Anderson	Edm., Tor., NYR, St.L.	15	225	93
Mike Bossy	NYI	10	129	85
Maurice Richard	Mtl.	15	133	82
Jean Beliveau	Mtl.	17	162	79
* Brett Hull	Cgy., St.L., Dal.	14	130	77
* Claude Lemieux	Mtl., N.J., Col.	14	198	76
Dino Ciccarelli	Min., Wsh., Det.	14	141	73
* Esa Tikkanen	Edm., NYR, St.L., Van., Wsh.	13	186	72
Bryan Trottier	NYI, Pit.	17	221	71
Mario Lemieux	Pit.	7	89	70
Gordie Howe	Det., Hfd.	20	157	68
Denis Savard	Chi., Mtl., T.B.	16	169	66
Yvan Cournoyer	Mtl.	12	147	64
Brian Propp	Phi., Bos., Min., Hfd.	13	160	64
Bobby Smith	Min., Mtl.	13	184	64
Bobby Hull	Chi., Wpg., Hfd.	14	119	62
Phil Esposito	Chi., Bos., NYR	15	130	61
Jacques Lemaire	Mtl.	11	145	61
* Steve Yzerman	Det.	14	145	61
Joe Mullen	St.L., Cgy., Pit., Bos.	15	143	60
Stan Mikita	Chi.	18	155	59
* Paul Coffey	Edm., Pit., L.A., Det., Phi., Car.	16	194	59
Guy Lafleur	Mtl., NYR, Que.	14	128	58
Bernie Geoffrion	Mtl., NYR	16	132	58
Cam Neely	Van., Bos.	9	93	57
Steve Larmer	Chi., NYR	13	140	56
Denis Potvin	NYI	14	185	56
* Jaromir Jagr	Pit.	9	113	55
Rick MacLeish	Phi., Hfd., Pit., Det.	11	114	54
* Doug Gilmour	St.L., Cgy., Tor., N.J.	14	152	54
Bill Barber	Phi.	11	129	53
* Stephane Richer	Mtl., N.J.	11	128	52
Frank Mahovlich	Tor., Det., Mtl.	14	137	51
* Brian Bellows	Min., Mtl., T.B., Ana., Wsh.	13	143	51
Steve Shutt	Mtl., L.A.	12	99	50
Henri Richard	Mtl.	18	180	49
Reggie Leach	Bos., Cal., Phi., Det.	8	94	47
* Luc Robitaille	L.A., Pit., NYR	11	115	47
* Rick Tocchet	Phi., Pit., Bos., Phx.	11	121	47
Ted Lindsay	Det., Chi.	16	133	47
Clark Gillies	NYI, Buf.	13	164	47
* Joe Nieuwendyk	Cgy., Dal.	11	97	46
Dickie Moore	Mtl., Tor., St.L.	14	135	46
Rick Middleton	NYR, Bos.	12	114	45
Lanny McDonald	Tor., Col., Cgy.	13	117	44
* Kevin Stevens	Pit.	6	86	43
Ken Linseman	Phi., Edm., Bos., Tor.	11	113	43
Mike Gartner	Wsh., Min., NYR, Tor., Phx.	15	122	43
* Jeremy Roenick	Chi., Phx.	11	95	42
Bernie Nicholls	L.A., NYR, Edm., N.J., Chi., S.J.	13	118	42
Bobby Clarke	Phi.	13	136	42
* Dale Hunter	Que., Wsh., Col.	18	186	42
* Joe Sakic	Que., Col.	6	76	41
John Bucyk	Det., Bos.	14	124	41
Tim Kerr	Phi., NYR, Hfd.	10	81	40
Peter McNab	Buf., Bos., Van., N.J.	10	107	40
* Ron Francis	Hfd., Pit., Car.	14	133	40
Bob Bourne	NYI, L.A.	13	139	40
John Tonelli	NYI, Cgy., L.A., Chi., Que.	13	172	40

All-Time Playoff Assist Leaders since 1918
(60 or more assists)

Player	Teams	Yrs.	GP	A
Wayne Gretzky	Edm., L.A., St.L., NYR	16	208	260
* Mark Messier	Edm., NYR	17	236	186
* Paul Coffey	Edm., Pit., L.A., Det., Phi., Car.	16	194	137
Jari Kurri	Edm., L.A., NYR, Ana., Col.	14	200	127
* Ray Bourque	Bos.	19	180	125
Glenn Anderson	Edm., Tor., NYR, St.L.	15	225	121
* Doug Gilmour	St.L., Cgy., Tor., N.J.	14	152	117
Larry Robinson	Mtl., L.A.	20	227	116
Bryan Trottier	NYI, Pit.	17	221	113
* Larry Murphy	L.A., Wsh., Min., Pit., Tor., Det.	18	200	111
Denis Savard	Chi., Mtl., T.B.	16	169	109
Denis Potvin	NYI	14	185	108
* Al MacInnis	Cgy., St.L.	15	142	102
* Adam Oates	Det., St.L., Bos., Wsh.	11	126	100
Jean Beliveau	Mtl.	17	162	97
Bobby Smith	Min., Mtl.	13	184	96
Gordie Howe	Det., Hfd.	20	157	92
* Chris Chelios	Mtl., Chi., Det.	15	173	92
Stan Mikita	Chi.	18	155	91
Brad Park	NYR, Bos., Det.	17	161	90
* Sergei Fedorov	Det.	9	120	88
* Steve Yzerman	Det.	14	145	87
* Craig Janney	Bos., St.L., S.J., Wpg., Phx.	11	120	86
Mario Lemieux	Pit.	7	89	85
Brian Propp	Phi., Bos., Min., Hfd.	13	160	84
* Ron Francis	Hfd., Pit., Car.	14	133	83
Henri Richard	Mtl.	18	180	80
Jacques Lemaire	Mtl.	11	145	78
Ken Linseman	Phi., Edm., Bos., Tor.	11	113	77
Bobby Clarke	Phi.	13	136	77
Guy Lafleur	Mtl., NYR, Que.	14	128	76
Phil Esposito	Chi., Bos., NYR	15	130	76
Dale Hunter	Que., Wsh., Col	18	186	76
Mike Bossy	NYI	10	129	75
Steve Larmer	Chi., NYR	13	140	75
John Tonelli	NYI, Cgy., L.A., Chi., Que.	13	172	75
Peter Stastny	Que., N.J., St.L.	12	93	72
Bernie Nicholls	L.A., NYR, Edm., N.J., Chi., S.J.	13	118	72
* Brian Bellows	Min., Mtl., T.B., Ana., Wsh.	13	143	71
* Scott Stevens	Wsh., St.L., N.J.	16	155	71
* Claude Lemieux	Mtl., N.J., Col.	14	198	71
Gilbert Perreault	Buf.	11	90	70
* Geoff Courtnall	Bos., Edm., Wsh., Van., St.L.	15	156	70
Dale Hawerchuk	Wpg., Buf., St.L., Phi.	15	97	69
Alex Delvecchio	Det.	14	121	69
Bobby Hull	Chi., Wpg., Hfd.	14	119	67
Frank Mahovlich	Tor., Det., Mtl.	14	137	67
Bobby Orr	Bos., Chi.	8	74	66
Bernie Federko	St.L., Det.	11	91	66
Jean Ratelle	NYR, Bos.	15	123	66
Charlie Huddy	Edm., L.A., Buf., St.L.	14	183	66
* Jaromir Jagr	Pit.	9	113	64
Dickie Moore	Mtl., Tor., St.L.	14	135	64
Doug Harvey	Mtl., NYR, Det., St.L.	15	137	64
Neal Broten	Min., Dal., N.J., L.A.	13	135	63
Yvan Cournoyer	Mtl.	12	147	63
John Bucyk	Det., Bos.,	14	124	62
* Brian Leetch	NYR	7	82	61
Doug Wilson	Chi., S.J.	12	95	61
Bernie Geoffrion	Mtl., NYR	16	132	60
* Esa Tikkanen	Edm., NYR, St.L., Van., Wsh.	13	186	60

All-Time Playoff Point Leaders since 1918
(100 or more points)

Player	Teams	Yrs.	GP	G	A	Pts.
Wayne Gretzky	Edm., L.A., St.L. NYR	16	208	122	260	382
* Mark Messier	Edm., NYR	17	236	109	186	295
Jari Kurri	Edm., L.A., NYR, Ana.,Col.	14	200	106	127	233
Glenn Anderson	Edm., Tor., NYR, St.L.	15	225	93	121	214
* Paul Coffey	Edm., Pit., L.A., Det.,Phi., Car.	16	194	59	137	196
Bryan Trottier	NYI, Pit.	17	221	71	113	184
Jean Beliveau	Mtl.	17	162	79	97	176
Denis Savard	Chi., Mtl., T.B.	16	169	66	109	175
* Doug Gilmour	St.L., Cgy., Tor., N.J.	14	152	54	117	171
Denis Potvin	NYI	14	185	56	108	164
* Ray Bourque	Bos.	19	180	36	125	161
Mike Bossy	NYI	10	129	85	75	160
Gordie Howe	Det., Hfd.	20	157	68	92	160
Bobby Smith	Min., Mtl.	13	184	64	96	160
Mario Lemieux	Pit.	7	89	70	85	155
Stan Mikita	Chi.	18	155	59	91	150
* Steve Yzerman	Det.	14	145	61	87	148
Brian Propp	Phi., Bos., Min., Hfd.	13	160	64	84	148
* Claude Lemieux	Mtl., N.J., Col.	14	198	76	71	147
* Larry Murphy	L.A., Wsh., Min., Pit.,Tor., Det.	18	200	35	111	146
Larry Robinson	Mtl., L.A.	20	227	28	116	144
Jacques Lemaire	Mtl	11	145	61	78	139
* Adam Oates	Det., St.L., Bos., Wsh.	11	126	38	100	138
* Al MacInnis	Cgy., St.L.	15	142	36	102	138
Phil Esposito	Chi., Bos., NYR	15	130	61	76	137
* Brett Hull	Cgy., St.L., Dal.	14	130	77	58	135
Guy Lafleur	Mtl., NYR, Que.	14	128	58	76	134
* Esa Tikkanen	Edm., NYR, St.L., Van.,Wsh.	13	186	72	60	132
Steve Larmer	Chi., NYR	13	140	56	75	131
Bobby Hull	Chi., Wpg., Hfd.	14	119	62	67	129
Henri Richard	Mtl.	18	180	49	80	129
Yvan Cournoyer	Mtl.	12	147	64	63	127
* Sergei Fedorov	Det.	9	120	38	88	126
Maurice Richard	Mtl.	15	133	82	44	126
Brad Park	NYR, Bos., Det.	17	161	35	90	125
* Ron Francis	Hfd., Pit., Car.	14	133	40	83	123
* Brian Bellows	Min., Mtl., T.B. Ana., Wsh.	13	143	51	71	122
Ken Linseman	Phi., Edm., Bos., Tor.	11	113	43	77	120
* Chris Chelios	Mtl., Chi.,Det.	15	173	28	92	120
* Jaromir Jagr	Pit.	9	113	55	64	119
Bobby Clarke	Phi.	13	136	42	77	119
Bernie Geoffrion	Mtl., NYR	16	132	58	60	118
Frank Mahovlich	Tor., Det., Mtl.	14	137	51	67	118
Dino Ciccarelli	Min., Wsh., Det.	14	141	73	45	118
John Tonelli	NYI, Cgy., L.A., Chi., Que.	13	172	40	75	115
Dale Hunter	Que., Wsh., Col.	18	186	42	76	118
Bernie Nicholls	L.A., NYR, Edm., N.J., Chi., S.J.	13	118	42	72	114
* Craig Janney	Bos., St.L., S.J., Wpg., Phx.	11	120	24	86	110
Dickie Moore	Mtl., Tor., St.L.	14	135	46	64	110
* Geoff Courtnall	Bos., Edm., Wsh., Van., St.L.	15	156	39	70	109
Bill Barber	Phi.	11	129	53	55	108
Rick MacLeish	Phi., Hfd., Pit., Det.	11	114	54	53	107
* Luc Robitaille	L.A., Pit., NYR	11	115	47	59	106
Joe Mullen	St.L., Cgy., Pit., Bos.	15	143	60	46	106
Peter Stastny	Que., N.J., St.L.	12	93	33	72	105
Alex Delvecchio	Det.	14	121	35	69	104
Gilbert Perreault	Buf.	11	90	33	70	103
John Bucyk	Det., Bos.,	14	124	41	62	103
Bernie Federko	St.L., Det.	11	91	35	66	101
* Kevin Stevens	Pit.	6	86	43	57	100
Rick Middleton	NYR, Bos.	12	114	45	55	100
* Rick Tocchet	Phi., Pit., Bos., Phx.	11	127	47	53	100

Three-or-more-Goal Games, Playoffs 1918–1999

Player	Team	Date	City	Total Goals	Opposing Goaltender	Score	
Wayne Gretzky (10)	Edm.	Apr. 11/81	Edm.	3	Richard Sevigny	Edm. 6	Mtl. 2
		Apr. 19/81	Edm.	3	Billy Smith	Edm. 5	NYI 2
		Apr. 6/83	Edm.	4	Brian Hayward	Edm. 6	Wpg. 3
		Apr. 17/83	Cgy.	4	Rejean Lemelin	Edm. 10	Cgy. 2
		Apr. 25/85	Wpg.	3	Bryan Hayward (2)		
					Marc Behrend (1)	Edm. 8	Wpg. 3
		May 25/85	Edm.	3	Pelle Lindbergh	Edm. 4	Phi. 3
		Apr. 24/86	Cgy.	3	Mike Vernon	Edm. 7	Cgy. 4
	L.A.	May 29/93	Tor.	3	Felix Potvin	L.A. 5	Tor. 4
	NYR	Apr. 23/97	NYR	3	John Vanbiesbrouck	NYR 3	Fla. 2
		May 18/97	Phi.	3	Garth Snow	NYR 5	Phi. 4
Maurice Richard (7)	Mtl.	Mar. 23/44	Mtl.	5	Paul Bibeault	Mtl. 5	Tor. 1
		Apr. 7/44	Chi.	3	Mike Karakas	Mtl. 3	Chi. 1
		Mar. 29/45	Mtl.	4	Frank McCool	Mtl. 10	Tor. 3
		Apr. 14/53	Bos.	3	Gord Henry	Mtl. 7	Bos. 3
		Mar. 20/56	Mtl.	3	Gump Worsley	Mtl. 7	NYR 1
		Apr. 6/57	Mtl.	4	Don Simmons	Mtl. 5	Bos. 1
		Apr. 1/58	Det.	3	Terry Sawchuk	Mtl. 4	Det. 3
Jari Kurri (7)	Edm.	Apr. 4/84	Edm.	3	Doug Soetaert (1)		
					Mike Veisor (2)	Edm. 9	Wpg. 2
		Apr. 25/85	Wpg.	3	Bryan Hayward (2)		
					Marc Behrend (1)	Edm. 8	Wpg. 3
		May 7/85	Edm.	3	Murray Bannerman	Edm. 7	Chi. 3
		May 14/85	Edm.	3	Murray Bannerman	Edm. 10	Chi. 5
		May 16/85	Chi.	4	Murray Bannerman	Edm. 8	Chi. 2
		Apr. 9/87	Edm.	4	Rollie Melanson (2)		
					Daren Eliot (2)	Edm. 13	L.A. 3
		May 18/90	Bos.	3	Andy Moog (2)		
					Rejean Lemelin (1)	Edm. 7	Bos. 2
Dino Ciccarelli (6)	Min.	May 5/81	Min.	3	Pat Riggin	Min. 7	Cgy. 4
		Apr. 10/82	Min.	3	Murray Bannerman	Min. 7	Chi. 1
	Wsh.	Apr. 5/90	N.J.	3	Sean Burke	Wsh. 5	N.J. 4
		Apr. 25/92	Pit.	4	Tom Barrasso (1)		
					Ken Wregget (3)	Wsh. 7	Pit. 2
	Det.	Apr. 29/93	Tor.	3	Felix Potvin (2)		
					Daren Puppa (1)	Det. 7	Tor. 3
		May 11/95	Dal.	3	Andy Moog (2)		
					Darcy Wakaluk (1)	Det. 5	Dal. 1
Mike Bossy (5)	NYI	Apr. 16/79	NYI	3	Tony Esposito	NYI 6	Chi. 2
		May 8/82	NYI	3	Richard Brodeur	NYI 6	Van. 5
		Apr. 10/83	Wsh.	3	Al Jensen	NYI 6	Wsh. 3
		May 3/83	NYI	3	Pete Peeters	NYI 8	Bos. 3
		May 7/83	NYI	4	Pete Peeters	NYI 8	Bos. 4
Phil Esposito (4)	Bos.	Apr. 2/69	Bos.	4	Bruce Gamble	Bos. 10	Tor. 0
		Apr. 8/70	Bos.	3	Ed Giacomin	Bos. 8	NYR 2
		Apr. 19/70	Chi.	3	Tony Esposito	Bos. 6	Chi. 3
		Apr. 8/75	Bos.	3	Tony Esposito (2)		
					Michel Dumas (1)	Bos. 8	Chi. 2
Mark Messier (4)	Edm.	Apr. 14/83	Edm.	4	Rejean Lemelin	Edm. 6	Cgy. 3
		Apr. 17/83	Cgy.	3	Rejean Lemelin (1)	Edm. 10	Cgy. 2
					Don Edwards (2)		
		Apr. 26/83	Edm.	3	Murray Bannerman	Edm. 8	Chi. 2
	NYR	May 25/94	N.J.	3	Martin Brodeur (2)	NYR 4	N.J. 2
					ENG (1)		
Steve Yzerman (4)	Det.	Apr. 6/89	Det.	3	Alain Chevrier	Chi. 5	Det. 4
		Apr. 4/91	St. L.	3	Vincent Riendeau (2)	Det. 6	St. L. 3
		May 8/96	St. L.	3	Jon Casey	St.L. 5	Det. 4
		Apr. 21/99	Det.	3	Guy Hebert (2)	Det.. 5	Ana. 3
					Pat Jablonski (1)		
Bernie Geoffrion (3)	Mtl.	Mar. 27/52	Mtl.	3	Jim Henry	Mtl. 4	Bos. 0
		Apr. 7/55	Mtl.	3	Terry Sawchuk	Mtl. 4	Det. 2
		Mar. 30/57	Mtl.	3	Gump Worsley	Mtl. 8	NYR 3
Norm Ullman (3)	Det.	Mar. 29/64	Chi.	3	Glenn Hall	Det. 5	Chi. 4
		Apr. 7/64	Det.	3	Glenn Hall (2)		
					Denis DeJordy (1)	Det. 7	Chi. 2
		Apr. 11/65	Det.	3	Glenn Hall	Det. 4	Chi. 2
John Bucyk (3)	Bos.	May 3/70	St. L.	3	Jacques Plante (1)		
					Ernie Wakely (2)	Bos. 6	St. L. 1
		Apr. 20/72	Bos.	3	Jacques Caron (1)		
					Ernie Wakely (2)	Bos. 10	St. L. 2
		Apr. 21/74	Bos.	3	Tony Esposito	Bos. 8	Chi. 6
Rick MacLeish (3)	Phi.	Apr. 11/74	Phi.	3	Phil Myre	Phi. 5	Atl. 1
		Apr. 13/75	Phi.	3	Gord McRae	Phi. 6	Tor. 3
		May 13/75	Phi.	3	Glenn Resch	Phi. 4	NYI 1
Denis Savard (3)	Chi.	Apr. 19/82	Chi.	3	Mike Liut	Chi. 7	StL. 4
		Apr. 10/86	Chi.	4	Ken Wregget	Tor. 6	Chi. 4
		Apr. 9/88	St. L.	3	Greg Millen	Chi. 6	St. L. 3
Tim Kerr (3)	Phi.	Apr. 13/85	NYR	4	Glen Hanlon	Phi. 6	NYR 5
		Apr. 20/87	Phi.	3	Kelly Hrudey	Phi. 4	NYI 2
		Apr. 19/89	Pit.	3	Tom Barrasso	Phi. 4	Pit. 2
Cam Neely (3)	Bos.	Apr. 9/87	Mtl.	3	Patrick Roy	Mtl. 4	Bos. 3
		Apr. 5/91	Bos.	3	Peter Sidorkiewicz	Bos. 4	Hfd. 3
		Apr. 25/91	Bos.	3	Patrick Roy	Bos. 4	Mtl. 1
Petr Klima (3)	Det.	Apr. 7/88	Tor.	3	Alan Bester (2)		
					Ken Wregett (1)	Det. 6	Tor. 2
		Apr. 21/88	St. L.	3	Greg Millen	Det. 6	St. L. 0
	Edm.	May 4/91	Edm.	3	Jon Casey	Edm. 7	Min. 2
Esa Tikkanen (3)	Edm.	May 22/88	Edm.	3	Rejean Lemelin	Edm. 6	Bos. 3
		Apr. 16/91	Cgy.	3	Mike Vernon	Edm. 5	Cgy. 4
		Apr. 26/92	L.A.	3	Kelly Hrudey	Edm. 5	L.A. 2
					Tom Askey (1)		
Mario Lemieux (3)	Pit.	Apr. 25/89	Pit.	5	Ron Hextall	Pit. 10	Phi. 7
		Apr. 23/92	Pit.	3	Don Beaupre	Pit. 6	Wsh. 4
		May 11/96	Pit.	3	Mike Richter	Pit. 7	NYR 3
Mike Gartner (3)	NYR	Apr. 13/90	NYR	3	Mark Fitzpatrick (2)		
					Glenn Healy (1)	NYR 6	NYI 5
		Apr. 27/92	NYR	3	Chris Terreri	NYR 8	N.J. 5
	Tor.	Apr. 25/96	Tor.	3	Jon Casey	Tor. 5	St.L. 4
Newsy Lalonde (2)	Mtl.	Mar. 1/19	Mtl.	5	Clint Benedict	Mtl. 6	Ott. 3
		Mar. 22/19	Sea.	4	Harry Holmes	Mtl. 4	Sea. 2
Howie Morenz (2)	Mtl.	Mar. 22/24	Mtl.	3	Charles Reid	Mtl. 6	Cgy.T. 1
		Mar. 27/25	Mtl.	3	Harry Holmes	Mtl. 4	Vic. 2
Toe Blake (2)	Mtl.	Mar. 22/38	Mtl.	3	Mike Karakas	Mtl. 6	Chi. 4
		Mar. 26/46	Chi.	3	Mike Karakas	Mtl. 7	Chi. 2
Doug Bentley (2)	Chi.	Mar. 28/44	Chi.	3	Connie Dion	Chi. 7	Det. 1
		Mar. 30/44	Det.	3	Connie Dion	Chi. 5	Det. 2
Ted Kennedy (2)	Tor.	Apr. 14/45	Tor.	3	Harry Lumley	Det. 5	Tor. 3
		Mar. 27/48	Tor.	4	Frank Brimsek	Tor. 5	Bos. 3
Bobby Hull (2)	Chi.	Apr. 7/63	Det.	3	Terry Sawchuk	Det. 7	Chi. 4
		Apr. 9/72	Pit.	3	Jim Rutherford	Chi. 6	Pit. 5
F. St. Marseille (2)	St. L.	Apr. 28/70	St. L.	3	Al Smith	St. L. 5	Pit. 0
		Apr. 6/72	Min	3	Cesare Maniago	Min. 6	St. L. 5
Pit Martin (2)	Chi.	Apr. 4/73	Chi.	3	Wayne Stephenson	Chi. 7	St. L. 1
		May 10/73	Chi.	3	Ken Dryden	Mtl. 6	Chi. 4
Yvan Cournoyer (2)	Mtl.	Apr. 5/73	Mtl.	3	Dave Dryden	Mtl. 7	Buf. 3
		Apr. 11/74	Mtl.	3	Ed Giacomin	Mtl. 4	NYR 1
Guy Lafleur (2)	Mtl.	May 1/75	Mtl.	3	Roger Crozier (1)		
					Gerry Desjardins (2)	Mtl. 7	Buf. 0
		Apr. 11/77	Mtl.	3	Ed Staniowski	Mtl. 7	St. L. 2
Lanny McDonald (2)	Tor.	Apr. 9/77	Pit.	3	Denis Herron	Tor. 5	Pit. 2
		Apr. 17/77	Tor.	4	Wayne Stephenson	Phi. 6	Tor. 5
Butch Goring (2)	L.A.	Apr. 9/77	L.A.	3	Phil Myre	L.A. 4	Atl. 2
	NYI	May 17/81	Min.	3	Gilles Meloche	NYI 7	Min. 5
Bryan Trottier (2)	NYI	Apr. 8/80	NYI	3	Doug Keans	NYI 8	L.A. 1
		Apr. 9/81	NYI	3	Michel Larocque	NYI 5	Tor. 1
Bill Barber (2)	Phi.	May 4/80	Min.	4	Gilles Meloche	Phi. 5	Min. 3
		Apr. 9/81	Phi.	3	Dan Bouchard	Phi. 8	Que. 5
Brian Propp (2)	Phi.	Apr. 22/81	Phi.	3	Pat Riggin	Phi. 9	Cgy. 4
		Apr. 21/85	Phi.	3	Billy Smith	Phi. 5	NYI 2
Paul Reinhart (2)	Cgy	Apr. 14/83	Edm.	3	Andy Moog	Edm. 6	Cgy. 3
		Apr. 8/84	Van	3	Richard Brodeur	Cgy. 5	Van. 1
Peter Stastny (2)	Que.	Apr. 5/83	Bos.	3	Pete Peeters	Bos. 4	Que. 3
		Apr. 11/87	Que.	3	Mike Liut (2)		
					Steve Weeks (1)	Que. 5	Hfd. 1
Glenn Anderson (2)	Edm.	Apr. 26/83	Edm.	4	Murray Bannerman	Edm. 8	Chi. 2
		Apr. 6/88	Wpg.	3	Daniel Berthiaume	Edm. 7	Wpg. 4
Michel Goulet (2)	Que.	Apr. 23/85	Que.	3	Steve Penney	Que. 7	Mtl. 6
		Apr. 12/87	Que.	3	Mike Liut	Que. 4	Hfd. 1
Peter Zezel (2)	Phi.	Apr. 13/86	NYR	3	John Vanbiesbrouck	Phi. 7	NYR 1
	St. L.	Apr. 11/89	St. L.	3	Jon Casey (2)		
					Kari Takko (1)	St. L. 6	Min. 1
Geoff Courtnall (2)	Van.	Apr. 4/91	L.A.	3	Kelly Hrudey	Van. 6	L.A. 5
		Apr. 30/92	Van.	3	Rick Tabaracci	Van. 5	Win. 0
Joe Sakic (2)	Que.	May 6/95	Que.	3	Mike Richter	Que. 5	NYR 4
	Col.	Apr. 25/96	Col.	3	Corey Hirsch	Col. 5	Van. 4
Daniel Alfredsson (2)	Ott.	Apr. 28/98	Ott.	3	Martin Brodeur	Ott. 4	N.J. 3
		May 11/98	Ott.	3	Olaf Kolzig	Ott. 4	Wsh. 3
Harry Meeking	Tor.	Mar. 11/18	Tor.	3	Georges Vezina	Tor. 7	Mtl. 3
Alf Skinner	Tor.	Mar. 23/18	Tor.	3	Hugh Lehman	Van.M. 6	Tor. 4
Joe Malone	Mtl.	Feb. 23/19	Mtl.	3	Clint Benedict	Mtl. 8	Ott. 4
Odie Cleghorn	Mtl.	Feb. 27/19	Ott.	3	Clint Benedict	Mtl. 5	Ott. 3
Jack Darragh	Ott.	Apr. 1/20	Tor.	3	Harry Holmes	Ott. 6	Sea. 1
George Boucher	Ott.	Mar. 10/21	Ott.	3	Jake Forbes	Ott. 5	Tor. 0
Babe Dye	Tor.	Mar. 28/22	Tor.	4	Hugh Lehman	Tor. 5	Van.M. 1
Percy Galbraith	Bos.	Mar. 31/27	Bos.	3	Hugh Lehman	Bos. 4	Chi. 4
Harvey Jackson	Tor.	Apr. 5/32	NYR	3	John Ross Roach	Tor. 6	NYR 4
Frank Boucher	NYR	Apr. 9/32	Tor.	3	Lorne Chabot	Tor. 6	NYR 4
Charlie Conacher	Tor.	Mar. 26/36	Tor.	3	Tiny Thompson	Tor. 8	Bos. 3
Syd Howe	Det.	Mar. 23/39	Det.	3	Claude Bourque	Det. 7	Mtl. 3
Bryan Hextall Sr.	NYR	Apr. 3/40	NYR	3	Turk Broda	NYR 6	Tor. 2
Joe Benoit	Mtl.	Mar. 22/41	Mtl.	3	Sam LoPresti	Mtl. 4	Chi. 3
Syl Apps Sr.	Tor.	Mar. 25/41	Tor.	3	Frank Brimsek	Tor. 7	Bos. 2
Jack McGill	Bos.	Mar. 29/42	Bos.	3	Johnny Mowers	Det. 6	Bos. 4
Don Metz	Tor.	Apr. 14/42	Tor.	3	Johnny Mowers	Tor. 9	Det. 3
Mud Bruneteau	Det.	Apr. 1/43	Det.	3	Frank Brimsek	Det. 6	Bos. 2
Don Grosso	Det.	Apr. 7/43	Bos.	3	Frank Brimsek	Det. 4	Bos. 0
Carl Liscombe	Det.	Apr. 3/45	Bos.	4	Paul Bibeault	Det. 5	Bos. 3
Billy Reay	Mtl.	Apr. 1/47	Bos.	4	Frank Brimsek	Mtl. 5	Bos. 1
Gerry Plamondon	Mtl.	Mar. 24/49	Det.	3	Harry Lumley	Mtl. 4	Det. 3
Sid Smith	Tor.	Apr. 10/49	Det.	3	Harry Lumley	Tor. 3	Det. 1
Pentti Lund	NYR	Apr. 2/50	NYR	3	Bill Durnan	NYR 4	Mtl. 1
Ted Lindsay	Det.	Apr. 5/55	Det.	4	Charlie Hodge (1)		
					Jacques Plante (3)	Det. 7	Mtl. 1
Gordie Howe	Det.	Apr. 10/55	Det.	3	Jacques Plante	Det. 5	Mtl. 1
Phil Goyette	Mtl.	Mar. 25/58	Mtl.	3	Terry Sawchuk	Mtl. 8	Det. 1
Jerry Toppazzini	Bos.	Apr. 5/58	Bos.	3	Gump Worsley	Bos. 8	NYR 2
Bob Pulford	Tor.	Apr. 19/62	Tor.	3	Glenn Hall	Tor. 8	Chi. 4
Dave Keon	Tor.	Apr. 9/64	Mtl.	3	Charlie Hodge	Tor. 3	Mtl. 1
Henri Richard	Mtl.	Apr. 20/67	Mtl.	3	Terry Sawchuk (2)		
					Johnny Bower (1)	Mtl. 6	Tor. 2
Rosaire Paiement	Phi.	Apr. 13/68	Phi.	3	Glenn Hall (1)		
					Seth Martin (2)	Phi. 6	St. L. 1
Jean Beliveau	Mtl.	Apr. 20/68	Mtl.	3	Denis DeJordy	Mtl. 4	Chi. 1
Red Berenson	St. L.	Apr. 15/69	St. L	3	Gerry Desjardins	St. L. 4	L.A. 0
Ken Schinkel	Pit.	Apr. 11/70	Oak.	3	Gary Smith	Pit. 5	Oak. 2
Jim Pappin	Chi.	Apr. 11/71	Phi.	3	Bruce Gamble	Chi. 6	Phi. 2
Bobby Orr	Bos.	Apr. 11/71	Mtl.	3	Ken Dryden	Bos. 5	Mtl. 2
Jacques Lemaire	Mtl.	Apr. 20/71	Mtl.	3	Gump Worsley	Mtl. 7	Min. 2

Player	Team	Date	City	Total Goals	Opposing Goaltender	Score	
Vic Hadfield	NYR	Apr. 22/71	NYR	3	Tony Esposito	NYR 4	Chi. 1
Fred Stanfield	Bos.	Apr. 18/72	Bos.	3	Jacques Caron	Bos. 6	St. L. 1
Ken Hodge	Bos.	Apr. 30/72	Bos.	3	Eddie Giacomin	Bos. 6	NYR 5
Steve Vickers	NYR	Apr. 10/73	Bos.	3	Ross Brooks (2) Eddie Johnston (1)	NYR 6	Bos. 3
Dick Redmond	Chi.	Apr. 4/73	Chi.	3	Wayne Stephenson	Chi. 7	St. L. 1
Tom Williams	L.A.	Apr. 14/74	L.A.	3	Mike Veisor	L.A. 5	Chi. 1
Marcel Dionne	L.A.	Apr. 15/76	L.A.	3	Gilles Gilbert	L.A. 6	Bos. 4
Don Saleski	Phi.	Apr. 20/76	Phi.	3	Wayne Thomas	Phi. 7	Tor. 1
Darryl Sittler	Tor.	Apr. 22/76	Tor.	5	Bernie Parent	Tor. 8	Phi. 5
Reggie Leach	Phi.	May 6/76	Phi.	5	Gilles Gilbert	Phi. 6	Bos. 3
Jim Lorentz	Buf.	Apr. 7/77	Min.	3	Pete LoPresti (2) Gary Smith (1)	Buf. 7	Min. 1
Bobby Schmautz	Bos.	Apr. 11/77	Bos.	3	Rogie Vachon	Bos. 8	L.A. 3
Billy Harris	NYI	Apr. 23/77	Mtl.	3	Ken Dryden	Mtl. 4	NYI 3
George Ferguson	Tor.	Apr. 11/78	Tor.	3	Rogie Vachon	Tor. 7	L.A. 3
Jean Ratelle	Bos.	May 3/79	Bos.	3	Ken Dryden	Bos. 4	Mtl. 3
Stan Jonathan	Bos.	May 8/79	Bos.	3	Ken Dryden	Bos. 5	Mtl. 2
Ron Duguay	NYR	Apr. 20/80	NYR	3	Pete Peeters	NYR 4	Phi. 2
Steve Shutt	Mtl.	Apr. 22/80	Mtl.	3	Gilles Meloche	Mtl. 6	Min. 2
Gilbert Perreault	Buf.	May 6/80	NYI	3	Billy Smith (2) ENG (1)	Buf. 7	NYI 4
Paul Holmgren	Phi.	May 15/80	Phil	3	Billy Smith	Phi. 8	NYI 3
Steve Payne	Min.	Apr. 8/81	Bos.	3	Rogie Vachon	Min. 5	Bos. 4
Denis Potvin	NYI	Apr. 17/81	NYI	3	Andy Moog	NYI 6	Edm. 3
Barry Pederson	Bos.	Apr. 8/82	Bos.	3	Don Edwards	Bos. 7	Buf. 3
Duane Sutter	NYI	Apr. 15/83	NYI	3	Glen Hanlon	NYI 5	NYR 0
Doug Halward	Van.	Apr. 7/84	Van.	3	Rejean Lemelin (2) Don Edwards (1)	Van. 7	Cgy. 0
Jorgen Pettersson	St. L.	Apr. 8/84	Det.	3	Eddie Mio	St. L. 3	Det. 2
Clark Gillies	NYI	May 12/84	NYI	3	Grant Fuhr	NYI 6	Edm. 1
Ken Linseman	Bos.	Apr. 14/85	Bos.	3	Steve Penney	Bos. 7	Mtl. 6
Dave Andreychuk	Buf.	Apr. 14/85	Buf.	3	Dan Bouchard	Buf. 7	Que. 4
Greg Paslawski	St. L.	Apr. 15/86	Min.	3	Don Beaupre	St. L. 6	Min. 3
Doug Risebrough	Cgy.	May 4/86	Cgy.	3	Rick Wamsley	Cgy. 8	St. L. 2
Mike McPhee	Mtl.	Apr. 11/87	Bos.	3	Doug Keans	Mtl. 5	Bos. 4
John Ogrodnick	Que.	Apr. 14/87	Hfd.	3	Mike Liut	Que. 7	Hfd. 5
Pelle Eklund	Phi.	May 10/87	Mtl.	3	Patrick Roy (1) Bryan Hayward (2)	Phi. 6	Mtl. 3
John Tucker	Buf.	Apr. 9/88	Bos.	4	Andy Moog	Buf. 6	Bos. 2
Tony Hrkac	St. L.	Apr. 10/88	St. L.	4	Darren Pang	St. L. 6	Chi. 5
Hakan Loob	Cgy.	Apr. 10/88	Cgy.	3	Glenn Healy	Cgy. 7	L.A. 3
Ed Olczyk	Tor.	Apr. 12/88	Tor.	3	Greg Stefan (2) Glen Hanlon (1)	Tor. 6	Det. 5
Aaron Broten	N.J.	Apr. 20/88	N.J.	3	Pete Peeters	N.J. 5	Wsh. 2
Mark Johnson	N.J.	Apr. 22/88	Wsh.	4	Pete Peeters	N.J. 10	Wsh. 4
Patrik Sundstrom	N.J.	Apr. 22/88	Wsh.	3	Pete Peeters (2) Clint Malarchuk (1)	N.J. 10	Wsh. 4
Bob Brooke	Min.	Apr. 5/89	St. L.	3	Greg Millen	St. L. 4	Min. 3
Chris Kontos	L.A.	Apr. 6/89	L.A.	3	Grant Fuhr	L.A. 5	Edm. 2
Wayne Presley	Chi.	Apr. 13/89	Chi.	3	Greg Stefan (1) Glen Hanlon (2)	Chi. 7	Det. 1
Tony Granato	L.A.	Apr. 10/90	L.A.	3	Mike Vernon (1) Rick Wamsley (2)	L.A. 12	Cgy. 4
Tomas Sandstrom	L.A.	Apr. 10/90	L.A.	3	Mike Vernon (1) Rick Wamsley (2)	L.A. 12	Cgy. 4
Dave Taylor	L.A.	Apr. 10/90	L.A.	3	Mike Vernon (1) Rick Wamsley (2)	L.A. 12	Cgy. 4
Bernie Nicholls	NYR	Apr. 19/90	NYR	3	Mike Liut	NYR 7	Wsh. 3
John Druce	Wsh.	Apr. 21/90	NYR	3	John Vanbiesbrouck	Wsh. 6	NYR 3
Adam Oates	St. L.	Apr. 12/91	St. L.	3	Tim Chevaldae	St. L. 6	Det. 1
Luc Robitaille	L.A.	Apr. 26/91	L.A.	3	Grant Fuhr	L.A. 5	Edm. 2
Ron Francis	Pit.	May 9/92	Pit.	3	Mike Richter (2) John V'brouck (1)	Pit. 5	NYR. 4
Dirk Graham	Chi.	June 1/92	Chi.	3	Tom Barrasso	Pit. 5	Chi. 2
Joe Murphy	Edm.	May 6/92	Edm.	3	Kirk McLean	Edm. 5	Van. 2
Ray Sheppard	Det.	Apr. 24/92	Min.	3	Jon Casey	Min. 5	Det. 2
Kevin Stevens	Pit.	May 21/92	Bos.	4	Andy Moog	Pit. 5	Bos. 2
Pavel Bure	Van.	Apr. 28/92	Wpg.	3	Rick Tabaracci	Van. 8	Wpg. 3
Brian Noonan	Chi.	Apr. 18/93	Chi.	3	Curtis Joseph	St. L. 4	Chi. 3
Dale Hunter	Wsh.	Apr. 20/93	Wsh.	3	Glenn Healy	NYI 5	Wsh. 4
Teemu Selanne	Wpg.	Apr. 23/93	Wpg.	3	Kirk McLean	Wpg. 5	Van. 4
Ray Ferraro	NYI	Apr. 26/93	Wsh.	4	Don Beaupre	Wsh. 6	NYI 4
Al Iafrate	Wsh.	Apr. 26/93	Wsh.	3	Glenn Healy (2) Mark Fitzpatrick (1)	Wsh. 6	NYI 4
Paul Di Pietro	Mtl.	Apr. 28/93	Mtl.	3	Ron Hextall	Mtl. 6	Que. 2
Wendel Clark	Tor.	May 27/93	L.A.	3	Kelly Hrudey	L.A. 5	Tor. 4
Eric Desjardins	Mtl.	Jun. 3/93	Mtl.	3	Kelly Hrudey	Mtl. 3	L.A. 2
Tony Amonte	Chi.	Apr. 23/94	Chi.	4	Felix Potvin	Chi. 5	Tor. 4
Gary Suter	Chi.	Apr. 24/94	Chi.	3	Felix Potvin	Chi. 4	Tor. 3
Ulf Dahlen	S.J.	May 6/94	S.J.	3	Felix Potvin	S.J. 5	Tor. 2
Mike Sullivan	Cgy.	May 11/95	S.J.	3	Arturs Irbe (2) Wade Flaherty (1)	Cgy. 9	S.J. 2
Theoren Fleury	Cgy.	May 13/95	S.J.	4	Arturs Irbe (3) ENG (1)	Cgy. 6	S.J. 4
Brendan Shanahan	St. L.	May 13/95	Van.	3	Kirk McLean	St. L. 5	Van. 2
John LeClair	Phi.	May 21/95	Phi.	3	Mike Richter	Phi. 5	NYR 4
Brian Leetch	NYR	May 22/95	Phi.	3	Ron Hextall	Phi. 4	NYR 3
Trevor Linden	Van.	Apr. 25/96	Col.	3	Patrick Roy	Col. 5	Van. 4
Jaromir Jagr	Pit.	May 11/96	Pit.	3	Mike Richter	Pit. 7	NYR 3
Peter Forsberg	Col.	Jun. 6/96	Col.	3	John Vanbiesbrouck	Col. 8	Fla. 1
Valeri Zelepukin	N.J.	Apr. 22/97	Mtl.	3	Jocelyn Thibault	N.J. 6	Mtl. 4
Valeri Kamensky	Col.	Apr. 24/97	Col.	3	Jeff Hackett (2) Chris Terreri (1)	Col. 7	Chi. 0
Eric Lindros	Phi.	May 20/97	NYR	3	Mike Richter	Phi. 6	NYR 3
Matthew Barnaby	Buf.	May 10/98	Buf.	3	Andy Moog (2) ENG (1)	Buf. 6	Mtl. 3
Martin Straka	Pit.	Apr. 25/99	Pit.	3	Martin Brodeur	Pit. 4	N.J. 2

Leading Playoff Scorers, 1918–1999

Season	Player and Club	Games Played	Goals	Assists	Points
1998-99	Peter Forsberg, Colorado	19	8	16	24
1997-98	Steve Yzerman, Detroit	22	6	18	24
1996-97	Eric Lindros, Philadelphia	19	12	14	26
1995-96	Joe Sakic, Colorado	22	18	16	34
1994-95	Sergei Fedorov, Detroit	17	7	17	24
1993-94	Brian Leetch, NY Rangers	23	11	23	34
1992-93	Wayne Gretzky, Los Angeles	24	15	25	40
1991-92	Mario Lemieux, Pittsburgh	15	16	18	34
1990-91	Mario Lemieux, Pittsburgh	23	16	28	44
1989-90	Craig Simpson, Edmonton	22	16	15	31
	Mark Messier, Edmonton	22	9	22	31
1988-89	Al MacInnis, Calgary	22	7	24	31
1987-88	Wayne Gretzky, Edmonton	19	12	31	43
1986-87	Wayne Gretzky, Edmonton	21	5	29	34
1985-86	Doug Gilmour, St. Louis	19	9	12	21
	Bernie Federko, St. Louis	19	7	14	21
1984-85	Wayne Gretzky, Edmonton	18	17	30	47
1983-84	Wayne Gretzky, Edmonton	19	13	22	35
1982-83	Wayne Gretzky, Edmonton	16	12	26	38
1981-82	Bryan Trottier, NY Islanders	19	6	23	29
1980-81	Mike Bossy, NY Islanders	18	17	18	35
1979-80	Bryan Trottier, NY Islanders	21	12	17	29
1978-79	Jacques Lemaire, Montreal	16	11	12	23
	Guy Lafleur, Montreal	16	10	13	23
1977-78	Guy Lafleur, Montreal	15	10	11	21
	Larry Robinson, Montreal	15	4	17	21
1976-77	Guy Lafleur, Montreal	14	9	17	26
1975-76	Reggie Leach, Philadelphia	16	19	5	24
1974-75	Rick MacLeish, Philadelphia	17	11	9	20
1973-74	Rick MacLeish, Philadelphia	17	13	9	22
1972-73	Yvan Cournoyer, Montreal	17	15	10	25
1971-72	Phil Esposito, Boston	15	9	15	24
	Bobby Orr, Boston	15	5	19	24
1970-71	Frank Mahovlich, Montreal	20	14	13	27
1969-70	Phil Esposito, Boston	14	13	14	27
1968-69	Phil Esposito, Boston	10	8	10	18
1967-68	Bill Goldsworthy, Minnesota	14	8	7	15
1966-67	Jim Pappin, Toronto	12	7	8	15
1965-66	Norm Ullman, Detroit	12	6	9	15
1964-65	Bobby Hull, Chicago	14	10	7	17
1963-64	Gordie Howe, Detroit	14	9	10	19
1962-63	Gordie Howe, Detroit	11	7	9	16
	Norm Ullman, Detroit	11	4	12	16
1961-62	Stan Mikita, Chicago	12	6	15	21
1960-61	Gordie Howe, Detroit	11	4	11	15
	Pierre Pilote, Chicago	12	3	12	15
1959-60	Henri Richard, Montreal	8	3	9	12
	Bernie Geoffrion, Montreal	8	2	10	12
1958-59	Dickie Moore, Montreal	11	5	12	17
1957-58	Fleming Mackell, Boston	12	5	14	19
1956-57	Bernie Geoffrion, Montreal	11	11	7	18
1955-56	Jean Béliveau, Montreal	10	12	7	19
1954-55	Gordie Howe, Detroit	11	9	11	20
1953-54	Dickie Moore, Montreal	11	5	8	13
1952-53	Ed Sanford, Boston	11	8	3	11
1951-52	Ted Lindsay, Detroit	8	5	2	7
	Floyd Curry, Montreal	11	4	3	7
	Metro Prystai, Detroit	8	2	5	7
	Gordie Howe, Detroit	8	2	5	7
1950-51	Maurice Richard, Montreal	11	9	4	13
	Max Bentley, Toronto	11	2	11	13
1949-50	Pentti Lund, NY Rangers	12	6	5	11
1948-49	Gordie Howe, Detroit	11	8	3	11
1947-48	Ted Kennedy, Toronto	9	8	6	14
1946-47	Maurice Richard, Montreal	10	6	5	11
1945-46	Elmer Lach, Montreal	9	5	12	17
1944-45	Joe Carveth, Detroit	14	5	6	11
1943-44	Toe Blake, Montreal	9	7	11	18
1942-43	Carl Liscombe, Detroit	10	6	8	14
1941-42	Don Grosso, Detroit	12	8	6	14
1940-41	Milt Schmidt, Boston	11	5	6	11
1939-40	Phil Watson, NY Rangers	12	3	6	9
	Neil Colville, NY Rangers	12	2	7	9
1938-39	Bill Cowley, Boston	12	3	11	14
1937-38	Johnny Gottselig, Chicago	10	5	3	8
1936-37	Marty Barry, Detroit	10	4	7	11
1935-36	Frank Boll, Toronto	9	7	3	10
1934-35	Baldy Northcott, Mtl. Maroons	7	4	1	5
	Harvey Jackson, Toronto	7	3	2	5
	Cy Wentworth, Mtl. Maroons	7	3	2	5
1933-34	Larry Aurie, Detroit	9	3	7	10
1932-33	Cecil Dillon, NY Rangers	8	8	2	10
1931-32	Frank Boucher, NY Rangers	7	3	6	9
1930-31	Cooney Weiland, Boston	5	6	3	9
1929-30	Marty Barry, Boston	6	3	3	6
	Cooney Weiland, Boston	6	1	5	6
1928-29	Andy Blair, Toronto	4	3	0	3
	Butch Keeling, NY Rangers	6	3	0	3
	Ace Bailey, Toronto	4	1	2	3
1927-28	Frank Boucher, NY Rangers	9	7	3	10
1926-27	Harry Oliver, Boston	8	4	2	6
	Percy Galbraith, Boston	8	3	3	6
	Frank Fredrickson, Boston	8	2	4	6
1925-26	Nels Stewart, Mtl. Maroons	8	6	3	9
1924-25	Howie Morenz, Montreal	6	7	1	8
1923-24	Howie Morenz, Montreal	6	7	2	9
1922-23	Punch Broadbent, Ottawa	8	6	1	7
1921-22	Babe Dye, Toronto	7	11	2	13
1920-21	Cy Denneny, Ottawa	7	4	2	6
1919-20	Frank Nighbor, Ottawa	5	6	1	7
	Jack Darragh, Ottawa	5	5	2	7
1918-19	Newsy Lalonde, Montreal	10	17	1	18
1917-18	Alf Skinner, Toronto	7	8	1	9

Overtime Games since 1918

Abbreviations: Teams/Cities: — **Ana.** - Anaheim; **Atl.** - Atlanta; **Bos.** - Boston; **Buf.** - Buffalo; **Cgy.** - Calgary; **Cgy. T.** - Calgary Tigers (Western Canada Hockey League); **Chi.** - Chicago; **Col.** - Colorado; **Dal.** - Dallas; **Det.** - Detroit; **Edm.** - Edmonton; **Edm. E.** - Edmonton Eskimos (WCHL); **Fla.** - Florida; **Hfd.** - Hartford; **K.C.** - Kansas City; **L.A.** - Los Angeles; **Min.** - Minnesota; **Mtl.** - Montreal; **Mtl.M.** - Montreal Maroons; **N.J.** - New Jersey; **NYA** - NY Americans; **NYI** - New York Islanders; **NYR** - New York Rangers; **Oak.** - Oakland; **Ott.** - Ottawa; **Phi.** - Philadelphia; **Phx.** - Phoenix; **Pit.** - Pittsburgh; **Que.** - Quebec; **St. L.** - St. Louis; **Sea.** - Seattle Metropolitans (Pacific Coast Hockey Association); **S.J.** - San Jose; **T.B.** - Tampa Bay; **Tor.** - Toronto; **Van.** - Vancouver; **Van. M** - Vancouver Millionaires (PCHA); **Vic.** - Victoria Cougars (WCHL); **Wpg.** - Winnipeg, **Wsh.** - Washington.

SERIES — **CF** - conference final; **CSF** - conference semi-final; **CQF** - conference quarter-final; **DF** - division final; **DSF** - division semi-final; **F** - final; **PR** - preliminary round; **QF** - quarter final; **SF** - semi-final.

Date	City	Series	Score		Scorer	Overtime	Series Winner
Mar. 26/19	Sea.	F	Mtl. 0	Sea. 0	no scorer	20:00	
Mar. 30/19	Sea.	F	Mtl. 4	Sea. 3	Odie Cleghorn	15:57	
Mar. 20/22	Tor.	F	Tor 2	Van.M. 1	Babe Dye	4:50	Tor.
Mar. 29/23	Van.	F	Ott. 2	Edm.E. 1	Cy Denneny	2:08	Ott.
Mar. 31/27	Mtl.	QF	Mtl. 1	Mtl. M. 0	Howie Morenz	12:05	Mtl.
Apr. 7/27	Bos.	F	Ott. 0	Bos. 0	no scorer	20:00	Ott.
Apr. 11/27	Ott.	F	Bos. 1	Ott. 1	no scorer	20:00	Ott.
Apr. 3/28	Mtl.	QF	Mtl. M. 1	Mtl. 0	Russ Oatman	8:20	Mtl. M.
Apr. 7/28	Mtl.	F	NYR 2	Mtl. M. 1	Frank Boucher	7:05	NYR
Mar. 21/29	NY	QF	NYR 1	NYA 0	Butch Keeling	29:50	NYR
Mar. 26/29	Tor.	SF	NYR 2	Tor. 1	Frank Boucher	2:03	NYR
Mar. 20/30	Mtl.	SF	Bos. 2	Mtl. M. 1	Harry Oliver	45:35	Bos.
Mar. 25/30	Bos.	SF	Mtl. M. 1	Bos. 0	Archie Wilcox	26:27	Bos.
Mar. 26/30	Mtl.	QF	Chi. 2	Mtl. 2	Howie Morenz (Mtl.)	51:43	Mtl.
Mar. 28/30	Mtl.	SF	Mtl. 2	NYR 1	Gus Rivers	68:52	Mtl.
Mar. 24/31	Bos.	SF	Bos. 5	Mtl. 4	Cooney Weiland	18:56	Mtl.
Mar. 26/31	Chi.	QF	Chi. 2	Tor. 1	Stew Adams	19:20	Chi.
Mar. 28/31	Mtl.	SF	Mtl. 4	Bos. 3	Georges Mantha	5:10	Mtl.
Apr. 1/31	Mtl.	SF	Mtl. 3	Bos. 2	Wildor Larochelle	19:00	Mtl.
Apr. 5/31	Chi.	F	Chi. 2	Mtl. 1	Johnny Gottselig	24:50	Mtl.
Apr. 9/31	Mtl.	F	Chi. 3	Mtl. 2	Cy Wentworth	53:50	Mtl.
Mar. 26/32	Mtl.	SF	NYR 4	Mtl. 3	Fred Cook	59:32	NYR
Apr. 2/32	Tor.	SF	Tor. 3	Mtl. M. 2	Bob Gracie	17:59	Tor.
Mar. 25/33	Bos.	SF	Bos. 2	Tor. 1	Marty Barry	14:14	Tor.
Mar. 28/33	Bos.	SF	Tor. 1	Bos. 0	Busher Jackson	15:03	Tor.
Mar. 30/33	Tor.	SF	Bos. 2	Tor. 1	Eddie Shore	4:23	Tor.
Apr. 3/33	Tor.	SF	Tor. 1	Bos. 0	Ken Doraty	104:46	Tor.
Apr. 13/33	Tor.	F	NYR 1	Tor. 0	Bill Cook	7:33	NYR
Mar. 22/34	Tor.	SF	Det. 2	Tor. 1	Herbie Lewis	1:33	Det.
Mar. 25/34	Chi.	QF	Chi. 1	Mtl. 1	Mush March (Chi)	11:05	Chi.
Apr. 3/34	Det	F	Chi. 2	Det. 1	Paul Thompson	21:10	Chi.
Apr. 10/34	Chi.	F	Chi. 1	Det. 0	Mush March	30:05	Chi.
Mar. 23/35	Bos.	SF	Bos. 1	Tor. 0	Dit Clapper	33:26	Tor.
Mar. 26/35	Chi.	QF	Mtl. M. 1	Chi. 0	Baldy Northcott	4:02	Mtl. M.
Mar. 30/35	Tor.	SF	Tor. 2	Bos. 1	Pep Kelly	1:36	Tor.
Apr. 4/35	Tor.	F	Mtl. M. 3	Tor. 2	Dave Trottier	5:28	Mtl. M.
Mar. 24/36	Mtl.	SF	Det. 1	Mtl. M. 0	Mud Bruneteau	116:30	Det.
Apr. 9/36	Tor.	F	Tor. 4	Det. 3	Buzz Boll	0:31	Det.
Mar. 25/37	NY	QF	NYR 2	Tor. 1	Babe Pratt	13:05	NYR
Apr. 1/37	Mtl.	SF	Det. 2	Mtl. 1	Hec Kilrea	51:49	Det.
Mar. 22/38	NY	QF	NYA 2	NYR 1	Johnny Sorrell	21:25	NYA
Mar. 24/38	Tor.	SF	Tor. 1	Bos. 0	George Parsons	21:31	Tor.
Mar. 26/38	Mtl.	QF	Chi. 3	Mtl. 2	Paul Thompson	11:49	Chi.
Mar. 27/38	NY	QF	NYA 3	NYR 2	Lorne Carr	60:40	NYA
Mar. 29/38	Bos.	SF	Tor. 3	Bos. 2	Gordie Drillon	10:04	Tor.
Mar. 31/38	Chi.	SF	Chi. 1	NYA 0	Cully Dahlstrom	33:01	Chi.
Mar. 21/39	NY	SF	Bos. 2	NYR 1	Mel Hill	59:25	Bos.
Mar. 23/39	Bos.	SF	Bos. 3	NYR 2	Mel Hill	8:24	Bos.
Mar. 26/39	Det.	QF	Det. 1	Mtl. 0	Marty Barry	7:47	Det.
Mar. 30/39	Bos.	SF	NYR 2	Bos. 1	Clint Smith	17:19	Bos.
Apr. 1/39	Tor.	SF	Tor. 5	Det. 4	Gordie Drillon	5:42	Tor.
Apr. 2/39	Bos.	SF	Bos. 2	NYR 1	Mel Hill	48:00	Bos.
Apr. 9/39	Bos.	F	Tor. 3	Bos. 2	Doc Romnes	10:38	Bos.
Mar. 19/40	Det.	QF	Det. 2	NYA 1	Syd Howe	0:25	Det.
Mar. 19/40	Tor.	QF	Tor. 3	Chi. 2	Syl Apps Sr.	6:35	Tor.
Apr. 2/40	NY	F	NYR 2	Tor. 1	Alf Pike	15:30	NYR
Apr. 11/40	Tor.	F	NYR 2	Tor. 1	Muzz Patrick	31:43	NYR
Apr. 13/40	Tor.	F	NYR 3	Tor. 2	Bryan Hextall Sr.	2:07	NYR
Mar. 20/41	Det.	QF	Det. 2	NYR 1	Gus Giesebrecht	12:01	Det.
Mar. 22/41	Mtl.	QF	Mtl. 4	Chi. 3	Charlie Sands	34:04	Chi.
Mar. 29/41	Bos.	SF	Tor. 2	Bos. 1	Pete Langelle	17:31	Bos.
Mar. 30/41	Chi.	SF	Det. 2	Chi. 1	Gus Giesebrecht	9:15	Det.
Mar. 22/42	Chi.	QF	Bos. 2	Chi. 1	Des Smith	6:51	Bos.
Mar. 21/43	Bos.	SF	Bos. 5	Mtl. 4	Don Gallinger	12:30	Bos.
Mar. 23/43	Det.	SF	Tor. 3	Det. 2	Jack McLean	70:18	Det.
Mar. 25/43	Mtl.	SF	Bos. 3	Mtl. 2	Harvey Jackson	3:20	Bos.
Mar. 30/43	Tor.	SF	Det. 3	Tor. 2	Adam Brown	9:21	Det.
Mar. 30/43	Bos.	SF	Bos. 5	Mtl. 4	Ab DeMarco	3:41	Bos.
Apr. 13/44	Mtl.	F	Mtl. 5	Chi. 4	Toe Blake	9:12	Mtl.
Mar. 27/45	Tor.	SF	Tor. 4	Mtl. 3	Gus Bodnar	12:36	Tor.
Mar. 29/45	Det.	SF	Det. 3	Bos. 2	Mud Bruneteau	17:12	Det.
Apr. 21/45	Tor.	F	Det. 1	Tor. 0	Ed Bruneteau	14:16	Tor.
Mar. 28/46	Bos	SF	Bos. 4	Det. 3	Don Gallinger	9:51	Bos.
Mar. 30/46	Mtl.	F	Mtl. 4	Bos. 3	Maurice Richard	9:08	Mtl.
Apr. 2/46	Mtl.	F	Mtl. 3	Bos. 2	Jim Peters	16:55	Mtl.
Apr. 7/46	Bos.	F	Bos. 3	Mtl. 2	Terry Reardon	15:13	Mtl.
Mar. 26/47	Tor.	SF	Tor. 3	Det. 2	Howie Meeker	3:05	Tor.
Mar. 27/47	Mtl.	SF	Mtl. 2	Bos. 1	Kenny Mosdell	5:38	Mtl.
Apr. 3/47	Mtl.	SF	Mtl. 4	Bos. 3	John Quilty	36:40	Mtl.
Apr. 15/47	Tor.	F	Tor. 2	Mtl. 1	Syl Apps Sr.	16:36	Tor.
Mar. 24/48	Tor.	SF	Tor. 5	Bos. 4	Nick Metz	17:03	Tor.
Mar. 22/49	Det.	SF	Det. 2	Mtl. 1	Max McNab	44:52	Det.
Mar. 24/49	Det.	SF	Mtl. 4	Det. 3	Gerry Plamondon	2:59	Det.
Mar. 26/49	Tor.	SF	Bos. 5	Tor. 4	Woody Dumart	16:14	Tor.
Apr. 8/49	Det.	F	Tor. 3	Det. 2	Joe Klukay	17:31	Tor.
Apr. 4/50	Tor.	SF	Det. 2	Tor. 1	Leo Reise Sr.	20:38	Det.
Apr. 4/50	Mtl.	SF	Mtl. 3	NYR 2	Elmer Lach	15:19	NYR
Apr. 9/50	Det.	SF	Det. 1	Tor. 0	Leo Reise	8:39	Det.
Apr. 18/50	Det.	F	NYR 4	Det. 3	Don Raleigh	8:34	Det.
Apr. 20/50	Det.	F	NYR 2	Det. 1	Don Raleigh	1:38	Det.
Apr. 23/50	Det.	F	Det. 4	NYR 3	Pete Babando	28:31	Det.
Mar. 27/51	Det.	SF	Mtl. 3	Det. 2	Maurice Richard	61:09	Mtl.
Mar. 29/51	Det.	SF	Mtl. 1	Det. 0	Maurice Richard	42:20	Mtl.
Mar. 31/51	Tor.	SF	Bos. 1	Tor. 1	no scorer	20:00	Tor.
Apr. 11/51	Tor.	F	Tor. 3	Mtl. 2	Sid Smith	5:51	Tor.
Apr. 14/51	Tor.	F	Mtl. 3	Tor. 2	Maurice Richard	2:55	Tor.
Apr. 17/51	Mtl.	F	Tor. 2	Mtl. 1	Ted Kennedy	4:47	Tor.
Apr. 19/51	Mtl.	F	Tor. 3	Mtl. 2	Harry Watson	5:15	Tor.
Apr. 21/51	Tor.	F	Tor. 3	Mtl. 2	Bill Barilko	2:53	Tor.
Apr. 6/52	Bos.	SF	Mtl. 3	Bos. 2	Paul Masnick	27:49	Mtl.
Mar. 29/53	Bos.	SF	Bos 2	Det. 1	Jack McIntyre	12:29	Bos.
Mar. 29/53	Chi.	SF	Chi. 2	Mtl. 1	Al Dewsbury	5:18	Mtl.
Apr. 16/53	Mtl.	F	Mtl. 1	Bos. 0	Elmer Lach	1:22	Mtl.
Apr. 1/54	Det.	SF	Det. 4	Tor. 3	Ted Lindsay	21:01	Det.
Apr. 11/54	Det.	F	Mtl. 1	Det. 0	Kenny Mosdell	5:45	Det.
Apr. 16/54	Det.	F	Det. 2	Mtl. 1	Tony Leswick	4:29	Det.
Mar. 29/55	Bos.	SF	Mtl. 4	Bos. 3	Don Marshall	3:05	Mtl.
Mar. 24/56	Tor.	SF	Det. 5	Tor. 4	Ted Lindsay	4:22	Det.
Mar. 28/57	NY	SF	NYR 4	Mtl. 3	Andy Hebenton	13:38	Mtl.
Apr. 4/57	Mtl.	SF	Mtl. 4	NYR 3	Maurice Richard	1:11	Mtl.
Mar. 27/58	NY	SF	Bos. 4	NYR 3	Jerry Toppazzini	4:46	Bos.
Mar. 30/58	Det.	SF	Mtl. 2	Det. 1	André Pronovost	11:52	Mtl.
Apr. 17/58	Mtl.	F	Mtl. 3	Bos. 2	Maurice Richard	5:45	Mtl.
Mar. 28/59	Tor.	SF	Tor. 3	Bos. 2	Gerry Ehman	5:02	Tor.
Mar. 31/59	Tor.	SF	Tor. 3	Bos. 2	Frank Mahovlich	11:21	Tor.
Apr. 14/59	Tor.	F	Tor. 3	Mtl. 2	Dick Duff	10:06	Mtl.
Mar. 26/60	Mtl.	SF	Mtl. 4	Chi. 3	Doug Harvey	8:38	Mtl.
Mar. 27/60	Det.	SF	Tor. 5	Det. 4	Frank Mahovlich	43:00	Tor.
Mar. 29/60	Det.	SF	Det. 2	Tor. 1	Gerry Melnyk	1:54	Tor.
Mar. 22/61	Tor.	SF	Tor. 3	Det. 2	George Armstrong	24:51	Det.
Mar. 26/61	Chi.	SF	Chi. 2	Mtl. 1	Murray Balfour	52:12	Chi.
Apr. 5/62	Tor.	SF	Tor. 3	NYR 2	Red Kelly	24:23	Tor.
Apr. 2/64	Det.	SF	Chi. 3	Det. 2	Murray Balfour	8:21	Det.
Apr. 14/64	Tor.	F	Det 4	Tor. 3	Larry Jeffrey	7:52	Tor.
Apr. 23/64	Det.	F	Tor. 4	Det. 3	Bob Baun	1:43	Tor.
Apr. 6/65	Tor.	SF	Tor. 3	Mtl. 2	Dave Keon	4:17	Mtl.
Apr. 13/65	Tor.	SF	Mtl. 4	Tor. 3	Claude Provost	16:33	Mtl.
May 5/66	Det.	F	Mtl. 3	Det. 2	Henri Richard	2:20	Mtl.
Apr. 13/67	NY	SF	Mtl. 2	NYR 1	John Ferguson	6:28	Mtl.
Apr. 25/67	Tor.	F	Tor. 3	Mtl. 2	Bob Pulford	28:26	Tor.
Apr. 10/68	St. L.	QF	St. L. 3	Phi. 2	Larry Keenan	24:10	St. L.
Apr. 16/68	St. L.	QF	Phi. 2	St. L. 1	Don Blackburn	31:18	St. L.
Apr. 16/68	Min.	QF	Min. 4	L.A. 3	Milan Marcetta	9:11	Min.
Apr. 22/68	Min.	SF	Min. 3	St. L. 2	Parker MacDonald	3:41	St. L.
Apr. 27/68	St. L.	SF	St. L. 4	Min. 3	Gary Sabourin	1:32	St. L.
Apr. 28/68	Mtl.	SF	Mtl 4	Chi. 3	Jacques Lemaire	2:14	Mtl.
Apr. 29/68	St. L.	SF	St. L. 3	Min. 2	Bill McCreary	17:27	St. L.
May 3/68	St. L.	SF	St. L. 2	Min. 1	Ron Schock	22:50	St. L.
May 5/68	St. L.	F	Mtl. 3	St. L. 2	Jacques Lemaire	1:41	Mtl.
May 9/68	Mtl.	F	Mtl. 4	St. L. 3	Bobby Rousseau	1:13	Mtl.
Apr. 2/69	Oak.	QF	L.A. 5	Oak. 4	Ted Irvine	0:19	L.A.
Apr. 10/69	Mtl.	SF	Mtl. 3	Bos. 2	Ralph Backstrom	0:42	Mtl.
Apr. 13/69	Mtl.	SF	Mtl. 4	Bos. 3	Mickey Redmond	4:55	Mtl.
Apr. 24/69	Bos.	SF	Mtl. 2	Bos. 1	Jean Béliveau	31:28	Mtl.
Apr. 12/70	Oak.	QF	Pit. 3	Oak. 2	Michel Briere	8:28	Pit.
May 10/70	Bos.	F	Bos. 4	St. L. 3	Bobby Orr	0:40	Bos.
Apr. 15/71	Tor.	QF	NYR 2	Tor. 1	Bob Nevin	9:07	NYR
Apr. 18/71	Chi.	SF	NYR 2	Chi. 1	Pete Stemkowski	1:37	Chi.
Apr. 27/71	Chi.	SF	Chi. 3	NYR 2	Bobby Hull	6:35	Chi.
Apr. 29/71	NY	SF	NYR 3	Chi. 2	Pete Stemkowski	41:29	Chi.
May 4/71	Chi.	F	Chi. 2	Mtl. 1	Jim Pappin	21:11	Mtl.
Apr. 6/72	Bos.	QF	Tor. 4	Bos. 3	Jim Harrison	2:58	Bos.
Apr. 6/72	Min.	QF	Min. 6	St. L. 5	Bill Goldsworthy	1:36	St. L.
Apr. 9/72	Pit.	QF	Chi. 6	Pit. 5	Pit Martin	0:12	Chi.
Apr. 16/72	Min.	QF	St. L. 2	Min. 1	Kevin O'Shea	10:07	St. L.
Apr. 1/73	Mtl.	QF	Buf. 3	Mtl. 2	René Robert	9:18	Mtl.
Apr. 10/73	Phi.	QF	Phi. 3	Min. 2	Gary Dornhoefer	8:35	Phi.
Apr. 14/73	Mtl.	SF	Phi. 5	Mtl. 4	Rick MacLeish	2:56	Mtl.
Apr. 17/73	Mtl.	SF	Mtl. 4	Phi. 3	Larry Robinson	6:45	Mtl.
Apr. 14/74	Tor.	QF	Bos 4	Tor. 3	Ken Hodge	1:27	Bos.
Apr. 14/74	Atl.	QF	Phi. 4	Atl. 3	Dave Schultz	5:40	Phi.
Apr. 16/74	Mtl.	QF	NYR 3	Mtl. 2	Ron Harris	4:07	NYR
Apr. 23/74	Chi.	SF	Chi. 4	Bos. 3	Jim Pappin	3:48	Bos.
Apr. 28/74	NY	SF	NYR 2	Phi. 1	Rod Gilbert	4:20	Phi.
May 9/74	Bos.	F	Phi. 3	Bos. 2	Bobby Clarke	12:01	Phi.
Apr. 8/75	L.A.	PR	L.A. 3	Tor. 2	Mike Murphy	8:53	Tor.
Apr. 10/75	Tor.	PR	Tor. 3	L.A. 2	Blaine Stoughton	10:19	Tor.
Apr. 10/75	Chi.	PR	Chi. 4	Bos. 3	Ivan Boldirev	7:33	Chi.
Apr. 11/75	NY	PR	NYI 4	NYR 3	Jean-Paul Parise	0:11	NYI
Apr. 19/75	Tor.	QF	Phi. 4	Tor. 3	André Dupont	1:45	Phi.
Apr. 17/75	Chi.	QF	Chi. 5	Buf. 4	Stan Mikita	2:31	Buf.
Apr. 22/75	Mtl.	QF	Mtl. 5	Van. 4	Guy Lafleur	17:06	Mtl.
May 1/75	Phi.	SF	Phi. 5	NYI 4	Bobby Clarke	2:56	Phi.
May 7/75	NYI	SF	NYI 4	Phi. 3	Jude Drouin	1:53	Phi.
Apr. 27/75	Buf.	SF	Buf. 6	Mtl. 5	Danny Gare	4:42	Buf.
May 6/75	Buf.	SF	Buf. 5	Mtl. 4	René Robert	5:56	Buf.
May 20/75	Buf.	F	Buf. 5	Phi. 4	René Robert	18:29	Phi.
Apr. 8/76	Buf.	PR	Buf. 3	St. L. 2	Danny Gare	11:43	Buf.
Apr. 9/76	Buf.	PR	Buf. 2	St. L. 1	Don Luce	14:27	Buf.
Apr. 13/76	Bos.	QF	L.A. 3	Bos. 2	Butch Goring	0:27	Bos.
Apr. 13/76	Buf.	QF	Buf. 3	NYI 2	Danny Gare	14:04	NYI
Apr. 22/76	L.A.	QF	L.A. 4	Bos. 3	Butch Goring	18:28	Bos.
Apr. 29/76	Phi.	SF	Phi. 2	Bos. 1	Reggie Leach	13:38	Phi.
Apr. 15/77	Tor.	QF	Phi. 4	Tor. 3	Rick MacLeish	2:55	Phi.
Apr. 17/77	Tor.	QF	Phi. 6	Tor. 5	Reggie Leach	19:10	Phi.
Apr. 24/77	Phi.	SF	Bos. 4	Phi. 3	Rick Middleton	2:57	Bos.
Apr. 26/77	Phi.	SF	Bos. 5	Phi. 4	Terry O'Reilly	30:07	Bos.
May 3/77	Mtl.	SF	NYI 4	Mtl. 3	Billy Harris	3:58	Mtl.
May 14/77	Bos.	F	Mtl. 2	Bos. 1	Jacques Lemaire	4:32	Mtl.

Date	City	Series	Score	Scorer		Overtime	Series Winner
Apr. 11/78	Phi.	PR	Phi. 3	Col. 2	Mel Bridgman	0:23	Phi.
Apr. 13/78	NY	PR	NYR 4	Buf. 3	Don Murdoch	1:37	Buf.
Apr. 19/78	Bos.	QF	Bos. 4	Chi. 3	Terry O'Reilly	1:50	Bos.
Apr. 19/78	NYI	QF	NYI 3	Tor. 2	Mike Bossy	2:50	Tor.
Apr. 21/78	Chi.	QF	Bos. 4	Chi. 3	Peter McNab	10:17	Bos.
Apr. 25/78	NYI	QF	NYI 2	Tor. 1	Bob Nystrom	8:02	Tor.
Apr. 29/78	NYI	QF	Tor. 2	NYI 1	Lanny McDonald	4:13	Tor.
May 2/78	Bos.	SF	Bos. 3	Phi. 2	Rick Middleton	1:43	Bos.
May 16/78	Mtl.	F	Mtl. 3	Bos. 2	Guy Lafleur	13:09	Mtl.
May 21/78	Bos.	F	Bos. 4	Mtl. 3	Bobby Schmautz	6:22	Mtl.
Apr. 12/79	L.A.	PR	NYR 2	L.A. 1	Phil Esposito	6:11	NYR
Apr. 14/79	Buf.	PR	Pit. 4	Buf. 3	George Ferguson	0:47	Pit.
Apr. 16/79	Phi.	QF	Phi. 3	NYR 2	Ken Linseman	0:44	NYR
Apr. 18/79	NYI	QF	NYI 1	Chi. 0	Mike Bossy	2:31	NYI
Apr. 21/79	Tor.	QF	Mtl. 4	Tor. 3	Cam Connor	25:25	Mtl.
Apr. 22/79	Tor.	QF	Mtl. 5	Tor. 4	Larry Robinson	4:14	Mtl.
Apr. 28/79	NYI	SF	NYI 4	NYR 3	Denis Potvin	8:02	NYR
May 3/79	NY	SF	NYI 3	NYR 2	Bob Nystrom	3:40	NYR
May 3/79	Bos.	SF	Bos. 4	Mtl. 3	Jean Ratelle	3:46	Mtl.
May 10/79	Mtl.	SF	Mtl. 5	Bos. 4	Yvon Lambert	9:33	Mtl.
May 19/79	NY	F	Mtl. 4	NYR 3	Serge Savard	7:25	Mtl.
Apr. 8/80	NY	PR	NYR 2	Atl. 1	Steve Vickers	0:33	NYR
Apr. 8/80	Phi.	PR	Phi. 4	Edm. 3	Bobby Clarke	8:06	Phi.
Apr. 8/80	Chi.	PR	Chi. 3	St. L. 2	Doug Lecuyer	12:34	Chi.
Apr. 11/80	Hfd.	PR	Mtl. 4	Hfd. 3	Yvon Lambert	0:29	Mtl.
Apr. 11/80	Tor.	PR	Min. 4	Tor. 3	Al MacAdam	0:32	Min.
Apr. 11/80	L.A.	PR	NYI 4	L.A. 3	Ken Morrow	6:55	NYI
Apr. 11/80	Edm.	PR	Phi. 3	Edm. 2	Ken Linseman	23:56	Phi.
Apr. 16/80	Bos.	QF	NYI 2	Bos. 1	Clark Gillies	1:02	NYI
Apr. 17/80	Bos.	QF	NYI 5	Bos. 4	Bob Bourne	1:24	NYI
Apr. 21/80	NYI	QF	Bos. 4	NYI 3	Terry O'Reilly	17:13	NYI
May 1/80	Buf.	SF	NYI 2	Buf. 1	Bob Nystrom	21:20	NYI
May 13/80	Phi.	F	NYI 4	Phi. 3	Denis Potvin	4:07	NYI
May 24/80	NYI	F	NYI 5	Phi. 4	Bob Nystrom	7:11	NYI
Apr. 8/81	Buf.	PR	Buf. 3	Van. 2	Alan Haworth	5:00	Buf.
Apr. 8/81	Bos.	PR	Min. 5	Bos. 4	Steve Payne	3:34	Min.
Apr. 11/81	Chi.	PR	Cgy. 5	Chi. 4	Willi Plett	35:17	Cgy.
Apr. 12/81	Que.	PR	Phi. 3	Que. 2	Dale Hunter	0:37	Phi.
Apr. 14/81	St. L.	PR	St. L. 4	Pit. 3	Mike Crombeen	25:16	St. L.
Apr. 16/81	Buf.	QF	Min. 4	Buf. 3	Steve Payne	0:22	Min.
Apr. 20/81	Min.	QF	Buf. 5	Min. 4	Craig Ramsay	16:32	Min.
Apr. 20/81	Edm.	QF	NYI 5	Edm. 4	Ken Morrow	5:41	NYI
Apr. 7/82	Min.	DSF	Chi. 3	Min. 2	Greg Fox	3:34	Chi.
Apr. 8/82	Edm.	DSF	Edm. 3	L.A. 2	Wayne Gretzky	6:20	L.A.
Apr. 8/82	Van.	DSF	Van. 2	Cgy. 1	Dave Williams	14:20	Van.
Apr. 10/82	Pit.	DSF	Pit. 2	NYI 1	Rick Kehoe	4:14	NYI
Apr. 10/82	L.A.	DSF	L.A. 6	Edm. 5	Daryl Evans	2:35	L.A.
Apr. 13/82	Mtl.	DSF	Que. 3	Mtl. 2	Dale Hunter	0:22	Que.
Apr. 13/82	NYI	DSF	NYI 4	Pit. 3	John Tonelli	6:19	NYI
Apr. 16/82	Van.	DF	L.A. 3	Van. 2	Steve Bozek	4:33	Van.
Apr. 18/82	Que.	DF	Que. 3	Bos. 2	Wilf Paiement	11:44	Que.
Apr. 18/82	NY	DF	NYI 4	NYR 3	Bryan Trottier	3:00	NYI
Apr. 18/82	L.A.	DF	Van. 4	L.A. 3	Colin Campbell	1:23	Van.
Apr. 21/82	St. L.	DF	St. L. 3	Chi. 2	Bernie Federko	3:28	Chi.
Apr. 23/82	Que.	DF	Bos. 6	Que. 5	Peter McNab	10:54	Que.
Apr. 27/82	Chi.	CF	Van. 2	Chi. 1	Jim Nill	28:58	Van.
May 1/82	Que.	CF	NYI 5	Que. 4	Wayne Merrick	16:52	NYI
May 8/82	NYI	F	NYI 6	Van. 5	Mike Bossy	19:58	NYI
Apr. 5/83	Bos.	DSF	Bos. 4	Que. 3	Barry Pederson	1:46	Bos.
Apr. 6/83	Cgy.	DSF	Cgy. 4	Van. 3	Eddy Beers	12:27	Cgy.
Apr. 7/83	Min.	DSF	Min. 5	Tor. 4	Bobby Smith	5:03	Min.
Apr. 10/83	Tor.	DSF	Min. 5	Tor. 4	Dino Ciccarelli	8:05	Min.
Apr. 10/83	Van.	DSF	Cgy. 4	Van. 3	Greg Meredith	1:06	Cgy.
Apr. 18/83	Min.	DF	Chi. 4	Min. 3	Rich Preston	10:34	Chi.
Apr. 24/83	Bos.	DF	Bos. 3	Buf. 2	Brad Park	1:52	Bos.
Apr. 5/84	Edm.	DSF	Edm. 5	Wpg. 4	Randy Gregg	0:21	Edm.
Apr. 7/84	Det.	DSF	St. L. 4	Det. 3	Mark Reeds	37:07	St. L.
Apr. 8/84	Det.	DSF	St. L. 3	Det. 2	Jorgen Pettersson	2:42	St. L.
Apr. 10/84	NYI	DSF	NYI 3	NYR 2	Ken Morrow	8:56	NYI
Apr. 13/84	Min.	DF	St. L. 4	Min. 3	Doug Gilmour	16:16	Min.
Apr. 13/84	Edm.	DF	Cgy. 6	Edm. 5	Carey Wilson	3:42	Edm.
Apr. 13/84	NYI	DF	NYI 5	Wsh. 4	Anders Kallur	7:35	NYI
Apr. 16/84	Mtl.	DF	Que. 4	Mtl. 3	Bo Berglund	3:00	Mtl.
Apr. 20/84	Cgy.	DF	Cgy. 5	Edm. 4	Lanny McDonald	1:04	Edm.
Apr. 22/84	Min.	DF	Min. 4	St. L. 3	Steve Payne	6:00	Min.
Apr. 10/85	Phi.	DSF	Phi. 5	NYR 4	Mark Howe	8:01	Phi.
Apr. 10/85	Wsh.	DSF	Wsh. 4	NYI 3	Alan Haworth	2:28	NYI
Apr. 10/85	Edm.	DSF	Edm. 3	L.A. 2	Lee Fogolin	3:01	Edm.
Apr. 10/85	Wpg.	DSF	Wpg. 5	Cgy. 4	Brian Mullen	7:56	Wpg.
Apr. 11/85	Wsh.	DSF	Wsh. 2	NYI 1	Mike Gartner	21:23	NYI
Apr. 13/85	L.A.	DF	Edm. 4	L.A. 3	Glenn Anderson	0:46	Edm.
Apr. 18/85	Mtl.	DF	Que. 2	Mtl. 1	Mark Kumpel	12:23	Que.
Apr. 23/85	Que.	DF	Que. 7	Mtl. 6	Dale Hunter	18:36	Que.
May 2/85	Mtl.	DF	Que. 3	Mtl. 2	Peter Stastny	2:22	Que.
Apr. 25/85	Min.	DF	Chi. 7	Min. 6	Darryl Sutter	21:57	Chi.
Apr. 28/85	Chi.	DF	Min. 5	Chi. 4	Dennis Maruk	1:14	Chi.
Apr. 30/85	Min.	DF	Chi. 6	Min. 5	Darryl Sutter	15:41	Chi.
May 5/85	Que.	CF	Que. 2	Phi. 1	Peter Stastny	6:20	Phi.
May 9/86	Que.	DSF	Hfd. 3	Que. 2	Sylvain Turgeon	2:36	Hfd.
Apr. 12/86	Wpg.	DSF	Cgy. 4	Wpg. 3	Lanny McDonald	8:25	Cgy.
Apr. 17/86	Wsh.	DF	NYR 4	Wsh. 3	Brian MacLellan	1:16	NYR
Apr. 20/86	Edm.	DF	Edm. 6	Cgy. 5	Glenn Anderson	1:04	Cgy.
Apr. 23/86	Hfd.	DF	Hfd. 2	Mtl. 1	Kevin Dineen	1:07	Mtl.
Apr. 23/86	NYR	DF	NYR 6	Wsh. 5	Bob Brooke	2:40	NYR
Apr. 26/86	St. L.	DF	St. L. 4	Tor. 3	Mark Reeds	7:11	St. L.
Apr. 29/86	Mtl.	DF	Mtl. 2	Hfd. 1	Claude Lemieux	5:55	Mtl.
May 5/86	NYR	CF	Mtl. 4	NYR 3	Claude Lemieux	9:41	Mtl.
May 12/86	St. L.	CF	St. L. 6	Cgy. 5	Doug Wickenheiser	7:30	Cgy.
May 18/86	Cgy.	F	Mtl. 3	Cgy. 2	Brian Skrudland	0:09	Mtl.
Apr. 8/87	Hfd.	DSF	Hfd. 3	Que. 2	Paul MacDermid	2:20	Que.
Apr. 9/87	Mtl.	DSF	Mtl. 4	Bos. 3	Mats Naslund	2:38	Mtl.
Apr. 9/87	St. L.	DSF	Tor. 3	St. L. 2	Rick Lanz	10:17	Tor.
Apr. 11/87	Wpg.	DSF	Cgy. 3	Wpg. 2	Mike Bullard	3:53	Wpg.
Apr. 11/87	Chi.	DSF	Det. 4	Chi. 3	Shawn Burr	4:51	Det.
Apr. 16/87	Que.	DSF	Que. 5	Hfd. 4	Peter Stastny	6:05	Que.
Apr. 18/87	Wsh.	DSF	NYI 3	Wsh. 2	Pat LaFontaine	68:47	NYI
Apr. 21/87	Edm.	DF	Edm. 3	Wpg. 2	Glenn Anderson	0:36	Edm.
Apr. 26/87	Que.	DF	Mtl. 3	Que. 2	Mats Naslund	5:30	Mtl.
Apr. 27/87	Tor.	DF	Tor. 3	Det. 2	Mike Allison	9:31	Det.
May 4/87	Phi.	CF	Phi. 4	Mtl. 3	Ilkka Sinisalo	9:11	Phi.
May 20/87	Edm.	F	Edm. 3	Phi. 2	Jari Kurri	6:50	Edm.
Apr. 6/88	NYI	DSF	NYI 4	N.J. 3	Pat LaFontaine	6:11	N.J.
Apr. 10/88	Phi.	DSF	Phi. 5	Wsh. 4	Murray Craven	1:18	Wsh.
Apr. 10/88	N.J.	DSF	NYI 5	N.J. 4	Brent Sutter	15:07	N.J.
Apr. 10/88	Buf.	DSF	Buf. 6	Bos. 5	John Tucker	5:32	Bos.
Apr. 12/88	Det.	DSF	Tor. 6	Det. 5	Ed Olczyk	0:34	Det.
Apr. 16/88	Wsh.	DSF	Wsh. 5	Phi. 4	Dale Hunter	5:57	Wsh.
Apr. 21/88	Cgy.	DF	Edm. 5	Cgy. 4	Wayne Gretzky	7:54	Edm
May 4/88	Bos.	CF	N.J. 3	Bos. 2	Doug Brown	17:46	Bos.
May 9/88	Det.	CF	Edm. 4	Det. 3	Jari Kurri	11:02	Edm.

Montreal celebrated a Stanley Cup victory in 1953 after Elmer Lach's goal at 1:22 of overtime gave the Canadiens a 1-0 win over the Boston Bruins in game five.

Date	City	Series	Score		Scorer	Overtime	Series Winner
Apr. 5/89	St. L.	DSF	St. L. 4	Min. 3	Brett Hull	11:55	St. L.
Apr. 5/89	Cgy.	DSF	Van. 4	Cgy. 3	Paul Reinhart	2:47	Cgy.
Apr. 6/89	St. L.	DSF	St. L. 4	Min. 3	Rick Meagher	5:30	St. L.
Apr. 6/89	Det.	DSF	Chi. 5	Det. 4	Duane Sutter	14:36	Chi.
Apr. 8/89	Hfd.	DSF	Mtl. 5	Hfd. 4	Stephane Richer	5:01	Mtl.
Apr. 8/89	Phi.	DSF	Wsh. 4	Phi. 3	Kelly Miller	0:51	Phi.
Apr. 9/89	Hfd.	DSF	Mtl. 4	Hfd. 3	Russ Courtnall	15:12	Mtl.
Apr. 15/89	Cgy.	DSF	Cgy. 4	Van. 3	Joel Otto	19:21	Cgy.
Apr. 18/89	Cgy.	DF	Cgy. 4	L.A. 3	Doug Gilmour	7:47	Cgy.
Apr. 19/89	Mtl.	DF	Mtl. 3	Bos. 2	Bobby Smith	12:24	Mtl.
Apr. 20/89	St. L.	DF	St. L. 5	Chi. 4	Tony Hrkac	33:49	Chi.
Apr. 21/89	Phi.	DF	Pit. 4	Phi. 3	Phil Bourque	12:08	Phi.
May 8/89	Chi.	CF	Cgy. 2	Chi. 1	Al MacInnis	15:05	Cgy.
May 9/89	Mtl.	CF	Phi. 2	Mtl. 1	Dave Poulin	5:02	Mtl.
May 19/89	Mtl.	F	Mtl. 4	Cgy. 3	Ryan Walter	38:08	Cgy.
Apr. 5/90	N.J.	DSF	Wsh. 5	N.J. 4	Dino Ciccarelli	5:34	Wsh.
Apr. 6/90	Edm.	DSF	Edm. 3	Wpg. 2	Mark Lamb	4:21	Edm.
Apr. 8/90	Tor.	DSF	St. L. 6	Tor. 5	Sergio Momesso	6:04	St. L.
Apr. 8/90	L.A.	DSF	L.A. 2	Cgy. 1	Tony Granato	8:37	L.A.
Apr. 9/90	Mtl.	DSF	Mtl. 2	Buf. 1	Brian Skrudland	12:35	Mtl.
Apr. 9/90	NYI	DSF	NYI 4	NYR 3	Brent Sutter	20:59	NYR
Apr. 10/90	Wpg.	DSF	Wpg. 4	Edm. 3	Dave Ellett	21:08	Edm.
Apr. 14/90	L.A.	DSF	L.A. 4	Cgy. 3	Mike Krushelnyski	23:14	L.A.
Apr. 15/90	Hfd.	DSF	Hfd. 3	Bos. 2	Kevin Dineen	12:30	Bos.
Apr. 21/90	Bos.	DF	Bos. 5	Mtl. 4	Garry Galley	3:42	Bos.
Apr. 24/90	L.A.	DF	Edm. 6	L.A. 5	Joe Murphy	4:42	Edm.
Apr. 25/90	Wsh.	DF	Wsh. 4	NYR 3	Rod Langway	0:34	Wsh.
Apr. 27/90	NYR	DF	Wsh. 2	NYR 1	John Druce	6:48	Wsh.
May 15/90	Bos.	F	Edm. 3	Bos. 2	Petr Klima	55:13	Edm.
Apr. 4/91	Chi.	DSF	Min. 4	Chi. 3	Brian Propp	4:14	Min.
Apr. 5/91	Pit.	DSF	Pit. 5	N.J. 4	Jaromir Jagr	8:52	Pit.
Apr. 6/91	L.A.	DSF	L.A. 3	Van. 2	Wayne Gretzky	11:08	L.A.
Apr. 8/91	Van.	DSF	Van. 2	L.A. 1	Cliff Ronning	3:12	L.A.
Apr. 11/91	NYR	DSF	Wsh. 5	NYR 4	Dino Ciccarelli	6:44	Wsh.
Apr. 11/91	Mtl.	DSF	Mtl. 4	Buf. 3	Russ Courtnall	5:56	Mtl.
Apr. 14/91	Edm.	DSF	Cgy. 2	Edm. 1	Theoren Fleury	4:40	Edm.
Apr. 16/91	Cgy.	DSF	Edm. 5	Cgy. 4	Esa Tikkanen	6:58	Edm.
Apr. 18/91	L.A.	DF	L.A. 4	Edm. 3	Luc Robitaille	2:13	Edm.
Apr. 19/91	Bos.	DF	Mtl. 4	Bos. 3	Stephane Richer	0:27	Bos.
Apr. 19/91	Pit.	DF	Pit. 7	Wsh. 6	Kevin Stevens	8:10	Pit.
Apr. 20/91	L.A.	DF	Edm. 4	L.A. 3	Petr Klima	24:48	Edm.
Apr. 22/91	Edm.	DF	Edm. 4	L.A. 3	Esa Tikkanen	20:48	Edm.
Apr. 27/91	Mtl.	DF	Mtl. 3	Bos. 2	Shayne Corson	17:47	Bos.
Apr. 28/91	Edm.	DF	Edm. 4	L.A. 3	Craig MacTavish	16:57	Edm.
May 3/91	Bos.	CF	Bos. 5	Pit. 4	Vladimir Ruzicka	8:14	Pit.
Apr. 21/92	Bos.	DSF	Bos. 3	Buf. 2	Adam Oates	11:14	Bos.
Apr. 22/92	Min.	DSF	Det. 5	Min. 4	Yves Racine	1:15	Det.
Apr. 22/92	St. L.	DSF	St. L. 5	Chi. 4	Brett Hull	23:33	Chi.
Apr. 25/92	Buf.	DSF	Bos. 5	Buf. 4	Ted Donato	2:08	Bos.
Apr. 28/92	Min.	DSF	Det. 1	Min. 0	Sergei Fedorov	16:13	Det.
Apr. 29/92	Hfd.	DSF	Hfd. 2	Mtl. 1	Yvon Corriveau	0:24	Mtl.
May 1/92	Mtl.	DSF	Mtl. 3	Hfd. 2	Russ Courtnall	25:26	Mtl.
May 3/92	Van.	DF	Edm. 4	Van. 3	Joe Murphy	8:36	Edm.
May 5/92	Mtl.	DF	Bos. 3	Mtl. 2	Peter Douris	3:12	Bos.
May 7/92	Pit.	DF	NYR 6	Pit. 5	Kris King	1:29	Pit.
May 9/92	Pit.	DF	Pit. 5	NYR 4	Ron Francis	2:47	Pit.
May 17/92	Pit.	CF	Pit. 4	Bos. 3	Jaromir Jagr	9:44	Pit.
May 20/92	Edm.	CF	Chi. 4	Edm. 3	Jeremy Roenick	2:45	Chi.
Apr. 18/93	Bos.	DSF	Buf. 5	Bos. 4	Bob Sweeney	11:03	Buf.
Apr. 18/93	Que.	DSF	Que. 3	Mtl. 2	Scott Young	16:49	Mtl.
Apr. 20/93	Wsh.	DSF	NYI 5	Wsh. 4	Brian Mullen	34:50	NYI
Apr. 22/93	Mtl.	DSF	Mtl. 2	Que. 1	Vincent Damphousse	10:30	Mtl.
Apr. 22/93	Buf.	DSF	Buf. 4	Bos. 3	Yuri Khmylev	1:05	Buf.
Apr. 22/93	NYI	DSF	NYI 4	Wsh. 3	Ray Ferraro	4:46	NYI
Apr. 24/93	Buf.	DSF	Buf. 6	Bos. 5	Brad May	4:48	Buf.
Apr. 24/93	NYI	DSF	NYI 4	Wsh. 3	Ray Ferraro	25:40	NYI
Apr. 25/93	St. L.	DSF	St. L. 4	Chi. 3	Craig Janney	10:43	St. L.
Apr. 26/93	Que.	DSF	Mtl. 5	Que. 4	Kirk Muller	8:17	Mtl.
Apr. 27/93	Det.	DSF	Tor. 5	Det. 4	Mike Foligno	2:05	Tor.
Apr. 27/93	Van.	DSF	Wpg. 4	Van. 3	Teemu Selanne	6:18	Van.
Apr. 29/93	Wpg.	DSF	Van. 4	Wpg. 3	Greg Adams	4:30	Van.
May 1/93	Det.	DSF	Tor. 4	Det. 3	Nikolai Borschevsky	2:35	Tor.
May 3/93	Tor.	DF	Tor. 2	St. L. 1	Doug Gilmour	23:16	Tor.
May 4/93	Mtl.	DF	Mtl. 4	Buf. 3	Guy Carbonneau	2:50	Mtl.
May 5/93	Tor.	DF	St. L. 2	Tor. 1	Jeff Brown	23:03	Tor.
May 6/93	Buf.	DF	Mtl. 4	Buf. 3	Gilbert Dionne	8:28	Mtl.
May 8/93	Buf.	DF	Mtl. 4	Buf. 3	Kirk Muller	11:37	Mtl.
May 11/93	Van.	DF	L.A. 4	Van. 3	Gary Shuchuk	26:31	L.A.
May 14/93	Pit.	DF	NYI 4	Pit. 3	Dave Volek	5:16	NYI
May 18/93	Mtl.	CF	Mtl. 4	NYI 3	Stephan Lebeau	26:21	Mtl.
May 20/93	NYI	CF	Mtl. 2	NYI 1	Guy Carbonneau	12:34	Mtl.
May 25/93	Tor.	CF	Tor. 3	L.A. 2	Glenn Anderson	19:20	L.A.
May 27/93	L.A.	CF	L.A. 5	Tor. 4	Wayne Gretzky	1:41	L.A.
Jun. 3/93	Mtl.	F	Mtl. 3	L.A. 2	Eric Desjardins	0:51	Mtl.
Jun. 5/93	L.A.	F	Mtl. 4	L.A. 3	John LeClair	0:34	Mtl.
Jun. 7/93	L.A.	F	Mtl. 3	L.A. 2	John LeClair	14:37	Mtl.
Apr. 20/94	Tor.	CQF	Tor. 1	Chi. 0	Todd Gill	2:15	Tor.
Apr. 22/94	St. L.	CQF	Dal. 5	St. L. 4	Paul Cavallini	8:34	Dal.
Apr. 24/94	Chi.	CQF	Chi. 4	Tor. 3	Jeremy Roenick	1:23	Tor.
Apr. 25/94	Bos.	CQF	Mtl. 2	Bos. 1	Kirk Muller	17:18	Bos.
Apr. 26/94	Cgy.	CQF	Van. 2	Cgy. 1	Geoff Courtnall	7:15	Van.
Apr. 27/94	Buf.	CQF	Buf. 1	N.J. 0	Dave Hannan	65:43	N.J.
Apr. 28/94	Van.	CQF	Van. 3	Cgy. 2	Trevor Linden	16:43	Van.
Apr. 30/94	Cgy.	CQF	Van. 4	Cgy. 3	Pavel Bure	22:20	Van.
May 3/94	N.J.	CSF	Bos. 6	N.J. 5	Don Sweeney	9:08	N.J.
May 7/94	Bos.	CSF	N.J. 5	Bos. 4	Stephane Richer	14:19	N.J.
May 8/94	Van.	CSF	Van. 2	Dal. 1	Sergio Momesso	11:01	Van.
May 12/94	Tor	CSF	Tor. 3	S.J. 2	Mike Gartner	8:53	Tor.
May 15/94	NYR	CF	N.J. 4	NYR 3	Stephane Richer	35:23	NYR
May 16/94	Tor.	CF	Tor. 3	Van. 2	Peter Zezel	16:55	Van.
May 19/94	N.J.	CF	NYR 3	N.J. 2	Stephane Matteau	26:13	NYR
May 24/94	Van.	CF	Van. 4	Tor. 3	Greg Adams	20:14	Van.
May 27/94	NYR	CF	NYR 2	N.J. 1	Stephane Matteau	24:24	NYR
May 31/94	NYR	F	Van. 3	NYR 2	Greg Adams	19:26	NYR
May 7/95	Phi.	CQF	Phi. 4	Buf. 3	Karl Dykhuis	10:06	Phi.
May 9/95	Cgy.	CQF	S.J. 5	Cgy. 4	Ulf Dahlen	12:21	S.J.
May 12/95	NYR	CQF	NYR 3	Que. 2	Steve Larmer	8:09	NYR
May 12/95	N.J.	CQF	N.J. 1	Bos. 0	Randy McKay	8:51	N.J.
May 14/95	Pit.	CQF	Pit. 6	Wsh. 5	Luc Robitaille	4:30	Pit.
May 15/95	St. L.	CQF	Van. 6	St. L. 5	Cliff Ronning	1:48	Van.
May 17/95	Tor.	CQF	Tor. 5	Chi. 4	Randy Wood	10:00	Chi.
May 19/95	Cgy.	CQF	S.J. 5	Cgy. 4	Ray Whitney	21:54	S.J.
May 21/95	Phi.	CSF	Phi. 5	NYR 4	Eric Desjardins	7:03	Phi.
May 21/95	Chi.	CSF	Chi. 2	Van. 1	Joe Murphy	9:04	Chi.
May 22/95	Phi.	CSF	Phi. 4	NYR 3	Kevin Haller	0:25	Phi.
May 25/95	Van.	CSF	Chi. 3	Van. 2	Chris Chelios	6:22	Chi.
May 26/95	N.J.	CSF	N.J. 2	Pit. 1	Neal Broten	18:36	N.J.
May 27/95	Van.	CSF	Chi. 4	Van. 3	Chris Chelios	5:35	Chi.
Jun. 1/95	Det.	CF	Det. 2	Chi. 1	Nicklas Lidstrom	1:01	Det.
Jun. 6/95	Chi.	CF	Det. 4	Chi. 3	Vladimir Konstantinov	29:25	Det.
Jun. 7/95	N.J.	CF	Phi. 3	N.J. 2	Eric Lindros	4:19	N.J.
Jun. 11/95	Det.	CF	Det. 2	Chi. 1	Vyacheslav Kozlov	22:25	Det.
Apr. 16/96	NYR	CQF	Mtl. 3	NYR 2	Vincent Damphousse	5:04	NYR
Apr. 18/96	Tor.	CQF	Tor. 5	St. L. 4	Mats Sundin	4:02	St. L.
Apr. 18/96	Phi.	CQF	T.B. 2	Phi. 1	Brian Bellows	9:05	Phi.
Apr. 21/96	St. L.	CQF	St. L. 3	Tor. 2	Glenn Anderson	1:24	St. L.
Apr. 21/96	T.B.	CQF	T.B. 5	Phi. 4	Alexander Selivanov	2:04	Phi.
Apr. 23/96	Cgy.	CQF	Chi. 2	Cgy. 1	Joe Murphy	50:02	Chi.
Apr. 24/96	Wsh.	CQF	Pit. 3	Wsh. 2	Petr Nedved	79:15	Pit.
Apr. 25/96	Col.	CQF	Col. 5	Van. 4	Joe Sakic	0:51	Col.
Apr. 25/96	Tor.	CQF	Tor. 5	St. L. 4	Mike Gartner	7:31	St. L.
May 2/96	Col.	CSF	Chi. 3	Col. 2	Jeremy Roenick	6:29	Col.
May 6/96	Chi.	CSF	Chi. 4	Col. 3	Sergei Krivokrasov	0:46	Col.
May 8/96	St. L.	CSF	St. L. 5	Det. 4	Igor Kravchuk	3:23	Det.
May 8/96	Chi.	CSF	Col. 3	Chi. 2	Joe Sakic	44:33	Col.
May 9/96	Fla.	CSF	Fla. 4	Phi. 3	Dave Lowry	4:06	Fla.
May 12/96	Phi.	CSF	Fla. 2	Phi. 1	Mike Hough	28:05	Fla.
May 13/96	Chi.	CSF	Col. 4	Chi. 3	Sandis Ozolinsh	25:18	Col.
May 16/96	Det.	CSF	Det. 1	St. L. 0	Steve Yzerman	21:15	Det.
May 19/96	Det.	CF	Col. 3	Det. 2	Mike Keane	17:31	Col.
Jun. 10/96	Fla.	F	Col. 1	Fla. 0	Uwe Krupp	44:31	Col.
Apr. 20/97	Chi.	CQF	Chi. 4	Col. 3	Sergei Krivokrasov	31:03	Col.
Apr. 20/97	Edm.	CQF	Edm. 4	Dal. 3	Kelly Buchberger	9:15	Edm.
Apr. 22/97	NYR	CQF	NYR 4	Fla. 3	Esa Tikkanen	16:29	NYR
Apr. 23/97	Ott.	CQF	Ott 1	Buf. 0	Daniel Alfredsson	2:34	Buf.
Apr. 24/97	Mtl.	CQF	Mtl. 4	N.J. 3	Patrice Brisebois	47:37	N.J.
Apr. 25/97	Fla.	CQF	NYR 3	Fla. 2	Esa Tikkanen	12:02	NYR
Apr. 25/97	Dal.	CQF	Edm. 1	Dal. 0	Ryan Smyth	20:22	Edm.
Apr. 27/97	Phx.	CQF	Ana. 3	Phx. 2	Paul Kariya	7:29	Ana.
Apr. 29/97	Buf.	CQF	Buf. 3	Ott. 2	Derek Plante	5:24	Buf.
Apr. 29/97	Dal.	CQF	Edm. 4	Dal. 3	Todd Marchant	12:26	Edm
May 2/97	Det.	CSF	Det. 2	Ana. 1	Martin Lapointe	0:59	Det.
May 4/97	Det.	CSF	Det 3	Ana. 2	Vyacheslav Kozlov	41:31	Det.
May 8/97	Ana.	CSF	Det. 3	Ana. 2	Brendan Shanahan	37:03	Det.
May 9/97	Phi.	CSF	Buf. 5	Phi. 4	Ed Ronan	6:24	Phi.
May 9/97	Edm.	CSF	Col. 3	Edm. 2	Claude Lemieux	8:35	Col.
May 11/97	N.J.	CSF	NYR 2	N.J. 1	Adam Graves	14:08	NYR
Apr. 22/98	N.J.	CQF	OTT. 2	N.J. 1	Bruce Gardiner	5:58	Ott.
Apr. 23/98	Pit.	CQF	Mtl. 3	Pit. 2	Benoit Brunet	18:43	Mtl.
Apr. 24/98	Wsh.	CQF	Bos. 4	Wsh. 3	Darren Van Impe	20:54	Wsh
Apr. 26/98	Ott.	CQF	Ott. 2	N.J. 1	Alexei Yashin	2:47	Ott.
Apr. 26/98	Bos.	CQF	Wsh. 3	Bos. 2	Joe Juneau	26:31	Wsh
Apr. 26/98	Edm.	CQF	Col. 5	Edm. 4	Joe Sakic	15:25	Edm.
Apr. 28/98	S.J.	CQF	S.J. 1	Dal. 0	Andrei Zyuzin	6:31	Dal.
May 1/98	Phi.	CQF	Buf 3	Phi. 2	Michal Grosek	5:40	Buf.
May 2/98	S.J.	CQF	Dal. 3	S.J. 2	Mike Keane	3:43	Dal.
May 3/98	Bos.	CQF	Wsh. 3	Bos. 2	Brian Bellows	15:24	Wsh.
May 3/98	Buf.	CSF	Buf 3	Mtl. 2	Geoff Sanderson	2:37	Buf.
May 11/98	Edm.	CSF	Dal. 1	Edm. 0	Benoit Hogue	13:07	Dal.
May 12/98	Mtl.	CSF	Buf 5	Mtl. 4	Michael Peca	21:24	Buf.
May 12/98	St.L.	CSF	Det 3	St.L. 2	Brendan Shanahan	31:12	Det.
May 25/98	Wsh.	CF	Wsh. 3	Buf. 2	Todd Krygier	3:01	Wsh.
May 28/98	Buf.	CF	Wsh. 4	Buf. 3	Peter Bondra	9:37	Wsh.
Jun. 3/98	Dal.	CF	Dal. 3	Det. 2	Jamie Langenbrunner	0:46	Det.
Jun. 4/98	Buf.	CF	Wsh. 3	Buf. 2	Joe Juneau	6:24	Wsh
Jun. 11/98	Det.	F	Det 5	Wsh. 4	Kris Draper	15:24	Det.
Apr. 23/99	Ott.	CQF	Buf 3	Ott. 2	Miroslav Satan	30:35	Buf.
Apr. 24/99	Car.	CQF	Car. 3	Bos. 2	Ray Sheppard	17:05	Bos.
Apr. 24/99	Phx.	CQF	Phx 4	St. L. 3	Shane Doan	8:58	St. L.
Apr. 26/99	S.J.	CQF	Col 2	S.J. 1	Milan Hejduk	7:53	Col.
Apr. 27/99	Edm.	CQF	Dal 3	Edm. 2	Joe Nieuwendyk	57:34	Dal.
Apr. 30/99	Tor.	CQF	Tor 2	Phi. 1	Yanic Perreault	11:51	Tor.
Apr. 30/99	Car.	CQF	Bos. 4	Car. 3	Anson Carter	34:45	Bos.
May 2/99	Pit.	CQF	Pit. 3	N.J. 2	Jaromir Jagr	8:59	Pit.
May 3/99	S.J.	CQF	Col. 3	S.J. 2	Milan Hejduk	13:12	Col.
May 4/99	Phx.	CQF	St. L. 1	Phx. 0	Pierre Turgeon	17:59	St. L.
May 7/99	Col.	CSF	Det 3	Col. 2	Kirk Maltby	4:18	Col.
May 8/99	Dal.	CSF	Dal. 5	St. L. 4	Joe Nieuwendyk	8:22	Dal.
May 10/99	St.L.	CSF	St. L. 3	Dal. 2	Pavol Demitra	2:43	Dal.
May 12/99	St.L.	CSF	St. L. 3	Dal. 2	Pierre Turgeon	5:52	Dal.
May 13/99	Pit.	CSF	Tor 3	Pit. 2	Sergei Berezin	2:18	Tor.
May 17/99	Pit.	CSF	Tor. 4	Pit. 3	Gary Valk	1:57	Tor.
May 17/99	St.L.	CSF	Dal 2	St. L. 1	Mike Mondano	2:21	Dal.
May 28/99	Col.	CF	Col 3	Dal. 2	Chris Drury	19:29	Dal.
Jun. 8/99	Dal.	F	Buf 3	Dal. 2	Jason Woolley	15:30	Dal.
Jun. 19/99	Buf.	F	Dal. 2	Buf. 1	Brett Hull	54:51	Dal.

NHL Playoff Coaching Records

Coach	Team	Games Coached	Wins	Losses	Ties	%Wins	Playoff Years	Cup Wins	Career
Abel, Sid	Chicago	7	3	4	0	.429	1		
	Detroit	69	29	40	0	.420	8		
	Total	76	32	44	0	.421	9		1952-76
Adams, Jack	Detroit	105	52	52	1	.500	15	3	1922-47
Allen, Keith	Philadelphia	11	3	8	0	.273	2		1967-69
Arbour, Al	St. Louis	11	4	7	0	.364	1		
	NY Islanders	198	119	79	0	.601	15	4	
	Total	209	123	86	0	.589	16	4	1970-94
Berenson, Red	St. Louis	14	5	9	0	.357	2		1979-82
Bergeron, Michel	Quebec	68	31	37	0	.456	7		1980-90
Berry, Bob	Los Angeles	10	2	8	0	.200	3		
	Montreal	8	2	6	0	.250	2		
	St. Louis	15	7	8	0	.467	2		
	Total	33	11	22	0	.333	7		1978-94
Beverley, Nick	Toronto	6	2	4	0	.333	1		1995-96
Blackburn, Don	Hartford	3	0	3	0	.000	1		1979-81
Blair, Wren	Minnesota	14	7	7	0	.500	1		1967-70
Blake, Toe	Montreal	119	82	37	0	.689	13	8	1955-68
Boileau, Marc	Pittsburgh	9	5	4	0	.556	1		1973-76
Boivin, Leo	St. Louis	3	1	2	0	.333	1		1975-78
Boucher, Frank	NY Rangers	27	13	14	0	.481	4	1	1939-54
Boucher, George	Mtl. Maroons	2	0	2	0	.000	1		1930-50
Bowman, Scotty	St. Louis	52	26	26	0	.500	4		
	Montreal	98	70	28	0	.714	8	5	
	Buffalo	36	18	18	0	.500	5		
	Pittsburgh	33	23	10	0	.697	2	1	
	Detroit	96	63	33	0	.656	7	2	
	Total	315	200	115	0	.635	25	8	1967-99
Bowness, Rick	Boston	15	8	7	0	.533	1		1988-98
Brooks, Herb	NY Rangers	24	12	12	0	.500	3		
	New Jersey	5	1	4	0	.200	1		
	Total	29	13	16	0	.448	4		1981-93
Brophy, John	Toronto	19	9	10	0	.474	2		1986-89
Burns, Charlie	Minnesota	6	2	4	0	.333	1		1969-75
Burns, Pat	Montreal	56	30	26	0	.536	4		
	Toronto	46	23	23	0	.500	3		
	Boston	18	8	10	0	.444	2		
	Total	120	61	59	0	.508	9		1988-99
Campbell, Colin	NY Rangers	36	18	18	0	.500	3		1994-98
Caroll, Dick	Toronto	9	4	5	0	.444	2	1	1917-21
Carpenter, Doug	Toronto	5	1	4	0	.200	1		1984-91
Cheevers, Gerry	Boston	34	15	19	0	.441	4		1980-85
Cherry, Don	Boston	55	31	24	0	.564	5		1974-80
Clancy, King	Toronto	19	3	16	0	.158	4		1937-72
Clapper, Dit	Boston	25	8	17	0	.320	4		1945-49
Cleghorn, Odie	Pittsburgh	4	1	3	1	.375	2		1925-29
Cleghorn, Sprague	Mtl. Maroons	4	1	1	2	.500	1		1931-32
Constantine, Kevin	San Jose	25	11	14	0	.440	2		
	Pittsburgh	19	8	11	0	.421	2		
	Total	44	19	25	0	.432	4		1993-99
Crawford, Marc	Quebec	6	2	4	0	.333	1		
	Colorado	46	29	17	0	.630	3	1	
	Total	52	31	21	0	.596	4	1	1994-98
Creighton, Fred	Atlanta	9	2	7	0	.222	4		1974-80
Crisp, Terry	Calgary	37	22	15	0	.595	3	1	
	Tampa Bay	6	2	4	0	.333	1		
	Total	43	24	19	0	.558	4	1	1987-98
Crozier, Joe	Buffalo	6	2	4	0	.333	1		1971-81
Cunniff, John	New Jersey	6	2	4	0	.333	1		1982-91
Dandurand, Leo	Montreal	16	10	6	0	.625	4	1	1921-35
Day, Hap	Toronto	80	49	31	0	.613	9	5	1940-50
Demers, Jacques	St. Louis	33	16	17	0	.485	3		
	Detroit	38	20	18	0	.526	3		
	Montreal	27	19	8	0	.704	2	1	
	Total	98	55	43	0	.561	8	1	1979-98
Denneny, Cy	Boston	5	5	0	0	1.000	1	1	1928-33
Dudley, Rick	Buffalo	12	4	8	0	.333	2		1989-92
Dugal, Jules	Montreal	3	1	2	0	.333	1		1938-39
Duncan, Art	Toronto	2	0	1	1	.250	1	1	1926-32
Dutton, Red	NY Americans	16	6	10	0	.375	4		1935-42
Esposito, Phil	NY Rangers	10	2	8	0	.200	2		1986-89
Evans, Jack	Hartford	16	8	8	0	.500	2		1975-88
Ferguson, John	Winnipeg	3	0	3	0	.000	1		1975-86
Francis, Emile	NY Rangers	75	34	41	0	.453	9		
	St. Louis	14	5	9	0	.357	2		
	Total	89	39	50	0	.438	11		1965-83
Ftorek, Robbie	Los Angeles	16	5	11	0	.313	2		
	New Jersey	7	3	4	0	.429	1		
	Total	23	8	15	0	.348	3		1987-99
Gainey, Bob	Minnesota	30	17	13	0	.567	2		
	Dallas	14	6	8	0	.429	2		
	Total	44	23	21	0	.523	4		1990-96
Geoffrion, Bernie	Atlanta	4	0	4	0	.000	1		1968-80
Gerard, Eddie	Mtl. Maroons	25	11	9	5	.540	5	1	1917-35
Gill, David	Ottawa	8	3	2	3	.563	2	1	1926-29
Glover, Fred	Oakland	11	3	8	0	.273	2		1968-74
Gordon, Jackie	Minnesota	25	11	14	0	.440	3		1970-75
Goring, Butch	Boston	3	0	3	0	.000	1		1985-87
Gorman, Tommy	NY Americans	2	0	1	1	.250	1		
	Chicago	8	6	1	1	.813	1	1	
	Mtl. Maroons	15	7	6	2	.533	3	1	
	Total	25	13	8	4	.600	5	2	1925-38
Gottselig, Johnny	Chicago	4	0	4	0	.000	1		1944-48
Green, Pete	Ottawa	26	14	9	3	.596	6	3	1919-26
Green, Ted	Edmonton	16	8	8	0	.500	1		1991-94
Guidolin, Bep	Boston	21	11	10	0	.524	2		1972-76
Harris, Ted	Minnesota	2	0	2	0	.000	1		1975-78
Hart, Cecil	Montreal	37	16	17	4	.486	8	2	1926-39
Hartley, Bob	Colorado	19	11	8	0	.579	1		1998-99
Hartsburg, Craig	Chicago	16	8	8	0	.500	2		
	Anaheim	4	0	4	0	.000	1		
	Total	20	8	12	0	.400	3		1995-99
Harvey, Doug	NY Rangers	6	2	4	0	.333	1		1961-62
Hay, Don	Phoenix	7	3	4	0	.429	1		1996-97
Henning, Lorne	Minnesota	5	2	3	0	.400	1		1985-95
Hitchcock, Ken	Dallas	47	29	18	0	.617	3	1	1995-99
Holmgren, Paul	Philadelphia	19	10	9	0	.526	1		1988-96
Imlach, Punch	Toronto	92	44	48	0	.478	11	4	1958-80
Inglis, Bill	Buffalo	3	1	2	0	.333	1		1978-79
Irvin, Dick	Chicago	9	5	3	1	.611	1		
	Toronto	66	33	32	1	.508	9	1	
	Montreal	115	62	53	0	.539	14	3	
	Total	190	100	88	2	.532	24	4	1930-56
Ivan, Tommy	Detroit	67	36	31	0	.537	7	3	1947-58
Johnson, Bob	Calgary	52	25	27	0	.481	5		
	Pittsburgh	24	16	8	0	.667	1	1	
	Total	76	41	35	0	.539	6	1	1982-91
Johnson, Tom	Boston	22	15	7	0	.682	2	1	1970-73
Johnston, Eddie	Chicago	7	3	4	0	.429	1		
	Pittsburgh	46	22	24	0	.478	5		
	Total	53	25	28	0	.472	6		1979-97
Kasper, Steve	Boston	5	1	4	0	.200	1		1995-97
Keenan, Mike	Philadelphia	57	32	25	0	.561	4		
	Chicago	60	33	27	0	.550	4		
	NY Rangers	23	16	7	0	.696	1	1	
	St. Louis	20	10	10	0	.500	2		
	Total	160	91	69	0	.569	11	1	1984-98
Kelly, Pat	Colorado	2	0	2	0	.000	1		1977-79
Kelly, Red	Los Angeles	18	7	11	0	.389	2		
	Pittsburgh	14	6	8	0	.429	2		
	Toronto	30	11	19	0	.367	4		
	Total	62	24	38	0	.387	8		1967-77
King, Dave	Calgary	20	8	12	0	.400	3		1992-95
Kromm, Bobby	Detroit	7	3	4	0	.429	1		1977-80
Lalonde, Newsy	Montreal	16	7	6	3	.531	4		
	Ottawa	2	0	1	1	.250	1		
	Total	18	7	7	4	.500	5		1917-35
Lemaire, Jacques	Montreal	27	15	12	0	.556	2		
	New Jersey	56	34	22	0	.607	4	1	
	Total	83	49	34	0	.590	6	1	1983-98
Ley, Rick	Hartford	13	5	8	0	.385	2		
	Vancouver	11	4	7	0	.364	1		
	Total	24	9	15	0	.375	3		1989-96
Long, Barry	Winnipeg	11	3	8	0	.273	2		1983-86
Loughlin, Clem	Chicago	4	1	2	1	.375	2		1934-37
Low, Ron	Edmonton	28	10	18	0	.357	3		1994-99
MacLean, Doug	Florida	27	13	14	0	.481	1		1995-98
MacNeil, Al	Montreal	20	12	8	0	.600	1	1	
	Atlanta	4	1	3	0	.250	1		
	Calgary	19	9	10	0	.474	2		
	Total	43	22	21	0	.512	4	1	1970-82
Magnuson, Keith	Chicago	3	0	3	0	.000	1		1980-82
Mahoney, Bill	Minnesota	16	7	9	0	.438	1		1983-85
Maloney, Dan	Toronto	10	6	4	0	.600	1		
	Winnipeg	15	5	10	0	.333	2		
	Total	25	11	14	0	.440	3		1984-89
Maloney, Phil	Vancouver	7	1	6	0	.143	2		1973-77
Martin, Jacques	St. Louis	16	7	9	0	.438	2		
	Ottawa	22	8	14	0	.364	3		
	Total	38	15	23	0	.395	5		1986-99
Maurice, Paul	Carolina	6	2	4	0	.333	1		1998-99
McCammon, Bob	Philadelphia	10	1	9	0	.100	3		
	Vancouver	7	3	4	0	.429	1		
	Total	17	4	13	0	.235	4		1978-91
McLellan, John	Toronto	6	2	4	0	.333	1		1969-73
McVie, Tom	New Jersey	14	6	8	0	.429	2		1975-92
Melrose, Barry	Los Angeles	24	13	11	0	.542	1		1992-95
Milbury, Mike	Boston	40	23	17	0	.575	2		1989-98
Muckler, John	Edmonton	40	25	15	0	.625	2	1	
	Buffalo	27	11	16	0	.407	4		
	Total	67	36	31	0	.537	6	1	1968-98
Muldoon, Pete	Chicago	2	0	1	1	.250	1		1926-27
Munro, Dunc	Mtl. Maroons	4	1	3	0	.250	1		1929-31
Murdoch, Bob	Winnipeg	7	3	4	0	.429	1		1989-91
Murphy, Mike	Los Angeles	5	1	4	0	.200	1		1986-98
Murray, Bryan	Washington	53	24	29	0	.453	7		
	Detroit	25	10	15	0	.400	3		
	Total	78	34	44	0	.436	10		1981-98
Murray, Terry	Washington	39	18	21	0	.462	4		
	Philadelphia	46	28	18	0	.609	3		
	Total	85	46	39	0	.541	7		1989-97
Neale, Harry	Vancouver	14	3	11	0	.214	4		1978-86

Coach	Team	Games Coached	Wins	Losses	Ties	%Wins	Playoff Years	Cup Wins	Career
Neilson, Roger	Toronto	19	8	11	0	.421	2		
	Buffalo	8	4	4	0	.500	1		
	Vancouver	21	12	9	0	.571	2		
	NY Rangers	29	13	16	0	.448	3		
	Philadelphia	11	3	8	0	.273	2		
	Total	88	40	48	0	.455	10		1977-99
Nolan, Ted	Buffalo	12	5	7	0	.417	1		1995-97
Nykoluk, Mike	Toronto	7	1	6	0	.143	2		1980-84
O'Donoghue, George	Toronto	7	4	2	1	.643	1	1	1921-22
O'Reilly, Terry	Boston	37	17	19	1	.473	3		1986-89
Oliver, Murray	Minnesota	13	5	8	0	.385	2		1981-83
Paddock, John	Winnipeg	13	5	8	0	.385	2		1991-95
Page, Pierre	Minnesota	12	4	8	0	.333	2		
	Quebec	6	2	4	0	.333	1		
	Calgary	4	0	4	0	.000	1		
	Total	22	6	16	0	.273	4		1988-98
Patrick, Craig	NY Rangers	17	7	10	0	.412	2		
	Pittsburgh	5	1	4	0	.200	1		
	Total	22	8	14	0	.364	3		1980-97
Patrick, Frank	Boston	6	2	4	0	.333	2		1934-36
Patrick, Lester	NY Rangers	65	32	26	7	.546	12	2	1926-39
Patrick, Lynn	NY Rangers	12	7	5	0	.583	1		
	Boston	28	9	18	1	.339	4		
	Total	40	16	23	1	.413	5		1948-76
Perron, Jean	Montreal	48	30	18	0	.625	3	1	1985-89
Perry, Don	Los Angeles	10	4	6	0	.400	1		1981-84
Pilous, Rudy	Chicago	41	19	22	0	.463	5	1	1957-63
Plager, Barclay	St. Louis	4	1	3	0	.250	1		1977-83
Pleau, Larry	Hartford	10	2	8	0	.200	2		1980-89
Polano, Nick	Detroit	7	1	6	0	.143	2		1982-85
Powers, Eddie	Toronto	2	0	2	0	.000	1		1924-25
Primeau, Joe	Toronto	15	8	6	1	.567	2	1	1950-53
Pronovost, Marcel	Buffalo	8	3	5	0	.375	1		1977-79
Pulford, Bob	Los Angeles	26	10	16	0	.385	4		
	Chicago	50	18	32	0	.360	7		
	Total	76	28	48	0	.368	11		1972-88
Quenneville, Joel	St. Louis	29	14	15	0	.483	3		1996-99
Quinn, Pat	Philadelphia	39	22	17	0	.564	3		
	Los Angeles	3	0	3	0	.000	1		
	Vancouver	61	31	30	0	.508	5		
	Toronto	15	9	6	0	.600	1		
	Total	120	62	58	0	.517	10		1978-99
Reay, Billy	Chicago	116	56	60	0	.483	12		1957-77
Risebrough, Doug	Calgary	7	3	4	0	.429	1		1990-92
Roberts, Jim	Hartford	7	3	4	0	.429	1		1981-97
Robinson, Larry	Los Angeles	4	0	4	0	.000	1		1995-98
Ross, Art	Boston	65	27	33	5	.454	11	1	1917-45
Ruel, Claude	Montreal	27	18	9	0	.667	3	2	1968-81
Ruff, Lindy	Buffalo	36	24	12	0	.667	2		1997-99
Sather, Glen	Edmonton	127	89	37	1	.705	10	4	1979-94

Coach	Team	Games Coached	Wins	Losses	Ties	%Wins	Playoff Years	Cup Wins	Career
Sator, Ted	NY Rangers	16	8	8	0	.500	1		
	Buffalo	11	3	8	0	.273	2		
	Total	27	11	16	0	.407	3		1985-89
Schinkel, Ken	Pittsburgh	6	2	4	0	.333	1		1972-77
Schmidt, Milt	Boston	34	15	19	0	.441	4		1954-76
Schoenfeld, Jim	New Jersey	20	11	9	0	.550	1		
	Washington	24	10	14	0	.417	3		
	Phoenix	13	5	8	0	.385	2		
	Total	57	26	31	0	.456	6		1985-99
Shero, Fred	Philadelphia	83	48	35	0	.578	6	2	
	NY Rangers	27	15	12	0	.556	2		
	Total	110	63	47	0	.573	8	2	1971-81
Simpson, Terry	NY Islanders	20	9	11	0	.450	2		
	Winnipeg	6	2	4	0	.333	1		
	Total	26	11	15	0	.423	3		1986-96
Sinden, Harry	Boston	43	24	19	0	.558	5	1	1966-85
Skinner, Jimmy	Detroit	26	14	12	0	.538	3	1	1954-58
Smith, Alf	Ottawa	5	1	4	0	.200	1		1918-19
Smith, Floyd	Buffalo	32	16	16	0	.500	3		1971-80
Smythe, Conn	Toronto	4	2	2	0	.500	1		1927-31
Sonmor, Glen	Minnesota	43	25	18	0	.581	3		1978-87
Stasiuk, Vic	Philadelphia	4	0	4	0	.000	1		1969-73
Stewart, Bill	Chicago	10	7	3	0	.700	1	1	1937-39
Stewart, Ron	Los Angeles	2	0	2	0	.000	1		1975-78
Sutter, Brian	St. Louis	41	20	21	0	.488	4		
	Boston	22	7	15	0	.318	3		
	Total	63	27	36	0	.429	7		1988-98
Sutter, Darryl	Chicago	26	11	15	0	.423	3		
	San Jose	12	4	8	0	.333	2		
	Total	38	15	23	0	.395	5		1992-99
Talbot, Jean-Guy	St. Louis	5	1	4	0	.200	1		
	NY Rangers	3	1	2	0	.333	1		
	Total	8	2	6	0	.250	2		1972-78
Tessier, Orval	Chicago	18	9	9	0	.500	2		1982-85
Thompson, Paul	Chicago	19	7	12	0	.368	4		1938-45
Tobin, Bill	Chicago	4	1	2	1	.375	2		1929-32
Tremblay, Mario	Montreal	11	3	8	0	.273	2		1995-97
Ubriaco, Gene	Pittsburgh	11	7	4	0	.636	1		1988-90
Vigneault, Alain	Montreal	10	4	6	0	.400	1		1997-98
Watson, Phil	NY Rangers	16	4	12	0	.250	3		1955-63
Watt, Tom	Winnipeg	7	1	6	0	.143	2		
	Vancouver	3	0	3	0	.000	1		
	Total	10	1	9	0	.100	3		1981-92
Webster, Tom	Los Angeles	28	12	16	0	.429	3		1986-92
Weiland, Cooney	Boston	17	10	7	0	.588	2	1	1939-41
White, Bill	Chicago	2	0	2	0	.000	1		1976-77
Wilson, Johnny	Pittsburgh	12	4	8	0	.333	2		1969-80
Wilson, Ron	Anaheim	11	4	7	0	.364	1		
	Washington	21	12	9	0	.571	1		
	Total	32	16	16	0	.500	2		1993-98
Young, Garry	St. Louis	2	0	2	0	.000	1		1972-76

Mervyn "Red" Dutton (left) became the coach of the New York Americans in 1935-36 and guided the team into the playoffs in four of his seven seasons behind the bench. Detroit bench-boss Sid Abel (below), seen here with (left to right) Larry Jeffrey, Norm Ullman, Paul Henderson, Alex Delvecchio and Roger Crozier, piloted the Red Wings into the Stanley Cup finals four times in the 1960s

Penalty Shots in Stanley Cup Playoff Games

Date	Player	Goaltender	Scored	Final Score	Series
Mar. 25/37	Lionel Conacher, Mtl. Maroons	Tiny Thompson, Boston	No	Mtl. M. 0 at Bos. 4	QF
Apr. 15/37	Alex Shibicky, NY Rangers	Earl Robertson, Detroit	No	NYR 0 at Det. 3	F
Apr. 13/44	Virgil Johnson, Chicago	Bill Durnan, Montreal	No	Chi. 4 at Mtl. 5*	F
Apr. 9/68	Wayne Connelly, Minnesota	Terry Sawchuk, Los Angeles	Yes	L.A. 5 at Min. 7	QF
Apr. 27/68	Jim Roberts, St. Louis	Cesare Maniago, Minnesota	No	St. L. 4 at Min. 3	SF
May 16/71	Frank Mahovlich, Montreal	Tony Esposito, Chicago	No	Chi. 3 at Mtl. 4	F
May 7/75	Bill Barber, Philadelphia	Glenn Resch, NY Islanders	No	Phi. 3 at NYI 4*	SF
Apr. 20/79	Mike Walton, Chicago	Glenn Resch, NY Islanders	No	NYI 4 at Chi. 0	QF
Apr. 9/81	Peter McNab, Boston	Don Beaupre, Minnesota	No	Min. 5 at Bos. 4*	PR
Apr. 17/81	Anders Hedberg, NY Rangers	Mike Liut, St. Louis	Yes	NYR 6 at St. L. 4	QF
Apr. 9/83	Denis Potvin, NY Islanders	Pat Riggin, Washington	No	NYI 6 at Wsh. 2	DSF
Apr. 28/84	Wayne Gretzky, Edmonton	Don Beaupre, Minnesota	Yes	Edm. 8 at Min. 5	CF
May 1/84	Mats Naslund, Montreal	Billy Smith, NY Islanders	No	Mtl. 1 at NYI 3	CF
Apr. 14/85	Bob Carpenter, Washington	Billy Smith, NY Islanders	No	Wsh. 4 at NYI 6	DF
May 28/85	Ron Sutter, Philadelphia	Grant Fuhr, Edmonton	No	Phi. 3 at Edm. 5	F
May 30/85	Dave Poulin, Philadelphia	Grant Fuhr, Edmonton	No	Phi. 3 at Edm. 8	F
Apr. 9/88	John Tucker, Buffalo	Andy Moog, Boston	Yes	Bos. 2 at Buf. 6	DSF
Apr. 9/88	Petr Klima, Detroit	Allan Bester, Toronto	Yes	Det. 6 at Tor. 3	DSF
Apr. 8/89	Neal Broten, Minnesota	Greg Millen, St. Louis	Yes	St. L. 5 at Min. 3	DSF
Apr. 4/90	Al MacInnis, Calgary	Kelly Hrudey, Los Angeles	Yes	L.A. 5 at Cgy. 3	DSF
Apr. 5/90	Randy Wood, NY Islanders	Mike Richter, NY Rangers	No	NYI 1 at NYR 2	DSF
May 3/90	Kelly Miller, Washington	Andy Moog, Boston	No	Wsh. 3 at Bos. 5	CF
May 18/90	Petr Klima, Edmonton	Rejean Lemelin, Boston	No	Edm. 7 at Bos. 2	F
Apr. 6/91	Basil McRae, Minnesota	Ed Belfour, Chicago	Yes	Min. 2 at Chi. 5	DSF
Apr. 10/91	Steve Duchesne, Los Angeles	Kirk McLean, Vancouver	Yes	L.A. 6 at Van. 1	DSF
May 11/92	Jaromir Jagr, Pittsburgh	John Vanbiesbrouck, NYR	Yes	Pit. 3 at NYR 2	DF
May 13/92	Shawn McEachern, Pittsburgh	John Vanbiesbrouck, NYR	No	NYR 1 at Pit. 5	DF
June 7/94	Pavel Bure, Vancouver	Mike Richter, NYR	No	NYR 4 at Van. 2	F
May 9/95	Patrick Poulin, Chicago	Felix Potvin, Toronto	No	Tor. 3 at Chi. 0	CQF
May 10/95	Michal Pivonka, Washington	Tom Barrasso, Pittsburgh	No	Pit. 2 at Wsh. 6	CQF
Apr. 24/96	Joe Juneau, Washington	Ken Wregget, Pittsburgh	No	Pit. 3 at Wsh. 2**	CQF
May 11/97	Eric Lindros, Philadelphia	Steve Shields, Buffalo	Yes	Phi. 6 at Buf. 3	CSF
Apr. 23/98	Alexei Morozov, Pittsburgh	Andy Moog, Montreal	No	Mtl. 3 at Pit. 2**	CQF
Apr. 22/99	Mats Sundin, Toronto	John Vanbiesbrouck, Phi.	No	Phi. 3 at Tor. 0	CQF
May 29/99	Mats Sundin, Toronto	Dominik Hasek, Buffalo	Yes	Tor. 2 at Buf. 5	CF

* Game was decided in overtime, but shot taken during regulation time.
** Shot taken in overtime.

Ten Longest Overtime Games

Date	City	Series	Score			Scorer	Overtime	Series Winner
Mar. 24/36	Mtl.	SF	Det. 1	Mtl. M. 0		Mud Bruneteau	116:30	Det.
Apr. 3/33	Tor.	SF	Tor. 1	Bos. 0		Ken Doraty	104:46	Tor.
Apr. 24/96	Wsh.	CQF	Pit. 3	Wsh. 2		Petr Nedved	79:15	Pit.
Mar. 23/43	Det.	SF	Tor. 3	Det. 2		Jack McLean	70:18	Det.
Mar. 28/30	Mtl.	SF	Mtl. 2	NYR 1		Gus Rivers	68:52	Mtl.
Apr. 18/87	Wsh.	DSF	NYI 3	Wsh. 2		Pat LaFontaine	68:47	NYI
Apr. 27/94	Buf.	CQF	Buf. 1	N.J. 0		Dave Hannan	65:43	N.J.
Mar. 27/51	Det.	SF	Mtl. 3	Det. 2		Maurice Richard	61:09	Mtl.
Mar. 27/38	NY	QF	NYA 3	NYR 2		Lorne Carr	60:40	NYA
Mar. 26/32	Mtl.	SF	NYR 4	Mtl. 3		Fred Cook	59:32	NYR

Mats Sundin (above) became the first player in NHL history to take two penalty shots in one playoff year. He was stopped by John Vanbiesbrouck, but beat Dominik Hasek (below). The Dominator's experience in long overtime games in the playoffs includes a 125-minute 1-0 shutout of New Jersey in 1994 and a triple-overtime loss to Dallas in 1999's Cup-clinching game.

Overtime Record of Current Teams

(Listed by number of OT games played)

Team	Overall				Home					Road				
	GP	W	L	T	GP	W	L	T	Last OT Game	GP	W	L	T	Last OT Game
Montreal	120	69	49	2	55	36	18	1	May 12/98	65	33	31	1	May 8/98
Boston	98	38	57	3	45	20	24	1	May 3/98	53	18	33	2	Apr. 30/99
Toronto	92	48	43	1	58	31	26	1	Apr. 30/99	34	17	17	0	May 13/99
NY Rangers	63	30	33	0	27	12	15	0	Apr. 22/97	36	18	18	0	May 11/97
Chicago	62	30	30	2	30	16	13	1	Apr. 20/97	32	14	17	1	May 2/96
Detroit	63	31	32	0	38	16	22	0	Jun. 11/98	25	15	10	0	Jun. 3/98
Philadelphia	45	22	23	0	20	11	9	0	May 1/98	25	11	14	0	Apr. 30/99
NY Islanders	38	29	9	0	17	14	3	0	May 20/93	21	15	6	0	May 18/93
St. Louis	44	24	20	0	22	17	5	0	May 12/99	22	7	15	0	May 8/99
* Dallas	42	18	24	0	19	7	12	0	Jun. 8/99	23	11	12	0	Jun. 1/99
Buffalo	40	21	19	0	22	13	9	0	Jun. 19/99	18	8	10	0	Jun. 8/99
Edmonton	34	20	14	0	19	10	9	0	Apr. 27/99	15	10	5	0	Apr. 29/97
** Colorado	32	20	12	0	14	8	6	0	May 28/99	18	12	6	0	May 3/99
Los Angeles	30	12	18	0	16	8	8	0	Jun. 7/93	14	4	10	0	Jun. 3/93
*** Calgary	30	11	19	0	14	4	10	0	Apr. 23/96	16	7	9	0	Apr. 28/94
Vancouver	29	13	16	0	12	5	7	0	May 27/95	17	8	9	0	Apr. 25/96
Washington	26	13	13	0	10	5	5	0	May 25/98	16	8	8	0	Jun. 11/98
Pittsburgh	20	11	9	0	12	7	5	0	May 13/99	8	4	4	0	Apr. 24/96
**** New Jersey	20	5	15	0	9	2	7	0	Apr. 22/98	11	3	8	0	May 2/99
***** Carolina	13	6	7	0	9	5	4	0	Apr. 30/99	4	1	3	0	May 1/92
****** Phoenix	12	5	7	0	8	3	5	0	May 4/99	4	2	2	0	Apr. 27/93
Florida	5	2	3	0	3	1	2	0	Apr. 25/97	2	1	1	0	Apr. 22/97
Anaheim	4	1	3	0	1	0	1	0	May 8/97	3	1	2	0	May 4/97
San Jose	7	3	4	0	4	1	3	0	May 3/99	3	2	1	0	May 19/95
Tampa Bay	2	2	0	0	1	1	0	0	Apr. 21/96	1	1	0	0	Apr. 18/96
Ottawa	3	2	1	0	2	1	1	0	Apr. 23/99	1	1	0	0	Apr. 22/98

*Totals include those of Minnesota 1967-93.
**Totals include those of Quebec 1979-95.
***Totals include those of Atlanta 1972-80.
****Totals include those of Kansas City and Colorado 1974-82.
*****Totals include those of Hartford 1979-97.
******Totals include those of Winnipeg 1979-96.

Late Additions

GRANT FUHR traded from St. Louis to Calgary for Calgary's 3rd round selection in the 2000 Entry Draft, September 5, 1999.

ALDRIDGE, Keith — DAL.

Defense. Shoots right. 5'11", 185 lbs. Born, Detroit, MI, July 20, 1973.

			Regular Season					Playoffs				
Season	Club	Lea	GP	G	A	TP	PIM	GP	G	A	TP	PIM
1992-93	Lake Superior	CCHA	37	3	1	14	30	....	....	....	....	....
1993-94	Lake Superior	CCHA	45	10	24	34	86	....	....	....	....	....
1994-95	Lake Superior	CCHA	40	10	31	41	89	....	....	....	....	....
1995-96	Lake Superior	CCHA	38	14	36	50	88	....	....	....	....	....
	Baltimore	AHL	7	0	2	2	2	....	....	....	....	....
1996-97	Baltimore	AHL	51	4	9	13	92	3	0	0	0	4
1997-98	Detroit	IHL	79	13	21	34	89	23	1	9	10	67
1998-99	Detroit	IHL	66	15	28	43	130	11	2	7	9	49

Signed as a free agent by **Dallas**, September, 1999.

COUTURE, Alexandre — CHI.

Left wing. Shoots left. 6'4", 217 lbs. Born, Sorel, Que., September 14, 1980.
(Chicago's 8th choice, 238th overall, in 1998 Entry Draft).

			Regular Season					Playoffs				
Season	Club	Lea	GP	G	A	TP	PIM	GP	G	A	TP	PIM
1998-99	Sherbrooke	QMJHL	35	9	18	27	52	....	....	....	....	....
	Drummondville	QMJHL	34	5	12	17	32	....	....	....	....	....

CULL, Trent — PHX.

Defense. Shoots left. 6'3", 210 lbs. Born, Brampton, Ont., September 27, 1973.

			Regular Season					Playoffs				
Season	Club	Lea	GP	G	A	TP	PIM	GP	G	A	TP	PIM
1989-90	Owen Sound	OHL	40	23	33	56	28	....	....	....	....	....
1990-91	Owen Sound	OHL	24	1	2	3	19	....	....	....	....	....
	Windsor	OHL	33	1	6	7	34	11	0	0	0	8
1991-92	Windsor	OHL	32	0	6	6	66	....	....	....	....	....
	Kingston	OHL	18	0	0	0	31	....	....	....	....	....
1992-93	Kingston	OHL	60	11	28	39	144	16	2	8	10	37
1993-94	Kingston	OHL	50	2	30	32	147	6	0	1	1	6
1994-95	St. John's	AHL	43	0	1	1	53	....	....	....	....	....
	Brantford	ColHL	4	0	0	0	14	....	....	....	....	....
1995-96	St. John's	AHL	46	2	1	3	118	4	0	0	0	6
1996-97	St. John's	AHL	75	4	5	9	219	8	0	1	1	18
1997-98	Houston	IHL	72	4	8	12	201	4	0	0	0	4
1998-99	Houston	IHL	72	2	14	16	232	19	0	2	2	34

Signed as a free agent by **Toronto**, June 4, 1994. Signed as a free agent by **Phoenix**, August, 1999.

DANDENAULT, Eric — CAR.

Defense. Shoots right. 6', 195 lbs. Born, Sherbrooke, Que., March 10, 1970.

			Regular Season					Playoffs				
Season	Club	Lea	GP	G	A	TP	PIM	GP	G	A	TP	PIM
1988-89	Drummondville	QMJHL	66	5	24	29	64	....	....	....	....	....
1989-90	Chicoutimi	QMJHL	67	14	38	52	238	6	0	2	2	65
1990-91	Drummondville	QMJHL	67	14	33	47	215	14	5	6	11	84
1991-92	Hershey	AHL	69	6	13	19	149	3	0	0	0	4
1992-93	Hershey	AHL	72	20	19	39	118	....	....	....	....	....
1993-94	Hershey	AHL	14	2	1	3	49	....	....	....	....	....
	Johnstown	ECHL	2	1	1	2	6	....	....	....	....	....
1994-95	HC Fassa	Italy	31	14	17	31	87	....	....	....	....	....
1995-96	Saginaw	ColHL	61	5	30	35	160	....	....	....	....	....
	Cincinnati	IHL	16	1	2	3	49	17	1	6	7	30
1996-97	Cincinnati	IHL	77	5	14	19	240	3	0	0	0	7
1997-98	Cincinnati	IHL	81	2	11	13	230	9	0	2	2	18
1998-99	Cincinnati	IHL	63	4	13	17	180	3	0	0	0	2

Signed as a free agent by **Philadelphia**, December 4, 1991. • Missed majority of 1993-94 season with hernia injury, October 31, 1993. Signed as a free agent by **Cincinnati** (IHL), March 11, 1996. Signed as a free agent by **Carolina**, August 31, 1999.

NHL Clubs and Minor-League Affiliates, 1999-2000

NHL Club	Minor-League Affiliate
Atlanta	Orlando Solar Bears (IHL) Greenville Grrrowl (ECHL)
Anaheim	Cincinnati Mighty Ducks (AHL)
Boston	Providence Bruins (AHL) Greenville Grrrowl (ECHL)
Buffalo	Rochester Americans (AHL) South Carolina Stingrays (ECHL) B.C. Iceman (UHL)
Calgary	Saint John Flames (AHL) Johnstown Chiefs (ECHL)
Carolina	Cincinnati Cyclones (IHL) Florida Everblades (ECHL)
Chicago	Cleveland Lumberjacks (IHL)
Colorado	Hershey Bears (AHL)
Dallas	Michigan K-Wings (IHL)
Detroit	Cincinnati Mighty Ducks (AHL) Toledo Storm (ECHL)
Edmonton	Hamilton Bulldogs (AHL) Tallahassee Tiger Sharks (ECHL)
Florida	Louisville Panthers (AHL) Port Huron Border Cats (UHL)
Los Angeles	Springfield Falcons (AHL) Long Beach Ice Dogs (IHL)
Montreal	Citadelles de Québec (AHL) New Orleans Brass (ECHL)
Nashville	Milwaukee Admirals (IHL) Hampton Roads Admirals (ECHL)
New Jersey	Albany River Rats (AHL) Augusta Lynx (ECHL)
NY Islanders	Lowell Lock Monsters (AHL) Chicago Wolves (IHL) Trenton Titans (ECHL)
NY Rangers	Hartford Wolf Pack (AHL)
Ottawa	Grand Rapids Griffins (IHL)
Philadelphia	Philadelphia Phantoms (AHL) Trenton Titans (ECHL)
Phoenix	Springfield Falcons (AHL) Las Vegas Thunder (IHL) Mississippi Sea Wolves (ECHL)
Pittsburgh	Wilkes-Barre/Scranton Penguins (AHL) Wheeling Nailers (ECHL)
St. Louis	Worcester IceCats (AHL) Peoria Rivermen (ECHL)
San Jose	Kentucky Thoroughblades (AHL) Richmond Renegades (ECHL)
Tampa Bay	Detroit Vipers (IHL) Toledo Storm (ECHL)
Toronto	St. John's Maple Leafs (AHL)
Vancouver	Syracuse Crunch (AHL)
Washington	Portland Pirates (AHL) Hampton Roads Admirals (ECHL)

ELORANTA, Mikko — BOS.

Left wing. Shoots left. 6', 185 lbs. Born, Aura, Finland, August 24, 1972.
(Boston's 9th choice, 247th overall, in 1999 Entry Draft).

			Regular Season					Playoffs				
Season	Club	Lea	GP	G	A	TP	PIM	GP	G	A	TP	PIM
1990-91	TPS Turku	Finn-Jr.	35	8	8	16	18	....	....	....	....	....
1991-92	TPS Turku	Finn-Jr.	19	3	1	4	8	8	0	0	0	0
1992-93	TPS Turku	Finn-Jr.	31	11	6	17	20	6	0	4	4	6
1993-94	Kiekko-67 Turku	Finland-2	45	3	4	7	24	....	....	....	....	....
1994-95	Kiekko-67 Turku	Finland-2	40	14	13	27	32	7	4	1	5	20
1995-96	Kiekko-67 Turku	Finland-2	8	6	7	13	2	....	....	....	....	....
	Ilves Tampere	Finland	43	18	15	33	86	3	0	2	2	2
1996-97	TPS Turku	EuroHL	6	3	1	4	6	1	0	0	0	0
	TPS Turku	Finland	31	6	15	21	52	10	5	2	7	6
1997-98	TPS Turku	EuroHL	3	1	0	1	12	....	....	....	....	....
	TPS Turku	Finland	46	23	14	37	82	2	0	0	0	8
1998-99	TPS Turku	Finland	52	19	21	40	103	10	1	6	7	26

FEDOTENKO, Ruslan — PHI.

Center. Shoots left. 6'2", 191 lbs. Born, Kiev, Ukraine, January 18, 1970.

			Regular Season					Playoffs				
Season	Club	Lea	GP	G	A	TP	PIM	GP	G	A	TP	PIM
1996-97	Sokol Kiev	Ukraine	STATISTICS NOT AVAILABLE									
1997-98	Melfort	SJHL	68	35	31	66	....	....	....	....	....	....
1998-99	Sioux City	USHL	55	43	34	77	139	5	5	1	6	9

Signed as a free agent by **Philadelphia**, August 3, 1999.

HEALEY, Eric — PHX.

Left wing. Shoots left. 6', 195 lbs. Born, Hull, MA, January 20, 1975.

			Regular Season					Playoffs				
Season	Club	Lea	GP	G	A	TP	PIM	GP	G	A	TP	PIM
1993-94	New England	NEJHL	37	61	76	137	....	....	....	....	....	....
1994-95	RPI Engineers	ECAC	37	13	11	24	35	....	....	....	....	....
1995-96	RPI Engineers	ECAC	35	18	22	40	57	....	....	....	....	....
1996-97	RPI Engineers	ECAC	36	30	26	56	63	....	....	....	....	....
1997-98	RPI Engineers	ECAC	35	21	27	48	42	....	....	....	....	....
1998-99	Saint John	AHL	64	14	24	38	77	....	....	....	....	....
	Orlando	IHL	13	5	4	9	13	8	1	0	1	12

ECAC Second All-Star Team (1997) • NCAA East Second All-American Team (1997) • ECAC First All-Star Team (1998)

Signed as a free agent by **Calgary**, September 22, 1998. Traded to **Orlando** (IHL) by **Saint John** (AHL) with Tyler Moss for Allan Egeland and Arttu Kayhla, March 22, 1999. Signed as a free agent by **Phoenix**, July 26, 1999.

LETANG, Alan — DAL.

Defense. Shoots left. 6'1", 205 lbs. Born, Renfrew, Ont., September 4, 1975.
(Montreal's 10th choice, 203rd overall, in 1993 Entry Draft).

			Regular Season					Playoffs				
Season	Club	Lea	GP	G	A	TP	PIM	GP	G	A	TP	PIM
1990-91	Ottawa Valley	OMHA	32	3	26	29	16	....	....	....	....	....
1991-92	Cornwall	OHL	47	1	4	5	16	6	0	0	0	2
1992-93	Newmarket	OHL	66	1	25	26	14	6	0	3	3	2
1993-94	Newmarket	OHL	58	3	21	24	30	....	....	....	....	....
1994-95	Sarnia	OHL	62	5	36	41	35	4	2	2	4	6
1995-96	Fredericton	AHL	71	0	26	26	40	....	....	....	....	....
1996-97	Fredericton	AHL	60	2	9	11	8	....	....	....	....	....
1997-98	Kaufenbeurer	Germany	15	1	5	6	8	....	....	....	....	....
	SC Langnau	Switz-2	11	4	3	7	6	....	....	....	....	....
	Augsburger	Germany	17	0	1	1	4	....	....	....	....	....
1998-99	Canada	Nat-Team	41	3	9	12	20	....	....	....	....	....
	Michigan	IHL	12	3	3	6	0	5	0	2	2	0

Signed as a free agent by **Dallas**, March 22, 1999.

McCANN, Sean — PHX.

Defense. Shoots right. 6', 195 lbs. Born, North York, Ont., September 18, 1971.
(Florida's 1st choice, 1st overall, in 1994 Supplemental Draft).

			Regular Season					Playoffs				
Season	Club	Lea	GP	G	A	TP	PIM	GP	G	A	TP	PIM
1990-91	Harvard	ECAC	28	2	9	11	88	....	....	....	....	....
1991-92	Harvard	ECAC	27	4	10	14	51	....	....	....	....	....
1992-93	Harvard	ECAC	31	4	5	9	38	....	....	....	....	....
1994-95	Cincinnati	IHL	76	10	12	22	58	10	0	2	2	8
1995-96	Carolina	AHL	80	14	33	47	61	....	....	....	....	....
1996-97	Grand Rapids	IHL	76	8	26	34	46	5	0	0	0	2
1997-98	Milwaukee	IHL	33	6	11	17	37	....	....	....	....	....
	Orlando	IHL	26	5	3	8	30	....	....	....	....	....
1998-99	Orlando	IHL	42	4	9	13	28	....	....	....	....	....
	Springfield	IHL	31	8	15	23	31	3	0	1	1	4

ECAC First All-Star Team (1994) • NCAA East First All-American Team (1994) • NCAA Final Four All-Tournament Team (1994) • NCAA Final Four Tournament Most Valuable Player (1994)

Signed as a free agent by **Phoenix**, August, 1999.

PETROCHININ, Evgeny (peht-roh-CHIH-nihn) — DAL.

Defense. Shoots left. 6'2", 190 lbs. Born, Murmansk, USSR, February 7, 1976.
(Dallas' 5th choice, 150th overall, in 1994 Entry Draft).

			Regular Season					Playoffs				
Season	Club	Lea	GP	G	A	TP	PIM	GP	G	A	TP	PIM
1993-94	SKA Spartak	CIS	2	0	0	0	0	....	....	....	....	....
1994-95	SKA Spartak	CIS	45	0	2	2	14	....	....	....	....	....
1995-96	SKA Spartak	CIS	50	5	17	22	18	5	3	0	3	0
1996-97	SKA Spartak	Russia	32	5	6	11	52	....	....	....	....	....
1997-98	SKA Spartak	Russia	46	12	6	18	100	....	....	....	....	....
1998-99	SKA Spartak	Russia	21	4	6	10	14	....	....	....	....	....
	Kazan	Russia	6	0	2	2	2	9	1	1	2	24

SCOVILLE, Darryl — CGY.

Defense. Shoots left. 6'3", 215 lbs. Born, Regina, SK, October 13, 1975.

			Regular Season					Playoffs				
Season	Club	Lea	GP	G	A	TP	PIM	GP	G	A	TP	PIM
1995-96	Merrimack	HE	34	6	20	26	54	....	....	....	....	....
1996-97	Merrimack	HE	35	7	16	23	71	....	....	....	....	....
1997-98	Merrimack	HE	38	4	26	30	84	....	....	....	....	....
1998-99	Saint John	AHL	61	1	7	8	66	7	1	2	3	13

Signed as a free agent by **Calgary**, June 12, 1998

1999-2000 Prospect Register

Note: The 1999-2000 Prospect Register lists forwards and defensemen only. Goaltenders are listed separately. The Prospect Register lists every player drafted in the first six rounds of the 1999 Entry Draft, players on NHL Reserve Lists and other players who have not yet played in the NHL. Trades and roster changes are current as of September 1, 1999.

Abbreviations: A – assists; **G** – goals; **GP** – games played; **Lea** – league; **PIM** – penalties in minutes; **TP** – total points; ***** – league-leading total; **♦** – member of Stanley Cup-winning team.

NHL Player Register begins on page 313.

Goaltender Register begins on page 545.

League Abbreviations are listed on page 313.

ABID, Ramzi
(a-BIHD, RAM-zee) **COL.**

Left wing. Shoots left. 6'2", 195 lbs.   Born, Montreal, Que., March 24, 1980.
(Colorado's 5th choice, 28th overall, in 1998 Entry Draft).

				Regular Season					Playoffs			
Season	Club	Lea	GP	G	A	TP	PIM	GP	G	A	TP	PIM
1996-97	Chicoutimi	QMJHL	65	13	24	37	141	21	2	12	14	28
1997-98	Chicoutimi	QMJHL	68	50	*85	*135	266	6	3	4	7	10
1998-99	Chicoutimi	QMJHL	21	11	15	26	97	....	....	....	....	....
	Bathurst	QMJHL	24	14	22	36	102	23	14	20	34	*84

QMJHL First All-Star Team (1998)

ABRAHAMSSON, Elias
(AH-brah-ham-suhn, eh-LEE-ahs) **BOS.**

Defense. Shoots left. 6'3", 240 lbs.   Born, Uppsala, Sweden, June 15, 1977.
(Boston's 6th choice, 132nd overall, in 1996 Entry Draft).

				Regular Season					Playoffs			
Season	Club	Lea	GP	G	A	TP	PIM	GP	G	A	TP	PIM
1994-95	Halifax	QMJHL	25	0	3	3	41	....	....	....	....	....
1995-96	Halifax	QMJHL	64	3	11	14	268	6	2	2	4	8
1996-97	Halifax	QMJHL	30	4	10	14	231	18	4	9	13	74
1997-98	Providence	AHL	29	0	1	1	47	....	....	....	....	....
1998-99	Providence	AHL	75	2	9	11	184	4	0	0	0	7

ADAMS, Bryan
ATL.

Left wing. Shoots left. 6', 185 lbs.   Born, Ft. St. James, B.C., March 20, 1977.

				Regular Season					Playoffs			
Season	Club	Lea	GP	G	A	TP	PIM	GP	G	A	TP	PIM
1994-95	Prince George	BCJHL	48	37	53	90	....	....	....	....	....	....
1995-96	Michigan State	CCHA	42	3	8	11	12	....	....	....	....	....
1996-97	Michigan State	CCHA	29	7	7	14	51	....	....	....	....	....
1997-98	Michigan State	CCHA	31	9	21	30	39	....	....	....	....	....
1998-99	Michigan State	CCHA	42	21	16	37	56	....	....	....	....	....

Signed as a free agent by **Atlanta**, July 6, 1999.

ADAMS, Craig
CAR.

Right wing. Shoots right. 6', 200 lbs.   Born, Calgary, Alta., April 26, 1977.
(Hartford's 9th choice, 223rd overall, in 1996 Entry Draft).

				Regular Season					Playoffs			
Season	Club	Lea	GP	G	A	TP	PIM	GP	G	A	TP	PIM
1995-96	Harvard University	ECAC	34	8	9	17	56	....	....	....	....	....
1996-97	Harvard University	ECAC	32	6	4	10	36	....	....	....	....	....
1997-98	Harvard University	ECAC	12	6	6	12	12	....	....	....	....	....
1998-99	Harvard University	ECAC	31	9	14	23	53	....	....	....	....	....

Rights transferred to **Carolina** after **Hartford** franchise relocated, June 25, 1997.

ADDUONO, Jeremy
(uh-DOO-noh) **BUF.**

Right wing. Shoots right. 6', 182 lbs.   Born, Thunder Bay, Ont., August 4, 1978.
(Buffalo's 8th choice, 184th overall, in 1997 Entry Draft).

				Regular Season					Playoffs			
Season	Club	Lea	GP	G	A	TP	PIM	GP	G	A	TP	PIM
1995-96	Sudbury	OHL	66	15	22	37	14	....	....	....	....	....
1996-97	Sudbury	OHL	66	29	40	69	24	....	....	....	....	....
1997-98	Sudbury	OHL	66	37	69	106	40	10	5	5	10	10
1998-99	Canada	Nat-Team	44	10	18	28	10	....	....	....	....	....

AFANASENKOV, Dmitri
(ah-fahn-AH-sehn-kahv) **T.B.**

Left wing. Shoots right. 6'1", 180 lbs.   Born, Arkhangelsk, USSR, May 12, 1980.
(Tampa Bay's 3rd choice, 72nd overall, in 1998 Entry Draft).

				Regular Season					Playoffs			
Season	Club	Lea	GP	G	A	TP	PIM	GP	G	A	TP	PIM
1995-96	Yaroslavl-2	Russia-2	25	10	5	15	10	....	....	....	....	....
	Yaroslavl	Russia-Jr.	35	28	16	44	8	....	....	....	....	....
1996-97	Yaroslavl-2	Russia-3	45	20	15	35	14	....	....	....	....	....
1997-98	Yaroslavl-2	Russia-2	48	14	7	21	20	....	....	....	....	....
1998-99	Moncton	QMJHL	15	5	5	10	12	....	....	....	....	....
	Sherbrooke	QMJHL	51	23	30	53	22	13	10	6	16	6

AFINOGENOV, Maxim
(ah-fihn-ah-GEHN-ahf) **BUF.**

Right wing. Shoots left. 5'11", 176 lbs.   Born, Moscow, USSR, September 4, 1979.
(Buffalo's 3rd choice, 69th overall, in 1997 Entry Draft).

				Regular Season					Playoffs			
Season	Club	Lea	GP	G	A	TP	PIM	GP	G	A	TP	PIM
1995-96	Moscow D'amo-2	Russia-2			STATISTICS NOT AVAILABLE							
	Moscow D'amo	CIS	1	0	0	0	0	....	....	....	....	....
1996-97	Moscow D'amo	Russia	29	6	5	11	10	4	0	2	2	0
1997-98	Moscow D'amo	Russia	35	10	5	15	53	....	....	....	....	....
	Moscow D'amo	EuroHL	6	3	1	4	27	....	....	....	....	....
1998-99	Moscow D'amo	Russia	38	8	13	21	24	16	10	6	16	14

AHMAOJA, Timo
(ahkh-mah-OH-yah) **ANA.**

Defense. Shoots right. 6'1", 180 lbs.   Born, Jyvaskyla, Finland, August 8, 1978.
(Anaheim's 5th choice, 172nd overall, in 1996 Entry Draft).

				Regular Season					Playoffs			
Season	Club	Lea	GP	G	A	TP	PIM	GP	G	A	TP	PIM
1995-96	JyP Jyvaskyla	Finn-Jr.	28	0	7	7	16	6	1	0	1	2
	JyP Jyvaskyla	Finland	4	0	0	0	4	....	....	....	....	....
1996-97	JyP Jyvaskyla	Finland	35	0	4	4	8	....	....	....	....	....
	JyP Jyvaskyla	Finn-Jr.	19	4	5	9	24	....	....	....	....	....
1997-98	JyP Jyvaskyla	Finland	10	0	0	0	4	....	....	....	....	....
	Lukko Rauma	Finland	10	0	0	0	0	....	....	....	....	....
	Diskos Jyvaskyla	Finland-2	23	1	2	3	14	....	....	....	....	....
1998-99	KalPa Kuopio	Finn-Jr.	3	0	1	1	10	....	....	....	....	....
	KalPa Kuopio	Finland	52	0	1	1	16	....	....	....	....	....

AHOSILTA, Marko
(ah-hoh-SIHL-tuh) **N.J.**

Center. Shoots left. 5'8", 165 lbs.   Born, Kuopio, Finland, January 24, 1980.
(New Jersey's 11th choice, 227th overall, in 1998 Entry Draft).

				Regular Season					Playoffs			
Season	Club	Lea	GP	G	A	TP	PIM	GP	G	A	TP	PIM
1995-96	KalPa Kuopio	Finn-Jr.	12	4	8	12	10	....	....	....	....	....
1996-97	KalPa Kuopio	Finn-Jr.	35	15	21	36	36	5	2	0	2	2
1997-98	KalPa Kuopio	Finn-Jr.	14	14	13	27	10	....	....	....	....	....
	KalPa Kuopio	Finland	2	0	0	0	0	....	....	....	....	....
1998-99	KalPa Kuopio	Finn-Jr.	24	7	7	14	10	....	....	....	....	....
	KalPa Kuopio	Finland	1	0	0	0	0	....	....	....	....	....

AITKEN, Johnathan
BOS.

Defense. Shoots left. 6'4", 215 lbs.   Born, Edmonton, Alta., May 24, 1978.
(Boston's 1st choice, 8th overall, in 1996 Entry Draft).

				Regular Season					Playoffs			
Season	Club	Lea	GP	G	A	TP	PIM	GP	G	A	TP	PIM
1994-95	Medicine Hat	WHL	53	0	5	5	71	5	0	0	0	0
1995-96	Medicine Hat	WHL	71	6	14	20	131	5	1	0	1	6
1996-97	Brandon	WHL	65	4	18	22	211	6	0	0	0	4
1997-98	Brandon	WHL	69	9	25	34	183	18	0	8	8	67
1998-99	Providence	AHL	65	2	9	11	92	13	0	0	0	17

WHL East Second All-Star Team (1998)

ALATALO, Mika
(a-luh-TAH-loh, MEE-kuh) **PHX.**

Left wing. Shoots left. 6', 190 lbs.   Born, Oulu, Finland, May 11, 1971.
(Winnipeg's 11th choice, 203rd overall, in 1990 Entry Draft)

				Regular Season					Playoffs			
Season	Club	Lea	GP	G	A	TP	PIM	GP	G	A	TP	PIM
1988-89	KooKoo	Finland	34	8	6	14	10	....	....	....	....	....
1989-90	KooKoo	Finland	41	3	5	8	22	....	....	....	....	....
1990-91	Lukko Rauma	Finland	39	10	1	11	10	....	....	....	....	....
1991-92	Lukko Rauma	Finland	43	20	17	37	32	2	0	0	0	0
1992-93	Lukko Rauma	Finland	48	16	19	35	38	3	0	0	0	0
1993-94	Lukko Rauma	Finland	45	19	15	34	77	9	2	2	4	4
1994-95	TPS Turku	Finland	44	23	13	36	79	13	2	5	7	8
1995-96	TPS Turku	Finland	49	19	18	37	44	11	3	4	7	8
1996-97	Lulea HF	Sweden	50	19	18	37	54	10	2	3	5	22
1997-98	Lulea HF	Sweden	45	14	10	24	22	2	0	0	0	0
1998-99	TPS Turku	Finland	53	14	23	37	44	10	6	3	9	6

Transferred to **Phoenix** after **Winnipeg** franchise relocated, July 1, 1996.

ALBERT, Chris — PHI.

Center. Shoots right. 5'11", 195 lbs. Born, Ottawa, Ont., October 12, 1972.

			Regular Season					Playoffs				
Season	Club	Lea	GP	G	A	TP	PIM	GP	G	A	TP	PIM
1991-92	Union College	ECAC	21	5	7	12	16	....	....	....	....	....
1992-93	Union College	ECAC	25	9	11	20	56	....	....	....	....	....
1993-94	Union College	ECAC	30	11	18	29	48	....	....	....	....	....
1994-95	Union College	ECAC	29	17	15	32	44	....	....	....	....	....
1995-96	San Antonio	CHL	37	8	12	20	54	13	3	1	4	35
1996-97	San Antonio	CHL	55	19	29	48	48	....	....	....	....	....
1997-98	Fort Worth	WPHL	68	21	29	50	205	13	7	5	12	20
	Detroit	IHL	2	0	0	0	2	....	....	....	....	....
1998-99	Cincinnati	AHL	17	4	3	7	109	....	....	....	....	....
	Michigan	IHL	23	3	3	6	44	....	....	....	....	....
	Philadelphia	AHL	22	1	3	4	88	15	5	5	10	22

Signed as a free agent by **Philadelphia**, July 14, 1999.

ALINC, Jan (AH-lihnch, YAHN) — PIT.

Center. Shoots left. 6'2", 190 lbs. Born, Louny, Czech., May 27, 1972.
(Pittsburgh's 7th choice, 163rd overall, in 1992 Entry Draft).

			Regular Season					Playoffs				
Season	Club	Lea	GP	G	A	TP	PIM	GP	G	A	TP	PIM
1990-91	CHZ Litvinov	Czech.	7	1	1	2	....	....	....	....	....	....
1991-92	CHZ Litvinov	Czech.	45	21	16	37	24	....	....	....	....	....
1992-93	CHZ Litvinov	Czech.	36	16	13	29	....	....	....	....	....	....
1993-94	CHZ Litvinov	Cze-Rep	36	16	25	41	....	4	1	4	5	....
	Czech Republic	Olympics	6	2	0	2	4	....	....	....	....	....
1994-95	CHZ Litvinov	Cze-Rep	42	16	32	48	50	4	3	2	5	2
1995-96	CHZ Litvinov	Cze-Rep	38	15	29	44	....	16	2	5	7	....
1996-97	Assat Pori	Finland	47	9	16	25	16	4	0	4	4	2
1997-98	Assat Pori	Finland	15	2	8	10	10	....	....	....	....	....
	CHZ Litvinov	Cze-Rep	33	12	32	44	14	4	1	2	3	12
1998-99	MoDo Hockey	Sweden	48	7	11	18	22	9	1	0	1	0

ALLAN, Brett — T.B.

Center. Shoots left. 6'3", 184 lbs. Born, Bentley, Alta., September 8, 1980.
(Tampa Bay's 7th choice, 174th overall, in 1998 Entry Draft).

			Regular Season					Playoffs				
Season	Club	Lea	GP	G	A	TP	PIM	GP	G	A	TP	PIM
1995-96	Red Deer	AAHA	36	25	46	71	36	....	....	....	....	....
1996-97	Swift Current	WHL	57	3	9	12	11	....	....	....	....	....
1997-98	Swift Current	WHL	68	17	9	26	42	....	....	....	....	....
1998-99	Swift Current	WHL	72	16	18	34	74	6	0	2	2	0

ALLAN, Chad

Defense. Shoots left. 6'1", 200 lbs. Born, Saskatoon, Sask., July 12, 1976.
(Vancouver's 4th choice, 65th overall, in 1994 Entry Draft).

			Regular Season					Playoffs				
Season	Club	Lea	GP	G	A	TP	PIM	GP	G	A	TP	PIM
1991-92	Saskatoon AA	AAHA	36	5	16	21	64	....	....	....	....	....
	Saskatoon	WHL	1	0	0	0	2	....	....	....	....	....
1992-93	Saskatoon	WHL	69	2	10	12	67	9	0	0	0	25
1993-94	Saskatoon	WHL	70	6	16	22	123	16	1	1	2	21
1994-95	Saskatoon	WHL	63	14	29	43	95	9	0	3	3	2
1995-96	Saskatoon	WHL	57	8	30	38	106	4	0	0	0	5
1996-97	Syracuse	AHL	73	3	10	13	83	3	0	1	1	0
1997-98	Syracuse	AHL	73	2	10	12	121	5	0	0	0	4
1998-99	Syracuse	AHL	60	2	8	10	98	....	....	....	....	....

WHL East First All-Star Team (1995) • WHL East Second All-Star Team (1996)

ALLEN, Bobby — BOS.

Defense. Shoots left. 6'1", 198 lbs. Born, Braintree, MA, November 14, 1978.
(Boston's 2nd choice, 52nd overall, in 1998 Entry Draft).

			Regular Season					Playoffs				
Season	Club	Lea	GP	G	A	TP	PIM	GP	G	A	TP	PIM
1996-97	Cushing Academy	H.S.	36	11	33	44	28	....	....	....	....	....
1997-98	Boston College	H.E.	40	7	21	28	49	....	....	....	....	....
1998-99	Boston College	H.E.	43	9	23	32	34	....	....	....	....	....

ALLEN, Bryan — VAN.

Defense. Shoots left. 6'4", 210 lbs. Born, Kingston, Ont., August 21, 1980.
(Vancouver's 1st choice, 4th overall, in 1998 Entry Draft).

			Regular Season					Playoffs				
Season	Club	Lea	GP	G	A	TP	PIM	GP	G	A	TP	PIM
1996-97	Oshawa	OHL	60	2	4	6	76	18	1	3	4	26
1997-98	Oshawa	OHL	48	6	13	19	126	5	0	5	5	18
1998-99	Oshawa	OHL	37	7	15	22	77	15	0	3	3	26

OHL First All-Star Team (1999)

ANDERSON, Craig

Defense. Shoots left. 6'1", 171 lbs. Born, Minneapolis, MN, January 6, 1976.
(NY Rangers' 10th choice, 208th overall, in 1994 Entry Draft).

			Regular Season					Playoffs				
Season	Club	Lea	GP	G	A	TP	PIM	GP	G	A	TP	PIM
1993-94	Park Center	H.S.	24	24	18	42	....	....	....	....	....	....
1994-95	U. of Wisconsin	WCHA	DID NOT PLAY – FRESHMAN									
1995-96	U. of Wisconsin	WCHA	16	1	3	4	2	....	....	....	....	....
1996-97	U. of Wisconsin	WCHA	34	3	8	11	22	....	....	....	....	....
1997-98	U. of Wisconsin	WCHA	41	12	30	42	24	....	....	....	....	....
1998-99	U. of Wisconsin	WCHA	9	2	4	6	6	....	....	....	....	....

WCHA First All-Star Team (1998)

ANDERSON, Michael

Right wing. Shoots right. 6'1", 186 lbs. Born, Edina, MN, December 24, 1976.
(Washington's 10th choice, 180th overall, in 1996 Entry Draft).

			Regular Season					Playoffs				
Season	Club	Lea	GP	G	A	TP	PIM	GP	G	A	TP	PIM
1995-96	U. of Minnesota	WCHA	28	3	6	9	51	....	....	....	....	....
1996-97	U. of Minnesota	WCHA	42	9	11	20	46	....	....	....	....	....
1997-98	U. of Minnesota	WCHA	31	12	13	25	62	....	....	....	....	....
1998-99	U. of Minnesota	WCHA	43	10	7	17	64	....	....	....	....	....

ANDERSSON, Jonas — NSH.

Right wing. Shoots left. 6'2", 189 lbs. Born, Lidingo, Sweden, February 24, 1981.
(Nashville's 2nd choice, 33rd overall, in 1999 Entry Draft).

			Regular Season					Playoffs				
Season	Club	Lea	GP	G	A	TP	PIM	GP	G	A	TP	PIM
1997-98	AIK Solna	Swede-Jr.	33	14	16	30	32	....	....	....	....	....
1998-99	AIK Solna	Swede-Jr.	16	3	7	10	18	....	....	....	....	....

ANDERSSON-JUNKKA, Jonas — PIT.

Defense. Shoots right. 6'2", 170 lbs. Born, Kiruna, Sweden, May 4, 1975.
(Pittsburgh's 4th choice, 104th overall, in 1993 Entry Draft).

			Regular Season					Playoffs				
Season	Club	Lea	GP	G	A	TP	PIM	GP	G	A	TP	PIM
1991-92	Kiruna IK	Sweden-2	1	0	0	0	0	....	....	....	....	....
1992-93	Kiruna IK	Sweden-2	30	3	7	10	32	....	....	....	....	....
1993-94	Kiruna IK	Sweden-2	32	6	10	16	84	....	....	....	....	....
1994-95	V. Frolunda	Sweden	19	0	2	2	2	....	....	....	....	....
1995-96	V. Frolunda	Sweden	31	3	1	4	20	13	1	0	1	6
1996-97	MoDo Hockey	Sweden	12	1	3	4	10	....	....	....	....	....
1997-98	MoDo Hockey	Sweden	35	5	5	10	12	1	0	0	0	0
1998-99	Kiekko-Espoo	Finland	34	4	4	8	20	....	....	....	....	....
	HPK Hameenlinna	Finland	16	1	5	6	16	8	3	1	4	8

ANDREWS, Daryl — N.J.

Defense. Shoots left. 6'2", 205 lbs. Born, Campbell River, B.C., April 27, 1977.
(New Jersey's 11th choice, 173rd overall, in 1996 Entry Draft).

			Regular Season					Playoffs				
Season	Club	Lea	GP	G	A	TP	PIM	GP	G	A	TP	PIM
1995-96	Melfort	SJHL	55	2	12	14	51	....	....	....	....	....
1996-97	Western Michigan	CCHA	37	6	20	26	86	....	....	....	....	....
1997-98	Western Michigan	CCHA	36	3	0	3	81	....	....	....	....	....
1998-99	Western Michigan	CCHA	33	3	11	14	42	....	....	....	....	....

ANDREYEV, Alexander (an-DRAY-ehv) — PHX.

Defense. Shoots left. 6'4", 220 lbs. Born, Riga, Latvia, September 14, 1979.
(Phoenix's 5th choice, 207th overall, in 1997 Entry Draft).

			Regular Season					Playoffs				
Season	Club	Lea	GP	G	A	TP	PIM	GP	G	A	TP	PIM
1996-97	Essamika Riga	Latvia	5	0	0	0	6	....	....	....	....	....
	Weyburn	SJHL	13	0	1	1	81	....	....	....	....	....
1997-98	Prince George	WHL	23	0	1	1	30	....	....	....	....	....
1998-99	Moose Jaw	WHL	60	11	11	22	80	5	0	0	0	4

ANGEL, Brett — NSH.

Defense. Shoots left. 6'5", 221 lbs. Born, Kingston, Ont., April 29, 1981.
(Nashville's 6th choice, 72nd overall, in 1999 Entry Draft).

			Regular Season					Playoffs				
Season	Club	Lea	GP	G	A	TP	PIM	GP	G	A	TP	PIM
1997-98	North Bay	OHL	61	1	3	4	131	....	....	....	....	....
1998-99	North Bay	OHL	55	5	9	14	139	....	....	....	....	....

ANGELSTAD, Mel (AN-gehl-stahd) — DAL.

Left wing. Shoots left. 6'2", 210 lbs. Born, Saskatoon, Sask., October 31, 1971.

			Regular Season					Playoffs				
Season	Club	Lea	GP	G	A	TP	PIM	GP	G	A	TP	PIM
1988-89	Allan AAA	MAHA	35	15	23	38	256	....	....	....	....	....
1989-90	Warman Valley	MJHL	38	1	5	6	411	....	....	....	....	....
1990-91	Flin Flon	MJHL	62	6	11	17	463	....	....	....	....	....
1991-92	Dauphin	MJHL	40	....	....	....	*345	....	....	....	....	....
1992-93	Thunder Bay	ColHL	42	2	5	7	256	....	....	....	....	....
	Nashville	ECHL	1	0	0	0	14	....	....	....	....	....
1993-94	Thunder Bay	ColHL	58	1	20	21	374	9	1	2	3	65
	P.E.I. Senators	AHL	1	0	0	0	5	....	....	....	....	....
1994-95	Thunder Bay	ColHL	46	0	8	8	317	7	0	3	3	62
	P.E.I. Senators	AHL	3	0	0	0	16	....	....	....	....	....
1995-96	Thunder Bay	ColHL	51	3	3	6	335	16	0	6	6	94
	Phoenix	IHL	5	0	0	0	43	....	....	....	....	....
1996-97	Thunder Bay	ColHL	66	10	21	31	422	7	0	1	1	21
1997-98	Fort Worth	WPHL	19	1	6	7	102	....	....	....	....	....
	Las Vegas	IHL	3	0	0	0	5	....	....	....	....	....
	Orlando	IHL	63	1	3	4	321	8	0	0	0	29
1998-99	Michigan	IHL	78	3	5	8	421	5	1	0	1	16

Signed as a free agent by **Dallas**, July 29, 1998.

ANGER, Niklas (AN-guhr) — MTL.

Right wing. Shoots left. 6'1", 185 lbs. Born, Gavle, Sweden, July 31, 1977.
(Montreal's 5th choice, 112th overall, in 1995 Entry Draft).

			Regular Season					Playoffs				
Season	Club	Lea	GP	G	A	TP	PIM	GP	G	A	TP	PIM
1994-95	Djurgardens IF	Swede-Jr.	30	14	12	26	26	....	....	....	....	....
	Djurgardens IF	Sweden	1	0	0	0	0	....	....	....	....	....
1995-96	Djurgardens IF	Sweden	10	0	0	0	2	....	....	....	....	....
1996-97	Djurgardens IF	Sweden	4	0	0	0	0	....	....	....	....	....
	Arlanda HK	Sweden-2	16	5	9	14	6	....	....	....	....	....
	Linkoping	Sweden-2	7	2	1	3	10	....	....	....	....	....
1997-98	Djurgardens IF	Sweden	45	2	5	7	37	12	0	1	1	2
1998-99	AIK Solna	Sweden	47	6	6	12	16	....	....	....	....	....

ANTROPOV, Nikolai (an-TROH-pahv) — TOR.

Center. Shoots left. 6'5", 203 lbs. Born, Vost, USSR, February 18, 1980.
(Toronto's 1st choice, 10th overall, in 1998 Entry Draft).

			Regular Season					Playoffs				
Season	Club	Lea	GP	G	A	TP	PIM	GP	G	A	TP	PIM
1995-96	Kamenogorsk	Russia-Jr.	20	18	20	38	30	....	....	....	....	....
1996-97	Kamenogorsk	Russia-2	8	2	1	3	6	....	....	....	....	....
1997-98	Kamenogorsk	Russia-2	42	15	24	39	62	....	....	....	....	....
1998-99	Moscow D'amo	Russia	30	5	9	14	30	11	0	1	1	4

APPS, Syl **TOR.**

Center. Shoots right. 6', 195 lbs. Born, Pittsburgh, PA, June 2, 1976.

			Regular Season					Playoffs				
Season	Club	Lea	GP	G	A	TP	PIM	GP	G	A	TP	PIM
1994-95	Upper Canada	H.S.	Statistics Not Available									
1995-96	Princeton	ECAC	26	4	6	10	30	....	....	....	....	....
1996-97	Princeton	ECAC	27	3	6	9	40	....	....	....	....	....
1997-98	Princeton	ECAC	35	10	8	18	65	....	....	....	....	....
1998-99	Princeton	ECAC	34	13	21	34	45	....	....	....	....	....

Signed as a free agent by **Toronto**, July 22, 1999.

ARCHAMBAULT, Daniel (ahr-sham-BOH)

Defense. Shoots left. 6', 200 lbs. Born, Ste-Agathe, Que., March 28, 1978.
(Montreal's 6th choice, 127th overall, in 1996 Entry Draft).

			Regular Season					Playoffs				
Season	Club	Lea	GP	G	A	TP	PIM	GP	G	A	TP	PIM
1994-95	Val d'Or	QMJHL	54	3	1	4	165	....	....	....	....	....
1995-96	Val d'Or	QMJHL	43	1	12	13	254	13	1	1	2	74
1996-97	Val d'Or	QMJHL	38	3	9	12	229	10	0	1	1	29
1997-98	Chicoutimi	QMJHL	66	11	34	45	318	5	1	1	2	28
1998-99	Quebec	QMJHL	70	4	24	28	382	13	0	3	3	16

ARKHIPOV, Denis (ahr-KHEE-pahv) **NSH.**

Right wing. Shoots left. 6'3", 196 lbs. Born, Kazan, USSR, May 19, 1979.
(Nashville's 2nd choice, 60th overall, in 1998 Entry Draft).

			Regular Season					Playoffs				
Season	Club	Lea	GP	G	A	TP	PIM	GP	G	A	TP	PIM
1994-95	Ak Bars Kazan	Russia-Jr	40	20	12	32	10	....	....	....	....	....
1995-96	Ak Bars Kazan	Russia-Jr.	40	15	8	23	30	....	....	....	....	....
	Ak Bars Kazan-2	Russia-2	15	10	8	18	10	....	....	....	....	....
1996-97	Ak Bars Kazan-2	Russia-3	50	17	23	40	20	....	....	....	....	....
	Ak Bars Kazan	Russia	1	1	0	1	0	....	....	....	....	....
1997-98	Ak Bars Kazan	Russia	29	2	2	4	2	....	....	....	....	....
1998-99	Ak Bars Kazan	Russia	34	12	1	13	22	9	2	3	5	6

ARMSTRONG, Chris

Defense. Shoots left. 6', 198 lbs. Born, Regina, Sask., June 26, 1975.
(Florida's 3rd choice, 57th overall, in 1993 Entry Draft).

			Regular Season					Playoffs				
Season	Club	Lea	GP	G	A	TP	PIM	GP	G	A	TP	PIM
1990-91	Whitewood	SAHA	40	25	30	55	40	....	....	....	....	....
1991-92	Moose Jaw	WHL	43	2	7	9	19	4	0	0	0	0
1992-93	Moose Jaw	WHL	67	9	35	44	104	....	....	....	....	....
1993-94	Moose Jaw	WHL	64	13	55	68	54	....	....	....	....	....
	Cincinnati	IHL	1	0	0	0	0	10	1	3	4	2
1994-95	Moose Jaw	WHL	66	17	54	71	61	10	2	12	14	22
	Cincinnati	IHL	....	....	....	....	....	9	1	3	4	10
1995-96	Carolina	AHL	78	9	33	42	65	....	....	....	....	....
1996-97	Carolina	AHL	66	9	23	32	38	....	....	....	....	....
1997-98	Fort Wayne	IHL	79	8	36	44	66	4	0	2	2	4
1998-99	Milwaukee	IHL	5	0	3	3	4	....	....	....	....	....
	Hershey	AHL	65	12	32	44	30	5	0	1	1	0

WHL East First All-Star Team (1994) • Canadian Major Junior Second All-Star Team (1994) • WHL East Second All-Star Team (1995)

Claimed by **Nashville** from **Florida** in Expansion Draft, June 26, 1998.

ARNASON, Tyler **CHI.**

Center. Shoots left. 5'11", 185 lbs. Born, Oklahoma City, OK, March 16, 1979.
(Chicago's 6th choice, 183rd overall, in 1998 Entry Draft).

			Regular Season					Playoffs				
Season	Club	Lea	GP	G	A	TP	PIM	GP	G	A	TP	PIM
1997-98	Fargo	USHL	52	37	45	82	16	....	....	....	....	....
1998-99	St. Cloud State	WCHA	38	14	17	31	16	....	....	....	....	....

ASTASHENKO, Kaspars (ahs-tuh-SHEHN-koh, KAHS-pars) **T.B.**

Defense. Shoots left. 6'2", 183 lbs. Born, Riga, Latvia, February 17, 1975.
(Tampa Bay's 5th choice, 127th overall, in 1999 Entry Draft).

			Regular Season					Playoffs				
Season	Club	Lea	GP	G	A	TP	PIM	GP	G	A	TP	PIM
1993-94	Pardaugava Riga	CIS	4	0	0	0	10	....	....	....	....	....
1994-95	Pardaugava Riga	CIS	25	0	0	0	24	....	....	....	....	....
1995-96	CSKA Moscow	CIS	26	0	1	1	10	....	....	....	....	....
1996-97	CSKA Moscow	Russia	41	0	0	0	48	2	0	1	1	4
1997-98	CSKA Moscow	Russia	25	1	3	4	6	....	....	....	....	....
1998-99	Cincinnati	IHL	74	3	11	14	166	3	0	2	2	6
	Dayton	ECHL	2	0	1	1	4	....	....	....	....	....

AUFIERO, Patrick (ow-fee-AIR-oh) **NYR**

Defense. Shoots right. 6'2", 186 lbs. Born, Winchester, MA, July 1, 1980.
(NY Rangers' 5th choice, 90th overall, in 1999 Entry Draft).

			Regular Season					Playoffs				
Season	Club	Lea	GP	G	A	TP	PIM	GP	G	A	TP	PIM
1997-98	Team USA	Under-18	56	10	11	21	111	....	....	....	....	....
1998-99	Boston University	H.E.	22	3	4	7	14	....	....	....	....	....

BABENKO, Yuri (bah-BEHN-koh) **COL.**

Center. Shoots left. 6', 185 lbs. Born, Penza, USSR, January 2, 1978.
(Colorado's 2nd choice, 51st overall, in 1996 Entry Draft).

			Regular Season					Playoffs				
Season	Club	Lea	GP	G	A	TP	PIM	GP	G	A	TP	PIM
1995-96	Soviet Wings	CIS	21	0	0	0	16	....	....	....	....	....
1996-97	Soviet Wings	Russia	4	1	0	1	4	....	....	....	....	....
	Soviet Wings-2	Russia-3	26	8	10	18	24	....	....	....	....	....
	CSKA Moscow	Russia-2	24	3	3	6	12	....	....	....	....	....
1997-98	Plymouth	OHL	59	22	34	56	22	15	3	7	10	24
1998-99	Hershey	AHL	74	11	15	26	47	2	0	1	1	0

BACKMAN, Christian **ST.L.**

Defense. Shoots left. 6'2", 187 lbs. Born, Alingsas, Sweden, April 28, 1980.
(St. Louis' 1st choice, 24th overall, in 1998 Entry Draft).

			Regular Season					Playoffs				
Season	Club	Lea	GP	G	A	TP	PIM	GP	G	A	TP	PIM
1996-97	V. Frolunda	Swede-Jr.	26	2	5	7	16	....	....	....	....	....
1997-98	V. Frolunda	Swede-Jr.	28	5	14	19	12	2	0	1	1	4
1998-99	V. Frolunda	Swede-Jr.	4	0	2	2	4	....	....	....	....	....
	V. Frolunda	Sweden	49	0	4	4	4	4	0	0	0	0

BALA, Chris (BA-la) **OTT.**

Left wing. Shoots left. 6'1", 180 lbs. Born, Alexandria, VA, September 24, 1978.
(Ottawa's 3rd choice, 58th overall, in 1998 Entry Draft).

			Regular Season					Playoffs				
Season	Club	Lea	GP	G	A	TP	PIM	GP	G	A	TP	PIM
1996-97	Hill-Murray School	H.S.	23	28	33	61	36	....	....	....	....	....
1997-98	Harvard University	ECAC	33	16	14	30	23	....	....	....	....	....
1998-99	Harvard University	ECAC	28	5	10	15	16	....	....	....	....	....

BALMOCHNYKH, Maxim (bahl-MAWCH-nihky, mahx-EEM) **ANA.**

Left wing. Shoots left. 6', 185 lbs. Born, Lipetsk, USSR, March 7, 1979.
(Anaheim's 2nd choice, 45th overall, in 1997 Entry Draft).

			Regular Season					Playoffs				
Season	Club	Lea	GP	G	A	TP	PIM	GP	G	A	TP	PIM
1994-95	Lipetsk	CIS-2	3	0	1	1	4	....	....	....	....	....
1995-96	Lipetsk	CIS-2	40	15	5	20	60	....	....	....	....	....
1996-97	Lada Togliatti	Russia	18	6	1	7	22	....	....	....	....	....
1997-98	Lada Togliatti	Russia	37	10	4	14	46	....	....	....	....	....
	Chelyabinsk	Russia	2	0	0	0	2	....	....	....	....	....
1998-99	Quebec	QMJHL	21	9	22	31	38	....	....	....	....	....
	Lada Togliatti	Russia	15	2	1	3	10	4	0	1	1	8

BARCH, Krys **WSH.**

Left wing. Shoots left. 6'2", 200 lbs. Born, Guelph, Ont., March 26, 1980.
(Washington's 3rd choice, 106th overall, in 1998 Entry Draft).

			Regular Season					Playoffs				
Season	Club	Lea	GP	G	A	TP	PIM	GP	G	A	TP	PIM
1996-97	Georgetown	OJHL	51	18	26	44	58	....	....	....	....	....
1997-98	London	OHL	65	9	27	36	62	16	4	3	7	16
1998-99	London	OHL	66	18	20	38	66	25	9	17	26	15

BARNES, Ryan **DET.**

Left wing. Shoots left. 6'1", 201 lbs. Born, Dunnville, Ont., January 30, 1980.
(Detroit's 2nd choice, 55th overall, in 1998 Entry Draft).

			Regular Season					Playoffs				
Season	Club	Lea	GP	G	A	TP	PIM	GP	G	A	TP	PIM
1996-97	Quinte Hawks	OJHL	46	15	19	34	245	....	....	....	....	....
1997-98	Sudbury	OHL	46	13	18	31	111	10	0	2	2	24
1998-99	Sudbury	OHL	8	2	0	2	*23	....	....	....	....	....
	Toronto	OHL	31	11	14	25	*215	....	....	....	....	....
	Barrie	OHL	24	16	14	30	*161	12	2	4	6	40

BARNEY, Scott **L.A.**

Center. Shoots right. 6'4", 198 lbs. Born, Oshawa, Ont., March 27, 1979.
(Los Angeles' 3rd choice, 29th overall, in 1997 Entry Draft).

			Regular Season					Playoffs				
Season	Club	Lea	GP	G	A	TP	PIM	GP	G	A	TP	PIM
1995-96	Peterborough	OHL	60	22	24	46	52	24	6	8	14	38
1996-97	Peterborough	OHL	64	21	33	54	110	9	0	3	3	16
1997-98	Peterborough	OHL	62	44	32	76	60	4	1	0	1	6
1998-99	Peterborough	OHL	44	41	26	67	80	5	4	1	5	4
	Springfield	AHL	5	0	0	0	2	1	0	0	0	2

BARTEK, Martin (BAHR-tehk) **NSH.**

Center. Shoots left. 6', 192 lbs. Born, Kindgssed Jill, Sweden, July 17, 1980.
(Nashville's 7th choice, 202nd overall, in 1998 Entry Draft).

			Regular Season					Playoffs				
Season	Club	Lea	GP	G	A	TP	PIM	GP	G	A	TP	PIM
1995-96	HKm Zvolen	Slovak-Jr.	46	75	43	118	....	....	....	....	....	....
1996-97	Kings Edgehill	H.S.	35	45	40	85	32	....	....	....	....	....
1997-98	Rouyn-Noranda	QMJHL	28	9	19	28	12	....	....	....	....	....
	Rimouski	QMJHL	13	3	4	7	6	....	....	....	....	....
	Sherbrooke	QMJHL	25	11	12	23	38	....	....	....	....	....
1998-99	HKm Zvolen	Slovak-Jr.	17	14	17	31	89	....	....	....	....	....
	HKm Zvolen	Slovakia	28	10	8	18	18	2	1	0	1	0

BARTOVIC, Milan (BAHR-tuh-vihch) **BUF.**

Right wing. Shoots left. 5'11", 183 lbs. Born, Trencin, Czech., April 9, 1981.
(Buffalo's 2nd choice, 35th overall, in 1999 Entry Draft).

			Regular Season					Playoffs				
Season	Club	Lea	GP	G	A	TP	PIM	GP	G	A	TP	PIM
1997-98	Dukla Trencin	Slovak-Jr.	26	2	6	8	27	....	....	....	....	....
1998-99	Dukla Trencin	Slovak-Jr.	46	36	35	71	62	6	9	3	12	10

BATEMAN, Jeff **DAL.**

Center. Shoots left. 5'11", 165 lbs. Born, Belleville, Ont., August 29, 1980.
(Dallas' 4th choice, 126th overall, in 1999 Entry Draft).

			Regular Season					Playoffs				
Season	Club	Lea	GP	G	A	TP	PIM	GP	G	A	TP	PIM
1997-98	Wellington	OJHL	50	26	35	61	68	....	....	....	....	....
1998-99	Brampton	OHL	68	23	35	58	27	....	....	....	....	....

BATHERSON, Norm

Left wing. Shoots left. 6'1", 198 lbs. Born, North Sydney, N.S., March 27, 1969.

			Regular Season					Playoffs				
Season	Club	Lea	GP	G	A	TP	PIM	GP	G	A	TP	PIM
1992-93	Acadia	AUAA	20	16	21	37	44	....	....	....	....	....
1993-94	P.E.I. Senators	AHL	67	14	23	37	85	....	....	....	....	....
1994-95	Portland	AHL	77	27	34	61	64	7	3	4	7	4
1995-96	Portland	AHL	45	6	21	27	72	24	11	8	19	16
1996-97	Portland	AHL	53	15	28	43	43	5	2	1	3	0
1997-98	Portland	AHL	17	3	5	8	4	....	....	....	....	....
	Fort Wayne	IHL	54	8	18	26	46	....	....	....	....	....
1998-99	Revier Lowen	Germany	50	18	12	30	57	....	....	....	....	....

Signed as a free agent by **Washington**, August 21, 1995.

BAUMGARTNER, Gregor (BAWM-gahr-nuhr) **DAL.**

Left wing. Shoots left. 6', 185 lbs. Born, Leoben, Austria, July 13, 1979.
(Dallas' 5th choice, 156th overall, in 1999 Entry Draft).

			Regular Season					Playoffs				
Season	Club	Lea	GP	G	A	TP	PIM	GP	G	A	TP	PIM
1996-97	Laval	QMJHL	68	19	45	64	15	3	0	0	0	0
1997-98	Laval	QMJHL	68	31	51	82	10	16	5	12	17	6
1998-99	Acadie-Bathurst	QMJHL	68	33	58	91	14	23	8	8	16	8

• Re-entered NHL draft. Originally, Montreal's 2nd choice, 37th overall, in 1997 Entry Draft.

BAXTER, Jim **CAR.**

Defense. Shoots right. 6'2", 186 lbs. Born, Brantford, Ont., August 24, 1979.
(Carolina's 6th choice, 202nd overall, in 1999 Entry Draft).

			Regular Season					Playoffs				
Season	Club	Lea	GP	G	A	TP	PIM	GP	G	A	TP	PIM
1996-97	Oshawa	OHL	47	3	6	9	4	15	0	0	0	0
1997-98	Oshawa	OHL	65	4	28	32	18	7	3	4	7	0
1998-99	Oshawa	OHL	66	22	52	74	20	12	4	8	12	4

• Re-entered NHL draft. Originally Boston's 9th choice, 180th overall, in 1997 Entry Draft.

BEAUCHEMIN, Francois (boh-sheh-MEH, frahn-SWUH) **MTL.**

Defense. Shoots left. 6', 193 lbs. Born, Sorel, Que., June 4, 1980.
(Montreal's 3rd choice, 75th overall, in 1998 Entry Draft).

			Regular Season					Playoffs				
Season	Club	Lea	GP	G	A	TP	PIM	GP	G	A	TP	PIM
1996-97	Laval	QMJHL	66	7	21	28	132	3	0	0	0	2
1997-98	Laval	QMJHL	70	12	35	47	132	16	1	3	4	23
1998-99	Acadie-Bathurst	QMJHL	31	4	17	21	53	23	2	16	18	55

BEAUCHESNE, Martin (boh-SHEHN) **NSH.**

Defense. Shoots left. 6', 200 lbs. Born, Cap-de-la-madaleine, Que., July 8, 1980.
(Nashville's 5th choice, 138th overall, in 1998 Entry Draft).

			Regular Season					Playoffs				
Season	Club	Lea	GP	G	A	TP	PIM	GP	G	A	TP	PIM
1996-97	Sherbrooke	QMJHL	65	1	2	3	125	3	0	0	0	4
1997-98	Sherbrooke	QMJHL	37	1	3	4	105	....	....	....	....	....
1998-99	Sherbrooke	QMJHL	46	1	8	9	76	13	0	2	2	27

BEAUDOIN, Eric (boh-DWEH) **T.B.**

Left wing. Shoots left. 6'3", 180 lbs. Born, Ottawa, Ont., May 3, 1980.
(Tampa Bay's 4th choice, 92nd overall, in 1998 Entry Draft).

			Regular Season					Playoffs				
Season	Club	Lea	GP	G	A	TP	PIM	GP	G	A	TP	PIM
1996-97	Ottawa	OJHL	54	12	19	31	55	....	....	....	....	....
1997-98	Guelph	OHL	62	9	13	22	43	12	3	2	5	4
1998-99	Guelph	OHL	66	28	43	71	79	11	5	3	8	12

BEAUDOIN, Nic (BOH-dwehn)

Left wing. Shoots left. 6'3", 205 lbs. Born, Ottawa, Ont., December 25, 1976.
(Colorado's 2nd choice, 51st overall, in 1995 Entry Draft).

			Regular Season					Playoffs				
Season	Club	Lea	GP	G	A	TP	PIM	GP	G	A	TP	PIM
1993-94	Detroit	OHL	63	9	18	27	32	17	1	2	3	13
1994-95	Detroit	OHL	11	1	3	4	16	21	5	7	12	16
1995-96	Detroit	OHL	60	26	33	59	78	16	8	10	18	35
1996-97	Hershey	AHL	34	4	3	7	51	....	....	....	....	....
1997-98	Canada	Nat-Team	49	10	16	26	107	....	....	....	....	....
1998-99	Roanoke	ECHL	22	6	7	13	38	....	....	....	....	....
	Lowell	AHL	49	9	9	18	18	3	1	0	1	7

Traded to **NY Islanders** by **Colorado** for cash, September 10, 1998.

BECKETT, Jason **PHI.**

Defense. Shoots right. 6'2", 203 lbs. Born, Lethbridge, Alta., July 23, 1980.
(Philadelphia's 2nd choice, 42nd overall, in 1998 Entry Draft).

			Regular Season					Playoffs				
Season	Club	Lea	GP	G	A	TP	PIM	GP	G	A	TP	PIM
1996-97	Lethbridge	AAHA	34	7	10	17	118	....	....	....	....	....
1997-98	Seattle	WHL	71	1	11	12	241	5	0	0	0	16
1998-99	Seattle	WHL	70	4	26	30	195	11	0	1	1	40

BEECH, Kris **WSH.**

Center. Shoots left. 6'2", 178 lbs. Born, Salmon Arm, B.C., February 5, 1981.
(Washington's 1st choice, 7th overall, in 1999 Entry Draft).

			Regular Season					Playoffs				
Season	Club	Lea	GP	G	A	TP	PIM	GP	G	A	TP	PIM
1996-97	Sicamous	BCAHA	49	34	36	70	80	....	....	....	....	....
	Calgary	WHL	8	1	1	2	0	....	....	....	....	....
1997-98	Calgary	WHL	58	10	25	35	24	12	4	5	9	32
1998-99	Calgary	WHL	68	26	41	67	103	6	1	4	5	8

BEKAR, Derek **ST.L.**

Left wing. Shoots left. 6'3", 194 lbs. Born, Burnaby, B.C., September 15, 1975.
(St. Louis' 7th choice, 205th overall, in 1995 Entry Draft).

			Regular Season					Playoffs				
Season	Club	Lea	GP	G	A	TP	PIM	GP	G	A	TP	PIM
1994-95	Powell River	BCJHL	46	33	29	62	35	....	....	....	....	....
1995-96	New Hampshire	H.E.	34	15	18	33	4	....	....	....	....	....
1996-97	New Hampshire	H.E.	39	18	21	39	34	....	....	....	....	....
1997-98	New Hampshire	H.E.	35	32	28	60	46	....	....	....	....	....
1998-99	Worcester	AHL	51	16	20	36	6	4	0	0	0	0

Hockey East Second All-Star Team (1998)

BELAK, Graham (BEE-lak)

Defense. Shoots left. 6'4", 210 lbs. Born, Battleford, Sask., August 1, 1979.
(Colorado's 2nd choice, 53rd overall, in 1997 Entry Draft).

			Regular Season					Playoffs				
Season	Club	Lea	GP	G	A	TP	PIM	GP	G	A	TP	PIM
1995-96	North Battleford	SJHL	55	3	14	17	110	....	....	....	....	....
1996-97	Edmonton	WHL	61	3	5	8	251	....	....	....	....	....
1997-98	Edmonton	WHL	47	5	5	10	168	....	....	....	....	....
	Hershey	AHL	1	0	0	0	15	....	....	....	....	....
1998-99	Kootenay	WHL	45	3	1	4	201	7	0	0	0	38

BELANGER, Eric (buh-LAWN-zhay) **L.A.**

Center. Shoots left. 6', 177 lbs. Born, Sherbrooke, Que., December 16, 1977.
(Los Angeles' 5th choice, 96th overall, in 1996 Entry Draft).

			Regular Season					Playoffs				
Season	Club	Lea	GP	G	A	TP	PIM	GP	G	A	TP	PIM
1994-95	Beauport	QMJHL	71	12	28	40	24	18	5	9	14	25
1995-96	Beauport	QMJHL	59	35	38	83	18	20	13	14	27	6
1996-97	Beauport	QMJHL	31	13	37	50	30	....	....	....	....	....
	Rimouski	QMJHL	31	26	41	67	36	4	2	3	5	10
1997-98	Fredericton	AHL	56	17	34	51	28	4	2	1	3	2
1998-99	Springfield	AHL	33	8	18	26	10	3	0	1	1	2
	Long Beach	IHL	1	0	0	0	0	....	....	....	....	....

BELANGER, Francis (buh-LAWN-zhay) **PHI.**

Left wing. Shoots left. 6'2", 216 lbs. Born, Bellefeuille, Que., January 15, 1978.
(Philadelphia's 5th choice, 124th overall, in 1998 Entry Draft)

			Regular Season					Playoffs				
Season	Club	Lea	GP	G	A	TP	PIM	GP	G	A	TP	PIM
1996-97	Hull	QMJHL	53	13	13	26	134	8	2	2	4	57
1997-98	Hull	QMJHL	33	22	23	45	133	....	....	....	....	....
	Rimouski	QMJHL	30	18	10	28	248	17	14	8	22	61
1998-99	Philadelphia	AHL	58	13	13	26	242	16	4	3	7	16

BELL, Mark **CHI.**

Center. Shoots left. 6'3", 198 lbs. Born, St. Paul's, Ont., August 5, 1980.
(Chicago's 1st choice, 8th overall, in 1998 Entry Draft).

			Regular Season					Playoffs				
Season	Club	Lea	GP	G	A	TP	PIM	GP	G	A	TP	PIM
1996-97	Ottawa	OHL	65	8	12	20	40	24	4	7	11	13
1997-98	Ottawa	OHL	55	34	26	60	87	13	6	5	11	14
1998-99	Ottawa	OHL	44	29	26	55	69	9	6	5	11	8

BEMBRIDGE, Garrett **NYR**

Right wing. Shoots right. 6', 164 lbs. Born, Melfort, Sask., July 6, 1981.
(NY Rangers' 6th choice, 137th overall, in 1999 Entry Draft).

			Regular Season					Playoffs				
Season	Club	Lea	GP	G	A	TP	PIM	GP	G	A	TP	PIM
1997-98	Saskatoon AA	AAHA	44	29	45	74	74	....	....	....	....	....
1998-99	Saskatoon	WHL	68	23	27	50	30	....	....	....	....	....

BENOIT, Mathieu (behn-WAH)

Right wing. Shoots right. 5'11", 200 lbs. Born, St. Clec, Que., July 12, 1979.
(New Jersey's 6th choice, 188th overall, in 1997 Entry Draft).

			Regular Season					Playoffs				
Season	Club	Lea	GP	G	A	TP	PIM	GP	G	A	TP	PIM
1995-96	Chicoutimi	QMJHL	61	6	14	20	17	17	0	0	0	0
1996-97	Chicoutimi	QMJHL	64	35	36	71	22	9	2	2	4	0
1997-98	Chicoutimi	QMJHL	59	56	61	117	32	6	2	3	5	2
1998-99	Chicoutimi	QMJHL	36	39	14	53	28	....	....	....	....	....
	Acadie-Bathurst	QMJHL	32	23	33	56	6	23	*20	*21	*41	16

QMJHL First All-Star Team (1998) • QMJHL Second All-Star Team (1999)

BERENZWEIG, Andy **NSH.**

Defense. Shoots left. 6'2", 195 lbs. Born, Chicago, IL, August 8, 1977.
(NY Islanders' 5th choice, 109th overall, in 1996 Entry Draft).

			Regular Season					Playoffs				
Season	Club	Lea	GP	G	A	TP	PIM	GP	G	A	TP	PIM
1992-93	Loomis-Chaffee	H.S.	22	5	13	18	....	....	....	....	....	....
1993-94	Loomis-Chaffee	H.S.	22	12	27	39	....	....	....	....	....	....
1994-95	Loomis-Chaffee	H.S.	23	19	23	42	10	....	....	....	....	....
1995-96	U. of Michigan	CCHA	42	4	8	12	4	....	....	....	....	....
1996-97	U. of Michigan	CCHA	38	7	12	19	49	....	....	....	....	....
1997-98	U. of Michigan	CCHA	45	8	11	19	32	....	....	....	....	....
1998-99	U. of Michigan	CCHA	42	7	24	31	38	....	....	....	....	....

CCHA Second All-Star Team (1998) • NCAA Championship All-Tournament Team (1998)

Traded to **Nashville** by **NY Islanders** for Nashville's 4th round choice (Jonathon Halvarson) in 1999 Entry Draft, April 14, 1999.

BERG, Reggie

Center. Shoots left. 5'10", 180 lbs. Born, Coon Rapids, MN, September 18, 1976.
(Toronto's 12th choice, 178th overall, in 1996 Entry Draft).

			Regular Season					Playoffs				
Season	Club	Lea	GP	G	A	TP	PIM	GP	G	A	TP	PIM
1995-96	U. of Minnesota	WCHA	40	23	11	34	69	....	....	....	....	....
1996-97	U. of Minnesota	WCHA	38	11	26	37	48	....	....	....	....	....
1997-98	U. of Minnesota	WCHA	39	20	19	39	53	....	....	....	....	....
1998-99	U. of Minnesota	WCHA	43	20	28	48	64	....	....	....	....	....

WCHA Second All-Star Team (1998)

BERGLUND, Christian **N.J.**

Right wing. Shoots left. 5'11", 183 lbs. Born, Orebro, Sweden, March 12, 1980.
(New Jersey's 3rd choice, 37th overall, in 1998 Entry Draft).

			Regular Season					Playoffs				
Season	Club	Lea	GP	G	A	TP	PIM	GP	G	A	TP	PIM
1994-95	Kariskoga	Sweden-4	20	14	13	27	....	....	....	....	....	....
1995-96	Kristinehamn	Sweden-3	23	8	8	16	12	....	....	....	....	....
1996-97	Farjestads BK	Swede-Jr.	21	2	3	5	24	....	....	....	....	....
1997-98	Farjestads BK	Swede-Jr.	29	23	19	42	88	2	0	0	0	0
	Farjestads BK	Sweden	1	0	0	0	0	....	....	....	....	....
1998-99	Farjestads BK	Swede-Jr.	5	3	4	7	22	....	....	....	....	....
	Farjestads BK	Sweden	37	2	4	6	37	4	1	0	1	4

BERNIER, David **ANA.**

Right wing. Shoots right. 6'3", 205 lbs. Born, St-Hyacinthe, Que., January 9, 1978.
(Anaheim's 6th choice, 205th overall, in 1998 Entry Draft).

			Regular Season					Playoffs				
Season	Club	Lea	GP	G	A	TP	PIM	GP	G	A	TP	PIM
1994-95	St-Hyacinthe	QMJHL	66	15	16	31	40	1	0	1	1	0
1995-96	St-Hyacinthe	QMJHL	65	10	18	28	64	....	....	....	....	....
1996-97	Rouyn-Noranda	QMJHL	21	2	9	11	11	....	....	....	....	....
	Beauport	QMJHL	38	7	17	24	37	4	2	1	3	5
1997-98	Quebec	QMJHL	70	35	53	88	88	14	7	8	15	12
1998-99	Quebec	QMJHL	50	34	50	84	69	13	6	10	16	12

BERRY, Rick — COL.

Defense. Shoots left. 6'1", 192 lbs. Born, Brandon, Man., November 4, 1978.
(Colorado's 3rd choice, 55th overall, in 1997 Entry Draft).

				Regular Season					Playoffs			
Season	Club	Lea	GP	G	A	TP	PIM	GP	G	A	TP	PIM
1995-96	Seattle	WHL	59	4	9	13	103	1	0	0	0	0
1996-97	Seattle	WHL	72	12	21	33	125	15	3	7	10	23
1997-98	Seattle	WHL	37	5	12	17	100	....	....	....	....	....
	Spokane	WHL	22	4	9	13	31	17	1	4	5	26
1998-99	Hershey	AHL	62	2	6	8	153	....	....	....	....	....

BERTRAN, Rick — VAN.

Defense. Shoots left. 6'3", 190 lbs. Born, Niagara Falls, Ont., March 12, 1980.
(Vancouver's 7th choice, 140th overall, in 1998 Entry Draft).

				Regular Season					Playoffs			
Season	Club	Lea	GP	G	A	TP	PIM	GP	G	A	TP	PIM
1997-98	Kitchener	OHL	56	0	9	9	149	6	0	0	0	11
1998-99	Kitchener	OHL	38	1	2	3	78	....	....	....	....	....
	Belleville	OHL	17	0	10	10	35	13	0	0	0	21

BERTRAND, Eric — N.J.

Left wing. Shoots left. 6'1", 205 lbs. Born, St. Ephrem, Que., April 16, 1975.
(New Jersey's 9th choice, 207th overall, in 1994 Entry Draft).

				Regular Season					Playoffs			
Season	Club	Lea	GP	G	A	TP	PIM	GP	G	A	TP	PIM
1992-93	Granby	QMJHL	64	10	15	25	82	....	....	....	....	....
1993-94	Granby	QMJHL	60	11	15	26	151	6	1	0	1	18
1994-95	Granby	QMJHL	56	14	26	40	268	13	3	8	11	50
1995-96	Albany	AHL	70	16	13	29	199	4	0	0	0	6
1996-97	Albany	AHL	77	16	27	43	204	8	3	3	6	15
1997-98	Albany	AHL	76	20	29	49	256	13	5	5	10	4
1998-99	Albany	AHL	78	34	31	65	160	5	4	2	6	0

BETTS, Blair — CGY.

Center. Shoots left. 6'1", 183 lbs. Born, Edmonton, Alta., February 16, 1980.
(Calgary's 2nd choice, 33rd overall, in 1998 Entry Draft).

				Regular Season					Playoffs			
Season	Club	Lea	GP	G	A	TP	PIM	GP	G	A	TP	PIM
1996-97	Prince George	WHL	58	12	18	30	19	15	2	2	4	6
1997-98	Prince George	WHL	71	35	41	76	38	11	4	6	10	8
1998-99	Prince George	WHL	42	20	22	42	39	7	3	2	5	8

BICEK, Jiri — (bee-CHEHK, YEH-ree) N.J.

Left wing. Shoots left. 5'10", 195 lbs. Born, Kosice, Czech., December 3, 1978.
(New Jersey's 4th choice, 131st overall, in 1997 Entry Draft).

				Regular Season					Playoffs			
Season	Club	Lea	GP	G	A	TP	PIM	GP	G	A	TP	PIM
1995-96	HC Kosice	Slovakia	30	10	15	25	16	9	2	4	6	0
1996-97	HC Kosice	Slovakia	44	11	14	25	20	7	1	3	4	....
1997-98	Albany	AHL	50	10	10	20	22	13	1	6	7	4
1998-99	Albany	AHL	79	15	45	60	102	5	2	2	4	2

BIENVENUE, Daniel — (bee-ehn-veh-nyoo) BUF.

Left wing. Shoots left. 6', 196 lbs. Born, Val d'Or, Que., June 10, 1977.
(Buffalo's 8th choice, 123rd overall, in 1995 Entry Draft).

				Regular Season					Playoffs			
Season	Club	Lea	GP	G	A	TP	PIM	GP	G	A	TP	PIM
1993-94	Chicoutimi	QMJHL	42	2	7	9	4	....	....	....	....	....
1994-95	Val d'Or	QMJHL	67	27	14	41	40	....	....	....	....	....
1995-96	Val d'Or	QMJHL	67	30	42	72	65	13	6	1	7	0
1996-97	Val d'Or	QMJHL	20	4	4	8	22	13	6	6	12	19
1997-98	Rochester	AHL	10	0	0	0	17	....	....	....	....	....
	South Carolina	ECHL	50	10	11	21	4	....	....	....	....	....
1998-99	Jacksonville	ECHL	2	0	0	0	2	....	....	....	....	....
	Baton Rouge	ECHL	37	3	3	6	19	....	....	....	....	....

BIRON, Mathieu — (BEE-rawn, mat-yoo) NYI

Defense. Shoots right. 6'6", 212 lbs. Born, Lac St. Charles, Que., April 29, 1980.
(Los Angeles' 1st choice, 21st overall, in 1998 Entry Draft).

				Regular Season					Playoffs			
Season	Club	Lea	GP	G	A	TP	PIM	GP	G	A	TP	PIM
1996-97	Ste-Foy	QAAA	40	4	22	26	49	....	....	....	....	....
1997-98	Shawinigan	QMJHL	59	8	28	36	60	....	....	....	....	....
1998-99	Shawinigan	QMJHL	69	13	32	45	116	6	0	2	2	6

Traded to **NY Islanders** by **Los Angeles** with Olli Jokinen, Josh Green and Los Angeles' 1st round choice (Taylor Pyatt) in 1999 Entry Draft for Zigmund Palffy, Brian Smolinski, Marcel Cousineau and New Jersey's 4th round choice (previously acquired, Los Angeles selected Daniel Johanssen) in 1999 Entry Draft, June 20, 1999.

BLAIS, Ben — NYI

Defense. Shoots left. 6'4", 195 lbs. Born, Berlin, NH, February 16, 1978.
(NY Islanders' 8th choice, 237th overall, in 1998 Entry Draft).

				Regular Season					Playoffs			
Season	Club	Lea	GP	G	A	TP	PIM	GP	G	A	TP	PIM
1997-98	Walpole High	H.S.	34	7	18	25	75	....	....	....	....	....
1998-99	St. Lawrence	ECAC	3	0	1	1	6	....	....	....	....	....

BLANCHARD, Sean — L.A.

Defense. Shoots left. 5'11", 198 lbs. Born, Sudbury, Ont., March 29, 1978.
(Los Angeles' 5th choice, 99th overall, in 1997 Entry Draft).

				Regular Season					Playoffs			
Season	Club	Lea	GP	G	A	TP	PIM	GP	G	A	TP	PIM
1994-95	Ottawa	OHL	59	2	5	7	24	....	....	....	....	....
1995-96	Ottawa	OHL	64	7	29	36	49	4	1	3	4	7
1996-97	Ottawa	OHL	66	11	57	68	64	24	3	15	18	34
1997-98	Ottawa	OHL	57	13	51	64	43	13	0	5	5	27
1998-99	Springfield	AHL	10	0	1	1	4	....	....	....	....	....
	Mississippi	ECHL	58	5	24	29	30	17	0	8	8	4

OHL First All-Star Team (1997, 1998) • Canadian Major Junior First All-Star Team (1997) • Canadian Major Junior Defenseman of the Year (1997)

BLATNY, Zdenek — (BLAT-nee, z-DEHN-ehk) ATL.

Center. Shoots left. 6'1", 187 lbs. Born, Brno, Czech., January 14, 1981.
(Atlanta's 3rd choice, 68th overall, in 1999 Entry Draft).

				Regular Season					Playoffs			
Season	Club	Lea	GP	G	A	TP	PIM	GP	G	A	TP	PIM
1997-98	Kometa Brno	Czech-Jr.	42	22	21	43	40	....	....	....	....	....
1998-99	Seattle	WHL	44	18	15	33	25	11	4	0	4	24

BODTKER, Stewart — (BAWD-kuhr) VAN.

Center. Shoots right. 6'1", 190 lbs. Born, Vancouver, B.C., September 15, 1976.
(Vancouver's 7th choice, 170th overall, in 1995 Entry Draft).

				Regular Season					Playoffs			
Season	Club	Lea	GP	G	A	TP	PIM	GP	G	A	TP	PIM
1994-95	Colorado	WCHA	27	6	4	10	22	....	....	....	....	....
1995-96	Colorado	WCHA	42	6	7	13	40	....	....	....	....	....
1996-97	Colorado	WCHA	43	19	17	36	71	....	....	....	....	....
1997-98	Colorado	WCHA	30	11	15	26	50	....	....	....	....	....
1998-99	Augusta	ECHL	47	17	15	32	58	....	....	....	....	....
	Syracuse	AHL	31	5	5	10	12	....	....	....	....	....

BOGAS, Chris — (BOH-GUHS) TOR.

Defense. Shoots right. 6'1", 202 lbs. Born, Cleveland, OH, November 12, 1976.
(Toronto's 10th choice, 148th overall, in 1996 Entry Draft).

				Regular Season					Playoffs			
Season	Club	Lea	GP	G	A	TP	PIM	GP	G	A	TP	PIM
1994-95	Calgary	AJHL	52	27	34	61	80	....	....	....	....	....
1995-96	Michigan State	CCHA	39	1	19	20	55	....	....	....	....	....
1996-97	Michigan State	CCHA	40	7	4	11	58	....	....	....	....	....
1997-98	Michigan State	CCHA	44	4	10	14	75	....	....	....	....	....
1998-99	Michigan State	CCHA	35	1	13	14	86	....	....	....	....	....

BOGUNIECKI, Eric — (BOH-guhn-ih-kee) FLA.

Center. Shoots right. 5'8", 192 lbs. Born, New Haven, CT, May 6, 1975.
(St. Louis' 6th choice, 193rd overall, in 1993 Entry Draft).

				Regular Season					Playoffs			
Season	Club	Lea	GP	G	A	TP	PIM	GP	G	A	TP	PIM
1992-93	Westminster High	H.S.	24	30	24	54	55	....	....	....	....	....
1993-94	New Hampshire	H.E.	40	17	16	33	66	....	....	....	....	....
1994-95	New Hampshire	H.E.	34	12	16	28	62	....	....	....	....	....
1995-96	New Hampshire	H.E.	32	23	28	51	46	....	....	....	....	....
1996-97	New Hampshire	H.E.	36	26	31	57	58	....	....	....	....	....
1997-98	Dayton	ECHL	26	19	18	37	36	....	....	....	....	....
	Fort Wayne	IHL	35	4	8	12	29	4	1	2	3	10
1998-99	Fort Wayne	IHL	72	32	34	66	100	2	0	1	1	2

Hockey East Second All-Star Team (1997)

Signed as a free agent by **Florida**, July 7, 1999.

BOIKOV, Alexander — (bohy-KAHV) NSH.

Defense. Shoots left. 6', 195 lbs. Born, Chelyabinsk, USSR, February 7, 1975

				Regular Season					Playoffs			
Season	Club	Lea	GP	G	A	TP	PIM	GP	G	A	TP	PIM
1993-94	Victoria	WHL	70	4	31	35	250	....	....	....	....	....
1994-95	Prince George	WHL	46	5	23	28	115	....	....	....	....	....
	Tri-City	WHL	24	3	13	16	63	17	1	7	8	30
1995-96	Tri-City	WHL	71	3	49	52	230	11	2	4	6	28
1996-97	Kentucky	AHL	61	1	19	20	182	4	0	1	1	4
1997-98	Kentucky	AHL	69	5	14	19	153	3	0	1	1	8
1998-99	Kentucky	AHL	55	5	13	18	116	....	....	....	....	....
	Rochester	AHL	13	0	1	1	15	17	1	3	4	24

Signed as a free agent by **San Jose**, April 22, 1996. Signed as a free agent by **Nashville**, July 24, 1999.

BOISVERT, Hugo — (bwuh-VAIR) ATL.

Center. Shoots left. 6', 195 lbs. Born, St-Eustache, Que., May 22, 1975.

				Regular Season					Playoffs			
Season	Club	Lea	GP	G	A	TP	PIM	GP	G	A	TP	PIM
1995-96	Cornwall	OJHL	54	40	90	130	102	15	15	20	35	44
1996-97	Ohio State	CCHA	38	11	27	38	44	....	....	....	....	....
1997-98	Ohio State	CCHA	42	23	*35	58	70	....	....	....	....	....
1998-99	Ohio State	CCHA	41	24	27	51	54	....	....	....	....	....

CCHA First All-Star Team (1998, 1999) • NCAA West First All-American Team (1998) • NCAA West Second All-American Team (1999)

Signed as a free agent by **Atlanta**, June 25, 1999.

BOLIBRUCK, Kevin — EDM.

Defense. Shoots left. 6'1", 200 lbs. Born, Peterborough, Ont., February 8, 1977.
(Edmonton's 7th choice, 176th overall, in 1997 Entry Draft).

				Regular Season					Playoffs			
Season	Club	Lea	GP	G	A	TP	PIM	GP	G	A	TP	PIM
1993-94	Thorold	OJHL-B	38	6	18	24	78	....	....	....	....	....
1994-95	Peterborough	OHL	66	2	16	18	88	11	1	1	2	14
1995-96	Peterborough	OHL	57	6	21	27	105	24	3	6	9	46
1996-97	Peterborough	OHL	46	4	26	30	63	11	3	3	6	14
1997-98	Canada	Nat-Team	49	2	5	7	65	....	....	....	....	....
1998-99	Hamilton	AHL	64	1	6	7	42	11	0	1	1	4

OHL First All-Star Team (1996)

Rights traded to **Chicago** by **Ottawa** with Denis Chasse and Ottawa's 6th round choice in 1998 Entry Draft for Mike Prokopec, March 18, 1997. Re-entered NHL Entry Draft. Originally Ottawa's 4th choice, 89th overall, in 1995 Entry Draft.

BONNI, Ryan — (baw-NEE) VAN.

Defense. Shoots left. 6'4", 190 lbs. Born, Winnipeg, Man., February 18, 1979.
(Vancouver's 2nd choice, 34th overall, in 1997 Entry Draft).

				Regular Season					Playoffs			
Season	Club	Lea	GP	G	A	TP	PIM	GP	G	A	TP	PIM
1995-96	Saskatoon	WHL	63	1	7	8	78	3	0	0	0	0
1996-97	Saskatoon	WHL	69	11	19	30	219	....	....	....	....	....
1997-98	Saskatoon	WHL	42	5	14	19	100	0	0	0	0	0
1998-99	Saskatoon	WHL	51	6	26	32	211	....	....	....	....	....
	Red Deer	WHL	20	3	10	13	41	9	0	4	4	25

BOOTLAND, Nick — COL.

Left wing. Shoots left. 6', 210 lbs. Born, Shelbourne, Ont., July 31, 1978.
(Dallas' 8th choice, 220th overall, in 1996 Entry Draft).

| | | | Regular Season | | | | | Playoffs | | | | |
Season	Club	Lea	GP	G	A	TP	PIM	GP	G	A	TP	PIM
1995-96	Guelph	OHL	64	8	7	15	90	16	1	0	1	21
1996-97	Guelph	OHL	64	35	23	58	117	18	11	7	18	36
1997-98	Guelph	OHL	64	23	37	60	128	12	7	6	13	22
1998-99	Hershey	AHL	62	3	6	9	122	....				

Signed as a free agent by Colorado, August 6, 1998.

BOUCHARD, Frederic — DAL.

Defense. Shoots right. 6', 181 lbs. Born, Beauport, Que., July 30, 1976.

| | | | Regular Season | | | | | Playoffs | | | | |
Season	Club	Lea	GP	G	A	TP	PIM	GP	G	A	TP	PIM
1993-94	Granby	QMJHL	45	1	9	10	67	7	1	3	4	8
1994-95	Granby	QMJHL	70	17	49	66	190	13	3	6	9	20
1995-96	Granby	QMJHL	43	13	37	50	152	....				
	St-Hyacinthe	QMJHL	23	7	10	17	48	12	3	8	11	38
1996-97	Rouyn-Noranda	QMJHL	6	1	5	6	6	....				
	Chicoutimi	QMJHL	50	33	62	95	87	21	22	29	51	42
1997-98	Michigan	IHL	53	2	12	14	46	....				
	Dayton	ECHL	3	1	2	3	0	5	1	5	6	2
1998-99	Dayton	ECHL	50	3	18	21	75	....				
	Michigan	IHL	3	0	1	1	17	....				

QMJHL Second All-Star Team (1997)
Signed as a free agent by Dallas, August 28, 1997.

BOUCK, Tyler (BOWK) — DAL.

Right wing. Shoots left. 6', 185 lbs. Born, Camrose, Alta., January 13, 1980.
(Dallas' 2nd choice, 57th overall, in 1998 Entry Draft).

| | | | Regular Season | | | | | Playoffs | | | | |
Season	Club	Lea	GP	G	A	TP	PIM	GP	G	A	TP	PIM
1996-97	Prince George	WHL	12	0	2	2	11	....				
1997-98	Prince George	WHL	65	11	26	37	90	11	1	0	1	21
1998-99	Prince George	WHL	56	22	25	47	178	2	0	2	2	10

BOUILLON, Francis — MTL.

Defense. Shoots left. 5'8", 186 lbs. Born, New York, NY, October 17, 1975.

| | | | Regular Season | | | | | Playoffs | | | | |
Season	Club	Lea	GP	G	A	TP	PIM	GP	G	A	TP	PIM
1992-93	Laval	QMJHL	46	0	7	7	45	....				
1993-94	Laval	QMJHL	68	3	15	18	129	19	2	9	11	48
1994-95	Laval	QMJHL	72	8	25	33	115	20	3	11	14	21
1995-96	Granby	QMJHL	68	11	35	46	156	21	2	12	14	30
1996-97	Wheeling	ECHL	69	10	32	42	77	3	0	2	2	10
1997-98	Quebec	IHL	71	8	27	35	76	....				
1998-99	Fredericton	AHL	79	19	36	55	174	5	2	1	3	0

Signed as a free agent by Montreal, June 28, 1998

BOULERICE, Jesse (BOO-luhr-ighs) — PHI.

Right wing. Shoots right. 6'1", 214 lbs. Born, Plattsburgh, NY, August 10, 1978.
(Philadelphia's 4th choice, 133rd overall, in 1996 Entry Draft).

| | | | Regular Season | | | | | Playoffs | | | | |
Season	Club	Lea	GP	G	A	TP	PIM	GP	G	A	TP	PIM
1995-96	Detroit	OHL	64	2	5	7	150	16	0	0	0	12
1996-97	Detroit	OHL	33	10	14	24	209	....				
1997-98	Plymouth	OHL	53	20	23	43	170	13	2	4	6	35
1998-99	Philadelphia	AHL	24	1	2	3	82	....				
	New Orleans	ECHL	12	0	1	1	38	....				

BOUMEDIENNE, Josef (BOO-mih-dyehn) — N.J.

Defense. Shoots left. 6'1", 190 lbs. Born, Stockholm, Sweden, January 12, 1978.
(New Jersey's 7th choice, 91st overall, in 1996 Entry Draft).

| | | | Regular Season | | | | | Playoffs | | | | |
Season	Club	Lea	GP	G	A	TP	PIM	GP	G	A	TP	PIM
1995-96	Huddinge IK	Swede-Jr.	25	2	4	6	66	....				
	Huddinge IK	Sweden-2	7	0	0	0	14	....				
1996-97	Sodertalje SK	Sweden	32	1	1	2	32	....				
1997-98	Sodertalje SK	Sweden	26	3	3	6	28	....				
1998-99	Tappara Tampere	Finland	51	6	8	14	119	....				

BOWEN, Curtis (BOW-ehn)

Left wing. Shoots left. 6'1", 195 lbs. Born, Kenora, Ont., March 24, 1974.
(Detroit's 1st choice, 22nd overall, in 1992 Entry Draft).

| | | | Regular Season | | | | | Playoffs | | | | |
Season	Club	Lea	GP	G	A	TP	PIM	GP	G	A	TP	PIM
1989-90	Kenora	OMHA	40	37	35	72		....				
1990-91	Ottawa	OHL	42	12	14	26	31	....				
1991-92	Ottawa	OHL	65	31	45	76	94	11	3	7	10	11
1992-93	Ottawa	OHL	21	9	19	28	51	....				
1993-94	Ottawa	OHL	52	25	37	62	98	17	8	13	21	14
1994-95	Adirondack	AHL	64	6	11	17	71	4	0	2	2	4
1995-96	Canada	Nat-Team	31	8	8	16	48	....				
	Adirondack	AHL	3	0	0	0	0	....				
1996-97	Adirondack	AHL	78	11	11	22	110	4	0	0	0	2
1997-98	Canada	Nat-Team	46	8	22	30	73	....				
1998-99	Manitoba	IHL	45	10	12	22	54	....				

BOYNTON, Nicholas (BOHYN-tuhn) — BOS.

Defense. Shoots right. 6'2", 210 lbs. Born, Nobleton, Ont., January 14, 1979.
(Boston's 1st choice, 21st overall, in 1999 Entry Draft).

| | | | Regular Season | | | | | Playoffs | | | | |
Season	Club	Lea	GP	G	A	TP	PIM	GP	G	A	TP	PIM
1994-95	Caledon	OJHL	44	10	35	45	139	....				
1995-96	Ottawa	OHL	64	10	14	24	90	4	0	3	3	10
1996-97	Ottawa	OHL	63	13	51	64	143	24	4	24	28	38
1997-98	Ottawa	OHL	40	7	31	38	94	13	0	4	4	24
1998-99	Ottawa	OHL	51	11	48	59	83	9	1	9	10	18

Memorial Cup All-Star Team (1999) • Won Stafford Smythe Memorial Trophy (Memorial Cup Tournament MVP) (1999)

• Re-entered NHL draft. Originally, Washington's 1st choice, 9th overall, in 1997 Entry Draft.

BRADLEY, Matt — S.J.

Right wing. Shoots right. 6'2", 195 lbs. Born, Stittsville, Ont., June 13, 1978.
(San Jose's 4th choice, 102nd overall, in 1996 Entry Draft).

| | | | Regular Season | | | | | Playoffs | | | | |
Season	Club	Lea	GP	G	A	TP	PIM	GP	G	A	TP	PIM
1994-95	Cumberland	OJHL	49	13	20	33	18	....				
1995-96	Kingston	OHL	55	10	14	24	17	6	0	1	1	6
1996-97	Kingston	OHL	65	24	24	48	41	5	0	4	4	2
	Kentucky	AHL	1	0	1	1	0	....				
1997-98	Kingston	OHL	55	33	50	83	24	8	3	4	7	7
1998-99	Kentucky	AHL	79	23	20	43	57	10	1	4	5	4

BRAND, Aaron

Center. Shoots left. 6', 190 lbs. Born, Toronto, Ont., June 14, 1975.

| | | | Regular Season | | | | | Playoffs | | | | |
Season	Club	Lea	GP	G	A	TP	PIM	GP	G	A	TP	PIM
1992-93	Pickering	OJHL	15	7	15	22	4	....				
	St. Michael's	OJHL	30	15	21	36	16	15	5	18	23	12
1993-94	Newmarket	OHL	65	19	45	64	55	....				
1994-95	Sarnia	OHL	66	33	42	75	58	3	0	2	2	4
1995-96	Sarnia	OHL	66	46	*73	*119	110	10	7	11	18	18
	St. John's	AHL	1	0	1	1	0	4	0	0	0	4
1996-97	St. John's	AHL	75	15	25	40	80	11	3	2	5	2
1997-98	St. John's	AHL	79	10	20	30	107	4	2	2	4	6
1998-99	St. John's	AHL	80	7	26	33	88	5	1	2	3	8

OHL Second All-Star Team (1996)
Signed as a free agent by Toronto, March 21, 1996.

BRENDL, Pavel (BREHN-duhl) — NYR

Right wing. Shoots right. 6', 204 lbs. Born, Opocno, Czech., March 23, 1981.
(NY Rangers' 1st choice, 4th overall, in 1999 Entry Draft).

| | | | Regular Season | | | | | Playoffs | | | | |
Season	Club	Lea	GP	G	A	TP	PIM	GP	G	A	TP	PIM
1996-97	HC Olomouc	Czech-Jr.	40	35	17	52		....				
1997-98	HC Olomouc	Czech-Jr.	38	29	23	52		....				
	HC Olomouc	Czech-2	12	1	1	2		....				
1998-99	Calgary	WHL	68	*73	61	*134	40	20	*21	*25	*46	18

BRENNAN, Kip — L.A.

Left wing. Shoots left. 6'4", 196 lbs. Born, Kingston, Ont., August 27, 1980.
(Los Angeles' 4th choice, 103rd overall, in 1998 Entry Draft).

| | | | Regular Season | | | | | Playoffs | | | | |
Season	Club	Lea	GP	G	A	TP	PIM	GP	G	A	TP	PIM
1996-97	Windsor	OHL	42	0	10	10	156	5	0	1	1	16
1997-98	Windsor	OHL	24	0	7	7	103	....				
	Sudbury	OHL	24	0	3	3	85	....				
1998-99	Sudbury	OHL	38	9	12	21	160	....				

BRISKE, Byron (BRIHS-kee) — MTL.

Defense. Shoots right. 6'3", 200 lbs. Born, Humboldt, Sask., January 23, 1976.
(Anaheim's 4th choice, 80th overall, in 1994 Entry Draft).

| | | | Regular Season | | | | | Playoffs | | | | |
Season	Club	Lea	GP	G	A	TP	PIM	GP	G	A	TP	PIM
1991-92	Saskatoon	AAHA	74	9	14	23	156	....				
1992-93	Victoria	WHL	66	1	10	11	110	....				
1993-94	Red Deer	WHL	61	6	21	27	174	....				
1994-95	Red Deer	WHL	48	4	17	21	116	....				
	Tri-City	WHL	15	0	1	1	22	13	0	0	0	18
1995-96	Tri-City	WHL	72	15	38	53	189	11	0	5	5	36
1996-97	Baltimore	AHL	69	0	6	6	131	1	0	0	0	0
1997-98	Cincinnati	AHL	59	0	9	9	95	....				
1998-99	Cincinnati	AHL	55	0	6	6	130	3	0	0	0	2

Signed as a free agent by Montreal, August 17, 1999.

BROS, Michal (BROHSH, MEE-khahl) — S.J.

Center. Shoots right. 6'1", 195 lbs. Born, Olomouc, Czech., January 25, 1976.
(San Jose's 6th choice, 130th overall, in 1995 Entry Draft).

| | | | Regular Season | | | | | Playoffs | | | | |
Season	Club	Lea	GP	G	A	TP	PIM	GP	G	A	TP	PIM
1994-95	HC Olomouc	Czech-Jr.	34	29	32	61		....				
1995-96	HC Olomouc	Cze-Rep	35	8	11	19		4	2	0	2	
1996-97	HC Olomouc	Cze-Rep	50	13	14	27	28	....				
1997-98	Petra Vsetin	EuroHL	9	3	0	3	2	....				
	Petra Vsetin	Cze-Rep	47	14	18	32	28	10	3	1	4	2
1998-99	Slovnaft Vsetin	Cze-Rep	42	10	18	28	18	12	1	3	4	

BROWN, Bobby

Center. Shoots right. 6', 200 lbs. Born, Winnipeg, Man., September 26, 1975.

| | | | Regular Season | | | | | Playoffs | | | | |
Season	Club	Lea	GP	G	A	TP	PIM	GP	G	A	TP	PIM
1990-91	Winnipeg AA	MAHA	48	46	49	95	32	....				
1991-92	Winnipeg	MJHL	46	30	16	46	36	....				
1992-93	Winnipeg	MJHL	28	14	17	31	84	....				
	Brandon	WHL	5	1	1	2	0	....				
1993-94	Brandon	WHL	71	18	19	37	138	14	5	0	5	12
1994-95	Brandon	WHL	72	23	28	51	128	18	3	3	6	31
1995-96	Brandon	WHL	59	42	46	88	106	19	14	13	27	38
1996-97	Roanoke	ECHL	39	9	14	23	61	....				
	Baton Rouge	ECHL	24	7	8	15	26	....				
1997-98	Saint John	AHL	2	0	0	0	0	....				
	Dayton	ECHL	65	25	28	53	117	5	3	2	5	6
1998-99	Dayton	ECHL	66	30	30	60	125	4	2	1	3	2
	Cincinnati	IHL	2	0	0	0	0	....				
	Manitoba	IHL	2	0	0	0	0	....				

Signed as a free agent by Calgary, August 6, 1996.

BROWN, Jeff NYR

Defense. Shoots right. 6'1", 217 lbs. Born, Mississauga, Ont., April 24, 1978.
(NY Rangers' 1st choice, 22nd overall, in 1996 Entry Draft).

			Regular Season					Playoffs				
Season	Club	Lea	GP	G	A	TP	PIM	GP	G	A	TP	PIM
1994-95	Sarnia	OHL	58	2	14	16	52	4	0	2	2	2
1995-96	Sarnia	OHL	65	8	20	28	111	10	1	2	3	12
1996-97	Sarnia	OHL	35	5	14	19	60	....	....	....	....	....
	London	OHL	28	1	17	18	32	....	....	....	....	....
1997-98	London	OHL	63	12	42	54	96	15	1	4	5	26
1998-99	Hartford	AHL	9	0	2	2	21	....	....	....	....	....
	Charlotte	ECHL	12	1	2	3	20	....	....	....	....	....

BROWN, Mike VAN.

Left wing. Shoots left. 6'5", 185 lbs. Born, Surrey, B.C., April 27, 1979.
(Florida's 1st choice, 20th overall, in 1997 Entry Draft).

			Regular Season					Playoffs				
Season	Club	Lea	GP	G	A	TP	PIM	GP	G	A	TP	PIM
1995-96	Red Deer	WHL	62	4	5	9	125	10	0	0	0	18
1996-97	Red Deer	WHL	70	19	13	32	243	16	1	2	3	47
1997-98	Kamloops	WHL	72	23	33	56	305	7	2	1	3	22
1998-99	Kamloops	WHL	69	28	16	44	*285	15	3	7	10	*68

Traded to **Vancouver** by **Florida** with Ed Jovanovski, Dave Gagner, Kevin Weekes and Florida's 1st round choice in 2000 Entry Draft for Pavel Bure, Bret Hedican, Brad Ference and Vancouver's 3rd round choice in 2000 Entry Draft, January 17, 1999.

BRULE, Steve (broo-LAY) N.J.

Right wing. Shoots right. 6', 200 lbs. Born, Montreal, Que., January 15, 1975.
(New Jersey's 6th choice, 143rd overall, in 1993 Entry Draft).

			Regular Season					Playoffs				
Season	Club	Lea	GP	G	A	TP	PIM	GP	G	A	TP	PIM
1991-92	Bourassa	QAAA	38	41	26	67	14					
1992-93	St-Jean	QMJHL	70	33	47	80	46	4	0	0	0	9
1993-94	St-Jean	QMJHL	66	41	64	105	46	5	2	1	3	0
1994-95	St-Jean	QMJHL	69	44	64	108	42	7	3	4	7	8
	Albany	AHL	3	1	4	5	0	14	9	5	14	4
1995-96	Albany	AHL	80	30	21	51	37	4	0	0	0	17
1996-97	Albany	AHL	79	28	48	76	27	16	7	7	14	12
1997-98	Albany	AHL	80	34	43	77	34	13	8	3	11	4
1998-99	Albany	AHL	78	32	52	84	35	5	3	1	4	4

QMJHL Second All-Star Team (1995)

BRUNEL, Craig BUF.

Right wing. Shoots right. 6', 201 lbs. Born, Winnipeg, Man., November 12, 1979.
(Buffalo's 12th choice, 263rd overall, in 1999 Entry Draft).

			Regular Season					Playoffs				
Season	Club	Lea	GP	G	A	TP	PIM	GP	G	A	TP	PIM
1996-97	Prince Albert	WHL	57	5	2	7	208	4	0	0	0	13
1997-98	Prince Albert	WHL	58	6	12	18	247	....	....	....	....	....
1998-99	Prince Albert	WHL	50	10	8	18	173	14	4	2	6	48

• Re-entered NHL draft. Originally Nashville's 6th choice, 147th overall, in 1998 Entry Draft.

BURNETT, Garrett S.J.

Left wing. Shoots left. 6'3", 225 lbs. Born, Coquitlam, B.C., September 23, 1975.

			Regular Season					Playoffs				
Season	Club	Lea	GP	G	A	TP	PIM	GP	G	A	TP	PIM
1993-94	Trail	RIJHL	26	2	1	3	248	....	....	....	....	....
1994-95	S.S. Marie	OHL	14	0	1	1	78	....	....	....	....	....
	Kitchener	OHL	22	0	1	1	74	....	....	....	....	....
1995-96	Utica	ColHL	15	0	1	1	78	....	....	....	....	....
	Oklahoma City	CHL	3	0	0	0	20	....	....	....	....	....
	Tulsa	CHL	6	1	0	1	94	....	....	....	....	....
	Nashville	ECHL	3	0	0	0	22	....	....	....	....	....
	Jacksonville	ECHL	3	0	1	1	38	....	....	....	....	....
1996-97	Knoxville	ECHL	50	5	11	16	321	....	....	....	....	....
1997-98	Johnstown	ECHL	34	1	1	2	331	....	....	....	....	....
	Philadelphia	AHL	14	1	2	3	129	....	....	....	....	....
1998-99	Kentucky	AHL	31	1	0	1	186	....	....	....	....	....

Signed as a free agent by **San Jose**, July 22, 1998.

BURNHAM, Andy NYI

Right wing. Shoots right. 6'5", 201 lbs. Born, New Liskeard, Ont., July 2, 1980.
(NY Islanders' 3rd choice, 95th overall, in 1998 Entry Draft).

			Regular Season					Playoffs				
Season	Club	Lea	GP	G	A	TP	PIM	GP	G	A	TP	PIM
1997-98	Plymouth	OHL	28	1	3	4	55	....	....	....	....	....
	Windsor	OHL	10	1	1	2	23	....	....	....	....	....
1998-99	Windsor	OHL	51	7	7	14	165	....	....	....	....	....

BUT, Anton (BOOT) N.J.

Left wing. Shoots left. 6'1", 187 lbs. Born, Kharkov, USSR, July 3, 1980.
(New Jersey's 7th choice, 119th overall, in 1998 Entry Draft).

			Regular Season					Playoffs				
Season	Club	Lea	GP	G	A	TP	PIM	GP	G	A	TP	PIM
1995-96	Yaroslavl-2	Russia-2	60	30	12	42	10	....	....	....	....	....
1996-97	Yaroslavl-2	Russia-3	70	30	20	50	20	....	....	....	....	....
1997-98	Yaroslavl-2	Russia-2	48	12	5	17	28	....	....	....	....	....
1998-99	Yaroslavl	Russia	5	0	0	0	0	....	....	....	....	....

BUTSAYEV, Yuri (buht-SIGH-ehv, YOO-ree) DET.

Center. Shoots left. 6'1", 183 lbs. Born, Togliatti, USSR, October 11, 1978.
(Detroit's 1st choice, 49th overall, in 1997 Entry Draft).

			Regular Season					Playoffs				
Season	Club	Lea	GP	G	A	TP	PIM	GP	G	A	TP	PIM
1995-96	Togliatti-2	CIS-2	STATISTICS NOT AVAILABLE									
	Togliatti	CIS	1	0	0	0	0	....	....	....	....	....
1996-97	Togliatti	Russia	42	13	11	24	38	11	2	2	4	8
1997-98	Togliatti	EuroHL	6	2	0	2	8	....	....	....	....	....
	Togliatti	Russia	44	8	9	17	63	....	....	....	....	....
1998-99	Moscow D'amo	Russia	1	0	1	1	0	....	....	....	....	....
	Togliatti	Russia	39	10	7	17	55	7	1	2	3	14

BUTURLIN, Alexander (boo-tuhr-LIHN) MTL.

Right wing. Shoots left. 5'11", 183 lbs. Born, Moscow, USSR, September 3, 1981.
(Montreal's 1st choice, 39th overall, in 1999 Entry Draft).

			Regular Season					Playoffs				
Season	Club	Lea	GP	G	A	TP	PIM	GP	G	A	TP	PIM
1997-98	CSKA-2 Moscow	Russia-3	50	12	15	27	46	....	....	....	....	....
	CSKA Moscow	Russia	2	0	0	0	0	....	....	....	....	....
1998-99	CSKA Moscow	Russia	16	1	0	1	6	3	1	0	1	2
	CSKA-2 Moscow	Russia-3	STATISTICS NOT AVAILABLE									

BYRNE, Trevor ST.L.

Defense. Shoots left. 6'3", 200 lbs. Born, Hingham, MA, May 7, 1980.
(St. Louis' 4th choice, 143rd overall, in 1999 Entry Draft).

			Regular Season					Playoffs				
Season	Club	Lea	GP	G	A	TP	PIM	GP	G	A	TP	PIM
1997-98	Deerfield Prep	H.S.	25	5	14	19	16	....	....	....	....	....
1998-99	Deerfield Prep	H.S.	25	9	19	28	22	....	....	....	....	....

CABANA, Chad FLA.

Left wing. Shoots left. 6'1", 205 lbs. Born, Bonnyville, Alta., October 1, 1974.
(Florida's 11th choice, 213th overall, in 1993 Entry Draft).

			Regular Season					Playoffs				
Season	Club	Lea	GP	G	A	TP	PIM	GP	G	A	TP	PIM
1990-91	Bonneyville	AJHL	65	28	42	70	150	....	....	....	....	....
1991-92	Tri-City	WHL	57	5	8	13	145	4	0	1	1	21
1992-93	Tri-City	WHL	68	19	23	42	104	4	1	0	1	10
1993-94	Tri-City	WHL	67	27	33	60	201	4	2	0	2	24
1994-95	Tri-City	WHL	68	25	34	59	252	17	10	11	21	47
1995-96	Carolina	AHL	54	4	9	13	159	....	....	....	....	....
1996-97	Carolina	AHL	55	8	5	13	221	....	....	....	....	....
	Port Huron	ColHL	14	7	9	16	49	....	....	....	....	....
1997-98	New Haven	AHL	34	5	5	10	163	2	0	0	0	7
	Fort Wayne	IHL	6	0	0	0	22	....	....	....	....	....
1998-99	New Haven	AHL	66	6	5	11	251	....	....	....	....	....

CABANA, Clint VAN.

Defense. Shoots right. 6'2", 195 lbs. Born, Bonnyville, Alta., April 28, 1978.
(Vancouver's 6th choice, 175th overall, in 1996 Entry Draft).

			Regular Season					Playoffs				
Season	Club	Lea	GP	G	A	TP	PIM	GP	G	A	TP	PIM
1993-94	Bonneyville	AJHL	7	1	0	1	4	....	....	....	....	....
1994-95	Medicine Hat	WHL	49	0	1	1	68	....	....	....	....	....
1995-96	Medicine Hat	WHL	71	1	11	12	156	5	0	1	1	35
1996-97	Medicine Hat	WHL	4	0	1	1	10	....	....	....	....	....
	Edmonton	WHL	67	3	12	15	302	....	....	....	....	....
	Syracuse	AHL	2	0	0	0	2	....	....	....	....	....
1997-98	Edmonton	WHL	17	1	5	6	60	....	....	....	....	....
	Regina	WHL	34	1	1	2	140	8	1	0	1	16
1998-99	Syracuse	AHL	19	0	1	1	86	....	....	....	....	....
	Augusta	ECHL	6	0	0	0	37	2	0	0	0	2

CABANA, Paul VAN.

Right wing. Shoots right. 6'1", 185 lbs. Born, Calgary, Alta., September 28, 1978.
(Vancouver's 8th choice, 149th overall, in 1998 Entry Draft).

			Regular Season					Playoffs				
Season	Club	Lea	GP	G	A	TP	PIM	GP	G	A	TP	PIM
1997-98	Fort McMurray	AJHL	52	48	32	80	111	....	....	....	....	....
1998-99	Michigan Tech	WCHA	38	12	9	21	50	....	....	....	....	....

CALDER, Kyle CHI.

Center. Shoots left. 5'11", 180 lbs. Born, Mannville, Alta., January 5, 1979.
(Chicago's 7th choice, 130th overall, in 1997 Entry Draft).

			Regular Season					Playoffs				
Season	Club	Lea	GP	G	A	TP	PIM	GP	G	A	TP	PIM
1995-96	Regina	WHL	27	1	7	8	10	11	0	0	0	0
1996-97	Regina	WHL	62	25	34	59	17	5	3	0	3	6
1997-98	Regina	WHL	62	27	50	77	58	2	0	1	1	0
1998-99	Regina	WHL	34	23	28	51	29	....	....	....	....	....
	Kamloops	WHL	27	19	18	37	30	15	6	10	16	6

CAMERON, David PIT.

Center. Shoots right. 6'1", 180 lbs. Born, Winnipeg, Man., April 27, 1980.
(Pittsburgh's 3rd choice, 80th overall, in 1998 Entry Draft).

			Regular Season					Playoffs				
Season	Club	Lea	GP	G	A	TP	PIM	GP	G	A	TP	PIM
1996-97	Lethbridge	WHL	38	3	3	6	5	....	....	....	....	....
	Prince Albert	WHL	18	3	4	7	11	3	0	2	2	0
1997-98	Prince Albert	WHL	69	20	36	56	42	....	....	....	....	....
1998-99	Prince Albert	WHL	41	9	30	39	25	....	....	....	....	....
	Saskatoon	WHL	24	6	14	20	12	....	....	....	....	....

CAMERON, Scott N.J.

Center. Shoots left. 6', 182 lbs. Born, Sudbury, Ont., April 11, 1981.
(New Jersey's 6th choice, 185th overall, in 1999 Entry Draft).

			Regular Season					Playoffs				
Season	Club	Lea	GP	G	A	TP	PIM	GP	G	A	TP	PIM
1998-99	Barrie	OHL	66	10	32	42	14	12	2	2	4	2

CAMPBELL, Brian BUF.

Defense. Shoots left. 5'11", 185 lbs Born, Strathroy, Ont., May 23, 1979.
(Buffalo's 7th choice, 156th overall, in 1997 Entry Draft).

			Regular Season					Playoffs				
Season	Club	Lea	GP	G	A	TP	PIM	GP	G	A	TP	PIM
1995-96	Ottawa	OHL	66	5	22	27	23	4	0	1	1	2
1996-97	Ottawa	OHL	66	7	36	43	12	24	2	11	13	8
1997-98	Ottawa	OHL	66	14	39	53	31	13	1	14	15	0
1998-99	Ottawa	OHL	62	12	75	87	27	9	2	10	12	6
	Rochester	AHL	....	....	....	....	....	2	0	0	0	0

OHL First All-Star Team (1999) • Canadian Major Junior First All-Star Team (1999) • Won George Parsons Trophy (Memorial Cup Tournament Most Sportsmanlike Player) (1999) • Canadian Major Junior Player of the Year (1999)

CARDARELLI, Joe — T.B.

Left wing. Shoots left. 6', 203 lbs. Born, Vancouver, B.C., June 13, 1977.
(Tampa Bay's 7th choice, 186th overall, in 1995 Entry Draft).

			Regular Season					Playoffs				
Season	Club	Lea	GP	G	A	TP	PIM	GP	G	A	TP	PIM
1992-93	Burnaby	BCAHA	66	133	102	235	30	....	....	....	....	....
1993-94	Spokane	WHL	51	7	11	18	9	2	0	0	0	0
1994-95	Spokane	WHL	71	27	22	49	20	11	4	9	13	0
1995-96	Spokane	WHL	44	25	19	44	21	18	4	0	4	4
1996-97	Spokane	WHL	66	34	37	71	39	9	6	1	7	0
1997-98	Adirondack	AHL	30	0	3	3	2	....	....	....	....	....
	Chesapeake	ECHL	8	2	4	6	4	3	0	1	1	0
1998-99	Chesapeake	ECHL	17	2	6	8	8	....	....	....	....	....
	Cleveland	IHL	50	7	7	14	8	....	....	....	....	....

CARKNER, Matt — MTL.

Defense. Shoots right. 6'4", 222 lbs. Born, Winchester, Ont., November 3, 1980.
(Montreal's 2nd choice, 58th overall, in 1999 Entry Draft).

			Regular Season					Playoffs				
Season	Club	Lea	GP	G	A	TP	PIM	GP	G	A	TP	PIM
1996-97	Winchester	OJHL-B	29	1	18	19	....	....	....	....	....	....
1997-98	Peterborough	OHL	57	0	6	6	121	4	0	0	0	2
1998-99	Peterborough	OHL	60	2	16	18	173	5	0	0	0	20

CARPENTIER, Benjamin (kar-PAWN-tyay) — NYR

Defense. Shoots left. 6'2", 195 lbs. Born, Grand-Mere, Que., June 13, 1978.

			Regular Season					Playoffs				
Season	Club	Lea	GP	G	A	TP	PIM	GP	G	A	TP	PIM
1994-95	Shawinigan	QMJHL	2	0	0	0	0	2	0	0	0	2
1995-96	Shawinigan	QMJHL	65	0	3	3	197	6	0	0	0	2
1996-97	Shawinigan	QMJHL	63	2	4	6	275	7	0	0	0	12
1997-98	Laval	QMJHL	64	1	8	9	279	14	1	3	4	30
1998-99	Charlotte	ECHL	23	4	6	10	68	....	....	....	....	....
	Hartford	AHL	21	0	1	1	31	....	....	....	....	....

Signed as a free agent by **NY Rangers**, October 3, 1996.

CARTER, Shawn

Center. Shoots left. 6'2", 210 lbs. Born, Eagle River, WI, April 16, 1973.

			Regular Season					Playoffs				
Season	Club	Lea	GP	G	A	TP	PIM	GP	G	A	TP	PIM
1992-93	U. of Wisconsin	WCHA	5	1	0	1	4	....	....	....	....	....
1993-94	U. of Wisconsin	WCHA	16	2	2	4	24	....	....	....	....	....
1994-95	U. of Wisconsin	WCHA	43	15	13	28	98	....	....	....	....	....
1995-96	U. of Wisconsin	WCHA	40	17	28	45	50	....	....	....	....	....
1996-97	Orlando	IHL	53	22	25	47	40	....	....	....	....	....
	St. John's	AHL	18	5	6	11	15	7	1	2	3	6
1997-98	St. John's	AHL	80	14	16	30	117	4	1	0	1	4
1998-99	Orlando	IHL	79	13	26	39	103	17	1	4	5	10

Signed as a free agent by **Toronto**, February 14, 1997.

CAULFIELD, Kevin — WSH.

Right wing. Shoots right. 6'2", 210 lbs. Born, Boston, MA, January 7, 1978.
(Washington's 4th choice, 116th overall, in 1997 Entry Draft).

			Regular Season					Playoffs				
Season	Club	Lea	GP	G	A	TP	PIM	GP	G	A	TP	PIM
1995-96	Thayer Academy	H.S.	31	12	23	35	45	....	....	....	....	....
1996-97	Boston College	H.E.	38	5	10	15	90	....	....	....	....	....
1997-98	Boston College	H.E.	41	9	6	15	82	....	....	....	....	....
1998-99	Boston College	H.E.	41	8	8	16	81	....	....	....	....	....

CAVA, Peter (KAH-va)

Center. Shoots left. 5'11", 175 lbs. Born, Thunder Bay, Ont., February 14, 1978.
(Toronto's 7th choice, 110th overall, in 1996 Entry Draft).

			Regular Season					Playoffs				
Season	Club	Lea	GP	G	A	TP	PIM	GP	G	A	TP	PIM
1995-96	S.S. Marie	OHL	40	14	17	31	44	4	1	1	2	4
1996-97	S.S. Marie	OHL	55	14	36	50	64	11	5	4	9	27
1997-98	S.S. Marie	OHL	64	30	60	90	86	....	....	....	....	....
	St. John's	AHL	2	0	0	0	0	....	....	....	....	....
	Thunder Bay	UHL	....	....	....	....	....	5	2	4	6	4
1998-99	Sarnia	OHL	62	33	48	81	63	5	1	5	6	8

CAVANAUGH, Dan — CGY.

Center. Shoots right. 6'1", 190 lbs. Born, Springfield, MA, March 3, 1980.
(Calgary's 2nd choice, 38th overall, in 1999 Entry Draft).

			Regular Season					Playoffs				
Season	Club	Lea	GP	G	A	TP	PIM	GP	G	A	TP	PIM
1997-98	New England	EJHL	51	39	59	98	58	....	....	....	....	....
1998-99	Boston University	H.E.	36	6	8	14	60	....	....	....	....	....

CECH, Vratislav (CHEHKH) — BOS.

Defense. Shoots left. 6'3", 196 lbs. Born, Tabor, Czech., January 28, 1979.
(Florida's 3rd choice, 56th overall, in 1997 Entry Draft).

			Regular Season					Playoffs				
Season	Club	Lea	GP	G	A	TP	PIM	GP	G	A	TP	PIM
1995-96	HC Brno	Czech-Jr.	37	10	13	23	....	....	....	....	....	....
1996-97	Kitchener	OHL	57	5	19	24	72	13	1	2	3	12
1997-98	Kitchener	OHL	63	9	33	42	66	6	2	2	4	13
1998-99	Kitchener	OHL	66	6	21	27	73	1	0	1	1	4

Signed as a free agent by **Boston**, July 22, 1999.

CEREDA, Luca (suh-REH-duh) — TOR.

Center. Shoots left. 6'2", 203 lbs. Born, Lugano, Switzerland, September 7, 1981.
(Toronto's 1st choice, 24th overall, in 1999 Entry Draft).

			Regular Season					Playoffs				
Season	Club	Lea	GP	G	A	TP	PIM	GP	G	A	TP	PIM
1996-97	Ambri-Piotta	Switz-Jr.	35	13	8	21	....	....	....	....	....	....
1997-98	Ambri-Piotta	Switz-Jr.	28	17	27	44	24	....	....	....	....	....
1998-99	Ambri-Piotta	Switz.	38	6	10	16	8	15	0	6	6	4

CERVEN, Martin (CHEHR-vehn) — PHI.

Center. Shoots left. 6'4", 200 lbs. Born, Trencin, Czech., March 7, 1977.
(Edmonton's 6th choice, 161st overall, in 1995 Entry Draft).

			Regular Season					Playoffs				
Season	Club	Lea	GP	G	A	TP	PIM	GP	G	A	TP	PIM
1994-95	Dukla Trencin	Slovak-Jr.	22	8	3	11	....	....	....	....	....	....
1995-96	Spokane	WHL	40	9	9	18	42	....	....	....	....	....
	Seattle	WHL	27	6	14	20	10	5	1	2	3	0
1996-97	Seattle	WHL	72	27	25	52	64	15	2	6	8	14
1997-98	Philadelphia	AHL	50	7	11	18	27	8	1	2	3	2
1998-99	Philadelphia	AHL	46	6	4	10	20	1	0	1	1	0
	Mohawk Valley	UHL	16	4	8	12	20	....	....	....	....	....

Traded to **Philadelphia** by **Edmonton** for Philadelphia's 7th round choice (Chad Hinz) in 1997 Entry Draft, June 18, 1997.

CHAGODAYEV, Alexander (cheh-goh-digh-ehv) — ANA.

Center. Shoots left. 6'1", 180 lbs. Born, Moscow, USSR, January 15, 1981.
(Anaheim's 3rd choice, 105th overall, in 1999 Entry Draft).

			Regular Season					Playoffs				
Season	Club	Lea	GP	G	A	TP	PIM	GP	G	A	TP	PIM
1997-98	CSKA Moscow	Russia	1	0	0	0	0	....	....	....	....	....
	CSKA Moscow	Russia-2	5	1	0	1	0	....	....	....	....	....
1998-99	CSKA Moscow	Russia-2	14	3	6	9	2	....	....	....	....	....

CHARRON, Craig — TOR.

Center. Shoots right. 5'10", 175 lbs. Born, North Easton, MA, November 15, 1967.

			Regular Season					Playoffs				
Season	Club	Lea	GP	G	A	TP	PIM	GP	G	A	TP	PIM
1986-87	U. Mass-Lowell	H.E.	36	11	16	27	48	....	....	....	....	....
1987-88	U. Mass-Lowell	H.E.	39	22	18	40	32	....	....	....	....	....
1988-89	U. Mass-Lowell	H.E.	32	14	21	35	32	....	....	....	....	....
1989-90	U. Mass-Lowell	H.E.	35	17	29	46	10	....	....	....	....	....
1990-91	Winston-Salem	ECHL	30	11	16	27	10	....	....	....	....	....
	Albany	IHL	5	0	2	2	0	....	....	....	....	....
	Fredericton	AHL	24	2	5	7	4	5	0	3	3	0
1991-92	Cincinnati	ECHL	64	41	55	96	97	9	5	5	10	10
1992-93	Birmingham	ECHL	23	9	17	26	18	....	....	....	....	....
	Cincinnati	IHL	27	6	8	14	8	....	....	....	....	....
1993-94	Holje BK	Sweden-2	33	49	40	89	....	....	....	....	....	....
1994-95	Dayton	ECHL	48	35	47	82	82	9	9	13	22	10
	Kalamazoo	IHL	2	0	0	0	0	....	....	....	....	....
	Fort Wayne	IHL	2	1	0	1	4	....	....	....	....	....
	Cornwall	AHL	6	5	0	5	0	2	0	0	0	0
1995-96	Rochester	AHL	72	43	52	95	79	19	7	10	17	12
1996-97	Rochester	AHL	72	24	41	65	42	10	8	8	16	2
1997-98	Rochester	AHL	75	25	53	78	51	4	1	1	2	0
1998-99	Lowell	AHL	71	22	39	61	41	3	1	2	3	8

Signed as a free agent by **NY Islanders**, August 24, 1998. Traded to **Toronto** by **NY Islanders** for Niklas Andersson, August 17, 1999.

CHARTRAND, Brad — L.A.

Right wing. Shoots left. 5'11", 185 lbs. Born, Winnipeg, Man., December 14, 1974.

			Regular Season					Playoffs				
Season	Club	Lea	GP	G	A	TP	PIM	GP	G	A	TP	PIM
1988-89	Winnipeg	MAHA	24	30	50	80	40	....	....	....	....	....
1989-90	Winnipeg	MAHA	24	26	55	81	40	....	....	....	....	....
1990-91	Winnipeg	MAHA	34	26	45	71	40	....	....	....	....	....
1991-92	St. James	MJHL	Statistics Not Available									
1992-93	Cornell	ECAC	26	10	6	16	16	....	....	....	....	....
1993-94	Cornell	ECAC	30	4	14	18	48	....	....	....	....	....
1994-95	Cornell	ECAC	28	9	9	18	10	....	....	....	....	....
1995-96	Cornell	ECAC	34	24	19	43	16	....	....	....	....	....
1996-97	Canada	Nat-Team	54	10	14	24	42	....	....	....	....	....
1997-98	Canada	Nat-Team	60	24	30	54	47	....	....	....	....	....
	HC Rapperswil	Switz.	8	2	3	5	4	....	....	....	....	....
1998-99	St. John's	AHL	64	16	14	30	48	5	0	2	2	2

Signed as a free agent by **Los Angeles**, July 21, 1999.

CHEECHOO, Jonathan (CHEE-choo) — S.J.

Right wing. Shoots right. 6', 205 lbs. Born, Moose Factory, Ont., July 15, 1980.
(San Jose's 2nd choice, 29th overall, in 1998 Entry Draft).

			Regular Season					Playoffs				
Season	Club	Lea	GP	G	A	TP	PIM	GP	G	A	TP	PIM
1996-97	Kitchener	OJHL	43	35	41	76	33	....	....	....	....	....
1997-98	Belleville	OHL	64	31	45	76	62	10	4	2	6	10
1998-99	Belleville	OHL	63	35	47	82	74	21	15	15	30	27

CHERNESKI, Stefan (chuhr-NEHS-kee) — NYR

Right wing. Shoots left. 6', 200 lbs. Born, Winnipeg, Man., September 19, 1978.
(NY Rangers' 1st choice, 19th overall, in 1997 Entry Draft).

			Regular Season					Playoffs				
Season	Club	Lea	GP	G	A	TP	PIM	GP	G	A	TP	PIM
1995-96	Brandon	WHL	58	8	21	29	62	19	3	1	4	11
1996-97	Brandon	WHL	56	39	29	68	83	....	....	....	....	....
1997-98	Brandon	WHL	65	43	38	81	127	18	*15	8	23	21
1998-99	Hartford	AHL	11	1	2	3	41	....	....	....	....	....

Canadian Major Junior Scholastic Player of the Year (1997)

• Missed majority of 1998-99 season recovering from knee injury suffered in game vs. Springfield, November 13, 1998.

CHERNOV, Mikhail (chair-NAHF) — PHI.

Defense. Shoots right. 6'2", 196 lbs. Born, Prokopjevsk, USSR, November 11, 1978.
(Philadelphia's 4th choice, 103rd overall, in 1997 Entry Draft).

			Regular Season					Playoffs				
Season	Club	Lea	GP	G	A	TP	PIM	GP	G	A	TP	PIM
1996-97	Yaroslavl-2	Russia-3	33	4	2	6	40	....	....	....	....	....
	Yaroslavl	Russia	5	0	0	0	0	....	....	....	....	....
1997-98	Yaroslavl	Russia	7	0	0	0	4	....	....	....	....	....
	Yaroslavl-2	Russia-2	Statistics Not Available									
1998-99	Philadelphia	AHL	56	4	3	7	98	14	1	0	1	8

CHIMERA, Jason (CHIHM-air-a) EDM.

Center. Shoots left. 6', 180 lbs. Born, Edmonton, Alta., May 2, 1979.
(Edmonton's 5th choice, 121st overall, in 1997 Entry Draft).

			Regular Season					Playoffs				
Season	Club	Lea	GP	G	A	TP	PIM	GP	G	A	TP	PIM
1996-97	Medicine Hat	WHL	71	16	23	39	64	4	0	1	1	4
1997-98	Medicine Hat	WHL	72	34	32	66	93	....	....	....	....	....
	Hamilton	AHL	4	0	0	0	8	....	....	....	....	....
1998-99	Medicine Hat	WHL	37	18	22	40	84	....	....	....	....	....
	Brandon	WHL	21	14	12	26	32	5	4	1	5	8

CHOUINARD, Eric (shwee-NAHR) MTL.

Center. Shoots left. 6'3", 198 lbs. Born, Atlanta, GA, July 8, 1980.
(Montreal's 1st choice, 16th overall, in 1998 Entry Draft).

			Regular Season					Playoffs				
Season	Club	Lea	GP	G	A	TP	PIM	GP	G	A	TP	PIM
1996-97	Ste-Foy	QAAA	40	29	41	70	40	....	....	....	....	....
1997-98	Quebec	QMJHL	68	41	42	83	18	14	7	10	17	6
1998-99	Quebec	QMJHL	62	50	59	109	56	13	8	10	18	8
	Fredericton	AHL	....	....	....	....	....	6	3	2	5	0

CHOUINARD, Marc (shwee-NAHR) ANA.

Center. Shoots right. 6'5", 200 lbs. Born, Charlesbourg, Ont., May 6, 1977.
(Winnipeg's 2nd choice, 32nd overall, in 1995 Entry Draft).

			Regular Season					Playoffs				
Season	Club	Lea	GP	G	A	TP	PIM	GP	G	A	TP	PIM
1993-94	Beauport	QMJHL	62	11	19	30	23	13	2	5	7	2
1994-95	Beauport	QMJHL	68	24	40	64	32	18	1	6	7	4
1995-96	Beauport	QMJHL	30	14	21	35	19	....	....	....	....	....
	Halifax	QMJHL	24	6	12	18	17	6	2	1	3	2
1996-97	Halifax	QMJHL	63	24	49	73	74	18	9	16	25	12
1997-98	Cincinnati	AHL	8	1	2	3	4	....	....	....	....	....
1998-99	New Orleans	ECHL	9	1	0	1	4	....	....	....	....	....
	Cincinnati	AHL	69	7	8	15	20	3	0	0	0	4

Traded to **Anaheim** by **Winnipeg** with Teemu Selanne and Winnipeg's 4th round choice (later traded to Toronto — later traded to Montreal — Montreal selected Kim Staal) in 1996 Entry Draft for Chad Kilger, Oleg Tverdovsky and Anaheim's 3rd round choice (Per-Anton Ludstrom) in 1996 Entry Draft, February 7, 1996.

CHRISTIE, Ryan DAL.

Left wing. Shoots left. 6'2", 175 lbs. Born, Beamsville, Ont., July 3, 1978.
(Dallas' 4th choice, 112th overall, in 1996 Entry Draft).

			Regular Season					Playoffs				
Season	Club	Lea	GP	G	A	TP	PIM	GP	G	A	TP	PIM
1995-96	Owen Sound	OHL	66	29	17	46	93	6	1	1	2	0
1996-97	Owen Sound	OHL	66	23	29	52	136	4	1	1	2	8
1997-98	Owen Sound	OHL	66	39	41	80	208	11	3	5	8	13
1998-99	Michigan	IHL	48	4	5	9	74	3	1	1	2	2

CHUBAROV, Artem (choo-BAH-rahf) VAN.

Center. Shoots left. 6'1", 189 lbs. Born, Gorky, USSR, December 12, 1979.
(Vancouver's 2nd choice, 31st overall, in 1998 Entry Draft).

			Regular Season					Playoffs				
Season	Club	Lea	GP	G	A	TP	PIM	GP	G	A	TP	PIM
1996-97	Nizhny Novgorod	Russia-3	40	24	5	29	16	....	....	....	....	....
	Nizhny Novgorod	Russia-2	15	1	1	2	8	....	....	....	....	....
1997-98	Moscow D'amo	Russia	30	1	4	5	4	....	....	....	....	....
1998-99	Moscow D'amo	Russia	34	8	2	10	10	12	0	0	0	4

CIBAK, Martin (TSEE-bak) T.B.

Center. Shoots left. 6', 183 lbs. Born, Liptovmikulas, Czech., May 17, 1980.
(Tampa Bay's 11th choice, 252nd overall, in 1998 Entry Draft).

			Regular Season					Playoffs				
Season	Club	Lea	GP	G	A	TP	PIM	GP	G	A	TP	PIM
1995-96	HK Liptovsky	Slovak-Jr.	48	38	35	73	....	....	....	....	....	....
1996-97	HK Liptovsky	Slovak-Jr.	45	22	18	40	....	....	....	....	....	....
1997-98	HK Liptovsky	Slovak-Jr.	42	31	21	52	....	....	....	....	....	....
	HK Liptovsky	Slovakia	28	1	3	4	10	....	....	....	....	....
1998-99	Medicine Hat	WHL	66	21	26	47	72	....	....	....	....	....

CISAR, Marian (SIH-sahr) NSH.

Right wing. Shoots right. 6', 176 lbs. Born, Bratislava, Czech., February 25, 1978.
(Los Angeles' 2nd choice, 37th overall, in 1996 Entry Draft).

			Regular Season					Playoffs				
Season	Club	Lea	GP	G	A	TP	PIM	GP	G	A	TP	PIM
1994-95	Bratislava	Slovak-Jr.	38	42	28	70	16	....	....	....	....	....
1995-96	Bratislava	Slovak-Jr.	16	26	17	43	2	....	....	....	....	....
	Bratislava	Slovakia	13	3	3	6	0	6	3	0	3	0
1996-97	Spokane	WHL	70	31	35	66	52	9	6	2	8	4
1997-98	Spokane	WHL	52	33	40	73	34	18	8	5	13	8
1998-99	Milwaukee	IHL	51	11	17	28	31	2	0	0	0	12

Traded to **Nashville** by **LA Kings** for future considerations, May 29, 1998.

CLARK, Chris CGY.

Right wing. Shoots right. 6', 190 lbs. Born, Manchester, CT, March 8, 1976.
(Calgary's 3rd choice, 77th overall, in 1994 Entry Draft).

			Regular Season					Playoffs				
Season	Club	Lea	GP	G	A	TP	PIM	GP	G	A	TP	PIM
1993-94	Springfield	NAJHL	35	31	26	57	185	....	....	....	....	....
1994-95	Clarkson	ECAC	32	12	11	23	92	....	....	....	....	....
1995-96	Clarkson	ECAC	38	10	8	18	108	....	....	....	....	....
1996-97	Clarkson	ECAC	37	23	25	48	*86	....	....	....	....	....
1997-98	Clarkson	ECAC	35	18	21	39	*106	....	....	....	....	....
1998-99	Saint John	AHL	73	13	27	40	123	7	2	4	6	15

ECAC Second All-Star Team (1998)

CLARK, Kyle WSH.

Right wing. Shoots right. 6'6", 210 lbs. Born, Burlington, VT, February 14, 1980.
(Washington's 7th choice, 175th overall, in 1999 Entry Draft).

			Regular Season					Playoffs				
Season	Club	Lea	GP	G	A	TP	PIM	GP	G	A	TP	PIM
1997-98	Team USA	Under-18	65	14	11	25	287	....	....	....	....	....
1998-99	Harvard University	ECAC	20	0	2	2	30	....	....	....	....	....

CLARK, Ryan NYI

Defense. Shoots left. 6'3", 205 lbs. Born, Edmonton, Alta., October 30, 1977.
(NY Islanders' 11th choice, 222nd overall, in 1997 Entry Draft).

			Regular Season					Playoffs				
Season	Club	Lea	GP	G	A	TP	PIM	GP	G	A	TP	PIM
1996-97	Lincoln Stars	USHL	35	6	7	13	94	....	....	....	....	....
1997-98	Notre Dame	CCHA	38	0	6	6	22	....	....	....	....	....
1998-99	Notre Dame	CCHA	14	1	2	3	26	....	....	....	....	....

CLAUSON, Kevin NYI

Defense. Shoots left. 6'5", 210 lbs. Born, Lebanon, NH, November 13, 1978.
(NY Islanders' 5th choice, 155th overall, in 1998 Entry Draft).

			Regular Season					Playoffs				
Season	Club	Lea	GP	G	A	TP	PIM	GP	G	A	TP	PIM
1997-98	Western Michigan	CCHA	36	1	1	2	56	....	....	....	....	....
1998-99	Western Michigan	CCHA	12	0	1	1	14	....	....	....	....	....

CLOUTHIER, Brett N.J.

Left wing. Shoots left. 6'4", 215 lbs. Born, Ottawa, Ont., June 9, 1981.
(New Jersey's 3rd choice, 50th overall, in 1999 Entry Draft).

			Regular Season					Playoffs				
Season	Club	Lea	GP	G	A	TP	PIM	GP	G	A	TP	PIM
1997-98	Kanata	OJHL	50	12	10	22	135	....	....	....	....	....
1998-99	Kingston	OHL	64	8	14	22	227	5	1	1	2	4

CLYMER, Ben BOS.

Defense. Shoots left. 6'1", 195 lbs. Born, Edina, MN, April 11, 1978.
(Boston's 3rd choice, 27th overall, in 1997 Entry Draft).

			Regular Season					Playoffs				
Season	Club	Lea	GP	G	A	TP	PIM	GP	G	A	TP	PIM
1995-96	Jefferson High	H.S.	23	12	34	46	34	....	....	....	....	....
1996-97	U. of Minnesota	WCHA	29	7	13	20	64	....	....	....	....	....
1997-98	U. of Minnesota	WCHA	1	0	0	0	2	....	....	....	....	....
1998-99	Seattle	WHL	70	12	44	56	93	11	1	5	6	12

• Missed majority of 1997-98 season after suffering shoulder injury in game vs. Michigan, October 10, 1997.

COALTER, Brandon S.J.

Left wing. Shoots left. 6'2", 200 lbs. Born, Richmond Hill, Ont., June 22, 1978.
(San Jose's 6th choice, 127th overall, in 1998 Entry Draft).

			Regular Season					Playoffs				
Season	Club	Lea	GP	G	A	TP	PIM	GP	G	A	TP	PIM
1995-96	Oshawa	OHL	37	1	5	6	40	5	0	0	0	0
1996-97	Oshawa	OHL	63	4	9	13	98	18	2	1	3	12
1997-98	Oshawa	OHL	64	8	13	21	143	7	3	3	6	6
1998-99	Oshawa	OHL	55	12	11	23	95	15	3	3	6	23

COLAGIACOMO, Adam (coh-lah-JAH-coh-moh) S.J.

Right wing. Shoots right. 6'2", 205 lbs. Born, Toronto, Ont., March 17, 1979.
(San Jose's 3rd choice, 82nd overall, in 1997 Entry Draft).

			Regular Season					Playoffs				
Season	Club	Lea	GP	G	A	TP	PIM	GP	G	A	TP	PIM
1995-96	London	OHL	66	28	38	66	88	....	....	....	....	....
1996-97	London	OHL	26	11	11	22	37	....	....	....	....	....
	Oshawa	OHL	23	14	10	24	32	13	1	5	6	4
1997-98	Oshawa	OHL	58	25	31	56	80	7	1	0	1	2
1998-99	Plymouth	OHL	67	40	68	108	89	10	6	9	15	14

COLE, Erik CAR.

Left wing. Shoots left. 6', 185 lbs. Born, Oswego, NY, November 6, 1978.
(Carolina's 3rd choice, 71st overall, in 1998 Entry Draft).

			Regular Season					Playoffs				
Season	Club	Lea	GP	G	A	TP	PIM	GP	G	A	TP	PIM
1996-97	Des Moines	USHL	48	30	34	64	140	....	....	....	....	....
1997-98	Clarkson	ECAC	34	11	20	31	55	....	....	....	....	....
1998-99	Clarkson	ECAC	36	*22	20	42	50	....	....	....	....	....

ECAC First All-Star Team (1999) • NCAA East Second All-American Team (1999)

COLEMAN, Jon

Defense. Shoots right. 6'1", 190 lbs. Born, Boston, MA, March 9, 1975.
(Detroit's 2nd choice, 48th overall, in 1993 Entry Draft).

			Regular Season					Playoffs				
Season	Club	Lea	GP	G	A	TP	PIM	GP	G	A	TP	PIM
1992-93	Phillips Academy	H.S.	24	14	33	47	40	....	....	....	....	....
1993-94	Boston University	H.E.	29	1	14	15	26	....	....	....	....	....
1994-95	Boston University	H.E.	40	5	23	28	42	....	....	....	....	....
1995-96	Boston University	H.E.	40	7	31	38	58	....	....	....	....	....
1996-97	Boston University	H.E.	39	5	27	32	20	....	....	....	....	....
1997-98	Detroit	IHL	1	0	0	0	0	....	....	....	....	....
	Adirondack	AHL	54	2	29	31	23	2	0	0	0	0
1998-99	Adirondack	AHL	72	12	26	38	32	3	0	0	0	0

Hockey East Second All-Star Team (1996, 1997) • NCAA East Second All-American Team (1996) • NCAA East First All-American Team (1997)

COLLINS, Brian NYI

Center. Shoots left. 6'1", 190 lbs. Born, Worcester, MA, September 13, 1980.
(NY Islanders' 6th choice, 87th overall, in 1999 Entry Draft).

			Regular Season					Playoffs				
Season	Club	Lea	GP	G	A	TP	PIM	GP	G	A	TP	PIM
1998-99	St. John's	H.S.	28	38	35	73	20	....	....	....	....	....

COMMODORE, Mike N.J.

Defense. Shoots right. 6'4", 225 lbs. Born, Fort Saskatchewan, Alta., November 4, 1979.
(New Jersey's 2nd choice, 42nd overall, in 1999 Entry Draft).

			Regular Season					Playoffs				
Season	Club	Lea	GP	G	A	TP	PIM	GP	G	A	TP	PIM
1996-97	Ft. Saskatchewan	AJHL	51	3	8	11	244	....	....	....	....	....
1997-98	North Dakota	WCHA	29	0	5	5	74	....	....	....	....	....
1998-99	North Dakota	WCHA	39	5	8	13	154	....	....	....	....	....

COMRIE, Mike   EDM.

Center. Shoots left. 5'9", 172 lbs.   Born, Edmonton, Alta., September 11, 1980.
(Edmonton's 5th choice, 91st overall, in 1999 Entry Draft).

			Regular Season					Playoffs				
Season	Club	Lea	GP	G	A	TP	PIM	GP	G	A	TP	PIM
1995-96	Edmonton CAC	AAHA	33	51	52	103	....	....	....	....	....	....
1996-97	St. Albert	AJHL	63	37	41	78	44	....	....	....	....	....
1997-98	St. Albert	AJHL	58	60	78	138	134	....	....	....	....	....
1998-99	U. of Michigan	CCHA	36	17	22	39	30	....	....	....	....	....

COMRIE, Paul   EDM.

Center. Shoots left. 5'11", 192 lbs.   Born, Edmonton, Alta., February 7, 1977.
(Tampa Bay's 12th choice, 224th overall, in 1997 Entry Draft)

			Regular Season					Playoffs				
Season	Club	Lea	GP	G	A	TP	PIM	GP	G	A	TP	PIM
1993-94	Ft. Saskatchewan	AJHL	55	7	23	30	50	6	0	1	1	2
1994-95	Ft. Saskatchewan	AJHL	51	30	37	67	121	....	....	....	....	....
1995-96	U. of Denver	WCHA	38	13	10	23	61	....	....	....	....	....
1996-97	U. of Denver	WCHA	40	21	28	49	72	....	....	....	....	....
1997-98	U. of Denver	WCHA	33	17	23	40	72	....	....	....	....	....
1998-99	U. of Denver	WCHA	40	18	31	49	84	....	....	....	....	....
	Hamilton	AHL	7	0	1	1	0	8	1	3	4	2

WCHA First All-Star Team (1999) • NCAA West Second All-American Team (1999)

Traded to **Edmonton** by **Tampa Bay** with Roman Hamrlik for Bryan Marchment, Steve Kelly and Jason Bonsignore, December 30, 1997.

CONCANNON, Mark   S.J.

Left wing. Shoots left. 6', 200 lbs.   Born, Boston, MA, June 12, 1980.
(San Jose's 2nd choice, 82nd overall, in 1999 Entry Draft).

			Regular Season					Playoffs				
Season	Club	Lea	GP	G	A	TP	PIM	GP	G	A	TP	PIM
1998-99	Winchendon	H.S.	26	23	38	51	11	....	....	....	....	....

CONNOLLY, Tim   NYI

Center. Shoots right. 6', 186 lbs.   Born, Baldwinsville, NY, May 7, 1980.
(NY Islanders' 1st choice, 5th overall, in 1999 Entry Draft).

			Regular Season					Playoffs				
Season	Club	Lea	GP	G	A	TP	PIM	GP	G	A	TP	PIM
1996-97	Syracuse	NEJHL	50	42	62	104	34	....	....	....	....	....
1997-98	Erie	OHL	59	30	32	62	32	7	1	6	7	6
1998-99	Erie	OHL	46	34	34	68	50	....	....	....	....	....

COOK, Jesse   CGY.

Defense. Shoots right. 6'6", 210 lbs.   Born, Denver, CO, October 11, 1979.
(Calgary's 6th choice, 153rd overall, in 1999 Entry Draft).

			Regular Season					Playoffs				
Season	Club	Lea	GP	G	A	TP	PIM	GP	G	A	TP	PIM
1997-98	Calgary	AJHL	34	5	24	29	35	....	....	....	....	....
1998-99	U. of Denver	WCHA	30	0	9	9	22	....	....	....	....	....

COPELAND, Adam   EDM.

Right wing. Shoots right. 6'1", 215 lbs.   Born, St. Catharines, Ont., June 5, 1976.
(Edmonton's 6th choice, 79th overall, in 1994 Entry Draft).

			Regular Season					Playoffs				
Season	Club	Lea	GP	G	A	TP	PIM	GP	G	A	TP	PIM
1993-94	Burlington	OJHL	39	28	44	72	55	....	....	....	....	....
1994-95	U. of Miami-Ohio	CCHA	39	6	4	10	28	....	....	....	....	....
1995-96	U. of Miami-Ohio	CCHA	36	10	4	14	38	....	....	....	....	....
1996-97	U. of Miami-Ohio	CCHA	40	18	22	40	62	....	....	....	....	....
1997-98	U. of Miami-Ohio	CCHA	37	19	14	33	52	....	....	....	....	....
1998-99	Hamilton	AHL	30	3	6	9	6	....	....	....	....	....
	New Orleans	ECHL	23	9	9	18	15	11	3	1	4	6

COPLEY, Randy   NYR

Right wing. Shoots right. 6'1", 205 lbs.   Born, Inverness, NS, October 4, 1979.
(NY Rangers' 2nd choice, 40th overall, in 1998 Entry Draft).

			Regular Season					Playoffs				
Season	Club	Lea	GP	G	A	TP	PIM	GP	G	A	TP	PIM
1996-97	Granby	QMJHL	70	7	14	21	114	5	0	0	0	5
1997-98	Cape Breton	QMJHL	69	34	42	76	194	4	0	0	0	16
1998-99	Cape Breton	QMJHL	25	8	22	30	60	....	....	....	....	....
	Rouyn-Noranda	QMJHL	38	7	25	32	87	11	3	5	8	14

CORRINET, Chris   WSH.

Right wing. Shoots right. 6'3", 220 lbs.   Born, Derby, CT, October 29, 1978.
(Washington's 4th choice, 107th overall, in 1998 Entry Draft)

			Regular Season					Playoffs				
Season	Club	Lea	GP	G	A	TP	PIM	GP	G	A	TP	PIM
1996-97	Deerfield High	H.S.	16	6	15	21	10	....	....	....	....	....
1997-98	Princeton	ECAC	31	3	6	9	22	....	....	....	....	....
1998-99	Princeton	ECAC	32	10	6	16	38	....	....	....	....	....

CORSO, Daniel   ST.L.

Center. Shoots left. 5'10", 183 lbs.   Born, Montreal, Que., April 3, 1978.
(St. Louis' 6th choice, 169th overall, in 1996 Entry Draft).

			Regular Season					Playoffs				
Season	Club	Lea	GP	G	A	TP	PIM	GP	G	A	TP	PIM
1994-95	Victoriaville	QMJHL	65	27	26	53	6	4	2	5	7	2
1995-96	Victoriaville	QMJHL	65	49	65	114	77	12	6	7	13	4
1996-97	Victoriaville	QMJHL	54	51	68	119	50	....	....	....	....	....
1997-98	Victoriaville	QMJHL	35	24	51	75	20	3	1	1	2	2
1998-99	Worcester	AHL	63	14	14	28	26	....	....	....	....	....

QMJHL First All-Star Team (1997)

CORVO, Joseph   L.A.

Defense. Shoots right. 6', 205 lbs.   Born, Oak Park, IL, June 20, 1977.
(Los Angeles' 4th choice, 83rd overall, in 1997 Entry Draft).

			Regular Season					Playoffs				
Season	Club	Lea	GP	G	A	TP	PIM	GP	G	A	TP	PIM
1995-96	Western Michigan	CCHA	41	5	25	30	38	....	....	....	....	....
1996-97	Western Michigan	CCHA	32	12	21	33	85	....	....	....	....	....
1997-98	Western Michigan	CCHA	32	5	12	17	93	....	....	....	....	....
1998-99	Springfield	AHL	50	5	15	20	32	....	....	....	....	....
	Hampton Roads	ECHL	5	0	0	0	15	4	0	1	1	0

CCHA Second All-Star Team (1997)

COWAN, Jeff   CGY.

Left wing. Shoots left. 6'2", 185 lbs.   Born, Scarborough, Ont., September 27, 1976.

			Regular Season					Playoffs				
Season	Club	Lea	GP	G	A	TP	PIM	GP	G	A	TP	PIM
1992-93	Guelph Fire	OJHL-B	45	8	8	16	22	....	....	....	....	....
1993-94	Guelph	OHL	17	1	0	1	5	....	....	....	....	....
1994-95	Guelph	OHL	51	10	7	17	14	14	1	1	2	0
1995-96	Barrie	OHL	66	38	14	52	29	5	1	2	3	6
1996-97	Saint John	AHL	22	5	5	10	8	....	....	....	....	....
	Roanoke	ECHL	47	21	13	34	42	....	....	....	....	....
1997-98	Saint John	AHL	69	15	13	28	23	13	4	1	5	14
1998-99	Saint John	AHL	71	7	12	19	117	4	0	1	1	10

Signed as a free agent by **Calgary**, October 2, 1995.

COX, Justin   DAL.

Right wing. Shoots right. 6', 160 lbs.   Born, Hinton, Alta., March 13, 1981.
(Dallas' 6th choice, 184th overall, in 1999 Entry Draft).

			Regular Season					Playoffs				
Season	Club	Lea	GP	G	A	TP	PIM	GP	G	A	TP	PIM
1997-98	Prince George	WHL	40	1	4	5	15	2	0	0	0	0
1998-99	Prince George	WHL	72	9	13	22	51	7	1	0	1	13

CRAIN, Jason   L.A.

Defense. Shoots left. 6'3", 190 lbs.   Born, Pittsburgh, PA, January 3, 1980.
(Los Angeles' 2nd choice, 74th overall, in 1999 Entry Draft).

			Regular Season					Playoffs				
Season	Club	Lea	GP	G	A	TP	PIM	GP	G	A	TP	PIM
1997-98	St. Thomas	OJHL-B	43	6	33	39	49	....	....	....	....	....
1998-99	Ohio State	CCHA	41	3	14	17	18	....	....	....	....	....

CROZIER, Greg   PIT.

Left wing. Shoots left. 6'4", 200 lbs.   Born, Calgary, Alta., July 6, 1976.
(Pittsburgh's 4th choice, 73rd overall, in 1994 Entry Draft).

			Regular Season					Playoffs				
Season	Club	Lea	GP	G	A	TP	PIM	GP	G	A	TP	PIM
1992-93	Lawrence Prep	H.S.	22	22	14	36	....	....	....	....	....	....
1993-94	Lawrence Prep	H.S.	18	22	26	48	12	....	....	....	....	....
1994-95	Lawrence Prep	H.S.	31	45	32	77	22	....	....	....	....	....
1995-96	U. of Michigan	CCHA	42	14	10	24	46	....	....	....	....	....
1996-97	U. of Michigan	CCHA	31	5	15	20	45	....	....	....	....	....
1997-98	U. of Michigan	CCHA	45	12	10	22	26	....	....	....	....	....
1998-99	U. of Michigan	CCHA	39	7	6	13	63	....	....	....	....	....

CULLEN, David   PHX.

Defense. Shoots right. 6'2", 209 lbs.   Born, St. Catharines, Ont., December 30, 1976.

			Regular Season					Playoffs				
Season	Club	Lea	GP	G	A	TP	PIM	GP	G	A	TP	PIM
1995-96	U. of Maine	H.E.	34	2	4	6	22	....	....	....	....	....
1996-97	U. of Maine	H.E.	35	5	25	30	8	....	....	....	....	....
1997-98	U. of Maine	H.E.	36	10	27	37	24	....	....	....	....	....
1998-99	U. of Maine	H.E.	41	11	33	44	24	....	....	....	....	....

Hockey East First All-Star Team (1999) • NCAA East First All-American Team (1999) • NCAA Championship All-Tournament Team (1999)

Signed as a free agent by **Phoenix**, April 16, 1999.

CUNNIFF, David

Left wing. Shoots left. 5'10", 185 lbs.   Born, South Boston, MA, October 9, 1973.

			Regular Season					Playoffs				
Season	Club	Lea	GP	G	A	TP	PIM	GP	G	A	TP	PIM
1995-96	Salem State	ECAC-2	27	12	17	29	62	....	....	....	....	....
1996-97	Jacksonville	ECHL	16	4	5	9	75	....	....	....	....	....
	Raleigh	ECHL	46	14	6	20	67	....	....	....	....	....
1997-98	Raleigh	ECHL	62	12	12	24	168	....	....	....	....	....
	Albany	AHL	4	0	0	0	13	....	....	....	....	....
1998-99	Albany	AHL	48	2	9	11	118	5	0	1	1	4

Signed as a free agent by **New Jersey**, October 1, 1997.

DAFOE, Kyle

Defense. Shoots right. 6'5", 195 lbs.   Born, Charlottetown, P.E.I., January 11, 1979.
(Carolina's 5th choice, 142nd overall, in 1997 Entry Draft).

			Regular Season					Playoffs				
Season	Club	Lea	GP	G	A	TP	PIM	GP	G	A	TP	PIM
1996-97	Owen Sound	OHL	41	1	1	2	58	3	0	0	0	0
1997-98	Owen Sound	OHL	30	1	3	4	55	....	....	....	....	....
	Sudbury	OHL	21	0	3	3	112	10	0	0	0	29
1998-99	Sudbury	OHL	66	3	6	9	239	4	0	0	0	4

DAGENAIS, Pierre   (da-ZHUH-nay)   N.J.

Left wing. Shoots left. 6'4", 215 lbs.   Born, Blainville, Que., March 4, 1978.
(New Jersey's 6th choice, 105th overall, in 1998 Entry Draft).

			Regular Season					Playoffs				
Season	Club	Lea	GP	G	A	TP	PIM	GP	G	A	TP	PIM
1995-96	Moncton	QMJHL	67	43	25	68	59	....	....	....	....	....
1996-97	Moncton	QMJHL	6	4	2	6	0	....	....	....	....	....
	Laval	QMJHL	37	16	14	30	40	....	....	....	....	....
	Rouyn-Noranda	QMJHL	27	21	8	29	22	....	....	....	....	....
1997-98	Rouyn-Noranda	QMJHL	60	*66	67	133	50	6	6	2	8	2
1998-99	Albany	AHL	69	17	13	30	37	4	0	0	0	0

QMJHL Second All-Star Team (1998)

• Re-entered NHL draft. Originally New Jersey's 4th choice, 47th overall, in 1996 Entry Draft.

DARBY, Regan — VAN.

Defense. Shoots left. 6'2", 200 lbs. Born, Estevan, Sask., July 17, 1980.
(Vancouver's 5th choice, 90th overall, in 1998 Entry Draft).

			Regular Season					Playoffs				
Season	Club	Lea	GP	G	A	TP	PIM	GP	G	A	TP	PIM
1997-98	Spokane	WHL	7	0	1	1	28	....	....	....	....	....
	Tri-City	WHL	32	1	2	3	125	....	....	....	....	....
1998-99	Tri-City	WHL	38	2	4	6	152	....	....	....	....	....
	Red Deer	WHL	19	1	6	7	90	9	0	1	1	18

DARDIS, Jay — NYR

Center. Shoots right. 6'3", 190 lbs. Born, Proctor, MN, July 4, 1981.
(NY Rangers' 7th choice, 177th overall, in 1999 Entry Draft).

			Regular Season					Playoffs				
Season	Club	Lea	GP	G	A	TP	PIM	GP	G	A	TP	PIM
1998-99	Proctor High	H.S.	26	23	36	59	32	....	....	....	....	....

DATSYUK, Pavel (daht-SOOK) — DET.

Center. Shoots left. 5'11", 180 lbs. Born, Sverdlovsk, USSR, July 20, 1978.
(Detroit's 8th choice, 171st overall, in 1998 Entry Draft).

			Regular Season					Playoffs				
Season	Club	Lea	GP	G	A	TP	PIM	GP	G	A	TP	PIM
1996-97	Yekaterinburg	Russia	18	2	2	4	4	....	....	....	....	....
	Yekaterinburg	Russia-2	36	12	10	22	12	....	....	....	....	....
1997-98	Yekaterinburg	Russia	24	3	5	8	4	....	....	....	....	....
	Yekaterinburg	Russia-2	22	7	8	15	4	....	....	....	....	....
1998-99	Yekaterinburg	Russia-2	22	12	15	27	12	....	....	....	....	....
	Yekaterinburg	Russia-2	13	9	8	17	2	9	3	7	10	10

DAVIDSON, Matt — BUF.

Right wing. Shoots right. 6'2", 190 lbs. Born, Flin Flon, Man., August 9, 1977.
(Buffalo's 5th choice, 94th overall, in 1995 Entry Draft).

			Regular Season					Playoffs				
Season	Club	Lea	GP	G	A	TP	PIM	GP	G	A	TP	PIM
1992-93	Saskatoon	SAHA	36	14	18	32	36	....	....	....	....	....
1993-94	Portland	WHL	59	4	12	16	18	10	0	0	0	4
1994-95	Portland	WHL	72	17	20	37	51	9	1	3	4	0
1995-96	Portland	WHL	70	24	26	50	96	7	2	2	4	2
1996-97	Portland	WHL	72	44	27	71	47	6	0	1	1	2
1997-98	Rochester	AHL	72	15	12	27	12	3	1	0	1	2
1998-99	Rochester	AHL	80	26	15	41	44	18	2	1	3	6

DAVIS, Justin

Right wing. Shoots right. 6'2", 175 lbs. Born, Burlington, Ont., March 1, 1978.
(Washington's 7th choice, 85th overall, in 1996 Entry Draft).

			Regular Season					Playoffs				
Season	Club	Lea	GP	G	A	TP	PIM	GP	G	A	TP	PIM
1995-96	Kingston	OHL	64	30	18	48	20	6	2	3	5	0
1996-97	Kingston	OHL	35	8	17	25	17	....	....	....	....	....
	S.S. Marie	OHL	20	1	5	6	2	3	0	1	1	0
1997-98	S.S. Marie	OHL	2	0	0	0	0	....	....	....	....	....
	Ottawa	OHL	58	32	23	55	14	9	5	5	10	0
1998-99	Ottawa	OHL	61	22	37	59	13	9	2	8	10	4

Won Ed Chynoweth Trophy (Memorial Cup Tournament Leading Scorer) (1999)

DAVISON, Rob — S.J.

Defense. Shoots left. 6'2", 210 lbs. Born, St. Catharines, Ont., May 1, 1980.
(San Jose's 4th choice, 98th overall, in 1998 Entry Draft).

			Regular Season					Playoffs				
Season	Club	Lea	GP	G	A	TP	PIM	GP	G	A	TP	PIM
1997-98	North Bay	OHL	59	0	11	11	200	....	....	....	....	....
1998-99	North Bay	OHL	59	2	17	19	150	4	0	1	1	12

DAW, Jeff — CHI.

Center. Shoots right. 6'3", 190 lbs. Born, Carlisle, Ont., February 28, 1972.

			Regular Season					Playoffs				
Season	Club	Lea	GP	G	A	TP	PIM	GP	G	A	TP	PIM
1992-93	U. Mass-Lowell	H.E.	37	12	18	30	14	....	....	....	....	....
1993-94	U. Mass-Lowell	H.E.	40	6	12	18	12	....	....	....	....	....
1994-95	U. Mass-Lowell	H.E.	40	27	15	42	24	....	....	....	....	....
1995-96	U. Mass-Lowell	H.E.	40	23	28	51	10	....	....	....	....	....
1996-97	Wheeling	ECHL	13	3	8	11	26	....	....	....	....	....
	Hamilton	AHL	56	11	8	19	39	19	4	5	9	0
1997-98	Hamilton	AHL	79	28	35	63	20	9	6	3	9	0
1998-99	Hamilton	AHL	66	18	29	47	10	11	0	3	3	4

Signed as a free agent by **Edmonton**, August 1, 1996. Signed as a free agent by **Chicago**, July 22, 1999.

DEFAUW, Brad — CAR.

Left wing. Shoots left. 6'2", 210 lbs. Born, Edina, MN, November 10, 1977.
(Carolina's 2nd choice, 28th overall, in 1997 Entry Draft).

			Regular Season					Playoffs				
Season	Club	Lea	GP	G	A	TP	PIM	GP	G	A	TP	PIM
1995-96	Apple Valley	H.S.	28	21	34	55	14	....	....	....	....	....
1996-97	North Dakota	WCHA	37	7	6	13	39	....	....	....	....	....
1997-98	North Dakota	WCHA	36	9	11	20	34	....	....	....	....	....
1998-99	North Dakota	WCHA	34	11	12	23	64	....	....	....	....	....

DEGERMAN, Tommi (DEH-guhr-mahn) — ANA.

Left wing. Shoots left. 6'2", 185 lbs. Born, Espoo, Finland, February 23, 1976.
(Anaheim's 8th choice, 235th overall, in 1997 Entry Draft).

			Regular Season					Playoffs				
Season	Club	Lea	GP	G	A	TP	PIM	GP	G	A	TP	PIM
1994-95	Kiekko-Espoo	Finn-Jr.	26	4	7	11	14	5	1	0	1	4
1995-96	Kiekko-Espoo	Finn-Jr.	36	11	15	26	14	....	....	....	....	....
1996-97	Kiekko-Espoo	Finn-Jr.	3	3	0	3	0	....	....	....	....	....
	Pelicans Lahti	Finland-2	4	0	4	4	0	....	....	....	....	....
	Kiekko-Espoo	Finland	23	2	0	2	2	....	....	....	....	....
	Boston University	H.E.	17	6	10	16	19	....	....	....	....	....
1997-98	Boston University	H.E.	35	12	20	32	37	....	....	....	....	....
1998-99	Boston University	H.E.	27	12	9	21	24	....	....	....	....	....

DELANEY, Keith — FLA.

Center. Shoots left. 6'1", 196 lbs. Born, Labrador City, Nfld., May 7, 1979.
(Florida's 7th choice, 155th overall, in 1997 Entry Draft).

			Regular Season					Playoffs				
Season	Club	Lea	GP	G	A	TP	PIM	GP	G	A	TP	PIM
1996-97	Barrie	OHL	64	5	5	10	19	9	0	1	1	0
1997-98	Barrie	OHL	66	24	30	54	28	6	4	1	5	2
1998-99	Barrie	OHL	38	12	21	33	10	....	....	....	....	....
	Toronto	OHL	28	9	17	26	12	....	....	....	....	....

DELEEUW, Adam — DET.

Left wing. Shoots left. 6', 206 lbs. Born, Brampton, Ont., February 29, 1980.
(Detroit's 7th choice, 151st overall, in 1998 Entry Draft).

			Regular Season					Playoffs				
Season	Club	Lea	GP	G	A	TP	PIM	GP	G	A	TP	PIM
1996-97	Brampton	OJHL	45	11	17	28	97	....	....	....	....	....
1997-98	Barrie	OHL	56	10	6	16	224	....	....	....	....	....
1998-99	Barrie	OHL	39	15	16	31	146	....	....	....	....	....
	Toronto	OHL	29	10	5	15	55	....	....	....	....	....

DEMIDOV, Ilja (deh-MEE-dahf, ihl-YA) — CGY.

Defense. Shoots left. 6'3", 185 lbs. Born, Moscow, USSR, April 14, 1979.
(Calgary's 10th choice, 140th overall, in 1997 Entry Draft).

			Regular Season					Playoffs				
Season	Club	Lea	GP	G	A	TP	PIM	GP	G	A	TP	PIM
1995-96	Moscow D'amo-2	CIS-2	10	0	14	14	....	....	....	....	....	....
1996-97	Moscow D'amo-2	Russia-3	32	1	0	1	60	....	....	....	....	....
1997-98	Oshawa	OHL	61	4	16	20	67	7	0	1	1	2
1998-99	Oshawa	OHL	62	4	23	27	72	15	2	5	7	24

DESCOTEAUX, Matthieu (DAY-koh-toh) — EDM.

Defense. Shoots left. 6'3", 220 lbs. Born, Pierreville, Que., September 23, 1977.
(Edmonton's 2nd choice, 19th overall, in 1996 Entry Draft).

			Regular Season					Playoffs				
Season	Club	Lea	GP	G	A	TP	PIM	GP	G	A	TP	PIM
1994-95	Shawinigan	QMJHL	50	3	2	5	28	15	1	1	2	19
1995-96	Shawinigan	QMJHL	69	2	13	15	129	6	0	0	0	6
1996-97	Shawinigan	QMJHL	38	6	18	24	121	....	....	....	....	....
	Hull	QMJHL	32	6	19	25	34	14	1	8	9	29
1997-98	Hamilton	AHL	67	2	8	10	70	2	0	0	0	0
1998-99	Hamilton	AHL	74	6	12	18	49	4	0	0	0	0

DESROCHES, Jonathan (deh-ROHSH)

Defense. Shoots left. 6', 206 lbs. Born, Granby, Que., May 23, 1979.
(Montreal's 7th choice, 145th overall, in 1997 Entry Draft).

			Regular Season					Playoffs				
Season	Club	Lea	GP	G	A	TP	PIM	GP	G	A	TP	PIM
1994-95	Magog	QAAA	42	6	15	21	38	....	....	....	....	....
1995-96	Granby	QMJHL	44	1	6	7	38	11	0	0	0	2
1996-97	Granby	QMJHL	58	7	15	22	30	5	0	1	1	2
1997-98	Moncton	QMJHL	63	4	27	31	56	10	0	2	2	4
1998-99	Moncton	QMJHL	70	5	29	34	54	4	1	0	1	0

DESSNER, Jeff — NYR

Defense. Shoots left. 6'2", 177 lbs. Born, Skokie, IL, April 16, 1977.
(NY Rangers' 6th choice, 185th overall, in 1996 Entry Draft).

			Regular Season					Playoffs				
Season	Club	Lea	GP	G	A	TP	PIM	GP	G	A	TP	PIM
1995-96	Taft High	H.S.	25	12	18	30	....	....	....	....	....	....
1996-97	U. of Wisconsin	WCHA	DID NOT PLAY – INJURED									
1997-98	U. of Wisconsin	WCHA	19	1	3	4	43	....	....	....	....	....
1998-99	U. of Wisconsin	WCHA	37	7	14	21	46	....	....	....	....	....

• Missed entire 1996-97 season recovering from back surgery, June, 1996.

DEWOLF, Josh (duh-WOOLF) — N.J.

Defense. Shoots left. 6'2", 200 lbs. Born, Bloomington, MN, July 25, 1977.
(New Jersey's 3rd choice, 41st overall, in 1996 Entry Draft).

			Regular Season					Playoffs				
Season	Club	Lea	GP	G	A	TP	PIM	GP	G	A	TP	PIM
1995-96	Twin Cities	USHL	40	11	15	26	38	....	....	....	....	....
1996-97	St. Cloud State	WCHA	31	3	11	14	62	....	....	....	....	....
1997-98	St. Cloud State	WCHA	37	9	9	18	78	....	....	....	....	....
	Albany	AHL	2	0	0	0	0	....	....	....	....	....
1998-99	Albany	AHL	75	1	17	18	111	5	0	0	0	2

DEYELL, Mark (digh-EHL) — TOR.

Center. Shoots right. 6', 180 lbs. Born, Regina, Sask., March 26, 1976.
(Toronto's 4th choice, 126th overall, in 1994 Entry Draft).

			Regular Season					Playoffs				
Season	Club	Lea	GP	G	A	TP	PIM	GP	G	A	TP	PIM
1992-93	Winnipeg	MAHA	35	45	56	101	125	....	....	....	....	....
1993-94	Saskatoon	WHL	66	17	36	53	52	16	5	2	7	20
1994-95	Saskatoon	WHL	70	34	68	102	56	10	2	5	7	14
1995-96	Saskatoon	WHL	69	61	*98	*159	122	4	0	5	5	8
1996-97	St. John's	AHL	58	15	27	42	30	10	1	5	6	6
1997-98	St. John's	AHL	72	20	43	63	75	4	1	1	2	4
1998-99	St. John's	AHL	44	20	27	47	39	3	0	3	3	0

WHL East First All-Star Team (1996)

DHADPHALE, Aniket (dahd-FAH-lee, AN-ih-keht) — S.J.

Left wing. Shoots left. 6'3", 185 lbs. Born, Ann Arbor, MI, April 2, 1976.
(San Jose's 11th choice, 245th overall, in 1994 Entry Draft).

			Regular Season					Playoffs				
Season	Club	Lea	GP	G	A	TP	PIM	GP	G	A	TP	PIM
1993-94	Marquette	USHL	50	58	36	94	95	....	....	....	....	....
1994-95	Stratford	OJHL-B	46	31	33	64	74	....	....	....	....	....
1995-96	Notre Dame	CCHA	34	13	7	20	34	....	....	....	....	....
1996-97	Notre Dame	CCHA	34	5	16	21	20	....	....	....	....	....
1997-98	Notre Dame	CCHA	41	25	10	35	34	....	....	....	....	....
1998-99	Notre Dame	CCHA	34	18	11	29	55	....	....	....	....	....

DIENER, Derek — ST.L.

Defense. Shoots left. 6'5", 200 lbs. Born, Burnaby, B.C., July 13, 1976.
(Philadelphia's 6th choice, 192nd overall, in 1994 Entry Draft).

			Regular Season					Playoffs				
Season	Club	Lea	GP	G	A	TP	PIM	GP	G	A	TP	PIM
1993-94	Lethbridge	WHL	62	1	8	9	64	3	0	0	0	7
1994-95	Lethbridge	WHL	68	13	29	42	104	....	....	....	....	....
1995-96	Lethbridge	WHL	56	6	27	33	78	4	0	1	1	4
1996-97	Kelowna	WHL	70	13	45	58	135	6	1	3	4	6
1997-98	Worcester	AHL	32	2	5	7	88	....	....	....	....	....
1998-99	Worcester	AHL	39	1	5	6	39	....	....	....	....	....

Signed as a free agent by **St. Louis**, March 20, 1997.

DIMITRAKOS, Nicholas — S.J.

Right wing. Shoots right. 5'11", 190 lbs. Born, Boston, MA, May 21, 1979.
(San Jose's 4th choice, 155th overall, in 1999 Entry Draft).

			Regular Season					Playoffs				
Season	Club	Lea	GP	G	A	TP	PIM	GP	G	A	TP	PIM
1997-98	Avon	H.S.	26	27	28	55	....	....	....	....	....	....
1998-99	U. of Marine	H.E.	35	8	19	27	33	....	....	....	....	....

DIPENTA, Joe — FLA.

Defense. Shoots right. 6'2", 221 lbs. Born, Barrie, Ont., February 25, 1979.
(Florida's 2nd choice, 61st overall, in 1998 Entry Draft).

			Regular Season					Playoffs				
Season	Club	Lea	GP	G	A	TP	PIM	GP	G	A	TP	PIM
1996-97	Smiths Falls	OJHL	54	13	22	35	92	....	....	....	....	....
1997-98	Boston University	H.E.	38	2	16	18	50	....	....	....	....	....
1998-99	Boston University	H.E.	36	2	15	17	72	....	....	....	....	....

DIROBERTO, Torrey (DIH-raw-buhr-toh) — ANA.

Center. Shoots left. 5'11", 180 lbs. Born, New York, NY, April 17, 1978.
(Buffalo's 6th choice, 128th overall, in 1997 Entry Draft).

			Regular Season					Playoffs				
Season	Club	Lea	GP	G	A	TP	PIM	GP	G	A	TP	PIM
1995-96	Seattle	WHL	70	16	19	35	118	5	0	2	2	8
1996-97	Seattle	WHL	72	37	44	81	91	15	9	5	14	8
1997-98	Seattle	WHL	43	14	21	35	48	5	0	2	2	14
1998-99	Seattle	WHL	66	25	42	67	100	11	4	4	8	14

Signed as a free agent by **Anaheim**, July 1, 1999.

DIVISEK, Tomas — PHI.

Left wing. Shoots left. 6'2", 194 lbs. Born, Most, Czech., July 19, 1979.
(Philadelphia's 9th choice, 195th overall, in 1998 Entry Draft).

			Regular Season					Playoffs				
Season	Club	Lea	GP	G	A	TP	PIM	GP	G	A	TP	PIM
1995-96	Slavia Praha	Czech-Jr.	36	20	27	47	12	....	....	....	....	....
1996-97	Slavia Praha	Czech-Jr.	41	17	25	42	18	....	....	....	....	....
	Slavia Praha	Cze-Rep	1	0	0	0	0	....	....	....	....	....
1997-98	Slavia Praha	Czech-Jr.	27	20	16	36	12	....	....	....	....	....
	Slavia Praha	Cze-Rep	22	2	0	2	8	....	....	....	....	....
1998-99	Slavia Praha	Cze-Rep	45	8	4	12	26	....	....	....	....	....

DIXON, Sean — MTL.

Defense. Shoots left. 6'3", 186 lbs. Born, Kitchener, Ont., February 22, 1981.
(Montreal's 8th choice, 167th overall, in 1999 Entry Draft).

			Regular Season					Playoffs				
Season	Club	Lea	GP	G	A	TP	PIM	GP	G	A	TP	PIM
1997-98	Erie	OHL	58	0	8	8	22	....	....	....	....	....
1998-99	Erie	OHL	55	2	12	14	57	....	....	....	....	....

DOBRYSHKIN, Yuri (doh-BRIHSH-kihn) — ATL.

Left wing. Shoots right. 6', 189 lbs. Born, Penza, USSR, July 19, 1979.
(Atlanta's 7th choice, 159th overall, in 1999 Entry Draft).

			Regular Season					Playoffs				
Season	Club	Lea	GP	G	A	TP	PIM	GP	G	A	TP	PIM
1996-97	Soviet Wings-2	Russia-3	35	13	5	18	42	....	....	....	....	....
	Soviet Wings	Russia	2	0	0	0	0	2	0	0	0	0
1997-98	Soviet Wings-2	Russia-3	26	12	5	17	68	....	....	....	....	....
	Soviet Wings	Russia	22	4	0	4	12	....	....	....	....	....
1998-99	Soviet Wings	Russia	37	6	4	10	30	....	....	....	....	....

DODGINGHORSE, Brent — CGY.

Center. Shoots left. 6', 180 lbs. Born, Calgary, Alta., February 17, 1978.

			Regular Season					Playoffs				
Season	Club	Lea	GP	G	A	TP	PIM	GP	G	A	TP	PIM
1997-98	Omaha	USHL	12	7	5	12	55	....	....	....	....	....
	Calgary	WHL	53	14	23	37	78	12	2	6	8	42
1998-99	Calgary	WHL	50	13	31	44	153	21	10	15	25	72

Signed as a free agent by **Calgary**, June 18, 1999.

DOELL, Curtis — FLA.

Defense. Shoots right. 5'11", 209 lbs. Born, Saskatoon, Sask., October 3, 1976.

			Regular Season					Playoffs				
Season	Club	Lea	GP	G	A	TP	PIM	GP	G	A	TP	PIM
1996-97	U. Minn-Duluth	WCHA	37	6	20	26	114	....	....	....	....	....
1997-98	U. Minn-Duluth	WCHA	39	9	23	32	120	....	....	....	....	....
1998-99	Kentucky	AHL	53	2	8	10	166	....	....	....	....	....

Signed as a free agent by **Florida**, June 5, 1998.

DOMAN, Matt — CGY.

Right wing. Shoots right. 6'1", 218 lbs. Born, St. Cloud, MN, February 10, 1980.
(Calgary's 5th choice, 135th overall, in 1999 Entry Draft).

			Regular Season					Playoffs				
Season	Club	Lea	GP	G	A	TP	PIM	GP	G	A	TP	PIM
1997-98	Team USA	Under-18	55	24	22	46	208	....	....	....	....	....
1998-99	U. of Wisconsin	WCHA	34	5	5	10	52	....	....	....	....	....

DOWNEY, Aaron — BOS.

Right wing. Shoots right. 6', 210 lbs. Born, Shelburne, Ont., August 27, 1974.

			Regular Season					Playoffs				
Season	Club	Lea	GP	G	A	TP	PIM	GP	G	A	TP	PIM
1995-96	Hampton Roads	ECHL	65	12	11	23	354	....	....	....	....	....
1996-97	Hampton Roads	ECHL	64	8	8	16	338	9	0	3	3	26
	Portland	AHL	3	0	0	0	19	....	....	....	....	....
	Manitoba	IHL	2	0	0	0	17	....	....	....	....	....
1997-98	Providence	AHL	78	5	10	15	*407	....	....	....	....	....
1998-99	Providence	AHL	75	10	12	22	*401	19	1	1	2	46

Signed as a free agent by **Boston**, January 20, 1998.

DOYLE, Jason (DOIL)

Right wing. Shoots right. 6'1", 200 lbs. Born, Toronto, Ont., May 15, 1978.
(NY Islanders' 9th choice, 242nd overall, in 1998 Entry Draft).

			Regular Season					Playoffs				
Season	Club	Lea	GP	G	A	TP	PIM	GP	G	A	TP	PIM
1994-95	London	OHL	45	4	10	14	7	4	1	1	2	0
1995-96	London	OHL	21	11	5	16	24	....	....	....	....	....
	S.S. Marie	OHL	44	17	17	34	30	4	1	1	2	6
1996-97	S.S. Marie	OHL	5	....	1	1	5	....	....	....	....	....
	Owen Sound	OHL	58	13	15	28	33	4	1	1	2	4
1997-98	Owen Sound	OHL	46	15	22	37	70	10	7	4	11	11
1998-99	Brampton	OHL	4	2	1	3	7	....	....	....	....	....
	London	OHL	54	20	31	51	61	25	12	22	34	24

• Re-entered NHL draft. Originally Boston's 4th choice, 80th overall, in 1996 Entry Draft.

DRANEY, Brett — DAL.

Left wing. Shoots left. 6', 179 lbs. Born, Kamloops, B.C., March 12, 1981.
(Dallas' 7th choice, 186th overall, in 1999 Entry Draft).

			Regular Season					Playoffs				
Season	Club	Lea	GP	G	A	TP	PIM	GP	G	A	TP	PIM
1997-98	Kamloops	WHL	42	2	2	4	16	7	0	0	0	0
1998-99	Kamloops	WHL	58	7	10	17	48	15	1	1	2	8

DRUKEN, Harold (DROO-kehn) — VAN.

Center. Shoots left. 6', 205 lbs. Born, St. John's, Nfld., January 26, 1979.
(Vancouver's 3rd choice, 36th overall, in 1997 Entry Draft).

			Regular Season					Playoffs				
Season	Club	Lea	GP	G	A	TP	PIM	GP	G	A	TP	PIM
1996-97	Detroit	OHL	63	27	31	58	14	5	3	2	5	0
1997-98	Plymouth	OHL	64	38	44	82	12	15	9	11	20	4
1998-99	Plymouth	OHL	60	*58	45	103	34	11	9	12	21	14

OHL Second All-Star Team (1999)

DUCE, Bryan — N.J.

Right wing. Shoots right. 6', 200 lbs. Born, Thunder Bay, Ont., January 15, 1978.

			Regular Season					Playoffs				
Season	Club	Lea	GP	G	A	TP	PIM	GP	G	A	TP	PIM
1995-96	Kitchener	OHL	55	14	9	23	16	11	0	0	0	2
1996-97	Kitchener	OHL	62	27	30	57	36	11	5	3	8	2
1997-98	Kitchener	OHL	37	9	20	29	12	....	....	....	....	....
	S.S. Marie	OHL	21	3	2	5	4	....	....	....	....	....
1998-99	Albany	AHL	2	0	0	0	2	....	....	....	....	....
	Augusta	ECHL	68	17	27	44	33	2	0	0	0	0

Signed as a free agent by **New Jersey**, August 12, 1997.

DUDA, Radek (DOO-duh) — CGY.

Right wing. Shoots left. 6'1", 190 lbs. Born, Skolov, Czech., January 28, 1979.
(Calgary's 7th choice, 192nd overall, in 1998 Entry Draft).

			Regular Season					Playoffs				
Season	Club	Lea	GP	G	A	TP	PIM	GP	G	A	TP	PIM
1994-95	Sokolov	Czech-Jr.	36	67	37	104	....	....	....	....	....	....
1995-96	Sparta Praha	Czech-Jr.	39	15	10	25	....	....	....	....	....	....
1996-97	Sparta Praha	Cezch-Jr.	21	9	14	23	....	....	....	....	....	....
	Sokolov	CRep-2	1	0	0	0	....	....	....	....	....	....
	Sparta Praha	Cze-Rep	....	....	....	....	....	1	0	0	0	0
1997-98	Sparta Praha	Czech-Jr.	39	3	3	6	41	10	0	2	2	6
1998-99	Regina	WHL	65	24	31	55	139	....	....	....	....	....

DUERDEN, Dave — FLA.

Left wing. Shoots left. 6'2", 201 lbs. Born, Oshawa, Ont., April 11, 1977.
(Florida's 4th choice, 80th overall, in 1995 Entry Draft).

			Regular Season					Playoffs				
Season	Club	Lea	GP	G	A	TP	PIM	GP	G	A	TP	PIM
1993-94	Wexford	OJHL	47	17	27	44	26	....	....	....	....	....
1994-95	Peterborough	OHL	66	20	33	53	21	11	6	2	8	6
1995-96	Peterborough	OHL	66	35	35	70	47	24	14	13	27	16
1996-97	Peterborough	OHL	66	36	48	84	34	4	2	4	6	0
1997-98	Port Huron	UHL	7	0	4	4	10	....	....	....	....	....
	New Haven	AHL	36	6	7	13	10	....	....	....	....	....
	Fort Wayne	IHL	7	0	1	1	0	....	....	....	....	....
1998-99	Miami	ECHL	13	10	7	17	0	....	....	....	....	....
	Kentucky	AHL	36	8	9	17	9	6	0	2	2	0

OHL Second All-Star Team (1997)

DUSABEK, Joe — S.J.

Right wing. Shoots right. 6'1", 200 lbs. Born, Fairbault, MN, May 1, 1978.
(San Jose's 5th choice, 163rd overall, in 1997 Entry Draft).

			Regular Season					Playoffs				
Season	Club	Lea	GP	G	A	TP	PIM	GP	G	A	TP	PIM
1996-97	Notre Dame	CCHA	35	13	12	25	74	....	....	....	....	....
1997-98	Notre Dame	CCHA	21	1	8	9	32	....	....	....	....	....
1998-99	Notre Dame	CCHA	34	4	10	14	36	....	....	....	....	....

DUTIAUME, Mark (doo-TEE-owm) **BUF.**

Left wing. Shoots left. 6', 200 lbs. Born, Winnipeg, Man., January 31, 1977.
(Buffalo's 3rd choice, 42nd overall, in 1995 Entry Draft).

			Regular Season					Playoffs				
Season	Club	Lea	GP	G	A	TP	PIM	GP	G	A	TP	PIM
1993-94	Tri-City	WHL	3	2	0	2	0	....	....	....	....	....
	Brandon	WHL	55	4	7	11	43	12	0	2	2	6
1994-95	Brandon	WHL	62	23	21	44	80	17	1	2	3	33
1995-96	Brandon	WHL	7	0	4	4	6	9	2	1	3	12
1996-97	Brandon	WHL	48	12	11	23	73	6	2	2	4	13
	Rochester	AHL	6	1	1	2	0	....	....	....	....	....
1997-98	Rochester	AHL	11	1	0	1	4	....	....	....	....	....
	South Carolina	ECHL	28	3	4	7	24	2	0	0	0	2
1998-99	Rochester	AHL	2	0	0	0	0	....	....	....	....	....
	Binghamton	UHL	67	27	35	62	43	1	1	0	1	0

DWYER, Gordie (DWIGHR) **MTL.**

Left wing. Shoots left. 6'2", 216 lbs. Born, Dalhousie, NB, January 25, 1978.
(Montreal's 5th choice, 152nd overall, in 1998 Entry Draft).

			Regular Season					Playoffs				
Season	Club	Lea	GP	G	A	TP	PIM	GP	G	A	TP	PIM
1994-95	Hull	QMJHL	57	3	7	10	204	17	1	3	4	54
1995-96	Hull	QMJHL	25	5	9	14	199	....	....	....	....	....
	Laval	QMJHL	22	5	17	22	72	....	....	....	....	....
	Beauport	QMJHL	22	4	9	13	87	20	3	5	8	104
1996-97	Drummondville	QMJHL	66	21	48	69	393	8	6	1	7	39
1997-98	Quebec	QMJHL	59	18	27	45	365	14	4	9	13	67
1998-99	Fredericton	AHL	14	0	0	0	46	....	....	....	....	....
	New Orleans	ECHL	36	1	3	4	163	11	0	0	0	27

• Re-entered NHL draft. Originally St. Louis' 2nd choice, 67th overall, in 1996 Entry Draft.

DYMENT, Chris **MTL.**

Defense. Shoots right. 6'3", 201 lbs. Born, Stoneham, MA, October 24, 1979.
(Montreal's 3rd choice, 97th overall, in 1999 Entry Draft).

			Regular Season					Playoffs				
Season	Club	Lea	GP	G	A	TP	PIM	GP	G	A	TP	PIM
1997-98	Reading High	H.S.	22	22	22	44	15	....	....	....	....	....
1998-99	Boston University	H.E.	25	1	5	6	16	....	....	....	....	....

EATON, Mark **PHI.**

Defense. Shoots left. 6'3", 195 lbs. Born, Wilmington, DE, May 6, 1977.

			Regular Season					Playoffs				
Season	Club	Lea	GP	G	A	TP	PIM	GP	G	A	TP	PIM
1996-97	Waterloo	USHL	50	6	32	38	62	....	....	....	....	....
1997-98	Notre Dame	CCHA	41	12	17	29	32	....	....	....	....	....
1998-99	Philadelphia	AHL	74	9	27	36	38	16	4	8	12	0

Signed as a free agent by **Philadelphia**, July 28, 1998.

EDINGER, Adam **NYI**

Center. Shoots left. 6'2", 210 lbs. Born, Toledo, OH, September 21, 1977.
(NY Islanders' 7th choice, 115th overall, in 1997 Entry Draft).

			Regular Season					Playoffs				
Season	Club	Lea	GP	G	A	TP	PIM	GP	G	A	TP	PIM
1994-95	Leamington	OJHL	38	19	62	81	100	....	....	....	....	....
1995-96	Leamington	OJHL	45	45	50	95	120	....	....	....	....	....
1996-97	Bowling Green	CCHA	34	11	18	29	42	....	....	....	....	....
1997-98	Bowling Green	CCHA	27	9	13	22	62	....	....	....	....	....
1998-99	Bowling Green	CCHA	38	23	25	48	36	....	....	....	....	....

CCHA First All-Star Team (1999)

EKLUND, Per (EHK-luhnd, PAIR)

Left wing. Shoots left. 5'11", 196 lbs. Born, Sollentuna, Sweden, July 9, 1970.
(Detroit's 8th choice, 182nd overall, in 1995 Entry Draft).

			Regular Season					Playoffs				
Season	Club	Lea	GP	G	A	TP	PIM	GP	G	A	TP	PIM
1991-92	Vasby	Sweden-2	29	13	24	37	26	....	....	....	....	....
1992-93	Huddinge IK	Sweden-2	36	22	23	45	14	....	....	....	....	....
1993-94	Huddinge IK	Sweden-2	35	20	11	31	40	....	....	....	....	....
1994-95	Djurgardens	Sweden	40	19	10	29	20	3	1	1	2	4
1995-96	Djurgardens	Sweden	39	17	10	27	10	1	0	0	0	0
1996-97	Djurgardens	Sweden	50	20	16	36	14	4	1	0	1	0
1997-98	Adirondack	AHL	73	21	29	50	12	3	0	0	0	0
1998-99	Djurgardens	Sweden	48	14	9	23	49	4	0	0	0	0

ELICH, Matt **T.B.**

Right wing. Shoots right. 6'3", 187 lbs. Born, Detroit, MI, September 22, 1979.
(Tampa Bay's 3rd choice, 61st overall, in 1997 Entry Draft).

			Regular Season					Playoffs				
Season	Club	Lea	GP	G	A	TP	PIM	GP	G	A	TP	PIM
1995-96	Windsor	OHL	52	10	2	12	17	5	1	0	1	2
1996-97	Windsor	OHL	58	15	13	28	19	5	0	1	1	6
1997-98	Windsor	OHL	20	9	12	21	8	....	....	....	....	....
	Kingston	OHL	34	14	4	18	2	12	2	4	6	2
1998-99	Kingston	OHL	67	44	30	74	32	5	3	5	8	0

ELICK, Mickey (EHL-ihk)

Defense. Shoots left. 6'1", 200 lbs. Born, Calgary, Alta., March 17, 1974.
(NY Rangers' 8th choice, 192nd overall, in 1992 Entry Draft).

			Regular Season					Playoffs				
Season	Club	Lea	GP	G	A	TP	PIM	GP	G	A	TP	PIM
1991-92	Calgary	AJHL	41	18	32	50	54	....	....	....	....	....
1992-93	U. of Wisconsin	WCHA	33	1	6	7	24	....	....	....	....	....
1993-94	U. of Wisconsin	WCHA	42	7	12	19	54	....	....	....	....	....
1994-95	U. of Wisconsin	WCHA	43	5	24	29	52	....	....	....	....	....
1995-96	U. of Wisconsin	WCHA	39	14	26	40	60	....	....	....	....	....
1996-97	Charlotte	ECHL	70	25	36	61	79	3	1	0	1	14
	Binghamton	AHL	1	0	1	1	2	....	....	....	....	....
1997-98	Canada	Nat-Team	61	20	28	48	60	....	....	....	....	....
1998-99	Saint John	AHL	62	2	11	13	50	....	....	....	....	....
	Grand Rapids	IHL	17	3	6	9	8	....	....	....	....	....

Signed as a free agent by **Calgary**, July 6, 1998.

ELLIOTT, Paul **EDM.**

Defense. Shoots left. 6', 202 lbs. Born, White Rock, B.C., June 2, 1980.
(Edmonton's 5th choice, 128th overall, in 1998 Entry Draft).

			Regular Season					Playoffs				
Season	Club	Lea	GP	G	A	TP	PIM	GP	G	A	TP	PIM
1995-96	Lethbridge	WHL	2	0	0	0	0	....	....	....	....	....
1996-97	Lethbridge	WHL	46	0	8	8	17	1	0	0	0	0
1997-98	Lethbridge	WHL	48	4	18	22	35	....	....	....	....	....
	Medicine Hat	WHL	24	7	9	16	12	....	....	....	....	....
1998-99	Medicine Hat	WHL	71	11	36	47	80	....	....	....	....	....

ELOFSSON, Jonas (EHL-uhf-suhn, YEW-nuhs) **CHI.**

Defense. Shoots left. 6'1", 180 lbs. Born, Ulricehamn, Sweden, January 31, 1979.
(Edmonton's 4th choice, 94th overall, in 1997 Entry Draft).

			Regular Season					Playoffs				
Season	Club	Lea	GP	G	A	TP	PIM	GP	G	A	TP	PIM
1995-96	Farjestads BK	Sweden	26	6	11	17	18	....	....	....	....	....
1996-97	Farjestads BK	Sweden	3	0	0	0	0	5	0	1	1	0
	Farjestads BK	EuroHL	2	1	1	2	0	....	....	....	....	....
1997-98	Farjestads BK	Sweden	29	3	2	5	14	12	0	1	1	6
	Farjestads BK	EuroHL	7	1	1	2	4	....	....	....	....	....
1998-99	Farjestads BK	Sweden	40	2	7	9	18	4	0	0	0	0
	Farjestads BK	EuroHL	5	1	0	1	4	....	....	....	....	....

Traded to **Chicago** by **Edmonton** with Boris Mironov and Dean McAmmond for Chad Kilger, Daniel Cleary, Ethan Moreau and Christian Laflamme, March 20, 1999.

ELOMO, Miika (eh-LOH-moh, MEE-ka) **WSH.**

Left wing. Shoots left. 6', 200 lbs. Born, Turku, Finland, April 21, 1977.
(Washington's 2nd choice, 23rd overall, in 1995 Entry Draft).

			Regular Season					Playoffs				
Season	Club	Lea	GP	G	A	TP	PIM	GP	G	A	TP	PIM
1994-95	TPS Turku	Finn-Jr.	14	3	8	11	24	....	....	....	....	....
	Kiekko-67	Finland-2	14	9	2	11	39	....	....	....	....	....
1995-96	TPS Turku	Finn-Jr.	6	0	2	2	18	....	....	....	....	....
	Kiekko-67	Finland-2	21	9	6	15	100	....	....	....	....	....
	TPS Turku	Finland	10	1	1	2	8	3	0	0	0	2
1996-97	Portland	AHL	52	8	9	17	37	....	....	....	....	....
1997-98	Portland	AHL	33	1	1	2	54	....	....	....	....	....
	HIFK Helsinki	Finland	16	4	1	5	6	9	4	3	7	6
1998-99	TPS Turku	Finland	36	5	10	15	76	10	3	5	8	6

ELOMO, Teemu (eh-LOH-moh, TEE-moo) **DAL.**

Left wing. Shoots left. 5'11", 176 lbs. Born, Turku, Finland, January 13, 1979.
(Dallas' 5th choice, 132nd overall, in 1997 Entry Draft).

			Regular Season					Playoffs				
Season	Club	Lea	GP	G	A	TP	PIM	GP	G	A	TP	PIM
1996-97	TPS Turku	Finn-Jr.	9	6	2	8	16	....	....	....	....	....
	Kiekko-67	Finland-2	15	4	3	7	24	....	....	....	....	....
	TPS Turku	Finland	6	0	1	1	0	3	0	0	0	2
1997-98	TPS Turku	Finland	26	3	3	6	14	3	1	0	1	2
	TPS Turku	EuroHL	3	0	0	0	2	....	....	....	....	....
1998-99	TPS Turku	Finland	34	4	8	12	16	5	0	0	0	2

EMMONS, John **OTT.**

Center. Shoots left. 6'2", 205 lbs. Born, San Jose, CA, August 17, 1974.
(Calgary's 7th choice, 122nd overall, in 1993 Entry Draft).

			Regular Season					Playoffs				
Season	Club	Lea	GP	G	A	TP	PIM	GP	G	A	TP	PIM
1992-93	Yale University	ECAC	28	3	5	8	66	....	....	....	....	....
1993-94	Yale University	ECAC	25	5	12	17	66	....	....	....	....	....
1994-95	Yale University	ECAC	28	4	16	20	57	....	....	....	....	....
1995-96	Yale University	ECAC	31	8	20	28	124	....	....	....	....	....
1996-97	Dayton	ECHL	69	20	37	57	62	....	....	....	....	....
1997-98	Michigan	IHL	81	9	25	34	85	4	1	1	2	10
1998-99	Detroit	IHL	75	13	22	35	172	11	4	5	9	22

Signed as a free agent by **Ottawa**, August 7, 1998.

ENGBLOM, David (EHNG-blahm) **DET.**

Center. Shoots left. 6'1", 183 lbs. Born, Vallentuna, Sweden, June 2, 1977.
(Detroit's 10th choice, 234th overall, in 1995 Entry Draft).

			Regular Season					Playoffs				
Season	Club	Lea	GP	G	A	TP	PIM	GP	G	A	TP	PIM
1993-94	Vallentuna IK	Sweden-2	27	0	0	0	4	....	....	....	....	....
1994-95	Vallentuna IK	Sweden-2	32	1	4	5	12	....	....	....	....	....
1995-96	AIK Solna	Sweden	39	0	4	4	6	....	....	....	....	....
1996-97	AIK Solna	Sweden	39	3	1	4	10	7	0	1	1	0
1997-98	AIK Solna	Sweden	44	4	2	6	24	....	....	....	....	....
1998-99	AIK Solna	Sweden	49	5	3	8	8	....	....	....	....	....

ERSKINE, John **DAL.**

Defense. Shoots left. 6'4", 197 lbs. Born, Kingston, Ont., June 26, 1980.
(Dallas' 1st choice, 39th overall, in 1998 Entry Draft).

			Regular Season					Playoffs				
Season	Club	Lea	GP	G	A	TP	PIM	GP	G	A	TP	PIM
1996-97	Quinte Hawks	OJHL	48	4	16	20	241	....	....	....	....	....
1997-98	London	OHL	55	0	9	9	205	16	0	5	5	25
1998-99	London	OHL	57	8	12	20	208	25	5	10	15	38

ETTINGER, Trevor **EDM.**

Defense. Shoots left. 6'5", 240 lbs. Born, Truro, N.S., July 13, 1980.
(Edmonton's 7th choice, 159th overall, in 1998 Entry Draft).

			Regular Season					Playoffs				
Season	Club	Lea	GP	G	A	TP	PIM	GP	G	A	TP	PIM
1997-98	Cape Breton	QMJHL	50	1	2	3	181	3	0	0	0	7
1998-99	Cape Breton	QMJHL	61	0	5	5	376	5	0	1	1	23

EVANS, Blake **WSH.**

Center. Shoots right. 6'1", 221 lbs. Born, Kindersley, Saskatchewan, July 2, 1980.
(Washington's 10th choice, 251st overall, in 1998 Entry Draft).

			Regular Season					Playoffs				
Season	Club	Lea	GP	G	A	TP	PIM	GP	G	A	TP	PIM
1995-96	Saskatoon	SAHA	41	15	23	38	84	....	....	....	....	....
1996-97	Spokane	WHL	53	4	7	11	19	7	0	0	0	0
1997-98	Spokane	WHL	16	6	5	11	29	....	....	....	....	....
	Tri-City	WHL	57	13	29	42	102	....	....	....	....	....
1998-99	Tri-City	WHL	72	18	29	47	131	12	0	4	4	16

FADRNY, Jan (FAHD-uhr-nee, YAN) PIT.

Center. Shoots right. 6', 176 lbs. Born, Brno, Czech., June 14, 1980.
(Pittsburgh's 6th choice, 169th overall, in 1998 Entry Draft).

			Regular Season					Playoffs				
Season	Club	Lea	GP	G	A	TP	PIM	GP	G	A	TP	PIM
1995-96	Kometa Brno	Czech-Jr.	36	22	15	37	26	....	....	....	....	....
1996-97	HC Olomouc	Czech-Jr.	38	16	24	40	32	....	....	....	....	....
1997-98	Slavia Praha	Czech-Jr.	14	7	4	11	12	....	....	....	....	....
	Slavia Praha	Cze-Rep	18	1	1	2	2	3	0	0	0	4
1998-99	Brandon	WHL	45	4	17	21	36	5	1	2	3	4

FAHEY, Jim S.J.

Defense. Shoots right. 6', 215 lbs. Born, Boston, MA, May 11, 1979.
(San Jose's 9th choice, 212th overall, in 1998 Entry Draft).

			Regular Season					Playoffs				
Season	Club	Lea	GP	G	A	TP	PIM	GP	G	A	TP	PIM
1997-98	Catholic Memorial	H.S.	24	12	32	44	28	....	....	....	....	....
1998-99	Northeastern	H.E.	32	5	13	18	34	....	....	....	....	....

FARKAS, Jeff (FAHR-kuhs) TOR.

Center. Shoots left. 6'1", 175 lbs. Born, Amherst, MA, January 24, 1978.
(Toronto's 1st choice, 57th overall, in 1997 Entry Draft).

			Regular Season					Playoffs				
Season	Club	Lea	GP	G	A	TP	PIM	GP	G	A	TP	PIM
1995-96	Niagara	OJHL-B	74	64	107	171	95	....	....	....	....	....
1996-97	Boston College	H.E.	35	13	23	36	34	....	....	....	....	....
1997-98	Boston College	H.E.	40	11	28	39	42	....	....	....	....	....
1998-99	Boston College	H.E.	43	32	25	57	56	....	....	....	....	....

FARRELL, Michael WSH.

Defense. Shoots right. 6'1", 205 lbs. Born, Edina, MN, October 20, 1978.
(Washington's 9th choice, 220th overall, in 1998 Entry Draft).

			Regular Season					Playoffs				
Season	Club	Lea	GP	G	A	TP	PIM	GP	G	A	TP	PIM
1996-97	Culver Academy	H.S.				STATISTICS NOT AVAILABLE						
1997-98	Providence	H.E.	33	5	8	13	32	....	....	....	....	....
1998-99	Providence	H.E.	29	3	12	15	51	....	....	....	....	....

FAST, Brad CAR.

Defense. Shoots left. 6', 185 lbs. Born, Fort St. John, B.C., February 21, 1980.
(Carolina's 2nd choice, 84th overall, in 1999 Entry Draft).

			Regular Season					Playoffs				
Season	Club	Lea	GP	G	A	TP	PIM	GP	G	A	TP	PIM
1994-95	Fort St. John	BCAHA	40	9	26	35	40	....	....	....	....	....
1995-96	Fort St. John	BCAHA	60	53	52	105	70	....	....	....	....	....
1996-97	Prince George	BCJHL	49	3	7	10	19	....	....	....	....	....
1997-98	Prince George	BCJHL	59	10	33	43	22	....	....	....	....	....
1998-99	Prince George	BCJHL	59	27	46	73	....					

FAUTEUX, Jonathan (foh-TOH) EDM.

Defense. Shoots right. 6'2", 232 lbs. Born, Terrebone, Que., December 3, 1980.
(Edmonton's 6th choice, 139th overall, in 1999 Entry Draft).

			Regular Season					Playoffs				
Season	Club	Lea	GP	G	A	TP	PIM	GP	G	A	TP	PIM
1996-97	Val d'Or	QMJHL	62	1	2	3	26	....	....	....	....	....
1997-98	Val d'Or	QMJHL	56	4	10	14	74	....	....	....	....	....
1998-99	Val d'Or	QMJHL	59	15	33	48	139	....	....	....	....	....

FEDOROV, Fedor (FEH-duh-rahf) T.B.

Center. Shoots left. 6'3", 187 lbs. Born, Moscow, USSR, June 11, 1981.
(Tampa Bay's 7th choice, 182nd overall, in 1999 Entry Draft).

			Regular Season					Playoffs				
Season	Club	Lea	GP	G	A	TP	PIM	GP	G	A	TP	PIM
1997-98	Little Caesars	MNHL	13	3	7	10	18	....	....	....	....	....
1998-99	Port Huron	UHL	42	2	5	7	20	....	....	....	....	....

FEDORUK, Todd PHI.

Left wing. Shoots left. 6'1", 205 lbs. Born, Redwater, Alta., February 13, 1979.
(Philadelphia's 6th choice, 164th overall, in 1997 Entry Draft).

			Regular Season					Playoffs				
Season	Club	Lea	GP	G	A	TP	PIM	GP	G	A	TP	PIM
1996-97	Kelowna	WHL	31	1	5	6	87	6	0	0	0	13
1997-98	Kelowna	WHL	31	3	5	8	120	....	....	....	....	....
	Regina	WHL	21	4	3	7	80	9	1	2	3	23
1998-99	Regina	WHL	39	12	12	24	107	....	....	....	....	....
	Prince Albert	WHL	28	6	4	10	75	13	1	6	7	49

FEDOTOV, Sergei (feh-DAW-tahf) CAR.

Defense. Shoots left. 6'1", 185 lbs. Born, Moscow, USSR, January 24, 1977.
(Hartford's 2nd choice, 35th overall, in 1995 Entry Draft).

			Regular Season					Playoffs				
Season	Club	Lea	GP	G	A	TP	PIM	GP	G	A	TP	PIM
1994-95	Moscow D'amo	CIS	8	0	0	0	2	....	....	....	....	....
1995-96	Moscow D'amo-2	CIS-2				STATISTICS NOT AVAILABLE						
	Moscow D'amo	CIS	4	0	0	0	24	....	....	....	....	....
1996-97	Detroit	OHL	52	10	27	37	60	5	0	2	2	9
	Springfield	AHL	2	0	0	0	2	....	....	....	....	....
1997-98	Plymouth	OHL	38	5	11	16	33	15	3	2	5	10
	New Haven	AHL	5	0	0	0	0	....	....	....	....	....
	Richmond	ECHL	5	1	1	2	4	....	....	....	....	....
1998-99	New Haven	AHL	3	0	0	0	2	....	....	....	....	....
	Florida	ECHL	47	9	15	24	28	3	1	0	1	2

FEIL, Chris CHI.

Defense. Shoots left. 6'2", 202 lbs. Born, Orland Park, IL, April 25, 1978.
(Chicago's 11th choice, 230th overall, in 1997 Entry Draft).

			Regular Season					Playoffs				
Season	Club	Lea	GP	G	A	TP	PIM	GP	G	A	TP	PIM
1996-97	Ohio State	CCHA	33	5	4	9	119	....	....	....	....	....
1997-98	Barrie	OHL	40	3	16	19	51	6	0	0	0	15
1998-99	Barrie	OHL	67	10	31	41	158	12	1	6	7	25

FENIAK, Jeff PHI.

Defense. Shoots left. 6'5", 210 lbs. Born, Edmonton, Alta., January 31, 1981.
(Philadelphia's 2nd choice, 119th overall, in 1999 Entry Draft).

			Regular Season					Playoffs				
Season	Club	Lea	GP	G	A	TP	PIM	GP	G	A	TP	PIM
1997-98	Calgary	WHL	48	0	2	2	25	....	....	....	....	....
1998-99	Calgary	WHL	39	1	4	5	81	....	....	....	....	....

FERENCE, Andrew (fuhr-EHNS) PIT.

Defense. Shoots left. 5'10", 190 lbs. Born, Edmonton, Alta., March 17, 1979.
(Pittsburgh's 8th choice, 208th overall, in 1997 Entry Draft).

			Regular Season					Playoffs				
Season	Club	Lea	GP	G	A	TP	PIM	GP	G	A	TP	PIM
1995-96	Portland	WHL	72	9	31	40	159	7	1	3	4	12
1996-97	Portland	WHL	72	12	32	44	163	6	1	2	3	12
1997-98	Portland	WHL	72	11	57	68	142	16	2	18	20	28
1998-99	Portland	WHL	40	11	21	32	104	4	1	4	5	10
	Kansas City	IHL	5	1	2	3	4	3	0	0	0	9

WHL West First All-Star Team (1998) • WHL West Second All-Star Team (1999)

FERENCE, Brad (fuhr-EHNS) FLA.

Defense. Shoots right. 6'3", 196 lbs. Born, Calgary, Alta., April 2, 1979.
(Vancouver's 1st choice, 10th overall, in 1997 Entry Draft).

			Regular Season					Playoffs				
Season	Club	Lea	GP	G	A	TP	PIM	GP	G	A	TP	PIM
1995-96	Spokane	WHL	5	0	2	2	18	....	....	....	....	....
1996-97	Spokane	WHL	67	6	20	26	324	9	0	4	4	21
1997-98	Spokane	WHL	54	9	30	39	213	18	0	7	7	59
1998-99	Spokane	WHL	31	3	22	25	125	....	....	....	....	....
	Tri-City	WHL	20	6	15	21	116	12	1	9	10	63

Memorial Cup All-Star Team (1998)

Traded to **Florida** by **Vancouver** with Pavel Bure, Bret Hedican and Vancouver's 3rd round choice in 2000 Entry Draft for Ed Jovanovski, Dave Gagner, Mike Brown, Kevin Weekes and Florida's 1st round choice in 2000 Entry Draft, January 17, 1999.

FERONE, Paul VAN.

Right wing. Shoots right. 5'11", 180 lbs. Born, Vancouver, B.C., April 2, 1976.

			Regular Season					Playoffs				
Season	Club	Lea	GP	G	A	TP	PIM	GP	G	A	TP	PIM
1995-96	Seattle	WHL	63	14	19	33	241	5	0	1	1	31
1996-97	Seattle	WHL	59	20	21	41	155	15	1	4	5	41
1997-98	Syracuse	AHL	20	1	3	4	85	....	....	....	....	....
	Raleigh	ECHL	50	1	3	4	152	4	0	0	0	8
1998-99	Syracuse	AHL	28	0	2	2	109	....	....	....	....	....

Signed as a free agent by **Vancouver**, September 19, 1997.

FIBIGER, Jesse ANA.

Defense. Shoots left. 6'3", 205 lbs. Born, Victoria, B.C., April 4, 1978.
(Anaheim's 5th choice, 178th overall, in 1998 Entry Draft).

			Regular Season					Playoffs				
Season	Club	Lea	GP	G	A	TP	PIM	GP	G	A	TP	PIM
1996-97	Victoria	BCJHL	53	6	18	24	88	....	....	....	....	....
1997-98	U. Minn-Duluth	WCHA	40	3	6	9	82	....	....	....	....	....
1998-99	U. Minn-Duluth	WCHA	36	4	16	20	61	....	....	....	....	....

FILATOV, Anatoli (fih-LAH-tohv) S.J.

Right wing. Shoots right. 5'10", 180 lbs. Born, Kamenogorsk, USSR, March 29, 1975.
(San Jose's 10th choice, 158th overall, in 1993 Entry Draft).

			Regular Season					Playoffs				
Season	Club	Lea	GP	G	A	TP	PIM	GP	G	A	TP	PIM
1992-93	UST Kamenogorsk	CIS	17	4	0	4	14	....	....	....	....	....
1993-94	UST Kamenogorsk	CIS	20	3	3	6	22	....	....	....	....	....
	Niagara Falls	OHL	4	3	1	4	0	....	....	....	....	....
1994-95	UST Kamenogorsk	CIS	33	6	6	12	30	....	....	....	....	....
	Niagara Falls	OHL	12	2	3	5	6	....	....	....	....	....
1995-96	UST Kamenogorsk	CIS	48	9	15	24	78	....	....	....	....	....
1996-97	UST Kamenogorsk	Russia-2	25	14	14	28	28	....	....	....	....	....
1997-98	Sibir Novosibirsk	Russia	25	2	4	6	26	....	....	....	....	....
1998-99	Nizhny Novgorod	Russia-2	11	7	6	13	10	....	....	....	....	....

FINNSTROM, Johan (FIHN-struhm) CGY.

Defense. Shoots left. 6'3", 205 lbs. Born, Broby, Sweden, March 27, 1976.
(Calgary's 5th choice, 97th overall, in 1994 Entry Draft).

			Regular Season					Playoffs				
Season	Club	Lea	GP	G	A	TP	PIM	GP	G	A	TP	PIM
1993-94	HC Rogle	Sweden	7	1	1	2	2	....	....	....	....	....
1994-95	HC Rogle	Sweden	19	0	0	0	10	....	....	....	....	....
1995-96	HC Rogle	Sweden	18	0	0	0	10	....	....	....	....	....
1996-97	HC Rogle	Sweden-2	31	1	5	6	59	....	....	....	....	....
1997-98	Lulea HF	EuroHL	6	0	0	0	4	....	....	....	....	....
	Lulea HF	Sweden	45	0	1	1	17	3	0	0	0	0
1998-99	Lulea HF	Sweden	49	1	8	9	63	9	0	4	4	12

FISCHER, Jiri (FIHSH-uhr, YIH-ree) DET.

Defense. Shoots left. 6'5", 210 lbs. Born, Horovice, Czech., July 31, 1980.
(Detroit's 1st choice, 25th overall, in 1998 Entry Draft).

			Regular Season					Playoffs				
Season	Club	Lea	GP	G	A	TP	PIM	GP	G	A	TP	PIM
1995-96	Poldi Kladno	Czech-Jr.	39	6	10	16	....	....	....	....	....	....
1996-97	Poldi Kladno	Czech-Jr.	38	7	21	28	....	....	....	....	....	....
1997-98	Hull	QMJHL	70	3	19	22	112	11	1	4	5	16
1998-99	Hull	QMJHL	65	22	56	78	141	23	6	17	23	44

QMJHL First All-Star Team (1999)

FISHER, Mike OTT.

Center. Shoots right. 6', 180 lbs. Born, Peterborough, Ont., June 5, 1980.
(Ottawa's 2nd choice, 44th overall, in 1998 Entry Draft).

			Regular Season					Playoffs				
Season	Club	Lea	GP	G	A	TP	PIM	GP	G	A	TP	PIM
1996-97	Peterborough	OJHL	51	26	30	56	35	....	....	....	....	....
1997-98	Sudbury	OHL	66	24	25	49	65	9	2	2	4	13
1998-99	Sudbury	OHL	68	41	65	106	55	4	2	1	3	4

FITZGERALD, Randy

Left wing. Shoots left. 5'9", 175 lbs. Born, Toronto, Ont., September 5, 1979.
(Carolina's 8th choice, 199th overall, in 1997 Entry Draft).

			Regular Season					Playoffs				
Season	Club	Lea	GP	G	A	TP	PIM	GP	G	A	TP	PIM
1996-97	Detroit	OHL	65	12	18	30	123	5	0	1	1	13
1997-98	Plymouth	OHL	54	11	24	35	104	15	6	3	9	46
1998-99	Plymouth	OHL	64	15	34	49	144	11	3	7	10	16

FLICHEL, Marty (FLICK-ehl)

Right wing. Shoots left. 5'11", 175 lbs. Born, Hodgeville, Sask., March 6, 1976.
(Dallas' 6th choice, 228th overall, in 1994 Entry Draft).

			Regular Season					Playoffs				
Season	Club	Lea	GP	G	A	TP	PIM	GP	G	A	TP	PIM
1991-92	Swift Current	SAHA	69	126	88	214	198	...	...	...	...	...
1992-93	Tacoma	WHL	61	21	20	41	19	7	0	0	0	8
1993-94	Tacoma	WHL	72	27	48	75	69	8	1	4	5	13
1994-95	Tacoma	WHL	67	25	53	78	81	4	2	3	5	8
1995-96	Kelowna	WHL	69	28	79	107	107	6	1	6	7	10
1996-97	Daytona	ECHL	28	17	16	33	24	2	0	1	1	4
	Michigan	IHL	19	2	3	5	10	...	...	...	...	...
1997-98	Michigan	IHL	74	18	16	34	56	4	0	0	0	23
1998-99	Michigan	IHL	70	15	28	43	57	1	0	0	0	0

FLINN, Ryan

Left wing. Shoots left. 6'4", 210 lbs. Born, Halifax, N.S., April 20, 1980.
(New Jersey's 8th choice, 143rd overall, in 1998 Entry Draft).

			Regular Season					Playoffs				
Season	Club	Lea	GP	G	A	TP	PIM	GP	G	A	TP	PIM
1996-97	Laval	QMJHL	23	3	2	5	56	2	0	0	0	0
1997-98	Laval	QMJHL	59	4	12	16	217	15	1	0	1	63
1998-99	Bathurst	QMJHL	44	3	4	7	195	23	2	0	2	37

FOCHT, Dan (FOHKT) **PHX.**

Defense. Shoots left. 6'6", 240 lbs. Born, Regina, Sask., December 31, 1977.
(Phoenix's 1st choice, 11th overall, in 1996 Entry Draft).

			Regular Season					Playoffs				
Season	Club	Lea	GP	G	A	TP	PIM	GP	G	A	TP	PIM
1995-96	Tri-City	WHL	63	6	12	18	161	11	1	1	2	23
1996-97	Tri-City	WHL	28	0	5	5	92	...	...	...	...	...
	Regina	WHL	22	2	2	4	59	5	0	2	2	8
	Springfield	AHL	1	0	0	0	2	...	...	...	...	...
1997-98	Springfield	AHL	61	2	5	7	125	3	0	0	0	4
1998-99	Mississippi	ECHL	2	0	0	0	6	...	...	...	...	...
	Springfield	AHL	30	0	2	2	58	3	1	0	1	10

FORBES, Ian **PHI.**

Defense. Shoots left. 6'6", 180 lbs. Born, Brampton, Ont., August 2, 1980.
(Philadelphia's 3rd choice, 51st overall, in 1998 Entry Draft).

			Regular Season					Playoffs				
Season	Club	Lea	GP	G	A	TP	PIM	GP	G	A	TP	PIM
1996-97	Mississauga	OJHL	39	10	32	42	178	...	...	...	...	...
1997-98	Guelph	OHL	61	2	3	5	164	12	0	0	0	16
1998-99	Guelph	OHL	60	1	8	9	182	5	0	1	1	8

FÖRSANDER, Johan (fohr-SAHN-duhr, YOO-hahn) **DET.**

Left wing. Shoots left. 6'1", 174 lbs. Born, Jonkoping, Sweden, April 28, 1978.
(Detroit's 3rd choice, 108th overall, in 1996 Entry Draft).

			Regular Season					Playoffs				
Season	Club	Lea	GP	G	A	TP	PIM	GP	G	A	TP	PIM
1995-96	HV Jonkoping	Swede-Jr.	27	15	8	23	12	...	...	...	...	...
	HV Jonkoping	Sweden	6	0	0	0	0	3	0	0	0	2
1996-97	HV Jonkoping	Sweden	44	3	2	5	6	5	0	0	0	0
1997-98	HV Jonkoping	Sweden	46	3	2	5	12	5	0	0	0	0
1998-99	HV Jonkoping	Sweden	48	5	4	9	6	...	...	...	...	...

FORSTER, Nathan **WSH.**

Defense. Shoots right. 6'1", 195 lbs. Born, Vancouver, B.C., July 3, 1980.
(Washington's 7th choice, 179th overall, in 1998 Entry Draft).

			Regular Season					Playoffs				
Season	Club	Lea	GP	G	A	TP	PIM	GP	G	A	TP	PIM
1996-97	Seattle	WHL	22	1	2	3	39	4	0	0	0	0
1997-98	Seattle	WHL	68	1	12	13	153	5	0	1	1	8
1998-99	Seattle	WHL	65	5	17	22	153	10	0	2	2	26

FORTIER, Francois **NYR**

Left wing. Shoots left. 5'11", 190 lbs. Born, Beauport, Que., June 13, 1979.

			Regular Season					Playoffs				
Season	Club	Lea	GP	G	A	TP	PIM	GP	G	A	TP	PIM
1996-97	Sherbrooke	QMJHL	62	21	16	37	74	3	0	2	2	2
1997-98	Sherbrooke	QMJHL	70	36	52	88	42	...	...	...	...	...
1998-99	Sherbrooke	QMJHL	48	36	40	76	8	13	6	9	15	4
	Hartford	AHL	1	0	0	0	0	...	...	...	...	...

Signed as a free agent by **NY Rangers**, October 1, 1998.

FORTIN, Jean-Francois (fohr-TEHN) **WSH.**

Defense. Shoots right. 6'2", 200 lbs. Born, Laval, Que., March 15, 1979.
(Washington's 2nd choice, 35th overall, in 1997 Entry Draft).

			Regular Season					Playoffs				
Season	Club	Lea	GP	G	A	TP	PIM	GP	G	A	TP	PIM
1995-96	Sherbrooke	QMJHL	69	7	15	22	40	7	2	6	8	2
1996-97	Sherbrooke	QMJHL	59	7	30	37	89	2	0	1	1	14
1997-98	Sherbrooke	QMJHL	55	12	25	37	37	...	...	...	...	...
1998-99	Sherbrooke	QMJHL	64	17	33	50	78	12	5	13	18	20

FRANCZ, Robert (FRANZ) **PHX.**

Left wing. Shoots left. 6'1", 194 lbs. Born, Bad Muskau, East Germany, March 30, 1978.
(Phoenix's 4th choice, 151st overall, in 1997 Entry Draft).

			Regular Season					Playoffs				
Season	Club	Lea	GP	G	A	TP	PIM	GP	G	A	TP	PIM
1995-96	Augsburger EV	German-Jr.	7	1	1	2	62	...	...	...	...	...
	Augsburger EV	Germany	36	0	1	1	43	6	0	0	0	0
1996-97	Peterborough	OHL	60	9	21	30	149	8	1	1	2	17
1997-98	Peterborough	OHL	60	24	27	51	135	4	1	0	1	10
1998-99	Peterborough	OHL	65	25	32	57	171	5	0	2	2	12
	Springfield	AHL	2	1	0	1	4	1	0	0	0	0

FREADRICH, Kyle (FREE-drihk) **T.B.**

Left wing. Shoots left. 6'6", 225 lbs. Born, Edmonton, Alta., December 28, 1978.
(Vancouver's 4th choice, 64th overall, in 1997 Entry Draft).

			Regular Season					Playoffs				
Season	Club	Lea	GP	G	A	TP	PIM	GP	G	A	TP	PIM
1995-96	Killam	AAHA	37	11	22	33	176	...	...	...	...	...
1996-97	Prince George	WHL	12	0	0	0	12	...	...	...	...	...
	Regina	WHL	50	1	3	4	152	4	0	0	0	8
1997-98	Regina	WHL	62	6	5	11	259	9	0	1	1	25
1998-99	Regina	WHL	52	2	2	4	215	...	...	...	...	...
	Syracuse	AHL	5	0	0	0	20	...	...	...	...	...
	Louisiana	ECHL	5	0	0	0	17	4	0	0	0	2

Signed as a free agent by **Tampa Bay**, July 16, 1999.

FROGREN, Jonas (FREW-grehn, YOH-nuhs) **CGY.**

Defense. Shoots left. 6'1", 190 lbs. Born, Falun, Sweden, August 28, 1980.
(Calgary's 8th choice, 206th overall, in 1998 Entry Draft).

			Regular Season					Playoffs				
Season	Club	Lea	GP	G	A	TP	PIM	GP	G	A	TP	PIM
1996-97	Farjestads BK	Swede-Jr.	20	2	7	9	4	...	...	...	...	...
1997-98	Farjestads BK	Swede-Jr.	28	5	6	11	12	...	...	...	...	...
1998-99	Farjestads BK	Swede-Jr.	14	1	5	6	12	...	...	...	...	...
	Farjestads BK	Sweden	22	0	0	0	2	...	...	...	...	...

FRYLEN, Edvin (FREE-ew-lihn) **ST.L.**

Defense. Shoots left. 6', 211 lbs. Born, Jarfalla, Sweden, December 23, 1975.
(St. Louis' 3rd choice, 120th overall, in 1994 Entry Draft).

			Regular Season					Playoffs				
Season	Club	Lea	GP	G	A	TP	PIM	GP	G	A	TP	PIM
1991-92	Vasteras IK	Sweden	2	0	0	0	0	...	...	...	...	...
1992-93	Vasteras IK	Sweden	29	0	2	2	14	3	0	0	0	0
1993-94	Vasteras IK	Sweden	32	1	0	1	26	...	...	...	...	...
1994-95	Vasteras IK	Sweden	25	2	1	3	14	4	0	0	0	4
1995-96	Vasteras IK	Sweden	39	8	5	13	16	...	...	...	...	...
1996-97	Vasteras IK	Sweden	47	8	3	11	32	...	...	...	...	...
1997-98	Vasteras IK	Sweden	46	4	7	11	36	...	...	...	...	...
1998-99	Vasteras IK	Sweden	50	6	20	26	36	...	...	...	...	...

GAFFANEY, Brian **PIT.**

Defense. Shoots left. 6'5", 205 lbs. Born, Alexandria, MN, October 4, 1977.
(Pittsburgh's 2nd choice, 44th overall, in 1997 Entry Draft).

			Regular Season					Playoffs				
Season	Club	Lea	GP	G	A	TP	PIM	GP	G	A	TP	PIM
1996-97	North Iowa	USHL	48	8	13	21	49	...	...	...	...	...
1997-98	St. Cloud State	WCHA	26	0	2	2	37	...	...	...	...	...
1998-99	St. Cloud State	WCHA	37	3	5	8	45	...	...	...	...	...

GAGNE, Simon (GAH nyay) **PHI.**

Center. Shoots left. 6', 175 lbs. Born, Ste. Foy, Que., February 29, 1980.
(Philadelphia's 1st choice, 22nd overall, in 1998 Entry Draft).

			Regular Season					Playoffs				
Season	Club	Lea	GP	G	A	TP	PIM	GP	G	A	TP	PIM
1996-97	Beauport	QMJHL	51	9	22	31	49	...	...	...	...	...
1997-98	Quebec	QMJHL	53	30	39	69	26	12	11	5	16	23
1998-99	Quebec	QMJHL	61	50	70	120	42	13	9	8	17	4

QMJHL Second All-Star Team (1999)

GAGNON, Jonathan (GAN-YAW) **TOR.**

Center. Shoots left. 6'1", 187 lbs. Born, Montreal, Que., May 20, 1980.
(Toronto's 7th choice, 181st overall, in 1998 Entry Draft).

			Regular Season					Playoffs				
Season	Club	Lea	GP	G	A	TP	PIM	GP	G	A	TP	PIM
1996-97	Val D'Or	QMJHL	65	5	15	20	35	13	1	0	1	2
1997-98	Val D'Or	QMJHL	40	9	19	28	54	...	...	...	...	...
	Cape Breton	QMJHL	29	6	7	13	25	4	2	3	5	12
1998-99	Cape Breton	QMJHL	68	27	37	64	39	5	2	4	6	2

GAINEY, Steve **DAL.**

Left wing. Shoots left. 6', 180 lbs. Born, Montreal, Que., January 26, 1979.
(Dallas' 3rd choice, 77th overall, in 1997 Entry Draft).

			Regular Season					Playoffs				
Season	Club	Lea	GP	G	A	TP	PIM	GP	G	A	TP	PIM
1995-96	Kamloops	WHL	49	1	4	5	40	3	0	0	0	0
1996-97	Kamloops	WHL	60	9	18	27	60	2	0	0	0	9
1997-98	Kamloops	WHL	68	21	34	55	93	7	1	7	8	15
1998-99	Kamloops	WHL	68	30	34	64	155	15	5	4	9	38

GARDINER, Peter **CHI.**

Right wing. Shoots right. 6'5", 220 lbs. Born, Toronto, Ont., September 29, 1977.
(Chicago's 6th choice, 120th overall, in 1997 Entry Draft).

			Regular Season					Playoffs				
Season	Club	Lea	GP	G	A	TP	PIM	GP	G	A	TP	PIM
1996-97	RPI Engineers	ECAC	36	10	21	31	47	...	...	...	...	...
1997-98	RPI Engineers	ECAC	35	10	9	19	52	...	...	...	...	...
1998-99	RPI Engineers	ECAC	37	17	21	38	76	...	...	...	...	...

GAUVREAU, Brent — CGY.

Right wing. Shoots right. 6'3", 191 lbs. Born, Sudbury, Ont., June 29, 1980.
(Calgary's 6th choice, 120th overall, in 1998 Entry Draft).

			Regular Season					Playoffs				
Season	Club	Lea	GP	G	A	TP	PIM	GP	G	A	TP	PIM
1996-97	Oshawa	OHL	59	8	13	21	13	18	1	5	6	2
1997-98	Oshawa	OHL	66	25	42	67	39	7	3	1	4	2
1998-99	Oshawa	OHL	68	33	62	95	57	15	9	11	20	15

GILLAM, Sean

Defense. Shoots right. 6'2", 187 lbs. Born, Lethbridge, Alta., May 7, 1976.
(Detroit's 3rd choice, 75th overall, in 1994 Entry Draft).

			Regular Season					Playoffs				
Season	Club	Lea	GP	G	A	TP	PIM	GP	G	A	TP	PIM
1992-93	Spokane	WHL	70	6	27	33	121	10	0	2	2	10
1993-94	Spokane	WHL	70	7	17	24	106	3	0	0	0	6
1994-95	Spokane	WHL	72	16	40	56	192	11	0	3	3	33
1995-96	Spokane	WHL	69	11	58	69	123	18	2	12	14	26
1996-97	Adirondack	AHL	64	1	7	8	50	....	....	....	....	....
1997-98	Adirondack	AHL	73	1	9	10	60	3	1	0	1	0
1998-99	Adirondack	AHL	68	1	10	11	75	3	1	0	1	6

WHL West Second All-Star Team (1995, 1996)

GILLIS, Nick — OTT.

Right wing. Shoots right. 6', 188 lbs. Born, Cambridge, MA, February 20, 1978.
(Ottawa's 7th choice, 203rd overall, in 1997 Entry Draft).

			Regular Season					Playoffs				
Season	Club	Lea	GP	G	A	TP	PIM	GP	G	A	TP	PIM
1992-93	Boston Jr. Bruins	USAHA	60	58	70	128	112	....	....	....	....	....
1993-94	Cushing Academy	H.S.	28	15	38	53	62	....	....	....	....	....
1994-95	Cushing Academy	H.S.	34	34	58	92	47	....	....	....	....	....
1996-97	Cushing Academy	H.S.	32	30	54	84	27	....	....	....	....	....
1997-98	Boston University	H.E.	34	8	12	20	43	....	....	....	....	....
1998-99	Boston University	H.E.	33	3	16	19	37	....	....	....	....	....

GIONTA, Brian (jee-OHN-tuh) — N.J.

Right wing. Shoots right. 5'7", 160 lbs. Born, Rochester, NY, January 18, 1979.
(New Jersey's 4th choice, 82nd overall, in 1998 Entry Draft).

			Regular Season					Playoffs				
Season	Club	Lea	GP	G	A	TP	PIM	GP	G	A	TP	PIM
1997-98	Boston College	H.E.	40	30	32	62	44	....	....	....	....	....
1998-99	Boston College	H.E.	39	27	33	60	46	....	....	....	....	....

Hockey East Second All-Star Team (1998) • NCAA East Second All-American Team (1998) • Hockey East First All-Star Team (1999) • NCAA East First All-American Team (1999)

GIROUX, Ray (zhih-ROO) — NYI

Defense. Shoots left. 6', 180 lbs. Born, North Bay, Ont., July 20, 1976.
(Philadelphia's 7th choice, 202nd overall, in 1994 Entry Draft).

			Regular Season					Playoffs				
Season	Club	Lea	GP	G	A	TP	PIM	GP	G	A	TP	PIM
1993-94	Powasson	OJHL	36	10	40	50	42	....	....	....	....	....
1994-95	Yale University	ECAC	27	1	3	4	8	....	....	....	....	....
1995-96	Yale University	ECAC	30	3	16	19	36	....	....	....	....	....
1996-97	Yale University	ECAC	32	9	12	21	38	....	....	....	....	....
1997-98	Yale University	ECAC	35	9	*30	39	62	....	....	....	....	....
1998-99	Lowell	AHL	59	13	19	32	92	3	1	1	2	0

ECAC First All-Star Team (1998) • NCAA East First All-American Team (1998)

Rights traded to **NY Islanders** by **Philadelphia** for NY Islanders' 6th round choice in 2000 Entry Draft, August 25, 1998.

GOC, Sascha (GAWCH, SA-shah) — N.J.

Defense. Shoots right. 6'1", 225 lbs. Born, Calw, West Germany, April 17, 1979.
(New Jersey's 5th choice, 159th overall, in 1997 Entry Draft).

			Regular Season					Playoffs				
Season	Club	Lea	GP	G	A	TP	PIM	GP	G	A	TP	PIM
1995-96	Schwenninger	German-Jr.	11	3	6	9	77	....	....	....	....	....
	Schwenninger	Germany	1	0	0	0	0	....	....	....	....	....
1996-97	Schwenningen	Germany	41	3	1	4	28	5	0	0	0	0
1997-98	Schwenningen	Germany	49	5	5	10	45	....	....	....	....	....
1998-99	Albany	AHL	55	1	12	13	24	2	0	0	0	0

GOETZINGER, Jeremy — DET.

Defense. Shoots left. 6'4", 200 lbs. Born, Calgary, Alta., June 26, 1980.
(Detroit's 9th choice, 198th overall, in 1998 Entry Draft).

			Regular Season					Playoffs				
Season	Club	Lea	GP	G	A	TP	PIM	GP	G	A	TP	PIM
1996-97	Prince Albert	WHL	57	0	4	4	19	4	0	0	0	0
1997-98	Prince Albert	WHL	69	4	6	10	78	....	....	....	....	....
1998-99	Prince Albert	WHL	51	2	17	19	42	14	0	3	3	4

GOLDADE, Aaron — BUF.

Center. Shoots left. 6', 180 lbs. Born, Prince Albert, Sask., July 30, 1980.
(Buffalo's 6th choice, 137th overall, in 1998 Entry Draft).

			Regular Season					Playoffs				
Season	Club	Lea	GP	G	A	TP	PIM	GP	G	A	TP	PIM
1996-97	Brandon	WHL	59	4	10	14	51	6	0	1	1	0
1997-98	Brandon	WHL	66	19	16	35	58	16	0	2	2	22
1998-99	Brandon	WHL	64	27	33	60	56	5	0	1	1	8

GOLDMANN, Erich (GOHLD-mahn, AIR-ihkh) — OTT.

Defense. Shoots left. 6'3", 196 lbs. Born, Dingolfing, West Germany, April 7, 1976.
(Ottawa's 5th choice, 212th overall, in 1996 Entry Draft).

			Regular Season					Playoffs				
Season	Club	Lea	GP	G	A	TP	PIM	GP	G	A	TP	PIM
1988-89	Cincinnati	IHL	5	0	1	1	7	....	....	....	....	....
1993-94	EV Landshut	Germany	33	0	0	0	4	7	0	0	0	0
1994-95	Mannheim	Germany	31	0	0	0	22	10	1	0	1	2
1995-96	Mannheim	Germany	47	0	3	3	40	8	0	0	0	4
1996-97	ESV Kaufbeuren	Germany	44	2	4	6	58	6	1	0	1	2
1997-98	Worcester	AHL	31	0	2	2	40	....	....	....	....	....
	Germany	Olympics	4	0	1	1	27	....	....	....	....	....
	Detroit	IHL	3	0	0	0	2	....	....	....	....	....
	Dayton	ECHL	3	0	2	2	5	5	0	0	0	8
1998-99	Hershey	AHL	21	1	1	2	23	....	....	....	....	....
	Cincinnati	AHL	32	0	2	2	18	3	0	0	0	2

GOMEZ, Scott (GOH-mehz) — N.J.

Center. Shoots left. 5'11", 200 lbs. Born, Anchorage, AK, December 23, 1979.
(New Jersey's 2nd choice, 27th overall, in 1998 Entry Draft).

			Regular Season					Playoffs				
Season	Club	Lea	GP	G	A	TP	PIM	GP	G	A	TP	PIM
1996-97	Surrey	BCJHL	56	48	76	124	94	....	....	....	....	....
1997-98	Tri-City	WHL	45	12	37	49	57	....	....	....	....	....
1998-99	Tri-City	WHL	58	30	78	108	55	10	6	13	19	31

WHL West First All-Star Team (1999)

GORDON, Heath — CHI.

Right wing. Shoots left. 6'2", 197 lbs. Born, Boston, MA, May 28, 1978.
(Chicago's 8th choice, 147th overall, in 1997 Entry Draft).

			Regular Season					Playoffs				
Season	Club	Lea	GP	G	A	TP	PIM	GP	G	A	TP	PIM
1996-97	Green Bay	USHL	52	16	28	44	71	....	....	....	....	....
1997-98	Providence	H.E.	18	2	2	4	22	....	....	....	....	....
1998-99	Providence	H.E.	30	7	10	17	16	....	....	....	....	....

GORDON, Rhett — PHX.

Right wing. Shoots right. 5'11", 175 lbs. Born, Regina, Sask., August 26, 1976.

			Regular Season					Playoffs				
Season	Club	Lea	GP	G	A	TP	PIM	GP	G	A	TP	PIM
1992-93	Regina	AAHA	33	21	16	37	69	....	....	....	....	....
	Regina	WHL	2	1	0	1	2	4	0	0	0	0
1993-94	Regina	WHL	60	19	28	47	14	4	0	0	0	7
1994-95	Regina	WHL	71	36	43	79	64	4	2	2	4	0
1995-96	Regina	WHL	66	53	50	103	68	11	9	4	13	10
	Springfield	AHL	2	0	0	0	2	1	0	0	0	0
1996-97	Springfield	AHL	54	11	11	22	54	8	1	2	3	6
1997-98	Springfield	AHL	75	17	11	28	54	4	1	1	2	0
1998-99	Manitoba	IHL	76	14	23	37	61	5	0	0	0	0

WHL West First All-Star Team (1996)

Signed as a free agent by **Winnipeg**, September 29, 1994. Rights transferred to **Phoenix** after **Winnipeg** franchise relocated, July 1, 1996.

GOREN, Lee — BOS.

Right wing. Shoots right. 6'3", 190 lbs. Born, Winnipeg, Man., December 26, 1977.
(Boston's 5th choice, 63rd overall, in 1997 Entry Draft).

			Regular Season					Playoffs				
Season	Club	Lea	GP	G	A	TP	PIM	GP	G	A	TP	PIM
1995-96	Minot	SJHL	64	31	55	86	....	....	....	....	....	....
1996-97	North Dakota	WCHA	DID NOT PLAY – FRESHMAN									
1997-98	North Dakota	WCHA	29	3	13	16	26	....	....	....	....	....
1998-99	North Dakota	WCHA	38	26	19	45	20	....	....	....	....	....

GOSSELIN, Christian (gawz-LEH) — S.J.

Defense. Shoots right. 6'5", 235 lbs. Born, Laval, Que., August 21, 1976.
(New Jersey's 5th choice, 129th overall, in 1994 Entry Draft).

			Regular Season					Playoffs				
Season	Club	Lea	GP	G	A	TP	PIM	GP	G	A	TP	PIM
1993-94	St-Hyacinthe	QMJHL	12	3	2	5	16	....	....	....	....	....
1994-95	St-Hyacinthe	QMJHL	60	5	10	15	202	5	0	0	0	11
1995-96	Laval	QMJHL	21	1	8	9	69	....	....	....	....	....
1996-97	Macon	CHL	63	8	10	18	229	....	....	....	....	....
1997-98	Pensacola	ECHL	42	6	5	11	181	18	0	1	1	52
	Fredericton	AHL	6	0	0	0	17	....	....	....	....	....
1998-99	Kentucky	AHL	31	1	1	2	107	....	....	....	....	....

Signed as a free agent by **San Jose**, July 15, 1998.

GOSSELIN, David (gawz-LEH) — NSH.

Right wing. Shoots right. 6', 175 lbs. Born, Levis, Que., June 22, 1977.
(New Jersey's 4th choice, 78th overall, in 1995 Entry Draft).

			Regular Season					Playoffs				
Season	Club	Lea	GP	G	A	TP	PIM	GP	G	A	TP	PIM
1994-95	Sherbrooke	QMJHL	58	8	8	16	36	7	0	0	0	2
1995-96	Sherbrooke	QMJHL	55	24	24	48	147	7	2	2	4	4
1996-97	Sherbrooke	QMJHL	23	11	15	26	52	....	....	....	....	....
	Chicoutimi	QMJHL	28	16	33	49	65	12	9	7	16	16
1997-98	Chicoutimi	QMJHL	69	46	64	110	139	6	1	4	5	8
1998-99	Milwaukee	IHL	74	17	11	28	78	2	0	2	2	2

Signed as a free agent by **Nashville**, July 1, 1998.

GRACHEV, Vladimir (grah-CHEHF) — NYI

Left wing. Shoots left. 6', 178 lbs. Born, Moscow, USSR, January 28, 1973.
(NY Islanders' 6th choice, 152nd overall, in 1992 Entry Draft).

			Regular Season					Playoffs				
Season	Club	Lea	GP	G	A	TP	PIM	GP	G	A	TP	PIM
1991-92	Moscow D'amo-2	CIS-3	62	13	3	16	26	....	....	....	....	....
1992-93	Moscow D'amo	CIS	33	2	1	3	26	7	0	0	0	2
1993-94	Moscow D'amo	CIS	36	4	3	7	10	6	0	0	0	4
1994-95	Moscow D'amo	CIS	48	13	8	21	20	14	7	2	9	10
1995-96	Moscow D'amo	CIS	44	5	9	14	16	11	2	1	3	2
1996-97	Moscow D'amo	Russia	35	2	8	10	14	4	0	2	2	2
1997-98	Nizhnekamsk	Russia	46	10	10	20	12	....	....	....	....	....
1998-99	Nizhnekamsk	Russia	DID NOT PLAY – INJURED									

GRENIER, Martin (GREH-nyay) — COL.

Defense. Shoots left. 6'5", 231 lbs. Born, Laval, Que., November 2, 1980.
(Colorado's 2nd choice, 45th overall, in 1999 Entry Draft).

			Regular Season					Playoffs				
Season	Club	Lea	GP	G	A	TP	PIM	GP	G	A	TP	PIM
1996-97	St. Jerome	QAAA	34	3	16	19	117	....	....	....	....	....
1997-98	Quebec	QMJHL	61	4	11	15	202	14	0	2	2	36
1998-99	Quebec	QMJHL	60	7	18	25	*479	13	0	4	4	29

GRIFFIN, Sean — CHI.

Defense. Shoots left. 6'3", 193 lbs. Born, Ottawa, Ont., April 18, 1980.
(Chicago's 7th choice, 210th overall, in 1998 Entry Draft).

			Regular Season					Playoffs				
Season	Club	Lea	GP	G	A	TP	PIM	GP	G	A	TP	PIM
1997-98	Kingston	OHL	63	0	6	6	97	12	0	0	0	13
1998-99	Kingston	OHL	59	1	19	20	151	5	0	0	0	10

GRIMES, Kevin — OTT.

Defense. Shoots left. 6'2", 205 lbs. Born, Ottawa, Ont., August 19, 1979.
(Colorado's 1st choice, 26th overall, in 1997 Entry Draft).

			Regular Season					Playoffs				
Season	Club	Lea	GP	G	A	TP	PIM	GP	G	A	TP	PIM
1996-97	Kingston	OHL	57	2	12	14	188	1	0	0	0	0
1997-98	Kingston	OHL	62	1	27	28	179	12	0	1	1	16
1998-99	Kingston	OHL	56	5	20	25	184	5	2	3	5	12

Signed as a free agent by **Ottawa**, August 24, 1999.

GRON, Stanislav — (GRAHN) — N.J.

Center. Shoots left. 6'2", 210 lbs. Born, Bratislava, Czech., October 28, 1978.
(New Jersey's 2nd choice, 38th overall, in 1997 Entry Draft).

			Regular Season					Playoffs				
Season	Club	Lea	GP	G	A	TP	PIM	GP	G	A	TP	PIM
1996-97	Bratislava	Slovak-Jr.	22	20	16	36	....	....	....	....	....	....
	Bratislava	Slovakia	7	0	0	0	....	....	....	....	....	....
1997-98	Seattle	WHL	61	9	29	38	21	5	1	5	6	0
1998-99	Kootenay	WHL	49	28	18	46	18	7	3	8	11	12
	Utah	IHL	4	0	3	3	0	....	....	....	....	....

GUITE, Ben — MTL.

Right wing. Shoots right. 6', 202 lbs. Born, Montreal, Que., July 17, 1978.
(Montreal's 8th choice, 172nd overall, in 1997 Entry Draft).

			Regular Season					Playoffs				
Season	Club	Lea	GP	G	A	TP	PIM	GP	G	A	TP	PIM
1996-97	U. of Maine	H.E.	34	7	7	14	21	....	....	....	....	....
1997-98	U. of Maine	H.E.	32	6	12	18	20	....	....	....	....	....
1998-99	U. of Maine	H.E.	40	12	16	28	30	....	....	....	....	....

GUNKO, Yuri — (goon-KOH, YOO-ree) — ST.L.

Defense. Shoots left. 6'1", 187 lbs. Born, Kiev, USSR, February 28, 1972.
(St. Louis' 11th choice, 230th overall, in 1992 Entry Draft).

			Regular Season					Playoffs				
Season	Club	Lea	GP	G	A	TP	PIM	GP	G	A	TP	PIM
1990-91	Sokol Kiev	USSR	14	0	0	0	8	....	....	....	....	....
1991-92	Sokol Kiev	CIS	22	1	0	1	16	....	....	....	....	....
1992-93	Sokol Kiev	CIS	40	2	3	5	28	....	....	....	....	....
1993-94	Sokol Kiev	CIS	42	0	8	8	28	....	....	....	....	....
1994-95	Sokol Kiev	CIS	25	4	0	4	18	....	....	....	....	....
1995-96	AK Bars Kazan	CIS	41	1	2	3	22	5	1	0	1	4
1996-97	AK Bars Kazan	Russia	42	6	7	13	42	3	1	0	1	4
1997-98	AK Bars Kazan	Russia	45	6	5	11	50	....	....	....	....	....
1998-99	AK Bars Kazan	Russia	9	0	3	3	0	....	....	....	....	....
	AK Bars Kazan	EuroHL	2	0	0	0	2	....	....	....	....	....

GUSTAFSSON, Juha — (GOOS-tahf-suhn, YOO-huh) — PHX.

Defense. Shoots left. 6'2", 200 lbs. Born, Helsinki, Finland, April 26, 1979.
(Phoenix's 1st choice, 43rd overall, in 1997 Entry Draft).

			Regular Season					Playoffs				
Season	Club	Lea	GP	G	A	TP	PIM	GP	G	A	TP	PIM
1995-96	Kiekko-Espoo	Finn-Jr.	33	1	5	6	28	4	0	0	0	2
	Kiekko-Espoo	Finland	1	0	0	0	0	....	....	....	....	....
1996-97	Kiekko-Espoo	Finn-Jr.	32	1	3	4	30	....	....	....	....	....
	Kiekko-Espoo	Finland	3	0	0	0	0	3	0	0	0	0
1997-98	Kiekko-Espoo	Finn-Jr.	33	3	3	6	18	....	....	....	....	....
	Kiekko-Espoo	Finland	2	0	0	0	0	....	....	....	....	....
1998-99	Ahmat Hyvinkaa	Finland-2	37	3	7	10	36	....	....	....	....	....

HAGLUND, Bobby — ST.L.

Left wing. Shoots left. 5'11", 195 lbs. Born, Worcester, MA, November 17, 1977.
(St. Louis' 7th choice, 206th overall, in 1997 Entry Draft).

			Regular Season					Playoffs				
Season	Club	Lea	GP	G	A	TP	PIM	GP	G	A	TP	PIM
1996-97	Des Moines	USHL	45	18	14	32	86	....	....	....	....	....
1997-98	Northeastern	H.E.	29	5	7	12	24	....	....	....	....	....
1998-99	Northeastern	H.E.	27	3	5	8	31	....	....	....	....	....

HAGMAN, Niklas — (HAG-muhn) — FLA.

Left wing. Shoots left. 5'11", 183 lbs. Born, Espoo, Finland, December 5, 1979.
(Florida's 3rd choice, 70th overall, in 1999 Entry Draft).

			Regular Season					Playoffs				
Season	Club	Lea	GP	G	A	TP	PIM	GP	G	A	TP	PIM
1996-97	HIFK Helsinki	Finn-Jr.	30	13	12	25	30	4	1	1	2	0
1997-98	HIFK Helsinki	Finn-Jr.	26	9	5	14	16	....	....	....	....	....
	HIFK Helsinki	Finland	8	1	0	1	0	....	....	....	....	....
1998-99	HIFK Helsinki	Finn-Jr.	14	4	9	13	43	....	....	....	....	....
	HIFK Helsinki	EuroHL	1	0	1	1	0	....	....	....	....	....
	HIFK Helsinki	Finland	17	1	1	2	14	....	....	....	....	....
	Kiekko-Espoo	Finland	14	1	1	2	2	4	1	0	1	0

HAHL, Riku — (HAHL, REE-koo) — COL.

Center. Shoots left. 6', 187 lbs. Born, Hameenlinna, Finland, November 1, 1980.
(Colorado's 9th choice, 183rd overall, in 1999 Entry Draft).

			Regular Season					Playoffs				
Season	Club	Lea	GP	G	A	TP	PIM	GP	G	A	TP	PIM
1996-97	Hameenlinna	Finn-Jr.	2	0	1	1	2	6	2	0	2	2
1997-98	Hameenlinna	Finn-Jr.	35	13	6	19	12	....	....	....	....	....
1998-99	Hameenlinna	Finn-Jr.	6	0	2	2	6	....	....	....	....	....
	Hameenlinna	Finland	28	0	1	1	0	8	0	0	0	2

HAJT, Chris — (HIGHT) — EDM.

Defense. Shoots left. 6'3", 206 lbs. Born, Saskatoon, Sask., July 5, 1978.
(Edmonton's 3rd choice, 32nd overall, in 1996 Entry Draft).

			Regular Season					Playoffs				
Season	Club	Lea	GP	G	A	TP	PIM	GP	G	A	TP	PIM
1994-95	Guelph	OHL	57	1	7	8	35	14	0	2	2	9
1995-96	Guelph	OHL	63	8	27	35	69	16	0	6	6	13
1996-97	Guelph	OHL	58	11	15	26	62	18	0	8	8	25
1997-98	Guelph	OHL	44	2	21	23	46	12	1	5	6	11
1998-99	Hamilton	AHL	64	0	4	4	36	....	....	....	....	....

OHL Second All-Star Team (1998)

HAKANEN, Timo — (HAW-kan-en, TEE-moo) — S.J.

Center. Shoots left. 6'2", 195 lbs. Born, Pori, Finland, March 26, 1977.
(San Jose's 7th choice, 140th overall, in 1995 Entry Draft).

			Regular Season					Playoffs				
Season	Club	Lea	GP	G	A	TP	PIM	GP	G	A	TP	PIM
1994-95	Assat Pori	Finn-Jr.	36	23	21	44	6	5	0	0	0	0
1995-96	Assat Pori	Finn-Jr.	28	8	24	32	6	....	....	....	....	....
	Assat Pori	Finland	12	0	2	2	0	3	0	0	0	0
1996-97	Assat Pori	Finn-Jr.	20	10	12	22	22	....	....	....	....	....
	Assat Pori	Finland	22	0	2	2	2	2	0	0	0	0
1997-98	Assat Pori	Finland	48	1	6	7	14	3	0	0	0	0
1998-99	Assat Pori	Finland	53	7	6	13	41	....	....	....	....	....

HALFNIGHT, Ashlin — (HAF-night, ASH-lihn)

Defense. Shoots left. 6', 180 lbs. Born, Toronto, Ont., March 14, 1975.
(Hartford's 5th choice, 213th overall, in 1994 Entry Draft).

			Regular Season					Playoffs				
Season	Club	Lea	GP	G	A	TP	PIM	GP	G	A	TP	PIM
1992-93	Canada	Nat-Team	3	1	0	1	2	....	....	....	....	....
1993-94	Harvard University	ECAC	30	2	8	10	24	....	....	....	....	....
1994-95	Harvard University	ECAC	24	5	15	20	42	....	....	....	....	....
1995-96	Harvard University	ECAC	30	2	10	12	12	....	....	....	....	....
1996-97	Harvard University	ECAC	31	6	6	12	50	....	....	....	....	....
1997-98	New Haven	AHL	64	3	11	14	26	3	0	1	1	2
1998-99	New Haven	AHL	71	2	9	11	45	....	....	....	....	....

Rights transferred to **Carolina** after **Hartford** franchise relocated, June 25, 1997.

HALL, Adam — NSH.

Right wing. Shoots right. 6'3", 200 lbs. Born, Kalamazoo, MI, August 14, 1980.
(Nashville's 3rd choice, 52nd overall, in 1999 Entry Draft).

			Regular Season					Playoffs				
Season	Club	Lea	GP	G	A	TP	PIM	GP	G	A	TP	PIM
1997-98	Team USA	Under-18	71	42	23	65	63	....	....	....	....	....
1998-99	Michigan State	CCHA	36	16	7	23	74	....	....	....	....	....

HALL, Todd — NYR

Left wing. Shoots left. 6'1", 212 lbs. Born, Hamden, CT, January 22, 1973.
(Hartford's 3rd choice, 53rd overall, in 1991 Entry Draft).

			Regular Season					Playoffs				
Season	Club	Lea	GP	G	A	TP	PIM	GP	G	A	TP	PIM
1990-91	Hamden High	H.S.	23	10	15	25	12	....	....	....	....	....
1991-92	Boston College	H.E.	33	2	10	12	14	....	....	....	....	....
1992-93	Boston College	H.E.	34	2	10	12	22	....	....	....	....	....
1993-94	New Hampshire	H.E.	DID NOT PLAY – TRANSFERRED COLLEGES									
1994-95	New Hampshire	H.E.	36	8	18	26	16	....	....	....	....	....
1995-96	New Hampshire	H.E.	31	4	26	30	10	....	....	....	....	....
1996-97	Binghamton	AHL	40	3	7	10	12	4	0	1	1	0
	Charlotte	ECHL	13	0	2	2	8	....	....	....	....	....
1997-98	Hartford	AHL	73	7	18	25	26	8	0	1	1	8
1998-99	Hartford	AHL	72	14	15	29	12	1	0	0	0	0

Hockey East Second All-Star Team (1996)

Signed as a free agent by **NY Rangers**, July 28, 1997.

HALPERN, Jeff — WSH.

Center. Shoots right. 6', 195 lbs. Born, Potomac, MD, May 3, 1976.

			Regular Season					Playoffs				
Season	Club	Lea	GP	G	A	TP	PIM	GP	G	A	TP	PIM
1995-96	Princeton	ECAC	29	3	11	14	30	....	....	....	....	....
1996-97	Princeton	ECAC	33	7	24	31	35	....	....	....	....	....
1997-98	Princeton	ECAC	36	*28	25	*53	46	....	....	....	....	....
1998-99	Princeton	ECAC	33	*22	22	44	32	....	....	....	....	....
	Portland	AHL	6	2	1	3	4	....	....	....	....	....

ECAC Second All-Star Team (1998, 1999)

Signed as a free agent by **Washington**, March 29, 1999.

HALVARDSSON, Johan — NYI

Defense. Shoots left. 6'3", 198 lbs. Born, Jonkoping, Sweden, December 26, 1979.
(NY Islanders' 8th choice, 102nd overall, in 1999 Entry Draft).

			Regular Season					Playoffs				
Season	Club	Lea	GP	G	A	TP	PIM	GP	G	A	TP	PIM
1997-98	HV Jonkoping	Swede-Jr.	28	5	5	10	65	....	....	....	....	....
1998-99	HV Jonkoping	Sweden	17	1	2	3	33	....	....	....	....	....

HAMEL, Denis — (ha-MEHL, deh-NEE) — BUF.

Left wing. Shoots left. 6'2", 200 lbs. Born, Lachute, Que., May 10, 1977.
(St. Louis' 5th choice, 153rd overall, in 1995 Entry Draft).

			Regular Season					Playoffs				
Season	Club	Lea	GP	G	A	TP	PIM	GP	G	A	TP	PIM
1994-95	Chicoutimi	QMJHL	66	15	12	27	155	12	2	0	2	27
1995-96	Chicoutimi	QMJHL	65	40	49	89	199	17	10	14	24	64
1996-97	Chicoutimi	QMJHL	70	50	50	100	357	20	15	10	25	58
1997-98	Rochester	AHL	74	10	15	25	98	4	1	2	3	0
1998-99	Rochester	AHL	74	16	17	33	121	20	3	4	7	10

Traded to **Buffalo** by **St. Louis** for Charlie Huddy and Buffalo's 7th round choice (Daniel Corso) in 1996 Entry Draft, March 19, 1996.

HAMILTON, Hugh — CAR.

Defense. Shoots left. 6'1", 175 lbs. Born, Saskatoon, Sask., February 11, 1977.
(Hartford's 5th choice, 113th overall, in 1995 Entry Draft).

			Regular Season					Playoffs				
Season	Club	Lea	GP	G	A	TP	PIM	GP	G	A	TP	PIM
1991-92	Shellbrook	SAHA	36	11	12	23	62	....	....	....	....	....
1992-93	Saskatoon AA	SAHA	36	5	13	18	54	....	....	....	....	....
1993-94	Spokane	WHL	64	5	9	14	70	3	0	0	0	0
1994-95	Spokane	WHL	60	5	28	33	102	11	3	5	8	16
1995-96	Spokane	WHL	72	11	49	60	92	18	3	5	8	26
1996-97	Spokane	WHL	57	8	37	45	69	9	1	6	7	14
1997-98	New Haven	AHL	51	3	3	6	17	3	0	0	0	2
1998-99	New Haven	AHL	1	0	0	0	0	....	....	....	....	....
	Florida	ECHL	65	8	25	33	57	6	0	4	4	6

WHL West Second All-Star Team (1997)

Rights transferred to **Carolina** after **Hartford** franchise relocated, June 25, 1997.

HAMILTON, Jason — CHI.

Defense. Shoots right. 6'2", 218 lbs. Born, Montreal, Que., January 25, 1977.

			Regular Season					Playoffs				
Season	Club	Lea	GP	G	A	TP	PIM	GP	G	A	TP	PIM
1995-96	Shawinigan	QMJHL	62	3	6	9	240	6	0	0	0	15
1996-97	Shawinigan	QMJHL	67	2	5	7	254	7	0	1	1	8
1997-98	Shawinigan	QMJHL	59	2	9	11	358	6	0	1	1	55
1998-99	Portland	AHL	4	0	0	0	0	....	....	....	....	....
	Greenville	ECHL	45	2	6	8	206	....	....	....	....	....

Signed as a free agent by **Chicago**, July 18, 1998.

HANKINSON, Casey (HAN-kihn-suhn) — CHI.

Left wing. Shoots left. 6'1", 187 lbs. Born, Edina, MN, May 8, 1976.
(Chicago's 9th choice, 201st overall, in 1995 Entry Draft).

			Regular Season					Playoffs				
Season	Club	Lea	GP	G	A	TP	PIM	GP	G	A	TP	PIM
1994-95	U. of Minnesota	WCHA	33	7	1	8	86	....	....	....	....	....
1995-96	U. of Minnesota	WCHA	39	16	19	35	101	....	....	....	....	....
1996-97	U. of Minnesota	WCHA	42	17	24	41	79	....	....	....	....	....
1997-98	U. of Minnesota	WCHA	35	10	12	22	81	....	....	....	....	....
1998-99	Portland	AHL	72	10	13	23	106	....	....	....	....	....

HANNUS, Tommi (HA-nuhs) — L.A.

Center. Shoots right. 6', 180 lbs. Born, Vantaa, Finland, June 27, 1980.
(Los Angeles' 7th choice, 190th overall, in 1998 Entry Draft).

			Regular Season					Playoffs				
Season	Club	Lea	GP	G	A	TP	PIM	GP	G	A	TP	PIM
1995-96	TPS Turku	Finn-Jr.	1	1	0	1	2	....	....	....	....	....
1996-97	TPS Turku	Finn-Jr.	45	14	13	27	10	6	4	2	6	10
1997-98	TPS Turku	Finn-Jr.	19	6	3	9	4	....	....	....	....	....
1998-99	TPS Turku	Finn-Jr.	8	5	4	9	22	....	....	....	....	....
	TuTo Turku	Finland-2	18	6	4	10	16	8	0	2	2	8

HANSEN, Justin — PHX.

Right wing. Shoots right. 6'1", 193 lbs. Born, Winnipeg, Man., June 11, 1980.
(Phoenix's 10th choice, 214th overall, in 1998 Entry Draft).

			Regular Season					Playoffs				
Season	Club	Lea	GP	G	A	TP	PIM	GP	G	A	TP	PIM
1995-96	Moose Jaw AAA	MAHA	41	20	15	35	26	....	....	....	....	....
	Moose Jaw	WHL	1	0	0	0	0	....	....	....	....	....
1996-97	Moose Jaw	WHL	23	1	3	4	7	1	0	0	0	0
1997-98	Moose Jaw	WHL	67	16	18	34	97	....	....	....	....	....
1998-99	Moose Jaw	WHL	10	4	3	7	11	....	....	....	....	....
	Prince George	WHL	32	13	7	20	29	4	0	0	0	0

HARDER, Mike — NYR

Center. Shoots right. 6', 180 lbs. Born, Winnipeg, Man., February 8, 1973.

			Regular Season					Playoffs				
Season	Club	Lea	GP	G	A	TP	PIM	GP	G	A	TP	PIM
1993-94	Colgate	ECAC	33	21	25	46	14	....	....	....	....	....
1994-95	Colgate	ECAC	36	22	36	58	13	....	....	....	....	....
1995-96	Colgate	ECAC	32	23	32	55	26	....	....	....	....	....
1996-97	Colgate	ECAC	33	22	33	55	20	....	....	....	....	....
	Hamilton	AHL	2	0	1	1	0	....	....	....	....	....
	Milwaukee	IHL	7	1	3	4	6	2	0	1	1	0
1997-98	Milwaukee	IHL	62	20	17	37	32	....	....	....	....	....
	Springfield	AHL	3	2	0	2	2	....	....	....	....	....
	Rochester	AHL	8	4	2	6	0	4	3	2	5	8
1998-99	Rochester	AHL	79	31	48	79	39	20	2	9	11	23

Signed as a free agent by **NY Rangers**, August 25, 1999.

HARIKKALA, Jaakko (HAHR-ee-kuh-lah, YAH-koh) — BOS.

Defense. Shoots left. 6'2", 215 lbs. Born, Kalanti, Finland, March 30, 1981.
(Boston's 4th choice, 118th overall, in 1999 Entry Draft).

			Regular Season					Playoffs				
Season	Club	Lea	GP	G	A	TP	PIM	GP	G	A	TP	PIM
1997-98	Jaa-Kotkat	Finland-2	45	2	6	8	65	....	....	....	....	....
1998-99	Lukko Rauma	Finn-Jr.	11	1	3	4	22	....	....	....	....	....
	Lukko Rauma	Finland	35	0	0	0	10	....	....	....	....	....

HARLTON, Tyler — ST.L.

Defense. Shoots left. 6'2", 212 lbs. Born, Pense, Sask., January 11, 1976.
(St. Louis' 2nd choice, 94th overall, in 1994 Entry Draft).

			Regular Season					Playoffs				
Season	Club	Lea	GP	G	A	TP	PIM	GP	G	A	TP	PIM
1993-94	Vernon	BCJHL	60	3	18	21	102	....	....	....	....	....
1994-95	Michigan State	CCHA	39	1	3	4	55	....	....	....	....	....
1995-96	Michigan State	CCHA	39	1	6	7	51	....	....	....	....	....
1996-97	Michigan State	CCHA	39	2	9	11	75	....	....	....	....	....
1997-98	Michigan State	CCHA	44	1	12	13	68	....	....	....	....	....
1998-99	Worcester	AHL	58	2	5	7	94	....	....	....	....	....
	Peoria	ECHL	6	0	2	2	40	....	....	....	....	....

CCHA First All-Star Team (1998) • NCAA West Second All-American Team (1998)

HARRIS, Darcy — MTL.

Right wing. Shoots right. 6'1", 194 lbs. Born, O'Leary, P.E.I., December 22, 1978.
(Montreal's 10th choice, 247th overall, in 1998 Entry Draft).

			Regular Season					Playoffs				
Season	Club	Lea	GP	G	A	TP	PIM	GP	G	A	TP	PIM
1995-96	Summerside	MJrHL	48	13	13	26	168	....	....	....	....	....
1996-97	Kitchener	OHL	55	4	8	12	134	4	0	0	0	4
1997-98	Kitchener	OHL	61	21	19	40	200	6	2	4	6	28
1998-99	Fredericton	AHL	31	3	3	6	97	3	0	0	0	0

HARVEY, Paul — FLA.

Right wing. Shoots right. 6'4", 196 lbs. Born, South Boston, MA, August 8, 1978.

			Regular Season					Playoffs				
Season	Club	Lea	GP	G	A	TP	PIM	GP	G	A	TP	PIM
1996-97	Syracuse	OJHL	23	18	31	49	196	....	....	....	....	....
1997-98	Erie	OHL	31	3	6	9	64	6	0	1	1	0
1998-99	Erie	OHL	61	16	17	33	132	5	1	0	1	15

Signed as a free agent by **Florida**, June 16, 1999

HAVELID, Niclas (HAHV-lihd) — ANA.

Defense. Shoots left. 5'11", 200 lbs. Born, Enkoping, Sweden, April 12, 1973.
(Anaheim's 2nd choice, 83rd overall, in 1999 Entry Draft).

			Regular Season					Playoffs				
Season	Club	Lea	GP	G	A	TP	PIM	GP	G	A	TP	PIM
1991-92	AIK Solna	Sweden	10	0	0	0	2	....	....	....	....	....
1992-93	AIK Solna	Sweden	22	1	0	1	16	....	....	....	....	....
1993-94	AIK Solna	Sweden-2	40	6	12	18	26	9	0	1	1	10
1994-95	AIK Solna	Sweden	40	3	7	10	38	....	....	....	....	....
1995-96	AIK Solna	Sweden	40	5	6	11	30	....	....	....	....	....
1996-97	AIK Solna	Sweden	49	3	6	9	42	7	1	2	3	8
1997-98	AIK Solna	Sweden	43	8	4	12	42	....	....	....	....	....
1998-99	Malmo	Sweden	50	10	12	22	42	8	0	4	4	10

HAVELKA, Petr (huh-VEHL-kah) — PIT.

Left wing. Shoots left. 6'2", 187 lbs. Born, Most, Czech., March 4, 1979.
(Pittsburgh's 6th choice, 152nd overall, in 1997 Entry Draft).

			Regular Season					Playoffs				
Season	Club	Lea	GP	G	A	TP	PIM	GP	G	A	TP	PIM
1995-96	Sparta Praha	Czech-Jr.	40	15	10	25	....	....	....	....	....	....
1996-97	Sparta Praha	Czech-Jr.	22	14	13	27	....	....	....	....	....	....
	Sparta Praha	Cze-Rep	....	....	....	....	....	1	0	0	0	0
1997-98	Sparta Praha	Czech-Jr.	DID NOT PLAY – INJURED									
1998-99	Velvana Kladno	Cze-Rep	5	0	0	0	0	....	....	....	....	....
	Sparta Praha	Cze-Rep	5	7	3	10	....	4	1	1	2	....

HAVLAT, Martin (hahv-lat) — OTT.

Center. Shoots left. 6'1", 178 lbs. Born, Mlada Boleslav, Czech., April 19, 1981.
(Ottawa's 1st choice, 26th overall, in 1999 Entry Draft).

			Regular Season					Playoffs				
Season	Club	Lea	GP	G	A	TP	PIM	GP	G	A	TP	PIM
1997-98	Ytong Brno	Czech-Jr.	32	38	29	67	....	....	....	....	....	....
1998-99	HC Trinec	Czech-Jr.	31	28	23	51	....	....	....	....	....	....
	HC Trinec	Cze-Rep	24	2	3	5	4	8	0	0	0	....

HEDSTROM, Jonathan (HEHD-struhm) — TOR.

Right wing. Shoots left. 6', 200 lbs. Born, Skelleftea, Sweden, December 27, 1977.
(Toronto's 8th choice, 221st overall, in 1997 Entry Draft).

			Regular Season					Playoffs				
Season	Club	Lea	GP	G	A	TP	PIM	GP	G	A	TP	PIM
1995-96	HV Skelleftea	Sweden-2	7	0	0	0	0	....	....	....	....	....
1996-97	HV Skelleftea	Sweden-2	12	1	1	2	10	6	0	0	0	2
	HV Skelleftea	Swede-Jr.	9	4	4	8	....	....	....	....	....	....
1997-98	HV Skelleftea	Sweden-2	16	2	3	5	....	....	....	....	....	....
	HV Skelleftea	Swede-Jr.	1	0	0	0	2	....	....	....	....	....
1998-99	Skelleftea AIK	Sweden-2	36	15	28	43	74	....	....	....	....	....

HEEREMA, Jeff (HEER-eh-muh) — CAR.

Right wing. Shoots right. 6'1", 171 lbs. Born, Thunder Bay, Ont., January 17, 1980.
(Carolina's 1st choice, 11th overall, in 1998 Entry Draft).

			Regular Season					Playoffs				
Season	Club	Lea	GP	G	A	TP	PIM	GP	G	A	TP	PIM
1996-97	Thunder Bay	USHL	54	42	29	71	112	....	....	....	....	....
1997-98	Sarnia	OHL	63	32	40	72	88	5	4	1	5	10
1998-99	Sarnia	OHL	62	31	39	70	113	6	5	1	6	0

HEISTEN, Barrett — BUF.

Left wing. Shoots left. 6'1", 189 lbs. Born, Anchorage, AK, March 19, 1980.
(Buffalo's 1st choice, 20th overall, in 1999 Entry Draft).

			Regular Season					Playoffs				
Season	Club	Lea	GP	G	A	TP	PIM	GP	G	A	TP	PIM
1996-97	Anchorage	USAHA	39	35	29	64	....	....	....	....	....	....
1997-98	Team USA	Under-18	50	11	26	37	245	....	....	....	....	....
1998-99	U. of Maine	H.E.	34	12	16	28	72	....	....	....	....	....

HELBLING, Timo (HEHL-blihng) — NSH.

Defense. Shoots right. 6'2", 183 lbs. Born, Basel, Switzerland, July 21, 1981.
(Nashville's 11th choice, 162nd overall, in 1999 Entry Draft).

			Regular Season					Playoffs				
Season	Club	Lea	GP	G	A	TP	PIM	GP	G	A	TP	PIM
1997-98	HC Davos	Switz-Jr.	34	6	6	12	38	....	....	....	....	....
1998-99	HC Davos	Switz-Jr.	22	8	10	18	108	....	....	....	....	....
	HC Davos	Switz.	44	0	0	0	8	4	0	0	0	0

HELD, Ryan — N.J.

Center. Shoots left. 6'2", 175 lbs. Born, London, Ont., January 30, 1980.
(New Jersey's 12th choice, 257th overall, in 1998 Entry Draft).

			Regular Season					Playoffs				
Season	Club	Lea	GP	G	A	TP	PIM	GP	G	A	TP	PIM
1997-98	Kitchener	OHL	59	15	16	31	35	6	1	0	1	7
1998-99	Kitchener	OHL	65	18	25	43	45	1	0	0	0	0

HENKEL, Jim — L.A.

Center. Shoots left. 6'2", 186 lbs. Born, Red Bank, NJ, May 25, 1979.
(Los Angeles' 8th choice, 217th overall, in 1998 Entry Draft).

			Regular Season					Playoffs				
Season	Club	Lea	GP	G	A	TP	PIM	GP	G	A	TP	PIM
1997-98	New England	EJHL	37	34	37	71	....	11	7	17	24	....
1998-99	RPI Engineers	ECAC	20	0	4	4	14	....	....	....	....	....

HENRICH, Michael — EDM.

Right wing. Shoots right. 6'2", 206 lbs. Born, Thornhill, Ont., March 3, 1980.
(Edmonton's 1st choice, 13th overall, in 1998 Entry Draft).

			Regular Season					Playoffs				
Season	Club	Lea	GP	G	A	TP	PIM	GP	G	A	TP	PIM
1996-97	Barrie	OHL	52	9	15	24	19	9	0	5	5	0
1997-98	Barrie	OHL	66	41	22	63	75	5	1	3	4	0
1998-99	Barrie	OHL	62	38	33	71	42	12	0	2	2	4

HENRY, Alex — EDM.

Defense. Shoots left. 6'5", 220 lbs. Born, Elliot Lake, Ont., October 18, 1979.
(Edmonton's 2nd choice, 67th overall, in 1998 Entry Draft).

			Regular Season					Playoffs				
Season	Club	Lea	GP	G	A	TP	PIM	GP	G	A	TP	PIM
1996-97	London	OHL	61	1	10	11	65	....	....	....	....	....
1997-98	London	OHL	62	5	9	14	97	16	0	3	3	14
1998-99	London	OHL	68	5	23	28	105	25	3	10	13	22

HENRY, Burke — NYR

Defense. Shoots left. 6'2", 190 lbs. Born, Ste. Rose, Man., January 21, 1979.
(NY Rangers' 3rd choice, 73rd overall, in 1997 Entry Draft).

			Regular Season					Playoffs				
Season	Club	Lea	GP	G	A	TP	PIM	GP	G	A	TP	PIM
1995-96	Brandon	WHL	50	6	11	17	58	19	0	4	4	19
1996-97	Brandon	WHL	55	6	25	31	81	6	1	3	4	4
1997-98	Brandon	WHL	72	18	65	83	153	18	3	16	19	37
1998-99	Brandon	WHL	68	18	58	76	151	5	1	6	7	9

WHL East First All-Star Team (1998) • WHL East Second All-Star Team (1999)

HERPERGER, Chris — CHI.

Left wing. Shoots left. 6', 190 lbs. Born, Esterhazy, Sask., February 24, 1974.
(Philadelphia's 9th choice, 223rd overall, in 1992 Entry Draft).

			Regular Season					Playoffs				
Season	Club	Lea	GP	G	A	TP	PIM	GP	G	A	TP	PIM
1990-91	Swift Current	WHL	10	0	1	1	5	....	....	....	....	....
1991-92	Swift Current	WHL	72	14	19	33	44	8	0	1	1	9
1992-93	Swift Current	WHL	20	9	7	16	31	....	....	....	....	....
	Seattle	WHL	46	20	11	31	30	5	1	1	2	6
1993-94	Seattle	WHL	71	44	51	95	110	9	12	10	22	12
1994-95	Seattle	WHL	59	49	52	101	106	4	4	0	4	6
	Hershey	AHL	4	0	0	0	0	....	....	....	....	....
1995-96	Hershey	AHL	46	8	12	20	36	....	....	....	....	....
	Baltimore	AHL	21	2	3	5	17	9	2	3	5	6
1996-97	Baltimore	AHL	67	19	22	41	88	3	0	0	0	0
1997-98	Canada	Nat-Team	63	20	30	50	102	....	....	....	....	....
1998-99	Indianapolis	IHL	79	19	29	48	81	7	0	4	4	4

WHL West Second All-Star Team (1995)

Traded to **Anaheim** by **Philadelphia** with Winnipeg's 7th round choice (previously acquired, Anaheim selected Tony Mohagen) in 1997 Entry Draft for Bob Corkum, February 6, 1996. Signed as a free agent by **Chicago**, September 2, 1998.

HEWER, Oak — T.B.

Center. Shoots right. 6'3", 210 lbs. Born, Ottawa, Ont., September 21, 1979.
(Tampa Bay's 8th choice, 194th overall, in 1998 Entry Draft).

			Regular Season					Playoffs				
Season	Club	Lea	GP	G	A	TP	PIM	GP	G	A	TP	PIM
1996-97	S.S. Marie	OHL	42	1	1	2	7	....	....	....	....	....
1997-98	S.S. Marie	OHL	62	8	11	19	68	....	....	....	....	....
1998-99	S.S. Marie	OHL	10	1	3	4	16	....	....	....	....	....
	North Bay	OHL	40	11	9	20	34	4	0	1	1	0

HILL, Ed — NSH.

Defense. Shoots left. 6'3", 215 lbs. Born, Newburyport, MA, October 24, 1980.
(Nashville's 5th choice, 61st overall, in 1999 Entry Draft).

			Regular Season					Playoffs				
Season	Club	Lea	GP	G	A	TP	PIM	GP	G	A	TP	PIM
1996-97	Green Bay	USHL	61	4	11	15	36	....	....	....	....	....
1997-98	Green Bay	USHL	51	1	16	17	76	....	....	....	....	....
1998-99	Barrie	OHL	53	7	17	24	42	12	0	2	2	8

HINOTE, Dan — COL.

Right wing. Shoots right. 6', 187 lbs. Born, Leesburg, FL, January 30, 1977.
(Colorado's 9th choice, 167th overall, in 1996 Entry Draft).

			Regular Season					Playoffs				
Season	Club	Lea	GP	G	A	TP	PIM	GP	G	A	TP	PIM
1994-95	Army	NCAA	33	20	24	44	20	....	....	....	....	....
1995-96	Army	NCAA	34	21	24	45	22	....	....	....	....	....
1996-97	Oshawa	OHL	60	15	13	28	58	18	4	5	9	8
1997-98	Oshawa	OHL	35	12	15	27	39	5	2	2	4	7
	Hershey	AHL	24	1	4	5	25	....	....	....	....	....
1998-99	Hershey	AHL	65	4	16	20	95	5	3	1	4	6

HINZ, Chad — EDM.

Right wing. Shoots right. 5'10", 190 lbs. Born, Saskatoon, Sask., March 21, 1979.
(Edmonton's 8th choice, 187th overall, in 1997 Entry Draft).

			Regular Season					Playoffs				
Season	Club	Lea	GP	G	A	TP	PIM	GP	G	A	TP	PIM
1995-96	Moose Jaw	WHL	70	22	32	54	65	....	....	....	....	....
1996-97	Moose Jaw	WHL	72	37	47	84	47	12	4	1	5	11
1997-98	Moose Jaw	WHL	72	20	57	77	45	4	1	2	3	2
1998-99	Moose Jaw	WHL	71	42	*75	117	40	11	4	12	16	12
	Hamilton	AHL	3	0	0	0	2	....	....	....	....	....

WHL East First All-Star Team (1999)

HIRVONEN, Tomi — (HIHR-voh-nehn) COL.

Center. Shoots left. 5'11", 185 lbs. Born, Tampere, Finland, January 11, 1977.
(Colorado's 8th choice, 207th overall, in 1995 Entry Draft).

			Regular Season					Playoffs				
Season	Club	Lea	GP	G	A	TP	PIM	GP	G	A	TP	PIM
1992-93	Ilves Tampere	Finn-Jr-C	34	32	20	52	71	....	....	....	....	....
1993-94	Ilves Tampere	Finn-Jr-B	28	13	14	27	96	....	....	....	....	....
	Ilves Tampere	Finn-Jr.	1	0	0	0	0	....	....	....	....	....
1994-95	Ilves Tampere	Finn-Jr-B	6	1	5	6	14	....	....	....	....	....
	Ilves Tampere	Finn-Jr.	28	9	13	22	30	8	4	2	6	14
1995-96	Ilves Tampere	Finn-Jr.	5	2	2	4	37	7	5	10	15	8
	KooVee	Finland-2	7	4	1	5	26	....	....	....	....	....
	Ilves Tampere	Finland	28	1	0	1	24	....	....	....	....	....
1996-97	Ilves Tampere	Finn-Jr.	5	2	2	4	37	4	1	3	4	8
	Ilves Tampere	Finland	40	0	7	7	22	6	0	0	0	4
1997-98	Ilves Tampere	Finland	48	10	12	22	54	9	0	0	0	2
	Ilves Tampere	Finn-Jr.	....	....	....	....	....	2	5	0	5	4
1998-99	Ilves Tampere	Finland	50	5	15	20	94	4	0	0	0	8
	Ilves Tampere	EuroHL	6	1	3	4	2	....	....	....	....	....

HLAVAC, Jan — (huh-LAH-vahch, YAHN) NYR

Left wing. Shoots left. 6', 183 lbs. Born, Prague, Czech., September 20, 1976.
(NY Islanders' 2nd choice, 28th overall, in 1995 Entry Draft).

			Regular Season					Playoffs				
Season	Club	Lea	GP	G	A	TP	PIM	GP	G	A	TP	PIM
1993-94	Sparta Praha	Cze-Rep	9	1	1	2	....	....	....	....	....	....
1994-95	Sparta Praha	Cze-Rep	38	7	6	13	18	5	0	2	2	0
1995-96	Sparta Praha	Cze-Rep	34	8	5	13	....	12	1	2	3	....
1996-97	Sparta Praha	Cze-Rep	38	8	13	21	24	10	5	2	7	2
	Sparta Praha	EuroHL	3	4	0	4	6	....	....	....	....	....
1997-98	Sparta Praha	EuroHL	5	0	3	3	4	....	....	....	....	....
	Sparta Praha	Cze-Rep	48	17	30	47	40	5	1	0	1	2
1998-99	Sparta Praha	Cze-Rep	49	*33	20	53	52	6	1	3	4	....
	Sparta Praha	EuroHL	5	4	2	6	0	1	1	1	2	0

Rights traded to **NY Rangers** by **Calgary** with Calgary's 1st (Jamie Lundmark) and 3rd (later traded back to Calgary - Calgary selected Craig Andersson) round choices in 1999 Entry Draft for Marc Savard and NY Rangers' 1st round choice (Oleg Saprykin) in 1999 Entry Draft, June 26, 1999.

HOBDAY, Brent — DET.

Center. Shoots left. 6'1", 192 lbs. Born, Winnipeg, Man., August 26, 1979.
(Detroit's 5th choice, 111th overall, in 1998 Entry Draft).

			Regular Season					Playoffs				
Season	Club	Lea	GP	G	A	TP	PIM	GP	G	A	TP	PIM
1997-98	Moose Jaw	WHL	68	21	22	43	122	4	2	0	2	4
1998-99	Moose Jaw	WHL	72	40	26	66	135	11	3	3	6	21

HOGAN, Peter — L.A.

Defense. Shoots right. 6'3", 183 lbs. Born, Oshawa, Ont., January 10, 1978.
(Los Angeles' 7th choice, 123rd overall, in 1996 Entry Draft).

			Regular Season					Playoffs				
Season	Club	Lea	GP	G	A	TP	PIM	GP	G	A	TP	PIM
1995-96	Oshawa	OHL	66	3	25	28	54	5	2	0	2	2
1996-97	Oshawa	OHL	65	13	37	50	56	18	1	11	12	22
1997-98	Oshawa	OHL	63	10	28	38	104	....	....	....	....	....
1998-99	Springfield	AHL	71	1	14	15	41	2	0	0	0	0

HOLDRIDGE, Kevin — CAR.

Defense. Shoots left. 6'2", 202 lbs. Born, Syracuse, NY, September 9, 1980.
(Carolina's 2nd choice, 70th overall, in 1998 Entry Draft).

			Regular Season					Playoffs				
Season	Club	Lea	GP	G	A	TP	PIM	GP	G	A	TP	PIM
1996-97	Detroit	OHL	55	0	9	9	49	5	0	0	0	2
1997-98	Plymouth	OHL	61	4	15	19	106	15	0	3	3	30
1998-99	Plymouth	OHL	64	2	17	19	118	11	0	1	1	15

HOLMQVIST, Mikael — (HOHLM-kvihst) ANA.

Center. Shoots left. 6'3", 189 lbs. Born, Stockholm, Sweden, June 8, 1979.
(Anaheim's 1st choice, 18th overall, in 1997 Entry Draft).

			Regular Season					Playoffs				
Season	Club	Lea	GP	G	A	TP	PIM	GP	G	A	TP	PIM
1995-96	Djurgardens IF	Swede-Jr.	24	7	2	9	4	....	....	....	....	....
1996-97	Djurgardens IF	Swede-Jr.	39	29	35	64	110	....	....	....	....	....
	Djurgardens IF	Sweden	9	0	0	0	0	....	....	....	....	....
1997-98	Farjestads BK	Sweden	41	2	3	5	6	7	0	0	0	0
	Farjestads BK	EuroHL	5	2	2	4	2	....	....	....	....	....
1998-99	Farjestads BK	Sweden	15	0	0	0	6	....	....	....	....	....
	Farjestads BK	EuroHL	3	0	0	0	0	1	0	0	0	0
	Farjestads BK	Swede-Jr.	2	2	2	4	2	....	....	....	....	....
	Hammarby IF	Sweden-2	3	2	0	2	0	....	....	....	....	....

HORACEK, Jan — (HOHR-uh-chehk) ST.L.

Defense. Shoots right. 6'4", 206 lbs. Born, Benesov, Czech., May 22, 1979.
(St. Louis' 3rd choice, 98th overall, in 1997 Entry Draft).

			Regular Season					Playoffs				
Season	Club	Lea	GP	G	A	TP	PIM	GP	G	A	TP	PIM
1996-97	Slavia Praha	Czech-Jr.	25	4	14	18	....	....	....	....	....	....
	Slavia Praha	Cze-Rep	9	0	0	0	6	3	0	0	0	0
	HC Beroun	Czech-2	2	0	0	0	....	....	....	....	....	....
1997-98	Moncton	QMJHL	54	3	18	21	146	10	1	5	6	20
1998-99	Slavia Praha	Cze-Rep	1	0	0	0	2	....	....	....	....	....
	Worcester	AHL	53	1	13	14	119	4	0	0	0	6

HORCOFF, Shawn — EDM.

Center. Shoots left. 6'1", 194 lbs. Born, Trail, B.C., September 17, 1978.
(Edmonton's 3rd choice, 99th overall, in 1998 Entry Draft).

			Regular Season					Playoffs				
Season	Club	Lea	GP	G	A	TP	PIM	GP	G	A	TP	PIM
1996-97	Michigan State	CCHA	40	10	13	23	20	....	....	....	....	....
1997-98	Michigan State	CCHA	34	14	13	27	50	....	....	....	....	....
1998-99	Michigan State	CCHA	39	12	25	37	70	....	....	....	....	....

HORNUNG, Todd — WSH.

Center. Shoots left. 6', 200 lbs. Born, Swift Current, Sask., September 3, 1980.
(Washington's 2nd choice, 59th overall, in 1998 Entry Draft).

			Regular Season					Playoffs				
Season	Club	Lea	GP	G	A	TP	PIM	GP	G	A	TP	PIM
1995-96	Swift Current	AA	59	71	55	126	276	....	....	....	....	....
	Portland	WHL	1	0	0	0	0	....	....	....	....	....
1996-97	Portland	WHL	59	3	3	6	51	6	0	0	0	0
1997-98	Portland	WHL	64	19	18	37	96	16	6	6	12	26
1998-99	Portland	WHL	45	15	15	30	86	....	....	....	....	....
	Lethbridge	WHL	13	1	1	2	26	....	....	....	....	....

HOULE, Jean-Francois — (HOOL) MTL.

Left wing. Shoots left. 5'9", 186 lbs. Born, Charlesbourg, Que., January 14, 1975.
(Montreal's 5th choice, 99th overall, in 1993 Entry Draft).

			Regular Season					Playoffs				
Season	Club	Lea	GP	G	A	TP	PIM	GP	G	A	TP	PIM
1992-93	Northwood Prep	H.S.	28	37	45	82	....	....	....	....	....	....
1993-94	Clarkson	ECAC	34	6	19	25	20	....	....	....	....	....
1994-95	Clarkson	ECAC	34	8	11	19	42	....	....	....	....	....
1995-96	Clarkson	ECAC	38	14	15	29	46	....	....	....	....	....
1996-97	Clarkson	ECAC	37	21	*36	57	40	....	....	....	....	....
1997-98	Fredericton	AHL	7	1	0	1	8	....	....	....	....	....
	New Orleans	ECHL	53	25	37	62	119	4	1	1	2	16
1998-99	Fredericton	AHL	62	7	22	29	101	12	1	7	8	10

HOUSE, Bobby — TOR.

Right wing. Shoots right. 6'1", 205 lbs. Born, Whitehorse, Yukon, January 7, 1973.
(Chicago's 4th choice, 66th overall, in 1991 Entry Draft).

			Regular Season					Playoffs				
Season	Club	Lea	GP	G	A	TP	PIM	GP	G	A	TP	PIM
1989-90	Spokane	WHL	64	18	16	34	74	5	0	0	0	6
1990-91	Spokane	WHL	38	11	19	30	63	....	....	....	....	....
	Brandon	WHL	23	18	7	25	14	....	....	....	....	....
1991-92	Brandon	WHL	71	35	42	77	133	....	....	....	....	....
1992-93	Brandon	WHL	61	57	39	96	87	4	2	2	4	0
1993-94	Indianapolis	IHL	42	10	8	18	51	....	....	....	....	....
	Flint	ColHL	4	3	3	6	0	....	....	....	....	....
1994-95	Columbus	ECHL	9	11	6	17	2	....	....	....	....	....
	Indianapolis	IHL	26	2	3	5	26	....	....	....	....	....
	Albany	AHL	26	4	7	11	12	8	1	1	2	0
1995-96	Albany	AHL	77	37	49	86	57	4	0	0	0	4
1996-97	Albany	AHL	68	18	16	34	65	16	3	2	5	23
1997-98	Albany	AHL	19	10	10	20	10	....	....	....	....	....
	Hershey	AHL	20	2	6	8	8	....	....	....	....	....
	Quebec	IHL	24	5	7	12	12	....	....	....	....	....
	Syracuse	AHL	9	5	6	11	6	5	2	0	2	4
1998-99	Augusta	ECHL	5	1	0	1	15	....	....	....	....	....
	Albany	AHL	1	0	0	0	0	....	....	....	....	....
	Springfield	AHL	56	11	18	29	27	3	1	0	1	2

WHL East Second All-Star Team (1993)

Traded to **New Jersey** by **Chicago** for cash, May 21, 1996. Signed as a free agent by **Toronto**, August 20, 1999.

HUBACEK, Petr (HOO-buh-chehk) — PHI.

Center. Shoots right. 6'2", 183 lbs. Born, Brno, Czech., September 2, 1979.
(Philadelphia's 11th choice, 243rd overall, in 1998 Entry Draft).

			Regular Season					Playoffs				
Season	Club	Lea	GP	G	A	TP	PIM	GP	G	A	TP	PIM
1997-98	HC Brno	Czech-Jr.	17	9	5	14		....	....	....	....	....
	Zetor Brno	Cze-Rep-2	48	6	10	16	....	....	....	....	....	....
1998-99	HC Vitkovice	Cze-Rep	25	0	4	4	2	4	0	0	0	....

HULAK, Daniel (HEW-lahk) — T.B.

Defense. Shoots left. 6'2", 182 lbs. Born, Saskatoon, Sask., August 9, 1980.
(Tampa Bay's 9th choice, 221st overall, in 1998 Entry Draft).

			Regular Season					Playoffs				
Season	Club	Lea	GP	G	A	TP	PIM	GP	G	A	TP	PIM
1997-98	Swift Current	WHL	70	3	14	17	32	....	....	....	....	....
1998-99	Swift Current	WHL	68	6	14	20	71	6	0	0	0	4

HUNTER, Trent — ANA.

Right wing. Shoots right. 6'3", 191 lbs. Born, Red Deer, Alta., July 5, 1980.
(Anaheim's 4th choice, 150th overall, in 1998 Entry Draft).

			Regular Season					Playoffs				
Season	Club	Lea	GP	G	A	TP	PIM	GP	G	A	TP	PIM
1996-97	Red Deer	AJHL	42	30	25	55	50	....	....	....	....	....
1997-98	Prince George	WHL	60	13	14	27	34	8	1	0	1	4
1998-99	Prince George	WHL	50	18	20	38	34	7	2	5	7	2

HUSELIUS, Kristian (hoo-SAY-lee-oos)

Left wing. Shoots left. 6'1", 183 lbs. Born, Stockholm, Sweden, November 10, 1978.
(Florida's 2nd choice, 47th overall, in 1997 Entry Draft).

			Regular Season					Playoffs				
Season	Club	Lea	GP	G	A	TP	PIM	GP	G	A	TP	PIM
1996-97	Farjestads BK	Sweden	13	2	0	2	4	5	1	0	1	0
1997-98	Farjestads BK	Sweden	34	2	1	3	2	11	0	0	0	0
	Farjestads BK	EuroHL	5	2	3	5	0	....	....	....	....	....
1998-99	Farjestads BK	Sweden	28	4	4	8	4	....	....	....	....	....
	Farjestads BK	EuroHL	6	2	2	4	8	1	0	0	0	0
	V. Frolunda	Sweden	20	2	2	4	2	4	1	0	1	0

HUSKINS, Kent — CHI.

Defense. Shoots left. 6'2", 190 lbs. Born, Ottawa, Ont., May 4, 1979.
(Chicago's 3rd choice, 156th overall, in 1998 Entry Draft).

			Regular Season					Playoffs				
Season	Club	Lea	GP	G	A	TP	PIM	GP	G	A	TP	PIM
1997-98	Clarkson	ECAC	35	2	8	10	46	....	....	....	....	....
1998-99	Clarkson	ECAC	37	5	11	16	28	....	....	....	....	....

HUSSEY, Marc

Defense. Shoots right. 6'4", 210 lbs. Born, Chatham, N.B., January 22, 1974.
(Pittsburgh's 2nd choice, 43rd overall, in 1992 Entry Draft).

			Regular Season					Playoffs				
Season	Club	Lea	GP	G	A	TP	PIM	GP	G	A	TP	PIM
1990-91	Moose Jaw	WHL	68	5	8	13	67	8	2	2	4	7
1991-92	Moose Jaw	WHL	72	7	27	34	203	4	1	1	2	0
1992-93	Moose Jaw	WHL	68	12	28	40	121	....	....	....	....	....
1993-94	Moose Jaw	WHL	17	4	5	9	33	....	....	....	....	....
	Tri-City	WHL	16	3	6	9	26	....	....	....	....	....
	Medicine Hat	WHL	41	6	24	30	90	3	0	1	1	4
1994-95	St. John's	AHL	11	0	1	1	20	....	....	....	....	....
	Canada	Nat-Team	36	2	7	9	42	....	....	....	....	....
1995-96	Saint John	AHL	68	10	21	31	120	5	0	0	0	8
1996-97	Saint John	AHL	46	6	18	24	62	....	....	....	....	....
	Utah	IHL	8	0	1	1	6	....	....	....	....	....
	Indianapolis	IHL	14	0	2	2	17	4	0	1	1	10
1997-98	Indianapolis	IHL	23	2	5	7	14	....	....	....	....	....
	Milwaukee	IHL	50	3	15	18	81	10	2	3	5	14
1998-99	Fredericton	AHL	51	3	5	8	105	....	....	....	....	....
	Grand Rapids	IHL	13	0	6	6	14	....	....	....	....	....

Signed as a free agent by **Calgary**, March 10, 1996. Traded to **Chicago** by **Calgary** for Ravil Gusmanov, March 18, 1997.

HUSSEY, Matt — PIT.

Center. Shoots left. 6'2", 195 lbs. Born, New Haven, CT, May 28, 1979.
(Pittsburgh's 10th choice, 254th overall, in 1998 Entry Draft).

			Regular Season					Playoffs				
Season	Club	Lea	GP	G	A	TP	PIM	GP	G	A	TP	PIM
1997-98	Avon Old Farm	H.S.	26	26	23	49	20	....	....	....	....	....
1998-99	U. of Wisconsin	WCHA	37	10	5	15	18	....	....	....	....	....

HUTCHINS, Tony — ST.L.

Center. Shoots left. 6', 196 lbs. Born, Wolfeboro, NH, January 11, 1977.
(St. Louis' 9th choice, 203rd overall, in 1996 Entry Draft).

			Regular Season					Playoffs				
Season	Club	Lea	GP	G	A	TP	PIM	GP	G	A	TP	PIM
1995-96	Lawrence Prep	H.S.	27	18	20	38	22	....	....	....	....	....
1996-97	Boston College	H.E.	26	8	0	8	10	....	....	....	....	....
1997-98	Boston College	H.E.	39	12	5	17	52	....	....	....	....	....
1998-99	Boston College	H.E.	39	4	9	13	42	....	....	....	....	....

HUTCHINSON, Andrew — NSH.

Defense. Shoots right. 6'2", 186 lbs. Born, Evaston, IL, March 24, 1980.
(Nashville's 4th choice, 54th overall, in 1999 Entry Draft).

			Regular Season					Playoffs				
Season	Club	Lea	GP	G	A	TP	PIM	GP	G	A	TP	PIM
1997-98	Team USA	Under-18	59	7	21	28	53	....	....	....	....	....
1998-99	Michigan State	CCHA	37	3	12	15	26	....	....	....	....	....

HYACINTHE, Seneque — BUF.

Left wing. Shoots left. 6', 180 lbs. Born, Montreal, Que., February 22, 1981.
(Buffalo's 9th choice, 178th overall, in 1999 Entry Draft).

			Regular Season					Playoffs				
Season	Club	Lea	GP	G	A	TP	PIM	GP	G	A	TP	PIM
1997-98	Laval	QMJHL	65	10	8	18	37	8	3	2	5	2
1998-99	Acadie-Bathurst	QMJHL	31	13	17	30	70	....	....	....	....	....
	Val d'Or	QMJHL	32	11	16	27	36	4	0	2	2	2

HYMOVITZ, David — L.A.

Left wing. Shoots left. 5'11", 188 lbs. Born, Boston, MA, May 30, 1973.
(Chicago's 9th choice, 209th overall, in 1992 Entry Draft).

			Regular Season					Playoffs				
Season	Club	Lea	GP	G	A	TP	PIM	GP	G	A	TP	PIM
1992-93	Boston College	H.E.	37	7	6	13	6	....	....	....	....	....
1993-94	Boston College	H.E.	36	18	14	32	18	....	....	....	....	....
1994-95	Boston College	H.E.	35	21	19	40	22	....	....	....	....	....
1995-96	Boston College	H.E.	36	26	18	44	32	....	....	....	....	....
1996-97	Columbus	ECHL	58	39	32	71	29	5	4	1	5	2
	Indianapolis	IHL	6	0	1	1	0	1	0	0	0	0
1997-98	Indianapolis	IHL	63	11	15	26	20	5	1	1	2	6
1998-99	Indianapolis	IHL	78	46	30	76	42	5	2	3	5	2

IHL Second All-Star Team (1999)

Signed as a free agent by **Los Angeles**, June 10, 1999.

IANIERO, Andrew (juh-NAIR-oh) — OTT.

Left wing. Shoots left. 6', 188 lbs. Born, St. Catharines, Ont., January 10, 1981.
(Ottawa's 5th choice, 154th overall, in 1999 Entry Draft).

			Regular Season					Playoffs				
Season	Club	Lea	GP	G	A	TP	PIM	GP	G	A	TP	PIM
1997-98	Brampton	OMHA	45	6	14	20	75	....	....	....	....	....
1998-99	Kingston	OHL	68	21	26	47	81	....	....	....	....	....

INMAN, David — NYR

Center. Shoots left. 6'1", 180 lbs. Born, New York, NY, June 13, 1980.
(NY Rangers' 3rd choice, 59th overall, in 1999 Entry Draft).

			Regular Season					Playoffs				
Season	Club	Lea	GP	G	A	TP	PIM	GP	G	A	TP	PIM
1996-97	Wexford	OJHL	43	32	56	88	59	....	....	....	....	....
1997-98	Wexford	OJHL	37	36	44	80	82	....	....	....	....	....
1998-99	Notre Dame	CCHA	38	10	10	20	74	....	....	....	....	....

IRVING, Joel — CGY.

Center. Shoots right. 6'3", 210 lbs. Born, Lumsden, Sask., January 2, 1976.
(Montreal's 8th choice, 148th overall, in 1994 Entry Draft).

			Regular Season					Playoffs				
Season	Club	Lea	GP	G	A	TP	PIM	GP	G	A	TP	PIM
1993-94	Regina	AJHL	32	16	46	62	22	....	....	....	....	....
1994-95	Western Michigan	CCHA	30	2	3	5	20	....	....	....	....	....
1995-96	Western Michigan	CCHA	39	7	6	13	58	....	....	....	....	....
1996-97	Western Michigan	CCHA	34	8	11	19	62	....	....	....	....	....
1997-98	Western Michigan	CCHA	36	8	10	18	82	....	....	....	....	....
1998-99	Saint John	AHL	5	0	0	0	2	....	....	....	....	....
	Johnstown	ECHL	65	26	20	46	112	....	....	....	....	....

Signed as a free agent by **Calgary**, July 28, 1998.

IVAN, Marek (EE-vahn, MAHR-ehk)

Center. Shoots left. 6'1", 182 lbs. Born, Uhreske Hradiste, Czech., November 17, 1978.
(St. Louis' 9th choice, 244th overall, in 1997 Entry Draft).

			Regular Season					Playoffs				
Season	Club	Lea	GP	G	A	TP	PIM	GP	G	A	TP	PIM
1996-97	Lethbridge	WHL	69	14	10	24	127	19	0	0	0	20
1997-98	Lethbridge	WHL	14	8	6	14	26	....	....	....	....	....
	Moose Jaw	WHL	56	16	13	29	133	4	2	0	2	4
1998-99	Worcester	AHL	7	0	2	2	4	....	....	....	....	....
	Peoria	ECHL	61	27	25	52	206	4	2	1	3	20

JACK, Justin

Right wing. Shoots right. 6'4", 195 lbs. Born, Melfort, Sask., July 11, 1979.
(Tampa Bay's 8th choice, 168th overall, in 1997 Entry Draft).

			Regular Season					Playoffs				
Season	Club	Lea	GP	G	A	TP	PIM	GP	G	A	TP	PIM
1996-97	Kelowna	WHL	37	2	0	2	125	....	....	....	....	....
1997-98	Kelowna	WHL	37	1	3	4	93	7	0	0	0	23
1998-99	Kelowna	WHL	22	0	0	0	43	....	....	....	....	....

JACKMAN, Barret — ST.L.

Defense. Shoots left. 6'1", 200 lbs. Born, Trail, B.C., March 5, 1981.
(St. Louis' 1st choice, 17th overall, in 1999 Entry Draft).

			Regular Season					Playoffs				
Season	Club	Lea	GP	G	A	TP	PIM	GP	G	A	TP	PIM
1996-97	Beaver Valley	BCAHA	32	22	25	47	180	....	....	....	....	....
1997-98	Regina	WHL	68	2	11	13	224	9	0	3	3	32
1998-99	Regina	WHL	70	8	36	44	259	....	....	....	....	....

JACKMAN, Richard — DAL.

Defense. Shoots right. 6'2", 180 lbs. Born, Toronto, Ont., June 28, 1978.
(Dallas' 1st choice, 5th overall, in 1996 Entry Draft).

			Regular Season					Playoffs				
Season	Club	Lea	GP	G	A	TP	PIM	GP	G	A	TP	PIM
1995-96	S.S. Marie	OHL	66	13	29	42	97	4	1	0	1	15
1996-97	S.S. Marie	OHL	53	13	34	47	116	10	2	6	8	24
1997-98	S.S. Marie	OHL	60	33	40	73	111	....	....	....	....	....
	Michigan	IHL	14	1	5	6	10	4	0	0	0	10
1998-99	Michigan	IHL	71	13	17	30	106	5	0	4	4	6

OHL Second All-Star Team (1998)

JACOBS, Ian — FLA.

Right wing. Shoots right. 6'4", 204 lbs. Born, Walpole Island, Ont., May 16, 1980.
(Florida's 8th choice, 203rd overall, in 1998 Entry Draft).

			Regular Season					Playoffs				
Season	Club	Lea	GP	G	A	TP	PIM	GP	G	A	TP	PIM
1997-98	Ottawa	OHL	61	7	8	15	23	9	0	0	0	4
1998-99	Ottawa	OHL	63	7	17	24	46	9	1	2	3	7

JACOBSEN, Michael — CHI.

Defense. Shoots left. 6'1", 207 lbs. Born, Thunder Bay, Ont., July 24, 1981.
(Chicago's 4th choice, 134th overall, in 1999 Entry Draft).

			Regular Season					Playoffs				
Season	Club	Lea	GP	G	A	TP	PIM	GP	G	A	TP	PIM
1997-98	Belleville	OHL	56	7	14	21	14	10	0	3	3	0
1998-99	Belleville	OHL	68	5	27	32	33	21	0	4	4	10

JACQUES, Alexandre (ZHAHK) — DET.

Center. Shoots right. 5'11", 165 lbs. Born, Laval, Que., September 27, 1977.
(Detroit's 6th choice, 162nd overall, in 1996 Entry Draft).

			Regular Season					Playoffs				
Season	Club	Lea	GP	G	A	TP	PIM	GP	G	A	TP	PIM
1994-95	Shawinigan	QMJHL	71	9	8	17	18	14	8	5	13	8
1995-96	Shawinigan	QMJHL	60	25	32	57	57	6	3	2	5	2
1996-97	Shawinigan	QMJHL	70	41	60	101	46	7	3	3	6	2
1997-98	Rimouski	QMJHL	24	17	23	40	47	10	12	10	22	6
	Adirondack	AHL	16	1	1	2	0	....	....	....	....	....
	Toledo	ECHL	9	6	4	10	6	....	....	....	....	....
1998-99	Adirondack	AHL	68	9	13	22	25	3	0	0	0	0

JAMIESON, Dustin — MTL.

Left wing. Shoots left. 6'2", 180 lbs. Born, Sarnia, Ont., May 26, 1981.
(Montreal's 5th choice, 136th overall, in 1999 Entry Draft).

			Regular Season					Playoffs				
Season	Club	Lea	GP	G	A	TP	PIM	GP	G	A	TP	PIM
1997-98	Guelph	OHL	48	3	4	7	0	....	....	....	....	....
1998-99	Guelph	OHL	12	2	7	9	0	....	....	....	....	....
	Sarnia	OHL	54	14	21	35	10	6	1	0	1	2

JANCEVSKI, Dan — DAL.

Defense. Shoots left. 6'2", 208 lbs. Born, Windsor, Ont., June 15, 1981.
(Dallas' 2nd choice, 66th overall, in 1999 Entry Draft).

			Regular Season					Playoffs				
Season	Club	Lea	GP	G	A	TP	PIM	GP	G	A	TP	PIM
1995-96	Riverside	OMHA	59	9	22	31	67	....	....	....	....	....
1996-97	Windsor	OMHA	47	6	20	26	99	....	....	....	....	....
1997-98	Tecumseh	OJHL-B	49	3	11	14	145	....	....	....	....	....
1998-99	London	OHL	68	2	12	14	115	....	....	....	....	....

JANIK, Doug — BUF.

Defense. Shoots left. 6'2", 198 lbs. Born, Agawam, MA, March 26, 1980.
(Buffalo's 3rd choice, 55th overall, in 1999 Entry Draft).

			Regular Season					Playoffs				
Season	Club	Lea	GP	G	A	TP	PIM	GP	G	A	TP	PIM
1996-97	Springfield	EJHL	48	17	33	50	....	....	....	....	....	....
1997-98	Team USA	Under-18	65	8	26	34	105	....	....	....	....	....
1998-99	U. of Maine	H.E.	35	3	13	16	44	....	....	....	....	....

JARDINE, Ryan — FLA.

Left wing. Shoots left. 6', 187 lbs. Born, Ottawa, Ont., March 15, 1980.
(Florida's 4th choice, 89th overall, in 1998 Entry Draft).

			Regular Season					Playoffs				
Season	Club	Lea	GP	G	A	TP	PIM	GP	G	A	TP	PIM
1997-98	S.S. Marie	OHL	65	28	32	60	16	....	....	....	....	....
1998-99	S.S. Marie	OHL	68	27	34	61	56	5	0	1	1	6

JARVIS, Wes — NYR

Defense. Shoots left. 6'4", 203 lbs. Born, Toronto, Ont., April 16, 1979.
(NY Rangers' 2nd choice, 46th overall, in 1997 Entry Draft).

			Regular Season					Playoffs				
Season	Club	Lea	GP	G	A	TP	PIM	GP	G	A	TP	PIM
1996-97	Kitchener	OHL	56	4	8	12	108	13	0	4	4	25
1997-98	Kitchener	OHL	47	10	18	28	112	1	0	0	0	2
1998-99	Kitchener	OHL	52	5	18	23	80	1	0	0	0	2
	Canada	Nat-Team	7	1	0	1	4	....	....	....	....	....

JASPERS, Jason — PHX.

Center/Left wing. Shoots left. 5'11", 185 lbs. Born, Thunder Bay, Ont., April 8, 1981.
(Phoenix's 4th choice, 71st overall, in 1999 Entry Draft).

			Regular Season					Playoffs				
Season	Club	Lea	GP	G	A	TP	PIM	GP	G	A	TP	PIM
1998-99	Sudbury	OHL	68	28	33	61	81	4	2	1	3	13

JENSEN, Erik — N.J.

Right wing. Shoots right. 6'1", 195 lbs. Born, Madison, WI, September 4, 1979.
(New Jersey's 10th choice, 199th overall, in 1998 Entry Draft).

			Regular Season					Playoffs				
Season	Club	Lea	GP	G	A	TP	PIM	GP	G	A	TP	PIM
1997-98	Des Moines	USHL	41	12	14	26	90	....	....	....	....	....
1998-99	Des Moines	USHL	26	5	11	16	62	14	4	3	7	35

JILLSON, Jeff — S.J.

Defense. Shoots right. 6'3", 219 lbs. Born, Providence, RI, July 24, 1980.
(San Jose's 1st choice, 14th overall, in 1999 Entry Draft).

			Regular Season					Playoffs				
Season	Club	Lea	GP	G	A	TP	PIM	GP	G	A	TP	PIM
1996-97	Mt. St. Charles	H.S.	15	16	14	30	20	....	....	....	....	....
1997-98	Mt. St. Charles	H.S.	15	10	13	23	32	....	....	....	....	....
1998-99	U. of Michigan	CCHA	38	5	19	24	71	....	....	....	....	....

JINDRICH, Robert (IHN-drihkh) — S.J.

Defense. Shoots left. 5'11", 190 lbs. Born, Plzen, Czech., October 14, 1976.
(San Jose's 10th choice, 168th overall, in 1995 Entry Draft).

			Regular Season					Playoffs				
Season	Club	Lea	GP	G	A	TP	PIM	GP	G	A	TP	PIM
1993-94	ZKZ Plzen	Cze-Rep	18	0	2	2	....	....	....	....	....	....
1994-95	ZKZ Plzen	Cze-Rep	11	1	0	1	4	....	....	....	....	....
1995-96	ZKZ Plzen	Cze-Rep	37	1	3	4	....	3	0	0	0	....
1996-97	ZKZ Plzen	Cze-Rep	49	7	9	16	44	....	....	....	....	....
1997-98	ZKZ Plzen	Cze-Rep	39	1	6	7	18	4	0	0	0	0
1998-99	ZKZ Plzen	Cze-Rep	52	6	12	18	24	5	1	0	1	....

JOHANSSON, Daniel (yoh-HAN-suhn) — NYI

Defense. Shoots left. 5'11", 180 lbs. Born, Glimakra, Sweden, September 10, 1974.
(NY Islanders' 9th choice, 222nd overall, in 1993 Entry Draft).

			Regular Season					Playoffs				
Season	Club	Lea	GP	G	A	TP	PIM	GP	G	A	TP	PIM
1991-92	HC Rogle	Sweden-2	33	4	9	13	30	....	....	....	....	....
1992-93	HC Rogle	Sweden	28	2	4	6	20	....	....	....	....	....
1993-94	HC Rogle	Sweden	37	5	10	15	34	3	0	0	0	0
1994-95	HC Rogle	Sweden	22	4	2	6	16	....	....	....	....	....
1995-96	HV Jonkoping	Sweden	40	3	5	8	24	4	0	1	1	0
1996-97	HV Jonkoping	Sweden	50	8	7	15	30	5	0	1	1	2
1997-98	HV Jonkoping	Sweden	46	3	9	12	32	5	2	0	2	6
1998-99	HV Jonkoping	Sweden	50	5	7	12	46	....	....	....	....	....

JOHANSSON, Daniel — L.A.

Center. Shoots left. 5'11", 176 lbs. Born, Ornskoldsvik, Sweden, July 5, 1981.
(Los Angeles' 6th choice, 125th overall, in 1999 Entry Draft).

			Regular Season					Playoffs				
Season	Club	Lea	GP	G	A	TP	PIM	GP	G	A	TP	PIM
1997-98	MoDo Hockey	Swede-Jr.	6	0	0	0	0	....	....	....	....	....
1998-99	MoDo Hockey	Swede-Jr.	43	10	19	29	....	....	....	....	....	....

JOHANSSON, Tobias (yoh-HAHN-suhn) — ANA.

Left wing. Shoots left. 5'11", 180 lbs. Born, Malmo, Sweden, October 22, 1977.
(Anaheim's 7th choice, 224th overall, in 1996 Entry Draft).

			Regular Season					Playoffs				
Season	Club	Lea	GP	G	A	TP	PIM	GP	G	A	TP	PIM
1995-96	Malmo IF	Swede-Jr.	30	7	13	20	38	....	....	....	....	....
1996-97	Malmo IF	Swede-Jr.	15	6	8	14	63	....	....	....	....	....
1997-98	Tranas AIF	Sweden-2	31	7	2	9	18	....	....	....	....	....
1998-99	Tranas AIF	Sweden-2	32	11	5	16	28	....	....	....	....	....

JOHNSON, Adam — NYI

Defense. Shoots left. 6'6", 220 lbs. Born, Minneapolis, MN, August 2, 1980.
(NY Islanders' 10th choice, 140th overall, in 1999 Entry Draft).

			Regular Season					Playoffs				
Season	Club	Lea	GP	G	A	TP	PIM	GP	G	A	TP	PIM
1998-99	Greenway High	H.S.	17	5	13	18	32	....	....	....	....	....

JOHNSON, Andy — CHI.

Defense. Shoots left. 6'3", 188 lbs. Born, Fredericton, N.B., March 6, 1978.
(Chicago's 4th choice, 130th overall, in 1996 Entry Draft).

			Regular Season					Playoffs				
Season	Club	Lea	GP	G	A	TP	PIM	GP	G	A	TP	PIM
1995-96	Peterborough	OHL	54	0	4	4	57	22	0	6	6	21
1996-97	Peterborough	OHL	57	4	24	28	82	7	1	2	3	10
1997-98	Peterborough	OHL	60	17	20	37	112	4	0	0	0	6
1998-99	Asheville	UHL	1	1	1	2	0	....	....	....	....	....
	Greenville	ECHL	42	2	5	7	30	....	....	....	....	....

JOHNSSON, Kim (YAWN-suhn) — NYR

Defense. Shoots left. 6'1", 175 lbs. Born, Malmo, Sweden, March 16, 1976.
(NY Rangers' 15th choice, 286th overall, in 1994 Entry Draft).

			Regular Season					Playoffs				
Season	Club	Lea	GP	G	A	TP	PIM	GP	G	A	TP	PIM
1993-94	Malmo IF	Sweden	2	0	0	0	0	....	....	....	....	....
1994-95	Malmo IF	Sweden	13	0	0	0	4	1	0	0	0	0
1995-96	Malmo IF	Sweden	38	2	0	2	30	4	0	1	1	8
1996-97	Malmo IF	Sweden	49	4	9	13	42	4	0	0	0	2
1997-98	Malmo IF	Sweden	45	5	9	14	29	....	....	....	....	....
1998-99	Malmo IF	Sweden	49	9	8	17	76	8	2	3	5	12

JOHNSTONE, Alex — N.J.

Defense. Shoots left. 6'1", 205 lbs. Born, Halifax, N.S., December 28, 1979.

			Regular Season					Playoffs				
Season	Club	Lea	GP	G	A	TP	PIM	GP	G	A	TP	PIM
1996-97	Halifax	QMJHL	39	1	5	6	213	18	1	0	1	48
1997-98	Halifax	QMJHL	66	3	10	13	390	5	0	2	2	8
1998-99	Halifax	QMJHL	60	1	8	9	248	5	0	1	1	4

Signed as a free agent by **New Jersey**, August 8, 1998.

JOKELA, Mikko (YOH-kih-lah, MIH-koh) — N.J.

Defense. Shoots right. 6'1", 212 lbs. Born, Lappeenranta, Finland, March 4, 1980.
(New Jersey's 5th choice, 96th overall, in 1998 Entry Draft).

			Regular Season					Playoffs				
Season	Club	Lea	GP	G	A	TP	PIM	GP	G	A	TP	PIM
1995-96	KalPa Kuopio	Finn-Jr.	11	2	1	3	20	....	....	....	....	....
1996-97	KalPa Kuopio	Finn-Jr.	45	5	7	12	26	5	1	1	2	4
1997-98	HIFK Helsinki	Finn-Jr.	22	2	5	7	14	....	....	....	....	....
	HIFK Helsinki	Finland	16	0	0	0	0	....	....	....	....	....
	Hermes HT	Finland-2	6	0	1	1	2	....	....	....	....	....
1998-99	HIFK Helsinki	Finland	3	0	0	0	2	....	....	....	....	....
	KalPa Kuopio	Finland	42	1	2	3	18	....	....	....	....	....

JONSSON, Hans (YAWN-suhn) PIT.

Defense. Shoots left. 6'1", 183 lbs. Born, Jarved, Sweden, August 2, 1973.
(Pittsburgh's 11th choice, 286th overall, in 1993 Entry Draft).

			Regular Season					Playoffs				
Season	Club	Lea	GP	G	A	TP	PIM	GP	G	A	TP	PIM
1991-92	MoDo Hockey	Sweden	6	0	1	1	4	....	....	....	....	....
1992-93	MoDo Hockey	Sweden	40	2	2	4	24	3	0	1	1	2
1993-94	MoDo Hockey	Sweden	23	4	1	5	18	10	0	1	1	12
1994-95	MoDo Hockey	Sweden	39	4	6	10	30	....	....	....	....	....
1995-96	MoDo Hockey	Sweden	36	10	6	16	30	8	2	1	3	24
1996-97	MoDo Hockey	Sweden	27	7	5	12	18	....	....	....	....	....
1997-98	MoDo Hockey	Sweden	40	8	6	14	40	8	1	1	2	12
1998-99	MoDo Hockey	Sweden	41	3	4	7	40	13	2	4	6	22

JONSSON, Jorgen (YAWN-suhn) NYI

Left wing. Shoots left. 6', 185 lbs. Born, Angelholm, Sweden, September 29, 1972.
(Calgary's 11th choice, 227th overall, in 1994 Entry Draft).

			Regular Season					Playoffs				
Season	Club	Lea	GP	G	A	TP	PIM	GP	G	A	TP	PIM
1992-93	Rogle BK	Sweden	40	17	11	28	28	....	....	....	....	....
1993-94	Rogle BK	Sweden	40	17	14	31	46	....	....	....	....	....
	Sweden	Olympics	6	0	0	0	0	....	....	....	....	....
1994-95	Rogle BK	Sweden	22	4	6	10	18	....	....	....	....	....
1995-96	Farjestads BK	Sweden	39	11	15	26	36	8	0	4	4	6
1996-97	Farjestads BK	Sweden	49	12	21	33	58	14	9	5	14	14
	Farjestads BK	EuroHL	4	2	1	3	2	....	....	....	....	....
1997-98	Farjestads BK	Sweden	45	22	25	47	53	12	2	*9	11	12
	Farjestads BK	EuroHL	7	2	4	6	6	....	....	....	....	....
	Sweden	Olympics	1	0	0	0	0	....	....	....	....	....
1998-99	Farjestads BK	Sweden	48	17	24	41	44	4	0	2	2	4
	Farjestads BK	EuroHL	5	2	4	6	4	2	1	0	1	4

KABERLE, Frantisek (KA-buhr-law) L.A.

Defense. Shoots left. 6', 185 lbs. Born, Kladno, Czech., November 8, 1973.
(Los Angeles' 3rd choice, 76th overall, in 1999 Entry Draft).

			Regular Season					Playoffs				
Season	Club	Lea	GP	G	A	TP	PIM	GP	G	A	TP	PIM
1991-92	Poldi Kladno	Czech.	37	1	4	5	8	8	0	1	1	0
1992-93	Poldi Kladno	Czech.	40	4	5	9	....	9	2	4	6	....
1993-94	HC Kladno	Cze-Rep	41	4	16	20	....	11	1	1	2	....
1994-95	HC Kladno	Cze-Rep	40	7	17	24	20	8	0	3	3	12
1995-96	MoDo Hockey	Sweden	40	5	7	12	34	8	0	1	1	0
1996-97	MoDo Hockey	Sweden	50	3	11	14	28	....	....	....	....	....
1997-98	MoDo Hockey	Sweden	46	5	4	9	22	9	1	1	2	4
1998-99	MoDo Hockey	Sweden	45	15	18	33	4	13	2	5	7	8

KACZOWKA, David (kuh-zow-kuk) ATL.

Left wing. Shoots left. 6'2", 205 lbs. Born, Regina, Sask., July 5, 1981.
(Atlanta's 3rd choice, 98th overall, in 1999 Entry Draft).

			Regular Season					Playoffs				
Season	Club	Lea	GP	G	A	TP	PIM	GP	G	A	TP	PIM
1998-99	Seattle	WHL	60	3	2	5	247	9	0	0	0	24

KALININ, Dimitri (kah-LIHN-ihn) BUF.

Defense. Shoots left. 6'2", 198 lbs. Born, Chelyabinsk, USSR, July 22, 1980.
(Buffalo's 1st choice, 18th overall, in 1998 Entry Draft).

			Regular Season					Playoffs				
Season	Club	Lea	GP	G	A	TP	PIM	GP	G	A	TP	PIM
1995-96	Chelyabinsk	Russia-Jr.	30	10	10	20	60	....	....	....	....	....
	Chelyabinsk	Russia-2	20	0	3	3	10	....	....	....	....	....
1996-97	Chelyabinsk	Russia	2	0	0	0	0	2	0	0	0	0
	Chelyabinsk-2	Russia-3	20	0	0	0	10	....	....	....	....	....
1997-98	Chelyabinsk	Russia	26	0	2	2	24	....	....	....	....	....
1998-99	Moncton	QMJHL	39	7	18	25	44	4	1	1	2	0
	Rochester	AHL	3	0	1	1	14	7	0	0	0	6

KALLARSSON, Tomi (KAL-ahr-suhn) NYR

Defense. Shoots left. 6'3", 194 lbs. Born, Lempaala, Finland, March 15, 1979.
(NY Rangers' 4th choice, 93rd overall, in 1997 Entry Draft).

			Regular Season					Playoffs				
Season	Club	Lea	GP	G	A	TP	PIM	GP	G	A	TP	PIM
1996-97	HPK Hameenlinna	Finn-Jr.	31	1	3	4	26	....	....	....	....	....
1997-98	HPK Hameenlinna	Finland	12	0	0	0	2	....	....	....	....	....
1998-99	HPK Hameenlinna	Finland	25	0	0	0	22	8	0	0	0	8
	HPK Hameenlinna	Finn-Jr.	2	0	1	1	6	....	....	....	....	....
	Ahmat Hyvinkaa	Finland-2	21	2	7	9	52	....	....	....	....	....

KALLIO, Tomi (KAL-ee-oh) ATL.

Left wing. Shoots left. 6'1", 180 lbs. Born, Turku, Finland, January 27, 1977.
(Colorado's 4th choice, 81st overall, in 1995 Entry Draft).

			Regular Season					Playoffs				
Season	Club	Lea	GP	G	A	TP	PIM	GP	G	A	TP	PIM
1994-95	TPS Turku	Finn-Jr.	14	5	12	17	24	....	....	....	....	....
	Kiekko-67	Finland-2	25	8	5	13	16	7	3	1	4	6
1995-96	TPS Turku	Finn-Jr.	8	8	3	11	14	....	....	....	....	....
	Kiekko-67	Finland-2	29	10	11	21	28	....	....	....	....	....
	TPS Turku	Finland	8	2	3	5	10	4	0	0	0	2
1996-97	TPS Turku	Finland	47	9	10	19	18	8	2	0	2	2
	TPS Turku	EuroHL	6	2	0	2	25	4	0	0	0	0
1997-98	TPS Turku	Finland	47	10	10	20	8	4	0	2	2	0
	TPS Turku	EuroHL	6	0	1	1	2	....	....	....	....	....
1998-99	TPS Turku	Finland	54	15	21	36	20	10	3	4	7	6

Claimed by **Atlanta** from **Colorado** in Expansion Draft, June 25, 1999.

KALMIKOV, Konstantin (kahl-mih-KAHV) TOR.

Left wing. Shoots right. 6'4", 211 lbs. Born, Kharkov, USSR, June 14, 1978.
(Toronto's 4th choice, 68th overall, in 1996 Entry Draft).

			Regular Season					Playoffs				
Season	Club	Lea	GP	G	A	TP	PIM	GP	G	A	TP	PIM
1994-95	Druzhba-78	Russia	65	51	55	106	45	....	....	....	....	....
1995-96	Flint	ColHL	38	4	12	16	16	....	....	....	....	....
	Detroit	ColHL	5	0	1	1	0	....	....	....	....	....
1996-97	Sudbury	OHL	66	22	34	56	25	....	....	....	....	....
	St. John's	AHL	2	0	0	0	0	....	....	....	....	....
1997-98	Sudbury	OHL	66	32	32	64	21	10	7	2	9	2
1998-99	St. John's	AHL	52	3	4	7	4	....	....	....	....	....

KAMINSKI, Erik (kay-MIHN-skee)

Right wing. Shoots right. 6'3", 205 lbs. Born, Hudson, OH, March 23, 1976.
(Ottawa's 9th choice, 231st overall, in 1995 Entry Draft).

			Regular Season					Playoffs				
Season	Club	Lea	GP	G	A	TP	PIM	GP	G	A	TP	PIM
1994-95	Cleveland	NAJHL	42	34	33	67	99	....	....	....	....	....
1995-96	Northeastern	H.E.	34	5	8	13	30	....	....	....	....	....
1996-97	Northeastern	H.E.	34	11	7	18	30	....	....	....	....	....
1997-98	Winston-Salem	UHL	3	0	0	0	0	....	....	....	....	....
	Brantford	UHL	21	3	3	6	11	6	1	0	1	2
1998-99	Chesapeake	ECHL	5	0	0	0	0	....	....	....	....	....

• Released by **Chesapeake** (ECHL), October 28, 1998.

KANE, Boyd NYR

Left wing. Shoots left. 6'1", 207 lbs. Born, Swift Current, Sask., April 18, 1978.
(NY Rangers' 4th choice, 114th overall, in 1998 Entry Draft).

			Regular Season					Playoffs				
Season	Club	Lea	GP	G	A	TP	PIM	GP	G	A	TP	PIM
1994-95	Regina	WHL	25	6	5	11	6	4	0	0	0	0
1995-96	Regina	WHL	72	21	42	63	155	11	5	7	12	12
1996-97	Regina	WHL	66	25	50	75	154	5	1	1	2	15
1997-98	Regina	WHL	68	48	45	93	133	9	5	7	12	29
1998-99	Hartford	AHL	56	3	5	8	23	....	....	....	....	....
	Charlotte	ECHL	12	5	6	11	14	....	....	....	....	....

• Re-entered NHL draft. Originally Pittsburgh's 3rd choice, 72nd overall, in 1996 Entry Draft.

KAPANEN, Niko (KA-pah-nehn) DAL.

Center. Shoots left. 5'9", 180 lbs. Born, Hattula, Finland, April 29, 1978
(Dallas' 5th choice, 173rd overall, in 1998 Entry Draft).

			Regular Season					Playoffs				
Season	Club	Lea	GP	G	A	TP	PIM	GP	G	A	TP	PIM
1993-94	HPK Hameenlinna	Finn-Jr.	31	17	33	50	34	....	....	....	....	....
1994-95	HPK Hameenlinna	Finn-Jr.	37	19	44	63	40	....	....	....	....	....
1995-96	HPK Hameenlinna	Finn-Jr.	26	15	22	37	34	....	....	....	....	....
	HPK Hameenlinna	Finland	7	1	0	1	0	....	....	....	....	....
1996-97	HPK Hameenlinna	Finn-Jr.	5	1	7	8	2	2	0	1	1	2
	HPK Hameenlinna	Finland	41	6	9	15	12	10	4	5	9	2
	HPK Hameenlinna	EuroHL	6	3	0	3	4	1	0	0	0	0
1997-98	HPK Hameenlinna	Finn-Jr.	2	1	1	2	0	....	....	....	....	....
	HPK Hameenlinna	Finland	48	8	18	26	44	....	....	....	....	....
1998-99	HPK Hameenlinna	Finland	53	14	29	43	49	8	3	4	7	4

KARALAHTI, Jere (kar-ah-LAHKH-tee, YEH-reh) L.A.

Defense. Shoots right. 6'2", 210 lbs. Born, Helsinki, Finland, March 25, 1975.
(Los Angeles' 7th choice, 146th overall, in 1993 Entry Draft).

			Regular Season					Playoffs				
Season	Club	Lea	GP	G	A	TP	PIM	GP	G	A	TP	PIM
1993-94	HIFK Helsinki	Finland	46	1	10	11	36	3	0	0	0	6
1994-95	HIFK Helsinki	Finland	37	1	7	8	42	3	0	0	0	0
1995-96	HIFK Helsinki	Finland	36	4	6	10	102	3	0	0	0	4
1996-97	HIFK Helsinki	Finland	18	3	5	8	20	....	....	....	....	....
1997-98	HIFK Helsinki	Finland	43	14	16	30	32	9	2	0	2	8
1998-99	HIFK Helsinki	Finland	49	11	22	33	65	11	1	1	2	10
	HIFK Helsinki	EuroHL	6	2	1	3	2	....	....	....	....	....

KARIYA, Steve (kah-REE-ah) VAN.

Left wing. Shoots right. 5'9", 165 lbs. Born, North Vancouver, B.C., December 22, 1977.

			Regular Season					Playoffs				
Season	Club	Lea	GP	G	A	TP	PIM	GP	G	A	TP	PIM
1995-96	U. of Maine	H.E.	39	7	16	23	8	....	....	....	....	....
1996-97	U. of Maine	H.E.	35	19	31	50	10	....	....	....	....	....
1997-98	U. of Maine	H.E.	35	25	25	50	22	....	....	....	....	....
1998-99	U. of Maine	H.E.	41	27	38	65	24	....	....	....	....	....

Hockey East First All-Star Team (1999) • NCAA East First All-American Team (1999)

Signed as a free agent by **Vancouver**, April 21, 1999.

KARLIN, Mattias (KAR-lihn) BOS.

Center/right wing. Shoots left. 5'11", 183 lbs. Born, Ornskoldsvik, Sweden, July 4, 1979.
(Boston's 4th choice, 54th overall, in 1997 Entry Draft).

			Regular Season					Playoffs				
Season	Club	Lea	GP	G	A	TP	PIM	GP	G	A	TP	PIM
1995-96	MoDo Hockey	Swede-Jr.	30	12	23	35	16	....	....	....	....	....
1996-97	MoDo Hockey	Sweden	6	0	0	0	0	....	....	....	....	....
1997-98	MoDo Hockey	Sweden	32	0	2	2	8	1	0	0	0	0
1998-99	MoDo Hockey	Sweden	50	2	5	7	14	13	1	1	2	4

KARLSSON, Andreas ATL.

Center. Shoots left. 6'3", 193 lbs. Born, Luvicka, Sweden, August 19, 1975.
(Calgary's 8th choice, 148th overall, in 1993 Entry Draft).

			Regular Season					Playoffs				
Season	Club	Lea	GP	G	A	TP	PIM	GP	G	A	TP	PIM
1992-93	Leksands IF	Sweden	13	0	0	0	6	....	....	....	....	....
1993-94	Leksands IF	Sweden	21	0	0	0	10	3	0	0	0	0
1994-95	Leksands IF	Sweden	24	7	8	15	0	4	0	1	1	0
1995-96	Leksands IF	Sweden	40	10	13	23	10	....	....	....	....	....
1996-97	Leksands IF	Sweden	49	13	11	24	39	9	2	0	2	2
1997-98	Leksands IF	Sweden	33	9	14	23	20	4	1	0	1	0
	Leksands IF	EuroHL	6	2	3	5	2	....	....	....	....	....
1998-99	Leksands IF	Sweden	49	18	15	33	18	4	1	0	1	6
	Leksands IF	EuroHL	6	1	3	4	2	2	1	1	2	2

Traded to **Atlanta** by **Calgary** for future considerations, June 25, 1999.

KARLSSON, Gabriel DAL.

Center. Shoots left. 6'1", 189 lbs. Born, Borlange, Sweden, January 22, 1980.
(Dallas' 3rd choice, 86th overall, in 1998 Entry Draft).

			Regular Season					Playoffs				
Season	Club	Lea	GP	G	A	TP	PIM	GP	G	A	TP	PIM
1996-97	HV Jonkoping	Swede-Jr.	25	7	9	16	....	....	....	....	....	....
1997-98	HV Jonkoping	Swede-Jr.	27	11	15	26	32	....	....	....	....	....
	HV Jonkoping	Sweden	1	0	0	0	0	....	....	....	....	....
1998-99	HV Jonkoping	Swede-Jr.	12	4	9	13	4	....	....	....	....	....
	HV Jonkoping	Sweden	33	2	1	3	2	....	....	....	....	....

KATCHER, Jeff

Defense. Shoots right. 6'4", 188 lbs. Born, Winnipeg, Man., April 16, 1979.
(Los Angeles' 7th choice, 150th overall, in 1997 Entry Draft).

			Regular Season					Playoffs				
Season	**Club**	**Lea**	**GP**	**G**	**A**	**TP**	**PIM**	**GP**	**G**	**A**	**TP**	**PIM**
1996-97	Brandon	WHL	48	2	2	4	31	....	....	....	....	....
1997-98	Brandon	WHL	9	0	0	0	13	....	....	....	....	....
	Tri-City	WHL	54	1	12	13	104	....	....	....	....	....
1998-99	Tri-City	WHL	60	4	14	18	136	8	2	0	2	20

KAUPPINEN, Marko (KOW-pih-nehn) PHI.

Defense. Shoots left. 6', 178 lbs. Born, Mikkeli, Finland, March 23, 1979.
(Philadelphia's 7th choice, 214th overall, in 1997 Entry Draft).

			Regular Season					Playoffs				
Season	**Club**	**Lea**	**GP**	**G**	**A**	**TP**	**PIM**	**GP**	**G**	**A**	**TP**	**PIM**
1996-97	JyP Jyvaskyla	Finn-Jr.	29	2	3	5	14	7	0	0	0	29
1997-98	JyP Jyvaskyla	Finn-Jr.	16	2	4	6	16	....	....	....	....	....
	Diskos Jyvaskyla	Finland-2	2	2	1	3	0	....	....	....	....	....
	JyP Jyvaskyla	Finland	33	2	6	8	26	....	....	....	....	....
1998-99	JyP Jyvaskyla	Finland	49	5	7	12	56	3	0	0	0	6
	JyP Jyvaskyla	Finn-Jr.	3	2	1	3	6	....	....	....	....	....

KAVANAGH, Pat (KA-vuh-naw) VAN.

Right wing. Shoots right. 6'3", 192 lbs. Born, Ottawa, Ont., March 14, 1979.
(Philadelphia's 2nd choice, 50th overall, in 1997 Entry Draft).

			Regular Season					Playoffs				
Season	**Club**	**Lea**	**GP**	**G**	**A**	**TP**	**PIM**	**GP**	**G**	**A**	**TP**	**PIM**
1996-97	Peterborough	OHL	43	6	8	14	53	11	1	1	2	12
1997-98	Peterborough	OHL	66	10	16	26	85	4	1	0	1	6
1998-99	Peterborough	OHL	68	26	43	69	118	5	0	5	5	10

Traded to **Vancouver** by **Philadelphia** for Vancouver's 6th round choice (Konstantin Rudenko) in 1999 Entry Draft, June 1, 1999.

KAZAKEVICH, Mikhail (kah-zak-KAY-vihch) PIT.

Left wing. Shoots left. 6'1", 187 lbs. Born, Murmansk, USSR, January 14, 1976.
(Pittsburgh's 13th choice, 258th overall, in 1994 Entry Draft).

			Regular Season					Playoffs				
Season	**Club**	**Lea**	**GP**	**G**	**A**	**TP**	**PIM**	**GP**	**G**	**A**	**TP**	**PIM**
1992-93	Yaroslavl	CIS	7	0	1	1	0	3	0	0	0	0
1993-94	Yaroslavl	CIS	4	0	0	0	2	....	....	....	....	....
1994-95	Yaroslavl	CIS	11	1	3	4	2	....	....	....	....	....
1995-96	Moncton	QMJHL	41	7	13	20	16	....	....	....	....	....
	Shawinigan	QMJHL	14	1	3	4	8	4	0	1	1	2
1996-97	Khimik	Russia	1	0	0	0	0	....	....	....	....	....
1997-98	Kristall Saratov	Russia	10	0	1	1	8	....	....	....	....	....
1998-99	St. Petersburg	Russia	2	0	0	0	0	....	....	....	....	....

KEEFE, Sheldon T.B.

Right wing. Shoots right. 5'10", 176 lbs. Born, Brampton, Ont., September 17, 1980.
(Tampa Bay's 1st choice, 47th overall, in 1999 Entry Draft).

			Regular Season					Playoffs				
Season	**Club**	**Lea**	**GP**	**G**	**A**	**TP**	**PIM**	**GP**	**G**	**A**	**TP**	**PIM**
1995-96	Toronto Nats	MTHL	45	66	71	134	....	....	....	....	....	....
1996-97	Quinte	OJHL	44	21	23	44	....	....	....	....	....	....
1997-98	Caledon	OJHL	43	41	40	81	117	....	....	....	....	....
1998-99	St. Michael's	OHL	38	37	37	74	00	....	....	....	....	....
	Barrie	OHL	28	14	28	42	60	10	5	5	10	31

KELLEHER, Chris (KEH-leh-huhr) PIT.

Defense. Shoots left. 6'1", 210 lbs. Born, Cambridge, MA, March 23, 1975.
(Pittsburgh's 5th choice, 130th overall, in 1993 Entry Draft).

			Regular Season					Playoffs				
Season	**Club**	**Lea**	**GP**	**G**	**A**	**TP**	**PIM**	**GP**	**G**	**A**	**TP**	**PIM**
1993-94	St. Sebastian's	H.S.	24	10	21	31	....	....	....	....	....	....
1994-95	Boston University	H.E.	35	3	17	20	62	....	....	....	....	....
1995-96	Boston University	H.E.	37	7	18	25	43	....	....	....	....	....
1996-97	Boston University	H.E.	39	10	24	34	54	....	....	....	....	....
1997-98	Boston University	H.E.	37	4	26	30	40	....	....	....	....	....
1998-99	Syracuse	AHL	45	1	4	5	43	....	....	....	....	....

NCAA East Second All-American Team (1997, 1998) • Hockey East Second All-Star Team (1998)

KELLY, Chris OTT.

Center/Left wing. Shoots left. 6', 179 lbs. Born, Toronto, Ont., November 11, 1980.
(Ottawa's 4th choice, 94th overall, in 1999 Entry Draft).

			Regular Season					Playoffs				
Season	**Club**	**Lea**	**GP**	**G**	**A**	**TP**	**PIM**	**GP**	**G**	**A**	**TP**	**PIM**
1995-96	Toronto Marlies	MTHL	42	25	45	70	25	....	....	....	....	....
1996-97	Aurora	OJHL	49	14	20	34	11	....	....	....	....	....
1997-98	London	OHL	54	15	14	29	4	....	....	....	....	....
1998-99	London	OHL	68	36	41	77	60	....	....	....	....	....

KELMAN, Scott PHX.

Center. Shoots left. 6'2", 185 lbs. Born, Winnipeg, Man., May 7, 1981.
(Phoenix's 1st choice, 15th overall, in 1999 Entry Draft).

			Regular Season					Playoffs				
Season	**Club**	**Lea**	**GP**	**G**	**A**	**TP**	**PIM**	**GP**	**G**	**A**	**TP**	**PIM**
1996-97	Winnipeg	MAHA	35	21	44	65	78	....	....	....	....	....
1997-98	Seattle	WHL	61	13	17	30	35	5	0	0	0	4
1998-99	Seattle	WHL	66	19	54	73	95	11	4	3	7	37

KESA, Teemu (KEH-sah, TA-moo) N.J.

Defense. Shoots right. 6'1", 189 lbs. Born, Helsinki, Finland, June 7, 1981.
(New Jersey's 5th choice, 100th overall, in 1999 Entry Draft).

			Regular Season					Playoffs				
Season	**Club**	**Lea**	**GP**	**G**	**A**	**TP**	**PIM**	**GP**	**G**	**A**	**TP**	**PIM**
1997-98	Ilves Tampere	Finn-Jr.	33	8	1	9	78	....	....	....	....	....
1998-99	Ilves Tampere	Finn-Jr.	31	4	5	9	139	....	....	....	....	....

KETCHESON, B.J. FLA.

Defense. Shoots left. 6'4", 210 lbs. Born, Napanee, Ont., January 29, 1980.
(Florida's 7th choice, 176th overall, in 1998 Entry Draft).

			Regular Season					Playoffs				
Season	**Club**	**Lea**	**GP**	**G**	**A**	**TP**	**PIM**	**GP**	**G**	**A**	**TP**	**PIM**
1996-97	Peterborough	OHL	61	1	3	4	32	9	0	1	1	8
1997-98	Peterborough	OHL	58	3	4	7	99	4	0	1	1	6
1998-99	Peterborough	OHL	62	1	20	21	86	5	0	1	1	4

KIDNEY, Kyle COL.

Left wing. Shoots left. 6'2", 223 lbs. Born, Ithaca, NY, January 11, 1978
(Colorado's 9th choice, 243rd overall, in 1997 Entry Draft).

			Regular Season					Playoffs				
Season	**Club**	**Lea**	**GP**	**G**	**A**	**TP**	**PIM**	**GP**	**G**	**A**	**TP**	**PIM**
1996-97	Salisbury High	H.S.	28	27	35	62	....	....	....	....	....	....
1997-98	U. Mass-Lowell	H.E.	33	3	8	11	38	....	....	....	....	....
1998-99	U. Mass-Lowell	H.E.	30	3	7	10	58	....	....	....	....	....

KINCH, Matthew BUF.

Defense. Shoots left. 5'11", 189 lbs. Born, Red Deer, Alta., February 17, 1980.
(Buffalo's 8th choice, 146th overall, in 1999 Entry Draft).

			Regular Season					Playoffs				
Season	**Club**	**Lea**	**GP**	**G**	**A**	**TP**	**PIM**	**GP**	**G**	**A**	**TP**	**PIM**
1996-97	Calgary	WHL	64	10	22	32	31	....	....	....	....	....
1997-98	Calgary	WHL	55	7	24	31	13	18	3	2	5	4
1998-99	Calgary	WHL	68	14	69	83	16	21	8	15	23	59

KLIMENTIEV, Sergei (klih-MEHN-tyehv) NSH.

Defense. Shoots left. 5'11", 200 lbs. Born, Kiev, USSR, April 5, 1975.
(Buffalo's 4th choice, 121st overall, in 1994 Entry Draft).

			Regular Season					Playoffs				
Season	**Club**	**Lea**	**GP**	**G**	**A**	**TP**	**PIM**	**GP**	**G**	**A**	**TP**	**PIM**
1991-92	SVSM Kiev	CIS-3	42	4	15	19	....	....	....	....	....	....
1992-93	Sokol Kiev	CIS	3	0	0	0	4	1	0	0	0	0
1993-94	Medicine Hat	WHL	72	16	26	42	165	3	0	0	0	4
1994-95	Medicine Hat	WHL	71	19	45	64	146	5	4	2	6	14
	Rochester	AHL	7	0	0	0	8	1	0	0	0	0
1995-96	Rochester	AHL	70	7	29	36	74	19	2	8	10	16
1996-97	Rochester	AHL	77	14	28	42	114	10	1	4	5	28
1997-98	Rochester	AHL	57	4	22	26	94	....	....	....	....	....
1998-99	Philadelphia	AHL	43	5	12	17	99	....	....	....	....	....
	Milwaukee	IHL	35	4	11	15	59	2	0	0	0	6

Signed as a free agent by **Philadelphia**, June 9, 1998. Traded to **Nashville** by **Philadelphia** for cash, January 26, 1999.

KLOUCEK, Tomas (KLOH-chehk, TAW-mahsh) NYR

Defense. Shoots left. 6'2", 205 lbs. Born, Prague, Czech., March 7, 1980.
(NY Rangers' 6th choice, 131st overall, in 1998 Entry Draft).

			Regular Season					Playoffs				
Season	**Club**	**Lea**	**GP**	**G**	**A**	**TP**	**PIM**	**GP**	**G**	**A**	**TP**	**PIM**
1995-96	Slavia Praha	Czech-Jr.	40	2	8	10	....	....	....	....	....	....
1996-97	Slavia Praha	Czech-Jr.	43	4	14	18	44	....	....	....	....	....
1997-98	Slavia Praha	Czech-Jr.	43	1	9	10	....	....	....	....	....	....
1998-99	Cape Breton	QMJHL	59	4	17	21	163	2	0	0	0	4

KOCH, Geoff NSH.

Left wing. Shoots left. 6'1", 190 lbs. Born, Exeter, NH, June 27, 1979.
(Nashville's 3rd choice, 85th overall, in 1998 Entry Draft).

			Regular Season					Playoffs				
Season	**Club**	**Lea**	**GP**	**G**	**A**	**TP**	**PIM**	**GP**	**G**	**A**	**TP**	**PIM**
1994-95	Exeter Academy	H.S.	24	32	20	52	51	....	....	....	....	....
1995-96	Exeter Academy	H.S.	28	37	40	77	48	....	....	....	....	....
1996-97	Exeter Academy	H.S.	22	30	30	60	62	....	....	....	....	....
1997-98	U. of Michigan	CCHA	43	5	6	11	51	....	....	....	....	....
1998-99	U. of Michigan	CCHA	40	4	12	16	101	....	....	....	....	....

KOEHLER, Greg CAR.

Center. Shoots left. 6'2", 195 lbs. Born, Scarborough, Ont., February 27, 1975.

			Regular Season					Playoffs				
Season	**Club**	**Lea**	**GP**	**G**	**A**	**TP**	**PIM**	**GP**	**G**	**A**	**TP**	**PIM**
1996-97	U. Mass-Lowell	H.E.	37	16	20	36	49	....	....	....	....	....
1997-98	U. Mass-Lowell	H.E.	33	20	17	37	62	....	....	....	....	....
	New Haven	AHL	3	0	0	0	2	....	....	....	....	....
1998-99	New Haven	AHL	26	4	0	4	29	....	....	....	....	....
	Florida	ECHL	29	13	14	27	62	6	2	3	5	12

Signed as a free agent by **Carolina**, March 31, 1998.

KOKOREV, Dmitri (KOH-koh-rehf) CGY.

Defense. Shoots left. 6'3", 198 lbs. Born, Moscow, USSR, January 9, 1979.
(Calgary's 4th choice, 51st overall, in 1997 Entry Draft).

			Regular Season					Playoffs				
Season	**Club**	**Lea**	**GP**	**G**	**A**	**TP**	**PIM**	**GP**	**G**	**A**	**TP**	**PIM**
1996-97	Moscow D'amo-2	Russia-3	27	2	4	6	24	....	....	....	....	....
	Moscow D'amo	Russia	1	0	0	0	0	....	....	....	....	....
1997-98	Moscow D'amo-2	Russia-2	24	1	2	3	20	....	....	....	....	....
1998-99	Moscow D'amo	Russia	26	0	1	1	20	8	1	0	1	0

KOLKUNOV, Alexei (kohl-koo-NAHV) PIT.

Center. Shoots right. 6', 201 lbs. Born, Belgorod, USSR, February 3, 1977.
(Pittsburgh's 5th choice, 154th overall, in 1995 Entry Draft).

			Regular Season					Playoffs				
Season	**Club**	**Lea**	**GP**	**G**	**A**	**TP**	**PIM**	**GP**	**G**	**A**	**TP**	**PIM**
1994-95	Soviet Wings	CIS	7	0	0	0	0	4	1	0	1	0
1995-96	Soviet Wings	CIS	43	9	3	12	35	....	....	....	....	....
1996-97	Soviet Wings	Russia	44	9	16	25	36	2	0	0	0	4
1997-98	Soviet Wings	Russia	20	6	4	10	22	....	....	....	....	....
1998-99	Syracuse	AHL	55	5	13	18	20	....	....	....	....	....

KOLNIK, Juraj (KOHL-nihk, YEW-igh) NYI

Right wing. Shoots right. 5'10", 182 lbs. Born, Nitra, Czech., November 13, 1980.
(NY Islanders' 7th choice, 101st overall, in 1999 Entry Draft).

			Regular Season					Playoffs				
Season	Club	Lea	GP	G	A	TP	PIM	GP	G	A	TP	PIM
1997-98	MHC Nitra	Slovak-Jr.	26	28	16	44	50	....	....	....	....	....
	MHC Nitra	Slovakia	28	1	3	4	6	....	....	....	....	....
1998-99	Quebec	QMJHL	12	6	5	11	6	....	....	....	....	....
	Rimouski	QMJHL	50	36	37	73	34	11	9	6	15	6

KOLTSOV, Konstantin (KOHLT-sahv) PIT.

Right wing. Shoots left. 6', 187 lbs. Born, Minsk, USSR, April 17, 1981.
(Pittsburgh's 1st choice, 18th overall, in 1999 Entry Draft).

			Regular Season					Playoffs				
Season	Club	Lea	GP	G	A	TP	PIM	GP	G	A	TP	PIM
1997-98	Cherepovets-2	Russia-3	44	11	12	23	16	....	....	....	....	....
	Cherepovets	Russia	2	0	0	0	2	....	....	....	....	....
1998-99	Cherepovets	Russia	33	3	0	3	8	1	0	0	0	2

KOMARNISKI, Zenith (KOH-mahr-NIHS-kee, ZEE-nihth) VAN.

Defense. Shoots left. 6', 200 lbs. Born, Edmonton, Alta., August 13, 1978.
(Vancouver's 2nd choice, 75th overall, in 1996 Entry Draft).

			Regular Season					Playoffs				
Season	Club	Lea	GP	G	A	TP	PIM	GP	G	A	TP	PIM
1994-95	Tri-City	WHL	66	5	19	24	110	17	1	2	3	47
1995-96	Tri-City	WHL	42	5	21	26	85	....	....	....	....	....
1996-97	Tri-City	WHL	58	12	44	56	112	....	....	....	....	....
1997-98	Tri-City	WHL	3	0	4	4	18	....	....	....	....	....
	Spokane	WHL	43	7	20	27	90	18	4	6	10	49
1998-99	Syracuse	AHL	58	9	19	28	89	....	....	....	....	....

WHL West First All-Star Team (1997)

KOMAROV, Alexei (KOH-muh-rahf) DAL.

Defense. Shoots left. 6'4", 194 lbs. Born, Moscow, USSR, June 11, 1978.
(Dallas' 8th choice, 216th overall, in 1997 Entry Draft).

			Regular Season					Playoffs				
Season	Club	Lea	GP	G	A	TP	PIM	GP	G	A	TP	PIM
1996-97	Moscow D'amo-2	Russia-3	32	2	3	5	12	....	....	....	....	....
1997-98	Yekaterinburg	Russia	19	0	0	0	6	....	....	....	....	....
	Yekaterinburg	Russia-2	22	0	1	1	14	....	....	....	....	....
1998-99	Spartak Moscow	Russia	21	1	0	1	6	....	....	....	....	....

KOPISCHKE, Jay (koh-PIHSH-kee) L.A.

Left wing. Shoots left. 6'3", 210 lbs. Born, Alexandria, MN, February 7, 1978.
(Los Angeles' 8th choice, 193rd overall, in 1997 Entry Draft).

			Regular Season					Playoffs				
Season	Club	Lea	GP	G	A	TP	PIM	GP	G	A	TP	PIM
1996-97	North Iowa	USHL	53	14	17	31	97	....	....	....	....	....
1997-98	Notre Dame	CCHA	40	2	4	6	24	....	....	....	....	....
1998-99	Notre Dame	CCHA	29	0	3	3	30	....	....	....	....	....

KOROBOLIN, Alexander (koh-roh-BOH-lihn) NYR

Defense. Shoots left. 6'2", 189 lbs. Born, Chelyabinsk, USSR, March 12, 1976.
(NY Rangers' 4th choice, 100th overall, in 1994 Entry Draft).

			Regular Season					Playoffs				
Season	Club	Lea	GP	G	A	TP	PIM	GP	G	A	TP	PIM
1993-94	Chelyabinsk	CIS	32	0	0	0	30	....	....	....	....	....
1994-95	Chelyabinsk	CIS-2	STATISTICS NOT AVAILABLE									
1995-96	Chelyabinsk	CIS-2	STATISTICS NOT AVAILABLE									
1996-97	Chelyabinsk	Russia-2	60	2	7	9	54	....	....	....	....	....
1997-98	Chelyabinsk	Russia	45	1	5	6	50	....	....	....	....	....
1998-99	Chelyabinsk	Russia	29	1	4	5	14	....	....	....	....	....

KOROLEV, Evgeny (koh-roh-LEHV) NYI

Defense. Shoots left. 6'1", 186 lbs. Born, Moscow, USSR, July 24, 1978.
(NY Islanders' 9th choice, 192nd overall, in 1996 Entry Draft).

			Regular Season					Playoffs				
Season	Club	Lea	GP	G	A	TP	PIM	GP	G	A	TP	PIM
1995-96	Peterborough	OHL	60	2	12	14	60	6	0	0	0	2
1996-97	Peterborough	OHL	64	5	17	22	60	11	1	1	2	8
1997-98	Peterborough	OHL	37	5	21	26	39	....	....	....	....	....
	London	OHL	27	4	10	14	36	15	2	7	9	29
1998-99	Roanoke	ECHL	2	0	1	1	0	....	....	....	....	....
	Lowell	AHL	54	2	6	8	48	2	0	1	1	0

KOS, Kyle (KOHS) T.B.

Defense. Shoots left. 6'3", 184 lbs. Born, Hope, B.C., May 25, 1979.
(Tampa Bay's 2nd choice, 33rd overall, in 1997 Entry Draft).

			Regular Season					Playoffs				
Season	Club	Lea	GP	G	A	TP	PIM	GP	G	A	TP	PIM
1996-97	Red Deer	WHL	64	2	18	20	40	10	0	0	0	8
1997-98	Red Deer	WHL	71	7	33	40	102	5	0	3	3	4
1998-99	Red Deer	WHL	37	3	17	20	56	....	....	....	....	....
	Kamloops	WHL	28	6	14	20	42	9	0	0	0	8

KOSICK, Mark CAR.

Center. Shoots left. 5'11", 187 lbs. Born, Victoria, B.C., March 25, 1979.
(Carolina's 9th choice, 211th overall, in 1998 Entry Draft).

			Regular Season					Playoffs				
Season	Club	Lea	GP	G	A	TP	PIM	GP	G	A	TP	PIM
1996-97	Victoria	BCJHL	54	21	37	58	12	....	....	....	....	....
1997-98	U. of Michigan	CCHA	45	14	32	46	18	....	....	....	....	....
1998-99	U. of Michigan	CCHA	42	12	23	35	14	....	....	....	....	....

KOTALIK, Ales (KOH-tuh-lihk, AH-lehsh) BUF.

Right wing. Shoots right. 6'1", 198 lbs. Born, Jindrichuv Hradec, Czech., December 23, 1978.
(Buffalo's 7th choice, 164th overall, in 1998 Entry Draft).

			Regular Season					Playoffs				
Season	Club	Lea	GP	G	A	TP	PIM	GP	G	A	TP	PIM
1993-94	HC Budejovice	Czech-Jr.	28	12	12	24	....	....	....	....	....	....
1994-95	HC Budejovice	Czech-Jr.	36	26	17	43	....	....	....	....	....	....
1995-96	HC Budejovice	Czech-Jr.	28	6	7	13	....	....	....	....	....	....
1996-97	HC Budejovice	Czech-Jr.	36	15	16	31	24	....	....	....	....	....
1997-98	HC Budejovice	Cze-Rep	47	9	7	16	14	....	....	....	....	....
1998-99	HC Budejovice	Cze-Rep	41	8	13	21	16	3	0	0	0	....

KOVAC, Kristian (KOH-vach) COL.

Right wing. Shoots right. 6'3", 213 lbs. Born, Kosice, Czech., January 1, 1981.
(Colorado's 5th choice, 122nd overall, in 1999 Entry Draft).

			Regular Season					Playoffs				
Season	Club	Lea	GP	G	A	TP	PIM	GP	G	A	TP	PIM
1997-98	HC Kosice	Slovak-Jr.	47	22	11	33	103	....	....	....	....	....
1998-99	HC Kosice	Slovak-Jr.	39	30	20	50	73	2	1	0	1	2
	HC Kosice	Slovakia	6	0	0	0	2	....	....	....	....	....

KRAFT, Milan (KRAFT) PIT.

Center. Shoots right. 6'3", 191 lbs. Born, Plzen, Czech., January 17, 1980.
(Pitsburgh's 1st choice, 23rd overall, in 1998 Entry Draft).

			Regular Season					Playoffs				
Season	Club	Lea	GP	G	A	TP	PIM	GP	G	A	TP	PIM
1995-96	ZKZ Plzen	Czech-Jr.	49	54	41	95	....	....	....	....	....	....
1996-97	ZKZ Plzen	Czech-Jr.	29	24	12	36	....	....	....	....	....	....
	ZKZ Plzen	Cze-Rep	9	0	1	1	2	....	....	....	....	....
1997-98	Keramika Plzen	Czech-Jr.	24	22	21	43	12	....	....	....	....	....
	Keramika Plzen	Cze-Rep	16	0	5	5	0	1	0	0	0	0
1998-99	Prince Albert	WHL	68	40	46	86	32	14	7	13	20	6

KRESTANOVICH, Jordan COL.

Left wing. Shoots left. 6', 168 lbs. Born, Surrey, B.C., June 14, 1981.
(Colorado's 7th choice, 152nd overall, in 1999 Entry Draft).

			Regular Season					Playoffs				
Season	Club	Lea	GP	G	A	TP	PIM	GP	G	A	TP	PIM
1997-98	Calgary	WHL	22	1	0	1	0	13	0	0	0	0
1998-99	Calgary	WHL	62	6	13	19	10	20	3	8	11	4

KREVSUN, Alexander (krehv-SOON) NSH.

Right wing. Shoots left. 5'11", 174 lbs. Born, Togliatti, USSR, June 2, 1980.
(Nashville's 9th choice, 124th overall, in 1999 Entry Draft).

			Regular Season					Playoffs				
Season	Club	Lea	GP	G	A	TP	PIM	GP	G	A	TP	PIM
1996-97	Lada Togliatti	Russia	2	0	0	0	0	....	....	....	....	....
1997-98	Lada Togliatti-2	Russia-3	37	10	5	15	24	....	....	....	....	....
1998-99	CSK Samara	Russia	5	0	2	2	4	2	0	0	0	0

KRISTEK, Jaroslav (KRIHSH-tehk, YAH-roh-slahv) BUF.

Right wing. Shoots left. 6', 183 lbs. Born, Zlin, Czech., March 16, 1980.
(Buffalo's 4th choice, 50th overall, in 1998 Entry Draft).

			Regular Season					Playoffs				
Season	Club	Lea	GP	G	A	TP	PIM	GP	G	A	TP	PIM
1995-96	ZPS Zlin	Czech-Jr.	34	33	20	53	....	....	....	....	....	....
1996-97	ZPS Zlin	Czech-Jr.	44	28	27	55	....	....	....	....	....	....
1997-98	ZPS Zlin	Czech-Jr.	7	8	5	13	....	....	....	....	....	....
	ZPS Zlin	Cze-Rep	37	2	8	10	20	....	....	....	....	....
	HC Prostejov	Czech-2	4	0	0	0	....	....	....	....	....	....
1998-99	Tri-City	WHL	70	38	48	86	55	12	4	3	7	2

KRISTOFFERSON, Marc DAL.

Right wing. Shoots left. 6'3", 200 lbs. Born, Ostersund, Sweden, January 22, 1979.
(Dallas' 4th choice, 105th overall, in 1997 Entry Draft).

			Regular Season					Playoffs				
Season	Club	Lea	GP	G	A	TP	PIM	GP	G	A	TP	PIM
1996-97	Mora IK	Sweden-2	33	1	5	6	26	....	....	....	....	....
1997-98	Mora IK	Sweden-2	27	7	6	13	40	....	....	....	....	....
1998-99	HV Jonkoping	Swede-Jr.	3	0	1	1	27	....	....	....	....	....
	HV Jonkoping	Sweden	34	0	1	1	65	....	....	....	....	....

KROG, Jason (KRAWG) NYI

Center. Shoots right. 5'11", 191 lbs. Born, Fernie, B.C., October 9, 1975.

			Regular Season					Playoffs				
Season	Club	Lea	GP	G	A	TP	PIM	GP	G	A	TP	PIM
1995-96	New Hampshire	H.E.	34	4	16	20	20	....	....	....	....	....
1996-97	New Hampshire	H.E.	39	23	44	67	28	....	....	....	....	....
1997-98	New Hampshire	H.E.	38	*33	33	66	44	....	....	....	....	....
1998-99	New Hampshire	H.E.	41	*34	*51	*85	38	....	....	....	....	....

Hockey East All-Star Team (1997) • NCAA East Second All-American Team (1997) • Hockey East First All-Star Team (1998, 1999) • NCAA East First All-American Team (1999) • NCAA Championship All-Tournament Team (1999) • Won Hobey Baker Memorial Award (Top U S Collegiate player) (1999)

Signed as a free agent by **NY Islanders**, May 14, 1999.

KROPAC, Radoslav (KRO-pahch) NYR

Right wing. Shoots left. 6', 187 lbs. Born, Bratislava, Czech., April 5, 1975.
(NY Rangers' 13th choice, 260th overall, in 1994 Entry Draft).

			Regular Season					Playoffs				
Season	Club	Lea	GP	G	A	TP	PIM	GP	G	A	TP	PIM
1993-94	HC Bratislava	Slovakia	33	7	6	13	12	....	....	....	....	....
1994-95	HC Bratislava	Slovakia	35	17	8	25	38	7	1	2	3	4
1995-96	HC Bratislava	Slovakia	31	5	9	14	8	13	4	3	7	....
1996-97	HC Bratislava	Slovakia	43	8	7	15		2	1	1	2	....
1997-98	HC Bratislava	Slovakia	33	12	12	24	8	11	3	3	6	4
	HC Bratislava	EuroHL	8	0	0	0	6	....	....	....	....	....
1998-99	HC Bratislava	Slovakia	41	27	17	44	24	9	3	6	9	6

KRUCHININ, Andrei (kroo-CHIHN-ihn) MTL.

Defense. Shoots left. 5'11", 176 lbs. Born, Karaganda, USSR, May 18, 1978.
(Montreal's 7th choice, 189th overall, in 1998 Entry Draft).

			Regular Season					Playoffs				
Season	Club	Lea	GP	G	A	TP	PIM	GP	G	A	TP	PIM
1996-97	Lada Togliatti	Russia	19	0	1	1	8	11	0	0	0	0
1997-98	Lada Togliatti	Russia	43	0	4	4	73	....	....	....	....	....
1998-99	Lada Togliatti	Russia	41	1	4	5	56	6	0	1	1	2

KUBOS, Petr (KOO-bawsh)

Defense. Shoots right. 6'2", 189 lbs. Born, Vsetin, Czech., September 10, 1979.
(Montreal's 9th choice, 197th overall, in 1997 Entry Draft).

			Regular Season					Playoffs				
Season	Club	Lea	GP	G	A	TP	PIM	GP	G	A	TP	PIM
1994-95	Petra Vsetin	Czech-Jr.	19	8	11	19	14	....	....	....	....	....
1995-96	Petra Vsetin	Czech-Jr.	37	21	17	38	18	....	....	....	....	....
	Petra Vsetin	Cze-Rep	2	0	0	0	0	....	....	....	....	....
1996-97	Petra Vsetin	Czech-Jr.	14	3	13	16	6	....	....	....	....	....
	Petra Vsetin	Cze-Rep	16	0	1	1	2	....	....	....	....	....
1997-98	Prince George	WHL	58	3	17	20	12	11	1	0	1	0
1998-99	Prince George	WHL	70	8	29	37	52	7	0	2	2	0

KUCERA, Jiri (kuh-CHEH-rah) PIT.

Center. Shoots left. 5'11", 180 lbs. Born, Bratislava, Czech., March 28, 1966.
(Pittsburgh's 8th choice, 152nd overall, in 1987 Entry Draft).

			Regular Season					Playoffs				
Season	Club	Lea	GP	G	A	TP	PIM	GP	G	A	TP	PIM
1986-87	Dukla Jihlava	Czech.	43	13	12	25	18	....	....	....	....	....
1987-88	Skoda Plzen	Czech.	41	21	24	45	22	....	....	....	....	....
1988-89	Skoda Plzen	Czech.	40	20	15	35	22	....	....	....	....	....
1989-89	Skoda Plzen	Czech.	47	13	24	37	....	....	....	....	....	....
1990-91	Tappara	Finland	44	23	34	57	26	3	0	2	2	4
1991-92	Tappara	Finland	44	22	20	42	8	....	....	....	....	....
1992-93	Tappara	Finland	48	22	32	54	20	....	....	....	....	....
1993-94	Tappara	Finland	47	16	26	42	37	10	7	5	12	4
1994-95	Lulea HF	Sweden	40	15	12	27	24	9	2	7	9	8
1995-96	Lulea HF	Sweden	39	15	19	34	38	12	4	6	10	6
1996-97	ZKZ Plzen	Cze-Rep	43	10	23	33	28	....	....	....	....	....
1997-98	EHC Kloten	Switz.	38	8	22	30	18	7	1	2	3	2
1998-99	Lulea HF	Sweden	44	7	21	28	52	5	2	1	3	4

KUDROC, Kristian (KOO-drawch) NYI

Defense. Shoots right. 6'6", 229 lbs. Born, Michalovce, Czech., May 21, 1981.
(NY Islanders' 4th choice, 28th overall, in 1999 Entry Draft).

			Regular Season					Playoffs				
Season	Club	Lea	GP	G	A	TP	PIM	GP	G	A	TP	PIM
1997-98	HK Michalovce	Slovak-Jr.	47	7	4	11	66	....	....	....	....	....
	HK Michalovce	Slovak-2	4	0	0	0	0	....	....	....	....	....
1998-99	HK Michalovce	Slovak-2	17	0	3	3	12	....	....	....	....	....

KUKI, Arto (KUH-kee) MTL.

Center. Shoots left. 6'3", 205 lbs. Born, Espoo, Finland, February 22, 1976.
(Montreal's 6th choice, 96th overall, in 1994 Entry Draft).

			Regular Season					Playoffs				
Season	Club	Lea	GP	G	A	TP	PIM	GP	G	A	TP	PIM
1993-94	Kiekko-Espoo	Finn-Jr.	26	1	10	11	28	....	....	....	....	....
1994-95	Kiekko-Espoo	Finland	4	0	1	1	0	....	....	....	....	....
1995-96	Kiekko-Espoo	Finland	47	6	3	9	16	....	....	....	....	....
1996-97	Kiekko-Espoo	Finland	50	6	15	21	20	4	0	1	1	2
1997-98	Kiekko-Espoo	Finland	17	2	1	3	0	8	1	1	2	2
1998-99	Kiekko-Espoo	Finland	27	2	1	3	22	4	0	1	1	0
	Ahmat Hyvinkaa	Finland-2	5	0	3	3	2	....	....	....	....	....

KULESHOV, Mikhail (koo-leh-SHAWV) COL.

Left wing. Shoots right. 6'2", 200 lbs. Born, Perm, USSR, January 7, 1981.
(Colorado's 1st choice, 25th overall, in 1999 Entry Draft).

			Regular Season					Playoffs				
Season	Club	Lea	GP	G	A	TP	PIM	GP	G	A	TP	PIM
1997-98	Omsk-2 VDV	Russia-3	12	12	3	15	12	....	....	....	....	....
	Omsk-2 VDV	Russia	4	1	0	1	4	....	....	....	....	....
1998-99	Cherepovets	Russia	15	2	0	2	8	3	0	0	0	4

KUPARINEN, Mikko T.B.

Defense. Shoots left. 6'3", 213 lbs. Born, Kerava, Finland, March 29, 1977.
(Tampa Bay's 10th choice, 244th overall, in 1999 Entry Draft).

			Regular Season					Playoffs				
Season	Club	Lea	GP	G	A	TP	PIM	GP	G	A	TP	PIM
1996-97	HPK Hameenlinna	Finn-Jr.	35	0	6	6	38	....	....	....	....	....
	HPK Hameenlinna	Finland	1	0	1	1	2	....	....	....	....	....
1997-98	HPK Hameenlinna	Finn-Jr.	28	2	4	6	18	....	....	....	....	....
1998-99	HPK Hameenlinna	Finland	33	0	3	3	52	....	....	....	....	....
	Ahmat Hyvinkas	Finland-2	3	0	0	0	2	....	....	....	....	....
	Grand Rapids	IHL	19	0	2	2	35	....	....	....	....	....

KUZNETSOV, Maxim (kooz-NEHT-zahv) DET.

Defense. Shoots left. 6'5", 198 lbs. Born, Pavlodar, USSR, March 24, 1977.
(Detroit's 1st choice, 26th overall, in 1995 Entry Draft).

			Regular Season					Playoffs				
Season	Club	Lea	GP	G	A	TP	PIM	GP	G	A	TP	PIM
1994-95	Moscow D'amo	CIS	11	0	0	0	8	....	....	....	....	....
1995-96	Moscow D'amo	CIS	9	1	1	2	22	4	0	0	0	0
1996-97	Moscow D'amo	Russia	23	0	2	2	16	....	....	....	....	....
	Adirondack	AHL	2	0	1	1	6	2	0	0	0	0
1997-98	Adirondack	AHL	51	5	5	10	43	3	0	1	1	4
1998-99	Adirondack	AHL	60	0	4	4	30	3	0	0	0	0

KUZNETSOV, Sergei (kooz-NEHT-zahv) T.B.

Center. Shoots left. 6', 180 lbs. Born, Yaroslavl, USSR, January 29, 1980.
(Tampa Bay's 6th choice, 146th overall, in 1998 Entry Draft).

			Regular Season					Playoffs				
Season	Club	Lea	GP	G	A	TP	PIM	GP	G	A	TP	PIM
1995-96	Yaroslavl	Russia-Jr.	28	14	14	28	20	....	....	....	....	....
1996-97	Yaroslavl-2	Russia-3	62	16	15	31	35	....	....	....	....	....
1997-98	Yaroslavl-2	Russia-2	42	10	13	23	30	....	....	....	....	....
1998-99	Peterborough	OHL	65	8	17	25	39	5	2	1	3	2

KUZNIK, Greg CAR.

Defense. Shoots left. 6', 182 lbs. Born, Prince George, B.C., June 12, 1978.
(Hartford's 7th choice, 171st overall, in 1996 Entry Draft).

			Regular Season					Playoffs				
Season	Club	Lea	GP	G	A	TP	PIM	GP	G	A	TP	PIM
1995-96	Seattle	WHL	70	2	13	15	149	5	0	0	0	6
1996-97	Seattle	WHL	70	4	9	13	161	14	0	2	2	26
1997-98	Seattle	WHL	72	5	12	17	197	5	0	0	0	4
1998-99	New Haven	AHL	27	1	0	1	33	....	....	....	....	....
	Florida	ECHL	50	6	8	14	110	5	1	0	1	0

KWIATKOWSKI, Joel (KWEE-at-KOW-skee) ANA.

Defense. Shoots left. 6'2", 200 lbs. Born, Kindersley, Sask., March 22, 1977.
(Dallas' 7th choice, 194th overall, in 1996 Entry Draft).

			Regular Season					Playoffs				
Season	Club	Lea	GP	G	A	TP	PIM	GP	G	A	TP	PIM
1995-96	Prince George	WHL	72	12	28	40	133	....	....	....	....	....
1996-97	Prince George	WHL	72	15	37	52	94	15	4	2	6	24
1997-98	Prince George	WHL	62	21	43	64	65	11	3	6	9	6
1998-99	Cincinnati	AHL	80	12	21	33	48	3	2	0	2	0

WHL West Second All-Star Team (1997) • WHL West First All-Star Team (1998)

LABRAATEN, Jan (la-BRA-tuhn) CGY.

Left wing. Shoots right. 6'2", 198 lbs. Born, Karlstad, Sweden, February 17, 1977.
(Calgary's 4th choice, 98th overall, in 1995 Entry Draft).

			Regular Season					Playoffs				
Season	Club	Lea	GP	G	A	TP	PIM	GP	G	A	TP	PIM
1994-95	Farjestads BK	Swede-Jr.	25	10	6	16	20	....	....	....	....	....
	Farjestads BK	Sweden	2	0	1	1	2	1	0	0	0	0
1995-96	Farjestads BK	Sweden	4	0	0	0	0	....	....	....	....	....
1996-97	Orebro IK	Sweden-2	30	9	6	15	51	....	....	....	....	....
1997-98	Raleigh	ECHL	41	5	12	17	26	....	....	....	....	....
1998-99	Jacksonville	ECHL	1	0	0	0	0	....	....	....	....	....
	Monroe	WPHL	54	11	21	32	39	6	0	0	0	0

LACHANCE, Bob (lah-CHANTS) ATL.

Right wing. Shoots right. 5'11", 180 lbs. Born, Northampton, MA, February 1, 1974.
(St. Louis' 5th choice, 134th overall, in 1992 Entry Draft).

			Regular Season					Playoffs				
Season	Club	Lea	GP	G	A	TP	PIM	GP	G	A	TP	PIM
1991-92	Springfield	NAJHL	46	40	98	138	87	....	....	....	....	....
1992-93	Boston University	H.E.	33	4	10	14	24	....	....	....	....	....
1993-94	Boston University	H.E.	32	13	19	32	42	....	....	....	....	....
1994-95	Boston University	H.E.	37	12	29	41	51	....	....	....	....	....
1995-96	Boston University	H.E.	39	15	37	52	67	....	....	....	....	....
	Worcester	AHL	7	1	0	1	6	....	....	....	....	....
1996-97	Worcester	AHL	74	21	35	56	66	5	0	2	2	4
1997-98	Worcester	AHL	70	15	33	48	56	11	6	10	16	12
1998-99	Indianapolis	IHL	70	17	46	63	59	7	1	5	6	16

Signed as a free agent by **Atlanta**, July 13, 1999.

LAING, Quintin DET.

Left wing. Shoots left. 6'2", 175 lbs. Born, Rosetown, Sask., June 8, 1979.
(Detroit's 3rd choice, 102nd overall, in 1997 Entry Draft).

			Regular Season					Playoffs				
Season	Club	Lea	GP	G	A	TP	PIM	GP	G	A	TP	PIM
1996-97	Kelowna	WHL	63	13	24	37	54	1	0	0	0	0
1997-98	Kelowna	WHL	59	11	24	35	47	7	0	1	1	8
1998-99	Kelowna	WHL	70	11	10	21	107	6	3	0	3	0

LAKOS, Andre (LA-kaws) N.J.

Defense. Shoots right. 6'6", 210 lbs. Born, Toronto, Ont., July 29, 1979.
(New Jersey's 4th choice, 95th overall, in 1999 Entry Draft).

			Regular Season					Playoffs				
Season	Club	Lea	GP	G	A	TP	PIM	GP	G	A	TP	PIM
1995-96	Montreal Bourassa	QAAA	40	2	13	15	68	....	....	....	....	....
1996-97	Shelburne	OJHL	36	5	12	17	47	....	....	....	....	....
1997-98	Toronto	OHL	49	2	10	12	54	....	....	....	....	....
1998-99	Barrie	OHL	62	4	23	27	40	12	3	3	6	8

LANGFELD, Josh OTT.

Right wing. Shoots right. 6'3", 205 lbs. Born, Fridley, MN, July 17, 1977.
(Ottawa's 3rd choice, 66th overall, in 1997 Entry Draft).

			Regular Season					Playoffs				
Season	Club	Lea	GP	G	A	TP	PIM	GP	G	A	TP	PIM
1995-96	Great Falls	AFJHL	45	45	40	85	105	....	....	....	....	....
1996-97	Lincoln Stars	USHL	38	35	23	58	100	4	3	3	6	....
1997-98	U. of Michigan	CCHA	46	19	17	36	66	....	....	....	....	....
1998-99	U. of Michigan	CCHA	41	21	14	35	84	....	....	....	....	....

NCAA Championship All-Tournament Team (1998)

LANK, Jeff PHI.

Defense. Shoots left. 6'3", 205 lbs. Born, Indian Head, Sask., March 1, 1975.
(Philadelphia's 9th choice, 230th overall, in 1995 Entry Draft).

			Regular Season					Playoffs				
Season	Club	Lea	GP	G	A	TP	PIM	GP	G	A	TP	PIM
1991-92	Prince Albert	WHL	56	2	8	10	26	9	0	0	0	2
1992-93	Prince Albert	WHL	63	1	11	12	60	....	....	....	....	....
1993-94	Prince Albert	WHL	72	9	38	47	62	....	....	....	....	....
1994-95	Prince Albert	WHL	68	12	25	37	60	13	2	10	12	8
1995-96	Hershey	AHL	72	7	13	20	70	5	0	0	0	8
1996-97	Philadelphia	AHL	44	2	12	14	49	7	2	1	3	4
1997-98	Philadelphia	AHL	69	7	9	16	59	20	1	4	5	22
1998-99	Philadelphia	AHL	51	5	10	15	36	2	0	0	0	2

• Re-entered NHL draft. Originally Montreal's 6th choice, 113th overall in 1993 Entry Draft.

LAPLANTE, Eric S.J.

Left wing. Shoots left. 6', 190 lbs. Born, St. Maurice, Que., December 1, 1979.
(San Jose's 3rd choice, 65th overall, in 1998 Entry Draft).

			Regular Season					Playoffs				
Season	Club	Lea	GP	G	A	TP	PIM	GP	G	A	TP	PIM
1996-97	Halifax	QMJHL	68	20	30	50	245	18	3	11	14	28
1997-98	Halifax	QMJHL	40	19	22	41	193	....	....	....	....	....
1998-99	Drummondville	QMJHL	42	14	25	39	258	....	....	....	....	....
	Quebec	QMJHL	23	4	17	21	58	13	8	7	15	45

LARIVIERE, Jacques

Left wing. Shoots left. 6'1", 210 lbs. Born, Sorel, Que., December 18, 1979.
(New Jersey's 9th choice, 172nd overall, in 1998 Entry Draft).

			Regular Season					Playoffs				
Season	Club	Lea	GP	G	A	TP	PIM	GP	G	A	TP	PIM
1996-97	Moncton	QMJHL	3	0	0	0	5	....	....	....	....	....
1997-98	Moncton	QMJHL	68	3	1	4	249	9	0	0	0	15
1998-99	Moncton	QMJHL	66	5	5	10	306	4	0	1	1	12

LAUZON, Ryan — PHX.

Center. Shoots left. 5'10", 185 lbs. Born, Halifax, N.S., October 8, 1980.
(Phoenix's 5th choice, 116th overall, in 1999 Entry Draft).

			Regular Season					Playoffs				
Season	Club	Lea	GP	G	A	TP	PIM	GP	G	A	TP	PIM
1996-97	Hull	QMJHL	65	8	10	18	16	14	1	0	1	0
1997-98	Hull	QMJHL	64	33	56	89	37	11	8	13	21	2
1998-99	Hull	QMJHL	57	21	47	68	36	23	3	20	23	10

LAW, Kirby — ATL.

Right wing. Shoots right. 6'1", 180 lbs. Born, McCreary, Man., March 11, 1977.

			Regular Season					Playoffs				
Season	Club	Lea	GP	G	A	TP	PIM	GP	G	A	TP	PIM
1992-93	Dauphin	MAHA	48	20	15	35	8	....	..	..	..	..
1993-94	Saskatoon	WHL	66	9	11	20	39	16	0	0	0	6
1994-95	Saskatoon	WHL	46	10	15	25	44	....	..	..	..	..
	Lethbridge	WHL	24	4	10	14	38	....	..	..	..	..
1995-96	Lethbridge	WHL	71	17	45	62	133	4	0	0	0	12
1996-97	Lethbridge	WHL	72	39	52	91	200	19	4	14	18	60
1997-98	Brandon	WHL	49	34	44	78	153	9	3	3	6	41
1998-99	Orlando	IHL	67	18	13	31	136	....	..	..	..	..
	Adirondack	AHL	11	2	3	5	40	3	1	0	1	2

Signed as a free agent by **Atlanta**, July 27, 1999.

LAZAREV, Yevgeny (LA-zahr-ehv, YEHV-geh-nee) — COL.

Right wing. Shoots left. 6'2", 215 lbs. Born, Kharkov, USSR, April 25, 1980.
(Colorado's 8th choice, 79th overall, in 1998 Entry Draft).

			Regular Season					Playoffs				
Season	Club	Lea	GP	G	A	TP	PIM	GP	G	A	TP	PIM
1995-96	Yaroslavl-2	Russia-2	60	32	30	62	45	....	..	..	..	..
1996-97	Yaroslavl-2	Russia-3	44	18	15	33	38	16	23	21	44	22
	Yaroslavl	Russia	1	0	0	0	0	....	..	..	..	..
1997-98	Kitchener	OJHL	11	9	13	22	19	5	5	2	7	17
1998-99	Hershey	AHL	53	6	15	21	18	....	..	..	..	..

LEACH, Jay — PHX.

Defense. Shoots left. 6'3", 202 lbs. Born, Syracuse, NY, September 2, 1979.
(Phoenix's 5th choice, 115th overall, in 1998 Entry Draft).

			Regular Season					Playoffs				
Season	Club	Lea	GP	G	A	TP	PIM	GP	G	A	TP	PIM
1996-97	Capital District	NAJHL	57	8	50	58	140	....	..	..	..	..
1997-98	Providence	H.E.	32	0	8	8	29	....	..	..	..	..
1998-99	Providence	H.E.	33	1	8	9	42	....	..	..	..	..

LEAHY, Patrick — NYR

Right wing. Shoots right. 6'3", 190 lbs. Born, Brighton, MA, June 9, 1979.
(NY Rangers' 5th choice, 122nd overall, in 1998 Entry Draft).

			Regular Season					Playoffs				
Season	Club	Lea	GP	G	A	TP	PIM	GP	G	A	TP	PIM
1997-98	U. of Miami-Ohio	CCHA	28	0	1	1	24	....	..	..	..	..
1998-99	U. of Miami-Ohio	CCHA	34	10	20	30	40	....	..	..	..	..

LeCOMPTE, Eric (luh-COMP)

Left wing. Shoots left. 6'4", 190 lbs. Born, Montreal, Que., April 4, 1975.
(Chicago's 1st choice, 24th overall, in 1993 Entry Draft).

			Regular Season					Playoffs				
Season	Club	Lea	GP	G	A	TP	PIM	GP	G	A	TP	PIM
1991-92	Hull	QMJHL	60	16	17	33	138	6	1	0	1	4
1992-93	Hull	QMJHL	66	33	38	71	149	10	4	4	8	52
1993-94	Hull	QMJHL	62	39	49	88	171	20	10	10	20	68
1994-95	Hull	QMJHL	12	11	9	20	58	....	..	..	..	..
	St-Jean	QMJHL	18	9	10	19	54	....	..	..	..	..
	Sherbrooke	QMJHL	34	22	29	51	111	4	2	2	4	4
	Indianapolis	IHL	3	2	0	2	2	....	..	..	..	..
1995-96	Indianapolis	IHL	79	24	20	44	131	....	..	..	..	..
1996-97	Worcester	AHL	8	0	1	1	4	....	..	..	..	..
	Indianapolis	IHL	35	2	3	5	74	....	..	..	..	..
	Fort Wayne	IHL	14	1	2	3	62	....	..	..	..	..
1997-98	Indianapolis	IHL	46	7	11	18	52	....	..	..	..	..
	Cincinnati	AHL	26	11	8	19	68	....	..	..	..	..
1998-99	Cincinnati	AHL	67	11	22	33	183	3	1	2	3	0

Signed as a free agent by **Anaheim**, August 18, 1998.

LEEB, Greg — DAL.

Center. Shoots left. 5'9", 160 lbs. Born, Red Deer, Alta., May 31, 1977.

			Regular Season					Playoffs				
Season	Club	Lea	GP	G	A	TP	PIM	GP	G	A	TP	PIM
1994-95	Spokane	WHL	72	21	34	55	48	11	5	10	15	10
1995-96	Spokane	WHL	64	33	21	54	54	18	1	7	8	16
1996-97	Spokane	WHL	72	27	59	86	69	9	3	3	6	4
1997-98	Spokane	WHL	68	46	50	96	54	18	10	10	20	10
1998-99	Michigan	IHL	77	16	27	43	18	5	0	3	3	4

WHL West Second All-Star Team (1998)

Signed as a free agent by **Dallas**, July 24, 1998.

LEGAULT, Jay (LEH-goh) — ANA.

Left wing. Shoots left. 6'4", 205 lbs. Born, Peterborough, Ont., May 15, 1979.
(Anaheim's 3rd choice, 72nd overall, in 1997 Entry Draft).

			Regular Season					Playoffs				
Season	Club	Lea	GP	G	A	TP	PIM	GP	G	A	TP	PIM
1995-96	Oshawa	OHL	61	2	11	13	37	5	0	1	1	8
1996-97	Oshawa	OHL	39	13	26	39	50	....	..	..	..	..
	London	OHL	28	6	13	19	37	....	..	..	..	..
1997-98	London	OHL	61	39	56	95	87	16	1	8	9	34
1998-99	London	OHL	65	43	51	94	99	25	8	18	26	40

LEGG, Chris — EDM.

Center. Shoots left. 5'11", 177 lbs. Born, London, Ont., February 19, 1980.
(Edmonton's 7th choice, 171st overall, in 1999 Entry Draft).

			Regular Season					Playoffs				
Season	Club	Lea	GP	G	A	TP	PIM	GP	G	A	TP	PIM
1997-98	London	OJHL-B	50	36	32	68	45	....	..	..	..	..
1998-99	London	OJHL-B	52	38	40	78	28	....	..	..	..	..

LENT, Nicholas — PHX.

Right wing. Shoots right. 6'3", 210 lbs. Born, Boston, MA, June 10, 1977.
(Phoenix's 7th choice, 200th overall, in 1996 Entry Draft).

			Regular Season					Playoffs				
Season	Club	Lea	GP	G	A	TP	PIM	GP	G	A	TP	PIM
1995-96	Omaha	USHL	42	7	9	16	65	6	2	1	3	8
1996-97	Providence	H.E.	27	6	6	12	16	....	..	..	..	..
1997-98	Providence	H.E.	33	6	8	14	30	....	..	..	..	..
1998-99	Providence	H.E.	36	8	3	11	31	....	..	..	..	..

LEOPOLD, Jordan — ANA.

Defense. Shoots left. 6', 193 lbs. Born, Golden Valley, MN, August 3, 1980.
(Anaheim's 1st choice, 44th overall, in 1999 Entry Draft).

			Regular Season					Playoffs				
Season	Club	Lea	GP	G	A	TP	PIM	GP	G	A	TP	PIM
1995-96	Armstrong High	H.S.	19	11	14	25	30	....	..	..	..	..
1996-97	Armstrong High	H.S.	30	24	36	60		....	..	..	..	..
1997-98	Team USA	Under-18	60	11	12	23	16	....	..	..	..	..
1998-99	U. of Minnesota	WCHA	39	7	16	23	20	....	..	..	..	..

LESSARD, Francis (leh-SAHR) — PHI.

Defense. Shoots right. 6'2", 184 lbs. Born, Montreal, Que., May 30, 1979.
(Carolina's 3rd choice, 80th overall, in 1997 Entry Draft).

			Regular Season					Playoffs				
Season	Club	Lea	GP	G	A	TP	PIM	GP	G	A	TP	PIM
1996-97	Val d'Or	QMJHL	66	1	9	10	287	....	..	..	..	..
1997-98	Val d'Or	QMJHL	63	3	20	23	338	19	1	6	7	*101
1998-99	Drummondville	QMJHL	53	12	36	48	295	....	..	..	..	..

Memorial Cup All-Star Team (1998)

Traded to **Philadelphia** by **Carolina** for Philadelphia's 8th round choice (Antti Jokella) in 1999 Entry Draft, May 25, 1999.

LEVESQUE, Willie (luh-VEHK) — S.J.

Right wing. Shoots right. 6', 195 lbs. Born, Oak Bluffs, MA, January 22, 1980.
(San Jose's 3rd choice, 111th overall, in 1999 Entry Draft).

			Regular Season					Playoffs				
Season	Club	Lea	GP	G	A	TP	PIM	GP	G	A	TP	PIM
1997-98	Team USA	Under-18	60	12	24	36	118	....	..	..	..	..
1998-99	Northeastern	H.E.	34	12	10	22	38	....	..	..	..	..

LEVINSKY, Dmitri (leh-VOHN-skee) — CHI.

Right wing. Shoots left. 6'1", 183 lbs. Born, Ust-Kamenogorsk, USSR, June 23, 1981.
(Chicago's 2nd choice, 46th overall, in 1999 Entry Draft).

			Regular Season					Playoffs				
Season	Club	Lea	GP	G	A	TP	PIM	GP	G	A	TP	PIM
1997-98	Omsk-2 VDV	Russia-3	18	5	2	7	8	....	..	..	..	..
1998-99	Cherepovets-2	Russia-3				STATISTICS NOT AVAILABLE						
	Cherepovets	Russia	1	0	0	0	0	....	..	..	..	..

LEVERSTROM, Erik (LEH-vuhr-struhm) — PHX.

Defense. Shoots left. 6'2", 198 lbs. Born, Grums, Sweden, May 2, 1980.
(Phoenix's 7th choice, 168th overall, in 1999 Entry Draft).

			Regular Season					Playoffs				
Season	Club	Lea	GP	G	A	TP	PIM	GP	G	A	TP	PIM
1996-97	Grums IK	Sweden-2	1	0	0	0	0	....	..	..	..	..
1997-98	Grums IK	Sweden-2	4	0	0	0	2	....	..	..	..	..
1998-99	Grums IK	Sweden-2	29	3	9	12	42	....	..	..	..	..

LIND, Eric — PIT.

Defense. Shoots right. 6'1", 198 lbs. Born, New Canaan, CT, March 12, 1978.
(Pittsburgh's 9th choice, 234th overall, in 1997 Entry Draft).

			Regular Season					Playoffs				
Season	Club	Lea	GP	G	A	TP	PIM	GP	G	A	TP	PIM
1996-97	Avon Old Farms	H.S.	55	18	39	57	50	....	..	..	..	..
1997-98	New Hampshire	H.E.	33	1	11	12	63	....	..	..	..	..
1998-99	New Hampshire	H.E.	41	3	9	12	20	....	..	..	..	..

LINDSTROM, Sanny (LIHND-struhm) — COL.

Defense. Shoots left. 6'2", 194 lbs. Born, Huddinge, Sweden, December 24, 1979.
(Colorado's 4th choice, 112th overall, in 1999 Entry Draft).

			Regular Season					Playoffs				
Season	Club	Lea	GP	G	A	TP	PIM	GP	G	A	TP	PIM
1997-98	Huddinge IF	Sweden-2	32	6	6	12	46	....	..	..	..	..
1998-99	Huddinge IF	Sweden-2	23	3	2	5	45	....	..	..	..	..

LINGREN, Steve

Defense. Shoots left. 6', 193 lbs. Born, Lake Cowachin, B.C., July 23, 1973.

			Regular Season					Playoffs				
Season	Club	Lea	GP	G	A	TP	PIM	GP	G	A	TP	PIM
1991-92	Victoria	WHL	70	4	14	18	103	....	..	..	..	..
1992-93	Victoria	WHL	72	10	43	53	148	....	..	..	..	..
1993-94	Victoria	WHL	56	14	21	35	118	....	..	..	..	..
	Kalamazoo	IHL	2	0	0	0	0	....	..	..	..	..
1994-95	Dayton	ECHL	64	11	23	34	128	9	2	8	10	16
1995-96	Dayton	ECHL	51	15	28	43	83	....	..	..	..	..
	Cornwall	AHL	1	0	1	1	0	....	..	..	..	..
1996-97	Dayton	ECHL	9	2	5	7	15	....	..	..	..	..
	Hershey	AHL	40	3	10	13	67	12	1	2	3	8
1997-98	Hershey	AHL	63	12	18	30	89	....	..	..	..	..
1998-99	Kentucky	AHL	74	11	19	30	60	12	0	4	4	0

ECHL First All-Star Team (1996)

Signed as a free agent by **San Jose**, July 23, 1998.

LINNIK, Maxim (LIH-nihk, mahx-EEM) — ST.L.

Defense. Shoots left. 6'4", 185 lbs. Born, Kiev, USSR, September 6, 1979.
(St. Louis' 2nd choice, 41st overall, in 1998 Entry Draft).

			Regular Season					Playoffs				
Season	Club	Lea	GP	G	A	TP	PIM	GP	G	A	TP	PIM
1996-97	Sokol Kiev	Russia-2	7	0	0	0	0	....	..	..	..	..
1997-98	St. Thomas	OJHL	35	4	14	18	130	....	..	..	..	..
1998-99	Plymouth	OHL	21	0	3	3	19	....	..	..	..	..
	Windsor	OHL	19	1	2	3	14	3	0	1	1	0

LINTNER, Richard (LIHNT-nuhr) NSH.

Defense. Shoots right. 6'3", 194 lbs. Born, Trencin, Czech., November 15, 1977.
(Phoenix's 4th choice, 119th overall, in 1996 Entry Draft).

			Regular Season					Playoffs				
Season	Club	Lea	GP	G	A	TP	PIM	GP	G	A	TP	PIM
1994-95	Dukla Trencin	Slovak-Jr.	42	12	13	25	20	....	....	....	....	....
1995-96	Dukla Trencin	Slovak-Jr.	30	15	17	32	210	....	....	....	....	....
	Dukla Trencin	Slovakia	2	0	0	0	0	....	....	....	....	....
1996-97	Spisska Nova	Slovakia	35	2	1	3	....	....	....	....	....	....
1997-98	Springfield	AHL	71	6	9	15	61	3	1	1	2	4
1998-99	Springfield	AHL	8	0	1	1	16	....	....	....	....	....
	Milwaukee	IHL	66	9	16	25	75	....	....	....	....	....

Traded to **Nashville** by **Phoenix** with Cliff Ronning for future considerations, October 31, 1998.

LOJKIN, Alexei (LOHZH-kihn)

Left wing. Shoots left. 5'9", 176 lbs. Born, Minsk, USSR, February 21, 1974.

			Regular Season					Playoffs				
Season	Club	Lea	GP	G	A	TP	PIM	GP	G	A	TP	PIM
1993-94	Chicoutimi	QMJHL	66	40	67	107	68	27	9	34	43	15
1994-95	Chicoutimi	QMJHL	57	43	58	101	26	11	6	5	11	2
1995-96	Fredericton	AHL	73	24	33	57	16	7	1	3	4	0
1996-97	Fredericton	AHL	79	33	56	89	41	....	....	....	....	....
1997-98	Fredericton	AHL	61	13	22	35	18	2	0	1	1	0
1998-99	Fredericton	AHL	71	20	20	40	16	....	....	....	....	....
	Grand Rapids	IHL	10	1	2	3	4	....	....	....	....	....

Signed as a free agent by **Montreal**, September 11, 1997.

LONG, Andrew FLA.

Center. Shoots right. 6'2", 181 lbs. Born, Toronto, Ont., August 10, 1978.
(Florida's 5th choice, 129th overall, in 1996 Entry Draft).

			Regular Season					Playoffs				
Season	Club	Lea	GP	G	A	TP	PIM	GP	G	A	TP	PIM
1994-95	Guelph	OHL	36	1	6	7	9	....	....	....	....	....
1995-96	Guelph	OHL	48	8	10	18	16	10	0	1	1	4
1996-97	Guelph	OHL	42	10	36	46	30	13	2	10	12	6
1997-98	Guelph	OHL	62	29	40	69	41	8	3	3	6	10
1998-99	New Haven	AHL	16	0	3	3	8	....	....	....	....	....
	Miami	ECHL	25	7	8	15	16	....	....	....	....	....

LOVDAHL, Anders (LUHV-duhl) COL.

Center. Shoots left. 6'3", 189 lbs. Born, Borlange, Sweden, February 4, 1981.
(Colorado's 8th choice, 158th overall, in 1999 Entry Draft).

			Regular Season					Playoffs				
Season	Club	Lea	GP	G	A	TP	PIM	GP	G	A	TP	PIM
1997-98	HV Jonkoping	Swede-Jr.	26	5	5	10	18	....	....	....	....	....
1998-99	HV Jonkoping	Swede-Jr.			STATISTICS NOT AVAILABLE							

LOVEN, Fredrik (LUH-vehn) PHX.

Center. Shoots left. 6'2", 183 lbs. Born, Stockholm, Sweden, March 14, 1977.
(Winnipeg's 10th choice, 189th overall, in 1995 Entry Draft).

			Regular Season					Playoffs				
Season	Club	Lea	GP	G	A	TP	PIM	GP	G	A	TP	PIM
1994-95	Djurgardens IF	Swede-Jr.	29	6	10	16	14	....	....	....		
1995-96	Djurgardens IF	Sweden	4	0	0	0	0	4	0	0	0	0
1996-97	Djurgardens IF	Sweden	7	0	0	0	0	....	....	....	....	....
	Djurgardens IF	Swede-Jr.	4	2	2	4	8	....	....	....	....	....
	Arlanda	Sweden-2	5	0	3	3	4	....	....	....	....	....
1997-98	Bjorkloven IF	Sweden-2	31	5	7	12	8	....	....	....	....	....
1998-99	Hammarby IF	Sweden-2	26	5	10	15	41	....	....	....	....	....

LOW, Reed (LŌH) ST.L.

Right wing. Shoots right. 6'5", 220 lbs. Born, Moose Jaw, Sask., June 21, 1976.
(St. Louis' 7th choice, 177th overall, in 1996 Entry Draft).

			Regular Season					Playoffs				
Season	Club	Lea	GP	G	A	TP	PIM	GP	G	A	TP	PIM
1995-96	Moose Jaw	WHL	61	12	7	19	221	....	....	....	....	....
1996-97	Moose Jaw	WHL	62	16	11	27	228	12	2	1	3	50
1997-98	Worcester	AHL	17	1	1	2	75	3	0	0	0	0
	Baton Rouge	ECHL	39	4	2	6	145	....	....	....	....	....
1998-99	Worcester	AHL	77	5	6	11	239	4	0	0	0	2

LUCHINKIN, Sergei (loo-CHIHN-kihn) DAL.

Left wing. Shoots left. 5'11", 172 lbs. Born, Dmitrov, USSR, October 16, 1976.
(Dallas' 9th choice, 202nd overall, in 1995 Entry Draft).

			Regular Season					Playoffs				
Season	Club	Lea	GP	G	A	TP	PIM	GP	G	A	TP	PIM
1994-95	Moscow D'amo	CIS	6	1	0	1	4	....	....	....	....	....
1995-96	Moscow D'amo	CIS	21	6	2	8	14	10	0	1	1	6
1996-97	Moscow D'amo	Russia	18	1	5	6	4	....	....	....	....	....
1997-98	Moscow D'amo	EuroHL	1	0	0	0	0	....	....	....	....	....
	Moscow D'amo	Russia	6	0	1	1	0	....	....	....	....	....
	SKA Spartak	Russia	10	0	1	1	4	....	....	....	....	....
1998-99	SKA Spartak	Russia	33	4	5	9	18	....	....	....	....	....

LUNDBOHM, Andy S.J.

Center. Shoots left. 6'4", 225 lbs. Born, Roseau, MN, March 24, 1977.

			Regular Season					Playoffs				
Season	Club	Lea	GP	G	A	TP	PIM	GP	G	A	TP	PIM
1994-95	Roseau High	H.S.	23	....	....	30	....	....	....	....	....	....
1995-96	Army	NCAA	37	21	25	46		....	....	....	....	....
1996-97	Army	NCAA	29	19	27	46	16	....	....	....	....	....
1997-98	Army	NCAA	31	19	25	44		....	....	....	....	....
1998-99	Army	NCAA	26	17	15	32	30	....	....	....	....	....

Signed as a free agent by **San Jose**, June 11, 1999.

LUNDMARK, Jamie NYR

Center. Shoots right. 6', 174 lbs. Born, Edmonton, Alta., January 16, 1981.
(NY Rangers' 2nd choice, 9th overall, in 1999 Entry Draft).

			Regular Season					Playoffs				
Season	Club	Lea	GP	G	A	TP	PIM	GP	G	A	TP	PIM
1996-97	St. Albert	AJHL	35	10	9	19	8	....	....	....	....	....
1997-98	St. Albert	AJHL	57	33	58	91	176	....	....	....	....	....
1998-99	Moose Jaw	WHL	70	40	51	91	121	11	5	4	9	24

LUNDQVIST, Stefan (LUHND-kvihst) NYR

Right wing. Shoots left. 6'3", 209 lbs. Born, Gavle, Sweden, February 18, 1978.
(NY Rangers' 7th choice, 180th overall, in 1998 Entry Draft).

			Regular Season					Playoffs				
Season	Club	Lea	GP	G	A	TP	PIM	GP	G	A	TP	PIM
1994-95	Avesta BK	Sweden-2	3	0	1	1	0	....	....	....	....	....
1995-96	Avesta BK	Sweden-3	27	24	13	37	10	....	....	....	....	....
1996-97	Avesta BK	Sweden-3	31	37	29	66	....	....	....	....	....	....
1997-98	Brynas Gavle	Swede-Jr.	21	23	15	38	2	....	....	....	....	....
	Brynas IF	Sweden	27	2	2	4	0	1	0	0	0	0
1998-99	Brynas IF	Sweden	13	0	0	0	0	....	....	....	....	....
	Uppsala ALF	Sweden-2	15	7	8	15	0	....	....	....	....	....
	Mora IK	Sweden-2	23	10	7	17	22	4	2	2	4	2

LUNDSTROM, Per-Anton (LUHND-struhm) PHX.

Defense. Shoots left. 6'2", 185 lbs. Born, Umea, Sweden, September 29, 1977.
(Phoenix's 3rd choice, 62nd overall, in 1996 Entry Draft).

			Regular Season					Playoffs				
Season	Club	Lea	GP	G	A	TP	PIM	GP	G	A	TP	PIM
1995-96	MoDo Hockey	Swede-Jr.	25	3	3	6	28	2	1	0	1	4
	MoDo Hockey	Sweden	19	1	1	2	29	4	0	0	0	2
1996-97	MoDo Hockey	Sweden	35	0	0	0	42	....	....	....	....	....
1997-98	Bjorkloven IF	Sweden-2	31	6	13	19	71	....	....	....	....	....
1998-99	Bjorkloven IF	Sweden	39	1	2	3	36	....	....	....	....	....

LUPASCHUK, Ross (LOO-puhs-chuhk) WSH.

Defense. Shoots right. 6'1", 211 lbs. Born, Edmonton, Alta., January 19, 1981.
(Washington's 4th choice, 34th overall, in 1999 Entry Draft).

			Regular Season					Playoffs				
Season	Club	Lea	GP	G	A	TP	PIM	GP	G	A	TP	PIM
1996-97	Edmonton	AAHA	65	5	22	27	87	....	....	....	....	....
1997-98	Prince Albert	WHL	67	6	12	18	170	....	....	....	....	....
1998-99	Prince Albert	WHL	67	8	20	28	127	14	4	9	13	16

LYASHENKO, Roman (LIGH-a-SHEHN-koh) DAL.

Center. Shoots right. 6', 174 lbs. Born, Murmansk, Russia, May 2, 1979.
(Dallas' 2nd choice, 52nd overall, in 1997 Entry Draft).

			Regular Season					Playoffs				
Season	Club	Lea	GP	G	A	TP	PIM	GP	G	A	TP	PIM
1995-96	Yaroslavl-2	CIS-2	60	7	10	17	12	....	....	....	....	....
1996-97	Yaroslavl	Russia	42	5	7	12	16	9	3	0	3	6
	Yaroslavl-2	Russia-3	2	1	1	2	8	....	....	....	....	....
1997-98	Yaroslavl	Russia	46	7	6	13	28	....	....	....	....	....
	Yaroslavl	EuroHL	10	1	1	2	2	....	....	....	....	....
1998-99	Yaroslavl	Russia	42	10	9	19	51	9	0	4	4	8

LYDMAN, Toni (LEED-man) CGY.

Defense. Shoots left. 6'1", 183 lbs. Born, Lahti, Finland, September 25, 1977.
(Calgary's 5th choice, 89th overall, in 1996 Entry Draft).

			Regular Season					Playoffs				
Season	Club	Lea	GP	G	A	TP	PIM	GP	G	A	TP	PIM
1995-96	Reipas Lahti	Finn-Jr.	9	2	2	4	6	....	....	....	....	....
	Reipas Lahti	Finland	39	5	2	7	30	3	0	1	1	0
1996-97	Tappara	Finland	49	1	2	3	65	3	0	0	0	6
1997-98	Tappara	Finland	48	4	10	14	48	4	0	2	2	0
1998-99	HIFK Helsinki	Finland	42	4	7	11	36	11	0	3	3	2

LYNESS, Chris T.B.

Defense. Shoots right. 6'1", 200 lbs. Born, Montreal, Que., March 2, 1980.
(Tampa Bay's 10th choice, 229th overall, in 1998 Entry Draft).

			Regular Season					Playoffs				
Season	Club	Lea	GP	G	A	TP	PIM	GP	G	A	TP	PIM
1997-98	Rouyn-Noranda	QMJHL	65	2	15	17	100	6	0	1	1	12
1998-99	Rouyn-Noranda	QMJHL	25	3	6	9	49	....	....	....	....	....
	Cape Breton	QMJHL	42	12	17	29	35	5	0	1	1	4

LYSAK, Brett CAR.

Center. Shoots left. 6', 190 lbs. Born, Edmonton, Alta., December 30, 1980.
(Carolina's 2nd choice, 49th overall, in 1999 Entry Draft).

			Regular Season					Playoffs				
Season	Club	Lea	GP	G	A	TP	PIM	GP	G	A	TP	PIM
1995-96	St. Albert	AAHA	35	20	23	43	68	....	....	....	....	....
1996-97	Regina	WHL	66	11	14	25	41	5	0	1	1	5
1997-98	Regina	WHL	70	22	38	60	82	9	6	2	8	8
1998-99	Regina	WHL	61	39	49	88	84	....	....	....	....	....

MacISAAC, Dave L.A.

Defense. Shoots left. 6'2", 225 lbs. Born, Arlington, MA, April 23, 1972.

			Regular Season					Playoffs				
Season	Club	Lea	GP	G	A	TP	PIM	GP	G	A	TP	PIM
1992-93	U. of Maine	H.E.	35	5	32	37	14	....	....	....	....	....
1993-94	U. of Maine	H.E.	31	4	20	24	22	....	....	....	....	....
1994-95	U. of Maine	H.E.	44	5	13	18	44	....	....	....	....	....
	Milwaukee	IHL	2	0	0	0	5	9	0	2	2	2
1995-96	Milwaukee	IHL	71	7	16	23	165	....	....	....	....	....
1996-97	Philadelphia	AHL	61	3	15	18	187	10	0	1	1	31
1997-98	Philadelphia	AHL	80	7	21	28	241	18	5	13	18	20
1998-99	Philadelphia	AHL	47	6	15	21	98	16	2	5	7	50

Signed as a free agent by **Philadelphia**, July 30, 1996. Signed as a free agent by **LA Kings**, August 27, 1999.

MACKENZIE, Derek ATL.

Center. Shoots left. 5'11", 169 lbs. Born, Sudbury, Ont., June 11, 1981.
(Atlanta's 6th choice, 128th overall, in 1999 Entry Draft).

			Regular Season					Playoffs				
Season	Club	Lea	GP	G	A	TP	PIM	GP	G	A	TP	PIM
1997-98	Sudbury	OHL	59	9	11	20	26	....	....	....	....	....
1998-99	Sudbury	OHL	68	22	65	87	74	....	....	....	....	....

MacNEIL, Ian — CAR.

Center. Shoots left. 6'2", 171 lbs. Born, Halifax, N.S., April 27, 1977.
(Hartford's 3rd choice, 85th overall, in 1995 Entry Draft).

				Regular Season					Playoffs			
Season	Club	Lea	GP	G	A	TP	PIM	GP	G	A	TP	PIM
1994-95	Oshawa	OHL	60	7	21	28	62	7	0	2	2	0
1995-96	Oshawa	OHL	49	15	17	32	54	5	1	2	3	8
1996-97	Oshawa	OHL	64	23	20	43	96	18	2	3	5	37
1997-98	New Haven	AHL	68	12	21	33	67	3	1	0	1	10
1998-99	New Haven	AHL	47	6	4	10	62	....	....	....	....	....

Rights transferred to **Carolina** after **Hartford** franchise relocated, June 25, 1997.

MacNEVIN, Josh — N.J.

Defense. Shoots right. 6'2", 185 lbs. Born, Calgary, Alta., July 14, 1977.
(New Jersey's 8th choice, 101st overall, in 1996 Entry Draft).

				Regular Season					Playoffs			
Season	Club	Lea	GP	G	A	TP	PIM	GP	G	A	TP	PIM
1995-96	Vernon	BCJHL	51	13	45	58	54	....	....	....	....	....
1996-97	Providence	H.E.	30	5	9	14	18	....	....	....	....	....
1997-98	Providence	H.E.	33	5	14	19	39	....	....	....	....	....
1998-99	Providence	H.E.	36	6	29	35	52	....	....	....	....	....

MADER, Mike — NYI

Right wing. Shoots right. 6'2", 180 lbs. Born, Manchester, CT, November 7, 1975.
(Winnipeg's 10th choice, 238th overall, in 1994 Entry Draft).

				Regular Season					Playoffs			
Season	Club	Lea	GP	G	A	TP	PIM	GP	G	A	TP	PIM
1993-94	Loomis High	H.S.	26	12	35	47	....	....	....	....	....	....
1994-95	Providence	H.E.	29	1	5	6	26	....	....	....	....	....
1995-96	Providence	H.E.	37	3	6	9	33	....	....	....	....	....
1996-97	Providence	H.E.	35	4	10	14	48	....	....	....	....	....
1997-98	Providence	H.E.	34	7	13	20	50	....	....	....	....	....
	Springfield	AHL	2	0	0	0	0	....	....	....	....	....
1998-99	Roanoke	ECHL	14	3	2	5	38	....	....	....	....	....
	Lowell	AHL	52	5	9	14	91	2	0	0	0	0

Signed as a free agent by **NY Islanders**, September 11, 1998.

MAGNUSON, William — COL.

Defense. Shoots right. 6'5", 232 lbs. Born, Anchorage, AK, February 19, 1980.
(Colorado's 6th choice, 142nd overall, in 1999 Entry Draft).

				Regular Season					Playoffs			
Season	Club	Lea	GP	G	A	TP	PIM	GP	G	A	TP	PIM
1997-98	Team USA	Under-18	69	2	15	17	62	....	....	....	....	....
1998-99	Lake Superior	CCHA	31	0	0	0	44	....	....	....	....	....

MAKINEN, Marko — (mya-KIH-nehn)

Right wing. Shoots right. 6'5", 200 lbs. Born, Turku, Finland, March 31, 1977.
(San Jose's 3rd choice, 64th overall, in 1995 Entry Draft).

				Regular Season					Playoffs			
Season	Club	Lea	GP	G	A	TP	PIM	GP	G	A	TP	PIM
1994-95	TPS Turku	Finn-Jr.	26	7	1	8	34	....	....	....	....	....
	Kiekko-67	Finland-2	4	0	0	0	6	....	....	....	....	....
1995-96	TPS Turku	Finn-Jr.	11	5	1	6	28	....	....	....	....	....
	Kiekko-67	Finn-Jr.	4	4	2	6	12	....	....	....	....	....
	Kiekko-67	Finland-2	21	6	2	8	98	6	2	2	4	6
1996-97	Kiekko-Espoo	Finland	15	2	1	3	34	4	0	0	0	0
	Kiekko-67	Finland-2	30	2	8	10	63	....	....	....	....	....
1997-98	Kentucky	AHL	26	2	2	4	15	....	....	....	....	....
	Louisville	ECHL	38	10	6	16	19	....	....	....	....	....
1998-99	Indianapolis	IHL	5	0	0	0	0	....	....	....	....	....
	Greenville	ECHL	20	3	5	8	14	....	....	....	....	....
	Lukko Rauma	Finland	21	1	0	1	30	....	....	....	....	....

Traded to **Chicago** by **San Jose** for cash, October 14, 1998.

MALENKYKH, Vladimir — (MAH-lihn-keh) — PIT.

Defense. Shoots left. 6'1", 187 lbs. Born, Togliatti, USSR, October 1, 1980.
(Pittsburgh's 7th choice, 157th overall, in 1999 Entry Draft).

				Regular Season					Playoffs			
Season	Club	Lea	GP	G	A	TP	PIM	GP	G	A	TP	PIM
1997-98	Lada Togliatti-2	Russia-3	39	6	4	10	112	....	....	....	....	....
1998-99	Lada Togliatti	Russia	9	0	0	0	2	....	....	....	....	....

MALONE, Ryan — PIT.

Left wing. Shoots left. 6'3", 190 lbs. Born, Pittsburgh, PA, December 1, 1979.
(Pittsburgh's 5th choice, 115th overall, in 1999 Entry Draft).

				Regular Season					Playoffs			
Season	Club	Lea	GP	G	A	TP	PIM	GP	G	A	TP	PIM
1997-98	Shattuck High	H.S.	50	41	44	85	69	....	....	....	....	....
1998-99	Omaha	USHL	51	14	22	36	81	....	....	....	....	....

MANNING, Paul — CGY.

Defense. Shoots left. 6'4", 193 lbs. Born, Red Deer, Alta., April 15, 1979.
(Calgary's 3rd choice, 62nd overall, in 1998 Entry Draft).

				Regular Season					Playoffs			
Season	Club	Lea	GP	G	A	TP	PIM	GP	G	A	TP	PIM
1996-97	Red Deer	HJHL-B	36	9	33	42	....	....	....	....	....	....
1997-98	Colorado College	WCHA	30	1	5	6	16	....	....	....	....	....
1998-99	Colorado College	WCHA	41	3	10	13	75	....	....	....	....	....

MAPLETOFT, Justin — NYI

Center. Shoots left. 6'1", 180 lbs. Born, Lloydminster, Sask., January 11, 1981.
(NY Islanders' 9th choice, 130th overall, in 1999 Entry Draft).

				Regular Season					Playoffs			
Season	Club	Lea	GP	G	A	TP	PIM	GP	G	A	TP	PIM
1997-98	Red Deer	WHL	65	9	4	13	41	....	....	....	....	....
1998-99	Red Deer	WHL	72	24	22	46	81	....	....	....	....	....

MARA, Rob — (MA-rah) — CHI.

Right wing. Shoots right. 6'2", 215 lbs. Born, Boston, MA, September 25, 1975.
(Chicago's 10th choice, 263rd overall, in 1994 Entry Draft).

				Regular Season					Playoffs			
Season	Club	Lea	GP	G	A	TP	PIM	GP	G	A	TP	PIM
1993-94	Belmont Hill	H.S.	28	18	28	46	....	....	....	....	....	....
1994-95	Colgate	ECAC	33	6	8	14	33	....	....	....	....	....
1995-96	Colgate	ECAC	33	8	6	14	36	....	....	....	....	....
1996-97	Colgate	ECAC	32	18	15	33	44	....	....	....	....	....
1997-98	Colgate	ECAC	32	13	11	24	66	....	....	....	....	....
1998-99	Indianapolis	IHL					DID NOT PLAY – INJURED					

• Missed entire 1998-99 season recovering from pre-season shoulder injury, October 3, 1998.

MARCHANT, Terry — (mahr-SHAHNT)

Left wing. Shoots left. 6'2", 205 lbs. Born, Buffalo, NY, February 24, 1976.
(Edmonton's 9th choice, 136th overall, in 1994 Entry Draft).

				Regular Season					Playoffs			
Season	Club	Lea	GP	G	A	TP	PIM	GP	G	A	TP	PIM
1993-94	Niagara Scenics	NAJHL	42	27	40	67	43	....	....	....	....	....
1994-95	Lake Superior	CCHA	23	2	5	7	12	....	....	....	....	....
1995-96	Lake Superior	CCHA	36	8	5	13	15	....	....	....	....	....
1996-97	Lake Superior	CCHA	38	12	14	26	26	....	....	....	....	....
1997-98	Lake Superior	CCHA	36	17	22	39	24	....	....	....	....	....
1998-99	Hamilton	AHL	47	12	8	20	10	2	1	0	1	0

CCHA Second All-Star Team (1998)

MARKKANEN, Mikko — (MAHR-kah-nehn, MEE-koh) — S.J.

Right wing. Shoots right. 5'9", 165 lbs. Born, Turku, Finland, January 9, 1977.
(San Jose's 12th choice, 220th overall, in 1995 Entry Draft).

				Regular Season					Playoffs			
Season	Club	Lea	GP	G	A	TP	PIM	GP	G	A	TP	PIM
1994-95	TPS Turku	Finn-Jr.	32	10	8	18	28	....	....	....	....	....
	Kiekko-67	Finland-2	1	0	1	1	0	....	....	....	....	....
1995-96	TPS Turku	Finn-Jr.	7	2	3	5	16	....	....	....	....	....
	Kiekko-67	Finland-2	38	9	11	20	34	6	1	1	2	6
1996-97	Kiekko-67	Finland-2	43	15	3	18	51	....	....	....	....	....
1997-98	TuTo Turku	Finland-2	24	2	4	6	12	....	....	....	....	....
	EHC Nordhorn	German-2	21	9	6	15	8	....	....	....	....	....
1998-99	Trondheim IK	Norway	40	7	7	14	12	3	0	1	1	0

MARKOV, Andrei — (MAHR-kahf) — MTL.

Defense. Shoots left. 6', 185 lbs. Born, Voskresensk, USSR, December 20, 1978.
(Montreal's 6th choice, 162nd overall, in 1998 Entry Draft).

				Regular Season					Playoffs			
Season	Club	Lea	GP	G	A	TP	PIM	GP	G	A	TP	PIM
1995-96	Khimik	CIS	38	0	0	0	14	....	....	....	....	....
1996-97	Khimik	Russia	43	8	4	12	32	2	1	1	2	0
1997-98	Khimik	Russia	43	10	5	15	83	....	....	....	....	....
1998-99	Moscow D'amo	Russia	38	10	11	21	32	16	3	6	9	6

MARTIN, Jeff — BUF.

Center. Shoots left. 6'1", 177 lbs. Born, Stratford, Ont., April 26, 1979.
(Buffalo's 4th choice, 75th overall, in 1997 Entry Draft).

				Regular Season					Playoffs			
Season	Club	Lea	GP	G	A	TP	PIM	GP	G	A	TP	PIM
1995-96	Windsor	OHL	63	9	5	14	8	7	1	1	2	4
1996-97	Windsor	OHL	65	24	23	47	37	5	2	0	2	2
1997-98	Windsor	OHL	65	40	54	94	48	....	....	....	....	....
1998-99	Windsor	OHL	65	30	38	68	38	5	2	0	2	2

MARTONE, Mike — (mahr-TOHN) — PHX.

Defense. Shoots right. 6'2", 200 lbs. Born, Sault Ste. Marie, Ont., September 26, 1977.
(Buffalo's 6th choice, 106th overall, in 1996 Entry Draft).

				Regular Season					Playoffs			
Season	Club	Lea	GP	G	A	TP	PIM	GP	G	A	TP	PIM
1994-95	Peterborough	OHL	62	3	9	12	99	10	0	2	2	4
1995-96	Peterborough	OHL	64	3	12	15	127	24	7	5	12	37
1996-97	Peterborough	OHL	50	9	21	30	104	10	0	6	6	30
1997-98	Peterborough	OHL	48	5	17	22	88	4	0	2	2	10
1998-99	Springfield	AHL	2	0	0	0	2	....	....	....	....	....
	Mississippi	ECHL	44	5	11	16	59	18	0	3	3	40

Signed as a free agent by **Phoenix**, August 12, 1998.

MARTYNYUK, Denis — (mahr-tih-nyook) — VAN.

Left wing. Shoots left. 6'3", 190 lbs. Born, Kapfenberg, Austria, July 26, 1979.
(Vancouver's 11th choice, 201st overall, in 1997 Entry Draft).

				Regular Season					Playoffs			
Season	Club	Lea	GP	G	A	TP	PIM	GP	G	A	TP	PIM
1994-95	CSKA Moscow	Russia-Jr.	34	25	25	50	20	....	....	....	....	....
1995-96	CSKA Moscow	Russia-Jr.	36	10	15	25	20	....	....	....	....	....
	CSKA Moscow-2	Russia-2	25	2	5	7	20	....	....	....	....	....
1996-97	CSKA Moscow-2	Russia-3	41	7	4	11	12	....	....	....	....	....
	CSKA Moscow	Russia	3	1	0	1	0	....	....	....	....	....
1997-98	SKA Spartak-2	Russia-3	45	9	5	14	34	....	....	....	....	....
1998-99	SKA Spartak	Russia	17	0	0	0	8	....	....	....	....	....

MATEJOVSKY, Radek — (ma-teh-YAHV-skee) — NYI

Right wing. Shoots right. 6'1", 187 lbs. Born, Praha, Czech., November 17, 1977.
(NY Islanders' 9th choice, 250th overall, in 1998 Entry Draft).

				Regular Season					Playoffs			
Season	Club	Lea	GP	G	A	TP	PIM	GP	G	A	TP	PIM
1992-93	HC Budejovice	Czech-Jr.	25	38	24	62	....	....	....	....	....	....
1993-94	Slavia Praha	Czech-Jr.	45	30	26	56	....	....	....	....	....	....
1994-95	Slavia Praha	Czech-Jr.	28	7	8	15	12	....	....	....	....	....
1995-96	Slavia Praha	Czech-Jr	47	37	21	58	24	....	....	....	....	....
1996-97	Slavia Praha	Cze-Rep	41	3	4	7	10	3	0	0	0	0
	HC Beroun	C-Rep-2	12	3	1	4	18	....	....	....	....	....
1997-98	Slavia Praha	Cze-Rep	52	9	4	13	24	3	0	0	0	0
1998-99	Dukla Jihla	Cze-Rep	52	12	10	22	57	....	....	....	....	....

MATHIEU, Alexandre (mah-TYOO) PIT.

Left wing. Shoots left. 6'2", 176 lbs. Born, Repentigny, Que., February 12, 1979.
(Pittsburgh's 4th choice, 97th overall, in 1997 Entry Draft).

			Regular Season					Playoffs				
Season	Club	Lea	GP	G	A	TP	PIM	GP	G	A	TP	PIM
1996-97	Halifax	QMJHL	70	12	22	34	16	18	2	5	7	2
1997-98	Halifax	QMJHL	68	35	41	76	52	5	1	1	2	4
1998-99	Halifax	QMJHL	69	21	27	48	90	5	0	1	1	4

MAXIMENKO, Andrei (max-EE-mehn-koh) DET.

Left wing. Shoots right. 5'11", 172 lbs. Born, Moscow, USSR, January 10, 1981.
(Detroit's 2nd choice, 149th overall, in 1999 Entry Draft).

			Regular Season					Playoffs				
Season	Club	Lea	GP	G	A	TP	PIM	GP	G	A	TP	PIM
1997-98	Soviet Wings-2	Russia-3	42	2	4	6	12	....	....	....	....	....
1998-99	Soviet Wings	Russia	15	0	1	1	16	....	....	....	....	....

MAXWELL, Dennis TOR.

Center. Shoots Right. 6'2", 210 lbs. Born, Dauphin, MAN., June 4, 1974.
(Tampa Bay's 8th choice, 170th overall, in 1992 Entry Draft).

			Regular Season					Playoffs				
Season	Club	Lea	GP	G	A	TP	PIM	GP	G	A	TP	PIM
1990-91	Hamilton	OJHL-B	42	8	29	37	161	....	....	....	....	....
1991-92	Niagara Falls	OHL	66	20	26	46	139	17	4	9	13	32
1992-93	Niagara Falls	OHL	12	5	9	14	21	....	....	....	....	....
	Sudbury	OHL	52	15	24	39	116	14	3	4	7	42
1993-94	Niagara Falls	OHL	17	2	14	16	41	....	....	....	....	....
	Newmarket	OHL	41	12	24	36	113	....	....	....	....	....
1994-95	Sarnia	OHL	55	16	30	46	227	....	....	....	....	....
1995-96	Binghamton	AHL	8	1	0	1	7	....	....	....	....	....
	Charlotte	ECHL	51	25	19	44	291	14	5	5	10	78
1996-97	Tallahassee	ECHL	30	13	22	35	175	....	....	....	....	....
	Carolina	AHL	2	0	0	0	2	....	....	....	....	....
	St. John's	AHL	22	2	2	4	97	....	....	....	....	....
	San Antonio	IHL	14	1	4	5	32	4	1	0	1	41
1997-98	San Antonio	IHL	6	0	0	0	49	....	....	....	....	....
	Quebec	IHL	55	9	13	22	249	....	....	....	....	....
1998-99	St. John's	AHL	41	9	16	25	212	5	0	3	3	8

Signed as a free agent by **Toronto**, September 28, 1998.

McCAMBRIDGE, Keith BOS.

Defense. Shoots left. 6'2", 205 lbs. Born, Thompson, Man., February 1, 1974.
(Calgary's 10th choice, 201st overall, in 1994 Entry Draft).

			Regular Season					Playoffs				
Season	Club	Lea	GP	G	A	TP	PIM	GP	G	A	TP	PIM
1991-92	Swift Current	WHL	72	1	4	5	84	8	0	0	0	2
1992-93	Swift Current	WHL	70	0	6	6	87	17	0	1	1	27
1993-94	Swift Current	WHL	71	0	10	10	179	7	0	0	0	4
1994-95	Swift Current	WHL	48	5	7	12	120	....	....	....	....	....
	Kamloops	WHL	21	0	6	6	90	21	0	5	5	49
1995-96	Saint John	AHL	48	1	3	4	89	16	0	0	0	6
1996-97	Saint John	AHL	56	2	1	3	109	....	....	....	....	....
1997-98	Saint John	AHL	56	4	4	8	118	....	....	....	....	....
	Las Vegas	IHL	10	0	1	1	16	4	0	0	0	9
1998-99	Las Vegas	IHL	18	1	2	3	56	....	....	....	....	....
	Long Beach	IHL	52	2	5	7	200	8	0	0	0	20

Signed as free agent by **Boston**, August 20, 1999.

McCARTHY, Steve CHI.

Defense. Shoots left. 6', 197 lbs. Born, Trail, B.C., February 3, 1981.
(Chicago's 1st choice, 23rd overall, in 1999 Entry Draft).

			Regular Season					Playoffs				
Season	Club	Lea	GP	G	A	TP	PIM	GP	G	A	TP	PIM
1996-97	Trail	BCAHA	57	25	52	77	81	....	....	....	....	....
	Edmonton	WHL	2	0	0	0	0	....	....	....	....	....
1997-98	Edmonton	WHL	58	11	29	40	59	....	....	....	....	....
1998-99	Kootenay	WHL	57	19	33	52	79	6	0	5	5	8

McCORMICK, Morgan FLA.

Right wing. Shoots right. 6'3", 199 lbs. Born, Guelph, Ont., February 21, 1981.
(Florida's 5th choice, 103rd overall, in 1999 Entry Draft).

			Regular Season					Playoffs				
Season	Club	Lea	GP	G	A	TP	PIM	GP	G	A	TP	PIM
1998-99	Kingston	OHL	34	6	5	11	43	5	0	0	0	13

McDONALD, Brent CAR.

Center. Shoots right. 5'11", 170 lbs. Born, Olds, Alta., October 7, 1979.
(Carolina's 10th choice, 239th overall, in 1998 Entry Draft).

			Regular Season					Playoffs				
Season	Club	Lea	GP	G	A	TP	PIM	GP	G	A	TP	PIM
1995-96	Red Deer	WHL	68	1	7	8	55	6	0	1	1	2
1996-97	Red Deer	WHL	69	11	17	28	94	16	4	3	7	38
1997-98	Red Deer	WHL	69	18	27	45	93	5	0	2	2	4
1998-99	Red Deer	WHL	38	17	18	35	64	....	....	....	....	....
	Prince George	WHL	34	13	13	26	40	7	1	1	2	18

McDONELL, Kent DET.

Right wing. Shoots right. 6'2", 195 lbs. Born, Williamstown, Ont., March 1, 1979.
(Detroit's 3rd choice, 181st overall, in 1999 Entry Draft).

			Regular Season					Playoffs				
Season	Club	Lea	GP	G	A	TP	PIM	GP	G	A	TP	PIM
1996-97	Guelph	OHL	56	7	5	12	57	16	0	2	2	4
1997-98	Guelph	OHL	64	28	23	51	76	12	7	4	11	18
1998-99	Guelph	OHL	60	31	38	69	110	11	4	3	7	36

• Re-entered NHL draft. Originally Carolina's 9th choice, 225th overall, in 1997 Entry Draft.

McGRATTAN, Brian L.A.

Right wing. Shoots right. 6'3", 210 lbs. Born, Hamilton, Ont., September 2, 1981.
(Los Angeles' 5th choice, 104th overall, in 1999 Entry Draft).

			Regular Season					Playoffs				
Season	Club	Lea	GP	G	A	TP	PIM	GP	G	A	TP	PIM
1997-98	Guelph	OHL	25	3	2	5	11	....	....	....	....	....
1998-99	Guelph	OHL	6	1	3	4	15	....	....	....	....	....
	Sudbury	OHL	53	7	10	17	153	4	0	0	0	8

McKERCHER, Jeff DAL.

Defense. Shoots right. 6'2", 197 lbs. Born, Cornwall, Ont., January 14, 1979.
(Dallas' 7th choice, 189th overall, in 1997 Entry Draft).

			Regular Season					Playoffs				
Season	Club	Lea	GP	G	A	TP	PIM	GP	G	A	TP	PIM
1996-97	Barrie	OHL	60	1	4	5	32	9	0	1	1	13
1997-98	Barrie	OHL	51	0	2	2	21	6	0	0	0	2
1998-99	S.S. Marie	OHL	8	0	0	0	0	....	....	....	....	....
	Peterborough	OHL	57	1	7	8	22	5	0	0	0	4

McLAREN, Steve PHI.

Left wing. Shoots left. 6', 194 lbs. Born, Owen Sound, Ont., February 3, 1975.
(Chicago's 3rd choice, 85th overall, in 1994 Entry Draft).

			Regular Season					Playoffs				
Season	Club	Lea	GP	G	A	TP	PIM	GP	G	A	TP	PIM
1993-94	North Bay	OHL	55	2	15	17	130	18	0	3	3	50
1994-95	North Bay	OHL	27	3	10	13	119	6	2	1	3	23
1995-96	Indianapolis	IHL	54	1	2	3	170	3	0	0	0	2
1996-97	Indianapolis	IHL	63	2	5	7	309	4	0	0	0	10
1997-98	Indianapolis	IHL	61	3	5	8	208	5	0	0	0	24
1998-99	Philadelphia	AHL	52	4	3	7	216	7	0	0	0	2

Signed as a free agent by **Philadelphia**, August 24, 1998.

McLEOD, Gavin OTT.

Defense. Shoots left. 6'4", 187 lbs. Born, Fort Sasaktchewan, Alta., January 1, 1980.
(Ottawa's 6th choice, 130th overall, in 1998 Entry Draft).

			Regular Season					Playoffs				
Season	Club	Lea	GP	G	A	TP	PIM	GP	G	A	TP	PIM
1996-97	Kelowna	WHL	60	0	6	6	44	....	....	....	....	....
1997-98	Kelowna	WHL	70	3	17	20	98	7	0	0	0	14
1998-99	Kelowna	WHL	49	5	15	20	140	6	1	0	1	6

McMAHON, Mark (muhk-MAN) CAR.

Defense. Shoots left. 6'1", 179 lbs. Born, Geralton, Ont., February 10, 1978.
(Hartford's 5th choice, 116th overall, in 1996 Entry Draft).

			Regular Season					Playoffs				
Season	Club	Lea	GP	G	A	TP	PIM	GP	G	A	TP	PIM
1994-95	Elmira	OJHL-B	41	3	10	13	91	....	....	....	....	....
1995-96	Kitchener	OHL	55	1	8	9	105	5	0	1	1	17
1996-97	Kitchener	OHL	63	4	18	22	155	13	0	6	6	31
1997-98	Kitchener	OHL	61	12	38	50	175	6	1	5	6	27
	New Haven	AHL	4	0	1	1	6	2	0	0	0	16
1998-99	Plymouth	OHL	34	2	12	14	91	11	0	1	1	25
	Florida	ECHL	13	1	4	5	59	....	....	....	....	....

McNEIL, Shawn

Center. Shoots left. 5'11", 175 lbs. Born, Pembroke, Ont., March 17, 1978.
(Washington's 6th choice, 78th overall, in 1996 Entry Draft).

			Regular Season					Playoffs				
Season	Club	Lea	GP	G	A	TP	PIM	GP	G	A	TP	PIM
1993-94	Bonneyville	AMHA	37	22	39	61	40	....	....	....	....	....
	Kamloops	WHL	1	0	0	0	0	....	....	....	....	....
1994-95	Kamloops	WHL	43	4	3	7	11	9	0	1	1	0
1995-96	Kamloops	WHL	67	15	30	45	21	10	4	12	16	17
1996-97	Kamloops	WHL	70	38	47	85	37	5	1	3	4	2
1997-98	Red Deer	WHL	72	47	62	109	69	5	1	3	4	9
1998-99	Red Deer	WHL	72	44	59	103	87	9	8	7	15	6

MELENOVSKY, Marek (meh-leh-NAHF-skee) TOR.

Center. Shoots left. 5'10", 180 lbs. Born, Humpolec, Czech., March 30, 1977.
(Toronto's 5th choice, 171st overall, in 1995 Entry Draft).

			Regular Season					Playoffs				
Season	Club	Lea	GP	G	A	TP	PIM	GP	G	A	TP	PIM
1993-94	Dukla Jihlava	Cze-Rep	1	0	0	0	....	....	....	....	....	....
1994-95	Dukla Jihlava	Czech-Jr	28	23	11	34	....	....	....	....	....	....
	Dukla Jihlava	Cze-Rep	3	0	0	0	0	5	1	3	4	0
1995-96	Dukla Jihlava	Cze-Rep	33	3	3	6	....	5	1	2	3	....
1996-97	Dukla Jihlava	Cze-Rep	46	5	13	18	22	....	....	....	....	....
	St. John's	AHL	2	1	2	3	0	2	0	0	0	0
1997-98	Dukla Jihlava	Cze-Rep	18	10	14	24	30	....	....	....	....	....
1998-99	Dukla Jihla	Cze-Rep	52	7	10	17	26	....	....	....	....	....

MELICHAR, Josef (mehl-ee-KHAHR, YOH-sehf) PIT.

Defense. Shoots left. 6'2", 204 lbs. Born, Budejovice, Czech., January 20, 1979.
(Pittsburgh's 3rd choice, 71st overall, in 1997 Entry Draft).

			Regular Season					Playoffs				
Season	Club	Lea	GP	G	A	TP	PIM	GP	G	A	TP	PIM
1995-96	HC Budejovice	Czech-Jr.	38	3	4	7	....	....	....	....	....	....
1996-97	HC Budejovice	Cze-Rep	41	2	3	5	10	....	....	....	....	....
1997-98	Tri-City	WHL	67	9	24	33	154	....	....	....	....	....
1998-99	Tri-City	WHL	65	8	28	36	125	11	1	0	1	15

MELIN, Bjorn (MEH-lihn, b-YUHRN) NYI

Right wing. Shoots right. 6'1", 178 lbs. Born, Jonkoping, Sweden, July 4, 1981.
(NY Islanders' 11th choice, 163rd overall, in 1999 Entry Draft).

			Regular Season					Playoffs				
Season	Club	Lea	GP	G	A	TP	PIM	GP	G	A	TP	PIM
1997-98	HV Jonkoping	Swede-Jr.	8	0	3	3	2	....	....	....	....	....
1998-99	HV Jonkoping	Swede-Jr.	30	12	7	19	50	....	....	....	....	....

MELOCHE, Eric (muh-LAWSH) PIT.

Right wing. Shoots right. 5'11", 195 lbs. Born, Montreal, Que., May 1, 1976.
(Pittsburgh's 7th choice, 186th overall, in 1996 Entry Draft).

			Regular Season					Playoffs				
Season	Club	Lea	GP	G	A	TP	PIM	GP	G	A	TP	PIM
1995-96	Cornwall	OJHL	64	68	53	121	162	....	....	....	....	....
1996-97	Ohio State	CCHA	39	12	11	23	78	....	....	....	....	....
1997-98	Ohio State	CCHA	42	26	22	48	86	....	....	....	....	....
1998-99	Ohio State	CCHA	35	11	16	27	87	....	....	....	....	....

MERRICK, Andrew CAR.

Center. Shoots left. 5'11", 202 lbs. Born, Syosset, NY, March 23, 1978.
(Carolina's 6th choice, 169th overall, in 1997 Entry Draft).

			Regular Season					Playoffs				
Season	Club	Lea	GP	G	A	TP	PIM	GP	G	A	TP	PIM
1996-97	U. of Michigan	CCHA	36	3	10	13	42	....	....	....	....	....
1997-98	U. of Michigan	CCHA	33	4	3	7	74	....	....	....	....	....
1998-99	U. of Michigan	CCHA	32	1	3	4	61	....	....	....	....	....

METHOT, Francois (meh-THOH) BUF.

Center. Shoots right. 6', 175 lbs. Born, Montreal, Que., April 26, 1978.
(Buffalo's 4th choice, 54th overall, in 1996 Entry Draft).

			Regular Season					Playoffs				
Season	Club	Lea	GP	G	A	TP	PIM	GP	G	A	TP	PIM
1994-95	St-Hyacinthe	QMJHL	60	14	38	52	22	5	0	1	1	0
1995-96	St-Hyacinthe	QMJHL	68	32	62	94	22	12	6	6	12	4
1996-97	Rouyn-Noranda	QMJHL	47	21	30	51	22	....	....	....	....	....
	Shawinigan	QMJHL	18	8	17	25	2	7	2	6	8	2
1997-98	Shawinigan	QMJHL	36	23	42	65	10	6	1	3	4	5
1998-99	Rochester	AHL	58	5	8	13	8	9	0	1	1	0

METROPOLIT, Glen WSH.

Right wing. Shoots right. 6', 185 lbs. Born, Toronto, Ont., June 25, 1974.

			Regular Season					Playoffs				
Season	Club	Lea	GP	G	A	TP	PIM	GP	G	A	TP	PIM
1992-93	Richmond Hill	OJHL-B	43	27	36	63	36	....	....	....	....	....
1993-94	Richmond Hill	OJHL-B	49	38	62	100	83	....	....	....	....	....
1994-95	Vernon	BCJHL	60	43	74	117	92	....	....	....	....	....
1995-96	Nashville	ECHL	58	30	31	61	62	5	3	8	11	2
	Atlanta	IHL	1	0	0	0	0	....	....	....	....	....
1996-97	Pensacola	ECHL	54	35	47	82	45	12	9	16	25	28
	Quebec	IHL	22	5	4	9	14	5	0	0	0	2
1997-98	Grand Rapids	IHL	79	20	35	55	90	3	1	1	2	0
1998-99	Grand Rapids	IHL	77	28	53	81	92	....	....	....	....	....

Signed as a free agent by **Washington**, July 19, 1999.

MEYER, Doug PIT.

Left wing. Shoots left. 6'2", 197 lbs. Born, Bloomington, MN, February 21, 1980.
(Pittsburgh's 8th choice, 176th overall, in 1999 Entry Draft).

			Regular Season					Playoffs				
Season	Club	Lea	GP	G	A	TP	PIM	GP	G	A	TP	PIM
1998-99	U. of Minnesota	WCHA	36	4	4	8	18	....	....	....	....	....

MEZEI, Branislav (MEH-zay) NYI

Defense. Shoots left. 6'4", 221 lbs. Born, Nitra, Czech., October 8, 1980.
(NY Islanders' 3rd choice, 10th overall, in 1999 Entry Draft).

			Regular Season					Playoffs				
Season	Club	Lea	GP	G	A	TP	PIM	GP	G	A	TP	PIM
1996-97	MHC Nitra	Slovak-Jr.	40	8	17	25	42	....	....	....	....	....
1997-98	Belleville	OHL	53	3	5	8	58	8	0	2	2	8
1998-99	Belleville	OHL	60	5	18	23	90	18	0	4	4	29

MIETTINEN, Tommi (mih-EHT-tih-nehn) ANA.

Center. Shoots left. 5'10", 165 lbs. Born, Kuopio, Finland, December 3, 1975.
(Anaheim's 9th choice, 236th overall, in 1994 Entry Draft).

			Regular Season					Playoffs				
Season	Club	Lea	GP	G	A	TP	PIM	GP	G	A	TP	PIM
1992-93	KalPa Kuopio	Finland	14	0	0	0	0	....	....	....	....	....
1993-94	KalPa Kuopio	Finland	47	5	7	12	14	....	....	....	....	....
1994-95	KalPa Kuopio	Finland	48	13	16	29	26	3	1	1	2	2
1995-96	TPS Turku	Finland	36	3	10	13	10	10	2	1	3	29
1996-97	TPS Turku	Finland	41	6	15	21	6	12	3	4	7	8
1997-98	TPS Turku	Finland	42	8	6	14	26	4	0	0	0	0
	TPS Turku	EuroHL	3	0	0	0	2	....	....	....	....	....
1998-99	TPS Turku	Finland	54	10	17	27	26	10	4	4	8	0

MIKA, Petr (MEE-kah) NYI

Left wing. Shoots right. 6'4", 194 lbs. Born, Prague, Czech., February 12, 1979.
(NY Islanders' 6th choice, 85th overall, in 1997 Entry Draft).

			Regular Season					Playoffs				
Season	Club	Lea	GP	G	A	TP	PIM	GP	G	A	TP	PIM
1996-97	Slavia Praha	Cze-Rep	15	8	0	8	....	....	....	....	....	....
	HC Beroun	Czech-2	9	1	0	1	....	....	....	....	....	....
	Slavia Praha	Cze-Rep	20	1	2	3	6	....	....	....	....	....
1997-98	Ottawa	OHL	41	10	8	18	28	....	....	....	....	....
1998-99	Slavia Praha	Cze-Rep	49	6	5	11	57	....	....	....	....	....

MIKKOLA, Ilkka (mih-KOHLA-, IHL-ka) MTL.

Defense. Shoots left. 6', 189 lbs. Born, Oulu, Finland, January 18, 1979.
(Montreal's 3rd choice, 65th overall, in 1997 Entry Draft).

			Regular Season					Playoffs				
Season	Club	Lea	GP	G	A	TP	PIM	GP	G	A	TP	PIM
1995-96	Karpat Oulu	Finn-Jr.	21	2	3	5	20	....	....	....	....	....
	Karpat Oulu	Finland-2	10	0	4	4	29	2	0	0	0	2
1996-97	Karpat Oulu	Finn-Jr.	40	7	12	19	32	6	0	0	0	4
1997-98	Karpat Oulu	Finland-2	27	7	2	9	34	....	....	....	....	....
	Karpat Oulu	Finn-Jr.	8	4	2	6	10	....	....	....	....	....
1998-99	TPS Turku	Finland	42	1	3	4	41	10	1	0	1	6

MILANOVIC, Ryan BOS.

Left wing. Shoots left. 6'2", 201 lbs. Born, Toronto, Ont., September 3, 1980.
(Boston's 5th choice, 165th overall, in 1998 Entry Draft).

			Regular Season					Playoffs				
Season	Club	Lea	GP	G	A	TP	PIM	GP	G	A	TP	PIM
1996-97	Kitchener	OHL	58	3	10	13	78	13	1	1	2	4
1997-98	Kitchener	OHL	42	1	8	9	72	6	1	3	4	19
1998-99	Kitchener	OHL	61	15	18	33	114	1	1	0	1	0

MILLER, Richard NYR

Defense. Shoots right. 6'3", 200 lbs. Born, Meriden, CT, January 12, 1978.
(NY Rangers' 12th choice, 236th overall, in 1997 Entry Draft).

			Regular Season					Playoffs				
Season	Club	Lea	GP	G	A	TP	PIM	GP	G	A	TP	PIM
1996-97	Providence	H.E.	12	1	4	5	6	....	....	....	....	....
1997-98	Providence	H.E.	27	1	5	6	32	....	....	....	....	....
1998-99	Providence	H.E.	13	1	3	4	12	....	....	....	....	....

MILLEY, Norman BUF.

Right wing. Shoots right. 5'11", 185 lbs. Born, Toronto, Ont., February 14, 1980.
(Buffalo's 3rd choice, 47th overall, in 1998 Entry Draft).

			Regular Season					Playoffs				
Season	Club	Lea	GP	G	A	TP	PIM	GP	G	A	TP	PIM
1996-97	Sudbury	OHL	61	30	32	62	15	....	....	....	....	....
1997-98	Sudbury	OHL	62	33	41	74	48	10	0	1	1	4
1998-99	Sudbury	OHL	68	52	68	120	47	4	2	3	5	4

OHL Second All-Star Team (1999)

MISCHLER, Graig VAN.

Center. Shoots left. 6'3", 174 lbs. Born, Holbrook, NY, September 15, 1978.
(Vancouver's 10th choice, 204th overall, in 1998 Entry Draft).

			Regular Season					Playoffs				
Season	Club	Lea	GP	G	A	TP	PIM	GP	G	A	TP	PIM
1996-97	Canterbury Prep	H.S.	Statistics Not Available									
1997-98	Northeastern	H.E.	39	7	13	20	22	....	....	....	....	....
1998-99	Northeastern	H.E.	33	8	15	23	36	....	....	....	....	....

MISKOVICH, Aaron (MIHS-kuh-vihch) COL.

Center. Shoots left. 5'10", 185 lbs. Born, Grand Rapids, MN, April 28, 1978.
(Colorado's 6th choice, 133rd overall, in 1997 Entry Draft).

			Regular Season					Playoffs				
Season	Club	Lea	GP	G	A	TP	PIM	GP	G	A	TP	PIM
1996-97	Green Bay	USHL	14	4	9	13	14	....	....	....	....	....
1997-98	U. of Minnesota	WCHA	28	4	8	12	14	....	....	....	....	....
1998-99	U. of Minnesota	WCHA	42	11	11	22	36	....	....	....	....	....

MITCHELL, Kevin CGY.

Defense. Shoots left. 5'11", 165 lbs. Born, Bronx, NY, June 5, 1980.
(Calgary's 9th choice, 234th overall, in 1998 Entry Draft).

			Regular Season					Playoffs				
Season	Club	Lea	GP	G	A	TP	PIM	GP	G	A	TP	PIM
1996-97	Cambridge	OJHL-B	47	30	28	58	140	....	....	....	....	....
1997-98	Guelph	OHL	65	10	46	56	73	12	1	7	8	14
1998-99	Guelph	OHL	68	26	52	78	107	11	3	10	13	29

MITCHELL, Willie N.J.

Defense. Shoots left. 6'3", 210 lbs. Born, Ft. McNeill, B.C., April 23, 1977.
(New Jersey's 12th choice, 199th overall, in 1996 Entry Draft).

			Regular Season					Playoffs				
Season	Club	Lea	GP	G	A	TP	PIM	GP	G	A	TP	PIM
1995-96	Melfort	SJHL	19	2	6	8	....	14	0	2	2	12
1996-97	Melfort	SJHL	64	14	42	56	227	4	0	1	1	23
1997-98	Clarkson	ECAC	34	9	17	26	105	....	....	....	....	....
1998-99	Clarkson	ECAC	34	10	19	29	40	....	....	....	....	....
	Albany	AHL	6	1	3	4	29	....	....	....	....	....

ECAC Second All-Star Team (1998) • ECAC First All-Star Team (1999) • NCAA East Second All-American Team (1999)

MIZZI, Preston (MIHZ-zee) PHX.

Center. Shoots left. 5'11", 193 lbs. Born, Sault Ste. Marie, Ont., December 22, 1980.
(Phoenix's 6th choice, 123rd overall, in 1999 Entry Draft).

			Regular Season					Playoffs				
Season	Club	Lea	GP	G	A	TP	PIM	GP	G	A	TP	PIM
1997-98	Peterborough	OHL	66	17	32	49	37	4	0	3	3	12
1998-99	Peterborough	OHL	67	29	29	58	74	5	2	3	5	15

MOHAGEN, Tony ANA.

Left wing. Shoots left. 6'4", 220 lbs. Born, Regina, Sask., July 13, 1978.
(Anaheim's 5th choice, 178th overall, in 1997 Entry Draft).

			Regular Season					Playoffs				
Season	Club	Lea	GP	G	A	TP	PIM	GP	G	A	TP	PIM
1995-96	Seattle	WHL	58	2	2	4	131	2	0	0	0	0
1996-97	Seattle	WHL	55	5	6	11	191	15	0	1	1	50
1997-98	Swift Current	WHL	62	7	11	18	299	11	3	0	3	*70
1998-99	Cincinnati	AHL	1	0	0	0	5	....	....	....	....	....

• Missed majority of 1998-99 season recovering from head injury suffered in game vs. Providence (AHL), October 8, 1998.

MOISE, Martin (MOIZ)

Left wing. Shoots left. 6', 197 lbs. Born, Valleyfield, Que., January 18, 1979.
(Calgary's 9th choice, 113th overall, in 1997 Entry Draft).

			Regular Season					Playoffs				
Season	Club	Lea	GP	G	A	TP	PIM	GP	G	A	TP	PIM
1995-96	St-Hyacinthe	QMJHL	67	6	19	25	11	10	1	1	2	0
1996-97	Beauport	QMJHL	70	21	23	44	23	4	4	1	5	0
1997-98	Quebec	QMJHL	70	32	43	75	37	14	3	3	6	17
1998-99	Quebec	QMJHL	67	36	38	74	34	13	2	10	12	2

MOKHOV, Stepan (MOH-khohv) CHI.

Defense. Shoots left. 6'1", 183 lbs. Born, Ust-Kamenogorsk, USSR, January 22, 1981.
(Chicago's 3rd choice, 63rd overall, in 1999 Entry Draft).

			Regular Season					Playoffs				
Season	Club	Lea	GP	G	A	TP	PIM	GP	G	A	TP	PIM
1997-98	Omsk-2 VDV	Russia-3	18	0	1	1	8	....	....	....	....	....
1998-99	Cherepovets-2	Russia-3	28	2	0	2	....	....	....	....	....	....
	Cherepovets	Russia	1	0	0	0	0	....	....	....	....	....

MOORE, Mark — PIT.

Defense. Shoots right. 6'3", 185 lbs. Born, Windsor, Ont., February 18, 1977.
(Pittsburgh's 7th choice, 179th overall, in 1997 Entry Draft).

			Regular Season					Playoffs				
Season	Club	Lea	GP	G	A	TP	PIM	GP	G	A	TP	PIM
1996-97	Harvard University	ECAC	22	5	2	7	16	....	....	....	....	....
1997-98	Harvard University	ECAC	32	1	3	4	90	....	....	....	....	....
1998-99	Harvard University	ECAC	32	1	2	3	82	....	....	....	....	....

MOORE, Steve — COL.

Center. Shoots right. 6'2", 190 lbs. Born, Windsor, Ont., September 22, 1978.
(Colorado's 7th choice, 53rd overall, in 1998 Entry Draft).

			Regular Season					Playoffs				
Season	Club	Lea	GP	G	A	TP	PIM	GP	G	A	TP	PIM
1996-97	Thornhill	OJHL	50	34	52	86	52	....	....	....	....	....
1997-98	Harvard University	ECAC	33	10	23	33	46	....	....	....	....	....
1998-99	Harvard University	ECAC	30	18	13	31	34	....	....	....	....	....

MORAN, Brad — BUF.

Center. Shoots left. 5'11", 175 lbs. Born, Abbotsford, B.C., March 20, 1979.
(Buffalo's 8th choice, 191st overall, in 1998 Entry Draft).

			Regular Season					Playoffs				
Season	Club	Lea	GP	G	A	TP	PIM	GP	G	A	TP	PIM
1995-96	Calgary	WHL	70	13	31	44	28	....	....	....	....	....
1996-97	Calgary	WHL	72	30	36	66	61	....	....	....	....	....
1997-98	Calgary	WHL	72	53	49	102	64	18	10	8	18	20
1998-99	Calgary	WHL	71	60	58	118	96	21	17	*25	42	26

MORAVEC, David — (muh-RAHV-ehts) — BUF.

Right wing. Shoots left. 6', 180 lbs. Born, Vitkovice, Czech., March 24, 1973.
(Buffalo's 9th choice, 218th overall, in 1998 Entry Draft).

			Regular Season					Playoffs				
Season	Club	Lea	GP	G	A	TP	PIM	GP	G	A	TP	PIM
1994-95	HC Vitkovice	Cze-Rep	38	4	13	17	12	6	1	7	8	0
1995-96	HC Vitkovice	Cze-Rep	39	5	3	8	....	4	0	0	0	....
1996-97	HC Vitkovice	Cze-Rep	52	18	22	40	30	9	6	3	9	0
1997-98	HC Vitkovice	Cze-Rep	51	*38	26	64	28	11	6	9	15	8
1998-99	HC Vitkovice	Cze-Rep	50	21	22	43	44	4	1	1	2	....

MORIN, Jean-Philippe — (moh-REH) — PHI.

Defense. Shoots left. 6'1", 188 lbs. Born, Gaspe, Que., February 6, 1980.
(Philadelphia's 4th choice, 109th overall, in 1998 Entry Draft).

			Regular Season					Playoffs				
Season	Club	Lea	GP	G	A	TP	PIM	GP	G	A	TP	PIM
1996-97	Victoriaville	QMJHL	56	3	5	8	20	1	0	0	0	0
1997-98	Victoriaville	QMJHL	35	3	11	14	79	....	....	....	....	....
	Drummondville	QMJHL	18	1	4	5	16	....	....	....	....	....
1998-99	Drummondville	QMJHL	69	2	31	33	158	....	....	....	....	....

MORIN, Olivier — (moh-REH) — MTL.

Right wing. Shoots right. 6', 177 lbs. Born, Montreal, Que., April 2, 1978.

			Regular Season					Playoffs				
Season	Club	Lea	GP	G	A	TP	PIM	GP	G	A	TP	PIM
1995-96	Chicoutimi	QMJHL	68	17	32	49	102	17	6	5	11	51
1996-97	Chicoutimi	QMJHL	70	22	44	66	152	21	5	8	13	24
1997-98	Val d'Or	QMJHL	56	20	31	51	73	4	4	3	7	4
1998-99	New Orleans	ECHL	54	9	8	17	61	9	0	0	0	2

Signed as a free agent by **Montreal**, October 3, 1996.

MOROZOV, Valentin — (moh-ROH-zohv) — PIT.

Center. Shoots left. 5'11", 196 lbs. Born, Moscow, USSR, June 1, 1975.
(Pittsburgh's 8th choice, 154th overall, in 1994 Entry Draft).

			Regular Season					Playoffs				
Season	Club	Lea	GP	G	A	TP	PIM	GP	G	A	TP	PIM
1992-93	CSKA Moscow	CIS	17	0	0	0	6	....	....	....	....	....
1993-94	CSKA Moscow	CIS	18	4	1	5	8	3	0	1	1	0
1994-95	CSKA Moscow	CIS	47	9	4	13	10	2	2	0	2	0
1995-96	CSKA Moscow	CIS	51	30	11	41	28	3	1	0	1	2
1996-97	CSKA Moscow	Russia	22	8	5	13	8	....	....	....	....	....
	CSKA Moscow	EuroHL	4	2	1	3	0	....	....	....	....	....
1997-98	Soviet Wings	Russia	34	5	15	20	8	....	....	....	....	....
1998-99	Syracuse	AHL	63	17	23	40	10	....	....	....	....	....

MORRISON, Justin — VAN.

Right wing. Shoots right. 6'3", 205 lbs. Born, Los Angeles, CA, September 10, 1979.
(Vancouver's 4th choice, 81st overall, in 1998 Entry Draft).

			Regular Season					Playoffs				
Season	Club	Lea	GP	G	A	TP	PIM	GP	G	A	TP	PIM
1996-97	Omaha	USHL	62	12	24	36	44	....	....	....	....	....
1997-98	Colorado College	WCHA	42	4	9	13	8	....	....	....	....	....
1998-99	Colorado College	WCHA	38	23	15	38	33	....	....	....	....	....

MORRONE, Mike — CAR.

Left wing. Shoots left. 5'11", 215 lbs. Born, Windsor, Ont., January 3, 1976.

			Regular Season					Playoffs				
Season	Club	Lea	GP	G	A	TP	PIM	GP	G	A	TP	PIM
1993-94	Owen Sound	OHL	57	0	7	7	99	6	0	0	0	4
1994-95	Owen Sound	OHL	8	1	1	2	14	0	0	0	0	0
	Detroit	OHL	47	4	21	25	129	21	1	1	2	11
1995-96	Detroit	OHL	65	9	20	29	207	17	3	6	9	42
1996-97	Detroit	OHL	46	5	13	18	164	5	1	1	2	42
1997-98	Richmond	ECHL	65	4	4	8	281	0	0	0	0	0
	New Haven	AHL	1	0	0	0	4	0	0	0	0	0
1998-99	New Orleans	ECHL	21	1	5	6	37	....	....	....	....	....

Signed as a free agent by **Carolina**, June 9, 1997.

MORROW, Brenden — DAL.

Left wing. Shoots left. 5'11", 196 lbs. Born, Carlisle, Sask., January 16, 1979.
(Dallas' 1st choice, 25th overall, in 1997 Entry Draft).

			Regular Season					Playoffs				
Season	Club	Lea	GP	G	A	TP	PIM	GP	G	A	TP	PIM
1995-96	Portland	WHL	65	13	12	25	61	7	0	0	0	8
1996-97	Portland	WHL	71	39	49	88	178	6	2	1	3	4
1997-98	Portland	WHL	68	34	52	86	184	16	10	8	18	65
1998-99	Portland	WHL	61	41	44	85	248	4	0	4	4	18

WHL West First All-Star Team (1999)

MOSOVSKY, Karel — (moh-SAWV-skee) — BUF.

Left wing. Shoots right. 6'2", 198 lbs. Born, Piesk, Czech., August 22, 1981.
(Buffalo's 6th choice, 117th overall, in 1999 Entry Draft).

			Regular Season					Playoffs				
Season	Club	Lea	GP	G	A	TP	PIM	GP	G	A	TP	PIM
1997-98	HC Budejovice	Czech-Jr.	36	15	17	32	52	....	....	....	....	....
1998-99	Regina	WHL	68	26	25	51	58	....	....	....	....	....

MOTTAU, Mike — (MAW-tuh) — NYR

Defense. Shoots left. 6', 188 lbs. Born, Quincy, MA, March 19, 1978.
(NY Rangers' 10th choice, 182nd overall, in 1997 Entry Draft).

			Regular Season					Playoffs				
Season	Club	Lea	GP	G	A	TP	PIM	GP	G	A	TP	PIM
1996-97	Boston College	H.E.	38	5	18	23	77	....	....	....	....	....
1997-98	Boston College	H.E.	40	13	36	49	50	....	....	....	....	....
1998-99	Boston College	H.E.	43	3	39	42	44	....	....	....	....	....

Hockey East First All-Star Team (1998) • NCAA East Second All-American Team (1998) • NCAA Championship All-Tournament Team (1998) • Hockey East Second All-Star Team (1999) • NCAA East First All-American Team (1999)

MRAZEK, Frantisek — (muh-RA-zehk) — TOR.

Left wing. Shoots left. 6'4", 220 lbs. Born, Ceske-Budejovice, Czech., May 16, 1979.
(Toronto's 3rd choice, 111th overall, in 1997 Entry Draft).

			Regular Season					Playoffs				
Season	Club	Lea	GP	G	A	TP	PIM	GP	G	A	TP	PIM
1996-97	HC Budejovice	Czech-Jr.	40	18	15	33	....	....	....	....	....	....
1997-98	Red Deer	WHL	65	30	24	54	71	5	1	0	1	2
1998-99	Red Deer	WHL	60	34	42	76	79	9	6	4	10	16

MULICK, Robert — S.J.

Defense. Shoots right. 6'2", 205 lbs. Born, Toronto, Ont., October 23, 1979.
(San Jose's 8th choice, 185th overall, in 1998 Entry Draft).

			Regular Season					Playoffs				
Season	Club	Lea	GP	G	A	TP	PIM	GP	G	A	TP	PIM
1995-96	S.S. Marie	OHL	54	0	3	3	58	....	....	....	....	....
1996-97	S.S. Marie	OHL	60	2	8	10	49	11	0	1	1	12
1997-98	S.S. Marie	OHL	61	0	10	10	109	....	....	....	....	....
1998-99	S.S. Marie	OHL	66	1	12	13	83	5	0	1	1	10

MURLEY, Matt — PIT.

Left wing. Shoots left. 6'1", 192 lbs. Born, Troy, NY, December 17, 1979.
(Pittsburgh's 2nd choice, 51st overall, in 1999 Entry Draft).

			Regular Season					Playoffs				
Season	Club	Lea	GP	G	A	TP	PIM	GP	G	A	TP	PIM
1996-97	Syracuse	OJHL	48	52	58	110	111	....	....	....	....	....
1997-98	Syracuse	OJHL	49	56	70	126	103	....	....	....	....	....
1998-99	RPI Engineers	ECAC	36	17	32	49	32	....	....	....	....	....

MUROVIC, Mirko — TOR.

Left wing. Shoots left. 6'3", 190 lbs. Born, Montreal, Que., February 2, 1981.
(Toronto's 3rd choice, 108th overall, in 1999 Entry Draft).

			Regular Season					Playoffs				
Season	Club	Lea	GP	G	A	TP	PIM	GP	G	A	TP	PIM
1997-98	Moncton	QMJHL	54	10	15	25	10	....	....	....	....	....
1998-99	Moncton	QMJHL	69	21	33	54	60	4	0	1	1	2

MURPHY, Mark

Left wing. Shoots left. 5'11", 200 lbs. Born, Stoughton, MA, August 6, 1976.
(Toronto's 6th choice, 197th overall, in 1995 Entry Draft).

			Regular Season					Playoffs				
Season	Club	Lea	GP	G	A	TP	PIM	GP	G	A	TP	PIM
1994-95	Stratford	OJHL-B	47	52	56	108	64	....	....	....	....	....
1995-96	Stratford	OJHL-B	1	0	0	0	0	....	....	....	....	....
	RPI Engineers	ECAC	32	1	1	2	50	....	....	....	....	....
1996-97	RPI Engineers	ECAC	34	9	18	27	56	....	....	....	....	....
1997-98	RPI Engineers	ECAC	35	8	27	35	63	....	....	....	....	....
1998-99	RPI Engineers	ECAC	37	11	30	41	76	....	....	....	....	....

MURPHY, Ryan — CAR.

Left wing. Shoots left. 6'1", 192 lbs. Born, Van Nuys, CA, March 21, 1979.
(Carolina's 4th choice, 113th overall, in 1999 Entry Draft).

			Regular Season					Playoffs				
Season	Club	Lea	GP	G	A	TP	PIM	GP	G	A	TP	PIM
1997-98	Bowling Green	CCHA	36	3	9	12	27	....	....	....	....	....
1998-99	Bowling Green	CCHA	34	19	23	33	38	....	....	....	....	....

MURRAY, Craig — MTL.

Center. Shoots left. 6', 175 lbs. Born, Souris, Man., February 22, 1979.
(Montreal's 8th choice, 201st overall, in 1998 Entry Draft).

			Regular Season					Playoffs				
Season	Club	Lea	GP	G	A	TP	PIM	GP	G	A	TP	PIM
1994-95	Penticton AA	BCAHA	60	74	76	150	42	....	....	....	....	....
1995-96	Penticton	BCJHL	55	14	6	20	54	....	....	....	....	....
1996-97	Penticton	BCJHL	45	25	31	56	39	....	....	....	....	....
1997-98	Penticton	BCJHL	57	45	52	97	50	7	6	8	14	14
1998-99	U. of Michigan	CCHA	16	0	1	1	6	....	....	....	....	....

NAGY, Ladislav (NA-gee, LA-dih-slahv) ST.L.

Center. Shoots left. 5'11", 183 lbs. Born, Saca, Czech., June 1, 1979.
(St. Louis' 6th choice, 177th overall, in 1997 Entry Draft).

			Regular Season					Playoffs				
Season	Club	Lea	GP	G	A	TP	PIM	GP	G	A	TP	PIM
1996-97	Dragon Presov	Slovak-2	11	6	5	11	....	....	....	....	....	....
1997-98	HC Kosice	Slovakia	29	19	15	34	41	11	2	4	6	6
1998-99	Halifax	QMJHL	63	71	55	126	148	5	3	3	6	18
	Worcester	AHL	....	....	....	....	....	3	2	2	4	0

NAUMENKO, Nick (NAH-mehn-koh)

Defense. Shoots right. 5'11", 180 lbs. Born, Chicago, IL, July 7, 1974.
(St. Louis' 9th choice, 182nd overall, in 1992 Entry Draft).

			Regular Season					Playoffs				
Season	Club	Lea	GP	G	A	TP	PIM	GP	G	A	TP	PIM
1991-92	Dubuque	USHL	24	6	19	25	4	....	....	....	....	....
1992-93	North Dakota	WCHA	38	10	24	34	26	....	....	....	....	....
1993-94	North Dakota	WCHA	32	4	22	26	22	....	....	....	....	....
1994-95	North Dakota	WCHA	39	13	26	39	78	....	....	....	....	....
1995-96	North Dakota	WCHA	37	11	30	41	32	....	....	....	....	....
1996-97	Worcester	AHL	54	6	22	28	72	1	0	0	0	0
1997-98	Worcester	AHL	71	12	34	46	63	11	1	7	8	8
1998-99	Utah	IHL	20	4	3	7	20	....	....	....	....	....
	Las Vegas	IHL	34	5	16	21	37	....	....	....	....	....
	Kansas City	IHL	21	3	8	11	4	3	1	2	3	4

WCHA First All-Star Team (1995, 1996)

NEHRLING, Lucas N.J.

Defense. Shoots right. 6'5", 225 lbs. Born, Peterborough, Ont., August 14, 1979.
(New Jersey's 3rd choice, 104th overall, in 1997 Entry Draft).

			Regular Season					Playoffs				
Season	Club	Lea	GP	G	A	TP	PIM	GP	G	A	TP	PIM
1996-97	Sarnia	OHL	63	3	12	15	74	12	0	2	2	23
1997-98	Sarnia	OHL	22	0	2	2	46	....	....	....	....	....
	Kingston	OHL	39	1	8	9	83	12	0	1	1	19
1998-99	Kingston	OHL	2	0	1	1	13	....	....	....	....	....
	Guelph	OHL	60	5	14	19	131	11	0	1	1	35

NEIL, Christopher OTT.

Right wing. Shoots right. 6', 210 lbs. Born, Markdale, Ont., June 18, 1979.
(Ottawa's 7th choice, 161st overall, in 1998 Entry Draft).

			Regular Season					Playoffs				
Season	Club	Lea	GP	G	A	TP	PIM	GP	G	A	TP	PIM
1996-97	North Bay	OHL	65	13	16	29	150	....	....	....	....	....
1997-98	North Bay	OHL	59	26	29	55	231	....	....	....	....	....
1998-99	North Bay	OHL	66	26	46	72	215	4	1	0	1	15

NIELSEN, Chris NYI

Center. Shoots right. 6'2", 185 lbs. Born, Moshi, Tanzania, February 16, 1980.
(NY Islanders' 2nd choice, 36th overall, in 1998 Entry Draft).

			Regular Season					Playoffs				
Season	Club	Lea	GP	G	A	TP	PIM	GP	G	A	TP	PIM
1995-96	Southwest	MAHA	39	37	35	72	59	....	....	....	....	....
	Calgary	WHL	6	0	0	0	0	....	....	....	....	....
1996-97	Calgary	WHL	62	11	19	30	39	....	....	....	....	....
1997-98	Calgary	WHL	68	22	29	51	31	18	2	4	6	10
1998-99	Calgary	WHL	70	22	24	46	45	21	11	5	16	28

NIEMI, Antti-Jussi (nee-mee, AN-tee-YOO-see) ANA.

Defense. Shoots left. 6'1", 183 lbs. Born, Vantaa, Finland, September 22, 1977.
(Ottawa's 2nd choice, 81st overall, in 1996 Entry Draft).

			Regular Season					Playoffs				
Season	Club	Lea	GP	G	A	TP	PIM	GP	G	A	TP	PIM
1995-96	Jokerit	Finn-Jr.	34	11	18	29	56	8	0	4	4	39
	Jarvenpaa HT	Finland-2	4	0	2	2	8	....	....	....	....	....
	Jokerit	Finland	6	0	2	2	6	1	0	0	0	0
1996-97	Jokerit	Finland	44	2	9	11	38	9	0	2	2	2
1997-98	Jokerit	Finland	46	2	6	8	24	8	0	1	1	0
	Jokerit	EuroHL	6	0	1	1	6	....	....	....	....	....
1998-99	Jokerit	Finland	53	3	7	10	107	3	0	0	0	2
	Jokerit	EuroHL	6	2	2	4	4	2	0	1	1	0

Traded to **Anaheim** by **Ottawa** with Ted Donato for Patrick Lalime and future considerations, June 18, 1999.

NIEMINEN, Ville (nee-EHM-ih-nehn, VIHL-ee) COL.

Left wing. Shoots left. 5'11", 205 lbs. Born, Tampere, Finland, April 6, 1977.
(Colorado's 4th choice, 78th overall, in 1997 Entry Draft).

			Regular Season					Playoffs				
Season	Club	Lea	GP	G	A	TP	PIM	GP	G	A	TP	PIM
1994-95	Tappara	Finn-Jr.	16	11	21	32	47	....	....	....	....	....
	Tappara	Finland	16	0	0	0	0	....	....	....	....	....
1995-96	Tappara	Finn-Jr.	20	20	23	43	63	....	....	....	....	....
	Tappara	Finland	4	0	1	1	8	....	....	....	....	....
	KooVee	Finland-2	7	2	1	3	4	....	....	....	....	....
1996-97	Tappara	Finland	49	10	13	23	120	3	1	0	1	8
1997-98	Hershey	AHL	74	14	22	36	85	....	....	....	....	....
1998-99	Hershey	AHL	67	24	19	43	127	3	0	1	1	0

NIKOLOV, Angel (NIH-koh-lohv) S.J.

Defense. Shoots left. 6'1", 185 lbs. Born, Most, Czech., November 18, 1975.
(San Jose's 2nd choice, 37th overall, in 1994 Entry Draft).

			Regular Season					Playoffs				
Season	Club	Lea	GP	G	A	TP	PIM	GP	G	A	TP	PIM
1993-94	CHZ Litvinov	Cze-Rep	10	2	2	4	....	3	0	0	0	....
1994-95	CHZ Litvinov	Cze-Rep	41	1	4	5	18	4	0	0	0	27
1995-96	CHZ Litvinov	Cze-Rep	40	1	7	8	....	10	0	1	1	....
1996-97	CHZ Litvinov	Cze-Rep	47	0	9	9	44	....	....	....	....	....
1997-98	CHZ Litvinov	Cze-Rep	51	1	4	5	53	4	0	3	3	27
1998-99	CHZ Litvinov	Cze-Rep	51	5	12	17	54	....	....	....	....	....

NILSSON, Magnus DET.

Right wing. Shoots left. 6'1", 187 lbs. Born, Finspang, Sweden, February 1, 1978.
(Detroit's 5th choice, 144th overall, in 1996 Entry Draft).

			Regular Season					Playoffs				
Season	Club	Lea	GP	G	A	TP	PIM	GP	G	A	TP	PIM
1995-96	Vita Hasten	Sweden-2	28	3	3	6	16	....	....	....	....	....
1996-97	Malmo IF	Swede-Jr.	14	10	9	19	45	....	....	....	....	....
	Malmo IF	Sweden	12	0	0	0	0	....	....	....	....	....
1997-98	Malmo IF	Sweden	45	6	1	7	6	....	....	....	....	....
1998-99	Malmo IF	Sweden	42	0	0	0	10	4	0	0	0	0

NITTEL, Adam (nih-TEHL) S.J.

Right wing. Shoots right. 6'2", 220 lbs. Born, Kitchener, Ont., July 17, 1978.
(San Jose's 4th choice, 107th overall, in 1997 Entry Draft).

			Regular Season					Playoffs				
Season	Club	Lea	GP	G	A	TP	PIM	GP	G	A	TP	PIM
1995-96	Niagara Falls	OHL	39	3	3	6	74	10	0	3	3	39
1996-97	Erie	OHL	46	8	11	19	194	....	....	....	....	....
1997-98	Erie	OHL	48	11	17	28	*309	7	0	0	0	19
1998-99	Mississauga	OHL	34	15	16	31	235	....	....	....	....	....
	S.S. Marie	OHL	21	3	8	11	101	5	1	2	3	30

NORDGREN, Niklas CAR.

Left wing. Shoots right. 5'11", 183 lbs. Born, Ornskoldsvik, Sweden, June 28, 1979.
(Carolina's 7th choice, 195th overall, in 1997 Entry Draft).

			Regular Season					Playoffs				
Season	Club	Lea	GP	G	A	TP	PIM	GP	G	A	TP	PIM
1996-97	MoDo Hockey	Swede-Jr.	22	14	6	20	....	....	....	....	....	....
	MoDo Hockey	Sweden	5	0	0	0	0	....	....	....	....	....
1997-98	MoDo Hockey	Swede-Jr.	28	15	15	30	52	....	....	....	....	....
1998-99	MoDo Hockey	Sweden	7	0	0	0	2	....	....	....	....	....
	Ornskoldsviks SK	Sweden-2	22	7	4	11	22	....	....	....	....	....

NORRIS, Clayton

Right wing. Shoots right. 6'2", 205 lbs. Born, Edmonton, Alta., March 8, 1972.
(Philadelphia's 5th choice, 116th overall, in 1991 Entry Draft).

			Regular Season					Playoffs				
Season	Club	Lea	GP	G	A	TP	PIM	GP	G	A	TP	PIM
1988-89	Medicine Hat	WHL	66	4	9	13	122	3	0	0	0	2
1989-90	Medicine Hat	WHL	72	13	18	31	176	3	0	0	0	15
1990-91	Medicine Hat	WHL	71	26	27	53	165	12	5	4	9	41
1991-92	Medicine Hat	WHL	69	26	39	65	300	2	0	0	0	9
1992-93	Medicine Hat	WHL	41	21	16	37	128	10	3	2	5	14
	Hershey	AHL	4	0	0	0	5					
	Roanoke	ECHL	4	0	0	0	0					
1993-94	Hershey	AHL	62	8	10	18	217	10	1	0	1	18
1994-95	Hershey	AHL	76	12	21	33	287	4	0	0	0	8
1995-96	Hershey	AHL	57	8	8	16	163	5	0	1	1	4
1996-97	Philadelphia	AHL	1	0	0	0	17	....	....	....	....	....
	Orlando	IHL	69	9	9	18	261	10	2	3	5	17
1997-98	St. John's	AHL	59	4	11	15	265	4	0	0	0	10
	Orlando	IHL	13	0	3	3	51	....	....	....	....	....
1998-99	Orlando	IHL	66	6	5	11	327	7	0	0	0	25

WHL East Second All-Star Team (1992)

NORTON, Brad EDM.

Defense. Shoots left. 6'4", 225 lbs. Born, Cambridge, MA, February 13, 1975.
(Edmonton's 9th choice, 215th overall, in 1993 Entry Draft).

			Regular Season					Playoffs				
Season	Club	Lea	GP	G	A	TP	PIM	GP	G	A	TP	PIM
1992-93	Cushing Academy	H.S.	31	10	26	36	....	....	....	....	....	....
1993-94	Cushing Academy	H.S.	STATISTICS NOT AVAILABLE									
1994-95	U. Mass-Amherst	H.E.	30	0	6	6	89	....	....	....	....	....
1995-96	U. Mass-Amherst	H.E.	34	4	12	16	99	....	....	....	....	....
1996-97	U. Mass-Amherst	H.E.	35	2	16	18	88	....	....	....	....	....
1997-98	U. Mass-Amherst	H.E.	20	2	13	15	28	....	....	....	....	....
	Detroit	IHL	33	1	4	5	56	22	0	2	2	87
1998-99	Hamilton	AHL	58	1	8	9	134	11	0	1	1	6

NOVOSELTSEV, Ivan (noh-voh-SEHLT-sehv, ee-VAHN) FLA.

Left wing. Shoots left. 6'1", 183 lbs. Born, Golitsino, USSR, January 23, 1979.
(Florida's 5th choice, 95th overall, in 1997 Entry Draft).

			Regular Season					Playoffs				
Season	Club	Lea	GP	G	A	TP	PIM	GP	G	A	TP	PIM
1995-96	Soviet Wings	CIS	1	0	0	0	2	....	....	....	....	....
1996-97	Soviet Wings	Russia	30	0	3	3	18	2	0	0	0	4
	Soviet Wings-2	Russia-3	19	5	3	8	39	....	....	....	....	....
1997-98	Sarnia	OHL	53	26	22	48	41	5	1	1	2	8
1998-99	Sarnia	OHL	68	57	39	96	45	5	2	4	6	6

OHL First All-Star Team (1999)

NUUTINEN, Sami (NOO-tih-nehn) EDM.

Defense. Shoots left. 6'1", 189 lbs. Born, Espoo, Finland, June 11, 1971.
(Edmonton's 12th choice, 248th overall, in 1990 Entry Draft).

			Regular Season					Playoffs				
Season	Club	Lea	GP	G	A	TP	PIM	GP	G	A	TP	PIM
1988-89	Kiekko-Espoo	Finland-2	39	18	10	28	46	....	....	....	....	....
1989-90	Kiekko-Espoo	Finland-2	40	8	15	23	....	....	....	....	....	....
1990-91	K-Kissat	Finland-2	3	1	0	1	0	....	....	....	....	....
	HIFK Helsinki	Finland	27	1	3	4	6	3	0	0	0	0
1991-92	HIFK Helsinki	Finland	44	5	6	11	10	9	0	1	1	4
1992-93	Kiekko-Espoo	Finland	48	7	11	18	59	....	....	....	....	....
1993-94	Kiekko-Espoo	Finland	46	9	15	24	36	....	....	....	....	....
1994-95	Kiekko-Espoo	Finland	50	8	24	32	38	4	0	1	1	0
1995-96	Kiekko-Espoo	Finland	49	7	7	14	54	....	....	....	....	....
1996-97	Vasteras IK	Sweden	50	7	7	14	22	....	....	....	....	....
1997-98	Kiekko-Espoo	Finland	48	4	17	21	51	8	0	2	2	6
1998-99	Jokerit	Finland	54	10	18	28	22	3	0	2	2	0

O'BRIEN, Sean — PHI.

Left wing. Shoots left. 6'1", 200 lbs. Born, Belmont, MA, February 9, 1972.

			Regular Season					Playoffs				
Season	Club	Lea	GP	G	A	TP	PIM	GP	G	A	TP	PIM
1990-91	Princeton	ECAC	24	0	6	6	12	....	....	....	....	....
1991-92	Princeton	ECAC	27	3	10	13	38	....	....	....	....	....
1992-93	Princeton	ECAC	29	2	22	24	54	....	....	....	....	....
1993-94	Princeton	ECAC	28	8	15	23	40	....	....	....	....	....
1994-95	Richmond	ECHL	52	5	18	23	147	17	2	5	7	77
	Houston	IHL	13	2	1	3	23	....	....	....	....	....
1995-96	Las Vegas	IHL	1	0	....	0	2	....	....	....	....	....
	Utah	IHL	7	2	2	4	12	....	....	....	....	....
	Houston	IHL	4	0	1	1	12	....	....	....	....	....
	Tallahasee	ECHL	54	9	19	28	179	8	0	2	2	23
1996-97	Tallahasee	ECHL	10	7	3	10	29	....	....	....	....	....
	Utah	IHL	50	21	10	31	135	....	....	....	....	....
	Phoenix	IHL	10	3	3	6	20	....	....	....	....	....
1997-98	Fayetteville	CHL	1	0	0	0	0	....	....	....	....	....
	Philadelphia	AHL	33	7	10	17	88	20	4	2	6	48
	Utah	IHL	36	3	8	11	77	....	....	....	....	....
1998-99	Syracuse	AHL	45	5	11	16	155	....	....	....	....	....
	Philadelphia	AHL	18	1	2	3	60	16	3	4	7	24

ECAC Second All-Star Team (1994)

Signed as a free agent by **LA Kings**, June 26, 1997. Signed as a free agent by **Pittsburgh**, August 11, 1998. Traded to **Philadelphia** by **Pittsburgh** for future considerations, February 10, 1999.

OBSUT, Jaroslav — (OHB-suht, YAHR-oh-slahv) ST.L.

Defense. Shoots left. 6'1", 200 lbs. Born, Presov, Czech., September 3, 1976.
(Winnipeg's 9th choice, 188th overall, in 1995 Entry Draft).

			Regular Season					Playoffs				
Season	Club	Lea	GP	G	A	TP	PIM	GP	G	A	TP	PIM
1995-96	Swift Current	WHL	72	10	11	21	57	6	0	0	0	2
1996-97	Edmonton	WHL	13	2	9	11	4	....	....	....	....	....
	Medicine Hat	WHL	50	8	26	34	42	4	0	2	2	2
	Toledo	ECHL	3	1	0	1	0	5	0	1	1	6
1997-98	Raleigh	ECHL	60	6	26	32	46	....	....	....	....	....
	Syracuse	AHL	4	0	1	1	4	....	....	....	....	....
1998-99	Augusta	ECHL	41	11	25	36	42	....	....	....	....	....
	Manitoba	IHL	2	0	0	0	0	....	....	....	....	....
	Worcester	AHL	31	2	8	10	14	4	0	1	1	2

Signed as a free agent by **St. Louis**, April 26, 1999.

O'CONNELL, Albert

Left wing. Shoots left. 6', 188 lbs. Born, Cambridge, MA, May 20, 1976.
(NY Islanders' 6th choice, 116th overall, in 1994 Entry Draft).

			Regular Season					Playoffs				
Season	Club	Lea	GP	G	A	TP	PIM	GP	G	A	TP	PIM
1993-94	St. Sebastian's	H.S.	24	16	23	39	26	....	....	....	....	....
1994-95	St. Sebastian's	H.S.	26	19	25	44	....	....	....	....	....	....
1995-96	Boston University	H.E.	38	9	8	17	34	....	....	....	....	....
1996-97	Boston University	H.E.	41	12	12	24	72	....	....	....	....	....
1997-98	Boston University	H.E.	34	12	16	28	60	....	....	....	....	....
1998-99	Boston University	H.E.	36	9	30	39	66	....	....	....	....	....

O'CONNOR, Tom — PIT.

Defence. Shoots left. 6'2", 190 lbs. Born, Springfield, MA, January 9, 1976.
(Pittsburgh's 6th choice, 102nd overall, in 1994 Entry Draft).

			Regular Season					Playoffs				
Season	Club	Lea	GP	G	A	TP	PIM	GP	G	A	TP	PIM
1993-94	Springfield	NEJHL	30	6	30	36	73	....	....	....	....	....
1994-95	U. Mass-Amherst	H.E.	34	1	2	3	44	....	....	....	....	....
1995-96	U. Mass-Amherst	H.E.	35	2	4	6	48	....	....	....	....	....
1996-97	U. Mass-Amherst	H.E.	30	3	8	11	42	....	....	....	....	....
1997-98	U. Mass-Amherst	H.E.	33	2	16	18	30	....	....	....	....	....
1998-99	Syracuse	AHL	16	0	1	1	8	....	....	....	....	....
	Wheeling	ECHL	54	5	20	25	58	....	....	....	....	....

ODUYA, Fredrik — (oh-DOO-yuh) CGY.

Left wing. Shoots left. 6'3", 220 lbs. Born, Stockholm, Sweden, May 31, 1975.
(San Jose's 8th choice, 154th overall, in 1993 Entry Draft).

			Regular Season					Playoffs				
Season	Club	Lea	GP	G	A	TP	PIM	GP	G	A	TP	PIM
1992-93	Guelph	OHL	23	2	4	6	29	....	....	....	....	....
	Ottawa	OHL	17	0	3	3	70	....	....	....	....	....
1993-94	Ottawa	OHL	51	11	12	23	181	17	0	3	3	22
1994-95	Ottawa	OHL	61	2	13	15	175	....	....	....	....	....
1995-96	Kansas City	IHL	56	2	6	8	235	3	0	0	0	2
1996-97	Kentucky	AHL	69	2	9	11	241	....	....	....	....	....
1997-98	Kentucky	AHL	72	6	10	16	300	....	....	....	....	....
1998-99	Orlando	IHL	64	2	14	16	259	....	....	....	....	....
	Saint John	AHL	12	0	2	2	48	6	0	0	0	22

Traded to **Calgary** by **San Jose** for Eric Landry, July 12, 1999.

OIKAWA, Matt — (oh-ee-kah-wah) WSH.

Right wing. Shoots right. 6'2", 205 lbs. Born, Hamilton, Ont., October 27, 1977.
(Washington's 7th choice, 226th overall, in 1997 Entry Draft).

			Regular Season					Playoffs				
Season	Club	Lea	GP	G	A	TP	PIM	GP	G	A	TP	PIM
1995-96	St. Lawrence	ECAC	13	3	1	4	15	....	....	....	....	....
1996-97	St. Lawrence	ECAC	34	9	10	19	18	....	....	....	....	....
1997-98	St. Lawrence	ECAC	16	2	5	7	6	....	....	....	....	....
1998-99	St. Lawrence	ECAC	35	6	8	14	14	....	....	....	....	....

O'LEARY, Pat — PHX.

Center. Shoots left. 6'2", 190 lbs. Born, Minneapolis, MN, September 2, 1979.
(Phoenix's 3rd choice, 73rd overall, in 1998 Entry Draft).

			Regular Season					Playoffs				
Season	Club	Lea	GP	G	A	TP	PIM	GP	G	A	TP	PIM
1996-97	Robbinsdale	H.S.	22	28	27	55	42	....	....	....	....	....
1997-98	Robbinsdale	H.S.	24	22	27	49	28	....	....	....	....	....
1998-99	U. of Minnesota	WCHA	17	0	2	2	8	....	....	....	....	....

OLSON, Boyd — MTL.

Center. Shoots left. 6'1", 188 lbs. Born, Edmonton, Alta., April 4, 1976.
(Montreal's 6th choice, 138th overall, in 1995 Entry Draft).

			Regular Season					Playoffs				
Season	Club	Lea	GP	G	A	TP	PIM	GP	G	A	TP	PIM
1993-94	Tri-City	WHL	2	0	1	1	0	....	....	....	....	....
1994-95	Tri-City	WHL	69	16	16	32	87	17	6	2	8	22
1995-96	Tri-City	WHL	62	13	12	25	105	11	1	4	5	16
	Fredericton	AHL	....	....	....	....	....	2	1	0	1	0
1996-97	Fredericton	AHL	74	8	12	20	43	....	....	....	....	....
1997-98	Fredericton	AHL	57	4	9	13	43	....	....	....	....	....
1998-99	Fredericton	AHL	61	10	16	26	60	13	1	3	4	16

OLVESTAD, Jimmie — (OHL-vuh-stahd) T.B.

Left wing. Shoots left. 6'1", 194 lbs. Born, Stockholm, Sweden, February 16, 1980.
(Tampa Bay's 4th choice, 88th overall, in 1999 Entry Draft).

			Regular Season					Playoffs				
Season	Club	Lea	GP	G	A	TP	PIM	GP	G	A	TP	PIM
1996-97	Huddinge IF	Swede-Jr.	40	15	16	31	....	....	....	....	....	....
1997-98	Djurgardens IF	Swede-Jr.	10	3	3	6	10	....	....	....	....	....
	Huddinge IF	Sweden-2	11	0	0	0	6	....	....	....	....	....
1998-99	Djurgardens IF	Sweden	44	2	4	6	18	4	0	0	0	8

OREKHOVSKY, Oleg — (oh-reh-KHOHV-skee) WSH.

Defense. Shoots right. 6', 183 lbs. Born, Krasnoyarsk, USSR, November 3, 1977.
(Washington's 11th choice, 206th overall, in 1996 Entry Draft).

			Regular Season					Playoffs				
Season	Club	Lea	GP	G	A	TP	PIM	GP	G	A	TP	PIM
1994-95	Moscow D'amo	CIS	30	0	1	1	18	....	....	....	....	....
1995-96	Moscow D'amo	CIS	22	1	2	3	14	8	0	0	0	6
1996-97	Moscow D'amo	Russia	32	4	2	6	16	4	2	1	3	2
1997-98	Moscow D'amo	EuroHL	7	2	1	3	12	....	....	....	....	....
	Moscow D'amo	Russia	40	4	5	9	34	....	....	....	....	....
1998-99	Moscow D'amo	Russia	42	1	1	2	22	16	1	2	3	6

OVINGTON, Chris — FLA.

Defense. Shoots right. 6'3", 182 lbs. Born, Vernon, B.C., August 15, 1980.
(Florida's 6th choice, 148th overall, in 1998 Entry Draft).

			Regular Season					Playoffs				
Season	Club	Lea	GP	G	A	TP	PIM	GP	G	A	TP	PIM
1996-97	Red Deer	WHL	33	0	3	3	17	7	0	1	1	2
1997-98	Red Deer	WHL	68	2	13	15	72	5	0	0	0	2
1998-99	Red Deer	WHL	49	1	10	11	73	....	....	....	....	....
	Saskatoon	WHL	19	2	1	3	37	....	....	....	....	....

PAHLSSON, Samual — (PAWL-suhn) COL.

Center. Shoots left. 5'11", 190 lbs. Born, Ornskoldsvik, Sweden, December 17, 1977.
(Colorado's 10th choice, 176th overall, in 1996 Entry Draft).

			Regular Season					Playoffs				
Season	Club	Lea	GP	G	A	TP	PIM	GP	G	A	TP	PIM
1994-95	MoDo Hockey	Swede-Jr.	30	10	11	21	26	....	....	....	....	....
	MoDo Hockey	Sweden	1	0	0	0	0	....	....	....	....	....
1995-96	MoDo Hockey	Swede-Jr.	5	2	6	8	2	....	....	....	....	....
	MoDo Hockey	Sweden	36	1	3	4	8	1	0	0	0	0
1996-97	MoDo Hockey	Sweden	49	8	9	17	83	....	....	....	....	....
1997-98	MoDo Hockey	Sweden	23	6	11	17	24	9	3	0	3	6
1998-99	MoDo Hockey	Sweden	50	17	17	34	44	13	3	3	6	10

PANDOLFO, Mike — (pan-DAHL-foh) BUF.

Left wing. Shoots left. 6'3", 226 lbs. Born, Winchester, MA, September 15, 1979.
(Buffalo's 5th choice, 77th overall, in 1998 Entry Draft)

			Regular Season					Playoffs				
Season	Club	Lea	GP	G	A	TP	PIM	GP	G	A	TP	PIM
1996-97	St. Sebastians	H.S.	32	27	28	55	30	....	....	....	....	....
1997-98	St. Sebastians	H.S.	28	29	23	52	18	....	....	....	....	....
1998-99	Boston University	H.E.	34	13	4	17	26	....	....	....	....	....

PANOV, Konstantin — (puh-NAWV) NSH.

Right wing. Shoots left. 5'11", 186 lbs. Born, Chelyabinsk, USSR, June 29, 1980.
(Nashville's 10th choice, 131st overall, in 1999 Entry Draft).

			Regular Season					Playoffs				
Season	Club	Lea	GP	G	A	TP	PIM	GP	G	A	TP	PIM
1997-98	Kurgan-T	Russia-3	20	7	3	10	6	....	....	....	....	....
1998-99	Kamloops	WHL	62	33	30	63	62	13	5	3	8	10

PAPINEAU, Justin — (PA-pih-noh) L.A.

Center. Shoots left. 5'10", 160 lbs. Born, Ottawa, Ont., January 15, 1980.
(Los Angeles' 2nd choice, 46th overall, in 1998 Entry Draft).

			Regular Season					Playoffs				
Season	Club	Lea	GP	G	A	TP	PIM	GP	G	A	TP	PIM
1996-97	Belleville	OHL	50	10	32	42	32	....	....	....	....	....
1997-98	Belleville	OHL	66	41	53	94	34	10	5	9	14	6
1998-99	Belleville	OHL	68	52	47	99	28	21	*21	*30	*51	20

PASTUKH, Yevgeny — (pas-TOOKH) ST.L.

Left wing. Shoots left. 5'11", 178 lbs. Born, Yaroslavl, USSR, January 18, 1979.
(St. Louis' 7th choice, 225th overall, in 1998 Entry Draft).

			Regular Season					Playoffs				
Season	Club	Lea	GP	G	A	TP	PIM	GP	G	A	TP	PIM
1995-96	Yaroslavl-2	Russia-2	4	0	0	0	0	....	....	....	....	....
1996-97	Yaroslavl-2	Russia-3	34	3	5	8	6	....	....	....	....	....
1997-98	Yaroslavl-2	Russia-2	26	6	6	12	14	....	....	....	....	....
	Yaroslavl	Russia	3	0	0	0	0	....	....	....	....	....
	Khimik	Russia	3	0	0	0	2	....	....	....	....	....
1998-99	Khimik	Russia	8	0	0	0	0	....	....	....	....	....

PATERA, Pavel (puh-TEHR-uh) DAL.

Center. Shoots left. 6'1", 172 lbs. Born, Kladno, Czech., September 6, 1971.
(Dallas' 4th choice, 153rd overall, in 1998 Entry Draft).

			Regular Season					Playoffs				
Season	Club	Lea	GP	G	A	TP	PIM	GP	G	A	TP	PIM
1990-91	Poldi Kladno	Czech.	3	0	0	0	....	....	....	....	....	....
1991-92	Poldi Kladno	Czech.	38	12	13	25	26	8	8	4	12	0
1992-93	Poldi Kladno	Czech.	42	9	23	32	....	....	....	....	....	....
1993-94	HC Kladno	Cze-Rep	43	21	39	60	....	11	5	10	15	....
1994-95	HC Kladno	Cze-Rep	43	26	49	75	24	11	5	7	12	6
1995-96	Poldi Kladno	Cze-Rep	40	24	31	55	38	8	3	1	4	34
1996-97	AIK Solna	Sweden	50	19	24	43	44	7	2	3	5	6
1997-98	AIK Solna	Sweden	46	8	17	25	50	....	....	....	....	....
1998-99	HC Vsetin	Cze-Rep	52	16	37	53	58	12	5	*10	15	....

PAUL, Dustin

Right wing. Shoots right. 5'11", 195 lbs. Born, Calgary, Alta., April 22, 1979.
(Calgary's 12th choice, 223rd overall, in 1997 Entry Draft).

			Regular Season					Playoffs				
Season	Club	Lea	GP	G	A	TP	PIM	GP	G	A	TP	PIM
1996-97	Moose Jaw	WHL	70	19	13	32	33	12	7	2	9	2
1997-98	Moose Jaw	WHL	71	36	31	67	46	4	1	2	3	8
1998-99	Moose Jaw	WHL	71	31	52	83	75	11	2	6	8	26

PAUL, Jeff CHI.

Defense. Shoots right. 6'3", 196 lbs. Born, London, Ont., March 1, 1978.
(Chicago's 2nd choice, 42nd overall, in 1996 Entry Draft).

			Regular Season					Playoffs				
Season	Club	Lea	GP	G	A	TP	PIM	GP	G	A	TP	PIM
1994-95	Niagara Falls	OHL	57	3	10	13	64	6	0	2	2	0
1995-96	Niagara Falls	OHL	48	1	7	8	81	10	0	4	4	37
1996-97	Erie	OHL	60	4	23	27	152	5	2	0	2	12
1997-98	Erie	OHL	48	3	17	20	108	7	0	2	2	13
1998-99	Portland	AHL	6	0	0	0	4	....	....	....	....	....
	Indianapolis	IHL	55	0	7	7	120	7	0	2	2	12

PAVLIKOVSKY, Rastisla (pahv-lih-KAWV-skee) OTT.

Center. Shoots left. 5'10", 195 lbs. Born, Dubnica, Czech., September 8, 1979.
(Ottawa's 10th choice, 246th overall, in 1998 Entry Draft).

			Regular Season					Playoffs				
Season	Club	Lea	GP	G	A	TP	PIM	GP	G	A	TP	PIM
1993-94	Dukla Trencin	Slovakia	3	0	1	1	0	....	....	....	....	....
1994-95	Dukla Trencin	Slovakia	14	0	7	7	4	6	1	1	2	0
1995-96	S.S. Marie	OHL	13	0	3	3	6	....	....	....	....	....
	Dukla Trencin	Slovakia	10	1	1	2	6	12	4	1	5	....
1996-97	Dukla Trencin	Slovakia	35	7	5	12	....	7	3	2	5	....
1997-98	Dukla Trencin	Slovakia	3	2	1	3	0	....	....	....	....	....
	Las Vegas	IHL	1	0	0	0	0	....	....	....	....	....
	Utah	IHL	74	17	29	46	54	2	0	0	0	6
1998-99	Cincinnati	IHL	31	4	12	16	28	....	....	....	....	....
	Cincinnati	AHL	36	12	23	35	59	2	0	1	1	4

PAVLOV, Yevgeny NSH.

Left wing. Shoots right. 6'1", 191 lbs. Born, Togliatti, USSR, January 10, 1981.
(Nashville's 8th choice, 121st overall, in 1999 Entry Draft).

			Regular Season					Playoffs				
Season	Club	Lea	GP	G	A	TP	PIM	GP	G	A	TP	PIM
1997-98	Lada Togliatti-2	Russia-3	27	8	1	9	4	....	....	....	....	....
1998-99	Lada Togliatti	Russia	9	0	1	1	2	....	....	....	....	....

PAYER, Serge FLA.

Center. Shoots left. 6', 173 lbs. Born, Rockland, Ont., May 7, 1979.

			Regular Season					Playoffs				
Season	Club	Lea	GP	G	A	TP	PIM	GP	G	A	TP	PIM
1995-96	Kitchener	OHL	66	8	16	24	18	12	0	2	2	2
1996-97	Kitchener	OHL	63	7	16	23	27	13	1	3	4	2
1997-98	Kitchener	OHL	44	20	21	41	51	6	3	0	3	7
1998-99	Kitchener	OHL	40	18	19	37	22	....	....	....	....	....

Signed as a free agent by **Florida**, September 30, 1997.

PAYETTE, Andre

Center. Shoots left. 6'2", 205 lbs. Born, Cornwall, Ont., July 29, 1976.
(Philadelphia's 9th choice, 244th overall, in 1994 Entry Draft).

			Regular Season					Playoffs				
Season	Club	Lea	GP	G	A	TP	PIM	GP	G	A	TP	PIM
1993-94	S.S. Marie	OHL	40	2	3	5	98	....	....	....	....	....
1994-95	S.S. Marie	OHL	50	15	15	30	177	....	....	....	....	....
1995-96	S.S. Marie	OHL	57	20	19	39	257	4	0	0	0	5
1996-97	S.S. Marie	OHL	4	3	....	3	19	....	....	....	....	....
	Kingston	OHL	29	10	13	23	143	2	0	0	0	2
1997-98	Philadelphia	AHL	56	5	5	10	209	4	0	0	0	9
1998-99	Philadelphia	AHL	12	0	1	1	34	....	....	....	....	....
	Mohawk	UHL	51	9	21	30	241	....	....	....	....	....

PEAT, Stephen ANA.

Defense. Shoots right. 6'3", 210 lbs. Born, Princeton, B.C., March 10, 1980.
(Anaheim's 2nd choice, 32nd overall, in 1998 Entry Draft).

			Regular Season					Playoffs				
Season	Club	Lea	GP	G	A	TP	PIM	GP	G	A	TP	PIM
1995-96	Red Deer	WHL	1	0	0	0	0	....	....	....	....	....
1996-97	Red Deer	WHL	68	3	14	17	161	16	0	2	2	22
1997-98	Red Deer	WHL	63	6	12	18	189	5	0	0	0	8
1998-99	Red Deer	WHL	31	2	6	8	98	....	....	....	....	....
	Tri-City	WHL	5	0	0	0	19	....	....	....	....	....

PECKER, Cory CGY.

Center. Shoots right. 6', 190 lbs. Born, Montreal, Que., March 20, 1981.
(Calgary's 7th choice, 166th overall, in 1999 Entry Draft).

			Regular Season					Playoffs				
Season	Club	Lea	GP	G	A	TP	PIM	GP	G	A	TP	PIM
1997-98	S.S. Marie	OHL	29	3	4	7	15	....	....	....	....	....
1998-99	S.S. Marie	OHL	68	25	34	59	24	5	1	2	3	2

PELUSO, Mike WSH.

Right wing. Shoots right. 6'1", 195 lbs. Born, Bismark, ND, September 2, 1974.
(Calgary's 12th choice, 253rd overall, in 1994 Entry Draft).

			Regular Season					Playoffs				
Season	Club	Lea	GP	G	A	TP	PIM	GP	G	A	TP	PIM
1993-94	Omaha	USHL	48	36	29	65	77	....	....	....	....	....
1994-95	U. Minn-Duluth	WCHA	38	11	23	34	38	....	....	....	....	....
1995-96	U. Minn-Duluth	WCHA	38	25	19	44	64	....	....	....	....	....
1996-97	U. Minn-Duluth	WCHA	37	20	20	40	53	....	....	....	....	....
1997-98	U. Minn-Duluth	WCHA	40	24	21	45	100	....	....	....	....	....
1998-99	Portland	AHL	26	7	6	13	6	....	....	....	....	....

Signed as a free agent by **Washington**, October 9,1998.

PEPPERALL, Colin (PEH-puhr-awl) CHI.

Left wing. Shoots left. 5'11", 160 lbs. Born, Niagara Falls, Ont., April 28, 1978.
(NY Rangers' 4th choice, 131st overall, in 1996 Entry Draft).

			Regular Season					Playoffs				
Season	Club	Lea	GP	G	A	TP	PIM	GP	G	A	TP	PIM
1995-96	Niagara Falls	OHL	66	26	26	52	47	10	3	4	7	8
1996-97	Erie	OHL	66	36	36	72	39	5	3	2	5	2
1997-98	Erie	OHL	60	31	60	91	151	7	4	4	8	16
	Hartford	AHL	3	1	0	1	2	....	....	....	....	....
1998-99	Portland	AHL	4	0	0	0	6	....	....	....	....	....
	Greenville	ECHL	55	15	20	35	128	....	....	....	....	....
	Indianapolis	IHL	9	2	2	4	12	....	....	....	....	....

OHL Second All-Star Team (1998)

PEPPERALL, Ryan (PEH-puhr-awl) TOR.

Right wing. Shoots right. 6'1", 185 lbs. Born, Niagara Falls, Ont., January 26, 1977.
(Toronto's 2nd choice, 54th overall, in 1995 Entry Draft).

			Regular Season					Playoffs				
Season	Club	Lea	GP	G	A	TP	PIM	GP	G	A	TP	PIM
1994-95	Kitchener	OHL	62	17	16	33	86	5	2	2	4	8
1995-96	Kitchener	OHL	66	31	26	57	173	12	3	4	7	34
1996-97	Kitchener	OHL	65	35	36	71	201	13	9	6	15	17
1997-98	St. John's	AHL	63	3	4	7	50	1	0	0	0	0
1998-99	St. John's	AHL	79	16	8	24	70	5	1	0	1	2

PERIARD, Michael (pair-EE-ahr)

Defense. Shoots left. 5'11", 175 lbs. Born, Montreal, Que., November 10, 1979.
(Ottawa's 8th choice, 188th overall, in 1998 Entry Draft).

			Regular Season					Playoffs				
Season	Club	Lea	GP	G	A	TP	PIM	GP	G	A	TP	PIM
1997-98	Shawinigan	QMJHL	68	14	30	44	64	5	0	0	0	18
1998-99	Shawinigan	QMJHL	64	14	40	54	90	6	1	2	3	4

PERROTT, Nathan CHI.

Right wing. Shoots right. 6', 215 lbs. Born, Owen Sound, Ont., December 8, 1976.
(New Jersey's 2nd choice, 44th overall, in 1995 Entry Draft).

			Regular Season					Playoffs				
Season	Club	Lea	GP	G	A	TP	PIM	GP	G	A	TP	PIM
1994-95	Oshawa	OHL	63	18	28	46	233	2	1	1	2	9
1995-96	Oshawa	OHL	59	30	32	62	158	5	2	3	5	8
	Albany	AHL	4	0	0	0	12	....	....	....	....	....
1996-97	Oshawa	OHL	5	1	0	1	17	....	....	....	....	....
	S.S. Marie	OHL	37	18	23	41	120	11	5	5	10	60
1997-98	Indianapolis	IHL	31	4	3	7	76	....	....	....	....	....
	Jacksonville	ECHL	30	6	8	14	135	....	....	....	....	....
1998-99	Indianapolis	IHL	72	14	11	25	307	7	3	1	4	45

Signed as a free agent by **Chicago**, August 27, 1997.

PERRY, Scott DAL.

Center. Shoots left. 6', 180 lbs. Born, Boston, MA, October 12, 1978.
(Dallas' 6th choice, 200th overall, in 1998 Entry Draft).

			Regular Season					Playoffs				
Season	Club	Lea	GP	G	A	TP	PIM	GP	G	A	TP	PIM
1996-97	Thayer Academy	H.S.			STATISTICS NOT AVAILABLE							
1997-98	Boston University	H.E.	38	5	12	17	18	....	....	....	....	....
1998-99	Boston University	H.E.	33	4	8	12	26	....	....	....	....	....

PERSHIN, Eduard (PEHR-shihn, ehd-WUHRD) T.B.

Right wing. Shoots left. 6', 191 lbs. Born, Nizhnekamsk, USSR, September 1, 1977.
(Tampa Bay's 5th choice, 134th overall, in 1995 Entry Draft).

			Regular Season					Playoffs				
Season	Club	Lea	GP	G	A	TP	PIM	GP	G	A	TP	PIM
1994-95	Moscow D'amo	CIS	4	1	1	2	2	3	0	0	0	2
1995-96	Moscow D'amo	CIS	38	4	10	14	18	2	0	0	0	0
1996-97	Moscow D'amo	Russia	31	4	9	13	16	3	0	2	2	0
1997-98	Chesapeake	ECHL	38	12	21	33	38	3	0	0	0	4
1998-99	Chesapeake	ECHL	2	0	1	1	2	....	....	....	....	....
	Cleveland	IHL	68	9	12	21	71	....	....	....	....	....

PETERS, Andrew BUF.

Left wing. Shoots left. 6'4", 195 lbs. Born, St. Catharines, Ont., May 5, 1980.
(Buffalo's 2nd choice, 34th overall, in 1998 Entry Draft).

			Regular Season					Playoffs				
Season	Club	Lea	GP	G	A	TP	PIM	GP	G	A	TP	PIM
1996-97	Georgetown	OJHL	46	11	16	27	65	....	....	....	....	....
1997-98	Oshawa	OHL	60	11	7	18	220	7	2	0	2	19
1998-99	Oshawa	OHL	54	14	10	24	137	15	2	7	9	36

PETERS, Geoff CHI.

Center. Shoots left. 6'1", 185 lbs. Born, Hamilton, Ont., April 30, 1978.
(Chicago's 3rd choice, 46th overall, in 1996 Entry Draft).

			Regular Season					Playoffs				
Season	Club	Lea	GP	G	A	TP	PIM	GP	G	A	TP	PIM
1994-95	Niagara Falls	OHL	57	11	9	20	37	6	2	0	2	4
1995-96	Niagara Falls	OHL	64	25	34	59	51	10	4	4	8	8
1996-97	Erie	OHL	28	12	10	22	39	5	1	3	4	7
1997-98	Erie	OHL	31	15	11	26	36	....	....	....	....	....
	North Bay	OHL	20	11	14	25	22	....	....	....	....	....
	Indianapolis	IHL	2	0	0	0	10	....	....	....	....	....
1998-99	Canada	Nat-Team	38	9	4	13	50	....	....	....	....	....
	Portland	AHL	4	1	1	2	9	....	....	....	....	....

PETERSON, Toby — PIT.

Center. Shoots left. 5'10", 196 lbs. Born, Minneapolis, MN, October 27, 1978.
(Pittsburgh's 9th choice, 244th overall, in 1998 Entry Draft).

			Regular Season					Playoffs				
Season	Club	Lea	GP	G	A	TP	PIM	GP	G	A	TP	PIM
1995-96	Jefferson High	H.S.	25	29	30	59	....	....	....	....	....	....
1996-97	Colorado	WCHA	40	17	21	38	18	....	....	....	....	....
1997-98	Colorado	WCHA	40	16	17	33	34	....	....	....	....	....
1998-99	Colorado	WCHA	21	12	12	24	2	....	....	....	....	....

PETRAKOV, Andrei (peh-trah-KAHF) — ST.L.

Right wing. Shoots left. 6', 204 lbs. Born, Sverdlovsk, USSR, April 26, 1976.
(St. Louis' 4th choice, 97th overall, in 1996 Entry Draft).

			Regular Season					Playoffs				
Season	Club	Lea	GP	G	A	TP	PIM	GP	G	A	TP	PIM
1992-93	Yekaterinburg	CIS	5	0	0	0	0	1	0	0	0	0
1993-94	Yekaterinburg	CIS	35	4	2	6	10	....	....	....	....	....
1994-95	Yekaterinburg	CIS	11	1	1	2	6	1	0	0	0	0
1995-96	Yekaterinburg	CIS-2	52	17	6	23	14	....	....	....	....	....
1996-97	Yekaterinburg	Russia	14	6	1	7	6	....	....	....	....	....
	Magnitogorsk	Russia	18	4	0	4	8	6	0	0	0	0
1997-98	CSK Samara	Russia	9	0	0	0	4	....	....	....	....	....
	Magnitogorsk	Russia	29	9	11	20	0	....	....	....	....	....
1998-99	Worcester	AHL	4	0	1	1	2	....	....	....	....	....
	Magnitogorsk	Russia	10	4	4	8	8	15	4	8	12	4
	Muskegon	UHL	5	4	3	7	0	....	....	....	....	....
	Fort Wayne	IHL	11	2	4	6	0	....	....	....	....	....

PETRASEK, David (PEH-truh-sehk) — DET.

Defense. Shoots right. 6', 187 lbs. Born, Jonkoping, Sweden, February 1, 1976.
(Detroit's 10th choice, 226th overall, in 1998 Entry Draft).

			Regular Season					Playoffs				
Season	Club	Lea	GP	G	A	TP	PIM	GP	G	A	TP	PIM
1993-94	HV Jonkoping	Swede-Jr.	14	3	3	6	26	....	....	....	....	....
1994-95	HV Jonkoping	Sweden	30	0	1	1	6	11	0	0	0	0
	HV Jonkoping	Swede-Jr.	19	8	9	17	55	....	....	....	....	....
1995-96	HV Jonkoping	Swede-Jr.	12	1	5	6	16	....	....	....	....	....
	HV Jonkoping	Swede-Jr.	12	1	5	6	16	....	....	....	....	....
1996-97	HV Jonkoping	Swede-Jr.	3	0	0	0	....	....	....	....	....	....
	HV Jonkoping	Sweden	49	2	4	6	14	5	0	0	0	4
1997-98	HV Jonkoping	Sweden	43	6	7	13	80	5	2	2	4	14
1998-99	HV Jonkoping	Sweden	45	3	4	7	48	....	....	....	....	....

PETRE, Henrik (PEH-truh) — WSH.

Defense. Shoots left. 6'1", 187 lbs. Born, Stockholm, Sweden, April 9, 1979.
(Washington's 5th choice, 143rd overall, in 1997 Entry Draft).

			Regular Season					Playoffs				
Season	Club	Lea	GP	G	A	TP	PIM	GP	G	A	TP	PIM
1995-96	Djurgardens IF	Swede-Jr.	21	6	4	10	8	....	....	....	....	....
1996-97	Djurgardens IF	Swede-Jr.	20	7	6	13	....	....	....	....	....	....
1997-98	Huddinge IF	Sweden-2	30	4	4	8	30	....	....	....	....	....
1998-99	Djurgardens IF	Sweden	9	0	0	0	10	....	....	....	....	....
	Huddinge IK	Sweden-2	14	0	1	1	20	....	....	....	....	....

PETRILAINEN, Pasi (peh-trih-LAI-nehn, PAH-see) — N.J.

Defense. Shoots left. 5'10", 185 lbs. Born, Tampere, Finland, May 5, 1978.
(New Jersey's 14th choice, 225th overall, in 1996 Entry Draft).

			Regular Season					Playoffs				
Season	Club	Lea	GP	G	A	TP	PIM	GP	G	A	TP	PIM
1994-95	Tappara	Finland	25	3	0	3	14	....	....	....	....	....
	Tappara	Finn-Jr.	14	3	4	7	6	....	....	....	....	....
1995-96	Tappara	Finland	40	0	4	4	18	4	0	0	0	2
	Tappara	Finn-Jr.	5	0	2	2	4	....	....	....	....	....
1996-97	Tappara	Finland	43	2	9	11	46	3	0	0	0	2
1997-98	Tappara	Finland	48	4	7	11	34	4	0	0	0	4
1998-99	Tappara	Finland	35	3	3	6	26	....	....	....	....	....

PETROVICKY, Ronald (PEHT-roh-vih-kee) — CGY.

Right wing. Shoots right. 5'11", 185 lbs. Born, Zilina, Czech., February 15, 1977.
(Calgary's 9th choice, 228th overall, in 1996 Entry Draft).

			Regular Season					Playoffs				
Season	Club	Lea	GP	G	A	TP	PIM	GP	G	A	TP	PIM
1993-94	Dukla Trencin	Slovak-Jr.	36	28	27	55	42	....	....	....	....	....
	Dukla Trencin	Slovakia	1	0	0	0	0	....	....	....	....	....
1994-95	Tri-City	WHL	39	4	11	15	86	....	....	....	....	....
	Prince George	WHL	21	4	6	10	37	....	....	....	....	....
1995-96	Prince George	WHL	39	19	21	40	61	....	....	....	....	....
1996-97	Prince George	WHL	72	32	37	69	119	15	4	9	13	31
1997-98	Regina	WHL	71	64	49	113	168	9	2	4	6	11
1998-99	Saint John	AHL	78	12	21	33	114	7	1	2	3	19

WHL East Second All-Star Team (1998)

PETRUNIN, Andrei (puh-TROO-nihn) — CAR.

Right wing. Shoots left. 5'9", 169 lbs. Born, Moscow, USSR, February 2, 1978.
(Hartford's 2nd choice, 61st overall, in 1996 Entry Draft).

			Regular Season					Playoffs				
Season	Club	Lea	GP	G	A	TP	PIM	GP	G	A	TP	PIM
1994-95	CSKA Moscow	CIS	7	0	1	1	0	2	0	0	0	0
1995-96	CSKA Moscow	CIS	52	12	8	20	22	2	0	0	0	2
1996-97	CSKA Moscow	Russia-2	55	36	32	68	73	....	....	....	....	....
1997-98	CSKA Moscow	Russia	45	7	13	20	71	....	....	....	....	....
1998-99	Muskegon	UHL	63	37	37	74	63	13	3	8	11	8

PHILLIPS, Greg — L.A.

Right wing. Shoots right. 6'2", 205 lbs. Born, Winnipeg, Man., March 27, 1978.
(Los Angeles' 3rd choice, 57th overall, in 1996 Entry Draft).

			Regular Season					Playoffs				
Season	Club	Lea	GP	G	A	TP	PIM	GP	G	A	TP	PIM
1994-95	Saskatoon	WHL	64	3	5	8	94	10	0	0	0	4
1995-96	Saskatoon	WHL	67	21	24	45	132	4	1	2	3	2
1996-97	Saskatoon	WHL	34	17	19	36	64	....	....	....	....	....
1997-98	Saskatoon	WHL	47	24	28	52	116	....	....	....	....	....
	Brandon	WHL	22	10	21	31	49	18	11	11	22	58
1998-99	Springfield	AHL	63	16	13	29	74	3	0	0	0	4

PIETILAINEN, Petja (pee-eh-tih-LIGH-nehn, PEHT-ya) — DET.

Left wing. Shoots left. 5'11", 177 lbs. Born, Vyvaskyla, Finland, March 24, 1980.
(Detroit's 11th choice, 256th overall, in 1998 Entry Draft).

			Regular Season					Playoffs				
Season	Club	Lea	GP	G	A	TP	PIM	GP	G	A	TP	PIM
1995-96	JyP Jyvaskyla	Finn-Jr.	19	8	3	11	36	....	....	....	....	....
1996-97	JyP Jyvaskyla	Finn-Jr.	30	5	8	13	100	2	0	0	0	0
1997-98	Saskatoon	WHL	66	16	11	27	63	6	2	1	3	4
1998-99	Saskatoon	WHL	53	1	10	11	58	....	....	....	....	....

PIETROPAULO, Didier (pee-EHT-roh-PAW-loh) — S.J.

Defense. Shoots left. 6'1", 200 lbs. Born, Laval, Que., February 9, 1979.

			Regular Season					Playoffs				
Season	Club	Lea	GP	G	A	TP	PIM	GP	G	A	TP	PIM
1995-96	St-Hyacinthe	QMJHL	55	0	1	1	124	....	....	....	....	....
1996-97	Rouyn-Noranda	QMJHL	33	1	2	3	145	....	....	....	....	....
1997-98	Rouyn-Noranda	QMJHL	60	7	18	25	320	6	0	2	2	26
1998-99	Rouyn-Noranda	QMJHL	37	3	19	22	190	11	2	2	4	20

Signed as a free agent by **San Jose**, September 19, 1997.

PIROS, Kamil (PIH-ruhsh, KA-mihl) — BUF.

Center. Shoots left. 6'1", 183 lbs. Born, Most, Czech., November 20, 1978.
(Buffalo's 9th choice, 212th overall, in 1997 Entry Draft).

			Regular Season					Playoffs				
Season	Club	Lea	GP	G	A	TP	PIM	GP	G	A	TP	PIM
1993-94	Most	Czech-Jr.	16	12	10	22	....	....	....	....	....	....
	CHZ Litvinov	Czech-Jr.	22	6	13	19	....	....	....	....	....	....
1994-95	CHZ Litvinov	Czech-Jr.	40	27	16	43	....	....	....	....	....	....
1995-96	CHZ Litvinov	Czech-Jr.	42	16	13	29	....	....	....	....	....	....
1996-97	CHZ Litvinov	Czech-Jr.	3	2	1	3	....	....	....	....	....	....
	CHZ Litvinov	Cze-Rep	38	4	9	13	10	....	....	....	....	....
1997-98	CHZ Litvinov	Cze-Rep	14	0	1	1	2	....	....	....	....	....
1998-99	CHZ Litvinov	Cze-Rep	41	7	9	16	10	....	....	....	....	....

PISANI, Fernando (pih-ZAN-ee) — EDM.

Center/left wing. Shoots left. 6'1", 180 lbs. Born, Edmonton, Alta., December 27, 1976.
(Edmonton's 9th choice, 195th overall, in 1996 Entry Draft).

			Regular Season					Playoffs				
Season	Club	Lea	GP	G	A	TP	PIM	GP	G	A	TP	PIM
1995-96	St. Albert	AJHL	58	40	63	103	134	18	7	22	29	28
1996-97	Providence	H.E.	35	12	18	30	36	....	....	....	....	....
1997-98	Providence	H.E.	36	16	18	34	20	....	....	....	....	....
1998-99	Providence	H.E.	38	14	37	51	42	....	....	....	....	....

PISTEK, Lubomir (pihsh-TEHK) — PHI.

Right wing. Shoots left. 6'2", 195 lbs. Born, Bratislava, Czech., August 7, 1980.
(Philadelphia's 10th choice, 222nd overall, in 1998 Entry Draft).

			Regular Season					Playoffs				
Season	Club	Lea	GP	G	A	TP	PIM	GP	G	A	TP	PIM
1995-96	HC Bratislava	Slovak-Jr.	45	31	29	60	40	....	....	....	....	....
1996-97	HC Bratislava	Slovak-Jr.	45	15	20	35	20	....	....	....	....	....
1997-98	HC Bratislava	Slovak-Jr.	49	16	35	51	50	11	1	5	6	25
1998-99	Kelowna	WHL	55	13	16	29	38	6	0	0	0	6

PLEKHANOV, Dmitri (plih-KHAH-nahv) — ST.L.

Defense. Shoots left. 6'2", 176 lbs. Born, Nizhnekamsk, USSR, March 13, 1978.
(St. Louis' 8th choice, 232nd overall, in 1997 Entry Draft).

			Regular Season					Playoffs				
Season	Club	Lea	GP	G	A	TP	PIM	GP	G	A	TP	PIM
1995-96	Nizhnekamsk	CIS	30	1	2	3	28	....	....	....	....	....
1996-97	Nizhnekamsk	Russia	26	0	0	0	18	2	0	0	0	2
1997-98	Nizhnekamsk	Russia	18	0	0	0	6	....	....	....	....	....
1998-99	Nizhnekamsk	Russia	3	0	0	0	2	....	....	....	....	....

PODKONICKY, Andrei (pohd-koh-NIHTZ-kee) — ST.L.

Center. Shoots left. 6'2", 202 lbs. Born, Zvolen, Czech., May 9, 1978.
(St. Louis' 8th choice, 196th overall, in 1996 Entry Draft).

			Regular Season					Playoffs				
Season	Club	Lea	GP	G	A	TP	PIM	GP	G	A	TP	PIM
1994-95	HKM Zvolen	Slovak-2	17	0	4	4	6	....	....	....	....	....
1995-96	HKM Zvolen	Slovak-2	38	18	12	30	18	....	....	....	....	....
1996-97	Portland	WHL	71	25	46	71	127	6	1	1	2	8
1997-98	Portland	WHL	64	30	44	74	81	16	4	12	16	20
1998-99	Worcester	AHL	61	19	24	43	52	4	0	0	0	4

Memorial Cup All-Star Team (1998) • Won Ed Chynoweth Award (Memorial Cup Tournament Top Scorer) (1998)

POHL, John (PAWL) — ST.L.

Center. Shoots right. 6', 173 lbs. Born, Rochester, MN, June 29, 1979.
(St. Louis' 8th choice, 255th overall, in 1998 Entry Draft).

			Regular Season					Playoffs				
Season	Club	Lea	GP	G	A	TP	PIM	GP	G	A	TP	PIM
1997-98	Red Wing High	H.S.	28	30	77	107	18	....	....	....	....	....
1998-99	U. of Minnesota	WCHA	42	7	10	17	18	....	....	....	....	....

POLLOCK, Jame — ST.L.

Defense. Shoots right. 6'3", 202 lbs. Born, Quebec City, Que., June 16, 1979.
(St. Louis' 4th choice, 106th overall, in 1997 Entry Draft).

			Regular Season					Playoffs				
Season	Club	Lea	GP	G	A	TP	PIM	GP	G	A	TP	PIM
1995-96	Seattle	WHL	32	0	1	1	15	....	....	....	....	....
1996-97	Seattle	WHL	66	15	19	34	94	15	3	5	8	16
1997-98	Seattle	WHL	66	11	36	47	78	5	0	1	1	17
1998-99	Seattle	WHL	59	10	32	42	78	11	3	4	7	8

PONIKAROVSKY, Alexei (poh-NIH-kahr-ohv-skee) **TOR.**

Right wing. Shoots left. 6'4", 196 lbs. Born, Kiev, USSR, April 9, 1980.
(Toronto's 4th choice, 87th overall, in 1998 Entry Draft).

			Regular Season					Playoffs				
Season	**Club**	**Lea**	**GP**	**G**	**A**	**TP**	**PIM**	**GP**	**G**	**A**	**TP**	**PIM**
1995-96	Moscow D'amo	Russia-Jr.	70	14	10	24	20	....	....	....	....	....
1996-97	Moscow D'amo	Russia-Jr.	60	12	15	27	30	....	....	....	....	....
	Moscow D'amo-2	Russia-3	2	0	0	0	2	....	....	....	....	....
1997-98	Moscow D'amo-2	Russia-2	24	1	2	3	30	....	....	....	....	....
1998-99	Soviet Wings	Russia	13	2	1	3	2	....	....	....	....	....
	Moscow D'amo	Russia	....	....	....	....	....	3	0	0	0	2

POSMYK, Marek (PAWZ-mihk) **TOR.**

Defense. Shoots right. 6'5", 228 lbs. Born, Jihlava, Czech., September 15, 1978.
(Toronto's 1st choice, 36th overall, in 1996 Entry Draft).

			Regular Season					Playoffs				
Season	**Club**	**Lea**	**GP**	**G**	**A**	**TP**	**PIM**	**GP**	**G**	**A**	**TP**	**PIM**
1994-95	Dukla Jihlava	Czech-Jr.	16	1	3	4	....	....	....	....	....	....
1995-96	Dukla Jihlava	Czech-Jr.	16	6	5	11	....	....	....	....	....	....
	Dukla Jihlava	Cze-Rep	18	1	2	3	....	1	0	0	0	....
1996-97	Dukla Jihlava	Cze-Rep	24	1	7	8	44	....	....	....	....	....
	St. John's	AHL	2	0	0	0	2	....	....	....	....	....
1997-98	Sarnia	OHL	48	8	16	24	94	5	0	2	2	6
	St. John's	AHL	3	0	0	0	4	....	....	....	....	....
1998-99	St. John's	AHL	41	1	0	1	36	....	....	....	....	....

PRESTBERG, Pelle **ANA.**

Left wing. Shoots left. 5'10", 170 lbs. Born, Jonkoping, Sweden, February 5, 1975.
(Anaheim's 7th choice, 233rd overall, in 1998 Entry Draft).

			Regular Season					Playoffs				
Season	**Club**	**Lea**	**GP**	**G**	**A**	**TP**	**PIM**	**GP**	**G**	**A**	**TP**	**PIM**
1991-92	IFK Munkfors	Sweden-3	26	6	10	16	18	....	....	....	....	....
1992-93	IFK Munkfors	Sweden-3	36	8	8	16	20	....	....	....	....	....
1993-94	Sunne IK	Sweden-3	32	8	6	14	16	....	....	....	....	....
1994-95	IFK Munkfors	Sweden-3	27	13	9	22	44	....	....	....	....	....
1995-96	IFK Munkfors	Sweden-3	30	20	11	31	32	....	....	....	....	....
1996-97	IFK Munkfors	Sweden-3	32	28	10	38	50	....	....	....	....	....
1997-98	Farjestads BK	Sweden	45	29	15	44	22	12	*9	2	11	8
1998-99	Farjestads BK	Sweden	48	18	15	33	28	4	0	1	1	4

PRESTON, Tim **BUF.**

Left wing. Shoots left. 6', 193 lbs. Born, Vancouver, B.C., June 30, 1981.
(Buffalo's 5th choice, 73rd overall, in 1999 Entry Draft).

			Regular Season					Playoffs				
Season	**Club**	**Lea**	**GP**	**G**	**A**	**TP**	**PIM**	**GP**	**G**	**A**	**TP**	**PIM**
1997-98	Seattle	WHL	55	11	5	16	49	5	0	0	0	0
1998-99	Seattle	WHL	60	12	15	27	98	11	0	1	1	11

PRIER, Bob (PRIGH-uhr) **OTT.**

Right wing. Shoots right. 6'1", 210 lbs. Born, Pembroke, Ont., August 5, 1976.
(Boston's 9th choice, 208th overall, in 1996 Entry Draft).

			Regular Season					Playoffs				
Season	**Club**	**Lea**	**GP**	**G**	**A**	**TP**	**PIM**	**GP**	**G**	**A**	**TP**	**PIM**
1995-96	St. Lawrence	ECAC	32	10	8	18	31	....	....	....	....	....
1996-97	St. Lawrence	ECAC	33	15	9	24	14	....	....	....	....	....
1997-98	St. Lawrence	ECAC	31	15	13	28	34	....	....	....	....	....
1998-99	St. Lawrence	ECAC	37	20	26	46	50	....	....	....	....	....

ECAC Second All-Star Team (1999)

Signed as a free agent by **Ottawa**, August 24, 1999.

PROCHAZKA, Libor (proh-HAHZ-kah) **ST.L.**

Defense. Shoots right. 6', 185 lbs. Born, Vlasim, Czech., April 25, 1974.
(St. Louis' 8th choice, 245th overall, in 1993 Entry Draft).

			Regular Season					Playoffs				
Season	**Club**	**Lea**	**GP**	**G**	**A**	**TP**	**PIM**	**GP**	**G**	**A**	**TP**	**PIM**
1991-92	Poldi Kladno	Czech.	7	0	0	0	0	....	....	....	....	....
1992-93	Poldi Kladno	Czech.	34	2	2	4	....	....	....	....	....	....
1993-94	Poldi Kladno	Cze-Rep	41	4	7	11	....	8	0	3	3	....
1994-95	Poldi Kladno	Cze-Rep	40	4	16	20	81	11	2	1	3	14
1995-96	Poldi Kladno	Cze-Rep	38	6	10	16	....	8	2	1	3	....
1996-97	Poldi Kladno	Cze-Rep	49	4	15	19	108	3	0	0	0	4
1997-98	AIK Solna	Sweden	43	3	4	7	92	....	....	....	....	....
	Czech Republic	Olympics	1	0	0	0	0	....	....	....	....	....
1998-99	HC Trinec	Cze-Rep	51	9	28	37	112	7	1	5	6	....

PROSKURNICKI, Andrew (praws-KUHR-nih-kee)

Left wing. Shoots left. 6'3", 201 lbs. Born, Hamilton, Ont., July 24, 1978.
(NY Rangers' 11th choice, 210th overall, in 1997 Entry Draft).

			Regular Season					Playoffs				
Season	**Club**	**Lea**	**GP**	**G**	**A**	**TP**	**PIM**	**GP**	**G**	**A**	**TP**	**PIM**
1995-96	Sarnia	OHL	60	3	11	14	96	10	1	3	4	12
1996-97	Sarnia	OHL	62	9	26	35	191	12	2	4	6	28
1997-98	Sarnia	OHL	66	20	33	53	229	5	1	1	2	28
	Hartford	AHL	4	0	1	1	7	....	....	....	....	....
1998-99	Sarnia	OHL	36	4	14	18	136	....	....	....	....	....
	Erie	OHL	15	6	5	11	39	5	2	2	4	16

PROSOFSKY, Garrett (proh-SAWF-skee) **PHI.**

Center. Shoots left. 5'11", 180 lbs. Born, Saskatoon, Sask., May 19, 1980.
(Philadelphia's 6th choice, 139th overall, in 1998 Entry Draft).

			Regular Season					Playoffs				
Season	**Club**	**Lea**	**GP**	**G**	**A**	**TP**	**PIM**	**GP**	**G**	**A**	**TP**	**PIM**
1995-96	Saskatoon AAA	SAHA	42	30	51	81	35	....	....	....	....	....
	Saskatoon	WHL	4	0	0	0	0	....	....	....	....	....
1996-97	Saskatoon	WHL	66	20	45	65	67	....	....	....	....	....
1997-98	Saskatoon	WHL	71	28	42	70	76	6	6	3	9	4
1998-99	Saskatoon	WHL	25	8	7	15	21	....	....	....	....	....
	Prince Albert	WHL	24	15	16	31	21	14	7	8	15	20

PROTSENKO, Boris (proht-SEHN-koh) **PIT.**

Right wing. Shoots right. 5'11", 197 lbs. Born, Kiev, USSR, August 21, 1978.
(Pittsburgh's 4th choice, 77th overall, in 1996 Entry Draft).

			Regular Season					Playoffs				
Season	**Club**	**Lea**	**GP**	**G**	**A**	**TP**	**PIM**	**GP**	**G**	**A**	**TP**	**PIM**
1995-96	Calgary	WHL	71	46	29	75	68	....	....	....	....	....
1996-97	Calgary	WHL	67	35	32	67	136	....	....	....	....	....
1997-98	Calgary	WHL	70	40	47	87	124	18	6	8	14	30
1998-99	Syracuse	AHL	65	24	24	48	84	....	....	....	....	....

PURINTON, Dale **NYR**

Defense. Shoots left. 6'2", 190 lbs. Born, Fort Wayne, IN, October 11, 1976.
(NY Rangers' 5th choice, 117th overall, in 1995 Entry Draft).

			Regular Season					Playoffs				
Season	**Club**	**Lea**	**GP**	**G**	**A**	**TP**	**PIM**	**GP**	**G**	**A**	**TP**	**PIM**
1994-95	Tacoma	WHL	65	0	8	8	291	3	0	0	0	13
1995-96	Kelowna	WHL	22	1	4	5	88	....	....	....	....	....
	Lethbridge	WHL	37	3	6	9	144	4	1	1	2	25
1996-97	Lethbridge	WHL	51	6	26	32	254	18	3	5	8	*88
1997-98	Hartford	AHL	17	0	0	0	95	....	....	....	....	....
	Charlotte	ECHL	34	3	5	8	186	....	....	....	....	....
1998-99	Hartford	AHL	45	1	3	4	306	7	0	2	2	24

PYATT, Taylor (PIGH-at) **NYI**

Left wing. Shoots left. 6'4", 220 lbs. Born, Thunder Bay, Ont., August 19, 1981.
(NY Islanders' 2nd choice, 8th overall, in 1999 Entry Draft).

			Regular Season					Playoffs				
Season	**Club**	**Lea**	**GP**	**G**	**A**	**TP**	**PIM**	**GP**	**G**	**A**	**TP**	**PIM**
1996-97	Thunder Bay	OMHA	60	52	61	113	72	....	....	....	....	....
1997-98	Sudbury	OHL	58	14	17	31	104	10	3	1	4	8
1998-99	Sudbury	OHL	68	37	38	75	95	4	0	4	4	6

RACHUNEK, Karel (ra-KHOO-nehk, KAH-rehl) **OTT.**

Defense. Shoots right. 6', 183 lbs. Born, Gottwaldov, Czech., August 27, 1979.
(Ottawa's 8th choice, 229th overall, in 1997 Entry Draft).

			Regular Season					Playoffs				
Season	**Club**	**Lea**	**GP**	**G**	**A**	**TP**	**PIM**	**GP**	**G**	**A**	**TP**	**PIM**
1995-96	ZPS Zlin	Czech-Jr.	38	8	11	19	....	....	....	....	....	....
1996-97	ZPS Zlin	Czech-Jr.	27	2	11	13	....	....	....	....	....	....
1997-98	ZPS Zlin	Cze-Rep	27	1	2	3	16	....	....	....	....	....
1998-99	ZPS Zlin	Cze-Rep	39	3	9	12	88	6	0	0	0	....

RADIVOJEVIC, Branko (ra-dih-VOI-uh-vihch) **COL.**

Right wing. Shoots right. 6', 183 lbs. Born, Piestany, Czech., November 24, 1980.
(Colorado's 3rd choice, 93rd overall, in 1999 Entry Draft).

			Regular Season					Playoffs				
Season	**Club**	**Lea**	**GP**	**G**	**A**	**TP**	**PIM**	**GP**	**G**	**A**	**TP**	**PIM**
1997-98	Dukla Trencin	Slovak-Jr.	52	30	31	61	50	....	....	....	....	....
	Dukla Trencin	Slovakia	1	0	0	0	2	....	....	....	....	....
1998-99	Belleville	OHL	68	20	38	58	61	21	7	17	24	18

RAFALSKI, Brian **N.J.**

Defense. Shoots right. 5'11", 200 lbs. Born, Dearborn, MI, September 28, 1973.

			Regular Season					Playoffs				
Season	**Club**	**Lea**	**GP**	**G**	**A**	**TP**	**PIM**	**GP**	**G**	**A**	**TP**	**PIM**
1991-92	U. of Wisconsin	WCHA	34	3	14	17	34	....	....	....	....	....
1992-93	U. of Wisconsin	WCHA	32	0	13	13	10	....	....	....	....	....
1993-94	U. of Wisconsin	WCHA	37	6	17	23	26	....	....	....	....	....
1994-95	U. of Wisconsin	WCHA	43	11	34	45	48	....	....	....	....	....
1995-96	Brynas Gavle	Sweden-2	18	3	6	9	12	9	0	1	1	2
	Brynas Gavle	Sweden	22	1	8	9	14	....	....	....	....	....
1996-97	Hameenlinna	Finland	49	11	24	35	26	10	6	5	11	4
1997-98	HIFK Helsinki	Finland	40	13	10	23	20	9	5	6	11	0
1998-99	HIFK Helsinki	Finland	53	19	34	53	18	11	5	*9	*14	4
	HIFK Helsinki	EuroHL	6	4	6	10	10	....	....	....	....	....

WCHA First All-Star Team (1995) • NCAA West First All-American Team (1995)

Signed as a free agent by **New Jersey**, May 7, 1999.

RAJNOHA, Pavel (righ-NOH-kha) **CGY.**

Defense. Shoots right. 6', 185 lbs. Born, Gottwaldov, Czech., February 23, 1974.
(Calgary's 8th choice, 150th overall, in 1992 Entry Draft).

			Regular Season					Playoffs				
Season	**Club**	**Lea**	**GP**	**G**	**A**	**TP**	**PIM**	**GP**	**G**	**A**	**TP**	**PIM**
1990-91	TJ Zlin	Czech.	6	0	0	0	4	....	....	....	....	....
1991-92	ZPS Zlin	Czech.	24	0	1	1	4	....	....	....	....	....
1992-93	ZPS Zlin	Czech.	26	2	1	3	....	....	....	....	....	....
1993-94	ZPS Zlin	Cze-Rep	28	2	1	3	0	3	0	4	4	....
1994-95	ZPS Zlin	Cze-Rep	29	0	6	6	22	....	....	....	....	....
1995-96	Dukla Jihlava	Cze-Rep	38	0	2	2	....	8	0	0	0	....
1996-97	ZPS Zlin	Cze-Rep	32	6	5	11	4	....	....	....	....	....
1997-98	ZPS Zlin	Cze-Rep	15	1	2	3	12	....	....	....	....	....
1998-99	Dukla Jihla	Cze-Rep	18	1	3	4	8	....	....	....	....	....

RAKHMATULLIN, Askhat (rahkh-ma-TOO-lihn, ahs-KHAHT) **CAR.**

Left wing. Shoots left. 5'11", 165 lbs. Born, Ufa, USSR, May 31, 1978.
(Hartford's 10th choice, 231st overall, in 1996 Entry Draft).

			Regular Season					Playoffs				
Season	**Club**	**Lea**	**GP**	**G**	**A**	**TP**	**PIM**	**GP**	**G**	**A**	**TP**	**PIM**
1996-97	Ufa Salavat	Russia	28	1	3	4	8	3	0	0	0	0
1997-98	Ufa Salavat	Russia	14	0	1	1	6	....	....	....	....	....
1998-99	Asheville	UHL	31	6	10	16	23	4	1	0	1	0
	Fayetteville	CHL	4	0	0	0	4	....	....	....	....	....

Rights transferred to **Carolina** after **Hartford** franchise relocated, June 25, 1997.

RALPH, Brad **PHX.**

Left wing. Shoots left. 6'2", 198 lbs. Born, Ottawa, Ont., October 17, 1980.
(Phoenix's 3rd choice, 53rd overall, in 1999 Entry Draft).

			Regular Season					Playoffs				
Season	**Club**	**Lea**	**GP**	**G**	**A**	**TP**	**PIM**	**GP**	**G**	**A**	**TP**	**PIM**
1996-97	Kanata Valley	OJHL	44	13	13	26	63	....	....	....	....	....
1997-98	Oshawa	OHL	59	20	17	37	45	7	2	1	3	8
1998-99	Oshawa	OHL	67	31	44	75	93	14	7	7	14	10

RAZIN, Gennady (RAH-zihn, gen-AH-dee) MTL.

Defense. Shoots left. 6'4", 201 lbs. Born, Kharkov, USSR, February 3, 1978.
(Montreal's 6th choice, 122nd overall, in 1997 Entry Draft).

			Regular Season					Playoffs				
Season	Club	Lea	GP	G	A	TP	PIM	GP	G	A	TP	PIM
1996-97	Kamloops	WHL	63	7	19	26	56	3	0	0	0	4
1997-98	Kamloops	WHL	70	2	11	13	64	7	0	0	0	4
1998-99	Fredericton	AHL	48	0	3	3	16	4	0	0	0	2

READY, Ryan

Left wing. Shoots left. 6'2", 185 lbs. Born, Peterborough, Ont., November 7, 1978.
(Calgary's 8th choice, 100th overall, in 1997 Entry Draft).

			Regular Season					Playoffs				
Season	Club	Lea	GP	G	A	TP	PIM	GP	G	A	TP	PIM
1995-96	Belleville	OHL	63	5	13	18	54	10	0	2	2	2
1996-97	Belleville	OHL	66	23	24	47	102	6	1	3	4	4
1997-98	Belleville	OHL	66	33	39	72	80	10	5	2	7	12
1998-99	Belleville	OHL	63	33	59	92	73	21	10	28	38	22

OHL First All-Star Team (1999)

REED, Josh VAN.

Defense. Shoots right. 6'2", 204 lbs. Born, Vernon, B.C., May 21, 1979.
(Vancouver's 5th choice, 172nd overall, in 1999 Entry Draft).

			Regular Season					Playoffs				
Season	Club	Lea	GP	G	A	TP	PIM	GP	G	A	TP	PIM
1994-95	Vernon	BCAHA	56	13	41	54	136	....	....	....	....	....
1995-96	Vernon	BCAHA	50	9	43	52	150	....	....	....	....	....
1996-97	Cowichan Valley	BCJHL	42	3	3	6	61	....	....	....	....	....
1997-98	Cowichan Valley	BCJHL	50	5	20	25	115	....	....	....	....	....
1998-99	Vernon	BCJHL	54	16	38	54	110	....	....	....	....	....

REGEHR, Robyn (reh-GUHR) CGY.

Defense. Shoots left. 6'2", 210 lbs. Born, Recife, Brazil, April 19, 1980.
(Colorado's 3rd choice, 19th overall, in 1998 Entry Draft).

			Regular Season					Playoffs				
Season	Club	Lea	GP	G	A	TP	PIM	GP	G	A	TP	PIM
1996-97	Kamloops	WHL	64	4	19	23	96	5	0	1	1	18
1997-98	Kamloops	WHL	65	4	10	14	120	5	0	3	3	8
1998-99	Kamloops	WHL	54	12	20	32	130	12	1	4	5	21

WHL West First All-Star Team (1999)

Traded to **Calgary** by **Colorado** to complete transaction that sent Theoren Fleury to Colorado (February 28, 1999), March 27, 1999.

REICH, Jeremy (RIGHK)

Center. Shoots left. 6'1", 198 lbs. Born, Craik, Sask., February 11, 1979.
(Chicago's 3rd choice, 39th overall, in 1997 Entry Draft).

			Regular Season					Playoffs				
Season	Club	Lea	GP	G	A	TP	PIM	GP	G	A	TP	PIM
1995-96	Seattle	WHL	65	11	11	22	88	5	0	1	1	10
1996-97	Seattle	WHL	62	19	31	50	134	15	2	5	7	36
1997-98	Seattle	WHL	43	24	23	47	121	....	....	....	....	....
	Swift Current	WHL	22	8	0	16	47	12	5	6	11	37
1998-99	Swift Current	WHL	67	21	28	49	220	6	0	3	3	26

REICHEL, Martin (RIGH-khul) EDM.

Right wing. Shoots left. 6'1", 183 lbs. Born, Most, Czech., November 7, 1973.
(Edmonton's 2nd choice, 37th overall, in 1992 Entry Draft).

			Regular Season					Playoffs				
Season	Club	Lea	GP	G	A	TP	PIM	GP	G	A	TP	PIM
1990-91	EHC Freiburg	Germany	23	7	8	15	19	....	....	....	....	....
1991-92	EHC Freiburg	Germany	27	15	16	31	8	4	1	1	2	4
1992-93	EHC Freiburg	Germany	37	13	9	22	27	9	4	4	8	11
1993-94	Rosenheim	Germany	20	5	15	20	6	....	....	....	....	....
1994-95	Rosenheim	Germany	43	11	26	37	36	7	3	3	6	37
1995-96	Rosenheim	Germany	50	17	28	45	40	4	3	0	3	2
1996-97	Rosenheim	Germany	45	8	14	22	30	3	0	0	0	4
1997-98	EHC Nurnberg	Germany	49	13	24	37	35	....	....	....	....	....
1998-99	EHC Nurnberg	Germany	50	11	23	34	16	13	2	3	5	6

RENNETTE, Tyler ST.L.

Center. Shoots right. 6'1", 175 lbs. Born, North Bay, Ont., April 16, 1979.
(St. Louis' 1st choice, 40th overall, in 1997 Entry Draft).

			Regular Season					Playoffs				
Season	Club	Lea	GP	G	A	TP	PIM	GP	G	A	TP	PIM
1996-97	North Bay	OHL	63	24	34	58	42	....	....	....	....	....
1997-98	North Bay	OHL	31	17	14	31	37	....	....	....	....	....
	Erie	OHL	24	16	17	33	20	6	3	3	6	2
1998-99	Erie	OHL	61	30	37	67	40	5	6	1	7	8

REYNOLDS, Peter TOR.

Defense. Shoots right. 6'3", 190 lbs. Born, Waterloo, Ont., April 27, 1981.
(Toronto's 2nd choice, 60th overall, in 1999 Entry Draft).

			Regular Season					Playoffs				
Season	Club	Lea	GP	G	A	TP	PIM	GP	G	A	TP	PIM
1996-97	Caledon	OJHL	45	1	10	11	69	....	....	....	....	....
1997-98	London	OHL	55	0	8	8	30	16	0	0	0	10
1998-99	London	OHL	59	2	25	27	55	23	2	3	5	24

RIBEIRO, Mike (rih-bee-AIR-roh) MTL.

Center. Shoots left. 5'11", 165 lbs. Born, Montreal, Que., February 10, 1980.
(Montreal's 2nd choice, 45th overall, in 1998 Entry Draft).

			Regular Season					Playoffs				
Season	Club	Lea	GP	G	A	TP	PIM	GP	G	A	TP	PIM
1996-97	Montreal	QAAA	43	32	57	89	48	....	....	....	....	....
1997-98	Rouyn Noranda	QMJHL	67	40	*85	125	55	6	3	1	4	0
1998-99	Rouyn-Noranda	QMJHL	69	*67	*100	*167	137	11	5	11	16	12
	Fredericton	AHL	....	....	....	....	....	5	0	1	1	2

QMJHL Second All-Star Team (1998) • QMJHL First All-Star Team (1999) • Canadian Major Junior First All-Star Team (1999)

RICH, Curtis T.B.

Defense. Shoots left. 6'4", 200 lbs. Born, Edmonton, Alta., October 6, 1979.
(Tampa Bay's 5th choice, 121st overall, in 1998 Entry Draft).

			Regular Season					Playoffs				
Season	Club	Lea	GP	G	A	TP	PIM	GP	G	A	TP	PIM
1995-96	Calgary	WHL	24	0	0	0	10	....	....	....	....	....
1996-97	Calgary	WHL	45	1	6	7	73	....	....	....	....	....
1997-98	Calgary	WHL	70	3	12	15	204	17	0	0	0	36
1998-99	Calgary	WHL	68	3	15	18	215	18	4	1	5	31

RICHARDS, Brad T.B.

Left wing. Shoots left. 6', 170 lbs. Born, Montague, P.E.I., May 2, 1980.
(Tampa Bay's 2nd choice, 64th overall, in 1998 Entry Draft).

			Regular Season					Playoffs				
Season	Club	Lea	GP	G	A	TP	PIM	GP	G	A	TP	PIM
1996-97	Notre Dame	SJHL	63	39	48	87	73	....	....	....	....	....
1997-98	Rimouski	QMJHL	68	33	82	115	44	19	8	24	32	2
1998-99	Rimouski	QMJHL	59	39	92	131	55	11	9	12	21	6

RIESEN, Michel (REE-sehn, MEE-shehl) EDM.

Right wing. Shoots right. 6'2", 190 lbs. Born, Oberbalm, Switzerland, April 11, 1979.
(Edmonton's 1st choice, 14th overall, in 1997 Entry Draft).

			Regular Season					Playoffs				
Season	Club	Lea	GP	G	A	TP	PIM	GP	G	A	TP	PIM
1994-95	EC Biel	Switz.	12	0	2	2	0	6	2	0	2	0
1995-96	EC Biel	Switz-2	34	9	6	15	2	3	1	0	1	0
1996-97	EC Biel	Switz-2	38	16	16	32	49	....	....	....	....	....
1997-98	HC Davos	Switz.	32	16	9	25	8	18	5	5	10	4
1998-99	Hamilton	AHL	60	6	17	23	6	3	0	0	0	0

RIIHIJARVI, Teemu (REE-ee-hee-jahr-vee) S.J.

Left wing. Shoots left. 6'6", 220 lbs. Born, Espoo, Finland, March 1, 1977.
(San Jose's 1st choice, 12th overall, in 1995 Entry Draft).

			Regular Season					Playoffs				
Season	Club	Lea	GP	G	A	TP	PIM	GP	G	A	TP	PIM
1993-94	Kiekko-Espoo	Finland	13	1	1	2	6	....	....	....	....	....
1994-95	Kiekko-Espoo	Finland	13	1	0	1	4	....	....	....	....	....
1995-96	Kiekko-Espoo	Finn-Jr.	19	2	4	6	46	4	0	2	2	6
	Kiekko-Espoo	Finland	2	0	0	0	0	....	....	....	....	....
	Haukat	Finland-2	4	0	0	0	2	....	....	....	....	....
1996-97	Kiekko-Espoo	Finland	47	3	1	4	8	4	0	0	0	2
1997-98	Kiekko-Espoo	Finland	12	0	1	1	6	....	....	....	....	....
	Lukko Rauma	Finland	37	5	3	8	61	....	....	....	....	....
1998-99	Kiekko-Espoo	Finland	53	2	4	6	75	4	0	0	0	0

RITA, Jani (REETA, YA-nee) EDM.

Right wing. Shoots right. 6'1", 206 lbs. Born, Helsinki, Finland, July 25, 1981.
(Edmonton's 1st choice, 13th overall, in 1999 Entry Draft).

			Regular Season					Playoffs				
Season	Club	Lea	GP	G	A	TP	PIM	GP	G	A	TP	PIM
1997-98	Jokerit	Finn-Jr.	36	15	9	24	2	8	4	1	5	0
	Jokerit	Finland	....	....	....	....	....	1	0	0	0	0
1998-99	Jokerit	Finn-Jr.	20	9	13	22	8	....	....	....	....	....
	Jokerit	Finland	41	3	2	5	39	....	....	....	....	....

RITCHLIN, Sean (RIHCH-lihn, SHAWN)

Right wing. Shoots right. 6', 200 lbs. Born, Rochester, NY, June 14, 1977.
(New Jersey's 10th choice, 145th overall, in 1996 Entry Draft).

			Regular Season					Playoffs				
Season	Club	Lea	GP	G	A	TP	PIM	GP	G	A	TP	PIM
1995-96	U. of Michigan	CCHA	27	7	7	14	24	....	....	....	....	....
1996-97	U. of Michigan	CCHA	38	10	10	20	48	....	....	....	....	....
1997-98	U. of Michigan	CCHA	27	3	3	6	29	....	....	....	....	....
1998-99	U. of Michigan	CCHA	42	12	5	17	55	....	....	....	....	....

RIVA, Danny (REE-vuh) NSH.

Center. Shoots right. 6', 190 lbs. Born, Framingham, MA, September 17, 1975.

			Regular Season					Playoffs				
Season	Club	Lea	GP	G	A	TP	PIM	GP	G	A	TP	PIM
1995-96	RPI Engineers	ECAC	35	3	7	10	30	....	....	....	....	....
1996-97	RPI Engineers	ECAC	36	12	14	26	30	....	....	....	....	....
1997-98	RPI Engineers	ECAC	35	10	18	28	16	....	....	....	....	....
1998-99	RPI Engineers	ECAC	36	*22	*35	*57	35	....	....	....	....	....

ECAC First All-Star Team (1999)

Signed as a free agent by **Nashville**, April 3, 1999.

ROBIDAS, Stephane (ROH-bih-dah) MTL.

Defense. Shoots right. 5'10", 180 lbs. Born, Sherbrooke, Que., March 3, 1977.
(Montreal's 7th choice, 164th overall, in 1995 Entry Draft).

			Regular Season					Playoffs				
Season	Club	Lea	GP	G	A	TP	PIM	GP	G	A	TP	PIM
1993-94	Shawinigan	QMJHL	67	3	18	21	33	1	0	0	0	0
1994-95	Shawinigan	QMJHL	71	13	56	69	44	15	7	12	19	4
1995-96	Shawinigan	QMJHL	67	23	56	79	53	6	1	5	6	10
1996-97	Shawinigan	QMJHL	67	24	51	75	59	7	4	6	10	14
1997-98	Fredericton	AHL	79	10	21	31	50	4	0	2	2	0
1998-99	Fredericton	AHL	79	8	33	41	59	15	1	5	6	10

QMJHL First All-Star Team (1996, 1997)

ROBINSON, Jason T.B.

Defense. Shoots left. 6'2", 190 lbs. Born, Goderich, Ont., August 22, 1978.
(Tampa Bay's 3rd choice, 125th overall, in 1996 Entry Draft).

			Regular Season					Playoffs				
Season	Club	Lea	GP	G	A	TP	PIM	GP	G	A	TP	PIM
1995-96	Niagara Falls	OHL	51	2	4	6	100	10	0	0	0	16
1996-97	Erie	OHL	19	....	7	7	58	....	....	....	....	....
1997-98	Erie	OHL	49	5	15	20	97	7	0	1	1	14
1998-99	Chesapeake	ECHL	37	1	5	6	57	....	....	....	....	....
	Cleveland	IHL	29	2	3	5	26	....	....	....	....	....

ROCHEFORT, Richard — N.J.

Center. Shoots right. 5'10", 195 lbs. Born, North Bay, Ont., January 7, 1977.
(New Jersey's 9th choice, 174th overall, in 1995 Entry Draft).

			Regular Season					Playoffs				
Season	Club	Lea	GP	G	A	TP	PIM	GP	G	A	TP	PIM
1993-94	Waterloo	OJHL	45	21	32	53	41	....	....	....	....	....
1994-95	Sudbury	OHL	57	21	44	65	26	13	3	7	10	6
1995-96	Sudbury	OHL	56	25	40	65	38	....	....	....	....	....
1996-97	Sudbury	OHL	28	18	24	42	40	....	....	....	....	....
	Sarnia	OHL	18	5	23	28	23	12	3	9	12	8
1997-98	Albany	AHL	59	7	14	21	16	13	1	0	1	4
1998-99	Albany	AHL	70	16	10	26	26	5	1	0	1	0

RODGERS, Marc — DET.

Right wing. Shoots right. 5'9", 185 lbs. Born, Shawville, Que., March 16, 1972.

			Regular Season					Playoffs				
Season	Club	Lea	GP	G	A	TP	PIM	GP	G	A	TP	PIM
1989-90	Granby	QMJHL	61	24	31	55	155	....	....	....	....	....
1990-91	Granby	QMJHL	64	28	49	77	41	....	....	....	....	....
1991-92	Granby	QMJHL	36	30	57	87	49	....	....	....	....	....
	Verdun	QMJHL	29	14	19	33	0	18	3	13	16	26
1992-93	Wheeling	ECHL	64	23	40	63	91	6	1	1	2	8
1993-94	Las Vegas	IHL	40	7	7	14	110	4	0	2	2	17
1994-95	Las Vegas	IHL	58	17	19	36	131	10	2	6	8	25
1995-96	Las Vegas	IHL	51	13	16	29	65	....	....	....	....	....
	Utah	IHL	31	6	14	20	51	21	4	4	8	16
1996-97	Utah	IHL	5	2	2	4	10	....	....	....	....	....
	Quebec	IHL	70	25	42	67	115	9	1	9	10	14
1997-98	Quebec	IHL	61	20	22	42	61	....	....	....	....	....
	Chicago	IHL	11	5	5	10	22	22	9	9	18	10
1998-99	Adirondack	AHL	80	19	38	57	66	3	0	0	0	10

Signed as a free agent by **Detroit**, August 3, 1998.

ROED, Peter — S.J.

Center. Shoots left. 5'11", 190 lbs. Born, St. Paul, MN, November 15, 1976.
(San Jose's 2nd choice, 38th overall, in 1995 Entry Draft).

			Regular Season					Playoffs				
Season	Club	Lea	GP	G	A	TP	PIM	GP	G	A	TP	PIM
1994-95	White Bear Lake	H.S.	28	20	39	59	22	....	....	....	....	....
1995-96	Prince George	WHL	66	18	19	37	36	....	....	....	....	....
1996-97	Prince George	WHL	51	21	16	37	8	14	5	2	7	9
	Louisville	ECHL	7	1	0	1	4	....	....	....	....	....
1997-98	Kentucky	AHL	67	6	7	13	44	....	....	....	....	....
	Louisville	ECHL	4	0	2	2	10	....	....	....	....	....
1998-99	Richmond	ECHL	60	26	24	50	68	18	6	10	16	14

ROHLOFF, Todd — CHI.

Defense. Shoots left. 6'3", 213 lbs. Born, Grand Rapids, IL, January 16, 1974.

			Regular Season					Playoffs				
Season	Club	Lea	GP	G	A	TP	PIM	GP	G	A	TP	PIM
1993-94	St. Paul	USHL	47	4	22	26	....	....	....	....	....	....
1994-95	U. of Miami-Ohio	CCHA	38	1	6	7	22	....	....	....	....	....
1995-96	U. of Miami-Ohio	CCHA	23	2	4	6	24	....	....	....	....	....
1997-98	U. of Miami-Ohio	CCHA	17	2	5	7	38	....	....	....	....	....
	Indianapolis	IHL	5	0	1	1	6	1	0	0	0	0
1998-99	Portland	AHL	58	1	6	7	58	....	....	....	....	....
	Indianapolis	IHL	12	2	0	2	8	5	1	1	2	6

Signed as a free agent by **Chicago**, March 24, 1998.

ROMINSKI, Dale — T.B.

Right wing. Shoots right. 6'2", 200 lbs. Born, Farmington Hills, MI, October 1, 1975.

			Regular Season					Playoffs				
Season	Club	Lea	GP	G	A	TP	PIM	GP	G	A	TP	PIM
1994-95	Detroit	NAHL	40	21	21	42	30	....	....	....	....	....
1995-96	U. of Michigan	CCHA	35	8	7	15	37	....	....	....	....	....
1996-97	U. of Michigan	CCHA	38	6	7	13	58	....	....	....	....	....
1997-98	U. of Michigan	CCHA	46	10	14	24	102	....	....	....	....	....
1998-99	U. of Michigan	CCHA	41	15	8	23	80	....	....	....	....	....

Signed as a free agent by **Tampa Bay**, August 31, 1999

ROSSITER, Kyle — FLA.

Defense. Shoots left. 6'2", 217 lbs. Born, Edmonton, Alta., June 9, 1980.
(Florida's 1st choice, 30th overall, in 1998 Entry Draft).

			Regular Season					Playoffs				
Season	Club	Lea	GP	G	A	TP	PIM	GP	G	A	TP	PIM
1996-97	Spokane	WHL	50	0	2	2	65	9	0	0	0	6
1997-98	Spokane	WHL	61	6	16	22	190	15	0	3	3	28
1998-99	Spokane	WHL	71	4	17	21	206	....	....	....	....	....

Canadian Major Junior Scholastic Player of the Year (1998)

ROSTOV, Sergei (roh-STOHV) — TOR.

Defense. Shoots left. 6'3", 194 lbs. Born, Murmansk, USSR, March 29, 1980.
(Toronto's 10th choice, 236th overall, in 1998 Entry Draft).

			Regular Season					Playoffs				
Season	Club	Lea	GP	G	A	TP	PIM	GP	G	A	TP	PIM
1995-96	Yaroslavl-2	Russia-2	80	1	3	4	60	....	....	....	....	....
1996-97	Yaroslavl-2	Russia-3	8	0	0	0	0	....	....	....	....	....
	CSKA Moscow	Russia-Jr.	45	8	10	18	70	....	....	....	....	....
1997-98	Mosc. D'amo-2	Russia-2	32	1	1	2	51	....	....	....	....	....
1998-99	HC Tver	Russia-2	11	3	1	4	8	....	....	....	....	....

ROURKE, Allan (RAWRK) — TOR.

Defense. Shoots left. 6'2", 210 lbs. Born, Mississauga, Ont., March 6, 1980.
(Toronto's 6th choice, 154th overall, in 1998 Entry Draft).

			Regular Season					Playoffs				
Season	Club	Lea	GP	G	A	TP	PIM	GP	G	A	TP	PIM
1996-97	Kitchener	OHL	25	1	1	2	12	6	0	0	0	0
1997-98	Kitchener	OHL	48	5	17	22	59	6	1	1	2	6
1998-99	Kitchener	OHL	66	11	28	39	79	1	0	0	0	2

ROY, Jimmy (ROI)

Center. Shoots right. 5'11", 170 lbs. Born, Sioux Lookout, Ont., September 22, 1975.
(Dallas' 7th choice, 254th overall, in 1994 Entry Draft).

			Regular Season					Playoffs				
Season	Club	Lea	GP	G	A	TP	PIM	GP	G	A	TP	PIM
1993-94	Thunder Bay	USHL	46	21	33	54	101	....	....	....	....	....
1994-95	Michigan Tech	WCHA	38	5	11	16	62	....	....	....	....	....
1995-96	Michigan Tech	WCHA	42	17	17	34	84	....	....	....	....	....
1996-97	Canada	Nat-Team	55	10	17	27	82	....	....	....	....	....
1997-98	Manitoba	IHL	61	8	10	18	133	3	0	0	0	6
1998-99	Manitoba	IHL	78	10	16	26	185	5	0	1	1	6

ROY, Stephane (WAH) — ST.L.

Center. Shoots left. 5'11", 191 lbs. Born, Ste-Martine, Que., January 26, 1976.
(St. Louis' 1st choice, 68th overall, in 1994 Entry Draft).

			Regular Season					Playoffs				
Season	Club	Lea	GP	G	A	TP	PIM	GP	G	A	TP	PIM
1993-94	Val d'Or	QMJHL	72	25	28	53	116	....	....	....	....	....
1994-95	Val d'Or	QMJHL	68	19	52	71	113	....	....	....	....	....
1995-96	Val d'Or	QMJHL	62	43	72	115	89	13	9	15	24	10
	Worcester	AHL	1	0	0	0	2	....	....	....	....	....
1996-97	Worcester	AHL	66	24	23	47	57	5	2	0	2	4
1997-98	Worcester	AHL	77	21	27	48	95	10	4	4	8	10
1998-99	Worcester	AHL	64	16	28	44	41	4	0	2	2	2

Canadian Major Junior Humanitarian Player of the Year (1994)

ROZAKOV, Rail (roh-zah-KAWF, righ-EEL) — CGY.

Defense. Shoots left. 6'1", 198 lbs. Born, Murmansk, USSR, March 29, 1981.
(Calgary's 4th choice, 106th overall, in 1999 Entry Draft).

			Regular Season					Playoffs				
Season	Club	Lea	GP	G	A	TP	PIM	GP	G	A	TP	PIM
1997-98	Lada Togliatti-2	Russia-3	36	0	2	2	43	....	....	....	....	....
1998-99	Lada Togliatti-2	Russia-4	7	1	0	1	2	....	....	....	....	....

ROZSIVAL, Michal (roh-ZIH-vahl, mee-KHUHL) — PIT.

Defense. Shoots right. 6'1", 200 lbs. Born, Vlasim, Czech., September 3, 1978.
(Pittsburgh's 5th choice, 105th overall, in 1996 Entry Draft).

			Regular Season					Playoffs				
Season	Club	Lea	GP	G	A	TP	PIM	GP	G	A	TP	PIM
1994-95	Dukla Jihlava	Czech-Jr.	31	8	13	21	....	....	....	....	....	....
1995-96	Dukla Jihlava	Cze-Rep	36	3	4	7	....	....	....	....	....	....
1996-97	Swift Current	WHL	63	8	31	39	80	10	0	6	6	15
1997-98	Swift Current	WHL	71	14	55	69	122	12	0	5	5	33
1998-99	Syracuse	AHL	49	3	22	25	72	....	....	....	....	....

WHL East First All-Star Team (1998)

RUDENKO, Konstantin (roo-DEHN-koh) — PHI.

Left wing. Shoots right. 5'10", 163 lbs. Born, Ust-Kamenogorsk, USSR, July 23, 1981.
(Philadelphia's 3rd choice, 160th overall, in 1999 Entry Draft).

			Regular Season					Playoffs				
Season	Club	Lea	GP	G	A	TP	PIM	GP	G	A	TP	PIM
1997-98	Omsk-2 VDV	Russia-3	22	7	8	15	4	....	....	....	....	....
1998-99	Cherepovets-2	Russia-3	28	15	9	24	....	....	....	....	....	....

RULLIER, Joe (ROO-yay) — L.A.

Defense. Shoots right. 6'3", 198 lbs. Born, Montreal, Que., January 28, 1980.
(Los Angeles' 5th choice, 133rd overall, in 1998 Entry Draft).

			Regular Season					Playoffs				
Season	Club	Lea	GP	G	A	TP	PIM	GP	G	A	TP	PIM
1996-97	Rimouski	QMJHL	23	0	3	3	87	4	0	0	0	11
1997-98	Rimouski	QMJHL	55	1	10	11	176	16	1	4	5	34
1998-99	Rimouski	QMJHL	54	7	32	39	202	11	2	3	5	26

RUPP, Michael — NYI

Left wing. Shoots left. 6'5", 218 lbs. Born, Cleveland, OH, January 13, 1980.
(NY Islanders' 1st choice, 9th overall, in 1998 Entry Draft).

			Regular Season					Playoffs				
Season	Club	Lea	GP	G	A	TP	PIM	GP	G	A	TP	PIM
1997-98	Windsor	OHL	38	9	8	17	60	....	....	....	....	....
	Erie	OHL	26	7	3	10	57	7	3	1	4	6
1998-99	Erie	OHL	63	22	25	47	102	5	0	2	2	25

RUUTU, Jarkko (ROO-too, YAHR-koh) — VAN.

Left wing. Shoots left. 6'2", 194 lbs. Born, Vantaa, Finland, August 23, 1975.
(Vancouver's 3rd choice, 68th overall, in 1998 Entry Draft).

			Regular Season					Playoffs				
Season	Club	Lea	GP	G	A	TP	PIM	GP	G	A	TP	PIM
1991-92	HIFK Helsinki	Finn-Jr.	1	0	0	0	0	....	....	....	....	....
1992-93	HIFK Helsinki	Finn-Jr.	34	26	21	47	53	....	....	....	....	....
1993-94	HIFK Helsinki	Finn-Jr.	19	9	12	21	44	....	....	....	....	....
1994-95	HIFK Helsinki	Finn-Jr.	35	26	22	48	117	....	....	....	....	....
1995-96	Michigan Tech	WCHA	39	12	10	22	96	....	....	....	....	....
1996-97	HIFK Helsinki	Finland	48	11	10	21	155	....	....	....	....	....
1997-98	HIFK Helsinki	Finland	37	10	10	20	87	8	*7	4	11	10
1998-99	HIFK Helsinki	Finland	25	10	4	14	136	9	0	2	2	43

RYAN, Michael — DAL.

Center. Shoots left. 6'1", 170 lbs. Born, Milton, MA, May 16, 1980.
(Dallas' 1st choice, 32nd overall, in 1999 Entry Draft).

			Regular Season					Playoffs				
Season	Club	Lea	GP	G	A	TP	PIM	GP	G	A	TP	PIM
1997-98	Boston College	H.S.	23	22	14	26	28	....	....	....	....	....
1998-99	Boston College	H.S.	21	20	24	44	22	....	....	....	....	....

RYAZANTSEV, Alexander (ree-ZAHNT-sehv) — COL.

Defense. Shoots right. 5'11", 200 lbs. Born, Moscow, USSR, March 15, 1980.
(Colorado's 10th choice, 167th overall, in 1998 Entry Draft).

			Regular Season					Playoffs				
Season	Club	Lea	GP	G	A	TP	PIM	GP	G	A	TP	PIM
1996-97	SKA Spartak	Russia	20	1	2	3	4	....	....	....	....	....
	SAK Moscow	Russia-3	18	0	0	0	8	....	....	....	....	....
1997-98	Spartak-2	Russia-3	31	3	8	11	26	....	....	....	....	....
	Victoriaville	QMJHL	22	6	9	15	14	....	....	....	....	....
1998-99	Victoriaville	QMJHL	64	17	40	57	57	6	0	3	3	10

RYBIN, Maxim (ray-bihn, max-EEM) ANA.

Left wing. Shoots right. 5'9", 176 lbs. Born, Moscow, USSR, June 15, 1981.
(Anaheim's 4th choice, 141st overall, in 1999 Entry Draft).

Season	Club	Lea	Regular Season GP	G	A	TP	PIM	Playoffs GP	G	A	TP	PIM
1996-97	Spartak-2	Russia-3	5	0	0	0	4	....	....	....	....	....
	Spartak	Russia	6	0	0	0	0	....	....	....	....	....
1997-98	Spartak-2	Russia-3	25	13	5	18	26	....	....	....	....	....
	Spartak	Russia	5	0	0	0	2	....	....	....	....	....
1998-99	Spartak	Russia	41	13	8	21	52	....	....	....	....	....

RYDER, Michael MTL.

Center. Shoots right. 6', 185 lbs. Born, St. John's, Nfld., March 31, 1980.
(Montreal's 9th choice, 216th overall, in 1998 Entry Draft).

Season	Club	Lea	Regular Season GP	G	A	TP	PIM	Playoffs GP	G	A	TP	PIM
1997-98	Hull	QMJHL	69	34	28	62	41	10	4	2	6	4
1998-99	Hull	QMJHL	69	44	43	87	65	23	*20	16	36	39

SAFRONOV, Kirill (sah-FRAW-nawf, kih-RIHL) PHX.

Defense. Shoots left. 6'2", 196 lbs. Born, Leningrad, USSR, February 26, 1981.
(Phoenix's 2nd choice, 19th overall, in 1999 Entry Draft).

Season	Club	Lea	Regular Season GP	G	A	TP	PIM	Playoffs GP	G	A	TP	PIM
1996-97	St. Petersburg-2	Russia-3	9	0	0	0	6	....	....	....	....	....
	St. Petersburg	Russia	1	0	0	0	0	....	....	....	....	....
1997-98	St. Petersburg-2	Russia-3	34	4	3	7	36	....	....	....	....	....
	St. Petersburg	Russia	9	0	1	1	4	....	....	....	....	....
1998-99	St. Petersburg	Russia	35	1	1	2	26	....	....	....	....	....

SAINOMAA, Teemu (SIGH-noh-muh, TA-moo) OTT.

Left wing. Shoots left. 6'3", 202 lbs. Born, Helsinki, Finland, May 15, 1981.
(Ottawa's 3rd choice, 62nd overall, in 1999 Entry Draft).

Season	Club	Lea	Regular Season GP	G	A	TP	PIM	Playoffs GP	G	A	TP	PIM
1997-98	Jokerit	Finn-Jr.	12	3	5	8	8	3	1	1	2	6
1998-99	Jokerit	Finn-Jr.	11	4	5	9	0	....	....	....	....	....

ST. CROIX, Chris (SAINT KWAH) CGY.

Defense. Shoots right. 6'1", 186 lbs. Born, Voorhees, NJ, May 2, 1979.
(Calgary's 7th choice, 92nd overall, in 1997 Entry Draft).

Season	Club	Lea	Regular Season GP	G	A	TP	PIM	Playoffs GP	G	A	TP	PIM
1995-96	Kamloops	WHL	61	4	5	9	29	13	0	2	2	4
1996-97	Kamloops	WHL	67	11	39	50	67	5	0	1	1	2
1997-98	Kamloops	WHL	46	3	13	16	51	7	1	1	2	6
1998-99	Kamloops	WHL	64	8	27	35	123	14	0	4	4	16

ST. JACQUES, Bruno (SAINT ZHAWK) PHI.

Defense. Shoots left. 6'2", 195 lbs. Born, Montreal, Que., August 22, 1980.
(Philadelphia's 12th choice, 253rd overall, in 1998 Entry Draft).

Season	Club	Lea	Regular Season GP	G	A	TP	PIM	Playoffs GP	G	A	TP	PIM
1996-97	Montreal AAA	QAAA			Statistics Not Available							
1997-98	Baie-Comeau	QMJHL	63	1	11	12	140	....	....	....	....	....
1998-99	Baie-Comeau	QMJHL	49	8	13	21	85	....	....	....	....	....

ST. PIERRE, Samuel T.B.

Right wing. Shoots right. 6'1", 170 lbs. Born, Laurierville, Que., June 28, 1979.
(Tampa Bay's 10th choice, 185th overall, in 1997 Entry Draft).

Season	Club	Lea	Regular Season GP	G	A	TP	PIM	Playoffs GP	G	A	TP	PIM
1996-97	Victoriaville	QMJHL	61	13	10	23	24	6	0	1	1	2
1997-98	Victoriaville	QMJHL	34	8	10	18	32	....	....	....	....	....
	Drummondville	QMJHL	35	28	15	43	16	....	....	....	....	....
1998-99	Drummondville	QMJHL	68	47	28	75	65	....	....	....	....	....
	Cleveland	IHL	13	2	5	7	4	....	....	....	....	....

SALMELAINEN, Tony (sal-meh-LIGH-nehn) EDM.

Left wing. Shoots right. 5'9", 176 lbs. Born, Espoo, Finland, August 8, 1981.
(Edmonton's 3rd choice, 41st overall, in 1999 Entry Draft).

Season	Club	Lea	Regular Season GP	G	A	TP	PIM	Playoffs GP	G	A	TP	PIM
1997-98	HIFK Helsinki	Finn-Jr.	33	23	16	39	30	....	....	....	....	....
1998-99	HIFK Helsinki	Finn-Jr.	30	21	17	38	53	....	....	....	....	....

SALVADOR, Bryce ST.L.

Defense. Shoots left. 6'2", 215 lbs. Born, Brandon, Man., February 11, 1976.
(Tampa Bay's 6th choice, 138th overall, in 1994 Entry Draft).

Season	Club	Lea	Regular Season GP	G	A	TP	PIM	Playoffs GP	G	A	TP	PIM
1992-93	Lethbridge	WHL	64	1	4	5	29	4	0	0	0	0
1993-94	Lethbridge	WHL	61	4	14	18	36	9	0	1	1	2
1994-95	Lethbridge	WHL	67	1	9	10	88	....	....	....	....	....
1995-96	Lethbridge	WHL	56	4	12	16	75	3	0	1	1	2
1996-97	Lethbridge	WHL	63	8	32	40	81	19	0	7	7	14
1997-98	Worcester	AHL	46	2	8	10	74	11	0	1	1	45
1998-99	Worcester	AHL	69	5	13	18	129	4	0	1	1	2

Signed as a free agent by **St. Louis**, December 16, 1996.

SAMUELSSON, Mikael (SAM-yuhl-suhn, MIH-kigh-ehl) S.J.

Right wing. Shoots left. 6'1", 195 lbs. Born, Mariefred, Sweden, December 23, 1976.
(San Jose's 7th choice, 145th overall, in 1998 Entry Draft).

Season	Club	Lea	Regular Season GP	G	A	TP	PIM	Playoffs GP	G	A	TP	PIM
1994-95	Sodertalje SK	Swede-Jr.	30	8	6	14	12	....	....	....	....	....
1995-96	Sodertalje SK	Swede-Jr.	22	13	12	25	20	....	....	....	....	....
	Sodertalje SK	Sweden-2	18	5	1	6	0	4	0	0	0	0
1996-97	Sodertalje SK	Swede-Jr.	2	2	1	3	....	....	....	....	....	....
	Sodertalje SK	Sweden	29	3	2	5	10	....	....	....	....	....
1997-98	Sodertalje SK	Sweden	31	8	8	16	47	....	....	....	....	....
1998-99	Sodertalje SK	Sweden-2	12	7	9	16	20	....	....	....	....	....
	V. Frolunda	Sweden	27	0	5	5	10	....	....	....	....	....

SANDSTROM, Jan ANA.

Defense. Shoots left. 6', 191 lbs. Born, Pitea, Sweden, January 24, 1978.
(Anaheim's 5th choice, 173rd overall, in 1999 Entry Draft).

Season	Club	Lea	Regular Season GP	G	A	TP	PIM	Playoffs GP	G	A	TP	PIM
1994-95	Pitea HC	Sweden-2	12	1	0	1	4	....	....	....	....	....
1995-96	Pitea HC	Sweden-2	29	1	11	12	18	....	....	....	....	....
1996-97	Pitea HC	Sweden-2	28	3	4	7	28	....	....	....	....	....
1997-98	AIK Solna	Sweden	38	0	2	2	16	....	....	....	....	....
1998-99	AIK Solna	Sweden	47	2	7	9	18	....	....	....	....	....

SAPRYKIN, Oleg (sah-PRIH-kihn) CGY.

Center. Shoots left. 6', 187 lbs. Born, Moscow, USSR, February 12, 1981.
(Calgary's 1st choice, 11th overall, in 1999 Entry Draft).

Season	Club	Lea	Regular Season GP	G	A	TP	PIM	Playoffs GP	G	A	TP	PIM
1997-98	CSKA Moscow	Russia	20	0	2	2	8	....	....	....	....	....
	CSKA Moscow	Russia-2	15	0	3	3	6	....	....	....	....	....
1998-99	Seattle	WHL	66	47	46	93	107	11	5	11	16	36

SARICH, Rod (SAHR-ihch) FLA.

Defense. Shoots left. 6'3", 178 lbs. Born, Davidson, Sask., March 3, 1981.
(Florida's 6th choice, 109th overall, in 1999 Entry Draft).

Season	Club	Lea	Regular Season GP	G	A	TP	PIM	Playoffs GP	G	A	TP	PIM
1996-97	Calgary	WHL	4	0	1	1	2	....	....	....	....	....
1997-98	Calgary	WHL	9	0	1	1	2	17	0	0	0	0
1998-99	Calgary	WHL	65	3	15	18	22	21	1	2	3	8

SARNO, Peter EDM.

Center. Shoots left. 5'11", 185 lbs. Born, Toronto, Ont., July 26, 1979.
(Edmonton's 6th choice, 141st overall, in 1997 Entry Draft).

Season	Club	Lea	Regular Season GP	G	A	TP	PIM	Playoffs GP	G	A	TP	PIM
1996-97	Windsor	OHL	66	20	63	83	59	5	0	3	3	6
1997-98	Windsor	OHL	64	33	88	121	18	....	....	....	....	....
	Hamilton	AHL	8	1	1	2	2	....	....	....	....	....
1998-99	Sarnia	OHL	68	37	*93	*130	49	6	1	7	8	2

SAUER, Kent NSH.

Defense. Shoots right. 6'2", 226 lbs. Born, St. Cloud, MN, May 10, 1979.
(Nashville's 4th choice, 88th overall, in 1998 Entry Draft).

Season	Club	Lea	Regular Season GP	G	A	TP	PIM	Playoffs GP	G	A	TP	PIM
1996-97	St. Cloud-Apollo	H.S.	23	14	15	29	20	....	....	....	....	....
1997-98	North Iowa	USHL	54	4	19	23	99	....	....	....	....	....
1998-99	U. of Minn-Duluth	WCHA	38	1	3	4	50	....	....	....	....	....

SCHASTLIVY, Petr (schust-LEE-vee, PEH-tuhr) OTT.

Left wing. Shoots left. 6', 191 lbs. Born, Angarsk, USSR, April 18, 1979.
(Ottawa's 5th choice, 101st overall, in 1998 Entry Draft).

Season	Club	Lea	Regular Season GP	G	A	TP	PIM	Playoffs GP	G	A	TP	PIM
1996-97	Yermak Angarsk	Russia-3			Statistics Not Available							
1997-98	Yaroslavl-2	Russia-2	47	15	9	24	34	....	....	....	....	....
	Yaroslavl	Russia	4	0	0	0	0	....	....	....	....	....
1998-99	Yaroslavl	Russia	40	6	1	7	28	6	0	0	0	2

SCHEFFELMAIER, Brett T.B.

Defense. Shoots right. 6'5", 200 lbs. Born, Coronation, Alta., March 31, 1981.
(Tampa Bay's 3rd choice, 75th overall, in 1999 Entry Draft).

Season	Club	Lea	Regular Season GP	G	A	TP	PIM	Playoffs GP	G	A	TP	PIM
1997-98	Medicine Hat	WHL	25	0	1	1	69	....	....	....	....	....
1998-99	Medicine Hat	WHL	69	3	10	13	252	....	....	....	....	....

SCHERBAN, Joel PIT.

Center. Shoots left. 6'2", 207 lbs. Born, Thunder Bay, Ont., April 22, 1980.
(Pittsburgh's 7th choice, 196th overall, in 1998 Entry Draft).

Season	Club	Lea	Regular Season GP	G	A	TP	PIM	Playoffs GP	G	A	TP	PIM
1996-97	London	OHL	65	8	13	21	2	....	....	....	....	....
1997-98	London	OHL	8	2	5	7	2	16	2	3	5	4
1998-99	London	OHL	68	22	32	54	14	25	5	11	16	4

SCHMIDT, Doug COL.

Defense. Shoots right. 5'10", 205 lbs. Born, Pompton Plains, NJ, January 19, 1978.
(Colorado's 8th choice, 217th overall, in 1997 Entry Draft).

Season	Club	Lea	Regular Season GP	G	A	TP	PIM	Playoffs GP	G	A	TP	PIM
1996-97	Waterloo	USHL	48	18	26	44	201	....	....	....	....	....
1997-98	North-Michigan	WCHA	34	7	12	19	100	....	....	....	....	....
1998-99	North-Michigan	CCHA	35	7	5	12	77	....	....	....	....	....

SCHNABEL, Robert SHNAH-buhl PHX.

Defense. Shoots left. 6'6", 216 lbs. Born, Prague, Czech., November 10, 1978.
(Phoenix's 7th choice, 129th overall, in 1998 Entry Draft).

Season	Club	Lea	Regular Season GP	G	A	TP	PIM	Playoffs GP	G	A	TP	PIM
1995-96	Slavia Praha	Czech-Jr.	38	3	5	8	....	....	....	....	....	....
1996-97	Slavia Praha	Czech-Jr.	36	5	2	7	....	....	....	....	....	....
	Slavia Praha	Cze-Rep	4	0	0	0	4	1	0	0	0	0
1997-98	Red Deer	WHL	61	1	22	23	143	5	0	0	0	16
1998-99	Springfield	AHL	77	1	7	8	155	3	1	0	1	4

• Re-entered NHL draft. Originally NY Islanders' 5th choice, 79th overall, in 1997 Entry Draft.

SCISSONS, Jeff (SKIH-zuhns) VAN.

Center. Shoots left. 6'1", 190 lbs. Born, Saskatoon, Sask., November 24, 1976.
(Vancouver's 7th choice, 201st overall, in 1996 Entry Draft).

			Regular Season					Playoffs				
Season	Club	Lea	GP	G	A	TP	PIM	GP	G	A	TP	PIM
1995-96	Vernon	BCJHL	60	26	48	74	28	....	....	....	....	....
1996-97	U. Minn-Duluth	WCHA	38	3	14	17	30	....	....	....	....	....
1997-98	U. Minn-Duluth	WCHA	40	17	24	41	50	....	....	....	....	....
1998-99	U. Minn-Duluth	WCHA	38	18	19	37	42	....	....	....	....	....

SCORSUNE, Matthew (SKOHR-soon) COL.

Defense. Shoots right. 6'3", 190 lbs. Born, Morristown, NJ, June 27, 1977.
(Colorado's 12th choice, 214th overall, in 1996 Entry Draft).

			Regular Season					Playoffs				
Season	Club	Lea	GP	G	A	TP	PIM	GP	G	A	TP	PIM
1995-96	Hotchkiss High	H.S.	24	7	22	29	24	....	....	....	....	....
1996-97	Harvard University	ECAC	30	3	8	11	28	....	....	....	....	....
1997-98	Harvard University	ECAC	33	9	10	19	30	....	....	....	....	....
1998-99	Harvard University	ECAC	31	8	9	17	34	....	....	....	....	....

SCUDERI, Robert PIT.

Defense. Shoots left. 6'1", 194 lbs. Born, Syosset, NY, December 30, 1978.
(Pittsburgh's 5th choice, 134th overall, in 1998 Entry Draft).

			Regular Season					Playoffs				
Season	Club	Lea	GP	G	A	TP	PIM	GP	G	A	TP	PIM
1996-97	Apple Collegiate	H.S.	80	42	70	112	52	....	....	....	....	....
1997-98	Boston College	H.E.	42	0	24	24	12	....	....	....	....	....
1998-99	Boston College	H.E.	41	2	8	10	20	....	....	....	....	....

SEDIN, Daniel (suh-DEEN) VAN.

Left wing. Shoots left. 6'1", 194 lbs. Born, Ornskoldsvik, Sweden, September 26, 1980.
(Vancouver's 1st choice, 2nd overall, in 1999 Entry Draft).

			Regular Season					Playoffs				
Season	Club	Lea	GP	G	A	TP	PIM	GP	G	A	TP	PIM
1996-97	MoDo Hockey	Swede-Jr.	26	26	14	40	....	....	....	....	....	....
1997-98	MoDo Hockey	Swede-Jr.	4	3	3	6	4	....	....	....	....	....
	MoDo Hockey	Sweden	45	4	8	12	26	9	0	0	0	2
1998-99	MoDo Hockey	Sweden	50	21	21	42	20	13	4	8	12	14

SEDIN, Henrik (suh-DEEN) VAN.

Center. Shoots left. 6'2", 196 lbs. Born, Ornskoldsvik, Sweden, September 26, 1980.
(Vancouver's 2nd choice, 3rd overall, in 1999 Entry Draft).

			Regular Season					Playoffs				
Season	Club	Lea	GP	G	A	TP	PIM	GP	G	A	TP	PIM
1996-97	MoDo Hockey	Swede-Jr.	26	14	22	36	....	....	....	....	....	....
1997-98	MoDo Hockey	Swede-Jr.	8	4	7	11	6	....	....	....	....	....
	MoDo Hockey	Sweden	39	1	4	5	8	7	0	0	0	0
1998-99	MoDo Hockey	Sweden	49	12	22	34	32	13	2	8	10	6

SEELEY, Richard L.A.

Defense. Shoots left. 6'2", 199 lbs. Born, Powell River, B.C., April 30, 1979.
(Los Angeles' 6th choice, 137th overall, in 1997 Entry Draft).

			Regular Season					Playoffs				
Season	Club	Lea	GP	G	A	TP	PIM	GP	G	A	TP	PIM
1995-96	Powell River	BCJHL	44	1	8	9	42	....	....	....	....	....
1996-97	Lethbridge	WHL	3	0	0	0	11	....	....	....	....	....
	Prince Albert	WHL	18	0	1	1	9	4	0	0	0	2
1997-98	Prince Albert	WHL	65	8	21	29	114	....	....	....	....	....
1998-99	Prince Albert	WHL	61	10	48	58	110	14	1	11	12	14

SEIKKULA, Timo (SAY-koo-lah, TEE-moh) PIT.

Center. Shoots left. 6'2", 183 lbs. Born, Kalajoki, Finland, May 27, 1978.
(Pittsburgh's 8th choice, 238th overall, in 1996 Entry Draft).

			Regular Season					Playoffs				
Season	Club	Lea	GP	G	A	TP	PIM	GP	G	A	TP	PIM
1994-95	Junkkarit HT	Finland-2	44	1	2	3	8	....	....	....	....	....
1995-96	Junkkarit HT	Finland-2	46	10	11	21	80	....	....	....	....	....
1996-97	Kiekko-Espoo	Finland-2	43	5	5	10	38	....	....	....	....	....
1997-98	TPS Turku	Finland	1	0	1	1	0	....	....	....	....	....
	TuTo Turku	Finland-2	17	4	4	8	29	....	....	....	....	....
1998-99	KalPa Kuopio	Finland	52	3	8	11	40	....	....	....	....	....
	KalPa Kuopio	Finland-2	....	....	....	....	....	6	0	0	0	0

SELLARS, Luke ATL.

Defense. Shoots left. 6'1", 195 lbs. Born, Toronto, Ont., May 21, 1981.
(Atlanta's 2nd choice, 30th overall, in 1999 Entry Draft).

			Regular Season					Playoffs				
Season	Club	Lea	GP	G	A	TP	PIM	GP	G	A	TP	PIM
1997-98	Wexford	OJHL	46	2	18	20	155	....	....	....	....	....
1998-99	Ottawa	OHL	56	4	19	23	87	....	....	....	....	....

SEMENOV, Alexei (seh-MEH-nahv) EDM.

Defense. Shoots left. 6'6", 210 lbs. Born, Murmansk, USSR, April 10, 1981.
(Edmonton's 2nd choice, 36th overall, in 1999 Entry Draft).

			Regular Season					Playoffs				
Season	Club	Lea	GP	G	A	TP	PIM	GP	G	A	TP	PIM
1997-98	Soviet Wings-2	Russia-3	52	1	2	3	48	....	....	....	....	....
1998-99	Sudbury	OHL	28	0	3	3	28	2	0	0	0	4

SESSA, Jason (SEH-sa) TOR.

Right wing. Shoots right. 6'1", 190 lbs. Born, Long Island, NY, July 17, 1977.
(Toronto's 5th choice, 86th overall, in 1996 Entry Draft).

			Regular Season					Playoffs				
Season	Club	Lea	GP	G	A	TP	PIM	GP	G	A	TP	PIM
1995-96	Lake Superior	CCHA	30	9	5	14	12	....	....	....	....	....
1996-97	Lake Superior	CCHA	34	22	22	44	91	....	....	....	....	....
1997-98	Lake Superior	CCHA	32	16	13	29	55	....	....	....	....	....
	St. John's	AHL	5	0	0	0	6	....	....	....	....	....
1998-99	St. John's	AHL	56	9	4	13	25	....	....	....	....	....

CCHA Second All-Star Team (1997)

SEVERSON, Cam S.J.

Left wing. Shoots left. 6'1", 215 lbs. Born, Canora, Sask., January 15, 1978.
(San Jose's 6th choice, 192nd overall, in 1997 Entry Draft).

			Regular Season					Playoffs				
Season	Club	Lea	GP	G	A	TP	PIM	GP	G	A	TP	PIM
1996-97	Lethbridge	WHL	45	12	13	25	169	....	....	....	....	....
	Prince Albert	WHL	16	5	13	18	54	4	4	0	4	8
1997-98	Prince Albert	WHL	41	23	25	48	129	....	....	....	....	....
	Spokane	WHL	23	9	11	20	88	18	11	4	15	51
1998-99	Spokane	WHL	46	16	17	33	190	....	....	....	....	....
	Oklahoma City	CHL	5	6	3	9	4	10	4	0	4	26

SHAFIKOV, Ruslan (SHAH-fee-kahv, roos-LAHN) PHI.

Center. Shoots right. 6'1", 176 lbs. Born, Ufa, USSR, May 11, 1976.
(Philadelphia's 8th choice, 204th overall, in 1995 Entry Draft).

			Regular Season					Playoffs				
Season	Club	Lea	GP	G	A	TP	PIM	GP	G	A	TP	PIM
1994-95	Ufa Salavat	CIS	30	2	0	2	10	7	1	1	2	4
1995-96	Ufa Salavat	CIS	51	9	2	11	18	3	0	0	0	4
1996-97	Ufa Salavat	Russia	31	11	7	18	22	10	3	2	5	12
1997-98	Ufa Salavat	Russia	40	12	4	16	16	....	....	....	....	....
1998-99	Yulayev	Russia	41	4	10	14	26	4	1	1	2	2

SHAPLEY, Larry (SHAP-lee) VAN.

Defense. Shoots right. 6'6", 215 lbs. Born, Dunnville, Ont., February 6, 1978.
(Vancouver's 9th choice, 148th overall, in 1997 Entry Draft).

			Regular Season					Playoffs				
Season	Club	Lea	GP	G	A	TP	PIM	GP	G	A	TP	PIM
1996-97	Welland	OJHL	35	3	10	13	270	....	....	....	....	....
1997-98	Peterborough	OHL	63	1	1	2	211	4	0	0	0	0
1998-99	Syracuse	AHL	50	1	1	2	254	....	....	....	....	....

SHASBY, Matt MTL.

Defense. Shoots left. 6'3", 188 lbs. Born, Sioux Falls, SD, July 2, 1980.
(Montreal's 6th choice, 150th overall, in 1999 Entry Draft).

			Regular Season					Playoffs				
Season	Club	Lea	GP	G	A	TP	PIM	GP	G	A	TP	PIM
1997-98	Lincoln	USHL	43	1	15	16	30	....	....	....	....	....
1998-99	Des Moines	USHL	49	4	22	26	34	....	....	....	....	....

SHAW, Lloyd ANA.

Defense. Shoots right. 6'3", 220 lbs. Born, Regina, Sask., September 26, 1976.
(Vancouver's 4th choice, 92nd overall, in 1995 Entry Draft).

			Regular Season					Playoffs				
Season	Club	Lea	GP	G	A	TP	PIM	GP	G	A	TP	PIM
1993-94	Seattle	WHL	47	0	4	4	107	8	0	0	0	23
1994-95	Seattle	WHL	66	3	12	15	313	3	0	0	0	13
1995-96	Seattle	WHL	27	0	1	1	92	....	....	....	....	....
	Red Deer	WHL	37	2	4	6	120	10	0	2	2	25
1996-97	Red Deer	WHL	66	8	16	24	257	16	0	6	6	60
1997-98	Cincinnati	AHL	60	1	2	3	138	....	....	....	....	....
	Columbus	ECHL	4	0	0	0	7	....	....	....	....	....
1998-99	Cincinnati	AHL	50	2	0	2	170	....	....	....	....	....
	Huntington	ECHL	2	0	0	0	4	....	....	....	....	....

Signed as a free agent by **Anaheim**, July 7, 1997.

SHEARER, Rob COL.

Center. Shoots right. 5'10", 190 lbs. Born, Kitchener, Ont., October 19, 1976.

			Regular Season					Playoffs				
Season	Club	Lea	GP	G	A	TP	PIM	GP	G	A	TP	PIM
1993-94	Windsor	OHL	66	17	25	42	46	4	0	2	2	6
1994-95	Windsor	OHL	59	28	28	56	48	10	4	4	8	10
1995-96	Windsor	OHL	63	40	53	93	74	7	6	3	9	8
1996-97	Hershey	AHL	78	12	16	28	88	23	0	4	4	9
1997-98	Hershey	AHL	79	30	30	60	44	7	0	5	5	6
1998-99	Hershey	AHL	77	24	42	66	43	3	0	0	0	6

Signed as a free agent by **Colorado**, October 5, 1995.

SHEFER, Andrei (SHEH-fuhr) L.A.

Right wing. Shoots left. 6'1", 194 lbs. Born, Sverdlovsk, USSR, July 26, 1981.
(Los Angeles' 1st choice, 43rd overall, in 1999 Entry Draft).

			Regular Season					Playoffs				
Season	Club	Lea	GP	G	A	TP	PIM	GP	G	A	TP	PIM
1997-98	Yekaterinburg	Russia-3	16	3	3	6	18	....	....	....	....	....
1998-99	Cherepovets	Russia	8	1	0	1	4	....	....	....	....	....

SHELLEY, Jody

Left wing. Shoots left. 6'3", 228 lbs. Born, Yarmouth, N.S., February 7, 1976.

			Regular Season					Playoffs				
Season	Club	Lea	GP	G	A	TP	PIM	GP	G	A	TP	PIM
1994-95	Halifax	QMJHL	72	10	12	22	194	7	0	1	1	12
1995-96	Halifax	QMJHL	50	13	19	32	319	6	0	2	2	36
1996-97	Halifax	QMJHL	58	25	19	44	448	17	6	6	12	123
1997-98	Dalhousie	AUAA	19	6	11	17	145	....	....	....	....	....
	Saint John	AHL	18	1	1	2	50	....	....	....	....	....
1998-99	Saint John	AHL	8	0	0	0	46	....	....	....	....	....
	Johnstown	ECHL	52	12	17	29	325	....	....	....	....	....

Signed as a free agent by **Calgary**, September 1, 1998.

SHIKHANOV, Sergei (shih-KHAHN-ohf) CHI.

Right wing. Shoots right. 6'2", 190 lbs. Born, Togliatti, USSR, April 8, 1978.
(Chicago's 10th choice, 204th overall, in 1997 Entry Draft).

			Regular Season					Playoffs				
Season	Club	Lea	GP	G	A	TP	PIM	GP	G	A	TP	PIM
1996-97	Togliatti	Russia	19	4	4	8	20	8	1	0	1	10
	Neftekhimik	Russia	5	1	1	2	2	....	....	....	....	....
1997-98	Togliatti	Russia	19	3	0	3	4	....	....	....	....	....
1998-99	Togliatti	Russia	29	4	5	9	65	3	0	0	0	2
	CSK Samara	Russia	11	3	4	7	10	3	1	0	1	2

SHIRREFFS, Steve (SHUHR-ehfs) **WSH.**

Defense. Shoots right. 6'3", 220 lbs. Born, Norwich, VT, February 18, 1976.
(Calgary's 7th choice, 233rd overall, in 1995 Entry Draft).

			Regular Season					Playoffs				
Season	Club	Lea	GP	G	A	TP	PIM	GP	G	A	TP	PIM
1995-96	Princeton	ECAC	25	0	3	3	6	....	....	....	....	....
1996-97	Princeton	ECAC	34	5	4	9	12	....	....	....	....	....
1997-98	Princeton	ECAC	36	9	24	33	54	....	....	....	....	....
1998-99	Princeton	ECAC	27	2	17	19	39	....	....	....	....	....

ECAC First All-Star Team (1998) • NCAA East Second All-American Team (1998) • ECAC Second All-Star Team (1999)

Traded to **Washington** by **Calgary** for Benoit Gratton, August 18, 1999.

SHMYR, Jason (SHMEER) **WSH.**

Left wing. Shoots left. 6'4", 220 lbs. Born, Fairview, Alta., July 27, 1975.

			Regular Season					Playoffs				
Season	Club	Lea	GP	G	A	TP	PIM	GP	G	A	TP	PIM
1995-96	Bonneyville	AJHL	42	10	22	32	270	....	....	....	....	....
1996-97	Anchorage	WCHL	51	8	12	20	388	9	1	1	2	50
	Pensacola	ECHL	1	0	0	0	2	....	....	....	....	....
1997-98	Anchorage	WCHL	31	4	6	10	177	....	....	....	....	....
	Utah	IHL	3	0	0	0	7	....	....	....	....	....
	San Diego	WCHL	14	0	3	3	50	11	3	3	6	78
1998-99	Long Beach	IHL	8	0	0	0	35	....	....	....	....	....
	San Diego	WCHL	2	0	0	0	7	....	....	....	....	....
	Manitoba	IHL	57	1	1	2	227	3	0	0	0	0

Signed as a free agent by **Washington**, April 27, 1999.

SHVIDKI, Denis (SHVIHD-kee) **FLA.**

Right wing. Shoots left. 6', 195 lbs. Born, Kharkov, USSR, November 21, 1980.
(Florida's 1st choice, 12th overall, in 1999 Entry Draft).

			Regular Season					Playoffs				
Season	Club	Lea	GP	G	A	TP	PIM	GP	G	A	TP	PIM
1996-97	Yaroslavl-2	Russia-3	35	21	12	33	32	....	....	....	....	....
	Yaroslavl	Russia	17	3	2	5	6	....	....	....	....	....
1997-98	Yaroslavl-2	Russia-2	32	20	13	33	20	....	....	....	....	....
	Yaroslavl	Russia	15	1	1	2	2	....	....	....	....	....
1998-99	Barrie	OHL	61	35	59	94	8	12	7	9	16	2

SIDULOV, Konstantin (sih-DOO-lahf) **MTL.**

Defense. Shoots right. 6'1", 176 lbs. Born, Chelyabinsk, USSR, January 1, 1977.
(Montreal's 5th choice, 118th overall, in 1997 Entry Draft).

			Regular Season					Playoffs				
Season	Club	Lea	GP	G	A	TP	PIM	GP	G	A	TP	PIM
1994-95	Chelyabinsk	CIS	2	0	0	0	0	....	....	....	....	....
1995-96	Chelyabinsk	CIS	52	1	0	1	58	....	....	....	....	....
1996-97	Chelyabinsk	Russia	42	0	0	0	28	2	0	0	0	0
1997-98	Chelyabinsk	Russia	43	1	3	4	36	....	....	....	....	....
1998-99	Fredericton	AHL	5	0	0	0	6	....	....	....	....	....
	Miami	ECHL	45	1	4	5	60	....	....	....	....	....

SIDYAKIN, Andrei (sihd-YA-kihn) **MTL.**

Right wing. Shoots left. 5'11", 169 lbs. Born, Ufa, USSR, January 20, 1979.
(Montreal's 10th choice, 202nd overall, in 1997 Entry Draft).

			Regular Season					Playoffs				
Season	Club	Lea	GP	G	A	TP	PIM	GP	G	A	TP	PIM
1994-95	Yulayev	CIS	7	0	1	1	0	....	....	....	....	....
1995-96	Yulayev	CIS	25	1	0	1	4	3	0	0	0	2
1996-97	Yulayev	Russia	29	3	5	8	4	....	....	....	....	....
1997-98	Yulayev	Russia	42	5	4	9	32	....	....	....	....	....
1998-99	Yulayev	Russia	36	6	4	10	14	2	0	0	0	2

SIKLENKA, Mike (sih-KLEHN-kuh) **WSH.**

Defense. Shoots right. 6'5", 224 lbs. Born, Meadow Lake, Sask., December 18, 1979.
(Washington's 5th choice, 118th overall, in 1998 Entry Draft).

			Regular Season					Playoffs				
Season	Club	Lea	GP	G	A	TP	PIM	GP	G	A	TP	PIM
1997-98	Lloydminster	SJHL	54	10	17	27	120	....	....	....	....	....
1998-99	Seattle	WHL	68	19	13	32	115	11	6	6	12	24

SIMON, Benjamin **CHI.**

Center. Shoots left. 5'11", 178 lbs. Born, Shaker Heights, OH, June 14, 1978.
(Chicago's 5th choice, 110th overall, in 1997 Entry Draft).

			Regular Season					Playoffs				
Season	Club	Lea	GP	G	A	TP	PIM	GP	G	A	TP	PIM
1996-97	Notre Dame	CCHA	30	4	15	19	79	....	....	....	....	....
1997-98	Notre Dame	CCHA	37	9	28	37	91	....	....	....	....	....
1998-99	Notre Dame	CCHA	37	18	24	42	65	....	....	....	....	....

CCHA Second All-Star Team (1999)

SIVEK, Michal (sih-VIHK, mee-KHAHL) **WSH.**

Center. Shoots left. 6'3", 209 lbs. Born, Nachod, Czech., January 21, 1981.
(Washington's 2nd choice, 29th overall, in 1999 Entry Draft).

			Regular Season					Playoffs				
Season	Club	Lea	GP	G	A	TP	PIM	GP	G	A	TP	PIM
1997-98	Sparta Praha	Czech-Jr.	31	13	8	21	....	....	....	....	....	....
	Sparta Praha	Cze-Rep	25	1	1	2	10	5	1	0	1	0
1998-99	Sparta Praha	Cze-Rep	1	1	0	1	....	....	....	....	....	....
	HC Kladno	Cze-Rep	34	3	8	11	24	....	....	....	....	....

SKOULA, Martin (SHKOH-la) **COL.**

Defense. Shoots left. 6'2", 195 lbs. Born, Litomerice, Czech., October 28, 1979.
(Colorado's 2nd choice, 17th overall, in 1998 Entry Draft).

			Regular Season					Playoffs				
Season	Club	Lea	GP	G	A	TP	PIM	GP	G	A	TP	PIM
1995-96	CHZ Litvinov	Czech-Jr.	38	0	4	4	....	....	....	....	....	....
	CHZ Litvinov	Cze-Rep	....	....	....	....	....	1	0	0	0	0
1996-97	CHZ Litvinov	Czech-Jr.	38	2	9	11	....	....	....	....	....	....
	CHZ Litvinov	Cze-Rep	1	0	0	0	0	....	....	....	....	....
1997-98	Barrie	OHL	66	8	36	44	36	6	1	3	4	4
1998-99	Barrie	OHL	67	13	46	59	46	12	3	10	13	13
	Hershey	AHL	....	....	....	....	....	1	0	0	0	0

OHL Second All-Star Team (1999)

SKRLAC, Rob (SKUHR-lak) **N.J.**

Left wing. Shoots left. 6'5", 240 lbs. Born, Campbell, B.C., June 10, 1976.
(Buffalo's 11th choice, 224th overall, in 1995 Entry Draft).

			Regular Season					Playoffs				
Season	Club	Lea	GP	G	A	TP	PIM	GP	G	A	TP	PIM
1994-95	Kamloops	WHL	23	0	1	1	177	....	....	....	....	....
1995-96	Kamloops	WHL	63	1	4	5	216	13	0	0	0	52
1996-97	Kamloops	WHL	61	8	10	18	278	5	0	0	0	35
1997-98	Albany	AHL	53	0	2	2	256	....	....	....	....	....
1998-99	Albany	AHL	61	1	1	2	213	1	0	0	0	0

Signed as a free agent by **New Jersey**, June 17, 1997.

SKROBOT, Sergei (SKROH-bawt) **PHI.**

Defense. Shoots right. 6'3", 191 lbs. Born, Moscow, USSR, March 19, 1980.
(Philadelphia's 13th choice, 258th overall, in 1998 Entry Draft).

			Regular Season					Playoffs				
Season	Club	Lea	GP	G	A	TP	PIM	GP	G	A	TP	PIM
1995-96	Moscow Dynamo	Russ-Jr	30	4	10	14	8	....	....	....	....	....
1996-97	Moscow D'amo	Russia-3	70	5	10	15	10	....	....	....	....	....
1997-98	Moscow D'amo-2	Russia-2	44	2	4	6	10	....	....	....	....	....
1998-99	Tverskoi HC	Russia-2	11	2	3	5	0	....	....	....	....	....

SKVARIDLO, Tomas (SHKVAHR-ihd-loh) **PIT.**

Left wing. Shoots left. 6'1", 180 lbs. Born, Zvolen, Czech., June 19, 1981.
(Pittsburgh's 6th choice, 144th overall, in 1999 Entry Draft).

			Regular Season					Playoffs				
Season	Club	Lea	GP	G	A	TP	PIM	GP	G	A	TP	PIM
1997-98	HKM Zvolen	Slovak-Jr.	51	11	11	22	22	....	....	....	....	....
1998-99	HKM Zvolen	Slovak-Jr.	35	21	11	32	18	6	0	4	4	2
	HKM Zvolen	Slovak-2	9	1	1	2	2	....	....	....	....	....
	HKM Zvolen	Slovakia	1	0	0	0	0	....	....	....	....	....

SMIRNOV, Oleg (smihr-NOHF) **EDM.**

Left wing. Shoots right. 5'11", 176 lbs. Born, Elektrostal, USSR, April 8, 1980.
(Edmonton's 6th choice, 144th overall, in 1998 Entry Draft).

			Regular Season					Playoffs				
Season	Club	Lea	GP	G	A	TP	PIM	GP	G	A	TP	PIM
1996-97	Kristall-2	Russia-3	38	2	2	4	8	....	....	....	....	....
1997-98	Kristall	Russia	6	0	2	2	0	....	....	....	....	....
	Kristall	Russia-2	10	0	0	0	2	....	....	....	....	....
1998-99	SKA Spartak	Russia	14	4	0	4	4	....	....	....	....	....
	Chelyabinsk	Russia	27	0	3	3	6	....	....	....	....	....

SMITH, Donald **CAR.**

Center. Shoots left. 6'3", 189 lbs. Born, Buffalo, NY, March 17, 1979.
(Carolina's 7th choice, 184th overall, in 1998 Entry Draft).

			Regular Season					Playoffs				
Season	Club	Lea	GP	G	A	TP	PIM	GP	G	A	TP	PIM
1996-97	Nichols High	H.S.	31	25	29	54	....	....	....	....	....	....
1997-98	Clarkson	ECAC	30	4	6	10	8	....	....	....	....	....
1998-99	Clarkson	ECAC	37	9	12	21	18	....	....	....	....	....

SMITH, Jarrett

Center. Shoots left. 6'1", 190 lbs. Born, Edmonton, Alta., June 15, 1979.
(NY Islanders' 4th choice, 59th overall, in 1997 Entry Draft).

			Regular Season					Playoffs				
Season	Club	Lea	GP	G	A	TP	PIM	GP	G	A	TP	PIM
1994-95	Prince George	WHL	1	0	0	0	0	....	....	....	....	....
1995-96	Prince George	WHL	18	2	0	2	6	....	....	....	....	....
1996-97	Prince George	WHL	67	20	22	42	58	15	2	2	4	5
1997-98	Prince George	WHL	42	12	22	34	21	11	3	1	4	8
1998-99	Prince George	WHL	49	20	37	57	54	3	0	2	2	2

SMITH, Mark **S.J.**

Center. Shoots left. 5'10", 190 lbs. Born, Edmonton, Alta., October 24, 1977.
(San Jose's 7th choice, 219th overall, in 1997 Entry Draft).

			Regular Season					Playoffs				
Season	Club	Lea	GP	G	A	TP	PIM	GP	G	A	TP	PIM
1995-96	Lethbridge	WHL	71	11	24	35	59	4	2	0	2	2
1996-97	Lethbridge	WHL	62	19	38	57	125	19	7	13	20	51
1997-98	Lethbridge	WHL	70	42	67	109	206	3	0	2	2	18
1998-99	Kentucky	AHL	78	18	21	39	101	12	2	7	9	16

WHL East Second All-Star Team (1998)

SMITH, Matt **ST.L.**

Defense. Shoots right. 6'6", 229 lbs. Born, Kent, England, December 23, 1976.

			Regular Season					Playoffs				
Season	Club	Lea	GP	G	A	TP	PIM	GP	G	A	TP	PIM
1997-98	U. Mass-Amherst	H.E.	33	5	8	13	48	....	....	....	....	....
	Worcester	AHL	4	1	0	1	4	3	0	0	0	10
1998-99	Peoria	ECHL	6	0	3	3	6	4	1	1	2	6
	Worcester	AHL	44	3	8	11	81	....	....	....	....	....

Signed as a free agent by **St. Louis**, March 27, 1998.

SMITH, Nick **FLA.**

Center. Shoots left. 6'2", 180 lbs. Born, Hamilton, Ont., March 23, 1979.
(Florida's 4th choice, 74th overall, in 1997 Entry Draft).

			Regular Season					Playoffs				
Season	Club	Lea	GP	G	A	TP	PIM	GP	G	A	TP	PIM
1995-96	Shelburne	OJHL-B	42	13	18	31	12	....	....	....	....	....
1996-97	Barrie	OHL	63	10	18	28	15	9	3	8	11	13
1997-98	Barrie	OHL	63	13	21	34	21	6	1	2	3	4
1998-99	Barrie	OHL	68	19	34	53	18	12	3	8	11	8

SMITH, Wyatt **PHX.**

Center. Shoots left. 5'11", 198 lbs. Born, Thief River Falls, MN, February 13, 1977.
(Phoenix's 6th choice, 233rd overall, in 1997 Entry Draft).

			Regular Season					Playoffs				
Season	Club	Lea	GP	G	A	TP	PIM	GP	G	A	TP	PIM
1995-96	U. of Minnesota	WCHA	32	4	5	9	32	....	....	....	....	....
1996-97	U. of Minnesota	WCHA	38	16	14	30	44	....	....	....	....	....
1997-98	U. of Minnesota	WCHA	39	24	23	47	62	....	....	....	....	....
1998-99	U. of Minnesota	WCHA	43	23	20	43	37	....	....	....	....	....

SMREK, Peter (SMUHR-ehk) ST.L.

Defense. Shoots left. 6'1", 215 lbs. Born, Martin, Czech., February 16, 1979.
(St. Louis' 2nd choice, 85th overall, in 1999 Entry Draft).

Season	Club	Lea	Regular Season					Playoffs				
			GP	G	A	TP	PIM	GP	G	A	TP	PIM
1996-97	ZTS Martin	Slovakia	12	1	0	1	....	3	0	0	0	....
1997-98	ZTS Martin	Slovak-Jr.	19	7	6	13	32	....	....	....	....	....
	ZTS Martin	Slovakia	23	0	5	5	24	1	0	0	0	0
1998-99	Des Moines	USHL	52	6	26	32	59	14	2	7	9	8

SNESRUD, Mat (SHEHS-rud) ANA.

Defense. Shoots right. 6'1", 205 lbs. Born, Minneapolis, MN, January 28, 1977.
(Anaheim's 6th choice, 181st overall, in 1997 Entry Draft).

Season	Club	Lea	Regular Season					Playoffs				
			GP	G	A	TP	PIM	GP	G	A	TP	PIM
1996-97	North Iowa	USHL	50	12	22	34	76	....	....	....	....	....
1997-98	Michigan Tech	WCHA	39	0	18	18	44	....	....	....	....	....
1998-99	Michigan Tech	WCHA	37	3	8	11	22	....	....	....	....	....

SNYDER, Dan ATL.

Center. Shoots left. 6', 185 lbs. Born, Elmira, Ont., February 23, 1978.

Season	Club	Lea	Regular Season					Playoffs				
			GP	G	A	TP	PIM	GP	G	A	TP	PIM
1995-96	Owen Sound	OHL	63	8	17	25	78	6	1	2	3	4
1996-97	Owen Sound	OHL	57	17	29	46	96	4	2	3	5	8
1997-98	Owen Sound	OHL	46	23	33	56	74	10	2	3	5	16
1998-99	Owen Sound	OHL	64	27	67	94	110	16	8	5	13	30

Signed as a free agent by **Atlanta**, June 28, 1999.

SOCHOR, Jan (soh-KHAWR, YAN) TOR.

Left wing. Shoots right. 6', 198 lbs. Born, Usti nad Labem, Czech., January 17, 1980.
(Toronto's 6th choice, 161st overall, in 1999 Entry Draft).

Season	Club	Lea	Regular Season					Playoffs				
			GP	G	A	TP	PIM	GP	G	A	TP	PIM
1996-97	Slavia Praha	Czech-Jr.	26	11	12	23	....	....	....	....	....	....
1997-98	Slavia Praha	Czech-Jr.	33	26	12	38	....	....	....	....	....	....
	Slavia Praha	Cze-Rep	14	1	1	2	2	1	0	0	0	0
1998-99	Slavia Praha	Czech-Jr.	7	2	1	3	2	....	....	....	....	....
	Slavia Praha	Cze-Rep	47	10	10	20	14	....	....	....	....	....

SODERBERG, Anders (SOH-dehr-buhrg) BOS.

Right wing. Shoots right. 5'6", 161 lbs. Born, Ornskoldsvik, Sweden, October 7, 1975.
(Boston's 10th choice, 234th overall, in 1996 Entry Draft).

Season	Club	Lea	Regular Season					Playoffs				
			GP	G	A	TP	PIM	GP	G	A	TP	PIM
1992-93	MoDo Hockey	Swede-Jr.	13	6	12	18	2	....	....	....	....	....
	MoDo Hockey	Sweden	1	0	0	0	0	....	....	....	....	....
1993-94	MoDo Hockey	Swede-Jr.	9	8	5	13	10	....	....	....	....	....
	MoDo Hockey	Sweden	19	0	0	0	2	9	0	0	0	0
1994-95	MoDo Hockey	Sweden	38	9	14	23	2	....	....	....	....	....
1995-96	MoDo Hockey	Sweden	40	10	18	28	10	8	3	3	6	0
1996-97	MoDo Hockey	Sweden	39	9	13	22	16	....	....	....	....	....
1997-98	MoDo Hockey	Sweden	44	15	10	25	4	9	5	1	6	2
1998-99	MoDo Hockey	Sweden	49	6	15	21	18	13	3	6	9	4

SOLING, Jonas (SOH-lihng, YOH-nahs) VAN.

Right wing. Shoots left. 6'4", 192 lbs. Born, Stockholm, Sweden, September 7, 1978.
(Vancouver's 3rd choice, 93rd overall, in 1996 Entry Draft).

Season	Club	Lea	Regular Season					Playoffs				
			GP	G	A	TP	PIM	GP	G	A	TP	PIM
1995-96	Huddinge IK	Swede-Jr.	24	8	4	12	18	....	....	....	....	....
	Huddinge IK	Sweden-2	5	0	0	0	0	....	....	....	....	....
1996-97	Sudbury	OHL	66	18	22	40	60	....	....	....	....	....
1997-98	Sudbury	OHL	56	9	25	34	67	10	0	7	7	10
1998-99	Syracuse	AHL	29	2	2	4	4	....	....	....	....	....
	Augusta	ECHL	50	27	20	47	71	....	....	....	....	....

SOMERVUORI, Eero (soh-muhr-VOH-ree, ai-AIR-oh) T.B.

Right wing. Shoots right. 5'10", 167 lbs. Born, Jarvenpaa, Finland, February 7, 1979.
(Tampa Bay's 9th choice, 170th overall, in 1997 Entry Draft).

Season	Club	Lea	Regular Season					Playoffs				
			GP	G	A	TP	PIM	GP	G	A	TP	PIM
1994-95	Jokerit	Finn-Jr.	26	9	12	21	6	....	....	....	....	....
1995-96	Jokerit	Finn-Jr.	28	14	12	26	10	9	4	1	5	4
	Jokerit	Finland	6	1	2	3	0	....	....	....	....	....
	Jarvenpaa	Finland-2	1	0	0	0	0	....	....	....	....	....
1996-97	Jokerit	Finland	35	1	1	2	2	5	0	0	0	0
	Jokerit	Finn-Jr.	28	20	19	39	30	5	3	0	3	4
1997-98	Jokerit	Finn-Jr.	14	4	8	12	2	....	....	....	....	....
	Jokerit	Finland	42	3	7	10	46	8	2	1	3	6
1998-99	Jokerit	Finn-Jr.	4	1	1	2	2	....	....	....	....	....
	Jokerit	Finland	50	7	8	15	24	3	1	0	1	6

SOMIK, Radovan (SAW-mihk, RAH-doh-vahn) PHI.

Left wing. Shoots right. 6'2", 194 lbs. Born, Martin, Czech., May 5, 1977.
(Philadelphia's 3rd choice, 100th overall, in 1995 Entry Draft).

Season	Club	Lea	Regular Season					Playoffs				
			GP	G	A	TP	PIM	GP	G	A	TP	PIM
1993-94	ZTS Martin	Slovakia	1	0	0	0	0	....	....	....	....	....
1994-95	ZTS Martin	Slovakia	25	3	0	3	39	3	1	0	1	2
1995-96	ZTS Martin	Slovakia	25	3	6	9	8	9	1	0	1	....
1996-97	ZTS Martin	Slovakia	35	3	5	8	....	3	0	0	0	....
1997-98	ZTS Martin	Slovakia	26	6	9	15	10	3	0	0	0	0
1998-99	Dukla Trencin	Slovakia	26	1	4	5	6	....	....	....	....	....

SOUZA, Mike (SOO-zah) CHI.

Left wing. Shoots left. 6'1", 190 lbs. Born, Melrose, MA, January 28, 1978.
(Chicago's 4th choice, 67th overall, in 1997 Entry Draft).

Season	Club	Lea	Regular Season					Playoffs				
			GP	G	A	TP	PIM	GP	G	A	TP	PIM
1996-97	New Hampshire	H.E.	39	15	11	26	20	....	....	....	....	....
1997-98	New Hampshire	H.E.	38	13	12	25	36	....	....	....	....	....
1998-99	New Hampshire	H.E.	41	23	42	65	38	....	....	....	....	....

NCAA Championship All-Tournament Team (1999)

SPIRIDONOV, Maxim (spih-rih-DAWN-uhv) EDM.

Left wing. Shoots left. 5'10", 185 lbs. Born, Moscow, USSR, April 7, 1978.
(Edmonton's 10th choice, 241st overall, in 1998 Entry Draft).

Season	Club	Lea	Regular Season					Playoffs				
			GP	G	A	TP	PIM	GP	G	A	TP	PIM
1993-94	CSKA Moscow	Russia-Jr.	35	20	20	40	16	....	....	....	....	....
1994-95	CSKA Moscow	Russia-Jr.	68	60	31	91	34	....	....	....	....	....
1995-96	Smiths Falls	OJHL	51	52	36	88	71	....	....	....	....	....
1996-97	London	OHL	55	31	22	53	99	....	....	....	....	....
1997-98	London	OHL	66	54	44	98	52	16	3	4	7	4
	Grand Rapids	IHL	....	....	....	....	....	3	0	0	0	0
1998-99	Grand Rapids	IHL	41	11	17	28	12	....	....	....	....	....
	Springfield	AHL	23	8	8	16	2	2	0	0	0	2

SRDINKO, Jan (suhr-DIHN-koh, YAN) N.J.

Defense. Shoots left. 5'11", 195 lbs. Born, Vsetin, Czech., February 22, 1974.
(New Jersey's 8th choice, 241st overall, in 1997 Entry Draft).

Season	Club	Lea	Regular Season					Playoffs				
			GP	G	A	TP	PIM	GP	G	A	TP	PIM
1994-95	Petra Vsetin	Cze-Rep	1	0	0	0	....	....	....	....	....	....
1995-96	Petra Vsetin	Cze-Rep	31	0	3	3	....	9	0	0	0	....
1996-97	Petra Vsetin	Cze-Rep	49	2	8	10	71	10	0	3	3	29
1997-98	Petra Vsetin	Cze-Rep	47	1	4	5	95	10	0	3	3	4
	Petra Vsetin	EuroHL	9	0	1	1	4	....	....	....	....	....
1998-99	Slovnaft Vsetin	Cze-Rep	50	2	7	9	58	12	0	1	1	....

STAAL, Kim (STOHL) MTL.

Center. Shoots right. 6', 185 lbs. Born, Herlev, Denmark, March 10, 1978.
(Montreal's 4th choice, 92nd overall, in 1996 Entry Draft).

Season	Club	Lea	Regular Season					Playoffs				
			GP	G	A	TP	PIM	GP	G	A	TP	PIM
1995-96	Malmo IF	Swede-Jr.	30	24	20	44	14	....	....	....	....	....
1996-97	Malmo IF	Sweden	4	0	1	1	2	....	....	....	....	....
	Malmo IF	Swede-Jr.	3	6	4	10	2	....	....	....	....	....
1997-98	Malmo IF	Swede-Jr.	20	13	11	24	36	....	....	....	....	....
	Malmo IF	Sweden	13	0	1	1	1	....	....	....	....	....
1998-99	Malmo IF	Sweden	48	1	5	6	14	4	0	0	0	0

STANLEY, Chris

Center. Shoots left. 6'1", 200 lbs. Born, Parry Sound, Ont., June 18, 1979.
(Vancouver's 5th choice, 90th overall, in 1997 Entry Draft).

Season	Club	Lea	Regular Season					Playoffs				
			GP	G	A	TP	PIM	GP	G	A	TP	PIM
1996-97	Belleville	OHL	66	19	24	43	16	6	1	0	1	0
1997-98	Belleville	OHL	66	21	23	44	31	10	3	2	5	4
1998-99	Belleville	OHL	51	29	40	69	32	8	1	0	1	0

STARLING, Chad ST.L.

Defense. Shoots left. 6'6", 210 lbs. Born, Saskatoon, Sask., September 16, 1980.
(St. Louis' 3rd choice, 114th overall, in 1999 Entry Draft).

Season	Club	Lea	Regular Season					Playoffs				
			GP	G	A	TP	PIM	GP	G	A	TP	PIM
1997-98	Saskatoon	SAHA	60	15	49	64	172	....	....	....	....	....
1998-99	Kamloops	WHL	65	4	13	17	101	14	0	0	0	8

STEEN, Calle DET.

Right wing. Shoots left. 5'11", 198 lbs. Born, Stockholm, Sweden, May 16, 1980.
(Detroit's 6th choice, 142nd overall, in 1998 Entry Draft).

Season	Club	Lea	Regular Season					Playoffs				
			GP	G	A	TP	PIM	GP	G	A	TP	PIM
1995-96	Hammarby IF	Swede-Jr.	5	0	0	0	....	....	....	....	....	....
1996-97	Hammarby IF	Swede-Jr.	24	4	9	13	....	....	....	....	....	....
1997-98	Hammarby IF	Swede-Jr.	STATISTICS NOT AVAILABLE									
1998-99	Hammarby IF	Sweden-2	22	2	8	10	14	....	....	....	....	....

STEFAN, Patrik (SHTEH-fan) ATL.

Center. Shoots left. 6'1", 205 lbs. Born, Pribram, Czech., September 16, 1980.
(Atlanta's 1st choice, 1st overall, in 1999 Entry Draft).

Season	Club	Lea	Regular Season					Playoffs				
			GP	G	A	TP	PIM	GP	G	A	TP	PIM
1996-97	Sparta Praha	Cze-Rep	5	0	1	1	2	7	1	0	1	0
1997-98	Sparta Praha	Cze-Rep	27	2	6	8	16	....	....	....	....	....
	Long Beach	IHL	25	5	10	15	10	10	1	1	2	2
1998-99	Long Beach	IHL	33	11	24	35	26	....	....	....	....	....

STEPHENS, Charlie WSH.

Center/Right wing. Shoots right. 6'4", 225 lbs. Born, Nilestown, Ont., April 5, 1981.
(Washington's 3rd choice, 31st overall, in 1999 Entry Draft).

Season	Club	Lea	Regular Season					Playoffs				
			GP	G	A	TP	PIM	GP	G	A	TP	PIM
1995-96	Elgin/Middlesex	OMHA	60	25	29	54	60	....	....	....	....	....
1996-97	Leamington	OJHL-B	50	26	36	62	103	....	....	....	....	....
1997-98	St. Michael's	OHL	58	9	21	30	38	....	....	....	....	....
1998-99	Toronto	OHL	7	2	4	6	8	....	....	....	....	....
	Guelph	OHL	61	24	28	52	72	11	3	5	8	19

STEWART, Jason NYI

Right wing. Shoots right. 5'11", 185 lbs. Born, St. Paul, MN, April 30, 1976.
(NY Islanders' 7th choice, 142nd overall, in 1994 Entry Draft).

Season	Club	Lea	Regular Season					Playoffs				
			GP	G	A	TP	PIM	GP	G	A	TP	PIM
1993-94	Simley High	H.S.	23	15	15	30	32	....	....	....	....	....
1994-95	St. Cloud State	WCHA	28	1	3	4	16	....	....	....	....	....
1995-96	St. Cloud State	WCHA	36	4	7	11	40	....	....	....	....	....
1996-97	St. Cloud State	WCHA	40	6	5	11	32	....	....	....	....	....
1997-98	St. Cloud State	WCHA	36	14	15	29	53	....	....	....	....	....
1998-99	Lowell	AHL	31	0	2	2	7	....	....	....	....	....
	Roanoke	ECHL	31	7	13	20	39	12	0	0	0	2

STOREY, Ben — COL.

Defense. Shoots left. 6'2", 180 lbs. Born, Ottawa, Ont., June 22, 1977.
(Colorado's 4th choice, 98th overall, in 1996 Entry Draft).

			Regular Season					Playoffs				
Season	Club	Lea	GP	G	A	TP	PIM	GP	G	A	TP	PIM
1994-95	Ottawa	OJHL	51	6	33	39	83	....	....	....	....	....
1995-96	Harvard University	ECAC	33	2	11	13	44	....	....	....	....	....
1996-97	Harvard University	ECAC	25	0	6	6	40	....	....	....	....	....
1997-98	Harvard University	ECAC	33	9	16	25	56	....	....	....	....	....
1998-99	Harvard University	ECAC	23	4	11	15	30	....	....	....	....	....
	Hershey	AHL	5	0	0	0	0	....	....	....	....	....

STORK, Dean — WSH.

Defense. Shoots left. 6'3", 205 lbs. Born, Edmonton, Alta., October 2, 1975.

			Regular Season					Playoffs				
Season	Club	Lea	GP	G	A	TP	PIM	GP	G	A	TP	PIM
1995-96	Penticton	BCJHL	45	24	30	54	....	....	....	....	....	....
1996-97	U. Mass-Amherst	H.E.	34	1	4	5	54	....	....	....	....	....
1997-98	U. Mass-Amherst	H.E.	33	3	6	9	66	....	....	....	....	....
1998-99	U. Mass-Amherst	H.E.	34	9	7	16	44	....	....	....	....	....
	Portland	AHL	10	0	2	2	13	....	....	....	....	....

Signed as a free agent by **Washington**, March 24, 1999.

STRAKA, Josef — (STRAH-kuh) CGY.

Center. Shoots right. 5'11", 183 lbs. Born, Jindrichuv Hradec, Czech., February 11, 1978.
(Calgary's 7th choice, 122nd overall, in 1996 Entry Draft).

			Regular Season					Playoffs				
Season	Club	Lea	GP	G	A	TP	PIM	GP	G	A	TP	PIM
1995-96	CHZ Litvinov	Cze-Rep	33	5	6	11	14	15	3	1	4	....
1996-97	CHZ Litvinov	Cze-Rep	52	14	16	30	32	....	....	....	....	....
1997-98	CHZ Litvinov	Cze-Rep	17	2	4	6	8	....	....	....	....	....
1998-99	CHZ Litvinov	Cze-Rep	50	5	17	22	48	....	....	....	....	....

STREIT, Martin — (STRIGHT) PHI.

Left wing. Shoots right. 6'2", 191 lbs. Born, Vyskov, Czech., February 2, 1977.
(Philadelphia's 7th choice, 178th overall, in 1995 Entry Draft).

			Regular Season					Playoffs				
Season	Club	Lea	GP	G	A	TP	PIM	GP	G	A	TP	PIM
1994-95	HC Olomouc	Czech-Jr.				STATISTICS NOT AVAILABLE						
1995-96	HC Olomouc	Czech-Jr.	19	10	6	16	....	....	....	....	....	....
	HC Olomouc	Cze-Rep	10	0	0	0	....	....	....	....	....	....
1996-97	HC Olomouc	Cze-Rep	18	1	2	3	14	....	....	....	....	....
1997-98	Karlovy Vary	Cze-Rep	48	5	13	18	24	....	....	....	....	....
1998-99	Karlovy Vary	Cze-Rep	48	9	4	13	34	....	....	....	....	....

STROM, Peter — (STRUHM) MTL.

Left wing. Shoots right. 6', 178 lbs. Born, Snotorp, Sweden, January 14, 1975.
(Montreal's 10th choice, 200th overall, in 1994 Entry Draft).

			Regular Season					Playoffs				
Season	Club	Lea	GP	G	A	TP	PIM	GP	G	A	TP	PIM
1993-94	V. Frolunda	Sweden	29	0	0	0	8	....	....	....	....	....
1994-95	V. Frolunda	Sweden	16	0	3	3	10	....	....	....	....	....
	V. Frolunda	Sweden-2	12	8	10	18	10	....	....	....	....	....
1995-96	V. Frolunda	Sweden	35	7	8	15	10	13	0	3	3	0
1996-97	V. Frolunda	Sweden	49	7	16	23	24	3	0	0	0	2
1997-98	V. Frolunda	Sweden	46	6	15	21	22	7	0	4	4	0
1998-99	V. Frolunda	Sweden	49	17	15	32	18	4	0	2	2	0

STUART, Brad — S.J.

Defense. Shoots left. 6'2", 210 lbs. Born, Rocky Mountain House, Alta., November 6, 1979.
(San Jose's 1st choice, 3rd overall, in 1998 Entry Draft).

			Regular Season					Playoffs				
Season	Club	Lea	GP	G	A	TP	PIM	GP	G	A	TP	PIM
1996-97	Regina	WHL	57	7	36	43	58	5	0	4	4	14
1997-98	Regina	WHL	72	20	45	65	82	9	3	4	7	10
1998-99	Regina	WHL	29	10	19	29	43	....	....	....	....	....
	Calgary	WHL	30	11	22	33	26	21	8	15	23	59

WHL East Second All-Star Team (1998) • WHL East First All-Star Team (1999) • Canadian Major Junior First All-Star Team (1999) • Canadian Major Junior Defenseman of the Year (1999)

STUSSI, Rene — (SHTOO-see) ANA.

Center. Shoots right. 5'11", 183 lbs. Born, Muri, Switzerland, December 13, 1978.
(Anaheim's 7th choice, 209th overall, in 1997 Entry Draft).

			Regular Season					Playoffs				
Season	Club	Lea	GP	G	A	TP	PIM	GP	G	A	TP	PIM
1995-96	HC Thurgau	Switz-2	34	2	4	6	10	7	3	0	3	2
1996-97	HC Thurgau	Switz-2	42	20	31	51	24	8	5	4	9	4
1997-98	HC Kloten	Switz.	38	9	8	17	10	7	1	0	1	4
1998-99	EHC Kloten	Switz.	36	5	5	10	14	....	....	....	....	....
	ZSC Zurich	Switz.	7	1	1	2	6	7	1	1	2	4

STYF, Par — (STOOF) PHI.

Defense. Shoots left. 6', 187 lbs. Born, Harnosand, Sweden, April 11, 1979.
(Philadelphia's 8th choice, 240th overall, in 1997 Entry Draft).

			Regular Season					Playoffs				
Season	Club	Lea	GP	G	A	TP	PIM	GP	G	A	TP	PIM
1996-97	MoDo Hockey	Swede-Jr.	11	2	4	6	....	....	....	....	....	....
1997-98	MoDo Hockey	Swede-Jr.	17	7	5	12	60	....	....	....	....	....
1998-99	Ornskoldsvik SK	Sweden-2	18	2	5	7	63	....	....	....	....	....

SUBBOTIN, Dmitri — (soo-BOH-tihn) NYR

Left wing. Shoots left. 6'1", 183 lbs. Born, Tomsk, USSR, October 20, 1977.
(NY Rangers' 3rd choice, 76th overall, in 1996 Entry Draft).

			Regular Season					Playoffs				
Season	Club	Lea	GP	G	A	TP	PIM	GP	G	A	TP	PIM
1993-94	Yekaterinburg	CIS	12	0	3	3	4	....	....	....	....	....
1994-95	Yekaterinburg	CIS	52	9	6	15	75	2	0	0	0	2
1995-96	CSKA Moscow	CIS	41	6	5	11	62	3	0	0	0	0
1996-97	CSKA Moscow	Russia	17	5	3	8	22	2	0	0	0	2
	CSKA Moscow	Russia-2	8	1	0	1	8	....	....	....	....	....
1997-98	CSKA Moscow	Russia	16	1	1	2	47	....	....	....	....	....
1998-99	Moscow D'amo	Russia	1	0	1	1	0	....	....	....	....	....
	Togliatti	Russia	31	8	3	11	47	7	0	0	0	4

SUCHY, Radoslav — (soo-KHEE) PHX.

Defense. Shoots left. 6'1", 185 lbs. Born, Poprad, Czech., April 7, 1976.

			Regular Season					Playoffs				
Season	Club	Lea	GP	G	A	TP	PIM	GP	G	A	TP	PIM
1993-94	SKP PS Poprad	Slovakia	3	0	0	0	0	....	....	....	....	....
1994-95	Sherbrooke	QMJHL	69	12	32	44	30	7	0	3	3	2
1995-96	Sherbrooke	QMJHL	68	15	53	68	68	7	0	3	3	2
1996-97	Sherbrooke	QMJHL	32	6	34	40	14	....	....	....	....	....
	Chicoutimi	QMJHL	28	5	24	29	26	19	6	15	21	12
1997-98	Las Vegas	IHL	26	1	4	5	10	....	....	....	....	....
	Springfield	AHL	41	6	15	21	16	4	0	1	1	2
1998-99	Springfield	AHL	69	4	32	36	10	3	0	1	1	0

QMJHL Second All-Star Team (1997) • Won George Parsons Trophy (Memorial Cup Tournament Most Sportsmanlike Player) (1997)

Signed as a free agent by **Phoenix**, September 26, 1997.

SULC, Jan — (SOOLTZ, YAN) T.B.

Center. Shoots right. 6'3", 180 lbs. Born, Litvinov, Czech., February 17, 1979.
(Tampa Bay's 5th choice, 109th overall, in 1997 Entry Draft).

			Regular Season					Playoffs				
Season	Club	Lea	GP	G	A	TP	PIM	GP	G	A	TP	PIM
1996-97	CHZ Litvinov	Cze-Rep	37	14	17	31	....	....	....	....	....	....
1997-98	St. Michael's	OHL	34	3	10	13	11	....	....	....	....	....
	Kingston	OHL	29	6	8	14	7	12	0	0	0	0
1998-99	Kingston	OHL	13	4	4	8	6	....	....	....	....	....
	Owen Sound	OHL	53	20	29	49	59	16	4	8	12	18

SULLIVAN, Jeff

Defense. Shoots left. 6'1", 185 lbs. Born, St. John's, Nfld., September 18, 1978.
(Ottawa's 5th choice, 146th overall, in 1997 Entry Draft).

			Regular Season					Playoffs				
Season	Club	Lea	GP	G	A	TP	PIM	GP	G	A	TP	PIM
1996-97	Granby	QMJHL	25	4	8	12	47	....	....	....	....	....
	Halifax	QMJHL	45	4	23	27	200	18	0	5	5	96
1997-98	Halifax	QMJHL	69	9	27	36	377	5	0	1	1	21
1998-99	Halifax	QMJHL	69	7	30	37	320	5	1	1	2	14

SURMA, Damian — CAR.

Left wing. Shoots left. 5'9", 202 lbs. Born, Lincoln Park, MI, June 22, 1981.
(Carolina's 5th choice, 174th overall, in 1999 Entry Draft).

			Regular Season					Playoffs				
Season	Club	Lea	GP	G	A	TP	PIM	GP	G	A	TP	PIM
1998-99	Plymouth	OHL	65	17	15	32	62	11	3	6	9	15

SUTER, Curtis — (SOO-tuhr)

Left wing. Shoots left. 6'4", 220 lbs. Born, Kerrobert, Sask., August 5, 1979.
(Phoenix's 3rd choice, 123rd overall, in 1997 Entry Draft).

			Regular Season					Playoffs				
Season	Club	Lea	GP	G	A	TP	PIM	GP	G	A	TP	PIM
1996-97	Spokane	WHL	56	2	2	4	133	2	0	0	0	0
1997-98	Spokane	WHL	62	9	8	17	216	10	0	1	1	9
1998-99	Spokane	WHL	65	7	13	20	221	....	....	....	....	....

SUTTER, Shaun — (SUH-tuhr) CGY.

Center. Shoots right. 5'11", 160 lbs. Born, Red Deer, Alta., June 2, 1980.
(Calgary's 4th choice, 102nd overall, in 1998 Entry Draft).

			Regular Season					Playoffs				
Season	Club	Lea	GP	G	A	TP	PIM	GP	G	A	TP	PIM
1996-97	Lethbridge	WHL	1	0	0	0	0	....	....	....	....	....
1997-98	Lethbridge	WHL	69	11	9	20	146	4	0	0	0	4
1998-99	Lethbridge	WHL	35	8	4	12	43	....	....	....	....	....
	Medicine Hat	WHL	23	9	5	14	38	....	....	....	....	....

SUURSOO, Toivo — (SUH-uhr-soh-oh) DET.

Left wing. Shoots right. 6', 175 lbs. Born, Tallinn, USSR, November 23, 1975.
(Detroit's 10th choice, 283rd overall, in 1994 Entry Draft).

			Regular Season					Playoffs				
Season	Club	Lea	GP	G	A	TP	PIM	GP	G	A	TP	PIM
1993-94	Soviet Wings	CIS	33	3	0	3	8	....	....	....	....	....
1994-95	Soviet Wings	CIS	47	10	5	15	36	4	0	0	0	4
1995-96	Soviet Wings	CIS	47	6	4	10	36	....	....	....	....	....
1996-97	TPS Turku	Finland	50	11	8	19	64	12	2	3	5	4
1997-98	TPS Turku	Finland	38	17	5	22	46	4	2	1	3	2
	TPS Turku	EuroHL	4	2	0	2	0	....	....	....	....	....
1998-99	Malmo IF	Sweden	29	8	6	14	57	8	4	3	7	12
	Adirondack	AHL	2	0	0	0	0	....	....	....	....	....

SVARTVADET, Per — (svahrt-VAH-deht) ATL.

Center. Shoots left. 6'1", 180 lbs. Born, Solleftea, Sweden, May 17, 1975.
(Dallas' 5th choice, 139th overall, in 1993 Entry Draft).

			Regular Season					Playoffs				
Season	Club	Lea	GP	G	A	TP	PIM	GP	G	A	TP	PIM
1992-93	MoDo Hockey	Sweden	2	0	0	0	0	....	....	....	....	....
1993-94	MoDo Hockey	Sweden	36	2	1	3	4	11	0	0	0	6
1994-95	MoDo Hockey	Sweden	40	6	9	15	31	....	....	....	....	....
1995-96	MoDo Hockey	Sweden	40	9	14	23	26	8	2	3	5	0
1996-97	MoDo Hockey	Sweden	50	7	18	25	38	....	....	....	....	....
1997-98	MoDo Hockey	Sweden	46	6	12	18	28	7	3	2	5	2
1998-99	MoDo Hockey	Sweden	50	9	23	32	30	13	3	6	9	6

Traded to **Atlanta** by **Dallas** for Ottawa's 6th round choice (previously acquired, Dallas selected Justin Cox) in 1999 Entry Draft, June 26, 1999.

SVOBODA, Jaroslav — (svah-BOH-duh) CAR.

Left wing. Shoots left. 6'1", 174 lbs. Born, Cervenka, Czech., June 1, 1980.
(Carolina's 8th choice, 208th overall, in 1998 Entry Draft).

			Regular Season					Playoffs				
Season	Club	Lea	GP	G	A	TP	PIM	GP	G	A	TP	PIM
1995-96	HC Olomouc	Czech-Jr.	40	13	15	28	....	....	....	....	....	....
1996-97	HC Olomouc	Czech-Jr.	39	19	14	33	....	....	....	....	....	....
1997-98	HC Olomouc	Czech-Jr.	43	15	18	33	....	....	....	....	....	....
	HC Olomouc	Czech-2	13	0	1	1	....	....	....	....	....	....
1998-99	Kootenay	WHL	54	26	33	59	46	7	2	2	4	11

SVOBODA, Petr   (svah-BOH-duh)   **TOR.**

Defense. Shoots right. 6'2", 194 lbs.   Born, Jihlava, Czech., June 20, 1980.
(Toronto's 2nd choice, 35th overall, in 1998 Entry Draft).

				Regular Season					Playoffs			
Season	Club	Lea	GP	G	A	TP	PIM	GP	G	A	TP	PIM
1995-96	SK Jihlava	Czech-Jr.	38	4	12	16	50	.....	....	....	....	....
1996-97	SK Jihlava	Czech-Jr.	29	1	3	4		.....	....	....	....	....
1997-98	Dukla Jihlava	Cze-Rep	1	0	0	0	0	.....	....	....	....	....
	Havlickuv Brod	Czech-2	18	1	2	3	16	.....	....	....	....	....
	SK Jihlava	Czech-Jr.	12	0	2	2		.....	....	....	....	....
1998-99	Dukla Jihla	Cze-Rep	40	1	5	6	28	.....	....	....	....	....

SWANSON, Brian

Center. Shoots left. 5'10", 180 lbs.   Born, Anchorage, AK, March 24, 1976.
(San Jose's 5th choice, 115th overall, in 1994 Entry Draft).

				Regular Season					Playoffs			
Season	Club	Lea	GP	G	A	TP	PIM	GP	G	A	TP	PIM
1993-94	Omaha	USHL	47	38	42	80	40	.....	....	....	....	....
1994-95	Omaha	USHL	33	14	35	49	12	.....	....	....	....	....
1995-96	Colorado	WCHA	40	26	33	59	24	.....	....	....	....	....
1996-97	Colorado	WCHA	43	19	32	51	47	.....	....	....	....	....
1997-98	Colorado	WCHA	42	18	*38	*56	26	.....	....	....	....	....
1998-99	Colorado	WCHA	42	25	*41	66	28	.....	....	....	....	....
	Hartford	AHL	4	0	0	0	4	.....	....	....	....	....

WCHA Second All-Star Team (1996) • WCHA First All-Star Team (1997, 1998, 1999) • NCAA West Second All-American Team (1998) • NCAA West First All-American Team (1999)

Traded to **NY Rangers** by **San Jose** with Jayson More and a conditional choice in 1998 Entry Draft for Marty McSorley, August 20, 1996.

SWANSON, Scott   **WSH.**

Defense. Shoots left. 6'2", 190 lbs.   Born, St. Paul, MN, February 15, 1975.
(Washington's 10th choice, 225th overall, in 1995 Entry Draft).

				Regular Season					Playoffs			
Season	Club	Lea	GP	G	A	TP	PIM	GP	G	A	TP	PIM
1994-95	Omaha	USHL	48	14	46	60	22	.....	....	....	....	....
1995-96	Omaha	USHL	1	0	0	0	0	.....	....	....	....	....
	Colorado	WCHA	42	13	35	48	16	.....	....	....	....	....
1996-97	Colorado	WCHA	44	4	16	20	22	.....	....	....	....	....
1997-98	Colorado	WCHA	42	7	32	39	24	.....	....	....	....	....
1998-99	Colorado	WCHA	42	11	*41	52	16	.....	....	....	....	....

WCHA Second All-Star Team (1996) • NCAA Championship All-Tournament Team (1996) • WCHA First All-Star Team (1999) • NCAA West First All-American Team (1999)

SZYSKY, Chris   **OTT.**

RIght wing. Shoots right. 5'11", 205 lbs.   Born, White City, Sask., June 8, 1976.

				Regular Season					Playoffs			
Season	Club	Lea	GP	G	A	TP	PIM	GP	G	A	TP	PIM
1993-94	Swift Current	WHL	60	6	10	16	82	7	0	1	1	12
1994-95	Swift Current	WHL	61	6	6	12	105	6	2	0	2	10
1995-96	Swift Current	WHL	63	19	16	35	115	6	3	2	5	21
1996-97	Swift Current	WHL	66	28	30	58	181	10	5	10	15	18
1997-98	Canada	Nat-Team	50	9	20	29	111	.....	....	....	....	....
1998-99	Canada	Nat-Team	41	9	13	22	56	.....	....	....	....	....
	Grand Rapids	IHL	6	1	1	2	10	.....	....	....	....	....

Signed as a free agent by **Ottawa**, June 20, 1999.

TALLINDER, Henrik   (tah-LIHN-duhr)   **BUF.**

Defense. Shoots left. 6'3", 194 lbs.   Born, Stockholm, Sweden, January 10, 1979.
(Buffalo's 2nd choice, 48th overall, in 1997 Entry Draft).

				Regular Season					Playoffs			
Season	Club	Lea	GP	G	A	TP	PIM	GP	G	A	TP	PIM
1996-97	AIK Solna	Swede-Jr.	40	4	13	17	55	.....	....	....	....	....
	AIK Solna	Sweden	1	0	0	0	0	.....	....	....	....	....
1997-98	AIK Solna	Sweden	34	0	0	0	26	.....	....	....	....	....
1998-99	AIK Solna	Sweden	36	0	0	0	30	.....	....	....	....	....

TANABE, David   **CAR.**

Defense. Shoots right. 6'1", 190 lbs.   Born, Minneapolis, MN, July 19, 1980.
(Carolina's 1st choice, 16th overall, in 1999 Entry Draft).

				Regular Season					Playoffs			
Season	Club	Lea	GP	G	A	TP	PIM	GP	G	A	TP	PIM
1996-97	Hill-Murray	H.S.	28	12	14	26	....	.....	....	....	....	....
1997-98	Team USA	Under-18	73	8	21	29	96	.....	....	....	....	....
1998-99	Wisconsin	WCHA	35	10	12	22	44	.....	....	....	....	....

TANGUAY, Alex   (TAN-guay)   **COL.**

Center. Shoots left. 6', 180 lbs.   Born, Ste-Justine, Que., November 21, 1979.
(Colorado's 1st choice, 12th overall, in 1998 Entry Draft).

				Regular Season					Playoffs			
Season	Club	Lea	GP	G	A	TP	PIM	GP	G	A	TP	PIM
1996-97	Halifax	QMJHL	70	27	41	68	60	12	5	8	13	8
1997-98	Halifax	QMJHL	51	47	38	85	32	5	7	6	13	4
1998-99	Hershey	AHL	5	1	2	3	2	5	0	2	2	0
	Halifax	QMJHL	31	27	34	61	30	5	1	2	3	2

TARDIF, Steve   (tahr-DIHF)   **CHI.**

Center. Shoots left. 6'1", 180 lbs.   Born, St-Agnes, Que., March 29, 1977.
(Chicago's 8th choice, 175th overall, in 1995 Entry Draft).

				Regular Season					Playoffs			
Season	Club	Lea	GP	G	A	TP	PIM	GP	G	A	TP	PIM
1993-94	Drummondville	QMJHL	71	5	16	21	117	10	0	1	1	19
1994-95	Drummondville	QMJHL	64	10	33	43	313	4	1	2	3	9
1995-96	Drummondville	QMJHL	54	17	33	50	291	6	2	3	5	58
1996-97	Drummondville	QMJHL	65	24	40	64	377	6	1	5	6	62
1997-98	Jacksonville	ECHL	15	4	3	7	48	.....	....	....	....	....
	Indianapolis	IHL	42	3	4	7	113	.....	....	....	....	....
1998-99	Portland	AHL	33	2	9	11	48	.....	....	....	....	....
	Indianapolis	IHL	6	0	0	0	40	.....	....	....	....	....
	Florida	ECHL	25	13	12	25	75	6	4	3	7	18

TARVAINEN, Jussi   (tahr-VIGH-nehn)   **EDM.**

Right wing. Shoots right. 6'3", 215 lbs.   Born, Lahti, Finland, May 31, 1976.
(Edmonton's 7th choice, 95th overall, in 1994 Entry Draft).

				Regular Season					Playoffs			
Season	Club	Lea	GP	G	A	TP	PIM	GP	G	A	TP	PIM
1993-94	KalPa Kuopio	Finland	42	3	4	7	20	.....	....	....	....	....
1994-95	KalPa Kuopio	Finland	45	10	7	17	34	3	0	0	0	2
1995-96	KalPa Kuopio	Finland	47	8	11	19	50	.....	....	....	....	....
1996-97	KalPa Kuopio	Finland	49	14	26	40	62	.....	....	....	....	....
1997-98	JyP Jyvaskyla	Finland	43	12	26	38	59	.....	....	....	....	....
1998-99	JyP Jyvaskyla	Finland	54	17	24	41	84	3	0	0	0	8

TERGLAV, Edo   (TAIR-glav, EH-doh)   **BUF.**

Right wing. Shoots left. 6', 195 lbs.   Born, Kranj, Czech., January 24, 1980.
(Buffalo's 10th choice, 249th overall, in 1998 Entry Draft).

				Regular Season					Playoffs			
Season	Club	Lea	GP	G	A	TP	PIM	GP	G	A	TP	PIM
1995-96	Lac St-Louis	QAAA	44	6	12	18	20	.....	....	....	....	....
1996-97	Lac St-Louis	QAAA	44	20	32	52	18	.....	....	....	....	....
1997-98	Baie-Comeau	QMJHL	46	17	27	44	40	.....	....	....	....	....
1998-99	Baie-Comeau	QMJHL	48	13	16	29	35	.....	....	....	....	....

TETARENKO, Joey   (teh-tar-EHN-koh)   **FLA.**

Defense. Shoots right. 6'2", 212 lbs.   Born, Prince Albert, Sask., March 3, 1978.
(Florida's 4th choice, 82nd overall, in 1996 Entry Draft).

				Regular Season					Playoffs			
Season	Club	Lea	GP	G	A	TP	PIM	GP	G	A	TP	PIM
1994-95	Portland	WHL	59	0	1	1	134	9	0	0	0	8
1995-96	Portland	WHL	71	4	11	15	190	7	0	1	1	17
1996-97	Portland	WHL	68	8	18	26	182	2	0	0	0	2
1997-98	Portland	WHL	49	2	12	14	148	16	0	2	2	30
1998-99	New Haven	AHL	65	4	10	14	154	.....	....	....	....	....

TETRAULT, Daniel   (teh-TROH)

Defense. Shoots right. 6', 198 lbs.   Born, St. Boniface, Man., September 4, 1979.
(Montreal's 4th choice, 91st overall, in 1997 Entry Draft).

				Regular Season					Playoffs			
Season	Club	Lea	GP	G	A	TP	PIM	GP	G	A	TP	PIM
1995-96	Brandon	WHL	72	6	13	19	91	19	1	1	2	25
1996-97	Brandon	WHL	64	5	24	29	136	6	0	0	0	14
1997-98	Brandon	WHL	16	2	3	5	32	18	0	5	5	25
1998-99	Brandon	WHL	57	10	36	46	91	4	0	0	0	9

THEORET, Luc   (THEE-ohr-eht)   **BUF.**

Defense. Shoots left. 6'1", 197 lbs.   Born, Winnipeg, Man., July 30, 1979.
(Buffalo's 5th choice, 101st overall, in 1997 Entry Draft).

				Regular Season					Playoffs			
Season	Club	Lea	GP	G	A	TP	PIM	GP	G	A	TP	PIM
1995-96	Lethbridge	WHL	47	4	13	17	41	4	0	0	0	6
1996-97	Lethbridge	WHL	43	3	7	10	51	19	1	5	6	8
1997-98	Lethbridge	WHL	65	12	37	49	98	4	0	1	1	8
1998-99	Lethbridge	WHL	46	13	39	52	92	.....	....	....	....	....
	Portland	WHL	3	0	0	0	10	.....	....	....	....	....

THIBEAULT, David   (TEE-boh)

Left wing. Shoots left. 6'1", 190 lbs.   Born, Trois-Rivieres, Que., May 12, 1978.
(San Jose's 8th choice, 217th overall, in 1996 Entry Draft).

				Regular Season					Playoffs			
Season	Club	Lea	GP	G	A	TP	PIM	GP	G	A	TP	PIM
1994-95	Drummondville	QMJHL	61	10	19	29	101	4	0	0	0	0
1995-96	Drummondville	QMJHL	57	23	35	58	99	6	0	3	3	12
1996-97	Victoriaville	QMJHL	58	39	38	77	37	6	3	3	6	4
	Kentucky	AHL	1	0	0	0	0	.....	....	....	....	....
1997-98	Victoriaville	QMJHL	70	46	56	102	95	6	3	4	7	6
1998-99	Victoriaville	QMJHL	63	43	59	102	72	6	5	2	7	8

QMJHL Second All-Star Team (1999)

THINEL, Marc-Andre   (tih-nehl)   **MTL.**

Right wing. Shoots left. 5'11", 170 lbs.   Born, St. Jerome, Que., March 24, 1981.
(Montreal's 5th choice, 145th overall, in 1999 Entry Draft).

				Regular Season					Playoffs			
Season	Club	Lea	GP	G	A	TP	PIM	GP	G	A	TP	PIM
1997-98	Victoriaville	QMJHL	58	7	10	17	20	.....	....	....	....	....
1998-99	Victoriaville	QMJHL	66	45	58	103	16	.....	....	....	....	....

THOMPSON, Chris   **N.J.**

Right wing. Shoots left. 6'1", 210 lbs.   Born, Prince Albert, Sask., April 10, 1978.

				Regular Season					Playoffs			
Season	Club	Lea	GP	G	A	TP	PIM	GP	G	A	TP	PIM
1995-96	Seattle	WHL	56	8	5	13	86	5	0	0	0	21
1996-97	Seattle	WHL	65	3	14	17	191	15	1	1	2	67
1997-98	Seattle	WHL	70	16	32	48	339	5	0	0	0	18
1998-99	Albany	AHL	9	0	0	0	14	.....	....	....	....	....
	Augusta	ECHL	57	16	14	30	221	2	0	0	0	4

Signed as a free agent by **New Jersey**, July 23, 1998.

THOMPSON, Mark   **T.B.**

Defense. Shoots right. 6'6", 205 lbs.   Born, St. Albert, Alta., April 26, 1979.
(Tampa Bay's 4th choice, 108th overall, in 1997 Entry Draft).

				Regular Season					Playoffs			
Season	Club	Lea	GP	G	A	TP	PIM	GP	G	A	TP	PIM
1996-97	Regina	WHL	32	1	5	6	20	3	0	1	1	2
1997-98	Regina	WHL	46	0	2	2	44	9	0	0	0	0
1998-99	Kootenay	WHL	36	2	7	9	76	4	0	0	0	2

THORNTON, Shawn   **TOR.**

Right wing. Shoots right. 6'1", 196 lbs.   Born, Oshawa, Ont., July 23, 1979.
(Toronto's 6th choice, 190th overall, in 1997 Entry Draft).

				Regular Season					Playoffs			
Season	Club	Lea	GP	G	A	TP	PIM	GP	G	A	TP	PIM
1995-96	Peterborough	OHL	63	4	10	14	192	24	3	0	3	25
1996-97	Peterborough	OHL	61	19	10	29	204	11	2	4	6	20
1997-98	St. John's	AHL	59	0	3	3	225	.....	....	....	....	....
1998-99	St. John's	AHL	78	8	11	19	354	5	0	0	0	9

THORPE, Ryan — VAN.

Left wing. Shoots left. 6'4", 202 lbs. Born, Vancouver, B.C., February 6, 1981.
(Vancouver's 4th choice, 129th overall, in 1999 Entry Draft).

			Regular Season					Playoffs				
Season	Club	Lea	GP	G	A	TP	PIM	GP	G	A	TP	PIM
1998-99	Spokane	WHL	41	12	4	16	60	....	....	....	....	....
	Kamloops	WHL	22	2	1	3	68	....	....	....	....	....

TIMKIN, Alexei — (TIHM-kihn) DAL.

Right wing. Shoots left. 6'2", 194 lbs. Born, Kirov, USSR, April 21, 1979.
(Dallas' 6th choice, 160th overall, in 1997 Entry Draft).

			Regular Season					Playoffs				
Season	Club	Lea	GP	G	A	TP	PIM	GP	G	A	TP	PIM
1996-97	Yaroslavl-2	Russia-3	47	16	6	22	54	....	....	....	....	....
	Yaroslavl	Russia	3	0	1	1	0	....	....	....	....	....
1997-98	Yaroslavl-2	Russia-2	16	4	5	9	14	....	....	....	....	....
1998-99			STATISTICS NOT AVAILABLE									

TIMMONS, K.C. — COL.

Left wing. Shoots left. 6'2", 205 lbs. Born, Victoria, B.C., April 6, 1980.
(Colorado's 9th choice, 141st overall, in 1998 Entry Draft).

			Regular Season					Playoffs				
Season	Club	Lea	GP	G	A	TP	PIM	GP	G	A	TP	PIM
1996-97	Tri-City	WHL	52	0	5	5	27	....	....	....	....	....
1997-98	Tri-City	WHL	72	11	7	18	139	....	....	....	....	....
1998-99	Tri-City	WHL	69	13	11	24	113	12	1	1	2	36

TIPLER, Curtis — T.B.

Right wing. Shoots right. 6'5", 205 lbs. Born, Wainwright, Alta., May 9, 1978.
(Tampa Bay's 2nd choice, 69th overall, in 1996 Entry Draft).

			Regular Season					Playoffs				
Season	Club	Lea	GP	G	A	TP	PIM	GP	G	A	TP	PIM
1995-96	Regina	WHL	69	27	38	65	65	11	3	1	4	4
1996-97	Regina	WHL	47	18	18	36	35	5	1	2	3	4
1997-98	Prince George	WHL	68	26	32	58	43	11	0	3	3	4
1998-99	Prince George	WHL	55	14	25	39	36	7	0	4	4	12

TJARNQVIST, Daniel — (TUH-yahrn-kvihst) ATL.

Defense. Shoots left. 6'2", 180 lbs. Born, Umea, Sweden, October 14, 1976.
(Florida's 5th choice, 88th overall, in 1995 Entry Draft).

			Regular Season					Playoffs				
Season	Club	Lea	GP	G	A	TP	PIM	GP	G	A	TP	PIM
1994-95	Rogle BK	Sweden	18	0	1	1	2	....	....	....	....	....
	Rogle BK	Sweden-2	15	2	3	5	0	....	....	....	....	....
1995-96	Rogle BK	Sweden	22	1	7	8	6	....	....	....	....	....
1996-97	Jokerit	Finland	44	3	8	11	4	9	0	3	3	4
1997-98	Djurgardens IF	Sweden	40	5	9	14	12	15	1	1	2	2
1998-99	Djurgardens IF	Sweden	40	4	3	7	16	4	0	0	0	2

Traded to **Atlanta** by **Florida** with Gord Murphy, Herbert Vasiljevs and Ottawa's 6th round choice (previously acquired, later traded to Dallas - Dallas selected Justin Cox) in 1999 Entry Draft for Trevor Kidd, June 25, 1999.

TJARNQVIST, Mathias — (TUH-yahrn-kvihst) DAL.

Right wing. Shoots left. 6'1", 183 lbs. Born, Umea, Sweden, April 15, 1979.
(Dallas' 3rd choice, 96th overall, in 1999 Entry Draft)

			Regular Season					Playoffs				
Season	Club	Lea	GP	G	A	TP	PIM	GP	G	A	TP	PIM
1995-96	Rogle BK	Swede-Jr.	4	2	0	2	0	....	....	....	....	....
1996-97	Rogle BK	Swede-Jr.	18	5	8	13	....	....	....	....	....	....
	Rogle BK	Sweden-2	15	1	4	5	4	....	....	....	....	....
1997-98	Rogle BK	Sweden-2	31	12	11	23	30	....	....	....	....	....
1998-99	Rogle BK	Sweden-2	13	7	5	12	14	5	4	1	5	4

TKACZUK, Daniel — (kuh-CHUK) CGY.

Center. Shoots left. 6', 190 lbs. Born, Toronto, Ont., June 10, 1979.
(Calgary's 1st choice, 6th overall, in 1997 Entry Draft).

			Regular Season					Playoffs				
Season	Club	Lea	GP	G	A	TP	PIM	GP	G	A	TP	PIM
1995-96	Barrie	OHL	61	22	39	61	38	7	1	2	3	8
1996-97	Barrie	OHL	62	45	48	93	49	9	7	2	9	2
1997-98	Barrie	OHL	57	35	40	75	38	6	2	3	5	8
1998-99	Barrie	OHL	58	43	62	105	58	12	7	8	15	10

OHL First All-Star Team (1999)

TOLSA, Jari — (TOHL-suh, YA-ree) DET.

Center. Shoots left. 6', 172 lbs. Born, Goteborg, Sweden, April 20, 1981.
(Detroit's 1st choice, 120th overall, in 1999 Entry Draft).

			Regular Season					Playoffs				
Season	Club	Lea	GP	G	A	TP	PIM	GP	G	A	TP	PIM
1997-98	V. Frolunda	Swede-Jr.	26	18	25	43	30	....	....	....	....	....
1998-99	V. Frolunda	Swede-Jr.	35	16	21	37	51	....	....	....	....	....

TORY, Jeff — PHI.

Defense. Shoots right. 5'11", 190 lbs. Born, Burnaby, B.C., May 9, 1973.

			Regular Season					Playoffs				
Season	Club	Lea	GP	G	A	TP	PIM	GP	G	A	TP	PIM
1993-94	U. of Maine	H.E.	3	0	0	0	4	....	....	....	....	....
1994-95	U. of Maine	H.E.	40	13	42	55	22	....	....	....	....	....
1995-96	U. of Maine	H.E.	37	4	36	40	36	....	....	....	....	....
1996-97	Canada	Nat-Team	54	8	37	45	30	....	....	....	....	....
	Kentucky	AHL	3	0	2	2	0	4	0	0	0	2
1997-98	Houston	IHL	74	11	27	38	35	4	0	1	1	2
1998-99	Houston	IHL	79	19	36	55	46	18	2	6	8	8

Hockey East First All-Star Team (1995) • NCAA East Second All-American Team (1995) • Hockey East All-Star Team (1996) • NCAA East First All-American Team (1996)

Signed as a free agent by **Philadelphia**, July 27, 1999.

TRATTNIG, Matthias — (TRAT-nihg, MAH-tee-uhs) CHI.

Center. Shoots left. 6'1", 208 lbs. Born, Graz, Austria, April 22, 1979.
(Chicago's 2nd choice, 94th overall, in 1998 Entry Draft).

			Regular Season					Playoffs				
Season	Club	Lea	GP	G	A	TP	PIM	GP	G	A	TP	PIM
1995-96	EC Graz	Austria	17	0	1	1	0	....	....	....	....	....
1996-97	Capital District	NYJHL	51	30	54	84	64	....	....	....	....	....
1997-98	U. of Maine	H.E.	34	8	9	17	30	....	....	....	....	....
1998-99	U. of Maine	H.E.	39	5	5	10	32	....	....	....	....	....

TRAVNICEK, Mihail — (TRAV-nih-chehk, MEE-khuhl) TOR.

Right wing. Shoots left. 6'1", 198 lbs. Born, Decin, Czech., March 14, 1980.
(Toronto's 9th choice, 228th overall, in 1998 Entry Draft).

			Regular Season					Playoffs				
Season	Club	Lea	GP	G	A	TP	PIM	GP	G	A	TP	PIM
1996-97	CHZ Litvinov	Czech-Jr.	45	35	22	57	....	....	....	....	....	....
1997-98	CHZ Litvinov	Czech-Jr.	43	18	20	38	....	....	....	....	....	....
1998-99	CHZ Litvinov	Cze-Rep	49	7	7	14	65	....	....	....	....	....

TREMBLAY, Didier — (TRAHM-blay) ST.L.

Defense. Shoots left. 6'1", 190 lbs. Born, Laval, Que., May 4, 1979.
(St. Louis' 2nd choice, 86th overall, in 1997 Entry Draft).

			Regular Season					Playoffs				
Season	Club	Lea	GP	G	A	TP	PIM	GP	G	A	TP	PIM
1995-96	Halifax	QMJHL	56	4	10	14	80	6	0	3	3	4
1996-97	Halifax	QMJHL	68	11	26	37	79	12	1	3	4	6
1997-98	Halifax	QMJHL	39	6	19	25	26	....	....	....	....	....
	Val d'Or	QMJHL	31	6	24	30	43	19	5	13	18	8
1998-99	Val d'Or	QMJHL	63	23	51	74	56	6	1	4	5	4

TRIPP, John — CGY.

Right wing. Shoots right. 6'2", 207 lbs. Born, Kingston, Ont., May 4, 1977.
(Calgary's 3rd choice, 42nd overall, in 1997 Entry Draft).

			Regular Season					Playoffs				
Season	Club	Lea	GP	G	A	TP	PIM	GP	G	A	TP	PIM
1994-95	Oshawa	OHL	58	6	11	17	53	7	0	1	1	4
1995-96	Oshawa	OHL	56	13	14	27	95	5	1	1	2	13
1996-97	Oshawa	OHL	59	28	20	48	126	18	*16	10	26	42
1997-98	Roanoke	ECHL	9	0	2	2	22	....	....	....	....	....
	Saint John	AHL	61	1	11	12	66	2	0	1	1	0
1998-99	Saint John	AHL	2	0	0	0	10	....	....	....	....	....
	Johnstown	ECHL	7	2	0	2	12	....	....	....	....	....

• Re-entered NHL draft. Originally Colorado's 3rd choice, 77th overall, in 1995 Entry Draft.

TROCHINSKY, Andrei — (troh-SCHIHN-skee) ST.L.

Center. Shoots left. 6'5", 187 lbs. Born, Ust-Kamenogorsk, USSR, February 14, 1978.
(St. Louis' 5th choice, 170th overall, in 1998 Entry Draft).

			Regular Season					Playoffs				
Season	Club	Lea	GP	G	A	TP	PIM	GP	G	A	TP	PIM
1996-97	Torpedo Ust	Russia-2	9	1	1	2	8	....	....	....	....	....
1997-98	Torpedo Ust	Russia-2	47	10	16	26	34	....	....	....	....	....

TROTTIER, Joel — BOS.

Right wing. Shoots right. 6', 190 lbs. Born, Alexandria, Ont., February 11, 1977.
(Boston's 8th choice, 162nd overall, in 1997 Entry Draft).

			Regular Season					Playoffs				
Season	Club	Lea	GP	G	A	TP	PIM	GP	G	A	TP	PIM
1994-95	Ottawa	OHL	53	7	10	17	13	....	....	....	....	....
1995-96	Ottawa	OHL	63	25	19	44	57	4	4	1	5	7
1996-97	Ottawa	OHL	56	41	39	80	57	22	14	12	26	23
1997-98	Plymouth	OHL	10	4	6	10	17	....	....	....	....	....
	Belleville	OHL	43	23	32	55	51	10	5	6	11	9
1998-99	Providence	AHL	7	3	0	3	17	....	....	....	....	....
	Greenville	ECHL	53	15	15	30	49	....	....	....	....	....

TSELIOS, Nikos — (TSEHL-ee-ohs) CAR.

Defense. Shoots left. 6'4", 187 lbs. Born, Oak Park, IL, January 20, 1979.
(Carolina's 1st choice, 22nd overall, in 1997 Entry Draft).

			Regular Season					Playoffs				
Season	Club	Lea	GP	G	A	TP	PIM	GP	G	A	TP	PIM
1996-97	Belleville	OHL	64	9	37	46	61	6	1	1	2	2
1997-98	Belleville	OHL	20	2	10	12	16	....	....	....	....	....
	Plymouth	OHL	41	8	20	28	27	15	1	8	9	27
1998-99	Plymouth	OHL	60	21	39	60	60	11	4	10	14	8

TSYBUK, Yevgeny — (tsee-BUHK) DAL.

Defense. Shoots left. 6', 183 lbs. Born, Chebarkul, USSR, February 2, 1978.
(Dallas' 5th choice, 113th overall, in 1996 Entry Draft).

			Regular Season					Playoffs				
Season	Club	Lea	GP	G	A	TP	PIM	GP	G	A	TP	PIM
1995-96	Yaroslavl-2	CIS-2	STATISTICS NOT AVAILABLE									
1996-97	Lethbridge	WHL	10	0	1	1	13	....	....	....	....	....
1997-98	Lethbridge	WHL	41	5	13	18	129	4	1	1	2	12
1998-99	Michigan	IHL	42	1	3	4	69	2	0	0	0	2

TVRDON, Roman — (t-vahr-DAWN) WSH.

Center. Shoots left. 6'1", 189 lbs. Born, Trencin, Czech., January 29, 1981.
(Washington's 6th choice, 132nd overall, in 1999 Entry Draft).

			Regular Season					Playoffs				
Season	Club	Lea	GP	G	A	TP	PIM	GP	G	A	TP	PIM
1997-98	Dukla Trencin	Slovak-Jr.	48	4	12	16	39	....	....	....	....	....
1998-99	Dukla Trencin	Slovak-Jr.	49	23	23	46	20	6	4	4	8	4

TWORDIK, Brad — (TWOHR-dihk) ST.L.

Center. Shoots left. 5'10", 201 lbs. Born, Saskatoon, Sask., November 20, 1979.
(St. Louis' 6th choice, 197th overall, in 1998 Entry Draft).

			Regular Season					Playoffs				
Season	Club	Lea	GP	G	A	TP	PIM	GP	G	A	TP	PIM
1995-96	Brandon	WHL	3	0	0	0	2	....	....	....	....	....
1996-97	Brandon	WHL	71	23	33	56	77	6	1	1	2	17
1997-98	Brandon	WHL	69	23	49	72	81	18	5	11	16	35
1998-99	Brandon	WHL	57	29	45	74	67	5	2	1	3	9

URICK, Brian (YOOR-ihk) EDM.

Right wing. Shoots right. 6'1", 195 lbs. Born, Minneapolis, MN, January 25, 1977.
(Edmonton's 5th choice, 114th overall, in 1996 Entry Draft).

			Regular Season					Playoffs				
Season	Club	Lea	GP	G	A	TP	PIM	GP	G	A	TP	PIM
1994-95	Minnetonka High	H.S.	24	30	29	59	28	....	....	....	....	....
1995-96	Notre Dame	CCHA	36	12	15	27	66	....	....	....	....	....
1996-97	Notre Dame	CCHA	34	13	12	25	88	....	....	....	....	....
1997-98	Notre Dame	CCHA	41	16	18	34	40	....	....	....	....	....
1998-99	Notre Dame	CCHA	35	16	25	41	45	....	....	....	....	....

VAANANEN, Ossi (VAN-ih-nehn, AW-see) PHX.

Defense. Shoots left. 6'3", 200 lbs. Born, Vantaa, Finland, August 18, 1980.
(Phoenix's 2nd choice, 43rd overall, in 1998 Entry Draft).

			Regular Season					Playoffs				
Season	Club	Lea	GP	G	A	TP	PIM	GP	G	A	TP	PIM
1995-96	Jokerit	Finn-Jr.	2	0	0	0	0	....	....	....	....	....
1996-97	Jokerit	Finn-Jr.	17	1	2	3	43	....	....	....	....	....
1997-98	Jokerit	Finn-Jr.	31	0	6	6	24	....	....	....	....	....
1998-99	Jokerit	Finn-Jr.	12	1	6	7	16	....	....	....	....	....
	Jokerit	Finland	48	0	1	1	42	3	0	1	1	2

VALENTINE, Curtis VAN.

Left wing. Shoots left. 6'5", 195 lbs. Born, Haileybury, Ont., July 22, 1979.
(Vancouver's 11th choice, 219th overall, in 1998 Entry Draft).

			Regular Season					Playoffs				
Season	Club	Lea	GP	G	A	TP	PIM	GP	G	A	TP	PIM
1996-97	Capital District	USA-Jr.	56	53	60	113	28	....	....	....	....	....
1997-98	Bowling Green	CCHA	38	7	8	15	34	....	....	....	....	....
1998-99	Bowling Green	CCHA	38	4	8	12	40	....	....	....	....	....

VALILA, Mika (VA-lih-lah, MEE-ka) PIT.

Center. Shoots left. 6', 187 lbs. Born, Sodertalje, Sweden, February 20, 1970.
(Pittsburgh's 7th choice, 130th overall, in 1990 Entry Draft).

			Regular Season					Playoffs				
Season	Club	Lea	GP	G	A	TP	PIM	GP	G	A	TP	PIM
1988-89	Tappara	Finland	14	2	5	7	8	3	1	0	1	2
1989-90	Tappara	Finland	44	8	16	24	16	7	2	2	4	4
1990-91	Tappara	Finland	41	10	9	19	16	3	0	1	1	0
1991-92	Jokerit	Finland	30	4	3	7	4	8	1	1	2	2
1992-93	Lukko Rauma	Finland	48	8	10	18	24	3	0	0	0	0
1993-94	Lukko Rauma	Finland	45	7	7	14	18	9	0	0	0	8
1994-95	Troja-Ljunby	Sweden-2	33	14	14	28	54	....	....	....	....	....
1995-96	Troja-Ljunby	Sweden-2	29	4	6	10	36	....	....	....	....	....
1996-97	Bodens IK	Sweden-2	19	6	8	14	47	....	....	....	....	....
1997-98	Boras HK	Sweden-3	34	12	13	25	7	....	....	....	....	....
1998-99			Statistics Not Available									

VALTONEN, Tomek (VAL-tuh-nehn) DET.

Left wing. Shoots left. 6'1", 198 lbs. Born, Piotrkow Trybunalski, Poland, January 8, 1980.
(Detroit's 3rd choice, 56th overall, in 1998 Entry Draft).

			Regular Season					Playoffs				
Season	Club	Lea	GP	G	A	TP	PIM	GP	G	A	TP	PIM
1995-96	Ilves Tampere	Finn-Jr.	12	7	7	14	28	....	....	....	....	....
1996-97	Ilves Tampere	Finn-Jr.	27	10	9	19	82	3	0	1	1	6
1997-98	Kiekko	Finland-2	6	1	2	3	39	....	....	....	....	....
	Ilves Tampere	Finn-Jr.	13	3	2	5	36	....	....	....	....	....
	Ilves Tampere	Finland	19	1	0	1	14	3	0	0	0	0
1998-99	Plymouth	OHL	43	8	16	24	53	7	1	0	1	0

VAN ACKER, Eric BOS.

Defense. Shoots left. 6'5", 220 lbs. Born, St-Jean, Que., March 1, 1979.
(Boston's 11th choice, 218th overall, in 1997 Entry Draft).

			Regular Season					Playoffs				
Season	Club	Lea	GP	G	A	TP	PIM	GP	G	A	TP	PIM
1996-97	Chicoutimi	QMJHL	69	2	5	7	153	16	0	0	0	4
1997-98	Chicoutimi	QMJHL	49	1	5	6	136	6	0	0	0	14
1998-99	Baie-Comeau	QMJHL	65	1	6	7	192	....	....	....	....	....

VANBUSKIRK, Ryan PHX.

Defense. Shoots left. 6'1", 190 lbs. Born, Sault Ste. Marie, MI, January 12, 1980.
(Phoenix's 4th choice, 100th overall, in 1998 Entry Draft).

			Regular Season					Playoffs				
Season	Club	Lea	GP	G	A	TP	PIM	GP	G	A	TP	PIM
1996-97	Petrolia	OJHL	43	7	28	35	133	....	....	....	....	....
1997-98	Sarnia	OHL	61	8	17	25	84	5	1	2	3	4
1998-99	Sarnia	OHL	66	15	33	48	85	6	1	2	3	4

VAN DRUNEN, David OTT.

Defense. Shoots right. 6', 200 lbs. Born, Sherwood Park, Alta., January 31, 1976.

			Regular Season					Playoffs				
Season	Club	Lea	GP	G	A	TP	PIM	GP	G	A	TP	PIM
1993-94	Prince Albert	WHL	63	3	10	13	95	....	....	....	....	....
1994-95	Prince Albert	WHL	71	2	14	16	132	15	3	4	7	36
1995-96	Prince Albert	WHL	70	10	23	33	172	18	1	5	6	37
1996-97	Prince Albert	WHL	72	18	47	65	218	4	0	4	4	24
1997-98	Hershey	AHL	5	0	0	0	2	....	....	....	....	....
	Portland	AHL	4	0	0	0	2	....	....	....	....	....
	Baton Rouge	ECHL	59	8	22	30	107	....	....	....	....	....
1998-99	Saginaw	UHL	63	5	17	22	107	....	....	....	....	....
	Cincinnati	IHL	1	0	0	0	0	....	....	....	....	....
	Dayton	ECHL	9	2	4	6	12	4	0	0	0	12

WHL East Second All-Star Team (1997)

Signed as a free agent by **Ottawa**, May 2, 1997.

VAN HOOF, Jeremy PIT.

Defense. Shoots left. 6'3", 200 lbs. Born, Lindsay, Ont., August 12, 1981.
(Pittsburgh's 3rd choice, 57th overall, in 1999 Entry Draft).

			Regular Season					Playoffs				
Season	Club	Lea	GP	G	A	TP	PIM	GP	G	A	TP	PIM
1997-98	Lindsay	OJHL	50	2	8	10	40	....	....	....	....	....
1998-99	Ottawa	OHL	54	0	13	13	46	5	1	0	1	2

VAN OENE, Darren (van OH-uhn) BUF.

Left wing. Shoots left. 6'3", 207 lbs. Born, Edmonton, Alta., January 18, 1978.
(Buffalo's 3rd choice, 33rd overall, in 1996 Entry Draft).

			Regular Season					Playoffs				
Season	Club	Lea	GP	G	A	TP	PIM	GP	G	A	TP	PIM
1994-95	Brandon	WHL	58	5	13	18	106	18	1	1	2	34
1995-96	Brandon	WHL	47	10	18	28	126	18	1	6	7	*78
1996-97	Brandon	WHL	56	21	27	48	139	6	2	3	5	19
1997-98	Brandon	WHL	51	23	24	47	161	18	6	8	14	51
1998-99	Rochester	AHL	73	11	20	31	143	12	2	4	6	8

VAN RYN, Mike (VAN RIHN) N.J.

Defense. Shoots right. 6'1", 190 lbs. Born, London, Ont., May 14, 1979.
(New Jersey's 1st choice, 26th overall, in 1998 Entry Draft).

			Regular Season					Playoffs				
Season	Club	Lea	GP	G	A	TP	PIM	GP	G	A	TP	PIM
1996-97	London	OJHL	46	14	31	45	32	....	....	....	....	....
1997-98	U. of Michigan	CCHA	38	4	14	18	44	....	....	....	....	....
1998-99	U. of Michigan	CCHA	37	10	13	23	52	....	....	....	....	....

VASICEK, Josef (VAHSH-ih-chehk, YOH-zehf) CAR.

Center. Shoots left. 6'4", 189 lbs. Born, Havlickuv Brod, Czech., September 12, 1980.
(Carolina's 4th choice, 91st overall, in 1998 Entry Draft).

			Regular Season					Playoffs				
Season	Club	Lea	GP	G	A	TP	PIM	GP	G	A	TP	PIM
1995-96	Havlickuv Brod	Czech-Jr.	36	25	25	50	....	....	....	....	....	....
1996-97	Slavia Praha	Czech-Jr.	37	20	40	60	....	....	....	....	....	....
1997-98	Slavia Praha	Czech-Jr.	34	13	20	33	....	....	....	....	....	....
1998-99	S.S. Marie	OHL	66	21	35	56	30	5	3	0	3	10

VASILIEV, Alexei (vah-SEE-lee-ehf) NYR

Defense. Shoots left. 6'1", 190 lbs. Born, Yaroslavl, USSR, September 1, 1977.
(NY Rangers' 4th choice, 110th overall, in 1995 Entry Draft).

			Regular Season					Playoffs				
Season	Club	Lea	GP	G	A	TP	PIM	GP	G	A	TP	PIM
1993-94	Yaroslavl	CIS	2	0	1	1	4	....	....	....	....	....
1994-95	Yaroslavl-2	CIS-2	Statistics Not Available									
1995-96	Yaroslavl	CIS	40	4	7	11	4	....	....	....	....	....
1996-97	Yaroslavl	Russia	44	2	8	10	10	9	1	1	2	8
1997-98	Hartford	AHL	Did Not Play – Injured									
1998-99	Hartford	AHL	75	8	19	27	24	6	0	1	1	2

• Missed entire 1997-98 season after suffering knee injury at conclusion of training camp, October, 1997.

VAUCLAIR, Julien (voh-KLAIR) OTT.

Defense. Shoots left. 6'1", 198 lbs. Born, Delemont, Switzerland, October 2, 1979.
(Ottawa's 4th choice, 74th overall, in 1998 Entry Draft).

			Regular Season					Playoffs				
Season	Club	Lea	GP	G	A	TP	PIM	GP	G	A	TP	PIM
1995-96	HC Ajoie	Switz-3	20	4	10	14	....	....	....	....	....	....
1996-97	HC Ajoie	Switz-2	40	0	6	6	24	9	0	2	2	8
1997-98	HC Lugano	Switz.	36	1	2	3	12	7	0	0	0	25
1998-99	HC Lugano	Switz.	38	0	3	3	8	....	....	....	....	....

VELLINGA, Mike CGY.

Defense. Shoots right. 6'1", 218 lbs. Born, Chatham, Ont., August 19, 1978.
(Chicago's 5th choice, 184th overall, in 1996 Entry Draft).

			Regular Season					Playoffs				
Season	Club	Lea	GP	G	A	TP	PIM	GP	G	A	TP	PIM
1995-96	Guelph	OHL	57	3	8	11	32	16	2	6	8	6
1996-97	Guelph	OHL	66	6	30	36	73	18	1	9	10	34
1997-98	Guelph	OHL	63	6	22	28	101	12	1	8	9	28
1998-99	Saint John	AHL	15	0	1	1	6	....	....	....	....	....
	Orlando	IHL	1	0	0	0	4	....	....	....	....	....
	Johnstown	ECHL	45	1	14	15	22	....	....	....	....	....

Signed as a free agent by **Calgary**, July 21, 1998.

VERCIK, Rudolf (VEHR-chihk) NYR

Left wing. Shoots left. 6'1", 189 lbs. Born, Bratislava, Czech., March 19, 1976.
(NY Rangers' 2nd choice, 52nd overall, in 1994 Entry Draft).

			Regular Season					Playoffs				
Season	Club	Lea	GP	G	A	TP	PIM	GP	G	A	TP	PIM
1993-94	HC Bratislava	Slovakia	17	1	4	5	14	....	....	....	....	....
1994-95	HC Bratislava	Slovakia	33	14	9	23	22	....	....	....	....	....
1995-96	HC Bratislava	Slovakia	28	7	3	10	61	13	1	0	1	....
1996-97	HC Bratislava	Slovakia	40	8	3	11	....	2	0	0	0	....
1997-98	Nova Ves	Slovakia	36	8	5	13	36	3	1	1	2	0
1998-99	HC Bratislava	Slovakia	35	6	7	13	53	7	1	0	1	4

VERENIKIN, Sergei (veh-rih-NEE-kihn) OTT.

Right wing. Shoots left. 5'11", 187 lbs. Born, Yaroslavl, USSR, September 8, 1979.
(Ottawa's 9th choice, 223rd overall, in 1998 Entry Draft).

			Regular Season					Playoffs				
Season	Club	Lea	GP	G	A	TP	PIM	GP	G	A	TP	PIM
1996-97	Yermak Angars	Russia-3	Statistics Not Available									
1997-98	Yaroslavl-2	Russia-2	44	11	4	15	100	....	....	....	....	....
	Yaroslavl	Russia	3	0	0	0	0	....	....	....	....	....
1998-99	Yaroslavl	Russia	37	2	5	7	16	8	0	0	0	18

VERTALA, Timo (vehr-TAH-lah, TEE-moh) MTL.

Left wing. Shoots left. 6'1", 180 lbs. Born, Jyvaskyla, Finland, May 2, 1978.
(Montreal's 8th choice, 181st overall, in 1996 Entry Draft).

			Regular Season					Playoffs				
Season	Club	Lea	GP	G	A	TP	PIM	GP	G	A	TP	PIM
1995-96	JyP Jyvaskyla	Finn-Jr.	35	15	10	25	54	6	1	1	2	6
	JyP Jyvaskyla	Finland	3	0	1	1	2	....	....	....	....	....
1996-97	JyP Jyvaskyla	Finn-Jr.	7	4	4	8	12	....	....	....	....	....
	JyP Jyvaskyla	Finland	46	8	5	13	39	4	0	0	0	0
1997-98	JyP Jyvaskyla	Finn-Jr.	2	2	1	3	4	....	....	....	....	....
	JyP Jyvaskyla	Finland	43	4	8	12	34	....	....	....	....	....
1998-99	JyP Jyvaskyla	Finland	48	5	5	10	60	3	0	0	0	2

VIKINGSTAD, Tore (VIH-kihng-stahd, TOO-reh) ST.L.

Center. Shoots left. 6'4", 202 lbs. Born, Trondheim, Norway, October 8, 1975.
(St. Louis' 5th choice, 180th overall, in 1999 Entry Draft).

			Regular Season					Playoffs				
Season	Club	Lea	GP	G	A	TP	PIM	GP	G	A	TP	PIM
1994-95	Viking IHK	Norway	28	5	3	8	8	....	....	....	....	....
1995-96	Viking IHK	Norway	27	12	11	23	....	....	....	....	....	....
1996-97	IL Stjernen	Norway	42	23	35	58	20	....	....	....	....	....
1997-98	IL Stjernen	Norway	42	26	31	57	18	....	....	....	....	....
1998-99	Farjestads BK	Sweden	49	9	11	20	18	4	2	3	5	0

VISHNEVSKI, Vitaly (vihsh-NEHV-skee, vih-TAL-ee) ANA.

Defense. Shoots left. 6'1", 190 lbs. Born, Kharkov, USSR, March 18, 1980.
(Anaheim's 1st choice, 5th overall, in 1998 Entry Draft).

			Regular Season					Playoffs				
Season	Club	Lea	GP	G	A	TP	PIM	GP	G	A	TP	PIM
1995-96	Yaroslavl-2	Russia-2	40	4	4	8	20	....	....	....	....	....
1996-97	Yaroslavl-2	Russia-3	45	0	2	2	30	....	....	....	....	....
1997-98	Yaroslavl-2	Russia-2	47	8	9	17	164	....	....	....	....	....
1998-99	Yaroslavl	Russia	34	3	4	7	38	10	0	0	0	4

VIUHKOLA, Jari (VEW-koh-lak, YA-ree)

Center. Shoots left. 6', 165 lbs. Born, Oulu, Finland, February 27, 1980.
(Chicago's 4th choice, 158th overall, in 1998 Entry Draft).

			Regular Season					Playoffs				
Season	Club	Lea	GP	G	A	TP	PIM	GP	G	A	TP	PIM
1996-97	Karpat Oulu	Finn-Jr.	32	8	11	19	74	....	....	....	....	....
1997-98	Karpat Oulu	Finn-Jr.	28	8	18	26	57	....	....	....	....	....
1998-99	Karpat Oulu	Finn-Jr.	21	8	14	22	6	....	....	....	....	....
	Karpat Oulu	Finland-2	14	5	5	10	6	....	....	....	....	....

VLASENKOV, Dmitri (vlah-SEHN-khahf) CGY.

Left wing. Shoots left. 5'11", 183 lbs. Born, Olenigorsk, USSR, January 1, 1978.
(Calgary's 4th choice, 73rd overall, in 1996 Entry Draft).

			Regular Season					Playoffs				
Season	Club	Lea	GP	G	A	TP	PIM	GP	G	A	TP	PIM
1995-96	Yaroslavl	CIS	17	1	1	2	4	1	0	0	0	0
1996-97	Yaroslavl-2	Russia-3	18	10	2	12	6	....	....	....	....	....
	Yaroslavl	Russia	28	3	2	5	10	8	1	1	2	2
1997-98	Yaroslavl	EuroHL	6	0	0	0	2	....	....	....	....	....
	Yaroslavl	Russia	44	10	3	13	12	....	....	....	....	....
1998-99	Yaroslavl	Russia	41	11	5	16	26	10	1	2	3	6

VOLCHKOV, Alexander (VOHLCH-kahf) WSH.

Center. Shoots left. 6'2", 204 lbs. Born, Moscow, USSR, September 25, 1977.
(Washington's 1st choice, 4th overall, in 1996 Entry Draft).

			Regular Season					Playoffs				
Season	Club	Lea	GP	G	A	TP	PIM	GP	G	A	TP	PIM
1994-95	CSKA Moscow	CIS	1	0	0	0	0	....	....	....	....	....
1995-96	Barrie	OHL	47	37	27	64	36	7	2	3	5	12
1996-97	Barrie	OHL	56	29	53	82	76	9	6	9	15	12
	Portland	AHL	....	....	....	....	....	4	0	0	0	0
1997-98	Portland	AHL	34	2	5	7	20	1	0	0	0	0
1998-99	Portland	AHL	27	3	8	11	24	....	....	....	....	....
	Cincinnati	IHL	25	1	3	4	8	....	....	....	....	....

OHL Second All-Star Team (1997)

VOTH, Brad ST.L.

Defense. Shoots right. 6'4", 223 lbs. Born, Saskatoon, Sask., February 25, 1980.
(St. Louis' 4th choice, 157th overall, in 1998 Entry Draft).

			Regular Season					Playoffs				
Season	Club	Lea	GP	G	A	TP	PIM	GP	G	A	TP	PIM
1996-97	Medicine Hat	WHL	2	0	0	0	2	....	....	....	....	....
1997-98	Medicine Hat	WHL	70	8	5	13	244	....	....	....	....	....
1998-99	Medicine Hat	WHL	40	4	6	10	102	....	....	....	....	....

VYDARENY, Rene (vih-DAH-reh-nay) VAN.

Defense. Shoots left. 6'1", 198 lbs. Born, Bratislava, Czech., May 6, 1981.
(Vancouver's 3rd choice, 69th overall, in 1999 Entry Draft).

			Regular Season					Playoffs				
Season	Club	Lea	GP	G	A	TP	PIM	GP	G	A	TP	PIM
1997-98	Bratislava	Slovak-Jr.	50	5	14	19	26	....	....	....	....	....
1998-99	Bratislava	Slovak-Jr.	42	4	7	11	65	2	0	0	0	2
	Trnava	Slovak-2	20	1	6	7	6	....	....	....	....	....

VYSHEDKEVICH, Sergei (vee-shehd-KAY-vihch) ATL.

Defense. Shoots left. 6', 195 lbs. Born, Dedovsk, USSR, January 3, 1975.
(New Jersey's 3rd choice, 70th overall, in 1995 Entry Draft).

			Regular Season					Playoffs				
Season	Club	Lea	GP	G	A	TP	PIM	GP	G	A	TP	PIM
1994-95	Moscow D'amo	CIS	49	6	7	13	67	14	2	0	2	12
1995-96	Moscow D'amo	CIS	49	5	4	9	12	13	1	1	2	6
1996-97	Albany	AHL	65	8	27	35	16	12	0	6	6	0
1997-98	Albany	AHL	54	12	16	28	12	13	0	10	10	4
1998-99	Albany	AHL	79	11	38	49	28	5	0	3	3	0

Traded to **Atlanta** by **New Jersey** for future considerations, June 25, 1999.

WALBY, Steffon

Right wing. Shoots right. 6'1", 198 lbs. Born, Madison, WI, November 22, 1972.

			Regular Season					Playoffs				
Season	Club	Lea	GP	G	A	TP	PIM	GP	G	A	TP	PIM
1992-93	Kelowna	BCJHL	59	53	68	121	76	....	....	....	....	....
1993-94	St. John's	AHL	63	15	22	37	79	2	0	0	0	2
1994-95	St. John's	AHL	70	23	23	46	30	5	1	1	2	4
1995-96	St. John's	AHL	57	23	31	54	61	4	2	2	4	17
1996-97	Hershey	AHL	74	24	23	47	61	19	7	3	10	34
1997-98	Fort Wayne	IHL	77	28	26	54	53	4	1	1	2	6
1998-99	Rochester	AHL	48	15	13	28	52	....	....	....	....	....
	Kentucky	AHL	11	8	4	12	6	12	3	2	5	14

Signed as a free agent by **Toronto**, August 20, 1993. Signed as a free agent by **Buffalo**, August 31, 1998.

WALKER, Matt ST.L.

Defense. Shoots right. 6'2", 222 lbs. Born, Beaverlodge, Alta., April 7, 1980.
(St. Louis' 3rd choice, 83rd overall, in 1998 Entry Draft).

			Regular Season					Playoffs				
Season	Club	Lea	GP	G	A	TP	PIM	GP	G	A	TP	PIM
1997-98	Portland	WHL	64	2	13	15	124	16	0	0	0	21
1998-99	Portland	WHL	64	1	10	11	151	4	0	1	1	6

WALLACE, Buddy OTT.

Center. Shoots left. 6'1", 195 lbs. Born, Palantine, IL, December 18, 1975.

			Regular Season					Playoffs				
Season	Club	Lea	GP	G	A	TP	PIM	GP	G	A	TP	PIM
1993-94	Hill-Murray School	H.S.	33	29	27	56	....	....	....	....	....	....
1994-95	Clarkson	ECAC	17	0	3	3	18	....	....	....	....	....
1995-96	Clarkson	ECAC	35	0	5	5	84	....	....	....	....	....
1996-97	Clarkson	ECAC	36	5	8	13	77	....	....	....	....	....
1997-98	Clarkson	ECAC	35	12	13	35	66	....	....	....	....	....
1998-99	Lowell	AHL	70	11	11	22	57	3	1	1	2	2

Signed as a free agent by **Ottawa**, August 31, 1999.

WALLIN, Jesse (WAHL-ihn) DET.

Defense. Shoots left. 6'2", 190 lbs. Born, Saskatoon, Sask., March 10, 1978.
(Detroit's 1st choice, 26th overall, in 1996 Entry Draft).

			Regular Season					Playoffs				
Season	Club	Lea	GP	G	A	TP	PIM	GP	G	A	TP	PIM
1994-95	Red Deer	WHL	72	4	20	24	72	....	....	....	....	....
1995-96	Red Deer	WHL	70	5	19	24	61	9	0	3	3	4
1996-97	Red Deer	WHL	59	6	33	39	70	16	1	4	5	10
1997-98	Red Deer	WHL	14	1	6	7	17	5	0	1	1	2
1998-99	Adirondack	AHL	76	4	12	16	34	3	0	2	2	2

Canadian Major Junior Humanitarian Player of the Year (1997)

WALLIN, Rickard (WAHL-in) PHX.

Center. Shoots left. 6'2", 183 lbs. Born, Stockholm, Sweden, April 19, 1980.
(Phoenix's 8th choice, 160th overall, in 1998 Entry Draft).

			Regular Season					Playoffs				
Season	Club	Lea	GP	G	A	TP	PIM	GP	G	A	TP	PIM
1996-97	Farjestads BK	Swede-Jr.	26	3	3	6	....	....	....	....	....	....
1997-98	Farjestads BK	Swede-Jr.	29	20	30	50	32	2	1	1	2	2
1998-99	Farjestads BK	Swede-Jr.	21	11	15	26	30	....	....	....	....	....
	Farjestads BK	Sweden	5	0	0	0	0	....	....	....	....	....

WALLIN, Viktor (WAHL-in) ANA.

Defense. Shoots left. 6'3", 200 lbs. Born, Jonkoping, Sweden, January 17, 1980.
(Anaheim's 3rd choice, 112th overall, in 1998 Entry Draft).

			Regular Season					Playoffs				
Season	Club	Lea	GP	G	A	TP	PIM	GP	G	A	TP	PIM
1996-97	HV Jonkoping	Swede-Jr.	16	1	2	3	....	....	....	....	....	....
1997-98	HV Jonkoping	Swede-Jr.	28	9	15	24	42	....	....	....	....	....
1998-99	HV Jonkoping	Sweden	23	0	0	0	4	....	....	....	....	....

WANSBOROUGH, Shawn (WEHNS-boh-roh) PHX.

Left wing. Shoots left. 6', 200 lbs. Born, Deseronto, Ont., June 3, 1974.

			Regular Season					Playoffs				
Season	Club	Lea	GP	G	A	TP	PIM	GP	G	A	TP	PIM
1993-94	Smiths Falls	OJHL			STATISTICS NOT AVAILABLE							
1994-95	U. of Maine	H.E.	36	14	21	35	20	....	....	....	....	....
1995-96	U. of Maine	H.E.	36	27	16	43	42	....	....	....	....	....
1996-97	U. of Maine	H.E.	35	18	21	39	62	....	....	....	....	....
1997-98	U. of Maine	H.E.	32	15	19	34	77	....	....	....	....	....
	Orlando	IHL	3	3	3	6	4	17	8	8	16	14
1998-99	Orlando	IHL	3	0	0	0	6	....	....	....	....	....
	Long Beach	IHL	8	1	5	6	16	....	....	....	....	....
	Las Vegas	IHL	62	7	20	27	144	....	....	....	....	....

Signed as a free agent by **Phoenix**, July 26, 1999.

WANVIG, Kyle (WEHN-vihg) BOS.

Right wing. Shoots right. 6'2", 197 lbs. Born, Calgary, Alta., January 29, 1981.
(Boston's 3rd choice, 89th overall, in 1999 Entry Draft).

			Regular Season					Playoffs				
Season	Club	Lea	GP	G	A	TP	PIM	GP	G	A	TP	PIM
1997-98	Edmonton	WHL	62	17	12	29	69	....	....	....	....	....
1998-99	Kootenay	WHL	71	12	20	32	119	....	....	....	....	....

WARD, Jason MTL.

Right wing. Shoots right. 6'2", 192 lbs. Born, Chapleau, Ont., January 16, 1979.
(Montreal's 1st choice, 11th overall, in 1997 Entry Draft).

			Regular Season					Playoffs				
Season	Club	Lea	GP	G	A	TP	PIM	GP	G	A	TP	PIM
1995-96	Niagara Falls	OHL	64	15	35	50	139	10	6	4	10	23
1996-97	Erie	OHL	58	25	39	64	137	5	1	2	3	2
1997-98	Erie	OHL	21	7	9	16	42	....	....	....	....	....
	Windsor	OHL	26	19	27	46	34	....	....	....	....	....
	Fredericton	AHL	7	1	0	1	2	1	0	0	0	2
1998-99	Windsor	OHL	12	8	11	19	25	....	....	....	....	....
	Plymouth	OHL	23	14	13	27	28	11	6	8	14	12
	Fredericton	AHL	....	....	....	....	....	10	4	2	6	22

WARD, Lance FLA.

Defense. Shoots left. 6'3", 215 lbs. Born, Lloydminster, Alta., June 2, 1978.
(Florida's 3rd choice, 63rd overall, in 1998 Entry Draft).

			Regular Season					Playoffs				
Season	Club	Lea	GP	G	A	TP	PIM	GP	G	A	TP	PIM
1994-95	Red Deer	WHL	28	0	0	0	57	....	....	....	....	....
1995-96	Red Deer	WHL	72	4	13	17	127	10	0	4	4	10
1996-97	Red Deer	WHL	70	5	34	39	229	16	0	3	3	36
1997-98	Red Deer	WHL	71	8	25	33	233	5	0	0	0	16
1998-99	Miami	ECHL	6	1	0	1	12	....	....	....	....	....
	Fort Wayne	IHL	13	0	2	2	28	....	....	....	....	....
	New Haven	AHL	43	2	5	7	51	....	....	....	....	....

• Re-entered NHL draft. Originally New Jersey's 1st choice, 10th overall, in 1996 Entry Draft.

WARREN, Morgan — TOR.

Right wing. Shoots right. 6'2", 185 lbs. Born, Summerside, P.E.I., March 6, 1980.
(Toronto's 5th choice, 126th overall, in 1998 Entry Draft).

			Regular Season					Playoffs				
Season	Club	Lea	GP	G	A	TP	PIM	GP	G	A	TP	PIM
1996-97	Quinte Hawks	OJHL	49	32	38	70	65	....	....	....	....	....
1997-98	Moncton	QMJHL	58	11	10	21	80	10	2	2	4	2
1998-99	Moncton	QMJHL	48	20	16	36	68	1	0	0	0	2

WEINHANDL, Mattias (vayn-hanh-duhl, mah-TEE-uhs) — NYI

Right wing. Shoots right. 6', 183 lbs. Born, Ljungby, Sweden, June 1, 1980.
(NY Islanders' 5th choice, 78th overall, in 1999 Entry Draft).

			Regular Season					Playoffs				
Season	Club	Lea	GP	G	A	TP	PIM	GP	G	A	TP	PIM
1995-96	Troja-Ljungby	Swede-Jr.	28	38	40	78	....	....	....	....	....	....
1996-97	Troja-Ljungby	Swede-Jr.	48	61	69	130	46	....	....	....	....	....
1997-98	Troja-Ljungby	Sweden-2	28	3	2	5	2	5	0	0	0	2
1998-99	Troja-Ljungby	Sweden-2	38	20	20	40	30	5	4	3	7	4

WENDELL, Erik — WSH.

Center. Shoots left. 6'1", 197 lbs. Born, Minneapolis, MN, August 23, 1979.
(Washington's 6th choice, 125th overall, in 1998 Entry Draft).

			Regular Season					Playoffs				
Season	Club	Lea	GP	G	A	TP	PIM	GP	G	A	TP	PIM
1997-98	Maple Grove	H.S.	24	24	23	47	38	....	....	....	....	....
1998-99	U. of Minnesota	WCHA	41	7	7	14	46	....	....	....	....	....

WESTLUND, Tommy — CAR.

Right wing. Shoots right. 6', 210 lbs. Born, Fors, Sweden, December 29, 1974.
(Carolina's 5th choice, 93rd overall, in 1998 Entry Draft).

			Regular Season					Playoffs				
Season	Club	Lea	GP	G	A	TP	PIM	GP	G	A	TP	PIM
1991-92	Avesta BK	Sweden-3	27	11	9	20	8	....	....	....	....	....
1992-93	Avesta BK	Sweden-2	32	9	5	14	32	....	....	....	....	....
1993-94	Avesta BK	Sweden-2	31	20	11	31	34	....	....	....	....	....
1994-95	Avesta BK	Sweden-2	32	17	13	30	22	....	....	....	....	....
1995-96	Brynas Gavle	Sweden	18	2	1	3	2	....	....	....	....	....
	Brynas Gavle	Sweden-2	18	10	10	20	4	8	1	0	1	4
1996-97	Brynas Gavle	Sweden	50	21	13	34	16	....	....	....	....	....
1997-98	Brynas Gavle	Sweden	46	29	9	38	45	3	0	1	1	0
1998-99	New Haven	AHL	50	8	18	26	31	....	....	....	....	....

WESTRUM, Erik — PHX.

Center. Shoots left. 5'11", 186 lbs. Born, Minneapolis, MN, July 26, 1979.
(Phoenix's 9th choice, 187th overall, in 1998 Entry Draft).

			Regular Season					Playoffs				
Season	Club	Lea	GP	G	A	TP	PIM	GP	G	A	TP	PIM
1996-97	Apple Valley High	H.S.	25	23	33	56	....	....	....	....	....	....
1997-98	U. of Minnesota	WCHA	39	6	12	18	43	....	....	....	....	....
1998-99	U. of Minnesota	WCHA	41	10	26	36	81	....	....	....	....	....

WHITE, Colin — N.J.

Defense. Shoots left. 6'3", 215 lbs. Born, New Glasgow, N.S., December 12, 1977.
(New Jersey's 5th choice, 49th overall, in 1996 Entry Draft).

			Regular Season					Playoffs				
Season	Club	Lea	GP	G	A	TP	PIM	GP	G	A	TP	PIM
1994-95	Laval	QMJHL	7	0	1	1	32	....	....	....	....	....
	Hull	QMJHL	5	0	1	1	4	12	0	0	0	23
1995-96	Hull	QMJHL	62	2	8	10	303	18	0	4	4	42
1996-97	Hull	QMJHL	63	3	12	15	297	14	3	12	15	65
1997-98	Albany	AHL	76	3	13	16	235	13	0	0	0	55
1998-99	Albany	AHL	77	2	12	14	265	5	0	1	1	8

WHITFIELD, Trent — WSH.

Center. Shoots left. 5'11", 190 lbs. Born, Estevan, Sask., June 17, 1977.
(Boston's 5th choice, 100th overall, in 1996 Entry Draft).

			Regular Season					Playoffs				
Season	Club	Lea	GP	G	A	TP	PIM	GP	G	A	TP	PIM
1993-94	Spokane	WHL	5	1	1	2	0	....	....	....	....	....
1994-95	Spokane	WHL	48	8	17	25	26	11	7	6	13	5
1995-96	Spokane	WHL	72	33	51	84	75	18	8	10	18	10
1996-97	Spokane	WHL	58	34	42	76	74	9	5	7	12	10
1997-98	Spokane	WHL	65	38	44	82	97	18	9	10	19	15
1998-99	Portland	AHL	50	10	8	18	20	....	....	....	....	....
	Hampton Roads	ECHL	19	13	12	25	12	4	2	0	2	14

WHL West First All-Star Team (1997) • WHL West Second All-Star Team (1998)

WIKSTROM, John — DET.

Defense. Shoots left. 6'3", 200 lbs. Born, Lulea, Sweden, January 30, 1979.
(Detroit's 4th choice, 129th overall, in 1997 Entry Draft).

			Regular Season					Playoffs				
Season	Club	Lea	GP	G	A	TP	PIM	GP	G	A	TP	PIM
1995-96	Lulea HF	Sweden	9	0	0	0	2	....	....	....	....	....
1996-97	Lulea HF	Sweden	9	0	0	0	0	3	0	0	0	0
1997-98	Lulea HF	Sweden	1	0	0	0	0	....	....	....	....	....
	Lulea HF	EuroHL	1	0	0	0	0	....	....	....	....	....
1998-99	Morrum IK	Sweden-2	18	0	1	1	24	....	....	....	....	....

WILFORD, Marty — CHI.

Defense. Shoots left. 6', 216 lbs. Born, Cobourg, Ont., April 17, 1977.
(Chicago's 7th choice, 149th overall, in 1995 Entry Draft).

			Regular Season					Playoffs				
Season	Club	Lea	GP	G	A	TP	PIM	GP	G	A	TP	PIM
1994-95	Oshawa	OHL	63	1	6	7	95	7	1	1	2	4
1995-96	Oshawa	OHL	65	3	24	27	107	5	0	1	1	4
1996-97	Oshawa	OHL	62	19	43	62	126	16	2	18	20	28
1997-98	Columbus	ECHL	46	8	27	35	123	....	....	....	....	....
	Indianapolis	IHL	26	0	4	4	16	....	....	....	....	....
1998-99	Indianapolis	IHL	80	3	13	16	116	7	0	1	1	16

OHL Second All-Star Team (1997)

WILLEJTO, Steve (wihl-EH-toh) — DET.

Center. Shoots left. 5'10", 178 lbs. Born, Burn's Lake, B.C., January 26, 1979.
(Detroit's 7th choice, 213th overall, in 1997 Entry Draft).

			Regular Season					Playoffs				
Season	Club	Lea	GP	G	A	TP	PIM	GP	G	A	TP	PIM
1996-97	Prince Albert	WHL	69	11	13	24	32	4	1	1	2	0
1997-98	Prince Albert	WHL	71	15	15	30	35	....	....	....	....	....
1998-99	Prince Albert	WHL	27	0	3	3	17	....	....	....	....	....
	Medicine Hat	WHL	33	2	6	8	18	....	....	....	....	....

WILLERS, Greg — DET.

Defense. Shoots right. 6'1", 195 lbs. Born, Scarborough, Ont., August 8, 1979.
(Detroit's 8th choice, 239th overall, in 1997 Entry Draft).

			Regular Season					Playoffs				
Season	Club	Lea	GP	G	A	TP	PIM	GP	G	A	TP	PIM
1996-97	Kingston	OHL	51	4	7	11	37	5	1	0	1	0
1997-98	Kingston	OHL	19	1	5	6	8	....	....	....	....	....
	Sarnia	OHL	40	12	16	28	26	5	2	1	3	6
1998-99	Sarnia	OHL	68	16	38	54	32	6	1	1	2	6

WILLIAMS, Jeff — N.J.

Center. Shoots left. 6'1", 200 lbs. Born, Pointe-Claire, Que., February 11, 1976.
(New Jersey's 8th choice, 181st overall, in 1994 Entry Draft).

			Regular Season					Playoffs				
Season	Club	Lea	GP	G	A	TP	PIM	GP	G	A	TP	PIM
1993-94	Guelph	OHL	62	14	12	26	19	9	2	1	3	4
1994-95	Guelph	OHL	52	15	32	47	21	14	5	5	10	0
1995-96	Guelph	OHL	63	15	49	64	42	16	13	15	28	10
1996-97	Raleigh	ECHL	20	4	8	12	8					
	Albany	AHL	46	13	20	33	12	15	1	2	3	15
1997-98	Albany	AHL	58	13	12	25	20	12	5	6	11	2
1998-99	Albany	AHL	74	*46	27	73	39	5	1	2	3	0

Canadian Major Junior Most Sportsmanlike Player of the Year (1996) • AHL Second All-Star Team (1999)

WILLIS, Tyler — ST.L.

Right wing. Shoots right. 5'9", 171 lbs. Born, Princeton, B.C., April 8, 1977.
(Vancouver's 8th choice, 196th overall, in 1995 Entry Draft).

			Regular Season					Playoffs				
Season	Club	Lea	GP	G	A	TP	PIM	GP	G	A	TP	PIM
1993-94	Swift Current	WHL	71	19	26	45	263	....	....	....	....	....
1994-95	Swift Current	WHL	71	21	29	50	284	6	0	0	0	20
1995-96	Swift Current	WHL	40	9	38	47	196	....	....	....	....	....
	Seattle	WHL	15	1	3	4	71	5	1	5	6	13
1996-97	Seattle	WHL	72	12	40	52	302	15	1	7	8	68
1997-98	Worcester	AHL	24	2	1	3	140	....	....	....	....	....
	Baton Rouge	ECHL	21	4	10	14	112	....	....	....	....	....
1998-99	Worcester	AHL	55	8	10	18	227	....	....	....	....	....

Signed as a free agent by **St. Louis**, October 3, 1997.

WILLSIE, Brian (WIHL-see) — COL.

Right wing. Shoots right. 6', 190 lbs. Born, London, Ont., March 16, 1978.
(Colorado's 7th choice, 146th overall, in 1996 Entry Draft).

			Regular Season					Playoffs				
Season	Club	Lea	GP	G	A	TP	PIM	GP	G	A	TP	PIM
1995-96	Guelph	OHL	65	13	21	34	18	16	4	2	6	6
1996-97	Guelph	OHL	64	37	31	68	37	18	15	4	19	10
1997-98	Guelph	OHL	57	45	31	76	41	12	9	5	14	18
1998-99	Hershey	AHL	72	19	10	29	28	3	1	0	1	0

OHL First All-Star Team (1998)

WOLFE, Dwight — TOR.

Defense. Shoots left. 6'5", 227 lbs. Born, Liverpool, N.S., February 12, 1980.
(Toronto's 8th choice, 215th overall, in 1998 Entry Draft).

			Regular Season					Playoffs				
Season	Club	Lea	GP	G	A	TP	PIM	GP	G	A	TP	PIM
1997-98	Halifax	QMJHL	52	0	2	2	72	5	0	0	0	0
1998-99	Halifax	QMJHL	1	0	0	0	9	....	....	....	....	....
	Val d'Or	QMJHL	52	2	5	7	57	....	....	....	....	....

WOODS, Brad — FLA.

Defense. Shoots right. 6'3", 198 lbs. Born, Cambridge, Ont., March 4, 1981.
(Florida's 6th choice, 169th overall, in 1999 Entry Draft).

			Regular Season					Playoffs				
Season	Club	Lea	GP	G	A	TP	PIM	GP	G	A	TP	PIM
1998-99	Brampton	OHL	58	1	5	6	42	....	....	....	....	....

YAKUSHIN, Dmitri (yah-KOO-shihn) — TOR.

Defense. Shoots left. 6', 200 lbs. Born, Kharkov, USSR, January 21, 1978.
(Toronto's 9th choice, 140th overall, in 1996 Entry Draft).

			Regular Season					Playoffs				
Season	Club	Lea	GP	G	A	TP	PIM	GP	G	A	TP	PIM
1995-96	Pembroke	OJHL	31	8	5	13	62	....	....	....	....	....
1996-97	Edmonton	WHL	63	3	14	17	103	....	....	....	....	....
1997-98	Edmonton	WHL	29	1	10	11	41	....	....	....	....	....
	Regina	WHL	13	0	14	14	16	9	2	8	10	12
1998-99	St. John's	AHL	71	2	6	8	65	4	0	0	0	0

YERKOVICH, Sergei (yehr-KOH-vihch) — EDM.

Defense. Shoots left. 6'3", 210 lbs. Born, Minsk, USSR, September 3, 1974.
(Edmonton's 3rd choice, 68th overall, in 1997 Entry Draft).

			Regular Season					Playoffs				
Season	Club	Lea	GP	G	A	TP	PIM	GP	G	A	TP	PIM
1993-94	Minsk	CIS	39	2	1	3	34	....	....	....	....	....
1994-95	Minsk	CIS	45	3	1	4	52	....	....	....	....	....
1995-96	Minsk	CIS	41	5	3	8	30	....	....	....	....	....
1996-97	Las Vegas	IHL	76	6	19	25	167	....	....	....	....	....
1997-98	Las Vegas	IHL	69	7	15	22	130	4	0	0	0	6
	Belarus	Olympics	6	2	0	2	16	....	....	....	....	....
1998-99	Hamilton	AHL	69	7	11	18	103	8	0	2	2	2

YERSHOV, Andrei   (yuhr-SHAWF)   CHI.
Defense. Shoots left. 6', 176 lbs. Born, Voskresensk, USSR, August 22, 1976.
(Chicago's 8th choice, 240th overall, in 1998 Entry Draft).

Season	Club	Lea	GP	G	A	TP	PIM	GP	G	A	TP	PIM
1994-95	Khimik	CIS	16	0	0	0	6	....	....	....	....	....
1995-96	Khimik	CIS	18	1	0	1	28	....	....	....	....	....
1996-97	Khimik	Russia	23	3	1	4	32	2	0	0	0	2
1997-98	Khimik	Russia	45	5	8	13	60	....	....	....	....	....
1998-99	Khimik	Russia	33	6	6	12	88	....	....	....	....	....

YONKMAN, Nolan   WSH.
Defense. Shoots right. 6'5", 218 lbs. Born, Punnicht, Sask., April 1, 1981.
(Washington's 5th choice, 37th overall, in 1999 Entry Draft).

Season	Club	Lea	GP	G	A	TP	PIM	GP	G	A	TP	PIM
1996-97	Naicam	SAHA	64	15	23	38	36	....	....	....	....	....
1997-98	Kelowna	WHL	65	0	2	2	36	7	0	0	0	2
1998-99	Kelowna	WHL	61	1	6	7	129	6	0	0	0	6

YORK, Michael   NYR
Center. Shoots right. 5'9", 179 lbs. Born, Pontiac, MI, January 3, 1978.
(NY Rangers' 7th choice, 136th overall, in 1997 Entry Draft).

Season	Club	Lea	GP	G	A	TP	PIM	GP	G	A	TP	PIM
1992-93	Michigan	MNHL	50	45	50	95	....					
1993-94	Detroit	MNHL	85	136	140	276	....					
1994-95	Thornhill	OJHL	49	39	54	93	....					
1995-96	Michigan State	CCHA	39	12	27	39	20					
1996-97	Michigan State	CCHA	37	18	29	47	42					
1997-98	Michigan State	CCHA	40	27	34	61	38					
1998-99	Michigan State	CCHA	42	22	32	*54	41					
	Hartford	AHL	3	2	2	4	0	6	3	1	4	0

CCHA Second All-Star Team (1998) • NCAA West First All-American Team (1998, 1999) • CCHA First All-Star Team (1999)

YOUNG, B.J.   DET.
Right wing. Shoots right. 5'10", 178 lbs. Born, Anchorage, AK, July 23, 1977.
(Detroit's 5th choice, 157th overall, in 1997 Entry Draft).

Season	Club	Lea	GP	G	A	TP	PIM	GP	G	A	TP	PIM
1993-94	Tri-City	WHL	54	19	24	43	66	2	1	1	2	2
1994-95	Tri-City	WHL	30	6	3	9	39	....				
	Red Deer	WHL	21	5	9	14	33	....				
1995-96	Red Deer	WHL	67	49	45	94	144	8	4	9	13	12
1996-97	Red Deer	WHL	63	58	56	114	97	16	8	14	22	26
1997-98	Adirondack	AHL	65	15	22	37	191	3	0	2	2	6
1998-99	Adirondack	AHL	58	13	17	30	150	3	1	0	1	6

WHL East First All-Star Team (1997)

YTFELDT, David   (YOOT-fehld)   VAN.
Defense. Shoots left. 6', 187 lbs. Born, Ornskoldsvik, Sweden, September 29, 1979.
(Vancouver's 6th choice, 136th overall, in 1998 Entry Draft).

Season	Club	Lea	GP	G	A	TP	PIM	GP	G	A	TP	PIM
1996-97	Leksands IF	Swede-Jr.	25	3	5	8	....	....	....	....	....	....
1997-98	Leksands IF	Sweden	10	0	0	0	2	....	....	....	....	....
	Leksands IF	Swede-Jr.	23	13	10	23	101					
1998-99	Leksands IF	Sweden	39	0	4	4	65	4	0	1	1	4

• Name when drafted was David Jonsson. His last name was legally changed to Ytfeldt.

ZALESAK, Miroslav   (zah-LIH-sahk)   S.J.
Right wing. Shoots left. 6', 185 lbs. Born, Skalica, Czech., January 2, 1980.
(San Jose's 5th choice, 104th overall, in 1998 Entry Draft).

Season	Club	Lea	GP	G	A	TP	PIM	GP	G	A	TP	PIM
1995-96	MHC Nitra	Slovak-Jr.	49	53	29	82	....					
1996-97	MHC Nitra	Slovak-Jr.	58	51	31	82	....					
1997-98	MHC Nitra	Slovak-Jr.	27	32	29	61	30					
	MHC Nitra	Slovakia	30	8	6	14	0					
1998-99	MHC Nitra	Slovakia	15	4	3	7	10					
	Drummondville	QMJHL	45	24	27	51	18					

ZANUTTO, Mike   BUF.
Center. Shoots left. 6', 190 lbs. Born, Burlington, Ont., January 1, 1977.
(Buffalo's 10th choice, 198th overall, in 1995 Entry Draft).

Season	Club	Lea	GP	G	A	TP	PIM	GP	G	A	TP	PIM
1994-95	North Bay	OHL	13	1	1	2	2	....				
	Oshawa	OHL	42	13	17	30	2	7	4	1	5	0
1995-96	Oshawa	OHL	66	32	38	70	6	5	0	2	2	0
1996-97	Oshawa	OHL	62	23	33	56	18	18	6	6	12	12
1997-98	Rochester	AHL	9	0	0	0	0	....				
	South Carolina	ECHL	49	18	17	35	6	5	0	0	0	0
1998-99	Canada	Nat-Team	10	2	1	3	0					

ZAVORAL, Vaclav   (ZA-vohr-uhl, VATS-lahf)   TOR.
Defense. Shoots left. 6'3", 198 lbs. Born, Teplice, Czech., May 22, 1981.
(Toronto's 5th choice, 151st overall, in 1999 Entry Draft).

Season	Club	Lea	GP	G	A	TP	PIM	GP	G	A	TP	PIM
1997-98	HC Litvinov	Czech-Jr.	46	0	5	5	....					
1998-99	HC Litvinov	Czech-Jr.	43	2	10	12	....					
	HC Litvinov	Cze-Rep	1	0	1	1	2					

ZEHR, Jeff   (ZAIR)   BOS.
Left wing. Shoots left. 6'3", 195 lbs. Born, Woodstock, Ont., December 10, 1978.
(NY Islanders' 3rd choice, 31st overall, in 1997 Entry Draft).

Season	Club	Lea	GP	G	A	TP	PIM	GP	G	A	TP	PIM
1995-96	Windsor	OHL	56	4	21	25	103	7	0	1	1	2
1996-97	Windsor	OHL	57	27	32	59	196	5	2	1	3	4
1997-98	Windsor	OHL	20	12	18	30	67	....				
	Erie	OHL	32	15	24	39	91	5	0	3	3	24
1998-99	Erie	OHL	28	20	23	43	78	....				
	Sarnia	OHL	14	4	10	14	43	6	3	4	7	27

ZEVAKHIN, Alexander   (zeh-VAH-khin)   PIT.
Right wing. Shoots left. 6', 187 lbs. Born, Perm, USSR, June 4, 1980.
(Pittsburgh's 2nd choice, 54th overall, in 1998 Entry Draft).

Season	Club	Lea	GP	G	A	TP	PIM	GP	G	A	TP	PIM
1995-96	CSKA Moscow	Russia-Jr.	65	52	30	82	30					
1996-97	CSKA Moscow	Russia	29	7	3	10	10					
	CSKA Moscow-2	Russia-3	30	15	18	33	10					
1997-98	CSKA Moscow-2	Russia-3	32	13	14	27	20					
	CSKA Moscow	Russia	10	1	0	1	0					
1998-99	CSKA Moscow	Russia	42	7	4	11	16	3	0	0	0	0

ZHURIK, Alexander   (ZHUH-rihk)
Defense. Shoots left. 6'3", 195 lbs. Born, Minsk, USSR, May 29, 1975.
(Edmonton's 7th choice, 163rd overall, in 1993 Entry Draft).

Season	Club	Lea	GP	G	A	TP	PIM	GP	G	A	TP	PIM
1993-94	Kingston	OHL	59	7	23	30	92	6	0	0	0	4
1994-95	Kingston	OHL	54	3	21	24	51	6	0	0	0	4
1995-96	Cape Breton	AHL	80	5	36	41	85	....				
1996-97	Hamilton	AHL	72	5	16	21	49	22	2	11	13	14
1997-98	Hamilton	AHL	63	1	23	24	84	9	0	4	4	8
	Belarus	Olympics	4	0	0	0	10	....				
1998-99	Moscow D'amo	Russia	42	1	7	8	88	15	0	0	0	12

ZIB, Lukas   (ZIHB, LOO-kahsh)   EDM.
Defense. Shoots right. 6'1", 200 lbs. Born, Ceske Budejovice, Czech., February 24, 1977.
(Edmonton's 3rd choice, 57th overall, in 1995 Entry Draft).

Season	Club	Lea	GP	G	A	TP	PIM	GP	G	A	TP	PIM
1994-95	HC Budejovice	Cze-Rep	13	2	0	2	16	9	1	0	1	6
1995-96	HC Budejovice	Czech-Rep	11	5	1	6	....					
	HC Budejovice	Cze-Rep	10	1	0	1	....	2	0	0	0	0
1996-97	HC Budejovice	Cze-Rep	13	0	0	0	4	2	0	0	0	0
1997-98	HC Budejovice	Cze-Rep	47	5	6	11	22	....				
1998-99	HC Budejovice	Cze-Rep	24	1	4	5	18	....				

ZIGOMANIS, Michael   (zih-goh-MAN-ihs)   BUF.
Center. Shoots right. 6', 183 lbs. Born, North York, Ont., January 17, 1981.
(Buffalo's 4th choice, 64th overall, in 1999 Entry Draft).

Season	Club	Lea	GP	G	A	TP	PIM	GP	G	A	TP	PIM
1996-97	Wexford	OMHA	10	37	48	84	23	....				
1997-98	Kingston	OHL	62	23	51	74	30	12	1	6	7	2
1998-99	Kingston	OHL	67	29	56	85	36	5	1	7	8	2

ZIMAKOV, Sergei   (zih-MAH-kahv)   WSH.
Defense. Shoots left. 6'1", 194 lbs. Born, Moscow, USSR, January 15, 1978.
(Washington's 4th choice, 58th overall, in 1996 Entry Draft).

Season	Club	Lea	GP	G	A	TP	PIM	GP	G	A	TP	PIM
1995-96	Soviet Wings	CIS	49	2	7	9	36	....				
1996-97	Soviet Wings	Russia	39	4	3	7	57	2	0	0	0	0
1997-98	Soviet Wings	Russia	42	4	1	5	48	....				
1998-99	Kazan	Russia	28	1	0	1	6	8	0	1	1	6

ZION, Jonathon   (ZIGH-awn)   TOR.
Defense. Shoots left. 6', 198 lbs. Born, Nepean, Ont., May 21, 1981.
(Toronto's 4th choice, 110th overall, in 1999 Entry Draft).

Season	Club	Lea	GP	G	A	TP	PIM	GP	G	A	TP	PIM
1997-98	Ottawa	OHL	53	4	19	23	20	....				
1998-99	Ottawa	OHL	60	8	33	41	10	9	2	3	5	8

ZIZKA, Tomas   (ZHIHZH-kuh, TAW-mahsh)   L.A.
Defense. Shoots left. 6'1", 198 lbs. Born, Sternberk, Czech., October 10, 1979.
(Los Angeles' 6th choice, 163rd overall, in 1998 Entry Draft).

Season	Club	Lea	GP	G	A	TP	PIM	GP	G	A	TP	PIM
1994-95	ZPS Zlin	Czech-Jr.	39	1	10	11	....					
1995-96	ZPS Zlin	Czech-Jr.	47	2	8	10	....					
1996-97	ZPS Zlin	Czech-Jr.	14	1	0	1	....					
1997-98	ZPS Zlin	Czech-Jr.	11	3	4	7	....					
	ZPS Zlin	Cze-Rep	33	0	3	3	2	....				
1998-99	ZPS Zlin	Cze-Rep	44	3	7	10	14	11	1	2	3	....

ZULTEK, Matt   (ZUHL-tehk)   BOS.
Center. Shoots left. 6'4", 222 lbs. Born, Windsor, Ont., March 12, 1979.
(Boston's 2nd choice, 56th overall, in 1999 Entry Draft).

Season	Club	Lea	GP	G	A	TP	PIM	GP	G	A	TP	PIM
1996-97	Ottawa	OHL	63	27	13	40	76	21	7	6	13	27
1997-98	Ottawa	OHL	62	28	28	56	156	13	6	12	18	20
1998-99	Ottawa	OHL	56	33	33	66	71	9	6	2	8	4

• Re-entered NHL draft. Originally, Los Angeles' 2nd choice, 15th overall, in 1997 Entry Draft.

Key to Prospect, NHL Player and Goaltender Registers

Demographics: Position, shooting side (catching hand for goaltenders), height, weight, place and date of birth as well as draft information, if any, is located on this line.

Tier II Junior, High School, Major Junior, NCAA, minor pro, junior and senior European and NHL clubs form a permanent part of each player's data panel. If a player sees action with more than one club in any of the above categories, a separate line is included for each one.

Olympic Team statistics are also listed.

Player's NHL organization as of September 1, 1999. This includes players under contract, unsigned draft choices and other players on reserve lists. Free agents as of September 1, 1999 show a blank here.

The complete career data panels of players with NHL experience who announced their retirement before the start of the 1999-2000 season are included in the 1999-2000 Player Register. These newly-retired players also show a blank here.

Each NHL club's minor-pro affiliates are listed on page 262.

				Regular Season																	Playoffs						
Season	Club	League	GP	G	A	Pts	PIM	PP	SH	GW	S	%	+/-	TF	F%	H	SB	Min	GP	G	A	Pts	PIM	PP	SH	GW
NIEUWENDYK, Joe																			(NOO-ihn-DIGHK)						**DAL.**	
Center. Shoots left. 6'1" 195 lbs. Born, Oshawa, Ont., September 10, 1966. Calgary's 2nd choice, 27th overall, in 1985 Entry Draft.																										
1983-84	Pickering	OJHL	38	30	28	58	35	....	....	....	....	....	....	....	....	....	....	....	....	....	....	....	....	....	....	....
1984-85	Cornell	ECAC	29	21	24	45	30	....	....	....	....	....	....	....	....	....	....	....	....	....	....	....	....	....	....	....
1985-86	Cornell	ECAC	29	26	28	54	67	....	....	....	....	....	....	....	....	....	....	....	....	....	....	....	....	....	....	....
1986-87	Cornell	ECAC	23	26	26	52	26	....	....	....	....	....	....	....	....	....	....	....	....	....	....	....	....	....	....	....
	Canada	Nat-Team	5	2	0	2	0	....	....	....	....	....	....	....	....	....	....	....	....	....	....	....	....	....	....	....
	Calgary	NHL	9	5	1	6	0	2	0	1	16	31.3	0	....	....	....	....	....	6	2	2	4	0	0	0	0
1987-88	Calgary	NHL	75	51	41	92	23	31	3	8	212	24.1	20	....	....	....	....	....	8	3	4	7	2	1	0	0
1988-89♦	Calgary	NHL	77	51	31	82	40	19	3	11	215	23.7	26	....	....	....	....	....	22	10	4	14	10	6	0	1
1989-90	Calgary	NHL	79	45	50	95	40	18	0	3	226	19.9	32	....	....	....	....	....	6	4	6	10	4	1	0	0
1990-91	Calgary	NHL	79	45	40	85	36	22	4	1	222	20.3	19	....	....	....	....	....	7	4	2	6	0	2	0	0
1991-92	Calgary	NHL	69	22	34	56	55	7	0	2	137	16.1	-1	....	....	....	....	....								
1992-93	Calgary	NHL	79	38	37	75	52	14	0	6	208	18.3	9	....	....	....	....	....	1	0	0	0	0			
1993-94	Calgary	NHL	64	36	39	75	51	14	1	7	191	18.8	19	....	....	....	....	....	1	1	0	1	0	1	0	0
1994-95	Calgary	NHL	46	21	29	50	33	3	0	4	122	17.2	11	....	....	....	....	....								
1995-96	Dallas	NHL	52	14	18	32	41	8	0	3	138	10.1	-17	....	....	....	....	....	5	4	3	7	0	2	0	1
1996-97	Dallas	NHL	66	30	21	51	32	8	0	2	173	17.3	-5	....	....	....	....	....	7	2	2	4	6	0	0	0
1997-98	Dallas	NHL	73	39	30	69	30	14	0	11	203	19.2	16	....	....	....	....	....	1	1	0	1	0	0	0	0
1998-99♦	Dallas	NHL	67	28	27	55	34	8	0	8	157	17.8	11	1170	63.2	42	9	15:33	23	*11	10	21	19	3	0	6
NHL Totals			835	425	398	823	467	168	11	67	2220	19.1		1170	63.2	42	9	15:33	97	46	40	86	61	17	0	8

NCAA East First All-American Team (1986, 1987) • ECAC First All-Star Team (1986, 1987) • NHL All-Rookie Team (1988) • Won Calder Memorial Trophy (1988) • Won Dodge Ram Tough Award (1998) • Won King Clancy Memorial Trophy (1995) • Won Conn Smythe Trophy (1999)
Played in NHL All-Star Game (1988, 1989, 1990, 1994)
Traded to **Dallas** by **Calgary** for Corey Millen and Jarome Iginla, December 19, 1995.

Diamond (♦) indicates Member of Stanley Cup-winning team.

Asterisk (*) indicates league leader in this statistical category.

Trade and free agent signing dates are based on when the player's contract is filed with NHL Central Registry. This date often differs from the date when the club announces that it has made a trade or come to terms with a free agent.

All-star team choices and awards are listed below player's year-by-year data.

NHL All-Star Game appearances are listed above trade notes.

All trades, free agent signings and other transactions involving NHL clubs are listed in chronological order. First draft choice for players who re-enter the NHL Entry Draft is noted here. Other special notes are also listed here. These are highlighted with a bullet (•).

BEGINNING WITH THIS EDITION OF THE *NHL Official Guide & Record Book*, additional statistical categories are included for forwards and defensemen in the National Hockey League. These new categories are, from left to right in the sample panel above, power-play goals (PP), shorthand goals (SH), game-winning goals (GW), shots on goal (S), percentage of shots that score (%), plus-minus rating (+/–), total faceoffs taken (TF), faceoff winning percentage (F%), hits (H), shots blocked (SB) and average time-on-ice per game played (Min).

To integrate this new data, the Player Register has been split into two sections. The Prospect Register presents data on players who have yet to play in the NHL. The NHL Player Register, containing more information and a photo of each player, lists all active players who have appeared in an NHL regular-season or playoff game at any time.

The Goaltender and Retired Player registers are unchanged except for their order. Both Retired Registers are now grouped together. The order of the Registers is as follows: Prospect, NHL Player, Goaltender, Retired Player and Retired Goaltender.

Pronunciation of Player Names

United Press International phonetic style.

AY	long A as in mate
A	short A as in cat
AI	nasal A as on air
AH	short A as in father
AW	broad A as in talk
EE	long E as in meat
EH	short E as in get
UH	hollow E as in "the"
AY	French long E with acute accent as in Pathe
IH	middle E as in pretty
EW	EW dipthong as in few
IGH	long I as in time
EE	French long I as in machine
IH	short I as in pity
OH	long O as in note
AH	short O as in hot
AW	broad O as in fought
OI	OI dipthong as in noise
OO	long double OO as in fool
UH	short double O as in ouch
OW	OW dipthong as in how
EW	long U as in mule
OO	long U as in rule
U	middle U as in put
UH	short U as in shut or hurt
K	hard C as in cat
S	soft C as in cease
SH	soft CH as in machine
CH	hard CH or TCH as in catch
Z	hard S as in bells
S	soft S as in sun
G	hard G as in gang
J	soft G as in general
ZH	soft J as in French version of Joliet
KH	gutteral CH as in Scottish version of Loch

Some information is unavailable at press time. Readers are encouraged to contribute.
See page 5 for contact names and addresses.

1999-2000 NHL Player Register

Note: The 1999-2000 NHL Player Register lists forwards and defensemen only. Goaltenders are listed separately. The NHL Player Register lists every skater who has played in the NHL. Trades and roster changes are current as of September 2, 1999.

Abbreviations: A – assists; **F%** – faceoff winning percentage; **G** – goals; **GP** – games played; **GT** – game-tying goals scored; **GW** – game-winning goals scored; **H** – HITS: any legal contact by one player on an opposing player that impedes the opposing player's progress; **Lea** – league; **MIN** – average time on ice; **PIM** – penalties in minutes; **+/–** – plus/minus rating; **PP** – powerplay goals scored; **Pts** – points; **S** – shots on goal; **S%** – shooting percentage; **SB** – shots blocked; **SH** – shorthand goal scored; **TF** – Total faceoffs taken; ***** – league-leading total; **♦** – member of Stanley Cup-winning team.

Prospect Register begins on page 263.

Goaltender Register begins on page 545.

LEAGUES:

AAHA	Alberta Amateur Hockey Association	GLJHL	Great Lakes Junior Hockey League	OHA	Ontario Hockey Association
ACHL	Atlantic Coast Hockey League	G.N.	Great Northern	OHL	Ontario Hockey League
AFHL	American Frontier Hockey League	GPAC	Great Plains Athletic Conference	OJHL	Ontario Junior Hockey Leagues
AHL	American Hockey League	H.E.	Hockey East	OMHA	Ontario Minor Hockey Association
AJHL	Alberta Junior Hockey League	HJHL	Heritage Junior Hockey League	OUAA	Ontario Universities Athletic Association
Alpenliga	Alpenliga	H.S.	High School	QAAA	Quebec Amateur Athletic Association
AMHA	Alberta Minor Hockey Association	IHL	International Hockey League	QJHL	Quebec Junior Hockey League
AUAA	Atlantic Universities Athletic Association	KIJHL	Kootenay International Jr. B Hockey League	QMJHL	Quebec Major Junior Hockey League
BCAHA	British Columbia Amateur Hockey Association	MAHA	Manitoba Amateur Hockey League	RMJHL	Rocky Mountain Junior Hockey League
BCJHL	British Columbia Junior Hockey League	MJHA	(New York) Metropolitan Junior Hockey Association	SAHA	Saskatchewan Amateur Hockey Association
CCHA	Central Collegiate Hockey Association			SJHL	Saskatchewan Junior Hockey League
CEGEP	Quebec Collegiate League	MJHL	Manitoba Junior Hockey League	SOHL	Southern Ontario Hockey League
CHL	Central Hockey League	MJrHL	Maritime Junior Hockey League	UHL	United Hockey League
CIAU	Canadian Interuniversity Athletic Union	MNHL	Michigan National Hockey League	Under-18	United States under-18 Hockey
CIS	Commonwealth of Independent States (former USSR)	NAHL	North American Hockey League		Development Program
		NAJHL	North American Junior Hockey League	USAHA	United States Amateur Hockey Association
COJHL	Central Ontario Junior Hockey League	Nat-Tm	National Team	USHL	United States Hockey League (Junior A)
ColHL	Colonial Hockey League	NBAHA	New Brunswick Amateur Hockey Association	WCHA	Western Collegiate Hockey Association
CWUAA	Canada West Universities Athletic Association	NCAA	National Collegiate Athletic Association	WCHL	West Coast Hockey League
ECAC	Eastern Collegiate Athletic Conference	NCHA	Northern Collegiate Hockey Association	WPHL	Western Professional Hockey League
ECHL	East Coast Hockey League	NEJHL	New England Junior Hockey League	WHA	World Hockey Association
EJHL	Eastern Junior Hockey League	**NHL**	**National Hockey League**	WHL	Western Hockey League
EuroHL	European Hockey League	NSAHA	Nova Scotia Amateur Hockey Association		

AALTO, Antti (AL-toh, AN-tee) ANA.

Center. Shoots left. 6'2", 210 lbs. Born, Lappeenranta, Finland, March 4, 1975. Anaheim's 6th choice, 134th overall, in 1993 Entry Draft.

								Regular Season												Playoffs						
Season	Club	League	GP	G	A	Pts	PIM	PP	SH	GW	S	%	+/–	TF	F%	H	SB	Min	GP	G	A	Pts	PIM	PP	SH	GW
1991-92	SaiPa	Finn-Jr.	19	10	10	20	38																			
	SaiPa	Finland-3	20	0	6	12	20																			
1992-93	TPS Turku	Finn-Jr.	14	6	8	14	18												6	2	2	4	8			
	TPS Turku	Finland	1	0	0	0	0																			
	SaiPa	Finland-2	23	6	8	14	14																			
1993-94	TPS Turku	Finn-Jr.	10	3	8	11	14												5	1	4	5	12			
	Kiekko 67	Finland-2	2	2	1	3	2																			
	TPS Turku	Finland	33	5	9	14	16												10	1	1	2	4			
1994-95	Kiekko 67	Finland-2	1	1	0	1	29																			
	TPS Turku	Finland	44	11	7	18	18												5	0	1	1	2			
1995-96	Kiekko-67	Finland-2	2	0	2	2	2																			
	TPS Turku	Finland	40	15	16	31	22												11	3	5	8	14			
1996-97	TPS Turku	Finland	44	15	19	34	60												11	5	6	11	31			
	TPS Turku	EuroHL	5	3	3	6	2												2	1	1	2	0			
1997-98	**Anaheim**	**NHL**	3	0	0	0	0	0	0	0	1	0.0	–1													
	Cincinnati	AHL	29	4	9	13	30																			
1998-99	**Anaheim**	**NHL**	73	3	5	8	24	2	0	0	61	4.9	–12	22	22.7	64	12	9:23	4	0	0	0	2	0	0	0
	NHL Totals		76	3	5	8	24	2	0	0	62	4.8		22	22.7	64	12	9:23	4	0	0	0	2	0	0	0

ADAMS, Greg PHX.

Left wing. Shoots left. 6'3", 195 lbs. Born, Nelson, B.C., August 15, 1963.

								Regular Season												Playoffs						
Season	Club	League	GP	G	A	Pts	PIM	PP	SH	GW	S	%	+/–	TF	F%	H	SB	Min	GP	G	A	Pts	PIM	PP	SH	GW
1980-81	Kelowna	BCJHL	48	40	50	90	16																			
1981-82	Kelowna	BCJHL	45	31	42	73	24																			
1982-83	North Arizona	NCAA	29	14	21	35	19																			
1983-84	North Arizona	NCAA	26	44	29	73	34																			
1984-85	**New Jersey**	**NHL**	36	12	9	21	14	5	0	0	63	19.0	–14													
	Maine	AHL	41	15	20	35	12												11	3	4	7	0			
1985-86	**New Jersey**	**NHL**	78	35	42	77	30	10	0	2	202	17.3	–7													
1986-87	**New Jersey**	**NHL**	72	20	27	47	19	6	0	1	143	14.0	–16													
1987-88	**Vancouver**	**NHL**	80	36	40	76	30	12	0	3	227	15.9	–24													
1988-89	**Vancouver**	**NHL**	61	19	14	33	24	9	0	2	144	13.2	–21						7	2	3	5	2	0	0	0
1989-90	**Vancouver**	**NHL**	65	30	20	50	18	13	0	1	181	16.6	–8													
1990-91	**Vancouver**	**NHL**	55	21	24	45	10	5	1	2	148	14.2	–5						5	0	0	0	2	0	0	0
1991-92	**Vancouver**	**NHL**	76	30	27	57	26	13	1	5	184	16.3	8						6	0	2	2	4	0	0	0
1992-93	**Vancouver**	**NHL**	53	25	31	56	14	6	1	3	124	20.2	31						12	7	6	13	6	5	0	1
1993-94	**Vancouver**	**NHL**	68	13	24	37	20	5	1	2	139	9.4	–1						23	6	8	14	2	2	0	2
1994-95	**Vancouver**	**NHL**	31	5	10	15	12	2	2	0	56	8.9	1						5	2	0	2	0	0	0	0
	Dallas	**NHL**	12	3	6	9	4	1	0	0	16	18.8	–4													
1995-96	**Dallas**	**NHL**	66	22	21	43	33	11	1	1	140	15.7	–21						3	0	1	1	0	0	0	0
1996-97	**Dallas**	**NHL**	50	21	15	36	2	5	0	4	113	18.6	27						12	2	2	4	0	0	0	2
1997-98	**Dallas**	**NHL**	49	14	18	32	20	7	0	1	75	18.7	11						3	0	1	1	0	0	0	0
1998-99	**Phoenix**	**NHL**	75	19	24	43	26	5	0	3	176	10.8	–1	295	52.9	26	15	17:22	3	0	1	1	0	0	0	0
	NHL Totals		927	325	349	674	302	115	7	30	2131	15.3		295	52.9	26	15	17:22	76	19	23	42	16	7	0	5

Played in NHL All-Star Game (1988)

Signed as a free agent by **New Jersey**, June 25, 1984. Traded to **Vancouver** by **New Jersey** with Kirk McLean and New Jersey's 2nd round choice (Leif Rohlin) in 1988 Entry Draft for Patrik Sundstrom and Vancouver's 2nd (Jeff Christian) and 4th (Matt Ruchty) round choices in 1988 Entry Draft, September 10, 1987. Traded to **Dallas** by **Vancouver** with Dan Kesa and Vancouver's 5th round choice (later traded to LA Kings — LA Kings selected Jason Morgan) in 1995 Entry Draft for Russ Courtnall, April 7, 1995. Signed as a free agent by **Phoenix**, September 1, 1998.

ADAMS, Kevyn — TOR.

Center. Shoots right. 6'1", 195 lbs. Born, Washington, D.C., October 8, 1974. Boston's 1st choice, 25th overall, in 1993 Entry Draft.

			Regular Season																Playoffs							
Season	Club	League	GP	G	A	Pts	PIM	PP	SH	GW	S	%	+/-	TF	F%	H	SB	Min	GP	G	A	Pts	PIM	PP	SH	GW
1990-91	Niagara Scenics	NAJHL	55	17	20	37	24	....	....	....	....	....	....	....	....	....	....	....	....	....	....	....	....	....	....	....
1991-92	Niagara Scenics	NAJHL	40	25	33	58	51	....	....	....	....	....	....	....	....	....	....	....	....	....	....	....	....	....	....	....
1992-93	U. of Miami-Ohio	CCHA	40	17	15	32	18	....	....	....	....	....	....	....	....	....	....	....	....	....	....	....	....	....	....	....
1993-94	U. of Miami-Ohio	CCHA	36	15	28	43	24	....	....	....	....	....	....	....	....	....	....	....	....	....	....	....	....	....	....	....
	United States	WJC-A	7	3	4	7	2	....	....	....	....	....	....	....	....	....	....	....	....	....	....	....	....	....	....	....
1994-95	U. of Miami-Ohio	CCHA	38	20	29	49	30	....	....	....	....	....	....	....	....	....	....	....	....	....	....	....	....	....	....	....
1995-96	U. of Miami-Ohio	CCHA	36	17	30	47	30	....	....	....	....	....	....	....	....	....	....	....	....	....	....	....	....	....	....	....
1996-97	Grand Rapids	IHL	82	22	25	47	47	....	....	....	....	....	....	....	....	....	....	....	5	1	1	2	4	....	....	....
1997-98	**Toronto**	**NHL**	**5**	**0**	**0**	**0**	**7**	**0**	**0**	**0**	**3**	**0.0**	**0**	....	....	....	....	....	....	....	....	....	....	....	....	....
	St. John's	AHL	59	17	20	37	99	....	....	....	....	....	....	....	....	....	....	....	4	0	0	0	4	....	....	....
1998-99	**Toronto**	**NHL**	**1**	**0**	**0**	**0**	**0**	**0**	**0**	**0**	**1**	**0.0**	**0**	**9**	**44.4**	**2**	**0**	**7:56**	**7**	**0**	**2**	**2**	**14**	**0**	**0**	**0**
	St. John's	AHL	80	15	35	50	85	....	....	....	....	....	....	....	....	....	....	....	5	2	0	2	4	....	....	....
	NHL Totals		**6**	**0**	**0**	**0**	**7**	**0**	**0**	**0**	**4**	**0.0**		**9**	**44.4**	**2**	**0**	**7:56**	**7**	**0**	**2**	**2**	**14**	**0**	**0**	**0**

CCHA Second All-Star Team (1995)

Signed as a free agent by **Toronto**, August 7, 1997.

AIVAZOFF, Micah

(A-vuh-zahf, MIGH-kuh)

Center. Shoots left. 6', 195 lbs. Born, Powell River, B.C., May 4, 1969. Los Angeles' 6th choice, 109th overall, in 1988 Entry Draft.

Season	Club	League	GP	G	A	Pts	PIM	PP	SH	GW	S	%	+/-	TF	F%	H	SB	Min	GP	G	A	Pts	PIM	PP	SH	GW
1985-86	Powell River	BCAHA	STATISTICS NOT AVAILABLE																							
	Victoria	WHL	25	3	4	7	25	....	....	....	....	....	....	....	....	....	....	....	....	....	....	....	....	....	....	....
1986-87	Victoria	WHL	72	18	39	57	112	....	....	....	....	....	....	....	....	....	....	....	5	1	0	1	2	....	....	....
1987-88	Victoria	WHL	69	26	57	83	79	....	....	....	....	....	....	....	....	....	....	....	8	3	4	7	14	....	....	....
1988-89	Victoria	WHL	70	35	65	100	136	....	....	....	....	....	....	....	....	....	....	....	8	5	7	12	2	....	....	....
1989-90	New Haven	AHL	77	20	39	59	71	....	....	....	....	....	....	....	....	....	....	....	....	....	....	....	....	....	....	....
1990-91	New Haven	AHL	79	11	29	40	84	....	....	....	....	....	....	....	....	....	....	....	....	....	....	....	....	....	....	....
1991-92	Adirondack	AHL	61	9	20	29	50	....	....	....	....	....	....	....	....	....	....	....	19	2	8	10	25	....	....	....
1992-93	Adirondack	AHL	79	32	53	85	100	....	....	....	....	....	....	....	....	....	....	....	11	8	6	14	10	....	....	....
1993-94	**Detroit**	**NHL**	**59**	**4**	**4**	**8**	**38**	**0**	**0**	**0**	**52**	**7.7**	**–1**	....	....	....	....	....	....	....	....	....	....	....	....	....
1994-95	**Edmonton**	**NHL**	**21**	**0**	**1**	**1**	**2**	**0**	**0**	**0**	**6**	**0.0**	**–2**	....	....	....	....	....	....	....	....	....	....	....	....	....
1995-96	**NY Islanders**	**NHL**	**12**	**0**	**1**	**1**	**6**	**0**	**0**	**0**	**8**	**0.0**	**–6**	....	....	....	....	....	....	....	....	....	....	....	....	....
	Utah	IHL	59	14	21	35	58	....	....	....	....	....	....	....	....	....	....	....	22	3	5	8	33	....	....	....
1996-97	Binghamton	AHL	75	12	36	48	70	....	....	....	....	....	....	....	....	....	....	....	4	1	1	2	0	....	....	....
1997-98	San Antonio	IHL	54	13	33	46	33	....	....	....	....	....	....	....	....	....	....	....	....	....	....	....	....	....	....	....
	ERC Ingolstadt	German-2	19	10	19	29	59	....	....	....	....	....	....	....	....	....	....	....	....	....	....	....	....	....	....	....
1998-99	Utah	IHL	79	25	22	47	67	....	....	....	....	....	....	....	....	....	....	....	....	....	....	....	....	....	....	....
	NHL Totals		**92**	**4**	**6**	**10**	**46**	**0**	**0**	**0**	**66**	**6.1**		....	....	....	....	....	....	....	....	....	....	....	....	....

Signed as a free agent by **Detroit**, March 18, 1993. Claimed by **Pittsburgh** from **Detroit** in Waiver Draft, January 18, 1995. Claimed by **Edmonton** from **Pittsburgh** in Waiver Draft, January 18, 1995. Signed as a free agent by **NY Islanders**, August 23, 1995. Signed as a free agent by **NY Rangers**, August 23, 1996.

ALBELIN, Tommy — CGY.

(AL-buh-LEEN)

Defense. Shoots left. 6'1", 195 lbs. Born, Stockholm, Sweden, May 21, 1964. Quebec's 7th choice, 158th overall, in 1983 Entry Draft.

Season	Club	League	GP	G	A	Pts	PIM	PP	SH	GW	S	%	+/-	TF	F%	H	SB	Min	GP	G	A	Pts	PIM	PP	SH	GW
1982-83	Djurgardens IF	Sweden	19	2	5	7	4	....	....	....	....	....	....	....	....	....	....	....	6	1	0	1	2	....	....	....
1983-84	Djurgardens IF	Sweden	30	9	5	14	26	....	....	....	....	....	....	....	....	....	....	....	4	0	1	1	2	....	....	....
1984-85	Djurgardens IF	Sweden	32	9	8	17	22	....	....	....	....	....	....	....	....	....	....	....	8	2	1	3	4	....	....	....
1985-86	Djurgardens IF	Sweden	35	4	8	12	26	....	....	....	....	....	....	....	....	....	....	....	....	....	....	....	....	....	....	....
1986-87	Djurgardens IF	Sweden	33	7	5	12	49	....	....	....	....	....	....	....	....	....	....	....	2	0	0	0	0	....	....	....
1987-88	**Quebec**	**NHL**	**60**	**3**	**23**	**26**	**47**	**0**	**0**	**0**	**98**	**3.1**	**–7**	....	....	....	....	....	....	....	....	....	....	....	....	....
1988-89	**Quebec**	**NHL**	**14**	**2**	**4**	**6**	**27**	**1**	**0**	**1**	**16**	**12.5**	**–6**	....	....	....	....	....	....	....	....	....	....	....	....	....
	Halifax	AHL	8	2	5	7	4	....	....	....	....	....	....	....	....	....	....	....	....	....	....	....	....	....	....	....
	New Jersey	**NHL**	**46**	**7**	**24**	**31**	**40**	**1**	**1**	**1**	**82**	**8.5**	**18**	....	....	....	....	....	....	....	....	....	....	....	....	....
1989-90	**New Jersey**	**NHL**	**68**	**6**	**23**	**29**	**63**	**4**	**0**	**0**	**125**	**4.8**	**–1**	....	....	....	....	....	....	....	....	....	....	....	....	....
1990-91	**New Jersey**	**NHL**	**47**	**2**	**12**	**14**	**44**	**1**	**0**	**0**	**66**	**3.0**	**1**	....	....	....	....	....	**3**	**0**	**1**	**1**	**2**	**0**	**0**	**0**
	Utica	AHL	14	4	2	6	10	....	....	....	....	....	....	....	....	....	....	....	....	....	....	....	....	....	....	....
1991-92	**New Jersey**	**NHL**	**19**	**0**	**4**	**4**	**4**	**0**	**0**	**0**	**18**	**0.0**	**7**	....	....	....	....	....	**1**	**1**	**1**	**2**	**0**	**0**	**0**	**0**
	Utica	AHL	11	4	6	10	4	....	....	....	....	....	....	....	....	....	....	....	....	....	....	....	....	....	....	....
1992-93	**New Jersey**	**NHL**	**36**	**1**	**5**	**6**	**14**	**1**	**0**	**1**	**33**	**3.0**	**0**	....	....	....	....	....	**5**	**2**	**0**	**2**	**0**	**1**	**0**	**1**
1993-94	**New Jersey**	**NHL**	**62**	**2**	**17**	**19**	**36**	**1**	**0**	**1**	**62**	**3.2**	**20**	....	....	....	....	....	**20**	**2**	**5**	**7**	**14**	**1**	**0**	**1**
	Albany	AHL	4	0	2	2	17	....	....	....	....	....	....	....	....	....	....	....	....	....	....	....	....	....	....	....
1994-95♦	**New Jersey**	**NHL**	**48**	**5**	**10**	**15**	**20**	**2**	**0**	**0**	**60**	**8.3**	**9**	....	....	....	....	....	**20**	**1**	**7**	**8**	**2**	**0**	**0**	**0**
1995-96	**New Jersey**	**NHL**	**53**	**1**	**12**	**13**	**14**	**0**	**0**	**0**	**90**	**1.1**	**0**	....	....	....	....	....	....	....	....	....	....	....	....	....
	Calgary	**NHL**	**20**	**0**	**1**	**1**	**4**	**0**	**0**	**0**	**31**	**0.0**	**1**	....	....	....	....	....	**4**	**0**	**0**	**0**	**0**	**0**	**0**	**0**
1996-97	**Calgary**	**NHL**	**72**	**4**	**11**	**15**	**14**	**2**	**0**	**0**	**103**	**3.9**	**–8**	....	....	....	....	....	....	....	....	....	....	....	....	....
1997-98	**Calgary**	**NHL**	**69**	**2**	**17**	**19**	**32**	**1**	**0**	**2**	**88**	**2.3**	**9**	....	....	....	....	....	....	....	....	....	....	....	....	....
	Sweden	Olympics	3	0	0	0	4	....	....	....	....	....	....	....	....	....	....	....	....	....	....	....	....	....	....	....
1998-99	**Calgary**	**NHL**	**60**	**1**	**5**	**6**	**8**	**0**	**0**	**0**	**54**	**1.9**	**–11**	**1**	**0.0**	**34**	**55**	**19:08**	....	....	....	....	....	....	....	....
	NHL Totals		**674**	**36**	**168**	**204**	**367**	**14**	**1**	**6**	**926**	**3.9**		**1**	**0.0**	**34**	**55**	**19:08**	**53**	**6**	**14**	**20**	**18**	**2**	**0**	**2**

Swedish World All-Star Team (1987, 1997)

Traded to **New Jersey** by **Quebec** for New Jersey's 4th round choice (Niclas Andersson) in 1989 Entry Draft, December 12, 1988. Traded to **Calgary** by **New Jersey** with Cale Hulse and Jocelyn Lemieux for Phil Housley and Dan Keczmer, February 26, 1996.

ALFREDSSON, Daniel — OTT.

(AHL-frehd-suhn)

Right wing. Shoots right. 5'11", 194 lbs. Born, Goteborg, Sweden, December 11, 1972. Ottawa's 5th choice, 133rd overall, in 1994 Entry Draft.

Season	Club	League	GP	G	A	Pts	PIM	PP	SH	GW	S	%	+/-	TF	F%	H	SB	Min	GP	G	A	Pts	PIM	PP	SH	GW
1990-91	IF Molndal	Sweden-2	3	0	0	0	2	....	....	....	....	....	....	....	....	....	....	....	8	4	4	8	4	....	....	....
1991-92	IF Molndal	Sweden-2	32	12	8	20	43	....	....	....	....	....	....	....	....	....	....	....	....	....	....	....	....	....	....	....
1992-93	V. Frolunda	Sweden	20	1	5	6	8	....	....	....	....	....	....	....	....	....	....	....	....	....	....	....	....	....	....	....
1993-94	V. Frolunda	Sweden	39	20	10	30	18	....	....	....	....	....	....	....	....	....	....	....	4	1	1	2	....	....	....	....
1994-95	V. Frolunda	Sweden	22	7	11	18	22	....	....	....	....	....	....	....	....	....	....	....	....	....	....	....	....	....	....	....
1995-96	**Ottawa**	**NHL**	**82**	**26**	**35**	**61**	**28**	**8**	**2**	**3**	**212**	**12.3**	**–18**	....	....	....	....	....	....	....	....	....	....	....	....	....
1996-97	**Ottawa**	**NHL**	**76**	**24**	**47**	**71**	**30**	**11**	**1**	**1**	**247**	**9.7**	**5**	....	....	....	....	....	**7**	**5**	**2**	**7**	**6**	**3**	**0**	**2**
1997-98	**Ottawa**	**NHL**	**55**	**17**	**28**	**45**	**18**	**7**	**0**	**7**	**149**	**11.4**	**7**	....	....	....	....	....	**11**	**7**	**2**	**9**	**20**	**2**	**1**	**1**
	Sweden	Olympics	4	2	3	5	2	....	....	....	....	....	....	....	....	....	....	....	....	....	....	....	....	....	....	....
1998-99	**Ottawa**	**NHL**	**58**	**11**	**22**	**33**	**14**	**3**	**0**	**5**	**163**	**6.7**	**8**	**7**	**57.1**	**67**	**21**	**17:22**	**4**	**1**	**2**	**3**	**4**	**1**	**0**	**0**
	NHL Totals		**271**	**78**	**132**	**210**	**90**	**29**	**3**	**16**	**771**	**10.1**		**7**	**57.1**	**67**	**21**	**17:22**	**22**	**13**	**6**	**19**	**30**	**6**	**1**	**3**

NHL All-Rookie Team (1996) • Won Calder Memorial Trophy (1996)

Played in NHL All-Star Game (1996, 1997, 1998)

ALLEN, Chris — FLA.

Defense. Shoots right. 6'2", 197 lbs. Born, Chatham, Ont., May 8, 1978. Florida's 2nd choice, 60th overall, in 1996 Entry Draft.

Season	Club	League	GP	G	A	Pts	PIM	PP	SH	GW	S	%	+/-	TF	F%	H	SB	Min	GP	G	A	Pts	PIM	PP	SH	GW
1992-93	Blenheim	OJHL-C	3	0	0	0	0	....	....	....	....	....	....	....	....	....	....	....	....	....	....	....	....	....	....	....
1993-94	Leamington	OJHL-B	52	6	20	26	38	....	....	....	....	....	....	....	....	....	....	....	....	....	....	....	....	....	....	....
1994-95	Kingston	OHL	43	3	5	8	15	....	....	....	....	....	....	....	....	....	....	....	2	0	0	0	0	....	....	....
1995-96	Kingston	OHL	55	21	18	39	58	....	....	....	....	....	....	....	....	....	....	....	6	0	2	2	8	....	....	....
1996-97	Kingston	OHL	61	14	29	43	81	....	....	....	....	....	....	....	....	....	....	....	5	1	2	3	4	....	....	....
	Carolina	AHL	9	0	0	0	2	....	....	....	....	....	....	....	....	....	....	....	....	....	....	....	....	....	....	....

Season	Club	League	GP	G	A	Pts	PIM	PP	SH	GW	S	%	+/–	TF	F%	H	SB	Min	GP	G	A	Pts	PIM	PP	SH	GW
			Regular Season																Playoffs							
1997-98	Kingston	OHL	66	38	57	95	91	....	....	....	....	....	....	....	....	....	....	....	10	4	2	6	6	....	....	....
	Florida	**NHL**	**1**	**0**	**0**	**0**	**2**	**0**	**0**	**0**	**1**	**0.0**	**0**	....	....	....	....	....	....	....	....	....	....	....	....	....
1998-99	**Florida**	**NHL**	**1**	**0**	**0**	**0**	**0**	**0**	**0**	**0**	**0**	**0.0**	**1**	**0**	**0.0**	**0**	**0**	**12:35**	....	....	....	....	....	....	....	....
	New Haven	AHL	58	8	27	35	43	....	....	....	....	....	....	....	....	....	....	....	....	....	....	....	....	....	....	....
	NHL Totals		**2**	**0**	**0**	**0**	**2**	**0**	**0**	**0**	**1**	**0.0**		**0**	**0.0**	**0**	**0**	**12:35**	....	....	....	....	....	....	....	....

OHL First All-Star Team (1998) • Canadian Major Junior First All-Star Team (1998)

ALLEN, Peter

Defense. Shoots right. 6'2", 200 lbs. Born, Calgary, Alta., March 6, 1970. Boston's 1st choice, 24th overall, in 1991 Supplemental Draft.

Season	Club	League	GP	G	A	Pts	PIM	PP	SH	GW	S	%	+/–	TF	F%	H	SB	Min	GP	G	A	Pts	PIM	PP	SH	GW
1989-90	Yale University	ECAC	26	2	4	6	16	....	....	....	....	....	....	....	....	....	....	....	....	....	....	....	....	....	....	....
1990-91	Yale University	ECAC	17	0	6	6	14	....	....	....	....	....	....	....	....	....	....	....	....	....	....	....	....	....	....	....
1991-92	Yale University	ECAC	26	5	13	18	26	....	....	....	....	....	....	....	....	....	....	....	....	....	....	....	....	....	....	....
1992-93	Yale University	ECAC	30	3	15	18	32	....	....	....	....	....	....	....	....	....	....	....	....	....	....	....	....	....	....	....
1993-94	Richmond	ECHL	52	2	16	18	62	....	....	....	....	....	....	....	....	....	....	....	....	....	....	....	....	....	....	....
	P.E.I. Senators	AHL	6	0	1	1	6	....	....	....	....	....	....	....	....	....	....	....	....	....	....	....	....	....	....	....
1994-95	Canada	Nat-Team	52	5	15	20	36	....	....	....	....	....	....	....	....	....	....	....	....	....	....	....	....	....	....	....
1995-96	**Pittsburgh**	**NHL**	**8**	**0**	**0**	**0**	**8**	**0**	**0**	**0**	**2**	**0.0**	**2**	....	....	....	....	....	....	....	....	....	....	....	....	....
	Cleveland	IHL	65	3	45	48	55	....	....	....	....	....	....	....	....	....	....	....	3	0	0	0	2	....	....	....
1996-97	Cleveland	IHL	81	14	31	45	75	....	....	....	....	....	....	....	....	....	....	....	14	0	6	6	24	....	....	....
1997-98	Kentucky	AHL	72	0	18	18	73	....	....	....	....	....	....	....	....	....	....	....	3	0	1	1	4	....	....	....
1998-99	Kentucky	AHL	72	3	17	20	48	....	....	....	....	....	....	....	....	....	....	....	12	1	1	2	8	....	....	....
	NHL Totals		**8**	**0**	**0**	**0**	**8**	**0**	**0**	**0**	**2**	**0.0**		....	....	....	....	....	....	....	....	....	....	....	....	....

Signed as a free agent by **Pittsburgh**, August 10, 1995. Signed as a free agent by **San Jose**, August 19, 1997.

ALLISON, Jamie — CHI.

Defense. Shoots left. 6'1", 195 lbs. Born, Lindsay, Ont., May 13, 1975. Calgary's 2nd choice, 44th overall, in 1993 Entry Draft.

Season	Club	League	GP	G	A	Pts	PIM	PP	SH	GW	S	%	+/–	TF	F%	H	SB	Min	GP	G	A	Pts	PIM	PP	SH	GW
1990-91	Waterloo	OJHL-B	45	3	8	11	91	....	....	....	....	....	....	....	....	....	....	....	....	....	....	....	....	....	....	....
1991-92	Windsor	OHL	59	4	8	12	70	....	....	....	....	....	....	....	....	....	....	....	4	1	1	2	2	....	....	....
1992-93	Detroit	OHL	61	0	13	13	64	....	....	....	....	....	....	....	....	....	....	....	15	2	5	7	23	....	....	....
1993-94	Detroit	OHL	40	2	22	24	69	....	....	....	....	....	....	....	....	....	....	....	17	2	9	11	35	....	....	....
1994-95	Detroit	OHL	50	1	14	15	119	....	....	....	....	....	....	....	....	....	....	....	18	2	7	9	35	....	....	....
	Calgary	**NHL**	**1**	**0**	**0**	**0**	**0**	**0**	**0**	**0**	**0**	**0.0**	**0**	....	....	....	....	....	....	....	....	....	....	....	....	....
1995-96	Saint John	AHL	71	3	16	19	223	....	....	....	....	....	....	....	....	....	....	....	14	0	2	2	16	....	....	....
1996-97	**Calgary**	**NHL**	**20**	**0**	**0**	**0**	**35**	**0**	**0**	**0**	**8**	**0.0**	**–4**	....	....	....	....	....	....	....	....	....	....	....	....	....
	Saint John	AHL	46	3	6	9	139	....	....	....	....	....	....	....	....	....	....	....	5	0	1	1	4	....	....	....
1997-98	**Calgary**	**NHL**	**43**	**3**	**8**	**11**	**104**	**0**	**0**	**1**	**27**	**11.1**	**3**	....	....	....	....	....	....	....	....	....	....	....	....	....
	Saint John	AHL	16	0	5	5	49	....	....	....	....	....	....	....	....	....	....	....	....	....	....	....	....	....	....	....
1998-99	Saint John	AHL	5	0	0	0	23	....	....	....	....	....	....	....	....	....	....	....	....	....	....	....	....	....	....	....
	Chicago	**NHL**	**39**	**2**	**2**	**4**	**62**	**0**	**0**	**0**	**24**	**8.3**	**0**	**0**	**0.0**	**50**	**12**	**14:01**	....	....	....	....	....	....	....	....
	Indianapolis	IHL	3	1	0	1	10	....	....	....	....	....	....	....	....	....	....	....	....	....	....	....	....	....	....	....
	NHL Totals		**103**	**5**	**10**	**15**	**201**	**0**	**0**	**1**	**59**	**8.5**		**0**	**0.0**	**50**	**12**	**14:01**	....	....	....	....	....	....	....	....

Traded to **Chicago** by **Calgary** with Marty McInnis and Eric Andersson for Jeff Shantz and Steve Dubinsky, October 27, 1998.

ALLISON, Jason — BOS.

Center. Shoots right. 6'3", 205 lbs. Born, North York, Ont., May 29, 1975. Washington's 2nd choice, 17th overall, in 1993 Entry Draft.

Season	Club	League	GP	G	A	Pts	PIM	PP	SH	GW	S	%	+/–	TF	F%	H	SB	Min	GP	G	A	Pts	PIM	PP	SH	GW
1990-91	North York	MTHL	63	53	41	94	....	....	....	....	....	....	....	....	....	....	....	....	....	....	....	....	....	....	....	....
1991-92	London	OHL	65	11	19	30	15	....	....	....	....	....	....	....	....	....	....	....	7	0	0	0	0	....	....	....
1992-93	London	OHL	66	42	76	118	50	....	....	....	....	....	....	....	....	....	....	....	12	7	13	20	8	....	....	....
1993-94	London	OHL	56	55	87	*142	68	....	....	....	....	....	....	....	....	....	....	....	5	2	13	15	13	....	....	....
	Washington	**NHL**	**2**	**0**	**1**	**1**	**0**	**0**	**0**	**0**	**5**	**0.0**	**1**	....	....	....	....	....	....	....	....	....	....	....	....	....
	Portland	AHL	....	....	....	....	....	....	....	....	....	....	....	....	....	....	....	....	6	2	1	3	0	....	....	....
1994-95	London	OHL	15	15	21	36	43	....	....	....	....	....	....	....	....	....	....	....	....	....	....	....	....	....	....	....
	Washington	**NHL**	**12**	**2**	**1**	**3**	**6**	**2**	**0**	**0**	**9**	**22.2**	**–3**	....	....	....	....	....	....	....	....	....	....	....	....	....
	Portland	AHL	8	5	4	9	2	....	....	....	....	....	....	....	....	....	....	....	7	3	8	11	2	....	....	....
1995-96	**Washington**	**NHL**	**19**	**0**	**3**	**3**	**2**	**0**	**0**	**0**	**18**	**0.0**	**–3**	....	....	....	....	....	....	....	....	....	....	....	....	....
	Portland	AHL	57	28	41	69	42	....	....	....	....	....	....	....	....	....	....	....	6	1	6	7	9	....	....	....
1996-97	**Washington**	**NHL**	**53**	**5**	**17**	**22**	**25**	**1**	**0**	**1**	**71**	**7.0**	**–3**	....	....	....	....	....	....	....	....	....	....	....	....	....
	Boston	**NHL**	**19**	**3**	**9**	**12**	**9**	**1**	**0**	**0**	**28**	**10.7**	**–3**	....	....	....	....	....	....	....	....	....	....	....	....	....
1997-98	**Boston**	**NHL**	**81**	**33**	**50**	**83**	**60**	**5**	**0**	**8**	**158**	**20.9**	**33**	....	....	....	....	....	**6**	**2**	**6**	**8**	**4**	**1**	**0**	**0**
1998-99	**Boston**	**NHL**	**82**	**23**	**53**	**76**	**68**	**5**	**1**	**3**	**158**	**14.6**	**5**	**1760**	**52.2**	**91**	**28**	**22:23**	**12**	**2**	**9**	**11**	**6**	**1**	**0**	**0**
	NHL Totals		**268**	**66**	**134**	**200**	**170**	**14**	**1**	**12**	**447**	**14.8**		**1760**	**52.2**	**91**	**28**	**22:23**	**18**	**4**	**15**	**19**	**10**	**2**	**0**	**0**

OHL First All-Star Team (1994) • Canadian Major Junior First All-Star Team (1994) • Canadian Major Junior Player of the Year (1994)
Traded to **Boston** by **Washington** with Jim Carey, Anson Carter and Washington's 3rd round choice (Lee Goren) in 1997 Entry Draft for Bill Ranford, Adam Oates and Rick Tocchet, March 1, 1997.

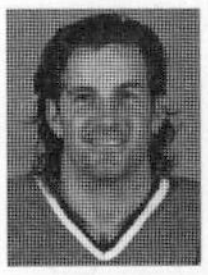

AMONTE, Tony — (eh-MAHN-tee) — CHI.

Right wing. Shoots left. 6', 200 lbs. Born, Hingham, MA, August 2, 1970. NY Rangers' 3rd choice, 68th overall, in 1988 Entry Draft.

Season	Club	League	GP	G	A	Pts	PIM	PP	SH	GW	S	%	+/–	TF	F%	H	SB	Min	GP	G	A	Pts	PIM	PP	SH	GW
1985-86	Thayer Academy	H.S.	2	0	0	0	0	....	....	....	....	....	....	....	....	....	....	....	....	....	....	....	....	....	....	....
1986-87	Thayer Academy	H.S.	25	25	32	57	....	....	....	....	....	....	....	....	....	....	....	....	....	....	....	....	....	....	....	....
1987-88	Thayer Academy	H.S.	28	30	38	68	....	....	....	....	....	....	....	....	....	....	....	....	....	....	....	....	....	....	....	....
1988-89	Thayer Academy	H.S.	25	35	38	73	....	....	....	....	....	....	....	....	....	....	....	....	....	....	....	....	....	....	....	....
1989-90	Boston University	H.E.	41	25	33	58	52	....	....	....	....	....	....	....	....	....	....	....	....	....	....	....	....	....	....	....
1990-91	Boston University	H.E.	38	31	37	68	82	....	....	....	....	....	....	....	....	....	....	....	....	....	....	....	....	....	....	....
	NY Rangers	**NHL**	....	....	....	....	....	....	....	....	....	....	....	....	....	....	....	....	**2**	**0**	**2**	**2**	**2**	....	....	....
1991-92	**NY Rangers**	**NHL**	**79**	**35**	**34**	**69**	**55**	**9**	**0**	**4**	**234**	**15.0**	**12**	....	....	....	....	....	**13**	**3**	**6**	**9**	**2**	**2**	**0**	**0**
1992-93	**NY Rangers**	**NHL**	**83**	**33**	**43**	**76**	**49**	**13**	**0**	**4**	**270**	**12.2**	**0**	....	....	....	....	....	....	....	....	....	....	....	....	....
1993-94	**NY Rangers**	**NHL**	**72**	**16**	**22**	**38**	**31**	**3**	**0**	**4**	**179**	**8.9**	**5**	....	....	....	....	....	....	....	....	....	....	....	....	....
	Chicago	**NHL**	**7**	**1**	**3**	**4**	**6**	**1**	**0**	**0**	**16**	**6.3**	**–5**	....	....	....	....	....	**6**	**4**	**2**	**6**	**4**	**1**	**0**	**1**
1994-95	Fassa	Italy	14	22	16	38	10	....	....	....	....	....	....	....	....	....	....	....	....	....	....	....	....	....	....	....
	Chicago	**NHL**	**48**	**15**	**20**	**35**	**41**	**6**	**1**	**3**	**105**	**14.3**	**7**	....	....	....	....	....	**16**	**3**	**3**	**6**	**10**	**0**	**0**	**0**
1995-96	**Chicago**	**NHL**	**81**	**31**	**32**	**63**	**62**	**5**	**4**	**5**	**216**	**14.4**	**10**	....	....	....	....	....	**7**	**2**	**4**	**6**	**6**	**1**	**0**	**0**
1996-97	**Chicago**	**NHL**	**81**	**41**	**36**	**77**	**64**	**9**	**2**	**4**	**266**	**15.4**	**35**	....	....	....	....	....	**6**	**4**	**2**	**6**	**8**	**0**	**0**	**0**
1997-98	**Chicago**	**NHL**	**82**	**31**	**42**	**73**	**66**	**7**	**3**	**5**	**296**	**10.5**	**21**	....	....	....	....	....	....	....	....	....	....	....	....	....
	United States	Olympics	4	0	1	1	4	....	....	....	....	....	....	....	....	....	....	....	....	....	....	....	....	....	....	....
1998-99	**Chicago**	**NHL**	**82**	**44**	**31**	**75**	**60**	**14**	**3**	**8**	**256**	**17.2**	**0**	**8**	**12.5**	**55**	**40**	**22:12**	....	....	....	....	....	....	....	....
	NHL Totals		**615**	**247**	**263**	**510**	**434**	**67**	**13**	**37**	**1838**	**13.4**		**8**	**12.5**	**55**	**40**	**22:12**	**50**	**16**	**19**	**35**	**32**	**4**	**0**	**1**

Hockey East Second All-Star Team (1991) • NCAA Championship All-Tournament Team (1991) • NHL/Upper Deck All-Rookie Team (1992)
Played in NHL All-Star Game (1997, 1998, 1999)
• Suffered season-ending knee injury in second game of season, October, 1985. Traded to **Chicago** by **NY Rangers** with the rights to Matt Oates for Stephane Matteau and Brian Noonan, March 21, 1994.

ANDERSSON, Erik — (AN-duhr-suhn)

Center. Shoots left. 6'3", 210 lbs. Born, Stockholm, Sweden, August 19, 1971. Calgary's 6th choice, 70th overall, in 1997 Entry Draft.

Season	Club	League	GP	G	A	Pts	PIM	PP	SH	GW	S	%	+/–	TF	F%	H	SB	Min	GP	G	A	Pts	PIM	PP	SH	GW
1989-90	Danderyd	Sweden-2	30	14	5	19	16	....	....	....	....	....	....	....	....	....	....	....	....	....	....	....	....	....	....	....
1990-91	AIK Solna	Sweden	32	1	1	2	10	....	....	....	....	....	....	....	....	....	....	....	....	....	....	....	....	....	....	....
1991-92	AIK Solna	Sweden	3	0	0	0	0	....	....	....	....	....	....	....	....	....	....	....	....	....	....	....	....	....	....	....
1992-93			DID NOT PLAY																							

			Regular Season																Playoffs							
Season	Club	League	GP	G	A	Pts	PIM	PP	SH	GW	S	%	+/-	TF	F%	H	SB	Min	GP	G	A	Pts	PIM	PP	SH	GW
1993-94	U. of Denver	WCHA	38	10	20	30	26																			
1994-95	U. of Denver	WCHA	42	12	19	31	42																			
1995-96	U. of Denver	WCHA	39	12	35	47	40																			
1996-97	U. of Denver	WCHA	39	17	17	34	42																			
1997-98	**Calgary**	**NHL**	**12**	**2**	**1**	**3**	**8**	**0**	**0**	**0**	**11**	**18.2**	**–4**													
	Saint John	AHL	29	5	9	14	29																			
1998-99	Saint John	AHL	5	0	0	0	4																			
	Indianapolis	IHL	48	5	7	12	24												4	0	0	0	44			
	NHL Totals		**12**	**2**	**1**	**3**	**8**	**0**	**0**	**0**	**11**	**18.2**														

• Re-entered NHL draft. Originally LA Kings' 5th choice, 112th overall, in 1990 Entry Draft. Traded to **Chicago** by **Calgary** with Marty McInnis and Jamie Allison for Jeff Shantz and Steve Dubinsky, October 27, 1998.

ANDERSSON, Mikael

(AN-duhr-suhn) **PHI.**

Left wing. Shoots left. 5'11", 181 lbs. Born, Malmo, Sweden, May 10, 1966. Buffalo's 1st choice, 18th overall, in 1984 Entry Draft.

			Regular Season																Playoffs							
Season	Club	League	GP	G	A	Pts	PIM	PP	SH	GW	S	%	+/-	TF	F%	H	SB	Min	GP	G	A	Pts	PIM	PP	SH	GW
1982-83	V. Frolunda	Sweden	1	1	0	1	0																			
1983-84	V. Frolunda	Sweden	18	0	3	3	6																			
1984-85	V. Frolunda	Sweden	30	16	11	27	18												6	3	2	5	2			
1985-86	**Buffalo**	**NHL**	**32**	**1**	**9**	**10**	**4**	**0**	**0**	**0**	**13**	**7.7**	**0**													
	Rochester	AHL	20	10	4	14	6																			
1986-87	**Buffalo**	**NHL**	**16**	**0**	**3**	**3**	**0**	**0**	**0**	**0**	**6**	**0.0**	**–2**													
	Rochester	AHL	42	6	20	26	14												9	1	2	3	2			
1987-88	**Buffalo**	**NHL**	**37**	**3**	**20**	**23**	**10**	**0**	**1**	**1**	**34**	**8.8**	**7**						**1**	**1**	**0**	**1**	**0**	**0**	**0**	**0**
	Rochester	AHL	35	12	24	36	16																			
1988-89	**Buffalo**	**NHL**	**14**	**0**	**1**	**1**	**4**	**0**	**0**	**0**	**12**	**0.0**	**–1**													
	Rochester	AHL	56	18	33	51	12																			
1989-90	**Hartford**	**NHL**	**50**	**13**	**24**	**37**	**6**	**1**	**2**	**2**	**86**	**15.1**	**0**						**5**	**0**	**3**	**3**	**2**	**0**	**0**	**0**
1990-91	**Hartford**	**NHL**	**41**	**4**	**7**	**11**	**8**	**0**	**0**	**0**	**57**	**7.0**	**0**													
	Springfield	AHL	26	7	22	29	10												18	*10	8	18	12			
1991-92	**Hartford**	**NHL**	**74**	**18**	**29**	**47**	**14**	**1**	**3**	**1**	**149**	**12.1**	**18**						**7**	**0**	**2**	**2**	**6**	**0**	**0**	**0**
1992-93	**Tampa Bay**	**NHL**	**77**	**16**	**11**	**27**	**14**	**3**	**2**	**4**	**169**	**9.5**	**–14**													
1993-94	**Tampa Bay**	**NHL**	**76**	**13**	**12**	**25**	**23**	**1**	**1**	**2**	**136**	**9.6**	**8**													
1994-95	V. Frolunda	Sweden	7	1	0	1	31																			
	Tampa Bay	**NHL**	**36**	**4**	**7**	**11**	**4**	**0**	**0**	**0**	**36**	**11.1**	**–3**													
1995-96	**Tampa Bay**	**NHL**	**64**	**8**	**11**	**19**	**2**	**0**	**0**	**1**	**104**	**7.7**	**0**						**6**	**1**	**1**	**2**	**0**	**0**	**0**	**0**
1996-97	**Tampa Bay**	**NHL**	**70**	**5**	**14**	**19**	**8**	**0**	**3**	**1**	**102**	**4.9**	**1**													
1997-98	**Tampa Bay**	**NHL**	**72**	**6**	**11**	**17**	**29**	**0**	**1**	**1**	**105**	**5.7**	**–4**													
	Sweden	Olympics	4	1	1	2	0																			
1998-99	**Tampa Bay**	**NHL**	**40**	**2**	**3**	**5**	**4**	**0**	**0**	**0**	**40**	**5.0**	**–8**	**38**	**34.2**	**10**	**13**	**12:39**								
	Philadelphia	**NHL**	**7**	**0**	**1**	**1**	**0**	**0**	**0**	**0**	**11**	**0.0**	**1**	**35**	**28.6**	**5**	**2**	**12:59**	**6**	**0**	**1**	**1**	**2**	**0**	**0**	**0**
	NHL Totals		**706**	**93**	**163**	**256**	**130**	**6**	**13**	**13**	**1060**	**8.8**		**73**	**31.5**	**15**	**15**	**12:42**	**25**	**2**	**7**	**9**	**10**	**0**	**0**	**0**

Claimed by **Hartford** from **Buffalo** in NHL Waiver Draft, October 2, 1989. Signed as a free agent by **Tampa Bay**, June 29, 1992. Traded to **Philadelphia** by **Tampa Bay** with Sandy McCarthy for Colin Forbes and Philadelphia's 4th round choice (Michal Lanisak) in 1999 Entry Draft, March 20, 1999.

ANDERSSON, Niklas

(AN-duhr-suhn) **NYI**

Left wing. Shoots left. 5'9", 175 lbs. Born, Kungalv, Sweden, May 20, 1971. Quebec's 5th choice, 68th overall, in 1989 Entry Draft.

			Regular Season																Playoffs							
Season	Club	League	GP	G	A	Pts	PIM	PP	SH	GW	S	%	+/-	TF	F%	H	SB	Min	GP	G	A	Pts	PIM	PP	SH	GW
1987-88	V. Frolunda	Sweden-2	15	5	5	10	6												8	6	4	10	4			
1988-89	V. Frolunda	Sweden-2	30	13	24	37	24												10	4	6	10	4			
1989-90	V. Frolunda	Sweden	38	10	21	31	14																			
1990-91	V. Frolunda	Sweden	22	6	10	16	16																			
1991-92	Halifax	AHL	57	8	26	34	41																			
1992-93	**Quebec**	**NHL**	**3**	**0**	**1**	**1**	**2**	**0**	**0**	**0**	**4**	**0.0**	**0**													
	Halifax	AHL	76	32	50	82	42																			
1993-94	Cornwall	AHL	42	18	34	52	8																			
1994-95	Denver	IHL	66	22	39	61	28												15	8	13	21	10			
1995-96	**NY Islanders**	**NHL**	**47**	**14**	**12**	**26**	**12**	**3**	**2**	**1**	**89**	**15.7**	**–3**													
	Utah	IHL	30	13	22	35	25																			
1996-97	**NY Islanders**	**NHL**	**74**	**12**	**31**	**43**	**57**	**1**	**1**	**1**	**122**	**9.8**	**4**													
1997-98	**San Jose**	**NHL**	**5**	**0**	**0**	**0**	**2**	**0**	**0**	**0**	**6**	**0.0**	**–1**													
	Kentucky	AHL	37	10	28	38	54																			
	Utah	IHL	21	6	20	26	24												4	3	1	4	4			
1998-99	Chicago	IHL	65	17	47	64	49												10	2	2	4	10			
	NHL Totals		**129**	**26**	**44**	**70**	**73**	**4**	**3**	**2**	**221**	**11.8**														

Signed as a free agent by **NY Islanders**, July 15, 1994. Signed as a free agent by **San Jose**, September 17, 1997. Signed as a free agent by **Toronto**, September 4, 1998. Traded to **NY Islanders** by **Toronto** for Craig Charron, August 17, 1999.

ANDREYCHUK, Dave

(AN-druh-chuhk) **BOS.**

Left wing. Shoots right. 6'4", 220 lbs. Born, Hamilton, Ont., September 29, 1963. Buffalo's 3rd choice, 16th overall, in 1982 Entry Draft.

			Regular Season																Playoffs							
Season	Club	League	GP	G	A	Pts	PIM	PP	SH	GW	S	%	+/-	TF	F%	H	SB	Min	GP	G	A	Pts	PIM	PP	SH	GW
1979-80	Hamilton	OMHA	21	25	24	49																				
1980-81	Oshawa	OHA	67	22	22	44	80												10	3	2	5	20			
1981-82	Oshawa	OHL	67	57	43	100	71												3	1	4	5	16			
1982-83	Oshawa	OHL	14	8	24	32	6																			
	Buffalo	**NHL**	**43**	**14**	**23**	**37**	**16**	**3**	**0**	**1**	**66**	**21.2**	**6**						**4**	**1**	**0**	**1**	**4**	**0**	**0**	**0**
1983-84	**Buffalo**	**NHL**	**78**	**38**	**42**	**80**	**42**	**10**	**0**	**7**	**178**	**21.3**	**20**						**2**	**0**	**1**	**1**	**2**	**0**	**0**	**0**
1984-85	**Buffalo**	**NHL**	**64**	**31**	**30**	**61**	**54**	**14**	**0**	**2**	**153**	**20.3**	**–4**						**5**	**4**	**2**	**6**	**4**	**0**	**0**	**2**
1985-86	**Buffalo**	**NHL**	**80**	**36**	**51**	**87**	**61**	**12**	**0**	**3**	**225**	**16.0**	**3**													
1986-87	**Buffalo**	**NHL**	**77**	**25**	**48**	**73**	**46**	**13**	**0**	**2**	**255**	**9.8**	**2**													
1987-88	**Buffalo**	**NHL**	**80**	**30**	**48**	**78**	**112**	**15**	**0**	**5**	**253**	**11.9**	**1**						**6**	**2**	**4**	**6**	**0**	**1**	**0**	**0**
1988-89	**Buffalo**	**NHL**	**56**	**28**	**24**	**52**	**40**	**7**	**0**	**3**	**145**	**19.3**	**0**						**5**	**0**	**3**	**3**	**0**	**0**	**0**	**0**
1989-90	**Buffalo**	**NHL**	**73**	**40**	**42**	**82**	**42**	**18**	**0**	**3**	**206**	**19.4**	**6**						**6**	**2**	**5**	**7**	**2**	**1**	**0**	**0**
1990-91	**Buffalo**	**NHL**	**80**	**36**	**33**	**69**	**32**	**13**	**0**	**4**	**234**	**15.4**	**11**						**6**	**2**	**2**	**4**	**8**	**1**	**0**	**0**
1991-92	**Buffalo**	**NHL**	**80**	**41**	**50**	**91**	**71**	**28**	**0**	**2**	**337**	**12.2**	**–9**						**7**	**1**	**3**	**4**	**12**	**0**	**0**	**0**
1992-93	**Buffalo**	**NHL**	**52**	**29**	**32**	**61**	**48**	**20**	**0**	**2**	**171**	**17.0**	**–8**													
	Toronto	**NHL**	**31**	**25**	**13**	**38**	**8**	**12**	**0**	**2**	**139**	**18.0**	**12**						**21**	**12**	**7**	**19**	**35**	**4**	**0**	**3**
1993-94	**Toronto**	**NHL**	**83**	**53**	**46**	**99**	**98**	**21**	**5**	**8**	**333**	**15.9**	**22**						**18**	**5**	**5**	**10**	**16**	**3**	**1**	**0**
1994-95	**Toronto**	**NHL**	**48**	**22**	**16**	**38**	**34**	**8**	**0**	**2**	**168**	**13.1**	**–7**						**7**	**3**	**2**	**5**	**25**	**2**	**0**	**0**
1995-96	**Toronto**	**NHL**	**61**	**20**	**24**	**44**	**54**	**12**	**2**	**3**	**200**	**10.0**	**–11**													
	New Jersey	**NHL**	**15**	**8**	**5**	**13**	**10**	**2**	**0**	**0**	**41**	**19.5**	**2**													
1996-97	**New Jersey**	**NHL**	**82**	**27**	**34**	**61**	**48**	**4**	**1**	**2**	**233**	**11.6**	**38**						**1**	**0**	**0**	**0**	**0**	**0**	**0**	**0**
1997-98	**New Jersey**	**NHL**	**75**	**14**	**34**	**48**	**26**	**4**	**0**	**2**	**180**	**7.8**	**19**						**6**	**1**	**0**	**1**	**4**	**1**	**0**	**0**
1998-99	**New Jersey**	**NHL**	**52**	**15**	**13**	**28**	**20**	**4**	**0**	**3**	**110**	**13.6**	**1**	**9**	**44.4**	**36**	**17**	**15:32**	**4**	**2**	**0**	**2**	**4**	**0**	**0**	**0**
	NHL Totals		**1210**	**532**	**608**	**1140**	**862**	**220**	**8**	**56**	**3627**	**14.7**		**9**	**44.4**	**36**	**17**	**15:32**	**98**	**35**	**34**	**69**	**116**	**13**	**1**	**5**

Played in NHL All-Star Game (1990, 1994)

Traded to **Toronto** by **Buffalo** with Daren Puppa and Buffalo's 1st round choice (Kenny Jonsson) in 1993 Entry Draft for Grant Fuhr and Toronto's 5th round choice (Kevin Popp) in 1995 Entry Draft, February 2, 1993. Traded to **New Jersey** by **Toronto** for New Jersey's 2nd round choice (Marek Posmyk) in 1996 Entry Draft and future considerations, March 13, 1996. Signed as a free agent by Boston, July 29, 1999

ANDRUSAK, Greg
(AN-druh-sak) **TOR.**

Defense. Shoots right. 6'1", 190 lbs. Born, Cranbrook, B.C., November 14, 1969. Pittsburgh's 5th choice, 88th overall, in 1988 Entry Draft.

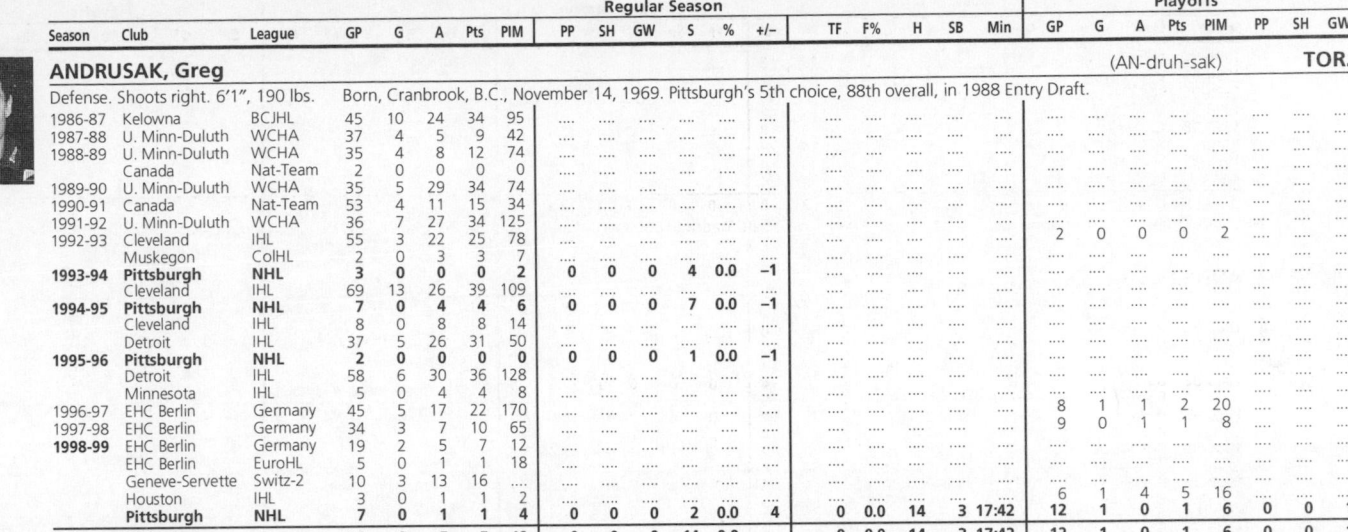

			Regular Season																Playoffs							
Season	Club	League	GP	G	A	Pts	PIM	PP	SH	GW	S	%	+/-	TF	F%	H	SB	Min	GP	G	A	Pts	PIM	PP	SH	GW
1986-87	Kelowna	BCJHL	45	10	24	34	95																			
1987-88	U. Minn-Duluth	WCHA	37	4	5	9	42																			
1988-89	U. Minn-Duluth	WCHA	35	4	8	12	74																			
	Canada	Nat-Team	2	0	0	0	0																			
1989-90	U. Minn-Duluth	WCHA	35	5	29	34	74																			
1990-91	Canada	Nat-Team	53	4	11	15	34																			
1991-92	U. Minn-Duluth	WCHA	36	7	27	34	125																			
1992-93	Cleveland	IHL	55	3	22	25	78												2	0	0	0	2			
	Muskegon	ColHL	2	0	3	3	7																			
1993-94	**Pittsburgh**	**NHL**	**3**	**0**	**0**	**0**	**2**	**0**	**0**	**0**	**4**	**0.0**	**–1**													
	Cleveland	IHL	69	13	26	39	109																			
1994-95	**Pittsburgh**	**NHL**	**7**	**0**	**4**	**4**	**6**	**0**	**0**	**0**	**7**	**0.0**	**–1**													
	Cleveland	IHL	8	0	8	8	14																			
	Detroit	IHL	37	5	26	31	50																			
1995-96	**Pittsburgh**	**NHL**	**2**	**0**	**0**	**0**	**0**	**0**	**0**	**0**	**1**	**0.0**	**–1**													
	Detroit	IHL	58	6	30	36	128																			
	Minnesota	IHL	5	0	4	4	8																			
1996-97	EHC Berlin	Germany	45	5	17	22	170												8	1	1	2	20			
1997-98	EHC Berlin	Germany	34	3	7	10	65												9	0	1	1	8			
1998-99	EHC Berlin	Germany	19	2	5	7	12																			
	EHC Berlin	EuroHL	5	0	1	1	18																			
	Geneve-Servette	Switz-2	10	3	13	16																				
	Houston	IHL	3	0	1	1	2												6	1	4	5	16			
	Pittsburgh	**NHL**	**7**	**0**	**1**	**1**	**4**	**0**	**0**	**0**	**2**	**0.0**	**4**	**0**	**0.0**	**14**	**3**	**17:42**	**12**	**1**	**0**	**1**	**6**	**0**	**0**	**1**
	NHL Totals		**19**	**0**	**5**	**5**	**12**	**0**	**0**	**0**	**14**	**0.0**		**0**	**0.0**	**14**	**3**	**17:42**	**12**	**1**	**0**	**1**	**6**	**0**	**0**	**1**

WCHA First All-Star Team (1992)

Signed as a free agent by **Pittsburgh**, March 19, 1999. Signed as a free agent by **Toronto**, July 19, 1999.

ARCHIBALD, Dave

Center/Left wing. Shoots left. 6'1", 210 lbs. Born, Chilliwack, B.C., April 14, 1969. Minnesota's 1st choice, 6th overall, in 1987 Entry Draft.

1983-84	Chilliwack	BCAHA	STATISTICS NOT AVAILABLE																							
	Portland	WHL	7	0	1	1	2																			
1984-85	Portland	WHL	47	7	11	18	10												3	0	2	2	0			
1985-86	Portland	WHL	70	29	35	64	56												15	6	7	13	11			
1986-87	Portland	WHL	65	50	57	107	40												20	10	18	28	11			
1987-88	**Minnesota**	**NHL**	**78**	**13**	**20**	**33**	**26**	**3**	**0**	**2**	**96**	**13.5**	**–17**													
1988-89	**Minnesota**	**NHL**	**72**	**14**	**19**	**33**	**14**	**7**	**0**	**2**	**105**	**13.3**	**–11**						**5**	**0**	**1**	**1**	**0**	**0**	**0**	**0**
1989-90	**Minnesota**	**NHL**	**12**	**1**	**5**	**6**	**6**	**1**	**0**	**1**	**26**	**3.8**	**1**													
	NY Rangers	**NHL**	**19**	**2**	**3**	**5**	**6**	**1**	**0**	**0**	**30**	**6.7**	**0**													
	Flint	IHL	41	14	38	52	16												4	3	2	5	0			
1990-91	Canada	Nat-Team	29	19	12	31	20																			
1991-92	Canada	Nat-Team	58	20	43	63	64																			
	Canada	Olympics	8	7	1	8	18																			
	HC Bolzano	Italy	5	4	3	7	16												7	8	5	13	7			
1992-93	Binghamton	AHL	8	6	3	9	10																			
	Ottawa	**NHL**	**44**	**9**	**6**	**15**	**32**	**6**	**0**	**0**	**93**	**9.7**	**–16**													
1993-94	**Ottawa**	**NHL**	**33**	**10**	**8**	**18**	**14**	**2**	**0**	**1**	**65**	**15.4**	**–7**													
1994-95	**Ottawa**	**NHL**	**14**	**2**	**2**	**4**	**10**	**0**	**0**	**1**	**27**	**7.4**	**–7**													
1995-96	**Ottawa**	**NHL**	**44**	**6**	**4**	**10**	**18**	**0**	**0**	**1**	**56**	**10.7**	**–14**													
	Utah	IHL	19	1	4	5	10																			
1996-97	**NY Islanders**	**NHL**	**7**	**0**	**0**	**0**	**4**	**0**	**0**	**0**	**4**	**0.0**	**–4**													
	Frankfurt	Germany	34	10	19	29	48												9	4	2	6	16			
1997-98	San Antonio	IHL	55	11	21	32	10																			
1998-99	Utah	IHL	76	23	25	48	32																			
	NHL Totals		**323**	**57**	**67**	**124**	**139**	**20**	**0**	**8**	**502**	**11.4**							**5**	**0**	**1**	**1**	**0**	**0**	**0**	**0**

Traded to **NY Rangers** by **Minnesota** for Jayson More, November 1, 1989. Traded to **Ottawa** by **NY Rangers** for Ottawa's 5th round choice (later traded to LA Kings — LA Kings selected Frederick Beaubien) in 1993 Entry Draft, November 5, 1992. Signed as a free agent by **NY Islanders**, October 10, 1996

ARMSTRONG, Derek
NYR

Center. Shoots right. 5'11", 188 lbs. Born, Ottawa, Ont., April 23, 1973. NY Islanders' 5th choice, 128th overall, in 1992 Entry Draft.

1989-90	Hawkesbury	OJHL	48	8	10	18	30																			
1990-91	Hawkesbury	OJHL	54	27	45	75	49																			
	Sudbury	OHL	2	0	2	2	0																			
1991-92	Sudbury	OHL	66	31	54	85	22												9	2	2	4	2			
1992-93	Sudbury	OHL	66	44	62	106	56												14	9	10	19	26			
1993-94	**NY Islanders**	**NHL**	**1**	**0**	**0**	**0**	**0**	**0**	**0**	**0**	**2**	**0.0**	**0**													
	Salt Lake	IHL	76	23	35	58	61																			
1994-95	Denver	IHL	59	13	18	31	65												6	0	2	2	0			
1995-96	**NY Islanders**	**NHL**	**19**	**1**	**3**	**4**	**14**	**0**	**0**	**0**	**23**	**4.3**	**–6**													
	Worcester	AHL	51	11	15	26	33												4	2	1	3	0			
1996-97	**NY Islanders**	**NHL**	**50**	**6**	**7**	**13**	**33**	**0**	**0**	**2**	**36**	**16.7**	**–8**													
	Utah	IHL	17	4	8	12	10												6	0	4	4	4			
1997-98	**Ottawa**	**NHL**	**9**	**2**	**0**	**2**	**9**	**0**	**0**	**1**	**8**	**25.0**	**1**													
	Detroit	IHL	10	0	1	1	2																			
	Hartford	AHL	54	16	30	46	40												15	2	6	8	22			
1998-99	**NY Rangers**	**NHL**	**3**	**0**	**0**	**0**	**0**	**0**	**0**	**0**	**1**	**0.0**	**0**	**0**	**0.0**	**0**	**0**	**2:50**								
	Hartford	AHL	59	29	51	80	73												7	5	4	9	10			
	NHL Totals		**82**	**9**	**10**	**19**	**56**	**0**	**0**	**3**	**70**	**12.9**		**0**	**0.0**	**0**	**0**	**2:50**								

Signed as a free agent by **Ottawa**, July 28, 1997. Signed as a free agent by **NY Rangers**, August 10, 1998.

ARNOTT, Jason
(AHR-nawt) **N.J.**

Center. Shoots right. 6'4", 220 lbs. Born, Collingwood, Ont., October 11, 1974. Edmonton's 1st choice, 7th overall, in 1993 Entry Draft.

1989-90	Stayner	OJHL-C	34	21	31	52	12																			
1990-91	Lindsay	OJHL-C	42	17	44	61	10																			
1991-92	Oshawa	OHL	57	9	15	24	12																			
1992-93	Oshawa	OHL	56	41	57	98	74												13	9	9	18	20			
1993-94	**Edmonton**	**NHL**	**78**	**33**	**35**	**68**	**104**	**10**	**0**	**4**	**194**	**17.0**	**1**													
1994-95	**Edmonton**	**NHL**	**42**	**15**	**22**	**37**	**128**	**7**	**0**	**1**	**156**	**9.6**	**–14**													
1995-96	**Edmonton**	**NHL**	**64**	**28**	**31**	**59**	**87**	**8**	**0**	**5**	**244**	**11.5**	**–6**													
1996-97	**Edmonton**	**NHL**	**67**	**19**	**38**	**57**	**92**	**10**	**1**	**2**	**248**	**7.7**	**–21**						**12**	**3**	**6**	**9**	**18**	**1**	**0**	**0**
1997-98	**Edmonton**	**NHL**	**35**	**5**	**13**	**18**	**78**	**1**	**0**	**0**	**100**	**5.0**	**–16**													
	New Jersey	**NHL**	**35**	**5**	**10**	**15**	**21**	**3**	**0**	**2**	**99**	**5.1**	**–8**						**5**	**0**	**2**	**2**	**0**	**0**	**0**	**0**

Season	Club	League	GP	G	A	Pts	PIM	PP	SH	GW	S	%	+/-	TF	F%	H	SB	Min	GP	G	A	Pts	PIM	PP	SH	GW
												Regular Season										Playoffs				
1998-99	New Jersey	NHL	74	27	27	54	79	8	0	3	200	13.5	10	872	49.3	196	16	15:24	7	2	2	4	4	1	0	0
	NHL Totals		395	132	176	308	589	47	1	17	1241	10.6		872	49.3	196	16	15:24	24	5	10	15	22	2	0	0

NHL/Upper Deck All-Rookie Team (1994)
Played in NHL All-Star Game (1997)
Traded to **New Jersey** by **Edmonton** with Bryan Muir for Valeri Zelepukin and Bill Guerin, January 4, 1998.

ARVEDSON, Magnus   (AHR-vehd-suhn, MAGH-nuhs)   OTT.

Center. Shoots left. 6'2", 198 lbs. Born, Karlstad, Swe., November 25, 1971. Ottawa's 4th choice, 119th overall, in 1997 Entry Draft.

Season	Club	League	GP	G	A	Pts	PIM	PP	SH	GW	S	%	+/-	TF	F%	H	SB	Min	GP	G	A	Pts	PIM	PP	SH	GW
1990-91	Orebro IK	Sweden-2	29	7	11	18	12												2	0	1	1	2			
1991-92	Orebro IK	Sweden-2	32	12	21	33	30												7	4	4	8	4			
1992-93	Orebro IK	Sweden-2	36	11	18	29	34												6	2	1	3	0			
1993-94	Farjestads BK	Sweden	16	1	7	8	10																			
1994-95	Farjestads BK	Sweden	36	1	6	7	45												4	0	0	0	6			
1995-96	Farjestads BK	Sweden	40	10	14	24	40												8	0	3	3	10			
1996-97	Farjestads BK	Sweden	48	13	11	24	36												14	4	7	11	8			
	Farjestads	EuroHL	5	1	0	1	2												2	0	1	1	2			
1997-98	**Ottawa**	**NHL**	61	11	15	26	36	0	1	0	90	12.2	2						11	0	1	1	6	0	0	0
1998-99	**Ottawa**	**NHL**	80	21	26	47	50	0	4	6	136	15.4	33	25	20.0	48	42	17:08	3	0	1	1	2	0	0	0
	NHL Totals		141	32	41	73	86	0	5	6	226	14.2		25	20.0	48	42	17:08	14	0	2	2	8	0	0	0

ASHAM, Arron   (ASH-uhm, AIR-uhn)   MTL.

Right wing. Shoots right. 5'11", 194 lbs. Born, Portage La Prairie, Man., April 13, 1978. Montreal's 3rd choice, 71st overall, in 1996 Entry Draft.

Season	Club	League	GP	G	A	Pts	PIM	PP	SH	GW	S	%	+/-	TF	F%	H	SB	Min	GP	G	A	Pts	PIM	PP	SH	GW
1993-94	Portage	MAHA	21	18	19	37	82																			
1994-95	Red Deer	WHL	62	11	16	27	126																			
1995-96	Red Deer	WHL	70	32	45	77	174												10	6	3	9	20			
1996-97	Red Deer	WHL	67	45	51	96	149												16	12	14	26	36			
1997-98	Red Deer	WHL	67	43	49	92	153												5	0	2	2	8			
	Fredericton	AHL	2	1	1	2	0												2	0	1	1	0			
1998-99	**Montreal**	**NHL**	7	0	0	0	0	0	0	0	5	0.0	-4	0	0.0	8	2	7:27								
	Fredericton	AHL	60	16	18	34	118												13	8	6	14	11			
	NHL Totals		7	0	0	0	0	0	0	0	5	0.0		0	0.0	8	2	7:27								

ATCHEYNUM, Blair   (ATCH-uh-num)

Right wing. Shoots right. 6'2", 210 lbs. Born, Estevan, Sask., April 20, 1969. Hartford's 2nd choice, 52nd overall, in 1989 Entry Draft.

Season	Club	League	GP	G	A	Pts	PIM	PP	SH	GW	S	%	+/-	TF	F%	H	SB	Min	GP	G	A	Pts	PIM	PP	SH	GW
1984-85	North Battleford	SAHA	25	25	21	46	106																			
1985-86	North Battleford	SJHL	33	16	14	30	41																			
	Saskatoon	WHL	19	1	4	5	22												6	2	0	2	6			
1986-87	Saskatoon	WHL	21	0	4	4	4																			
	Swift Current	WHL	5	2	1	3	0																			
	Moose Jaw	WHL	12	3	0	3	2																			
1987-88	Moose Jaw	WHL	60	32	16	48	52																			
1988-89	Moose Jaw	WHL	71	70	68	138	70												7	2	5	7	13			
1989-90	Binghamton	AHL	78	20	21	41	45																			
1990-91	Springfield	AHL	72	25	27	52	42												13	0	6	6	6			
1991-92	Springfield	AHL	62	16	21	37	64												6	1	1	2	2			
1992-93	**Ottawa**	**NHL**	4	0	1	1	0	0	0	0	2	0.0	-3													
	New Haven	AHL	51	16	18	34	47																			
1993-94	Columbus	ECHL	16	15	12	27	10																			
	Portland	AHL	2	0	0	0	0																			
	Springfield	AHL	40	18	22	40	13												6	0	2	2	0			
1994-95	Minnesota	IHL	17	4	6	10	7																			
	Worcester	AHL	55	17	29	46	26																			
1995-96	Cape Breton	AHL	79	30	42	72	65																			
1996-97	Hershey	AHL	77	42	45	87	57												13	6	11	17	6			
1997-98	**St. Louis**	**NHL**	61	11	15	26	10	0	1	3	103	10.7	5						10	0	0	0	2	0	0	0
1998-99	**Nashville**	**NHL**	53	8	6	14	16	2	0	1	70	11.4	-10	5	40.0	28	26	14:54								
	St. Louis	NHL	12	2	2	4	2	0	0	1	23	8.7	2	2	0.0	12	5	15:38	13	1	3	4	6	0	0	0
	NHL Totals		130	21	24	45	28	2	1	5	198	10.6		7	28.6	40	31	15:02	23	1	3	4	8	0	0	0

WHL First All-Star Team (1989) • AHL First All-Star Team (1997)
Claimed by **Ottawa** from **Hartford** in Expansion Draft, June 18, 1992. Signed as a free agent by **St. Louis**, September 15, 1997. Claimed by **Nashville** from **St. Louis** in Expansion Draft, June 26, 1998. Traded to **St. Louis** by **Nashville** for St. Louis' 6th round choice in 2000 Entry Draft, March 23, 1999.

AUBIN, Serge   (oh-BEHN)   COL.

Center. Shoots left. 6'1", 194 lbs. Born, Val d'Or, Que., February 15, 1975. Pittsburgh's 9th choice, 161st overall, in 1994 Entry Draft.

Season	Club	League	GP	G	A	Pts	PIM	PP	SH	GW	S	%	+/-	TF	F%	H	SB	Min	GP	G	A	Pts	PIM	PP	SH	GW
1990-91	Temiscaminque	QAAA	27	2	4	6	10																			
1991-92	Temiscaminque	QAAA	42	28	32	60	36																			
1992-93	Drummondville	QMJHL	65	16	34	50	30												8	0	1	1	16			
1993-94	Granby	QMJHL	63	42	32	74	80												7	2	3	5	8			
1994-95	Granby	QMJHL	60	37	73	110	55												11	8	15	23	4			
1995-96	Hampton Roads	ECHL	62	24	62	86	74												3	1	4	5	10			
	Cleveland	IHL	2	0	0	0	0												2	0	0	0	0			
1996-97	Cleveland	IHL	57	9	16	25	38												2	0	0	0	0			
1997-98	Syracuse	AHL	55	6	14	20	57																			
	Hershey	AHL	5	2	1	3	0												7	1	3	4	6			
1998-99	Hershey	AHL	64	30	39	69	58												3	0	1	1	2			
	Colorado	**NHL**	1	0	0	0	0	0	0	0	1	0.0	0	1	0.0	0	0	4:16								
	NHL Totals		1	0	0	0	0	0	0	0	1	0.0		1	0.0	0	0	4:16								

Signed as a free agent by **Hershey** (AHL), July 24, 1998. Signed as a free agent by **Colorado**, December 22, 1998.

AUCOIN, Adrian   (oh-KWEHN)   VAN.

Defense. Shoots right. 6'2", 210 lbs. Born, Ottawa, Ont., July 3, 1973. Vancouver's 7th choice, 117th overall, in 1992 Entry Draft.

Season	Club	League	GP	G	A	Pts	PIM	PP	SH	GW	S	%	+/-	TF	F%	H	SB	Min	GP	G	A	Pts	PIM	PP	SH	GW
1989-90	Nepean	OJHL	54	2	14	16													4	0	1	1				
1990-91	Nepean	OJHL	56	17	33	50	125																			
1991-92	Boston University	H.E.	32	2	10	12	60																			
1992-93	Canada	Nat-Team	42	8	10	18	71																			
1993-94	Canada	Nat-Team	59	5	12	17	80																			
	Canada	Olympics	4	0	0	0	2																			
	Hamilton	AHL	13	1	2	3	19												4	0	2	2	6			
1994-95	**Vancouver**	**NHL**	1	1	0	1	0	0	0	0	2	50.0	1						4	1	0	1	0	1	0	0
	Syracuse	AHL	71	13	18	31	52																			
1995-96	**Vancouver**	**NHL**	49	4	14	18	34	2	0	0	85	4.7	8						6	0	0	0	2	0	0	0
	Syracuse	AHL	29	5	13	18	47																			
1996-97	**Vancouver**	**NHL**	70	5	16	21	63	1	0	0	116	4.3	0													

Season	Club	League	Regular Season GP	G	A	Pts	PIM	PP	SH	GW	S	%	+/-	TF	F%	H	SB	Min	Playoffs GP	G	A	Pts	PIM	PP	SH	GW
1997-98	Vancouver	NHL	35	3	3	6	21	1	0	1	44	6.8	-4	....	....	....	....	....	....	....	....	....	....	....	....	....
1998-99	Vancouver	NHL	82	23	11	34	77	18	2	3	174	13.2	-14	1	100.0	208	50	23:52	....	....	....	....	....	....	....	....
	NHL Totals		237	36	44	80	195	22	2	4	421	8.6		1	100.0	208	50	23:52	10	1	0	1	2	1	0	0

AUDET, Philippe

(aw-DEHT) **DET.**

Left wing. Shoots left. 6'2", 175 lbs. Born, Ottawa, Ont., June 4, 1977. Detroit's 2nd choice, 52nd overall, in 1995 Entry Draft.

Season	Club	League	GP	G	A	Pts	PIM	PP	SH	GW	S	%	+/-	TF	F%	H	SB	Min	GP	G	A	Pts	PIM	PP	SH	GW
1992-93	Beauce-Amiante	QAAA	28	21	24	45	75	....	....	....	....	....	....	....	....	....	....	....	....	....	....	....	....	....	....	....
1993-94	Trois-Rivieres	QAAA	34	22	21	43	90	....	....	....	....	....	....	....	....	....	....	....	....	....	....	....	....	....	....	....
1994-95	Granby	QMJHL	62	19	17	36	93	....	....	....	....	....	....	....	....	....	....	....	13	2	5	7	10	....	....	....
1995-96	Granby	QMJHL	67	40	43	83	162	....	....	....	....	....	....	....	....	....	....	....	21	12	18	30	32	....	....	....
1996-97	Granby	QMJHL	67	52	56	108	138	....	....	....	....	....	....	....	....	....	....	....	4	4	1	5	35	....	....	....
	Adirondack	AHL	3	1	1	2	0	....	....	....	....	....	....	....	....	....	....	....	1	1	0	1	0	....	....	....
1997-98	Adirondack	AHL	50	7	8	15	43	....	....	....	....	....	....	....	....	....	....	....	1	0	0	0	0	....	....	....
1998-99	**Detroit**	**NHL**	**4**	**0**	**0**	**0**	**0**	0	0	0	3	0.0	-2	0	0.0	4	1	4:19	....	....	....	....	....	....	....	....
	Adirondack	AHL	70	20	20	40	77	....	....	....	....	....	....	....	....	....	....	....	2	1	0	1	4	....	....	....
	NHL Totals		**4**	**0**	**0**	**0**	**0**	0	0	0	3	0.0		0	0.0	4	1	4:19	....	....	....	....	....	....	....	....

Memorial Cup All-Star Team (1996) • QMJHL First All-Star Team (1997)

AUDETTE, Donald

(aw-DEHT) **L.A.**

Right wing. Shoots right. 5'8", 184 lbs. Born, Laval, Que., September 23, 1969. Buffalo's 8th choice, 183rd overall, in 1989 Entry Draft.

Season	Club	League	GP	G	A	Pts	PIM	PP	SH	GW	S	%	+/-	TF	F%	H	SB	Min	GP	G	A	Pts	PIM	PP	SH	GW
1985-86	Laval	QAAA	41	32	38	70	....	....	....	....	....	....	....	....	....	....	....	....	....	....	....	....	....	....	....	....
1986-87	Laval	QMJHL	66	17	22	39	36	....	....	....	....	....	....	....	....	....	....	....	14	2	6	8	10	....	....	....
1987-88	Laval	QMJHL	63	48	61	109	56	....	....	....	....	....	....	....	....	....	....	....	14	7	12	19	20	....	....	....
1988-89	Laval	QMJHL	70	76	85	161	123	....	....	....	....	....	....	....	....	....	....	....	17	17	12	29	43	....	....	....
1989-90	Rochester	AHL	70	42	46	88	78	....	....	....	....	....	....	....	....	....	....	....	15	9	8	17	29	....	....	....
	Buffalo	**NHL**	....	....	....	....	....	....	....	....	....	....	....	....	....	....	....	....	**2**	**0**	**0**	**0**	**0**	....	....	....
1990-91	**Buffalo**	**NHL**	**8**	**4**	**3**	**7**	**4**	2	0	1	17	23.5	-1	....	....	....	....	....	....	....	....	....	....	....	....	....
	Rochester	AHL	5	4	0	4	2	....	....	....	....	....	....	....	....	....	....	....	....	....	....	....	....	....	....	....
1991-92	**Buffalo**	**NHL**	**63**	**31**	**17**	**48**	**75**	5	0	6	153	20.3	-1	....	....	....	....	....	....	....	....	....	....	....	....	....
1992-93	**Buffalo**	**NHL**	**44**	**12**	**7**	**19**	**51**	2	0	0	92	13.0	-8	....	....	....	....	....	**8**	**2**	**2**	**4**	**6**	**0**	**0**	**0**
	Rochester	AHL	6	8	4	12	10	....	....	....	....	....	....	....	....	....	....	....	....	....	....	....	....	....	....	....
1993-94	**Buffalo**	**NHL**	**77**	**29**	**30**	**59**	**41**	16	1	4	207	14.0	2	....	....	....	....	....	**7**	**0**	**1**	**1**	**6**	**0**	**0**	**0**
1994-95	**Buffalo**	**NHL**	**46**	**24**	**13**	**37**	**27**	13	0	7	124	19.4	-3	....	....	....	....	....	**5**	**1**	**1**	**2**	**4**	**1**	**0**	**0**
1995-96	**Buffalo**	**NHL**	**23**	**12**	**13**	**25**	**18**	8	0	1	92	13.0	0	....	....	....	....	....	....	....	....	....	....	....	....	....
1996-97	**Buffalo**	**NHL**	**73**	**28**	**22**	**50**	**48**	8	0	5	182	15.4	-6	....	....	....	....	....	**11**	**4**	**5**	**9**	**6**	**0**	**0**	**0**
1997-98	**Buffalo**	**NHL**	**75**	**24**	**20**	**44**	**59**	10	0	5	198	12.1	10	....	....	....	....	....	**15**	**5**	**8**	**13**	**10**	**3**	**0**	**2**
1998-99	**Los Angeles**	**NHL**	**49**	**18**	**18**	**36**	**51**	6	0	2	152	11.8	7	4	50.0	28	9	16:50	....	....	....	....	....	....	....	....
	NHL Totals		**458**	**182**	**143**	**325**	**374**	70	1	31	1217	15.0		4	50.0	28	9	16:50	48	12	17	29	32	4	0	2

QMJHL First All-Star Team (1989) • AHL First All-Star Team (1990) • Won Dudley "Red" Garret Memorial Trophy (Top Rookie - AHL) (1990)

Traded to **Los Angeles** by **Buffalo** for Los Angeles' 2nd round choice (Milan Bartovic) in 1999 Entry Draft, December 18, 1998.

AUGUSTA, Patrik

(ah-GOOS-tuh, pa-TREEK)

Right wing. Shoots left. 5'10", 170 lbs. Born, Jihlava, Czech., November 13, 1969. Toronto's 8th choice, 149th overall, in 1992 Entry Draft.

Season	Club	League	GP	G	A	Pts	PIM	PP	SH	GW	S	%	+/-	TF	F%	H	SB	Min	GP	G	A	Pts	PIM	PP	SH	GW
1988-89	Dukla Jihlava	Czech.	15	3	1	4	4	....	....	....	....	....	....	....	....	....	....	....	....	....	....	....	....	....	....	....
1989-90	Dukla Jihlava	Czech.	46	12	12	24		....	....	....	....	....	....	....	....	....	....	....	....	....	....	....	....	....	....	....
1990-91	Dukla Jihlava	Czech.	51	20	23	43	....	....	....	....	....	....	....	....	....	....	....	....	....	....	....	....	....	....	....	....
1991-92	Dukla Jihlava	Czech.	42	16	16	32	26	....	....	....	....	....	....	....	....	....	....	....	....	....	....	....	....	....	....	....
	Czech Republic	Olympics	8	3	2	5	0	....	....	....	....	....	....	....	....	....	....	....	....	....	....	....	....	....	....	....
1992-93	St. John's	AHL	75	32	45	77	74	....	....	....	....	....	....	....	....	....	....	....	8	3	3	6	23	....	....	....
1993-94	**Toronto**	**NHL**	**2**	**0**	**0**	**0**	**0**	0	0	0	3	0.0	0	....	....	....	....	....	....	....	....	....	....	....	....	....
	St. John's	AHL	77	*53	43	96	105	....	....	....	....	....	....	....	....	....	....	....	11	4	8	12	4	....	....	....
1994-95	St. John's	AHL	71	37	32	69	98	....	....	....	....	....	....	....	....	....	....	....	4	2	0	2	7	....	....	....
1995-96	Los Angeles	IHL	79	34	51	85	83	....	....	....	....	....	....	....	....	....	....	....	....	....	....	....	....	....	....	....
1996-97	Long Beach	IHL	82	45	42	87	96	....	....	....	....	....	....	....	....	....	....	....	18	4	4	8	33	....	....	....
1997-98	Long Beach	IHL	82	41	40	81	84	....	....	....	....	....	....	....	....	....	....	....	17	11	7	18	20	....	....	....
1998-99	Long Beach	IHL	68	24	35	59	125	....	....	....	....	....	....	....	....	....	....	....	8	4	6	10	4	....	....	....
	Washington	**NHL**	**2**	**0**	**0**	**0**	**0**	0	0	0	4	0.0	0	0	0.0	0	1	13:38	....	....	....	....	....	....	....	....
	NHL Totals		**4**	**0**	**0**	**0**	**0**	0	0	0	7	0.0		0	0.0	0	1	13:38	....	....	....	....	....	....	....	....

AHL Second All-Star Team (1994) • IHL Second All-Star Team (1997)

Signed as a free agent by **Washington**, December 11, 1998.

AXELSSON, Per-Johan

(AHX-ehl-suhn, PAIR, YEW-hahn) **BOS.**

Left wing. Shoots left. 6'1", 174 lbs. Born, Kungalv, Sweden, February 26, 1975. Boston's 7th choice, 177th overall, in 1995 Entry Draft.

Season	Club	League	GP	G	A	Pts	PIM	PP	SH	GW	S	%	+/-	TF	F%	H	SB	Min	GP	G	A	Pts	PIM	PP	SH	GW
1992-93	V. Frolunda	Swede-Jr.	16	9	5	14	12	....	....	....	....	....	....	....	....	....	....	....	....	....	....	....	....	....	....	....
1993-94	V. Frolunda	Sweden	11	0	0	0	4	....	....	....	....	....	....	....	....	....	....	....	4	0	0	0	0	....	....	....
1994-95	V. Frolunda	Sweden	8	2	1	3	6	....	....	....	....	....	....	....	....	....	....	....	....	....	....	....	....	....	....	....
1995-96	V. Frolunda	Sweden	36	15	5	20	10	....	....	....	....	....	....	....	....	....	....	....	13	3	0	3	10	....	....	....
1996-97	V. Frolunda	Sweden	50	19	15	34	34	....	....	....	....	....	....	....	....	....	....	....	3	0	2	2	0	....	....	....
	V. Frolunda	EuroHL	3	1	1	2	0	....	....	....	....	....	....	....	....	....	....	....	3	0	0	0	2	....	....	....
1997-98	**Boston**	**NHL**	**82**	**8**	**19**	**27**	**38**	2	0	1	144	5.6	-14	....	....	....	....	....	**6**	**1**	**0**	**1**	**0**	**0**	**0**	**0**
1998-99	**Boston**	**NHL**	**77**	**7**	**10**	**17**	**18**	0	0	2	146	4.8	-14	8	75.0	66	22	16:38	**12**	**1**	**1**	**2**	**4**	**0**	**0**	**0**
	NHL Totals		**159**	**15**	**29**	**44**	**56**	2	0	3	290	5.2		8	75.0	66	22	16:38	18	2	1	3	4	0	0	0

BABYCH, Dave

(BAB-itch)

Defense. Shoots left. 6'2", 215 lbs. Born, Edmonton, Alta., May 23, 1961. Winnipeg's 1st choice, 2nd overall, in 1980 Entry Draft.

Season	Club	League	GP	G	A	Pts	PIM	PP	SH	GW	S	%	+/-	TF	F%	H	SB	Min	GP	G	A	Pts	PIM	PP	SH	GW
1977-78	Ft. Saskatchewan	AJHL	56	31	69	100	37	....	....	....	....	....	....	....	....	....	....	....	....	....	....	....	....	....	....	....
	Portland	WCJHL	6	1	3	4	4	....	....	....	....	....	....	....	....	....	....	....	....	....	....	....	....	....	....	....
1978-79	Portland	WHL	67	20	59	79	63	....	....	....	....	....	....	....	....	....	....	....	25	7	22	29	22	....	....	....
1979-80	Portland	WHL	50	22	60	82	71	....	....	....	....	....	....	....	....	....	....	....	8	1	10	11	2	....	....	....
1980-81	**Winnipeg**	**NHL**	**69**	**6**	**38**	**44**	**90**	3	0	0	209	2.9	-61	....	....	....	....	....	....	....	....	....	....	....	....	....
1981-82	**Winnipeg**	**NHL**	**79**	**19**	**49**	**68**	**92**	11	0	2	262	7.3	-11	....	....	....	....	....	**4**	**1**	**2**	**3**	**29**	**1**	**0**	**0**
1982-83	**Winnipeg**	**NHL**	**79**	**13**	**61**	**74**	**56**	7	0	1	253	5.1	-10	....	....	....	....	....	**3**	**0**	**0**	**0**	**0**	**0**	**0**	**0**
1983-84	**Winnipeg**	**NHL**	**66**	**18**	**39**	**57**	**62**	10	0	4	233	7.7	-31	....	....	....	....	....	**3**	**1**	**1**	**2**	**0**	**1**	**0**	**0**
1984-85	**Winnipeg**	**NHL**	**78**	**13**	**49**	**62**	**78**	6	0	1	239	5.4	-16	....	....	....	....	....	**8**	**2**	**7**	**9**	**6**	**2**	**0**	**0**
1985-86	**Winnipeg**	**NHL**	**19**	**4**	**12**	**16**	**14**	2	0	0	53	7.5	-1	....	....	....	....	....	....	....	....	....	....	....	....	....
	Hartford	**NHL**	**62**	**10**	**43**	**53**	**36**	7	1	2	152	6.6	2	....	....	....	....	....	**8**	**1**	**3**	**4**	**14**	**0**	**0**	**0**
1986-87	**Hartford**	**NHL**	**66**	**8**	**33**	**41**	**44**	7	0	1	157	5.1	-18	....	....	....	....	....	**6**	**1**	**1**	**2**	**14**	**1**	**0**	**0**
1987-88	**Hartford**	**NHL**	**71**	**14**	**36**	**50**	**54**	10	0	2	233	6.0	-25	....	....	....	....	....	**6**	**3**	**2**	**5**	**2**	**0**	**0**	**0**
1988-89	**Hartford**	**NHL**	**70**	**6**	**41**	**47**	**54**	4	0	2	172	3.5	-5	....	....	....	....	....	**4**	**1**	**5**	**6**	**2**	**0**	**0**	**0**
1989-90	**Hartford**	**NHL**	**72**	**6**	**37**	**43**	**62**	4	0	1	164	3.7	-16	....	....	....	....	....	**7**	**1**	**2**	**3**	**0**	**0**	**0**	**0**
1990-91	**Hartford**	**NHL**	**8**	**0**	**6**	**6**	**4**	0	0	0	15	0.0	-4	....	....	....	....	....	....	....	....	....	....	....	....	....
1991-92	**Vancouver**	**NHL**	**75**	**5**	**24**	**29**	**63**	4	0	1	148	3.4	-2	....	....	....	....	....	**13**	**2**	**6**	**8**	**10**	**1**	**0**	**1**
1992-93	**Vancouver**	**NHL**	**43**	**3**	**16**	**19**	**44**	3	0	0	78	3.8	6	....	....	....	....	....	**12**	**2**	**5**	**7**	**6**	**1**	**0**	**0**
1993-94	**Vancouver**	**NHL**	**73**	**4**	**28**	**32**	**52**	0	0	2	96	4.2	0	....	....	....	....	....	**24**	**3**	**5**	**8**	**12**	**0**	**0**	**1**
1994-95	**Vancouver**	**NHL**	**40**	**3**	**11**	**14**	**18**	1	0	0	58	5.2	-13	....	....	....	....	....	**11**	**2**	**2**	**4**	**14**	**1**	**1**	**0**
1995-96	**Vancouver**	**NHL**	**53**	**3**	**21**	**24**	**38**	3	0	0	69	4.3	-5	....	....	....	....	....	....	....	....	....	....	....	....	....
1996-97	**Vancouver**	**NHL**	**78**	**5**	**22**	**27**	**38**	2	0	1	105	4.8	-2	....	....	....	....	....	....	....	....	....	....	....	....	....

			Regular Season																Playoffs							
Season	Club	League	GP	G	A	Pts	PIM	PP	SH	GW	S	%	+/-	TF	F%	H	SB	Min	GP	G	A	Pts	PIM	PP	SH	GW
1997-98	Vancouver	NHL	47	0	9	9	37	0	0	0	40	0.0	-11													
	Philadelphia	NHL	6	0	0	0	12	0	0	0	6	0.0	2						5	1	0	1	4	1	0	0
1998-99	Philadelphia	NHL	33	2	4	6	20	2	0	0	44	4.5	0	0	0.0	39	45	17:44								
	Los Angeles	NHL	8	0	2	2	2	0	0	0	5	0.0	-2	0	0.0	13	10	17:48								
	NHL Totals		1195	142	581	723	970	86	1	20	2791	5.1		0	0.0	52	55	17:45	114	21	41	62	113	9	1	2

WHL First All-Star Team (1980)

Played in NHL All-Star Game (1983, 1984)

Traded to **Hartford** by **Winnipeg** for Ray Neufeld, November 21, 1985. Claimed by **Minnesota** from **Hartford** in Expansion Draft, May 30, 1991. Traded to **Vancouver** by **Minnesota** for Tom Kurvers, June 22, 1991. Traded to **Philadelphia** by **Vancouver** with Philadelphia's 5th round choice (previously acquired, Philadelphia selected Garrett Prosofsky) in 1998 Entry Draft for Philadelphia's 3rd round choice (Justin Morrison) in 1998 Entry Draft, March 24, 1998. Traded to **Los Angeles** by **Philadelphia** with Philadelphia's 5th round choice in 2000 Entry Draft for Steve Duchesne, March 23, 1999.

BAKER, Jamie

Center. Shoots left. 6', 195 lbs. Born, Ottawa, Ont., August 31, 1966. Quebec's 2nd choice, 8th overall, in 1988 Supplemental Draft.

Season	Club	League	GP	G	A	Pts	PIM	PP	SH	GW	S	%	+/-	TF	F%	H	SB	Min	GP	G	A	Pts	PIM	PP	SH	GW
1985-86	St. Lawrence	ECAC	31	9	16	25	52																			
1986-87	St. Lawrence	ECAC	32	8	24	32	59																			
1987-88	St. Lawrence	ECAC	34	26	24	50	38																			
1988-89	St. Lawrence	ECAC	13	11	16	27	16																			
1989-90	Quebec	NHL	1	0	0	0	0	0	0	0	0	0.0	-1													
	Halifax	AHL	74	17	43	60	47												6	0	0	0	7			
1990-91	Quebec	NHL	18	2	0	2	8	0	1	0	18	11.1	-4													
	Halifax	AHL	50	14	22	36	85																			
1991-92	Quebec	NHL	52	7	10	17	32	3	0	1	77	9.1	-5													
	Halifax	AHL	9	5	0	5	12																			
1992-93	Ottawa	NHL	76	19	29	48	54	10	0	2	160	11.9	-20													
1993-94	San Jose	NHL	65	12	5	17	38	0	0	2	68	17.6	2						14	3	2	5	30	0	0	1
1994-95	San Jose	NHL	43	7	4	11	22	0	1	0	60	11.7	-7						11	2	2	4	12	0	0	1
1995-96	San Jose	NHL	77	16	17	33	79	2	6	0	117	13.7	-19													
1996-97	Toronto	NHL	58	8	8	16	28	1	0	3	69	11.6	2													
1997-98	Toronto	NHL	13	0	5	5	10	0	0	0	16	0.0	1													
	Chicago	IHL	53	11	34	45	80												22	4	5	9	42			
1998-99	San Jose	NHL	1	0	1	1	0	0	0	0	1	0.0	1													
	HIFK	Finland	11	1	5	6	22												6	0	3	3	35			
	NHL Totals		404	71	79	150	271	16	8	8	586	12.1							25	5	4	9	42	0	0	2

Signed as a free agent by **Ottawa**, September 2, 1992. Signed as a free agent by **San Jose**, September 11, 1993. Traded to **Toronto** by **San Jose** with San Jose's 5th round choice (Peter Cava) in 1996 Entry Draft for Todd Gill, June 14, 1996. • Lone 1998-99 NHL appearance October 10 vs. Calgary in Japan. Real-Time statistics not kept for this game.

BANCROFT, Steve

CAR.

Defense. Shoots left. 6'1", 214 lbs. Born, Toronto, Ont., October 6, 1970. Toronto's 3rd choice, 21st overall, in 1989 Entry Draft.

Season	Club	League	GP	G	A	Pts	PIM	PP	SH	GW	S	%	+/-	TF	F%	H	SB	Min	GP	G	A	Pts	PIM	PP	SH	GW
1986-87	St. Catharines	OJHL-B	11	5	8	13	20																			
1987-88	Belleville	OHL	56	1	8	9	42																			
1988-89	Belleville	OHL	66	7	30	37	99												5	0	2	2	10			
1989-90	Belleville	OHL	53	10	33	43	135												11	3	9	12	38			
1990-91	Newmarket	AHL	9	0	3	3	22																			
	Maine	AHL	53	2	12	14	46												2	0	0	0	2			
1991-92	Maine	AHL	26	1	3	4	45																			
	Indianapolis	IHL	36	8	23	31	49																			
1992-93	Chicago	NHL	1	0	0	0	0	0	0	0	0	0.0	0													
	Indianapolis	IHL	53	10	35	45	138																			
	Moncton	AHL	21	3	13	16	16												5	0	0	0	16			
1993-94	Cleveland	IHL	33	2	12	14	58																			
1994-95	Detroit	IHL	6	1	3	4	0																			
	Fort Wayne	IHL	50	7	17	24	100																			
	St. John's	AHL	4	2	0	2	2												5	0	3	3	8			
1995-96	Los Angeles	IHL	15	3	10	13	22																			
	Chicago	IHL	64	9	41	50	91												9	1	7	8	22			
1996-97	Chicago	IHL	39	6	10	16	66																			
	Las Vegas	IHL	36	9	28	37	64												3	0	0	0	2			
1997-98	Las Vegas	IHL	70	15	44	59	148																			
	Saint John	AHL	9	0	4	4	12												19	2	11	13	30			
1998-99	Saint John	AHL	8	1	4	5	22																			
	Providence	AHL	62	7	34	41	78												15	0	6	6	28			
	NHL Totals		1	0	0	0	0	0	0	0	0	0.0														

Traded to **Boston** by **Toronto** for Rob Cimetta, November 9, 1990. Traded to **Chicago** by **Boston** with Boston's 11th round choice (later traded to Winnipeg — Winnipeg selected Russel Hewson) in 1993 Entry Draft for Chicago's 11th round choice (Eugene Pavlov) in 1992 Entry Draft, January 9, 1992. Traded to **Winnipeg** by **Chicago** with future considerations for Troy Murray, February 21, 1993. Claimed by **Florida** from **Winnipeg** in Expansion Draft, June 24, 1993. Signed as a free agent by **Pittsburgh**, August 2, 1993. Signed as a free agent by **Carolina**, August 4, 1999.

BANHAM, Frank

ANA.

Right wing. Shoots right. 6', 190 lbs. Born, Calahoo, Alta., April 14, 1975. Washington's 4th choice, 147th overall, in 1993 Entry Draft.

Season	Club	League	GP	G	A	Pts	PIM	PP	SH	GW	S	%	+/-	TF	F%	H	SB	Min	GP	G	A	Pts	PIM	PP	SH	GW
1991-92	Fernie	RMJHL	47	45	45	90	120																			
1992-93	Saskatoon	WHL	71	29	33	62	55												9	2	7	9	8			
1993-94	Saskatoon	WHL	65	28	39	67	99												16	8	11	19	36			
1994-95	Saskatoon	WHL	70	50	39	89	63												8	2	6	8	12			
1995-96	Saskatoon	WHL	72	*83	69	152	116												4	6	0	6	2			
	Baltimore	AHL	9	1	4	5	0												7	1	1	2	2			
1996-97	Anaheim	NHL	3	0	0	0	0	0	0	0	1	0.0	-2													
	Baltimore	AHL	21	11	13	24	4																			
1997-98	Anaheim	NHL	21	9	2	11	12	1	0	0	43	20.9	-6													
	Cincinnati	AHL	35	7	8	15	39																			
1998-99	Cincinnati	AHL	66	22	27	49	20												3	0	1	1	0			
	NHL Totals		24	9	2	11	12	1	0	0	44	20.5														

WHL East First All-Star Team (1996)

Signed as a free agent by **Anaheim**, January 27, 1996.

BANNISTER, Drew

T.B.

Defense. Shoots right. 6'2", 200 lbs. Born, Belleville, Ont., September 4, 1974. Tampa Bay's 2nd choice, 26th overall, in 1992 Entry Draft.

Season	Club	League	GP	G	A	Pts	PIM	PP	SH	GW	S	%	+/-	TF	F%	H	SB	Min	GP	G	A	Pts	PIM	PP	SH	GW
1989-90	Sudbury	OMHA	26	13	14	27	98																			
1990-91	S.S. Marie	OHL	41	2	8	10	51												4	0	0	0	0			
1991-92	S.S. Marie	OHL	64	4	21	25	122												16	3	10	13	36			
1992-93	S.S. Marie	OHL	59	5	28	33	114												18	2	7	9	12			
1993-94	S.S. Marie	OHL	58	7	43	50	108												14	6	9	15	20			
1994-95	Atlanta	IHL	72	5	7	12	74												5	0	2	2	22			
1995-96	Tampa Bay	NHL	13	0	1	1	4	0	0	0	10	0.0	-1													
	Atlanta	IHL	61	3	13	16	105												3	0	0	0	4			
1996-97	Tampa Bay	NHL	64	4	13	17	44	1	0	0	57	7.0	-21													
	Edmonton	NHL	1	0	1	1	0	0	0	0	2	0.0	-2						12	0	0	0	30	0	0	0
1997-98	Edmonton	NHL	34	0	2	2	42	0	0	0	27	0.0	-7													
	Anaheim	NHL	27	0	6	6	47	0	0	0	23	0.0	-2													

			Regular Season																Playoffs							
Season	Club	League	GP	G	A	Pts	PIM	PP	SH	GW	S	%	+/-	TF	F%	H	SB	Min	GP	G	A	Pts	PIM	PP	SH	GW
1998-99	**Tampa Bay**	**NHL**	**21**	**1**	**2**	**3**	**24**	**0**	**0**	**0**	**29**	**3.4**	**–4**	**0**	**0.0**	**25**	**11**	**15:49**								
	Las Vegas	IHL	16	2	1	3	73																			
	NHL Totals		**160**	**5**	**25**	**30**	**161**	**1**	**0**	**0**	**148**	**3.4**		**0**	**0.0**	**25**	**11**	**15:49**	**12**	**0**	**0**	**0**	**30**	**0**	**0**	**0**

Memorial Cup All-Star Team (1993) • OHL Second All-Star Team (1994)

Traded to **Edmonton** by **Tampa Bay** with Tampa Bay's 6th round choice (Peter Sarno) in 1997 Entry Draft for Jeff Norton, March 18, 1997. Traded to **Anaheim** by **Edmonton** for Bobby Dollas, January 9, 1998. Traded to **Tampa Bay** by **Anaheim** for Tampa Bay's 5th round choice in 2000 Entry Draft, December 10, 1998.

BARNABY, Matthew — PIT.

Right wing. Shoots left. 6', 188 lbs. Born, Ottawa, Ont., May 4, 1973. Buffalo's 5th choice, 83rd overall, in 1992 Entry Draft.

1989-90	Hull	QAAA	50	43	50	93	149																			
1990-91	Beauport	QMJHL	52	9	5	14	262																			
1991-92	Beauport	QMJHL	63	29	37	66	*476																			
1992-93	Victoriaville	QMJHL	65	44	67	111	*448												6	2	4	6	44			
	Buffalo	**NHL**	**2**	**1**	**0**	**1**	**10**	**1**	**0**	**0**	**8**	**12.5**	**0**						**1**	**0**	**1**	**1**	**4**	**0**	**0**	**0**
1993-94	**Buffalo**	**NHL**	**35**	**2**	**4**	**6**	**106**	**1**	**0**	**0**	**13**	**15.4**	**–7**						**3**	**0**	**0**	**0**	**17**	**0**	**0**	**0**
	Rochester	AHL	42	10	32	42	153																			
1994-95	**Buffalo**	**NHL**	**23**	**1**	**1**	**2**	**116**	**0**	**0**	**0**	**27**	**3.7**	**–2**													
	Rochester	AHL	56	21	29	50	274																			
1995-96	**Buffalo**	**NHL**	**73**	**15**	**16**	**31**	***335**	**0**	**0**	**0**	**131**	**11.5**	**–2**													
1996-97	**Buffalo**	**NHL**	**68**	**19**	**24**	**43**	**249**	**2**	**0**	**1**	**121**	**15.7**	**16**						**8**	**0**	**4**	**4**	**36**	**0**	**0**	**0**
1997-98	**Buffalo**	**NHL**	**72**	**5**	**20**	**25**	**289**	**0**	**0**	**2**	**96**	**5.2**	**8**						**15**	**7**	**6**	**13**	**22**	**3**	**0**	**1**
1998-99	**Buffalo**	**NHL**	**44**	**4**	**14**	**18**	**143**	**0**	**0**	**3**	**52**	**7.7**	**–2**	**6**	**16.7**	**45**	**8**	**13:56**								
	Pittsburgh	**NHL**	**18**	**2**	**2**	**4**	**34**	**1**	**0**	**0**	**27**	**7.4**	**–10**	**3**	**66.7**	**40**	**6**	**13:33**	**13**	**0**	**0**	**0**	**35**	**0**	**0**	**0**
	NHL Totals		**335**	**49**	**81**	**130**	**1282**	**5**	**0**	**6**	**475**	**10.3**		**9**	**33.3**	**85**	**14**	**13:49**	**40**	**7**	**11**	**18**	**114**	**3**	**0**	**1**

Traded to **Pittsburgh** by **Buffalo** for Stu Barnes, March 11, 1999.

BARNES, Stu — BUF.

Center. Shoots right. 5'11", 174 lbs. Born, Spruce Grove, Alta., December 25, 1970. Winnipeg's 1st choice, 4th overall, in 1989 Entry Draft.

1986-87	St. Albert	AJHL	53	41	34	*75	103												3	2	2	4	0			
1987-88	New Westminster	WHL	71	37	64	101	88												5	2	3	5	6			
1988-89	Tri-City	WHL	70	59	82	141	117												7	6	5	11	10			
1989-90	Tri-City	WHL	63	52	92	144	165												7	1	5	6	26			
1990-91	Canada	Nat-Team	53	22	27	49	68																			
1991-92	**Winnipeg**	**NHL**	**46**	**8**	**9**	**17**	**26**	**4**	**0**	**0**	**75**	**10.7**	**–2**													
	Moncton	AHL	30	13	19	32	10												11	3	9	12	6			
1992-93	**Winnipeg**	**NHL**	**38**	**12**	**10**	**22**	**10**	**3**	**0**	**3**	**73**	**16.4**	**–3**						**6**	**1**	**3**	**4**	**2**	**0**	**0**	**0**
	Moncton	AHL	42	23	31	54	58																			
1993-94	**Winnipeg**	**NHL**	**18**	**5**	**4**	**9**	**8**	**2**	**0**	**0**	**24**	**20.8**	**–1**													
	Florida	**NHL**	**59**	**18**	**20**	**38**	**30**	**6**	**1**	**3**	**148**	**12.2**	**5**													
1994-95	**Florida**	**NHL**	**41**	**10**	**19**	**29**	**8**	**1**	**0**	**2**	**93**	**10.8**	**7**													
1995-96	**Florida**	**NHL**	**72**	**19**	**25**	**44**	**46**	**8**	**0**	**5**	**158**	**12.0**	**–12**						**22**	**6**	**10**	**16**	**4**	**2**	**0**	**2**
1996-97	**Florida**	**NHL**	**19**	**2**	**8**	**10**	**10**	**1**	**0**	**0**	**44**	**4.5**	**–3**													
	Pittsburgh	**NHL**	**62**	**17**	**22**	**39**	**16**	**4**	**0**	**3**	**132**	**12.9**	**–20**						**5**	**0**	**1**	**1**	**0**	**0**	**0**	**0**
1997-98	**Pittsburgh**	**NHL**	**78**	**30**	**35**	**65**	**30**	**15**	**1**	**5**	**196**	**15.3**	**15**						**6**	**3**	**3**	**6**	**2**	**0**	**0**	**1**
1998-99	**Pittsburgh**	**NHL**	**64**	**20**	**12**	**32**	**20**	**13**	**0**	**3**	**155**	**12.9**	**–12**	**720**	**51.9**	**57**	**13**	**17:52**								
	Buffalo	**NHL**	**17**	**0**	**4**	**4**	**10**	**0**	**0**	**0**	**25**	**0.0**	**1**	**236**	**51.3**	**15**	**4**	**18:20**	**21**	**7**	**3**	**10**	**6**	**4**	**0**	**1**
	NHL Totals		**514**	**141**	**168**	**309**	**214**	**57**	**2**	**24**	**1123**	**12.6**		**956**	**51.8**	**72**	**17**	**17:58**	**60**	**17**	**20**	**37**	**14**	**6**	**0**	**4**

WHL West Second All-Star Team (1988, 1989)

Traded to **Florida** by **Winnipeg** with St. Louis' 6th round choice (previously acquired by Winnipeg — later traded to Edmonton — later traded to Winnipeg — Winnipeg selected Chris Kibermanis) in 1994 Entry Draft for Randy Gilhen, November 25, 1993. Traded to **Pittsburgh** by **Florida** with Jason Woolley for Chris Wells, November 19, 1996. Traded to **Buffalo** by **Pittsburgh** for Matthew Barnaby, March 11, 1999.

BARON, Murray (BAIR-uhn) — VAN.

Defense. Shoots left. 6'3", 215 lbs. Born, Prince George, B.C., June 1, 1967. Philadelphia's 7th choice, 167th overall, in 1986 Entry Draft.

1984-85	Vernon	BCJHL	37	5	9	14	93												13	5	6	11	107			
1985-86	Vernon	BCJHL	46	12	32	44	179												7	1	2	3	13			
1986-87	North Dakota	WCHA	41	4	10	14	62																			
1987-88	North Dakota	WCHA	41	1	10	11	95																			
1988-89	North Dakota	WCHA	40	2	6	8	92																			
	Hershey	AHL	9	0	3	3	8																			
1989-90	**Philadelphia**	**NHL**	**16**	**2**	**2**	**4**	**12**	**0**	**0**	**0**	**18**	**11.1**	**–1**													
	Hershey	AHL	50	0	10	10	101																			
1990-91	**Philadelphia**	**NHL**	**67**	**8**	**8**	**16**	**74**	**3**	**0**	**1**	**86**	**9.3**	**–3**													
	Hershey	AHL	6	2	3	5	0																			
1991-92	**St. Louis**	**NHL**	**67**	**3**	**8**	**11**	**94**	**0**	**0**	**0**	**55**	**5.5**	**–3**						**2**	**0**	**0**	**0**	**2**	**0**	**0**	**0**
1992-93	**St. Louis**	**NHL**	**53**	**2**	**2**	**4**	**59**	**0**	**0**	**1**	**42**	**4.8**	**–5**						**11**	**0**	**0**	**0**	**12**	**0**	**0**	**0**
1993-94	**St. Louis**	**NHL**	**77**	**5**	**9**	**14**	**123**	**0**	**0**	**0**	**73**	**6.8**	**–14**						**4**	**0**	**0**	**0**	**10**	**0**	**0**	**0**
1994-95	**St. Louis**	**NHL**	**39**	**0**	**5**	**5**	**93**	**0**	**0**	**0**	**28**	**0.0**	**9**						**7**	**1**	**1**	**2**	**2**	**0**	**0**	**0**
1995-96	**St. Louis**	**NHL**	**82**	**2**	**9**	**11**	**190**	**0**	**0**	**0**	**86**	**2.3**	**3**						**13**	**1**	**0**	**1**	**20**	**0**	**1**	**0**
1996-97	**St. Louis**	**NHL**	**11**	**0**	**2**	**2**	**11**	**0**	**0**	**0**	**7**	**0.0**	**–4**													
	Montreal	**NHL**	**60**	**1**	**5**	**6**	**107**	**0**	**0**	**0**	**52**	**1.9**	**–16**													
	Phoenix	**NHL**	**8**	**0**	**0**	**0**	**4**	**0**	**0**	**0**	**5**	**0.0**	**0**						**1**	**0**	**0**	**0**	**0**	**0**	**0**	**0**
1997-98	**Phoenix**	**NHL**	**45**	**1**	**5**	**6**	**106**	**0**	**0**	**0**	**23**	**4.3**	**–10**						**6**	**0**	**2**	**2**	**6**	**0**	**0**	**0**
1998-99	**Vancouver**	**NHL**	**81**	**2**	**6**	**8**	**115**	**0**	**0**	**0**	**53**	**3.8**	**–23**	**0**	**0.0**	**192**	**100**	**18:14**								
	NHL Totals		**606**	**26**	**61**	**87**	**988**	**3**	**0**	**2**	**528**	**4.9**		**0**	**0.0**	**192**	**100**	**18:14**	**44**	**2**	**3**	**5**	**52**	**0**	**1**	**0**

Traded to **St. Louis** by **Philadelphia** with Ron Sutter for Dan Quinn and Rod Brind'Amour, September 22, 1991. Traded to **Montreal** by **St. Louis** with Shayne Corson and St. Louis' 5th round choice (Gennady Razin) in 1997 Entry Draft for Pierre Turgeon, Rory Fitzpatrick and Craig Conroy, October 29, 1996. Traded to **Phoenix** by **Montreal** with Chris Murray for Dave Manson, March 18, 1997. Signed as a free agent by **Vancouver**, July 15, 1998.

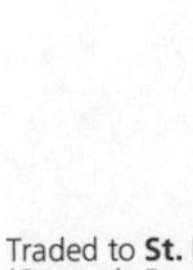

BARRIE, Len — L.A.

Center. Shoots left. 6', 200 lbs. Born, Kimberley, B.C., June 4, 1969. Edmonton's 7th choice, 124th overall, in 1988 Entry Draft.

1984-85	Kelowna	BCAHA	20	51	55	106	24																			
1985-86	Calgary	AJHL	23	7	14	21	86																			
	Calgary	WHL	32	3	0	3	18																			
1986-87	Calgary	WHL	34	13	13	26	81																			
	Victoria	WHL	34	7	6	13	92												5	0	1	1	15			
1987-88	Victoria	WHL	70	37	49	86	192												8	2	0	2	29			
1988-89	Victoria	WHL	67	39	48	87	157												7	5	2	7	23			
1989-90	Kamloops	WHL	70	*85	*100	*185	108												17	*14	23	*37	24			
	Philadelphia	**NHL**	**1**	**0**	**0**	**0**	**0**	**0**	**0**	**0**	**0**	**0.0**	**–2**													
1990-91	Hershey	AHL	63	26	32	58	60												7	4	0	4	12			
1991-92	Hershey	AHL	75	42	43	85	78												3	0	2	2	32			
1992-93	**Philadelphia**	**NHL**	**8**	**2**	**2**	**4**	**9**	**0**	**0**	**0**	**14**	**14.3**	**2**													
	Hershey	AHL	61	31	45	76	162																			
1993-94	**Florida**	**NHL**	**2**	**0**	**0**	**0**	**0**	**0**	**0**	**0**	**0**	**0.0**	**–2**													
	Cincinnati	IHL	77	45	71	116	246												11	8	13	21	60			
1994-95	Cleveland	IHL	28	13	30	43	137																			
	Pittsburgh	**NHL**	**48**	**3**	**11**	**14**	**66**	**0**	**0**	**1**	**37**	**8.1**	**–4**						**4**	**1**	**0**	**1**	**8**	**1**	**0**	**0**

Season	Club	League	GP	G	A	Pts	PIM	PP	SH	GW	S	%	+/-	TF	F%	H	SB	Min	GP	G	A	Pts	PIM	PP	SH	GW
1995-96	Pittsburgh	NHL	5	0	0	0	18	0	0	0	5	0.0	-1													
	Cleveland	IHL	55	29	43	72	178												3	2	3	5	6			
1996-97	San Antonio	IHL	57	26	40	66	196												9	5	5	10	20			
1997-98	San Antonio	IHL	32	7	13	20	90																			
	Frankfurt	Germany	25	11	19	30	32												6	2	3	5	35			
1998-99	Frankfurt	Germany	41	24	35	59	105												8	2	4	6	43			
	Frankfurt	EuroHL	5	3	1	4	10																			
	NHL Totals		64	5	13	18	93	0	0	1	56	8.9							4	1	0	1	8	1	0	0

WHL West First All-Star Team (1990) • IHL Second All-Star Team (1994)

Signed as a free agent by **Philadelphia**, February 28, 1990. Signed as a free agent by **Florida**, July 20, 1993. Signed as a free agent by **Pittsburgh**, August 15, 1994. Signed as a free agent by **LA Kings**, July 9, 1999.

BARTECKO, Lubos

(bahr-TEHK-oh, LOO-bohsh) **ST.L.**

Left wing. Shoots left. 6'1", 200 lbs. Born, Kezmarok, Czech., July 14, 1976.

Season	Club	League	GP	G	A	Pts	PIM	PP	SH	GW	S	%	+/-	TF	F%	H	SB	Min	GP	G	A	Pts	PIM	PP	SH	GW
1994-95	SKP Propad	Slovakia	3	1	0	1	0																			
	SKP Propad	Slovak-Jr.	STATISTICS NOT AVAILABLE																							
1995-96	Chicoutimi	QMJHL	70	32	41	73	50												17	8	15	23	10			
1996-97	Drummondville	QMJHL	58	40	51	91	49												8	1	8	9	4			
1997-98	Worcester	AHL	34	10	12	22	24												10	4	2	6	2			
1998-99	SKP Poprad	Slovakia	1	1	0	1	0																			
	St. Louis	**NHL**	32	5	11	16	6	0	0	1	37	13.5	4	0	0.0	34	5	13:13	5	0	0	0	2	0	0	0
	Worcester	AHL	49	14	24	38	22																			
	NHL Totals		32	5	11	16	6	0	0	1	37	13.5		0	0.0	34	5	13:13	5	0	0	0	2	0	0	0

Signed as a free agent by **St. Louis**, October 3, 1997.

BASHKIROV, Andrei

(bahsh-KIHR-ahf) **MTL.**

Left wing. Shoots left. 6', 198 lbs. Born, Shelekhov, USSR, June 22, 1970. Montreal's 4th choice, 132nd overall, in 1998 Entry Draft.

Season	Club	League	GP	G	A	Pts	PIM	PP	SH	GW	S	%	+/-	TF	F%	H	SB	Min	GP	G	A	Pts	PIM	PP	SH	GW
1990-91	Yermak Angarsk	USSR-3	STATISTICS NOT AVAILABLE																							
1991-92	Khimik	CIS	11	2	0	2	4																			
1992-93	Yermak Angarsk	CIS-3	STATISTICS NOT AVAILABLE																							
1993-94	Charlotte	ECHL	62	28	42	70	25												3	1	0	1	0			
	Providence	AHL	1	0	0	0	2																			
1994-95	Charlotte	ECHL	61	19	27	46	20												3	0	0	0	0			
1995-96	Huntington	ECHL	55	19	39	58	35																			
1996-97	Huntington	ECHL	47	29	41	70	12																			
	Detroit	IHL	2	0	0	0	0																			
	Las Vegas	IHL	27	10	12	22	0												2	0	0	0	0			
1997-98	Las Vegas	IHL	15	2	3	5	5																			
	Port Huron	UHL	3	1	3	4	0																			
	Fort Wayne	IHL	65	28	48	76	16												4	2	2	4	2			
1998-99	**Montreal**	**NHL**	10	0	0	0	0	0	0	0	4	0.0	-3	0	0.0	3	3	6:57								
	Fredericton	AHL	13	7	5	12	4																			
	Fort Wayne	IHL	34	11	25	36	10																			
	NHL Totals		10	0	0	0	0	0	0	0	4	0.0		0	0.0	3	3	6:57								

BASSEN, Bob

Center. Shoots left. 5'10", 185 lbs. Born, Calgary, Alta., May 6, 1965.

Season	Club	League	GP	G	A	Pts	PIM	PP	SH	GW	S	%	+/-	TF	F%	H	SB	Min	GP	G	A	Pts	PIM	PP	SH	GW
1982-83	Calgary	AJHL	STATISTICS NOT AVAILABLE																							
	Medicine Hat	WHL	4	3	2	5	0												3	0	0	0	4			
1983-84	Medicine Hat	WHL	72	29	29	58	93												14	5	11	16	12			
1984-85	Medicine Hat	WHL	65	32	50	82	143												10	2	8	10	39			
1985-86	**NY Islanders**	**NHL**	11	2	1	3	6	0	0	0	5	40.0	0						3	0	1	1	0	0	0	0
	Springfield	AHL	54	13	21	34	111																			
1986-87	**NY Islanders**	**NHL**	77	7	10	17	89	0	0	1	59	11.9	-17						14	1	2	3	21	0	0	0
1987-88	**NY Islanders**	**NHL**	77	6	16	22	99	1	0	2	65	9.2	8						6	0	1	1	23	0	0	0
1988-89	**NY Islanders**	**NHL**	19	1	4	5	21	0	0	0	14	7.1	0													
	Chicago	**NHL**	49	4	12	16	62	0	0	1	37	10.8	5						10	1	1	2	34	0	0	0
1989-90	**Chicago**	**NHL**	6	1	1	2	8	0	0	0	7	14.3	1						1	0	0	0	2	0	0	0
	Indianapolis	IHL	73	22	32	54	179												12	3	8	11	33			
1990-91	**St. Louis**	**NHL**	79	16	18	34	183	0	2	1	117	13.7	17						13	1	3	4	24	0	0	0
1991-92	**St. Louis**	**NHL**	79	7	25	32	167	0	0	1	101	6.9	12						6	0	2	2	4	0	0	0
1992-93	**St. Louis**	**NHL**	53	9	10	19	63	0	1	0	61	14.8	0						11	0	0	0	10	0	0	0
1993-94	**St. Louis**	**NHL**	46	2	7	9	44	0	0	0	73	2.7	-14													
	Quebec	**NHL**	37	11	8	19	55	1	0	0	56	19.6	-3													
1994-95	**Quebec**	**NHL**	47	12	15	27	33	0	1	1	66	18.2	14						5	2	4	6	0	0	0	0
1995-96	**Dallas**	**NHL**	13	0	1	1	15	0	0	0	9	0.0	-6													
	Michigan	IHL	1	0	0	0	4																			
1996-97	**Dallas**	**NHL**	46	5	7	12	41	0	0	2	50	10.0	5						7	3	1	4	0	0	0	0
1997-98	**Dallas**	**NHL**	58	3	4	7	57	0	0	1	40	7.5	-4						17	1	0	1	12	0	0	0
1998-99	**Calgary**	**NHL**	41	1	2	3	35	0	0	0	47	2.1	-13	20	40.0	108	17	12:36								
	NHL Totals		738	87	141	228	978	2	5	10	807	10.8		20	40.0	108	17	12:36	93	9	15	24	134	0	0	0

WHL First All-Star Team (1985) • IHL First All-Star Team (1990)

Signed as a free agent by **NY Islanders**, October 19, 1984. Traded to **Chicago** by **NY Islanders** with Steve Konroyd for Marc Bergevin and Gary Nylund, November 25, 1988. Claimed by **St. Louis** from **Chicago** in NHL Waiver Draft, October 1, 1990. Traded to **Quebec** by **St. Louis** with Garth Butcher and Ron Sutter for Steve Duchesne and Denis Chasse, January 23, 1994. Signed as a free agent by **Dallas**, August 10, 1995. Traded to **Calgary** by **Dallas** for Aaron Gavey, July 14, 1998.

BAST, Ryan

(Bast) **PHI.**

Defense. Shoots left. 6'2", 190 lbs. Born, Spruce Grove, Alta., August 27, 1975.

Season	Club	League	GP	G	A	Pts	PIM	PP	SH	GW	S	%	+/-	TF	F%	H	SB	Min	GP	G	A	Pts	PIM	PP	SH	GW
1992-93	St. Albert	AAHA	35	1	18	19	51																			
1993-94	Prince Albert	WHL	47	2	8	10	139																			
	Portland	WHL	6	0	0	0	4																			
1994-95	Prince Albert	WHL	42	1	10	11	149												14	0	3	3	13			
1995-96	Swift Current	WHL	72	9	18	27	203												6	1	0	1	21			
1996-97	Las Vegas	IHL	49	2	3	5	266																			
	Saint John	AHL	12	0	0	0	21												5	0	0	0	4			
1997-98	Saint John	AHL	77	3	8	11	187												21	0	1	1	55			
1998-99	Saint John	AHL	2	0	0	0	5																			
	Philadelphia	**NHL**	2	0	1	1	0	0	0	0	1	0.0		0	0.0	0	0	13:24								
	Philadelphia	AHL	69	0	11	11	160												16	0	0	0	30			
	NHL Totals		2	0	1	1	0	0	0	0	1	0.0		0	0.0	0	0	13:24								

AHL Second All-Star Team (1998)

Signed as a free agent by **Las Vegas** (IHL), September 30, 1996. Traded to **Saint John** (AHL) by **Las Vegas** (IHL) for loan of Sasha Lakovic, March 20, 1997. Signed as a free agent by **Philadelphia**, May 18, 1998. • Calgary Flames filed official protest to NHL contesting Philadelphia's signing of Bast under the contention that he was property of AHL's Saint John Flames, May 20, 1998. • NHL ruled that Bast was not under contract to Calgary since he was never drafted and had no NHL clause in contract, May 22, 1998. NHL also ruled that Bast was not property of Philadelphia because Flyers' contract offer exceeded NHL rookie salary cap, May 22, 1998. A compromise was reached that traded Bast to **Philadelphia** by **Calgary** with Calgary's 8th round choice (David Nystrom) in 1999 Entry Draft for Calgary's 3rd round choice (later traded to NY Rangers, NY Rangers selected Patrik Aufiero) in 1999 Entry Draft, October 13, 1998.

			Regular Season																Playoffs							
Season	Club	League	GP	G	A	Pts	PIM	PP	SH	GW	S	%	+/-	TF	F%	H	SB	Min	GP	G	A	Pts	PIM	PP	SH	GW

BATES, Shawn — BOS.

Center. Shoots right. 5'11", 205 lbs. Born, Melrose, MA, April 3, 1975. Boston's 4th choice, 103rd overall, in 1993 Entry Draft.

1990-91	Medford High	H.S.	22	18	43	61	6	....	....	....	....	....	....	....	....	....	....	....	....	....	....	....	....	....	....	....
1991-92	Medford High	H.S.	22	38	41	79	10	....	....	....	....	....	....	....	....	....	....	....	....	....	....	....	....	....	....	....
1992-93	Medford High	H.S.	25	49	46	95	20	....	....	....	....	....	....	....	....	....	....	....	....	....	....	....	....	....	....	....
1993-94	Boston University	H.E.	41	10	19	29	24	....	....	....	....	....	....	....	....	....	....	....	....	....	....	....	....	....	....	....
1994-95	Boston University	H.E.	38	18	12	30	48	....	....	....	....	....	....	....	....	....	....	....	....	....	....	....	....	....	....	....
1995-96	Boston University	H.E.	40	28	22	50	54	....	....	....	....	....	....	....	....	....	....	....	....	....	....	....	....	....	....	....
1996-97	Boston University	H.E.	41	17	18	35	64	....	....	....	....	....	....	....	....	....	....	....	....	....	....	....	....	....	....	....
1997-98	**Boston**	**NHL**	**13**	**2**	**0**	**2**	**2**	**0**	**0**	**0**	**12**	**16.7**	**–3**	....	....	....	....	....	....	....	....	....	....	....	....	....
	Providence	AHL	50	15	19	34	22	....	....	....	....	....	....	....	....	....	....	....	....	....	....	....	....	....	....	....
1998-99	**Boston**	**NHL**	**33**	**5**	**4**	**9**	**2**	**0**	**0**	**0**	**30**	**16.7**	**3**	**178**	**51.1**	**47**	**5**	**8:35**	**12**	**0**	**0**	**0**	**4**	**0**	**0**	**0**
	Providence	AHL	37	25	21	46	39	....	....	....	....	....	....	....	....	....	....	....	....	....	....	....	....	....	....	....
	NHL Totals		**46**	**7**	**4**	**11**	**4**	**0**	**0**	**0**	**42**	**16.7**		**178**	**51.1**	**47**	**5**	**8:35**	**12**	**0**	**0**	**0**	**4**	**0**	**0**	**0**

NCAA Championship All-Tournament Team (1995)

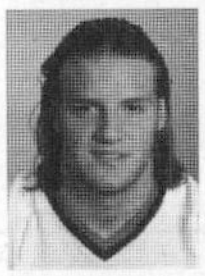

BATTAGLIA, Bates — (buh-TAG-lee-ah) — CAR.

Left wing. Shoots left. 6'2", 185 lbs. Born, Chicago, IL, December 13, 1975. Anaheim's 6th choice, 132nd overall, in 1994 Entry Draft.

1992-93	Team Illinois	USAHA	60	42	42	84	68	....	....	....	....	....	....	....	....	....	....	....	....	....	....	....	....	....	....	....
1993-94	Caledon	OJHL	47	35	39	74	212	....	....	....	....	....	....	....	....	....	....	....	....	....	....	....	....	....	....	....
1994-95	Lake Superior	CCHA	38	6	14	20	34	....	....	....	....	....	....	....	....	....	....	....	....	....	....	....	....	....	....	....
	United States	WJC-A	7	3	2	5	2	....	....	....	....	....	....	....	....	....	....	....	....	....	....	....	....	....	....	....
1995-96	Lake Superior	CCHA	40	13	22	35	48	....	....	....	....	....	....	....	....	....	....	....	....	....	....	....	....	....	....	....
1996-97	Lake Superior	CCHA	38	12	27	39	80	....	....	....	....	....	....	....	....	....	....	....	....	....	....	....	....	....	....	....
1997-98	**Carolina**	**NHL**	**33**	**2**	**4**	**6**	**10**	**0**	**0**	**1**	**21**	**9.5**	**–1**	....	....	....	....	....	....	....	....	....	....	....	....	....
	New Haven	AHL	48	15	21	36	48	....	....	....	....	....	....	....	....	....	....	....	1	0	0	0	0	....	....	....
1998-99	**Carolina**	**NHL**	**60**	**7**	**11**	**18**	**97**	**0**	**0**	**0**	**52**	**13.5**	**7**	**144**	**39.6**	**67**	**9**	**9:53**	**6**	**0**	**3**	**3**	**8**	**0**	**0**	**0**
	NHL Totals		**93**	**9**	**15**	**24**	**107**	**0**	**0**	**1**	**73**	**12.3**		**144**	**39.6**	**67**	**9**	**9:53**	**6**	**0**	**3**	**3**	**8**	**0**	**0**	**0**

Traded to **Hartford** by **Anaheim** with Anaheim's 4th round choice (Josef Vasicek) in 1998 Entry Draft for Mark Janssens, March 18, 1997. Rights transferred to **Carolina** after **Hartford** franchise relocated, June 25, 1997.

BAUMGARTNER, Ken — (BAWM-gahrt-nuhr)

Left wing. Shoots left. 6'1", 205 lbs. Born, Flin Flon, Man., March 11, 1966. Buffalo's 12th choice, 245th overall, in 1985 Entry Draft.

1983-84	Prince Albert	WHL	57	1	6	7	203	....	....	....	....	....	....	....	....	....	....	....	4	0	0	0	23	....	....	....
1984-85	Prince Albert	WHL	60	3	9	12	252	....	....	....	....	....	....	....	....	....	....	....	13	1	3	4	89	....	....	....
1985-86	Prince Albert	WHL	70	4	23	27	277	....	....	....	....	....	....	....	....	....	....	....	20	3	9	12	112	....	....	....
1986-87	EHC Chur	Switz.	STATISTICS NOT AVAILABLE																								
	New Haven	AHL	13	0	3	3	99	....	....	....	....	....	....	....	....	....	....	....	6	0	0	0	60	....	....	....
1987-88	**Los Angeles**	**NHL**	**30**	**2**	**3**	**5**	**189**	**0**	**0**	**0**	**17**	**11.8**	**5**	....	....	....	....	....	**5**	**0**	**1**	**1**	**28**	**0**	**0**	**0**
	New Haven	AHL	48	1	5	6	181	....	....	....	....	....	....	....	....	....	....	....	....	....	....	....	....	....	....	....
1988-89	**Los Angeles**	**NHL**	**49**	**1**	**3**	**4**	**288**	**0**	**0**	**0**	**15**	**6.7**	**–9**	....	....	....	....	....	**5**	**0**	**0**	**0**	**8**	**0**	**0**	**0**
	New Haven	AHL	10	1	3	4	26	....	....	....	....	....	....	....	....	....	....	....	....	....	....	....	....	....	....	....
1989-90	**Los Angeles**	**NHL**	**12**	**1**	**0**	**1**	**28**	**0**	**0**	**0**	**7**	**14.3**	**–10**	....	....	....	....	....	....	....	....	....	....	....	....	....
	NY Islanders	**NHL**	**53**	**0**	**5**	**5**	**194**	**0**	**0**	**0**	**41**	**0.0**	**6**	....	....	....	....	....	**4**	**0**	**0**	**0**	**27**	**0**	**0**	**0**
1990-91	**NY Islanders**	**NHL**	**78**	**1**	**6**	**7**	**282**	**0**	**0**	**0**	**41**	**2.4**	**–14**	....	....	....	....	....	....	....	....	....	....	....	....	....
1991-92	**NY Islanders**	**NHL**	**44**	**0**	**1**	**1**	**202**	**0**	**0**	**0**	**11**	**0.0**	**–10**	....	....	....	....	....	....	....	....	....	....	....	....	....
	Toronto	**NHL**	**11**	**0**	**0**	**0**	**23**	**0**	**0**	**0**	**5**	**0.0**	**1**	....	....	....	....	....	....	....	....	....	....	....	....	....
1992-93	**Toronto**	**NHL**	**63**	**1**	**0**	**1**	**155**	**0**	**0**	**0**	**23**	**4.3**	**–11**	....	....	....	....	....	**7**	**1**	**0**	**1**	**0**	**0**	**0**	**0**
1993-94	**Toronto**	**NHL**	**64**	**4**	**4**	**8**	**185**	**0**	**0**	**0**	**34**	**11.8**	**–6**	....	....	....	....	....	**10**	**0**	**0**	**0**	**18**	**0**	**0**	**0**
1994-95	**Toronto**	**NHL**	**2**	**0**	**0**	**0**	**5**	**0**	**0**	**0**	**1**	**0.0**	**0**	....	....	....	....	....	....	....	....	....	....	....	....	....
1995-96	**Toronto**	**NHL**	**60**	**2**	**3**	**5**	**152**	**0**	**0**	**1**	**27**	**7.4**	**–5**	....	....	....	....	....	....	....	....	....	....	....	....	....
	Anaheim	**NHL**	**12**	**0**	**1**	**1**	**41**	**0**	**0**	**0**	**5**	**0.0**	**0**	....	....	....	....	....	....	....	....	....	....	....	....	....
1996-97	**Anaheim**	**NHL**	**67**	**0**	**11**	**11**	**182**	**0**	**0**	**0**	**20**	**0.0**	**0**	....	....	....	....	....	**11**	**0**	**1**	**1**	**11**	**0**	**0**	**0**
1997-98	**Boston**	**NHL**	**82**	**0**	**1**	**1**	**199**	**0**	**0**	**0**	**28**	**0.0**	**–14**	....	....	....	....	....	**6**	**0**	**0**	**0**	**14**	**0**	**0**	**0**
1998-99	**Boston**	**NHL**	**69**	**1**	**3**	**4**	**119**	**0**	**0**	**0**	**15**	**6.7**	**–6**	**0**	**0.0**	**82**	**10**	**5:08**	**3**	**0**	**0**	**0**	**0**	**0**	**0**	**0**
	NHL Totals		**696**	**13**	**41**	**54**	**2244**	**0**	**0**	**1**	**290**	**4.5**		**0**	**0.0**	**82**	**10**	**5:08**	**51**	**1**	**2**	**3**	**106**	**0**	**0**	**0**

Traded to **LA Kings** by **Buffalo** with Sean McKenna and Larry Playfair for Brian Engblom and Doug Smith, January 29, 1986. Traded to **NY Islanders** by **LA Kings** with Hubie McDonough for Mikko Makela, November 29, 1989. Traded to **Toronto** by **NY Islanders** with Dave McLlwain for Daniel Marois and Claude Loiselle, March 10, 1992. Traded to **Anaheim** by **Toronto** for Winnipeg's 4th round choice (previously acquired by Anaheim — later traded to Montreal — Montreal selected Kim Staal) in 1996 Entry Draft, March 20, 1996. Signed as a free agent by **Boston**, July 14, 1997.

BAUMGARTNER, Nolan — (BAWM-gahrt-nuhr) — WSH.

Defense. Shoots right. 6'1", 200 lbs. Born, Calgary, Alta., March 23, 1976. Washington's 1st choice, 10th overall, in 1994 Entry Draft.

1991-92	Calgary	AAHA	39	11	29	40	38	....	....	....	....	....	....	....	....	....	....	....	....	....	....	....	....	....	....	....
1992-93	Kamloops	WHL	43	0	5	5	30	....	....	....	....	....	....	....	....	....	....	....	11	1	1	2	0	....	....	....
1993-94	Kamloops	WHL	69	13	42	55	109	....	....	....	....	....	....	....	....	....	....	....	19	3	14	17	33	....	....	....
1994-95	Kamloops	WHL	62	8	36	44	71	....	....	....	....	....	....	....	....	....	....	....	21	4	13	17	16	....	....	....
1995-96	Kamloops	WHL	28	13	15	28	45	....	....	....	....	....	....	....	....	....	....	....	16	1	9	10	26	....	....	....
	Washington	**NHL**	**1**	**0**	**0**	**0**	**0**	**0**	**0**	**0**	**0**	**0.0**	**–1**	....	....	....	....	....	**1**	**0**	**0**	**0**	**10**	**0**	**0**	**0**
1996-97	Portland	AHL	8	2	2	4	4	....	....	....	....	....	....	....	....	....	....	....	....	....	....	....	....	....	....	....
1997-98	**Washington**	**NHL**	**4**	**0**	**1**	**1**	**0**	**0**	**0**	**0**	**4**	**0.0**	**0**	....	....	....	....	....	....	....	....	....	....	....	....	....
	Portland	AHL	70	2	24	26	70	....	....	....	....	....	....	....	....	....	....	....	10	1	4	5	10	....	....	....
1998-99	**Washington**	**NHL**	**5**	**0**	**0**	**0**	**0**	**0**	**0**	**0**	**1**	**0.0**	**–3**	**0**	**0.0**	**1**	**0**	**8:41**	....	....	....	....	....	....	....	....
	Portland	AHL	38	5	14	19	62	....	....	....	....	....	....	....	....	....	....	....	....	....	....	....	....	....	....	....
	NHL Totals		**10**	**0**	**1**	**1**	**0**	**0**	**0**	**0**	**5**	**0.0**		**0**	**0.0**	**1**	**0**	**8:41**	**1**	**0**	**0**	**0**	**10**	**0**	**0**	**0**

Memorial Cup All-Star Team (1994, 1995) • WHL West First All-Star Team (1995, 1996) • Canadian Major Junior First All-Star Team (1995) • Canadian Major Junior Defenseman of the Year (1995)

BEAUFAIT, Mark

Center. Shoots right. 5'9", 170 lbs. Born, Livonia, MI, May 13, 1970. San Jose's 2nd choice, 7th overall, in 1991 Supplemental Draft.

1988-89	North-Michigan	WCHA	11	2	1	3	2	....	....	....	....	....	....	....	....	....	....	....	....	....	....	....	....	....	....	....
1989-90	North-Michigan	WCHA	34	10	14	24	12	....	....	....	....	....	....	....	....	....	....	....	....	....	....	....	....	....	....	....
1990-91	North-Michigan	WCHA	47	19	30	49	18	....	....	....	....	....	....	....	....	....	....	....	....	....	....	....	....	....	....	....
1991-92	North-Michigan	WCHA	39	31	44	75	43	....	....	....	....	....	....	....	....	....	....	....	....	....	....	....	....	....	....	....
1992-93	**San Jose**	**NHL**	**5**	**1**	**0**	**1**	**0**	**0**	**0**	**0**	**3**	**33.3**	**–1**	....	....	....	....	....	....	....	....	....	....	....	....	....
	Kansas City	IHL	66	19	40	59	22	....	....	....	....	....	....	....	....	....	....	....	9	1	1	2	8	....	....	....
1993-94	United States	Nat-Team	51	22	29	51	36	....	....	....	....	....	....	....	....	....	....	....	....	....	....	....	....	....	....	....
	United States	Olympics	8	1	4	5	2	....	....	....	....	....	....	....	....	....	....	....	....	....	....	....	....	....	....	....
	Kansas City	IHL	21	12	9	21	18	....	....	....	....	....	....	....	....	....	....	....	....	....	....	....	....	....	....	....
1994-95	San Diego	IHL	68	24	39	63	22	....	....	....	....	....	....	....	....	....	....	....	5	2	2	4	2	....	....	....
1995-96	Orlando	IHL	77	30	79	109	87	....	....	....	....	....	....	....	....	....	....	....	22	9	*19	*28	22	....	....	....
1996-97	Orlando	IHL	80	26	65	91	63	....	....	....	....	....	....	....	....	....	....	....	10	5	8	13	18	....	....	....
1997-98	Orlando	IHL	76	24	61	85	56	....	....	....	....	....	....	....	....	....	....	....	17	6	16	22	10	....	....	....
1998-99	Orlando	IHL	71	28	43	71	38	....	....	....	....	....	....	....	....	....	....	....	15	2	12	14	14	....	....	....
	NHL Totals		**5**	**1**	**0**	**1**	**0**	**0**	**0**	**0**	**3**	**33.3**		....	....	....	....	....	....	....	....	....	....	....	....	....

IHL Second All-Star Team (1997)

Regular Season | Playoffs

BEDDOES, Clayton

Center. Shoots left. 5'11", 190 lbs. Born, Bentley, Alta., November 10, 1970.

Season	Club	League	GP	G	A	Pts	PIM	PP	SH	GW	S	%	+/-	TF	F%	H	SB	Min	GP	G	A	Pts	PIM	PP	SH	GW
1989-90	Weyburn	MJHL	63	34	60	94	69	....	....	....	....	....	....	....	....	....	....	....	....	....	....	....	....	....	....	....
1990-91	Lake Superior	CCHA	45	14	28	42	26	....	....	....	....	....	....	....	....	....	....	....	....	....	....	....	....	....	....	....
1991-92	Lake Superior	CCHA	38	14	26	40	24	....	....	....	....	....	....	....	....	....	....	....	....	....	....	....	....	....	....	....
1992-93	Lake Superior	CCHA	43	18	40	58	30	....	....	....	....	....	....	....	....	....	....	....	....	....	....	....	....	....	....	....
1993-94	Lake Superior	CCHA	44	23	31	54	56	....	....	....	....	....	....	....	....	....	....	....	....	....	....	....	....	....	....	....
1994-95	Providence	AHL	65	16	20	36	39	....	....	....	....	....	....	....	....	....	....	....	13	3	1	4	18	....	....	....
1995-96	**Boston**	**NHL**	**39**	**1**	**6**	**7**	**44**	**0**	**0**	**0**	**18**	**5.6**	**-5**	....	....	....	....	....	....	....	....	....	....	....	....	....
	Providence	AHL	32	10	15	25	24	....	....	....	....	....	....	....	....	....	....	....	4	2	3	5	0	....	....	....
1996-97	**Boston**	**NHL**	**21**	**1**	**2**	**3**	**13**	**0**	**0**	**0**	**11**	**9.1**	**-1**	....	....	....	....	....	....	....	....	....	....	....	....	....
	Providence	AHL	36	11	23	34	60	....	....	....	....	....	....	....	....	....	....	....	7	2	0	2	4	....	....	....
1997-98	Detroit	IHL	65	22	24	46	63	....	....	....	....	....	....	....	....	....	....	....	22	5	10	15	16	....	....	....
1998-99	EHC Berlin	Germany	52	17	26	43	12	....	....	....	....	....	....	....	....	....	....	....	....	....	....	....	....	....	....	....
	NHL Totals		**60**	**2**	**8**	**10**	**57**	**0**	**0**	**0**	**29**	**6.9**		....	....	....	....	....	....	....	....	....	....	....	....	....

CCHA Second All-Star Team (1994) • NCAA West Second All-American Team (1994) • NCAA Championship All-Tournament Team (1994)

Signed as a free agent by **Boston**, June 2, 1994. Signed as a free agent by **Ottawa**, July 28, 1997.

BEGIN, Steve

(bay-ZHIN) **CGY.**

Center. Shoots left. 5'11", 185 lbs. Born, Trois-Rivieres, Que., June 14, 1978. Calgary's 3rd choice, 40th overall, in 1996 Entry Draft.

Season	Club	League	GP	G	A	Pts	PIM	PP	SH	GW	S	%	+/-	TF	F%	H	SB	Min	GP	G	A	Pts	PIM	PP	SH	GW
1994-95	Cap-de-Madelaine	QAAA	35	9	15	24	48	....	....	....	....	....	....	....	....	....	....	....	....	....	....	....	....	....	....	....
1995-96	Val d'Or	QMJHL	64	13	23	36	218	....	....	....	....	....	....	....	....	....	....	....	13	1	3	4	33	....	....	....
1996-97	Val d'Or	QMJHL	58	13	33	46	229	....	....	....	....	....	....	....	....	....	....	....	10	0	3	3	8	....	....	....
	Saint John	AHL	....	....	....	....	....	....	....	....	....	....	....	....	....	....	....	....	4	0	2	2	6	....	....	....
1997-98	Val d'Or	QMJHL	35	18	17	35	73	....	....	....	....	....	....	....	....	....	....	....	15	2	12	14	34	....	....	....
	Calgary	**NHL**	**5**	**0**	**0**	**0**	**23**	**0**	**0**	**0**	**2**	**0.0**	**0**	....	....	....	....	....	....	....	....	....	....	....	....	....
1998-99	Saint John	AHL	73	11	9	20	156	....	....	....	....	....	....	....	....	....	....	....	7	2	0	2	18	....	....	....
	NHL Totals		**5**	**0**	**0**	**0**	**23**	**0**	**0**	**0**	**2**	**0.0**		....	....	....	....	....	....	....	....	....	....	....	....	....

BELAK, Wade

(BEE-lak) **CGY.**

Defense. Shoots right. 6'5", 225 lbs. Born, Saskatoon, Sask., July 3, 1976. Quebec's 1st choice, 12th overall, in 1994 Entry Draft.

Season	Club	League	GP	G	A	Pts	PIM	PP	SH	GW	S	%	+/-	TF	F%	H	SB	Min	GP	G	A	Pts	PIM	PP	SH	GW
1991-92	North Battleford	SAHA	57	6	20	26	186	....	....	....	....	....	....	....	....	....	....	....	....	....	....	....	....	....	....	....
1992-93	North Battleford	SJHL	50	5	15	20	146	....	....	....	....	....	....	....	....	....	....	....	....	....	....	....	....	....	....	....
	Saskatoon	WHL	7	0	0	0	23	....	....	....	....	....	....	....	....	....	....	....	7	0	0	0	0	....	....	....
1993-94	Saskatoon	WHL	69	4	13	17	226	....	....	....	....	....	....	....	....	....	....	....	16	2	2	4	43	....	....	....
1994-95	Saskatoon	WHL	72	4	14	18	290	....	....	....	....	....	....	....	....	....	....	....	9	0	0	0	36	....	....	....
	Cornwall	AHL	....	....	....	....	....	....	....	....	....	....	....	....	....	....	....	....	11	1	2	3	40	....	....	....
1995-96	Saskatoon	WHL	63	3	15	18	207	....	....	....	....	....	....	....	....	....	....	....	4	0	0	0	9	....	....	....
	Cornwall	AHL	5	0	0	0	18	....	....	....	....	....	....	....	....	....	....	....	2	0	0	0	2	....	....	....
1996-97	**Colorado**	**NHL**	**5**	**0**	**0**	**0**	**11**	**0**	**0**	**0**	**1**	**0.0**	**-1**	....	....	....	....	....	....	....	....	....	....	....	....	....
	Hershey	AHL	65	1	7	8	320	....	....	....	....	....	....	....	....	....	....	....	16	0	1	1	61	....	....	....
1997-98	**Colorado**	**NHL**	**8**	**1**	**1**	**2**	**27**	**0**	**0**	**1**	**2**	**50.0**	**-3**	....	....	....	....	....	....	....	....	....	....	....	....	....
	Hershey	AHL	11	0	0	0	30	....	....	....	....	....	....	....	....	....	....	....	....	....	....	....	....	....	....	....
1998-99	**Colorado**	**NHL**	**22**	**0**	**0**	**0**	**71**	**0**	**0**	**0**	**5**	**0.0**	**-2**	**0**	**0.0**	**18**	**10**	**6:48**	....	....	....	....	....	....	....	....
	Hershey	AHL	17	0	1	1	49	....	....	....	....	....	....	....	....	....	....	....	....	....	....	....	....	....	....	....
	Calgary	**NHL**	**9**	**0**	**1**	**1**	**23**	**0**	**0**	**0**	**2**	**0.0**	**3**	**0**	**0.0**	**9**	**7**	**10:46**	....	....	....	....	....	....	....	....
	Saint John	AHL	12	0	2	2	43	....	....	....	....	....	....	....	....	....	....	....	6	0	1	1	23	....	....	....
	NHL Totals		**44**	**1**	**2**	**3**	**132**	**0**	**0**	**1**	**10**	**10.0**		**0**	**0.0**	**27**	**17**	**7:57**	....	....	....	....	....	....	....	....

Rights transferred to **Colorado** after **Quebec** franchise relocated, June 21, 1995. Traded to **Calgary** by **Colorado** with Rene Corbet and future considerations (Robyn Regehr, March 27, 1999) for Theoren Fleury and Chris Dingman, February 28, 1999.

BELANGER, Jesse

(buh-LAWN-zhay) **MTL.**

Center. Shoots right. 6'1", 190 lbs. Born, St. Georges de Beauce, Que., June 15, 1969.

Season	Club	League	GP	G	A	Pts	PIM	PP	SH	GW	S	%	+/-	TF	F%	H	SB	Min	GP	G	A	Pts	PIM	PP	SH	GW
1987-88	Granby	QMJHL	69	33	43	76	10	....	....	....	....	....	....	....	....	....	....	....	5	3	3	6	0	....	....	....
1988-89	Granby	QMJHL	67	40	63	103	26	....	....	....	....	....	....	....	....	....	....	....	4	0	5	5	0	....	....	....
1989-90	Granby	QMJHL	67	53	54	107	53	....	....	....	....	....	....	....	....	....	....	....	....	....	....	....	....	....	....	....
	Canada	Nat-Team	1	0	0	0	0	....	....	....	....	....	....	....	....	....	....	....	....	....	....	....	....	....	....	....
1990-91	Fredericton	AHL	75	40	58	98	30	....	....	....	....	....	....	....	....	....	....	....	6	2	4	6	0	....	....	....
1991-92	**Montreal**	**NHL**	**4**	**0**	**0**	**0**	**0**	**0**	**0**	**0**	**4**	**0.0**	**-1**	....	....	....	....	....	....	....	....	....	....	....	....	....
	Fredericton	AHL	65	30	41	71	26	....	....	....	....	....	....	....	....	....	....	....	7	3	3	6	2	....	....	....
1992-93♦	**Montreal**	**NHL**	**19**	**4**	**2**	**6**	**4**	**0**	**0**	**0**	**24**	**16.7**	**1**	....	....	....	....	....	**9**	**0**	**1**	**1**	**0**	**0**	**0**	**0**
	Fredericton	AHL	39	19	32	51	24	....	....	....	....	....	....	....	....	....	....	....	....	....	....	....	....	....	....	....
1993-94	**Florida**	**NHL**	**70**	**17**	**33**	**50**	**16**	**11**	**0**	**3**	**104**	**16.3**	**-4**	....	....	....	....	....	....	....	....	....	....	....	....	....
1994-95	**Florida**	**NHL**	**47**	**15**	**14**	**29**	**18**	**6**	**0**	**3**	**89**	**16.9**	**-5**	....	....	....	....	....	....	....	....	....	....	....	....	....
1995-96	**Florida**	**NHL**	**63**	**17**	**21**	**38**	**10**	**7**	**0**	**1**	**140**	**12.1**	**-5**	....	....	....	....	....	....	....	....	....	....	....	....	....
	Vancouver	**NHL**	**9**	**3**	**0**	**3**	**4**	**1**	**0**	**1**	**11**	**27.3**	**0**	....	....	....	....	....	**3**	**0**	**2**	**2**	**2**	**0**	**0**	**0**
1996-97	**Edmonton**	**NHL**	**6**	**0**	**0**	**0**	**0**	**0**	**0**	**0**	**8**	**0.0**	**-3**	....	....	....	....	....	....	....	....	....	....	....	....	....
	Hamilton	AHL	6	4	3	7	0	....	....	....	....	....	....	....	....	....	....	....	....	....	....	....	....	....	....	....
	Quebec	IHL	47	34	28	62	18	....	....	....	....	....	....	....	....	....	....	....	9	3	5	8	13	....	....	....
1997-98	SC Herisau	Switz.	5	4	3	7	4	....	....	....	....	....	....	....	....	....	....	....	....	....	....	....	....	....	....	....
	Las Vegas	IHL	54	32	36	68	20	....	....	....	....	....	....	....	....	....	....	....	4	0	1	1	0	....	....	....
1998-99	Cleveland	IHL	22	9	13	22	10	....	....	....	....	....	....	....	....	....	....	....	....	....	....	....	....	....	....	....
	NHL Totals		**218**	**56**	**70**	**126**	**52**	**25**	**0**	**8**	**380**	**14.7**		....	....	....	....	....	**12**	**0**	**3**	**3**	**2**	**0**	**0**	**0**

Signed as a free agent by **Montreal**, October 3, 1990. Claimed by **Florida** from **Montreal** in Expansion Draft, June 24, 1993. Traded to **Vancouver** by **Florida** for Vancouver's 3rd round choice (Oleg Kvasha) in 1996 Entry Draft and future considerations, March 20, 1996. Signed as a free agent by **Edmonton**, September 16, 1996. Signed as a free agent by **Tampa Bay**, August 18, 1998. Signed as a free agent by **Montreal**, July 23, 1999.

BELANGER, Ken

(buh-LAWN-zhay) **BOS.**

Left wing. Shoots left. 6'4", 225 lbs. Born, Sault Ste. Marie, Ont., May 14, 1974. Hartford's 7th choice, 153rd overall, in 1992 Entry Draft.

Season	Club	League	GP	G	A	Pts	PIM	PP	SH	GW	S	%	+/-	TF	F%	H	SB	Min	GP	G	A	Pts	PIM	PP	SH	GW
1990-91	S.S. Marie	OMHA	43	24	29	53	169	....	....	....	....	....	....	....	....	....	....	....	....	....	....	....	....	....	....	....
1991-92	Ottawa	OHL	51	4	4	8	174	....	....	....	....	....	....	....	....	....	....	....	11	0	0	0	24	....	....	....
1992-93	Ottawa	OHL	34	6	12	18	139	....	....	....	....	....	....	....	....	....	....	....	....	....	....	....	....	....	....	....
	Guelph	OHL	29	10	14	24	86	....	....	....	....	....	....	....	....	....	....	....	5	2	1	3	14	....	....	....
1993-94	Guelph	OHL	55	11	22	33	185	....	....	....	....	....	....	....	....	....	....	....	9	2	3	5	30	....	....	....
1994-95	St. John's	AHL	47	5	5	10	246	....	....	....	....	....	....	....	....	....	....	....	4	0	0	0	30	....	....	....
	Toronto	**NHL**	**3**	**0**	**0**	**0**	**9**	**0**	**0**	**0**	**1**	**0.0**	**0**	....	....	....	....	....	....	....	....	....	....	....	....	....
1995-96	St. John's	AHL	40	16	14	30	222	....	....	....	....	....	....	....	....	....	....	....	....	....	....	....	....	....	....	....
	NY Islanders	**NHL**	**7**	**0**	**0**	**0**	**27**	**0**	**0**	**0**	**0**	**0.0**	**-2**	....	....	....	....	....	....	....	....	....	....	....	....	....
1996-97	**NY Islanders**	**NHL**	**18**	**0**	**2**	**2**	**102**	**0**	**0**	**0**	**5**	**0.0**	**-1**	....	....	....	....	....	....	....	....	....	....	....	....	....
	Kentucky	AHL	38	10	12	22	164	....	....	....	....	....	....	....	....	....	....	....	4	0	1	1	27	....	....	....
1997-98	**NY Islanders**	**NHL**	**37**	**3**	**1**	**4**	**101**	**0**	**0**	**1**	**10**	**30.0**	**1**	....	....	....	....	....	....	....	....	....	....	....	....	....
1998-99	**NY Islanders**	**NHL**	**9**	**1**	**1**	**2**	**30**	**0**	**0**	**0**	**3**	**33.3**	**1**	**0**	**0.0**	**15**	**1**	**5:05**	....	....	....	....	....	....	....	....
	Boston	**NHL**	**45**	**1**	**4**	**5**	**152**	**0**	**0**	**0**	**16**	**6.3**	**-2**	**1**	**0.0**	**66**	**4**	**4:38**	**12**	**1**	**0**	**1**	**16**	**0**	**0**	**0**
	NHL Totals		**119**	**5**	**8**	**13**	**421**	**0**	**0**	**1**	**35**	**14.3**		**1**	**0.0**	**81**	**5**	**4:42**	**12**	**1**	**0**	**1**	**16**	**0**	**0**	**0**

Traded to **Toronto** by **Hartford** for Toronto's 9th round choice (Matt Ball) in 1994 Entry Draft, March 18, 1994. Traded to **NY Islanders** by **Toronto** with Damian Rhodes for future considerations (Kirk Muller and Don Beaupre, January 23, 1996), January 23, 1996. Traded to **Boston** by **NY Islanders** for Ted Donato, November 7, 1998.

BELLOWS, Brian

Left wing. Shoots right. 5'11", 210 lbs. Born, St. Catharines, Ont., September 1, 1964. Minnesota's 1st choice, 2nd overall, in 1982 Entry Draft.

			Regular Season																Playoffs							
Season	Club	League	GP	G	A	Pts	PIM	PP	SH	GW	S	%	+/–	TF	F%	H	SB	Min	GP	G	A	Pts	PIM	PP	SH	GW
1979-80	St. Catharines	OJHL-B	44	50	80	130	24	....	....	....	....	....	....	....	....	....	....	....	....	....	....	....	....	....	....	....
1980-81	Kitchener	OHA	66	49	67	116	23	....	....	....	....	....	....	....	....	....	....	....	16	14	13	27	13	....	....	....
1981-82	Kitchener	OHL	47	45	52	97	23	....	....	....	....	....	....	....	....	....	....	....	15	16	13	29	11	....	....	....
1982-83	**Minnesota**	**NHL**	78	35	30	65	27	15	1	3	184	19.0	–12	....	....	....	....	....	9	5	4	9	18	2	0	0
1983-84	**Minnesota**	**NHL**	78	41	42	83	66	14	5	5	236	17.4	–2	....	....	....	....	....	16	2	12	14	6	0	1	0
1984-85	**Minnesota**	**NHL**	78	26	36	62	72	8	1	3	211	12.3	–18	....	....	....	....	....	9	2	4	6	9	0	1	0
1985-86	**Minnesota**	**NHL**	77	31	48	79	46	11	2	2	256	12.1	16	....	....	....	....	....	5	5	0	5	16	3	0	0
1986-87	**Minnesota**	**NHL**	65	26	27	53	34	8	1	2	200	13.0	–13	....	....	....	....	....	....	....	....	....	....	....	....	....
1987-88	**Minnesota**	**NHL**	77	40	41	81	81	21	1	4	283	14.1	–8	....	....	....	....	....	....	....	....	....	....	....	....	....
1988-89	**Minnesota**	**NHL**	60	23	27	50	55	7	0	4	196	11.7	–14	....	....	....	....	....	5	2	3	5	8	2	0	0
1989-90	**Minnesota**	**NHL**	80	55	44	99	72	21	1	9	300	18.3	–3	....	....	....	....	....	7	4	3	7	10	3	0	1
1990-91	**Minnesota**	**NHL**	80	35	40	75	43	17	0	4	296	11.8	–13	....	....	....	....	....	23	10	19	29	30	6	0	1
1991-92	**Minnesota**	**NHL**	80	30	45	75	41	12	1	4	255	11.8	–20	....	....	....	....	....	7	4	4	8	14	2	0	1
1992-93♦	**Montreal**	**NHL**	82	40	48	88	44	16	0	5	260	15.4	4	....	....	....	....	....	18	6	9	15	18	2	0	0
1993-94	**Montreal**	**NHL**	77	33	38	71	36	13	0	2	251	13.1	9	....	....	....	....	....	6	1	2	3	2	0	0	0
1994-95	**Montreal**	**NHL**	41	8	8	16	8	1	0	1	110	7.3	–7	....	....	....	....	....	....	....	....	....	....	....	....	....
1995-96	**Tampa Bay**	**NHL**	79	23	26	49	39	13	0	4	190	12.1	–14	....	....	....	....	....	6	2	0	2	4	0	0	1
1996-97	**Tampa Bay**	**NHL**	7	1	2	3	0	0	0	0	17	5.9	–4	....	....	....	....	....	....	....	....	....	....	....	....	....
	Anaheim	**NHL**	62	15	13	28	22	8	0	1	151	9.9	–11	....	....	....	....	....	11	2	4	6	2	1	0	0
1997-98	EHC Berlin	Germany	31	15	17	32	18	....	....	....	....	....	....	....	....	....	....	....	....	....	....	....	....	....	....	....
	Washington	**NHL**	11	6	3	9	6	5	0	2	26	23.1	–3	....	....	....	....	....	21	6	7	13	6	2	0	1
1998-99	**Washington**	**NHL**	76	17	19	36	26	8	0	3	166	10.2	–12	2	0.0	36	13	15:14	....	....	....	....	....	....	....	....
	NHL Totals		**1188**	**485**	**537**	**1022**	**718**	**198**	**13**	**58**	**3588**	**13.5**		**2**	**0.0**	**36**	**13**	**15:14**	**143**	**51**	**71**	**122**	**143**	**23**	**2**	**5**

OHL First All-Star Team (1982) • Won George Parsons Trophy (Memorial Cup Tournament Most Sportsmanlike Player) (1982) • NHL Second All-Star Team (1990)

Played in NHL All-Star Game (1984, 1988, 1992)

Traded to **Montreal** by **Minnesota** for Russ Courtnall, August 31, 1992. Traded to **Tampa Bay** by **Montreal** for Marc Bureau, June 30, 1995. Traded to **Anaheim** by **Tampa Bay** for Anaheim's 6th round choice (Andrei Skopintsev) in 1997 Entry Draft, November 19, 1996. Signed as a free agent by **Washington**, March 21, 1998.

BENDA, Jan

(BEHN-duh, YAHN)

Center. Shoots right. 6'2", 208 lbs. Born, Reef, Belgium, March 28, 1972.

			Regular Season																Playoffs							
Season	Club	League	GP	G	A	Pts	PIM	PP	SH	GW	S	%	+/–	TF	F%	H	SB	Min	GP	G	A	Pts	PIM	PP	SH	GW
1989-90	Oshawa	OJHL-B	44	50	80	130	24	....	....	....	....	....	....	....	....	....	....	....	....	....	....	....	....	....	....	....
	Oshawa	OHL	1	0	1	1	0	....	....	....	....	....	....	....	....	....	....	....	....	....	....	....	....	....	....	....
1990-91	Oshawa	OHL	51	4	11	15	64	....	....	....	....	....	....	....	....	....	....	....	16	2	4	6	19	....	....	....
	Grefrather EC	German-3	13	0	0	0	2	....	....	....	....	....	....	....	....	....	....	....	....	....	....	....	....	....	....	....
1991-92	Oshawa	OHL	61	12	23	35	68	....	....	....	....	....	....	....	....	....	....	....	7	1	1	2	12	....	....	....
1992-93	FEHC reiburg	Germany	41	6	11	17	49	....	....	....	....	....	....	....	....	....	....	....	9	3	3	6	12	....	....	....
1993-94	EC Munchen	Germany	43	16	11	27	67	....	....	....	....	....	....	....	....	....	....	....	10	3	2	5	21	....	....	....
	Germany	Olympics	8	0	1	1	6	....	....	....	....	....	....	....	....	....	....	....	....	....	....	....	....	....	....	....
	Germany	WC-A	5	0	0	0	24	....	....	....	....	....	....	....	....	....	....	....	....	....	....	....	....	....	....	....
1994-95	Binghamton	AHL	4	0	0	0	0	....	....	....	....	....	....	....	....	....	....	....	....	....	....	....	....	....	....	....
	Richmond	ECHL	62	21	39	60	187	....	....	....	....	....	....	....	....	....	....	....	17	8	5	13	50	....	....	....
1995-96	ESC Essen	German-2	2	1	0	1	6	....	....	....	....	....	....	....	....	....	....	....	....	....	....	....	....	....	....	....
	Slavia Praha	Cze-Rep	28	8	11	19	....	....	....	....	....	....	....	....	....	....	....	....	7	1	5	6	....	....	....	....
	Germany	WC-A	6	1	1	2	33	....	....	....	....	....	....	....	....	....	....	....	....	....	....	....	....	....	....	....
1996-97	Germany	W Cup	4	2	1	3	0	....	....	....	....	....	....	....	....	....	....	....	....	....	....	....	....	....	....	....
	Sparta Praha	Cze-Rep	49	7	21	28	61	....	....	....	....	....	....	....	....	....	....	....	10	1	1	2	12	....	....	....
	Sparta Praha	EuroHL	5	1	0	1	4	....	....	....	....	....	....	....	....	....	....	....	4	0	1	1	2	....	....	....
	Germany	WC-A	8	0	2	2	18	....	....	....	....	....	....	....	....	....	....	....	....	....	....	....	....	....	....	....
1997-98	Sparta Praha	Cze-Rep	1	0	1	1	4	....	....	....	....	....	....	....	....	....	....	....	....	....	....	....	....	....	....	....
	Washington	**NHL**	**9**	**0**	**3**	**3**	**6**	....	....	....	....	....	....	....	....	....	....	....	....	....	....	....	....	....	....	....
	Portland	AHL	62	25	29	54	90	....	....	....	....	....	....	....	....	....	....	....	8	0	7	7	6	....	....	....
	Germany	Olympics	4	3	0	3	8	....	....	....	....	....	....	....	....	....	....	....	....	....	....	....	....	....	....	....
1998-99	Assat Pori	Finland	52	21	22	43	139	....	....	....	....	....	....	....	....	....	....	....	....	....	....	....	....	....	....	....
	NHL Totals		**9**	**0**	**3**	**3**	**6**	....	....	....	....	....	....	....	....	....	....	....	....	....	....	....	....	....	....	....

Signed as a free agent by **Washington**, October 1, 1997.

BENYSEK, Ladislav

(BEHN-ih-sihk)

Defense. Shoots left. 6'2", 190 lbs. Born, Olomouc, Czech., March 24, 1975. Edmonton's 16th choice, 266th overall, in 1994 Entry Draft.

			Regular Season																Playoffs							
Season	Club	League	GP	G	A	Pts	PIM	PP	SH	GW	S	%	+/–	TF	F%	H	SB	Min	GP	G	A	Pts	PIM	PP	SH	GW
1993-94	HC Olomouc	Czech-Jr.	STATISTICS NOT AVAILABLE																							
1994-95	Cape Breton	AHL	58	2	7	9	54	....	....	....	....	....	....	....	....	....	....	....	....	....	....	....	....	....	....	....
1995-96	HC Olomouc	Cze-Rep	33	1	4	5	....	....	....	....	....	....	....	....	....	....	....	....	4	0	0	0	....	....	....	....
1996-97	Sparta Praha	Cze-Rep	36	5	5	10	28	....	....	....	....	....	....	....	....	....	....	....	5	0	1	1	2	....	....	....
	Sparta Praha	EuroHL	3	0	0	0	4	....	....	....	....	....	....	....	....	....	....	....	4	0	0	0	0	....	....	....
1997-98	Sparta Praha	Cze-Rep	1	0	0	0	0	....	....	....	....	....	....	....	....	....	....	....	....	....	....	....	....	....	....	....
	Edmonton	**NHL**	**2**	**0**	**0**	**0**	**0**	....	....	....	....	....	....	....	....	....	....	....	....	....	....	....	....	....	....	....
	Hamilton	AHL	53	2	14	16	29	....	....	....	....	....	....	....	....	....	....	....	9	1	1	2	2	....	....	....
1998-99	Sparta Praha	Cze-Rep	52	8	11	19	47	....	....	....	....	....	....	....	....	....	....	....	8	0	1	1	....	....	....	....
	NHL Totals		**2**	**0**	**0**	**0**	**0**	....	....	....	....	....	....	....	....	....	....	....	....	....	....	....	....	....	....	....

BERANEK, Josef

(buh-RAH-nehk, JOH-sehf) **EDM.**

Left wing/Center. Shoots left. 6'2", 195 lbs. Born, Litvinov, Czech., October 25, 1969. Edmonton's 3rd choice, 78th overall, in 1989 Entry Draft.

			Regular Season																Playoffs							
Season	Club	League	GP	G	A	Pts	PIM	PP	SH	GW	S	%	+/–	TF	F%	H	SB	Min	GP	G	A	Pts	PIM	PP	SH	GW
1987-88	CHZ Litvinov	Czech.	14	7	4	11	12	....	....	....	....	....	....	....	....	....	....	....	....	....	....	....	....	....	....	....
1988-89	CHZ Litvinov	Czech.	32	18	10	28	47	....	....	....	....	....	....	....	....	....	....	....	....	....	....	....	....	....	....	....
1989-90	Dukla Trencin	Czech.	49	19	23	42	....	....	....	....	....	....	....	....	....	....	....	....	....	....	....	....	....	....	....	....
1990-91	CHZ Litvinov	Czech.	58	29	31	60	98	....	....	....	....	....	....	....	....	....	....	....	....	....	....	....	....	....	....	....
1991-92	**Edmonton**	**NHL**	58	12	16	28	18	0	0	1	79	15.2	–2	....	....	....	....	....	12	2	1	3	0	1	0	1
1992-93	**Edmonton**	**NHL**	26	2	6	8	28	0	0	0	44	4.5	–7	....	....	....	....	....	....	....	....	....	....	....	....	....
	Cape Breton	AHL	6	1	2	3	8	....	....	....	....	....	....	....	....	....	....	....	....	....	....	....	....	....	....	....
	Philadelphia	**NHL**	40	13	12	25	50	1	0	0	86	15.1	–1	....	....	....	....	....	....	....	....	....	....	....	....	....
1993-94	**Philadelphia**	**NHL**	80	28	21	49	85	6	0	2	182	15.4	–2	....	....	....	....	....	....	....	....	....	....	....	....	....
1994-95	Petra Vsetin	Cze-Rep	16	7	7	14	26	....	....	....	....	....	....	....	....	....	....	....	....	....	....	....	....	....	....	....
	Philadelphia	**NHL**	14	5	5	10	2	1	0	0	39	12.8	3	....	....	....	....	....	....	....	....	....	....	....	....	....
	Vancouver	**NHL**	37	8	13	21	28	2	0	0	95	8.4	–10	....	....	....	....	....	11	1	1	2	12	0	0	0
1995-96	**Vancouver**	**NHL**	61	6	14	20	60	0	0	1	131	4.6	–11	....	....	....	....	....	3	2	1	3	0	0	0	0
1996-97	Petra Vsetin	Cze-Rep	39	19	24	43	115	....	....	....	....	....	....	....	....	....	....	....	3	3	2	5	4	....	....	....
	Pittsburgh	**NHL**	8	3	1	4	4	1	0	0	15	20.0	–1	....	....	....	....	....	5	0	0	0	2	0	0	0
1997-98	Petra Vsetin	Cze-Rep	45	24	27	51	92	....	....	....	....	....	....	....	....	....	....	....	10	2	8	10	14	....	....	....
	Petra Vsetin	EuroHL	8	5	4	9	10	....	....	....	....	....	....	....	....	....	....	....	....	....	....	....	....	....	....	....
	Czech Republic	Olympics	6	1	0	1	4	....	....	....	....	....	....	....	....	....	....	....	....	....	....	....	....	....	....	....
1998-99	**Edmonton**	**NHL**	66	19	30	49	23	7	0	2	160	11.9	6	1261	50.2	47	21	16:25	2	0	0	0	4	0	0	0
	NHL Totals		**390**	**96**	**118**	**214**	**298**	**18**	**0**	**6**	**831**	**11.6**		**1261**	**50.2**	**47**	**21**	**16:25**	**33**	**5**	**3**	**8**	**18**	**1**	**0**	**1**

Traded to **Philadelphia** by **Edmonton** with Greg Hawgood for Brian Benning, January 16, 1993. Traded to **Vancouver** by **Philadelphia** for Shawn Antoski, February 15, 1995. Traded to **Pittsburgh** by **Vancouver** for future considerations, March 18, 1997. Traded to **Edmonton** by **Pittsburgh** for Bobby Dollas and Tony Hrkac, June 16, 1998.

			Regular Season																Playoffs							
Season	Club	League	GP	G	A	Pts	PIM	PP	SH	GW	S	%	+/-	TF	F%	H	SB	Min	GP	G	A	Pts	PIM	PP	SH	GW

BERARD, Bryan

(buh-RAHRD) **TOR.**

Defense. Shoots left. 6'1", 190 lbs. Born, Woonsocket, RI, March 5, 1977. Ottawa's 1st choice, 1st overall, in 1995 Entry Draft.

Season	Club	League	GP	G	A	Pts	PIM	PP	SH	GW	S	%	+/-	TF	F%	H	SB	Min	GP	G	A	Pts	PIM	PP	SH	GW
1991-92	Mt. St. Charles	H.S.	32	3	15	18	10	....	....	....	....	....	....	....	....	....	....	....	....	....	....	....	....	....	....	....
1992-93	Mt. St. Charles	H.S.	32	8	12	20	18	....	....	....	....	....	....	....	....	....	....	....	....	....	....	....	....	....	....	....
1993-94	Mt. St. Charles	H.S.	32	11	36	47	97	....	....	....	....	....	....	....	....	....	....	....	....	....	....	....	....	....	....	....
1994-95	Detroit	OHL	58	20	55	75	97	....	....	....	....	....	....	....	....	....	....	....	21	4	20	24	38	....	....	....
1995-96	Detroit	OHL	56	31	58	89	116	....	....	....	....	....	....	....	....	....	....	....	17	7	18	25	41	....	....	....
1996-97	**NY Islanders**	**NHL**	**82**	**8**	**40**	**48**	**86**	**3**	**0**	**1**	**172**	**4.7**	**1**	....	....	....	....	....	....	....	....	....	....	....	....	....
1997-98	**NY Islanders**	**NHL**	**75**	**14**	**32**	**46**	**59**	**8**	**1**	**2**	**192**	**7.3**	**-32**	....	....	....	....	....	....	....	....	....	....	....	....	....
	United States	Olympics	2	0	0	0	0	....	....	....	....	....	....	....	....	....	....	....	....	....	....	....	....	....	....	....
1998-99	**NY Islanders**	**NHL**	**31**	**4**	**11**	**15**	**26**	**2**	**0**	**3**	**72**	**5.6**	**-6**	**0**	**0.0**	**16**	**32**	**24:45**	....	....	....	....	....	....	....	....
	Toronto	**NHL**	**38**	**5**	**14**	**19**	**22**	**2**	**0**	**2**	**63**	**7.9**	**7**	**0**	**0.0**	**34**	**42**	**22:38**	**17**	**1**	**8**	**9**	**8**	**1**	**0**	**0**
	NHL Totals		**226**	**31**	**97**	**128**	**193**	**15**	**1**	**8**	**499**	**6.2**		**0**	**0.0**	**50**	**74**	**23:35**	**17**	**1**	**8**	**9**	**8**	**1**	**0**	**0**

OHL First All-Star Team (1995, 1996) • Canadian Major Junior First All-Star Team (1995, 1996) • Canadian Major Junior Rookie of the Year (1995) • Canadian Major Junior Defenseman of the Year (1996) • NHL All-Rookie Team (1997) • Won Calder Memorial Trophy (1997)

Traded to **NY Islanders** by **Ottawa** with Don Beaupre and Martin Straka for Damian Rhodes and Wade Redden, January 23, 1996. Traded to **Toronto** by **NY Islanders** with NY Islanders' 6th round choice (Jan Socher) in 1999 Entry Draft for Felix Potvin and Toronto's 6th round choice (later traded to Tampa Bay - Tampa Bay selected Fedor Fedorov) in 1999 Entry Draft, January 9, 1999.

BEREHOWSKY, Drake

(beh-reh-HOW-skee)

Defense. Shoots right. 6'2", 212 lbs. Born, Toronto, Ont., January 3, 1972. Toronto's 1st choice, 10th overall, in 1990 Entry Draft.

Season	Club	League	GP	G	A	Pts	PIM	PP	SH	GW	S	%	+/-	TF	F%	H	SB	Min	GP	G	A	Pts	PIM	PP	SH	GW
1987-88	Barrie	OJHL-B	40	10	36	46	81	....	....	....	....	....	....	....	....	....	....	....	....	....	....	....	....	....	....	....
1988-89	Kingston	OHL	63	7	39	46	85	....	....	....	....	....	....	....	....	....	....	....	....	....	....	....	....	....	....	....
	Canada	Nat-Team	1	0	0	0	0	....	....	....	....	....	....	....	....	....	....	....	....	....	....	....	....	....	....	....
1989-90	Kingston	OHL	9	3	11	14	28	....	....	....	....	....	....	....	....	....	....	....	....	....	....	....	....	....	....	....
1990-91	Kingston	OHL	13	5	13	18	38	....	....	....	....	....	....	....	....	....	....	....	....	....	....	....	....	....	....	....
	Toronto	**NHL**	**8**	**0**	**1**	**1**	**25**	**0**	**0**	**0**	**4**	**0.0**	**-6**	....	....	....	....	....	....	....	....	....	....	....	....	....
	North Bay	OHL	26	7	23	30	51	....	....	....	....	....	....	....	....	....	....	....	10	2	7	9	21	....	....	....
1991-92	North Bay	OHL	62	19	63	82	147	....	....	....	....	....	....	....	....	....	....	....	21	7	24	31	22	....	....	....
	Toronto	**NHL**	**1**	**0**	**0**	**0**	**0**	**0**	**0**	**0**	**0**	**0.0**	**0**	....	....	....	....	....	....	....	....	....	....	....	....	....
	St. John's	AHL	....	....	....	....	....	....	....	....	....	....	....	....	....	....	....	....	6	0	5	5	21	....	....	....
1992-93	**Toronto**	**NHL**	**41**	**4**	**15**	**19**	**61**	**1**	**0**	**1**	**41**	**9.8**	**1**	....	....	....	....	....	....	....	....	....	....	....	....	....
	St. John's	AHL	28	10	17	27	38	....	....	....	....	....	....	....	....	....	....	....	....	....	....	....	....	....	....	....
1993-94	**Toronto**	**NHL**	**49**	**2**	**8**	**10**	**63**	**2**	**0**	**2**	**29**	**6.9**	**-3**	....	....	....	....	....	....	....	....	....	....	....	....	....
	St. John's	AHL	18	3	12	15	40	....	....	....	....	....	....	....	....	....	....	....	....	....	....	....	....	....	....	....
1994-95	**Toronto**	**NHL**	**25**	**0**	**2**	**2**	**15**	**0**	**0**	**0**	**12**	**0.0**	**-10**	....	....	....	....	....	....	....	....	....	....	....	....	....
	Pittsburgh	**NHL**	**4**	**0**	**0**	**0**	**13**	**0**	**0**	**0**	**2**	**0.0**	**1**	....	....	....	....	....	**1**	**0**	**0**	**0**	**0**	**0**	**0**	**0**
1995-96	**Pittsburgh**	**NHL**	**1**	**0**	**0**	**0**	**0**	**0**	**0**	**0**	**0**	**0.0**	**1**	....	....	....	....	....	....	....	....	....	....	....	....	....
	Cleveland	IHL	74	6	28	34	141	....	....	....	....	....	....	....	....	....	....	....	3	0	3	3	6	....	....	....
1996-97	Carolina	AHL	49	2	15	17	55	....	....	....	....	....	....	....	....	....	....	....	....	....	....	....	....	....	....	....
	San Antonio	IHL	16	3	4	7	36	....	....	....	....	....	....	....	....	....	....	....	....	....	....	....	....	....	....	....
1997-98	**Edmonton**	**NHL**	**67**	**1**	**6**	**7**	**169**	**1**	**0**	**1**	**58**	**1.7**	**1**	....	....	....	....	....	**12**	**1**	**2**	**3**	**14**	**0**	**0**	**1**
	Hamilton	AHL	8	2	0	2	21	....	....	....	....	....	....	....	....	....	....	....	....	....	....	....	....	....	....	....
1998-99	**Nashville**	**NHL**	**74**	**2**	**15**	**17**	**140**	**0**	**0**	**0**	**79**	**2.5**	**-9**	**1**	**100.0**	**140**	**109**	**21:43**	....	....	....	....	....	....	....	....
	NHL Totals		**270**	**9**	**47**	**56**	**486**	**4**	**0**	**4**	**225**	**4.0**		**1**	**100.0**	**140**	**109**	**21:43**	**13**	**1**	**2**	**3**	**14**	**0**	**0**	**1**

Canadian Major Junior Defenseman of the Year (1992) • OHL First All-Star Team (1992)

Traded to **Pittsburgh** by **Toronto** for Grant Jennings, April 7, 1995. Signed as a free agent by **Edmonton**, September 30, 1997. Traded to **Nashville** by **Edmonton** with Eric Fichaud and Greg de Vries for Mikhail Shtalenkov and Jim Dowd, October 1, 1998.

BEREZIN, Sergei

(BEH-reh-zihn) **TOR.**

Left wing. Shoots right. 5'10", 200 lbs. Born, Voskresensk, USSR, November 5, 1971. Toronto's 8th choice, 256th overall, in 1994 Entry Draft.

Season	Club	League	GP	G	A	Pts	PIM	PP	SH	GW	S	%	+/-	TF	F%	H	SB	Min	GP	G	A	Pts	PIM	PP	SH	GW
1990-91	Khimik	USSR	30	6	2	8	4	....	....	....	....	....	....	....	....	....	....	....	....	....	....	....	....	....	....	....
	Soviet Union	WJC-A	7	3	1	4	6	....	....	....	....	....	....	....	....	....	....	....	....	....	....	....	....	....	....	....
1991-92	Khimik	CIS	36	7	5	12	10	....	....	....	....	....	....	....	....	....	....	....	....	....	....	....	....	....	....	....
1992-93	Khimik	CIS	38	9	3	12	12	....	....	....	....	....	....	....	....	....	....	....	2	1	0	1	0	....	....	....
1993-94	Khimik	CIS	40	31	10	41	16	....	....	....	....	....	....	....	....	....	....	....	3	2	0	2	2	....	....	....
	Russia	Olympics	8	3	2	5	2	....	....	....	....	....	....	....	....	....	....	....	....	....	....	....	....	....	....	....
1994-95	Kolner Haie	Germany	43	38	19	57	8	....	....	....	....	....	....	....	....	....	....	....	18	17	8	25	14	....	....	....
1995-96	Kolner Haie	Germany	45	49	31	80	8	....	....	....	....	....	....	....	....	....	....	....	14	13	9	22	10	....	....	....
1996-97	**Toronto**	**NHL**	**73**	**25**	**16**	**41**	**2**	**7**	**0**	**2**	**177**	**14.1**	**-3**	....	....	....	....	....	....	....	....	....	....	....	....	....
1997-98	**Toronto**	**NHL**	**68**	**16**	**15**	**31**	**10**	**3**	**0**	**3**	**167**	**9.6**	**-3**	....	....	....	....	....	....	....	....	....	....	....	....	....
1998-99	**Toronto**	**NHL**	**76**	**37**	**22**	**59**	**12**	**9**	**1**	**4**	**263**	**14.1**	**16**	**26**	**57.7**	**24**	**11**	**15:32**	**17**	**6**	**6**	**12**	**4**	**2**	**0**	**2**
	NHL Totals		**217**	**78**	**53**	**131**	**24**	**19**	**1**	**9**	**607**	**12.9**		**26**	**57.7**	**24**	**11**	**15:32**	**17**	**6**	**6**	**12**	**4**	**2**	**0**	**2**

NHL All-Rookie Team (1997)

BERG, Aki-Petteri

(BUHRG, AH-kee-PEHT-uhr-ee) **L.A.**

Defense. Shoots left. 6'3", 203 lbs. Born, Turku, Finland, February 28, 1977. Los Angeles' 1st choice, 3rd overall, in 1995 Entry Draft.

Season	Club	League	GP	G	A	Pts	PIM	PP	SH	GW	S	%	+/-	TF	F%	H	SB	Min	GP	G	A	Pts	PIM	PP	SH	GW
1992-93	TPS Turku	Finn-Jr.	39	18	24	42	24	....	....	....	....	....	....	....	....	....	....	....	....	....	....	....	....	....	....	....
1993-94	TPS Turku	Finn-Jr.	21	3	11	14	24	....	....	....	....	....	....	....	....	....	....	....	7	0	0	0	10	....	....	....
	Kiekko-67	Finland-2	12	1	1	2	16	....	....	....	....	....	....	....	....	....	....	....	....	....	....	....	....	....	....	....
	TPS Turku	Finland	6	0	3	3	4	....	....	....	....	....	....	....	....	....	....	....	....	....	....	....	....	....	....	....
1994-95	TPS Turku	Finn-Jr.	8	1	0	1	30	....	....	....	....	....	....	....	....	....	....	....	....	....	....	....	....	....	....	....
	Kiekko-67	Finland-2	21	3	9	12	24	....	....	....	....	....	....	....	....	....	....	....	7	0	0	0	10	....	....	....
	TPS Turku	Finland	5	0	0	0	4	....	....	....	....	....	....	....	....	....	....	....	....	....	....	....	....	....	....	....
1995-96	**Los Angeles**	**NHL**	**51**	**0**	**7**	**7**	**29**	**0**	**0**	**0**	**56**	**0.0**	**-13**	....	....	....	....	....	....	....	....	....	....	....	....	....
	Phoenix	IHL	20	0	3	3	18	....	....	....	....	....	....	....	....	....	....	....	2	0	0	0	4	....	....	....
1996-97	**Los Angeles**	**NHL**	**41**	**2**	**6**	**8**	**24**	**2**	**0**	**0**	**65**	**3.1**	**-9**	....	....	....	....	....	....	....	....	....	....	....	....	....
	Phoenix	IHL	23	1	3	4	21	....	....	....	....	....	....	....	....	....	....	....	....	....	....	....	....	....	....	....
1997-98	**Los Angeles**	**NHL**	**72**	**0**	**8**	**8**	**61**	**0**	**0**	**0**	**58**	**0.0**	**3**	....	....	....	....	....	**4**	**0**	**3**	**3**	**0**	**0**	**0**	**0**
	Finland	Olympics	6	0	0	0	6	....	....	....	....	....	....	....	....	....	....	....	....	....	....	....	....	....	....	....
1998-99	TPS Turku	Finland	48	8	7	15	137	....	....	....	....	....	....	....	....	....	....	....	9	1	1	2	45	....	....	....
	NHL Totals		**164**	**2**	**21**	**23**	**114**	**2**	**0**	**0**	**179**	**1.1**		....	....	....	....	....	**4**	**0**	**3**	**3**	**0**	**0**	**0**	**0**

BERG, Bill

Left wing. Shoots left. 6'1", 205 lbs. Born, St. Catharines, Ont., October 21, 1967. NY Islanders' 3rd choice, 59th overall, in 1986 Entry Draft.

Season	Club	League	GP	G	A	Pts	PIM	PP	SH	GW	S	%	+/-	TF	F%	H	SB	Min	GP	G	A	Pts	PIM	PP	SH	GW
1984-85	Grimsby	OJHL-B	42	10	22	32	153	....	....	....	....	....	....	....	....	....	....	....	....	....	....	....	....	....	....	....
1985-86	Toronto	OHL	64	3	35	38	143	....	....	....	....	....	....	....	....	....	....	....	4	0	0	0	19	....	....	....
	Springfield	AHL	4	1	1	2	4	....	....	....	....	....	....	....	....	....	....	....	....	....	....	....	....	....	....	....
1986-87	Toronto	OHL	57	3	15	18	138	....	....	....	....	....	....	....	....	....	....	....	....	....	....	....	....	....	....	....
1987-88	Springfield	AHL	76	6	26	32	148	....	....	....	....	....	....	....	....	....	....	....	....	....	....	....	....	....	....	....
	Peoria	IHL	5	0	1	1	8	....	....	....	....	....	....	....	....	....	....	....	7	0	3	3	31	....	....	....
1988-89	**NY Islanders**	**NHL**	**7**	**1**	**2**	**3**	**10**	**1**	**0**	**0**	**10**	**10.0**	**-2**	....	....	....	....	....	....	....	....	....	....	....	....	....
	Springfield	AHL	69	17	32	49	122	....	....	....	....	....	....	....	....	....	....	....	....	....	....	....	....	....	....	....
1989-90	Springfield	AHL	74	12	42	54	74	....	....	....	....	....	....	....	....	....	....	....	15	5	12	17	35	....	....	....
1990-91	**NY Islanders**	**NHL**	**78**	**9**	**14**	**23**	**67**	**0**	**0**	**0**	**95**	**9.5**	**-3**	....	....	....	....	....	....	....	....	....	....	....	....	....
1991-92	**NY Islanders**	**NHL**	**47**	**5**	**9**	**14**	**28**	**1**	**0**	**1**	**60**	**8.3**	**-18**	....	....	....	....	....	....	....	....	....	....	....	....	....
	Capital District	AHL	3	0	2	2	16	....	....	....	....	....	....	....	....	....	....	....	....	....	....	....	....	....	....	....

			Regular Season																Playoffs							
Season	Club	League	GP	G	A	Pts	PIM	PP	SH	GW	S	%	+/–	TF	F%	H	SB	Min	GP	G	A	Pts	PIM	PP	SH	GW
1992-93	NY Islanders	NHL	22	6	3	9	49	0	2	0	30	20.0	4													
	Toronto	NHL	58	7	8	15	54	0	1	2	83	8.4	–1						21	1	1	2	18	0	0	0
1993-94	Toronto	NHL	83	8	11	19	93	0	0	1	99	8.1	–3						18	1	2	3	10	0	0	0
1994-95	Toronto	NHL	32	5	1	6	26	0	0	2	57	8.8	–11						7	0	1	1	4	0	0	0
1995-96	Toronto	NHL	23	1	1	2	33	0	0	0	33	3.0	–6													
	NY Rangers	NHL	18	2	1	3	8	0	1	0	27	7.4	0						10	1	0	1	0	0	0	0
1996-97	NY Rangers	NHL	67	8	6	14	37	0	2	3	84	9.5	2						3	0	0	0	2	0	0	0
1997-98	NY Rangers	NHL	67	1	9	10	55	0	0	0	74	1.4	–15													
1998-99	Ottawa	NHL	44	2	2	4	28	0	0	0	40	5.0	4	5	20.0	49	11	10:21	2	0	0	0	0	0	0	0
	Hartford	AHL	16	4	7	11	23																			
	NHL Totals		546	55	67	122	488	2	6	9	692	7.9		5	20.0	49	11	10:21	61	3	4	7	34	0	0	0

Claimed on waivers by **Toronto** from **NY Islanders**, December 3, 1992. Traded to **NY Rangers** by **Toronto** for Nick Kypreos, February 29, 1996. Traded to **Ottawa** by **NY Rangers** with NY Rangers' 2nd round choice (later traded to Anaheim, Anaheim selected Jordan Leopold) in 1999 Entry Draft for Stan Neckar, November 27, 1998.

BERGEVIN, Marc

(BUHR-zheh-vihn) **ST.L.**

Defense. Shoots left. 6'1", 214 lbs. Born, Montreal, Que., August 11, 1965. Chicago's 3rd choice, 60th overall, in 1983 Entry Draft.

Season	Club	League	GP	G	A	Pts	PIM	PP	SH	GW	S	%	+/–	TF	F%	H	SB	Min	GP	G	A	Pts	PIM	PP	SH	GW
1981-82	Montreal	QAAA	44	10	20	30																				
1982-83	Chicoutimi	QMJHL	64	3	27	30	113																			
1983-84	Chicoutimi	QMJHL	70	10	35	45	125																			
	Springfield	AHL	7	0	1	1	2																			
1984-85	Chicago	NHL	60	0	6	6	54	0	0	0	41	0.0	–9						6	0	3	3	2	0	0	0
	Springfield	AHL																	4	0	0	0	0			
1985-86	Chicago	NHL	71	7	7	14	60	0	0	1	50	14.0	0						3	0	0	0	0	0	0	0
1986-87	Chicago	NHL	66	4	10	14	66	0	0	0	56	7.1	4						3	1	0	1	2	0	0	0
1987-88	Chicago	NHL	58	1	6	7	85	0	0	0	51	2.0	–19													
	Saginaw	IHL	10	2	7	9	20																			
1988-89	Chicago	NHL	11	0	0	0	18	0	0	0	9	0.0	–3													
	NY Islanders	NHL	58	2	13	15	62	1	0	0	56	3.6	2													
1989-90	NY Islanders	NHL	18	0	4	4	30	0	0	0	12	0.0	–8													
	Springfield	AHL	47	7	16	23	66												17	2	11	13	16			
1990-91	Capital District	AHL	7	0	5	5	6																			
	Hartford	NHL	4	0	0	0	4	0	0	0	2	0.0	–3													
	Springfield	AHL	58	4	23	27	85												18	0	7	7	26			
1991-92	Hartford	NHL	75	7	17	24	64	4	1	1	96	7.3	–13						5	0	0	0	2	0	0	0
1992-93	Tampa Bay	NHL	78	2	12	14	66	0	0	0	69	2.9	–16													
1993-94	Tampa Bay	NHL	83	1	15	16	87	0	0	1	76	1.3	–5													
1994-95	Tampa Bay	NHL	44	2	4	6	51	0	1	0	32	6.3	–6													
1995-96	Detroit	NHL	70	1	9	10	33	0	0	0	26	3.8	7						17	1	0	1	14	1	0	0
1996-97	St. Louis	NHL	82	0	4	4	53	0	0	0	30	0.0	–9						6	1	0	1	8	0	0	0
1997-98	St. Louis	NHL	81	3	7	10	90	0	0	0	40	7.5	–2						10	0	1	1	8	0	0	0
1998-99	St. Louis	NHL	52	1	1	2	99	0	0	0	40	2.5	–14	0	0.0	90	40	16:09								
	NHL Totals		911	31	115	146	922	5	2	3	686	4.5		0	0.0	90	40	16:09	50	3	4	7	36	1	0	0

Traded to **NY Islanders** by **Chicago** with Gary Nylund for Steve Konroyd and Bob Bassen, November 25, 1988. Traded to **Hartford** by **NY Islanders** for Hartford's 5th round choice (Ryan Duthie) in 1992 Entry Draft, October 30, 1990. Signed as a free agent by **Tampa Bay**, July 9, 1992. Traded to **Detroit** by **Tampa Bay** with Ben Hankinson for Shawn Burr and Detroit's 3rd round choice (later traded to Boston — Boston selected Jason Doyle) in 1996 Entry Draft, August 17, 1995. Signed as a free agent by **St. Louis**, July 31, 1996.

BERGKVIST, Stefan

(BUHRG-kvihst, STEH-fan)

Defense. Shoots left. 6'2", 224 lbs. Born, Leksand, Sweden, March 10, 1975. Pittsburgh's 1st choice, 26th overall, in 1993 Entry Draft.

Season	Club	League	GP	G	A	Pts	PIM	PP	SH	GW	S	%	+/–	TF	F%	H	SB	Min	GP	G	A	Pts	PIM	PP	SH	GW
1992-93	Leksands IF	Sweden	15	0	0	0	6																			
1993-94	Leksands IF	Sweden	6	0	0	0	0																			
1994-95	London	OHL	64	[illegible]	17	20	33												4	0	0	0	5			
1995-96	Pittsburgh	NHL	2	0	0	0	2	0	0	0	4	0.0	0						4	0	0	0	2	0	0	0
	Cleveland	IHL	61	2	8	10	58												3	0	0	0	14			
1996-97	Pittsburgh	NHL	5	0	0	0	7	0	0	0	0	0.0	–1													
	Cleveland	IHL	33	0	1	1	54												4	0	0	0	0			
1997-98	Cleveland	IHL	71	3	6	9	129												10	0	2	2	24			
1998-99	Leksands IF	Sweden	42	0	2	2	167												3	0	0	0	4			
	Leksands IK	EuroHL	6	0	2	2	28												1	0	0	0	0			
	NHL Totals		7	0	0	0	9	0	0	0	4	0.0							4	0	0	0	2	0	0	0

BERTUZZI, Todd

(buhr-TOO-zee) **VAN.**

Center. Shoots left. 6'3", 224 lbs. Born, Sudbury, Ont., February 2, 1975. NY Islanders' 1st choice, 23rd overall, in 1993 Entry Draft.

Season	Club	League	GP	G	A	Pts	PIM	PP	SH	GW	S	%	+/–	TF	F%	H	SB	Min	GP	G	A	Pts	PIM	PP	SH	GW
1990-91	Sudbury Legion	OMHA	48	25	46	71	247																			
	Sudbury	OHL	3	3	2	5	10																			
1991-92	Guelph	OHL	47	7	14	21	145																			
1992-93	Guelph	OHL	59	27	32	59	164												5	2	2	4	6			
1993-94	Guelph	OHL	61	28	54	82	165												9	2	6	8	30			
1994-95	Guelph	OHL	62	54	65	119	58												14	*15	18	33	41			
1995-96	NY Islanders	NHL	76	18	21	39	83	4	0	2	127	14.2	–14													
1996-97	NY Islanders	NHL	64	10	13	23	68	3	0	1	79	12.7	–3													
	Utah	IHL	13	5	5	10	16																			
1997-98	NY Islanders	NHL	52	7	11	18	58	1	0	1	63	11.1	–19													
	Vancouver	NHL	22	6	9	15	63	1	1	1	39	15.4	2													
1998-99	Vancouver	NHL	32	8	8	16	44	1	0	3	72	11.1	–6	191	43.5	53	12	18:28								
	NHL Totals		246	49	62	111	316	10	1	8	380	12.9		191	43.5	53	12	18:28								

OHL Second All-Star team (1995)

Traded to **Vancouver** by **NY Islanders** with Bryan McCabe and NY Islanders' 3rd round choice (Jarkko Ruutu) in 1998 Entry Draft for Trevor Linden, February 6, 1998.

BERUBE, Craig

(buh-ROO-bee)

Left wing. Shoots left. 6'1", 205 lbs. Born, Calahoo, Alta., December 17, 1965.

Season	Club	League	GP	G	A	Pts	PIM	PP	SH	GW	S	%	+/–	TF	F%	H	SB	Min	GP	G	A	Pts	PIM	PP	SH	GW
1981-82	Williams Lake	PCJHL	33	9	24	33	99																			
1982-83	Kamloops	WHL	4	0	0	0	0																			
1983-84	New Westminster	WHL	70	11	20	31	104												8	1	2	3	5			
1984-85	New Westminster	WHL	70	25	44	69	191												10	3	2	5	4			
1985-86	Kamloops	WHL	32	17	14	31	119																			
	Medicine Hat	WHL	34	14	16	30	95												25	7	8	15	102			
1986-87	Philadelphia	NHL	7	0	0	0	57	0	0	0	4	0.0	2						5	0	0	0	17			
	Hershey	AHL	63	7	17	24	325																			
1987-88	Philadelphia	NHL	27	3	2	5	108	0	0	2	13	23.1	1													
	Hershey	AHL	31	5	9	14	119																			
1988-89	Philadelphia	NHL	53	1	1	2	199	0	0	0	31	3.2	–15						16	0	0	0	56	0	0	0
	Hershey	AHL	7	0	2	2	19																			
1989-90	Philadelphia	NHL	74	4	14	18	291	0	0	0	52	7.7	–7													
1990-91	Philadelphia	NHL	74	8	9	17	293	0	0	0	46	17.4	–6													
1991-92	Toronto	NHL	40	5	7	12	109	1	0	1	42	11.9	–2													
	Calgary	NHL	36	1	4	5	155	0	0	0	27	3.7	–3													
1992-93	Calgary	NHL	77	4	8	12	209	0	0	2	58	6.9	–6						6	0	1	1	21	0	0	0
1993-94	Washington	NHL	84	7	7	14	305	0	0	0	48	14.6	–4						8	0	0	0	21	0	0	0
1994-95	Washington	NHL	43	2	4	6	173	0	0	0	22	9.1	–5						7	0	0	0	29	0	0	0
1995-96	Washington	NHL	50	2	10	12	151	1	0	1	28	7.1	1						2	0	0	0	19	0	0	0

Season	Club	League	Regular Season GP	G	A	Pts	PIM	PP	SH	GW	S	%	+/-	TF	F%	H	SB	Min	Playoffs GP	G	A	Pts	PIM	PP	SH	GW
1996-97	**Washington**	**NHL**	**80**	**4**	**3**	**7**	**218**	**0**	**0**	**1**	**55**	**7.3**	**–11**						....	....	....	....	....	....	....	....
1997-98	**Washington**	**NHL**	**74**	**6**	**9**	**15**	**189**	**0**	**0**	**0**	**68**	**8.8**	**–3**	....	....	....	....	....	**21**	**1**	**0**	**1**	**21**	**0**	**0**	**1**
1998-99	**Washington**	**NHL**	**66**	**5**	**4**	**9**	**166**	**0**	**0**	**0**	**45**	**11.1**	**–7**	**14**	**42.9**	**85**	**10**	**6:47**	....	....	....	....	....	....	....	....
	Philadelphia	**NHL**	**11**	**0**	**0**	**0**	**28**	**0**	**0**	**0**	**7**	**0.0**	**–3**	**0**	**0.0**	**8**	**1**	**8:15**	**6**	**1**	**0**	**1**	**4**	**0**	**0**	**0**
	NHL Totals		**796**	**52**	**82**	**134**	**2651**	**2**	**0**	**7**	**546**	**9.5**		**14**	**42.9**	**93**	**11**	**6:60**	**71**	**2**	**1**	**3**	**188**	**0**	**0**	**1**

Signed as a free agent by **Philadelphia**, March 19, 1986. Traded to **Edmonton** by **Philadelphia** with Craig Fisher and Scott Mellanby for Dave Brown, Corey Foster and Jari Kurri, May 30, 1991. Traded to **Toronto** by **Edmonton** with Grant Fuhr and Glenn Anderson for Vincent Damphousse, Peter Ing, Scott Thornton, Luke Richardson, future considerations and cash, September 19, 1991. Traded to **Calgary** by **Toronto** with Alexander Godynyuk, Gary Leeman, Michel Petit and Jeff Reese for Doug Gilmour, Jamie Macoun, Ric Nattress, Rick Wamsley and Kent Manderville, January 2, 1992. Traded to **Washington** by **Calgary** for Washington's 5th round choice (Darryl Lafrance) in 1993 Entry Draft, June 26, 1993. Traded to **Philadelphia** by **Washington** for cash, March 23, 1999.

BETIK, Karel

(BEH-tihk, KAHR-ehl) **T.B.**

Defense. Shoots left. 6'2", 208 lbs. Born, Karvina, Czech., October 28, 1978. Tampa Bay's 6th choice, 112th overall, in 1997 Entry Draft.

Season	Club	League	GP	G	A	Pts	PIM	PP	SH	GW	S	%	+/-	TF	F%	H	SB	Min	GP	G	A	Pts	PIM	PP	SH	GW
1995-96	HC Vitkovice	Czech-Jr.	48	3	12	15	88	....	....	....	....	....	....	....	....	....	....	....	....	....	....	....	....	....	....	....
1996-97	Kelowna	WHL	56	3	10	13	76	....	....	....	....	....	....	....	....	....	....	....	6	1	1	2	2	....	....	....
1997-98	Kelowna	WHL	61	5	25	30	121	....	....	....	....	....	....	....	....	....	....	....	7	1	2	3	8	....	....	....
1998-99	**Tampa Bay**	**NHL**	**3**	**0**	**2**	**2**	**2**	**0**	**0**	**0**	**2**	**0.0**	**–3**	**0**	**0.0**	**2**	**2**	**13:28**	....	....	....	....	....	....	....	....
	Cleveland	IHL	74	5	11	16	97	....	....	....	....	....	....	....	....	....	....	....	....	....	....	....	....	....	....	....
	NHL Totals		**3**	**0**	**2**	**2**	**2**	**0**	**0**	**0**	**2**	**0.0**		**0**	**0.0**	**2**	**2**	**13:28**	....	....	....	....	....	....	....	....

BEUKEBOOM, Jeff

(BOO-kuh-BOOM)

Defense. Shoots right. 6'5", 230 lbs. Born, Ajax, Ont., March 28, 1965. Edmonton's 1st choice, 19th overall, in 1983 Entry Draft.

Season	Club	League	GP	G	A	Pts	PIM	PP	SH	GW	S	%	+/-	TF	F%	H	SB	Min	GP	G	A	Pts	PIM	PP	SH	GW
1981-82	Newmarket	OJHL-B	49	5	30	35	218	....	....	....	....	....	....	....	....	....	....	....	....	....	....	....	....	....	....	....
1982-83	S.S. Marie	OHL	70	0	25	25	143	....	....	....	....	....	....	....	....	....	....	....	16	1	4	5	46	....	....	....
1983-84	S.S. Marie	OHL	61	6	30	36	178	....	....	....	....	....	....	....	....	....	....	....	16	1	7	8	43	....	....	....
1984-85	S.S. Marie	OHL	37	4	20	24	85	....	....	....	....	....	....	....	....	....	....	....	16	4	6	10	47	....	....	....
1985-86	Nova Scotia	AHL	77	9	20	29	175	....	....	....	....	....	....	....	....	....	....	....	....	....	....	....	....	....	....	....
	Edmonton	**NHL**	....	....	....	....	....	....	....	....	....	....	....	....	....	....	....	....	**1**	**0**	**0**	**0**	**4**	....	....	....
1986-87♦	**Edmonton**	**NHL**	**44**	**3**	**8**	**11**	**124**	**1**	**0**	**1**	**24**	**12.5**	**7**	....	....	....	....	....	....	....	....	....	....	....	....	....
	Nova Scotia	AHL	14	1	7	8	35	....	....	....	....	....	....	....	....	....	....	....	....	....	....	....	....	....	....	....
1987-88♦	**Edmonton**	**NHL**	**73**	**5**	**20**	**25**	**201**	**1**	**0**	**1**	**76**	**6.6**	**27**	....	....	....	....	....	**7**	**0**	**0**	**0**	**16**	**0**	**0**	**0**
1988-89	**Edmonton**	**NHL**	**36**	**0**	**5**	**5**	**94**	**0**	**0**	**0**	**26**	**0.0**	**2**	....	....	....	....	....	**1**	**0**	**0**	**0**	**2**	**0**	**0**	**0**
	Cape Breton	AHL	8	0	4	4	36	....	....	....	....	....	....	....	....	....	....	....	....	....	....	....	....	....	....	....
1989-90♦	**Edmonton**	**NHL**	**46**	**1**	**12**	**13**	**86**	**0**	**0**	**0**	**36**	**2.8**	**5**	....	....	....	....	....	**2**	**0**	**0**	**0**	**0**	**0**	**0**	**0**
1990-91	**Edmonton**	**NHL**	**67**	**3**	**7**	**10**	**150**	**0**	**0**	**0**	**48**	**6.3**	**6**	....	....	....	....	....	**18**	**1**	**3**	**4**	**28**	**0**	**0**	**0**
1991-92	**Edmonton**	**NHL**	**18**	**0**	**5**	**5**	**78**	**0**	**0**	**0**	**7**	**0.0**	**4**	....	....	....	....	....	....	....	....	....	....	....	....	....
	NY Rangers	**NHL**	**56**	**1**	**10**	**11**	**122**	**0**	**0**	**0**	**41**	**2.4**	**19**	....	....	....	....	....	**13**	**2**	**3**	**5**	**47**	**0**	**0**	**0**
1992-93	**NY Rangers**	**NHL**	**82**	**2**	**17**	**19**	**153**	**0**	**0**	**0**	**54**	**3.7**	**9**	....	....	....	....	....	....	....	....	....	....	....	....	....
1993-94♦	**NY Rangers**	**NHL**	**68**	**8**	**8**	**16**	**170**	**1**	**0**	**0**	**58**	**13.8**	**18**	....	....	....	....	....	**22**	**0**	**6**	**6**	**50**	**0**	**0**	**0**
1994-95	**NY Rangers**	**NHL**	**44**	**1**	**3**	**4**	**70**	**0**	**0**	**0**	**29**	**3.4**	**3**	....	....	....	....	....	**9**	**0**	**0**	**0**	**10**	**0**	**0**	**0**
1995-96	**NY Rangers**	**NHL**	**82**	**3**	**11**	**14**	**220**	**0**	**0**	**1**	**65**	**4.6**	**19**	....	....	....	....	....	**11**	**0**	**3**	**3**	**6**	**0**	**0**	**0**
1996-97	**NY Rangers**	**NHL**	**80**	**3**	**9**	**12**	**167**	**0**	**0**	**0**	**55**	**5.5**	**22**	....	....	....	....	....	**15**	**0**	**1**	**1**	**34**	**0**	**0**	**0**
1997-98	**NY Rangers**	**NHL**	**63**	**0**	**5**	**5**	**195**	**0**	**0**	**0**	**23**	**0.0**	**–25**	....	....	....	....	....	....	....	....	....	....	....	....	....
1998-99	**NY Rangers**	**NHL**	**45**	**0**	**9**	**9**	**60**	**0**	**0**	**0**	**8**	**0.0**	**–2**	**0**	**0.0**	**129**	**50**	**13:57**	....	....	....	....	....	....	....	....
	NHL Totals		**804**	**30**	**129**	**159**	**1890**	**3**	**0**	**3**	**550**	**5.5**		**0**	**0.0**	**129**	**50**	**13:57**	**99**	**3**	**16**	**19**	**197**	**0**	**0**	**0**

OHL First All-Star Team (1985)

Traded to **NY Rangers** by **Edmonton** for David Shaw, November 12, 1991.

BIALOWAS, Frank

(bigh-uh-LOH-uhs)

Left wing. Shoots left. 5'11", 220 lbs. Born, Winnipeg, Man., September 25, 1969.

Season	Club	League	GP	G	A	Pts	PIM	PP	SH	GW	S	%	+/-	TF	F%	H	SB	Min	GP	G	A	Pts	PIM	PP	SH	GW
1991-92	Roanoke	ECHL	23	4	2	6	150	....	....	....	....	....	....	....	....	....	....	....	3	0	0	0	4	....	....	....
1992-93	Richmond	ECHL	60	3	18	21	261	....	....	....	....	....	....	....	....	....	....	....	1	0	0	0	2	....	....	....
	St. John's	AHL	7	1	0	1	28	....	....	....	....	....	....	....	....	....	....	....	1	0	0	0	0	....	....	....
1993-94	**Toronto**	**NHL**	**3**	**0**	**0**	**0**	**12**	**0**	**0**	**0**	**1**	**0.0**	**0**	....	....	....	....	....	....	....	....	....	....	....	....	....
	St. John's	AHL	69	2	8	10	352	....	....	....	....	....	....	....	....	....	....	....	7	0	3	3	25	....	....	....
1994-95	St. John's	AHL	51	2	3	5	277	....	....	....	....	....	....	....	....	....	....	....	4	0	0	0	12	....	....	....
1995-96	Portland	AHL	65	4	3	7	211	....	....	....	....	....	....	....	....	....	....	....	7	0	0	0	42	....	....	....
1996-97	Philadelphia	AHL	67	7	6	13	254	....	....	....	....	....	....	....	....	....	....	....	6	0	2	2	41	....	....	....
1997-98	Philadelphia	AHL	65	5	7	12	259	....	....	....	....	....	....	....	....	....	....	....	19	0	0	0	26	....	....	....
1998-99	Philadelphia	AHL	24	0	3	3	42	....	....	....	....	....	....	....	....	....	....	....	....	....	....	....	....	....	....	....
	Portland	AHL	6	0	0	0	10	....	....	....	....	....	....	....	....	....	....	....	....	....	....	....	....	....	....	....
	Indianapolis	IHL	16	1	0	1	27	....	....	....	....	....	....	....	....	....	....	....	2	0	0	0	6	....	....	....
	NHL Totals		**3**	**0**	**0**	**0**	**12**	**0**	**0**	**0**	**1**	**0.0**		....	....	....	....	....	....	....	....	....	....	....	....	....

Signed as a free agent by **Toronto**, March 20, 1994. Signed as a free agent by **Washington**, September 8, 1995. Traded to **Philadelphia** by **Washington** for future considerations, July 18, 1996. Traded to **Chicago** by **Philadelphia** for Dennis Bonvie, January 8, 1999.

BICANEK, Radim

(BEE-chah-nehk) **CHI.**

Defense. Shoots left. 6'1", 195 lbs. Born, Uherske Hradiste, Czech., January 18, 1975. Ottawa's 2nd choice, 27th overall, in 1993 Entry Draft.

Season	Club	League	GP	G	A	Pts	PIM	PP	SH	GW	S	%	+/-	TF	F%	H	SB	Min	GP	G	A	Pts	PIM	PP	SH	GW
1992-93	Dukla Jihlava	Czech.	43	2	3	5	....	....	....	....	....	....	....	....	....	....	....	....	....	....	....	....	....	....	....	....
1993-94	Belleville	OHL	63	16	27	43	49	....	....	....	....	....	....	....	....	....	....	....	12	2	8	10	21	....	....	....
1994-95	Belleville	OHL	49	13	26	39	61	....	....	....	....	....	....	....	....	....	....	....	16	6	5	11	30	....	....	....
	Ottawa	**NHL**	**6**	**0**	**0**	**0**	**0**	**0**	**0**	**0**	**6**	**0.0**	**3**	....	....	....	....	....	....	....	....	....	....	....	....	....
	P.E.I. Senators	AHL	....	....	....	....	....	....	....	....	....	....	....	....	....	....	....	....	3	0	1	1	0	....	....	....
1995-96	P.E.I. Senators	AHL	74	7	19	26	87	....	....	....	....	....	....	....	....	....	....	....	5	0	2	2	6	....	....	....
1996-97	**Ottawa**	**NHL**	**21**	**0**	**1**	**1**	**8**	**0**	**0**	**0**	**27**	**0.0**	**–4**	....	....	....	....	....	**7**	**0**	**0**	**0**	**8**	**0**	**0**	**0**
	Worcester	AHL	44	1	15	16	22	....	....	....	....	....	....	....	....	....	....	....	....	....	....	....	....	....	....	....
1997-98	**Ottawa**	**NHL**	**1**	**0**	**0**	**0**	**0**	**0**	**0**	**0**	**0**	**0.0**	**0**	....	....	....	....	....	....	....	....	....	....	....	....	....
	Detroit	IHL	9	1	3	4	16	....	....	....	....	....	....	....	....	....	....	....	....	....	....	....	....	....	....	....
	Manitoba	IHL	42	1	7	8	52	....	....	....	....	....	....	....	....	....	....	....	....	....	....	....	....	....	....	....
1998-99	**Ottawa**	**NHL**	**7**	**0**	**0**	**0**	**4**	**0**	**0**	**0**	**6**	**0.0**	**–1**	**0**	**0.0**	**11**	**4**	**10:51**	....	....	....	....	....	....	....	....
	Grand Rapids	IHL	46	8	17	25	48	....	....	....	....	....	....	....	....	....	....	....	....	....	....	....	....	....	....	....
	Chicago	**NHL**	**7**	**0**	**0**	**0**	**6**	**0**	**0**	**0**	**7**	**0.0**	**–3**	**0**	**0.0**	**7**	**8**	**15:57**	....	....	....	....	....	....	....	....
	NHL Totals		**42**	**0**	**1**	**1**	**18**	**0**	**0**	**0**	**46**	**0.0**		**0**	**0.0**	**18**	**12**	**13:24**	**7**	**0**	**0**	**0**	**8**	**0**	**0**	**0**

Traded to **Chicago** by **Ottawa** for Los Angeles' 6th round choice (previously acquired, Ottawa selected Martin Prusek) in 1999 Entry Draft, March 12, 1999.

BLACK, James

WSH.

Left wing. Shoots left. 6', 202 lbs. Born, Regina, Sask., August 15, 1969. Hartford's 4th choice, 94th overall, in 1989 Entry Draft.

Season	Club	League	GP	G	A	Pts	PIM	PP	SH	GW	S	%	+/-	TF	F%	H	SB	Min	GP	G	A	Pts	PIM	PP	SH	GW
1986-87	Edmonton Pats	AAHA	41	36	48	84	58	....	....	....	....	....	....	....	....	....	....	....	....	....	....	....	....	....	....	....
1987-88	Portland	WHL	72	30	50	80	50	....	....	....	....	....	....	....	....	....	....	....	....	....	....	....	....	....	....	....
1988-89	Portland	WHL	71	45	51	96	57	....	....	....	....	....	....	....	....	....	....	....	19	13	6	19	28	....	....	....
1989-90	**Hartford**	**NHL**	**1**	**0**	**0**	**0**	**0**	**0**	**0**	**0**	**0**	**0.0**	**0**	....	....	....	....	....	....	....	....	....	....	....	....	....
	Binghamton	AHL	80	37	35	72	34	....	....	....	....	....	....	....	....	....	....	....	....	....	....	....	....	....	....	....
1990-91	**Hartford**	**NHL**	**1**	**0**	**0**	**0**	**0**	**0**	**0**	**0**	**0**	**0.0**	**0**	....	....	....	....	....	....	....	....	....	....	....	....	....
	Springfield	AHL	79	35	61	96	34	....	....	....	....	....	....	....	....	....	....	....	18	9	9	18	6	....	....	....
1991-92	**Hartford**	**NHL**	**30**	**4**	**6**	**10**	**10**	**1**	**0**	**1**	**54**	**7.4**	**–4**	....	....	....	....	....	....	....	....	....	....	....	....	....
	Springfield	AHL	47	15	25	40	33	....	....	....	....	....	....	....	....	....	....	....	10	3	2	5	18	....	....	....
1992-93	**Minnesota**	**NHL**	**10**	**2**	**1**	**3**	**4**	**0**	**0**	**0**	**10**	**20.0**	**0**	....	....	....	....	....	....	....	....	....	....	....	....	....
	Kalamazoo	IHL	63	25	45	70	40	....	....	....	....	....	....	....	....	....	....	....	....	....	....	....	....	....	....	....

Season	Club	League	GP	G	A	Pts	PIM	PP	SH	GW	S	%	+/-	TF	F%	H	SB	Min	GP	G	A	Pts	PIM	PP	SH	GW
1993-94	Dallas	NHL	13	2	3	5	2	2	0	0	16	12.5	-4	....	....	....	....	....	....							
	Buffalo	NHL	2	0	0	0	0	2	0	0	2	0.0	0													
	Rochester	AHL	45	19	32	51	28												4	2	3	5	0			
1994-95	Las Vegas	IHL	78	29	44	73	54												10	1	6	7	4			
1995-96	**Chicago**	NHL	13	3	3	6	16	0	0	1	23	13.0	1						8	1	0	1	2	0	0	0
	Indianapolis	IHL	67	32	50	82	56																			
1996-97	**Chicago**	NHL	64	12	11	23	20	0	0	3	122	9.8	6						5	1	1	2	2	0	0	0
1997-98	**Chicago**	NHL	52	10	5	15	8	2	1	3	90	11.1	-8													
1998-99	Chicago	IHL	5	6	0	6	0																			
	Washington	NHL	75	16	14	30	14	1	1	3	135	11.9	5	10	50.0	42	30	15:04								
	NHL Totals		261	49	43	92	74	8	2	11	452	10.8		10	50.0	42	30	15:04	13	2	1	3	4	0	0	0

Traded to **Minnesota** by **Hartford** for Mark Janssens, September 3, 1992. Transferred to **Dallas** after **Minnesota** franchise relocated, June 9, 1993. Traded to **Buffalo** by **Dallas** with Dallas' 7th round choice (Steve Webb) in 1994 Entry Draft for Gord Donnelly, December 15, 1993. Signed as a free agent by **Chicago**, September 18, 1995. Traded to **Washington** by **Chicago** for future considerations, October 15, 1998.

BLAKE, Jason   L.A.

Center. Shoots left. 5'10", 180 lbs.   Born, Moorhead, MN, September 2, 1973.

Season	Club	League	GP	G	A	Pts	PIM	PP	SH	GW	S	%	+/-	TF	F%	H	SB	Min	GP	G	A	Pts	PIM	PP	SH	GW
1993-94	Moorehead High	H.S.	25	30	30	60	....																			
1994-95	Ferris State	CCHA	36	16	16	32	46																			
1995-96							DID NOT PLAY – TRANSFERRED COLLEGES																		
1996-97	North Dakota	WCHA	43	19	32	51	44																			
1997-98	North Dakota	WCHA	38	24	27	51	62																			
1998-99	North Dakota	WCHA	38	*28	*41	*69	49																			
	LA Kings	NHL	1	1	0	1	0	0	0	0	5	20.0	1	14	35.7	1	0	17:13								
	Orlando	IHL	5	3	5	8	6												13	3	4	7	20			
	NHL Totals		1	1	0	1	0	0	0	0	5	20.0		14	35.7	1	0	17:13								

WCHA First All-Star Team (1997, 1998, 1999) • NCAA West Second All-American Team (1998) • NCAA West First All-American Team (1999)
Signed as a free agent by **Los Angeles**, April 20, 1999.

BLAKE, Rob   L.A.

Defense. Shoots right. 6'4", 220 lbs.   Born, Simcoe, Ont., December 10, 1969. Los Angeles' 4th choice, 70th overall, in 1988 Entry Draft.

Season	Club	League	GP	G	A	Pts	PIM	PP	SH	GW	S	%	+/-	TF	F%	H	SB	Min	GP	G	A	Pts	PIM	PP	SH	GW
1986-87	Stratford	OJHL-B	31	11	20	31	115																			
1987-88	Bowling Green	CCHA	43	5	8	13	88																			
1988-89	Bowling Green	CCHA	46	11	21	32	140																			
1989-90	Bowling Green	CCHA	42	23	36	59	140																			
	Los Angeles	NHL	4	0	0	0	4	0	0	0	3	0.0	0						8	1	3	4	4	1	0	0
1990-91	**Los Angeles**	NHL	75	12	34	46	125	9	0	2	150	8.0	3						12	1	4	5	26	1	0	0
1991-92	**Los Angeles**	NHL	57	7	13	20	102	5	0	0	131	5.3	-5						6	2	1	3	12	0	0	0
1992-93	**Los Angeles**	NHL	76	16	43	59	152	10	0	4	243	6.6	18						23	4	6	10	46	1	1	0
1993-94	**Los Angeles**	NHL	84	20	48	68	137	7	0	6	304	6.6	-7													
1994-95	**Los Angeles**	NHL	24	4	7	11	38	4	0	1	76	5.3	-16													
1995-96	**Los Angeles**	NHL	6	1	2	3	8	0	0	0	13	7.7	0													
1996-97	**Los Angeles**	NHL	62	8	23	31	82	4	0	1	169	4.7	-28													
1997-98	**Los Angeles**	NHL	81	23	27	50	94	11	0	4	261	8.8	-3						4	0	0	0	6	0	0	0
	Canada	Olympics	6	1	1	2	2																			
1998-99	**Los Angeles**	NHL	62	12	23	35	128	5	1	2	216	5.6	-7	0	0.0	132	139	24:52								
	NHL Totals		531	103	220	323	870	55	1	20	1566	6.6		0	0.0	132	139	24:52	53	8	14	22	94	3	1	0

CCHA Second All-Star Team (1989) • CCHA First All-Star Team (1990) • NCAA West First All-American Team (1990) • NHL/Upper Deck All-Rookie Team (1991) • NHL First All-Star Team (1998) • Won James Norris Memorial Trophy (1998)
Played in NHL All-Star Game (1994, 1999)

BLOEMBERG, Jeff   (BLOOM-buhrg)

Defense. Shoots right. 6'2", 205 lbs.   Born, Listowel, Ont., January 31, 1968. NY Rangers' 5th choice, 93rd overall, in 1986 Entry Draft.

Season	Club	League	GP	G	A	Pts	PIM	PP	SH	GW	S	%	+/-	TF	F%	H	SB	Min	GP	G	A	Pts	PIM	PP	SH	GW
1984-85	Listowel	OJHL-B	31	7	14	21																			
1985-86	North Bay	OHL	60	7	11	13	76												8	1	2	3	9			
1986-87	North Bay	OHL	60	5	13	18	91												21	1	6	7	13			
1987-88	North Bay	OHL	46	9	26	35	60												4	1	4	5	2			
	Colorado	IHL	5	0	0	0	0												11	1	0	1	8			
1988-89	**NY Rangers**	NHL	9	0	0	0	0	0	0	0	9	0.0	2													
	Denver	IHL	64	7	22	29	55												1	0	0	0	0			
1989-90	**NY Rangers**	NHL	28	3	3	6	25	2	0	1	20	15.0	-8						7	0	3	3	5	0	0	0
	Flint	IHL	41	7	14	21	24																			
1990-91	**NY Rangers**	NHL	3	0	2	2	0	0	0	0	4	0.0	3													
	Binghamton	AHL	77	16	46	62	28												10	0	6	6	10			
1991-92	**NY Rangers**	NHL	3	0	1	1	0	0	0	0	5	0.0	1													
	Binghamton	AHL	66	6	41	47	22												11	1	10	11	10			
1992-93	Cape Breton	AHL	76	6	45	51	34												16	5	10	15	10			
1993-94	Springfield	AHL	78	8	28	36	36												6	0	3	3	8			
1994-95	Adirondack	AHL	44	5	19	24	10												4	0	0	0	0			
1995-96	Adirondack	AHL	72	10	28	38	32												3	0	1	1	4			
1996-97	Adirondack	AHL	69	5	31	36	24												4	0	3	3	2			
1997-98	EHC Berlin	Germany	27	3	7	10	16																			
1998-99	Revier Lowen	Germany	52	3	17	20	54																			
	NHL Totals		43	3	6	9	25	2	0	1	38	7.9							7	0	3	3	5	0	0	0

AHL Second All-Star Team (1991)
Claimed by **Tampa Bay** from **NY Rangers** in Expansion Draft, June 18, 1992. Traded to **Edmonton** by **Tampa Bay** for future considerations, September 25, 1992. Signed as a free agent by **Hartford**, August 9, 1993. Signed as a free agent by **Detroit**, May 9, 1995.

BLOUIN, Sylvain   (bluh-WEHN)   ST.L.

Left wing. Shoots left. 6'2", 207 lbs.   Born, Montreal, Que., May 21, 1974. NY Rangers' 5th choice, 104th overall, in 1994 Entry Draft.

Season	Club	League	GP	G	A	Pts	PIM	PP	SH	GW	S	%	+/-	TF	F%	H	SB	Min	GP	G	A	Pts	PIM	PP	SH	GW
1991-92	Laval	QMJHL	28	0	0	0	23												9	0	0	0	35			
1992-93	Laval	QMJHL	68	0	10	10	373												13	1	0	1	*66			
1993-94	Laval	QMJHL	62	18	22	40	*492												21	4	13	17	*177			
1994-95	Chicago	IHL	1	0	0	0	2																			
	Charlotte	ECHL	50	5	7	12	280												3	0	0	0	6			
	Binghamton	AHL	10	1	0	1	46												2	0	0	0	24			
1995-96	Binghamton	AHL	71	5	8	13	*352												4	0	3	3	4			
1996-97	**NY Rangers**	NHL	6	0	0	0	18	0	0	0	1	0.0	-1													
	Binghamton	AHL	62	13	17	30	301												4	2	1	3	16			
1997-98	**NY Rangers**	NHL	1	0	0	0	5	0	0	0	0	0.0	0													
	Hartford	AHL	53	8	9	17	286												9	0	1	1	63			
1998-99	**Montreal**	NHL	5	0	0	0	19	0	0	0	1	0.0	0	0	0.0	2	0	3:37								
	Fredericton	AHL	67	6	10	16	333												15	2	0	2	*87			
	NHL Totals		12	0	0	0	42	0	0	0	2	0.0		0	0.0	2	0	3:37								

Traded to **Montreal** by **NY Rangers** with NY Rangers' 6th round choice (later traded to Phoenix, Phoenix selected Erik Leverstrom) in 1999 Entry Draft for Peter Popovic, June 30, 1998. Signed as a free agent by **St. Louis**, August 25, 1999

BODGER, Doug (BAW-juhr) VAN.

Defense. Shoots left. 6'2", 210 lbs. Born, Chemainus, B.C., June 18, 1966. Pittsburgh's 2nd choice, 9th overall, in 1984 Entry Draft.

			Regular Season																Playoffs							
Season	Club	League	GP	G	A	Pts	PIM	PP	SH	GW	S	%	+/-	TF	F%	H	SB	Min	GP	G	A	Pts	PIM	PP	SH	GW
1981-82	Cowichan Valley	BCAHA	STATISTICS NOT AVAILABLE																							
1982-83	Chemainus	BCAHA	STATISTICS NOT AVAILABLE																							
	Kamloops	WHL	72	26	66	92	98	....	....	....	....	....	....	....	....	....	....	....	7	0	5	5	2	....	....	....
1983-84	Kamloops	WHL	70	21	77	98	90	....	....	....	....	....	....	....	....	....	....	....	17	2	15	17	12	....	....	....
1984-85	**Pittsburgh**	**NHL**	**65**	**5**	**26**	**31**	**67**	**3**	**0**	**1**	**119**	**4.2**	**–24**	....	....	....	....	....	....	....	....	....	....	....	....	....
1985-86	**Pittsburgh**	**NHL**	**79**	**4**	**33**	**37**	**63**	**1**	**0**	**1**	**140**	**2.9**	**3**	....	....	....	....	....	....	....	....	....	....	....	....	....
1986-87	**Pittsburgh**	**NHL**	**76**	**11**	**38**	**49**	**52**	**5**	**0**	**1**	**176**	**6.3**	**6**	....	....	....	....	....	....	....	....	....	....	....	....	....
1987-88	**Pittsburgh**	**NHL**	**69**	**14**	**31**	**45**	**103**	**13**	**0**	**1**	**184**	**7.6**	**–4**	....	....	....	....	....	....	....	....	....	....	....	....	....
1988-89	**Pittsburgh**	**NHL**	**10**	**1**	**4**	**5**	**7**	**0**	**0**	**0**	**22**	**4.5**	**6**	....	....	....	....	....	....	....	....	....	....	....	....	....
	Buffalo	**NHL**	**61**	**7**	**40**	**47**	**52**	**6**	**0**	**1**	**134**	**5.2**	**9**	....	....	....	....	....	**5**	**1**	**1**	**2**	**11**	**1**	**0**	**0**
1989-90	**Buffalo**	**NHL**	**71**	**12**	**36**	**48**	**64**	**8**	**0**	**1**	**167**	**7.2**	**0**	....	....	....	....	....	**6**	**1**	**5**	**6**	**6**	**0**	**0**	**0**
1990-91	**Buffalo**	**NHL**	**58**	**5**	**23**	**28**	**54**	**2**	**0**	**0**	**139**	**3.6**	**–8**	....	....	....	....	....	**4**	**0**	**1**	**1**	**0**	**0**	**0**	**0**
1991-92	**Buffalo**	**NHL**	**73**	**11**	**35**	**46**	**108**	**4**	**0**	**1**	**180**	**6.1**	**1**	....	....	....	....	....	**7**	**2**	**1**	**3**	**2**	**2**	**0**	**1**
1992-93	**Buffalo**	**NHL**	**81**	**9**	**45**	**54**	**87**	**6**	**0**	**0**	**154**	**5.8**	**14**	....	....	....	....	....	**8**	**2**	**3**	**5**	**0**	**2**	**0**	**0**
1993-94	**Buffalo**	**NHL**	**75**	**7**	**32**	**39**	**76**	**5**	**1**	**1**	**144**	**4.9**	**8**	....	....	....	....	....	**7**	**0**	**3**	**3**	**6**	**0**	**0**	**0**
1994-95	**Buffalo**	**NHL**	**44**	**3**	**17**	**20**	**47**	**2**	**0**	**0**	**87**	**3.4**	**–3**	....	....	....	....	....	**5**	**0**	**4**	**4**	**0**	**0**	**0**	**0**
1995-96	**Buffalo**	**NHL**	**16**	**0**	**5**	**5**	**18**	**0**	**0**	**0**	**27**	**0.0**	**–6**	....	....	....	....	....	....	....	....	....	....	....	....	....
	San Jose	**NHL**	**57**	**4**	**19**	**23**	**50**	**3**	**0**	**0**	**94**	**4.3**	**–18**	....	....	....	....	....	....	....	....	....	....	....	....	....
1996-97	**San Jose**	**NHL**	**81**	**1**	**15**	**16**	**64**	**0**	**0**	**1**	**96**	**1.0**	**–14**	....	....	....	....	....	....	....	....	....	....	....	....	....
1997-98	**San Jose**	**NHL**	**28**	**4**	**6**	**10**	**32**	**0**	**0**	**1**	**41**	**9.8**	**0**	....	....	....	....	....	....	....	....	....	....	....	....	....
	New Jersey	**NHL**	**49**	**5**	**5**	**10**	**25**	**3**	**0**	**0**	**55**	**9.1**	**–1**	....	....	....	....	....	**5**	**0**	**0**	**0**	**0**	**0**	**0**	**0**
1998-99	**Los Angeles**	**NHL**	**65**	**3**	**11**	**14**	**34**	**0**	**0**	**0**	**67**	**4.5**	**1**	**0**	**0.0**	**75**	**101**	**19:27**	....	....	....	....	....	....	....	....
	NHL Totals		**1058**	**106**	**421**	**527**	**1003**	**61**	**1**	**10**	**2026**	**5.2**		**0**	**0.0**	**75**	**101**	**19:27**	**47**	**6**	**18**	**24**	**25**	**5**	**0**	**1**

WHL Second All-Star Team (1983)

Traded to **Buffalo** by **Pittsburgh** wih Darrin Shannon for Tom Barrasso and Buffalo's 3rd round choice (Joe Dziedzic) in 1990 Entry Draft, November 12, 1988. Traded to **San Jose** by **Buffalo** for Vaclav Varada, Martin Spanhel and Philadelphia's 1st (previously acquired by San Jose — later traded to Phoenix — Phoenix selected Daniel Briere) and 4th (previously acquired, Buffalo selected Mike Martone) round choices in 1996 Entry Draft, November 16, 1995. Traded to **New Jersey** by **San Jose** with Dody Wood for John MacLean and Ken Sutton, December 7, 1997. Traded to **LA Kings** by **New Jersey** for Boston's 4th round choice (previously acquired, New Jersey selected Pierre Dagenais) in 1998 Entry Draft, June 18, 1998. Signed as a free agent by **Vancouver**, August 18, 1999.

BOHONOS, Lonny (boh-HOH-nohz) TOR.

Right wing. Shoots right. 5'11", 190 lbs. Born, Winnipeg, Man., May 20, 1973.

			Regular Season																Playoffs							
Season	Club	League	GP	G	A	Pts	PIM	PP	SH	GW	S	%	+/-	TF	F%	H	SB	Min	GP	G	A	Pts	PIM	PP	SH	GW
1990-91	Winnipeg Blues	MJHL	46	33	22	55	70	....	....	....	....	....	....	....	....	....	....	....	....	....	....	....	....	....	....	....
1991-92	Winnipeg Blues	MJHL	40	53	36	89	42	....	....	....	....	....	....	....	....	....	....	....	....	....	....	....	....	....	....	....
	Moose Jaw	WHL	8	1	1	2	0	....	....	....	....	....	....	....	....	....	....	....	....	....	....	....	....	....	....	....
1992-93	Seattle	WHL	46	13	13	26	27	....	....	....	....	....	....	....	....	....	....	....	....	....	....	....	....	....	....	....
	Portland	WHL	27	20	17	37	16	....	....	....	....	....	....	....	....	....	....	....	15	8	13	21	19	....	....	....
1993-94	Portland	WHL	70	*62	*90	*152	80	....	....	....	....	....	....	....	....	....	....	....	10	8	11	19	13	....	....	....
1994-95	Syracuse	AHL	67	30	45	75	71	....	....	....	....	....	....	....	....	....	....	....	....	....	....	....	....	....	....	....
1995-96	**Vancouver**	**NHL**	**3**	**0**	**1**	**1**	**0**	**0**	**0**	**0**	**3**	**0.0**	**1**	....	....	....	....	....	....	....	....	....	....	....	....	....
	Syracuse	AHL	74	40	39	79	82	....	....	....	....	....	....	....	....	....	....	....	16	14	8	22	16	....	....	....
1996-97	**Vancouver**	**NHL**	**36**	**11**	**11**	**22**	**10**	**2**	**0**	**1**	**67**	**16.4**	**–3**	....	....	....	....	....	....	....	....	....	....	....	....	....
	Syracuse	AHL	41	22	30	52	28	....	....	....	....	....	....	....	....	....	....	....	3	2	2	4	4	....	....	....
1997-98	**Vancouver**	**NHL**	**31**	**2**	**1**	**3**	**4**	**0**	**0**	**0**	**37**	**5.4**	**–9**	....	....	....	....	....	....	....	....	....	....	....	....	....
	Syracuse	AHL	17	12	12	24	8	....	....	....	....	....	....	....	....	....	....	....	....	....	....	....	....	....	....	....
	Toronto	**NHL**	**6**	**3**	**3**	**6**	**4**	**0**	**0**	**0**	**13**	**23.1**	**1**	....	....	....	....	....	....	....	....	....	....	....	....	....
	St. John's	AHL	11	7	9	16	10	....	....	....	....	....	....	....	....	....	....	....	2	1	1	2	2	....	....	....
1998-99	**Toronto**	**NHL**	**7**	**3**	**0**	**3**	**4**	**0**	**0**	**0**	**13**	**23.1**	**3**	**2**	**50.0**	**3**	**2**	**13:47**	**9**	**3**	**6**	**9**	**2**	**0**	**0**	**0**
	St. John's	AHL	70	34	48	82	40	....	....	....	....	....	....	....	....	....	....	....	5	2	4	6	2	....	....	....
	NHL Totals		**83**	**19**	**16**	**35**	**22**	**2**	**0**	**1**	**133**	**14.3**		**2**	**50.0**	**3**	**2**	**13:47**	**9**	**3**	**6**	**9**	**2**	**0**	**0**	**0**

WHL West First All-Star Team (1994) • Canadian Major Junior First All-Star Team (1994)

Signed as a free agent by **Vancouver**, May 31, 1994. Traded to **Toronto** by **Vancouver** for Brandon Convery, March 7, 1998.

BOILEAU, Patrick (BWOI-loh) WSH.

Defense. Shoots right. 6', 190 lbs. Born, Montreal, Que., February 22, 1975. Washington's 3rd choice, 69th overall, in 1993 Entry Draft.

			Regular Season																Playoffs							
Season	Club	League	GP	G	A	Pts	PIM	PP	SH	GW	S	%	+/-	TF	F%	H	SB	Min	GP	G	A	Pts	PIM	PP	SH	GW
1991-92	Laval Regents	QAAA	42	9	36	45	94	....	....	....	....	....	....	....	....	....	....	....	....	....	....	....	....	....	....	....
1992-93	Laval	QMJHL	69	4	19	23	73	....	....	....	....	....	....	....	....	....	....	....	13	1	2	3	10	....	....	....
1993-94	Laval	QMJHL	64	13	57	70	56	....	....	....	....	....	....	....	....	....	....	....	21	1	7	8	24	....	....	....
1994-95	Laval	QMJHL	38	8	25	33	46	....	....	....	....	....	....	....	....	....	....	....	20	4	16	20	24	....	....	....
1995-96	Portland	AHL	78	10	28	38	41	....	....	....	....	....	....	....	....	....	....	....	19	1	3	4	12	....	....	....
1996-97	**Washington**	**NHL**	**1**	**0**	**0**	**0**	**0**	**0**	**0**	**0**	**0**	**0.0**	**0**	....	....	....	....	....	....	....	....	....	....	....	....	....
	Portland	AHL	67	16	28	44	63	....	....	....	....	....	....	....	....	....	....	....	5	1	1	2	4	....	....	....
1997-98	Portland	AHL	47	6	21	27	53	....	....	....	....	....	....	....	....	....	....	....	10	0	1	1	8	....	....	....
1998-99	**Washington**	**NHL**	**4**	**0**	**1**	**1**	**2**	**0**	**0**	**0**	**7**	**0.0**	**–4**	**0**	**0.0**	**8**	**2**	**15:56**	....	....	....	....	....	....	....	....
	Portland	AHL	52	6	18	24	52	....	....	....	....	....	....	....	....	....	....	....	....	....	....	....	....	....	....	....
	Indianapolis	IHL	29	8	13	21	27	....	....	....	....	....	....	....	....	....	....	....	4	0	1	1	2	....	....	....
	NHL Totals		**5**	**0**	**1**	**1**	**2**	**0**	**0**	**0**	**7**	**0.0**		**0**	**0.0**	**8**	**2**	**15:56**	....	....	....	....	....	....	....	....

Canadian Major Junior Scholastic Player of the Year (1994)

BOMBARDIR, Brad (bawm-bahr-DEER) N.J.

Defense. Shoots left. 6'1", 205 lbs. Born, Powell River, B.C., May 5, 1972. New Jersey's 5th choice, 56th overall, in 1990 Entry Draft.

			Regular Season																Playoffs							
Season	Club	League	GP	G	A	Pts	PIM	PP	SH	GW	S	%	+/-	TF	F%	H	SB	Min	GP	G	A	Pts	PIM	PP	SH	GW
1988-89	Powell River	BCJHL	30	6	5	11	24	....	....	....	....	....	....	....	....	....	....	....	6	0	0	0	0	....	....	....
1989-90	Powell River	BCJHL	60	10	35	45	93	....	....	....	....	....	....	....	....	....	....	....	8	2	3	5	4	....	....	....
1990-91	North Dakota	WCHA	33	3	6	9	18	....	....	....	....	....	....	....	....	....	....	....	....	....	....	....	....	....	....	....
1991-92	North Dakota	WCHA	35	3	14	17	54	....	....	....	....	....	....	....	....	....	....	....	....	....	....	....	....	....	....	....
1992-93	North Dakota	WCHA	38	8	15	23	34	....	....	....	....	....	....	....	....	....	....	....	....	....	....	....	....	....	....	....
1993-94	North Dakota	WCHA	38	5	17	22	38	....	....	....	....	....	....	....	....	....	....	....	....	....	....	....	....	....	....	....
1994-95	Albany	AHL	77	5	22	27	22	....	....	....	....	....	....	....	....	....	....	....	14	0	3	3	6	....	....	....
1995-96	Albany	AHL	80	6	25	31	63	....	....	....	....	....	....	....	....	....	....	....	3	0	1	1	4	....	....	....
1996-97	Albany	AHL	32	0	8	8	6	....	....	....	....	....	....	....	....	....	....	....	16	1	3	4	8	....	....	....
1997-98	**New Jersey**	**NHL**	**43**	**1**	**5**	**6**	**8**	**0**	**0**	**0**	**16**	**6.3**	**11**	....	....	....	....	....	....	....	....	....	....	....	....	....
	Albany	AHL	5	0	0	0	0	....	....	....	....	....	....	....	....	....	....	....	....	....	....	....	....	....	....	....
1998-99	**New Jersey**	**NHL**	**56**	**1**	**7**	**8**	**16**	**0**	**0**	**0**	**47**	**2.1**	**–4**	**1**	**0.0**	**48**	**57**	**15:03**	**5**	**0**	**0**	**0**	**0**	**0**	**0**	**0**
	NHL Totals		**99**	**2**	**12**	**14**	**24**	**0**	**0**	**0**	**63**	**3.2**		**1**	**0.0**	**48**	**57**	**15:03**	**5**	**0**	**0**	**0**	**0**	**0**	**0**	**0**

AHL Second All-Star Team (1996)

BONDRA, Peter (BAWN-druh) WSH.

Right wing. Shoots left. 6'1", 200 lbs. Born, Luck, USSR, February 7, 1968. Washington's 9th choice, 156th overall, in 1990 Entry Draft.

			Regular Season																Playoffs							
Season	Club	League	GP	G	A	Pts	PIM	PP	SH	GW	S	%	+/-	TF	F%	H	SB	Min	GP	G	A	Pts	PIM	PP	SH	GW
1986-87	VSZ Kosice	Czech.	32	4	5	9	24	....	....	....	....	....	....	....	....	....	....	....	....	....	....	....	....	....	....	....
1987-88	VSZ Kosice	Czech.	45	27	11	38	20	....	....	....	....	....	....	....	....	....	....	....	....	....	....	....	....	....	....	....
1988-89	VSZ Kosice	Czech.	40	30	10	40	20	....	....	....	....	....	....	....	....	....	....	....	....	....	....	....	....	....	....	....
1989-90	VSZ Kosice	Czech.	49	36	19	55	....	....	....	....	....	....	....	....	....	....	....	....	....	....	....	....	....	....	....	....
1990-91	**Washington**	**NHL**	**54**	**12**	**16**	**28**	**47**	**4**	**0**	**1**	**95**	**12.6**	**–10**	....	....	....	....	....	**4**	**0**	**1**	**1**	**2**	**0**	**0**	**0**
1991-92	**Washington**	**NHL**	**71**	**28**	**28**	**56**	**42**	**4**	**0**	**3**	**158**	**17.7**	**16**	....	....	....	....	....	**7**	**6**	**2**	**8**	**4**	**1**	**0**	**0**
1992-93	**Washington**	**NHL**	**83**	**37**	**48**	**85**	**70**	**10**	**0**	**7**	**239**	**15.5**	**8**	....	....	....	....	....	**6**	**0**	**6**	**6**	**0**	**0**	**0**	**0**
1993-94	**Washington**	**NHL**	**69**	**24**	**19**	**43**	**40**	**4**	**0**	**2**	**200**	**12.0**	**22**	....	....	....	....	....	**9**	**2**	**4**	**6**	**4**	**0**	**0**	**1**

			Regular Season																Playoffs							
Season	Club	League	GP	G	A	Pts	PIM	PP	SH	GW	S	%	+/–	TF	F%	H	SB	Min	GP	G	A	Pts	PIM	PP	SH	GW
1994-95	VSZ Kosice	Slovakia	2	1	0	1	0																			
	Washington	NHL	47	*34	9	43	24	12	6	3	177	19.2	9						7	5	3	8	10	2	0	1
1995-96	Detroit	IHL	7	8	1	9	0																			
	Washington	NHL	67	52	28	80	40	11	4	7	322	16.1	18						6	3	2	5	8	2	0	1
1996-97	Washington	NHL	77	46	31	77	72	10	4	3	314	14.6	7													
1997-98	Washington	NHL	76	*52	26	78	44	11	5	13	284	18.3	14						17	7	5	12	12	3	0	2
1998-99	Washington	NHL	66	31	24	55	56	6	3	5	284	10.9	–1	1	0.0	87	22	20:35								
	NHL Totals		610	316	229	545	435	72	22	44	2073	15.2		1	0.0	87	22	20:35	56	23	23	46	40	8	0	5

Played in NHL All-Star Game (1993, 1996, 1997, 1998, 1999)

BONIN, Brian

Center. Shoots left. 5'10", 185 lbs. Born, St. Paul, MN, November 28, 1973. Pittsburgh's 9th choice, 211th overall, in 1992 Entry Draft.

Season	Club	League	GP	G	A	Pts	PIM	PP	SH	GW	S	%	+/–	TF	F%	H	SB	Min	GP	G	A	Pts	PIM	PP	SH	GW
1991-92	White Bear Lake	H.S.	23	22	35	57	8																			
1992-93	U. of Minnesota	WCHA	38	10	18	28	10																			
1993-94	U. of Minnesota	WCHA	42	24	20	44	14																			
1994-95	U. of Minnesota	WCHA	44	32	31	*63	28																			
1995-96	U. of Minnesota	WCHA	42	34	*47	*81	30																			
1996-97	Cleveland	IHL	60	13	26	39	18												1	1	0	1	0			
1997-98	Syracuse	AHL	67	31	38	69	46												5	1	3	4	6			
1998-99	Pittsburgh	NHL	5	0	0	0	0	0	0	0	2	0.0	–2	28	39.3	4	2	12:19	3	0	0	0	0	0	0	0
	Kansas City	IHL	19	2	5	7	10																			
	Adirondack	AHL	54	19	16	35	31												2	0	0	0	0			
	NHL Totals		5	0	0	0	0	0	0	0	2	0.0		28	39.3	4	2	12:19	3	0	0	0	0	0	0	0

WCHA First All-Star Team (1995, 1996) • NCAA West First All-American Team (1995, 1996) • Won Hobey Baker Memorial Award (Top U.S. Collegiate Player) (1996)

BONK, Radek (BOHNK) OTT.

Center. Shoots left. 6'3", 210 lbs. Born, Krnov, Czech., January 9, 1976. Ottawa's 1st choice, 3rd overall, in 1994 Entry Draft.

Season	Club	League	GP	G	A	Pts	PIM	PP	SH	GW	S	%	+/–	TF	F%	H	SB	Min	GP	G	A	Pts	PIM	PP	SH	GW
1990-91	HC Opava	Czech-Jr.	35	47	42	89	25																			
1991-92	ZPS Zlin	Czech-Jr.	45	47	36	83	30																			
1992-93	ZPS Zlin	Czech.	30	5	5	10	10																			
1993-94	Las Vegas	IHL	76	42	45	87	208												5	1	2	3	10			
1994-95	Las Vegas	IHL	33	7	13	20	62																			
	Ottawa	NHL	42	3	8	11	28	1	0	0	40	7.5	–5													
	P.E.I. Senators	AHL																	1	0	0	0	0			
1995-96	Ottawa	NHL	76	16	19	35	36	5	0	1	161	9.9	–5													
1996-97	Ottawa	NHL	53	5	13	18	14	0	1	0	82	6.1	–4						7	0	1	1	4	0	0	0
1997-98	Ottawa	NHL	65	7	9	16	16	1	0	0	93	7.5	–13						5	0	0	0	2	0	0	0
1998-99	Ottawa	NHL	81	16	16	32	48	0	1	6	110	14.5	15	1184	50.1	225	30	13:44	4	0	0	0	6	0	0	0
	NHL Totals		317	47	65	112	142	7	2	7	486	9.7		1184	50.1	225	30	13:44	16	0	1	1	12	0	0	0

Won Garry F. Longman Memorial Trophy (Top Rookie - IHL) (1994)

BONSIGNORE, Jason (bohn-SEE-nohr) TOR.

Center. Shoots right. 6'4", 220 lbs. Born, Rochester, NY, April 15, 1976. Edmonton's 1st choice, 4th overall, in 1994 Entry Draft.

Season	Club	League	GP	G	A	Pts	PIM	PP	SH	GW	S	%	+/–	TF	F%	H	SB	Min	GP	G	A	Pts	PIM	PP	SH	GW
1990-91	Greece High	H.S.	18	24	18	42																				
1991-92	Rochester	NAJHL	18	31	29	60	42																			
1992-93	Newmarket	OHL	66	22	20	42	6												7	0	3	3	0			
1993-94	Newmarket	OHL	17	7	17	24	22																			
	United States	Nat-Team	5	0	2	2	0																			
	Niagara Falls	OHL	41	15	47	62	41																			
1994-95	Niagara Falls	OHL	26	12	21	33	51																			
	Sudbury	OHL	23	15	14	29	45												17	13	10	23	12			
	Edmonton	NHL	1	1	0	1	0	0	0	0	3	33.3	–1													
1995-96	Sudbury	OHL	18	10	16	26	37																			
	Edmonton	NHL	20	0	2	2	4	0	0	0	13	0.0	–6													
	Cape Breton	AHL	12	1	4	5	12																			
1996-97	Hamilton	AHL	78	21	33	54	78												7	0	0	0	4			
1997-98	Hamilton	AHL	8	0	2	2	14																			
	San Antonio	IHL	22	3	8	11	34																			
	Tampa Bay	NHL	35	2	8	10	22	0	0	0	29	6.9	–11													
	Cleveland	IHL	6	4	0	4	32												8	1	1	2	20			
1998-99	Tampa Bay	NHL	23	0	3	3	8	0	0	0	12	0.0	–4	179	57.0	45	2	7:25								
	Cleveland	IHL	48	14	19	33	68																			
	NHL Totals		79	3	13	16	34	0	0	0	57	5.3		179	57.0	45	2	7:25								

Traded to **Tampa Bay** by **Edmonton** with Bryan Marchment and Steve Kelly for Roman Hamrlik and Paul Comrie, December 30, 1997. Signed as a free agent by **Toronto**, July 15, 1999.

BONVIE, Dennis (BOHN-vee)

Right wing/Defense. Shoots right. 5'11", 205 lbs. Born, Antigonish, N.S., July 23, 1973.

Season	Club	League	GP	G	A	Pts	PIM	PP	SH	GW	S	%	+/–	TF	F%	H	SB	Min	GP	G	A	Pts	PIM	PP	SH	GW
1989-90	Antigonish AA	NSAHA	50	15	30	45	52																			
1990-91	Antigonish	MJrHL	40	1	8	9	347																			
1991-92	Kitchener	OHL	7	1	1	2	23																			
	North Bay	OHL	49	0	12	12	261												21	0	1	1	91			
1992-93	North Bay	OHL	64	3	21	24	*316												5	0	0	0	34			
1993-94	Cape Breton	AHL	63	1	10	11	278												4	0	0	0	11			
1994-95	Edmonton	NHL	2	0	0	0	0	0	0	0	0	0.0	0													
	Cape Breton	AHL	74	5	15	20	422																			
1995-96	Edmonton	NHL	8	0	0	0	47	0	0	0	0	0.0	–3													
	Cape Breton	AHL	38	13	14	27	269																			
1996-97	Hamilton	AHL	73	9	20	29	*522												22	3	11	14	*91			
1997-98	Edmonton	NHL	4	0	0	0	27	0	0	0	0	0.0	0													
	Hamilton	AHL	57	11	19	30	295												9	0	5	5	18			
1998-99	Chicago	NHL	11	0	0	0	44	0	0	0	1	0.0	–4	0	0.0	10	0	3:59								
	Portland	AHL	3	1	0	1	16																			
	Philadelphia	AHL	37	4	10	14	158												14	3	3	6	26			
	NHL Totals		25	0	0	0	118	0	0	0	1	0.0		0	0.0	10	0	3:59								

Signed as a free agent by **Edmonton**, August 25, 1994. Claimed by **Chicago** from **Edmonton** in NHL Waiver Draft, October 5, 1998. Traded to **Philadelphia** by **Chicago** for Frank Bialowas, January 8, 1999.

BORDELEAU, Sebastien (BOHR-duh-loh) NSH.

Center. Shoots right. 5'11", 187 lbs. Born, Vancouver, B.C., February 15, 1975. Montreal's 3rd choice, 73rd overall, in 1993 Entry Draft.

Season	Club	League	GP	G	A	Pts	PIM	PP	SH	GW	S	%	+/–	TF	F%	H	SB	Min	GP	G	A	Pts	PIM	PP	SH	GW
1990-91	Laval	QAAA	39	27	36	63																				
1991-92	Hull	QMJHL	62	26	32	58	91												5	0	3	3	23			
1992-93	Hull	QMJHL	60	18	39	57	95												10	3	8	11	20			
1993-94	Hull	QMJHL	60	26	57	83	147												17	6	14	20	26			
1994-95	Hull	QMJHL	68	52	76	128	142												18	*13	19	*32	25			
	Fredericton	AHL																	1	0	0	0	0			
1995-96	Montreal	NHL	4	0	0	0	0	0	0	0	0	0.0	–1													
	Fredericton	AHL	43	17	29	46	68												7	0	2	2	8			

Season	Club	League	Regular Season GP	G	A	Pts	PIM	PP	SH	GW	S	%	+/-	TF	F%	H	SB	Min	Playoffs GP	G	A	Pts	PIM	PP	SH	GW
1996-97	Montreal	NHL	28	2	9	11	2	0	0	0	27	7.4	–3	....	....	....	....	....	....	....	....	....	....	....	....	....
	Fredericton	AHL	34	18	22	40	50	....	....	....	....	....	....	....	....	....	....	....	....	....	....	....	....	....	....	....
1997-98	Montreal	NHL	53	6	8	14	36	2	1	0	55	10.9	5	....	....	....	....	....	5	0	0	0	2	0	0	0
1998-99	Nashville	NHL	72	16	24	40	26	1	2	3	168	9.5	–14	1368	57.1	76	22	15:18	....	....	....	....	....	....	....	....
	NHL Totals		157	24	41	65	64	3	3	3	250	9.6		1368	57.1	76	22	15:18	5	0	0	0	2	0	0	0

QMJHL First All-Star Team (1995)
Traded to **Nashville** by **Montreal** for future considerations, June 26, 1998.

BOTTERILL, Jason (BOH-tuhr-ihl) ATL.

Left wing. Shoots left. 6'4", 220 lbs. Born, Edmonton, Alta., May 19, 1976. Dallas' 1st choice, 20th overall, in 1994 Entry Draft.

Season	Club	League	GP	G	A	Pts	PIM	PP	SH	GW	S	%	+/-	TF	F%	H	SB	Min	GP	G	A	Pts	PIM	PP	SH	GW
1992-93	St. Paul's Prep	H.S.	22	22	26	48	....	....	....	....	....	....	....	....	....	....	....	....	....	....	....	....	....	....	....	....
1993-94	U. of Michigan	CCHA	36	20	19	39	94	....	....	....	....	....	....	....	....	....	....	....	....	....	....	....	....	....	....	....
1994-95	U. of Michigan	CCHA	34	14	14	28	117	....	....	....	....	....	....	....	....	....	....	....	....	....	....	....	....	....	....	....
1995-96	U. of Michigan	CCHA	37	*32	25	57	*143	....	....	....	....	....	....	....	....	....	....	....	....	....	....	....	....	....	....	....
1996-97	U. of Michigan	CCHA	42	*37	24	61	129	....	....	....	....	....	....	....	....	....	....	....	....	....	....	....	....	....	....	....
1997-98	Dallas	NHL	4	0	0	0	19	0	0	0	2	0.0	–1	....	....	....	....	....	....	....	....	....	....	....	....	....
	Michigan	IHL	50	11	11	22	82	....	....	....	....	....	....	....	....	....	....	....	4	0	0	0	5	....	....	....
1998-99	Dallas	NHL	17	0	0	0	23	0	0	0	8	0.0	–2	0	0.0	27	0	8:19	....	....	....	....	....	....	....	....
	Michigan	IHL	56	13	25	38	106	....	....	....	....	....	....	....	....	....	....	....	5	2	1	3	4	....	....	....
	NHL Totals		21	0	0	0	42	0	0	0	10	0.0		0	0.0	27	0	8:19	....	....	....	....	....	....	....	....

CCHA Second All-Star Team (1996) • NCAA West Second All-American Team (1997)
Traded to **Atlanta** by **Dallas** for Jamie Pushor, July 15, 1999.

BOUCHARD, Joel (BOO-shahrd) NSH.

Defense. Shoots left. 6', 190 lbs. Born, Montreal, Que., January 23, 1974. Calgary's 7th choice, 129th overall, in 1992 Entry Draft.

Season	Club	League	GP	G	A	Pts	PIM	PP	SH	GW	S	%	+/-	TF	F%	H	SB	Min	GP	G	A	Pts	PIM	PP	SH	GW
1989-90	Montreal AAA	QAAA	41	7	17	24	10	....	....	....	....	....	....	....	....	....	....	....	1	1	0	1	0	....	....	....
1990-91	Longueuil	QMJHL	53	3	19	22	34	....	....	....	....	....	....	....	....	....	....	....	8	1	0	1	11	....	....	....
1991-92	Verdun	QMJHL	70	9	20	29	55	....	....	....	....	....	....	....	....	....	....	....	19	1	7	8	20	....	....	....
1992-93	Verdun	QMJHL	60	10	49	59	126	....	....	....	....	....	....	....	....	....	....	....	4	0	2	2	4	....	....	....
1993-94	Verdun	QMJHL	60	15	55	70	62	....	....	....	....	....	....	....	....	....	....	....	4	1	0	1	6	....	....	....
	Saint John	AHL	1	0	0	0	0	....	....	....	....	....	....	....	....	....	....	....	2	0	0	0	0	....	....	....
1994-95	Calgary	NHL	2	0	0	0	0	0	0	0	0	0.0	0	....	....	....	....	....	....	....	....	....	....	....	....	....
	Saint John	AHL	77	6	25	31	63	....	....	....	....	....	....	....	....	....	....	....	5	1	0	1	4	....	....	....
1995-96	Calgary	NHL	4	0	0	0	4	0	0	0	0	0.0	0	....	....	....	....	....	....	....	....	....	....	....	....	....
	Saint John	AHL	74	8	25	33	104	....	....	....	....	....	....	....	....	....	....	....	16	1	4	5	10	....	....	....
1996-97	Calgary	NHL	76	4	5	9	49	0	1	0	61	6.6	–23	....	....	....	....	....	....	....	....	....	....	....	....	....
1997-98	Calgary	NHL	44	5	7	12	57	0	1	1	51	9.8	0	....	....	....	....	....	....	....	....	....	....	....	....	....
	Saint John	AHL	3	2	1	3	6	....	....	....	....	....	....	....	....	....	....	....	....	....	....	....	....	....	....	....
1998-99	Nashville	NHL	64	4	11	15	60	0	0	0	78	5.1	–10	0	0.0	109	67	22:34	....	....	....	....	....	....	....	....
	NHL Totals		190	13	23	36	170	0	2	1	190	6.8		0	0.0	109	67	22:34	....	....	....	....	....	....	....	....

QMJHL First All-Star Team (1994)
Claimed by **Nashville** from **Calgary** in Expansion Draft, June 26, 1998.

BOUCHER, Philippe (boo-SHAY, fihl-EEP) L.A.

Defense. Shoots right. 6'2", 214 lbs. Born, St. Apollinaire, Que., March 24, 1973. Buffalo's 1st choice, 13th overall, in 1991 Entry Draft.

Season	Club	League	GP	G	A	Pts	PIM	PP	SH	GW	S	%	+/-	TF	F%	H	SB	Min	GP	G	A	Pts	PIM	PP	SH	GW
1989-90	Ste-Foy	QAAA	33	18	47	65	64	....	....	....	....	....	....	....	....	....	....	....	9	8	13	21	12	....	....	....
1990-91	Granby	QMJHL	69	21	46	67	92	....	....	....	....	....	....	....	....	....	....	....	....	....	....	....	....	....	....	....
1991-92	Granby	QMJHL	49	22	37	59	47	....	....	....	....	....	....	....	....	....	....	....	....	....	....	....	....	....	....	....
	Laval	QMJHL	16	7	11	18	36	....	....	....	....	....	....	....	....	....	....	....	10	5	6	11	8	....	....	....
1992-93	Laval	QMJHL	16	12	15	27	37	....	....	....	....	....	....	....	....	....	....	....	13	6	15	21	12	....	....	....
	Buffalo	NHL	18	0	4	4	14	0	0	0	28	0.0	1	....	....	....	....	....	....	....	....	....	....	....	....	....
	Rochester	AHL	5	4	3	7	8	....	....	....	....	....	....	....	....	....	....	....	3	0	1	1	2	....	....	....
1993-94	Buffalo	NHL	38	6	8	14	29	4	0	1	67	9.0	–1	....	....	....	....	....	7	1	1	2	2	1	0	0
	Rochester	AHL	31	10	22	32	51	....	....	....	....	....	....	....	....	....	....	....	....	....	....	....	....	....	....	....
1994-95	Buffalo	NHL	9	1	4	5	0	0	0	0	15	6.7	6	....	....	....	....	....	....	....	....	....	....	....	....	....
	Rochester	AHL	43	14	27	41	26	....	....	....	....	....	....	....	....	....	....	....	....	....	....	....	....	....	....	....
	Los Angeles	NHL	6	1	0	1	4	0	0	0	15	6.7	–3	....	....	....	....	....	....	....	....	....	....	....	....	....
1995-96	Los Angeles	NHL	53	7	16	23	31	5	0	1	145	4.8	–26	....	....	....	....	....	....	....	....	....	....	....	....	....
	Phoenix	IHL	10	4	3	7	4	....	....	....	....	....	....	....	....	....	....	....	....	....	....	....	....	....	....	....
1996-97	Los Angeles	NHL	60	7	18	25	25	2	0	1	159	4.4	0	....	....	....	....	....	....	....	....	....	....	....	....	....
1997-98	Los Angeles	NHL	45	6	10	16	49	1	0	0	80	7.5	6	....	....	....	....	....	....	....	....	....	....	....	....	....
	Long Beach	IHL	2	0	1	1	4	....	....	....	....	....	....	....	....	....	....	....	....	....	....	....	....	....	....	....
1998-99	Los Angeles	NHL	45	2	6	8	32	1	0	0	87	2.3	–12	0	0.0	58	63	17:51	....	....	....	....	....	....	....	....
	NHL Totals		274	30	66	96	184	13	0	3	596	5.0		0	0.0	58	63	17:51	7	1	1	2	2	1	0	0

Canadian Major Junior Rookie of the Year (1991) • QMJHL Second All-Star Team (1991, 1992)
Traded to **LA Kings** by **Buffalo** with Denis Tsygurov and Grant Fuhr for Alexei Zhitnik, Robb Stauber, Charlie Huddy and LA Kings' 5th round choice (Marian Menhart) in 1995 Entry Draft, February 14, 1995.

BOUGHNER, Bob (BOOG-nuhr) NSH.

Defense. Shoots right. 6', 206 lbs. Born, Windsor, Ont., March 8, 1971. Detroit's 2nd choice, 32nd overall, in 1989 Entry Draft.

Season	Club	League	GP	G	A	Pts	PIM	PP	SH	GW	S	%	+/-	TF	F%	H	SB	Min	GP	G	A	Pts	PIM	PP	SH	GW
1986-87	Belle River	OJHL-C	37	3	11	14	88	....	....	....	....	....	....	....	....	....	....	....	....	....	....	....	....	....	....	....
1987-88	St. Mary's	OJHL-B	36	4	18	22	177	....	....	....	....	....	....	....	....	....	....	....	....	....	....	....	....	....	....	....
1988-89	S.S. Marie	OHL	64	6	15	21	182	....	....	....	....	....	....	....	....	....	....	....	....	....	....	....	....	....	....	....
1989-90	S.S. Marie	OHL	49	7	23	30	122	....	....	....	....	....	....	....	....	....	....	....	....	....	....	....	....	....	....	....
1990-91	S.S. Marie	OHL	64	13	33	46	156	....	....	....	....	....	....	....	....	....	....	....	14	2	9	11	35	....	....	....
1991-92	Toledo	ECHL	28	3	10	13	79	....	....	....	....	....	....	....	....	....	....	....	5	2	0	2	15	....	....	....
	Adirondack	AHL	1	0	0	0	7	....	....	....	....	....	....	....	....	....	....	....	....	....	....	....	....	....	....	....
1992-93	Adirondack	AHL	69	1	16	17	190	....	....	....	....	....	....	....	....	....	....	....	....	....	....	....	....	....	....	....
1993-94	Adirondack	AHL	72	8	14	22	292	....	....	....	....	....	....	....	....	....	....	....	10	1	1	2	18	....	....	....
1994-95	Cincinnati	IHL	81	2	14	16	192	....	....	....	....	....	....	....	....	....	....	....	10	0	0	0	18	....	....	....
1995-96	Carolina	AHL	46	2	15	17	127	....	....	....	....	....	....	....	....	....	....	....	....	....	....	....	....	....	....	....
	Buffalo	NHL	31	0	1	1	104	0	0	0	14	0.0	3	....	....	....	....	....	....	....	....	....	....	....	....	....
1996-97	Buffalo	NHL	77	1	7	8	225	0	0	0	34	2.9	12	....	....	....	....	....	11	0	1	1	9	0	0	0
1997-98	Buffalo	NHL	69	1	3	4	165	0	0	0	26	3.8	5	....	....	....	....	....	14	0	4	4	15	0	0	0
1998-99	Nashville	NHL	79	3	10	13	137	0	0	1	59	5.1	–6	0	0.0	233	91	18:31	....	....	....	....	....	....	....	....
	NHL Totals		256	5	21	26	631	0	0	1	133	3.8		0	0.0	233	91	18:31	25	0	5	5	24	0	0	0

Signed as a free agent by **Florida**, July 25, 1994. Traded to **Buffalo** by **Florida** for Buffalo's 3rd round choice (Chris Allen) in 1996 Entry Draft, February 1, 1996. Claimed by **Nashville** from **Buffalo** in Expansion Draft, June 26, 1998.

BOURQUE, Ray (BOHRK) BOS.

Defense. Shoots left. 5'11", 219 lbs. Born, Montreal, Que., December 28, 1960. Boston's 1st choice, 8th overall, in 1979 Entry Draft.

Season	Club	League	GP	G	A	Pts	PIM	PP	SH	GW	S	%	+/-	TF	F%	H	SB	Min	GP	G	A	Pts	PIM	PP	SH	GW
1976-77	Sorel	QMJHL	69	12	36	48	61	....	....	....	....	....	....	....	....	....	....	....	....	....	....	....	....	....	....	....
1977-78	Verdun	QMJHL	72	22	57	79	90	....	....	....	....	....	....	....	....	....	....	....	4	2	1	3	0	....	....	....
1978-79	Verdun	QMJHL	63	22	71	93	44	....	....	....	....	....	....	....	....	....	....	....	11	3	16	19	18	....	....	....
1979-80	Boston	NHL	80	17	48	65	73	3	2	1	185	9.2	52	....	....	....	....	....	10	2	9	11	27	0	0	0
1980-81	Boston	NHL	67	27	29	56	96	9	1	6	207	13.0	29	....	....	....	....	....	3	0	1	1	2	0	0	0
1981-82	Boston	NHL	65	17	49	66	51	4	0	2	211	8.1	22	....	....	....	....	....	9	1	5	6	16	0	0	1

			Regular Season																Playoffs							
Season	**Club**	**League**	**GP**	**G**	**A**	**Pts**	**PIM**	**PP**	**SH**	**GW**	**S**	**%**	**+/–**	**TF**	**F%**	**H**	**SB**	**Min**	**GP**	**G**	**A**	**Pts**	**PIM**	**PP**	**SH**	**GW**
1982-83	**Boston**	**NHL**	**65**	**22**	**51**	**73**	**20**	**7**	**0**	**5**	**205**	**10.7**	**49**						**17**	**8**	**15**	**23**	**10**	**2**	**0**	**1**
1983-84	**Boston**	**NHL**	**78**	**31**	**65**	**96**	**57**	**12**	**1**	**5**	**340**	**9.1**	**51**						**3**	**0**	**2**	**2**	**0**	**0**	**0**	**0**
1984-85	**Boston**	**NHL**	**73**	**20**	**66**	**86**	**53**	**10**	**1**	**1**	**333**	**6.0**	**30**						**5**	**0**	**3**	**3**	**4**	**0**	**0**	**0**
1985-86	**Boston**	**NHL**	**74**	**19**	**58**	**77**	**68**	**11**	**0**	**3**	**289**	**6.6**	**17**						**3**	**0**	**0**	**0**	**0**	**0**	**0**	**0**
1986-87	**Boston**	**NHL**	**78**	**23**	**72**	**95**	**36**	**6**	**1**	**3**	**334**	**6.9**	**44**						**4**	**1**	**2**	**3**	**0**	**0**	**0**	**0**
1987-88	**Boston**	**NHL**	**78**	**17**	**64**	**81**	**72**	**7**	**1**	**5**	**344**	**4.9**	**34**						**23**	**3**	**18**	**21**	**26**	**0**	**0**	**1**
1988-89	**Boston**	**NHL**	**60**	**18**	**43**	**61**	**52**	**6**	**0**	**0**	**243**	**7.4**	**20**						**10**	**0**	**4**	**4**	**6**	**0**	**0**	**0**
1989-90	**Boston**	**NHL**	**76**	**19**	**65**	**84**	**50**	**8**	**0**	**3**	**310**	**6.1**	**31**						**17**	**5**	**12**	**17**	**16**	**1**	**0**	**0**
1990-91	**Boston**	**NHL**	**76**	**21**	**73**	**94**	**75**	**7**	**0**	**3**	**323**	**6.5**	**33**						**19**	**7**	**18**	**25**	**12**	**3**	**0**	**0**
1991-92	**Boston**	**NHL**	**80**	**21**	**60**	**81**	**56**	**7**	**1**	**2**	**334**	**6.3**	**11**						**12**	**3**	**6**	**9**	**12**	**2**	**0**	**0**
1992-93	**Boston**	**NHL**	**78**	**19**	**63**	**82**	**40**	**8**	**0**	**7**	**330**	**5.8**	**38**						**4**	**1**	**0**	**1**	**2**	**1**	**0**	**0**
1993-94	**Boston**	**NHL**	**72**	**20**	**71**	**91**	**58**	**10**	**3**	**1**	**386**	**5.2**	**26**						**13**	**2**	**8**	**10**	**0**	**1**	**0**	**0**
1994-95	**Boston**	**NHL**	**46**	**12**	**31**	**43**	**20**	**9**	**0**	**2**	**210**	**5.7**	**3**						**5**	**0**	**3**	**3**	**0**	**0**	**0**	**0**
1995-96	**Boston**	**NHL**	**82**	**20**	**62**	**82**	**58**	**9**	**2**	**2**	**390**	**5.1**	**31**						**5**	**1**	**6**	**7**	**2**	**1**	**0**	**0**
1996-97	**Boston**	**NHL**	**62**	**19**	**31**	**50**	**18**	**8**	**1**	**3**	**230**	**8.3**	**–11**													
1997-98	**Boston**	**NHL**	**82**	**13**	**35**	**48**	**80**	**9**	**0**	**3**	**264**	**4.9**	**2**						**6**	**1**	**4**	**5**	**2**	**1**	**0**	**0**
	Canada	Olympics	6	1	2	3	4																			
1998-99	**Boston**	**NHL**	**81**	**10**	**47**	**57**	**34**	**8**	**0**	**3**	**262**	**3.8**	**–7**	**2**	**0.0**	**173**	**113**	**29:31**	**12**	**1**	**9**	**10**	**14**	**0**	**0**	**0**
	NHL Totals		**1453**	**385**	**1083**	**1468**	**1067**	**158**	**14**	**60**	**5730**	**6.7**		**2**	**0.0**	**173**	**113**	**29:31**	**180**	**36**	**125**	**161**	**151**	**12**	**0**	**3**

QMJHL First All-Star Team (1978, 1979) • Won Calder Memorial Trophy (1980) • NHL First All-Star Team (1980, 1982, 1984, 1985, 1987, 1988, 1990, 1991, 1992, 1993, 1994, 1996) • NHL Second All-Star Team (1981, 1983, 1986, 1989, 1995, 1999) • Won James Norris Memorial Trophy (1987, 1988, 1990, 1991, 1994) • Won King Clancy Memorial Trophy (1992)

Played in NHL All-Star Game (1981, 1982, 1983, 1984, 1985, 1986, 1988, 1989, 1990, 1991, 1992, 1993, 1994, 1996, 1997, 1998, 1999)

BOWEN, Jason (BOW-ehn) COL.

Defense. Shoots left. 6'4", 220 lbs. Born, Port Alice, B.C., November 9, 1973. Philadelphia's 2nd choice, 15th overall, in 1992 Entry Draft.

1988-89	Notre Dame	AAHA	56	10	29	39	40																			
1989-90	Tri-City	WHL	61	8	5	13	129												7	0	3	3	4			
1990-91	Tri-City	WHL	60	7	13	20	252												6	2	2	4	18			
1991-92	Tri-City	WHL	19	5	3	8	135												5	0	1	1	42			
1992-93	Tri-City	WHL	62	10	12	22	219												3	1	1	2	18			
	Philadelphia	**NHL**	**7**	**1**	**0**	**1**	**2**	**0**	**0**	**0**	**3**	**33.3**	**1**													
1993-94	**Philadelphia**	**NHL**	**56**	**1**	**5**	**6**	**87**	**0**	**0**	**1**	**50**	**2.0**	**12**													
1994-95	**Philadelphia**	**NHL**	**4**	**0**	**0**	**0**	**0**	**0**	**0**	**0**	**2**	**0.0**	**–2**													
	Hershey	AHL	55	5	5	10	116												6	0	0	0	46			
1995-96	**Philadelphia**	**NHL**	**2**	**0**	**0**	**0**	**2**	**0**	**0**	**0**	**2**	**0.0**	**0**													
	Hershey	AHL	72	6	7	13	128												4	2	0	2	13			
1996-97	**Philadelphia**	**NHL**	**4**	**0**	**1**	**1**	**8**	**0**	**0**	**0**	**1**	**0.0**	**1**													
	Philadelphia	AHL	61	10	12	22	160												6	0	1	1	10			
1997-98	Philadelphia	AHL	3	0	0	0	19																			
	Edmonton	**NHL**	**4**	**0**	**0**	**0**	**10**	**0**	**0**	**0**	**3**	**0.0**	**0**													
	Hamilton	AHL	51	5	14	19	108												7	1	1	2	22			
1998-99	Hamilton	AHL	58	3	3	6	178												11	0	1	1	16			
	NHL Totals		**77**	**2**	**6**	**8**	**109**	**0**	**0**	**1**	**61**	**3.3**														

Traded to **Edmonton** by **Philadelphia** for Brantt Myhres, October 15, 1997. Signed as a free agent by **Colorado**, August 26, 1999.

BOYLE, Dan (BOIL) FLA.

Defense. Shoots right. 5'11", 190 lbs. Born, Ottawa, Ont., July 12, 1976.

1994-95	U. of Miami-Ohio	CCHA	35	8	18	26	24																			
1995-96	U. of Miami-Ohio	CCHA	36	7	20	27	70																			
1996-97	U. of Miami-Ohio	CCHA	40	11	43	54	52																			
1997-98	U. of Miami-Ohio	CCHA	37	14	26	40	58																			
1998-99	**Florida**	**NHL**	**22**	**3**	**5**	**8**	**6**	**1**	**0**	**1**	**31**	**9.7**	**0**	**1**	**100.0**	**27**	**14**	**18:50**								
	Kentucky	AHL	53	8	34	42	87												12	3	5	8	16			
	NHL Totals		**22**	**3**	**5**	**8**	**6**	**1**	**0**	**1**	**31**	**9.7**		**1**	**100.0**	**27**	**14**	**18:50**								

CCHA First All-Star Team (1997, 1998) • NCAA West First All-American Team (1997, 1998) • AHL Second All-Star Team (1999)

Signed as a free agent by **Florida**, March 30, 1998.

BRASHEAR, Donald (bra-SHEER) VAN.

Left wing. Shoots left. 6'2", 225 lbs. Born, Bedford, IN, January 7, 1972.

1988-89	Ste-Foy	QAAA	10	1	2	3	10																			
1989-90	Longueuil	QMJHL	64	12	14	26	169												7	0	0	0	11			
1990-91	Longueuil	QMJHL	68	12	26	38	195												8	0	3	3	33			
1991-92	Verdun	QMJHL	65	18	24	42	283												18	4	2	6	98			
1992-93	Fredericton	AHL	76	11	3	14	261												5	0	0	0	8			
1993-94	**Montreal**	**NHL**	**14**	**2**	**2**	**4**	**34**	**0**	**0**	**0**	**15**	**13.3**	**0**						**2**	**0**	**0**	**0**	**0**	**0**	**0**	**0**
	Fredericton	AHL	62	38	28	66	250																			
1994-95	Fredericton	AHL	29	10	9	19	182												17	7	5	12	77			
	Montreal	**NHL**	**20**	**1**	**1**	**2**	**63**	**0**	**0**	**1**	**10**	**10.0**	**–5**													
1995-96	**Montreal**	**NHL**	**67**	**0**	**4**	**4**	**223**	**0**	**0**	**0**	**25**	**0.0**	**–10**						**6**	**0**	**0**	**0**	**2**	**0**	**0**	**0**
1996-97	**Montreal**	**NHL**	**10**	**0**	**0**	**0**	**38**	**0**	**0**	**0**	**6**	**0.0**	**–2**													
	Vancouver	**NHL**	**59**	**8**	**5**	**13**	**207**	**0**	**0**	**2**	**55**	**14.5**	**–6**													
1997-98	**Vancouver**	**NHL**	**77**	**9**	**9**	**18**	***372**	**0**	**0**	**1**	**64**	**14.1**	**–9**													
1998-99	**Vancouver**	**NHL**	**82**	**8**	**10**	**18**	**209**	**2**	**0**	**1**	**112**	**7.1**	**–25**	**6**	**16.7**	**126**	**20**	**13:25**								
	NHL Totals		**329**	**28**	**31**	**59**	**1146**	**2**	**0**	**5**	**287**	**9.8**		**6**	**16.7**	**126**	**20**	**13:25**	**8**	**0**	**0**	**0**	**2**	**0**	**0**	**0**

Signed as a free agent by **Montreal**, July 28, 1992. Traded to **Vancouver** by **Montreal** for Jassen Cullimore, November 13, 1996.

BRENNAN, Rich

Defense. Shoots right. 6'2", 200 lbs. Born, Schenectady, NY, November 26, 1972. Quebec's 3rd choice, 46th overall, in 1991 Entry Draft.

1988-89	Albany Academy	H.S.	25	17	30	47	57																			
1989-90	Tabor Academy	H.S.	33	12	14	26	68																			
1990-91	Tabor Academy	H.S.	34	13	37	50	91																			
1991-92	Boston University	H.E.	30	4	13	17	50																			
1992-93	Boston University	H.E.	40	9	11	20	68																			
1993-94	Boston University	H.E.	41	8	27	35	82																			
1994-95	Boston University	H.E.	31	5	22	27	56																			
1995-96	Brantford	ColHL	5	1	2	3	2																			
	Cornwall	AHL	36	4	8	12	61												7	0	0	0	6			
1996-97	**Colorado**	**NHL**	**2**	**0**	**0**	**0**	**0**	**0**	**0**	**0**	**0**	**0.0**	**0**													
	Hershey	AHL	74	11	45	56	88												23	2	16	18	22			
1997-98	**San Jose**	**NHL**	**11**	**1**	**2**	**3**	**2**	**1**	**0**	**0**	**24**	**4.2**	**–4**													
	Kentucky	AHL	42	11	17	28	71																			
	Hartford	AHL	9	2	4	6	12												15	4	5	9	14			
1998-99	**NY Rangers**	**NHL**	**24**	**1**	**3**	**4**	**23**	**0**	**0**	**0**	**36**	**2.8**	**–4**	**0**	**0.0**	**40**	**22**	**13:02**								
	Hartford	AHL	47	4	24	28	42																			
	NHL Totals		**37**	**2**	**5**	**7**	**25**	**1**	**0**	**0**	**60**	**3.3**		**0**	**0.0**	**40**	**22**	**13:02**								

Hockey East First All-Star Team (1994) • NCAA East Second All-American Team (1994)

Rights transferred to **Colorado** after **Quebec** franchise relocated, June 21, 1995. Signed as a free agent by **San Jose**, July 9, 1997. Traded to **NY Rangers** by **San Jose** for Jason Muzzatti, March 24, 1998.

BREWER, Eric — NYI

Defense. Shoots left. 6'3", 195 lbs. Born, Vernon, B.C., April 17, 1979. NY Islanders' 2nd choice, 5th overall, in 1997 Entry Draft.

			Regular Season																Playoffs							
Season	Club	League	GP	G	A	Pts	PIM	PP	SH	GW	S	%	+/–	TF	F%	H	SB	Min	GP	G	A	Pts	PIM	PP	SH	GW
1994-95	Kamloops	BCAHA	40	19	19	38	62	....	....	....	....	....	....	....	....	....	....	....	....	....	....	....	....	....	....	....
1995-96	Prince George	WHL	63	4	10	14	25	....	....	....	....	....	....	....	....	....	....	....	....	....	....	....	....	....	....	....
1996-97	Prince George	WHL	71	5	24	29	81	....	....	....	....	....	....	....	....	....	....	....	15	2	4	6	16	....	....	....
1997-98	Prince George	WHL	34	5	28	33	45	....	....	....	....	....	....	....	....	....	....	....	11	4	2	6	19	....	....	....
1998-99	**NY Islanders**	**NHL**	**63**	**5**	**6**	**11**	**32**	**2**	**0**	**0**	**63**	**7.9**	**–14**	**0**	**0.0**	**89**	**32**	**15:28**	....	....	....	....	....	....	....	....
	NHL Totals		**63**	**5**	**6**	**11**	**32**	**2**	**0**	**0**	**63**	**7.9**		**0**	**0.0**	**89**	**32**	**15:28**	....	....	....	....	....	....	....	....

WHL West Second All-Star Team (1998)

BRIERE, Daniel (bree-AIR) — PHX.

Center. Shoots left. 5'9", 185 lbs. Born, Gatineau, Que., October 6, 1977. Phoenix's 2nd choice, 24th overall, in 1996 Entry Draft.

Season	Club	League	GP	G	A	Pts	PIM	PP	SH	GW	S	%	+/–	TF	F%	H	SB	Min	GP	G	A	Pts	PIM	PP	SH	GW
1993-94	Gatineau	QAAA	44	56	47	103	56	....	....	....	....	....	....	....	....	....	....	....	....	....	....	....	....	....	....	....
1994-95	Drummondville	QMJHL	72	51	72	123	54	....	....	....	....	....	....	....	....	....	....	....	4	2	3	5	2	....	....	....
1995-96	Drummondville	QMJHL	67	*67	*96	*163	84	....	....	....	....	....	....	....	....	....	....	....	6	6	12	18	8	....	....	....
1996-97	Drummondville	QMJHL	59	52	78	130	94	....	....	....	....	....	....	....	....	....	....	....	8	7	7	14	14	....	....	....
1997-98	**Phoenix**	**NHL**	**5**	**1**	**0**	**1**	**2**	**0**	**0**	**0**	**4**	**25.0**	**1**	....	....	....	....	....	....	....	....	....	....	....	....	....
	Springfield	AHL	68	36	56	92	42	....	....	....	....	....	....	....	....	....	....	....	4	1	2	3	4	....	....	....
1998-99	**Phoenix**	**NHL**	**64**	**8**	**14**	**22**	**30**	**2**	**0**	**2**	**90**	**8.9**	**–3**	**484**	**47.5**	**15**	**8**	**11:13**	....	....	....	....	....	....	....	....
	Las Vegas	IHL	1	1	1	2	0	....	....	....	....	....	....	....	....	....	....	....	....	....	....	....	....	....	....	....
	Springfield	AHL	13	2	6	8	20	....	....	....	....	....	....	....	....	....	....	....	3	0	1	1	2	....	....	....
	NHL Totals		**69**	**9**	**14**	**23**	**32**	**2**	**0**	**2**	**94**	**9.6**		**484**	**47.5**	**15**	**8**	**11:13**	....	....	....	....	....	....	....	....

QMJHL Second All-Star Team (1996, 1997) • AHL First All-Star Team (1998) • Won Dudley "Red" Garrett Memorial Trophy (Top Rookie - AHL) (1998)

BRIGLEY, Travis — CGY.

Left wing. Shoots left. 6'1", 195 lbs. Born, Coronation, Alta., June 16, 1977. Calgary's 2nd choice, 39th overall, in 1996 Entry Draft.

Season	Club	League	GP	G	A	Pts	PIM	PP	SH	GW	S	%	+/–	TF	F%	H	SB	Min	GP	G	A	Pts	PIM	PP	SH	GW
1992-93	Leduc	AAHA	32	36	24	60	56	....	....	....	....	....	....	....	....	....	....	....	....	....	....	....	....	....	....	....
1993-94	Leduc	AAHA	34	29	44	73	141	....	....	....	....	....	....	....	....	....	....	....	....	....	....	....	....	....	....	....
	Lethbridge	WHL	1	0	0	0	0	....	....	....	....	....	....	....	....	....	....	....	....	....	....	....	....	....	....	....
1994-95	Lethbridge	WHL	64	14	18	32	14	....	....	....	....	....	....	....	....	....	....	....	....	....	....	....	....	....	....	....
1995-96	Lethbridge	WHL	69	34	43	77	94	....	....	....	....	....	....	....	....	....	....	....	4	2	3	5	8	....	....	....
1996-97	Lethbridge	WHL	71	43	47	90	56	....	....	....	....	....	....	....	....	....	....	....	19	9	9	18	31	....	....	....
1997-98	**Calgary**	**NHL**	**2**	**0**	**0**	**0**	**2**	**0**	**0**	**0**	**1**	**0.0**	**0**	....	....	....	....	....	....	....	....	....	....	....	....	....
	Saint John	AHL	79	17	15	32	28	....	....	....	....	....	....	....	....	....	....	....	8	0	0	0	0	....	....	....
1998-99	Saint John	AHL	74	15	35	50	48	....	....	....	....	....	....	....	....	....	....	....	7	3	1	4	2	....	....	....
	NHL Totals		**2**	**0**	**0**	**0**	**2**	**0**	**0**	**0**	**1**	**0.0**		....	....	....	....	....	....	....	....	....	....	....	....	....

BRIMANIS, Aris (brih-MAN-ihs, AR-ihs) — NYI

Defense. Shoots right. 6'3", 210 lbs. Born, Cleveland, OH, March 14, 1972. Philadelphia's 3rd choice, 86th overall, in 1991 Entry Draft.

Season	Club	League	GP	G	A	Pts	PIM	PP	SH	GW	S	%	+/–	TF	F%	H	SB	Min	GP	G	A	Pts	PIM	PP	SH	GW
1988-89	Culver Academy	H.S.	38	10	13	23	24	....	....	....	....	....	....	....	....	....	....	....	....	....	....	....	....	....	....	....
1989-90	Culver Academy	H.S.	37	15	10	25	52	....	....	....	....	....	....	....	....	....	....	....	....	....	....	....	....	....	....	....
1990-91	Bowling Green	CCHA	38	3	6	9	42	....	....	....	....	....	....	....	....	....	....	....	....	....	....	....	....	....	....	....
1991-92	Bowling Green	CCHA	32	2	9	11	38	....	....	....	....	....	....	....	....	....	....	....	....	....	....	....	....	....	....	....
1992-93	Brandon	WHL	71	8	50	58	110	....	....	....	....	....	....	....	....	....	....	....	4	2	1	3	7	....	....	....
1993-94	**Philadelphia**	**NHL**	**1**	**0**	**0**	**0**	**0**	**0**	**0**	**0**	**1**	**0.0**	**–1**	....	....	....	....	....	....	....	....	....	....	....	....	....
	Hershey	AHL	75	8	15	23	65	....	....	....	....	....	....	....	....	....	....	....	11	2	3	5	12	....	....	....
1994-95	Hershey	AHL	76	8	17	25	68	....	....	....	....	....	....	....	....	....	....	....	6	1	1	2	14	....	....	....
1995-96	**Philadelphia**	**NHL**	**17**	**0**	**2**	**2**	**12**	**0**	**0**	**0**	**11**	**0.0**	**–1**	....	....	....	....	....	....	....	....	....	....	....	....	....
	Hershey	AHL	54	9	22	31	64	....	....	....	....	....	....	....	....	....	....	....	5	1	2	3	4	....	....	....
1996-97	**Philadelphia**	**NHL**	**3**	**0**	**1**	**1**	**0**	**0**	**0**	**0**	**1**	**0.0**	**0**	....	....	....	....	....	....	....	....	....	....	....	....	....
	Philadelphia	AHL	65	14	18	32	69	....	....	....	....	....	....	....	....	....	....	....	10	2	2	4	13	....	....	....
1997-98	Philadelphia	AHL	30	1	11	12	26	....	....	....	....	....	....	....	....	....	....	....	....	....	....	....	....	....	....	....
	Michigan	IHL	35	3	9	12	24	....	....	....	....	....	....	....	....	....	....	....	4	1	0	1	4	....	....	....
1998-99	Grand Rapids	IHL	66	16	21	37	70	....	....	....	....	....	....	....	....	....	....	....	....	....	....	....	....	....	....	....
	Fredericton	AHL	8	2	4	6	6	....	....	....	....	....	....	....	....	....	....	....	15	3	10	13	18	....	....	....
	NHL Totals		**21**	**0**	**3**	**3**	**12**	**0**	**0**	**0**	**13**	**0.0**		....	....	....	....	....	....	....	....	....	....	....	....	....

Signed as a free agent by **NY Islanders**, August 16, 1999.

BRIND'AMOUR, Rod (BRIHND-uh-MOHR) — PHI.

Center. Shoots left. 6'1", 202 lbs. Born, Ottawa, Ont., August 9, 1970. St. Louis' 1st choice, 9th overall, in 1988 Entry Draft.

Season	Club	League	GP	G	A	Pts	PIM	PP	SH	GW	S	%	+/–	TF	F%	H	SB	Min	GP	G	A	Pts	PIM	PP	SH	GW
1986-87	Notre Dame	AAHA	33	38	50	88	66	....	....	....	....	....	....	....	....	....	....	....	....	....	....	....	....	....	....	....
1987-88	Notre Dame	SJHL	56	46	61	107	136	....	....	....	....	....	....	....	....	....	....	....	....	....	....	....	....	....	....	....
1988-89	Michigan State	CCHA	42	27	32	59	63	....	....	....	....	....	....	....	....	....	....	....	....	....	....	....	....	....	....	....
	St. Louis	**NHL**	....	....	....	....	....	....	....	....	....	....	....	....	....	....	....	....	**5**	**2**	**0**	**2**	**4**	....	....	....
1989-90	**St. Louis**	**NHL**	**79**	**26**	**35**	**61**	**46**	**10**	**0**	**1**	**160**	**16.3**	**23**	....	....	....	....	....	**12**	**5**	**8**	**13**	**6**	**1**	**0**	**0**
1990-91	**St. Louis**	**NHL**	**78**	**17**	**32**	**49**	**93**	**4**	**0**	**3**	**169**	**10.1**	**2**	....	....	....	....	....	**13**	**2**	**5**	**7**	**10**	**1**	**0**	**0**
1991-92	**Philadelphia**	**NHL**	**80**	**33**	**44**	**77**	**100**	**8**	**4**	**5**	**202**	**16.3**	**–3**	....	....	....	....	....	....	....	....	....	....	....	....	....
1992-93	**Philadelphia**	**NHL**	**81**	**37**	**49**	**86**	**89**	**13**	**4**	**4**	**206**	**18.0**	**–8**	....	....	....	....	....	....	....	....	....	....	....	....	....
1993-94	**Philadelphia**	**NHL**	**84**	**35**	**62**	**97**	**85**	**14**	**1**	**4**	**230**	**15.2**	**–9**	....	....	....	....	....	....	....	....	....	....	....	....	....
1994-95	**Philadelphia**	**NHL**	**48**	**12**	**27**	**39**	**33**	**4**	**1**	**2**	**86**	**14.0**	**–4**	....	....	....	....	....	**15**	**6**	**9**	**15**	**8**	**2**	**1**	**1**
1995-96	**Philadelphia**	**NHL**	**82**	**26**	**61**	**87**	**110**	**4**	**4**	**5**	**213**	**12.2**	**20**	....	....	....	....	....	**12**	**2**	**5**	**7**	**6**	**1**	**0**	**0**
1996-97	**Philadelphia**	**NHL**	**82**	**27**	**32**	**59**	**41**	**8**	**2**	**3**	**205**	**13.2**	**2**	....	....	....	....	....	**19**	***13**	**8**	**21**	**10**	**4**	**2**	**1**
1997-98	**Philadelphia**	**NHL**	**82**	**36**	**38**	**74**	**54**	**10**	**2**	**8**	**205**	**17.6**	**–2**	....	....	....	....	....	**5**	**2**	**2**	**4**	**7**	**0**	**0**	**0**
	Canada	Olympics	6	1	2	3	0	....	....	....	....	....	....	....	....	....	....	....	....	....	....	....	....	....	....	....
1998-99	**Philadelphia**	**NHL**	**82**	**24**	**50**	**74**	**47**	**10**	**0**	**3**	**191**	**12.6**	**3**	**1773**	**56.5**	**90**	**31**	**21:29**	**6**	**1**	**3**	**4**	**0**	**0**	**0**	**0**
	NHL Totals		**778**	**273**	**430**	**703**	**698**	**85**	**18**	**38**	**1867**	**14.6**		**1773**	**56.5**	**90**	**31**	**21:29**	**87**	**33**	**40**	**73**	**51**	**9**	**3**	**2**

NHL All-Rookie Team (1990)
Played in NHL All-Star Game (1992)
Traded to **Philadelphia** by **St. Louis** with Dan Quinn for Ron Sutter and Murray Baron, September 22, 1991.

BRISEBOIS, Patrice (BREES-bwah, pa-TREEZ) — MTL.

Defense. Shoots right. 6'2", 204 lbs. Born, Montreal, Que., January 27, 1971. Montreal's 2nd choice, 30th overall, in 1989 Entry Draft.

Season	Club	League	GP	G	A	Pts	PIM	PP	SH	GW	S	%	+/–	TF	F%	H	SB	Min	GP	G	A	Pts	PIM	PP	SH	GW
1986-87	Montreal AAA	QAAA	39	15	19	34	66	....	....	....	....	....	....	....	....	....	....	....	....	....	....	....	....	....	....	....
1987-88	Laval	QMJHL	48	10	34	44	95	....	....	....	....	....	....	....	....	....	....	....	6	0	2	2	2	....	....	....
1988-89	Laval	QMJHL	50	20	45	65	95	....	....	....	....	....	....	....	....	....	....	....	17	8	14	22	45	....	....	....
1989-90	Laval	QMJHL	56	18	70	88	108	....	....	....	....	....	....	....	....	....	....	....	13	7	9	16	26	....	....	....
1990-91	Drummondville	QMJHL	54	17	44	61	72	....	....	....	....	....	....	....	....	....	....	....	14	6	18	24	49	....	....	....
	Montreal	**NHL**	**10**	**0**	**2**	**2**	**4**	**0**	**0**	**0**	**11**	**0.0**	**1**	....	....	....	....	....	....	....	....	....	....	....	....	....
1991-92	**Montreal**	**NHL**	**26**	**2**	**8**	**10**	**20**	**0**	**0**	**1**	**37**	**5.4**	**9**	....	....	....	....	....	**11**	**2**	**4**	**6**	**6**	**1**	**0**	**1**
	Fredericton	AHL	53	12	27	39	51	....	....	....	....	....	....	....	....	....	....	....	....	....	....	....	....	....	....	....
1992-93♦	**Montreal**	**NHL**	**70**	**10**	**21**	**31**	**79**	**4**	**0**	**2**	**123**	**8.1**	**6**	....	....	....	....	....	**20**	**0**	**4**	**4**	**18**	**0**	**0**	**0**
1993-94	**Montreal**	**NHL**	**53**	**2**	**21**	**23**	**63**	**1**	**0**	**0**	**71**	**2.8**	**5**	....	....	....	....	....	**7**	**0**	**4**	**4**	**6**	**0**	**0**	**0**
1994-95	**Montreal**	**NHL**	**35**	**4**	**8**	**12**	**26**	**0**	**0**	**2**	**67**	**6.0**	**–2**	....	....	....	....	....	....	....	....	....	....	....	....	....
1995-96	**Montreal**	**NHL**	**69**	**9**	**27**	**36**	**65**	**3**	**0**	**1**	**127**	**7.1**	**10**	....	....	....	....	....	**6**	**1**	**2**	**3**	**6**	**0**	**0**	**0**
1996-97	**Montreal**	**NHL**	**49**	**2**	**13**	**15**	**24**	**0**	**0**	**1**	**72**	**2.8**	**–7**	....	....	....	....	....	**3**	**1**	**1**	**2**	**24**	**0**	**0**	**1**

Season	Club	League	GP	G	A	Pts	PIM	PP	SH	GW	S	%	+/-	TF	F%	H	SB	Min	GP	G	A	Pts	PIM	PP	SH	GW
																				Playoffs						
1997-98	Montreal	NHL	79	10	27	37	67	5	0	1	125	8.0	16						10	1	0	1	0	0	0	0
1998-99	Montreal	NHL	54	3	9	12	28	1	0	1	90	3.3	-8	0	0.0	62	80	22:26								
	NHL Totals		445	42	136	178	376	14	0	9	723	5.8		0	0.0	62	80	22:26	57	5	15	20	60	1	0	2

QMJHL Second All-Star Team (1990) • Canadian Major Junior Defenseman of the Year (1991) • QMJHL First All-Star Team (1991) • Memorial Cup All-Star Team (1991)

BROUSSEAU, Paul

(BROO-soh)

Right wing. Shoots right. 6'2", 203 lbs. Born, Pierrefonds, Que., September 18, 1973. Quebec's 2nd choice, 28th overall, in 1992 Entry Draft.

Season	Club	League	GP	G	A	Pts	PIM	PP	SH	GW	S	%	+/-	TF	F%	H	SB	Min	GP	G	A	Pts	PIM	PP	SH	GW
1988-89	Lac St-Louis	QAAA	37	6	17	23	....																			
1989-90	Chicoutimi	QMJHL	57	17	24	41	32											7	0	3	3	0			
1990-91	Trois-Rivieres	QMJHL	67	30	66	96	48												6	3	2	5	2			
1991-92	Hull	QMJHL	57	35	61	96	54											6	3	5	8	10			
1992-93	Hull	QMJHL	59	27	48	75	49											10	7	8	15	6			
1993-94	Cornwall	AHL	69	18	26	44	35											1	0	0	0	0			
1994-95	Cornwall	AHL	57	19	17	36	29											7	2	1	3	10			
1995-96	**Colorado**	**NHL**	8	1	1	2	2	0	0	0	10	10.0	1													
	Cornwall	AHL	63	21	22	43	60											8	4	0	4	2			
1996-97	**Tampa Bay**	**NHL**	6	0	0	0	0	0	0	0	3	0.0	-4													
	Adirondack	AHL	66	35	31	66	25											4	1	2	3	0			
1997-98	**Tampa Bay**	**NHL**	11	0	2	2	27	0	0	0	6	0.0														
	Adirondack	AHL	67	45	20	65	18											3	1	1	2	0			
1998-99	Milwaukee	IHL	5	1	1	2	2																			
	Hershey	AHL	39	11	21	32	15											5	1	1	2	0			
	NHL Totals		25	1	3	4	29	0	0	0	19	5.3														

AHL Second All-Star Team (1998)

Rights transferred to **Colorado** after **Quebec** franchise relocated, June 21, 1995. Signed as a free agent by **Tampa Bay**, September 10, 1996. Claimed by **Nashville** from **Tampa Bay** in Expansion Draft, June 26, 1998.

BROWN, Brad

CHI.

Defense. Shoots right. 6'4", 218 lbs. Born, Baie Verte, Nfld., December 27, 1975. Montreal's 1st choice, 18th overall, in 1994 Entry Draft.

Season	Club	League	GP	G	A	Pts	PIM	PP	SH	GW	S	%	+/-	TF	F%	H	SB	Min	GP	G	A	Pts	PIM	PP	SH	GW
1990-91	Toronto	MTHL	80	15	45	60	105																			
	St. Michael's	OJHL-B	2	0	0	0	0																			
1991-92	North Bay	OHL	49	2	9	11	170											18	0	6	6	43			
1992-93	North Bay	OHL	61	4	9	13	228											2	0	2	2	13			
1993-94	North Bay	OHL	66	8	24	32	196											18	3	12	15	33			
1994-95	North Bay	OHL	64	8	38	46	172											6	1	4	5	8			
1995-96	Barrie	OHL	27	3	13	16	82																		
	Fredericton	AHL	38	0	3	3	148											10	2	1	3	6			
1996-97	**Montreal**	**NHL**	8	0	0	0	22	0	0	0	0	0.0	-1													
	Fredericton	AHL	64	3	7	10	368																		
1997-98	Fredericton	AHL	64	1	8	9	297											4	0	0	0	29			
1998-99	**Montreal**	**NHL**	5	0	0	0	21	0	0	0	0	0.0	0	0	0.0	1	5	6:02								
	Chicago	**NHL**	61	1	7	8	184	0	0	0	26	3.8	-4	0	0.0	145	63	15:08								
	NHL Totals		74	1	7	8	227	0	0	0	26	3.8		0	0.0	146	68	14:27								

Traded to **Chicago** by **Montreal** with Jocelyn Thibault and Dave Manson for Jeff Hackett, Eric Weinrich, Alain Nasreddine and Tampa Bay's 4th round choice (previously acquired, Montreal selected Chris Dyment) in 1999 Entry Draft, November 16, 1998.

BROWN, Curtis

BUF.

Center. Shoots left. 6', 190 lbs. Born, Unity, Sask., February 12, 1976. Buffalo's 2nd choice, 43rd overall, in 1994 Entry Draft.

Season	Club	League	GP	G	A	Pts	PIM	PP	SH	GW	S	%	+/-	TF	F%	H	SB	Min	GP	G	A	Pts	PIM	PP	SH	GW
1990-91	Unity	SAHA	60	93	104	197	55																			
1991-92	Moose Jaw	SAHA	36	35	30	65	44																			
1992-93	Moose Jaw	WHL	71	13	16	29	30																			
1993-94	Moose Jaw	WHL	72	27	38	65	82																			
1994-95	Moose Jaw	WHL	70	51	53	104	63											10	8	7	15	20			
	Buffalo	**NHL**	1	1	1	2	2	0	0	0	4	25.0	2													
1995-96	Moose Jaw	WHL	25	20	18	38	30											18	10	15	25	18			
	Prince Albert	WHL	19	12	21	33	8																		
	Buffalo	**NHL**	4	0	0	0	0	0	0	0	1	0.0	0													
	Rochester	AHL																12	0	1	1	2			
1996-97	**Buffalo**	**NHL**	28	4	3	7	18	0	0	1	31	12.9	4													
	Rochester	AHL	51	22	21	43	30											10	4	6	10	4			
1997-98	**Buffalo**	**NHL**	63	12	12	24	34	1	1	2	91	13.2	11						13	1	2	3	10	1	0	0
1998-99	**Buffalo**	**NHL**	78	16	31	47	56	5	1	3	128	12.5	23	1198	45.0	83	64	17:30	21	7	6	13	10	3	0	3
	NHL Totals		174	33	47	80	110	6	2	6	255	12.9		1198	45.0	83	64	17:30	34	8	8	16	20	4	0	3

WHL East First All-Star Team (1995) • WHL East Second All-Star Team (1996)

BROWN, Doug

DET.

Right wing. Shoots right. 5'10", 185 lbs. Born, Southborough, MA, June 12, 1964.

Season	Club	League	GP	G	A	Pts	PIM	PP	SH	GW	S	%	+/-	TF	F%	H	SB	Min	GP	G	A	Pts	PIM	PP	SH	GW
1981-82	St. Mark's	H.S.	STATISTICS NOT AVAILABLE																							
1982-83	Boston College	ECAC	22	9	8	17	0																			
1983-84	Boston College	ECAC	38	11	10	21	6																			
1984-85	Boston College	H.E.	45	37	31	68	10																			
1985-86	Boston College	H.E.	38	16	40	56	16																			
1986-87	**New Jersey**	**NHL**	4	0	1	1	0	0	0	0	10	0.0	-4													
	Maine	AHL	73	24	34	58	15																			
1987-88	**New Jersey**	**NHL**	70	14	11	25	20	1	4	2	112	12.5	7						19	5	1	6	6	0	1	1
	Utica	AHL	2	0	2	2	2																			
1988-89	**New Jersey**	**NHL**	63	15	10	25	15	4	0	2	110	13.6	-7													
	Utica	AHL	4	1	4	5	0																			
1989-90	**New Jersey**	**NHL**	69	14	20	34	16	1	3	3	135	10.4	7						6	0	1	1	2	0	0	0
1990-91	**New Jersey**	**NHL**	58	14	16	30	4	0	2	2	122	11.5	18						7	2	2	4	2	0	1	0
1991-92	**New Jersey**	**NHL**	71	11	17	28	27	1	2	1	140	7.9	17													
1992-93	**New Jersey**	**NHL**	15	0	5	5	2	0	0	0	17	0.0	3													
	Utica	AHL	25	11	17	28	8																			
1993-94	**Pittsburgh**	**NHL**	77	18	37	55	18	2	0	1	152	11.8	19						6	0	0	0	2	0	0	0
1994-95	**Detroit**	**NHL**	45	9	12	21	16	1	1	2	69	13.0	14						18	4	8	12	2	0	1	1
1995-96	**Detroit**	**NHL**	62	12	15	27	4	1	0	1	115	10.4	11						13	3	3	6	4	0	1	0
1996-97 ♦	**Detroit**	**NHL**	49	6	7	13	8	1	0	0	69	8.7	-3						14	3	3	6	2	0	0	0
1997-98 ♦	**Detroit**	**NHL**	80	19	23	42	12	6	1	5	145	13.1	7						9	4	2	6	4	3	0	1
1998-99	**Detroit**	**NHL**	80	9	19	28	42	3	1	1	180	5.0	5	235	52.8	33	27	13:47	10	2	2	4	4	1	0	1
	NHL Totals		743	141	193	334	184	20	15	20	1376	10.2		235	52.8	33	27	13:47	102	23	22	45	24	4	4	4

Hockey East Second All-Star Team (1985, 1986)

Signed as a free agent by **New Jersey**, August 6, 1986. Signed as a free agent by **Pittsburgh**, September 28, 1993. Claimed by **Detroit** from **Pittsburgh** in NHL Waiver Draft, January 18, 1995. Claimed by **Nashville** from **Detroit** in Expansion Draft, June 26, 1998. Traded to **Detroit** by **Nashville** for Petr Sykora and Detroit's 3rd round choice (later traded to Edmonton, Edmonton selected Mike Comrie) in 1999 Entry Draft, July 14, 1998.

BROWN, Kevin

Right wing. Shoots right. 6'1", 212 lbs. Born, Birmingham, England, May 11, 1974. Los Angeles' 3rd choice, 87th overall, in 1992 Entry Draft.

Season	Club	League	GP	G	A	Pts	PIM	PP	SH	GW	S	%	+/–	TF	F%	H	SB	Min	GP	G	A	Pts	PIM	PP	SH	GW
			Regular Season																Playoffs							
1989-90	Georgetown	OJHL-B	31	3	8	11	59																			
1990-91	Waterloo	OJHL-B	46	25	33	58	116																			
1991-92	Belleville	OHL	66	24	24	48	52												5	1	4	5	8			
1992-93	Belleville	OHL	6	2	5	7	4																			
	Detroit	OHL	56	48	86	134	76												15	10	18	28	18			
1993-94	Detroit	OHL	57	54	81	135	85												17	14	*26	*40	28			
1994-95	Los Angeles	NHL	23	2	3	5	18	0	0	0	25	8.0	–7													
	Phoenix	IHL	48	19	31	50	64																			
1995-96	Los Angeles	NHL	7	1	0	1	4	0	0	0	9	11.1	–2													
	Phoenix	IHL	45	10	16	26	39																			
	P.E.I. Senators	AHL	8	3	6	9	2												3	1	3	4	0			
1996-97	Hartford	NHL	11	0	4	4	6	0	0	0	12	0.0	–6													
	Springfield	AHL	48	32	16	48	45												17	*11	6	17	24			
1997-98	Carolina	NHL	4	0	0	0	0	0	0	0	0	0.0	–2													
	New Haven	AHL	67	28	44	72	65												3	0	2	2	0			
1998-99	Edmonton	NHL	12	4	2	6	0	2	0	0	13	30.8	–2	1	0.0	19	3	9:11								
	Hamilton	AHL	32	9	14	23	47																			
	Hartford	AHL	9	3	2	5	14												5	1	3	4	4			
	NHL Totals		57	7	9	16	28	2	0	0	59	11.9		1	0.0	19	3	9:11								

OHL Second All-Star Team (1993) • OHL First All-Star Team (1994) • Canadian Major Junior Second All-Star Team (1994)

Traded to **Ottawa** by **LA Kings** for Jaroslav Modry and Ottawa's 8th round choice (Stephen Valiquette) in 1996 Entry Draft, March 20, 1996. Traded to **Anaheim** by **Ottawa** for Mike Maneluk, July 1, 1996. Traded to **Hartford** by **Anaheim** for the rights to Espen Knutsen, October 1, 1996. Transferred to **Carolina** after **Hartford** franchise relocated, June 25, 1997. Signed as a free agent by **Edmonton**, August 14, 1998. Traded to **NY Rangers** by **Edmonton** for Vladimir Vorobiev, March 23, 1999.

BROWN, Rob — PIT.

Right wing. Shoots left. 5'10", 177 lbs. Born, Kingston, Ont., April 10, 1968. Pittsburgh's 4th choice, 67th overall, in 1986 Entry Draft.

Season	Club	League	GP	G	A	Pts	PIM	PP	SH	GW	S	%	+/–	TF	F%	H	SB	Min	GP	G	A	Pts	PIM	PP	SH	GW
1982-83	St. Albert	AAHA	61	137	122	259	200																			
1983-84	St. Albert	AJHL	1	0	0	0	0																			
	Kamloops	WHL	50	16	42	58	80												15	1	2	3	17			
1984-85	Kamloops	WHL	60	29	50	79	95												15	8	8	26	28			
1985-86	Kamloops	WHL	69	58	*115	*173	171												16	*18	*28	*46	14			
1986-87	Kamloops	WHL	63	*76	*136	*212	101												5	6	5	11	6			
1987-88	Pittsburgh	NHL	51	24	20	44	56	13	0	1	80	30.0	8													
1988-89	Pittsburgh	NHL	68	49	66	115	118	24	0	6	169	29.0	27						11	5	3	8	22	1	0	3
1989-90	Pittsburgh	NHL	80	33	47	80	102	12	0	3	157	21.0	–10													
1990-91	Pittsburgh	NHL	25	6	10	16	31	2	0	0	32	18.8	0													
	Hartford	NHL	44	18	24	42	101	10	0	2	94	19.1	–7						5	1	0	1	7	1	0	1
1991-92	Hartford	NHL	42	16	15	31	39	13	0	2	65	24.6	–14													
	Chicago	NHL	25	5	11	16	34	3	0	1	41	12.2	–1						8	2	4	6	4	1	0	0
1992-93	Chicago	NHL	15	1	6	7	33	0	0	0	16	6.3	6													
	Indianapolis	IHL	19	14	19	33	32												2	0	1	1	2			
1993-94	Dallas	NHL	1	0	0	0	0	0	0	0	1	0.0	–1													
	Kalamazoo	IHL	79	42	*113	*155	188												5	1	3	4	6			
1994-95	Phoenix	IHL	69	34	73	107	135												9	4	12	16	0			
	Los Angeles	NHL	2	0	0	0	0	0	0	0	1	0.0	–2													
1995-96	Chicago	IHL	79	52	*91	*143	100												9	4	11	15	6			
1996-97	Chicago	IHL	76	37	*80	*117	98												4	2	4	6	16			
1997-98	Pittsburgh	NHL	82	15	25	40	59	4	0	4	172	8.7	–1						6	1	0	1	4	1	0	0
1998-99	Pittsburgh	NHL	58	13	11	24	16	9	0	1	78	16.7	–15	18	38.9	115	18	12:35	13	2	5	7	8	2	0	0
	NHL Totals		493	180	235	415	589	90	0	20	906	19.9		18	38.9	115	18	12:35	43	11	12	23	45	6	0	4

WHL First All-Star Team (1986, 1987) • Canadian Major Junior Player of the Year (1987) • IHL First All-Star Team (1994, 1996, 1997) • Won Leo P. Lamoureux Memorial Trophy (Top Scorer - IHL) (1994, 1996, 1997) • Won James Gatschene Memorial Trophy (MVP - IHL) (1994) • IHL Second All-Star Team (1995)

Played in NHL All-Star Game (1989)

Traded to **Hartford** by **Pittsburgh** for Scott Young, December 21, 1990. Traded to **Chicago** by **Hartford** for Steve Konroyd, January 24, 1992. Signed as a free agent by **Dallas**, August 12, 1993. Signed as a free agent by **LA Kings**, June 14, 1994. Signed as a free agent by **Pittsburgh**, October 1, 1997.

BROWN, Sean — EDM.

Defense. Shoots left. 6'3", 205 lbs. Born, Oshawa, Ont., November 5, 1976. Boston's 2nd choice, 21st overall, in 1995 Entry Draft.

Season	Club	League	GP	G	A	Pts	PIM	PP	SH	GW	S	%	+/–	TF	F%	H	SB	Min	GP	G	A	Pts	PIM	PP	SH	GW
1992-93	Oshawa	OMHA	15	0	1	1	9																			
1993-94	Wellington	OJHL	32	5	14	19	155																			
	Belleville	OHL	28	1	2	3	53												8	0	0	0	17			
1994-95	Belleville	OHL	58	2	16	18	200												16	4	2	6	*67			
1995-96	Belleville	OHL	37	10	23	33	150																			
	Sarnia	OHL	26	8	17	25	112												10	1	0	1	38			
1996-97	Edmonton	NHL	5	0	0	0	4	0	0	0	2	0.0	–1													
	Hamilton	AHL	61	1	7	8	238												19	1	0	1	47			
1997-98	Edmonton	NHL	18	0	1	1	43	0	0	0	9	0.0	–1													
1998-99	Edmonton	NHL	51	0	7	7	188	0	0	0	27	0.0	1	0	0.0	104	29	12:14	1	0	0	0	10	0	0	0
	NHL Totals		74	0	8	8	235	0	0	0	38	0.0		0	0.0	104	29	12:14	1	0	0	0	10	0	0	0

OHL Second All-Star Team (1996)

Rights traded to **Edmonton** by **Boston** with Mariusz Czerkawski and Boston's 1st round choice (Matthieu Descoteaux) in 1996 Entry Draft for Bill Ranford, January 11, 1996.

BRUNET, Benoit — (broo-NAY, BEHN-wah) — MTL.

Left wing. Shoots left. 6', 198 lbs. Born, Ste-Anne-de-Bellevue, Que., August 24, 1968. Montreal's 2nd choice, 27th overall, in 1986 Entry Draft.

Season	Club	League	GP	G	A	Pts	PIM	PP	SH	GW	S	%	+/–	TF	F%	H	SB	Min	GP	G	A	Pts	PIM	PP	SH	GW
1985-86	Hull	QMJHL	71	33	37	70	81																			
1986-87	Hull	QMJHL	60	43	67	110	105												6	7	5	12	8			
1987-88	Hull	QMJHL	62	54	89	143	131												10	3	10	13	11			
1988-89	Montreal	NHL	2	0	1	1	0	0	0	0	1	0.0	0													
	Sherbrooke	AHL	73	41	76	117	95												6	2	0	2	4			
1989-90	Sherbrooke	AHL	72	32	35	67	82												12	8	7	15	20			
1990-91	Montreal	NHL	17	1	3	4	0	0	0	0	12	8.3	–1													
	Fredericton	AHL	24	13	18	31	16												6	5	6	11	2			
1991-92	Montreal	NHL	18	4	6	10	14	0	0	0	37	10.8	4													
	Fredericton	AHL	6	7	9	16	27																			
1992-93♦	Montreal	NHL	47	10	15	25	19	0	0	1	71	14.1	13						20	2	8	10	8	1	0	1
1993-94	Montreal	NHL	71	10	20	30	20	0	3	1	92	10.9	14						7	1	4	5	16	0	0	0
1994-95	Montreal	NHL	45	7	18	25	16	1	1	2	80	8.8	7													
1995-96	Montreal	NHL	26	7	8	15	17	3	1	4	48	14.6	–4						3	0	2	2	0	0	0	0
	Fredericton	AHL	3	2	1	3	6																			
1996-97	Montreal	NHL	39	10	13	23	14	2	0	2	63	15.9	6						4	1	3	4	4	0	1	0
1997-98	Montreal	NHL	68	12	20	32	61	1	2	2	87	13.8	11						8	1	0	1	4	0	0	1
1998-99	Montreal	NHL	60	14	17	31	31	4	2	0	115	12.2	–1	375	41.6	27	37	17:47								
	NHL Totals		393	75	121	196	192	11	9	12	606	12.4		375	41.6	27	37	17:47	42	5	17	22	32	1	1	2

QMJHL Second All-Star Team (1987) • AHL First All-Star Team (1989)

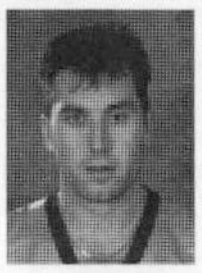

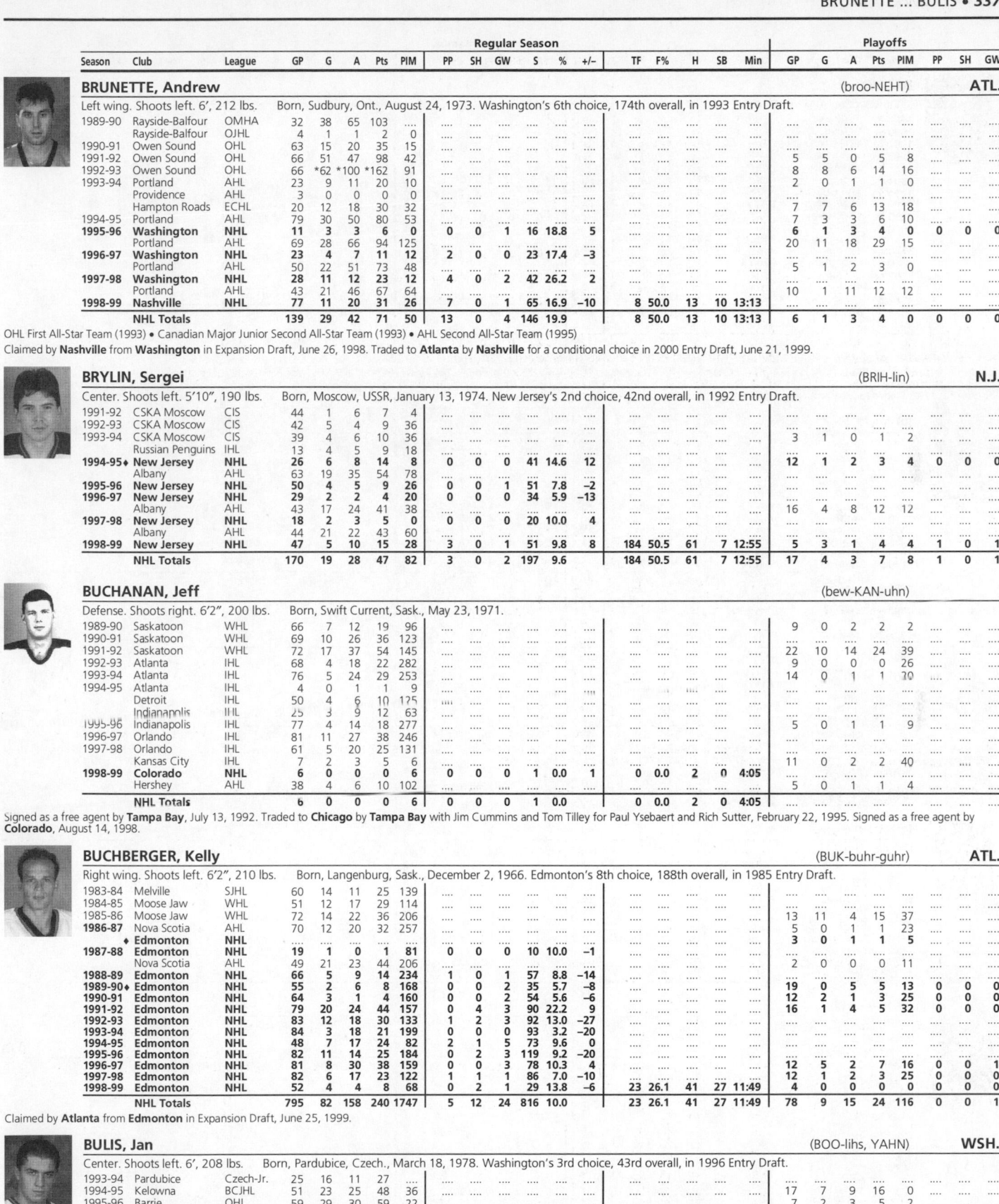

BRUNETTE, Andrew (broo-NEHT) ATL.

Left wing. Shoots left. 6', 212 lbs. Born, Sudbury, Ont., August 24, 1973. Washington's 6th choice, 174th overall, in 1993 Entry Draft.

Season	Club	League	GP	G	A	Pts	PIM	PP	SH	GW	S	%	+/–	TF	F%	H	SB	Min	Playoffs GP	G	A	Pts	PIM	PP	SH	GW
1989-90	Rayside-Balfour	OMHA	32	38	65	103																				
	Rayside-Balfour	OJHL	4	1	1	2	0																			
1990-91	Owen Sound	OHL	63	15	20	35	15																			
1991-92	Owen Sound	OHL	66	51	47	98	42												5	5	0	5	8			
1992-93	Owen Sound	OHL	66	*62	*100	*162	91												8	8	6	14	16			
1993-94	Portland	AHL	23	9	11	20	10												2	0	1	1	0			
	Providence	AHL	3	0	0	0	0																			
	Hampton Roads	ECHL	20	12	18	30	32												7	7	6	13	18			
1994-95	Portland	AHL	79	30	50	80	53												7	3	3	6	10			
1995-96	**Washington**	**NHL**	**11**	**3**	**3**	**6**	**0**	**0**	**0**	**1**	**16**	**18.8**	**5**						**6**	**1**	**3**	**4**	**0**	**0**	**0**	**0**
	Portland	AHL	69	28	66	94	125												20	11	18	29	15			
1996-97	**Washington**	**NHL**	**23**	**4**	**7**	**11**	**12**	**2**	**0**	**0**	**23**	**17.4**	**–3**													
	Portland	AHL	50	22	51	73	48												5	1	2	3	0			
1997-98	**Washington**	**NHL**	**28**	**11**	**12**	**23**	**12**	**4**	**0**	**2**	**42**	**26.2**	**2**													
	Portland	AHL	43	21	46	67	64												10	1	11	12	12			
1998-99	**Nashville**	**NHL**	**77**	**11**	**20**	**31**	**26**	**7**	**0**	**1**	**65**	**16.9**	**–10**	**8**	**50.0**	**13**	**10**	**13:13**								
	NHL Totals		**139**	**29**	**42**	**71**	**50**	**13**	**0**	**4**	**146**	**19.9**		**8**	**50.0**	**13**	**10**	**13:13**	**6**	**1**	**3**	**4**	**0**	**0**	**0**	**0**

OHL First All-Star Team (1993) • Canadian Major Junior Second All-Star Team (1993) • AHL Second All-Star Team (1995)

Claimed by **Nashville** from **Washington** in Expansion Draft, June 26, 1998. Traded to **Atlanta** by **Nashville** for a conditional choice in 2000 Entry Draft, June 21, 1999.

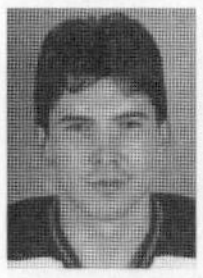

BRYLIN, Sergei (BRIH-lin) N.J.

Center. Shoots left. 5'10", 190 lbs. Born, Moscow, USSR, January 13, 1974. New Jersey's 2nd choice, 42nd overall, in 1992 Entry Draft.

Season	Club	League	GP	G	A	Pts	PIM	PP	SH	GW	S	%	+/–	TF	F%	H	SB	Min	Playoffs GP	G	A	Pts	PIM	PP	SH	GW
1991-92	CSKA Moscow	CIS	44	1	6	7	4																			
1992-93	CSKA Moscow	CIS	42	5	4	9	36																			
1993-94	CSKA Moscow	CIS	39	4	6	10	36												3	1	0	1	2			
	Russian Penguins	IHL	13	4	5	9	18																			
1994-95◆	**New Jersey**	**NHL**	**26**	**6**	**8**	**14**	**8**	**0**	**0**	**0**	**41**	**14.6**	**12**						**12**	**1**	**2**	**3**	**4**	**0**	**0**	**0**
	Albany	AHL	63	19	35	54	78																			
1995-96	**New Jersey**	**NHL**	**50**	**4**	**5**	**9**	**26**	**0**	**0**	**1**	**51**	**7.8**	**–2**													
1996-97	**New Jersey**	**NHL**	**29**	**2**	**2**	**4**	**20**	**0**	**0**	**0**	**34**	**5.9**	**–13**													
	Albany	AHL	43	17	24	41	38												16	4	8	12	12			
1997-98	**New Jersey**	**NHL**	**18**	**2**	**3**	**5**	**0**	**0**	**0**	**0**	**20**	**10.0**	**4**													
	Albany	AHL	44	21	22	43	60																			
1998-99	**New Jersey**	**NHL**	**47**	**5**	**10**	**15**	**28**	**3**	**0**	**1**	**51**	**9.8**	**8**	**184**	**50.5**	**61**	**7**	**12:55**	**5**	**3**	**1**	**4**	**4**	**1**	**0**	**1**
	NHL Totals		**170**	**19**	**28**	**47**	**82**	**3**	**0**	**2**	**197**	**9.6**		**184**	**50.5**	**61**	**7**	**12:55**	**17**	**4**	**3**	**7**	**8**	**1**	**0**	**1**

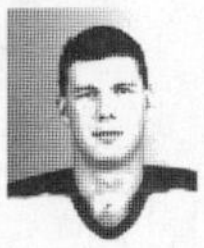

BUCHANAN, Jeff (bew-KAN-uhn)

Defense. Shoots right. 6'2", 200 lbs. Born, Swift Current, Sask., May 23, 1971.

Season	Club	League	GP	G	A	Pts	PIM	PP	SH	GW	S	%	+/–	TF	F%	H	SB	Min	Playoffs GP	G	A	Pts	PIM	PP	SH	GW
1989-90	Saskatoon	WHL	66	7	12	19	96												9	0	2	2	2			
1990-91	Saskatoon	WHL	69	10	26	36	123																			
1991-92	Saskatoon	WHL	72	17	37	54	145												22	10	14	24	39			
1992-93	Atlanta	IHL	68	4	18	22	282												9	0	0	0	26			
1993-94	Atlanta	IHL	76	5	24	29	253												14	0	1	1	20			
1994-95	Atlanta	IHL	4	0	1	1	9																			
	Detroit	IHL	50	4	6	10	125																			
	Indianapolis	IHL	25	3	9	12	63																			
1995-96	Indianapolis	IHL	77	4	14	18	277												5	0	1	1	9			
1996-97	Orlando	IHL	81	11	27	38	246																			
1997-98	Orlando	IHL	61	5	20	25	131																			
	Kansas City	IHL	7	2	3	5	6												11	0	2	2	40			
1998-99	**Colorado**	**NHL**	**6**	**0**	**0**	**0**	**6**	**0**	**0**	**0**	**1**	**0.0**	**1**	**0**	**0.0**	**2**	**0**	**4:05**								
	Hershey	AHL	38	4	6	10	102												5	0	1	1	4			
	NHL Totals		**6**	**0**	**0**	**0**	**6**	**0**	**0**	**0**	**1**	**0.0**		**0**	**0.0**	**2**	**0**	**4:05**								

Signed as a free agent by **Tampa Bay**, July 13, 1992. Traded to **Chicago** by **Tampa Bay** with Jim Cummins and Tom Tilley for Paul Ysebaert and Rich Sutter, February 22, 1995. Signed as a free agent by **Colorado**, August 14, 1998.

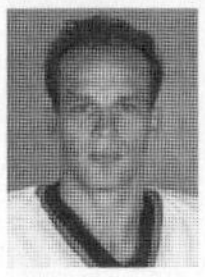

BUCHBERGER, Kelly (BUK-buhr-guhr) ATL.

Right wing. Shoots left. 6'2", 210 lbs. Born, Langenburg, Sask., December 2, 1966. Edmonton's 8th choice, 188th overall, in 1985 Entry Draft.

Season	Club	League	GP	G	A	Pts	PIM	PP	SH	GW	S	%	+/–	TF	F%	H	SB	Min	Playoffs GP	G	A	Pts	PIM	PP	SH	GW
1983-84	Melville	SJHL	60	14	11	25	139																			
1984-85	Moose Jaw	WHL	51	12	17	29	114																			
1985-86	Moose Jaw	WHL	72	14	22	36	206												13	11	4	15	37			
1986-87	Nova Scotia	AHL	70	12	20	32	257												5	0	1	1	23			
	◆ **Edmonton**	**NHL**																	**3**	**0**	**1**	**1**	**5**			
1987-88	**Edmonton**	**NHL**	**19**	**1**	**0**	**1**	**81**	**0**	**0**	**0**	**10**	**10.0**	**–1**													
	Nova Scotia	AHL	49	21	23	44	206												2	0	0	0	11			
1988-89	**Edmonton**	**NHL**	**66**	**5**	**9**	**14**	**234**	**1**	**0**	**1**	**57**	**8.8**	**–14**													
1989-90◆	**Edmonton**	**NHL**	**55**	**2**	**6**	**8**	**168**	**0**	**0**	**2**	**35**	**5.7**	**–8**						**19**	**0**	**5**	**5**	**13**	**0**	**0**	**0**
1990-91	**Edmonton**	**NHL**	**64**	**3**	**1**	**4**	**160**	**0**	**0**	**2**	**54**	**5.6**	**–6**						**12**	**2**	**1**	**3**	**25**	**0**	**0**	**0**
1991-92	**Edmonton**	**NHL**	**79**	**20**	**24**	**44**	**157**	**0**	**4**	**3**	**90**	**22.2**	**9**						**16**	**1**	**4**	**5**	**32**	**0**	**0**	**0**
1992-93	**Edmonton**	**NHL**	**83**	**12**	**18**	**30**	**133**	**1**	**2**	**3**	**92**	**13.0**	**–27**													
1993-94	**Edmonton**	**NHL**	**84**	**3**	**18**	**21**	**199**	**0**	**0**	**0**	**93**	**3.2**	**–20**													
1994-95	**Edmonton**	**NHL**	**48**	**7**	**17**	**24**	**82**	**2**	**1**	**5**	**73**	**9.6**	**0**													
1995-96	**Edmonton**	**NHL**	**82**	**11**	**14**	**25**	**184**	**0**	**2**	**3**	**119**	**9.2**	**–20**													
1996-97	**Edmonton**	**NHL**	**81**	**8**	**30**	**38**	**159**	**0**	**0**	**3**	**78**	**10.3**	**4**						**12**	**5**	**2**	**7**	**16**	**0**	**0**	**1**
1997-98	**Edmonton**	**NHL**	**82**	**6**	**17**	**23**	**122**	**1**	**1**	**1**	**86**	**7.0**	**–10**						**12**	**1**	**2**	**3**	**25**	**0**	**0**	**0**
1998-99	**Edmonton**	**NHL**	**52**	**4**	**4**	**8**	**68**	**0**	**2**	**1**	**29**	**13.8**	**–6**	**23**	**26.1**	**41**	**27**	**11:49**	**4**	**0**	**0**	**0**	**0**	**0**	**0**	**0**
	NHL Totals		**795**	**82**	**158**	**240**	**1747**	**5**	**12**	**24**	**816**	**10.0**		**23**	**26.1**	**41**	**27**	**11:49**	**78**	**9**	**15**	**24**	**116**	**0**	**0**	**1**

Claimed by **Atlanta** from **Edmonton** in Expansion Draft, June 25, 1999.

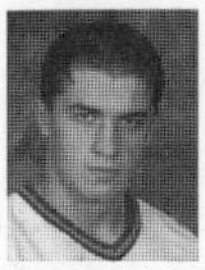

BULIS, Jan (BOO-lihs, YAHN) WSH.

Center. Shoots left. 6', 208 lbs. Born, Pardubice, Czech., March 18, 1978. Washington's 3rd choice, 43rd overall, in 1996 Entry Draft.

Season	Club	League	GP	G	A	Pts	PIM	PP	SH	GW	S	%	+/–	TF	F%	H	SB	Min	Playoffs GP	G	A	Pts	PIM	PP	SH	GW
1993-94	Pardubice	Czech-Jr.	25	16	11	27																				
1994-95	Kelowna	BCJHL	51	23	25	48	36												17	7	9	16	0			
1995-96	Barrie	OHL	59	29	30	59	22												7	2	3	5	2			
1996-97	Barrie	OHL	64	42	61	103	42												9	3	7	10	10			
1997-98	Kingston	OHL	2	0	1	1	0												12	8	10	18	12			
	Washington	**NHL**	**48**	**5**	**11**	**16**	**18**	**0**	**0**	**0**	**37**	**13.5**	**–5**													
	Portland	AHL	3	1	4	5	12																			
1998-99	**Washington**	**NHL**	**38**	**7**	**16**	**23**	**6**	**3**	**0**	**3**	**57**	**12.3**	**3**	**599**	**48.9**	**48**	**3**	**14:27**								
	Cincinnati	IHL	10	2	2	4	14																			
	NHL Totals		**86**	**12**	**27**	**39**	**24**	**3**	**0**	**3**	**94**	**12.8**		**599**	**48.9**	**48**	**3**	**14:27**								

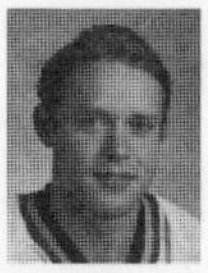

BURE, Pavel

(boo-RAY) **FLA.**

Right wing. Shoots left. 5'10", 189 lbs. Born, Moscow, USSR, March 31, 1971. Vancouver's 4th choice, 113th overall, in 1989 Entry Draft.

			Regular Season																Playoffs							
Season	Club	League	GP	G	A	Pts	PIM	PP	SH	GW	S	%	+/-	TF	F%	H	SB	Min	GP	G	A	Pts	PIM	PP	SH	GW
1987-88	CSKA Moscow	USSR	5	1	1	2	0																			
1988-89	CSKA Moscow	USSR	32	17	9	26	8																			
1989-90	CSKA Moscow	USSR	46	14	10	24	20																			
1990-91	CSKA Moscow	USSR	44	35	11	46	24																			
	Soviet Union	WJC-A	7	*12	3	15	*31																			
1991-92	**Vancouver**	**NHL**	**65**	**34**	**26**	**60**	**30**	**7**	**3**	**6**	**268**	**12.7**	**0**						**13**	**6**	**4**	**10**	**14**	**0**	**0**	**0**
1992-93	**Vancouver**	**NHL**	**83**	**60**	**50**	**110**	**69**	**13**	**7**	**9**	**407**	**14.7**	**35**						**12**	**5**	**7**	**12**	**8**	**0**	**0**	**1**
1993-94	**Vancouver**	**NHL**	**76**	***60**	**47**	**107**	**86**	**25**	**4**	**9**	**374**	**16.0**	**1**						**24**	***16**	**15**	**31**	**40**	**3**	**0**	**2**
1994-95	EV Landshut	Germany	1	3	0	3	2																			
	SKA Spartak	CIS	1	2	0	2	2																			
	Vancouver	**NHL**	**44**	**20**	**23**	**43**	**47**	**6**	**2**	**2**	**198**	**10.1**	**-8**						**11**	**7**	**6**	**13**	**10**	**2**	**2**	**0**
1995-96	**Vancouver**	**NHL**	**15**	**6**	**7**	**13**	**8**	**1**	**1**	**0**	**78**	**7.7**	**-2**													
1996-97	**Vancouver**	**NHL**	**63**	**23**	**32**	**55**	**40**	**4**	**1**	**2**	**265**	**8.7**	**-14**													
1997-98	**Vancouver**	**NHL**	**82**	**51**	**39**	**90**	**48**	**13**	**6**	**4**	**329**	**15.5**	**5**													
	Russia	Olympics	6	*9	0	9	2																			
1998-99	**Florida**	**NHL**	**11**	**13**	**3**	**16**	**4**	**5**	**1**	**0**	**44**	**29.5**	**3**	**1**	**0.0**	**2**	**5**	**21:41**								
	NHL Totals		**439**	**267**	**227**	**494**	**332**	**74**	**25**	**32**	**1963**	**13.6**		**1**	**0.0**	**2**	**5**	**21:41**	**60**	**34**	**32**	**66**	**72**	**5**	**2**	**3**

• Named Soviet National League Rookie-of-the-Year (1989) • Won Calder Memorial Trophy (1992) • NHL First All-Star Team (1994)

Played in NHL All-Star Game (1993, 1994, 1997, 1998)

Traded to **Florida** by **Vancouver** with Bret Hedican, Brad Ference and Vancouver's 3rd round choice in 2000 Entry Draft for Ed Jovanovski, Dave Gagner, Mike Brown, Kevin Weekes and Florida's 1st round choice in 2000 Entry Draft, January 17, 1999. • Missed majority of 1998-99 season due to trade demands (August 10, 1998) and knee injury suffered in game vs. Pittsburgh, February 5, 1999.

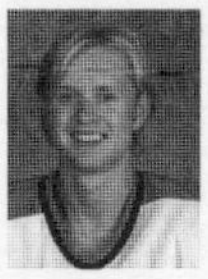

BURE, Valeri

(boo-RAY) **CGY.**

Right wing. Shoots right. 5'10", 180 lbs. Born, Moscow, USSR, June 13, 1974. Montreal's 2nd choice, 33rd overall, in 1992 Entry Draft.

			Regular Season																Playoffs							
Season	Club	League	GP	G	A	Pts	PIM	PP	SH	GW	S	%	+/-	TF	F%	H	SB	Min	GP	G	A	Pts	PIM	PP	SH	GW
1990-91	CSKA Moscow	USSR	3	0	0	0	0																			
1991-92	Spokane	WHL	53	27	22	49	78												10	11	6	17	10			
1992-93	Spokane	WHL	66	68	79	147	49												9	6	11	17	14			
1993-94	Spokane	WHL	59	40	62	102	48												3	5	3	8	2			
1994-95	**Montreal**	**NHL**	**24**	**3**	**1**	**4**	**6**	**0**	**0**	**1**	**39**	**7.7**	**-1**													
	Fredericton	AHL	45	23	25	48	32																			
1995-96	**Montreal**	**NHL**	**77**	**22**	**20**	**42**	**28**	**5**	**0**	**1**	**143**	**15.4**	**10**						**6**	**0**	**1**	**1**	**6**	**0**	**0**	**0**
1996-97	**Montreal**	**NHL**	**64**	**14**	**21**	**35**	**6**	**4**	**0**	**2**	**131**	**10.7**	**4**						**5**	**0**	**1**	**1**	**2**	**0**	**0**	**0**
1997-98	**Montreal**	**NHL**	**50**	**7**	**22**	**29**	**33**	**2**	**0**	**1**	**134**	**5.2**	**-5**													
	Calgary	**NHL**	**16**	**5**	**4**	**9**	**2**	**0**	**0**	**1**	**45**	**11.1**	**0**													
	Russia	Olympics	6	1	0	1	0																			
1998-99	**Calgary**	**NHL**	**80**	**26**	**27**	**53**	**22**	**7**	**0**	**4**	**260**	**10.0**	**0**	**15**	**40.0**	**25**	**8**	**16:11**								
	NHL Totals		**311**	**77**	**95**	**172**	**97**	**18**	**0**	**10**	**752**	**10.2**		**15**	**40.0**	**25**	**8**	**16:11**	**11**	**0**	**2**	**2**	**8**	**0**	**0**	**0**

WHL West First All-Star Team (1993) • WHL West Second All-Star Team (1994)

Traded to **Calgary** by **Montreal** with Montreal's 4th round choice (Shaun Sutter) in 1998 Entry Draft for Jonas Hoglund and Zarley Zalapski, February 1, 1998.

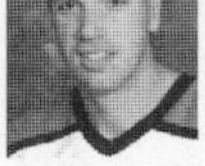

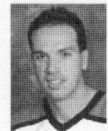

BUREAU, Marc

(BEWR-oh) **PHI.**

Center. Shoots right. 6'1", 198 lbs. Born, Trois-Rivières, Que., May 19, 1966.

			Regular Season																Playoffs							
Season	Club	League	GP	G	A	Pts	PIM	PP	SH	GW	S	%	+/-	TF	F%	H	SB	Min	GP	G	A	Pts	PIM	PP	SH	GW
1983-84	Chicoutimi	QMJHL	56	6	16	22	14																			
1984-85	Chicoutimi	QMJHL	41	30	25	55	15																			
	Granby	QMJHL	27	20	45	65	14																			
1985-86	Granby	QMJHL	19	6	17	23	36																			
	Chicoutimi	QMJHL	44	30	45	75	33												9	3	7	10	10			
1986-87	Longueuil	QMJHL	66	54	58	112	68												20	17	20	37	12			
1987-88	Salt Lake	IHL	69	7	20	27	86												7	0	3	3	8			
1988-89	Salt Lake	IHL	76	28	36	64	119												14	7	5	12	31			
1989-90	**Calgary**	**NHL**	**5**	**0**	**0**	**0**	**4**	**0**	**0**	**0**	**3**	**0.0**	**-1**													
	Salt Lake	IHL	67	43	48	91	173												11	4	8	12	0			
1990-91	**Calgary**	**NHL**	**5**	**0**	**0**	**0**	**2**	**0**	**0**	**0**	**4**	**0.0**	**-4**													
	Salt Lake	IHL	54	40	48	88	101																			
	Minnesota	**NHL**	**9**	**0**	**6**	**6**	**4**	**0**	**0**	**0**	**8**	**0.0**	**-3**						**23**	**3**	**2**	**5**	**20**	**0**	**1**	**0**
1991-92	**Minnesota**	**NHL**	**46**	**6**	**4**	**10**	**50**	**0**	**0**	**0**	**53**	**11.3**	**-5**						**5**	**0**	**0**	**0**	**14**	**0**	**0**	**0**
	Kalamazoo	IHL	7	2	8	10	2																			
1992-93	**Tampa Bay**	**NHL**	**63**	**10**	**21**	**31**	**111**	**1**	**2**	**1**	**132**	**7.6**	**-12**													
1993-94	**Tampa Bay**	**NHL**	**75**	**8**	**7**	**15**	**30**	**0**	**1**	**1**	**110**	**7.3**	**-9**													
1994-95	**Tampa Bay**	**NHL**	**48**	**2**	**12**	**14**	**30**	**0**	**1**	**0**	**72**	**2.8**	**-8**													
1995-96	**Montreal**	**NHL**	**65**	**3**	**7**	**10**	**46**	**0**	**0**	**1**	**43**	**7.0**	**-3**						**6**	**1**	**1**	**2**	**4**	**0**	**0**	**0**
1996-97	**Montreal**	**NHL**	**43**	**6**	**9**	**15**	**16**	**1**	**1**	**2**	**56**	**10.7**	**4**													
1997-98	**Montreal**	**NHL**	**74**	**13**	**6**	**19**	**12**	**0**	**0**	**2**	**82**	**15.9**	**0**						**10**	**1**	**2**	**3**	**6**	**0**	**0**	**0**
1998-99	**Philadelphia**	**NHL**	**71**	**4**	**6**	**10**	**10**	**0**	**0**	**0**	**52**	**7.7**	**-2**	**776**	**53.5**	**74**	**28**	**11:02**	**6**	**0**	**2**	**2**	**2**	**0**	**0**	**0**
	NHL Totals		**504**	**52**	**78**	**130**	**315**	**2**	**5**	**7**	**615**	**8.5**		**776**	**53.5**	**74**	**28**	**11:02**	**50**	**5**	**7**	**12**	**46**	**0**	**1**	**0**

IHL Second All-Star Team (1990, 1991)

Signed as a free agent by **Calgary**, May 19, 1987. Traded to **Minnesota** by **Calgary** for Minnesota's 3rd round choice (Sandy McCarthy) in 1991 Entry Draft, March 5, 1991. Claimed on waivers by **Tampa Bay** from **Minnesota**, October 16, 1992. Traded to **Montreal** by **Tampa Bay** for Brian Bellows, June 30, 1995. Signed as a free agent by **Philadelphia**, July 20, 1998.

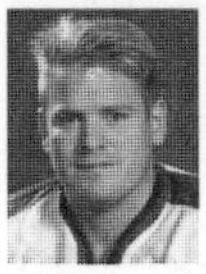

BURR, Shawn

T.B.

Left wing/Center. Shoots left. 6'1", 205 lbs. Born, Sarnia, Ont., July 1, 1966. Detroit's 1st choice, 7th overall, in 1984 Entry Draft.

			Regular Season																Playoffs							
Season	Club	League	GP	G	A	Pts	PIM	PP	SH	GW	S	%	+/-	TF	F%	H	SB	Min	GP	G	A	Pts	PIM	PP	SH	GW
1982-83	Sarnia	OJHL	52	50	85	135	125																			
1983-84	Kitchener	OHL	68	41	44	85	50												16	5	12	17	22			
1984-85	Kitchener	OHL	48	24	42	66	50												4	3	3	6	2			
	Detroit	**NHL**	**9**	**0**	**0**	**0**	**2**	**0**	**0**	**0**	**4**	**0.0**	**-4**													
	Adirondack	AHL	4	0	0	0	2																			
1985-86	Kitchener	OHL	59	60	67	127	104												5	2	3	5	8			
	Detroit	**NHL**	**5**	**1**	**0**	**1**	**4**	**1**	**0**	**0**	**6**	**16.7**	**1**													
	Adirondack	AHL	3	2	2	4	2												17	5	7	12	32			
1986-87	**Detroit**	**NHL**	**80**	**22**	**25**	**47**	**107**	**1**	**2**	**1**	**153**	**14.4**	**2**						**16**	**7**	**2**	**9**	**20**	**0**	**0**	**2**
1987-88	**Detroit**	**NHL**	**78**	**17**	**23**	**40**	**97**	**5**	**3**	**3**	**124**	**13.7**	**7**						**9**	**3**	**1**	**4**	**14**	**0**	**0**	**1**
1988-89	**Detroit**	**NHL**	**79**	**19**	**27**	**46**	**78**	**1**	**4**	**2**	**149**	**12.8**	**5**						**6**	**1**	**2**	**3**	**6**	**0**	**0**	**0**
1989-90	**Detroit**	**NHL**	**76**	**24**	**32**	**56**	**82**	**4**	**3**	**2**	**173**	**13.9**	**14**													
	Adirondack	AHL	3	4	2	6	2																			
1990-91	**Detroit**	**NHL**	**80**	**20**	**30**	**50**	**112**	**6**	**0**	**4**	**164**	**12.2**	**14**						**7**	**0**	**4**	**4**	**15**	**0**	**0**	**0**
1991-92	**Detroit**	**NHL**	**79**	**19**	**32**	**51**	**118**	**2**	**0**	**3**	**140**	**13.6**	**26**						**11**	**1**	**5**	**6**	**10**	**0**	**0**	**0**
1992-93	**Detroit**	**NHL**	**80**	**10**	**25**	**35**	**74**	**1**	**0**	**2**	**99**	**10.1**	**18**						**7**	**2**	**1**	**3**	**2**	**0**	**1**	**0**
1993-94	**Detroit**	**NHL**	**51**	**10**	**12**	**22**	**31**	**0**	**1**	**1**	**64**	**15.6**	**12**						**7**	**2**	**0**	**2**	**6**	**0**	**0**	**2**
1994-95	**Detroit**	**NHL**	**42**	**6**	**8**	**14**	**60**	**0**	**0**	**3**	**65**	**9.2**	**13**						**16**	**0**	**2**	**2**	**6**	**0**	**0**	**0**
1995-96	**Tampa Bay**	**NHL**	**81**	**13**	**15**	**28**	**119**	**1**	**0**	**2**	**122**	**10.7**	**4**						**6**	**0**	**2**	**2**	**8**	**0**	**0**	**0**
1996-97	**Tampa Bay**	**NHL**	**74**	**14**	**21**	**35**	**106**	**1**	**0**	**3**	**128**	**10.9**	**5**													
1997-98	**San Jose**	**NHL**	**42**	**6**	**6**	**12**	**50**	**0**	**0**	**0**	**63**	**9.5**	**2**						**6**	**0**	**0**	**0**	**8**	**0**	**0**	**0**

			Regular Season																Playoffs							
Season	Club	League	GP	G	A	Pts	PIM	PP	SH	GW	S	%	+/–	TF	F%	H	SB	Min	GP	G	A	Pts	PIM	PP	SH	GW
1998-99	**San Jose**	**NHL**	**18**	**0**	**1**	**1**	**29**	**0**	**0**	**0**	**22**	**0.0**	**–3**	**22**	**50.0**	**17**	**6**	**8:42**	....	....	....	....	....	....	....	....
	Kentucky	AHL	26	10	14	24	29	....	....	....	....	....	....	....	....	....	....	....	12	4	9	13	10	....	....	....
	NHL Totals		**874**	**181**	**257**	**438**	**1069**	**23**	**14**	**26**	**1476**	**12.3**		**22**	**50.0**	**17**	**6**	**8:42**	**91**	**16**	**19**	**35**	**95**	**0**	**1**	**5**

OHL Second All-Star Team (1986)

Traded to **Tampa Bay** by **Detroit** with Detroit's 3rd round choice (later traded to Boston — Boston selected Jason Doyle) in 1996 Entry Draft for Marc Bergevin and Ben Hankinson, August 17, 1995. Traded to **San Jose** by **Tampa Bay** for San Jose's 5th round choice (Mark Thompson) in 1997 Entry Draft, June 21, 1997. Traded to **Tampa Bay** by **San Jose** with Andrei Zyuzin, Bill Houlder and Steve Guolla for Niklas Sundstrom and NY Rangers' 3rd round choice (previously acquired) in 2000 Entry Draft, August 4, 1999.

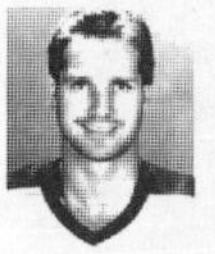

BURRIDGE, Randy

Left wing. Shoots left. 5'9", 188 lbs. Born, Fort Erie, Ont., January 7, 1966. Boston's 7th choice, 157th overall, in 1985 Entry Draft.

Season	Club	League	GP	G	A	Pts	PIM	PP	SH	GW	S	%	+/–	TF	F%	H	SB	Min	GP	G	A	Pts	PIM	PP	SH	GW
1982-83	Fort Erie	OJHL-B	42	32	56	88	32	....	....	....	....	....	....	....	....	....	....	....	....	....	....	....	....	....	....	....
1983-84	Peterborough	OHL	55	6	7	13	44	....	....	....	....	....	....	....	....	....	....	....	8	3	2	5	7	....	....	....
1984-85	Peterborough	OHL	66	49	57	106	88	....	....	....	....	....	....	....	....	....	....	....	17	9	16	25	18	....	....	....
1985-86	Peterborough	OHL	17	15	11	26	23	....	....	....	....	....	....	....	....	....	....	....	3	1	3	4	2	....	....	....
	Boston	**NHL**	**52**	**17**	**25**	**42**	**28**	**1**	**0**	**2**	**90**	**18.9**	**17**	....	....	....	....	....	**3**	**0**	**4**	**4**	**12**	**0**	**0**	**0**
	Moncton	AHL	....	....	....	....	....	....	....	....	....	....	....	....	....	....	....	....	3	0	2	2	2	....	....	....
1986-87	**Boston**	**NHL**	**23**	**1**	**4**	**5**	**16**	**0**	**0**	**1**	**27**	**3.7**	**–6**	....	....	....	....	....	**2**	**1**	**0**	**1**	**2**	**0**	**0**	**0**
	Moncton	AHL	47	26	41	67	139	....	....	....	....	....	....	....	....	....	....	....	3	1	2	3	30	....	....	....
1987-88	**Boston**	**NHL**	**79**	**27**	**28**	**55**	**105**	**5**	**3**	**3**	**159**	**17.0**	**0**	....	....	....	....	....	**23**	**2**	**10**	**12**	**16**	**0**	**0**	**0**
1988-89	**Boston**	**NHL**	**80**	**31**	**30**	**61**	**39**	**6**	**2**	**6**	**189**	**16.4**	**19**	....	....	....	....	....	**10**	**5**	**2**	**7**	**6**	**1**	**1**	**0**
1989-90	**Boston**	**NHL**	**63**	**17**	**15**	**32**	**47**	**7**	**0**	**1**	**118**	**14.4**	**9**	....	....	....	....	....	**21**	**4**	**11**	**15**	**14**	**0**	**1**	**0**
1990-91	**Boston**	**NHL**	**62**	**15**	**13**	**28**	**40**	**1**	**0**	**4**	**108**	**13.9**	**17**	....	....	....	....	....	**19**	**0**	**3**	**3**	**39**	**0**	**0**	**0**
1991-92	**Washington**	**NHL**	**66**	**23**	**44**	**67**	**50**	**9**	**0**	**3**	**131**	**17.6**	**–4**	....	....	....	....	....	**2**	**0**	**1**	**1**	**0**	**0**	**0**	**0**
1992-93	**Washington**	**NHL**	**4**	**0**	**0**	**0**	**0**	**0**	**0**	**0**	**7**	**0.0**	**1**	....	....	....	....	....	**4**	**1**	**0**	**1**	**0**	**0**	**0**	**0**
	Baltimore	AHL	2	0	1	1	2	....	....	....	....	....	....	....	....	....	....	....	....	....	....	....	....	....	....	....
1993-94	**Washington**	**NHL**	**78**	**25**	**17**	**42**	**73**	**8**	**1**	**5**	**150**	**16.7**	**–1**	....	....	....	....	....	**11**	**0**	**2**	**2**	**12**	**0**	**0**	**0**
1994-95	**Washington**	**NHL**	**2**	**0**	**0**	**0**	**2**	**0**	**0**	**0**	**2**	**0.0**	**0**	....	....	....	....	....	....	....	....	....	....	....	....	....
	Los Angeles	**NHL**	**38**	**4**	**15**	**19**	**8**	**2**	**0**	**0**	**50**	**8.0**	**–4**	....	....	....	....	....	....	....	....	....	....	....	....	....
1995-96	**Buffalo**	**NHL**	**74**	**25**	**33**	**58**	**30**	**6**	**0**	**3**	**154**	**16.2**	**0**	....	....	....	....	....	....	....	....	....	....	....	....	....
1996-97	**Buffalo**	**NHL**	**55**	**10**	**21**	**31**	**20**	**1**	**3**	**0**	**85**	**11.8**	**17**	....	....	....	....	....	**12**	**5**	**1**	**6**	**2**	**0**	**0**	**0**
1997-98	**Buffalo**	**NHL**	**30**	**4**	**6**	**10**	**0**	**1**	**0**	**1**	**40**	**10.0**	**0**	....	....	....	....	....	....	....	....	....	....	....	....	....
	Rochester	AHL	6	0	1	1	19	....	....	....	....	....	....	....	....	....	....	....	1	0	1	1	0	....	....	....
1998-99	EC Hannover	Germany	14	7	6	13	35	....	....	....	....	....	....	....	....	....	....	....	....	....	....	....	....	....	....	....
	Las Vegas	IHL	25	7	12	19	8	....	....	....	....	....	....	....	....	....	....	....	....	....	....	....	....	....	....	....
	NHL Totals		**706**	**199**	**251**	**450**	**458**	**47**	**9**	**29**	**1310**	**15.2**		....	....	....	....	....	**107**	**18**	**34**	**52**	**103**	**1**	**2**	**0**

Played in NHL All-Star Game (1992)

Traded to **Washington** by **Boston** for Stephen Leach, June 21, 1991. Traded to **LA Kings** by **Washington** for Warren Rychel, February 10, 1995. Signed as a free agent by **Buffalo**, October 5, 1995.

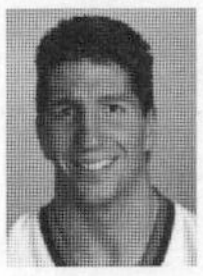

BURT, Adam — PHI.

Defense. Shoots left. 6'2", 207 lbs. Born, Detroit, MI, January 15, 1969. Hartford's 2nd choice, 39th overall, in 1987 Entry Draft.

Season	Club	League	GP	G	A	Pts	PIM	PP	SH	GW	S	%	+/–	TF	F%	H	SB	Min	GP	G	A	Pts	PIM	PP	SH	GW
1985-86	North Bay	OHL	49	0	11	11	81	....	....	....	....	....	....	....	....	....	....	....	10	0	0	0	24	....	....	....
1986-87	North Bay	OHL	57	4	27	31	138	....	....	....	....	....	....	....	....	....	....	....	24	1	6	7	68	....	....	....
1987-88	North Bay	OHL	66	17	53	70	176	....	....	....	....	....	....	....	....	....	....	....	2	0	3	3	6	....	....	....
	Binghamton	AHL	....	....	....	....	....	....	....	....	....	....	....	....	....	....	....	....	2	1	1	2	0	....	....	....
1988-89	North Bay	OHL	23	4	11	15	45	....	....	....	....	....	....	....	....	....	....	....	12	2	12	14	12	....	....	....
	Hartford	**NHL**	**5**	**0**	**0**	**0**	**6**	**0**	**0**	**0**	**1**	**0.0**	**–1**	....	....	....	....	....	....	....	....	....	....	....	....	....
	Binghamton	AHL	5	0	2	2	13	....	....	....	....	....	....	....	....	....	....	....	....	....	....	....	....	....	....	....
1989-90	**Hartford**	**NHL**	**63**	**4**	**8**	**12**	**105**	**1**	**0**	**0**	**83**	**4.8**	**3**	....	....	....	....	....	**2**	**0**	**0**	**0**	**0**	**0**	**0**	**0**
1990-91	**Hartford**	**NHL**	**42**	**2**	**7**	**9**	**63**	**1**	**0**	**1**	**43**	**4.7**	**–4**	....	....	....	....	....	....	....	....	....	....	....	....	....
	Springfield	AHL	9	1	3	4	22	....	....	....	....	....	....	....	....	....	....	....	....	....	....	....	....	....	....	....
1991-92	**Hartford**	**NHL**	**66**	**9**	**15**	**24**	**93**	**4**	**0**	**1**	**89**	**10.1**	**–16**	....	....	....	....	....	**2**	**0**	**0**	**0**	**0**	**0**	**0**	**0**
1992-93	**Hartford**	**NHL**	**65**	**6**	**14**	**20**	**116**	**0**	**0**	**0**	**81**	**7.4**	**–11**	....	....	....	....	....	....	....	....	....	....	....	....	....
1993-94	**Hartford**	**NHL**	**63**	**1**	**17**	**18**	**75**	**0**	**0**	**0**	**91**	**1.1**	**–4**	....	....	....	....	....	....	....	....	....	....	....	....	....
1994-95	**Hartford**	**NHL**	**46**	**7**	**11**	**18**	**65**	**3**	**0**	**1**	**73**	**9.6**	**0**	....	....	....	....	....	....	....	....	....	....	....	....	....
1995-96	**Hartford**	**NHL**	**78**	**4**	**9**	**13**	**121**	**0**	**0**	**1**	**90**	**4.4**	**–4**	....	....	....	....	....	....	....	....	....	....	....	....	....
1996-97	**Hartford**	**NHL**	**71**	**2**	**11**	**13**	**79**	**0**	**0**	**0**	**85**	**2.4**	**–13**	....	....	....	....	....	....	....	....	....	....	....	....	....
1997-98	**Carolina**	**NHL**	**76**	**1**	**11**	**12**	**106**	**0**	**1**	**0**	**51**	**2.0**	**–6**	....	....	....	....	....	....	....	....	....	....	....	....	....
1998-99	**Carolina**	**NHL**	**51**	**0**	**3**	**3**	**46**	**0**	**0**	**0**	**37**	**0.0**	**3**	**0**	**0.0**	**78**	**60**	**18:39**	....	....	....	....	....	....	....	....
	Philadelphia	**NHL**	**17**	**0**	**1**	**1**	**14**	**0**	**0**	**0**	**24**	**0.0**	**1**	**0**	**0.0**	**16**	**16**	**17:25**	**6**	**0**	**0**	**0**	**4**	**0**	**0**	**0**
	NHL Totals		**643**	**36**	**107**	**143**	**889**	**9**	**1**	**4**	**748**	**4.8**		**0**	**0.0**	**94**	**76**	**18:20**	**10**	**0**	**0**	**0**	**4**	**0**	**0**	**0**

OHL Second All-Star Team (1988)

Transferred to **Carolina** after **Hartford** franchise relocated, June 25, 1997. Traded to **Philadelphia** by **Carolina** for Andrei Kovalenko, March 6, 1999.

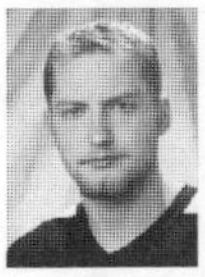

BUTENSCHON, Sven (BUH-tehn-shohn) — PIT.

Defense. Shoots left. 6'4", 215 lbs. Born, Itzehoe, West Germany, March 22, 1976. Pittsburgh's 3rd choice, 57th overall, in 1994 Entry Draft.

Season	Club	League	GP	G	A	Pts	PIM	PP	SH	GW	S	%	+/–	TF	F%	H	SB	Min	GP	G	A	Pts	PIM	PP	SH	GW
1991-92	Eastman Selects	MAHA	36	2	10	12	110	....	....	....	....	....	....	....	....	....	....	....	....	....	....	....	....	....	....	....
1992-93	Eastman Selects	MAHA	35	14	22	36	101	....	....	....	....	....	....	....	....	....	....	....	....	....	....	....	....	....	....	....
1993-94	Brandon	WHL	70	3	19	22	51	....	....	....	....	....	....	....	....	....	....	....	4	0	0	0	6	....	....	....
1994-95	Brandon	WHL	21	1	5	6	44	....	....	....	....	....	....	....	....	....	....	....	18	1	2	3	11	....	....	....
1995-96	Brandon	WHL	70	4	37	41	99	....	....	....	....	....	....	....	....	....	....	....	19	1	12	13	18	....	....	....
1996-97	Cleveland	IHL	75	3	12	15	68	....	....	....	....	....	....	....	....	....	....	....	10	0	1	1	4	....	....	....
1997-98	**Pittsburgh**	**NHL**	**8**	**0**	**0**	**0**	**6**	**0**	**0**	**0**	**4**	**0.0**	**–1**	....	....	....	....	....	....	....	....	....	....	....	....	....
	Syracuse	AHL	65	14	23	37	66	....	....	....	....	....	....	....	....	....	....	....	5	1	2	3	0	....	....	....
1998-99	**Pittsburgh**	**NHL**	**17**	**0**	**0**	**0**	**6**	**0**	**0**	**0**	**8**	**0.0**	**–7**	**0**	**0.0**	**13**	**12**	**13:08**	....	....	....	....	....	....	....	....
	Houston	IHL	57	1	4	5	81	....	....	....	....	....	....	....	....	....	....	....	....	....	....	....	....	....	....	....
	NHL Totals		**25**	**0**	**0**	**0**	**12**	**0**	**0**	**0**	**12**	**0.0**		**0**	**0.0**	**13**	**12**	**13:08**	....	....	....	....	....	....	....	....

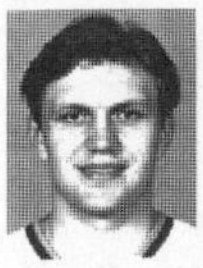

BUTSAYEV, Viacheslav (boot-SIGH-yehf) — OTT.

Center. Shoots left. 6'2", 200 lbs. Born, Togliatti, USSR, June 13, 1970. Philadelphia's 10th choice, 109th overall, in 1990 Entry Draft.

Season	Club	League	GP	G	A	Pts	PIM	PP	SH	GW	S	%	+/–	TF	F%	H	SB	Min	GP	G	A	Pts	PIM	PP	SH	GW
1987-88	Togliatti	USSR-2	10	1	7	8	....	....	....	....	....	....	....	....	....	....	....	....	....	....	....	....	....	....	....	....
1988-89	Lada Togliatti	USSR-3	60	14	7	21	32	....	....	....	....	....	....	....	....	....	....	....	....	....	....	....	....	....	....	....
1989-90	CSKA Moscow	USSR	48	14	4	18	30	....	....	....	....	....	....	....	....	....	....	....	....	....	....	....	....	....	....	....
	Soviet Union	WJC-A	7	3	4	7	14	....	....	....	....	....	....	....	....	....	....	....	....	....	....	....	....	....	....	....
1990-91	CSKA Moscow	USSR	46	14	9	23	32	....	....	....	....	....	....	....	....	....	....	....	....	....	....	....	....	....	....	....
1991-92	CSKA Moscow	CIS	36	12	13	25	26	....	....	....	....	....	....	....	....	....	....	....	....	....	....	....	....	....	....	....
	Russia	Olympics	8	1	1	2	4	....	....	....	....	....	....	....	....	....	....	....	....	....	....	....	....	....	....	....
1992-93	CSKA Moscow	CIS	5	3	4	7	6	....	....	....	....	....	....	....	....	....	....	....	....	....	....	....	....	....	....	....
	Philadelphia	**NHL**	**52**	**2**	**14**	**16**	**61**	**0**	**0**	**0**	**58**	**3.4**	**3**	....	....	....	....	....	....	....	....	....	....	....	....	....
	Hershey	AHL	24	8	10	18	51	....	....	....	....	....	....	....	....	....	....	....	....	....	....	....	....	....	....	....
1993-94	**Philadelphia**	**NHL**	**47**	**12**	**9**	**21**	**58**	**0**	**0**	**3**	**79**	**15.2**	**2**	....	....	....	....	....	....	....	....	....	....	....	....	....
	San Jose	**NHL**	**12**	**0**	**2**	**2**	**10**	**2**	**0**	**0**	**6**	**0.0**	**–2**	....	....	....	....	....	....	....	....	....	....	....	....	....
1994-95	Lada Togliatti	CIS	9	2	6	8	6	....	....	....	....	....	....	....	....	....	....	....	....	....	....	....	....	....	....	....
	San Jose	**NHL**	**6**	**2**	**0**	**2**	**0**	**0**	**0**	**0**	**6**	**33.3**	**–2**	....	....	....	....	....	....	....	....	....	....	....	....	....
	Kansas City	IHL	13	3	4	7	12	....	....	....	....	....	....	....	....	....	....	....	3	0	0	0	2	....	....	....
1995-96	**Anaheim**	**NHL**	**7**	**1**	**0**	**1**	**0**	**0**	**0**	**0**	**9**	**11.1**	**–4**	....	....	....	....	....	....	....	....	....	....	....	....	....
	Baltimore	AHL	62	23	42	65	70	....	....	....	....	....	....	....	....	....	....	....	12	4	8	12	28	....	....	....

Season	Club	League	GP	G	A	Pts	PIM	PP	SH	GW	S	%	+/-	TF	F%	H	SB	Min	GP	G	A	Pts	PIM	PP	SH	GW
			Regular Season																Playoffs							
1996-97	Sodertalje SK	Sweden	16	2	4	6	61	....	....	....	....	....	....	....	....	....	....	....	....	....	....	....	....	....	....	....
	Farjestads BK	Sweden	24	4	3	7	47	....	....	....	....	....	....	....	....	....	....	....	8	3	4	7	41	....	....	....
	Farjestads BK	EuroHL	1	0	0	0	0	....	....	....	....	....	....	....	....	....	....	....	....	....	....	....	....	....	....	....
1997-98	Fort Wayne	IHL	76	36	51	87	128	....	....	....	....	....	....	....	....	....	....	....	4	2	2	4	4	....	....	....
1998-99	**Florida**	**NHL**	**1**	**0**	**0**	**0**	**2**	**0**	**0**	**0**	**0**	**0.0**	**–1**	**20**	**60.0**	**0**	**0**	**16:21**	....	....	....	....	....	....	....	....
	Fort Wayne	IHL	71	28	44	72	123	....	....	....	....	....	....	....	....	....	....	....	2	1	0	1	4	....	....	....
	Ottawa	**NHL**	**2**	**0**	**1**	**1**	**2**	**0**	**0**	**0**	**5**	**0.0**	**0**	**6**	**33.3**	**2**	**0**	**11:08**	....	....	....	....	....	....	....	....
	NHL Totals		**127**	**17**	**26**	**43**	**133**	**2**	**0**	**3**	**163**	**10.4**		**26**	**53.8**	**2**	**0**	**12:52**	....	....	....	....	....	....	....	....

IHL Second All-Star Team (1998)

Traded to **San Jose** by **Philadelphia** for Rob Zettler, February 1, 1994. Signed as a free agent by **Anaheim**, October 19, 1995. Signed as a free agent by **Florida**, August 12, 1998. Traded to **Ottawa** by **Florida** for Ottawa's 6th round choice (later traded to Dallas, Dallas selected Justin Cox) in 1999 Entry Draft, March 8, 1999.

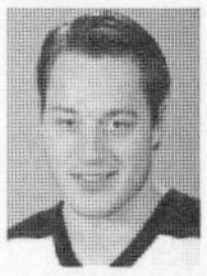

BUZEK, Petr (BOO-zehk) ATL.

Defense. Shoots left. 6', 205 lbs. Born, Jihlava, Czech., April 26, 1977. Dallas' 3rd choice, 63rd overall, in 1995 Entry Draft.

Season	Club	League	GP	G	A	Pts	PIM	PP	SH	GW	S	%	+/-	TF	F%	H	SB	Min	GP	G	A	Pts	PIM	PP	SH	GW
1993-94	Dukla Jihlava	Cze-Rep	3	0	0	0		....	....	....	....	....	....	....	....	....	....	....	....	....	....	....	....	....	....	....
1994-95	Dukla Jihlava	Cze-Rep	43	2	5	7	47	....	....	....	....	....	....	....	....	....	....	....	2	0	0	0	2	....	....	....
1995-96	Michigan	IHL	DID NOT PLAY – INJURED																							
1996-97	Michigan	IHL	67	4	6	10	48	....	....	....	....	....	....	....	....	....	....	....	....	....	....	....	....	....	....	....
1997-98	**Dallas**	**NHL**	**2**	**0**	**0**	**0**	**2**	**0**	**0**	**0**	**0**	**0.0**	**1**	....	....	....	....	....	....	....	....	....	....	....	....	....
	Michigan	IHL	60	10	15	25	58	....	....	....	....	....	....	....	....	....	....	....	2	0	1	1	17	....	....	....
1998-99	**Dallas**	**NHL**	**2**	**0**	**0**	**0**	**2**	**0**	**0**	**0**	**0**	**0.0**	**0**	**0**	**0.0**	**3**	**0**	**13:50**	....	....	....	....	....	....	....	....
	Michigan	IHL	74	5	14	19	68	....	....	....	....	....	....	....	....	....	....	....	5	0	0	0	10	....	....	....
	NHL Totals		**4**	**0**	**0**	**0**	**4**	**0**	**0**	**0**	**0**	**0.0**		**0**	**0.0**	**3**	**0**	**13:50**	....	....	....	....	....	....	....	....

• Missed entire 1995-96 season recovering from injuries suffered in automobile accident, July, 1995. Claimed by **Atlanta** from **Dallas** in Expansion Draft, June 25, 1999.

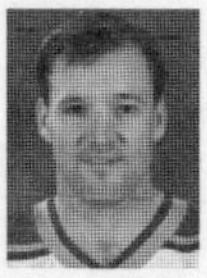

BYLSMA, Dan (BEEL-smah)

Right wing. Shoots left. 6'2", 209 lbs. Born, Grand Haven, MI, September 19, 1970. Winnipeg's 7th choice, 109th overall, in 1989 Entry Draft.

Season	Club	League	GP	G	A	Pts	PIM	PP	SH	GW	S	%	+/-	TF	F%	H	SB	Min	GP	G	A	Pts	PIM	PP	SH	GW
1987-88	St. Mary's	OJHL-B	40	30	39	69	33	....	....	....	....	....	....	....	....	....	....	....	....	....	....	....	....	....	....	....
1988-89	Bowling Green	CCHA	32	3	7	10	10	....	....	....	....	....	....	....	....	....	....	....	....	....	....	....	....	....	....	....
1989-90	Bowling Green	CCHA	44	13	17	30	30	....	....	....	....	....	....	....	....	....	....	....	....	....	....	....	....	....	....	....
1990-91	Bowling Green	CCHA	40	9	12	21	48	....	....	....	....	....	....	....	....	....	....	....	....	....	....	....	....	....	....	....
1991-92	Bowling Green	CCHA	34	11	14	25	24	....	....	....	....	....	....	....	....	....	....	....	....	....	....	....	....	....	....	....
1992-93	Greensboro	ECHL	60	25	35	60	66	....	....	....	....	....	....	....	....	....	....	....	1	0	1	1	10	....	....	....
	Rochester	AHL	2	0	1	1	0	....	....	....	....	....	....	....	....	....	....	....	....	....	....	....	....	....	....	....
1993-94	Greensboro	ECHL	25	14	16	30	52	....	....	....	....	....	....	....	....	....	....	....	....	....	....	....	....	....	....	....
	Albany	AHL	3	0	1	1	2	....	....	....	....	....	....	....	....	....	....	....	....	....	....	....	....	....	....	....
	Moncton	AHL	50	12	16	28	25	....	....	....	....	....	....	....	....	....	....	....	21	3	4	7	31	....	....	....
1994-95	Phoenix	IHL	81	19	23	42	41	....	....	....	....	....	....	....	....	....	....	....	9	4	4	8	4	....	....	....
1995-96	**Los Angeles**	**NHL**	**4**	**0**	**0**	**0**	**0**	**0**	**0**	**0**	**6**	**0.0**	**0**	....	....	....	....	....	....	....	....	....	....	....	....	....
	Phoenix	IHL	78	22	20	42	48	....	....	....	....	....	....	....	....	....	....	....	4	1	0	1	2	....	....	....
1996-97	**Los Angeles**	**NHL**	**79**	**3**	**6**	**9**	**32**	**0**	**0**	**0**	**86**	**3.5**	**–15**	....	....	....	....	....	....	....	....	....	....	....	....	....
1997-98	**Los Angeles**	**NHL**	**65**	**3**	**9**	**12**	**33**	**0**	**0**	**0**	**57**	**5.3**	**9**	....	....	....	....	....	**2**	**0**	**0**	**0**	**0**	**0**	**0**	**0**
	Long Beach	IHL	8	2	3	5	0	....	....	....	....	....	....	....	....	....	....	....	....	....	....	....	....	....	....	....
1998-99	**Los Angeles**	**NHL**	**8**	**0**	**0**	**0**	**2**	**0**	**0**	**0**	**3**	**0.0**	**–1**	**0**	**0.0**	**15**	**4**	**9:51**	....	....	....	....	....	....	....	....
	Springfield	AHL	2	0	2	2	2	....	....	....	....	....	....	....	....	....	....	....	....	....	....	....	....	....	....	....
	Long Beach	IHL	58	10	8	18	53	....	....	....	....	....	....	....	....	....	....	....	4	0	0	0	8	....	....	....
	NHL Totals		**156**	**6**	**15**	**21**	**67**	**0**	**0**	**0**	**152**	**3.9**		**0**	**0.0**	**15**	**4**	**9:51**	**2**	**0**	**0**	**0**	**0**	**0**	**0**	**0**

Signed as a free agent by **LA Kings**, July 7, 1994.

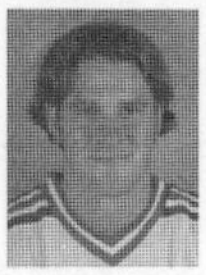

CAIRNS, Eric (KAIRNZ) NYI

Defense. Shoots left. 6'6", 230 lbs. Born, Oakville, Ont., June 27, 1974. NY Rangers' 3rd choice, 72nd overall, in 1992 Entry Draft.

Season	Club	League	GP	G	A	Pts	PIM	PP	SH	GW	S	%	+/-	TF	F%	H	SB	Min	GP	G	A	Pts	PIM	PP	SH	GW
1990-91	Burlington	OJHL-B	37	5	16	21	120	....	....	....	....	....	....	....	....	....	....	....	....	....	....	....	....	....	....	....
1991-92	Detroit	OHL	64	1	11	12	232	....	....	....	....	....	....	....	....	....	....	....	7	0	0	0	31	....	....	....
1992-93	Detroit	OHL	64	3	13	16	194	....	....	....	....	....	....	....	....	....	....	....	15	0	3	3	24	....	....	....
1993-94	Detroit	OHL	59	7	35	42	204	....	....	....	....	....	....	....	....	....	....	....	17	0	4	4	46	....	....	....
1994-95	Birmingham	ECHL	11	1	3	4	49	....	....	....	....	....	....	....	....	....	....	....	....	....	....	....	....	....	....	....
	Binghamton	AHL	27	0	3	3	134	....	....	....	....	....	....	....	....	....	....	....	9	1	1	2	28	....	....	....
1995-96	Binghamton	AHL	46	1	13	14	192	....	....	....	....	....	....	....	....	....	....	....	4	0	0	0	37	....	....	....
	Charlotte	ECHL	6	0	1	1	34	....	....	....	....	....	....	....	....	....	....	....	....	....	....	....	....	....	....	....
1996-97	**NY Rangers**	**NHL**	**40**	**0**	**1**	**1**	**147**	**0**	**0**	**0**	**17**	**0.0**	**–7**	....	....	....	....	....	**3**	**0**	**0**	**0**	**0**	**0**	**0**	**0**
	Binghamton	AHL	10	1	1	2	96	....	....	....	....	....	....	....	....	....	....	....	....	....	....	....	....	....	....	....
1997-98	**NY Rangers**	**NHL**	**39**	**0**	**3**	**3**	**92**	**0**	**0**	**0**	**17**	**0.0**	**–3**	....	....	....	....	....	....	....	....	....	....	....	....	....
	Hartford	AHL	7	1	2	3	43	....	....	....	....	....	....	....	....	....	....	....	....	....	....	....	....	....	....	....
1998-99	Hartford	AHL	11	0	2	2	49	....	....	....	....	....	....	....	....	....	....	....	....	....	....	....	....	....	....	....
	NY Islanders	**NHL**	**9**	**0**	**3**	**3**	**23**	**0**	**0**	**0**	**2**	**0.0**	**1**	**0**	**0.0**	**13**	**5**	**10:15**	....	....	....	....	....	....	....	....
	Lowell	AHL	24	0	0	0	91	....	....	....	....	....	....	....	....	....	....	....	3	1	0	1	32	....	....	....
	NHL Totals		**88**	**0**	**7**	**7**	**262**	**0**	**0**	**0**	**36**	**0.0**		**0**	**0.0**	**13**	**5**	**10:15**	**3**	**0**	**0**	**0**	**0**	**0**	**0**	**0**

Claimed on waivers by **NY Islanders** from **NY Rangers**, December 22, 1998.

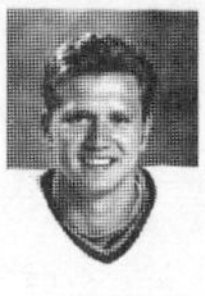

CALOUN, Jan (CHAH-loon, YAHN)

Right wing. Shoots right. 5'10", 190 lbs. Born, Usti-Nad-Labem, Czech., December 20, 1972. San Jose's 4th choice, 75th overall, in 1992 Entry Draft.

Season	Club	League	GP	G	A	Pts	PIM	PP	SH	GW	S	%	+/-	TF	F%	H	SB	Min	GP	G	A	Pts	PIM	PP	SH	GW
1990-91	CHZ Litvinov	Czech.	50	28	19	47	12	....	....	....	....	....	....	....	....	....	....	....	....	....	....	....	....	....	....	....
1991-92	CHZ Litvinov	Czech.	46	39	13	52	24	....	....	....	....	....	....	....	....	....	....	....	....	....	....	....	....	....	....	....
1992-93	CHZ Litvinov	Czech.	47	45	22	67		....	....	....	....	....	....	....	....	....	....	....	....	....	....	....	....	....	....	....
1993-94	CHZ Litvinov	Cze-Rep	38	25	17	42	....	....	....	....	....	....	....	....	....	....	....	....	4	2	2	4		....	....	....
1994-95	Kansas City	IHL	76	34	39	73	50	....	....	....	....	....	....	....	....	....	....	....	21	13	10	23	18	....	....	....
1995-96	**San Jose**	**NHL**	**11**	**8**	**3**	**11**	**0**	**2**	**0**	**0**	**20**	**40.0**	**4**	....	....	....	....	....	....	....	....	....	....	....	....	....
	Kansas City	IHL	61	38	30	68	58	....	....	....	....	....	....	....	....	....	....	....	5	0	1	1	6	....	....	....
1996-97	**San Jose**	**NHL**	**2**	**0**	**0**	**0**	**0**	**0**	**0**	**0**	**3**	**0.0**	**–2**	....	....	....	....	....	....	....	....	....	....	....	....	....
	Kentucky	AHL	66	43	43	86	68	....	....	....	....	....	....	....	....	....	....	....	4	0	1	1	4	....	....	....
1997-98	HIFK Helsinki	Finland	41	22	26	48	73	....	....	....	....	....	....	....	....	....	....	....	9	6	*11	*17	6	....	....	....
	Czech Republic	Olympics	3	0	0	0	6	....	....	....	....	....	....	....	....	....	....	....	....	....	....	....	....	....	....	....
1998-99	HIFK Helsinki	Finland	51	24	*57	*81	95	....	....	....	....	....	....	....	....	....	....	....	8	*8	6	*14	31	....	....	....
	HIFK Helsinki	EuroHL	5	4	2	6	26	....	....	....	....	....	....	....	....	....	....	....	....	....	....	....	....	....	....	....
	NHL Totals		**13**	**8**	**3**	**11**	**0**	**2**	**0**	**0**	**23**	**34.8**		....	....	....	....	....	....	....	....	....	....	....	....	....

AHL Second All-Star Team (1997)

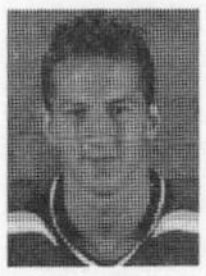

CAMPBELL, Jim ST.L.

Right wing. Shoots right. 6'2", 205 lbs. Born, Worcester, MA, April 3, 1973. Montreal's 2nd choice, 28th overall, in 1991 Entry Draft.

Season	Club	League	GP	G	A	Pts	PIM	PP	SH	GW	S	%	+/-	TF	F%	H	SB	Min	GP	G	A	Pts	PIM	PP	SH	GW
1988-89	Northwood	H.S.	12	12	8	20	6	....	....	....	....	....	....	....	....	....	....	....	....	....	....	....	....	....	....	....
1989-90	Northwood	H.S.	8	14	7	21	8	....	....	....	....	....	....	....	....	....	....	....	....	....	....	....	....	....	....	....
1990-91	Northwood	H.S.	26	36	47	83	36	....	....	....	....	....	....	....	....	....	....	....	....	....	....	....	....	....	....	....
1991-92	Hull	QMJHL	64	41	44	85	51	....	....	....	....	....	....	....	....	....	....	....	6	7	3	10	8	....	....	....
1992-93	Hull	QMJHL	50	42	29	71	66	....	....	....	....	....	....	....	....	....	....	....	8	11	4	15	43	....	....	....

			Regular Season																Playoffs							
Season	Club	League	GP	G	A	Pts	PIM	PP	SH	GW	S	%	+/-	TF	F%	H	SB	Min	GP	G	A	Pts	PIM	PP	SH	GW
1993-94	United States	Nat-Team	56	24	33	57	59	....	....	....	....	....	....	....	....	....	....	....	....	....	....	....	....	....	....	....
	United States	Olympics	8	0	0	0	6	....	....	....	....	....	....	....	....	....	....	....	....	....	....	....	....	....	....	....
	Fredericton	AHL	19	6	17	23	6	....	....	....	....	....	....	....	....	....	....	....	....	....	....	....	....	....	....	....
1994-95	Fredericton	AHL	77	27	24	51	103	....	....	....	....	....	....	....	....	....	....	....	12	0	7	7	8	....	....	....
1995-96	Fredericton	AHL	44	28	23	51	24	....	....	....	....	....	....	....	....	....	....	....	....	....	....	....	....	....	....	....
	Anaheim	**NHL**	**16**	**2**	**3**	**5**	**36**	**1**	**0**	**0**	**25**	**8.0**	**0**	....	....	....	....	....	....	....	....	....	....	....	....	....
	Baltimore	AHL	16	13	7	20	8	....	....	....	....	....	....	....	....	....	....	....	12	7	5	12	10	....	....	....
1996-97	**St. Louis**	**NHL**	**68**	**23**	**20**	**43**	**68**	**5**	**0**	**6**	**169**	**13.6**	**3**	....	....	....	....	....	**4**	**1**	**0**	**1**	**6**	**1**	**0**	**0**
1997-98	**St. Louis**	**NHL**	**76**	**22**	**19**	**41**	**55**	**7**	**0**	**6**	**147**	**15.0**	**0**	....	....	....	....	....	**10**	**7**	**3**	**10**	**12**	**4**	**0**	**2**
1998-99	**St. Louis**	**NHL**	**55**	**4**	**21**	**25**	**41**	**1**	**0**	**0**	**99**	**4.0**	**–8**	**7**	**42.9**	**65**	**7**	**13:34**	....	....	....	....	....	....	....	....
	NHL Totals		**215**	**51**	**63**	**114**	**200**	**14**	**0**	**12**	**440**	**11.6**		**7**	**42.9**	**65**	**7**	**13:34**	**14**	**8**	**3**	**11**	**18**	**5**	**0**	**2**

NHL All-Rookie Team (1997)

Traded to **Anaheim** by **Montreal** for Robert Dirk, January 21, 1996. Signed as a free agent by **St. Louis**, July 11, 1996.

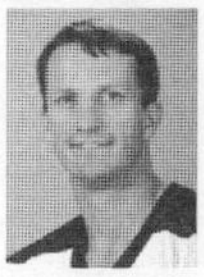

CARBONNEAU, Guy

(KAR-buhn-oh, GEE) **DAL.**

Center. Shoots right. 5'11", 186 lbs. Born, Sept-Iles, Que., March 18, 1960. Montreal's 4th choice, 44th overall, in 1979 Entry Draft.

Season	Club	League	GP	G	A	Pts	PIM	PP	SH	GW	S	%	+/-	TF	F%	H	SB	Min	GP	G	A	Pts	PIM	PP	SH	GW
1976-77	Chicoutimi	QMJHL	59	9	20	29	8	....	....	....	....	....	....	....	....	....	....	....	4	1	0	1	0	....	....	....
1977-78	Chicoutimi	QMJHL	70	28	55	83	60	....	....	....	....	....	....	....	....	....	....	....	....	....	....	....	....	....	....	....
1978-79	Chicoutimi	QMJHL	72	62	79	141	47	....	....	....	....	....	....	....	....	....	....	....	4	2	1	3	4	....	....	....
1979-80	Chicoutimi	QMJHL	72	72	110	182	66	....	....	....	....	....	....	....	....	....	....	....	12	9	15	24	28	....	....	....
	Nova Scotia	AHL	....	....	....	....	....	....	....	....	....	....	....	....	....	....	....	....	2	1	1	2	2	....	....	....
1980-81	**Montreal**	**NHL**	**2**	**0**	**1**	**1**	**0**	**0**	**0**	**0**	**1**	**0.0**	**0**	....	....	....	....	....	....	....	....	....	....	....	....	....
	Nova Scotia	AHL	78	35	53	88	87	....	....	....	....	....	....	....	....	....	....	....	6	1	3	4	9	....	....	....
1981-82	Nova Scotia	AHL	77	27	67	94	124	....	....	....	....	....	....	....	....	....	....	....	9	2	7	9	8	....	....	....
1982-83	**Montreal**	**NHL**	**77**	**18**	**29**	**47**	**68**	**0**	**5**	**2**	**109**	**16.5**	**18**	....	....	....	....	....	**3**	**0**	**0**	**0**	**2**	**0**	**0**	**0**
1983-84	**Montreal**	**NHL**	**78**	**24**	**30**	**54**	**75**	**3**	**7**	**2**	**166**	**14.5**	**5**	....	....	....	....	....	**15**	**4**	**3**	**7**	**12**	**0**	**0**	**1**
1984-85	**Montreal**	**NHL**	**79**	**23**	**34**	**57**	**43**	**0**	**4**	**2**	**163**	**14.1**	**28**	....	....	....	....	....	**12**	**4**	**3**	**7**	**8**	**0**	**1**	**1**
1985-86♦	**Montreal**	**NHL**	**80**	**20**	**36**	**56**	**57**	**1**	**2**	**3**	**147**	**13.6**	**18**	....	....	....	....	....	**20**	**7**	**5**	**12**	**35**	**0**	**2**	**1**
1986-87	**Montreal**	**NHL**	**79**	**18**	**27**	**45**	**68**	**0**	**0**	**2**	**120**	**15.0**	**9**	....	....	....	....	....	**17**	**3**	**8**	**11**	**20**	**0**	**0**	**0**
1987-88	**Montreal**	**NHL**	**80**	**17**	**21**	**38**	**61**	**0**	**3**	**1**	**109**	**15.6**	**14**	....	....	....	....	....	**11**	**0**	**4**	**4**	**2**	**0**	**0**	**0**
1988-89	**Montreal**	**NHL**	**79**	**26**	**30**	**56**	**44**	**1**	**2**	**10**	**142**	**18.3**	**37**	....	....	....	....	....	**21**	**4**	**5**	**9**	**10**	**0**	**1**	**0**
1989-90	**Montreal**	**NHL**	**68**	**19**	**36**	**55**	**37**	**1**	**1**	**3**	**125**	**15.2**	**21**	....	....	....	....	....	**11**	**2**	**3**	**5**	**6**	**0**	**0**	**0**
1990-91	**Montreal**	**NHL**	**78**	**20**	**24**	**44**	**63**	**4**	**1**	**3**	**131**	**15.3**	**–1**	....	....	....	....	....	**13**	**1**	**5**	**6**	**10**	**0**	**0**	**1**
1991-92	**Montreal**	**NHL**	**72**	**18**	**21**	**39**	**39**	**1**	**1**	**4**	**120**	**15.0**	**2**	....	....	....	....	....	**11**	**1**	**1**	**2**	**6**	**0**	**0**	**0**
1992-93♦	**Montreal**	**NHL**	**61**	**4**	**13**	**17**	**20**	**0**	**1**	**0**	**73**	**5.5**	**–9**	....	....	....	....	....	**20**	**3**	**3**	**6**	**10**	**0**	**1**	**2**
1993-94	**Montreal**	**NHL**	**79**	**14**	**24**	**38**	**48**	**0**	**0**	**1**	**120**	**11.7**	**16**	....	....	....	....	....	**7**	**1**	**3**	**4**	**4**	**0**	**0**	**0**
1994-95	**St. Louis**	**NHL**	**42**	**5**	**11**	**16**	**16**	**1**	**0**	**1**	**33**	**15.2**	**11**	....	....	....	....	....	**7**	**1**	**2**	**3**	**6**	**0**	**0**	**0**
1995-96	**Dallas**	**NHL**	**71**	**8**	**15**	**23**	**38**	**0**	**2**	**1**	**54**	**14.8**	**–2**	....	....	....	....	....	....	....	....	....	....	....	....	....
1996-97	**Dallas**	**NHL**	**73**	**5**	**16**	**21**	**36**	**0**	**1**	**0**	**99**	**5.1**	**9**	....	....	....	....	....	**7**	**0**	**1**	**1**	**6**	**0**	**0**	**0**
1997-98	**Dallas**	**NHL**	**77**	**7**	**17**	**24**	**40**	**0**	**1**	**1**	**81**	**8.6**	**3**	....	....	....	....	....	**16**	**3**	**1**	**4**	**6**	**0**	**0**	**0**
1998-99♦	**Dallas**	**NHL**	**74**	**4**	**12**	**16**	**31**	**0**	**0**	**2**	**60**	**6.7**	**–3**	**1055**	**53.3**	**83**	**57**	**13:21**	**17**	**2**	**4**	**6**	**6**	**0**	**0**	**1**
	NHL Totals		**1249**	**250**	**397**	**647**	**784**	**12**	**31**	**38**	**1853**	**13.5**		**1055**	**53.3**	**83**	**57**	**13:21**	**208**	**36**	**51**	**87**	**149**	**0**	**5**	**7**

QMJHL Second All-Star Team (1980) • Won Frank J. Selke Trophy (1988, 1989, 1992)

Traded to **St. Louis** by **Montreal** for Jim Montgomery, August 19, 1994. Traded to **Dallas** by **St. Louis** for Paul Broten, October 2, 1995.

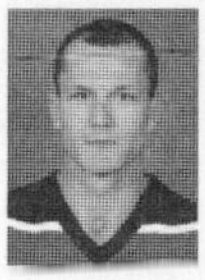

CARKNER, Terry

Defense. Shoots left. 6'3", 210 lbs. Born, Smiths Falls, Ont., March 7, 1966. NY Rangers' 1st choice, 14th overall, in 1984 Entry Draft.

Season	Club	League	GP	G	A	Pts	PIM	PP	SH	GW	S	%	+/-	TF	F%	H	SB	Min	GP	G	A	Pts	PIM	PP	SH	GW
1982-83	Brockville	OJHL	47	8	32	40	94	....	....	....	....	....	....	....	....	....	....	....	....	....	....	....	....	....	....	....
1983-84	Peterborough	OHL	58	4	19	23	77	....	....	....	....	....	....	....	....	....	....	....	8	0	6	6	13	....	....	....
1984-85	Peterborough	OHL	64	14	47	61	125	....	....	....	....	....	....	....	....	....	....	....	17	2	10	12	11	....	....	....
1985-86	Peterborough	OHL	54	12	32	44	106	....	....	....	....	....	....	....	....	....	....	....	16	1	7	8	17	....	....	....
1986-87	**NY Rangers**	**NHL**	**52**	**2**	**13**	**15**	**118**	**0**	**0**	**0**	**33**	**6.1**	**–1**	....	....	....	....	....	**1**	**0**	**0**	**0**	**0**	**0**	**0**	**0**
	New Haven	AHL	12	2	6	8	56	....	....	....	....	....	....	....	....	....	....	....	3	1	0	1	0	....	....	....
1987-88	**Quebec**	**NHL**	**63**	**3**	**24**	**27**	**159**	**2**	**0**	**1**	**54**	**5.6**	**–8**	....	....	....	....	....	....	....	....	....	....	....	....	....
1988-89	**Philadelphia**	**NHL**	**78**	**11**	**32**	**43**	**149**	**2**	**1**	**1**	**84**	**13.1**	**–6**	....	....	....	....	....	**19**	**1**	**5**	**6**	**28**	**0**	**1**	**0**
1989-90	**Philadelphia**	**NHL**	**63**	**4**	**18**	**22**	**169**	**1**	**0**	**1**	**60**	**6.7**	**–8**	....	....	....	....	....	....	....	....	....	....	....	....	....
1990-91	**Philadelphia**	**NHL**	**79**	**7**	**25**	**32**	**204**	**6**	**0**	**1**	**97**	**7.2**	**15**	....	....	....	....	....	....	....	....	....	....	....	....	....
1991-92	**Philadelphia**	**NHL**	**73**	**4**	**12**	**16**	**195**	**0**	**1**	**0**	**70**	**5.7**	**–14**	....	....	....	....	....	....	....	....	....	....	....	....	....
1992-93	**Philadelphia**	**NHL**	**83**	**3**	**16**	**19**	**150**	**0**	**0**	**0**	**45**	**6.7**	**18**	....	....	....	....	....	....	....	....	....	....	....	....	....
1993-94	**Detroit**	**NHL**	**68**	**1**	**6**	**7**	**130**	**0**	**0**	**0**	**32**	**3.1**	**13**	....	....	....	....	....	**7**	**0**	**0**	**0**	**4**	**0**	**0**	**0**
1994-95	**Detroit**	**NHL**	**20**	**1**	**2**	**3**	**21**	**0**	**0**	**0**	**9**	**11.1**	**7**	....	....	....	....	....	....	....	....	....	....	....	....	....
1995-96	**Florida**	**NHL**	**73**	**3**	**10**	**13**	**80**	**1**	**0**	**0**	**42**	**7.1**	**10**	....	....	....	....	....	**22**	**0**	**4**	**4**	**10**	**0**	**0**	**0**
1996-97	**Florida**	**NHL**	**70**	**0**	**14**	**14**	**96**	**0**	**0**	**0**	**38**	**0.0**	**–4**	....	....	....	....	....	**5**	**0**	**0**	**0**	**6**	**0**	**0**	**0**
1997-98	**Florida**	**NHL**	**74**	**1**	**7**	**8**	**63**	**0**	**0**	**1**	**34**	**2.9**	**6**	....	....	....	....	....	....	....	....	....	....	....	....	....
1998-99	**Florida**	**NHL**	**62**	**2**	**9**	**11**	**54**	**0**	**0**	**0**	**25**	**8.0**	**0**	**0**	**0.0**	**66**	**57**	**18:14**	....	....	....	....	....	....	....	....
	NHL Totals		**858**	**42**	**188**	**230**	**1588**	**12**	**2**	**5**	**623**	**6.7**		**0**	**0.0**	**66**	**57**	**18:14**	**54**	**1**	**9**	**10**	**48**	**0**	**1**	**0**

OHL Second All-Star Team (1985) • OHL First All-Star Team (1986)

Traded to **Quebec** by **NY Rangers** with Jeff Jackson for John Ogrodnick and David Shaw, September 30, 1987. Traded to **Philadelphia** by **Quebec** for Greg Smyth and Philadelphia's 3rd round choice (John Tanner) in the 1989 Entry Draft, July 25, 1988. Traded to **Detroit** by **Philadelphia** for Yves Racine and Detroit's 4th round choice (Sebastien Vallee) in 1994 Entry Draft, October 5, 1993. Signed as a free agent by **Florida**, August 8, 1995.

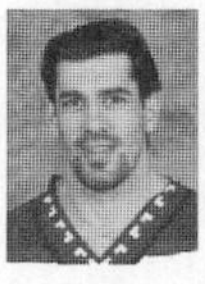

CARNEY, Keith

PHX.

Defense. Shoots left. 6'2", 205 lbs. Born, Providence, RI, February 3, 1970. Buffalo's 3rd choice, 76th overall, in 1988 Entry Draft.

Season	Club	League	GP	G	A	Pts	PIM	PP	SH	GW	S	%	+/-	TF	F%	H	SB	Min	GP	G	A	Pts	PIM	PP	SH	GW
1987-88	Mt. St. Charles	H.S.	23	12	43	55		....	....	....	....	....	....	....	....	....	....	....	....	....	....	....	....	....	....	....
1988-89	U. of Maine	H.E.	40	4	22	26	24	....	....	....	....	....	....	....	....	....	....	....	....	....	....	....	....	....	....	....
1989-90	U. of Maine	H.E.	41	3	41	44	43	....	....	....	....	....	....	....	....	....	....	....	....	....	....	....	....	....	....	....
1990-91	U. of Maine	H.E.	40	7	49	56	38	....	....	....	....	....	....	....	....	....	....	....	....	....	....	....	....	....	....	....
1991-92	United States	Nat-Team	49	2	17	19	16	....	....	....	....	....	....	....	....	....	....	....	....	....	....	....	....	....	....	....
	Buffalo	**NHL**	**14**	**1**	**2**	**3**	**18**	**1**	**0**	**0**	**17**	**5.9**	**–3**	....	....	....	....	....	**7**	**0**	**3**	**3**	**0**	**0**	**0**	**0**
	Rochester	AHL	24	1	10	11	2	....	....	....	....	....	....	....	....	....	....	....	2	0	2	2	0	....	....	....
1992-93	**Buffalo**	**NHL**	**30**	**2**	**4**	**6**	**55**	**0**	**0**	**1**	**26**	**7.7**	**3**	....	....	....	....	....	**8**	**0**	**3**	**3**	**6**	**0**	**0**	**0**
	Rochester	AHL	41	5	21	26	32	....	....	....	....	....	....	....	....	....	....	....	....	....	....	....	....	....	....	....
1993-94	**Buffalo**	**NHL**	**7**	**1**	**3**	**4**	**4**	**0**	**0**	**0**	**6**	**16.7**	**–1**	....	....	....	....	....	....	....	....	....	....	....	....	....
	Chicago	**NHL**	**30**	**3**	**5**	**8**	**35**	**0**	**0**	**0**	**31**	**9.7**	**15**	....	....	....	....	....	**6**	**0**	**1**	**1**	**4**	**0**	**0**	**0**
	Indianapolis	IHL	28	0	14	14	20	....	....	....	....	....	....	....	....	....	....	....	....	....	....	....	....	....	....	....
1994-95	**Chicago**	**NHL**	**18**	**1**	**0**	**1**	**11**	**0**	**0**	**1**	**14**	**7.1**	**–1**	....	....	....	....	....	**4**	**0**	**1**	**1**	**0**	**0**	**0**	**0**
1995-96	**Chicago**	**NHL**	**82**	**5**	**14**	**19**	**94**	**1**	**0**	**1**	**69**	**7.2**	**31**	....	....	....	....	....	**10**	**0**	**3**	**3**	**4**	**0**	**0**	**0**
1996-97	**Chicago**	**NHL**	**81**	**3**	**15**	**18**	**62**	**0**	**0**	**1**	**77**	**3.9**	**26**	....	....	....	....	....	**6**	**1**	**1**	**2**	**2**	**0**	**0**	**0**
1997-98	**Chicago**	**NHL**	**60**	**2**	**13**	**15**	**73**	**0**	**1**	**0**	**53**	**3.8**	**–7**	....	....	....	....	....	....	....	....	....	....	....	....	....
	United States	Olympics	4	0	0	0	2	....	....	....	....	....	....	....	....	....	....	....	....	....	....	....	....	....	....	....
	Phoenix	**NHL**	**20**	**1**	**6**	**7**	**18**	**1**	**0**	**0**	**18**	**5.6**	**5**	....	....	....	....	....	**6**	**0**	**0**	**0**	**4**	**0**	**0**	**0**
1998-99	**Phoenix**	**NHL**	**82**	**2**	**14**	**16**	**62**	**0**	**2**	**0**	**62**	**3.2**	**15**	**0**	**0.0**	**133**	**87**	**22:46**	**7**	**1**	**2**	**3**	**10**	**0**	**0**	**0**
	NHL Totals		**424**	**21**	**76**	**97**	**432**	**3**	**3**	**4**	**373**	**5.6**		**0**	**0.0**	**133**	**87**	**22:46**	**54**	**2**	**14**	**16**	**30**	**0**	**0**	**0**

Hockey East Second All-Star Team (1990) • NCAA East Second All-American Team (1990) • Hockey East First All-Star Team (1991) • NCAA East First All-American Team (1991)

Traded to **Chicago** by **Buffalo** with Buffalo's 6th round choice (Marc Magliarditi) in 1995 Entry Draft for Craig Muni and Chicago's 5th round choice (Daniel Bienvenue) in 1995 Entry Draft, October 26, 1993. Traded to **Phoenix** by **Chicago** with Jim Cummins for Chad Kilger and Jayson More, March 4, 1998.

			Regular Season																Playoffs							
Season	Club	League	GP	G	A	Pts	PIM	PP	SH	GW	S	%	+/-	TF	F%	H	SB	Min	GP	G	A	Pts	PIM	PP	SH	GW

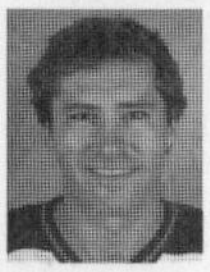

CARPENTER, Bob

Center. Shoots left. 6', 200 lbs. Born, Beverly, MA, July 13, 1963. Washington's 1st choice, 3rd overall, in 1981 Entry Draft.

Season	Club	League	GP	G	A	Pts	PIM	PP	SH	GW	S	%	+/-	TF	F%	H	SB	Min	GP	G	A	Pts	PIM	PP	SH	GW
1979-80	St. John's Prep	H.S.	33	28	37	65	....	....	....	....	....	....	....	....	....	....	....	....	....	....	....	....	....	....	....	....
1980-81	St. John's Prep	H.S.	18	14	24	38	....	....	....	....	....	....	....	....	....	....	....	....	....	....	....	....	....	....	....	....
1981-82	**Washington**	**NHL**	**80**	**32**	**35**	**67**	**69**	**7**	**1**	**3**	**263**	**12.2**	**-23**	....	....	....	....	....	....	....	....	....	....	....	....	....
1982-83	**Washington**	**NHL**	**80**	**32**	**37**	**69**	**64**	**14**	**0**	**4**	**197**	**16.2**	**0**	....	....	....	....	....	**4**	**1**	**0**	**1**	**2**	**0**	**0**	**0**
1983-84	**Washington**	**NHL**	**80**	**28**	**40**	**68**	**51**	**8**	**0**	**5**	**228**	**12.3**	**0**	....	....	....	....	....	**8**	**2**	**1**	**3**	**25**	**1**	**0**	**0**
1984-85	**Washington**	**NHL**	**80**	**53**	**42**	**95**	**87**	**12**	**0**	**7**	**260**	**20.4**	**20**	....	....	....	....	....	**5**	**1**	**4**	**5**	**8**	**0**	**0**	**0**
1985-86	**Washington**	**NHL**	**80**	**27**	**29**	**56**	**105**	**7**	**0**	**3**	**205**	**13.2**	**-12**	....	....	....	....	....	**9**	**5**	**4**	**9**	**12**	**2**	**0**	**1**
1986-87	**Washington**	**NHL**	**22**	**5**	**7**	**12**	**21**	**4**	**0**	**0**	**47**	**10.6**	**-7**	....	....	....	....	....	....	....	....	....	....	....	....	....
	NY Rangers	**NHL**	**28**	**2**	**8**	**10**	**20**	**1**	**0**	**0**	**41**	**4.9**	**-12**	....	....	....	....	....	....	....	....	....	....	....	....	....
	Los Angeles	**NHL**	**10**	**2**	**3**	**5**	**6**	**0**	**0**	**0**	**23**	**8.7**	**-8**	....	....	....	....	....	**5**	**1**	**2**	**3**	**2**	**0**	**0**	**0**
1987-88	**Los Angeles**	**NHL**	**71**	**19**	**33**	**52**	**84**	**10**	**0**	**2**	**176**	**10.8**	**-21**	....	....	....	....	....	**5**	**1**	**1**	**2**	**0**	**0**	**0**	**0**
1988-89	**Los Angeles**	**NHL**	**39**	**11**	**15**	**26**	**16**	**3**	**0**	**1**	**91**	**12.1**	**3**	....	....	....	....	....	....	....	....	....	....	....	....	....
	Boston	**NHL**	**18**	**5**	**9**	**14**	**10**	**1**	**0**	**2**	**46**	**10.9**	**4**	....	....	....	....	....	**8**	**1**	**1**	**2**	**4**	**1**	**0**	**1**
1989-90	**Boston**	**NHL**	**80**	**25**	**31**	**56**	**97**	**5**	**0**	**5**	**220**	**11.4**	**-3**	....	....	....	....	....	**21**	**4**	**6**	**10**	**39**	**2**	**0**	**1**
1990-91	**Boston**	**NHL**	**29**	**8**	**8**	**16**	**22**	**2**	**0**	**0**	**54**	**14.8**	**2**	....	....	....	....	....	**1**	**0**	**1**	**1**	**2**	**0**	**0**	**0**
1991-92	**Boston**	**NHL**	**60**	**25**	**23**	**48**	**46**	**6**	**1**	**6**	**171**	**14.6**	**-3**	....	....	....	....	....	**8**	**0**	**1**	**1**	**6**	**0**	**0**	**0**
1992-93	**Washington**	**NHL**	**68**	**11**	**17**	**28**	**65**	**2**	**0**	**0**	**141**	**7.8**	**-16**	....	....	....	....	....	**6**	**1**	**4**	**5**	**6**	**0**	**0**	**0**
1993-94	**New Jersey**	**NHL**	**76**	**10**	**23**	**33**	**51**	**0**	**2**	**1**	**125**	**8.0**	**7**	....	....	....	....	....	**20**	**1**	**7**	**8**	**20**	**0**	**0**	**0**
1994-95♦	**New Jersey**	**NHL**	**41**	**5**	**11**	**16**	**19**	**0**	**0**	**0**	**69**	**7.2**	**-1**	....	....	....	....	....	**17**	**1**	**4**	**5**	**6**	**1**	**0**	**0**
1995-96	**New Jersey**	**NHL**	**52**	**5**	**5**	**10**	**14**	**0**	**1**	**0**	**63**	**7.9**	**-10**	....	....	....	....	....	....	....	....	....	....	....	....	....
1996-97	**New Jersey**	**NHL**	**62**	**4**	**15**	**19**	**14**	**0**	**1**	**0**	**76**	**5.3**	**6**	....	....	....	....	....	**10**	**1**	**2**	**3**	**2**	**0**	**0**	**0**
1997-98	**New Jersey**	**NHL**	**66**	**9**	**9**	**18**	**22**	**0**	**1**	**1**	**81**	**11.1**	**-4**	....	....	....	....	....	**6**	**1**	**0**	**1**	**0**	**0**	**0**	**0**
1998-99	**New Jersey**	**NHL**	**56**	**2**	**8**	**10**	**36**	**0**	**0**	**0**	**69**	**2.9**	**-3**	**987**	**51.4**	**52**	**33**	**15:17**	**7**	**0**	**0**	**0**	**2**	**0**	**0**	**0**
	NHL Totals		**1178**	**320**	**408**	**728**	**919**	**82**	**7**	**40**	**2646**	**12.1**		**987**	**51.4**	**52**	**33**	**15:17**	**140**	**21**	**38**	**59**	**136**	**7**	**0**	**3**

Played in NHL All-Star Game (1985)

Traded to **NY Rangers** by **Washington** with Washington's 2nd round choice (Jason Prosofsky) in 1989 Entry Draft for Bob Crawford, Kelly Miller and Mike Ridley, January 1, 1987. Traded to **LA Kings** by **NY Rangers** with Tom Laidlaw for Jeff Crossman, Marcel Dionne and LA Kings' 3rd round choice (later traded to Minnesota — Minnesota selected Murray Garbutt) in 1989 Entry Draft. Traded to **Boston** by **LA Kings** for Steve Kasper, January 23, 1989. Signed as a free agent by **Washington**, June 30, 1992. Signed as a free agent by **New Jersey**, September 30, 1993.

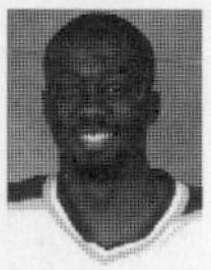

CARTER, Anson **BOS.**

Center. Shoots right. 6'1", 185 lbs. Born, Toronto, Ont., June 6, 1974. Quebec's 11th choice, 220th overall, in 1992 Entry Draft.

Season	Club	League	GP	G	A	Pts	PIM	PP	SH	GW	S	%	+/-	TF	F%	H	SB	Min	GP	G	A	Pts	PIM	PP	SH	GW
1989-90	Don Mills	MTHL	40	15	47	62	105	....	....	....	....	....	....	....	....	....	....	....	....	....	....	....	....	....	....	....
1990-91	Don Mills	MTHL	67	69	73	142	43	....	....	....	....	....	....	....	....	....	....	....	....	....	....	....	....	....	....	....
1991-92	Wexford	OJHL-B	42	18	22	40	24	....	....	....	....	....	....	....	....	....	....	....	....	....	....	....	....	....	....	....
1992-93	Michigan State	CCHA	34	15	7	22	20	....	....	....	....	....	....	....	....	....	....	....	....	....	....	....	....	....	....	....
1993-94	Michigan State	CCHA	39	30	24	54	36	....	....	....	....	....	....	....	....	....	....	....	....	....	....	....	....	....	....	....
1994-95	Michigan State	CCHA	39	34	17	51	40	....	....	....	....	....	....	....	....	....	....	....	....	....	....	....	....	....	....	....
1995-96	Michigan State	CCHA	42	23	20	43	36	....	....	....	....	....	....	....	....	....	....	....	....	....	....	....	....	....	....	....
1996-97	**Washington**	**NHL**	**19**	**3**	**2**	**5**	**7**	**1**	**0**	**1**	**28**	**10.7**	**0**	....	....	....	....	....	....	....	....	....	....	....	....	....
	Portland	AHL	27	19	19	38	11	....	....	....	....	....	....	....	....	....	....	....	....	....	....	....	....	....	....	....
	Boston	**NHL**	**19**	**8**	**5**	**13**	**2**	**1**	**1**	**1**	**51**	**15.7**	**-7**	....	....	....	....	....	....	....	....	....	....	....	....	....
1997-98	**Boston**	**NHL**	**78**	**16**	**27**	**43**	**31**	**6**	**0**	**4**	**179**	**8.9**	**7**	....	....	....	....	....	**6**	**1**	**1**	**2**	**0**	**0**	**0**	**0**
1998-99	**Boston**	**NHL**	**55**	**24**	**16**	**40**	**22**	**6**	**0**	**6**	**123**	**19.5**	**7**	**172**	**43.0**	**62**	**5**	**18:44**	**12**	**4**	**3**	**7**	**0**	**1**	**0**	**1**
	Utah	IHL	6	1	1	2	0	....	....	....	....	....	....	....	....	....	....	....	....	....	....	....	....	....	....	....
	NHL Totals		**171**	**51**	**50**	**101**	**62**	**14**	**1**	**12**	**381**	**13.4**		**172**	**43.0**	**62**	**5**	**18:44**	**18**	**5**	**4**	**9**	**0**	**1**	**0**	**1**

CCHA First All-Star Team (1994, 1995) • NCAA West Second All-American Team (1995) • CCHA Second All-Star Team (1996)

Rights transferred to **Colorado** after **Quebec** franchise relocated, June 21, 1995. Traded to **Washington** by **Colorado** for Washington's 4th round choice (Ben Storey) in 1996 Entry Draft, April 3, 1996. Traded to **Boston** by **Washington** with Jim Carey, Jason Allison and Washington's 3rd round choice (Lee Goren) in 1997 Entry Draft for Bill Ranford, Adam Oates and Rick Tocchet, March 1, 1997.

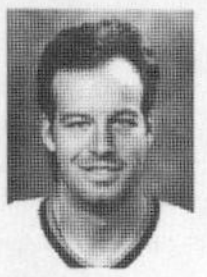

CASSELMAN, Mike

Center. Shoots left. 5'11", 190 lbs. Born, Morrisburg, Ont., August 23, 1968. Detroit's 1st choice, 3rd overall, in 1990 Supplemental Draft.

Season	Club	League	GP	G	A	Pts	PIM	PP	SH	GW	S	%	+/-	TF	F%	H	SB	Min	GP	G	A	Pts	PIM	PP	SH	GW
1987-88	Clarkson	ECAC	24	4	1	5	....	....	....	....	....	....	....	....	....	....	....	....	....	....	....	....	....	....	....	....
1988-89	Clarkson	ECAC	31	3	14	17	....	....	....	....	....	....	....	....	....	....	....	....	....	....	....	....	....	....	....	....
1989-90	Clarkson	ECAC	34	22	21	43	69	....	....	....	....	....	....	....	....	....	....	....	....	....	....	....	....	....	....	....
1990-91	Clarkson	ECAC	40	19	35	54	44	....	....	....	....	....	....	....	....	....	....	....	....	....	....	....	....	....	....	....
1991-92	Toledo	ECHL	61	39	60	99	83	....	....	....	....	....	....	....	....	....	....	....	5	0	1	1	6	....	....	....
	Adirondack	AHL	1	0	0	0	0	....	....	....	....	....	....	....	....	....	....	....	....	....	....	....	....	....	....	....
1992-93	Adirondack	AHL	60	12	19	31	27	....	....	....	....	....	....	....	....	....	....	....	8	3	3	6	0	....	....	....
	Toledo	ECHL	3	0	1	1	2	....	....	....	....	....	....	....	....	....	....	....	....	....	....	....	....	....	....	....
1993-94	Adirondack	AHL	77	17	38	55	34	....	....	....	....	....	....	....	....	....	....	....	12	2	4	6	10	....	....	....
1994-95	Adirondack	AHL	60	17	43	60	42	....	....	....	....	....	....	....	....	....	....	....	4	0	0	0	2	....	....	....
1995-96	**Florida**	**NHL**	**3**	**0**	**0**	**0**	**0**	**0**	**0**	**0**	**2**	**0.0**	**-1**	....	....	....	....	....	....	....	....	....	....	....	....	....
	Carolina	AHL	70	34	68	102	46	....	....	....	....	....	....	....	....	....	....	....	....	....	....	....	....	....	....	....
1996-97	Cincinnati	IHL	68	30	34	64	54	....	....	....	....	....	....	....	....	....	....	....	3	1	0	1	2	....	....	....
1997-98	Cincinnati	IHL	55	19	28	47	44	....	....	....	....	....	....	....	....	....	....	....	....	....	....	....	....	....	....	....
	Rochester	AHL	25	8	7	15	14	....	....	....	....	....	....	....	....	....	....	....	4	1	1	2	2	....	....	....
1998-99	EV Landshut	Germany	49	20	29	49	64	....	....	....	....	....	....	....	....	....	....	....	3	0	1	1	0	....	....	....
	NHL Totals		**3**	**0**	**0**	**0**	**0**	**0**	**0**	**0**	**2**	**0.0**		....	....	....	....	....	....	....	....	....	....	....	....	....

ECHL Second All-Star Team (1992)

Signed as a free agent by **Florida**, October 31, 1995. Signed as a free agent by **San Jose**, September 24, 1997.

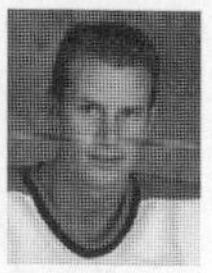

CASSELS, Andrew (KAS-uhls) **VAN.**

Center. Shoots left. 6'1", 185 lbs. Born, Bramalea, Ont., July 23, 1969. Montreal's 1st choice, 17th overall, in 1987 Entry Draft.

Season	Club	League	GP	G	A	Pts	PIM	PP	SH	GW	S	%	+/-	TF	F%	H	SB	Min	GP	G	A	Pts	PIM	PP	SH	GW
1985-86	Bramalea	OJHL-B	33	18	25	43	26	....	....	....	....	....	....	....	....	....	....	....	....	....	....	....	....	....	....	....
1986-87	Ottawa	OHL	66	26	66	92	28	....	....	....	....	....	....	....	....	....	....	....	11	5	9	14	7	....	....	....
1987-88	Ottawa	OHL	61	48	*103	*151	39	....	....	....	....	....	....	....	....	....	....	....	16	8	*24	*32	13	....	....	....
1988-89	Ottawa	OHL	56	37	97	134	66	....	....	....	....	....	....	....	....	....	....	....	12	5	10	15	10	....	....	....
1989-90	**Montreal**	**NHL**	**6**	**2**	**0**	**2**	**2**	**0**	**0**	**1**	**5**	**40.0**	**1**	....	....	....	....	....	....	....	....	....	....	....	....	....
	Sherbrooke	AHL	55	22	45	67	25	....	....	....	....	....	....	....	....	....	....	....	12	2	11	13	6	....	....	....
1990-91	**Montreal**	**NHL**	**54**	**6**	**19**	**25**	**20**	**1**	**0**	**3**	**55**	**10.9**	**2**	....	....	....	....	....	**8**	**0**	**2**	**2**	**2**	**0**	**0**	**0**
1991-92	**Hartford**	**NHL**	**67**	**11**	**30**	**41**	**18**	**2**	**2**	**3**	**99**	**11.1**	**3**	....	....	....	....	....	**7**	**2**	**4**	**6**	**6**	**1**	**0**	**0**
1992-93	**Hartford**	**NHL**	**84**	**21**	**64**	**85**	**62**	**8**	**3**	**1**	**134**	**15.7**	**-11**	....	....	....	....	....	....	....	....	....	....	....	....	....
1993-94	**Hartford**	**NHL**	**79**	**16**	**42**	**58**	**37**	**8**	**1**	**3**	**126**	**12.7**	**-21**	....	....	....	....	....	....	....	....	....	....	....	....	....
1994-95	**Hartford**	**NHL**	**46**	**7**	**30**	**37**	**18**	**1**	**0**	**1**	**74**	**9.5**	**-3**	....	....	....	....	....	....	....	....	....	....	....	....	....
1995-96	**Hartford**	**NHL**	**81**	**20**	**43**	**63**	**39**	**6**	**0**	**1**	**135**	**14.8**	**8**	....	....	....	....	....	....	....	....	....	....	....	....	....
1996-97	**Hartford**	**NHL**	**81**	**22**	**44**	**66**	**46**	**8**	**0**	**2**	**142**	**15.5**	**-16**	....	....	....	....	....	....	....	....	....	....	....	....	....
1997-98	**Calgary**	**NHL**	**81**	**17**	**27**	**44**	**32**	**6**	**1**	**2**	**138**	**12.3**	**-7**	....	....	....	....	....	....	....	....	....	....	....	....	....
1998-99	**Calgary**	**NHL**	**70**	**12**	**25**	**37**	**18**	**4**	**1**	**3**	**97**	**12.4**	**-12**	**1322**	**51.1**	**25**	**40**	**18:58**	....	....	....	....	....	....	....	....
	NHL Totals		**649**	**134**	**324**	**458**	**292**	**44**	**8**	**20**	**1005**	**13.3**		**1322**	**51.1**	**25**	**40**	**18:58**	**15**	**2**	**6**	**8**	**8**	**1**	**0**	**0**

OHL First All-Star Team (1988,1989)

Traded to **Hartford** by **Montreal** for Hartford's 2nd round choice (Valeri Bure) in 1992 Entry Draft, September 17, 1991. Transferred to **Carolina** after **Hartford** franchise relocated, June 25, 1997. Traded to **Calgary** by **Carolina** with Jean-Sebastien Giguere for Gary Roberts and Trevor Kidd, August 25, 1997. Signed as a free agent by **Vancouver**, August 19, 1999.

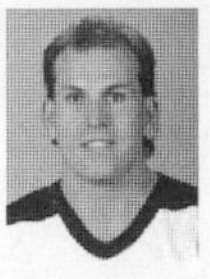

CHAMBERS, Shawn — DAL.

Defense. Shoots left. 6'2", 200 lbs. Born, Sterling Hts., MI, October 11, 1966. Minnesota's 1st choice, 4th overall, in 1987 Supplemental Draft.

			Regular Season																Playoffs							
Season	Club	League	GP	G	A	Pts	PIM	PP	SH	GW	S	%	+/–	TF	F%	H	SB	Min	GP	G	A	Pts	PIM	PP	SH	GW
1985-86	Alaska-Fairbanks	G.N.	25	15	21	36	34	....	....	....	....	....	....	....	....	....	....	....	....	....	....	....	....	....	....	....
1986-87	Alaska-Fairbanks	G.N.	17	11	19	30	84	....	....	....	....	....	....	....	....	....	....	....	....	....	....	....	....	....	....	....
	Seattle	WHL	28	8	25	33	58	....	....	....	....	....	....	....	....	....	....	....	....	....	....	....	....	....	....	....
	Fort Wayne	IHL	12	2	6	8	0	....	....	....	....	....	....	....	....	....	....	....	10	1	4	5	5	....	....	....
1987-88	**Minnesota**	**NHL**	**19**	**1**	**7**	**8**	**21**	**1**	**0**	**0**	**28**	**3.6**	**–6**	....	....	....	....	....	....	....	....	....	....	....	....	....
	Kalamazoo	IHL	19	1	6	7	22	....	....	....	....	....	....	....	....	....	....	....	....	....	....	....	....	....	....	....
1988-89	**Minnesota**	**NHL**	**72**	**5**	**19**	**24**	**80**	**1**	**2**	**0**	**131**	**3.8**	**–4**	....	....	....	....	....	**3**	**0**	**2**	**2**	**0**	**0**	**0**	**0**
1989-90	**Minnesota**	**NHL**	**78**	**8**	**18**	**26**	**81**	**0**	**1**	**2**	**116**	**6.9**	**–2**	....	....	....	....	....	**7**	**2**	**1**	**3**	**10**	**1**	**0**	**0**
1990-91	**Minnesota**	**NHL**	**29**	**1**	**3**	**4**	**24**	**0**	**0**	**0**	**55**	**1.8**	**2**	....	....	....	....	....	**23**	**0**	**7**	**7**	**16**	**0**	**0**	**0**
	Kalamazoo	IHL	3	1	1	2	0	....	....	....	....	....	....	....	....	....	....	....	....	....	....	....	....	....	....	....
1991-92	**Washington**	**NHL**	**2**	**0**	**0**	**0**	**2**	**0**	**0**	**0**	**1**	**0.0**	**–3**	....	....	....	....	....	....	....	....	....	....	....	....	....
	Baltimore	AHL	5	2	3	5	9	....	....	....	....	....	....	....	....	....	....	....	....	....	....	....	....	....	....	....
1992-93	**Tampa Bay**	**NHL**	**55**	**10**	**29**	**39**	**36**	**5**	**0**	**1**	**152**	**6.6**	**–21**	....	....	....	....	....	....	....	....	....	....	....	....	....
	Atlanta	IHL	6	0	2	2	18	....	....	....	....	....	....	....	....	....	....	....	....	....	....	....	....	....	....	....
1993-94	**Tampa Bay**	**NHL**	**66**	**11**	**23**	**34**	**23**	**6**	**1**	**1**	**142**	**7.7**	**–6**	....	....	....	....	....	....	....	....	....	....	....	....	....
1994-95	**Tampa Bay**	**NHL**	**24**	**2**	**12**	**14**	**6**	**1**	**0**	**0**	**44**	**4.5**	**0**	....	....	....	....	....	....	....	....	....	....	....	....	....
	♦ New Jersey	**NHL**	**21**	**2**	**5**	**7**	**6**	**1**	**0**	**0**	**23**	**8.7**	**2**	....	....	....	....	....	**20**	**4**	**5**	**9**	**2**	**2**	**0**	**0**
1995-96	**New Jersey**	**NHL**	**64**	**2**	**21**	**23**	**18**	**2**	**0**	**1**	**112**	**1.8**	**1**	....	....	....	....	....	....	....	....	....	....	....	....	....
1996-97	**New Jersey**	**NHL**	**73**	**4**	**17**	**21**	**19**	**1**	**0**	**0**	**114**	**3.5**	**17**	....	....	....	....	....	**10**	**1**	**6**	**7**	**6**	**1**	**0**	**0**
1997-98	**Dallas**	**NHL**	**57**	**2**	**22**	**24**	**26**	**1**	**1**	**0**	**73**	**2.7**	**11**	....	....	....	....	....	**14**	**0**	**3**	**3**	**20**	**0**	**0**	**0**
1998-99♦	**Dallas**	**NHL**	**61**	**2**	**9**	**11**	**18**	**1**	**0**	**1**	**82**	**2.4**	**6**	**0**	**0.0**	**59**	**76**	**17:23**	**17**	**0**	**2**	**2**	**18**	**0**	**0**	**0**
	NHL Totals		**621**	**50**	**185**	**235**	**360**	**20**	**5**	**6**	**1073**	**4.7**		**0**	**0.0**	**59**	**76**	**17:23**	**94**	**7**	**26**	**33**	**72**	**4**	**0**	**0**

Traded to **Washington** by **Minnesota** for Steve Maltais and Trent Klatt, June 21, 1991. •Missed majority of 1991-92 season after re-injuring knee that required surgery in May, 1991. Claimed by **Tampa Bay** from **Washington** in Expansion Draft, June 18, 1992. Traded to **New Jersey** by **Tampa Bay** with Danton Cole for Alexander Semak and Ben Hankinson, March 14, 1995. Signed as a free agent by **Dallas**, July 17, 1997.

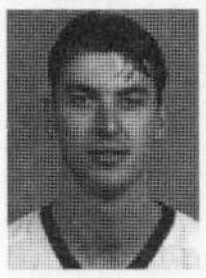

CHARA, Zdeno — (KHAH-rah, ZDEH-noh) — NYI

Defense. Shoots left. 6'9", 255 lbs. Born, Trencin, Czech., March 18, 1977. NY Islanders' 3rd choice, 56th overall, in 1996 Entry Draft.

			Regular Season																Playoffs							
Season	Club	League	GP	G	A	Pts	PIM	PP	SH	GW	S	%	+/–	TF	F%	H	SB	Min	GP	G	A	Pts	PIM	PP	SH	GW
1994-95	Dukla Trencin	Slovak-Jr.	2	0	0	0	0	....	....	....	....	....	....	....	....	....	....	....	....	....	....	....	....	....	....	....
	Dukla Trencin	Slovak-Jr.	30	22	22	44	113	....	....	....	....	....	....	....	....	....	....	....	....	....	....	....	....	....	....	....
1995-96	Dukla Trencin	Slovak-Jr.	22	1	13	14	80	....	....	....	....	....	....	....	....	....	....	....	....	....	....	....	....	....	....	....
	Piestany	Slovak-2	10	1	3	4	10	....	....	....	....	....	....	....	....	....	....	....	....	....	....	....	....	....	....	....
	Sparta Praha	Czech-Jr.	15	1	2	3	42	....	....	....	....	....	....	....	....	....	....	....	....	....	....	....	....	....	....	....
	Sparta Praha	Cze-Rep	1	0	0	0	0	....	....	....	....	....	....	....	....	....	....	....	....	....	....	....	....	....	....	....
1996-97	Prince George	WHL	49	3	19	22	120	....	....	....	....	....	....	....	....	....	....	....	15	1	7	8	45	....	....	....
1997-98	**NY Islanders**	**NHL**	**25**	**0**	**1**	**1**	**50**	**0**	**0**	**0**	**10**	**0.0**	**1**	....	....	....	....	....	....	....	....	....	....	....	....	....
	Kentucky	AHL	48	4	9	13	125	....	....	....	....	....	....	....	....	....	....	....	1	0	0	0	4	....	....	....
1998-99	**NY Islanders**	**NHL**	**59**	**2**	**6**	**8**	**83**	**0**	**1**	**0**	**56**	**3.6**	**–8**	**0**	**0.0**	**214**	**55**	**18:54**	....	....	....	....	....	....	....	....
	Lowell	AHL	23	2	2	4	47	....	....	....	....	....	....	....	....	....	....	....	....	....	....	....	....	....	....	....
	NHL Totals		**84**	**2**	**7**	**9**	**133**	**0**	**1**	**0**	**66**	**3.0**		**0**	**0.0**	**214**	**55**	**18:54**	....	....	....	....	....	....	....	....

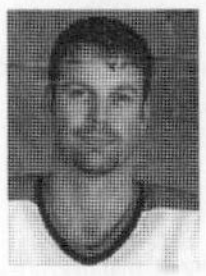

CHARRON, Eric — (shah-ROHN) — CGY.

Defense. Shoots left. 6'3", 195 lbs. Born, Verdun, Que., January 14, 1970. Montreal's 1st choice, 20th overall, in 1988 Entry Draft.

			Regular Season																Playoffs							
Season	Club	League	GP	G	A	Pts	PIM	PP	SH	GW	S	%	+/–	TF	F%	H	SB	Min	GP	G	A	Pts	PIM	PP	SH	GW
1986-87	Lac St-Louis	QAAA	41	1	8	9	92	....	....	....	....	....	....	....	....	....	....	....	....	....	....	....	....	....	....	....
1987-88	Trois-Rivieres	QMJHL	67	3	13	16	135	....	....	....	....	....	....	....	....	....	....	....	....	....	....	....	....	....	....	....
1988-89	Trois-Rivieres	QMJHL	38	2	16	18	111	....	....	....	....	....	....	....	....	....	....	....	....	....	....	....	....	....	....	....
	Verdun	QMJHL	28	2	15	17	66	....	....	....	....	....	....	....	....	....	....	....	....	....	....	....	....	....	....	....
	Sherbrooke	AHL	1	0	0	0	0	....	....	....	....	....	....	....	....	....	....	....	....	....	....	....	....	....	....	....
1989-90	St-Hyacinthe	QMJHL	68	13	38	51	152	....	....	....	....	....	....	....	....	....	....	....	11	3	4	7	67	....	....	....
	Sherbrooke	AHL	....	....	....	....	....	....	....	....	....	....	....	....	....	....	....	....	2	0	0	0	0	....	....	....
1990-91	Fredericton	AHL	71	1	11	12	108	....	....	....	....	....	....	....	....	....	....	....	2	1	0	1	29	....	....	....
1991-92	Fredericton	AHL	59	2	11	13	98	....	....	....	....	....	....	....	....	....	....	....	6	1	0	1	4	....	....	....
1992-93	**Montreal**	**NHL**	**3**	**0**	**0**	**0**	**2**	**0**	**0**	**0**	**0**	**0.0**	**0**	....	....	....	....	....	....	....	....	....	....	....	....	....
	Fredericton	AHL	54	3	13	16	93	....	....	....	....	....	....	....	....	....	....	....	....	....	....	....	....	....	....	....
	Atlanta	IHL	11	0	2	2	12	....	....	....	....	....	....	....	....	....	....	....	3	0	1	1	6	....	....	....
1993-94	**Tampa Bay**	**NHL**	**4**	**0**	**0**	**0**	**2**	**0**	**0**	**0**	**1**	**0.0**	**0**	....	....	....	....	....	....	....	....	....	....	....	....	....
	Atlanta	IHL	66	5	18	23	144	....	....	....	....	....	....	....	....	....	....	....	14	1	4	5	28	....	....	....
1994-95	**Tampa Bay**	**NHL**	**45**	**1**	**4**	**5**	**26**	**0**	**0**	**0**	**33**	**3.0**	**1**	....	....	....	....	....	....	....	....	....	....	....	....	....
1995-96	**Tampa Bay**	**NHL**	**14**	**0**	**0**	**0**	**18**	**0**	**0**	**0**	**11**	**0.0**	**–6**	....	....	....	....	....	....	....	....	....	....	....	....	....
	Washington	**NHL**	**4**	**0**	**1**	**1**	**4**	**0**	**0**	**0**	**2**	**0.0**	**3**	....	....	....	....	....	**6**	**0**	**0**	**0**	**8**	**0**	**0**	**0**
	Portland	AHL	45	0	8	8	88	....	....	....	....	....	....	....	....	....	....	....	20	1	1	2	33	....	....	....
1996-97	**Washington**	**NHL**	**25**	**1**	**1**	**2**	**20**	**0**	**0**	**0**	**11**	**9.1**	**1**	....	....	....	....	....	....	....	....	....	....	....	....	....
	Portland	AHL	29	6	8	14	55	....	....	....	....	....	....	....	....	....	....	....	5	0	3	3	0	....	....	....
1997-98	**Calgary**	**NHL**	**2**	**0**	**0**	**0**	**4**	**0**	**0**	**0**	**1**	**0.0**	**0**	....	....	....	....	....	....	....	....	....	....	....	....	....
	Saint John	AHL	56	8	20	28	136	....	....	....	....	....	....	....	....	....	....	....	20	1	7	8	55	....	....	....
1998-99	**Calgary**	**NHL**	**12**	**0**	**1**	**1**	**14**	**0**	**0**	**0**	**9**	**0.0**	**–6**	**0**	**0.0**	**12**	**13**	**13:45**	....	....	....	....	....	....	....	....
	Saint John	AHL	50	10	12	22	148	....	....	....	....	....	....	....	....	....	....	....	3	1	0	1	22	....	....	....
	NHL Totals		**109**	**2**	**7**	**9**	**90**	**0**	**0**	**0**	**68**	**2.9**		**0**	**0.0**	**12**	**13**	**13:45**	**6**	**0**	**0**	**0**	**8**	**0**	**0**	**0**

Traded to **Tampa Bay** by **Montreal** with Alain Cote and future considerations (Donald Dufresne, June 18, 1993) for Rob Ramage, March 20, 1993. Traded to **Washington** by **Tampa Bay** for Washington's 7th round choice (Eero Somervuori) in 1997 Entry Draft, November 16, 1995. Traded to **Calgary** by **Washington** for Calgary's 7th round choice (Nathan Forster) in 1998 Entry Draft, September 4, 1997.

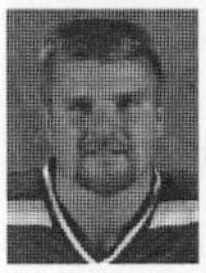

CHASE, Kelly — (CHAYS) — ST.L.

Right wing. Shoots right. 5'11", 201 lbs. Born, Porcupine Plain, Sask., October 25, 1967.

			Regular Season																Playoffs							
Season	Club	League	GP	G	A	Pts	PIM	PP	SH	GW	S	%	+/–	TF	F%	H	SB	Min	GP	G	A	Pts	PIM	PP	SH	GW
1985-86	Saskatoon	WHL	57	7	18	25	172	....	....	....	....	....	....	....	....	....	....	....	10	3	4	7	37	....	....	....
1986-87	Saskatoon	WHL	68	17	29	46	285	....	....	....	....	....	....	....	....	....	....	....	11	2	8	10	37	....	....	....
1987-88	Saskatoon	WHL	70	21	34	55	*343	....	....	....	....	....	....	....	....	....	....	....	9	3	5	8	32	....	....	....
1988-89	Peoria	IHL	38	14	7	21	278	....	....	....	....	....	....	....	....	....	....	....	....	....	....	....	....	....	....	....
1989-90	**St. Louis**	**NHL**	**43**	**1**	**3**	**4**	**244**	**0**	**0**	**0**	**9**	**11.1**	**–1**	....	....	....	....	....	**9**	**1**	**0**	**1**	**46**	**0**	**0**	**0**
	Peoria	IHL	10	1	2	3	76	....	....	....	....	....	....	....	....	....	....	....	....	....	....	....	....	....	....	....
1990-91	**St. Louis**	**NHL**	**2**	**1**	**0**	**1**	**15**	**0**	**0**	**1**	**1**	**100.0**	**1**	....	....	....	....	....	**6**	**0**	**0**	**0**	**18**	**0**	**0**	**0**
	Peoria	IHL	61	20	34	54	406	....	....	....	....	....	....	....	....	....	....	....	10	4	3	7	61	....	....	....
1991-92	**St. Louis**	**NHL**	**46**	**1**	**2**	**3**	**264**	**0**	**0**	**0**	**29**	**3.4**	**–6**	....	....	....	....	....	**1**	**0**	**0**	**0**	**7**	**0**	**0**	**0**
1992-93	**St. Louis**	**NHL**	**49**	**2**	**5**	**7**	**204**	**0**	**0**	**0**	**28**	**7.1**	**–9**	....	....	....	....	....	....	....	....	....	....	....	....	....
1993-94	**St. Louis**	**NHL**	**68**	**2**	**5**	**7**	**278**	**0**	**0**	**0**	**57**	**3.5**	**–5**	....	....	....	....	....	**4**	**0**	**1**	**1**	**6**	**0**	**0**	**0**
1994-95	**Hartford**	**NHL**	**28**	**0**	**4**	**4**	**141**	**0**	**0**	**0**	**15**	**0.0**	**1**	....	....	....	....	....	....	....	....	....	....	....	....	....
1995-96	**Hartford**	**NHL**	**55**	**2**	**4**	**6**	**230**	**0**	**0**	**1**	**19**	**10.5**	**–4**	....	....	....	....	....	....	....	....	....	....	....	....	....
1996-97	**Hartford**	**NHL**	**28**	**1**	**2**	**3**	**122**	**0**	**0**	**0**	**5**	**20.0**	**2**	....	....	....	....	....	....	....	....	....	....	....	....	....
	Toronto	**NHL**	**2**	**0**	**0**	**0**	**27**	**0**	**0**	**0**	**1**	**0.0**	**0**	....	....	....	....	....	....	....	....	....	....	....	....	....
1997-98	**St. Louis**	**NHL**	**67**	**4**	**3**	**7**	**231**	**0**	**0**	**1**	**29**	**13.8**	**10**	....	....	....	....	....	**7**	**0**	**0**	**0**	**23**	**0**	**0**	**0**
1998-99	**St. Louis**	**NHL**	**45**	**3**	**7**	**10**	**143**	**0**	**0**	**1**	**25**	**12.0**	**2**	**4**	**50.0**	**28**	**1**	**5:56**	....	....	....	....	....	....	....	....
	NHL Totals		**433**	**17**	**35**	**52**	**1899**	**0**	**0**	**4**	**218**	**7.8**		**4**	**50.0**	**28**	**1**	**5:56**	**27**	**1**	**1**	**2**	**100**	**0**	**0**	**0**

Won King Clancy Memorial Trophy (1998)

Signed as a free agent by **St. Louis**, February 23, 1988. Claimed by **Hartford** from **St. Louis** in NHL Waiver Draft, January 18, 1995. Traded to **Toronto** by **Hartford** for Toronto's 8th round choice (Hartford/Carolina selected Jaroslav Svoboda) in 1998 Entry Draft, March 18, 1997. Traded to **St. Louis** by **Toronto** for future considerations, September 30, 1997.

Season	Club	League	GP	G	A	Pts	PIM	PP	SH	GW	S	%	+/–	TF	F%	H	SB	Min	GP	G	A	Pts	PIM	PP	SH	GW
			Regular Season																Playoffs							

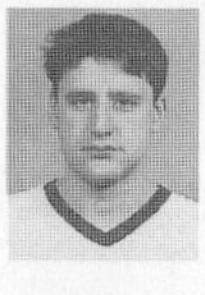

CHEBATURKIN, Vladimir

(cheh-bah-TOOR-kihn) **NYI**

Defense. Shoots left. 6'2", 213 lbs. Born, Tyumen, USSR, April 23, 1975. NY Islanders' 3rd choice, 66th overall, in 1993 Entry Draft.

Season	Club	League	GP	G	A	Pts	PIM	PP	SH	GW	S	%	+/–	TF	F%	H	SB	Min	GP	G	A	Pts	PIM	PP	SH	GW
1992-93	Kristal	CIS-2	Statistics Not Available																							
	Russia	WEC-A	6	0	1	1	0	....	....	....	....	....	....	....	....	....	....	....	....	....	....	....	....	....	....	....
1993-94	Kristall	CIS-2	42	4	4	8	38	....	....	....	....	....	....	....	....	....	....	....	....	....	....	....	....	....	....	....
1994-95	Kristall	CIS	52	2	6	8	90	....	....	....	....	....	....	....	....	....	....	....	....	....	....	....	....	....	....	....
1995-96	Kristall	CIS	44	1	6	7	30	....	....	....	....	....	....	....	....	....	....	....	....	....	....	....	....	....	....	....
1996-97	Utah	IHL	68	0	4	4	34	....	....	....	....	....	....	....	....	....	....	....	1	0	0	0	0	....	....	....
1997-98	**NY Islanders**	**NHL**	**2**	**0**	**2**	**2**	**0**	**0**	**0**	**0**	**0**	**0.0**	**–1**	....	....	....	....	....	....	....	....	....	....	....	....	....
	Kentucky	AHL	54	6	8	14	52	....	....	....	....	....	....	....	....	....	....	....	2	0	0	0	4	....	....	....
1998-99	**NY Islanders**	**NHL**	**8**	**0**	**0**	**0**	**12**	**0**	**0**	**0**	**4**	**0.0**	**6**	**0**	**0.0**	**27**	**8**	**17:12**	....	....	....	....	....	....	....	....
	Lowell	AHL	69	2	12	14	85	....	....	....	....	....	....	....	....	....	....	....	3	0	0	0	0	....	....	....
	NHL Totals		**10**	**0**	**2**	**2**	**12**	**0**	**0**	**0**	**4**	**0.0**		**0**	**0.0**	**27**	**8**	**17:12**	....	....	....	....	....	....	....	....

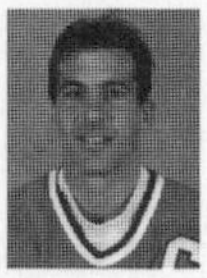

CHELIOS, Chris

(CHELL-EE-ohs) **DET.**

Defense. Shoots right. 6'1", 190 lbs. Born, Chicago, IL, January 25, 1962. Montreal's 5th choice, 40th overall, in 1981 Entry Draft.

Season	Club	League	GP	G	A	Pts	PIM	PP	SH	GW	S	%	+/–	TF	F%	H	SB	Min	GP	G	A	Pts	PIM	PP	SH	GW
1979-80	Moose Jaw	SJHL	53	12	31	43	118	....	....	....	....	....	....	....	....	....	....	....	....	....	....	....	....	....	....	....
1980-81	Moose Jaw	SJHL	54	23	64	87	175	....	....	....	....	....	....	....	....	....	....	....	....	....	....	....	....	....	....	....
1981-82	U. of Wisconsin	WCHA	43	6	43	49	50	....	....	....	....	....	....	....	....	....	....	....	....	....	....	....	....	....	....	....
1982-83	U. of Wisconsin	WCHA	26	9	17	26	50	....	....	....	....	....	....	....	....	....	....	....	....	....	....	....	....	....	....	....
1983-84	United States	Nat-Team	60	14	35	49	58	....	....	....	....	....	....	....	....	....	....	....	....	....	....	....	....	....	....	....
	United States	Olympics	6	0	4	4	8	....	....	....	....	....	....	....	....	....	....	....	....	....	....	....	....	....	....	....
	Montreal	**NHL**	**12**	**0**	**2**	**2**	**12**	**0**	**0**	**0**	**23**	**0.0**	**–5**	....	....	....	....	....	**15**	**1**	**9**	**10**	**17**	**1**	**0**	**0**
1984-85	**Montreal**	**NHL**	**74**	**9**	**55**	**64**	**87**	**2**	**1**	**0**	**199**	**4.5**	**11**	....	....	....	....	....	**9**	**2**	**8**	**10**	**17**	**2**	**0**	**0**
1985-86♦	**Montreal**	**NHL**	**41**	**8**	**26**	**34**	**67**	**2**	**0**	**0**	**101**	**7.9**	**4**	....	....	....	....	....	**20**	**2**	**9**	**11**	**49**	**1**	**0**	**0**
1986-87	**Montreal**	**NHL**	**71**	**11**	**33**	**44**	**124**	**6**	**0**	**2**	**141**	**7.8**	**–5**	....	....	....	....	....	**17**	**4**	**9**	**13**	**38**	**2**	**1**	**0**
1987-88	**Montreal**	**NHL**	**71**	**20**	**41**	**61**	**172**	**10**	**1**	**5**	**199**	**10.1**	**14**	....	....	....	....	....	**11**	**3**	**1**	**4**	**29**	**1**	**0**	**0**
1988-89	**Montreal**	**NHL**	**80**	**15**	**58**	**73**	**185**	**8**	**0**	**6**	**206**	**7.3**	**35**	....	....	....	....	....	**21**	**4**	**15**	**19**	**28**	**1**	**0**	**2**
1989-90	**Montreal**	**NHL**	**53**	**9**	**22**	**31**	**136**	**1**	**2**	**1**	**123**	**7.3**	**20**	....	....	....	....	....	**5**	**0**	**1**	**1**	**8**	**0**	**0**	**0**
1990-91	**Chicago**	**NHL**	**77**	**12**	**52**	**64**	**192**	**5**	**2**	**2**	**187**	**6.4**	**23**	....	....	....	....	....	**6**	**1**	**7**	**8**	**46**	**1**	**0**	**0**
1991-92	**Chicago**	**NHL**	**80**	**9**	**47**	**56**	**245**	**2**	**2**	**2**	**239**	**3.8**	**24**	....	....	....	....	....	**18**	**6**	**15**	**21**	**37**	**3**	**0**	**1**
1992-93	**Chicago**	**NHL**	**84**	**15**	**58**	**73**	**282**	**8**	**0**	**2**	**290**	**5.2**	**14**	....	....	....	....	....	**4**	**0**	**2**	**2**	**14**	**0**	**0**	**0**
1993-94	**Chicago**	**NHL**	**76**	**16**	**44**	**60**	**212**	**7**	**1**	**2**	**219**	**7.3**	**12**	....	....	....	....	....	**6**	**1**	**1**	**2**	**8**	**1**	**0**	**0**
1994-95	EC Biel	Switz.	3	0	3	3	4	....	....	....	....	....	....	....	....	....	....	....	....	....	....	....	....	....	....	....
	Chicago	**NHL**	**48**	**5**	**33**	**38**	**72**	**3**	**1**	**0**	**166**	**3.0**	**17**	....	....	....	....	....	**16**	**4**	**7**	**11**	**12**	**0**	**1**	**3**
1995-96	**Chicago**	**NHL**	**81**	**14**	**58**	**72**	**140**	**7**	**0**	**3**	**219**	**6.4**	**25**	....	....	....	....	....	**9**	**0**	**3**	**3**	**8**	**0**	**0**	**0**
1996-97	**Chicago**	**NHL**	**72**	**10**	**38**	**48**	**112**	**2**	**0**	**2**	**194**	**5.2**	**16**	....	....	....	....	....	**6**	**0**	**1**	**1**	**8**	**0**	**0**	**0**
1997-98	**Chicago**	**NHL**	**81**	**3**	**39**	**42**	**151**	**1**	**0**	**0**	**205**	**1.5**	**–7**	....	....	....	....	....	....	....	....	....	....	....	....	....
	United States	Olympics	4	2	0	2	2	....	....	....	....	....	....	....	....	....	....	....	....	....	....	....	....	....	....	....
1998-99	**Chicago**	**NHL**	**65**	**8**	**26**	**34**	**89**	**2**	**1**	**0**	**172**	**4.7**	**–4**	**4**	**25.0**	**72**	**109**	**27:19**	....	....	....	....	....	....	....	....
	Detroit	**NHL**	**10**	**1**	**1**	**2**	**4**	**1**	**0**	**1**	**15**	**6.7**	**5**	**0**	**0.0**	**11**	**7**	**22:21**	**10**	**0**	**4**	**4**	**14**	**0**	**0**	**0**
	NHL Totals		**1076**	**165**	**633**	**798**	**2282**	**67**	**11**	**28**	**2898**	**5.7**		**4**	**25.0**	**83**	**116**	**26:39**	**173**	**28**	**92**	**120**	**333**	**13**	**2**	**6**

WCHA Second All-Star Team (1983) • NCAA Championship All-Tournament Team (1983) • NHL All-Rookie Team (1985) • NHL First All-Star Team (1989, 1993, 1995, 1996) • Won James Norris Memorial Trophy (1989, 1993, 1996) • NHL Second All-Star Team (1991, 1997)

Played in NHL All-Star Game (1985, 1990, 1991, 1992, 1993, 1994, 1996, 1997, 1998)

Traded to **Chicago** by **Montreal** with Montreal's 2nd round choice (Michael Pomichter) in 1991 Entry Draft for Denis Savard, June 29, 1990. Traded to **Detroit** by **Chicago** for Anders Eriksson and Detroit's 1st round choices in 1999 (Steve McCarthy) and 2001 Entry Drafts, March 23, 1999.

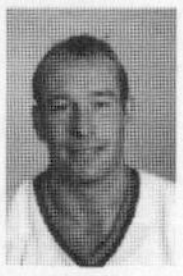

CHIASSON, Steve

(CHAY-sahn)

Defense. Shoots left. 6'1", 205 lbs. Born, Barrie, Ont., April 14, 1967. Detroit's 3rd choice, 50th overall, in 1985 Entry Draft.

Season	Club	League	GP	G	A	Pts	PIM	PP	SH	GW	S	%	+/–	TF	F%	H	SB	Min	GP	G	A	Pts	PIM	PP	SH	GW
1982-83	Peterborough	OMHA	40	25	35	60	120	....	....	....	....	....	....	....	....	....	....	....	....	....	....	....	....	....	....	....
1983-84	Guelph	OHL	55	1	9	10	112	....	....	....	....	....	....	....	....	....	....	....	....	....	....	....	....	....	....	....
1984-85	Guelph	OHL	61	8	22	30	139	....	....	....	....	....	....	....	....	....	....	....	....	....	....	....	....	....	....	....
1985-86	Guelph	OHL	54	12	30	42	126	....	....	....	....	....	....	....	....	....	....	....	18	10	10	20	37	....	....	....
1986-87	**Detroit**	**NHL**	**45**	**1**	**4**	**5**	**73**	**0**	**0**	**0**	**44**	**2.3**	**–7**	....	....	....	....	....	**2**	**0**	**0**	**0**	**19**	**0**	**0**	**0**
1987-88	**Detroit**	**NHL**	**29**	**2**	**9**	**11**	**57**	**0**	**0**	**0**	**45**	**4.4**	**15**	....	....	....	....	....	**9**	**2**	**2**	**4**	**31**	**1**	**0**	**0**
	Adirondack	AHL	23	6	11	17	58	....	....	....	....	....	....	....	....	....	....	....	....	....	....	....	....	....	....	....
1988-89	**Detroit**	**NHL**	**65**	**12**	**35**	**47**	**149**	**5**	**2**	**0**	**187**	**6.4**	**–6**	....	....	....	....	....	**5**	**2**	**1**	**3**	**6**	**1**	**0**	**0**
1989-90	**Detroit**	**NHL**	**67**	**14**	**28**	**42**	**114**	**4**	**0**	**2**	**190**	**7.4**	**–16**	....	....	....	....	....	....	....	....	....	....	....	....	....
1990-91	**Detroit**	**NHL**	**42**	**3**	**17**	**20**	**80**	**1**	**0**	**1**	**101**	**3.0**	**0**	....	....	....	....	....	**5**	**3**	**1**	**4**	**19**	**1**	**0**	**0**
1991-92	**Detroit**	**NHL**	**62**	**10**	**24**	**34**	**136**	**5**	**0**	**2**	**143**	**7.0**	**22**	....	....	....	....	....	**11**	**1**	**5**	**6**	**12**	**1**	**0**	**0**
1992-93	**Detroit**	**NHL**	**79**	**12**	**50**	**62**	**155**	**6**	**0**	**1**	**227**	**5.3**	**14**	....	....	....	....	....	**7**	**2**	**2**	**4**	**19**	**1**	**0**	**1**
1993-94	**Detroit**	**NHL**	**82**	**13**	**33**	**46**	**122**	**4**	**1**	**2**	**238**	**5.5**	**17**	....	....	....	....	....	**7**	**2**	**3**	**5**	**2**	**2**	**0**	**1**
1994-95	**Calgary**	**NHL**	**45**	**2**	**23**	**25**	**39**	**1**	**0**	**0**	**110**	**1.8**	**10**	....	....	....	....	....	**7**	**1**	**2**	**3**	**9**	**1**	**0**	**0**
1995-96	**Calgary**	**NHL**	**76**	**8**	**25**	**33**	**62**	**5**	**0**	**2**	**175**	**4.6**	**3**	....	....	....	....	....	**4**	**2**	**1**	**3**	**0**	**0**	**0**	**0**
1996-97	**Calgary**	**NHL**	**47**	**5**	**11**	**16**	**32**	**1**	**2**	**1**	**112**	**4.5**	**–11**	....	....	....	....	....	....	....	....	....	....	....	....	....
	Hartford	**NHL**	**18**	**3**	**11**	**14**	**7**	**3**	**0**	**0**	**56**	**5.4**	**–10**	....	....	....	....	....	....	....	....	....	....	....	....	....
1997-98	**Carolina**	**NHL**	**66**	**7**	**27**	**34**	**65**	**6**	**0**	**0**	**173**	**4.0**	**–2**	....	....	....	....	....	....	....	....	....	....	....	....	....
1998-99	**Carolina**	**NHL**	**28**	**1**	**8**	**9**	**16**	**1**	**0**	**0**	**74**	**1.4**	**7**	**0**	**0.0**	**37**	**25**	**23:11**	**6**	**1**	**2**	**3**	**2**	**1**	**0**	**0**
	NHL Totals		**751**	**93**	**305**	**398**	**1107**	**42**	**5**	**11**	**1875**	**5.0**		**0**	**0.0**	**37**	**25**	**23:11**	**63**	**16**	**19**	**35**	**119**	**9**	**0**	**2**

Won Stafford Smythe Memorial Trophy (Memorial Cup Tournament MVP) (1986)

Played in NHL All-Star Game (1993)

Traded to **Calgary** by **Detroit** for Mike Vernon, June 29, 1994. Traded to **Hartford** by **Calgary** with Colorado's 3rd round choice (previously acquired, Hartford/Carolina selected Francis Lessard) in 1997 Entry Draft for Hnat Domenichelli, Glen Featherstone, New Jersey's 2nd round choice (previously acquired, Calgary selected Dimitri Kokorev) in 1997 Entry Draft and Vancouver's 3rd round choice (previously acquired, Calgary selected Paul Manning) in 1998 Entry Draft, March 5, 1997. Transferred to **Carolina** after **Hartford** franchise relocated, June 25, 1997. • Died of injuries suffered in single vehicle automobile accident, May 3, 1999.

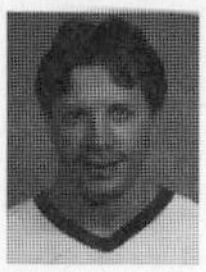

CHORSKE, Tom

(CHOHR-skee)

Left wing. Shoots right. 6'1", 212 lbs. Born, Minneapolis, MN, September 18, 1966. Montreal's 2nd choice, 16th overall, in 1985 Entry Draft.

Season	Club	League	GP	G	A	Pts	PIM	PP	SH	GW	S	%	+/–	TF	F%	H	SB	Min	GP	G	A	Pts	PIM	PP	SH	GW
1984-85	Minn-Southwest	H.S.	23	44	26	70	....	....	....	....	....	....	....	....	....	....	....	....	....	....	....	....	....	....	....	....
1985-86	U. of Minnesota	WCHA	39	6	4	10	16	....	....	....	....	....	....	....	....	....	....	....	....	....	....	....	....	....	....	....
1986-87	U. of Minnesota	WCHA	47	20	22	42	20	....	....	....	....	....	....	....	....	....	....	....	....	....	....	....	....	....	....	....
1987-88	United States	Nat-Team	36	9	16	25	24	....	....	....	....	....	....	....	....	....	....	....	....	....	....	....	....	....	....	....
1988-89	U. of Minnesota	WCHA	37	25	24	49	28	....	....	....	....	....	....	....	....	....	....	....	....	....	....	....	....	....	....	....
1989-90	**Montreal**	**NHL**	**14**	**3**	**1**	**4**	**2**	**0**	**0**	**0**	**19**	**15.8**	**2**	....	....	....	....	....	....	....	....	....	....	....	....	....
	Sherbrooke	AHL	59	22	24	46	54	....	....	....	....	....	....	....	....	....	....	....	12	4	4	8	8	....	....	....
1990-91	**Montreal**	**NHL**	**57**	**9**	**11**	**20**	**32**	**3**	**0**	**1**	**82**	**11.0**	**–8**	....	....	....	....	....	....	....	....	....	....	....	....	....
1991-92	**New Jersey**	**NHL**	**76**	**19**	**17**	**36**	**32**	**0**	**3**	**2**	**143**	**13.3**	**8**	....	....	....	....	....	**7**	**0**	**3**	**3**	**4**	**0**	**0**	**0**
1992-93	**New Jersey**	**NHL**	**50**	**7**	**12**	**19**	**25**	**0**	**0**	**1**	**63**	**11.1**	**–1**	....	....	....	....	....	**1**	**0**	**0**	**0**	**0**	**0**	**0**	**0**
	Utica	AHL	6	1	4	5	2	....	....	....	....	....	....	....	....	....	....	....	....	....	....	....	....	....	....	....
1993-94	**New Jersey**	**NHL**	**76**	**21**	**20**	**41**	**32**	**1**	**1**	**4**	**131**	**16.0**	**14**	....	....	....	....	....	**20**	**4**	**3**	**7**	**0**	**0**	**0**	**1**
1994-95	HC Milano	Italy	7	11	5	16	6	....	....	....	....	....	....	....	....	....	....	....	....	....	....	....	....	....	....	....
	♦ New Jersey	**NHL**	**42**	**10**	**8**	**18**	**16**	**0**	**0**	**2**	**59**	**16.9**	**–4**	....	....	....	....	....	**17**	**1**	**5**	**6**	**4**	**0**	**0**	**0**
1995-96	**Ottawa**	**NHL**	**72**	**15**	**14**	**29**	**21**	**0**	**2**	**1**	**118**	**12.7**	**–9**	....	....	....	....	....	....	....	....	....	....	....	....	....
1996-97	**Ottawa**	**NHL**	**68**	**18**	**8**	**26**	**16**	**1**	**1**	**1**	**116**	**15.5**	**–1**	....	....	....	....	....	**5**	**0**	**1**	**1**	**2**	**0**	**0**	**0**
1997-98	**NY Islanders**	**NHL**	**82**	**12**	**23**	**35**	**39**	**1**	**4**	**2**	**132**	**9.1**	**7**	....	....	....	....	....	....	....	....	....	....	....	....	....

			Regular Season																Playoffs							
Season	Club	League	GP	G	A	Pts	PIM	PP	SH	GW	S	%	+/-	TF	F%	H	SB	Min	GP	G	A	Pts	PIM	PP	SH	GW
1998-99	**NY Islanders**	**NHL**	**2**	**0**	**1**	**1**	**2**	0	0	0	9	0.0	1	0	0.0	2	0	12:54	....	....	....	....	....	....	....	....
	Washington	**NHL**	**17**	**0**	**2**	**2**	**4**	0	0	0	22	0.0	–4	4	50.0	15	5	11:26	....	....	....	....	....	....	....	....
	Calgary	**NHL**	**7**	**0**	**0**	**0**	**2**	0	0	0	0	13.0	–5	7	71.4	7	2	13:48	....	....	....	....	....	....	....	....
	NHL Totals		**563**	**114**	**117**	**231**	**223**	**6**	**11**	**14**	**894**	**12.8**		**11**	**63.6**	**24**	**7**	**12:11**	**50**	**5**	**12**	**17**	**10**	**0**	**0**	**1**

WCHA First All-Star Team (1989)

Traded to **New Jersey** by **Montreal** with Stephane Richer for Kirk Muller and Roland Melanson, September 20, 1991. Claimed on waivers by **Ottawa** from **New Jersey**, October 5, 1995. Claimed by **NY Islanders** from **Ottawa** in NHL Waiver Draft, September 28, 1997. Traded to **Washington** by **NY Islanders** with NY Islanders' 8th round choice (Maxim Orlov) in 1999 Entry Draft for Washington's 6th round choice (Bjorn Melin) in 1999 Entry Draft, October 16, 1998. Traded to **Calgary** by **Washington** for Calgary's 7th round choice in 2000 Entry Draft and Washington's 9th round choice (previously acquired) in 2000 Entry Draft, March 22, 1999.

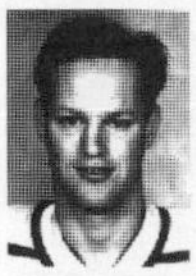

CHRISTIAN, Jeff — CHI.

Left wing. Shoots left. 6'2", 210 lbs. Born, Burlington, Ont., July 30, 1970. New Jersey's 2nd choice, 23rd overall, in 1988 Entry Draft.

1986-87	Dundas	OJHL-C	29	20	34	54	42	....	....	....	....	....	....	....	....	....	....	....	....	....	....	....	....	....	....	....
1987-88	London	OHL	64	15	29	44	154	....	....	....	....	....	....	....	....	....	....	....	9	1	5	6	27	....	....	....
1988-89	London	OHL	60	27	30	57	221	....	....	....	....	....	....	....	....	....	....	....	20	3	4	7	56	....	....	....
1989-90	London	OHL	18	14	7	21	64	....	....	....	....	....	....	....	....	....	....	....	....	....	....	....	....	....	....	....
	Owen Sound	OHL	37	19	26	45	145	....	....	....	....	....	....	....	....	....	....	....	10	6	7	13	43	....	....	....
1990-91	Utica	AHL	80	24	42	66	165	....	....	....	....	....	....	....	....	....	....	....	....	....	....	....	....	....	....	....
1991-92	**New Jersey**	**NHL**	**2**	**0**	**0**	**0**	**2**	**0**	**0**	**0**	**1**	**0.0**	**0**	....	....	....	....	....	....	....	....	....	....	....	....	....
	Utica	AHL	76	27	24	51	198	....	....	....	....	....	....	....	....	....	....	....	4	0	0	0	16	....	....	....
1992-93	Utica	AHL	22	4	6	10	39	....	....	....	....	....	....	....	....	....	....	....	....	....	....	....	....	....	....	....
	Hamilton	AHL	11	2	5	7	35	....	....	....	....	....	....	....	....	....	....	....	....	....	....	....	....	....	....	....
	Cincinnati	IHL	36	5	12	17	113	....	....	....	....	....	....	....	....	....	....	....	....	....	....	....	....	....	....	....
1993-94	Albany	AHL	76	34	43	77	227	....	....	....	....	....	....	....	....	....	....	....	5	1	2	3	19	....	....	....
1994-95	**Pittsburgh**	**NHL**	**1**	**0**	**0**	**0**	**0**	**0**	**0**	**0**	**2**	**0.0**	**0**	....	....	....	....	....	....	....	....	....	....	....	....	....
	Cleveland	IHL	56	13	24	37	126	....	....	....	....	....	....	....	....	....	....	....	2	0	1	1	8	....	....	....
1995-96	**Pittsburgh**	**NHL**	**3**	**0**	**0**	**0**	**2**	**0**	**0**	**0**	**0**	**0.0**	**0**	....	....	....	....	....	....	....	....	....	....	....	....	....
	Cleveland	IHL	66	23	32	55	131	....	....	....	....	....	....	....	....	....	....	....	3	0	1	1	8	....	....	....
1996-97	**Pittsburgh**	**NHL**	**11**	**2**	**2**	**4**	**13**	**0**	**0**	**0**	**18**	**11.1**	**–3**	....	....	....	....	....	....	....	....	....	....	....	....	....
	Cleveland	IHL	69	40	40	80	262	....	....	....	....	....	....	....	....	....	....	....	12	6	8	14	44	....	....	....
1997-98	**Phoenix**	**NHL**	**1**	**0**	**0**	**0**	**0**	**0**	**0**	**0**	**0**	**0.0**	**–1**	....	....	....	....	....	....	....	....	....	....	....	....	....
	Las Vegas	IHL	30	12	15	27	90	....	....	....	....	....	....	....	....	....	....	....	4	2	2	4	20	....	....	....
1998-99	Houston	IHL	80	45	41	86	252	....	....	....	....	....	....	....	....	....	....	....	18	4	12	16	32	....	....	....
	NHL Totals		**18**	**2**	**2**	**4**	**17**	**0**	**0**	**0**	**21**	**9.5**		....	....	....	....	....	....	....	....	....	....	....	....	....

Signed as a free agent by **Pittsburgh**, August 2, 1994. Signed as a free agent by **Phoenix**, July 28, 1997. Signed as a free agent by **Chicago**, August 25, 1999.

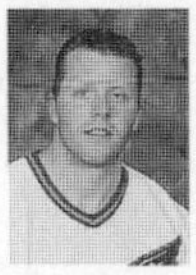

CHURCH, Brad — EDM.

Left wing. Shoots left. 6'1", 210 lbs. Born, Dauphin, Man., November 14, 1976. Washington's 1st choice, 17th overall, in 1995 Entry Draft.

1991-92	Parkland	MAHA	26	15	17	32	62	....	....	....	....	....	....	....	....	....	....	....	....	....	....	....	....	....	....	....
1992-93	Dauphin	MJHL	45	15	23	38	80	....	....	....	....	....	....	....	....	....	....	....	....	....	....	....	....	....	....	....
1993-94	Prince Albert	WHL	71	33	20	53	197	....	....	....	....	....	....	....	....	....	....	....	....	....	....	....	....	....	....	....
1994-95	Prince Albert	WHL	62	26	24	50	184	....	....	....	....	....	....	....	....	....	....	....	15	6	9	15	32	....	....	....
1995-96	Prince Albert	WHL	69	42	46	88	123	....	....	....	....	....	....	....	....	....	....	....	18	15	*20	*35	74	....	....	....
1996-97	Portland	AHL	50	4	8	12	92	....	....	....	....	....	....	....	....	....	....	....	1	0	0	0	0	....	....	....
1997-98	**Washington**	**NHL**	**2**	**0**	**0**	**0**	**0**	**0**	**0**	**0**	**4**	**0.0**	**0**	....	....	....	....	....	....	....	....	....	....	....	....	....
	Portland	AHL	59	6	5	11	98	....	....	....	....	....	....	....	....	....	....	....	9	2	4	6	14	....	....	....
1998-99	Portland	AHL	10	1	3	4	18	....	....	....	....	....	....	....	....	....	....	....	....	....	....	....	....	....	....	....
	Hampton Roads	ECHL	24	10	9	19	129	....	....	....	....	....	....	....	....	....	....	....	....	....	....	....	....	....	....	....
	Hamilton	AHL	9	0	2	2	4	....	....	....	....	....	....	....	....	....	....	....	....	....	....	....	....	....	....	....
	New Orleans	ECHL	5	3	4	7	4	....	....	....	....	....	....	....	....	....	....	....	11	1	1	2	22	....	....	....
	NHL Totals		**2**	**0**	**0**	**0**	**0**	**0**	**0**	**0**	**4**	**0.0**		....	....	....	....	....	....	....	....	....	....	....	....	....

Traded to **Edmonton** by **Washington** for the rights to Barrie Moore, February 3, 1999.

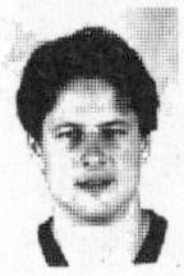

CHYZOWSKI, Dave (chih-ZOW-skee)

Left wing. Shoots left. 6'1", 190 lbs. Born, Edmonton, Alta., July 11, 1971. NY Islanders' 1st choice, 2nd overall, in 1989 Entry Draft.

1987-88	Kamloops	WHL	66	16	17	33	117	....	....	....	....	....	....	....	....	....	....	....	18	2	4	6	26	....	....	....
1988-89	Kamloops	WHL	68	56	48	104	139	....	....	....	....	....	....	....	....	....	....	....	16	15	13	28	32	....	....	....
1989-90	Kamloops	WHL	4	5	2	7	17	....	....	....	....	....	....	....	....	....	....	....	17	11	6	17	46	....	....	....
	NY Islanders	**NHL**	**34**	**8**	**6**	**14**	**45**	**3**	**0**	**1**	**59**	**13.6**	**–4**	....	....	....	....	....	....	....	....	....	....	....	....	....
	Springfield	AHL	4	0	0	0	7	....	....	....	....	....	....	....	....	....	....	....	....	....	....	....	....	....	....	....
1990-91	**NY Islanders**	**NHL**	**56**	**5**	**9**	**14**	**61**	**0**	**0**	**0**	**66**	**7.6**	**–19**	....	....	....	....	....	....	....	....	....	....	....	....	....
	Capital District	AHL	7	3	6	9	22	....	....	....	....	....	....	....	....	....	....	....	....	....	....	....	....	....	....	....
1991-92	**NY Islanders**	**NHL**	**12**	**1**	**1**	**2**	**17**	**0**	**0**	**0**	**18**	**5.6**	**–4**	....	....	....	....	....	....	....	....	....	....	....	....	....
	Capital District	AHL	55	15	18	33	121	....	....	....	....	....	....	....	....	....	....	....	6	1	1	2	23	....	....	....
1992-93	Capital District	AHL	66	15	21	36	177	....	....	....	....	....	....	....	....	....	....	....	3	2	0	2	0	....	....	....
1993-94	**NY Islanders**	**NHL**	**3**	**1**	**0**	**1**	**4**	**0**	**0**	**0**	**4**	**25.0**	**–1**	....	....	....	....	....	**2**	**0**	**0**	**0**	**0**	**0**	**0**	**0**
	Salt Lake	IHL	66	27	13	40	151	....	....	....	....	....	....	....	....	....	....	....	....	....	....	....	....	....	....	....
1994-95	**NY Islanders**	**NHL**	**13**	**0**	**0**	**0**	**11**	**0**	**0**	**0**	**11**	**0.0**	**–2**	....	....	....	....	....	....	....	....	....	....	....	....	....
	Kalamazoo	IHL	4	0	4	4	8	....	....	....	....	....	....	....	....	....	....	....	16	9	5	14	27	....	....	....
1995-96	Adirondack	AHL	80	44	39	83	160	....	....	....	....	....	....	....	....	....	....	....	3	0	0	0	6	....	....	....
1996-97	**Chicago**	**NHL**	**8**	**0**	**0**	**0**	**6**	**0**	**0**	**0**	**6**	**0.0**	**1**	....	....	....	....	....	....	....	....	....	....	....	....	....
	Indianapolis	IHL	76	34	40	74	261	....	....	....	....	....	....	....	....	....	....	....	4	0	2	2	38	....	....	....
1997-98	Orlando	IHL	17	9	7	16	32	....	....	....	....	....	....	....	....	....	....	....	....	....	....	....	....	....	....	....
	San Antonio	IHL	10	1	5	6	39	....	....	....	....	....	....	....	....	....	....	....	....	....	....	....	....	....	....	....
	Kansas City	IHL	38	19	14	33	88	....	....	....	....	....	....	....	....	....	....	....	11	5	4	9	11	....	....	....
1998-99	Kansas City	IHL	67	24	15	39	147	....	....	....	....	....	....	....	....	....	....	....	....	....	....	....	....	....	....	....
	NHL Totals		**126**	**15**	**16**	**31**	**144**	**3**	**0**	**1**	**164**	**9.1**		....	....	....	....	....	**2**	**0**	**0**	**0**	**0**	**0**	**0**	**0**

WHL West All-Star Team (1989)

Signed as a free agent by **Detroit**, August 29, 1995. Signed as a free agent by **Chicago**, September 26, 1996.

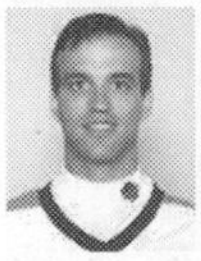

CIAVAGLIA, Peter (see-a-VIHG-lee-a)

Center. Shoots left. 5'10", 173 lbs. Born, Albany, NY, July 15, 1969. Calgary's 8th choice, 145th overall, in 1987 Entry Draft.

1985-86	N. Wheatfield	NYJHL	60	84	113	197	....	....	....	....	....	....	....	....	....	....	....	....	....	....	....	....	....	....	....	....
1986-87	N. Wheatfield	NYJHL	58	53	84	137	....	....	....	....	....	....	....	....	....	....	....	....	....	....	....	....	....	....	....	....
1987-88	Harvard University	ECAC	30	10	23	33	16	....	....	....	....	....	....	....	....	....	....	....	....	....	....	....	....	....	....	....
1988-89	Harvard University	ECAC	34	15	48	63	36	....	....	....	....	....	....	....	....	....	....	....	....	....	....	....	....	....	....	....
1989-90	Harvard University	ECAC	28	17	18	35	22	....	....	....	....	....	....	....	....	....	....	....	....	....	....	....	....	....	....	....
1990-91	Harvard University	ECAC	27	24	*38	*62	2	....	....	....	....	....	....	....	....	....	....	....	....	....	....	....	....	....	....	....
1991-92	**Buffalo**	**NHL**	**2**	**0**	**0**	**0**	**0**	**0**	**0**	**0**	**1**	**0.0**	**1**	....	....	....	....	....	....	....	....	....	....	....	....	....
	Rochester	AHL	77	37	61	98	16	....	....	....	....	....	....	....	....	....	....	....	6	2	5	7	6	....	....	....
1992-93	**Buffalo**	**NHL**	**3**	**0**	**0**	**0**	**0**	**0**	**0**	**0**	**2**	**0.0**	**0**	....	....	....	....	....	....	....	....	....	....	....	....	....
	Rochester	AHL	64	35	67	102	32	....	....	....	....	....	....	....	....	....	....	....	17	9	16	25	12	....	....	....
1993-94	United States	Nat-Team	18	2	9	11	6	....	....	....	....	....	....	....	....	....	....	....	....	....	....	....	....	....	....	....
	Leksands IF	Sweden	39	14	18	32	34	....	....	....	....	....	....	....	....	....	....	....	4	1	2	3	0	....	....	....
	United States	Olympics	8	2	4	6	0	....	....	....	....	....	....	....	....	....	....	....	....	....	....	....	....	....	....	....
1994-95	Detroit	IHL	73	22	59	81	83	....	....	....	....	....	....	....	....	....	....	....	5	1	1	2	6	....	....	....
1995-96	Detroit	IHL	75	22	56	78	38	....	....	....	....	....	....	....	....	....	....	....	12	6	11	17	12	....	....	....

			Regular Season																Playoffs							
Season	Club	League	GP	G	A	Pts	PIM	PP	SH	GW	S	%	+/-	TF	F%	H	SB	Min	GP	G	A	Pts	PIM	PP	SH	GW
1996-97	Detroit	IHL	72	21	51	72	54	....	....	....	....	....	....	....	....	....	....	....	21	*14	19	*33	32	....	....	....
1997-98	Detroit	IHL	35	11	30	41	10	....	....	....	....	....	....	....	....	....	....	....	23	8	11	19	12	....	....	....
1998-99	Detroit	IHL	59	27	31	58	33	....	....	....	....	....	....	....	....	....	....	....	11	1	8	9	10	....	....	....
	NHL Totals		**5**	**0**	**0**	**0**	**0**	**0**	**0**	**0**	**3**	**0.0**		....	....	....	....	....	....	....	....	....	....	....	....	....

ECAC Second All-Star Team (1989, 1991) • NCAA East Second All-American Team (1991) • Won "Bud" Poile Trophy (Playoff MVP - IHL) (1997)

Signed as a free agent by **Buffalo**, August 30, 1991.

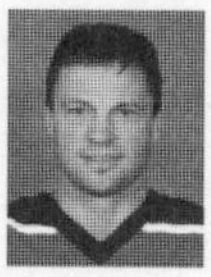

CICCARELLI, Dino

(sih-sih-REHL-ee)

Right wing. Shoots right. 5'10", 185 lbs. Born, Sarnia, Ont., February 8, 1960.

Season	Club	League	GP	G	A	Pts	PIM	PP	SH	GW	S	%	+/-	TF	F%	H	SB	Min	GP	G	A	Pts	PIM	PP	SH	GW
1975-76	Sarnia	OJHL-B	40	45	43	88		....	....	....	....	....	....	....	....	....	....	....	....	....	....	....	....	....	....	....
1976-77	London	OHA	66	39	43	82	45	....	....	....	....	....	....	....	....	....	....	....	....	....	....	....	....	....	....	....
1977-78	London	OHA	68	72	70	142	49	....	....	....	....	....	....	....	....	....	....	....	9	6	10	16	6	....	....	....
1978-79	London	OHA	30	8	11	19	35	....	....	....	....	....	....	....	....	....	....	....	7	3	5	8	0	....	....	....
1979-80	London	OHA	62	50	53	103	72	....	....	....	....	....	....	....	....	....	....	....	5	2	6	8	15	....	....	....
	Oklahoma City	CHL	6	3	2	5	0	....	....	....	....	....	....	....	....	....	....	....	....	....	....	....	....	....	....	....
1980-81	**Minnesota**	**NHL**	**32**	**18**	**12**	**30**	**29**	**8**	**0**	**0**	**126**	**14.3**	**2**	....	....	....	....	....	**19**	**14**	**7**	**21**	**25**	**5**	**0**	**3**
	Oklahoma City	CHL	48	32	25	57	45	....	....	....	....	....	....	....	....	....	....	....	....	....	....	....	....	....	....	....
1981-82	**Minnesota**	**NHL**	**76**	**55**	**51**	**106**	**138**	**20**	**0**	**4**	**289**	**19.0**	**14**	....	....	....	....	....	**4**	**3**	**1**	**4**	**2**	**2**	**0**	**1**
1982-83	**Minnesota**	**NHL**	**77**	**37**	**38**	**75**	**94**	**14**	**0**	**4**	**210**	**17.6**	**16**	....	....	....	....	....	**9**	**4**	**6**	**10**	**11**	**1**	**0**	**2**
1983-84	**Minnesota**	**NHL**	**79**	**38**	**33**	**71**	**58**	**16**	**0**	**2**	**211**	**18.0**	**1**	....	....	....	....	....	**16**	**4**	**5**	**9**	**27**	**1**	**0**	**1**
1984-85	**Minnesota**	**NHL**	**51**	**15**	**17**	**32**	**41**	**5**	**0**	**0**	**133**	**11.3**	**-10**	....	....	....	....	....	**9**	**3**	**3**	**6**	**8**	**1**	**0**	**0**
1985-86	**Minnesota**	**NHL**	**75**	**44**	**45**	**89**	**51**	**19**	**0**	**5**	**262**	**16.8**	**12**	....	....	....	....	....	**5**	**0**	**1**	**1**	**6**	**0**	**0**	**0**
1986-87	**Minnesota**	**NHL**	**80**	**52**	**51**	**103**	**88**	**22**	**0**	**5**	**255**	**20.4**	**10**	....	....	....	....	....	....	....	....	....	....	....	....	....
1987-88	**Minnesota**	**NHL**	**67**	**41**	**45**	**86**	**79**	**13**	**1**	**2**	**262**	**15.6**	**-29**	....	....	....	....	....	....	....	....	....	....	....	....	....
1988-89	**Minnesota**	**NHL**	**65**	**32**	**27**	**59**	**64**	**13**	**0**	**5**	**208**	**15.4**	**-16**	....	....	....	....	....	....	....	....	....	....	....	....	....
	Washington	**NHL**	**11**	**12**	**3**	**15**	**12**	**3**	**0**	**3**	**39**	**30.8**	**10**	....	....	....	....	....	**6**	**3**	**3**	**6**	**12**	**3**	**0**	**0**
1989-90	**Washington**	**NHL**	**80**	**41**	**38**	**79**	**122**	**10**	**0**	**6**	**267**	**15.4**	**-5**	....	....	....	....	....	**8**	**8**	**3**	**11**	**6**	**1**	**0**	**1**
1990-91	**Washington**	**NHL**	**54**	**21**	**18**	**39**	**66**	**2**	**0**	**2**	**186**	**11.3**	**-17**	....	....	....	....	....	**11**	**5**	**4**	**9**	**22**	**3**	**0**	**2**
1991-92	**Washington**	**NHL**	**78**	**38**	**38**	**76**	**78**	**13**	**0**	**7**	**279**	**13.6**	**-10**	....	....	....	....	....	**7**	**5**	**4**	**9**	**14**	**1**	**0**	**0**
1992-93	**Detroit**	**NHL**	**82**	**41**	**56**	**97**	**81**	**21**	**0**	**8**	**200**	**20.5**	**12**	....	....	....	....	....	**7**	**4**	**2**	**6**	**16**	**3**	**0**	**0**
1993-94	**Detroit**	**NHL**	**66**	**28**	**29**	**57**	**73**	**12**	**0**	**1**	**153**	**18.3**	**10**	....	....	....	....	....	**7**	**5**	**2**	**7**	**14**	**1**	**0**	**0**
1994-95	**Detroit**	**NHL**	**42**	**16**	**27**	**43**	**39**	**6**	**0**	**3**	**106**	**15.1**	**12**	....	....	....	....	....	**16**	**9**	**2**	**11**	**22**	**6**	**0**	**2**
1995-96	**Detroit**	**NHL**	**64**	**22**	**21**	**43**	**99**	**13**	**0**	**5**	**107**	**20.6**	**14**	....	....	....	....	....	**17**	**6**	**2**	**8**	**26**	**6**	**0**	**1**
1996-97	**Tampa Bay**	**NHL**	**77**	**35**	**25**	**60**	**116**	**12**	**0**	**6**	**229**	**15.3**	**-11**	....	....	....	....	....	....	....	....	....	....	....	....	....
1997-98	**Tampa Bay**	**NHL**	**34**	**11**	**6**	**17**	**42**	**3**	**0**	**3**	**104**	**10.6**	**-14**	....	....	....	....	....	....	....	....	....	....	....	....	....
	Florida	**NHL**	**28**	**5**	**11**	**16**	**28**	**2**	**0**	**1**	**57**	**8.8**	**-2**	....	....	....	....	....	....	....	....	....	....	....	....	....
1998-99	**Florida**	**NHL**	**14**	**6**	**1**	**7**	**27**	**5**	**0**	**1**	**23**	**26.1**	**-1**	**1**	**0.0**	**8**	**1**	**13:15**	....	....	....	....	....	....	....	....
	NHL Totals		**1232**	**608**	**592**	**1200**	**1425**	**232**	**1**	**73**	**3706**	**16.4**		**1**	**0.0**	**8**	**1**	**13:15**	**141**	**73**	**45**	**118**	**211**	**34**	**0**	**13**

OHA Second All-Star Team (1978)

Played in NHL All-Star Game (1982, 1983, 1989, 1997)

Signed as a free agent by **Minnesota**, September 28, 1979. Traded to **Washington** by **Minnesota** with Bob Rouse for Mike Gartner and Larry Murphy, March 7, 1989. Traded to **Detroit** by **Washington** for Kevin Miller, June 20, 1992. Traded to **Tampa Bay** by **Detroit** for future considerations, August 27, 1996. Traded to **Florida** by **Tampa Bay** with Jeff Norton for Mark Fitzpatrick and Jody Hull, January 15, 1998. • Missed majority of 1998-99 season with back injury suffered in game vs. Chicago, November 4, 1998.

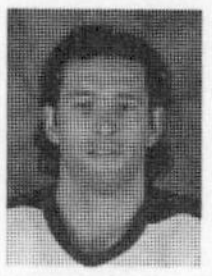

CICCONE, Enrico

(CHIH-koh-nee)

Defense. Shoots left. 6'5", 220 lbs. Born, Montreal, Que., April 10, 1970. Minnesota's 5th choice, 92nd overall, in 1990 Entry Draft.

Season	Club	League	GP	G	A	Pts	PIM	PP	SH	GW	S	%	+/-	TF	F%	H	SB	Min	GP	G	A	Pts	PIM	PP	SH	GW
1986-87	Lac St-Louis	QAAA	38	10	20	30	172	....	....	....	....	....	....	....	....	....	....	....	....	....	....	....	....	....	....	....
1987-88	Shawinigan	QMJHL	61	2	12	14	324	....	....	....	....	....	....	....	....	....	....	....	....	....	....	....	....	....	....	....
1988-89	Shawinigan	QMJHL	34	7	11	18	132	....	....	....	....	....	....	....	....	....	....	....	....	....	....	....	....	....	....	....
	Trois-Rivieres	QMJHL	24	0	7	7	153	....	....	....	....	....	....	....	....	....	....	....	....	....	....	....	....	....	....	....
1989-90	Trois-Rivieres	QMJHL	40	4	24	28	227	....	....	....	....	....	....	....	....	....	....	....	3	0	0	0	15	....	....	....
1990-91	Kalamazoo	IHL	57	4	9	13	384	....	....	....	....	....	....	....	....	....	....	....	4	0	1	1	32	....	....	....
1991-92	**Minnesota**	**NHL**	**11**	**0**	**0**	**0**	**48**	**0**	**0**	**0**	**2**	**0.0**	**-2**	....	....	....	....	....	....	....	....	....	....	....	....	....
	Kalamazoo	IHL	53	4	16	20	406	....	....	....	....	....	....	....	....	....	....	....	10	0	1	1	58	....	....	....
1992-93	**Minnesota**	**NHL**	**31**	**0**	**1**	**1**	**115**	**0**	**0**	**0**	**13**	**0.0**	**2**	....	....	....	....	....	....	....	....	....	....	....	....	....
	Kalamazoo	IHL	13	1	3	4	50	....	....	....	....	....	....	....	....	....	....	....	....	....	....	....	....	....	....	....
	Hamilton	AHL	6	1	3	4	44	....	....	....	....	....	....	....	....	....	....	....	....	....	....	....	....	....	....	....
1993-94	**Washington**	**NHL**	**46**	**1**	**1**	**2**	**174**	**0**	**0**	**0**	**23**	**4.3**	**-2**	....	....	....	....	....	....	....	....	....	....	....	....	....
	Portland	AHL	6	0	0	0	27	....	....	....	....	....	....	....	....	....	....	....	....	....	....	....	....	....	....	....
	Tampa Bay	**NHL**	**11**	**0**	**1**	**1**	**52**	**0**	**0**	**0**	**10**	**0.0**	**-2**	....	....	....	....	....	....	....	....	....	....	....	....	....
1994-95	**Tampa Bay**	**NHL**	**41**	**2**	**4**	**6**	***225**	**0**	**0**	**0**	**43**	**4.7**	**3**	....	....	....	....	....	....	....	....	....	....	....	....	....
1995-96	**Tampa Bay**	**NHL**	**55**	**2**	**3**	**5**	**258**	**0**	**0**	**0**	**48**	**4.2**	**-4**	....	....	....	....	....	....	....	....	....	....	....	....	....
	Chicago	**NHL**	**11**	**0**	**1**	**1**	**48**	**0**	**0**	**0**	**12**	**0.0**	**5**	....	....	....	....	....	**9**	**1**	**0**	**1**	**30**	**0**	**0**	**0**
1996-97	**Chicago**	**NHL**	**67**	**2**	**2**	**4**	**233**	**0**	**0**	**1**	**65**	**3.1**	**-1**	....	....	....	....	....	**4**	**0**	**0**	**0**	**18**	**0**	**0**	**0**
1997-98	**Carolina**	**NHL**	**14**	**0**	**3**	**3**	**83**	**0**	**0**	**0**	**8**	**0.0**	**3**	....	....	....	....	....	....	....	....	....	....	....	....	....
	Vancouver	**NHL**	**13**	**0**	**1**	**1**	**47**	**0**	**0**	**0**	**7**	**0.0**	**-2**	....	....	....	....	....	....	....	....	....	....	....	....	....
	Tampa Bay	**NHL**	**12**	**0**	**0**	**0**	**45**	**0**	**0**	**0**	**7**	**0.0**	**-3**	....	....	....	....	....	....	....	....	....	....	....	....	....
1998-99	**Tampa Bay**	**NHL**	**16**	**1**	**1**	**2**	**24**	**0**	**0**	**0**	**9**	**11.1**	**-1**	**0**	**0.0**	**20**	**7**	**10:18**	....	....	....	....	....	....	....	....
	Cleveland	IHL	6	0	0	0	23	....	....	....	....	....	....	....	....	....	....	....	....	....	....	....	....	....	....	....
	Washington	**NHL**	**43**	**2**	**0**	**2**	**103**	**0**	**0**	**0**	**43**	**4.7**	**-6**	**0**	**0.0**	**58**	**21**	**11:29**	....	....	....	....	....	....	....	....
	NHL Totals		**371**	**10**	**18**	**28**	**1455**	**0**	**0**	**1**	**290**	**3.4**		**0**	**0.0**	**78**	**28**	**11:010**	**13**	**1**	**0**	**1**	**48**	**0**	**0**	**0**

Traded to **Washington** by **Dallas** to complete transaction that sent Paul Cavallini to Dallas (June 20, 1993), June 25, 1993. Traded to **Tampa Bay** by **Washington** with Washington's 3rd round choice (later traded to Anaheim — Anaheim selected Craig Reichert) in 1994 Entry Draft and the return of future draft choices transferred in the Pat Elynuik trade for Joe Reekie, March 21, 1994. Traded to **Chicago** by **Tampa Bay** with Tampa Bay's 2nd round choice (Jeff Paul) in 1996 Entry Draft for Patrick Poulin, Igor Ulanov and Chicago's 2nd round choice (later traded to New Jersey — New Jersey selected Pierre Dagenais) in 1996 Entry Draft, March 20, 1996. Traded to **Carolina** by **Chicago** for Ryan Risidore and Carolina's 5th round choice in 1998 Entry Draft, July 25, 1997. Traded to **Vancouver** by **Carolina** with Sean Burke and Geoff Sanderson for Kirk McLean and Martin Gelinas, January 3, 1998. Traded to **Tampa Bay** by **Vancouver** for Jamie Huscroft, March 14, 1998. Traded to **Washington** by **Tampa Bay** for cash, December 28, 1998.

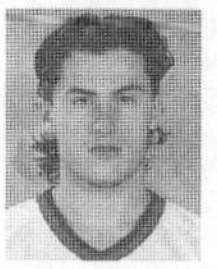

CIERNIK, Ivan

(CHAIR-nihk, ee-VAHN) **OTT.**

Left wing. Shoots left. 6'1", 198 lbs. Born, Levice, Czech., October 30, 1977. Ottawa's 6th choice, 216th overall, in 1996 Entry Draft.

Season	Club	League	GP	G	A	Pts	PIM	PP	SH	GW	S	%	+/-	TF	F%	H	SB	Min	GP	G	A	Pts	PIM	PP	SH	GW
1994-95	MHC Nitra	Slovak-Jr.	30	22	15	37	36	....	....	....	....	....	....	....	....	....	....	....	....	....	....	....	....	....	....	....
	MHC Nitra	Slovakia	7	1	0	1	2	....	....	....	....	....	....	....	....	....	....	....	....	....	....	....	....	....	....	....
1995-96	MHC Nitra	Slovakia	35	9	7	16	36	....	....	....	....	....	....	....	....	....	....	....	8	3	3	6	....	....	....	....
1996-97	MHC Nitra	Slovakia	41	11	19	30	....	....	....	....	....	....	....	....	....	....	....	....	....	....	....	....	....	....	....	....
1997-98	**Ottawa**	**NHL**	**2**	**0**	**0**	**0**	**0**	**0**	**0**	**0**	**0**	**0.0**	**0**	....	....	....	....	....	....	....	....	....	....	....	....	....
	Worcester	AHL	53	9	12	21	38	....	....	....	....	....	....	....	....	....	....	....	1	0	0	0	2	....	....	....
1998-99	Adirondack	AHL	21	1	4	5	4	....	....	....	....	....	....	....	....	....	....	....	....	....	....	....	....	....	....	....
	Cincinnati	AHL	32	10	3	13	10	....	....	....	....	....	....	....	....	....	....	....	2	0	0	0	2	....	....	....
	NHL Totals		**2**	**0**	**0**	**0**	**0**	**0**	**0**	**0**	**0**	**0.0**		....	....	....	....	....	....	....	....	....	....	....	....	....

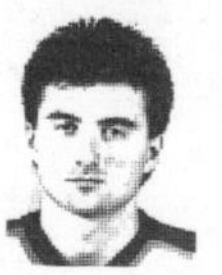

CIERNY, Jozef

(chee-ER-nee) **EDM.**

Left wing. Shoots left. 6'2", 185 lbs. Born, Zvolen, Czech., May 13, 1974. Buffalo's 2nd choice, 35th overall, in 1992 Entry Draft.

Season	Club	League	GP	G	A	Pts	PIM	PP	SH	GW	S	%	+/-	TF	F%	H	SB	Min	GP	G	A	Pts	PIM	PP	SH	GW
1991-92	ZTK Zvolen	Czech-2	26	10	3	13	8	....	....	....	....	....	....	....	....	....	....	....	....	....	....	....	....	....	....	....
1992-93	Rochester	AHL	54	27	27	54	36	....	....	....	....	....	....	....	....	....	....	....	....	....	....	....	....	....	....	....
1993-94	**Edmonton**	**NHL**	**1**	**0**	**0**	**0**	**0**	**0**	**0**	**0**	**0**	**0.0**	**-1**	....	....	....	....	....	....	....	....	....	....	....	....	....
	Cape Breton	AHL	73	30	27	57	88	....	....	....	....	....	....	....	....	....	....	....	4	1	1	2	4	....	....	....
1994-95	Cape Breton	AHL	73	28	24	52	58	....	....	....	....	....	....	....	....	....	....	....	....	....	....	....	....	....	....	....

			Regular Season																Playoffs							
Season	Club	League	GP	G	A	Pts	PIM	PP	SH	GW	S	%	+/-	TF	F%	H	SB	Min	GP	G	A	Pts	PIM	PP	SH	GW
1995-96	Detroit	IHL	20	2	5	7	16	....	....	....	....	....	....	....	....	....	....	....	....	....	....	....	....	....	....	....
	Los Angeles	IHL	43	23	16	39	36	....	....	....	....	....	....	....	....	....	....	....	....	....	....	....	....	....	....	....
1996-97	Long Beach	IHL	68	27	27	54	106	....	....	....	....	....	....	....	....	....	....	....	16	8	5	13	7	....	....	....
1997-98	EHC Nurnberg	Germany	45	20	22	42	61	....	....	....	....	....	....	....	....	....	....	....	....	....	....	....	....	....	....	....
1998-99	EHC Nurnberg	Germany	47	22	21	43	65	....	....	....	....	....	....	....	....	....	....	....	13	3	2	5	37	....	....	....
	NHL Totals		**1**	**0**	**0**	**0**	**0**	**0**	**0**	**0**	**0**	**0.0**		....	....	....	....	....	....	....	....	....	....	....	....	....

Traded to **Edmonton** by **Buffalo** with Buffalo's 4th round choice (Jussi Tarvainen) in 1994 Entry Draft for Craig Simpson, September 1, 1993.

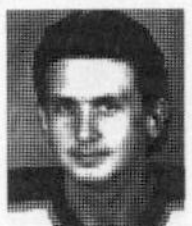

CIGER, Zdeno

(SEE-gu, ZDEH-noh)

Left wing. Shoots left. 6'1", 190 lbs. Born, Martin, Czech., October 19, 1969. New Jersey's 3rd choice, 54th overall, in 1988 Entry Draft.

Season	Club	League	GP	G	A	Pts	PIM	PP	SH	GW	S	%	+/-	TF	F%	H	SB	Min	GP	G	A	Pts	PIM	PP	SH	GW
1987-88	Dukla Trencin	Czech.	8	3	4	7	2	....	....	....	....	....	....	....	....	....	....	....	....	....	....	....	....	....	....	....
	Czechoslovakia	WJC-A	7	5	0	5	0	....	....	....	....	....	....	....	....	....	....	....	....	....	....	....	....	....	....	....
1988-89	Dukla Trencin	Czech.	43	18	13	31	18	....	....	....	....	....	....	....	....	....	....	....	....	....	....	....	....	....	....	....
1989-90	Dukla Trencin	Czech.	53	18	28	46	....	....	....	....	....	....	....	....	....	....	....	....	....	....	....	....	....	....	....	....
1990-91	**New Jersey**	**NHL**	**45**	**8**	**17**	**25**	**8**	**2**	**0**	**1**	**82**	**9.8**	**3**	....	....	....	....	....	**6**	**0**	**2**	**2**	**4**	**0**	**0**	**0**
	Utica	AHL	8	5	4	9	2	....	....	....	....	....	....	....	....	....	....	....	....	....	....	....	....	....	....	....
1991-92	**New Jersey**	**NHL**	**20**	**6**	**5**	**11**	**10**	**1**	**0**	**0**	**33**	**18.2**	**–2**	....	....	....	....	....	**7**	**2**	**4**	**6**	**0**	**0**	**0**	**1**
1992-93	**New Jersey**	**NHL**	**27**	**4**	**8**	**12**	**2**	**2**	**0**	**1**	**39**	**10.3**	**–8**	....	....	....	....	....	....	....	....	....	....	....	....	....
	Edmonton	**NHL**	**37**	**9**	**15**	**24**	**6**	**0**	**0**	**1**	**67**	**13.4**	**–5**	....	....	....	....	....	....	....	....	....	....	....	....	....
1993-94	**Edmonton**	**NHL**	**84**	**22**	**35**	**57**	**8**	**8**	**0**	**1**	**158**	**13.9**	**–11**	....	....	....	....	....	....	....	....	....	....	....	....	....
1994-95	Dukla Trencin	Slovakia	34	23	25	48	8	....	....	....	....	....	....	....	....	....	....	....	9	2	9	11	2	....	....	....
	Edmonton	**NHL**	**5**	**2**	**2**	**4**	**0**	**1**	**0**	**1**	**10**	**20.0**	**–1**	....	....	....	....	....	....	....	....	....	....	....	....	....
1995-96	**Edmonton**	**NHL**	**78**	**31**	**39**	**70**	**41**	**12**	**0**	**3**	**184**	**16.8**	**–15**	....	....	....	....	....	....	....	....	....	....	....	....	....
1996-97	HC Bratislava	Slovakia	44	26	27	53	....	....	....	....	....	....	....	....	....	....	....	....	2	1	3	4	....	....	....	....
	HC Bratislava	EuroHL	6	4	5	9	2	....	....	....	....	....	....	....	....	....	....	....	2	1	1	2	2	....	....	....
1997-98	HC Bratislava	Slovakia	36	14	*31	45	2	....	....	....	....	....	....	....	....	....	....	....	11	6	*10	*16	4	....	....	....
	HC Bratislava	EuroHL	8	1	5	6	6	....	....	....	....	....	....	....	....	....	....	....	....	....	....	....	....	....	....	....
	Slovakia	Olympics	4	1	1	2	4	....	....	....	....	....	....	....	....	....	....	....	....	....	....	....	....	....	....	....
1998-99	HC Bratislava	Slovakia	40	26	32	*58	8	....	....	....	....	....	....	....	....	....	....	....	9	3	*10	13	2	....	....	....
	Slovan Bratislava	EuroHL	6	4	5	9	8	....	....	....	....	....	....	....	....	....	....	....	....	....	....	....	....	....	....	....
	NHL Totals		**296**	**82**	**121**	**203**	**75**	**26**	**0**	**8**	**573**	**14.3**		....	....	....	....	....	**13**	**2**	**6**	**8**	**4**	**0**	**0**	**1**

Czechoslovakian Rookie of the Year (1989)

Traded to **Edmonton** by **New Jersey** with Kevin Todd for Bernie Nicholls, January 13, 1993. Claimed by **Nashville** from **Edmonton** in NHL Waiver Draft, October 5, 1998.

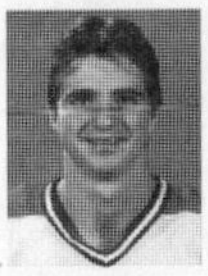

CLARK, Brett

ATL.

Defense. Shoots left. 6'1", 182 lbs. Born, Wapella, Sask., December 23, 1976. Montreal's 7th choice, 154th overall, in 1996 Entry Draft.

Season	Club	League	GP	G	A	Pts	PIM	PP	SH	GW	S	%	+/-	TF	F%	H	SB	Min	GP	G	A	Pts	PIM	PP	SH	GW
1994-95	Melville	SJHL	62	19	32	51	77	....	....	....	....	....	....	....	....	....	....	....	....	....	....	....	....	....	....	....
1995-96	U. of Maine	H.E.	39	7	31	38	22	....	....	....	....	....	....	....	....	....	....	....	....	....	....	....	....	....	....	....
1996-97	Canada	Nat-Team	57	6	21	27	52	....	....	....	....	....	....	....	....	....	....	....	....	....	....	....	....	....	....	....
1997-98	**Montreal**	**NHL**	**41**	**1**	**0**	**1**	**20**	**0**	**0**	**0**	**26**	**3.8**	**–3**	....	....	....	....	....	....	....	....	....	....	....	....	....
	Fredericton	AHL	20	0	6	6	6	....	....	....	....	....	....	....	....	....	....	....	4	0	1	1	17	....	....	....
1998-99	**Montreal**	**NHL**	**61**	**2**	**2**	**4**	**16**	**0**	**0**	**0**	**36**	**5.6**	**–3**	**0**	**0.0**	**62**	**43**	**13:11**	....	....	....	....	....	....	....	....
	Fredericton	AHL	3	1	0	1	0	....	....	....	....	....	....	....	....	....	....	....	....	....	....	....	....	....	....	....
	NHL Totals		**102**	**3**	**2**	**5**	**36**	**0**	**0**	**0**	**62**	**4.8**		**0**	**0.0**	**62**	**43**	**13:11**	....	....	....	....	....	....	....	....

Claimed by **Atlanta** from **Montreal** in Expansion Draft, June 25, 1999.

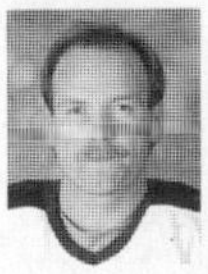

CLARK, Wendel

CHI.

Left wing/defense. Shoots left. 5'11", 194 lbs. Born, Kelvington, Sask., October 25, 1966. Toronto's 1st choice, 1st overall, in 1985 Entry Draft.

Season	Club	League	GP	G	A	Pts	PIM	PP	SH	GW	S	%	+/-	TF	F%	H	SB	Min	GP	G	A	Pts	PIM	PP	SH	GW
1982-83	Notre Dame	SAHA	27	21	28	49	83	....	....	....	....	....	....	....	....	....	....	....	....	....	....	....	....	....	....	....
1983-84	Saskatoon	WHL	72	23	45	68	225	....	....	....	....	....	....	....	....	....	....	....	....	....	....	....	....	....	....	....
1984-85	Saskatoon	WHL	64	32	55	87	253	....	....	....	....	....	....	....	....	....	....	....	3	3	3	6	7	....	....	....
1985-86	**Toronto**	**NHL**	**66**	**34**	**11**	**45**	**227**	**4**	**0**	**3**	**164**	**20.7**	**–27**	....	....	....	....	....	**10**	**5**	**1**	**6**	**47**	**1**	**0**	**1**
1986-87	**Toronto**	**NHL**	**80**	**37**	**23**	**60**	**271**	**15**	**0**	**1**	**246**	**15.0**	**–23**	....	....	....	....	....	**13**	**6**	**5**	**11**	**38**	**3**	**0**	**1**
1987-88	**Toronto**	**NHL**	**28**	**12**	**11**	**23**	**80**	**4**	**0**	**1**	**93**	**12.9**	**–13**	....	....	....	....	....	....	....	....	....	....	....	....	....
1988-89	**Toronto**	**NHL**	**15**	**7**	**4**	**11**	**66**	**3**	**0**	**1**	**30**	**23.3**	**–3**	....	....	....	....	....	....	....	....	....	....	....	....	....
1989-90	**Toronto**	**NHL**	**38**	**18**	**8**	**26**	**116**	**7**	**0**	**2**	**85**	**21.2**	**2**	....	....	....	....	....	**5**	**1**	**1**	**2**	**19**	**0**	**0**	**0**
1990-91	**Toronto**	**NHL**	**63**	**18**	**16**	**34**	**152**	**4**	**0**	**2**	**181**	**9.9**	**–5**	....	....	....	....	....	....	....	....	....	....	....	....	....
1991-92	**Toronto**	**NHL**	**43**	**19**	**21**	**40**	**123**	**7**	**0**	**4**	**158**	**12.0**	**–14**	....	....	....	....	....	....	....	....	....	....	....	....	....
1992-93	**Toronto**	**NHL**	**66**	**17**	**22**	**39**	**193**	**2**	**0**	**5**	**146**	**11.6**	**2**	....	....	....	....	....	**21**	**10**	**10**	**20**	**51**	**2**	**0**	**1**
1993-94	**Toronto**	**NHL**	**64**	**46**	**30**	**76**	**115**	**21**	**0**	**8**	**275**	**16.7**	**10**	....	....	....	....	....	**18**	**9**	**7**	**16**	**24**	**2**	**0**	**1**
1994-95	**Quebec**	**NHL**	**37**	**12**	**18**	**30**	**45**	**5**	**0**	**0**	**95**	**12.6**	**–1**	....	....	....	....	....	**6**	**1**	**2**	**3**	**6**	**0**	**0**	**0**
1995-96	**NY Islanders**	**NHL**	**58**	**24**	**19**	**43**	**60**	**6**	**0**	**2**	**192**	**12.5**	**–12**	....	....	....	....	....	....	....	....	....	....	....	....	....
	Toronto	**NHL**	**13**	**8**	**7**	**15**	**16**	**2**	**0**	**1**	**45**	**17.8**	**7**	....	....	....	....	....	**6**	**2**	**2**	**4**	**2**	**1**	**0**	**0**
1996-97	**Toronto**	**NHL**	**65**	**30**	**19**	**49**	**75**	**6**	**0**	**6**	**212**	**14.2**	**–2**	....	....	....	....	....	....	....	....	....	....	....	....	....
1997-98	**Toronto**	**NHL**	**47**	**12**	**7**	**19**	**80**	**4**	**0**	**3**	**140**	**8.6**	**–21**	....	....	....	....	....	....	....	....	....	....	....	....	....
1998-99	**Tampa Bay**	**NHL**	**65**	**28**	**14**	**42**	**35**	**11**	**0**	**2**	**171**	**16.4**	**–25**	**5**	**40.0**	**54**	**11**	**15:38**	....	....	....	....	....	....	....	....
	Detroit	**NHL**	**12**	**4**	**2**	**6**	**2**	**0**	**0**	**1**	**44**	**9.1**	**1**	**2**	**50.0**	**11**	**5**	**17:01**	**10**	**2**	**3**	**5**	**10**	**1**	**0**	**0**
	NHL Totals		**760**	**326**	**232**	**558**	**1656**	**101**	**0**	**42**	**2277**	**14.3**		**7**	**42.9**	**65**	**16**	**15:51**	**89**	**36**	**31**	**67**	**197**	**10**	**0**	**4**

WHL East First All-Star Team (1985) • NHL All-Rookie Team (1986)

Played in NHL All-Star Game (1986, 1999)

Traded to **Quebec** by **Toronto** with Sylvain Lefebvre, Landon Wilson and Toronto's 1st round choice (Jeffrey Kealty) in 1994 Entry Draft for Mats Sundin, Garth Butcher, Todd Warriner and Philadelphia's 1st round choice (previously acquired by Quebec — later traded to Washington — Washington selected Nolan Baumgartner) in 1994 Entry Draft, June 28, 1994. Transferred to **Colorado** after **Quebec** franchise relocated, June 21, 1995. Traded to **NY Islanders** by **Colorado** for Claude Lemieux, October 3, 1995. Traded to **Toronto** by **NY Islanders** with Mathieu Schneider and D.J. Smith for Darby Hendrickson, Sean Haggerty, Kenny Jonsson and Toronto's 1st round choice (Roberto Luongo) in 1997 Entry Draft, March 13, 1996. Signed as a free agent by **Tampa Bay**, July 31, 1998. Traded to **Detroit** by **Tampa Bay** with Detroit's 6th round choice (previously acquired, Detroit selected Kent McDonnell) in 1999 Entry Draft for Kevin Hodson and San Jose's 2nd round choice (previously acquired, Tampa Bay selected Sheldon Keefe) in 1999 Entry Draft, March 23, 1999. Signed as a free agent by **Chicago**, August 2, 1999.

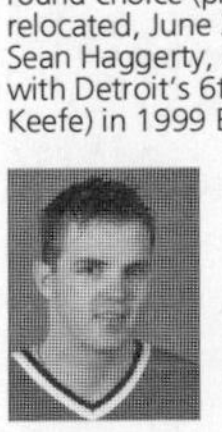

CLEARY, Daniel

(KLIH-ree) **EDM.**

Left wing. Shoots left. 6', 203 lbs. Born, Carbonear, Nfld., December 18, 1978. Chicago's 1st choice, 13th overall, in 1997 Entry Draft.

Season	Club	League	GP	G	A	Pts	PIM	PP	SH	GW	S	%	+/-	TF	F%	H	SB	Min	GP	G	A	Pts	PIM	PP	SH	GW
1993-94	Kingston	OJHL	41	18	28	49	83	....	....	....	....	....	....	....	....	....	....	....	....	....	....	....	....	....	....	....
1994-95	Belleville	OHL	62	26	55	81	62	....	....	....	....	....	....	....	....	....	....	....	16	7	10	17	23	....	....	....
1995-96	Belleville	OHL	64	53	62	115	74	....	....	....	....	....	....	....	....	....	....	....	14	10	17	27	40	....	....	....
1996-97	Belleville	OHL	64	32	48	80	88	....	....	....	....	....	....	....	....	....	....	....	6	3	4	7	6	....	....	....
1997-98	Belleville	OHL	30	16	31	47	14	....	....	....	....	....	....	....	....	....	....	....	10	6	*17	*23	10	....	....	....
	Chicago	**NHL**	**6**	**0**	**0**	**0**	**0**	**0**	**0**	**0**	**4**	**0.0**	**–2**	....	....	....	....	....	....	....	....	....	....	....	....	....
	Indianapolis	IHL	4	2	1	3	6	....	....	....	....	....	....	....	....	....	....	....	....	....	....	....	....	....	....	....
1998-99	**Chicago**	**NHL**	**35**	**4**	**5**	**9**	**24**	**0**	**0**	**0**	**49**	**8.2**	**–1**	**13**	**46.2**	**28**	**9**	**14:21**	....	....	....	....	....	....	....	....
	Portland	AHL	30	9	17	26	74	....	....	....	....	....	....	....	....	....	....	....	....	....	....	....	....	....	....	....
	Hamilton	AHL	9	0	1	1	7	....	....	....	....	....	....	....	....	....	....	....	3	0	0	0	0	....	....	....
	NHL Totals		**41**	**4**	**5**	**9**	**24**	**0**	**0**	**0**	**53**	**7.5**		**13**	**46.2**	**28**	**9**	**14:21**	....	....	....	....	....	....	....	....

OHL First All-Star Team (1996, 1997)

Traded to **Edmonton** by **Chicago** with Chad Kilger, Ethan Moreau and Christian Laflamme for Boris Mironov, Dean McAmmond and Jonas Elofsson, March 20, 1999.

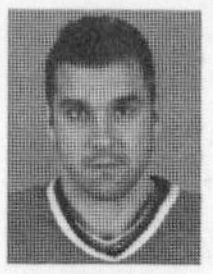

CLOUTIER, Sylvain

(klootz-YAY) **ATL.**

Center. Shoots left. 6', 195 lbs. Born, Mont-Laurier, Que., February 13, 1974. Detroit's 3rd choice, 70th overall, in 1992 Entry Draft.

			Regular Season																Playoffs							
Season	Club	League	GP	G	A	Pts	PIM	PP	SH	GW	S	%	+/–	TF	F%	H	SB	Min	GP	G	A	Pts	PIM	PP	SH	GW
1990-91	S.S. Marie	OMHA	34	51	40	91	92	....	....	....	....	....	....	....	....	....	....	....	....	....	....	....	....	....	....	....
1991-92	Guelph	OHL	62	35	31	66	74	....	....	....	....	....	....	....	....	....	....	....	....	....	....	....	....	....	....	....
1992-93	Guelph	OHL	44	26	29	55	78	....	....	....	....	....	....	....	....	....	....	....	5	0	5	5	14	....	....	....
1993-94	Guelph	OHL	66	45	71	116	127	....	....	....	....	....	....	....	....	....	....	....	9	7	9	16	32	....	....	....
	Adirondack	AHL	2	0	2	2	2	....	....	....	....	....	....	....	....	....	....	....	....	....	....	....	....	....	....	....
1994-95	Adirondack	AHL	71	7	26	33	144	....	....	....	....	....	....	....	....	....	....	....	....	....	....	....	....	....	....	....
1995-96	Adirondack	AHL	65	11	17	28	118	....	....	....	....	....	....	....	....	....	....	....	3	0	0	0	4	....	....	....
	Toledo	ECHL	6	4	2	6	4	....	....	....	....	....	....	....	....	....	....	....	....	....	....	....	....	....	....	....
1996-97	Adirondack	AHL	77	13	36	49	190	....	....	....	....	....	....	....	....	....	....	....	4	0	2	2	4	....	....	....
1997-98	Adirondack	AHL	72	14	22	36	155	....	....	....	....	....	....	....	....	....	....	....	....	....	....	....	....	....	....	....
	Detroit	IHL	8	0	1	1	18	....	....	....	....	....	....	....	....	....	....	....	21	7	5	12	31	....	....	....
1998-99	**Chicago**	**NHL**	**7**	**0**	**0**	**0**	**0**	**0**	**0**	**0**	**3**	**0.0**	**–1**	**35**	**51.4**	**4**	**0**	**5:28**	....	....	....	....	....	....	....	....
	Indianapolis	IHL	73	21	33	54	128	....	....	....	....	....	....	....	....	....	....	....	7	3	2	5	12	....	....	....
	NHL Totals		**7**	**0**	**0**	**0**	**0**	**0**	**0**	**0**	**3**	**0.0**		**35**	**51.4**	**4**	**0**	**5:28**	....	....	....	....	....	....	....	....

Signed as a free agent by **Chicago**, August 17, 1998. Claimed by **Atlanta** from **Chicago** in Expansion Draft, June 25, 1999.

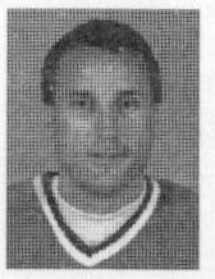

COFFEY, Paul

CAR.

Defense. Shoots left. 6', 190 lbs. Born, Weston, Ont., June 1, 1961. Edmonton's 1st choice, 6th overall, in 1980 Entry Draft.

1977-78	North York	MTHL	50	14	33	47	64	....	....	....	....	....	....	....	....	....	....	....	....	....	....	....	....	....	....	....
	Kingston	OJHL	8	2	2	4	11	....	....	....	....	....	....	....	....	....	....	....	....	....	....	....	....	....	....	....
1978-79	S.S. Marie	OHA	68	17	72	89	103	....	....	....	....	....	....	....	....	....	....	....	....	....	....	....	....	....	....	....
1979-80	S.S. Marie	OHA	23	10	21	31	63	....	....	....	....	....	....	....	....	....	....	....	....	....	....	....	....	....	....	....
	Kitchener	OHA	52	19	52	71	130	....	....	....	....	....	....	....	....	....	....	....	....	....	....	....	....	....	....	....
1980-81	**Edmonton**	**NHL**	**74**	**9**	**23**	**32**	**130**	**2**	**0**	**0**	**113**	**8.0**	**4**	....	....	....	....	....	**9**	**4**	**3**	**7**	**22**	**1**	**0**	**0**
1981-82	**Edmonton**	**NHL**	**80**	**29**	**60**	**89**	**106**	**13**	**0**	**1**	**234**	**12.4**	**35**	....	....	....	....	....	**5**	**1**	**1**	**2**	**6**	**1**	**0**	**0**
1982-83	**Edmonton**	**NHL**	**80**	**29**	**67**	**96**	**87**	**9**	**1**	**2**	**259**	**11.2**	**52**	....	....	....	....	....	**16**	**7**	**7**	**14**	**14**	**2**	**2**	**0**
1983-84♦	**Edmonton**	**NHL**	**80**	**40**	**86**	**126**	**104**	**14**	**1**	**4**	**258**	**15.5**	**52**	....	....	....	....	....	**19**	**8**	**14**	**22**	**21**	**2**	**0**	**1**
1984-85♦	**Edmonton**	**NHL**	**80**	**37**	**84**	**121**	**97**	**12**	**2**	**6**	**284**	**13.0**	**55**	....	....	....	....	....	**18**	**12**	**25**	**37**	**44**	**3**	**1**	**4**
1985-86	**Edmonton**	**NHL**	**79**	**48**	**90**	**138**	**120**	**9**	**9**	**3**	**307**	**15.6**	**61**	....	....	....	....	....	**10**	**1**	**9**	**10**	**30**	**1**	**0**	**0**
1986-87♦	**Edmonton**	**NHL**	**59**	**17**	**50**	**67**	**49**	**10**	**2**	**3**	**165**	**10.3**	**12**	....	....	....	....	....	**17**	**3**	**8**	**11**	**30**	**1**	**0**	**1**
1987-88	**Pittsburgh**	**NHL**	**46**	**15**	**52**	**67**	**93**	**6**	**2**	**2**	**193**	**7.8**	**–1**	....	....	....	....	....	....	....	....	....	....	....	....	....
1988-89	**Pittsburgh**	**NHL**	**75**	**30**	**83**	**113**	**195**	**11**	**0**	**2**	**342**	**8.8**	**–10**	....	....	....	....	....	**11**	**2**	**13**	**15**	**31**	**2**	**0**	**1**
1989-90	**Pittsburgh**	**NHL**	**80**	**29**	**74**	**103**	**95**	**10**	**0**	**3**	**324**	**9.0**	**–25**	....	....	....	....	....	....	....	....	....	....	....	....	....
1990-91♦	**Pittsburgh**	**NHL**	**76**	**24**	**69**	**93**	**128**	**8**	**0**	**3**	**240**	**10.0**	**–18**	....	....	....	....	....	**12**	**2**	**9**	**11**	**6**	**0**	**0**	**0**
1991-92	**Pittsburgh**	**NHL**	**54**	**10**	**54**	**64**	**62**	**5**	**0**	**1**	**207**	**4.8**	**4**	....	....	....	....	....	....	....	....	....	....	....	....	....
	Los Angeles	**NHL**	**10**	**1**	**4**	**5**	**25**	**0**	**0**	**0**	**25**	**4.0**	**–3**	....	....	....	....	....	**6**	**4**	**3**	**7**	**2**	**3**	**0**	**0**
1992-93	**Los Angeles**	**NHL**	**50**	**8**	**49**	**57**	**50**	**2**	**0**	**0**	**182**	**4.4**	**9**	....	....	....	....	....	....	....	....	....	....	....	....	....
	Detroit	**NHL**	**30**	**4**	**26**	**30**	**27**	**3**	**0**	**0**	**72**	**5.6**	**7**	....	....	....	....	....	**7**	**2**	**9**	**11**	**2**	**0**	**0**	**0**
1993-94	**Detroit**	**NHL**	**80**	**14**	**63**	**77**	**106**	**5**	**0**	**3**	**278**	**5.0**	**28**	....	....	....	....	....	**7**	**1**	**6**	**7**	**8**	**0**	**0**	**0**
1994-95	**Detroit**	**NHL**	**45**	**14**	**44**	**58**	**72**	**4**	**1**	**2**	**181**	**7.7**	**18**	....	....	....	....	....	**18**	**6**	**12**	**18**	**10**	**2**	**1**	**0**
1995-96	**Detroit**	**NHL**	**76**	**14**	**60**	**74**	**90**	**3**	**1**	**3**	**234**	**6.0**	**19**	....	....	....	....	....	**17**	**5**	**9**	**14**	**30**	**3**	**2**	**1**
1996-97	**Hartford**	**NHL**	**20**	**3**	**5**	**8**	**18**	**1**	**0**	**1**	**39**	**7.7**	**0**	....	....	....	....	....	....	....	....	....	....	....	....	....
	Philadelphia	**NHL**	**37**	**6**	**20**	**26**	**20**	**0**	**1**	**1**	**71**	**8.5**	**11**	....	....	....	....	....	**17**	**1**	**8**	**9**	**6**	**0**	**0**	**0**
1997-98	**Philadelphia**	**NHL**	**57**	**2**	**27**	**29**	**30**	**1**	**0**	**1**	**107**	**1.9**	**3**	....	....	....	....	....	....	....	....	....	....	....	....	....
1998-99	**Chicago**	**NHL**	**10**	**0**	**4**	**4**	**0**	**0**	**0**	**0**	**8**	**0.0**	**–6**	**0**	**0.0**	**1**	**8**	**15:22**	....	....	....	....	....	....	....	....
	Carolina	**NHL**	**44**	**2**	**8**	**10**	**28**	**1**	**0**	**0**	**79**	**2.5**	**–1**	**0**	**0.0**	**16**	**31**	**19:41**	**5**	**0**	**1**	**1**	**2**	**0**	**0**	**0**
	NHL Totals		**1322**	**385**	**1102**	**1487**	**1732**	**129**	**20**	**41**	**4202**	**9.2**		**0**	**0.0**	**17**	**39**	**18:53**	**194**	**59**	**137**	**196**	**264**	**21**	**6**	**8**

OHA Second All-Star Team (1980) • NHL Second All-Star Team (1982, 1983, 1984, 1990) • Won James Norris Memorial Trophy (1985, 1986, 1995) • NHL First All-Star Team (1985, 1986, 1989, 1995)
Played in NHL All-Star Game (1982, 1983, 1984, 1985, 1986, 1988, 1989, 1990, 1991, 1992, 1993, 1994, 1996, 1997)

Traded to **Pittsburgh** by **Edmonton** with Dave Hunter and Wayne Van Dorp for Craig Simpson, Dave Hannan, Moe Mantha and Chris Joseph, November 24, 1987. Traded to **LA Kings** by **Pittsburgh** for Brian Benning, Jeff Chychrun and LA Kings' 1st round choice (later traded to Philadelphia — Philadelphia selected Jason Bowen) in 1992 Entry Draft, February 19, 1992. Traded to **Detroit** by **LA Kings** with Sylvain Couturier and Jim Hiller for Jimmy Carson, Marc Potvin and Gary Shuchuk, January 29, 1993. Traded to **Hartford** by **Detroit** with Keith Primeau and Detroit's 1st round choice (Nikos Tselios) in 1997 Entry Draft for Brendan Shanahan and Brian Glynn, October 9, 1996. Traded to **Philadelphia** by **Hartford** with Hartford-Carolina's 3rd round choice (Kris Mallette) in 1997 Entry Draft for Kevin Haller, Philadelphia's 1st round choice (later traded to San Jose — San Jose selected Scott Hannan) in 1997 Entry Draft and Hartford's 7th round choice (previously acquired, Carolina selected Andrew Merrick) in 1997 Entry Draft, December 15, 1996. Traded to **Chicago** by **Philadelphia** for NY Islanders' 5th round choice (previously acquired, Philadelphia selected Francis Belanger) in 1998 Entry Draft, June 27, 1998. Traded to **Carolina** by **Chicago** for Nelson Emerson, December 29, 1998.

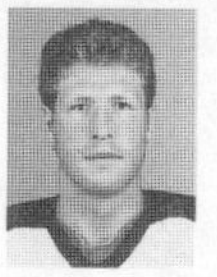

COLE, Danton

Center/Right wing. Shoots right. 5'11", 185 lbs. Born, Pontiac, MI, January 10, 1967. Winnipeg's 6th choice, 123rd overall, in 1985 Entry Draft.

1984-85	Aurora	OJHL	41	51	44	95	91	....	....	....	....	....	....	....	....	....	....	....	....	....	....	....	....	....	....	....
1985-86	Michigan State	CCHA	43	11	10	21	22	....	....	....	....	....	....	....	....	....	....	....	....	....	....	....	....	....	....	....
1986-87	Michigan State	CCHA	44	9	15	24	16	....	....	....	....	....	....	....	....	....	....	....	....	....	....	....	....	....	....	....
1987-88	Michigan State	CCHA	46	20	36	56	38	....	....	....	....	....	....	....	....	....	....	....	....	....	....	....	....	....	....	....
1988-89	Michigan State	CCHA	47	29	33	62	46	....	....	....	....	....	....	....	....	....	....	....	....	....	....	....	....	....	....	....
1989-90	**Winnipeg**	**NHL**	**2**	**1**	**1**	**2**	**0**	**0**	**0**	**0**	**2**	**50.0**	**–1**	....	....	....	....	....	....	....	....	....	....	....	....	....
	Moncton	AHL	80	31	42	73	18	....	....	....	....	....	....	....	....	....	....	....	....	....	....	....	....	....	....	....
1990-91	**Winnipeg**	**NHL**	**66**	**13**	**11**	**24**	**24**	**1**	**1**	**1**	**109**	**11.9**	**–14**	....	....	....	....	....	....	....	....	....	....	....	....	....
	Moncton	AHL	3	1	1	2	0	....	....	....	....	....	....	....	....	....	....	....	....	....	....	....	....	....	....	....
1991-92	**Winnipeg**	**NHL**	**52**	**7**	**5**	**12**	**32**	**1**	**2**	**0**	**65**	**10.8**	**–15**	....	....	....	....	....	....	....	....	....	....	....	....	....
1992-93	**Tampa Bay**	**NHL**	**67**	**12**	**15**	**27**	**23**	**0**	**1**	**1**	**100**	**12.0**	**–2**	....	....	....	....	....	....	....	....	....	....	....	....	....
	Atlanta	IHL	1	1	0	1	2	....	....	....	....	....	....	....	....	....	....	....	....	....	....	....	....	....	....	....
1993-94	**Tampa Bay**	**NHL**	**81**	**20**	**23**	**43**	**32**	**8**	**1**	**4**	**149**	**13.4**	**7**	....	....	....	....	....	....	....	....	....	....	....	....	....
1994-95	**Tampa Bay**	**NHL**	**26**	**3**	**3**	**6**	**6**	**1**	**0**	**0**	**56**	**5.4**	**–1**	....	....	....	....	....	....	....	....	....	....	....	....	....
	♦ New Jersey	**NHL**	**12**	**1**	**2**	**3**	**8**	**0**	**0**	**0**	**20**	**5.0**	**0**	....	....	....	....	....	**1**	**0**	**0**	**0**	**0**	**0**	**0**	**0**
1995-96	**NY Islanders**	**NHL**	**10**	**1**	**0**	**1**	**0**	**0**	**0**	**0**	**5**	**20.0**	**0**	....	....	....	....	....	....	....	....	....	....	....	....	....
	Utah	IHL	34	28	15	43	22	....	....	....	....	....	....	....	....	....	....	....	....	....	....	....	....	....	....	....
	Chicago	**NHL**	**2**	**0**	**0**	**0**	**0**	**0**	**0**	**0**	**1**	**0.0**	**0**	....	....	....	....	....	....	....	....	....	....	....	....	....
	Indianapolis	IHL	32	9	13	22	20	....	....	....	....	....	....	....	....	....	....	....	5	1	5	6	8	....	....	....
1996-97	Krefelder EV	Germany	28	7	12	19	14	....	....	....	....	....	....	....	....	....	....	....	....	....	....	....	....	....	....	....
	Grand Rapids	IHL	35	8	18	26	24	....	....	....	....	....	....	....	....	....	....	....	5	3	1	4	2	....	....	....
1997-98	Grand Rapids	IHL	81	13	13	26	36	....	....	....	....	....	....	....	....	....	....	....	3	1	1	2	0	....	....	....
1998-99	Grand Rapids	IHL	72	14	11	25	50	....	....	....	....	....	....	....	....	....	....	....	....	....	....	....	....	....	....	....
	NHL Totals		**318**	**58**	**60**	**118**	**125**	**11**	**5**	**6**	**507**	**11.4**		....	....	....	....	....	**1**	**0**	**0**	**0**	**0**	**0**	**0**	**0**

Traded to **Tampa Bay** by **Winnipeg** for future considerations, June 19, 1992. Traded to **New Jersey** by **Tampa Bay** with Shawn Chambers for Alexander Semak and Ben Hankinson, March 14, 1995. Signed as a free agent by **NY Islanders**, August 26, 1995. Traded to **Chicago** by **NY Islanders** for Bob Halkidis, February 2, 1996.

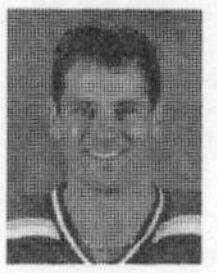

CONROY, Craig

ST.L.

Center. Shoots right. 6'2", 198 lbs. Born, Potsdam, NY, September 4, 1971. Montreal's 7th choice, 123rd overall, in 1990 Entry Draft.

1989-90	Northwood Prep	H.S.	31	33	43	76	....	....	....	....	....	....	....	....	....	....	....	....	....	....	....	....	....	....	....	....
1990-91	Clarkson	ECAC	40	8	21	29	24	....	....	....	....	....	....	....	....	....	....	....	....	....	....	....	....	....	....	....
1991-92	Clarkson	ECAC	31	19	17	36	36	....	....	....	....	....	....	....	....	....	....	....	....	....	....	....	....	....	....	....
1992-93	Clarkson	ECAC	35	10	23	33	26	....	....	....	....	....	....	....	....	....	....	....	....	....	....	....	....	....	....	....
1993-94	Clarkson	ECAC	34	26	*40	*66	46	....	....	....	....	....	....	....	....	....	....	....	....	....	....	....	....	....	....	....
1994-95	**Montreal**	**NHL**	**6**	**1**	**0**	**1**	**0**	**0**	**0**	**0**	**4**	**25.0**	**–1**	....	....	....	....	....	....	....	....	....	....	....	....	....
	Fredericton	AHL	55	26	18	44	29	....	....	....	....	....	....	....	....	....	....	....	11	7	3	10	6	....	....	....
1995-96	**Montreal**	**NHL**	**7**	**0**	**0**	**0**	**2**	**0**	**0**	**0**	**1**	**0.0**	**–4**	....	....	....	....	....	....	....	....	....	....	....	....	....
	Fredericton	AHL	67	31	38	69	65	....	....	....	....	....	....	....	....	....	....	....	10	5	7	12	6	....	....	....

Season	Club	League	GP	G	A	Pts	PIM	PP	SH	GW	S	%	+/-	TF	F%	H	SB	Min	GP	G	A	Pts	PIM	PP	SH	GW
1996-97	Fredericton	AHL	9	10	6	16	10																			
	St. Louis	**NHL**	61	6	11	17	43	0	0	1	74	8.1	0						6	0	0	0	8	0	0	0
	Worcester	AHL	5	5	6	11	2																			
1997-98	**St. Louis**	**NHL**	81	14	29	43	46	0	3	1	118	11.9	20						10	1	2	3	8	0	0	1
1998-99	**St. Louis**	**NHL**	69	14	25	39	38	0	1	1	134	10.4	14	1190	54.6	77	35	16:39	13	2	1	3	6	0	0	0
	NHL Totals		224	35	65	100	129	0	4	3	331	10.6		1190	54.6	77	35	16:39	29	3	3	6	22	0	0	1

ECAC First All-Star Team (1994) • NCAA East First All-American Team (1994) • NCAA Final Four All-Tournament Team (1994)
Traded to **St. Louis** by **Montreal** with Pierre Turgeon and Rory Fitzpatrick for Murray Baron, Shayne Corson and St. Louis' 5th round choice (Gennady Razin) in 1997 Entry Draft, October 29, 1996.

CONVERY, Brandon (KOHN-vehr-ee)
Center. Shoots right. 6'1", 195 lbs.   Born, Kingston, Ont., February 4, 1974. Toronto's 1st choice, 8th overall, in 1992 Entry Draft.

Season	Club	League	GP	G	A	Pts	PIM	PP	SH	GW	S	%	+/-	TF	F%	H	SB	Min	GP	G	A	Pts	PIM	PP	SH	GW
1989-90	Kingston	OJHL	42	13	25	38	4																			
1990-91	Sudbury	OHL	56	26	22	48	18												5	1	1	2	2			
1991-92	Sudbury	OHL	44	40	26	66	44												5	3	2	5	4			
1992-93	Sudbury	OHL	7	7	9	16	6																			
	Niagara Falls	OHL	51	38	39	77	24												4	1	3	4	4			
	St. John's	AHL	3	0	0	0	0												5	0	1	1	0			
1993-94	Niagara Falls	OHL	29	24	29	53	30																			
	Belleville	OHL	23	16	19	35	22												12	4	10	14	13			
	St. John's	AHL																	1	0	0	0	0			
1994-95	St. John's	AHL	76	34	37	71	43												5	2	2	4	4			
1995-96	**Toronto**	**NHL**	11	5	2	7	4	3	0	1	16	31.3	-7						5	0	0	0	2	0	0	0
	St. John's	AHL	57	22	23	45	28																			
1996-97	**Toronto**	**NHL**	39	2	8	10	20	0	0	0	41	4.9	-9													
	St. John's	AHL	25	14	14	28	15																			
1997-98	St. John's	AHL	49	27	36	63	35																			
	Vancouver	**NHL**	7	0	2	2	0	0	0	0	2	0.0	0													
	Syracuse	AHL	2	1	2	3	5																			
1998-99	**Vancouver**	**NHL**	12	2	7	9	8	0	0	1	12	16.7	5	111	52.3	4	1	10:37								
	Los Angeles	**NHL**	3	0	0	0	4	0	0	0	2	0.0	-1	33	51.5	3	0	9:39								
	Long Beach	IHL	14	3	7	10	8																			
	Springfield	AHL	31	9	14	23	45																			
	NHL Totals		72	9	19	28	36	3	0	2	73	12.3		144	52.1	7	1	10:25	5	0	0	0	2	0	0	0

Traded to **Vancouver** by **Toronto** for Lonny Bohonos, March 7, 1998. Claimed on waivers by **Los Angeles** from **Vancouver**, November 21, 1998.

COOKE, Matt   VAN.
Left wing. Shoots left. 5'11", 200 lbs.   Born, Belleville, Ont., September 7, 1978. Vancouver's 8th choice, 144th overall, in 1997 Entry Draft.

Season	Club	League	GP	G	A	Pts	PIM	PP	SH	GW	S	%	+/-	TF	F%	H	SB	Min	GP	G	A	Pts	PIM	PP	SH	GW
1995-96	Windsor	OHL	61	8	11	19	102												7	1	3	4	6			
1996-97	Windsor	OHL	65	45	50	95	146												5	5	5	10	10			
1997-98	Windsor	OHL	23	14	19	33	50																			
	Kingston	OHL	25	8	13	21	49												12	8	8	16	20			
1998-99	**Vancouver**	**NHL**	30	0	2	2	27	0	0	0	22	0.0	-12	189	40.2	43	7	8:07								
	Syracuse	AHL	37	15	18	33	119																			
	NHL Totals		30	0	2	2	27	0	0	0	22	0.0		189	40.2	43	7	8:07								

COOPER, David
Defense. Shoots left. 6'2", 204 lbs.   Born, Ottawa, Ont., November 2, 1973. Buffalo's 1st choice, 11th overall, in 1992 Entry Draft.

Season	Club	League	GP	G	A	Pts	PIM	PP	SH	GW	S	%	+/-	TF	F%	H	SB	Min	GP	G	A	Pts	PIM	PP	SH	GW
1988-89	Edmonton Mets	AAHA	32	24	22	46	151																			
1989-90	Medicine Hat	WHL	61	4	11	15	65												3	0	2	2	2			
1990-91	Medicine Hat	WHL	64	12	31	43	66												11	1	3	4	23			
1991-92	Medicine Hat	WHL	72	17	47	64	176												4	1	4	5	8			
1992-93	Medicine Hat	WHL	63	15	50	65	88												10	2	2	4	32			
	Rochester	AHL																	2	0	0	0	2			
1993-94	Rochester	AHL	68	10	25	35	82												4	1	1	2	2			
1994-95	Rochester	AHL	21	2	4	6	48																			
	South Carolina	ECHL	39	9	19	28	90												9	3	8	11	24			
1995-96	Rochester	AHL	67	9	18	27	79												8	0	1	1	12			
1996-97	**Toronto**	**NHL**	19	3	3	6	16	2	0	0	23	13.0	-3													
	St. John's	AHL	44	16	19	35	65																			
1997-98	**Toronto**	**NHL**	9	0	4	4	8	0	0	0	13	0.0	2													
	St. John's	AHL	60	19	23	42	117												4	0	1	1	6			
1998-99	Saint John	AHL	65	18	24	42	121												7	1	4	5	10			
	NHL Totals		28	3	7	10	24	2	0	0	36	8.3														

WHL East First All-Star Team (1992) • AHL Second All-Star Team (1998)
Signed as a free agent by **Toronto**, September 26, 1996. Traded to **Calgary** by **Toronto** for Ladislav Kohn, July 2, 1998.

CORBET, Rene (cohr-BAY, ruh-NAY)   CGY.
Left wing. Shoots left. 6', 190 lbs.   Born, St-Hyacinthe, Que., June 25, 1973. Quebec's 2nd choice, 24th overall, in 1991 Entry Draft.

Season	Club	League	GP	G	A	Pts	PIM	PP	SH	GW	S	%	+/-	TF	F%	H	SB	Min	GP	G	A	Pts	PIM	PP	SH	GW
1989-90	Richelieu	QAAA	42	53	63	116	34																			
1990-91	Drummondville	QMJHL	45	25	40	65	34												14	11	6	17	15			
1991-92	Drummondville	QMJHL	56	46	50	96	90												4	1	2	3	17			
1992-93	Drummondville	QMJHL	63	*79	69	*148	143												10	7	13	20	16			
1993-94	**Quebec**	**NHL**	9	1	1	2	0	0	0	0	14	7.1	1													
	Cornwall	AHL	68	37	40	77	56												13	7	2	9	18			
1994-95	**Quebec**	**NHL**	8	0	3	3	2	0	0	0	4	0.0	3						2	0	1	1	0	0	0	0
	Cornwall	AHL	65	33	24	57	79												12	3	8	10	27			
1995-96♦	**Colorado**	**NHL**	33	3	6	9	33	0	0	0	35	8.6	10						8	3	2	5	2	1	0	1
	Cornwall	AHL	9	5	6	11	10																			
1996-97	**Colorado**	**NHL**	76	12	15	27	67	1	0	3	128	9.4	14						17	2	2	4	27	0	0	0
1997-98	**Colorado**	**NHL**	68	16	12	28	133	4	0	4	117	13.7	8						2	0	0	0	2	0	0	0
1998-99	**Colorado**	**NHL**	53	8	14	22	58	2	0	1	82	9.8	3	211	45.0	37	16	11:39								
	Calgary	**NHL**	20	5	4	9	10	1	0	0	45	11.1	-2	4	50.0	39	6	18:05								
	NHL Totals		267	45	55	100	303	8	0	8	425	10.6		215	45.1	76	22	13:25	29	5	5	10	31	1	0	1

QMJHL First All-Star Team (1993) • Canadian Major Junior First All-Star Team (1993) • Won Dudley "Red" Garrett Memorial Trophy (Top Rookie - AHL) (1994)
Transferred to **Colorado** after **Quebec** franchise relocated, June 21, 1995. Traded to **Calgary** by **Colorado** with Wade Belak and future considerations (Robyn Regehr, March 27, 1999) for Theoren Fleury and Chris Dingman, February 28, 1999.

CORKUM, Bob (KOHR-kuhm)
Center. Shoots right. 6', 222 lbs.   Born, Salisbury, MA, December 18, 1967. Buffalo's 3rd choice, 47th overall, in 1986 Entry Draft.

Season	Club	League	GP	G	A	Pts	PIM	PP	SH	GW	S	%	+/-	TF	F%	H	SB	Min	GP	G	A	Pts	PIM	PP	SH	GW
1984-85	Triton Regional	H.S.	18	35	36	71																				
1985-86	U. of Maine	H.E.	39	7	26	33	53																			
1986-87	U. of Maine	H.E.	35	18	11	29	24																			
1987-88	U. of Maine	H.E.	40	14	18	32	64																			
1988-89	U. of Maine	H.E.	45	17	31	48	64																			

			Regular Season																Playoffs							
Season	Club	League	GP	G	A	Pts	PIM	PP	SH	GW	S	%	+/–	TF	F%	H	SB	Min	GP	G	A	Pts	PIM	PP	SH	GW
1989-90	**Buffalo**	**NHL**	8	2	0	2	4	0	0	1	6	33.3	2	....	....	....	....	....	5	1	0	1	4	0	0	0
	Rochester	AHL	43	8	11	19	45	....	....	....	....	....	....	....	....	....	....	....	12	2	5	7	16	....	....	....
1990-91	Rochester	AHL	69	13	21	34	77	....	....	....	....	....	....	....	....	....	....	....	15	4	4	8	4	....	....	....
1991-92	**Buffalo**	**NHL**	20	2	4	6	21	0	0	0	23	8.7	–9	....	....	....	....	....	4	1	0	1	0	1	0	0
	Rochester	AHL	52	16	12	28	47	....	....	....	....	....	....	....	....	....	....	....	8	0	6	6	8	....	....	....
1992-93	**Buffalo**	**NHL**	68	6	4	10	38	0	1	1	69	8.7	–3	....	....	....	....	....	5	0	0	0	2	0	0	0
1993-94	**Anaheim**	**NHL**	76	23	28	51	18	3	3	0	180	12.8	4	....	....	....	....	....	....	....	....	....	....	....	....	....
1994-95	**Anaheim**	**NHL**	44	10	9	19	25	0	0	1	100	10.0	–7	....	....	....	....	....	....	....	....	....	....	....	....	....
1995-96	**Anaheim**	**NHL**	48	5	7	12	26	0	0	1	88	5.7	0	....	....	....	....	....	....	....	....	....	....	....	....	....
	Philadelphia	**NHL**	28	4	3	7	8	0	0	2	38	10.5	3	....	....	....	....	....	12	1	2	3	6	0	0	0
1996-97	**Phoenix**	**NHL**	80	9	11	20	40	0	1	3	119	7.6	–7	....	....	....	....	....	7	2	2	4	4	0	0	1
1997-98	**Phoenix**	**NHL**	76	12	9	21	28	0	5	0	105	11.4	–7	....	....	....	....	....	6	1	0	1	4	0	0	0
1998-99	**Phoenix**	**NHL**	77	9	10	19	17	0	0	0	146	6.2	–9	1644	51.6	116	28	17:15	7	0	1	1	4	0	0	0
	NHL Totals		525	82	85	167	225	3	10	9	874	9.4		1644	51.6	116	28	17:15	46	6	5	11	24	1	0	1

Claimed by **Anaheim** from **Buffalo** in Expansion Draft, June 24, 1993. Traded to **Philadelphia** by **Anaheim** for Chris Herperger and Winnipeg's 7th round choice (previously acquired, Anaheim selected Tony Monahan) in 1997 Entry Draft, February 6, 1996. Claimed by **Phoenix** from **Philadelphia** in Waiver Draft, September 30, 1996.

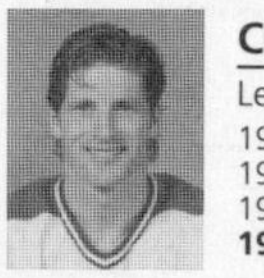

CORSON, Shayne — MTL.

Left wing. Shoots left. 6'1", 202 lbs. Born, Barrie, Ont., August 13, 1966. Montreal's 2nd choice, 8th overall, in 1984 Entry Draft.

Season	Club	League	GP	G	A	Pts	PIM	PP	SH	GW	S	%	+/–	TF	F%	H	SB	Min	GP	G	A	Pts	PIM	PP	SH	GW
1982-83	Barrie	OJHL	23	13	29	42	87	....	....	....	....	....	....	....	....	....	....	....	....	....	....	....	....	....	....	....
1983-84	Brantford	OHL	66	25	46	71	165	....	....	....	....	....	....	....	....	....	....	....	6	4	1	5	26	....	....	....
1984-85	Hamilton	OHL	54	27	63	90	154	....	....	....	....	....	....	....	....	....	....	....	11	3	7	10	19	....	....	....
1985-86	Hamilton	OHL	47	41	57	98	153	....	....	....	....	....	....	....	....	....	....	....	....	....	....	....	....	....	....	....
	Montreal	**NHL**	3	0	0	0	2	0	0	0	1	0.0	–3	....	....	....	....	....	....	....	....	....	....	....	....	....
1986-87	**Montreal**	**NHL**	55	12	11	23	144	0	1	3	69	17.4	10	....	....	....	....	....	17	6	5	11	30	1	1	1
1987-88	**Montreal**	**NHL**	71	12	27	39	152	2	0	2	90	13.3	22	....	....	....	....	....	3	1	0	1	12	0	0	0
1988-89	**Montreal**	**NHL**	80	26	24	50	193	10	0	3	133	19.5	–1	....	....	....	....	....	21	4	5	9	65	2	0	2
1989-90	**Montreal**	**NHL**	76	31	44	75	144	7	0	6	192	16.1	33	....	....	....	....	....	11	2	8	10	20	0	0	0
1990-91	**Montreal**	**NHL**	71	23	24	47	138	7	0	2	164	14.0	9	....	....	....	....	....	13	9	6	15	36	4	1	3
1991-92	**Montreal**	**NHL**	64	17	36	53	118	3	0	2	165	10.3	15	....	....	....	....	....	10	2	5	7	15	0	0	0
1992-93	**Edmonton**	**NHL**	80	16	31	47	209	9	2	1	164	9.8	–19	....	....	....	....	....	....	....	....	....	....	....	....	....
1993-94	**Edmonton**	**NHL**	64	25	29	54	118	11	0	3	171	14.6	–8	....	....	....	....	....	....	....	....	....	....	....	....	....
1994-95	**Edmonton**	**NHL**	48	12	24	36	86	2	0	1	131	9.2	–17	....	....	....	....	....	....	....	....	....	....	....	....	....
1995-96	**St. Louis**	**NHL**	77	18	28	46	192	13	0	0	150	12.0	3	....	....	....	....	....	13	8	6	14	22	6	1	1
1996-97	**St. Louis**	**NHL**	11	2	1	3	24	1	0	0	19	10.5	–4	....	....	....	....	....	....	....	....	....	....	....	....	....
	Montreal	**NHL**	47	6	15	21	80	2	0	2	96	6.3	–5	....	....	....	....	....	5	1	0	1	4	0	1	0
1997-98	**Montreal**	**NHL**	62	21	34	55	108	14	1	1	142	14.8	2	....	....	....	....	....	10	3	6	9	26	1	0	1
	Canada	Olympics	6	1	1	2	2	....	....	....	....	....	....	....	....	....	....	....	....	....	....	....	....	....	....	....
1998-99	**Montreal**	**NHL**	63	12	20	32	147	7	0	4	142	8.5	–10	184	45.1	71	38	20:42	....	....	....	....	....	....	....	....
	NHL Totals		872	233	348	581	1855	88	4	30	1829	12.7		184	45.1	71	38	20:42	103	36	41	77	230	14	4	8

WJC-A All-Star Team (1986)

Played in NHL All-Star Game (1990, 1994, 1998)

Traded to **Edmonton** by **Montreal** with Brent Gilchrist and Vladimir Vujtek for Vincent Damphousse and Edmonton's 4th round choice (Adam Wiesel) in 1993 Entry Draft, August 27, 1992. Signed as a free agent by **St. Louis**, July 28, 1995. Traded to **Montreal** by **St. Louis** with Murray Baron and St. Louis' 5th round choice (Gennady Razin) in 1997 Entry Draft for Pierre Turgeon, Rory Fitzpatrick and Craig Conroy, October 29, 1996.

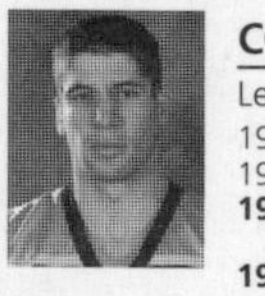

COTE, Patrick — (KOH-tay) — NSH.

Left wing. Shoots left. 6'3", 199 lbs. Born, Lasalle, Que., January 24, 1975. Dallas' 2nd choice, 37th overall, in 1995 Entry Draft.

Season	Club	League	GP	G	A	Pts	PIM	PP	SH	GW	S	%	+/–	TF	F%	H	SB	Min	GP	G	A	Pts	PIM	PP	SH	GW
1993-94	Beauport	QMJHL	48	2	4	6	230	....	....	....	....	....	....	....	....	....	....	....	12	1	0	1	61	....	....	....
1994-95	Beauport	QMJHL	56	20	20	40	314	....	....	....	....	....	....	....	....	....	....	....	17	8	8	16	115	....	....	....
1995-96	**Dallas**	**NHL**	2	0	0	0	5	0	0	0	0	0.0	–2	....	....	....	....	....	....	....	....	....	....	....	....	....
	Michigan	IHL	57	4	6	10	239	....	....	....	....	....	....	....	....	....	....	....	3	0	0	0	2	....	....	....
1996-97	**Dallas**	**NHL**	3	0	0	0	27	0	0	0	1	0.0	0	....	....	....	....	....	....	....	....	....	....	....	....	....
	Michigan	IHL	58	14	10	24	237	....	....	....	....	....	....	....	....	....	....	....	4	2	0	2	6	....	....	....
1997-98	**Dallas**	**NHL**	3	0	0	0	15	0	0	0	3	0.0	–1	....	....	....	....	....	....	....	....	....	....	....	....	....
	Michigan	IHL	4	2	0	2	4	....	....	....	....	....	....	....	....	....	....	....	....	....	....	....	....	....	....	....
1998-99	**Nashville**	**NHL**	70	1	2	3	242	0	0	0	21	4.8	–7	0	0.0	47	7	4:14	....	....	....	....	....	....	....	....
	NHL Totals		78	1	2	3	289	0	0	0	25	4.0		0	0.0	47	7	4:14	....	....	....	....	....	....	....	....

Claimed by **Nashville** from **Dallas** in Expansion Draft, June 26, 1998.

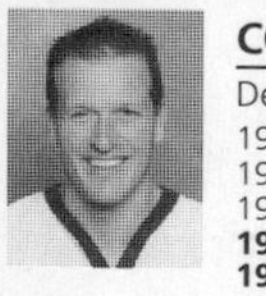

COTE, Sylvain — (KOH-tay) — TOR.

Defense. Shoots right. 6', 190 lbs. Born, Quebec City, Que., January 19, 1966. Hartford's 1st choice, 11th overall, in 1984 Entry Draft.

Season	Club	League	GP	G	A	Pts	PIM	PP	SH	GW	S	%	+/–	TF	F%	H	SB	Min	GP	G	A	Pts	PIM	PP	SH	GW
1981-82	Ste-Foy	QAAA	37	1	6	7	....	....	....	....	....	....	....	....	....	....	....	....	....	....	....	....	....	....	....	....
1982-83	Quebec	QMJHL	66	10	24	34	50	....	....	....	....	....	....	....	....	....	....	....	....	....	....	....	....	....	....	....
1983-84	Quebec	QMJHL	66	15	50	65	89	....	....	....	....	....	....	....	....	....	....	....	5	1	1	2	0	....	....	....
1984-85	**Hartford**	**NHL**	67	3	9	12	17	1	0	1	90	3.3	–30	....	....	....	....	....	....	....	....	....	....	....	....	....
1985-86	Hull	QMJHL	26	10	33	43	14	....	....	....	....	....	....	....	....	....	....	....	13	6	*28	34	22	....	....	....
	Hartford	**NHL**	2	0	0	0	0	0	0	0	0	0.0	1	....	....	....	....	....	....	....	....	....	....	....	....	....
	Binghamton	AHL	12	2	4	6	0	....	....	....	....	....	....	....	....	....	....	....	....	....	....	....	....	....	....	....
1986-87	**Hartford**	**NHL**	67	2	8	10	20	0	0	0	100	2.0	11	....	....	....	....	....	2	0	2	2	2	0	0	0
1987-88	**Hartford**	**NHL**	67	7	21	28	30	0	1	0	142	4.9	–8	....	....	....	....	....	6	1	1	2	4	1	0	0
1988-89	**Hartford**	**NHL**	78	8	9	17	49	1	0	0	130	6.2	–7	....	....	....	....	....	3	0	1	1	4	0	0	0
1989-90	**Hartford**	**NHL**	28	4	2	6	14	1	0	1	50	8.0	2	....	....	....	....	....	5	0	0	0	2	0	0	0
1990-91	**Hartford**	**NHL**	73	7	12	19	17	1	0	0	154	4.5	–17	....	....	....	....	....	6	0	2	2	2	0	0	0
1991-92	**Washington**	**NHL**	78	11	29	40	31	6	0	2	151	7.3	7	....	....	....	....	....	7	1	2	3	4	0	0	0
1992-93	**Washington**	**NHL**	77	21	29	50	34	8	2	3	206	10.2	28	....	....	....	....	....	6	1	1	2	4	0	0	0
1993-94	**Washington**	**NHL**	84	16	35	51	66	3	2	2	212	7.5	30	....	....	....	....	....	9	1	8	9	6	0	0	0
1994-95	**Washington**	**NHL**	47	5	14	19	53	1	0	2	124	4.0	2	....	....	....	....	....	7	1	3	4	2	0	0	0
1995-96	**Washington**	**NHL**	81	5	33	38	40	3	0	2	212	2.4	5	....	....	....	....	....	6	2	0	2	12	1	0	0
1996-97	**Washington**	**NHL**	57	6	18	24	28	2	0	0	131	4.6	11	....	....	....	....	....	....	....	....	....	....	....	....	....
1997-98	**Washington**	**NHL**	59	1	15	16	36	0	0	0	83	1.2	–5	....	....	....	....	....	....	....	....	....	....	....	....	....
	Toronto	**NHL**	12	3	6	9	6	1	0	1	20	15.0	2	....	....	....	....	....	....	....	....	....	....	....	....	....
1998-99	**Toronto**	**NHL**	79	5	24	29	28	0	0	1	119	4.2	22	1	0.0	76	95	21:04	17	2	1	3	10	0	0	0
	NHL Totals		956	104	264	368	469	28	5	15	1924	5.4		1	0.0	76	95	21:04	74	9	21	30	52	2	0	0

QMJHL Second All-Star Team (1984) • QMJHL First All-Star Team (1986)

Traded to **Washington** by **Hartford** for Washington's 2nd round choice (Andrei Nikolishin) in 1992 Entry Draft, September 8, 1991. Traded to **Toronto** by **Washington** for Jeff Brown, March 24, 1998.

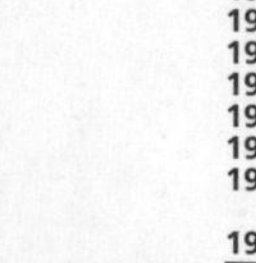

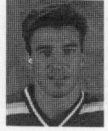

COURTNALL, Geoff — ST.L.

Left wing. Shoots left. 6'1", 204 lbs. Born, Duncan, B.C., August 18, 1962.

Season	Club	League	GP	G	A	Pts	PIM	PP	SH	GW	S	%	+/–	TF	F%	H	SB	Min	GP	G	A	Pts	PIM	PP	SH	GW
1980-81	Victoria	WHL	11	3	4	7	6	....	....	....	....	....	....	....	....	....	....	....	15	2	1	3	7	....	....	....
1981-82	Victoria	WHL	72	35	57	92	100	....	....	....	....	....	....	....	....	....	....	....	4	1	0	1	2	....	....	....
1982-83	Victoria	WHL	71	41	73	114	186	....	....	....	....	....	....	....	....	....	....	....	12	6	7	13	42	....	....	....
1983-84	**Boston**	**NHL**	4	0	0	0	0	0	0	0	1	0.0	–1	....	....	....	....	....	....	....	....	....	....	....	....	....
	Hershey	AHL	74	14	12	26	51	....	....	....	....	....	....	....	....	....	....	....	....	....	....	....	....	....	....	....
1984-85	**Boston**	**NHL**	64	12	16	28	82	0	0	1	91	13.2	–3	....	....	....	....	....	5	0	2	2	7	0	0	0
	Hershey	AHL	9	8	4	12	4	....	....	....	....	....	....	....	....	....	....	....	....	....	....	....	....	....	....	....
1985-86	**Boston**	**NHL**	64	21	16	37	61	2	0	4	161	13.0	1	....	....	....	....	....	3	0	0	0	2	0	0	0
	Moncton	AHL	12	8	8	16	6	....	....	....	....	....	....	....	....	....	....	....	....	....	....	....	....	....	....	....
1986-87	**Boston**	**NHL**	65	13	23	36	117	2	0	1	178	7.3	–4	....	....	....	....	....	1	0	0	0	0	0	0	0

			Regular Season																Playoffs							
Season	**Club**	**League**	**GP**	**G**	**A**	**Pts**	**PIM**	**PP**	**SH**	**GW**	**S**	**%**	**+/–**	**TF**	**F%**	**H**	**SB**	**Min**	**GP**	**G**	**A**	**Pts**	**PIM**	**PP**	**SH**	**GW**
1987-88	**Boston**	**NHL**	**62**	**32**	**26**	**58**	**108**	**8**	**0**	**4**	**220**	**14.5**	**24**	....	....	....	....	....	....	....	....	....	....	....	....	....
	♦ **Edmonton**	**NHL**	**12**	**4**	**4**	**8**	**15**	**0**	**0**	**1**	**32**	**12.5**	**1**	....	....	....	....	....	**19**	**0**	**3**	**3**	**23**	**0**	**0**	**0**
1988-89	**Washington**	**NHL**	**79**	**42**	**38**	**80**	**112**	**16**	**0**	**6**	**239**	**17.6**	**11**	....	....	....	....	....	**6**	**2**	**5**	**7**	**12**	**1**	**0**	**0**
1989-90	**Washington**	**NHL**	**80**	**35**	**39**	**74**	**104**	**9**	**0**	**2**	**307**	**11.4**	**27**	....	....	....	....	....	**15**	**4**	**9**	**13**	**32**	**1**	**0**	**2**
1990-91	**St. Louis**	**NHL**	**66**	**27**	**30**	**57**	**56**	**9**	**0**	**6**	**216**	**12.5**	**19**	....	....	....	....	....	....	....	....	....	....	....	....	....
	Vancouver	**NHL**	**11**	**6**	**2**	**8**	**8**	**3**	**0**	**2**	**47**	**12.8**	**–3**	....	....	....	....	....	**6**	**3**	**5**	**8**	**4**	**0**	**0**	**0**
1991-92	**Vancouver**	**NHL**	**70**	**23**	**34**	**57**	**116**	**12**	**0**	**3**	**281**	**8.2**	**–6**	....	....	....	....	....	**12**	**6**	**8**	**14**	**20**	**2**	**0**	**1**
1992-93	**Vancouver**	**NHL**	**84**	**31**	**46**	**77**	**167**	**9**	**0**	**11**	**214**	**14.5**	**27**	....	....	....	....	....	**12**	**4**	**10**	**14**	**12**	**1**	**0**	**1**
1993-94	**Vancouver**	**NHL**	**82**	**26**	**44**	**70**	**123**	**12**	**1**	**2**	**264**	**9.8**	**15**	....	....	....	....	....	**24**	**9**	**10**	**19**	**51**	**0**	**1**	**3**
1994-95	**Vancouver**	**NHL**	**45**	**16**	**18**	**34**	**81**	**7**	**0**	**1**	**144**	**11.1**	**2**	....	....	....	....	....	**11**	**4**	**2**	**6**	**34**	**3**	**1**	**1**
1995-96	**St. Louis**	**NHL**	**69**	**24**	**16**	**40**	**101**	**7**	**1**	**1**	**228**	**10.5**	**–9**	....	....	....	....	....	**13**	**0**	**3**	**3**	**14**	**0**	**0**	**0**
1996-97	**St. Louis**	**NHL**	**82**	**17**	**40**	**57**	**86**	**4**	**0**	**2**	**203**	**8.4**	**3**	....	....	....	....	....	**6**	**3**	**1**	**4**	**23**	**1**	**0**	**2**
1997-98	**St. Louis**	**NHL**	**79**	**31**	**31**	**62**	**94**	**6**	**0**	**5**	**189**	**16.4**	**12**	....	....	....	....	....	**10**	**2**	**8**	**10**	**18**	**1**	**0**	**0**
1998-99	**St. Louis**	**NHL**	**24**	**5**	**7**	**12**	**28**	**1**	**0**	**2**	**60**	**8.3**	**2**	**1**	**100.0**	**21**	**4**	**14:48**	**13**	**2**	**4**	**6**	**10**	**2**	**0**	**0**
	NHL Totals		**1042**	**365**	**430**	**795**	**1459**	**107**	**2**	**54**	**3075**	**11.9**		**1**	**100.0**	**21**	**4**	**14:48**	**156**	**39**	**70**	**109**	**262**	**12**	**2**	**10**

Signed as a free agent by **Boston**, July 6, 1983. Traded to **Edmonton** by **Boston** with Bill Ranford and future considerations for Andy Moog, March 8, 1988. Rights traded to **Washington** by **Edmonton** for Greg C. Adams, July 22, 1988. Traded to **St. Louis** by **Washington** for Peter Zezel and Mike Lalor, July 13, 1990. Traded to **Vancouver** by **St. Louis** with Robert Dirk, Sergio Momesso, Cliff Ronning and St. Louis' 5th round choice (Brian Loney) in 1992 Entry Draft for Dan Quinn and Garth Butcher, March 5, 1991. Signed as a free agent by **St. Louis**, July 14, 1995. •Missed majority of 1998-99 season recovering from head injury suffered in game vs. San Jose, November 27, 1998.

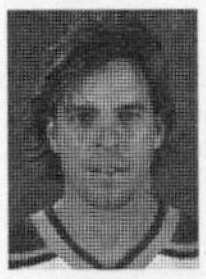

COURTNALL, Russ

Right wing. Shoots right. 5'11", 185 lbs. Born, Duncan, B.C., June 2, 1965. Toronto's 1st choice, 7th overall, in 1983 Entry Draft.

1982-83	Victoria	WHL	60	36	61	97	33	....	....	....	....	....	....	....	....	....	....	....	12	11	7	18	6	....	....	....
1983-84	Victoria	WHL	32	29	37	66	63	....	....	....	....	....	....	....	....	....	....	....	....	....	....	....	....	....	....	....
	Canada	Nat-Team	16	4	7	11	10	....	....	....	....	....	....	....	....	....	....	....	....	....	....	....	....	....	....	....
	Canada	Olympics	7	1	3	4	2	....	....	....	....	....	....	....	....	....	....	....	....	....	....	....	....	....	....	....
	Toronto	**NHL**	**14**	**3**	**9**	**12**	**6**	**1**	**0**	**0**	**29**	**10.3**	**0**	....	....	....	....	....	....	....	....	....	....	....	....	....
1984-85	**Toronto**	**NHL**	**69**	**12**	**10**	**22**	**44**	**0**	**2**	**1**	**130**	**9.2**	**–23**	....	....	....	....	....	....	....	....	....	....	....	....	....
1985-86	**Toronto**	**NHL**	**73**	**22**	**38**	**60**	**52**	**3**	**1**	**4**	**203**	**10.8**	**0**	....	....	....	....	....	**10**	**3**	**6**	**9**	**8**	**1**	**0**	**0**
1986-87	**Toronto**	**NHL**	**79**	**29**	**44**	**73**	**90**	**3**	**6**	**3**	**282**	**10.3**	**–20**	....	....	....	....	....	**13**	**3**	**4**	**7**	**11**	**1**	**0**	**0**
1987-88	**Toronto**	**NHL**	**65**	**23**	**26**	**49**	**47**	**6**	**3**	**1**	**212**	**10.8**	**–16**	....	....	....	....	....	**6**	**2**	**1**	**3**	**0**	**0**	**0**	**0**
1988-89	**Toronto**	**NHL**	**9**	**1**	**1**	**2**	**4**	**0**	**1**	**0**	**11**	**9.1**	**–2**	....	....	....	....	....	....	....	....	....	....	....	....	....
	Montreal	**NHL**	**64**	**22**	**17**	**39**	**15**	**7**	**0**	**3**	**136**	**16.2**	**11**	....	....	....	....	....	**21**	**8**	**5**	**13**	**18**	**1**	**0**	**2**
1989-90	**Montreal**	**NHL**	**80**	**27**	**32**	**59**	**27**	**3**	**0**	**2**	**294**	**9.2**	**14**	....	....	....	....	....	**11**	**5**	**1**	**6**	**10**	**0**	**0**	**0**
1990-91	**Montreal**	**NHL**	**79**	**26**	**50**	**76**	**29**	**5**	**1**	**5**	**279**	**9.3**	**5**	....	....	....	....	....	**13**	**8**	**3**	**11**	**7**	**2**	**2**	**1**
1991-92	**Montreal**	**NHL**	**27**	**7**	**14**	**21**	**6**	**0**	**1**	**1**	**63**	**11.1**	**6**	....	....	....	....	....	**10**	**1**	**1**	**2**	**4**	**0**	**0**	**1**
1992-93	**Minnesota**	**NHL**	**84**	**36**	**43**	**79**	**49**	**14**	**2**	**3**	**294**	**12.2**	**1**	....	....	....	....	....	....	....	....	....	....	....	....	....
1993-94	**Dallas**	**NHL**	**84**	**23**	**57**	**80**	**59**	**5**	**0**	**4**	**231**	**10.0**	**6**	....	....	....	....	....	**9**	**1**	**8**	**9**	**0**	**0**	**0**	**0**
1994-95	**Dallas**	**NHL**	**32**	**7**	**10**	**17**	**13**	**2**	**0**	**1**	**90**	**7.8**	**–8**	....	....	....	....	....	....	....	....	....	....	....	....	....
	Vancouver	**NHL**	**13**	**4**	**14**	**18**	**4**	**0**	**2**	**1**	**42**	**9.5**	**10**	....	....	....	....	....	**11**	**4**	**8**	**12**	**21**	**0**	**2**	**1**
1995-96	**Vancouver**	**NHL**	**81**	**26**	**39**	**65**	**40**	**6**	**4**	**4**	**205**	**12.7**	**25**	....	....	....	....	....	**6**	**1**	**3**	**4**	**2**	**0**	**0**	**0**
1996-97	**Vancouver**	**NHL**	**47**	**9**	**19**	**28**	**24**	**1**	**0**	**1**	**101**	**8.9**	**4**	....	....	....	....	....	....	....	....	....	....	....	....	....
	NY Rangers	**NHL**	**14**	**2**	**5**	**7**	**2**	**1**	**1**	**1**	**24**	**8.3**	**–3**	....	....	....	....	....	**15**	**3**	**4**	**7**	**0**	**1**	**0**	**0**
1997-98	**Los Angeles**	**NHL**	**58**	**12**	**6**	**18**	**27**	**1**	**4**	**4**	**97**	**12.4**	**–2**	....	....	....	....	....	**4**	**0**	**0**	**0**	**2**	**0**	**0**	**0**
1998-99	**Los Angeles**	**NHL**	**57**	**6**	**13**	**19**	**19**	**0**	**1**	**1**	**77**	**7.8**	**–9**	**152**	**44.1**	**46**	**14**	**15:03**	....	....	....	....	....	....	....	....
	NHL Totals		**1029**	**297**	**447**	**744**	**557**	**58**	**29**	**40**	**2800**	**10.6**		**152**	**44.1**	**46**	**14**	**15:03**	**129**	**39**	**44**	**83**	**83**	**6**	**4**	**5**

Played in NHL All-Star Game (1994)

Traded to **Montreal** by **Toronto** for John Kordic and Montreal's 6th round choice (Michael Doers) in 1989 Entry Draft, November 7, 1988. Traded to **Minnesota** by **Montreal** for Brian Bellows, August 31, 1992. Transferred to **Dallas** after **Minnesota** franchise relocated, June 9, 1993. Traded to **Vancouver** by **Dallas** for Greg Adams, Dan Kesa and Vancouver's 5th round choice (later traded to LA Kings — LA Kings selected Jason Morgan) in 1995 Entry Draft, April 7, 1995. Traded to **NY Rangers** by **Vancouver** with Esa Tikkanen for Sergei Nemchinov and Brian Noonan, March 8, 1997. Signed as a free agent by **LA Kings**, November 7, 1997.

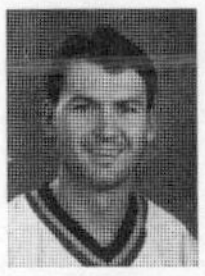

COURVILLE, Larry

(KOOR-vihl)

Left wing. Shoots left. 6'1", 195 lbs. Born, Timmins, Ont., April 2, 1975. Vancouver's 2nd choice, 61st overall, in 1995 Entry Draft.

1990-91	Waterloo	OJHL	47	20	18	38	144	....	....	....	....	....	....	....	....	....	....	....	....	....	....	....	....	....	....	....
1991-92	Cornwall	OHL	60	8	12	20	80	....	....	....	....	....	....	....	....	....	....	....	6	0	0	0	8	....	....	....
1992-93	Newmarket	OHL	64	21	18	39	181	....	....	....	....	....	....	....	....	....	....	....	7	0	6	6	14	....	....	....
1993-94	Newmarket	OHL	39	20	19	39	134	....	....	....	....	....	....	....	....	....	....	....	....	....	....	....	....	....	....	....
	Moncton	AHL	8	2	0	2	37	....	....	....	....	....	....	....	....	....	....	....	10	2	2	4	27	....	....	....
1994-95	Sarnia	OHL	16	9	9	18	58	....	....	....	....	....	....	....	....	....	....	....	....	....	....	....	....	....	....	....
	Oshawa	OHL	28	25	30	55	72	....	....	....	....	....	....	....	....	....	....	....	7	4	10	14	10	....	....	....
1995-96	**Vancouver**	**NHL**	**3**	**1**	**0**	**1**	**0**	**0**	**0**	**1**	**2**	**50.0**	**1**	....	....	....	....	....	....	....	....	....	....	....	....	....
	Syracuse	AHL	71	17	32	49	127	....	....	....	....	....	....	....	....	....	....	....	14	5	3	8	10	....	....	....
1996-97	**Vancouver**	**NHL**	**19**	**0**	**2**	**2**	**11**	**0**	**0**	**0**	**11**	**0.0**	**–4**	....	....	....	....	....	....	....	....	....	....	....	....	....
	Syracuse	AHL	54	20	24	44	103	....	....	....	....	....	....	....	....	....	....	....	3	0	1	1	20	....	....	....
1997-98	**Vancouver**	**NHL**	**11**	**0**	**0**	**0**	**5**	**0**	**0**	**0**	**3**	**0.0**	**–7**	....	....	....	....	....	....	....	....	....	....	....	....	....
	Syracuse	AHL	29	6	12	18	84	....	....	....	....	....	....	....	....	....	....	....	....	....	....	....	....	....	....	....
1998-99	Syracuse	AHL	71	13	28	41	155	....	....	....	....	....	....	....	....	....	....	....	....	....	....	....	....	....	....	....
	NHL Totals		**33**	**1**	**2**	**3**	**16**	**0**	**0**	**1**	**16**	**6.3**		....	....	....	....	....	....	....	....	....	....	....	....	....

OHL Second All-Star Team (1995)

• Re-entered NHL Entry Draft. Originally Winnipeg's 6th choice, 119th overall in 1993 Entry Draft.

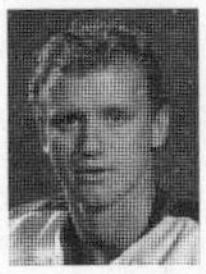

CRAIG, Mike

Right wing. Shoots right. 6'1", 180 lbs. Born, St. Mary's, Ont., June 6, 1971. Minnesota's 2nd choice, 28th overall, in 1989 Entry Draft.

1986-87	Woodstock	OJHL-C	32	29	19	48	64	....	....	....	....	....	....	....	....	....	....	....	....	....	....	....	....	....	....	....
1987-88	Oshawa	OHL	61	6	10	16	39	....	....	....	....	....	....	....	....	....	....	....	7	7	0	1	11	....	....	....
1988-89	Oshawa	OHL	63	36	36	72	34	....	....	....	....	....	....	....	....	....	....	....	6	3	1	4	6	....	....	....
1989-90	Oshawa	OHL	43	36	40	76	85	....	....	....	....	....	....	....	....	....	....	....	17	10	16	26	46	....	....	....
1990-91	**Minnesota**	**NHL**	**39**	**8**	**4**	**12**	**32**	**1**	**0**	**2**	**59**	**13.6**	**–11**	....	....	....	....	....	**10**	**1**	**1**	**2**	**20**	**1**	**0**	**1**
1991-92	**Minnesota**	**NHL**	**67**	**15**	**16**	**31**	**155**	**4**	**0**	**4**	**136**	**11.0**	**–12**	....	....	....	....	....	**4**	**1**	**0**	**1**	**7**	**0**	**0**	**0**
1992-93	**Minnesota**	**NHL**	**70**	**15**	**23**	**38**	**106**	**7**	**0**	**0**	**131**	**11.5**	**–11**	....	....	....	....	....	....	....	....	....	....	....	....	....
1993-94	**Dallas**	**NHL**	**72**	**13**	**24**	**37**	**139**	**3**	**0**	**2**	**150**	**8.7**	**–14**	....	....	....	....	....	**4**	**0**	**0**	**0**	**2**	**0**	**0**	**0**
1994-95	**Toronto**	**NHL**	**37**	**5**	**5**	**10**	**12**	**1**	**0**	**1**	**61**	**8.2**	**–21**	....	....	....	....	....	**2**	**0**	**1**	**1**	**2**	**0**	**0**	**0**
1995-96	**Toronto**	**NHL**	**70**	**8**	**12**	**20**	**42**	**1**	**0**	**1**	**108**	**7.4**	**–8**	....	....	....	....	....	**6**	**0**	**0**	**0**	**18**	**0**	**0**	**0**
1996-97	**Toronto**	**NHL**	**65**	**7**	**13**	**20**	**62**	**1**	**0**	**0**	**128**	**5.5**	**–20**	....	....	....	....	....	....	....	....	....	....	....	....	....
1997-98	San Antonio	IHL	12	4	1	5	18	....	....	....	....	....	....	....	....	....	....	....	....	....	....	....	....	....	....	....
	Kansas City	IHL	59	14	33	47	68	....	....	....	....	....	....	....	....	....	....	....	11	5	5	10	28	....	....	....
1998-99	**San Jose**	**NHL**	**1**	**0**	**0**	**0**	**0**	**0**	**0**	**0**	**1**	**0.0**	**–1**	**0**	**0.0**	**1**	**1**	**11:25**	....	....	....	....	....	....	....	....
	Kentucky	AHL	52	27	17	44	72	....	....	....	....	....	....	....	....	....	....	....	12	5	4	9	18	....	....	....
	NHL Totals		**421**	**71**	**97**	**168**	**548**	**18**	**0**	**10**	**774**	**9.2**		**0**	**0.0**	**1**	**1**	**11:25**	**26**	**2**	**2**	**4**	**49**	**1**	**0**	**1**

Transferred to **Dallas** after **Minnesota** franchise relocated, June 9, 1993. Signed as a free agent by **Toronto**, July 29, 1994. Signed as a free agent by **San Jose**, July 13, 1998.

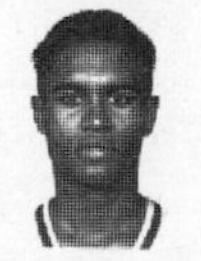

CRAIGWELL, Dale

Center. Shoots left. 5'11", 180 lbs. Born, Toronto, Ont., April 24, 1971. San Jose's 11th choice, 199th overall, in 1991 Entry Draft.

1987-88	Oshawa Majors	OMHA	60	49	57	106	42	....	....	....	....	....	....	....	....	....	....	....	....	....	....	....	....	....	....	....
1988-89	Oshawa	OHL	55	9	14	23	15	....	....	....	....	....	....	....	....	....	....	....	....	....	....	....	....	....	....	....
1989-90	Oshawa	OHL	64	22	41	63	39	....	....	....	....	....	....	....	....	....	....	....	17	7	7	14	11	....	....	....
1990-91	Oshawa	OHL	56	27	68	95	34	....	....	....	....	....	....	....	....	....	....	....	16	7	16	23	9	....	....	....
1991-92	**San Jose**	**NHL**	**32**	**5**	**11**	**16**	**8**	**4**	**0**	**2**	**38**	**13.2**	**–3**	....	....	....	....	....	....	....	....	....	....	....	....	....
	Kansas City	IHL	48	6	19	25	29	....	....	....	....	....	....	....	....	....	....	....	12	4	7	11	4	....	....	....

			Regular Season																Playoffs							
Season	Club	League	GP	G	A	Pts	PIM	PP	SH	GW	S	%	+/–	TF	F%	H	SB	Min	GP	G	A	Pts	PIM	PP	SH	GW
1992-93	**San Jose**	**NHL**	**8**	**3**	**1**	**4**	**4**	**0**	**0**	**0**	**7**	**42.9**	**–4**													
	Kansas City	IHL	60	15	38	53	24												12	*7	5	12	2			
1993-94	**San Jose**	**NHL**	**58**	**3**	**6**	**9**	**16**	**0**	**1**	**0**	**35**	**8.6**	**–13**													
	Kansas City	IHL	5	3	1	4	0																			
1994-95			DID NOT PLAY – INJURED																							
1995-96	San Francisco	IHL	75	11	49	60	38												4	2	0	2	0			
1996-97	Kansas City	IHL	82	17	51	68	34												3	1	0	1	0			
1997-98	Kansas City	IHL	81	13	42	55	12												11	2	9	11	2			
1998-99	Augsburg	Germany	16	1	4	5	4																			
	Kansas City	IHL	61	11	28	39	14												3	0	2	2	2			
	NHL Totals		**98**	**11**	**18**	**29**	**28**	**4**	**1**	**2**	**80**	**13.8**														

• Missed entire 1994-95 season recovering from broken ankle, September, 1994.

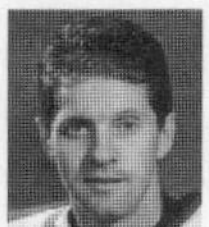

CRAVEN, Murray — S.J.

Left wing. Shoots left. 6'3", 190 lbs. Born, Medicine Hat, Alta., July 20, 1964. Detroit's 1st choice, 17th overall, in 1982 Entry Draft.

Season	Club	League	GP	G	A	Pts	PIM	PP	SH	GW	S	%	+/–	TF	F%	H	SB	Min	GP	G	A	Pts	PIM	PP	SH	GW
1980-81	Medicine Hat	WHL	69	5	10	15	18												5	0	0	0	2			
1981-82	Medicine Hat	WHL	72	35	46	81	49																			
1982-83	Medicine Hat	WHL	28	17	29	46	35																			
	Detroit	**NHL**	**31**	**4**	**7**	**11**	**6**	**0**	**0**	**1**	**21**	**19.0**	**4**													
1983-84	Medicine Hat	WHL	48	38	56	94	53												4	5	3	8	4			
	Detroit	**NHL**	**15**	**0**	**4**	**4**	**6**	**0**	**0**	**0**	**8**	**0.0**	**2**													
1984-85	**Philadelphia**	**NHL**	**80**	**26**	**35**	**61**	**30**	**2**	**2**	**5**	**142**	**18.3**	**45**						**19**	**4**	**6**	**10**	**11**	**1**	**1**	**1**
1985-86	**Philadelphia**	**NHL**	**78**	**21**	**33**	**54**	**34**	**2**	**0**	**6**	**182**	**11.5**	**24**						**5**	**0**	**3**	**3**	**4**	**0**	**0**	**0**
1986-87	**Philadelphia**	**NHL**	**77**	**19**	**30**	**49**	**38**	**5**	**3**	**2**	**98**	**19.4**	**1**						**12**	**3**	**1**	**4**	**9**	**2**	**0**	**0**
1987-88	**Philadelphia**	**NHL**	**72**	**30**	**46**	**76**	**58**	**6**	**2**	**2**	**184**	**16.3**	**25**						**7**	**2**	**5**	**7**	**4**	**0**	**0**	**1**
1988-89	**Philadelphia**	**NHL**	**51**	**9**	**28**	**37**	**52**	**0**	**0**	**2**	**89**	**10.1**	**4**						**1**	**0**	**0**	**0**	**0**	**0**	**0**	**0**
1989-90	**Philadelphia**	**NHL**	**76**	**25**	**50**	**75**	**42**	**7**	**2**	**3**	**175**	**14.3**	**2**													
1990-91	**Philadelphia**	**NHL**	**77**	**19**	**47**	**66**	**53**	**6**	**0**	**0**	**170**	**11.2**	**–2**													
1991-92	**Philadelphia**	**NHL**	**12**	**3**	**3**	**6**	**8**	**1**	**0**	**0**	**19**	**15.8**	**2**													
	Hartford	**NHL**	**61**	**24**	**30**	**54**	**38**	**8**	**4**	**1**	**133**	**18.0**	**–4**						**7**	**3**	**3**	**6**	**6**	**0**	**1**	**0**
1992-93	**Hartford**	**NHL**	**67**	**25**	**42**	**67**	**20**	**6**	**3**	**2**	**139**	**18.0**	**–4**													
	Vancouver	**NHL**	**10**	**0**	**10**	**10**	**12**	**0**	**0**	**0**	**12**	**0.0**	**3**						**12**	**4**	**6**	**10**	**4**	**1**	**0**	**1**
1993-94	**Vancouver**	**NHL**	**78**	**15**	**40**	**55**	**30**	**2**	**1**	**3**	**115**	**13.0**	**5**						**22**	**4**	**9**	**13**	**18**	**0**	**0**	**1**
1994-95	**Chicago**	**NHL**	**16**	**4**	**3**	**7**	**2**	**1**	**0**	**2**	**29**	**13.8**	**2**						**16**	**5**	**5**	**10**	**4**	**0**	**0**	**1**
1995-96	**Chicago**	**NHL**	**66**	**18**	**29**	**47**	**36**	**5**	**1**	**7**	**86**	**20.9**	**20**						**9**	**1**	**4**	**5**	**2**	**1**	**0**	**0**
1996-97	**Chicago**	**NHL**	**75**	**8**	**27**	**35**	**12**	**2**	**0**	**1**	**122**	**6.6**	**0**						**2**	**0**	**0**	**0**	**2**	**0**	**0**	**0**
1997-98	**San Jose**	**NHL**	**67**	**12**	**17**	**29**	**25**	**2**	**3**	**3**	**107**	**11.2**	**4**						**6**	**1**	**1**	**2**	**0**	**0**	**0**	**0**
1998-99	**San Jose**	**NHL**	**43**	**4**	**10**	**14**	**18**	**0**	**1**	**1**	**55**	**7.3**	**–3**	**244**	**42.2**	**20**	**21**	**14:26**								
	NHL Totals		**1052**	**266**	**491**	**757**	**520**	**55**	**22**	**41**	**1886**	**14.1**		**244**	**42.2**	**20**	**21**	**14:26**	**118**	**27**	**43**	**70**	**64**	**5**	**2**	**5**

Traded to **Philadelphia** by **Detroit** with Joe Paterson for Darryl Sittler, October 10, 1984. Traded to **Hartford** by **Philadelphia** with Philadelphia's 4th round choice (Kevin Smyth) in 1992 Entry Draft for Kevin Dineen, November 13, 1991. Traded to **Vancouver** by **Hartford** with Vancouver's 5th round choice (previously acquired, Vancouver selected Scott Walker) in 1993 Entry Draft for Robert Kron, Vancouver's 3rd round choice (Marek Malik) in 1993 Entry Draft and future considerations (Jim Sandlak, May 17, 1993), March 22, 1993. Traded to **Chicago** by **Vancouver** for Christian Ruutu, March 10, 1995. Traded to **San Jose** by **Chicago** for the rights to Petri Varis and San Jose's 6th round choice (Jari Viuhkola) in 1998 Entry Draft, July 25, 1997.

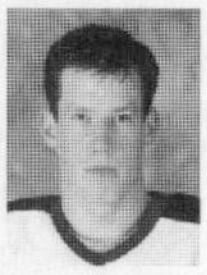

CROSS, Cory — T.B.

Defense. Shoots left. 6'5", 219 lbs. Born, Lloydminster, Alta., January 3, 1971. Tampa Bay's 1st choice, 1st overall, in 1992 Supplemental Draft.

Season	Club	League	GP	G	A	Pts	PIM	PP	SH	GW	S	%	+/–	TF	F%	H	SB	Min	GP	G	A	Pts	PIM	PP	SH	GW
1990-91	U. of Alberta	CWUAA	20	2	5	7	16																			
1991-92	U. of Alberta	CWUAA	41	4	11	15	82																			
1992-93	U. of Alberta	CWUAA	43	11	28	39	105																			
	Atlanta	IHL	7	0	1	1	2												4	0	0	0	6			
1993-94	**Tampa Bay**	**NHL**	**5**	**0**	**0**	**0**	**6**	**0**	**0**	**0**	**5**	**0.0**	**–3**													
	Atlanta	IHL	70	4	14	18	72												9	1	2	3	14			
1994-95	**Tampa Bay**	**NHL**	**43**	**1**	**5**	**6**	**41**	**0**	**0**	**1**	**35**	**2.9**	**–6**													
	Atlanta	IHL	41	5	10	15	67																			
1995-96	**Tampa Bay**	**NHL**	**75**	**2**	**14**	**16**	**66**	**0**	**0**	**0**	**57**	**3.5**	**4**						**6**	**0**	**0**	**0**	**22**	**0**	**0**	**0**
1996-97	**Tampa Bay**	**NHL**	**72**	**4**	**5**	**9**	**95**	**0**	**0**	**2**	**75**	**5.3**	**6**													
1997-98	**Tampa Bay**	**NHL**	**74**	**3**	**6**	**9**	**77**	**0**	**1**	**0**	**72**	**4.2**	**–24**													
1998-99	**Tampa Bay**	**NHL**	**67**	**2**	**16**	**18**	**92**	**0**	**0**	**0**	**96**	**2.1**	**–25**	**0**	**0.0**	**127**	**82**	**22:38**								
	NHL Totals		**336**	**12**	**46**	**58**	**377**	**0**	**1**	**3**	**340**	**3.5**		**0**	**0.0**	**127**	**82**	**22:38**	**6**	**0**	**0**	**0**	**22**	**0**	**0**	**0**

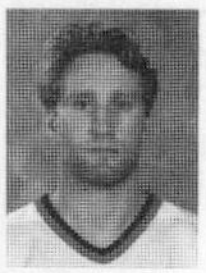

CROWE, Philip (KROH) — NSH.

Left wing. Shoots left. 6'2", 215 lbs. Born, Nanton, Alta., April 14, 1970.

Season	Club	League	GP	G	A	Pts	PIM	PP	SH	GW	S	%	+/–	TF	F%	H	SB	Min	GP	G	A	Pts	PIM	PP	SH	GW
1989-90	Olds Grizzlies	AJHL	47	8	21	29	248																			
1990-91	Olds Grizzlies	AJHL	50	16	24	40	290																			
1991-92	Adirondack	AHL	6	1	0	1	29																			
	Columbus	ECHL	32	4	7	11	145																			
	Toledo	ECHL	2	0	0	0	0												5	0	0	0	58			
1992-93	Phoenix	IHL	53	3	3	6	190																			
1993-94	Fort Wayne	IHL	5	0	1	1	26																			
	Los Angeles	**NHL**	**31**	**0**	**2**	**2**	**77**	**0**	**0**	**0**	**5**	**0.0**	**4**													
	Phoenix	IHL	2	0	0	0	0																			
1994-95	Hershey	AHL	46	11	6	17	132												6	0	1	1	19			
1995-96	**Philadelphia**	**NHL**	**16**	**1**	**1**	**2**	**28**	**0**	**0**	**0**	**6**	**16.7**	**0**													
	Hershey	AHL	39	6	8	14	105												5	1	2	3	19			
1996-97	**Ottawa**	**NHL**	**26**	**0**	**1**	**1**	**30**	**0**	**0**	**0**	**8**	**0.0**	**0**						**3**	**0**	**0**	**0**	**16**	**0**	**0**	**0**
	Detroit	IHL	41	7	7	14	83																			
1997-98	**Ottawa**	**NHL**	**9**	**3**	**0**	**3**	**24**	**0**	**0**	**1**	**6**	**50.0**	**3**													
	Detroit	IHL	55	6	13	19	160												20	5	2	7	48			
1998-99	**Ottawa**	**NHL**	**8**	**0**	**1**	**1**	**4**	**0**	**0**	**0**	**2**	**0.0**	**1**	**0**	**0.0**	**5**	**1**	**4:10**								
	Cincinnati	IHL	39	2	6	8	62																			
	Detroit	IHL	2	0	0	0	9																			
	Las Vegas	IHL	14	1	3	4	18																			
	NHL Totals		**90**	**4**	**5**	**9**	**163**	**0**	**0**	**1**	**27**	**14.8**		**0**	**0.0**	**5**	**1**	**4:10**	**3**	**0**	**0**	**0**	**16**	**0**	**0**	**0**

Signed as a free agent by **LA Kings**, November 8, 1993. Signed as a free agent by **Philadelphia**, July 19, 1994. Signed as a free agent by **Ottawa**, July 29, 1996. Claimed by **Atlanta** from **Ottawa** in Expansion Draft, June 25, 1999. Traded to **Nashville** by **Atlanta** for future considerations, June 26, 1999.

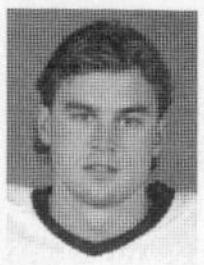

CROWLEY, Mike — ANA.

Defense. Shoots left. 5'11", 190 lbs. Born, Bloomington, MN, July 4, 1975. Philadelphia's 5th choice, 140th overall, in 1993 Entry Draft.

Season	Club	League	GP	G	A	Pts	PIM	PP	SH	GW	S	%	+/–	TF	F%	H	SB	Min	GP	G	A	Pts	PIM	PP	SH	GW
1990-91	Jefferson High	H.S.	20	3	9	12	2																			
1991-92	Jefferson High	H.S.	28	5	18	23	8																			
1992-93	Jefferson High	H.S.	22	10	32	42	18																			
1993-94	Jefferson High	H.S.	28	23	54	77	26																			
1994-95	U. of Minnesota	WCHA	41	11	27	38	60																			
1995-96	U. of Minnesota	WCHA	42	17	46	63	28																			
1996-97	U. of Minnesota	WCHA	42	9	*47	*56	24																			
1997-98	**Anaheim**	**NHL**	**8**	**2**	**2**	**4**	**8**	**0**	**0**	**1**	**17**	**11.8**	**0**													
	Cincinnati	AHL	76	12	26	38	91																			

			Regular Season																Playoffs							
Season	Club	League	GP	G	A	Pts	PIM	PP	SH	GW	S	%	+/-	TF	F%	H	SB	Min	GP	G	A	Pts	PIM	PP	SH	GW
1998-99	Anaheim	NHL	20	2	3	5	16	1	0	1	41	4.9	-10	0	0.0	8	20	16:36	....	....	....	....	....			
	Cincinnati	AHL	44	5	23	28	42												3	0	3	3	2			
	NHL Totals		28	4	5	9	24	1	0	2	58	6.9		0	0.0	8	20	16:36								

WCHA First All-Star Team (1996, 1997) • NCAA West First All-American Team (1996, 1997)
Traded to **Anaheim** by Philadelphia with Anatoli Semenov for Brian Wesenberg, March 19, 1996.

CROWLEY, Ted — CHI.
Defense. Shoots right. 6'2", 188 lbs. Born, Concord, MA, May 3, 1970. Toronto's 4th choice, 69th overall, in 1988 Entry Draft.

Season	Club	League	GP	G	A	Pts	PIM	PP	SH	GW	S	%	+/-	TF	F%	H	SB	Min	GP	G	A	Pts	PIM
1987-88	Lawrence Prep	H.S.	23	11	23	34																	
1988-89	Lawrence Prep	H.S.	23	12	24	36																	
1989-90	Boston College	H.E.	39	7	24	31	34																
1990-91	Boston College	H.E.	39	12	24	36	61																
1991-92	United States	Nat-Team	42	6	7	13	65																
	St. John's	AHL	29	5	4	9	33												10	3	1	4	11
1992-93	St. John's	AHL	79	19	38	57	41												9	2	2	4	4
1993-94	United States	Nat-Team	48	9	13	22	80																
	United States	Olympics	8	0	2	2	8																
	Hartford	**NHL**	21	1	2	3	10	1	0	0	28	3.6	-1										
1994-95	Chicago	IHL	53	8	23	31	68																
	Houston	IHL	23	4	9	13	35												3	0	1	1	0
1995-96	Providence	AHL	72	12	30	42	47												4	1	2	3	2
1996-97	Cincinnati	IHL	39	9	9	18	24																
	Phoenix	IHL	30	5	8	13	21																
1997-98	Springfield	AHL	78	14	35	49	55												4	1	1	2	2
1998-99	**Colorado**	**NHL**	7	0	1	1	2	0	0	0	10	0.0	-1	0	0.0	1	0	7:00					
	Hershey	AHL	18	1	5	6	27																
	NY Islanders	**NHL**	6	1	1	2	0	1	0	0	10	10.0	0	0	0.0	3	2	15:11					
	Lowell	AHL	41	3	22	25	51												3	0	0	0	6
	NHL Totals		34	2	4	6	12	2	0	0	48	4.2		0	0.0	4	2	10:47					

Hockey East First All-Star Team (1991) • NCAA East Second All-American Team (1991)

Traded to **Hartford** by **Toronto** for Mark Greig and Hartford's 6th round choice (later traded to NY Rangers — NY Rangers selected Yuri Litvinov) in 1994 Entry Draft, January 25, 1994. Signed as a free agent by **Boston**, August 9, 1995. Signed as a free agent by **Phoenix**, June 27, 1997. Signed as a free agent by **Colorado**, August 14, 1998. Traded to **NY Islanders** by **Colorado** for Michael Gaul, December 15, 1998. Signed as a free agent by **Chicago**, July 22, 1999.

CULLEN, John
Center. Shoots right. 5'10", 182 lbs. Born, Fort Erie, Ont., August 2, 1964. Buffalo's 2nd choice, 10th overall, in 1986 Supplemental Draft.

Season	Club	League	GP	G	A	Pts	PIM	PP	SH	GW	S	%	+/-	TF	F%	H	SB	Min	GP	G	A	Pts	PIM	PP	SH	GW
1983-84	Boston University	ECAC	40	23	33	56	28																			
1984-85	Boston University	H.E.	41	27	32	59	46																			
1985-86	Boston University	H.E.	43	25	49	74	54																			
1986-87	Boston University	H.E.	36	23	29	52	35																			
1987-88	Flint	IHL	81	48	*109	*157	113												16	11	*15	26	16			
1988-89	**Pittsburgh**	**NHL**	79	12	37	49	112	8	0	0	121	9.9	-25						11	3	6	9	28	0	0	0
1989-90	**Pittsburgh**	**NHL**	72	32	60	92	138	9	0	4	197	16.2	-13													
1990-91	**Pittsburgh**	**NHL**	65	31	63	94	83	10	0	2	171	18.1	0													
	Hartford	**NHL**	13	8	8	16	18	4	0	1	34	23.5	-6						6	2	7	9	10	0	0	0
1991-92	**Hartford**	**NHL**	77	26	51	77	141	10	0	4	173	15.0	-28						7	2	1	3	12	1	0	1
1992-93	**Hartford**	**NHL**	19	5	4	9	58	3	0	0	38	13.2	-15													
	Toronto	**NHL**	47	13	28	41	53	10	0	1	86	15.1	-8						11	3	5	8	0	1	0	0
1993-94	**Toronto**	**NHL**	53	13	17	30	67	2	0	4	80	16.2	2						3	0	0	0	0	0	0	0
1994-95	**Pittsburgh**	**NHL**	46	13	24	37	68	2	0	1	88	14.8	-4						9	0	2	2	8	0	0	0
1995-96	**Tampa Bay**	**NHL**	76	16	34	50	65	8	0	3	152	10.5	1						5	3	3	6	0	1	0	0
1996-97	**Tampa Bay**	**NHL**	70	18	37	55	95	5	0	2	116	15.5	-14													
1997-98	**Tampa Bay**	**NHL**	DID NOT PLAY																						
1998-99	**Tampa Bay**	**NHL**	4	0	0	0	2	0	0	0	3	0.0	-2	23	30.4	1	0	12:42								
	Cleveland	IHL	6	2	7	9	0																			
	NHL Totals		621	187	363	550	898	71	0	22	1259	14.9		23	30.4	1	0	12:42	53	12	22	34	58	2	1	1

Hockey East First All-Star Team (1985, 1986) • NCAA East Second All-American Team (1986) • Hockey East Second All-Star Team (1987) • IHL First All-Star Team (1988) • Won James Gatschene Memorial Trophy (MVP - IHL) (1988) • Shared Garry F. Longman Memorial Trophy (Top Rookie - IHL) with Ed Belfour (1988) • Won Leo P. Lamoureux Memorial Trophy (Top Scorer - IHL) (1988) • Won Bill Masterton Memorial Trophy (1999)
Played in NHL All-Star Game (1991, 1992)

Signed as a free agent by **Pittsburgh**, June 21, 1988. Traded to **Hartford** by **Pittsburgh** with Jeff Parker and Zarley Zalapski for Ron Francis, Grant Jennings and Ulf Samuelsson, March 4, 1991. Traded to **Toronto** by **Hartford** for future considerations, November 24, 1992. Signed as a free agent by **Pittsburgh**, August 3, 1994. Signed as a free agent by **Tampa Bay**, September 11, 1995. • Missed entire 1997-98 season recovering from treatment and surgery for non-Hodgkins Lymphoma. • Retired to become assistant coach with Tampa Bay, November 27, 1998.

CULLEN, Matt — ANA.
Center. Shoots left. 6'1", 195 lbs. Born, Virginia, MN, November 2, 1976. Anaheim's 2nd choice, 35th overall, in 1996 Entry Draft.

Season	Club	League	GP	G	A	Pts	PIM	PP	SH	GW	S	%	+/-	TF	F%	H	SB	Min	GP	G	A	Pts	PIM	PP	SH	GW
1994-95	Moorehead High	H.S.	28	47	42	89	78																			
1995-96	St. Cloud State	WCHA	39	12	29	41	28																			
1996-97	St. Cloud State	WCHA	36	15	30	45	70																			
	Baltimore	AHL	6	3	3	6	7												3	0	2	2	0			
1997-98	**Anaheim**	**NHL**	61	6	21	27	23	2	0	0	75	8.0	-4													
	Cincinnati	AHL	18	15	12	27	2																			
1998-99	**Anaheim**	**NHL**	75	11	14	25	47	5	1	1	112	9.8	-12	1047	47.7	41	22	15:31	4	0	0	0	0	0	0	0
	Cincinnati	AHL	3	1	2	3	8																			
	NHL Totals		136	17	35	52	70	7	1	1	187	9.1		1047	47.7	41	22	15:31	4	0	0	0	0	0	0	0

WCHA Second All-Star Team (1997)

CULLIMORE, Jassen — (KUHL-ih-mohr) — T.B.
Defense. Shoots left. 6'5", 225 lbs. Born, Simcoe, Ont., December 4, 1972. Vancouver's 2nd choice, 29th overall, in 1991 Entry Draft.

Season	Club	League	GP	G	A	Pts	PIM	PP	SH	GW	S	%	+/-	TF	F%	H	SB	Min	GP	G	A	Pts	PIM	PP	SH	GW
1986-87	Caledonia	OJHL-C	18	2	0	2	9																			
1987-88	Simcoe	OJHL-C	35	11	14	25	92																			
1988-89	Peterborough	OJHL-B	29	11	15	26	146																			
	Peterborough	OHL	20	2	1	3	6																			
1989-90	Peterborough	OHL	59	2	6	8	61												11	0	2	2	8			
1990-91	Peterborough	OHL	62	8	16	24	74												4	1	0	1	7			
1991-92	Peterborough	OHL	54	9	37	46	65												10	3	6	9	8			
1992-93	Hamilton	AHL	56	5	7	12	60																			
1993-94	Hamilton	AHL	71	8	20	28	86												3	0	1	1	2			
1994-95	**Vancouver**	**NHL**	34	1	2	3	39	0	0	0	30	3.3	-2						11	0	0	0	12	0	0	0
	Syracuse	AHL	33	2	7	9	66																			
1995-96	**Vancouver**	**NHL**	27	1	1	2	21	0	0	1	12	8.3	4													
1996-97	**Vancouver**	**NHL**	3	0	0	0	2	0	0	0	2	0.0	-2						2	0	0	0	0	0	0	0
	Montreal	**NHL**	49	2	6	8	42	0	1	1	52	3.8	4													
1997-98	**Montreal**	**NHL**	3	0	0	0	4	0	0	0	1	0.0	0													
	Fredericton	AHL	5	1	0	1	8																			
	Tampa Bay	**NHL**	25	1	2	3	22	1	0	0	17	5.9	-4													

								Regular Season											Playoffs							
Season	Club	League	GP	G	A	Pts	PIM	PP	SH	GW	S	%	+/–	TF	F%	H	SB	Min	GP	G	A	Pts	PIM	PP	SH	GW
1998-99	**Tampa Bay**	**NHL**	**78**	**5**	**12**	**17**	**81**	**1**	**1**	**1**	**73**	**6.8**	**–22**	**0**	**0.0**	**161**	**67**	**20:14**	....	....	....	....	....	....	....	....
	NHL Totals		**219**	**10**	**23**	**33**	**211**	**2**	**2**	**3**	**187**	**5.3**		**0**	**0.0**	**161**	**67**	**20:14**	**13**	**0**	**0**	**0**	**14**	**0**	**0**	**0**

OHL Second All-Star Team (1992)

Traded to **Montreal** by **Vancouver** for Donald Brashear, November 13, 1996. Claimed on waivers by **Tampa Bay** from **Montreal**, January 22, 1998.

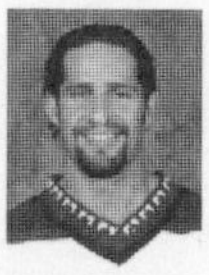

CUMMINS, Jim — MTL.

Right wing. Shoots right. 6'2", 219 lbs. Born, Dearborn, MI, May 17, 1970. NY Rangers' 5th choice, 67th overall, in 1989 Entry Draft.

1987-88	Detroit	NAJHL	31	11	15	26	146	....	....	....	....	....	....	....	....	....	....	....	....	....	....	....	....	....	....	....
1988-89	Michigan State	CCHA	30	3	8	11	98	....	....	....	....	....	....	....	....	....	....	....	....	....	....	....	....	....	....	....
1989-90	Michigan State	CCHA	41	8	7	15	94	....	....	....	....	....	....	....	....	....	....	....	....	....	....	....	....	....	....	....
1990-91	Michigan State	CCHA	34	9	6	15	110	....	....	....	....	....	....	....	....	....	....	....	....	....	....	....	....	....	....	....
1991-92	**Detroit**	**NHL**	**1**	**0**	**0**	**0**	**7**	**0**	**0**	**0**	**0**	**0.0**	**0**	....	....	....	....	....	....	....	....	....	....	....	....	....
	Adirondack	AHL	65	7	13	20	338	....	....	....	....	....	....	....	....	....	....	....	5	0	0	0	19	....	....	....
1992-93	**Detroit**	**NHL**	**7**	**1**	**1**	**2**	**58**	**0**	**0**	**0**	**5**	**20.0**	**0**	....	....	....	....	....	....	....	....	....	....	....	....	....
	Adirondack	AHL	43	16	4	20	179	....	....	....	....	....	....	....	....	....	....	....	9	3	1	4	4	....	....	....
1993-94	**Philadelphia**	**NHL**	**22**	**1**	**2**	**3**	**71**	**0**	**0**	**0**	**17**	**5.9**	**0**	....	....	....	....	....	....	....	....	....	....	....	....	....
	Hershey	AHL	17	6	6	12	70	....	....	....	....	....	....	....	....	....	....	....	....	....	....	....	....	....	....	....
	Tampa Bay	**NHL**	**4**	**0**	**0**	**0**	**13**	**0**	**0**	**0**	**3**	**0.0**	**–1**	....	....	....	....	....	....	....	....	....	....	....	....	....
	Atlanta	IHL	7	4	5	9	14	....	....	....	....	....	....	....	....	....	....	....	13	1	2	3	90	....	....	....
1994-95	**Tampa Bay**	**NHL**	**10**	**1**	**0**	**1**	**41**	**0**	**0**	**1**	**3**	**33.3**	**–3**	....	....	....	....	....	....	....	....	....	....	....	....	....
	Chicago	**NHL**	**27**	**3**	**1**	**4**	**117**	**0**	**0**	**0**	**20**	**15.0**	**–3**	....	....	....	....	....	**14**	**1**	**1**	**2**	**4**	**0**	**0**	**1**
1995-96	**Chicago**	**NHL**	**52**	**2**	**4**	**6**	**180**	**0**	**0**	**2**	**34**	**5.9**	**–1**	....	....	....	....	....	**10**	**0**	**0**	**0**	**2**	**0**	**0**	**0**
1996-97	**Chicago**	**NHL**	**65**	**6**	**6**	**12**	**199**	**0**	**0**	**0**	**61**	**9.8**	**4**	....	....	....	....	....	**6**	**0**	**0**	**0**	**24**	**0**	**0**	**0**
1997-98	**Chicago**	**NHL**	**55**	**0**	**2**	**2**	**178**	**0**	**0**	**0**	**33**	**0.0**	**–9**	....	....	....	....	....	....	....	....	....	....	....	....	....
	Phoenix	**NHL**	**20**	**0**	**0**	**0**	**47**	**0**	**0**	**0**	**10**	**0.0**	**–7**	....	....	....	....	....	**3**	**0**	**0**	**0**	**4**	**0**	**0**	**0**
1998-99	**Phoenix**	**NHL**	**55**	**1**	**7**	**8**	**190**	**0**	**0**	**0**	**26**	**3.8**	**3**	**0**	**0.0**	**74**	**7**	**7:07**	**3**	**0**	**1**	**1**	**0**	**0**	**0**	**0**
	NHL Totals		**318**	**15**	**23**	**38**	**1101**	**0**	**0**	**3**	**212**	**7.1**		**0**	**0.0**	**74**	**7**	**7:07**	**36**	**1**	**2**	**3**	**34**	**0**	**0**	**1**

Traded to **Detroit** by **NY Rangers** with Kevin Miller and Dennis Vial for Joey Kocur and Per Djoos, March 5, 1991. Traded to **Philadelphia** by **Detroit** with Philadelphia's 4th round choice (previously acquired by Detroit — later traded to Boston — Boston selected Charles Paquette) in 1993 Entry Draft for Greg Johnson and Philadelphia's 5th round choice (Frederic Deschenes) in 1994 Entry Draft, June 20, 1993. Traded to **Tampa Bay** by **Philadelphia** with Philadelphia's 4th round choice (later traded back to Philadelphia — Philadelphia selected Radovan Somik) in 1995 Entry Draft for Rob DiMaio, March 18, 1994. Traded to **Chicago** by **Tampa Bay** with Tom Tilley and Jeff Buchanan for Paul Ysebaert and Rich Sutter, February 22, 1995. Traded to **Phoenix** by **Chicago** with Keith Carney for Chad Kilger and Jayson More, March 4, 1998. Traded to **Montreal** by **Phoenix** for NY Rangers' 6th round choice (previously acquired, Phoenix selected Erik Leverstrom) in 1999 Entry Draft, June 26, 1999.

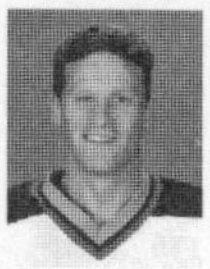

CUNNEYWORTH, Randy — (KUH-nee-wuhrth) — BUF.

Left wing. Shoots left. 6', 198 lbs. Born, Etobicoke, Ont., May 10, 1961. Buffalo's 9th choice, 167th overall, in 1980 Entry Draft.

1978-79	Dixie	MTHL	44	17	14	31	127	....	....	....	....	....	....	....	....	....	....	....	....	....	....	....	....	....	....	....
1979-80	Ottawa	OHA	63	16	25	41	145	....	....	....	....	....	....	....	....	....	....	....	11	0	1	1	13	....	....	....
1980-81	Ottawa	OHA	67	54	74	128	240	....	....	....	....	....	....	....	....	....	....	....	15	5	8	13	35	....	....	....
	Buffalo	**NHL**	**1**	**0**	**0**	**0**	**2**	**0**	**0**	**0**	**1**	**0.0**	**0**	....	....	....	....	....	....	....	....	....	....	....	....	....
	Rochester	AHL	1	0	1	1	2	....	....	....	....	....	....	....	....	....	....	....	....	....	....	....	....	....	....	....
1981-82	**Buffalo**	**NHL**	**20**	**2**	**4**	**6**	**47**	**0**	**0**	**0**	**33**	**6.1**	**–3**	....	....	....	....	....	....	....	....	....	....	....	....	....
	Rochester	AHL	57	12	15	27	86	....	....	....	....	....	....	....	....	....	....	....	9	4	0	4	30	....	....	....
1982-83	Rochester	AHL	78	23	33	56	111	....	....	....	....	....	....	....	....	....	....	....	16	4	4	8	35	....	....	....
1983-84	Rochester	AHL	54	18	17	35	85	....	....	....	....	....	....	....	....	....	....	....	17	5	5	10	55	....	....	....
1984-85	Rochester	AHL	72	30	38	68	148	....	....	....	....	....	....	....	....	....	....	....	5	2	1	3	16	....	....	....
1985-86	**Pittsburgh**	**NHL**	**75**	**15**	**30**	**45**	**74**	**2**	**2**	**2**	**134**	**11.2**	**12**	....	....	....	....	....	....	....	....	....	....	....	....	....
1986-87	**Pittsburgh**	**NHL**	**79**	**26**	**27**	**53**	**142**	**3**	**2**	**5**	**169**	**15.4**	**14**	....	....	....	....	....	....	....	....	....	....	....	....	....
1987-88	**Pittsburgh**	**NHL**	**71**	**35**	**39**	**74**	**141**	**14**	**0**	**6**	**229**	**15.3**	**13**	....	....	....	....	....	....	....	....	....	....	....	....	....
1988-89	**Pittsburgh**	**NHL**	**70**	**25**	**19**	**44**	**156**	**10**	**0**	**1**	**163**	**15.3**	**–22**	....	....	....	....	....	**11**	**3**	**5**	**8**	**26**	**1**	**0**	**1**
1989-90	**Winnipeg**	**NHL**	**28**	**5**	**6**	**11**	**34**	**2**	**0**	**1**	**51**	**9.8**	**–7**	....	....	....	....	....	....	....	....	....	....	....	....	....
	Hartford	**NHL**	**43**	**9**	**9**	**18**	**41**	**2**	**0**	**1**	**70**	**12.9**	**–4**	....	....	....	....	....	**4**	**0**	**0**	**0**	**2**	**0**	**0**	**0**
1990-91	**Hartford**	**NHL**	**32**	**9**	**5**	**14**	**49**	**0**	**0**	**1**	**56**	**16.1**	**–6**	....	....	....	....	....	**1**	**0**	**0**	**0**	**0**	**0**	**0**	**0**
	Springfield	AHL	2	0	0	0	5	....	....	....	....	....	....	....	....	....	....	....	....	....	....	....	....	....	....	....
1991-92	**Hartford**	**NHL**	**39**	**7**	**10**	**17**	**71**	**0**	**0**	**1**	**63**	**11.1**	**–5**	....	....	....	....	....	**7**	**3**	**0**	**3**	**9**	**1**	**1**	**1**
1992-93	**Hartford**	**NHL**	**39**	**5**	**4**	**9**	**63**	**0**	**0**	**1**	**47**	**10.6**	**–1**	....	....	....	....	....	....	....	....	....	....	....	....	....
1993-94	**Hartford**	**NHL**	**63**	**9**	**8**	**17**	**87**	**0**	**1**	**1**	**121**	**7.4**	**–2**	....	....	....	....	....	....	....	....	....	....	....	....	....
	Chicago	**NHL**	**16**	**4**	**3**	**7**	**13**	**0**	**0**	**1**	**33**	**12.1**	**1**	....	....	....	....	....	**6**	**0**	**0**	**0**	**8**	**0**	**0**	**0**
1994-95	**Ottawa**	**NHL**	**48**	**5**	**5**	**10**	**68**	**2**	**0**	**0**	**71**	**7.0**	**–19**	....	....	....	....	....	....	....	....	....	....	....	....	....
1995-96	**Ottawa**	**NHL**	**81**	**17**	**19**	**36**	**130**	**4**	**0**	**2**	**142**	**12.0**	**–31**	....	....	....	....	....	....	....	....	....	....	....	....	....
1996-97	**Ottawa**	**NHL**	**76**	**12**	**24**	**36**	**99**	**6**	**0**	**3**	**115**	**10.4**	**–7**	....	....	....	....	....	**7**	**1**	**1**	**2**	**10**	**0**	**0**	**0**
1997-98	**Ottawa**	**NHL**	**71**	**2**	**11**	**13**	**63**	**1**	**0**	**0**	**81**	**2.5**	**–14**	....	....	....	....	....	**6**	**0**	**1**	**1**	**6**	**0**	**0**	**0**
1998-99	**Buffalo**	**NHL**	**14**	**2**	**2**	**4**	**0**	**0**	**0**	**1**	**12**	**16.7**	**1**	**35**	**54.3**	**27**	**2**	**8:58**	**3**	**0**	**0**	**0**	**0**	**0**	**0**	**0**
	Rochester	AHL	52	10	18	28	55	....	....	....	....	....	....	....	....	....	....	....	20	3	14	17	58	....	....	....
	NHL Totals		**866**	**189**	**225**	**414**	**1280**	**46**	**5**	**27**	**1591**	**11.9**		**35**	**54.3**	**27**	**2**	**8:58**	**45**	**7**	**7**	**14**	**61**	**2**	**1**	**2**

Traded to **Pittsburgh** by **Buffalo** with Mike Moller for Pat Hughes, October 4, 1985. Traded to **Winnipeg** by **Pittsburgh** with Rick Tabaracci and Dave McLlwain for Jim Kyte, Andrew McBain and Randy Gilhen, June 17, 1989. Traded to **Hartford** by **Winnipeg** for Paul MacDermid, December 13, 1989. Traded to **Chicago** by **Hartford** with Gary Suter and Hartford's 3rd round choice (later traded to Vancouver — Vancouver selected Larry Courville) in 1995 Entry Draft for Frantisek Kucera and Jocelyn Lemieux, March 11, 1994. Signed as a free agent by **Ottawa**, July 15, 1994. Signed as a free agent by **Buffalo**, August 27, 1998.

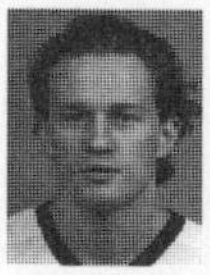

CZERKAWSKI, Mariusz — (chehr-KAWV-skee) — NYI

Right wing. Shoots left. 6', 195 lbs. Born, Radomsko, Poland, April 13, 1972. Boston's 5th choice, 106th overall, in 1991 Entry Draft.

1989-90	GKS Tychy	Poland-Jr.	....	....	....	....	....	....	....	....	....	....	....	....	....	....	....	....	....	....	....	....	....	....	....	....
1990-91	GKS Tychy	Poland	24	25	15	40	....	....	....	....	....	....	....	....	....	....	....	....	....	....	....	....	....	....	....	....
1991-92	Djurgardens IF	Sweden	39	8	5	13	4	....	....	....	....	....	....	....	....	....	....	....	3	0	0	0	2	....	....	....
	Poland	Olympics	5	0	1	1	4	....	....	....	....	....	....	....	....	....	....	....	....	....	....	....	....	....	....	....
1992-93	SC Hammarby	Sweden-2	32	*39	30	*69	74	....	....	....	....	....	....	....	....	....	....	....	13	*16	7	*23	34	....	....	....
1993-94	Djurgardens IF	Sweden	39	13	21	34	20	....	....	....	....	....	....	....	....	....	....	....	6	3	1	4	2	....	....	....
	Boston	**NHL**	**4**	**2**	**1**	**3**	**0**	**1**	**0**	**0**	**11**	**18.2**	**–2**	....	....	....	....	....	**13**	**3**	**3**	**6**	**4**	**1**	**0**	**0**
1994-95	Kiekko-Espoo	Finland	7	9	3	12	10	....	....	....	....	....	....	....	....	....	....	....	....	....	....	....	....	....	....	....
	Boston	**NHL**	**47**	**12**	**14**	**26**	**31**	**1**	**0**	**2**	**126**	**9.5**	**4**	....	....	....	....	....	**5**	**1**	**0**	**1**	**0**	**0**	**0**	**0**
1995-96	**Boston**	**NHL**	**33**	**5**	**6**	**11**	**10**	**1**	**0**	**0**	**63**	**7.9**	**–11**	....	....	....	....	....	....	....	....	....	....	....	....	....
	Edmonton	**NHL**	**37**	**12**	**17**	**29**	**8**	**2**	**0**	**1**	**79**	**15.2**	**7**	....	....	....	....	....	....	....	....	....	....	....	....	....
1996-97	**Edmonton**	**NHL**	**76**	**26**	**21**	**47**	**16**	**4**	**0**	**3**	**182**	**14.3**	**0**	....	....	....	....	....	**12**	**2**	**1**	**3**	**10**	**0**	**0**	**0**
1997-98	**NY Islanders**	**NHL**	**68**	**12**	**13**	**25**	**23**	**2**	**0**	**1**	**136**	**8.8**	**11**	....	....	....	....	....	....	....	....	....	....	....	....	....
	Poland	WC-B	3	2	1	3	0	....	....	....	....	....	....	....	....	....	....	....	....	....	....	....	....	....	....	....
1998-99	**NY Islanders**	**NHL**	**78**	**21**	**17**	**38**	**14**	**4**	**0**	**1**	**205**	**10.2**	**–10**	**2**	**0.0**	**47**	**14**	**14:18**	....	....	....	....	....	....	....	....
	NHL Totals		**343**	**90**	**89**	**179**	**102**	**15**	**0**	**8**	**802**	**11.2**		**2**	**0.0**	**47**	**14**	**14:18**	**30**	**6**	**4**	**10**	**14**	**1**	**0**	**0**

Traded to **Edmonton** by **Boston** with Sean Brown and Boston's 1st round choice (Matthieu Descoteaux) in 1996 Entry Draft for Bill Ranford, January 11, 1996. Traded to **NY Islanders** by **Edmonton** for Dan Lacouture, August 25, 1997.

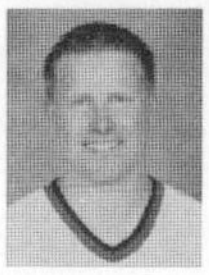

DACKELL, Andreas — (DA-kuhl, an-DRAY-uhs) — OTT.

Right wing. Shoots right. 5'11", 191 lbs. Born, Gavle, Sweden, December 29, 1972. Ottawa's 3rd choice, 136th overall, in 1996 Entry Draft.

1990-91	Stomsbro HC	Sweden-2	29	21	9	30	12	....	....	....	....	....	....	....	....	....	....	....	....	....	....	....	....	....	....	....
	Brynas IF	Sweden	3	0	1	1	2	....	....	....	....	....	....	....	....	....	....	....	....	....	....	....	....	....	....	....
1991-92	Gavle HF	Sweden-2	26	17	24	41	42	....	....	....	....	....	....	....	....	....	....	....	2	3	1	4	2	....	....	....
	Brynas IF	Sweden	4	0	0	0	2	....	....	....	....	....	....	....	....	....	....	....	2	0	1	1	4	....	....	....
1992-93	Brynas IF	Sweden	40	12	15	27	12	....	....	....	....	....	....	....	....	....	....	....	10	4	5	9	2	....	....	....
1993-94	Brynas IF	Sweden	38	12	17	29	47	....	....	....	....	....	....	....	....	....	....	....	7	2	2	4	8	....	....	....
	Sweden	Olympics	4	0	0	0	0	....	....	....	....	....	....	....	....	....	....	....	....	....	....	....	....	....	....	....

Season	Club	League	GP	G	A	Pts	PIM	PP	SH	GW	S	%	+/–	TF	F%	H	SB	Min	GP	G	A	Pts	PIM	PP	SH	GW
					Regular Season																Playoffs					
1994-95	Brynas IF	Sweden	39	17	16	33	34	....	....	....	....	....	....	....	....	....	....	....	14	3	3	6	14	....	....	....
1995-96	Brynas IF	Sweden	22	6	6	12	8	....	....	....	....	....	....	....	....	....	....	....	....	....	....	....	....	....	....	....
1996-97	**Ottawa**	**NHL**	79	12	19	31	8	2	0	3	79	15.2	–6	....	....	....	....	....	7	1	0	1	0	0	0	0
1997-98	**Ottawa**	**NHL**	82	15	18	33	24	3	2	2	130	11.5	–11	....	....	....	....	....	11	1	1	2	2	1	0	0
1998-99	**Ottawa**	**NHL**	77	15	35	50	30	6	0	3	107	14.0	9	5	40.0	34	29	17:18	4	0	1	1	0	0	0	0
	NHL Totals		238	42	72	114	62	11	2	8	316	13.3		5	40.0	34	29	17:18	22	2	2	4	2	1	0	0

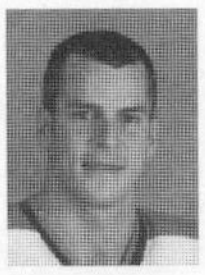

DAHL, Kevin

(DAHL)

Defense. Shoots right. 5'11", 190 lbs. Born, Regina, Sask., December 30, 1968. Montreal's 12th choice, 230th overall, in 1988 Entry Draft.

Season	Club	League	GP	G	A	Pts	PIM	PP	SH	GW	S	%	+/–	TF	F%	H	SB	Min	GP	G	A	Pts	PIM	PP	SH	GW
1986-87	Bowling Green	CCHA	32	2	6	8	54	....	....	....	....	....	....	....	....	....	....	....	....	....	....	....	....	....	....	....
1987-88	Bowling Green	CCHA	44	2	23	25	78	....	....	....	....	....	....	....	....	....	....	....	....	....	....	....	....	....	....	....
1988-89	Bowling Green	CCHA	46	9	26	35	51	....	....	....	....	....	....	....	....	....	....	....	....	....	....	....	....	....	....	....
1989-90	Bowling Green	CCHA	43	8	22	30	74	....	....	....	....	....	....	....	....	....	....	....	....	....	....	....	....	....	....	....
1990-91	Fredericton	AHL	32	1	15	16	45	....	....	....	....	....	....	....	....	....	....	....	9	0	1	1	11	....	....	....
	Winston-Salem	ECHL	36	7	17	24	58	....	....	....	....	....	....	....	....	....	....	....	....	....	....	....	....	....	....	....
1991-92	Canada	Nat-Team	45	2	15	17	44	....	....	....	....	....	....	....	....	....	....	....	....	....	....	....	....	....	....	....
	Canada	Olympics	8	2	0	2	6	....	....	....	....	....	....	....	....	....	....	....	....	....	....	....	....	....	....	....
	Salt Lake	IHL	13	0	2	2	12	....	....	....	....	....	....	....	....	....	....	....	5	0	0	0	13	....	....	....
1992-93	**Calgary**	**NHL**	61	2	9	11	56	1	0	0	40	5.0	9	....	....	....	....	....	6	0	2	2	8	0	0	0
1993-94	**Calgary**	**NHL**	33	0	3	3	23	0	0	0	20	0.0	–2	....	....	....	....	....	6	0	0	0	4	0	0	0
	Saint John	AHL	2	0	0	0	0	....	....	....	....	....	....	....	....	....	....	....	....	....	....	....	....	....	....	....
1994-95	**Calgary**	**NHL**	34	4	8	12	38	0	0	0	30	13.3	8	....	....	....	....	....	3	0	0	0	0	0	0	0
1995-96	**Calgary**	**NHL**	32	1	1	2	26	0	0	1	17	5.9	–2	....	....	....	....	....	1	0	0	0	0	0	0	0
	Saint John	AHL	23	4	11	15	37	....	....	....	....	....	....	....	....	....	....	....	....	....	....	....	....	....	....	....
1996-97	**Phoenix**	**NHL**	2	0	0	0	0	0	0	0	2	0.0	0	....	....	....	....	....	....	....	....	....	....	....	....	....
	Las Vegas	IHL	73	10	21	31	101	....	....	....	....	....	....	....	....	....	....	....	3	0	0	0	2	....	....	....
1997-98	**Calgary**	**NHL**	19	0	1	1	6	0	0	0	17	0.0	–3	....	....	....	....	....	....	....	....	....	....	....	....	....
	Chicago	IHL	45	8	9	17	61	....	....	....	....	....	....	....	....	....	....	....	20	1	8	9	32	....	....	....
1998-99	**Toronto**	**NHL**	3	0	0	0	2	0	0	0	0	0.0	0	0	0.0	6	1	15:19	....	....	....	....	....	....	....	....
	Chicago	IHL	34	3	6	9	61	....	....	....	....	....	....	....	....	....	....	....	10	2	3	5	8	....	....	....
	NHL Totals		184	7	22	29	151	1	0	1	126	5.6		0	0.0	6	1	15:19	16	0	2	2	12	0	0	0

Signed as a free agent by **Calgary**, July 27, 1991. Signed as a free agent by **Phoenix**, September 4, 1996. Signed as a free agent by **Calgary**, September 8, 1997. Signed as a free agent by **St. Louis**, September 4, 1998. Claimed by **Toronto** from **St. Louis** in NHL Waiver Draft, October 5, 1998.

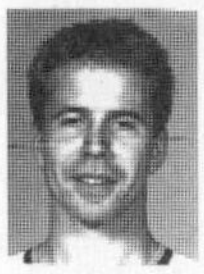

DAHLEN, Ulf

(DAH-lehn) **WSH.**

Right wing. Shoots left. 6'2", 195 lbs. Born, Ostersund, Sweden, January 12, 1967. NY Rangers' 1st choice, 7th overall, in 1985 Entry Draft.

Season	Club	League	GP	G	A	Pts	PIM	PP	SH	GW	S	%	+/–	TF	F%	H	SB	Min	GP	G	A	Pts	PIM	PP	SH	GW
1983-84	Ostersunds IK	Sweden-2	36	15	11	26	10	....	....	....	....	....	....	....	....	....	....	....	....	....	....	....	....	....	....	....
1984-85	Ostersunds IK	Sweden-2	31	27	*26	53	20	....	....	....	....	....	....	....	....	....	....	....	5	6	0	6	4	....	....	....
1985-86	IF Bjorkloven	Sweden	22	4	3	7	8	....	....	....	....	....	....	....	....	....	....	....	....	....	....	....	....	....	....	....
1986-87	IF Bjorkloven	Sweden	31	9	12	21	20	....	....	....	....	....	....	....	....	....	....	....	6	6	2	8	4	....	....	....
1987-88	**NY Rangers**	**NHL**	70	29	23	52	26	11	0	4	159	18.2	5	....	....	....	....	....	....	....	....	....	....	....	....	....
	Colorado	IHL	2	2	2	4	0	....	....	....	....	....	....	....	....	....	....	....	....	....	....	....	....	....	....	....
1988-89	**NY Rangers**	**NHL**	56	24	19	43	50	8	0	1	147	16.3	–6	....	....	....	....	....	4	0	0	0	0	0	0	0
1989-90	**NY Rangers**	**NHL**	63	18	18	36	30	13	0	4	111	16.2	–4	....	....	....	....	....	....	....	....	....	....	....	....	....
	Minnesota	**NHL**	13	2	4	6	0	0	0	0	24	8.3	1	....	....	....	....	....	7	1	4	5	2	0	0	0
1990-91	**Minnesota**	**NHL**	66	21	18	39	6	4	0	3	133	15.8	7	....	....	....	....	....	15	2	6	8	4	0	0	0
1991-92	**Minnesota**	**NHL**	79	36	30	66	10	16	1	5	216	16.7	–5	....	....	....	....	....	7	0	3	3	2	0	0	0
1992-93	**Minnesota**	**NHL**	83	35	39	74	6	13	0	6	223	15.7	–20	....	....	....	....	....	....	....	....	....	....	....	....	....
1993-94	**Dallas**	**NHL**	65	19	38	57	10	12	0	3	147	12.9	–1	....	....	....	....	....	....	....	....	....	....	....	....	....
	San Jose	**NHL**	13	6	6	12	0	3	0	[illegible]	[illegible]	[illegible]	[illegible]	....	....	....	....	....	14	6	2	8	0	3	0	1
1994-95	**San Jose**	**NHL**	[illegible]	11	[illegible]	34	11	4	1	4	85	12.9	–2	....	....	....	....	....	11	5	4	9	0	3	0	1
1995-96	**San Jose**	**NHL**	59	16	12	28	27	5	0	2	103	15.5	–21	....	....	....	....	....	....	....	....	....	....	....	....	....
1996-97	**San Jose**	**NHL**	43	8	11	19	8	3	0	1	78	10.3	–11	....	....	....	....	....	....	....	....	....	....	....	....	....
	Chicago	**NHL**	30	6	8	14	10	1	0	3	53	11.3	9	....	....	....	....	....	5	0	1	1	0	0	0	0
1997-98	HV Jonkoping	Sweden	29	9	22	31	16	....	....	....	....	....	....	....	....	....	....	....	5	1	3	4	12	....	....	....
	Sweden	Olympics	4	1	0	1	2	....	....	....	....	....	....	....	....	....	....	....	....	....	....	....	....	....	....	....
1998-99	HV Jonkoping	Sweden	25	14	15	29	4	....	....	....	....	....	....	....	....	....	....	....	....	....	....	....	....	....	....	....
	NHL Totals		686	231	249	480	194	93	2	38	1522	15.2		....	....	....	....	....	63	14	20	34	8	6	0	2

Traded to **Minnesota** by **NY Rangers** with LA Kings' 4th round choice (previously acquired by NY Rangers — Minnesota selected Cal McGowan) in 1990 Entry Draft and future considerations for Mike Gartner, March 6, 1990. Transferred to **Dallas** after **Minnesota** franchise relocated, June 9, 1993. Traded to **San Jose** by **Dallas** with Dallas' 7th round choice (Brad Mehalko) in 1995 Entry Draft for Doug Zmolek, Mike Lalor and cash, March 19, 1994. Traded to **Chicago** by **San Jose** with Chris Terreri and Michal Sykora for Ed Belfour, January 25, 1997. Signed as a free agent by **Washington**, August 16, 1999.

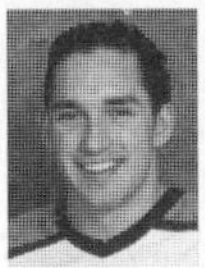

DAIGLE, Alexandre

(DAYG) **T.B.**

Center. Shoots left. 6', 195 lbs. Born, Montreal, Que., February 7, 1975. Ottawa's 1st choice, 1st overall, in 1993 Entry Draft.

Season	Club	League	GP	G	A	Pts	PIM	PP	SH	GW	S	%	+/–	TF	F%	H	SB	Min	GP	G	A	Pts	PIM	PP	SH	GW
1990-91	Laval	QAAA	42	50	60	110	98	....	....	....	....	....	....	....	....	....	....	....	....	....	....	....	....	....	....	....
1991-92	Victoriaville	QMJHL	66	35	75	110	63	....	....	....	....	....	....	....	....	....	....	....	....	....	....	....	....	....	....	....
1992-93	Victoriaville	QMJHL	53	45	92	137	85	....	....	....	....	....	....	....	....	....	....	....	6	5	6	11	4	....	....	....
1993-94	**Ottawa**	**NHL**	84	20	31	51	40	4	0	2	168	11.9	–45	....	....	....	....	....	....	....	....	....	....	....	....	....
1994-95	Victoriaville	QMJHL	18	14	20	34	16	....	....	....	....	....	....	....	....	....	....	....	....	....	....	....	....	....	....	....
	Ottawa	**NHL**	47	16	21	37	14	4	1	2	105	15.2	–22	....	....	....	....	....	....	....	....	....	....	....	....	....
1995-96	**Ottawa**	**NHL**	50	5	12	17	24	1	0	0	77	6.5	–30	....	....	....	....	....	....	....	....	....	....	....	....	....
1996-97	**Ottawa**	**NHL**	82	26	25	51	33	4	0	5	203	12.8	–33	....	....	....	....	....	7	0	0	0	2	0	0	0
1997-98	**Ottawa**	**NHL**	38	7	9	16	8	4	0	2	68	10.3	–7	....	....	....	....	....	....	....	....	....	....	....	....	....
	Philadelphia	**NHL**	37	9	17	26	6	4	0	3	78	11.5	–1	....	....	....	....	....	5	0	2	2	0	0	0	0
1998-99	**Philadelphia**	**NHL**	31	3	2	5	2	1	0	1	26	11.5	–1	53	39.6	5	3	7:59	....	....	....	....	....	....	....	....
	Tampa Bay	**NHL**	32	6	6	12	2	3	0	0	56	10.7	–12	4	50.0	6	8	13:59	....	....	....	....	....	....	....	....
	NHL Totals		401	92	123	215	129	25	1	15	781	11.8		57	40.4	11	11	11:02	12	0	2	2	2	0	0	0

QMJHL Second All-Star Team (1992) • Canadian Major Junior Rookie of the Year (1992) • QMJHL First All-Star Team (1993)

Traded to **Philadelphia** by **Ottawa** for Vaclav Prospal, Pat Falloon and Dallas' 2nd round choice (previously acquired, Ottawa selected Chris Bala) in 1998 Entry Draft, January 17, 1998. Traded to **Edmonton** by **Philadelphia** for Andrei Kovalenko, January 29, 1998. Traded to **Tampa Bay** by **Edmonton** for Alexnader Selinov, January 29, 1998.

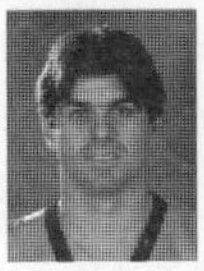

DAIGNEAULT, J.J.

(DAYN-yoh) **PHX.**

Defense. Shoots left. 5'10", 192 lbs. Born, Montreal, Que., October 12, 1965. Vancouver's 1st choice, 10th overall, in 1984 Entry Draft.

Season	Club	League	GP	G	A	Pts	PIM	PP	SH	GW	S	%	+/–	TF	F%	H	SB	Min	GP	G	A	Pts	PIM	PP	SH	GW
1980-81	Montreal AAA	QAAA	48	7	48	55	....	....	....	....	....	....	....	....	....	....	....	....	....	....	....	....	....	....	....	....
1981-82	Laval	QMJHL	64	4	25	29	41	....	....	....	....	....	....	....	....	....	....	....	18	1	3	4	2	....	....	....
1982-83	Longueuil	QMJHL	70	26	58	84	58	....	....	....	....	....	....	....	....	....	....	....	15	4	11	15	35	....	....	....
1983-84	Longueuil	QMJHL	10	2	11	13	6	....	....	....	....	....	....	....	....	....	....	....	14	3	13	16	30	....	....	....
	Canada	Nat-Team	55	5	14	19	40	....	....	....	....	....	....	....	....	....	....	....	....	....	....	....	....	....	....	....
	Canada	Olympics	7	1	1	2	0	....	....	....	....	....	....	....	....	....	....	....	....	....	....	....	....	....	....	....
1984-85	**Vancouver**	**NHL**	67	4	23	27	69	2	0	0	93	4.3	–14	....	....	....	....	....	....	....	....	....	....	....	....	....
1985-86	**Vancouver**	**NHL**	64	5	23	28	45	4	0	0	114	4.4	–20	....	....	....	....	....	3	0	2	2	0	0	0	0
1986-87	**Philadelphia**	**NHL**	77	6	16	22	56	0	0	1	82	7.3	12	....	....	....	....	....	9	1	0	1	0	0	0	1
1987-88	**Philadelphia**	**NHL**	28	2	2	4	12	2	0	0	20	10.0	–8	....	....	....	....	....	....	....	....	....	....	....	....	....
	Hershey	AHL	10	1	5	6	8	....	....	....	....	....	....	....	....	....	....	....	....	....	....	....	....	....	....	....
1988-89	Hershey	AHL	12	0	10	10	13	....	....	....	....	....	....	....	....	....	....	....	....	....	....	....	....	....	....	....
	Sherbrooke	AHL	63	10	33	43	48	....	....	....	....	....	....	....	....	....	....	....	6	1	3	4	2	....	....	....
1989-90	**Montreal**	**NHL**	36	2	10	12	14	0	0	1	40	5.0	11	....	....	....	....	....	9	0	0	0	2	0	0	0
	Sherbrooke	AHL	28	8	19	27	18	....	....	....	....	....	....	....	....	....	....	....	....	....	....	....	....	....	....	....

			Regular Season																Playoffs							
Season	Club	League	GP	G	A	Pts	PIM	PP	SH	GW	S	%	+/–	TF	F%	H	SB	Min	GP	G	A	Pts	PIM	PP	SH	GW
1990-91	**Montreal**	**NHL**	**51**	**3**	**16**	**19**	**31**	**2**	**0**	**0**	**68**	**4.4**	**–2**	....	....	....	....	....	**5**	**0**	**1**	**1**	**0**	**0**	**0**	**0**
1991-92	**Montreal**	**NHL**	**79**	**4**	**14**	**18**	**36**	**2**	**0**	**0**	**108**	**3.7**	**16**	....	....	....	....	....	**11**	**0**	**3**	**3**	**4**	**0**	**0**	**0**
1992-93♦	**Montreal**	**NHL**	**66**	**8**	**10**	**18**	**57**	**0**	**0**	**1**	**68**	**11.8**	**25**	....	....	....	....	....	**20**	**1**	**3**	**4**	**22**	**0**	**0**	**0**
1993-94	**Montreal**	**NHL**	**68**	**2**	**12**	**14**	**73**	**0**	**0**	**1**	**61**	**3.3**	**16**	....	....	....	....	....	**7**	**0**	**1**	**1**	**12**	**0**	**0**	**0**
1994-95	**Montreal**	**NHL**	**45**	**3**	**5**	**8**	**40**	**0**	**0**	**0**	**36**	**8.3**	**2**	....	....	....	....	....	....	....	....	....	....	....	....	....
1995-96	**Montreal**	**NHL**	**7**	**0**	**1**	**1**	**6**	**0**	**0**	**0**	**3**	**0.0**	**0**	....	....	....	....	....	....	....	....	....	....	....	....	....
	St. Louis	**NHL**	**37**	**1**	**3**	**4**	**24**	**0**	**0**	**0**	**45**	**2.2**	**–6**	....	....	....	....	....	....	....	....	....	....	....	....	....
	Worcester	AHL	9	1	10	11	10	....	....	....	....	....	....	....	....	....	....	....	....	....	....	....	....	....	....	....
	Pittsburgh	**NHL**	**13**	**3**	**3**	**6**	**23**	**2**	**0**	**0**	**13**	**23.1**	**0**	....	....	....	....	....	**17**	**1**	**9**	**10**	**36**	**1**	**0**	**1**
1996-97	**Pittsburgh**	**NHL**	**53**	**3**	**14**	**17**	**36**	**0**	**0**	**1**	**49**	**6.1**	**–5**	....	....	....	....	....	....	....	....	....	....	....	....	....
	Anaheim	**NHL**	**13**	**2**	**9**	**11**	**22**	**0**	**0**	**0**	**13**	**15.4**	**5**	....	....	....	....	....	**11**	**2**	**7**	**9**	**16**	**1**	**0**	**1**
1997-98	**Anaheim**	**NHL**	**53**	**2**	**15**	**17**	**28**	**1**	**0**	**1**	**74**	**2.7**	**–10**	....	....	....	....	....	....	....	....	....	....	....	....	....
	NY Islanders	**NHL**	**18**	**0**	**6**	**6**	**21**	**0**	**0**	**0**	**18**	**0.0**	**1**	....	....	....	....	....	....	....	....	....	....	....	....	....
1998-99	**Nashville**	**NHL**	**35**	**2**	**2**	**4**	**38**	**1**	**0**	**1**	**38**	**5.3**	**–4**	**1**	**100.0**	**46**	**29**	**20:47**	....	....	....	....	....	....	....	....
	Phoenix	**NHL**	**35**	**0**	**7**	**7**	**32**	**0**	**0**	**0**	**27**	**0.0**	**–8**	**0**	**0.0**	**58**	**34**	**18:00**	**6**	**0**	**0**	**0**	**8**	**0**	**0**	**0**
	NHL Totals		**845**	**52**	**191**	**243**	**663**	**16**	**0**	**7**	**970**	**5.4**		**1**	**100.0**	**104**	**63**	**19:23**	**98**	**5**	**26**	**31**	**100**	**2**	**0**	**3**

QMJHL First All-Star Team (1983)

Traded to **Philadelphia** by **Vancouver** with Vancouver's 2nd round choice (Kent Hawley) in 1986 Entry Draft for Dave Richter, Rich Sutter and Vancouver's 3rd round choice (previously acquired, Vancouver selected Don Gibson) in 1986 Entry Draft, June 6, 1986. Traded to **Montreal** by **Philadelphia** for Scott Sandelin, November 7, 1988. Traded to **St. Louis** by **Montreal** for Pat Jablonski, November 7, 1995. Traded to **Pittsburgh** by **St. Louis** for Pittsburgh's 6th round choice (Stephen Wagner) in 1996 Entry Draft, March 20, 1996. Traded to **Anaheim** by **Pittsburgh** for Garry Valk, February 21, 1997. Traded to **NY Islanders** by **Anaheim** with Joe Sacco and Mark Janssens for Travis Green, Doug Houda and Tony Tuzzolino, February 6, 1998. Claimed by **Nashville** from **NY Islanders** in Expansion Draft, June 26, 1998. Traded to **Phoenix** by **Nashville** for future considerations, January 13, 1999.

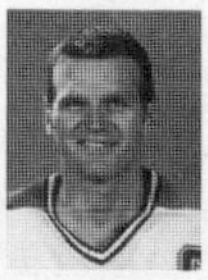

DAMPHOUSSE, Vincent

(DAHM-fooz) **S.J.**

Center. Shoots left. 6'1", 191 lbs. Born, Montreal, Que., December 17, 1967. Toronto's 1st choice, 6th overall, in 1986 Entry Draft.

Season	Club	League	GP	G	A	Pts	PIM	PP	SH	GW	S	%	+/–	TF	F%	H	SB	Min	GP	G	A	Pts	PIM	PP	SH	GW
1982-83	Bourassa	QAAA	48	33	45	78	....	....	....	....	....	....	....	....	....	....	....	....	....	....	....	....	....	....	....	....
1983-84	Laval	QMJHL	66	29	36	65	25	....	....	....	....	....	....	....	....	....	....	....	....	....	....	....	....	....	....	....
1984-85	Laval	QMJHL	68	35	68	103	62	....	....	....	....	....	....	....	....	....	....	....	....	....	....	....	....	....	....	....
1985-86	Laval	QMJHL	69	45	110	155	70	....	....	....	....	....	....	....	....	....	....	....	14	9	27	36	12	....	....	....
1986-87	**Toronto**	**NHL**	**80**	**21**	**25**	**46**	**26**	**4**	**0**	**1**	**142**	**14.8**	**–6**	....	....	....	....	....	**12**	**1**	**5**	**6**	**8**	**1**	**0**	**0**
1987-88	**Toronto**	**NHL**	**75**	**12**	**36**	**48**	**40**	**1**	**0**	**2**	**111**	**10.8**	**2**	....	....	....	....	....	**6**	**0**	**1**	**1**	**10**	**0**	**0**	**0**
1988-89	**Toronto**	**NHL**	**80**	**26**	**42**	**68**	**75**	**6**	**0**	**4**	**190**	**13.7**	**–8**	....	....	....	....	....	....	....	....	....	....	....	....	....
1989-90	**Toronto**	**NHL**	**80**	**33**	**61**	**94**	**56**	**9**	**0**	**5**	**229**	**14.4**	**2**	....	....	....	....	....	**5**	**0**	**2**	**2**	**2**	**0**	**0**	**0**
1990-91	**Toronto**	**NHL**	**79**	**26**	**47**	**73**	**65**	**10**	**1**	**4**	**247**	**10.5**	**–31**	....	....	....	....	....	....	....	....	....	....	....	....	....
1991-92	**Edmonton**	**NHL**	**80**	**38**	**51**	**89**	**53**	**12**	**1**	**8**	**247**	**15.4**	**10**	....	....	....	....	....	**16**	**6**	**8**	**14**	**8**	**1**	**0**	**0**
1992-93♦	**Montreal**	**NHL**	**84**	**39**	**58**	**97**	**98**	**9**	**3**	**8**	**287**	**13.6**	**5**	....	....	....	....	....	**20**	**11**	**12**	**23**	**16**	**5**	**0**	**3**
1993-94	**Montreal**	**NHL**	**84**	**40**	**51**	**91**	**75**	**13**	**0**	**10**	**274**	**14.6**	**0**	....	....	....	....	....	**7**	**1**	**2**	**3**	**8**	**0**	**0**	**0**
1994-95	Ratingen Lowen	Germany	11	5	7	12	24	....	....	....	....	....	....	....	....	....	....	....	....	....	....	....	....	....	....	....
	Montreal	**NHL**	**48**	**10**	**30**	**40**	**42**	**4**	**0**	**4**	**123**	**8.1**	**15**	....	....	....	....	....	....	....	....	....	....	....	....	....
1995-96	**Montreal**	**NHL**	**80**	**38**	**56**	**94**	**158**	**11**	**4**	**3**	**254**	**15.0**	**5**	....	....	....	....	....	**6**	**4**	**4**	**8**	**0**	**0**	**1**	**2**
1996-97	**Montreal**	**NHL**	**82**	**27**	**54**	**81**	**82**	**7**	**2**	**3**	**244**	**11.1**	**–6**	....	....	....	....	....	**5**	**0**	**0**	**0**	**2**	**0**	**0**	**0**
1997-98	**Montreal**	**NHL**	**76**	**18**	**41**	**59**	**58**	**2**	**1**	**5**	**164**	**11.0**	**14**	....	....	....	....	....	**10**	**3**	**6**	**9**	**22**	**1**	**0**	**0**
1998-99	**Montreal**	**NHL**	**65**	**12**	**24**	**36**	**46**	**3**	**2**	**2**	**147**	**8.2**	**–7**	**1425**	**48.4**	**41**	**37**	**20:27**	....	....	....	....	....	....	....	....
	San Jose	**NHL**	**12**	**7**	**6**	**13**	**4**	**3**	**0**	**1**	**43**	**16.3**	**3**	**230**	**51.3**	**9**	**1**	**19:21**	**6**	**3**	**2**	**5**	**6**	**0**	**2**	**0**
	NHL Totals		**1005**	**347**	**582**	**929**	**878**	**94**	**14**	**60**	**2702**	**12.8**		**1655**	**48.8**	**50**	**38**	**20:17**	**93**	**29**	**42**	**71**	**82**	**8**	**3**	**5**

QMJHL Second All-Star Team (1986)

Played in NHL All-Star Game (1991, 1992)

Traded to **Edmonton** by **Toronto** with Peter Ing, Scott Thornton, Luke Richardson, future considerations and cash for Grant Fuhr, Glenn Anderson and Craig Berube, September 19, 1991. Traded to **Montreal** by **Edmonton** with Edmonton's 4th round choice (Adam Wiesel) in 1993 Entry Draft for Shayne Corson, Brent Gilchrist and Vladimir Vujtek, August 27, 1992. Traded to **San Jose** by **Montreal** for Phoenix's 5th round choice (previously acquired, Montreal selected Marc-Andre Thinel) in 1999 Entry Draft and San Jose's 2nd round choice in 2000 Entry Draft, March 23, 1999.

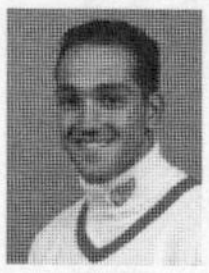

DANDENAULT, Mathieu

(DAHN-deh-noh) **DET.**

Right wing/defense. Shoots right. 6', 174 lbs. Born, Sherbrooke, Que., February 3, 1976. Detroit's 2nd choice, 49th overall, in 1994 Entry Draft.

Season	Club	League	GP	G	A	Pts	PIM	PP	SH	GW	S	%	+/–	TF	F%	H	SB	Min	GP	G	A	Pts	PIM	PP	SH	GW
1990-91	Gloucester	OMHA	44	52	50	102	30	....	....	....	....	....	....	....	....	....	....	....	....	....	....	....	....	....	....	....
1991-92	Vanier	OJHL	33	27	31	58	20	....	....	....	....	....	....	....	....	....	....	....	....	....	....	....	....	....	....	....
	Gloucester	OJHL	6	3	4	7	0	....	....	....	....	....	....	....	....	....	....	....	....	....	....	....	....	....	....	....
1992-93	Gloucester	OJHL	52	14	28	42	75	....	....	....	....	....	....	....	....	....	....	....	....	....	....	....	....	....	....	....
1993-94	Sherbrooke	QMJHL	67	17	36	53	67	....	....	....	....	....	....	....	....	....	....	....	12	4	10	14	12	....	....	....
1994-95	Sherbrooke	QMJHL	67	37	70	107	76	....	....	....	....	....	....	....	....	....	....	....	7	1	7	8	10	....	....	....
1995-96	**Detroit**	**NHL**	**34**	**5**	**7**	**12**	**6**	**1**	**0**	**0**	**32**	**15.6**	**6**	....	....	....	....	....	....	....	....	....	....	....	....	....
	Adirondack	AHL	4	0	0	0	0	....	....	....	....	....	....	....	....	....	....	....	....	....	....	....	....	....	....	....
1996-97♦	**Detroit**	**NHL**	**65**	**3**	**9**	**12**	**28**	**0**	**0**	**0**	**81**	**3.7**	**–10**	....	....	....	....	....	....	....	....	....	....	....	....	....
1997-98♦	**Detroit**	**NHL**	**68**	**5**	**12**	**17**	**43**	**0**	**0**	**0**	**75**	**6.7**	**5**	....	....	....	....	....	**3**	**1**	**0**	**1**	**0**	**1**	**0**	**0**
1998-99	**Detroit**	**NHL**	**75**	**4**	**10**	**14**	**59**	**0**	**0**	**0**	**94**	**4.3**	**17**	**3**	**0.0**	**109**	**37**	**15:10**	**10**	**0**	**1**	**1**	**0**	**0**	**0**	**0**
	NHL Totals		**242**	**17**	**38**	**55**	**136**	**1**	**0**	**0**	**282**	**6.0**		**3**	**0.0**	**109**	**3715:010**		**13**	**1**	**1**	**2**	**0**	**1**	**0**	**0**

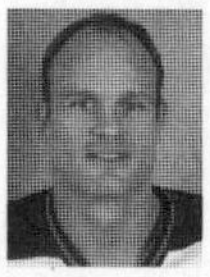

DANEYKO, Ken

(DAN-ee-KOH) **N.J.**

Defense. Shoots left. 6'1", 215 lbs. Born, Windsor, Ont., April 17, 1964. New Jersey's 2nd choice, 18th overall, in 1982 Entry Draft.

Season	Club	League	GP	G	A	Pts	PIM	PP	SH	GW	S	%	+/–	TF	F%	H	SB	Min	GP	G	A	Pts	PIM	PP	SH	GW
1980-81	St. Albert	AJHL	1	0	0	0	4	....	....	....	....	....	....	....	....	....	....	....	....	....	....	....	....	....	....	....
	Spokane	WHL	62	6	13	19	140	....	....	....	....	....	....	....	....	....	....	....	4	0	0	0	6	....	....	....
1981-82	Spokane	WHL	26	1	11	12	147	....	....	....	....	....	....	....	....	....	....	....	....	....	....	....	....	....	....	....
	Seattle	WHL	38	1	22	23	151	....	....	....	....	....	....	....	....	....	....	....	14	1	9	10	49	....	....	....
1982-83	Seattle	WHL	69	17	43	60	150	....	....	....	....	....	....	....	....	....	....	....	4	1	3	4	14	....	....	....
1983-84	Kamloops	WHL	19	6	28	34	52	....	....	....	....	....	....	....	....	....	....	....	17	4	9	13	28	....	....	....
	New Jersey	**NHL**	**11**	**1**	**4**	**5**	**17**	**0**	**0**	**0**	**17**	**5.9**	**–1**	....	....	....	....	....	....	....	....	....	....	....	....	....
1984-85	**New Jersey**	**NHL**	**1**	**0**	**0**	**0**	**10**	**0**	**0**	**0**	**1**	**0.0**	**–1**	....	....	....	....	....	....	....	....	....	....	....	....	....
	Maine	AHL	80	4	9	13	206	....	....	....	....	....	....	....	....	....	....	....	11	1	3	4	36	....	....	....
1985-86	**New Jersey**	**NHL**	**44**	**0**	**10**	**10**	**100**	**0**	**0**	**0**	**48**	**0.0**	**0**	....	....	....	....	....	....	....	....	....	....	....	....	....
	Maine	AHL	21	3	2	5	75	....	....	....	....	....	....	....	....	....	....	....	....	....	....	....	....	....	....	....
1986-87	**New Jersey**	**NHL**	**79**	**2**	**12**	**14**	**183**	**0**	**0**	**0**	**113**	**1.8**	**–13**	....	....	....	....	....	....	....	....	....	....	....	....	....
1987-88	**New Jersey**	**NHL**	**80**	**5**	**7**	**12**	**239**	**1**	**0**	**0**	**82**	**6.1**	**–3**	....	....	....	....	....	**20**	**1**	**6**	**7**	**83**	**0**	**0**	**1**
1988-89	**New Jersey**	**NHL**	**80**	**5**	**5**	**10**	**283**	**1**	**0**	**0**	**108**	**4.6**	**–22**	....	....	....	....	....	....	....	....	....	....	....	....	....
1989-90	**New Jersey**	**NHL**	**74**	**6**	**15**	**21**	**219**	**0**	**1**	**1**	**64**	**9.4**	**15**	....	....	....	....	....	**6**	**2**	**0**	**2**	**21**	**0**	**0**	**0**
1990-91	**New Jersey**	**NHL**	**80**	**4**	**16**	**20**	**249**	**1**	**2**	**1**	**106**	**3.8**	**–10**	....	....	....	....	....	**7**	**0**	**1**	**1**	**10**	**0**	**0**	**0**
1991-92	**New Jersey**	**NHL**	**80**	**1**	**7**	**8**	**170**	**0**	**0**	**0**	**57**	**1.8**	**7**	....	....	....	....	....	**7**	**0**	**3**	**3**	**16**	**0**	**0**	**0**
1992-93	**New Jersey**	**NHL**	**84**	**2**	**11**	**13**	**236**	**0**	**0**	**0**	**71**	**2.8**	**4**	....	....	....	....	....	**5**	**0**	**0**	**0**	**8**	**0**	**0**	**0**
1993-94	**New Jersey**	**NHL**	**78**	**1**	**9**	**10**	**176**	**0**	**0**	**1**	**60**	**1.7**	**27**	....	....	....	....	....	**20**	**0**	**1**	**1**	**45**	**0**	**0**	**0**
1994-95♦	**New Jersey**	**NHL**	**25**	**1**	**2**	**3**	**54**	**0**	**0**	**0**	**27**	**3.7**	**4**	....	....	....	....	....	**20**	**1**	**0**	**1**	**22**	**0**	**0**	**0**
1995-96	**New Jersey**	**NHL**	**80**	**2**	**4**	**6**	**115**	**0**	**0**	**0**	**67**	**3.0**	**–10**	....	....	....	....	....	....	....	....	....	....	....	....	....
1996-97	**New Jersey**	**NHL**	**77**	**2**	**7**	**9**	**70**	**0**	**0**	**0**	**63**	**3.2**	**24**	....	....	....	....	....	**10**	**0**	**0**	**0**	**28**	**0**	**0**	**0**
1997-98	**New Jersey**	**NHL**	**37**	**0**	**1**	**1**	**57**	**0**	**0**	**0**	**18**	**0.0**	**3**	....	....	....	....	....	**6**	**0**	**1**	**1**	**10**	**0**	**0**	**0**
1998-99	**New Jersey**	**NHL**	**82**	**2**	**9**	**11**	**63**	**0**	**0**	**0**	**63**	**3.2**	**27**	**1**	**0.0**	**182**	**159**	**20:03**	**7**	**0**	**0**	**0**	**8**	**0**	**0**	**0**
	NHL Totals		**992**	**34**	**119**	**153**	**2241**	**3**	**3**	**3**	**965**	**3.5**		**1**	**0.0**	**182**	**159**	**20:03**	**108**	**4**	**12**	**16**	**251**	**0**	**0**	**1**

			Regular Season																	Playoffs							
Season	Club	League	GP	G	A	Pts	PIM	PP	SH	GW	S	%	+/-	TF	F%	H	SB	Min	GP	G	A	Pts	PIM	PP	SH	GW

DANIELS, Jeff — CAR.

Left wing. Shoots left. 6'1", 200 lbs. Born, Oshawa, Ont., June 24, 1968. Pittsburgh's 6th choice, 109th overall, in 1986 Entry Draft.

Season	Club	League	GP	G	A	Pts	PIM	PP	SH	GW	S	%	+/-	TF	F%	H	SB	Min	GP	G	A	Pts	PIM	PP	SH	GW
1983-84	Oshawa Majors	OMHA	57	59	72	131	22																			
1984-85	Oshawa	OHL	59	7	11	18	16																			
1985-86	Oshawa	OHL	62	13	19	32	23											6	0	1	1	0			
1986-87	Oshawa	OHL	54	14	9	23	22											15	3	2	5	5			
1987-88	Oshawa	OHL	64	29	39	68	59											4	2	3	5	0			
1988-89	Muskegon	IHL	58	21	21	42	58											11	3	5	8	11			
1989-90	Muskegon	IHL	80	30	47	77	39											6	1	1	2	7			
1990-91	**Pittsburgh**	**NHL**	**11**	**0**	**2**	**2**	**2**	0	0	0	6	0.0	0												
	Muskegon	IHL	62	23	29	52	18											5	1	3	4	2			
1991-92	**Pittsburgh**	**NHL**	**2**	**0**	**0**	**0**	**0**	0	0	0	0	0.0	0												
	Muskegon	IHL	44	19	16	35	38											10	5	4	9	9			
1992-93	**Pittsburgh**	**NHL**	**58**	**5**	**4**	**9**	**14**	0	0	1	30	16.7	−5						12	3	2	5	0	0	0	1
	Cleveland	IHL	3	2	1	3	0																		
1993-94	**Pittsburgh**	**NHL**	**63**	**3**	**5**	**8**	**20**	0	0	1	46	6.5	−1												
	Florida	**NHL**	**7**	**0**	**0**	**0**	**0**	0	0	0	6	0.0	0												
1994-95	**Florida**	**NHL**	**3**	**0**	**0**	**0**	**0**	0	0	0	0	0.0	0												
	Detroit	IHL	25	8	12	20	6											5	1	0	1	0			
1995-96	Springfield	AHL	72	22	20	42	32											10	3	0	3	2			
1996-97	**Hartford**	**NHL**	**10**	**0**	**2**	**2**	**0**	0	0	0	6	0.0	2												
	Springfield	AHL	38	18	14	32	19											16	7	3	10	4			
1997-98	**Carolina**	**NHL**	**2**	**0**	**0**	**0**	**0**	0	0	0	1	0.0	0												
	New Haven	AHL	71	24	27	51	34											3	0	1	1	0			
1998-99	**Nashville**	**NHL**	**9**	**1**	**3**	**4**	**2**	0	0	0	8	12.5	−1	1	0.0	9	1	10:56							
	Milwaukee	IHL	62	12	31	43	19											2	1	1	2	0			
	NHL Totals		**165**	**9**	**16**	**25**	**38**	**0**	**0**	**2**	**103**	**8.7**		**1**	**0.0**	**9**	**1**	**10:56**	**12**	**3**	**2**	**5**	**0**	**0**	**0**	**1**

Traded to **Florida** by **Pittsburgh** for Greg Hawgood, March 19, 1994. Signed as a free agent by **Hartford**, August 18, 1995. Transferred to **Carolina** after **Hartford** franchise relocated, June 25, 1997. Claimed by **Nashville** from **Carolina** in Expansion Draft, June 26, 1998. Signed as a free agent by **Carolina**, August, 1999.

DANIELS, Scott

Left wing. Shoots left. 6'3", 215 lbs. Born, Prince Albert, Sask., September 19, 1969. Hartford's 6th choice, 136th overall, in 1989 Entry Draft.

Season	Club	League	GP	G	A	Pts	PIM	PP	SH	GW	S	%	+/-	TF	F%	H	SB	Min	GP	G	A	Pts	PIM	PP	SH	GW
1985-86	Notre Dame	SJHL	25	13	17	30	51																			
1986-87	Kamloops	WHL	43	6	4	10	68																			
	New Westminster	WHL	19	4	7	11	30																			
1987-88	New Westminster	WHL	37	6	11	17	157																			
	Regina	WHL	19	2	3	5	83																			
1988-89	Regina	WHL	64	21	26	47	241																			
1989-90	Regina	WHL	52	28	31	59	171																			
1990-91	Springfield	AHL	40	2	6	8	121																			
	Louisville	ECHL	9	5	3	8	34											1	0	2	2	0			
1991-92	Springfield	AHL	54	7	15	22	213											10	0	0	0	32			
1992-93	**Hartford**	**NHL**	**1**	**0**	**0**	**0**	**19**	0	0	0	0	0.0	0												
	Springfield	AHL	60	11	12	23	181											12	2	7	9	12			
1993-94	Springfield	AHL	52	9	11	20	185											6	0	1	1	53			
1994-95	**Hartford**	**NHL**	**12**	**0**	**2**	**2**	**55**	0	0	0	7	0.0	1												
	Springfield	AHL	48	9	5	14	277																			
1995-96	**Hartford**	**NHL**	**53**	**3**	**4**	**7**	**254**	0	0	0	43	7.0	−4												
	Springfield	AHL	6	4	1	5	17																			
1996-97	**Philadelphia**	**NHL**	**56**	**5**	**3**	**8**	**237**	0	0	2	48	10.4	2												
1997-98	**New Jersey**	**NHL**	**26**	**0**	**3**	**3**	**102**	0	0	0	17	0.0	1						1	0	0	0	0	0	0	0
1998-99	**New Jersey**	**NHL**	**1**	**0**	**0**	**0**	**0**	0	0	0	0	0.0	0	0	0.0	1	1	2:11							
	Albany	AHL	13	1	5	6	97																			
	NHL Totals		**149**	**8**	**12**	**20**	**667**	**0**	**0**	**2**	**115**	**7.0**		**0**	**0.0**	**1**	**1**	**2:11**	**1**	**0**	**0**	**0**	**0**	**0**	**0**	**0**

Signed as a free agent by **Philadelphia**, June 27, 1996. Claimed by **New Jersey** from **Philadelphia** in NHL Waiver Draft, September 28, 1997.

DARBY, Craig — MTL.

Center. Shoots right. 6'3", 200 lbs. Born, Oneida, NY, September 26, 1972. Montreal's 3rd choice, 43rd overall, in 1991 Entry Draft.

Season	Club	League	GP	G	A	Pts	PIM	PP	SH	GW	S	%	+/-	TF	F%	H	SB	Min	GP	G	A	Pts	PIM	PP	SH	GW
1989-90	Albany Academy	H.S.	29	32	53	95																			
1990-91	Albany Academy	H.S.	29	33	61	94																			
1991-92	Providence	H.E.	35	17	24	41	47																			
1992-93	Providence	H.E.	35	11	21	32	62																			
1993-94	Fredericton	AHL	66	23	33	56	51																			
1994-95	**Montreal**	**NHL**	**10**	**0**	**2**	**2**	**0**	0	0	0	4	0.0	−5												
	Fredericton	AHL	64	21	47	68	82																			
	NY Islanders	**NHL**	**3**	**0**	**0**	**0**	**0**	0	0	0	1	0.0	−1												
1995-96	**NY Islanders**	**NHL**	**10**	**0**	**2**	**2**	**0**	0	0	0	1	0.0	−1												
	Worcester	AHL	68	22	28	50	47											4	1	1	2	2			
1996-97	**Philadelphia**	**NHL**	**9**	**1**	**4**	**5**	**2**	0	1	0	13	7.7	2						10	3	6	9	0			
	Philadelphia	AHL	59	26	33	59	24																			
1997-98	**Philadelphia**	**NHL**	**3**	**1**	**0**	**1**	**0**	0	0	0	3	33.3	0												
	Philadelphia	AHL	77	*42	45	87	34											20	5	9	14	4			
1998-99	Milwaukee	IHL	81	32	22	54	33											2	3	0	3	0			
	NHL Totals		**35**	**2**	**8**	**10**	**2**	**0**	**1**	**0**	**22**	**9.1**														

AHL First All-Star Team (1998)

Traded to **NY Islanders** by **Montreal** with Kirk Muller and Mathieu Schneider for Pierre Turgeon and Vladimir Malakhov, April 5, 1995. Claimed on waivers by **Philadelphia** from **NY Islanders**, June 4, 1996. Claimed by **Nashville** from **Philadelphia** in Expansion Draft, June 26, 1998. Signed as a free agent by **Montreal**, August 4, 1999.

DAVIDSSON, Johan (DAH-vihd-suhn, YOH-hahn) ANA.

Center. Shoots right. 6'1", 190 lbs. Born, Jonkoping, Sweden, January 6, 1976. Anaheim's 2nd choice, 28th overall, in 1994 Entry Draft.

Season	Club	League	GP	G	A	Pts	PIM	PP	SH	GW	S	%	+/-	TF	F%	H	SB	Min	GP	G	A	Pts	PIM	PP	SH	GW
1992-93	HV Jonkoping	Sweden	8	1	0	1	0																			
1993-94	HV Jonkoping	Sweden	38	2	5	7	4																			
1994-95	HV Jonkoping	Sweden	37	4	7	11	20											13	3	2	5	0			
1995-96	HV Jonkoping	Sweden	39	7	11	18	20											4	0	2	2	0			
1996-97	HV Jonkoping	Sweden	50	18	21	39	18											5	0	3	3	2			
1997-98	HIFK Helsinki	Finland	43	10	30	40	8											9	3	10	13	0			
1998-99	**Anaheim**	**NHL**	**64**	**3**	**5**	**8**	**14**	1	0	1	48	6.3	−9	516	37.0	34	7	10:37	1	0	0	0	0	0	0	0
	Cincinnati	AHL	9	1	6	7	2																			
	NHL Totals		**64**	**3**	**5**	**8**	**14**	**1**	**0**	**1**	**48**	**6.3**		**516**	**37.0**	**34**	**7**	**10:37**	**1**	**0**	**0**	**0**	**0**	**0**	**0**	**0**

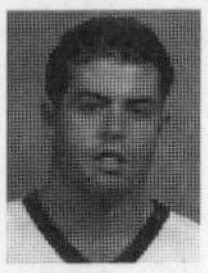

DAWE, Jason (DAW)

Right wing. Shoots left. 5'10", 189 lbs. Born, North York, Ont., May 29, 1973. Buffalo's 2nd choice, 35th overall, in 1991 Entry Draft.

			Regular Season																Playoffs							
Season	Club	League	GP	G	A	Pts	PIM	PP	SH	GW	S	%	+/–	TF	F%	H	SB	Min	GP	G	A	Pts	PIM	PP	SH	GW
1988-89	Don Mills	OMHA	44	43	28	63	103	....	....	....	....	....	....	....	....	....	....	....	....	....	....	....	....	....	....	....
1989-90	Peterborough	OHL	50	15	18	33	19	....	....	....	....	....	....	....	....	....	....	....	12	4	7	11	4	....	....	....
1990-91	Peterborough	OHL	66	43	27	70	43	....	....	....	....	....	....	....	....	....	....	....	4	3	1	4	0	....	....	....
1991-92	Peterborough	OHL	66	53	55	108	55	....	....	....	....	....	....	....	....	....	....	....	4	5	0	5	0	....	....	....
1992-93	Peterborough	OHL	59	58	68	126	80	....	....	....	....	....	....	....	....	....	....	....	21	18	33	51	18	....	....	....
	Rochester	AHL	....	....	....	....	....	....	....	....	....	....	....	....	....	....	....	....	3	1	0	1	0	....	....	....
1993-94	**Buffalo**	**NHL**	**32**	**6**	**7**	**13**	**12**	**3**	**0**	**1**	**35**	**17.1**	**1**	....	....	....	....	....	**6**	**0**	**1**	**1**	**6**	**0**	**0**	**0**
	Rochester	AHL	48	22	14	36	44	....	....	....	....	....	....	....	....	....	....	....	....	....	....	....	....	....	....	....
1994-95	Rochester	AHL	44	27	19	46	24	....	....	....	....	....	....	....	....	....	....	....	....	....	....	....	....	....	....	....
	Buffalo	**NHL**	**42**	**7**	**4**	**11**	**19**	**0**	**1**	**2**	**51**	**13.7**	**–6**	....	....	....	....	....	**5**	**2**	**1**	**3**	**6**	**0**	**0**	**0**
1995-96	**Buffalo**	**NHL**	**67**	**25**	**25**	**50**	**33**	**8**	**1**	**0**	**130**	**19.2**	**–8**	....	....	....	....	....	....	....	....	....	....	....	....	....
	Rochester	AHL	7	5	4	9	2	....	....	....	....	....	....	....	....	....	....	....	....	....	....	....	....	....	....	....
1996-97	**Buffalo**	**NHL**	**81**	**22**	**26**	**48**	**32**	**4**	**1**	**3**	**136**	**16.2**	**14**	....	....	....	....	....	**11**	**2**	**1**	**3**	**6**	**0**	**0**	**0**
1997-98	**Buffalo**	**NHL**	**68**	**19**	**17**	**36**	**36**	**4**	**1**	**3**	**115**	**16.5**	**10**	....	....	....	....	....	....	....	....	....	....	....	....	....
	NY Islanders	**NHL**	**13**	**1**	**2**	**3**	**6**	**0**	**0**	**0**	**19**	**5.3**	**–2**	....	....	....	....	....	....	....	....	....	....	....	....	....
1998-99	**NY Islanders**	**NHL**	**22**	**2**	**3**	**5**	**8**	**0**	**0**	**0**	**29**	**6.9**	**0**	**4**	**25.0**	**27**	**5**	**11:55**	....	....	....	....	....	....	....	....
	Montreal	**NHL**	**37**	**4**	**5**	**9**	**14**	**1**	**0**	**1**	**52**	**7.7**	**0**	**4**	**0.0**	**44**	**4**	**11:00**	....	....	....	....	....	....	....	....
	NHL Totals		**362**	**86**	**89**	**175**	**160**	**20**	**4**	**10**	**567**	**15.2**		**8**	**12.5**	**71**	**9**	**11:21**	**22**	**4**	**3**	**7**	**18**	**0**	**0**	**0**

OHL First All-Star Team (1993) • Canadian Major Junior Second All-Star Team (1993) • Won George Parsons Trophy (Memorial Cup Tournament Most Sportsmanlike Player) (1993)

Traded to **NY Islanders** by **Buffalo** for Jason Holland and Paul Kruse, March 24, 1998. Claimed on waivers by **Montreal** from **NY Islanders**, December 15, 1998.

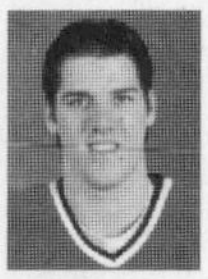

DAZE, Eric (dah-ZAY) CHI.

Left wing. Shoots left. 6'6", 234 lbs. Born, Montreal, Que., July 2, 1975. Chicago's 5th choice, 90th overall, in 1993 Entry Draft.

			Regular Season																Playoffs							
Season	Club	League	GP	G	A	Pts	PIM	PP	SH	GW	S	%	+/–	TF	F%	H	SB	Min	GP	G	A	Pts	PIM	PP	SH	GW
1990-91	Laval	QAAA	30	25	20	45	30	....	....	....	....	....	....	....	....	....	....	....	....	....	....	....	....	....	....	....
1991-92	Laval	QAAA	35	30	29	59	40	....	....	....	....	....	....	....	....	....	....	....	....	....	....	....	....	....	....	....
1992-93	Beauport	QMJHL	68	19	36	55	24	....	....	....	....	....	....	....	....	....	....	....	....	....	....	....	....	....	....	....
1993-94	Beauport	QMJHL	66	59	48	107	31	....	....	....	....	....	....	....	....	....	....	....	15	16	8	24	2	....	....	....
1994-95	Beauport	QMJHL	57	54	45	99	20	....	....	....	....	....	....	....	....	....	....	....	16	9	12	21	23	....	....	....
	Chicago	**NHL**	**4**	**1**	**1**	**2**	**2**	**0**	**0**	**0**	**1**	**100.0**	**2**	....	....	....	....	....	**16**	**0**	**1**	**1**	**4**	**0**	**0**	**0**
1995-96	**Chicago**	**NHL**	**80**	**30**	**23**	**53**	**18**	**2**	**0**	**2**	**167**	**18.0**	**16**	....	....	....	....	....	**10**	**3**	**5**	**8**	**0**	**0**	**0**	**1**
1996-97	**Chicago**	**NHL**	**71**	**22**	**19**	**41**	**16**	**11**	**0**	**4**	**176**	**12.5**	**–4**	....	....	....	....	....	**6**	**2**	**1**	**3**	**2**	**0**	**0**	**0**
1997-98	**Chicago**	**NHL**	**80**	**31**	**11**	**42**	**22**	**10**	**0**	**7**	**216**	**14.4**	**4**	....	....	....	....	....	....	....	....	....	....	....	....	....
1998-99	**Chicago**	**NHL**	**72**	**22**	**20**	**42**	**22**	**8**	**0**	**2**	**189**	**11.6**	**–13**	**4**	**0.0**	**92**	**22**	**16:16**	....	....	....	....	....	....	....	....
	NHL Totals		**307**	**106**	**74**	**180**	**80**	**31**	**0**	**15**	**749**	**14.2**		**4**	**0.0**	**92**	**22**	**16:16**	**32**	**5**	**7**	**12**	**6**	**0**	**0**	**1**

QMJHL First All-Star Team (1994, 1995) • Canadian Major Junior Most Sportsmanlike Player of the Year (1995) • NHL All-Rookie Team (1996)

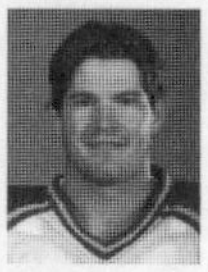

DEADMARSH, Adam COL.

Center. Shoots right. 6', 195 lbs. Born, Trail, B.C., May 10, 1975. Quebec's 2nd choice, 14th overall, in 1993 Entry Draft.

			Regular Season																Playoffs							
Season	Club	League	GP	G	A	Pts	PIM	PP	SH	GW	S	%	+/–	TF	F%	H	SB	Min	GP	G	A	Pts	PIM	PP	SH	GW
1990-91	Beaver Valley	KIJHL	35	28	44	72	95	....	....	....	....	....	....	....	....	....	....	....	....	....	....	....	....	....	....	....
1991-92	Portland	WHL	68	30	30	60	81	....	....	....	....	....	....	....	....	....	....	....	6	3	3	6	13	....	....	....
1992-93	Portland	WHL	58	33	36	69	126	....	....	....	....	....	....	....	....	....	....	....	16	7	8	15	29	....	....	....
1993-94	Portland	WHL	65	43	56	99	212	....	....	....	....	....	....	....	....	....	....	....	10	9	8	17	33	....	....	....
1994-95	Portland	WHL	29	28	20	48	129	....	....	....	....	....	....	....	....	....	....	....	....	....	....	....	....	....	....	....
	Quebec	**NHL**	**48**	**9**	**8**	**17**	**56**	**0**	**0**	**0**	**48**	**18.8**	**16**	....	....	....	....	....	**6**	**0**	**1**	**1**	**0**	**0**	**0**	**0**
1995-96♦	**Colorado**	**NHL**	**78**	**21**	**27**	**48**	**142**	**3**	**0**	**2**	**151**	**13.9**	**20**	....	....	....	....	....	**22**	**5**	**12**	**17**	**25**	**1**	**0**	**0**
1996-97	**Colorado**	**NHL**	**78**	**33**	**27**	**60**	**136**	**10**	**3**	**4**	**198**	**16.7**	**8**	....	....	....	....	....	**17**	**3**	**6**	**9**	**24**	**1**	**0**	**1**
1997-98	**Colorado**	**NHL**	**73**	**22**	**21**	**43**	**125**	**10**	**0**	**6**	**187**	**11.8**	**0**	....	....	....	....	....	**7**	**2**	**0**	**2**	**4**	**1**	**0**	**0**
	United States	Olympics	4	1	0	1	2	....	....	....	....	....	....	....	....	....	....	....	....	....	....	....	....	....	....	....
1998-99	**Colorado**	**NHL**	**66**	**22**	**27**	**49**	**99**	**10**	**0**	**3**	**152**	**14.5**	**–2**	**621**	**45.9**	**121**	**51**	**20:46**	**19**	**8**	**4**	**12**	**20**	**3**	**0**	**0**
	NHL Totals		**343**	**107**	**110**	**217**	**558**	**33**	**3**	**15**	**736**	**14.5**		**621**	**45.9**	**121**	**51**	**20:46**	**71**	**18**	**23**	**41**	**73**	**6**	**0**	**1**

Transferred to **Colorado** after **Quebec** franchise relocated, June 21, 1995.

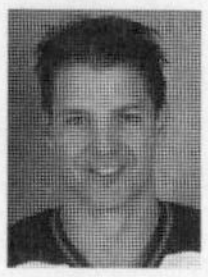

DEAN, Kevin ATL.

Defense. Shoots left. 6'3", 205 lbs. Born, Madison, WI, April 1, 1969. New Jersey's 4th choice, 86th overall, in 1987 Entry Draft.

			Regular Season																Playoffs							
Season	Club	League	GP	G	A	Pts	PIM	PP	SH	GW	S	%	+/–	TF	F%	H	SB	Min	GP	G	A	Pts	PIM	PP	SH	GW
1985-86	Culver Academy	H.S.	35	28	44	72	48	....	....	....	....	....	....	....	....	....	....	....	....	....	....	....	....	....	....	....
1986-87	Culver Academy	H.S.	25	19	25	44	30	....	....	....	....	....	....	....	....	....	....	....	....	....	....	....	....	....	....	....
1987-88	New Hampshire	H.E.	27	1	6	7	34	....	....	....	....	....	....	....	....	....	....	....	....	....	....	....	....	....	....	....
1988-89	New Hampshire	H.E.	34	1	12	13	28	....	....	....	....	....	....	....	....	....	....	....	....	....	....	....	....	....	....	....
1989-90	New Hampshire	H.E.	39	2	6	8	42	....	....	....	....	....	....	....	....	....	....	....	....	....	....	....	....	....	....	....
1990-91	New Hampshire	H.E.	31	10	12	22	22	....	....	....	....	....	....	....	....	....	....	....	....	....	....	....	....	....	....	....
	Utica	AHL	7	0	1	1	2	....	....	....	....	....	....	....	....	....	....	....	....	....	....	....	....	....	....	....
1991-92	Utica	AHL	23	0	3	3	6	....	....	....	....	....	....	....	....	....	....	....	....	....	....	....	....	....	....	....
	Cincinnati	ECHL	30	3	22	25	43	....	....	....	....	....	....	....	....	....	....	....	9	1	6	7	8	....	....	....
1992-93	Cincinnati	IHL	13	2	1	3	15	....	....	....	....	....	....	....	....	....	....	....	....	....	....	....	....	....	....	....
	Utica	AHL	57	2	16	18	76	....	....	....	....	....	....	....	....	....	....	....	5	1	0	1	8	....	....	....
1993-94	Albany	AHL	70	9	33	42	92	....	....	....	....	....	....	....	....	....	....	....	5	0	2	2	7	....	....	....
1994-95♦	**New Jersey**	**NHL**	**17**	**0**	**1**	**1**	**4**	**0**	**0**	**0**	**11**	**0.0**	**6**	....	....	....	....	....	**3**	**0**	**2**	**2**	**0**	**0**	**0**	**0**
	Albany	AHL	68	5	37	42	66	....	....	....	....	....	....	....	....	....	....	....	8	0	4	4	4	....	....	....
1995-96	**New Jersey**	**NHL**	**41**	**0**	**6**	**6**	**28**	**0**	**0**	**0**	**29**	**0.0**	**4**	....	....	....	....	....	....	....	....	....	....	....	....	....
	Albany	AHL	1	1	0	1	2	....	....	....	....	....	....	....	....	....	....	....	....	....	....	....	....	....	....	....
1996-97	**New Jersey**	**NHL**	**28**	**2**	**4**	**6**	**6**	**0**	**0**	**0**	**21**	**9.5**	**2**	....	....	....	....	....	**1**	**1**	**0**	**1**	**0**	**0**	**0**	**1**
	Albany	AHL	2	0	1	1	4	....	....	....	....	....	....	....	....	....	....	....	....	....	....	....	....	....	....	....
1997-98	**New Jersey**	**NHL**	**50**	**1**	**8**	**9**	**12**	**1**	**0**	**0**	**28**	**3.6**	**12**	....	....	....	....	....	**5**	**1**	**0**	**1**	**2**	**0**	**0**	**0**
	Albany	AHL	2	0	1	1	2	....	....	....	....	....	....	....	....	....	....	....	....	....	....	....	....	....	....	....
1998-99	**New Jersey**	**NHL**	**62**	**1**	**10**	**11**	**22**	**1**	**0**	**0**	**51**	**2.0**	**4**	**0**	**0.0**	**77**	**59**	**15:42**	**7**	**0**	**0**	**0**	**0**	**0**	**0**	**0**
	NHL Totals		**198**	**4**	**29**	**33**	**72**	**2**	**0**	**0**	**140**	**2.9**		**0**	**0.0**	**77**	**59**	**15:42**	**16**	**2**	**2**	**4**	**2**	**0**	**0**	**1**

AHL First All-Star Team (1995)

Claimed by **Atlanta** from **New Jersey** in Expansion Draft, June 25, 1999.

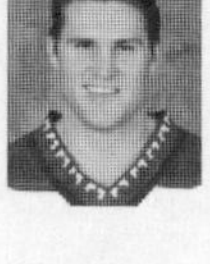

DeBRUSK, Louie (duh-BRUHSK) PHX.

Left wing. Shoots left. 6'2", 230 lbs. Born, Cambridge, Ont., March 19, 1971. NY Rangers' 4th choice, 49th overall, in 1989 Entry Draft.

			Regular Season																Playoffs							
Season	Club	League	GP	G	A	Pts	PIM	PP	SH	GW	S	%	+/–	TF	F%	H	SB	Min	GP	G	A	Pts	PIM	PP	SH	GW
1986-87	Port Elgin	OJHL-C	10	2	1	3	4	....	....	....	....	....	....	....	....	....	....	....	....	....	....	....	....	....	....	....
1987-88	Stratford	OJHL-B	45	13	14	27	205	....	....	....	....	....	....	....	....	....	....	....	....	....	....	....	....	....	....	....
1988-89	London	OHL	59	11	11	22	149	....	....	....	....	....	....	....	....	....	....	....	19	1	1	2	43	....	....	....
1989-90	London	OHL	61	21	19	40	198	....	....	....	....	....	....	....	....	....	....	....	6	2	2	4	24	....	....	....
1990-91	London	OHL	61	31	33	64	*223	....	....	....	....	....	....	....	....	....	....	....	7	2	2	4	14	....	....	....
	Binghamton	AHL	2	0	0	0	7	....	....	....	....	....	....	....	....	....	....	....	2	0	0	0	9	....	....	....
1991-92	**Edmonton**	**NHL**	**25**	**2**	**1**	**3**	**124**	**0**	**0**	**1**	**7**	**28.6**	**4**	....	....	....	....	....	....	....	....	....	....	....	....	....
	Cape Breton	AHL	28	2	2	4	73	....	....	....	....	....	....	....	....	....	....	....	....	....	....	....	....	....	....	....
1992-93	**Edmonton**	**NHL**	**51**	**8**	**2**	**10**	**205**	**0**	**0**	**1**	**33**	**24.2**	**–16**	....	....	....	....	....	....	....	....	....	....	....	....	....
1993-94	**Edmonton**	**NHL**	**48**	**4**	**6**	**10**	**185**	**0**	**0**	**0**	**27**	**14.8**	**–9**	....	....	....	....	....	....	....	....	....	....	....	....	....
	Cape Breton	AHL	5	3	1	4	58	....	....	....	....	....	....	....	....	....	....	....	....	....	....	....	....	....	....	....
1994-95	**Edmonton**	**NHL**	**34**	**2**	**0**	**2**	**93**	**0**	**0**	**0**	**14**	**14.3**	**–4**	....	....	....	....	....	....	....	....	....	....	....	....	....
1995-96	**Edmonton**	**NHL**	**38**	**1**	**3**	**4**	**96**	**0**	**0**	**0**	**17**	**5.9**	**–7**	....	....	....	....	....	....	....	....	....	....	....	....	....
1996-97	**Edmonton**	**NHL**	**32**	**2**	**0**	**2**	**94**	**0**	**0**	**0**	**10**	**20.0**	**–6**	....	....	....	....	....	**6**	**0**	**0**	**0**	**4**	**0**	**0**	**0**

			Regular Season																Playoffs							
Season	Club	League	GP	G	A	Pts	PIM	PP	SH	GW	S	%	+/-	TF	F%	H	SB	Min	GP	G	A	Pts	PIM	PP	SH	GW
1997-98	Tampa Bay	NHL	54	1	2	3	166	0	0	0	14	7.1	-2	....	....	....	....	....	....							
	San Antonio	IHL	17	7	4	11	130																		
1998-99	Phoenix	NHL	15	0	0	0	34	0	0	0	6	0.0	-2	0	0.0	16	0	5:57	6	2	0	2	6	0	0	0
	Las Vegas	IHL	26	3	6	9	160																		
	Springfield	AHL	3	1	0	1	0																		
	Long Beach	IHL	24	5	5	10	134																		
	NHL Totals		297	20	14	34	997	0	0	2	128	15.6		0	0.0	16	0	5:57	12	2	0	2	10	0	0	0

Traded to **Edmonton** by **NY Rangers** with Bernie Nicholls and Steven Rice for Mark Messier and future considerations, October 4, 1991. Signed as a free agent by **Tampa Bay**, September 23, 1997. Traded to **Phoenix** by **Tampa Bay** with Tampa Bay's 5th round choice (Jay Leach) in 1998 Entry Draft for Craig Janney, June 11, 1998.

DELISLE, Jonathan
(duh-LIGHL)　　**MTL.**

Right wing. Shoots right. 5'10", 180 lbs.　　Born, Ste-Anne-des-Plaines, Que., June 30, 1977. Montreal's 4th choice, 86th overall, in 1995 Entry Draft.

Season	Club	League	GP	G	A	Pts	PIM	PP	SH	GW	S	%	+/-	TF	F%	H	SB	Min	GP	G	A	Pts	PIM	PP	SH	GW
1992-93	Laval	QAAA	14	3	3	6	12	....												13	2	5	7	24			
1993-94	Verdun	QMJHL	61	16	17	33	130	....												4	0	1	1	14			
1994-95	Hull	QMJHL	60	21	38	59	218	....												19	11	8	19	43			
1995-96	Hull	QMJHL	62	31	57	88	193	....												18	6	13	19	64			
1996-97	Hull	QMJHL	61	35	54	89	228	....												14	11	13	24	46			
1997-98	Fredericton	AHL	78	15	21	36	138	....												4	0	1	1	7			
1998-99	**Montreal**	**NHL**	1	0	0	0	0	0	0	0	0	0.0	0	0	0.0	1	0	4:32	....							
	Fredericton	AHL	78	7	29	36	118	....												15	3	6	9	39			
	NHL Totals		1	0	0	0	0	0	0	0	0	0.0		0	0.0	1	0	4:32	....							

DELISLE, Xavier
(duh-LIGHL)　　**T.B.**

Center. Shoots right. 5'11", 182 lbs.　　Born, Quebec City, Que., May 24, 1977. Tampa Bay's 5th choice, 157th overall, in 1996 Entry Draft.

Season	Club	League	GP	G	A	Pts	PIM	PP	SH	GW	S	%	+/-	TF	F%	H	SB	Min	GP	G	A	Pts	PIM	PP	SH	GW
1992-93	Ste-Foy	QAAA	41	20	23	43	....																				
1993-94	Granby	QMJHL	46	11	22	33	25	....												7	2	0	2	0			
1994-95	Granby	QMJHL	72	18	36	54	48	....												13	2	6	8	4			
1995-96	Granby	QMJHL	67	45	75	120	45	....												20	13	*27	*40	12			
1996-97	Granby	QMJHL	59	36	56	92	20	....												5	1	4	5	6			
1997-98	Adirondack	AHL	76	10	19	29	47	....												3	0	0	0	0			
1998-99	**Tampa Bay**	**NHL**	2	0	0	0	0	0	0	0	1	0.0	0	11	45.5	1	0	5:51	....							
	Cleveland	IHL	77	15	29	44	36	....												....							
	NHL Totals		2	0	0	0	0	0	0	0	1	0.0		11	45.5	1	0	5:51	....							

QMJHL Second All-Star Team (1996) • Memorial Cup All-Star Team (1996)

DELMORE, Andy
PHI.

Defense. Shoots right. 6'1", 192 lbs.　　Born, LaSalle, Ont., December 26, 1976.

Season	Club	League	GP	G	A	Pts	PIM	PP	SH	GW	S	%	+/-	TF	F%	H	SB	Min	GP	G	A	Pts	PIM	PP	SH	GW
1992-93	Chatham	OJHL-B	47	4	21	25	38	....												....							
1993-94	North Bay	OHL	45	2	7	9	33	....												17	0	0	0	2			
1994-95	North Bay	OHL	40	2	14	16	21	....												3	0	0	0	2			
	Sarnia	OHL	27	5	13	18	27	....												3	0	0	0	2			
1995-96	Sarnia	OHL	64	21	38	59	45	....												10	3	7	10	2			
1996-97	Sarnia	OHL	64	18	60	78	39	....												12	2	10	12	10			
	Fredericton	AHL	4	0	1	1	0	....												....							
1997-98	Philadelphia	AHL	73	9	30	39	46	....												18	4	4	8	21			
1998-99	**Philadelphia**	**NHL**	2	0	1	1	0	0	0	0	2	0.0	-1	0	0.0	1	1	20:42	....							
	Philadelphia	AHL	70	5	18	23	51													15	1	4	5	6			
	NHL Totals		2	0	1	1	0	0	0	0	2	0.0		0	0.0	1	1	20:42	....							

OHL First All-Star Team (1997)
Signed as a free agent by **Philadelphia**, June 9, 1997.

DEMITRA, Pavol
(deh-MIHT-rah)　　**ST.L.**

Left wing. Shoots left. 6', 196 lbs.　　Born, Dubnica, Czech., November 29, 1974. Ottawa's 8th choice, 227th overall, in 1993 Entry Draft.

Season	Club	League	GP	G	A	Pts	PIM	PP	SH	GW	S	%	+/-	TF	F%	H	SB	Min	GP	G	A	Pts	PIM	PP	SH	GW
1991-92	Dubnica	Czech-2	28	13	10	23	12	....												....							
1992-93	Dubnica	Czech-2	4	3	0	3	....													....							
	Dukla Trencin	Czech.	46	10	18	28	....													....							
1993-94	**Ottawa**	**NHL**	12	1	1	2	4	1	0	0	10	10.0	-7	....	....	....	....	....	....							
	P.E.I. Senators	AHL	41	18	23	41	8	....												....							
1994-95	**Ottawa**	**NHL**	16	4	3	7	0	1	0	0	21	19.0	-4	....	....	....	....	....	....							
	P.E.I. Senators	AHL	61	26	48	74	23	....												5	0	7	7	0			
1995-96	**Ottawa**	**NHL**	31	7	10	17	6	2	0	1	66	10.6	-3	....	....	....	....	....	....							
	P.E.I. Senators	AHL	48	28	53	81	44	....												....							
1996-97	Dukla Trencin	Slovakia	1	1	1	2	....													....							
	St. Louis	**NHL**	8	3	0	3	2	2	0	1	15	20.0	0	....	....	....	....	....	6	1	3	4	6	0	0	0
	Las Vegas	IHL	22	8	13	21	10	....												....							
	Grand Rapids	IHL	42	20	30	50	24	....												....							
1997-98	**St. Louis**	**NHL**	61	22	30	52	22	4	4	6	147	15.0	11	....	....	....	....	....	10	3	3	6	2	0	0	0
1998-99	**St. Louis**	**NHL**	82	37	52	89	16	14	0	10	259	14.3	13	250	44.0	31	15	20:10	13	5	4	9	4	3	0	1
	NHL Totals		210	74	96	170	50	24	4	18	518	14.3		250	44.0	31	15	20:10	29	9	10	19	12	3	0	1

Played in NHL All-Star Game (1999)
Traded to **St. Louis** by **Ottawa** for Christer Olsson, November 27, 1996.

DEMPSEY, Nathan
TOR.

Defense. Shoots left. 6', 170 lbs.　　Born, Spruce Grove, Alta., July 14, 1974. Toronto's 12th choice, 245th overall, in 1992 Entry Draft.

Season	Club	League	GP	G	A	Pts	PIM	PP	SH	GW	S	%	+/-	TF	F%	H	SB	Min	GP	G	A	Pts	PIM	PP	SH	GW
1990-91	St. Albert	AJHL	34	11	20	31	73	....												....							
1991-92	Regina	WHL	70	4	22	26	72	....												....							
1992-93	Regina	WHL	72	12	29	41	95	....												13	3	8	11	14			
	St. John's	AHL	....																	2	0	0	0	0			
1993-94	Regina	WHL	56	14	36	50	100	....												4	0	0	0	4			
1994-95	St. John's	AHL	74	7	30	37	91	....												5	1	0	1	11			
1995-96	St. John's	AHL	73	5	15	20	103	....												4	1	0	1	9			
1996-97	**Toronto**	**NHL**	14	1	1	2	2	0	0	0	11	9.1	-2	....	....	....	....	....	....							
	St. John's	AHL	52	8	18	26	108	....												6	1	0	1	4			
1997-98	St. John's	AHL	68	12	16	28	85	....												4	0	0	0	0			
1998-99	St. John's	AHL	67	2	29	31	70	....												5	0	1	1	2			
	NHL Totals		14	1	1	2	2	0	0	0	11	9.1		....	....	....	....	....	....							

WHL East Second All-Star Team (1994)

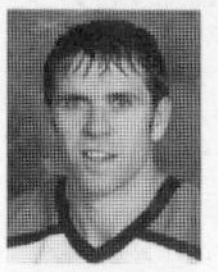

DESJARDINS, Eric

(deh-ZHAHR-dai) **PHI.**

Defense. Shoots right. 6'1", 200 lbs. Born, Rouyn, Que., June 14, 1969. Montreal's 3rd choice, 38th overall, in 1987 Entry Draft.

Season	Club	League	GP	G	A	Pts	PIM	PP	SH	GW	S	%	+/-	TF	F%	H	SB	Min	GP	G	A	Pts	PIM	PP	SH	GW
			Regular Season																Playoffs							
1985-86	Laval	QAAA	42	6	30	36	54	....	....	....	....	....	....	....	....	....	....	....	....	....	....	....	....	....	....	....
1986-87	Granby	QMJHL	66	14	24	38	178	....	....	....	....	....	....	....	....	....	....	....	8	3	2	5	10	....	....	....
1987-88	Granby	QMJHL	62	18	49	67	138	....	....	....	....	....	....	....	....	....	....	....	5	0	3	3	10	....	....	....
	Sherbrooke	AHL	3	0	0	0	6	....	....	....	....	....	....	....	....	....	....	....	4	0	2	2	2	....	....	....
1988-89	**Montreal**	**NHL**	**36**	**2**	**12**	**14**	**26**	**1**	**0**	**0**	**39**	**5.1**	**9**	....	....	....	....	....	**14**	**1**	**1**	**2**	**6**	**1**	**0**	**0**
1989-90	**Montreal**	**NHL**	**55**	**3**	**13**	**16**	**51**	**1**	**0**	**0**	**48**	**6.3**	**1**	....	....	....	....	....	**6**	**0**	**0**	**0**	**10**	**0**	**0**	**0**
1990-91	**Montreal**	**NHL**	**62**	**7**	**18**	**25**	**27**	**0**	**0**	**1**	**114**	**6.1**	**7**	....	....	....	....	....	**13**	**1**	**4**	**5**	**8**	**1**	**0**	**0**
1991-92	**Montreal**	**NHL**	**77**	**6**	**32**	**38**	**50**	**4**	**0**	**2**	**141**	**4.3**	**17**	....	....	....	....	....	**11**	**3**	**3**	**6**	**4**	**1**	**0**	**0**
1992-93♦	**Montreal**	**NHL**	**82**	**13**	**32**	**45**	**98**	**7**	**0**	**1**	**163**	**8.0**	**20**	....	....	....	....	....	**20**	**4**	**10**	**14**	**23**	**1**	**0**	**1**
1993-94	**Montreal**	**NHL**	**84**	**12**	**23**	**35**	**97**	**6**	**1**	**3**	**193**	**6.2**	**–1**	....	....	....	....	....	**7**	**0**	**2**	**2**	**4**	**0**	**0**	**0**
1994-95	**Montreal**	**NHL**	**9**	**0**	**6**	**6**	**2**	**0**	**0**	**0**	**14**	**0.0**	**2**	....	....	....	....	....	....	....	....	....	....	....	....	....
	Philadelphia	**NHL**	**34**	**5**	**18**	**23**	**12**	**1**	**0**	**1**	**79**	**6.3**	**10**	....	....	....	....	....	**15**	**4**	**4**	**8**	**10**	**1**	**0**	**2**
1995-96	**Philadelphia**	**NHL**	**80**	**7**	**40**	**47**	**45**	**5**	**0**	**2**	**184**	**3.8**	**19**	....	....	....	....	....	**12**	**0**	**6**	**6**	**2**	**0**	**0**	**0**
1996-97	**Philadelphia**	**NHL**	**82**	**12**	**34**	**46**	**50**	**5**	**1**	**1**	**183**	**6.6**	**25**	....	....	....	....	....	**19**	**2**	**8**	**10**	**12**	**0**	**0**	**0**
1997-98	**Philadelphia**	**NHL**	**77**	**6**	**27**	**33**	**36**	**2**	**1**	**0**	**150**	**4.0**	**11**	....	....	....	....	....	**5**	**0**	**1**	**1**	**0**	**0**	**0**	**0**
	Canada	Olympics	6	0	0	0	2	....	....	....	....	....	....	....	....	....	....	....	....	....	....	....	....	....	....	....
1998-99	**Philadelphia**	**NHL**	**68**	**15**	**36**	**51**	**38**	**6**	**0**	**2**	**190**	**7.9**	**18**	**0**	**0.0**	**36**	**108**	**25:48**	**6**	**2**	**2**	**4**	**4**	**1**	**0**	**1**
	NHL Totals		**746**	**88**	**291**	**379**	**532**	**38**	**3**	**13**	**1498**	**5.9**		**0**	**0.0**	**36**	**108**	**25:48**	**128**	**17**	**41**	**58**	**83**	**6**	**0**	**4**

QMJHL Second All-Star Team (1987) • QMJHL First All-Star Team (1988) • NHL Second All-Star Team (1999)
Played in NHL All-Star Game (1992, 1996)
Traded to **Philadelphia** by **Montreal** with Gilbert Dionne and John LeClair for Mark Recchi and Philadelphia's 3rd round choice (Martin Hohenberger) in 1995 Entry Draft, February 9, 1995.

DEULING, Jarrett

S.J.

Left wing. Shoots left. 6', 200 lbs. Born, Vernon, B.C., March 4, 1974. NY Islanders' 2nd choice, 56th overall, in 1992 Entry Draft.

Season	Club	League	GP	G	A	Pts	PIM	PP	SH	GW	S	%	+/-	TF	F%	H	SB	Min	GP	G	A	Pts	PIM	PP	SH	GW
1990-91	Kamloops	WHL	48	4	12	16	43	....	....	....	....	....	....	....	....	....	....	....	12	5	2	7	7	....	....	....
1991-92	Kamloops	WHL	68	28	26	54	79	....	....	....	....	....	....	....	....	....	....	....	17	10	6	16	18	....	....	....
1992-93	Kamloops	WHL	68	31	32	63	93	....	....	....	....	....	....	....	....	....	....	....	13	6	7	13	14	....	....	....
1993-94	Kamloops	WHL	70	44	59	103	171	....	....	....	....	....	....	....	....	....	....	....	18	*13	8	21	43	....	....	....
1994-95	Worcester	AHL	63	11	8	19	37	....	....	....	....	....	....	....	....	....	....	....	....	....	....	....	....	....	....	....
1995-96	**NY Islanders**	**NHL**	**14**	**0**	**1**	**1**	**11**	**0**	**0**	**0**	**11**	**0.0**	**–1**	....	....	....	....	....	....	....	....	....	....	....	....	....
	Worcester	AHL	57	16	7	23	57	....	....	....	....	....	....	....	....	....	....	....	4	1	2	3	2	....	....	....
1996-97	**NY Islanders**	**NHL**	**1**	**0**	**0**	**0**	**0**	**0**	**0**	**0**	**0**	**0.0**	**0**	....	....	....	....	....	....	....	....	....	....	....	....	....
	Kentucky	AHL	58	15	31	46	57	....	....	....	....	....	....	....	....	....	....	....	4	3	0	3	8	....	....	....
1997-98	Milwaukee	IHL	64	18	18	36	84	....	....	....	....	....	....	....	....	....	....	....	10	4	3	7	36	....	....	....
1998-99	Kentucky	AHL	60	22	31	53	68	....	....	....	....	....	....	....	....	....	....	....	12	3	6	9	8	....	....	....
	NHL Totals		**15**	**0**	**1**	**1**	**11**	**0**	**0**	**0**	**11**	**0.0**		....	....	....	....	....	....	....	....	....	....	....	....	....

Signed as a free agent by **San Jose**, August 27, 1998.

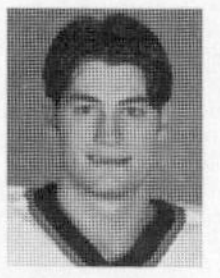

DEVEREAUX, Boyd

(DEH-vuhr-oh) **EDM.**

Center. Shoots left. 6'2", 195 lbs. Born, Seaforth, Ont., April 16, 1978. Edmonton's 1st choice, 6th overall, in 1996 Entry Draft.

Season	Club	League	GP	G	A	Pts	PIM	PP	SH	GW	S	%	+/-	TF	F%	H	SB	Min	GP	G	A	Pts	PIM	PP	SH	GW
1993-94	Stratford	OJHL-B	46	12	27	39	8	....	....	....	....	....	....	....	....	....	....	....	....	....	....	....	....	....	....	....
1994-95	Stratford	OJHL-B	45	31	74	105	21	....	....	....	....	....	....	....	....	....	....	....	....	....	....	....	....	....	....	....
1995-96	Kitchener	OHL	66	20	38	58	35	....	....	....	....	....	....	....	....	....	....	....	12	3	7	10	4	....	....	....
1996-97	Kitchener	OHL	54	28	41	69	37	....	....	....	....	....	....	....	....	....	....	....	13	4	11	15	8	....	....	....
	Hamilton	AHL	....	....	....	....	....	....	....	....	....	....	....	....	....	....	....	....	1	0	1	1	0	....	....	....
1997-98	**Edmonton**	**NHL**	**38**	**1**	**4**	**5**	**6**	**0**	**0**	**0**	**27**	**3.7**	**–5**	....	....	....	....	....	....	....	....	....	....	....	....	....
	Hamilton	AHL	14	5	6	11	6	....	....	....	....	....	....	....	....	....	....	....	9	1	1	2	8	....	....	....
1998-99	**Edmonton**	**NHL**	**61**	**6**	**8**	**14**	**23**	**0**	**1**	**4**	**39**	**15.4**	**2**	**409**	**42.8**	**32**	**32**	**10:09**	**1**	**0**	**0**	**0**	**0**	**0**	**0**	**0**
	Hamilton	AHL	7	4	6	10	2	....	....	....	....	....	....	....	....	....	....	....	8	0	3	3	4	....	....	....
	NHL Totals		**99**	**7**	**12**	**19**	**29**	**0**	**1**	**4**	**66**	**10.6**		**409**	**42.8**	**32**	**32**	**10:09**	**1**	**0**	**0**	**0**	**0**	**0**	**0**	**0**

Canadian Major Junior Scholastic Player of the Year (1996)

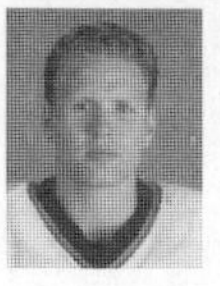

de VRIES, Greg

(deh-VREES) **COL.**

Defense. Shoots left. 6'3", 215 lbs. Born, Sundridge, Ont., January 4, 1973.

Season	Club	League	GP	G	A	Pts	PIM	PP	SH	GW	S	%	+/-	TF	F%	H	SB	Min	GP	G	A	Pts	PIM	PP	SH	GW
1988-89	Cortina Astros	OMHA	35	28	40	68	....	....	....	....	....	....	....	....	....	....	....	....	....	....	....	....	....	....	....	....
1989-90	Aurora	OJHL-B	40	7	28	35	....	....	....	....	....	....	....	....	....	....	....	....	....	....	....	....	....	....	....	....
1990-91	Stratford	OJHL-B	43	10	33	43	....	....	....	....	....	....	....	....	....	....	....	....	....	....	....	....	....	....	....	....
1991-92	Bowling Green	CCHA	24	0	3	3	20	....	....	....	....	....	....	....	....	....	....	....	....	....	....	....	....	....	....	....
1992-93	Niagara Falls	OHL	62	3	23	26	86	....	....	....	....	....	....	....	....	....	....	....	4	0	1	1	6	....	....	....
1993-94	Niagara Falls	OHL	64	5	40	45	135	....	....	....	....	....	....	....	....	....	....	....	....	....	....	....	....	....	....	....
	Cape Breton	AHL	9	0	0	0	11	....	....	....	....	....	....	....	....	....	....	....	1	0	0	0	0	....	....	....
1994-95	Cape Breton	AHL	77	5	19	24	68	....	....	....	....	....	....	....	....	....	....	....	....	....	....	....	....	....	....	....
1995-96	**Edmonton**	**NHL**	**13**	**1**	**1**	**2**	**12**	**0**	**0**	**0**	**8**	**12.5**	**–2**	....	....	....	....	....	....	....	....	....	....	....	....	....
	Cape Breton	AHL	58	9	30	39	174	....	....	....	....	....	....	....	....	....	....	....	....	....	....	....	....	....	....	....
1996-97	**Edmonton**	**NHL**	**37**	**0**	**4**	**4**	**52**	**0**	**0**	**0**	**31**	**0.0**	**–2**	....	....	....	....	....	**12**	**0**	**1**	**1**	**8**	**0**	**0**	**0**
	Hamilton	AHL	34	4	14	18	26	....	....	....	....	....	....	....	....	....	....	....	....	....	....	....	....	....	....	....
1997-98	**Edmonton**	**NHL**	**65**	**7**	**4**	**11**	**80**	**1**	**0**	**0**	**53**	**13.2**	**–17**	....	....	....	....	....	**7**	**0**	**0**	**0**	**21**	**0**	**0**	**0**
1998-99	**Nashville**	**NHL**	**6**	**0**	**0**	**0**	**4**	**0**	**0**	**0**	**1**	**1.0**	**–4**	**0**	**0.0**	**12**	**7**	**18:11**	....	....	....	....	....	....	....	....
	Colorado	**NHL**	**67**	**1**	**3**	**4**	**60**	**0**	**0**	**0**	**56**	**56.0**	**–3**	**1**	**100.0**	**85**	**69**	**16:23**	**19**	**0**	**2**	**2**	**22**	**0**	**0**	**0**
	NHL Totals		**188**	**9**	**12**	**21**	**208**	**1**	**0**	**0**	**149**	**6.0**		**1**	**100.0**	**97**	**76**	**16:32**	**38**	**0**	**3**	**3**	**51**	**0**	**0**	**0**

Signed as a free agent by **Edmonton**, March 20, 1994. Traded to **Nashville** by **Edmonton** with Eric Fichaud and Drake Berehowsky for Mikhail Shtalenkov and Jim Dowd, October 1, 1998. Traded to **Colorado** by **Nashville** for Colorado's 2nd round choice (Ed Hill) in 1999 Entry Draft, October 24, 1998.

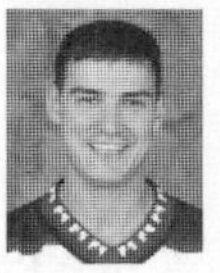

DIDUCK, Gerald

(DIH-duhk)

Defense. Shoots right. 6'2", 217 lbs. Born, Edmonton, Alta., April 6, 1965. NY Islanders' 2nd choice, 16th overall, in 1983 Entry Draft.

Season	Club	League	GP	G	A	Pts	PIM	PP	SH	GW	S	%	+/-	TF	F%	H	SB	Min	GP	G	A	Pts	PIM	PP	SH	GW
1981-82	Lethbridge	WHL	71	1	15	16	81	....	....	....	....	....	....	....	....	....	....	....	12	0	3	3	27	....	....	....
1982-83	Lethbridge	WHL	67	8	16	24	151	....	....	....	....	....	....	....	....	....	....	....	20	3	12	15	49	....	....	....
1983-84	Lethbridge	WHL	65	10	24	34	133	....	....	....	....	....	....	....	....	....	....	....	5	1	4	5	27	....	....	....
	Indianapolis	CHL	....	....	....	....	....	....	....	....	....	....	....	....	....	....	....	....	10	1	6	7	19	....	....	....
1984-85	**NY Islanders**	**NHL**	**65**	**2**	**8**	**10**	**80**	**0**	**0**	**0**	**52**	**3.8**	**2**	....	....	....	....	....	....	....	....	....	....	....	....	....
1985-86	**NY Islanders**	**NHL**	**10**	**1**	**2**	**3**	**2**	**0**	**0**	**0**	**6**	**16.7**	**5**	....	....	....	....	....	....	....	....	....	....	....	....	....
	Springfield	AHL	61	6	14	20	173	....	....	....	....	....	....	....	....	....	....	....	....	....	....	....	....	....	....	....
1986-87	**NY Islanders**	**NHL**	**30**	**2**	**3**	**5**	**67**	**0**	**0**	**0**	**54**	**3.7**	**–3**	....	....	....	....	....	**14**	**0**	**1**	**1**	**35**	**0**	**0**	**0**
	Springfield	AHL	45	6	8	14	120	....	....	....	....	....	....	....	....	....	....	....	....	....	....	....	....	....	....	....
1987-88	**NY Islanders**	**NHL**	**68**	**7**	**12**	**19**	**113**	**4**	**0**	**1**	**128**	**5.5**	**22**	....	....	....	....	....	**6**	**1**	**0**	**1**	**42**	**1**	**0**	**0**
1988-89	**NY Islanders**	**NHL**	**65**	**11**	**21**	**32**	**155**	**6**	**0**	**0**	**132**	**8.3**	**9**	....	....	....	....	....	....	....	....	....	....	....	....	....
1989-90	**NY Islanders**	**NHL**	**76**	**3**	**17**	**20**	**163**	**1**	**0**	**0**	**102**	**2.9**	**2**	....	....	....	....	....	**5**	**0**	**0**	**0**	**12**	**0**	**0**	**0**
1990-91	**Montreal**	**NHL**	**32**	**1**	**2**	**3**	**39**	**0**	**0**	**0**	**34**	**2.9**	**3**	....	....	....	....	....	....	....	....	....	....	....	....	....
	Vancouver	**NHL**	**31**	**3**	**7**	**10**	**66**	**0**	**0**	**1**	**66**	**4.5**	**–8**	....	....	....	....	....	**6**	**1**	**0**	**1**	**11**	**1**	**0**	**0**
1991-92	**Vancouver**	**NHL**	**77**	**6**	**21**	**27**	**229**	**2**	**0**	**1**	**128**	**4.7**	**–3**	....	....	....	....	....	**5**	**0**	**0**	**0**	**10**	**0**	**0**	**0**
1992-93	**Vancouver**	**NHL**	**80**	**6**	**14**	**20**	**171**	**0**	**1**	**0**	**92**	**6.5**	**32**	....	....	....	....	....	**12**	**4**	**2**	**6**	**12**	**0**	**0**	**0**
1993-94	**Vancouver**	**NHL**	**55**	**1**	**10**	**11**	**72**	**0**	**0**	**0**	**50**	**2.0**	**2**	....	....	....	....	....	**24**	**1**	**7**	**8**	**22**	**0**	**0**	**0**
1994-95	**Vancouver**	**NHL**	**22**	**1**	**3**	**4**	**15**	**1**	**0**	**0**	**25**	**4.0**	**–8**	....	....	....	....	....	....	....	....	....	....	....	....	....
	Chicago	**NHL**	**13**	**1**	**0**	**1**	**48**	**1**	**0**	**0**	**42**	**2.4**	**3**	....	....	....	....	....	**16**	**1**	**3**	**4**	**22**	**0**	**0**	**0**
1995-96	**Hartford**	**NHL**	**79**	**1**	**9**	**10**	**88**	**0**	**0**	**0**	**93**	**1.1**	**7**	....	....	....	....	....	....	....	....	....	....	....	....	....

			Regular Season																Playoffs							
Season	Club	League	GP	G	A	Pts	PIM	PP	SH	GW	S	%	+/-	TF	F%	H	SB	Min	GP	G	A	Pts	PIM	PP	SH	GW
1996-97	Hartford	NHL	56	1	10	11	40	0	0	1	59	1.7	–9	....	....	....	....	....	....	....	....	....	....	....	....	....
	Phoenix	NHL	11	1	2	3	23	1	0	0	21	4.8	2	....	....	....	....	....	7	0	0	0	10	0	0	0
1997-98	Phoenix	NHL	78	8	10	18	118	1	0	4	104	7.7	14	....	....	....	....	....	6	0	2	2	20	0	0	0
1998-99	Phoenix	NHL	44	0	2	2	72	0	0	0	39	0.0	9	0	0.0	127	50	18:32	3	0	0	0	2	0	0	0
	NHL Totals		892	56	153	209	1561	17	1	8	1227	4.6		0	0.0	127	50	18:32	104	8	15	23	198	2	0	0

Traded to **Montreal** by **NY Islanders** for Craig Ludwig, September 4, 1990. Traded to **Vancouver** by **Montreal** for Vancouver's 4th round choice (Vladimir Vujtek) in 1991 Entry Draft, January 12, 1991. Traded to **Chicago** by **Vancouver** for Bogdan Savenko and Hartford's 3rd round choice (previously acquired, Vancouver selected Larry Courville) in 1995 Entry Draft, April 7, 1995. Signed as a free agent by **Hartford**, August 24, 1995. Traded to **Phoenix** by **Hartford** for Chris Murray, March 18, 1997.

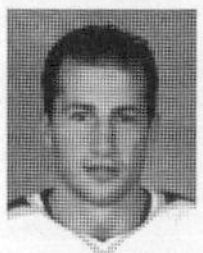

DiMAIO, Rob
(duh-MIGH-oh) **BOS.**

Center. Shoots right. 5'10", 190 lbs. Born, Calgary, Alta., February 19, 1968. NY Islanders' 6th choice, 118th overall, in 1987 Entry Draft.

Season	Club	League	GP	G	A	Pts	PIM	PP	SH	GW	S	%	+/-	TF	F%	H	SB	Min	GP	G	A	Pts	PIM	PP	SH	GW
1983-84	Calgary	AAHA	STATISTICS NOT AVAILABLE																							
1984-85	Kamloops	WHL	55	9	18	27	29	....	....	....	....	....	....	....	....	....	....	....	7	1	3	4	2	....	....	....
1985-86	Kamloops	WHL	6	1	0	1	0	....	....	....	....	....	....	....	....	....	....	....	....	....	....	....	....	....	....	....
	Medicine Hat	WHL	55	20	30	50	82	....	....	....	....	....	....	....	....	....	....	....	22	6	6	12	39	....	....	....
1986-87	Medicine Hat	WHL	70	27	43	70	130	....	....	....	....	....	....	....	....	....	....	....	20	7	11	18	46	....	....	....
1987-88	Medicine Hat	WHL	54	47	43	90	120	....	....	....	....	....	....	....	....	....	....	....	14	12	19	*31	59	....	....	....
1988-89	NY Islanders	NHL	16	1	0	1	30	0	0	1	16	6.3	–6	....	....	....	....	....	....	....	....	....	....	....	....	....
	Springfield	AHL	40	13	18	31	67	....	....	....	....	....	....	....	....	....	....	....	....	....	....	....	....	....	....	....
1989-90	NY Islanders	NHL	7	0	0	0	2	0	0	0	2	0.0	0	....	....	....	....	....	1	1	0	1	4	0	0	0
	Springfield	AHL	54	25	27	52	69	....	....	....	....	....	....	....	....	....	....	....	16	4	7	11	45	....	....	....
1990-91	NY Islanders	NHL	1	0	0	0	0	0	0	0	0	0.0	0	....	....	....	....	....	....	....	....	....	....	....	....	....
	Capital District	AHL	12	3	4	7	22	....	....	....	....	....	....	....	....	....	....	....	....	....	....	....	....	....	....	....
1991-92	NY Islanders	NHL	50	5	2	7	43	0	2	0	43	11.6	–23	....	....	....	....	....	....	....	....	....	....	....	....	....
1992-93	Tampa Bay	NHL	54	9	15	24	62	2	0	0	75	12.0	0	....	....	....	....	....	....	....	....	....	....	....	....	....
1993-94	Tampa Bay	NHL	39	8	7	15	40	2	0	1	51	15.7	–5	....	....	....	....	....	....	....	....	....	....	....	....	....
	Philadelphia	NHL	14	3	5	8	6	0	0	1	30	10.0	1	....	....	....	....	....	....	....	....	....	....	....	....	....
1994-95	Philadelphia	NHL	36	3	1	4	53	0	0	0	34	8.8	8	....	....	....	....	....	15	2	4	6	4	0	1	1
1995-96	Philadelphia	NHL	59	6	15	21	58	1	1	0	49	12.2	0	....	....	....	....	....	3	0	0	0	0	0	0	0
1996-97	Boston	NHL	72	13	15	28	82	0	3	2	152	8.6	–21	....	....	....	....	....	....	....	....	....	....	....	....	....
1997-98	Boston	NHL	79	10	17	27	82	0	0	4	112	8.9	–13	....	....	....	....	....	6	1	0	1	8	0	0	0
1998-99	Boston	NHL	71	7	14	21	95	1	0	0	121	5.8	–14	83	45.8	106	26	16:41	12	2	0	2	8	0	0	1
	NHL Totals		498	65	91	156	553	6	6	9	685	9.5		83	45.8	106	26	16:41	37	6	4	10	24	0	1	2

Won Stafford Smythe Memorial Trophy (Memorial Cup Tournament MVP) (1988)

Claimed by **Tampa Bay** from **NY Islanders** in Expansion Draft, June 18, 1992. Traded to **Philadelphia** by **Tampa Bay** for Jim Cummins and Philadelphia's 4th round choice (later traded back to Philadelphia — Philadelphia selected Radovan Somik) in 1995 Entry Draft, March 18, 1994. Claimed by **San Jose** from **Philadelphia** in NHL Waiver Draft, September 30, 1996. Traded to **Boston** by **San Jose** for Boston's 5th round choice (Adam Nittel) in 1997 Entry Draft, September 30, 1996.

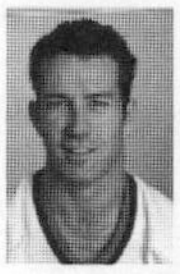

DINEEN, Kevin
OTT.

Right wing. Shoots right. 5'11", 190 lbs. Born, Quebec City, Que., October 28, 1963. Hartford's 3rd choice, 56th overall, in 1982 Entry Draft.

Season	Club	League	GP	G	A	Pts	PIM	PP	SH	GW	S	%	+/-	TF	F%	H	SB	Min	GP	G	A	Pts	PIM	PP	SH	GW
1980-81	St. Michael's	OJHL-B	40	15	28	43	167	....	....	....	....	....	....	....	....	....	....	....	....	....	....	....	....	....	....	....
1981-82	U. of Denver	WCHA	26	10	10	20	70	....	....	....	....	....	....	....	....	....	....	....	....	....	....	....	....	....	....	....
1982-83	U. of Denver	WCHA	36	16	13	29	108	....	....	....	....	....	....	....	....	....	....	....	....	....	....	....	....	....	....	....
1983-84	Canada	Nat-Team	52	5	11	16	2	....	....	....	....	....	....	....	....	....	....	....	....	....	....	....	....	....	....	....
	Canada	Olympics	7	0	0	0	8	....	....	....	....	....	....	....	....	....	....	....	....	....	....	....	....	....	....	....
1984-85	Hartford	NHL	57	25	16	41	120	8	4	2	141	17.7	–6	....	....	....	....	....	....	....	....	....	....	....	....	....
	Binghamton	AHL	25	15	8	23	41	....	....	....	....	....	....	....	....	....	....	....	....	....	....	....	....	....	....	....
1985-86	Hartford	NHL	57	33	35	68	124	6	0	8	167	19.8	16	....	....	....	....	....	10	6	7	13	18	1	0	1
1986-87	Hartford	NHL	78	40	39	79	110	11	0	7	234	17.1	7	....	....	....	....	....	6	2	1	3	31	1	0	0
1987-88	Hartford	NHL	74	25	25	50	217	5	0	4	223	11.2	–14	....	....	....	....	....	6	4	4	8	8	1	0	1
1988-89	Hartford	NHL	79	45	44	89	167	20	1	4	294	15.3	–6	....	....	....	....	....	4	1	0	1	10	0	0	0
1989-90	Hartford	NHL	67	25	41	66	164	8	2	2	214	11.7	7	....	....	....	....	....	6	3	2	5	18	0	0	1
1990-91	Hartford	NHL	61	17	30	47	104	4	0	2	161	10.6	–15	....	....	....	....	....	6	1	0	1	16	0	0	0
1991-92	Hartford	NHL	16	4	2	6	23	1	0	1	28	14.3	–6	....	....	....	....	....	....	....	....	....	....	....	....	....
	Philadelphia	NHL	64	26	30	56	130	5	3	4	197	13.2	1	....	....	....	....	....	....	....	....	....	....	....	....	....
1992-93	Philadelphia	NHL	83	35	28	63	201	6	3	7	241	14.5	14	....	....	....	....	....	....	....	....	....	....	....	....	....
1993-94	Philadelphia	NHL	71	19	23	42	113	5	1	2	156	12.2	–9	....	....	....	....	....	....	....	....	....	....	....	....	....
1994-95	Philadelphia	NHL	40	8	5	13	39	4	0	2	55	14.5	–1	....	....	....	....	....	15	6	4	10	18	1	0	1
	Houston	IHL	17	6	4	10	42	....	....	....	....	....	....	....	....	....	....	....	....	....	....	....	....	....	....	....
1995-96	Philadelphia	NHL	26	0	2	2	50	0	0	0	31	0.0	–8	....	....	....	....	....	....	....	....	....	....	....	....	....
	Hartford	NHL	20	2	7	9	67	0	0	0	35	5.7	7	....	....	....	....	....	....	....	....	....	....	....	....	....
1996-97	Hartford	NHL	78	19	29	48	141	8	0	5	185	10.3	–6	....	....	....	....	....	....	....	....	....	....	....	....	....
1997-98	Carolina	NHL	54	7	16	23	105	0	0	1	96	7.3	–7	....	....	....	....	....	....	....	....	....	....	....	....	....
1998-99	Carolina	NHL	67	8	10	18	97	0	0	1	86	9.3	5	6	16.7	77	6	9:58	6	0	0	0	8	0	0	0
	NHL Totals		992	338	382	720	1972	91	14	52	2544	13.3		6	16.7	77	6	9:58	59	23	18	41	127	4	0	5

Won Bud Light/NHL Man of the Year Award (1991)

Played in NHL All-Star Game (1988, 1989)

Traded to **Philadelphia** by **Hartford** for Murray Craven and Philadelphia's 4th round choice (Kevin Smyth) in 1992 Entry Draft, November 13, 1991. Traded to **Hartford** by **Philadelphia** for Hartford's 3rd round choice (Kris Mallette) in 1997 Entry Draft, December 28, 1995. Transferred to **Carolina** after **Hartford** franchise relocated, June 25, 1997. Signed as a free agent by **Ottawa**, September 1, 1999.

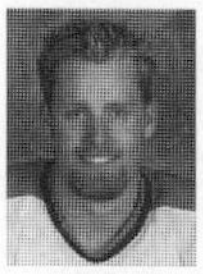

DINGMAN, Chris
COL.

Left wing. Shoots left. 6'4", 245 lbs. Born, Edmonton, Alta., July 6, 1976. Calgary's 1st choice, 19th overall, in 1994 Entry Draft.

Season	Club	League	GP	G	A	Pts	PIM	PP	SH	GW	S	%	+/-	TF	F%	H	SB	Min	GP	G	A	Pts	PIM	PP	SH	GW
1991-92	Edmonton AC	AAHA	36	23	18	41	72	....	....	....	....	....	....	....	....	....	....	....	....	....	....	....	....	....	....	....
1992-93	Brandon	WHL	50	10	17	27	64	....	....	....	....	....	....	....	....	....	....	....	4	0	0	0	0	....	....	....
1993-94	Brandon	WHL	45	21	20	41	77	....	....	....	....	....	....	....	....	....	....	....	13	1	7	8	39	....	....	....
1994-95	Brandon	WHL	66	40	43	83	201	....	....	....	....	....	....	....	....	....	....	....	3	1	0	1	9	....	....	....
1995-96	Brandon	WHL	40	16	29	45	109	....	....	....	....	....	....	....	....	....	....	....	19	12	11	23	60	....	....	....
	Saint John	AHL	....	....	....	....	....	....	....	....	....	....	....	....	....	....	....	....	1	0	0	0	0	....	....	....
1996-97	Saint John	AHL	71	5	6	11	195	....	....	....	....	....	....	....	....	....	....	....	....	....	....	....	....	....	....	....
1997-98	Calgary	NHL	70	3	3	6	149	1	0	0	47	6.4	–11	....	....	....	....	....	....	....	....	....	....	....	....	....
1998-99	Calgary	NHL	2	0	0	0	17	0	0	0	1	0.0	–2	0	0.0	3	1	8:11	....	....	....	....	....	....	....	....
	Saint John	AHL	50	5	7	12	140	....	....	....	....	....	....	....	....	....	....	....	....	....	....	....	....	....	....	....
	Colorado	NHL	1	0	0	0	7	0	0	0	0	0.0	0	0	0.0	0	0	0:30	....	....	....	....	....	....	....	....
	Hershey	AHL	17	1	3	4	102	....	....	....	....	....	....	....	....	....	....	....	5	0	2	2	6	....	....	....
	NHL Totals		73	3	3	6	173	1	0	0	48	6.3		0	0.0	3	1	5:37	....	....	....	....	....	....	....	....

Traded to **Colorado** by **Calgary** with Theoren Fleury for Rene Corbet, Wade Belak and future considerations (Robyn Regehr, March 27, 1999), February 28, 1999.

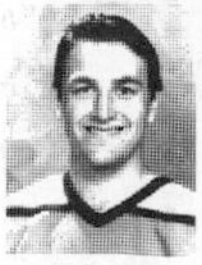

DIONNE, Gilbert
(dee-AHN, ZHIHL-bair) **CAR.**

Left wing. Shoots left. 6', 194 lbs. Born, Drummondville, Que., September 19, 1970. Montreal's 5th choice, 81st overall, in 1990 Entry Draft.

Season	Club	League	GP	G	A	Pts	PIM	PP	SH	GW	S	%	+/-	TF	F%	H	SB	Min	GP	G	A	Pts	PIM	PP	SH	GW
1987-88	Niagara Falls	OJHL	36	36	48	84	60	....	....	....	....	....	....	....	....	....	....	....	....	....	....	....	....	....	....	....
1988-89	Kitchener	OHL	66	11	33	44	13	....	....	....	....	....	....	....	....	....	....	....	5	1	1	2	4	....	....	....
1989-90	Kitchener	OHL	64	48	57	105	85	....	....	....	....	....	....	....	....	....	....	....	17	13	10	23	22	....	....	....
1990-91	Montreal	NHL	2	0	0	0	0	0	0	0	0	0.0	–2	....	....	....	....	....	....	....	....	....	....	....	....	....
	Fredericton	AHL	77	40	47	87	62	....	....	....	....	....	....	....	....	....	....	....	9	6	5	11	8	....	....	....
1991-92	Montreal	NHL	39	21	13	34	10	7	0	2	90	23.3	7	....	....	....	....	....	11	3	4	7	10	1	0	1
	Fredericton	AHL	29	19	27	46	20	....	....	....	....	....	....	....	....	....	....	....	....	....	....	....	....	....	....	....
1992-93♦	Montreal	NHL	75	20	28	48	63	6	1	2	145	13.8	5	....	....	....	....	....	20	6	6	12	20	1	0	1
	Fredericton	AHL	3	4	3	7	0	....	....	....	....	....	....	....	....	....	....	....	....	....	....	....	....	....	....	....
1993-94	Montreal	NHL	74	19	26	45	31	3	0	5	162	11.7	–9	....	....	....	....	....	5	1	2	3	0	0	0	0

											Regular Season									Playoffs							
Season	Club	League	GP	G	A	Pts	PIM	PP	SH	GW	S	%	+/-	TF	F%	H	SB	Min	GP	G	A	Pts	PIM	PP	SH	GW
1994-95	Montreal	NHL	6	0	3	3	2	0	0	0	4	0.0	-3	....	....	....	....	....	....	....	....	....	....	....	....	....
	Philadelphia	NHL	20	0	6	6	2	0	0	0	29	0.0	-1	....	....	....	....	....	3	0	0	0	4	0	0	0
1995-96	Philadelphia	NHL	2	0	1	1	0	0	0	0	0	0.0	0	....	....	....	....	....	....	....	....	....	....	....	....	....
	Florida	NHL	5	1	2	3	0	0	0	0	12	8.3	0	....	....	....	....	....	....	....	....	....	....	....	....	....
	Carolina	AHL	55	43	58	101	29	....	....	....	....	....	....	....	....	....	....	....	....	....	....	....	....	....	....	....
1996-97	Carolina	AHL	72	41	47	88	69	....	....	....	....	....	....	....	....	....	....	....	....	....	....	....	....	....	....	....
1997-98	Cincinnati	IHL	76	42	57	99	54	....	....	....	....	....	....	....	....	....	....	....	9	3	4	7	28	....	....	....
1998-99	Cincinnati	IHL	76	35	53	88	123	....	....	....	....	....	....	....	....	....	....	....	3	0	2	2	6	....	....	....
	NHL Totals		223	61	79	140	108	16	1	9	442	13.8		....	....	....	....	....	39	10	12	22	34	2	0	2

NHL/Upper Deck All-Rookie Team (1992) • AHL Second All-Star Team (1996) • IHL First All-Star Team (1998)

Traded to **Philadelphia** by **Montreal** with Eric Desjardins and John LeClair for Mark Recchi and Philadelphia's 3rd round choice (Martin Hohenberger) in 1995 Entry Draft, February 9, 1995. Signed as a free agent by **Florida**, January 29, 1996. Signed as a free agent by **Carolina**, August, 1999.

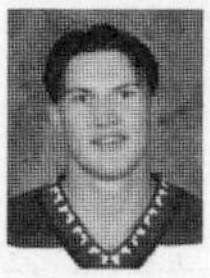

DOAN, Shane

(DOHN) **PHX.**

Right wing. Shoots right. 6'2", 217 lbs. Born, Halkirk, Alta., October 10, 1976. Winnipeg's 1st choice, 7th overall, in 1995 Entry Draft.

Season	Club	League	GP	G	A	Pts	PIM	PP	SH	GW	S	%	+/-	TF	F%	H	SB	Min	GP	G	A	Pts	PIM	PP	SH	GW
1991-92	Killam Selects	AAHA	56	80	84	164	74	....	....	....	....	....	....	....	....	....	....	....	....	....	....	....	....	....	....	....
1992-93	Kamloops	WHL	51	7	12	19	65	....	....	....	....	....	....	....	....	....	....	....	13	0	1	1	8	....	....	....
1993-94	Kamloops	WHL	52	24	24	48	88	....	....	....	....	....	....	....	....	....	....	....	....	....	....	....	....	....	....	....
1994-95	Kamloops	WHL	71	37	57	94	106	....	....	....	....	....	....	....	....	....	....	....	21	6	10	16	16	....	....	....
1995-96	Winnipeg	NHL	74	7	10	17	101	1	0	3	106	6.6	-9	....	....	....	....	....	6	0	0	0	6	0	0	0
1996-97	Phoenix	NHL	63	4	8	12	49	0	0	1	100	4.0	-3	....	....	....	....	....	4	0	0	0	2	0	0	0
1997-98	Phoenix	NHL	33	5	6	11	35	0	0	3	42	11.9	-3	....	....	....	....	....	6	1	0	1	6	0	0	0
	Springfield	AHL	39	21	21	42	64	....	....	....	....	....	....	....	....	....	....	....	....	....	....	....	....	....	....	....
1998-99	Phoenix	NHL	79	6	16	22	54	0	0	0	156	3.8	-5	6	16.7	161	15	12:42	7	2	2	4	6	0	0	2
	NHL Totals		249	22	40	62	239	1	0	6	404	5.4		6	16.7	161	15	12:42	23	3	2	5	20	0	0	2

Memorial Cup All-Star Team (1995) • Won Stafford Smythe Memorial Trophy (Memorial Cup Tournament MVP) (1995)

Transferred to **Phoenix** after **Winnipeg** franchise relocated, July 1, 1996.

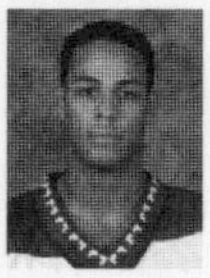

DOIG, Jason

(DOIG) **NYR**

Defense. Shoots right. 6'3", 220 lbs. Born, Montreal, Que., January 29, 1977. Winnipeg's 3rd choice, 34th overall, in 1995 Entry Draft.

Season	Club	League	GP	G	A	Pts	PIM	PP	SH	GW	S	%	+/-	TF	F%	H	SB	Min	GP	G	A	Pts	PIM	PP	SH	GW
1990-91	North Shore	QAAA	31	30	33	63	53	....	....	....	....	....	....	....	....	....	....	....	....	....	....	....	....	....	....	....
1991-92	North Shore	QAAA	29	11	11	22	20	....	....	....	....	....	....	....	....	....	....	....	....	....	....	....	....	....	....	....
1992-93	Lac St-Louis	QAAA	35	11	10	21	40	....	....	....	....	....	....	....	....	....	....	....	7	5	5	10	16	....	....	....
1993-94	St-Jean	QMJHL	63	8	17	25	65	....	....	....	....	....	....	....	....	....	....	....	5	0	2	2	2	....	....	....
1994-95	Laval	QMJHL	55	13	42	55	259	....	....	....	....	....	....	....	....	....	....	....	20	4	13	17	39	....	....	....
1995-96	Laval	QMJHL	5	3	6	9	20	....	....	....	....	....	....	....	....	....	....	....	....	....	....	....	....	....	....	....
	Granby	QMJHL	24	4	30	34	91	....	....	....	....	....	....	....	....	....	....	....	20	10	22	32	*110	....	....	....
	Winnipeg	NHL	15	1	1	2	28	0	0	0	7	14.3	-2	....	....	....	....	....	....	....	....	....	....	....	....	....
	Springfield	AHL	5	0	0	0	28	....	....	....	....	....	....	....	....	....	....	....	....	....	....	....	....	....	....	....
1996-97	Granby	QMJHL	39	14	33	47	211	....	....	....	....	....	....	....	....	....	....	....	5	0	4	4	27	....	....	....
	Las Vegas	IHL	6	0	1	1	19	....	....	....	....	....	....	....	....	....	....	....	....	....	....	....	....	....	....	....
	Springfield	AHL	5	0	3	3	2	....	....	....	....	....	....	....	....	....	....	....	17	1	4	5	37	....	....	....
1997-98	Phoenix	NHL	4	0	1	1	12	0	0	0	1	0.0	-4	....	....	....	....	....	....	....	....	....	....	....	....	....
	Springfield	AHL	46	2	25	27	153	....	....	....	....	....	....	....	....	....	....	....	3	0	0	0	2	....	....	....
1998-99	Phoenix	NHL	9	0	1	1	10	0	0	0	0	0.0	2	0	0.0	1	2	5:08	....	....	....	....	....	....	....	....
	Springfield	AHL	32	3	5	8	67	....	....	....	....	....	....	....	....	....	....	....	....	....	....	....	....	....	....	....
	Hartford	AHL	8	1	4	5	40	....	....	....	....	....	....	....	....	....	....	....	7	1	1	2	39	....	....	....
	NHL Totals		28	1	3	4	50	0	0	0	8	12.5		0	0.0	1	2	5:08	....	....	....	....	....	....	....	....

Memorial Cup All-Star Team (1996)

Transferred to **Phoenix** after **Winnipeg** franchise relocated, July 1, 1996. Traded to **NY Rangers** by **Phoenix** with Phoenix's 6th round choice (Jay Dardis) in 1999 Entry Draft for Stan Neckar, March 23, 1999.

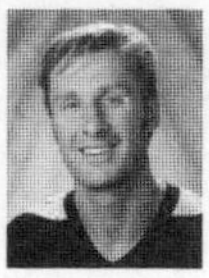

DOLLAS, Bobby

(DAW-luhs)

Defense. Shoots left. 6'2", 212 lbs. Born, Montreal, Que., January 31, 1965. Winnipeg's 2nd choice, 14th overall, in 1983 Entry Draft.

Season	Club	League	GP	G	A	Pts	PIM	PP	SH	GW	S	%	+/-	TF	F%	H	SB	Min	GP	G	A	Pts	PIM	PP	SH	GW
1980-81	Lac-St-Louis	QAAA	46	9	14	23	....	....	....	....	....	....	....	....	....	....	....	....	....	....	....	....	....	....	....	....
1981-82	Lac St-Louis	QAAA	44	9	31	40	138	....	....	....	....	....	....	....	....	....	....	....	....	....	....	....	....	....	....	....
1982-83	Laval	QMJHL	63	16	45	61	144	....	....	....	....	....	....	....	....	....	....	....	11	5	5	10	23	....	....	....
1983-84	Laval	QMJHL	54	12	33	45	80	....	....	....	....	....	....	....	....	....	....	....	14	1	8	9	23	....	....	....
	Winnipeg	NHL	1	0	0	0	0	0	0	0	0	0.0	-2	....	....	....	....	....	....	....	....	....	....	....	....	....
1984-85	Winnipeg	NHL	9	0	0	0	0	0	0	0	2	0.0	4	....	....	....	....	....	....	....	....	....	....	....	....	....
	Sherbrooke	AHL	8	1	3	4	4	....	....	....	....	....	....	....	....	....	....	....	17	3	6	9	17	....	....	....
1985-86	Winnipeg	NHL	46	0	5	5	66	0	0	0	50	0.0	-3	....	....	....	....	....	3	0	0	0	2	0	0	0
	Sherbrooke	AHL	25	4	7	11	29	....	....	....	....	....	....	....	....	....	....	....	....	....	....	....	....	....	....	....
1986-87	Sherbrooke	AHL	75	6	18	24	87	....	....	....	....	....	....	....	....	....	....	....	16	2	4	6	13	....	....	....
1987-88	Quebec	NHL	9	0	0	0	2	0	0	0	5	0.0	-4	....	....	....	....	....	....	....	....	....	....	....	....	....
	Moncton	AHL	26	4	10	14	20	....	....	....	....	....	....	....	....	....	....	....	....	....	....	....	....	....	....	....
	Fredericton	AHL	33	4	8	12	27	....	....	....	....	....	....	....	....	....	....	....	15	2	2	4	24	....	....	....
1988-89	Quebec	NHL	16	0	3	3	16	0	0	0	11	0.0	-11	....	....	....	....	....	....	....	....	....	....	....	....	....
	Halifax	AHL	57	5	19	24	65	....	....	....	....	....	....	....	....	....	....	....	4	1	0	1	14	....	....	....
1989-90	Canada	Nat-Team	68	8	29	37	60	....	....	....	....	....	....	....	....	....	....	....	....	....	....	....	....	....	....	....
1990-91	Detroit	NHL	56	3	5	8	20	0	0	1	59	5.1	6	....	....	....	....	....	7	1	0	1	13	0	0	0
1991-92	Detroit	NHL	27	3	1	4	20	0	1	0	26	11.5	4	....	....	....	....	....	2	0	1	1	0	0	0	0
	Adirondack	AHL	19	1	6	7	33	....	....	....	....	....	....	....	....	....	....	....	18	7	4	11	22	....	....	....
1992-93	Detroit	NHL	6	0	0	0	2	0	0	0	5	0.0	-1	....	....	....	....	....	....	....	....	....	....	....	....	....
	Adirondack	AHL	64	7	36	43	54	....	....	....	....	....	....	....	....	....	....	....	11	3	8	11	8	....	....	....
1993-94	Anaheim	NHL	77	9	11	20	55	1	0	1	121	7.4	20	....	....	....	....	....	....	....	....	....	....	....	....	....
1994-95	Anaheim	NHL	45	7	13	20	12	3	1	1	70	10.0	-3	....	....	....	....	....	....	....	....	....	....	....	....	....
1995-96	Anaheim	NHL	82	8	22	30	64	0	1	1	117	6.8	9	....	....	....	....	....	....	....	....	....	....	....	....	....
1996-97	Anaheim	NHL	79	4	14	18	55	1	0	1	96	4.2	17	....	....	....	....	....	11	0	0	0	4	0	0	0
1997-98	Anaheim	NHL	22	0	1	1	27	0	0	0	11	0.0	-12	....	....	....	....	....	....	....	....	....	....	....	....	....
	Edmonton	NHL	30	2	5	7	22	0	0	0	27	7.4	6	....	....	....	....	....	11	0	0	0	16	0	0	0
1998-99	Pittsburgh	NHL	70	2	8	10	60	0	0	0	34	5.9	-3	0	0.0	47	56	15:35	13	1	0	1	6	0	0	0
	NHL Totals		575	38	88	126	421	5	3	5	634	6.0		0	0.0	47	56	15:35	47	2	1	3	41	0	0	0

QMJHL Second All-Star Team (1983) • Won Eddie Shore Award (AHL's Outstanding Defenseman) (1993) • AHL First All-Star Team (1993)

Traded to **Quebec** by **Winnipeg** for Stu Kulak, December 17, 1987. Signed as a free agent by **Detroit**, October 18, 1990. Claimed by **Anaheim** from **Detroit** in Expansion Draft, June 24, 1993. Traded to **Edmonton** by **Anaheim** for Drew Bannister, January 9, 1998. Traded to **Pittsburgh** by **Edmonton** with Tony Hrkac for Josef Beranek, June 16, 1998.

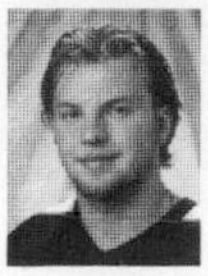

DOME, Robert

(doh-MAY) **PIT.**

Right wing. Shoots left. 6', 215 lbs. Born, Skalica, Czech., January 29, 1979. Pittsburgh's 1st choice, 17th overall, in 1997 Entry Draft.

Season	Club	League	GP	G	A	Pts	PIM	PP	SH	GW	S	%	+/-	TF	F%	H	SB	Min	GP	G	A	Pts	PIM	PP	SH	GW
1994-95	HC Dukla	Slovak-Jr.	36	36	43	79	39	....	....	....	....	....	....	....	....	....	....	....	....	....	....	....	....	....	....	....
1995-96	Utah	IHL	56	10	9	19	28	....	....	....	....	....	....	....	....	....	....	....	....	....	....	....	....	....	....	....
1996-97	Long Beach	IHL	13	4	6	10	14	....	....	....	....	....	....	....	....	....	....	....	....	....	....	....	....	....	....	....
	Las Vegas	IHL	43	10	7	17	22	....	....	....	....	....	....	....	....	....	....	....	....	....	....	....	....	....	....	....
1997-98	Pittsburgh	NHL	30	5	2	7	12	1	0	0	29	17.2	-1	....	....	....	....	....	....	....	....	....	....	....	....	....
	Syracuse	AHL	36	21	25	46	77	....	....	....	....	....	....	....	....	....	....	....	....	....	....	....	....	....	....	....

			Regular Season																Playoffs							
Season	Club	League	GP	G	A	Pts	PIM	PP	SH	GW	S	%	+/-	TF	F%	H	SB	Min	GP	G	A	Pts	PIM	PP	SH	GW
1998-99	Syracuse	AHL	48	18	17	35	70	....	....	....	....	....	....	....	....	....	....	....	....	....	....	....	....	....	....	....
	Houston	IHL	20	2	4	6	24	....	....	....	....	....	....	....	....	....	....	....	....	....	....	....	....	....	....	....
	NHL Totals		**30**	**5**	**2**	**7**	**12**	**1**	**0**	**0**	**29**	**17.2**	....	....	....	....	....	....	....	....	....	....	....	....	....	....

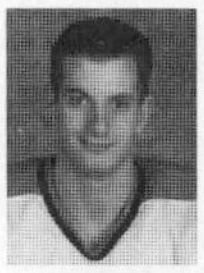

DOMENICHELLI, Hnat

(daw-mehn-ih-CHEHL-ee, NAT) **CGY.**

Center. Shoots left. 6', 190 lbs. Born, Edmonton, Alta., February 17, 1976. Hartford's 2nd choice, 83rd overall, in 1994 Entry Draft.

Season	Club	League	GP	G	A	Pts	PIM	PP	SH	GW	S	%	+/-	TF	F%	H	SB	Min	GP	G	A	Pts	PIM	PP	SH	GW
1991-92	Edmonton AA	AAHA	34	34	49	83	101	....	....	....	....	....	....	....	....	....	....	....	....	....	....	....	....	....	....	....
1992-93	Kamloops	WHL	45	12	8	20	15	....	....	....	....	....	....	....	....	....	....	....	11	1	1	2	2	....	....	....
1993-94	Kamloops	WHL	69	27	40	67	31	....	....	....	....	....	....	....	....	....	....	....	19	10	12	22	0	....	....	....
1994-95	Kamloops	WHL	72	52	62	114	34	....	....	....	....	....	....	....	....	....	....	....	19	9	9	18	9	....	....	....
1995-96	Kamloops	WHL	62	59	89	148	37	....	....	....	....	....	....	....	....	....	....	....	16	7	9	16	29	....	....	....
1996-97	**Hartford**	**NHL**	**13**	**2**	**1**	**3**	**7**	**1**	**0**	**0**	**14**	**14.3**	**–4**	....	....	....	....	....	....	....	....	....	....	....	....	....
	Springfield	AHL	39	24	24	48	12	....	....	....	....	....	....	....	....	....	....	....	....	....	....	....	....	....	....	....
	Calgary	**NHL**	**10**	**1**	**2**	**3**	**2**	**1**	**0**	**0**	**16**	**6.3**	**1**	....	....	....	....	....	....	....	....	....	....	....	....	....
	Saint John	AHL	1	1	1	2	0	....	....	....	....	....	....	....	....	....	....	....	5	5	0	5	2	....	....	....
1997-98	**Calgary**	**NHL**	**31**	**9**	**7**	**16**	**6**	**1**	**0**	**1**	**70**	**12.9**	**4**	....	....	....	....	....	....	....	....	....	....	....	....	....
	Saint John	AHL	48	33	13	46	24	....	....	....	....	....	....	....	....	....	....	....	19	7	8	15	14	....	....	....
1998-99	**Calgary**	**NHL**	**23**	**5**	**5**	**10**	**11**	**3**	**0**	**0**	**45**	**11.1**	**–4**	**3**	**0.0**	**27**	**0**	**12:59**	....	....	....	....	....	....	....	....
	Saint John	AHL	51	25	21	46	26	....	....	....	....	....	....	....	....	....	....	....	7	4	4	8	2	....	....	....
	NHL Totals		**77**	**17**	**15**	**32**	**26**	**6**	**0**	**1**	**145**	**11.7**		**3**	**0.0**	**27**	**0**	**12:59**	....	....	....	....	....	....	....	....

WHL West Second All-Star Team (1995) • WHL West First All-Star Team (1996) • Canadian Major Junior First All-Star Team (1996) • Canadian Major Junior Most Sportsmanlike Player of the Year (1996)

Traded to **Calgary** by **Hartford** with Glen Featherstone, New Jersey's 2nd round choice (previously acquired, Calgary selected Dimitri Kokorev) in 1997 Entry Draft and Vancouver's 3rd round choice (previously acquired, Calgary selected Paul Manning) in 1998 Entry Draft for Steve Chiasson and Colorado's 3rd round choice (previously acquired, Carolina selected Francis Lessard) in 1997 Entry Draft, March 5, 1997.

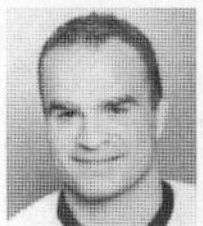

DOMI, Tie

(DOH-mee) **TOR.**

Right wing. Shoots right. 5'10", 200 lbs. Born, Windsor, Ont., November 1, 1969. Toronto's 2nd choice, 27th overall, in 1988 Entry Draft.

Season	Club	League	GP	G	A	Pts	PIM	PP	SH	GW	S	%	+/-	TF	F%	H	SB	Min	GP	G	A	Pts	PIM	PP	SH	GW
1985-86	Windsor	OJHL-B	42	8	17	25	346	....	....	....	....	....	....	....	....	....	....	....	....	....	....	....	....	....	....	....
1986-87	Peterborough	OHL	18	1	1	2	79	....	....	....	....	....	....	....	....	....	....	....	....	....	....	....	....	....	....	....
1987-88	Peterborough	OHL	60	22	21	43	292	....	....	....	....	....	....	....	....	....	....	....	12	3	9	12	24	....	....	....
1988-89	Peterborough	OHL	43	14	16	30	175	....	....	....	....	....	....	....	....	....	....	....	17	10	9	19	70	....	....	....
1989-90	**Toronto**	**NHL**	**2**	**0**	**0**	**0**	**42**	**0**	**0**	**0**	**0**	**0.0**	**0**	....	....	....	....	....	....	....	....	....	....	....	....	....
	Newmarket	AHL	57	14	11	25	285	....	....	....	....	....	....	....	....	....	....	....	....	....	....	....	....	....	....	....
1990-91	**NY Rangers**	**NHL**	**28**	**1**	**0**	**1**	**185**	**0**	**0**	**0**	**5**	**20.0**	**–5**	....	....	....	....	....	....	....	....	....	....	....	....	....
	Binghamton	AHL	25	11	6	17	219	....	....	....	....	....	....	....	....	....	....	....	7	3	2	5	16	....	....	....
1991-92	**NY Rangers**	**NHL**	**42**	**2**	**4**	**6**	**246**	**0**	**0**	**1**	**20**	**10.0**	**–4**	....	....	....	....	....	**6**	**1**	**1**	**2**	**32**	**0**	**0**	**0**
1992-93	**NY Rangers**	**NHL**	**12**	**2**	....	**2**	**95**	**0**	**0**	**0**	**11**	**18.2**	**–1**	....	....	....	....	....	....	....	....	....	....	....	....	....
	Winnipeg	**NHL**	**49**	**3**	**10**	**13**	**249**	**0**	**0**	**0**	**29**	**10.3**	**2**	....	....	....	....	....	**6**	**1**	**0**	**1**	**23**	**0**	**0**	**0**
1993-94	**Winnipeg**	**NHL**	**81**	**8**	**11**	**19**	***347**	**0**	**0**	**1**	**98**	**8.2**	**–8**	....	....	....	....	....	....	....	....	....	....	....	....	....
1994-95	**Winnipeg**	**NHL**	**31**	**4**	**4**	**8**	**128**	**0**	**0**	**0**	**34**	**11.8**	**–6**	....	....	....	....	....	....	....	....	....	....	....	....	....
	Toronto	**NHL**	**9**	**0**	**1**	**1**	**31**	**0**	**0**	**0**	**12**	**0.0**	**1**	....	....	....	....	....	**7**	**1**	**0**	**1**	**0**	**0**	**0**	**0**
1995-96	**Toronto**	**NHL**	**72**	**7**	**6**	**13**	**297**	**0**	**0**	**1**	**61**	**11.5**	**–3**	....	....	....	....	....	**6**	**0**	**2**	**2**	**4**	**0**	**0**	**0**
1996-97	**Toronto**	**NHL**	**80**	**11**	**17**	**28**	**275**	**2**	**0**	**1**	**98**	**11.2**	**–17**	....	....	....	....	....	....	....	....	....	....	....	....	....
1997-98	**Toronto**	**NHL**	**80**	**4**	**10**	**14**	**365**	**0**	**0**	**0**	**72**	**5.6**	**–5**	....	....	....	....	....	....	....	....	....	....	....	....	....
1998-99	**Toronto**	**NHL**	**72**	**8**	**14**	**22**	**198**	**0**	**0**	**1**	**65**	**12.3**	**5**	**9**	**44.4**	**100**	**3**	**9:42**	**14**	**0**	**2**	**2**	**24**	**0**	**0**	**0**
	NHL Totals		**558**	**50**	**77**	**127**	**2458**	**2**	**0**	**5**	**505**	**9.9**		**9**	**44.4**	**100**	**3**	**9:42**	**39**	**3**	**5**	**8**	**83**	**0**	**0**	**0**

Traded to **NY Rangers** by **Toronto** with Mark LaForest for Greg Johnston, June 28, 1990. Traded to **Winnipeg** by **NY Rangers** with Kris King for Ed Olczyk, December 28, 1992. Traded to **Toronto** by **Winnipeg** for Mike Eastwood and Toronto's 3rd round choice (Brad Isbister) in 1995 Entry Draft, April 7, 1995.

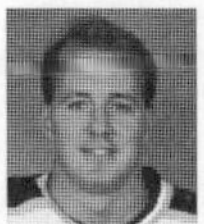

DONATO, Ted

(duh-NAH-toh) **ANA.**

Left wing. Shoots left. 5'10", 181 lbs. Born, Boston, MA, April 28, 1969. Boston's 6th choice, 98th overall, in 1987 Entry Draft.

Season	Club	League	GP	G	A	Pts	PIM	PP	SH	GW	S	%	+/-	TF	F%	H	SB	Min	GP	G	A	Pts	PIM	PP	SH	GW
1986-87	Catholic Memorial	H.S.	22	29	34	63	30	....	....	....	....	....	....	....	....	....	....	....	....	....	....	....	....	....	....	....
1987-88	Harvard University	ECAC	28	12	14	26	24	....	....	....	....	....	....	....	....	....	....	....	....	....	....	....	....	....	....	....
1988-89	Harvard University	ECAC	34	14	37	51	30	....	....	....	....	....	....	....	....	....	....	....	....	....	....	....	....	....	....	....
1989-90	Harvard University	ECAC	16	5	6	11	34	....	....	....	....	....	....	....	....	....	....	....	....	....	....	....	....	....	....	....
1990-91	Harvard University	ECAC	27	19	*37	56	26	....	....	....	....	....	....	....	....	....	....	....	....	....	....	....	....	....	....	....
1991-92	United States	Nat-Team	52	11	22	33	24	....	....	....	....	....	....	....	....	....	....	....	....	....	....	....	....	....	....	....
	United States	Olympics	8	4	3	7	8	....	....	....	....	....	....	....	....	....	....	....	....	....	....	....	....	....	....	....
	Boston	**NHL**	**10**	**1**	**2**	**3**	**8**	**0**	**0**	**0**	**13**	**7.7**	**–1**	....	....	....	....	....	**15**	**3**	**4**	**7**	**4**	**0**	**0**	**1**
1992-93	**Boston**	**NHL**	**82**	**15**	**20**	**35**	**61**	**3**	**2**	**5**	**118**	**12.7**	**2**	....	....	....	....	....	**4**	**0**	**1**	**1**	....	**0**	**0**	**0**
1993-94	**Boston**	**NHL**	**84**	**22**	**32**	**54**	**59**	**9**	**2**	**1**	**158**	**13.9**	**0**	....	....	....	....	....	**13**	**4**	**2**	**6**	**10**	**2**	**0**	**1**
1994-95	TuTo Turku	Finland	14	5	5	10	47	....	....	....	....	....	....	....	....	....	....	....	....	....	....	....	....	....	....	....
	Boston	**NHL**	**47**	**10**	**10**	**20**	**10**	**1**	**0**	**1**	**71**	**14.1**	**3**	....	....	....	....	....	**5**	**0**	**0**	**0**	**4**	**0**	**0**	**0**
1995-96	**Boston**	**NHL**	**82**	**23**	**26**	**49**	**46**	**7**	**0**	**1**	**152**	**15.1**	**6**	....	....	....	....	....	**5**	**1**	**2**	**3**	**2**	**1**	**0**	**0**
1996-97	**Boston**	**NHL**	**67**	**25**	**26**	**51**	**37**	**6**	**2**	**2**	**172**	**14.5**	**–9**	....	....	....	....	....	....	....	....	....	....	....	....	....
1997-98	**Boston**	**NHL**	**79**	**16**	**23**	**39**	**54**	**3**	**0**	**5**	**129**	**12.4**	**6**	....	....	....	....	....	**5**	**0**	**0**	**0**	**2**	**0**	**0**	**0**
1998-99	**Boston**	**NHL**	**14**	**1**	**3**	**4**	**4**	**0**	**0**	**0**	**22**	**4.5**	**0**	**18**	**44.4**	**6**	**1**	**15:21**	....	....	....	....	....	....	....	....
	NY Islanders	**NHL**	**55**	**7**	**11**	**18**	**27**	**2**	**0**	**0**	**68**	**10.3**	**–10**	**142**	**45.8**	**23**	**2**	**12:09**	....	....	....	....	....	....	....	....
	Ottawa	**NHL**	**13**	**3**	**2**	**5**	**10**	**1**	**0**	**0**	**16**	**18.8**	**2**	**4**	**25.0**	**7**	**5**	**11:10**	**1**	**0**	**0**	**0**	**0**	**0**	**0**	**0**
	NHL Totals		**533**	**123**	**155**	**278**	**316**	**32**	**6**	**15**	**919**	**13.4**		**164**	**45.1**	**36**	**8**	**12:32**	**48**	**8**	**9**	**17**	**22**	**3**	**0**	**2**

NCAA Championship All-Tournament Team (1989) • NCAA Championship Tournament MVP (1989) • ECAC First All-Star Team (1991)

Traded to **NY Islanders** by **Boston** for Ken Belanger, November 7, 1998. Traded to **Ottawa** by **NY Islanders** for Ottawa's 4th round choice (later traded to Phoenix - Phoenix selected Preston Mizzi) in 1999 Entry Draft, March 20, 1999. Traded to **Anaheim** by **Ottawa** with Antti-Jussi Niemi for Patrick Lalime and future considerations, June 18, 1999.

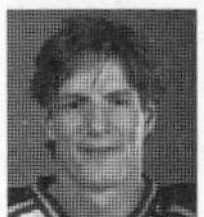

DONOVAN, Shean

(DAW-nuh-vuhn, SHAWN) **COL.**

Right wing. Shoots right. 6'3", 210 lbs. Born, Timmins, Ont., January 22, 1975. San Jose's 2nd choice, 28th overall, in 1993 Entry Draft.

Season	Club	League	GP	G	A	Pts	PIM	PP	SH	GW	S	%	+/-	TF	F%	H	SB	Min	GP	G	A	Pts	PIM	PP	SH	GW
1990-91	Kanata	OJHL	44	8	5	13	8	....	....	....	....	....	....	....	....	....	....	....	....	....	....	....	....	....	....	....
1991-92	Ottawa	OHL	58	11	8	19	14	....	....	....	....	....	....	....	....	....	....	....	11	1	0	1	5	....	....	....
1992-93	Ottawa	OHL	66	29	23	52	33	....	....	....	....	....	....	....	....	....	....	....	....	....	....	....	....	....	....	....
1993-94	Ottawa	OHL	62	35	49	84	63	....	....	....	....	....	....	....	....	....	....	....	17	10	11	21	14	....	....	....
1994-95	Ottawa	OHL	29	22	19	41	41	....	....	....	....	....	....	....	....	....	....	....	....	....	....	....	....	....	....	....
	San Jose	**NHL**	**14**	**0**	**0**	**0**	**6**	**0**	**0**	**0**	**13**	**0.0**	**–6**	....	....	....	....	....	**7**	**0**	**1**	**1**	**6**	**0**	**0**	**0**
	Kansas City	IHL	5	0	2	2	7	....	....	....	....	....	....	....	....	....	....	....	14	5	3	8	23	....	....	....
1995-96	**San Jose**	**NHL**	**74**	**13**	**8**	**21**	**39**	**0**	**1**	**2**	**73**	**17.8**	**–17**	....	....	....	....	....	....	....	....	....	....	....	....	....
	Kansas City	IHL	4	0	0	0	8	....	....	....	....	....	....	....	....	....	....	....	5	0	0	0	8	....	....	....
1996-97	**San Jose**	**NHL**	**73**	**9**	**6**	**15**	**42**	**0**	**1**	**0**	**115**	**7.8**	**–18**	....	....	....	....	....	....	....	....	....	....	....	....	....
	Kentucky	AHL	3	1	3	4	18	....	....	....	....	....	....	....	....	....	....	....	....	....	....	....	....	....	....	....
1997-98	**San Jose**	**NHL**	**20**	**3**	**3**	**6**	**22**	**0**	**0**	**0**	**24**	**12.5**	**3**	....	....	....	....	....	....	....	....	....	....	....	....	....
	Colorado	**NHL**	**47**	**5**	**7**	**12**	**48**	**0**	**0**	**0**	**57**	**8.8**	**3**	....	....	....	....	....	....	....	....	....	....	....	....	....
1998-99	**Colorado**	**NHL**	**68**	**7**	**12**	**19**	**37**	**1**	**0**	**1**	**81**	**8.6**	**4**	**9**	**22.2**	**35**	**8**	**8:46**	**5**	**0**	**0**	**0**	**2**	**0**	**0**	**0**
	NHL Totals		**296**	**37**	**36**	**73**	**194**	**1**	**2**	**3**	**363**	**10.2**		**9**	**22.2**	**35**	**8**	**8:46**	**12**	**0**	**1**	**1**	**8**	**0**	**0**	**0**

Traded to **Colorado** by **San Jose** with San Jose's 1st round choice (Alex Tanguay) in 1998 Entry Draft for Mike Ricci and Colorado's 2nd round choice (later traded to Buffalo — Buffalo selected Jaroslav Kristek), in 1998 Entry Draft, November 21, 1997.

			Regular Season																Playoffs							
Season	Club	League	GP	G	A	Pts	PIM	PP	SH	GW	S	%	+/–	TF	F%	H	SB	Min	GP	G	A	Pts	PIM	PP	SH	GW

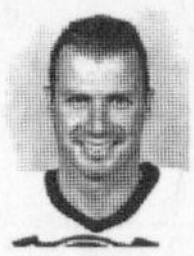

DOURIS, Peter

(DOOR-ihs)

Right wing. Shoots right. 6'1", 195 lbs. Born, Toronto, Ont., February 19, 1966. Winnipeg's 1st choice, 30th overall, in 1984 Entry Draft.

Season	Club	League	GP	G	A	Pts	PIM	PP	SH	GW	S	%	+/–	TF	F%	H	SB	Min	GP	G	A	Pts	PIM	PP	SH	GW
1983-84	New Hampshire	ECAC	37	19	15	34	14																			
1984-85	New Hampshire	H.E.	42	27	24	51	34																			
1985-86	Canada	Nat-Team	33	16	7	23	18																			
	Winnipeg	NHL	11	0	0	0	0	0	0	0	0	0.0	–1													
1986-87	Winnipeg	NHL	6	0	0	0	0	0	0	0	3	0.0	–1													
	Sherbrooke	AHL	62	14	28	42	24												17	7	*15	*22	16			
1987-88	Winnipeg	NHL	4	0	2	2	0	0	0	0	2	0.0	–1						1	0	0	0	0	0	0	0
	Moncton	AHL	73	42	37	79	53																			
1988-89	Peoria	IHL	81	28	41	69	32												4	1	2	3	0			
1989-90	Boston	NHL	36	5	6	11	15	1	0	0	63	7.9	8						8	0	1	1	8	0	0	0
	Maine	AHL	38	17	20	37	14																			
1990-91	Boston	NHL	39	5	2	7	9	1	0	1	46	10.9	–12						7	0	1	1	6	0	0	0
	Maine	AHL	35	16	15	31	9												2	3	0	3	2			
1991-92	Boston	NHL	54	10	13	23	10	0	0	1	107	9.3	9						7	2	3	5	0	0	0	1
	Maine	AHL	12	4	3	7	2																			
1992-93	Boston	NHL	19	4	4	8	4	0	1	0	33	12.1	5						4	1	0	1	0	0	0	0
	Providence	AHL	50	29	26	55	12																			
1993-94	Anaheim	NHL	74	12	22	34	21	1	0	1	142	8.5	–5													
1994-95	Anaheim	NHL	46	10	11	21	12	0	0	4	69	14.5	4													
1995-96	Anaheim	NHL	31	8	7	15	9	2	0	3	45	17.8	–3													
1996-97	Milwaukee	IHL	80	36	36	72	14												3	2	2	4	2			
1997-98	Dallas	NHL	1	0	0	0	0	0	0	0	3	0.0	–1													
	Michigan	IHL	78	26	31	57	29												4	0	5	5	2			
1998-99	EV Landshut	Germany	51	17	26	43	59												3	1	0	1	0			
	NHL Totals		321	54	67	121	80	5	1	10	513	10.5							27	3	5	8	14	0	0	1

Traded to **St. Louis** by **Winnipeg** for Kent Carlson and St. Louis' 12th round choice (Sergei Kharin) in 1989 Entry Draft and St. Louis' 4th round choice (Scott Levins) in 1990 Entry Draft, September 29, 1988. Signed as a free agent by **Boston**, June 27, 1989. Signed as a free agent by **Anaheim**, July 22, 1993. Signed as a free agent by **Dallas**, July 16, 1997.

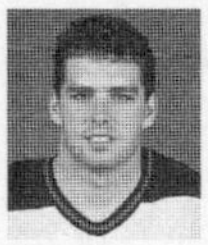

DOWD, Jim

(DOWD) **EDM.**

Center. Shoots right. 6'1", 190 lbs. Born, Brick, NJ, December 25, 1968. New Jersey's 7th choice, 149th overall, in 1987 Entry Draft.

Season	Club	League	GP	G	A	Pts	PIM	PP	SH	GW	S	%	+/–	TF	F%	H	SB	Min	GP	G	A	Pts	PIM	PP	SH	GW
1983-84	Brick High	H.S.	20	19	30	49																				
1984-85	Brick High	H.S.	24	58	55	113																				
1985-86	Brick High	H.S.	24	47	51	98																				
1986-87	Brick High	H.S.	24	22	33	55																				
1987-88	Lake Superior	CCHA	45	18	27	45	16																			
1988-89	Lake Superior	CCHA	46	24	35	59	40																			
1989-90	Lake Superior	CCHA	46	25	*67	92	30																			
1990-91	Lake Superior	CCHA	44	24	*54	*78	53																			
1991-92	New Jersey	NHL	1	0	0	0	0	0	0	0	0	0.0	0													
	Utica	AHL	78	17	42	59	47												4	2	2	4	4			
1992-93	New Jersey	NHL	1				0	0	0	0	1	0.0	–1													
	Utica	AHL	78	27	45	72	62												5	1	7	8	10			
1993-94	New Jersey	NHL	15	5	10	15	0	2	0	0	26	19.2	8						19	2	6	8	8	0	0	0
	Albany	AHL	58	26	37	63	76																			
1994-95♦	New Jersey	NHL	10	1	4	5	0	1	0	0	14	7.1	–5						11	2	1	3	8	0	0	1
1995-96	New Jersey	NHL	28	4	9	13	17	0	0	0	41	9.8	–1													
	Vancouver	NHL	38	1	6	7	6	0	0	0	35	2.9	–8						1	0	0	0	0	0	0	0
1996-97	NY Islanders	NHL	3	0	0	0	0	0	0	0	0	0.0	–1													
	Utah	IHL	48	10	21	31	27																			
	Saint John	AHL	24	5	11	16	18												5	1	2	3	0			
1997-98	Calgary	NHL	48	6	8	14	12	0	1	0	58	10.3	10													
	Saint John	AHL	35	8	30	38	20												19	3	13	16	10			
1998-99	Edmonton	NHL	1	0	0	0	0	0	0	0	1	0.0	0	7	14.3	1	0	9:47								
	Hamilton	AHL	51	15	29	44	82												11	3	6	9	8			
	NHL Totals		145	17	37	54	35	3	1	0	176	9.7		7	14.3	1	0	9:47	31	4	7	11	16	0	0	1

CCHA Second All-Star Team (1990) • NCAA West Second All-American Team (1990) • CCHA First All-Star Team (1991) • NCAA West First All-American Team (1991)

Traded to **Hartford** by **New Jersey** with New Jersey's 2nd round choice (later traded to Calgary – Calgary selected Dmitri Kokorev) in 1997 Entry Draft for Jocelyn Lemieux and Hartford's 2nd round choice in 1998 Entry Draft, December 19, 1995. Traded to **Vancouver** by **Hartford** with Frantisek Kucera and Hartford's 2nd round choice (Ryan Bonni) in 1997 Entry Draft for Jeff Brown and Vancouver's 3rd round choice in 1998 Entry Draft, December 19, 1995. Claimed by **NY Islanders** from **Vancouver** in NHL Waiver Draft, September 30, 1996. Signed as a free agent by **Calgary**, August, 1997. Traded to **Nashville** by **Calgary** for future considerations, June 26, 1998. Traded to **Edmonton** by **Nashville** with Mikhail Shtalenkov for Eric Fichaud, Drake Berehowsky and Greg de Vries, October 1, 1998.

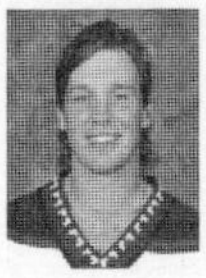

DRAKE, Dallas

PHX.

Right wing. Shoots left. 6'1", 185 lbs. Born, Trail, B.C., February 4, 1969. Detroit's 6th choice, 116th overall, in 1989 Entry Draft.

Season	Club	League	GP	G	A	Pts	PIM	PP	SH	GW	S	%	+/–	TF	F%	H	SB	Min	GP	G	A	Pts	PIM	PP	SH	GW
1984-85	Rossland	KIJHL	30	13	37	50																				
1985-86	Rossland	KIJHL	41	53	73	126																				
1986-87	Rossland	KIJHL	40	55	80	135																				
1987-88	Vernon	BCJHL	47	39	85	124	50												11	9	17	26	30			
1988-89	North. Michigan	WCHA	38	17	22	39	22																			
1989-90	North. Michigan	WCHA	46	13	24	37	42																			
1990-91	North. Michigan	WCHA	44	22	36	58	89																			
1991-92	North. Michigan	WCHA	38	*39	41	*80	46																			
1992-93	Detroit	NHL	72	18	26	44	93	3	2	5	89	20.2	15						7	3	3	6	6	1	0	0
1993-94	Detroit	NHL	47	10	22	32	37	0	1	2	78	12.8	5													
	Adirondack	AHL	1	2	0	2	0																			
	Winnipeg	NHL	15	3	5	8	12	1	1	1	34	8.8	–6													
1994-95	Winnipeg	NHL	43	8	18	26	30	0	0	1	66	12.1	–6													
1995-96	Winnipeg	NHL	69	19	20	39	36	4	4	2	121	15.7	–7						3	0	0	0	0	0	0	0
1996-97	Phoenix	NHL	63	17	19	36	52	5	1	1	113	15.0	–11						7	0	1	1	2	0	0	0
1997-98	Phoenix	NHL	60	11	29	40	71	3	0	2	112	9.8	17						4	0	1	1	2	0	0	0
1998-99	Phoenix	NHL	53	9	22	31	65	0	0	3	105	8.6	17	5	60.0	105	17	15:38	7	4	3	7	4	2	0	1
	NHL Totals		422	95	161	256	396	16	9	17	718	13.2		5	60.0	105	17	15:38	28	7	8	15	14	3	0	1

WCHA First All-Star Team (1992) • NCAA West First All-American Team (1992)

Traded to **Winnipeg** by **Detroit** with Tim Cheveldae for Bob Essensa and Sergei Bautin, March 8, 1994. Transferred to **Phoenix** after **Winnipeg** franchise relocated, July 1, 1996.

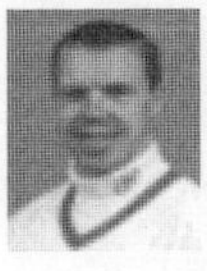

DRAPER, Kris

(DRAY-puhr) **DET.**

Center. Shoots left. 5'11", 185 lbs. Born, Toronto, Ont., May 24, 1971. Winnipeg's 4th choice, 62nd overall, in 1989 Entry Draft.

Season	Club	League	GP	G	A	Pts	PIM	PP	SH	GW	S	%	+/–	TF	F%	H	SB	Min	GP	G	A	Pts	PIM	PP	SH	GW
1987-88	Don Mills	MTHL	40	35	32	67	46																			
1988-89	Canada	Nat-Team	60	11	15	26	16																			
1989-90	Canada	Nat-Team	61	12	22	34	44																			
1990-91	Ottawa	OHL	39	19	42	61	35												17	8	11	19	20			
	Winnipeg	NHL	3	1	0	1	5	0	0	0	1	100.0	0													
	Moncton	AHL	7	2	1	3	2																			
1991-92	Winnipeg	NHL	10	2	0	2	2	0	0	0	19	10.5	0						2	0	0	0	0	0	0	0
	Moncton	AHL	61	11	18	29	113												4	0	1	1	6			
1992-93	Winnipeg	NHL	7	0	0	0	2	0	0	0	5	0.0	–6													
	Moncton	AHL	67	12	23	35	40												5	2	2	4	18			

Season	Club	League	GP	G	A	Pts	PIM	PP	SH	GW	S	%	+/-	TF	F%	H	SB	Min	GP	G	A	Pts	PIM	PP	SH	GW
																								Regular Season / Playoffs		
1993-94	Detroit	NHL	39	5	8	13	31	0	1	0	55	9.1	11	....	....	....	....	....	7	2	2	4	4	0	1	0
	Adirondack	AHL	46	20	23	43	49												....							
1994-95	Detroit	NHL	36	2	6	8	22	0	0	0	44	4.5	1						18	4	1	5	12	0	1	1
1995-96	Detroit	NHL	52	7	9	16	32	0	1	0	51	13.7	2						18	4	2	6	18	0	1	0
1996-97♦	Detroit	NHL	76	8	5	13	73	1	0	1	85	9.4	-11						20	2	4	6	12	0	1	0
1997-98♦	Detroit	NHL	64	13	10	23	45	1	0	4	96	13.5	5						19	1	3	4	12	0	0	1
1998-99	Detroit	NHL	80	4	14	18	79	0	1	1	78	5.1	2	887	54.6	82	18	12:43	10	0	1	1	6	0	0	0
	NHL Totals		367	42	52	94	291	2	3	6	434	9.7		887	54.6	82	18	12:43	94	13	13	26	64	0	4	2

Traded to **Detroit** by **Winnipeg** for future considerations, June 30, 1993.

DROUIN, P.C.   (droo-IHN)

Left wing. Shoots left. 6'2", 208 lbs.   Born, St. Lambert, Que., April 22, 1974.

Season	Club	League	GP	G	A	Pts	PIM	PP	SH	GW	S	%	+/-						GP	G	A	Pts	PIM
1991-92	Gloucester	OJHL	42	21	28	49	....																
1992-93	Cornell	ECAC	23	3	6	9	30																
1993-94	Cornell	ECAC	21	6	13	19	32																
1994-95	Cornell	ECAC	26	4	16	20	48																
1995-96	Cornell	ECAC	31	18	14	32	60																
1996-97	**Boston**	**NHL**	3	0	0	0	0	0	0	0	1	0.0	1										
	Providence	AHL	42	12	11	23	10																
1997-98	Providence	AHL	7	0	2	2	4																
	Charlotte	ECHL	62	21	46	67	57												7	2	4	6	4
1998-99	Bracknell	Britain	42	12	21	33	12												2	3	0	3	0
	NHL Totals		3	0	0	0	0	0	0	0	1	0.0											

Signed as a free agent by **Boston**, October 14, 1996.

DRUCE, John   (DROOS)

Right wing. Shoots right. 6'2", 195 lbs.   Born, Peterborough, Ont., February 23, 1966. Washington's 2nd choice, 40th overall, in 1985 Entry Draft.

Season	Club	League	GP	G	A	Pts	PIM	PP	SH	GW	S	%	+/-	GP	G	A	Pts	PIM	PP	SH	GW
1983-84	Peterborough	OJHL-B	40	15	18	33	69														
	Peterborough	OHL	1	0	0	0	0														
1984-85	Peterborough	OHL	54	12	14	26	90							17	6	2	8	21			
1985-86	Peterborough	OHL	49	22	24	46	84							16	0	5	5	34			
1986-87	Binghamton	AHL	77	13	9	22	131							12	0	3	3	28			
1987-88	Binghamton	AHL	68	32	29	61	82							1	0	0	0	0			
1988-89	**Washington**	**NHL**	48	8	7	15	62	0	0	0	59	13.6	7	1	0	0	0	0	0	0	0
	Baltimore	AHL	16	2	11	13	10														
1989-90	**Washington**	**NHL**	45	8	3	11	52	1	0	0	66	12.1	-3	15	14	3	17	23	8	1	4
	Baltimore	AHL	26	15	16	31	38														
1990-91	**Washington**	**NHL**	80	22	36	58	46	7	1	4	209	10.5	4	11	1	1	2	7	1	0	0
1991-92	**Washington**	**NHL**	67	19	18	37	39	1	0	3	129	14.7	14	7	1	0	1	2	0	0	1
1992-93	**Winnipeg**	**NHL**	50	6	14	20	37	0	0	0	60	10.0	-4	2	0	0	0	0	0	0	0
1993-94	**Los Angeles**	**NHL**	55	14	17	31	50	1	1	0	104	13.5	16								
	Phoenix	IHL	8	5	6	11	9														
1994-95	**Los Angeles**	**NHL**	43	15	5	20	20	3	0	1	75	20.0	-3								
1995-96	**Los Angeles**	**NHL**	64	9	12	21	14	0	0	0	103	8.7	-26								
	Philadelphia	**NHL**	13	4	4	8	13	0	0	0	25	16.0	6	2	0	2	2	2	0	0	0
1996-97	**Philadelphia**	**NHL**	43	7	8	15	12	1	0	0	73	9.6	-5	13	1	0	1	2	0	1	0
1997-98	**Philadelphia**	**NHL**	23	1	2	3	2	0	0	0	18	5.6	0	2	0	0	0	2	0	0	0
	Philadelphia	AHL	39	21	28	49	45														
1998-99	EHC Hannover	Germany	36	15	7	22	34														
	NHL Totals		531	113	126	239	347	14	2	10	921	12.3		53	17	6	23	38	9	2	5

Traded to **Winnipeg** by **Washington** with Toronto's 4th round choice (previously acquired by Washington — later traded to Detroit — Detroit selected John Jakopin) in 1993 Entry Draft for Pat Elynuik, October 1, 1992. Signed as a free agent by **LA Kings**, August 2, 1993. Traded to **Philadelphia** by **LA Kings** with LA Kings' 7th round choice (Todd Fedoruk) in 1997 Entry Draft for LA Kings' 4th round choice (previously acquired, LA Kings selected Mikael Simons) in 1996 Entry Draft, March 19, 1996.

DRURY, Chris   COL.

Center. Shoots right. 5'10", 180 lbs.   Born, Trumbull, CT, August 20, 1976. Quebec's 5th choice, 72nd overall, in 1994 Entry Draft.

Season	Club	League	GP	G	A	Pts	PIM	PP	SH	GW	S	%	+/-	TF	F%	H	SB	Min	GP	G	A	Pts	PIM	PP	SH	GW
1991-92	Fairfield Prep	H.S.	25	22	27	49	....																			
1992-93	Fairfield Prep	H.S.	24	25	32	57	15																			
1993-94	Fairfield Prep	H.S.	24	37	18	55																				
1994-95	Boston University	H.E.	39	12	15	27	38																			
1995-96	Boston University	H.E.	37	35	33	*68	46																			
1996-97	Boston University	H.E.	41	*38	24	62	64																			
1997-98	Boston University	H.E.	38	28	29	57	88																			
1998-99	**Colorado**	**NHL**	79	20	24	44	62	6	0	3	138	14.5	9	418	46.9	88	39	13:15	19	6	2	8	4	0	0	4
	NHL Totals		79	20	24	44	62	6	0	3	138	14.5		418	46.9	88	39	13:15	19	6	2	8	4	0	0	4

Hockey East Second All-Star Team (1996, 1997) • NCAA East Second All-American Team (1996) • NCAA East First All-American Team (1997, 1998) • NCAA Championship All-Tournament Team (1997) • Hockey East First All-Star Team (1998) • Won Hobey Baker Memorial Award (Top U.S. Collegiate Player) (1998) • NHL All-Rookie Team (1999) • Won Calder Memorial Trophy (1999)
Rights transferred to **Colorado** after **Quebec** franchise relocated, June 21, 1995.

DRURY, Ted   (DROO-ree)   ANA.

Center. Shoots left. 6', 208 lbs.   Born, Boston, MA, September 13, 1971. Calgary's 2nd choice, 42nd overall, in 1989 Entry Draft.

Season	Club	League	GP	G	A	Pts	PIM	PP	SH	GW	S	%	+/-	TF	F%	H	SB	Min	GP	G	A	Pts	PIM	PP	SH	GW
1987-88	Fairfield Prep	H.S.	24	21	28	49	....																			
1988-89	Fairfield Prep	H.S.	25	35	31	66	....																			
1989-90	Harvard University	ECAC	17	9	13	22	10																			
1990-91	Harvard University	ECAC	25	18	18	36	22																			
	United States	WJC-A	8	5	7	12	2																			
1991-92	United States	Nat-Team	53	11	23	34	30																			
	United States	Olympics	7	1	1	2	0																			
1992-93	Harvard University	ECAC	31	22	*41	*63	28																			
1993-94	**Calgary**	**NHL**	34	5	7	12	26	0	1	1	43	11.6	-5													
	United States	Nat-Team	11	1	4	5	11																			
	United States	Olympics	7	1	2	3	2																			
	Hartford	**NHL**	16	1	5	6	10	0	0	0	37	2.7	-10													
1994-95	**Hartford**	**NHL**	34	3	6	9	21	0	0	0	31	9.7	-3													
	Springfield	AHL	2	0	1	1	0																			
1995-96	**Ottawa**	**NHL**	42	9	7	16	54	1	0	1	80	11.3	-19													
1996-97	**Anaheim**	**NHL**	73	9	9	18	54	1	0	2	114	7.9	-10						10	1	0	1	4	0	0	0
1997-98	**Anaheim**	**NHL**	73	6	10	16	82	0	1	0	110	5.5	-10													
1998-99	**Anaheim**	**NHL**	75	5	6	11	83	0	0	0	79	6.3	2	449	47.9	77	13	8:15	4	0	0	0	0	0	0	0
	NHL Totals		347	38	50	88	330	2	2	4	494	7.7		449	47.9	77	13	8:15	14	1	0	1	4	0	0	0

ECAC First All-Star Team (1993) • NCAA East First All-America Team (1993)
Traded to **Hartford** by **Calgary** with Gary Suter and Paul Ranheim for James Patrick, Zarley Zalapski and Michael Nylander, March 10, 1994. Claimed by **Ottawa** from **Hartford** in NHL Waiver Draft, October 2, 1995. Traded to **Anaheim** by **Ottawa** with the rights to Marc Moro for Jason York and Shaun Van Allen, October 1, 1996.

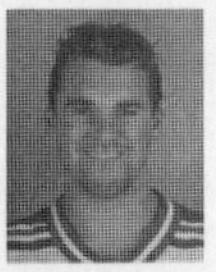

DUBE, Christian

(doo-BAY)

Center. Shoots right. 5'11", 170 lbs. Born, Sherbrooke, Que., April 25, 1977. NY Rangers' 1st choice, 39th overall, in 1995 Entry Draft.

			Regular Season																Playoffs							
Season	**Club**	**League**	**GP**	**G**	**A**	**Pts**	**PIM**	**PP**	**SH**	**GW**	**S**	**%**	**+/–**	**TF**	**F%**	**H**	**SB**	**Min**	**GP**	**G**	**A**	**Pts**	**PIM**	**PP**	**SH**	**GW**
1992-93	HC Martigny	Switz-2	27	36	40	76	34	....	....	....	....	....	....	....	....	....	....	....	....	....	....	....	....	....	....	....
1993-94	Sherbrooke	QMJHL	72	31	41	72	22	....	....	....	....	....	....	....	....	....	....	....	11	3	2	5	8	....	....	....
1994-95	Sherbrooke	QMJHL	71	36	65	101	43	....	....	....	....	....	....	....	....	....	....	....	7	1	7	8	8	....	....	....
1995-96	Sherbrooke	QMJHL	62	52	93	145	105	....	....	....	....	....	....	....	....	....	....	....	7	5	5	10	6	....	....	....
1996-97	Hull	QMJHL	19	15	22	37	37	....	....	....	....	....	....	....	....	....	....	....	14	7	16	23	14	....	....	....
	NY Rangers	**NHL**	**27**	**1**	**1**	**2**	**4**	**1**	**0**	**0**	**14**	**7.1**	**–4**	....	....	....	....	....	**3**	**0**	**0**	**0**	**0**	**0**	**0**	**0**
1997-98	Hartford	AHL	79	11	46	57	46	....	....	....	....	....	....	....	....	....	....	....	9	0	4	4	6	....	....	....
1998-99	**NY Rangers**	**NHL**	**6**	**0**	**0**	**0**	**0**	**0**	**0**	**0**	**0**	**0.0**	**0**	**13**	**38.5**	**2**	**1**	**2:39**	....	....	....	....	....	....	....	....
	Hartford	AHL	58	21	30	51	20	....	....	....	....	....	....	....	....	....	....	....	6	0	3	3	4	....	....	....
	NHL Totals		**33**	**1**	**1**	**2**	**4**	**1**	**0**	**0**	**14**	**7.1**		**13**	**38.5**	**2**	**1**	**2:39**	**3**	**0**	**0**	**0**	**0**	**0**	**0**	**0**

QMJHL First All-Star Team (1996) • Canadian Major Junior First All-Star Team (1996) • Canadian Major Junior Player of the Year (1996) • Won Stafford Smythe Memorial Trophy (Memorial Cup Tournament MVP) (1997)

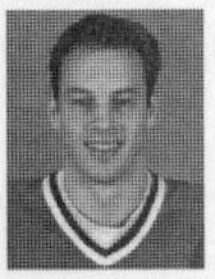

DUBINSKY, Steve

(doo-BIHN-skee) **CGY.**

Center. Shoots left. 6', 190 lbs. Born, Montreal, Que., July 9, 1970. Chicago's 9th choice, 226th overall, in 1990 Entry Draft.

Season	Club	League	GP	G	A	Pts	PIM	PP	SH	GW	S	%	+/–	TF	F%	H	SB	Min	GP	G	A	Pts	PIM	PP	SH	GW
1989-90	Clarkson	ECAC	35	7	10	17	24	....	....	....	....	....	....	....	....	....	....	....	....	....	....	....	....	....	....	....
1990-91	Clarkson	ECAC	39	13	23	36	26	....	....	....	....	....	....	....	....	....	....	....	....	....	....	....	....	....	....	....
1991-92	Clarkson	ECAC	32	20	31	51	40	....	....	....	....	....	....	....	....	....	....	....	....	....	....	....	....	....	....	....
1992-93	Clarkson	ECAC	35	18	26	44	58	....	....	....	....	....	....	....	....	....	....	....	....	....	....	....	....	....	....	....
1993-94	**Chicago**	**NHL**	**27**	**2**	**6**	**8**	**16**	**0**	**0**	**0**	**20**	**10.0**	**1**	....	....	....	....	....	**6**	**0**	**0**	**0**	**10**	**0**	**0**	**0**
	Indianapolis	IHL	54	15	25	40	63	....	....	....	....	....	....	....	....	....	....	....	....	....	....	....	....	....	....	....
1994-95	**Chicago**	**NHL**	**16**	**0**	**0**	**0**	**8**	**0**	**0**	**0**	**16**	**0.0**	**–5**	....	....	....	....	....	....	....	....	....	....	....	....	....
	Indianapolis	IHL	62	16	11	27	29	....	....	....	....	....	....	....	....	....	....	....	....	....	....	....	....	....	....	....
1995-96	**Chicago**	**NHL**	**43**	**2**	**3**	**5**	**14**	**0**	**0**	**0**	**33**	**6.1**	**3**	....	....	....	....	....	....	....	....	....	....	....	....	....
	Indianapolis	IHL	16	8	8	16	10	....	....	....	....	....	....	....	....	....	....	....	....	....	....	....	....	....	....	....
1996-97	**Chicago**	**NHL**	**5**	**0**	**0**	**0**	**0**	**0**	**0**	**0**	**4**	**0.0**	**2**	....	....	....	....	....	**4**	**1**	**0**	**1**	**4**	**0**	**0**	**0**
	Indianapolis	IHL	77	32	40	72	53	....	....	....	....	....	....	....	....	....	....	....	1	3	1	4	0	....	....	....
1997-98	**Chicago**	**NHL**	**82**	**5**	**13**	**18**	**57**	**0**	**1**	**0**	**112**	**4.5**	**–6**	....	....	....	....	....	....	....	....	....	....	....	....	....
1998-99	**Chicago**	**NHL**	**1**	**0**	**0**	**0**	**0**	**0**	**0**	**0**	**1**	**0.0**	**0**	**5**	**60.0**	**1**	**0**	**5:11**	....	....	....	....	....	....	....	....
	Calgary	**NHL**	**61**	**4**	**10**	**14**	**14**	**0**	**2**	**0**	**69**	**5.8**	**–7**	**223**	**46.6**	**161**	**75**	**14:38**	....	....	....	....	....	....	....	....
	NHL Totals		**235**	**13**	**32**	**45**	**109**	**0**	**3**	**0**	**255**	**5.1**		**228**	**46.9**	**162**	**75**	**14:29**	**10**	**1**	**0**	**1**	**14**	**0**	**0**	**0**

Traded to **Calgary** by **Chicago** with Jeff Shantz for Marty McInnis, Jamie Allison and Eric Andersson, October 27, 1998.

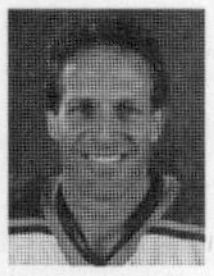

DUCHESNE, Steve

(doo-SHAYN)

Defense. Shoots left. 5'11", 195 lbs. Born, Sept-Iles, Que., June 30, 1965.

Season	Club	League	GP	G	A	Pts	PIM	PP	SH	GW	S	%	+/–	TF	F%	H	SB	Min	GP	G	A	Pts	PIM	PP	SH	GW
1983-84	Drummondville	QMJHL	67	1	34	35	79	....	....	....	....	....	....	....	....	....	....	....	....	....	....	....	....	....	....	....
1984-85	Drummondville	QMJHL	65	22	54	76	94	....	....	....	....	....	....	....	....	....	....	....	5	4	7	11	8	....	....	....
1985-86	New Haven	AHL	75	14	35	49	76	....	....	....	....	....	....	....	....	....	....	....	5	0	2	2	9	....	....	....
1986-87	**Los Angeles**	**NHL**	**75**	**13**	**25**	**38**	**74**	**5**	**0**	**2**	**113**	**11.5**	**8**	....	....	....	....	....	**5**	**2**	**2**	**4**	**4**	**1**	**0**	**0**
1987-88	**Los Angeles**	**NHL**	**71**	**16**	**39**	**55**	**109**	**5**	**0**	**4**	**190**	**8.4**	**0**	....	....	....	....	....	**5**	**1**	**3**	**4**	**14**	**1**	**0**	**0**
1988-89	**Los Angeles**	**NHL**	**79**	**25**	**50**	**75**	**92**	**8**	**5**	**2**	**215**	**11.6**	**31**	....	....	....	....	....	**11**	**4**	**4**	**8**	**12**	**2**	**0**	**0**
1989-90	**Los Angeles**	**NHL**	**79**	**20**	**42**	**62**	**36**	**6**	**0**	**1**	**224**	**8.9**	**–3**	....	....	....	....	....	**10**	**2**	**9**	**11**	**6**	**1**	**0**	**0**
1990-91	**Los Angeles**	**NHL**	**78**	**21**	**41**	**62**	**66**	**8**	**0**	**3**	**171**	**12.3**	**19**	....	....	....	....	....	**12**	**4**	**8**	**12**	**8**	**1**	**0**	**0**
1991-92	**Philadelphia**	**NHL**	**78**	**18**	**38**	**56**	**86**	**7**	**2**	**3**	**229**	**7.9**	**–7**	....	....	....	....	....	....	....	....	....	....	....	....	....
1992-93	**Quebec**	**NHL**	**82**	**20**	**62**	**82**	**57**	**8**	**0**	**2**	**227**	**8.8**	**15**	....	....	....	....	....	**6**	**0**	**5**	**5**	**6**	**0**	**0**	**0**
1993-94	**St. Louis**	**NHL**	**36**	**12**	**19**	**31**	**14**	**8**	**0**	**1**	**115**	**10.4**	**1**	....	....	....	....	....	**4**	**0**	**2**	**2**	**2**	**0**	**0**	**0**
1994-95	**St. Louis**	**NHL**	**47**	**12**	**26**	**38**	**36**	**1**	**0**	**1**	**116**	**10.3**	**29**	....	....	....	....	....	**7**	**0**	**4**	**4**	**2**	**0**	**0**	**0**
1995-96	**Ottawa**	**NHL**	**62**	**12**	**24**	**36**	**42**	**7**	**0**	**2**	**163**	**7.4**	**–23**	....	....	....	....	....	....	....	....	....	....	....	....	....
1996-97	**Ottawa**	**NHL**	**78**	**19**	**28**	**47**	**38**	**10**	**2**	**3**	**208**	**9.1**	**–9**	....	....	....	....	....	**7**	**1**	**4**	**5**	**0**	**1**	**0**	**1**
1997-98	**St. Louis**	**NHL**	**80**	**14**	**42**	**56**	**32**	**5**	**1**	**1**	**153**	**9.2**	**9**	....	....	....	....	....	**10**	**0**	**4**	**4**	**6**	**0**	**0**	**0**
1998-99	**Los Angeles**	**NHL**	**60**	**4**	**19**	**23**	**22**	**1**	**0**	**1**	**99**	**4.0**	**–6**	**2**	**50.0**	**38**	**95**	**21:11**	....	....	....	....	....	....	....	....
	Philadelphia	**NHL**	**11**	**2**	**5**	**7**	**2**	**1**	**0**	**1**	**19**	**10.5**	**0**	**0**	**0.0**	**5**	**14**	**22:28**	**6**	**0**	**2**	**2**	**2**	**0**	**0**	**0**
	NHL Totals		**916**	**208**	**460**	**668**	**706**	**80**	**10**	**27**	**2242**	**9.3**		**2**	**50.0**	**43**	**109**	**21:23**	**83**	**14**	**47**	**61**	**62**	**7**	**0**	**1**

QMJHL First All-Star Team (1985) • NHL All-Rookie Team (1987)

Played in NHL All-Star Game (1989, 1990, 1993)

Signed as a free agent by **LA Kings**, October 1, 1984. Traded to **Philadelphia** by **LA Kings** with Steve Kasper and LA Kings' 4th round choice (Aris Brimanis) in 1991 Entry Draft for Jari Kurri and Jeff Chychrun, May 30, 1991. Traded to **Quebec** by **Philadelphia** with Peter Forsberg, Kerry Huffman, Mike Ricci, Ron Hextall, Chris Simon, Philadelphia's 1st round choice in the 1993 (Jocelyn Thibault) and 1994 (later traded to Toronto — later traded to Washington — Washington selected Nolan Baumgartner) Entry Drafts and cash for Eric Lindros, June 30, 1992. Traded to **St. Louis** by **Quebec** with Denis Chasse for Garth Butcher, Ron Sutter and Bob Bassen, January 23, 1994. Traded to **Ottawa** by **St. Louis** for Ottawa's 2nd round choice (later traded to Buffalo — Buffalo selected Cory Sarich) in 1996 Entry Draft, August 4, 1995. Traded to **St. Louis** by **Ottawa** for Igor Kravchuk, August 25, 1997. Signed as a free agent by **LA Kings**, July 2, 1998. Traded to **Philadelphia** by **Los Angeles** for Dave Babych and Philadelphia's 5th round choice in 2000 Entry Draft, March 23, 1999.

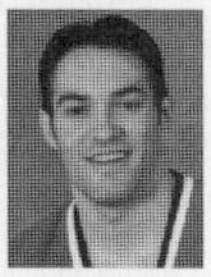

DUMONT, Jean-Pierre

(doo-MAWNT) **CHI.**

Right wing. Shoots left. 6'2", 200 lbs. Born, Montreal, Que., April 1, 1978. NY Islanders' 1st choice, 3rd overall, in 1996 Entry Draft.

Season	Club	League	GP	G	A	Pts	PIM	PP	SH	GW	S	%	+/–	TF	F%	H	SB	Min	GP	G	A	Pts	PIM	PP	SH	GW
1993-94	Val d'Or	QMJHL	25	9	11	20	10	....	....	....	....	....	....	....	....	....	....	....	....	....	....	....	....	....	....	....
1994-95	Val d'Or	QMJHL	48	5	14	19	24	....	....	....	....	....	....	....	....	....	....	....	....	....	....	....	....	....	....	....
1995-96	Val d'Or	QMJHL	66	48	57	105	109	....	....	....	....	....	....	....	....	....	....	....	13	12	8	20	22	....	....	....
1996-97	Val d'Or	QMJHL	62	44	64	108	86	....	....	....	....	....	....	....	....	....	....	....	13	9	7	16	12	....	....	....
1997-98	Val d'Or	QMJHL	55	57	42	99	63	....	....	....	....	....	....	....	....	....	....	....	19	31	15	46	18	....	....	....
1998-99	**Chicago**	**NHL**	**25**	**9**	**6**	**15**	**10**	**0**	**0**	**2**	**42**	**21.4**	**7**	**10**	**50.0**	**22**	**8**	**14:14**	....	....	....	....	....	....	....	....
	Portland	AHL	50	32	14	46	39	....	....	....	....	....	....	....	....	....	....	....	....	....	....	....	....	....	....	....
	Chicago	IHL	....	....	....	....	....	....	....	....	....	....	....	....	....	....	....	....	10	4	1	5	6	....	....	....
	NHL Totals		**25**	**9**	**6**	**15**	**10**	**0**	**0**	**2**	**42**	**21.4**		**10**	**50.0**	**22**	**8**	**14:14**	....	....	....	....	....	....	....	....

QMJHL Second All-Star Team (1997)

Rights traded to **Chicago** by **NY Islanders** for Dmitri Nabokov, May 30, 1998.

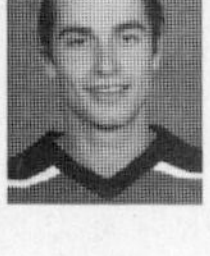

DVORAK, Radek

(duh-VOHR-ak) **FLA.**

Right wing. Shoots right. 6'1", 194 lbs. Born, Tabor, Czech., March 9, 1977. Florida's 1st choice, 10th overall, in 1995 Entry Draft.

Season	Club	League	GP	G	A	Pts	PIM	PP	SH	GW	S	%	+/–	TF	F%	H	SB	Min	GP	G	A	Pts	PIM	PP	SH	GW
1992-93	HC Budejovice	Czech-Jr.	35	44	46	90	....	....	....	....	....	....	....	....	....	....	....	....	....	....	....	....	....	....	....	....
1993-94	HC Budejovice	Czech-Jr.	20	17	18	35	....	....	....	....	....	....	....	....	....	....	....	....	....	....	....	....	....	....	....	....
	HC Budejovice	Cze-Rep	8	0	0	0	0	....	....	....	....	....	....	....	....	....	....	....	....	....	....	....	....	....	....	....
1994-95	HC Budejovice	Cze-Rep	10	3	5	8	2	....	....	....	....	....	....	....	....	....	....	....	9	5	1	6	....	....	....	....
1995-96	**Florida**	**NHL**	**77**	**13**	**14**	**27**	**20**	**0**	**0**	**4**	**126**	**10.3**	**5**	....	....	....	....	....	**16**	**1**	**3**	**4**	**0**	**0**	**0**	**0**
1996-97	**Florida**	**NHL**	**78**	**18**	**21**	**39**	**30**	**2**	**0**	**1**	**139**	**12.9**	**–2**	....	....	....	....	....	**3**	**0**	**0**	**0**	**0**	**0**	**0**	**0**
1997-98	**Florida**	**NHL**	**64**	**12**	**24**	**36**	**33**	**2**	**3**	**0**	**112**	**10.7**	**–1**	....	....	....	....	....	....	....	....	....	....	....	....	....
1998-99	**Florida**	**NHL**	**82**	**19**	**24**	**43**	**29**	**0**	**4**	**0**	**182**	**10.4**	**7**	**98**	**46.9**	**30**	**33**	**16:13**	....	....	....	....	....	....	....	....
	NHL Totals		**301**	**62**	**83**	**145**	**112**	**4**	**7**	**5**	**559**	**11.1**		**98**	**46.9**	**30**	**33**	**16:13**	**19**	**1**	**3**	**4**	**0**	**0**	**0**	**0**

						Regular Season													Playoffs						
Season	Club	League	GP	G	A	Pts	PIM	PP	SH	GW	S	%	+/–	TF	F%	H	SB	Min	GP	G	A	Pts	PIM	PP	SH	GW

DYKHUIS, Karl (DIGH-kowz) **PHI.**

Defense. Shoots left. 6'3", 214 lbs.   Born, Sept-Iles, Que., July 8, 1972. Chicago's 1st choice, 16th overall, in 1990 Entry Draft.

Season	Club	League	GP	G	A	Pts	PIM	PP	SH	GW	S	%	+/–	TF	F%	H	SB	Min	GP	G	A	Pts	PIM	PP	SH	GW
1987-88	Lac St-Jean	QAAA	37	2	12	14	....	....	....	....	....	....	....	....	....	....	....	....	....	....	....	....	....	....	....	....	....
1988-89	Hull	QMJHL	63	2	29	31	59	....	....	....	....	....	....							9	1	9	10	6	....	....	....
1989-90	Hull	QMJHL	69	10	46	56	119	....	....	....	....	....	....							11	2	5	7	2	....	....	....
1990-91	Longueuil	QMJHL	3	1	4	5	6	....	....	....	....	....	....							8	2	5	7	6	....	....	....
	Canada	Nat-Team	37	2	9	11	16	....	....	....	....	....	....							....	....	....	....	....	....	....	....
1991-92	Verdun	QMJHL	29	5	19	24	55	....	....	....	....	....	....							17	0	12	12	14	....	....	....
	Canada	Nat-Team	19	1	2	3	16	....	....	....	....	....	....							....	....	....	....	....	....	....	....
	Chicago	**NHL**	6	1	3	4	4	1	0	0	12	8.3	–1							....	....	....	....	....	....	....	....
1992-93	Chicago	NHL	12	0	5	5	0	0	0	0	10	0.0	2							....	....	....	....	....	....	....	....
	Indianapolis	IHL	59	5	18	23	76	....	....	....	....	....	....							5	1	1	2	8	....	....	....
1993-94	Indianapolis	IHL	73	7	25	32	132	....	....	....	....	....	....							....	....	....	....	....	....	....	....
1994-95	Indianapolis	IHL	52	2	21	23	63	....	....	....	....	....	....							....	....	....	....	....	....	....	....
	Philadelphia	**NHL**	33	2	6	8	37	1	0	1	46	4.3	7							15	4	4	8	14	2	0	2
	Hershey	AHL	1	0	0	0	0	....	....	....	....	....	....							....	....	....	....	....	....	....	....
1995-96	Philadelphia	NHL	82	5	15	20	101	1	0	0	104	4.8	12							12	2	2	4	22	1	0	0
1996-97	Philadelphia	NHL	62	4	15	19	35	2	0	1	101	4.0	6							18	0	3	3	2	0	0	0
1997-98	Tampa Bay	NHL	78	5	9	14	110	0	1	0	91	5.5	–8							....	....	....	....	....	....	....	....
1998-99	Tampa Bay	NHL	33	2	1	3	18	0	0	0	27	7.4	–21	0	0.0	44	39	20:14		....	....	....	....	....	....	....	....
	Philadelphia	NHL	45	2	4	6	32	1	0	0	61	3.3	–2	0	0.0	38	47	18:15		5	1	0	1	4	0	0	0
	NHL Totals		351	21	58	79	337	6	1	2	452	4.6		0	0.0	82	86	19:05		50	7	9	16	42	3	0	2

QMJHL First All-Star Team (1990)

Traded to **Philadelphia** by **Chicago** for Bob Wilkie and future considerations, February 16, 1995. Traded to **Tampa Bay** by **Philadelphia** with Mikael Renberg for Philadelphia's 1st round choices in 1998 (Simon Gagne), 1999, 2000, and 2001 Entry Drafts (previously acquired by Tampa Bay), August 20, 1997. Traded to **Philadelphia** by **Tampa Bay** for Petr Svoboda, December 28, 1998.

DZIEDZIC, Joe (zeed-ZIHK)

Left wing. Shoots left. 6'3", 227 lbs.   Born, Minneapolis, MN, December 18, 1971. Pittsburgh's 2nd choice, 61st overall, in 1990 Entry Draft.

Season	Club	League	GP	G	A	Pts	PIM	PP	SH	GW	S	%	+/–	TF	F%	H	SB	Min	GP	G	A	Pts	PIM	PP	SH	GW
1988-89	Edison High	H.S.	22	46	27	73	34	....	....	....	....	....	....							....	....	....	....	....	....	....	....
1989-90	Edison High	H.S.	17	29	19	48	10	....	....	....	....	....	....							....	....	....	....	....	....	....	....
1990-91	U. of Minnesota	WCHA	20	6	4	10	26	....	....	....	....	....	....							....	....	....	....	....	....	....	....
1991-92	U. of Minnesota	WCHA	34	8	9	17	68	....	....	....	....	....	....							....	....	....	....	....	....	....	....
1992-93	U. of Minnesota	WCHA	41	11	14	25	62	....	....	....	....	....	....							....	....	....	....	....	....	....	....
1993-94	U. of Minnesota	WCHA	18	7	10	17	48	....	....	....	....	....	....							....	....	....	....	....	....	....	....
1994-95	Cleveland	IHL	68	15	15	30	74	....	....	....	....	....	....							4	1	0	1	10	....	....	....
1995-96	Pittsburgh	NHL	69	5	5	10	68	0	0	3	44	11.4	–5							16	1	2	3	19	0	0	0
1996-97	Pittsburgh	NHL	59	9	9	18	63	0	0	1	85	10.6	–4							5	0	1	1	4	0	0	0
1997-98	Cleveland	IHL	65	21	20	41	176	....	....	....	....	....	....							10	3	4	7	28	....	....	....
1998-99	**Phoenix**	**NHL**	2	0	0	0	0	0	0	0	1	0.0	–2	3	100.0	3	0	8:09		....	....	....	....	....	....	....	....
	Springfield	AHL	61	18	27	45	128	....	....	....	....	....	....							3	1	1	2	20	....	....	....
	NHL Totals		130	14	14	28	131	0	0	4	130	10.8		3	100.0	3	0	8:09		21	1	3	4	23	0	0	0

Signed as a free agent by **Phoenix**, August 27, 1998.

EAGLES, Mike **WSH.**

Center/Left wing. Shoots left. 5'10", 190 lbs.   Born, Sussex, N.B., March 7, 1963. Quebec's 5th choice, 116th overall, in 1981 Entry Draft.

Season	Club	League	GP	G	A	Pts	PIM	PP	SH	GW	S	%	+/–	TF	F%	H	SB	Min	GP	G	A	Pts	PIM	PP	SH	GW
1979-80	Melville	SJHL	55	46	30	76	77	....	....	....	....	....	....							....	....	....	....	....	....	....	....
	Billings	WHL	5	0	1	1	0	....	....	....	....	....	....							....	....	....	....	....	....	....	....
1980-81	Kitchener	OHA	56	11	27	38	64	....	....	....	....	....	....							18	4	2	6	36	....	....	....
1981-82	Kitchener	OHL	62	26	40	66	148	....	....	....	....	....	....							15	3	11	14	27	....	....	....
1982-83	Kitchener	OHL	58	26	36	62	133	....	....	....	....	....	....							12	5	7	12	27	....	....	....
	Quebec	**NHL**	2	0	0	0	2	0	0	0	1	0.0	–1							....	....	....	....	....	....	....	....
1983-84	Fredericton	AHL	68	13	29	42	85	....	....	....	....	....	....							4	0	0	0	5	....	....	....
1984-85	Fredericton	AHL	36	4	20	24	80	....	....	....	....	....	....							3	0	0	0	2	....	....	....
1985-86	Quebec	NHL	73	11	12	23	49	1	0	1	68	16.2	3							3	0	0	0	2	0	0	0
1986-87	Quebec	NHL	73	13	19	32	55	0	2	2	95	13.7	–15							4	1	0	1	10	0	0	0
1987-88	Quebec	NHL	76	10	10	20	74	1	2	2	89	11.2	–18							....	....	....	....	....	....	....	....
1988-89	Chicago	NHL	47	5	11	16	44	0	0	0	39	12.8	–8							....	....	....	....	....	....	....	....
1989-90	Chicago	NHL	23	1	2	3	34	0	0	0	23	4.3	–4							....	....	....	....	....	....	....	....
	Indianapolis	IHL	24	11	13	24	47	....	....	....	....	....	....							13	*10	10	20	34	....	....	....
1990-91	Winnipeg	NHL	44	0	9	9	79	0	0	0	51	0.0	–10							....	....	....	....	....	....	....	....
	Indianapolis	IHL	25	15	14	29	47	....	....	....	....	....	....							....	....	....	....	....	....	....	....
1991-92	Winnipeg	NHL	65	7	10	17	118	0	1	0	60	11.7	–17							7	0	0	0	8	0	0	0
1992-93	Winnipeg	NHL	84	8	18	26	131	1	0	1	67	11.9	–1							5	0	1	1	6	0	0	0
1993-94	Winnipeg	NHL	73	4	8	12	96	0	1	0	53	7.5	–20							....	....	....	....	....	....	....	....
1994-95	Winnipeg	NHL	27	2	1	3	40	0	0	0	13	15.4	–13							....	....	....	....	....	....	....	....
	Washington	NHL	13	1	3	4	8	0	0	0	15	6.7	2							7	0	2	2	4	0	0	0
1995-96	Washington	NHL	70	4	7	11	75	0	0	0	70	5.7	–1							6	1	1	2	2	0	0	0
1996-97	Washington	NHL	70	1	7	8	42	0	0	0	38	2.6	–4							....	....	....	....	....	....	....	....
1997-98	Washington	NHL	36	1	3	4	16	0	0	0	25	4.0	–2							12	0	2	2	2	0	0	0
1998-99	Washington	NHL	52	4	2	6	50	0	0	0	41	9.8	–5	298	53.0	94	25	9:34		....	....	....	....	....	....	....	....
	NHL Totals		828	72	122	194	913	3	6	6	748	9.6		298	53.0	94	25	9:34		44	2	6	8	34	0	0	0

Traded to **Chicago** by **Quebec** for Bob Mason, July 5, 1988. Traded to **Winnipeg** by **Chicago** for Winnipeg's 4th round choice (Igor Kravchuk) in 1991 Entry Draft, December 14, 1990. Traded to **Washington** by **Winnipeg** with Igor Ulanov for Washington's 3rd (later traded to Dallas — Dallas selected Sergei Gusev) and 5th (Brian Elder) round choices in 1995 Entry Draft, April 7, 1995.

EAKINS, Dallas (EE-kins) **NYI**

Defense. Shoots left. 6'2", 195 lbs.   Born, Dade City, FL, February 27, 1967. Washington's 11th choice, 208th overall, in 1985 Entry Draft.

Season	Club	League	GP	G	A	Pts	PIM	PP	SH	GW	S	%	+/–	TF	F%	H	SB	Min	GP	G	A	Pts	PIM	PP	SH	GW
1983-84	Peterborough AA	OMHA	29	7	20	27	67	....	....	....	....	....	....							....	....	....	....	....	....	....	....
1984-85	Peterborough	OHL	48	0	8	8	96	....	....	....	....	....	....							7	0	0	0	18	....	....	....
1985-86	Peterborough	OHL	60	6	16	22	134	....	....	....	....	....	....							16	0	1	1	30	....	....	....
1986-87	Peterborough	OHL	54	3	11	14	145	....	....	....	....	....	....							12	1	4	5	37	....	....	....
1987-88	Peterborough	OHL	64	11	27	38	129	....	....	....	....	....	....							12	3	12	15	16	....	....	....
1988-89	Baltimore	AHL	62	0	10	10	139	....	....	....	....	....	....							....	....	....	....	....	....	....	....
1989-90	Moncton	AHL	75	2	11	13	189	....	....	....	....	....	....							....	....	....	....	....	....	....	....
1990-91	Moncton	AHL	75	1	12	13	132	....	....	....	....	....	....							9	0	1	1	44	....	....	....
1991-92	Moncton	AHL	67	3	13	16	136	....	....	....	....	....	....							11	2	1	3	16	....	....	....
1992-93	**Winnipeg**	**NHL**	14	0	2	2	38	0	0	0	9	0.0	2							....	....	....	....	....	....	....	....
	Moncton	AHL	55	4	6	10	132	....	....	....	....	....	....							....	....	....	....	....	....	....	....
1993-94	Florida	NHL	1	0	0	0	0	0	0	0	2	0.0	0							....	....	....	....	....	....	....	....
	Cincinnati	IHL	80	1	18	19	143	....	....	....	....	....	....							8	0	1	1	41	....	....	....
1994-95	Florida	NHL	17	0	1	1	35	0	0	0	3	0.0	2							....	....	....	....	....	....	....	....
	Cincinnati	IHL	59	6	12	18	69	....	....	....	....	....	....							....	....	....	....	....	....	....	....
1995-96	St. Louis	NHL	16	0	1	1	34	0	0	0	6	0.0	–2							....	....	....	....	....	....	....	....
	Worcester	AHL	4	0	0	0	12	....	....	....	....	....	....							....	....	....	....	....	....	....	....
	Winnipeg	NHL	2	0	0	0	0	0	0	0	0	0.0	1							....	....	....	....	....	....	....	....
1996-97	Phoenix	NHL	4	0	0	0	10	0	0	0	2	0.0	–3							....	....	....	....	....	....	....	....
	Springfield	AHL	38	6	7	13	63	....	....	....	....	....	....							....	....	....	....	....	....	....	....
	NY Rangers	**NHL**	3	0	0	0	6	0	0	0	2	0.0	–1							4	0	0	0	4	0	0	0
	Binghamton	AHL	19	1	7	8	15	....	....	....	....	....	....							....	....	....	....	....	....	....	....

Season	Club	League	GP	G	A	Pts	PIM	PP	SH	GW	S	%	+/-	TF	F%	H	SB	Min	GP	G	A	Pts	PIM	PP	SH	GW
			Regular Season																Playoffs							
1997-98	**Florida**	**NHL**	**23**	**0**	**1**	**1**	**44**	**0**	**0**	**0**	**16**	**0.0**	**1**	....	....	....	....	....	....	....	....	....	....	....	....	....
	New Haven	AHL	4	0	1	1	7	....	....	....	....	....	....	....	....	....	....	....	....	....	....	....	....	....	....	....
1998-99	**Toronto**	**NHL**	**18**	**0**	**2**	**2**	**24**	**0**	**0**	**0**	**11**	**0.0**	**3**	**0**	**0.0**	**20**	**10**	**16:28**	**1**	**0**	**0**	**0**	**0**	**0**	**0**	**0**
	Chicago	IHL	2	0	0	0	0	....	....	....	....	....	....	....	....	....	....	....	....	....	....	....	....	....	....	....
	St. John's	AHL	20	3	7	10	16	....	....	....	....	....	....	....	....	....	....	....	5	0	1	1	6	....	....	....
	NHL Totals		**98**	**0**	**7**	**7**	**191**	**0**	**0**	**0**	**51**	**0.0**		**0**	**0.0**	**20**	**10**	**16:28**	**5**	**0**	**0**	**0**	**4**	**0**	**0**	**0**

Signed as a free agent by **Winnipeg**, October 17, 1989. Signed as a free agent by **Florida**, July 8, 1993. Traded to **St. Louis** by **Florida** for St. Louis' 4th round choice (Ivan Novoseltsev) in 1997 Entry Draft, September 28, 1995. Claimed on waivers by **Winnipeg** from **St. Louis**, March 20, 1996. Transferred to **Phoenix** after **Winnipeg** franchise relocated, July 1, 1996. Traded to **NY Rangers** by **Phoenix** with Mike Eastwood for Jayson More, February 6, 1997. Signed as a free agent by **Florida**, July 30, 1997. Signed as a free agent by **Toronto**, July 28, 1998. Signed as a free agent by **NY Islanders**, August 12, 1999.

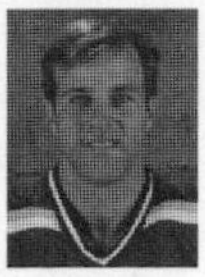

EASTWOOD, Mike — ST.L.

Center. Shoots right. 6'3", 209 lbs. Born, Ottawa, Ont., July 1, 1967. Toronto's 5th choice, 91st overall, in 1987 Entry Draft.

Season	Club	League	GP	G	A	Pts	PIM	PP	SH	GW	S	%	+/-	TF	F%	H	SB	Min	GP	G	A	Pts	PIM	PP	SH	GW
1986-87	Pembroke	OJHL	STATISTICS NOT AVAILABLE																							
1987-88	Western Michigan	CCHA	42	5	8	13	14	....	....	....	....	....	....	....	....	....	....	....	....	....	....	....	....	....	....	....
1988-89	Western Michigan	CCHA	40	10	13	23	87	....	....	....	....	....	....	....	....	....	....	....	....	....	....	....	....	....	....	....
1989-90	Western Michigan	CCHA	40	25	27	52	36	....	....	....	....	....	....	....	....	....	....	....	....	....	....	....	....	....	....	....
1990-91	Western Michigan	CCHA	42	29	32	61	84	....	....	....	....	....	....	....	....	....	....	....	....	....	....	....	....	....	....	....
1991-92	**Toronto**	**NHL**	**9**	**0**	**2**	**2**	**4**	**0**	**0**	**0**	**6**	**0.0**	**-4**	....	....	....	....	....	....	....	....	....	....	....	....	....
	St. John's	AHL	61	18	25	43	28	....	....	....	....	....	....	....	....	....	....	....	16	9	10	19	16	....	....	....
1992-93	**Toronto**	**NHL**	**12**	**1**	**6**	**7**	**21**	**0**	**0**	**0**	**11**	**9.1**	**-2**	....	....	....	....	....	**10**	**1**	**2**	**3**	**8**	**0**	**0**	**0**
	St. John's	AHL	60	24	35	59	32	....	....	....	....	....	....	....	....	....	....	....	....	....	....	....	....	....	....	....
1993-94	**Toronto**	**NHL**	**54**	**8**	**10**	**18**	**28**	**1**	**0**	**2**	**41**	**19.5**	**2**	....	....	....	....	....	**18**	**3**	**2**	**5**	**12**	**1**	**0**	**1**
1994-95	**Toronto**	**NHL**	**36**	**5**	**5**	**10**	**32**	**0**	**0**	**0**	**38**	**13.2**	**-12**	....	....	....	....	....	....	....	....	....	....	....	....	....
	Winnipeg	**NHL**	**13**	**3**	**6**	**9**	**4**	**0**	**0**	**0**	**17**	**17.6**	**3**	....	....	....	....	....	....	....	....	....	....	....	....	....
1995-96	**Winnipeg**	**NHL**	**80**	**14**	**14**	**28**	**20**	**2**	**0**	**3**	**94**	**14.9**	**-14**	....	....	....	....	....	**6**	**0**	**1**	**1**	**2**	**0**	**0**	**0**
1996-97	**Phoenix**	**NHL**	**33**	**1**	**3**	**4**	**4**	**0**	**0**	**0**	**22**	**4.5**	**-3**	....	....	....	....	....	....	....	....	....	....	....	....	....
	NY Rangers	**NHL**	**27**	**1**	**7**	**8**	**10**	**0**	**0**	**0**	**22**	**4.5**	**2**	....	....	....	....	....	**15**	**1**	**2**	**3**	**22**	**0**	**0**	**0**
1997-98	**NY Rangers**	**NHL**	**48**	**5**	**5**	**10**	**16**	**0**	**0**	**0**	**34**	**14.7**	**-2**	....	....	....	....	....	....	....	....	....	....	....	....	....
	St. Louis	**NHL**	**10**	**1**	**0**	**1**	**6**	**0**	**0**	**1**	**4**	**25.0**	**0**	....	....	....	....	....	**3**	**1**	**0**	**1**	**0**	**0**	**0**	**1**
1998-99	**St. Louis**	**NHL**	**82**	**9**	**21**	**30**	**36**	**0**	**0**	**0**	**76**	**11.8**	**6**	**1235**	**56.6**	**40**	**35**	**14:59**	**13**	**1**	**1**	**2**	**6**	**0**	**0**	**0**
	NHL Totals		**404**	**48**	**79**	**127**	**181**	**3**	**0**	**6**	**365**	**13.2**		**1235**	**56.6**	**40**	**35**	**14:59**	**65**	**7**	**8**	**15**	**50**	**1**	**0**	**2**

CCHA Second All-Star Team (1991)

Traded to **Winnipeg** by **Toronto** with Toronto's 3rd round choice (Brad Isbister) in 1995 Entry Draft for Tie Domi, April 7, 1995. Transferred to **Phoenix** after **Winnipeg** franchise relocated, July 1, 1996. Traded to **NY Rangers** by **Phoenix** with Dallas Eakins for Jayson More, February 6, 1997. Traded to **St. Louis** by **NY Rangers** for Harry York, March 24, 1998.

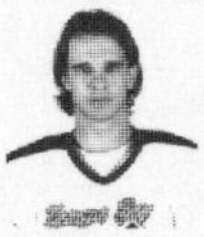

EGELAND, Allan — (eh-GUH-luhnd) — CGY.

Center. Shoots left. 6', 175 lbs. Born, Lethbridge, Alta., January 31, 1973. Tampa Bay's 3rd choice, 55th overall, in 1993 Entry Draft.

Season	Club	League	GP	G	A	Pts	PIM	PP	SH	GW	S	%	+/-	TF	F%	H	SB	Min	GP	G	A	Pts	PIM	PP	SH	GW
1989-90	Lethbridge Y	AAHA	36	21	30	51	52	....	....	....	....	....	....	....	....	....	....	....	....	....	....	....	....	....	....	....
1990-91	Lethbridge	WHL	67	2	16	18	57	....	....	....	....	....	....	....	....	....	....	....	9	0	0	0	0	....	....	....
1991-92	Tacoma	WHL	72	35	39	74	135	....	....	....	....	....	....	....	....	....	....	....	4	0	1	1	18	....	....	....
1992-93	Tacoma	WHL	71	56	57	113	119	....	....	....	....	....	....	....	....	....	....	....	7	9	7	16	18	....	....	....
1993-94	Tacoma	WHL	70	47	76	123	204	....	....	....	....	....	....	....	....	....	....	....	8	5	3	8	26	....	....	....
1994-95	Atlanta	IHL	60	8	16	24	112	....	....	....	....	....	....	....	....	....	....	....	5	0	1	1	16	....	....	....
1995-96	**Tampa Bay**	**NHL**	**5**	**0**	**0**	**0**	**2**	**0**	**0**	**0**	**1**	**0.0**	**0**	....	....	....	....	....	....	....	....	....	....	....	....	....
	Atlanta	IHL	68	22	22	44	182	....	....	....	....	....	....	....	....	....	....	....	3	0	1	1	0	....	....	....
1996-97	**Tampa Bay**	**NHL**	**4**	**0**	**0**	**0**	**5**	**0**	**0**	**0**	**1**	**0.0**	**-3**	....	....	....	....	....	....	....	....	....	....	....	....	....
	Adirondack	AHL	52	18	32	50	184	....	....	....	....	....	....	....	....	....	....	....	2	0	1	1	4	....	....	....
1997-98	**Tampa Bay**	**NHL**	**8**	**0**	**0**	**0**	**9**	**0**	**0**	**0**	**4**	**0.0**	**0**	....	....	....	....	....	....	....	....	....	....	....	....	....
	Adirondack	AHL	35	11	22	33	78	....	....	....	....	....	....	....	....	....	....	....	3	0	2	2	10	....	....	....
1998-99	Orlando	IHL	62	7	23	30	182	....	....	....	....	....	....	....	....	....	....	....	....	....	....	....	....	....	....	....
	Saint John	AHL	14	5	5	10	49	....	....	....	....	....	....	....	....	....	....	....	7	1	4	5	21	....	....	....
	NHL Totals		**17**	**0**	**0**	**0**	**16**	**0**	**0**	**0**	**6**	**0.0**		....	....	....	....	....	....	....	....	....	....	....	....	....

WHL West First All-Star Team (1993) • WHL West Second All-Star Team (1994)

Signed as a free agent by **Calgary**, July 20, 1999.

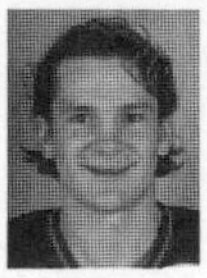

ELIAS, Patrik — (EH-lih-ahsh) — N.J.

Left wing. Shoots left. 6'1", 200 lbs. Born, Trebic, Czech., April 13, 1976. New Jersey's 2nd choice, 51st overall, in 1994 Entry Draft.

Season	Club	League	GP	G	A	Pts	PIM	PP	SH	GW	S	%	+/-	TF	F%	H	SB	Min	GP	G	A	Pts	PIM	PP	SH	GW
1992-93	Poldi Kladno	Czech.	2	0	0	0	....	....	....	....	....	....	....	....	....	....	....	....	....	....	....	....	....	....	....	....
1993-94	Poldi Kladno	Cze-Rep	15	1	2	3	....	....	....	....	....	....	....	....	....	....	....	....	11	2	2	4	....	....	....	....
1994-95	Poldi Kladno	Cze-Rep	28	4	3	7	37	....	....	....	....	....	....	....	....	....	....	....	7	1	2	3	12	....	....	....
1995-96	**New Jersey**	**NHL**	**1**	**0**	**0**	**0**	**0**	**0**	**0**	**0**	**2**	**0.0**	**-1**	....	....	....	....	....	....	....	....	....	....	....	....	....
	Albany	AHL	74	27	36	63	83	....	....	....	....	....	....	....	....	....	....	....	4	1	1	2	2	....	....	....
1996-97	**New Jersey**	**NHL**	**17**	**2**	**3**	**5**	**2**	**0**	**0**	**0**	**23**	**8.7**	**-4**	....	....	....	....	....	**8**	**2**	**3**	**5**	**4**	**1**	**0**	**0**
	Albany	AHL	57	24	43	67	76	....	....	....	....	....	....	....	....	....	....	....	6	1	2	3	8	....	....	....
1997-98	**New Jersey**	**NHL**	**74**	**18**	**19**	**37**	**28**	**5**	**0**	**6**	**147**	**12.2**	**18**	....	....	....	....	....	**4**	**0**	**1**	**1**	**0**	**0**	**0**	**0**
	Albany	AHL	3	3	0	3	2	....	....	....	....	....	....	....	....	....	....	....	....	....	....	....	....	....	....	....
1998-99	**New Jersey**	**NHL**	**74**	**17**	**33**	**50**	**34**	**3**	**0**	**2**	**157**	**10.8**	**19**	**99**	**38.4**	**86**	**13**	**15:50**	**7**	**0**	**5**	**5**	**6**	**0**	**0**	**0**
	NHL Totals		**166**	**37**	**55**	**92**	**64**	**8**	**0**	**8**	**329**	**11.2**		**99**	**38.4**	**86**	**13**	**15:50**	**19**	**2**	**9**	**11**	**10**	**1**	**0**	**0**

NHL All-Rookie Team (1998)

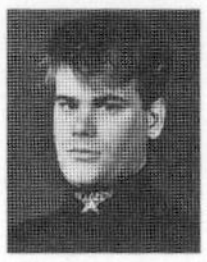

ELIK, Todd — (EHL-ihk)

Center. Shoots left. 6'2", 195 lbs. Born, Brampton, Ont., April 15, 1966.

Season	Club	League	GP	G	A	Pts	PIM	PP	SH	GW	S	%	+/-	TF	F%	H	SB	Min	GP	G	A	Pts	PIM	PP	SH	GW
1982-83	St. Michael's	OJHL-B	35	25	26	51	55	....	....	....	....	....	....	....	....	....	....	....	....	....	....	....	....	....	....	....
1983-84	Kingston	OHL	64	5	16	21	17	....	....	....	....	....	....	....	....	....	....	....	....	....	....	....	....	....	....	....
1984-85	Kingston	OHL	34	14	11	25	6	....	....	....	....	....	....	....	....	....	....	....	....	....	....	....	....	....	....	....
	North Bay	OHL	23	4	6	10	2	....	....	....	....	....	....	....	....	....	....	....	4	2	0	2	0	....	....	....
1985-86	North Bay	OHL	40	12	34	46	20	....	....	....	....	....	....	....	....	....	....	....	10	7	6	13	0	....	....	....
1986-87	U. of Regina	CWUAA	27	26	34	60	137	....	....	....	....	....	....	....	....	....	....	....	....	....	....	....	....	....	....	....
	Canada	Nat-Team	1	0	0	0	0	....	....	....	....	....	....	....	....	....	....	....	....	....	....	....	....	....	....	....
1987-88	Colorado	IHL	81	44	56	100	83	....	....	....	....	....	....	....	....	....	....	....	12	8	12	20	9	....	....	....
1988-89	Denver	IHL	28	20	15	35	22	....	....	....	....	....	....	....	....	....	....	....	....	....	....	....	....	....	....	....
	New Haven	AHL	43	11	25	36	31	....	....	....	....	....	....	....	....	....	....	....	17	10	12	22	44	....	....	....
1989-90	**Los Angeles**	**NHL**	**48**	**10**	**23**	**33**	**41**	**1**	**0**	**0**	**86**	**11.6**	**4**	....	....	....	....	....	**10**	**3**	**9**	**12**	**10**	**1**	**0**	**0**
	New Haven	AHL	32	20	23	43	42	....	....	....	....	....	....	....	....	....	....	....	....	....	....	....	....	....	....	....
1990-91	**Los Angeles**	**NHL**	**74**	**21**	**37**	**58**	**58**	**2**	**0**	**4**	**153**	**13.7**	**20**	....	....	....	....	....	**12**	**2**	**7**	**9**	**6**	**0**	**0**	**0**
1991-92	**Minnesota**	**NHL**	**62**	**14**	**32**	**46**	**125**	**4**	**3**	**1**	**118**	**11.9**	**0**	....	....	....	....	....	**5**	**1**	**1**	**2**	**2**	**0**	**0**	**1**
1992-93	**Minnesota**	**NHL**	**46**	**13**	**18**	**31**	**48**	**4**	**0**	**1**	**76**	**17.1**	**-5**	....	....	....	....	....	....	....	....	....	....	....	....	....
	Edmonton	**NHL**	**14**	**1**	**9**	**10**	**8**	**0**	**0**	**0**	**28**	**3.6**	**1**	....	....	....	....	....	....	....	....	....	....	....	....	....
1993-94	**Edmonton**	**NHL**	**4**	**0**	**0**	**0**	**6**	**0**	**0**	**0**	**5**	**0.0**	**0**	....	....	....	....	....	....	....	....	....	....	....	....	....
	San Jose	**NHL**	**75**	**25**	**41**	**66**	**89**	**9**	**0**	**4**	**180**	**13.9**	**-3**	....	....	....	....	....	**14**	**5**	**5**	**10**	**12**	**1**	**0**	**0**
1994-95	**San Jose**	**NHL**	**22**	**7**	**10**	**17**	**18**	**4**	**0**	**0**	**50**	**14.0**	**3**	....	....	....	....	....	....	....	....	....	....	....	....	....
	St. Louis	**NHL**	**13**	**2**	**4**	**6**	**4**	**0**	**0**	**0**	**26**	**7.7**	**5**	....	....	....	....	....	**7**	**4**	**3**	**7**	**2**	**1**	**1**	**0**
1995-96	**Boston**	**NHL**	**59**	**13**	**33**	**46**	**40**	**6**	**0**	**2**	**108**	**12.0**	**2**	....	....	....	....	....	**4**	**0**	**2**	**2**	**16**	**0**	**0**	**0**
	Providence	AHL	7	2	7	9	10	....	....	....	....	....	....	....	....	....	....	....	....	....	....	....	....	....	....	....
1996-97	**Boston**	**NHL**	**31**	**4**	**12**	**16**	**16**	**1**	**0**	**0**	**72**	**5.6**	**-12**	....	....	....	....	....	....	....	....	....	....	....	....	....
	Providence	AHL	37	16	29	45	63	....	....	....	....	....	....	....	....	....	....	....	10	1	6	7	33	....	....	....
1997-98	HC Lugano	Switz.	39	30	36	66	22	....	....	....	....	....	....	....	....	....	....	....	7	6	5	11	12	....	....	....

			Regular Season																	Playoffs							
Season	Club	League	GP	G	A	Pts	PIM	PP	SH	GW	S	%	+/–	TF	F%	H	SB	Min	GP	G	A	Pts	PIM	PP	SH	GW
1998-99	SC Langnau	Switz.	36	14	42	56	180	....	....	....	....	....	....	....	....	....	....	....	8	6	17	23	53	....	....	....
	NHL Totals		**448**	**110**	**219**	**329**	**453**	**31**	**3**	**12**	**902**	**12.2**		....	....	....	....	....	**52**	**15**	**27**	**42**	**48**	**3**	**1**	**1**

Signed as a free agent by **NY Rangers**, February 26, 1988. Traded to **LA Kings** by **NY Rangers** with Igor Liba, Michael Boyce and future considerations for Dean Kennedy and Denis Larocque, December 12, 1988. Traded to **Minnesota** by **LA Kings** for Randy Gilhen, Charlie Huddy, Jim Thomson and NY Rangers' 4th round choice (previously acquired, LA Kings selected Alexei Zhitnik) in 1991 Entry Draft, June 22, 1991. Traded to **Edmonton** by **Minnesota** for Brent Gilchrist, March 5, 1993. Claimed on waivers by **San Jose** from **Edmonton**, October 26, 1993. Traded to **St. Louis** by **San Jose** for Kevin Miller, March 23, 1995. Signed as a free agent by **Boston**, August 8, 1995.

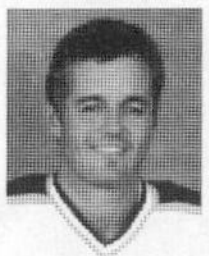

ELLETT, Dave

Defense. Shoots left. 6'2", 205 lbs. Born, Cleveland, OH, March 30, 1964. Winnipeg's 3rd choice, 75th overall, in 1982 Entry Draft.

Season	Club	League	GP	G	A	Pts	PIM	PP	SH	GW	S	%	+/–	TF	F%	H	SB	Min	GP	G	A	Pts	PIM	PP	SH	GW
1981-82	Ottawa	OJHL	50	9	35	44	....	....	....	....	....	....	....	....	....	....	....	....	....	....	....	....	....	....	....	....
1982-83	Bowling Green	CCHA	40	4	13	17	34	....	....	....	....	....	....	....	....	....	....	....	....	....	....	....	....	....	....	....
1983-84	Bowling Green	CCHA	43	15	39	54	96	....	....	....	....	....	....	....	....	....	....	....	....	....	....	....	....	....	....	....
1984-85	**Winnipeg**	**NHL**	**80**	**11**	**27**	**38**	**85**	**3**	**0**	**0**	**146**	**7.5**	**20**	....	....	....	....	....	**8**	**1**	**5**	**6**	**4**	**1**	**0**	**0**
1985-86	**Winnipeg**	**NHL**	**80**	**15**	**31**	**46**	**96**	**2**	**0**	**1**	**168**	**8.9**	**–38**	....	....	....	....	....	**3**	**0**	**1**	**1**	**0**	**0**	**0**	**0**
1986-87	**Winnipeg**	**NHL**	**78**	**13**	**31**	**44**	**53**	**5**	**0**	**2**	**159**	**8.2**	**19**	....	....	....	....	....	**10**	**0**	**8**	**8**	**2**	**0**	**0**	**0**
1987-88	**Winnipeg**	**NHL**	**68**	**13**	**45**	**58**	**106**	**5**	**0**	**1**	**198**	**6.6**	**–8**	....	....	....	....	....	**5**	**1**	**2**	**3**	**10**	**1**	**0**	**0**
1988-89	**Winnipeg**	**NHL**	**75**	**22**	**34**	**56**	**62**	**9**	**2**	**5**	**209**	**10.5**	**–18**	....	....	....	....	....	....	....	....	....	....	....	....	....
1989-90	**Winnipeg**	**NHL**	**77**	**17**	**29**	**46**	**96**	**8**	**0**	**1**	**205**	**8.3**	**–15**	....	....	....	....	....	**7**	**2**	**0**	**2**	**6**	**2**	**0**	**1**
1990-91	**Winnipeg**	**NHL**	**17**	**4**	**7**	**11**	**6**	**1**	**1**	**0**	**41**	**9.8**	**–4**	....	....	....	....	....	....	....	....	....	....	....	....	....
	Toronto	**NHL**	**60**	**8**	**30**	**38**	**69**	**5**	**0**	**1**	**154**	**5.2**	**–4**	....	....	....	....	....	....	....	....	....	....	....	....	....
1991-92	**Toronto**	**NHL**	**79**	**18**	**33**	**51**	**95**	**9**	**1**	**4**	**225**	**8.0**	**–13**	....	....	....	....	....	....	....	....	....	....	....	....	....
1992-93	**Toronto**	**NHL**	**70**	**6**	**34**	**40**	**46**	**4**	**0**	**1**	**186**	**3.2**	**19**	....	....	....	....	....	**21**	**4**	**8**	**12**	**8**	**2**	**0**	**0**
1993-94	**Toronto**	**NHL**	**68**	**7**	**36**	**43**	**42**	**5**	**0**	**1**	**146**	**4.8**	**6**	....	....	....	....	....	**18**	**3**	**15**	**18**	**31**	**3**	**0**	**0**
1994-95	**Toronto**	**NHL**	**33**	**5**	**10**	**15**	**26**	**3**	**0**	**1**	**84**	**6.0**	**–6**	....	....	....	....	....	**7**	**0**	**2**	**2**	**0**	**0**	**0**	**0**
1995-96	**Toronto**	**NHL**	**80**	**3**	**19**	**22**	**59**	**1**	**1**	**0**	**153**	**2.0**	**–10**	....	....	....	....	....	**6**	**0**	**0**	**0**	**4**	**0**	**0**	**0**
1996-97	**Toronto**	**NHL**	**56**	**4**	**10**	**14**	**34**	**0**	**0**	**1**	**83**	**4.8**	**–8**	....	....	....	....	....	....	....	....	....	....	....	....	....
	New Jersey	**NHL**	**20**	**2**	**5**	**7**	**6**	**1**	**0**	**1**	**22**	**9.1**	**2**	....	....	....	....	....	**10**	**0**	**3**	**3**	**10**	**0**	**0**	**0**
1997-98	**Boston**	**NHL**	**82**	**3**	**20**	**23**	**67**	**2**	**0**	**1**	**129**	**2.3**	**3**	....	....	....	....	....	**6**	**0**	**1**	**1**	**6**	**0**	**0**	**0**
1998-99	**Boston**	**NHL**	**54**	**0**	**6**	**6**	**25**	**0**	**0**	**0**	**45**	**0.0**	**11**	**0**	**0.0**	**41**	**56**	**14:48**	**8**	**0**	**0**	**0**	**4**	**0**	**0**	**0**
	NHL Totals		**1077**	**151**	**407**	**558**	**973**	**63**	**5**	**21**	**2353**	**6.4**		**0**	**0.0**	**41**	**56**	**14:48**	**109**	**11**	**45**	**56**	**85**	**9**	**0**	**1**

CCHA Second All-Star Team (1984) • NCAA Championship All-Tournament Team (1984)

Played in NHL All-Star Game (1989, 1992)

Traded to **Toronto** by **Winnipeg** with Paul Fenton for Ed Olczyk and Mark Osborne, November 10, 1990. Traded to **New Jersey** by **Toronto** with Doug Gilmour and future considerations for Jason Smith, Steve Sullivan and the rights to Alyn McCauley, February 25, 1997. Signed as a free agent by **Boston**, July 29, 1997.

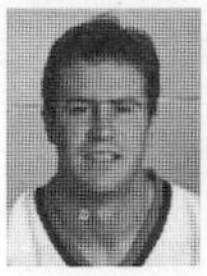

EMERSON, Nelson — ATL.

Right wing. Shoots right. 5'11", 180 lbs. Born, Hamilton, Ont., August 17, 1967. New Jersey's 4th choice, 45th overall, in 1985 Entry Draft.

Season	Club	League	GP	G	A	Pts	PIM	PP	SH	GW	S	%	+/–	TF	F%	H	SB	Min	GP	G	A	Pts	PIM	PP	SH	GW
1984-85	Stratford	OJHL-B	40	23	38	61	70	....	....	....	....	....	....	....	....	....	....	....	....	....	....	....	....	....	....	....
1985-86	Stratford	OJHL-B	39	54	58	112	91	....	....	....	....	....	....	....	....	....	....	....	....	....	....	....	....	....	....	....
1986-87	Bowling Green	CCHA	45	26	35	61	28	....	....	....	....	....	....	....	....	....	....	....	....	....	....	....	....	....	....	....
1987-88	Bowling Green	CCHA	45	34	49	83	54	....	....	....	....	....	....	....	....	....	....	....	....	....	....	....	....	....	....	....
1988-89	Bowling Green	CCHA	44	22	46	68	46	....	....	....	....	....	....	....	....	....	....	....	....	....	....	....	....	....	....	....
1989-90	Bowling Green	CCHA	44	30	52	82	42	....	....	....	....	....	....	....	....	....	....	....	....	....	....	....	....	....	....	....
	Peoria	IHL	3	1	1	2	0	....	....	....	....	....	....	....	....	....	....	....	....	....	....	....	....	....	....	....
1990-91	**St. Louis**	**NHL**	**4**	**0**	**3**	**3**	**2**	**0**	**0**	**0**	**3**	**0.0**	**–2**	....	....	....	....	....	....	....	....	....	....	....	....	....
	Peoria	IHL	73	36	79	115	91	....	....	....	....	....	....	....	....	....	....	....	17	9	12	21	16	....	....	....
1991-92	**St. Louis**	**NHL**	**79**	**23**	**36**	**59**	**66**	**3**	**0**	**2**	**143**	**16.1**	**–5**	....	....	....	....	....	**6**	**3**	**3**	**6**	**21**	**2**	**0**	**0**
1992-93	**St. Louis**	**NHL**	**82**	**22**	**51**	**73**	**62**	**5**	**2**	**4**	**196**	**11.2**	**2**	....	....	....	....	....	**11**	**1**	**6**	**7**	**6**	**0**	**0**	**0**
1993-94	**Winnipeg**	**NHL**	**83**	**33**	**41**	**74**	**80**	**4**	**5**	**6**	**282**	**11.7**	**–38**	....	....	....	....	....	....	....	....	....	....	....	....	....
1994-95	**Winnipeg**	**NHL**	**48**	**14**	**23**	**37**	**26**	**4**	**1**	**1**	**122**	**11.5**	**–12**	....	....	....	....	....	....	....	....	....	....	....	....	....
1995-96	**Hartford**	**NHL**	**81**	**29**	**29**	**58**	**78**	**12**	**2**	**5**	**247**	**11.7**	**–7**	....	....	....	....	....	....	....	....	....	....	....	....	....
1996-97	**Hartford**	**NHL**	**66**	**9**	**29**	**38**	**34**	**2**	**1**	**2**	**194**	**4.6**	**–21**	....	....	....	....	....	....	....	....	....	....	....	....	....
1997-98	**Carolina**	**NHL**	**81**	**21**	**24**	**45**	**50**	**6**	**0**	**4**	**203**	**10.3**	**–17**	....	....	....	....	....	....	....	....	....	....	....	....	....
1998-99	**Carolina**	**NHL**	**35**	**8**	**13**	**21**	**36**	**3**	**0**	**0**	**84**	**9.5**	**1**	**7**	**42.9**	**6**	**7**	**14:30**	....	....	....	....	....	....	....	....
	Chicago	**NHL**	**27**	**4**	**10**	**14**	**13**	**0**	**0**	**1**	**94**	**4.3**	**8**	**169**	**41.4**	**8**	**9**	**19:37**	....	....	....	....	....	....	....	....
	Ottawa	**NHL**	**3**	**1**	**1**	**2**	**2**	**0**	**0**	**0**	**10**	**10.0**	**–1**	**5**	**60.0**	**1**	**0**	**17:05**	**4**	**1**	**3**	**4**	**0**	**0**	**0**	**0**
	NHL Totals		**589**	**164**	**260**	**424**	**449**	**39**	**11**	**25**	**1578**	**10.4**		**181**	**42.0**	**15**	**16**	**16:45**	**21**	**5**	**12**	**17**	**27**	**2**	**0**	**0**

NCAA West Second All-American Team (1988) • CCHA First All-Star Team (1988, 1990) • CCHA Second All-Star Team (1989) • NCAA West First All-American Team (1990) • IHL First All-Star Team (1991) • Won Garry F. Longman Memorial Trophy (Top Rookie - IHL) (1991)

Traded to **Winnipeg** by **St. Louis** with Stephane Quintal for Phil Housley, September 24, 1993. Traded to **Hartford** by **Winnipeg** for Darren Turcotte, October 6, 1995. Transferred to **Carolina** after **Hartford** franchise relocated, June 25, 1997. Traded to **Chicago** by **Carolina** for Paul Coffey, December 29, 1998. Traded to **Ottawa** by **Chicago** for Chris Murray, March 23, 1999. Signed as a free agent by **Atlanta**, August 3, 1999.

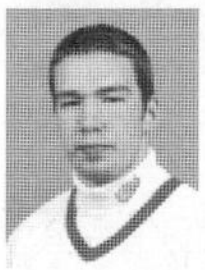

ERIKSSON, Anders — (AIR-ihk-suhn, AND-uhrs) — CHI.

Defense. Shoots left. 6'3", 218 lbs. Born, Bollnas, Sweden, January 9, 1975. Detroit's 1st choice, 22nd overall, in 1993 Entry Draft.

Season	Club	League	GP	G	A	Pts	PIM	PP	SH	GW	S	%	+/–	TF	F%	H	SB	Min	GP	G	A	Pts	PIM	PP	SH	GW
1992-93	MoDo AIK	Swede-Jr.	10	5	3	8	14	....	....	....	....	....	....	....	....	....	....	....	....	....	....	....	....	....	....	....
	MoDo AIK	Sweden	20	0	2	2	2	....	....	....	....	....	....	....	....	....	....	....	1	0	0	0	0	....	....	....
1993-94	MoDo AIK	Swede-Jr.	3	1	2	3	34	....	....	....	....	....	....	....	....	....	....	....	....	....	....	....	....	....	....	....
	MoDo AIK	Sweden	38	2	8	10	42	....	....	....	....	....	....	....	....	....	....	....	11	0	0	0	8	....	....	....
1994-95	MoDo AIK	Sweden	39	3	6	9	54	....	....	....	....	....	....	....	....	....	....	....	....	....	....	....	....	....	....	....
1995-96	**Detroit**	**NHL**	**1**	**0**	**0**	**0**	**2**	**0**	**0**	**0**	**0**	**0.0**	**1**	....	....	....	....	....	**3**	**0**	**0**	**0**	**0**	**0**	**0**	**0**
	Adirondack	AHL	75	6	36	42	64	....	....	....	....	....	....	....	....	....	....	....	3	0	0	0	0	....	....	....
1996-97	**Detroit**	**NHL**	**23**	**0**	**6**	**6**	**10**	**0**	**0**	**0**	**27**	**0.0**	**5**	....	....	....	....	....	....	....	....	....	....	....	....	....
	Adirondack	AHL	44	3	25	28	36	....	....	....	....	....	....	....	....	....	....	....	4	0	1	1	4	....	....	....
1997-98♦	**Detroit**	**NHL**	**66**	**7**	**14**	**21**	**32**	**1**	**0**	**2**	**91**	**7.7**	**21**	....	....	....	....	....	**18**	**0**	**5**	**5**	**16**	**0**	**0**	**0**
1998-99	**Detroit**	**NHL**	**61**	**2**	**10**	**12**	**34**	**0**	**0**	**1**	**67**	**3.0**	**5**	**0**	**0.0**	**72**	**60**	**15:54**	....	....	....	....	....	....	....	....
	Chicago	**NHL**	**11**	**0**	**8**	**8**	**0**	**0**	**0**	**0**	**12**	**0.0**	**6**	**0**	**0.0**	**15**	**20**	**22:51**	....	....	....	....	....	....	....	....
	NHL Totals		**162**	**9**	**38**	**47**	**78**	**1**	**0**	**3**	**197**	**4.6**		**0**	**0.0**	**87**	**80**	**16:58**	**21**	**0**	**5**	**5**	**16**	**0**	**0**	**0**

Traded to **Chicago** by **Detroit** with Detroit's 1st round choices in 1999 (Steve McCarthy) and 2001 Entry Drafts for Chris Chelios, March 23, 1999.

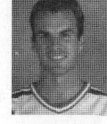

ERREY, Bob — (AIRY)

Left wing. Shoots left. 5'10", 185 lbs. Born, Montreal, Que., September 21, 1964. Pittsburgh's 1st choice, 15th overall, in 1983 Entry Draft.

Season	Club	League	GP	G	A	Pts	PIM	PP	SH	GW	S	%	+/–	TF	F%	H	SB	Min	GP	G	A	Pts	PIM	PP	SH	GW
1979-80	Peterborough	OJHL-B	29	13	11	24	12	....	....	....	....	....	....	....	....	....	....	....	....	....	....	....	....	....	....	....
1980-81	Peterborough B's	OJHL-B	42	28	42	70	93	....	....	....	....	....	....	....	....	....	....	....	....	....	....	....	....	....	....	....
	Peterborough	OHA	6	0	0	0	0	....	....	....	....	....	....	....	....	....	....	....	....	....	....	....	....	....	....	....
1981-82	Peterborough	OHL	68	29	31	60	39	....	....	....	....	....	....	....	....	....	....	....	9	3	1	4	9	....	....	....
1982-83	Peterborough	OHL	67	53	47	100	74	....	....	....	....	....	....	....	....	....	....	....	4	1	3	4	7	....	....	....
1983-84	**Pittsburgh**	**NHL**	**65**	**9**	**13**	**22**	**29**	**1**	**0**	**0**	**84**	**10.7**	**–20**	....	....	....	....	....	....	....	....	....	....	....	....	....
1984-85	**Pittsburgh**	**NHL**	**16**	**0**	**2**	**2**	**7**	**0**	**0**	**0**	**12**	**0.0**	**–8**	....	....	....	....	....	....	....	....	....	....	....	....	....
	Baltimore	AHL	59	17	24	41	14	....	....	....	....	....	....	....	....	....	....	....	8	3	4	7	11	....	....	....
1985-86	**Pittsburgh**	**NHL**	**37**	**11**	**6**	**17**	**8**	**1**	**0**	**2**	**57**	**19.3**	**1**	....	....	....	....	....	....	....	....	....	....	....	....	....
	Baltimore	AHL	18	8	7	15	28	....	....	....	....	....	....	....	....	....	....	....	....	....	....	....	....	....	....	....
1986-87	**Pittsburgh**	**NHL**	**72**	**16**	**18**	**34**	**46**	**2**	**1**	**1**	**138**	**11.6**	**–5**	....	....	....	....	....	....	....	....	....	....	....	....	....
1987-88	**Pittsburgh**	**NHL**	**17**	**3**	**6**	**9**	**18**	**0**	**0**	**0**	**18**	**16.7**	**6**	....	....	....	....	....	....	....	....	....	....	....	....	....
1988-89	**Pittsburgh**	**NHL**	**76**	**26**	**32**	**58**	**124**	**0**	**3**	**5**	**130**	**20.0**	**40**	....	....	....	....	....	**11**	**1**	**2**	**3**	**12**	**0**	**0**	**0**
1989-90	**Pittsburgh**	**NHL**	**78**	**20**	**19**	**39**	**109**	**0**	**1**	**1**	**127**	**15.7**	**3**	....	....	....	....	....	....	....	....	....	....	....	....	....
1990-91♦	**Pittsburgh**	**NHL**	**79**	**20**	**22**	**42**	**115**	**0**	**1**	**2**	**131**	**15.3**	**11**	....	....	....	....	....	**24**	**5**	**2**	**7**	**29**	**0**	**1**	**0**
1991-92♦	**Pittsburgh**	**NHL**	**78**	**19**	**16**	**35**	**119**	**0**	**3**	**1**	**122**	**15.6**	**1**	....	....	....	....	....	**14**	**3**	**0**	**3**	**10**	**0**	**1**	**0**

			Regular Season																	Playoffs							
Season	Club	League	GP	G	A	Pts	PIM	PP	SH	GW	S	%	+/–	TF	F%	H	SB	Min	GP	G	A	Pts	PIM	PP	SH	GW
1992-93	**Pittsburgh**	**NHL**	**54**	**8**	**6**	**14**	**76**	**0**	**0**	**2**	**79**	**10.1**	**–2**	....	....	....	....	....	....	....	....	....	....	....	....	....
	Buffalo	**NHL**	**8**	**1**	**3**	**4**	**4**	**0**	**0**	**0**	**9**	**11.1**	**2**	....	....	....	....	....	**4**	**0**	**1**	**1**	**10**	**0**	**0**	**0**
1993-94	**San Jose**	**NHL**	**64**	**12**	**18**	**30**	**126**	**5**	**0**	**2**	**89**	**13.5**	**–11**	....	....	....	....	....	**14**	**3**	**2**	**5**	**10**	**1**	**0**	**0**
1994-95	**San Jose**	**NHL**	**13**	**2**	**2**	**4**	**27**	**0**	**0**	**0**	**19**	**10.5**	**4**	....	....	....	....	....	....	....	....	....	....	....	....	....
	Detroit	**NHL**	**30**	**6**	**11**	**17**	**31**	**0**	**0**	**1**	**53**	**11.3**	**9**	....	....	....	....	....	**18**	**1**	**5**	**6**	**30**	**1**	**0**	**0**
1995-96	**Detroit**	**NHL**	**71**	**11**	**21**	**32**	**66**	**2**	**2**	**2**	**85**	**12.9**	**30**	....	....	....	....	....	**14**	**0**	**4**	**4**	**8**	**0**	**0**	**0**
1996-97	**Detroit**	**NHL**	**36**	**1**	**2**	**3**	**27**	**0**	**0**	**0**	**34**	**2.9**	**–3**	....	....	....	....	....	....	....	....	....	....	....	....	....
	San Jose	**NHL**	**30**	**3**	**6**	**9**	**20**	**0**	**0**	**0**	**38**	**7.9**	**–2**	....	....	....	....	....	....	....	....	....	....	....	....	....
1997-98	**Dallas**	**NHL**	**59**	**2**	**9**	**11**	**46**	**0**	**0**	**0**	**34**	**5.9**	**7**	....	....	....	....	....	....	....	....	....	....	....	....	....
	NY Rangers	**NHL**	**12**	**0**	**0**	**0**	**7**	**0**	**0**	**0**	**11**	**0.0**	**–5**	....	....	....	....	....	....	....	....	....	....	....	....	....
1998-99	Hartford	AHL	69	18	27	45	59	....	....	....	....	....	....	....	....	....	....	....	7	0	3	3	8	....	....	....
	NHL Totals		**895**	**170**	**212**	**382**	**1005**	**11**	**11**	**19**	**1270**	**13.4**		....	....	....	....	....	**99**	**13**	**16**	**29**	**109**	**2**	**2**	**0**

OHL First All-Star Team (1983)

Traded to **Buffalo** by **Pittsburgh** for Mike Ramsey, March 22, 1993. Signed as a free agent by **San Jose**, August 17, 1993. Traded to **Detroit** by **San Jose** for Detroit's 5th round choice (Michal Bros) in 1995 Entry Draft, February 27, 1995. Claimed on waivers by **San Jose** from **Detroit**, February 8, 1997. Signed as a free agent by **Dallas**, July 28, 1997. Traded to **NY Rangers** by **Dallas** with Todd Harvey and Dallas' 4th round choice (Boyd Kane) in 1998 Entry Draft for Brian Skrudland, Mike Keane and NY Rangers' 6th round choice (Pavel Patera) in 1998 Entry Draft, March 24, 1998.

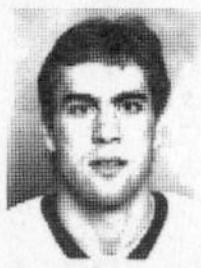

FAIRCHILD, Kelly — DAL.

Center. Shoots left. 5'11", 180 lbs. Born, Hibbing, MN, April 9, 1973. Los Angeles' 6th choice, 152nd overall, in 1991 Entry Draft.

Season	Club	League	GP	G	A	Pts	PIM	PP	SH	GW	S	%	+/–	TF	F%	H	SB	Min	GP	G	A	Pts	PIM	PP	SH	GW
1988-89	Hibbing High	H.S.	22	9	8	17	24	....	....	....	....	....	....	....	....	....	....	....	....	....	....	....	....	....	....	....
1989-90	Grand Rapids	H.S.	28	12	17	29	73	....	....	....	....	....	....	....	....	....	....	....	....	....	....	....	....	....	....	....
1990-91	Grand Rapids	H.S.	28	28	45	73	25	....	....	....	....	....	....	....	....	....	....	....	....	....	....	....	....	....	....	....
1991-92	U. of Wisconsin	WCHA	37	11	10	21	45	....	....	....	....	....	....	....	....	....	....	....	....	....	....	....	....	....	....	....
1992-93	U. of Wisconsin	WCHA	42	25	29	54	54	....	....	....	....	....	....	....	....	....	....	....	....	....	....	....	....	....	....	....
1993-94	U. of Wisconsin	WCHA	42	20	44	*64	81	....	....	....	....	....	....	....	....	....	....	....	....	....	....	....	....	....	....	....
1994-95	St. John's	AHL	53	27	23	50	51	....	....	....	....	....	....	....	....	....	....	....	4	0	2	2	4	....	....	....
1995-96	**Toronto**	**NHL**	**1**	**0**	**1**	**1**	**2**	**0**	**0**	**0**	**1**	**0.0**	**1**	....	....	....	....	....	....	....	....	....	....	....	....	....
	St. John's	AHL	78	29	49	78	85	....	....	....	....	....	....	....	....	....	....	....	2	0	1	1	4	....	....	....
1996-97	**Toronto**	**NHL**	**22**	**0**	**2**	**2**	**2**	**0**	**0**	**0**	**14**	**0.0**	**–5**	....	....	....	....	....	....	....	....	....	....	....	....	....
	St. John's	AHL	29	9	22	31	36	....	....	....	....	....	....	....	....	....	....	....	....	....	....	....	....	....	....	....
	Orlando	IHL	25	9	6	15	20	....	....	....	....	....	....	....	....	....	....	....	9	6	5	11	16	....	....	....
1997-98	St. John's	AHL	17	5	2	7	24	....	....	....	....	....	....	....	....	....	....	....	....	....	....	....	....	....	....	....
	Orlando	IHL	22	2	6	8	20	....	....	....	....	....	....	....	....	....	....	....	....	....	....	....	....	....	....	....
	Milwaukee	IHL	40	20	24	44	32	....	....	....	....	....	....	....	....	....	....	....	10	5	2	7	4	....	....	....
1998-99	**Dallas**	**NHL**	**1**	**0**	**0**	**0**	**0**	**0**	**0**	**0**	**4**	**0.0**	**0**	**12**	**25.0**	**1**	**1**	**12:37**	....	....	....	....	....	....	....	....
	Michigan	IHL	74	17	33	50	88	....	....	....	....	....	....	....	....	....	....	....	5	2	2	4	16	....	....	....
	NHL Totals		**24**	**0**	**3**	**3**	**4**	**0**	**0**	**0**	**19**	**0.0**		**12**	**25.0**	**1**	**1**	**12:37**	....	....	....	....	....	....	....	....

WCHA First All-Star Team (1994)

Traded to **Toronto** by **LA Kings** with Dixon Ward, Guy Leveque and Shayne Toporowski for Eric Lacroix, Chris Snell and Toronto's 4th round choice (Eric Belanger) in 1996 Entry Draft, October 3, 1994. Signed as a free agent by **Dallas**, July 2, 1998.

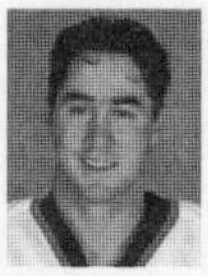

FALLOON, Pat (fah-LOON) — EDM.

Right wing. Shoots right. 5'11", 190 lbs. Born, Foxwarren, Man., September 22, 1972. San Jose's 1st choice, 2nd overall, in 1991 Entry Draft.

Season	Club	League	GP	G	A	Pts	PIM	PP	SH	GW	S	%	+/–	TF	F%	H	SB	Min	GP	G	A	Pts	PIM	PP	SH	GW
1987-88	Yellowhead	AAHA	52	74	69	143	50	....	....	....	....	....	....	....	....	....	....	....	....	....	....	....	....	....	....	....
1988-89	Spokane	WHL	72	22	56	78	41	....	....	....	....	....	....	....	....	....	....	....	....	....	....	....	....	....	....	....
1989-90	Spokane	WHL	71	60	64	124	48	....	....	....	....	....	....	....	....	....	....	....	6	5	8	13	4	....	....	....
1990-91	Spokane	WHL	61	64	74	138	33	....	....	....	....	....	....	....	....	....	....	....	15	10	14	24	10	....	....	....
	Canada	WJC-A	7	3	3	6	2	....	....	....	....	....	....	....	....	....	....	....	....	....	....	....	....	....	....	....
1991-92	**San Jose**	**NHL**	**79**	**25**	**34**	**59**	**16**	**5**	**0**	**1**	**181**	**13.8**	**–32**	....	....	....	....	....	....	....	....	....	....	....	....	....
1992-93	**San Jose**	**NHL**	**41**	**14**	**14**	**28**	**12**	**5**	**1**	**1**	**131**	**10.7**	**–25**	....	....	....	....	....	....	....	....	....	....	....	....	....
1993-94	**San Jose**	**NHL**	**83**	**22**	**31**	**53**	**18**	**6**	**0**	**1**	**193**	**11.4**	**–3**	....	....	....	....	....	**14**	**1**	**2**	**3**	**6**	**0**	**0**	**0**
1994-95	**San Jose**	**NHL**	**46**	**12**	**7**	**19**	**25**	**0**	**0**	**3**	**91**	**13.2**	**–4**	....	....	....	....	....	**11**	**3**	**1**	**4**	**0**	**0**	**0**	**0**
1995-96	**San Jose**	**NHL**	**9**	**3**	**0**	**3**	**4**	**0**	**0**	**0**	**18**	**16.7**	**–1**	....	....	....	....	....	....	....	....	....	....	....	....	....
	Philadelphia	**NHL**	**62**	**22**	**26**	**48**	**6**	**9**	**0**	**2**	**152**	**14.5**	**15**	....	....	....	....	....	**12**	**3**	**2**	**5**	**2**	**2**	**0**	**0**
1996-97	**Philadelphia**	**NHL**	**52**	**11**	**12**	**23**	**10**	**2**	**0**	**4**	**124**	**8.9**	**–8**	....	....	....	....	....	**14**	**3**	**1**	**4**	**2**	**1**	**0**	**0**
1997-98	**Philadelphia**	**NHL**	**30**	**5**	**7**	**12**	**8**	**1**	**0**	**0**	**63**	**7.9**	**3**	....	....	....	....	....	....	....	....	....	....	....	....	....
	Ottawa	**NHL**	**28**	**3**	**3**	**6**	**8**	**2**	**0**	**0**	**73**	**4.1**	**–11**	....	....	....	....	....	**1**	**0**	**0**	**0**	**0**	**0**	**0**	**0**
1998-99	**Edmonton**	**NHL**	**82**	**17**	**23**	**40**	**20**	**8**	**0**	**2**	**152**	**11.2**	**–4**	**29**	**48.3**	**49**	**11**	**14:42**	**4**	**0**	**1**	**1**	**4**	**0**	**0**	**0**
	NHL Totals		**512**	**134**	**157**	**291**	**127**	**38**	**1**	**14**	**1178**	**11.4**		**29**	**48.3**	**49**	**11**	**14:42**	**56**	**10**	**7**	**17**	**14**	**3**	**0**	**0**

WHL West Second All-Star Team (1989) • WHL West First All-Star Team (1991) • Canadian Major Junior Most Sportsmanlike Player of the Year (1991) • Memorial Cup All-Star Team (1991) • Won Stafford Smythe Memorial Trophy (Memorial Cup Tournament MVP) (1991)

Traded to **Philadelphia** by **San Jose** for Martin Spanhel, Philadelphia's 1st round choice (later traded to Phoenix — Phoenix selected Daniel Briere) in 1996 Entry Draft and Philadelphia's 4th round choice (later traded to Buffalo — Buffalo selected Mike Martone), in 1996 Entry Draft, November 16, 1995. Traded to **Ottawa** by **Philadelphia** with Vaclav Prospal and Dallas' 2nd round choice (previously acquired, Ottawa selected Chris Bala) in 1998 Entry Draft for Alexandre Daigle, January 17, 1998. Signed as a free agent by **Edmonton**, August 21, 1998.

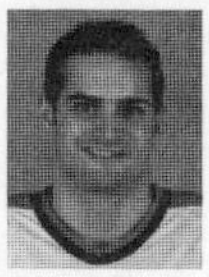

FATA, Rico (FA-tuh, REE-koh) — CGY.

Center. Shoots left. 5'11", 202 lbs. Born, Sault Ste. Marie, Ont., February 12, 1980. Calgary's 1st choice, 6th overall, in 1998 Entry Draft.

Season	Club	League	GP	G	A	Pts	PIM	PP	SH	GW	S	%	+/–	TF	F%	H	SB	Min	GP	G	A	Pts	PIM	PP	SH	GW
1995-96	S.S. Marie	OHL	62	11	15	26	52	....	....	....	....	....	....	....	....	....	....	....	4	0	0	0	0	....	....	....
1996-97	London	OHL	59	19	34	53	76	....	....	....	....	....	....	....	....	....	....	....	....	....	....	....	....	....	....	....
1997-98	London	OHL	64	43	33	76	110	....	....	....	....	....	....	....	....	....	....	....	16	9	5	14	*49	....	....	....
1998-99	London	OHL	23	15	18	33	41	....	....	....	....	....	....	....	....	....	....	....	25	10	12	22	42	....	....	....
	Calgary	**NHL**	**20**	**0**	**1**	**1**	**4**	**0**	**0**	**0**	**13**	**0.0**	**0**	**2**	**50.0**	**10**	**5**	**7:36**	....	....	....	....	....	....	....	....
	NHL Totals		**20**	**0**	**1**	**1**	**4**	**0**	**0**	**0**	**13**	**0.0**		**2**	**50.0**	**10**	**5**	**7:36**	....	....	....	....	....	....	....	....

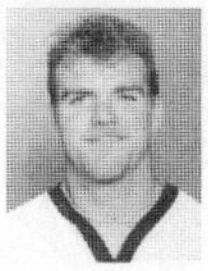

FEATHERSTONE, Glen

Defense. Shoots left. 6'4", 209 lbs. Born, Toronto, Ont., July 8, 1968. St. Louis' 4th choice, 73rd overall, in 1986 Entry Draft.

Season	Club	League	GP	G	A	Pts	PIM	PP	SH	GW	S	%	+/–	TF	F%	H	SB	Min	GP	G	A	Pts	PIM	PP	SH	GW
1984-85	Toronto	MTHL	45	7	24	31	94	....	....	....	....	....	....	....	....	....	....	....	....	....	....	....	....	....	....	....
1985-86	Windsor	OHL	49	0	6	6	135	....	....	....	....	....	....	....	....	....	....	....	14	1	1	2	23	....	....	....
1986-87	Windsor	OHL	47	6	11	17	154	....	....	....	....	....	....	....	....	....	....	....	14	2	6	8	19	....	....	....
1987-88	Windsor	OHL	53	7	27	34	201	....	....	....	....	....	....	....	....	....	....	....	12	6	9	15	47	....	....	....
1988-89	**St. Louis**	**NHL**	**18**	**0**	**2**	**2**	**22**	**0**	**0**	**0**	**9**	**0.0**	**–3**	....	....	....	....	....	**6**	**0**	**0**	**0**	**25**	**0**	**0**	**0**
	Peoria	IHL	37	5	19	24	97	....	....	....	....	....	....	....	....	....	....	....	....	....	....	....	....	....	....	....
1989-90	**St. Louis**	**NHL**	**58**	**0**	**12**	**12**	**145**	**0**	**0**	**0**	**34**	**0.0**	**–1**	....	....	....	....	....	**12**	**0**	**2**	**2**	**47**	**0**	**0**	**0**
	Peoria	IHL	15	1	4	5	43	....	....	....	....	....	....	....	....	....	....	....	....	....	....	....	....	....	....	....
1990-91	**St. Louis**	**NHL**	**68**	**5**	**15**	**20**	**204**	**1**	**0**	**1**	**59**	**8.5**	**19**	....	....	....	....	....	**9**	**0**	**0**	**0**	**31**	**0**	**0**	**0**
1991-92	**Boston**	**NHL**	**7**	**1**	**0**	**1**	**20**	**0**	**0**	**0**	**8**	**12.5**	**–2**	....	....	....	....	....	....	....	....	....	....	....	....	....
1992-93	**Boston**	**NHL**	**34**	**5**	**5**	**10**	**102**	**1**	**0**	**0**	**33**	**15.2**	**6**	....	....	....	....	....	....	....	....	....	....	....	....	....
	Providence	AHL	8	3	4	7	60	....	....	....	....	....	....	....	....	....	....	....	....	....	....	....	....	....	....	....
1993-94	**Boston**	**NHL**	**58**	**1**	**8**	**9**	**152**	**0**	**0**	**1**	**55**	**1.8**	**–5**	....	....	....	....	....	**1**	**0**	**0**	**0**	**0**	**0**	**0**	**0**
1994-95	**NY Rangers**	**NHL**	**6**	**1**	**0**	**1**	**18**	**0**	**0**	**0**	**6**	**16.7**	**0**	....	....	....	....	....	....	....	....	....	....	....	....	....
	Hartford	**NHL**	**13**	**1**	**1**	**2**	**32**	**0**	**0**	**0**	**16**	**6.3**	**–7**	....	....	....	....	....	....	....	....	....	....	....	....	....
1995-96	**Hartford**	**NHL**	**68**	**2**	**10**	**12**	**138**	**0**	**0**	**1**	**62**	**3.2**	**10**	....	....	....	....	....	....	....	....	....	....	....	....	....
1996-97	**Hartford**	**NHL**	**41**	**2**	**5**	**7**	**87**	**0**	**0**	**0**	**40**	**5.0**	**0**	....	....	....	....	....	....	....	....	....	....	....	....	....
	Calgary	**NHL**	**13**	**1**	**3**	**4**	**19**	**0**	**0**	**0**	**27**	**3.7**	**–1**	....	....	....	....	....	....	....	....	....	....	....	....	....
1997-98	Indianapolis	IHL	73	10	28	38	187	....	....	....	....	....	....	....	....	....	....	....	5	0	3	3	16	....	....	....

			Regular Season																Playoffs							
Season	Club	League	GP	G	A	Pts	PIM	PP	SH	GW	S	%	+/–	TF	F%	H	SB	Min	GP	G	A	Pts	PIM	PP	SH	GW
1998-99	Chicago	IHL	62	5	21	26	191												10	0	3	3	26			
	NHL Totals		384	19	61	80	939	2	0	3	349	5.4							28	0	2	2	103	0	0	0

Signed as a free agent by **Boston**, July 25, 1991. Traded to **NY Rangers** by **Boston** for Daniel Lacroix, August 19, 1994. Traded to **Hartford** by **NY Rangers** with Michael Stewart, NY Rangers' 1st round choice (Jean-Sebastien Giguere) in 1995 Entry Draft and 4th round choice (Steve Wasylko) in 1996 Entry Draft for Pat Verbeek, March 23, 1995. Traded to **Calgary** by **Hartford** with Hnat Domenichelli, New Jersey's 2nd round choice (previously acquired, Calgary selected Dimitri Kokorev) in 1997 Entry Draft and Vancouver's 3rd round choice (previously acquired, Calgary selected Paul Manning) in 1998 Entry Draft for Steve Chiasson and Colorado's 3rd round choice (previously acquired, Carolina selected Francis Lessard) in 1997 Entry Draft, March 5, 1997.

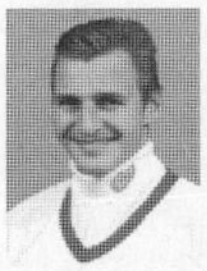

FEDOROV, Sergei (FEH-duh-rahf) DET.

Center. Shoots left. 6'1", 200 lbs. Born, Pskov, USSR, December 13, 1969. Detroit's 4th choice, 74th overall, in 1989 Entry Draft.

Season	Club	League	GP	G	A	Pts	PIM	PP	SH	GW	S	%	+/–	TF	F%	H	SB	Min	GP	G	A	Pts	PIM	PP	SH	GW
1985-86	Dynamo Minsk	USSR	15	6	1	7	10																			
1986-87	CSKA Moscow	USSR	29	6	6	12	12																			
1987-88	CSKA Moscow	USSR	48	7	9	16	20																			
1988-89	CSKA Moscow	USSR	44	9	8	17	35																			
1989-90	CSKA Moscow	USSR	48	19	10	29	22																			
1990-91	Detroit	NHL	77	31	48	79	66	11	3	5	259	12.0	11						7	1	5	6	4	0	0	1
1991-92	Detroit	NHL	80	32	54	86	72	7	2	5	249	12.9	26						11	5	5	10	8	1	2	1
1992-93	Detroit	NHL	73	34	53	87	72	13	4	3	217	15.7	33						7	3	6	9	23	1	1	0
1993-94	Detroit	NHL	82	56	64	120	34	13	4	10	337	16.6	48						7	1	7	8	6	0	0	0
1994-95	Detroit	NHL	42	20	30	50	24	7	3	5	147	13.6	6						17	7	*17	*24	6	3	0	0
1995-96	Detroit	NHL	78	39	68	107	48	11	3	11	306	12.7	49						19	2	*18	20	10	0	0	2
1996-97♦	Detroit	NHL	74	30	33	63	30	9	2	4	273	11.0	29						20	8	12	20	12	3	0	4
1997-98♦	Detroit	NHL	21	6	11	17	25	2	0	2	68	8.8	10						22	*10	10	20	12	2	1	1
	Russia	Olympics	6	1	5	6	8																			
1998-99	Detroit	NHL	77	26	37	63	66	6	2	3	224	11.6	9	1414	51.7	77	24	19:21	10	1	8	9	8	0	0	0
	NHL Totals		604	274	398	672	437	79	23	48	2080	13.2		1414	51.7	77	24	19:21	120	38	88	126	89	10	4	9

NHL/Upper Deck All-Rookie Team (1991) • NHL First All-Star Team (1994) • Won Frank J. Selke Trophy (1994, 1996) • Won Lester B. Pearson Award (1994) • Won Hart Trophy (1994)
Played in NHL All-Star Game (1992, 1994, 1996)

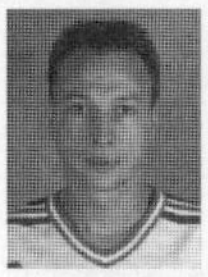

FEDYK, Brent (FEH-dihk)

Left wing. Shoots right. 6', 194 lbs. Born, Yorkton, Sask., March 8, 1967. Detroit's 1st choice, 8th overall, in 1985 Entry Draft.

Season	Club	League	GP	G	A	Pts	PIM	PP	SH	GW	S	%	+/–	TF	F%	H	SB	Min	GP	G	A	Pts	PIM	PP	SH	GW
1982-83	Regina AAA	SAHA	70	78	65	143	20																			
	Regina	WHL	1	0	0	0	0																			
1983-84	Regina	WHL	63	15	28	43	30												23	8	7	15	6			
1984-85	Regina	WHL	66	35	35	70	48												8	5	4	9	0			
1985-86	Regina	WHL	50	43	34	77	47												5	0	1	1	0			
1986-87	Regina	WHL	12	9	6	15	9																			
	Seattle	WHL	13	5	11	16	9																			
	Portland	WHL	11	5	4	9	6												14	5	6	11	0			
1987-88	Detroit	NHL	2	0	1	1	2	0	0	0	2	0.0	–1													
	Adirondack	AHL	34	9	11	20	22												5	0	2	2	6			
1988-89	Detroit	NHL	5	2	0	2	0	1	0	0	6	33.3	–1													
	Adirondack	AHL	66	40	28	68	33												15	7	8	15	23			
1989-90	Detroit	NHL	27	1	4	5	6	0	0	0	28	3.6	–1													
	Adirondack	AHL	33	14	15	29	24												6	2	1	3	4			
1990-91	Detroit	NHL	67	16	19	35	38	0	0	1	74	21.6	20						6	1	0	1	2	0	0	1
1991-92	Detroit	NHL	61	5	8	13	42	0	0	1	60	8.3	–5						1	0	0	0	2	0	0	0
	Adirondack	AHL	1	0	2	2	0																			
1992-93	Philadelphia	NHL	74	21	38	59	48	4	1	2	167	12.6	14													
1993-94	Philadelphia	NHL	72	20	18	38	74	5	0	1	104	19.2	–14													
1994-95	Philadelphia	NHL	30	8	4	12	14	3	0	2	41	19.5	–2						9	2	2	4	8	0	0	0
1995-96	Philadelphia	NHL	24	10	5	15	24	4	0	0	42	23.8	1													
	Dallas	NHL	41	10	9	19	30	4	0	0	71	14.1	–17													
1996-97	Michigan	IHL	9	1	2	3	4																			
1997-98	Detroit	IHL	40	18	23	41	24																			
	Cincinnati	IHL	26	21	13	34	14												9	5	5	10	7			
1998-99	NY Rangers	NHL	67	4	6	10	30	0	1	0	47	8.5	–11	2	0.0	63	21	11:06								
	NHL Totals		470	97	112	209	308	21	2	7	642	15.1		2	0.0	63	21	11:06	16	3	2	5	12	0	0	1

Traded to **Philadelphia** by **Detroit** for Philadelphia's 4th round choice (later traded to Boston — Boston selected Charles Paquette) in 1993 Entry Draft, October 1, 1992. Traded to **Dallas** by **Philadelphia** for Trent Klatt, December 13, 1995. Signed as a free agent by **NY Rangers**, August 13, 1998.

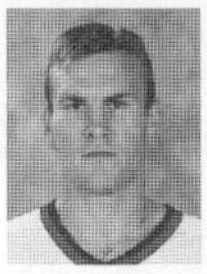

FELSNER, Brian (FEHLZ-nuhr)

Left wing. Shoots left. 5'11", 189 lbs. Born, Mt. Clemens, MI, November 11, 1972.

Season	Club	League	GP	G	A	Pts	PIM	PP	SH	GW	S	%	+/–	TF	F%	H	SB	Min	GP	G	A	Pts	PIM	PP	SH	GW
1993-94	Lake Superior	CCHA	6	1	1	2	6																			
1994-95	Lake Superior	CCHA	41	24	28	52	51																			
1995-96	Lake Superior	CCHA	38	16	36	52	40																			
1996-97	Orlando	IHL	75	29	41	70	38												7	2	3	5	6			
1997-98	Chicago	NHL	12	1	3	4	12																			
	Indianapolis	IHL	53	17	36	53	36																			
	Milwaukee	IHL	15	7	8	15	20												10	3	9	12	12			
1998-99	Detroit	IHL	72	20	35	55	49												11	4	6	10	12			
	NHL Totals		12	1	3	4	12																			

Signed as a free agent by **Chicago**, September 5, 1997. Traded to **Ottawa** by **Chicago** for Justin Hocking, August 21, 1998.

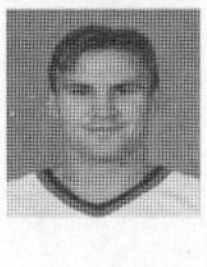

FERGUSON, Craig FLA.

Center. Shoots left. 5'11", 190 lbs. Born, Castro Valley, CA, April 8, 1970. Montreal's 8th choice, 146th overall, in 1989 Entry Draft.

Season	Club	League	GP	G	A	Pts	PIM	PP	SH	GW	S	%	+/–	TF	F%	H	SB	Min	GP	G	A	Pts	PIM	PP	SH	GW
1988-89	Yale University	ECAC	24	11	6	17	20																			
1989-90	Yale University	ECAC	28	6	13	19	36																			
1990-91	Yale University	ECAC	29	11	10	21	34																			
1991-92	Yale University	ECAC	27	9	16	25	26																			
1992-93	Fredericton	AHL	55	15	13	28	20												5	0	1	1	2			
	Wheeling	ECHL	9	6	5	11	24																			
1993-94	Montreal	NHL	2	0	1	1	0	0	0	0	0	0.0	1													
	Fredericton	AHL	57	29	32	61	60																			
1994-95	Fredericton	AHL	80	27	35	62	62												17	6	2	8	6			
	Montreal	NHL	1	0	0	0	0	0	0	0	3	0.0	0													
1995-96	Montreal	NHL	10	1	0	1	2	0	0	0	9	11.1	–5													
	Calgary	NHL	8	0	0	0	4	0	0	0	11	0.0	–4													
	Saint John	AHL	18	5	13	18	8																			
	Phoenix	IHL	31	6	9	15	25												4	0	2	2	6			
1996-97	Florida	NHL	3	0	0	0	0	0	0	0	5	0.0	–1													
	Carolina	AHL	74	29	41	70	57																			
1997-98	New Haven	AHL	64	24	28	52	41												3	2	1	3	2			
1998-99	New Haven	AHL	61	18	27	45	76																			
	NHL Totals		24	1	1	2	6	0	0	0	28	3.6														

Traded to **Calgary** by **Montreal** with Yves Sarault for Calgary's 8th round choice (Petr Kubos) in 1997 Entry Draft, November 26, 1995. Traded to **LA Kings** by **Calgary** for Pat Conacher, February 10, 1996. Signed as a free agent by **Florida**, July 24, 1996.

FERGUSON, Scott — ANA.

Defense. Shoots left. 6'1", 195 lbs. Born, Camrose, Alta., January 6, 1973.

Season	Club	League	GP	G	A	Pts	PIM	PP	SH	GW	S	%	+/-	TF	F%	H	SB	Min	GP	G	A	Pts	PIM	PP	SH	GW
1990-91	Sherwood Park	AJHL	32	2	9	11	91																			
	Kamloops	WHL	4	0	0	0	0																			
1991-92	Kamloops	WHL	62	4	10	14	138												12	0	2	2	21			
1992-93	Kamloops	WHL	71	4	19	23	206												13	0	2	2	24			
1993-94	Kamloops	WHL	68	5	49	54	180												19	5	11	16	48			
1994-95	Cape Breton	AHL	58	4	6	10	103																			
	Wheeling	ECHL	5	1	5	6	16																			
1995-96	Cape Breton	AHL	80	5	16	21	196																			
1996-97	Hamilton	AHL	74	6	14	20	115												21	5	7	12	59			
1997-98	**Edmonton**	**NHL**	1	0	0	0	0	0	0	0	0	0.0	1												
	Hamilton	AHL	77	7	17	24	150												9	0	3	3	16			
1998-99	**Anaheim**	**NHL**	2	0	1	1	0	0	0	0	1	0.0	0	0	0.0	1	4	15:09								
	Cincinnati	AHL	78	4	31	35	59												3	0	0	0	4			
	NHL Totals		3	0	1	1	0	0	0	0	1	0.0		0	0.0	1	4	15:09								

WHL West Second All-Star Team (1994)

Signed as a free agent by **Edmonton**, June 2, 1994. Traded to **Ottawa** by **Edmonton** for Frantisek Musil, March 9, 1998. Signed as a free agent by **Anaheim**, July 27, 1998.

FERRARO, Chris — (fuh-RAHR-oh) — NYI

Center/Right wing. Shoots right. 5'10", 180 lbs. Born, Port Jefferson, NY, January 24, 1973. NY Rangers' 4th choice, 85th overall, in 1992 Entry Draft.

Season	Club	League	GP	G	A	Pts	PIM	PP	SH	GW	S	%	+/-	TF	F%	H	SB	Min	GP	G	A	Pts	PIM	PP	SH	GW
1990-91	Dubuque	USHL	45	53	44	97	84												8	3	9	12	12			
1991-92	Dubuque	USHL	20	30	19	49	52																			
	Waterloo	USHL	18	19	31	50	54												4	5	6	11	14			
1992-93	U. of Maine	H.E.	39	25	26	51	46																			
1993-94	U. of Maine	H.E.	4	0	1	1	8																			
	United States	Nat-Team	48	8	34	42	58																			
1994-95	Atlanta	IHL	54	13	14	27	72																			
	Binghamton	AHL	13	6	4	10	38												10	2	3	5	16			
1995-96	**NY Rangers**	**NHL**	2	1	0	1	0	1	0	0	4	25.0	-3													
	Binghamton	AHL	77	32	67	99	208												4	4	2	6	13			
1996-97	**NY Rangers**	**NHL**	12	1	1	2	6	0	0	0	23	4.3	1													
	Binghamton	AHL	53	29	34	63	94																			
1997-98	**Pittsburgh**	**NHL**	46	3	4	7	43	0	0	0	42	7.1	-2													
1998-99	**Edmonton**	**NHL**	2	1	0	1	0	0	0	0	1	100.0	1	19	52.6	0	0	8:33								
	Hamilton	AHL	72	35	41	76	104												11	8	5	13	20			
	NHL Totals		62	6	5	11	49	1	0	0	70	8.6		19	52.6	0	0	8:33								

Claimed on waivers by **Pittsburgh** from **NY Rangers**, October 1, 1997. Signed as a free agent by **Edmonton**, August 13, 1998. Signed as a free agent by **NY Islanders**, July 22, 1999.

FERRARO, Peter — (fuh-RAHR-oh) — BOS.

Center. Shoots right. 5'10", 180 lbs. Born, Port Jefferson, NY, January 24, 1973. NY Rangers' 1st choice, 24th overall, in 1992 Entry Draft.

Season	Club	League	GP	G	A	Pts	PIM	PP	SH	GW	S	%	+/-	TF	F%	H	SB	Min	GP	G	A	Pts	PIM	PP	SH	GW
1990-91	Dubuque	USHL	29	21	31	52	83												8	7	5	12	10			
1991-92	Dubuque	USHL	21	25	25	50	92																			
	Waterloo	USHL	21	23	28	51	76												4	8	5	13	16			
1992-93	U. of Maine	H.E.	36	18	32	50	106																			
1993-94	U. of Maine	H.E.	4	3	6	9	16																			
	United States	Nat-Team	60	30	34	64	87																			
	United States	Olympics	8	6	0	6	6																			
1994-95	Atlanta	IHL	61	15	24	39	118																			
	Binghamton	AHL	12	2	6	8	67												11	4	3	7	51			
1995-96	**NY Rangers**	**NHL**	5	0	1	1	0	0	0	0	6	0.0	-5													
	Binghamton	AHL	68	48	53	101	157												4	1	6	7	22			
1996-97	**NY Rangers**	**NHL**	2	0	0	0	0	0	0	0	3	0.0	0						2	0	0	0	0	0	0	0
	Binghamton	AHL	75	38	39	77	171												4	3	1	4	18			
1997-98	**Pittsburgh**	**NHL**	29	3	4	7	12	0	0	0	34	8.8	-2													
	NY Rangers	**NHL**	1	0	0	0	2	0	0	0	3	0.0	-2													
	Hartford	AHL	36	17	23	40	54												15	8	6	14	59			
1998-99	**Boston**	**NHL**	46	6	8	14	44	1	0	1	61	9.8	10	70	37.1	52	21	10:12	19	9	12	21	38			
	Providence	AHL	16	15	10	25	14																			
	NHL Totals		83	9	13	22	58	1	0	1	107	8.4		70	37.1	52	21	10:12	2	0	0	0	0	0	0	0

• AHL First All-Star Team (1996) • Won Jack A. Butterfield Trophy (Playoff MVP - AHL) (1999)

Claimed on waivers by **Pittsburgh** from **NY Rangers**, October 1, 1997. Claimed on waivers by **NY Rangers** from **Pittsburgh**, January 9, 1998. Signed as a free agent by **Boston**, August 5, 1998. Claimed by **Atlanta** from **Boston** in Expansion Draft, June 25, 1999. Traded to **Boston** by **Atlanta** for Randy Robitaille, June 25, 1999.

FERRARO, Ray — (fuh-RAHR-oh) — ATL.

Center. Shoots left. 5'9", 193 lbs. Born, Trail, B.C., August 23, 1964. Hartford's 5th choice, 88th overall, in 1982 Entry Draft.

Season	Club	League	GP	G	A	Pts	PIM	PP	SH	GW	S	%	+/-	TF	F%	H	SB	Min	GP	G	A	Pts	PIM	PP	SH	GW
1981-82	Penticton	BCJHL	40	65	67	132	90																			
1982-83	Portland	WHL	50	41	49	90	39												14	14	10	24	13			
1983-84	Brandon	WHL	72	*108	84	*192	84												11	13	15	28	20			
1984-85	**Hartford**	**NHL**	44	11	17	28	40	6	0	2	59	18.6	-1													
	Binghamton	AHL	37	20	13	33	29																			
1985-86	**Hartford**	**NHL**	76	30	47	77	57	14	0	0	132	22.7	10						10	3	6	9	4	3	0	0
1986-87	**Hartford**	**NHL**	80	27	32	59	42	14	0	2	96	28.1	-9						6	1	1	2	8	0	0	0
1987-88	**Hartford**	**NHL**	68	21	29	50	81	6	0	2	105	20.0	1						6	1	1	2	6	1	0	0
1988-89	**Hartford**	**NHL**	80	41	35	76	86	11	0	4	169	24.3	1						4	2	0	2	4	0	0	0
1989-90	**Hartford**	**NHL**	79	25	29	54	109	7	0	4	138	18.1	-15						7	0	3	3	2	0	0	0
1990-91	**Hartford**	**NHL**	15	2	5	7	18	1	0	0	18	11.1	-1													
	NY Islanders	**NHL**	61	19	16	35	52	5	0	1	91	20.9	-11													
1991-92	**NY Islanders**	**NHL**	80	40	40	80	92	7	0	4	154	26.0	25													
1992-93	**NY Islanders**	**NHL**	46	14	13	27	40	3	0	1	72	19.4	0						18	13	7	20	18	0	0	0
	Capital District	AHL	1	0	2	2	2																			
1993-94	**NY Islanders**	**NHL**	82	21	32	53	83	5	0	3	136	15.4	1						4	1	0	1	6	0	0	0
1994-95	**NY Islanders**	**NHL**	47	22	21	43	30	2	0	1	94	23.4	1													
1995-96	**NY Rangers**	**NHL**	65	25	29	54	82	8	0	4	160	15.6	13													
	Los Angeles	**NHL**	11	4	2	6	10	1	0	0	18	22.2	-13													
1996-97	**Los Angeles**	**NHL**	81	25	21	46	112	11	0	2	152	16.4	-22													
1997-98	**Los Angeles**	**NHL**	40	6	9	15	42	0	0	2	45	13.3	-10						3	0	1	1	2	0	0	0
1998-99	**Los Angeles**	**NHL**	65	13	18	31	59	4	0	4	84	15.5	0	979	47.8	58	24	14:34								
	NHL Totals		1020	346	395	741	1035	105	0	39	1723	20.1		979	47.8	58	24	14:34	58	21	19	40	50	4	0	0

WHL First All-Star Team (1984)
Played in NHL All-Star Game (1992)

Traded to **NY Islanders** by **Hartford** for Doug Crossman, November 13, 1990. Signed as a free agent by **NY Rangers**, August 9, 1995. Traded to **LA Kings** by **NY Rangers** with Ian Laperriere, Mattias Norstrom, Nathan Lafayette and NY Rangers' 4th round choice (Sean Blanchard) in 1997 Entry Draft for Marty McSorley, Jari Kurri and Shane Churla, March 14, 1996. Signed as a free agent by **Atlanta**, August 9, 1999.

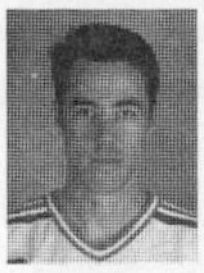

FINLEY, Jeff — ST.L.

Defense. Shoots left. 6'2", 205 lbs. Born, Edmonton, Alta., April 14, 1967. NY Islanders' 4th choice, 55th overall, in 1985 Entry Draft.

			Regular Season																Playoffs							
Season	Club	League	GP	G	A	Pts	PIM	PP	SH	GW	S	%	+/–	TF	F%	H	SB	Min	GP	G	A	Pts	PIM	PP	SH	GW
1983-84	Summerland	BCJHL	49	0	21	21	14	....	....	....	....	....	....	....	....	....	....	....	....	....	....	....	....	....	....	....
	Portland	WHL	5	0	0	0	5	....	....	....	....	....	....	....	....	....	....	....	5	0	1	1	4	....	....	....
1984-85	Portland	WHL	69	6	44	50	57	....	....	....	....	....	....	....	....	....	....	....	6	1	2	3	2	....	....	....
1985-86	Portland	WHL	70	11	59	70	83	....	....	....	....	....	....	....	....	....	....	....	15	1	7	8	16	....	....	....
1986-87	Portland	WHL	72	13	53	66	113	....	....	....	....	....	....	....	....	....	....	....	20	1	*21	22	27	....	....	....
1987-88	**NY Islanders**	**NHL**	**10**	**0**	**5**	**5**	**15**	**0**	**0**	**0**	**9**	**0.0**	**5**	....	....	....	....	....	**1**	**0**	**0**	**0**	**2**	**0**	**0**	**0**
	Springfield	AHL	52	5	18	23	50	....	....	....	....	....	....	....	....	....	....	....	....	....	....	....	....	....	....	....
1988-89	**NY Islanders**	**NHL**	**4**	**0**	**0**	**0**	**6**	**0**	**0**	**0**	**1**	**0.0**	**1**	....	....	....	....	....	....	....	....	....	....	....	....	....
	Springfield	AHL	65	3	16	19	55	....	....	....	....	....	....	....	....	....	....	....	....	....	....	....	....	....	....	....
1989-90	**NY Islanders**	**NHL**	**11**	**0**	**1**	**1**	**0**	**0**	**0**	**0**	**7**	**0.0**	**0**	....	....	....	....	....	**5**	**0**	**2**	**2**	**2**	**0**	**0**	**0**
	Springfield	AHL	57	1	15	16	41	....	....	....	....	....	....	....	....	....	....	....	13	1	4	5	23	....	....	....
1990-91	**NY Islanders**	**NHL**	**11**	**0**	**0**	**0**	**4**	**0**	**0**	**0**	**0**	**0.0**	**–1**	....	....	....	....	....	....	....	....	....	....	....	....	....
	Capital District	AHL	67	10	34	44	34	....	....	....	....	....	....	....	....	....	....	....	....	....	....	....	....	....	....	....
1991-92	**NY Islanders**	**NHL**	**51**	**1**	**10**	**11**	**26**	**0**	**0**	**0**	**25**	**4.0**	**–6**	....	....	....	....	....	....	....	....	....	....	....	....	....
	Capital District	AHL	20	1	9	10	6	....	....	....	....	....	....	....	....	....	....	....	....	....	....	....	....	....	....	....
1992-93	Capital District	AHL	61	6	29	35	34	....	....	....	....	....	....	....	....	....	....	....	4	0	1	1	0	....	....	....
1993-94	**Philadelphia**	**NHL**	**55**	**1**	**8**	**9**	**24**	**0**	**0**	**0**	**43**	**2.3**	**16**	....	....	....	....	....	....	....	....	....	....	....	....	....
1994-95	Hershey	AHL	36	2	9	11	33	....	....	....	....	....	....	....	....	....	....	....	6	0	1	1	8	....	....	....
1995-96	**Winnipeg**	**NHL**	**65**	**1**	**5**	**6**	**81**	**0**	**0**	**0**	**27**	**3.7**	**–2**	....	....	....	....	....	**6**	**0**	**0**	**0**	**4**	**0**	**0**	**0**
	Springfield	AHL	14	3	12	15	22	....	....	....	....	....	....	....	....	....	....	....	....	....	....	....	....	....	....	....
1996-97	**Phoenix**	**NHL**	**65**	**3**	**7**	**10**	**40**	**1**	**0**	**1**	**38**	**7.9**	**–8**	....	....	....	....	....	**1**	**0**	**0**	**0**	**2**	**0**	**0**	**0**
1997-98	**NY Rangers**	**NHL**	**63**	**1**	**6**	**7**	**55**	**0**	**0**	**0**	**32**	**3.1**	**–3**	....	....	....	....	....	....	....	....	....	....	....	....	....
1998-99	**NY Rangers**	**NHL**	**2**	**0**	**0**	**0**	**0**	**0**	**0**	**0**	**0**	**0.0**	**–1**	**0**	**0.0**	**2**	**2**	**11:40**	....	....	....	....	....	....	....	....
	St. Louis	**NHL**	**30**	**1**	**2**	**3**	**20**	**0**	**0**	**0**	**16**	**6.3**	**12**	**0**	**0.0**	**35**	**28**	**17:36**	**13**	**1**	**2**	**3**	**8**	**0**	**0**	**1**
	Hartford	AHL	42	2	10	12	28	....	....	....	....	....	....	....	....	....	....	....	....	....	....	....	....	....	....	....
	NHL Totals		**367**	**8**	**44**	**52**	**271**	**1**	**0**	**1**	**198**	**4.0**		**0**	**0.0**	**37**	**30**	**17:14**	**26**	**1**	**4**	**5**	**18**	**0**	**0**	**1**

Traded to **Ottawa** by **NY Islanders** for Chris Luongo, June 30, 1993. Signed as a free agent by **Philadelphia**, July 30, 1993. Traded to **Winnipeg** by **Philadelphia** for Russ Romaniuk, June 27, 1995. Transferred to **Phoenix** after **Winnipeg** franchise relocated, July 1, 1996. Signed as a free agent by **NY Rangers**, August 18, 1997. Traded to **St. Louis** by **NY Rangers** with Geoff Smith for future considerations (Chris Kenady, February 22, 1999), February 13, 1999.

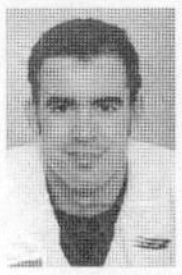

FISHER, Craig — BUF.

Center. Shoots left. 6'3", 180 lbs. Born, Oshawa, Ont., June 30, 1970. Philadelphia's 3rd choice, 56th overall, in 1988 Entry Draft.

			Regular Season																Playoffs							
Season	Club	League	GP	G	A	Pts	PIM	PP	SH	GW	S	%	+/–	TF	F%	H	SB	Min	GP	G	A	Pts	PIM	PP	SH	GW
1986-87	Ottawa	OJHL-B	34	22	26	48	18	....	....	....	....	....	....	....	....	....	....	....	....	....	....	....	....	....	....	....
1987-88	Oshawa	OJHL	36	42	34	76	48	....	....	....	....	....	....	....	....	....	....	....	....	....	....	....	....	....	....	....
1988-89	U. of Miami-Ohio	CCHA	37	22	20	42	37	....	....	....	....	....	....	....	....	....	....	....	....	....	....	....	....	....	....	....
1989-90	U. of Miami-Ohio	CCHA	39	37	29	66	38	....	....	....	....	....	....	....	....	....	....	....	....	....	....	....	....	....	....	....
	Philadelphia	**NHL**	**2**	**0**	**0**	**0**	**0**	**0**	**0**	**0**	**5**	**0.0**	**0**	....	....	....	....	....	....	....	....	....	....	....	....	....
1990-91	**Philadelphia**	**NHL**	**2**	**0**	**0**	**0**	**0**	**0**	**0**	**0**	**2**	**0.0**	**0**	....	....	....	....	....	....	....	....	....	....	....	....	....
	Hershey	AHL	77	43	36	79	46	....	....	....	....	....	....	....	....	....	....	....	7	5	3	8	2	....	....	....
1991-92	Cape Breton	AHL	60	20	25	45	28	....	....	....	....	....	....	....	....	....	....	....	1	0	0	0	0	....	....	....
1992-93	Cape Breton	AHL	75	32	29	61	74	....	....	....	....	....	....	....	....	....	....	....	1	0	0	0	2	....	....	....
1993-94	Cape Breton	AHL	16	5	5	10	11	....	....	....	....	....	....	....	....	....	....	....	....	....	....	....	....	....	....	....
	Winnipeg	**NHL**	**4**	**0**	**0**	**0**	**2**	**0**	**0**	**0**	**5**	**0.0**	**–1**	....	....	....	....	....	....	....	....	....	....	....	....	....
	Moncton	AHL	46	26	35	61	36	....	....	....	....	....	....	....	....	....	....	....	21	11	11	22	28	....	....	....
1994-95	Indianapolis	IHL	77	53	40	93	65	....	....	....	....	....	....	....	....	....	....	....	....	....	....	....	....	....	....	....
1995-96	Orlando	IHL	82	*74	56	130	81	....	....	....	....	....	....	....	....	....	....	....	14	10	7	17	6	....	....	....
1996-97	Utah	IHL	15	6	7	13	4	....	....	....	....	....	....	....	....	....	....	....	....	....	....	....	....	....	....	....
	Florida	**NHL**	**4**	**0**	**0**	**0**	**0**	**0**	**0**	**0**	**2**	**0.0**	**–2**	....	....	....	....	....	....	....	....	....	....	....	....	....
	Carolina	AHL	42	33	29	62	16	....	....	....	....	....	....	....	....	....	....	....	....	....	....	....	....	....	....	....
1997-98	Kolner Haie	Germany	34	9	8	17	34	....	....	....	....	....	....	....	....	....	....	....	....	....	....	....	....	....	....	....
	Kolner Haie	EuroHL	4	0	0	0	4	....	....	....	....	....	....	....	....	....	....	....	....	....	....	....	....	....	....	....
1998-99	Rochester	AHL	70	29	52	81	28	....	....	....	....	....	....	....	....	....	....	....	20	9	11	20	10	....	....	....
	NHL Totals		**12**	**0**	**0**	**0**	**2**	**0**	**0**	**0**	**14**	**0.0**		....	....	....	....	....	....	....	....	....	....	....	....	....

CCHA First All-Star Team (1990) • IHL First All-Star Team (1996)

Traded to **Edmonton** by **Philadelphia** with Scott Mellanby and Craig Berube for Dave Brown, Corey Foster and Jari Kurri, May 30, 1991. Traded to **Winnipeg** by **Edmonton** for cash, December 9, 1993. Signed as a free agent by **Chicago**, June 9, 1994. Signed as a free agent by **NY Islanders**, July 29, 1996. Traded to **Florida** by **NY Islanders** for cash, December 7, 1996. Signed as a free agent by **Buffalo**, July 30, 1998.

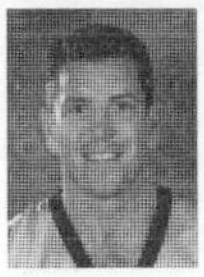

FITZGERALD, Tom

Right wing/Center. Shoots right. 6'1", 191 lbs. Born, Melrose, MA, August 28, 1968. NY Islanders' 1st choice, 17th overall, in 1986 Entry Draft.

			Regular Season																Playoffs							
Season	Club	League	GP	G	A	Pts	PIM	PP	SH	GW	S	%	+/–	TF	F%	H	SB	Min	GP	G	A	Pts	PIM	PP	SH	GW
1984-85	Austin Prep	H.S.	18	20	21	41	....	....	....	....	....	....	....	....	....	....	....	....	....	....	....	....	....	....	....	....
1985-86	Austin Prep	H.S.	24	35	38	73	....	....	....	....	....	....	....	....	....	....	....	....	....	....	....	....	....	....	....	....
1986-87	Providence	H.E.	27	8	14	22	22	....	....	....	....	....	....	....	....	....	....	....	....	....	....	....	....	....	....	....
1987-88	Providence	H.E.	36	19	15	34	50	....	....	....	....	....	....	....	....	....	....	....	....	....	....	....	....	....	....	....
1988-89	**NY Islanders**	**NHL**	**23**	**3**	**5**	**8**	**10**	**0**	**0**	**1**	**24**	**12.5**	**1**	....	....	....	....	....	....	....	....	....	....	....	....	....
	Springfield	AHL	61	24	18	42	43	....	....	....	....	....	....	....	....	....	....	....	....	....	....	....	....	....	....	....
1989-90	**NY Islanders**	**NHL**	**19**	**2**	**5**	**7**	**4**	**0**	**0**	**1**	**24**	**8.3**	**–3**	....	....	....	....	....	**4**	**1**	**0**	**1**	**4**	**0**	**0**	**0**
	Springfield	AHL	53	30	23	53	32	....	....	....	....	....	....	....	....	....	....	....	14	2	9	11	13	....	....	....
1990-91	**NY Islanders**	**NHL**	**41**	**5**	**5**	**10**	**24**	**0**	**0**	**2**	**60**	**8.3**	**–9**	....	....	....	....	....	....	....	....	....	....	....	....	....
	Capital District	AHL	27	7	7	14	50	....	....	....	....	....	....	....	....	....	....	....	....	....	....	....	....	....	....	....
1991-92	**NY Islanders**	**NHL**	**45**	**6**	**11**	**17**	**28**	**0**	**2**	**2**	**71**	**8.5**	**–3**	....	....	....	....	....	....	....	....	....	....	....	....	....
	Capital District	AHL	4	1	1	2	4	....	....	....	....	....	....	....	....	....	....	....	....	....	....	....	....	....	....	....
1992-93	**NY Islanders**	**NHL**	**77**	**9**	**18**	**27**	**34**	**0**	**3**	**1**	**83**	**10.8**	**–2**	....	....	....	....	....	**18**	**2**	**5**	**7**	**18**	**0**	**0**	**0**
1993-94	**Florida**	**NHL**	**83**	**18**	**14**	**32**	**54**	**0**	**3**	**1**	**144**	**12.5**	**–3**	....	....	....	....	....	....	....	....	....	....	....	....	....
1994-95	**Florida**	**NHL**	**48**	**3**	**13**	**16**	**31**	**0**	**0**	**0**	**78**	**3.8**	**–3**	....	....	....	....	....	....	....	....	....	....	....	....	....
1995-96	**Florida**	**NHL**	**82**	**13**	**21**	**34**	**75**	**1**	**6**	**2**	**141**	**9.2**	**–3**	....	....	....	....	....	**22**	**4**	**4**	**8**	**34**	**0**	**0**	**2**
1996-97	**Florida**	**NHL**	**71**	**10**	**14**	**24**	**64**	**0**	**2**	**1**	**135**	**7.4**	**7**	....	....	....	....	....	**5**	**0**	**1**	**1**	**0**	**0**	**0**	**0**
1997-98	**Florida**	**NHL**	**69**	**10**	**5**	**15**	**57**	**0**	**1**	**1**	**105**	**9.5**	**–4**	....	....	....	....	....	....	....	....	....	....	....	....	....
	Colorado	**NHL**	**11**	**2**	**1**	**3**	**22**	**0**	**1**	**0**	**14**	**14.3**	**0**	....	....	....	....	....	**7**	**0**	**1**	**1**	**20**	**0**	**0**	**0**
1998-99	**Nashville**	**NHL**	**80**	**13**	**19**	**32**	**48**	**0**	**0**	**1**	**180**	**7.2**	**–18**	**155**	**52.3**	**70**	**49**	**17:17**	....	....	....	....	....	....	....	....
	NHL Totals		**649**	**94**	**131**	**225**	**451**	**1**	**18**	**13**	**1059**	**8.9**		**155**	**52.3**	**70**	**49**	**17:17**	**56**	**7**	**11**	**18**	**76**	**0**	**0**	**2**

Claimed by **Florida** from **NY Islanders** in Expansion Draft, June 24, 1993. Traded to **Colorado** by **Florida** for the rights to Mark Parrish and Anaheim's 3rd round choice (previously acquired, Florida selected Lance Ward) in 1998 Entry Draft, March 24, 1998. Signed as a free agent by **Nashville**, July 6, 1998.

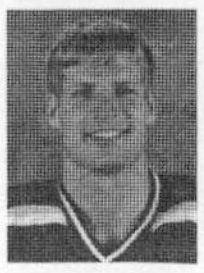

FITZPATRICK, Rory — ST.L.

Defense. Shoots right. 6'2", 208 lbs. Born, Rochester, NY, January 11, 1975. Montreal's 2nd choice, 47th overall, in 1993 Entry Draft.

			Regular Season																Playoffs							
Season	Club	League	GP	G	A	Pts	PIM	PP	SH	GW	S	%	+/–	TF	F%	H	SB	Min	GP	G	A	Pts	PIM	PP	SH	GW
1990-91	Rochester	USHL-B	40	0	5	5	....	....	....	....	....	....	....	....	....	....	....	....	....	....	....	....	....	....	....	....
1991-92	Rochester	USHL-B	28	8	28	36	141	....	....	....	....	....	....	....	....	....	....	....	....	....	....	....	....	....	....	....
1992-93	Sudbury	OHL	58	4	20	24	68	....	....	....	....	....	....	....	....	....	....	....	14	0	0	0	17	....	....	....
1993-94	Sudbury	OHL	65	12	34	46	112	....	....	....	....	....	....	....	....	....	....	....	10	2	5	7	10	....	....	....
1994-95	Sudbury	OHL	56	12	36	48	72	....	....	....	....	....	....	....	....	....	....	....	18	3	15	18	21	....	....	....
	Fredericton	AHL	....	....	....	....	....	....	....	....	....	....	....	....	....	....	....	....	10	1	2	3	5	....	....	....
1995-96	**Montreal**	**NHL**	**42**	**0**	**2**	**2**	**18**	**0**	**0**	**0**	**31**	**0.0**	**–7**	....	....	....	....	....	**6**	**1**	**1**	**2**	**0**	**0**	**0**	**0**
	Fredericton	AHL	18	4	6	10	36	....	....	....	....	....	....	....	....	....	....	....	....	....	....	....	....	....	....	....
1996-97	**Montreal**	**NHL**	**6**	**0**	**1**	**1**	**6**	**0**	**0**	**0**	**5**	**0.0**	**–2**	....	....	....	....	....	....	....	....	....	....	....	....	....
	St. Louis	**NHL**	**2**	**0**	**0**	**0**	**2**	**0**	**0**	**0**	**1**	**0.0**	**–2**	....	....	....	....	....	....	....	....	....	....	....	....	....
	Worcester	AHL	49	4	13	17	78	....	....	....	....	....	....	....	....	....	....	....	5	1	2	3	0	....	....	....

Season	Club	League	GP	G	A	Pts	PIM	PP	SH	GW	S	%	+/-	TF	F%	H	SB	Min	GP (Playoffs)	G	A	Pts	PIM	PP	SH	GW
1997-98	Worcester	AHL	62	8	22	30	111												11	0	3	3	26			
1998-99	**St. Louis**	**NHL**	**1**	**0**	**0**	**0**	**2**	**0**	**0**	**0**	**0**	**0.0**	**-3**	**0**	**0.0**	**0**	**0**	**4:49**								
	Worcester	AHL	53	5	16	21	82												4	0	1	1	17			
	NHL Totals		**51**	**0**	**3**	**3**	**28**	**0**	**0**	**0**	**37**	**0.0**		**0**	**0.0**	**0**	**0**	**4:49**	**6**	**1**	**1**	**2**	**0**	**0**	**0**	**0**

Traded to **St. Louis** by **Montreal** with Pierre Turgeon and Craig Conroy for Murray Baron, Shayne Corson and St. Louis' 5th round choice (Gennady Razin) in 1997 Entry Draft, October 29, 1996. Claimed by **Boston** from **St. Louis** in NHL Waiver Draft, October 5, 1998. Claimed on waivers by **St. Louis** from **Boston**, October 7, 1998.

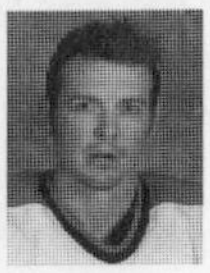

FLEURY, Theoren

(FLUH-ree, THAIR-ihn) **NYR**

Right wing. Shoots right. 5'6", 180 lbs. Born, Oxbow, Sask., June 29, 1968. Calgary's 9th choice, 166th overall, in 1987 Entry Draft.

Season	Club	League	GP	G	A	Pts	PIM	PP	SH	GW	S	%	+/-	TF	F%	H	SB	Min	GP (Playoffs)	G	A	Pts	PIM	PP	SH	GW
1983-84	St. James	MAHA	22	33	31	64	88																			
1984-85	Moose Jaw	WHL	71	29	46	75	82																			
1985-86	Moose Jaw	WHL	72	43	65	108	124																			
1986-87	Moose Jaw	WHL	66	61	68	129	110												9	7	9	16	34			
1987-88	Moose Jaw	WHL	65	68	92	*160	235																			
	Salt Lake	IHL	2	3	4	7	7												8	11	5	16	16			
1988-89♦	**Calgary**	**NHL**	**36**	**14**	**20**	**34**	**46**	**5**	**0**	**3**	**89**	**15.7**	**5**						**22**	**5**	**6**	**11**	**24**	**3**	**0**	**3**
	Salt Lake	IHL	40	37	37	74	81																			
1989-90	**Calgary**	**NHL**	**80**	**31**	**35**	**66**	**157**	**9**	**3**	**6**	**200**	**15.5**	**22**						**6**	**2**	**3**	**5**	**10**	**0**	**0**	**0**
1990-91	**Calgary**	**NHL**	**79**	**51**	**53**	**104**	**136**	**9**	**7**	**9**	**249**	**20.5**	**48**						**7**	**2**	**5**	**7**	**14**	**0**	**0**	**1**
1991-92	**Calgary**	**NHL**	**80**	**33**	**40**	**73**	**133**	**11**	**1**	**6**	**225**	**14.7**	**0**													
1992-93	**Calgary**	**NHL**	**83**	**34**	**66**	**100**	**88**	**12**	**2**	**4**	**250**	**13.6**	**14**						**6**	**5**	**7**	**12**	**27**	**3**	**1**	**0**
1993-94	**Calgary**	**NHL**	**83**	**40**	**45**	**85**	**186**	**16**	**1**	**6**	**278**	**14.4**	**30**						**7**	**6**	**4**	**10**	**5**	**1**	**0**	**2**
1994-95	Tappara	Finland	10	8	9	17	22																			
	Calgary	**NHL**	**47**	**29**	**29**	**58**	**112**	**9**	**2**	**5**	**173**	**16.8**	**6**						**7**	**7**	**7**	**14**	**2**	**2**	**1**	**0**
1995-96	**Calgary**	**NHL**	**80**	**46**	**50**	**96**	**112**	**17**	**5**	**4**	**353**	**13.0**	**17**						**4**	**2**	**1**	**3**	**14**	**0**	**0**	**0**
1996-97	**Calgary**	**NHL**	**81**	**29**	**38**	**67**	**104**	**9**	**2**	**3**	**336**	**8.6**	**-12**													
1997-98	**Calgary**	**NHL**	**82**	**27**	**51**	**78**	**197**	**3**	**2**	**4**	**282**	**9.6**	**0**													
	Canada	Olympics	6	1	3	4	2																			
1998-99	**Calgary**	**NHL**	**60**	**30**	**39**	**69**	**68**	**7**	**3**	**3**	**250**	**12.0**	**18**	**517**	**59.2**	**51**	**25**	**23:33**								
	Colorado	**NHL**	**15**	**10**	**14**	**24**	**18**	**1**	**0**	**2**	**51**	**19.6**	**8**	**150**	**58.7**	**12**	**3**	**22:33**	**18**	**5**	**12**	**17**	**20**	**2**	**0**	**0**
	NHL Totals		**806**	**374**	**480**	**854**	**1357**	**108**	**28**	**55**	**2736**	**13.7**		**667**	**59.1**	**63**	**28**	**23:21**	**77**	**34**	**45**	**79**	**116**	**11**	**2**	**6**

WJC-A All-Star Team (1988) • WHL East Second All-Star Team (1988) • Co-winner of Alka-Seltzer Plus Award with Marty McSorley (1991) • NHL Second All-Star Team (1995)

Played in NHL All-Star Game (1991, 1992, 1996, 1997, 1998, 1999)

Traded to **Colorado** by **Calgary** with Chris Dingman for Rene Corbet, Wade Belak and future considerations (Robyn Regehr, March 27, 1999), February 28, 1999. Signed as a free agent by **NY Rangers**, July 8, 1999.

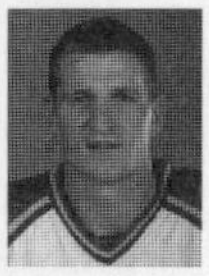

FOOTE, Adam

(FUT) **COL.**

Defense. Shoots right. 6'1", 205 lbs. Born, Toronto, Ont., July 10, 1971. Quebec's 2nd choice, 22nd overall, in 1989 Entry Draft.

Season	Club	League	GP	G	A	Pts	PIM	PP	SH	GW	S	%	+/-	TF	F%	H	SB	Min	GP (Playoffs)	G	A	Pts	PIM	PP	SH	GW
1987-88	Whitby	OMHA	65	25	43	68	108																			
1988-89	S.S. Marie	OHL	66	7	32	39	120																			
1989-90	S.S. Marie	OHL	61	12	43	55	199																			
	Canada	Nat-Team	3	1	0	1	0																			
1990-91	S.S. Marie	OHL	59	18	51	69	93												14	5	12	17	28			
1991-92	**Quebec**	**NHL**	**46**	**2**	**5**	**7**	**44**	**0**	**0**	**0**	**55**	**3.6**	**-4**													
	Halifax	AHL	6	0	1	1	2																			
1992-93	**Quebec**	**NHL**	**81**	**4**	**12**	**16**	**168**	**0**	**1**	**0**	**54**	**7.4**	**6**						**6**	**0**	**1**	**1**	**2**	**0**	**0**	**0**
1993-94	**Quebec**	**NHL**	**45**	**2**	**6**	**8**	**67**	**0**	**0**	**0**	**42**	**4.8**	**3**													
1994-95	**Quebec**	**NHL**	**35**	**0**	**7**	**7**	**52**	**0**	**0**	**0**	**24**	**0.0**	**17**						**6**	**0**	**1**	**1**	**14**	**0**	**0**	**0**
1995-96♦	**Colorado**	**NHL**	**73**	**5**	**11**	**16**	**88**	**1**	**0**	**1**	**49**	**10.2**	**27**						**22**	**1**	**3**	**4**	**36**	**0**	**0**	**0**
1996-97	**Colorado**	**NHL**	**78**	**2**	**19**	**21**	**135**	**1**	**0**	**0**	**60**	**3.3**	**16**						**17**	**0**	**4**	**4**	**62**	**0**	**0**	**0**
1997-98	**Colorado**	**NHL**	**77**	**3**	**14**	**17**	**124**	**0**	**0**	**1**	**64**	**4.7**	**-3**						**7**	**0**	**0**	**0**	**23**	**0**	**0**	**0**
	Canada	Olympics	6	0	1	1	4																			
1998-99	**Colorado**	**NHL**	**64**	**5**	**16**	**21**	**92**	**3**	**0**	**0**	**83**	**6.0**	**20**	**0**	**0.0**	**125**	**93**	**24:50**	**19**	**2**	**3**	**5**	**24**	**1**	**0**	**0**
	NHL Totals		**499**	**23**	**90**	**113**	**770**	**4**	**1**	**2**	**431**	**5.3**		**0**	**0.0**	**125**	**93**	**24:50**	**77**	**3**	**12**	**15**	**161**	**1**	**0**	**0**

OHL First All-Star Team (1991)

Transferred to **Colorado** after **Quebec** franchise relocated, June 21, 1995.

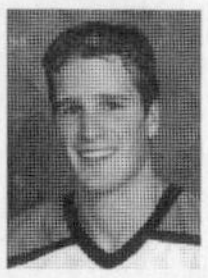

FORBES, Colin

T.B.

Left wing. Shoots left. 6'3", 205 lbs. Born, New Westminster, B.C., February 16, 1976. Philadelphia's 5th choice, 166th overall, in 1994 Entry Draft.

Season	Club	League	GP	G	A	Pts	PIM	PP	SH	GW	S	%	+/-	TF	F%	H	SB	Min	GP (Playoffs)	G	A	Pts	PIM	PP	SH	GW
1993-94	Sherwood Park	AJHL	47	18	22	40	76																			
1994-95	Portland	WHL	72	24	31	55	108												9	1	3	4	10			
1995-96	Portland	WHL	72	33	44	77	137												7	2	5	7	14			
	Hershey	AHL	2	1	0	1	2												4	0	2	2	2			
1996-97	**Philadelphia**	**NHL**	**3**	**1**	**0**	**1**	**0**	**0**	**0**	**0**	**3**	**33.3**	**0**						**3**	**0**	**0**	**0**	**0**	**0**	**0**	**0**
	Philadelphia	AHL	74	21	28	49	108												10	5	5	10	33			
1997-98	**Philadelphia**	**NHL**	**63**	**12**	**7**	**19**	**59**	**2**	**0**	**2**	**93**	**12.9**	**2**						**5**	**0**	**0**	**0**	**2**	**0**	**0**	**0**
	Philadelphia	AHL	13	7	4	11	22																			
1998-99	**Philadelphia**	**NHL**	**66**	**9**	**7**	**16**	**51**	**0**	**0**	**4**	**92**	**9.8**	**0**	**2**	**50.0**	**46**	**10**	**12:35**								
	Tampa Bay	**NHL**	**14**	**3**	**1**	**4**	**10**	**0**	**1**	**0**	**25**	**12.0**	**-5**	**0**	**0.0**	**21**	**4**	**17:30**								
	NHL Totals		**146**	**25**	**15**	**40**	**120**	**2**	**1**	**6**	**213**	**11.7**		**2**	**50.0**	**67**	**14**	**13:27**	**8**	**0**	**0**	**0**	**2**	**0**	**0**	**0**

Traded to **Tampa Bay** by **Philadelphia** with Philadelphia's 4th round choice (Michal Lanisak) in 1999 Entry Draft for Mikael Andersson and Sandy McCarthy, March 20, 1999.

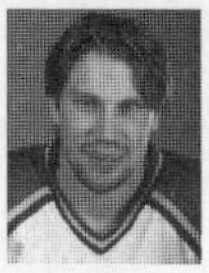

FORSBERG, Peter

(FOHRS-buhrg) **COL.**

Center. Shoots left. 6', 190 lbs. Born, Ornskoldsvik, Sweden, July 20, 1973. Philadelphia's 1st choice, 6th overall, in 1991 Entry Draft.

Season	Club	League	GP	G	A	Pts	PIM	PP	SH	GW	S	%	+/-	TF	F%	H	SB	Min	GP (Playoffs)	G	A	Pts	PIM	PP	SH	GW
1989-90	MoDo AIK	Swede-Jr.	30	15	12	27	42																			
	MoDo AIK	Sweden	1	0	1	1	4																			
1990-91	MoDo AIK	Swede-Jr.	39	38	64	102	56																			
	MoDo AIK	Sweden	23	7	10	17	22																			
1991-92	MoDo AIK	Sweden	39	9	18	27	78																			
1992-93	MoDo AIK	Swede-Jr.	2	0	3	3	4																			
	MoDo Domsjo	Sweden	39	23	24	47	92												3	4	1	5	0			
1993-94	MoDo AIK	Sweden	39	18	26	44	82												11	9	7	16	14			
	Sweden	Olympics	8	2	6	8	6																			
1994-95	MoDo AIK	Sweden	11	5	9	14	20																			
	Quebec	**NHL**	**47**	**15**	**35**	**50**	**16**	**3**	**0**	**3**	**86**	**17.4**	**17**						**6**	**2**	**4**	**6**	**4**	**1**	**0**	**0**
1995-96♦	**Colorado**	**NHL**	**82**	**30**	**86**	**116**	**47**	**7**	**3**	**3**	**217**	**13.8**	**26**						**22**	**10**	**11**	**21**	**18**	**3**	**0**	**1**
1996-97	**Colorado**	**NHL**	**65**	**28**	**58**	**86**	**73**	**5**	**4**	**4**	**188**	**14.9**	**31**						**14**	**5**	**12**	**17**	**10**	**3**	**0**	**0**
1997-98	**Colorado**	**NHL**	**72**	**25**	**66**	**91**	**94**	**7**	**3**	**7**	**202**	**12.4**	**6**						**7**	**6**	**5**	**11**	**12**	**2**	**0**	**0**
	Sweden	Olympics	4	1	4	5	6																			
1998-99	**Colorado**	**NHL**	**78**	**30**	**67**	**97**	**108**	**9**	**2**	**7**	**217**	**13.8**	**27**	**895**	**54.4**	**108**	**31**	**23:29**	**19**	**8**	**16**	***24**	**31**	**1**	**1**	**0**
	NHL Totals		**344**	**128**	**312**	**440**	**338**	**31**	**12**	**24**	**910**	**14.1**		**895**	**54.4**	**108**	**31**	**23:29**	**68**	**31**	**48**	**79**	**75**	**10**	**1**	**1**

NHL/Upper Deck All-Rookie Team (1995) • Won Calder Memorial Trophy (1995) • NHL First All-Star Team (1998, 1999)

Played in NHL All-Star Game (1996, 1998, 1999)

Traded to **Quebec** by **Philadelphia** with Steve Duchesne, Kerry Huffman, Mike Ricci, Ron Hextall, Chris Simon, Philadelphia's 1st round choice in the 1993 (Jocelyn Thibault) and 1994 (later traded to Toronto — later traded to Washington — Washington selected Nolan Baumgartner) Entry Drafts and cash for Eric Lindros, June 30, 1992. Transferred to **Colorado** after **Quebec** franchise relocated, June 21, 1995.

						Regular Season														Playoffs						
Season	Club	League	GP	G	A	Pts	PIM	PP	SH	GW	S	%	+/−	TF	F%	H	SB	Min	GP	G	A	Pts	PIM	PP	SH	GW

FRANCIS, Ron — CAR.

Center. Shoots left. 6'3", 200 lbs. Born, Sault Ste. Marie, Ont., March 1, 1963. Hartford's 1st choice, 4th overall, in 1981 Entry Draft.

Season	Club	League	GP	G	A	Pts	PIM	PP	SH	GW	S	%	+/−	TF	F%	H	SB	Min	GP	G	A	Pts	PIM	PP	SH	GW
1979-80	S.S. Marie Legion	OMHA	45	57	92	149	....																			
1980-81	S.S. Marie	OHA	64	26	43	69	33												19	7	8	15	34			
1981-82	S.S. Marie	OHL	25	18	30	48	46																			
	Hartford	NHL	59	25	43	68	51	12	0	1	163	15.3	−13													
1982-83	Hartford	NHL	79	31	59	90	60	4	2	4	212	14.6	−25													
1983-84	Hartford	NHL	72	23	60	83	45	5	0	5	202	11.4	−10													
1984-85	Hartford	NHL	80	24	57	81	66	4	0	1	195	12.3	−23													
1985-86	Hartford	NHL	53	24	53	77	24	7	1	4	120	20.0	8						10	1	2	3	4	0	0	0
1986-87	Hartford	NHL	75	30	63	93	45	7	0	7	189	15.9	10						6	2	2	4	6	1	0	0
1987-88	Hartford	NHL	80	25	50	75	87	11	1	3	172	14.5	−8						6	2	5	7	2	1	0	0
1988-89	Hartford	NHL	69	29	48	77	36	8	0	1	156	18.6	4						4	0	2	2	0	0	0	0
1989-90	Hartford	NHL	80	32	69	101	73	15	1	5	170	18.8	13						7	3	3	6	8	1	0	0
1990-91	Hartford	NHL	67	21	55	76	51	10	1	6	149	14.1	−2													
♦	Pittsburgh	NHL	14	2	9	11	21	0	0	1	25	8.0	0						24	7	10	17	24	0	0	4
1991-92 ♦	Pittsburgh	NHL	70	21	33	54	30	5	1	2	121	17.4	−7						21	8	*19	27	6	2	0	2
1992-93	Pittsburgh	NHL	84	24	76	100	68	9	2	4	215	11.2	6						12	6	11	17	19	1	0	1
1993-94	Pittsburgh	NHL	82	27	66	93	62	8	0	2	216	12.5	−3						6	0	2	2	6	0	0	0
1994-95	Pittsburgh	NHL	44	11	*48	59	18	3	0	1	94	11.7	30						12	6	13	19	4	2	0	0
1995-96	Pittsburgh	NHL	77	27	*92	119	56	12	1	4	158	17.1	25						11	3	6	9	4	2	0	1
1996-97	Pittsburgh	NHL	81	27	63	90	20	10	1	5	183	14.8	7						5	1	2	3	2	1	0	0
1997-98	Pittsburgh	NHL	81	25	62	87	20	7	0	5	189	13.2	12						6	1	5	6	2	0	0	0
1998-99	Carolina	NHL	82	21	31	52	34	8	0	2	133	15.8	−2	1589	51.5	36	57	21:55	3	0	1	1	0	0	0	0
	NHL Totals		1329	449	1037	1486	867	145	11	63	3062	14.7		1589	51.5	36	57	21:55	133	40	83	123	87	11	0	8

Won Alka-Seltzer Plus Award (1995) • Won Frank J. Selke Trophy (1995) • Won Lady Byng Trophy (1995, 1998)
Played in NHL All-Star Game (1983, 1985, 1990, 1998)
Traded to **Pittsburgh** by **Hartford** with Grant Jennings and Ulf Samuelsson for John Cullen, Jeff Parker and Zarley Zalapski, March 4, 1991. Signed as a free agent by **Carolina**, July 13, 1998.

FRASER, Scott

Center. Shoots right. 6'1", 178 lbs. Born, Moncton, N.B., May 3, 1972. Montreal's 12th choice, 193rd overall, in 1991 Entry Draft.

Season	Club	League	GP	G	A	Pts	PIM	PP	SH	GW	S	%	+/−	TF	F%	H	SB	Min	GP	G	A	Pts	PIM	PP	SH	GW
1989-90	Moncton	NBAHA	STATISTICS NOT AVAILABLE																							
1990-91	Dartmouth	ECAC	24	10	10	20	30																			
1991-92	Dartmouth	ECAC	24	11	7	18	60																			
1992-93	Dartmouth	ECAC	26	21	23	44	13																			
	Canada	Nat-Team	5	1	0	1	0																			
1993-94	Dartmouth	ECAC	24	17	13	30	34																			
	Canada	Nat-Team	4	0	1	1	4																			
1994-95	Fredericton	AHL	65	23	25	48	36												16	3	5	8	14			
	Wheeling	ECHL	8	4	2	6	8																			
1995-96	**Montreal**	**NHL**	15	2	0	2	4	0	0	0	9	22.2	−1													
	Fredericton	AHL	58	37	37	74	43												10	9	7	16	2			
1996-97	Fredericton	AHL	7	3	8	11	0																			
	Saint John	AHL	37	22	10	32	24																			
	San Antonio	IHL	8	0	1	1	2																			
	Carolina	AHL	18	9	19	28	12																			
1997-98	**Edmonton**	**NHL**	29	12	11	23	6	6	0	2	61	19.7	6						11	1	1	2	0	0	0	0
	Hamilton	AHL	50	29	32	61	26																			
1998-99	**NY Rangers**	**NHL**	28	2	4	6	14	1	0	0	35	5.7	−12	1	0.0	21	9	10:06								
	Hartford	AHL	36	13	24	37	30												6	4	3	7	4			
	NHL Totals		72	16	15	31	24	7	0	2	105	15.2		1	0.0	21	9	10:06	11	1	1	2	0	0	0	0

ECAC Second All-Star Team (1993)
Traded to **Calgary** by **Montreal** for David Ling and Calgary's 6th round choice in 1998 Entry Draft, October 24, 1996. Signed as a free agent by **Edmonton**, July 28, 1997. Signed as a free agent by **NY Rangers**, July 2, 1998.

FREER, Mark — (FRIHR)

Center. Shoots left. 5'10", 180 lbs. Born, Peterborough, Ont., July 14, 1968.

Season	Club	League	GP	G	A	Pts	PIM	PP	SH	GW	S	%	+/−	TF	F%	H	SB	Min	GP	G	A	Pts	PIM	PP	SH	GW
1984-85	Peterborough	OMHA	49	53	68	121	63																			
1985-86	Peterborough	OHL	65	16	28	44	24												14	3	4	7	13			
1986-87	Peterborough	OHL	65	39	43	82	44												12	2	6	8	5			
	Philadelphia	**NHL**	1	0	1	1	0	0	0	0	0	0.0	1													
1987-88	Peterborough	OHL	63	38	70	108	63												12	5	12	17	4			
	Philadelphia	**NHL**	1	0	0	0	0	0	0	0	0	0.0	−2													
1988-89	**Philadelphia**	**NHL**	5	0	1	1	0	0	0	0	1	0.0	0													
	Hershey	AHL	75	30	49	79	77												12	4	6	10	2			
1989-90	**Philadelphia**	**NHL**	2	0	0	0	0	0	0	0	2	0.0	0													
	Hershey	AHL	65	28	36	64	31												7	1	3	4	17			
1990-91	Hershey	AHL	77	18	44	62	45																			
1991-92	**Philadelphia**	**NHL**	50	6	7	13	18	0	0	2	41	14.6	−1													
	Hershey	AHL	31	13	11	24	38												6	0	3	3	2			
1992-93	**Ottawa**	**NHL**	63	10	14	24	39	3	3	0	80	12.5	−35													
1993-94	**Calgary**	**NHL**	2	0	0	0	4	0	0	0	0	0.0	0													
	Saint John	AHL	77	33	53	86	45												7	2	4	6	16			
1994-95	Houston	IHL	80	38	42	80	54												4	0	1	4	4			
1995-96	Houston	IHL	80	22	31	53	67																			
1996-97	Houston	IHL	81	21	36	57	43												12	2	3	5	4			
1997-98	Houston	IHL	74	14	38	52	41												4	2	2	4	4			
1998-99	Houston	IHL	79	17	28	45	66												19	*11	11	*22	12			
	NHL Totals		124	16	23	39	61	3	3	2	124	12.9														

Won "Bud" Poile Trophy (Playoff MVP - IHL) (1999)
Signed as a free agent by **Philadelphia**, October 7, 1986. Claimed by **Ottawa** from **Philadelphia** in Expansion Draft, June 18, 1992. Signed as a free agent by **Calgary**, August 10, 1993.

FRIEDMAN, Doug

Left wing. Shoots left. 6'1", 195 lbs. Born, Cape Elizabeth, ME, September 1, 1971. Quebec's 13th choice, 222nd overall, in 1991 Entry Draft.

Season	Club	League	GP	G	A	Pts	PIM	PP	SH	GW	S	%	+/−	TF	F%	H	SB	Min	GP	G	A	Pts	PIM	PP	SH	GW
1989-90	Lawrence Acad.	H.S.	20	9	26	35	....																			
1990-91	Boston University	H.E.	36	6	6	12	37																			
1991-92	Boston University	H.E.	34	11	8	19	42																			
1992-93	Boston University	H.E.	38	17	24	41	62																			
1993-94	Boston University	H.E.	41	9	23	32	110																			
1994-95	Cornwall	AHL	55	6	9	15	56												3	0	0	0	0			
1995-96	Cornwall	AHL	80	12	22	34	178												8	1	1	2	17			
1996-97	Hershey	AHL	61	12	21	33	245												23	6	9	15	49			
1997-98	**Edmonton**	**NHL**	16	0	0	0	20	0	0	0	8	0.0	0													
	Hamilton	AHL	55	19	27	46	235												9	4	4	8	40			

			Regular Season																Playoffs							
Season	Club	League	GP	G	A	Pts	PIM	PP	SH	GW	S	%	+/–	TF	F%	H	SB	Min	GP	G	A	Pts	PIM	PP	SH	GW
1998-99	Nashville	NHL	2	0	1	1	14	0	0	0	3	0.0	0	0	0.0	2	1	6:60								
	Milwaukee	IHL	69	26	25	51	251												2	1	2	3	8			
	NHL Totals		18	0	1	1	34	0	0	0	11	0.0		0	0.0	2	1	7:00								

Rights transferred to **Colorado** after **Quebec** franchise relocated, June 21, 1995. Signed as a free agent by **Edmonton**, July 14, 1997. Claimed by **Nashville** from **Edmonton** in Expansion Draft, June 26, 1998.

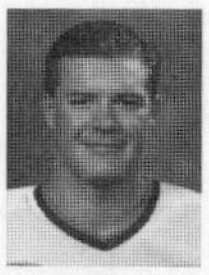

FRIESEN, Jeff

(FREE-zuhn) **S.J.**

Center. Shoots left. 6'1", 200 lbs. Born, Meadow Lake, Sask., August 5, 1976. San Jose's 1st choice, 11th overall, in 1994 Entry Draft.

1991-92	Saskatoon	SAHA	35	37	51	88	75																			
	Regina	WHL	4	3	1	4	2																			
1992-93	Regina	WHL	70	45	38	83	23												13	7	10	17	8			
1993-94	Regina	WHL	66	51	67	118	48												4	3	2	5	2			
	Canada	WJC-A	5	0	2	2	0																			
1994-95	Regina	WHL	25	21	23	44	22																			
	San Jose	NHL	48	15	10	25	14	5	1	2	86	17.4	–8						11	1	5	6	4	0	0	0
1995-96	San Jose	NHL	79	15	31	46	42	2	0	0	123	12.2	–19													
1996-97	San Jose	NHL	82	28	34	62	75	6	2	5	200	14.0	–8													
1997-98	San Jose	NHL	79	31	32	63	40	7	6	7	186	16.7	8						6	0	1	1	2	0	0	0
1998-99	San Jose	NHL	78	22	35	57	42	10	1	3	215	10.2	3	24	33.3	99	22	19:25	6	2	2	4	14	1	0	0
	NHL Totals		366	111	142	253	213	30	10	17	810	13.7		24	33.3	99	22	19:25	23	3	8	11	20	1	0	0

Canadian Major Junior Rookie of the Year (1993) • NHL/Upper Deck All-Rookie Team (1995)

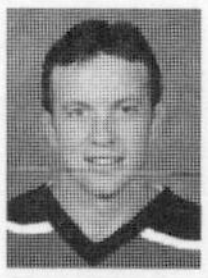

GAGNER, Dave

(GAH-nyay)

Center. Shoots left. 5'10", 188 lbs. Born, Chatham, Ont., December 11, 1964. NY Rangers' 1st choice, 12th overall, in 1983 Entry Draft.

1980-81	Newmarket	OJHL	41	33	55	88	42																			
1981-82	Brantford	OHL	68	30	46	76	31												11	3	6	9	6			
1982-83	Brantford	OHL	70	55	66	121	57												8	5	5	10	4			
1983-84	Brantford	OHL	12	7	13	20	4												6	0	4	4	6			
	Canada	Nat-Team	50	19	18	37	26																			
	Canada	Olympics	7	5	2	7	6																			
1984-85	NY Rangers	NHL	38	6	6	12	16	0	1	0	52	11.5	–16													
	New Haven	AHL	38	13	20	33	23																			
1985-86	NY Rangers	NHL	32	4	6	10	19	0	0	0	41	9.8	1													
	New Haven	AHL	16	10	11	21	11												4	1	2	3	2			
1986-87	NY Rangers	NHL	10	1	4	5	12	0	0	0	16	6.3	–1													
	New Haven	AHL	56	22	41	63	50												7	1	5	6	18			
1987-88	Minnesota	NHL	51	8	11	19	55	0	2	0	87	9.2	–14													
	Kalamazoo	IHL	14	16	10	26	26																			
1988-89	Minnesota	NHL	75	35	43	78	104	11	3	3	183	19.1	13													
	Kalamazoo	IHL	1	0	1	1	4																			
1989-90	Minnesota	NHL	79	40	38	78	54	10	0	3	238	16.8	–1						7	2	3	5	16	1	0	0
1990-91	Minnesota	NHL	73	40	42	82	114	20	0	5	223	17.9	9						23	12	15	27	28	6	1	1
1991-92	Minnesota	NHL	78	31	40	71	107	17	0	3	229	13.5	–4						7	2	4	6	8	2	0	0
1992-93	Minnesota	NHL	84	33	43	76	143	17	0	5	230	14.3	–13													
1993-94	Dallas	NHL	76	32	29	61	83	10	0	6	213	15.0	13						9	5	1	6	2	3	0	0
1994-95	Courmaosta	Italy	3	0	0	0	0																			
	Courmaosta	EuroHL	1	0	4	4	0																			
	Dallas	NHL	48	14	28	42	42	7	0	2	138	10.1	2						5	1	1	2	4	1	0	0
1995-96	Dallas	NHL	45	14	13	27	44	6	0	2	145	9.7	–17													
	Toronto	NHL	28	7	15	22	59	1	0	1	70	10.0	–2						6	0	2	2	6	0	0	0
1996-97	Calgary	NHL	82	27	33	60	48	9	0	4	228	11.8	2													
1997-98	Florida	NHL	78	20	28	48	55	5	1	1	165	12.1	–21													
1998-99	Florida	NHL	36	4	10	14	39	2	0	0	50	8.0	–7	236	55.5	17	11	13:36								
	Vancouver	NHL	33	2	12	14	24	0	0	1	50	4.0	–9	381	49.1	29	8	14:14								
	NHL Totals		946	318	401	719	1018	115	7	36	2358	13.5		617	51.5	46	19	13:54	57	22	26	48	64	13	1	1

OHL Second All-Star Team (1983)

Played in NHL All-Star Game (1991)

Traded to **Minnesota** by **NY Rangers** with Jay Caulfield for Jari Gronstrand and Paul Boutilier, October 8, 1987. Transferred to **Dallas** after **Minnesota** franchise relocated, June 9, 1993. Traded to **Toronto** by **Dallas** with Dallas' 6th round choice (Dmitriy Yakushin) in 1996 Entry Draft for Benoit Hogue and Randy Wood, January 29, 1996. Traded to **Calgary** by **Toronto** for Calgary's 3rd round choice (Mike Lankshear) in 1996 Entry Draft, June 22, 1996. Signed as a free agent by **Florida**, July 12, 1997. Traded to **Vancouver** by **Florida** with Ed Jovanovski, Mike Brown, Kevin Weekes and Florida's 1st round choice in 2000 Entry Draft for Pavel Bure, Bret Hedican, Brad Ference and Vancouver's 3rd round choice in 2000 Entry Draft, January 17, 1999.

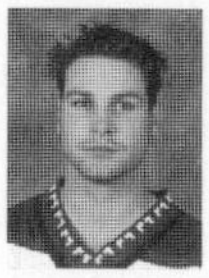

GAGNON, Sean

(gah-NYAWN) **PHX.**

Defense. Shoots left. 6'2", 219 lbs. Born, Sault Ste. Marie, Ont., September 11, 1973.

1989-90	S.S. Marie Elks	OMHA	46	21	26	47	218																			
1991-92	Sudbury	OHL	44	3	4	7	60												5	0	1	1	0			
1992-93	Sudbury	OHL	6	1	1	2	16																			
	Ottawa	OHL	33	2	10	12	68																			
	S.S. Marie	OHL	24	1	5	6	65												15	2	2	4	25			
1993-94	S.S. Marie	OHL	42	4	12	16	147												14	1	1	2	52			
1994-95	Dayton	ECHL	68	9	23	32	339												8	0	3	3	69			
1995-96	Dayton	ECHL	68	7	22	29	326												3	0	1	1	33			
1996-97	Fort Wayne	IHL	72	7	7	14	457																			
1997-98	Phoenix	NHL	5	0	1	1	14	0	0	0	3	0.0	1													
	Springfield	AHL	54	4	13	17	330												2	0	1	1	17			
1998-99	Phoenix	NHL	2	0	0	0	7	0	0	0	1	0.0	–2	0	0.0	1	2	7:56								
	Springfield	AHL	68	8	14	22	331												3	0	0	0	14			
	NHL Totals		7	0	1	1	21	0	0	0	4	0.0		0	0.0	1	2	7:56								

Signed as a free agent by **Phoenix**, May 14, 1997.

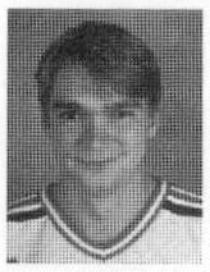

GALANOV, Maxim

(gah-LAH-nahf, mahx-EEM) **ATL.**

Defense. Shoots left. 6'1", 205 lbs. Born, Krasnoyarsk, USSR, March 13, 1974. NY Rangers' 3rd choice, 61st overall, in 1993 Entry Draft.

1992-93	Lada	CIS	41	4	2	6	12												10	1	1	2	12			
1993-94	Lada	CIS	7	1	0	1	4												12	1	0	1	8			
1994-95	Lada	CIS	45	5	6	11	54												9	0	1	1	12			
1995-96	Binghamton	AHL	72	17	36	53	24												4	1	1	2	0			
1996-97	Binghamton	AHL	73	13	30	43	30												3	0	0	0	2			
1997-98	NY Rangers	NHL	6	0	1	1	2	0	0	0	5	0.0	1													
	Hartford	AHL	61	6	24	30	22												13	3	6	9	2			
1998-99	Pittsburgh	NHL	51	4	3	7	14	2	0	0	44	9.1	–8	1	0.0	32	49	15:13	1	0	0	0	0	0	0	0
	NHL Totals		57	4	4	8	16	2	0	0	49	8.2		1	0.0	32	49	15:13	1	0	0	0	0	0	0	0

Claimed by **Pittsburgh** from **NY Rangers** in NHL Waiver Draft, October 5, 1998. Claimed by **Atlanta** from **Pittsburgh** in Expansion Draft, June 25, 1999.

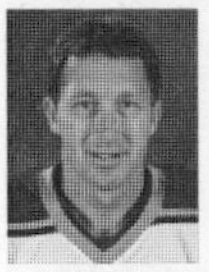

GALLEY, Garry

(GA-lee) **L.A.**

Defense. Shoots left. 6', 207 lbs. Born, Montreal, Que., April 16, 1963. Los Angeles' 4th choice, 103rd overall, in 1983 Entry Draft.

			Regular Season																Playoffs							
Season	Club	League	GP	G	A	Pts	PIM	PP	SH	GW	S	%	+/-	TF	F%	H	SB	Min	GP	G	A	Pts	PIM	PP	SH	GW
1979-80	Ottawa	OJHL	2	1	0	1	4	....	....	....	....	....	....	....	....	....	....	....	....	....	....	....	....	....	....	....
1980-81	Gloucester	OJHL	49	18	26	44	103	....	....	....	....	....	....	....	....	....	....	....	....	....	....	....	....	....	....	....
1981-82	Bowling Green	CCHA	42	3	36	39	48	....	....	....	....	....	....	....	....	....	....	....	....	....	....	....	....	....	....	....
1982-83	Bowling Green	CCHA	40	17	29	46	40	....	....	....	....	....	....	....	....	....	....	....	....	....	....	....	....	....	....	....
1983-84	Bowling Green	CCHA	44	15	52	67	61	....	....	....	....	....	....	....	....	....	....	....	....	....	....	....	....	....	....	....
1984-85	**Los Angeles**	**NHL**	**78**	**8**	**30**	**38**	**82**	**1**	**1**	**2**	**131**	**6.1**	**3**	....	....	....	....	....	**3**	**1**	**0**	**1**	**2**	**0**	**0**	**0**
1985-86	**Los Angeles**	**NHL**	**49**	**9**	**13**	**22**	**46**	**1**	**0**	**1**	**57**	**15.8**	**–9**	....	....	....	....	....	....	....	....	....	....	....	....	....
	New Haven	AHL	4	2	6	8	6	....	....	....	....	....	....	....	....	....	....	....	....	....	....	....	....	....	....	....
1986-87	**Los Angeles**	**NHL**	**30**	**5**	**11**	**16**	**57**	**2**	**0**	**1**	**43**	**11.6**	**–9**	....	....	....	....	....	....	....	....	....	....	....	....	....
	Washington	**NHL**	**18**	**1**	**10**	**11**	**10**	**1**	**0**	**0**	**27**	**3.7**	**3**	....	....	....	....	....	**2**	**0**	**0**	**0**	**0**	**0**	**0**	**0**
1987-88	**Washington**	**NHL**	**58**	**7**	**23**	**30**	**44**	**3**	**0**	**0**	**100**	**7.0**	**11**	....	....	....	....	....	**13**	**2**	**4**	**6**	**13**	**0**	**0**	**0**
1988-89	**Boston**	**NHL**	**78**	**8**	**22**	**30**	**80**	**2**	**1**	**0**	**145**	**5.5**	**–7**	....	....	....	....	....	**9**	**0**	**1**	**1**	**33**	**0**	**0**	**0**
1989-90	**Boston**	**NHL**	**71**	**8**	**27**	**35**	**75**	**1**	**0**	**0**	**142**	**5.6**	**2**	....	....	....	....	....	**21**	**3**	**3**	**6**	**34**	**1**	**0**	**2**
1990-91	**Boston**	**NHL**	**70**	**6**	**21**	**27**	**84**	**1**	**0**	**0**	**128**	**4.7**	**0**	....	....	....	....	....	**16**	**1**	**5**	**6**	**17**	**0**	**0**	**0**
1991-92	**Boston**	**NHL**	**38**	**2**	**12**	**14**	**83**	**1**	**0**	**0**	**51**	**3.9**	**–3**	....	....	....	....	....	....	....	....	....	....	....	....	....
	Philadelphia	**NHL**	**39**	**3**	**15**	**18**	**34**	**2**	**0**	**1**	**74**	**4.1**	**1**	....	....	....	....	....	....	....	....	....	....	....	....	....
1992-93	**Philadelphia**	**NHL**	**83**	**13**	**49**	**62**	**115**	**4**	**1**	**3**	**231**	**5.6**	**18**	....	....	....	....	....	....	....	....	....	....	....	....	....
1993-94	**Philadelphia**	**NHL**	**81**	**10**	**60**	**70**	**91**	**5**	**1**	**0**	**186**	**5.4**	**–11**	....	....	....	....	....	....	....	....	....	....	....	....	....
1994-95	**Philadelphia**	**NHL**	**33**	**2**	**20**	**22**	**20**	**1**	**0**	**0**	**66**	**3.0**	**0**	....	....	....	....	....	....	....	....	....	....	....	....	....
	Buffalo	**NHL**	**14**	**1**	**9**	**10**	**10**	**2**	**0**	**0**	**31**	**3.2**	**4**	....	....	....	....	....	**5**	**0**	**3**	**3**	**4**	**0**	**0**	**0**
1995-96	**Buffalo**	**NHL**	**78**	**10**	**44**	**54**	**81**	**7**	**1**	**2**	**175**	**5.7**	**–2**	....	....	....	....	....	....	....	....	....	....	....	....	....
1996-97	**Buffalo**	**NHL**	**71**	**4**	**34**	**38**	**102**	**1**	**1**	**1**	**84**	**4.8**	**10**	....	....	....	....	....	**12**	**0**	**6**	**6**	**14**	**0**	**0**	**0**
1997-98	**Los Angeles**	**NHL**	**74**	**9**	**28**	**37**	**63**	**7**	**0**	**0**	**128**	**7.0**	**–5**	....	....	....	....	....	**4**	**0**	**1**	**1**	**2**	**0**	**0**	**0**
1998-99	**Los Angeles**	**NHL**	**60**	**4**	**12**	**16**	**30**	**3**	**0**	**0**	**77**	**5.2**	**–9**	**0**	**0.0**	**100**	**59**	**17:16**	....	....	....	....	....	....	....	....
	NHL Totals		**1023**	**110**	**440**	**550**	**1107**	**45**	**6**	**11**	**1876**	**5.9**		**0**	**0.0**	**100**	**59**	**17:16**	**85**	**7**	**23**	**30**	**119**	**1**	**0**	**2**

CCHA First All-Star Team (1983, 1984) • NCAA East First All-American Team (1984) • NCAA Championship All-Tournament Team (1984)

Played in NHL All-Star Game (1991, 1994)

Traded to **Washington** by **LA Kings** for Al Jensen, February 14, 1987. Signed as a free agent by **Boston**, July 8, 1988. Traded to **Philadelphia** by **Boston** with Wes Walz and Boston's 3rd round choice (Milos Holan) in 1993 Entry Draft for Gord Murphy, Brian Dobbin, Philadelphia's 3rd round choice (Sergei Zholtok) in 1992 Entry Draft and 4th round choice (Charles Paquette) in 1993 Entry Draft, January 2, 1992. Traded to **Buffalo** by **Philadelphia** for Petr Svoboda, April 7, 1995. Signed as a free agent by **LA Kings**, July 15, 1997.

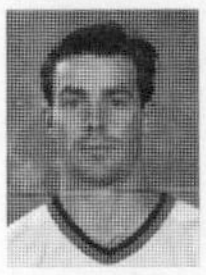

GARDINER, Bruce

OTT.

Center. Shoots right. 6'1", 193 lbs. Born, Barrie, Ont., February 11, 1972. St. Louis' 6th choice, 131st overall, in 1991 Entry Draft.

			Regular Season																Playoffs							
Season	Club	League	GP	G	A	Pts	PIM	PP	SH	GW	S	%	+/-	TF	F%	H	SB	Min	GP	G	A	Pts	PIM	PP	SH	GW
1990-91	Colgate	ECAC	27	4	9	13	72	....	....	....	....	....	....	....	....	....	....	....	....	....	....	....	....	....	....	....
1991-92	Colgate	ECAC	23	7	8	15	77	....	....	....	....	....	....	....	....	....	....	....	....	....	....	....	....	....	....	....
1992-93	Colgate	ECAC	33	17	12	29	64	....	....	....	....	....	....	....	....	....	....	....	....	....	....	....	....	....	....	....
1993-94	Colgate	ECAC	33	23	23	46	68	....	....	....	....	....	....	....	....	....	....	....	....	....	....	....	....	....	....	....
	Peoria	IHL	3	0	0	0	0	....	....	....	....	....	....	....	....	....	....	....	....	....	....	....	....	....	....	....
1994-95	P.E.I. Senators	AHL	72	17	20	37	132	....	....	....	....	....	....	....	....	....	....	....	7	4	1	5	4	....	....	....
1995-96	P.E.I. Senators	AHL	38	11	13	24	87	....	....	....	....	....	....	....	....	....	....	....	5	2	4	6	4	....	....	....
1996-97	**Ottawa**	**NHL**	**67**	**11**	**10**	**21**	**49**	**0**	**1**	**2**	**94**	**11.7**	**4**	....	....	....	....	....	**7**	**0**	**1**	**1**	**2**	**0**	**0**	**0**
1997-98	**Ottawa**	**NHL**	**55**	**7**	**11**	**18**	**50**	**0**	**0**	**0**	**64**	**10.9**	**2**	....	....	....	....	....	**11**	**1**	**3**	**4**	**2**	**0**	**0**	**1**
1998-99	**Ottawa**	**NHL**	**59**	**4**	**8**	**12**	**43**	**0**	**0**	**1**	**70**	**5.7**	**6**	**278**	**45.7**	**88**	**17**	**12:52**	**3**	**0**	**0**	**0**	**4**	**0**	**0**	**0**
	NHL Totals		**181**	**22**	**29**	**51**	**142**	**0**	**1**	**3**	**228**	**9.6**		**278**	**45.7**	**88**	**17**	**12:52**	**21**	**1**	**4**	**5**	**8**	**0**	**0**	**1**

ECAC Second All-Star Team (1994)

Signed as a free agent by **Ottawa**, June 14, 1994.

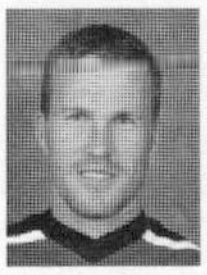

GARPENLOV, Johan

(GAHR-pehn-LAHV, YOH-hahn) **ATL.**

Left wing. Shoots left. 5'11", 185 lbs. Born, Stockholm, Sweden, March 21, 1968. Detroit's 5th choice, 85th overall, in 1986 Entry Draft.

			Regular Season																Playoffs							
Season	Club	League	GP	G	A	Pts	PIM	PP	SH	GW	S	%	+/-	TF	F%	H	SB	Min	GP	G	A	Pts	PIM	PP	SH	GW
1984-85	Hacka HK	Sweden-2	4	1	2	3	2	....	....	....	....	....	....	....	....	....	....	....	....	....	....	....	....	....	....	....
1985-86	Hacka HK	Sweden-2	20	8	12	20	22	....	....	....	....	....	....	....	....	....	....	....	....	....	....	....	....	....	....	....
1986-87	Djurgardens IF	Sweden	29	5	8	13	22	....	....	....	....	....	....	....	....	....	....	....	2	0	0	0	0	....	....	....
1987-88	Djurgardens IF	Sweden	30	7	10	17	12	....	....	....	....	....	....	....	....	....	....	....	3	1	3	4	4	....	....	....
1988-89	Djurgardens IF	Sweden	36	17	19	31	20	....	....	....	....	....	....	....	....	....	....	....	8	3	4	7	10	....	....	....
1989-90	Djurgardens IF	Sweden	39	20	13	33	35	....	....	....	....	....	....	....	....	....	....	....	8	2	4	6	4	....	....	....
1990-91	**Detroit**	**NHL**	**71**	**18**	**22**	**40**	**18**	**2**	**0**	**3**	**91**	**19.8**	**–4**	....	....	....	....	....	**6**	**0**	**1**	**1**	**4**	**0**	**0**	**0**
1991-92	**Detroit**	**NHL**	**16**	**1**	**1**	**2**	**4**	**0**	**0**	**0**	**13**	**7.7**	**2**	....	....	....	....	....	....	....	....	....	....	....	....	....
	Adirondack	AHL	9	3	3	6	6	....	....	....	....	....	....	....	....	....	....	....	....	....	....	....	....	....	....	....
	San Jose	**NHL**	**12**	**5**	**6**	**11**	**4**	**1**	**0**	**1**	**21**	**23.8**	**–2**	....	....	....	....	....	....	....	....	....	....	....	....	....
1992-93	**San Jose**	**NHL**	**79**	**22**	**44**	**66**	**56**	**14**	**0**	**1**	**171**	**12.9**	**–26**	....	....	....	....	....	....	....	....	....	....	....	....	....
1993-94	**San Jose**	**NHL**	**80**	**18**	**35**	**53**	**28**	**7**	**0**	**3**	**125**	**14.4**	**9**	....	....	....	....	....	**14**	**4**	**6**	**10**	**6**	**0**	**0**	**2**
1994-95	**San Jose**	**NHL**	**13**	**1**	**1**	**2**	**2**	**0**	**0**	**0**	**16**	**6.3**	**–3**	....	....	....	....	....	....	....	....	....	....	....	....	....
	Florida	**NHL**	**27**	**3**	**9**	**12**	**0**	**0**	**0**	**0**	**28**	**10.7**	**4**	....	....	....	....	....	....	....	....	....	....	....	....	....
1995-96	**Florida**	**NHL**	**82**	**23**	**28**	**51**	**36**	**8**	**0**	**7**	**130**	**17.7**	**–10**	....	....	....	....	....	**20**	**4**	**2**	**6**	**8**	**0**	**0**	**0**
1996-97	**Florida**	**NHL**	**53**	**11**	**25**	**36**	**47**	**1**	**0**	**1**	**83**	**13.3**	**10**	....	....	....	....	....	**4**	**2**	**0**	**2**	**4**	**2**	**0**	**1**
1997-98	**Florida**	**NHL**	**39**	**2**	**3**	**5**	**8**	**0**	**0**	**0**	**43**	**4.7**	**–6**	....	....	....	....	....	....	....	....	....	....	....	....	....
1998-99	**Florida**	**NHL**	**64**	**8**	**9**	**17**	**42**	**0**	**1**	**0**	**71**	**11.3**	**–9**	**3**	**0.0**	**23**	**13**	**13:14**	....	....	....	....	....	....	....	....
	NHL Totals		**536**	**112**	**183**	**295**	**245**	**33**	**1**	**16**	**792**	**14.1**		**3**	**0.0**	**23**	**13**	**13:14**	**44**	**10**	**9**	**19**	**22**	**2**	**0**	**3**

Traded to **San Jose** by **Detroit** for Bob McGill and Vancouver's 8th round choice (previously acquired, San Jose selected C.J. Denomme) in 1992 Entry Draft, March 9, 1992. Traded to **Florida** by **San Jose** for future considerations, March 3, 1995. Claimed by **Atlanta** from **Florida** in Expansion Draft, June 25, 1999.

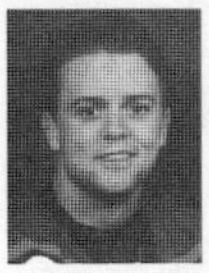

GAUL, Michael

(GAWL) **COL.**

Defense. Shoots right. 6'1", 200 lbs. Born, Lachine, Que., April 22, 1973. Los Angeles' 10th choice, 262nd overall, in 1991 Entry Draft.

			Regular Season																Playoffs							
Season	Club	League	GP	G	A	Pts	PIM	PP	SH	GW	S	%	+/-	TF	F%	H	SB	Min	GP	G	A	Pts	PIM	PP	SH	GW
1989-90	Lac St-Louis	QAAA	39	5	9	14	....	....	....	....	....	....	....	....	....	....	....	....	....	....	....	....	....	....	....	....
1990-91	St. Lawrence	ECAC	31	1	3	4	46	....	....	....	....	....	....	....	....	....	....	....	....	....	....	....	....	....	....	....
1991-92	Laval	QMJHL	50	6	38	44	44	....	....	....	....	....	....	....	....	....	....	....	10	0	2	2	20	....	....	....
1992-93	Laval	QMJHL	57	16	57	73	66	....	....	....	....	....	....	....	....	....	....	....	13	3	10	13	10	....	....	....
1993-94	Laval	QMJHL	22	10	17	27	24	....	....	....	....	....	....	....	....	....	....	....	21	5	15	20	14	....	....	....
1994-95	Phoenix	IHL	4	0	1	1	2	....	....	....	....	....	....	....	....	....	....	....	....	....	....	....	....	....	....	....
	Knoxville	ECHL	68	13	41	54	51	....	....	....	....	....	....	....	....	....	....	....	4	2	1	3	2	....	....	....
1995-96	Knoxville	ECHL	54	13	48	61	44	....	....	....	....	....	....	....	....	....	....	....	....	....	....	....	....	....	....	....
1996-97	ETC Timmendorf	German-2	51	40	52	92	100	....	....	....	....	....	....	....	....	....	....	....	....	....	....	....	....	....	....	....
1997-98	Hershey	AHL	60	12	47	59	69	....	....	....	....	....	....	....	....	....	....	....	7	0	7	7	6	....	....	....
	Mobile	ECHL	5	0	7	7	0	....	....	....	....	....	....	....	....	....	....	....	....	....	....	....	....	....	....	....
1998-99	Lowell	AHL	18	3	5	8	14	....	....	....	....	....	....	....	....	....	....	....	....	....	....	....	....	....	....	....
	Colorado	**NHL**	**1**	**0**	**0**	**0**	**0**	**0**	**0**	**0**	**1**	**0.0**	**0**	**0**	**0.0**	**2**	**0**	**10:46**	....	....	....	....	....	....	....	....
	Hershey	AHL	43	9	31	40	22	....	....	....	....	....	....	....	....	....	....	....	5	1	1	2	6	....	....	....
	NHL Totals		**1**	**0**	**0**	**0**	**0**	**0**	**0**	**0**	**1**	**0.0**		**0**	**0.0**	**2**	**0**	**10:46**	....	....	....	....	....	....	....	....

Signed as a free agent by **NY Islanders**, July 16, 1998. Traded to **Colorado** by **NY Islanders** for Ted Crowley, December 15, 1998.

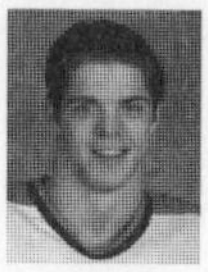

GAUTHIER, Denis

(GOH-tyay) **CGY.**

Defense. Shoots left. 6'2", 205 lbs. Born, Montreal, Que., October 1, 1976. Calgary's 1st choice, 20th overall, in 1995 Entry Draft.

			Regular Season																Playoffs							
Season	Club	League	GP	G	A	Pts	PIM	PP	SH	GW	S	%	+/-	TF	F%	H	SB	Min	GP	G	A	Pts	PIM	PP	SH	GW
1992-93	Drummondville	QMJHL	60	1	7	8	136	....	....	....	....	....	....	....	....	....	....	....	10	0	5	5	40	....	....	....
1993-94	Drummondville	QMJHL	60	0	7	7	176	....	....	....	....	....	....	....	....	....	....	....	9	2	0	2	41	....	....	....
1994-95	Drummondville	QMJHL	64	9	31	40	190	....	....	....	....	....	....	....	....	....	....	....	4	0	5	5	12	....	....	....
1995-96	Drummondville	QMJHL	53	25	49	74	140	....	....	....	....	....	....	....	....	....	....	....	6	4	4	8	32	....	....	....
	Saint John	AHL	5	2	0	2	8	....	....	....	....	....	....	....	....	....	....	....	16	1	6	7	20	....	....	....
1996-97	Saint John	AHL	73	3	28	31	74	....	....	....	....	....	....	....	....	....	....	....	5	0	0	0	6	....	....	....
1997-98	**Calgary**	**NHL**	**10**	**0**	**0**	**0**	**16**	**0**	**0**	**0**	**3**	**0.0**	**–5**	....	....	....	....	....	....	....	....	....	....	....	....	....
	Saint John	AHL	68	4	20	24	154	....	....	....	....	....	....	....	....	....	....	....	21	0	4	4	83	....	....	....
1998-99	**Calgary**	**NHL**	**55**	**3**	**4**	**7**	**68**	**0**	**0**	**0**	**40**	**7.5**	**3**	**0**	**0.0**	**162**	**51**	**12:41**	....	....	....	....	....	....	....	....
	Saint John	AHL	16	0	3	3	31	....	....	....	....	....	....	....	....	....	....	....	....	....	....	....	....	....	....	....
	NHL Totals		**65**	**3**	**4**	**7**	**84**	**0**	**0**	**0**	**43**	**7.0**		**0**	**0.0**	**162**	**51**	**12:41**	....	....	....	....	....	....	....	....

QMJHL First All-Star Team (1996) • Canadian Major Junior First All-Star Team (1996)

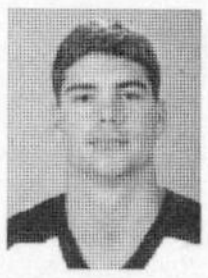

GAVEY, Aaron

(GAY-vee) **DAL.**

Center. Shoots left. 6'2", 200 lbs. Born, Sudbury, Ont., February 22, 1974. Tampa Bay's 4th choice, 74th overall, in 1992 Entry Draft.

Season	Club	League	GP	G	A	Pts	PIM	PP	SH	GW	S	%	+/-	TF	F%	H	SB	Min	GP	G	A	Pts	PIM	PP	SH	GW
1990-91	Peterborough	OJHL-B	42	26	30	56	68	....	....	....	....	....	....	....	....	....	....	....	....	....	....	....	....	....	....	....
1991-92	S.S. Marie	OHL	48	7	11	18	27	....	....	....	....	....	....	....	....	....	....	....	19	5	1	6	10	....	....	....
1992-93	S.S. Marie	OHL	62	45	39	84	116	....	....	....	....	....	....	....	....	....	....	....	18	5	9	14	36	....	....	....
1993-94	S.S. Marie	OHL	60	42	60	102	116	....	....	....	....	....	....	....	....	....	....	....	14	11	10	21	22	....	....	....
1994-95	Atlanta	IHL	66	18	17	35	85	....	....	....	....	....	....	....	....	....	....	....	5	0	1	1	9	....	....	....
1995-96	**Tampa Bay**	**NHL**	**73**	**8**	**4**	**12**	**56**	**1**	**1**	**2**	**65**	**12.3**	**–6**	....	....	....	....	....	**6**	**0**	**0**	**0**	**4**	**0**	**0**	**0**
1996-97	**Tampa Bay**	**NHL**	**16**	**1**	**2**	**3**	**12**	**0**	**0**	**0**	**8**	**12.5**	**–1**	....	....	....	....	....	....	....	....	....	....	....	....	....
	Calgary	**NHL**	**41**	**7**	**9**	**16**	**34**	**3**	**0**	**1**	**54**	**13.0**	**–11**	....	....	....	....	....	....	....	....	....	....	....	....	....
1997-98	**Calgary**	**NHL**	**26**	**2**	**3**	**5**	**24**	**0**	**0**	**1**	**27**	**7.4**	**–5**	....	....	....	....	....	....	....	....	....	....	....	....	....
	Saint John	AHL	8	4	3	7	28	....	....	....	....	....	....	....	....	....	....	....	....	....	....	....	....	....	....	....
1998-99	**Dallas**	**NHL**	**7**	**0**	**0**	**0**	**10**	**0**	**0**	**0**	**4**	**0.0**	**–1**	**43**	**48.8**	**13**	**0**	**8:09**	....	....	....	....	....	....	....	....
	Michigan	IHL	67	24	33	57	128	....	....	....	....	....	....	....	....	....	....	....	5	2	3	5	4	....	....	....
	NHL Totals		**163**	**18**	**18**	**36**	**136**	**4**	**1**	**4**	**158**	**11.4**		**43**	**48.8**	**13**	**0**	**8:09**	**6**	**0**	**0**	**0**	**4**	**0**	**0**	**0**

Traded to **Calgary** by **Tampa Bay** for Rick Tabaracci, November 19, 1996. Traded to **Dallas** by **Calgary** for Bob Bassen, July 14, 1998.

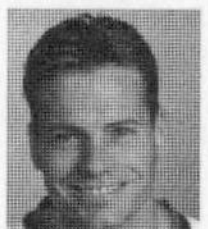

GELINAS, Martin

(ZHEHL-in-nuh, MAHR-ta) **CAR.**

Left wing. Shoots left. 5'11", 195 lbs. Born, Shawinigan, Que., June 5, 1970. Los Angeles' 1st choice, 7th overall, in 1988 Entry Draft.

Season	Club	League	GP	G	A	Pts	PIM	PP	SH	GW	S	%	+/-	TF	F%	H	SB	Min	GP	G	A	Pts	PIM	PP	SH	GW
1986-87	Montreal West	QAAA	41	36	42	78	36	....	....	....	....	....	....	....	....	....	....	....	....	....	....	....	....	....	....	....
1987-88	Hull	QMJHL	65	63	68	131	74	....	....	....	....	....	....	....	....	....	....	....	17	15	18	33	32	....	....	....
1988-89	Hull	QMJHL	41	38	39	77	31	....	....	....	....	....	....	....	....	....	....	....	9	5	4	9	14	....	....	....
	Edmonton	**NHL**	**6**	**1**	**2**	**3**	**0**	**0**	**0**	**0**	**14**	**7.1**	**–1**	....	....	....	....	....	....	....	....	....	....	....	....	....
1989-90♦	**Edmonton**	**NHL**	**46**	**17**	**8**	**25**	**30**	**5**	**0**	**2**	**71**	**23.9**	**0**	....	....	....	....	....	**20**	**2**	**3**	**5**	**6**	**0**	**0**	**0**
1990-91	**Edmonton**	**NHL**	**73**	**20**	**20**	**40**	**34**	**4**	**0**	**2**	**124**	**16.1**	**–7**	....	....	....	....	....	**18**	**3**	**6**	**9**	**25**	**0**	**0**	**1**
1991-92	**Edmonton**	**NHL**	**68**	**11**	**18**	**29**	**62**	**1**	**0**	**0**	**94**	**11.7**	**14**	....	....	....	....	....	**15**	**1**	**3**	**4**	**10**	**0**	**0**	**0**
1992-93	**Edmonton**	**NHL**	**65**	**11**	**12**	**23**	**30**	**0**	**0**	**1**	**93**	**11.8**	**3**	....	....	....	....	....	....	....	....	....	....	....	....	....
1993-94	**Quebec**	**NHL**	**31**	**6**	**6**	**12**	**8**	**0**	**0**	**0**	**53**	**11.3**	**–2**	....	....	....	....	....	....	....	....	....	....	....	....	....
	Vancouver	**NHL**	**33**	**8**	**8**	**16**	**26**	**3**	**0**	**1**	**54**	**14.8**	**–6**	....	....	....	....	....	**24**	**5**	**4**	**9**	**14**	**2**	**0**	**1**
1994-95	**Vancouver**	**NHL**	**46**	**13**	**10**	**23**	**36**	**1**	**0**	**4**	**75**	**17.3**	**8**	....	....	....	....	....	**3**	**0**	**1**	**1**	**0**	**0**	**0**	**0**
1995-96	**Vancouver**	**NHL**	**81**	**30**	**26**	**56**	**59**	**3**	**4**	**5**	**181**	**16.6**	**8**	....	....	....	....	....	**6**	**1**	**1**	**2**	**12**	**1**	**0**	**0**
1996-97	**Vancouver**	**NHL**	**74**	**35**	**33**	**68**	**42**	**6**	**1**	**3**	**177**	**19.8**	**6**	....	....	....	....	....	....	....	....	....	....	....	....	....
1997-98	**Vancouver**	**NHL**	**24**	**4**	**4**	**8**	**10**	**1**	**1**	**1**	**49**	**8.2**	**–6**	....	....	....	....	....	....	....	....	....	....	....	....	....
	Carolina	**NHL**	**40**	**12**	**14**	**26**	**30**	**2**	**1**	**4**	**98**	**12.2**	**1**	....	....	....	....	....	....	....	....	....	....	....	....	....
1998-99	**Carolina**	**NHL**	**76**	**13**	**15**	**28**	**67**	**0**	**0**	**2**	**111**	**11.7**	**3**	**6**	**50.0**	**70**	**13**	**13:13**	**6**	**0**	**3**	**3**	**2**	**0**	**0**	**0**
	NHL Totals		**663**	**181**	**176**	**357**	**434**	**26**	**7**	**25**	**1194**	**15.2**		**6**	**50.0**	**70**	**13**	**13:13**	**92**	**12**	**21**	**33**	**69**	**3**	**0**	**2**

QMJHL First All-Star Team (1988) • Canadian Major Junior Rookie of the Year (1988) • Won George Parsons Trophy (Memorial Cup Tournament Most Sportsmanlike Player) (1988)

Traded to **Edmonton** by **LA Kings** with Jimmy Carson and LA Kings' 1st round choices in 1989 (previously acquired, New Jersey selected Jason Miller), 1991 (Martin Rucinsky) and 1993 (Nick Stajduhar) Entry Drafts and cash for Wayne Gretzky, Mike Krushelnyski and Marty McSorley, August 9, 1988. Traded to **Quebec** by **Edmonton** with Edmonton's 6th round choice (Nicholas Checco) in 1993 Entry Draft for Scott Pearson, June 20, 1993. Claimed on waivers by **Vancouver** from **Quebec**, January 15, 1994. Traded to **Carolina** by **Vancouver** with Kirk McLean for Sean Burke, Geoff Sanderson and Enrico Ciccone, January 3, 1998.

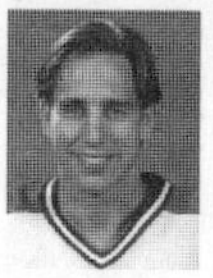

GENDRON, Martin

(ZHEHN-drawn) **VAN.**

Right wing. Shoots right. 5'9", 190 lbs. Born, Valleyfield, Que., February 15, 1974. Washington's 4th choice, 71st overall, in 1992 Entry Draft.

Season	Club	League	GP	G	A	Pts	PIM	PP	SH	GW	S	%	+/-	TF	F%	H	SB	Min	GP	G	A	Pts	PIM	PP	SH	GW
1989-90	Lac St-Louis	QAAA	42	42	32	74	26	....	....	....	....	....	....	....	....	....	....	....	2	3	1	4	0	....	....	....
1990-91	St-Hyacinthe	QMJHL	55	34	23	57	33	....	....	....	....	....	....	....	....	....	....	....	4	1	2	3	0	....	....	....
1991-92	St-Hyacinthe	QMJHL	69	*71	66	137	45	....	....	....	....	....	....	....	....	....	....	....	6	7	4	11	14	....	....	....
1992-93	St-Hyacinthe	QMJHL	63	73	61	134	44	....	....	....	....	....	....	....	....	....	....	....	....	....	....	....	....	....	....	....
	Baltimore	AHL	10	1	2	3	2	....	....	....	....	....	....	....	....	....	....	....	3	0	0	0	0	....	....	....
1993-94	Hull	QMJHL	37	39	36	75	18	....	....	....	....	....	....	....	....	....	....	....	20	*21	17	38	8	....	....	....
	Canada	Nat-Team	19	4	5	9	2	....	....	....	....	....	....	....	....	....	....	....	....	....	....	....	....	....	....	....
1994-95	**Washington**	**NHL**	**8**	**2**	**1**	**3**	**2**	**0**	**0**	**0**	**11**	**18.2**	**3**	....	....	....	....	....	....	....	....	....	....	....	....	....
	Portland	AHL	72	36	32	68	54	....	....	....	....	....	....	....	....	....	....	....	4	5	1	6	2	....	....	....
1995-96	**Washington**	**NHL**	**20**	**2**	**1**	**3**	**8**	**0**	**0**	**0**	**22**	**9.1**	**–5**	....	....	....	....	....	....	....	....	....	....	....	....	....
	Portland	AHL	48	38	29	67	39	....	....	....	....	....	....	....	....	....	....	....	22	*15	18	33	8	....	....	....
1996-97	Las Vegas	IHL	81	51	39	90	20	....	....	....	....	....	....	....	....	....	....	....	3	2	1	3	0	....	....	....
1997-98	**Chicago**	**NHL**	**2**	**0**	**0**	**0**	**0**	**0**	**0**	**0**	**3**	**0.0**	**–1**	....	....	....	....	....	....	....	....	....	....	....	....	....
	Indianapolis	IHL	17	8	6	14	16	....	....	....	....	....	....	....	....	....	....	....	....	....	....	....	....	....	....	....
	Milwaukee	IHL	40	20	19	39	14	....	....	....	....	....	....	....	....	....	....	....	....	....	....	....	....	....	....	....
	Fredericton	AHL	10	5	10	15	4	....	....	....	....	....	....	....	....	....	....	....	2	0	0	0	4	....	....	....
1998-99	Fredericton	AHL	65	33	34	67	26	....	....	....	....	....	....	....	....	....	....	....	15	*12	5	17	2	....	....	....
	NHL Totals		**30**	**4**	**2**	**6**	**10**	**0**	**0**	**0**	**36**	**11.1**		....	....	....	....	....	....	....	....	....	....	....	....	....

QMJHL First All-Star Team (1992) • Canadian Major Junior Most Sportsmanlike Player of the Year (1992) • QMJHL Second All-Star Team (1993) • Canadian Major Junior First All-Star Team (1993)

Traded to **Chicago** by **Washington** with Washington's 6th round choice (Jonathan Pelletier) in 1998 Entry Draft for Chicago's 5th round choice (Erik Wendell) in 1998 Entry Draft, October 10, 1997. Traded to **Montreal** by **Chicago** for David Ling, March 14, 1998. Signed as a free agent **Vancouver**, August 25, 1999.

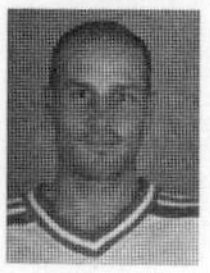

GERNANDER, Ken

(guhr-NAN-duhr) **NYR**

Center. Shoots left. 5'10", 180 lbs. Born, Coleraine, MN, June 30, 1969. Winnipeg's 4th choice, 96th overall, in 1987 Entry Draft.

Season	Club	League	GP	G	A	Pts	PIM	PP	SH	GW	S	%	+/-	TF	F%	H	SB	Min	GP	G	A	Pts	PIM	PP	SH	GW
1985-86	Greenway High	H.S.	23	14	23	37		....	....	....	....	....	....	....	....	....	....	....	....	....	....	....	....	....	....	....
1986-87	Greenway High	H.S.	26	35	34	69	....	....	....	....	....	....	....	....	....	....	....	....	....	....	....	....	....	....	....	....
1987-88	U. of Minnesota	WCHA	44	14	14	28	14	....	....	....	....	....	....	....	....	....	....	....	....	....	....	....	....	....	....	....
1988-89	U. of Minnesota	WCHA	44	9	11	20	2	....	....	....	....	....	....	....	....	....	....	....	....	....	....	....	....	....	....	....
1989-90	U. of Minnesota	WCHA	44	32	17	49	24	....	....	....	....	....	....	....	....	....	....	....	....	....	....	....	....	....	....	....
1990-91	U. of Minnesota	WCHA	44	23	20	43	24	....	....	....	....	....	....	....	....	....	....	....	....	....	....	....	....	....	....	....
1991-92	Fort Wayne	IHL	13	7	6	13	2	....	....	....	....	....	....	....	....	....	....	....	....	....	....	....	....	....	....	....
	Moncton	AHL	43	8	18	26	9	....	....	....	....	....	....	....	....	....	....	....	8	1	1	2	2	....	....	....
1992-93	Moncton	AHL	71	18	29	47	20	....	....	....	....	....	....	....	....	....	....	....	5	1	4	5	0	....	....	....
1993-94	Moncton	AHL	71	22	25	47	12	....	....	....	....	....	....	....	....	....	....	....	19	6	1	7	0	....	....	....
1994-95	Binghamton	AHL	80	28	25	53	24	....	....	....	....	....	....	....	....	....	....	....	11	2	2	4	6	....	....	....
1995-96	**NY Rangers**	**NHL**	**10**	**2**	**3**	**5**	**4**	**2**	**0**	**0**	**10**	**20.0**	**–3**	....	....	....	....	....	**6**	**0**	**0**	**0**	**0**	**0**	**0**	**0**
	Binghamton	AHL	63	44	29	73	38	....	....	....	....	....	....	....	....	....	....	....	....	....	....	....	....	....	....	....

			Regular Season																Playoffs							
Season	Club	League	GP	G	A	Pts	PIM	PP	SH	GW	S	%	+/–	TF	F%	H	SB	Min	GP	G	A	Pts	PIM	PP	SH	GW
1996-97	Binghamton	AHL	46	13	18	31	30	....	....	....	....	....	....	....	....	....	....	....	2	0	1	1	0	....	....	....
	NY Rangers	**NHL**	....	....	....	....	....	....	....	....	....	....	....	....	....	....	....	....	**9**	**0**	**0**	**0**	**0**	**0**	**0**	**0**
1997-98	Hartford	AHL	80	35	28	63	26	....	....	....	....	....	....	....	....	....	....	....	12	5	6	11	4	....	....	....
1998-99	Hartford	AHL	70	23	26	49	32	....	....	....	....	....	....	....	....	....	....	....	7	1	2	3	2	....	....	....
	NHL Totals		**10**	**2**	**3**	**5**	**4**	**2**	**0**	**0**	**10**	**20.0**		....	....	....	....	....	**15**	**0**	**0**	**0**	**0**	**0**	**0**	**0**

Won Fred Hunt Memorial Trophy (Sportsmanship — AHL) (1996)
Signed as a free agent by **NY Rangers**, July 4, 1994.

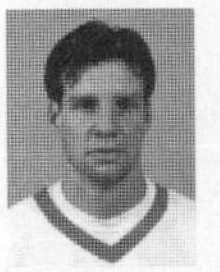

GILCHRIST, Brent — DET.

Left wing. Shoots left. 5'11", 180 lbs. Born, Moose Jaw, Sask., April 3, 1967. Montreal's 6th choice, 79th overall, in 1985 Entry Draft.

Season	Club	League	GP	G	A	Pts	PIM	PP	SH	GW	S	%	+/–	TF	F%	H	SB	Min	GP	G	A	Pts	PIM	PP	SH	GW
1983-84	Kelowna	WHL	69	16	11	27	16	....	....	....	....	....	....	....	....	....	....	....	....	....	....	....	....	....	....	....
1984-85	Kelowna	WHL	51	35	38	73	58	....	....	....	....	....	....	....	....	....	....	....	6	5	2	7	8	....	....	....
1985-86	Spokane	WHL	52	45	45	90	57	....	....	....	....	....	....	....	....	....	....	....	9	6	7	13	19	....	....	....
1986-87	Spokane	WHL	46	45	55	100	71	....	....	....	....	....	....	....	....	....	....	....	5	2	7	9	6	....	....	....
	Sherbrooke	AHL	....	....	....	....	....	....	....	....	....	....	....	....	....	....	....	....	10	2	7	9	2	....	....	....
1987-88	Sherbrooke	AHL	77	26	48	74	83	....	....	....	....	....	....	....	....	....	....	....	6	1	3	4	6	....	....	....
1988-89	**Montreal**	**NHL**	**49**	**8**	**16**	**24**	**16**	**0**	**0**	**2**	**68**	**11.8**	**9**	....	....	....	....	....	**9**	**1**	**1**	**2**	**10**	**0**	**0**	**0**
	Sherbrooke	AHL	7	6	5	11	7	....	....	....	....	....	....	....	....	....	....	....	....	....	....	....	....	....	....	....
1989-90	**Montreal**	**NHL**	**57**	**9**	**15**	**24**	**28**	**1**	**0**	**0**	**80**	**11.3**	**3**	....	....	....	....	....	**8**	**2**	**0**	**2**	**2**	**0**	**0**	**0**
1990-91	**Montreal**	**NHL**	**51**	**6**	**9**	**15**	**10**	**1**	**0**	**1**	**81**	**7.4**	**–3**	....	....	....	....	....	**13**	**5**	**3**	**8**	**6**	**0**	**0**	**1**
1991-92	**Montreal**	**NHL**	**79**	**23**	**27**	**50**	**57**	**2**	**0**	**3**	**146**	**15.8**	**29**	....	....	....	....	....	**11**	**2**	**4**	**6**	**6**	**1**	**0**	**0**
1992-93	**Edmonton**	**NHL**	**60**	**10**	**10**	**20**	**47**	**2**	**0**	**0**	**94**	**10.6**	**–10**	....	....	....	....	....	....	....	....	....	....	....	....	....
	Minnesota	**NHL**	**8**	**0**	**1**	**1**	**2**	**0**	**0**	**0**	**12**	**0.0**	**–2**	....	....	....	....	....	....	....	....	....	....	....	....	....
1993-94	**Dallas**	**NHL**	**76**	**17**	**14**	**31**	**31**	**3**	**1**	**5**	**103**	**16.5**	**0**	....	....	....	....	....	**9**	**3**	**1**	**4**	**2**	**1**	**0**	**0**
1994-95	**Dallas**	**NHL**	**32**	**9**	**4**	**13**	**16**	**1**	**3**	**1**	**70**	**12.9**	**–3**	....	....	....	....	....	**5**	**0**	**1**	**1**	**2**	**0**	**0**	**0**
1995-96	**Dallas**	**NHL**	**77**	**20**	**22**	**42**	**36**	**6**	**1**	**2**	**164**	**12.2**	**–11**	....	....	....	....	....	....	....	....	....	....	....	....	....
1996-97	**Dallas**	**NHL**	**67**	**10**	**20**	**30**	**24**	**2**	**0**	**2**	**116**	**8.6**	**6**	....	....	....	....	....	**6**	**2**	**2**	**4**	**2**	**0**	**0**	**0**
1997-98♦	**Detroit**	**NHL**	**61**	**13**	**14**	**27**	**40**	**5**	**0**	**3**	**124**	**10.5**	**4**	....	....	....	....	....	**15**	**2**	**1**	**3**	**12**	**0**	**0**	**0**
1998-99	**Detroit**	**NHL**	**5**	**1**	**0**	**1**	**0**	**0**	**0**	**1**	**4**	**25.0**	**–1**	**28**	**42.9**	**1**	**2**	**11:58**	**3**	**0**	**0**	**0**	**0**	**0**	**0**	**0**
	NHL Totals		**622**	**126**	**152**	**278**	**307**	**23**	**5**	**20**	**1062**	**11.9**		**28**	**42.9**	**1**	**2**	**11:58**	**79**	**17**	**13**	**30**	**42**	**2**	**0**	**1**

Traded to **Edmonton** by **Montreal** with Shayne Corson and Vladimir Vujtek for Vincent Damphousse and Edmonton's 4th round choice (Adam Wiesel) in 1993 Entry Draft, August 27, 1992. Traded to **Minnesota** by **Edmonton** for Todd Elik, March 5, 1993. Transferred to **Dallas** after **Minnesota** franchise relocated, June 9, 1993. Signed as a free agent by **Detroit**, August 1, 1997. Claimed by **Tampa Bay** from **Detroit** in NHL Waiver Draft, October 5, 1998. Traded to **Detroit** by **Tampa Bay** for future considerations, October 5, 1998. • Missed majority of 1998-99 season recovering from hernia surgery, September 22, 1998.

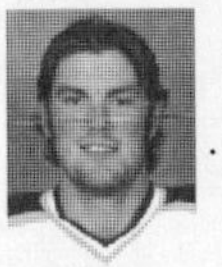

GILL, Hal (GIHL) — BOS.

Defense. Shoots left. 6'7", 240 lbs. Born, Concord, MA, April 6, 1975. Boston's 8th choice, 207th overall, in 1993 Entry Draft.

Season	Club	League	GP	G	A	Pts	PIM	PP	SH	GW	S	%	+/–	TF	F%	H	SB	Min	GP	G	A	Pts	PIM	PP	SH	GW
1992-93	Nashoba High	H.S.	20	25	25	50	....	....	....	....	....	....	....	....	....	....	....	....	....	....	....	....	....	....	....	....
1993-94	Providence	H.E.	31	1	2	3	26	....	....	....	....	....	....	....	....	....	....	....	....	....	....	....	....	....	....	....
1994-95	Providence	H.E.	26	1	3	4	22	....	....	....	....	....	....	....	....	....	....	....	....	....	....	....	....	....	....	....
1995-96	Providence	H.E.	39	5	12	17	54	....	....	....	....	....	....	....	....	....	....	....	....	....	....	....	....	....	....	....
1996-97	Providence	H.E.	35	5	16	21	52	....	....	....	....	....	....	....	....	....	....	....	....	....	....	....	....	....	....	....
1997-98	**Boston**	**NHL**	**68**	**2**	**4**	**6**	**47**	**0**	**0**	**0**	**56**	**3.6**	**4**	....	....	....	....	....	**6**	**0**	**0**	**0**	**4**	**0**	**0**	**0**
	Providence	AHL	4	1	0	1	23	....	....	....	....	....	....	....	....	....	....	....	....	....	....	....	....	....	....	....
1998-99	**Boston**	**NHL**	**80**	**3**	**7**	**10**	**63**	**0**	**0**	**2**	**102**	**2.9**	**–10**	**1**	**100.0**	**144**	**102**	**20:54**	**12**	**0**	**0**	**0**	**14**	**0**	**0**	**0**
	NHL Totals		**148**	**5**	**11**	**16**	**110**	**0**	**0**	**2**	**158**	**3.2**		**1**	**100.0**	**144**	**102**	**20:54**	**18**	**0**	**0**	**0**	**18**	**0**	**0**	**0**

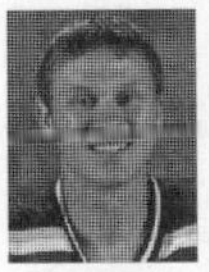

GILL, Todd (GIHL) — PHX.

Defense. Shoots left. 6', 185 lbs. Born, Cardinal, Ont., November 9, 1965. Toronto's 2nd choice, 25th overall, in 1984 Entry Draft.

Season	Club	League	GP	G	A	Pts	PIM	PP	SH	GW	S	%	+/–	TF	F%	H	SB	Min	GP	G	A	Pts	PIM	PP	SH	GW
1981-82	Brockville	OJHL	48	5	16	21	169	....	....	....	....	....	....	....	....	....	....	....	....	....	....	....	....	....	....	....
1982-83	Windsor	OHL	70	12	24	36	108	....	....	....	....	....	....	....	....	....	....	....	3	0	0	0	11	....	....	....
1983-84	Windsor	OHL	68	9	48	57	184	....	....	....	....	....	....	....	....	....	....	....	3	1	1	2	10	....	....	....
1984-85	Windsor	OHL	53	17	40	57	148	....	....	....	....	....	....	....	....	....	....	....	4	0	1	1	14	....	....	....
	Toronto	**NHL**	**10**	**1**	**0**	**1**	**13**	**0**	**0**	**0**	**9**	**11.1**	**–1**	....	....	....	....	....	....	....	....	....	....	....	....	....
1985-86	**Toronto**	**NHL**	**15**	**1**	**2**	**3**	**28**	**0**	**0**	**0**	**9**	**11.1**	**0**	....	....	....	....	....	**1**	**0**	**0**	**0**	**0**	**0**	**0**	**0**
	St. Catharines	AHL	58	8	25	33	90	....	....	....	....	....	....	....	....	....	....	....	10	1	6	7	17	....	....	....
1986-87	**Toronto**	**NHL**	**61**	**4**	**27**	**31**	**92**	**1**	**0**	**0**	**51**	**7.8**	**–3**	....	....	....	....	....	**13**	**2**	**2**	**4**	**42**	**0**	**0**	**0**
	Newmarket	AHL	11	1	8	9	33	....	....	....	....	....	....	....	....	....	....	....	....	....	....	....	....	....	....	....
1987-88	**Toronto**	**NHL**	**65**	**8**	**17**	**25**	**131**	**1**	**0**	**3**	**109**	**7.3**	**–20**	....	....	....	....	....	**6**	**1**	**3**	**4**	**20**	**1**	**0**	**0**
	Newmarket	AHL	2	0	1	1	2	....	....	....	....	....	....	....	....	....	....	....	....	....	....	....	....	....	....	....
1988-89	**Toronto**	**NHL**	**59**	**11**	**14**	**25**	**72**	**0**	**0**	**1**	**92**	**12.0**	**–3**	....	....	....	....	....	....	....	....	....	....	....	....	....
1989-90	**Toronto**	**NHL**	**48**	**1**	**14**	**15**	**92**	**0**	**0**	**0**	**44**	**2.3**	**–8**	....	....	....	....	....	**5**	**0**	**3**	**3**	**16**	**0**	**0**	**0**
1990-91	**Toronto**	**NHL**	**72**	**2**	**22**	**24**	**113**	**0**	**0**	**0**	**90**	**2.2**	**–4**	....	....	....	....	....	....	....	....	....	....	....	....	....
1991-92	**Toronto**	**NHL**	**74**	**2**	**15**	**17**	**91**	**1**	**0**	**0**	**82**	**2.4**	**–22**	....	....	....	....	....	....	....	....	....	....	....	....	....
1992-93	**Toronto**	**NHL**	**69**	**11**	**32**	**43**	**66**	**5**	**0**	**2**	**113**	**9.7**	**4**	....	....	....	....	....	**21**	**1**	**10**	**11**	**26**	**0**	**0**	**0**
1993-94	**Toronto**	**NHL**	**45**	**4**	**24**	**28**	**44**	**2**	**0**	**1**	**74**	**5.4**	**8**	....	....	....	....	....	**18**	**1**	**5**	**6**	**37**	**0**	**0**	**1**
1994-95	**Toronto**	**NHL**	**47**	**7**	**25**	**32**	**64**	**3**	**1**	**2**	**82**	**8.5**	**–8**	....	....	....	....	....	**7**	**0**	**3**	**3**	**6**	**0**	**0**	**0**
1995-96	**Toronto**	**NHL**	**74**	**7**	**18**	**25**	**116**	**1**	**0**	**2**	**109**	**6.4**	**–15**	....	....	....	....	....	**6**	**0**	**0**	**0**	**24**	**0**	**0**	**0**
1996-97	**San Jose**	**NHL**	**79**	**0**	**21**	**21**	**101**	**0**	**0**	**0**	**101**	**0.0**	**–20**	....	....	....	....	....	....	....	....	....	....	....	....	....
1997-98	**San Jose**	**NHL**	**64**	**8**	**13**	**21**	**31**	**4**	**0**	**1**	**100**	**8.0**	**–13**	....	....	....	....	....	....	....	....	....	....	....	....	....
	St. Louis	**NHL**	**11**	**5**	**4**	**9**	**10**	**3**	**0**	**1**	**22**	**22.7**	**2**	....	....	....	....	....	**10**	**2**	**2**	**4**	**10**	**1**	**1**	**0**
1998-99	**St. Louis**	**NHL**	**28**	**2**	**3**	**5**	**16**	**1**	**0**	**0**	**36**	**5.6**	**–6**	**0**	**0.0**	**34**	**16**	**17:36**	....	....	....	....	....	....	....	....
	Detroit	**NHL**	**23**	**2**	**2**	**4**	**11**	**0**	**0**	**1**	**25**	**8.0**	**–4**	**0**	**0.0**	**32**	**13**	**18:45**	**2**	**0**	**1**	**1**	**0**	**0**	**0**	**0**
	NHL Totals		**844**	**76**	**253**	**329**	**1091**	**22**	**1**	**14**	**1148**	**6.6**		**0**	**0.0**	**66**	**29**	**18:07**	**89**	**7**	**29**	**36**	**181**	**2**	**1**	**1**

Traded to **San Jose** by **Toronto** for Jamie Baker and San Jose's 5th round choice (Peter Cava) in 1996 Entry Draft, June 14, 1996. Traded to **St. Louis** by **San Jose** for Joe Murphy, March 24, 1998. Claimed on waivers by **Detroit** from **St. Louis**, December 30, 1998. Signed as a free agent by **Phoenix**, July 21, 1999.

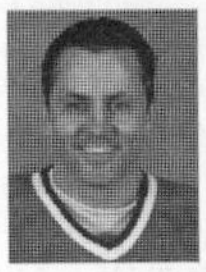

GILMOUR, Doug (GIHL-mohr) — CHI.

Center. Shoots left. 5'11", 175 lbs. Born, Kingston, Ont., June 25, 1963. St. Louis' 4th choice, 134th overall, in 1982 Entry Draft.

Season	Club	League	GP	G	A	Pts	PIM	PP	SH	GW	S	%	+/–	TF	F%	H	SB	Min	GP	G	A	Pts	PIM	PP	SH	GW
1979-80	Kingston	OJHL-B	15	2	5	7	26	....	....	....	....	....	....	....	....	....	....	....	....	....	....	....	....	....	....	....
	Belleville	OJHL	25	9	14	23	18	....	....	....	....	....	....	....	....	....	....	....	....	....	....	....	....	....	....	....
1980-81	Cornwall	QMJHL	51	12	23	35	35	....	....	....	....	....	....	....	....	....	....	....	....	....	....	....	....	....	....	....
1981-82	Cornwall	OHL	67	46	73	119	42	....	....	....	....	....	....	....	....	....	....	....	5	6	9	15	2	....	....	....
1982-83	Cornwall	OHL	68	70	*107	*177	62	....	....	....	....	....	....	....	....	....	....	....	8	8	10	18	16	....	....	....
1983-84	**St. Louis**	**NHL**	**80**	**25**	**28**	**53**	**57**	**3**	**1**	**1**	**157**	**15.9**	**6**	....	....	....	....	....	**11**	**2**	**9**	**11**	**10**	**1**	**0**	**1**
1984-85	**St. Louis**	**NHL**	**78**	**21**	**36**	**57**	**49**	**3**	**1**	**3**	**162**	**13.0**	**3**	....	....	....	....	....	**3**	**1**	**1**	**2**	**2**	**0**	**0**	**0**
1985-86	**St. Louis**	**NHL**	**74**	**25**	**28**	**53**	**41**	**2**	**1**	**5**	**183**	**13.7**	**–3**	....	....	....	....	....	**19**	**9**	**12**	***21**	**25**	**1**	**2**	**2**
1986-87	**St. Louis**	**NHL**	**80**	**42**	**63**	**105**	**58**	**17**	**1**	**2**	**207**	**20.3**	**–2**	....	....	....	....	....	**6**	**2**	**2**	**4**	**16**	**1**	**0**	**1**
1987-88	**St. Louis**	**NHL**	**72**	**36**	**50**	**86**	**59**	**19**	**2**	**4**	**163**	**22.1**	**–13**	....	....	....	....	....	**10**	**3**	**14**	**17**	**18**	**1**	**0**	**0**
1988-89♦	**Calgary**	**NHL**	**72**	**26**	**59**	**85**	**44**	**11**	**0**	**5**	**161**	**16.1**	**45**	....	....	....	....	....	**22**	**11**	**11**	**22**	**20**	**3**	**0**	**3**
1989-90	**Calgary**	**NHL**	**78**	**24**	**67**	**91**	**54**	**12**	**1**	**3**	**152**	**15.8**	**20**	....	....	....	....	....	**6**	**3**	**1**	**4**	**8**	**0**	**0**	**1**
1990-91	**Calgary**	**NHL**	**78**	**20**	**61**	**81**	**144**	**2**	**2**	**5**	**135**	**14.8**	**27**	....	....	....	....	....	**7**	**1**	**1**	**2**	**0**	**0**	**0**	**1**
1991-92	**Calgary**	**NHL**	**38**	**11**	**27**	**38**	**46**	**4**	**1**	**1**	**64**	**17.2**	**12**	....	....	....	....	....	....	....	....	....	....	....	....	....
	Toronto	**NHL**	**40**	**15**	**34**	**49**	**32**	**6**	**0**	**3**	**104**	**14.4**	**13**	....	....	....	....	....	....	....	....	....	....	....	....	....
1992-93	**Toronto**	**NHL**	**83**	**32**	**95**	**127**	**100**	**15**	**3**	**2**	**211**	**15.2**	**32**	....	....	....	....	....	**21**	**10**	***25**	**35**	**30**	**4**	**0**	**1**
1993-94	**Toronto**	**NHL**	**83**	**27**	**84**	**111**	**105**	**10**	**1**	**3**	**167**	**16.2**	**25**	....	....	....	....	....	**18**	**6**	**22**	**28**	**42**	**5**	**0**	**1**
1994-95	HC Rapperswil	Switz.	9	2	13	15	16	....	....	....	....	....	....	....	....	....	....	....	....	....	....	....	....	....	....	....
	Toronto	**NHL**	**44**	**10**	**23**	**33**	**26**	**3**	**0**	**1**	**73**	**13.7**	**–5**	....	....	....	....	....	**7**	**0**	**6**	**6**	**6**	**0**	**0**	**0**
1995-96	**Toronto**	**NHL**	**81**	**32**	**40**	**72**	**77**	**10**	**2**	**3**	**180**	**17.8**	**–5**	....	....	....	....	....	**6**	**1**	**7**	**8**	**12**	**1**	**0**	**0**

			Regular Season																Playoffs							
Season	Club	League	GP	G	A	Pts	PIM	PP	SH	GW	S	%	+/-	TF	F%	H	SB	Min	GP	G	A	Pts	PIM	PP	SH	GW
1996-97	Toronto	NHL	61	15	45	60	46	2	1	1	103	14.6	-5	....	....	....	....	....	....	....	....	....	....	....	....	....
	New Jersey	NHL	20	7	15	22	22	2	0	0	40	17.5	7	....	....	....	....	....	10	0	4	4	14	0	0	0
1997-98	New Jersey	NHL	63	13	40	53	68	3	0	5	94	13.8	10	....	....	....	....	....	6	5	2	7	4	1	0	1
1998-99	Chicago	NHL	72	16	40	56	56	7	1	4	110	14.5	-16	1619	53.6	37	45	22:29	....	....	....	....	....	....	....	....
	NHL Totals		1197	397	835	1232	1084	131	18	51	2466	16.1		1619	53.6	37	45	22:29	152	54	117	171	207	18	2	12

OHL First All-Star Team (1983) • Won Frank J. Selke Trophy (1993)

Played in NHL All-Star Game (1993, 1994)

Traded to **Calgary** by **St. Louis** with Mark Hunter, Steve Bozek and Michael Dark for Mike Bullard, Craig Coxe and Tim Corkery, September 6, 1988. Traded to **Toronto** by **Calgary** with Jamie Macoun, Ric Nattress, Kent Manderville and Rick Wamsley for Gary Leeman, Alexander Godynyuk, Jeff Reese, Michel Petit and Craig Berube, January 2, 1992. Traded to **New Jersey** by **Toronto** with Dave Ellett and future considerations for Jason Smith, Steve Sullivan and the rights to Alyn McCauley, February 25, 1997. Signed as a free agent by **Chicago**, July 28, 1998.

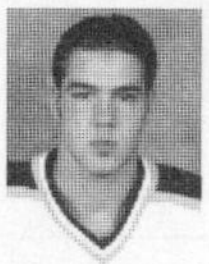

GIRARD, Jonathan

(zhih-RAHR) **BOS.**

Defense. Shoots right. 5'11", 192 lbs. Born, Joliette, Que., May 27, 1980. Boston's 1st choice, 48th overall, in 1998 Entry Draft.

1994-95	St-Hyacinthe	QMJHL	6	0	0	0	0	....	....	....	....	....	....	....	....	....	....	....	....	....	....	....	....	....	....	....
1995-96	Laval Lauren	QAAA	39	11	22	33	44	....	....	....	....	....	....	....	....	....	....	....	....	....	....	....	....	....	....	....
	St-Hyacinthe	QMJHL	8	0	1	1	2	....	....	....	....	....	....	....	....	....	....	....	....	....	....	....	....	....	....	....
	Laval	QMJHL	26	2	3	5	23	....	....	....	....	....	....	....	....	....	....	....	....	....	....	....	....	....	....	....
1996-97	Laval	QMJHL	39	11	23	34	13	....	....	....	....	....	....	....	....	....	....	....	3	0	3	3	0	....	....	....
1997-98	Laval	QMJHL	64	20	47	67	44	....	....	....	....	....	....	....	....	....	....	....	16	2	16	18	13	....	....	....
1998-99	Bathurst	QMJHL	50	9	58	67	60	....	....	....	....	....	....	....	....	....	....	....	23	13	18	31	22	....	....	....
	Boston	NHL	3	0	0	0	0	0	0	0	3	0.0	1	0	0.0	0	0	9:28	....	....	....	....	....	....	....	....
	NHL Totals		3	0	0	0	0	0	0	0	3	0.0		0	0.0	0	0	9:28	....	....	....	....	....	....	....	....

QMJHL Second All-Star Team (1998) • QMJHL First All-Star Team (1999)

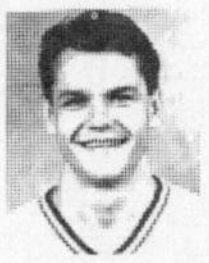

GODYNYUK, Alexander

(goh-dih-NYOOK)

Defense. Shoots left. 6', 207 lbs. Born, Kiev, Ukraine, January 27, 1970. Toronto's 5th choice, 115th overall, in 1990 Entry Draft.

1986-87	Sokol Kiev	USSR	9	0	1	1	2	....	....	....	....	....	....	....	....	....	....	....	....	....	....	....	....	....	....	....
1987-88	Sokol Kiev	USSR	2	0	0	0	2	....	....	....	....	....	....	....	....	....	....	....	....	....	....	....	....	....	....	....
1988-89	Sokol Kiev	USSR	30	3	3	6	12	....	....	....	....	....	....	....	....	....	....	....	....	....	....	....	....	....	....	....
1989-90	Sokol Kiev	USSR	37	3	2	5	31	....	....	....	....	....	....	....	....	....	....	....	....	....	....	....	....	....	....	....
1990-91	Sokol Kiev	USSR	19	3	1	4	20	....	....	....	....	....	....	....	....	....	....	....	....	....	....	....	....	....	....	....
	Toronto	NHL	18	0	3	3	16	0	0	0	15	0.0	-3	....	....	....	....	....	....	....	....	....	....	....	....	....
	Newmarket	AHL	11	0	1	1	29	....	....	....	....	....	....	....	....	....	....	....	....	....	....	....	....	....	....	....
1991-92	Toronto	NHL	31	3	6	9	59	1	0	1	30	10.0	-12	....	....	....	....	....	....	....	....	....	....	....	....	....
	Calgary	NHL	6	0	1	1	4	0	0	0	12	0.0	-2	....	....	....	....	....	....	....	....	....	....	....	....	....
	Salt Lake	IHL	17	2	1	3	24	....	....	....	....	....	....	....	....	....	....	....	....	....	....	....	....	....	....	....
1992-93	Calgary	NHL	27	3	4	7	19	0	0	0	35	8.6	6	....	....	....	....	....	....	....	....	....	....	....	....	....
1993-94	Florida	NHL	26	0	10	10	35	0	0	0	43	0.0	5	....	....	....	....	....	....	....	....	....	....	....	....	....
	Hartford	NHL	43	3	9	12	40	0	0	1	67	4.5	8	....	....	....	....	....	....	....	....	....	....	....	....	....
1994-95	Hartford	NHL	14	0	0	0	8	0	0	0	16	0.0	1	....	....	....	....	....	....	....	....	....	....	....	....	....
1995-96	Hartford	NHL	3	0	0	0	2	0	0	0	1	0.0	-1	....	....	....	....	....	....	....	....	....	....	....	....	....
	Springfield	AHL	14	1	3	4	19	....	....	....	....	....	....	....	....	....	....	....	....	....	....	....	....	....	....	....
	Detroit	IHL	7	0	3	3	12	....	....	....	....	....	....	....	....	....	....	....	....	....	....	....	....	....	....	....
	Minnesota	IHL	45	9	17	26	81	....	....	....	....	....	....	....	....	....	....	....	....	....	....	....	....	....	....	....
1996-97	Hartford	NHL	55	1	6	7	41	0	0	1	34	2.9	-10	....	....	....	....	....	....	....	....	....	....	....	....	....
1997-98	Chicago	IHL	50	5	11	16	85	....	....	....	....	....	....	....	....	....	....	....	1	0	0	0	0	....	....	....
1998-99	SC Bern	Switz.	43	9	16	25	20	....	....	....	....	....	....	....	....	....	....	....	5	1	0	1	2	....	....	....
	NHL Totals		223	10	39	49	224	1	0	3	253	4.0		....	....	....	....	....	....	....	....	....	....	....	....	....

Traded to **Calgary** by **Toronto** with Craig Berube, Gary Leeman, Michel Petit and Jeff Reese for Doug Gilmour, Jamie Macoun, Ric Nattress, Rick Wamsley and Kent Manderville, January 2, 1992. Claimed by **Florida** from **Calgary** in Expansion Draft, June 24, 1993. Traded to **Hartford** by **Florida** for Jim McKenzie, December 16, 1993. Transferred to **Carolina** after **Hartford** franchise relocated, June 25, 1997. Traded to **St. Louis** by **Carolina** with Carolina's 6th round choice (Brad Vott) in 1998 Entry Draft for Stephen Leach, June 27, 1997.

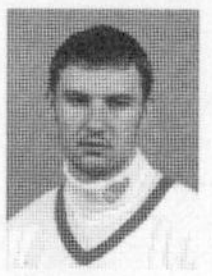

GOLUBOVSKY, Yan

(goh-luh-BOHV-skee) **DET.**

Defense. Shoots right. 6'3", 183 lbs. Born, Novosibirsk, USSR, March 9, 1976. Detroit's 1st choice, 23rd overall, in 1994 Entry Draft.

1993-94	Moscow D'amo	CIS-3	10	0	1	1	....	....	....	....	....	....	....	....	....	....	....	....	....	....	....	....	....	....	....	....
	Russian Penguins	IHL	8	0	0	0	23	....	....	....	....	....	....	....	....	....	....	....	....	....	....	....	....	....	....	....
1994-95	Adirondack	AHL	57	4	2	6	39	....	....	....	....	....	....	....	....	....	....	....	....	....	....	....	....	....	....	....
1995-96	Adirondack	AHL	71	5	16	21	97	....	....	....	....	....	....	....	....	....	....	....	3	0	0	0	2	....	....	....
1996-97	Adirondack	AHL	62	2	11	13	67	....	....	....	....	....	....	....	....	....	....	....	4	0	0	0	0	....	....	....
1997-98	Detroit	NHL	12	0	2	2	6	0	0	0	9	0.0	1	....	....	....	....	....	....	....	....	....	....	....	....	....
	Adirondack	AHL	52	1	15	16	57	....	....	....	....	....	....	....	....	....	....	....	3	0	0	0	2	....	....	....
1998-99	Detroit	NHL	17	0	1	1	16	0	0	0	10	0.0	4	0	0.0	9	4	9:39	....	....	....	....	....	....	....	....
	Adirondack	AHL	43	2	2	4	32	....	....	....	....	....	....	....	....	....	....	....	2	0	0	0	4	....	....	....
	NHL Totals		29	0	3	3	22	0	0	0	19	0.0		0	0.0	9	4	9:39	....	....	....	....	....	....	....	....

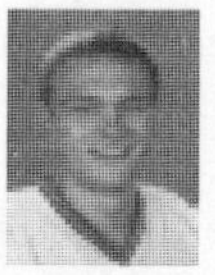

GONCHAR, Sergei

(gohn-CHAR) **WSH.**

Defense. Shoots left. 6'2", 212 lbs. Born, Chelyabinsk, USSR, April 13, 1974. Washington's 1st choice, 14th overall, in 1992 Entry Draft.

1991-92	Chelyabinsk	CIS	31	1	0	1	6	....	....	....	....	....	....	....	....	....	....	....	....	....	....	....	....	....	....	....
1992-93	Moscow D'amo	CIS	31	1	3	4	70	....	....	....	....	....	....	....	....	....	....	....	10	0	0	0	12	....	....	....
1993-94	Moscow D'amo	CIS	44	4	5	9	36	....	....	....	....	....	....	....	....	....	....	....	10	0	3	3	14	....	....	....
	Portland	AHL	....	....	....	....	....	....	....	....	....	....	....	....	....	....	....	....	2	0	0	0	0	....	....	....
1994-95	Portland	AHL	61	10	32	42	67	....	....	....	....	....	....	....	....	....	....	....	....	....	....	....	....	....	....	....
	Washington	NHL	31	2	5	7	22	0	0	0	38	5.3	4	....	....	....	....	....	7	2	2	4	2	0	0	1
1995-96	Washington	NHL	78	15	26	41	60	4	0	4	139	10.8	25	....	....	....	....	....	6	2	4	6	4	1	0	0
1996-97	Washington	NHL	57	13	17	30	36	3	0	3	129	10.1	-11	....	....	....	....	....	....	....	....	....	....	....	....	....
1997-98	Lada	Russia	7	3	2	5	4	....	....	....	....	....	....	....	....	....	....	....	....	....	....	....	....	....	....	....
	Lada	EuroHL	1	1	0	1	2	....	....	....	....	....	....	....	....	....	....	....	....	....	....	....	....	....	....	....
	Washington	NHL	72	5	16	21	66	2	0	0	134	3.7	2	....	....	....	....	....	21	7	4	11	30	3	1	2
	Russia	Olympics	6	0	2	2	0	....	....	....	....	....	....	....	....	....	....	....	....	....	....	....	....	....	....	....
1998-99	Washington	NHL	53	21	10	31	57	13	1	3	180	11.7	1	0	0.0	72	31	23:55	....	....	....	....	....	....	....	....
	NHL Totals		291	56	74	130	241	22	1	10	620	9.0		0	0.0	72	31	23:55	34	11	10	21	36	4	1	3

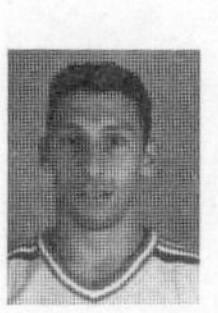

GONEAU, Daniel

(guh-NOH) **NYR**

Left wing. Shoots left. 6', 194 lbs. Born, Montreal, Que., January 16, 1976. NY Rangers' 2nd choice, 48th overall, in 1996 Entry Draft.

1990-91	Laval Leafs	QAAA	32	16	18	34	20	....	....	....	....	....	....	....	....	....	....	....	....	....	....	....	....	....	....	....
1991-92	Lac St-Louis	QAAA	42	21	14	35	52	....	....	....	....	....	....	....	....	....	....	....	....	....	....	....	....	....	....	....
1992-93	Laval	QMJHL	62	16	25	41	44	....	....	....	....	....	....	....	....	....	....	....	13	0	4	4	4	....	....	....
1993-94	Laval	QMJHL	68	29	57	86	81	....	....	....	....	....	....	....	....	....	....	....	19	8	21	29	45	....	....	....
1994-95	Laval	QMJHL	56	16	31	47	78	....	....	....	....	....	....	....	....	....	....	....	20	5	10	15	33	....	....	....
1995-96	Granby	QMJHL	67	54	51	105	115	....	....	....	....	....	....	....	....	....	....	....	21	11	22	33	40	....	....	....
1996-97	NY Rangers	NHL	41	10	3	13	10	3	0	2	44	22.7	-5	....	....	....	....	....	....	....	....	....	....	....	....	....
	Binghamton	AHL	39	15	15	30	10	....	....	....	....	....	....	....	....	....	....	....	....	....	....	....	....	....	....	....
1997-98	NY Rangers	NHL	11	2	0	2	4	0	0	1	13	15.4	-4	....	....	....	....	....	....	....	....	....	....	....	....	....
	Hartford	AHL	66	21	26	47	44	....	....	....	....	....	....	....	....	....	....	....	13	1	4	5	18	....	....	....

			Regular Season																Playoffs							
Season	Club	League	GP	G	A	Pts	PIM	PP	SH	GW	S	%	+/–	TF	F%	H	SB	Min	GP	G	A	Pts	PIM	PP	SH	GW
1998-99	Hartford	AHL	72	20	19	39	56	....	....	....	....	....	....	....	....	....	....	....	2	1	0	1	0	....	....	....
	NHL Totals		**52**	**12**	**3**	**15**	**14**	**3**	**0**	**3**	**57**	**21.1**		....	....	....	....	....	....	....	....	....	....	....	....	....

QMJHL First All-Star Team (1996)
•Re-entered NHL Entry Draft. Originally Boston's 2nd choice, 47th overall, in 1994 Entry Draft.

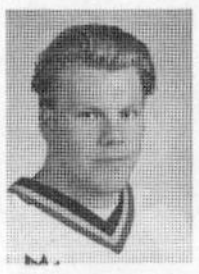

GORDON, Robb

Center. Shoots right. 5'11", 190 lbs. Born, Murrayville, B.C., January 13, 1976. Vancouver's 2nd choice, 39th overall, in 1994 Entry Draft.

Season	Club	League	GP	G	A	Pts	PIM	PP	SH	GW	S	%	+/–	TF	F%	H	SB	Min	GP	G	A	Pts	PIM	PP	SH	GW
1992-93	Powell River	BCJHL	60	55	38	93	76	....	....	....	....	....	....	....	....	....	....	....	....	....	....	....	....	....	....	....
1993-94	Powell River	BCJHL	60	69	89	158	141	....	....	....	....	....	....	....	....	....	....	....	....	....	....	....	....	....	....	....
1994-95	U. of Michigan	CCHA	39	15	26	41	72	....	....	....	....	....	....	....	....	....	....	....	....	....	....	....	....	....	....	....
1995-96	Kelowna	WHL	58	51	63	114	84	....	....	....	....	....	....	....	....	....	....	....	6	3	6	9	19	....	....	....
1996-97	Syracuse	AHL	63	11	14	25	72	....	....	....	....	....	....	....	....	....	....	....	3	0	0	0	7	....	....	....
1997-98	Syracuse	AHL	40	4	6	10	35	....	....	....	....	....	....	....	....	....	....	....	....	....	....	....	....	....	....	....
	Raleigh	ECHL	7	3	10	13	28	....	....	....	....	....	....	....	....	....	....	....	....	....	....	....	....	....	....	....
1998-99	**Vancouver**	**NHL**	**4**	**0**	**0**	**0**	**2**	**0**	**0**	**0**	**1**	**0.0**	**0**	**25**	**52.0**	**2**	**0**	**8:50**	....	....	....	....	....	....	....	....
	Syracuse	AHL	68	16	22	38	98	....	....	....	....	....	....	....	....	....	....	....	....	....	....	....	....	....	....	....
	NHL Totals		**4**	**0**	**0**	**0**	**2**	**0**	**0**	**0**	**1**	**0.0**		**25**	**52.0**	**2**	**0**	**8:50**	....	....	....	....	....	....	....	....

WHL West First All-Star Team (1996)

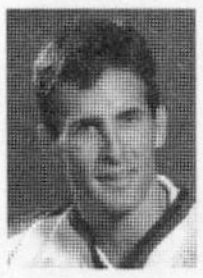

GRANATO, Tony (gruh-NA-toh) S.J.

Right wing. Shoots right. 5'10", 185 lbs. Born, Downers Grove, IL, July 25, 1964. NY Rangers' 5th choice, 120th overall, in 1982 Entry Draft.

Season	Club	League	GP	G	A	Pts	PIM	PP	SH	GW	S	%	+/–	TF	F%	H	SB	Min	GP	G	A	Pts	PIM	PP	SH	GW
1982-83	Northwood Prep	H.S.	34	32	60	92	....	....	....	....	....	....	....	....	....	....	....	....	....	....	....	....	....	....	....	....
1983-84	U. of Wisconsin	WCHA	35	14	17	31	48	....	....	....	....	....	....	....	....	....	....	....	....	....	....	....	....	....	....	....
1984-85	U. of Wisconsin	WCHA	42	33	34	67	94	....	....	....	....	....	....	....	....	....	....	....	....	....	....	....	....	....	....	....
1985-86	U. of Wisconsin	WCHA	33	25	24	49	36	....	....	....	....	....	....	....	....	....	....	....	....	....	....	....	....	....	....	....
1986-87	U. of Wisconsin	WCHA	42	28	45	73	64	....	....	....	....	....	....	....	....	....	....	....	....	....	....	....	....	....	....	....
1987-88	United States	Nat-Team	49	40	31	71	55	....	....	....	....	....	....	....	....	....	....	....	....	....	....	....	....	....	....	....
	United States	Olympics	6	1	7	8	4	....	....	....	....	....	....	....	....	....	....	....	....	....	....	....	....	....	....	....
	Colorado	IHL	22	13	14	27	36	....	....	....	....	....	....	....	....	....	....	....	8	9	4	13	16	....	....	....
1988-89	**NY Rangers**	**NHL**	**78**	**36**	**27**	**63**	**140**	**4**	**4**	**3**	**234**	**15.4**	**17**	....	....	....	....	....	**4**	**1**	**1**	**2**	**21**	**0**	**0**	**0**
1989-90	**NY Rangers**	**NHL**	**37**	**7**	**18**	**25**	**77**	**1**	**0**	**0**	**79**	**8.9**	**1**	....	....	....	....	....	....	....	....	....	....	....	....	....
	Los Angeles	**NHL**	**19**	**5**	**6**	**11**	**45**	**1**	**0**	**0**	**41**	**12.2**	**–2**	....	....	....	....	....	**10**	**5**	**4**	**9**	**12**	**2**	**1**	**2**
1990-91	**Los Angeles**	**NHL**	**68**	**30**	**34**	**64**	**154**	**11**	**1**	**3**	**197**	**15.2**	**22**	....	....	....	....	....	**12**	**1**	**4**	**5**	**28**	**0**	**0**	**0**
1991-92	**Los Angeles**	**NHL**	**80**	**39**	**29**	**68**	**187**	**7**	**2**	**8**	**223**	**17.5**	**4**	....	....	....	....	....	**6**	**1**	**5**	**6**	**10**	**0**	**0**	**0**
1992-93	**Los Angeles**	**NHL**	**81**	**37**	**45**	**82**	**171**	**14**	**2**	**6**	**247**	**15.0**	**–1**	....	....	....	....	....	**24**	**6**	**11**	**17**	**50**	**1**	**0**	**1**
1993-94	**Los Angeles**	**NHL**	**50**	**7**	**14**	**21**	**150**	**2**	**0**	**0**	**117**	**6.0**	**–2**	....	....	....	....	....	....	....	....	....	....	....	....	....
1994-95	**Los Angeles**	**NHL**	**33**	**13**	**11**	**24**	**68**	**2**	**0**	**3**	**106**	**12.3**	**9**	....	....	....	....	....	....	....	....	....	....	....	....	....
1995-96	**Los Angeles**	**NHL**	**49**	**17**	**18**	**35**	**46**	**5**	**0**	**1**	**156**	**10.9**	**–5**	....	....	....	....	....	....	....	....	....	....	....	....	....
1996-97	**San Jose**	**NHL**	**76**	**25**	**15**	**40**	**159**	**5**	**1**	**4**	**231**	**10.8**	**–7**	....	....	....	....	....	....	....	....	....	....	....	....	....
1997-98	**San Jose**	**NHL**	**59**	**16**	**9**	**25**	**70**	**3**	**0**	**2**	**119**	**13.4**	**3**	....	....	....	....	....	**1**	**0**	**0**	**0**	**0**	**0**	**0**	**0**
1998-99	**San Jose**	**NHL**	**35**	**6**	**6**	**12**	**54**	**0**	**1**	**1**	**65**	**9.2**	**4**	**3**	**100.0**	**31**	**4**	**10:29**	**6**	**1**	**1**	**2**	**2**	**0**	**0**	**0**
	NHL Totals		**665**	**238**	**232**	**470**	**1321**	**55**	**11**	**31**	**1815**	**13.1**		**3**	**100.0**	**31**	**4**	**10:29**	**63**	**15**	**26**	**41**	**123**	**3**	**1**	**3**

WCHA Second All-Star Team (1985, 1987) • NCAA West Second All-American Team (1985, 1987) • NHL All-Rookie Team (1989) • Won Bill Masterton Memorial Trophy (1997)
Played in NHL All-Star Game (1997)
Traded to **LA Kings** by **NY Rangers** with Tomas Sandstrom for Bernie Nicholls, January 20, 1990. Signed as a free agent by **San Jose**, September 1, 1996.

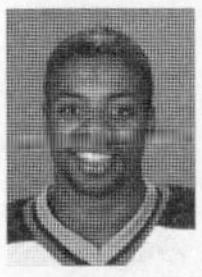

GRAND PIERRE, Jean-Luc (GRAHN pee-AIR, ZHAH LOOK) BUF.

Defense. Shoots right. 6'3", 207 lbs. Born, Montreal, Que., February 2, 1977. St. Louis' 6th choice, 179th overall, in 1995 Entry Draft.

Season	Club	League	GP	G	A	Pts	PIM	PP	SH	GW	S	%	+/–	TF	F%	H	SB	Min	GP	G	A	Pts	PIM	PP	SH	GW
1993-94	Beauport	QMJHL	46	1	4	5	27	....	....	....	....	....	....	....	....	....	....	....	1	0	0	0	0	....	....	....
1994-95	Val d'Or	QMJHL	59	10	13	23	126	....	....	....	....	....	....	....	....	....	....	....	....	....	....	....	....	....	....	....
1995-96	Val d'Or	QMJHL	67	13	21	34	209	....	....	....	....	....	....	....	....	....	....	....	13	1	4	5	47	....	....	....
1996-97	Val d'Or	QMJHL	58	9	24	33	186	....	....	....	....	....	....	....	....	....	....	....	13	5	8	13	46	....	....	....
1997-98	Rochester	AHL	75	4	6	10	211	....	....	....	....	....	....	....	....	....	....	....	4	0	0	0	2	....	....	....
1998-99	**Buffalo**	**NHL**	**16**	**0**	**1**	**1**	**17**	**0**	**0**	**0**	**11**	**0.0**	**0**	**0**	**0.0**	**46**	**13**	**13:36**	....	....	....	....	....	....	....	....
	Rochester	AHL	55	5	4	9	90	....	....	....	....	....	....	....	....	....	....	....	....	....	....	....	....	....	....	....
	NHL Totals		**16**	**0**	**1**	**1**	**17**	**0**	**0**	**0**	**11**	**0.0**		**0**	**0.0**	**46**	**13**	**13:36**	....	....	....	....	....	....	....	....

Traded to **Buffalo** by **St. Louis** with Ottawa's 2nd round choice (previously acquired, Buffalo selected Cory Sarich) in 1996 Entry Draft and St. Louis' 3rd round choice (Maxim Afinogenov) in 1997 Entry Draft for Yuri Khmylev and Buffalo's 8th round choice (Andrei Podkonicky) in 1996 Entry Draft, March 20, 1996.

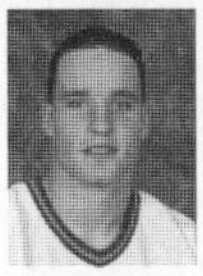

GRATTON, Benoit (grah-TOHN) CGY.

Left wing. Shoots left. 5'10", 182 lbs. Born, Montreal, Que., December 28, 1976. Washington's 6th choice, 105th overall, in 1995 Entry Draft.

Season	Club	League	GP	G	A	Pts	PIM	PP	SH	GW	S	%	+/–	TF	F%	H	SB	Min	GP	G	A	Pts	PIM	PP	SH	GW
1992-93	Laval Regents	QAAA	40	19	38	57	74	....	....	....	....	....	....	....	....	....	....	....	13	1	9	10	27	....	....	....
1993-94	Laval	QMJHL	51	9	14	23	70	....	....	....	....	....	....	....	....	....	....	....	20	2	1	3	19	....	....	....
1994-95	Laval	QMJHL	71	30	58	88	199	....	....	....	....	....	....	....	....	....	....	....	20	8	*21	29	42	....	....	....
1995-96	Laval	QMJHL	38	21	39	60	130	....	....	....	....	....	....	....	....	....	....	....	....	....	....	....	....	....	....	....
	Granby	QMJHL	27	12	46	58	97	....	....	....	....	....	....	....	....	....	....	....	21	13	26	39	68	....	....	....
1996-97	Portland	AHL	76	6	40	46	140	....	....	....	....	....	....	....	....	....	....	....	5	2	1	3	14	....	....	....
1997-98	**Washington**	**NHL**	**6**	**0**	**1**	**1**	**6**	**0**	**0**	**0**	**5**	**0.0**	**1**	....	....	....	....	....	....	....	....	....	....	....	....	....
	Portland	AHL	58	19	31	50	137	....	....	....	....	....	....	....	....	....	....	....	8	4	2	6	24	....	....	....
1998-99	**Washington**	**NHL**	**16**	**4**	**3**	**7**	**16**	**0**	**0**	**0**	**24**	**16.7**	**–1**	**136**	**54.4**	**26**	**7**	**13:28**	....	....	....	....	....	....	....	....
	Portland	AHL	64	18	42	60	135	....	....	....	....	....	....	....	....	....	....	....	....	....	....	....	....	....	....	....
	NHL Totals		**22**	**4**	**4**	**8**	**22**	**0**	**0**	**0**	**29**	**13.8**		**136**	**54.4**	**26**	**7**	**13:28**	....	....	....	....	....	....	....	....

Traded to **Calgary** by **Washington** for Steve Shirreffs, August 18, 1999.

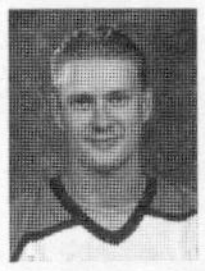

GRATTON, Chris (GRA-tuhn) T.B.

Center. Shoots left. 6'4", 218 lbs. Born, Brantford, Ont., July 5, 1975. Tampa Bay's 1st choice, 3rd overall, in 1993 Entry Draft.

Season	Club	League	GP	G	A	Pts	PIM	PP	SH	GW	S	%	+/–	TF	F%	H	SB	Min	GP	G	A	Pts	PIM	PP	SH	GW
1990-91	Brantford	OJHL	31	30	30	60	28	....	....	....	....	....	....	....	....	....	....	....	....	....	....	....	....	....	....	....
1991-92	Kingston	OHL	62	27	29	66	37	....	....	....	....	....	....	....	....	....	....	....	....	....	....	....	....	....	....	....
1992-93	Kingston	OHL	58	55	54	109	125	....	....	....	....	....	....	....	....	....	....	....	16	11	18	29	42	....	....	....
1993-94	**Tampa Bay**	**NHL**	**84**	**13**	**29**	**42**	**123**	**5**	**1**	**2**	**161**	**8.1**	**–25**	....	....	....	....	....	....	....	....	....	....	....	....	....
1994-95	**Tampa Bay**	**NHL**	**46**	**7**	**20**	**27**	**89**	**2**	**0**	**0**	**91**	**7.7**	**–2**	....	....	....	....	....	....	....	....	....	....	....	....	....
1995-96	**Tampa Bay**	**NHL**	**82**	**17**	**21**	**38**	**105**	**7**	**0**	**3**	**183**	**9.3**	**–13**	....	....	....	....	....	**6**	**0**	**2**	**2**	**27**	**0**	**0**	**0**
1996-97	**Tampa Bay**	**NHL**	**82**	**30**	**32**	**62**	**201**	**9**	**0**	**4**	**230**	**13.0**	**–28**	....	....	....	....	....	....	....	....	....	....	....	....	....
1997-98	**Philadelphia**	**NHL**	**82**	**22**	**40**	**62**	**159**	**5**	**0**	**2**	**182**	**12.1**	**11**	....	....	....	....	....	**5**	**2**	**0**	**2**	**10**	**0**	**0**	**0**
1998-99	**Philadelphia**	**NHL**	**26**	**1**	**7**	**8**	**41**	**0**	**0**	**0**	**54**	**1.9**	**–8**	**38**	**42.1**	**35**	**0**	**14:25**	....	....	....	....	....	....	....	....
	Tampa Bay	**NHL**	**52**	**7**	**19**	**26**	**102**	**1**	**0**	**1**	**127**	**5.5**	**–20**	**1032**	**53.9**	**74**	**12**	**18:20**	....	....	....	....	....	....	....	....
	NHL Totals		**454**	**97**	**168**	**265**	**820**	**29**	**1**	**12**	**1028**	**9.4**		**1070**	**53.5**	**109**	**12**	**17:02**	**11**	**2**	**2**	**4**	**37**	**0**	**0**	**0**

Signed as a free agent by **Philadelphia**, August 14, 1997. Traded to **Tampa Bay** by **Philadelphia** with Mike Sillinger for Mikael Renberg and Daymond Langkow, December 12, 1998.

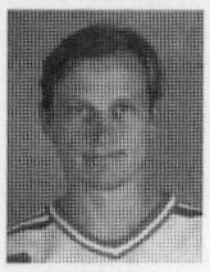

GRAVES, Adam

NYR

Center. Shoots left. 6', 205 lbs. Born, Toronto, Ont., April 12, 1968. Detroit's 2nd choice, 22nd overall, in 1986 Entry Draft.

			Regular Season																Playoffs							
Season	Club	League	GP	G	A	Pts	PIM	PP	SH	GW	S	%	+/-	TF	F%	H	SB	Min	GP	G	A	Pts	PIM	PP	SH	GW
1984-85	King City	OJHL-B	25	23	33	56	29	....	....	....	....	....	....	....	....	....	....	....	....	....	....	....	....	....	....	....
1985-86	Windsor	OHL	62	27	37	64	35	....	....	....	....	....	....	....	....	....	....	....	16	5	11	16	10	....	....	....
1986-87	Windsor	OHL	66	45	55	100	70	....	....	....	....	....	....	....	....	....	....	....	14	9	8	17	32	....	....	....
	Adirondack	AHL	....	....	....	....	....	....	....	....	....	....	....	....	....	....	....	....	5	0	1	1	0	....	....	....
1987-88	Windsor	OHL	37	28	32	60	107	....	....	....	....	....	....	....	....	....	....	....	12	14	18	*32	16	....	....	....
	Detroit	**NHL**	**9**	**0**	**1**	**1**	**8**	**0**	**0**	**0**	**9**	**0.0**	**–2**	....	....	....	....	....	....	....	....	....	....	....	....	....
1988-89	**Detroit**	**NHL**	**56**	**7**	**5**	**12**	**60**	**0**	**0**	**1**	**60**	**11.7**	**–5**	....	....	....	....	....	**5**	**0**	**0**	**0**	**4**	**0**	**0**	**0**
	Adirondack	AHL	14	10	11	21	28	....	....	....	....	....	....	....	....	....	....	....	14	11	7	18	17	....	....	....
1989-90	**Detroit**	**NHL**	**13**	**0**	**1**	**1**	**13**	**0**	**0**	**0**	**10**	**0.0**	**–5**	....	....	....	....	....	....	....	....	....	....	....	....	....
	♦ **Edmonton**	**NHL**	**63**	**9**	**12**	**21**	**123**	**1**	**0**	**1**	**84**	**10.7**	**5**	....	....	....	....	....	**22**	**5**	**6**	**11**	**17**	**0**	**0**	**1**
1990-91	**Edmonton**	**NHL**	**76**	**7**	**18**	**25**	**127**	**2**	**0**	**1**	**126**	**5.6**	**–21**	....	....	....	....	....	**18**	**2**	**4**	**6**	**22**	**0**	**0**	**0**
1991-92	**NY Rangers**	**NHL**	**80**	**26**	**33**	**59**	**139**	**4**	**4**	**4**	**228**	**11.4**	**19**	....	....	....	....	....	**10**	**5**	**3**	**8**	**22**	**1**	**0**	**1**
1992-93	**NY Rangers**	**NHL**	**84**	**36**	**29**	**65**	**148**	**12**	**1**	**6**	**275**	**13.1**	**–4**	....	....	....	....	....	....	....	....	....	....	....	....	....
1993-94♦	**NY Rangers**	**NHL**	**84**	**52**	**27**	**79**	**127**	**20**	**4**	**4**	**291**	**17.9**	**27**	....	....	....	....	....	**23**	**10**	**7**	**17**	**24**	**3**	**0**	**0**
1994-95	**NY Rangers**	**NHL**	**47**	**17**	**14**	**31**	**51**	**9**	**0**	**3**	**185**	**9.2**	**9**	....	....	....	....	....	**10**	**4**	**4**	**8**	**8**	**2**	**0**	**0**
1995-96	**NY Rangers**	**NHL**	**82**	**22**	**36**	**58**	**100**	**9**	**1**	**2**	**266**	**8.3**	**18**	....	....	....	....	....	**10**	**7**	**1**	**8**	**4**	**6**	**0**	**2**
1996-97	**NY Rangers**	**NHL**	**82**	**33**	**28**	**61**	**66**	**10**	**4**	**3**	**269**	**12.3**	**10**	....	....	....	....	....	**15**	**2**	**1**	**3**	**12**	**1**	**0**	**2**
1997-98	**NY Rangers**	**NHL**	**72**	**23**	**12**	**35**	**41**	**10**	**0**	**2**	**226**	**10.2**	**–30**	....	....	....	....	....	....	....	....	....	....	....	....	....
1998-99	**NY Rangers**	**NHL**	**82**	**38**	**15**	**53**	**47**	**14**	**2**	**7**	**239**	**15.9**	**–12**	**347**	**51.3**	**162**	**28**	**20:33**	....	....	....	....	....	....	....	....
	NHL Totals		**830**	**270**	**231**	**501**	**1050**	**91**	**16**	**34**	**2268**	**11.9**		**347**	**51.3**	**162**	**28**	**20:33**	**113**	**35**	**26**	**61**	**113**	**13**	**0**	**6**

NHL Second All-Star Team (1994) • Won King Clancy Memorial Trophy (1994)
Played in NHL All-Star Game (1994)

Traded to **Edmonton** by **Detroit** with Petr Klima, Joe Murphy and Jeff Sharples for Jimmy Carson, Kevin McClelland and Edmonton's 5th round choice (later traded to Montreal — Montreal selected Brad Layzell) in 1991 Entry Draft, November 2, 1989. Signed as a free agent by **NY Rangers**, September 3, 1991.

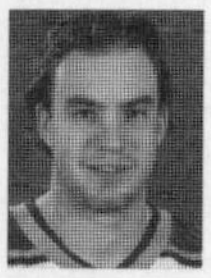

GREEN, Josh

NYI

Left wing. Shoots left. 6'4", 212 lbs. Born, Camrose, Alta., November 16, 1977. Los Angeles' 1st choice, 30th overall, in 1996 Entry Draft.

Season	Club	League	GP	G	A	Pts	PIM	PP	SH	GW	S	%	+/-	TF	F%	H	SB	Min	GP	G	A	Pts	PIM	PP	SH	GW
1992-93	Camrose	AAHA	60	55	45	100	80	....	....	....	....	....	....	....	....	....	....	....	....	....	....	....	....	....	....	....
1993-94	Medicine Hat	WHL	63	22	22	44	43	....	....	....	....	....	....	....	....	....	....	....	3	0	0	0	4	....	....	....
1994-95	Medicine Hat	WHL	68	32	23	55	64	....	....	....	....	....	....	....	....	....	....	....	5	5	1	6	2	....	....	....
1995-96	Medicine Hat	WHL	46	18	25	43	55	....	....	....	....	....	....	....	....	....	....	....	5	2	2	4	4	....	....	....
1996-97	Medicine Hat	WHL	51	25	32	57	61	....	....	....	....	....	....	....	....	....	....	....	....	....	....	....	....	....	....	....
	Swift Current	WHL	23	10	15	25	33	....	....	....	....	....	....	....	....	....	....	....	10	9	7	16	19	....	....	....
1997-98	Swift Current	WHL	5	9	1	10	9	....	....	....	....	....	....	....	....	....	....	....	....	....	....	....	....	....	....	....
	Portland	WHL	26	26	18	44	27	....	....	....	....	....	....	....	....	....	....	....	....	....	....	....	....	....	....	....
	Fredericton	AHL	43	16	15	31	14	....	....	....	....	....	....	....	....	....	....	....	4	1	3	4	6	....	....	....
1998-99	**Los Angeles**	**NHL**	**27**	**1**	**3**	**4**	**8**	**1**	**0**	**0**	**35**	**2.9**	**–5**	**2**	**50.0**	**30**	**1**	**11:44**	....	....	....	....	....	....	....	....
	Springfield	AHL	41	15	15	30	29	....	....	....	....	....	....	....	....	....	....	....	....	....	....	....	....	....	....	....
	NHL Totals		**27**	**1**	**3**	**4**	**8**	**1**	**0**	**0**	**35**	**2.9**		**2**	**50.0**	**30**	**1**	**11:44**	....	....	....	....	....	....	....	....

Traded to **NY Islanders** by **Los Angeles** with Olli Jokinen, Mathieu Biron and Los Angeles' 1st round choice (Taylor Pyatt) in 1999 Entry Draft for Zigmund Palffy, Brian Smolinski, Marcel Cousineau and New Jersey's 4th round choice (previously acquired, Los Angeles selected Daniel Johanssen) in 1999 Entry Draft, June 20, 1999.

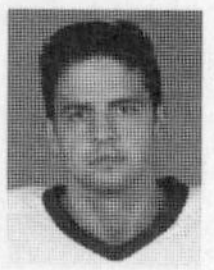

GREEN, Travis

PHX.

Center. Shoots right. 6'2", 196 lbs. Born, Castlegar, B.C., December 20, 1970. NY Islanders' 2nd choice, 23rd overall, in 1989 Entry Draft.

Season	Club	League	GP	G	A	Pts	PIM	PP	SH	GW	S	%	+/-	TF	F%	H	SB	Min	GP	G	A	Pts	PIM	PP	SH	GW
1985-86	Castlegar	KIJHL	35	30	40	70	41	....	....	....	....	....	....	....	....	....	....	....	....	....	....	....	....	....	....	....
1986-87	Spokane	WHL	64	8	17	25	27	....	....	....	....	....	....	....	....	....	....	....	3	0	0	0	0	....	....	....
1987-88	Spokane	WHL	72	33	54	87	42	....	....	....	....	....	....	....	....	....	....	....	15	10	10	20	13	....	....	....
1988-89	Spokane	WHL	75	51	51	102	79	....	....	....	....	....	....	....	....	....	....	....	....	....	....	....	....	....	....	....
1989-90	Spokane	WHL	50	45	44	89	80	....	....	....	....	....	....	....	....	....	....	....	....	....	....	....	....	....	....	....
	Medicine Hat	WHL	25	15	24	39	19	....	....	....	....	....	....	....	....	....	....	....	3	0	0	0	2	....	....	....
1990-91	Capital District	AHL	73	21	34	55	26	....	....	....	....	....	....	....	....	....	....	....	....	....	....	....	....	....	....	....
1991-92	Capital District	AHL	71	23	27	50	10	....	....	....	....	....	....	....	....	....	....	....	7	0	4	4	21	....	....	....
1992-93	**NY Islanders**	**NHL**	**61**	**7**	**18**	**25**	**43**	**1**	**0**	**0**	**115**	**6.1**	**4**	....	....	....	....	....	**12**	**3**	**1**	**4**	**6**	**0**	**0**	**0**
	Capital District	AHL	20	12	11	23	39	....	....	....	....	....	....	....	....	....	....	....	....	....	....	....	....	....	....	....
1993-94	**NY Islanders**	**NHL**	**83**	**18**	**22**	**40**	**44**	**1**	**0**	**2**	**164**	**11.0**	**16**	....	....	....	....	....	**4**	**0**	**0**	**0**	**2**	**0**	**0**	**0**
1994-95	**NY Islanders**	**NHL**	**42**	**5**	**7**	**12**	**25**	**0**	**0**	**0**	**59**	**8.5**	**–10**	....	....	....	....	....	....	....	....	....	....	....	....	....
1995-96	**NY Islanders**	**NHL**	**69**	**25**	**45**	**70**	**42**	**14**	**1**	**2**	**186**	**13.4**	**–20**	....	....	....	....	....	....	....	....	....	....	....	....	....
1996-97	**NY Islanders**	**NHL**	**79**	**23**	**41**	**64**	**38**	**10**	**0**	**3**	**177**	**13.0**	**–5**	....	....	....	....	....	....	....	....	....	....	....	....	....
1997-98	**NY Islanders**	**NHL**	**54**	**14**	**12**	**26**	**66**	**8**	**0**	**2**	**99**	**14.1**	**–19**	....	....	....	....	....	....	....	....	....	....	....	....	....
	Anaheim	**NHL**	**22**	**5**	**11**	**16**	**16**	**1**	**0**	**0**	**42**	**11.9**	**–10**	....	....	....	....	....	....	....	....	....	....	....	....	....
1998-99	**Anaheim**	**NHL**	**79**	**13**	**17**	**30**	**81**	**3**	**1**	**2**	**165**	**7.9**	**–7**	**1325**	**52.8**	**97**	**24**	**17:17**	**4**	**0**	**1**	**1**	**4**	**0**	**0**	**0**
	NHL Totals		**489**	**110**	**173**	**283**	**355**	**38**	**2**	**11**	**1007**	**10.9**		**1325**	**52.8**	**97**	**24**	**17:17**	**20**	**3**	**2**	**5**	**12**	**0**	**0**	**0**

Traded to **Anaheim** by **NY Islanders** with Doug Houda and Tony Tuzzolino for Joe Sacco, J.J. Daigneault and Mark Janssens, February 6, 1998. Traded to **Phoenix** by **Anaheim** with Anaheim's 1st round choice (Scott Kelman) in 1999 Entry Draft for Oleg Tverdovsky, June 26, 1999.

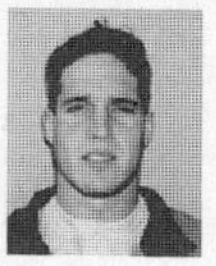

GREIG, Mark

(GREG) **PHI.**

Right wing. Shoots right. 5'11", 190 lbs. Born, High River, Alta., January 25, 1970. Hartford's 1st choice, 15th overall, in 1990 Entry Draft.

Season	Club	League	GP	G	A	Pts	PIM	PP	SH	GW	S	%	+/-	TF	F%	H	SB	Min	GP	G	A	Pts	PIM	PP	SH	GW
1985-86	Blackie Bisons	AAHA	31	12	43	55	44	....	....	....	....	....	....	....	....	....	....	....	....	....	....	....	....	....	....	....
1986-87	Calgary Stars	AAHA	18	9	28	37	30	....	....	....	....	....	....	....	....	....	....	....	....	....	....	....	....	....	....	....
	Calgary	WHL	5	0	0	0	0	....	....	....	....	....	....	....	....	....	....	....	....	....	....	....	....	....	....	....
1987-88	Lethbridge	WHL	65	9	18	27	38	....	....	....	....	....	....	....	....	....	....	....	....	....	....	....	....	....	....	....
1988-89	Lethbridge	WHL	71	36	72	108	113	....	....	....	....	....	....	....	....	....	....	....	8	5	5	10	16	....	....	....
1989-90	Lethbridge	WHL	65	55	80	135	149	....	....	....	....	....	....	....	....	....	....	....	18	11	21	32	35	....	....	....
1990-91	**Hartford**	**NHL**	**4**	**0**	**0**	**0**	**0**	**0**	**0**	**0**	**1**	**0.0**	**–1**	....	....	....	....	....	....	....	....	....	....	....	....	....
	Springfield	AHL	73	32	55	87	73	....	....	....	....	....	....	....	....	....	....	....	17	2	6	8	22	....	....	....
1991-92	**Hartford**	**NHL**	**17**	**0**	**5**	**5**	**6**	**0**	**0**	**0**	**18**	**0.0**	**7**	....	....	....	....	....	....	....	....	....	....	....	....	....
	Springfield	AHL	50	20	27	47	38	....	....	....	....	....	....	....	....	....	....	....	9	1	1	2	20	....	....	....
1992-93	**Hartford**	**NHL**	**22**	**1**	**7**	**8**	**27**	**0**	**0**	**0**	**16**	**6.3**	**–11**	....	....	....	....	....	....	....	....	....	....	....	....	....
	Springfield	AHL	55	20	38	58	86	....	....	....	....	....	....	....	....	....	....	....	....	....	....	....	....	....	....	....
1993-94	**Hartford**	**NHL**	**31**	**4**	**5**	**9**	**31**	**0**	**0**	**0**	**41**	**9.8**	**–6**	....	....	....	....	....	....	....	....	....	....	....	....	....
	Springfield	AHL	4	0	4	4	21	....	....	....	....	....	....	....	....	....	....	....	....	....	....	....	....	....	....	....
	Toronto	**NHL**	**13**	**2**	**2**	**4**	**10**	**0**	**0**	**0**	**14**	**14.3**	**1**	....	....	....	....	....	....	....	....	....	....	....	....	....
	St. John's	AHL	9	4	6	10	0	....	....	....	....	....	....	....	....	....	....	....	11	4	2	6	26	....	....	....
1994-95	**Calgary**	**NHL**	**8**	**1**	**1**	**2**	**2**	**0**	**0**	**0**	**5**	**20.0**	**1**	....	....	....	....	....	....	....	....	....	....	....	....	....
	Saint John	AHL	67	31	50	81	82	....	....	....	....	....	....	....	....	....	....	....	2	0	1	1	0	....	....	....
1995-96	Atlanta	IHL	71	25	48	73	104	....	....	....	....	....	....	....	....	....	....	....	3	2	1	3	4	....	....	....
1996-97	Quebec	IHL	5	1	2	3	0	....	....	....	....	....	....	....	....	....	....	....	....	....	....	....	....	....	....	....
	Houston	IHL	59	12	30	42	59	....	....	....	....	....	....	....	....	....	....	....	13	5	8	13	2	....	....	....
1997-98	Grand Rapids	IHL	69	26	36	62	103	....	....	....	....	....	....	....	....	....	....	....	3	0	4	4	4	....	....	....
1998-99	**Philadelphia**	**NHL**	**7**	**1**	**3**	**4**	**2**	**0**	**0**	**0**	**9**	**11.1**	**1**	**0**	**0.0**	**5**	**3**	**9:55**	**2**	**0**	**1**	**1**	**0**	**0**	**0**	**0**
	Philadelphia	AHL	67	23	46	69	102	....	....	....	....	....	....	....	....	....	....	....	7	1	5	6	14	....	....	....
	NHL Totals		**102**	**9**	**23**	**32**	**78**	**0**	**0**	**0**	**104**	**8.7**		**0**	**0.0**	**5**	**3**	**9:55**	**2**	**0**	**1**	**1**	**0**	**0**	**0**	**0**

WHL East First All-Star Team (1990)

Traded to **Toronto** by **Hartford** with Hartford's 6th round choice (later traded to NY Rangers — NY Rangers selected Yuri Litvinov) in 1994 Entry Draft for Ted Crowley, January 25, 1994. Signed as a free agent by **Calgary**, August 9, 1994. Signed as a free agent by **Philadelphia**, July 28, 1998.

						Regular Season															Playoffs						
Season	Club	League	GP	G	A	Pts	PIM	PP	SH	GW	S	%	+/−		TF	F%	H	SB	Min		GP	G	A	Pts	PIM	PP	SH	GW

GRETZKY, Wayne
(GRETZ-kee)

Center. Shoots left. 6', 185 lbs.   Born, Brantford, Ont., January 26, 1961.

Season	Club	League	GP	G	A	Pts	PIM	PP	SH	GW	S	%	+/−	TF	F%	H	SB	Min	GP	G	A	Pts	PIM	PP	SH	GW
1974-75	Brantford	OMHA		STATISTICS NOT AVAILABLE																						
1975-76	Vaughn Nats	OJHL-B	28	27	33	60	7																			
1976-77	Seneca Nats	OJHL-B	32	36	36	72	35													23	40	35	75				
	Peterborough	OHA	3	0	3	3	0																				
1977-78	S.S. Marie	OHA	64	70	112	182	14													13	6	20	26	0			
1978-79	Indianapolis	WHA	8	3	3	6	0																				
	Edmonton	WHA	72	43	61	104	19													13	*10	10	*20	2			
1979-80	Edmonton	NHL	79	51	*86	*137	21	13	1	6	284	18.0	15						3	2	1	3	0	0	0	0
1980-81	Edmonton	NHL	80	55	*109	*164	28	15	4	3	261	21.1	41						9	7	14	21	4	2	1	1
1981-82	Edmonton	NHL	80	*92	*120	*212	26	18	6	12	369	24.9	81						5	5	7	12	8	1	1	1
1982-83	Edmonton	NHL	80	*71	*125	*196	59	18	6	9	348	20.4	60						16	12	*26	*38	4	2	3	3
1983-84◆	Edmonton	NHL	74	*87	*118	*205	39	20	12	11	324	26.9	76						19	13	*22	*35	12	2	0	3
1984-85◆	Edmonton	NHL	80	*73	*135	*208	52	8	11	7	358	20.4	98						18	17	*30	*47	4	4	2	3
1985-86	Edmonton	NHL	80	52	*163	*215	46	11	3	6	350	14.9	71						10	8	11	19	2	4	1	2
1986-87◆	Edmonton	NHL	79	*62	*121	*183	28	13	7	4	288	21.5	70						21	5	*29	*34	6	2	0	0
1987-88◆	Edmonton	NHL	64	40	*109	149	24	9	5	3	211	19.0	39						19	12	*31	*43	16	5	1	3
1988-89	Los Angeles	NHL	78	54	*114	168	26	11	5	5	303	17.8	15						11	5	17	22	0	1	1	0
1989-90	Los Angeles	NHL	73	40	*102	*142	42	10	4	4	236	16.9	8						7	3	7	10	0	1	0	0
1990-91	Los Angeles	NHL	78	41	*122	*163	16	8	0	5	212	19.3	30						12	4	11	15	2	1	0	0
1991-92	Los Angeles	NHL	74	31	*90	121	34	12	2	2	215	14.4	−12						6	2	5	7	2	1	0	0
1992-93	Los Angeles	NHL	45	16	49	65	6	0	2	1	141	11.3	6						24	*15	*25	*40	4	4	1	3
1993-94	Los Angeles	NHL	81	38	*92	*130	20	14	4	0	233	16.3	−25													
1994-95	Los Angeles	NHL	48	11	37	48	6	3	0	1	142	7.7	−20													
1995-96	Los Angeles	NHL	62	15	66	81	32	5	0	2	144	10.4	−7													
	St. Louis	NHL	18	8	13	21	2	1	1	1	51	15.7	−6						13	2	14	16	0	1	0	1
1996-97	NY Rangers	NHL	82	25	*72	97	28	6	0	2	286	8.7	12						15	10	10	20	2	3	0	2
1997-98	NY Rangers	NHL	82	23	*67	90	28	6	0	4	201	11.4	−11													
	Canada	Olympics	6	0	4	4	2																			
1998-99	NY Rangers	NHL	70	9	53	62	14	3	0	3	132	6.8	−23	1137	52.0	7	11	21:04								
	NHL Totals		1487	*894	*1963	*2857	577	204	73	91	5089	17.6		1137	52.0	7	11	21:04	208	*122	*260	*382	66	34	11	24

OHA Second All-Star Team (1978) • WHA Second All-Star Team (1979) • Won Lou Kaplan Trophy (WHA Rookie of the Year) (1979) • Won Hart Trophy (1980, 1981, 1982, 1983, 1984, 1985, 1986, 1987, 1989) • Won Lady Byng Trophy (1980, 1991, 1992, 1994, 1999) • NHL Second All-Star Team (1980, 1988, 1989, 1990, 1994, 1997, 1998) • NHL First All-Star Team (1981, 1982, 1983, 1984, 1985, 1986, 1987, 1991) • Won Art Ross Trophy (1981, 1982, 1983, 1984, 1985, 1986, 1987, 1990, 1991, 1994) • NHL record for assists in regular season (1981, 1982, 1983, 1985, 1986) • NHL record for points in regular season (1981, 1982, 1986) • NHL record for goals in regular season (1982) • Won Lester B. Pearson Award (1982, 1983, 1984, 1985, 1987) • NHL record for assists in one playoff year (1983, 1985, 1988) • NHL record for points in one playoff year (1983, 1985) • Won Conn Smythe Trophy (1985, 1988) • NHL Plus/Minus Leader (1982, 1984, 1985, 1987) • Selected Chrysler-Dodge/NHL Performer of the Year (1985, 1986, 1987) • Won Dodge Performance of the Year Award (1989) • Won Lester Patrick Trophy (1994)

Played in NHL All-Star Game (1980, 1981, 1982, 1983, 1984, 1985, 1986, 1988, 1989, 1990, 1991, 1992, 1994, 1996, 1997, 1998, 1999)

Signed as an underage free agent by **Indianapolis** (WHA), June 12, 1978. Traded to **Edmonton** (WHA) by **Indianapolis** (WHA) with Eddie Mio and Peter Driscoll for cash, November, 1978. Reclaimed by **Edmonton** as an under-age junior prior to Expansion Draft, June 9, 1979. Claimed as priority selection by **Edmonton**, June 9, 1979. Traded to **LA Kings** by **Edmonton** with Mike Krushelnyski and Marty McSorley for Jimmy Carson, Martin Gelinas, LA Kings' 1st round choices in 1989 (acquired by New Jersey — New Jersey selected Jason Miller), 1991 (Martin Rucinsky) and 1993 (Nick Stajduhar) Entry Drafts and cash, August 9, 1988. Traded to **St. Louis** by **LA Kings** for Craig Johnson, Patrice Tardif, Roman Vopat, St. Louis 5th round choice (Peter Hogan) in 1996 Entry Draft and 1st round choice (Matt Zultek) in 1997 Entry Draft, February 27, 1996. Signed as a free agent by **NY Rangers**, July 21, 1996.

GRIER, Michael
(GREER)   **EDM.**

Right wing. Shoots right. 6'1", 227 lbs.   Born, Detroit, MI, January 5, 1975. St. Louis' 7th choice, 219th overall, in 1993 Entry Draft.

Season	Club	League	GP	G	A	Pts	PIM	PP	SH	GW	S	%	+/−	TF	F%	H	SB	Min	GP	G	A	Pts	PIM	PP	SH	GW
1992-93	St. Sebastian's	H.S.	22	16	27	43	32																			
1993-94	Boston University	H.E.	39	9	9	18	56																			
1994-95	Boston University	H.E.	37	*29	26	55	85																			
1995-96	Boston University	H.E.	38	21	25	46	82																			
1996-97	Edmonton	NHL	79	15	17	32	45	4	0	2	89	16.9	7						12	3	1	4	4	1	0	1
1997-98	Edmonton	NHL	66	9	6	15	73	1	0	1	90	10.0	−3						12	2	2	4	13	0	0	1
1998-99	Edmonton	NHL	82	20	24	44	54	3	2	1	143	14.0	5	34	20.6	188	49	15:57	4	1	1	2	6	0	0	2
	NHL Totals		227	44	47	91	172	8	2	4	322	13.7		34	20.6	188	49	15:57	28	6	4	10	23	1	0	2

Hockey East First All-Star Team (1995) • NCAA East First All-American Team (1995)

Rights traded to **Edmonton** by **St. Louis** with Curtis Joseph for St. Louis' 1st round choices in 1996 (previously acquired, St. Louis selected Marty Reasoner) and 1997 (later traded to LA Kings — LA Kings selected Matt Zultek) Entry Drafts, August 4, 1995.

GRIMSON, Stu
ANA.

Left wing. Shoots left. 6'5", 227 lbs.   Born, Kamloops, B.C., May 20, 1965. Calgary's 8th choice, 143rd overall, in 1985 Entry Draft.

Season	Club	League	GP	G	A	Pts	PIM	PP	SH	GW	S	%	+/−	TF	F%	H	SB	Min	GP	G	A	Pts	PIM	PP	SH	GW
1982-83	Regina	WHL	48	0	1	1	105												5	0	0	0	14			
1983-84	Regina	WHL	63	8	8	16	131												21	0	1	1	29			
1984-85	Regina	WHL	71	24	32	56	248												8	1	2	3	14			
1985-86	U. of Manitoba	CWUAA	12	7	4	11	113												8	1	1	2	24			
1986-87	U. of Manitoba	CWUAA	29	8	8	16	67												14	4	2	6	28			
1987-88	Salt Lake	IHL	38	9	5	14	268																			
1988-89	Calgary	NHL	1	0	0	0	5	0	0	0	0	0.0	0													
	Salt Lake	IHL	72	9	18	27	397												14	2	3	5	86			
1989-90	Calgary	NHL	3	0	0	0	17	0	0	0	0	0.0	−1						4	0	0	0	8			
	Salt Lake	IHL	62	8	8	16	319												5	0	0	0	46	0	0	0
1990-91	Chicago	NHL	35	0	1	1	183	0	0	0	14	0.0	−3						14	0	1	1	10	0	0	0
1991-92	Chicago	NHL	54	2	2	4	234	0	0	0	23	8.7	−2													
	Indianapolis	IHL	5	1	1	2	17												2	0	0	0	4	0	0	0
1992-93	Chicago	NHL	78	1	1	2	193	1	0	0	14	7.1	2													
1993-94	Anaheim	NHL	77	1	5	6	199	0	0	0	34	2.9	−6													
1994-95	Anaheim	NHL	31	0	1	1	110	0	0	0	14	0.0	−7													
	Detroit	NHL	11	0	0	0	37	0	0	0	4	0.0	−4						11	1	0	1	26	0	0	0
1995-96	Detroit	NHL	56	0	1	1	128	0	0	0	19	0.0	−10						2	0	0	0	0	0	0	0
1996-97	Detroit	NHL	1	0	0	0	0	0	0	0	0	0.0	−1													
	Hartford	NHL	75	2	2	4	218	0	0	0	17	11.8	−7													
1997-98	Carolina	NHL	82	3	4	7	204	0	0	1	17	17.6	0						3	0	0	0	30	0	0	0
1998-99	Anaheim	NHL	73	3	0	3	158	0	0	0	10	30.0	0	0	0.0	25	4	3:25								
	NHL Totals		577	12	17	29	1686	1	0	2	166	7.2		0	0.0	25	4	3:25	37	1	1	2	116	0	0	0

• Re-entered NHL draft. Originally Detroit's 11th choice, 193rd overall, in 1983 Entry Draft.

Claimed on waivers by **Chicago** from **Calgary**, October 1, 1990. Claimed by **Anaheim** from **Chicago** in Expansion Draft, June 24, 1993. Traded to **Detroit** by **Anaheim** with Mark Ferner and Anaheim's 6th round choice (Magnus Nilsson) in 1996 Entry Draft for Mike Sillinger and Jason York, April 4, 1995. Claimed on waivers by **Hartford** from **Detroit**, October 13, 1996. Transferred to **Carolina** after **Hartford** franchise relocated, June 25, 1997. Traded to **Anaheim** by **Carolina** with Kevin Haller for David Karpa and a 4th round choice in 2000 Entry Draft, August 11, 1998.

GROLEAU, Francois
(groh-LOH)

Defense. Shoots left. 6', 197 lbs.   Born, Longueuil, Que., January 23, 1973. Calgary's 2nd choice, 41st overall, in 1991 Entry Draft.

Season	Club	League	GP	G	A	Pts	PIM	PP	SH	GW	S	%	+/−	TF	F%	H	SB	Min	GP	G	A	Pts	PIM	PP	SH	GW
1988-89	Ste-Foy	QAAA	42	3	24	27	42												6	0	1	1	12			
1989-90	Shawinigan	QMJHL	65	11	54	65	80												6	0	3	3	2			
1990-91	Shawinigan	QMJHL	70	9	60	69	70												10	5	15	20	8			
1991-92	Shawinigan	QMJHL	65	8	70	78	74												4	0	1	1	14			
1992-93	St-Jean	QMJHL	48	7	38	45	66												7	0	1	1	2			
1993-94	Saint John	AHL	73	8	14	22	49																			
1994-95	Saint John	AHL	65	6	34	40	28												14	2	7	9	16			
	Cornwall	AHL	8	1	2	3	7																			

			Regular Season																	Playoffs							
Season	Club	League	GP	G	A	Pts	PIM	PP	SH	GW	S	%	+/–	TF	F%	H	SB	Min	GP	G	A	Pts	PIM	PP	SH	GW
1995-96	**Montreal**	**NHL**	**2**	**0**	**1**	**1**	**2**	**0**	**0**	**0**	**1**	**0.0**	**2**	....	....	....	....	....	....	....	....	....	....	....	....	....
	San Francisco	IHL	63	6	26	32	60	....	....	....	....	....	....	....	....	....	....	....	....	....	....	....	....	....	....	....
	Fredericton	AHL	12	3	5	8	10	....	....	....	....	....	....	....	....	....	....	....	10	1	6	7	14	....	....	....
1996-97	**Montreal**	**NHL**	**5**	**0**	**0**	**0**	**4**	**0**	**0**	**0**	**3**	**0.0**	**0**	....	....	....	....	....	....	....	....	....	....	....	....	....
	Fredericton	AHL	47	8	24	32	43	....	....	....	....	....	....	....	....	....	....	....	....	....	....	....	....	....	....	....
1997-98	**Montreal**	**NHL**	**1**	**0**	**0**	**0**	**0**	**0**	**0**	**0**	**3**	**0.0**	**1**	....	....	....	....	....	....	....	....	....	....	....	....	....
	Fredericton	AHL	63	14	26	40	70	....	....	....	....	....	....	....	....	....	....	....	4	0	2	2	4	....	....	....
1998-99	Augsburg	Germany	52	9	21	30	67	....	....	....	....	....	....	....	....	....	....	....	5	0	4	4	4	....	....	....
	NHL Totals		**8**	**0**	**1**	**1**	**6**	**0**	**0**	**0**	**7**	**0.0**		....	....	....	....	....	....	....	....	....	....	....	....	....

QMJHL Second All-Star Team (1990) • QMJHL First All-Star Team (1992)
Traded to **Quebec** by **Calgary** for Ed Ward, March 23, 1995. Signed as a free agent by **Montreal**, June 17, 1995.

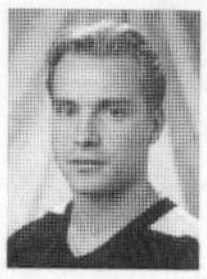

GRONMAN, Tuomas

(GROHN-mahn)

Defense. Shoots right. 6'3", 219 lbs. Born, Viitasaari, Finland, March 22, 1974. Quebec's 3rd choice, 29th overall, in 1992 Entry Draft.

1990-91	Lukko Rauma	Finn-Jr.	21	8	7	15	14	....	....	....	....	....	....	....	....	....	....	....	14	2	8	10	0	....	....	....
1991-92	Tacoma	WHL	61	5	18	23	102	....	....	....	....	....	....	....	....	....	....	....	4	0	1	1	2	....	....	....
1992-93	Lukko Rauma	Finn-Jr.	1	0	0	0	0	....	....	....	....	....	....	....	....	....	....	....	....	....	....	....	....	....	....	....
	Lukko Rauma	Finland	45	2	11	13	46	....	....	....	....	....	....	....	....	....	....	....	3	1	0	1	2	....	....	....
1993-94	Lukko Rauma	Finland	44	4	12	16	60	....	....	....	....	....	....	....	....	....	....	....	9	0	1	1	14	....	....	....
1994-95	TPS Turku	Finn-Jr.	1	0	0	0	0	....	....	....	....	....	....	....	....	....	....	....	....	....	....	....	....	....	....	....
	TPS Turku	Finland	47	4	20	24	66	....	....	....	....	....	....	....	....	....	....	....	13	2	2	4	43	....	....	....
1995-96	TPS Turku	Finland	32	5	7	12	85	....	....	....	....	....	....	....	....	....	....	....	11	1	4	5	16	....	....	....
	Finland	Nat-Team	2	0	0	0	4	....	....	....	....	....	....	....	....	....	....	....	....	....	....	....	....	....	....	....
1996-97	**Chicago**	**NHL**	**16**	**0**	**1**	**1**	**13**	**0**	**0**	**0**	**9**	**0.0**	**–4**	....	....	....	....	....	....	....	....	....	....	....	....	....
	Indianapolis	IHL	51	5	16	21	89	....	....	....	....	....	....	....	....	....	....	....	4	1	1	2	6	....	....	....
1997-98	Indianapolis	IHL	6	0	3	3	6	....	....	....	....	....	....	....	....	....	....	....	....	....	....	....	....	....	....	....
	Pittsburgh	**NHL**	**22**	**1**	**2**	**3**	**25**	**1**	**0**	**1**	**33**	**3.0**	**3**	....	....	....	....	....	**1**	**0**	**0**	**0**	**0**	**0**	**0**	**0**
	Syracuse	AHL	33	6	14	20	45	....	....	....	....	....	....	....	....	....	....	....	....	....	....	....	....	....	....	....
	Finland	Nat-Team	2	0	0	0	0	....	....	....	....	....	....	....	....	....	....	....	....	....	....	....	....	....	....	....
	Finland	Olympics	4	0	0	0	2	....	....	....	....	....	....	....	....	....	....	....	....	....	....	....	....	....	....	....
1998-99	Kansas City	IHL	4	0	0	0	0	....	....	....	....	....	....	....	....	....	....	....	....	....	....	....	....	....	....	....
	NHL Totals		**38**	**1**	**3**	**4**	**38**	**1**	**0**	**1**	**42**	**2.4**		....	....	....	....	....	**1**	**0**	**0**	**0**	**0**	**0**	**0**	**0**

Rights traded to **Chicago** by **Colorado** for Chicago's 2nd round choice (Phillippe Sauve) in 1998 Entry Draft, July 10, 1996. Traded to **Pittsburgh** by **Chicago** for Greg Johnson, October 27, 1997.

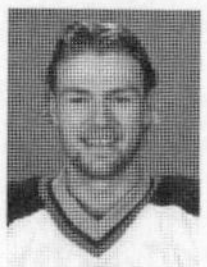

GROSEK, Michal

(GROH-shehk) **BUF.**

Left wing. Shoots right. 6'2", 207 lbs. Born, Vyskov, Czech., June 1, 1975. Winnipeg's 7th choice, 145th overall, in 1993 Entry Draft.

1992-93	ZPS Zlin	Czech.	17	1	3	4	....	....	....	....	....	....	....	....	....	....	....	....	....	....	....	....	....	....	....	....
1993-94	Tacoma	WHL	30	25	20	45	106	....	....	....	....	....	....	....	....	....	....	....	7	2	2	4	30	....	....	....
	Winnipeg	**NHL**	**3**	**1**	**0**	**1**	**0**	**0**	**0**	**0**	**4**	**25.0**	**–1**	....	....	....	....	....	....	....	....	....	....	....	....	....
	Moncton	AHL	20	1	2	3	47	....	....	....	....	....	....	....	....	....	....	....	2	0	0	0	0	....	....	....
1994-95	**Winnipeg**	**NHL**	**24**	**2**	**2**	**4**	**21**	**0**	**0**	**1**	**27**	**7.4**	**–3**	....	....	....	....	....	....	....	....	....	....	....	....	....
	Springfield	AHL	45	10	22	32	98	....	....	....	....	....	....	....	....	....	....	....	....	....	....	....	....	....	....	....
1995-96	**Winnipeg**	**NHL**	**1**	**0**	**0**	**0**	**0**	**0**	**0**	**0**	**1**	**0.0**	**–1**	....	....	....	....	....	....	....	....	....	....	....	....	....
	Springfield	AHL	39	16	19	35	68	....	....	....	....	....	....	....	....	....	....	....	....	....	....	....	....	....	....	....
	Buffalo	**NHL**	**22**	**6**	**4**	**10**	**31**	**2**	**0**	**1**	**33**	**18.2**	**0**	....	....	....	....	....	....	....	....	....	....	....	....	....
1996-97	**Buffalo**	**NHL**	**82**	**15**	**21**	**36**	**71**	**1**	**0**	**2**	**117**	**12.8**	**25**	....	....	....	....	....	**12**	**3**	**3**	**6**	**8**	**0**	**0**	**0**
1997-98	**Buffalo**	**NHL**	**67**	**10**	**20**	**30**	**60**	**2**	**0**	**1**	**114**	**8.8**	**9**	....	....	....	....	....	**15**	**6**	**4**	**10**	**28**	**2**	**0**	**3**
1998-99	**Buffalo**	**NHL**	**76**	**20**	**30**	**50**	**102**	**4**	**0**	**3**	**140**	**14.3**	**21**	**5**	**60.0**	**98**	**20**	**17:14**	**13**	**0**	**4**	**4**	**28**	**0**	**0**	**0**
	NHL Totals		**275**	**54**	**77**	**131**	**285**	**9**	**0**	**8**	**436**	**12.4**		**5**	**60.0**	**98**	**20**	**17:14**	**40**	**9**	**11**	**20**	**64**	**2**	**0**	**3**

Traded to **Buffalo** by **Winnipeg** with Darryl Shannon for Craig Muni, February 15, 1996.

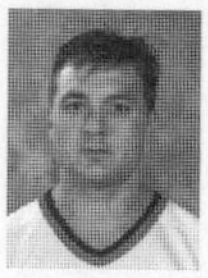

GRUDEN, John

(GROO-duhn) **OTT.**

Defense. Shoots left. 6', 190 lbs. Born, Virginia, MN, June 4, 1970. Boston's 7th choice, 168th overall, in 1990 Entry Draft.

1989-90	Waterloo	USHL	47	7	39	46	35	....	....	....	....	....	....	....	....	....	....	....	....	....	....	....	....	....	....	....
1990-91	Ferris State	CCHA	37	4	11	15	27	....	....	....	....	....	....	....	....	....	....	....	....	....	....	....	....	....	....	....
1991-92	Ferris State	CCHA	37	9	14	23	24	....	....	....	....	....	....	....	....	....	....	....	....	....	....	....	....	....	....	....
1992-93	Ferris State	CCHA	41	16	14	30	58	....	....	....	....	....	....	....	....	....	....	....	....	....	....	....	....	....	....	....
1993-94	Ferris State	CCHA	38	11	25	36	52	....	....	....	....	....	....	....	....	....	....	....	....	....	....	....	....	....	....	....
	Boston	**NHL**	**7**	**0**	**1**	**1**	**2**	**0**	**0**	**0**	**8**	**0.0**	**–3**	....	....	....	....	....	....	....	....	....	....	....	....	....
1994-95	**Boston**	**NHL**	**38**	**0**	**6**	**6**	**22**	**0**	**0**	**0**	**30**	**0.0**	**3**	....	....	....	....	....	....	....	....	....	....	....	....	....
	Providence	AHL	1	0	1	1	0	....	....	....	....	....	....	....	....	....	....	....	....	....	....	....	....	....	....	....
1995-96	**Boston**	**NHL**	**14**	**0**	**0**	**0**	**4**	**0**	**0**	**0**	**12**	**0.0**	**–3**	....	....	....	....	....	**3**	**0**	**1**	**1**	**0**	**0**	**0**	**0**
	Providence	AHL	39	5	19	24	29	....	....	....	....	....	....	....	....	....	....	....	....	....	....	....	....	....	....	....
1996-97	Providence	AHL	78	18	27	45	52	....	....	....	....	....	....	....	....	....	....	....	10	3	6	9	4	....	....	....
1997-98	Detroit	IHL	76	13	42	55	74	....	....	....	....	....	....	....	....	....	....	....	21	1	8	9	14	....	....	....
1998-99	**Ottawa**	**NHL**	**13**	**0**	**1**	**1**	**8**	**0**	**0**	**0**	**10**	**0.0**	**0**	**0**	**0.0**	**16**	**4**	**13:07**	....	....	....	....	....	....	....	....
	Detroit	IHL	59	10	28	38	52	....	....	....	....	....	....	....	....	....	....	....	10	0	1	1	6	....	....	....
	NHL Totals		**72**	**0**	**8**	**8**	**36**	**0**	**0**	**0**	**60**	**0.0**		**0**	**0.0**	**16**	**4**	**13:07**	**3**	**0**	**1**	**1**	**0**	**0**	**0**	**0**

CCHA First All-Star Team (1994) • NCAA West First All-American Team (1994) • IHL Second All-Star Team (1998)
Signed as a free agent by **Ottawa**, August 7, 1998.

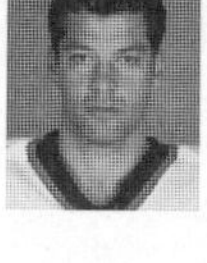

GUERIN, Bill

(GAIR-ihn) **EDM.**

Right wing. Shoots right. 6'2", 210 lbs. Born, Wilbraham, MA, November 9, 1970. New Jersey's 1st choice, 5th overall, in 1989 Entry Draft.

1985-86	Springfield	NEJHL	48	26	19	45	71	....	....	....	....	....	....	....	....	....	....	....	....	....	....	....	....	....	....	....
1986-87	Springfield	NEJHL	32	34	20	54	40	....	....	....	....	....	....	....	....	....	....	....	....	....	....	....	....	....	....	....
1987-88	Springfield	NEJHL	38	31	44	75	146	....	....	....	....	....	....	....	....	....	....	....	....	....	....	....	....	....	....	....
1988-89	Springfield	NEJHL	31	32	35	67	90	....	....	....	....	....	....	....	....	....	....	....	....	....	....	....	....	....	....	....
1989-90	Boston College	H.E.	39	14	11	25	54	....	....	....	....	....	....	....	....	....	....	....	....	....	....	....	....	....	....	....
1990-91	Boston College	H.E.	38	26	19	45	102	....	....	....	....	....	....	....	....	....	....	....	....	....	....	....	....	....	....	....
	United States	Nat-Team	46	12	15	27	67	....	....	....	....	....	....	....	....	....	....	....	....	....	....	....	....	....	....	....
1991-92	**New Jersey**	**NHL**	**5**	**0**	**1**	**1**	**9**	**0**	**0**	**0**	**8**	**0.0**	**1**	....	....	....	....	....	**6**	**3**	**0**	**3**	**4**	**0**	**0**	**0**
	Utica	AHL	22	13	10	23	6	....	....	....	....	....	....	....	....	....	....	....	4	1	3	4	14	....	....	....
1992-93	**New Jersey**	**NHL**	**65**	**14**	**20**	**34**	**63**	**0**	**0**	**2**	**123**	**11.4**	**14**	....	....	....	....	....	**5**	**1**	**1**	**2**	**4**	**0**	**0**	**0**
	Utica	AHL	18	10	7	17	47	....	....	....	....	....	....	....	....	....	....	....	....	....	....	....	....	....	....	....
1993-94	**New Jersey**	**NHL**	**81**	**25**	**19**	**44**	**101**	**2**	**0**	**3**	**195**	**12.8**	**14**	....	....	....	....	....	**17**	**2**	**1**	**3**	**35**	**0**	**0**	**1**
1994-95♦	**New Jersey**	**NHL**	**48**	**12**	**13**	**25**	**72**	**4**	**0**	**3**	**96**	**12.5**	**6**	....	....	....	....	....	**20**	**3**	**8**	**11**	**30**	**1**	**0**	**0**
1995-96	**New Jersey**	**NHL**	**80**	**23**	**30**	**53**	**116**	**8**	**0**	**6**	**216**	**10.6**	**7**	....	....	....	....	....	....	....	....	....	....	....	....	....
1996-97	**New Jersey**	**NHL**	**82**	**29**	**18**	**47**	**95**	**7**	**0**	**9**	**177**	**16.4**	**–2**	....	....	....	....	....	**8**	**2**	**1**	**3**	**18**	**1**	**0**	**1**
1997-98	**New Jersey**	**NHL**	**19**	**5**	**5**	**10**	**13**	**1**	**0**	**2**	**48**	**10.4**	**0**	....	....	....	....	....	....	....	....	....	....	....	....	....
	Edmonton	**NHL**	**40**	**13**	**16**	**29**	**80**	**8**	**0**	**2**	**130**	**10.0**	**1**	....	....	....	....	....	**12**	**7**	**1**	**8**	**17**	**4**	**0**	**0**
	United States	Olympics	4	0	3	3	2	....	....	....	....	....	....	....	....	....	....	....	....	....	....	....	....	....	....	....
1998-99	**Edmonton**	**NHL**	**80**	**30**	**34**	**64**	**133**	**13**	**0**	**2**	**261**	**11.5**	**7**	**74**	**40.5**	**131**	**20**	**19:42**	**3**	**0**	**2**	**2**	**2**	**0**	**0**	**0**
	NHL Totals		**500**	**151**	**156**	**307**	**682**	**43**	**0**	**29**	**1254**	**12.0**		**74**	**40.5**	**131**	**20**	**19:42**	**71**	**18**	**14**	**32**	**110**	**6**	**0**	**2**

Traded to **Edmonton** by **New Jersey** with Valeri Zelepukin for Jason Arnott and Bryan Muir, January 4, 1998.

GUOLLA, Stephen (GUH-wah-lah) T.B.

Left wing. Shoots left. 6', 190 lbs. Born, Scarborough, Ont., March 15, 1973. Ottawa's 1st choice, 3rd overall, in 1994 Supplemental Draft.

Season	Club	League	GP	G	A	Pts	PIM	PP	SH	GW	S	%	+/-	TF	F%	H	SB	Min	GP	G	A	Pts	PIM	PP	SH	GW
1988-89	Toronto	MTHL	25	14	20	34	....																			
1989-90	Toronto	MTHL	40	42	47	89	....																			
1990-91	Wexford	OJHL	47	37	42	79	....												12	12	16	28				
1991-92	Michigan State	CCHA	33	4	9	13	8																			
1992-93	Michigan State	CCHA	39	19	35	54	6																			
1993-94	Michigan State	CCHA	41	23	46	69	16																			
1994-95	Michigan State	CCHA	40	16	35	51	16																			
1995-96	P.E.I. Senators	AHL	72	32	48	80	28												3	0	0	0	0			
1996-97	**San Jose**	**NHL**	43	13	8	21	14	2	0	1	81	16.0	–10													
	Kentucky	AHL	34	22	22	44	10												4	2	1	3	0			
1997-98	**San Jose**	**NHL**	7	1	1	2	0	0	0	0	9	11.1	–2													
	Kentucky	AHL	69	37	63	100	45												3	0	0	0	0			
1998-99	**San Jose**	**NHL**	14	2	2	4	6	0	0	1	22	9.1	3	172	36.6	19	6	13:54								
	Kentucky	AHL	53	29	47	76	33																			
	NHL Totals		64	16	11	27	20	2	0	2	112	14.3		172	36.6	19	6	13:54								

CCHA Second All-Star Team (1994) • NCAA West Second All-American Team (1994) • AHL Second All-Star Team (1998, 1999) • Won Les Cunningham Plaque (MVP - AHL) (1998)

Signed as a free agent by **San Jose**, August 22, 1996. Traded to **Tampa Bay** by **San Jose** with Bill Houlder, Shawn Burr and Andrei Zyuzin for Niklas Sundstrom and NY Rangers' 3rd round choice (previously acquired) in 2000 Entry Draft, August 4, 1999.

GUREN, Miloslav (GOO-rihn) MTL.

Defense. Shoots left. 6'2", 209 lbs. Born, Uherske Hradiste, Czech., September 24, 1976. Montreal's 2nd choice, 60th overall, in 1995 Entry Draft.

Season	Club	League	GP	G	A	Pts	PIM	PP	SH	GW	S	%	+/-	TF	F%	H	SB	Min	GP	G	A	Pts	PIM	PP	SH	GW
1993-94	ZPS Zlin	Cze-Rep	22	1	5	6	....												3	0	0	0				
1994-95	ZPS Zlin	Cze-Rep	33	3	7	10	10												12	1	0	1	6			
1995-96	ZPS Zlin	Cze-Rep	28	1	2	3													7	1	0	1				
1996-97	Fredericton	AHL	79	6	26	32	26												....							
1997-98	Fredericton	AHL	78	15	36	51	36												4	1	2	3	0			
1998-99	**Montreal**	**NHL**	12	0	1	1	4	0	0	0	11	0.0	–1	0	0.0	4	10	12:02								
	Fredericton	AHL	63	5	16	21	24												15	4	7	11	10			
	NHL Totals		12	0	1	1	4	0	0	0	11	0.0		0	0.0	4	10	12:02								

GUSAROV, Alexei (goo-SAH-rahf)

Defense. Shoots left. 6'3", 185 lbs. Born, Leningrad, USSR, July 8, 1964. Quebec's 11th choice, 213th overall, in 1988 Entry Draft.

Season	Club	League	GP	G	A	Pts	PIM	PP	SH	GW	S	%	+/-	TF	F%	H	SB	Min	GP	G	A	Pts	PIM	PP	SH	GW
1981-82	Leningrad	USSR	20	1	2	3	16																			
1982-83	Leningrad	USSR	42	2	1	3	32																			
1983-84	Leningrad	USSR	43	2	3	5	32																			
1984-85	CSKA Moscow	USSR	36	3	2	5	26																			
1985-86	CSKA Moscow	USSR	40	3	5	8	30																			
1986-87	CSKA Moscow	USSR	38	4	7	11	24																			
1987-88	CSKA Moscow	USSR	39	3	2	5	28																			
	Soviet Union	Olympics	8	1	3	4	6																			
1988-89	CSKA Moscow	USSR	42	5	4	9	37																			
1989-90	CSKA Moscow	USSR	42	4	7	11	42																			
1990-91	CSKA Moscow	USSR	15	0	0	0	12																			
	Quebec	**NHL**	36	3	9	12	12	1	0	0	36	8.3	–4													
	Halifax	AHL	2	0	3	3	2												....							
1991-92	**Quebec**	**NHL**	68	5	18	23	22	3	0	1	66	7.6	–9													
	Halifax	AHL	3	0	0	0	0																			
1992-93	**Quebec**	**NHL**	79	8	22	30	57	0	2	1	60	13.3	18						5	0	1	1	0	0	0	0
1993-94	**Quebec**	**NHL**	76	5	20	25	38	0	1	0	84	6.0	3													
1994-95	**Quebec**	**NHL**	14	1	2	3	6	0	0	1	7	14.3	–1													
1995-96♦	**Colorado**	**NHL**	65	5	15	20	56	0	0	0	42	11.9	29						21	0	9	9	12	0	0	0
1996-97	**Colorado**	**NHL**	58	2	12	14	28	0	0	0	33	6.1	–4						17	0	3	3	14	0	0	0
1997-98	**Colorado**	**NHL**	72	4	10	14	42	0	1	1	47	8.5	9						7	0	1	1	6	0	0	0
	Russia	Olympics	6	0	1	1	8																			
1998-99	**Colorado**	**NHL**	54	3	10	13	24	1	0	0	28	10.7	12	1	0.0	22	65	19:57	5	0	0	0	2	0	0	0
	NHL Totals		522	36	118	154	285	5	4	4	403	8.9		1	0.0	22	65	19:57	55	0	14	14	34	0	0	0

Transferred to **Colorado** after **Quebec** franchise relocated, June 21, 1995.

GUSEV, Sergey (GOO-sehv) T.B.

Defense. Shoots left. 6'1", 195 lbs. Born, Nizhny Tagil, USSR, July 31, 1975. Dallas' 4th choice, 69th overall, in 1995 Entry Draft.

Season	Club	League	GP	G	A	Pts	PIM	PP	SH	GW	S	%	+/-	TF	F%	H	SB	Min	GP	G	A	Pts	PIM	PP	SH	GW
1994-95	CSK Samara	CIS	50	3	5	8	58												....							
1995-96	Michigan	IHL	73	11	17	28	76												....							
1996-97	Michigan	IHL	51	7	8	15	44												4	0	4	4	6			
1997-98	**Dallas**	**NHL**	9	0	0	0	2	0	0	0	5	0.0	–5													
	Michigan	IHL	36	3	6	9	36												4	0	2	2	6			
1998-99	**Dallas**	**NHL**	22	1	4	5	6	0	0	1	30	3.3	5	0	0.0	12	16	12:04								
	Michigan	IHL	12	0	6	6	14																			
	Tampa Bay	**NHL**	14	0	3	3	10	0	0	0	16	0.0	–8	0	0.0	13	28	21:30								
	NHL Totals		45	1	7	8	18	0	0	1	51	2.0		0	0.0	25	44	15:44								

Traded to **Tampa Bay** by **Dallas** for Benoit Hogue and a conditional choice in 2001 Entry Draft, March 21, 1999.

GUSTAFSSON, Per (GOOS-tahf-suhn)

Defense. Shoots left. 6'2", 190 lbs. Born, Osterham, Sweden, June 6, 1970. Florida's 10th choice, 261st overall, in 1994 Entry Draft.

Season	Club	League	GP	G	A	Pts	PIM	PP	SH	GW	S	%	+/-	TF	F%	H	SB	Min	GP	G	A	Pts	PIM	PP	SH	GW
1988-89	HV Jonkoping	Swede-Jr.	14	1	4	5	8												3	0	0	0	2			
1989-90	HV Jonkoping	Swede-Jr.	27	4	3	7	16												....							
1990-91	HV Jonkoping	Sweden	31	3	5	8	16												2	0	0	0	4			
1991-92	HV Jonkoping	Sweden	39	9	8	17	22												3	0	0	0	0			
1992-93	HV Jonkoping	Sweden	40	6	3	9	28												....							
1993-94	HV Jonkoping	Sweden	34	9	7	16	10												....							
1994-95	HV Jonkoping	Sweden	38	10	6	16	14												13	7	5	12	8			
1995-96	HV Jonkoping	Sweden	34	8	13	21	12												4	3	1	4	2			
1996-97	**Florida**	**NHL**	58	7	22	29	22	2	0	1	105	6.7	11													
1997-98	**Toronto**	**NHL**	22	1	4	5	10	0	0	0	24	4.2	–5													
	St. John's	AHL	25	7	18	25	10												1	0	0	0	0			
	Ottawa	**NHL**	9	0	1	1	6	0	0	0	12	0.0	3						1	0	0	0	0	0	0	0
1998-99	HV Jonkoping	Sweden	50	12	16	28	52																			
	NHL Totals		89	8	27	35	38	2	0	1	141	5.7							1	0	0	0	0	0	0	0

Swedish World All-Star Team (1996)

Traded to **Toronto** by **Florida** for Mike Lankshear, June 13, 1997. Traded to **Ottawa** by **Toronto** for Ottawa's 8th round choice (Dwight Wolfe) in 1998 Entry Draft, March 17, 1998.

HAGGERTY, Sean — NYI

Left wing. Shoots left. 6'1", 186 lbs. Born, Rye, NY, February 11, 1976. Toronto's 2nd choice, 48th overall, in 1994 Entry Draft.

						Regular Season														Playoffs						
Season	Club	League	GP	G	A	Pts	PIM	PP	SH	GW	S	%	+/-	TF	F%	H	SB	Min	GP	G	A	Pts	PIM	PP	SH	GW
1990-91	Westminster	H.S.	25	20	22	42	....																			
1991-92	Westminster	H.S.	25	24	36	64	....																			
1992-93	Boston	USAHA	72	70	111	181	80																			
1993-94	Detroit	OHL	60	31	32	63	21												17	9	10	19	11			
1994-95	Detroit	OHL	61	40	49	89	37												21	13	24	37	18			
1995-96	Detroit	OHL	66	*60	51	111	78												17	15	9	24	30			
	Toronto	**NHL**	1	0	0	0	0	0	0	0	0	0.0	0						1	0	0	0	0			
	Worcester	AHL	....	....	....	....	....												4	1	0	1	4			
1996-97	Kentucky	AHL	77	13	22	35	60												4	1	0	1	4			
1997-98	NY Islanders	**NHL**	5	0	0	0	0	0	0	0	2	0.0	-3						....	....	....	....	....			
	Kentucky	AHL	63	33	20	53	64												3	0	2	2	4			
1998-99	Lowell	AHL	77	19	27	46	40												3	0	1	1	0			
	NHL Totals		6	0	0	0	0	0	0	0	2	0.0							....	....	....	....	....			

Memorial Cup All-Star Team (1995) • OHL Second All-Star Team (1996) • AHL Second All-Star Team (1998)

Traded to **NY Islanders** by **Toronto** with Darby Hendrickson, Kenny Jonsson and Toronto's 1st round choice (Roberto Luongo) in 1997 Entry Draft for Wendel Clark, Mathieu Schneider and D.J. Smith, March 13, 1996.

HALKO, Steven — (HAL-koh) CAR.

Defense. Shoots right. 6'1", 195 lbs. Born, Etobicoke, Ont., March 8, 1974. Hartford's 10th choice, 225th overall, in 1992 Entry Draft.

Season	Club	League	GP	G	A	Pts	PIM	PP	SH	GW	S	%	+/-	TF	F%	H	SB	Min	GP	G	A	Pts	PIM	PP	SH	GW
1991-92	Thornhill	OJHL	44	15	46	61	43																			
1992-93	U. of Michigan	CCHA	39	1	12	13	12																			
1993-94	U. of Michigan	CCHA	41	2	13	15	32																			
1994-95	U. of Michigan	CCHA	39	2	14	16	20																			
1995-96	U. of Michigan	CCHA	43	4	16	20	32																			
1996-97	Springfield	AHL	70	1	5	6	37												11	0	2	2	8			
1997-98	Carolina	**NHL**	18	0	2	2	10	0	0	0	7	0.0	-1						1	0	0	0	0			
	New Haven	AHL	65	1	19	20	44																			
1998-99	Carolina	**NHL**	20	0	3	3	24	0	0	0	6	0.0	5	0	0.0	32	11	15:57	4	0	0	0	2	0	0	0
	New Haven	AHL	42	2	7	9	58																			
	NHL Totals		38	0	5	5	34	0	0	0	13	0.0		0	0.0	32	11	15:57	4	0	0	0	2	0	0	0

CCHA Second All-Star Team (1995, 1996) • NCAA Championship All-Tournament Team (1996)

Transferred to **Carolina** after **Hartford** franchise relocated, June 25, 1997.

HALLER, Kevin — (HAHL-ehr) ANA.

Defense. Shoots left. 6'2", 195 lbs. Born, Trochu, Alta., December 5, 1970. Buffalo's 1st choice, 14th overall, in 1989 Entry Draft.

Season	Club	League	GP	G	A	Pts	PIM	PP	SH	GW	S	%	+/-	TF	F%	H	SB	Min	GP	G	A	Pts	PIM	PP	SH	GW
1986-87	Three Hills	AAHA	12	10	11	21	8																			
1987-88	Olds Grizzlies	AJHL	53	13	31	44	66																			
1988-89	Regina	WHL	72	10	31	41	99																			
1989-90	Regina	WHL	58	16	37	53	93												11	2	9	11	16			
	Buffalo	**NHL**	2	0	0	0	0	0	0	0	1	0.0	0													
1990-91	**Buffalo**	**NHL**	21	1	8	9	20	1	0	0	42	2.4	9						6	1	4	5	10	0	0	0
	Rochester	AHL	52	0	8	10	53												10	2	1	3	6			
1991-92	**Buffalo**	**NHL**	58	6	15	21	75	2	0	1	76	7.9	-13													
	Rochester	AHL	4	0	0	0	18																			
	Montreal	**NHL**	8	2	2	4	17	1	0	0	9	22.2	4						9	0	0	0	6	0	0	0
1992-93 ♦	Montreal	NHL	73	11	14	25	117	6	0	1	126	8.7	7						17	1	6	7	16	1	0	0
1993-94	Montreal	NHL	68	4	9	13	118	0	0	1	72	5.6	3						7	1	1	2	19	0	0	0
1994-95	Philadelphia	NHL	36	2	8	10	48	0	0	0	26	7.7	16						15	4	4	8	10	0	1	1
1995-96	Philadelphia	NHL	69	5	9	14	92	0	2	2	89	5.6	18						6	0	1	1	8	0	0	0
1996-97	Philadelphia	NHL	27	0	5	5	37	0	0	0	34	0.0	-1													
	Hartford	NHL	35	2	6	8	48	0	0	0	43	4.7	-11													
1997-98	Carolina	NHL	65	3	5	8	94	0	0	0	67	4.5	-5													
1998-99	Anaheim	NHL	82	1	6	7	122	0	0	0	64	1.6	-1	0	0.0	95	110	20:39	4	0	0	0	2	0	0	0
	NHL Totals		544	37	87	124	788	10	2	5	649	5.7		0	0.0	95	110	20:39	64	7	16	23	71	1	1	1

WHL East First All-Star Team (1990)

Traded to **Montreal** by **Buffalo** for Petr Svoboda, March 10, 1992. Traded to **Philadelphia** by **Montreal** for Yves Racine, June 29, 1994. Traded to **Hartford** by **Philadelphia** with Philadelphia's 1st round choice (later traded to San Jose — San Jose selected Scott Hannan) in 1997 Entry Draft and Hartford/Carolina's 7th round choice (previously acquired, Carolina selected Andrew Merrick) in 1997 Entry Draft for Paul Coffey and Hartford's 3rd round choice (Kris Mallette) in 1997 Entry Draft, December 15, 1996. Transferred to **Carolina** after **Hartford** franchise relocated, June 25, 1997. Traded to **Anaheim** by **Carolina** with Stu Grimson for David Karpa and a 4th round choice in 2000 Entry Draft, August 11, 1998.

HALVERSON, Trevor — WSH.

Left wing. Shoots left. 6', 194 lbs. Born, White River, Ont., April 6, 1971. Washington's 2nd choice, 21st overall, in 1991 Entry Draft.

Season	Club	League	GP	G	A	Pts	PIM	PP	SH	GW	S	%	+/-	TF	F%	H	SB	Min	GP	G	A	Pts	PIM	PP	SH	GW
1987-88	S.S. Marie	NOHA	33	29	35	64	34																			
1988-89	North Bay	OHL	52	8	10	18	7																			
1989-90	North Bay	OHL	54	22	20	42	162												2	2	1	3	2			
1990-91	North Bay	OHL	54	22	20	42	172												2	2	1	3	2			
1991-92	North Bay	OHL	64	59	36	95	128												10	3	6	9	4			
1992-93	Hampton Roads	ECHL	9	7	5	12	6																			
	Baltimore	AHL	67	19	21	40	170												2	1	0	1	0			
1993-94	San Diego	IHL	58	4	9	13	115																			
	Milwaukee	IHL	4	1	0	1	8												2	0	0	0	17			
1994-95	Portland	AHL	5	0	1	1	9																			
	Hampton Roads	ECHL	42	14	26	40	194																			
1995-96	Las Vegas	IHL	22	6	9	15	86																			
	Utah	IHL	1	0	1	1	0																			
	Hampton Roads	ECHL	38	34	27	61	152												5	0	0	0	4			
	Portland	AHL	3	0	1	1	0																			
	Indianapolis	IHL	12	0	1	1	18																			
1996-97	Portland	AHL	50	9	8	17	157												3	1	1	2	4			
1997-98	Fort Wayne	IHL	14	1	4	5	34																			
	Manitoba	IHL	7	0	1	1	20																			
	Portland	AHL	43	14	13	27	181												10	2	4	6	20			
1998-99	Washington	**NHL**	17	0	4	4	28	0	0	0	16	0.0	-5	3	66.7	19	8	11:57								
	Portland	AHL	57	24	25	49	153																			
	NHL Totals		17	0	4	4	28	0	0	0	16	0.0		3	66.7	19	8	11:57								

HAMRLIK, Roman — (HAHM-reh-lik) EDM.

Defense. Shoots left. 6'2", 215 lbs. Born, Gottwaldov, Czech., April 12, 1974. Tampa Bay's 1st choice, 1st overall, in 1992 Entry Draft.

Season	Club	League	GP	G	A	Pts	PIM	PP	SH	GW	S	%	+/-	TF	F%	H	SB	Min	GP	G	A	Pts	PIM	PP	SH	GW
1990-91	ZPS Zlin	Czech.	14	2	2	4	18																			
1991-92	ZPS Zlin	Czech.	34	5	5	10	50																			
1992-93	Tampa Bay	**NHL**	67	6	15	21	71	1	0	1	113	5.3	-21													
	Atlanta	IHL	2	1	1	2	2																			
1993-94	Tampa Bay	**NHL**	64	3	18	21	135	0	0	0	158	1.9	-14													

			Regular Season																Playoffs							
Season	Club	League	GP	G	A	Pts	PIM	PP	SH	GW	S	%	+/-	TF	F%	H	SB	Min	GP	G	A	Pts	PIM	PP	SH	GW
1994-95	ZPS Zlin	Cze-Rep	2	1	0	1	10	....	....	....	....	....	....	....	....	....	....	....	....	....	....	....	....	....	....	....
	Tampa Bay	**NHL**	**48**	**12**	**11**	**23**	**86**	**7**	**1**	**2**	**134**	**9.0**	**−18**	....	....	....	....	....	....	....	....	....	....	....	....	....
1995-96	**Tampa Bay**	**NHL**	**82**	**16**	**49**	**65**	**103**	**12**	**0**	**2**	**281**	**5.7**	**−24**	....	....	....	....	....	**5**	**0**	**1**	**1**	**4**	**0**	**0**	**0**
1996-97	**Tampa Bay**	**NHL**	**79**	**12**	**28**	**40**	**57**	**6**	**0**	**0**	**238**	**5.0**	**−29**	....	....	....	....	....	....	....	....	....	....	....	....	....
1997-98	**Tampa Bay**	**NHL**	**37**	**3**	**12**	**15**	**22**	**1**	**0**	**0**	**86**	**3.5**	**−18**	....	....	....	....	....	....	....	....	....	....	....	....	....
	Edmonton	**NHL**	**41**	**6**	**20**	**26**	**48**	**4**	**1**	**3**	**112**	**5.4**	**3**	....	....	....	....	....	**12**	**0**	**6**	**6**	**12**	**0**	**0**	**0**
	Czech Republic	Olympics	6	1	0	1	2	....	....	....	....	....	....	....	....	....	....	....	....	....	....	....	....	....	....	....
1998-99	**Edmonton**	**NHL**	**75**	**8**	**24**	**32**	**70**	**3**	**0**	**0**	**172**	**4.7**	**9**	**0**	**0.0**	**144**	**121**	**23:49**	**3**	**0**	**0**	**0**	**2**	**0**	**0**	**0**
	NHL Totals		**493**	**66**	**177**	**243**	**592**	**34**	**2**	**8**	**1294**	**5.1**		**0**	**0.0**	**144**	**121**	**23:49**	**20**	**0**	**7**	**7**	**18**	**0**	**0**	**0**

Played in NHL All-Star Game (1996, 1999)

Traded to **Edmonton** by **Tampa Bay** with Paul Comrie for Bryan Marchment, Steve Kelly and Jason Bonsignore, December 30, 1997.

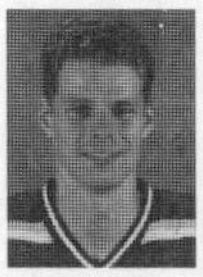

HANDZUS, Michal (HAHND-zuhs, MEE-chal) ST.L.

Center. Shoots left. 6'5", 210 lbs. Born, Banska Bystrica, Czech., March 11, 1977. St. Louis' 3rd choice, 101st overall, in 1995 Entry Draft.

Season	Club	League	GP	G	A	Pts	PIM	PP	SH	GW	S	%	+/-	TF	F%	H	SB	Min	GP	G	A	Pts	PIM	PP	SH	GW
1993-94	Banska Bystrica	Slov-Jr.	40	23	36	59	....	....	....	....	....	....	....	....	....	....	....	....	....	....	....	....	....	....	....	....
1994-95	Banska Bystrica	Slovak-2	22	15	14	29	10	....	....	....	....	....	....	....	....	....	....	....	....	....	....	....	....	....	....	....
1995-96	Banska Bystrica	Slovakia	19	3	1	4	8	....	....	....	....	....	....	....	....	....	....	....	....	....	....	....	....	....	....	....
1996-97	Poprad	Slovakia	44	15	18	33	....	....	....	....	....	....	....	....	....	....	....	....	....	....	....	....	....	....	....	....
1997-98	Worcester	AHL	69	27	36	63	54	....	....	....	....	....	....	....	....	....	....	....	11	2	6	8	10	....	....	....
1998-99	**St. Louis**	**NHL**	**66**	**4**	**12**	**16**	**30**	**0**	**0**	**0**	**78**	**5.1**	**−9**	**794**	**49.9**	**56**	**38**	**14:48**	**11**	**0**	**2**	**2**	**8**	**0**	**0**	**0**
	NHL Totals		**66**	**4**	**12**	**16**	**30**	**0**	**0**	**0**	**78**	**5.1**		**794**	**49.9**	**56**	**38**	**14:48**	**11**	**0**	**2**	**2**	**8**	**0**	**0**	**0**

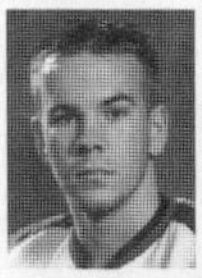

HANNAN, Scott S.J.

Defense. Shoots left. 6'2", 215 lbs. Born, Richmond, B.C., January 23, 1979. San Jose's 2nd choice, 23rd overall, in 1997 Entry Draft.

Season	Club	League	GP	G	A	Pts	PIM	PP	SH	GW	S	%	+/-	TF	F%	H	SB	Min	GP	G	A	Pts	PIM	PP	SH	GW
1994-95	Surrey	BCAHA	70	54	54	108	200	....	....	....	....	....	....	....	....	....	....	....	....	....	....	....	....	....	....	....
	Tacoma	WHL	2	0	0	0	0	....	....	....	....	....	....	....	....	....	....	....	....	....	....	....	....	....	....	....
1995-96	Kelowna	WHL	69	4	5	9	76	....	....	....	....	....	....	....	....	....	....	....	6	0	1	1	4	....	....	....
1996-97	Kelowna	WHL	70	17	26	43	101	....	....	....	....	....	....	....	....	....	....	....	6	0	0	0	8	....	....	....
1997-98	Kelowna	WHL	47	10	30	40	70	....	....	....	....	....	....	....	....	....	....	....	7	2	7	9	14	....	....	....
1998-99	Kelowna	WHL	47	15	30	45	92	....	....	....	....	....	....	....	....	....	....	....	6	1	2	3	14	....	....	....
	San Jose	**NHL**	**5**	**0**	**2**	**2**	**6**	**0**	**0**	**0**	**4**	**0.0**	**0**	**0**	**0.0**	**2**	**0**	**7:15**	....	....	....	....	....	....	....	....
	Kentucky	AHL	2	0	0	0	2	....	....	....	....	....	....	....	....	....	....	....	12	0	2	2	10	....	....	....
	NHL Totals		**5**	**0**	**2**	**2**	**6**	**0**	**0**	**0**	**4**	**0.0**		**0**	**0.0**	**2**	**0**	**7:15**	....	....	....	....	....	....	....	....

WHL West First All-Star Team (1999)

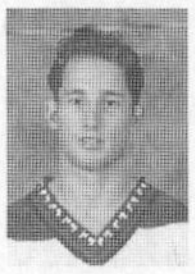

HANSEN, Tavis PHX.

Center. Shoots right. 6'2", 204 lbs. Born, Prince Albert, Sask., June 17, 1975. Winnipeg's 3rd choice, 58th overall, in 1994 Entry Draft.

Season	Club	League	GP	G	A	Pts	PIM	PP	SH	GW	S	%	+/-	TF	F%	H	SB	Min	GP	G	A	Pts	PIM	PP	SH	GW
1992-93	Shellbrook	SAHA	42	42	63	105	107	....	....	....	....	....	....	....	....	....	....	....	....	....	....	....	....	....	....	....
1993-94	Tacoma	WHL	71	23	31	54	122	....	....	....	....	....	....	....	....	....	....	....	8	1	3	4	17	....	....	....
1994-95	Tacoma	WHL	71	32	41	73	142	....	....	....	....	....	....	....	....	....	....	....	4	1	1	2	8	....	....	....
	Winnipeg	**NHL**	**1**	**0**	**0**	**0**	**0**	**0**	**0**	**0**	**0**	**0.0**	**0**	....	....	....	....	....	....	....	....	....	....	....	....	....
1995-96	Springfield	AHL	67	6	16	22	85	....	....	....	....	....	....	....	....	....	....	....	5	1	2	3	2	....	....	....
1996-97	**Phoenix**	**NHL**	**1**	**0**	**0**	**0**	**0**	**0**	**0**	**0**	**0**	**0.0**	**0**	....	....	....	....	....	....	....	....	....	....	....	....	....
	Springfield	AHL	12	3	1	4	23	....	....	....	....	....	....	....	....	....	....	....	....	....	....	....	....	....	....	....
1997-98	Springfield	AHL	73	20	14	34	70	....	....	....	....	....	....	....	....	....	....	....	4	1	2	3	18	....	....	....
1998-99	**Phoenix**	**NHL**	**20**	**2**	**1**	**3**	**12**	**0**	**0**	**0**	**14**	**14.3**	**−4**	**5**	**80.0**	**26**	**3**	**8:07**	**2**	**0**	**0**	**0**	**0**	**0**	**0**	**0**
	Springfield	AHL	63	23	11	34	85	....	....	....	....	....	....	....	....	....	....	....	3	0	1	1	5	....	....	....
	NHL Totals		**22**	**2**	**1**	**3**	**12**	**0**	**0**	**0**	**14**	**14.3**		**5**	**80.0**	**26**	**3**	**8:07**	**2**	**0**	**0**	**0**	**0**	**0**	**0**	**0**

Transferred to **Phoenix** after **Winnipeg** franchise relocated, July 1, 1996.

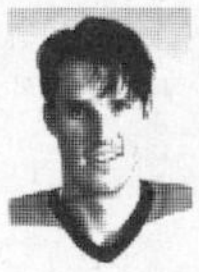

HARKINS, Brett

Left wing. Shoots left. 6'1", 185 lbs. Born, North Ridgeville, OH, July 2, 1970. NY Islanders' 9th choice, 133rd overall, in 1989 Entry Draft.

Season	Club	League	GP	G	A	Pts	PIM	PP	SH	GW	S	%	+/-	TF	F%	H	SB	Min	GP	G	A	Pts	PIM	PP	SH	GW
1987-88	Brockville	OJHL	55	21	55	76	36	....	....	....	....	....	....	....	....	....	....	....	....	....	....	....	....	....	....	....
1988-89	Detroit	NAJHL	38	23	46	69	94	....	....	....	....	....	....	....	....	....	....	....	....	....	....	....	....	....	....	....
1989-90	Bowling Green	CCHA	41	11	43	54	45	....	....	....	....	....	....	....	....	....	....	....	....	....	....	....	....	....	....	....
1990-91	Bowling Green	CCHA	40	22	38	60	30	....	....	....	....	....	....	....	....	....	....	....	....	....	....	....	....	....	....	....
1991-92	Bowling Green	CCHA	34	8	39	47	32	....	....	....	....	....	....	....	....	....	....	....	....	....	....	....	....	....	....	....
1992-93	Bowling Green	CCHA	35	19	28	47	28	....	....	....	....	....	....	....	....	....	....	....	....	....	....	....	....	....	....	....
1993-94	Adirondack	AHL	80	22	47	69	23	....	....	....	....	....	....	....	....	....	....	....	10	1	5	6	4	....	....	....
1994-95	**Boston**	**NHL**	**1**	**0**	**1**	**1**	**0**	**0**	**0**	**0**	**1**	**0.0**	**0**	....	....	....	....	....	....	....	....	....	....	....	....	....
	Providence	AHL	80	23	*69	92	32	....	....	....	....	....	....	....	....	....	....	....	13	8	14	22	4	....	....	....
1995-96	**Florida**	**NHL**	**8**	**0**	**3**	**3**	**6**	**0**	**0**	**0**	**4**	**0.0**	**−2**	....	....	....	....	....	....	....	....	....	....	....	....	....
	Carolina	AHL	55	23	*71	94	44	....	....	....	....	....	....	....	....	....	....	....	....	....	....	....	....	....	....	....
1996-97	**Boston**	**NHL**	**44**	**4**	**14**	**18**	**8**	**3**	**0**	**2**	**52**	**7.7**	**−3**	....	....	....	....	....	....	....	....	....	....	....	....	....
	Providence	AHL	28	9	31	40	32	....	....	....	....	....	....	....	....	....	....	....	10	2	10	12	0	....	....	....
1997-98	Cleveland	IHL	80	32	62	94	82	....	....	....	....	....	....	....	....	....	....	....	10	4	13	17	14	....	....	....
1998-99	Cleveland	IHL	74	20	67	87	84	....	....	....	....	....	....	....	....	....	....	....	....	....	....	....	....	....	....	....
	NHL Totals		**53**	**4**	**18**	**22**	**14**	**3**	**0**	**2**	**57**	**7.0**		....	....	....	....	....	....	....	....	....	....	....	....	....

Signed as a free agent by **Boston**, July 1, 1994. Signed as a free agent by **Florida**, July 24, 1995. Signed as a free agent by **Boston**, September 4, 1996.

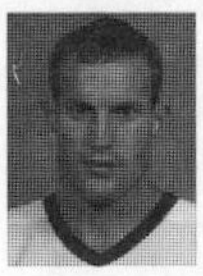

HARLOCK, David (HAHR-lahk) ATL.

Defense. Shoots left. 6'2", 205 lbs. Born, Toronto, Ont., March 16, 1971. New Jersey's 2nd choice, 24th overall, in 1990 Entry Draft.

Season	Club	League	GP	G	A	Pts	PIM	PP	SH	GW	S	%	+/-	TF	F%	H	SB	Min	GP	G	A	Pts	PIM	PP	SH	GW
1986-87	Toronto	MTHL	86	17	55	72	60	....	....	....	....	....	....	....	....	....	....	....	....	....	....	....	....	....	....	....
1987-88	Toronto	MTHL	70	16	56	72	100	....	....	....	....	....	....	....	....	....	....	....	....	....	....	....	....	....	....	....
	Henry Carr	OJHL-B	3	0	0	0	4	....	....	....	....	....	....	....	....	....	....	....	....	....	....	....	....	....	....	....
1988-89	St. Michael's	OJHL-B	25	4	16	20	34	....	....	....	....	....	....	....	....	....	....	....	27	3	12	15	14	....	....	....
1989-90	U. of Michigan	CCHA	42	2	13	15	44	....	....	....	....	....	....	....	....	....	....	....	....	....	....	....	....	....	....	....
1990-91	U. of Michigan	CCHA	39	2	8	10	70	....	....	....	....	....	....	....	....	....	....	....	....	....	....	....	....	....	....	....
1991-92	U. of Michigan	CCHA	44	1	6	7	80	....	....	....	....	....	....	....	....	....	....	....	....	....	....	....	....	....	....	....
1992-93	U. of Michigan	CCHA	38	3	9	12	58	....	....	....	....	....	....	....	....	....	....	....	....	....	....	....	....	....	....	....
	Canada	Nat-Team	4	0	0	0	2	....	....	....	....	....	....	....	....	....	....	....	....	....	....	....	....	....	....	....
1993-94	Canada	Nat-Team	41	0	3	3	28	....	....	....	....	....	....	....	....	....	....	....	....	....	....	....	....	....	....	....
	Canada	Olympics	8	0	0	0	8	....	....	....	....	....	....	....	....	....	....	....	....	....	....	....	....	....	....	....
	Toronto	**NHL**	**6**	**0**	**0**	**0**	**0**	**0**	**0**	**0**	**2**	**0.0**	**−2**	....	....	....	....	....	....	....	....	....	....	....	....	....
	St. John's	AHL	10	0	3	3	2	....	....	....	....	....	....	....	....	....	....	....	9	0	0	0	6	....	....	....
1994-95	**Toronto**	**NHL**	**1**	**0**	**0**	**0**	**0**	**0**	**0**	**0**	**0**	**0.0**	**−1**	....	....	....	....	....	....	....	....	....	....	....	....	....
	St. John's	AHL	58	0	6	6	44	....	....	....	....	....	....	....	....	....	....	....	5	0	0	0	0	....	....	....
1995-96	**Toronto**	**NHL**	**1**	**0**	**0**	**0**	**0**	**0**	**0**	**0**	**0**	**0.0**	**0**	....	....	....	....	....	....	....	....	....	....	....	....	....
	St. John's	AHL	77	0	12	12	92	....	....	....	....	....	....	....	....	....	....	....	4	0	1	1	2	....	....	....
1996-97	San Antonio	IHL	69	3	10	13	82	....	....	....	....	....	....	....	....	....	....	....	9	0	0	0	10	....	....	....
1997-98	**Washington**	**NHL**	**6**	**0**	**0**	**0**	**4**	**0**	**0**	**0**	**2**	**0.0**	**2**	....	....	....	....	....	....	....	....	....	....	....	....	....
	Portland	AHL	71	3	15	18	66	....	....	....	....	....	....	....	....	....	....	....	10	2	2	4	6	....	....	....

			Regular Season																Playoffs							
Season	Club	League	GP	G	A	Pts	PIM	PP	SH	GW	S	%	+/–	TF	F%	H	SB	Min	GP	G	A	Pts	PIM	PP	SH	GW
1998-99	NY Islanders	NHL	70	2	6	8	68	0	0	0	35	5.7	–16	0	0.0	172	65	18:15								
	NHL Totals		84	2	6	8	72	0	0	0	39	5.1		0	0.0	172	65	18:15								

Signed as a free agent by **Toronto**, August 20, 1993. Signed as a free agent by **Washington**, August 20, 1997. Signed as a free agent by **NY Islanders**, August 24, 1998. Claimed by **Atlanta** from **NY Islanders** in Expansion Draft, June 25, 1999.

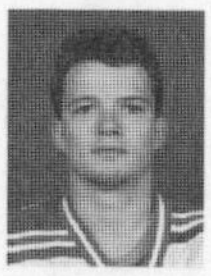

HARVEY, Todd — NYR

Center. Shoots right. 6', 200 lbs. Born, Hamilton, Ont., February 17, 1975. Dallas' 1st choice, 9th overall, in 1993 Entry Draft.

1989-90	Cambridge	OJHL	41	35	27	62	213																			
1990-91	Cambridge	OJHL	35	32	39	71	174																			
1991-92	Detroit	OHL	58	21	43	64	141												7	3	5	8	30			
1992-93	Detroit	OHL	55	50	50	100	83												15	9	12	21	39			
1993-94	Detroit	OHL	49	34	51	85	75												17	10	12	22	26			
1994-95	Detroit	OHL	11	8	14	22	12																			
	Dallas	**NHL**	**40**	**11**	**9**	**20**	**67**	**2**	**0**	**1**	**64**	**17.2**	**–3**						**5**	**0**	**0**	**0**	**8**	**0**	**0**	**0**
1995-96	**Dallas**	**NHL**	**69**	**9**	**20**	**29**	**136**	**3**	**0**	**1**	**101**	**8.9**	**–13**													
	Michigan	IHL	5	1	3	4	8																			
1996-97	**Dallas**	**NHL**	**71**	**9**	**22**	**31**	**142**	**1**	**0**	**2**	**99**	**9.1**	**19**						**7**	**0**	**1**	**1**	**10**	**0**	**0**	**0**
1997-98	**Dallas**	**NHL**	**59**	**9**	**10**	**19**	**104**	**0**	**0**	**1**	**88**	**10.2**	**5**													
1998-99	**NY Rangers**	**NHL**	**37**	**11**	**17**	**28**	**72**	**6**	**0**	**2**	**58**	**19.0**	**–1**	**175**	**50.3**	**126**	**22**	**17:19**								
	NHL Totals		**276**	**49**	**78**	**127**	**521**	**12**	**0**	**7**	**410**	**12.0**		**175**	**50.3**	**126**	**22**	**17:19**	**12**	**0**	**1**	**1**	**18**	**0**	**0**	**0**

Traded to **NY Rangers** by **Dallas** with Bob Errey and Dallas' 4th round choice (Boyd Kane) in 1998 Entry Draft for Brian Skrudland, Mike Keane and NY Rangers' 6th round choice (Pavel Patera) in 1998 Entry Draft, March 24, 1998.

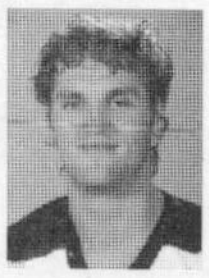

HATCHER, Derian — DAL.

Defense. Shoots left. 6'5", 225 lbs. Born, Sterling Heights, MI, June 4, 1972. Minnesota's 1st choice, 8th overall, in 1990 Entry Draft.

1987-88	Detroit AAA	MNHL	25	5	13	18	52																			
1988-89	Detroit AAA	MNHL	51	19	35	54	100																			
1989-90	North Bay	OHL	64	14	38	52	81												5	2	3	5	8			
1990-91	North Bay	OHL	64	13	49	62	163												10	2	10	12	28			
1991-92	**Minnesota**	**NHL**	**43**	**8**	**4**	**12**	**88**	**0**	**0**	**2**	**51**	**15.7**	**7**						**5**	**0**	**2**	**2**	**8**	**0**	**0**	**0**
1992-93	**Minnesota**	**NHL**	**67**	**4**	**15**	**19**	**178**	**0**	**0**	**1**	**73**	**5.5**	**–27**													
	Kalamazoo	IHL	2	1	2	3	21																			
1993-94	**Dallas**	**NHL**	**83**	**12**	**19**	**31**	**211**	**2**	**1**	**2**	**132**	**9.1**	**19**						**9**	**0**	**2**	**2**	**14**	**0**	**0**	**0**
1994-95	**Dallas**	**NHL**	**43**	**5**	**11**	**16**	**105**	**2**	**0**	**2**	**74**	**6.8**	**3**													
1995-96	**Dallas**	**NHL**	**79**	**8**	**23**	**31**	**129**	**2**	**0**	**1**	**125**	**6.4**	**–12**													
1996-97	**Dallas**	**NHL**	**63**	**3**	**19**	**22**	**97**	**0**	**0**	**0**	**96**	**3.1**	**8**						**7**	**0**	**2**	**2**	**20**	**0**	**0**	**0**
1997-98	**Dallas**	**NHL**	**70**	**6**	**25**	**31**	**132**	**3**	**0**	**2**	**74**	**8.1**	**9**						**17**	**3**	**3**	**6**	**39**	**2**	**0**	**0**
	United States	Olympics	4	0	0	0	0																			
1998-99♦	**Dallas**	**NHL**	**80**	**9**	**21**	**30**	**102**	**3**	**0**	**2**	**125**	**7.2**	**21**	**0**	**0.0**	**204**	**97**	**24:44**	**18**	**1**	**6**	**7**	**24**	**0**	**0**	**0**
	NHL Totals		**528**	**55**	**137**	**192**	**1042**	**12**	**1**	**12**	**750**	**7.3**		**0**	**0.0**	**204**	**97**	**24:44**	**56**	**4**	**15**	**19**	**105**	**2**	**0**	**0**

Played in NHL All-Star Game (1997)

Transferred to **Dallas** after **Minnesota** franchise relocated, June 9, 1993.

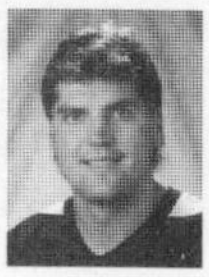

HATCHER, Kevin — PIT.

Defense. Shoots right. 6'3", 230 lbs. Born, Detroit, MI, September 9, 1966. Washington's 1st choice, 17th overall, in 1984 Entry Draft.

1982-83	Detroit	MNHL	75	30	45	75	120																			
1983-84	North Bay	OHL	67	10	39	49	61												4	2	2	4	11			
1984-85	North Bay	OHL	58	26	37	63	75												8	3	8	11	9			
	Washington	**NHL**	**2**	**1**	**0**	**1**	**0**	**0**	**1**	**0**	**3**	**33.3**	**1**						**1**	**0**	**0**	**0**	**0**	**0**	**0**	**0**
1985-86	**Washington**	**NHL**	**79**	**9**	**10**	**19**	**119**	**1**	**0**	**1**	**132**	**6.8**	**6**						**9**	**1**	**1**	**2**	**19**	**0**	**0**	**0**
1986-87	**Washington**	**NHL**	**78**	**8**	**16**	**24**	**144**	**1**	**0**	**2**	**100**	**8.0**	**–29**						**7**	**1**	**0**	**1**	**20**	**0**	**0**	**0**
1987-88	**Washington**	**NHL**	**71**	**14**	**27**	**41**	**137**	**5**	**0**	**3**	**181**	**7.7**	**1**						**14**	**5**	**7**	**12**	**55**	**1**	**0**	**1**
1988-89	**Washington**	**NHL**	**62**	**13**	**27**	**40**	**101**	**3**	**0**	**2**	**148**	**8.8**	**19**						**6**	**1**	**4**	**5**	**20**	**1**	**0**	**0**
1989-90	**Washington**	**NHL**	**80**	**13**	**41**	**54**	**102**	**4**	**0**	**2**	**240**	**5.4**	**4**						**11**	**0**	**8**	**8**	**32**	**0**	**0**	**0**
1990-91	**Washington**	**NHL**	**79**	**24**	**50**	**74**	**69**	**9**	**2**	**3**	**267**	**9.0**	**–10**						**11**	**3**	**3**	**6**	**8**	**2**	**0**	**0**
1991-92	**Washington**	**NHL**	**79**	**17**	**37**	**54**	**105**	**8**	**1**	**2**	**246**	**6.9**	**18**						**7**	**2**	**4**	**6**	**19**	**0**	**1**	**0**
1992-93	**Washington**	**NHL**	**83**	**34**	**45**	**79**	**114**	**13**	**1**	**6**	**329**	**10.3**	**–7**						**6**	**0**	**1**	**1**	**14**	**0**	**0**	**0**
1993-94	**Washington**	**NHL**	**72**	**16**	**24**	**40**	**108**	**6**	**0**	**3**	**217**	**7.4**	**–13**						**11**	**3**	**4**	**7**	**37**	**0**	**1**	**0**
1994-95	**Dallas**	**NHL**	**47**	**10**	**19**	**29**	**66**	**3**	**0**	**2**	**138**	**7.2**	**–4**						**5**	**2**	**1**	**3**	**2**	**1**	**0**	**1**
1995-96	**Dallas**	**NHL**	**74**	**15**	**26**	**41**	**58**	**7**	**0**	**3**	**237**	**6.3**	**–24**													
1996-97	**Pittsburgh**	**NHL**	**80**	**15**	**39**	**54**	**103**	**9**	**0**	**1**	**199**	**7.5**	**11**						**5**	**1**	**1**	**2**	**4**	**1**	**0**	**0**
1997-98	**Pittsburgh**	**NHL**	**74**	**19**	**29**	**48**	**66**	**13**	**1**	**3**	**169**	**11.2**	**–3**						**6**	**1**	**0**	**1**	**12**	**1**	**0**	**0**
	United States	Olympics	3	0	2	2	0																			
1998-99	**Pittsburgh**	**NHL**	**66**	**11**	**27**	**38**	**24**	**4**	**2**	**3**	**131**	**8.4**	**11**	**2**	**50.0**	**87**	**102**	**24:38**	**13**	**2**	**3**	**5**	**4**	**1**	**0**	**0**
	NHL Totals		**1026**	**219**	**417**	**636**	**1316**	**86**	**8**	**36**	**2737**	**8.0**		**2**	**50.0**	**87**	**102**	**24:38**	**112**	**22**	**37**	**59**	**246**	**8**	**2**	**2**

OHL Second All-Star Team (1985)

Played in NHL All-Star Game (1990, 1991, 1992, 1996, 1997)

Traded to **Dallas** by **Washington** for Mark Tinordi and Rick Mrozik, January 18, 1995. Traded to **Pittsburgh** by **Dallas** for Sergei Zubov, June 22, 1996.

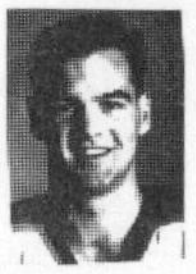

HAUER, Brett (HOW-uhr) — EDM.

Defense. Shoots right. 6'2", 200 lbs. Born, Richfield, MN, July 11, 1971. Vancouver's 3rd choice, 71st overall, in 1989 Entry Draft.

1987-88	Richfield High	H.S.	24	3	3	6	....																			
1988-89	Richfield High	H.S.	24	8	15	23	70																			
1989-90	U. Minn-Duluth	WCHA	37	2	6	8	44																			
1990-91	U. Minn-Duluth	WCHA	30	1	7	8	54																			
1991-92	U. Minn-Duluth	WCHA	33	8	14	22	40																			
1992-93	U. Minn-Duluth	WCHA	40	10	46	56	52																			
1993-94	United States	Nat-Team	57	6	14	20	88																			
	United States	Olympics	8	0	0	0	10																			
	Las Vegas	IHL	21	0	7	7	8												1	0	0	0	0			
1994-95	AIK Solna	Sweden	37	1	3	4	38																			
1995-96	**Edmonton**	**NHL**	**29**	**4**	**2**	**6**	**30**	**2**	**0**	**1**	**53**	**7.5**	**–11**													
	Cape Breton	AHL	17	3	5	8	29																			
1996-97	Chicago	IHL	81	10	30	40	50												4	2	0	2	4			
1997-98	Manitoba	IHL	82	13	48	61	58												3	0	0	0	2			
1998-99	Manitoba	IHL	81	15	56	71	66												5	0	5	5	4			
	NHL Totals		**29**	**4**	**2**	**6**	**30**	**2**	**0**	**1**	**53**	**7.5**														

WCHA First All-Star Team (1993) • NCAA West First All-American Team (1993) • IHL First All-Star Team (1999)

Traded to **Edmonton** by **Vancouver** for Edmonton's 7th round choice (Larry Shapley) in 1997 Entry Draft, August 24, 1995.

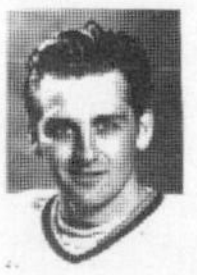

HAWGOOD, Greg (HAW-guhd)

Defense. Shoots left. 5'10", 190 lbs. Born, Edmonton, Alta., August 10, 1968. Boston's 9th choice, 202nd overall, in 1986 Entry Draft.

1982-83	St. Albert	AJHL	STATISTICS NOT AVAILABLE																							
1983-84	Kamloops	WHL	49	10	23	33	39																			
1984-85	Kamloops	WHL	66	25	40	65	72																			
1985-86	Kamloops	WHL	71	34	85	119	86												16	9	22	31	16			

			Regular Season																Playoffs							
Season	Club	League	GP	G	A	Pts	PIM	PP	SH	GW	S	%	+/–	TF	F%	H	SB	Min	GP	G	A	Pts	PIM	PP	SH	GW
1986-87	Kamloops	WHL	61	30	93	123	139	....	....	....	....	....	....	....	....	....	....	....	....	....	....	....	....	....	....	....
1987-88	Kamloops	WHL	63	48	85	133	142	....	....	....	....	....	....	....	....	....	....	....	16	10	16	26	33	....	....	....
	Boston	**NHL**	**1**	**0**	**0**	**0**	**0**	**0**	**0**	**0**	**1**	**0.0**	**–1**	....	....	....	....	....	**3**	**1**	**0**	**1**	**0**	**0**	**0**	**0**
1988-89	**Boston**	**NHL**	**56**	**16**	**24**	**40**	**84**	**5**	**0**	**0**	**132**	**12.1**	**4**	....	....	....	....	....	**10**	**0**	**2**	**2**	**2**	**0**	**0**	**0**
	Maine	AHL	21	2	9	11	41	....	....	....	....	....	....	....	....	....	....	....	....	....	....	....	....	....	....	....
1989-90	**Boston**	**NHL**	**77**	**11**	**27**	**38**	**76**	**2**	**0**	**1**	**127**	**8.7**	**12**	....	....	....	....	....	**15**	**1**	**3**	**4**	**12**	**1**	**0**	**0**
1990-91	HC Asiago	Italy	2	3	0	3	9	....	....	....	....	....	....	....	....	....	....	....	....	....	....	....	....	....	....	....
	Maine	AHL	5	0	1	1	13	....	....	....	....	....	....	....	....	....	....	....	....	....	....	....	....	....	....	....
	Edmonton	**NHL**	**6**	**0**	**1**	**1**	**6**	**0**	**0**	**0**	**9**	**0.0**	**–2**	....	....	....	....	....	....	....	....	....	....	....	....	....
	Cape Breton	AHL	55	10	32	42	73	....	....	....	....	....	....	....	....	....	....	....	4	0	3	3	23	....	....	....
1991-92	**Edmonton**	**NHL**	**20**	**2**	**11**	**13**	**22**	**0**	**0**	**0**	**24**	**8.3**	**19**	....	....	....	....	....	**13**	**0**	**3**	**3**	**23**	**0**	**0**	**0**
	Cape Breton	AHL	56	20	55	75	26	....	....	....	....	....	....	....	....	....	....	....	3	2	2	4	0	....	....	....
1992-93	**Edmonton**	**NHL**	**29**	**5**	**13**	**18**	**35**	**2**	**0**	**0**	**47**	**10.6**	**–1**	....	....	....	....	....	....	....	....	....	....	....	....	....
	Philadelphia	**NHL**	**40**	**6**	**22**	**28**	**39**	**5**	**0**	**1**	**91**	**6.6**	**–7**	....	....	....	....	....	....	....	....	....	....	....	....	....
1993-94	**Philadelphia**	**NHL**	**19**	**3**	**12**	**15**	**19**	**3**	**0**	**0**	**37**	**8.1**	**2**	....	....	....	....	....	....	....	....	....	....	....	....	....
	Florida	**NHL**	**33**	**2**	**14**	**16**	**9**	**0**	**0**	**1**	**55**	**3.6**	**8**	....	....	....	....	....	....	....	....	....	....	....	....	....
	Pittsburgh	**NHL**	**12**	**1**	**2**	**3**	**8**	**1**	**0**	**1**	**20**	**5.0**	**–1**	....	....	....	....	....	**1**	**0**	**0**	**0**	**0**	**0**	**0**	**0**
1994-95	**Pittsburgh**	**NHL**	**21**	**1**	**4**	**5**	**25**	**1**	**0**	**0**	**17**	**5.9**	**2**	....	....	....	....	....	....	....	....	....	....	....	....	....
	Cleveland	IHL	....	....	....	....	....	....	....	....	....	....	....	....	....	....	....	....	3	1	0	1	4	....	....	....
1995-96	Las Vegas	IHL	78	20	65	85	101	....	....	....	....	....	....	....	....	....	....	....	15	5	11	16	24	....	....	....
1996-97	**San Jose**	**NHL**	**63**	**6**	**12**	**18**	**69**	**3**	**0**	**0**	**83**	**7.2**	**–22**	....	....	....	....	....	....	....	....	....	....	....	....	....
1997-98	Kolner Haie	Germany	4	0	1	1	16	....	....	....	....	....	....	....	....	....	....	....	....	....	....	....	....	....	....	....
	Houston	IHL	81	19	52	71	75	....	....	....	....	....	....	....	....	....	....	....	4	0	4	4	0	....	....	....
	Kolner Haie	EuroHL	1	0	0	0	2	....	....	....	....	....	....	....	....	....	....	....	....	....	....	....	....	....	....	....
1998-99	Houston	IHL	76	17	57	74	90	....	....	....	....	....	....	....	....	....	....	....	19	4	8	12	24	....	....	....
	NHL Totals		**377**	**53**	**142**	**195**	**392**	**22**	**0**	**4**	**643**	**8.2**		....	....	....	....	....	**42**	**2**	**8**	**10**	**37**	**1**	**0**	**0**

WHL West All-Star Team (1986, 1987, 1988) • Canadian Major Junior Defenseman of the Year (1988) • AHL First All-Star Team (1992) • Won Eddie Shore Award (Top Defenseman - AHL) (1992) • IHL First All-Star Team (1996, 1998, 1999) • Won Governors' Trophy (Top Defenseman — IHL) (1996, 1999)

Traded to **Edmonton** by **Boston** for Vladimir Ruzicka, October 22, 1990. Traded to **Philadelphia** by **Edmonton** with Josef Beranek for Brian Benning, January 16, 1993. Traded to **Florida** by **Philadelphia** for cash, November 30, 1993. Traded to **Pittsburgh** by **Florida** for Jeff Daniels, March 19, 1994. Signed as a free agent by **San Jose**, September 25, 1996.

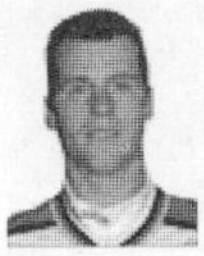

HAWKINS, Todd

Left/Right wing. Shoots right. 6'1", 195 lbs. Born, Kingston, Ont., August 2, 1966. Vancouver's 10th choice, 217th overall, in 1986 Entry Draft.

1983-84	Pembroke	OJHL	53	28	22	50	117	....	....	....	....	....	....	....	....	....	....	....	....	....	....	....	....	....	....	....
1984-85	Belleville	OHL	58	7	16	23	117	....	....	....	....	....	....	....	....	....	....	....	12	1	0	1	10	....	....	....
1985-86	Belleville	OHL	60	14	13	27	172	....	....	....	....	....	....	....	....	....	....	....	24	9	7	16	60	....	....	....
1986-87	Belleville	OHL	60	47	40	87	187	....	....	....	....	....	....	....	....	....	....	....	6	3	5	8	16	....	....	....
1987-88	Flint	IHL	50	13	13	26	337	....	....	....	....	....	....	....	....	....	....	....	16	3	5	8	*174	....	....	....
	Fredericton	AHL	2	0	4	4	11	....	....	....	....	....	....	....	....	....	....	....	....	....	....	....	....	....	....	....
1988-89	**Vancouver**	**NHL**	**4**	**0**	**0**	**0**	**9**	**0**	**0**	**0**	**2**	**0.0**	**–1**	....	....	....	....	....	....	....	....	....	....	....	....	....
	Milwaukee	IHL	63	12	14	26	307	....	....	....	....	....	....	....	....	....	....	....	9	1	0	1	33	....	....	....
1989-90	**Vancouver**	**NHL**	**4**	**0**	**0**	**0**	**6**	**0**	**0**	**0**	**3**	**0.0**	**–1**	....	....	....	....	....	....	....	....	....	....	....	....	....
	Milwaukee	IHL	61	23	17	40	273	....	....	....	....	....	....	....	....	....	....	....	5	4	1	5	19	....	....	....
1990-91	Newmarket	AHL	22	2	5	7	66	....	....	....	....	....	....	....	....	....	....	....	....	....	....	....	....	....	....	....
	Milwaukee	IHL	39	9	11	20	134	....	....	....	....	....	....	....	....	....	....	....	....	....	....	....	....	....	....	....
1991-92	**Toronto**	**NHL**	**2**	**0**	**0**	**0**	**0**	**0**	**0**	**0**	**0**	**0.0**	**0**	....	....	....	....	....	....	....	....	....	....	....	....	....
	St. John's	AHL	66	30	27	57	139	....	....	....	....	....	....	....	....	....	....	....	7	1	0	1	10	....	....	....
1992-93	St. John's	AHL	72	21	41	62	103	....	....	....	....	....	....	....	....	....	....	....	9	1	3	4	10	....	....	....
1993-94	Cleveland	IHL	76	19	14	33	115	....	....	....	....	....	....	....	....	....	....	....	....	....	....	....	....	....	....	....
1994-95	Cleveland	IHL	4	2	0	2	29	....	....	....	....	....	....	....	....	....	....	....	....	....	....	....	....	....	....	....
	Minnesota	IHL	47	10	8	18	95	....	....	....	....	....	....	....	....	....	....	....	3	0	1	1	12	....	....	....
1995-96	Cincinnati	IHL	73	16	12	28	65	....	....	....	....	....	....	....	....	....	....	....	17	7	4	11	32	....	....	....
1996-97	Cincinnati	IHL	81	13	13	26	162	....	....	....	....	....	....	....	....	....	....	....	3	0	1	1	2	....	....	....
1997-98	Cincinnati	IHL	71	13	23	36	168	....	....	....	....	....	....	....	....	....	....	....	9	0	3	3	36	....	....	....
1998-99	Cincinnati	IHL	82	20	32	52	171	....	....	....	....	....	....	....	....	....	....	....	3	2	1	3	8	....	....	....
	NHL Totals		**10**	**0**	**0**	**0**	**15**	**0**	**0**	**0**	**5**	**0.0**		....	....	....	....	....	....	....	....	....	....	....	....	....

OHL Second All-Star Team (1987)

Traded to **Toronto** by **Vancouver** for Brian Blad, January 22, 1991. Signed as a free agent by **Pittsburgh**, August 20, 1993.

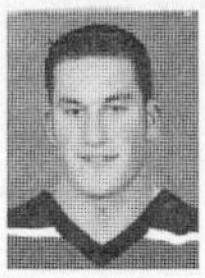

HAY, Dwayne — FLA.

Left wing. Shoots left. 6', 219 lbs. Born, London, Ont., February 11, 1977. Washington's 3rd choice, 43rd overall, in 1995 Entry Draft.

1993-94	Listowel	OJHL	48	10	24	34	56	....	....	....	....	....	....	....	....	....	....	....	....	....	....	....	....	....	....	....
1994-95	Guelph	OHL	65	26	28	54	37	....	....	....	....	....	....	....	....	....	....	....	14	5	7	12	6	....	....	....
1995-96	Guelph	OHL	60	28	30	58	49	....	....	....	....	....	....	....	....	....	....	....	16	4	9	13	18	....	....	....
1996-97	Guelph	OHL	32	17	17	34	21	....	....	....	....	....	....	....	....	....	....	....	11	4	6	10	0	....	....	....
1997-98	**Washington**	**NHL**	**2**	**0**	**0**	**0**	**2**	**0**	**0**	**0**	**1**	**0.0**	**0**	....	....	....	....	....	....	....	....	....	....	....	....	....
	Portland	AHL	58	6	7	13	35	....	....	....	....	....	....	....	....	....	....	....	....	....	....	....	....	....	....	....
	New Haven	AHL	10	3	2	5	4	....	....	....	....	....	....	....	....	....	....	....	2	0	0	0	0	....	....	....
1998-99	**Florida**	**NHL**	**9**	**0**	**0**	**0**	**0**	**0**	**0**	**0**	**3**	**0.0**	**–1**	**1**	**0.0**	**5**	**0**	**6:35**	....	....	....	....	....	....	....	....
	New Haven	AHL	46	18	17	35	22	....	....	....	....	....	....	....	....	....	....	....	....	....	....	....	....	....	....	....
	NHL Totals		**11**	**0**	**0**	**0**	**2**	**0**	**0**	**0**	**4**	**0.0**		**1**	**0.0**	**5**	**0**	**6:35**	....	....	....	....	....	....	....	....

Traded to **Florida** by **Washington** with future considerations for Esa Tikkanen, March 9, 1998.

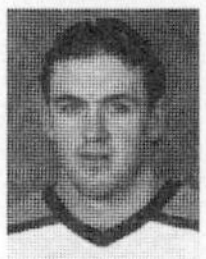

HEALEY, Paul — PHI.

Right wing. Shoots right. 6'2", 196 lbs. Born, Edmonton, Alta., March 20, 1975. Philadelphia's 7th choice, 192nd overall, in 1993 Entry Draft.

1991-92	Ft. Saskatchewan	AJHL	52	11	19	30	40	....	....	....	....	....	....	....	....	....	....	....	....	....	....	....	....	....	....	....
1992-93	Prince Albert	WHL	72	12	20	32	66	....	....	....	....	....	....	....	....	....	....	....	....	....	....	....	....	....	....	....
1993-94	Prince Albert	WHL	63	23	26	49	70	....	....	....	....	....	....	....	....	....	....	....	....	....	....	....	....	....	....	....
1994-95	Prince Albert	WHL	71	43	50	93	67	....	....	....	....	....	....	....	....	....	....	....	12	3	4	7	2	....	....	....
1995-96	Hershey	AHL	60	7	15	22	35	....	....	....	....	....	....	....	....	....	....	....	....	....	....	....	....	....	....	....
1996-97	**Philadelphia**	**NHL**	**2**	**0**	**0**	**0**	**0**	**0**	**0**	**0**	**0**	**0.0**	**0**	....	....	....	....	....	....	....	....	....	....	....	....	....
	Philadelphia	AHL	64	21	19	40	56	....	....	....	....	....	....	....	....	....	....	....	10	4	1	5	10	....	....	....
1997-98	**Philadelphia**	**NHL**	**4**	**0**	**0**	**0**	**12**	**0**	**0**	**0**	**0**	**0.0**	**0**	....	....	....	....	....	....	....	....	....	....	....	....	....
	Philadelphia	AHL	71	34	18	52	48	....	....	....	....	....	....	....	....	....	....	....	20	6	2	8	4	....	....	....
1998-99	Philadelphia	AHL	72	26	20	46	39	....	....	....	....	....	....	....	....	....	....	....	15	4	6	10	11	....	....	....
	NHL Totals		**6**	**0**	**0**	**0**	**12**	**0**	**0**	**0**	**0**	**0.0**		....	....	....	....	....	....	....	....	....	....	....	....	....

WHL East Second All-Star Team (1995)

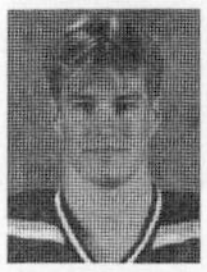

HECHT, Jochen (HEHKHT, yoh-HEHN) — ST.L.

Center. Shoots left. 6'3", 196 lbs. Born, Mannheim, West Germany, June 21, 1977. St. Louis' 1st choice, 49th overall, in 1995 Entry Draft.

1994-95	Mannheim	Germany	43	11	12	23	68	....	....	....	....	....	....	....	....	....	....	....	10	5	4	9	12	....	....	....
1995-96	Mannheim	Germany	44	12	16	28	68	....	....	....	....	....	....	....	....	....	....	....	8	3	2	5	6	....	....	....
1996-97	Mannheim	Germany	46	21	21	42	36	....	....	....	....	....	....	....	....	....	....	....	9	3	3	6	4	....	....	....
1997-98	Mannheim	Germany	44	7	19	26	42	....	....	....	....	....	....	....	....	....	....	....	10	1	1	2	14	....	....	....
	Mannheim	EuroHL	5	0	4	4	8	....	....	....	....	....	....	....	....	....	....	....	....	....	....	....	....	....	....	....
	Germany	Olympics	4	1	0	1	6	....	....	....	....	....	....	....	....	....	....	....	....	....	....	....	....	....	....	....

			Regular Season																Playoffs							
Season	Club	League	GP	G	A	Pts	PIM	PP	SH	GW	S	%	+/-	TF	F%	H	SB	Min	GP	G	A	Pts	PIM	PP	SH	GW
1998-99	**St. Louis**	**NHL**	**3**	**0**	**0**	**0**	**0**	**0**	**0**	**0**	**4**	**0.0**	**–2**	**19**	**21.1**	**1**	**0**	**13:16**	**5**	**2**	**0**	**2**	**0**	**0**	**0**	**0**
	Worcester	AHL	74	21	35	56	48	....	....	....	....	....	....	....	....	....	....	....	4	1	1	2	2	....	....	....
	NHL Totals		**3**	**0**	**0**	**0**	**0**	**0**	**0**	**0**	**4**	**0.0**		**19**	**21.1**	**1**	**0**	**13:16**	**5**	**2**	**0**	**2**	**0**	**0**	**0**	**0**

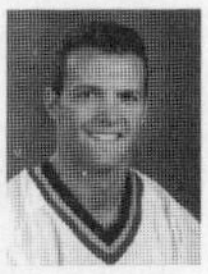

HEDICAN, Bret

(HEH-dih-kan) **FLA.**

Defense. Shoots left. 6'2", 205 lbs. Born, St. Paul, MN, August 10, 1970. St. Louis' 10th choice, 198th overall, in 1988 Entry Draft.

Season	Club	League	GP	G	A	Pts	PIM	PP	SH	GW	S	%	+/-	TF	F%	H	SB	Min	GP	G	A	Pts	PIM	PP	SH	GW
1987-88	St. Paul High	H.S.	23	15	19	34	16	....	....	....	....	....	....	....	....	....	....	....	....	....	....	....	....	....	....	....
1988-89	St. Cloud State	NCAA	28	5	3	8	28	....	....	....	....	....	....	....	....	....	....	....	....	....	....	....	....	....	....	....
1989-90	St. Cloud State	NCAA	36	4	17	21	37	....	....	....	....	....	....	....	....	....	....	....	....	....	....	....	....	....	....	....
1990-91	St. Cloud State	WCHA	41	21	26	47	26	....	....	....	....	....	....	....	....	....	....	....	....	....	....	....	....	....	....	....
1991-92	United States	Nat-Team	54	1	8	9	59	....	....	....	....	....	....	....	....	....	....	....	....	....	....	....	....	....	....	....
	United States	Olympics	8	0	0	0	4	....	....	....	....	....	....	....	....	....	....	....	....	....	....	....	....	....	....	....
	St. Louis	**NHL**	**4**	**1**	**0**	**1**	**0**	**0**	**0**	**0**	**1**	**100.0**	**1**	....	....	....	....	....	**5**	**0**	**0**	**0**	**0**	**0**	**0**	**0**
1992-93	**St. Louis**	**NHL**	**42**	**0**	**8**	**8**	**30**	**0**	**0**	**0**	**40**	**0.0**	**–2**	....	....	....	....	....	**10**	**0**	**0**	**0**	**14**	**0**	**0**	**0**
	Peoria	IHL	19	0	8	8	10	....	....	....	....	....	....	....	....	....	....	....	....	....	....	....	....	....	....	....
1993-94	**St. Louis**	**NHL**	**61**	**0**	**11**	**11**	**64**	**0**	**0**	**0**	**78**	**0.0**	**–8**	....	....	....	....	....	....	....	....	....	....	....	....	....
	Vancouver	**NHL**	**8**	**0**	**1**	**1**	**0**	**0**	**0**	**0**	**10**	**0.0**	**1**	....	....	....	....	....	**24**	**1**	**6**	**7**	**16**	**0**	**0**	**0**
1994-95	**Vancouver**	**NHL**	**45**	**2**	**11**	**13**	**34**	**0**	**0**	**0**	**56**	**3.6**	**–3**	....	....	....	....	....	**11**	**0**	**2**	**2**	**6**	**0**	**0**	**0**
1995-96	**Vancouver**	**NHL**	**77**	**6**	**23**	**29**	**83**	**1**	**0**	**0**	**113**	**5.3**	**8**	....	....	....	....	....	**6**	**0**	**1**	**1**	**10**	**0**	**0**	**0**
1996-97	**Vancouver**	**NHL**	**67**	**4**	**15**	**19**	**51**	**2**	**0**	**1**	**93**	**4.3**	**–3**	....	....	....	....	....	....	....	....	....	....	....	....	....
1997-98	**Vancouver**	**NHL**	**71**	**3**	**24**	**27**	**79**	**1**	**0**	**0**	**84**	**3.6**	**3**	....	....	....	....	....	....	....	....	....	....	....	....	....
1998-99	**Vancouver**	**NHL**	**42**	**2**	**11**	**13**	**34**	**0**	**2**	**0**	**52**	**3.8**	**7**	**0**	**0.0**	**60**	**32**	**18:40**	....	....	....	....	....	....	....	....
	Florida	**NHL**	**25**	**3**	**7**	**10**	**17**	**0**	**0**	**1**	**38**	**7.9**	**–2**	**0**	**0.0**	**46**	**42**	**22:24**	....	....	....	....	....	....	....	....
	NHL Totals		**442**	**21**	**111**	**132**	**392**	**4**	**2**	**2**	**565**	**3.7**		**0**	**0.0**	**106**	**74**	**20:04**	**56**	**1**	**9**	**10**	**46**	**0**	**0**	**0**

WCHA First All-Star Team (1991)

Traded to **Vancouver** by **St. Louis** with Jeff Brown and Nathan Lafayette for Craig Janney, March 21, 1994. Traded to **Florida** by **Vancouver** with Pavel Bure, Brad Ference and Vancouver's 3rd round choice in 2000 Entry Draft for Ed Jovanovski, Dave Gagner, Mike Brown, Kevin Weekes and Florida's 1st round choice in 2000 Entry Draft, January 17, 1999.

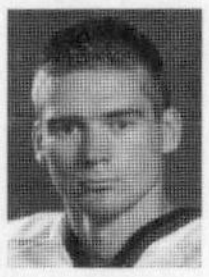

HEINS, Shawn

(HIGHNS) **S.J.**

Defense. Shoots left. 6'4", 220 lbs. Born, Eganville, Ont., December 24, 1973.

Season	Club	League	GP	G	A	Pts	PIM	PP	SH	GW	S	%	+/-	TF	F%	H	SB	Min	GP	G	A	Pts	PIM	PP	SH	GW
1990-91	Renfrew	OJHL-B	....	....	....	....	....	....	....	....	....	....	....	....	....	....	....	....	7	0	0	0	5	....	....	....
1991-92	Peterborough	OHL	49	1	1	2	73	....	....	....	....	....	....	....	....	....	....	....	....	....	....	....	....	....	....	....
1992-93	Peterborough	OHL	5	0	0	0	10	....	....	....	....	....	....	....	....	....	....	....	....	....	....	....	....	....	....	....
	Windsor	OHL	53	7	10	17	107	....	....	....	....	....	....	....	....	....	....	....	....	....	....	....	....	....	....	....
1993-94	Renfrew	OJHL-B	32	16	34	50	250	....	....	....	....	....	....	....	....	....	....	....	....	....	....	....	....	....	....	....
1994-95	Renfrew	OJHL-B	35	30	49	79	188	....	....	....	....	....	....	....	....	....	....	....	....	....	....	....	....	....	....	....
1995-96	Mobile	ECHL	62	7	20	27	152	....	....	....	....	....	....	....	....	....	....	....	....	....	....	....	....	....	....	....
	Cape Breton	AHL	1	0	0	0	0	....	....	....	....	....	....	....	....	....	....	....	....	....	....	....	....	....	....	....
1996-97	Mobile	ECHL	56	6	17	23	253	....	....	....	....	....	....	....	....	....	....	....	3	0	2	2	2	....	....	....
	Kansas City	IHL	6	0	0	0	9	....	....	....	....	....	....	....	....	....	....	....	....	....	....	....	....	....	....	....
1997-98	Kansas City	IHL	82	22	28	50	303	....	....	....	....	....	....	....	....	....	....	....	11	1	0	1	49	....	....	....
1998-99	Canada	Nat-Team	36	5	16	21	66	....	....	....	....	....	....	....	....	....	....	....	....	....	....	....	....	....	....	....
	San Jose	**NHL**	**5**	**0**	**0**	**0**	**13**	**0**	**0**	**0**	**4**	**0.0**	**0**	**0**	**0.0**	**4**	**1**	**13:38**	....	....	....	....	....	....	....	....
	Kentucky	AHL	18	2	2	4	108	....	....	....	....	....	....	....	....	....	....	....	12	2	7	9	10	....	....	....
	NHL Totals		**5**	**0**	**0**	**0**	**13**	**0**	**0**	**0**	**4**	**0.0**		**0**	**0.0**	**4**	**1**	**13:38**	....	....	....	....	....	....	....	....

Signed as a free agent by **San Jose**, January 5, 1997.

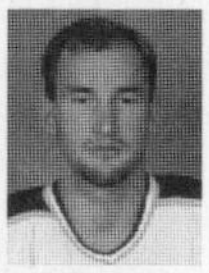

HEINZE, Steve

(HIGHNS) **BOS.**

Right wing. Shoots right. 5'11", 202 lbs. Born, Lawrence, MA, January 30, 1970. Boston's 2nd choice, 60th overall, in 1988 Entry Draft.

Season	Club	League	GP	G	A	Pts	PIM	PP	SH	GW	S	%	+/-	TF	F%	H	SB	Min	GP	G	A	Pts	PIM	PP	SH	GW
1986-87	Lawrence Acad.	H.S.	23	26	24	50	....	....	....	....	....	....	....	....	....	....	....	....	....	....	....	....	....	....	....	....
1987-88	Lawrence Acad.	H.S.	23	30	25	55	....	....	....	....	....	....	....	....	....	....	....	....	....	....	....	....	....	....	....	....
1988-89	Boston College	H.E.	36	26	23	49	26	....	....	....	....	....	....	....	....	....	....	....	....	....	....	....	....	....	....	....
1989-90	Boston College	H.E.	40	27	36	63	41	....	....	....	....	....	....	....	....	....	....	....	....	....	....	....	....	....	....	....
1990-91	Boston College	H.E.	35	21	26	47	35	....	....	....	....	....	....	....	....	....	....	....	....	....	....	....	....	....	....	....
1991-92	United States	Nat-Team	49	18	15	33	38	....	....	....	....	....	....	....	....	....	....	....	....	....	....	....	....	....	....	....
	United States	Olympics	8	1	3	4	8	....	....	....	....	....	....	....	....	....	....	....	....	....	....	....	....	....	....	....
	Boston	**NHL**	**14**	**3**	**4**	**7**	**6**	**0**	**0**	**2**	**29**	**10.3**	**–1**	....	....	....	....	....	**7**	**0**	**3**	**3**	**17**	**0**	**0**	**0**
1992-93	**Boston**	**NHL**	**73**	**18**	**13**	**31**	**24**	**0**	**2**	**4**	**146**	**12.3**	**20**	....	....	....	....	....	**4**	**1**	**1**	**2**	**2**	**0**	**0**	**0**
1993-94	**Boston**	**NHL**	**77**	**10**	**11**	**21**	**32**	**0**	**2**	**1**	**183**	**5.5**	**–2**	....	....	....	....	....	**13**	**2**	**3**	**5**	**7**	**0**	**0**	**0**
1994-95	**Boston**	**NHL**	**36**	**7**	**9**	**16**	**23**	**0**	**1**	**0**	**70**	**10.0**	**0**	....	....	....	....	....	**5**	**0**	**0**	**0**	**0**	**0**	**0**	**0**
1995-96	**Boston**	**NHL**	**76**	**16**	**12**	**28**	**43**	**0**	**1**	**3**	**129**	**12.4**	**–3**	....	....	....	....	....	**5**	**1**	**1**	**2**	**4**	**0**	**1**	**0**
1996-97	**Boston**	**NHL**	**30**	**17**	**8**	**25**	**27**	**4**	**2**	**2**	**96**	**17.7**	**–8**	....	....	....	....	....	....	....	....	....	....	....	....	....
1997-98	**Boston**	**NHL**	**61**	**26**	**20**	**46**	**54**	**9**	**0**	**6**	**160**	**16.3**	**8**	....	....	....	....	....	**6**	**0**	**0**	**0**	**6**	**0**	**0**	**0**
1998-99	**Boston**	**NHL**	**73**	**22**	**18**	**40**	**30**	**9**	**0**	**3**	**146**	**15.1**	**7**	**2**	**0.0**	**91**	**13**	**15:48**	**12**	**4**	**3**	**7**	**0**	**2**	**0**	**0**
	NHL Totals		**440**	**119**	**95**	**214**	**239**	**22**	**8**	**21**	**959**	**12.4**		**2**	**0.0**	**91**	**13**	**15:48**	**52**	**8**	**11**	**19**	**36**	**2**	**1**	**0**

Hockey East First All-Star Team (1990) • NCAA East First All-American Team (1990)

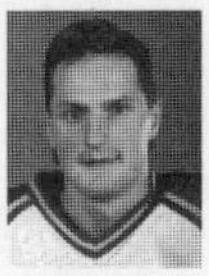

HEJDUK, Milan

(HAY-dook) **COL.**

Right wing. Shoots right. 5'11", 165 lbs. Born, Usti-nad-Labem, Czech., February 14, 1976. Quebec's 6th choice, 87th overall, in 1994 Entry Draft.

Season	Club	League	GP	G	A	Pts	PIM	PP	SH	GW	S	%	+/-	TF	F%	H	SB	Min	GP	G	A	Pts	PIM	PP	SH	GW
1993-94	Pardubice	Cze-Rep	22	6	3	9	....	....	....	....	....	....	....	....	....	....	....	....	10	5	1	6	....	....	....	....
1994-95	Pardubice	Cze-Rep	43	11	13	24	6	....	....	....	....	....	....	....	....	....	....	....	6	3	1	4	0	....	....	....
1995-96	Pardubice	Cze-Rep	37	13	7	20	....	....	....	....	....	....	....	....	....	....	....	....	....	....	....	....	....	....	....	....
1996-97	Pardubice	Cze-Rep	51	27	11	38	10	....	....	....	....	....	....	....	....	....	....	....	10	6	0	6	27	....	....	....
1997-98	Pardubice	Cze-Rep	48	26	19	45	20	....	....	....	....	....	....	....	....	....	....	....	3	0	0	0	2	....	....	....
	Czech Republic	Olympics	4	0	0	0	2	....	....	....	....	....	....	....	....	....	....	....	....	....	....	....	....	....	....	....
1998-99	**Colorado**	**NHL**	**82**	**14**	**34**	**48**	**26**	**4**	**0**	**5**	**178**	**7.9**	**8**	**2**	**50.0**	**50**	**30**	**15:45**	**16**	**6**	**6**	**12**	**4**	**1**	**0**	**3**
	NHL Totals		**82**	**14**	**34**	**48**	**26**	**4**	**0**	**5**	**178**	**7.9**		**2**	**50.0**	**50**	**30**	**15:45**	**16**	**6**	**6**	**12**	**4**	**1**	**0**	**3**

NHL All-Rookie Team (1999)

Rights transferred to **Colorado** after **Quebec** franchise relocated, June 21, 1995.

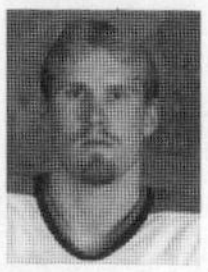

HELENIUS, Sami

(huh-LEHN-ee-uhs) **COL.**

Defense. Shoots left. 6'5", 225 lbs. Born, Helsinki, Finland, January 22, 1974. Calgary's 5th choice, 102nd overall, in 1992 Entry Draft.

Season	Club	League	GP	G	A	Pts	PIM	PP	SH	GW	S	%	+/-	TF	F%	H	SB	Min	GP	G	A	Pts	PIM	PP	SH	GW
1991-92	Jokerit Helsinki	Finn-Jr.	14	3	3	6	24	....	....	....	....	....	....	....	....	....	....	....	....	....	....	....	....	....	....	....
	Jokerit Helsinki	Finland-2	13	4	4	8	24	....	....	....	....	....	....	....	....	....	....	....	....	....	....	....	....	....	....	....
1992-93	Vantaa HT	Finland-2	21	3	2	5	50	....	....	....	....	....	....	....	....	....	....	....	....	....	....	....	....	....	....	....
	Jokerit Helsinki	Finland	1	0	0	0	0	....	....	....	....	....	....	....	....	....	....	....	....	....	....	....	....	....	....	....
1993-94	Reipas Lahti	Finland	37	2	3	5	46	....	....	....	....	....	....	....	....	....	....	....	....	....	....	....	....	....	....	....
1994-95	Saint John	AHL	69	2	5	7	217	....	....	....	....	....	....	....	....	....	....	....	....	....	....	....	....	....	....	....
1995-96	Saint John	AHL	68	0	3	3	231	....	....	....	....	....	....	....	....	....	....	....	10	0	0	0	9	....	....	....
1996-97	**Calgary**	**NHL**	**3**	**0**	**1**	**1**	**0**	**0**	**0**	**0**	**1**	**0.0**	**1**	....	....	....	....	....	....	....	....	....	....	....	....	....
	Saint John	AHL	72	5	10	15	218	....	....	....	....	....	....	....	....	....	....	....	2	0	0	0	0	....	....	....
1997-98	Saint John	AHL	63	1	2	3	185	....	....	....	....	....	....	....	....	....	....	....	....	....	....	....	....	....	....	....
	Las Vegas	IHL	10	0	1	1	19	....	....	....	....	....	....	....	....	....	....	....	4	0	0	0	25	....	....	....

			Regular Season																Playoffs							
Season	Club	League	GP	G	A	Pts	PIM	PP	SH	GW	S	%	+/-	TF	F%	H	SB	Min	GP	G	A	Pts	PIM	PP	SH	GW
1998-99	Calgary	NHL	4	0	0	0	8	0	0	0	1	0.0	-2	0	0.0	6	6	10:16	....	....	....	....	....	....	....	....
	Las Vegas	IHL	42	2	3	5	193	....	....	....	....	....	....	....	....	....	....	....	....	....	....	....	....	....	....	....
	Tampa Bay	NHL	4	1	0	1	15	0	1	0	3	33.3	-3	0	0.0	6	3	16:53	....	....	....	....	....	....	....	....
	Chicago	IHL	4	0	0	0	11	....	....	....	....	....	....	....	....	....	....	....	....	....	....	....	....	....	....	....
	Hershey	AHL	8	0	0	0	29	....	....	....	....	....	....	....	....	....	....	....	5	0	0	0	16	....	....	....
	NHL Totals		11	1	1	2	23	0	1	0	5	20.0		0	0.0	12	9	13:34	....	....	....	....	....	....	....	....

Traded to **Tampa Bay** by **Calgary** for future considerations, January 29, 1999. Traded to **Colorado** by **Tampa Bay** for future considerations, March 23, 1999.

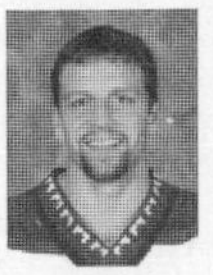

HELMER, Bryan — ST.L.

Defense. Shoots right. 6'1", 200 lbs. Born, Sault Ste. Marie, Ont., July 15, 1972.

1989-90	Wellington	OJHL	51	6	22	28	204	....	....	....	....	....	....	....	....	....	....	....	....	....	....	....	....	....	....	....
	Belleville	OHL	6	0	1	1	0	....	....	....	....	....	....	....	....	....	....	....	....	....	....	....	....	....	....	....
1990-91	Wellington	OJHL	50	11	14	25	109	....	....	....	....	....	....	....	....	....	....	....	....	....	....	....	....	....	....	....
1991-92	Wellington	OJHL	45	19	32	51	66	....	....	....	....	....	....	....	....	....	....	....	....	....	....	....	....	....	....	....
1992-93	Wellington	OJHL	57	25	62	87	62	....	....	....	....	....	....	....	....	....	....	....	....	....	....	....	....	....	....	....
1993-94	Albany	AHL	65	4	19	23	79	....	....	....	....	....	....	....	....	....	....	....	5	0	0	0	9	....	....	....
1994-95	Albany	AHL	77	7	36	43	101	....	....	....	....	....	....	....	....	....	....	....	7	1	0	1	0	....	....	....
1995-96	Albany	AHL	80	14	30	44	107	....	....	....	....	....	....	....	....	....	....	....	4	2	0	2	6	....	....	....
1996-97	Albany	AHL	77	12	27	39	113	....	....	....	....	....	....	....	....	....	....	....	16	1	7	8	10	....	....	....
1997-98	Albany	AHL	80	14	49	63	101	....	....	....	....	....	....	....	....	....	....	....	13	4	9	13	18	....	....	....
1998-99	Phoenix	NHL	11	0	0	0	23	0	0	0	11	0.0	2	0	0.0	1	2	7:43	....	....	....	....	....	....	....	....
	Las Vegas	IHL	8	1	3	4	28	....	....	....	....	....	....	....	....	....	....	....	....	....	....	....	....	....	....	....
	St. Louis	NHL	29	0	4	4	19	0	0	0	38	0.0	3	1	100.0	34	28	19:08	....	....	....	....	....	....	....	....
	Worcester	AHL	16	7	8	15	18	....	....	....	....	....	....	....	....	....	....	....	4	0	0	0	12	....	....	....
	NHL Totals		40	0	4	4	42	0	0	0	49	0.0		1	100.0	35	30	15:60	....	....	....	....	....	....	....	....

AHL First All-Star Team (1998)

Signed as a free agent by **New Jersey**, July 10, 1994. Signed as a free agent by **Phoenix**, July 17, 1998. Claimed on waivers by **St. Louis** from **Phoenix**, December 19, 1998.

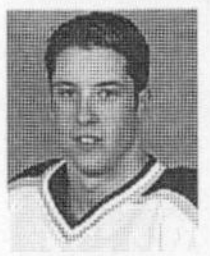

HENDERSON, Jay — BOS.

Left wing. Shoots left. 5'11", 188 lbs. Born, Edmonton, Alta., September 17, 1978. Boston's 12th choice, 246th overall, in 1997 Entry Draft.

1993-94	Sherwood Park	AAHA	31	12	21	33	36	....	....	....	....	....	....	....	....	....	....	....	....	....	....	....	....	....	....	....
1994-95	Red Deer	WHL	54	3	9	12	80	....	....	....	....	....	....	....	....	....	....	....	....	....	....	....	....	....	....	....
1995-96	Red Deer	WHL	71	15	13	28	139	....	....	....	....	....	....	....	....	....	....	....	10	1	1	2	11	....	....	....
1996-97	Edmonton	WHL	66	28	32	60	127	....	....	....	....	....	....	....	....	....	....	....	....	....	....	....	....	....	....	....
1997-98	Edmonton	WHL	72	49	45	94	130	....	....	....	....	....	....	....	....	....	....	....	....	....	....	....	....	....	....	....
1998-99	Boston	NHL	4	0	0	0	2	0	0	0	4	0.0	-1	0	0.0	1	1	5:39	....	....	....	....	....	....	....	....
	Providence	AHL	55	7	9	16	172	....	....	....	....	....	....	....	....	....	....	....	2	0	0	0	2	....	....	....
	NHL Totals		4	0	0	0	2	0	0	0	4	0.0		0	0.0	1	1	5:39	....	....	....	....	....	....	....	....

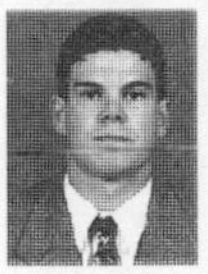

HENDERSON, Matt — NSH.

Right wing. Shoots left. 6'1", 200 lbs. Born, White Bear Lake, MN, June 22, 1974.

1993-94	St. Paul	USHL	48	27	24	51	....	....	....	....	....	....	....	....	....	....	....	....	....	....	....	....	....	....	....	....
1994-95	North Dakota	WCHA	19	1	3	4	16	....	....	....	....	....	....	....	....	....	....	....	....	....	....	....	....	....	....	....
1995-96	North Dakota	WCHA	36	9	10	19	34	....	....	....	....	....	....	....	....	....	....	....	2	0	1	1	0	....	....	....
1996-97	North Dakota	WCHA	42	14	17	31	71	....	....	....	....	....	....	....	....	....	....	....	7	5	4	9	10	....	....	....
1997-98	North Dakota	WCHA	38	24	14	38	74	....	....	....	....	....	....	....	....	....	....	....	5	2	2	4	4	....	....	....
1998-99	Nashville	NHL	2	0	0	0	2	0	0	0	0	0.0	-1	0	0.0	4	0	6:23	....	....	....	....	....	....	....	....
	Milwaukee	IHL	77	19	19	38	117	....	....	....	....	....	....	....	....	....	....	....	2	0	0	0	0	....	....	....
	NHL Totals		2	0	0	0	2	0	0	0	0	0.0		0	0.0	4	0	6:23	....	....	....	....	....	....	....	....

NCAA Championship All-Tournament Team (1997) • NCAA Championship Tournament MVP (1997)

Signed as a free agent by **Nashville**, August, 1998.

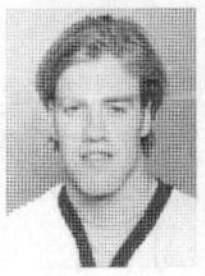

HENDRICKSON, Darby — VAN.

Center. Shoots left. 6', 195 lbs. Born, Richfield, MN, August 28, 1972. Toronto's 3rd choice, 73rd overall, in 1990 Entry Draft.

1987-88	Richfield High	H.S.	22	12	9	21	10	....	....	....	....	....	....	....	....	....	....	....	....	....	....	....	....	....	....	....
1988-89	Richfield High	H.S.	22	22	20	42	12	....	....	....	....	....	....	....	....	....	....	....	....	....	....	....	....	....	....	....
1989-90	Richfield High	H.S.	24	23	27	50	49	....	....	....	....	....	....	....	....	....	....	....	....	....	....	....	....	....	....	....
1990-91	Richfield High	H.S.	27	32	29	61	....	....	....	....	....	....	....	....	....	....	....	....	....	....	....	....	....	....	....	....
1991-92	U. of Minnesota	WCHA	41	25	28	53	61	....	....	....	....	....	....	....	....	....	....	....	....	....	....	....	....	....	....	....
1992-93	U. of Minnesota	WCHA	31	12	15	27	35	....	....	....	....	....	....	....	....	....	....	....	....	....	....	....	....	....	....	....
1993-94	United States	Nat-Team	59	12	16	28	30	....	....	....	....	....	....	....	....	....	....	....	....	....	....	....	....	....	....	....
	United States	Olympics	8	0	0	0	6	....	....	....	....	....	....	....	....	....	....	....	....	....	....	....	....	....	....	....
	Toronto	NHL	....	....	....	....	....	....	....	....	....	....	....	....	....	....	....	....	2	0	0	0	0	....	....	....
	St. John's	AHL	6	4	1	5	4	....	....	....	....	....	....	....	....	....	....	....	3	1	1	2	0	....	....	....
1994-95	Toronto	NHL	8	0	1	1	4	0	0	0	4	0.0	0	....	....	....	....	....	....	....	....	....	....	....	....	....
	St. John's	AHL	59	16	20	36	48	....	....	....	....	....	....	....	....	....	....	....	....	....	....	....	....	....	....	....
1995-96	Toronto	NHL	46	6	6	12	47	0	0	0	43	14.0	-2	....	....	....	....	....	....	....	....	....	....	....	....	....
	NY Islanders	NHL	16	1	4	5	33	0	0	1	30	3.3	-6	....	....	....	....	....	....	....	....	....	....	....	....	....
1996-97	Toronto	NHL	64	11	6	17	47	0	1	0	105	10.5	-20	....	....	....	....	....	....	....	....	....	....	....	....	....
	St. John's	AHL	12	5	4	9	21	....	....	....	....	....	....	....	....	....	....	....	....	....	....	....	....	....	....	....
1997-98	Toronto	NHL	80	8	4	12	67	0	0	0	115	7.0	-20	....	....	....	....	....	....	....	....	....	....	....	....	....
1998-99	Toronto	NHL	35	2	3	5	30	0	0	0	34	5.9	-4	278	46.0	35	8	10:16	....	....	....	....	....	....	....	....
	Vancouver	NHL	27	2	2	4	22	1	0	0	36	5.6	-15	427	46.8	24	23	17:15	....	....	....	....	....	....	....	....
	NHL Totals		276	30	26	56	250	1	1	1	367	8.2		705	46.5	59	31	13:18	2	0	0	0	0	....	....	....

Traded to **NY Islanders** by **Toronto** with Sean Haggerty, Kenny Jonsson and Toronto's 1st round choice (Roberto Luongo) in 1997 Entry Draft for Wendel Clark, Mathieu Schneider and D.J. Smith, March 13, 1996. Traded to **Toronto** by **NY Islanders** for a conditional choice in 1998 Entry Draft, October 11, 1996. Traded to **Vancouver** by **Toronto** for Chris McAllister, February 16, 1999.

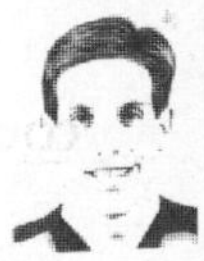

HERBERS, Ian

Defense. Shoots left. 6'4", 225 lbs. Born, Jasper, Alta., July 18, 1967. Buffalo's 11th choice, 190th overall, in 1987 Entry Draft.

1984-85	Kelowna	WHL	68	3	14	17	120	....	....	....	....	....	....	....	....	....	....	....	6	0	1	1	9	....	....	....
1985-86	Spokane	WHL	29	1	6	7	85	....	....	....	....	....	....	....	....	....	....	....	....	....	....	....	....	....	....	....
	Lethbridge	WHL	32	1	4	5	109	....	....	....	....	....	....	....	....	....	....	....	10	1	0	1	37	....	....	....
1986-87	Swift Current	WHL	72	5	8	13	230	....	....	....	....	....	....	....	....	....	....	....	4	1	1	2	12	....	....	....
1987-88	Swift Current	WHL	56	5	14	19	238	....	....	....	....	....	....	....	....	....	....	....	4	0	2	2	4	....	....	....
1988-89	U. of Alberta	CWUAA	47	4	22	26	137	....	....	....	....	....	....	....	....	....	....	....	....	....	....	....	....	....	....	....
1989-90	U. of Alberta	CWUAA	45	5	31	36	83	....	....	....	....	....	....	....	....	....	....	....	....	....	....	....	....	....	....	....
1990-91	U. of Alberta	CWUAA	45	6	24	30	87	....	....	....	....	....	....	....	....	....	....	....	....	....	....	....	....	....	....	....
1991-92	U. of Alberta	CWUAA	43	14	34	48	86	....	....	....	....	....	....	....	....	....	....	....	....	....	....	....	....	....	....	....
1992-93	Cape Breton	AHL	77	7	15	22	129	....	....	....	....	....	....	....	....	....	....	....	10	0	1	1	16	....	....	....
1993-94	Edmonton	NHL	22	0	2	2	32	0	0	0	16	0.0	-6	....	....	....	....	....	....	....	....	....	....	....	....	....
	Cape Breton	AHL	53	7	16	23	122	....	....	....	....	....	....	....	....	....	....	....	5	0	3	3	12	....	....	....
1994-95	Cape Breton	AHL	36	1	11	12	104	....	....	....	....	....	....	....	....	....	....	....	....	....	....	....	....	....	....	....
	Detroit	IHL	37	1	5	6	46	....	....	....	....	....	....	....	....	....	....	....	5	1	1	2	6	....	....	....
1995-96	Detroit	IHL	73	3	11	14	140	....	....	....	....	....	....	....	....	....	....	....	12	3	5	8	29	....	....	....
1996-97	Detroit	IHL	67	3	16	19	129	....	....	....	....	....	....	....	....	....	....	....	21	0	4	4	34	....	....	....

			Regular Season																Playoffs							
Season	Club	League	GP	G	A	Pts	PIM	PP	SH	GW	S	%	+/-	TF	F%	H	SB	Min	GP	G	A	Pts	PIM	PP	SH	GW
1997-98	Detroit	IHL	70	6	6	12	100	....	....	....	....	....	....	....	....	....	....	....	23	0	3	3	54	....	....	....
1998-99	Detroit	IHL	82	8	16	24	142	....	....	....	....	....	....	....	....	....	....	....	11	1	3	4	18	....	....	....
	NHL Totals		**22**	**0**	**2**	**2**	**32**	**0**	**0**	**0**	**16**	**0.0**		....	....	....	....	....	....	....	....	....	....	....	....	....

a ABCIAU All-Canadian Team (1991, 1992)

Signed as a free agent by **Edmonton**, September 9, 1992.

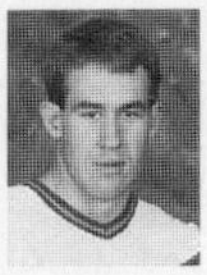

HERR, Matt — WSH.

Center. Shoots left. 6'2", 204 lbs. Born, Hackensack, NJ, May 26, 1976. Washington's 4th choice, 93rd overall, in 1994 Entry Draft.

Season	Club	League	GP	G	A	Pts	PIM	PP	SH	GW	S	%	+/-	TF	F%	H	SB	Min	GP	G	A	Pts	PIM	PP	SH	GW
1990-91	Hotchkiss High	H.S.	26	9	5	14	....	....	....	....	....	....	....	....	....	....	....	....	....	....	....	....	....	....	....	....
1991-92	Hotchkiss High	H.S.	25	17	16	33	....	....	....	....	....	....	....	....	....	....	....	....	....	....	....	....	....	....	....	....
1992-93	Hotchkiss High	H.S.	24	48	30	78	....	....	....	....	....	....	....	....	....	....	....	....	....	....	....	....	....	....	....	....
1993-94	Hotchkiss High	H.S.	24	28	19	47	....	....	....	....	....	....	....	....	....	....	....	....	....	....	....	....	....	....	....	....
1994-95	U. of Michigan	CCHA	37	11	8	19	51	....	....	....	....	....	....	....	....	....	....	....	....	....	....	....	....	....	....	....
1995-96	U. of Michigan	CCHA	40	18	13	31	55	....	....	....	....	....	....	....	....	....	....	....	....	....	....	....	....	....	....	....
1996-97	U. of Michigan	CCHA	43	29	23	52	67	....	....	....	....	....	....	....	....	....	....	....	....	....	....	....	....	....	....	....
1997-98	U. of Michigan	CCHA	31	14	17	31	62	....	....	....	....	....	....	....	....	....	....	....	....	....	....	....	....	....	....	....
1998-99	**Washington**	**NHL**	**30**	**2**	**2**	**4**	**8**	**1**	**0**	**0**	**40**	**5.0**	**-7**	**176**	**52.8**	**42**	**10**	**11:05**	....	....	....	....	....	....	....	....
	Portland	AHL	46	15	14	29	29	....	....	....	....	....	....	....	....	....	....	....	....	....	....	....	....	....	....	....
	NHL Totals		**30**	**2**	**2**	**4**	**8**	**1**	**0**	**0**	**40**	**5.0**		**176**	**52.8**	**42**	**10**	**11:05**	....	....	....	....	....	....	....	....

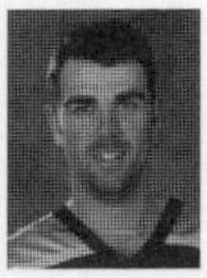

HEWARD, Jamie (HEW-uhrd) — NYI

Defense. Shoots right. 6'2", 207 lbs. Born, Regina, Sask., March 30, 1971. Pittsburgh's 1st choice, 16th overall, in 1989 Entry Draft.

Season	Club	League	GP	G	A	Pts	PIM	PP	SH	GW	S	%	+/-	TF	F%	H	SB	Min	GP	G	A	Pts	PIM	PP	SH	GW
1987-88	Regina	WHL	68	10	17	27	17	....	....	....	....	....	....	....	....	....	....	....	4	1	1	2	2	....	....	....
1988-89	Regina	WHL	52	31	28	59	29	....	....	....	....	....	....	....	....	....	....	....	....	....	....	....	....	....	....	....
1989-90	Regina	WHL	72	14	44	58	42	....	....	....	....	....	....	....	....	....	....	....	11	2	2	4	10	....	....	....
1990-91	Regina	WHL	71	23	61	84	41	....	....	....	....	....	....	....	....	....	....	....	8	2	9	11	6	....	....	....
1991-92	Muskegon	IHL	54	6	21	27	37	....	....	....	....	....	....	....	....	....	....	....	14	1	4	5	4	....	....	....
1992-93	Cleveland	IHL	58	9	18	27	64	....	....	....	....	....	....	....	....	....	....	....	....	....	....	....	....	....	....	....
1993-94	Cleveland	IHL	73	8	16	24	72	....	....	....	....	....	....	....	....	....	....	....	....	....	....	....	....	....	....	....
1994-95	Canada	Nat-Team	51	11	35	46	32	....	....	....	....	....	....	....	....	....	....	....	....	....	....	....	....	....	....	....
1995-96	**Toronto**	**NHL**	**5**	**0**	**0**	**0**	**0**	**0**	**0**	**0**	**8**	**0.0**	**-1**	....	....	....	....	....	....	....	....	....	....	....	....	....
	St. John's	AHL	73	22	34	56	33	....	....	....	....	....	....	....	....	....	....	....	3	1	1	2	6	....	....	....
1996-97	**Toronto**	**NHL**	**20**	**1**	**4**	**5**	**6**	**0**	**0**	**0**	**23**	**4.3**	**-6**	....	....	....	....	....	....	....	....	....	....	....	....	....
	St. John's	AHL	27	8	19	27	26	....	....	....	....	....	....	....	....	....	....	....	9	1	3	4	6	....	....	....
1997-98	Philadelphia	AHL	72	17	48	65	54	....	....	....	....	....	....	....	....	....	....	....	20	3	16	19	10	....	....	....
1998-99	**Nashville**	**NHL**	**63**	**6**	**12**	**18**	**44**	**4**	**0**	**1**	**124**	**4.8**	**-24**	**0**	**0.0**	**80**	**35**	**16:12**	....	....	....	....	....	....	....	....
	NHL Totals		**88**	**7**	**16**	**23**	**50**	**4**	**0**	**1**	**155**	**4.5**		**0**	**0.0**	**80**	**35**	**16:12**	....	....	....	....	....	....	....	....

WHL East First All-Star Team (1991) • AHL First All-Star Team (1996, 1998) • Won Eddie Shore Award (Outstanding Defenseman - AHL) (1998)

Signed as a free agent by **Toronto**, May 4, 1995. Signed as a free agent by **Philadelphia**, July 31, 1997. Signed as a free agent by **Nashville**, August 10, 1998. Signed as a free agent by **NY Islanders**, July 27, 1999.

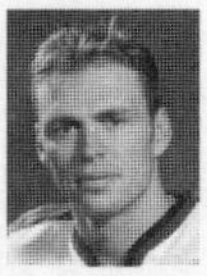

HICKS, Alex — FLA.

Left wing. Shoots left. 6', 190 lbs. Born, Calgary, Alta., September 4, 1969.

Season	Club	League	GP	G	A	Pts	PIM	PP	SH	GW	S	%	+/-	TF	F%	H	SB	Min	GP	G	A	Pts	PIM	PP	SH	GW
1988-89	Wisc.-Eau Claire	NCHA	30	21	26	47	42	....	....	....	....	....	....	....	....	....	....	....	....	....	....	....	....	....	....	....
1989-90	Wisc.-Eau Claire	NCHA	34	31	48	79	30	....	....	....	....	....	....	....	....	....	....	....	....	....	....	....	....	....	....	....
1990-91	Wisc.-Eau Claire	NCHA	26	22	35	57	43	....	....	....	....	....	....	....	....	....	....	....	....	....	....	....	....	....	....	....
1991-92	Wisc.-Eau Claire	NCHA	26	24	42	66	63	....	....	....	....	....	....	....	....	....	....	....	....	....	....	....	....	....	....	....
1992-93	Toledo	ECHL	50	26	34	60	100	....	....	....	....	....	....	....	....	....	....	....	16	5	10	15	79	....	....	....
	Adirondack	AHL	3	0	0	0	0	....	....	....	....	....	....	....	....	....	....	....	....	....	....	....	....	....	....	....
1993-94	Toledo	ECHL	60	31	49	80	240	....	....	....	....	....	....	....	....	....	....	....	14	10	10	20	56	....	....	....
	Adirondack	AHL	8	1	3	4	2	....	....	....	....	....	....	....	....	....	....	....	5	0	2	2	2	....	....	....
1994-95	Las Vegas	IHL	79	24	42	66	212	....	....	....	....	....	....	....	....	....	....	....	9	2	4	6	47	....	....	....
1995-96	**Anaheim**	**NHL**	**64**	**10**	**11**	**21**	**37**	**0**	**0**	**2**	**83**	**12.0**	**11**	....	....	....	....	....	....	....	....	....	....	....	....	....
	Baltimore	AHL	13	2	10	12	23	....	....	....	....	....	....	....	....	....	....	....	....	....	....	....	....	....	....	....
1996-97	**Anaheim**	**NHL**	**18**	**2**	**6**	**8**	**14**	**0**	**0**	**0**	**21**	**9.5**	**1**	....	....	....	....	....	....	....	....	....	....	....	....	....
	Pittsburgh	**NHL**	**55**	**5**	**15**	**20**	**76**	**0**	**0**	**3**	**57**	**8.8**	**-6**	....	....	....	....	....	**5**	**0**	**1**	**1**	**2**	**0**	**0**	**0**
1997-98	**Pittsburgh**	**NHL**	**58**	**7**	**13**	**20**	**54**	**0**	**0**	**1**	**78**	**9.0**	**4**	....	....	....	....	....	**6**	**0**	**0**	**0**	**2**	**0**	**0**	**0**
1998-99	**San Jose**	**NHL**	**4**	**0**	**1**	**1**	**4**	**0**	**0**	**0**	**4**	**0.0**	**-1**	**0**	**0.0**	**3**	**0**	**4:33**	....	....	....	....	....	....	....	....
	Florida	**NHL**	**51**	**0**	**6**	**6**	**58**	**0**	**0**	**0**	**47**	**0.0**	**-4**	**33**	**42.4**	**89**	**17**	**10:21**	....	....	....	....	....	....	....	....
	NHL Totals		**250**	**24**	**52**	**76**	**243**	**0**	**0**	**6**	**290**	**8.3**		**33**	**42.4**	**92**	**17**	**9:56**	**11**	**0**	**1**	**1**	**4**	**0**	**0**	**0**

NCAA (College Div.) West First All-American Team (1991, 1992)

Signed as a free agent by **Anaheim**, August 17, 1995. Traded to **Pittsburgh** by **Anaheim** with Fredrik Olausson for Shawn Antoski and Dmitri Mironov, November 19, 1996. Traded to **Florida** by **San Jose** with San Jose's 5th round choice (later traded to NY Islanders, NY Islanders selected Adam Johnson) in 1999 Entry Draft for Jeff Norton, November 11, 1998.

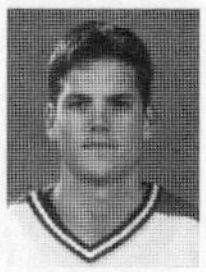

HIGGINS, Matt — MTL.

Center. Shoots left. 6'2", 188 lbs. Born, Calgary, Alta., October 29, 1977. Montreal's 1st choice, 18th overall, in 1996 Entry Draft.

Season	Club	League	GP	G	A	Pts	PIM	PP	SH	GW	S	%	+/-	TF	F%	H	SB	Min	GP	G	A	Pts	PIM	PP	SH	GW
1992-93	Vernon	BCAHA	70	53	76	129	54	....	....	....	....	....	....	....	....	....	....	....	....	....	....	....	....	....	....	....
1993-94	Moose Jaw	WHL	64	6	10	16	10	....	....	....	....	....	....	....	....	....	....	....	....	....	....	....	....	....	....	....
1994-95	Moose Jaw	WHL	72	36	34	70	26	....	....	....	....	....	....	....	....	....	....	....	10	1	2	3	2	....	....	....
1995-96	Moose Jaw	WHL	67	30	33	63	43	....	....	....	....	....	....	....	....	....	....	....	....	....	....	....	....	....	....	....
1996-97	Moose Jaw	WHL	71	33	57	90	51	....	....	....	....	....	....	....	....	....	....	....	12	3	5	8	2	....	....	....
1997-98	**Montreal**	**NHL**	**1**	**0**	**0**	**0**	**0**	**0**	**0**	**0**	**1**	**0.0**	**-1**	....	....	....	....	....	....	....	....	....	....	....	....	....
	Fredericton	AHL	50	5	22	27	12	....	....	....	....	....	....	....	....	....	....	....	4	1	2	3	2	....	....	....
1998-99	**Montreal**	**NHL**	**25**	**1**	**0**	**1**	**0**	**0**	**0**	**0**	**12**	**8.3**	**-2**	**108**	**45.4**	**9**	**4**	**5:41**	....	....	....	....	....	....	....	....
	Fredericton	AHL	11	3	4	7	6	....	....	....	....	....	....	....	....	....	....	....	5	0	2	2	0	....	....	....
	NHL Totals		**26**	**1**	**0**	**1**	**0**	**0**	**0**	**0**	**13**	**7.7**		**108**	**45.4**	**9**	**4**	**5:41**	....	....	....	....	....	....	....	....

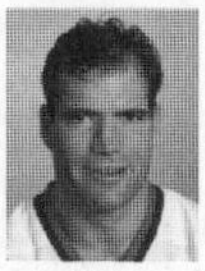

HILL, Sean (HIHL, SHAWN) — CAR.

Defense. Shoots right. 6', 203 lbs. Born, Duluth, MN, February 14, 1970. Montreal's 9th choice, 167th overall, in 1988 Entry Draft.

Season	Club	League	GP	G	A	Pts	PIM	PP	SH	GW	S	%	+/-	TF	F%	H	SB	Min	GP	G	A	Pts	PIM	PP	SH	GW
1987-88	East Duluth	H.S.	24	10	17	27		....	....	....	....	....	....	....	....	....	....	....	....	....	....	....	....	....	....	....
1988-89	U. of Wisconsin	WCHA	45	2	23	25	69	....	....	....	....	....	....	....	....	....	....	....	....	....	....	....	....	....	....	....
1989-90	U. of Wisconsin	WCHA	42	14	39	53	78	....	....	....	....	....	....	....	....	....	....	....	....	....	....	....	....	....	....	....
1990-91	U. of Wisconsin	WCHA	37	19	32	51	122	....	....	....	....	....	....	....	....	....	....	....	....	....	....	....	....	....	....	....
	Montreal	**NHL**	....	....	....	....	....	**0**	**0**	**0**	**0**	**0.0**	**0**	....	....	....	....	....	**1**	**0**	**0**	**0**	**0**	**0**	**0**	**0**
	Fredericton	AHL	....	....	....	....	....	....	....	....	....	....	....	....	....	....	....	....	3	0	2	2	2	....	....	....
1991-92	Fredericton	AHL	42	7	20	27	65	....	....	....	....	....	....	....	....	....	....	....	7	1	3	4	6	....	....	....
	United States	Olympics	8	2	0	2	6	....	....	....	....	....	....	....	....	....	....	....	....	....	....	....	....	....	....	....
	United States	Nat-Team	12	4	3	7	16	....	....	....	....	....	....	....	....	....	....	....	....	....	....	....	....	....	....	....
	Montreal	**NHL**	....	....	....	....	....	....	....	....	....	....	....	....	....	....	....	....	**4**	**1**	**0**	**1**	**2**	....	....	....
1992-93♦	**Montreal**	**NHL**	**31**	**2**	**6**	**8**	**54**	**1**	**0**	**1**	**37**	**5.4**	**-5**	....	....	....	....	....	**3**	**0**	**0**	**0**	**4**	**0**	**0**	**0**
	Fredericton	AHL	6	1	3	4	10	....	....	....	....	....	....	....	....	....	....	....	....	....	....	....	....	....	....	....
1993-94	**Anaheim**	**NHL**	**68**	**7**	**20**	**27**	**78**	**2**	**1**	**1**	**165**	**4.2**	**-12**	....	....	....	....	....	....	....	....	....	....	....	....	....
1994-95	**Ottawa**	**NHL**	**45**	**1**	**14**	**15**	**30**	**0**	**0**	**0**	**107**	**0.9**	**-11**	....	....	....	....	....	....	....	....	....	....	....	....	....
1995-96	**Ottawa**	**NHL**	**80**	**7**	**14**	**21**	**94**	**2**	**0**	**2**	**157**	**4.5**	**-26**	....	....	....	....	....	....	....	....	....	....	....	....	....
1996-97	**Ottawa**	**NHL**	**5**	**0**	**0**	**0**	**4**	**0**	**0**	**0**	**9**	**0.0**	**1**	....	....	....	....	....	....	....	....	....	....	....	....	....

			Regular Season																Playoffs							
Season	Club	League	GP	G	A	Pts	PIM	PP	SH	GW	S	%	+/–	TF	F%	H	SB	Min	GP	G	A	Pts	PIM	PP	SH	GW
1997-98	Ottawa	NHL	13	1	1	2	6	0	0	0	16	6.3	–3	....	....	....	....	....	....	....	....	....	....	....	....	....
	Carolina	NHL	42	0	5	5	48	0	0	0	37	0.0	–2	....	....	....	....	....	....	....	....	....	....	....	....	....
1998-99	Carolina	NHL	54	0	10	10	48	0	0	0	44	0.0	9	0	0.0	194	79	19:02	....	....	....	....	....	....	....	....
	NHL Totals		338	18	70	88	362	5	1	4	572	3.1		0	0.0	194	79	19:02	8	1	0	1	6	0	0	0

WCHA Second All-Star Team (1990, 1991) • NCAA West Second All-American Team (1991)

Claimed by **Anaheim** from **Montreal** in Expansion Draft, June 24, 1993. Traded to **Ottawa** by **Anaheim** with Anaheim's 9th round choice (Frederic Cassivi) in 1994 Entry Draft for Ottawa's 3rd round choice (later traded to Tampa Bay — Tampa Bay selected Vadim Epanchintsev) in 1994 Entry Draft, June 29, 1994. Traded to **Carolina** by **Ottawa** for Chris Murray, November 18, 1997.

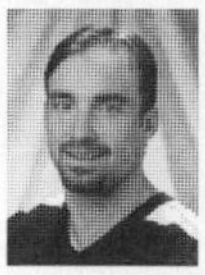

HLUSHKO, Todd

(huh-LUSH-koh)

Center. Shoots left. 5'11", 185 lbs. Born, Toronto, Ont., February 7, 1970. Washington's 14th choice, 240th overall, in 1990 Entry Draft.

Season	Club	League	GP	G	A	Pts	PIM	PP	SH	GW	S	%	+/–	TF	F%	H	SB	Min	GP	G	A	Pts	PIM	PP	SH	GW
1987-88	Guelph Jr. Bees	OJHL-B	44	36	47	83	94	....	....	....	....	....	....	....	....	....	....	....	....	....	....	....	....	....	....	....
1988-89	Guelph	OHL	66	28	18	46	71	....	....	....	....	....	....	....	....	....	....	....	7	5	3	8	18	....	....	....
1989-90	Owen Sound	OHL	25	9	17	26	31	....	....	....	....	....	....	....	....	....	....	....	....	....	....	....	....	....	....	....
	London	OHL	40	27	17	44	39	....	....	....	....	....	....	....	....	....	....	....	6	2	4	6	10	....	....	....
1990-91	Baltimore	AHL	66	9	14	23	55	....	....	....	....	....	....	....	....	....	....	....	....	....	....	....	....	....	....	....
1991-92	Baltimore	AHL	74	16	35	51	113	....	....	....	....	....	....	....	....	....	....	....	....	....	....	....	....	....	....	....
1992-93	Canada	Nat-Team	58	22	26	48	10	....	....	....	....	....	....	....	....	....	....	....	....	....	....	....	....	....	....	....
1993-94	Canada	Nat-Team	55	22	6	28	61	....	....	....	....	....	....	....	....	....	....	....	....	....	....	....	....	....	....	....
	Canada	Olympics	8	5	0	5	6	....	....	....	....	....	....	....	....	....	....	....	....	....	....	....	....	....	....	....
	Philadelphia	NHL	2	1	0	1	0	0	0	0	2	50.0	1	....	....	....	....	....	....	....	....	....	....	....	....	....
	Hershey	AHL	9	6	0	6	4	....	....	....	....	....	....	....	....	....	....	....	6	2	1	3	4	....	....	....
1994-95	Calgary	NHL	2	0	1	1	2	0	0	0	3	0.0	1	....	....	....	....	....	1	0	0	0	2	0	0	0
	Saint John	AHL	46	22	10	32	36	....	....	....	....	....	....	....	....	....	....	....	4	2	2	4	22	....	....	....
1995-96	Calgary	NHL	4	0	0	0	6	0	0	0	6	0.0	0	....	....	....	....	....	....	....	....	....	....	....	....	....
	Saint John	AHL	35	14	13	27	70	....	....	....	....	....	....	....	....	....	....	....	16	8	1	9	26	....	....	....
1996-97	Calgary	NHL	58	7	11	18	49	0	0	0	76	9.2	–2	....	....	....	....	....	....	....	....	....	....	....	....	....
1997-98	Calgary	NHL	13	0	1	1	27	0	0	0	7	0.0	0	....	....	....	....	....	....	....	....	....	....	....	....	....
	Saint John	AHL	33	10	14	24	48	....	....	....	....	....	....	....	....	....	....	....	21	*13	4	17	61	....	....	....
1998-99	Grand Rapids	IHL	82	24	26	50	78	....	....	....	....	....	....	....	....	....	....	....	....	....	....	....	....	....	....	....
	Pittsburgh	NHL	....	....	....	....	....	....	....	....	....	....	....	....	....	....	....	....	2	0	0	0	0	0	0	0
	NHL Totals		79	8	13	21	84	0	0	0	94	8.5		....	....	....	....	....	3	0	0	0	2	0	0	0

Signed as a free agent by **Philadelphia**, March 7, 1994. Signed as a free agent by **Calgary**, June 17, 1994. Traded to **Pittsburgh** by **Calgary** with German Titov for Ken Wregget and Dave Roche, June 17, 1998.

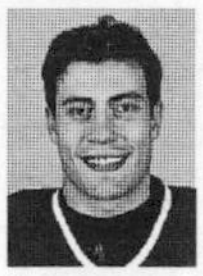

HOCKING, Justin

Defense. Shoots right. 6'4", 205 lbs. Born, Stettler, Alta., January 9, 1974. Los Angeles' 1st choice, 39th overall, in 1992 Entry Draft.

Season	Club	League	GP	G	A	Pts	PIM	PP	SH	GW	S	%	+/–	TF	F%	H	SB	Min	GP	G	A	Pts	PIM	PP	SH	GW
1990-91	Ft. Saskatchewan	AJHL	38	4	6	10	84	....	....	....	....	....	....	....	....	....	....	....	....	....	....	....	....	....	....	....
1991-92	Spokane	WHL	71	4	6	10	309	....	....	....	....	....	....	....	....	....	....	....	10	0	3	3	28	....	....	....
1992-93	Spokane	WHL	16	0	1	1	75	....	....	....	....	....	....	....	....	....	....	....	....	....	....	....	....	....	....	....
	Medicine Hat	WHL	54	1	9	10	119	....	....	....	....	....	....	....	....	....	....	....	10	0	1	1	13	....	....	....
1993-94	Medicine Hat	WHL	68	7	26	33	236	....	....	....	....	....	....	....	....	....	....	....	3	0	0	0	6	....	....	....
	Los Angeles	NHL	1	0	0	0	0	0	0	0	0	0.0	0	....	....	....	....	....	....	....	....	....	....	....	....	....
	Phoenix	IHL	3	0	0	0	15	....	....	....	....	....	....	....	....	....	....	....	....	....	....	....	....	....	....	....
1994-95	Syracuse	AHL	7	0	0	0	24	....	....	....	....	....	....	....	....	....	....	....	....	....	....	....	....	....	....	....
	Portland	AHL	9	0	1	1	34	....	....	....	....	....	....	....	....	....	....	....	....	....	....	....	....	....	....	....
	Knoxville	ECHL	20	0	6	6	70	....	....	....	....	....	....	....	....	....	....	....	4	0	0	0	26	....	....	....
	Phoenix	IHL	20	1	1	2	50	....	....	....	....	....	....	....	....	....	....	....	1	0	0	0	0	....	....	....
1995-96	P.E.I. Senators	AHL	74	4	8	12	251	....	....	....	....	....	....	....	....	....	....	....	4	0	2	2	5	....	....	....
1996-97	Worcester	AHL	68	1	10	11	198	....	....	....	....	....	....	....	....	....	....	....	5	0	3	3	2	....	....	....
1997-98	Worcester	AHL	79	5	12	17	198	....	....	....	....	....	....	....	....	....	....	....	11	1	2	3	19	....	....	....
1998-99	Indianapolis	IHL	34	2	4	6	111	....	....	....	....	....	....	....	....	....	....	....	....	....	....	....	....	....	....	....
	St. John's	AHL	44	4	6	10	99	....	....	....	....	....	....	....	....	....	....	....	5	0	0	0	2	....	....	....
	NHL Totals		1	0	0	0	0	0	0	0	0	0.0		....	....	....	....	....	....	....	....	....	....	....	....	....

WHL East Second All-Star Team (1994)

Claimed by **Ottawa** from **LA Kings** in Waiver Draft, October 2, 1995. Traded to **Chicago** by **Ottawa** for Brian Felsner, August 21, 1998.

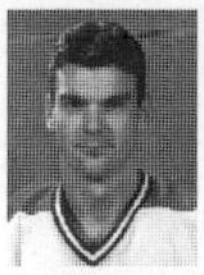

HOGLUND, Jonas

(HOHG-lund, YOH-nuhs) **TOR.**

Right wing. Shoots right. 6'3", 215 lbs. Born, Hammaro, Swe., August 29, 1972. Calgary's 11th choice, 222nd overall, in 1992 Entry Draft.

Season	Club	League	GP	G	A	Pts	PIM	PP	SH	GW	S	%	+/–	TF	F%	H	SB	Min	GP	G	A	Pts	PIM	PP	SH	GW
1988-89	Farjestads BK	Sweden	1	0	0	0	0	....	....	....	....	....	....	....	....	....	....	....	....	....	....	....	....	....	....	....
1989-90	Farjestads BK	Sweden	1	0	0	....	0	....	....	....	....	....	....	....	....	....	....	....	....	....	....	....	....	....	....	....
1990-91	Farjestads BK	Sweden	40	5	5	10	4	....	....	....	....	....	....	....	....	....	....	....	8	1	0	1	0	....	....	....
1991-92	Farjestads BK	Sweden	40	14	11	25	6	....	....	....	....	....	....	....	....	....	....	....	6	2	4	6	2	....	....	....
1992-93	Farjestads BK	Sweden	40	13	13	26	14	....	....	....	....	....	....	....	....	....	....	....	3	1	0	1	0	....	....	....
1993-94	Farjestads BK	Sweden	22	7	2	9	10	....	....	....	....	....	....	....	....	....	....	....	....	....	....	....	....	....	....	....
1994-95	Farjestads BK	Sweden	40	14	12	26	16	....	....	....	....	....	....	....	....	....	....	....	4	3	2	5	0	....	....	....
1995-96	Farjestads BK	Sweden	40	32	11	43	18	....	....	....	....	....	....	....	....	....	....	....	8	2	1	3	6	....	....	....
1996-97	Calgary	NHL	68	19	16	35	12	3	0	6	189	10.1	–4	....	....	....	....	....	....	....	....	....	....	....	....	....
1997-98	Calgary	NHL	50	6	8	14	16	0	0	0	124	4.8	–9	....	....	....	....	....	....	....	....	....	....	....	....	....
	Montreal	NHL	28	6	5	11	6	4	0	0	62	9.7	2	....	....	....	....	....	10	2	0	2	0	0	0	0
1998-99	Montreal	NHL	74	8	10	18	16	1	0	0	122	6.6	–5	17	29.4	41	15	11:50	....	....	....	....	....	....	....	....
	NHL Totals		220	39	39	78	50	8	0	6	497	7.8		17	29.4	41	15	11:50	10	2	0	2	0	0	0	0

Traded to **Montreal** by **Calgary** with Zarley Zalapski for Valeri Bure and Montreal's 4th round choice (Shaun Sutter) in 1998 Entry Draft, February 1, 1998. Signed as a free agent by **Toronto**, July 13, 1999.

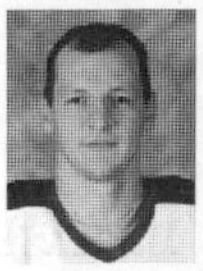

HOGUE, Benoit

(HOHG)

Center. Shoots left. 5'10", 194 lbs. Born, Repentigny, Que., October 28, 1966. Buffalo's 2nd choice, 35th overall, in 1985 Entry Draft.

Season	Club	League	GP	G	A	Pts	PIM	PP	SH	GW	S	%	+/–	TF	F%	H	SB	Min	GP	G	A	Pts	PIM	PP	SH	GW
1982-83	Bourassa	QAAA	40	20	20	40	....	....	....	....	....	....	....	....	....	....	....	....	....	....	....	....	....	....	....	....
1983-84	St-Jean	QMJHL	59	14	11	25	42	....	....	....	....	....	....	....	....	....	....	....	....	....	....	....	....	....	....	....
1984-85	St-Jean	QMJHL	63	46	44	90	92	....	....	....	....	....	....	....	....	....	....	....	....	....	....	....	....	....	....	....
1985-86	St-Jean	QMJHL	65	54	54	108	115	....	....	....	....	....	....	....	....	....	....	....	9	6	4	10	26	....	....	....
1986-87	Rochester	AHL	52	14	20	34	52	....	....	....	....	....	....	....	....	....	....	....	12	5	4	9	8	....	....	....
1987-88	Buffalo	NHL	3	1	1	2	0	0	0	1	3	33.3	3	....	....	....	....	....	....	....	....	....	....	....	....	....
	Rochester	AHL	62	24	31	55	141	....	....	....	....	....	....	....	....	....	....	....	7	6	1	7	46	....	....	....
1988-89	Buffalo	NHL	69	14	30	44	120	1	2	0	114	12.3	–5	....	....	....	....	....	5	0	0	0	17	0	0	0
1989-90	Buffalo	NHL	45	11	7	18	79	1	0	1	73	15.1	0	....	....	....	....	....	3	0	0	0	10	0	0	0
1990-91	Buffalo	NHL	76	19	28	47	76	1	0	2	134	14.2	–8	....	....	....	....	....	5	3	1	4	10	0	0	0
1991-92	Buffalo	NHL	3	0	1	1	0	0	0	0	6	0.0	0	....	....	....	....	....	....	....	....	....	....	....	....	....
	NY Islanders	NHL	72	30	45	75	67	8	0	5	143	21.0	30	....	....	....	....	....	....	....	....	....	....	....	....	....
1992-93	NY Islanders	NHL	70	33	42	75	108	5	3	5	147	22.4	13	....	....	....	....	....	18	6	6	12	31	0	0	0
1993-94	NY Islanders	NHL	83	36	33	69	73	9	5	3	218	16.5	–7	....	....	....	....	....	4	0	1	1	4	0	0	0
1994-95	NY Islanders	NHL	33	6	4	10	34	1	0	1	50	12.0	0	....	....	....	....	....	....	....	....	....	....	....	....	....
	Toronto	NHL	12	3	3	6	0	1	0	1	16	18.8	0	....	....	....	....	....	7	0	0	0	6	0	0	0
1995-96	Toronto	NHL	44	12	25	37	68	3	0	5	94	12.8	6	....	....	....	....	....	....	....	....	....	....	....	....	....
	Dallas	NHL	34	7	20	27	36	2	0	0	61	11.5	4	....	....	....	....	....	....	....	....	....	....	....	....	....
1996-97	Dallas	NHL	73	19	24	43	54	5	0	5	131	14.5	8	....	....	....	....	....	7	2	2	4	6	1	0	0
1997-98	Dallas	NHL	53	6	16	22	35	3	0	1	55	10.9	7	....	....	....	....	....	17	4	2	6	16	1	0	2

			Regular Season																Playoffs							
Season	Club	League	GP	G	A	Pts	PIM	PP	SH	GW	S	%	+/-	TF	F%	H	SB	Min	GP	G	A	Pts	PIM	PP	SH	GW
1998-99	**Tampa Bay**	**NHL**	**62**	**11**	**14**	**25**	**50**	**2**	**0**	**3**	**101**	**10.9**	**−12**	**63**	**42.9**	**89**	**24**	**16:23**	....	....	....	....	....	....	....	....
	♦ Dallas	**NHL**	**12**	**1**	**3**	**4**	**4**	**0**	**0**	**0**	**20**	**5.0**	**2**	**52**	**46.2**	**31**	**4**	**15:04**	**14**	**0**	**2**	**2**	**16**	**0**	**0**	**0**
	NHL Totals		**744**	**209**	**296**	**505**	**804**	**42**	**10**	**33**	**1366**	**15.3**		**115**	**44.3**	**120**	**28**	**16:10**	**80**	**15**	**14**	**29**	**116**	**2**	**0**	**2**

Traded to **NY Islanders** by **Buffalo** with Pierre Turgeon, Uwe Krupp and Dave McLlwain for Pat Lafontaine, Randy Hillier, Randy Wood and NY Islanders' 4th round choice (Dean Melanson) in 1992 Entry Draft, October 25, 1991. Traded to **Toronto** by **NY Islanders** with NY Islanders' 3rd round choice (Ryan Pepperall) in 1995 Entry Draft and 5th round choice (Brandon Sugden) in 1996 Entry Draft for Eric Fichaud, April 6, 1995. Traded to **Dallas** by **Toronto** with Randy Wood for Dave Gagner and Dallas' 6th round choice (Dmitriy Yakushin) in 1996 Entry Draft, January 29, 1996. Signed as a free agent by **Tampa Bay**, August 19, 1998. Traded to **Dallas** by **Tampa Bay** with a conditional choice in 2001 Entry Draft for Sergey Gusev, March 21, 1999.

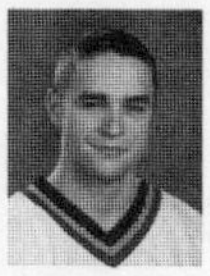

HOLDEN, Josh — VAN.

Center. Shoots left. 6', 190 lbs. Born, Calgary, Alta., January 18, 1978. Vancouver's 1st choice, 12th overall, in 1996 Entry Draft.

Season	Club	League	GP	G	A	Pts	PIM	PP	SH	GW	S	%	+/-	TF	F%	H	SB	Min	GP	G	A	Pts	PIM	PP	SH	GW
1993-94	Calgary	AAHA	34	14	15	29	82	....	....	....	....	....	....	....	....	....	....	....	....	....	....	....	....	....	....	....
1994-95	Regina	WHL	62	20	23	43	45	....	....	....	....	....	....	....	....	....	....	....	4	3	1	4	0	....	....	....
1995-96	Regina	WHL	70	57	55	112	105	....	....	....	....	....	....	....	....	....	....	....	11	4	5	9	23	....	....	....
1996-97	Regina	WHL	58	49	49	98	148	....	....	....	....	....	....	....	....	....	....	....	5	3	2	5	10	....	....	....
1997-98	Regina	WHL	56	41	58	99	134	....	....	....	....	....	....	....	....	....	....	....	2	2	2	4	10	....	....	....
1998-99	**Vancouver**	**NHL**	**30**	**2**	**4**	**6**	**10**	**1**	**0**	**0**	**44**	**4.5**	**−10**	**269**	**39.0**	**38**	**6**	**12:44**	....	....	....	....	....	....	....	....
	Syracuse	AHL	38	14	15	29	48	....	....	....	....	....	....	....	....	....	....	....	....	....	....	....	....	....	....	....
	NHL Totals		**30**	**2**	**4**	**6**	**10**	**1**	**0**	**0**	**44**	**4.5**		**269**	**39.0**	**38**	**6**	**12:44**	....	....	....	....	....	....	....	....

WHL East Second All-Star Team (1998)

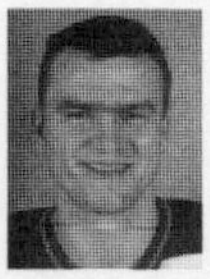

HOLIK, Bobby (HOH-leek) — N.J.

Left wing. Shoots right. 6'4", 230 lbs. Born, Jihlava, Czech., January 1, 1971. Hartford's 1st choice, 10th overall, in 1989 Entry Draft.

Season	Club	League	GP	G	A	Pts	PIM	PP	SH	GW	S	%	+/-	TF	F%	H	SB	Min	GP	G	A	Pts	PIM	PP	SH	GW
1987-88	Dukla Jihlava	Czech.	31	5	9	14	16	....	....	....	....	....	....	....	....	....	....	....	....	....	....	....	....	....	....	....
1988-89	Dukla Jihlava	Czech.	24	7	10	17	32	....	....	....	....	....	....	....	....	....	....	....	....	....	....	....	....	....	....	....
1989-90	Dukla Jihlava	Czech.	42	15	26	41	....	....	....	....	....	....	....	....	....	....	....	....	....	....	....	....	....	....	....	....
1990-91	**Hartford**	**NHL**	**78**	**21**	**22**	**43**	**113**	**8**	**0**	**3**	**173**	**12.1**	**−3**	....	....	....	....	....	**6**	**0**	**0**	**0**	**7**	**0**	**0**	**0**
1991-92	**Hartford**	**NHL**	**76**	**21**	**24**	**45**	**44**	**1**	**0**	**2**	**207**	**10.1**	**4**	....	....	....	....	....	**7**	**0**	**1**	**1**	**6**	**0**	**0**	**0**
1992-93	**New Jersey**	**NHL**	**61**	**20**	**19**	**39**	**76**	**7**	**0**	**4**	**180**	**11.1**	**−6**	....	....	....	....	....	**5**	**1**	**1**	**2**	**6**	**0**	**0**	**0**
	Utica	AHL	1	....	....	....	2	....	....	....	....	....	....	....	....	....	....	....	....	....	....	....	....	....	....	....
1993-94	**New Jersey**	**NHL**	**70**	**13**	**20**	**33**	**72**	**2**	**0**	**3**	**130**	**10.0**	**28**	....	....	....	....	....	**20**	**0**	**3**	**3**	**6**	**0**	**0**	**0**
1994-95♦	**New Jersey**	**NHL**	**48**	**10**	**10**	**20**	**18**	**0**	**0**	**2**	**84**	**11.9**	**9**	....	....	....	....	....	**20**	**4**	**4**	**8**	**22**	**2**	**0**	**1**
1995-96	**New Jersey**	**NHL**	**63**	**13**	**17**	**30**	**58**	**1**	**0**	**1**	**157**	**8.3**	**9**	....	....	....	....	....	....	....	....	....	....	....	....	....
1996-97	**New Jersey**	**NHL**	**82**	**23**	**39**	**62**	**54**	**5**	**0**	**6**	**192**	**12.0**	**24**	....	....	....	....	....	**10**	**2**	**3**	**5**	**4**	**1**	**0**	**0**
1997-98	**New Jersey**	**NHL**	**82**	**29**	**36**	**65**	**100**	**8**	**0**	**8**	**238**	**12.2**	**23**	....	....	....	....	....	**5**	**0**	**0**	**0**	**8**	**0**	**0**	**0**
1998-99	**New Jersey**	**NHL**	**78**	**27**	**37**	**64**	**119**	**5**	**0**	**8**	**253**	**10.7**	**16**	**1350**	**53.6**	**217**	**24**	**17:34**	**7**	**0**	**7**	**7**	**6**	**0**	**0**	**0**
	NHL Totals		**638**	**177**	**224**	**401**	**654**	**37**	**0**	**37**	**1614**	**11.0**		**1350**	**53.6**	**217**	**24**	**17:34**	**80**	**7**	**19**	**26**	**65**	**3**	**0**	**1**

Played in NHL All-Star Game (1998, 1999)

Traded to **New Jersey** by **Hartford** with Hartford's 2nd round choice (Jay Pandolfo) in 1993 Entry Draft and future considerations for Sean Burke and Eric Weinrich, August 28, 1992.

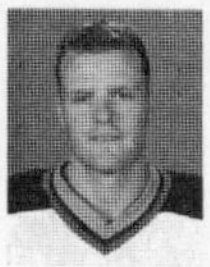

HOLLAND, Jason — BUF.

Defense. Shoots right. 6'2", 193 lbs. Born, Morinville, Alta., April 30, 1976. NY Islanders' 2nd choice, 38th overall, in 1994 Entry Draft.

Season	Club	League	GP	G	A	Pts	PIM	PP	SH	GW	S	%	+/-	TF	F%	H	SB	Min	GP	G	A	Pts	PIM	PP	SH	GW
1991-92	St. Albert	AAHA	38	9	29	38	94	....	....	....	....	....	....	....	....	....	....	....	....	....	....	....	....	....	....	....
1992-93	St. Albert	AAHA	31	11	25	36	36	....	....	....	....	....	....	....	....	....	....	....	....	....	....	....	....	....	....	....
	Kamloops	WHL	4	0	0	0	2	....	....	....	....	....	....	....	....	....	....	....	....	....	....	....	....	....	....	....
1993-94	Kamloops	WHL	59	14	15	29	80	....	....	....	....	....	....	....	....	....	....	....	18	2	3	5	4	....	....	....
1994-95	Kamloops	WHL	71	9	32	41	65	....	....	....	....	....	....	....	....	....	....	....	21	2	7	9	9	....	....	....
1995-96	Kamloops	WHL	63	24	33	57	98	....	....	....	....	....	....	....	....	....	....	....	16	4	9	13	22	....	....	....
1996-97	**NY Islanders**	**NHL**	**4**	**1**	**0**	**1**	**0**	**0**	**0**	**0**	**3**	**33.3**	**1**	....	....	....	....	....	....	....	....	....	....	....	....	....
	Kentucky	AHL	72	14	25	39	46	....	....	....	....	....	....	....	....	....	....	....	4	0	2	2	0	....	....	....
1997-98	**NY Islanders**	**NHL**	**8**	**0**	**0**	**0**	**4**	**0**	**0**	**0**	**6**	**0.0**	**−4**	....	....	....	....	....	....	....	....	....	....	....	....	....
	Kentucky	AHL	50	10	16	26	29	....	....	....	....	....	....	....	....	....	....	....	....	....	....	....	....	....	....	....
	Rochester	AHL	9	0	4	4	10	....	....	....	....	....	....	....	....	....	....	....	4	0	3	3	4	....	....	....
1998-99	**Buffalo**	**NHL**	**3**	**0**	**0**	**0**	**8**	**0**	**0**	**0**	**2**	**0.0**	**−1**	**0**	**0.0**	**0**	**2**	**10:58**	....	....	....	....	....	....	....	....
	Rochester	AHL	74	4	25	29	36	....	....	....	....	....	....	....	....	....	....	....	20	2	5	7	8	....	....	....
	NHL Totals		**15**	**1**	**0**	**1**	**12**	**0**	**0**	**0**	**11**	**9.1**		**0**	**0.0**	**0**	**2**	**10:58**	....	....	....	....	....	....	....	....

WHL West First All-Star Team (1996)

Traded to **Buffalo** by **NY Islanders** with Paul Kruse for Jason Dawe, March 24, 1998.

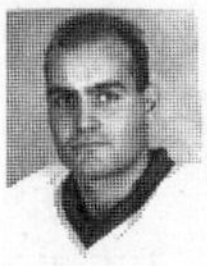

HOLLINGER, Terry

Defense. Shoots left. 6'1", 200 lbs. Born, Regina, Sask., February 24, 1971. St. Louis' 7th choice, 153rd overall, in 1991 Entry Draft.

Season	Club	League	GP	G	A	Pts	PIM	PP	SH	GW	S	%	+/-	TF	F%	H	SB	Min	GP	G	A	Pts	PIM	PP	SH	GW
1987-88	Regina	AAHA	30	13	36	49	74	....	....	....	....	....	....	....	....	....	....	....	....	....	....	....	....	....	....	....
	Regina	WHL	7	1	1	2	4	....	....	....	....	....	....	....	....	....	....	....	....	....	....	....	....	....	....	....
1988-89	Regina	WHL	65	2	27	29	49	....	....	....	....	....	....	....	....	....	....	....	....	....	....	....	....	....	....	....
1989-90	Regina	WHL	70	14	43	57	40	....	....	....	....	....	....	....	....	....	....	....	11	1	3	4	10	....	....	....
1990-91	Regina	WHL	8	1	6	7	6	....	....	....	....	....	....	....	....	....	....	....	....	....	....	....	....	....	....	....
	Lethbridge	WHL	62	9	32	41	113	....	....	....	....	....	....	....	....	....	....	....	16	3	14	17	22	....	....	....
1991-92	Lethbridge	WHL	65	23	62	85	155	....	....	....	....	....	....	....	....	....	....	....	5	1	2	3	13	....	....	....
	Peoria	IHL	1	0	2	2	0	....	....	....	....	....	....	....	....	....	....	....	5	0	1	1	0	....	....	....
1992-93	Peoria	IHL	72	2	28	30	67	....	....	....	....	....	....	....	....	....	....	....	4	1	1	2	0	....	....	....
1993-94	**St. Louis**	**NHL**	**2**	**0**	**0**	**0**	**0**	**0**	**0**	**0**	**0**	**0.0**	**1**	....	....	....	....	....	....	....	....	....	....	....	....	....
	Peoria	IHL	78	12	31	43	96	....	....	....	....	....	....	....	....	....	....	....	6	0	3	3	31	....	....	....
1994-95	**St. Louis**	**NHL**	**5**	**0**	**0**	**0**	**2**	**0**	**0**	**0**	**1**	**0.0**	**−1**	....	....	....	....	....	....	....	....	....	....	....	....	....
	Peoria	IHL	69	7	25	32	137	....	....	....	....	....	....	....	....	....	....	....	4	2	4	6	8	....	....	....
1995-96	Rochester	AHL	62	5	50	55	71	....	....	....	....	....	....	....	....	....	....	....	19	3	11	14	12	....	....	....
1996-97	Rochester	AHL	73	12	51	63	54	....	....	....	....	....	....	....	....	....	....	....	10	2	7	9	27	....	....	....
1997-98	Worcester	AHL	55	8	24	32	34	....	....	....	....	....	....	....	....	....	....	....	....	....	....	....	....	....	....	....
	Houston	IHL	8	1	1	2	6	....	....	....	....	....	....	....	....	....	....	....	4	1	2	3	11	....	....	....
1998-99	Utah	IHL	58	4	19	23	40	....	....	....	....	....	....	....	....	....	....	....	....	....	....	....	....	....	....	....
	Orlando	IHL	21	9	9	18	18	....	....	....	....	....	....	....	....	....	....	....	17	3	5	8	14	....	....	....
	NHL Totals		**7**	**0**	**0**	**0**	**2**	**0**	**0**	**0**	**1**	**0.0**		....	....	....	....	....	....	....	....	....	....	....	....	....

AHL Second All-Star Team (1996) • AHL First All-Star Team (1997)

Signed as a free agent by **Buffalo**, August 23, 1995. Signed as a free agent by **St. Louis**, July 28, 1997.

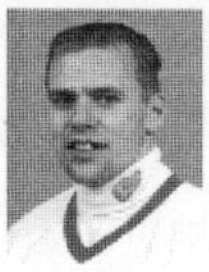

HOLMSTROM, Tomas (HOHLM-struhm) — DET.

Left wing. Shoots left. 6', 200 lbs. Born, Pitea, Sweden, January 23, 1973. Detroit's 9th choice, 257th overall, in 1994 Entry Draft.

Season	Club	League	GP	G	A	Pts	PIM	PP	SH	GW	S	%	+/-	TF	F%	H	SB	Min	GP	G	A	Pts	PIM	PP	SH	GW
1994-95	Lulea HF	Sweden	40	14	14	28	56	....	....	....	....	....	....	....	....	....	....	....	8	1	2	3	20	....	....	....
1995-96	Lulea HF	Sweden	34	12	11	23	78	....	....	....	....	....	....	....	....	....	....	....	11	6	2	8	22	....	....	....
1996-97♦	**Detroit**	**NHL**	**47**	**6**	**3**	**9**	**33**	**3**	**0**	**0**	**53**	**11.3**	**−10**	....	....	....	....	....	**1**	**0**	**0**	**0**	**0**	**0**	**0**	**0**
	Adirondack	AHL	6	3	1	4	7	....	....	....	....	....	....	....	....	....	....	....	....	....	....	....	....	....	....	....
1997-98♦	**Detroit**	**NHL**	**57**	**5**	**17**	**22**	**44**	**1**	**0**	**1**	**48**	**10.4**	**6**	....	....	....	....	....	**22**	**7**	**12**	**19**	**16**	**2**	**0**	**0**
1998-99	**Detroit**	**NHL**	**82**	**13**	**21**	**34**	**69**	**5**	**0**	**4**	**100**	**13.0**	**−11**	**0**	**0.0**	**94**	**9**	**12:22**	**10**	**4**	**3**	**7**	**4**	**2**	**0**	**1**
	NHL Totals		**186**	**24**	**41**	**65**	**146**	**9**	**0**	**5**	**201**	**11.9**		**0**	**0.0**	**94**	**9**	**12:22**	**33**	**11**	**15**	**26**	**20**	**4**	**0**	**1**

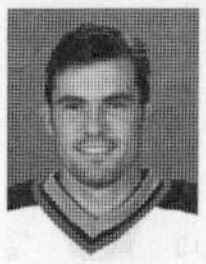

HOLZINGER, Brian

(HOHL-zihn-guhr) **BUF.**

Center. Shoots right. 5'11", 190 lbs. Born, Parma, OH, October 10, 1972. Buffalo's 7th choice, 124th overall, in 1991 Entry Draft.

			Regular Season																Playoffs							
Season	Club	League	GP	G	A	Pts	PIM	PP	SH	GW	S	%	+/–	TF	F%	H	SB	Min	GP	G	A	Pts	PIM	PP	SH	GW
1990-91	Detroit	NAJHL	37	45	41	86	16																			
1991-92	Bowling Green	CCHA	30	14	8	22	36																			
1992-93	Bowling Green	CCHA	41	31	26	57	44																			
1993-94	Bowling Green	CCHA	38	22	15	37	24																			
1994-95	Bowling Green	CCHA	38	35	33	68	42																			
	Buffalo	**NHL**	**4**	**0**	**3**	**3**	**0**	**0**	**0**	**0**	**3**	**0.0**	**2**						**4**	**2**	**1**	**3**	**2**	**1**	**0**	**0**
1995-96	**Buffalo**	**NHL**	**58**	**10**	**10**	**20**	**37**	**5**	**0**	**1**	**71**	**14.1**	**–21**													
	Rochester	AHL	17	10	11	21	14												19	10	14	24	10			
1996-97	**Buffalo**	**NHL**	**81**	**22**	**29**	**51**	**54**	**2**	**2**	**6**	**142**	**15.5**	**9**						**12**	**2**	**5**	**7**	**8**	**0**	**0**	**0**
1997-98	**Buffalo**	**NHL**	**69**	**14**	**21**	**35**	**36**	**4**	**2**	**1**	**116**	**12.1**	**–2**						**15**	**4**	**7**	**11**	**18**	**1**	**1**	**0**
1998-99	**Buffalo**	**NHL**	**81**	**17**	**17**	**34**	**45**	**5**	**0**	**2**	**143**	**11.9**	**2**	**852**	**50.4**	**72**	**23**	**16:31**	**21**	**3**	**5**	**8**	**33**	**1**	**0**	**0**
	NHL Totals		**293**	**63**	**80**	**143**	**172**	**16**	**4**	**10**	**475**	**13.3**		**852**	**50.4**	**72**	**23**	**16:31**	**52**	**11**	**18**	**29**	**61**	**3**	**1**	**0**

CCHA Second All-Star Team (1993) • CCHA First All-Star Team (1995) • NCAA West First All-American Team (1995) • Won Hobey Baker Memorial Award (Top U.S. Collegiate Player) (1995)

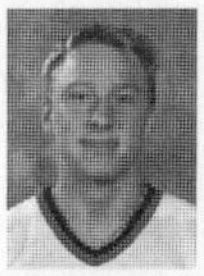

HOSSA, Marian

(HOH-sah) **OTT.**

Left wing. Shoots left. 6'1", 194 lbs. Born, Stara Lubovna, Czech., January 12, 1979. Ottawa's 1st choice, 12th overall, in 1997 Entry Draft.

Season	Club	League	GP	G	A	Pts	PIM	PP	SH	GW	S	%	+/–	TF	F%	H	SB	Min	GP	G	A	Pts	PIM	PP	SH	GW
1995-96	Dukla Trencin	Slovak-Jr.	53	42	49	91	26																			
1996-97	Dukla Trencin	Slovakia	46	25	19	44	33												7	5	5	10				
1997-98	Portland	WHL	53	45	40	85	50												16	13	6	19	6			
	Ottawa	**NHL**	**7**	**0**	**1**	**1**	**0**	**0**	**0**	**0**	**10**	**0.0**	**–1**													
1998-99	**Ottawa**	**NHL**	**60**	**15**	**15**	**30**	**37**	**1**	**0**	**2**	**124**	**12.1**	**18**	**4**	**25.0**	**59**	**6**	**13:59**	**4**	**0**	**2**	**2**	**4**	**0**	**0**	**0**
	NHL Totals		**67**	**15**	**16**	**31**	**37**	**1**	**0**	**2**	**134**	**11.2**		**4**	**25.0**	**59**	**6**	**13:59**	**4**	**0**	**2**	**2**	**4**	**0**	**0**	**0**

WHL West First All-Star Team (1998) • Canadian Major Junior First All-Star Team (1998) • Memorial Cup All-Star Team (1998) • NHL All-Rookie Team (1999)

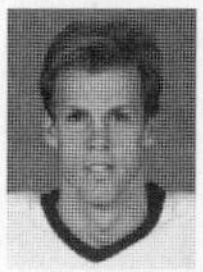

HOUDA, Doug

(HOO-duh) **BUF.**

Defense. Shoots right. 6'2", 190 lbs. Born, Blairmore, Alta., June 3, 1966. Detroit's 2nd choice, 28th overall, in 1984 Entry Draft.

Season	Club	League	GP	G	A	Pts	PIM	PP	SH	GW	S	%	+/–	TF	F%	H	SB	Min	GP	G	A	Pts	PIM	PP	SH	GW
1981-82	Calgary	AAHA	STATISTICS NOT AVAILABLE																							
	Calgary	WHL	3	0	0	0	0																			
1982-83	Calgary	WHL	71	5	23	28	99												16	1	3	4	44			
1983-84	Calgary	WHL	69	6	30	36	195												4	0	0	0	7			
1984-85	Calgary	WHL	65	20	54	74	182												8	3	4	7	29			
	Kalamazoo	IHL																	7	0	2	2	10			
1985-86	Calgary	WHL	16	4	10	14	60																			
	Medicine Hat	WHL	35	9	23	32	80												25	4	19	23	64			
	Detroit	**NHL**	**6**	**0**	**0**	**0**	**4**	**0**	**0**	**0**	**5**	**0.0**	**–7**													
1986-87	Adirondack	AHL	77	6	23	29	142												11	1	8	9	50			
1987-88	**Detroit**	**NHL**	**11**	**1**	**1**	**2**	**10**	**0**	**0**	**0**	**10**	**10.0**	**0**													
	Adirondack	AHL	71	10	32	42	169												11	0	3	3	44			
1988-89	**Detroit**	**NHL**	**57**	**2**	**11**	**13**	**67**	**0**	**0**	**0**	**38**	**5.3**	**17**						**6**	**0**	**1**	**1**	**0**	**0**	**0**	**0**
	Adirondack	AHL	7	0	3	3	8																			
1989-90	**Detroit**	**NHL**	**73**	**2**	**9**	**11**	**127**	**0**	**0**	**0**	**59**	**3.4**	**–5**													
1990-91	**Detroit**	**NHL**	**22**	**0**	**4**	**4**	**43**	**0**	**0**	**0**	**21**	**0.0**	**–2**													
	Adirondack	AHL	38	9	17	26	67																			
	Hartford	**NHL**	**19**	**1**	**2**	**3**	**41**	**0**	**0**	**0**	**21**	**4.8**	**–3**						**6**	**0**	**0**	**0**	**8**	**0**	**0**	**0**
1991-92	**Hartford**	**NHL**	**56**	**3**	**6**	**9**	**125**	**1**	**0**	**1**	**40**	**7.5**	**–2**						**6**	**0**	**2**	**2**	**13**	**0**	**0**	**0**
1992-93	**Hartford**	**NHL**	**60**	**2**	**6**	**8**	**167**	**0**	**0**	**0**	**43**	**4.7**	**–19**													
1993-94	**Hartford**	**NHL**	**7**	**0**	**0**	**0**	**23**	**0**	**0**	**0**	**1**	**0.0**	**–4**													
	Los Angeles	**NHL**	**54**	**2**	**6**	**8**	**165**	**0**	**0**	**0**	**31**	**6.5**	**–15**													
1994-95	**Buffalo**	**NHL**	**28**	**1**	**2**	**3**	**68**	**0**	**0**	**0**	**21**	**4.8**	**1**													
1995-96	**Buffalo**	**NHL**	**38**	**1**	**3**	**4**	**52**	**0**	**0**	**0**	**21**	**4.8**	**3**													
	Rochester	AHL	21	1	6	7	41												19	3	5	8	30			
1996-97	**NY Islanders**	**NHL**	**70**	**2**	**8**	**10**	**99**	**0**	**0**	**0**	**29**	**6.9**	**1**													
	Utah	IHL	3	0	0	0	7																			
1997-98	**NY Islanders**	**NHL**	**31**	**1**	**2**	**3**	**47**	**0**	**0**	**0**	**15**	**6.7**	**–6**													
	Anaheim	**NHL**	**24**	**1**	**2**	**3**	**52**	**0**	**1**	**0**	**9**	**11.1**	**–5**													
1998-99	**Detroit**	**NHL**	**3**	**0**	**1**	**1**	**0**	**0**	**0**	**0**	**1**	**0.0**	**–2**	**0**	**0.0**	**4**	**1**	**6:51**								
	Adirondack	AHL	73	7	21	28	122												3	0	1	1	4			
	NHL Totals		**559**	**19**	**63**	**82**	**1090**	**1**	**1**	**1**	**365**	**5.2**		**0**	**0.0**	**4**	**1**	**6:51**	**18**	**0**	**3**	**3**	**21**	**0**	**0**	**0**

WHL East Second All-Star Team (1985) • AHL First All-Star Team (1988)

Traded to **Hartford** by **Detroit** for Doug Crossman, February 20, 1991. Traded to **LA Kings** by **Hartford** for Marc Potvin, November 3, 1993. Traded to **Buffalo** by **LA Kings** for Sean O'Donnell, July 26, 1994. Signed as a free agent by **NY Islanders**, October 26, 1996. Traded to **Anaheim** by **NY Islanders** with Travis Green and Tony Tuzzolino for Joe Sacco, J.J. Daigneault and Mark Janssens, February 6, 1998. Traded to **Detroit** by **Anaheim** for future considerations, October 9, 1998. Signed as a free agent by **Buffalo**, July 13, 1999.

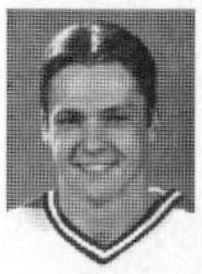

HOUDE, Eric

(OOD) **EDM.**

Center. Shoots left. 5'11", 191 lbs. Born, Montreal, Que., December 19, 1976. Montreal's 9th choice, 216th overall, in 1995 Entry Draft.

Season	Club	League	GP	G	A	Pts	PIM	PP	SH	GW	S	%	+/–	TF	F%	H	SB	Min	GP	G	A	Pts	PIM	PP	SH	GW
1992-93	St-Hubert	QAAA	35	45	40	85																				
1993-94	St-Jean	QMJHL	71	16	16	32	14												5	1	1	2	4			
1994-95	St-Jean	QMJHL	40	10	13	23	23																			
	Halifax	QMJHL	28	13	23	36	8												3	2	1	3	4			
1995-96	Halifax	QMJHL	69	40	48	88	35												6	3	4	7	2			
1996-97	**Montreal**	**NHL**	**13**	**0**	**2**	**2**	**2**	**0**	**0**	**0**	**1**	**0.0**	**1**													
	Fredericton	AHL	66	30	36	66	20																			
1997-98	**Montreal**	**NHL**	**9**	**1**	**0**	**1**	**0**	**0**	**0**	**1**	**4**	**25.0**	**–3**													
	Fredericton	AHL	71	28	42	70	24												4	5	2	7	4			
1998-99	**Montreal**	**NHL**	**8**	**1**	**1**	**2**	**2**	**0**	**0**	**1**	**4**	**25.0**	**–2**	**41**	**46.3**	**4**	**0**	**7:11**								
	Fredericton	AHL	69	27	37	64	32												14	2	7	9	4			
	NHL Totals		**30**	**2**	**3**	**5**	**4**	**0**	**0**	**2**	**9**	**22.2**		**41**	**46.3**	**4**	**0**	**7:11**								

Signed as a free agent by **Edmonton**, August 11, 1999.

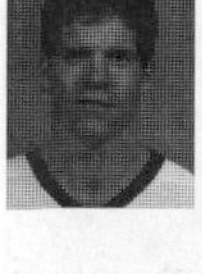

HOUGH, Mike

(HUHF)

Left wing. Shoots left. 6'1", 197 lbs. Born, Montreal, Que., February 6, 1963. Quebec's 7th choice, 181st overall, in 1982 Entry Draft.

Season	Club	League	GP	G	A	Pts	PIM	PP	SH	GW	S	%	+/–	TF	F%	H	SB	Min	GP	G	A	Pts	PIM	PP	SH	GW
1979-80	Toronto	MTHL	44	20	50	70																				
1980-81	Dixie	OJHL	24	15	20	35	84																			
1981-82	Kitchener	OHL	58	14	24	38	172												14	4	1	5	16			
1982-83	Kitchener	OHL	61	17	27	44	156												12	5	4	9	30			
1983-84	Fredericton	AHL	69	11	16	27	142												1	0	0	0	7			
1984-85	Fredericton	AHL	76	21	27	48	49												6	1	1	2	2			
1985-86	Fredericton	AHL	74	21	33	54	68												6	0	3	3	8			
1986-87	**Quebec**	**NHL**	**56**	**6**	**8**	**14**	**79**	**1**	**1**	**0**	**60**	**10.0**	**–8**						**9**	**0**	**3**	**3**	**26**	**0**	**0**	**0**
	Fredericton	AHL	10	1	3	4	20																			
1987-88	**Quebec**	**NHL**	**17**	**3**	**2**	**5**	**2**	**0**	**0**	**1**	**23**	**13.0**	**–8**													
	Fredericton	AHL	46	16	25	41	133												15	4	8	12	55			
1988-89	**Quebec**	**NHL**	**46**	**9**	**10**	**19**	**39**	**1**	**3**	**3**	**51**	**17.6**	**–7**													
	Halifax	AHL	22	11	10	21	87																			
1989-90	**Quebec**	**NHL**	**43**	**13**	**13**	**26**	**84**	**3**	**1**	**0**	**93**	**14.0**	**–24**													

			Regular Season																Playoffs							
Season	Club	League	GP	G	A	Pts	PIM	PP	SH	GW	S	%	+/–	TF	F%	H	SB	Min	GP	G	A	Pts	PIM	PP	SH	GW
1990-91	**Quebec**	**NHL**	**63**	**13**	**20**	**33**	**111**	**1**	**1**	**1**	**106**	**12.3**	**–7**	....	....	....	....	....	....	....	....	....	....	....	....	....
1991-92	**Quebec**	**NHL**	**61**	**16**	**22**	**38**	**77**	**6**	**2**	**1**	**92**	**17.4**	**–1**	....	....	....	....	....	....	....	....	....	....	....	....	....
1992-93	**Quebec**	**NHL**	**77**	**8**	**22**	**30**	**69**	**2**	**1**	**2**	**98**	**8.2**	**–11**	....	....	....	....	....	**6**	**0**	**1**	**1**	**2**	**0**	**0**	**0**
1993-94	**Florida**	**NHL**	**78**	**6**	**23**	**29**	**62**	**0**	**1**	**1**	**106**	**5.7**	**3**	....	....	....	....	....	....	....	....	....	....	....	....	....
1994-95	**Florida**	**NHL**	**48**	**6**	**7**	**13**	**38**	**0**	**0**	**2**	**58**	**10.3**	**1**	....	....	....	....	....	....	....	....	....	....	....	....	....
1995-96	**Florida**	**NHL**	**64**	**7**	**16**	**23**	**37**	**0**	**1**	**1**	**66**	**10.6**	**4**	....	....	....	....	....	**22**	**4**	**1**	**5**	**8**	**0**	**0**	**2**
1996-97	**Florida**	**NHL**	**69**	**8**	**6**	**14**	**48**	**0**	**0**	**2**	**85**	**9.4**	**12**	....	....	....	....	....	**5**	**1**	**0**	**1**	**2**	**0**	**0**	**0**
1997-98	**NY Islanders**	**NHL**	**74**	**5**	**7**	**12**	**27**	**0**	**0**	**0**	**44**	**11.4**	**–4**	....	....	....	....	....	....	....	....	....	....	....	....	....
1998-99	**NY Islanders**	**NHL**	**11**	**0**	**0**	**0**	**2**	**0**	**0**	**0**	**4**	**0.0**	**–2**	**0**	**0.0**	**8**	**5**	**8:21**	....	....	....	....	....	....	....	....
	Utah	IHL	26	5	7	12	8	....	....	....	....	....	....	....	....	....	....	....	....	....	....	....	....	....	....	....
	Lowell	AHL	11	0	3	3	21	....	....	....	....	....	....	....	....	....	....	....	....	....	....	....	....	....	....	....
	NHL Totals		**707**	**100**	**156**	**256**	**675**	**14**	**11**	**14**	**886**	**11.3**		**0**	**0.0**	**8**	**5**	**8:21**	**42**	**5**	**5**	**10**	**38**	**0**	**0**	**2**

Traded to **Washington** by **Quebec** for Reggie Savage and Paul MacDermid, June 20, 1993. Claimed by **Florida** from **Washington** in Expansion Draft, June 24, 1993. Signed as a free agent by **NY Islanders**, July 21, 1997.

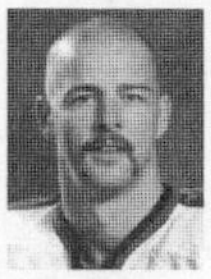

HOULDER, Bill (HOHL-duhr) T.B.

Defense. Shoots left. 6'2", 210 lbs. Born, Thunder Bay, Ont., March 11, 1967. Washington's 4th choice, 82nd overall, in 1985 Entry Draft.

			Regular Season																Playoffs							
Season	Club	League	GP	G	A	Pts	PIM	PP	SH	GW	S	%	+/–	TF	F%	H	SB	Min	GP	G	A	Pts	PIM	PP	SH	GW
1983-84	Thunder Bay	TBJHL	23	4	18	22	37	....	....	....	....	....	....	....	....	....	....	....	....	....	....	....	....	....	....	....
1984-85	North Bay	OHL	66	4	20	24	37	....	....	....	....	....	....	....	....	....	....	....	8	0	0	0	2	....	....	....
1985-86	North Bay	OHL	59	5	30	35	97	....	....	....	....	....	....	....	....	....	....	....	10	1	6	7	12	....	....	....
1986-87	North Bay	OHL	62	17	51	68	68	....	....	....	....	....	....	....	....	....	....	....	22	4	19	23	20	....	....	....
1987-88	**Washington**	**NHL**	**30**	**1**	**2**	**3**	**10**	**0**	**0**	**0**	**20**	**5.0**	**–2**	....	....	....	....	....	....	....	....	....	....	....	....	....
	Fort Wayne	IHL	43	10	14	24	32	....	....	....	....	....	....	....	....	....	....	....	....	....	....	....	....	....	....	....
1988-89	**Washington**	**NHL**	**8**	**0**	**3**	**3**	**4**	**0**	**0**	**0**	**5**	**0.0**	**7**	....	....	....	....	....	....	....	....	....	....	....	....	....
	Baltimore	AHL	65	10	36	46	50	....	....	....	....	....	....	....	....	....	....	....	....	....	....	....	....	....	....	....
1989-90	**Washington**	**NHL**	**41**	**1**	**11**	**12**	**28**	**0**	**0**	**0**	**49**	**2.0**	**8**	....	....	....	....	....	....	....	....	....	....	....	....	....
	Baltimore	AHL	26	3	7	10	12	....	....	....	....	....	....	....	....	....	....	....	7	0	2	2	2	....	....	....
1990-91	**Buffalo**	**NHL**	**7**	**0**	**2**	**2**	**4**	**0**	**0**	**0**	**7**	**0.0**	**–2**	....	....	....	....	....	....	....	....	....	....	....	....	....
	Rochester	AHL	69	13	53	66	28	....	....	....	....	....	....	....	....	....	....	....	15	5	13	18	4	....	....	....
1991-92	**Buffalo**	**NHL**	**10**	**1**	**0**	**1**	**8**	**0**	**0**	**0**	**18**	**5.6**	**–2**	....	....	....	....	....	....	....	....	....	....	....	....	....
	Rochester	AHL	42	8	26	34	16	....	....	....	....	....	....	....	....	....	....	....	16	5	6	11	4	....	....	....
1992-93	**Buffalo**	**NHL**	**15**	**3**	**5**	**8**	**6**	**0**	**0**	**0**	**29**	**10.3**	**5**	....	....	....	....	....	**8**	**0**	**2**	**2**	**4**	**0**	**0**	**0**
	San Diego	IHL	64	24	48	72	39	....	....	....	....	....	....	....	....	....	....	....	....	....	....	....	....	....	....	....
1993-94	**Anaheim**	**NHL**	**80**	**14**	**25**	**39**	**40**	**3**	**0**	**3**	**187**	**7.5**	**–18**	....	....	....	....	....	....	....	....	....	....	....	....	....
1994-95	**St. Louis**	**NHL**	**41**	**5**	**13**	**18**	**20**	**1**	**0**	**0**	**59**	**8.5**	**16**	....	....	....	....	....	**4**	**1**	**1**	**2**	**0**	**0**	**0**	**0**
1995-96	**Tampa Bay**	**NHL**	**61**	**5**	**23**	**28**	**22**	**3**	**0**	**0**	**90**	**5.6**	**1**	....	....	....	....	....	**6**	**0**	**1**	**1**	**4**	**0**	**0**	**0**
1996-97	**Tampa Bay**	**NHL**	**79**	**4**	**21**	**25**	**30**	**0**	**0**	**2**	**116**	**3.4**	**16**	....	....	....	....	....	....	....	....	....	....	....	....	....
1997-98	**San Jose**	**NHL**	**82**	**7**	**25**	**32**	**48**	**4**	**0**	**2**	**102**	**6.9**	**13**	....	....	....	....	....	**6**	**1**	**2**	**3**	**2**	**0**	**0**	**0**
1998-99	**San Jose**	**NHL**	**76**	**9**	**23**	**32**	**40**	**7**	**0**	**5**	**115**	**7.8**	**8**	**0**	**0.0**	**70**	**83**	**22:08**	**6**	**3**	**0**	**3**	**4**	**3**	**0**	**0**
	NHL Totals		**530**	**50**	**153**	**203**	**260**	**18**	**0**	**12**	**797**	**6.3**		**0**	**0.0**	**70**	**83**	**22:08**	**30**	**5**	**6**	**11**	**14**	**3**	**0**	**0**

AHL First All-Star Team (1991) • Won Governor's Trophy (Outstanding Defenseman - IHL) (1993) • IHL First All-Star Team (1993)

Traded to **Buffalo** by **Washington** for Shawn Anderson, September 30, 1990. Claimed by **Anaheim** from **Buffalo** in Expansion Draft, June 24, 1993. Traded to **St. Louis** by **Anaheim** for Jason Marshall, August 29, 1994. Signed as a free agent by **Tampa Bay**, July 26, 1995. Signed as a free agent by **San Jose**, July 16, 1997. Traded to **Tampa Bay** by **San Jose** with Andrei Zyuzin, Shawn Burr and Steve Guolla for Niklas Sundstrom and NY Rangers' 3rd round choice (previously acquired) in 2000 Entry Draft, August 4, 1999.

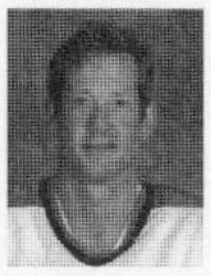

HOUSLEY, Phil (HOWZ-lee) CGY.

Defense. Shoots left. 5'10", 185 lbs. Born, St. Paul, MN, March 9, 1964. Buffalo's 1st choice, 6th overall, in 1982 Entry Draft.

			Regular Season																Playoffs							
Season	Club	League	GP	G	A	Pts	PIM	PP	SH	GW	S	%	+/–	TF	F%	H	SB	Min	GP	G	A	Pts	PIM	PP	SH	GW
1980-81	St. Paul High	H.S.	STATISTICS NOT AVAILABLE																							
	St. Paul Vulcans	USHL	6	7	7	14	6	....	....	....	....	....	....	....	....	....	....	....	10	5	5	10	0	....	....	....
1981-82	St. Paul High	H.S.	22	31	34	65	18	....	....	....	....	....	....	....	....	....	....	....	....	....	....	....	....	....	....	....
1982-83	**Buffalo**	**NHL**	**77**	**19**	**47**	**66**	**39**	**11**	**0**	**2**	**183**	**10.4**	**–4**	....	....	....	....	....	**10**	**3**	**4**	**7**	**2**	**1**	**0**	**0**
1983-84	**Buffalo**	**NHL**	**75**	**31**	**46**	**77**	**33**	**13**	**2**	**6**	**234**	**13.2**	**3**	....	....	....	....	....	**3**	**0**	**0**	**0**	**6**	**0**	**0**	**0**
1984-85	**Buffalo**	**NHL**	**73**	**16**	**53**	**69**	**28**	**3**	**0**	**4**	**188**	**8.5**	**15**	....	....	....	....	....	**5**	**3**	**2**	**5**	**2**	**0**	**0**	**0**
1985-86	**Buffalo**	**NHL**	**79**	**15**	**47**	**62**	**54**	**7**	**0**	**2**	**180**	**8.3**	**–9**	....	....	....	....	....	....	....	....	....	....	....	....	....
1986-87	**Buffalo**	**NHL**	**78**	**21**	**46**	**67**	**57**	**8**	**1**	**2**	**202**	**10.4**	**–2**	....	....	....	....	....	....	....	....	....	....	....	....	....
1987-88	**Buffalo**	**NHL**	**74**	**29**	**37**	**66**	**96**	**6**	**0**	**1**	**231**	**12.6**	**–17**	....	....	....	....	....	**6**	**2**	**4**	**6**	**6**	**1**	**0**	**0**
1988-89	**Buffalo**	**NHL**	**72**	**26**	**44**	**70**	**47**	**5**	**0**	**3**	**178**	**14.6**	**6**	....	....	....	....	....	**5**	**1**	**3**	**4**	**2**	**0**	**0**	**0**
1989-90	**Buffalo**	**NHL**	**80**	**21**	**60**	**81**	**32**	**8**	**1**	**4**	**201**	**10.4**	**11**	....	....	....	....	....	**6**	**1**	**4**	**5**	**4**	**1**	**0**	**0**
1990-91	**Winnipeg**	**NHL**	**78**	**23**	**53**	**76**	**24**	**12**	**1**	**3**	**206**	**11.2**	**–13**	....	....	....	....	....	....	....	....	....	....	....	....	....
1991-92	**Winnipeg**	**NHL**	**74**	**23**	**63**	**86**	**92**	**11**	**0**	**4**	**234**	**9.8**	**–5**	....	....	....	....	....	**7**	**1**	**4**	**5**	**0**	**1**	**0**	**1**
1992-93	**Winnipeg**	**NHL**	**80**	**18**	**79**	**97**	**52**	**6**	**0**	**2**	**249**	**7.2**	**–14**	....	....	....	....	....	**6**	**0**	**7**	**7**	**2**	**0**	**0**	**0**
1993-94	**St. Louis**	**NHL**	**26**	**7**	**15**	**22**	**12**	**4**	**0**	**1**	**60**	**11.7**	**–5**	....	....	....	....	....	**4**	**2**	**1**	**3**	**4**	**2**	**0**	**0**
1994-95	Zurcher SC	Switz.	10	6	8	14	34	....	....	....	....	....	....	....	....	....	....	....	....	....	....	....	....	....	....	....
	Calgary	**NHL**	**43**	**8**	**35**	**43**	**18**	**3**	**0**	**0**	**135**	**5.9**	**17**	....	....	....	....	....	**7**	**0**	**9**	**9**	**0**	**0**	**0**	**0**
1995-96	**Calgary**	**NHL**	**59**	**16**	**36**	**52**	**22**	**6**	**0**	**1**	**155**	**10.3**	**–2**	....	....	....	....	....	....	....	....	....	....	....	....	....
	New Jersey	**NHL**	**22**	**1**	**15**	**16**	**8**	**0**	**0**	**0**	**50**	**2.0**	**–4**	....	....	....	....	....	....	....	....	....	....	....	....	....
1996-97	**Washington**	**NHL**	**77**	**11**	**29**	**40**	**24**	**3**	**1**	**2**	**167**	**6.6**	**–10**	....	....	....	....	....	....	....	....	....	....	....	....	....
1997-98	**Washington**	**NHL**	**64**	**6**	**25**	**31**	**24**	**4**	**1**	**0**	**116**	**5.2**	**–10**	....	....	....	....	....	**18**	**0**	**4**	**4**	**4**	**0**	**0**	**0**
1998-99	**Calgary**	**NHL**	**79**	**11**	**43**	**54**	**52**	**4**	**0**	**1**	**193**	**5.7**	**14**	**0**	**0.0**	**21**	**52**	**20:52**	....	....	....	....	....	....	....	....
	NHL Totals		**1210**	**302**	**773**	**1075**	**714**	**114**	**7**	**38**	**3162**	**9.6**		**0**	**0.0**	**21**	**52**	**20:52**	**77**	**13**	**42**	**55**	**32**	**6**	**0**	**1**

NHL All-Rookie Team (1983) • NHL Second All-Star Team (1992)

Played in NHL All-Star Game (1984, 1989, 1990, 1991, 1992, 1993)

Traded to **Winnipeg** by **Buffalo** with Scott Arniel, Jeff Parker and Buffalo's 1st round choice (Keith Tkachuk) in 1990 Entry Draft for Dale Hawerchuk, Winnipeg's 1st round choice (Brad May) in 1990 Entry Draft and future considerations, June 16, 1990. Traded to **St. Louis** by **Winnipeg** for Nelson Emerson and Stephane Quintal, September 24, 1993. Traded to **Calgary** by **St. Louis** with St. Louis' 2nd round choice (Steve Begin) in 1996 Entry Draft and 2nd round choice (John Tripp) in 1997 Entry Draft for Al MacInnis and Calgary's 4th round choice (Didier Tremblay) in 1997 Entry Draft, July 4, 1994. Traded to **New Jersey** by **Calgary** with Dan Keczmer for Tommy Albelin, Cale Hulse and Jocelyn Lemieux, February 26, 1996. Signed as a free agent by **Washington**, July 22, 1996. Claimed on waivers by **Calgary** from **Washington**, July 21, 1998.

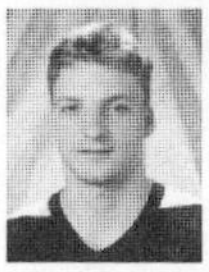

HRDINA, Jan (hir-DEE-nah) PIT.

Center. Shoots right. 6', 197 lbs. Born, Hradec Kralove, Czech., February 5, 1976. Pittsburgh's 4th choice, 128th overall, in 1995 Entry Draft.

			Regular Season																Playoffs							
Season	Club	League	GP	G	A	Pts	PIM	PP	SH	GW	S	%	+/–	TF	F%	H	SB	Min	GP	G	A	Pts	PIM	PP	SH	GW
1993-94	HC Stadion	Czech-Jr.	10	1	6	7	0	....	....	....	....	....	....	....	....	....	....	....	....	....	....	....	....	....	....	....
	HC Stadion	Cze-Rep	23	1	5	6	....	....	....	....	....	....	....	....	....	....	....	....	4	0	1	1	....	....	....	....
1994-95	Seattle	WHL	69	41	59	100	79	....	....	....	....	....	....	....	....	....	....	....	4	0	1	1	8	....	....	....
1995-96	Seattle	WHL	30	19	28	47	37	....	....	....	....	....	....	....	....	....	....	....	....	....	....	....	....	....	....	....
	Spokane	WHL	18	10	16	26	25	....	....	....	....	....	....	....	....	....	....	....	18	5	14	19	49	....	....	....
1996-97	Cleveland	IHL	68	23	31	54	82	....	....	....	....	....	....	....	....	....	....	....	13	1	2	3	8	....	....	....
1997-98	Syracuse	AHL	72	20	24	44	82	....	....	....	....	....	....	....	....	....	....	....	5	1	3	4	10	....	....	....
1998-99	**Pittsburgh**	**NHL**	**82**	**13**	**29**	**42**	**40**	**3**	**0**	**2**	**94**	**13.8**	**–2**	**1461**	**56.7**	**104**	**26**	**16:26**	**13**	**4**	**1**	**5**	**12**	**1**	**0**	**1**
	NHL Totals		**82**	**13**	**29**	**42**	**40**	**3**	**0**	**2**	**94**	**13.8**		**1461**	**56.7**	**104**	**26**	**16:26**	**13**	**4**	**1**	**5**	**12**	**1**	**0**	**1**

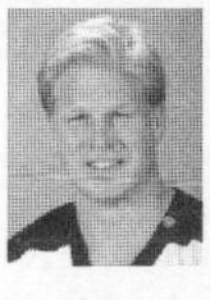

HRKAC, Tony (HUHR-kuhz) NYI

Center. Shoots left. 5'11", 170 lbs. Born, Thunder Bay, Ont., July 7, 1966. St. Louis' 2nd choice, 32nd overall, in 1984 Entry Draft.

			Regular Season																Playoffs							
Season	Club	League	GP	G	A	Pts	PIM	PP	SH	GW	S	%	+/–	TF	F%	H	SB	Min	GP	G	A	Pts	PIM	PP	SH	GW
1983-84	Orillia	OJHL	42	*52	54	*106	20	....	....	....	....	....	....	....	....	....	....	....	....	....	....	....	....	....	....	....
1984-85	North Dakota	WCHA	36	18	36	54	16	....	....	....	....	....	....	....	....	....	....	....	....	....	....	....	....	....	....	....
1985-86	Canada	Nat-Team	62	19	30	49	36	....	....	....	....	....	....	....	....	....	....	....	....	....	....	....	....	....	....	....
1986-87	North Dakota	WCHA	48	46	79	125	48	....	....	....	....	....	....	....	....	....	....	....	....	....	....	....	....	....	....	....
	St. Louis	**NHL**	....	....	....	....	....	....	....	....	....	....	....	....	....	....	....	....	**3**	**0**	**0**	**0**	**0**	....	....	....
1987-88	**St. Louis**	**NHL**	**67**	**11**	**37**	**48**	**22**	**2**	**1**	**3**	**86**	**12.8**	**5**	....	....	....	....	....	**10**	**6**	**1**	**7**	**4**	**3**	**1**	**1**
1988-89	**St. Louis**	**NHL**	**70**	**17**	**28**	**45**	**8**	**5**	**0**	**1**	**133**	**12.8**	**–10**	....	....	....	....	....	**4**	**1**	**1**	**2**	**0**	**0**	**0**	**1**

			Regular Season																Playoffs							
Season	Club	League	GP	G	A	Pts	PIM	PP	SH	GW	S	%	+/–	TF	F%	H	SB	Min	GP	G	A	Pts	PIM	PP	SH	GW
1989-90	**St. Louis**	**NHL**	**28**	**5**	**12**	**17**	**8**	**1**	**0**	**0**	**41**	**12.2**	**1**													
	Quebec	**NHL**	**22**	**4**	**8**	**12**	**2**	**2**	**0**	**0**	**29**	**13.8**	**–5**													
	Halifax	AHL	20	12	21	33	4												6	5	9	14	4			
1990-91	**Quebec**	**NHL**	**70**	**16**	**32**	**48**	**16**	**6**	**0**	**0**	**122**	**13.1**	**–22**													
	Halifax	AHL	3	4	1	5	2																			
1991-92	**San Jose**	**NHL**	**22**	**2**	**10**	**12**	**4**	**0**	**0**	**0**	**31**	**6.5**	**–2**													
	Chicago	**NHL**	**18**	**1**	**2**	**3**	**6**	**0**	**0**	**0**	**22**	**4.5**	**4**						**3**	**0**	**0**	**0**	**2**	**0**	**0**	**0**
1992-93	Indianapolis	IHL	80	45	*87	*132	70												5	0	2	2	2			
1993-94	**St. Louis**	**NHL**	**36**	**6**	**5**	**11**	**8**	**1**	**1**	**1**	**43**	**14.0**	**–11**						**4**	**0**	**0**	**0**	**0**	**0**	**0**	**0**
	Peoria	IHL	45	30	51	81	25												1	1	2	3	0			
1994-95	Milwaukee	IHL	71	24	67	91	26												15	4	9	13	16			
1995-96	Milwaukee	IHL	43	14	28	42	18												5	1	3	4	4			
1996-97	Milwaukee	IHL	81	27	61	88	20												3	1	1	2	2			
1997-98	**Dallas**	**NHL**	**13**	**5**	**3**	**8**	**0**	**3**	**0**	**0**	**14**	**35.7**	**0**													
	Michigan	IHL	20	7	15	22	6																			
	Edmonton	**NHL**	**36**	**8**	**11**	**19**	**10**	**4**	**0**	**1**	**43**	**18.6**	**3**						**12**	**0**	**3**	**3**	**2**	**0**	**0**	**0**
1998-99♦	**Dallas**	**NHL**	**69**	**13**	**14**	**27**	**26**	**2**	**0**	**2**	**67**	**19.4**	**2**	**666**	**48.0**	**49**	**13**	**12:02**	**5**	**0**	**2**	**2**	**4**	**0**	**0**	**0**
	NHL Totals		**451**	**88**	**162**	**250**	**110**	**26**	**2**	**8**	**631**	**13.9**		**666**	**48.0**	**49**	**13**	**12:02**	**41**	**7**	**7**	**14**	**12**	**3**	**1**	**2**

WCHA First All-Star Team (1987) • NCAA West First All-American Team (1987) • NCAA Championship All-Tournament Team (1987) • NCAA Championship Tournament MVP (1987) • Won 1987 Hobey Baker Memorial Award (Top U.S. Collegiate Player) (1987) • Won James Gatschene Memorial Trophy (MVP - IHL) (1993) • Won Leo P. Lamoureux Memorial Trophy (Leading Scorer - IHL) (1993) • IHL First All-Star Team (1993)

Traded to **Quebec** by **St. Louis** with Greg Millen for Jeff Brown, December 13, 1989. Traded to **San Jose** by **Quebec** for Greg Paslawski, May 31, 1991. Traded to **Chicago** by **San Jose** for future considerations, February 7, 1992. Signed as a free agent by **St. Louis**, July 30, 1993. Signed as a free agent by **Dallas**, August 12, 1997. Claimed on waivers by **Edmonton** from **Dallas**, January 6, 1998. Traded to **Pittsburgh** by **Edmonton** with Bobby Dollas for Josef Beranek, June 16, 1998. Claimed by **Nashville** from **Pittsburgh** in Expansion Draft, June 26, 1998. Traded to **Dallas** by **Nashville** for future considerations, July 9, 1998. Signed as a free agent by **NY Islanders**, July 29, 1999.

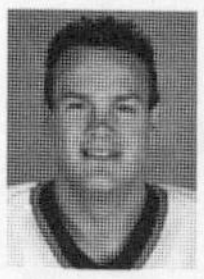

HUARD, Bill

(HEW-ahrd) **L.A.**

Left wing. Shoots left. 6'1", 215 lbs. Born, Welland, Ont., June 24, 1967.

Season	Club	League	GP	G	A	Pts	PIM	PP	SH	GW	S	%	+/–	TF	F%	H	SB	Min	GP	G	A	Pts	PIM	PP	SH	GW
1985-86	Welland	OJHL-B	28	8	17	25	123																			
	Peterborough	OHL	7	1	1	2	2																			
1986-87	Peterborough	OHL	61	14	11	25	61												12	5	2	7	19			
1987-88	Peterborough	OHL	66	28	33	61	132												12	7	8	15	33			
1988-89	Carolina	ECHL	40	27	21	48	177												10	7	2	9	70			
1989-90	Utica	AHL	27	1	7	8	67												5	0	1	1	33			
	Nashville	ECHL	34	24	27	51	212																			
1990-91	Utica	AHL	72	11	16	27	359																			
1991-92	Utica	AHL	62	9	11	20	233												4	1	1	2	4			
1992-93	**Boston**	**NHL**	**2**	**0**	**0**	**0**	**0**	**0**	**0**	**0**	**0**	**0.0**	**0**													
	Providence	AHL	72	18	19	37	302												6	3	0	3	9			
1993-94	**Ottawa**	**NHL**	**63**	**2**	**2**	**4**	**162**	**0**	**0**	**0**	**24**	**8.3**	**–19**													
1994-95	**Ottawa**	**NHL**	**26**	**1**	**1**	**2**	**64**	**0**	**0**	**0**	**15**	**6.7**	**–2**													
	Quebec	**NHL**	**7**	**2**	**2**	**4**	**13**	**0**	**0**	**0**	**6**	**33.3**	**2**						**1**	**0**	**0**	**0**	**0**	**0**	**0**	**0**
1995-96	**Dallas**	**NHL**	**51**	**6**	**6**	**12**	**176**	**0**	**0**	**0**	**34**	**17.6**	**3**													
	Michigan	IHL	12	1	1	2	74																			
1996-97	**Dallas**	**NHL**	**40**	**5**	**6**	**11**	**105**	**0**	**0**	**0**	**34**	**14.7**	**5**													
1997-98	**Edmonton**	**NHL**	**30**	**0**	**1**	**1**	**72**	**0**	**0**	**0**	**12**	**0.0**	**–5**						**4**	**0**	**0**	**0**	**2**	**0**	**0**	**0**
1998-99	**Edmonton**	**NHL**	**3**	**0**	**0**	**0**	**0**	**0**	**0**	**0**	**2**	**0.0**	**0**	**1**	**100.0**	**5**	**0**	**5:36**								
	Houston	IHL	38	9	5	14	201												10	0	0	0	8			
	NHL Totals		**222**	**16**	**18**	**34**	**592**	**0**	**0**	**0**	**127**	**12.6**		**1**	**100.0**	**5**	**0**	**5:36**	**5**	**0**	**0**	**0**	**2**	**0**	**0**	**0**

Signed as a free agent by **New Jersey**, October 1, 1989. Signed as a free agent by **Boston**, December 4, 1992. Signed as a free agent by **Ottawa**, June 30, 1993. Traded to **Quebec** by **Ottawa** for Mika Stromberg and Quebec's 4th round choice (Kevin Boyd) in 1995 Entry Draft, April 7, 1995. Transferred to **Colorado** after **Quebec** franchise relocated, July 1, 1995. Claimed by **Dallas** from **Colorado** in NHL Waiver Draft, October 2, 1995. Signed as a free agent by **Edmonton**, July 22, 1997. Signed as a free agent by **Houston** (IHL), January 23, 1999. Signed as a free agent by **LA Kings**, July 19, 1999.

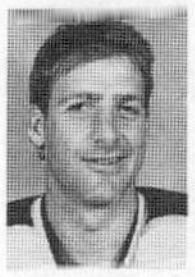

HUGHES, Brent

(HEWS)

Left wing. Shoots left. 5'11", 195 lbs. Born, New Westminster, B.C., April 5, 1966.

Season	Club	League	GP	G	A	Pts	PIM	PP	SH	GW	S	%	+/–	TF	F%	H	SB	Min	GP	G	A	Pts	PIM	PP	SH	GW
1983-84	New Westminster	WHL	67	21	18	39	133												9	2	2	4	27			
1984-85	New Westminster	WHL	64	25	32	57	135												11	2	1	3	37			
1985-86	New Westminster	WHL	71	28	52	80	180																			
1986-87	New Westminster	WHL	8	5	4	9	22																			
	Victoria	WHL	61	38	61	99	146												5	4	1	5	8			
1987-88	Moncton	AHL	73	13	19	32	206																			
1988-89	**Winnipeg**	**NHL**	**28**	**3**	**2**	**5**	**82**	**0**	**1**	**0**	**37**	**8.1**	**–7**													
	Moncton	AHL	54	34	34	68	286												10	9	4	13	40			
1989-90	**Winnipeg**	**NHL**	**11**	**1**	**2**	**3**	**33**	**0**	**0**	**1**	**7**	**14.3**	**–4**													
	Moncton	AHL	65	31	29	60	277																			
1990-91	Moncton	AHL	63	21	22	43	144												3	0	0	0	7			
1991-92	Baltimore	AHL	55	25	29	54	190																			
	Boston	**NHL**	**8**	**1**	**1**	**2**	**38**	**0**	**0**	**1**	**10**	**10.0**	**1**						**10**	**2**	**0**	**2**	**20**	**0**	**0**	**0**
	Maine	AHL	12	6	4	10	34																			
1992-93	**Boston**	**NHL**	**62**	**5**	**4**	**9**	**191**	**0**	**0**	**0**	**54**	**9.3**	**–4**						**1**	**0**	**0**	**0**	**2**	**0**	**0**	**0**
1993-94	**Boston**	**NHL**	**77**	**13**	**11**	**24**	**143**	**1**	**0**	**1**	**100**	**13.0**	**10**						**13**	**2**	**1**	**3**	**27**	**0**	**0**	**1**
	Providence	AHL	6	2	5	7	4																			
1994-95	**Boston**	**NHL**	**44**	**6**	**6**	**12**	**139**	**0**	**0**	**0**	**75**	**8.0**	**6**						**5**	**0**	**0**	**0**	**4**	**0**	**0**	**0**
1995-96	**Buffalo**	**NHL**	**76**	**5**	**10**	**15**	**148**	**0**	**0**	**0**	**56**	**8.9**	**–9**													
1996-97	**NY Islanders**	**NHL**	**51**	**7**	**3**	**10**	**57**	**0**	**0**	**0**	**47**	**14.9**	**–4**													
	Utah	IHL	5	2	2	4	11																			
1997-98	Houston	IHL	79	19	12	31	128												4	0	3	3	20			
1998-99	Houston	IHL	29	4	2	6	87																			
	Utah	IHL	51	13	11	24	80																			
	NHL Totals		**357**	**41**	**39**	**80**	**831**	**1**	**1**	**3**	**386**	**10.6**							**29**	**4**	**1**	**5**	**53**	**0**	**0**	**1**

Signed as a free agent by **Winnipeg**, June 13, 1988. Traded to **Washington** by **Winnipeg** with Craig Duncanson and Simon Wheeldon for Bob Joyce, Tyler Larter and Kent Paynter, May 21, 1991. Traded to **Boston** by **Washington** with future considerations for John Byce and Dennis Smith, February 24, 1992. Claimed By **Buffalo** from **Boston** in NHL Waiver Draft, October 2, 1995. Signed as a free agent by **NY Islanders**, August 9, 1996.

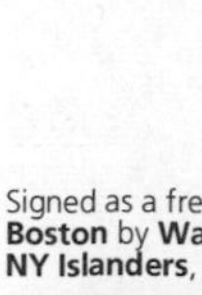

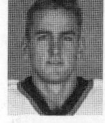

HULBIG, Joe

(HUHL-bihg) **BOS.**

Left wing. Shoots left. 6'3", 215 lbs. Born, Norwood, MA, September 29, 1973. Edmonton's 1st choice, 13th overall, in 1992 Entry Draft.

Season	Club	League	GP	G	A	Pts	PIM	PP	SH	GW	S	%	+/–	TF	F%	H	SB	Min	GP	G	A	Pts	PIM	PP	SH	GW
1989-90	St. Sebastian's	H.S.	30	13	12	25																				
1990-91	St. Sebastian's	H.S.	30	23	19	42																				
1991-92	St. Sebastian's	H.S.	17	19	24	43	30																			
1992-93	Providence	H.E.	26	3	13	16	22																			
1993-94	Providence	H.E.	28	6	4	10	36																			
1994-95	Providence	H.E.	37	14	21	35	36																			
1995-96	Providence	H.E.	31	14	22	36	56																			
1996-97	**Edmonton**	**NHL**	**6**	**0**	**0**	**0**	**0**	**0**	**0**	**0**	**4**	**0.0**	**–1**						**6**	**0**	**1**	**1**	**2**	**0**	**0**	**0**
	Hamilton	AHL	73	18	28	46	59												16	6	10	16	6			
1997-98	**Edmonton**	**NHL**	**17**	**2**	**2**	**4**	**2**	**0**	**0**	**1**	**8**	**25.0**	**–1**													
	Hamilton	AHL	46	15	16	31	52												3	0	1	1	2			

			Regular Season																Playoffs							
Season	Club	League	GP	G	A	Pts	PIM	PP	SH	GW	S	%	+/-	TF	F%	H	SB	Min	GP	G	A	Pts	PIM	PP	SH	GW
1998-99	Edmonton	NHL	1	0	0	0	2	0	0	0	2	0.0	1	0	0.0	0	1	8:20								
	Hamilton	AHL	76	22	24	46	68												11	4	2	6	18			
	NHL Totals		24	2	2	4	4	0	0	1	14	14.3		0	0.0	0	1	8:20	6	0	1	1	2	0	0	0

Signed as a free agent by **Boston**, July 23, 1999.

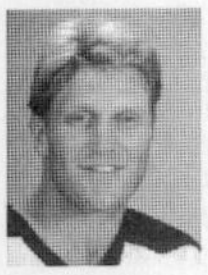

HULL, Brett — DAL.

Right wing. Shoots right. 5'10", 201 lbs. Born, Belleville, Ont., August 9, 1964. Calgary's 6th choice, 117th overall, in 1984 Entry Draft.

Season	Club	League	GP	G	A	Pts	PIM	PP	SH	GW	S	%	+/-	TF	F%	H	SB	Min	GP	G	A	Pts	PIM	PP	SH	GW
1982-83	Penticton	BCJHL	50	48	56	104	27																			
1983-84	Penticton	BCJHL	56	*105	88	*188	20																			
1984-85	U. Minn-Duluth	WCHA	48	32	28	60	24																			
1985-86	U. Minn-Duluth	WCHA	42	52	32	84	46																			
	Calgary	NHL																	2	0	0	0	0			
1986-87	Calgary	NHL	5	1	0	1	0	0	0	1	5	20.0	–1						4	2	1	3	0	0	0	0
	Moncton	AHL	67	50	42	92	16												3	2	2	4	2			
1987-88	Calgary	NHL	52	26	24	50	12	4	0	3	153	17.0	10													
	St. Louis	NHL	13	6	8	14	4	2	0	0	58	10.3	4						10	7	2	9	4	4	0	3
1988-89	St. Louis	NHL	78	41	43	84	33	16	0	6	305	13.4	–17						10	5	5	10	6	1	0	2
1989-90	St. Louis	NHL	80	*72	41	113	24	27	0	12	385	18.7	–1						12	13	8	21	17	7	0	3
1990-91	St. Louis	NHL	78	*86	45	131	22	29	0	11	389	22.1	23						13	11	8	19	4	3	0	2
1991-92	St. Louis	NHL	73	*70	39	109	48	20	5	9	408	17.2	–2						6	4	4	8	4	1	1	1
1992-93	St. Louis	NHL	80	54	47	101	41	29	0	2	390	13.8	–27						11	8	5	13	2	5	0	2
1993-94	St. Louis	NHL	81	57	40	97	38	25	3	6	392	14.5	–3						4	2	1	3	0	1	0	0
1994-95	St. Louis	NHL	48	29	21	50	10	9	3	6	200	14.5	13						7	6	2	8	0	2	0	0
1995-96	St. Louis	NHL	70	43	40	83	30	16	5	6	327	13.1	4						13	6	5	11	10	2	1	1
1996-97	St. Louis	NHL	77	42	40	82	10	12	2	6	302	13.9	–9						6	2	7	9	2	0	0	0
1997-98	St. Louis	NHL	66	27	45	72	26	10	0	6	211	12.8	–1						10	3	3	6	2	1	0	1
	United States	Olympics	4	2	1	3	0																			
1998-99♦	Dallas	NHL	60	32	26	58	30	15	0	11	192	16.7	19	12	50.0	9	18	17:24	22	8	7	15	4	3	0	2
	NHL Totals		861	586	459	1045	328	214	18	85	3717	15.8		12	50.0	9	18	17:24	130	77	58	135	55	30	2	17

WCHA First All-Star Team (1986) • AHL First All-Star Team (1987) • Won Dudley "Red" Garrett Memorial Trophy (Top Rookie - AHL) (1987) • NHL First All-Star Team (1990, 1991, 1992) • Won Lady Byng Trophy (1990) • Won Dodge Ram Tough Award (1990, 1991) • Won Hart Memorial Trophy (1991) • Won Lester B. Pearson Award (1991) • Won ProSet/NHL Player of the Year Award (1991)

Played in NHL All-Star Game (1989, 1990, 1992, 1993, 1994, 1996, 1997, 1998)

Traded to **St. Louis** by **Calgary** with Steve Bozek for Rob Ramage and Rick Wamsley, March 7, 1988. Signed as a free agent by **Dallas**, July 3, 1998.

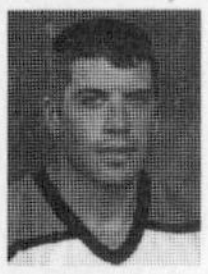

HULL, Jody — ATL.

Right wing. Shoots right. 6'2", 200 lbs. Born, Petrolia, Ont., February 2, 1969. Hartford's 1st choice, 18th overall, in 1987 Entry Draft.

Season	Club	League	GP	G	A	Pts	PIM	PP	SH	GW	S	%	+/-	TF	F%	H	SB	Min	GP	G	A	Pts	PIM	PP	SH	GW
1984-85	Cambridge	OJHL-B	38	13	17	30	39																			
1985-86	Peterborough	OHL	61	20	22	42	29												16	1	5	6	4			
1986-87	Peterborough	OHL	49	18	34	52	22												12	4	9	13	14			
1987-88	Peterborough	OHL	60	50	44	94	33												12	10	8	18	8			
1988-89	Hartford	NHL	60	16	18	34	10	6	0	2	82	19.5	6						1	0	0	0	2	0	0	0
1989-90	Hartford	NHL	38	7	10	17	21	2	0	0	46	15.2	–6						5	0	1	1	2	0	0	0
	Binghamton	AHL	21	7	10	17	6																			
1990-91	NY Rangers	NHL	47	5	8	13	10	0	0	0	57	8.8	2													
1991-92	NY Rangers	NHL	3	0	0	0	2	0	0	0	4	0.0	–4													
	Binghamton	AHL	69	34	31	65	28												11	5	2	7	4			
1992-93	Ottawa	NHL	69	13	21	34	14	5	1	0	134	9.7	–24													
1993-94	Florida	NHL	69	13	13	26	8	0	1	5	100	13.0	6													
1994-95	Florida	NHL	46	11	8	19	8	0	0	4	63	17.5	–1													
1995-96	Florida	NHL	78	20	17	37	25	2	0	3	120	16.7	5						14	3	2	5	0	0	0	0
1996-97	Florida	NHL	67	10	6	16	4	0	1	2	92	10.9	1						5	0	0	0	0	0	0	0
1997-98	Florida	NHL	21	2	0	2	4	0	1	0	23	8.7	1													
	Tampa Bay	NHL	28	2	4	6	4	0	0	2	28	7.1	2													
1998-99	Philadelphia	NHL	72	3	11	14	12	0	0	1	73	4.1	–2	15	53.3	34	28	12:59	6	0	0	0	4	0	0	0
	NHL Totals		598	102	116	218	122	15	4	19	822	12.4		15	53.3	34	28	12:59	31	3	3	6	8	0	0	0

OHL Second All-Star Team (1988)

Traded to **NY Rangers** by **Hartford** for Carey Wilson and NY Rangers' 3rd round choice (Mikael Nylander) in the 1991 Entry Draft, July 9, 1990. Traded to **Ottawa** by **NY Rangers** for future considerations, July 28, 1992. Signed as a free agent by **Florida**, August 10, 1993. Traded to **Tampa Bay** by **Florida** with Mark Fitzpatrick for Dino Ciccarelli and Jeff Norton, January 15, 1998. Claimed by **Atlanta** from **Philadelphia** in Expansion Draft, June 25, 1999.

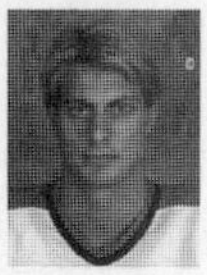

HULSE, Cale (HULS) — CGY.

Defense. Shoots right. 6'3", 215 lbs. Born, Edmonton, Alta., November 10, 1973. New Jersey's 3rd choice, 66th overall, in 1992 Entry Draft.

Season	Club	League	GP	G	A	Pts	PIM	PP	SH	GW	S	%	+/-	TF	F%	H	SB	Min	GP	G	A	Pts	PIM	PP	SH	GW
1990-91	Calgary	AJHL	49	3	23	26	220																			
1991-92	Portland	WHL	70	4	18	22	250												6	0	2	2	27			
1992-93	Portland	WHL	72	10	26	36	284												16	4	4	8	65			
1993-94	Albany	AHL	79	7	14	21	186												5	0	3	3	11			
1994-95	Albany	AHL	77	5	13	18	215												12	1	1	2	17			
1995-96	New Jersey	NHL	8	0	0	0	15	0	0	0	5	0.0	–2													
	Albany	AHL	42	4	23	27	107																			
	Calgary	NHL	3	0	0	0	5	0	0	0	4	0.0	3						1	0	0	0	0	0	0	0
	Saint John	AHL	13	2	7	9	39																			
1996-97	Calgary	NHL	63	1	6	7	91	0	1	0	58	1.7	–2													
1997-98	Calgary	NHL	79	5	22	27	169	1	1	0	117	4.3	1													
1998-99	Calgary	NHL	73	3	9	12	117	0	0	0	83	3.6	–8	1	0.0	113	74	16:38								
	NHL Totals		226	9	37	46	397	1	2	0	267	3.4		1	0.0	113	74	16:38	1	0	0	0	0	0	0	0

Traded to **Calgary** by **New Jersey** with Tommy Albelin and Jocelyn Lemieux for Phil Housley and Dan Keczmer, February 26, 1996.

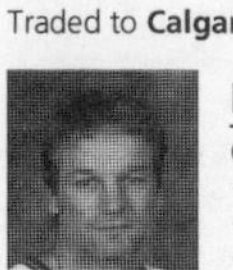

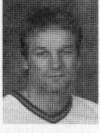

HUNTER, Dale

Center. Shoots left. 5'10", 198 lbs. Born, Petrolia, Ont., July 31, 1960. Quebec's 2nd choice, 41st overall, in 1979 Entry Draft.

Season	Club	League	GP	G	A	Pts	PIM	PP	SH	GW	S	%	+/-	TF	F%	H	SB	Min	GP	G	A	Pts	PIM	PP	SH	GW
1976-77	Strathroy	OJHL-B	42	25	30	55																				
1977-78	Kitchener	OHA	68	22	42	64	115																			
1978-79	Sudbury	OHA	59	42	68	110	188												10	4	12	16	47			
1979-80	Sudbury	OHA	61	34	51	85	189												9	6	9	15	45			
1980-81	Quebec	NHL	80	19	44	63	226	2	0	2	152	12.5	5						5	4	2	6	34	0	0	1
1981-82	Quebec	NHL	80	22	50	72	272	0	2	1	124	17.7	26						16	3	7	10	52	1	0	2
1982-83	Quebec	NHL	80	17	46	63	206	1	2	1	125	13.6	10						4	2	1	3	24	0	1	0
1983-84	Quebec	NHL	77	24	55	79	232	7	2	1	123	19.5	35						9	2	3	5	41	0	0	0
1984-85	Quebec	NHL	80	20	52	72	209	3	3	3	115	17.4	23						17	4	6	10	*97	0	1	2
1985-86	Quebec	NHL	80	28	42	70	265	7	0	4	152	18.4	6						3	0	0	0	15	0	0	0
1986-87	Quebec	NHL	46	10	29	39	135	0	0	0	53	18.9	4						13	1	7	8	56	1	0	0
1987-88	Washington	NHL	79	22	37	59	240	11	0	1	126	17.5	7						14	7	5	12	98	4	0	1
1988-89	Washington	NHL	80	20	37	57	219	9	0	3	138	14.5	–3						6	0	4	4	29	0	0	0
1989-90	Washington	NHL	80	23	39	62	233	9	1	6	123	18.7	17						15	4	8	12	61	1	0	0
1990-91	Washington	NHL	76	16	30	46	234	9	0	2	106	15.1	–22						11	1	9	10	41	0	0	0
1991-92	Washington	NHL	80	28	50	78	205	13	0	4	110	25.5	–2						7	1	4	5	16	0	0	0
1992-93	Washington	NHL	84	20	59	79	198	10	0	2	120	16.7	3						6	7	1	8	35	4	0	1
1993-94	Washington	NHL	52	9	29	38	131	1	0	1	61	14.8	–4						7	0	3	3	14	0	0	0
1994-95	Washington	NHL	45	8	15	23	101	3	0	1	73	11.0	–4						7	4	4	8	24	2	0	0
1995-96	Washington	NHL	82	13	24	37	112	4	0	3	128	10.2	5						6	1	5	6	24	0	0	0
1996-97	Washington	NHL	82	14	32	46	125	3	0	5	110	12.7	–2													

Season	Club	League	GP	G	A	Pts	PIM	PP	SH	GW	S	%	+/-	TF	F%	H	SB	Min	GP	G	A	Pts	PIM	PP	SH	GW
1997-98	Washington	NHL	82	8	18	26	103	0	0	1	82	9.8	1						21	0	4	4	30	0	0	0
1998-99	Washington	NHL	50	0	5	5	102	0	0	0	18	0.0	-7	442	56.1	54	17	8:42								
	Colorado	NHL	12	2	4	6	17	0	0	0	6	33.3	0	123	53.7	13	5	10:40	19	1	3	4	38	0	0	0
	NHL Totals		1407	323	697	1020	3565	92	10	41	2045	15.8		565	55.6	67	22	9:05	186	42	76	118	729	13	2	7

Played in NHL All-Star Game (1997)

Traded to **Washington** by **Quebec** with Clint Malarchuk for Gaetan Duchesne, Alan Haworth and Washington's 1st round choice (Joe Sakic) in 1987 Entry Draft, June 13, 1987. Traded to **Colorado** by **Washington** with Washington's 3rd round choice in 2000 Entry Draft for Vancouver's 2nd round choice (previously acquired, Washington selected Charlie Stephens) in 1999 Entry Draft, March 23, 1999.

HURLBUT, Mike

(HUHRL-buht)

Defense. Shoots left. 6'2", 200 lbs. Born, Massena, NY, October 7, 1966. NY Rangers' 1st choice, 5th overall, in 1988 Supplemental Draft.

Season	Club	League	GP	G	A	Pts	PIM	PP	SH	GW	S	%	+/-	TF	F%	H	SB	Min	GP	G	A	Pts	PIM	PP	SH	GW
1983-84	Massena High	H.S.	27	22	31	53	15																			
1984-85	Northwood Prep	H.S.	34	20	27	47	30																			
1985-86	St. Lawrence	ECAC	25	2	10	12	40																			
1986-87	St. Lawrence	ECAC	35	8	15	23	44																			
1987-88	St. Lawrence	ECAC	38	6	12	18	18																			
1988-89	St. Lawrence	ECAC	36	8	25	33	30																			
	Denver	IHL	8	0	2	2	13																			
1989-90	Flint	IHL	74	3	34	37	38												4	1	2	3	2			
1990-91	San Diego	IHL	2	1	0	1	0												3	0	1	1	2			
	Binghamton	AHL	33	2	11	13	27												3	0	1	1	0			
1991-92	Binghamton	AHL	79	16	39	55	64												11	2	7	9	8			
1992-93	**NY Rangers**	**NHL**	23	1	8	9	16	1	0	0	26	3.8	4													
	Binghamton	AHL	45	11	25	36	46												14	2	5	7	12			
1993-94	**Quebec**	**NHL**	1	0	0	0	0	0	0	0	1	0.0	-1													
	Cornwall	AHL	77	13	33	46	100												13	3	7	10	12			
1994-95	Cornwall	AHL	74	11	49	60	69												3	1	0	1	15			
1995-96	Minnesota	IHL	22	1	4	5	22																			
	Houston	IHL	38	3	12	15	33																			
1996-97	Houston	IHL	70	11	24	35	62												13	5	8	13	12			
1997-98	**Buffalo**	**NHL**	3	0	0	0	2	0	0	0	3	0.0	-1													
	Rochester	AHL	45	10	20	30	48												4	1	1	2	2			
1998-99	**Buffalo**	**NHL**	1	0	0	0	0	0	0	0	2	0.0	2	0	0.0	1	2	17:53								
	Rochester	AHL	72	15	39	54	46												20	4	5	9	12			
	NHL Totals		28	1	8	9	18	1	0	0	32	3.1		0	0.0	1	2	17:53								

ECAC First All-Star Team (1989) • NCAA East First All-American Team (1989) • AHL Second All-Star Team (1995)

Traded to **Quebec** by **NY Rangers** for Alexander Karpovtsev, September 7, 1993. Signed as a free agent by **Buffalo**, September 9, 1997.

HUSCROFT, Jamie

(HUHS-krawft)   **WSH.**

Defense. Shoots right. 6'2", 210 lbs. Born, Creston, B.C., January 9, 1967. New Jersey's 9th choice, 171st overall, in 1985 Entry Draft.

Season	Club	League	GP	G	A	Pts	PIM	PP	SH	GW	S	%	+/-	TF	F%	H	SB	Min	GP	G	A	Pts	PIM	PP	SH	GW
1982-83	Cresent	RMJHL	STATISTICS NOT AVAILABLE																							
1983-84	Portland	WHL	45	0	7	7	62																			
	Seattle	WHL	45	0	7	7	62												5	0	0	0	15			
1984-85	Seattle	WHL	69	3	13	16	273																			
1985-86	Seattle	WHL	66	6	20	26	394												5	0	1	1	18			
1986-87	Seattle	WHL	21	1	18	19	99																			
	Medicine Hat	WHL	35	4	21	25	170												20	0	3	3	*125			
1987-88	Utica	AHL	71	5	7	12	316												16	0	1	1	110			
	Flint	IHL	3	1	0	1	2																			
1988-89	**New Jersey**	**NHL**	15	0	2	2	51	0	0	0	9	0.0	-3													
	Utica	AHL	41	2	10	12	215												5	0	0	0	40			
1989-90	**New Jersey**	**NHL**	42	2	3	5	149	0	0	0	19	10.5	-2						5	0	0	0	0	0	0	0
	Utica	AHL	22	3	6	9	122																			
1990-91	**New Jersey**	**NHL**	8	0	1	1	27	0	0	0	3	0.0	1						3	0	0	0	6	0	0	0
	Utica	AHL	59	3	15	18	339																			
1991-92	Utica	AHL	50	4	7	11	224																			
1992-93	Providence	AHL	69	2	15	17	257												2	0	1	1	6			
1993-94	**Boston**	**NHL**	36	0	1	1	144	0	0	0	13	0.0	-2						4	0	0	0	9	0	0	0
	Providence	AHL	32	1	10	11	157																			
1994-95	**Boston**	**NHL**	34	0	6	6	103	0	0	0	30	0.0	-3						5	0	0	0	11	0	0	0
	Fresno	SunHL	3	1	1	2	7																			
1995-96	**Calgary**	**NHL**	70	3	9	12	162	0	0	1	57	5.3	14						4	0	1	1	4	0	0	0
1996-97	**Calgary**	**NHL**	39	0	4	4	117	0	0	0	33	0.0	2													
	Tampa Bay	NHL	13	0	1	1	34	0	0	0	7	0.0	-4													
1997-98	**Tampa Bay**	**NHL**	44	0	3	3	122	0	0	0	21	0.0	-4													
	Vancouver	NHL	7	0	1	1	55	0	0	0	5	0.0	2													
1998-99	**Vancouver**	**NHL**	26	0	1	1	63	0	0	0	20	0.0	-3	0	0.0	36	15	8:54								
	Phoenix	NHL	11	0	1	1	27	0	0	0	7	0.0	-1	0	0.0	27	3	11:02								
	NHL Totals		345	5	33	38	1054	0	0	1	224	2.2		0	0.0	63	18	9:32	21	0	1	1	46	0	0	0

Signed as a free agent by **Boston**, July 23, 1992. Signed as a free agent by **Calgary**, August 22, 1995. Traded to **Tampa Bay** by **Calgary** for Tyler Moss, March 18, 1997. Traded to **Vancouver** by **Tampa Bay** for Enrico Ciccone, March 14, 1998. Traded to **Phoenix** by **Vancouver** for future considerations, March 8, 1999. Signed as a free agent by **Washington**, August 9,1999.

HUSKA, Ryan

(HUHS-kuh)   **PHX.**

Left wing. Shoots left. 6'2", 194 lbs. Born, Cranbrook, B.C., July 2, 1975. Chicago's 4th choice, 76th overall, in 1993 Entry Draft.

Season	Club	League	GP	G	A	Pts	PIM	PP	SH	GW	S	%	+/-	TF	F%	H	SB	Min	GP	G	A	Pts	PIM	PP	SH	GW
1990-91	Trail AAA	BCAHA	37	65	70	135	18																			
1991-92	Kamloops	WHL	44	4	5	9	23												6	0	1	1	0			
1992-93	Kamloops	WHL	68	17	15	32	50												13	2	6	8	4			
1993-94	Kamloops	WHL	69	23	31	54	66												19	9	5	14	23			
1994-95	Kamloops	WHL	66	27	40	67	78												17	7	8	15	12			
1995-96	Indianapolis	IHL	28	2	3	5	15												5	1	1	2	27			
1996-97	Indianapolis	IHL	80	18	12	30	100												4	0	0	0	4			
1997-98	**Chicago**	**NHL**	1	0	0	0	0	0	0	0	0	0.0														
	Indianapolis	IHL	80	19	16	35	115												5	0	3	3	10			
1998-99	Lowell	AHL	60	5	13	18	70												2	0	0	0	0			
	NHL Totals		1	0	0	0	0	0	0	0	0	0.0														

Signed as a free agent by **Pheonix**, August 15, 1999.

IGINLA, Jarome

(ih-GIHN-lah, jah-ROHM)   **CGY.**

Right wing. Shoots right. 6'1", 205 lbs. Born, Edmonton, Alta., July 1, 1977. Dallas' 1st choice, 11th overall, in 1995 Entry Draft.

Season	Club	League	GP	G	A	Pts	PIM	PP	SH	GW	S	%	+/-	TF	F%	H	SB	Min	GP	G	A	Pts	PIM	PP	SH	GW
1991-92	St. Albert	AAHA	36	26	30	56	22																			
1992-93	St. Albert	AAHA	34	33	54	87	20																			
1993-94	Kamloops	WHL	48	6	23	39	33												19	3	6	9	10			
1994-95	Kamloops	WHL	72	33	38	71	111												21	7	11	18	34			
1995-96	Kamloops	WHL	63	63	73	136	120												16	16	13	29	44			
	Calgary	NHL																	2	1	1	2	0			
1996-97	Calgary	NHL	82	21	29	50	37	8	1	3	169	12.4	-4													
1997-98	Calgary	NHL	70	13	19	32	29	0	2	1	154	8.4	-10													

			Regular Season																Playoffs							
Season	Club	League	GP	G	A	Pts	PIM	PP	SH	GW	S	%	+/–	TF	F%	H	SB	Min	GP	G	A	Pts	PIM	PP	SH	GW
1998-99	**Calgary**	**NHL**	**82**	**28**	**23**	**51**	**58**	**7**	**0**	**4**	**211**	**13.3**	**1**	**111**	**51.4**	**119**	**25**	**16:30**	....	....	....	....	....	....	....	....
	NHL Totals		**234**	**62**	**71**	**133**	**124**	**15**	**3**	**8**	**534**	**11.6**		**111**	**51.4**	**119**	**25**	**16:30**	**2**	**1**	**1**	**2**	**0**	....	....	....

Won George Parsons Trophy (Memorial Cup Tournament Most Sportsmanlike Player) (1995) • WHL West First All-Star Team (1996) • Canadian Major Junior First All-Star Team (1996) • NHL All-Rookie Team (1997)

Traded to **Calgary** by **Dallas** with Corey Millen for Joe Nieuwendyk, December 19, 1995.

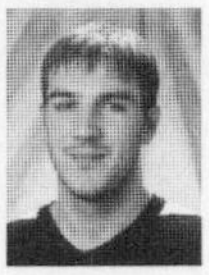

IGNATJEV, Victor

(ihg_NYAT-ee-ehv)

Defense. Shoots left. 6'4", 215 lbs. Born, Riga, USSR, April 26, 1970. San Jose's 11th choice, 243rd overall, in 1992 Entry Draft.

Season	Club	League	GP	G	A	Pts	PIM	PP	SH	GW	S	%	+/–	TF	F%	H	SB	Min	GP	G	A	Pts	PIM	PP	SH	GW
1989-90	Riga	USSR	40	0	0	0	26	....	....	....	....	....	....	....	....	....	....	....	....	....	....	....	....	....	....	....
1990-91	Riga	USSR	10	0	0	0	2	....	....	....	....	....	....	....	....	....	....	....	....	....	....	....	....	....	....	....
1991-92	Riga	CIS	22	4	5	9	22	....	....	....	....	....	....	....	....	....	....	....	....	....	....	....	....	....	....	....
1992-93	Kansas City	IHL	64	5	16	21	68	....	....	....	....	....	....	....	....	....	....	....	4	1	2	3	24	....	....	....
1993-94	Kansas City	IHL	67	1	24	25	123	....	....	....	....	....	....	....	....	....	....	....	....	....	....	....	....	....	....	....
1994-95	Oklahoma City	CHL	47	11	35	46	66	....	....	....	....	....	....	....	....	....	....	....	....	....	....	....	....	....	....	....
	Denver	IHL	23	2	11	13	4	....	....	....	....	....	....	....	....	....	....	....	17	3	8	11	8	....	....	....
1995-96	Utah	IHL	73	9	29	38	67	....	....	....	....	....	....	....	....	....	....	....	21	3	8	11	22	....	....	....
1996-97	Long Beach	IHL	82	16	53	69	112	....	....	....	....	....	....	....	....	....	....	....	16	3	4	7	26	....	....	....
1997-98	Long Beach	IHL	71	12	33	45	102	....	....	....	....	....	....	....	....	....	....	....	17	3	11	14	16	....	....	....
1998-99	**Pittsburgh**	**NHL**	**11**	**0**	**1**	**1**	**6**	**0**	**0**	**0**	**15**	**0.0**	**–3**	**0**	**0.0**	**10**	**6**	**12:14**	**1**	**0**	**0**	**0**	**2**	**0**	**0**	**0**
	NHL Totals		**11**	**0**	**1**	**1**	**6**	**0**	**0**	**0**	**15**	**0.0**		**0**	**0.0**	**10**	**6**	**12:14**	**1**	**0**	**0**	**0**	**2**	**0**	**0**	**0**

IHL Second All-Star Team (1997)

Signed as a free agent by **Pittsburgh**, August 11, 1998. • Suffered shoulder injury that required rotator-cuff surgery, November, 1998.

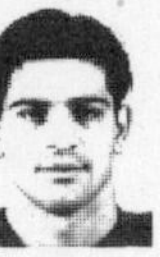

INTRANUOVO, Ralph

(ihn-trah-NOO-voh)

Center. Shoots left. 5'8", 185 lbs. Born, East York, Ont., December 11, 1973. Edmonton's 5th choice, 96th overall, in 1992 Entry Draft.

Season	Club	League	GP	G	A	Pts	PIM	PP	SH	GW	S	%	+/–	TF	F%	H	SB	Min	GP	G	A	Pts	PIM	PP	SH	GW
1989-90	Toronto	MTHL	37	33	26	59	20	....	....	....	....	....	....	....	....	....	....	....	....	....	....	....	....	....	....	....
1990-91	S.S. Marie	OHL	63	25	42	67	22	....	....	....	....	....	....	....	....	....	....	....	14	7	13	20	17	....	....	....
1991-92	S.S. Marie	OHL	65	50	63	113	44	....	....	....	....	....	....	....	....	....	....	....	18	10	14	24	12	....	....	....
1992-93	S.S. Marie	OHL	54	31	47	78	61	....	....	....	....	....	....	....	....	....	....	....	18	10	16	26	30	....	....	....
1993-94	Cape Breton	AHL	66	21	31	52	39	....	....	....	....	....	....	....	....	....	....	....	4	1	2	3	2	....	....	....
1994-95	**Edmonton**	**NHL**	**1**	**0**	**1**	**1**	**0**	**0**	**0**	**0**	**1**	**0.0**	**1**	....	....	....	....	....	....	....	....	....	....	....	....	....
	Cape Breton	AHL	70	46	47	93	62	....	....	....	....	....	....	....	....	....	....	....	....	....	....	....	....	....	....	....
1995-96	**Edmonton**	**NHL**	**13**	**1**	**2**	**3**	**4**	**0**	**0**	**1**	**19**	**5.3**	**–3**	....	....	....	....	....	....	....	....	....	....	....	....	....
	Cape Breton	AHL	52	34	39	73	84	....	....	....	....	....	....	....	....	....	....	....	....	....	....	....	....	....	....	....
1996-97	**Toronto**	**NHL**	**3**	**0**	**1**	**1**	**0**	**0**	**0**	**0**	**4**	**0.0**	**–1**	....	....	....	....	....	....	....	....	....	....	....	....	....
	Edmonton	**NHL**	**5**	**1**	**0**	**1**	**0**	**0**	**0**	**0**	**2**	**50.0**	**0**	....	....	....	....	....	....	....	....	....	....	....	....	....
	Hamilton	AHL	68	36	40	76	88	....	....	....	....	....	....	....	....	....	....	....	22	8	4	12	30	....	....	....
1997-98	Manitoba	IHL	81	26	35	61	68	....	....	....	....	....	....	....	....	....	....	....	3	2	0	2	4	....	....	....
1998-99	Manitoba	IHL	71	29	31	60	70	....	....	....	....	....	....	....	....	....	....	....	5	2	1	3	4	....	....	....
	NHL Totals		**22**	**2**	**4**	**6**	**4**	**0**	**0**	**1**	**26**	**7.7**		....	....	....	....	....	....	....	....	....	....	....	....	....

Memorial Cup All-Star Team (1993) • Won Stafford Smythe Memorial Trophy (Memorial Cup Tournament MVP) (1993) • AHL Second All-Star Team (1995, 1997)

Claimed by **Toronto** from **Edmonton** in Waiver Draft, September 30, 1996. Claimed on waivers by **Edmonton** from **Toronto**, October 25, 1996.

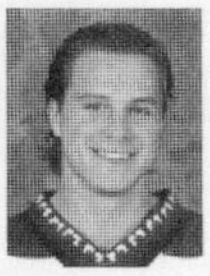

ISBISTER, Brad

(IHZ-bihs-tuhr) **NYI**

Right wing. Shoots right. 6'3", 222 lbs. Born, Edmonton, Alta., May 7, 1977. Winnipeg's 4th choice, 67th overall, in 1995 Entry Draft.

Season	Club	League	GP	G	A	Pts	PIM	PP	SH	GW	S	%	+/–	TF	F%	H	SB	Min	GP	G	A	Pts	PIM	PP	SH	GW
1992-93	Calgary AA	AAHA	35	24	25	49	74	....	....	....	....	....	....	....	....	....	....	....	....	....	....	....	....	....	....	....
1993-94	Portland	WHL	64	7	10	17	45	....	....	....	....	....	....	....	....	....	....	....	10	0	2	2	0	....	....	....
1994-95	Portland	WHL	67	16	20	36	123	....	....	....	....	....	....	....	....	....	....	....	....	....	....	....	....	....	....	....
1995-96	Portland	WHL	71	45	44	89	184	....	....	....	....	....	....	....	....	....	....	....	7	2	4	6	20	....	....	....
1996-97	Portland	WHL	24	15	18	33	45	....	....	....	....	....	....	....	....	....	....	....	6	2	1	3	16	....	....	....
	Springfield	AHL	7	3	1	4	14	....	....	....	....	....	....	....	....	....	....	....	9	1	2	3	10	....	....	....
1997-98	**Phoenix**	**NHL**	**66**	**9**	**8**	**17**	**102**	**1**	**0**	**1**	**115**	**7.8**	**4**	....	....	....	....	....	**5**	**0**	**0**	**0**	**2**	**0**	**0**	**0**
	Springfield	AHL	9	8	2	10	36	....	....	....	....	....	....	....	....	....	....	....	....	....	....	....	....	....	....	....
1998-99	**Phoenix**	**NHL**	**32**	**4**	**4**	**8**	**46**	**0**	**0**	**2**	**48**	**8.3**	**1**	**3**	**0.0**	**39**	**3**	**11:33**	....	....	....	....	....	....	....	....
	Springfield	AHL	4	1	1	2	12	....	....	....	....	....	....	....	....	....	....	....	....	....	....	....	....	....	....	....
	Las Vegas	IHL	2	0	0	0	9	....	....	....	....	....	....	....	....	....	....	....	....	....	....	....	....	....	....	....
	NHL Totals		**98**	**13**	**12**	**25**	**148**	**1**	**0**	**3**	**163**	**8.0**		**3**	**0.0**	**39**	**3**	**11:33**	**5**	**0**	**0**	**0**	**2**	**0**	**0**	**0**

WHL West Second All-Star Team (1997)

Rights transferred to **Phoenix** after **Winnipeg** franchise relocated, July 1, 1996. Traded to **NY Islanders** by **Phoenix** with Phoenix's 3rd round choice (Brian Collins) in 1999 Entry Draft for Robert Reichel, NY Islanders' 3rd round choice (Jason Jaspers) in 1999 Entry Draft and Ottawa's 4th round choice (previously acquired, Phoenix selected Preston Mizzi) in 1999 Entry Draft, March 20, 1999.

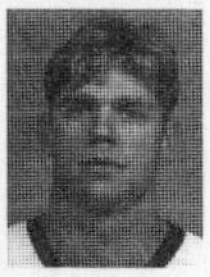

JACKSON, Dane

Right wing. Shoots right. 6'1", 200 lbs. Born, Castlegar, B.C., May 17, 1970. Vancouver's 3rd choice, 44th overall, in 1988 Entry Draft.

Season	Club	League	GP	G	A	Pts	PIM	PP	SH	GW	S	%	+/–	TF	F%	H	SB	Min	GP	G	A	Pts	PIM	PP	SH	GW
1985-86	Castlegard	KIJHL	39	22	38	60	53	....	....	....	....	....	....	....	....	....	....	....	....	....	....	....	....	....	....	....
1986-87	Castlegard	KIJHL	STATISTICS NOT AVAILABLE																							
1987-88	Vernon	BCJHL	49	24	30	54	95	....	....	....	....	....	....	....	....	....	....	....	13	7	10	17	49	....	....	....
1988-89	North Dakota	WCHA	30	4	5	9	33	....	....	....	....	....	....	....	....	....	....	....	....	....	....	....	....	....	....	....
1989-90	North Dakota	WCHA	44	15	11	26	56	....	....	....	....	....	....	....	....	....	....	....	....	....	....	....	....	....	....	....
1990-91	North Dakota	WCHA	37	17	9	26	79	....	....	....	....	....	....	....	....	....	....	....	....	....	....	....	....	....	....	....
1991-92	North Dakota	WCHA	39	23	19	42	81	....	....	....	....	....	....	....	....	....	....	....	....	....	....	....	....	....	....	....
1992-93	Hamilton	AHL	68	23	20	43	59	....	....	....	....	....	....	....	....	....	....	....	....	....	....	....	....	....	....	....
1993-94	**Vancouver**	**NHL**	**12**	**5**	**1**	**6**	**9**	**0**	**0**	**0**	**18**	**27.8**	**3**	....	....	....	....	....	....	....	....	....	....	....	....	....
	Hamilton	AHL	60	25	35	60	75	....	....	....	....	....	....	....	....	....	....	....	4	2	2	4	16	....	....	....
1994-95	**Vancouver**	**NHL**	**3**	**1**	**0**	**1**	**4**	**0**	**0**	**0**	**6**	**16.7**	**0**	....	....	....	....	....	**6**	**0**	**0**	**0**	**10**	**0**	**0**	**0**
	Syracuse	AHL	78	30	28	58	162	....	....	....	....	....	....	....	....	....	....	....	....	....	....	....	....	....	....	....
1995-96	**Buffalo**	**NHL**	**22**	**5**	**4**	**9**	**41**	**0**	**0**	**1**	**20**	**25.0**	**3**	....	....	....	....	....	....	....	....	....	....	....	....	....
	Rochester	AHL	50	27	19	46	132	....	....	....	....	....	....	....	....	....	....	....	19	4	6	10	53	....	....	....
1996-97	Rochester	AHL	78	24	34	58	111	....	....	....	....	....	....	....	....	....	....	....	10	7	4	11	14	....	....	....
1997-98	**NY Islanders**	**NHL**	**8**	**1**	**1**	**2**	**4**	**0**	**0**	**1**	**5**	**20.0**	**1**	....	....	....	....	....	....	....	....	....	....	....	....	....
	Rochester	AHL	28	10	13	23	55	....	....	....	....	....	....	....	....	....	....	....	3	2	2	4	4	....	....	....
1998-99	Lowell	AHL	80	16	27	43	103	....	....	....	....	....	....	....	....	....	....	....	3	0	1	1	16	....	....	....
	NHL Totals		**45**	**12**	**6**	**18**	**58**	**0**	**0**	**2**	**49**	**24.5**		....	....	....	....	....	**6**	**0**	**0**	**0**	**10**	**0**	**0**	**0**

Signed as a free agent by **Buffalo**, September 20, 1995. Signed as a free agent by **NY Islanders**, July 21, 1997.

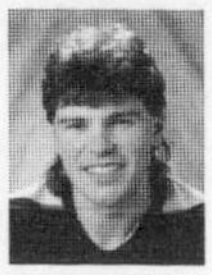

JAGR, Jaromir

(YAH-guhr) **PIT.**

Right wing. Shoots left. 6'2", 230 lbs. Born, Kladno, Czech., February 15, 1972. Pittsburgh's 1st choice, 5th overall, in 1990 Entry Draft.

Season	Club	League	GP	G	A	Pts	PIM	PP	SH	GW	S	%	+/–	TF	F%	H	SB	Min	GP	G	A	Pts	PIM	PP	SH	GW
1984-85	Poldi Kladno	Czech-B	34	24	17	41	....	....	....	....	....	....	....	....	....	....	....	....	....	....	....	....	....	....	....	....
1985-86	Poldi Kladno	Czech-B	36	41	29	70	....	....	....	....	....	....	....	....	....	....	....	....	....	....	....	....	....	....	....	....
1986-87	Poldi Kladno	Czech-Jr.	30	35	35	70	....	....	....	....	....	....	....	....	....	....	....	....	....	....	....	....	....	....	....	....
1987-88	Poldi Kladno	Czech-Jr.	35	57	27	84	....	....	....	....	....	....	....	....	....	....	....	....	....	....	....	....	....	....	....	....
1988-89	Poldi Kladno	Czech.	39	8	10	18	4	....	....	....	....	....	....	....	....	....	....	....	....	....	....	....	....	....	....	....
1989-90	Poldi Kladno	Czech.	51	30	29	59	....	....	....	....	....	....	....	....	....	....	....	....	....	....	....	....	....	....	....	....
1990-91♦	**Pittsburgh**	**NHL**	**80**	**27**	**30**	**57**	**42**	**7**	**0**	**4**	**136**	**19.9**	**–4**	....	....	....	....	....	**24**	**3**	**10**	**13**	**6**	**1**	**0**	**1**
1991-92♦	**Pittsburgh**	**NHL**	**70**	**32**	**37**	**69**	**34**	**4**	**0**	**4**	**194**	**16.5**	**12**	....	....	....	....	....	**21**	**11**	**13**	**24**	**6**	**2**	**0**	**4**
1992-93	**Pittsburgh**	**NHL**	**81**	**34**	**60**	**94**	**61**	**10**	**1**	**9**	**242**	**14.0**	**30**	....	....	....	....	....	**12**	**5**	**4**	**9**	**23**	**1**	**0**	**1**

Season	Club	League	GP	G	A	Pts	PIM	PP	SH	GW	S	%	+/–	TF	F%	H	SB	Min	Playoffs GP	G	A	Pts	PIM	PP	SH	GW
1993-94	Pittsburgh	NHL	80	32	67	99	61	9	0	6	298	10.7	15	....	....	....	....	....	6	2	4	6	16	0	0	1
1994-95	Poldi Kladno	Cze-Rep	11	8	14	22	10	....	....	....	....	....	....	....	....	....	....	....	....	....	....	....	....	....	....	....
	HC Bolzano	EuroHL	5	8	8	16	4	....	....	....	....	....	....	....	....	....	....	....	....	....	....	....	....	....	....	....
	HC Bolzano	Italy	1	0	0	0	0	....	....	....	....	....	....	....	....	....	....	....	....	....	....	....	....	....	....	....
	EHC Schalke	German-2	1	1	10	11	0	....	....	....	....	....	....	....	....	....	....	....	....	....	....	....	....	....	....	....
	Pittsburgh	NHL	48	32	38	*70	37	8	3	7	192	16.7	23	....	....	....	....	....	12	10	5	15	6	2	1	1
1995-96	Pittsburgh	NHL	82	62	87	149	96	20	1	12	403	15.4	31	....	....	....	....	....	18	11	12	23	18	5	1	1
1996-97	Pittsburgh	NHL	63	47	48	95	40	11	2	6	234	20.1	22	....	....	....	....	....	5	4	4	8	4	2	0	0
1997-98	Pittsburgh	NHL	77	35	*67	*102	64	7	0	8	262	13.4	17	....	....	....	....	....	6	4	5	9	2	1	0	0
	Czech Republic	Olympics	6	1	4	5	2	....	....	....	....	....	....	....	....	....	....	....	....	....	....	....	....	....	....	....
1998-99	Pittsburgh	NHL	81	44	*83	*127	66	10	1	7	343	12.8	17	4	50.0	27	23	25:51	9	5	7	12	16	1	0	1
	NHL Totals		662	345	517	862	501	86	8	63	2304	15.0		4	50.0	27	23	25:51	113	55	64	119	97	15	2	10

NHL/Upper Deck All-Rookie Team (1991) • NHL First All-Star Team (1995, 1996, 1998, 1999) • Won Art Ross Trophy (1995, 1998, 1999) • NHL Second All-Star Team (1997) • Won Lester B. Pearson Award (1999) • Won Hart Trophy (1999)

Played in NHL All-Star Game (1992, 1993, 1996, 1998, 1999)

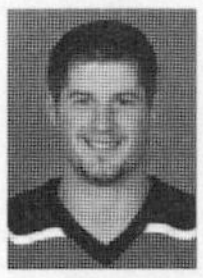

JAKOPIN, John

(JA-koh-pihn) **FLA.**

Defense. Shoots right. 6'5", 239 lbs. Born, Toronto, Ont., May 16, 1975. Detroit's 4th choice, 97th overall, in 1993 Entry Draft.

Season	Club	League	GP	G	A	Pts	PIM	PP	SH	GW	S	%	+/–	TF	F%	H	SB	Min	Playoffs GP	G	A	Pts	PIM	PP	SH	GW
1992-93	St. Michael's	OJHL-B	45	9	21	30	42	....	....	....	....	....	....	....	....	....	....	....	13	3	2	5	4	....	....	....
1993-94	Merrimack	H.E.	36	2	8	10	64	....	....	....	....	....	....	....	....	....	....	....	....	....	....	....	....	....	....	....
1994-95	Merrimack	H.E.	37	4	10	14	42	....	....	....	....	....	....	....	....	....	....	....	....	....	....	....	....	....	....	....
1995-96	Merrimack	H.E.	32	10	15	25	68	....	....	....	....	....	....	....	....	....	....	....	....	....	....	....	....	....	....	....
1996-97	Merrimack	H.E.	31	4	12	16	68	....	....	....	....	....	....	....	....	....	....	....	....	....	....	....	....	....	....	....
	Adirondack	AHL	3	0	0	0	9	....	....	....	....	....	....	....	....	....	....	....	....	....	....	....	....	....	....	....
1997-98	Florida	NHL	2	0	0	0	4	0	0	0	1	0.0	–3	....	....	....	....	....	....	....	....	....	....	....	....	....
	New Haven	AHL	60	2	18	20	151	....	....	....	....	....	....	....	....	....	....	....	3	0	0	0	0	....	....	....
1998-99	Florida	NHL	3	0	0	0	0	0	0	0	0	0.0	–1	0	0.0	8	2	13:32	....	....	....	....	....	....	....	....
	New Haven	AHL	60	2	7	9	154	....	....	....	....	....	....	....	....	....	....	....	....	....	....	....	....	....	....	....
	NHL Totals		5	0	0	0	4	0	0	0	1	0.0		0	0.0	8	2	13:32	....	....	....	....	....	....	....	....

Signed as a free agent by **Florida**, May 14, 1997.

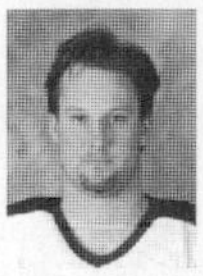

JANNEY, Craig

(JA-nee)

Center. Shoots left. 6'1", 190 lbs. Born, Hartford, CT, September 26, 1967. Boston's 1st choice, 13th overall, in 1986 Entry Draft.

Season	Club	League	GP	G	A	Pts	PIM	PP	SH	GW	S	%	+/–	TF	F%	H	SB	Min	Playoffs GP	G	A	Pts	PIM	PP	SH	GW
1983-84	Deerfield Prep	H.S.	17	33	35	68	6	....	....	....	....	....	....	....	....	....	....	....	....	....	....	....	....	....	....	....
1985-86	Boston College	H.E.	34	13	14	27	8	....	....	....	....	....	....	....	....	....	....	....	....	....	....	....	....	....	....	....
1986-87	Boston College	H.E.	37	26	55	81	6	....	....	....	....	....	....	....	....	....	....	....	....	....	....	....	....	....	....	....
1987-88	United States	Nat-Team	52	26	44	70	6	....	....	....	....	....	....	....	....	....	....	....	....	....	....	....	....	....	....	....
	United States	Olympics	5	3	3	6	2	....	....	....	....	....	....	....	....	....	....	....	....	....	....	....	....	....	....	....
	Boston	NHL	15	7	9	16	0	1	0	1	29	24.1	6	....	....	....	....	....	23	6	10	16	11	4	0	1
1988-89	Boston	NHL	62	16	46	62	12	2	0	2	95	16.8	20	....	....	....	....	....	10	4	9	13	21	0	0	0
1989-90	Boston	NHL	55	24	38	62	4	11	0	5	105	22.9	3	....	....	....	....	....	18	3	19	22	2	1	0	2
1990-91	Boston	NHL	77	26	66	92	8	9	1	5	133	19.5	15	....	....	....	....	....	18	4	18	22	11	4	0	0
1991-92	St. Louis	NHL	25	6	30	36	2	3	0	1	37	16.2	5	....	....	....	....	....	6	0	6	6	0	0	0	0
	Boston	NHL	53	12	39	51	20	3	0	1	90	13.3	1	....	....	....	....	....	....	....	....	....	....	....	....	....
1992-93	St. Louis	NHL	84	24	82	106	12	8	0	6	137	17.5	–4	....	....	....	....	....	11	2	9	11	0	1	0	2
1993-94	St. Louis	NHL	69	16	68	84	24	8	0	7	95	16.8	–14	....	....	....	....	....	4	1	3	4	0	0	0	0
1994-95	St. Louis	NHL	8	2	5	7	0	1	0	0	9	22.2	3	....	....	....	....	....	....	....	....	....	....	....	....	....
	San Jose	NHL	27	5	15	20	10	2	0	1	31	16.1	–4	....	....	....	....	....	11	3	4	7	4	0	0	1
1995-96	San Jose	NHL	71	13	49	62	26	5	0	1	78	16.7	–35	....	....	....	....	....	....	....	....	....	....	....	....	....
	Winnipeg	NHL	13	7	13	20	0	2	0	1	91	7.7	2	....	....	....	....	....	6	1	2	3	0	0	0	0
1996-97	Phoenix	NHL	77	15	38	53	26	5	0	1	88	17.0	–1	....	....	....	....	....	7	0	3	3	4	0	0	0
1997-98	Phoenix	NHL	68	10	43	53	12	4	0	0	72	13.9	5	....	....	....	....	....	6	0	3	3	0	0	0	0
1998-99	Tampa Bay	NHL	38	4	18	22	10	2	0	0	36	11.1	–13	599	45.4	3	9	15:46	....	....	....	....	....	....	....	....
	NY Islanders	NHL	18	1	4	5	4	0	0	0	9	11.1	–2	116	49.1	0	2	11:07	....	....	....	....	....	....	....	....
	NHL Totals		760	188	563	751	170	66	1	32	1135	16.6		715	46.0	3	11	14:16	120	24	86	110	53	10	0	6

Hockey East First All-Star Team (1987) • NCAA East First All-American Team (1987)

Traded to **St. Louis** by **Boston** with Stephane Quintal for Adam Oates, February 7, 1992. Acquired by **Vancouver** from **St. Louis** with St. Louis' 2nd round choice (Dave Scathard) in 1994 Entry Draft as compensation for St. Louis' signing of free agent Petr Nedved, March 14, 1994. Traded to **St. Louis** by **Vancouver** for Jeff Brown, Bret Hedican and Nathan Lafayette, March 21, 1994. Traded to **San Jose** by **St. Louis** with cash for Jeff Norton and future considerations, March 6, 1995. Traded to **Winnipeg** by **San Jose** for Darren Turcotte and Dallas' 2nd round choice (previously acquired, later traded to Chicago — Chicago selected Remi Royer) in 1996 Entry Draft, March 18, 1996. Transferred to **Phoenix** after **Winnipeg** franchise relocated, July 1, 1996. Traded to **Tampa Bay** by **Phoenix** for Louie Debrusk and Tampa Bay's 5th round choice (Jay Leach) in 1998 Entry Draft, June 11, 1998. Traded to **NY Islanders** by **Tampa Bay** for Toronto's 6th round choice (previously acquired, Tampa Bay selected Fedor Fedorov) in 1999 Entry Draft, January 18, 1999.

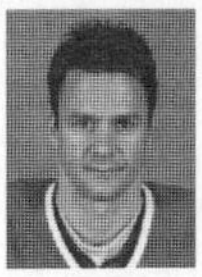

JANSSENS, Mark

CHI.

Center. Shoots left. 6'3", 212 lbs. Born, Surrey, B.C., May 19, 1968. NY Rangers' 4th choice, 72nd overall, in 1986 Entry Draft.

Season	Club	League	GP	G	A	Pts	PIM	PP	SH	GW	S	%	+/–	TF	F%	H	SB	Min	Playoffs GP	G	A	Pts	PIM	PP	SH	GW
1983-84	Surrey	BCAHA	40	40	58	98	64	....	....	....	....	....	....	....	....	....	....	....	....	....	....	....	....	....	....	....
1984-85	Regina	WHL	70	8	22	30	51	....	....	....	....	....	....	....	....	....	....	....	....	....	....	....	....	....	....	....
1985-86	Regina	WHL	71	25	38	63	146	....	....	....	....	....	....	....	....	....	....	....	9	0	2	2	17	....	....	....
1986-87	Regina	WHL	68	24	38	62	209	....	....	....	....	....	....	....	....	....	....	....	3	0	1	1	14	....	....	....
1987-88	Regina	WHL	71	39	51	90	202	....	....	....	....	....	....	....	....	....	....	....	4	3	4	7	6	....	....	....
	NY Rangers	NHL	1	0	0	0	0	0	0	0	0	0.0	0	....	....	....	....	....	....	....	....	....	....	....	....	....
	Colorado	IHL	6	2	2	4	24	....	....	....	....	....	....	....	....	....	....	....	12	3	2	5	20	....	....	....
1988-89	NY Rangers	NHL	5	0	0	0	0	0	0	0	4	0.0	–4	....	....	....	....	....	....	....	....	....	....	....	....	....
	Denver	IHL	38	19	19	38	104	....	....	....	....	....	....	....	....	....	....	....	4	3	0	3	18	....	....	....
1989-90	NY Rangers	NHL	80	5	8	13	161	0	0	0	61	8.2	–26	....	....	....	....	....	9	2	1	3	10	0	0	1
1990-91	NY Rangers	NHL	67	9	7	16	172	0	0	1	45	20.0	–1	....	....	....	....	....	6	3	0	3	6	0	0	0
1991-92	NY Rangers	NHL	4	0	0	0	5	0	0	0	0	0.0	–1	....	....	....	....	....	....	....	....	....	....	....	....	....
	Binghamton	AHL	55	10	23	33	109	....	....	....	....	....	....	....	....	....	....	....	....	....	....	....	....	....	....	....
	Minnesota	NHL	3	0	0	0	0	0	0	0	1	0.0	–1	....	....	....	....	....	....	....	....	....	....	....	....	....
	Kalamazoo	IHL	2	0	0	0	2	....	....	....	....	....	....	....	....	....	....	....	11	1	2	3	22	....	....	....
1992-93	Hartford	NHL	76	12	17	29	237	0	0	1	63	19.0	–15	....	....	....	....	....	....	....	....	....	....	....	....	....
1993-94	Hartford	NHL	84	2	10	12	137	0	0	0	52	3.8	–13	....	....	....	....	....	....	....	....	....	....	....	....	....
1994-95	Hartford	NHL	46	2	5	7	93	0	0	0	33	6.1	–8	....	....	....	....	....	....	....	....	....	....	....	....	....
1995-96	Hartford	NHL	81	2	7	9	155	0	0	0	63	3.2	–13	....	....	....	....	....	....	....	....	....	....	....	....	....
1996-97	Hartford	NHL	54	2	4	6	90	0	0	0	30	6.7	–10	....	....	....	....	....	....	....	....	....	....	....	....	....
	Anaheim	NHL	12	0	2	2	47	0	0	0	9	0.0	–3	....	....	....	....	....	11	0	0	0	15	0	0	0
1997-98	Anaheim	NHL	55	4	5	9	116	0	0	1	43	9.3	–22	....	....	....	....	....	....	....	....	....	....	....	....	....
	NY Islanders	NHL	12	0	0	0	34	0	0	0	4	0.0	–3	....	....	....	....	....	....	....	....	....	....	....	....	....
	Phoenix	NHL	7	1	2	3	4	0	0	0	6	16.7	4	....	....	....	....	....	1	0	0	0	2	0	0	0
1998-99	Chicago	NHL	60	1	0	1	65	0	0	0	27	3.7	–11	594	57.9	34	19	8:17	....	....	....	....	....	....	....	....
	NHL Totals		647	40	67	107	1316	0	0	3	441	9.1		594	57.9	34	19	8:17	27	5	1	6	33	0	0	1

Traded to **Minnesota** by **NY Rangers** for Mario Thyer and Minnesota's 3rd round choice (Maxim Galanov) in 1993 Entry Draft, March 10, 1992. Traded to **Hartford** by **Minnesota** for James Black, September 3, 1992. Traded to **Anaheim** by **Hartford** for Bates Battaglia and Anaheim's 4th round choice (Carolina selected Josef Vasicek) in 1998 Entry Draft, March 18, 1997. Traded to **NY Islanders** by **Anaheim** with Joe Sacco and J.J. Daigneault for Travis Green, Doug Houda and Tony Tuzzolino, February 6, 1998. Traded to **Phoenix** by **NY Islanders** for Phoenix's 9th round choice (Jason Doyle) in 1998 Entry Draft, March 24, 1998. Signed as a free agent by **Chicago**, July 28, 1998.

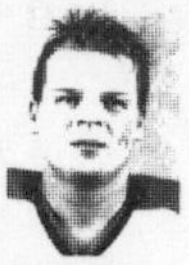

JANTUNEN, Marko
(YAN-too-nehn)

Center. Shoots left. 5'10", 185 lbs. Born, Lahti, Finland, February 14, 1971. Calgary's 13th choice, 239th overall, in 1991 Entry Draft.

			Regular Season																Playoffs							
Season	Club	League	GP	G	A	Pts	PIM	PP	SH	GW	S	%	+/-	TF	F%	H	SB	Min	GP	G	A	Pts	PIM	PP	SH	GW
1989-90	Army Sport	Finn-Jr.	8	4	9	13	6	....	....	....	....	....	....	....	....	....	....	....	....	....	....	....	....	....	....	....
	Reipas Lahti	Finn-Jr.	8	6	5	11	40	....	....	....	....	....	....	....	....	....	....	....	....	....	....	....	....	....	....	....
	Reipas Lahti	Finland-2	31	11	19	30	20	....	....	....	....	....	....	....	....	....	....	....	4	1	2	3	6	....	....	....
1990-91	Reipas Lahti	Finland	39	9	20	29	20	....	....	....	....	....	....	....	....	....	....	....	....	....	....	....	....	....	....	....
1991-92	Reipas Lahti	Finland	42	10	14	24	46	....	....	....	....	....	....	....	....	....	....	....	....	....	....	....	....	....	....	....
1992-93	KalPa Kuopio	Finland	48	21	27	48	63	....	....	....	....	....	....	....	....	....	....	....	....	....	....	....	....	....	....	....
1993-94	TPS Turku	Finland	48	29	29	58	22	....	....	....	....	....	....	....	....	....	....	....	11	2	6	8	12	....	....	....
	Finland	Nat-Team	5	0	0	0	2	....	....	....	....	....	....	....	....	....	....	....	....	....	....	....	....	....	....	....
1994-95	V. Frolunda	Sweden	45	33	28	61	49	....	....	....	....	....	....	....	....	....	....	....	....	....	....	....	....	....	....	....
	Finland	Nat-Team	17	3	4	7	12	....	....	....	....	....	....	....	....	....	....	....	....	....	....	....	....	....	....	....
1995-96	V. Frolunda	Sweden	40	17	14	31	66	....	....	....	....	....	....	....	....	....	....	....	13	8	8	16	10	....	....	....
	Finland	Nat-Team	8	4	1	5	12	....	....	....	....	....	....	....	....	....	....	....	....	....	....	....	....	....	....	....
1996-97	V. Frolunda	Sweden	13	4	7	11	16	....	....	....	....	....	....	....	....	....	....	....	3	2	0	2	16	....	....	....
	V. Frolunda	EuroHL	2	0	0	0	0	....	....	....	....	....	....	....	....	....	....	....	....	....	....	....	....	....	....	....
	Calgary	**NHL**	**3**	**0**	**0**	**0**	**0**	**0**	**0**	**0**	**7**	**0.0**	**–1**	....	....	....	....	....	....	....	....	....	....	....	....	....
	Saint John	AHL	23	8	16	24	18	....	....	....	....	....	....	....	....	....	....	....	....	....	....	....	....	....	....	....
1997-98	V. Frolunda	Sweden	43	14	20	34	61	....	....	....	....	....	....	....	....	....	....	....	7	1	2	3	2	....	....	....
1998-99	V. Frolunda	Sweden	47	12	21	33	57	....	....	....	....	....	....	....	....	....	....	....	4	4	0	4	4	....	....	....
	NHL Totals		**3**	**0**	**0**	**0**	**0**	**0**	**0**	**0**	**7**	**0.0**		....	....	....	....	....	....	....	....	....	....	....	....	....

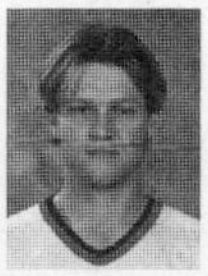

JOHANSSON, Andreas
(yoh-HAHN-suhn, ahn-DRAY-uhs) **T.B.**

Center. Shoots left. 6', 205 lbs. Born, Hofors, Sweden, May 19, 1973. NY Islanders' 7th choice, 136th overall, in 1991 Entry Draft.

Season	Club	League	GP	G	A	Pts	PIM	PP	SH	GW	S	%	+/-	TF	F%	H	SB	Min	GP	G	A	Pts	PIM	PP	SH	GW
1990-91	Falun	Sweden-2	31	12	10	22	38	....	....	....	....	....	....	....	....	....	....	....	....	....	....	....	....	....	....	....
1991-92	Farjestads BK	Sweden	30	3	1	4	10	....	....	....	....	....	....	....	....	....	....	....	6	0	0	0	4	....	....	....
1992-93	Farjestads BK	Sweden	38	4	7	11	38	....	....	....	....	....	....	....	....	....	....	....	2	0	0	0	0	....	....	....
1993-94	Farjestads BK	Sweden	20	3	6	9	6	....	....	....	....	....	....	....	....	....	....	....	....	....	....	....	....	....	....	....
1994-95	Farjestads BK	Sweden	36	9	10	19	42	....	....	....	....	....	....	....	....	....	....	....	4	0	0	0	10	....	....	....
1995-96	**NY Islanders**	**NHL**	**3**	**0**	**1**	**1**	**0**	**0**	**0**	**0**	**6**	**0.0**	**1**	....	....	....	....	....	....	....	....	....	....	....	....	....
	Worcester	AHL	29	5	5	10	32	....	....	....	....	....	....	....	....	....	....	....	....	....	....	....	....	....	....	....
	Utah	IHL	22	4	13	17	28	....	....	....	....	....	....	....	....	....	....	....	12	0	5	5	6	....	....	....
1996-97	**NY Islanders**	**NHL**	**15**	**2**	**2**	**4**	**0**	**1**	**0**	**0**	**21**	**9.5**	**–6**	....	....	....	....	....	....	....	....	....	....	....	....	....
	Pittsburgh	**NHL**	**27**	**2**	**7**	**9**	**20**	**0**	**0**	**0**	**38**	**5.3**	**–6**	....	....	....	....	....	....	....	....	....	....	....	....	....
	Cleveland	IHL	10	2	4	6	42	....	....	....	....	....	....	....	....	....	....	....	11	1	5	6	8	....	....	....
1997-98	**Pittsburgh**	**NHL**	**50**	**5**	**10**	**15**	**20**	**0**	**1**	**0**	**49**	**10.2**	**4**	....	....	....	....	....	**1**	**0**	**0**	**0**	**0**	**0**	**0**	**0**
	Sweden	Olympics	3	0	0	0	2	....	....	....	....	....	....	....	....	....	....	....	....	....	....	....	....	....	....	....
1998-99	**Ottawa**	**NHL**	**69**	**21**	**16**	**37**	**34**	**7**	**0**	**6**	**144**	**14.6**	**1**	**9**	**22.2**	**48**	**8**	**14:39**	**2**	**0**	**0**	**0**	**0**	**0**	**0**	**0**
	NHL Totals		**164**	**30**	**36**	**66**	**74**	**8**	**1**	**6**	**258**	**11.6**		**9**	**22.2**	**48**	**8**	**14:39**	**3**	**0**	**0**	**0**	**0**	**0**	**0**	**0**

Swedish World All-Star Team (1995)

Traded to **Pittsburgh** by **NY Islanders** with Darius Kasparaitis for Bryan Smolinski, November 17, 1996. Traded to **Tampa Bay** by **Ottawa** for Rob Zamuner and future considerations, June 29, 1999.

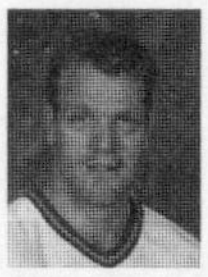

JOHANSSON, Calle
(yoh-HAHN-suhn, KAL-ee) **WSH.**

Defense. Shoots left. 5'11", 200 lbs. Born, Goteborg, Sweden, February 14, 1967. Buffalo's 1st choice, 14th overall, in 1985 Entry Draft.

Season	Club	League	GP	G	A	Pts	PIM	PP	SH	GW	S	%	+/-	TF	F%	H	SB	Min	GP	G	A	Pts	PIM	PP	SH	GW
1983-84	V. Frolunda	Sweden	28	4	4	8	10	....	....	....	....	....	....	....	....	....	....	....	....	....	....	....	....	....	....	....
1984-85	V. Frolunda	Sweden-2	25	8	13	21	16	....	....	....	....	....	....	....	....	....	....	....	6	1	2	3	4	....	....	....
1985-86	Bjorkloven	Sweden	17	1	2	3	4	....	....	....	....	....	....	....	....	....	....	....	....	....	....	....	....	....	....	....
1986-87	Bjorkloven	Sweden	30	2	13	15	20	....	....	....	....	....	....	....	....	....	....	....	6	1	3	4	6	....	....	....
1987-88	**Buffalo**	**NHL**	**71**	**4**	**38**	**42**	**37**	**2**	**0**	**0**	**93**	**4.3**	**12**	....	....	....	....	....	**6**	**0**	**1**	**1**	**0**	**0**	**0**	**0**
1988-89	**Buffalo**	**NHL**	**47**	**2**	**11**	**13**	**33**	**0**	**0**	**1**	**53**	**3.8**	**–7**	....	....	....	....	....	....	....	....	....	....	....	....	....
	Washington	**NHL**	**12**	**1**	**7**	**8**	**4**	**1**	**0**	**0**	**22**	**4.5**	**1**	....	....	....	....	....	**6**	**1**	**2**	**3**	**0**	**1**	**0**	**0**
1989-90	**Washington**	**NHL**	**70**	**8**	**31**	**39**	**25**	**4**	**0**	**2**	**103**	**7.8**	**7**	....	....	....	....	....	**15**	**1**	**6**	**7**	**4**	**0**	**0**	**0**
1990-91	**Washington**	**NHL**	**80**	**11**	**41**	**52**	**23**	**2**	**1**	**2**	**128**	**8.6**	**–2**	....	....	....	....	....	**10**	**2**	**7**	**9**	**8**	**1**	**0**	**0**
1991-92	**Washington**	**NHL**	**80**	**14**	**42**	**56**	**49**	**5**	**2**	**2**	**119**	**11.8**	**2**	....	....	....	....	....	**7**	**0**	**5**	**5**	**4**	**0**	**0**	**0**
1992-93	**Washington**	**NHL**	**77**	**7**	**38**	**45**	**56**	**6**	**0**	**0**	**133**	**5.3**	**3**	....	....	....	....	....	**6**	**0**	**5**	**5**	**4**	**0**	**0**	**0**
1993-94	**Washington**	**NHL**	**84**	**9**	**33**	**42**	**59**	**4**	**0**	**1**	**141**	**6.4**	**3**	....	....	....	....	....	**6**	**1**	**3**	**4**	**4**	**0**	**0**	**1**
1994-95	EHC Kloten	Switz.	5	1	2	3	8	....	....	....	....	....	....	....	....	....	....	....	....	....	....	....	....	....	....	....
	Washington	**NHL**	**46**	**5**	**26**	**31**	**35**	**4**	**0**	**2**	**112**	**4.5**	**–6**	....	....	....	....	....	**7**	**3**	**1**	**4**	**0**	**1**	**0**	**0**
1995-96	**Washington**	**NHL**	**78**	**10**	**25**	**35**	**50**	**4**	**0**	**0**	**182**	**5.5**	**13**	....	....	....	....	....	....	....	....	....	....	....	....	....
1996-97	**Washington**	**NHL**	**65**	**6**	**11**	**17**	**16**	**2**	**0**	**0**	**133**	**4.5**	**–2**	....	....	....	....	....	....	....	....	....	....	....	....	....
1997-98	**Washington**	**NHL**	**73**	**15**	**20**	**35**	**30**	**10**	**1**	**1**	**163**	**9.2**	**–11**	....	....	....	....	....	**21**	**2**	**8**	**10**	**16**	**0**	**0**	**0**
	Sweden	Olympics	4	0	0	0	2	....	....	....	....	....	....	....	....	....	....	....	....	....	....	....	....	....	....	....
1998-99	**Washington**	**NHL**	**67**	**8**	**21**	**29**	**22**	**2**	**0**	**2**	**145**	**5.5**	**10**	**0**	**0.0**	**51**	**140**	**23:58**	....	....	....	....	....	....	....	....
	NHL Totals		**850**	**100**	**344**	**444**	**439**	**46**	**4**	**13**	**1527**	**6.5**		**0**	**0.0**	**51**	**140**	**23:58**	**84**	**10**	**38**	**48**	**40**	**3**	**0**	**1**

• NHL All-Rookie Team (1988)

Traded to **Washington** by **Buffalo** with Buffalo's 2nd round choice (Byron Dafoe) in 1989 Entry Draft for Clint Malarchuk, Grant Ledyard and Washington's 6th round choice (Brian Holzinger) in 1991 Entry Draft, March 7, 1989.

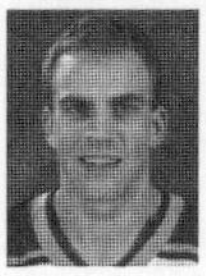

JOHNSON, Craig
L.A.

Left wing. Shoots left. 6'2", 197 lbs. Born, St. Paul, MN, March 8, 1972. St. Louis' 1st choice, 33rd overall, in 1990 Entry Draft.

Season	Club	League	GP	G	A	Pts	PIM	PP	SH	GW	S	%	+/-	TF	F%	H	SB	Min	GP	G	A	Pts	PIM	PP	SH	GW
1987-88	Hill-Murray	H.S.	28	14	20	34	4	....	....	....	....	....	....	....	....	....	....	....	....	....	....	....	....	....	....	....
1988-89	Hill-Murray	H.S.	24	22	30	52	10	....	....	....	....	....	....	....	....	....	....	....	....	....	....	....	....	....	....	....
1989-90	Hill-Murray	H.S.	23	15	36	51	0	....	....	....	....	....	....	....	....	....	....	....	....	....	....	....	....	....	....	....
1990-91	U. of Minnesota	WCHA	33	13	18	31	34	....	....	....	....	....	....	....	....	....	....	....	....	....	....	....	....	....	....	....
1991-92	U. of Minnesota	WCHA	41	17	38	55	66	....	....	....	....	....	....	....	....	....	....	....	....	....	....	....	....	....	....	....
1992-93	U. of Minnesota	WCHA	42	22	24	46	70	....	....	....	....	....	....	....	....	....	....	....	....	....	....	....	....	....	....	....
	Jacksonville	SunHL	23	2	9	11	38	....	....	....	....	....	....	....	....	....	....	....	....	....	....	....	....	....	....	....
1993-94	United States	Nat-Team	54	25	26	51	64	....	....	....	....	....	....	....	....	....	....	....	....	....	....	....	....	....	....	....
	United States	Olympics	8	0	4	4	4	....	....	....	....	....	....	....	....	....	....	....	....	....	....	....	....	....	....	....
1994-95	**St. Louis**	**NHL**	**15**	**3**	**3**	**6**	**6**	**0**	**0**	**0**	**19**	**15.8**	**4**	....	....	....	....	....	**1**	**0**	**0**	**0**	**2**	**0**	**0**	**0**
	Peoria	IHL	16	2	6	8	25	....	....	....	....	....	....	....	....	....	....	....	9	0	4	4	10	....	....	....
1995-96	**St. Louis**	**NHL**	**49**	**8**	**7**	**15**	**30**	**1**	**0**	**0**	**69**	**11.6**	**–4**	....	....	....	....	....	....	....	....	....	....	....	....	....
	Worcester	AHL	5	3	0	3	2	....	....	....	....	....	....	....	....	....	....	....	....	....	....	....	....	....	....	....
	Los Angeles	**NHL**	**11**	**5**	**4**	**9**	**6**	**3**	**0**	**0**	**28**	**17.9**	**–4**	....	....	....	....	....	....	....	....	....	....	....	....	....
1996-97	**Los Angeles**	**NHL**	**31**	**4**	**3**	**7**	**26**	**1**	**0**	**0**	**30**	**13.3**	**–7**	....	....	....	....	....	....	....	....	....	....	....	....	....
1997-98	**Los Angeles**	**NHL**	**74**	**17**	**21**	**38**	**42**	**6**	**0**	**2**	**125**	**13.6**	**9**	....	....	....	....	....	**4**	**1**	**0**	**1**	**4**	**0**	**0**	**0**
1998-99	**Los Angeles**	**NHL**	**69**	**7**	**12**	**19**	**32**	**2**	**0**	**2**	**94**	**7.4**	**–12**	**2**	**50.0**	**70**	**11**	**12:02**	....	....	....	....	....	....	....	....
	NHL Totals		**249**	**44**	**50**	**94**	**142**	**13**	**0**	**4**	**365**	**12.1**		**2**	**50.0**	**70**	**11**	**12:02**	**5**	**1**	**0**	**1**	**6**	**0**	**0**	**0**

Traded to **LA Kings** by **St. Louis** with Patrice Tardif, Roman Vopat, St. Louis 5th round choice (Peter Hogan) in 1996 Entry Draft and 1st round choice (Matt Zultek) in 1997 Entry Draft for Wayne Gretzky, February 27, 1996.

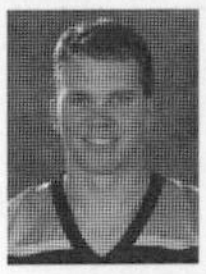

JOHNSON, Greg — NSH.

Center. Shoots left. 5'10", 185 lbs. Born, Thunder Bay, Ont., March 16, 1971. Philadelphia's 1st choice, 33rd overall, in 1989 Entry Draft.

			Regular Season																Playoffs							
Season	Club	League	GP	G	A	Pts	PIM	PP	SH	GW	S	%	+/–	TF	F%	H	SB	Min	GP	G	A	Pts	PIM	PP	SH	GW
1988-89	Thunder Bay	USHL	47	32	64	96	4	....	....	....	....	....	....	....	....	....	....	....	12	5	13	18	0	....	....	....
1989-90	North Dakota	WCHA	44	17	38	55	11	....	....	....	....	....	....	....	....	....	....	....	....	....	....	....	....	....	....	....
1990-91	North Dakota	WCHA	38	18	*61	79	6	....	....	....	....	....	....	....	....	....	....	....	....	....	....	....	....	....	....	....
1991-92	North Dakota	WCHA	39	20	*54	74	8	....	....	....	....	....	....	....	....	....	....	....	....	....	....	....	....	....	....	....
1992-93	North Dakota	WCHA	34	19	45	64	18	....	....	....	....	....	....	....	....	....	....	....	....	....	....	....	....	....	....	....
	Canada	Nat-Team	23	6	14	20	2	....	....	....	....	....	....	....	....	....	....	....	....	....	....	....	....	....	....	....
1993-94	**Detroit**	**NHL**	**52**	**6**	**11**	**17**	**22**	**1**	**1**	**0**	**48**	**12.5**	**–7**	....	....	....	....	....	**7**	**2**	**2**	**4**	**2**	**1**	**0**	**0**
	Adirondack	AHL	3	2	4	6	0	....	....	....	....	....	....	....	....	....	....	....	4	0	4	4	2	....	....	....
	Canada	Nat-Team	6	2	6	8	4	....	....	....	....	....	....	....	....	....	....	....	....	....	....	....	....	....	....	....
	Canada	Olympics	8	0	3	3	0	....	....	....	....	....	....	....	....	....	....	....	....	....	....	....	....	....	....	....
1994-95	**Detroit**	**NHL**	**22**	**3**	**5**	**8**	**14**	**2**	**0**	**0**	**32**	**9.4**	**1**	....	....	....	....	....	**1**	**0**	**0**	**0**	**0**	**0**	**0**	**0**
1995-96	**Detroit**	**NHL**	**60**	**18**	**22**	**40**	**30**	**5**	**0**	**2**	**87**	**20.7**	**6**	....	....	....	....	....	**13**	**3**	**1**	**4**	**8**	**0**	**0**	**0**
1996-97	**Detroit**	**NHL**	**43**	**6**	**10**	**16**	**12**	**0**	**0**	**0**	**56**	**10.7**	**–5**	....	....	....	....	....	....	....	....	....	....	....	....	....
	Pittsburgh	**NHL**	**32**	**7**	**9**	**16**	**14**	**1**	**0**	**0**	**52**	**13.5**	**–13**	....	....	....	....	....	**5**	**1**	**0**	**1**	**2**	**0**	**0**	**0**
1997-98	**Pittsburgh**	**NHL**	**5**	**1**	**0**	**1**	**2**	**0**	**0**	**0**	**4**	**25.0**	**0**	....	....	....	....	....	....	....	....	....	....	....	....	....
	Chicago	**NHL**	**69**	**11**	**22**	**33**	**38**	**4**	**0**	**3**	**85**	**12.9**	**–2**	....	....	....	....	....	....	....	....	....	....	....	....	....
1998-99	**Nashville**	**NHL**	**68**	**16**	**34**	**50**	**24**	**2**	**3**	**0**	**120**	**13.3**	**–8**	**1441**	**53.6**	**28**	**36**	**19:26**	....	....	....	....	....	....	....	....
	NHL Totals		**351**	**68**	**113**	**181**	**156**	**15**	**4**	**5**	**484**	**14.0**		**1441**	**53.6**	**28**	**36**	**19:26**	**26**	**6**	**3**	**9**	**12**	**1**	**0**	**0**

WCHA First All-Star Team (1991, 1992, 1993) • NCAA West First All-American Team (1991, 1993) • NCAA West Second All-American Team (1992)

Traded to **Detroit** by **Philadelphia** with Philadelphia's 5th round choice (Frederic Deschenes) in 1994 Entry Draft for Jim Cummins and Philadelphia's 4th round choice (previously acquired by Detroit — later traded to Boston — Boston selected Charles Paquette) in 1993 Entry Draft, June 20, 1993. Traded to **Pittsburgh** by **Detroit** for Tomas Sandstrom, January 27, 1997. Traded to **Chicago** by **Pittsburgh** for Tuomas Gronman, October 27, 1997. Claimed by **Nashville** from **Chicago** in Expansion Draft, June 26, 1998.

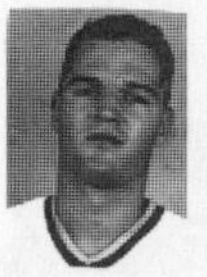

JOHNSON, Matt — ATL.

Left wing. Shoots left. 6'5", 232 lbs. Born, Welland, Ont., November 23, 1975. Los Angeles' 2nd choice, 33rd overall, in 1994 Entry Draft.

Season	Club	League	GP	G	A	Pts	PIM	PP	SH	GW	S	%	+/–	TF	F%	H	SB	Min	GP	G	A	Pts	PIM	PP	SH	GW
1991-92	Welland	OJHL	38	6	19	25	214	....	....	....	....	....	....	....	....	....	....	....	....	....	....	....	....	....	....	....
1992-93	Peterborough	OHL	66	8	17	25	211	....	....	....	....	....	....	....	....	....	....	....	16	1	1	2	56	....	....	....
1993-94	Peterborough	OHL	50	13	24	37	233	....	....	....	....	....	....	....	....	....	....	....	....	....	....	....	....	....	....	....
1994-95	Peterborough	OHL	14	1	2	3	43	....	....	....	....	....	....	....	....	....	....	....	....	....	....	....	....	....	....	....
	Los Angeles	**NHL**	**14**	**1**	**0**	**1**	**102**	**0**	**0**	**0**	**4**	**25.0**	**0**	....	....	....	....	....	....	....	....	....	....	....	....	....
1995-96	**Los Angeles**	**NHL**	**1**	**0**	**0**	**0**	**5**	**0**	**0**	**0**	**1**	**0.0**	**0**	....	....	....	....	....	....	....	....	....	....	....	....	....
	Phoenix	IHL	29	4	4	8	87	....	....	....	....	....	....	....	....	....	....	....	....	....	....	....	....	....	....	....
1996-97	**Los Angeles**	**NHL**	**52**	**1**	**3**	**4**	**194**	**0**	**0**	**0**	**20**	**5.0**	**–4**	....	....	....	....	....	....	....	....	....	....	....	....	....
1997-98	**Los Angeles**	**NHL**	**66**	**2**	**4**	**6**	**249**	**0**	**0**	**0**	**18**	**11.1**	**–8**	....	....	....	....	....	**4**	**0**	**0**	**0**	**6**	**0**	**0**	**0**
1998-99	**Los Angeles**	**NHL**	**49**	**2**	**1**	**3**	**131**	**0**	**0**	**0**	**14**	**14.3**	**–5**	**1**	**0.0**	**62**	**4**	**5:55**	....	....	....	....	....	....	....	....
	NHL Totals		**182**	**6**	**8**	**14**	**681**	**0**	**0**	**0**	**57**	**10.5**		**1**	**0.0**	**62**	**4**	**5:55**	**4**	**0**	**0**	**0**	**6**	**0**	**0**	**0**

Claimed by **Atlanta** from **Los Angeles** in Expansion Draft, June 25, 1999.

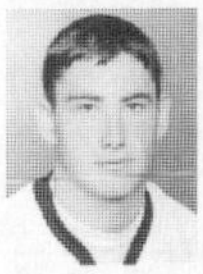

JOHNSON, Mike — TOR.

Right wing. Shoots right. 6'2", 197 lbs. Born, Scarborough, Ont., October 3, 1974.

Season	Club	League	GP	G	A	Pts	PIM	PP	SH	GW	S	%	+/–	TF	F%	H	SB	Min	GP	G	A	Pts	PIM	PP	SH	GW
1992-93	Aurora	OJHL	48	25	40	65	18	....	....	....	....	....	....	....	....	....	....	....	....	....	....	....	....	....	....	....
1993-94	Bowling Green	CCHA	38	6	14	20	18	....	....	....	....	....	....	....	....	....	....	....	....	....	....	....	....	....	....	....
1994-95	Bowling Green	CCHA	37	16	33	49	35	....	....	....	....	....	....	....	....	....	....	....	....	....	....	....	....	....	....	....
1995-96	Bowling Green	CCHA	30	12	19	31	22	....	....	....	....	....	....	....	....	....	....	....	....	....	....	....	....	....	....	....
1996-97	Bowling Green	CCHA	38	30	32	62	46	....	....	....	....	....	....	....	....	....	....	....	....	....	....	....	....	....	....	....
	Toronto	**NHL**	**13**	**2**	**2**	**4**	**4**	**0**	**1**	**1**	**27**	**7.4**	**–2**	....	....	....	....	....	....	....	....	....	....	....	....	....
1997-98	**Toronto**	**NHL**	**82**	**15**	**32**	**47**	**24**	**5**	**0**	**0**	**143**	**10.5**	**–4**	....	....	....	....	....	....	....	....	....	....	....	....	....
1998-99	**Toronto**	**NHL**	**79**	**20**	**24**	**44**	**35**	**5**	**3**	**2**	**149**	**13.4**	**13**	**15**	**53.3**	**70**	**17**	**16:16**	**17**	**3**	**2**	**5**	**4**	**0**	**0**	**1**
	NHL Totals		**174**	**37**	**58**	**95**	**63**	**10**	**4**	**3**	**319**	**11.6**		**15**	**53.3**	**70**	**17**	**16:16**	**17**	**3**	**2**	**5**	**4**	**0**	**0**	**1**

NHL All-Rookie Team (1998)

Signed as a free agent by **Toronto**, March 16, 1997.

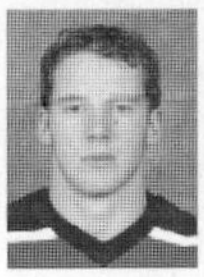

JOHNSON, Ryan — FLA.

Center. Shoots left. 6'1", 200 lbs. Born, Thunder Bay, Ont., June 14, 1976. Florida's 4th choice, 36th overall, in 1994 Entry Draft.

Season	Club	League	GP	G	A	Pts	PIM	PP	SH	GW	S	%	+/–	TF	F%	H	SB	Min	GP	G	A	Pts	PIM	PP	SH	GW
1992-93	Thunder Bay	TBAHA	60	25	33	58	....	....	....	....	....	....	....	....	....	....	....	....	....	....	....	....	....	....	....	....
1993-94	Thunder Bay	USHL	48	14	36	50	28	....	....	....	....	....	....	....	....	....	....	....	....	....	....	....	....	....	....	....
1994-95	North Dakota	WCHA	38	6	22	28	39	....	....	....	....	....	....	....	....	....	....	....	....	....	....	....	....	....	....	....
1995-96	North Dakota	WCHA	21	2	17	19	14	....	....	....	....	....	....	....	....	....	....	....	....	....	....	....	....	....	....	....
	Canada	Nat-Team	28	5	12	17	14	....	....	....	....	....	....	....	....	....	....	....	....	....	....	....	....	....	....	....
1996-97	Carolina	AHL	79	18	24	42	28	....	....	....	....	....	....	....	....	....	....	....	....	....	....	....	....	....	....	....
1997-98	**Florida**	**NHL**	**10**	**0**	**2**	**2**	**0**	**0**	**0**	**0**	**6**	**0.0**	**–4**	....	....	....	....	....	....	....	....	....	....	....	....	....
	New Haven	AHL	64	19	48	67	12	....	....	....	....	....	....	....	....	....	....	....	3	0	1	1	0	....	....	....
1998-99	**Florida**	**NHL**	**1**	**1**	**0**	**1**	**0**	**0**	**0**	**0**	**1**	**100.0**	**0**	**16**	**37.5**	**1**	**0**	**15:26**	....	....	....	....	....	....	....	....
	New Haven	AHL	37	8	19	27	18	....	....	....	....	....	....	....	....	....	....	....	....	....	....	....	....	....	....	....
	NHL Totals		**11**	**1**	**2**	**3**	**0**	**0**	**0**	**0**	**7**	**14.3**		**16**	**37.5**	**1**	**0**	**15:26**	....	....	....	....	....	....	....	....

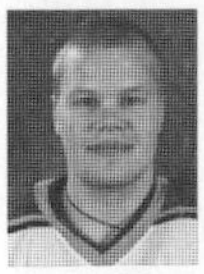

JOKINEN, Olli — NYI

(YOH-kih-nihn, OH-lee)

Center. Shoots left. 6'3", 208 lbs. Born, Kuopio, Finland, December 5, 1978. Los Angeles' 1st choice, 3rd overall, in 1997 Entry Draft.

Season	Club	League	GP	G	A	Pts	PIM	PP	SH	GW	S	%	+/–	TF	F%	H	SB	Min	GP	G	A	Pts	PIM	PP	SH	GW
1994-95	KaiPa Kuopio	Finn-Jr.	6	0	1	1	6	....	....	....	....	....	....	....	....	....	....	....	....	....	....	....	....	....	....	....
	KaiPa Kuopio	Finland-2	30	22	28	50	92	....	....	....	....	....	....	....	....	....	....	....	....	....	....	....	....	....	....	....
1995-96	KaiPa Kuopio	Finn-Jr.	25	20	14	34	47	....	....	....	....	....	....	....	....	....	....	....	7	4	4	8	20	....	....	....
	KalPa Kuopio	Finland	15	1	1	2	2	....	....	....	....	....	....	....	....	....	....	....	....	....	....	....	....	....	....	....
1996-97	HIFK Helsinki	Finland	50	14	27	41	88	....	....	....	....	....	....	....	....	....	....	....	....	....	....	....	....	....	....	....
	Finland	Nat-Team	12	4	3	7	4	....	....	....	....	....	....	....	....	....	....	....	....	....	....	....	....	....	....	....
1997-98	**Los Angeles**	**NHL**	**8**	**0**	**0**	**0**	**6**	**0**	**0**	**0**	**12**	**0.0**	**–5**	....	....	....	....	....	....	....	....	....	....	....	....	....
	HIFK Helsinki	Finland	30	11	28	39	8	....	....	....	....	....	....	....	....	....	....	....	9	*7	2	9	2	....	....	....
	Finland	Nat-Team	5	1	1	2	33	....	....	....	....	....	....	....	....	....	....	....	....	....	....	....	....	....	....	....
1998-99	**Los Angeles**	**NHL**	**66**	**9**	**12**	**21**	**44**	**3**	**1**	**1**	**87**	**10.3**	**–10**	**779**	**43.9**	**109**	**26**	**14:42**	....	....	....	....	....	....	....	....
	Springfield	AHL	9	3	6	9	6	....	....	....	....	....	....	....	....	....	....	....	....	....	....	....	....	....	....	....
	NHL Totals		**74**	**9**	**12**	**21**	**50**	**3**	**1**	**1**	**99**	**9.1**		**779**	**43.9**	**109**	**26**	**14:42**	....	....	....	....	....	....	....	....

Finnish Rookie of the Year (1997)

Traded to **NY Islanders** by **Los Angeles** with Josh Green, Mathieu Biron and Los Angeles' 1st round choice (Taylor Pyatt) in 1999 Entry Draft for Zigmund Palffy, Brian Smolinski, Marcel Cousineau and New Jersey's 4th round choice (previously acquired, Los Angeles selected Daniel Johanssen) in 1999 Entry Draft, June 20, 1999.

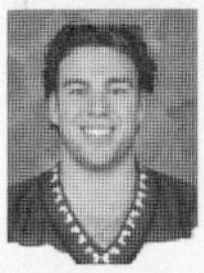

JOMPHE, Jean-Francois

(ZHAWMF)

Center. Shoots left. 6'1", 195 lbs. Born, Harve' St. Pierre, Que., December 28, 1972.

Season	Club	League	GP	G	A	Pts	PIM	PP	SH	GW	S	%	+/–	TF	F%	H	SB	Min	GP	G	A	Pts	PIM	PP	SH	GW
1990-91	Shawinigan	QMJHL	42	17	22	39	14	....	....	....	....	....	....	....	....	....	....	....	6	2	1	3	2	....	....	....
1991-92	Shawinigan	QMJHL	44	28	33	61	69	....	....	....	....	....	....	....	....	....	....	....	10	6	10	16	10	....	....	....
1992-93	Sherbrooke	QMJHL	60	43	43	86	86	....	....	....	....	....	....	....	....	....	....	....	15	10	13	23	18	....	....	....
1993-94	San Diego	IHL	29	2	3	5	12	....	....	....	....	....	....	....	....	....	....	....	....	....	....	....	....	....	....	....
	Greensboro	ECHL	25	9	9	18	41	....	....	....	....	....	....	....	....	....	....	....	1	1	0	1	0	....	....	....
1994-95	Canada	Nat-Team	52	33	25	58	85	....	....	....	....	....	....	....	....	....	....	....	....	....	....	....	....	....	....	....

Season	Club	League	GP	G	A	Pts	PIM	PP	SH	GW	S	%	+/-	TF	F%	H	SB	Min	GP	G	A	Pts	PIM	PP	SH	GW
1995-96	Anaheim	NHL	31	2	12	14	39	2	0	0	46	4.3	7	....	....	....	....	....	....	....	....	....	....	....	....	....
	Baltimore	AHL	47	21	34	55	75																		
1996-97	Anaheim	NHL	64	7	14	21	53	0	1	0	81	8.6	-9												
1997-98	Anaheim	NHL	9	1	3	4	8	0	0	0	8	12.5	1												
	Cincinnati	AHL	38	9	19	28	32																		
	Quebec	IHL	17	6	4	10	24																		
1998-99	Phoenix	NHL	1	0	0	0	2	0	0	0	0	0.0	0	3	66.7	3	0	7:36								
	Las Vegas	IHL	32	6	14	20	63																		
	Montreal	NHL	6	0	0	0	0	0	0	0	4	0.0	0	41	48.8	10	1	9:01								
	NHL Totals		111	10	29	39	102	2	1	0	139	7.2		44	50.0	13	1	8:49								

Signed as a free agent by **Anaheim**, September 7, 1993. Traded to **Phoenix** by **Anaheim** for Jim McKenzie, June 18, 1998. Traded to **Montreal** by Phoenix for cash, March 23, 1999.

JONES, Keith   PHI.

Right wing. Shoots left. 6'2", 200 lbs.   Born, Brantford, Ont., November 8, 1968. Washington's 7th choice, 141st overall, in 1988 Entry Draft.

Season	Club	League	GP	G	A	Pts	PIM	PP	SH	GW	S	%	+/-	TF	F%	H	SB	Min	GP	G	A	Pts	PIM	PP	SH	GW
1987-88	Niagara Falls	OJHL-B	40	50	80	130	113																		
1988-89	Western Michigan	CCHA	37	9	12	21	51																		
1989-90	Western Michigan	CCHA	40	19	18	37	82																		
1990-91	Western Michigan	CCHA	41	30	19	49	106																		
1991-92	Western Michigan	CCHA	35	25	31	56	77																		
	Baltimore	AHL	6	2	4	6	0																		
1992-93	**Washington**	NHL	71	12	14	26	124	0	0	3	73	16.4	18						6	0	0	0	10	0	0	0
	Baltimore	AHL	8	7	3	10	4																		
1993-94	**Washington**	NHL	68	16	19	35	149	5	0	1	97	16.5	4						11	0	1	1	36	0	0	0
	Portland	AHL	6	5	7	12	4																		
1994-95	**Washington**	NHL	40	14	6	20	65	1	0	5	85	16.5	-2						7	4	4	8	22	1	0	0
1995-96	**Washington**	NHL	68	18	23	41	103	5	0	2	155	11.6	8						2	0	0	0	7	0	0	0
1996-97	**Washington**	NHL	11	2	3	5	13	1	0	0	12	16.7	-2													
	Colorado	NHL	67	23	20	43	105	13	1	7	158	14.6	5						6	3	3	6	4	1	0	0
1997-98	**Colorado**	NHL	23	3	7	10	22	1	0	2	31	9.7	-4						7	0	0	0	13	0	0	0
	Hershey	AHL	4	2	1	3	2																		
1998-99	**Colorado**	NHL	12	2	2	4	20	1	0	0	11	18.2	-6	2	100.0	16	2	13:48								
	Philadelphia	NHL	66	18	31	49	78	2	0	3	124	14.5	29	78	44.9	40	18	16:59	6	2	1	3	14	0	0	0
	NHL Totals		426	108	125	233	679	29	1	22	746	14.5		80	46.3	56	20	16:30	45	9	9	18	106	2	0	0

CCHA First All-Star Team (1992)

Traded to **Colorado** by **Washington** with Washington's 1st round choice (Scott Parker) in 1998 Entry Draft and future considerations for Curtis Leschyshyn and Chris Simon, November 2, 1996. Traded to **Philadelphia** by **Colorado** for Shjon Podein, November 12, 1998.

JONES, Ty   CHI.

Right wing. Shoots right. 6'3", 218 lbs.   Born, Richland, WA, February 22, 1979. Chicago's 2nd choice, 16th overall, in 1997 Entry Draft.

Season	Club	League	GP	G	A	Pts	PIM	PP	SH	GW	S	%	+/-	TF	F%	H	SB	Min	GP	G	A	Pts	PIM	PP	SH	GW
1993-94	Alaska Stars	USAHA	64	84	104	188	126																		
1994-95	Alaska Stars	USAHA	42	33	35	68	98																		
1995-96	Spokane	WHL	34	1	0	1	77												3	0	0	0	6			
1996-97	Spokane	WHL	67	20	34	54	202												9	2	4	6	10			
1997-98	Spokane	WHL	60	36	48	84	161												18	2	14	16	35			
1998-99	Spokane	WHL	26	15	12	27	98																		
	Kamloops	WHL	20	3	16	19	84												14	5	3	8	22			
	Chicago	NHL	8	0	0	0	12	0	0	0	3	0.0	-1	0	0.0	5	1	7:53								
	NHL Totals		8	0	0	0	12	0	0	0	3	0.0		0	0.0	5	1	7:53								

JONSSON, Kenny   (YAWN-suhn)   NYI

Defense. Shoots left. 6'3", 195 lbs.   Born, Angelholm, Sweden, October 6, 1974. Toronto's 1st choice, 12th overall, in 1993 Entry Draft.

Season	Club	League	GP	G	A	Pts	PIM	PP	SH	GW	S	%	+/-	TF	F%	H	SB	Min	GP	G	A	Pts	PIM	PP	SH	GW
1991-92	Rogle BK	Sweden-2	30	4	11	15	24																		
1992-93	Rogle BK	Swede-Jr.	2	1	2	3	25																		
	Rogle BK	Sweden	39	3	10	13	42																		
1993-94	Rogle BK	Sweden	36	4	13	17	40												3	1	1	2	2			
	Sweden	Olympics	3	1	0	1	0																		
1994-95	Rogle BK	Sweden	8	3	1	4	20																		
	Toronto	NHL	39	2	7	9	16	0	0	1	50	4.0	-8						4	0	0	0	0	0	0	0
	St. John's	AHL	10	2	5	7	2																		
1995-96	**Toronto**	NHL	50	4	22	26	22	3	0	1	90	4.4	12													
	NY Islanders	NHL	16	0	4	4	10	0	0	0	40	0.0	-5													
1996-97	**NY Islanders**	NHL	81	3	18	21	24	1	0	0	92	3.3	10													
1997-98	**NY Islanders**	NHL	81	14	26	40	58	6	0	2	108	13.0	-2													
1998-99	**NY Islanders**	NHL	63	8	18	26	34	6	0	0	91	8.8	-18	0	0.0	57	90	24:59								
	NHL Totals		330	31	95	126	164	16	0	4	471	6.6		0	0.0	57	90	24:59	4	0	0	0	0	0	0	0

Swedish Rookie of the Year (1993) • NHL/Upper Deck All-Rookie Team (1995)

Traded to **NY Islanders** by **Toronto** with Sean Haggerty, Darby Hendrickson and Toronto's 1st round choice (Roberto Luongo) in 1997 Entry Draft for Wendel Clark, Mathieu Schneider and D.J. Smith, March 13, 1996.

JOSEPH, Chris   OTT.

Defense. Shoots right. 6'2", 212 lbs.   Born, Burnaby, B.C., September 10, 1969. Pittsburgh's 1st choice, 5th overall, in 1987 Entry Draft.

Season	Club	League	GP	G	A	Pts	PIM	PP	SH	GW	S	%	+/-	TF	F%	H	SB	Min	GP	G	A	Pts	PIM	PP	SH	GW
1984-85	Burnaby	BCAHA	52	18	48	66	52																		
1985-86	Seattle	WHL	72	4	8	12	50												5	0	3	3	12			
1986-87	Seattle	WHL	67	13	45	58	155																		
1987-88	**Pittsburgh**	NHL	17	0	4	4	12	0	0	0	13	0.0	2													
	Edmonton	NHL	7	0	4	4	6	0	0	0	1	0.0	-3													
	Seattle	WHL	23	5	14	19	49																		
	Nova Scotia	AHL	8	0	2	2	8												4	0	0	0	9			
1988-89	**Edmonton**	NHL	44	4	5	9	54	0	0	0	36	11.1	-9													
	Cape Breton	AHL	5	1	1	2	18																		
1989-90	**Edmonton**	NHL	4	0	2	2	2	0	0	0	5	0.0	-2													
	Cape Breton	AHL	61	10	20	30	69												6	2	1	3	4			
1990-91	**Edmonton**	NHL	49	5	17	22	59	2	0	0	74	6.8	3													
1991-92	**Edmonton**	NHL	7	0	0	0	8	0	0	0	5	0.0	-1						5	1	3	4	2	0	0	0
	Cape Breton	AHL	63	14	29	43	72												5	0	2	2	8			
1992-93	**Edmonton**	NHL	33	2	10	12	48	1	0	0	49	4.1	-9													
1993-94	**Edmonton**	NHL	10	1	1	2	28	1	0	0	25	4.0	-8													
	Tampa Bay	NHL	66	10	19	29	108	7	0	0	154	6.5	-13													
1994-95	**Pittsburgh**	NHL	33	5	10	15	46	3	0	0	73	6.8	3						10	1	1	2	12	0	0	0
1995-96	**Pittsburgh**	NHL	70	5	14	19	71	0	0	1	94	5.3	6						15	1	0	1	8	0	0	0
1996-97	**Vancouver**	NHL	63	3	13	16	62	2	0	1	99	3.0	-21													
1997-98	**Philadelphia**	NHL	15	1	0	1	19	0	0	1	20	5.0	1						1	0	0	0	2	0	0	0
	Philadelphia	AHL	6	2	3	5	2																		

			Regular Season																Playoffs							
Season	Club	League	GP	G	A	Pts	PIM	PP	SH	GW	S	%	+/–	TF	F%	H	SB	Min	GP	G	A	Pts	PIM	PP	SH	GW
1998-99	**Philadelphia**	**NHL**	**2**	**0**	**0**	**0**	**2**	**0**	**0**	**0**	**1**	**0.0**	**0**	**0**	**0.0**	**0**	**0**	**9:36**	....	....	....	....	....	....	....	....
	Cincinnati	IHL	27	11	19	30	38	....	....	....	....	....	....	....	....	....	....	....	....	....	....	....	....	....	....	....
	Philadelphia	AHL	51	9	29	38	26	....	....	....	....	....	....	....	....	....	....	....	16	3	10	13	8	....	....	....
	NHL Totals		**420**	**36**	**99**	**135**	**525**	**16**	**0**	**3**	**649**	**5.5**		**0**	**0.0**	**0**	**0**	**9:36**	**31**	**3**	**4**	**7**	**24**	**0**	**0**	**0**

WHL West Second All-Star Team (1987)

Traded to **Edmonton** by **Pittsburgh** with Craig Simpson, Dave Hannan and Moe Mantha for Paul Coffey, Dave Hunter and Wayne Van Dorp, November 24, 1987. Traded to **Tampa Bay** by **Edmonton** for Bob Beers, November 11, 1993. Claimed by **Pittsburgh** from **Tampa Bay** in NHL Waiver Draft, January 18, 1995. Claimed by **Vancouver** from **Pittsburgh** in NHL Waiver Draft, September 30, 1996. Signed as a free agent by **Philadelphia**, September 11, 1997. Signed as a free agent by **Ottawa**, August 18, 1999.

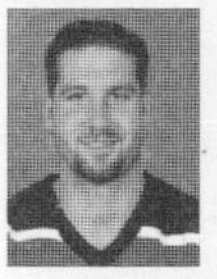

JOVANOVSKI, Ed (joh-van-OHV-skee) VAN.

Defense. Shoots left. 6'2", 210 lbs. Born, Windsor, Ont., June 26, 1976. Florida's 1st choice, 1st overall, in 1994 Entry Draft.

Season	Club	League	GP	G	A	Pts	PIM	PP	SH	GW	S	%	+/–	TF	F%	H	SB	Min	GP	G	A	Pts	PIM	PP	SH	GW
1991-92	Windsor AA	OMHA	50	25	40	65	88	....	....	....	....	....	....	....	....	....	....	....	....	....	....	....	....	....	....	....
1992-93	Windsor	OJHL	48	7	46	53	88	....	....	....	....	....	....	....	....	....	....	....	....	....	....	....	....	....	....	....
1993-94	Windsor	OHL	62	15	36	51	221	....	....	....	....	....	....	....	....	....	....	....	4	0	0	0	15	....	....	....
1994-95	Windsor	OHL	50	23	42	65	198	....	....	....	....	....	....	....	....	....	....	....	9	2	7	9	39	....	....	....
1995-96	**Florida**	**NHL**	**70**	**10**	**11**	**21**	**137**	**2**	**0**	**2**	**116**	**8.6**	**–3**	....	....	....	....	....	**22**	**1**	**8**	**9**	**52**	**0**	**0**	**0**
1996-97	**Florida**	**NHL**	**61**	**7**	**16**	**23**	**172**	**3**	**0**	**1**	**80**	**8.8**	**–1**	....	....	....	....	....	**5**	**0**	**0**	**0**	**4**	**0**	**0**	**0**
1997-98	**Florida**	**NHL**	**81**	**9**	**14**	**23**	**158**	**2**	**1**	**3**	**142**	**6.3**	**–12**	....	....	....	....	....	....	....	....	....	....	....	....	....
1998-99	**Florida**	**NHL**	**41**	**3**	**13**	**16**	**82**	**1**	**0**	**1**	**68**	**4.4**	**–4**	**0**	**0.0**	**88**	**36**	**22:35**	....	....	....	....	....	....	....	....
	Vancouver	**NHL**	**31**	**2**	**9**	**11**	**44**	**0**	**0**	**0**	**41**	**4.9**	**–5**	**0**	**0.0**	**68**	**35**	**21:16**	....	....	....	....	....	....	....	....
	NHL Totals		**284**	**31**	**63**	**94**	**593**	**8**	**1**	**7**	**447**	**6.9**		**0**	**0.0**	**156**	**71**	**22:01**	**27**	**1**	**8**	**9**	**56**	**0**	**0**	**0**

OHL Second All-Star Team (1994) • OHL First All-Star Team (1995) • NHL All-Rookie Team (1996)

Traded to **Vancouver** by **Florida** with Dave Gagner, Mike Brown, Kevin Weekes and Florida's 1st round choice in 2000 Entry Draft for Pavel Bure, Bret Hedican, Brad Ference and Vancouver's 3rd round choice in 2000 Entry Draft, January 17, 1999.

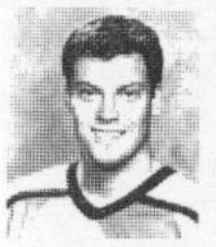

JUHLIN, Patrik (ew-LEEN)

Left wing. Shoots left. 6', 194 lbs. Born, Huddinge, Sweden, April 24, 1970. Philadelphia's 2nd choice, 34th overall, in 1989 Entry Draft.

Season	Club	League	GP	G	A	Pts	PIM	PP	SH	GW	S	%	+/–	TF	F%	H	SB	Min	GP	G	A	Pts	PIM	PP	SH	GW
1987-88	Vasteras IK	Sweden-2	2	0	0	0	0	....	....	....	....	....	....	....	....	....	....	....	....	....	....	....	....	....	....	....
1988-89	Vasteras IK	Sweden-2	30	29	13	42	....	....	....	....	....	....	....	....	....	....	....	....	....	....	....	....	....	....	....	....
1989-90	Vasteras IK	Sweden	35	10	13	23	18	....	....	....	....	....	....	....	....	....	....	....	2	0	0	0	0	....	....	....
1990-91	Vasteras IK	Sweden	40	13	9	22	24	....	....	....	....	....	....	....	....	....	....	....	4	3	1	4	0	....	....	....
1991-92	Vasteras IK	Sweden	39	15	12	27	40	....	....	....	....	....	....	....	....	....	....	....	....	....	....	....	....	....	....	....
1992-93	Vasteras IK	Sweden	34	14	12	26	22	....	....	....	....	....	....	....	....	....	....	....	3	0	1	1	2	....	....	....
1993-94	Vasteras IK	Sweden	40	15	16	31	20	....	....	....	....	....	....	....	....	....	....	....	4	1	1	2	2	....	....	....
	Sweden	Olympics	8	7	1	8	16	....	....	....	....	....	....	....	....	....	....	....	....	....	....	....	....	....	....	....
1994-95	Vasteras IK	Sweden	11	5	9	14	8	....	....	....	....	....	....	....	....	....	....	....	....	....	....	....	....	....	....	....
	Philadelphia	**NHL**	**42**	**4**	**3**	**7**	**6**	**0**	**0**	**1**	**44**	**9.1**	**–13**	....	....	....	....	....	**13**	**1**	**0**	**1**	**2**	**0**	**0**	**0**
1995-96	**Philadelphia**	**NHL**	**14**	**3**	**3**	**6**	**17**	**1**	**0**	**0**	**14**	**21.4**	**4**	....	....	....	....	....	....	....	....	....	....	....	....	....
	Hershey	AHL	14	5	2	7	8	....	....	....	....	....	....	....	....	....	....	....	1	0	0	0	0	....	....	....
1996-97	Philadelphia	AHL	78	31	60	91	24	....	....	....	....	....	....	....	....	....	....	....	9	7	6	13	4	....	....	....
1997-98	Jokerit	Finland	47	19	9	28	14	....	....	....	....	....	....	....	....	....	....	....	7	5	0	5	4	....	....	....
	Jokerit	EuroHL	6	2	3	5	2	....	....	....	....	....	....	....	....	....	....	....	....	....	....	....	....	....	....	....
1998-99	Jokerit	Finland	54	17	12	29	30	....	....	....	....	....	....	....	....	....	....	....	3	0	0	0	2	....	....	....
	Jokerit Heksinki	EuroHL	....	....	....	....	....	....	....	....	....	....	....	....	....	....	....	....	2	0	0	0	0	....	....	....
	NHL Totals		**56**	**7**	**6**	**13**	**23**	**1**	**0**	**1**	**58**	**12.1**		....	....	....	....	....	**13**	**1**	**0**	**1**	**2**	**0**	**0**	**0**

AHL First All-Star Team (1997)

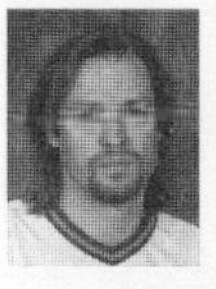

JUNEAU, Joe (ZHOO-noh, ZHOH-ay)

Center. Shoots left. 6', 195 lbs. Born, Pont-Rouge, Que., January 5, 1968. Boston's 3rd choice, 81st overall, in 1988 Entry Draft.

Season	Club	League	GP	G	A	Pts	PIM	PP	SH	GW	S	%	+/–	TF	F%	H	SB	Min	GP	G	A	Pts	PIM	PP	SH	GW
1983-84	Ste-Foy	QAAA	30	3	7	10	....	....	....	....	....	....	....	....	....	....	....	....	....	....	....	....	....	....	....	....
1984-85	Ste-Foy	QAAA	41	25	46	71	....	....	....	....	....	....	....	....	....	....	....	....	....	....	....	....	....	....	....	....
1985-86	Levis-Lauzon	CEGEP	STATISTICS NOT AVAILABLE																							
1986-87	Levis-Lauzon	CEGEP	38	27	57	84	....	....	....	....	....	....	....	....	....	....	....	....	....	....	....	....	....	....	....	....
1987-88	RPI Engineers	ECAC	31	16	29	45	18	....	....	....	....	....	....	....	....	....	....	....	....	....	....	....	....	....	....	....
1988-89	RPI Engineers	ECAC	30	12	23	35	40	....	....	....	....	....	....	....	....	....	....	....	....	....	....	....	....	....	....	....
1989-90	RPI Engineers	ECAC	34	18	*52	*70	31	....	....	....	....	....	....	....	....	....	....	....	....	....	....	....	....	....	....	....
	Canada	Nat-Team	3	0	2	2	4	....	....	....	....	....	....	....	....	....	....	....	....	....	....	....	....	....	....	....
1990-91	RPI Engineers	ECAC	29	23	40	63	68	....	....	....	....	....	....	....	....	....	....	....	....	....	....	....	....	....	....	....
	Canada	Nat-Team	7	2	3	5	0	....	....	....	....	....	....	....	....	....	....	....	....	....	....	....	....	....	....	....
1991-92	Canada	Nat-Team	60	20	49	69	35	....	....	....	....	....	....	....	....	....	....	....	....	....	....	....	....	....	....	....
	Canada	Olympics	8	6	9	15	4	....	....	....	....	....	....	....	....	....	....	....	....	....	....	....	....	....	....	....
	Boston	**NHL**	**14**	**5**	**14**	**19**	**4**	**2**	**0**	**0**	**38**	**13.2**	**6**	....	....	....	....	....	**15**	**4**	**8**	**12**	**21**	**2**	**0**	**0**
1992-93	**Boston**	**NHL**	**84**	**32**	**70**	**102**	**33**	**9**	**0**	**3**	**229**	**14.0**	**23**	....	....	....	....	....	**4**	**2**	**4**	**6**	**6**	**2**	**0**	**0**
1993-94	**Boston**	**NHL**	**63**	**14**	**58**	**72**	**35**	**4**	**0**	**2**	**142**	**9.9**	**11**	....	....	....	....	....	....	....	....	....	....	....	....	....
	Washington	**NHL**	**11**	**5**	**8**	**13**	**6**	**2**	**0**	**0**	**22**	**22.7**	**0**	....	....	....	....	....	**11**	**4**	**5**	**9**	**6**	**2**	**0**	**1**
1994-95	**Washington**	**NHL**	**44**	**5**	**38**	**43**	**8**	**3**	**0**	**0**	**70**	**7.1**	**–1**	....	....	....	....	....	**7**	**2**	**6**	**8**	**2**	**0**	**0**	**0**
1995-96	**Washington**	**NHL**	**80**	**14**	**50**	**64**	**30**	**7**	**2**	**2**	**176**	**8.0**	**–3**	....	....	....	....	....	**5**	**0**	**7**	**7**	**6**	**0**	**0**	**0**
1996-97	**Washington**	**NHL**	**58**	**15**	**27**	**42**	**8**	**9**	**1**	**3**	**124**	**12.1**	**–11**	....	....	....	....	....	....	....	....	....	....	....	....	....
1997-98	**Washington**	**NHL**	**56**	**9**	**22**	**31**	**26**	**4**	**1**	**1**	**87**	**10.3**	**–8**	....	....	....	....	....	**21**	**7**	**10**	**17**	**8**	**1**	**1**	**4**
1998-99	**Washington**	**NHL**	**63**	**14**	**27**	**41**	**20**	**2**	**1**	**3**	**142**	**9.9**	**–3**	**437**	**48.1**	**34**	**26**	**19:28**	....	....	....	....	....	....	....	....
	Buffalo	**NHL**	**9**	**1**	**1**	**2**	**2**	**0**	**0**	**0**	**8**	**12.5**	**–1**	**8**	**12.5**	**3**	**2**	**17:11**	**20**	**3**	**8**	**11**	**10**	**0**	**1**	**0**
	NHL Totals		**482**	**114**	**315**	**429**	**172**	**42**	**5**	**14**	**1038**	**11.0**		**445**	**47.4**	**37**	**28**	**19:11**	**83**	**22**	**48**	**70**	**59**	**7**	**2**	**5**

NCAA East First All-American Team (1990) • ECAC Second All-Star Team (1991) • NCAA East Second All-American Team (1991) • NHL/Upper Deck All-Rookie Team (1993)

Traded to **Washington** by **Boston** for Al Iafrate, March 21, 1994. Traded to **Buffalo** by **Washington** with Washington's 3rd round choice (Tim Preston) in 1999 Entry Draft for Alexei Tezikov and future considerations, March 22, 1999.

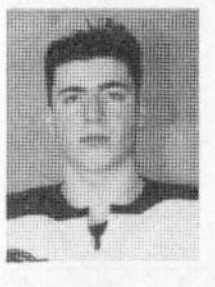

KABERLE, Tomas (ka-buhr-LAY) TOR.

Defense. Shoots left. 6'2", 200 lbs. Born, Rakovnik, Czech., March 2, 1978. Toronto's 13th choice, 204th overall, in 1996 Entry Draft.

Season	Club	League	GP	G	A	Pts	PIM	PP	SH	GW	S	%	+/–	TF	F%	H	SB	Min	GP	G	A	Pts	PIM	PP	SH	GW
1995-96	Poldi Kladno	Czech-Jr.	23	6	13	19		....	....	....	....	....	....	....	....	....	....	....	....	....	....	....	....	....	....	....
	Poldi Kladno	Cze-Rep	23	0	1	1	2	....	....	....	....	....	....	....	....	....	....	....	2	0	0	0	0	....	....	....
1996-97	Poldi Kladno	Cze-Rep	49	0	5	5	26	....	....	....	....	....	....	....	....	....	....	....	3	0	0	0	0	....	....	....
1997-98	Poldi Kladno	Cze-Rep	47	4	19	23	12	....	....	....	....	....	....	....	....	....	....	....	....	....	....	....	....	....	....	....
	St. John's	AHL	2	0	0	0	0	....	....	....	....	....	....	....	....	....	....	....	....	....	....	....	....	....	....	....
1998-99	**Toronto**	**NHL**	**57**	**4**	**18**	**22**	**12**	**0**	**0**	**2**	**71**	**5.6**	**3**	**0**	**0.0**	**27**	**46**	**18:42**	**14**	**0**	**3**	**3**	**2**	**0**	**0**	**0**
	NHL Totals		**57**	**4**	**18**	**22**	**12**	**0**	**0**	**2**	**71**	**5.6**		**0**	**0.0**	**27**	**46**	**18:42**	**14**	**0**	**3**	**3**	**2**	**0**	**0**	**0**

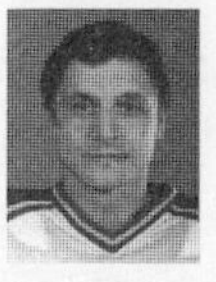

KAMENSKY, Valeri (kah-MEHN-skee) NYR

Left wing. Shoots right. 6'2", 198 lbs. Born, Voskresensk, USSR, April 18, 1966. Quebec's 8th choice, 129th overall, in 1988 Entry Draft.

Season	Club	League	GP	G	A	Pts	PIM	PP	SH	GW	S	%	+/–	TF	F%	H	SB	Min	GP	G	A	Pts	PIM	PP	SH	GW
1982-83	Khimik	USSR	5	0	0	0	0	....	....	....	....	....	....	....	....	....	....	....	....	....	....	....	....	....	....	....
1983-84	Khimik	USSR	20	2	2	4	6	....	....	....	....	....	....	....	....	....	....	....	....	....	....	....	....	....	....	....
1984-85	Khimik	USSR	45	9	3	12	24	....	....	....	....	....	....	....	....	....	....	....	....	....	....	....	....	....	....	....
1985-86	CSKA Moscow	USSR	40	15	9	24	8	....	....	....	....	....	....	....	....	....	....	....	....	....	....	....	....	....	....	....
1986-87	CSKA Moscow	USSR	37	13	8	21	16	....	....	....	....	....	....	....	....	....	....	....	....	....	....	....	....	....	....	....
1987-88	CSKA Moscow	USSR	51	26	20	46	40	....	....	....	....	....	....	....	....	....	....	....	....	....	....	....	....	....	....	....
	Soviet Union	Olympics	8	4	2	6	4	....	....	....	....	....	....	....	....	....	....	....	....	....	....	....	....	....	....	....

			Regular Season																Playoffs							
Season	Club	League	GP	G	A	Pts	PIM	PP	SH	GW	S	%	+/-	TF	F%	H	SB	Min	GP	G	A	Pts	PIM	PP	SH	GW
1988-89	CSKA Moscow	USSR	40	18	10	28	30																			
1989-90	CSKA Moscow	USSR	45	19	18	37	40																			
1990-91	CSKA Moscow	USSR	46	20	26	46	66																			
1991-92	**Quebec**	**NHL**	**23**	**7**	**14**	**21**	**14**	**2**	**0**	**1**	**42**	**16.7**	**-1**													
1992-93	**Quebec**	**NHL**	**32**	**15**	**22**	**37**	**14**	**2**	**3**	**0**	**94**	**16.0**	**13**						**6**	**0**	**1**	**1**	**6**	**0**	**0**	**0**
1993-94	**Quebec**	**NHL**	**76**	**28**	**37**	**65**	**42**	**6**	**0**	**1**	**170**	**16.5**	**12**													
1994-95	Ambri Piotta	Switz.	12	13	6	19	2																			
	Quebec	**NHL**	**40**	**10**	**20**	**30**	**22**	**5**	**1**	**5**	**70**	**14.3**	**3**						**2**	**1**	**0**	**1**	**0**	**0**	**0**	**0**
1995-96♦	**Colorado**	**NHL**	**81**	**38**	**47**	**85**	**85**	**18**	**1**	**5**	**220**	**17.3**	**14**						**22**	**10**	**12**	**22**	**28**	**3**	**0**	**2**
1996-97	**Colorado**	**NHL**	**68**	**28**	**38**	**66**	**38**	**8**	**0**	**4**	**165**	**17.0**	**5**						**17**	**8**	**14**	**22**	**16**	**5**	**0**	**2**
1997-98	**Colorado**	**NHL**	**75**	**26**	**40**	**66**	**60**	**8**	**0**	**4**	**173**	**15.0**	**-2**						**7**	**2**	**3**	**5**	**18**	**1**	**0**	**0**
	Russia	Olympics	6	1	2	3	0																			
1998-99	**Colorado**	**NHL**	**65**	**14**	**30**	**44**	**28**	**2**	**0**	**2**	**123**	**11.4**	**1**	**4**	**25.0**	**32**	**9**	**17:35**	**10**	**4**	**5**	**9**	**4**	**1**	**0**	**1**
	NHL Totals		**460**	**166**	**248**	**414**	**303**	**51**	**5**	**22**	**1057**	**15.7**		**4**	**25.0**	**32**	**9**	**17:35**	**64**	**25**	**35**	**60**	**72**	**10**	**0**	**5**

USSR First All-Star Team (1990, 1991) • USSR Player of the Year (1991)
Played in NHL All-Star Game (1998)
Transferred to **Colorado** after **Quebec** franchise relocated, June 21, 1995. Signed as a free agent by **NY Rangers**, July 7, 1999.

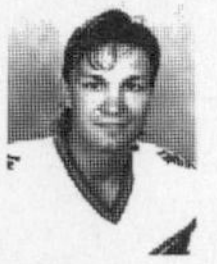

KAMINSKI, Kevin
(kah-MIHN-skee)

Center. Shoots left. 5'10", 190 lbs. Born, Churchbridge, Sask., March 13, 1969. Minnesota's 3rd choice, 48th overall, in 1987 Entry Draft.

1985-86	Saskatoon	SAHA	32	39	64	103	106																			
	Saskatoon	WHL	4	1	1	2	35																			
1986-87	Saskatoon	WHL	67	26	44	70	325												11	5	6	11	45			
1987-88	Saskatoon	WHL	55	38	61	99	247												10	5	7	12	37			
1988-89	Saskatoon	WHL	52	25	43	68	199												8	4	9	13	25			
	Minnesota	**NHL**	**1**	**0**	**0**	**0**	**0**	**0**	**0**	**0**	**0**	**0.0**	**0**													
1989-90	**Quebec**	**NHL**	**1**	**0**	**0**	**0**	**0**	**0**	**0**	**0**	**0**	**0.0**	**-1**													
	Halifax	AHL	19	3	4	7	128												2	0	0	0	5			
1990-91	Halifax	AHL	7	1	0	1	44																			
	Fort Wayne	IHL	56	9	15	24	*455												19	4	2	6	*169			
1991-92	**Quebec**	**NHL**	**5**	**0**	**0**	**0**	**45**	**0**	**0**	**0**	**6**	**0.0**	**-2**													
	Halifax	AHL	63	18	27	45	329																			
1992-93	Halifax	AHL	79	27	37	64	*345																			
1993-94	**Washington**	**NHL**	**13**	**0**	**5**	**5**	**87**	**0**	**0**	**0**	**9**	**0.0**	**2**													
	Portland	AHL	39	10	22	32	263												16	4	5	9	*91			
1994-95	**Washington**	**NHL**	**27**	**1**	**1**	**2**	**102**	**0**	**0**	**1**	**12**	**8.3**	**-6**						**5**	**0**	**0**	**0**	**36**	**0**	**0**	**0**
	Portland	AHL	34	15	20	35	292																			
1995-96	**Washington**	**NHL**	**54**	**1**	**2**	**3**	**164**	**0**	**0**	**0**	**17**	**5.9**	**-1**						**3**	**0**	**0**	**0**	**16**	**0**	**0**	**0**
1996-97	**Washington**	**NHL**	**38**	**1**	**2**	**3**	**130**	**0**	**0**	**0**	**12**	**8.3**	**0**													
1997-98	Portland	AHL	40	8	12	20	242												8	2	1	3	69			
1998-99	Las Vegas	IHL	39	7	10	17	217																			
	NHL Totals		**139**	**3**	**10**	**13**	**528**	**0**	**0**	**1**	**56**	**5.4**							**8**	**0**	**0**	**0**	**52**	**0**	**0**	**0**

Traded to **Quebec** by **Minnesota** for Gaetan Duchesne, June 19, 1989. Traded to **Washington** by **Quebec** for Mark Matier, June 15, 1993. Signed as a free agent by **Las Vegas** (IHL), September 4, 1999.

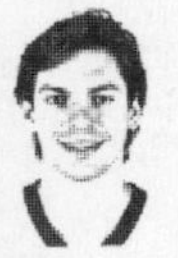

KAMINSKY, Yan
(kah-MIHN-skee)

Right wing. Shoots left. 6'1", 176 lbs. Born, Penza, USSR, July 28, 1971. Winnipeg's 4th choice, 99th overall, in 1991 Entry Draft.

1989-90	Moscow D'amo	USSR	6	1	0	1	4																			
1990-91	Moscow D'amo	USSR	25	10	5	15	2																			
1991-92	Moscow D'amo	CIS	42	9	7	16	22																			
1992-93	Moscow D'amo	CIS	39	15	14	29	12												10	2	5	7	8			
1993-94	**Winnipeg**	**NHL**	**1**	**0**	**0**	**0**	**0**	**0**	**0**	**0**	**0**	**0.0**	**1**													
	Moncton	AHL	33	9	13	22	6																			
	NY Islanders	**NHL**	**23**	**2**	**1**	**3**	**4**	**0**	**0**	**0**	**23**	**8.7**	**4**						**2**	**0**	**0**	**0**	**4**	**0**	**0**	**0**
1994-95	Denver	IHL	38	17	16	33	14												15	6	6	12	0			
	NY Islanders	**NHL**	**2**	**1**	**1**	**2**	**0**	**0**	**0**	**0**	**4**	**25.0**	**2**													
1995-96	Utah	IHL	16	3	3	6	8												21	3	5	8	4			
1996-97	Utah	IHL	77	28	27	55	18												7	1	4	5	0			
1997-98	Lukko Rauma	Finland	38	5	8	13	33																			
1998-99	Utah	IHL	56	11	17	28	12																			
	Grand Rapids	IHL	7	0	2	2	0																			
	NHL Totals		**26**	**3**	**2**	**5**	**4**	**0**	**0**	**0**	**27**	**11.1**							**2**	**0**	**0**	**0**	**4**	**0**	**0**	**0**

Traded to **NY Islanders** by **Winnipeg** for Wayne McBean, February 1, 1994.

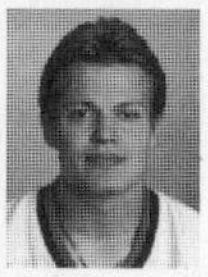

KAPANEN, Sami
(KA-pah-nehn) **CAR.**

Left wing. Shoots left. 5'10", 170 lbs. Born, Vantaa, Finland, June 14, 1973. Hartford's 4th choice, 87th overall, in 1995 Entry Draft.

1989-90	KalPa Kuopio	Finn-Jr.	30	14	13	27	4																			
1990-91	KalPa Kuopio	Finn-Jr.	31	9	27	36	10																			
	KalPa Kuopio	Finland	14	1	2	3	2												8	2	1	3	2			
1991-92	KalPa Kuopio	Finn-Jr.	8	1	3	4	12																			
	KalPa Kuopio	Finland	42	15	10	25	8																			
1992-93	KalPa Kuopio	Finland	37	4	17	21	12																			
1993-94	KalPa Kuopio	Finland	48	23	32	55	16																			
	Finland	Nat-Team	20	9	3	12	0																			
	Finland	Olympics	8	1	0	1	2																			
1994-95	HIFK Helsinki	Finland	49	14	28	42	42												3	0	0	0	0			
	Finland	Nat-Team	19	3	1	4	8																			
1995-96	**Hartford**	**NHL**	**35**	**5**	**4**	**9**	**6**	**0**	**0**	**0**	**46**	**10.9**	**0**													
	Springfield	AHL	28	14	17	31	4												3	1	2	3	0			
	Finland	Nat-Team	2	0	1	1	0																			
1996-97	**Hartford**	**NHL**	**45**	**13**	**12**	**25**	**2**	**3**	**0**	**2**	**82**	**15.9**	**6**													
	Finland	Nat-Team	4	1	0	1	4																			
1997-98	**Carolina**	**NHL**	**81**	**26**	**37**	**63**	**16**	**4**	**0**	**5**	**190**	**13.7**	**9**													
	Finland	Olympics	6	0	1	1	0																			
1998-99	**Carolina**	**NHL**	**81**	**24**	**35**	**59**	**10**	**5**	**0**	**7**	**254**	**9.4**	**-1**	**10**	**50.0**	**123**	**28**	**19:25**	**5**	**1**	**1**	**2**	**0**	**0**	**0**	**0**
	NHL Totals		**242**	**68**	**88**	**156**	**34**	**12**	**0**	**14**	**572**	**11.9**		**10**	**50.0**	**123**	**28**	**19:25**	**5**	**1**	**1**	**2**	**0**	**0**	**0**	**0**

Finnish First All-Star Team (1994)
Transferred to **Carolina** after **Hartford** franchise relocated, June 25, 1997.

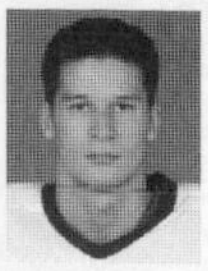

KARIYA, Paul
(kah-REE-ah) **ANA.**

Left wing. Shoots left. 5'11", 180 lbs. Born, Vancouver, B.C., October 16, 1974. Anaheim's 1st choice, 4th overall, in 1993 Entry Draft.

1990-91	Penticton	BCJHL	54	45	67	112	8																			
1991-92	Penticton	BCJHL	40	46	86	132	18																			
1992-93	U. of Maine	H.E.	39	25	*75	*100	12																			
1993-94	U. of Maine	H.E.	12	8	16	24	4																			
	Canada	Nat-Team	23	7	34	41	2																			
	Canada	Olympics	8	3	4	7	2																			
1994-95	**Anaheim**	**NHL**	**47**	**18**	**21**	**39**	**4**	**7**	**1**	**3**	**134**	**13.4**	**-17**													

			Regular Season																Playoffs							
Season	Club	League	GP	G	A	Pts	PIM	PP	SH	GW	S	%	+/-	TF	F%	H	SB	Min	GP	G	A	Pts	PIM	PP	SH	GW
1995-96	**Anaheim**	**NHL**	**82**	**50**	**58**	**108**	**20**	**20**	**3**	**9**	**349**	**14.3**	**9**	....	....	....	....	....	....	....	....	....	....	....	....	....
1996-97	**Anaheim**	**NHL**	**69**	**44**	**55**	**99**	**6**	**15**	**3**	**10**	**340**	**12.9**	**36**	....	....	....	....	....	**11**	**7**	**6**	**13**	**4**	**4**	**0**	**1**
1997-98	**Anaheim**	**NHL**	**22**	**17**	**14**	**31**	**23**	**3**	**0**	**2**	**103**	**16.5**	**12**	....	....	....	....	....	....	....	....	....	....	....	....	....
1998-99	**Anaheim**	**NHL**	**82**	**39**	**62**	**101**	**40**	**11**	**2**	**4**	**429**	**9.1**	**17**	**91**	**48.4**	**35**	**65**	**25:32**	**3**	**1**	**3**	**4**	**0**	**0**	**0**	**0**
	NHL Totals		**302**	**168**	**210**	**378**	**93**	**56**	**9**	**28**	**1355**	**12.4**		**91**	**48.4**	**35**	**65**	**25:32**	**14**	**8**	**9**	**17**	**4**	**4**	**0**	**1**

• Hockey East First All-Star Team (1993) • NCAA East First All-American Team (1993) • NCAA Championship All-Tournament Team (1993) • Won Hobey Baker Memorial Award (Top U.S. Collegiate Player) (1993) • NHL/Upper Deck All-Rookie Team (1995) • NHL First All-Star Team (1996, 1997) • Won Lady Byng Trophy (1996, 1997) • NHL First All-Star Team (1999)

Played in NHL All-Star Game (1996, 1997, 1999)

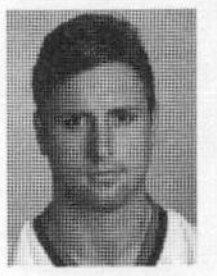

KARPA, Dave (KAHR-puh) CAR.

Defense. Shoots right. 6'1", 210 lbs. Born, Regina, Sask., May 7, 1971. Quebec's 4th choice, 68th overall, in 1991 Entry Draft.

Season	Club	League	GP	G	A	Pts	PIM	PP	SH	GW	S	%	+/-	TF	F%	H	SB	Min	GP	G	A	Pts	PIM	PP	SH	GW
1988-89	Notre Dame	SAHA	41	16	37	53	....	....	....	....	....	....	....	....	....	....	....	....	....	....	....	....	....	....	....	....
1989-90	Notre Dame	SJHL	43	9	19	28	271	....	....	....	....	....	....	....	....	....	....	....	....	....	....	....	....	....	....	....
1990-91	Ferris State	CCHA	41	6	19	25	109	....	....	....	....	....	....	....	....	....	....	....	....	....	....	....	....	....	....	....
1991-92	Ferris State	CCHA	34	7	12	19	124	....	....	....	....	....	....	....	....	....	....	....	....	....	....	....	....	....	....	....
	Quebec	**NHL**	**4**	**0**	**0**	**0**	**14**	**0**	**0**	**0**	**2**	**0.0**	**2**	....	....	....	....	....	....	....	....	....	....	....	....	....
	Halifax	AHL	2	0	0	0	4	....	....	....	....	....	....	....	....	....	....	....	....	....	....	....	....	....	....	....
1992-93	**Quebec**	**NHL**	**12**	**0**	**1**	**1**	**13**	**0**	**0**	**0**	**2**	**0.0**	**-6**	....	....	....	....	....	**3**	**0**	**0**	**0**	**0**	**0**	**0**	**0**
	Halifax	AHL	71	4	27	31	167	....	....	....	....	....	....	....	....	....	....	....	....	....	....	....	....	....	....	....
1993-94	**Quebec**	**NHL**	**60**	**5**	**12**	**17**	**148**	**2**	**0**	**0**	**48**	**10.4**	**0**	....	....	....	....	....	....	....	....	....	....	....	....	....
	Cornwall	AHL	1	0	0	0	0	....	....	....	....	....	....	....	....	....	....	....	12	2	2	4	27	....	....	....
1994-95	**Quebec**	**NHL**	**2**	**0**	**0**	**0**	**0**	**0**	**0**	**0**	**1**	**0.0**	**-1**	....	....	....	....	....	....	....	....	....	....	....	....	....
	Cornwall	AHL	6	0	2	2	19	....	....	....	....	....	....	....	....	....	....	....	....	....	....	....	....	....	....	....
	Anaheim	**NHL**	**26**	**1**	**5**	**6**	**91**	**0**	**0**	**0**	**32**	**3.1**	**0**	....	....	....	....	....	....	....	....	....	....	....	....	....
1995-96	**Anaheim**	**NHL**	**72**	**3**	**16**	**19**	**270**	**0**	**1**	**1**	**62**	**4.8**	**-3**	....	....	....	....	....	....	....	....	....	....	....	....	....
1996-97	**Anaheim**	**NHL**	**69**	**2**	**11**	**13**	**210**	**0**	**0**	**1**	**90**	**2.2**	**11**	....	....	....	....	....	**8**	**1**	**1**	**2**	**20**	**0**	**0**	**1**
1997-98	**Anaheim**	**NHL**	**78**	**1**	**11**	**12**	**217**	**0**	**0**	**0**	**64**	**1.6**	**-3**	....	....	....	....	....	....	....	....	....	....	....	....	....
1998-99	**Carolina**	**NHL**	**33**	**0**	**2**	**2**	**55**	**0**	**0**	**0**	**21**	**0.0**	**1**	**0**	**0.0**	**62**	**45**	**16:55**	**2**	**0**	**0**	**0**	**2**	**0**	**0**	**0**
	NHL Totals		**356**	**12**	**58**	**70**	**1018**	**2**	**1**	**2**	**322**	**3.7**		**0**	**0.0**	**62**	**45**	**16:55**	**13**	**1**	**1**	**2**	**22**	**0**	**0**	**1**

Traded to **Anaheim** by **Quebec** for Anaheim's 4th round choice (later traded to St. Louis — St. Louis selected Jan Horacek) in 1997 Entry Draft, March 9, 1995. Traded to **Carolina** by **Anaheim** with a 4th round choice in 2000 Entry Draft for Stu Grimson and Kevin Haller, August 11, 1998.

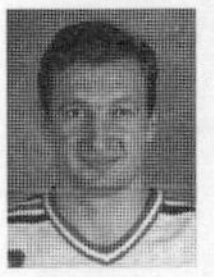

KARPOVTSEV, Alexander (kar-POHV-tzehv) TOR.

Defense. Shoots right. 6'1", 205 lbs. Born, Moscow, USSR, April 7, 1970. Quebec's 7th choice, 158th overall, in 1990 Entry Draft.

Season	Club	League	GP	G	A	Pts	PIM	PP	SH	GW	S	%	+/-	TF	F%	H	SB	Min	GP	G	A	Pts	PIM	PP	SH	GW
1989-90	Moscow D'amo	USSR	35	1	1	2	27	....	....	....	....	....	....	....	....	....	....	....	....	....	....	....	....	....	....	....
1990-91	Moscow D'amo	USSR	40	0	5	5	15	....	....	....	....	....	....	....	....	....	....	....	....	....	....	....	....	....	....	....
1991-92	Moscow D'amo	CIS	35	4	2	6	26	....	....	....	....	....	....	....	....	....	....	....	....	....	....	....	....	....	....	....
1992-93	Moscow D'amo	CIS	36	3	11	14	100	....	....	....	....	....	....	....	....	....	....	....	7	2	1	3	0	....	....	....
1993-94♦	**NY Rangers**	**NHL**	**67**	**3**	**15**	**18**	**58**	**1**	**0**	**1**	**78**	**3.8**	**12**	....	....	....	....	....	**17**	**0**	**4**	**4**	**12**	**0**	**0**	**0**
1994-95	Moscow D'amo	CIS	13	0	2	2	10	....	....	....	....	....	....	....	....	....	....	....	....	....	....	....	....	....	....	....
	NY Rangers	**NHL**	**47**	**4**	**8**	**12**	**30**	**1**	**0**	**1**	**82**	**4.9**	**-4**	....	....	....	....	....	**8**	**1**	**0**	**1**	**0**	**0**	**0**	**0**
1995-96	**NY Rangers**	**NHL**	**40**	**2**	**16**	**18**	**26**	**1**	**0**	**1**	**71**	**2.8**	**12**	....	....	....	....	....	**6**	**0**	**1**	**1**	**4**	**0**	**0**	**0**
1996-97	**NY Rangers**	**NHL**	**77**	**9**	**29**	**38**	**59**	**6**	**1**	**0**	**84**	**10.7**	**1**	....	....	....	....	....	**13**	**1**	**3**	**4**	**20**	**1**	**0**	**0**
1997-98	**NY Rangers**	**NHL**	**47**	**3**	**7**	**10**	**38**	**1**	**0**	**1**	**46**	**6.5**	**-1**	....	....	....	....	....	....	....	....	....	....	....	....	....
1998-99	**NY Rangers**	**NHL**	**2**	**1**	**0**	**1**	**0**	**0**	**0**	**0**	**4**	**25.0**	**1**	**0**	**0.0**	**2**	**3**	**22:38**	....	....	....	....	....	....	....	....
	Toronto	**NHL**	**56**	**2**	**25**	**27**	**52**	**1**	**0**	**1**	**61**	**3.3**	**38**	**0**	**0.0**	**79**	**103**	**20:58**	**14**	**1**	**3**	**4**	**12**	**1**	**0**	**0**
	NHL Totals		**336**	**24**	**100**	**124**	**263**	**11**	**1**	**5**	**426**	**5.6**		**0**	**0.0**	**81**	**106**	**21:01**	**58**	**3**	**11**	**14**	**48**	**2**	**0**	**0**

Traded to **NY Rangers** by **Quebec** for Mike Hurlbut, September 7, 1993. Traded to **Toronto** by **NY Rangers** with NY Rangers' 4th round choice (Mirko Murovic) in 1999 Entry Draft for Mathieu Schneider, October 14, 1998.

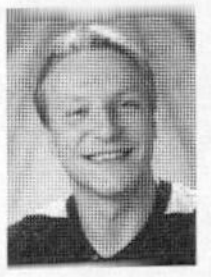

KASPARAITIS, Darius (KAZ-puhr-IGH-tihz) PIT.

Defense. Shoots left. 5'11", 212 lbs. Born, Elektrenai, USSR, October 16, 1972. NY Islanders' 1st choice, 5th overall, in 1992 Entry Draft.

Season	Club	League	GP	G	A	Pts	PIM	PP	SH	GW	S	%	+/-	TF	F%	H	SB	Min	GP	G	A	Pts	PIM	PP	SH	GW
1988-89	Moscow D'amo	USSR	3	0	0	0	0	....	....	....	....	....	....	....	....	....	....	....	....	....	....	....	....	....	....	....
1989-90	Moscow D'amo	USSR	1	0	0	0	0	....	....	....	....	....	....	....	....	....	....	....	....	....	....	....	....	....	....	....
1990-91	Moscow D'amo	USSR	17	0	1	1	10	....	....	....	....	....	....	....	....	....	....	....	....	....	....	....	....	....	....	....
1991-92	Moscow D'amo	CIS	31	2	10	12	14	....	....	....	....	....	....	....	....	....	....	....	....	....	....	....	....	....	....	....
1992-93	Moscow D'amo	CIS	7	1	3	4	8	....	....	....	....	....	....	....	....	....	....	....	....	....	....	....	....	....	....	....
	NY Islanders	**NHL**	**79**	**4**	**17**	**21**	**166**	**0**	**0**	**0**	**92**	**4.3**	**15**	....	....	....	....	....	**18**	**0**	**5**	**5**	**31**	**0**	**0**	**0**
1993-94	**NY Islanders**	**NHL**	**76**	**1**	**10**	**11**	**142**	**0**	**0**	**0**	**81**	**1.2**	**-6**	....	....	....	....	....	**4**	**0**	**0**	**0**	**8**	**0**	**0**	**0**
1994-95	**NY Islanders**	**NHL**	**13**	**0**	**1**	**1**	**22**	**0**	**0**	**0**	**8**	**0.0**	**-11**	....	....	....	....	....	....	....	....	....	....	....	....	....
1995-96	**NY Islanders**	**NHL**	**46**	**1**	**7**	**8**	**93**	**0**	**0**	**0**	**34**	**2.9**	**-12**	....	....	....	....	....	....	....	....	....	....	....	....	....
1996-97	**NY Islanders**	**NHL**	**18**	**0**	**5**	**5**	**16**	**0**	**0**	**0**	**12**	**0.0**	**-7**	....	....	....	....	....	....	....	....	....	....	....	....	....
	Pittsburgh	**NHL**	**57**	**2**	**16**	**18**	**84**	**0**	**0**	**0**	**46**	**4.3**	**24**	....	....	....	....	....	**5**	**0**	**0**	**0**	**6**	**0**	**0**	**0**
1997-98	**Pittsburgh**	**NHL**	**81**	**4**	**8**	**12**	**127**	**0**	**2**	**0**	**71**	**5.6**	**3**	....	....	....	....	....	**5**	**0**	**0**	**0**	**8**	**0**	**0**	**0**
	Russia	Olympics	6	0	2	2	6	....	....	....	....	....	....	....	....	....	....	....	....	....	....	....	....	....	....	....
1998-99	**Pittsburgh**	**NHL**	**48**	**1**	**4**	**5**	**70**	**0**	**0**	**0**	**32**	**3.1**	**12**	**0**	**0.0**	**173**	**48**	**16:01**	....	....	....	....	....	....	....	....
	NHL Totals		**418**	**13**	**68**	**81**	**720**	**0**	**2**	**0**	**376**	**3.5**		**0**	**0.0**	**173**	**48**	**16:01**	**32**	**0**	**5**	**5**	**53**	**0**	**0**	**0**

Traded to **Pittsburgh** by **NY Islanders** with Andreas Johansson for Bryan Smolinski, November 17, 1996.

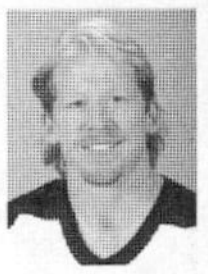

KEANE, Mike (KEEN) DAL.

Right wing. Shoots right. 6', 185 lbs. Born, Winnipeg, Man., May 29, 1967.

Season	Club	League	GP	G	A	Pts	PIM	PP	SH	GW	S	%	+/-	TF	F%	H	SB	Min	GP	G	A	Pts	PIM	PP	SH	GW
1983-84	Winnipeg Blues	MJHL	STATISTICS NOT AVAILABLE																							
	Winnipeg	WHL	1	0	0	0	0	....	....	....	....	....	....	....	....	....	....	....	....	....	....	....	....	....	....	....
1984-85	Moose Jaw	WHL	65	17	26	43	141	....	....	....	....	....	....	....	....	....	....	....	....	....	....	....	....	....	....	....
1985-86	Moose Jaw	WHL	67	34	49	83	162	....	....	....	....	....	....	....	....	....	....	....	13	6	8	14	9	....	....	....
1986-87	Moose Jaw	WHL	53	25	45	70	107	....	....	....	....	....	....	....	....	....	....	....	9	3	9	12	11	....	....	....
	Sherbrooke	AHL	....	....	....	....	....	....	....	....	....	....	....	....	....	....	....	....	9	2	2	4	16	....	....	....
1987-88	Sherbrooke	AHL	78	25	43	68	70	....	....	....	....	....	....	....	....	....	....	....	6	1	1	2	18	....	....	....
1988-89	**Montreal**	**NHL**	**69**	**16**	**19**	**35**	**69**	**5**	**0**	**1**	**90**	**17.8**	**9**	....	....	....	....	....	**21**	**4**	**3**	**7**	**17**	**2**	**0**	**0**
1989-90	**Montreal**	**NHL**	**74**	**9**	**15**	**24**	**78**	**1**	**0**	**1**	**92**	**9.8**	**0**	....	....	....	....	....	**11**	**0**	**1**	**1**	**8**	**0**	**0**	**0**
1990-91	**Montreal**	**NHL**	**73**	**13**	**23**	**36**	**50**	**2**	**1**	**2**	**109**	**11.9**	**6**	....	....	....	....	....	**12**	**3**	**2**	**5**	**6**	**0**	**0**	**0**
1991-92	**Montreal**	**NHL**	**67**	**11**	**30**	**41**	**64**	**2**	**0**	**2**	**116**	**9.5**	**16**	....	....	....	....	....	**8**	**1**	**1**	**2**	**16**	**0**	**0**	**0**
1992-93♦	**Montreal**	**NHL**	**77**	**15**	**45**	**60**	**95**	**0**	**0**	**1**	**120**	**12.5**	**29**	....	....	....	....	....	**19**	**2**	**13**	**15**	**6**	**0**	**0**	**0**
1993-94	**Montreal**	**NHL**	**80**	**16**	**30**	**46**	**119**	**6**	**2**	**2**	**129**	**12.4**	**6**	....	....	....	....	....	**6**	**3**	**1**	**4**	**4**	**0**	**0**	**0**
1994-95	**Montreal**	**NHL**	**48**	**10**	**10**	**20**	**15**	**1**	**0**	**0**	**75**	**13.3**	**5**	....	....	....	....	....	....	....	....	....	....	....	....	....
1995-96	**Montreal**	**NHL**	**18**	**0**	**7**	**7**	**6**	**0**	**0**	**0**	**17**	**0.0**	**-6**	....	....	....	....	....	....	....	....	....	....	....	....	....
♦	**Colorado**	**NHL**	**55**	**10**	**10**	**20**	**40**	**0**	**2**	**2**	**67**	**14.9**	**1**	....	....	....	....	....	**22**	**3**	**2**	**5**	**16**	**0**	**0**	**1**
1996-97	**Colorado**	**NHL**	**81**	**10**	**17**	**27**	**63**	**0**	**1**	**1**	**91**	**11.0**	**2**	....	....	....	....	....	**17**	**3**	**1**	**4**	**24**	**0**	**0**	**1**
1997-98	**NY Rangers**	**NHL**	**70**	**8**	**10**	**18**	**47**	**2**	**0**	**0**	**113**	**7.1**	**-12**	....	....	....	....	....	....	....	....	....	....	....	....	....
	Dallas	**NHL**	**13**	**2**	**3**	**5**	**5**	**0**	**0**	**1**	**15**	**13.3**	**0**	....	....	....	....	....	**17**	**4**	**4**	**8**	**0**	**0**	**1**	**1**
1998-99♦	**Dallas**	**NHL**	**81**	**6**	**23**	**29**	**62**	**1**	**1**	**1**	**106**	**5.7**	**-2**	**11**	**27.3**	**126**	**36**	**13:57**	**23**	**5**	**2**	**7**	**6**	**0**	**1**	**1**
	NHL Totals		**806**	**126**	**242**	**368**	**713**	**20**	**7**	**14**	**1140**	**11.1**		**11**	**27.3**	**126**	**36**	**13:57**	**156**	**28**	**30**	**58**	**103**	**2**	**2**	**4**

Signed as a free agent by **Montreal**, September 25, 1985. Traded to **Colorado** by **Montreal** with Patrick Roy for Andrei Kovalenko, Martin Rucinsky and Jocelyn Thibault, December 6, 1995. Signed as a free agent by **NY Rangers**, July 30, 1997. Traded to **Dallas** by **NY Rangers** with Brian Skrudland and NY Rangers' 6th round choice (Pavel Patera) in 1998 Entry Draft for Todd Harvey, Bob Errey and Dallas' 4th round choice (Boyd Kane) in 1998 Entry Draft, March 24, 1998.

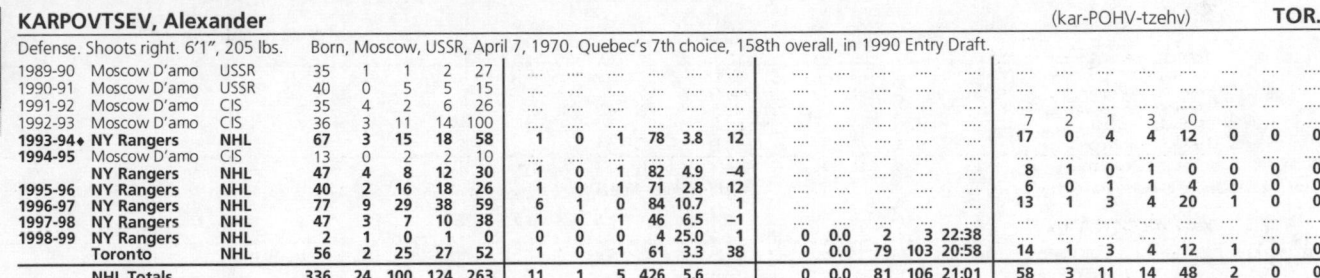

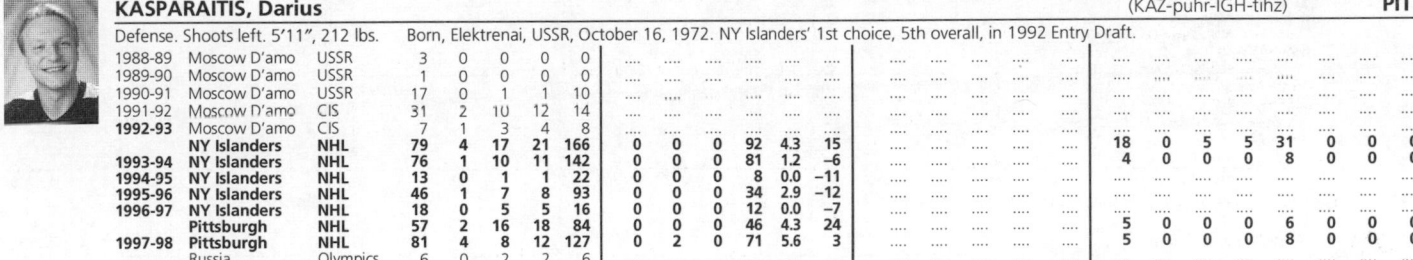

KECZMER, Dan (KEHS-muhr) NSH.

Defense. Shoots left. 6'1", 190 lbs. Born, Mt. Clemens, MI, May 25, 1968. Minnesota's 11th choice, 201st overall, in 1986 Entry Draft.

			Regular Season																Playoffs							
Season	Club	League	GP	G	A	Pts	PIM	PP	SH	GW	S	%	+/-	TF	F%	H	SB	Min	GP	G	A	Pts	PIM	PP	SH	GW
1985-86	Detroit	MNHL	65	6	48	54	116																			
1986-87	Lake Superior	CCHA	38	3	5	8	26																			
1987-88	Lake Superior	CCHA	41	2	15	17	34																			
1988-89	Lake Superior	CCHA	46	3	26	29	68																			
1989-90	Lake Superior	CCHA	43	13	23	36	48																			
1990-91	**Minnesota**	**NHL**	**9**	**0**	**1**	**1**	**6**	**0**	**0**	**0**	**6**	**0.0**	**0**													
	Kalamazoo	IHL	60	4	20	24	60												9	1	2	3	10			
1991-92	United States	Nat-Team	51	3	11	14	56																			
	Hartford	**NHL**	**1**	**0**	**0**	**0**	**0**	**0**	**0**	**0**	**2**	**0.0**	**–1**													
	Springfield	AHL	18	3	4	7	10												4	0	0	0	6			
1992-93	**Hartford**	**NHL**	**23**	**4**	**4**	**8**	**28**	**2**	**0**	**1**	**38**	**10.5**	**–3**													
	Springfield	AHL	37	1	13	14	38												12	0	4	4	14			
1993-94	**Hartford**	**NHL**	**12**	**0**	**1**	**1**	**12**	**0**	**0**	**0**	**12**	**0.0**	**–6**													
	Springfield	AHL	7	0	1	1	4																			
	Calgary	**NHL**	**57**	**1**	**20**	**21**	**48**	**0**	**0**	**0**	**104**	**1.0**	**–2**						**3**	**0**	**0**	**0**	**4**	**0**	**0**	**0**
1994-95	**Calgary**	**NHL**	**28**	**2**	**3**	**5**	**10**	**0**	**0**	**0**	**33**	**6.1**	**7**						**7**	**0**	**1**	**1**	**2**	**0**	**0**	**0**
1995-96	**Calgary**	**NHL**	**13**	**0**	**0**	**0**	**14**	**0**	**0**	**0**	**13**	**0.0**	**–6**													
	Saint John	AHL	22	3	11	14	14																			
	Albany	AHL	17	0	4	4	4												1	0	0	0	0			
1996-97	**Dallas**	**NHL**	**13**	**0**	**1**	**1**	**6**	**0**	**0**	**0**	**10**	**0.0**	**3**													
	Michigan	IHL	42	3	17	20	24																			
1997-98	**Dallas**	**NHL**	**17**	**1**	**2**	**3**	**26**	**0**	**0**	**0**	**9**	**11.1**	**5**						**2**	**0**	**0**	**0**	**2**	**0**	**0**	**0**
	Michigan	IHL	44	1	11	12	29																			
1998-99	**Dallas**	**NHL**	**22**	**0**	**1**	**1**	**22**	**0**	**0**	**0**	**12**	**0.0**	**–2**	**1**	**100.0**	**28**	**1**	**7:08**								
	Michigan	IHL	5	0	1	1	2																			
	Nashville	**NHL**	**16**	**0**	**0**	**0**	**12**	**0**	**0**	**0**	**12**	**0.0**	**–3**	**0**	**0.0**	**21**	**22**	**16:20**								
	NHL Totals		**211**	**8**	**33**	**41**	**184**	**2**	**0**	**1**	**251**	**3.2**		**1**	**100.0**	**49**	**23**	**11:00**	**12**	**0**	**1**	**1**	**8**	**0**	**0**	**0**

CCHA Second All-Star Team (1990)

Claimed by **San Jose** from **Minnesota** in Dispersal Draft, May 30, 1991. Traded to **Hartford** by **San Jose** for Dean Evason, October 2, 1991. Traded to **Calgary** by **Hartford** for Jeff Reese, November 19, 1993. Traded to **New Jersey** by **Calgary** with Phil Housley for Tommy Albelin, Cale Hulse and Jocelyn Lemieux, February 26, 1996. Signed as a free agent by **Dallas**, August 19, 1996. Claimed on waivers by **Nashville** from **Dallas**, March 12, 1999.

KELLY, Steve T.B.

Center. Shoots left. 6'1", 190 lbs. Born, Vancouver, B.C., October 26, 1976. Edmonton's 1st choice, 6th overall, in 1995 Entry Draft.

			Regular Season																Playoffs							
Season	Club	League	GP	G	A	Pts	PIM	PP	SH	GW	S	%	+/-	TF	F%	H	SB	Min	GP	G	A	Pts	PIM	PP	SH	GW
1991-92	Westside AA	BCAHA	30	25	60	85	75																			
1992-93	Prince Albert	WHL	65	11	9	20	75																			
1993-94	Prince Albert	WHL	65	19	42	61	106																			
1994-95	Prince Albert	WHL	68	31	41	72	153												15	7	9	16	35			
1995-96	Prince Albert	WHL	70	27	74	101	203												18	13	18	31	47			
1996-97	**Edmonton**	**NHL**	**8**	**1**	**0**	**1**	**6**	**0**	**0**	**1**	**6**	**16.7**	**–1**						**6**	**0**	**0**	**0**	**2**	**0**	**0**	**0**
	Hamilton	AHL	48	9	29	38	111												11	3	3	6	24			
1997-98	**Edmonton**	**NHL**	**19**	**0**	**2**	**2**	**8**	**0**	**0**	**0**	**5**	**0.0**	**–4**													
	Hamilton	AHL	11	2	8	10	18																			
	Tampa Bay	**NHL**	**24**	**2**	**1**	**3**	**15**	**1**	**0**	**0**	**17**	**11.8**	**–9**													
	Milwaukee	IHL	5	0	1	1	19																			
	Cleveland	IHL	5	1	1	2	29												1	0	1	1	0			
1998-99	**Tampa Bay**	**NHL**	**34**	**1**	**3**	**4**	**27**	**0**	**0**	**1**	**15**	**6.7**	**–15**	**11**	**54.5**	**12**	**13**	**10:51**								
	Cleveland	IHL	18	6	7	13	36																			
	NHL Totals		**85**	**4**	**6**	**10**	**56**	**1**	**0**	**2**	**43**	**9.3**		**11**	**54.5**	**12**	**13**	**10:51**	**6**	**0**	**0**	**0**	**2**	**0**	**0**	**0**

Traded to **Tampa Bay** by **Edmonton** with Bryan Marchment and Jason Bonsignore for Roman Hamrlik and Paul Comrie, December 30, 1997.

KENADY, Chris NYR

Right wing. Shoots right. 6'2", 195 lbs. Born, Mound, MN, April 10, 1973. St. Louis' 8th choice, 175th overall, in 1991 Entry Draft.

			Regular Season																Playoffs							
Season	Club	League	GP	G	A	Pts	PIM	PP	SH	GW	S	%	+/-	TF	F%	H	SB	Min	GP	G	A	Pts	PIM	PP	SH	GW
1990-91	St. Paul	USHL	45	16	20	36	57																			
1991-92	U. of Denver	WCHA	36	8	5	13	56																			
1992-93	U. of Denver	WCHA	38	8	16	24	95																			
1993-94	U. of Denver	WCHA	37	14	11	25	125																			
1994-95	U. of Denver	WCHA	39	21	17	38	113																			
1995-96	Worcester	AHL	43	9	10	19	58												2	0	0	0	0			
1996-97	Worcester	AHL	73	23	26	49	131												5	0	1	1	2			
1997-98	**St. Louis**	**NHL**	**5**	**0**	**2**	**2**	**0**	**0**	**0**	**0**	**3**	**0.0**	**1**													
	Worcester	AHL	63	23	22	45	84												11	1	5	6	26			
1998-99	Utah	IHL	35	7	6	13	68																			
	Long Beach	IHL	19	1	6	7	47																			
	Hartford	AHL	22	2	6	8	52												2	0	1	1	6			
	NHL Totals		**5**	**0**	**2**	**2**	**0**	**0**	**0**	**0**	**3**	**0.0**														

Traded to **NY Rangers** by **St. Louis** to complete transaction that sent sent Jeff Finley and Geoff Smith to St. Louis (February 13, 1999), February 22, 1999.

KENNEDY, Mike

Center. Shoots right. 6'1", 195 lbs. Born, Vancouver, B.C., April 13, 1972. Minnesota's 3rd choice, 97th overall, in 1991 Entry Draft.

			Regular Season																Playoffs							
Season	Club	League	GP	G	A	Pts	PIM	PP	SH	GW	S	%	+/-	TF	F%	H	SB	Min	GP	G	A	Pts	PIM	PP	SH	GW
1989-90	U.B.C.	CWUAA	9	5	7	12	0																			
1990-91	U.B.C.	CWUAA	28	17	17	34	18																			
1991-92	Seattle	WHL	71	42	47	89	134												15	11	6	17	20			
1992-93	Kalamazoo	IHL	77	21	30	51	39																			
1993-94	Kalamazoo	IHL	63	20	18	38	42												3	1	2	3	2			
1994-95	**Dallas**	**NHL**	**44**	**6**	**12**	**18**	**33**	**2**	**0**	**0**	**76**	**7.9**	**4**						**5**	**0**	**0**	**0**	**9**	**0**	**0**	**0**
	Kalamazoo	IHL	42	20	28	48	29																			
1995-96	**Dallas**	**NHL**	**61**	**9**	**17**	**26**	**48**	**4**	**0**	**1**	**111**	**8.1**	**–7**													
1996-97	**Dallas**	**NHL**	**24**	**1**	**6**	**7**	**13**	**0**	**0**	**1**	**26**	**3.8**	**3**													
	Michigan	IHL	2	0	1	1	2																			
1997-98	**Toronto**	**NHL**	**13**	**0**	**1**	**1**	**14**	**0**	**0**	**0**	**12**	**0.0**	**–2**													
	St. John's	AHL	49	11	17	28	86																			
	Dallas	**NHL**	**2**	**0**	**0**	**0**	**2**	**0**	**0**	**0**	**0**	**0.0**	**1**													
1998-99	**NY Islanders**	**NHL**	**1**	**0**	**0**	**0**	**2**	**0**	**0**	**0**	**0**	**0.0**	**0**	**0**	**0.0**	**4**	**0**	**10:50**								
	Lowell	AHL	62	14	26	40	52												3	1	0	1	0			
	NHL Totals		**145**	**16**	**36**	**52**	**112**	**6**	**0**	**2**	**225**	**7.1**		**0**	**0.0**	**4**	**0**	**10:50**	**5**	**0**	**0**	**0**	**9**	**0**	**0**	**0**

WHL West Second All-Star Team (1992)

Rights transferred to **Dallas** after **Minnesota** franchise relocated, June 9, 1993. Signed as a free agent by **Toronto**, July 2, 1997. Traded to **Dallas** by **Toronto** for Dallas' 8th round choice (Mikhail Travnicek) in 1998 Entry Draft, March 24, 1998. Signed as a free agent by **NY Islanders**, July 1, 1998.

KESA, Dan
(KEH-suh)

Right wing. Shoots right. 6', 198 lbs. Born, Vancouver, B.C., November 23, 1971. Vancouver's 4th choice, 95th overall, in 1991 Entry Draft.

			Regular Season																Playoffs							
Season	Club	League	GP	G	A	Pts	PIM	PP	SH	GW	S	%	+/–	TF	F%	H	SB	Min	GP	G	A	Pts	PIM	PP	SH	GW
1988-89	Richmond	BCJHL	44	21	21	42	71	....	....	....	....	....	....	....	....	....	....	....	....	....	....	....	....	....	....	....
1989-90	Richmond	BCJHL	54	39	38	77	103	....	....	....	....	....	....	....	....	....	....	....	....	....	....	....	....	....	....	....
1990-91	Prince Albert	WHL	69	30	23	53	116	....	....	....	....	....	....	....	....	....	....	....	3	1	1	2	0	....	....	....
1991-92	Prince Albert	WHL	62	46	51	97	201	....	....	....	....	....	....	....	....	....	....	....	10	9	10	19	27	....	....	....
1992-93	Hamilton	AHL	62	16	24	40	76	....	....	....	....	....	....	....	....	....	....	....	....	....	....	....	....	....	....	....
1993-94	**Vancouver**	**NHL**	**19**	**2**	**4**	**6**	**18**	**1**	**0**	**1**	**18**	**11.1**	**–3**	....	....	....	....	....	....	....	....	....	....	....	....	....
	Hamilton	AHL	53	37	33	70	33	....	....	....	....	....	....	....	....	....	....	....	4	1	4	5	4	....	....	....
1994-95	Syracuse	AHL	70	34	44	78	81	....	....	....	....	....	....	....	....	....	....	....	....	....	....	....	....	....	....	....
1995-96	**Dallas**	**NHL**	**3**	**0**	**0**	**0**	**0**	**0**	**0**	**0**	**0**	**0.0**	**–1**	....	....	....	....	....	....	....	....	....	....	....	....	....
	Michigan	IHL	15	4	11	15	33	....	....	....	....	....	....	....	....	....	....	....	....	....	....	....	....	....	....	....
	Springfield	AHL	22	10	5	15	13	....	....	....	....	....	....	....	....	....	....	....	....	....	....	....	....	....	....	....
	Detroit	IHL	27	9	6	15	22	....	....	....	....	....	....	....	....	....	....	....	12	6	4	10	4	....	....	....
1996-97	Detroit	IHL	60	22	21	43	19	....	....	....	....	....	....	....	....	....	....	....	20	7	5	12	20	....	....	....
1997-98	Detroit	IHL	76	40	37	77	40	....	....	....	....	....	....	....	....	....	....	....	20	*13	5	18	14	....	....	....
1998-99	Detroit	IHL	8	3	5	8	12	....	....	....	....	....	....	....	....	....	....	....	....	....	....	....	....	....	....	....
	Pittsburgh	**NHL**	**67**	**2**	**8**	**10**	**27**	**0**	**0**	**0**	**33**	**6.1**	**–9**	**392**	**48.2**	**91**	**46**	**10:07**	**13**	**1**	**0**	**1**	**0**	**1**	**0**	**1**
	NHL Totals		**89**	**4**	**12**	**16**	**45**	**1**	**0**	**1**	**51**	**7.8**		**392**	**48.2**	**91**	**46**	**10:07**	**13**	**1**	**0**	**1**	**0**	**1**	**0**	**1**

Traded to **Dallas** by **Vancouver** with Greg Adams and Vancouver's 5th round choice (later traded to LA Kings — LA Kings selected Jason Morgan) in 1995 Entry Draft for Russ Courtnall, April 7, 1995. Traded to **Hartford** by **Dallas** with future considerations for Robert Petrovicky, November 29, 1995. Signed as a free agent by **Pittsburgh**, August 20, 1998.

KHRISTICH, Dmitri
(KRIH-stihch)

Left wing/Center. Shoots right. 6'2", 195 lbs. Born, Kiev, USSR, July 23, 1969. Washington's 6th choice, 120th overall, in 1988 Entry Draft.

Season	Club	League	GP	G	A	Pts	PIM	PP	SH	GW	S	%	+/–	TF	F%	H	SB	Min	GP	G	A	Pts	PIM	PP	SH	GW
1985-86	Sokol Kiev	USSR	4	0	0	0	0	....	....	....	....	....	....	....	....	....	....	....	....	....	....	....	....	....	....	....
1986-87	Sokol Kiev	USSR	20	3	0	3	4	....	....	....	....	....	....	....	....	....	....	....	....	....	....	....	....	....	....	....
1987-88	Sokol Kiev	USSR	37	9	1	10	18	....	....	....	....	....	....	....	....	....	....	....	....	....	....	....	....	....	....	....
1988-89	Sokol Kiev	USSR	42	17	10	27	15	....	....	....	....	....	....	....	....	....	....	....	....	....	....	....	....	....	....	....
1989-90	Sokol Kiev	USSR	47	14	22	36	32	....	....	....	....	....	....	....	....	....	....	....	....	....	....	....	....	....	....	....
1990-91	Sokol Kiev	USSR	28	10	12	22	20	....	....	....	....	....	....	....	....	....	....	....	....	....	....	....	....	....	....	....
	Washington	**NHL**	**40**	**13**	**14**	**27**	**21**	**1**	**0**	**0**	**77**	**16.9**	**–1**	....	....	....	....	....	**11**	**1**	**3**	**4**	**6**	**0**	**0**	**0**
	Baltimore	AHL	3	0	0	0	0	....	....	....	....	....	....	....	....	....	....	....	....	....	....	....	....	....	....	....
1991-92	**Washington**	**NHL**	**80**	**36**	**37**	**73**	**35**	**14**	**1**	**7**	**188**	**19.1**	**24**	....	....	....	....	....	**7**	**3**	**2**	**5**	**15**	**3**	**0**	**1**
1992-93	**Washington**	**NHL**	**64**	**31**	**35**	**66**	**28**	**9**	**1**	**1**	**127**	**24.4**	**29**	....	....	....	....	....	**6**	**2**	**5**	**7**	**2**	**1**	**0**	**0**
1993-94	**Washington**	**NHL**	**83**	**29**	**29**	**58**	**73**	**10**	**0**	**4**	**195**	**14.9**	**–2**	....	....	....	....	....	**11**	**2**	**3**	**5**	**10**	**0**	**0**	**0**
1994-95	**Washington**	**NHL**	**48**	**12**	**14**	**26**	**41**	**8**	**0**	**2**	**92**	**13.0**	**0**	....	....	....	....	....	**7**	**1**	**4**	**5**	**0**	**0**	**0**	**0**
1995-96	**Los Angeles**	**NHL**	**76**	**27**	**37**	**64**	**44**	**12**	**0**	**3**	**204**	**13.2**	**0**	....	....	....	....	....	....	....	....	....	....	....	....	....
1996-97	**Los Angeles**	**NHL**	**75**	**19**	**37**	**56**	**38**	**3**	**0**	**2**	**135**	**14.1**	**8**	....	....	....	....	....	....	....	....	....	....	....	....	....
1997-98	**Boston**	**NHL**	**82**	**29**	**37**	**66**	**42**	**13**	**2**	**1**	**144**	**20.1**	**25**	....	....	....	....	....	**6**	**2**	**2**	**4**	**2**	**2**	**0**	**0**
1998-99	**Boston**	**NHL**	**79**	**29**	**42**	**71**	**48**	**13**	**1**	**6**	**144**	**20.1**	**11**	**76**	**44.7**	**80**	**39**	**19:46**	**12**	**3**	**4**	**7**	**6**	**0**	**0**	**1**
	NHL Totals		**627**	**225**	**282**	**507**	**370**	**83**	**5**	**26**	**1306**	**17.2**		**76**	**44.7**	**80**	**39**	**19:46**	**60**	**14**	**23**	**37**	**41**	**6**	**0**	**2**

Played in NHL All-Star Game (1997, 1999)

Traded to **LA Kings** by **Washington** with Byron Dafoe for LA Kings' 1st round choice (Alexander Volchkov) and Dallas' 4th round choice (previously acquired, Washington selected Justin Davis) in 1996 Entry Draft, July 8, 1995. Traded to **Boston** by **LA Kings** with Byron Dafoe for Jozef Stumpel, Sandy Moger and Boston's 4th round choice (later traded to New Jersey - New Jersey selected Pierre Dagenais) in 1998 Entry Draft, August 29, 1997.

KILGER, Chad
(KIHL-guhr) **EDM.**

Center. Shoots left. 6'3", 215 lbs. Born, Cornwall, Ont., November 27, 1976. Anaheim's 1st choice, 4th overall, in 1995 Entry Draft

Season	Club	League	GP	G	A	Pts	PIM	PP	SH	GW	S	%	+/–	TF	F%	H	SB	Min	GP	G	A	Pts	PIM	PP	SH	GW
1992-93	Cornwall	OJHL	55	30	36	66	26	....	....	....	....	....	....	....	....	....	....	....	6	0	0	0	0	....	....	....
1993-94	Kingston	OHL	66	17	35	52	23	....	....	....	....	....	....	....	....	....	....	....	6	7	2	9	8	....	....	....
1994-95	Kingston	OHL	65	42	53	95	95	....	....	....	....	....	....	....	....	....	....	....	6	5	2	7	10	....	....	....
1995-96	**Anaheim**	**NHL**	**45**	**5**	**7**	**12**	**22**	**0**	**0**	**1**	**38**	**13.2**	**–2**	....	....	....	....	....	....	....	....	....	....	....	....	....
	Winnipeg	**NHL**	**29**	**2**	**3**	**5**	**12**	**0**	**0**	**0**	**19**	**10.5**	**–2**	....	....	....	....	....	**4**	**1**	**0**	**1**	**0**	**0**	**0**	**1**
1996-97	**Phoenix**	**NHL**	**24**	**4**	**3**	**7**	**13**	**1**	**0**	**0**	**30**	**13.3**	**–5**	....	....	....	....	....	....	....	....	....	....	....	....	....
	Springfield	AHL	52	17	28	45	36	....	....	....	....	....	....	....	....	....	....	....	16	5	7	12	56	....	....	....
1997-98	**Phoenix**	**NHL**	**10**	**0**	**1**	**1**	**4**	**0**	**0**	**0**	**9**	**0.0**	**–2**	....	....	....	....	....	....	....	....	....	....	....	....	....
	Springfield	AHL	35	14	14	28	33	....	....	....	....	....	....	....	....	....	....	....	....	....	....	....	....	....	....	....
	Chicago	**NHL**	**22**	**3**	**8**	**11**	**6**	**2**	**0**	**1**	**23**	**13.0**	**2**	....	....	....	....	....	....	....	....	....	....	....	....	....
1998-99	**Chicago**	**NHL**	**64**	**14**	**11**	**25**	**30**	**2**	**1**	**1**	**68**	**20.6**	**–1**	**488**	**56.6**	**124**	**27**	**14:03**	....	....	....	....	....	....	....	....
	Edmonton	**NHL**	**13**	**1**	**1**	**2**	**4**	**0**	**0**	**0**	**13**	**7.7**	**–3**	**82**	**53.7**	**33**	**3**	**11:22**	**4**	**0**	**0**	**0**	**4**	**0**	**0**	**0**
	NHL Totals		**207**	**29**	**34**	**63**	**91**	**5**	**1**	**3**	**200**	**14.5**		**570**	**56.1**	**157**	**30**	**13:36**	**8**	**1**	**0**	**1**	**4**	**0**	**0**	**1**

Traded to **Winnipeg** by **Anaheim** with Oleg Tverdovsky and Anaheim's 3rd round choice (Per-Anton Lundstrom) in 1996 Entry Draft for Teemu Selanne, Marc Chouinard and Winnipeg's 4th round choice (later traded to Toronto — later traded to Montreal — Montreal selected Kim Staal) in 1996 Entry Draft, February 7, 1996. Transferred to **Phoenix** after **Winnipeg** franchise relocated, July 1, 1996. Traded to **Chicago** by **Phoenix** with Jayson More for Keith Carney and Jim Cummins, March 4, 1998. Traded to **Edmonton** by **Chicago** with Daniel Cleary, Ethan Moreau and Christian Laflamme for Boris Mironov, Dean McAmmond and Jonas Elofsson, March 20, 1999.

KING, Derek
TOR.

Left wing. Shoots left. 6', 210 lbs. Born, Hamilton, Ont., February 11, 1967. NY Islanders' 2nd choice, 13th overall, in 1985 Entry Draft.

Season	Club	League	GP	G	A	Pts	PIM	PP	SH	GW	S	%	+/–	TF	F%	H	SB	Min	GP	G	A	Pts	PIM	PP	SH	GW
1983-84	Hamilton	OJHL	37	10	14	24	142	....	....	....	....	....	....	....	....	....	....	....	....	....	....	....	....	....	....	....
1984-85	S.S. Marie	OHL	63	35	38	73	106	....	....	....	....	....	....	....	....	....	....	....	16	3	13	16	11	....	....	....
1985-86	S.S. Marie	OHL	25	12	17	29	33	....	....	....	....	....	....	....	....	....	....	....	....	....	....	....	....	....	....	....
	Oshawa	OHL	19	8	13	21	15	....	....	....	....	....	....	....	....	....	....	....	6	3	2	5	13	....	....	....
1986-87	Oshawa	OHL	57	53	53	106	74	....	....	....	....	....	....	....	....	....	....	....	17	14	10	24	40	....	....	....
	NY Islanders	**NHL**	**2**	**0**	**0**	**0**	**0**	**0**	**0**	**0**	**5**	**0.0**	**0**	....	....	....	....	....	....	....	....	....	....	....	....	....
1987-88	**NY Islanders**	**NHL**	**55**	**12**	**24**	**36**	**30**	**1**	**0**	**4**	**94**	**12.8**	**7**	....	....	....	....	....	**5**	**0**	**2**	**2**	**2**	**0**	**0**	**0**
	Springfield	AHL	10	7	6	13	6	....	....	....	....	....	....	....	....	....	....	....	....	....	....	....	....	....	....	....
1988-89	**NY Islanders**	**NHL**	**60**	**14**	**29**	**43**	**14**	**4**	**0**	**0**	**103**	**13.6**	**10**	....	....	....	....	....	....	....	....	....	....	....	....	....
	Springfield	AHL	4	4	0	4	0	....	....	....	....	....	....	....	....	....	....	....	....	....	....	....	....	....	....	....
1989-90	**NY Islanders**	**NHL**	**46**	**13**	**27**	**40**	**20**	**5**	**0**	**1**	**91**	**14.3**	**2**	....	....	....	....	....	**4**	**0**	**0**	**0**	**4**	**0**	**0**	**0**
	Springfield	AHL	21	11	12	23	33	....	....	....	....	....	....	....	....	....	....	....	....	....	....	....	....	....	....	....
1990-91	**NY Islanders**	**NHL**	**66**	**19**	**26**	**45**	**44**	**2**	**0**	**2**	**130**	**14.6**	**1**	....	....	....	....	....	....	....	....	....	....	....	....	....
1991-92	**NY Islanders**	**NHL**	**80**	**40**	**38**	**78**	**46**	**21**	**0**	**6**	**189**	**21.2**	**–10**	....	....	....	....	....	....	....	....	....	....	....	....	....
1992-93	**NY Islanders**	**NHL**	**77**	**38**	**38**	**76**	**47**	**21**	**0**	**7**	**201**	**18.9**	**–4**	....	....	....	....	....	**18**	**3**	**11**	**14**	**14**	**0**	**0**	**0**
1993-94	**NY Islanders**	**NHL**	**78**	**30**	**40**	**70**	**59**	**10**	**0**	**7**	**171**	**17.5**	**18**	....	....	....	....	....	**4**	**0**	**1**	**1**	**0**	**0**	**0**	**0**
1994-95	**NY Islanders**	**NHL**	**43**	**10**	**16**	**26**	**41**	**7**	**0**	**0**	**118**	**8.5**	**–5**	....	....	....	....	....	....	....	....	....	....	....	....	....
1995-96	**NY Islanders**	**NHL**	**61**	**12**	**20**	**32**	**23**	**5**	**1**	**0**	**154**	**7.8**	**–10**	....	....	....	....	....	....	....	....	....	....	....	....	....
1996-97	**NY Islanders**	**NHL**	**70**	**23**	**30**	**53**	**20**	**5**	**0**	**3**	**153**	**15.0**	**–6**	....	....	....	....	....	....	....	....	....	....	....	....	....
	Hartford	**NHL**	**12**	**3**	**3**	**6**	**2**	**1**	**0**	**0**	**28**	**10.7**	**0**	....	....	....	....	....	....	....	....	....	....	....	....	....
1997-98	**Toronto**	**NHL**	**77**	**21**	**25**	**46**	**43**	**4**	**0**	**3**	**166**	**12.7**	**–7**	....	....	....	....	....	....	....	....	....	....	....	....	....
1998-99	**Toronto**	**NHL**	**81**	**24**	**28**	**52**	**20**	**8**	**0**	**4**	**150**	**16.0**	**15**	**1**	**0.0**	**36**	**20**	**14:02**	**16**	**1**	**3**	**4**	**4**	**0**	**0**	**0**
	NHL Totals		**808**	**259**	**344**	**603**	**409**	**94**	**1**	**37**	**1753**	**14.8**		**1**	**0.0**	**36**	**20**	**14:02**	**47**	**4**	**17**	**21**	**24**	**0**	**0**	**0**

OHL First All-Star Team (1987)

Traded to **Hartford** by **NY Islanders** for Hartford's 5th round choice (Adam Edinger) in 1997 Entry Draft, March 18, 1997. Signed as a free agent by **Toronto**, July 4, 1997.

KING, Kris — TOR.

Left wing. Shoots left. 5'11", 208 lbs. Born, Bracebridge, Ont., February 18, 1966. Washington's 4th choice, 80th overall, in 1984 Entry Draft.

Season	Club	League	GP	G	A	Pts	PIM	PP	SH	GW	S	%	+/-	TF	F%	H	SB	Min	Playoffs GP	G	A	Pts	PIM	PP	SH	GW
1982-83	Gravenhurst	OJHL-C	32	72	53	125	115																			
1983-84	Peterborough	OHL	62	13	18	31	168												8	3	3	6	14			
1984-85	Peterborough	OHL	61	18	35	53	222												16	2	8	10	28			
1985-86	Peterborough	OHL	58	19	40	59	254												8	4	0	4	21			
1986-87	Peterborough	OHL	46	23	33	56	160												12	5	8	13	41			
	Binghamton	AHL	7	0	0	0	18																			
1987-88	**Detroit**	**NHL**	**3**	**1**	**0**	**1**	**2**	**0**	**0**	**0**	**3**	**33.3**	**1**													
	Adirondack	AHL	76	21	32	53	337												10	4	4	8	53			
1988-89	**Detroit**	**NHL**	**55**	**2**	**3**	**5**	**168**	**0**	**0**	**0**	**34**	**5.9**	**–7**						**2**	**0**	**0**	**0**	**2**	**0**	**0**	**0**
1989-90	**NY Rangers**	**NHL**	**68**	**6**	**7**	**13**	**286**	**0**	**0**	**0**	**49**	**12.2**	**2**						**10**	**0**	**1**	**1**	**38**	**0**	**0**	**0**
1990-91	**NY Rangers**	**NHL**	**72**	**11**	**14**	**25**	**154**	**0**	**0**	**0**	**107**	**10.3**	**–1**						**6**	**2**	**0**	**2**	**36**	**0**	**0**	**1**
1991-92	**NY Rangers**	**NHL**	**79**	**10**	**9**	**19**	**224**	**0**	**0**	**2**	**97**	**10.3**	**13**						**13**	**4**	**1**	**5**	**14**	**0**	**0**	**3**
1992-93	**NY Rangers**	**NHL**	**30**	**0**	**3**	**3**	**67**	**0**	**0**	**0**	**23**	**0.0**	**–1**													
	Winnipeg	**NHL**	**48**	**8**	**8**	**16**	**136**	**0**	**0**	**1**	**51**	**15.7**	**5**						**6**	**1**	**1**	**2**	**4**	**0**	**0**	**0**
1993-94	**Winnipeg**	**NHL**	**83**	**4**	**8**	**12**	**205**	**0**	**0**	**1**	**86**	**4.7**	**–22**													
1994-95	**Winnipeg**	**NHL**	**48**	**4**	**2**	**6**	**85**	**0**	**0**	**0**	**58**	**6.9**	**0**													
1995-96	**Winnipeg**	**NHL**	**81**	**9**	**11**	**20**	**151**	**0**	**1**	**2**	**89**	**10.1**	**–7**						**5**	**0**	**1**	**1**	**4**	**0**	**0**	**0**
1996-97	**Phoenix**	**NHL**	**81**	**3**	**11**	**14**	**185**	**0**	**0**	**0**	**57**	**5.3**	**–7**						**7**	**0**	**0**	**0**	**17**	**0**	**0**	**0**
1997-98	**Toronto**	**NHL**	**82**	**3**	**3**	**6**	**199**	**0**	**0**	**2**	**53**	**5.7**	**–13**													
1998-99	**Toronto**	**NHL**	**67**	**2**	**2**	**4**	**105**	**0**	**1**	**1**	**34**	**5.9**	**–16**	**6**	**50.0**	**116**	**14**	**9:22**	**17**	**1**	**1**	**2**	**25**	**0**	**0**	**0**
	NHL Totals		**797**	**63**	**81**	**144**	**1967**	**0**	**2**	**9**	**741**	**8.5**		**6**	**50.0**	**116**	**14**	**9:22**	**66**	**8**	**5**	**13**	**140**	**0**	**0**	**4**

Won King Clancy Memorial Trophy (1996)

Signed as a free agent by **Detroit**, March 23, 1987. Traded to **NY Rangers** by **Detroit** for Chris McRae and Detroit's 5th round choice (previously acquired, Detroit selected Tony Burns) in 1990 Entry Draft, September 7, 1989. Traded to **Winnipeg** by **NY Rangers** with Tie Domi for Ed Olczyk, December 28, 1992. Transferred to **Phoenix** after **Winnipeg** franchise relocated, July 1, 1996. Signed as a free agent by **Toronto**, July 23, 1997.

KING, Steven — PHX.

Right wing. Shoots right. 6', 195 lbs. Born, Greenwich, RI, July 22, 1969. NY Rangers' 1st choice, 21st overall, in 1991 Supplemental Draft.

Season	Club	League	GP	G	A	Pts	PIM	PP	SH	GW	S	%	+/-	TF	F%	H	SB	Min	Playoffs GP	G	A	Pts	PIM	PP	SH	GW
1987-88	Brown University	ECAC	24	10	5	15	30																			
1988-89	Brown University	ECAC	26	8	5	13	73																			
1989-90	Brown University	ECAC	27	19	8	27	53																			
1990-91	Brown University	ECAC	27	19	15	34	76																			
1991-92	Binghamton	AHL	66	27	15	42	56												10	2	0	2	14			
1992-93	**NY Rangers**	**NHL**	**24**	**7**	**5**	**12**	**16**	**5**	**0**	**2**	**42**	**16.7**	**4**													
	Binghamton	AHL	53	35	33	68	100												14	7	9	16	26			
1993-94	**Anaheim**	**NHL**	**36**	**8**	**3**	**11**	**44**	**3**	**0**	**1**	**50**	**16.0**	**–7**													
1994-95			DID NOT PLAY – INJURED																							
1995-96	**Anaheim**	**NHL**	**7**	**2**	**0**	**2**	**15**	**1**	**0**	**1**	**5**	**40.0**	**–1**													
	Baltimore	AHL	68	40	21	61	95												12	7	5	12	20			
1996-97	Philadelphia	AHL	39	17	10	27	47																			
	Michigan	IHL	39	15	11	26	39												4	1	2	3	12			
1997-98	Cincinnati	IHL	41	17	9	26	22																			
	Rochester	AHL	28	15	15	30	28												4	1	1	2	4			
1998-99	Providence	AHL	3	1	0	1	0												13	7	4	11	12			
	NHL Totals		**67**	**17**	**8**	**25**	**75**	**9**	**0**	**4**	**97**	**17.5**														

Claimed by **Anaheim** from **NY Rangers** in Expansion Draft, June 24, 1993. • Missed entire 1994-95 season after having reconstructive surgery on shoulder, January 5, 1994. Signed as a free agent by **Philadelphia**, July 31, 1996. • Missed majority of 1998-99 season recovering from off-season shoulder surgery, August, 1998. Signed as a free agent by **Phoenix**, July 28, 1999.

KJELLBERG, Patrik (CHEHL-buhrg) — NSH.

Left wing. Shoots left. 6'2", 196 lbs. Born, Falun, Sweden, June 17, 1969. Montreal's 4th choice, 83rd overall, in 1988 Entry Draft.

Season	Club	League	GP	G	A	Pts	PIM	PP	SH	GW	S	%	+/-	TF	F%	H	SB	Min	Playoffs GP	G	A	Pts	PIM	PP	SH	GW
1985-86	Falun IF	Sweden-2	5	0	2	2	0																			
1986-87	Falun IF	Sweden-2	32	11	13	24	16																			
1987-88	Falun IF	Sweden-2	29	15	10	25	6																			
1988-89	AIK Solna	Sweden	25	7	9	16	8																			
1989-90	AIK Solna	Sweden	33	8	16	24	6												3	1	0	1	0			
1990-91	AIK Solna	Sweden	38	4	11	15	18																			
1991-92	AIK Solna	Sweden	40	20	13	33	14												3	1	0	1	2			
	Sweden	Olympics	8	1	3	4	0																			
1992-93	**Montreal**	**NHL**	**7**	**0**	**0**	**0**	**2**	**0**	**0**	**0**	**7**	**0.0**	**–3**													
	Fredericton	AHL	41	10	27	37	14												5	2	2	4	0			
1993-94	HV Jonkoping	Sweden	40	11	17	28	18																			
	Sweden	Olympics	8	0	1	1	2																			
1994-95	HV Jonkoping	Sweden	29	5	15	20	12																			
1995-96	Djurgardens IF	Sweden	40	9	7	16	10												4	0	2	2	2			
1996-97	Djurgardens IF	Sweden	49	29	11	40	18												4	2	3	5	4			
1997-98	Djurgardens IF	Sweden	46	*30	18	48	16												15	7	3	10	12			
1998-99	**Nashville**	**NHL**	**71**	**11**	**20**	**31**	**24**	**2**	**0**	**2**	**103**	**10.7**	**–13**	**83**	**37.3**	**44**	**18**	**17:41**								
	NHL Totals		**78**	**11**	**20**	**31**	**26**	**2**	**0**	**2**	**110**	**10.0**		**83**	**37.3**	**44**	**18**	**17:41**								

Signed as a free agent by **Nashville**, July 7, 1998.

KLATT, Trent (KLAT) — VAN.

Right wing. Shoots right. 6'1", 205 lbs. Born, Robbinsdale, MN, January 30, 1971. Washington's 5th choice, 82nd overall, in 1989 Entry Draft.

Season	Club	League	GP	G	A	Pts	PIM	PP	SH	GW	S	%	+/-	TF	F%	H	SB	Min	Playoffs GP	G	A	Pts	PIM	PP	SH	GW
1987-88	Odessa High	H.S.	22	19	17	36	....																			
1988-89	Ossea High	H.S.	22	24	39	63	....																			
1989-90	U. of Minnesota	WCHA	38	22	14	36	16																			
1990-91	U. of Minnesota	WCHA	39	16	28	44	58																			
1991-92	U. of Minnesota	WCHA	41	27	36	63	76																			
	Minnesota	**NHL**	**1**	**0**	**0**	**0**	**0**	**0**	**0**	**0**	**1**	**0.0**	**0**						**6**	**0**	**0**	**0**	**2**	**0**	**0**	**0**
1992-93	**Minnesota**	**NHL**	**47**	**4**	**19**	**23**	**38**	**1**	**0**	**0**	**69**	**5.8**	**2**													
	Kalamazoo	IHL	31	8	11	19	18																			
1993-94	**Dallas**	**NHL**	**61**	**14**	**24**	**38**	**30**	**3**	**0**	**2**	**86**	**16.3**	**13**						**9**	**2**	**1**	**3**	**4**	**1**	**0**	**0**
	Kalamazoo	IHL	6	3	2	5	4																			
1994-95	**Dallas**	**NHL**	**47**	**12**	**10**	**22**	**26**	**5**	**0**	**3**	**91**	**13.2**	**–2**						**5**	**1**	**0**	**1**	**0**	**1**	**0**	**0**
1995-96	**Dallas**	**NHL**	**22**	**4**	**4**	**8**	**23**	**0**	**0**	**1**	**37**	**10.8**	**0**													
	Michigan	IHL	2	1	2	3	5																			
	Philadelphia	**NHL**	**49**	**3**	**8**	**11**	**21**	**0**	**0**	**1**	**64**	**4.7**	**2**						**12**	**4**	**1**	**5**	**0**	**0**	**0**	**0**
1996-97	**Philadelphia**	**NHL**	**76**	**24**	**21**	**45**	**20**	**5**	**5**	**5**	**131**	**18.3**	**9**						**19**	**4**	**3**	**7**	**12**	**0**	**0**	**2**
1997-98	**Philadelphia**	**NHL**	**82**	**14**	**28**	**42**	**16**	**5**	**0**	**3**	**143**	**9.8**	**2**						**5**	**0**	**0**	**0**	**0**	**0**	**0**	**0**
1998-99	**Philadelphia**	**NHL**	**2**	**0**	**0**	**0**	**0**	**0**	**0**	**0**	**2**	**0.0**	**0**	**0**	**0.0**	**3**	**2**	**11:11**								
	Vancouver	**NHL**	**73**	**4**	**10**	**14**	**12**	**0**	**0**	**0**	**58**	**6.9**	**–3**	**37**	**32.4**	**73**	**29**	**11:21**								
	NHL Totals		**460**	**79**	**124**	**203**	**186**	**19**	**5**	**15**	**682**	**11.6**		**37**	**32.4**	**76**	**31**	**11:21**	**56**	**11**	**5**	**16**	**18**	**2**	**0**	**2**

Traded to **Minnesota** by **Washington** with Steve Maltais for Shawn Chambers, June 21, 1991. Transferred to **Dallas** after **Minnesota** franchise relocated, June 9, 1993. Traded to **Philadelphia** by **Dallas** for Brent Fedyk, December 13, 1995. Traded to **Vancouver** by **Philadelphia** for Vancouver's 6th round choice in 2000 Entry Draft, October 19, 1998.

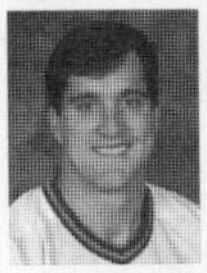

KLEE, Ken — WSH.

Right wing. Shoots right. 6'1", 212 lbs. Born, Indianapolis, IN, April 24, 1971. Washington's 11th choice, 177th overall, in 1990 Entry Draft.

			Regular Season																Playoffs							
Season	Club	League	GP	G	A	Pts	PIM	PP	SH	GW	S	%	+/–	TF	F%	H	SB	Min	GP	G	A	Pts	PIM	PP	SH	GW
1988-89	St. Michael's	OJHL-B	40	9	23	32	64	....	....	....	....	....	....	....	....	....	....	....	27	5	12	17	54	....	....	....
1989-90	Bowling Green	CCHA	39	0	5	5	52	....	....	....	....	....	....	....	....	....	....	....	....	....	....	....	....	....	....	....
1990-91	Bowling Green	CCHA	37	7	28	35	50	....	....	....	....	....	....	....	....	....	....	....	....	....	....	....	....	....	....	....
1991-92	Bowling Green	CCHA	10	0	1	1	14	....	....	....	....	....	....	....	....	....	....	....	....	....	....	....	....	....	....	....
1992-93	Baltimore	AHL	77	4	14	18	93	....	....	....	....	....	....	....	....	....	....	....	7	0	1	1	15	....	....	....
1993-94	Portland	AHL	65	2	9	11	87	....	....	....	....	....	....	....	....	....	....	....	17	1	2	3	14	....	....	....
1994-95	**Washington**	**NHL**	**23**	**3**	**1**	**4**	**41**	**0**	**0**	**0**	**18**	**16.7**	**2**	....	....	....	....	....	**7**	**0**	**0**	**0**	**4**	**0**	**0**	**0**
	Portland	AHL	49	5	7	12	89	....	....	....	....	....	....	....	....	....	....	....	....	....	....	....	....	....	....	....
1995-96	**Washington**	**NHL**	**66**	**8**	**3**	**11**	**60**	**0**	**1**	**2**	**76**	**10.5**	**–1**	....	....	....	....	....	**1**	**0**	**0**	**0**	**0**	**0**	**0**	**0**
1996-97	**Washington**	**NHL**	**80**	**3**	**8**	**11**	**115**	**0**	**0**	**2**	**108**	**2.8**	**–5**	....	....	....	....	....	....	....	....	....	....	....	....	....
1997-98	**Washington**	**NHL**	**51**	**4**	**2**	**6**	**46**	**0**	**0**	**1**	**44**	**9.1**	**–3**	....	....	....	....	....	**9**	**1**	**0**	**1**	**10**	**0**	**0**	**0**
1998-99	**Washington**	**NHL**	**78**	**7**	**13**	**20**	**80**	**0**	**0**	**1**	**132**	**5.3**	**–9**	**0**	**0.0**	**248**	**71**	**19:07**	....	....	....	....	....	....	....	....
	NHL Totals		**298**	**25**	**27**	**52**	**342**	**0**	**1**	**6**	**378**	**6.6**		**0**	**0.0**	**248**	**71**	**19:07**	**17**	**1**	**0**	**1**	**14**	**0**	**0**	**0**

KLEMM, Jon — COL.

Defense. Shoots right. 6'3", 200 lbs. Born, Cranbrook, B.C., January 8, 1970.

			Regular Season																Playoffs							
Season	Club	League	GP	G	A	Pts	PIM	PP	SH	GW	S	%	+/–	TF	F%	H	SB	Min	GP	G	A	Pts	PIM	PP	SH	GW
1987-88	Seattle	WHL	68	6	7	13	24	....	....	....	....	....	....	....	....	....	....	....	....	....	....	....	....	....	....	....
1988-89	Seattle	WHL	2	1	1	2	0	....	....	....	....	....	....	....	....	....	....	....	....	....	....	....	....	....	....	....
	Spokane	WHL	66	6	34	40	42	....	....	....	....	....	....	....	....	....	....	....	....	....	....	....	....	....	....	....
1989-90	Spokane	WHL	66	3	28	31	100	....	....	....	....	....	....	....	....	....	....	....	6	1	1	2	5	....	....	....
1990-91	Spokane	WHL	72	7	58	65	65	....	....	....	....	....	....	....	....	....	....	....	15	3	6	9	8	....	....	....
1991-92	**Quebec**	**NHL**	**4**	**0**	**1**	**1**	**0**	**0**	**0**	**0**	**2**	**0.0**	**2**	....	....	....	....	....	....	....	....	....	....	....	....	....
	Halifax	AHL	70	6	13	19	40	....	....	....	....	....	....	....	....	....	....	....	....	....	....	....	....	....	....	....
1992-93	Halifax	AHL	80	3	20	23	32	....	....	....	....	....	....	....	....	....	....	....	....	....	....	....	....	....	....	....
1993-94	**Quebec**	**NHL**	**7**	**0**	**0**	**0**	**4**	**0**	**0**	**0**	**11**	**0.0**	**–1**	....	....	....	....	....	....	....	....	....	....	....	....	....
	Cornwall	AHL	66	4	26	30	78	....	....	....	....	....	....	....	....	....	....	....	13	1	2	3	6	....	....	....
1994-95	**Quebec**	**NHL**	**4**	**1**	**0**	**1**	**2**	**0**	**0**	**0**	**5**	**20.0**	**3**	....	....	....	....	....	....	....	....	....	....	....	....	....
	Cornwall	AHL	65	6	13	19	84	....	....	....	....	....	....	....	....	....	....	....	....	....	....	....	....	....	....	....
1995-96♦	**Colorado**	**NHL**	**56**	**3**	**12**	**15**	**20**	**0**	**1**	**1**	**61**	**4.9**	**12**	....	....	....	....	....	**15**	**2**	**1**	**3**	**0**	**1**	**0**	**0**
1996-97	**Colorado**	**NHL**	**80**	**9**	**15**	**24**	**37**	**1**	**2**	**1**	**103**	**8.7**	**12**	....	....	....	....	....	**17**	**1**	**1**	**2**	**6**	**0**	**0**	**0**
1997-98	**Colorado**	**NHL**	**67**	**6**	**8**	**14**	**30**	**0**	**0**	**0**	**60**	**10.0**	**–3**	....	....	....	....	....	**4**	**0**	**0**	**0**	**0**	**0**	**0**	**0**
1998-99	**Colorado**	**NHL**	**39**	**1**	**2**	**3**	**31**	**0**	**0**	**0**	**28**	**3.6**	**4**	**14**	**35.7**	**38**	**21**	**13:43**	**19**	**0**	**1**	**1**	**10**	**0**	**0**	**0**
	NHL Totals		**257**	**20**	**38**	**58**	**124**	**1**	**3**	**2**	**270**	**7.4**		**14**	**35.7**	**38**	**21**	**13:43**	**55**	**3**	**3**	**6**	**16**	**1**	**0**	**0**

WHL West Second All-Star Team (1991)

Signed as a free agent by **Quebec**, May 14, 1991. Transferred to **Colorado** after **Quebec** franchise relocated, June 21, 1995.

KLIMA, Petr

(KLEE-muh)

Right/Left wing. Shoots right. 6', 190 lbs. Born, Chomutov, Czech., December 23, 1964. Detroit's 5th choice, 88th overall, in 1983 Entry Draft.

			Regular Season																Playoffs							
Season	Club	League	GP	G	A	Pts	PIM	PP	SH	GW	S	%	+/–	TF	F%	H	SB	Min	GP	G	A	Pts	PIM	PP	SH	GW
1981-82	CHZ Litvinov	Czech.	18	7	3	10	8	....	....	....	....	....	....	....	....	....	....	....	....	....	....	....	....	....	....	....
1982-83	CHZ Litvinov	Czech.	44	19	17	36	74	....	....	....	....	....	....	....	....	....	....	....	....	....	....	....	....	....	....	....
1983-84	Dukla Jihlava	Czech.	41	20	16	36	46	....	....	....	....	....	....	....	....	....	....	....	....	....	....	....	....	....	....	....
1984-85	Dukla Jihlava	Czech.	35	23	22	45	76	....	....	....	....	....	....	....	....	....	....	....	....	....	....	....	....	....	....	....
1985-86	**Detroit**	**NHL**	**74**	**32**	**24**	**56**	**16**	**8**	**0**	**4**	**174**	**18.4**	**–39**	....	....	....	....	....	....	....	....	....	....	....	....	....
1986-87	**Detroit**	**NHL**	**77**	**30**	**23**	**53**	**42**	**6**	**0**	**5**	**209**	**14.4**	**–9**	....	....	....	....	....	**13**	**1**	**2**	**3**	**4**	**0**	**0**	**0**
1987-88	**Detroit**	**NHL**	**78**	**37**	**25**	**62**	**46**	**6**	**5**	**5**	**174**	**21.3**	**4**	....	....	....	....	....	**12**	**10**	**8**	**18**	**10**	[illegible]	**1**	**4**
1988-89	**Detroit**	**NHL**	**51**	**25**	**16**	**41**	**44**	**1**	**0**	**3**	**145**	**17.2**	**5**	....	....	....	....	....	**6**	**2**	**4**	**6**	**19**	**1**	**0**	**0**
	Adirondack	AHL	5	5	1	[illegible]	[illegible]	....	....	....	....	....	....	....	....	....	....	....	....	....	....	....	....	....	....	....
1989-90	**Detroit**	**NHL**	**13**	**5**	**5**	**10**	**6**	**2**	**0**	**0**	**37**	**13.5**	**–8**	....	....	....	....	....	....	....	....	....	....	....	....	....
♦	**Edmonton**	**NHL**	**63**	**25**	**28**	**53**	**66**	**7**	**0**	**3**	**149**	**16.8**	**–1**	....	....	....	....	....	**21**	**5**	**0**	**5**	**8**	**1**	**0**	**1**
1990-91	**Edmonton**	**NHL**	**70**	**40**	**28**	**68**	**113**	**7**	**1**	**5**	**204**	**19.6**	**24**	....	....	....	....	....	**18**	**7**	**6**	**13**	**16**	**1**	**0**	**3**
1991-92	**Edmonton**	**NHL**	**57**	**21**	**13**	**34**	**52**	**5**	**0**	**0**	**107**	**19.6**	**–18**	....	....	....	....	....	**15**	**1**	**4**	**5**	**8**	**0**	**0**	**0**
1992-93	**Edmonton**	**NHL**	**68**	**32**	**16**	**48**	**100**	**13**	**0**	**2**	**175**	**18.3**	**–15**	....	....	....	....	....	....	....	....	....	....	....	....	....
1993-94	**Tampa Bay**	**NHL**	**75**	**28**	**27**	**55**	**76**	**10**	**0**	**2**	**167**	**16.8**	**–15**	....	....	....	....	....	....	....	....	....	....	....	....	....
1994-95	EHC Wolfsburg	German-2	12	27	11	38	28	....	....	....	....	....	....	....	....	....	....	....	....	....	....	....	....	....	....	....
	ZPS Zlin	Cze-Rep	1	1	0	1	0	....	....	....	....	....	....	....	....	....	....	....	....	....	....	....	....	....	....	....
	Tampa Bay	**NHL**	**47**	**13**	**13**	**26**	**26**	**4**	**0**	**3**	**75**	**17.3**	**–13**	....	....	....	....	....	....	....	....	....	....	....	....	....
1995-96	**Tampa Bay**	**NHL**	**67**	**22**	**30**	**52**	**68**	**8**	**0**	**3**	**164**	**13.4**	**–25**	....	....	....	....	....	**4**	**2**	**0**	**2**	**14**	**2**	**0**	**0**
1996-97	**Los Angeles**	**NHL**	**8**	**0**	**4**	**4**	**2**	**0**	**0**	**0**	**12**	**0.0**	**–7**	....	....	....	....	....	....	....	....	....	....	....	....	....
	Pittsburgh	**NHL**	**9**	**1**	**3**	**4**	**4**	**0**	**0**	**0**	**21**	**4.8**	**–4**	....	....	....	....	....	....	....	....	....	....	....	....	....
	Cleveland	IHL	19	7	14	21	6	....	....	....	....	....	....	....	....	....	....	....	....	....	....	....	....	....	....	....
	Edmonton	**NHL**	**16**	**1**	**5**	**6**	**6**	**0**	**0**	**0**	**22**	**4.5**	**–1**	....	....	....	....	....	**6**	**0**	**0**	**0**	**4**	**0**	**0**	**0**
1997-98	Krefeld	Germany	38	7	12	19	18	....	....	....	....	....	....	....	....	....	....	....	....	....	....	....	....	....	....	....
1998-99	**Detroit**	**NHL**	**13**	**1**	**0**	**1**	**4**	**0**	**0**	**1**	**12**	**8.3**	**–3**	**1**	**0.0**	**3**	**1**	**5:58**	....	....	....	....	....	....	....	....
	Adirondack	AHL	15	2	6	8	8	....	....	....	....	....	....	....	....	....	....	....	....	....	....	....	....	....	....	....
	NHL Totals		**786**	**313**	**260**	**573**	**671**	**77**	**6**	**36**	**1847**	**16.9**		**1**	**0.0**	**3**	**1**	**5:58**	**95**	**28**	**24**	**52**	**83**	**7**	**1**	**8**

Traded to **Edmonton** by **Detroit** with Joe Murphy, Adam Graves and Jeff Sharples for Jimmy Carson, Kevin McClelland and Edmonton's 5th round choice (later traded to Montreal — Montreal selected Brad Layzell) in 1991 Entry Draft, November 2, 1989. Traded to **Tampa Bay** by **Edmonton** for Tampa Bay's 3rd round choice (Brad Symes) in 1994 Entry Draft, June 16, 1993. Traded to **LA Kings** by **Tampa Bay** for LA Kings' 5th round choice (Jan Sulc) in 1997 Entry Draft, August 22, 1996. Traded to **Pittsburgh** by **LA Kings** for conditional draft pick, October 25, 1996. Klima failed to meet conditions specified in the trade agreement and conditional pick was forfeited. Signed as a free agent by **Edmonton**, February 26, 1997. Signed as a free agent by **Detroit**, January 11, 1999.

KNIPSCHEER, Fred

(kuh-NIHP-sheer)

Center. Shoots left. 5'11", 185 lbs. Born, Ft. Wayne, IN, September 3, 1969.

			Regular Season																Playoffs							
Season	Club	League	GP	G	A	Pts	PIM	PP	SH	GW	S	%	+/–	TF	F%	H	SB	Min	GP	G	A	Pts	PIM	PP	SH	GW
1988-89	Omaha	USHL	47	32	33	65	123	....	....	....	....	....	....	....	....	....	....	....	....	....	....	....	....	....	....	....
1989-90	Omaha	USHL	48	38	46	84	66	....	....	....	....	....	....	....	....	....	....	....	....	....	....	....	....	....	....	....
1990-91	St. Cloud State	WCHA	40	9	10	19	57	....	....	....	....	....	....	....	....	....	....	....	....	....	....	....	....	....	....	....
1991-92	St. Cloud State	WCHA	33	15	17	32	48	....	....	....	....	....	....	....	....	....	....	....	....	....	....	....	....	....	....	....
1992-93	St. Cloud State	WCHA	36	34	26	60	68	....	....	....	....	....	....	....	....	....	....	....	....	....	....	....	....	....	....	....
1993-94	**Boston**	**NHL**	**11**	**3**	**2**	**5**	**14**	**0**	**0**	**1**	**15**	**20.0**	**3**	....	....	....	....	....	**12**	**2**	**1**	**3**	**6**	**0**	**0**	**1**
	Providence	AHL	62	26	13	39	50	....	....	....	....	....	....	....	....	....	....	....	....	....	....	....	....	....	....	....
1994-95	**Boston**	**NHL**	**16**	**3**	**1**	**4**	**2**	**0**	**0**	**1**	**20**	**15.0**	**1**	....	....	....	....	....	**4**	**0**	**0**	**0**	**0**	**0**	**0**	**0**
	Providence	AHL	71	29	34	63	81	....	....	....	....	....	....	....	....	....	....	....	....	....	....	....	....	....	....	....
1995-96	**St. Louis**	**NHL**	**1**	**0**	**0**	**0**	**2**	**0**	**0**	**0**	**2**	**0.0**	**0**	....	....	....	....	....	....	....	....	....	....	....	....	....
	Worcester	AHL	68	36	37	73	93	....	....	....	....	....	....	....	....	....	....	....	3	0	0	0	2	....	....	....
1996-97	Phoenix	IHL	24	5	11	16	19	....	....	....	....	....	....	....	....	....	....	....	....	....	....	....	....	....	....	....
	Indianapolis	IHL	41	10	9	19	46	....	....	....	....	....	....	....	....	....	....	....	4	0	2	2	10	....	....	....
1997-98	Kentucky	AHL	17	0	7	7	8	....	....	....	....	....	....	....	....	....	....	....	3	0	1	1	7	....	....	....
	Utah	IHL	58	21	32	53	69	....	....	....	....	....	....	....	....	....	....	....	2	0	0	0	4	....	....	....
1998-99	Utah	IHL	21	4	9	13	20	....	....	....	....	....	....	....	....	....	....	....	....	....	....	....	....	....	....	....
	Cincinnati	IHL	43	14	15	29	44	....	....	....	....	....	....	....	....	....	....	....	3	2	1	3	4	....	....	....
	NHL Totals		**28**	**6**	**3**	**9**	**18**	**0**	**0**	**2**	**37**	**16.2**		....	....	....	....	....	**16**	**2**	**1**	**3**	**6**	**0**	**0**	**1**

WCHA First All-Star Team (1993) • NCAA West Second All-American Team (1993)

Signed as a free agent by **Boston**, April 30, 1993. Traded to **St. Louis** by **Boston** for Rick Zombo, October 2, 1995. Signed as a free agent by **Chicago**, August 16, 1996.

KNUBLE, Mike

(NOO-buhl) **NYR**

Right wing. Shoots right. 6'3", 208 lbs. Born, Toronto, Ont., July 4, 1972. Detroit's 4th choice, 76th overall, in 1991 Entry Draft.

Season	Club	League	Regular Season GP	G	A	Pts	PIM	PP	SH	GW	S	%	+/-	TF	F%	H	SB	Min	Playoffs GP	G	A	Pts	PIM	PP	SH	GW
1988-89	East Kentwood	H.S.	28	52	37	89	60	....	....	....	....	....	....	....	....	....	....	....	....	....	....	....	....	....	....	....
1989-90	East Kentwood	H.S.	29	63	40	103	40	....	....	....	....	....	....	....	....	....	....	....	....	....	....	....	....	....	....	....
1990-91	Kalamazoo	NAJHL	36	18	24	42	30	....	....	....	....	....	....	....	....	....	....	....	....	....	....	....	....	....	....	....
1991-92	U. of Michigan	CCHA	43	7	8	15	48	....	....	....	....	....	....	....	....	....	....	....	....	....	....	....	....	....	....	....
1992-93	U. of Michigan	CCHA	39	26	16	42	57	....	....	....	....	....	....	....	....	....	....	....	....	....	....	....	....	....	....	....
1993-94	U. of Michigan	CCHA	41	32	26	58	71	....	....	....	....	....	....	....	....	....	....	....	....	....	....	....	....	....	....	....
1994-95	U. of Michigan	CCHA	34	*38	22	60	62	....	....	....	....	....	....	....	....	....	....	....	....	....	....	....	....	....	....	....
	Adirondack	AHL	....	....	....	....	....	....	....	....	....	....	....	....	....	....	....	....	3	0	0	0	0	....	....	....
1995-96	Adirondack	AHL	80	22	23	45	59	....	....	....	....	....	....	....	....	....	....	....	3	1	0	1	0	....	....	....
1996-97	**Detroit**	**NHL**	**9**	**1**	**0**	**1**	**0**	**0**	**0**	**0**	**10**	**10.0**	**−1**	....	....	....	....	....	....	....	....	....	....	....	....	....
	Adirondack	AHL	68	28	35	63	54	....	....	....	....	....	....	....	....	....	....	....	....	....	....	....	....	....	....	....
1997-98◆	**Detroit**	**NHL**	**53**	**7**	**6**	**13**	**16**	**0**	**0**	**0**	**54**	**13.0**	**2**	....	....	....	....	....	**3**	**0**	**1**	**1**	**0**	**0**	**0**	**0**
1998-99	**NY Rangers**	**NHL**	**82**	**15**	**20**	**35**	**26**	**3**	**0**	**1**	**113**	**13.3**	**−7**	**1**	**100.0**	**180**	**32**	**14:52**	....	....	....	....	....	....	....	....
	NHL Totals		**144**	**23**	**26**	**49**	**42**	**3**	**0**	**1**	**177**	**13.0**		**1**	**100.0**	**180**	**32**	**14:52**	**3**	**0**	**1**	**1**	**0**	**0**	**0**	**0**

CCHA Second All-Star Team (1994, 1995) • NCAA West Second All-American Team (1995)

Traded to **NY Rangers** by **Detroit** for NY Rangers' 3rd round choice in 2000 Entry Draft, October 1, 1998.

KNUTSEN, Espen

(kuh-NOOT-suhn)

Center. Shoots left. 5'11", 180 lbs. Born, Oslo, Norway, January 12, 1972. Hartford's 9th choice, 204th overall, in 1990 Entry Draft.

Season	Club	League	Regular Season GP	G	A	Pts	PIM	PP	SH	GW	S	%	+/-	TF	F%	H	SB	Min	Playoffs GP	G	A	Pts	PIM	PP	SH	GW
1988-89	Valerengen IF	Norway-Jr.	36	14	7	21	18	....	....	....	....	....	....	....	....	....	....	....	....	....	....	....	....	....	....	....
1989-90	Valerengen IF	Norway	40	25	28	53	44	....	....	....	....	....	....	....	....	....	....	....	....	....	....	....	....	....	....	....
1990-91	Valerengen IF	Norway	31	30	24	54	42	....	....	....	....	....	....	....	....	....	....	....	5	3	4	7	....	....	....	....
1991-92	Valerengen IF	Norway	30	28	26	54	37	....	....	....	....	....	....	....	....	....	....	....	8	7	8	15	....	....	....	....
1992-93	Valerengen IF	Norway	13	11	13	24	4	....	....	....	....	....	....	....	....	....	....	....	....	....	....	....	....	....	....	....
1993-94	Valerengen IF	Norway	38	32	26	58	20	....	....	....	....	....	....	....	....	....	....	....	....	....	....	....	....	....	....	....
	Norway	Olympics	7	1	3	4	2	....	....	....	....	....	....	....	....	....	....	....	....	....	....	....	....	....	....	....
1994-95	Djurgardens IF	Sweden	30	6	14	20	18	....	....	....	....	....	....	....	....	....	....	....	3	0	1	1	0	....	....	....
1995-96	Djurgardens IF	Sweden	32	10	23	33	50	....	....	....	....	....	....	....	....	....	....	....	4	1	0	1	2	....	....	....
1996-97	Djurgardens IF	Sweden	39	16	33	49	20	....	....	....	....	....	....	....	....	....	....	....	4	2	4	6	6	....	....	....
1997-98	**Anaheim**	**NHL**	**19**	**3**	**0**	**3**	**6**	**1**	**0**	**0**	**21**	**14.3**	**−10**	....	....	....	....	....	....	....	....	....	....	....	....	....
	Cincinnati	AHL	41	4	13	17	18	....	....	....	....	....	....	....	....	....	....	....	....	....	....	....	....	....	....	....
1998-99	Djurgardens IF	Sweden	39	18	24	42	32	....	....	....	....	....	....	....	....	....	....	....	4	0	1	1	2	....	....	....
	Djurgardens IF	EuroHL	4	2	2	4	2	....	....	....	....	....	....	....	....	....	....	....	....	....	....	....	....	....	....	....
	NHL Totals		**19**	**3**	**0**	**3**	**6**	**1**	**0**	**0**	**21**	**14.3**		....	....	....	....	....	....	....	....	....	....	....	....	....

Norwegian Player of the Year (1994)

Rights traded to **Anaheim** by **Hartford** for Kevin Brown, October 1, 1996.

KOCUR, Joe

(KOH-suhr) **DET.**

Right wing. Shoots right. 6', 205 lbs. Born, Calgary, Alta., December 21, 1964. Detroit's 6th choice, 91st overall, in 1983 Entry Draft.

Season	Club	League	Regular Season GP	G	A	Pts	PIM	PP	SH	GW	S	%	+/-	TF	F%	H	SB	Min	Playoffs GP	G	A	Pts	PIM	PP	SH	GW
1980-81	Yorkton	SJHL	48	6	9	15	307	....	....	....	....	....	....	....	....	....	....	....	....	....	....	....	....	....	....	....
1981-82	Yorkton	SJHL	47	20	21	41	199	....	....	....	....	....	....	....	....	....	....	....	....	....	....	....	....	....	....	....
1982-83	Saskatoon	WHL	62	23	17	40	289	....	....	....	....	....	....	....	....	....	....	....	6	2	3	5	25	....	....	....
1983-84	Saskatoon	WHL	69	40	41	81	258	....	....	....	....	....	....	....	....	....	....	....	....	....	....	....	....	....	....	....
	Adirondack	AHL	....	....	....	....	....	....	....	....	....	....	....	....	....	....	....	....	5	0	0	0	20	....	....	....
1984-85	**Detroit**	**NHL**	**17**	**1**	**0**	**1**	**64**	**0**	**0**	**0**	**7**	**14.3**	**−4**	....	....	....	....	....	**3**	**1**	**0**	**1**	**5**	**0**	**0**	**0**
	Adirondack	AHL	47	12	7	19	171	....	....	....	....	....	....	....	....	....	....	....	....	....	....	....	....	....	....	....
1985-86	**Detroit**	**NHL**	**59**	**9**	**6**	**15**	***377**	**2**	**0**	**0**	**65**	**13.8**	**−24**	....	....	....	....	....	....	....	....	....	....	....	....	....
	Adirondack	AHL	9	6	2	8	34	....	....	....	....	....	....	....	....	....	....	....	....	....	....	....	....	....	....	....
1986-87	**Detroit**	**NHL**	**77**	**9**	**9**	**18**	**276**	**2**	**0**	**2**	**81**	**11.1**	**−10**	....	....	....	....	....	**16**	**2**	**3**	**5**	**71**	**1**	**0**	**2**
1987-88	**Detroit**	**NHL**	**63**	**7**	**7**	**14**	**263**	**0**	**0**	**1**	**41**	**17.1**	**−11**	....	....	....	....	....	**10**	**0**	**1**	**1**	**13**	**0**	**0**	**0**
1988-89	**Detroit**	**NHL**	**60**	**9**	**9**	**18**	**213**	**1**	**0**	**1**	**76**	**11.8**	**−4**	....	....	....	....	....	**3**	**0**	**1**	**1**	**6**	**0**	**0**	**0**
1989-90	**Detroit**	**NHL**	**71**	**16**	**20**	**36**	**268**	**1**	**0**	**5**	**128**	**12.5**	**−4**	....	....	....	....	....	....	....	....	....	....	....	....	....
1990-91	**Detroit**	**NHL**	**52**	**5**	**4**	**9**	**253**	**0**	**0**	**0**	**67**	**7.5**	**−6**	....	....	....	....	....	....	....	....	....	....	....	....	....
	NY Rangers	**NHL**	**5**	**0**	**0**	**0**	**36**	**0**	**0**	**0**	**6**	**0.0**	**−1**	....	....	....	....	....	**6**	**0**	**2**	**2**	**21**	**0**	**0**	**0**
1991-92	**NY Rangers**	**NHL**	**51**	**7**	**4**	**11**	**121**	**0**	**0**	**2**	**72**	**9.7**	**−4**	....	....	....	....	....	**12**	**1**	**1**	**2**	**38**	**0**	**0**	**0**
1992-93	**NY Rangers**	**NHL**	**65**	**3**	**6**	**9**	**131**	**2**	**0**	**0**	**43**	**7.0**	**−9**	....	....	....	....	....	....	....	....	....	....	....	....	....
1993-94◆	**NY Rangers**	**NHL**	**71**	**2**	**1**	**3**	**129**	**0**	**0**	**0**	**43**	**4.7**	**−9**	....	....	....	....	....	**20**	**1**	**1**	**2**	**17**	**0**	**0**	**0**
1994-95	**NY Rangers**	**NHL**	**48**	**1**	**2**	**3**	**71**	**0**	**0**	**0**	**25**	**4.0**	**−4**	....	....	....	....	....	**10**	**0**	**0**	**0**	**8**	**0**	**0**	**0**
1995-96	**NY Rangers**	**NHL**	**38**	**1**	**2**	**3**	**49**	**0**	**0**	**0**	**19**	**5.3**	**−4**	....	....	....	....	....	....	....	....	....	....	....	....	....
	Vancouver	**NHL**	**7**	**0**	**1**	**1**	**19**	**0**	**0**	**0**	**1**	**0.0**	**−3**	....	....	....	....	....	**1**	**0**	**0**	**0**	**0**	**0**	**0**	**0**
1996-97	San Antonio	IHL	5	1	1	2	24	....	....	....	....	....	....	....	....	....	....	....	....	....	....	....	....	....	....	....
	◆ Detroit	**NHL**	**34**	**2**	**1**	**3**	**70**	**0**	**0**	**1**	**38**	**5.3**	**−7**	....	....	....	....	....	**19**	**1**	**3**	**4**	**22**	**0**	**0**	**0**
1997-98◆	**Detroit**	**NHL**	**63**	**6**	**5**	**11**	**92**	**0**	**0**	**2**	**53**	**11.3**	**7**	....	....	....	....	....	**18**	**4**	**0**	**4**	**30**	**0**	**0**	**0**
1998-99	**Detroit**	**NHL**	**39**	**2**	**5**	**7**	**87**	**0**	**0**	**0**	**20**	**10.0**	**0**	**7**	**14.3**	**41**	**7**	**6:44**	....	....	....	....	....	....	....	....
	NHL Totals		**820**	**80**	**82**	**162**	**2519**	**8**	**0**	**14**	**785**	**10.2**		**7**	**14.3**	**41**	**7**	**6:44**	**118**	**10**	**12**	**22**	**231**	**1**	**0**	**2**

Traded to **NY Rangers** by **Detroit** with Per Djoos for Kevin Miller, Jim Cummins and Dennis Vial, March 5, 1991. Traded to **Vancouver** by **NY Rangers** for Kay Whitmore, March 20, 1996. Signed as a free agent by **Detroit**, December 27, 1996.

KOHN, Ladislav

(KOHN) **TOR.**

Right wing. Shoots left. 5'11", 194 lbs. Born, Uherske Hradiste, Czech., March 4, 1975. Calgary's 9th choice, 175th overall, in 1994 Entry Draft.

Season	Club	League	Regular Season GP	G	A	Pts	PIM	PP	SH	GW	S	%	+/-	TF	F%	H	SB	Min	Playoffs GP	G	A	Pts	PIM	PP	SH	GW
1993-94	Brandon	WHL	2	0	0	0	0	....	....	....	....	....	....	....	....	....	....	....	....	....	....	....	....	....	....	....
	Swift Current	WHL	69	33	35	68	68	....	....	....	....	....	....	....	....	....	....	....	7	5	4	9	8	....	....	....
1994-95	Swift Current	WHL	65	32	60	92	122	....	....	....	....	....	....	....	....	....	....	....	6	2	6	8	14	....	....	....
	Saint John	AHL	1	0	0	0	0	....	....	....	....	....	....	....	....	....	....	....	....	....	....	....	....	....	....	....
1995-96	**Calgary**	**NHL**	**5**	**1**	**0**	**1**	**2**	**0**	**0**	**0**	**8**	**12.5**	**−1**	....	....	....	....	....	....	....	....	....	....	....	....	....
	Saint John	AHL	73	28	45	73	97	....	....	....	....	....	....	....	....	....	....	....	16	6	5	11	12	....	....	....
1996-97	Saint John	AHL	76	28	29	57	81	....	....	....	....	....	....	....	....	....	....	....	5	0	0	0	0	....	....	....
1997-98	**Calgary**	**NHL**	**4**	**0**	**1**	**1**	**0**	**0**	**0**	**0**	**2**	**0.0**	**2**	....	....	....	....	....	....	....	....	....	....	....	....	....
	Saint John	AHL	65	25	31	56	90	....	....	....	....	....	....	....	....	....	....	....	21	14	6	20	20	....	....	....
1998-99	**Toronto**	**NHL**	**16**	**1**	**3**	**4**	**4**	**0**	**0**	**0**	**23**	**4.3**	**1**	**16**	**18.8**	**15**	**3**	**12:34**	**2**	**0**	**0**	**0**	**5**	**0**	**0**	**0**
	St. John's	AHL	61	27	42	69	90	....	....	....	....	....	....	....	....	....	....	....	....	....	....	....	....	....	....	....
	NHL Totals		**25**	**2**	**4**	**6**	**6**	**0**	**0**	**0**	**33**	**6.1**		**16**	**18.8**	**15**	**3**	**12:34**	**2**	**0**	**0**	**0**	**5**	**0**	**0**	**0**

Traded to **Toronto** by **Calgary** for David Cooper, July 2, 1998.

KOIVU, Saku

(KOY-voo, SA-koo) **MTL.**

Center. Shoots left. 5'10", 183 lbs. Born, Turku, Finland, November 23, 1974. Montreal's 1st choice, 21st overall, in 1993 Entry Draft.

Season	Club	League	Regular Season GP	G	A	Pts	PIM	PP	SH	GW	S	%	+/-	TF	F%	H	SB	Min	Playoffs GP	G	A	Pts	PIM	PP	SH	GW
1990-91	TPS Turku	Finn-Jr.	24	20	28	48	26	....	....	....	....	....	....	....	....	....	....	....	....	....	....	....	....	....	....	....
1991-92	TPS Turku	Finn-Jr.	34	25	28	53	57	....	....	....	....	....	....	....	....	....	....	....	8	5	*9	*14	6	....	....	....
	TPS Turku	Finland-2	12	3	7	10	6	....	....	....	....	....	....	....	....	....	....	....	....	....	....	....	....	....	....	....
1992-93	TPS Turku	Finland	46	3	7	10	28	....	....	....	....	....	....	....	....	....	....	....	11	3	2	5	2	....	....	....
	Finland	Nat-Team	4	2	2	4	2	....	....	....	....	....	....	....	....	....	....	....	....	....	....	....	....	....	....	....

			Regular Season																Playoffs							
Season	Club	League	GP	G	A	Pts	PIM	PP	SH	GW	S	%	+/–	TF	F%	H	SB	Min	GP	G	A	Pts	PIM	PP	SH	GW
1993-94	TPS Turku	Finland	47	23	30	53	42	....	....	....	....	....	....	....	....	....	....	....	11	4	8	12	16	....	....	....
	Finland	Nat-Team	7	2	3	5	12	....	....	....	....	....	....	....	....	....	....	....	....	....	....	....	....	....	....	....
	Finland	Olympics	8	4	3	7	12	....	....	....	....	....	....	....	....	....	....	....	....	....	....	....	....	....	....	....
1994-95	TPS Turku	Finland	45	27	47	74	73	....	....	....	....	....	....	....	....	....	....	....	13	7	10	17	16	....	....	....
	Finland	Nat-Team	7	1	5	6	8	....	....	....	....	....	....	....	....	....	....	....	....	....	....	....	....	....	....	....
1995-96	**Montreal**	**NHL**	**82**	**20**	**25**	**45**	**40**	**8**	**3**	**2**	**136**	**14.7**	**–7**	....	....	....	....	....	**6**	**3**	**1**	**4**	**8**	**0**	**0**	**0**
1996-97	**Montreal**	**NHL**	**50**	**17**	**39**	**56**	**38**	**5**	**0**	**3**	**135**	**12.6**	**7**	....	....	....	....	....	**5**	**1**	**3**	**4**	**10**	**0**	**0**	**0**
	Finland	Nat-Team	7	1	5	6	8	....	....	....	....	....	....	....	....	....	....	....	....	....	....	....	....	....	....	....
1997-98	**Montreal**	**NHL**	**69**	**14**	**43**	**57**	**48**	**2**	**2**	**3**	**145**	**9.7**	**8**	....	....	....	....	....	**6**	**2**	**3**	**5**	**2**	**1**	**0**	**0**
	Finland	Olympics	6	2	*8	*10	4	....	....	....	....	....	....	....	....	....	....	....	....	....	....	....	....	....	....	....
1998-99	**Montreal**	**NHL**	**65**	**14**	**30**	**44**	**38**	**4**	**2**	**0**	**145**	**9.7**	**–7**	**1427**	**52.6**	**53**	**12**	**20:02**	....	....	....	....	....	....	....	....
	NHL Totals		**266**	**65**	**137**	**202**	**164**	**19**	**7**	**8**	**561**	**11.6**		**1427**	**52.6**	**53**	**12**	**20:02**	**17**	**6**	**7**	**13**	**20**	**1**	**0**	**0**

Finnish First All-Star Team (1995) • Finnish Player of the Year (1995)
Played in NHL All-Star Game (1998)

KONOWALCHUK, Steve
(kahn-uh-WAHL-chuhk) **WSH.**

Center. Shoots left. 6'2", 207 lbs. Born, Salt Lake City, UT, November 11, 1972. Washington's 5th choice, 58th overall, in 1991 Entry Draft.

Season	Club	League	GP	G	A	Pts	PIM	PP	SH	GW	S	%	+/–	TF	F%	H	SB	Min	GP	G	A	Pts	PIM	PP	SH	GW
1989-90	Prince Albert	AAHA	36	30	28	58	22	....	....	....	....	....	....	....	....	....	....	....	....	....	....	....	....	....	....	....
1990-91	Portland	WHL	72	43	49	92	78	....	....	....	....	....	....	....	....	....	....	....	....	....	....	....	....	....	....	....
1991-92	Portland	WHL	64	51	53	104	95	....	....	....	....	....	....	....	....	....	....	....	6	3	6	9	12	....	....	....
	Washington	**NHL**	**1**	**0**	**0**	**0**	**0**	**0**	**0**	**0**	**1**	**0.0**	**0**	....	....	....	....	....	....	....	....	....	....	....	....	....
	Baltimore	AHL	3	1	1	2	0	....	....	....	....	....	....	....	....	....	....	....	....	....	....	....	....	....	....	....
1992-93	**Washington**	**NHL**	**36**	**4**	**7**	**11**	**16**	**1**	**0**	**1**	**34**	**11.8**	**4**	....	....	....	....	....	**2**	**0**	**1**	**1**	**0**	**0**	**0**	**0**
	Baltimore	AHL	37	18	28	46	74	....	....	....	....	....	....	....	....	....	....	....	....	....	....	....	....	....	....	....
1993-94	**Washington**	**NHL**	**62**	**12**	**14**	**26**	**33**	**0**	**0**	**0**	**63**	**19.0**	**9**	....	....	....	....	....	**11**	**0**	**1**	**1**	**10**	**0**	**0**	**0**
	Portland	AHL	8	11	4	15	4	....	....	....	....	....	....	....	....	....	....	....	....	....	....	....	....	....	....	....
1994-95	**Washington**	**NHL**	**46**	**11**	**14**	**25**	**44**	**3**	**3**	**3**	**88**	**12.5**	**7**	....	....	....	....	....	**7**	**2**	**5**	**7**	**12**	**0**	**1**	**0**
1995-96	**Washington**	**NHL**	**70**	**23**	**22**	**45**	**92**	**7**	**1**	**3**	**197**	**11.7**	**13**	....	....	....	....	....	**2**	**0**	**2**	**2**	**0**	**0**	**0**	**0**
1996-97	**Washington**	**NHL**	**78**	**17**	**25**	**42**	**67**	**2**	**1**	**3**	**155**	**11.0**	**–3**	....	....	....	....	....	....	....	....	....	....	....	....	....
1997-98	**Washington**	**NHL**	**80**	**10**	**24**	**34**	**80**	**2**	**0**	**2**	**131**	**7.6**	**9**	....	....	....	....	....	....	....	....	....	....	....	....	....
1998-99	**Washington**	**NHL**	**45**	**12**	**12**	**24**	**26**	**4**	**1**	**2**	**98**	**12.2**	**0**	**124**	**51.6**	**125**	**13**	**17:50**	....	....	....	....	....	....	....	....
	NHL Totals		**418**	**89**	**118**	**207**	**358**	**19**	**6**	**14**	**767**	**11.6**		**124**	**51.6**	**125**	**13**	**17:50**	**22**	**2**	**9**	**11**	**22**	**0**	**1**	**0**

WHL First All-Star Team (1992)

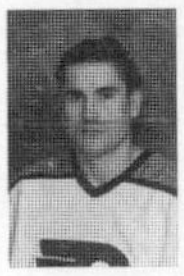

KORDIC, Dan
(KOHR-dihk)

Left wing. Shoots left. 6'5", 234 lbs. Born, Edmonton, Alta., April 18, 1971. Philadelphia's 9th choice, 88th overall, in 1990 Entry Draft.

Season	Club	League	GP	G	A	Pts	PIM	PP	SH	GW	S	%	+/–	TF	F%	H	SB	Min	GP	G	A	Pts	PIM	PP	SH	GW
1986-87	Edmonton	AAHA	42	1	16	17	88	....	....	....	....	....	....	....	....	....	....	....	....	....	....	....	....	....	....	....
1987-88	Medicine Hat	WHL	63	1	5	6	75	....	....	....	....	....	....	....	....	....	....	....	....	....	....	....	....	....	....	....
1988-89	Medicine Hat	WHL	70	1	13	14	190	....	....	....	....	....	....	....	....	....	....	....	....	....	....	....	....	....	....	....
1989-90	Medicine Hat	WHL	59	4	12	16	182	....	....	....	....	....	....	....	....	....	....	....	3	0	0	0	9	....	....	....
1990-91	Medicine Hat	WHL	67	8	15	23	150	....	....	....	....	....	....	....	....	....	....	....	12	2	6	8	42	....	....	....
1991-92	**Philadelphia**	**NHL**	**46**	**1**	**3**	**4**	**126**	**0**	**0**	**0**	**27**	**3.7**	**1**	....	....	....	....	....	....	....	....	....	....	....	....	....
1992-93	Hershey	AHL	14	0	2	2	17	....	....	....	....	....	....	....	....	....	....	....	....	....	....	....	....	....	....	....
1993-94	**Philadelphia**	**NHL**	**4**	**0**	**0**	**0**	**5**	**0**	**0**	**0**	**0**	**0.0**	**0**	....	....	....	....	....	....	....	....	....	....	....	....	....
	Hershey	AHL	64	0	4	4	164	....	....	....	....	....	....	....	....	....	....	....	11	0	3	3	26	....	....	....
1994-95	Hershey	AHL	37	0	2	2	121	....	....	....	....	....	....	....	....	....	....	....	6	0	1	1	21	....	....	....
1995-96	**Philadelphia**	**NHL**	**9**	**1**	**0**	**1**	**31**	**0**	**0**	**0**	**2**	**50.0**	**1**	....	....	....	....	....	....	....	....	....	....	....	....	....
	Hershey	AHL	52	2	6	8	101	....	....	....	....	....	....	....	....	....	....	....	....	....	....	....	....	....	....	....
1996-97	**Philadelphia**	**NHL**	**75**	**1**	**4**	**5**	**210**	**0**	**0**	**0**	**21**	**4.8**	**–1**	....	....	....	....	....	**12**	**1**	**0**	**1**	**22**	**0**	**0**	**0**
1997-98	**Philadelphia**	**NHL**	**61**	**1**	**1**	**2**	**210**	**0**	**0**	**0**	**12**	**8.3**	**–4**	....	....	....	....	....	....	....	....	....	....	....	....	....
1998-99	**Philadelphia**	**NHL**	**2**	**0**	**0**	**0**	**2**	**0**	**0**	**0**	**0**	**0.0**	**–1**	**0**	**0.0**	**0**	**0**	**2:27**	....	....	....	....	....	....	....	....
	Grand Rapids	IHL	3	0	0	0	0	....	....	....	....	....	....	....	....	....	....	....	....	....	....	....	....	....	....	....
	Philadelphia	AHL	9	1	1	2	43	....	....	....	....	....	....	....	....	....	....	....	1	0	0	0	0	....	....	....
	NHL Totals		**197**	**4**	**8**	**12**	**584**	**0**	**0**	**0**	**62**	**6.5**		**0**	**0.0**	**0**	**0**	**2:27**	**12**	**1**	**0**	**1**	**22**	**0**	**0**	**0**

KOROLEV, Igor
(koh-roh-LEHV) **TOR.**

Center/left wing. Shoots left. 6'1", 195 lbs. Born, Moscow, USSR, September 6, 1970. St. Louis' 1st choice, 38th overall, in 1992 Entry Draft.

Season	Club	League	GP	G	A	Pts	PIM	PP	SH	GW	S	%	+/–	TF	F%	H	SB	Min	GP	G	A	Pts	PIM	PP	SH	GW
1988-89	Moscow D'amo	USSR	1	0	0	0	2	....	....	....	....	....	....	....	....	....	....	....	....	....	....	....	....	....	....	....
1989-90	Moscow D'amo	USSR	17	3	2	5	2	....	....	....	....	....	....	....	....	....	....	....	....	....	....	....	....	....	....	....
1990-91	Moscow D'amo	USSR	38	12	4	16	12	....	....	....	....	....	....	....	....	....	....	....	....	....	....	....	....	....	....	....
1991-92	Moscow D'amo	CIS	39	15	12	27	16	....	....	....	....	....	....	....	....	....	....	....	....	....	....	....	....	....	....	....
1992-93	Moscow D'amo	CIS	5	1	2	3	4	....	....	....	....	....	....	....	....	....	....	....	....	....	....	....	....	....	....	....
	St. Louis	**NHL**	**74**	**4**	**23**	**27**	**20**	**2**	**0**	**0**	**76**	**5.3**	**–1**	....	....	....	....	....	**3**	**0**	**0**	**0**	**0**	**0**	**0**	**0**
1993-94	**St. Louis**	**NHL**	**73**	**6**	**10**	**16**	**40**	**0**	**0**	**1**	**93**	**6.5**	**–12**	....	....	....	....	....	**2**	**0**	**0**	**0**	**0**	**0**	**0**	**0**
1994-95	Moscow D'amo	CIS	13	4	6	10	18	....	....	....	....	....	....	....	....	....	....	....	....	....	....	....	....	....	....	....
	Winnipeg	**NHL**	**45**	**8**	**22**	**30**	**10**	**1**	**0**	**1**	**85**	**9.4**	**1**	....	....	....	....	....	....	....	....	....	....	....	....	....
1995-96	**Winnipeg**	**NHL**	**73**	**22**	**29**	**51**	**42**	**8**	**0**	**5**	**165**	**13.3**	**1**	....	....	....	....	....	**6**	**0**	**3**	**3**	**0**	**0**	**0**	**0**
1996-97	**Phoenix**	**NHL**	**41**	**3**	**7**	**10**	**28**	**2**	**0**	**0**	**41**	**7.3**	**–5**	....	....	....	....	....	**1**	**0**	**0**	**0**	**0**	**0**	**0**	**0**
	Michigan	IHL	4	2	2	4	0	....	....	....	....	....	....	....	....	....	....	....	....	....	....	....	....	....	....	....
	Phoenix	IHL	4	2	6	8	4	....	....	....	....	....	....	....	....	....	....	....	....	....	....	....	....	....	....	....
1997-98	**Toronto**	**NHL**	**78**	**17**	**22**	**39**	**22**	**6**	**3**	**5**	**97**	**17.5**	**–18**	....	....	....	....	....	....	....	....	....	....	....	....	....
1998-99	**Toronto**	**NHL**	**66**	**13**	**34**	**47**	**46**	**1**	**0**	**2**	**99**	**13.1**	**11**	**973**	**42.0**	**23**	**13**	**18:06**	**1**	**0**	**0**	**0**	**0**	**0**	**0**	**0**
	NHL Totals		**450**	**73**	**147**	**220**	**208**	**20**	**3**	**14**	**656**	**11.1**		**973**	**42.0**	**23**	**13**	**18:06**	**13**	**0**	**3**	**3**	**0**	**0**	**0**	**0**

Claimed by **Winnipeg** from **St. Louis** in NHL Waiver Draft, January 18, 1995. Transferred to **Phoenix** after **Winnipeg** franchise relocated, July 1, 1996. Signed as a free agent by **Toronto**, September 29, 1997.

KOROLYUK, Alexander
(koh-roh-LYUHK) **S.J.**

Right wing. Shoots left. 5'9", 190 lbs. Born, Moscow, USSR, January 15, 1976. San Jose's 6th choice, 141st overall, in 1994 Entry Draft.

Season	Club	League	GP	G	A	Pts	PIM	PP	SH	GW	S	%	+/–	TF	F%	H	SB	Min	GP	G	A	Pts	PIM	PP	SH	GW
1993-94	Soviet Wings	CIS	22	4	4	8	20	....	....	....	....	....	....	....	....	....	....	....	3	1	0	1	4	....	....	....
1994-95	Soviet Wings	CIS	52	16	13	29	62	....	....	....	....	....	....	....	....	....	....	....	4	1	2	3	4	....	....	....
1995-96	Soviet Wings	CIS	50	30	19	49	77	....	....	....	....	....	....	....	....	....	....	....	....	....	....	....	....	....	....	....
1996-97	Soviet Wings	Russia	17	8	5	13	46	....	....	....	....	....	....	....	....	....	....	....	....	....	....	....	....	....	....	....
	Manitoba	IHL	42	20	16	36	71	....	....	....	....	....	....	....	....	....	....	....	....	....	....	....	....	....	....	....
1997-98	**San Jose**	**NHL**	**19**	**2**	**3**	**5**	**6**	**1**	**0**	**0**	**23**	**8.7**	**–5**	....	....	....	....	....	....	....	....	....	....	....	....	....
	Kentucky	AHL	44	16	23	39	96	....	....	....	....	....	....	....	....	....	....	....	3	0	0	0	0	....	....	....
1998-99	**San Jose**	**NHL**	**55**	**12**	**18**	**30**	**26**	**2**	**0**	**0**	**96**	**12.5**	**3**	**4**	**50.0**	**66**	**7**	**13:53**	**6**	**1**	**3**	**4**	**2**	**0**	**0**	**1**
	Kentucky	AHL	23	9	13	22	16	....	....	....	....	....	....	....	....	....	....	....	....	....	....	....	....	....	....	....
	NHL Totals		**74**	**14**	**21**	**35**	**32**	**3**	**0**	**0**	**119**	**11.8**		**4**	**50.0**	**66**	**7**	**13:53**	**6**	**1**	**3**	**4**	**2**	**0**	**0**	**1**

KOVALENKO, Andrei
(koh-vah-LEHN-koh) **CAR.**

Right wing. Shoots left. 5'10", 215 lbs. Born, Balakovo, USSR, June 7, 1970. Quebec's 6th choice, 148th overall, in 1990 Entry Draft.

Season	Club	League	GP	G	A	Pts	PIM	PP	SH	GW	S	%	+/–	TF	F%	H	SB	Min	GP	G	A	Pts	PIM	PP	SH	GW
1987-88	Torpedo Gorky	USSR	2	1	0	1	0	....	....	....	....	....	....	....	....	....	....	....	....	....	....	....	....	....	....	....
1988-89	Kalinin	USSR-2	30	8	7	15	29	....	....	....	....	....	....	....	....	....	....	....	....	....	....	....	....	....	....	....
	CSKA Moscow	USSR	10	1	0	1	0	....	....	....	....	....	....	....	....	....	....	....	....	....	....	....	....	....	....	....
1989-90	CSKA Moscow	USSR	48	8	5	13	20	....	....	....	....	....	....	....	....	....	....	....	....	....	....	....	....	....	....	....
1990-91	CSKA Moscow	USSR	45	13	8	21	26	....	....	....	....	....	....	....	....	....	....	....	....	....	....	....	....	....	....	....

			Regular Season																Playoffs							
Season	Club	League	GP	G	A	Pts	PIM	PP	SH	GW	S	%	+/-	TF	F%	H	SB	Min	GP	G	A	Pts	PIM	PP	SH	GW
1991-92	CSKA Moscow	CIS	44	19	13	32	32	....	....	....	....	....	....	....	....	....	....	....	....	....	....	....	....	....	....	....
	Russia	Olympics	8	1	1	2	2	....	....	....	....	....	....	....	....	....	....	....	....	....	....	....	....	....	....	....
1992-93	CSKA Moscow	CIS	3	3	1	4	4	....	....	....	....	....	....	....	....	....	....	....	....	....	....	....	....	....	....	....
	Quebec	NHL	81	27	41	68	57	8	1	4	153	17.6	13	....	....	....	....	....	4	1	0	1	2	0	0	0
1993-94	Quebec	NHL	58	16	17	33	46	5	0	4	92	17.4	-5	....	....	....	....	....	....	....	....	....	....	....	....	....
1994-95	Lada	CIS	11	9	2	11	14	....	....	....	....	....	....	....	....	....	....	....	....	....	....	....	....	....	....	....
	Quebec	NHL	45	14	10	24	31	1	0	3	63	22.2	-4	....	....	....	....	....	6	0	1	1	2	0	0	0
1995-96	Colorado	NHL	26	11	11	22	16	3	0	3	46	23.9	11	....	....	....	....	....	....	....	....	....	....	....	....	....
	Montreal	NHL	51	17	17	34	33	3	0	3	85	20.0	9	....	....	....	....	....	6	0	0	0	6	0	0	0
1996-97	Edmonton	NHL	74	32	27	59	81	14	0	2	163	19.6	-5	....	....	....	....	....	12	4	3	7	6	3	0	0
1997-98	Edmonton	NHL	59	6	17	23	28	1	0	2	89	6.7	-14	....	....	....	....	....	1	0	0	0	2	0	0	0
	Russia	Olympics	6	4	1	5	14	....	....	....	....	....	....	....	....	....	....	....	....	....	....	....	....	....	....	....
1998-99	Edmonton	NHL	43	13	14	27	30	2	0	3	75	17.3	-4	0	0.0	40	7	16:19	....	....	....	....	....	....	....	....
	Philadelphia	NHL	13	0	1	1	2	0	0	0	8	0.0	-5	0	0.0	12	1	8:02	....	....	....	....	....	....	....	....
	Carolina	NHL	18	6	6	12	0	1	0	1	21	28.6	3	1	0.0	40	2	13:53	4	0	2	2	2	0	0	0
	NHL Totals		468	142	161	303	324	38	1	25	795	17.9		1	0.0	92	10	14:16	33	5	6	11	20	3	0	0

Transferred to **Colorado** after **Quebec** franchise relocated, June 21, 1995. Traded to **Montreal** by **Colorado** with Martin Rucinsky and Jocelyn Thibault for Patrick Roy and Mike Keane, December 6, 1995. Traded to **Edmonton** by **Montreal** for Scott Thornton, September 6, 1996. Traded to **Philadelphia** by **Edmonton** for Alexandre Daigle, January 29, 1999. Traded to **Carolina** by **Philadelphia** for Adam Burt, March 6, 1999.

KOVALEV, Alexei

(koh-VAH-lehv) **PIT.**

Right wing. Shoots left. 6'2", 215 lbs. Born, Togliatti, USSR, February 24, 1973. NY Rangers' 1st choice, 15th overall, in 1991 Entry Draft.

Season	Club	League	GP	G	A	Pts	PIM	PP	SH	GW	S	%	+/-	TF	F%	H	SB	Min	GP	G	A	Pts	PIM	PP	SH	GW
1989-90	Moscow D'amo	USSR	1	0	0	0	0	....	....	....	....	....	....	....	....	....	....	....	....	....	....	....	....	....	....	....
1990-91	Moscow D'amo	USSR	18	1	2	3	4	....	....	....	....	....	....	....	....	....	....	....	....	....	....	....	....	....	....	....
1991-92	Moscow D'amo	CIS	33	16	9	25	20	....	....	....	....	....	....	....	....	....	....	....	....	....	....	....	....	....	....	....
	Russia	Olympics	8	1	2	3	14	....	....	....	....	....	....	....	....	....	....	....	....	....	....	....	....	....	....	....
1992-93	NY Rangers	NHL	65	20	18	38	79	3	0	3	134	14.9	-10	....	....	....	....	....	....	....	....	....	....	....	....	....
	Binghamton	AHL	13	13	11	24	35	....	....	....	....	....	....	....	....	....	....	....	9	3	5	8	14	....	....	....
1993-94♦	NY Rangers	NHL	76	23	33	56	154	7	0	3	184	12.5	18	....	....	....	....	....	23	9	12	21	18	5	0	2
1994-95	Lada	CIS	12	8	8	16	49	....	....	....	....	....	....	....	....	....	....	....	....	....	....	....	....	....	....	....
	NY Rangers	NHL	48	13	15	28	30	1	1	1	103	12.6	-6	....	....	....	....	....	10	4	7	11	10	0	0	0
1995-96	NY Rangers	NHL	81	24	34	58	98	8	1	7	206	11.7	5	....	....	....	....	....	11	3	4	7	14	0	0	1
1996-97	NY Rangers	NHL	45	13	22	35	42	1	0	0	110	11.8	11	....	....	....	....	....	....	....	....	....	....	....	....	....
1997-98	NY Rangers	NHL	73	23	30	53	44	8	0	3	173	13.3	-22	....	....	....	....	....	....	....	....	....	....	....	....	....
1998-99	NY Rangers	NHL	14	3	4	7	12	1	0	1	35	8.6	-6	18	44.4	13	5	19:53	....	....	....	....	....	....	....	....
	Pittsburgh	NHL	63	20	26	46	37	5	1	4	156	12.8	8	226	43.4	82	40	20:30	10	5	7	12	14	0	0	1
	NHL Totals		465	139	182	321	496	34	3	22	1101	12.6		244	43.4	95	45	20:23	54	21	30	51	56	5	0	4

Traded to **Pittsburgh** by **NY Rangers** with Harry York for Petr Nedved, Chris Tamer and Sean Pronger, November 25, 1998.

KOZLOV, Viktor

(KAHS-lahf) **FLA.**

Center. Shoots right. 6'5", 232 lbs. Born, Togliatti, USSR, February 14, 1975. San Jose's 1st choice, 6th overall, in 1993 Entry Draft.

Season	Club	League	GP	G	A	Pts	PIM	PP	SH	GW	S	%	+/-	TF	F%	H	SB	Min	GP	G	A	Pts	PIM	PP	SH	GW
1990-91	Lada	USSR-2	2	2	0	2	0	....	....	....	....	....	....	....	....	....	....	....	....	....	....	....	....	....	....	....
1991-92	Lada	CIS	3	0	0	0	0	....	....	....	....	....	....	....	....	....	....	....	....	....	....	....	....	....	....	....
1992-93	Moscow D'amo	CIS	30	6	5	11	4	....	....	....	....	....	....	....	....	....	....	....	10	3	0	3	0	....	....	....
1993-94	Moscow D'amo	CIS	42	16	9	25	14	....	....	....	....	....	....	....	....	....	....	....	7	3	2	5	0	....	....	....
1994-95	Moscow D'amo	CIS	3	1	1	2	2	....	....	....	....	....	....	....	....	....	....	....	....	....	....	....	....	....	....	....
	San Jose	NHL	16	2	0	2	2	0	0	0	23	8.7	-5	....	....	....	....	....	....	....	....	....	....	....	....	....
	Kansas City	IHL	4	1	1	2	0	....	....	....	....	....	....	....	....	....	....	....	13	4	5	9	12	....	....	....
1995-96	San Jose	NHL	62	6	13	19	6	1	0	0	107	5.6	-15	....	....	....	....	....	....	....	....	....	....	....	....	....
	Kansas City	IHL	15	4	7	11	12	....	....	....	....	....	....	....	....	....	....	....	....	....	....	....	....	....	....	....
1996-97	San Jose	NHL	78	16	25	41	40	4	0	4	184	8.7	-16	....	....	....	....	....	....	....	....	....	....	....	....	....
1997-98	San Jose	NHL	18	5	2	7	2	2	0	0	51	9.8	-2	....	....	....	....	....	....	....	....	....	....	....	....	....
	Florida	NHL	46	12	11	23	14	3	2	0	114	10.5	-1	....	....	....	....	....	....	....	....	....	....	....	....	....
1998-99	Florida	NHL	65	16	35	51	24	5	1	1	209	7.7	13	985	41.2	32	30	19:03	....	....	....	....	....	....	....	....
	NHL Totals		285	57	86	143	88	15	3	5	688	8.3		985	41.2	32	30	19:03	....	....	....	....	....	....	....	....

Traded to **Florida** by **San Jose** with Florida's 5th round choice (previously acquired, Florida selected Jaroslav Spacek) in 1998 Entry Draft for Dave Lowry and Florida's 1st round choice (later traded to Tampa Bay - Tampa Bay selected Vincent Lecavalier) in 1998 Entry Draft, November 13, 1997.

KOZLOV, Vyacheslav

(KAHS-lahf, VYACH-ih-slav) **DET.**

Center. Shoots left. 5'10", 180 lbs. Born, Voskresensk, USSR, May 3, 1972. Detroit's 2nd choice, 45th overall, in 1990 Entry Draft.

Season	Club	League	GP	G	A	Pts	PIM	PP	SH	GW	S	%	+/-	TF	F%	H	SB	Min	GP	G	A	Pts	PIM	PP	SH	GW
1987-88	Khimik	USSR	2	0	0	0	0	....	....	....	....	....	....	....	....	....	....	....	....	....	....	....	....	....	....	....
1988-89	Khimik	USSR	14	0	1	1	2	....	....	....	....	....	....	....	....	....	....	....	....	....	....	....	....	....	....	....
1989-90	Khimik	USSR	45	14	12	26	38	....	....	....	....	....	....	....	....	....	....	....	....	....	....	....	....	....	....	....
1990-91	Khimik	USSR	45	11	13	24	46	....	....	....	....	....	....	....	....	....	....	....	....	....	....	....	....	....	....	....
1991-92	CSKA Moscow	CIS	11	6	5	11	12	....	....	....	....	....	....	....	....	....	....	....	....	....	....	....	....	....	....	....
	Detroit	NHL	7	0	2	2	2	0	0	0	9	0.0	-2	....	....	....	....	....	....	....	....	....	....	....	....	....
1992-93	Detroit	NHL	17	4	1	5	14	0	0	0	26	15.4	-1	....	....	....	....	....	4	0	2	2	2	0	0	0
	Adirondack	AHL	45	23	36	59	54	....	....	....	....	....	....	....	....	....	....	....	4	1	1	2	4	....	....	....
1993-94	Detroit	NHL	77	34	39	73	50	8	2	6	202	16.8	27	....	....	....	....	....	7	2	5	7	12	0	0	0
	Adirondack	AHL	3	0	1	1	15	....	....	....	....	....	....	....	....	....	....	....	....	....	....	....	....	....	....	....
1994-95	CSKA Moscow	CIS	10	3	4	7	14	....	....	....	....	....	....	....	....	....	....	....	....	....	....	....	....	....	....	....
	Detroit	NHL	46	13	20	33	45	5	0	3	97	13.4	12	....	....	....	....	....	18	9	7	16	10	1	0	4
1995-96	Detroit	NHL	82	36	37	73	70	9	0	7	237	15.2	33	....	....	....	....	....	19	5	7	12	10	2	0	1
1996-97♦	Detroit	NHL	75	23	22	45	46	3	0	6	211	10.9	21	....	....	....	....	....	20	8	5	13	14	4	0	2
1997-98♦	Detroit	NHL	80	25	27	52	46	6	0	1	221	11.3	14	....	....	....	....	....	22	6	8	14	10	1	0	4
1998-99	Detroit	NHL	79	29	29	58	45	6	1	4	209	13.9	10	38	36.8	41	20	16:02	10	6	1	7	4	3	0	0
	NHL Totals		463	164	177	341	318	37	3	27	1212	13.5		38	36.8	41	20	16:02	100	36	35	71	62	11	0	11

USSR Rookie of the Year (1990)

KRAVCHUK, Igor

(krahv-CHOOK) **OTT.**

Defense. Shoots left. 6'1", 200 lbs. Born, Ufa, USSR, September 13, 1966. Chicago's 5th choice, 71st overall, in 1991 Entry Draft.

Season	Club	League	GP	G	A	Pts	PIM	PP	SH	GW	S	%	+/-	TF	F%	H	SB	Min	GP	G	A	Pts	PIM	PP	SH	GW
1984-85	Yulayev	USSR-2	50	3	2	5	22	....	....	....	....	....	....	....	....	....	....	....	....	....	....	....	....	....	....	....
1985-86	Yulayev	USSR	21	2	2	4	6	....	....	....	....	....	....	....	....	....	....	....	....	....	....	....	....	....	....	....
1986-87	Yulayev	USSR	22	0	1	1	8	....	....	....	....	....	....	....	....	....	....	....	....	....	....	....	....	....	....	....
1987-88	CSKA Moscow	USSR	48	1	8	9	12	....	....	....	....	....	....	....	....	....	....	....	....	....	....	....	....	....	....	....
	Soviet Union	Olympics	6	1	0	1	0	....	....	....	....	....	....	....	....	....	....	....	....	....	....	....	....	....	....	....
1988-89	CSKA Moscow	USSR	22	3	3	6	2	....	....	....	....	....	....	....	....	....	....	....	....	....	....	....	....	....	....	....
1989-90	CSKA Moscow	USSR	48	1	3	4	16	....	....	....	....	....	....	....	....	....	....	....	....	....	....	....	....	....	....	....
1990-91	CSKA Moscow	USSR	41	6	5	11	16	....	....	....	....	....	....	....	....	....	....	....	....	....	....	....	....	....	....	....
1991-92	CSKA Moscow	CIS	30	3	8	11	6	....	....	....	....	....	....	....	....	....	....	....	....	....	....	....	....	....	....	....
	Russia	Olympics	8	3	2	5	6	....	....	....	....	....	....	....	....	....	....	....	....	....	....	....	....	....	....	....
	Chicago	NHL	18	1	8	9	4	0	0	1	40	2.5	-3	....	....	....	....	....	18	2	6	8	8	1	0	0
1992-93	Chicago	NHL	38	6	9	15	30	3	0	0	101	5.9	11	....	....	....	....	....	....	....	....	....	....	....	....	....
	Edmonton	NHL	17	4	8	12	2	1	0	0	42	9.5	-8	....	....	....	....	....	....	....	....	....	....	....	....	....
1993-94	Edmonton	NHL	81	12	38	50	16	5	0	2	197	6.1	-12	....	....	....	....	....	....	....	....	....	....	....	....	....
1994-95	Edmonton	NHL	36	7	11	18	29	3	1	0	93	7.5	-15	....	....	....	....	....	....	....	....	....	....	....	....	....
1995-96	Edmonton	NHL	26	4	4	8	10	3	0	0	59	6.8	-13	....	....	....	....	....	....	....	....	....	....	....	....	....
	St. Louis	NHL	40	3	12	15	24	0	0	1	114	2.6	-6	....	....	....	....	....	10	1	5	6	4	0	0	1

					Regular Season														Playoffs							
Season	Club	League	GP	G	A	Pts	PIM	PP	SH	GW	S	%	+/–	TF	F%	H	SB	Min	GP	G	A	Pts	PIM	PP	SH	GW
1996-97	St. Louis	NHL	82	4	24	28	35	1	0	0	142	2.8	7	....	....	....	....	....	2	0	0	0	2	0	0	0
1997-98	Ottawa	NHL	81	8	27	35	8	3	1	1	191	4.2	–19	....	....	....	....	....	11	2	3	5	4	0	0	0
	Russia	Olympics	6	0	2	2	2	....	....	....	....	....	....	....	....	....	....	....	....	....	....	....	....	....	....	....
1998-99	Ottawa	NHL	79	4	21	25	32	3	0	0	171	2.3	14	0	0.0	89	115	23:51	4	0	0	0	0	0	0	0
	NHL Totals		498	53	162	215	190	22	2	5	1150	4.6		0	0.0	89	115	23:51	45	5	14	19	18	1	0	1

Played in NHL All-Star Game (1998)

Traded to **Edmonton** by **Chicago** with Dean McAmmond for Joe Murphy, February 24, 1993. Traded to **St. Louis** by **Edmonton** with Ken Sutton for Jeff Norton and Donald Dufresne, January 4, 1996. Traded to **Ottawa** by **St. Louis** for Steve Duchesne, August 25, 1997.

KRIVOKRASOV, Sergei (krih-vuh-KRA-sahf) NSH.

Right wing. Shoots left. 5'11", 185 lbs. Born, Angarsk, USSR, April 15, 1974. Chicago's 1st choice, 12th overall, in 1992 Entry Draft.

1990-91	CSKA Moscow	USSR	41	4	0	4	8	....	....	....	....	....	....	....	....	....	....	....	....	....	....	....	....	....	....	....
1991-92	CSKA Moscow	CIS	42	10	8	18	35	....	....	....	....	....	....	....	....	....	....	....	....	....	....	....	....	....	....	....
1992-93	Chicago	NHL	4	0	0	0	2	0	0	0	0	0.0	–2	....	....	....	....	....	....	....	....	....	....	....	....	....
	Indianapolis	IHL	78	36	33	69	157	....	....	....	....	....	....	....	....	....	....	....	5	3	1	4	2	....	....	....
1993-94	Chicago	NHL	9	1	0	1	4	0	0	0	7	14.3	–2	....	....	....	....	....	....	....	....	....	....	....	....	....
	Indianapolis	IHL	53	19	26	45	145	....	....	....	....	....	....	....	....	....	....	....	....	....	....	....	....	....	....	....
1994-95	Indianapolis	IHL	29	12	15	27	41	....	....	....	....	....	....	....	....	....	....	....	....	....	....	....	....	....	....	....
	Chicago	NHL	41	12	7	19	33	6	0	2	72	16.7	9	....	....	....	....	....	10	0	0	0	8	0	0	0
1995-96	Chicago	NHL	46	6	10	16	32	0	0	1	52	11.5	10	....	....	....	....	....	5	1	0	1	2	0	0	1
	Indianapolis	IHL	9	4	5	9	28	....	....	....	....	....	....	....	....	....	....	....	....	....	....	....	....	....	....	....
1996-97	Chicago	NHL	67	13	11	24	42	2	0	3	104	12.5	–1	....	....	....	....	....	6	1	0	1	4	0	0	0
1997-98	Chicago	NHL	58	10	13	23	33	1	0	2	127	7.9	–1	....	....	....	....	....	....	....	....	....	....	....	....	....
	Russia	Olympics	6	0	0	0	4	....	....	....	....	....	....	....	....	....	....	....	....	....	....	....	....	....	....	....
1998-99	Nashville	NHL	70	25	23	48	42	10	0	6	208	12.0	–5	0	0.0	19	7	16:08	....	....	....	....	....	....	....	....
	NHL Totals		295	67	64	131	188	19	0	14	570	11.8		0	0.0	19	7	16:08	21	2	0	2	14	0	0	1

Played in NHL All-Star Game (1999)

Traded to **Nashville** by **Chicago** for future considerations, June 26, 1998.

KRON, Robert (KROHN) CAR.

Left wing. Shoots left. 5'11", 185 lbs. Born, Brno, Czech., February 27, 1967. Vancouver's 5th choice, 88th overall, in 1985 Entry Draft.

1983-84	Ingstav Brno	Czech-2	3	0	1	1	0	....	....	....	....	....	....	....	....	....	....	....	....	....	....	....	....	....	....	....
1984-85	Zetor Brno	Czech.	40	6	8	14	6	....	....	....	....	....	....	....	....	....	....	....	....	....	....	....	....	....	....	....
1985-86	Zetor Brno	Czech.	44	5	6	11	....	....	....	....	....	....	....	....	....	....	....	....	....	....	....	....	....	....	....	....
1986-87	Zetor Brno	Czech.	34	18	11	29	10	....	....	....	....	....	....	....	....	....	....	....	....	....	....	....	....	....	....	....
1987-88	Zetor Brno	Czech.	44	14	7	21	30	....	....	....	....	....	....	....	....	....	....	....	....	....	....	....	....	....	....	....
1988-89	Dukla Trencin	Czech.	43	28	19	47	26	....	....	....	....	....	....	....	....	....	....	....	....	....	....	....	....	....	....	....
1989-90	Dukla Trencin	Czech.	39	22	22	44	....	....	....	....	....	....	....	....	....	....	....	....	....	....	....	....	....	....	....	....
1990-91	Vancouver	NHL	76	12	20	32	21	2	3	0	124	9.7	–11	....	....	....	....	....	....	....	....	....	....	....	....	....
1991-92	Vancouver	NHL	36	2	2	4	2	0	0	0	49	4.1	–9	....	....	....	....	....	11	1	2	3	2	0	1	0
1992-93	Vancouver	NHL	32	10	11	21	14	2	2	2	60	16.7	10	....	....	....	....	....	....	....	....	....	....	....	....	....
	Hartford	NHL	13	4	2	6	4	2	0	0	37	10.8	–5	....	....	....	....	....	....	....	....	....	....	....	....	....
1993-94	Hartford	NHL	77	24	26	50	8	2	1	3	194	12.4	0	....	....	....	....	....	....	....	....	....	....	....	....	....
1994-95	Hartford	NHL	37	10	8	18	10	3	1	1	88	11.4	–3	....	....	....	....	....	....	....	....	....	....	....	....	....
1995-96	Hartford	NHL	77	22	28	50	6	8	1	3	203	10.8	–1	....	....	....	....	....	....	....	....	....	....	....	....	....
1996-97	Hartford	NHL	68	10	12	22	10	2	0	4	182	5.5	–18	....	....	....	....	....	....	....	....	....	....	....	....	....
1997-98	Carolina	NHL	81	16	20	36	12	4	0	2	175	9.1	–8	....	....	....	....	....	....	....	....	....	....	....	....	....
1998-99	Carolina	NHL	75	9	16	25	10	3	1	2	134	6.7	–13	244	38.9	88	27	16:14	5	2	0	2	0	0	0	1
	NHL Totals		572	119	145	264	97	28	9	17	1246	9.6		244	38.9	88	27	16:14	16	3	2	5	2	0	1	1

Traded to **Hartford** by **Vancouver** with Vancouver's 3rd round choice (Marek Malik) in 1993 Entry Draft and future considerations (Jim Sandlak, May 17, 1993) for Murray Craven and Vancouver's 5th round choice (previously acquired, Vancouver selected Scott Walker) in 1993 Entry Draft, March 22, 1993. Transferred to **Carolina** after **Hartford** franchise relocated, June 25, 1997.

KROUPA, Vlastimil (KROO-pah, VLAS-tuh-meel) N.J.

Defense. Shoots left. 6'3", 215 lbs. Born, Most, Czech., April 27, 1975. San Jose's 3rd choice, 45th overall, in 1993 Entry Draft.

1991-92	HC Litvinov	Czech-Jr.	37	9	16	25	....	....	....	....	....	....	....	....	....	....	....	....	....	....	....	....	....	....	....	....
1992-93	HC Litvinov	Czech	9	0	1	1	....	....	....	....	....	....	....	....	....	....	....	....	....	....	....	....	....	....	....	....
1993-94	San Jose	NHL	27	1	3	4	20	0	0	0	16	6.3	–6	....	....	....	....	....	14	1	2	3	21	0	0	1
	Kansas City	IHL	39	3	12	15	12	....	....	....	....	....	....	....	....	....	....	....	....	....	....	....	....	....	....	....
1994-95	San Jose	NHL	14	0	2	2	16	0	0	0	4	0.0	–7	....	....	....	....	....	6	0	0	0	4	0	0	0
	Kansas City	IHL	51	4	8	12	49	....	....	....	....	....	....	....	....	....	....	....	12	2	4	6	22	....	....	....
1995-96	San Jose	NHL	27	1	7	8	18	0	0	0	11	9.1	–17	....	....	....	....	....	....	....	....	....	....	....	....	....
	Kansas City	IHL	39	5	22	27	44	....	....	....	....	....	....	....	....	....	....	....	5	0	1	1	6	....	....	....
1996-97	San Jose	NHL	35	2	6	8	12	2	0	1	24	8.3	–17	....	....	....	....	....	....	....	....	....	....	....	....	....
	Kentucky	AHL	5	0	3	3	0	....	....	....	....	....	....	....	....	....	....	....	....	....	....	....	....	....	....	....
1997-98	New Jersey	NHL	2	0	1	1	0	0	0	0	1	0.0	1	....	....	....	....	....	....	....	....	....	....	....	....	....
	Albany	AHL	71	5	29	34	48	....	....	....	....	....	....	....	....	....	....	....	12	0	3	3	6	....	....	....
1998-99	Kansas City	IHL	77	6	32	38	52	....	....	....	....	....	....	....	....	....	....	....	3	0	1	1	0	....	....	....
	Albany	AHL	2	0	1	1	4	....	....	....	....	....	....	....	....	....	....	....	....	....	....	....	....	....	....	....
	NHL Totals		105	4	19	23	66	2	0	1	56	7.1		....	....	....	....	....	20	1	2	3	25	0	0	1

Traded to **New Jersey** by **San Jose** for New Jersey's 3rd round choice (later traded to Nashville — Nashville selected Geoff Koch) in 1998 Entry Draft, August 22, 1997.

KRUPP, Uwe (KROOP, OO-VAY) DET.

Defense. Shoots right. 6'6", 235 lbs. Born, Cologne, West Germany, June 24, 1965. Buffalo's 13th choice, 223rd overall, in 1983 Entry Draft.

1982-83	Kolner Haie	Germany	11	0	0	0	0	....	....	....	....	....	....	....	....	....	....	....	....	....	....	....	....	....	....	....
1983-84	Kolner Haie	Germany	26	0	4	4	22	....	....	....	....	....	....	....	....	....	....	....	....	....	....	....	....	....	....	....
1984-85	Kolner Haie	Germany	39	11	8	19	36	....	....	....	....	....	....	....	....	....	....	....	....	....	....	....	....	....	....	....
1985-86	Kolner Haie	Germany	45	10	21	31	83	....	....	....	....	....	....	....	....	....	....	....	....	....	....	....	....	....	....	....
1986-87	Buffalo	NHL	26	1	4	5	23	0	0	0	34	2.9	–9	....	....	....	....	....	....	....	....	....	....	....	....	....
	Rochester	AHL	42	3	19	22	50	....	....	....	....	....	....	....	....	....	....	....	17	1	11	12	16	....	....	....
1987-88	Buffalo	NHL	75	2	9	11	151	0	0	0	84	2.4	–1	....	....	....	....	....	6	0	0	0	15	0	0	0
1988-89	Buffalo	NHL	70	5	13	18	55	0	1	0	51	9.8	0	....	....	....	....	....	5	0	1	1	4	0	0	0
1989-90	Buffalo	NHL	74	3	20	23	85	0	1	1	69	4.3	15	....	....	....	....	....	6	0	0	0	4	0	0	0
1990-91	Buffalo	NHL	74	12	32	44	66	6	0	0	138	8.7	14	....	....	....	....	....	6	1	1	2	6	1	0	0
1991-92	Buffalo	NHL	8	2	0	2	6	0	0	0	13	15.4	0	....	....	....	....	....	....	....	....	....	....	....	....	....
	NY Islanders	NHL	59	6	29	35	43	2	0	0	115	5.2	13	....	....	....	....	....	....	....	....	....	....	....	....	....
1992-93	NY Islanders	NHL	80	9	29	38	67	2	0	2	116	7.8	6	....	....	....	....	....	18	1	5	6	12	0	0	0
1993-94	NY Islanders	NHL	41	7	14	21	30	3	0	0	82	8.5	11	....	....	....	....	....	4	0	1	1	4	0	0	0
1994-95	EV Landshut	Germany	5	1	2	3	6	....	....	....	....	....	....	....	....	....	....	....	....	....	....	....	....	....	....	....
	Quebec	NHL	44	6	17	23	20	3	0	1	102	5.9	14	....	....	....	....	....	5	0	2	2	2	0	0	0
1995-96♦	Colorado	NHL	6	0	3	3	4	0	0	0	9	0.0	4	....	....	....	....	....	22	4	12	16	33	1	0	2
1996-97	Colorado	NHL	60	4	17	21	48	2	0	1	107	3.7	12	....	....	....	....	....	....	....	....	....	....	....	....	....
1997-98	Colorado	NHL	78	9	22	31	38	5	0	2	149	6.0	21	....	....	....	....	....	7	0	1	1	4	0	0	0
	Germany	Olympics	2	0	2	2	4	....	....	....	....	....	....	....	....	....	....	....	....	....	....	....	....	....	....	....

Season	Club	League	Regular Season GP	G	A	Pts	PIM	PP	SH	GW	S	%	+/-	TF	F%	H	SB	Min	Playoffs GP	G	A	Pts	PIM	PP	SH	GW
1998-99	**Detroit**	**NHL**	**22**	**3**	**2**	**5**	**6**	**0**	**0**	**0**	**32**	**9.4**	**0**	**0**	**0.0**	**41**	**37**	**21:23**	....	....	....	....	....	....	....	....
	NHL Totals		**717**	**69**	**211**	**280**	**642**	**23**	**2**	**7**	**1101**	**6.3**		**0**	**0.0**	**41**	**37**	**21:23**	**79**	**6**	**23**	**29**	**84**	**2**	**0**	**2**

Played in NHL All-Star Game (1991)

Traded to **NY Islanders** by **Buffalo** with Pierre Turgeon, Benoit Hogue and Dave McLlwain for Pat Lafontaine, Randy Hillier, Randy Wood and NY Islanders' 4th round choice (Dean Melanson) in 1992 Entry Draft, October 25, 1991. Traded to **Quebec** by **NY Islanders** with NY Islanders' 1st round choice (Wade Belak) in 1994 Entry Draft for Ron Sutter and Quebec's 1st round choice (Brett Lindros) in 1994 Entry Draft, June 28, 1994. Transferred to **Colorado** after **Quebec** franchise relocated, June 21, 1995. Claimed by **Nashville** from **Colorado** in Expansion Draft, June 26, 1998. Signed as a free agent by **Detroit**, July 7, 1998.

KRUSE, Paul

(KROOZ) **BUF.**

Left wing. Shoots left. 6', 202 lbs. Born, Merritt, B.C., March 15, 1970. Calgary's 6th choice, 83rd overall, in 1990 Entry Draft.

Season	Club	League	GP	G	A	Pts	PIM	PP	SH	GW	S	%	+/-	TF	F%	H	SB	Min	GP	G	A	Pts	PIM	PP	SH	GW
1986-87	Merritt	BCJHL	35	8	15	23	120	....	....	....	....	....	....	....	....	....	....	....	....	....	....	....	....	....	....	....
1987-88	Merritt	BCJHL	44	12	32	44	227	....	....	....	....	....	....	....	....	....	....	....	4	1	4	5	18	....	....	....
	Moose Jaw	WHL	1	0	0	0	0	....	....	....	....	....	....	....	....	....	....	....	....	....	....	....	....	....	....	....
1988-89	Kamloops	WHL	68	8	15	23	209	....	....	....	....	....	....	....	....	....	....	....	....	....	....	....	....	....	....	....
1989-90	Kamloops	WHL	67	22	23	45	291	....	....	....	....	....	....	....	....	....	....	....	17	3	5	8	79	....	....	....
1990-91	**Calgary**	**NHL**	**1**	**0**	**0**	**0**	**7**	**0**	**0**	**0**	**0**	**0.0**	**–1**	....	....	....	....	....	....	....	....	....	....	....	....	....
	Salt Lake	IHL	83	24	20	44	313	....	....	....	....	....	....	....	....	....	....	....	4	1	1	2	4	....	....	....
1991-92	**Calgary**	**NHL**	**16**	**3**	**1**	**4**	**65**	**0**	**0**	**0**	**12**	**25.0**	**1**	....	....	....	....	....	....	....	....	....	....	....	....	....
	Salt Lake	IHL	57	14	15	29	267	....	....	....	....	....	....	....	....	....	....	....	5	1	2	3	19	....	....	....
1992-93	**Calgary**	**NHL**	**27**	**2**	**3**	**5**	**41**	**0**	**0**	**0**	**17**	**11.8**	**2**	....	....	....	....	....	....	....	....	....	....	....	....	....
	Salt Lake	IHL	35	1	4	5	206	....	....	....	....	....	....	....	....	....	....	....	....	....	....	....	....	....	....	....
1993-94	**Calgary**	**NHL**	**68**	**3**	**8**	**11**	**185**	**0**	**0**	**0**	**52**	**5.8**	**–6**	....	....	....	....	....	**7**	**0**	**0**	**0**	**14**	**0**	**0**	**0**
1994-95	**Calgary**	**NHL**	**45**	**11**	**5**	**16**	**141**	**0**	**0**	**2**	**52**	**21.2**	**13**	....	....	....	....	....	**7**	**4**	**2**	**6**	**10**	**0**	**1**	**0**
1995-96	**Calgary**	**NHL**	**75**	**3**	**12**	**15**	**145**	**0**	**0**	**0**	**83**	**3.6**	**–5**	....	....	....	....	....	**3**	**0**	**0**	**0**	**4**	**0**	**0**	**0**
1996-97	**Calgary**	**NHL**	**14**	**2**	**0**	**2**	**30**	**0**	**0**	**1**	**10**	**20.0**	**–4**	....	....	....	....	....	....	....	....	....	....	....	....	....
	NY Islanders	**NHL**	**48**	**4**	**2**	**6**	**111**	**0**	**0**	**0**	**39**	**10.3**	**–5**	....	....	....	....	....	....	....	....	....	....	....	....	....
1997-98	**NY Islanders**	**NHL**	**62**	**6**	**1**	**7**	**138**	**0**	**0**	**2**	**44**	**13.6**	**–12**	....	....	....	....	....	....	....	....	....	....	....	....	....
	Buffalo	**NHL**	**12**	**1**	**1**	**2**	**49**	**0**	**0**	**0**	**8**	**12.5**	**1**	....	....	....	....	....	**1**	**1**	**0**	**1**	**4**	**0**	**0**	**0**
1998-99	**Buffalo**	**NHL**	**43**	**3**	**0**	**3**	**114**	**0**	**0**	**0**	**33**	**9.1**	**0**	**3**	**33.3**	**56**	**8**	**6:24**	**10**	**0**	**0**	**0**	**4**	**0**	**0**	**0**
	NHL Totals		**411**	**38**	**33**	**71**	**1026**	**0**	**0**	**5**	**350**	**10.9**		**3**	**33.3**	**56**	**8**	**6:24**	**28**	**5**	**2**	**7**	**36**	**0**	**1**	**0**

Traded to **NY Islanders** by **Calgary** for Colorado's 3rd round choice (previously acquired by NY Islanders — later traded to Hartford — Hartford selected Francis Lessard) in 1997 Entry Draft, November 27, 1996. Traded to **Buffalo** by **NY Islanders** with Jason Holland for Jason Dawe, March 24, 1998.

KRYGIER, Todd

(KREE-guhr)

Left wing. Shoots left. 6', 185 lbs. Born, Chicago Heights, IL, October 12, 1965. Hartford's 1st choice, 16th overall, in 1988 Supplemental Draft.

Season	Club	League	GP	G	A	Pts	PIM	PP	SH	GW	S	%	+/-	TF	F%	H	SB	Min	GP	G	A	Pts	PIM	PP	SH	GW
1984-85	U. of Connecticut	ECAC-2	14	14	11	25	12	....	....	....	....	....	....	....	....	....	....	....	....	....	....	....	....	....	....	....
1985-86	U. of Connecticut	ECAC-2	32	29	27	56	46	....	....	....	....	....	....	....	....	....	....	....	....	....	....	....	....	....	....	....
1986-87	U. of Connecticut	ECAC-2	28	24	24	48	44	....	....	....	....	....	....	....	....	....	....	....	....	....	....	....	....	....	....	....
1987-88	U. of Connecticut	ECAC-2	27	32	39	71	28	....	....	....	....	....	....	....	....	....	....	....	....	....	....	....	....	....	....	....
	New Haven	AHL	13	1	5	6	34	....	....	....	....	....	....	....	....	....	....	....	....	....	....	....	....	....	....	....
1988-89	Binghamton	AHL	76	26	42	68	77	....	....	....	....	....	....	....	....	....	....	....	....	....	....	....	....	....	....	....
1989-90	**Hartford**	**NHL**	**58**	**18**	**12**	**30**	**52**	**5**	**1**	**3**	**103**	**17.5**	**4**	....	....	....	....	....	**7**	**2**	**1**	**3**	**4**	**0**	**0**	**0**
	Binghamton	AHL	12	1	9	10	16	....	....	....	....	....	....	....	....	....	....	....	....	....	....	....	....	....	....	....
1990-91	**Hartford**	**NHL**	**72**	**13**	**17**	**30**	**95**	**3**	**0**	**2**	**113**	**11.5**	**1**	....	....	....	....	....	**6**	**0**	**2**	**2**	**0**	**0**	**0**	**0**
1991-92	**Washington**	**NHL**	**67**	**13**	**17**	**30**	**107**	**1**	**0**	**1**	**127**	**10.2**	**–1**	....	....	....	....	....	**5**	**2**	**1**	**3**	**4**	**0**	**0**	**0**
1992-93	**Washington**	**NHL**	**77**	**11**	**12**	**23**	**60**	**0**	**2**	**0**	**133**	**8.3**	**–13**	....	....	....	....	....	**6**	**1**	**1**	**2**	**4**	**0**	**1**	**0**
1993-94	**Washington**	**NHL**	**66**	**12**	**18**	**30**	**60**	**0**	**1**	**3**	**146**	**8.2**	**–4**	....	....	....	....	....	**5**	**2**	**0**	**2**	**10**	**0**	**0**	**0**
1994-95	**Anaheim**	**NHL**	**35**	**11**	**11**	**22**	**10**	**1**	**0**	**1**	**90**	**12.2**	**1**	....	....	....	....	....	....	....	....	....	....	....	....	....
1995-96	**Anaheim**	**NHL**	**60**	**9**	**28**	**37**	**70**	**2**	**1**	**0**	**153**	**5.9**	**–9**	....	....	....	....	....	....	....	....	....	....	....	....	....
	Washington	**NHL**	**16**	**6**	**5**	**11**	**12**	**1**	**0**	**0**	**28**	**21.4**	**8**	....	....	....	....	....	**6**	**2**	**0**	**2**	**12**	**0**	**0**	**1**
1996-97	**Washington**	**NHL**	**47**	**5**	**11**	**16**	**37**	**1**	**0**	**1**	**121**	**4.1**	**–10**	....	....	....	....	....	....	....	....	....	....	....	....	....
1997-98	**Washington**	**NHL**	**45**	**2**	**12**	**14**	**30**	**0**	**0**	**1**	**71**	**2.8**	**–3**	....	....	....	....	....	**13**	**1**	**2**	**3**	**6**	**0**	**0**	**1**
	Portland	AHL	6	3	4	7	6	....	....	....	....	....	....	....	....	....	....	....	....	....	....	....	....	....	....	....
1998-99	Orlando	IHL	65	19	40	59	82	....	....	....	....	....	....	....	....	....	....	....	17	9	10	19	16	....	....	....
	NHL Totals		**543**	**100**	**143**	**243**	**533**	**14**	**5**	**12**	**1085**	**9.2**		....	....	....	....	....	**48**	**10**	**7**	**17**	**40**	**0**	**1**	**2**

NCAA (College Div.) East Second All-American Team (1987)

Traded to **Washington** by **Hartford** for Washington's 4th round choice (later traded to Calgary — Calgary selected Jason Smith) in 1993 Entry Draft, October 3, 1991. Traded to **Anaheim** by **Washington** for Anaheim's 4th round choice (later traded to Dallas — Dallas selected Mike Hurley) in 1996 Entry Draft, February 2, 1995. Traded to **Washington** by **Anaheim** for Mike Torchia, March 8, 1996.

KUBA, Filip

(KOO-bah, FIHL-ihp) **FLA.**

Defense. Shoots left. 6'3", 202 lbs. Born, Ostrava, Czech., December 29, 1976. Florida's 8th choice, 192nd overall, in 1995 Entry Draft.

Season	Club	League	GP	G	A	Pts	PIM	PP	SH	GW	S	%	+/-	TF	F%	H	SB	Min	GP	G	A	Pts	PIM	PP	SH	GW
1994-95	HC Vitkovice	Czech-Jr.	35	10	15	25	....	....	....	....	....	....	....	....	....	....	....	....	....	....	....	....	....	....	....	....
	HC Vitkovice	Cze-Rep	....	....	....	....	....	....	....	....	....	....	....	....	....	....	....	....	4	0	0	0	2	....	....	....
1995-96	HC Vitkovice	Cze-Rep	19	0	1	1	....	....	....	....	....	....	....	....	....	....	....	....	....	....	....	....	....	....	....	....
1996-97	Carolina	AHL	51	0	12	12	38	....	....	....	....	....	....	....	....	....	....	....	....	....	....	....	....	....	....	....
1997-98	New Haven	AHL	77	4	13	17	58	....	....	....	....	....	....	....	....	....	....	....	3	1	1	2	0	....	....	....
1998-99	**Florida**	**NHL**	**5**	**0**	**1**	**1**	**0**	**0**	**0**	**0**	**5**	**0.0**	**2**	**0**	**0.0**	**7**	**6**	**22:29**	....	....	....	....	....	....	....	....
	Kentucky	AHL	45	2	8	10	33	....	....	....	....	....	....	....	....	....	....	....	10	0	1	1	4	....	....	....
	NHL Totals		**5**	**0**	**1**	**1**	**0**	**0**	**0**	**0**	**5**	**0.0**		**0**	**0.0**	**7**	**6**	**22:29**	....	....	....	....	....	....	....	....

KUBINA, Pavel

(koo-BEE-nuh) **T.B.**

Defense. Shoots right. 6'3", 213 lbs. Born, Celadna, Czech., April 15, 1977. Tampa Bay's 6th choice, 179th overall, in 1996 Entry Draft.

Season	Club	League	GP	G	A	Pts	PIM	PP	SH	GW	S	%	+/-	TF	F%	H	SB	Min	GP	G	A	Pts	PIM	PP	SH	GW
1993-94	TJ Vitkovice	Czech-Jr.	35	4	3	7	....	....	....	....	....	....	....	....	....	....	....	....	....	....	....	....	....	....	....	....
	TJ Vitkovice	Cze-Rep	1	0	0	0	....	....	....	....	....	....	....	....	....	....	....	....	....	....	....	....	....	....	....	....
1994-95	TJ Vitkovice	Czech-Jr.	20	6	10	16	....	....	....	....	....	....	....	....	....	....	....	....	....	....	....	....	....	....	....	....
	TJ Vitkovice	Cze-Rep	8	2	0	2	10	....	....	....	....	....	....	....	....	....	....	....	4	0	0	0	0	....	....	....
1995-96	TJ Vitkovice	Cze-Rep	33	3	4	7	32	....	....	....	....	....	....	....	....	....	....	....	4	0	0	0	0	....	....	....
	TJ Vitkovice	Czech-Jr.	16	5	10	15	....	....	....	....	....	....	....	....	....	....	....	....	....	....	....	....	....	....	....	....
1996-97	TJ Vitkovice	Cze-Rep	1	0	0	0	0	....	....	....	....	....	....	....	....	....	....	....	....	....	....	....	....	....	....	....
	Moose Jaw	WHL	61	12	32	44	116	....	....	....	....	....	....	....	....	....	....	....	11	2	5	7	27	....	....	....
1997-98	**Tampa Bay**	**NHL**	**10**	**1**	**2**	**3**	**22**	**0**	**0**	**0**	**8**	**12.5**	**–1**	....	....	....	....	....	....	....	....	....	....	....	....	....
	Adirondack	AHL	55	4	8	12	86	....	....	....	....	....	....	....	....	....	....	....	1	1	0	1	14	....	....	....
1998-99	**Tampa Bay**	**NHL**	**68**	**9**	**12**	**21**	**80**	**3**	**1**	**1**	**119**	**7.6**	**–33**	**2**	**0.0**	**156**	**82**	**22:47**	....	....	....	....	....	....	....	....
	Cleveland	IHL	6	2	2	4	16	....	....	....	....	....	....	....	....	....	....	....	....	....	....	....	....	....	....	....
	NHL Totals		**78**	**10**	**14**	**24**	**102**	**3**	**1**	**1**	**127**	**7.9**		**2**	**0.0**	**156**	**82**	**22:47**	....	....	....	....	....	....	....	....

KUCERA, Frantisek

(koo-CHAIR-uh)

Defense. Shoots right. 6'2", 205 lbs. Born, Prague, Czech., February 3, 1968. Chicago's 3rd choice, 77th overall, in 1986 Entry Draft.

Season	Club	League	GP	G	A	Pts	PIM	PP	SH	GW	S	%	+/-	TF	F%	H	SB	Min	GP	G	A	Pts	PIM	PP	SH	GW
1985-86	Sparta Praha	Czech.	15	0	0	0	....	....	....	....	....	....	....	....	....	....	....	....	....	....	....	....	....	....	....	....
1986-87	Sparta Praha	Czech.	40	5	2	7	14	....	....	....	....	....	....	....	....	....	....	....	....	....	....	....	....	....	....	....
1987-88	Sparta Praha	Czech.	46	7	2	9	30	....	....	....	....	....	....	....	....	....	....	....	....	....	....	....	....	....	....	....
1988-89	Dukla Jihlava	Czech.	45	10	9	19	28	....	....	....	....	....	....	....	....	....	....	....	....	....	....	....	....	....	....	....
1989-90	Dukla Jihlava	Czech.	42	8	10	18	....	....	....	....	....	....	....	....	....	....	....	....	1	1	0	1	....	....	....	....
1990-91	**Chicago**	**NHL**	**40**	**2**	**12**	**14**	**32**	**1**	**0**	**0**	**65**	**3.1**	**3**	....	....	....	....	....	....	....	....	....	....	....	....	....
	Indianapolis	IHL	35	8	19	27	23	....	....	....	....	....	....	....	....	....	....	....	7	0	1	1	15	....	....	....

Season	Club	League	Regular Season GP	G	A	Pts	PIM	PP	SH	GW	S	%	+/-	TF	F%	H	SB	Min	Playoffs GP	G	A	Pts	PIM	PP	SH	GW
1991-92	**Chicago**	**NHL**	61	3	10	13	36	1	0	1	82	3.7	3	....	....	....	....	....	6	0	0	0	0	0	0	0
	Indianapolis	IHL	7	1	2	3	4																			
1992-93	**Chicago**	**NHL**	71	5	14	19	59	1	0	1	117	4.3	7													
1993-94	**Chicago**	**NHL**	60	4	13	17	34	2	0	0	90	4.4	9													
	Hartford	**NHL**	16	1	3	4	14	1	0	0	32	3.1	−12													
1994-95	Sparta Praha	Cze-Rep	16	1	2	3	14																			
	Hartford	**NHL**	48	3	17	20	30	0	0	1	73	4.1	3													
1995-96	**Hartford**	**NHL**	30	2	6	8	10	0	0	1	43	4.7	−3													
	Vancouver	**NHL**	24	1	0	1	10	0	0	0	34	2.9	5						6	0	1	1	0	0	0	0
1996-97	**Vancouver**	**NHL**	2	0	0	0	0	0	0	0	3	0.0	0													
	Syracuse	AHL	42	6	29	35	36																			
	Houston	IHL	12	0	3	3	20																			
	Philadelphia	**NHL**	2	0	0	0	2	0	0	0	2	0.0	−2													
	Philadelphia	AHL	9	1	5	6	2												10	1	6	7	20			
1997-98	Sparta Praha	EuroHL	4	0	1	1	2																			
	Sparta Praha	Cze-Rep	43	8	12	20	49												9	3	1	4	*53			
	Czech Republic	Olympics	6	0	0	0	0																			
1998-99	Sparta Praha	Cze-Rep	42	3	12	15	92												8	0	2	2				
	HC Sparta Praha	EuroHL	6	0	2	2	10												2	0	0	0	2			
	NHL Totals		354	21	75	96	227	6	0	4	541	3.9							12	0	1	1	0	0	0	0

Traded to **Hartford** by **Chicago** with Jocelyn Lemieux for Gary Suter, Randy Cunneyworth and Hartford's 3rd round choice (later traded to Vancouver — Vancouver selected Larry Courville) in 1995 Entry Draft, March 11, 1994. Traded to **Vancouver** by **Hartford** with Jim Dowd and Hartford's 2nd round choice (Ryan Bonni) in 1997 Entry Draft for Jeff Brown and Vancouver's 3rd round choice (later traded to Calgary — Calgary selected Paul Manning) in 1998 Entry Draft, December 19, 1995. Traded to **Philadelphia** by **Vancouver** for future considerations, March 18, 1997.

KVASHA, Oleg   (kuh-VAH-shah)   FLA.

Left wing. Shoots right. 6'5", 216 lbs. Born, Moscow, USSR, July 26, 1978. Florida's 3rd choice, 65th overall, in 1996 Entry Draft.

Season	Club	League	GP	G	A	Pts	PIM	PP	SH	GW	S	%	+/-	TF	F%	H	SB	Min	GP	G	A	Pts	PIM	PP	SH	GW
1995-96	CSKA Moscow	CIS	38	2	3	5	14							....	....	....	....	....	2	0	0	0	0	....		
1996-97	CSKA Moscow	Russia	44	20	22	42	115												3	2	1	3	0			
1997-98	New Haven	AHL	57	13	16	29	46																			
1998-99	**Florida**	**NHL**	68	12	13	25	45	4	0	2	138	8.7	5	373	28.4	21	13	12:48	....							
	NHL Totals		68	12	13	25	45	4	0	2	138	8.7		373	28.4	21	13	12:48								

LAAKSONEN, Antti   (lah-AHK-soh-nehn, AHN-tee)   BOS.

Left wing. Shoots left. 6', 180 lbs. Born, Tammela, Finland, October 3, 1973. Boston's 10th choice, 191st overall, in 1997 Entry Draft.

Season	Club	League	GP	G	A	Pts	PIM	PP	SH	GW	S	%	+/-	TF	F%	H	SB	Min	GP	G	A	Pts	PIM	PP	SH	GW
1990-91	FoPS Forssa	Finland-B	3	0	0	0	0												2	0	0	0	0			
1991-92	FoPS Forssa	Finn-Jr.	24	19	23	42	22																			
	FoPS Forssa	Finland-2	41	16	15	31	8																			
1992-93	Hameenlinna	Finn-Jr.	1	1	1	2	0																			
	Hameenlinna	Finn-Jr.	1	1	1	2	0																			
	FoPS Forssa	Finland-2	34	11	19	30	36																			
	Hameenlinna	Finland	2	0	0	0	0																			
1993-94	U. of Denver	WCHA	36	12	9	21	38																			
1994-95	U. of Denver	WCHA	40	17	18	35	42																			
1995-96	U. of Denver	WCHA	39	25	28	53	71																			
1996-97	U. of Denver	WCHA	39	21	17	38	63																			
1997-98	Providence	AHL	38	3	2	5	14																			
	Charlotte	ECHL	15	4	3	7	12												6	0	3	3	0			
1998-99	**Boston**	**NHL**	11	1	2	3	2	0	0	0	8	12.5	−1	0	0.0	5	3	9:20	19	7	2	9	28			
	Providence	AHL	66	25	33	58	52																			
	NHL Totals		11	1	2	3	2	0	0	0	8	12.5		0	0.0	5	3	9:20								

WCHA Second All-Star Team (1996)

LACHANCE, Scott   MTL.

Defense. Shoots left. 6'1", 209 lbs. Born, Charlottesville, VA, October 22, 1972. NY Islanders' 1st choice, 4th overall, in 1991 Entry Draft.

Season	Club	League	GP	G	A	Pts	PIM	PP	SH	GW	S	%	+/-	TF	F%	H	SB	Min	GP	G	A	Pts	PIM	PP	SH	GW
1988-89	Springfield	NEJHL	36	8	28	36	20																			
1989-90	Springfield	NEJHL	34	25	41	66	62																			
1990-91	Boston University	H.E.	31	5	19	24	48																			
1991-92	United States	Nat-Team	36	1	10	11	34																			
	United States	Olympics	8	0	1	1	6																			
	NY Islanders	**NHL**	17	1	4	5	9	0	0	0	20	5.0	13													
1992-93	**NY Islanders**	**NHL**	75	7	17	24	67	0	1	2	62	11.3	−1													
1993-94	**NY Islanders**	**NHL**	74	3	11	14	70	0	0	1	59	5.1	−5						3	0	0	0	0	0	0	0
1994-95	**NY Islanders**	**NHL**	26	6	7	13	26	3	0	0	56	10.7	2													
1995-96	**NY Islanders**	**NHL**	55	3	10	13	54	1	0	0	81	3.7	−19													
1996-97	**NY Islanders**	**NHL**	81	3	11	14	47	1	0	0	97	3.1	−7													
1997-98	**NY Islanders**	**NHL**	63	2	11	13	45	1	0	0	62	3.2	−11													
1998-99	**NY Islanders**	**NHL**	59	1	8	9	30	1	0	0	37	2.7	−19	0	0.0	67	92	21:34								
	Montreal	**NHL**	17	1	1	2	11	0	0	0	22	4.5	−2	0	0.0	19	47	22:29								
	NHL Totals		467	27	80	107	359	7	1	3	496	5.4		0	0.0	86	139	21:46	3	0	0	0	0	0	0	0

Played in NHL All-Star Game (1997)

Traded to **Montreal** by **NY Islanders** for Montreal's 3rd round choice (Mattias Weinhandl) in 1999 Entry Draft, March 9, 1999.

LaCOUTURE, Dan   (la-koo-TUHR)   EDM.

Left wing. Shoots left. 6'3", 210 lbs. Born, Hyannis, MA, April 18, 1977. NY Islanders' 2nd choice, 29th overall, in 1996 Entry Draft.

Season	Club	League	GP	G	A	Pts	PIM	PP	SH	GW	S	%	+/-	TF	F%	H	SB	Min	GP	G	A	Pts	PIM	PP	SH	GW
1991-92	Natick Academy	H.S.	20	38	34	72	46																			
1994-95	Springfield	IJHL-B	49	37	39	76	100																			
1995-96	Springfield	NAJHL	29	24	35	59	79												13	12	13	25	23			
1996-97	Boston University	H.E.	31	13	12	25	18																			
1997-98	Hamilton	AHL	77	15	10	25	31												5	1	0	1	0			
1998-99	**Edmonton**	**NHL**	3	0	0	0	0	0	0	0	0	0.0	1	0	0.0	3	0	6:30								
	Hamilton	AHL	72	17	14	31	73												9	2	1	3	2			
	NHL Totals		3	0	0	0	0	0	0	0	0	0.0		0	0.0	3	0	6:30								

Traded to **Edmonton** by **NY Islanders** for Mariusz Czerkawski, August 25, 1997.

LACROIX, Daniel   (luh-KWAH)   NYI

Left wing. Shoots left. 6'2", 205 lbs. Born, Montreal, Que., March 11, 1969. NY Rangers' 2nd choice, 31st overall, in 1987 Entry Draft.

Season	Club	League	GP	G	A	Pts	PIM	PP	SH	GW	S	%	+/-	TF	F%	H	SB	Min	GP	G	A	Pts	PIM	PP	SH	GW
1985-86	Hull	QAAA	37	10	13	23	46												8	1	2	3	22			
1986-87	Granby	QMJHL	54	9	16	25	311												5	0	4	4	12			
1987-88	Granby	QMJHL	58	24	50	74	468																			
1988-89	Granby	QMJHL	70	45	49	94	320												4	1	1	2	57			
	Denver	IHL	2	0	1	1	0												2	0	1	1	0			
1989-90	Flint	IHL	61	12	16	28	128												4	2	0	2	24			
1990-91	Binghamton	AHL	54	7	12	19	237												5	1	0	1	24			
1991-92	Binghamton	AHL	52	12	20	32	149												11	2	4	6	28			
1992-93	Binghamton	AHL	73	21	22	43	255																			

			Regular Season																Playoffs							
Season	Club	League	GP	G	A	Pts	PIM	PP	SH	GW	S	%	+/–	TF	F%	H	SB	Min	GP	G	A	Pts	PIM	PP	SH	GW
1993-94	NY Rangers	NHL	4	0	0	0	0	0	0	0	0	0.0	0													
	Binghamton	AHL	59	20	23	43	278																			
1994-95	Providence	AHL	40	15	11	26	266																			
	Boston	NHL	23	1	0	1	38	0	0	0	14	7.1	–2													
	NY Rangers	NHL	1	0	0	0	0	0	0	0	0	0.0	0													
1995-96	NY Rangers	NHL	25	2	2	4	30	0	0	0	14	14.3	–1													
	Binghamton	AHL	26	12	15	27	155																			
1996-97	Philadelphia	NHL	74	7	1	8	163	1	0	0	54	13.0	–1						12	0	1	1	22	0	0	0
1997-98	Philadelphia	NHL	56	1	4	5	135	0	0	0	28	3.6	0						4	0	0	0	4	0	0	0
1998-99	Edmonton	NHL	4	0	0	0	13	0	0	0	5	0.0	0	10	40.0	5	0	6:22								
	Hamilton	AHL	46	13	9	22	260												11	3	1	4	65			
	NHL Totals		187	11	7	18	379	1	0	0	115	9.6		10	40.0	5	0	6:22	16	0	1	1	26	0	0	0

Traded to **Boston** by **NY Rangers** for Glen Featherstone, August 19, 1994. Claimed on waivers by **NY Rangers** from **Boston**, March 23, 1995. Signed as a free agent by **Philadelphia**, July 18, 1996. Traded to **Edmonton** by **Philadelphia** for Valeri Zelepukin, October 5, 1998. Signed as a free agent by **NY Islanders**, August 11, 1999.

LACROIX, Eric

(luh-KWAH) **NYR**

Left wing. Shoots left. 6'2", 210 lbs. Born, Montreal, Que., July 15, 1971. Toronto's 6th choice, 136th overall, in 1990 Entry Draft.

Season	Club	League	GP	G	A	Pts	PIM	PP	SH	GW	S	%	+/–	TF	F%	H	SB	Min	GP	G	A	Pts	PIM	PP	SH	GW
1989-90	Gov-Dummer	H.S.	25	23	18	41																				
1990-91	St. Lawrence	ECAC	35	13	11	24	35																			
1991-92	St. Lawrence	ECAC	34	11	20	31	40																			
1992-93	St. John's	AHL	76	15	19	34	59												9	5	3	8	4			
1993-94	Toronto	NHL	3	0	0	0	2	0	0	0	3	0.0	0						2	0	0	0	0	0	0	0
	St. John's	AHL	59	17	22	39	69												11	5	3	8	6			
1994-95	St. John's	AHL	1	0	0	0	2																			
	Phoenix	IHL	25	7	1	8	31																			
	Los Angeles	NHL	45	9	7	16	54	2	1	1	64	14.1	2													
1995-96	Los Angeles	NHL	72	16	16	32	110	3	0	1	107	15.0	–11													
1996-97	Colorado	NHL	81	18	18	36	26	2	0	4	141	12.8	16						17	1	4	5	19	0	0	0
1997-98	Colorado	NHL	82	16	15	31	84	5	0	6	126	12.7	0						7	0	0	0	6	0	0	0
1998-99	Colorado	NHL	7	0	0	0	2	0	0	0	4	0.0	–2	1	0.0	14	5	11:58								
	Los Angeles	NHL	27	0	1	1	12	0	0	0	17	0.0	–5	2	50.0	82	10	8:37								
	NY Rangers	NHL	30	2	1	3	4	0	0	1	17	11.8	–5	14	100.0	49	12	4:05								
	NHL Totals		347	61	58	119	294	12	1	13	479	12.7		17	88.2	145	27	6:51	26	1	4	5	25	0	0	0

Traded to **LA Kings** by **Toronto** with Chris Snell and Toronto's 4th round choice (Eric Belanger) in 1996 Entry Draft for Dixon Ward, Guy Leveque, Kelly Fairchild and Shayne Toporowski, October 3, 1994. Traded to **Colorado** by **LA Kings** with LA Kings' 1st round choice (Martin Skoula) in 1998 Entry Draft for Stephane Fiset and Colorado's 1st round choice (Mathieu Biron) in 1998 Entry Draft, June 20, 1996. Traded to **Los Angeles** by **Colorado** for Roman Vopat and Los Angeles' 6th round choice (later traded to Ottawa - Ottawa selected Martin Brusek) in 1999 Entry Draft, October 29, 1998. Traded to **NY Rangers** by **Los Angeles** for Sean Pronger, February 12, 1999.

LaFAYETTE, Nathan

(LAH-fay-eht) **L.A.**

Center. Shoots right. 6'1", 200 lbs. Born, New Westminster, B.C., February 17, 1973. St. Louis' 3rd choice, 65th overall, in 1991 Entry Draft.

Season	Club	League	GP	G	A	Pts	PIM	PP	SH	GW	S	%	+/–	TF	F%	H	SB	Min	GP	G	A	Pts	PIM	PP	SH	GW
1988-89	Toronto	MTHL	69	38	68	106	24																			
1989-90	Kingston	OHL	53	6	8	14	14												7	0	1	1	0			
1990-91	Kingston	OHL	35	13	13	26	10																			
	Cornwall	OHL	28	16	22	38	25																			
1991-92	Cornwall	OHL	66	28	45	73	26												6	2	5	7	15			
1992-93	Newmarket	OHL	58	49	38	87	26												7	4	5	9	19			
1993-94	St. Louis	NHL	38	2	3	5	14	0	0	0	23	8.7	–9													
	Peoria	IHL	27	13	11	24	20																			
	Vancouver	NHL	11	1	1	2	4	0	0	0	11	9.1	2						20	2	7	9	4	0	0	0
1994-95	Syracuse	AHL	27	9	9	18	10																			
	Vancouver	NHL	27	4	4	8	2	0	1	0	30	13.3	2													
	NY Rangers	NHL	12	0	0	0	0	0	0	0	5	0.0	1						8	0	0	0	2	0	0	0
1995-96	NY Rangers	NHL	5	0	0	0	2	0	0	0	5	0.0	–1													
	Binghamton	AHL	57	21	27	48	32																			
	Los Angeles	NHL	12	2	4	6	6	1	0	0	23	8.7	–3													
1996-97	Los Angeles	NHL	15	1	3	4	8	0	1	1	26	3.8	–8													
	Phoenix	IHL	31	2	5	7	16																			
	Syracuse	AHL	26	14	11	25	18												3	1	0	1	2			
1997-98	Los Angeles	NHL	34	5	3	8	32	1	0	1	60	8.3	2						4	0	0	0	2	0	0	0
	Fredericton	AHL	28	7	8	15	36																			
1998-99	Los Angeles	NHL	33	2	2	4	35	0	1	1	42	4.8	0	276	45.7	49	14	11:50								
	Long Beach	IHL	41	9	13	22	24												7	1	0	1	8			
	NHL Totals		187	17	20	37	103	2	3	3	225	7.6		276	45.7	49	14	11:50	32	2	7	9	8	0	0	0

Canadian Major Junior Scholastic Player of the Year (1992)

Traded to **Vancouver** by **St. Louis** with Jeff Brown and Bret Hedican for Craig Janney, March 21, 1994. Traded to **NY Rangers** by **Vancouver** for Corey Hirsch, April 7, 1995. Traded to **LA Kings** by **NY Rangers** with Ray Ferraro, Mattias Norstrom, Ian Laperriere and NY Rangers' 4th round choice (Sean Blanchard) in 1997 Entry Draft for Marty McSorley, Jari Kurri and Shane Churla, March 14, 1996.

LAFLAMME, Christian

(lah-FLAM) **EDM.**

Defense. Shoots right. 6'1", 210 lbs. Born, St. Charles, Que., November 24, 1976. Chicago's 2nd choice, 45th overall, in 1995 Entry Draft.

Season	Club	League	GP	G	A	Pts	PIM	PP	SH	GW	S	%	+/–	TF	F%	H	SB	Min	GP	G	A	Pts	PIM	PP	SH	GW
1991-92	Ste-Foy	QAAA	42	5	27	32	100																			
1992-93	Verdun	QMJHL	69	2	17	19	85												3	0	2	2	6			
1993-94	Verdun	QMJHL	72	4	34	38	85												4	0	3	3	4			
1994-95	Beauport	QMJHL	67	6	41	47	82												8	1	4	5	6			
1995-96	Beauport	QMJHL	41	13	23	36	63												20	7	17	24	32			
1996-97	Chicago	NHL	4	0	1	1	2	0	0	0	3	0.0	3													
	Indianapolis	IHL	62	5	15	20	60												4	1	1	2	16			
1997-98	Chicago	NHL	72	0	11	11	59	0	0	0	75	0.0	14													
1998-99	Chicago	NHL	62	2	11	13	70	0	0	0	53	3.8	0	0	0.0	154	58	18:51								
	Portland	AHL	2	0	1	1	2																			
	Edmonton	NHL	11	0	1	1	0	0	0	0	15	0.0	–3	0	0.0	22	14	16:33	4	0	1	1	2	0	0	0
	NHL Totals		149	2	24	26	131	0	0	0	146	1.4		0	0.0	176	72	18:30	4	0	1	1	2	0	0	0

QMJHL Second All-Star Team (1995)

Traded to **Edmonton** by **Chicago** with Daniel Cleary, Ethan Moreau and Chad Kilger for Boris Mironov, Dean McAmmond and Jonas Elofsson, March 20, 1999.

LAKOVIC, Sasha

(LA-koh-vik) **N.J.**

Right wing. Shoots left. 6', 210 lbs. Born, Vancouver, B.C., September 7, 1971.

Season	Club	League	GP	G	A	Pts	PIM	PP	SH	GW	S	%	+/–	TF	F%	H	SB	Min	GP	G	A	Pts	PIM	PP	SH	GW
1991-92	Kelowna	BCJHL	4	1	0	1	14																			
	Bellingham	BCJHL	24	8	3	11	67																			
1992-93	Chatham	ColHL	28	7	5	12	235																			
	Columbus	ECHL	27	7	9	16	162																			
	Binghamton	AHL	3	0	0	0	0																			
	Brantford	ColHL																								
1993-94	Toledo	ECHL	24	5	10	15	198												5	2	1	3	66			
	Chatham	ColHL	13	11	7	18	61																			
1994-95	Tulsa	CHL	40	20	24	44	214												5	1	3	4	88			
1995-96	Las Vegas	IHL	49	1	2	3	416												13	1	1	2	*57			

Season	Club	League	GP	G	A	Pts	PIM	PP	SH	GW	S	%	+/–	TF	F%	H	SB	Min	GP	G	A	Pts	PIM	PP	SH	GW
								Regular Season											**Playoffs**							
1996-97	**Calgary**	**NHL**	**19**	**0**	**1**	**1**	**54**	**0**	**0**	**0**	**10**	**0.0**	**–1**	....	....	....	....	....	....	....	....	....	....	....	....	....
	St. John's	AHL	18	1	8	9	182	....	....	....	....	....	....	....	....	....	....	....	....	....	....	....	....	....	....	....
	Las Vegas	IHL	10	0	0	0	81	....	....	....	....	....	....	....	....	....	....	....	2	0	0	0	14	....	....	....
1997-98	**New Jersey**	**NHL**	**2**	**0**	**0**	**0**	**5**	**0**	**0**	**0**	**2**	**0.0**	**0**	....	....	....	....	....	....	....	....	....	....	....	....	....
	Albany	AHL	30	7	6	13	158	....	....	....	....	....	....	....	....	....	....	....	13	3	4	7	*84	....	....	....
1998-99	**New Jersey**	**NHL**	**16**	**0**	**3**	**3**	**59**	**0**	**0**	**0**	**10**	**0.0**	**0**	**0**	**0.0**	**41**	**1**	**6:20**	....	....	....	....	....	....	....	....
	Albany	AHL	10	1	1	2	93	....	....	....	....	....	....	....	....	....	....	....	....	....	....	....	....	....	....	....
	NHL Totals		**37**	**0**	**4**	**4**	**118**	**0**	**0**	**0**	**22**	**0.0**		**0**	**0.0**	**41**	**1**	**6:20**	....	....	....	....	....	....	....	....

Signed as a free agent by **Calgary**, October 10, 1996. Signed as a free agent by **New Jersey**, September 24, 1997.

LAMBERT, Denny (lahm-BAIR) ATL.

Left wing. Shoots left. 5'11", 200 lbs. Born, Wawa, Ont., January 7, 1970.

Season	Club	League	GP	G	A	Pts	PIM	PP	SH	GW	S	%	+/–	TF	F%	H	SB	Min	GP	G	A	Pts	PIM	PP	SH	GW
1986-87	S.S. Marie Legion	OMHA	22	8	13	21	129	....	....	....	....	....	....	....	....	....	....	....	....	....	....	....	....	....	....	....
1987-88	S.S. Marie Legion	OMHA	32	25	27	54	184	....	....	....	....	....	....	....	....	....	....	....	....	....	....	....	....	....	....	....
1988-89	S.S. Marie	OHL	61	14	15	29	203	....	....	....	....	....	....	....	....	....	....	....	....	....	....	....	....	....	....	....
1989-90	S.S. Marie	OHL	61	23	29	52	276	....	....	....	....	....	....	....	....	....	....	....	....	....	....	....	....	....	....	....
1990-91	S.S. Marie	OHL	59	28	39	67	169	....	....	....	....	....	....	....	....	....	....	....	14	7	9	16	48	....	....	....
1991-92	San Diego	IHL	71	17	14	31	229	....	....	....	....	....	....	....	....	....	....	....	3	0	0	0	10	....	....	....
	St. Thomas	ColHL	5	2	6	8	9	....	....	....	....	....	....	....	....	....	....	....	....	....	....	....	....	....	....	....
1992-93	San Diego	IHL	56	18	12	30	277	....	....	....	....	....	....	....	....	....	....	....	14	1	1	2	44	....	....	....
1993-94	San Diego	IHL	79	13	14	27	314	....	....	....	....	....	....	....	....	....	....	....	6	1	0	1	55	....	....	....
1994-95	San Diego	IHL	75	25	35	60	222	....	....	....	....	....	....	....	....	....	....	....	....	....	....	....	....	....	....	....
	Anaheim	**NHL**	**13**	**1**	**3**	**4**	**4**	**0**	**0**	**0**	**14**	**7.1**	**3**	....	....	....	....	....	....	....	....	....	....	....	....	....
1995-96	**Anaheim**	**NHL**	**33**	**0**	**8**	**8**	**55**	**0**	**0**	**0**	**28**	**0.0**	**–2**	....	....	....	....	....	....	....	....	....	....	....	....	....
	Baltimore	AHL	44	14	28	42	126	....	....	....	....	....	....	....	....	....	....	....	12	3	9	12	39	....	....	....
1996-97	**Ottawa**	**NHL**	**80**	**4**	**16**	**20**	**217**	**0**	**0**	**1**	**58**	**6.9**	**–4**	....	....	....	....	....	**6**	**0**	**1**	**1**	**9**	**0**	**0**	**0**
1997-98	**Ottawa**	**NHL**	**72**	**9**	**10**	**19**	**250**	**0**	**0**	**1**	**76**	**11.8**	**4**	....	....	....	....	....	**11**	**0**	**0**	**0**	**19**	**0**	**0**	**0**
1998-99	**Nashville**	**NHL**	**76**	**5**	**11**	**16**	**218**	**1**	**0**	**0**	**66**	**7.6**	**–3**	**1100.0**		**57**	**17**	**10:20**	....	....	....	....	....	....	....	....
	NHL Totals		**274**	**19**	**48**	**67**	**744**	**1**	**0**	**2**	**242**	**7.9**		**1100.0**		**57**	**17**	**10:20**	**17**	**0**	**1**	**1**	**28**	**0**	**0**	**0**

Signed as a free agent by **Anaheim**, August 16, 1993. Signed as a free agent by **Ottawa**, July 29, 1996. Claimed by **Nashville** from **Ottawa** in Expansion Draft, June 26, 1998. Traded to **Atlanta** by **Nashville** for the rights to Randy Robitaille, August 16, 1999.

LANDRY, Eric S.J.

Center. Shoots left. 5'11", 190 lbs. Born, Gatineau, Que., January 20, 1975.

Season	Club	League	GP	G	A	Pts	PIM	PP	SH	GW	S	%	+/–	TF	F%	H	SB	Min	GP	G	A	Pts	PIM	PP	SH	GW
1993-94	St-Hyacinthe	QMJHL	69	42	34	76	128	....	....	....	....	....	....	....	....	....	....	....	7	4	2	6	13	....	....	....
1994-95	St-Hyacinthe	QMJHL	68	38	36	74	249	....	....	....	....	....	....	....	....	....	....	....	5	2	1	3	10	....	....	....
1995-96	Cape Breton	AHL	74	19	33	52	187	....	....	....	....	....	....	....	....	....	....	....	....	....	....	....	....	....	....	....
1996-97	Hamilton	AHL	74	15	17	32	139	....	....	....	....	....	....	....	....	....	....	....	22	6	7	13	43	....	....	....
1997-98	**Calgary**	**NHL**	**12**	**1**	**0**	**1**	**4**	**0**	**0**	**0**	**7**	**14.3**	**–2**	....	....	....	....	....	....	....	....	....	....	....	....	....
	Saint John	AHL	61	17	21	38	194	....	....	....	....	....	....	....	....	....	....	....	20	4	6	10	58	....	....	....
1998-99	**Calgary**	**NHL**	**3**	**0**	**1**	**1**	**0**	**0**	**0**	**0**	**1**	**0.0**	**1**	**15**	**46.7**	**8**	**0**	**9:54**	....	....	....	....	....	....	....	....
	Saint John	AHL	56	19	22	41	158	....	....	....	....	....	....	....	....	....	....	....	7	2	5	7	12	....	....	....
	NHL Totals		**15**	**1**	**1**	**2**	**4**	**0**	**0**	**0**	**8**	**12.5**		**15**	**46.7**	**8**	**0**	**9:54**	....	....	....	....	....	....	....	....

Signed as a free agent by **Calgary**, August 20, 1997. Traded to **San Jose** by **Calgary** for Fredrik Oduya, July 12, 1999.

LANG, Robert (LUHNG) PIT.

Center. Shoots right. 6'2", 216 lbs. Born, Teplice, Czech., December 19, 1970. Los Angeles' 6th choice, 133rd overall, in 1988 Entry Draft.

Season	Club	League	GP	G	A	Pts	PIM	PP	SH	GW	S	%	+/–	TF	F%	H	SB	Min	GP	G	A	Pts	PIM	PP	SH	GW
1988-89	CHZ Litvinov	Czech.	7	[illegible]	[illegible]	[illegible]	0	....	....	....	....	....	....	....	....	....	....	....	....	....	....	....	....	....	....	....
1989-90	CHZ Litvinov	Czech.	32	8	7	15	....	....	....	....	....	....	....	....	....	....	....	....	8	3	3	6	....	....	....	....
1990-91	CHZ Litvinov	Czech.	56	26	26	52	38	....	....	....	....	....	....	....	....	....	....	....	....	....	....	....	....	....	....	....
1991-92	CHZ Litvinov	Czech.	43	12	31	43	34	....	....	....	....	....	....	....	....	....	....	....	....	....	....	....	....	....	....	....
	Czechoslovakia	Olympics	8	5	8	13	8	....	....	....	....	....	....	....	....	....	....	....	....	....	....	....	....	....	....	....
1992-93	**Los Angeles**	**NHL**	**11**	**0**	**5**	**5**	**2**	**0**	**0**	**0**	**3**	**0.0**	**–3**	....	....	....	....	....	....	....	....	....	....	....	....	....
	Phoenix	IHL	38	9	21	30	20	....	....	....	....	....	....	....	....	....	....	....	....	....	....	....	....	....	....	....
1993-94	**Los Angeles**	**NHL**	**32**	**9**	**10**	**19**	**10**	**0**	**0**	**0**	**41**	**22.0**	**7**	....	....	....	....	....	....	....	....	....	....	....	....	....
	Phoenix	IHL	44	11	24	35	34	....	....	....	....	....	....	....	....	....	....	....	....	....	....	....	....	....	....	....
1994-95	CHZ Litvinov	Cze-Rep	16	4	19	23	28	....	....	....	....	....	....	....	....	....	....	....	....	....	....	....	....	....	....	....
	Los Angeles	**NHL**	**36**	**4**	**8**	**12**	**4**	**0**	**0**	**0**	**38**	**10.5**	**–7**	....	....	....	....	....	....	....	....	....	....	....	....	....
1995-96	**Los Angeles**	**NHL**	**68**	**6**	**16**	**22**	**10**	**0**	**2**	**0**	**71**	**8.5**	**–15**	....	....	....	....	....	....	....	....	....	....	....	....	....
1996-97	HC Sparta	Cze-Rep	38	14	27	41	30	....	....	....	....	....	....	....	....	....	....	....	5	1	2	3	4	....	....	....
	HC Sparta	EuroHL	4	2	2	4	0	....	....	....	....	....	....	....	....	....	....	....	4	2	1	3	2	....	....	....
1997-98	**Boston**	**NHL**	**3**	**0**	**0**	**0**	**2**	**0**	**0**	**0**	**2**	**0.0**	**1**	....	....	....	....	....	....	....	....	....	....	....	....	....
	Czech Republic	Olympics	6	0	3	3	0	....	....	....	....	....	....	....	....	....	....	....	....	....	....	....	....	....	....	....
	Pittsburgh	**NHL**	**51**	**9**	**13**	**22**	**14**	**1**	**1**	**2**	**64**	**14.1**	**6**	....	....	....	....	....	**6**	**0**	**3**	**3**	**2**	**0**	**0**	**0**
	Houston	IHL	9	1	7	8	4	....	....	....	....	....	....	....	....	....	....	....	....	....	....	....	....	....	....	....
1998-99	**Pittsburgh**	**NHL**	**72**	**21**	**23**	**44**	**24**	**7**	**0**	**3**	**137**	**15.3**	**–10**	**964**	**44.8**	**84**	**22**	**16:24**	**12**	**0**	**2**	**2**	**0**	**0**	**0**	**0**
	NHL Totals		**273**	**49**	**75**	**124**	**66**	**8**	**3**	**5**	**356**	**13.8**		**964**	**44.8**	**84**	**22**	**16:24**	**18**	**0**	**5**	**5**	**2**	**0**	**0**	**0**

Signed as a free agent by **Pittsburgh**, September 2, 1997. Claimed by **Boston** from **Pittsburgh** in NHL Waiver Draft, September 28, 1997. Claimed on waivers by **Pittsburgh** from **Boston**, October 25, 1997.

LANGDON, Darren NYR

Left wing. Shoots left. 6'1", 200 lbs. Born, Deer Lake, Nfld., January 8, 1971.

Season	Club	League	GP	G	A	Pts	PIM	PP	SH	GW	S	%	+/–	TF	F%	H	SB	Min	GP	G	A	Pts	PIM	PP	SH	GW
1991-92	Summerside	MJrHL	44	34	49	83	441	....	....	....	....	....	....	....	....	....	....	....	....	....	....	....	....	....	....	....
1992-93	Binghamton	AHL	18	3	4	7	115	....	....	....	....	....	....	....	....	....	....	....	8	0	1	1	14	....	....	....
	Dayton	ECHL	54	23	22	45	429	....	....	....	....	....	....	....	....	....	....	....	3	0	1	1	40	....	....	....
1993-94	Binghamton	AHL	54	2	7	9	327	....	....	....	....	....	....	....	....	....	....	....	....	....	....	....	....	....	....	....
1994-95	Binghamton	AHL	55	6	14	20	296	....	....	....	....	....	....	....	....	....	....	....	11	1	3	4	*84	....	....	....
	NY Rangers	**NHL**	**18**	**1**	**1**	**2**	**62**	**0**	**0**	**0**	**6**	**16.7**	**0**	....	....	....	....	....	....	....	....	....	....	....	....	....
1995-96	**NY Rangers**	**NHL**	**64**	**7**	**4**	**11**	**175**	**0**	**0**	**1**	**29**	**24.1**	**2**	....	....	....	....	....	**2**	**0**	**0**	**0**	**0**	**0**	**0**	**0**
	Binghamton	AHL	1	0	0	0	12	....	....	....	....	....	....	....	....	....	....	....	....	....	....	....	....	....	....	....
1996-97	**NY Rangers**	**NHL**	**60**	**3**	**6**	**9**	**195**	**0**	**0**	**1**	**24**	**12.5**	**–1**	....	....	....	....	....	**10**	**0**	**0**	**0**	**2**	**0**	**0**	**0**
1997-98	**NY Rangers**	**NHL**	**70**	**3**	**3**	**6**	**197**	**0**	**0**	**0**	**15**	**20.0**	**0**	....	....	....	....	....	....	....	....	....	....	....	....	....
1998-99	**NY Rangers**	**NHL**	**44**	**0**	**0**	**0**	**80**	**0**	**0**	**0**	**8**	**0.0**	**–3**	**0**	**0.0**	**37**	**5**	**3:33**	....	....	....	....	....	....	....	....
	NHL Totals		**256**	**14**	**14**	**28**	**709**	**0**	**0**	**2**	**82**	**17.1**		**0**	**0.0**	**37**	**5**	**3:33**	**12**	**0**	**0**	**0**	**2**	**0**	**0**	**0**

Signed as a free agent by **NY Rangers**, August 16, 1993.

LANGENBRUNNER, Jamie (lan-gehn-BRUH-nuhr) DAL.

Center. Shoots right. 6'1", 208 lbs. Born, Duluth, MN, July 24, 1975. Dallas' 2nd choice, 35th overall, in 1993 Entry Draft.

Season	Club	League	GP	G	A	Pts	PIM	PP	SH	GW	S	%	+/–	TF	F%	H	SB	Min	GP	G	A	Pts	PIM	PP	SH	GW
1990-91	Cloquet High	H.S.	20	6	16	22	8	....	....	....	....	....	....	....	....	....	....	....	....	....	....	....	....	....	....	....
1991-92	Cloquet High	H.S.	23	16	23	39	24	....	....	....	....	....	....	....	....	....	....	....	....	....	....	....	....	....	....	....
1992-93	Cloquet High	H.S.	27	27	62	89	18	....	....	....	....	....	....	....	....	....	....	....	....	....	....	....	....	....	....	....
1993-94	Peterborough	OHL	62	33	58	91	53	....	....	....	....	....	....	....	....	....	....	....	7	4	6	10	2	....	....	....
1994-95	Peterborough	OHL	62	42	57	99	84	....	....	....	....	....	....	....	....	....	....	....	11	8	14	22	12	....	....	....
	Dallas	**NHL**	**2**	**0**	**0**	**0**	**2**	**0**	**0**	**0**	**1**	**0.0**	**0**	....	....	....	....	....	....	....	....	....	....	....	....	....
	Kalamazoo	IHL	....	....	....	....	....	....	....	....	....	....	....	....	....	....	....	....	11	1	3	4	2	....	....	....

Season	Club	League	GP	G	A	Pts	PIM	PP	SH	GW	S	%	+/-	TF	F%	H	SB	Min	GP	G	A	Pts	PIM	PP	SH	GW
1995-96	**Dallas**	**NHL**	12	2	2	4	6	1	0	0	15	13.3	-2	....	....	....	....	....	....	....	....	....	....			
	Michigan	IHL	59	25	40	65	129	....						....					10	3	10	13	8			
1996-97	**Dallas**	**NHL**	76	13	26	39	51	3	0	3	112	11.6	-2	....					5	1	1	2	14	0	0	1
1997-98	**Dallas**	**NHL**	81	23	29	52	61	8	0	6	159	14.5	9	....					16	1	4	5	14	0	0	1
	United States	Olympics	3	0	0	0	4	....																			
1998-99 ♦	**Dallas**	**NHL**	75	12	33	45	62	4	0	1	145	8.3	10	217	46.1	129	21	15:51	23	10	7	17	16	4	0	3
	NHL Totals		246	50	90	140	182	16	0	10	432	11.6		217	46.1	129	21	15:51	44	12	12	24	44	4	0	5

LANGKOW, Daymond (LAING-kow) PHI.

Center. Shoots left. 5'11", 175 lbs.   Born, Edmonton, Alta, September 27, 1976. Tampa Bay's 1st choice, 5th overall, in 1995 Entry Draft.

Season	Club	League	GP	G	A	Pts	PIM	PP	SH	GW	S	%	+/-	TF	F%	H	SB	Min	GP	G	A	Pts	PIM	PP	SH	GW
1991-92	Edmonton	AAHA	35	36	45	81	100	....						....						....							
	Tri-City	WHL	1	0	0	0	0	....																			
1992-93	Tri-City	WHL	64	22	42	64	100	....												4	1	0	1	4			
1993-94	Tri-City	WHL	61	40	43	83	174	....												4	2	2	4	15			
1994-95	Tri-City	WHL	72	*67	73	*140	142	....												17	12	15	27	52			
1995-96	Tri-City	WHL	48	30	61	91	103	....												11	14	13	27	20			
	Tampa Bay	**NHL**	4	0	1	1	0	0	0	0	4	0.0	-1													
1996-97	**Tampa Bay**	**NHL**	79	15	13	28	35	3	1	1	170	8.8	1													
	Adirondack	AHL	2	1	1	2	0	....																			
1997-98	**Tampa Bay**	**NHL**	68	8	14	22	62	2	0	1	156	5.1	-9													
1998-99	**Tampa Bay**	**NHL**	22	4	6	10	15	1	0	1	40	10.0	0	399	48.4	20	8	17:10								
	Cleveland	IHL	4	1	1	2	18	....																			
	Philadelphia	**NHL**	56	10	13	23	24	3	1	4	109	9.2	-8	738	48.0	35	12	15:12	6	0	2	2	2	0	0	0
	NHL Totals		229	37	47	84	136				479	7.7		1137	48.1	55	20	15:45	6	0	2	2	2	0	0	0

WHL West First All-Star Team (1995) • Canadian Major Junior First All-Star Team (1995) • WHL West Second All-Star Team (1996)
Traded to **Philadelphia** by **Tampa Bay** with Mikael Renberg for Chris Gratton and Mike Sillinger, December 12, 1998.

LAPERRIERE, Ian (luh-PAIR-ee-YAIR, EE-ihn) L.A.

Center. Shoots right. 6'1", 197 lbs.   Born, Montreal, Que., January 19, 1974. St. Louis' 6th choice, 158th overall, in 1992 Entry Draft.

Season	Club	League	GP	G	A	Pts	PIM	PP	SH	GW	S	%	+/-	TF	F%	H	SB	Min	GP	G	A	Pts	PIM	PP	SH	GW
1989-90	Monteal AAA	QAAA	22	4	10	14	10	....						....						3	0	1	1	0			
1990-91	Drummondville	QMJHL	65	19	29	48	117	....												14	2	9	11	48			
1991-92	Drummondville	QMJHL	70	28	49	77	160	....												4	2	2	4	9			
1992-93	Drummondville	QMJHL	60	44	*96	140	188	....												10	6	13	19	20			
1993-94	Drummondville	QMJHL	62	41	72	113	150	....												9	4	6	10	35			
	St. Louis	**NHL**	1	0	0	0	0	0	0	0	1	0.0	0													
	Peoria	IHL	....																	5	1	3	4	2			
1994-95	Peoria	IHL	51	16	32	48	111	....																			
	St. Louis	**NHL**	37	13	14	27	85	1	0	1	53	24.5	12						7	0	4	4	21	0	0	0
1995-96	**St. Louis**	**NHL**	33	3	6	9	87	1	0	1	31	9.7	-4													
	Worcester	AHL	3	2	1	3	22	....																			
	NY Rangers	**NHL**	28	1	2	3	53	0	0	0	21	4.8	-5													
	Los Angeles	**NHL**	10	2	3	5	15	0	0	0	18	11.1	-2													
1996-97	**Los Angeles**	**NHL**	62	8	15	23	102	0	1	2	84	9.5	-25													
1997-98	**Los Angeles**	**NHL**	77	6	15	21	131	0	1	1	74	8.1	0						4	1	0	1	6	0	0	0
1998-99	**Los Angeles**	**NHL**	72	3	10	13	138	0	0	1	62	4.8	-5	643	47.3	149	60	11:47	11	1	4	5	27	0	0	0
	NHL Totals		320	36	65	101	611	2	2	6	344	10.5		643	47.3	149	60	11:47	11	1	4	5	27	0	0	0

QMJHL Second All-Star Team (1993)
Traded to **NY Rangers** by **St. Louis** for Stephane Matteau, December 28, 1995. Traded to **LA Kings** by **NY Rangers** with Ray Ferraro, Mattias Norstrom, Nathan Lafayette and NY Rangers' 4th round choice (Sean Blanchard) in 1997 Entry Draft for Marty McSorley, Jari Kurri and Shane Churla, March 14, 1996.

LAPLANTE, Darryl DET.

Center. Shoots left. 6'1", 185 lbs.   Born, Calgary, Alta., March 28, 1977. Detroit's 3rd choice, 58th overall, in 1995 Entry Draft.

Season	Club	League	GP	G	A	Pts	PIM	PP	SH	GW	S	%	+/-	TF	F%	H	SB	Min	GP	G	A	Pts	PIM	PP	SH	GW
1992-93	Calgary AA	AAHA	32	20	26	46	60	....						....						....							
1993-94	Calgary AAA	AAHA	35	24	27	51	50	....																			
1994-95	Moose Jaw	WHL	71	22	24	46	66	....												10	2	2	4	7			
1995-96	Moose Jaw	WHL	72	42	40	82	76	....												12	2	4	6	15			
1996-97	Moose Jaw	WHL	69	38	42	80	79	....																			
1997-98	**Detroit**	**NHL**	2	0	0	0	0	0	0	0	2	0.0	0													
	Adirondack	AHL	77	15	10	25	51	....												3	0	1	1	4			
1998-99	**Detroit**	**NHL**	3	0	0	0	0	0	0	0	0	0.0	0	0	0.0	0	1	1:59								
	Adirondack	AHL	71	17	15	32	96	....												3	0	1	1	0			
	NHL Totals		5	0	0	0	0	0	0	0	2	0.0		0	0.0	0	1	1:59								

LAPOINTE, Claude (luh-PWAH, KLOHD) NYI

Center. Shoots left. 5'9", 181 lbs.   Born, Lachine, Que., October 11, 1968. Quebec's 12th choice, 234th overall, in 1988 Entry Draft.

Season	Club	League	GP	G	A	Pts	PIM	PP	SH	GW	S	%	+/-	TF	F%	H	SB	Min	GP	G	A	Pts	PIM	PP	SH	GW
1983-84	Lac St-Louis	QAAA	42	28	29	57	....	....						....						....							
1984-85	Lac St-Louis	QAAA	42	20	32	52	....	....																			
1985-86	Trois-Rivieres	QMJHL	63	14	32	46	70	....												9	5	6	11	4			
1986-87	Trois-Rivieres	QMJHL	70	47	57	104	123	....																			
1987-88	Laval	QMJHL	69	37	83	120	143	....												13	2	17	19	53			
1988-89	Laval	QMJHL	63	32	72	104	158	....												17	5	14	19	66			
1989-90	Halifax	AHL	63	18	19	37	51	....												6	1	1	2	34			
1990-91	**Quebec**	**NHL**	13	2	2	4	4	0	0	0	7	28.6	3													
	Halifax	AHL	43	17	17	34	46	....																			
1991-92	**Quebec**	**NHL**	78	13	20	33	86	0	2	2	95	13.7	-8													
1992-93	**Quebec**	**NHL**	74	10	26	36	98	0	0	1	91	11.0	5						6	2	4	6	8	0	0	0
1993-94	**Quebec**	**NHL**	59	11	17	28	70	1	1	1	73	15.1	2													
1994-95	**Quebec**	**NHL**	29	4	8	12	41	0	0	0	40	10.0	5						5	0	0	0	8	0	0	0
1995-96	**Colorado**	**NHL**	3	0	0	0	0	0	0	0	0	0.0	-1													
	Calgary	**NHL**	32	4	5	9	20	0	2	1	44	9.1	2						2	0	0	0	0	0	0	0
	Saint John	AHL	12	5	3	8	10	....																			
1996-97	**NY Islanders**	**NHL**	73	13	5	18	49	0	3	3	80	16.3	-12													
	Utah	IHL	9	7	6	13	14	....																			
1997-98	**NY Islanders**	**NHL**	78	10	10	20	47	0	1	3	82	12.2	-9													
1998-99	**NY Islanders**	**NHL**	82	14	23	37	62	2	2	1	134	10.4	-19	1218	56.6	168	60	19:21								
	NHL Totals		521	81	116	197	477	3	11	12	646	12.5		1218	56.6	168	60	19:21	13	2	4	6	16	0	0	0

Transferred to **Colorado** after **Quebec** franchise relocated, June 21, 1995. Traded to **Calgary** by **Colorado** for Calgary's 7th round choice (Samuel Pahlsson) in 1996 Entry Draft, November 1, 1995. Signed as a free agent by **NY Islanders**, August 14, 1996.

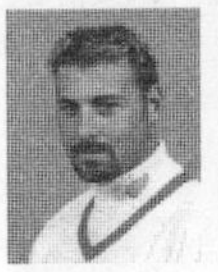

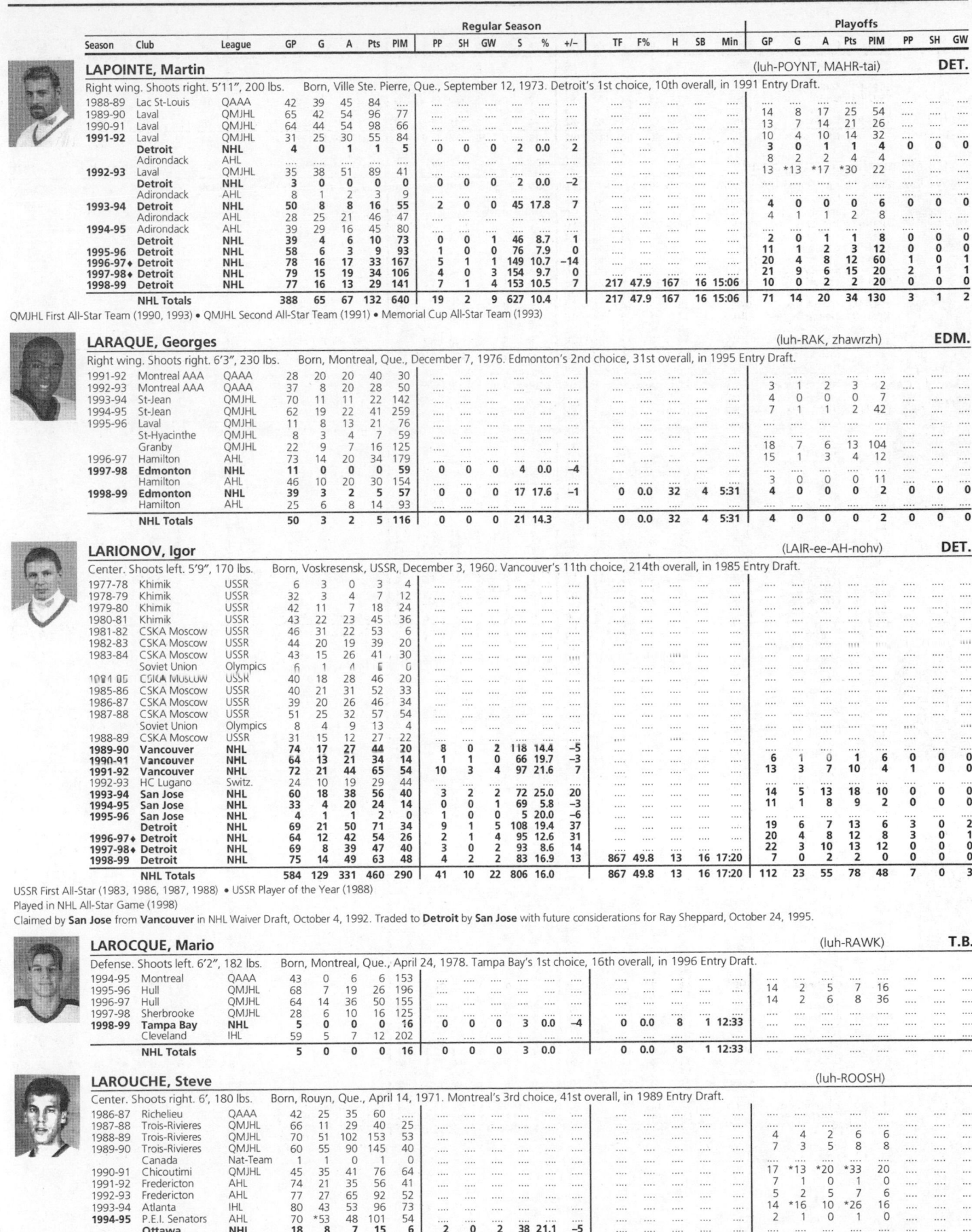

LAPOINTE, Martin
(luh-POYNT, MAHR-tai) **DET.**

Right wing. Shoots right. 5'11", 200 lbs. Born, Ville Ste. Pierre, Que., September 12, 1973. Detroit's 1st choice, 10th overall, in 1991 Entry Draft.

Season	Club	League	GP	G	A	Pts	PIM	PP	SH	GW	S	%	+/–	TF	F%	H	SB	Min	Playoffs GP	G	A	Pts	PIM	PP	SH	GW
1988-89	Lac St-Louis	QAAA	42	39	45	84	....	....	....	....	....	....	....	....	....	....	....	....	....	....	....	....	....	....	....	....
1989-90	Laval	QMJHL	65	42	54	96	77	....	....	....	....	....	....	....	....	....	....	....	14	8	17	25	54	....	....	....
1990-91	Laval	QMJHL	64	44	54	98	66	....	....	....	....	....	....	....	....	....	....	....	13	7	14	21	26	....	....	....
1991-92	Laval	QMJHL	31	25	30	55	84	....	....	....	....	....	....	....	....	....	....	....	10	4	10	14	32	....	....	....
	Detroit	**NHL**	**4**	**0**	**1**	**1**	**5**	**0**	**0**	**0**	**2**	**0.0**	**2**	....	....	....	....	....	**3**	**0**	**1**	**1**	**4**	**0**	**0**	**0**
	Adirondack	AHL	....	....	....	....	....	....	....	....	....	....	....	....	....	....	....	....	8	2	2	4	4	....	....	....
1992-93	Laval	QMJHL	35	38	51	89	41	....	....	....	....	....	....	....	....	....	....	....	13	*13	*17	*30	22	....	....	....
	Detroit	**NHL**	**3**	**0**	**0**	**0**	**0**	**0**	**0**	**0**	**2**	**0.0**	**–2**	....	....	....	....	....	....	....	....	....	....	....	....	....
	Adirondack	AHL	8	1	2	3	9	....	....	....	....	....	....	....	....	....	....	....	....	....	....	....	....	....	....	....
1993-94	**Detroit**	**NHL**	**50**	**8**	**8**	**16**	**55**	**2**	**0**	**0**	**45**	**17.8**	**7**	....	....	....	....	....	**4**	**0**	**0**	**0**	**6**	**0**	**0**	**0**
	Adirondack	AHL	28	25	21	46	47	....	....	....	....	....	....	....	....	....	....	....	4	1	1	2	8	....	....	....
1994-95	Adirondack	AHL	39	29	16	45	80	....	....	....	....	....	....	....	....	....	....	....	....	....	....	....	....	....	....	....
	Detroit	**NHL**	**39**	**4**	**6**	**10**	**73**	**0**	**0**	**1**	**46**	**8.7**	**1**	....	....	....	....	....	**2**	**0**	**1**	**1**	**8**	**0**	**0**	**0**
1995-96	**Detroit**	**NHL**	**58**	**6**	**3**	**9**	**93**	**1**	**0**	**0**	**76**	**7.9**	**0**	....	....	....	....	....	**11**	**1**	**2**	**3**	**12**	**0**	**0**	**0**
1996-97♦	**Detroit**	**NHL**	**78**	**16**	**17**	**33**	**167**	**5**	**1**	**1**	**149**	**10.7**	**–14**	....	....	....	....	....	**20**	**4**	**8**	**12**	**60**	**1**	**0**	**1**
1997-98♦	**Detroit**	**NHL**	**79**	**15**	**19**	**34**	**106**	**4**	**0**	**3**	**154**	**9.7**	**0**	....	....	....	....	....	**21**	**9**	**6**	**15**	**20**	**2**	**1**	**1**
1998-99	**Detroit**	**NHL**	**77**	**16**	**13**	**29**	**141**	**7**	**1**	**4**	**153**	**10.5**	**7**	**217**	**47.9**	**167**	**16**	**15:06**	**10**	**0**	**2**	**2**	**20**	**0**	**0**	**0**
	NHL Totals		**388**	**65**	**67**	**132**	**640**	**19**	**2**	**9**	**627**	**10.4**		**217**	**47.9**	**167**	**16**	**15:06**	**71**	**14**	**20**	**34**	**130**	**3**	**1**	**2**

QMJHL First All-Star Team (1990, 1993) • QMJHL Second All-Star Team (1991) • Memorial Cup All-Star Team (1993)

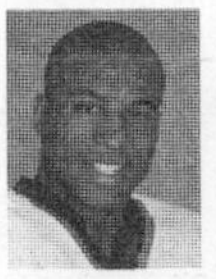

LARAQUE, Georges
(luh-RAK, zhawrzh) **EDM.**

Right wing. Shoots right. 6'3", 230 lbs. Born, Montreal, Que., December 7, 1976. Edmonton's 2nd choice, 31st overall, in 1995 Entry Draft.

Season	Club	League	GP	G	A	Pts	PIM	PP	SH	GW	S	%	+/–	TF	F%	H	SB	Min	Playoffs GP	G	A	Pts	PIM	PP	SH	GW
1991-92	Montreal AAA	QAAA	28	20	20	40	30	....	....	....	....	....	....	....	....	....	....	....	....	....	....	....	....	....	....	....
1992-93	Montreal AAA	QAAA	37	8	20	28	50	....	....	....	....	....	....	....	....	....	....	....	3	1	2	3	2	....	....	....
1993-94	St-Jean	QMJHL	70	11	11	22	142	....	....	....	....	....	....	....	....	....	....	....	4	0	0	0	7	....	....	....
1994-95	St-Jean	QMJHL	62	19	22	41	259	....	....	....	....	....	....	....	....	....	....	....	7	1	1	2	42	....	....	....
1995-96	Laval	QMJHL	11	8	13	21	76	....	....	....	....	....	....	....	....	....	....	....	....	....	....	....	....	....	....	....
	St-Hyacinthe	QMJHL	8	3	4	7	59	....	....	....	....	....	....	....	....	....	....	....	....	....	....	....	....	....	....	....
	Granby	QMJHL	22	9	7	16	125	....	....	....	....	....	....	....	....	....	....	....	18	7	6	13	104	....	....	....
1996-97	Hamilton	AHL	73	14	20	34	179	....	....	....	....	....	....	....	....	....	....	....	15	1	3	4	12	....	....	....
1997-98	**Edmonton**	**NHL**	**11**	**0**	**0**	**0**	**59**	**0**	**0**	**0**	**4**	**0.0**	**–4**	....	....	....	....	....	....	....	....	....	....	....	....	....
	Hamilton	AHL	46	10	20	30	154	....	....	....	....	....	....	....	....	....	....	....	3	0	0	0	11	....	....	....
1998-99	**Edmonton**	**NHL**	**39**	**3**	**2**	**5**	**57**	**0**	**0**	**0**	**17**	**17.6**	**–1**	**0**	**0.0**	**32**	**4**	**5:31**	**4**	**0**	**0**	**0**	**2**	**0**	**0**	**0**
	Hamilton	AHL	25	6	8	14	93	....	....	....	....	....	....	....	....	....	....	....	....	....	....	....	....	....	....	....
	NHL Totals		**50**	**3**	**2**	**5**	**116**	**0**	**0**	**0**	**21**	**14.3**		**0**	**0.0**	**32**	**4**	**5:31**	**4**	**0**	**0**	**0**	**2**	**0**	**0**	**0**

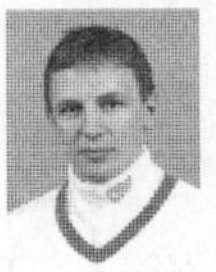

LARIONOV, Igor
(LAIR-ee-AH-nohv) **DET.**

Center. Shoots left. 5'9", 170 lbs. Born, Voskresensk, USSR, December 3, 1960. Vancouver's 11th choice, 214th overall, in 1985 Entry Draft.

Season	Club	League	GP	G	A	Pts	PIM	PP	SH	GW	S	%	+/–	TF	F%	H	SB	Min	Playoffs GP	G	A	Pts	PIM	PP	SH	GW
1977-78	Khimik	USSR	6	3	0	3	4	....	....	....	....	....	....	....	....	....	....	....	....	....	....	....	....	....	....	....
1978-79	Khimik	USSR	32	3	4	7	12	....	....	....	....	....	....	....	....	....	....	....	....	....	....	....	....	....	....	....
1979-80	Khimik	USSR	42	11	7	18	24	....	....	....	....	....	....	....	....	....	....	....	....	....	....	....	....	....	....	....
1980-81	Khimik	USSR	43	22	23	45	36	....	....	....	....	....	....	....	....	....	....	....	....	....	....	....	....	....	....	....
1981-82	CSKA Moscow	USSR	46	31	22	53	6	....	....	....	....	....	....	....	....	....	....	....	....	....	....	....	....	....	....	....
1982-83	CSKA Moscow	USSR	44	20	19	39	20	....	....	....	....	....	....	....	....	....	....	....	....	....	....	....	....	....	....	....
1983-84	CSKA Moscow	USSR	43	15	26	41	30	....	....	....	....	....	....	....	....	....	....	....	....	....	....	....	....	....	....	....
	Soviet Union	Olympics	6	1	4	5	6	....	....	....	....	....	....	....	....	....	....	....	....	....	....	....	....	....	....	....
1984-85	CSKA Moscow	USSR	40	18	28	46	20	....	....	....	....	....	....	....	....	....	....	....	....	....	....	....	....	....	....	....
1985-86	CSKA Moscow	USSR	40	21	31	52	33	....	....	....	....	....	....	....	....	....	....	....	....	....	....	....	....	....	....	....
1986-87	CSKA Moscow	USSR	39	20	26	46	34	....	....	....	....	....	....	....	....	....	....	....	....	....	....	....	....	....	....	....
1987-88	CSKA Moscow	USSR	51	25	32	57	54	....	....	....	....	....	....	....	....	....	....	....	....	....	....	....	....	....	....	....
	Soviet Union	Olympics	8	4	9	13	4	....	....	....	....	....	....	....	....	....	....	....	....	....	....	....	....	....	....	....
1988-89	CSKA Moscow	USSR	31	15	12	27	22	....	....	....	....	....	....	....	....	....	....	....	....	....	....	....	....	....	....	....
1989-90	**Vancouver**	**NHL**	**74**	**17**	**27**	**44**	**20**	**8**	**0**	**2**	**118**	**14.4**	**–5**	....	....	....	....	....	....	....	....	....	....	....	....	....
1990-91	**Vancouver**	**NHL**	**64**	**13**	**21**	**34**	**14**	**1**	**1**	**0**	**66**	**19.7**	**–3**	....	....	....	....	....	**6**	**1**	**0**	**1**	**6**	**0**	**0**	**0**
1991-92	**Vancouver**	**NHL**	**72**	**21**	**44**	**65**	**54**	**10**	**3**	**4**	**97**	**21.6**	**7**	....	....	....	....	....	**13**	**3**	**7**	**10**	**4**	**1**	**0**	**0**
1992-93	HC Lugano	Switz.	24	10	19	29	44	....	....	....	....	....	....	....	....	....	....	....	....	....	....	....	....	....	....	....
1993-94	**San Jose**	**NHL**	**60**	**18**	**38**	**56**	**40**	**3**	**2**	**2**	**72**	**25.0**	**20**	....	....	....	....	....	**14**	**5**	**13**	**18**	**10**	**0**	**0**	**0**
1994-95	**San Jose**	**NHL**	**33**	**4**	**20**	**24**	**14**	**0**	**0**	**1**	**69**	**5.8**	**–3**	....	....	....	....	....	**11**	**1**	**8**	**9**	**2**	**0**	**0**	**0**
1995-96	**San Jose**	**NHL**	**4**	**1**	**1**	**2**	**0**	**1**	**0**	**0**	**5**	**20.0**	**–6**	....	....	....	....	....	....	....	....	....	....	....	....	....
	Detroit	**NHL**	**69**	**21**	**50**	**71**	**34**	**9**	**1**	**5**	**108**	**19.4**	**37**	....	....	....	....	....	**19**	**6**	**7**	**13**	**6**	**3**	**0**	**2**
1996-97♦	**Detroit**	**NHL**	**64**	**12**	**42**	**54**	**26**	**2**	**1**	**4**	**95**	**12.6**	**31**	....	....	....	....	....	**20**	**4**	**8**	**12**	**8**	**3**	**0**	**1**
1997-98♦	**Detroit**	**NHL**	**69**	**8**	**39**	**47**	**40**	**3**	**0**	**2**	**93**	**8.6**	**14**	....	....	....	....	....	**22**	**3**	**10**	**13**	**12**	**0**	**0**	**0**
1998-99	**Detroit**	**NHL**	**75**	**14**	**49**	**63**	**48**	**4**	**2**	**2**	**83**	**16.9**	**13**	**867**	**49.8**	**13**	**16**	**17:20**	**7**	**0**	**2**	**2**	**0**	**0**	**0**	**0**
	NHL Totals		**584**	**129**	**331**	**460**	**290**	**41**	**10**	**22**	**806**	**16.0**		**867**	**49.8**	**13**	**16**	**17:20**	**112**	**23**	**55**	**78**	**48**	**7**	**0**	**3**

USSR First All-Star (1983, 1986, 1987, 1988) • USSR Player of the Year (1988)

Played in NHL All-Star Game (1998)

Claimed by **San Jose** from **Vancouver** in NHL Waiver Draft, October 4, 1992. Traded to **Detroit** by **San Jose** with future considerations for Ray Sheppard, October 24, 1995.

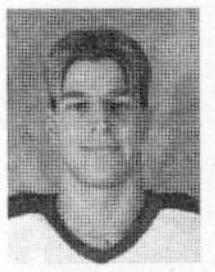

LAROCQUE, Mario
(luh-RAWK) **T.B.**

Defense. Shoots left. 6'2", 182 lbs. Born, Montreal, Que., April 24, 1978. Tampa Bay's 1st choice, 16th overall, in 1996 Entry Draft.

Season	Club	League	GP	G	A	Pts	PIM	PP	SH	GW	S	%	+/–	TF	F%	H	SB	Min	Playoffs GP	G	A	Pts	PIM	PP	SH	GW
1994-95	Montreal	QAAA	43	0	6	6	153	....	....	....	....	....	....	....	....	....	....	....	....	....	....	....	....	....	....	....
1995-96	Hull	QMJHL	68	7	19	26	196	....	....	....	....	....	....	....	....	....	....	....	14	2	5	7	16	....	....	....
1996-97	Hull	QMJHL	64	14	36	50	155	....	....	....	....	....	....	....	....	....	....	....	14	2	6	8	36	....	....	....
1997-98	Sherbrooke	QMJHL	28	6	10	16	125	....	....	....	....	....	....	....	....	....	....	....	....	....	....	....	....	....	....	....
1998-99	**Tampa Bay**	**NHL**	**5**	**0**	**0**	**0**	**16**	**0**	**0**	**0**	**3**	**0.0**	**–4**	**0**	**0.0**	**8**	**1**	**12:33**	....	....	....	....	....	....	....	....
	Cleveland	IHL	59	5	7	12	202	....	....	....	....	....	....	....	....	....	....	....	....	....	....	....	....	....	....	....
	NHL Totals		**5**	**0**	**0**	**0**	**16**	**0**	**0**	**0**	**3**	**0.0**		**0**	**0.0**	**8**	**1**	**12:33**	....	....	....	....	....	....	....	....

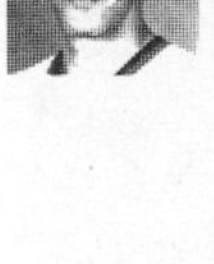

LAROUCHE, Steve
(luh-ROOSH)

Center. Shoots right. 6', 180 lbs. Born, Rouyn, Que., April 14, 1971. Montreal's 3rd choice, 41st overall, in 1989 Entry Draft.

Season	Club	League	GP	G	A	Pts	PIM	PP	SH	GW	S	%	+/–	TF	F%	H	SB	Min	Playoffs GP	G	A	Pts	PIM	PP	SH	GW
1986-87	Richelieu	QAAA	42	25	35	60	....	....	....	....	....	....	....	....	....	....	....	....	....	....	....	....	....	....	....	....
1987-88	Trois-Rivieres	QMJHL	66	11	29	40	25	....	....	....	....	....	....	....	....	....	....	....	....	....	....	....	....	....	....	....
1988-89	Trois-Rivieres	QMJHL	70	51	102	153	53	....	....	....	....	....	....	....	....	....	....	....	4	4	2	6	6	....	....	....
1989-90	Trois-Rivieres	QMJHL	60	55	90	145	40	....	....	....	....	....	....	....	....	....	....	....	7	3	5	8	8	....	....	....
	Canada	Nat-Team	1	1	0	1	0	....	....	....	....	....	....	....	....	....	....	....	....	....	....	....	....	....	....	....
1990-91	Chicoutimi	QMJHL	45	35	41	76	64	....	....	....	....	....	....	....	....	....	....	....	17	*13	*20	*33	20	....	....	....
1991-92	Fredericton	AHL	74	21	35	56	41	....	....	....	....	....	....	....	....	....	....	....	7	1	0	1	0	....	....	....
1992-93	Fredericton	AHL	77	27	65	92	52	....	....	....	....	....	....	....	....	....	....	....	5	2	5	7	6	....	....	....
1993-94	Atlanta	IHL	80	43	53	96	73	....	....	....	....	....	....	....	....	....	....	....	14	*16	10	*26	16	....	....	....
1994-95	P.E.I. Senators	AHL	70	*53	48	101	54	....	....	....	....	....	....	....	....	....	....	....	2	1	0	1	0	....	....	....
	Ottawa	**NHL**	**18**	**8**	**7**	**15**	**6**	**2**	**0**	**2**	**38**	**21.1**	**–5**	....	....	....	....	....	....	....	....	....	....	....	....	....

			Regular Season																Playoffs							
Season	Club	League	GP	G	A	Pts	PIM	PP	SH	GW	S	%	+/-	TF	F%	H	SB	Min	GP	G	A	Pts	PIM	PP	SH	GW
1995-96	**NY Rangers**	**NHL**	**1**	**0**	**0**	**0**	**0**	**0**	**0**	**0**	**1**	**0.0**	**0**	....	....	....	....	....	....	....	....	....	....	....	....	....
	Binghamton	AHL	39	20	46	66	47	....	....	....	....	....	....	....	....	....	....	....	....	....	....	....	....	....	....	....
	Los Angeles	**NHL**	**7**	**1**	**2**	**3**	**4**	**1**	**0**	**0**	**13**	**7.7**	**0**	....	....	....	....	....	....	....	....	....	....	....	....	....
	Phoenix	IHL	33	19	17	36	14	....	....	....	....	....	....	....	....	....	....	....	4	0	1	1	8	....	....	....
1996-97	Quebec	IHL	79	49	53	102	78	....	....	....	....	....	....	....	....	....	....	....	9	3	10	13	18	....	....	....
1997-98	Quebec	IHL	68	23	44	67	40	....	....	....	....	....	....	....	....	....	....	....	....	....	....	....	....	....	....	....
	Quebec Aces	QSPHL	2	0	0	0	0	....	....	....	....	....	....	....	....	....	....	....	....	....	....	....	....	....	....	....
	Chicago	IHL	13	9	10	19	20	....	....	....	....	....	....	....	....	....	....	....	22	9	11	20	14	....	....	....
1998-99	Chicago	IHL	33	13	25	38	18	....	....	....	....	....	....	....	....	....	....	....	....	....	....	....	....	....	....	....
	NHL Totals		**26**	**9**	**9**	**18**	**10**	**3**	**0**	**2**	**52**	**17.3**		....	....	....	....	....	....	....	....	....	....	....	....	....

QMJHL Second All-Star Team (1990) • AHL First All-Star Team (1995) • Won Fred Hunt Memorial Trophy (Sportsmanship - AHL) (1995) • Won Les Cunningham Plaque (MVP - AHL) (1995) • IHL First All-Star Team (1997)

Signed as a free agent by **Ottawa**, September 11, 1994. Traded to **NY Rangers** by **Ottawa** for Jean-Yves Roy, October 5, 1995. Traded to **LA Kings** by **NY Rangers** for Chris Snell, January 14, 1996. • Suffered season-ending knee injury in game vs. Detroit (IHL), December 29, 1998.

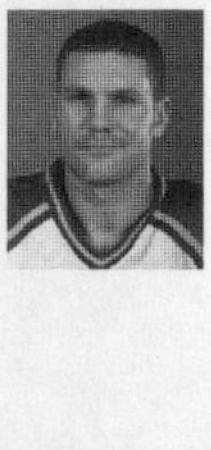

LARSEN, Brad — COL.

Left wing. Shoots left. 5'11", 212 lbs. Born, Nakusp, B.C., January 28, 1977. Colorado's 5th choice, 87th overall, in 1997 Entry Draft.

Season	Club	League	GP	G	A	Pts	PIM	PP	SH	GW	S	%	+/-	TF	F%	H	SB	Min	GP	G	A	Pts	PIM	PP	SH	GW
1992-93	Nelson	RMJHL	42	31	37	68	164	....	....	....	....	....	....	....	....	....	....	....	....	....	....	....	....	....	....	....
1993-94	Swift Current	WHL	64	15	18	33	32	....	....	....	....	....	....	....	....	....	....	....	7	1	2	3	4	....	....	....
1994-95	Swift Current	WHL	62	24	33	57	73	....	....	....	....	....	....	....	....	....	....	....	6	0	1	1	2	....	....	....
1995-96	Swift Current	WHL	51	30	47	77	67	....	....	....	....	....	....	....	....	....	....	....	6	3	2	5	13	....	....	....
1996-97	Swift Current	WHL	61	36	46	82	61	....	....	....	....	....	....	....	....	....	....	....	....	....	....	....	....	....	....	....
1997-98	**Colorado**	**NHL**	**1**	**0**	**0**	**0**	**0**	**0**	**0**	**0**	**0**	**0.0**	**0**	....	....	....	....	....	....	....	....	....	....	....	....	....
	Hershey	AHL	65	12	10	22	80	....	....	....	....	....	....	....	....	....	....	....	7	3	2	5	2	....	....	....
1998-99	Hershey	AHL	18	3	4	7	11	....	....	....	....	....	....	....	....	....	....	....	5	0	1	1	6	....	....	....
	NHL Totals		**1**	**0**	**0**	**0**	**0**	**0**	**0**	**0**	**0**	**0.0**		....	....	....	....	....	....	....	....	....	....	....	....	....

WHL East Second All-Star Team (1997)

• Re-entered NHL draft. Originally Ottawa's 3rd choice, 53rd overall, in 1995 Entry Draft.

Rights traded to **Colorado** by **Ottawa** for Janne Laukkanen, January 26, 1996. • Missed majority of 1998-99 season recovering from abdominal inury suffered in game vs. Albany (AHL), November 20, 1998.

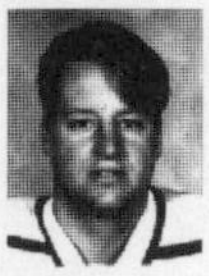

LAUER, Brad — (LAU-er)

Left wing. Shoots left. 6', 195 lbs. Born, Humboldt, Sask., October 27, 1966. NY Islanders' 3rd choice, 34th overall, in 1985 Entry Draft.

Season	Club	League	GP	G	A	Pts	PIM	PP	SH	GW	S	%	+/-	TF	F%	H	SB	Min	GP	G	A	Pts	PIM	PP	SH	GW
1982-83	Notre Dame	SAHA	STATISTICS NOT AVAILABLE																							
1983-84	Regina	WHL	60	5	7	12	51	....	....	....	....	....	....	....	....	....	....	....	16	0	1	1	24	....	....	....
1984-85	Regina	WHL	72	33	46	79	57	....	....	....	....	....	....	....	....	....	....	....	8	6	6	12	9	....	....	....
1985-86	Regina	WHL	57	36	38	74	69	....	....	....	....	....	....	....	....	....	....	....	10	4	5	9	2	....	....	....
1986-87	**NY Islanders**	**NHL**	**61**	**7**	**14**	**21**	**65**	**1**	**0**	**1**	**75**	**9.3**	**0**	....	....	....	....	....	**6**	**2**	**0**	**2**	**4**	**0**	**0**	**0**
1987-88	**NY Islanders**	**NHL**	**69**	**17**	**18**	**35**	**67**	**3**	**0**	**4**	**94**	**18.1**	**13**	....	....	....	....	....	**5**	**3**	**1**	**4**	**4**	**0**	**0**	**0**
1988-89	**NY Islanders**	**NHL**	**14**	**3**	**2**	**5**	**2**	**0**	**0**	**0**	**21**	**14.3**	**−2**	....	....	....	....	....	....	....	....	....	....	....	....	....
	Springfield	AHL	8	1	5	6	0	....	....	....	....	....	....	....	....	....	....	....	....	....	....	....	....	....	....	....
1989-90	**NY Islanders**	**NHL**	**63**	**6**	**18**	**24**	**19**	**0**	**0**	**2**	**86**	**7.0**	**5**	....	....	....	....	....	**4**	**0**	**2**	**2**	**10**	**0**	**0**	**0**
	Springfield	AHL	7	4	2	6	0	....	....	....	....	....	....	....	....	....	....	....	....	....	....	....	....	....	....	....
1990-91	**NY Islanders**	**NHL**	**44**	**4**	**8**	**12**	**45**	**0**	**1**	**0**	**70**	**5.7**	**−6**	....	....	....	....	....	....	....	....	....	....	....	....	....
	Capital District	AHL	11	5	11	16	14	....	....	....	....	....	....	....	....	....	....	....	....	....	....	....	....	....	....	....
1991-92	**NY Islanders**	**NHL**	**8**	**1**	**0**	**1**	**2**	**0**	**1**	**0**	**12**	**8.3**	**−2**	....	....	....	....	....	....	....	....	....	....	....	....	....
	Chicago	**NHL**	**6**	**0**	**0**	**0**	**4**	**0**	**0**	**0**	**6**	**0.0**	**−3**	....	....	....	....	....	**7**	**1**	**1**	**2**	**2**	**0**	**0**	**0**
	Indianapolis	IHL	57	24	30	54	46	....	....	....	....	....	....	....	....	....	....	....	....	....	....	....	....	....	....	....
1992-93	**Chicago**	**NHL**	**7**	**0**	**1**	**1**	**2**	**0**	**0**	**0**	**8**	**0.0**	**−1**	....	....	....	....	....	....	....	....	....	....	....	....	....
	Indianapolis	IHL	62	*50	41	91	80	....	....	....	....	....	....	....	....	....	....	....	5	3	1	4	6	....	....	....
1993-94	**Ottawa**	**NHL**	**30**	**2**	**5**	**7**	**6**	**0**	**1**	**0**	**45**	**4.4**	**−15**	....	....	....	....	....	....	....	....	....	....	....	....	....
	Las Vegas	IHL	32	21	21	42	30	....	....	....	....	....	....	....	....	....	....	....	4	1	0	1	2	....	....	....
1994-95	Cleveland	IHL	51	32	27	59	48	....	....	....	....	....	....	....	....	....	....	....	4	4	2	6	6	....	....	....
1995-96	**Pittsburgh**	**NHL**	**21**	**4**	**1**	**5**	**6**	**1**	**0**	**1**	**29**	**13.8**	**−5**	....	....	....	....	....	**12**	**1**	**1**	**2**	**4**	**0**	**0**	**0**
	Cleveland	IHL	53	25	27	52	44	....	....	....	....	....	....	....	....	....	....	....	....	....	....	....	....	....	....	....
1996-97	Cleveland	IHL	64	27	21	48	61	....	....	....	....	....	....	....	....	....	....	....	14	4	6	10	8	....	....	....
1997-98	Cleveland	IHL	68	22	33	55	74	....	....	....	....	....	....	....	....	....	....	....	10	0	3	3	12	....	....	....
1998-99	Utah	IHL	78	31	30	61	68	....	....	....	....	....	....	....	....	....	....	....	....	....	....	....	....	....	....	....
	NHL Totals		**323**	**44**	**67**	**111**	**218**	**5**	**3**	**8**	**446**	**9.9**		....	....	....	....	....	**34**	**7**	**5**	**12**	**24**	**0**	**0**	**0**

IHL First All-Star Team (1993)

Traded to **Chicago** by **NY Islanders** with Brent Sutter for Adam Creighton and Steve Thomas, October 25, 1991. Signed as a free agent by **Ottawa**, January 3, 1994. Signed as a free agent by **Pittsburgh**, August 10, 1995.

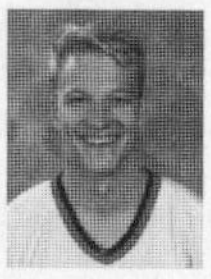

LAUKKANEN, Janne — (LOW-kah-nehn) — OTT.

Defense. Shoots left. 6', 180 lbs. Born, Lahti, Finland, March 19, 1970. Quebec's 8th choice, 156th overall, in 1991 Entry Draft.

Season	Club	League	GP	G	A	Pts	PIM	PP	SH	GW	S	%	+/-	TF	F%	H	SB	Min	GP	G	A	Pts	PIM	PP	SH	GW
1988-89	K-Reipas	Finland-2	33	1	7	8	24	....	....	....	....	....	....	....	....	....	....	....	....	....	....	....	....	....	....	....
1989-90	H-Reipas	Finn-Jr.	2	2	2	4	2	....	....	....	....	....	....	....	....	....	....	....	....	....	....	....	....	....	....	....
	H-Reipas	Finland-2	44	8	22	30	60	....	....	....	....	....	....	....	....	....	....	....	....	....	....	....	....	....	....	....
1990-91	Reipas Lahti	Finland	44	8	14	22	56	....	....	....	....	....	....	....	....	....	....	....	....	....	....	....	....	....	....	....
1991-92	Hameelinna	Finland	43	5	14	19	62	....	....	....	....	....	....	....	....	....	....	....	....	....	....	....	....	....	....	....
	Finland	Olympics	8	0	1	1	6	....	....	....	....	....	....	....	....	....	....	....	....	....	....	....	....	....	....	....
1992-93	Hameelinna	Finland	47	8	21	29	76	....	....	....	....	....	....	....	....	....	....	....	12	1	4	5	10	....	....	....
1993-94	Hameelinna	Finland	48	5	24	29	46	....	....	....	....	....	....	....	....	....	....	....	....	....	....	....	....	....	....	....
	Finland	Olympics	8	0	2	2	12	....	....	....	....	....	....	....	....	....	....	....	....	....	....	....	....	....	....	....
	HC Budejovice	Cze-Rep	....	....	....	....	....	....	....	....	....	....	....	....	....	....	....	....	3	0	1	1	0	....	....	....
1994-95	Cornwall	AHL	55	8	26	34	41	....	....	....	....	....	....	....	....	....	....	....	....	....	....	....	....	....	....	....
	Quebec	**NHL**	**11**	**0**	**3**	**3**	**4**	**0**	**0**	**0**	**12**	**0.0**	**3**	....	....	....	....	....	**6**	**1**	**0**	**1**	**2**	**0**	**0**	**0**
1995-96	**Colorado**	**NHL**	**3**	**1**	**0**	**1**	**0**	**1**	**0**	**0**	**4**	**25.0**	**−1**	....	....	....	....	....	....	....	....	....	....	....	....	....
	Cornwall	AHL	35	7	20	27	60	....	....	....	....	....	....	....	....	....	....	....	....	....	....	....	....	....	....	....
	Ottawa	**NHL**	**20**	**0**	**2**	**2**	**14**	**0**	**0**	**0**	**31**	**0.0**	**0**	....	....	....	....	....	....	....	....	....	....	....	....	....
1996-97	**Ottawa**	**NHL**	**76**	**3**	**18**	**21**	**76**	**2**	**0**	**0**	**109**	**2.8**	**−14**	....	....	....	....	....	**7**	**0**	**1**	**1**	**6**	**0**	**0**	**0**
1997-98	**Ottawa**	**NHL**	**60**	**4**	**17**	**21**	**64**	**2**	**0**	**2**	**69**	**5.8**	**−15**	....	....	....	....	....	**11**	**2**	**2**	**4**	**8**	**1**	**0**	**1**
	Finland	Olympics	6	0	0	0	4	....	....	....	....	....	....	....	....	....	....	....	....	....	....	....	....	....	....	....
1998-99	**Ottawa**	**NHL**	**50**	**1**	**11**	**12**	**40**	**0**	**0**	**0**	**46**	**2.2**	**18**	**0**	**0.0**	**87**	**80**	**18:37**	**4**	**0**	**0**	**0**	**4**	**0**	**0**	**0**
	NHL Totals		**220**	**9**	**51**	**60**	**198**	**5**	**0**	**2**	**271**	**3.3**		**0**	**0.0**	**87**	**80**	**18:37**	**28**	**3**	**3**	**6**	**20**	**1**	**0**	**1**

Finnish First All-Star Team (1993)

Transferred to **Colorado** after **Quebec** franchise relocated, June 21, 1995. Traded to **Ottawa** by **Colorado** for the rights to Brad Larsen, January 26, 1996.

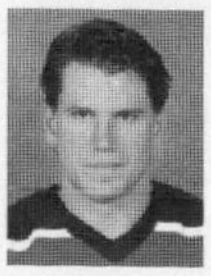

LAUS, Paul — (LOWZ) — FLA.

Defense. Shoots right. 6'1", 212 lbs. Born, Beamsville, Ont., September 26, 1970. Pittsburgh's 2nd choice, 37th overall, in 1989 Entry Draft.

Season	Club	League	GP	G	A	Pts	PIM	PP	SH	GW	S	%	+/-	TF	F%	H	SB	Min	GP	G	A	Pts	PIM	PP	SH	GW
1986-87	St. Catherines	OJHL	40	1	8	9	56	....	....	....	....	....	....	....	....	....	....	....	....	....	....	....	....	....	....	....
1987-88	Hamilton	OHL	56	1	9	10	171	....	....	....	....	....	....	....	....	....	....	....	14	0	0	0	28	....	....	....
1988-89	Niagara Falls	OHL	49	1	10	11	225	....	....	....	....	....	....	....	....	....	....	....	15	0	5	5	56	....	....	....
1989-90	Niagara Falls	OHL	60	13	35	48	231	....	....	....	....	....	....	....	....	....	....	....	16	6	16	22	71	....	....	....
1990-91	Albany	IHL	7	0	0	0	7	....	....	....	....	....	....	....	....	....	....	....	....	....	....	....	....	....	....	....
	Knoxville	ECHL	20	6	12	18	83	....	....	....	....	....	....	....	....	....	....	....	....	....	....	....	....	....	....	....
	Muskegon	IHL	35	3	4	7	103	....	....	....	....	....	....	....	....	....	....	....	4	0	0	0	13	....	....	....
1991-92	Muskegon	IHL	75	0	21	21	248	....	....	....	....	....	....	....	....	....	....	....	14	2	5	7	70	....	....	....

			Regular Season																Playoffs							
Season	Club	League	GP	G	A	Pts	PIM	PP	SH	GW	S	%	+/–	TF	F%	H	SB	Min	GP	G	A	Pts	PIM	PP	SH	GW
1992-93	Cleveland	IHL	76	8	18	26	427	....	....	....	....	....	....	....	....	....	....	....	4	1	0	1	27	....	....	....
1993-94	**Florida**	**NHL**	**39**	**2**	**0**	**2**	**109**	**0**	**0**	**1**	**15**	**13.3**	**9**	....	....	....	....	....	....	....	....	....	....	....	....	....
1994-95	**Florida**	**NHL**	**37**	**0**	**7**	**7**	**138**	**0**	**0**	**0**	**18**	**0.0**	**12**	....	....	....	....	....	....	....	....	....	....	....	....	....
1995-96	**Florida**	**NHL**	**78**	**3**	**6**	**9**	**236**	**0**	**0**	**0**	**45**	**6.7**	**–2**	....	....	....	....	....	**21**	**2**	**6**	**8**	***62**	**0**	**0**	**0**
1996-97	**Florida**	**NHL**	**77**	**0**	**12**	**12**	**313**	**0**	**0**	**0**	**63**	**0.0**	**13**	....	....	....	....	....	**5**	**0**	**1**	**1**	**4**	**0**	**0**	**0**
1997-98	**Florida**	**NHL**	**77**	**0**	**11**	**11**	**293**	**0**	**0**	**0**	**64**	**0.0**	**–5**	....	....	....	....	....	....	....	....	....	....	....	....	....
1998-99	**Florida**	**NHL**	**75**	**1**	**9**	**10**	**218**	**0**	**0**	**0**	**54**	**1.9**	**–1**	**0**	**0.0**	**93**	**20**	**11:09**	....	....	....	....	....	....	....	....
	NHL Totals		**383**	**6**	**45**	**51**	**1307**	**0**	**0**	**1**	**259**	**2.3**		**0**	**0.0**	**93**	**20**	**11:09**	**26**	**2**	**7**	**9**	**66**	**0**	**0**	**0**

Claimed by **Florida** from **Pittsburgh** in Expansion Draft, June 24, 1993.

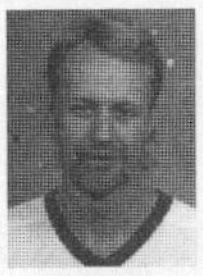

LAWRENCE, Mark — NYI

Right wing. Shoots right. 6'4", 215 lbs. Born, Burlington, Ont., January 27, 1972. Minnesota's 4th choice, 118th overall, in 1991 Entry Draft.

1987-88	Burlington	OJHL	40	11	12	23	90	....	....	....	....	....	....	....	....	....	....	....	....	....	....	....	....	....	....	....
1988-89	Niagara Falls	OHL	63	9	27	36	142	....	....	....	....	....	....	....	....	....	....	....	....	....	....	....	....	....	....	....
1989-90	Niagara Falls	OHL	54	15	18	33	123	....	....	....	....	....	....	....	....	....	....	....	16	2	5	7	42	....	....	....
1990-91	Detroit	OHL	66	27	38	65	53	....	....	....	....	....	....	....	....	....	....	....	....	....	....	....	....	....	....	....
1991-92	Detroit	OHL	28	19	26	45	54	....	....	....	....	....	....	....	....	....	....	....	....	....	....	....	....	....	....	....
	North Bay	OHL	24	13	14	27	21	....	....	....	....	....	....	....	....	....	....	....	21	*23	12	35	36	....	....	....
1992-93	Dayton	ECHL	20	8	14	22	46	....	....	....	....	....	....	....	....	....	....	....	....	....	....	....	....	....	....	....
	Kalamazoo	IHL	57	22	13	35	47	....	....	....	....	....	....	....	....	....	....	....	....	....	....	....	....	....	....	....
1993-94	Kalamazoo	IHL	64	17	20	37	90	....	....	....	....	....	....	....	....	....	....	....	....	....	....	....	....	....	....	....
1994-95	Kalamazoo	IHL	77	21	29	50	92	....	....	....	....	....	....	....	....	....	....	....	16	3	7	10	28	....	....	....
	Dallas	**NHL**	**2**	**0**	**0**	**0**	**0**	**0**	**0**	**0**	**3**	**0.0**	**0**	....	....	....	....	....	....	....	....	....	....	....	....	....
1995-96	**Dallas**	**NHL**	**13**	**0**	**1**	**1**	**17**	**0**	**0**	**0**	**13**	**0.0**	**0**	....	....	....	....	....	....	....	....	....	....	....	....	....
	Michigan	IHL	55	15	14	29	92	....	....	....	....	....	....	....	....	....	....	....	10	3	4	7	30	....	....	....
1996-97	Michigan	IHL	68	15	21	36	141	....	....	....	....	....	....	....	....	....	....	....	4	0	0	0	18	....	....	....
1997-98	**NY Islanders**	**NHL**	**2**	**0**	**0**	**0**	**2**	**0**	**0**	**0**	**4**	**0.0**	**0**	....	....	....	....	....	....	....	....	....	....	....	....	....
	Utah	IHL	80	36	28	64	102	....	....	....	....	....	....	....	....	....	....	....	4	1	1	2	4	....	....	....
1998-99	**NY Islanders**	**NHL**	**60**	**14**	**16**	**30**	**38**	**4**	**0**	**2**	**88**	**15.9**	**–8**	**0**	**0.0**	**99**	**10**	**14:08**	....	....	....	....	....	....	....	....
	Lowell	AHL	21	10	6	16	28	....	....	....	....	....	....	....	....	....	....	....	....	....	....	....	....	....	....	....
	NHL Totals		**77**	**14**	**17**	**31**	**57**	**4**	**0**	**2**	**108**	**13.0**		**0**	**0.0**	**99**	**10**	**14:08**	....	....	....	....	....	....	....	....

Rights transferred to **Dallas** after **Minnesota** franchise relocated, June 9, 1993. Signed as a free agent by **NY Islanders**, August 25, 1997.

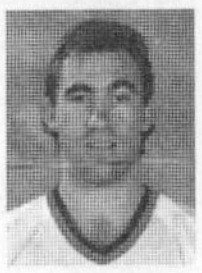

LEACH, Stephen

Right wing. Shoots right. 5'11", 197 lbs. Born, Cambridge, MA, January 16, 1966. Washington's 2nd choice, 34th overall, in 1984 Entry Draft.

1982-83	Matignon High	H.S.	23	17	21	38		....	....	....	....	....	....	....	....	....	....	....	....	....	....	....	....	....	....	....
1983-84	Matignon High	H.S.	21	27	22	49	49	....	....	....	....	....	....	....	....	....	....	....	....	....	....	....	....	....	....	....
1984-85	New Hampshire	H.E.	41	12	25	37	53	....	....	....	....	....	....	....	....	....	....	....	....	....	....	....	....	....	....	....
1985-86	New Hampshire	H.E.	25	22	6	28	30	....	....	....	....	....	....	....	....	....	....	....	....	....	....	....	....	....	....	....
	Washington	**NHL**	**11**	**1**	**1**	**2**	**2**	**0**	**0**	**0**	**4**	**25.0**	**0**	....	....	....	....	....	**6**	**0**	**1**	**1**	**0**	**0**	**0**	**0**
1986-87	**Washington**	**NHL**	**15**	**1**	**0**	**1**	**6**	**0**	**0**	**0**	**17**	**5.9**	**–4**	....	....	....	....	....	....	....	....	....	....	....	....	....
	Binghamton	AHL	54	18	21	39	39	....	....	....	....	....	....	....	....	....	....	....	13	3	1	4	6	....	....	....
1987-88	United States	Nat-Team	49	26	20	46	30	....	....	....	....	....	....	....	....	....	....	....	....	....	....	....	....	....	....	....
	United States	Olympics	6	1	2	3	0	....	....	....	....	....	....	....	....	....	....	....	....	....	....	....	....	....	....	....
	Washington	**NHL**	**8**	**1**	**1**	**2**	**17**	**0**	**0**	**1**	**5**	**20.0**	**2**	....	....	....	....	....	**9**	**2**	**1**	**3**	**0**	**0**	**0**	**1**
1988-89	**Washington**	**NHL**	**74**	**11**	**19**	**30**	**94**	**4**	**0**	**0**	**145**	**7.6**	**–4**	....	....	....	....	....	**6**	**1**	**0**	**1**	**12**	**1**	**0**	**0**
1989-90	**Washington**	**NHL**	**70**	**18**	**14**	**32**	**104**	**0**	**0**	**2**	**122**	**14.8**	**10**	....	....	....	....	....	**14**	**2**	**2**	**4**	**8**	**0**	**0**	**0**
1990-91	**Washington**	**NHL**	**68**	**11**	**19**	**30**	**99**	**4**	**0**	**1**	**134**	**8.2**	**–9**	....	....	....	....	....	**9**	**1**	**2**	**3**	**8**	**0**	**0**	**0**
1991-92	**Boston**	**NHL**	**78**	**31**	**29**	**60**	**147**	**12**	**0**	**4**	**243**	**12.8**	**–8**	....	....	....	....	....	**15**	**4**	**0**	**4**	**10**	**0**	**0**	**1**
1992-93	**Boston**	**NHL**	**79**	**26**	**25**	**51**	**126**	**9**	**0**	**4**	**256**	**10.2**	**–6**	....	....	....	....	....	**4**	**1**	**1**	**2**	**2**	**0**	**0**	**0**
1993-94	**Boston**	**NHL**	**42**	**5**	**10**	**15**	**74**	**1**	**0**	**1**	**89**	**5.6**	**–10**	....	....	....	....	....	**5**	**0**	**1**	**1**	**2**	**0**	**0**	**0**
1994-95	**Boston**	**NHL**	**35**	**5**	**6**	**11**	**68**	**1**	**0**	**1**	**82**	**6.1**	**–3**	....	....	....	....	....	....	....	....	....	....	....	....	....
1995-96	**Boston**	**NHL**	**59**	**9**	**13**	**22**	**86**	**1**	**0**	**2**	**124**	**7.3**	**–4**	....	....	....	....	....	....	....	....	....	....	....	....	....
	St. Louis	**NHL**	**14**	**2**	**4**	**6**	**22**	**0**	**0**	**0**	**33**	**6.1**	**–3**	....	....	....	....	....	**11**	**3**	**2**	**5**	**10**	**1**	**0**	**1**
1996-97	**St. Louis**	**NHL**	**17**	**2**	**1**	**3**	**24**	**0**	**0**	**0**	**33**	**6.1**	**–2**	....	....	....	....	....	**6**	**0**	**0**	**0**	**33**	**0**	**0**	**0**
1997-98	**Carolina**	**NHL**	**45**	**4**	**5**	**9**	**42**	**1**	**1**	**2**	**60**	**6.7**	**–19**	....	....	....	....	....	....	....	....	....	....	....	....	....
1998-99	**Ottawa**	**NHL**	**9**	**0**	**2**	**2**	**6**	**0**	**0**	**0**	**4**	**0.0**	**–1**	**2**	**50.0**	**10**	**0**	**11:00**	....	....	....	....	....	....	....	....
	Detroit	IHL	4	0	0	0	2	....	....	....	....	....	....	....	....	....	....	....	....	....	....	....	....	....	....	....
	Phoenix	**NHL**	**22**	**1**	**1**	**2**	**37**	**0**	**0**	**0**	**23**	**4.3**	**–6**	**0**	**0.0**	**17**	**4**	**7:18**	**7**	**1**	**1**	**2**	**2**	**0**	**0**	**0**
	Springfield	AHL	13	5	3	8	10	....	....	....	....	....	....	....	....	....	....	....	....	....	....	....	....	....	....	....
	NHL Totals		**646**	**128**	**150**	**278**	**954**	**33**	**1**	**18**	**1374**	**9.3**		**2**	**50.0**	**27**	**4**	**8:22**	**92**	**15**	**11**	**26**	**87**	**2**	**0**	**3**

Traded to **Boston** by **Washington** for Randy Burridge, June 21, 1991. Traded to **St. Louis** by **Boston** for Kevin Sawyer and Steve Staios, March 8, 1996. Traded to **Carolina** by **St. Louis** for Alexander Godynyuk and Carolina's 6th round choice in 1998 Entry Draft, June 27, 1997. Signed as a free agent by **Ottawa**, October 4, 1998. Signed as a free agent by **Phoenix**, December 3, 1998.

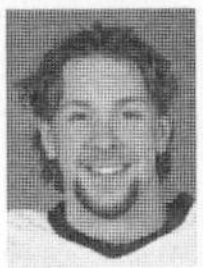

LeBOUTILLIER, Peter (lih-BOO-tihl-eer) — ANA.

Right wing. Shoots right. 6'1", 205 lbs. Born, Minnedosa, Man., January 11, 1975. Anaheim's 5th choice, 133rd overall, in 1995 Entry Draft.

1989-90	Souris	MAHA	55	91	109	200	64	....	....	....	....	....	....	....	....	....	....	....	....	....	....	....	....	....	....	....
1990-91	Souris	MAHA	10	7	12	19	6	....	....	....	....	....	....	....	....	....	....	....	....	....	....	....	....	....	....	....
1991-92	Neepawa	MJHL	35	11	14	25	99	....	....	....	....	....	....	....	....	....	....	....	....	....	....	....	....	....	....	....
1992-93	Red Deer	WHL	67	8	26	34	284	....	....	....	....	....	....	....	....	....	....	....	2	0	1	1	5	....	....	....
1993-94	Red Deer	WHL	66	19	20	39	300	....	....	....	....	....	....	....	....	....	....	....	2	0	1	1	4	....	....	....
1994-95	Red Deer	WHL	59	27	16	43	159	....	....	....	....	....	....	....	....	....	....	....	....	....	....	....	....	....	....	....
1995-96	Baltimore	AHL	68	7	9	16	228	....	....	....	....	....	....	....	....	....	....	....	11	0	0	0	33	....	....	....
1996-97	**Anaheim**	**NHL**	**23**	**1**	**0**	**1**	**121**	**0**	**0**	**0**	**5**	**20.0**	**0**	....	....	....	....	....	....	....	....	....	....	....	....	....
	Baltimore	AHL	47	6	12	18	175	....	....	....	....	....	....	....	....	....	....	....	....	....	....	....	....	....	....	....
1997-98	**Anaheim**	**NHL**	**12**	**1**	**1**	**2**	**55**	**0**	**0**	**0**	**6**	**16.7**	**–1**	....	....	....	....	....	....	....	....	....	....	....	....	....
	Cincinnati	AHL	51	9	11	20	143	....	....	....	....	....	....	....	....	....	....	....	....	....	....	....	....	....	....	....
1998-99	Cincinnati	AHL	63	12	12	24	189	....	....	....	....	....	....	....	....	....	....	....	3	0	0	0	2	....	....	....
	NHL Totals		**35**	**2**	**1**	**3**	**176**	**0**	**0**	**0**	**11**	**18.2**		....	....	....	....	....	....	....	....	....	....	....	....	....

• Re-entered NHL draft. Originally NY Islanders' 6th choice, 144th overall, in 1993 Entry Draft.

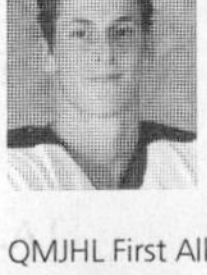

LECAVALIER, Vincent (luh-KAV-uhl-YAY) — T.B.

Center. Shoots left. 6'4", 180 lbs. Born, Ile Bizard, Que., April 21, 1980. Tampa Bay's 1st choice, 1st overall, in 1998 Entry Draft.

1995-96	Notre Dame	SAHA	22	52	52	104	....	....	....	....	....	....	....	....	....	....	....	....	....	....	....	....	....	....	....	....
1996-97	Rimouski	QMJHL	64	42	61	103	38	....	....	....	....	....	....	....	....	....	....	....	4	4	3	7	2	....	....	....
1997-98	Rimouski	QMJHL	58	44	71	115	117	....	....	....	....	....	....	....	....	....	....	....	18	*15	*26	*41	46	....	....	....
1998-99	**Tampa Bay**	**NHL**	**82**	**13**	**15**	**28**	**23**	**2**	**0**	**2**	**125**	**10.4**	**–19**	**953**	**40.3**	**52**	**15**	**13:40**	....	....	....	....	....	....	....	....
	NHL Totals		**82**	**13**	**15**	**28**	**23**	**2**	**0**	**2**	**125**	**10.4**		**953**	**40.3**	**52**	**15**	**13:40**	....	....	....	....	....	....	....	....

QMJHL First All-Star Team (1998) • Canadian Major Junior First All-Star Team (1998) • Canadian Major Junior Rookie of the Year (1997)

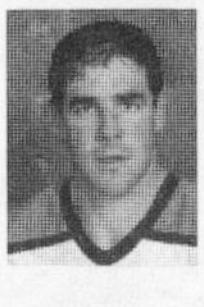

LeCLAIR, John (luh-KLAIR) — PHI.

Left wing. Shoots left. 6'3", 226 lbs. Born, St. Albans, VT, July 5, 1969. Montreal's 2nd choice, 33rd overall, in 1987 Entry Draft.

1985-86	Bellows Academy	H.S.	22	41	28	69	14	....	....	....	....	....	....	....	....	....	....	....	....	....	....	....	....	....	....	....
1986-87	Bellows Academy	H.S.	23	44	40	84	14	....	....	....	....	....	....	....	....	....	....	....	....	....	....	....	....	....	....	....
1987-88	U. of Vermont	ECAC	31	12	22	34	62	....	....	....	....	....	....	....	....	....	....	....	....	....	....	....	....	....	....	....
1988-89	U. of Vermont	ECAC	18	9	12	21	40	....	....	....	....	....	....	....	....	....	....	....	....	....	....	....	....	....	....	....
1989-90	U. of Vermont	ECAC	10	10	6	16	38	....	....	....	....	....	....	....	....	....	....	....	....	....	....	....	....	....	....	....

Season	Club	League	Regular Season																Playoffs							
			GP	G	A	Pts	PIM	PP	SH	GW	S	%	+/–	TF	F%	H	SB	Min	GP	G	A	Pts	PIM	PP	SH	GW
1990-91	U. of Vermont	ECAC	33	25	20	45	58	....	....	....	....	....	....	....	....	....	....	....	....	....	....	....	....	....	....	....
	Montreal	**NHL**	**10**	**2**	**5**	**7**	**2**	**0**	**0**	**1**	**12**	**16.7**	**1**	....	....	....	....	....	**3**	**0**	**0**	**0**	**0**	**0**	**0**	**0**
1991-92	**Montreal**	**NHL**	**59**	**8**	**11**	**19**	**14**	**3**	**0**	**0**	**73**	**11.0**	**5**	....	....	....	....	....	**8**	**1**	**1**	**2**	**4**	**0**	**0**	**0**
	Fredericton	AHL	8	7	7	14	10	....	....	....	....	....	....	....	....	....	....	....	2	0	0	0	4	....	....	....
1992-93♦	**Montreal**	**NHL**	**72**	**19**	**25**	**44**	**33**	**2**	**0**	**2**	**139**	**13.7**	**11**	....	....	....	....	....	**20**	**4**	**6**	**10**	**14**	**0**	**0**	**3**
1993-94	**Montreal**	**NHL**	**74**	**19**	**24**	**43**	**32**	**1**	**0**	**1**	**153**	**12.4**	**17**	....	....	....	....	....	**7**	**2**	**1**	**3**	**8**	**1**	**0**	**0**
1994-95	**Montreal**	**NHL**	**9**	**1**	**4**	**5**	**10**	**1**	**0**	**0**	**18**	**5.6**	**–1**	....	....	....	....	....	....	....	....	....	....	....	....	....
	Philadelphia	**NHL**	**37**	**25**	**24**	**49**	**20**	**5**	**0**	**7**	**113**	**22.1**	**21**	....	....	....	....	....	**15**	**5**	**7**	**12**	**4**	**1**	**0**	**1**
1995-96	**Philadelphia**	**NHL**	**82**	**51**	**46**	**97**	**64**	**19**	**0**	**10**	**270**	**18.9**	**21**	....	....	....	....	....	**11**	**6**	**5**	**11**	**6**	**4**	**0**	**1**
1996-97	**Philadelphia**	**NHL**	**82**	**50**	**47**	**97**	**58**	**10**	**0**	**5**	**324**	**15.4**	**44**	....	....	....	....	....	**19**	**9**	**12**	**21**	**10**	**4**	**0**	**3**
1997-98	**Philadelphia**	**NHL**	**82**	**51**	**36**	**87**	**32**	**16**	**0**	**9**	**303**	**16.8**	**30**	....	....	....	....	....	**5**	**1**	**1**	**2**	**8**	**1**	**0**	**1**
	United States	Olympics	4	0	1	1	0	....	....	....	....	....	....	....	....	....	....	....	....	....	....	....	....	....	....	....
1998-99	**Philadelphia**	**NHL**	**76**	**43**	**47**	**90**	**30**	**16**	**0**	**7**	**246**	**17.5**	**36**	**7**	**14.3**	**86**	**10**	**21:03**	**6**	**3**	**0**	**3**	**12**	**2**	**0**	**0**
	NHL Totals		**583**	**269**	**269**	**538**	**295**	**73**	**0**	**42**	**1651**	**16.3**		**7**	**14.3**	**86**	**10**	**21:03**	**94**	**31**	**33**	**64**	**66**	**13**	**0**	**9**

ECAC Second All-Star Team (1991) • NHL First All-Star Team (1995, 1998) • NHL Second All-Star Team (1996, 1997, 1999) • Won Bud Light Plus/Minus Award (1997) • Won Bud Ice Plus/Minus Award (1999)
Played in NHL All-Star Game (1996, 1997, 1998, 1999)

Traded to **Philadelphia** by **Montreal** with Eric Desjardins and Gilbert Dionne for Mark Recchi and Philadelphia's 3rd round choice (Martin Hohenberger) in 1995 Entry Draft, February 9, 1995.

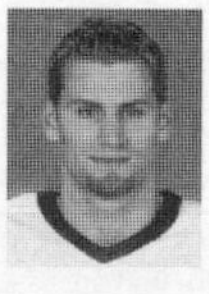

LECLERC, Mike — ANA.

Left wing. Shoots left. 6'1", 205 lbs. Born, Winnipeg, Man., November 10, 1976. Anaheim's 3rd choice, 55th overall, in 1995 Entry Draft.

Season	Club	League	GP	G	A	Pts	PIM	PP	SH	GW	S	%	+/–	TF	F%	H	SB	Min	GP	G	A	Pts	PIM	PP	SH	GW
1991-92	St. Boniface	MJHL	43	16	12	28	25	....	....	....	....	....	....	....	....	....	....	....	....	....	....	....	....	....	....	....
	Victoria	WHL	2	0	0	0	0	....	....	....	....	....	....	....	....	....	....	....	....	....	....	....	....	....	....	....
1992-93	Victoria	WHL	70	4	11	15	118	....	....	....	....	....	....	....	....	....	....	....	....	....	....	....	....	....	....	....
1993-94	Victoria	WHL	68	29	11	40	112	....	....	....	....	....	....	....	....	....	....	....	....	....	....	....	....	....	....	....
1994-95	Prince George	WHL	43	20	36	56	78	....	....	....	....	....	....	....	....	....	....	....	....	....	....	....	....	....	....	....
	Brandon	WHL	23	5	8	13	50	....	....	....	....	....	....	....	....	....	....	....	18	10	6	16	33	....	....	....
1995-96	Brandon	WHL	71	58	53	111	161	....	....	....	....	....	....	....	....	....	....	....	19	6	19	25	25	....	....	....
1996-97	**Anaheim**	**NHL**	**5**	**1**	**1**	**2**	**0**	**0**	**0**	**1**	**3**	**33.3**	**2**	....	....	....	....	....	**1**	**0**	**0**	**0**	**0**	**0**	**0**	**0**
	Baltimore	AHL	71	29	27	56	134	....	....	....	....	....	....	....	....	....	....	....	....	....	....	....	....	....	....	....
1997-98	**Anaheim**	**NHL**	**7**	**0**	**0**	**0**	**6**	**0**	**0**	**0**	**11**	**0.0**	**–6**	....	....	....	....	....	....	....	....	....	....	....	....	....
	Cincinnati	AHL	48	18	22	40	83	....	....	....	....	....	....	....	....	....	....	....	....	....	....	....	....	....	....	....
1998-99	**Anaheim**	**NHL**	**7**	**0**	**0**	**0**	**4**	**0**	**0**	**0**	**1**	**0.0**	**–2**	**0**	**0.0**	**9**	**2**	**5:52**	**1**	**0**	**0**	**0**	**0**	**0**	**0**	**0**
	Cincinnati	AHL	65	25	28	53	153	....	....	....	....	....	....	....	....	....	....	....	3	0	1	1	19	....	....	....
	NHL Totals		**19**	**1**	**1**	**2**	**10**	**0**	**0**	**1**	**15**	**6.7**		**0**	**0.0**	**9**	**2**	**5:52**	**2**	**0**	**0**	**0**	**0**	**0**	**0**	**0**

WHL East Second All-Star Team (1996)

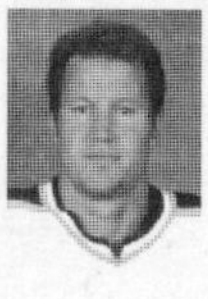

LEDYARD, Grant

Defense. Shoots left. 6'2", 195 lbs. Born, Winnipeg, Man., November 19, 1961.

Season	Club	League	GP	G	A	Pts	PIM	PP	SH	GW	S	%	+/–	TF	F%	H	SB	Min	GP	G	A	Pts	PIM	PP	SH	GW
1979-80	Fort Garry	MJHL	49	13	24	37	90	....	....	....	....	....	....	....	....	....	....	....	....	....	....	....	....	....	....	....
1980-81	Saskatoon	WHL	71	9	28	37	148	....	....	....	....	....	....	....	....	....	....	....	....	....	....	....	....	....	....	....
1981-82	Fort Garry	MJHL	63	25	45	70	150	....	....	....	....	....	....	....	....	....	....	....	....	....	....	....	....	....	....	....
1982-83	Tulsa	CHL	80	13	29	42	115	....	....	....	....	....	....	....	....	....	....	....	....	....	....	....	....	....	....	....
1983-84	Tulsa	CHL	58	9	17	26	71	....	....	....	....	....	....	....	....	....	....	....	9	5	4	9	10	....	....	....
1984-85	**NY Rangers**	**NHL**	**42**	**8**	**12**	**20**	**53**	**1**	**0**	**1**	**91**	**8.8**	**8**	....	....	....	....	....	**3**	**0**	**2**	**2**	**4**	**0**	**0**	**0**
	New Haven	AHL	36	6	20	26	18	....	....	....	....	....	....	....	....	....	....	....	....	....	....	....	....	....	....	....
1985-86	**NY Rangers**	**NHL**	**27**	**2**	**9**	**11**	**20**	**0**	**0**	**0**	**57**	**3.5**	**–7**	....	....	....	....	....	....	....	....	....	....	....	....	....
	Los Angeles	**NHL**	**52**	**7**	**18**	**25**	**78**	**4**	**0**	**2**	**113**	**6.2**	**–22**	....	....	....	....	....	....	....	....	....	....	....	....	....
1986-87	**Los Angeles**	**NHL**	**67**	**14**	**23**	**37**	**93**	**5**	**0**	**1**	**144**	**9.7**	**–40**	....	....	....	....	....	**5**	**0**	**0**	**0**	**10**	**0**	**0**	**0**
1987-88	**Los Angeles**	**NHL**	**23**	**1**	**7**	**8**	**52**	**1**	**0**	**0**	**40**	**2.5**	**–7**	....	....	....	....	....	....	....	....	....	....	....	....	....
	New Haven	AHL	3	2	1	3	4	....	....	....	....	....	....	....	....	....	....	....	....	....	....	....	....	....	....	....
	Washington	**NHL**	**21**	**4**	**3**	**7**	**14**	**1**	**0**	**1**	**41**	**9.8**	**–4**	....	....	....	....	....	**14**	**1**	**0**	**1**	**30**	**0**	**0**	**0**
1988-89	**Washington**	**NHL**	**61**	**3**	**11**	**14**	**43**	**1**	**0**	**1**	**81**	**3.7**	**1**	....	....	....	....	....	....	....	....	....	....	....	....	....
	Buffalo	**NHL**	**13**	**1**	**5**	**6**	**8**	**0**	**0**	**1**	**25**	**4.0**	**1**	....	....	....	....	....	**5**	**1**	**2**	**3**	**2**	**0**	**0**	**0**
1989-90	**Buffalo**	**NHL**	**67**	**2**	**13**	**15**	**37**	**0**	**0**	**1**	**91**	**2.2**	**2**	....	....	....	....	....	....	....	....	....	....	....	....	....
1990-91	**Buffalo**	**NHL**	**60**	**8**	**23**	**31**	**46**	**2**	**1**	**1**	**118**	**6.8**	**13**	....	....	....	....	....	**6**	**3**	**3**	**6**	**10**	**0**	**0**	**0**
1991-92	**Buffalo**	**NHL**	**50**	**5**	**16**	**21**	**45**	**0**	**0**	**0**	**87**	**5.7**	**–4**	....	....	....	....	....	....	....	....	....	....	....	....	....
1992-93	**Buffalo**	**NHL**	**50**	**2**	**14**	**16**	**45**	**1**	**0**	**0**	**79**	**2.5**	**–2**	....	....	....	....	....	**8**	**0**	**0**	**0**	**8**	**0**	**0**	**0**
	Rochester	AHL	5	0	2	2	8	....	....	....	....	....	....	....	....	....	....	....	....	....	....	....	....	....	....	....
1993-94	**Dallas**	**NHL**	**84**	**9**	**37**	**46**	**42**	**6**	**0**	**1**	**177**	**5.1**	**7**	....	....	....	....	....	**9**	**1**	**2**	**3**	**6**	**0**	**0**	**1**
1994-95	**Dallas**	**NHL**	**38**	**5**	**13**	**18**	**20**	**4**	**0**	**0**	**79**	**6.3**	**6**	....	....	....	....	....	**3**	**0**	**0**	**0**	**2**	**0**	**0**	**0**
1995-96	**Dallas**	**NHL**	**73**	**5**	**19**	**24**	**20**	**2**	**0**	**1**	**123**	**4.1**	**–15**	....	....	....	....	....	....	....	....	....	....	....	....	....
1996-97	**Dallas**	**NHL**	**67**	**1**	**15**	**16**	**61**	**0**	**0**	**0**	**99**	**1.0**	**31**	....	....	....	....	....	**7**	**0**	**2**	**2**	**0**	**0**	**0**	**0**
1997-98	**Vancouver**	**NHL**	**49**	**2**	**13**	**15**	**14**	**1**	**0**	**0**	**57**	**3.5**	**–2**	....	....	....	....	....	....	....	....	....	....	....	....	....
	Boston	**NHL**	**22**	**2**	**7**	**9**	**6**	**1**	**0**	**0**	**33**	**6.1**	**–2**	....	....	....	....	....	**6**	**0**	**0**	**0**	**2**	**0**	**0**	**0**
1998-99	**Boston**	**NHL**	**47**	**4**	**8**	**12**	**33**	**1**	**0**	**2**	**47**	**8.5**	**–8**	**1**	**0.0**	**65**	**49**	**17:31**	**2**	**0**	**0**	**0**	**2**	**0**	**0**	**0**
	NHL Totals		**913**	**85**	**266**	**351**	**730**	**31**	**1**	**13**	**1582**	**5.4**		**1**	**0.0**	**65**	**49**	**17:31**	**68**	**6**	**11**	**17**	**76**	**0**	**0**	**1**

Won Bob Gassoff Trophy (CHL's Most Improved Defenseman) (1984)

Signed as a free agent by **NY Rangers**, July 7, 1982. Traded to **LA Kings** by **NY Rangers** with Roland Melanson for LA Kings' 4th round choice (Mike Sullivan) in 1987 Entry Draft and Brian MacLellan, December 7, 1985. Traded to **Washington** by **LA Kings** for Craig Laughlin, February 9, 1988. Traded to **Buffalo** by **Washington** with Clint Malarchuk and Washington's 6th round choice (Brian Holzinger) in 1991 Entry Draft for Calle Johansson and Buffalo's 2nd round choice (Byron Dafoe) in 1989 Entry Draft, March 7, 1989. Signed as a free agent by **Dallas**, August 12, 1993. Signed as a free agent by **Vancouver**, July 17, 1997. Traded to **Boston** by **Vancouver** for Boston's 8th round choice (Curtis Valentine) in 1998 Entry Draft, March 3, 1998.

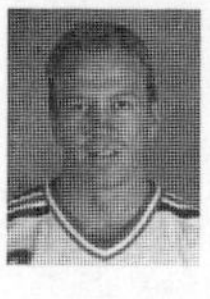

LEETCH, Brian — NYR

Defense. Shoots left. 6'1", 190 lbs. Born, Corpus Christi, TX, March 3, 1968. NY Rangers' 1st choice, 9th overall, in 1986 Entry Draft.

Season	Club	League	GP	G	A	Pts	PIM	PP	SH	GW	S	%	+/–	TF	F%	H	SB	Min	GP	G	A	Pts	PIM	PP	SH	GW
1984-85	Avon Old Farms	H.S.	26	30	46	76	15	....	....	....	....	....	....	....	....	....	....	....	....	....	....	....	....	....	....	....
1985-86	Avon Old Farms	H.S.	28	40	44	84	18	....	....	....	....	....	....	....	....	....	....	....	....	....	....	....	....	....	....	....
1986-87	Boston College	H.E.	37	9	38	47	10	....	....	....	....	....	....	....	....	....	....	....	....	....	....	....	....	....	....	....
1987-88	United States	Nat-Team	50	13	61	74	38	....	....	....	....	....	....	....	....	....	....	....	....	....	....	....	....	....	....	....
	United States	Olympics	6	1	5	6	4	....	....	....	....	....	....	....	....	....	....	....	....	....	....	....	....	....	....	....
	NY Rangers	**NHL**	**17**	**2**	**12**	**14**	**0**	**1**	**0**	**1**	**40**	**5.0**	**5**	....	....	....	....	....	....	....	....	....	....	....	....	....
1988-89	**NY Rangers**	**NHL**	**68**	**23**	**48**	**71**	**50**	**8**	**3**	**1**	**268**	**8.6**	**8**	....	....	....	....	....	....	....	....	....	....	....	....	....
1989-90	**NY Rangers**	**NHL**	**72**	**11**	**45**	**56**	**26**	**5**	**0**	**2**	**222**	**5.0**	**–18**	....	....	....	....	....	**4**	**3**	**2**	**5**	**2**	**2**	**0**	**0**
1990-91	**NY Rangers**	**NHL**	**80**	**16**	**72**	**88**	**42**	**6**	**0**	**4**	**206**	**7.8**	**2**	....	....	....	....	....	**6**	**1**	**3**	**4**	**0**	**0**	**0**	**0**
1991-92	**NY Rangers**	**NHL**	**80**	**22**	**80**	**102**	**26**	**10**	**1**	**3**	**245**	**9.0**	**25**	....	....	....	....	....	**13**	**4**	**11**	**15**	**4**	**1**	**1**	**0**
1992-93	**NY Rangers**	**NHL**	**36**	**6**	**30**	**36**	**26**	**2**	**1**	**1**	**150**	**4.0**	**2**	....	....	....	....	....	....	....	....	....	....	....	....	....
1993-94♦	**NY Rangers**	**NHL**	**84**	**23**	**56**	**79**	**67**	**17**	**1**	**4**	**328**	**7.0**	**28**	....	....	....	....	....	**23**	**11**	***23**	***34**	**6**	**4**	**0**	**4**
1994-95	**NY Rangers**	**NHL**	**48**	**9**	**32**	**41**	**18**	**3**	**0**	**2**	**182**	**4.9**	**0**	....	....	....	....	....	**10**	**6**	**8**	**14**	**8**	**3**	**0**	**1**
1995-96	**NY Rangers**	**NHL**	**82**	**15**	**70**	**85**	**30**	**7**	**0**	**3**	**276**	**5.4**	**12**	....	....	....	....	....	**11**	**1**	**6**	**7**	**4**	**1**	**0**	**0**
1996-97	**NY Rangers**	**NHL**	**82**	**20**	**58**	**78**	**40**	**9**	**0**	**2**	**256**	**7.8**	**31**	....	....	....	....	....	**15**	**2**	**8**	**10**	**6**	**1**	**0**	**1**
1997-98	**NY Rangers**	**NHL**	**76**	**17**	**33**	**50**	**32**	**11**	**0**	**2**	**230**	**7.4**	**–36**	....	....	....	....	....	....	....	....	....	....	....	....	....
	United States	Olympics	4	1	1	2	0	....	....	....	....	....	....	....	....	....	....	....	....	....	....	....	....	....	....	....
1998-99	**NY Rangers**	**NHL**	**82**	**13**	**42**	**55**	**42**	**4**	**0**	**1**	**184**	**7.1**	**–7**	**0**	**0.0**	**173**	**212**	**29:52**	....	....	....	....	....	....	....	....
	NHL Totals		**807**	**177**	**578**	**755**	**399**	**83**	**6**	**26**	**2587**	**6.8**		**0**	**0.0**	**173**	**212**	**29:52**	**82**	**28**	**61**	**89**	**30**	**12**	**1**	**6**

Hockey East First All-Star Team (1987) • NCAA East First All-American Team (1987) • NHL All-Rookie Team (1989) • Won Calder Memorial Trophy (1989) • NHL Second All-Star Team (1991, 1994, 1996) • Won James Norris Memorial Trophy (1992, 1997) • NHL First All-Star Team (1992, 1997) • Won Conn Smythe Trophy (1994)
Played in NHL All-Star Game (1990, 1991, 1992, 1994, 1996, 1997, 1998)

LEFEBVRE, Patrice

(luh-FAYV, put-trees)

Right wing. Shoots left. 5'6", 160 lbs. Born, Montreal, Que., June 28, 1967.

			Regular Season																Playoffs							
Season	Club	League	GP	G	A	Pts	PIM	PP	SH	GW	S	%	+/–	TF	F%	H	SB	Min	GP	G	A	Pts	PIM	PP	SH	GW
1983-84	Montreal	QAAA	42	36	45	81																				
1984-85	Shawinigan	QMJHL	68	28	52	80	63																			
1985-86	Shawinigan	QMJHL	69	38	98	136	119																			
1986-87	Shawinigan	QMJHL	69	57	122	179	144												12	9	16	25	19			
1987-88	Shawinigan	QMJHL	70	64	136	200	142																			
1988-89	Paris	France	20	26	17	43	24												19	13	23	36	24			
1989-90	HC Ajoie	Switz	32	23	23	46																				
1990-91	HC Langnau	Switz	3	1	8	9																				
	Louisville	ECHL	26	17	26	43	32																			
	Milwaukee	IHL	16	6	4	10	13																			
	Springfield	AHL	1	0	0	0	2																			
1991-92	HC Kloten	Switz	10	4	12	16																				
	HC Sierre	Switz	3	3	2	5																				
1992-93	Billingham	Britain	36	56	109	165	75												6	5	13	18	26			
1993-94	Las Vegas	IHL	76	31	67	98	71												5	3	4	7	4			
1994-95	Las Vegas	IHL	75	32	62	94	74												10	2	3	5	2			
1995-96	Las Vegas	IHL	77	36	78	114	85												15	9	11	20	12			
1996-97	Las Vegas	IHL	82	21	73	94	94												3	0	2	2	2			
1997-98	Las Vegas	IHL	77	27	*89	*116	113												4	2	0	2	2			
1998-99	Las Vegas	IHL	42	11	26	37	40																			
	Washington	**NHL**	**3**	**0**	**0**	**0**	**2**	**0**	**0**	**0**	**2**	**0.0**	**–2**	**0**	**0.0**	**0**	**1**	**11:11**								
	Long Beach	IHL	14	1	12	13	8												8	0	3	3	2			
	NHL Totals		**3**	**0**	**0**	**0**	**2**	**0**	**0**	**0**	**2**	**0.0**		**0**	**0.0**	**0**	**1**	**11:11**								

QMJHL Second All-Star Team (1986) • QMJHL First All-Star Team (1987, 1988) • IHL First All-Star Team (1998) • Won Leo P. Lamoureux Memorial Trophy (Top Scorer - IHL) (1998) • Won James Gatschene Memorial Trophy (MVP - IHL) (1998)

Signed as a free agent by **Washington**, December 18, 1998.

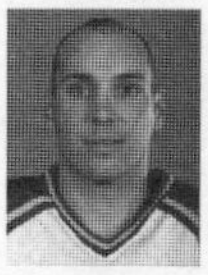

LEFEBVRE, Sylvain

(luh-FAYV) **NYR**

Defense. Shoots left. 6'2", 205 lbs. Born, Richmond, Que., October 14, 1967.

Season	Club	League	GP	G	A	Pts	PIM	PP	SH	GW	S	%	+/–	TF	F%	H	SB	Min	GP	G	A	Pts	PIM	PP	SH	GW
1984-85	Laval	QMJHL	66	7	5	12	31																			
1985-86	Laval	QMJHL	71	8	17	25	48												14	1	0	1	25			
1986-87	Laval	QMJHL	70	10	36	46	44												15	1	6	7	12			
1987-88	Sherbrooke	AHL	79	3	24	27	73												6	2	3	5	4			
1988-89	Sherbrooke	AHL	77	15	32	47	119												6	1	3	4	4			
1989-90	**Montreal**	**NHL**	**68**	**3**	**10**	**13**	**61**	**0**	**0**	**0**	**89**	**3.4**	**18**						**6**	**0**	**0**	**0**	**2**	**0**	**0**	**0**
1990-91	**Montreal**	**NHL**	**63**	**5**	**18**	**23**	**30**	**1**	**0**	**1**	**76**	**6.6**	**–11**						**11**	**1**	**0**	**1**	**6**	**0**	**0**	**0**
1991-92	**Montreal**	**NHL**	**69**	**3**	**14**	**17**	**91**	**0**	**0**	**0**	**85**	**3.5**	**9**						**2**	**0**	**0**	**0**	**2**	**0**	**0**	**0**
1992-93	**Toronto**	**NHL**	**81**	**2**	**12**	**14**	**90**	**0**	**0**	**0**	**81**	**2.5**	**8**						**21**	**3**	**3**	**6**	**20**	**0**	**0**	**0**
1993-94	**Toronto**	**NHL**	**84**	**2**	**9**	**11**	**79**	**0**	**0**	**0**	**96**	**2.1**	**33**						**18**	**0**	**3**	**3**	**16**	**0**	**0**	**0**
1994-95	**Quebec**	**NHL**	**48**	**2**	**11**	**13**	**17**	**0**	**0**	**0**	**81**	**2.5**	**13**						**6**	**0**	**2**	**2**	**2**	**0**	**0**	**0**
1995-96♦	**Colorado**	**NHL**	**75**	**5**	**11**	**16**	**49**	**2**	**0**	**0**	**115**	**4.3**	**26**						**22**	**0**	**5**	**5**	**12**	**0**	**0**	**0**
1996-97	**Colorado**	**NHL**	**71**	**2**	**11**	**13**	**30**	**1**	**0**	**0**	**77**	**2.6**	**12**						**17**	**0**	**0**	**0**	**25**	**0**	**0**	**0**
1997-98	**Colorado**	**NHL**	**81**	**0**	**10**	**10**	**48**	**0**	**0**	**0**	**66**	**0.0**	**2**						**7**	**0**	**0**	**0**	**4**	**0**	**0**	**0**
1998-99	**Colorado**	**NHL**	**76**	**2**	**18**	**20**	**48**	**0**	**0**	**0**	**64**	**3.1**	**18**	**0**	**0.0**	**120**	**79**	**20:56**	**19**	**0**	**1**	**1**	**12**	**0**	**0**	**0**
	NHL Totals		**716**	**26**	**124**	**150**	**543**	**4**	**0**	**1**	**830**	**3.1**		**0**	**0.0**	**120**	**79**	**20:56**	**129**	**4**	**14**	**18**	**101**	**0**	**0**	**0**

AHL Second All-Star Team (1989)

Signed as a free agent by **Montreal**, September 24, 1986. Traded to **Toronto** by **Montreal** for Toronto's 3rd round choice (Martin Belanger) in 1994 Entry Draft, August 20, 1992. Traded to **Quebec** by **Toronto** with Wendel Clark, Landon Wilson and Toronto's 1st round choice (Jeffrey Kealty) in 1994 Entry Draft for Mats Sundin, Garth Butcher, Todd Warriner and Philadelphia's 1st round choice (previously acquired by Quebec — later traded to Washington — Washington selected Nolan Baumgartner) in 1994 Entry Draft, June 28, 1994. Transferred to **Colorado** after **Quebec** franchise relocated, June 21, 1995. Signed as a free agent by **NY Rangers**, July 22, 1999.

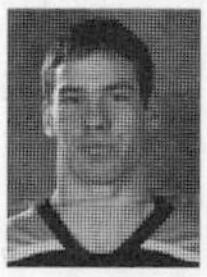

LEGWAND, David

(LEHG-wuhnd) **NSH.**

Center. Shoots left. 6'1", 175 lbs. Born, Detroit, MI, August 17, 1980. Nashville's 1st choice, 2nd overall, in 1998 Entry Draft.

Season	Club	League	GP	G	A	Pts	PIM	PP	SH	GW	S	%	+/–	TF	F%	H	SB	Min	GP	G	A	Pts	PIM	PP	SH	GW
1996-97	Detroit	MNHL	44	21	41	62	58																			
1997-98	Plymouth	OHL	59	54	51	105	56												15	8	12	20	24			
	United States	WJC-A	7	0	0	0	2																			
1998-99	**Nashville**	**NHL**	**1**	**0**	**0**	**0**	**0**	**0**	**0**	**0**	**2**	**0.0**	**0**	**9**	**55.6**	**0**	**1**	**12:50**								
	Plymouth	OHL	55	31	49	80	65												11	3	8	11	8			
	NHL Totals		**1**	**0**	**0**	**0**	**0**	**0**	**0**	**0**	**2**	**0.0**		**9**	**55.6**	**0**	**1**	**12:50**								

OHL First All-Star Team (1998) • Canadian Major Junior Rookie of the Year (1998)

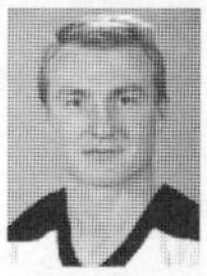

LEHTINEN, Jere

(lehkh-TIH-nehn) **DAL.**

Right wing. Shoots right. 6', 192 lbs. Born, Espoo, Finland, June 24, 1973. Minnesota's 3rd choice, 88th overall, in 1992 Entry Draft.

Season	Club	League	GP	G	A	Pts	PIM	PP	SH	GW	S	%	+/–	TF	F%	H	SB	Min	GP	G	A	Pts	PIM	PP	SH	GW
1989-90	Kiekoo-67	Finn-Jr.	32	23	23	46	6												5	0	3	3	0			
1990-91	Kiekko-Espoo	Finland-2	32	15	9	24	12																			
1991-92	Kiekoo-67	Finn-Jr.	8	5	4	9	2																			
	Kiekko-Espoo	Finland-2	43	32	17	49	6																			
1992-93	Kiekoo-67	Finn-Jr.	4	5	3	8	8																			
	Kiekko-Espoo	Finland	45	13	14	27	6																			
1993-94	TPS Turku	Finland	42	19	20	39	6												11	11	2	13	2			
	Finland	Olympics	8	3	0	3	0																			
1994-95	TPS Turku	Finland	39	19	23	42	33												13	8	6	14	4			
1995-96	**Dallas**	**NHL**	**57**	**6**	**22**	**28**	**16**	**0**	**0**	**1**	**109**	**5.5**	**5**													
	Michigan	IHL	1	1	0	1	0																			
1996-97	**Dallas**	**NHL**	**63**	**16**	**27**	**43**	**2**	**3**	**1**	**2**	**134**	**11.9**	**26**						**7**	**2**	**2**	**4**	**0**	**0**	**0**	**0**
1997-98	**Dallas**	**NHL**	**72**	**23**	**19**	**42**	**20**	**7**	**2**	**6**	**201**	**11.4**	**19**						**12**	**3**	**5**	**8**	**2**	**1**	**0**	**0**
	Finland	Olympics	6	4	2	6	2																			
1998-99♦	**Dallas**	**NHL**	**74**	**20**	**32**	**52**	**18**	**7**	**1**	**2**	**173**	**11.6**	**29**	**9**	**33.3**	**72**	**47**	**19:36**	**23**	**10**	**3**	**13**	**2**	**1**	**1**	**0**
	NHL Totals		**266**	**65**	**100**	**165**	**56**	**17**	**4**	**11**	**617**	**10.5**		**9**	**33.3**	**72**	**47**	**19:36**	**42**	**15**	**10**	**25**	**4**	**2**	**1**	**0**

Finnish First All-Star Team (1995) • Won Frank J. Selke Trophy (1998, 1999)

Played in NHL All-Star Game (1998)

Rights transferred to **Dallas** after **Minnesota** franchise relocated, June 9, 1993.

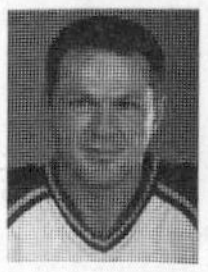

LEMIEUX, Claude

(lehm-YOO) **COL.**

Right wing. Shoots right. 6'1", 215 lbs. Born, Buckingham, Que., July 16, 1965. Montreal's 2nd choice, 26th overall, in 1983 Entry Draft.

Season	Club	League	GP	G	A	Pts	PIM	PP	SH	GW	S	%	+/–	TF	F%	H	SB	Min	GP	G	A	Pts	PIM	PP	SH	GW
1981-82	Richelieu	QAAA	48	24	48	72	96																			
1982-83	Trois-Rivieres	QMJHL	62	28	38	66	187												4	1	0	1	30			
1983-84	Verdun	QMJHL	51	41	45	86	225												9	8	12	20	63			
	Montreal	**NHL**	**8**	**1**	**1**	**2**	**12**	**0**	**0**	**0**	**7**	**14.3**	**–2**													
	Nova Scotia	AHL																	2	1	0	1	0			
1984-85	Verdun	QMJHL	52	58	66	124	152												14	23	17	40	38			
	Montreal	**NHL**	**1**	**0**	**1**	**1**	**7**	**0**	**0**	**0**	**0**	**0.0**	**1**													
1985-86♦	**Montreal**	**NHL**	**10**	**1**	**2**	**3**	**22**	**1**	**0**	**0**	**16**	**6.3**	**–6**						**20**	**10**	**6**	**16**	**68**	**4**	**0**	**4**
	Sherbrooke	AHL	58	21	32	53	145																			

			Regular Season																Playoffs							
Season	Club	League	GP	G	A	Pts	PIM	PP	SH	GW	S	%	+/-	TF	F%	H	SB	Min	GP	G	A	Pts	PIM	PP	SH	GW
1986-87	**Montreal**	**NHL**	**76**	**27**	**26**	**53**	**156**	**5**	**0**	**1**	**184**	**14.7**	**0**	....	....	....	....	....	**17**	**4**	**9**	**13**	**41**	**2**	**0**	**0**
1987-88	**Montreal**	**NHL**	**78**	**31**	**30**	**61**	**137**	**6**	**0**	**3**	**241**	**12.9**	**16**	....	....	....	....	....	**11**	**3**	**2**	**5**	**20**	**0**	**0**	**2**
1988-89	**Montreal**	**NHL**	**69**	**29**	**22**	**51**	**136**	**7**	**0**	**3**	**220**	**13.2**	**14**	....	....	....	....	....	**18**	**4**	**3**	**7**	**58**	**0**	**0**	**0**
1989-90	**Montreal**	**NHL**	**39**	**8**	**10**	**18**	**106**	**3**	**0**	**1**	**104**	**7.7**	**–8**	....	....	....	....	....	**11**	**1**	**3**	**4**	**38**	**0**	**0**	**1**
1990-91	**New Jersey**	**NHL**	**78**	**30**	**17**	**47**	**105**	**10**	**0**	**2**	**271**	**11.1**	**–8**	....	....	....	....	....	**7**	**4**	**0**	**4**	**34**	**2**	**0**	**1**
1991-92	**New Jersey**	**NHL**	**74**	**41**	**27**	**68**	**109**	**13**	**1**	**8**	**296**	**13.9**	**9**	....	....	....	....	....	**7**	**4**	**3**	**7**	**26**	**1**	**0**	**0**
1992-93	**New Jersey**	**NHL**	**77**	**30**	**51**	**81**	**155**	**13**	**0**	**3**	**311**	**9.6**	**3**	....	....	....	....	....	**5**	**2**	**0**	**2**	**19**	**1**	**0**	**0**
1993-94	**New Jersey**	**NHL**	**79**	**18**	**26**	**44**	**86**	**5**	**0**	**5**	**181**	**9.9**	**13**	....	....	....	....	....	**20**	**7**	**11**	**18**	**44**	**0**	**0**	**2**
1994-95♦	**New Jersey**	**NHL**	**45**	**6**	**13**	**19**	**86**	**1**	**0**	**1**	**117**	**5.1**	**2**	....	....	....	....	....	**20**	***13**	**3**	**16**	**20**	**0**	**0**	**3**
1995-96♦	**Colorado**	**NHL**	**79**	**39**	**32**	**71**	**117**	**9**	**2**	**10**	**315**	**12.4**	**14**	....	....	....	....	....	**19**	**5**	**7**	**12**	**55**	**3**	**0**	**0**
1996-97	**Colorado**	**NHL**	**45**	**11**	**17**	**28**	**43**	**5**	**0**	**4**	**168**	**6.5**	**–4**	....	....	....	....	....	**17**	***13**	**10**	**23**	**32**	**4**	**0**	**4**
1997-98	**Colorado**	**NHL**	**78**	**26**	**27**	**53**	**115**	**11**	**1**	**1**	**261**	**10.0**	**–7**	....	....	....	....	....	**7**	**3**	**3**	**6**	**8**	**1**	**0**	**1**
1998-99	**Colorado**	**NHL**	**82**	**27**	**24**	**51**	**102**	**11**	**0**	**8**	**292**	**9.2**	**0**	**43**	**41.9**	**110**	**26**	**21:14**	**19**	**3**	**11**	**14**	**26**	**1**	**0**	**0**
	NHL Totals		**918**	**325**	**326**	**651**	**1494**	**100**	**4**	**50**	**2984**	**10.9**		**43**	**41.9**	**110**	**26**	**21:14**	**198**	**76**	**71**	**147**	**489**	**19**	**0**	**18**

QMJHL Second All-Star Team (1984) • QMJHL First All-Star Team (1985) • Won Conn Smythe Trophy (1995)

Traded to **New Jersey** by **Montreal** for Sylvain Turgeon, September 4, 1990. Traded to **NY Islanders** by **New Jersey** for Steve Thomas, October 3, 1995. Traded to **Colorado** by **NY Islanders** for Wendel Clark, October 3, 1995.

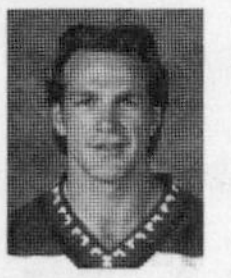

LEMIEUX, Jocelyn (lehm-YOO)

Right wing. Shoots left. 5'11", 220 lbs. Born, Mont-Laurier, Que., November 18, 1967. St. Louis' 1st choice, 10th overall, in 1986 Entry Draft.

			Regular Season																Playoffs							
Season	Club	League	GP	G	A	Pts	PIM	PP	SH	GW	S	%	+/-	TF	F%	H	SB	Min	GP	G	A	Pts	PIM	PP	SH	GW
1983-84	Montreal	QAAA	40	15	36	51		....	....	....	....	....	....	....	....	....	....	....	....	....	....	....	....	....	....	....
1984-85	Laval	QMJHL	68	13	19	32	92	....	....	....	....	....	....	....	....	....	....	....	....	....	....	....	....	....	....	....
1985-86	Laval	QMJHL	71	57	68	125	131	....	....	....	....	....	....	....	....	....	....	....	14	9	15	24	37	....	....	....
1986-87	**St. Louis**	**NHL**	**53**	**10**	**8**	**18**	**94**	**1**	**0**	**1**	**48**	**20.8**	**1**	....	....	....	....	....	**5**	**0**	**1**	**1**	**6**	**0**	**0**	**0**
1987-88	**St. Louis**	**NHL**	**23**	**1**	**0**	**1**	**42**	**0**	**0**	**0**	**19**	**5.3**	**–5**	....	....	....	....	....	**5**	**0**	**0**	**0**	**15**	**0**	**0**	**0**
	Peoria	IHL	8	0	5	5	35	....	....	....	....	....	....	....	....	....	....	....	....	....	....	....	....	....	....	....
1988-89	**Montreal**	**NHL**	**1**	**0**	**1**	**1**	**0**	**0**	**0**	**0**	**0**	**0.0**	**–1**	....	....	....	....	....	....	....	....	....	....	....	....	....
	Sherbrooke	AHL	73	25	28	53	134	....	....	....	....	....	....	....	....	....	....	....	4	3	1	4	6	....	....	....
1989-90	**Montreal**	**NHL**	**34**	**4**	**2**	**6**	**61**	**0**	**0**	**1**	**34**	**11.8**	**–1**	....	....	....	....	....	....	....	....	....	....	....	....	....
	Chicago	**NHL**	**39**	**10**	**11**	**21**	**47**	**1**	**0**	**1**	**78**	**12.8**	**0**	....	....	....	....	....	**18**	**1**	**8**	**9**	**28**	**0**	**0**	**0**
1990-91	**Chicago**	**NHL**	**67**	**6**	**7**	**13**	**119**	**1**	**1**	**2**	**89**	**6.7**	**–7**	....	....	....	....	....	**4**	**0**	**0**	**0**	**0**	**0**	**0**	**0**
1991-92	**Chicago**	**NHL**	**78**	**6**	**10**	**16**	**80**	**0**	**0**	**1**	**103**	**5.8**	**–2**	....	....	....	....	....	**18**	**3**	**1**	**4**	**33**	**0**	**0**	**2**
1992-93	**Chicago**	**NHL**	**81**	**10**	**21**	**31**	**111**	**1**	**0**	**2**	**117**	**8.5**	**5**	....	....	....	....	....	**4**	**1**	**0**	**1**	**2**	**0**	**0**	**0**
1993-94	**Chicago**	**NHL**	**66**	**12**	**8**	**20**	**63**	**0**	**0**	**0**	**129**	**9.3**	**5**	....	....	....	....	....	....	....	....	....	....	....	....	....
	Hartford	**NHL**	**16**	**6**	**1**	**7**	**19**	**0**	**0**	**2**	**22**	**27.3**	**–8**	....	....	....	....	....	....	....	....	....	....	....	....	....
1994-95	**Hartford**	**NHL**	**41**	**6**	**5**	**11**	**32**	**0**	**0**	**1**	**78**	**7.7**	**–7**	....	....	....	....	....	....	....	....	....	....	....	....	....
1995-96	**Hartford**	**NHL**	**29**	**1**	**2**	**3**	**31**	**0**	**0**	**0**	**43**	**2.3**	**–11**	....	....	....	....	....	....	....	....	....	....	....	....	....
	New Jersey	**NHL**	**18**	**0**	**1**	**1**	**4**	**0**	**0**	**0**	**20**	**0.0**	**–7**	....	....	....	....	....	....	....	....	....	....	....	....	....
	Calgary	**NHL**	**20**	**4**	**4**	**8**	**10**	**0**	**0**	**0**	**27**	**14.8**	**–1**	....	....	....	....	....	**4**	**0**	**0**	**0**	**0**	**0**	**0**	**0**
1996-97	Long Beach	IHL	28	4	10	14	54	....	....	....	....	....	....	....	....	....	....	....	....	....	....	....	....	....	....	....
	Phoenix	**NHL**	**2**	**1**	**0**	**1**	**0**	**0**	**0**	**1**	**4**	**25.0**	**0**	....	....	....	....	....	**2**	**0**	**0**	**0**	**4**	**0**	**0**	**0**
1997-98	**Phoenix**	**NHL**	**30**	**3**	**3**	**6**	**27**	**1**	**0**	**0**	**32**	**9.4**	**0**	....	....	....	....	....	....	....	....	....	....	....	....	....
	Long Beach	IHL	10	3	5	8	24	....	....	....	....	....	....	....	....	....	....	....	....	....	....	....	....	....	....	....
	Springfield	AHL	6	3	1	4	0	....	....	....	....	....	....	....	....	....	....	....	4	2	2	4	2	....	....	....
1998-99	Long Beach	IHL	17	4	4	8	16	....	....	....	....	....	....	....	....	....	....	....	8	0	2	2	15	....	....	....
	NHL Totals		**598**	**80**	**84**	**164**	**740**	**5**	**1**	**12**	**843**	**9.5**		....	....	....	....	....	**60**	**5**	**10**	**15**	**88**	**0**	**0**	**2**

QMJHL First All-Star Team (1986)

Traded to **Montreal** by **St. Louis** with Darrell May and St. Louis' 2nd round choice (Patrice Brisebois) in the 1989 Entry Draft for Sergio Momesso and Vincent Riendeau, August 9, 1988. Traded to **Chicago** by **Montreal** for Chicago's 3rd round choice (Charles Poulin) in 1990 Entry Draft, January 5, 1990. Traded to **Hartford** by **Chicago** with Frantisek Kucera for Gary Suter, Randy Cunneyworth and Hartford's 3rd round choice (later traded to Vancouver — Vancouver selected Larry Courville) in 1995 Entry Draft, March 11, 1994. Traded to **New Jersey** by **Hartford** with Hartford's 2nd round choice in 1998 Entry Draft for Jim Dowd and New Jersey's 2nd round choice (later traded to Calgary — Calgary selected Dmitri Kokorev) in 1997 Entry Draft, December 19, 1995. Traded to **Calgary** by **New Jersey** with Tommy Albelin and Cale Hulse for Phil Housley and Dan Keczmer, February 26, 1996. Signed as a free agent by **Phoenix**, March 18, 1997.

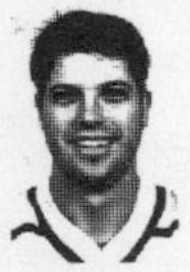

LEROUX, Francois (leh-ROO) PHX.

Defense. Shoots left. 6'6", 235 lbs. Born, Ste.-Adele, Que., April 18, 1970. Edmonton's 1st choice, 19th overall, in 1988 Entry Draft.

			Regular Season																Playoffs							
Season	Club	League	GP	G	A	Pts	PIM	PP	SH	GW	S	%	+/-	TF	F%	H	SB	Min	GP	G	A	Pts	PIM	PP	SH	GW
1986-87	Laval	QAAA	42	5	11	16	76	....	....	....	....	....	....	....	....	....	....	....	....	....	....	....	....	....	....	....
1987-88	St-Jean	QMJHL	58	3	8	11	143	....	....	....	....	....	....	....	....	....	....	....	7	2	0	2	21	....	....	....
1988-89	St-Jean	QMJHL	57	8	34	42	185	....	....	....	....	....	....	....	....	....	....	....	....	....	....	....	....	....	....	....
	Edmonton	**NHL**	**2**	**0**	**0**	**0**	**0**	**0**	**0**	**0**	**0**	**0.0**	**1**	....	....	....	....	....	....	....	....	....	....	....	....	....
1989-90	Victoriaville	QMJHL	54	4	33	37	169	....	....	....	....	....	....	....	....	....	....	....	....	....	....	....	....	....	....	....
	Edmonton	**NHL**	**3**	**0**	**1**	**1**	**0**	**0**	**0**	**0**	**0**	**0.0**	**–2**	....	....	....	....	....	....	....	....	....	....	....	....	....
1990-91	**Edmonton**	**NHL**	**1**	**0**	**2**	**2**	**0**	**0**	**0**	**0**	**1**	**0.0**	**1**	....	....	....	....	....	....	....	....	....	....	....	....	....
	Cape Breton	AHL	71	2	7	9	124	....	....	....	....	....	....	....	....	....	....	....	4	0	1	1	19	....	....	....
1991-92	**Edmonton**	**NHL**	**4**	**0**	**0**	**0**	**7**	**0**	**0**	**0**	**0**	**0.0**	**–1**	....	....	....	....	....	....	....	....	....	....	....	....	....
	Cape Breton	AHL	61	7	22	29	114	....	....	....	....	....	....	....	....	....	....	....	5	0	0	0	8	....	....	....
1992-93	**Edmonton**	**NHL**	**1**	**0**	**0**	**0**	**4**	**0**	**0**	**0**	**0**	**0.0**	**0**	....	....	....	....	....	....	....	....	....	....	....	....	....
	Cape Breton	AHL	55	10	24	34	139	....	....	....	....	....	....	....	....	....	....	....	16	0	5	5	29	....	....	....
1993-94	**Ottawa**	**NHL**	**23**	**0**	**1**	**1**	**70**	**0**	**0**	**0**	**8**	**0.0**	**–4**	....	....	....	....	....	....	....	....	....	....	....	....	....
	P.E.I. Senators	AHL	25	4	6	10	52	....	....	....	....	....	....	....	....	....	....	....	....	....	....	....	....	....	....	....
1994-95	P.E.I. Senators	AHL	45	4	14	18	137	....	....	....	....	....	....	....	....	....	....	....	....	....	....	....	....	....	....	....
	Pittsburgh	**NHL**	**40**	**0**	**2**	**2**	**114**	**0**	**0**	**0**	**19**	**0.0**	**7**	....	....	....	....	....	**12**	**0**	**2**	**2**	**14**	**0**	**0**	**0**
1995-96	**Pittsburgh**	**NHL**	**66**	**2**	**9**	**11**	**161**	**0**	**0**	**0**	**43**	**4.7**	**2**	....	....	....	....	....	**18**	**1**	**1**	**2**	**20**	**0**	**0**	**1**
1996-97	**Pittsburgh**	**NHL**	**59**	**0**	**3**	**3**	**81**	**0**	**0**	**0**	**5**	**0.0**	**–3**	....	....	....	....	....	**3**	**0**	**0**	**0**	**0**	**0**	**0**	**0**
1997-98	**Colorado**	**NHL**	**50**	**1**	**2**	**3**	**140**	**0**	**0**	**0**	**14**	**7.1**	**–3**	....	....	....	....	....	....	....	....	....	....	....	....	....
1998-99	Grand Rapids	IHL	13	1	1	2	22	....	....	....	....	....	....	....	....	....	....	....	....	....	....	....	....	....	....	....
	NHL Totals		**249**	**3**	**20**	**23**	**577**	**0**	**0**	**0**	**90**	**3.3**		....	....	....	....	....	**33**	**1**	**3**	**4**	**34**	**0**	**0**	**1**

Claimed on waivers by **Ottawa** from **Edmonton**, October 6, 1993. Claimed by **Pittsburgh** from **Ottawa** in Waiver Draft, January 18, 1995. Traded to **Colorado** by **Pittsburgh** for Colorado's 3rd round choice (David Cameron) in 1998 Entry Draft, September 28, 1997. Signed as a free agent by **Grand Rapids** (IHL), February 18, 1999. Signed as a free agent by **Phoenix**, July 20, 1999.

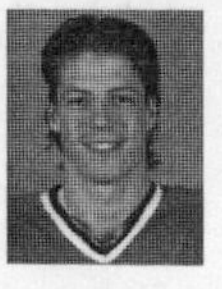

LEROUX, Jean-Yves (leh-ROO) CHI.

Left wing. Shoots left. 6'2", 211 lbs. Born, Montreal, Que., June 24, 1976. Chicago's 2nd choice, 40th overall, in 1994 Entry Draft.

			Regular Season																Playoffs							
Season	Club	League	GP	G	A	Pts	PIM	PP	SH	GW	S	%	+/-	TF	F%	H	SB	Min	GP	G	A	Pts	PIM	PP	SH	GW
1991-92	Montreal	QAAA	35	14	31	45	29	....	....	....	....	....	....	....	....	....	....	....	....	....	....	....	....	....	....	....
1992-93	Beauport	QMJHL	62	20	25	45	33	....	....	....	....	....	....	....	....	....	....	....	....	....	....	....	....	....	....	....
1993-94	Beauport	QMJHL	45	14	25	39	43	....	....	....	....	....	....	....	....	....	....	....	15	7	6	13	33	....	....	....
1994-95	Beauport	QMJHL	59	19	33	52	125	....	....	....	....	....	....	....	....	....	....	....	17	4	6	10	39	....	....	....
1995-96	Beauport	QMJHL	54	41	41	82	176	....	....	....	....	....	....	....	....	....	....	....	20	5	18	23	20	....	....	....
1996-97	**Chicago**	**NHL**	**1**	**0**	**1**	**1**	**5**	**0**	**0**	**0**	**0**	**0.0**	**1**	....	....	....	....	....	....	....	....	....	....	....	....	....
	Indianapolis	IHL	69	14	17	31	112	....	....	....	....	....	....	....	....	....	....	....	4	1	0	1	2	....	....	....
1997-98	**Chicago**	**NHL**	**66**	**6**	**7**	**13**	**55**	**0**	**0**	**0**	**57**	**10.5**	**–2**	....	....	....	....	....	....	....	....	....	....	....	....	....
1998-99	**Chicago**	**NHL**	**40**	**3**	**5**	**8**	**21**	**0**	**0**	**0**	**47**	**6.4**	**–7**	**10**	**50.0**	**98**	**8**	**12:43**	....	....	....	....	....	....	....	....
	Chicago	IHL	....	....	....	....	....	....	....	....	....	....	....	....	....	....	....	....	10	1	1	2	18	....	....	....
	NHL Totals		**107**	**9**	**13**	**22**	**81**	**0**	**0**	**0**	**104**	**8.7**		**10**	**50.0**	**98**	**8**	**12:43**	....	....	....	....	....	....	....	....

QMJHL Second All-Star Team (1994)

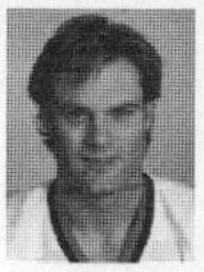

LESCHYSHYN, Curtis
(luh-SIH-shuhn) **CAR.**

Defense. Shoots left. 6'1", 205 lbs. Born, Thompson, Man., September 21, 1969. Quebec's 1st choice, 3rd overall, in 1988 Entry Draft.

			Regular Season																Playoffs							
Season	Club	League	GP	G	A	Pts	PIM	PP	SH	GW	S	%	+/–	TF	F%	H	SB	Min	GP	G	A	Pts	PIM	PP	SH	GW
1985-86	Saskatoon	SAHA	34	9	34	43	52																			
	Saskatoon	WHL	1	0	0	0	0																			
1986-87	Saskatoon	WHL	70	14	26	40	107												11	1	5	6	14			
1987-88	Saskatoon	WHL	56	14	41	55	86												10	2	5	7	16			
1988-89	Quebec	NHL	71	4	9	13	71	1	1	0	58	6.9	–32													
1989-90	Quebec	NHL	68	2	6	8	44	1	0	0	42	4.8	–41													
1990-91	Quebec	NHL	55	3	7	10	49	2	0	1	57	5.3	–19													
1991-92	Quebec	NHL	42	5	12	17	42	3	0	1	61	8.2	–28													
	Halifax	AHL	6	0	2	2	4																			
1992-93	Quebec	NHL	82	9	23	32	61	4	0	2	73	12.3	25						6	1	1	2	6	1	0	0
1993-94	Quebec	NHL	72	5	17	22	65	3	0	2	97	5.2	–2													
1994-95	Quebec	NHL	44	2	13	15	20	0	0	0	43	4.7	29						3	0	1	1	4	0	0	0
1995-96♦	Colorado	NHL	77	4	15	19	73	0	0	1	76	5.3	32						17	1	2	3	8	0	0	0
1996-97	Colorado	NHL	11	0	5	5	6	0	0	0	8	0.0	1													
	Washington	NHL	2	0	0	0	2	0	0	0	0	0.0	0													
	Hartford	NHL	64	4	13	17	30	1	1	1	94	4.3	–19													
1997-98	Carolina	NHL	73	2	10	12	45	1	0	1	53	3.8	–2													
1998-99	Carolina	NHL	65	2	7	9	50	0	0	0	35	5.7	–1	0	0.0	208	103	19:18	6	0	0	0	6	0	0	0
	NHL Totals		**726**	**42**	**137**	**179**	**558**	**16**	**2**	**9**	**697**	**6.0**		**0**	**0.0**	**208**	**103**	**19:18**	**32**	**2**	**4**	**6**	**24**	**1**	**0**	**0**

Transferred to **Colorado** after **Quebec** franchise relcoated, June 21, 1995. Traded to **Washington** by **Colorado** with Chris Simon for Keith Jones, Washington's 1st and 4th round choices in 1998 Entry Draft, November 2, 1996. Traded to **Hartford** by **Washington** for Andrei Nikolishin, November 9, 1996. Transferred to **Carolina** after **Hartford** franchise relocated, June 25, 1997.

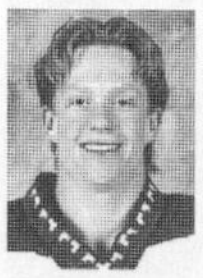

LETOWSKI, Trevor
(leh-TOW-skee) **PHX.**

Center. Shoots right. 5'10", 173 lbs. Born, Thunder Bay, Ont., April 5, 1977. Phoenix's 6th choice, 174th overall, in 1996 Entry Draft.

Season	Club	League	GP	G	A	Pts	PIM	PP	SH	GW	S	%	+/–	TF	F%	H	SB	Min	GP	G	A	Pts	PIM	PP	SH	GW
1993-94	Thunder Bay	OMHA	64	41	60	101	48																			
1994-95	Sarnia	OHL	66	22	19	41	33												4	0	1	1	9			
1995-96	Sarnia	OHL	66	36	63	99	66												10	9	5	14	10			
1996-97	Sarnia	OHL	55	35	73	108	51												12	9	12	21	20			
1997-98	Springfield	AHL	75	11	20	31	26												4	1	0	1	2			
1998-99	Phoenix	NHL	14	2	2	4	2	0	0	0	8	25.0	1	49	55.1	4	3	6:01								
	Springfield	AHL	67	32	35	67	46												3	1	0	1	2			
	NHL Totals		**14**	**2**	**2**	**4**	**2**	**0**	**0**	**0**	**8**	**25.0**		**49**	**55.1**	**4**	**3**	**6:01**								

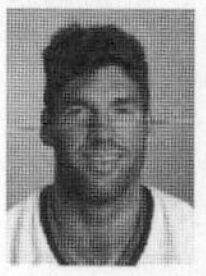

LEVINS, Scott

Center/Right wing. Shoots right. 6'4", 210 lbs. Born, Spokane, WA, January 30, 1970. Winnipeg's 4th choice, 75th overall, in 1990 Entry Draft.

Season	Club	League	GP	G	A	Pts	PIM	PP	SH	GW	S	%	+/–	TF	F%	H	SB	Min	GP	G	A	Pts	PIM	PP	SH	GW
1987-88	Spokane	KIJHL	42	49	59	108	180																			
1988-89	Penticton	BCJHL	50	27	58	85	154																			
1989-90	Tri-City	WHL	71	25	37	62	132												6	2	3	5	18			
1990-91	Moncton	AHL	74	12	26	38	133												4	0	0	0	4			
1991-92	Moncton	AHL	69	15	18	33	271												11	3	4	7	30			
1992-93	Winnipeg	NHL	9	0	1	1	18	0	0	0	8	0.0	–2													
	Moncton	AHL	54	22	26	48	158												5	1	3	4	14			
1993-94	Florida	NHL	29	5	6	11	69	2	0	1	38	13.2	0													
	Ottawa	NHL	33	3	5	8	93	2	0	0	39	7.7	–26													
1994-95	Ottawa	NHL	24	5	6	11	51	0	0	0	34	14.7	4													
	P.E.I. Senators	AHL	6	0	4	4	14																			
1995-96	Ottawa	NHL	27	0	2	2	80	0	0	0	6	0.0	–3													
	Detroit	IHL	9	0	0	0	9																			
1996-97	Springfield	AHL	60	24	23	47	267												11	5	4	9	37			
1997-98	Phoenix	NHL	2	0	0	0	5	0	0	0	2	0.0	–1													
	Springfield	AHL	79	28	39	67	177												4	2	0	2	24			
1998-99	New Haven	AHL	80	32	26	58	189																			
	NHL Totals		**124**	**13**	**20**	**33**	**316**	**4**	**0**	**1**	**127**	**10.2**														

WHL West Second All-Star Team (1990)

Claimed by **Florida** from **Winnipeg** in Expansion Draft, June 24, 1993. Traded to **Ottawa** by **Florida** with Evgeny Davydov, Florida's 6th round choice (Mike Gaffney) in 1994 Entry Draft and Dallas' 4th round choice (previously acquired, Ottawa selected Kevin Bolibruck) in 1995 Entry Draft for Bob Kudelski, January 6, 1994. Signed as a free agent by **Phoenix**, October 3, 1996. Signed as a free agent by **Carolina**, August 18, 1998.

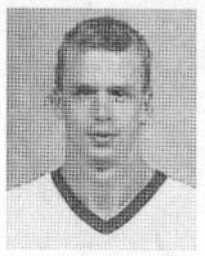

LIBBY, Jeff

Defense. Shoots left. 6'3", 215 lbs. Born, Waterville, ME, March 1, 1974.

Season	Club	League	GP	G	A	Pts	PIM	PP	SH	GW	S	%	+/–	TF	F%	H	SB	Min	GP	G	A	Pts	PIM	PP	SH	GW
1993-94	New Hampton	H.S.	STATISTICS NOT AVAILABLE																							
1994-95	U. of Maine	H.E.	22	2	4	6	6																			
1995-96	U. of Maine	H.E.	39	0	9	9	42																			
1996-97	U. of Maine	H.E.	34	6	25	31	41																			
1997-98	NY Islanders	NHL	1	0	0	0	0	0	0	0	0	0.0	0													
	Kentucky	AHL	8	0	3	3	4												3	0	0	0	4			
	Utah	IHL	47	1	5	6	25												1	0	0	0	0			
1998-99	Lowell	AHL	5	0	0	0	2																			
	NHL Totals		**1**	**0**	**0**	**0**	**0**	**0**	**0**	**0**	**0**	**0.0**														

Signed as a free agent by **NY Islanders**, May 12, 1997. • Suffered career-ending eye injury in game vs. St. John's, November 7, 1998.

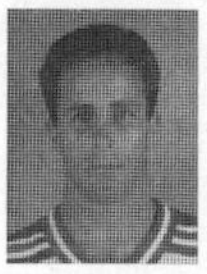

LIDSTER, Doug

Defense. Shoots right. 6'1", 190 lbs. Born, Kamloops, B.C., October 18, 1960. Vancouver's 6th choice, 133rd overall, in 1980 Entry Draft.

Season	Club	League	GP	G	A	Pts	PIM	PP	SH	GW	S	%	+/–	TF	F%	H	SB	Min	GP	G	A	Pts	PIM	PP	SH	GW
1977-78	Kamloops	BCJHL	64	24	39	63	46																			
	Seattle	WCJHL	2	0	0	0	0																			
1978-79	Kamloops	BCJHL	59	36	47	83	50																			
1979-80	Colorado	WCHA	39	18	25	43	52																			
1980-81	Colorado	WCHA	36	10	30	40	54																			
1981-82	Colorado	WCHA	36	13	22	35	32																			
1982-83	Colorado	WCHA	34	15	41	56	30																			
1983-84	Canada	Nat-Team	59	6	20	26	28																			
	Canada	Olympics	7	0	2	2	2																			
	Vancouver	NHL	8	0	0	0	4	0	0	0	7	0.0	–7						2	0	1	1	0	0	0	0
1984-85	Vancouver	NHL	78	6	24	30	55	2	0	0	125	4.8	–11													
1985-86	Vancouver	NHL	78	12	16	28	56	1	1	0	151	7.9	–12						3	0	1	1	2	0	0	0
1986-87	Vancouver	NHL	80	12	51	63	40	3	0	0	176	6.8	–35													
1987-88	Vancouver	NHL	64	4	32	36	105	2	1	0	133	3.0	–19													
1988-89	Vancouver	NHL	63	5	17	22	78	3	0	0	116	4.3	–4						7	1	1	2	9	0	0	0
1989-90	Vancouver	NHL	80	8	28	36	36	1	0	0	143	5.6	–16													
1990-91	Vancouver	NHL	78	6	32	38	77	4	0	1	157	3.8	–6						6	0	2	2	6	0	0	0
1991-92	Vancouver	NHL	66	6	23	29	39	3	0	2	89	6.7	9						11	1	2	3	11	0	0	0
1992-93	Vancouver	NHL	71	6	19	25	36	3	0	0	76	7.9	9						12	0	3	3	8	0	0	0
1993-94♦	NY Rangers	NHL	34	0	2	2	33	0	0	0	25	0.0	–12						9	2	0	2	10	0	0	0
1994-95	St. Louis	NHL	37	2	7	9	12	1	0	0	37	5.4	9						4	0	0	0	2	0	0	0
1995-96	NY Rangers	NHL	59	5	9	14	50	0	0	0	73	6.8	11						7	1	0	1	6	1	0	0
1996-97	NY Rangers	NHL	48	3	4	7	24	0	0	0	42	7.1	10						15	1	5	6	8	0	0	0

			Regular Season																Playoffs							
Season	Club	League	GP	G	A	Pts	PIM	PP	SH	GW	S	%	+/–	TF	F%	H	SB	Min	GP	G	A	Pts	PIM	PP	SH	GW
1997-98	**NY Rangers**	**NHL**	36	0	4	4	24	0	0	0	25	0.0	2	....	....	....	....	....	....	....	....	....	....	....	....	....
1998-99	Canada	Nat-Team	38	4	15	19	64	....	....	....	....	....	....	....	....	....	....	....	....	....	....	....	....	....	....	....
	♦ **Dallas**	**NHL**	17	0	0	0	10	0	0	0	7	0.0	0	1	0.0	16	16	13:16	4	0	0	0	2	0	0	0
	NHL Totals		897	75	268	343	679	23	2	3	1382	5.4		1	0.0	16	16	13:16	80	6	15	21	64	1	0	0

WCHA First All-Star Team (1982, 1983) • NCAA West First All-American Team (1983)

Traded to **NY Rangers** by **Vancouver** to complete transaction that sent John Vanbiesbrouck to Vancouver (June 30, 1993), June 25, 1993. Traded to **St. Louis** by **NY Rangers** with Esa Tikkanen for Petr Nedved, July 24, 1994. Traded to **NY Rangers** by **St. Louis** for Jay Wells, July 28, 1995. Signed as a free agent by **Dallas**, February 26, 1999.

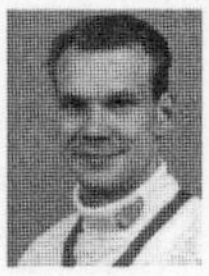

LIDSTROM, Nicklas
(LID-struhm) **DET.**

Defense. Shoots left. 6'2", 185 lbs. Born, Vasteras, Sweden, April 28, 1970. Detroit's 3rd choice, 53rd overall, in 1989 Entry Draft.

Season	Club	League	GP	G	A	Pts	PIM	PP	SH	GW	S	%	+/–	TF	F%	H	SB	Min	GP	G	A	Pts	PIM	PP	SH	GW
1988-89	Vasteras IK	Sweden	19	0	2	2	4	....	....	....	....	....	....	....	....	....	....	....	....	....	....	....	....	....	....	....
1989-90	Vasteras IK	Sweden	39	8	8	16	14	....	....	....	....	....	....	....	....	....	....	....	2	0	1	1	2	....	....	....
1990-91	Vasteras IK	Sweden	38	4	19	23	2	....	....	....	....	....	....	....	....	....	....	....	4	0	0	0	4	....	....	....
1991-92	**Detroit**	**NHL**	80	11	49	60	22	5	0	1	168	6.5	36	....	....	....	....	....	11	1	2	3	0	1	0	0
1992-93	**Detroit**	**NHL**	84	7	34	41	28	3	0	2	156	4.5	7	....	....	....	....	....	7	1	0	1	0	1	0	0
1993-94	**Detroit**	**NHL**	84	10	46	56	26	4	0	3	200	5.0	43	....	....	....	....	....	7	3	2	5	0	1	1	0
1994-95	Vasteras IK	Sweden	13	2	10	12	4	....	....	....	....	....	....	....	....	....	....	....	....	....	....	....	....	....	....	....
	Detroit	**NHL**	43	10	16	26	6	7	0	0	90	11.1	15	....	....	....	....	....	18	4	12	16	8	3	0	2
1995-96	**Detroit**	**NHL**	81	17	50	67	20	8	1	1	211	8.1	29	....	....	....	....	....	19	5	9	14	10	1	0	0
1996-97♦	**Detroit**	**NHL**	79	15	42	57	30	8	0	1	214	7.0	11	....	....	....	....	....	20	2	6	8	2	0	0	0
1997-98♦	**Detroit**	**NHL**	80	17	42	59	18	7	1	1	205	8.3	22	....	....	....	....	....	22	6	13	19	8	2	0	2
1998-99	**Detroit**	**NHL**	81	14	43	57	14	6	2	3	205	6.8	14	0	0.0	53	88	26:31	10	2	9	11	4	2	0	0
	NHL Totals		612	101	322	423	164	48	4	12	1449	7.0		0	0.0	53	88	26:31	114	24	53	77	32	11	1	4

NHL/Upper Deck All-Rookie Team (1992) • NHL First All-Star Team (1998, 1999)

Played in NHL All-Star Game (1996, 1998, 1999)

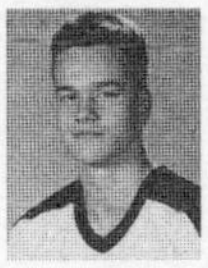

LIND, Juha
(LIHND, YOO-huh) **DAL.**

Center. Shoots left. 5'11", 180 lbs. Born, Helsinki, Finland, January 2, 1974. Minnesota's 6th choice, 178th overall, in 1992 Entry Draft.

Season	Club	League	GP	G	A	Pts	PIM	PP	SH	GW	S	%	+/–	TF	F%	H	SB	Min	GP	G	A	Pts	PIM	PP	SH	GW
1991-92	Jokerit	Finn-Jr.	14	9	16	25	2	....	....	....	....	....	....	....	....	....	....	....	14	7	8	15	8	....	....	....
1992-93	Vantaa HT	Finland-2	25	8	12	20	8	....	....	....	....	....	....	....	....	....	....	....	....	....	....	....	....	....	....	....
	Helsinki	Finland-2	3	2	4	6	2	....	....	....	....	....	....	....	....	....	....	....	....	....	....	....	....	....	....	....
	Jokerit	Finland	6	0	0	0	2	....	....	....	....	....	....	....	....	....	....	....	1	0	0	0	0	....	....	....
1993-94	Jokerit	Finland-2	11	6	7	13	4	....	....	....	....	....	....	....	....	....	....	....	....	....	....	....	....	....	....	....
	Jokerit	Finland	47	17	11	28	37	....	....	....	....	....	....	....	....	....	....	....	11	2	5	7	4	....	....	....
1994-95	Helsinki	Finn-Jr.	3	2	1	3	2	....	....	....	....	....	....	....	....	....	....	....	....	....	....	....	....	....	....	....
	Jokerit	Finland	50	10	8	18	12	....	....	....	....	....	....	....	....	....	....	....	11	1	2	3	6	....	....	....
1995-96	Jokerit	Finland	50	15	22	37	32	....	....	....	....	....	....	....	....	....	....	....	11	4	5	9	4	....	....	....
1996-97	Jokerit	Finland	50	16	22	38	28	....	....	....	....	....	....	....	....	....	....	....	9	5	3	8	0	....	....	....
	Jokerit	EuroHL	6	4	1	5	6	....	....	....	....	....	....	....	....	....	....	....	2	1	0	1	0	....	....	....
1997-98	**Dallas**	**NHL**	39	2	3	5	6	0	0	0	27	7.4	4	....	....	....	....	....	15	2	2	4	8	0	0	1
	Michigan	IHL	8	2	2	4	2	....	....	....	....	....	....	....	....	....	....	....	....	....	....	....	....	....	....	....
	Finland	Olympics	6	0	1	1	6	....	....	....	....	....	....	....	....	....	....	....	....	....	....	....	....	....	....	....
1998-99	Jokerit	Finland	50	20	19	39	22	....	....	....	....	....	....	....	....	....	....	....	3	3	1	4	2	....	....	....
	Jokerit	EuroHL	6	6	2	8	14	....	....	....	....	....	....	....	....	....	....	....	2	0	2	2	0	....	....	....
	NHL Totals		39	2	3	5	6	0	0	0	27	7.4		....	....	....	....	....	15	2	2	4	8	0	0	1

Rights transferred to **Dallas** after **Minnesota** franchise relocated, June 9, 1993.

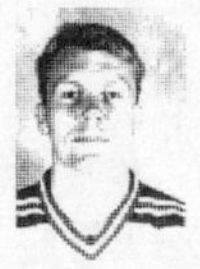

LINDBOM, Johan
(LIHND-buhm, YOO-hahn)

Left wing. Shoots left. 6'2", 216 lbs. Born, Alvesta, Sweden, July 8, 1971. NY Rangers' 6th choice, 134th overall, in 1997 Entry Draft.

Season	Club	League	GP	G	A	Pts	PIM	PP	SH	GW	S	%	+/–	TF	F%	H	SB	Min	GP	G	A	Pts	PIM	PP	SH	GW
1991-92	SC Tyngsryd	Sweden-2	30	10	11	21	68	....	....	....	....	....	....	....	....	....	....	....	....	....	....	....	....	....	....	....
1992-93	Troja-Ljungby	Sweden-2	30	10	16	26	20	....	....	....	....	....	....	....	....	....	....	....	10	6	3	9	18	....	....	....
1993-94	Troja-Ljungby	Sweden-2	33	16	11	27	30	....	....	....	....	....	....	....	....	....	....	....	11	6	6	12	2	....	....	....
1994-95	HV Jonkoping	Sweden	39	9	7	16	30	....	....	....	....	....	....	....	....	....	....	....	13	2	5	7	12	....	....	....
1995-96	HV Jonkoping	Sweden	37	12	14	26	30	....	....	....	....	....	....	....	....	....	....	....	4	0	0	0	4	....	....	....
1996-97	HV Jonkoping	Sweden	49	20	14	34	26	....	....	....	....	....	....	....	....	....	....	....	5	1	0	1	6	....	....	....
1997-98	**NY Rangers**	**NHL**	38	1	3	4	28	0	0	0	38	2.6	4	....	....	....	....	....	....	....	....	....	....	....	....	....
	Hartford	AHL	7	1	5	6	6	....	....	....	....	....	....	....	....	....	....	....	....	....	....	....	....	....	....	....
1998-99	HV Jonkoping	Sweden	49	9	17	26	40	....	....	....	....	....	....	....	....	....	....	....	....	....	....	....	....	....	....	....
	NHL Totals		38	1	3	4	28	0	0	0	38	2.6		....	....	....	....	....	....	....	....	....	....	....	....	....

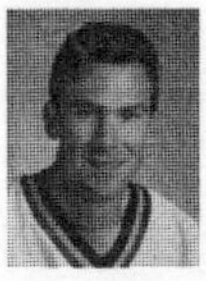

LINDEN, Trevor
MTL.

Center/Right wing. Shoots right. 6'4", 220 lbs. Born, Medicine Hat, Alta., April 11, 1970. Vancouver's 1st choice, 2nd overall, in 1988 Entry Draft.

Season	Club	League	GP	G	A	Pts	PIM	PP	SH	GW	S	%	+/–	TF	F%	H	SB	Min	GP	G	A	Pts	PIM	PP	SH	GW
1985-86	Medicine Hat	AAHA	40	14	22	36	14	....	....	....	....	....	....	....	....	....	....	....	....	....	....	....	....	....	....	....
	Medicine Hat	WHL	5	2	0	2	0	....	....	....	....	....	....	....	....	....	....	....	....	....	....	....	....	....	....	....
1986-87	Medicine Hat	WHL	72	14	22	36	59	....	....	....	....	....	....	....	....	....	....	....	20	5	4	9	17	....	....	....
1987-88	Medicine Hat	WHL	67	46	64	110	76	....	....	....	....	....	....	....	....	....	....	....	16	*13	12	25	19	....	....	....
1988-89	**Vancouver**	**NHL**	80	30	29	59	41	10	1	2	186	16.1	–10	....	....	....	....	....	7	3	4	7	8	2	1	0
1989-90	**Vancouver**	**NHL**	73	21	30	51	43	6	2	3	171	12.3	–17	....	....	....	....	....	....	....	....	....	....	....	....	....
1990-91	**Vancouver**	**NHL**	80	33	37	70	65	16	2	4	229	14.4	–25	....	....	....	....	....	6	0	7	7	2	0	0	0
1991-92	**Vancouver**	**NHL**	80	31	44	75	101	6	1	6	201	15.4	3	....	....	....	....	....	13	4	8	12	6	2	0	1
1992-93	**Vancouver**	**NHL**	84	33	39	72	64	8	0	3	209	15.8	19	....	....	....	....	....	12	5	8	13	16	2	0	1
1993-94	**Vancouver**	**NHL**	84	32	29	61	73	10	2	3	234	13.7	6	....	....	....	....	....	24	12	13	25	18	5	1	1
1994-95	**Vancouver**	**NHL**	48	18	22	40	40	9	0	1	129	14.0	–5	....	....	....	....	....	11	2	6	8	12	1	0	0
1995-96	**Vancouver**	**NHL**	82	33	47	80	42	12	1	2	202	16.3	6	....	....	....	....	....	6	4	4	8	6	2	0	0
1996-97	**Vancouver**	**NHL**	49	9	31	40	27	2	2	2	84	10.7	5	....	....	....	....	....	....	....	....	....	....	....	....	....
1997-98	**Vancouver**	**NHL**	42	7	14	21	49	2	0	1	74	9.5	–13	....	....	....	....	....	....	....	....	....	....	....	....	....
	NY Islanders	**NHL**	25	10	7	17	33	3	2	1	59	16.9	–1	....	....	....	....	....	....	....	....	....	....	....	....	....
	Canada	Olympics	6	1	0	1	10	....	....	....	....	....	....	....	....	....	....	....	....	....	....	....	....	....	....	....
1998-99	**NY Islanders**	**NHL**	82	18	29	47	32	8	1	1	167	10.8	–14	261	50.2	144	47	21:29	....	....	....	....	....	....	....	....
	NHL Totals		809	275	358	633	610	92	14	29	1945	14.1		261	50.2	144	47	21:29	79	30	50	80	68	14	2	3

WHL East Second All-Star Team (1988) • NHL All-Rookie Team (1989) • Won King Clancy Memorial Trophy (1997)

Played in NHL All-Star Game (1991, 1992)

Traded to **NY Islanders** by **Vancouver** for Todd Bertuzzi, Bryan McCabe and NY Islanders' 3rd round choice (Jarkko Ruutu) in 1998 Entry Draft, February 6, 1998. Traded to **Montreal** by **NY Islanders** for Montreal's 1st round choice (Branislav Mezel) in 1999 Entry Draft, May 29, 1999.

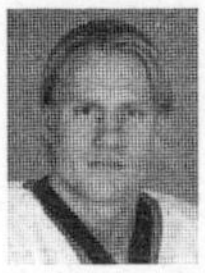

LINDGREN, Mats
(LIHND-gruhn)

Center. Shoots left. 6'2", 202 lbs. Born, Skelleftea, Sweden, October 1, 1974. Winnipeg's 1st choice, 15th overall, in 1993 Entry Draft.

Season	Club	League	GP	G	A	Pts	PIM	PP	SH	GW	S	%	+/–	TF	F%	H	SB	Min	GP	G	A	Pts	PIM	PP	SH	GW
1990-91	Skelleftea AIK	Sweden-2	10	0	1	1	0	....	....	....	....	....	....	....	....	....	....	....	....	....	....	....	....	....	....	....
1991-92	Skelleftea AIK	Sweden-2	29	14	188	32	12	....	....	....	....	....	....	....	....	....	....	....	3	3	2	5	2	....	....	....
1992-93	Skelleftea AIK	Sweden-2	32	20	18	38	18	....	....	....	....	....	....	....	....	....	....	....	3	0	0	0	2	....	....	....
1993-94	Farjestads BK	Sweden	22	11	6	17	26	....	....	....	....	....	....	....	....	....	....	....	....	....	....	....	....	....	....	....
1994-95	Farjestads BK	Sweden	37	17	15	32	20	....	....	....	....	....	....	....	....	....	....	....	3	0	0	0	4	....	....	....
1995-96	Cape Breton	AHL	13	7	5	12	6	....	....	....	....	....	....	....	....	....	....	....	....	....	....	....	....	....	....	....
1996-97	**Edmonton**	**NHL**	69	11	14	25	12	2	3	1	71	15.5	–7	....	....	....	....	....	12	0	4	4	0	0	0	0
	Hamilton	AHL	9	6	7	13	6	....	....	....	....	....	....	....	....	....	....	....	....	....	....	....	....	....	....	....

			Regular Season																Playoffs							
Season	Club	League	GP	G	A	Pts	PIM	PP	SH	GW	S	%	+/-	TF	F%	H	SB	Min	GP	G	A	Pts	PIM	PP	SH	GW
1997-98	Edmonton	NHL	82	13	13	26	42	1	3	3	131	9.9	0	....	....	....	....	....	12	1	1	2	10	0	0	0
	Sweden	Olympics	4	0	0	0	2	....	....	....	....	....	....	....	....	....	....	....	....	....	....	....	....	....	....	....
1998-99	Edmonton	NHL	48	5	12	17	22	0	1	0	53	9.4	4	363	47.9	44	16	11:31	....	....	....	....	....	....	....	....
	NY Islanders	NHL	12	5	3	8	2	3	0	1	30	16.7	2	180	48.9	18	4	20:08	....	....	....	....	....	....	....	....
	NHL Totals		211	34	42	76	78	6	7	5	285	11.9		543	48.3	62	20	13:14	24	1	5	6	10	0	0	0

Swedish Rookie of the Year (1994)

Traded to **Edmonton** by **Winnipeg** with Boris Mironov, Winnipeg's 1st round choice (Jason Bonsignore) in 1994 Entry Draft and Florida's 4th round choice (previously acquired, Edmonton selected Adam Copeland) in 1994 Entry Draft for Dave Manson and St. Louis' 6th round choice (previously acquired, Winnipeg selected Chris Kibermanis) in 1994 Entry Draft, March 15, 1994. Traded to **NY Islanders** by **Edmonton** with Edmonton's 8th round choice (Radek Martinek) in 1999 Entry Draft for Tommy Salo, March 20, 1999.

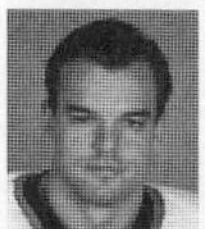

LINDQUIST, Fredrik (LIHND-kvihst) EDM.

Center. Shoots left. 6', 190 lbs. Born, Sodertalje, Sweden, June 21, 1973. New Jersey's 4th choice, 55th overall, in 1991 Entry Draft.

1989-90	Huddinge IF	Sweden-2	2	0	0	0	0	....	....	....	....	....	....	....	....	....	....	....	....	....	....	....	....	....	....	....
1990-91	Djurgardens IF	Sweden	28	6	4	10	0	....	....	....	....	....	....	....	....	....	....	....	7	1	0	1	2	....	....	....
1991-92	Djurgardens IF	Sweden	39	9	6	15	14	....	....	....	....	....	....	....	....	....	....	....	10	1	1	2	2	....	....	....
1992-93	Djurgardens IF	Sweden	39	9	11	20	8	....	....	....	....	....	....	....	....	....	....	....	4	1	2	3	2	....	....	....
1993-94	Djurgardens IF	Sweden	25	5	8	13	8	....	....	....	....	....	....	....	....	....	....	....	6	2	1	3	2	....	....	....
1994-95	Djurgardens IF	Sweden	40	11	16	27	14	....	....	....	....	....	....	....	....	....	....	....	3	0	0	0	2	....	....	....
1995-96	Djurgardens IF	Sweden	33	12	19	31	16	....	....	....	....	....	....	....	....	....	....	....	1	0	0	0	0	....	....	....
1996-97	Djurgardens IF	Sweden	44	19	28	47	20	....	....	....	....	....	....	....	....	....	....	....	4	0	3	3	2	....	....	....
1997-98	Djurgardens IF	Sweden	42	10	*32	42	30	....	....	....	....	....	....	....	....	....	....	....	13	3	6	9	4	....	....	....
1998-99	Edmonton	NHL	8	0	0	0	2	0	0	0	6	0.0	–2	0	0.0	1	1	12:18	....	....	....	....	....	....	....	....
	Hamilton	AHL	57	18	36	54	20	....	....	....	....	....	....	....	....	....	....	....	11	2	2	4	2	....	....	....
	NHL Totals		8	0	0	0	2	0	0	0	6	0.0		0	0.0	1	1	12:18	....	....	....	....	....	....	....	....

Traded to **Edmonton** by **New Jersey** with New Jersey's 4th (Kristian Antila) and 5th (Oleg Smirnov) round choices in 1998 Entry Draft for Pittsburgh's 3rd round choice (previously acquired, New Jersey selected Brian Gionta) in 1998 Entry Draft, June 27, 1998.

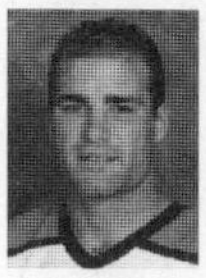

LINDROS, Eric (LIHND-rahz) PHI.

Center. Shoots right. 6'4", 236 lbs. Born, London, Ont., February 28, 1973. Quebec's 1st choice, 1st overall, in 1991 Entry Draft.

1988-89	St. Michael's	OJHL-B	37	24	43	67	193	....	....	....	....	....	....	....	....	....	....	....	27	23	25	48	155	....	....	....
	Canada	Nat-Team	2	1	0	1	0	....	....	....	....	....	....	....	....	....	....	....	....	....	....	....	....	....	....	....
1989-90	Detroit	USHL	14	23	29	52	123	....	....	....	....	....	....	....	....	....	....	....	....	....	....	....	....	....	....	....
	Canada	Nat-Team	3	1	0	1	4	....	....	....	....	....	....	....	....	....	....	....	....	....	....	....	....	....	....	....
	Oshawa	OHL	25	17	19	36	61	....	....	....	....	....	....	....	....	....	....	....	17	18	18	36	76	....	....	....
1990-91	Oshawa	OHL	57	*71	78	*149	189	....	....	....	....	....	....	....	....	....	....	....	16	*18	20	*38	*93	....	....	....
1991-92	Oshawa	OHL	13	9	22	31	54	....	....	....	....	....	....	....	....	....	....	....	....	....	....	....	....	....	....	....
	Canada	Nat-Team	24	19	16	35	34	....	....	....	....	....	....	....	....	....	....	....	....	....	....	....	....	....	....	....
	Canada	Olympics	8	5	6	11	5	....	....	....	....	....	....	....	....	....	....	....	....	....	....	....	....	....	....	....
1992-93	Philadelphia	NHL	61	41	34	75	147	8	1	5	180	22.8	28	....	....	....	....	....	....	....	....	....	....	....	....	....
1993-94	Philadelphia	NHL	65	44	53	97	103	13	2	9	197	22.3	16	....	....	....	....	....	....	....	....	....	....	....	....	....
1994-95	Philadelphia	NHL	46	29	41	*70	60	7	0	4	144	20.1	27	....	....	....	....	....	12	4	11	15	18	0	0	1
1995-96	Philadelphia	NHL	73	47	68	115	163	15	0	4	294	16.0	26	....	....	....	....	....	12	6	6	12	43	3	0	2
1996-97	Philadelphia	NHL	52	32	47	79	136	9	0	7	198	16.2	31	....	....	....	....	....	19	12	14	*26	40	4	0	1
1997-98	Philadelphia	NHL	63	30	41	71	134	10	1	4	202	14.9	14	....	....	....	....	....	5	1	2	3	17	0	0	0
	Canada	Olympics	6	2	3	5	2	....	....	....	....	....	....	....	....	....	....	....	....	....	....	....	....	....	....	....
1998-99	Philadelphia	NHL	71	40	53	93	120	10	1	2	242	16.5	35	1529	60.0	117	17	22:56	....	....	....	....	....	....	....	....
	NHL Totals		431	263	337	600	863	72	5	35	1457	18.1		1529	60.0	117	17	22:56	48	23	33	56	118	7	0	4

Memorial Cup All-Star Team (1990) • OHL First All-Star Team (1991) • Canadian Major Junior Player of the Year (1991) • NHL/Upper Deck All-Rookie Team (1993) • NHL First All-Star Team (1995) • Won Lester B. Pearson Award (1995) • Won Hart Trophy (1995) • NHL Second All-Star Team (1996)

Played in NHL All-Star Game (1994, 1996, 1997, 1998, 1999)

Rights traded to Oshawa (OHL) by Sault Ste. Marie (OHL) for Mike DeCoff, Jason Denomme, Mike Lenarduzzi and Oshawa's 2nd round choice in 1991 and 4th round choice (Joe Vanvolsen) in 1992 OHL Priority Draft, December 17, 1989. Traded to **Philadelphia** by **Quebec** for Peter Forsberg, Steve Duchesne, Kerry Huffman, Mike Ricci, Ron Hextall, Chris Simon, Philadelphia's 1st round choice in the 1993 (Jocelyn Thibault) and 1994 (later traded to Toronto — later traded to Washington — Washington selected Nolan Baumgartner) Entry Drafts and cash, June 30, 1992.

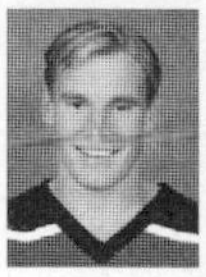

LINDSAY, Bill FLA.

Left wing. Shoots left. 6', 195 lbs. Born, Big Fork, MT, May 17, 1971. Quebec's 6th choice, 103rd overall, in 1991 Entry Draft.

198-89	Vernon	BCJHL	56	24	29	53	166	....	....	....	....	....	....	....	....	....	....	....	....	....	....	....	....	....	....	....
1989-90	Tri-City	WHL	72	40	45	85	84	....	....	....	....	....	....	....	....	....	....	....	7	3	0	3	17	....	....	....
1990-91	Tri-City	WHL	63	46	47	93	151	....	....	....	....	....	....	....	....	....	....	....	5	3	6	9	10	....	....	....
1991-92	Tri-City	WHL	42	34	59	93	111	....	....	....	....	....	....	....	....	....	....	....	3	2	3	5	16	....	....	....
	Quebec	NHL	23	2	4	6	14	0	0	1	35	5.7	–6	....	....	....	....	....	....	....	....	....	....	....	....	....
1992-93	Quebec	NHL	44	4	9	13	16	0	0	0	58	6.9	0	....	....	....	....	....	....	....	....	....	....	....	....	....
	Halifax	AHL	20	11	13	24	18	....	....	....	....	....	....	....	....	....	....	....	....	....	....	....	....	....	....	....
1993-94	Florida	NHL	84	6	6	12	97	0	0	0	90	6.7	–2	....	....	....	....	....	....	....	....	....	....	....	....	....
1994-95	Florida	NHL	48	10	9	19	46	0	1	0	63	15.9	1	....	....	....	....	....	....	....	....	....	....	....	....	....
1995-96	Florida	NHL	73	12	22	34	57	0	3	2	118	10.2	13	....	....	....	....	....	22	5	5	10	18	0	1	1
1996-97	Florida	NHL	81	11	23	34	120	0	1	3	168	6.5	1	....	....	....	....	....	3	0	1	1	8	0	0	0
1997-98	Florida	NHL	82	12	16	28	80	0	2	5	150	8.0	–2	....	....	....	....	....	....	....	....	....	....	....	....	....
1998-99	Florida	NHL	75	12	15	27	92	0	1	2	135	8.9	–1	57	40.4	149	20	13:37	....	....	....	....	....	....	....	....
	NHL Totals		510	69	104	173	522	0	8	13	817	8.4		57	40.4	149	20	13:37	25	5	6	11	26	0	1	1

WHL West Second All-Star Team (1992)

Claimed by **Florida** from **Quebec** in Expansion Draft, June 24, 1993.

LING, David

Right wing. Shoots right. 5'9", 185 lbs. Born, Halifax, N.S., January 9, 1975. Quebec's 9th choice, 179th overall, in 1993 Entry Draft.

1991-92	Charlottetown	MJrHL	30	33	42	75	270	....	....	....	....	....	....	....	....	....	....	....	....	....	....	....	....	....	....	....
	St. Michael's	OJHL-B	8	5	14	19	25	....	....	....	....	....	....	....	....	....	....	....	....	....	....	....	....	....	....	....
1992-93	Kingston	OHL	64	17	46	63	275	....	....	....	....	....	....	....	....	....	....	....	16	3	12	15	*72	....	....	....
1993-94	Kingston	OHL	61	37	40	77	*254	....	....	....	....	....	....	....	....	....	....	....	6	4	2	6	16	....	....	....
1994-95	Kingston	OHL	62	*61	74	135	136	....	....	....	....	....	....	....	....	....	....	....	6	7	8	15	12	....	....	....
1995-96	Saint John	AHL	75	24	32	56	179	....	....	....	....	....	....	....	....	....	....	....	9	0	5	5	12	....	....	....
1996-97	Saint John	AHL	5	0	2	2	19	....	....	....	....	....	....	....	....	....	....	....	....	....	....	....	....	....	....	....
	Montreal	NHL	2	0	0	0	0	0	0	0	0	0.0	0	....	....	....	....	....	....	....	....	....	....	....	....	....
	Fredericton	AHL	48	22	36	58	229	....	....	....	....	....	....	....	....	....	....	....	....	....	....	....	....	....	....	....
1997-98	Montreal	NHL	1	0	0	0	0	0	0	0	1	0.0	–1	....	....	....	....	....	....	....	....	....	....	....	....	....
	Fredericton	AHL	67	25	41	66	148	....	....	....	....	....	....	....	....	....	....	....	....	....	....	....	....	....	....	....
	Indianapolis	IHL	12	8	6	14	30	....	....	....	....	....	....	....	....	....	....	....	5	4	1	5	31	....	....	....
1998-99	Kansas City	IHL	82	30	42	72	112	....	....	....	....	....	....	....	....	....	....	....	3	1	0	1	20	....	....	....
	NHL Totals		3	0	0	0	0	0	0	0	1	0.0		....	....	....	....	....	....	....	....	....	....	....	....	....

OHL First All-Star Team (1995) • Canadian Major Junior First All-Star Team (1995) • Canadian Junior Player of the Year (1995)

Rights transferred to **Colorado** after **Quebec** franchise relocated, June 21, 1995. Traded to **Calgary** by **Colorado** with Colorado's 9th round choice (Steve Shirreffs) in 1995 Entry Draft for Calgary's 9th round choice (Chris George) in 1995 Entry Draft, July 7, 1995. Traded to **Montreal** by **Calgary** with Calgary's 6th round choice (Gordie Dwyer) in 1998 Entry Draft for Scott Fraser, October 24, 1996. Traded to **Chicago** by **Montreal** for Martin Gendron, March 14, 1998.

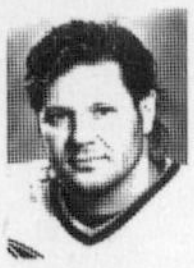

LIPUMA, Chris
(lih-POO-muh)

Defense. Shoots left. 6', 183 lbs. Born, Bridgeview, IL, March 23, 1971.

Season	Club	League	GP	G	A	Pts	PIM	PP	SH	GW	S	%	+/-	TF	F%	H	SB	Min	GP	G	A	Pts	PIM	PP	SH	GW
			Regular Season																Playoffs							
1987-88	Chicago	USAHA	19	6	16	22	31	....	....	....	....	....	....	....	....	....	....	....	....	....	....	....	....	....	....	....
1988-89	Kitchener	OJHL	2	0	0	0	17	....	....	....	....	....	....	....	....	....	....	....	....	....	....	....	....	....	....	....
	Kitchener	OHL	59	7	13	20	101	....	....	....	....	....	....	....	....	....	....	....	....	....	....	....	....	....	....	....
1989-90	Kitchener	OHL	63	11	26	37	125	....	....	....	....	....	....	....	....	....	....	....	17	1	4	5	6	....	....	....
1990-91	Kitchener	OHL	61	6	30	36	145	....	....	....	....	....	....	....	....	....	....	....	4	0	1	1	4	....	....	....
1991-92	Kitchener	OHL	61	13	59	72	115	....	....	....	....	....	....	....	....	....	....	....	14	4	9	13	34	....	....	....
1992-93	**Tampa Bay**	**NHL**	15	0	5	5	34	0	0	0	17	0.0	1	....	....	....	....	....	....	....	....	....	....	....	....	....
	Atlanta	IHL	66	4	14	18	379	....	....	....	....	....	....	....	....	....	....	....	9	1	1	2	35	....	....	....
1993-94	**Tampa Bay**	**NHL**	27	0	4	4	77	0	0	0	20	0.0	1	....	....	....	....	....	....	....	....	....	....	....	....	....
	Atlanta	IHL	42	2	10	12	254	....	....	....	....	....	....	....	....	....	....	....	11	1	1	2	28	....	....	....
1994-95	Atlanta	IHL	41	5	12	17	191	....	....	....	....	....	....	....	....	....	....	....	....	....	....	....	....	....	....	....
	Tampa Bay	**NHL**	1	0	0	0	0	0	0	0	1	0.0	2	....	....	....	....	....	....	....	....	....	....	....	....	....
	Nashville	ECHL	1	0	0	0	0	....	....	....	....	....	....	....	....	....	....	....	....	....	....	....	....	....	....	....
1995-96	**Tampa Bay**	**NHL**	21	0	0	0	13	0	0	0	8	0.0	-7	....	....	....	....	....	....	....	....	....	....	....	....	....
	Atlanta	IHL	48	5	11	16	146	....	....	....	....	....	....	....	....	....	....	....	....	....	....	....	....	....	....	....
1996-97	**San Jose**	**NHL**	8	0	0	0	22	0	0	0	4	0.0	-2	....	....	....	....	....	....	....	....	....	....	....	....	....
	Kentucky	AHL	48	6	17	23	93	....	....	....	....	....	....	....	....	....	....	....	4	0	3	3	6	....	....	....
1997-98	Orlando	IHL	13	1	4	5	63	....	....	....	....	....	....	....	....	....	....	....	....	....	....	....	....	....	....	....
	San Antonio	IHL	60	1	10	11	116	....	....	....	....	....	....	....	....	....	....	....	....	....	....	....	....	....	....	....
1998-99	Chicago	IHL	34	0	10	10	186	....	....	....	....	....	....	....	....	....	....	....	....	....	....	....	....	....	....	....
	NHL Totals		**72**	**0**	**9**	**9**	**146**	**0**	**0**	**0**	**50**	**0.0**		....	....	....	....	....	....	....	....	....	....	....	....	....

Signed as a free agent by **Tampa Bay**, June 29, 1992. Signed as a free agent by **San Jose**, August 23, 1996. Claimed on waivers by **New Jersey** from **San Jose**, March 18, 1997. Signed as a free agent by **Chicago** (IHL), September 8, 1998.

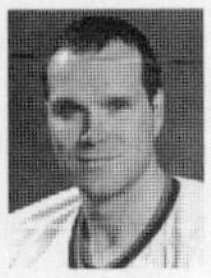

LOWRY, Dave
(LOW-ree)

Left wing. Shoots left. 6'1", 200 lbs. Born, Sudbury, Ont., February 14, 1965. Vancouver's 6th choice, 114th overall, in 1983 Entry Draft.

Season	Club	League	GP	G	A	Pts	PIM	PP	SH	GW	S	%	+/-	TF	F%	H	SB	Min	GP	G	A	Pts	PIM	PP	SH	GW
1981-82	Nepean	OMHA	60	50	64	114	46	....	....	....	....	....	....	....	....	....	....	....	....	....	....	....	....	....	....	....
1982-83	London	OHL	42	11	16	27	48	....	....	....	....	....	....	....	....	....	....	....	3	0	0	0	14	....	....	....
1983-84	London	OHL	66	29	47	76	125	....	....	....	....	....	....	....	....	....	....	....	8	6	6	12	41	....	....	....
1984-85	London	OHL	61	60	60	120	94	....	....	....	....	....	....	....	....	....	....	....	8	6	5	11	10	....	....	....
1985-86	**Vancouver**	**NHL**	73	10	8	18	143	1	0	1	66	15.2	-21	....	....	....	....	....	3	0	0	0	0	0	0	0
1986-87	**Vancouver**	**NHL**	70	8	10	18	176	0	0	1	74	10.8	-23	....	....	....	....	....	....	....	....	....	....	....	....	....
1987-88	**Vancouver**	**NHL**	22	1	3	4	38	0	0	0	14	7.1	-2	....	....	....	....	....	....	....	....	....	....	....	....	....
	Fredericton	AHL	46	18	27	45	59	....	....	....	....	....	....	....	....	....	....	....	14	7	3	10	72	....	....	....
1988-89	**St. Louis**	**NHL**	21	3	3	6	11	0	1	0	22	13.6	1	....	....	....	....	....	10	0	5	5	4	0	0	0
	Peoria	IHL	58	31	35	66	45	....	....	....	....	....	....	....	....	....	....	....	....	....	....	....	....	....	....	....
1989-90	**St. Louis**	**NHL**	78	19	6	25	75	0	2	1	98	19.4	1	....	....	....	....	....	12	2	1	3	39	0	0	0
1990-91	**St. Louis**	**NHL**	79	19	21	40	168	0	2	5	123	15.4	19	....	....	....	....	....	13	1	4	5	35	0	0	0
1991-92	**St. Louis**	**NHL**	75	7	13	20	77	0	0	1	85	8.2	-11	....	....	....	....	....	6	0	1	1	20	0	0	0
1992-93	**St. Louis**	**NHL**	58	5	8	13	101	0	0	0	59	8.5	-18	....	....	....	....	....	11	2	0	2	14	0	1	0
1993-94	**Florida**	**NHL**	80	15	22	37	64	3	0	3	122	12.3	-4	....	....	....	....	....	....	....	....	....	....	....	....	....
1994-95	**Florida**	**NHL**	45	10	10	20	25	2	0	3	70	14.3	-3	....	....	....	....	....	....	....	....	....	....	....	....	....
1995-96	**Florida**	**NHL**	63	10	14	24	36	0	0	1	83	12.0	-2	....	....	....	....	....	22	10	7	17	39	4	0	2
1996-97	**Florida**	**NHL**	77	15	14	29	51	2	0	2	96	15.6	2	....	....	....	....	....	5	0	0	0	0	0	0	0
1997-98	**Florida**	**NHL**	7	0	0	0	2	0	0	0	4	0.0	-1	....	....	....	....	....	....	....	....	....	....	....	....	....
	San Jose	**NHL**	50	4	4	8	51	0	0	1	47	8.5	0	....	....	....	....	....	6	0	0	0	18	0	0	0
1998-99	**San Jose**	**NHL**	61	6	9	15	24	2	0	0	58	10.3	-5	6	50.0	70	7	9:14	1	0	0	0	0	0	0	0
	NHL Totals		**859**	**132**	**145**	**277**	**1042**	**10**	**5**	**19**	**1021**	**12.9**		**6**	**50.0**	**70**	**7**	**9:14**	**89**	**15**	**18**	**33**	**169**	**4**	**1**	**2**

OHL First All-Star Team (1985)

Traded to **St. Louis** by **Vancouver** for Ernie Vargas, September 29, 1988. Claimed by **Florida** from **St. Louis** in Expansion Draft, June 24, 1993. Traded to **San Jose** by **Florida** with Florida's 1st round choice (later traded to Tampa Bay - Tampa Bay selected Vincent Lecavalier) for Viktor Kozlov and Florida's 5th round choice (previously acquired, Florida selected Jaroslav Spacek) in 1998 Entry Draft, November 13, 1997.

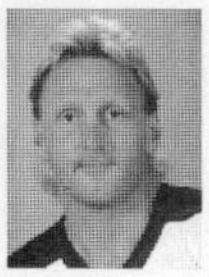

LUDWIG, Craig
(LUHD-wihg)

Defense. Shoots left. 6'3", 220 lbs. Born, Rhinelander, WI, March 15, 1961. Montreal's 5th choice, 61st overall, in 1980 Entry Draft.

Season	Club	League	GP	G	A	Pts	PIM	PP	SH	GW	S	%	+/-	TF	F%	H	SB	Min	GP	G	A	Pts	PIM	PP	SH	GW
1979-80	North Dakota	WCHA	33	1	8	9	32	....	....	....	....	....	....	....	....	....	....	....	....	....	....	....	....	....	....	....
1980-81	North Dakota	WCHA	34	4	8	12	48	....	....	....	....	....	....	....	....	....	....	....	....	....	....	....	....	....	....	....
1981-82	North Dakota	WCHA	37	4	17	21	42	....	....	....	....	....	....	....	....	....	....	....	....	....	....	....	....	....	....	....
1982-83	**Montreal**	**NHL**	80	0	25	25	59	0	0	0	81	0.0	4	....	....	....	....	....	3	0	0	0	2	0	0	0
1983-84	**Montreal**	**NHL**	80	7	18	25	52	0	0	1	116	6.0	-10	....	....	....	....	....	15	0	3	3	23	0	0	0
1984-85	**Montreal**	**NHL**	72	5	14	19	90	1	0	0	73	6.8	5	....	....	....	....	....	12	0	2	2	6	0	0	0
1985-86♦	**Montreal**	**NHL**	69	2	4	6	63	0	0	0	58	3.4	7	....	....	....	....	....	20	0	1	1	48	0	0	0
1986-87	**Montreal**	**NHL**	75	4	12	16	105	0	0	0	55	7.3	3	....	....	....	....	....	17	2	3	5	30	0	0	1
1987-88	**Montreal**	**NHL**	74	4	10	14	69	0	0	0	82	4.9	17	....	....	....	....	....	11	1	1	2	6	0	0	0
1988-89	**Montreal**	**NHL**	74	3	13	16	73	0	1	1	83	3.6	33	....	....	....	....	....	21	0	2	2	24	0	0	0
1989-90	**Montreal**	**NHL**	73	1	15	16	108	0	0	0	49	2.0	24	....	....	....	....	....	11	0	1	1	16	0	0	0
1990-91	**NY Islanders**	**NHL**	75	1	8	9	77	0	0	0	46	2.2	-24	....	....	....	....	....	....	....	....	....	....	....	....	....
1991-92	**Minnesota**	**NHL**	73	2	9	11	54	0	0	0	51	3.9	0	....	....	....	....	....	7	0	1	1	19	0	0	0
1992-93	**Minnesota**	**NHL**	78	1	10	11	153	0	0	0	66	1.5	1	....	....	....	....	....	....	....	....	....	....	....	....	....
1993-94	**Dallas**	**NHL**	84	1	13	14	123	1	0	0	65	1.5	-1	....	....	....	....	....	9	0	3	3	8	0	0	0
1994-95	**Dallas**	**NHL**	47	2	7	9	61	0	0	0	55	3.6	-6	....	....	....	....	....	4	0	1	1	2	0	0	0
1995-96	**Dallas**	**NHL**	65	1	2	3	70	0	0	0	47	2.1	-17	....	....	....	....	....	....	....	....	....	....	....	....	....
1996-97	**Dallas**	**NHL**	77	2	11	13	62	0	0	1	59	3.4	17	....	....	....	....	....	7	0	2	2	18	0	0	0
1997-98	**Dallas**	**NHL**	80	0	7	7	131	0	0	0	46	0.0	21	....	....	....	....	....	17	0	1	1	22	0	0	0
1998-99♦	**Dallas**	**NHL**	80	2	6	8	87	0	0	0	39	5.1	5	0	0.0	151	122	14:31	23	1	4	5	20	0	0	0
	NHL Totals		**1256**	**38**	**184**	**222**	**1437**	**2**	**1**	**3**	**1071**	**3.5**		**0**	**0.0**	**151**	**122**	**14:31**	**177**	**4**	**25**	**29**	**244**	**0**	**0**	**1**

WCHA Second All-Star Team (1982)

Traded to **NY Islanders** by **Montreal** for Gerald Diduck, September 4, 1990. Traded to **Minnesota** by **NY Islanders** for Tom Kurvers, June 22, 1991. Transferred to **Dallas** after **Minnesota** franchise relocated, June 9, 1993.

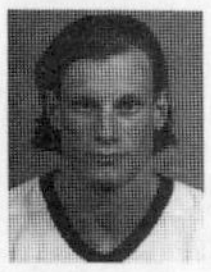

LUHNING, Warren
(LOO-nihng) **DAL.**

Right wing. Shoots right. 6'2", 185 lbs. Born, Edmonton, Alta., July 3, 1975. NY Islanders' 4th choice, 92nd overall, in 1993 Entry Draft.

Season	Club	League	GP	G	A	Pts	PIM	PP	SH	GW	S	%	+/-	TF	F%	H	SB	Min	GP	G	A	Pts	PIM	PP	SH	GW
1992-93	Calgary	AJHL	46	18	25	43	287	....	....	....	....	....	....	....	....	....	....	....	....	....	....	....	....	....	....	....
1993-94	U. of Michigan	CCHA	38	13	6	19	83	....	....	....	....	....	....	....	....	....	....	....	....	....	....	....	....	....	....	....
1994-95	U. of Michigan	CCHA	36	17	23	40	80	....	....	....	....	....	....	....	....	....	....	....	....	....	....	....	....	....	....	....
1995-96	U. of Michigan	CCHA	40	20	32	52	123	....	....	....	....	....	....	....	....	....	....	....	....	....	....	....	....	....	....	....
1996-97	U. of Michigan	CCHA	43	22	23	45	106	....	....	....	....	....	....	....	....	....	....	....	....	....	....	....	....	....	....	....
1997-98	**NY Islanders**	**NHL**	8	0	0	0	0	0	0	0	6	0.0	-4	....	....	....	....	....	....	....	....	....	....	....	....	....
	Kentucky	AHL	51	6	7	13	82	....	....	....	....	....	....	....	....	....	....	....	....	....	....	....	....	....	....	....
1998-99	**NY Islanders**	**NHL**	11	0	0	0	8	0	0	0	11	0.0	-4	0	0.0	11	2	9:17	....	....	....	....	....	....	....	....
	Lowell	AHL	56	20	20	40	67	....	....	....	....	....	....	....	....	....	....	....	3	0	3	3	16	....	....	....
	NHL Totals		**19**	**0**	**0**	**0**	**8**	**0**	**0**	**0**	**17**	**0.0**		**0**	**0.0**	**11**	**2**	**9:17**	....	....	....	....	....	....	....	....

Traded to **Dallas** by **NY Islanders** for Dallas' 3rd round choice (previously acquired, Dallas selected Mathias Tjarnqvist) in 1999 Entry Draft, June 25, 1999.

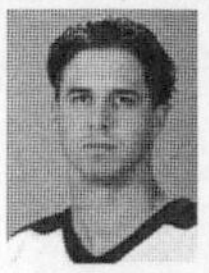

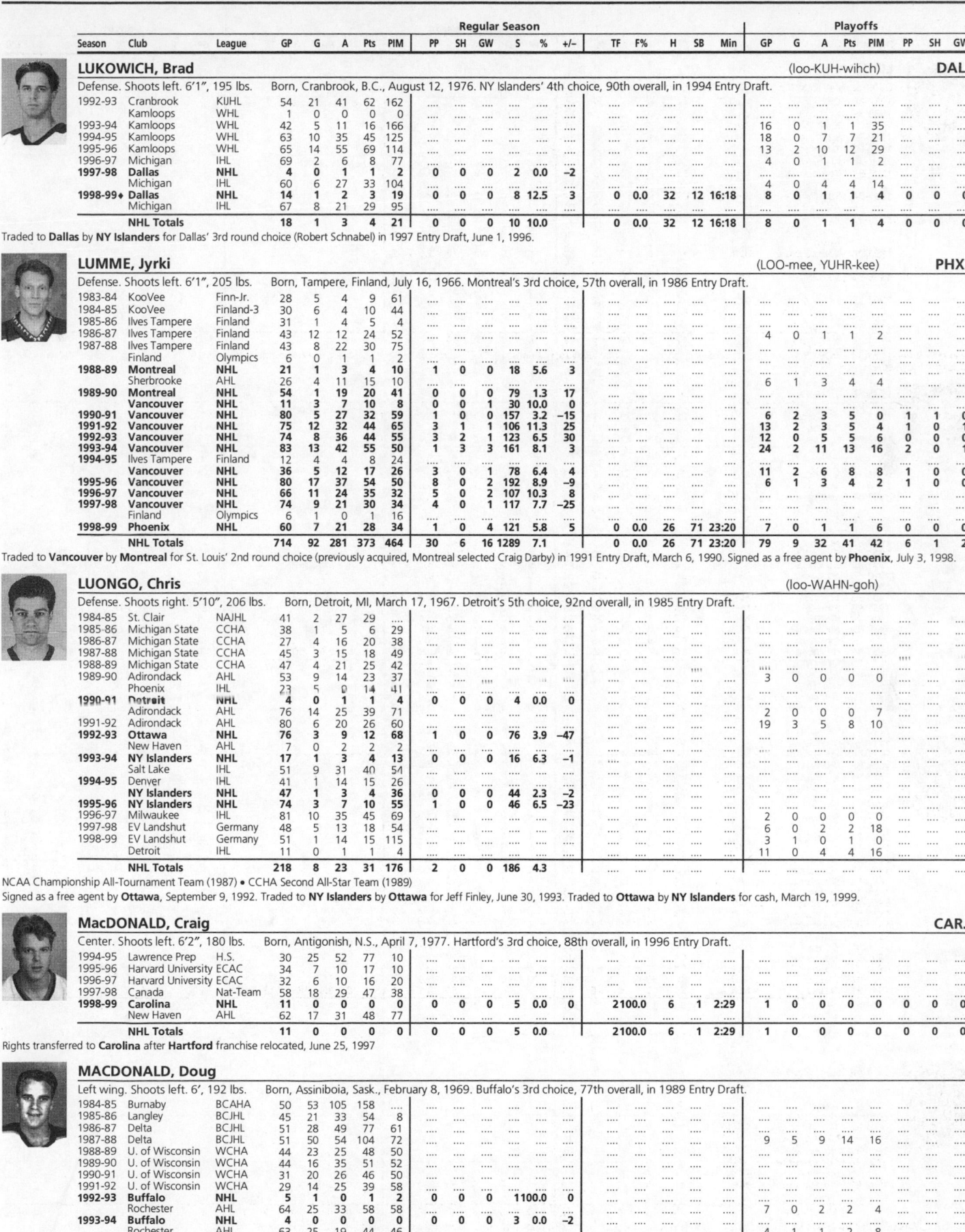

LUKOWICH, Brad
(loo-KUH-wihch) **DAL.**

Defense. Shoots left. 6'1", 195 lbs. Born, Cranbrook, B.C., August 12, 1976. NY Islanders' 4th choice, 90th overall, in 1994 Entry Draft.

			Regular Season																Playoffs							
Season	Club	League	GP	G	A	Pts	PIM	PP	SH	GW	S	%	+/-	TF	F%	H	SB	Min	GP	G	A	Pts	PIM	PP	SH	GW
1992-93	Cranbrook	KIJHL	54	21	41	62	162	....	....	....	....	....	....	....	....	....	....	....	....	....	....	....	....	....	....	....
	Kamloops	WHL	1	0	0	0	0	....	....	....	....	....	....	....	....	....	....	....	....	....	....	....	....	....	....	....
1993-94	Kamloops	WHL	42	5	11	16	166	....	....	....	....	....	....	....	....	....	....	....	16	0	1	1	35	....	....	....
1994-95	Kamloops	WHL	63	10	35	45	125	....	....	....	....	....	....	....	....	....	....	....	18	0	7	7	21	....	....	....
1995-96	Kamloops	WHL	65	14	55	69	114	....	....	....	....	....	....	....	....	....	....	....	13	2	10	12	29	....	....	....
1996-97	Michigan	IHL	69	2	6	8	77	....	....	....	....	....	....	....	....	....	....	....	4	0	1	1	2	....	....	....
1997-98	**Dallas**	**NHL**	**4**	**0**	**1**	**1**	**2**	**0**	**0**	**0**	**2**	**0.0**	**–2**	....	....	....	....	....	....	....	....	....	....	....	....	....
	Michigan	IHL	60	6	27	33	104	....	....	....	....	....	....	....	....	....	....	....	4	0	4	4	14	....	....	....
1998-99♦	**Dallas**	**NHL**	**14**	**1**	**2**	**3**	**19**	**0**	**0**	**0**	**8**	**12.5**	**3**	**0**	**0.0**	**32**	**12**	**16:18**	**8**	**0**	**1**	**1**	**4**	**0**	**0**	**0**
	Michigan	IHL	67	8	21	29	95	....	....	....	....	....	....	....	....	....	....	....	....	....	....	....	....	....	....	....
	NHL Totals		**18**	**1**	**3**	**4**	**21**	**0**	**0**	**0**	**10**	**10.0**		**0**	**0.0**	**32**	**12**	**16:18**	**8**	**0**	**1**	**1**	**4**	**0**	**0**	**0**

Traded to **Dallas** by **NY Islanders** for Dallas' 3rd round choice (Robert Schnabel) in 1997 Entry Draft, June 1, 1996.

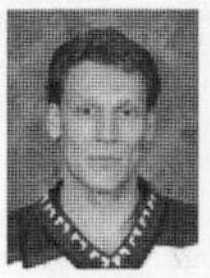

LUMME, Jyrki
(LOO-mee, YUHR-kee) **PHX.**

Defense. Shoots left. 6'1", 205 lbs. Born, Tampere, Finland, July 16, 1966. Montreal's 3rd choice, 57th overall, in 1986 Entry Draft.

			Regular Season																Playoffs							
Season	Club	League	GP	G	A	Pts	PIM	PP	SH	GW	S	%	+/-	TF	F%	H	SB	Min	GP	G	A	Pts	PIM	PP	SH	GW
1983-84	KooVee	Finn-Jr.	28	5	4	9	61	....	....	....	....	....	....	....	....	....	....	....	....	....	....	....	....	....	....	....
1984-85	KooVee	Finland-3	30	6	4	10	44	....	....	....	....	....	....	....	....	....	....	....	....	....	....	....	....	....	....	....
1985-86	Ilves Tampere	Finland	31	1	4	5	4	....	....	....	....	....	....	....	....	....	....	....	....	....	....	....	....	....	....	....
1986-87	Ilves Tampere	Finland	43	12	12	24	52	....	....	....	....	....	....	....	....	....	....	....	4	0	1	1	2	....	....	....
1987-88	Ilves Tampere	Finland	43	8	22	30	75	....	....	....	....	....	....	....	....	....	....	....	....	....	....	....	....	....	....	....
	Finland	Olympics	6	0	1	1	2	....	....	....	....	....	....	....	....	....	....	....	....	....	....	....	....	....	....	....
1988-89	**Montreal**	**NHL**	**21**	**1**	**3**	**4**	**10**	**1**	**0**	**0**	**18**	**5.6**	**3**	....	....	....	....	....	....	....	....	....	....	....	....	....
	Sherbrooke	AHL	26	4	11	15	10	....	....	....	....	....	....	....	....	....	....	....	6	1	3	4	4	....	....	....
1989-90	**Montreal**	**NHL**	**54**	**1**	**19**	**20**	**41**	**0**	**0**	**1**	**79**	**1.3**	**17**	....	....	....	....	....	....	....	....	....	....	....	....	....
	Vancouver	**NHL**	**11**	**3**	**7**	**10**	**8**	**0**	**0**	**1**	**30**	**10.0**	**0**	....	....	....	....	....	....	....	....	....	....	....	....	....
1990-91	**Vancouver**	**NHL**	**80**	**5**	**27**	**32**	**59**	**1**	**0**	**0**	**157**	**3.2**	**–15**	....	....	....	....	....	**6**	**2**	**3**	**5**	**0**	**1**	**1**	**0**
1991-92	**Vancouver**	**NHL**	**75**	**12**	**32**	**44**	**65**	**3**	**1**	**1**	**106**	**11.3**	**25**	....	....	....	....	....	**13**	**2**	**3**	**5**	**4**	**1**	**0**	**1**
1992-93	**Vancouver**	**NHL**	**74**	**8**	**36**	**44**	**55**	**3**	**2**	**1**	**123**	**6.5**	**30**	....	....	....	....	....	**12**	**0**	**5**	**5**	**6**	**0**	**0**	**0**
1993-94	**Vancouver**	**NHL**	**83**	**13**	**42**	**55**	**50**	**1**	**3**	**3**	**161**	**8.1**	**3**	....	....	....	....	....	**24**	**2**	**11**	**13**	**16**	**2**	**0**	**1**
1994-95	Ilves Tampere	Finland	12	4	4	8	24	....	....	....	....	....	....	....	....	....	....	....	....	....	....	....	....	....	....	....
	Vancouver	**NHL**	**36**	**5**	**12**	**17**	**26**	**3**	**0**	**1**	**78**	**6.4**	**4**	....	....	....	....	....	**11**	**2**	**6**	**8**	**8**	**1**	**0**	**0**
1995-96	**Vancouver**	**NHL**	**80**	**17**	**37**	**54**	**50**	**8**	**0**	**2**	**192**	**8.9**	**–9**	....	....	....	....	....	**6**	**1**	**3**	**4**	**2**	**1**	**0**	**0**
1996-97	**Vancouver**	**NHL**	**66**	**11**	**24**	**35**	**32**	**5**	**0**	**2**	**107**	**10.3**	**8**	....	....	....	....	....	....	....	....	....	....	....	....	....
1997-98	**Vancouver**	**NHL**	**74**	**9**	**21**	**30**	**34**	**4**	**0**	**1**	**117**	**7.7**	**–25**	....	....	....	....	....	....	....	....	....	....	....	....	....
	Finland	Olympics	6	1	0	1	16	....	....	....	....	....	....	....	....	....	....	....	....	....	....	....	....	....	....	....
1998-99	**Phoenix**	**NHL**	**60**	**7**	**21**	**28**	**34**	**1**	**0**	**4**	**121**	**5.8**	**5**	**0**	**0.0**	**26**	**71**	**23:20**	**7**	**0**	**1**	**1**	**6**	**0**	**0**	**0**
	NHL Totals		**714**	**92**	**281**	**373**	**464**	**30**	**6**	**16**	**1289**	**7.1**		**0**	**0.0**	**26**	**71**	**23:20**	**79**	**9**	**32**	**41**	**42**	**6**	**1**	**2**

Traded to **Vancouver** by **Montreal** for St. Louis' 2nd round choice (previously acquired, Montreal selected Craig Darby) in 1991 Entry Draft, March 6, 1990. Signed as a free agent by **Phoenix**, July 3, 1998.

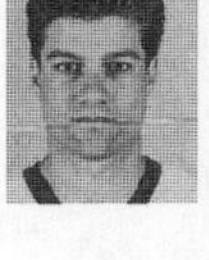

LUONGO, Chris
(loo-WAHN-goh)

Defense. Shoots right. 5'10", 206 lbs. Born, Detroit, MI, March 17, 1967. Detroit's 5th choice, 92nd overall, in 1985 Entry Draft.

			Regular Season																Playoffs							
Season	Club	League	GP	G	A	Pts	PIM	PP	SH	GW	S	%	+/-	TF	F%	H	SB	Min	GP	G	A	Pts	PIM	PP	SH	GW
1984-85	St. Clair	NAJHL	41	2	27	29	....	....	....	....	....	....	....	....	....	....	....	....	....	....	....	....	....	....	....	....
1985-86	Michigan State	CCHA	38	1	5	6	29	....	....	....	....	....	....	....	....	....	....	....	....	....	....	....	....	....	....	....
1986-87	Michigan State	CCHA	27	4	16	20	38	....	....	....	....	....	....	....	....	....	....	....	....	....	....	....	....	....	....	....
1987-88	Michigan State	CCHA	45	3	15	18	49	....	....	....	....	....	....	....	....	....	....	....	....	....	....	....	....	....	....	....
1988-89	Michigan State	CCHA	47	4	21	25	42	....	....	....	....	....	....	....	....	....	....	....	....	....	....	....	....	....	....	....
1989-90	Adirondack	AHL	53	9	14	23	37	....	....	....	....	....	....	....	....	....	....	....	3	0	0	0	0	....	....	....
	Phoenix	IHL	23	5	9	14	41	....	....	....	....	....	....	....	....	....	....	....	....	....	....	....	....	....	....	....
1990-91	**Detroit**	**NHL**	**4**	**0**	**1**	**1**	**4**	**0**	**0**	**0**	**4**	**0.0**	**0**	....	....	....	....	....	....	....	....	....	....	....	....	....
	Adirondack	AHL	76	14	25	39	71	....	....	....	....	....	....	....	....	....	....	....	2	0	0	0	7	....	....	....
1991-92	Adirondack	AHL	80	6	20	26	60	....	....	....	....	....	....	....	....	....	....	....	19	3	5	8	10	....	....	....
1992-93	**Ottawa**	**NHL**	**76**	**3**	**9**	**12**	**68**	**1**	**0**	**0**	**76**	**3.9**	**–47**	....	....	....	....	....	....	....	....	....	....	....	....	....
	New Haven	AHL	7	0	2	2	2	....	....	....	....	....	....	....	....	....	....	....	....	....	....	....	....	....	....	....
1993-94	**NY Islanders**	**NHL**	**17**	**1**	**3**	**4**	**13**	**0**	**0**	**0**	**16**	**6.3**	**–1**	....	....	....	....	....	....	....	....	....	....	....	....	....
	Salt Lake	IHL	51	9	31	40	54	....	....	....	....	....	....	....	....	....	....	....	....	....	....	....	....	....	....	....
1994-95	Denver	IHL	41	1	14	15	26	....	....	....	....	....	....	....	....	....	....	....	....	....	....	....	....	....	....	....
	NY Islanders	**NHL**	**47**	**1**	**3**	**4**	**36**	**0**	**0**	**0**	**44**	**2.3**	**–2**	....	....	....	....	....	....	....	....	....	....	....	....	....
1995-96	**NY Islanders**	**NHL**	**74**	**3**	**7**	**10**	**55**	**1**	**0**	**0**	**46**	**6.5**	**–23**	....	....	....	....	....	....	....	....	....	....	....	....	....
1996-97	Milwaukee	IHL	81	10	35	45	69	....	....	....	....	....	....	....	....	....	....	....	2	0	0	0	0	....	....	....
1997-98	EV Landshut	Germany	48	5	13	18	54	....	....	....	....	....	....	....	....	....	....	....	6	0	2	2	18	....	....	....
1998-99	EV Landshut	Germany	51	1	14	15	115	....	....	....	....	....	....	....	....	....	....	....	3	1	0	1	0	....	....	....
	Detroit	IHL	11	0	1	1	4	....	....	....	....	....	....	....	....	....	....	....	11	0	4	4	16	....	....	....
	NHL Totals		**218**	**8**	**23**	**31**	**176**	**2**	**0**	**0**	**186**	**4.3**							....	....	....	....	....	....	....	....

NCAA Championship All-Tournament Team (1987) • CCHA Second All-Star Team (1989)

Signed as a free agent by **Ottawa**, September 9, 1992. Traded to **NY Islanders** by **Ottawa** for Jeff Finley, June 30, 1993. Traded to **Ottawa** by **NY Islanders** for cash, March 19, 1999.

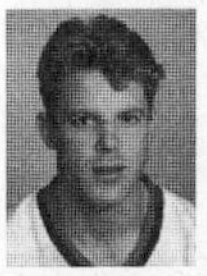

MacDONALD, Craig
CAR.

Center. Shoots left. 6'2", 180 lbs. Born, Antigonish, N.S., April 7, 1977. Hartford's 3rd choice, 88th overall, in 1996 Entry Draft.

			Regular Season																Playoffs							
Season	Club	League	GP	G	A	Pts	PIM	PP	SH	GW	S	%	+/-	TF	F%	H	SB	Min	GP	G	A	Pts	PIM	PP	SH	GW
1994-95	Lawrence Prep	H.S.	30	25	52	77	10	....	....	....	....	....	....	....	....	....	....	....	....	....	....	....	....	....	....	....
1995-96	Harvard University	ECAC	34	7	10	17	10	....	....	....	....	....	....	....	....	....	....	....	....	....	....	....	....	....	....	....
1996-97	Harvard University	ECAC	32	6	10	16	20	....	....	....	....	....	....	....	....	....	....	....	....	....	....	....	....	....	....	....
1997-98	Canada	Nat-Team	58	18	29	47	38	....	....	....	....	....	....	....	....	....	....	....	....	....	....	....	....	....	....	....
1998-99	**Carolina**	**NHL**	**11**	**0**	**0**	**0**	**0**	**0**	**0**	**0**	**5**	**0.0**	**0**	**2**	**100.0**	**6**	**1**	**2:29**	**1**	**0**	**0**	**0**	**0**	**0**	**0**	**0**
	New Haven	AHL	62	17	31	48	77	....	....	....	....	....	....	....	....	....	....	....	....	....	....	....	....	....	....	....
	NHL Totals		**11**	**0**	**0**	**0**	**0**	**0**	**0**	**0**	**5**	**0.0**		**2**	**100.0**	**6**	**1**	**2:29**	**1**	**0**	**0**	**0**	**0**	**0**	**0**	**0**

Rights transferred to **Carolina** after **Hartford** franchise relocated, June 25, 1997

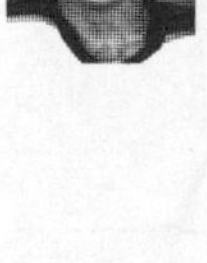

MACDONALD, Doug

Left wing. Shoots left. 6', 192 lbs. Born, Assiniboia, Sask., February 8, 1969. Buffalo's 3rd choice, 77th overall, in 1989 Entry Draft.

			Regular Season																Playoffs							
Season	Club	League	GP	G	A	Pts	PIM	PP	SH	GW	S	%	+/-	TF	F%	H	SB	Min	GP	G	A	Pts	PIM	PP	SH	GW
1984-85	Burnaby	BCAHA	50	53	105	158	....	....	....	....	....	....	....	....	....	....	....	....	....	....	....	....	....	....	....	....
1985-86	Langley	BCJHL	45	21	33	54	8	....	....	....	....	....	....	....	....	....	....	....	....	....	....	....	....	....	....	....
1986-87	Delta	BCJHL	51	28	49	77	61	....	....	....	....	....	....	....	....	....	....	....	....	....	....	....	....	....	....	....
1987-88	Delta	BCJHL	51	50	54	104	72	....	....	....	....	....	....	....	....	....	....	....	9	5	9	14	16	....	....	....
1988-89	U. of Wisconsin	WCHA	44	23	25	48	50	....	....	....	....	....	....	....	....	....	....	....	....	....	....	....	....	....	....	....
1989-90	U. of Wisconsin	WCHA	44	16	35	51	52	....	....	....	....	....	....	....	....	....	....	....	....	....	....	....	....	....	....	....
1990-91	U. of Wisconsin	WCHA	31	20	26	46	50	....	....	....	....	....	....	....	....	....	....	....	....	....	....	....	....	....	....	....
1991-92	U. of Wisconsin	WCHA	29	14	25	39	58	....	....	....	....	....	....	....	....	....	....	....	....	....	....	....	....	....	....	....
1992-93	**Buffalo**	**NHL**	**5**	**1**	**0**	**1**	**2**	**0**	**0**	**0**	**1**	**100.0**	**0**	....	....	....	....	....	....	....	....	....	....	....	....	....
	Rochester	AHL	64	25	33	58	58	....	....	....	....	....	....	....	....	....	....	....	7	0	2	2	4	....	....	....
1993-94	**Buffalo**	**NHL**	**4**	**0**	**0**	**0**	**0**	**0**	**0**	**0**	**3**	**0.0**	**–2**	....	....	....	....	....	....	....	....	....	....	....	....	....
	Rochester	AHL	63	25	19	44	46	....	....	....	....	....	....	....	....	....	....	....	4	1	1	2	8	....	....	....
1994-95	Rochester	AHL	58	21	25	46	73	....	....	....	....	....	....	....	....	....	....	....	5	0	1	1	0	....	....	....
	Buffalo	**NHL**	**2**	**0**	**0**	**0**	**0**	**0**	**0**	**0**	**0**	**0.0**	**–1**	....	....	....	....	....	....	....	....	....	....	....	....	....
1995-96	Cincinnati	IHL	71	19	40	59	66	....	....	....	....	....	....	....	....	....	....	....	15	1	3	4	14	....	....	....

			Regular Season																Playoffs							
Season	Club	League	GP	G	A	Pts	PIM	PP	SH	GW	S	%	+/-	TF	F%	H	SB	Min	GP	G	A	Pts	PIM	PP	SH	GW
1996-97	Cincinnati	IHL	65	20	34	54	36	....	....	....	....	....	....	....	....	....	....	....	3	0	0	0	0	....	....	....
1997-98	Cincinnati	IHL	70	17	19	36	64	....	....	....	....	....	....	....	....	....	....	....	4	0	4	4	0	....	....	....
1998-99	Cincinnati	IHL	33	7	11	18	22	....	....	....	....	....	....	....	....	....	....	....	....	....	....	....	....	....	....	....
	NHL Totals		**11**	**1**	**0**	**1**	**2**	**0**	**0**	**0**	**4**	**25.0**		....	....	....	....	....	....	....	....	....	....	....	....	....

Signed as a free agent by **Cincinnati** (IHL), July 26, 1998.

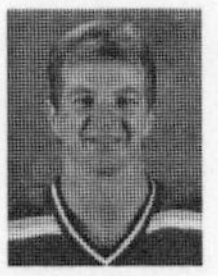

MacINNIS, Al — ST.L.

Defense. Shoots right. 6'2", 209 lbs. Born, Inverness, N.S., July 11, 1963. Calgary's 1st choice, 15th overall, in 1981 Entry Draft.

			Regular Season																Playoffs							
Season	Club	League	GP	G	A	Pts	PIM	PP	SH	GW	S	%	+/-	TF	F%	H	SB	Min	GP	G	A	Pts	PIM	PP	SH	GW
1979-80	Regina	SJHL	59	20	28	48	110	....	....	....	....	....	....	....	....	....	....	....	....	....	....	....	....	....	....	....
1980-81	Kitchener	OHA	47	11	28	39	59	....	....	....	....	....	....	....	....	....	....	....	18	4	12	16	20	....	....	....
1981-82	Kitchener	OHL	59	25	50	75	145	....	....	....	....	....	....	....	....	....	....	....	15	5	10	15	44	....	....	....
	Calgary	**NHL**	**2**	**0**	**0**	**0**	**0**	**0**	**0**	**0**	**2**	**0.0**	**0**	....	....	....	....	....	....	....	....	....	....	....	....	....
1982-83	Kitchener	OHL	51	38	46	84	67	....	....	....	....	....	....	....	....	....	....	....	8	3	8	11	9	....	....	....
	Calgary	**NHL**	**14**	**1**	**3**	**4**	**9**	**0**	**0**	**0**	**7**	**14.3**	**0**	....	....	....	....	....	....	....	....	....	....	....	....	....
1983-84	**Calgary**	**NHL**	**51**	**11**	**34**	**45**	**42**	**7**	**0**	**2**	**160**	**6.9**	**0**	....	....	....	....	....	**11**	**2**	**12**	**14**	**13**	**2**	**0**	**1**
	Colorado	CHL	19	5	14	19	22	....	....	....	....	....	....	....	....	....	....	....	....	....	....	....	....	....	....	....
1984-85	**Calgary**	**NHL**	**67**	**14**	**52**	**66**	**75**	**8**	**0**	**0**	**259**	**5.4**	**7**	....	....	....	....	....	**4**	**1**	**2**	**3**	**8**	**1**	**0**	**0**
1985-86	**Calgary**	**NHL**	**77**	**11**	**57**	**68**	**76**	**4**	**0**	**0**	**241**	**4.6**	**38**	....	....	....	....	....	**21**	**4**	***15**	**19**	**30**	**2**	**0**	**0**
1986-87	**Calgary**	**NHL**	**79**	**20**	**56**	**76**	**97**	**7**	**0**	**2**	**262**	**7.6**	**20**	....	....	....	....	....	**4**	**1**	**0**	**1**	**0**	**1**	**0**	**0**
1987-88	**Calgary**	**NHL**	**80**	**25**	**58**	**83**	**114**	**7**	**2**	**2**	**245**	**10.2**	**13**	....	....	....	....	....	**7**	**3**	**6**	**9**	**18**	**2**	**0**	**0**
1988-89◆	**Calgary**	**NHL**	**79**	**16**	**58**	**74**	**126**	**8**	**0**	**3**	**277**	**5.8**	**38**	....	....	....	....	....	**22**	**7**	***24**	***31**	**46**	**5**	**0**	**4**
1989-90	**Calgary**	**NHL**	**79**	**28**	**62**	**90**	**82**	**14**	**1**	**3**	**304**	**9.2**	**20**	....	....	....	....	....	**6**	**2**	**3**	**5**	**8**	**1**	**0**	**0**
1990-91	**Calgary**	**NHL**	**78**	**28**	**75**	**103**	**90**	**17**	**0**	**1**	**305**	**9.2**	**42**	....	....	....	....	....	**7**	**2**	**3**	**5**	**8**	**2**	**0**	**0**
1991-92	**Calgary**	**NHL**	**72**	**20**	**57**	**77**	**83**	**11**	**0**	**0**	**304**	**6.6**	**13**	....	....	....	....	....	....	....	....	....	....	....	....	....
1992-93	**Calgary**	**NHL**	**50**	**11**	**43**	**54**	**61**	**7**	**0**	**4**	**201**	**5.5**	**15**	....	....	....	....	....	**6**	**1**	**6**	**7**	**10**	**1**	**0**	**0**
1993-94	**Calgary**	**NHL**	**75**	**28**	**54**	**82**	**95**	**12**	**1**	**5**	**324**	**8.6**	**35**	....	....	....	....	....	**7**	**2**	**6**	**8**	**12**	**1**	**0**	**0**
1994-95	**St. Louis**	**NHL**	**32**	**8**	**20**	**28**	**43**	**2**	**0**	**0**	**110**	**7.3**	**19**	....	....	....	....	....	**7**	**1**	**5**	**6**	**10**	**0**	**0**	**0**
1995-96	**St. Louis**	**NHL**	**82**	**17**	**44**	**61**	**88**	**9**	**1**	**1**	**317**	**5.4**	**5**	....	....	....	....	....	**13**	**3**	**4**	**7**	**20**	**1**	**0**	**0**
1996-97	**St. Louis**	**NHL**	**72**	**13**	**30**	**43**	**65**	**6**	**1**	**1**	**296**	**4.4**	**2**	....	....	....	....	....	**6**	**1**	**2**	**3**	**4**	**1**	**0**	**0**
1997-98	**St. Louis**	**NHL**	**71**	**19**	**30**	**49**	**80**	**9**	**1**	**2**	**227**	**8.4**	**6**	....	....	....	....	....	**8**	**2**	**6**	**8**	**12**	**1**	**0**	**0**
	Canada	Olympics	6	2	0	2	2	....	....	....	....	....	....	....	....	....	....	....	....	....	....	....	....	....	....	....
1998-99	**St. Louis**	**NHL**	**82**	**20**	**42**	**62**	**70**	**11**	**1**	**2**	**314**	**6.4**	**33**	**0**	**0.0**	**56**	**128**	**29:07**	**13**	**4**	**8**	**12**	**20**	**2**	**0**	**0**
	NHL Totals		**1142**	**290**	**775**	**1065**	**1296**	**139**	**8**	**28**	**4155**	**7.0**		**0**	**0.0**	**56**	**128**	**29:07**	**142**	**36**	**102**	**138**	**219**	**23**	**0**	**5**

OHL First All-Star Team (1982, 1983) • NHL Second All-Star Team (1987, 1989, 1994) • Won Conn Smythe Trophy (1989) • NHL First All-Star Team (1990, 1991, 1999) • Won James Norris Memorial Trophy (1999)

Played in NHL All-Star Game (1985, 1988, 1990, 1991, 1992, 1994, 1996, 1997, 1998, 1999)

Traded to **St. Louis** by **Calgary** with Calgary's 4th round choice (Didier Tremblay) in 1997 Entry Draft for Phil Housley, St. Louis' 2nd round choice (Steve Begin) in 1996 Entry Draft and 2nd round choice (John Tripp) in 1997 Entry Draft, July 4, 1994.

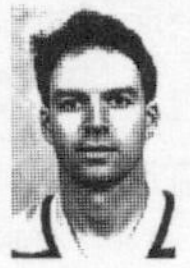

MACIVER, Norm — (mac-IGH-ver)

Defense. Shoots left. 5'11", 180 lbs. Born, Thunder Bay, Ont., September 8, 1964.

			Regular Season																Playoffs							
Season	Club	League	GP	G	A	Pts	PIM	PP	SH	GW	S	%	+/-	TF	F%	H	SB	Min	GP	G	A	Pts	PIM	PP	SH	GW
1982-83	U. Minn-Duluth	WCHA	45	1	26	27	40	....	....	....	....	....	....	....	....	....	....	....	6	0	2	2	2	....	....	....
1983-84	U. Minn-Duluth	WCHA	31	13	28	41	28	....	....	....	....	....	....	....	....	....	....	....	8	1	10	11	8	....	....	....
1984-85	U. Minn-Duluth	WCHA	47	14	47	61	63	....	....	....	....	....	....	....	....	....	....	....	10	3	3	6	6	....	....	....
1985-86	U. Minn-Duluth	WCHA	42	11	51	62	36	....	....	....	....	....	....	....	....	....	....	....	4	2	3	5	2	....	....	....
1986-87	**NY Rangers**	**NHL**	**3**	**0**	**1**	**1**	**0**	**0**	**0**	**0**	**2**	**0.0**	**–5**	....	....	....	....	....	....	....	....	....	....	....	....	....
	New Haven	AHL	71	6	30	36	73	....	....	....	....	....	....	....	....	....	....	....	7	0	0	0	9	....	....	....
1987-88	**NY Rangers**	**NHL**	**37**	**9**	**15**	**24**	**14**	**1**	**0**	**2**	**65**	**13.8**	**10**	....	....	....	....	....	....	....	....	....	....	....	....	....
	Colorado	IHL	27	6	20	26	22	....	....	....	....	....	....	....	....	....	....	....	....	....	....	....	....	....	....	....
1988-89	**NY Rangers**	**NHL**	**26**	**0**	**10**	**10**	**14**	**0**	**0**	**0**	**36**	**0.0**	**–3**	....	....	....	....	....	....	....	....	....	....	....	....	....
	Hartford	**NHL**	**37**	**1**	**22**	**23**	**24**	**1**	**0**	**0**	**51**	**2.0**	**0**	....	....	....	....	....	**1**	**0**	**0**	**0**	**2**	**0**	**0**	**0**
1989-90	Binghamton	AHL	2	0	0	0	0	....	....	....	....	....	....	....	....	....	....	....	....	....	....	....	....	....	....	....
	Edmonton	**NHL**	**1**	**0**	**0**	**0**	**0**	**0**	**0**	**0**	**0**	**0.0**	**–1**	....	....	....	....	....	....	....	....	....	....	....	....	....
	Cape Breton	AHL	68	13	37	50	55	....	....	....	....	....	....	....	....	....	....	....	6	0	7	7	10	....	....	....
1990-91	**Edmonton**	**NHL**	**21**	**2**	**5**	**7**	**14**	**1**	**0**	**0**	**25**	**8.0**	**1**	....	....	....	....	....	**18**	**0**	**4**	**4**	**8**	**0**	**0**	**0**
	Cape Breton	AHL	56	13	46	59	60	....	....	....	....	....	....	....	....	....	....	....	....	....	....	....	....	....	....	....
1991-92	**Edmonton**	**NHL**	**57**	**6**	**34**	**40**	**38**	**2**	**0**	**3**	**69**	**8.7**	**20**	....	....	....	....	....	**13**	**1**	**2**	**3**	**10**	**0**	**0**	**0**
1992-93	**Ottawa**	**NHL**	**80**	**17**	**46**	**63**	**84**	**7**	**1**	**2**	**184**	**9.2**	**–46**	....	....	....	....	....	....	....	....	....	....	....	....	....
1993-94	**Ottawa**	**NHL**	**53**	**3**	**20**	**23**	**26**	**0**	**0**	**0**	**88**	**3.4**	**–26**	....	....	....	....	....	....	....	....	....	....	....	....	....
1994-95	**Ottawa**	**NHL**	**28**	**4**	**7**	**11**	**10**	**0**	**0**	**0**	**30**	**13.3**	**–9**	....	....	....	....	....	....	....	....	....	....	....	....	....
	Pittsburgh	**NHL**	**13**	**0**	**9**	**9**	**6**	**2**	**0**	**0**	**20**	**0.0**	**7**	....	....	....	....	....	**12**	**1**	**4**	**5**	**8**	**0**	**0**	**1**
1995-96	**Pittsburgh**	**NHL**	**32**	**2**	**21**	**23**	**32**	**1**	**0**	**0**	**30**	**6.7**	**12**	....	....	....	....	....	....	....	....	....	....	....	....	....
	Winnipeg	**NHL**	**39**	**5**	**25**	**30**	**26**	**2**	**0**	**0**	**49**	**10.2**	**–6**	....	....	....	....	....	**6**	**1**	**0**	**1**	**2**	**0**	**0**	**0**
1996-97	**Phoenix**	**NHL**	**32**	**4**	**9**	**13**	**24**	**1**	**0**	**1**	**40**	**10.0**	**–11**	....	....	....	....	....	....	....	....	....	....	....	....	....
1997-98	**Phoenix**	**NHL**	**41**	**2**	**6**	**8**	**38**	**0**	**1**	**0**	**37**	**5.4**	**–11**	....	....	....	....	....	**6**	**0**	**1**	**1**	**2**	**0**	**0**	**0**
1998-99	Houston	IHL	49	6	25	31	48	....	....	....	....	....	....	....	....	....	....	....	10	0	5	5	14	....	....	....
	NHL Totals		**500**	**55**	**230**	**285**	**350**	**18**	**2**	**8**	**726**	**7.6**							**56**	**3**	**11**	**14**	**32**	**0**	**0**	**1**

WCHA First All-Star Team (1985, 1986) • NCAA West First All-American Team (1985, 1986) • AHL First All-Star Team (1991) • Won Eddie Shore Award (Top Defenseman - AHL) (1991)

Signed as a free agent by **NY Rangers**, September 8, 1986. Traded to **Hartford** by **NY Rangers** with Brian Lawton and Don Maloney for Carey Wilson and Hartford's 5th round choice (Lubos Rob) in 1990 Entry Draft, December 26, 1988. Traded to **Edmonton** by **Hartford** for Jim Ennis, October 10, 1989. Claimed by **Ottawa** from **Edmonton** in NHL Waiver Draft, October 4, 1992. Traded to **Pittsburgh** by **Ottawa** with Troy Murray for Martin Straka, April 7, 1995. Traded to **Winnipeg** by **Pittsburgh** for Neil Wilkinson, December 28, 1995. Transferred to **Phoenix** after **Winnipeg** franchise relocated, July 1, 1996.

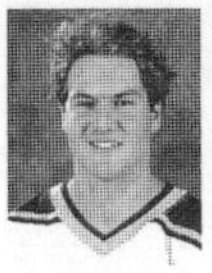

MacLEAN, Donald — L.A.

Center. Shoots left. 6'2", 199 lbs. Born, Sydney, N.S., January 14, 1977. Los Angeles' 2nd choice, 33rd overall, in 1995 Entry Draft.

			Regular Season																Playoffs							
Season	Club	League	GP	G	A	Pts	PIM	PP	SH	GW	S	%	+/-	TF	F%	H	SB	Min	GP	G	A	Pts	PIM	PP	SH	GW
1992-93	Halifax	NSAHA	27	15	25	40	34	....	....	....	....	....	....	....	....	....	....	....	....	....	....	....	....	....	....	....
1993-94	Halifax	NSAHA	25	35	35	70	151	....	....	....	....	....	....	....	....	....	....	....	....	....	....	....	....	....	....	....
1994-95	Beauport	QMJHL	64	15	27	42	37	....	....	....	....	....	....	....	....	....	....	....	17	4	4	8	6	....	....	....
1995-96	Beauport	QMJHL	1	0	1	1	0	....	....	....	....	....	....	....	....	....	....	....	....	....	....	....	....	....	....	....
	Laval	QMJHL	21	17	11	28	29	....	....	....	....	....	....	....	....	....	....	....	....	....	....	....	....	....	....	....
	Hull	QMJHL	39	26	34	60	44	....	....	....	....	....	....	....	....	....	....	....	17	6	7	13	14	....	....	....
1996-97	Hull	QMJHL	69	34	47	81	67	....	....	....	....	....	....	....	....	....	....	....	14	11	10	21	39	....	....	....
1997-98	**Los Angeles**	**NHL**	**22**	**5**	**2**	**7**	**4**	**2**	**0**	**0**	**25**	**20.0**	**–1**	....	....	....	....	....	....	....	....	....	....	....	....	....
	Fredericton	AHL	39	9	5	14	32	....	....	....	....	....	....	....	....	....	....	....	4	1	3	4	2	....	....	....
1998-99	Springfield	AHL	41	5	14	19	31	....	....	....	....	....	....	....	....	....	....	....	....	....	....	....	....	....	....	....
	Grand Rapids	IHL	28	6	13	19	8	....	....	....	....	....	....	....	....	....	....	....	....	....	....	....	....	....	....	....
	NHL Totals		**22**	**5**	**2**	**7**	**4**	**2**	**0**	**0**	**25**	**20.0**														

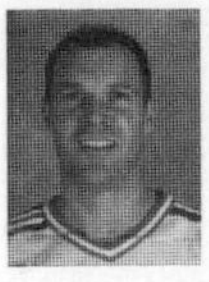

MacLEAN, John — NYR

Right wing. Shoots right. 6', 200 lbs. Born, Oshawa, Ont., November 20, 1964. New Jersey's 1st choice, 6th overall, in 1983 Entry Draft.

			Regular Season																Playoffs							
Season	Club	League	GP	G	A	Pts	PIM	PP	SH	GW	S	%	+/-	TF	F%	H	SB	Min	GP	G	A	Pts	PIM	PP	SH	GW
1980-81	Oshawa	OJHL	41	35	35	70	151	....	....	....	....	....	....	....	....	....	....	....	....	....	....	....	....	....	....	....
1981-82	Oshawa	OHL	67	17	22	39	197	....	....	....	....	....	....	....	....	....	....	....	12	3	6	9	63	....	....	....
1982-83	Oshawa	OHL	66	47	51	98	138	....	....	....	....	....	....	....	....	....	....	....	17	*18	20	*38	35	....	....	....
1983-84	Oshawa	OHL	30	23	36	59	58	....	....	....	....	....	....	....	....	....	....	....	7	2	5	7	18	....	....	....
	New Jersey	**NHL**	**23**	**1**	**0**	**1**	**10**	**0**	**0**	**0**	**22**	**4.5**	**–7**	....	....	....	....	....	....	....	....	....	....	....	....	....
1984-85	**New Jersey**	**NHL**	**61**	**13**	**20**	**33**	**44**	**1**	**0**	**4**	**92**	**14.1**	**–11**	....	....	....	....	....	....	....	....	....	....	....	....	....
1985-86	**New Jersey**	**NHL**	**74**	**21**	**36**	**57**	**112**	**1**	**0**	**4**	**139**	**15.1**	**–3**	....	....	....	....	....	....	....	....	....	....	....	....	....
1986-87	**New Jersey**	**NHL**	**80**	**31**	**36**	**67**	**120**	**9**	**0**	**4**	**197**	**15.7**	**–23**	....	....	....	....	....	....	....	....	....	....	....	....	....
1987-88	**New Jersey**	**NHL**	**76**	**23**	**16**	**39**	**147**	**12**	**0**	**4**	**204**	**11.3**	**–10**	....	....	....	....	....	**20**	**7**	**11**	**18**	**60**	**2**	**0**	**2**

Season	Club	League	GP	G	A	Pts	PIM	PP	SH	GW	S	%	+/-	TF	F%	H	SB	Min	GP	G	A	Pts	PIM	PP	SH	GW
											Regular Season											**Playoffs**				
1988-89	New Jersey	NHL	74	42	45	87	122	14	0	4	266	15.8	26	....	....	....		....								
1989-90	New Jersey	NHL	80	41	38	79	80	10	3	11	322	12.7	17						6	4	1	5	12	2	1	0
1990-91	New Jersey	NHL	78	45	33	78	150	19	2	7	292	15.4	8						7	5	3	8	20	1	0	0
1991-92			DID NOT PLAY – INJURED																							
1992-93	New Jersey	NHL	80	24	24	48	102	7	1	3	195	12.3	–6						5	0	1	1	10	0	0	0
1993-94	New Jersey	NHL	80	37	33	70	95	8	0	4	277	13.4	30						20	6	10	16	22	2	0	1
1994-95♦	New Jersey	NHL	46	17	12	29	32	2	1	0	139	12.2	13						20	5	13	18	14	2	0	1
1995-96	New Jersey	NHL	76	20	28	48	91	3	3	3	237	8.4	3						....							
1996-97	New Jersey	NHL	80	29	25	54	49	5	0	6	254	11.4	11						10	4	5	9	4	2	1	1
1997-98	New Jersey	NHL	26	3	8	11	14	1	0	1	74	4.1	–6													
	San Jose	NHL	51	13	19	32	28	5	0	2	139	9.4	0						6	2	3	5	4	1	0	0
1998-99	NY Rangers	NHL	82	28	27	55	46	11	1	2	231	12.1	5	20	35.0	120	30	20:43								
	NHL Totals		1067	388	400	788	1242	108	11	59	3080	12.6		20	35.0	120	30	20:43	94	33	47	80	146	12	2	4

Memorial Cup All-Star Team (1983)
Played in NHL All-Star Game (1989, 1991)
• Missed entire 1991-92 season with torn ligament in right knee. Traded to **San Jose** by **New Jersey** with Ken Sutton for Doug Bodger and Dody Wood, December 7, 1997. Signed as a free agent by **NY Rangers**, July 22, 1998.

MACOUN, Jamie
(muh-KOW-uhn)

Defense. Shoots left. 6'2", 200 lbs.   Born, Newmarket, Ont., August 17, 1961.

Season	Club	League	GP	G	A	Pts	PIM	PP	SH	GW	S	%	+/-	TF	F%	H	SB	Min	GP	G	A	Pts	PIM	PP	SH	GW
1978-79	Newmarket	OJHL	49	9	14	23	33																			
1979-80	Newmarket	OJHL	13	1	11	12	26																			
	Aurora	OJHL	30	9	19	28	30																			
1980-81	Ohio State	CCHA	38	9	20	29	83																			
1981-82	Ohio State	CCHA	25	2	18	20	89																			
1982-83	Ohio State	CCHA	19	6	21	27	54																			
	Calgary	NHL	22	1	4	5	25	0	0	0	18	5.6	3						9	0	2	2	8	0	0	0
1983-84	Calgary	NHL	72	9	23	32	97	0	1	0	165	5.5	3						11	1	0	1	0	1	0	0
1984-85	Calgary	NHL	70	9	30	39	67	0	0	2	129	7.0	44						4	1	0	1	4	0	0	0
1985-86	Calgary	NHL	77	11	21	32	81	0	2	1	133	8.3	14						22	1	6	7	23	0	0	0
1986-87	Calgary	NHL	79	7	33	40	111	1	0	0	137	5.1	33						3	0	1	1	8	0	0	0
1987-88	Calgary	NHL	DID NOT PLAY – INJURED																							
1988-89♦	Calgary	NHL	72	8	19	27	76	0	0	2	89	9.0	40						22	3	6	9	30	0	0	1
1989-90	Calgary	NHL	78	8	27	35	70	1	0	1	120	6.7	34						6	0	3	3	10	0	0	0
1990-91	Calgary	NHL	79	7	15	22	84	1	1	0	117	6.0	29						7	0	1	1	4	0	0	0
1991-92	Calgary	NHL	37	2	12	14	53	1	0	0	58	3.4	10													
	Toronto	NHL	39	3	13	16	18	2	0	0	71	4.2	0													
1992-93	Toronto	NHL	77	4	15	19	55	2	0	1	114	3.5	3						21	0	6	6	36	0	0	0
1993-94	Toronto	NHL	82	3	27	30	115	1	0	1	122	2.5	–5						18	1	1	2	12	0	0	0
1994-95	Toronto	NHL	46	2	8	10	75	1	0	0	84	2.4	–6						7	1	2	3	8	0	0	0
1995-96	Toronto	NHL	82	0	8	8	87	0	0	0	74	0.0	1						6	0	2	2	8	0	0	0
1996-97	Toronto	NHL	73	1	10	11	93	0	0	0	64	1.6	–14													
1997-98	Toronto	NHL	67	0	7	7	63	0	0	0	67	0.0	–17													
	♦ Detroit	NHL	7	0	0	0	2	0	0	0	11	0.0	0						22	2	2	4	18	0	0	2
1998-99	Detroit	NHL	69	1	10	11	36	0	0	0	62	1.6	–1	1	0.0	70	85	17:30	1	0	0	0	0	0	0	0
	NHL Totals		1128	76	282	358	1208	10	4	9	1635	4.6		1	0.0	70	85	17:30	159	10	32	42	169	1	0	3

NHL All-Rookie Team (1984)
Signed as a free agent by **Calgary**, January 30, 1983. • Missed entire 1987-88 season recovering from nerve damage to arm after automobile accident, May, 1987. Traded to **Toronto** by **Calgary** with Doug Gilmour, Ric Natress, Kent Manderville and Rick Wamsley for Gary Leeman, Alexander Godynyuk, Jeff Reese, Michel Petit and Craig Berube, January 2, 1992. Traded to **Detroit** by **Toronto** for Tampa Bay's 4th round choice (previously acquired, Toronto selected Alexei Ponikarovsky) in 1998 Entry Draft, March 24, 1998.

MADDEN, John
N.J.

Left Wing. Shoots left. 5'11", 195 lbs.   Born, Barrie, Ont., May 4, 1975.

Season	Club	League	GP	G	A	Pts	PIM	PP	SH	GW	S	%	+/-	TF	F%	H	SB	Min	GP	G	A	Pts	PIM	PP	SH	GW
1993-94	U. of Michigan	CCHA	36	6	11	17	14																			
1994-95	U. of Michigan	CCHA	39	21	22	43	8																			
1995-96	U. of Michigan	CCHA	43	27	30	57	45																			
1996-97	U. of Michigan	CCHA	42	26	37	63	56																			
1997-98	Albany	AHL	74	20	36	56	40												13	3	13	16	14			
1998-99	New Jersey	NHL	4	0	1	1	0	0	0	0	4	0.0	–2	0	0.0	3	1	9:13								
	Albany	AHL	75	38	60	98	44												5	2	2	4	6			
	NHL Totals		4	0	1	1	0	0	0	0	4	0.0		0	0.0	3	1	9:13								

CCHA First All-Star Team (1997) • NCAA West First All-American Team (1997)
Signed as a free agent by **New Jersey**, June 26, 1997.

MAIR, Adam
(MAIR)   TOR.

Center. Shoots right. 6'1", 195 lbs.   Born, Hamilton, Ont., February 15, 1979. Toronto's 2nd choice, 84th overall, in 1997 Entry Draft.

Season	Club	League	GP	G	A	Pts	PIM	PP	SH	GW	S	%	+/-	TF	F%	H	SB	Min	GP	G	A	Pts	PIM	PP	SH	GW
1994-95	Ohsweken	OJHL-B	39	21	23	44	91																			
1995-96	Owen Sound	OHL	62	12	15	27	63												6	0	0	0	2			
1996-97	Owen Sound	OHL	65	16	35	51	113												4	1	0	1	2			
1997-98	Owen Sound	OHL	56	25	27	52	179												11	6	3	9	31			
1998-99	Owen Sound	OHL	43	23	41	64	109												16	10	10	20	*47			
	Toronto	NHL	....																	5	1	0	1	14	0	0	0
	St. John's	AHL	....																	3	1	0	1	6			
	NHL Totals		....																	5	1	0	1	14	0	0	0

MAJOR, Mark

Left wing. Shoots left. 6'3", 223 lbs.   Born, Toronto, Ont., March 20, 1970. Pittsburgh's 2nd choice, 25th overall, in 1988 Entry Draft.

Season	Club	League	GP	G	A	Pts	PIM	PP	SH	GW	S	%	+/-	TF	F%	H	SB	Min	GP	G	A	Pts	PIM	PP	SH	GW
1986-87	Don Mills	MTHL	36	12	14	26	81																			
1987-88	North Bay	OHL	57	16	17	33	272												4	0	2	2	8			
1988-89	North Bay	OHL	11	3	2	5	58																			
	Kingston	OHL	53	22	29	51	193																			
1989-90	Kingston	OHL	62	29	32	61	168												6	3	3	6	12			
1990-91	Muskegon	IHL	60	8	10	18	160												5	0	0	0	0			
1991-92	Muskegon	IHL	80	13	18	31	302												12	1	3	4	29			
1992-93	Cleveland	IHL	82	13	15	28	155												3	0	0	0	0			
1993-94	Providence	AHL	61	17	9	26	176																			
1994-95	Detroit	IHL	78	17	19	36	229												5	0	1	1	23			
1995-96	Adirondack	AHL	78	10	19	29	234												3	0	0	0	21			
1996-97	Detroit	NHL	2	0	0	0	5	0	0	0	0	0.0	0													
	Adirondack	AHL	78	17	18	35	213												4	0	0	0	13			
1997-98	Portland	AHL	79	13	2	15	355												10	2	1	3	52			
1998-99	Portland	AHL	66	5	4	9	250																			
	NHL Totals		2	0	0	0	5	0	0	0	0	0.0														

Signed as a free agent by **Boston**, July 22, 1993. Signed as a free agent by **Detroit**, June 26, 1995. Signed as a free agent by **Washington**, August 20, 1997.

			Regular Season																Playoffs						
Season	Club	League	GP	G	A	Pts	PIM	PP	SH	GW	S	%	+/-	TF	F%	H	SB	Min	GP	G	A	Pts	PIM	PP	SH	GW

MALAKHOV, Vladimir (mah-LAH-kahf) **MTL.**

Defense. Shoots left. 6'4", 227 lbs.   Born, Ekaterinburg, USSR, August 30, 1968. NY Islanders' 12th choice, 191st overall, in 1989 Entry Draft.

Season	Club	League	GP	G	A	Pts	PIM	PP	SH	GW	S	%	+/-	TF	F%	H	SB	Min	GP	G	A	Pts	PIM	PP	SH	GW
1986-87	SKA Spartak	USSR	22	0	1	1	12	....	....	....	....	....	....						....	....	....	....	....	....	....	....
1987-88	SKA Spartak	USSR	28	2	2	4	26	....	....	....	....	....	....						....	....	....	....	....	....	....	....
1988-89	CSKA Moscow	USSR	34	6	2	8	16	....	....	....	....	....	....						....	....	....	....	....	....	....	....
1989-90	CSKA Moscow	USSR	48	2	10	12	34	....	....	....	....	....	....						....	....	....	....	....	....	....	....
1990-91	CSKA Moscow	USSR	46	5	13	18	22	....	....	....	....	....	....						....	....	....	....	....	....	....	....
1991-92	CSKA Moscow	CIS	40	1	9	10	12	....	....	....	....	....	....						....	....	....	....	....	....	....	....
	Russia	Olympics	8	3	0	3	4	....	....	....	....	....	....						....	....	....	....	....	....	....	....
1992-93	**NY Islanders**	**NHL**	64	14	38	52	59	7	0	0	178	7.9	14						17	3	6	9	12	0	0	0
	Capital District	AHL	3	2	1	3	11	....	....	....	....	....	....						....	....	....	....	....	....	....	....
1993-94	**NY Islanders**	**NHL**	76	10	47	57	80	4	0	2	235	4.3	29						4	0	0	0	6	0	0	0
1994-95	**NY Islanders**	**NHL**	26	3	13	16	32	1	0	0	61	4.9	−1						....	....	....	....	....	....	....	....
	Montreal	NHL	14	1	4	5	14	0	0	0	30	3.3	−2						....	....	....	....	....	....	....	....
1995-96	**Montreal**	**NHL**	61	5	23	28	79	2	0	0	122	4.1	7						....	....	....	....	....	....	....	....
1996-97	**Montreal**	**NHL**	65	10	20	30	43	5	0	1	177	5.6	3						5	0	0	0	6	0	0	0
1997-98	**Montreal**	**NHL**	74	13	31	44	70	8	0	2	166	7.8	16						9	3	4	7	10	2	0	0
1998-99	**Montreal**	**NHL**	62	13	21	34	77	8	0	3	143	9.1	−7	0	0.0	74	88	23:29	....	....	....	....	....	....	....	....
	NHL Totals		442	69	197	266	454	35	0	8	1112	6.2		0	0.0	74	88	23:29	35	6	10	16	34	2	0	0

NHL/Upper Deck All-Rookie Team (1993)
Traded to **Montreal** by **NY Islanders** with Pierre Turgeon for Kirk Muller, Mathieu Schneider and Craig Darby, April 5, 1995.

MALGUNAS, Stewart (mal-GOO-nuhs)

Defense. Shoots left. 6', 200 lbs.   Born, Prince George, B.C., April 21, 1970. Detroit's 3rd choice, 66th overall, in 1990 Entry Draft.

Season	Club	League	GP	G	A	Pts	PIM	PP	SH	GW	S	%	+/-	TF	F%	H	SB	Min	GP	G	A	Pts	PIM	PP	SH	GW
1985-86	Prince George	BCAHA	49	10	25	35	85	....	....	....	....	....	....						....	....	....	....	....	....	....	....
1986-87	Prince George	BCAHA	50	11	31	42	102	....	....	....	....	....	....						....	....	....	....	....	....	....	....
1987-88	Prince George	BCAHA	54	12	34	46	99	....	....	....	....	....	....						....	....	....	....	....	....	....	....
	New Westminster	WHL	6	0	0	0	0	....	....	....	....	....	....						....	....	....	....	....	....	....	....
1988-89	Seattle	WHL	72	11	41	52	51	....	....	....	....	....	....						....	....	....	....	....	....	....	....
1989-90	Seattle	WHL	63	15	48	63	116	....	....	....	....	....	....						13	2	9	11	32			
1990-91	Adirondack	AHL	78	5	19	24	70	....	....	....	....	....	....						2	0	0	0	4			
1991-92	Adirondack	AHL	69	4	28	32	82	....	....	....	....	....	....						18	2	6	8	28			
1992-93	Adirondack	AHL	45	3	12	15	39	....	....	....	....	....	....						11	3	3	6	8			
1993-94	**Philadelphia**	**NHL**	67	1	3	4	86	0	0	0	54	1.9	2						....	....	....	....	....			
1994-95	**Philadelphia**	**NHL**	4	0	0	0	4	0	0	0	1	0.0	−1						....	....	....	....	....			
	Hershey	AHL	32	3	5	8	28	....	....	....	....	....	....						6	2	1	3	31			
1995-96	**Winnipeg**	**NHL**	29	0	1	1	32	0	0	0	13	0.0	−10						....	....	....	....	....			
	Washington	**NHL**	1	0	0	0	0	0	0	0	0	0.0	0						....	....	....	....	....			
	Portland	AHL	16	2	5	7	18	....	....	....	....	....	....						13	1	3	4	12			
1996-97	**Washington**	**NHL**	6	0	0	0	2	0	0	0	3	0.0	2						....	....	....	....	....			
	Portland	AHL	68	6	12	18	59	....	....	....	....	....	....						5	0	0	0	8			
1997-98	**Washington**	**NHL**	8	0	0	0	12	0	0	0	5	0.0	1						....	....	....	....	....			
	Portland	AHL	69	14	25	39	73	....	....	....	....	....	....						9	1	1	2	19			
1998-99	**Washington**	**NHL**	10	0	0	0	6	0	0	0	2	0.0	−5	0	0.0	12	9	9:02	....	....	....	....	....			
	Portland	AHL	33	2	10	12	49	....	....	....	....	....	....						....	....	....	....	....			
	Detroit	IHL	9	0	2	2	10	....	....	....	....	....	....						11	0	1	1	21			
	NHL Totals		125	1	4	5	142	0	0	0	78	1.3		0	0.0	12	9	9:02	....	....	....	....	....			

WHL West First All-Star Team (1990)
Traded to **Philadelphia** by **Detroit** for Philadelphia's 5th round choice (David Arsenault) in 1995 Entry Draft, September 9, 1993. Signed as a free agent by **Winnipeg**, August 9, 1995. Traded to **Washington** by **Winnipeg** for Denis Chasse, February 15, 1996.

MALHOTRA, Manny (mal-HOH-truh) **NYR**

Center. Shoots left. 6'2", 210 lbs.   Born, Mississauga, Ont., May 18, 1980. NY Rangers' 1st choice, 7th overall, in 1998 Entry Draft.

Season	Club	League	GP	G	A	Pts	PIM	PP	SH	GW	S	%	+/-	TF	F%	H	SB	Min	GP	G	A	Pts	PIM	PP	SH	GW
1995-96	Mississauga	MTHL	54	27	44	71	62	....	....	....	....	....	....						....	....	....	....	....			
1996-97	Guelph	OHL	61	16	28	44	26	....	....	....	....	....	....						18	7	7	14	11			
1997-98	Guelph	OHL	57	16	35	51	29	....	....	....	....	....	....						12	7	6	13	8			
1998-99	**NY Rangers**	**NHL**	73	8	8	16	13	1	0	2	61	13.1	−2	588	43.9	115	17	8:36	....	....	....	....	....			
	NHL Totals		73	8	8	16	13	1	0	2	61	13.1		588	43.9	115	17	8:36	....	....	....	....	....			

Memorial Cup All-Star Team (1998) • Won George Parsons Trophy (Memorial Cup Tournament Most Sportsmanlike Player) (1998)

MALIK, Marek (MAW-leck)

Defense. Shoots left. 6'5", 190 lbs.   Born, Ostrava, Czech., June 24, 1975. Hartford's 2nd choice, 72nd overall, in 1993 Entry Draft.

Season	Club	League	GP	G	A	Pts	PIM	PP	SH	GW	S	%	+/-	TF	F%	H	SB	Min	GP	G	A	Pts	PIM	PP	SH	GW
1992-93	TJ Vitkovice	Czech-Jr.	20	5	10	15	16	....	....	....	....	....	....						....	....	....	....	....			
1993-94	TJ Vitkovice	Cze-Rep	38	3	3	6	0	....	....	....	....	....	....						3	0	1	1	0			
1994-95	Springfield	AHL	58	11	30	41	91	....	....	....	....	....	....						....	....	....	....	....			
	Hartford	**NHL**	1	0	1	1	0	0	0	0	0	0.0	1						....	....	....	....	....			
1995-96	**Hartford**	**NHL**	7	0	0	0	4	0	0	0	2	0.0	−3						....	....	....	....	....			
	Springfield	AHL	68	8	14	22	135	....	....	....	....	....	....						8	1	3	4	20			
1996-97	**Hartford**	**NHL**	47	1	5	6	50	0	0	1	33	3.0	5						....	....	....	....	....			
	Springfield	AHL	3	0	3	3	4	....	....	....	....	....	....						....	....	....	....	....			
1997-98	Malmo IF	Sweden	37	1	5	6	21	....	....	....	....	....	....						....	....	....	....	....			
1998-99	TJ Vitkovice	Cze-Rep	1	1	0	1	6	....	....	....	....	....	....						....	....	....	....	....			
	Carolina	**NHL**	52	2	9	11	36	1	0	0	36	5.6	−6	0	0.0	101	76	21:14	4	0	0	0	4	0	0	0
	New Haven	AHL	21	2	8	10	28	....	....	....	....	....	....						....	....	....	....	....			
	NHL Totals		107	3	15	18	90	1	0	1	71	4.2		0	0.0	101	76	21:14	4	0	0	0	4	0	0	0

Transferred to **Carolina** after **Hartford** franchise relocated, June 25, 1997.

MALKOC, Dean (mal-KAWK) **NYI**

Defense. Shoots left. 6'3", 215 lbs.   Born, Vancouver, B.C., January 26, 1970. New Jersey's 7th choice, 95th overall, in 1990 Entry Draft.

Season	Club	League	GP	G	A	Pts	PIM	PP	SH	GW	S	%	+/-	TF	F%	H	SB	Min	GP	G	A	Pts	PIM	PP	SH	GW
1987-88	Williams Lake	PCJHL	55	6	32	38	215	....	....	....	....	....	....						....	....	....	....	....			
1988-89	Powell River	BCJHL	55	10	32	42	370	....	....	....	....	....	....						....	....	....	....	....			
1989-90	Kamloops	WHL	48	3	18	21	209	....	....	....	....	....	....						17	0	3	3	56			
1990-91	Kamloops	WHL	8	1	4	5	47	....	....	....	....	....	....						....	....	....	....	....			
	Swift Current	WHL	56	10	23	33	248	....	....	....	....	....	....						3	0	2	2	5			
	Utica	AHL	1	0	0	0	0	....	....	....	....	....	....						....	....	....	....	....			
1991-92	Utica	AHL	66	1	11	12	274	....	....	....	....	....	....						4	0	2	2	6			
1992-93	Utica	AHL	73	5	19	24	255	....	....	....	....	....	....						5	0	1	1	8			
1993-94	Albany	AHL	79	0	9	9	296	....	....	....	....	....	....						5	0	0	0	21			
1994-95	Albany	AHL	9	0	1	1	52	....	....	....	....	....	....						....	....	....	....	....			
	Indianapolis	IHL	62	1	3	4	193	....	....	....	....	....	....						....	....	....	....	....			
1995-96	**Vancouver**	**NHL**	41	0	2	2	136	0	0	0	8	0.0	−10						....	....	....	....	....			
1996-97	**Boston**	**NHL**	33	0	0	0	70	0	0	0	7	0.0	−14						....	....	....	....	....			
	Providence	AHL	4	0	2	2	28	....	....	....	....	....	....						....	....	....	....	....			
1997-98	**Boston**	**NHL**	40	1	0	1	86	0	0	0	15	6.7	−12						....	....	....	....	....			

			Regular Season																Playoffs							
Season	Club	League	GP	G	A	Pts	PIM	PP	SH	GW	S	%	+/−	TF	F%	H	SB	Min	GP	G	A	Pts	PIM	PP	SH	GW
1998-99	NY Islanders	NHL	2	0	1	1	7	0	0	0	1	0.0	3	0	0.0	2	6	15:22	....					....		
	Lowell	AHL	61	2	8	10	193												3	0	0	0	8			
	NHL Totals		**116**	**1**	**3**	**4**	**299**	**0**	**0**	**0**	**31**	**3.2**		**0**	**0.0**	**2**	**6**	**15:22**	....					....		

Traded to **Chicago** by **New Jersey** for Rob Conn, January 30, 1995. Signed as a free agent by **Vancouver**, September 8, 1995. Claimed by **Boston** from **Vancouver** in NHL Waiver Draft, September 30, 1996. Signed as a free agent by **NY Islanders**, August 19, 1998.

MALTAIS, Steve (MAHL-tay)

Left wing. Shoots left. 6'2", 205 lbs. Born, Arvida, Que., January 25, 1969. Washington's 2nd choice, 57th overall, in 1987 Entry Draft.

Season	Club	League	GP	G	A	Pts	PIM	PP	SH	GW	S	%	+/−	TF	F%	H	SB	Min	GP	G	A	Pts	PIM	PP	SH	GW
1985-86	Wexford	MTHL	33	35	19	54	38																			
1986-87	Cornwall	OHL	65	32	12	44	29												5	0	0	0	2			
1987-88	Cornwall	OHL	59	39	46	85	30												11	9	6	15	33			
1988-89	Cornwall	OHL	58	53	70	123	67												18	14	16	30	16			
	Fort Wayne	IHL	....																4	2	1	3	0			
1989-90	**Washington**	**NHL**	8	0	0	0	2	0	0	0	11	0.0	−2						1	0	0	0	0	0	0	0
	Baltimore	AHL	67	29	37	66	54												12	6	10	16	6			
1990-91	**Washington**	**NHL**	7	0	0	0	2	0	0	0	3	0.0	−1													
	Baltimore	AHL	73	36	43	79	97												6	1	4	5	10			
1991-92	**Minnesota**	**NHL**	12	2	1	3	2	0	0	0	6	33.3	−1													
	Kalamazoo	IHL	48	25	31	56	51																			
	Halifax	AHL	10	3	3	6	0																			
1992-93	**Tampa Bay**	**NHL**	63	7	13	20	35	4	0	1	96	7.3	−20													
	Atlanta	IHL	16	14	10	24	22																			
1993-94	**Detroit**	**NHL**	4	0	1	1	0	0	0	0	2	0.0	−1													
	Adirondack	AHL	73	35	49	84	79												12	5	11	16	14			
1994-95	Chicago	IHL	79	*57	40	97	145												3	1	1	2	0			
1995-96	Chicago	IHL	81	56	66	122	161												9	7	7	14	20			
1996-97	Chicago	IHL	81	*60	54	114	62												4	2	0	2	4			
1997-98	Chicago	IHL	82	*46	57	103	120												22	8	11	19	28			
1998-99	Chicago	IHL	82	*56	44	100	164												10	4	6	10	2			
	NHL Totals		**94**	**9**	**15**	**24**	**41**	**4**	**0**	**1**	**118**	**7.6**							**1**	**0**	**0**	**0**	**0**	**0**	**0**	**0**

OHL Second All-Star Team (1989) • IHL First All-Star Team (1995, 1999) • IHL Second All-Star Team (1996, 1997)

Traded to **Minnesota** by **Washington** with Trent Klatt for Shawn Chambers, June 21, 1991. Traded to **Quebec** by **Minnesota** for Kip Miller, March 8, 1992. Claimed by **Tampa Bay** from **Quebec** in Expansion Draft, June 18, 1992. Traded to **Detroit** by **Tampa Bay** for Dennis Vial, June 8, 1993.

MALTBY, Kirk (MAHLT-bee)   DET.

Right wing. Shoots right. 6', 180 lbs. Born, Guelph, Ont., December 22, 1972. Edmonton's 4th choice, 65th overall, in 1992 Entry Draft.

Season	Club	League	GP	G	A	Pts	PIM	PP	SH	GW	S	%	+/−	TF	F%	H	SB	Min	GP	G	A	Pts	PIM	PP	SH	GW
1988-89	Cambridge	OJHL-B	48	28	18	46	138																			
1989-90	Owen Sound	OHL	61	12	15	27	90												12	1	6	7	15			
1990-91	Owen Sound	OHL	66	34	32	66	100																			
1991-92	Owen Sound	OHL	66	50	41	91	99												5	3	3	6	18			
1992-93	Cape Breton	AHL	73	22	23	45	130												16	3	3	6	45			
1993-94	**Edmonton**	**NHL**	68	11	8	19	74	0	1	1	89	12.4	−2													
1994-95	**Edmonton**	**NHL**	47	8	3	11	49	0	2	1	73	11.0	−11													
1995-96	**Edmonton**	**NHL**	49	2	6	8	61	0	0	1	51	3.9	−16													
	Cape Breton	AHL	4	1	2	3	6																			
	Detroit	**NHL**	6	1	0	1	6	0	0	0	4	25.0	0						8	0	1	1	4	0	0	0
1996-97♦	Detroit	NHL	66	3	5	8	75	0	0	0	62	4.8	3						20	5	2	7	24	0	1	1
1997-98♦	Detroit	NHL	65	14	9	23	89	2	1	3	106	13.2	11						22	3	1	4	30	0	1	0
1998-99♦	Detroit	NHL	53	8	6	14	34	0	1	2	76	10.5	−6	10	40.0	129	33	13:13	10	1	1	1	8	0	0	1
	NHL Totals		**354**	**47**	**37**	**84**	**388**	**2**	**5**	**8**	**461**	**10.1**		**10**	**40.0**	**129**	**33**	**13:13**	**60**	**9**	**4**	**13**	**66**	**0**	**2**	**2**

Traded to **Detroit** by **Edmonton** for Dan McGillis, March 20, 1996.

MANDERVILLE, Kent   CAR.

Left wing. Shoots left. 6'3", 210 lbs. Born, Edmonton, Alta., April 12, 1971. Calgary's 1st choice, 24th overall, in 1989 Entry Draft.

Season	Club	League	GP	G	A	Pts	PIM	PP	SH	GW	S	%	+/−	TF	F%	H	SB	Min	GP	G	A	Pts	PIM	PP	SH	GW
1987-88	Notre Dame	SAHA	32	22	18	40	42																			
1988-89	Notre Dame	SJHL	58	39	36	75	165																			
1989-90	Cornell	ECAC	26	11	15	26	28																			
1990-91	Cornell	ECAC	28	17	14	31	60																			
	Canada	Nat-Team	3	1	2	3	0																			
1991-92	Canada	Nat-Team	63	16	24	40	78																			
	Canada	Olympics	8	1	2	3	0																			
	Toronto	**NHL**	15	0	4	4	0	0	0	0	14	0.0	1													
	St. John's	AHL	....																12	5	9	14	14			
1992-93	Toronto	NHL	18	1	1	2	17	0	0	1	15	6.7	−9						18	1	0	1	8	0	0	0
	St. John's	AHL	56	19	28	47	86												2	0	2	2	0			
1993-94	Toronto	NHL	67	7	9	16	63	0	0	1	81	8.6	5						12	1	0	1	4	0	1	0
1994-95	Toronto	NHL	36	0	1	1	22	0	0	0	43	0.0	−2						7	0	0	0	6	0	0	0
1995-96	Edmonton	NHL	37	3	5	8	38	0	2	0	63	4.8	−5													
	St. John's	AHL	27	16	12	28	26																			
1996-97	Hartford	NHL	44	6	5	11	18	0	0	1	51	11.8	3													
	Springfield	AHL	23	5	20	25	18																			
1997-98	Carolina	NHL	77	4	4	8	31	0	0	0	80	5.0	−6													
1998-99	Carolina	NHL	81	5	11	16	38	0	0	0	71	7.0	9	609	46.3	140	28	8:07	6	0	0	0	2	0	0	0
	NHL Totals		**375**	**26**	**40**	**66**	**227**	**0**	**2**	**3**	**418**	**6.2**		**609**	**46.3**	**140**	**28**	**8:07**	**43**	**2**	**0**	**2**	**20**	**0**	**1**	**0**

Traded to **Toronto** by **Calgary** with Doug Gilmour, Jamie Macoun, Rick Wamsley and Ric Nattress for Gary Leeman, Alexander Godynyuk, Jeff Reese, Michel Petit and Craig Berube, January 2, 1992. Traded to **Edmonton** by **Toronto** for Peter White and Edmonton's 4th round choice (Jason Sessa) in 1996 Entry Draft, December 4, 1995. Signed as a free agent by **Hartford**, October 2, 1996. Transferred to **Carolina** after **Hartford** franchise relocated, June 25, 1997.

MANELUK, Mike (MAN-uh-luhk)   PHI.

Left wing. Shoots right. 5'11", 188 lbs. Born, Winnipeg, Man., October 1, 1973.

Season	Club	League	GP	G	A	Pts	PIM	PP	SH	GW	S	%	+/−	TF	F%	H	SB	Min	GP	G	A	Pts	PIM	PP	SH	GW
1989-90	Winnipeg	MAHA	40	49	38	87	92																			
1990-91	St. Boniface	MJHL	45	29	41	70	199																			
1991-92	Brandon	WHL	68	23	30	53	102																			
1992-93	Brandon	WHL	72	36	51	87	75												4	2	1	3	2			
1993-94	Brandon	WHL	63	50	47	97	112												13	11	3	14	23			
	San Diego	IHL	....																1	0	0	0	0			
1994-95	Canada	Na-Team	44	36	24	60	34																			
	San Diego	IHL	10	0	1	1	4																			
1995-96	Baltimore	AHL	74	33	38	71	73												6	4	3	7	14			
1996-97	Worcester	AHL	70	27	27	54	89												5	1	2	3	14			
1997-98	Worcester	AHL	5	3	3	6	4																			
	Philadelphia	AHL	66	27	35	62	62												20	*13	*21	*34	30			

Season	Club	League	GP	G	A	Pts	PIM	PP	SH	GW	S	%	+/-	TF	F%	H	SB	Min	GP	G	A	Pts	PIM	PP	SH	GW
			Regular Season																Playoffs							
1998-99	Philadelphia	NHL	13	2	6	8	8	0	0	0	23	8.7	4	0	0.0	8	1	14:02								
	Chicago	NHL	28	4	3	7	8	1	0	1	29	13.8	2	0	0.0	19	7	11:28								
	NY Rangers	NHL	45	6	9	15	20	1	0	1	55	10.9	5	0	0.0	3	0	7:18								
	NHL Totals		86	12	18	30	36	2	0	2	107	11.2		0	0.0	30	8	9:40								

Won Jack A. Butterfield Trophy (Playoff MVP - AHL) (1998)

Signed as a free agent by **Anaheim**, January 28, 1994. Traded to **Ottawa** by **Anaheim** for Kevin Brown, July 1, 1996. Traded to **Philadelphia** by **Ottawa** for future considerations, October 21, 1997. Traded to **Chicago** by **Philadelphia** for Roman Vopat, November 17, 1998. Claimed on waivers by **NY Rangers** from **Chicago**, March 4, 1999. Signed as a free agent by **Philadelphia**, July 30, 1999. Signed as a free agent by **Philadelphia**, August 17, 1999.

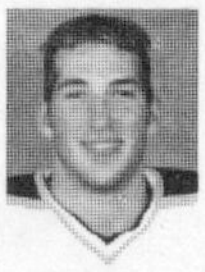

MANN, Cameron — BOS.

Right wing. Shoots right. 6', 194 lbs. Born, Thompson, Man., April 20, 1977. Boston's 5th choice, 99th overall, in 1995 Entry Draft.

Season	Club	League	GP	G	A	Pts	PIM	PP	SH	GW	S	%	+/-	TF	F%	H	SB	Min	GP	G	A	Pts	PIM	PP	SH	GW
1992-93	Kenora	NOHA	35	23	25	47	49																			
1993-94	Peterborough B's	OJHL-B	16	3	14	17	23																			
	Peterborough	OHL	49	8	17	25	18												7	1	1	2	2			
1994-95	Peterborough	OHL	64	19	24	43	40												11	3	8	11	4			
1995-96	Peterborough	OHL	66	42	60	102	108												24	*27	16	*43	33			
1996-97	Peterborough	OHL	51	33	50	83	91												11	10	18	28	16			
1997-98	**Boston**	**NHL**	**9**	**0**	**1**	**1**	**4**	**0**	**0**	**0**	**6**	**0.0**	**1**													
	Providence	AHL	71	21	26	47	99																			
1998-99	**Boston**	**NHL**	**33**	**5**	**2**	**7**	**17**	**1**	**0**	**1**	**42**	**11.9**	**0**	**22**	**36.4**	**28**	**4**	**10:40**	**1**	**0**	**0**	**0**	**0**	**0**	**0**	**0**
	Providence	AHL	43	21	25	46	65												11	7	7	14	4			
	NHL Totals		**42**	**5**	**3**	**8**	**21**	**1**	**0**	**1**	**48**	**10.4**		**22**	**36.4**	**28**	**4**	**10:40**	**1**	**0**	**0**	**0**	**0**	**0**	**0**	**0**

OHL First All-Star Team (1996, 1997) • Memorial Cup All-Star Team (1996) • Won Stafford Smythe Memorial Trophy (Memorial Cup Tournament MVP) (1996)

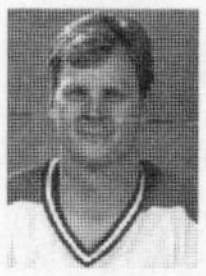

MANSON, Dave — CHI.

Defense. Shoots left. 6'2", 219 lbs. Born, Prince Albert, Sask., January 27, 1967. Chicago's 1st choice, 11th overall, in 1985 Entry Draft.

Season	Club	League	GP	G	A	Pts	PIM	PP	SH	GW	S	%	+/-	TF	F%	H	SB	Min	GP	G	A	Pts	PIM	PP	SH	GW
1982-83	Prince Albert AA	SAHA	28	11	11	22	170																			
	Prince Albert	WHL	6	0	1	1	9																			
1983-84	Prince Albert	WHL	70	2	7	9	233												5	0	0	0	4			
1984-85	Prince Albert	WHL	72	8	30	38	247												13	1	0	1	34			
1985-86	Prince Albert	WHL	70	14	34	48	177												20	1	8	9	63			
1986-87	**Chicago**	**NHL**	**63**	**1**	**8**	**9**	**146**	**0**	**0**	**0**	**42**	**2.4**	**–2**						**3**	**0**	**0**	**0**	**10**	**0**	**0**	**0**
1987-88	**Chicago**	**NHL**	**54**	**1**	**6**	**7**	**185**	**0**	**0**	**0**	**47**	**2.1**	**–12**						**5**	**0**	**0**	**0**	**27**	**0**	**0**	**0**
	Saginaw	IHL	6	0	3	3	37																			
1988-89	**Chicago**	**NHL**	**79**	**18**	**36**	**54**	**352**	**8**	**1**	**0**	**224**	**8.0**	**5**						**16**	**0**	**8**	**8**	**84**	**0**	**0**	**0**
1989-90	**Chicago**	**NHL**	**59**	**5**	**23**	**28**	**301**	**1**	**0**	**1**	**126**	**4.0**	**4**						**20**	**2**	**4**	**6**	**46**	**1**	**0**	**0**
1990-91	**Chicago**	**NHL**	**75**	**14**	**15**	**29**	**191**	**6**	**1**	**2**	**154**	**9.1**	**20**						**6**	**0**	**1**	**1**	**36**	**0**	**0**	**0**
1991-92	**Edmonton**	**NHL**	**79**	**15**	**32**	**47**	**220**	**7**	**0**	**2**	**206**	**7.3**	**9**						**16**	**3**	**9**	**12**	**44**	**1**	**0**	**0**
1992-93	**Edmonton**	**NHL**	**83**	**15**	**30**	**45**	**210**	**9**	**1**	**1**	**244**	**6.1**	**–28**													
1993-94	**Edmonton**	**NHL**	**57**	**3**	**13**	**16**	**140**	**1**	**0**	**0**	**144**	**2.1**	**–4**													
	Winnipeg	**NHL**	**13**	**1**	**4**	**5**	**51**	**1**	**0**	**0**	**36**	**2.8**	**–10**													
1994-95	**Winnipeg**	**NHL**	**44**	**3**	**15**	**18**	**139**	**2**	**0**	**1**	**104**	**2.9**	**–20**													
1995-96	**Winnipeg**	**NHL**	**82**	**7**	**23**	**30**	**205**	**3**	**0**	**0**	**189**	**3.7**	**8**						**6**	**2**	**1**	**3**	**30**	**0**	**0**	**1**
1996-97	**Phoenix**	**NHL**	**66**	**3**	**17**	**20**	**164**	**2**	**0**	**0**	**153**	**2.0**	**–25**													
	Montreal	**NHL**	**9**	**1**	**1**	**2**	**23**	**0**	**0**	**0**	**22**	**4.5**	**–1**						**5**	**0**	**0**	**0**	**17**	**0**	**0**	**0**
1997-98	**Montreal**	**NHL**	**81**	**4**	**30**	**34**	**122**	**2**	**0**	**0**	**148**	**2.7**	**22**						**10**	**0**	**1**	**1**	**14**	**0**	**0**	**0**
1998-99	**Montreal**	**NHL**	**11**	**0**	**2**	**2**	**48**	**0**	**0**	**0**	**11**	**0.0**	**–3**	**0**	**0.0**	**14**	**8**	**17:19**								
	Chicago	**NHL**	**64**	**6**	**15**	**21**	**107**	**2**	**0**	**0**	**134**	**4.5**	**4**	**0**	**0.0**	**127**	**51**	**22:37**								
	NHL Totals		**919**	**97**	**270**	**367**	**2604**	**43**	**3**	**7**	**1984**	**4.9**		**0**	**0.0**	**141**	**59**	**21:50**	**87**	**7**	**24**	**31**	**308**	**2**	**0**	**1**

WHL East Second All-Star Team (1986)

Played in NHL All-Star Game (1989, 1993)

Traded to **Edmonton** by **Chicago** with Chicago's 3rd round choice (Kirk Maltby) in 1992 Entry Draft for Steve Smith, October 2, 1991. Traded to **Winnipeg** by **Edmonton** with St. Louis' 6th round choice (previously acquired, Winnipeg selected Chris Kibermanis) in 1994 Entry Draft for Boris Mironov, Mats Lindgren, Winnipeg's 1st round choice (Jason Bonsignore) in 1994 Entry Draft and Florida's 4th round choice (previously acquired, Edmonton selected Adam Copeland) in 1994 Entry Draft, March 15, 1994. Transferred to **Phoenix** after **Winnipeg** franchise relocated, July 1, 1996. Traded to **Montreal** by **Phoenix** for Murray Baron and Chris Murray, March 18, 1997. Traded to **Chicago** by **Montreal** with Jocelyn Thibault and Brad Brown for Jeff Hackett, Eric Weinrich, Alain Nasreddine and Tampa Bay's 4th round choice (previously acquired, Montreal selected Chris Dyment) in 1999 Entry Draft, November 16, 1998.

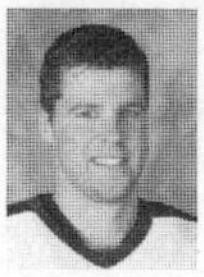

MARA, Paul — (MAIR-uh) — T.B.

Defense. Shoots left. 6'4", 202 lbs. Born, Ridgewood, NJ, September 7, 1979. Tampa Bay's 1st choice, 7th overall, in 1997 Entry Draft.

Season	Club	League	GP	G	A	Pts	PIM	PP	SH	GW	S	%	+/-	TF	F%	H	SB	Min	GP	G	A	Pts	PIM	PP	SH	GW
1994-95	Belmont Hill	H.S.	28	5	17	22	28																			
1995-96	Belmont Hill	H.S.	28	18	20	38	40																			
1996-97	Sudbury	OHL	44	9	34	43	61																			
1997-98	Sudbury	OHL	25	8	18	26	79																			
	Plymouth	OHL	25	8	15	23	30												15	3	14	17	30			
1998-99	**Tampa Bay**	**NHL**	**1**	**1**	**1**	**2**	**0**	**1**	**0**	**0**	**1**	**100.0**	**–3**	**0**	**0.0**	**1**	**3**	**19:34**								
	Plymouth	OHL	52	13	41	54	95												11	5	7	12	28			
	NHL Totals		**1**	**1**	**1**	**2**	**0**	**1**	**0**	**0**	**1**	**100.0**		**0**	**0.0**	**1**	**3**	**19:34**								

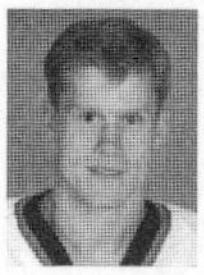

MARCHANT, Todd — (mahr-SHAHNT) — EDM.

Center. Shoots left. 5'10", 178 lbs. Born, Buffalo, NY, August 12, 1973. NY Rangers' 8th choice, 164th overall, in 1993 Entry Draft.

Season	Club	League	GP	G	A	Pts	PIM	PP	SH	GW	S	%	+/-	TF	F%	H	SB	Min	GP	G	A	Pts	PIM	PP	SH	GW
1991-92	Clarkson	ECAC	32	20	12	32	32																			
1992-93	Clarkson	ECAC	33	18	28	46	38																			
1993-94	United States	Nat-Team	59	28	39	67	48																			
	United States	Olympics	8	1	1	2	6																			
	NY Rangers	**NHL**	**1**	**0**	**0**	**0**	**0**	**0**	**0**	**0**	**1**	**0.0**	**–1**													
	Binghamton	AHL	8	2	7	9	6																			
	Edmonton	**NHL**	**3**	**0**	**1**	**1**	**2**	**0**	**0**	**0**	**5**	**0.0**	**–1**													
	Cape Breton	AHL	3	1	4	5	2												5	1	1	2	0			
1994-95	Cape Breton	AHL	38	22	25	47	25																			
	Edmonton	**NHL**	**45**	**13**	**14**	**27**	**32**	**3**	**2**	**2**	**95**	**13.7**	**–3**													
1995-96	**Edmonton**	**NHL**	**81**	**19**	**19**	**38**	**66**	**2**	**3**	**2**	**221**	**8.6**	**–19**													
1996-97	**Edmonton**	**NHL**	**79**	**14**	**19**	**33**	**44**	**0**	**4**	**3**	**202**	**6.9**	**11**						**12**	**4**	**2**	**6**	**12**	**0**	**3**	**1**
1997-98	**Edmonton**	**NHL**	**76**	**14**	**21**	**35**	**71**	**2**	**1**	**3**	**194**	**7.2**	**9**						**12**	**1**	**1**	**2**	**10**	**0**	**0**	**0**
1998-99	**Edmonton**	**NHL**	**82**	**14**	**22**	**36**	**65**	**3**	**1**	**2**	**183**	**7.7**	**3**	**1449**	**50.0**	**133**	**57**	**16:47**	**4**	**1**	**1**	**2**	**12**	**0**	**0**	**0**
	NHL Totals		**367**	**74**	**96**	**170**	**280**	**10**	**11**	**12**	**901**	**8.2**		**1449**	**50.0**	**133**	**57**	**16:47**	**28**	**6**	**4**	**10**	**34**	**0**	**3**	**1**

ECAC Second All-Star Team (1993)

Traded to **Edmonton** by **NY Rangers** for Craig MacTavish, March 21, 1994.

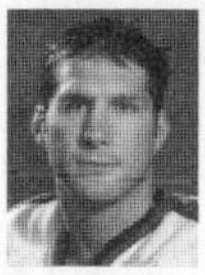

MARCHMENT, Bryan — (MAHRCH-mehnt) — S.J.

Defense. Shoots left. 6'1", 200 lbs. Born, Scarborough, Ont., May 1, 1969. Winnipeg's 1st choice, 16th overall, in 1987 Entry Draft.

Season	Club	League	GP	G	A	Pts	PIM	PP	SH	GW	S	%	+/-	TF	F%	H	SB	Min	GP	G	A	Pts	PIM	PP	SH	GW
1984-85	Toronto	MTHL	69	14	35	49	229																			
1985-86	Belleville	OHL	57	5	15	20	225												21	0	7	7	83			
1986-87	Belleville	OHL	52	6	38	44	238												6	0	4	4	17			
1987-88	Belleville	OHL	56	7	51	58	200												6	1	3	4	19			
1988-89	Belleville	OHL	43	14	36	50	118												5	0	1	1	12			
	Winnipeg	**NHL**	**2**	**0**	**0**	**0**	**2**	**0**	**0**	**0**	**1**	**0.0**	**0**													

			Regular Season																Playoffs							
Season	Club	League	GP	G	A	Pts	PIM	PP	SH	GW	S	%	+/–	TF	F%	H	SB	Min	GP	G	A	Pts	PIM	PP	SH	GW
1989-90	**Winnipeg**	**NHL**	**7**	**0**	**2**	**2**	**28**	**0**	**0**	**0**	**5**	**0.0**	**0**	....	....	....	....	....	....	....	....	....	....	....	....	....
	Moncton	AHL	56	4	19	23	217	....	....	....	....	....	....	....	....	....	....	....	....	....	....	....	....	....	....	....
1990-91	**Winnipeg**	**NHL**	**28**	**2**	**2**	**4**	**91**	**0**	**0**	**0**	**24**	**8.3**	**–5**	....	....	....	....	....	....	....	....	....	....	....	....	....
	Moncton	AHL	33	2	11	13	101	....	....	....	....	....	....	....	....	....	....	....	....	....	....	....	....	....	....	....
1991-92	**Chicago**	**NHL**	**58**	**5**	**10**	**15**	**168**	**2**	**0**	**0**	**55**	**9.1**	**–4**	....	....	....	....	....	**16**	**1**	**0**	**1**	**36**	**0**	**0**	**0**
1992-93	**Chicago**	**NHL**	**78**	**5**	**15**	**20**	**313**	**1**	**0**	**1**	**75**	**6.7**	**15**	....	....	....	....	....	**4**	**0**	**0**	**0**	**12**	**0**	**0**	**0**
1993-94	**Chicago**	**NHL**	**13**	**1**	**4**	**5**	**42**	**0**	**0**	**0**	**18**	**5.6**	**–2**	....	....	....	....	....	....	....	....	....	....	....	....	....
	Hartford	**NHL**	**42**	**3**	**7**	**10**	**124**	**0**	**1**	**1**	**74**	**4.1**	**–12**	....	....	....	....	....	....	....	....	....	....	....	....	....
1994-95	**Edmonton**	**NHL**	**40**	**1**	**5**	**6**	**184**	**0**	**0**	**0**	**57**	**1.8**	**–11**	....	....	....	....	....	....	....	....	....	....	....	....	....
1995-96	**Edmonton**	**NHL**	**78**	**3**	**15**	**18**	**202**	**0**	**0**	**0**	**96**	**3.1**	**–7**	....	....	....	....	....	....	....	....	....	....	....	....	....
1996-97	**Edmonton**	**NHL**	**71**	**3**	**13**	**16**	**132**	**1**	**0**	**0**	**89**	**3.4**	**13**	....	....	....	....	....	**3**	**0**	**0**	**0**	**4**	**0**	**0**	**0**
1997-98	**Edmonton**	**NHL**	**27**	**0**	**4**	**4**	**58**	**0**	**0**	**0**	**23**	**0.0**	**–2**	....	....	....	....	....	....	....	....	....	....	....	....	....
	Tampa Bay	**NHL**	**22**	**2**	**4**	**6**	**43**	**0**	**0**	**0**	**20**	**10.0**	**–3**	....	....	....	....	....	....	....	....	....	....	....	....	....
	San Jose	**NHL**	**12**	**0**	**3**	**3**	**43**	**0**	**0**	**0**	**13**	**0.0**	**2**	....	....	....	....	....	**6**	**0**	**0**	**0**	**10**	**0**	**0**	**0**
1998-99	**San Jose**	**NHL**	**59**	**2**	**6**	**8**	**101**	**0**	**0**	**0**	**49**	**4.1**	**–7**	**0**	**0.0**	**108**	**64**	**17:43**	**6**	**0**	**0**	**0**	**4**	**0**	**0**	**0**
	NHL Totals		**537**	**27**	**90**	**117**	**1531**	**4**	**1**	**2**	**599**	**4.5**		**0**	**0.0**	**108**	**64**	**17:43**	**35**	**1**	**0**	**1**	**66**	**0**	**0**	**0**

OHL Second All-Star Team (1989)

Traded to **Chicago** by **Winnipeg** with Chris Norton for Troy Murray and Warren Rychel, July 22, 1991. Traded to **Hartford** by **Chicago** with Steve Larmer for Eric Weinrich and Patrick Poulin, November 2, 1993. Transferred to **Edmonton** from **Hartford** as compensation for Hartford's signing of free agent Steven Rice, August 30, 1994. Traded to **Tampa Bay** by **Edmonton** with Steve Kelly and Jason Bonsignore for Roman Hamrlik and Paul Comrie, December 30, 1997. Traded to **San Jose** by **Tampa Bay** with David Shaw and Tampa Bay's 1st round choice (later traded to Nashville - Nashville selected David Legwand) in 1998 Entry Draft for Andrei Nazarov and Florida's 1st round choice (previously acquired, Tampa Bay selected Vincent Lecavallier) in 1998 Entry Draft, March 24, 1998.

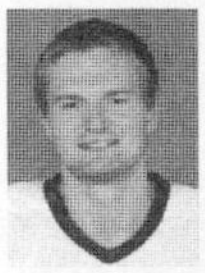

MARHA, Josef (MAHR-hah) CHI.

Center. Shoots left. 6', 176 lbs. Born, Havlickuv, Czech., June 2, 1976. Quebec's 3rd choice, 35th overall, in 1994 Entry Draft.

1991-92	Dukla Jihlava	Czech-Jr.	25	12	13	25	0	....	....	....	....	....	....	....	....	....	....	....	....	....	....	....	....	....	....	....
1992-93	Dukla Jihlava	Czech.	7	2	2	4	....	....	....	....	....	....	....	....	....	....	....	....	....	....	....	....	....	....	....	....
1993-94	Dukla Jihlava	Cze-Rep	41	7	2	9	....	....	....	....	....	....	....	....	....	....	....	....	3	0	1	1	....	....	....	....
1994-95	Dukla Jihlava	Cze-Rep	35	3	7	10	6	....	....	....	....	....	....	....	....	....	....	....	....	....	....	....	....	....	....	....
1995-96	**Colorado**	**NHL**	**2**	**0**	**1**	**1**	**0**	**0**	**0**	**0**	**2**	**0.0**	**1**	....	....	....	....	....	....	....	....	....	....	....	....	....
	Cornwall	AHL	74	18	30	48	30	....	....	....	....	....	....	....	....	....	....	....	8	1	2	3	10	....	....	....
1996-97	**Colorado**	**NHL**	**6**	**0**	**1**	**1**	**0**	**0**	**0**	**0**	**6**	**0.0**	**0**	....	....	....	....	....	....	....	....	....	....	....	....	....
	Hershey	AHL	67	23	49	72	44	....	....	....	....	....	....	....	....	....	....	....	19	6	*16	*22	10	....	....	....
1997-98	**Colorado**	**NHL**	**11**	**2**	**5**	**7**	**4**	**0**	**0**	**0**	**10**	**20.0**	**0**	....	....	....	....	....	....	....	....	....	....	....	....	....
	Hershey	AHL	55	6	46	52	30	....	....	....	....	....	....	....	....	....	....	....	....	....	....	....	....	....	....	....
	Anaheim	**NHL**	**12**	**7**	**4**	**11**	**0**	**3**	**0**	**0**	**21**	**33.3**	**4**	....	....	....	....	....	....	....	....	....	....	....	....	....
1998-99	**Anaheim**	**NHL**	**10**	**0**	**1**	**1**	**0**	**0**	**0**	**0**	**13**	**0.0**	**–4**	**107**	**40.2**	**3**	**1**	**12:02**	....	....	....	....	....	....	....	....
	Cincinnati	AHL	3	1	0	1	4	....	....	....	....	....	....	....	....	....	....	....	....	....	....	....	....	....	....	....
	Chicago	**NHL**	**22**	**2**	**5**	**7**	**4**	**1**	**0**	**1**	**32**	**6.3**	**5**	**275**	**50.9**	**6**	**10**	**14:37**	....	....	....	....	....	....	....	....
	Portland	AHL	8	0	8	8	2	....	....	....	....	....	....	....	....	....	....	....	....	....	....	....	....	....	....	....
	NHL Totals		**63**	**11**	**17**	**28**	**8**	**4**	**0**	**1**	**84**	**13.1**		**382**	**47.9**	**9**	**11**	**13:49**	....	....	....	....	....	....	....	....

Rights transferred to **Colorado** after **Quebec** franchise relocated, June 21, 1995. Traded to **Anaheim** by **Colorado** for Warren Rychel and future considerations, March 24, 1998. Traded to **Chicago** by **Anaheim** for Chicago's 4th round choice (Alexandr Chagodayev) in 1999 Entry Draft, January 28, 1999.

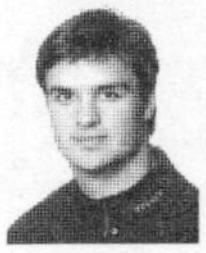

MARINUCCI, Chris (mair-ihn-OO-chee)

Center. Shoots left. 6', 188 lbs. Born, Grand Rapids, MN, December 29, 1971. NY Islanders' 4th choice, 90th overall, in 1990 Entry Draft.

1988-89	Grand Rapids	H.S.	25	24	18	42	....	....	....	....	....	....	....	....	....	....	....	....	....	....	....	....	....	....	....	....
1989-90	Grand Rapids	H.S.	28	24	39	63	12	....	....	....	....	....	....	....	....	....	....	....	....	....	....	....	....	....	....	....
1990-91	U. Minn-Duluth	WCHA	36	6	10	16	20	....	....	....	....	....	....	....	....	....	....	....	....	....	....	....	....	....	....	....
1991-92	U. Minn-Duluth	WCHA	37	6	13	19	41	....	....	....	....	....	....	....	....	....	....	....	....	....	....	....	....	....	....	....
1992-93	U. Minn-Duluth	WCHA	40	35	42	77	52	....	....	....	....	....	....	....	....	....	....	....	....	....	....	....	....	....	....	....
1993-94	U. Minn-Duluth	WCHA	38	*30	31	61	65	....	....	....	....	....	....	....	....	....	....	....	....	....	....	....	....	....	....	....
1994-95	**NY Islanders**	**NHL**	**12**	**1**	**4**	**5**	**2**	**0**	**0**	**0**	**11**	**9.1**	**–1**	....	....	....	....	....	....	....	....	....	....	....	....	....
	Denver	IHL	74	29	40	69	42	....	....	....	....	....	....	....	....	....	....	....	14	3	4	7	12	....	....	....
1995-96	Utah	IHL	8	3	5	8	8	....	....	....	....	....	....	....	....	....	....	....	....	....	....	....	....	....	....	....
1996-97	Utah	IHL	21	3	13	16	6	....	....	....	....	....	....	....	....	....	....	....	....	....	....	....	....	....	....	....
	Los Angeles	**NHL**	**1**	**0**	**0**	**0**	**0**	**0**	**0**	**0**	**1**	**0.0**	**–2**	....	....	....	....	....	....	....	....	....	....	....	....	....
	Phoenix	IHL	62	23	29	52	26	....	....	....	....	....	....	....	....	....	....	....	....	....	....	....	....	....	....	....
1997-98	Chicago	IHL	78	27	48	75	35	....	....	....	....	....	....	....	....	....	....	....	22	7	6	13	12	....	....	....
1998-99	Chicago	IHL	82	41	40	81	24	....	....	....	....	....	....	....	....	....	....	....	10	3	5	8	10	....	....	....
	NHL Totals		**13**	**1**	**4**	**5**	**2**	**0**	**0**	**0**	**12**	**8.3**		....	....	....	....	....	....	....	....	....	....	....	....	....

WCHA Second All-Star Team (1993) • WCHA First All-Star Team (1994) • NCAA West First All-American Team (1994) • Won Hobey Baker Memorial Award (Top U.S. Collegiate Player) (1994) • IHL Second All-Star Team (1999)

Traded to **LA Kings** by **NY Islanders** for Nick Vachon, November 19, 1996.

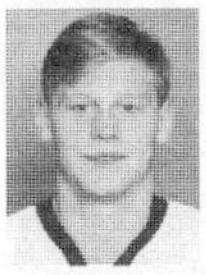

MARKOV, Daniil (MAHR-kahf, dan-EEL) TOR.

Defense. Shoots left. 6'1", 196 lbs. Born, Moscow, USSR, July 11, 1976. Toronto's 7th choice, 223rd overall, in 1995 Entry Draft.

1993-94	SKA Spartak	CIS	13	1	0	1	6	....	....	....	....	....	....	....	....	....	....	....	1	0	0	0	0	....	....	....
1994-95	SKA Spartak	CIS	39	0	1	1	36	....	....	....	....	....	....	....	....	....	....	....	....	....	....	....	....	....	....	....
1995-96	SKA Spartak	CIS	38	2	0	2	12	....	....	....	....	....	....	....	....	....	....	....	2	0	0	0	2	....	....	....
1996-97	SKA Spartak	Russia	39	3	6	9	41	....	....	....	....	....	....	....	....	....	....	....	....	....	....	....	....	....	....	....
	St. John's	AHL	10	2	4	6	18	....	....	....	....	....	....	....	....	....	....	....	11	2	6	8	14	....	....	....
1997-98	**Toronto**	**NHL**	**25**	**2**	**5**	**7**	**28**	**1**	**0**	**0**	**15**	**13.3**	**0**	....	....	....	....	....	....	....	....	....	....	....	....	....
	St. John's	AHL	52	3	23	26	124	....	....	....	....	....	....	....	....	....	....	....	2	0	1	1	0	....	....	....
1998-99	**Toronto**	**NHL**	**57**	**4**	**8**	**12**	**47**	**0**	**0**	**0**	**34**	**11.8**	**5**	**0**	**0.0**	**92**	**66**	**18:41**	**17**	**0**	**6**	**6**	**18**	**0**	**0**	**0**
	NHL Totals		**82**	**6**	**13**	**19**	**75**	**1**	**0**	**0**	**49**	**12.2**		**0**	**0.0**	**92**	**66**	**18:41**	**17**	**0**	**6**	**6**	**18**	**0**	**0**	**0**

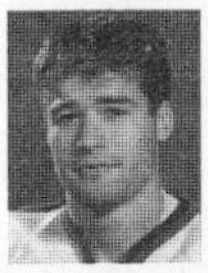

MARLEAU, Patrick (mahr-LOH) S.J.

Center. Shoots left. 6'2", 205 lbs. Born, Swift Current, Sask., September 15, 1979. San Jose's 1st choice, 2nd overall, in 1997 Entry Draft.

1993-94	Swift Current	SAHA	53	72	95	167	....	....	....	....	....	....	....	....	....	....	....	....	....	....	....	....	....	....	....	....
1994-95	Swift Current	SAHA	30	30	22	52	....	....	....	....	....	....	....	....	....	....	....	....	....	....	....	....	....	....	....	....
1995-96	Seattle	WHL	72	32	42	74	22	....	....	....	....	....	....	....	....	....	....	....	5	3	4	7	4	....	....	....
1996-97	Seattle	WHL	71	51	74	125	37	....	....	....	....	....	....	....	....	....	....	....	15	7	16	23	12	....	....	....
1997-98	**San Jose**	**NHL**	**74**	**13**	**19**	**32**	**14**	**1**	**0**	**2**	**90**	**14.4**	**5**	....	....	....	....	....	**5**	**0**	**1**	**1**	**0**	**0**	**0**	**0**
1998-99	**San Jose**	**NHL**	**81**	**21**	**24**	**45**	**24**	**4**	**0**	**4**	**134**	**15.7**	**10**	**1121**	**43.4**	**59**	**15**	**15:11**	**6**	**2**	**1**	**3**	**4**	**2**	**0**	**0**
	NHL Totals		**155**	**34**	**43**	**77**	**38**	**5**	**0**	**6**	**224**	**15.2**		**1121**	**43.4**	**59**	**15**	**15:11**	**11**	**2**	**2**	**4**	**4**	**2**	**0**	**0**

WHL West First All-Star Team (1997)

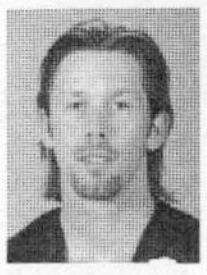

MARSHALL, Grant DAL.

Right wing. Shoots right. 6'1", 193 lbs. Born, Mississauga, Ont., June 9, 1973. Toronto's 2nd choice, 23rd overall, in 1992 Entry Draft.

1989-90	Toronto	MTHL	39	15	28	43	56	....	....	....	....	....	....	....	....	....	....	....	....	....	....	....	....	....	....	....
1990-91	Ottawa	OHL	26	6	11	17	25	....	....	....	....	....	....	....	....	....	....	....	1	0	0	0	0	....	....	....
1991-92	Ottawa	OHL	61	32	51	83	132	....	....	....	....	....	....	....	....	....	....	....	11	6	11	17	11	....	....	....
1992-93	Ottawa	OHL	30	14	29	43	83	....	....	....	....	....	....	....	....	....	....	....	....	....	....	....	....	....	....	....
	Newmarket	OHL	31	11	25	36	89	....	....	....	....	....	....	....	....	....	....	....	7	4	7	11	20	....	....	....
	St. John's	AHL	2	0	0	0	0	....	....	....	....	....	....	....	....	....	....	....	2	0	0	0	2	....	....	....
1993-94	St. John's	AHL	67	11	29	40	155	....	....	....	....	....	....	....	....	....	....	....	11	1	5	6	17	....	....	....

			Regular Season																Playoffs							
Season	Club	League	GP	G	A	Pts	PIM	PP	SH	GW	S	%	+/–	TF	F%	H	SB	Min	GP	G	A	Pts	PIM	PP	SH	GW
1994-95	**Dallas**	**NHL**	**2**	**0**	**1**	**1**	**0**	**0**	**0**	**0**	**0**	**0.0**	**1**	....	....	....	....	....	....	....	....	....	....	....	....	....
	Kalamazoo	IHL	61	17	29	46	96	....	....	....	....	....	....	....	....	....	....	....	16	9	3	12	27	....	....	....
1995-96	**Dallas**	**NHL**	**70**	**9**	**19**	**28**	**111**	**0**	**0**	**0**	**62**	**14.5**	**0**	....	....	....	....	....	....	....	....	....	....	....	....	....
1996-97	**Dallas**	**NHL**	**56**	**6**	**4**	**10**	**98**	**0**	**0**	**0**	**0**	**0.0**	**5**	....	....	....	....	....	**5**	**0**	**2**	**2**	**8**	**0**	**0**	**0**
1997-98	**Dallas**	**NHL**	**72**	**9**	**10**	**19**	**96**	**3**	**0**	**1**	**91**	**9.9**	**–2**	....	....	....	....	....	**17**	**0**	**2**	**2**	***47**	**0**	**0**	**0**
1998-99♦	**Dallas**	**NHL**	**82**	**13**	**18**	**31**	**85**	**2**	**0**	**4**	**112**	**11.6**	**1**	**2**	**50.0**	**172**	**12**	**12:39**	**14**	**0**	**3**	**3**	**20**	**0**	**0**	**0**
	NHL Totals		**282**	**37**	**52**	**89**	**390**	**5**	**0**	**5**	**265**	**14.0**		**2**	**50.0**	**172**	**12**	**12:39**	**36**	**0**	**7**	**7**	**75**	**0**	**0**	**0**

Transferred to **Dallas** from **Toronto** with Peter Zezel as compensation for Toronto's signing of free agent Mike Craig, August 10, 1994.

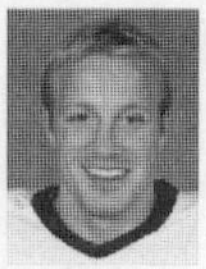

MARSHALL, Jason

ANA.

Defense. Shoots right. 6'2", 200 lbs. Born, Cranbrook, B.C., February 22, 1971. St. Louis' 1st choice, 9th overall, in 1989 Entry Draft.

Season	Club	League	GP	G	A	Pts	PIM	PP	SH	GW	S	%	+/–	TF	F%	H	SB	Min	GP	G	A	Pts	PIM	PP	SH	GW
1987-88	Columbia Valley	RMJHL	40	4	28	32	150	....	....	....	....	....	....	....	....	....	....	....	....	....	....	....	....	....	....	....
1988-89	Vernon	BCJHL	48	10	30	40	197	....	....	....	....	....	....	....	....	....	....	....	31	6	6	12	14	....	....	....
	Canada	Nat-Team	2	0	1	1	0	....	....	....	....	....	....	....	....	....	....	....	....	....	....	....	....	....	....	....
1989-90	Canada	Nat-Team	73	1	11	12	57	....	....	....	....	....	....	....	....	....	....	....	....	....	....	....	....	....	....	....
1990-91	Tri-City	WHL	59	10	34	44	236	....	....	....	....	....	....	....	....	....	....	....	7	1	2	3	20	....	....	....
	Peoria	IHL	....	....	....	....	....	....	....	....	....	....	....	....	....	....	....	....	18	0	1	1	48	....	....	....
1991-92	**St. Louis**	**NHL**	**2**	**1**	**0**	**1**	**4**	**0**	**0**	**0**	**2**	**50.0**	**0**	....	....	....	....	....	....	....	....	....	....	....	....	....
	Peoria	IHL	78	4	18	22	178	....	....	....	....	....	....	....	....	....	....	....	10	0	1	1	16	....	....	....
1992-93	Peoria	IHL	77	4	16	20	229	....	....	....	....	....	....	....	....	....	....	....	4	0	0	0	20	....	....	....
1993-94	Canada	Nat-Team	41	3	10	13	60	....	....	....	....	....	....	....	....	....	....	....	....	....	....	....	....	....	....	....
	Peoria	IHL	20	1	1	2	72	....	....	....	....	....	....	....	....	....	....	....	3	2	0	2	2	....	....	....
1994-95	**Anaheim**	**NHL**	**1**	**0**	**0**	**0**	**0**	**0**	**0**	**0**	**1**	**0.0**	**–2**	....	....	....	....	....	....	....	....	....	....	....	....	....
	San Diego	IHL	80	7	18	25	218	....	....	....	....	....	....	....	....	....	....	....	5	0	1	1	8	....	....	....
1995-96	**Anaheim**	**NHL**	**24**	**0**	**1**	**1**	**42**	**0**	**0**	**0**	**9**	**0.0**	**3**	....	....	....	....	....	....	....	....	....	....	....	....	....
	Baltimore	AHL	57	1	13	14	150	....	....	....	....	....	....	....	....	....	....	....	....	....	....	....	....	....	....	....
1996-97	**Anaheim**	**NHL**	**73**	**1**	**9**	**10**	**140**	**0**	**0**	**0**	**34**	**2.9**	**6**	....	....	....	....	....	**7**	**0**	**1**	**1**	**4**	**0**	**0**	**0**
1997-98	**Anaheim**	**NHL**	**72**	**3**	**6**	**9**	**189**	**1**	**0**	**0**	**68**	**4.4**	**–8**	....	....	....	....	....	....	....	....	....	....	....	....	....
1998-99	**Anaheim**	**NHL**	**72**	**1**	**7**	**8**	**142**	**0**	**0**	**0**	**63**	**1.6**	**–5**	**0**	**0.0**	**150**	**95**	**19:06**	**4**	**1**	**0**	**1**	**10**	**1**	**0**	**0**
	NHL Totals		**244**	**6**	**23**	**29**	**517**	**1**	**0**	**0**	**177**	**3.4**		**0**	**0.0**	**150**	**95**	**19:06**	**11**	**1**	**1**	**2**	**14**	**1**	**0**	**0**

Traded to **Anaheim** by **St. Louis** for Bill Houlder, August 29, 1994.

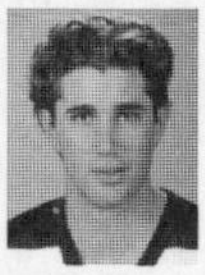

MARTIN, Matt

DAL.

Defense. Shoots left. 6'3", 205 lbs. Born, Hamden, CT, April 30, 1971. Toronto's 4th choice, 66th overall, in 1989 Entry Draft.

Season	Club	League	GP	G	A	Pts	PIM	PP	SH	GW	S	%	+/–	TF	F%	H	SB	Min	GP	G	A	Pts	PIM	PP	SH	GW
1987-88	S. Connecticut	USAHA	23	3	7	10	....	....	....	....	....	....	....	....	....	....	....	....	....	....	....	....	....	....	....	....
1988-89	Avon Old Farms	H.S.	25	9	23	32	....	....	....	....	....	....	....	....	....	....	....	....	....	....	....	....	....	....	....	....
1989-90	Avon Old Farms	H.S.	STATISTICS NOT AVAILABLE											....	....	....	....	....	....	....	....	....	....	....	....	....
1990-91	U. of Maine	H.E.	35	3	12	15	48	....	....	....	....	....	....	....	....	....	....	....	....	....	....	....	....	....	....	....
1991-92	U. of Maine	H.E.	30	4	14	18	46	....	....	....	....	....	....	....	....	....	....	....	....	....	....	....	....	....	....	....
1992-93	U. of Maine	H.E.	44	6	26	32	88	....	....	....	....	....	....	....	....	....	....	....	....	....	....	....	....	....	....	....
	St. John's	AHL	2	0	0	0	2	....	....	....	....	....	....	....	....	....	....	....	9	1	5	6	4	....	....	....
1993-94	United States	Nat-Team	39	7	8	15	127	....	....	....	....	....	....	....	....	....	....	....	....	....	....	....	....	....	....	....
	United States	Olympics	8	0	2	2	8	....	....	....	....	....	....	....	....	....	....	....	....	....	....	....	....	....	....	....
	Toronto	**NHL**	**12**	**0**	**1**	**1**	**6**	**0**	**0**	**0**	**6**	**0.0**	**0**	....	....	....	....	....	....	....	....	....	....	....	....	....
	St. John's	AHL	12	1	5	6	9	....	....	....	....	....	....	....	....	....	....	....	11	1	5	6	33	....	....	....
1994-95	**Toronto**	**NHL**	**15**	**0**	**0**	**0**	**13**	**0**	**0**	**0**	**14**	**0.0**	**2**	....	....	....	....	....	....	....	....	....	....	....	....	....
	St. John's	AHL	49	2	16	18	54	....	....	....	....	....	....	....	....	....	....	....	....	....	....	....	....	....	....	....
1995-96	**Toronto**	**NHL**	**13**	**0**	**0**	**0**	**14**	**0**	**0**	**0**	**3**	**0.0**	**–1**	....	....	....	....	....	....	....	....	....	....	....	....	....
1996-97	**Toronto**	**NHL**	**36**	**0**	**4**	**4**	**38**	**0**	**0**	**0**	**30**	**0.0**	**–12**	....	....	....	....	....	....	....	....	....	....	....	....	....
	St. John's	AHL	12	1	3	4	4	....	....	....	....	....	....	....	....	....	....	....	....	....	....	....	....	....	....	....
1997-98	Chicago	IHL	78	7	22	29	95	....	....	....	....	....	....	....	....	....	....	....	19	0	5	5	24	....	....	....
1998-99	Michigan	IHL	76	3	12	15	114	....	....	....	....	....	....	....	....	....	....	....	5	0	0	0	10	....	....	....
	NHL Totals		**76**	**0**	**5**	**5**	**71**	**0**	**0**	**0**	**53**	**0.0**		....	....	....	....	....	....	....	....	....	....	....	....	....

Signed as a free agent by **Dallas**, July 24, 1998.

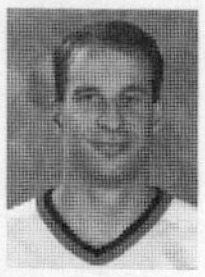

MARTINS, Steve

OTT.

Center. Shoots left. 5'9", 175 lbs. Born, Gatineau, Que., April 13, 1972. Hartford's 1st choice, 5th overall, in 1994 Supplemental Draft.

Season	Club	League	GP	G	A	Pts	PIM	PP	SH	GW	S	%	+/–	TF	F%	H	SB	Min	GP	G	A	Pts	PIM	PP	SH	GW
1988-89	L'Outaoais	QAAA	38	18	33	51	....	....	....	....	....	....	....	....	....	....	....	....	....	....	....	....	....	....	....	....
1989-90	Choate-Rosemary	H.S.	STATISTICS NOT AVAILABLE																							
1990-91	Choate-Rosemary	H.S.	STATISTICS NOT AVAILABLE																							
1991-92	Harvard University	ECAC	20	13	14	27	26	....	....	....	....	....	....	....	....	....	....	....	....	....	....	....	....	....	....	....
1992-93	Harvard University	ECAC	18	6	8	14	40	....	....	....	....	....	....	....	....	....	....	....	....	....	....	....	....	....	....	....
1993-94	Harvard University	ECAC	32	25	35	60	*93	....	....	....	....	....	....	....	....	....	....	....	....	....	....	....	....	....	....	....
1994-95	Harvard University	ECAC	28	15	23	38	93	....	....	....	....	....	....	....	....	....	....	....	....	....	....	....	....	....	....	....
1995-96	**Hartford**	**NHL**	**23**	**1**	**3**	**4**	**8**	**0**	**0**	**0**	**27**	**3.7**	**–3**	....	....	....	....	....	....	....	....	....	....	....	....	....
	Springfield	AHL	30	9	20	29	10	....	....	....	....	....	....	....	....	....	....	....	....	....	....	....	....	....	....	....
1996-97	**Hartford**	**NHL**	**2**	**0**	**1**	**1**	**0**	**0**	**0**	**0**	**2**	**0.0**	**0**	....	....	....	....	....	....	....	....	....	....	....	....	....
	Springfield	AHL	63	12	31	43	78	....	....	....	....	....	....	....	....	....	....	....	17	1	3	4	26	....	....	....
1997-98	**Carolina**	**NHL**	**3**	**0**	**0**	**0**	**0**	**0**	**0**	**0**	**0**	**0.0**	**0**	....	....	....	....	....	....	....	....	....	....	....	....	....
	Chicago	IHL	78	20	41	61	122	....	....	....	....	....	....	....	....	....	....	....	21	6	14	20	28	....	....	....
1998-99	**Ottawa**	**NHL**	**36**	**4**	**3**	**7**	**10**	**1**	**0**	**1**	**27**	**14.8**	**4**	**191**	**56.0**	**23**	**2**	**8:28**	....	....	....	....	....	....	....	....
	Detroit	IHL	4	1	6	7	16	....	....	....	....	....	....	....	....	....	....	....	....	....	....	....	....	....	....	....
	NHL Totals		**64**	**5**	**7**	**12**	**18**	**1**	**0**	**1**	**56**	**8.9**		**191**	**56.0**	**23**	**2**	**8:28**	....	....	....	....	....	....	....	....

ECAC First All-Star Team (1994) • NCAA East First All-American Team (1994) • NCAA Final Four All-Tournament Team (1994)

Transferred to **Carolina** after **Hartford** franchise relocated, June 25, 1997. Signed as a free agent by **Ottawa**, July 20, 1998.

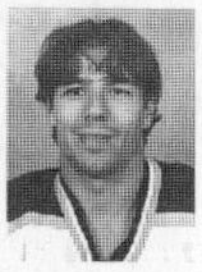

MATHIEU, Marquis

(MA-thew, MAHR-kwihs) **BOS.**

Center. Shoots right. 5'11", 190 lbs. Born, Hartford, CT, May 31, 1973.

Season	Club	League	GP	G	A	Pts	PIM	PP	SH	GW	S	%	+/–	TF	F%	H	SB	Min	GP	G	A	Pts	PIM	PP	SH	GW
1990-91	Beauport	QMJHL	26	4	13	17	73	....	....	....	....	....	....	....	....	....	....	....	....	....	....	....	....	....	....	....
1991-92	St-Jean	QMJHL	70	20	36	56	166	....	....	....	....	....	....	....	....	....	....	....	....	....	....	....	....	....	....	....
1992-93	St-Jean	QMJHL	61	31	36	67	115	....	....	....	....	....	....	....	....	....	....	....	2	1	0	1	33	....	....	....
1993-94	Wheeling	ECHL	42	12	11	23	75	....	....	....	....	....	....	....	....	....	....	....	9	1	3	4	23	....	....	....
	Fredericton	AHL	22	4	6	10	28	....	....	....	....	....	....	....	....	....	....	....	....	....	....	....	....	....	....	....
1994-95	Toledo	ECHL	33	13	22	35	168	....	....	....	....	....	....	....	....	....	....	....	....	....	....	....	....	....	....	....
	Raleigh	ECHL	33	15	17	32	181	....	....	....	....	....	....	....	....	....	....	....	....	....	....	....	....	....	....	....
	Worcester	AHL	2	0	0	0	0	....	....	....	....	....	....	....	....	....	....	....	....	....	....	....	....	....	....	....
1995-96	Johnstown	ECHL	25	4	17	21	89	....	....	....	....	....	....	....	....	....	....	....	....	....	....	....	....	....	....	....
	Worcester	AHL	17	3	10	13	26	....	....	....	....	....	....	....	....	....	....	....	....	....	....	....	....	....	....	....
	Houston	IHL	2	1	0	1	9	....	....	....	....	....	....	....	....	....	....	....	....	....	....	....	....	....	....	....
	Birmingham	ECHL	18	5	7	12	87	....	....	....	....	....	....	....	....	....	....	....	....	....	....	....	....	....	....	....
1996-97	Worcester	AHL	30	8	16	24	88	....	....	....	....	....	....	....	....	....	....	....	1	0	0	0	0	....	....	....
1997-98	Wheeling	ECHL	58	26	29	55	276	....	....	....	....	....	....	....	....	....	....	....	15	1	10	11	38	....	....	....
1998-99	**Boston**	**NHL**	**9**	**0**	**0**	**0**	**8**	**0**	**0**	**0**	**4**	**0.0**	**–1**	**84**	**63.1**	**9**	**1**	**7:20**	....	....	....	....	....	....	....	....
	Providence	AHL	64	15	15	30	166	....	....	....	....	....	....	....	....	....	....	....	19	4	7	11	30	....	....	....
	NHL Totals		**9**	**0**	**0**	**0**	**8**	**0**	**0**	**0**	**4**	**0.0**		**84**	**63.1**	**9**	**1**	**7:20**	....	....	....	....	....	....	....	....

Signed as a free agent by **Boston**, October 26, 1998.

			Regular Season																Playoffs							
Season	Club	League	GP	G	A	Pts	PIM	PP	SH	GW	S	%	+/-	TF	F%	H	SB	Min	GP	G	A	Pts	PIM	PP	SH	GW

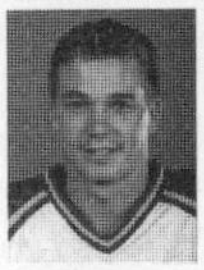

MATTE, Christian

(MA-teh) **COL.**

Right wing. Shoots right. 5'11", 170 lbs. Born, Hull, Que., January 20, 1975. Quebec's 8th choice, 153rd overall, in 1993 Entry Draft.

Season	Club	League	GP	G	A	Pts	PIM	PP	SH	GW	S	%	+/-	TF	F%	H	SB	Min	GP	G	A	Pts	PIM	PP	SH	GW
1991-92	Timiscaminque	QAAA	42	18	27	45	30	....	....	....	....	....	....	....	....	....	....	....	....	....	....	....	....	....	....	....
1992-93	Granby	QMJHL	68	17	36	53	59	....	....	....	....	....	....	....	....	....	....	....	....	....	....	....	....	....	....	....
1993-94	Granby	QMJHL	59	50	47	97	103	....	....	....	....	....	....	....	....	....	....	....	7	5	5	10	12	....	....	....
	Cornwall	AHL	1	0	0	0	0	....	....	....	....	....	....	....	....	....	....	....	....	....	....	....	....	....	....	....
1994-95	Granby	QMJHL	66	50	66	116	86	....	....	....	....	....	....	....	....	....	....	....	13	11	7	18	12	....	....	....
	Cornwall	AHL	....	....	....	....	....	....	....	....	....	....	....	....	....	....	....	....	3	0	1	1	2	....	....	....
1995-96	Cornwall	AHL	64	20	32	52	51	....	....	....	....	....	....	....	....	....	....	....	7	1	1	2	6	....	....	....
1996-97	**Colorado**	**NHL**	**5**	**1**	**1**	**2**	**0**	**0**	**0**	**0**	**6**	**16.7**	**1**	....	....	....	....	....	....	....	....	....	....	....	....	....
	Hershey	AHL	49	18	18	36	78	....	....	....	....	....	....	....	....	....	....	....	22	8	3	11	25	....	....	....
1997-98	**Colorado**	**NHL**	**5**	**0**	**0**	**0**	**6**	**0**	**0**	**0**	**5**	**0.0**	**0**	....	....	....	....	....	....	....	....	....	....	....	....	....
	Hershey	AHL	71	33	40	73	109	....	....	....	....	....	....	....	....	....	....	....	7	3	2	5	4	....	....	....
1998-99	**Colorado**	**NHL**	**7**	**1**	**1**	**2**	**0**	**0**	**0**	**0**	**9**	**11.1**	**–2**	**13**	**30.8**	**4**	**1**	**7:45**	....	....	....	....	....	....	....	....
	Hershey	AHL	60	31	47	78	48	....	....	....	....	....	....	....	....	....	....	....	5	2	1	3	8	....	....	....
	NHL Totals		**17**	**2**	**2**	**4**	**6**	**0**	**0**	**0**	**20**	**10.0**		**13**	**30.8**	**4**	**1**	**7:45**	....	....	....	....	....	....	....	....

QMJHL Second All-Star Team (1994)

Rights transferred to **Colorado** after **Quebec** franchise relocated, June 21, 1995.

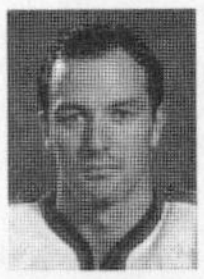

MATTEAU, Stephane

(mah-TOH) **S.J.**

Left wing. Shoots left. 6'4", 220 lbs. Born, Rouyn-Noranda, Que., September 2, 1969. Calgary's 2nd choice, 25th overall, in 1987 Entry Draft.

Season	Club	League	GP	G	A	Pts	PIM	PP	SH	GW	S	%	+/-	TF	F%	H	SB	Min	GP	G	A	Pts	PIM	PP	SH	GW
1985-86	Hull	QMJHL	60	6	8	14	19	....	....	....	....	....	....	....	....	....	....	....	4	0	0	0	0	....	....	....
1986-87	Hull	QMJHL	69	27	48	75	113	....	....	....	....	....	....	....	....	....	....	....	8	3	7	10	8	....	....	....
1987-88	Hull	QMJHL	57	17	40	57	179	....	....	....	....	....	....	....	....	....	....	....	18	5	14	19	94	....	....	....
1988-89	Hull	QMJHL	59	44	45	89	202	....	....	....	....	....	....	....	....	....	....	....	9	8	6	14	30	....	....	....
	Salt Lake	IHL	....	....	....	....	....	....	....	....	....	....	....	....	....	....	....	....	9	0	4	4	13	....	....	....
1989-90	Salt Lake	IHL	81	23	35	58	130	....	....	....	....	....	....	....	....	....	....	....	10	6	3	9	38	....	....	....
1990-91	**Calgary**	**NHL**	**78**	**15**	**19**	**34**	**93**	**0**	**1**	**1**	**114**	**13.2**	**17**	....	....	....	....	....	**5**	**0**	**1**	**1**	**0**	**0**	**0**	**0**
1991-92	**Calgary**	**NHL**	**4**	**1**	**0**	**1**	**19**	**0**	**0**	**0**	**7**	**14.3**	**2**	....	....	....	....	....	....	....	....	....	....	....	....	....
	Chicago	**NHL**	**20**	**5**	**8**	**13**	**45**	**1**	**0**	**0**	**31**	**16.1**	**3**	....	....	....	....	....	**18**	**4**	**6**	**10**	**24**	**1**	**1**	**0**
1992-93	**Chicago**	**NHL**	**79**	**15**	**18**	**33**	**98**	**2**	**0**	**4**	**95**	**15.8**	**6**	....	....	....	....	....	**3**	**0**	**1**	**1**	**2**	**0**	**0**	**0**
1993-94	**Chicago**	**NHL**	**65**	**15**	**16**	**31**	**55**	**2**	**0**	**2**	**113**	**13.3**	**10**	....	....	....	....	....	....	....	....	....	....	....	....	....
	♦ **NY Rangers**	**NHL**	**12**	**4**	**3**	**7**	**2**	**1**	**0**	**0**	**22**	**18.2**	**5**	....	....	....	....	....	**23**	**6**	**3**	**9**	**20**	**1**	**0**	**2**
1994-95	**NY Rangers**	**NHL**	**41**	**3**	**5**	**8**	**25**	**0**	**0**	**0**	**37**	**8.1**	**–8**	....	....	....	....	....	**9**	**0**	**1**	**1**	**10**	**0**	**0**	**0**
1995-96	**NY Rangers**	**NHL**	**32**	**4**	**2**	**6**	**22**	**1**	**0**	**0**	**39**	**10.3**	**–4**	....	....	....	....	....	....	....	....	....	....	....	....	....
	St. Louis	**NHL**	**46**	**7**	**13**	**20**	**65**	**3**	**0**	**2**	**70**	**10.0**	**–4**	....	....	....	....	....	**11**	**0**	**2**	**2**	**8**	**0**	**0**	**0**
1996-97	**St. Louis**	**NHL**	**74**	**16**	**20**	**36**	**50**	**1**	**2**	**2**	**98**	**16.3**	**11**	....	....	....	....	....	**5**	**0**	**0**	**0**	**0**	**0**	**0**	**0**
1997-98	**San Jose**	**NHL**	**73**	**15**	**14**	**29**	**60**	**1**	**0**	**2**	**79**	**19.0**	**4**	....	....	....	....	....	**4**	**0**	**1**	**1**	**0**	**0**	**0**	**0**
1998-99	**San Jose**	**NHL**	**68**	**8**	**15**	**23**	**73**	**0**	**0**	**0**	**72**	**11.1**	**2**	**13**	**38.5**	**58**	**20**	**13:34**	**5**	**0**	**0**	**0**	**6**	**0**	**0**	**0**
	NHL Totals		**592**	**108**	**133**	**241**	**607**	**12**	**3**	**13**	**777**	**13.9**		**13**	**38.5**	**58**	**20**	**13:34**	**83**	**10**	**15**	**25**	**70**	**2**	**1**	**2**

Traded to **Chicago** by **Calgary** for Trent Yawney, December 16, 1991. Traded to **NY Rangers** by **Chicago** with Brian Noonan for Tony Amonte and the rights to Matt Oates, March 21, 1994. Traded to **St. Louis** by **NY Rangers** for Ian Laperriere, December 28, 1995. Traded to **San Jose** by **St. Louis** for Darren Turcotte, July 24, 1997.

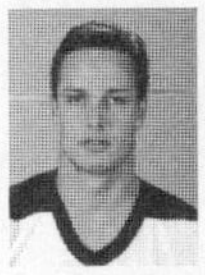

MATVICHUK, Richard

(MAT-vih-chuhk) **DAL.**

Defense. Shoots left. 6'2", 200 lbs. Born, Edmonton, Alta., February 5, 1973. Minnesota's 1st choice, 8th overall, in 1991 Entry Draft.

Season	Club	League	GP	G	A	Pts	PIM	PP	SH	GW	S	%	+/-	TF	F%	H	SB	Min	GP	G	A	Pts	PIM	PP	SH	GW
1988-89	Ft. Saskatchewan	AJHL	58	7	36	43	147	....	....	....	....	....	....	....	....	....	....	....	....	....	....	....	....	....	....	....
1989-90	Saskatoon	WHL	56	8	24	32	126	....	....	....	....	....	....	....	....	....	....	....	10	2	8	10	16	....	....	....
1990-91	Saskatoon	WHL	68	13	36	49	117	....	....	....	....	....	....	....	....	....	....	....	....	....	....	....	....	....	....	....
1991-92	Saskatoon	WHL	58	14	40	54	126	....	....	....	....	....	....	....	....	....	....	....	22	1	9	10	61	....	....	....
1992-93	**Minnesota**	**NHL**	**53**	**2**	**3**	**5**	**26**	**1**	**0**	**0**	**51**	**3.9**	**–8**	....	....	....	....	....	....	....	....	....	....	....	....	....
	Kalamazoo	IHL	3	0	1	1	6	....	....	....	....	....	....	....	....	....	....	....	....	....	....	....	....	....	....	....
1993-94	**Dallas**	**NHL**	**25**	**0**	**3**	**3**	**22**	**0**	**0**	**0**	**18**	**0.0**	**1**	....	....	....	....	....	**7**	**1**	**1**	**2**	**12**	**1**	**0**	**0**
	Kalamazoo	IHL	43	8	17	25	84	....	....	....	....	....	....	....	....	....	....	....	....	....	....	....	....	....	....	....
1994-95	**Dallas**	**NHL**	**14**	**0**	**2**	**2**	**14**	**0**	**0**	**0**	**21**	**0.0**	**–7**	....	....	....	....	....	**5**	**0**	**2**	**2**	**4**	**0**	**0**	**0**
	Kalamazoo	IHL	17	0	6	6	16	....	....	....	....	....	....	....	....	....	....	....	....	....	....	....	....	....	....	....
1995-96	**Dallas**	**NHL**	**73**	**6**	**16**	**22**	**71**	**0**	**0**	**1**	**81**	**7.4**	**4**	....	....	....	....	....	....	....	....	....	....	....	....	....
1996-97	**Dallas**	**NHL**	**57**	**5**	**7**	**12**	**87**	**0**	**2**	**0**	**83**	**6.0**	**1**	....	....	....	....	....	**7**	**0**	**1**	**1**	**20**	**0**	**0**	**0**
1997-98	**Dallas**	**NHL**	**74**	**3**	**15**	**18**	**63**	**0**	**0**	**0**	**71**	**4.2**	**7**	....	....	....	....	....	**16**	**1**	**1**	**2**	**14**	**0**	**0**	**0**
1998-99	♦ **Dallas**	**NHL**	**64**	**3**	**9**	**12**	**51**	**1**	**0**	**0**	**54**	**5.6**	**23**	**0**	**0.0**	**186**	**153**	**21:19**	**22**	**1**	**5**	**6**	**20**	**0**	**0**	**0**
	NHL Totals		**360**	**19**	**55**	**74**	**334**	**2**	**2**	**1**	**379**	**5.0**		**0**	**0.0**	**186**	**153**	**21:19**	**57**	**3**	**10**	**13**	**70**	**1**	**0**	**0**

WHL East First All-Star Team (1992)

Transferred to **Dallas** after **Minnesota** franchise relocated, June 9, 1993.

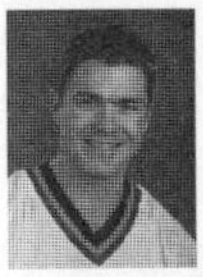

MAY, Brad

VAN.

Left wing. Shoots left. 6'1", 210 lbs. Born, Toronto, Ont., November 29, 1971. Buffalo's 1st choice, 14th overall, in 1990 Entry Draft.

Season	Club	League	GP	G	A	Pts	PIM	PP	SH	GW	S	%	+/-	TF	F%	H	SB	Min	GP	G	A	Pts	PIM	PP	SH	GW
1987-88	Markham AAA	OHA	31	22	37	65	58	....	....	....	....	....	....	....	....	....	....	....	....	....	....	....	....	....	....	....
	Markham	OJHL	6	1	1	2	21	....	....	....	....	....	....	....	....	....	....	....	....	....	....	....	....	....	....	....
1988-89	Niagara Falls	OHL	65	8	14	22	304	....	....	....	....	....	....	....	....	....	....	....	17	0	1	1	55	....	....	....
1989-90	Niagara Falls	OHL	61	32	58	90	223	....	....	....	....	....	....	....	....	....	....	....	16	9	13	22	64	....	....	....
1990-91	Niagara Falls	OHL	34	37	32	69	93	....	....	....	....	....	....	....	....	....	....	....	14	11	14	25	53	....	....	....
1991-92	**Buffalo**	**NHL**	**69**	**11**	**6**	**17**	**309**	**1**	**0**	**3**	**82**	**13.4**	**–12**	....	....	....	....	....	**7**	**1**	**4**	**5**	**2**	**0**	**0**	**1**
1992-93	**Buffalo**	**NHL**	**82**	**13**	**13**	**26**	**242**	**0**	**0**	**1**	**114**	**11.4**	**3**	....	....	....	....	....	**8**	**1**	**1**	**2**	**14**	**0**	**0**	**1**
1993-94	**Buffalo**	**NHL**	**84**	**18**	**27**	**45**	**171**	**3**	**0**	**3**	**166**	**10.8**	**–6**	....	....	....	....	....	**7**	**0**	**2**	**2**	**9**	**0**	**0**	**0**
1994-95	**Buffalo**	**NHL**	**33**	**3**	**3**	**6**	**87**	**1**	**0**	**0**	**42**	**7.1**	**5**	....	....	....	....	....	**4**	**0**	**0**	**0**	**2**	**0**	**0**	**0**
1995-96	**Buffalo**	**NHL**	**79**	**15**	**29**	**44**	**295**	**3**	**0**	**4**	**168**	**8.9**	**6**	....	....	....	....	....	....	....	....	....	....	....	....	....
1996-97	**Buffalo**	**NHL**	**42**	**3**	**4**	**7**	**106**	**1**	**0**	**1**	**75**	**4.0**	**–8**	....	....	....	....	....	**10**	**1**	**1**	**2**	**32**	**0**	**0**	**0**
1997-98	**Buffalo**	**NHL**	**36**	**4**	**7**	**11**	**113**	**0**	**0**	**0**	**41**	**9.8**	**2**	....	....	....	....	....	....	....	....	....	....	....	....	....
	Vancouver	**NHL**	**27**	**9**	**3**	**12**	**41**	**4**	**0**	**2**	**56**	**16.1**	**0**	....	....	....	....	....	....	....	....	....	....	....	....	....
1998-99	**Vancouver**	**NHL**	**66**	**6**	**11**	**17**	**102**	**1**	**0**	**1**	**91**	**6.6**	**–14**	**8**	**12.5**	**109**	**14**	**13:04**	....	....	....	....	....	....	....	....
	NHL Totals		**518**	**82**	**103**	**185**	**1466**	**14**	**0**	**15**	**835**	**9.8**		**8**	**12.5**	**109**	**14**	**13:04**	**36**	**3**	**8**	**11**	**59**	**0**	**0**	**2**

OHL Second All-Star Team (1990, 1991)

Traded to **Vancouver** by **Buffalo** with future considerations for Geoff Sanderson, February 4, 1998.

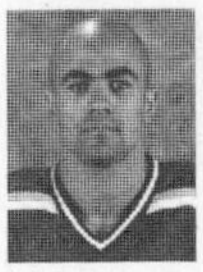

MAYERS, Jamal

(MAI-uhz, JUH-MAHL) **ST.L.**

Center. Shoots right. 6'1", 212 lbs. Born, Toronto, Ont., October 24, 1974. St. Louis' 3rd choice, 89th overall, in 1993 Entry Draft.

Season	Club	League	GP	G	A	Pts	PIM	PP	SH	GW	S	%	+/-	TF	F%	H	SB	Min	GP	G	A	Pts	PIM	PP	SH	GW
1990-91	Thornhill	OJHL	44	12	24	36	78	....	....	....	....	....	....	....	....	....	....	....	....	....	....	....	....	....	....	....
1991-92	Thornhill	OJHL	56	38	69	107	36	....	....	....	....	....	....	....	....	....	....	....	....	....	....	....	....	....	....	....
1992-93	Western Michigan	CCHA	38	8	17	25	26	....	....	....	....	....	....	....	....	....	....	....	....	....	....	....	....	....	....	....
1993-94	Western Michigan	CCHA	40	17	32	49	40	....	....	....	....	....	....	....	....	....	....	....	....	....	....	....	....	....	....	....
1994-95	Western Michigan	CCHA	39	13	32	45	40	....	....	....	....	....	....	....	....	....	....	....	....	....	....	....	....	....	....	....
1995-96	Western Michigan	CCHA	38	17	22	39	75	....	....	....	....	....	....	....	....	....	....	....	....	....	....	....	....	....	....	....
1996-97	**St. Louis**	**NHL**	**6**	**0**	**1**	**1**	**2**	**0**	**0**	**0**	**7**	**0.0**	**–3**	....	....	....	....	....	....	....	....	....	....	....	....	....
	Worcester	AHL	62	12	14	26	104	....	....	....	....	....	....	....	....	....	....	....	5	4	5	9	4	....	....	....
1997-98	Worcester	AHL	61	19	24	43	117	....	....	....	....	....	....	....	....	....	....	....	11	3	4	7	10	....	....	....
1998-99	**St. Louis**	**NHL**	**34**	**4**	**5**	**9**	**40**	**0**	**0**	**0**	**48**	**8.3**	**–3**	**2**	**50.0**	**56**	**3**	**8:08**	**11**	**0**	**1**	**1**	**8**	**0**	**0**	**0**
	Worcester	AHL	20	9	7	16	34	....	....	....	....	....	....	....	....	....	....	....	....	....	....	....	....	....	....	....
	NHL Totals		**40**	**4**	**6**	**10**	**42**	**0**	**0**	**0**	**55**	**7.3**		**2**	**50.0**	**56**	**3**	**8:08**	**11**	**0**	**1**	**1**	**8**	**0**	**0**	**0**

			Regular Season																Playoffs						
Season	Club	League	GP	G	A	Pts	PIM	PP	SH	GW	S	%	+/−	TF	F%	H	SB	Min	GP	G	A	Pts	PIM	PP	SH	GW

McALLISTER, Chris TOR.

Defense. Shoots left. 6'7", 235 lbs.   Born, Saskatoon, Sask., June 16, 1975. Vancouver's 1st choice, 40th overall, in 1995 Entry Draft.

Season	Club	League	GP	G	A	Pts	PIM	PP	SH	GW	S	%	+/−	TF	F%	H	SB	Min	GP	G	A	Pts	PIM	PP	SH	GW
1993-94	Humboldt	SJHL	50	3	5	8	150	....	....	....	....	....	....						....	....	....	....	....			
	Saskatoon	WHL	2	0	0	0	5	....	....	....	....	....	....						....	....	....	....	....			
1994-95	Saskatoon	WHL	65	2	8	10	134	....	....	....	....	....	....						10	0	0	0	28			
1995-96	Syracuse	AHL	68	0	2	2	142	....	....	....	....	....	....						16	0	0	0	34			
1996-97	Syracuse	AHL	43	3	1	4	108	....	....	....	....	....	....						3	0	0	0	6			
1997-98	**Vancouver**	**NHL**	36	1	2	3	106	0	0	0	15	6.7	−12						....	....	....	....	....			
	Syracuse	AHL	23	0	1	1	71	....	....	....	....	....	....						5	0	0	0	21			
1998-99	**Vancouver**	**NHL**	28	1	1	2	63	0	0	0	6	16.7	−7	0	0.0	19	5	5:53	....	....	....	....	....			
	Syracuse	AHL	5	0	0	0	24																			
	Toronto	**NHL**	20	0	2	2	39	0	0	0	12	0.0	4	0	0.0	37	17	13:59	6	0	1	1	4	0	0	0
	NHL Totals		84	2	5	7	208	0	0	0	33	6.1		0	0.0	56	22	9:15	6	0	1	1	4	0	0	0

Traded to **Toronto** by **Vancouver** for Darby Hendrickson, February 16, 1999.

McALPINE, Chris ST.L.

Defense. Shoots right. 6', 210 lbs.   Born, Roseville, MN, December 1, 1971. New Jersey's 10th choice, 137th overall, in 1990 Entry Draft.

Season	Club	League	GP	G	A	Pts	PIM	PP	SH	GW	S	%	+/−	TF	F%	H	SB	Min	GP	G	A	Pts	PIM	PP	SH	GW
1989-90	Roseville Prep	H.S.	25	15	13	28		....	....	....	....	....	....						....	....	....	....	....			
1990-91	U. of Minnesota	WCHA	38	7	9	16	112	....	....	....	....	....	....						....	....	....	....	....			
1991-92	U. of Minnesota	WCHA	39	3	9	12	126	....	....	....	....	....	....						....	....	....	....	....			
1992-93	U. of Minnesota	WCHA	41	14	9	23	82	....	....	....	....	....	....						....	....	....	....	....			
1993-94	U. of Minnesota	WCHA	36	12	18	30	121	....	....	....	....	....	....						....	....	....	....	....			
1994-95	Albany	AHL	48	4	18	22	49	....	....	....	....	....	....						....	....	....	....	....			
◆	**New Jersey**	**NHL**	24	0	3	3	17	0	0	0	19	0.0	4						....	....	....	....	....			
1995-96	Albany	AHL	57	5	14	19	72	....	....	....	....	....	....						4	0	0	0	13			
1996-97	Albany	AHL	44	1	9	10	48	....	....	....	....	....	....						....	....	....	....	....			
	St. Louis	**NHL**	15	0	0	0	24	0	0	0	3	0.0	−2						4	0	1	1	0	0	0	0
1997-98	**St. Louis**	**NHL**	54	3	7	10	36	0	0	0	35	8.6	14						10	0	0	0	16	0	0	0
1998-99	**St. Louis**	**NHL**	51	1	1	2	50	0	0	0	56	1.8	−10	0	0.0	75	42	12:51	13	0	0	0	2	0	0	0
	NHL Totals		144	4	11	15	127	0	0	0	113	3.5		0	0.0	75	42	12:51	27	0	1	1	18	0	0	0

WCHA First All-Star Team (1994) • NCAA West Second All-American Team (1994)
Traded to **St. Louis** by **New Jersey** with New Jersey's 9th round choice in 1999 Entry Draft for Peter Zezel, February 11, 1997.

McAMMOND, Dean CHI.

Center. Shoots left. 5'11", 200 lbs.   Born, Grand Cache, Alta., June 15, 1973. Chicago's 1st choice, 22nd overall, in 1991 Entry Draft.

Season	Club	League	GP	G	A	Pts	PIM	PP	SH	GW	S	%	+/−	TF	F%	H	SB	Min	GP	G	A	Pts	PIM	PP	SH	GW
1988-89	St. Albert	AJHL	36	33	44	77	132	....	....	....	....	....	....						14	2	3	5	18			
1989-90	Prince Albert	WHL	53	11	11	22	49	....	....	....	....	....	....						2	0	1	1	6			
1990-91	Prince Albert	WHL	71	33	35	68	108	....	....	....	....	....	....						10	12	11	23	26			
1991-92	Prince Albert	WHL	63	37	54	91	189	....	....	....	....	....	....						....	....	....	....	....			
	Chicago	**NHL**	5	0	2	2	0	0	0	0	4	0.0	−2						3	0	0	0	2	0	0	0
1992-93	Prince Albert	WHL	30	19	29	48	44	....	....	....	....	....	....						....	....	....	....	....			
	Swift Current	WHL	18	10	13	23	24	....	....	....	....	....	....						17	*16	19	35	20			
1993-94	**Edmonton**	**NHL**	45	6	21	27	16	2	0	0	52	11.5	12						....	....	....	....	....			
	Cape Breton	AHL	28	9	12	21	38	....	....	....	....	....	....						....	....	....	....	....			
1994-95	**Edmonton**	**NHL**	6	0	0	0	0	0	0	0	3	0.0	−1						....	....	....	....	....			
1995-96	**Edmonton**	**NHL**	53	15	15	30	23	4	0	0	79	19.0	6						....	....	....	....	....			
	Cape Breton	AHL	22	9	15	24	55	....	....	....	....	....	....						....	....	....	....	....			
1996-97	**Edmonton**	**NHL**	57	12	17	29	28	4	0	6	106	11.3	−15						12	1	4	5	12	0	0	0
1997-98	**Edmonton**	**NHL**	77	19	31	50	46	8	0	3	128	14.8	9						....	....	....	....	....			
1998-99	**Edmonton**	**NHL**	65	9	16	25	36	1	0	0	122	7.4	5	26	38.5	116	21	14:15	....	....	....	....	....			
	Chicago	**NHL**	12	1	4	5	2	0	0	1	16	6.3	3	37	48.6	22	4	15:43	....	....	....	....	....			
	NHL Totals		320	62	106	168	151	19	0	10	510	12.2		63	44.4	138	25	14:29	15	1	4	5	14	0	0	0

Traded to **Edmonton** by **Chicago** with Igor Kravchuk for Joe Murphy, February 24, 1993. Traded to **Chicago** by **Edmonton** with Boris Mironov and Jonas Elofsson for Chad Kilger, Daniel Cleary, Ethan Moreau and Christian Laflamme, March 20, 1999.

McBAIN, Jason

Defense. Shoots left. 6'2", 180 lbs.   Born, Ilion, NY, April 12, 1974. Hartford's 5th choice, 81st overall, in 1992 Entry Draft.

Season	Club	League	GP	G	A	Pts	PIM	PP	SH	GW	S	%	+/−	TF	F%	H	SB	Min	GP	G	A	Pts	PIM	PP	SH	GW
1989-90	Kimberley	BCAHA	37	20	38	58	77	....	....	....	....	....	....						....	....	....	....	....			
1990-91	Lethbridge	WHL	52	2	7	9	39	....	....	....	....	....	....						1	0	0	0	0			
1991-92	Lethbridge	WHL	13	0	1	1	12	....	....	....	....	....	....						....	....	....	....	....			
	Portland	WHL	54	9	23	32	95	....	....	....	....	....	....						6	1	0	1	13			
1992-93	Portland	WHL	71	9	35	44	76	....	....	....	....	....	....						16	2	12	14	14			
1993-94	Portland	WHL	63	15	51	66	86	....	....	....	....	....	....						10	2	7	9	14			
1994-95	Springfield	AHL	77	16	28	44	92	....	....	....	....	....	....						....	....	....	....	....			
1995-96	**Hartford**	**NHL**	3	0	0	0	0	0	0	0	0	0.0	−1						....	....	....	....	....			
	Springfield	AHL	73	11	33	44	43	....	....	....	....	....	....						8	1	1	2	2			
1996-97	**Hartford**	**NHL**	6	0	0	0	0	0	0	0	1	0.0	−4						....	....	....	....	....			
	Springfield	AHL	58	8	26	34	40	....	....	....	....	....	....						16	0	8	8	12			
1997-98	Cleveland	IHL	65	8	22	30	62	....	....	....	....	....	....						3	0	2	2	2			
1998-99	Las Vegas	IHL	65	9	37	46	54	....	....	....	....	....	....						19	1	8	9	16			
	Providence	AHL	9	1	7	8	10	....	....	....	....	....	....						....	....	....	....	....			
	NHL Totals		9	0	0	0	0	0	0	0	1	0.0							....	....	....	....	....			

Transferred to **Carolina** after **Hartford** franchise relocated, June 25, 1997.

McBAIN, Mike T.B.

Defense. Shoots left. 6'2", 195 lbs.   Born, Kimberley, B.C., January 12, 1977. Tampa Bay's 2nd choice, 30th overall, in 1995 Entry Draft.

Season	Club	League	GP	G	A	Pts	PIM	PP	SH	GW	S	%	+/−	TF	F%	H	SB	Min	GP	G	A	Pts	PIM	PP	SH	GW
1991-92	Kimberley	BCAHA	35	25	62	87	39	....	....	....	....	....	....						....	....	....	....	....			
1992-93	Kimberley	RMJHL	35	0	4	4	48	....	....	....	....	....	....						....	....	....	....	....			
1993-94	Red Deer	WHL	58	4	13	17	41	....	....	....	....	....	....						4	0	0	0	0			
1994-95	Red Deer	WHL	68	6	28	34	55	....	....	....	....	....	....						....	....	....	....	....			
1995-96	Red Deer	WHL	68	7	34	41	68	....	....	....	....	....	....						10	1	7	8	10			
1996-97	Red Deer	WHL	59	14	35	49	55	....	....	....	....	....	....						15	1	6	7	9			
1997-98	**Tampa Bay**	**NHL**	27	0	1	1	8	0	0	0	17	0.0	−10						....	....	....	....	....			
	Adirondack	AHL	42	2	13	15	28	....	....	....	....	....	....						....	....	....	....	....			
1998-99	**Tampa Bay**	**NHL**	37	0	6	6	14	0	0	0	22	0.0	−11	0	0.0	22	30	14:49	....	....	....	....	....			
	Cleveland	IHL	28	2	4	6	15	....	....	....	....	....	....						....	....	....	....	....			
	NHL Totals		64	0	7	7	22	0	0	0	39	0.0		0	0.0	22	30	14:49	....	....	....	....	....			

McCABE, Bryan CHI.

Defense. Shoots left. 6'1", 210 lbs.   Born, St. Catharines, Ont., June 8, 1975. NY Islanders' 2nd choice, 40th overall, in 1993 Entry Draft.

Season	Club	League	GP	G	A	Pts	PIM	PP	SH	GW	S	%	+/−	TF	F%	H	SB	Min	GP	G	A	Pts	PIM	PP	SH	GW
1990-91	Calgary	AAHA	33	14	34	48	55	....	....	....	....	....	....						....	....	....	....	....			
1991-92	Medicine Hat	WHL	68	6	24	30	157	....	....	....	....	....	....						4	0	0	0	6			
1992-93	Medicine Hat	WHL	14	0	13	13	83	....	....	....	....	....	....						....	....	....	....	....			
	Spokane	WHL	46	3	44	47	134	....	....	....	....	....	....						6	1	5	6	28			
1993-94	Spokane	WHL	64	22	62	84	218	....	....	....	....	....	....						3	0	4	4	4			

			Regular Season																Playoffs							
Season	Club	League	GP	G	A	Pts	PIM	PP	SH	GW	S	%	+/-	TF	F%	H	SB	Min	GP	G	A	Pts	PIM	PP	SH	GW
1994-95	Spokane	WHL	42	14	39	53	115	....	....	....	....	....	....	....	....	....	....	....	....	....	....	....	....	....	....	....
	Brandon	WHL	20	6	10	16	38	....	....	....	....	....	....	....	....	....	....	....	18	4	13	17	59	....	....	....
1995-96	**NY Islanders**	**NHL**	**82**	**7**	**16**	**23**	**156**	**3**	**0**	**1**	**130**	**5.4**	**–24**	....	....	....	....	....	....	....	....	....	....	....	....	....
1996-97	**NY Islanders**	**NHL**	**82**	**8**	**20**	**28**	**165**	**2**	**1**	**2**	**117**	**6.8**	**–2**	....	....	....	....	....	....	....	....	....	....	....	....	....
1997-98	**NY Islanders**	**NHL**	**56**	**3**	**9**	**12**	**145**	**1**	**0**	**0**	**81**	**3.7**	**9**	....	....	....	....	....	....	....	....	....	....	....	....	....
	Vancouver	**NHL**	**26**	**1**	**11**	**12**	**64**	**0**	**1**	**0**	**42**	**2.4**	**10**	....	....	....	....	....	....	....	....	....	....	....	....	....
1998-99	**Vancouver**	**NHL**	**69**	**7**	**14**	**21**	**120**	**1**	**2**	**0**	**98**	**7.1**	**–11**	**1**	**0.0**	**107**	**117**	**24:13**	....	....	....	....	....	....	....	....
	NHL Totals		**315**	**26**	**70**	**96**	**650**	**7**	**4**	**3**	**468**	**5.6**		**1**	**0.0**	**107**	**117**	**24:13**	....	....	....	....	....	....	....	....

WHL West Second All-Star Team (1993) • WHL West First All-Star Team (1994) • WHL East First All-Star Team (1995) • Memorial Cup All-Star Team (1995)

Traded to **Vancouver** by **NY Islanders** with Todd Bertuzzi and NY Islanders' 3rd round choice (Jarkko Ruutu) in 1998 Entry Draft for Trevor Linden, February 6, 1998. Traded to **Chicago** by **Vancouver** with Vancouver's 1st round choice in either the 2000 or 2001 Entry Draft for Chicago's 1st round choice (later traded to Tampa Bay - later traded to NY Rangers - NY Rangers selected Pavel Brendl) in 1999 Entry Draft, June 25, 1999.

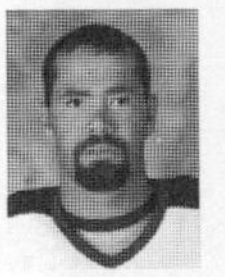

McCARTHY, Sandy — PHI.

Right wing. Shoots right. 6'3", 225 lbs. Born, Toronto, Ont., June 15, 1972. Calgary's 3rd choice, 52nd overall, in 1991 Entry Draft.

Season	Club	League	GP	G	A	Pts	PIM	PP	SH	GW	S	%	+/-	TF	F%	H	SB	Min	GP	G	A	Pts	PIM	PP	SH	GW
1987-88	Midland	OJHL-C	18	2	1	3	70	....	....	....	....	....	....	....	....	....	....	....	....	....	....	....	....	....	....	....
1989-90	Laval	QMJHL	65	10	11	21	269	....	....	....	....	....	....	....	....	....	....	....	14	3	3	6	60	....	....	....
1990-91	Laval	QMJHL	68	21	19	40	297	....	....	....	....	....	....	....	....	....	....	....	13	6	5	11	67	....	....	....
1991-92	Laval	QMJHL	62	39	51	90	326	....	....	....	....	....	....	....	....	....	....	....	8	4	5	9	81	....	....	....
1992-93	Salt Lake	IHL	77	18	20	38	220	....	....	....	....	....	....	....	....	....	....	....	....	....	....	....	....	....	....	....
1993-94	**Calgary**	**NHL**	**79**	**5**	**5**	**10**	**173**	**0**	**0**	**0**	**39**	**12.8**	**–3**	....	....	....	....	....	**7**	**0**	**0**	**0**	**34**	**0**	**0**	**0**
1994-95	**Calgary**	**NHL**	**37**	**5**	**3**	**8**	**101**	**0**	**0**	**2**	**29**	**17.2**	**1**	....	....	....	....	....	**6**	**0**	**1**	**1**	**17**	**0**	**0**	**0**
1995-96	**Calgary**	**NHL**	**75**	**9**	**7**	**16**	**173**	**3**	**0**	**1**	**98**	**9.2**	**–8**	....	....	....	....	....	**4**	**0**	**0**	**0**	**10**	**0**	**0**	**0**
1996-97	**Calgary**	**NHL**	**33**	**3**	**5**	**8**	**113**	**1**	**0**	**1**	**38**	**7.9**	**–8**	....	....	....	....	....	....	....	....	....	....	....	....	....
1997-98	**Calgary**	**NHL**	**52**	**8**	**5**	**13**	**170**	**1**	**0**	**1**	**68**	**11.8**	**–18**	....	....	....	....	....	....	....	....	....	....	....	....	....
	Tampa Bay	**NHL**	**14**	**0**	**5**	**5**	**71**	**0**	**0**	**0**	**26**	**0.0**	**–1**	....	....	....	....	....	....	....	....	....	....	....	....	....
1998-99	**Tampa Bay**	**NHL**	**67**	**5**	**7**	**12**	**135**	**1**	**0**	**0**	**89**	**5.6**	**–22**	**0**	**0.0**	**118**	**13**	**11:02**	....	....	....	....	....	....	....	....
	Philadelphia	**NHL**	**13**	**0**	**1**	**1**	**25**	**0**	**0**	**0**	**18**	**0.0**	**–2**	**2**	**50.0**	**26**	**2**	**11:09**	**6**	**0**	**1**	**1**	**0**	**0**	**0**	**0**
	NHL Totals		**370**	**35**	**38**	**73**	**961**	**6**	**0**	**5**	**405**	**8.6**		**2**	**50.0**	**144**	**15**	**11:03**	**23**	**0**	**2**	**2**	**61**	**0**	**0**	**0**

Traded to **Tampa Bay** by **Calgary** with Calgary's 3rd (Brad Richards) and 5th (Curtis Rich) round choices in 1998 Entry Draft for Jason Wiemer, March 24, 1998. Traded to **Philadelphia** by **Tampa Bay** with Mikael Andersson for Colin Forbes and Philadelphia's 4th round choice (Michal Lanisak) in 1999 Entry Draft, March 20, 1999.

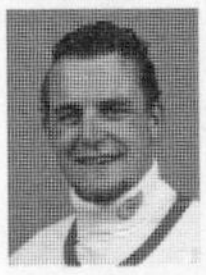

McCARTY, Darren — DET.

Right wing. Shoots right. 6'1", 210 lbs. Born, Burnaby, B.C., April 1, 1972. Detroit's 2nd choice, 46th overall, in 1992 Entry Draft.

Season	Club	League	GP	G	A	Pts	PIM	PP	SH	GW	S	%	+/-	TF	F%	H	SB	Min	GP	G	A	Pts	PIM	PP	SH	GW
1988-89	Peterborough	OJHL-B	34	18	17	35	35	....	....	....	....	....	....	....	....	....	....	....	....	....	....	....	....	....	....	....
1989-90	Belleville	OHL	63	12	15	27	142	....	....	....	....	....	....	....	....	....	....	....	11	1	1	2	21	....	....	....
1990-91	Belleville	OHL	60	30	37	67	151	....	....	....	....	....	....	....	....	....	....	....	6	2	2	4	13	....	....	....
1991-92	Belleville	OHL	65	*55	72	127	177	....	....	....	....	....	....	....	....	....	....	....	5	1	4	5	13	....	....	....
1992-93	Adirondack	AHL	73	17	19	36	278	....	....	....	....	....	....	....	....	....	....	....	11	0	1	1	33	....	....	....
1993-94	**Detroit**	**NHL**	**67**	**9**	**17**	**26**	**181**	**0**	**0**	**2**	**81**	**11.1**	**12**	....	....	....	....	....	**7**	**2**	**2**	**4**	**8**	**0**	**0**	**0**
1994-95	**Detroit**	**NHL**	**31**	**5**	**8**	**13**	**88**	**1**	**0**	**2**	**27**	**18.5**	**5**	....	....	....	....	....	**18**	**3**	**2**	**5**	**14**	**0**	**0**	**0**
1995-96	**Detroit**	**NHL**	**63**	**15**	**14**	**29**	**158**	**8**	**0**	**1**	**102**	**14.7**	**14**	....	....	....	....	....	**19**	**3**	**2**	**5**	**20**	**0**	**0**	**1**
1996-97♦	**Detroit**	**NHL**	**68**	**19**	**30**	**49**	**126**	**5**	**0**	**6**	**171**	**11.1**	**14**	....	....	....	....	....	**20**	**3**	**4**	**7**	**34**	**0**	**0**	**2**
1997-98♦	**Detroit**	**NHL**	**71**	**15**	**22**	**37**	**157**	**5**	**1**	**2**	**166**	**9.0**	**0**	....	....	....	....	....	**22**	**3**	**8**	**11**	**34**	**0**	**0**	**1**
1998-99	**Detroit**	**NHL**	**69**	**14**	**26**	**40**	**108**	**6**	**0**	**1**	**140**	**10.0**	**10**	**15**	**33.3**	**217**	**34**	**17:04**	**10**	**1**	**1**	**2**	**23**	**0**	**0**	**0**
	NHL Totals		**369**	**77**	**117**	**194**	**818**	**25**	**1**	**14**	**687**	**11.2**		**15**	**33.3**	**217**	**34**	**17:04**	**96**	**15**	**19**	**34**	**133**	**0**	**0**	**4**

OHL First All-Star Team (1992)

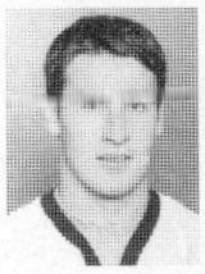

McCAULEY, Alyn — TOR.

Center. Shoots left. 5'11", 191 lbs. Born, Brockville, Ont., May 29, 1977. New Jersey's 5th choice, 79th overall, in 1995 Entry Draft.

Season	Club	League	GP	G	A	Pts	PIM	PP	SH	GW	S	%	+/-	TF	F%	H	SB	Min	GP	G	A	Pts	PIM	PP	SH	GW
1992-93	Kingston	OJHL	38	31	29	60	18	....	....	....	....	....	....	....	....	....	....	....	....	....	....	....	....	....	....	....
1993-94	Ottawa	OHL	38	13	23	36	10	....	....	....	....	....	....	....	....	....	....	....	13	5	14	19	4	....	....	....
1994-95	Ottawa	OHL	65	16	38	54	20	....	....	....	....	....	....	....	....	....	....	....	....	....	....	....	....	....	....	....
1995-96	Ottawa	OHL	55	34	48	82	24	....	....	....	....	....	....	....	....	....	....	....	2	0	0	0	0	....	....	....
1996-97	Ottawa	OHL	50	*56	56	112	16	....	....	....	....	....	....	....	....	....	....	....	22	14	22	36	14	....	....	....
	St. John's	AHL	....	....	....	....	....	....	....	....	....	....	....	....	....	....	....	....	3	0	1	1	0	....	....	....
1997-98	**Toronto**	**NHL**	**60**	**6**	**10**	**16**	**6**	**0**	**0**	**1**	**77**	**7.8**	**–7**	....	....	....	....	....	....	....	....	....	....	....	....	....
1998-99	**Toronto**	**NHL**	**39**	**9**	**15**	**24**	**2**	**1**	**0**	**1**	**76**	**11.8**	**7**	**591**	**46.4**	**10**	**4**	**15:10**	....	....	....	....	....	....	....	....
	NHL Totals		**99**	**15**	**25**	**40**	**8**	**1**	**0**	**2**	**153**	**9.8**		**591**	**46.4**	**10**		**415:010**	....	....	....	....	....	....	....	....

OHL First All-Star Team (1996, 1997) • Canadian Major Junior First All-Star Team (1997) • Canadian Major Junior Player of the Year (1997)

Rights traded to **Toronto** by **New Jersey** with Jason Smith and Steve Sullivan for Doug Gilmour, Dave Ellett and future considerations, February 25, 1997.

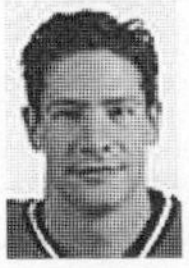

McCLEARY, Trent — MTL.

Right wing. Shoots right. 6', 180 lbs. Born, Swift Current, Sask., September 8, 1972.

Season	Club	League	GP	G	A	Pts	PIM	PP	SH	GW	S	%	+/-	TF	F%	H	SB	Min	GP	G	A	Pts	PIM	PP	SH	GW
1989-90	Swift Current	WHL	70	3	15	18	43	....	....	....	....	....	....	....	....	....	....	....	4	1	0	1	0	....	....	....
1990-91	Swift Current	WHL	70	16	24	40	53	....	....	....	....	....	....	....	....	....	....	....	3	0	0	0	2	....	....	....
1991-92	Swift Current	WHL	72	23	22	45	240	....	....	....	....	....	....	....	....	....	....	....	8	1	2	3	16	....	....	....
1992-93	Swift Current	WHL	63	17	33	50	138	....	....	....	....	....	....	....	....	....	....	....	17	5	4	9	16	....	....	....
	New Haven	AHL	2	1	0	1	6	....	....	....	....	....	....	....	....	....	....	....	....	....	....	....	....	....	....	....
1993-94	P.E.I. Senators	AHL	4	0	0	0	6	....	....	....	....	....	....	....	....	....	....	....	....	....	....	....	....	....	....	....
	Thunder Bay	ColHL	51	23	17	40	123	....	....	....	....	....	....	....	....	....	....	....	9	2	11	13	15	....	....	....
1994-95	P.E.I. Senators	AHL	51	9	20	29	60	....	....	....	....	....	....	....	....	....	....	....	9	2	3	5	26	....	....	....
1995-96	**Ottawa**	**NHL**	**75**	**4**	**10**	**14**	**68**	**0**	**1**	**0**	**58**	**6.9**	**–15**	....	....	....	....	....	....	....	....	....	....	....	....	....
1996-97	**Boston**	**NHL**	**59**	**3**	**5**	**8**	**33**	**0**	**0**	**1**	**41**	**7.3**	**–16**	....	....	....	....	....	....	....	....	....	....	....	....	....
1997-98	Detroit	IHL	21	1	1	2	45	....	....	....	....	....	....	....	....	....	....	....	....	....	....	....	....	....	....	....
	Las Vegas	IHL	54	7	6	13	120	....	....	....	....	....	....	....	....	....	....	....	3	1	0	1	2	....	....	....
1998-99	**Montreal**	**NHL**	**46**	**0**	**0**	**0**	**29**	**0**	**0**	**0**	**18**	**0.0**	**–1**	**113**	**45.1**	**81**	**15**	**5:50**	....	....	....	....	....	....	....	....
	NHL Totals		**180**	**7**	**15**	**22**	**130**	**0**	**1**	**1**	**117**	**6.0**		**113**	**45.1**	**81**	**15**	**5:50**	....	....	....	....	....	....	....	....

Signed as a free agent by **Ottawa**, October 9, 1992. Traded to **Boston** by **Ottawa** with Ottawa's 3rd round choice (Eric Naud) in 1996 Entry Draft for Shawn McEachern, June 22, 1996. Signed as a free agent by **Montreal**, October 9, 1998.

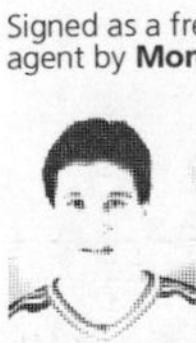

McCOSH, Shawn

Center. Shoots right. 6', 197 lbs. Born, Oshawa, Ont., June 5, 1969. Detroit's 5th choice, 95th overall, in 1989 Entry Draft.

Season	Club	League	GP	G	A	Pts	PIM	PP	SH	GW	S	%	+/-	TF	F%	H	SB	Min	GP	G	A	Pts	PIM	PP	SH	GW
1985-86	Oshawa	OMHA	68	67	81	148	145	....	....	....	....	....	....	....	....	....	....	....	....	....	....	....	....	....	....	....
1986-87	Hamilton	OHL	50	11	17	28	49	....	....	....	....	....	....	....	....	....	....	....	6	1	0	1	2	....	....	....
1987-88	Hamilton	OHL	64	17	36	53	96	....	....	....	....	....	....	....	....	....	....	....	14	6	8	14	14	....	....	....
1988-89	Niagara Falls	OHL	56	41	62	103	75	....	....	....	....	....	....	....	....	....	....	....	14	4	13	17	23	....	....	....
1989-90	Niagara Falls	OHL	9	6	10	16	24	....	....	....	....	....	....	....	....	....	....	....	....	....	....	....	....	....	....	....
	Hamilton	OHL	39	24	28	52	65	....	....	....	....	....	....	....	....	....	....	....	....	....	....	....	....	....	....	....
	Canada	Nat-Team	3	0	0	0	0	....	....	....	....	....	....	....	....	....	....	....	....	....	....	....	....	....	....	....
1990-91	New Haven	AHL	66	16	21	37	104	....	....	....	....	....	....	....	....	....	....	....	....	....	....	....	....	....	....	....
1991-92	**Los Angeles**	**NHL**	**4**	**0**	**0**	**0**	**4**	**0**	**0**	**0**	**2**	**0.0**	**0**	....	....	....	....	....	....	....	....	....	....	....	....	....
	Phoenix	IHL	71	21	32	53	118	....	....	....	....	....	....	....	....	....	....	....	....	....	....	....	....	....	....	....
	New Haven	AHL	....	....	....	....	....	....	....	....	....	....	....	....	....	....	....	....	5	0	1	1	0	....	....	....

								Regular Season											Playoffs							
Season	Club	League	GP	G	A	Pts	PIM	PP	SH	GW	S	%	+/-	TF	F%	H	SB	Min	GP	G	A	Pts	PIM	PP	SH	GW
1992-93	Phoenix	IHL	22	9	8	17	36	....	....	....	....	....	....	....	....	....	....	....	....	....	....	....	....	....	....	....
	New Haven	AHL	46	22	32	54	54	....	....	....	....	....	....	....	....	....	....	....	....	....	....	....	....	....	....	....
1993-94	Binghamton	AHL	75	31	44	75	68	....	....	....	....	....	....	....	....	....	....	....	....	....	....	....	....	....	....	....
1994-95	**NY Rangers**	**NHL**	**5**	**1**	**0**	**1**	**2**	**0**	**0**	**0**	**2**	**50.0**	**1**	....	....	....	....	....	....	....	....	....	....	....	....	....
	Binghamton	AHL	67	23	60	83	73	....	....	....	....	....	....	....	....	....	....	....	8	3	9	12	6	....	....	....
1995-96	Hershey	AHL	71	31	52	83	82	....	....	....	....	....	....	....	....	....	....	....	5	1	5	6	8	....	....	....
1996-97	Philadelphia	AHL	79	30	51	81	110	....	....	....	....	....	....	....	....	....	....	....	10	3	9	12	23	....	....	....
1997-98	Philadelphia	AHL	80	24	54	78	102	....	....	....	....	....	....	....	....	....	....	....	20	6	13	19	14	....	....	....
1998-99	Philadelphia	AHL	38	12	25	37	43	....	....	....	....	....	....	....	....	....	....	....	....	....	....	....	....	....	....	....
	Michigan	IHL	12	4	9	13	18	....	....	....	....	....	....	....	....	....	....	....	5	1	2	3	6	....	....	....
	NHL Totals		**9**	**1**	**0**	**1**	**6**	**0**	**0**	**0**	**4**	**25.0**		....	....	....	....	....	....	....	....	....	....	....	....	....

Traded to **LA Kings** by **Detroit** for LA Kings' 8th round choice (Justin Krall) in 1992 Entry Draft, August 15, 1990. Traded to **Ottawa** by **LA Kings** with Bob Kudelski for Marc Fortier and Jim Thomson, December 19, 1992. Signed as a free agent by **NY Rangers**, July 30, 1993. Signed as a free agent by **Philadelphia**, July 31, 1995.

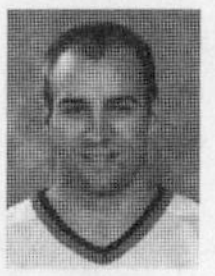

McEACHERN, Shawn

(muh-GEH-kruhn) **OTT.**

Left wing. Shoots left. 5'11", 195 lbs. Born, Waltham, MA, February 28, 1969. Pittsburgh's 6th choice, 110th overall, in 1987 Entry Draft.

1985-86	Matignon High	H.S.	20	32	20	52	....	....	....	....	....	....	....	....	....	....	....	....	....	....	....	....	....	....	....	....
1986-87	Matignon High	H.S.	16	29	28	57	....	....	....	....	....	....	....	....	....	....	....	....	....	....	....	....	....	....	....	....
1987-88	Matignon High	H.S.	22	52	40	92	....	....	....	....	....	....	....	....	....	....	....	....	....	....	....	....	....	....	....	....
1988-89	Boston University	H.E.	36	20	28	48	32	....	....	....	....	....	....	....	....	....	....	....	....	....	....	....	....	....	....	....
1989-90	Boston University	H.E.	43	25	31	56	78	....	....	....	....	....	....	....	....	....	....	....	....	....	....	....	....	....	....	....
1990-91	Boston University	H.E.	41	34	48	82	43	....	....	....	....	....	....	....	....	....	....	....	....	....	....	....	....	....	....	....
1991-92	United States	Nat-Team	57	26	23	49	38	....	....	....	....	....	....	....	....	....	....	....	....	....	....	....	....	....	....	....
	United States	Olympics	8	1	0	1	10	....	....	....	....	....	....	....	....	....	....	....	....	....	....	....	....	....	....	....
	♦ **Pittsburgh**	**NHL**	**15**	**0**	**4**	**4**	**0**	**0**	**0**	**0**	**14**	**0.0**	**1**	....	....	....	....	....	**19**	**2**	**7**	**9**	**4**	**0**	**0**	**0**
1992-93	**Pittsburgh**	**NHL**	**84**	**28**	**33**	**61**	**46**	**7**	**0**	**6**	**196**	**14.3**	**21**	....	....	....	....	....	**12**	**3**	**2**	**5**	**10**	**0**	**0**	**1**
1993-94	**Los Angeles**	**NHL**	**49**	**8**	**13**	**21**	**24**	**0**	**3**	**0**	**81**	**9.9**	**1**	....	....	....	....	....	....	....	....	....	....	....	....	....
	Pittsburgh	**NHL**	**27**	**12**	**9**	**21**	**10**	**0**	**2**	**1**	**78**	**15.4**	**13**	....	....	....	....	....	**6**	**1**	**0**	**1**	**2**	**0**	**0**	**0**
1994-95	Kiekko-Espoo	Finland	8	1	3	4	6	....	....	....	....	....	....	....	....	....	....	....	....	....	....	....	....	....	....	....
	Pittsburgh	**NHL**	**44**	**13**	**13**	**26**	**22**	**1**	**2**	**1**	**97**	**13.4**	**4**	....	....	....	....	....	**11**	**0**	**2**	**2**	**8**	**0**	**0**	**0**
1995-96	**Boston**	**NHL**	**82**	**24**	**29**	**53**	**34**	**3**	**2**	**3**	**238**	**10.1**	**–5**	....	....	....	....	....	**5**	**2**	**1**	**3**	**8**	**0**	**0**	**0**
1996-97	**Ottawa**	**NHL**	**65**	**11**	**20**	**31**	**18**	**0**	**1**	**2**	**150**	**7.3**	**–5**	....	....	....	....	....	**7**	**2**	**0**	**2**	**8**	**1**	**0**	**0**
1997-98	**Ottawa**	**NHL**	**81**	**24**	**24**	**48**	**42**	**8**	**2**	**4**	**229**	**10.5**	**1**	....	....	....	....	....	**11**	**0**	**4**	**4**	**8**	**0**	**0**	**0**
1998-99	**Ottawa**	**NHL**	**77**	**31**	**25**	**56**	**46**	**7**	**0**	**4**	**223**	**13.9**	**8**	**441**	**48.5**	**37**	**23**	**18:45**	**4**	**2**	**0**	**2**	**6**	**1**	**0**	**0**
	NHL Totals		**524**	**151**	**170**	**321**	**242**	**26**	**12**	**21**	**1306**	**11.6**		**441**	**48.5**	**37**	**23**	**18:45**	**75**	**12**	**16**	**28**	**54**	**2**	**0**	**1**

Hockey East Second All-Star Team (1990) • Hockey East First All-Star Team (1991) • NCAA East First All-American Team (1991)

Traded to **LA Kings** by **Pittsburgh** for Marty McSorley, August 27, 1993. Traded to **Pittsburgh** by **LA Kings** with Tomas Sandstrom for Marty McSorley and Jim Paek, February 16, 1994. Traded to **Boston** by **Pittsburgh** with Kevin Stevens for Glen Murray, Bryan Smolinski and Boston's 3rd round choice (Boyd Kane) in 1996 Entry Draft, August 2, 1995. Traded to **Ottawa** by **Boston** for Trent McCleary and Ottawa's 3rd round choice (Eric Naud) in 1996 Entry Draft, June 22, 1996.

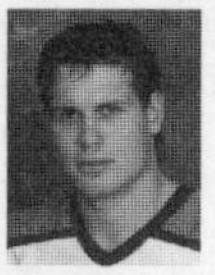

McGILLIS, Daniel

PHI.

Defense. Shoots left. 6'2", 225 lbs. Born, Hawkesbury, Ont., July 1, 1972. Detroit's 10th choice, 238th overall, in 1992 Entry Draft.

1991-92	Hawkesbury	OJHL	36	5	19	24	106	....	....	....	....	....	....	....	....	....	....	....	....	....	....	....	....	....	....	....
1992-93	Northeastern	H.E.	35	5	12	17	42	....	....	....	....	....	....	....	....	....	....	....	....	....	....	....	....	....	....	....
1993-94	Northeastern	H.E.	38	4	25	29	82	....	....	....	....	....	....	....	....	....	....	....	....	....	....	....	....	....	....	....
1994-95	Northeastern	H.E.	34	9	22	31	70	....	....	....	....	....	....	....	....	....	....	....	....	....	....	....	....	....	....	....
1995-96	Northeastern	H.E.	34	12	24	36	50	....	....	....	....	....	....	....	....	....	....	....	....	....	....	....	....	....	....	....
1996-97	**Edmonton**	**NHL**	**73**	**6**	**16**	**22**	**52**	**2**	**1**	**2**	**139**	**4.3**	**2**	....	....	....	....	....	**12**	**0**	**5**	**5**	**24**	**0**	**0**	**0**
1997-98	**Edmonton**	**NHL**	**67**	**10**	**15**	**25**	**74**	**5**	**0**	**3**	**119**	**8.4**	**–17**	....	....	....	....	....	....	....	....	....	....	....	....	....
	Philadelphia	**NHL**	**13**	**1**	**5**	**6**	**35**	**1**	**0**	**0**	**18**	**5.6**	**–4**	....	....	....	....	....	**5**	**1**	**2**	**3**	**10**	**1**	**0**	**0**
1998-99	**Philadelphia**	**NHL**	**78**	**8**	**37**	**45**	**61**	**6**	**0**	**4**	**164**	**4.9**	**16**	**0**	**0.0**	**220**	**71**	**21:41**	**6**	**0**	**1**	**1**	**12**	**0**	**0**	**0**
	NHL Totals		**231**	**25**	**73**	**98**	**222**	**14**	**1**	**9**	**440**	**5.7**		**0**	**0.0**	**220**	**71**	**21:41**	**23**	**1**	**8**	**9**	**46**	**1**	**0**	**0**

Hockey East First All-Star Team (1995, 1996) • NCAA East First All-American Team (1996)

Traded to **Edmonton** by **Detroit** for Kirk Maltby, March 20, 1996. Traded to **Philadelphia** by **Edmonton** with Edmonton's 2nd round choice (Jason Beckett) in 1998 Entry Draft for Janne Niinimaa, March 24, 1998.

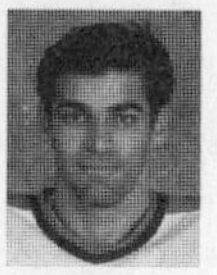

McINNIS, Marty

ANA.

Left wing. Shoots right. 5'11", 190 lbs. Born, Weymouth, MA., June 2, 1970. NY Islanders' 10th choice, 163rd overall, in 1988 Entry Draft.

1986-87	Milton Academy	H.S.	25	21	19	40	....	....	....	....	....	....	....	....	....	....	....	....	....	....	....	....	....	....	....	....
1987-88	Milton Academy	H.S.	25	26	25	51	....	....	....	....	....	....	....	....	....	....	....	....	....	....	....	....	....	....	....	....
1988-89	Boston College	H.E.	39	13	19	32	8	....	....	....	....	....	....	....	....	....	....	....	....	....	....	....	....	....	....	....
1989-90	Boston College	H.E.	41	24	29	53	43	....	....	....	....	....	....	....	....	....	....	....	....	....	....	....	....	....	....	....
1990-91	Boston College	H.E.	38	21	36	57	40	....	....	....	....	....	....	....	....	....	....	....	....	....	....	....	....	....	....	....
1991-92	United States	Nat-Team	54	15	19	34	20	....	....	....	....	....	....	....	....	....	....	....	....	....	....	....	....	....	....	....
	United States	Olympics	8	5	2	7	4	....	....	....	....	....	....	....	....	....	....	....	....	....	....	....	....	....	....	....
	NY Islanders	**NHL**	**15**	**3**	**5**	**8**	**0**	**0**	**0**	**0**	**24**	**12.5**	**6**	....	....	....	....	....	....	....	....	....	....	....	....	....
1992-93	**NY Islanders**	**NHL**	**56**	**10**	**20**	**30**	**24**	**0**	**1**	**0**	**60**	**16.7**	**7**	....	....	....	....	....	**3**	**0**	**1**	**1**	**0**	**0**	**0**	**0**
	Capital District	AHL	10	4	12	16	2	....	....	....	....	....	....	....	....	....	....	....	....	....	....	....	....	....	....	....
1993-94	**NY Islanders**	**NHL**	**81**	**25**	**31**	**56**	**24**	**3**	**5**	**3**	**136**	**18.4**	**31**	....	....	....	....	....	**4**	**0**	**0**	**0**	**0**	**0**	**0**	**0**
1994-95	**NY Islanders**	**NHL**	**41**	**9**	**7**	**16**	**8**	**0**	**0**	**1**	**68**	**13.2**	**–1**	....	....	....	....	....	....	....	....	....	....	....	....	....
1995-96	**NY Islanders**	**NHL**	**74**	**12**	**34**	**46**	**39**	**2**	**0**	**1**	**167**	**7.2**	**–11**	....	....	....	....	....	....	....	....	....	....	....	....	....
1996-97	**NY Islanders**	**NHL**	**70**	**20**	**22**	**42**	**20**	**4**	**1**	**4**	**163**	**12.3**	**–7**	....	....	....	....	....	....	....	....	....	....	....	....	....
	Calgary	**NHL**	**10**	**3**	**4**	**7**	**2**	**1**	**0**	**0**	**19**	**15.8**	**–1**	....	....	....	....	....	....	....	....	....	....	....	....	....
1997-98	**Calgary**	**NHL**	**75**	**19**	**25**	**44**	**34**	**5**	**4**	**0**	**128**	**14.8**	**1**	....	....	....	....	....	....	....	....	....	....	....	....	....
1998-99	**Calgary**	**NHL**	**6**	**1**	**1**	**2**	**6**	**0**	**0**	**0**	**7**	**14.3**	**–1**	**28**	**32.1**	**5**	**0**	**13:51**	....	....	....	....	....	....	....	....
	Anaheim	**NHL**	**75**	**18**	**34**	**52**	**36**	**11**	**1**	**5**	**139**	**12.9**	**–14**	**390**	**46.9**	**52**	**15**	**18:59**	**4**	**2**	**0**	**2**	**2**	**2**	**0**	**0**
	NHL Totals		**503**	**120**	**183**	**303**	**193**	**26**	**12**	**14**	**911**	**13.2**		**418**	**45.9**	**57**	**15**	**18:36**	**11**	**2**	**1**	**3**	**2**	**2**	**0**	**0**

Traded to **Calgary** by **NY Islanders** with Tyrone Garner and Calgary's 6th round choice (previously acquired, Calgary selected Ilja Demidov) in 1997 Entry Draft for Robert Reichel, March 18, 1997. Traded to **Chicago** by **Calgary** with Eric Andersson and Jamie Allison for Jeff Shantz and Steve Dubinsky, October 27, 1998. Traded to **Anaheim** by **Chicago** for Toronto's 4th round choice (previously acquired) in 2000 Entry Draft, October 27, 1998.

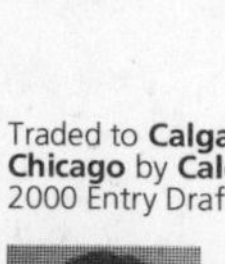

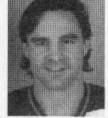

McKAY, Randy

N.J.

Right wing. Shoots right. 6'2", 210 lbs. Born, Montreal, Que., January 25, 1967. Detroit's 6th choice, 113th overall, in 1985 Entry Draft.

1983-84	Lac St-Louis	QAAA	38	18	28	46	62	....	....	....	....	....	....	....	....	....	....	....	....	....	....	....	....	....	....	....
1984-85	Michigan Tech	WCHA	25	4	5	9	32	....	....	....	....	....	....	....	....	....	....	....	....	....	....	....	....	....	....	....
1985-86	Michigan Tech	WCHA	40	12	22	34	46	....	....	....	....	....	....	....	....	....	....	....	....	....	....	....	....	....	....	....
1986-87	Michigan Tech	WCHA	39	5	11	16	46	....	....	....	....	....	....	....	....	....	....	....	....	....	....	....	....	....	....	....
1987-88	Michigan Tech	WCHA	41	17	24	41	70	....	....	....	....	....	....	....	....	....	....	....	....	....	....	....	....	....	....	....
	Adirondack	AHL	10	0	3	3	12	....	....	....	....	....	....	....	....	....	....	....	6	0	4	4	0	....	....	....
1988-89	**Detroit**	**NHL**	**3**	**0**	**0**	**0**	**0**	**0**	**0**	**0**	**2**	**0.0**	**–1**	....	....	....	....	....	**2**	**0**	**0**	**0**	**2**	**0**	**0**	**0**
	Adirondack	AHL	58	29	34	63	170	....	....	....	....	....	....	....	....	....	....	....	14	4	7	11	60	....	....	....
1989-90	**Detroit**	**NHL**	**33**	**3**	**6**	**9**	**51**	**0**	**0**	**0**	**33**	**9.1**	**1**	....	....	....	....	....	....	....	....	....	....	....	....	....
	Adirondack	AHL	36	16	23	39	99	....	....	....	....	....	....	....	....	....	....	....	6	3	0	3	35	....	....	....
1990-91	**Detroit**	**NHL**	**47**	**1**	**7**	**8**	**183**	**0**	**0**	**0**	**22**	**4.5**	**–15**	....	....	....	....	....	**5**	**0**	**1**	**1**	**41**	**0**	**0**	**0**
1991-92	**New Jersey**	**NHL**	**80**	**17**	**16**	**33**	**246**	**2**	**0**	**1**	**111**	**15.3**	**6**	....	....	....	....	....	**7**	**1**	**3**	**4**	**10**	**1**	**0**	**0**
1992-93	**New Jersey**	**NHL**	**73**	**11**	**11**	**22**	**206**	**1**	**0**	**2**	**94**	**11.7**	**0**	....	....	....	....	....	**5**	**0**	**0**	**0**	**16**	**0**	**0**	**0**
1993-94	**New Jersey**	**NHL**	**78**	**12**	**15**	**27**	**244**	**0**	**0**	**1**	**77**	**15.6**	**24**	....	....	....	....	....	**20**	**1**	**2**	**3**	**24**	**0**	**0**	**0**
1994-95♦	**New Jersey**	**NHL**	**33**	**5**	**7**	**12**	**44**	**0**	**0**	**0**	**44**	**11.4**	**10**	....	....	....	....	....	**19**	**8**	**4**	**12**	**11**	**2**	**0**	**2**
1995-96	**New Jersey**	**NHL**	**76**	**11**	**10**	**21**	**145**	**3**	**0**	**3**	**97**	**11.3**	**7**	....	....	....	....	....	....	....	....	....	....	....	....	....

			Regular Season																Playoffs							
Season	Club	League	GP	G	A	Pts	PIM	PP	SH	GW	S	%	+/-	TF	F%	H	SB	Min	GP	G	A	Pts	PIM	PP	SH	GW
1996-97	**New Jersey**	**NHL**	**77**	**9**	**18**	**27**	**109**	**0**	**0**	**2**	**92**	**9.8**	**15**	....	....	....	....	....	**10**	**1**	**1**	**2**	**0**	**0**	**0**	**0**
1997-98	**New Jersey**	**NHL**	**74**	**24**	**24**	**48**	**86**	**8**	**0**	**5**	**141**	**17.0**	**30**	....	....	....	....	....	**6**	**0**	**1**	**1**	**0**	**0**	**0**	**0**
1998-99	**New Jersey**	**NHL**	**70**	**17**	**20**	**37**	**143**	**3**	**0**	**5**	**136**	**12.5**	**10**	**1**	**0.0**	**124**	**11**	**16:06**	**7**	**3**	**2**	**5**	**2**	**0**	**0**	**1**
	NHL Totals		**644**	**110**	**134**	**244**	**1457**	**17**	**0**	**19**	**849**	**13.0**		**1**	**0.0**	**124**	**11**	**16:06**	**81**	**14**	**14**	**28**	**106**	**3**	**0**	**3**

Transferred to **New Jersey** by **Detroit** with Dave Barr as compensation for Detroit's signing of free agent Troy Crowder, September 9, 1991.

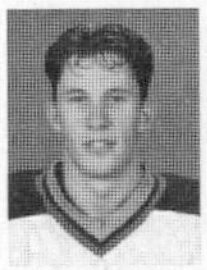

McKEE, Jay — BUF.

Defense. Shoots left. 6'3", 195 lbs. Born, Kingston, Ont., September 8, 1977. Buffalo's 1st choice, 14th overall, in 1995 Entry Draft.

Season	Club	League	GP	G	A	Pts	PIM	PP	SH	GW	S	%	+/-	TF	F%	H	SB	Min	GP	G	A	Pts	PIM	PP	SH	GW
1992-93	Ernestown	OJHL-C	36	0	17	17	37	....	....	....	....	....	....	....	....	....	....	....	....	....	....	....	....	....	....	....
1993-94	Sudbury	OHL	51	0	1	1	51	....	....	....	....	....	....	....	....	....	....	....	3	0	0	0	0	....	....	....
1994-95	Sudbury	OHL	39	6	6	12	91	....	....	....	....	....	....	....	....	....	....	....	....	....	....	....	....	....	....	....
	Niagara Falls	OHL	26	3	13	16	60	....	....	....	....	....	....	....	....	....	....	....	6	2	3	5	10	....	....	....
1995-96	Niagara Falls	OHL	64	5	41	46	129	....	....	....	....	....	....	....	....	....	....	....	10	1	5	6	16	....	....	....
	Buffalo	**NHL**	**1**	**0**	**1**	**1**	**2**	**0**	**0**	**0**	**2**	**0.0**	**1**	....	....	....	....	....	....	....	....	....	....	....	....	....
	Rochester	AHL	4	0	1	1	15	....	....	....	....	....	....	....	....	....	....	....	....	....	....	....	....	....	....	....
1996-97	**Buffalo**	**NHL**	**43**	**1**	**9**	**10**	**35**	**0**	**0**	**0**	**29**	**3.4**	**3**	....	....	....	....	....	**3**	**0**	**0**	**0**	**0**	**0**	**0**	**0**
	Rochester	AHL	7	2	5	7	4	....	....	....	....	....	....	....	....	....	....	....	....	....	....	....	....	....	....	....
1997-98	**Buffalo**	**NHL**	**56**	**1**	**13**	**14**	**42**	**0**	**0**	**0**	**55**	**1.8**	**–1**	....	....	....	....	....	**1**	**0**	**0**	**0**	**0**	**0**	**0**	**0**
	Rochester	AHL	13	1	7	8	11	....	....	....	....	....	....	....	....	....	....	....	....	....	....	....	....	....	....	....
1998-99	**Buffalo**	**NHL**	**72**	**0**	**6**	**6**	**75**	**0**	**0**	**0**	**57**	**0.0**	**20**	**0**	**0.0**	**204**	**129**	**20:28**	**21**	**0**	**3**	**3**	**24**	**0**	**0**	**0**
	NHL Totals		**172**	**2**	**29**	**31**	**154**	**0**	**0**	**0**	**143**	**1.4**		**0**	**0.0**	**204**	**129**	**20:28**	**25**	**0**	**3**	**3**	**24**	**0**	**0**	**0**

OHL Second All-Star Team (1996)

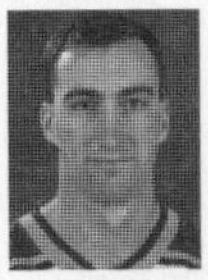

McKENNA, Steve — L.A.

Left wing. Shoots left. 6'8", 247 lbs. Born, Toronto, Ont., August 21, 1973.

Season	Club	League	GP	G	A	Pts	PIM	PP	SH	GW	S	%	+/-	TF	F%	H	SB	Min	GP	G	A	Pts	PIM	PP	SH	GW
1993-94	Merrimack	H.E.	37	1	2	3	74	....	....	....	....	....	....	....	....	....	....	....	....	....	....	....	....	....	....	....
1994-95	Merrimack	H.E.	37	1	9	10	74	....	....	....	....	....	....	....	....	....	....	....	....	....	....	....	....	....	....	....
1995-96	Merrimack	H.E.	33	3	11	14	67	....	....	....	....	....	....	....	....	....	....	....	....	....	....	....	....	....	....	....
1996-97	**Los Angeles**	**NHL**	**9**	**0**	**0**	**0**	**37**	**0**	**0**	**0**	**6**	**0.0**	**1**	....	....	....	....	....	....	....	....	....	....	....	....	....
	Phoenix	IHL	66	6	5	11	187	....	....	....	....	....	....	....	....	....	....	....	....	....	....	....	....	....	....	....
1997-98	**Los Angeles**	**NHL**	**62**	**4**	**4**	**8**	**150**	**1**	**0**	**0**	**42**	**9.5**	**–9**	....	....	....	....	....	**3**	**0**	**1**	**1**	**8**	**0**	**0**	**0**
	Fredericton	AHL	6	2	1	3	48	....	....	....	....	....	....	....	....	....	....	....	....	....	....	....	....	....	....	....
1998-99	**Los Angeles**	**NHL**	**20**	**1**	**0**	**1**	**36**	**0**	**0**	**0**	**12**	**8.3**	**–3**	**0**	**0.0**	**35**	**4**	**8:24**	....	....	....	....	....	....	....	....
	NHL Totals		**91**	**5**	**4**	**9**	**223**	**1**	**0**	**0**	**60**	**8.3**		**0**	**0.0**	**35**	**4**	**8:24**	**3**	**0**	**1**	**1**	**8**	**0**	**0**	**0**

Signed as a free agent by **LA Kings**, May 23, 1996.

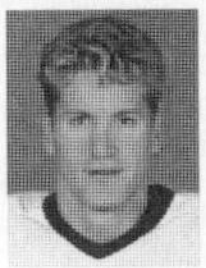

McKENZIE, Jim — ANA.

Left wing. Shoots left. 6'3", 229 lbs. Born, Gull Lake, Sask., November 3, 1969. Hartford's 3rd choice, 73rd overall, in 1989 Entry Draft.

Season	Club	League	GP	G	A	Pts	PIM	PP	SH	GW	S	%	+/-	TF	F%	H	SB	Min	GP	G	A	Pts	PIM	PP	SH	GW
1985-86	Moose Jaw AA	SAHA	36	18	26	44	86	....	....	....	....	....	....	....	....	....	....	....	....	....	....	....	....	....	....	....
	Moose Jaw	WHL	3	0	2	2	0	....	....	....	....	....	....	....	....	....	....	....	....	....	....	....	....	....	....	....
1986-87	Moose Jaw	WHL	65	5	3	8	125	....	....	....	....	....	....	....	....	....	....	....	9	0	0	0	7	....	....	....
1987-88	Moose Jaw	WHL	62	1	17	18	134	....	....	....	....	....	....	....	....	....	....	....	....	....	....	....	....	....	....	....
1988-89	Victoria	WHL	67	15	27	42	176	....	....	....	....	....	....	....	....	....	....	....	8	1	4	5	30	....	....	....
1989-90	**Hartford**	**NHL**	**5**	**0**	**0**	**0**	**4**	**0**	**0**	**0**	**0**	**0.0**	**0**	....	....	....	....	....	....	....	....	....	....	....	....	....
	Binghamton	AHL	56	4	12	16	149	....	....	....	....	....	....	....	....	....	....	....	....	....	....	....	....	....	....	....
1990-91	**Hartford**	**NHL**	**41**	**4**	**3**	**7**	**108**	**0**	**0**	**0**	**16**	**25.0**	**–7**	....	....	....	....	....	**6**	**0**	**0**	**0**	**8**	**0**	**0**	**0**
	Springfield	AHL	24	3	4	7	102	....	....	....	....	....	....	....	....	....	....	....	....	....	....	....	....	....	....	....
1991-92	**Hartford**	**NHL**	**67**	**5**	**1**	**6**	**87**	**0**	**0**	**0**	**34**	**14.7**	**–6**	....	....	....	....	....	....	....	....	....	....	....	....	....
1992-93	**Hartford**	**NHL**	**64**	**3**	**6**	**9**	**202**	**0**	**0**	**0**	**36**	**8.3**	**–10**	....	....	....	....	....	....	....	....	....	....	....	....	....
1993-94	**Hartford**	**NHL**	**26**	**1**	**2**	**3**	**67**	**0**	**0**	**0**	**9**	**11.1**	**–6**	....	....	....	....	....	....	....	....	....	....	....	....	....
	Dallas	**NHL**	**34**	**2**	**3**	**5**	**63**	**0**	**0**	**1**	**18**	**11.1**	**4**	....	....	....	....	....	....	....	....	....	....	....	....	....
	Pittsburgh	**NHL**	**11**	**0**	**0**	**0**	**16**	**0**	**0**	**0**	**6**	**0.0**	**–5**	....	....	....	....	....	**3**	**0**	**0**	**0**	**0**	**0**	**0**	**0**
1994-95	**Pittsburgh**	**NHL**	**39**	**2**	**1**	**3**	**63**	**0**	**0**	**1**	**16**	**12.5**	**–7**	....	....	....	....	....	**5**	**0**	**0**	**0**	**4**	**0**	**0**	**0**
1995-96	**Winnipeg**	**NHL**	**73**	**4**	**2**	**6**	**202**	**0**	**0**	**0**	**28**	**14.3**	**–4**	....	....	....	....	....	**1**	**0**	**0**	**0**	**2**	**0**	**0**	**0**
1996-97	**Phoenix**	**NHL**	**65**	**5**	**3**	**8**	**200**	**0**	**0**	**1**	**38**	**13.2**	**–5**	....	....	....	....	....	**7**	**0**	**0**	**0**	**2**	**0**	**0**	**0**
1997-98	**Phoenix**	**NHL**	**64**	**3**	**4**	**7**	**146**	**0**	**0**	**0**	**35**	**8.6**	**–7**	....	....	....	....	....	**1**	**0**	**0**	**0**	**0**	**0**	**0**	**0**
1998-99	**Anaheim**	**NHL**	**73**	**5**	**4**	**9**	**99**	**1**	**0**	**1**	**59**	**8.5**	**–18**	**8**	**50.0**	**85**	**8**	**10:22**	**4**	**0**	**0**	**0**	**4**	**0**	**0**	**0**
	NHL Totals		**562**	**34**	**29**	**63**	**1257**	**1**	**0**	**4**	**295**	**11.5**		**8**	**50.0**	**85**	**8**	**10:22**	**27**	**0**	**0**	**0**	**20**	**0**	**0**	**0**

Traded to **Florida** by **Hartford** for Alexander Godynyuk, December 16, 1993. Traded to **Dallas** by **Florida** for Dallas' 4th round choice (later traded to Ottawa — Ottawa selected Kevin Bolibruck) in 1995 Entry Draft, December 16, 1993. Traded to **Pittsburgh** by **Dallas** for Mike Needham, March 21, 1994. Signed as a free agent by **NY Islanders**, August 2, 1995. Claimed by **Winnipeg** from **NY Islanders** in NHL Waiver Draft, October 2, 1995. Transferred to **Phoenix** after **Winnipeg** franchise relocated, July 1, 1996. Traded to **Anaheim** by **Phoenix** for J.F. Jomphe, June 18, 1998.

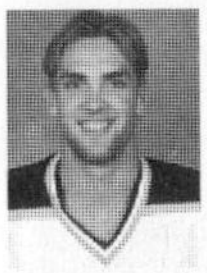

McLAREN, Kyle — BOS.

Defense. Shoots left. 6'4", 219 lbs. Born, Humboldt, Sask., June 18, 1977. Boston's 1st choice, 9th overall, in 1995 Entry Draft.

Season	Club	League	GP	G	A	Pts	PIM	PP	SH	GW	S	%	+/-	TF	F%	H	SB	Min	GP	G	A	Pts	PIM	PP	SH	GW
1992-93	Lethbridge	AAHA	60	28	28	56	84	....	....	....	....	....	....	....	....	....	....	....	....	....	....	....	....	....	....	....
	Lethbridge	AAHA	60	28	28	56	84	....	....	....	....	....	....	....	....	....	....	....	....	....	....	....	....	....	....	....
1993-94	Tacoma	WHL	62	1	9	10	53	....	....	....	....	....	....	....	....	....	....	....	6	1	4	5	6	....	....	....
1994-95	Tacoma	WHL	47	13	19	32	68	....	....	....	....	....	....	....	....	....	....	....	4	1	1	2	4	....	....	....
1995-96	**Boston**	**NHL**	**74**	**5**	**12**	**17**	**73**	**0**	**0**	**0**	**74**	**6.8**	**16**	....	....	....	....	....	**5**	**0**	**0**	**0**	**14**	**0**	**0**	**0**
1996-97	**Boston**	**NHL**	**58**	**5**	**9**	**14**	**54**	**0**	**0**	**1**	**68**	**7.4**	**–9**	....	....	....	....	....	....	....	....	....	....	....	....	....
1997-98	**Boston**	**NHL**	**66**	**5**	**20**	**25**	**56**	**2**	**0**	**0**	**101**	**5.0**	**13**	....	....	....	....	....	**6**	**1**	**0**	**1**	**4**	**1**	**0**	**0**
1998-99	**Boston**	**NHL**	**52**	**6**	**18**	**24**	**48**	**3**	**0**	**0**	**97**	**6.2**	**1**	**0**	**0.0**	**205**	**69**	**23:25**	**12**	**0**	**3**	**3**	**10**	**0**	**0**	**0**
	NHL Totals		**250**	**21**	**59**	**80**	**231**	**5**	**0**	**1**	**340**	**6.2**		**0**	**0.0**	**205**	**69**	**23:25**	**23**	**1**	**3**	**4**	**28**	**1**	**0**	**0**

NHL All-Rookie Team (1996)

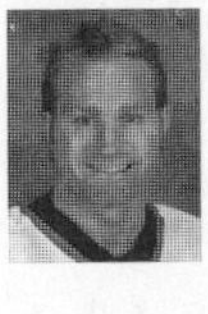

McSORLEY, Marty

Defense. Shoots right. 6'1", 235 lbs. Born, Hamilton, Ont., May 18, 1963.

Season	Club	League	GP	G	A	Pts	PIM	PP	SH	GW	S	%	+/-	TF	F%	H	SB	Min	GP	G	A	Pts	PIM	PP	SH	GW
1980-81	Hamilton	OJHL-B	40	16	17	33	72	....	....	....	....	....	....	....	....	....	....	....	....	....	....	....	....	....	....	....
1981-82	Belleville	OHL	58	6	13	19	234	....	....	....	....	....	....	....	....	....	....	....	....	....	....	....	....	....	....	....
1982-83	Belleville	OHL	70	10	41	51	183	....	....	....	....	....	....	....	....	....	....	....	4	0	0	0	7	....	....	....
	Baltimore	AHL	2	0	0	0	22	....	....	....	....	....	....	....	....	....	....	....	....	....	....	....	....	....	....	....
1983-84	**Pittsburgh**	**NHL**	**72**	**2**	**7**	**9**	**224**	**0**	**0**	**0**	**75**	**2.7**	**–39**	....	....	....	....	....	....	....	....	....	....	....	....	....
1984-85	**Pittsburgh**	**NHL**	**15**	**0**	**0**	**0**	**15**	**0**	**0**	**0**	**11**	**0.0**	**–3**	....	....	....	....	....	....	....	....	....	....	....	....	....
	Baltimore	AHL	58	6	24	30	154	....	....	....	....	....	....	....	....	....	....	....	14	0	7	7	47	....	....	....
1985-86	**Edmonton**	**NHL**	**59**	**11**	**12**	**23**	**265**	**0**	**0**	**2**	**72**	**15.3**	**9**	....	....	....	....	....	**8**	**0**	**2**	**2**	**50**	**0**	**0**	**0**
	Nova Scotia	AHL	9	2	4	6	34	....	....	....	....	....	....	....	....	....	....	....	....	....	....	....	....	....	....	....
1986-87♦	**Edmonton**	**NHL**	**41**	**2**	**4**	**6**	**159**	**0**	**0**	**0**	**32**	**6.3**	**–4**	....	....	....	....	....	**21**	**4**	**3**	**7**	**65**	**0**	**0**	**1**
	Nova Scotia	AHL	7	2	2	4	48	....	....	....	....	....	....	....	....	....	....	....	....	....	....	....	....	....	....	....
1987-88♦	**Edmonton**	**NHL**	**60**	**9**	**17**	**26**	**223**	**0**	**0**	**1**	**66**	**13.6**	**23**	....	....	....	....	....	**16**	**0**	**3**	**3**	**67**	**0**	**0**	**0**
1988-89	**Los Angeles**	**NHL**	**66**	**10**	**17**	**27**	**350**	**2**	**0**	**1**	**87**	**11.5**	**3**	....	....	....	....	....	**11**	**0**	**2**	**2**	**33**	**0**	**0**	**0**
1989-90	**Los Angeles**	**NHL**	**75**	**15**	**21**	**36**	**322**	**2**	**1**	**0**	**127**	**11.8**	**2**	....	....	....	....	....	**10**	**1**	**3**	**4**	**18**	**1**	**0**	**0**
1990-91	**Los Angeles**	**NHL**	**61**	**7**	**32**	**39**	**221**	**1**	**1**	**1**	**100**	**7.0**	**48**	....	....	....	....	....	**12**	**0**	**0**	**0**	**58**	**0**	**0**	**0**
1991-92	**Los Angeles**	**NHL**	**71**	**7**	**22**	**29**	**268**	**2**	**1**	**0**	**119**	**5.9**	**–13**	....	....	....	....	....	**6**	**1**	**0**	**1**	**21**	**0**	**0**	**0**
1992-93	**Los Angeles**	**NHL**	**81**	**15**	**26**	**41**	***399**	**3**	**3**	**0**	**197**	**7.6**	**1**	....	....	....	....	....	**24**	**4**	**6**	**10**	***60**	**2**	**0**	**1**
1993-94	**Pittsburgh**	**NHL**	**47**	**3**	**18**	**21**	**139**	**0**	**0**	**0**	**122**	**2.5**	**–9**	....	....	....	....	....	....	....	....	....	....	....	....	....
	Los Angeles	**NHL**	**18**	**4**	**6**	**10**	**55**	**1**	**0**	**1**	**38**	**10.5**	**–3**	....	....	....	....	....	....	....	....	....	....	....	....	....
1994-95	**Los Angeles**	**NHL**	**41**	**3**	**18**	**21**	**83**	**1**	**0**	**0**	**75**	**4.0**	**–14**	....	....	....	....	....	....	....	....	....	....	....	....	....

Season	Club	League	GP	G	A	Pts	PIM	PP	SH	GW	S	%	+/-	TF	F%	H	SB	Min	GP	G	A	Pts	PIM	PP	SH	GW
1995-96	Los Angeles	NHL	59	10	21	31	148	1	1	1	118	8.5	−14	....	....	....	....	....								
	NY Rangers	NHL	9	0	2	2	21	0	0	0	12	0.0	−6	....	....	....	....	....	4	0	0	0	0	0	0	0
1996-97	San Jose	NHL	57	4	12	16	186	0	1	1	74	5.4	−6	....	....	....	....	....								
1997-98	San Jose	NHL	56	2	10	12	140	0	0	0	46	4.3	10	....	....	....	....	....								
1998-99	Edmonton	NHL	46	2	3	5	101	0	0	0	29	6.9	−5	0	0.0	47	55	16:58	3	0	0	0	2	0	0	0
	NHL Totals		934	106	248	354	3319	13	8	8	1400	7.6		0	0.0	47	55	16:58	115	10	19	29	374	3	0	2

Co-winner of Alka-Seltzer Plus Award with Theoren Fleury (1991)

Signed as a free agent by **Pittsburgh**, July 30, 1982. Traded to **Edmonton** by **Pittsburgh** with Tim Hrynewich and future considerations (Craig Muni, October 6, 1986) for Gilles Meloche, September 12, 1985. Traded to **LA Kings** by **Edmonton** with Wayne Gretzky and Mike Krushelnyski for Jimmy Carson, Martin Gelinas, LA Kings' 1st round choices in 1989 (later traded to New Jersey — New Jersey selected Jason Miller), 1991 (Martin Rucinsky) and 1993 (Nick Stajduhar) Entry Drafts and cash, August 9, 1988. Traded to **Pittsburgh** by **LA Kings**, for Shawn McEachern, August 27, 1993. Traded to **LA Kings** by **Pittsburgh** with Jim Paek for Tomas Sandstrom and Shawn McEachern, February 16, 1994. Traded to **NY Rangers** by **LA Kings** with Jari Kurri and Shane Churla for Ray Ferraro, Ian Laperriere, Mattias Norstrom, Nathan Lafayette and NY Rangers' 4th round choice (Sean Blanchard) in 1997 Entry Draft, March 14, 1996. Traded to **San Jose** by **NY Rangers** for Jayson More, Brian Swanson and future considerations, August 20, 1996. Signed as a free agent by **Edmonton**, October 1, 1999.

McTAVISH, Dale

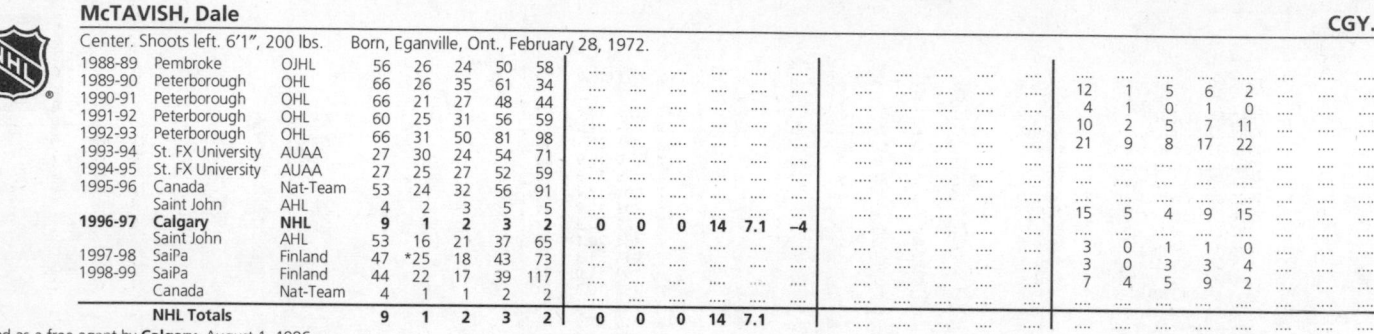

CGY.

Center. Shoots left. 6'1", 200 lbs.   Born, Eganville, Ont., February 28, 1972.

Season	Club	League	GP	G	A	Pts	PIM	PP	SH	GW	S	%	+/-						GP	G	A	Pts	PIM
1988-89	Pembroke	OJHL	56	26	24	50	58												....	....	....	....	....
1989-90	Peterborough	OHL	66	26	35	61	34												12	1	5	6	2
1990-91	Peterborough	OHL	66	21	27	48	44												4	1	0	1	0
1991-92	Peterborough	OHL	60	25	31	56	59												10	2	5	7	11
1992-93	Peterborough	OHL	66	31	50	81	98												21	9	8	17	22
1993-94	St. FX University	AUAA	27	30	24	54	71												....	....	....	....	....
1994-95	St. FX University	AUAA	27	25	27	52	59												....	....	....	....	....
1995-96	Canada	Nat-Team	53	24	32	56	91												....	....	....	....	....
	Saint John	AHL	4	2	3	5	5												15	5	4	9	15
1996-97	**Calgary**	**NHL**	9	1	2	3	2	0	0	0	14	7.1	−4						....	....	....	....	....
	Saint John	AHL	53	16	21	37	65												3	0	1	1	0
1997-98	SaiPa	Finland	47	*25	18	43	73												3	0	3	3	4
1998-99	SaiPa	Finland	44	22	17	39	117												7	4	5	9	2
	Canada	Nat-Team	4	1	1	2	2																
	NHL Totals		9	1	2	3	2	0	0	0	14	7.1							....	....	....	....	....

Signed as a free agent by **Calgary**, August 1, 1996.

MELANSON, Dean

(meh-LAHN-suhn)   PHI.

Defense. Shoots right. 5'11", 211 lbs.   Born, Antigonish, N.S., November 19, 1973. Buffalo's 4th choice, 80th overall, in 1992 Entry Draft.

Season	Club	League	GP	G	A	Pts	PIM	PP	SH	GW	S	%	+/-						GP	G	A	Pts	PIM
1989-90	Antigonish	NSAHA		STATISTICS NOT AVAILABLE																			
1990-91	St-Hyacinthe	QMJHL	69	10	17	27	110												4	0	1	1	2
1991-92	St-Hyacinthe	QMJHL	42	8	19	27	158												6	1	2	3	25
1992-93	St-Hyacinthe	QMJHL	57	13	29	42	253												14	1	6	7	18
	Rochester	AHL	8	0	1	1	6												4	0	1	1	2
1994-95	**Buffalo**	**NHL**	5	0	0	0	4	0	0	0	1	0.0	−1						....	....	....	....	....
	Rochester	AHL	43	4	7	11	84																
1995-96	Rochester	AHL	70	3	13	16	204												14	3	3	6	22
1996-97	Quebec	IHL	72	3	21	24	95												7	0	2	2	12
1997-98	Rochester	AHL	73	7	9	16	228												4	0	2	2	0
1998-99	Rochester	AHL	79	7	27	34	192												17	3	2	5	32
	NHL Totals		5	0	0	0	4	0	0	0	1	0.0							....	....	....	....	....

Signed as a free agent by **Philadelphia**, July 22, 1999.

MELLANBY, Scott

FLA.

Right wing. Shoots right. 6'1", 205 lbs.   Born, Montreal, Que., June 11, 1966. Philadelphia's 2nd choice, 27th overall, in 1984 Entry Draft.

Season	Club	League	GP	G	A	Pts	PIM	PP	SH	GW	S	%	+/-	TF	F%	H	SB	Min	GP	G	A	Pts	PIM	PP	SH	GW
1982-83	Don Mills	MTHL	72	66	52	118	38																				
1983-84	Henry Carr	OJHL-B	39	37	37	74	97																				
1984-85	U. of Wisconsin	WCHA	40	14	24	38	60																				
1985-86	U. of Wisconsin	WCHA	32	21	23	44	89																				
	Philadelphia	NHL	2	0	0	0	0	0	0	0	0	0.0	−1													
1986-87	Philadelphia	NHL	71	11	21	32	94	1	0	0	118	9.3	8						24	5	5	10	46	0	0	1
1987-88	Philadelphia	NHL	75	25	26	51	185	7	0	2	190	13.2	−7						7	0	1	1	16	0	0	0
1988-89	Philadelphia	NHL	76	21	29	50	183	11	0	3	202	10.4	−13						19	4	5	9	28	0	0	0
1989-90	Philadelphia	NHL	57	6	17	23	77	0	0	1	104	5.8	−4													
1990-91	Philadelphia	NHL	74	20	21	41	155	5	0	6	165	12.1	8													
1991-92	Edmonton	NHL	80	23	27	50	197	7	0	5	159	14.5	5						16	2	1	3	29	1	0	1
1992-93	Edmonton	NHL	69	15	17	32	147	6	0	3	114	13.2	−4													
1993-94	Florida	NHL	80	30	30	60	149	17	0	4	204	14.7	0													
1994-95	Florida	NHL	48	13	12	25	90	4	0	5	130	10.0	−16													
1995-96	Florida	NHL	79	32	38	70	160	19	0	3	225	14.2	4						22	3	6	9	44	2	0	0
1996-97	Florida	NHL	82	27	29	56	170	9	1	4	221	12.2	7						5	0	2	2	4	0	0	0
1997-98	Florida	NHL	79	15	24	39	127	6	0	1	188	8.0	−14													
1998-99	Florida	NHL	67	18	27	45	85	4	0	3	136	13.2	5	11	27.3	64	15	16:14								
	NHL Totals		939	256	318	574	1819	96	1	40	2156	11.9		11	27.3	64	15	16:14	93	14	20	34	167	3	0	2

Played in NHL All-Star Game (1996)

Traded to **Edmonton** by **Philadelphia** with Craig Fisher and Craig Berube for Dave Brown, Corey Foster and Jari Kurri, May 30, 1991. Claimed by **Florida** from **Edmonton** in Expansion Draft, June 24, 1993.

MERTZIG, Jan

(MUHR-tzihg, YAN)

Defense. Shoots left. 6'4", 218 lbs.   Born, Huddinge, Sweden, July 18, 1970. NY Rangers' 9th choice, 235th overall, in 1998 Entry Draft.

Season	Club	League	GP	G	A	Pts	PIM	PP	SH	GW	S	%	+/-	TF	F%	H	SB	Min	GP	G	A	Pts	PIM
1991-92	Huddinge IF	Sweden-2	28	1	6	7	10												4	2	0	2	4
1992-93	Huddinge IF	Sweden-2	35	3	7	10	18												9	1	0	1	10
1993-94	Huddinge IF	Sweden-2	35	5	7	12	26												2	1	0	1	4
1994-95	Huddinge IF	Sweden-2	34	10	8	18	16												2	0	1	1	0
1995-96	Lulea HF	Sweden	38	7	10	17	14												13	3	3	6	6
1996-97	Lulea HF	Sweden	47	15	10	25	30												9	0	2	2	4
1997-98	Lulea HF	Sweden	45	7	8	15	27												3	1	0	1	4
1998-99	**NY Rangers**	**NHL**	23	0	2	2	8	0	0	0	10	0.0	−5	0	0.0	16	17	12:02	....	....	....	....	....
	Hartford	AHL	35	3	2	5	14																
	Utah	IHL	5	0	1	1	6																
	NHL Totals		23	0	2	2	8	0	0	0	10	0.0		0	0.0	16	17	12:02	....	....	....	....	....

MESSIER, Eric

(MEHS-see-ay)   COL.

Defense. Shoots left. 6'2", 200 lbs.   Born, Drummondville, Que., October 29, 1973.

Season	Club	League	GP	G	A	Pts	PIM												GP	G	A	Pts	PIM
1990-91	Swift Textile	QAAA		STATISTICS NOT AVAILABLE																			
1991-92	Trois-Rivieres	QMJHL	58	2	10	12	28												15	2	2	4	13
1992-93	Sherbrooke	QMJHL	51	4	17	21	82												15	0	4	4	18
1993-94	Sherbrooke	QMJHL	67	4	24	28	69												12	1	7	8	14
1994-95	U. of Quebec	OUAA	13	8	5	13	20												4	0	3	3	8
1995-96	Cornwall	AHL	72	5	9	14	111												8	1	1	2	20

			Regular Season																Playoffs							
Season	Club	League	GP	G	A	Pts	PIM	PP	SH	GW	S	%	+/–	TF	F%	H	SB	Min	GP	G	A	Pts	PIM	PP	SH	GW
1996-97	**Colorado**	**NHL**	**21**	**0**	**0**	**0**	**4**	**0**	**0**	**0**	**11**	**0.0**	**7**	....	....	....	....	....	**6**	**0**	**0**	**0**	**4**	**0**	**0**	**0**
	Hershey	AHL	55	16	26	42	69	....	....	....	....	....	....	....	....	....	....	....	9	3	8	11	14	....	....	....
1997-98	**Colorado**	**NHL**	**62**	**4**	**12**	**16**	**20**	**0**	**0**	**0**	**66**	**6.1**	**4**	....	....	....	....	....	....	....	....	....	....	....	....	....
1998-99	**Colorado**	**NHL**	**31**	**4**	**2**	**6**	**14**	**1**	**0**	**1**	**30**	**13.3**	**0**	**0**	**0.0**	**29**	**22**	**13:43**	**3**	**0**	**0**	**0**	**0**	**0**	**0**	**0**
	Hershey	AHL	6	1	3	4	4	....	....	....	....	....	....	....	....	....	....	....	....	....	....	....	....	....	....	....
	NHL Totals		**114**	**8**	**14**	**22**	**38**	**1**	**0**	**1**	**107**	**7.5**		**0**	**0.0**	**29**	**22**	**13:43**	**9**	**0**	**0**	**0**	**4**	**0**	**0**	**0**

QMJHL Second All-Star Team (1994)

Signed as a free agent by **Colorado**, June 14, 1995. • Missed majority of 1998-99 season recovering from broken elbow suffered in game vs. Ottawa, October 10, 1998.

MESSIER, Mark

(MEHS-see-ay) **VAN.**

Center. Shoots left. 6'1", 205 lbs. Born, Edmonton, Alta., January 18, 1961. Edmonton's 2nd choice, 48th overall, in 1979 Entry Draft.

Season	Club	League	GP	G	A	Pts	PIM	PP	SH	GW	S	%	+/–	TF	F%	H	SB	Min	GP	G	A	Pts	PIM	PP	SH	GW
1976-77	Spruce Grove	AJHL	57	27	39	55	91	....	....	....	....	....	....	....	....	....	....	....	....	....	....	....	....	....	....	....
1977-78	St. Albert	AJHL	54	25	49	74	194	....	....	....	....	....	....	....	....	....	....	....	....	....	....	....	....	....	....	....
	Portland	WHL	....	....	....	....	....	....	....	....	....	....	....	....	....	....	....	....	7	4	1	5	2	....	....	....
1978-79	Indianapolis	WHA	5	0	0	0	0	....	....	....	....	....	....	....	....	....	....	....	....	....	....	....	....	....	....	....
	Cincinnati	WHA	47	1	10	11	58	....	....	....	....	....	....	....	....	....	....	....	....	....	....	....	....	....	....	....
1979-80	**Edmonton**	**NHL**	**75**	**12**	**21**	**33**	**120**	**1**	**1**	**1**	**113**	**10.6**	**–10**	....	....	....	....	....	**3**	**1**	**2**	**3**	**2**	**0**	**1**	**0**
	Houston	CHL	4	0	3	3	4	....	....	....	....	....	....	....	....	....	....	....	....	....	....	....	....	....	....	....
1980-81	**Edmonton**	**NHL**	**72**	**23**	**40**	**63**	**102**	**4**	**0**	**1**	**179**	**12.8**	**–12**	....	....	....	....	....	**9**	**2**	**5**	**7**	**13**	**0**	**0**	**0**
1981-82	**Edmonton**	**NHL**	**78**	**50**	**38**	**88**	**119**	**10**	**0**	**3**	**235**	**21.3**	**21**	....	....	....	....	....	**5**	**1**	**2**	**3**	**8**	**0**	**0**	**0**
1982-83	**Edmonton**	**NHL**	**77**	**48**	**58**	**106**	**72**	**12**	**1**	**2**	**237**	**20.3**	**19**	....	....	....	....	....	**15**	**15**	**6**	**21**	**14**	**4**	**2**	**0**
1983-84♦	**Edmonton**	**NHL**	**73**	**37**	**64**	**101**	**165**	**7**	**4**	**7**	**219**	**16.9**	**40**	....	....	....	....	....	**19**	**8**	**18**	**26**	**19**	**1**	**1**	**2**
1984-85♦	**Edmonton**	**NHL**	**55**	**23**	**31**	**54**	**57**	**4**	**5**	**1**	**136**	**16.9**	**8**	....	....	....	....	....	**18**	**12**	**13**	**25**	**12**	**1**	**1**	**1**
1985-86	**Edmonton**	**NHL**	**63**	**35**	**49**	**84**	**68**	**10**	**5**	**7**	**201**	**17.4**	**36**	....	....	....	....	....	**10**	**4**	**6**	**10**	**18**	**0**	**2**	**0**
1986-87♦	**Edmonton**	**NHL**	**77**	**37**	**70**	**107**	**73**	**7**	**4**	**5**	**208**	**17.8**	**21**	....	....	....	....	....	**21**	**12**	**16**	**28**	**16**	**1**	**2**	**1**
1987-88♦	**Edmonton**	**NHL**	**77**	**37**	**74**	**111**	**103**	**12**	**3**	**7**	**182**	**20.3**	**21**	....	....	....	....	....	**19**	**11**	**23**	**34**	**29**	**7**	**1**	**0**
1988-89	**Edmonton**	**NHL**	**72**	**33**	**61**	**94**	**130**	**6**	**6**	**4**	**164**	**20.1**	**–5**	....	....	....	....	....	**7**	**1**	**11**	**12**	**8**	**0**	**0**	**0**
1989-90♦	**Edmonton**	**NHL**	**79**	**45**	**84**	**129**	**79**	**13**	**6**	**3**	**211**	**21.3**	**19**	....	....	....	....	....	**22**	**9**	***22**	**31**	**20**	**1**	**1**	**1**
1990-91	**Edmonton**	**NHL**	**53**	**12**	**52**	**64**	**34**	**3**	**1**	**2**	**109**	**11.0**	**15**	....	....	....	....	....	**18**	**4**	**11**	**15**	**16**	**1**	**0**	**0**
1991-92	**NY Rangers**	**NHL**	**79**	**35**	**72**	**107**	**76**	**12**	**4**	**6**	**212**	**16.5**	**31**	....	....	....	....	....	**11**	**7**	**7**	**14**	**6**	**2**	**2**	**0**
1992-93	**NY Rangers**	**NHL**	**75**	**25**	**66**	**91**	**72**	**7**	**2**	**2**	**215**	**11.6**	**–6**	....	....	....	....	....	....	....	....	....	....	....	....	....
1993-94♦	**NY Rangers**	**NHL**	**76**	**26**	**58**	**84**	**76**	**6**	**2**	**5**	**216**	**12.0**	**25**	....	....	....	....	....	**23**	**12**	**18**	**30**	**33**	**2**	**1**	**4**
1994-95	**NY Rangers**	**NHL**	**46**	**14**	**39**	**53**	**40**	**3**	**3**	**2**	**126**	**11.1**	**8**	....	....	....	....	....	**10**	**3**	**10**	**13**	**8**	**2**	**0**	**1**
1995-96	**NY Rangers**	**NHL**	**74**	**47**	**52**	**99**	**122**	**14**	**1**	**5**	**241**	**19.5**	**29**	....	....	....	....	....	**11**	**4**	**7**	**11**	**16**	**2**	**0**	**1**
1996-97	**NY Rangers**	**NHL**	**71**	**36**	**48**	**84**	**88**	**7**	**5**	**9**	**227**	**15.9**	**12**	....	....	....	....	....	**15**	**3**	**9**	**12**	**6**	**0**	**0**	**1**
1997-98	**Vancouver**	**NHL**	**82**	**22**	**38**	**60**	**58**	**8**	**2**	**2**	**139**	**15.8**	**–10**	....	....	....	....	....	....	....	....	....	....	....	....	....
1998-99	**Vancouver**	**NHL**	**59**	**13**	**35**	**48**	**33**	**4**	**2**	**2**	**97**	**13.4**	**–12**	**1536**	**53.9**	**29**	**35**	**22:36**	....	....	....	....	....	....	....	....
	NHL Totals		**1413**	**610**	**1050**	**1660**	**1687**	**150**	**57**	**76**	**3667**	**16.6**		**1536**	**53.9**	**29**	**35**	**22:36**	**236**	**109**	**186**	**295**	**244**	**24**	**14**	**12**

NHL First All-Star Team (1982, 1983, 1990, 1992) • NHL Second All-Star Team (1984) • Won Conn Smythe Trophy (1984) • Won Hart Trophy (1990, 1992) • Won Lester B. Pearson Award (1990, 1992)

Played in NHL All-Star Game (1982, 1983, 1984, 1986, 1988, 1989, 1990, 1991, 1992, 1994, 1996, 1997, 1998)

Signed as an underage free agent by **Indianapolis** (WHA) to 10-game tryout contract, November 5, 1978. Signed as a free agent by **Cincinnati** (WHA) after **Indianapolis** (WHA) franchise folded, December, 1978. Traded to **NY Rangers** by **Edmonton** with future considerations for Bernie Nicholls, Steven Rice and Louie DeBrusk, October 4, 1991. Signed as a free agent by **Vancouver**, July 30, 1997.

MILLAR, Craig

EDM.

Defense. Shoots left. 6'2", 205 lbs. Born, Winnipeg, Man., July 12, 1976. Buffalo's 10th choice, 225th overall, in 1994 Entry Draft.

Season	Club	League	GP	G	A	Pts	PIM	PP	SH	GW	S	%	+/–	TF	F%	H	SB	Min	GP	G	A	Pts	PIM	PP	SH	GW
1992-93	Swift Current	WHL	43	2	1	3	8	....	....	....	....	....	....	....	....	....	....	....	....	....	....	....	....	....	....	....
1993-94	Swift Current	WHL	66	2	9	11	53	....	....	....	....	....	....	....	....	....	....	....	7	0	3	3	4	....	....	....
1994-95	Swift Current	WHL	72	8	42	50	80	....	....	....	....	....	....	....	....	....	....	....	6	1	1	2	10	....	....	....
1995-96	Swift Current	WHL	72	31	46	77	151	....	....	....	....	....	....	....	....	....	....	....	6	1	0	1	22	....	....	....
1996-97	Rochester	AHL	64	7	10	25	65	....	....	....	....	....	....	....	....	....	....	....	....	....	....	....	....	....	....	....
	Edmonton	**NHL**	**1**	**0**	**0**	**0**	**2**	**0**	**0**	**0**	**1**	**0.0**	**0**	....	....	....	....	....	....	....	....	....	....	....	....	....
	Hamilton	AHL	10	1	3	4	10	....	....	....	....	....	....	....	....	....	....	....	22	4	4	8	21	....	....	....
1997-98	**Edmonton**	**NHL**	**11**	**4**	**0**	**4**	**8**	**1**	**0**	**0**	**10**	**40.0**	**–3**	....	....	....	....	....	....	....	....	....	....	....	....	....
	Hamilton	AHL	60	10	22	32	113	....	....	....	....	....	....	....	....	....	....	....	9	3	1	4	22	....	....	....
1998-99	**Edmonton**	**NHL**	**24**	**0**	**2**	**2**	**19**	**0**	**0**	**0**	**18**	**0.0**	**–6**	**0**	**0.0**	**23**	**24**	**15:09**	....	....	....	....	....	....	....	....
	Hamilton	AHL	43	3	17	20	38	....	....	....	....	....	....	....	....	....	....	....	11	1	5	6	18	....	....	....
	NHL Totals		**36**	**4**	**2**	**6**	**29**	**1**	**0**	**0**	**29**	**13.8**		**0**	**0.0**	**23**	**24**	**15:09**	....	....	....	....	....	....	....	....

WHL East First All-Star Team (1996)

Traded to **Edmonton** by **Buffalo** with Barrie Moore for Miroslav Satan, March 18, 1997. Traded to **Nashville** by **Edmonton** for Detroit's 3rd round choice (previously acquired, Edmonton selected Mike Comrie) in 1999 Entry Draft, June 26, 1999.

MILLEN, Corey

Center. Shoots right. 5'7", 170 lbs. Born, Cloquet, MN, March 30, 1964. NY Rangers' 3rd choice, 57th overall, in 1982 Entry Draft.

Season	Club	League	GP	G	A	Pts	PIM	PP	SH	GW	S	%	+/–	TF	F%	H	SB	Min	GP	G	A	Pts	PIM	PP	SH	GW
1981-82	Cloquet High	H.S.	18	46	35	81	....	....	....	....	....	....	....	....	....	....	....	....	....	....	....	....	....	....	....	....
1982-83	U. of Minnesota	WCHA	21	14	15	29	18	....	....	....	....	....	....	....	....	....	....	....	....	....	....	....	....	....	....	....
1983-84	United States	Nat-Team	45	15	11	26	10	....	....	....	....	....	....	....	....	....	....	....	....	....	....	....	....	....	....	....
	United States	Olympics	6	0	0	0	2	....	....	....	....	....	....	....	....	....	....	....	....	....	....	....	....	....	....	....
1984-85	U. of Minnesota	WCHA	38	28	36	64	60	....	....	....	....	....	....	....	....	....	....	....	....	....	....	....	....	....	....	....
1985-86	U. of Minnesota	WCHA	48	41	42	83	64	....	....	....	....	....	....	....	....	....	....	....	....	....	....	....	....	....	....	....
1986-87	U. of Minnesota	WCHA	42	36	29	65	62	....	....	....	....	....	....	....	....	....	....	....	....	....	....	....	....	....	....	....
1987-88	United States	Nat-Team	47	41	43	84	26	....	....	....	....	....	....	....	....	....	....	....	....	....	....	....	....	....	....	....
	United States	Olympics	6	6	5	11	4	....	....	....	....	....	....	....	....	....	....	....	....	....	....	....	....	....	....	....
	Ambri Piotta	Switz.	5	4	3	7	....	....	....	....	....	....	....	....	....	....	....	....	6	*8	5	13	....	....	....	....
1988-89	Ambri Piotta	Switz.	36	32	22	54	18	....	....	....	....	....	....	....	....	....	....	....	6	4	3	7	0	....	....	....
1989-90	**NY Rangers**	**NHL**	**4**	**0**	**0**	**0**	**2**	**0**	**0**	**0**	**4**	**0.0**	**–2**	....	....	....	....	....	....	....	....	....	....	....	....	....
	Flint	IHL	11	4	5	9	2	....	....	....	....	....	....	....	....	....	....	....	....	....	....	....	....	....	....	....
1990-91	**NY Rangers**	**NHL**	**4**	**3**	**1**	**4**	**0**	**2**	**0**	**0**	**8**	**37.5**	**1**	....	....	....	....	....	**6**	**1**	**2**	**3**	**0**	**1**	**0**	**0**
	Binghamton	AHL	40	19	37	56	68	....	....	....	....	....	....	....	....	....	....	....	6	0	7	7	6	....	....	....
1991-92	**NY Rangers**	**NHL**	**11**	**1**	**4**	**5**	**10**	**0**	**0**	**0**	**20**	**5.0**	**–1**	....	....	....	....	....	....	....	....	....	....	....	....	....
	Binghamton	AHL	15	8	7	15	44	....	....	....	....	....	....	....	....	....	....	....	....	....	....	....	....	....	....	....
	Los Angeles	**NHL**	**46**	**20**	**21**	**41**	**44**	**8**	**1**	**3**	**89**	**22.5**	**3**	....	....	....	....	....	**6**	**0**	**1**	**1**	**6**	**0**	**0**	**0**
1992-93	**Los Angeles**	**NHL**	**42**	**23**	**16**	**39**	**42**	**9**	**2**	**1**	**100**	**23.0**	**16**	....	....	....	....	....	**23**	**2**	**4**	**6**	**12**	**0**	**0**	**0**
1993-94	**New Jersey**	**NHL**	**78**	**20**	**30**	**50**	**52**	**4**	**0**	**3**	**132**	**15.2**	**24**	....	....	....	....	....	**7**	**1**	**0**	**1**	**2**	**0**	**0**	**1**
1994-95	**New Jersey**	**NHL**	**17**	**2**	**3**	**5**	**8**	**0**	**0**	**0**	**30**	**6.7**	**2**	....	....	....	....	....	....	....	....	....	....	....	....	....
	Dallas	**NHL**	**28**	**3**	**15**	**18**	**28**	**1**	**0**	**0**	**44**	**6.8**	**4**	....	....	....	....	....	**5**	**1**	**0**	**1**	**2**	**0**	**0**	**0**
1995-96	**Dallas**	**NHL**	**13**	**3**	**4**	**7**	**8**	**1**	**0**	**0**	**25**	**12.0**	**0**	....	....	....	....	....	....	....	....	....	....	....	....	....
	Michigan	IHL	11	8	11	19	14	....	....	....	....	....	....	....	....	....	....	....	....	....	....	....	....	....	....	....
	Calgary	**NHL**	**31**	**4**	**10**	**14**	**10**	**1**	**0**	**1**	**48**	**8.3**	**8**	....	....	....	....	....	....	....	....	....	....	....	....	....
1996-97	**Calgary**	**NHL**	**61**	**11**	**15**	**26**	**32**	**1**	**0**	**0**	**82**	**13.4**	**–19**	....	....	....	....	....	....	....	....	....	....	....	....	....
1997-98	Kolner Haie	Germany	30	17	17	34	52	....	....	....	....	....	....	....	....	....	....	....	3	2	1	3	6	....	....	....
	Kolner Haie	EuroHL	5	1	5	6	10	....	....	....	....	....	....	....	....	....	....	....	....	....	....	....	....	....	....	....
1998-99	Kolner Haie	Germany	48	26	39	65	143	....	....	....	....	....	....	....	....	....	....	....	5	2	2	4	37	....	....	....
	NHL Totals		**335**	**90**	**119**	**209**	**236**	**27**	**3**	**8**	**582**	**15.5**		....	....	....	....	....	**47**	**5**	**7**	**12**	**22**	**1**	**0**	**1**

WCHA Second All-Star Team (1985, 1986, 1987) • NCAA West Second All-American Team (1986) • NCAA Championship All-Tournament Team (1987)

Traded to **LA Kings** by **NY Rangers** for Randy Gilhen, December 23, 1991. Traded to **New Jersey** by **LA Kings** for New Jersey's 5th round choice (Jason Saal) in 1993 Entry Draft, June 26, 1993. Traded to **Dallas** by **New Jersey** for Neal Broten, February 27, 1995. Traded to **Calgary** by **Dallas** with Jarome Iginla for Joe Nieuwendyk, December 19, 1995.

MILLER, Aaron

COL.

Defense. Shoots right. 6'3", 200 lbs. Born, Buffalo, NY, August 11, 1971. NY Rangers' 6th choice, 88th overall, in 1989 Entry Draft.

Season	Club	League	Regular Season GP	G	A	Pts	PIM	PP	SH	GW	S	%	+/-	TF	F%	H	SB	Min	Playoffs GP	G	A	Pts	PIM	PP	SH	GW
1987-88	Niagara Scenics	NAJHL	30	4	9	13	2																			
1988-89	Niagara Scenics	NAJHL	59	24	38	62	60																			
1989-90	U. of Vermont	ECAC	31	1	15	16	24																			
1990-91	U. of Vermont	ECAC	30	3	7	10	22																			
1991-92	U. of Vermont	ECAC	31	3	16	19	28																			
1992-93	U. of Vermont	ECAC	30	4	13	17	16																			
1993-94	Quebec	NHL	1	0	0	0	0	0	0	0	0	0.0	-1													
	Cornwall	AHL	64	4	10	14	49												13	0	2	2	10			
1994-95	Quebec	NHL	9	0	3	3	6	0	0	0	12	0.0	2													
	Cornwall	AHL	76	4	18	22	69																			
1995-96	Colorado	NHL	5	0	0	0	0	0	0	0	2	0.0	0													
	Cornwall	AHL	62	4	23	27	77												8	0	1	1	6			
1996-97	Colorado	NHL	56	5	12	17	15	0	0	3	47	10.6	15						17	1	2	3	10	0	0	0
1997-98	Colorado	NHL	55	2	2	4	51	0	0	0	29	6.9	0						7	0	0	0	8	0	0	0
1998-99	Colorado	NHL	76	5	13	18	42	1	0	2	87	5.7	3	0	0.0	115	128	21:49	19	1	5	6	10	0	0	0
	NHL Totals		202	12	30	42	114	1	0	5	177	6.8		0	0.0	115	128	21:49	43	2	7	9	28	0	0	0

ECAC First All-Star Team (1993) • NCAA East Second All-American Team (1993)

Traded to **Quebec** by **NY Rangers** with NY Rangers' 5th round choice (Bill Lindsay) in 1991 Entry Draft for Joe Cirella, January 17, 1991. Transferred to **Colorado** after **Quebec** franchise relocated, June 21, 1996.

MILLER, Kelly

Left wing. Shoots left. 5'11", 197 lbs. Born, Lansing, MI, March 3, 1963. NY Rangers' 9th choice, 183rd overall, in 1982 Entry Draft.

Season	Club	League	Regular Season GP	G	A	Pts	PIM	PP	SH	GW	S	%	+/-	TF	F%	H	SB	Min	Playoffs GP	G	A	Pts	PIM	PP	SH	GW
1979-80	Redford	GLJHL	45	31	37	68	16																			
1980-81	Redford	GLJHL	48	39	51	90	8																			
1981-82	Michigan State	CCHA	38	11	18	29	17																			
1982-83	Michigan State	CCHA	36	16	19	35	12																			
1983-84	Michigan State	CCHA	46	28	21	49	12																			
1984-85	Michigan State	CCHA	43	27	23	50	21																			
	NY Rangers	NHL	5	0	2	2	2	0	0	0	5	0.0	-2						3	0	0	0	2	0	0	0
1985-86	NY Rangers	NHL	74	13	20	33	52	0	1	3	112	11.6	3						16	3	4	7	4	0	1	0
1986-87	NY Rangers	NHL	38	6	14	20	22	2	0	1	58	10.3	-5													
	Washington	NHL	39	10	12	22	26	3	1	0	50	20.0	10						7	2	2	4	0	0	0	0
1987-88	Washington	NHL	80	9	23	32	35	0	1	3	96	9.4	9						14	4	4	8	10	0	1	1
1988-89	Washington	NHL	78	19	21	40	45	2	1	3	121	15.7	13						6	1	0	1	2	0	0	1
1989-90	Washington	NHL	80	18	22	40	49	3	2	2	107	16.8	-2						15	3	5	8	23	0	1	0
1990-91	Washington	NHL	80	24	26	50	29	4	2	3	155	15.5	10						11	4	2	6	6	0	1	0
1991-92	Washington	NHL	78	14	38	52	49	0	1	3	144	9.7	20						7	1	2	3	4	0	0	0
1992-93	Washington	NHL	84	18	27	45	32	3	0	3	144	12.5	-2						6	0	3	3	2	0	0	0
1993-94	Washington	NHL	84	14	25	39	32	0	1	3	138	10.1	8						11	2	7	9	0	1	1	0
1994-95	Washington	NHL	48	10	13	23	6	2	0	1	70	14.3	5						7	0	3	3	4	0	0	0
1995-96	Washington	NHL	74	7	13	20	30	0	2	1	93	7.5	7						6	0	1	1	4	0	0	0
1996-97	Washington	NHL	77	10	14	24	33	0	1	3	95	10.5	4													
1997-98	Washington	NHL	76	7	7	14	41	0	3	3	68	10.3	-2						10	0	1	1	4	0	0	0
1998-99	Washington	NHL	62	2	5	7	29	0	0	1	49	4.1	-5	5	0.0	111	34	11:11								
	NHL Totals		1057	181	282	463	512	19	16	33	1505	12.0		5	0.0	111	34	11:11	119	20	34	54	65	1	5	2

CCHA First All-Star Team (1985) • NCAA West First All-American Team (1985)

Traded to **Washington** by **NY Rangers** with Bob Crawford and Mike Ridley for Bob Carpenter and Washington's 2nd round choice (Jason Prosofsky) in 1989 Entry Draft, January 1, 1987.

MILLER, Kevin

OTT.

Center. Shoots right. 5'11", 190 lbs. Born, Lansing, MI, September 2, 1965. NY Rangers' 10th choice, 202nd overall, in 1984 Entry Draft.

Season	Club	League	Regular Season GP	G	A	Pts	PIM	PP	SH	GW	S	%	+/-	TF	F%	H	SB	Min	Playoffs GP	G	A	Pts	PIM	PP	SH	GW
1983-84	Redford	GLJHL	44	28	57	85																				
1984-85	Michigan State	CCHA	44	11	29	40	84																			
1985-86	Michigan State	CCHA	45	19	52	71	112																			
1986-87	Michigan State	CCHA	42	25	56	81	63																			
1987-88	Michigan State	CCHA	9	6	3	9	18																			
	United States	Nat-Team	48	31	32	63	33																			
	United States	Olympics	5	1	3	4	4																			
1988-89	NY Rangers	NHL	24	3	5	8	2	0	0	1	40	7.5	-1													
	Denver	IHL	55	29	47	76	19												4	2	1	3	2			
1989-90	NY Rangers	NHL	16	0	5	5	2	0	0	0	9	0.0	-1						1	0	0	0	0	0	0	0
	Flint	IHL	48	19	23	42	41																			
1990-91	NY Rangers	NHL	63	17	27	44	63	1	2	3	113	15.0	1													
	Detroit	NHL	11	5	2	7	4	0	1	0	23	21.7	-4						7	3	2	5	20	0	1	0
1991-92	Detroit	NHL	80	20	26	46	53	3	1	4	130	15.4	6						9	0	2	2	4	0	0	0
1992-93	Washington	NHL	10	0	3	3	35	0	0	0	10	0.0	-4													
	St. Louis	NHL	72	24	22	46	65	8	3	4	153	15.7	6						10	0	3	3	11	0	0	0
1993-94	St. Louis	NHL	75	23	25	48	83	6	3	5	154	14.9	6						3	1	0	1	4	0	1	0
1994-95	St. Louis	NHL	15	2	5	7	0	0	0	0	19	10.5	4													
	San Jose	NHL	21	6	7	13	13	1	1	2	41	14.6	0						6	0	0	0	2	0	0	0
1995-96	San Jose	NHL	68	22	20	42	41	2	2	2	146	15.1	-8													
	Pittsburgh	NHL	13	6	5	11	4	1	0	0	33	18.2	4						18	3	2	5	8	0	0	0
1996-97	Chicago	NHL	69	14	17	31	41	5	1	2	139	10.1	-10						6	0	1	1	0	0	0	0
1997-98	Chicago	NHL	37	4	7	11	8	0	0	1	37	10.8	-4													
	Indianapolis	IHL	26	11	11	22	41												2	1	1	2	0			
1998-99	NY Islanders	NHL	33	1	5	6	13	0	0	0	37	2.7	-5	114	49.1	42	11	10:19								
	Chicago	IHL	30	11	20	31	8												10	2	7	9	22			
	NHL Totals		607	147	181	328	427	27	14	24	1084	13.6		114	49.1	42	11	10:19	60	7	10	17	49	0	2	0

Traded to **Detroit** by **NY Rangers** with Jim Cummins and Dennis Vial for Joey Kocur and Per Djoos, March 5, 1991. Traded to **Washington** by **Detroit** for Dino Ciccarelli, June 20, 1992. Traded to **St. Louis** by **Washington** for Paul Cavallini, November 2, 1992. Traded to **San Jose** by **St. Louis** for Todd Elik, March 23, 1995. Traded to **Pittsburgh** by **San Jose** for Pittsburgh's 5th round choice (later traded to Boston — Boston selected Elias Abrahamsson) in 1996 Entry Draft and future considerations, March 20, 1996. Signed as a free agent by **Chicago**, July 18, 1996. Signed as a free agent by **NY Islanders**, October 9, 1998. Signed as a free agent by **Ottawa**, August 24, 1999.

MILLER, Kip

PIT.

Center. Shoots left. 5'10", 190 lbs. Born, Lansing, MI, June 11, 1969. Quebec's 4th choice, 72nd overall, in 1987 Entry Draft.

Season	Club	League	Regular Season GP	G	A	Pts	PIM	PP	SH	GW	S	%	+/-	TF	F%	H	SB	Min	Playoffs GP	G	A	Pts	PIM	PP	SH	GW
1984-85	Detroit	MNHL	65	69	63	132																				
1985-86	Detroit	GLJHL	30	25	28	53																				
1986-87	Michigan State	CCHA	41	20	19	39	92																			
1987-88	Michigan State	CCHA	39	16	25	41	51																			
1988-89	Michigan State	CCHA	47	32	45	77	94																			
1989-90	Michigan State	CCHA	45	*48	53	*101	60																			
1990-91	Quebec	NHL	13	4	3	7	7	0	0	0	16	25.0	-1													
	Halifax	AHL	66	36	33	69	40																			
1991-92	Quebec	NHL	36	5	10	15	12	1	0	2	46	10.9	-21													
	Halifax	AHL	24	9	17	26	8																			
	Minnesota	NHL	3	1	2	3	2	1	0	0	3	33.3	-1													
	Kalamazoo	IHL	6	1	8	9	4												12	3	9	12	12			
1992-93	Kalamazoo	IHL	61	17	39	56	59																			

			Regular Season																Playoffs							
Season	Club	League	GP	G	A	Pts	PIM	PP	SH	GW	S	%	+/–	TF	F%	H	SB	Min	GP	G	A	Pts	PIM	PP	SH	GW
1993-94	**San Jose**	**NHL**	**11**	**2**	**2**	**4**	**6**	**0**	**0**	**0**	**21**	**9.5**	**–1**	....	....	....	....	....	....	....	....	....	....	....	....	....
	Kansas City	IHL	71	38	54	92	51	....	....	....	....	....	....	....	....	....	....	....	....	....	....	....	....	....	....	....
1994-95	Denver	IHL	71	46	60	106	54	....	....	....	....	....	....	....	....	....	....	....	17	*15	14	29	8	....	....	....
	NY Islanders	**NHL**	**8**	**0**	**1**	**1**	**0**	**0**	**0**	**0**	**11**	**0.0**	**1**	....	....	....	....	....	....	....	....	....	....	....	....	....
1995-96	**Chicago**	**NHL**	**10**	**1**	**4**	**5**	**2**	**0**	**0**	**0**	**12**	**8.3**	**1**	....	....	....	....	....	....	....	....	....	....	....	....	....
	Indianapolis	IHL	73	32	59	91	46	....	....	....	....	....	....	....	....	....	....	....	5	2	6	8	2	....	....	....
1996-97	Chicago	IHL	43	11	41	52	32	....	....	....	....	....	....	....	....	....	....	....	....	....	....	....	....	....	....	....
	Indianapolis	IHL	37	17	24	41	18	....	....	....	....	....	....	....	....	....	....	....	4	2	2	4	2	....	....	....
1997-98	Utah	IHL	72	38	59	97	30	....	....	....	....	....	....	....	....	....	....	....	4	3	2	5	10	....	....	....
	NY Islanders	**NHL**	**9**	**1**	**3**	**4**	**2**	**0**	**0**	**0**	**11**	**9.1**	**–2**	....	....	....	....	....	....	....	....	....	....	....	....	....
1998-99	**Pittsburgh**	**NHL**	**77**	**19**	**23**	**42**	**22**	**1**	**0**	**4**	**125**	**15.2**	**1**	**150**	**44.7**	**67**	**25**	**16:55**	**13**	**2**	**7**	**9**	**19**	**1**	**0**	**0**
	NHL Totals		**167**	**33**	**48**	**81**	**53**	**3**	**0**	**6**	**245**	**13.5**		**150**	**44.7**	**67**	**25**	**16:55**	**13**	**2**	**7**	**9**	**19**	**1**	**0**	**0**

CCHA First All-Star Team (1989, 1990) • NCAA West First All-American Team (1989, 1990) • Won Hobey Baker Memorial Award (Top U.S. Collegiate Player) (1990)

Traded to **Minnesota** by **Quebec** for Steve Maltais, March 8, 1992. Signed as a free agent by **San Jose**, August 10, 1993. Signed as a free agent by **NY Islanders**, July 7, 1994. Signed as a free agent by **Chicago**, July 21, 1995. Signed as a free agent by **NY Islanders**, November 26, 1997. Claimed by **Pittsburgh** from **NY Islanders** in NHL Waiver Draft, October 5, 1998.

MILLS, Craig — CHI.

Right wing. Shoots right. 6', 190 lbs. Born, Toronto, Ont., August 27, 1976. Winnipeg's 5th choice, 108th overall, in 1994 Entry Draft.

1992-93	St. Michael's	OJHL-B	44	9	21	30	42	....	....	....	....	....	....	....	....	....	....	....	15	1	6	7	8	....	....	....
1993-94	Belleville	OHL	63	15	18	33	88	....	....	....	....	....	....	....	....	....	....	....	12	2	1	3	11	....	....	....
1994-95	Belleville	OHL	62	39	41	80	104	....	....	....	....	....	....	....	....	....	....	....	13	7	9	16	8	....	....	....
1995-96	Belleville	OHL	48	10	19	29	113	....	....	....	....	....	....	....	....	....	....	....	14	4	5	9	32	....	....	....
	Winnipeg	**NHL**	**4**	**0**	**2**	**2**	**0**	**0**	**0**	**0**	**0**	**0.0**	**0**	....	....	....	....	....	**1**	**0**	**0**	**0**	**0**	**0**	**0**	**0**
	Springfield	AHL	....	....	....	....	....	....	....	....	....	....	....	....	....	....	....	....	2	0	0	0	0	....	....	....
1996-97	Indianapolis	IHL	80	12	7	19	199	....	....	....	....	....	....	....	....	....	....	....	4	0	0	0	4	....	....	....
1997-98	**Chicago**	**NHL**	**20**	**0**	**3**	**3**	**34**	**0**	**0**	**0**	**5**	**0.0**	**1**	....	....	....	....	....	....	....	....	....	....	....	....	....
	Indianapolis	IHL	42	8	11	19	119	....	....	....	....	....	....	....	....	....	....	....	5	0	0	0	27	....	....	....
1998-99	**Chicago**	**NHL**	**7**	**0**	**0**	**0**	**2**	**0**	**0**	**0**	**1**	**0.0**	**–2**	**0**	**0.0**	**4**	**0**	**5:48**	....	....	....	....	....	....	....	....
	Chicago	IHL	5	0	0	0	14	....	....	....	....	....	....	....	....	....	....	....	....	....	....	....	....	....	....	....
	Portland	AHL	48	7	11	18	59	....	....	....	....	....	....	....	....	....	....	....	....	....	....	....	....	....	....	....
	Indianapolis	IHL	12	2	3	5	14	....	....	....	....	....	....	....	....	....	....	....	6	1	0	1	5	....	....	....
	NHL Totals		**31**	**0**	**5**	**5**	**36**	**0**	**0**	**0**	**6**	**0.0**		**0**	**0.0**	**4**	**0**	**5:48**	**1**	**0**	**0**	**0**	**0**	**0**	**0**	**0**

Canadian Major Junior Humanitarian Player of the Year (1996)

Rights transferred to **Phoenix** after **Winnipeg** franchise relocated, July 1, 1996. Traded to **Chicago** by **Phoenix** with Alexei Zhamnov and Phoenix's 1st round choice (Ty Jones) in 1997 Entry Draft for Jeremy Roenick, August 16, 1996.

MIRONOV, Boris (mih-RAWN-ohv) — CHI.

Defense. Shoots right. 6'3", 223 lbs. Born, Moscow, USSR, March 21, 1972. Winnipeg's 2nd choice, 27th overall, in 1992 Entry Draft.

1988-89	CSKA Moscow	USSR	1	0	0	0	0	....	....	....	....	....	....	....	....	....	....	....	....	....	....	....	....	....	....	....
1989-90	CSKA Moscow	USSR	7	0	0	0	0	....	....	....	....	....	....	....	....	....	....	....	....	....	....	....	....	....	....	....
1990-91	CSKA Moscow	USSR	36	1	5	6	16	....	....	....	....	....	....	....	....	....	....	....	....	....	....	....	....	....	....	....
1991-92	CSKA Moscow	CIS	36	2	1	3	22	....	....	....	....	....	....	....	....	....	....	....	....	....	....	....	....	....	....	....
1992-93	CSKA Moscow	CIS	19	0	5	5	20	....	....	....	....	....	....	....	....	....	....	....	....	....	....	....	....	....	....	....
1993-94	**Winnipeg**	**NHL**	**65**	**7**	**22**	**29**	**96**	**5**	**0**	**0**	**122**	**5.7**	**–29**	....	....	....	....	....	....	....	....	....	....	....	....	....
	Edmonton	**NHL**	**14**	**0**	**2**	**2**	**14**	**0**	**0**	**0**	**23**	**0.0**	**–4**	....	....	....	....	....	....	....	....	....	....	....	....	....
1994-95	**Edmonton**	**NHL**	**29**	**1**	**7**	**8**	**40**	**0**	**0**	**0**	**48**	**2.1**	**–9**	....	....	....	....	....	....	....	....	....	....	....	....	....
	Cape Breton	AHL	4	2	5	7	23	....	....	....	....	....	....	....	....	....	....	....	....	....	....	....	....	....	....	....
1995-96	**Edmonton**	**NHL**	**78**	**8**	**24**	**32**	**101**	**7**	**0**	**1**	**158**	**5.1**	**–23**	....	....	....	....	....	....	....	....	....	....	....	....	....
1996-97	**Edmonton**	**NHL**	**55**	**6**	**26**	**32**	**85**	**2**	**0**	**1**	**147**	**4.1**	**2**	....	....	....	....	....	**12**	**2**	**8**	**10**	**16**	**2**	**0**	**0**
1997-98	**Edmonton**	**NHL**	**81**	**16**	**30**	**46**	**100**	**10**	**1**	**1**	**203**	**7.9**	**–8**	....	....	....	....	....	**12**	**3**	**3**	**6**	**27**	**1**	**0**	**1**
	Russia	Olympics	6	0	2	2	2	....	....	....	....	....	....	....	....	....	....	....	....	....	....	....	....	....	....	....
1998-99	**Edmonton**	**NHL**	**63**	**11**	**29**	**40**	**104**	**5**	**0**	**4**	**138**	**8.0**	**6**	**0**	**0.0**	**142**	**103**	**25:55**	....	....	....	....	....	....	....	....
	Chicago	**NHL**	**12**	**0**	**9**	**9**	**27**	**0**	**0**	**0**	**35**	**0.0**	**7**	**0**	**0.0**	**32**	**17**	**24:17**	....	....	....	....	....	....	....	....
	NHL Totals		**397**	**49**	**149**	**198**	**567**	**29**	**1**	**7**	**874**	**5.6**		**0**	**0.0**	**174**	**120**	**25:39**	**24**	**5**	**11**	**16**	**43**	**3**	**0**	**1**

NHL/Upper Deck All-Rookie Team (1994)

Traded to **Edmonton** by **Winnipeg** with Mats Lindgren, Winnipeg's 1st round choice (Jason Bonsignore) in 1994 Entry Draft and Florida's 4th round choice (previously acquired, Edmonton selected Adam Copeland) in 1994 Entry Draft for Dave Manson and St. Louis' 6th round choice (previously acquired, Winnipeg selected Chris Kibermanis) in 1994 Entry Draft, March 15, 1994. Traded to **Chicago** by **Edmonton** with Dean McAmmond and Jonas Elofsson for Chad Kilger, Daniel Cleary, Ethan Moreau and Christian Laflamme, March 20, 1999.

MIRONOV, Dmitri (mih-RAWN-ohv) — WSH.

Defense. Shoots right. 6'3", 224 lbs. Born, Moscow, USSR, December 25, 1965. Toronto's 7th choice, 160th overall, in 1991 Entry Draft.

1985-86	CSKA Moscow	USSR	9	0	1	1	8	....	....	....	....	....	....	....	....	....	....	....	....	....	....	....	....	....	....	....
1986-87	CSKA Moscow	USSR	20	1	3	4	10	....	....	....	....	....	....	....	....	....	....	....	....	....	....	....	....	....	....	....
1987-88	Soviet Wings	USSR	44	12	6	18	30	....	....	....	....	....	....	....	....	....	....	....	....	....	....	....	....	....	....	....
1988-89	Soviet Wings	USSR	44	5	6	11	44	....	....	....	....	....	....	....	....	....	....	....	....	....	....	....	....	....	....	....
1989-90	Soviet Wings	USSR	45	4	11	15	34	....	....	....	....	....	....	....	....	....	....	....	....	....	....	....	....	....	....	....
1990-91	Soviet Wings	USSR	45	16	12	28	22	....	....	....	....	....	....	....	....	....	....	....	....	....	....	....	....	....	....	....
1991-92	Soviet Wings	CIS	35	15	16	31	62	....	....	....	....	....	....	....	....	....	....	....	....	....	....	....	....	....	....	....
	Toronto	**NHL**	**7**	**1**	**0**	**1**	**0**	**0**	**0**	**1**	**7**	**14.3**	**–4**	....	....	....	....	....	....	....	....	....	....	....	....	....
	Russia	Olympics	8	3	1	4	6	....	....	....	....	....	....	....	....	....	....	....	....	....	....	....	....	....	....	....
1992-93	**Toronto**	**NHL**	**59**	**7**	**24**	**31**	**40**	**4**	**0**	**1**	**105**	**6.7**	**–1**	....	....	....	....	....	**14**	**1**	**2**	**3**	**2**	**1**	**0**	**0**
1993-94	**Toronto**	**NHL**	**76**	**9**	**27**	**36**	**78**	**3**	**0**	**0**	**147**	**6.1**	**5**	....	....	....	....	....	**18**	**6**	**9**	**15**	**6**	**6**	**0**	**0**
1994-95	**Toronto**	**NHL**	**33**	**5**	**12**	**17**	**28**	**2**	**0**	**0**	**68**	**7.4**	**6**	....	....	....	....	....	**6**	**2**	**1**	**3**	**2**	**1**	**0**	**0**
1995-96	**Pittsburgh**	**NHL**	**72**	**3**	**31**	**34**	**88**	**1**	**0**	**1**	**86**	**3.5**	**19**	....	....	....	....	....	**15**	**0**	**1**	**1**	**10**	**0**	**0**	**0**
1996-97	**Pittsburgh**	**NHL**	**15**	**1**	**5**	**6**	**24**	**0**	**0**	**1**	**19**	**5.3**	**–4**	....	....	....	....	....	....	....	....	....	....	....	....	....
	Anaheim	**NHL**	**62**	**12**	**34**	**46**	**77**	**3**	**1**	**1**	**158**	**7.6**	**20**	....	....	....	....	....	**11**	**1**	**10**	**11**	**10**	**1**	**0**	**0**
1997-98	**Anaheim**	**NHL**	**66**	**6**	**30**	**36**	**115**	**2**	**0**	**1**	**142**	**4.2**	**–7**	....	....	....	....	....	....	....	....	....	....	....	....	....
	Russia	Olympics	6	0	3	3	0	....	....	....	....	....	....	....	....	....	....	....	....	....	....	....	....	....	....	....
	♦ **Detroit**	**NHL**	**11**	**2**	**5**	**7**	**4**	**1**	**0**	**0**	**28**	**7.1**	**0**	....	....	....	....	....	**7**	**0**	**3**	**3**	**14**	**0**	**0**	**0**
1998-99	**Washington**	**NHL**	**46**	**2**	**14**	**16**	**80**	**2**	**0**	**0**	**86**	**2.3**	**–5**	**0**	**0.0**	**47**	**37**	**19:51**	....	....	....	....	....	....	....	....
	NHL Totals		**447**	**48**	**182**	**230**	**534**	**18**	**1**	**6**	**846**	**5.7**		**0**	**0.0**	**47**	**37**	**19:51**	**71**	**10**	**26**	**36**	**44**	**9**	**0**	**0**

Played in NHL All-Star Game (1998)

Traded to **Pittsburgh** by **Toronto** with Toronto's 2nd round choice (later traded to New Jersey — New Jersey selected Joshua Dewolf) in 1996 Entry Draft for Larry Murphy, July 8, 1995. Traded to **Anaheim** by **Pittsburgh** with Shawn Antoski for Alex Hicks and Fredrik Olausson, November 19, 1996. Traded to **Detroit** by **Anaheim** for Jamie Pushor and Detroit's 4th round choice (Viktor Wallin) in 1998 Entry Draft, March 24, 1998. Signed as a free agent by **Washington**, July 29, 1998.

MITCHELL, Jeff

Center/Right wing. Shoots right. 6'1", 190 lbs. Born, Wayne, MI, May 16, 1975. Los Angeles' 2nd choice, 68th overall, in 1993 Entry Draft.

1990-91	Fruehauf	MNHL	62	52	63	115	196	....	....	....	....	....	....	....	....	....	....	....	....	....	....	....	....	....	....	....
1991-92	Fraser	MNHL	65	65	52	117	114	....	....	....	....	....	....	....	....	....	....	....	....	....	....	....	....	....	....	....
1992-93	Detroit	OHL	62	10	15	25	100	....	....	....	....	....	....	....	....	....	....	....	15	3	3	6	16	....	....	....
1993-94	Detroit	OHL	59	25	18	43	99	....	....	....	....	....	....	....	....	....	....	....	17	3	5	8	22	....	....	....
1994-95	Detroit	OHL	61	30	30	60	121	....	....	....	....	....	....	....	....	....	....	....	21	9	12	21	48	....	....	....
1995-96	Michigan	IHL	50	5	4	9	119	....	....	....	....	....	....	....	....	....	....	....	....	....	....	....	....	....	....	....
1996-97	Michigan	IHL	24	0	3	3	40	....	....	....	....	....	....	....	....	....	....	....	....	....	....	....	....	....	....	....
	Philadelphia	AHL	31	7	5	12	103	....	....	....	....	....	....	....	....	....	....	....	10	1	1	2	20	....	....	....

Season	Club	League	GP	G	A	Pts	PIM	PP	SH	GW	S	%	+/-	TF	F%	H	SB	Min	GP	G	A	Pts	PIM	PP	SH	GW
										Regular Season												Playoffs				
1997-98	Dallas	NHL	7	0	0	0	7	0	0	0	3	0.0	0	....	....	....	....	....								
	Michigan	IHL	62	9	8	17	206	....	....	....	....	....	....	....	....	....	....	....	4	0	0	0	30			
1998-99	Michigan	IHL	50	4	4	8	122	....	....	....	....	....	....	....	....	....	....	....	2	0	0	0	0			
	NHL Totals		7	0	0	0	7	0	0	0	3	0.0														

Rights traded to **Dallas** by **LA Kings** for Vancouver's 5th round choice (previously acquired, LA Kings selected Jason Morgan) in 1995 Entry Draft, June 7, 1995.

MODANO, Mike (moh-DA-noh) **DAL.**

Center. Shoots left. 6'3", 200 lbs.   Born, Livonia, MI, June 7, 1970. Minnesota's 1st choice, 1st overall, in 1988 Entry Draft.

Season	Club	League	GP	G	A	Pts	PIM	PP	SH	GW	S	%	+/-	TF	F%	H	SB	Min	GP	G	A	Pts	PIM	PP	SH	GW
1985-86	Detroit	MNHL	69	66	65	131	32																			
1986-87	Prince Albert	WHL	70	32	30	62	96	....	....	....	....	....	....													
1987-88	Prince Albert	WHL	65	47	80	127	80	....	....	....	....	....	....						8	1	4	5	4			
1988-89	Prince Albert	WHL	41	39	66	105	74	....	....	....	....	....	....						9	7	11	18	18			
	Minnesota	**NHL**																		2	0	0	0	0			
1989-90	Minnesota	NHL	80	29	46	75	63	12	0	2	172	16.9	-7						7	1	1	2	12	0	0	0
1990-91	Minnesota	NHL	79	28	36	64	65	9	0	2	232	12.1	2						23	8	12	20	16	3	0	1
1991-92	Minnesota	NHL	76	33	44	77	46	5	0	8	256	12.9	-9						7	3	2	5	4	1	0	0
1992-93	Minnesota	NHL	82	33	60	93	83	9	0	7	307	10.7	-7													
1993-94	Dallas	NHL	76	50	43	93	54	18	0	4	281	17.8	-8						9	7	3	10	16	2	0	2
1994-95	Dallas	NHL	30	12	17	29	8	4	1	0	100	12.0	7													
1995-96	Dallas	NHL	78	36	45	81	63	8	4	4	320	11.3	-12													
1996-97	Dallas	NHL	80	35	48	83	42	9	5	9	291	12.0	43						7	4	1	5	0	1	1	2
1997-98	Dallas	NHL	52	21	38	59	32	7	5	2	191	11.0	25						17	4	10	14	12	1	0	1
	United States	Olympics	4	2	0	2	0																				
1998-99♦	Dallas	NHL	77	34	47	81	44	6	4	7	224	15.2	29	1572	51.1	15	33	20:50	23	5	*18	23	16	1	1	1
	NHL Totals		710	311	424	735	500	87	19	45	2374	13.1		1572	51.1	15	33	20:50	95	32	47	79	76	9	2	7

WHL East All-Star Team (1989) • NHL All-Rookie Team (1990)
Played in NHL All-Star Game (1993, 1998, 1999)
Transferred to **Dallas** after **Minnesota** franchise relocated, June 9, 1993.

MODIN, Fredrik (muh-DEEN) **TOR.**

Left wing. Shoots left. 6'4", 220 lbs.   Born, Sundsvall, Sweden, October 8, 1974. Toronto's 3rd choice, 64th overall, in 1994 Entry Draft.

Season	Club	League	GP	G	A	Pts	PIM	PP	SH	GW	S	%	+/-	TF	F%	H	SB	Min	GP	G	A	Pts	PIM	PP	SH	GW
1991-92	Sundsvall	Sweden-2	11	1	0	1	0	....	....	....	....	....	....													
1992-93	Sundsvall	Sweden-2	30	5	7	12	12	....	....	....	....	....	....						5	1	0	1	0			
1993-94	Sundsvall	Sweden-2	30	16	15	31	36	....	....	....	....	....	....													
1994-95	Brynas IF	Sweden	38	9	10	19	33	....	....	....	....	....	....						14	4	4	8	6			
1995-96	Brynas IF	Sweden	22	4	8	12	22	....	....	....	....	....	....													
1996-97	**Toronto**	**NHL**	76	6	7	13	24	0	0	0	85	7.1	-14													
1997-98	**Toronto**	**NHL**	74	16	16	32	32	1	0	4	137	11.7	-5													
1998-99	**Toronto**	**NHL**	67	16	15	31	35	1	0	3	108	14.8	14	2	50.0	77	12	13:34	8	0	0	0	6	0	0	0
	NHL Totals		217	38	38	76	91	2	0	7	330	11.5		2	50.0	77	12	13:34	8	0	0	0	6	0	0	0

MODRY, Jaroslav (MOHD-ree) **L.A.**

Defense. Shoots left. 6'2", 219 lbs.   Born, Ceske-Budejovice, Czech., February 27, 1971. New Jersey's 11th choice, 179th overall, in 1990 Entry Draft.

Season	Club	League	GP	G	A	Pts	PIM	PP	SH	GW	S	%	+/-	TF	F%	H	SB	Min	GP	G	A	Pts	PIM	PP	SH	GW
1987-88	MC Budejovice	Czech.	3	0	0	0	0	....	....	....	....	....	....													
1988-89	MC Budejovice	Czech.	28	0	1	1	8	....	....	....	....	....	....													
1989-90	MC Budejovice	Czech.	41	2	2	4		....	....	....	....	....	....													
1990-91	Dukla Trencin	Czech.	33	1	9	10	6	....	....	....	....	....	....													
1991-92	Dukla Trencin	Czech.	18	0	4	4	6	....	....	....	....	....	....													
	MC Budejovice	Czech-2	14	4	10	14	....	....	....	....	....	....	....													
1992-93	Utica	AHL	80	7	35	42	62	....	....	....	....	....	....						5	0	2	2	2			
1993-94	**New Jersey**	**NHL**	41	2	15	17	18	2	0	0	35	5.7	10													
	Albany	AHL	19	1	5	6	25																			
1994-95	HC Budejovice	Cze-Rep	19	1	3	4	30																			
	New Jersey	**NHL**	11	0	0	0	0	0	0	0	10	0.0	-1													
	Albany	AHL	18	5	6	11	14												14	3	3	6	4			
1995-96	**Ottawa**	**NHL**	64	4	14	18	38	1	0	1	89	4.5	-17													
	Los Angeles	**NHL**	9	0	3	3	6	0	0	0	17	0.0	-4													
1996-97	**Los Angeles**	**NHL**	30	3	3	6	25	1	1	0	32	9.4	-13													
	Phoenix	IHL	23	3	12	15	17																			
	Utah	IHL	11	1	4	5	20												7	0	1	1	6			
1997-98	Utah	IHL	74	12	21	33	72												4	0	2	2	6			
1998-99	**Los Angeles**	**NHL**	5	0	1	1	0	0	0	0	11	0.0	1	0	0.0	6	7	25:60								
	Long Beach	IHL	64	6	29	35	44												8	4	2	6	4			
	NHL Totals		160	9	36	45	87	4	1	1	194	4.6		0	0.0	6	7	26:00								

Traded to **Ottawa** by **New Jersey** for Ottawa's 4th round choice (Alyn McCauley) in 1995 Entry Draft, July 8, 1995. Traded to **LA Kings** by **Ottawa** with Ottawa's 8th round choice (Stephen Valiquette) in 1996 Entry Draft for Kevin Brown, March 20, 1996.

MOGER, Sandy (MOH-guhr)

Center. Shoots right. 6'4", 220 lbs.   Born, 100 Mile House, B.C., March 21, 1969. Vancouver's 7th choice, 176th overall, in 1989 Entry Draft.

Season	Club	League	GP	G	A	Pts	PIM	PP	SH	GW	S	%	+/-	TF	F%	H	SB	Min	GP	G	A	Pts	PIM	PP	SH	GW
1986-87	Vernon	BCJHL	13	5	4	9	10	....	....	....	....	....	....													
1987-88	Yorkton	SJHL	60	39	41	80	144	....	....	....	....	....	....						16	7	6	13	....	....	....	....
1988-89	Lake Superior	CCHA	21	3	5	8	26	....	....	....	....	....	....													
1989-90	Lake Superior	CCHA	46	17	15	32	76	....	....	....	....	....	....													
1990-91	Lake Superior	CCHA	45	27	21	48	*172	....	....	....	....	....	....													
1991-92	Lake Superior	CCHA	38	24	24	48	93	....	....	....	....	....	....													
1992-93	Hamilton	AHL	78	23	26	49	57	....	....	....	....	....	....													
1993-94	Hamilton	AHL	29	9	8	17	41	....	....	....	....	....	....													
1994-95	**Boston**	**NHL**	18	2	6	8	6	2	0	0	32	6.3	-1													
	Providence	AHL	63	32	29	61	105																			
1995-96	Boston	NHL	80	15	14	29	65	4	0	6	103	14.6	-9						5	2	2	4	12	1	0	0
1996-97	Boston	NHL	34	10	3	13	45	3	0	0	54	18.5	-12													
	Providence	AHL	3	0	2	2	19																			
1997-98	Los Angeles	NHL	62	11	13	24	70	1	0	2	89	12.4	4													
1998-99	Los Angeles	NHL	42	3	2	5	26	0	0	2	28	10.7	-9	2	50.0	80	5	10:19								
	NHL Totals		236	41	38	79	212	10	0	10	306	13.4		2	50.0	80	5	10:19	5	2	2	4	12	1	0	0

CCHA Second All-Star Team (1992)
Signed as a free agent by **Boston**, June 22, 1994. Traded to **LA Kings** by **Boston** with Jozef Stumpel and Boston's 4th round choice (later traded to New Jersey — New Jersey selected Pierre Dagenais) in 1998 Entry Draft for Dimitri Khristich and Byron Dafoe, August 29, 1997.

MOGILNY, Alexander (moh-GIHL-nee) VAN.

Right wing. Shoots left. 5'11", 200 lbs. Born, Khabarovsk, USSR, February 18, 1969. Buffalo's 4th choice, 89th overall, in 1988 Entry Draft.

			Regular Season																Playoffs							
Season	Club	League	GP	G	A	Pts	PIM	PP	SH	GW	S	%	+/–	TF	F%	H	SB	Min	GP	G	A	Pts	PIM	PP	SH	GW
1986-87	CSKA Moscow	USSR	28	15	1	16	4	....	....	....	....	....	....	....	....	....	....	....	....	....	....	....	....	....	....	....
1987-88	CSKA Moscow	USSR	39	12	8	20	14	....	....	....	....	....	....	....	....	....	....	....	....	....	....	....	....	....	....	....
	Soviet Union	Olympics	6	3	2	5	2	....	....	....	....	....	....	....	....	....	....	....	....	....	....	....	....	....	....	....
1988-89	CSKA Moscow	USSR	31	11	11	22	24	....	....	....	....	....	....	....	....	....	....	....	....	....	....	....	....	....	....	....
1989-90	**Buffalo**	**NHL**	**65**	**15**	**28**	**43**	**16**	**4**	**0**	**2**	**130**	**11.5**	**8**	....	....	....	....	....	**4**	**0**	**1**	**1**	**2**	**0**	**0**	**0**
1990-91	**Buffalo**	**NHL**	**62**	**30**	**34**	**64**	**16**	**3**	**3**	**5**	**201**	**14.9**	**14**	....	....	....	....	....	**6**	**0**	**6**	**6**	**2**	**0**	**0**	**0**
1991-92	**Buffalo**	**NHL**	**67**	**39**	**45**	**84**	**73**	**15**	**0**	**2**	**236**	**16.5**	**7**	....	....	....	....	....	**2**	**0**	**2**	**2**	**0**	**0**	**0**	**0**
1992-93	**Buffalo**	**NHL**	**77**	***76**	**51**	**127**	**40**	**27**	**0**	**11**	**360**	**21.1**	**7**	....	....	....	....	....	**7**	**7**	**3**	**10**	**6**	**2**	**0**	**0**
1993-94	**Buffalo**	**NHL**	**66**	**32**	**47**	**79**	**22**	**17**	**0**	**7**	**258**	**12.4**	**8**	....	....	....	....	....	**7**	**4**	**2**	**6**	**6**	**1**	**0**	**0**
1994-95	SKA Spartak	CIS	1	0	1	1	0	....	....	....	....	....	....	....	....	....	....	....	....	....	....	....	....	....	....	....
	Buffalo	**NHL**	**44**	**19**	**28**	**47**	**36**	**12**	**0**	**2**	**148**	**12.8**	**0**	....	....	....	....	....	**5**	**3**	**2**	**5**	**2**	**0**	**0**	**0**
1995-96	**Vancouver**	**NHL**	**79**	**55**	**52**	**107**	**16**	**10**	**5**	**6**	**292**	**18.8**	**14**	....	....	....	....	....	**6**	**1**	**8**	**9**	**8**	**0**	**0**	**0**
1996-97	**Vancouver**	**NHL**	**76**	**31**	**42**	**73**	**18**	**7**	**1**	**4**	**174**	**17.8**	**9**	....	....	....	....	....	....	....	....	....	....	....	....	....
1997-98	**Vancouver**	**NHL**	**51**	**18**	**27**	**45**	**36**	**5**	**4**	**1**	**118**	**15.3**	**–6**	....	....	....	....	....	....	....	....	....	....	....	....	....
1998-99	**Vancouver**	**NHL**	**59**	**14**	**31**	**45**	**58**	**3**	**2**	**1**	**110**	**12.7**	**0**	**47**	**23.4**	**34**	**10**	**20:35**	....	....	....	....	....	....	....	....
	NHL Totals		**646**	**329**	**385**	**714**	**331**	**103**	**15**	**41**	**2027**	**16.2**		**47**	**23.4**	**34**	**10**	**20:35**	**37**	**15**	**24**	**39**	**26**	**3**	**0**	**0**

NHL Second All-Star Team (1993, 1996)

Played in NHL All-Star Game (1992, 1993, 1994, 1996)

Traded to **Vancouver** by **Buffalo** with Buffalo's 5th round choice (Todd Norman) in 1995 Entry Draft for Mike Peca, Mike Wilson and Vancouver's 1st round choice (Jay McKee) in 1995 Entry Draft, July 8, 1995.

MONTGOMERY, Jim PHI.

Center. Shoots right. 5'10", 185 lbs. Born, Montreal, Que., June 30, 1969.

Season	Club	League	GP	G	A	Pts	PIM	PP	SH	GW	S	%	+/–	TF	F%	H	SB	Min	GP	G	A	Pts	PIM	PP	SH	GW
1989-90	U. of Maine	H.E.	45	26	34	60	35	....	....	....	....	....	....	....	....	....	....	....	....	....	....	....	....	....	....	....
1990-91	U. of Maine	H.E.	43	24	*57	81	44	....	....	....	....	....	....	....	....	....	....	....	....	....	....	....	....	....	....	....
1991-92	U. of Maine	H.E.	37	21	44	65	46	....	....	....	....	....	....	....	....	....	....	....	....	....	....	....	....	....	....	....
1992-93	U. of Maine	H.E.	45	32	63	95	40	....	....	....	....	....	....	....	....	....	....	....	....	....	....	....	....	....	....	....
1993-94	**St. Louis**	**NHL**	**67**	**6**	**14**	**20**	**44**	**0**	**0**	**1**	**67**	**9.0**	**–1**	....	....	....	....	....	....	....	....	....	....	....	....	....
	Peoria	IHL	12	7	8	15	10	....	....	....	....	....	....	....	....	....	....	....	....	....	....	....	....	....	....	....
1994-95	**Montreal**	**NHL**	**5**	**0**	**0**	**0**	**2**	**0**	**0**	**0**	**3**	**0.0**	**–2**	....	....	....	....	....	....	....	....	....	....	....	....	....
	Philadelphia	**NHL**	**8**	**1**	**1**	**2**	**6**	**0**	**0**	**0**	**10**	**10.0**	**–2**	....	....	....	....	....	**7**	**1**	**0**	**1**	**2**	**0**	**0**	**0**
	Hershey	AHL	16	8	6	14	14	....	....	....	....	....	....	....	....	....	....	....	6	3	2	5	25	....	....	....
1995-96	**Philadelphia**	**NHL**	**5**	**1**	**2**	**3**	**9**	**0**	**0**	**0**	**4**	**25.0**	**1**	....	....	....	....	....	**1**	**0**	**0**	**0**	**0**	**0**	**0**	**0**
	Hershey	AHL	78	34	*71	105	95	....	....	....	....	....	....	....	....	....	....	....	4	3	2	5	6	....	....	....
1996-97	Kolner Haie	Germany	50	12	35	47	111	....	....	....	....	....	....	....	....	....	....	....	4	0	1	1	6	....	....	....
	Kolner Haie	EuroHL	6	0	1	1	16	....	....	....	....	....	....	....	....	....	....	....	....	....	....	....	....	....	....	....
1997-98	Philadelphia	AHL	68	19	43	62	75	....	....	....	....	....	....	....	....	....	....	....	20	*13	16	29	55	....	....	....
1998-99	Philadelphia	AHL	78	29	58	87	89	....	....	....	....	....	....	....	....	....	....	....	16	4	11	15	20	....	....	....
	NHL Totals		**85**	**8**	**17**	**25**	**61**	**0**	**0**	**1**	**84**	**9.5**		....	....	....	....	....	**8**	**1**	**0**	**1**	**2**	**0**	**0**	**0**

Hockey East Second All-Star Team (1991, 1992) • Hockey East First All-Star Team (1993) • NCAA East Second All-American Team (1993) • NCAA Championship All-Tournament Team (1993) • NCAA Championship Tournament MVP (1993) • AHL Second All-Star Team (1996)

Signed as a free agent by **St. Louis**, June 2, 1993. Traded to **Montreal** by **St. Louis** for Guy Carbonneau, August 19, 1994. Claimed on waivers by **Philadelphia** from **Montreal**, February 10, 1995.

MOORE, Barrie WSH.

Left wing. Shoots left. 5'11", 175 lbs. Born, London, Ont., May 22, 1975. Buffalo's 7th choice, 220th overall, in 1993 Entry Draft.

Season	Club	League	GP	G	A	Pts	PIM	PP	SH	GW	S	%	+/–	TF	F%	H	SB	Min	GP	G	A	Pts	PIM	PP	SH	GW
1990-91	Strathroy	OJHL-B	24	9	10	19	14	....	....	....	....	....	....	....	....	....	....	....	....	....	....	....	....	....	....	....
1991-92	Sudbury	OHL	62	15	38	53	57	....	....	....	....	....	....	....	....	....	....	....	11	0	7	7	12	....	....	....
1992-93	Sudbury	OHL	57	13	26	39	71	....	....	....	....	....	....	....	....	....	....	....	14	4	3	7	19	....	....	....
1993-94	Sudbury	OHL	65	36	49	85	69	....	....	....	....	....	....	....	....	....	....	....	10	3	5	8	14	....	....	....
1994-95	Sudbury	OHL	60	47	42	89	67	....	....	....	....	....	....	....	....	....	....	....	18	*15	14	29	24	....	....	....
1995-96	**Buffalo**	**NHL**	**3**	**0**	**0**	**0**	**0**	**0**	**0**	**0**	**3**	**0.0**	**0**	....	....	....	....	....	....	....	....	....	....	....	....	....
	Rochester	AHL	64	26	30	56	40	....	....	....	....	....	....	....	....	....	....	....	18	3	6	9	18	....	....	....
1996-97	**Buffalo**	**NHL**	**31**	**2**	**6**	**8**	**18**	**1**	**0**	**0**	**42**	**4.8**	**1**	....	....	....	....	....	....	....	....	....	....	....	....	....
	Rochester	AHL	32	14	15	29	14	....	....	....	....	....	....	....	....	....	....	....	....	....	....	....	....	....	....	....
	Edmonton	**NHL**	**4**	**0**	**0**	**0**	**0**	**0**	**0**	**0**	**1**	**0.0**	**0**	....	....	....	....	....	....	....	....	....	....	....	....	....
	Hamilton	AHL	9	5	2	7	0	....	....	....	....	....	....	....	....	....	....	....	22	2	6	8	15	....	....	....
1997-98	Hamilton	AHL	70	22	29	51	64	....	....	....	....	....	....	....	....	....	....	....	8	0	1	1	4	....	....	....
1998-99	Indianapolis	IHL	43	9	10	19	18	....	....	....	....	....	....	....	....	....	....	....	....	....	....	....	....	....	....	....
	Portland	AHL	23	3	7	10	4	....	....	....	....	....	....	....	....	....	....	....	....	....	....	....	....	....	....	....
	NHL Totals		**38**	**2**	**6**	**8**	**18**	**1**	**0**	**0**	**46**	**4.3**		....	....	....	....	....	....	....	....	....	....	....	....	....

Traded to **Edmonton** by **Buffalo** with Craig Millar for Miroslav Satan, March 18, 1997. Rights traded to **Washington** by **Edmonton** for Brad Church, February 3, 1999.

MORAN, Ian (moh-RAN) PIT.

Right wing. Shoots right. 6', 206 lbs. Born, Cleveland, OH, August 24, 1972. Pittsburgh's 5th choice, 107th overall, in 1990 Entry Draft.

Season	Club	League	GP	G	A	Pts	PIM	PP	SH	GW	S	%	+/–	TF	F%	H	SB	Min	GP	G	A	Pts	PIM	PP	SH	GW
1987-88	Belmont Hll	H.S.	25	3	13	16	15	....	....	....	....	....	....	....	....	....	....	....	....	....	....	....	....	....	....	....
1988-89	Belmont Hill	H.S.	23	7	25	32	8	....	....	....	....	....	....	....	....	....	....	....	....	....	....	....	....	....	....	....
1989-90	Belmont Hill	H.S.	23	10	36	46	....	....	....	....	....	....	....	....	....	....	....	....	....	....	....	....	....	....	....	....
1990-91	Belmont Hill	H.S.	23	7	44	51	12	....	....	....	....	....	....	....	....	....	....	....	....	....	....	....	....	....	....	....
1991-92	Boston College	H.E.	30	2	16	18	44	....	....	....	....	....	....	....	....	....	....	....	....	....	....	....	....	....	....	....
1992-93	Boston College	H.E.	31	8	12	20	32	....	....	....	....	....	....	....	....	....	....	....	....	....	....	....	....	....	....	....
1993-94	United States	Nat-Team	50	8	15	23	69	....	....	....	....	....	....	....	....	....	....	....	....	....	....	....	....	....	....	....
	Cleveland	IHL	33	5	13	18	39	....	....	....	....	....	....	....	....	....	....	....	....	....	....	....	....	....	....	....
1994-95	Cleveland	IHL	64	7	31	38	94	....	....	....	....	....	....	....	....	....	....	....	4	0	1	1	2	....	....	....
	Pittsburgh	**NHL**	....	....	....	....	....	....	....	....	....	....	....	....	....	....	....	....	**8**	**0**	**0**	**0**	**0**			
1995-96	**Pittsburgh**	**NHL**	**51**	**1**	**1**	**2**	**47**	**0**	**0**	**0**	**44**	**2.3**	**–1**	....	....	....	....	....	....	....	....	....	....	....	....	....
1996-97	**Pittsburgh**	**NHL**	**36**	**4**	**5**	**9**	**22**	**0**	**0**	**0**	**50**	**8.0**	**–11**	....	....	....	....	....	**5**	**1**	**2**	**3**	**4**	**0**	**0**	**0**
	Cleveland	IHL	36	6	23	29	26	....	....	....	....	....	....	....	....	....	....	....	....	....	....	....	....	....	....	....
1997-98	**Pittsburgh**	**NHL**	**37**	**1**	**6**	**7**	**19**	**0**	**0**	**1**	**33**	**3.0**	**0**	....	....	....	....	....	**6**	**0**	**0**	**0**	**2**	**0**	**0**	**0**
1998-99	**Pittsburgh**	**NHL**	**62**	**4**	**5**	**9**	**37**	**0**	**1**	**0**	**65**	**6.2**	**1**	**32**	**34.4**	**48**	**98**	**16:34**	**13**	**0**	**2**	**2**	**8**	**0**	**0**	**0**
	NHL Totals		**186**	**10**	**17**	**27**	**125**	**0**	**1**	**1**	**192**	**5.2**		**32**	**34.4**	**48**	**98**	**16:34**	**32**	**1**	**4**	**5**	**14**	**0**	**0**	**0**

MORE, Jayson (MOHR) NSH.

Defense. Shoots right. 6'1", 210 lbs. Born, Souris, Man., January 12, 1969. NY Rangers' 1st choice, 10th overall, in 1987 Entry Draft.

Season	Club	League	GP	G	A	Pts	PIM	PP	SH	GW	S	%	+/–	TF	F%	H	SB	Min	GP	G	A	Pts	PIM	PP	SH	GW
1984-85	Lethbridge	WHL	71	3	9	12	101	....	....	....	....	....	....	....	....	....	....	....	4	1	0	1	7	....	....	....
1985-86	Lethbridge	WHL	61	7	18	25	155	....	....	....	....	....	....	....	....	....	....	....	9	0	2	2	36	....	....	....
1986-87	Brandon	WHL	21	4	6	10	62	....	....	....	....	....	....	....	....	....	....	....	....	....	....	....	....	....	....	....
	New Westminster	WHL	43	4	23	27	155	....	....	....	....	....	....	....	....	....	....	....	....	....	....	....	....	....	....	....
1987-88	New Westminster	WHL	70	13	47	60	270	....	....	....	....	....	....	....	....	....	....	....	5	0	2	2	26	....	....	....
1988-89	**NY Rangers**	**NHL**	**1**	**0**	**0**	**0**	**0**	**0**	**0**	**0**	**0**	**0.0**	**–1**	....	....	....	....	....	....	....	....	....	....	....	....	....
	Denver	IHL	62	7	15	22	138	....	....	....	....	....	....	....	....	....	....	....	3	0	1	1	26	....	....	....
1989-90	Flint	IHL	9	1	5	6	41	....	....	....	....	....	....	....	....	....	....	....	....	....	....	....	....	....	....	....
	Minnesota	**NHL**	**5**	**0**	**0**	**0**	**16**	**0**	**0**	**0**	**4**	**0.0**	**1**	....	....	....	....	....	....	....	....	....	....	....	....	....
	Kalamazoo	IHL	64	9	25	34	316	....	....	....	....	....	....	....	....	....	....	....	10	0	3	3	13	....	....	....

Season	Club	League	GP	G	A	Pts	PIM	PP	SH	GW	S	%	+/-	TF	F%	H	SB	Min	Playoffs GP	G	A	Pts	PIM	PP	SH	GW
1990-91	Kalamazoo	IHL	10	0	5	5	46	....	....	....	....	....	....	....	....	....	....	....	....	....	....	....	....	....	....	....
	Fredericton	AHL	57	7	17	24	152	....	....	....	....	....	....	....	....	....	....	....	9	1	1	2	34	....	....	....
1991-92	**San Jose**	**NHL**	**46**	**4**	**13**	**17**	**85**	**1**	**0**	**1**	**60**	**6.7**	**-32**	....	....	....	....	....	....	....	....	....	....	....	....	....
	Kansas City	IHL	2	0	2	2	4	....	....	....	....	....	....	....	....	....	....	....	....	....	....	....	....	....	....	....
1992-93	**San Jose**	**NHL**	**73**	**5**	**6**	**11**	**179**	**0**	**1**	**0**	**107**	**4.7**	**-35**	....	....	....	....	....	....	....	....	....	....	....	....	....
1993-94	**San Jose**	**NHL**	**49**	**1**	**6**	**7**	**63**	**0**	**0**	**0**	**38**	**2.6**	**-5**	....	....	....	....	....	**13**	**0**	**2**	**2**	**32**	**0**	**0**	**0**
	Kansas City	IHL	2	1	0	1	25	....	....	....	....	....	....	....	....	....	....	....	....	....	....	....	....	....	....	....
1994-95	**San Jose**	**NHL**	**45**	**0**	**6**	**6**	**71**	**0**	**0**	**0**	**25**	**0.0**	**7**	....	....	....	....	....	**11**	**0**	**4**	**4**	**6**	**0**	**0**	**0**
1995-96	**San Jose**	**NHL**	**74**	**2**	**7**	**9**	**147**	**0**	**0**	**0**	**67**	**3.0**	**-32**	....	....	....	....	....	....	....	....	....	....	....	....	....
1996-97	**NY Rangers**	**NHL**	**14**	**0**	**1**	**1**	**25**	**0**	**0**	**0**	**10**	**0.0**	**0**	....	....	....	....	....	....	....	....	....	....	....	....	....
	Phoenix	**NHL**	**23**	**1**	**6**	**7**	**37**	**0**	**0**	**1**	**18**	**5.6**	**10**	....	....	....	....	....	**7**	**0**	**0**	**0**	**7**	**0**	**0**	**0**
1997-98	**Phoenix**	**NHL**	**41**	**5**	**5**	**10**	**53**	**0**	**1**	**0**	**40**	**12.5**	**0**	....	....	....	....	....	....	....	....	....	....	....	....	....
	Chicago	**NHL**	**17**	**0**	**2**	**2**	**8**	**0**	**0**	**0**	**17**	**0.0**	**7**	....	....	....	....	....	....	....	....	....	....	....	....	....
1998-99	**Nashville**	**NHL**	**18**	**0**	**2**	**2**	**18**	**0**	**0**	**0**	**24**	**0.0**	**2**	**0**	**0.0**	**34**	**9**	**16:30**	....	....	....	....	....	....	....	....
	NHL Totals		**406**	**18**	**54**	**72**	**702**	**1**	**2**	**2**	**410**	**4.4**		**0**	**0.0**	**34**	**9**	**16:30**	**31**	**0**	**6**	**6**	**45**	**0**	**0**	**0**

WHL All-Star Team (1988)

Traded to **Minnesota** by **NY Rangers** for Dave Archibald, November 1, 1989. Traded to **Montreal** by **Minnesota** for Brian Hayward, November 7, 1990. Claimed by **San Jose** from **Montreal** in Expansion Draft, May 30, 1991. Traded to **NY Rangers** by **San Jose** with Brian Swanson and future considerations for Marty McSorley, August 20, 1996. Traded to **Phoenix** by **NY Rangers** for Mike Eastwood and Dallas Eakins, February 6, 1997. Traded to **Chicago** by **Phoenix** with Chad Kilger for Keith Carney and Jim Cummins, March 4, 1998. Signed as a free agent by **Nashville**, June 4, 1998.

MOREAU, Ethan (moh-ROH, EE-than) EDM.

Left wing. Shoots left. 6'2", 211 lbs. Born, Huntsville, Ont., September 22, 1975. Chicago's 1st choice, 14th overall, in 1994 Entry Draft.

Season	Club	League	GP	G	A	Pts	PIM	PP	SH	GW	S	%	+/-	TF	F%	H	SB	Min	Playoffs GP	G	A	Pts	PIM	PP	SH	GW
1990-91	Orillia	OJHL-B	42	17	22	39	26	....	....	....	....	....	....	....	....	....	....	....	....	....	....	....	....	....	....	....
1991-92	Niagara Falls	OHL	62	20	35	55	39	....	....	....	....	....	....	....	....	....	....	....	17	4	6	10	4	....	....	....
1992-93	Niagara Falls	OHL	65	32	41	73	69	....	....	....	....	....	....	....	....	....	....	....	4	0	3	3	4	....	....	....
1993-94	Niagara Falls	OHL	59	44	54	98	100	....	....	....	....	....	....	....	....	....	....	....	....	....	....	....	....	....	....	....
1994-95	Niagara Falls	OHL	39	25	41	66	69	....	....	....	....	....	....	....	....	....	....	....	....	....	....	....	....	....	....	....
	Sudbury	OHL	23	13	17	30	22	....	....	....	....	....	....	....	....	....	....	....	18	6	12	18	26	....	....	....
1995-96	**Chicago**	**NHL**	**8**	**0**	**1**	**1**	**4**	**0**	**0**	**0**	**1**	**0.0**	**1**	....	....	....	....	....	....	....	....	....	....	....	....	....
	Indianapolis	IHL	71	21	20	41	126	....	....	....	....	....	....	....	....	....	....	....	5	4	0	4	8	....	....	....
1996-97	**Chicago**	**NHL**	**82**	**15**	**16**	**31**	**123**	**0**	**0**	**1**	**114**	**13.2**	**13**	....	....	....	....	....	**6**	**1**	**0**	**1**	**9**	**0**	**0**	**0**
1997-98	**Chicago**	**NHL**	**54**	**9**	**9**	**18**	**73**	**2**	**0**	**0**	**87**	**10.3**	**0**	....	....	....	....	....	....	....	....	....	....	....	....	....
1998-99	**Chicago**	**NHL**	**66**	**9**	**6**	**15**	**84**	**0**	**0**	**1**	**80**	**11.3**	**-5**	**3**	**33.3**	**113**	**15**	**12:30**	....	....	....	....	....	....	....	....
	Edmonton	**NHL**	**14**	**1**	**5**	**6**	**8**	**0**	**0**	**1**	**16**	**6.3**	**2**	**1**	**0.0**	**26**	**9**	**11:47**	**4**	**0**	**3**	**3**	**6**	**0**	**0**	**0**
	NHL Totals		**224**	**34**	**37**	**71**	**292**	**2**	**0**	**3**	**298**	**11.4**		**4**	**25.0**	**139**	**24**	**12:22**	**10**	**1**	**3**	**4**	**15**	**0**	**0**	**0**

Traded to **Edmonton** by **Chicago** with Daniel Cleary, Chad Kilger and Christian Laflamme for Boris Mironov, Dean McAmmond and Jonas Elofsson, March 20, 1999.

MORGAN, Jason

Center. Shoots left. 6'1", 200 lbs. Born, St. John's, Nfld., October 9, 1976. Los Angeles' 5th choice, 118th overall, in 1995 Entry Draft.

Season	Club	League	GP	G	A	Pts	PIM	PP	SH	GW	S	%	+/-	TF	F%	H	SB	Min	Playoffs GP	G	A	Pts	PIM	PP	SH	GW
1992-93	Kitchener AAA	OMHA	69	44	40	84	85	....	....	....	....	....	....	....	....	....	....	....	....	....	....	....	....	....	....	....
1993-94	Kitchener	OHL	65	6	15	21	16	....	....	....	....	....	....	....	....	....	....	....	5	1	0	1	0	....	....	....
1994-95	Kitchener	OHL	35	3	15	18	25	....	....	....	....	....	....	....	....	....	....	....	....	....	....	....	....	....	....	....
	Kingston	OHL	20	0	3	3	14	....	....	....	....	....	....	....	....	....	....	....	6	0	2	2	0	....	....	....
1995-96	Kingston	OHL	66	16	38	54	50	....	....	....	....	....	....	....	....	....	....	....	6	1	2	3	0	....	....	....
1996-97	**Los Angeles**	**NHL**	**3**	**0**	**0**	**0**	**0**	**0**	**0**	**0**	**4**	**0.0**	**-3**	....	....	....	....	....	....	....	....	....	....	....	....	....
	Phoenix	IHL	57	3	6	9	29	....	....	....	....	....	....	....	....	....	....	....	....	....	....	....	....	....	....	....
	Mississippi	ECHL	6	3	0	3	0	....	....	....	....	....	....	....	....	....	....	....	3	1	1	2	6	....	....	....
1997-98	**Los Angeles**	**NHL**	**11**	**1**	**0**	**1**	**4**	**0**	**0**	**0**	**5**	**20.0**	**-7**	....	....	....	....	....	....	....	....	....	....	....	....	....
	Springfield	AHL	58	13	22	35	66	....	....	....	....	....	....	....	....	....	....	....	3	1	0	1	18	....	....	....
1998-99	Long Beach	IHL	13	4	6	10	18	....	....	....	....	....	....	....	....	....	....	....	....	....	....	....	....	....	....	....
	Springfield	AHL	46	6	16	22	51	....	....	....	....	....	....	....	....	....	....	....	3	0	0	0	6	....	....	....
	NHL Totals		**14**	**1**	**0**	**1**	**4**	**0**	**0**	**0**	**9**	**11.1**		....	....	....	....	....	....	....	....	....	....	....	....	....

MORISSETTE, Dave MTL.

Left wing. Shoots left. 6'1", 224 lbs. Born, Baie Comeau, Que., December 24, 1971. Washington's 7th choice, 146th overall, in 1991 Entry Draft.

Season	Club	League	GP	G	A	Pts	PIM	PP	SH	GW	S	%	+/-	TF	F%	H	SB	Min	Playoffs GP	G	A	Pts	PIM	PP	SH	GW
1987-88	Lac St-Jean	QAAA	41	11	25	36	....	....	....	....	....	....	....	....	....	....	....	....	....	....	....	....	....	....	....	....
1988-89	Shawinigan	QMJHL	66	4	11	15	298	....	....	....	....	....	....	....	....	....	....	....	....	....	....	....	....	....	....	....
1989-90	Shawinigan	QMJHL	66	2	9	11	269	....	....	....	....	....	....	....	....	....	....	....	....	....	....	....	....	....	....	....
1990-91	Shawinigan	QMJHL	64	20	26	46	224	....	....	....	....	....	....	....	....	....	....	....	6	1	1	2	17	....	....	....
1991-92	Hampton Roads	ECHL	47	6	10	16	293	....	....	....	....	....	....	....	....	....	....	....	13	1	3	4	74	....	....	....
	Baltimore	AHL	2	0	0	0	6	....	....	....	....	....	....	....	....	....	....	....	....	....	....	....	....	....	....	....
1992-93	Hampton Roads	ECHL	54	9	13	22	226	....	....	....	....	....	....	....	....	....	....	....	2	0	0	0	2	....	....	....
1993-94	Roanoke	ECHL	45	8	10	18	278	....	....	....	....	....	....	....	....	....	....	....	2	0	1	1	4	....	....	....
1994-95	Minnesota	IHL	50	1	4	5	174	....	....	....	....	....	....	....	....	....	....	....	....	....	....	....	....	....	....	....
1995-96	Minnesota	IHL	33	3	2	5	104	....	....	....	....	....	....	....	....	....	....	....	....	....	....	....	....	....	....	....
1996-97	Houston	IHL	59	2	1	3	214	....	....	....	....	....	....	....	....	....	....	....	2	0	0	0	0	....	....	....
	Austin	WPHL	5	2	3	5	10	....	....	....	....	....	....	....	....	....	....	....	....	....	....	....	....	....	....	....
1997-98	Houston	IHL	67	4	4	8	254	....	....	....	....	....	....	....	....	....	....	....	2	0	0	0	2	....	....	....
1998-99	**Montreal**	**NHL**	**10**	**0**	**0**	**0**	**52**	**0**	**0**	**0**	**2**	**0.0**	**1**	**0**	**0.0**	**5**	**2**	**2:13**	....	....	....	....	....	....	....	....
	Fredericton	AHL	39	4	4	8	152	....	....	....	....	....	....	....	....	....	....	....	12	0	1	1	31	....	....	....
	NHL Totals		**10**	**0**	**0**	**0**	**52**	**0**	**0**	**0**	**2**	**0.0**		**0**	**0.0**	**5**	**2**	**2:13**	....	....	....	....	....	....	....	....

Signed as a free agent by **Montreal**, June 10, 1998.

MORO, Marc (MOH-roh) NSH.

Defense. Shoots left. 6'1", 225 lbs. Born, Toronto, Ont., July 17, 1977. Ottawa's 2nd choice, 27th overall, in 1995 Entry Draft.

Season	Club	League	GP	G	A	Pts	PIM	PP	SH	GW	S	%	+/-	TF	F%	H	SB	Min	Playoffs GP	G	A	Pts	PIM	PP	SH	GW
1992-93	Mississauga	MTHL	42	9	18	27	56	....	....	....	....	....	....	....	....	....	....	....	....	....	....	....	....	....	....	....
	Mississauga	OJHL	2	0	0	0	0	....	....	....	....	....	....	....	....	....	....	....	....	....	....	....	....	....	....	....
1993-94	Kingston	OJHL	12	0	2	2	10	....	....	....	....	....	....	....	....	....	....	....	....	....	....	....	....	....	....	....
	Kingston	OHL	43	0	3	3	81	....	....	....	....	....	....	....	....	....	....	....	....	....	....	....	....	....	....	....
1994-95	Kingston	OHL	64	4	12	16	255	....	....	....	....	....	....	....	....	....	....	....	6	0	0	0	23	....	....	....
1995-96	Kingston	OHL	66	4	17	21	261	....	....	....	....	....	....	....	....	....	....	....	6	0	0	0	12	....	....	....
	P.E.I. Senators	AHL	2	0	0	0	7	....	....	....	....	....	....	....	....	....	....	....	2	0	0	0	4	....	....	....
1996-97	Kingston	OHL	37	4	8	12	97	....	....	....	....	....	....	....	....	....	....	....	....	....	....	....	....	....	....	....
	S.S. Marie	OHL	26	0	5	5	74	....	....	....	....	....	....	....	....	....	....	....	11	1	6	7	38	....	....	....
1997-98	**Anaheim**	**NHL**	**1**	**0**	**0**	**0**	**0**	**0**	**0**	**0**	**0**	**0.0**	**0**	....	....	....	....	....	....	....	....	....	....	....	....	....
	Cincinnati	AHL	74	1	6	7	181	....	....	....	....	....	....	....	....	....	....	....	....	....	....	....	....	....	....	....
1998-99	Milwaukee	IHL	80	0	5	5	264	....	....	....	....	....	....	....	....	....	....	....	2	0	0	0	4	....	....	....
	NHL Totals		**1**	**0**	**0**	**0**	**0**	**0**	**0**	**0**	**0**	**0.0**		....	....	....	....	....	....	....	....	....	....	....	....	....

Rights traded to **Anaheim** by **Ottawa** with Ted Drury for Jason York and Shaun Van Allen, October 1, 1996. Traded to **Nashville** by **Anaheim** with Chris Mason for Dominic Roussel, October 5, 1998.

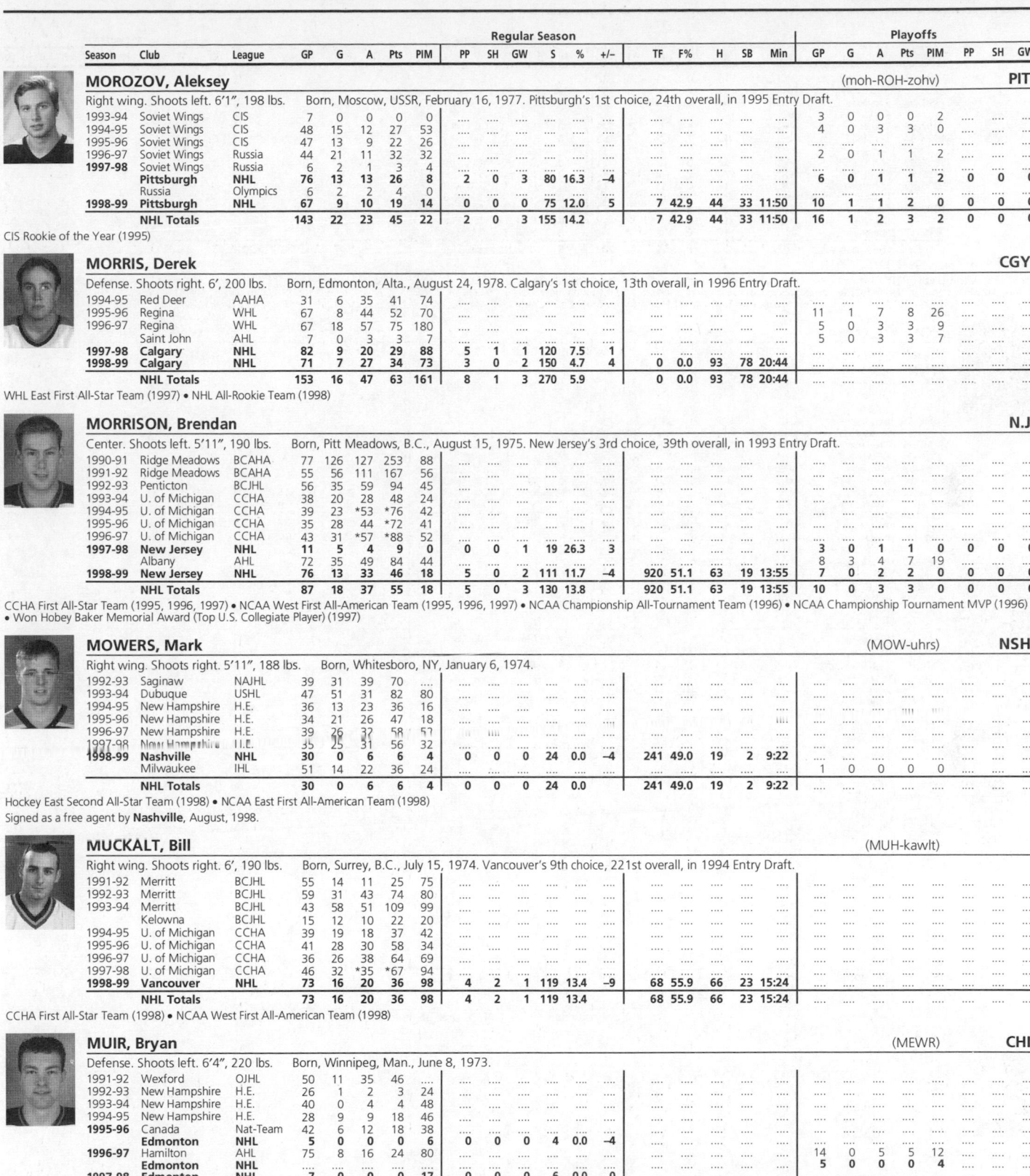

MOROZOV, Aleksey
(moh-ROH-zohv) **PIT.**

Right wing. Shoots left. 6'1", 198 lbs. Born, Moscow, USSR, February 16, 1977. Pittsburgh's 1st choice, 24th overall, in 1995 Entry Draft.

			Regular Season																Playoffs							
Season	Club	League	GP	G	A	Pts	PIM	PP	SH	GW	S	%	+/–	TF	F%	H	SB	Min	GP	G	A	Pts	PIM	PP	SH	GW
1993-94	Soviet Wings	CIS	7	0	0	0	0	....	....	....	....	....	....	....	....	....	....	....	3	0	0	0	2	....	....	....
1994-95	Soviet Wings	CIS	48	15	12	27	53	....	....	....	....	....	....	....	....	....	....	....	4	0	3	3	0	....	....	....
1995-96	Soviet Wings	CIS	47	13	9	22	26	....	....	....	....	....	....	....	....	....	....	....	....	....	....	....	....	....	....	....
1996-97	Soviet Wings	Russia	44	21	11	32	32	....	....	....	....	....	....	....	....	....	....	....	2	0	1	1	2	....	....	....
1997-98	Soviet Wings	Russia	6	2	1	3	4	....	....	....	....	....	....	....	....	....	....	....	....	....	....	....	....	....	....	....
	Pittsburgh	**NHL**	**76**	**13**	**13**	**26**	**8**	**2**	**0**	**3**	**80**	**16.3**	**–4**	....	....	....	....	....	**6**	**0**	**1**	**1**	**2**	**0**	**0**	**0**
	Russia	Olympics	6	2	2	4	0	....	....	....	....	....	....	....	....	....	....	....	....	....	....	....	....	....	....	....
1998-99	**Pittsburgh**	**NHL**	**67**	**9**	**10**	**19**	**14**	**0**	**0**	**0**	**75**	**12.0**	**5**	**7**	**42.9**	**44**	**33**	**11:50**	**10**	**1**	**1**	**2**	**0**	**0**	**0**	**0**
	NHL Totals		**143**	**22**	**23**	**45**	**22**	**2**	**0**	**3**	**155**	**14.2**		**7**	**42.9**	**44**	**33**	**11:50**	**16**	**1**	**2**	**3**	**2**	**0**	**0**	**0**

CIS Rookie of the Year (1995)

MORRIS, Derek
CGY.

Defense. Shoots right. 6', 200 lbs. Born, Edmonton, Alta., August 24, 1978. Calgary's 1st choice, 13th overall, in 1996 Entry Draft.

			Regular Season																Playoffs							
Season	Club	League	GP	G	A	Pts	PIM	PP	SH	GW	S	%	+/–	TF	F%	H	SB	Min	GP	G	A	Pts	PIM	PP	SH	GW
1994-95	Red Deer	AAHA	31	6	35	41	74	....	....	....	....	....	....	....	....	....	....	....	....	....	....	....	....	....	....	....
1995-96	Regina	WHL	67	8	44	52	70	....	....	....	....	....	....	....	....	....	....	....	11	1	7	8	26	....	....	....
1996-97	Regina	WHL	67	18	57	75	180	....	....	....	....	....	....	....	....	....	....	....	5	0	3	3	9	....	....	....
	Saint John	AHL	7	0	3	3	7	....	....	....	....	....	....	....	....	....	....	....	5	0	3	3	7	....	....	....
1997-98	**Calgary**	**NHL**	**82**	**9**	**20**	**29**	**88**	**5**	**1**	**1**	**120**	**7.5**	**1**	....	....	....	....	....	....	....	....	....	....	....	....	....
1998-99	**Calgary**	**NHL**	**71**	**7**	**27**	**34**	**73**	**3**	**0**	**2**	**150**	**4.7**	**4**	**0**	**0.0**	**93**	**78**	**20:44**	....	....	....	....	....	....	....	....
	NHL Totals		**153**	**16**	**47**	**63**	**161**	**8**	**1**	**3**	**270**	**5.9**		**0**	**0.0**	**93**	**78**	**20:44**	....	....	....	....	....	....	....	....

WHL East First All-Star Team (1997) • NHL All-Rookie Team (1998)

MORRISON, Brendan
N.J.

Center. Shoots left. 5'11", 190 lbs. Born, Pitt Meadows, B.C., August 15, 1975. New Jersey's 3rd choice, 39th overall, in 1993 Entry Draft.

			Regular Season																Playoffs							
Season	Club	League	GP	G	A	Pts	PIM	PP	SH	GW	S	%	+/–	TF	F%	H	SB	Min	GP	G	A	Pts	PIM	PP	SH	GW
1990-91	Ridge Meadows	BCAHA	77	126	127	253	88	....	....	....	....	....	....	....	....	....	....	....	....	....	....	....	....	....	....	....
1991-92	Ridge Meadows	BCAHA	55	56	111	167	56	....	....	....	....	....	....	....	....	....	....	....	....	....	....	....	....	....	....	....
1992-93	Penticton	BCJHL	56	35	59	94	45	....	....	....	....	....	....	....	....	....	....	....	....	....	....	....	....	....	....	....
1993-94	U. of Michigan	CCHA	38	20	28	48	24	....	....	....	....	....	....	....	....	....	....	....	....	....	....	....	....	....	....	....
1994-95	U. of Michigan	CCHA	39	23	*53	*76	42	....	....	....	....	....	....	....	....	....	....	....	....	....	....	....	....	....	....	....
1995-96	U. of Michigan	CCHA	35	28	44	*72	41	....	....	....	....	....	....	....	....	....	....	....	....	....	....	....	....	....	....	....
1996-97	U. of Michigan	CCHA	43	31	*57	*88	52	....	....	....	....	....	....	....	....	....	....	....	....	....	....	....	....	....	....	....
1997-98	**New Jersey**	**NHL**	**11**	**5**	**4**	**9**	**0**	**0**	**0**	**1**	**19**	**26.3**	**3**	....	....	....	....	....	**3**	**0**	**1**	**1**	**0**	**0**	**0**	**0**
	Albany	AHL	72	35	49	84	44	....	....	....	....	....	....	....	....	....	....	....	8	3	4	7	19	....	....	....
1998-99	**New Jersey**	**NHL**	**76**	**13**	**33**	**46**	**18**	**5**	**0**	**2**	**111**	**11.7**	**–4**	**920**	**51.1**	**63**	**19**	**13:55**	**7**	**0**	**2**	**2**	**0**	**0**	**0**	**0**
	NHL Totals		**87**	**18**	**37**	**55**	**18**	**5**	**0**	**3**	**130**	**13.8**		**920**	**51.1**	**63**	**19**	**13:55**	**10**	**0**	**3**	**3**	**0**	**0**	**0**	**0**

CCHA First All-Star Team (1995, 1996, 1997) • NCAA West First All-American Team (1995, 1996, 1997) • NCAA Championship All-Tournament Team (1996) • NCAA Championship Tournament MVP (1996) • Won Hobey Baker Memorial Award (Top U.S. Collegiate Player) (1997)

MOWERS, Mark
(MOW-uhrs) **NSH.**

Right wing. Shoots right. 5'11", 188 lbs. Born, Whitesboro, NY, January 6, 1974.

			Regular Season																Playoffs							
Season	Club	League	GP	G	A	Pts	PIM	PP	SH	GW	S	%	+/–	TF	F%	H	SB	Min	GP	G	A	Pts	PIM	PP	SH	GW
1992-93	Saginaw	NAJHL	39	31	39	70	....	....	....	....	....	....	....	....	....	....	....	....	....	....	....	....	....	....	....	....
1993-94	Dubuque	USHL	47	51	31	82	80	....	....	....	....	....	....	....	....	....	....	....	....	....	....	....	....	....	....	....
1994-95	New Hampshire	H.E.	36	13	23	36	16	....	....	....	....	....	....	....	....	....	....	....	....	....	....	....	....	....	....	....
1995-96	New Hampshire	H.E.	34	21	26	47	18	....	....	....	....	....	....	....	....	....	....	....	....	....	....	....	....	....	....	....
1996-97	New Hampshire	H.E.	39	26	32	58	52	....	....	....	....	....	....	....	....	....	....	....	....	....	....	....	....	....	....	....
1997-98	New Hampshire	H.E.	35	25	31	56	32	....	....	....	....	....	....	....	....	....	....	....	....	....	....	....	....	....	....	....
1998-99	**Nashville**	**NHL**	**30**	**0**	**6**	**6**	**4**	**0**	**0**	**0**	**24**	**0.0**	**–4**	**241**	**49.0**	**19**	**2**	**9:22**	....	....	....	....	....	....	....	....
	Milwaukee	IHL	51	14	22	36	24	....	....	....	....	....	....	....	....	....	....	....	1	0	0	0	0	....	....	....
	NHL Totals		**30**	**0**	**6**	**6**	**4**	**0**	**0**	**0**	**24**	**0.0**		**241**	**49.0**	**19**	**2**	**9:22**	....	....	....	....	....	....	....	....

Hockey East Second All-Star Team (1998) • NCAA East First All-American Team (1998)

Signed as a free agent by **Nashville**, August, 1998.

MUCKALT, Bill
(MUH-kawlt)

Right wing. Shoots right. 6', 190 lbs. Born, Surrey, B.C., July 15, 1974. Vancouver's 9th choice, 221st overall, in 1994 Entry Draft.

			Regular Season																Playoffs							
Season	Club	League	GP	G	A	Pts	PIM	PP	SH	GW	S	%	+/–	TF	F%	H	SB	Min	GP	G	A	Pts	PIM	PP	SH	GW
1991-92	Merritt	BCJHL	55	14	11	25	75	....	....	....	....	....	....	....	....	....	....	....	....	....	....	....	....	....	....	....
1992-93	Merritt	BCJHL	59	31	43	74	80	....	....	....	....	....	....	....	....	....	....	....	....	....	....	....	....	....	....	....
1993-94	Merritt	BCJHL	43	58	51	109	99	....	....	....	....	....	....	....	....	....	....	....	....	....	....	....	....	....	....	....
	Kelowna	BCJHL	15	12	10	22	20	....	....	....	....	....	....	....	....	....	....	....	....	....	....	....	....	....	....	....
1994-95	U. of Michigan	CCHA	39	19	18	37	42	....	....	....	....	....	....	....	....	....	....	....	....	....	....	....	....	....	....	....
1995-96	U. of Michigan	CCHA	41	28	30	58	34	....	....	....	....	....	....	....	....	....	....	....	....	....	....	....	....	....	....	....
1996-97	U. of Michigan	CCHA	36	26	38	64	69	....	....	....	....	....	....	....	....	....	....	....	....	....	....	....	....	....	....	....
1997-98	U. of Michigan	CCHA	46	32	*35	*67	94	....	....	....	....	....	....	....	....	....	....	....	....	....	....	....	....	....	....	....
1998-99	**Vancouver**	**NHL**	**73**	**16**	**20**	**36**	**98**	**4**	**2**	**1**	**119**	**13.4**	**–9**	**68**	**55.9**	**66**	**23**	**15:24**	....	....	....	....	....	....	....	....
	NHL Totals		**73**	**16**	**20**	**36**	**98**	**4**	**2**	**1**	**119**	**13.4**		**68**	**55.9**	**66**	**23**	**15:24**	....	....	....	....	....	....	....	....

CCHA First All-Star Team (1998) • NCAA West First All-American Team (1998)

MUIR, Bryan
(MEWR) **CHI.**

Defense. Shoots left. 6'4", 220 lbs. Born, Winnipeg, Man., June 8, 1973.

			Regular Season																Playoffs							
Season	Club	League	GP	G	A	Pts	PIM	PP	SH	GW	S	%	+/–	TF	F%	H	SB	Min	GP	G	A	Pts	PIM	PP	SH	GW
1991-92	Wexford	OJHL	50	11	35	46	....	....	....	....	....	....	....	....	....	....	....	....	....	....	....	....	....	....	....	....
1992-93	New Hampshire	H.E.	26	1	2	3	24	....	....	....	....	....	....	....	....	....	....	....	....	....	....	....	....	....	....	....
1993-94	New Hampshire	H.E.	40	0	4	4	48	....	....	....	....	....	....	....	....	....	....	....	....	....	....	....	....	....	....	....
1994-95	New Hampshire	H.E.	28	9	9	18	46	....	....	....	....	....	....	....	....	....	....	....	....	....	....	....	....	....	....	....
1995-96	Canada	Nat-Team	42	6	12	18	38	....	....	....	....	....	....	....	....	....	....	....	....	....	....	....	....	....	....	....
	Edmonton	**NHL**	**5**	**0**	**0**	**0**	**6**	**0**	**0**	**0**	**4**	**0.0**	**–4**	....	....	....	....	....	....	....	....	....	....	....	....	....
1996-97	Hamilton	AHL	75	8	16	24	80	....	....	....	....	....	....	....	....	....	....	....	14	0	5	5	12	....	....	....
	Edmonton	**NHL**	....	....	....	....	....	....	....	....	....	....	....	....	....	....	....	....	**5**	**0**	**0**	**0**	**4**	....	....	....
1997-98	**Edmonton**	**NHL**	**7**	**0**	**0**	**0**	**17**	**0**	**0**	**0**	**6**	**0.0**	**0**	....	....	....	....	....	....	....	....	....	....	....	....	....
	Hamilton	AHL	28	3	10	13	62	....	....	....	....	....	....	....	....	....	....	....	....	....	....	....	....	....	....	....
	Albany	AHL	41	3	10	13	67	....	....	....	....	....	....	....	....	....	....	....	13	3	0	3	12	....	....	....
1998-99	**New Jersey**	**NHL**	**1**	**0**	**0**	**0**	**0**	**0**	**0**	**0**	**4**	**0.0**	**0**	**0**	**0.0**	**0**	**0**	**9:54**	....	....	....	....	....	....	....	....
	Albany	AHL	10	0	0	0	29	....	....	....	....	....	....	....	....	....	....	....	....	....	....	....	....	....	....	....
	Chicago	**NHL**	**53**	**1**	**4**	**5**	**50**	**0**	**0**	**0**	**78**	**1.3**	**1**	**0**	**0.0**	**82**	**59**	**18:49**	....	....	....	....	....	....	....	....
	Portland	AHL	2	1	1	2	2	....	....	....	....	....	....	....	....	....	....	....	....	....	....	....	....	....	....	....
	NHL Totals		**66**	**1**	**4**	**5**	**73**	**0**	**0**	**0**	**92**	**1.1**		**0**	**0.0**	**82**	**59**	**18:39**	**5**	**0**	**0**	**0**	**4**	....	....	....

Signed as a free agent by **Edmonton**, April 30, 1996.

Traded to **New Jersey** by **Edmonton** with Jason Arnott for Valeri Zelepukin and Bill Guerin, January 4, 1998. Traded to **Chicago** by **New Jersey** for future considerations, November 13, 1998.

			Regular Season																		Playoffs							
Season	Club	League	GP	G	A	Pts	PIM	PP	SH	GW	S	%	+/−	TF	F%	H	SB	Min	GP	G	A	Pts	PIM	PP	SH	GW

MULHERN, Ryan   (muhl-HUHRN)   **WSH.**

Center. Shoots right. 6'1", 180 lbs.   Born, Philadelphia, PA, January 11, 1973. Calgary's 9th choice, 174th overall, in 1992 Entry Draft.

Season	Club	League	GP	G	A	Pts	PIM	PP	SH	GW	S	%	+/−	TF	F%	H	SB	Min	GP	G	A	Pts	PIM	PP	SH	GW
1991-92	Canterbury Prep	H.S.	37	51	27	78	50	....	....	....	....	....	....	....	....	....	....	....	....	....	....	....	....	....	....	....
1992-93	Brown University	ECAC	31	15	9	24	46	....	....	....	....	....	....	....	....	....	....	....	....	....	....	....	....	....	....	....
1993-94	Brown University	ECAC	27	18	17	35	48	....	....	....	....	....	....	....	....	....	....	....	....	....	....	....	....	....	....	....
1994-95	Brown University	ECAC	30	18	16	34	*108	....	....	....	....	....	....	....	....	....	....	....	....	....	....	....	....	....	....	....
1995-96	Brown University	ECAC	32	10	16	26	78	....	....	....	....	....	....	....	....	....	....	....	....	....	....	....	....	....	....	....
1996-97	Hampton Roads	ECHL	40	22	16	38	52	....	....	....	....	....	....	....	....	....	....	....	....	....	....	....	....	....	....	....
	Portland	AHL	38	19	15	34	16	....	....	....	....	....	....	....	....	....	....	....	5	1	1	2	2	....	....	....
1997-98	**Washington**	**NHL**	**3**	**0**	**0**	**0**	**0**	0	0	0	1	0.0	0	....	....	....	....	....	....	....	....	....	....	....	....	....
	Portland	AHL	71	25	40	65	85	....	....	....	....	....	....	....	....	....	....	....	6	1	0	1	12	....	....	....
1998-99	Kansas City	IHL	59	7	11	18	82	....	....	....	....	....	....	....	....	....	....	....	....	....	....	....	....	....	....	....
	Las Vegas	IHL	23	9	6	15	8	....	....	....	....	....	....	....	....	....	....	....	....	....	....	....	....	....	....	....
	NHL Totals		**3**	**0**	**0**	**0**	**0**	0	0	0	1	0.0		....	....	....	....	....								

AHL First All-Star Team (1998)
Signed as a free agent by **Washington**, March 17, 1997.

MULLER, Kirk

Left wing. Shoots left. 6', 205 lbs.   Born, Kingston, Ont., February 8, 1966. New Jersey's 1st choice, 2nd overall, in 1984 Entry Draft.

Season	Club	League	GP	G	A	Pts	PIM	PP	SH	GW	S	%	+/−	TF	F%	H	SB	Min	GP	G	A	Pts	PIM	PP	SH	GW
1981-82	Kingston	OHL	67	12	39	51	27	....	....	....	....	....	....	....	....	....	....	....	4	5	1	6	4	....	....	....
1982-83	Guelph	OHL	66	52	60	112	41	....	....	....	....	....	....	....	....	....	....	....	....	....	....	....	....	....	....	....
1983-84	Guelph	OHL	49	31	63	94	27	....	....	....	....	....	....	....	....	....	....	....	....	....	....	....	....	....	....	....
	Canada	Nat-Team	15	2	2	4	16	....	....	....	....	....	....	....	....	....	....	....	....	....	....	....	....	....	....	....
	Canada	Olympics	6	2	1	3	0	....	....	....	....	....	....	....	....	....	....	....	....	....	....	....	....	....	....	....
1984-85	**New Jersey**	**NHL**	80	17	37	54	69	9	1	0	157	10.8	−31	....	....	....	....	....	....	....	....	....	....	....	....	....
1985-86	**New Jersey**	**NHL**	77	25	41	66	45	5	1	1	168	14.9	−20	....	....	....	....	....	....	....	....	....	....	....	....	....
1986-87	**New Jersey**	**NHL**	79	26	50	76	75	10	1	4	193	13.5	−7	....	....	....	....	....	....	....	....	....	....	....	....	....
1987-88	**New Jersey**	**NHL**	80	37	57	94	114	6	1	1	215	17.2	19	....	....	....	....	....	20	4	8	12	37	0	0	0
1988-89	**New Jersey**	**NHL**	80	31	43	74	119	12	1	4	182	17.0	−23	....	....	....	....	....	....	....	....	....	....	....	....	....
1989-90	**New Jersey**	**NHL**	80	30	56	86	74	9	0	6	200	15.0	−1	....	....	....	....	....	6	1	3	4	11	0	0	0
1990-91	**New Jersey**	**NHL**	80	19	51	70	76	7	0	3	221	8.6	−3	....	....	....	....	....	7	0	2	2	10	0	0	0
1991-92	**Montreal**	**NHL**	78	36	41	77	86	15	1	7	191	18.8	15	....	....	....	....	....	11	4	3	7	31	2	1	1
1992-93♦	**Montreal**	**NHL**	80	37	57	94	77	12	0	4	231	16.0	8	....	....	....	....	....	20	10	7	17	18	3	0	3
1993-94	**Montreal**	**NHL**	76	23	34	57	96	9	2	3	168	13.7	−1	....	....	....	....	....	7	6	2	8	4	3	0	2
1994-95	**Montreal**	**NHL**	33	8	11	19	33	3	0	1	81	9.9	−21	....	....	....	....	....	....	....	....	....	....	....	....	....
	NY Islanders	**NHL**	12	3	5	8	14	1	1	1	16	18.8	3	....	....	....	....	....	....	....	....	....	....	....	....	....
1995-96	**NY Islanders**	**NHL**	15	4	3	7	15	0	0	0	23	17.4	−10	....	....	....	....	....	....	....	....	....	....	....	....	....
	Toronto	**NHL**	36	9	16	25	42	7	0	1	79	11.4	−3	....	....	....	....	....	6	3	2	5	0	2	0	0
1996-97	**Toronto**	**NHL**	66	20	17	37	85	9	1	3	153	13.1	−23	....	....	....	....	....	....	....	....	....	....	....	....	....
	Florida	**NHL**	10	1	2	3	4	1	0	1	21	4.8	−2	....	....	....	....	....	5	1	2	3	4	1	0	0
1997-98	**Florida**	**NHL**	70	8	21	29	54	1	0	3	115	7.0	−14	....	....	....	....	....	....	....	....	....	....	....	....	....
1998-99	**Florida**	**NHL**	82	4	11	15	49	0	0	1	107	3.7	−11	1157	49.1	68	39	14:28	....	....	....	....	....	....	....	....
	NHL Totals		**1114**	**338**	**553**	**891**	**1127**	116	10	44	2521	13.4		1157	49.1	68	39	14:28	82	29	29	58	115	11	1	6

Played in NHL All-Star Game (1985, 1986, 1988, 1990, 1992, 1993)
Traded to **Montreal** by **New Jersey** with Roland Melanson for Stephane Richer and Tom Chorske, September 20, 1991. Traded to **NY Islanders** by **Montreal** with Mathieu Schneider and Craig Darby for Pierre Turgeon and Vladimir Malakhov, April 5, 1995. Traded to **Toronto** by **NY Islanders** with Don Beaupre to complete transaction that sent Damian Rhodes and Ken Belanger to NY Islanders (January 23, 1996), January 23, 1996. Traded to **Florida** by **Toronto** for Jason Podollan, March 18, 1997.

MURPHY, Gord   **ATL.**

Defense. Shoots right. 6'2", 195 lbs.   Born, Willowdale, Ont., March 23, 1967. Philadelphia's 10th choice, 189th overall, in 1985 Entry Draft.

Season	Club	League	GP	G	A	Pts	PIM	PP	SH	GW	S	%	+/−	TF	F%	H	SB	Min	GP	G	A	Pts	PIM	PP	SH	GW
1983-84	Don Mills	MTHL	65	24	42	66	130	....	....	....	....	....	....	....	....	....	....	....	....	....	....	....	....	....	....	....
1984-85	Oshawa	OHL	59	3	12	15	25	....	....	....	....	....	....	....	....	....	....	....	....	....	....	....	....	....	....	....
1985-86	Oshawa	OHL	64	7	15	22	56	....	....	....	....	....	....	....	....	....	....	....	6	1	1	2	6	....	....	....
1986-87	Oshawa	OHL	56	7	30	37	95	....	....	....	....	....	....	....	....	....	....	....	24	6	16	22	22	....	....	....
1987-88	Hershey	AHL	62	8	20	28	44	....	....	....	....	....	....	....	....	....	....	....	12	0	8	8	12	....	....	....
1988-89	**Philadelphia**	**NHL**	75	4	31	35	68	3	0	1	116	3.4	−3	....	....	....	....	....	19	2	7	9	13	1	0	1
1989-90	**Philadelphia**	**NHL**	75	14	27	41	95	4	0	1	160	8.8	−7	....	....	....	....	....	....	....	....	....	....	....	....	....
1990-91	**Philadelphia**	**NHL**	80	11	31	42	58	6	0	2	203	5.4	−7	....	....	....	....	....	....	....	....	....	....	....	....	....
1991-92	**Philadelphia**	**NHL**	31	2	8	10	33	0	0	0	50	4.0	−4	....	....	....	....	....	....	....	....	....	....	....	....	....
	Boston	**NHL**	42	3	6	9	51	0	0	0	82	3.7	2	....	....	....	....	....	15	1	0	1	12	0	0	0
1992-93	**Boston**	**NHL**	49	5	12	17	62	3	0	2	68	7.4	−13	....	....	....	....	....	....	....	....	....	....	....	....	....
	Providence	AHL	2	1	3	4	2	....	....	....	....	....	....	....	....	....	....	....	....	....	....	....	....	....	....	....
1993-94	**Florida**	**NHL**	84	14	29	43	71	9	0	2	172	8.1	−11	....	....	....	....	....	....	....	....	....	....	....	....	....
1994-95	**Florida**	**NHL**	46	6	16	22	24	5	0	0	94	6.4	−14	....	....	....	....	....	....	....	....	....	....	....	....	....
1995-96	**Florida**	**NHL**	70	8	22	30	30	4	0	0	125	6.4	5	....	....	....	....	....	14	0	4	4	6	0	0	0
1996-97	**Florida**	**NHL**	80	8	15	23	51	2	0	0	137	5.8	3	....	....	....	....	....	5	0	5	5	4	0	0	0
1997-98	**Florida**	**NHL**	79	6	11	17	46	0	0	0	123	4.9	−3	....	....	....	....	....	....	....	....	....	....	....	....	....
1998-99	**Florida**	**NHL**	51	0	7	7	16	0	0	0	56	0.0	4	1	0.0	44	58	19:57	....	....	....	....	....	....	....	....
	NHL Totals		**762**	**81**	**215**	**296**	**605**	39	0	8	1386	5.8		1	0.0	44	58	19:57	53	3	16	19	35	1	0	1

Traded to **Boston** by **Philadelphia** with Brian Dobbin, Philadelphia's 3rd round choice (Sergei Zholtok) in 1992 Entry Draft and Philadelphia's 4th round choice (Charles Paquette) in 1993 Entry Draft, for Garry Galley, Wes Walz and Boston's 3rd round choice (Milos Holan) in 1993 Entry Draft, January 2, 1992. Traded to **Dallas** by **Boston** for future considerations (Jon Casey, June 25, 1993), June 20, 1993. Claimed by **Florida** from **Dallas** in Expansion Draft, June 24, 1993. Traded to **Atlanta** by **Florida** with Herbert Vasiljevs, Daniel Tjarnqvist and Ottawa's 6th round choice (previously acquired, later traded to Dallas - Dallas selected Justin Cox) in 1999 Entry Draft for Trevor Kidd, June 25, 1999.

MURPHY, Joe

Right wing. Shoots left. 6', 190 lbs.   Born, London, Ont., October 16, 1967. Detroit's 1st choice, 1st overall, in 1986 Entry Draft.

Season	Club	League	GP	G	A	Pts	PIM	PP	SH	GW	S	%	+/−	TF	F%	H	SB	Min	GP	G	A	Pts	PIM	PP	SH	GW
1984-85	Penticton	BCJHL	51	68	84	*152	92	....	....	....	....	....	....	....	....	....	....	....	....	....	....	....	....	....	....	....
1985-86	Michigan State	CCHA	35	24	37	61	50	....	....	....	....	....	....	....	....	....	....	....	....	....	....	....	....	....	....	....
	Canada	Nat-Team	8	3	3	6	2	....	....	....	....	....	....	....	....	....	....	....	....	....	....	....	....	....	....	....
1986-87	**Detroit**	**NHL**	5	0	1	1	2	0	0	0	3	0.0	0	....	....	....	....	....	....	....	....	....	....	....	....	....
	Adirondack	AHL	71	21	38	59	61	....	....	....	....	....	....	....	....	....	....	....	10	2	1	3	33	....	....	....
1987-88	**Detroit**	**NHL**	50	10	9	19	37	1	0	2	82	12.2	−4	....	....	....	....	....	8	0	1	1	6	0	0	0
	Adirondack	AHL	6	5	6	11	4	....	....	....	....	....	....	....	....	....	....	....	....	....	....	....	....	....	....	....
1988-89	**Detroit**	**NHL**	26	1	7	8	28	0	0	0	29	3.4	−7	....	....	....	....	....	....	....	....	....	....	....	....	....
	Adirondack	AHL	47	31	35	66	66	....	....	....	....	....	....	....	....	....	....	....	16	6	11	17	17	....	....	....
1989-90	**Detroit**	**NHL**	9	3	1	4	4	0	0	1	16	18.8	4	....	....	....	....	....	....	....	....	....	....	....	....	....
	♦ Edmonton	**NHL**	62	7	18	25	56	2	0	0	101	6.9	1	....	....	....	....	....	22	6	8	14	16	0	0	2
1990-91	**Edmonton**	**NHL**	80	27	35	62	35	4	1	4	141	19.1	17	....	....	....	....	....	15	2	5	7	14	1	0	1
1991-92	**Edmonton**	**NHL**	80	35	47	82	52	10	2	2	193	18.1	17	....	....	....	....	....	16	8	16	24	12	4	0	2
1992-93	**Chicago**	**NHL**	19	7	11	18	18	5	0	1	43	16.3	−3	....	....	....	....	....	4	0	0	0	6	0	0	0
1993-94	**Chicago**	**NHL**	81	31	39	70	111	7	4	4	222	14.0	1	....	....	....	....	....	6	1	3	4	25	0	0	0
1994-95	**Chicago**	**NHL**	40	23	18	41	89	7	0	3	120	19.2	7	....	....	....	....	....	16	9	3	12	29	3	0	3
1995-96	**Chicago**	**NHL**	70	22	29	51	86	8	0	3	212	10.4	−3	....	....	....	....	....	10	6	2	8	33	0	0	2
1996-97	**St. Louis**	**NHL**	75	20	25	45	69	4	1	2	151	13.2	−1	....	....	....	....	....	6	1	1	2	10	1	0	0
1997-98	**St. Louis**	**NHL**	27	4	9	13	22	2	0	0	52	7.7	8	....	....	....	....	....	....	....	....	....	....	....	....	....
	San Jose	**NHL**	10	5	4	9	14	2	0	0	29	17.2	1	....	....	....	....	....	6	1	1	2	20	1	0	0

										Regular Season									Playoffs							
Season	Club	League	GP	G	A	Pts	PIM	PP	SH	GW	S	%	+/–	TF	F%	H	SB	Min	GP	G	A	Pts	PIM	PP	SH	GW
1998-99	San Jose	NHL	76	25	23	48	73	7	0	2	176	14.2	10	15	40.0	29	9	14:45	6	0	3	3	4	0	0	0
	NHL Totals		**710**	**220**	**275**	**495**	**696**	**59**	**8**	**24**	**1570**	**14.0**		**15**	**40.0**	**29**	**9**	**14:45**	**115**	**34**	**43**	**77**	**177**	**10**	**0**	**10**

Traded to **Edmonton** by **Detroit** with Petr Klima, Adam Graves and Jeff Sharples for Jimmy Carson, Kevin McClelland and Edmonton's 5th round choice (later traded to Montreal — Montreal selected Brad Layzell) in 1991 Entry Draft, November 2, 1989. Traded to **Chicago** by **Edmonton** for Igor Kravchuk and Dean McAmmond, February 24, 1993. Signed as a free agent by **St. Louis**, July 8, 1996. Traded to **San Jose** by **St. Louis** for Todd Gill, March 24, 1998.

MURPHY, Larry

Defense. Shoots right. 6'2", 210 lbs. Born, Scarborough, Ont., March 8, 1961. Los Angeles' 1st choice, 4th overall, in 1980 Entry Draft.

1978-79	Peterborough	OHA	66	6	21	27	82	....	....	....	....	....	....	....	....	....	....	....	19	1	9	10	42	....	....	....
1979-80	Peterborough	OHA	68	21	68	89	88	....	....	....	....	....	....	....	....	....	....	....	14	4	13	17	20	....	....	....
1980-81	**Los Angeles**	**NHL**	**80**	**16**	**60**	**76**	**79**	**5**	**1**	**1**	**153**	**10.5**	**17**	....	....	....	....	....	**4**	**3**	**0**	**3**	**2**	**1**	**0**	**0**
1981-82	**Los Angeles**	**NHL**	**79**	**22**	**44**	**66**	**95**	**8**	**1**	**2**	**191**	**11.5**	**–13**	....	....	....	....	....	**10**	**2**	**8**	**10**	**12**	**1**	**0**	**0**
1982-83	**Los Angeles**	**NHL**	**77**	**14**	**48**	**62**	**81**	**9**	**0**	**2**	**172**	**8.1**	**2**	....	....	....	....	....	....	....	....	....	....	....	....	....
1983-84	**Los Angeles**	**NHL**	**6**	**0**	**3**	**3**	**0**	**0**	**0**	**0**	**11**	**0.0**	**–4**	....	....	....	....	....	....	....	....	....	....	....	....	....
	Washington	**NHL**	**72**	**13**	**33**	**46**	**50**	**2**	**0**	**2**	**138**	**9.4**	**12**	....	....	....	....	....	**8**	**0**	**3**	**3**	**6**	**0**	**0**	**0**
1984-85	**Washington**	**NHL**	**79**	**13**	**42**	**55**	**51**	**3**	**0**	**0**	**153**	**8.5**	**21**	....	....	....	....	....	**5**	**2**	**3**	**5**	**0**	**2**	**0**	**0**
1985-86	**Washington**	**NHL**	**78**	**21**	**44**	**65**	**50**	**8**	**1**	**2**	**180**	**11.7**	**2**	....	....	....	....	....	**9**	**1**	**5**	**6**	**6**	**1**	**0**	**0**
1986-87	**Washington**	**NHL**	**80**	**23**	**58**	**81**	**39**	**8**	**0**	**4**	**226**	**10.2**	**25**	....	....	....	....	....	**7**	**2**	**2**	**4**	**6**	**0**	**0**	**1**
1987-88	**Washington**	**NHL**	**79**	**8**	**53**	**61**	**72**	**7**	**0**	**1**	**201**	**4.0**	**2**	....	....	....	....	....	**13**	**4**	**4**	**8**	**33**	**2**	**0**	**1**
1988-89	**Washington**	**NHL**	**65**	**7**	**29**	**36**	**70**	**3**	**0**	**0**	**129**	**5.4**	**–5**	....	....	....	....	....	....	....	....	....	....	....	....	....
	Minnesota	**NHL**	**13**	**4**	**6**	**10**	**12**	**3**	**0**	**1**	**31**	**12.9**	**5**	....	....	....	....	....	**5**	**0**	**2**	**2**	**8**	**0**	**0**	**0**
1989-90	**Minnesota**	**NHL**	**77**	**10**	**58**	**68**	**44**	**4**	**0**	**1**	**173**	**5.8**	**–13**	....	....	....	....	....	**7**	**1**	**2**	**3**	**31**	**0**	**0**	**1**
1990-91	**Minnesota**	**NHL**	**31**	**4**	**11**	**15**	**38**	**1**	**0**	**2**	**103**	**3.9**	**–8**	....	....	....	....	....	....	....	....	....	....	....	....	....
	♦ **Pittsburgh**	**NHL**	**44**	**5**	**23**	**28**	**30**	**2**	**0**	**0**	**85**	**5.9**	**2**	....	....	....	....	....	**23**	**5**	**18**	**23**	**44**	**4**	**0**	**0**
1991-92♦	**Pittsburgh**	**NHL**	**77**	**21**	**56**	**77**	**48**	**7**	**2**	**3**	**206**	**10.2**	**33**	....	....	....	....	....	**21**	**6**	**10**	**16**	**19**	**3**	**0**	**1**
1992-93	**Pittsburgh**	**NHL**	**83**	**22**	**63**	**85**	**73**	**6**	**2**	**2**	**230**	**9.6**	**45**	....	....	....	....	....	**12**	**2**	**11**	**13**	**10**	**2**	**0**	**1**
1993-94	**Pittsburgh**	**NHL**	**84**	**17**	**56**	**73**	**44**	**7**	**0**	**4**	**236**	**7.2**	**10**	....	....	....	....	....	**6**	**0**	**5**	**5**	**0**	**0**	**0**	**0**
1994-95	**Pittsburgh**	**NHL**	**48**	**13**	**25**	**38**	**18**	**4**	**0**	**3**	**124**	**10.5**	**12**	....	....	....	....	....	**12**	**2**	**13**	**15**	**0**	**1**	**0**	**0**
1995-96	**Toronto**	**NHL**	**82**	**12**	**49**	**61**	**34**	**8**	**0**	**1**	**182**	**6.6**	**–2**	....	....	....	....	....	**6**	**0**	**2**	**2**	**4**	**0**	**0**	**0**
1996-97	**Toronto**	**NHL**	**69**	**7**	**32**	**39**	**20**	**4**	**0**	**0**	**137**	**5.1**	**1**	....	....	....	....	....	....	....	....	....	....	....	....	....
	♦ **Detroit**	**NHL**	**12**	**2**	**4**	**6**	**0**	**1**	**0**	**1**	**21**	**9.5**	**2**	....	....	....	....	....	**20**	**2**	**9**	**11**	**8**	**1**	**0**	**1**
1997-98♦	**Detroit**	**NHL**	**82**	**11**	**41**	**52**	**37**	**2**	**1**	**2**	**129**	**8.5**	**35**	....	....	....	....	....	**22**	**3**	**12**	**15**	**2**	**1**	**2**	**1**
1998-99	**Detroit**	**NHL**	**80**	**10**	**42**	**52**	**42**	**5**	**1**	**2**	**168**	**6.0**	**21**	**0**	**0.0**	**36**	**100**	**24:15**	**10**	**0**	**2**	**2**	**8**	**0**	**0**	**0**
	NHL Totals		**1477**	**275**	**880**	**1155**	**1027**	**107**	**9**	**36**	**3379**	**8.1**		**0**	**0.0**	**36**	**100**	**24:15**	**200**	**35**	**111**	**146**	**199**	**19**	**2**	**7**

OHA First All-Star Team (1980) • NHL Second All-Star Team (1987, 1993, 1995)

Played in NHL All-Star Game (1994, 1996, 1999)

Traded to **Washington** by **LA Kings** for Ken Houston and Brian Engblom, October 18, 1983. Traded to **Minnesota** by **Washington** with Mike Gartner for Dino Ciccarelli and Bob Rouse, March 7, 1989. Traded to **Pittsburgh** by **Minnesota** with Peter Taglianetti for Chris Dahlquist and Jim Johnson, December 11, 1990. Traded to **Toronto** by **Pittsburgh** for Dmitri Mironov and Toronto's 2nd round choice (later traded to New Jersey — New Jersey selected Joshua Dewolf) in 1996 Entry Draft, July 8, 1995. Traded to **Detroit** by **Toronto** for future considerations, March 18, 1997.

MURRAY, Chris — CHI.

Right wing. Shoots right. 6'2", 209 lbs. Born, Port Hardy, B.C., October 25, 1974. Montreal's 3rd choice, 54th overall, in 1994 Entry Draft.

1990-91	Bellingham	BCJHL	54	4	8	13	150	....	....	....	....	....	....	....	....	....	....	....	....	....	....	....	....	....	....	....
1991-92	Kamloops	WHL	33	1	1	2	218	....	....	....	....	....	....	....	....	....	....	....	5	0	0	0	10	....	....	....
1992-93	Kamloops	WHL	62	6	10	16	217	....	....	....	....	....	....	....	....	....	....	....	13	0	4	4	34	....	....	....
1993-94	Kamloops	WHL	59	14	16	30	260	....	....	....	....	....	....	....	....	....	....	....	15	4	2	6	*107	....	....	....
1994-95	**Montreal**	**NHL**	**3**	**0**	**0**	**0**	**4**	**0**	**0**	**0**	**0**	**0.0**	**0**	....	....	....	....	....	....	....	....	....	....	....	....	....
	Fredericton	AHL	55	6	12	18	234	....	....	....	....	....	....	....	....	....	....	....	12	1	1	2	50	....	....	....
1995-96	**Montreal**	**NHL**	**48**	**3**	**4**	**7**	**163**	**0**	**0**	**1**	**32**	**9.4**	**5**	....	....	....	....	....	**4**	**0**	**0**	**0**	**4**	**0**	**0**	**0**
	Fredericton	AHL	30	13	13	26	217	....	....	....	....	....	....	....	....	....	....	....	....	....	....	....	....	....	....	....
1996-97	**Montreal**	**NHL**	**56**	**4**	**2**	**6**	**114**	**0**	**0**	**0**	**32**	**12.5**	**–8**	....	....	....	....	....	....	....	....	....	....	....	....	....
	Hartford	**NHL**	**8**	**1**	**1**	**2**	**10**	**0**	**0**	**0**	**9**	**11.1**	**1**	....	....	....	....	....	....	....	....	....	....	....	....	....
1997-98	**Carolina**	**NHL**	**7**	**0**	**1**	**1**	**22**	**0**	**0**	**0**	**3**	**0.0**	**2**	....	....	....	....	....	....	....	....	....	....	....	....	....
	Ottawa	**NHL**	**46**	**5**	**3**	**8**	**96**	**0**	**0**	**2**	**48**	**10.4**	**1**	....	....	....	....	....	**11**	**1**	**0**	**1**	**8**	**0**	**0**	**0**
1998-99	**Ottawa**	**NHL**	**38**	**1**	**6**	**7**	**65**	**0**	**0**	**0**	**33**	**3.0**	**–2**	**1**	**100.0**	**30**	**5**	**7:06**	....	....	....	....	....	....	....	....
	Chicago	**NHL**	**4**	**0**	**0**	**0**	**14**	**0**	**0**	**0**	**4**	**0.0**	**0**	**1**	**100.0**	**3**	**0**	**7:20**	....	....	....	....	....	....	....	....
	NHL Totals		**210**	**14**	**17**	**31**	**488**	**0**	**0**	**3**	**161**	**8.7**		**2**	**100.0**	**33**	**5**	**7:07**	**15**	**1**	**0**	**1**	**12**	**0**	**0**	**0**

Traded to **Phoenix** by **Montreal** with Murray Baron for Dave Manson, March 18, 1997. Traded to **Hartford** by **Phoenix** for Gerald Diduck, March 18, 1997. Transferred to **Carolina** after **Hartford** franchise relocated, June 25, 1997. Traded to **Ottawa** by **Carolina** for Sean Hill, November 18, 1997. Traded to **Chicago** by **Ottawa** for Nelson Emerson, March 23, 1999.

MURRAY, Glen — L.A.

Right wing. Shoots right. 6'3", 222 lbs. Born, Halifax, N.S., November 1, 1972. Boston's 1st choice, 18th overall, in 1991 Entry Draft.

1988-89	Bridgewater	NSAHA	45	50	56	106	62	....	....	....	....	....	....	....	....	....	....	....	....	....	....	....	....	....	....	....
1989-90	Sudbury	OHL	62	8	28	36	17	....	....	....	....	....	....	....	....	....	....	....	7	0	0	0	4	....	....	....
1990-91	Sudbury	OHL	66	27	38	65	82	....	....	....	....	....	....	....	....	....	....	....	5	8	4	12	10	....	....	....
1991-92	Sudbury	OHL	54	37	47	84	93	....	....	....	....	....	....	....	....	....	....	....	11	7	4	11	18	....	....	....
	Boston	**NHL**	**5**	**3**	**1**	**4**	**0**	**1**	**0**	**0**	**20**	**15.0**	**2**	....	....	....	....	....	**15**	**4**	**2**	**6**	**10**	**1**	**0**	**0**
1992-93	**Boston**	**NHL**	**27**	**3**	**4**	**7**	**8**	**2**	**0**	**1**	**28**	**10.7**	**–6**	....	....	....	....	....	....	....	....	....	....	....	....	....
	Providence	AHL	48	30	26	56	42	....	....	....	....	....	....	....	....	....	....	....	6	1	4	5	4	....	....	....
1993-94	**Boston**	**NHL**	**81**	**18**	**13**	**31**	**48**	**0**	**0**	**4**	**114**	**15.8**	**–1**	....	....	....	....	....	**13**	**4**	**5**	**9**	**14**	**0**	**0**	**0**
1994-95	**Boston**	**NHL**	**35**	**5**	**2**	**7**	**46**	**0**	**0**	**2**	**64**	**7.8**	**–11**	....	....	....	....	....	**2**	**0**	**0**	**0**	**2**	**0**	**0**	**0**
1995-96	**Pittsburgh**	**NHL**	**69**	**14**	**15**	**29**	**57**	**0**	**0**	**2**	**100**	**14.0**	**4**	....	....	....	....	....	**18**	**2**	**6**	**8**	**10**	**0**	**0**	**1**
1996-97	**Pittsburgh**	**NHL**	**66**	**11**	**11**	**22**	**24**	**3**	**0**	**1**	**127**	**8.7**	**–19**	....	....	....	....	....	....	....	....	....	....	....	....	....
	Los Angeles	**NHL**	**11**	**5**	**3**	**8**	**8**	**0**	**0**	**0**	**26**	**19.2**	**–2**	....	....	....	....	....	....	....	....	....	....	....	....	....
1997-98	**Los Angeles**	**NHL**	**81**	**29**	**31**	**60**	**54**	**7**	**3**	**7**	**193**	**15.0**	**6**	....	....	....	....	....	**4**	**2**	**0**	**2**	**6**	**0**	**0**	**0**
1998-99	**Los Angeles**	**NHL**	**61**	**16**	**15**	**31**	**36**	**3**	**3**	**3**	**173**	**9.2**	**–14**	**12**	**25.0**	**63**	**15**	**20:33**	....	....	....	....	....	....	....	....
	NHL Totals		**436**	**104**	**95**	**199**	**281**	**16**	**6**	**20**	**845**	**12.3**		**12**	**25.0**	**63**	**15**	**20:33**	**52**	**12**	**13**	**25**	**42**	**1**	**0**	**1**

Traded to **Pittsburgh** by **Boston** with Bryan Smolinski and Boston's 3rd round choice (Boyd Kane) in 1996 Entry Draft for Kevin Stevens and Shawn McEachern, August 2, 1995. Traded to **LA Kings** by **Pittsburgh** for Ed Olczyk, March 18, 1997.

MURRAY, Marty — CGY.

Center. Shoots left. 5'9", 178 lbs. Born, Deloraine, Man., February 16, 1975. Calgary's 5th choice, 96th overall, in 1993 Entry Draft.

1990-91	Southwset	MAHA	36	46	47	95	50	....	....	....	....	....	....	....	....	....	....	....	....	....	....	....	....	....	....	....
1991-92	Brandon	WHL	68	20	36	56	22	....	....	....	....	....	....	....	....	....	....	....	....	....	....	....	....	....	....	....
1992-93	Brandon	WHL	67	29	65	94	50	....	....	....	....	....	....	....	....	....	....	....	4	1	3	4	0	....	....	....
1993-94	Brandon	WHL	64	43	71	114	33	....	....	....	....	....	....	....	....	....	....	....	14	6	14	20	14	....	....	....
1994-95	Brandon	WHL	65	40	*88	128	53	....	....	....	....	....	....	....	....	....	....	....	18	9	*20	29	16	....	....	....
1995-96	**Calgary**	**NHL**	**15**	**3**	**3**	**6**	**0**	**2**	**0**	**0**	**22**	**13.6**	**–4**	....	....	....	....	....	....	....	....	....	....	....	....	....
	Saint John	AHL	58	25	31	56	20	....	....	....	....	....	....	....	....	....	....	....	14	2	4	6	4	....	....	....
1996-97	**Calgary**	**NHL**	**2**	**0**	**0**	**0**	**4**	**0**	**0**	**0**	**2**	**0.0**	**0**	....	....	....	....	....	....	....	....	....	....	....	....	....
	Saint John	AHL	67	19	39	58	40	....	....	....	....	....	....	....	....	....	....	....	5	2	3	5	4	....	....	....
1997-98	**Calgary**	**NHL**	**2**	**0**	**0**	**0**	**2**	**0**	**0**	**0**	**2**	**0.0**	**1**	....	....	....	....	....	....	....	....	....	....	....	....	....
	Saint John	AHL	41	10	30	40	16	....	....	....	....	....	....	....	....	....	....	....	21	10	10	20	12	....	....	....
1998-99	VSV Villach	Alpenliga	34	27	42	69	12	....	....	....	....	....	....	....	....	....	....	....	....	....	....	....	....	....	....	....
	VSV Villach	Austria	6	1	4	5	0	....	....	....	....	....	....	....	....	....	....	....	....	....	....	....	....	....	....	....
	Canada	Nat-Team	5	1	3	4	2	....	....	....	....	....	....	....	....	....	....	....	....	....	....	....	....	....	....	....
	NHL Totals		**19**	**3**	**3**	**6**	**6**	**2**	**0**	**0**	**26**	**11.5**		....	....	....	....	....	....	....	....	....	....	....	....	....

WHL East First All-Star Team (1994, 1995) • Canadian Major Junior Second All-Star Team (1994)

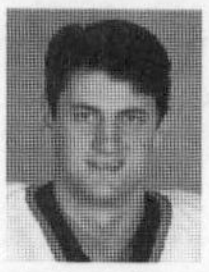

MURRAY, Rem — EDM.

Center/Left wing. Shoots left. 6'2", 195 lbs. Born, Stratford, Ont., October 9, 1972. Los Angeles' 5th choice, 135th overall, in 1992 Entry Draft.

			Regular Season																Playoffs							
Season	Club	League	GP	G	A	Pts	PIM	PP	SH	GW	S	%	+/-	TF	F%	H	SB	Min	GP	G	A	Pts	PIM	PP	SH	GW
1990-91	Stratford	OJHL-B	48	39	59	98	22	....	....	....	....	....	....	....	....	....	....	....	....	....	....	....	....	....	....	....
1991-92	Michigan State	CCHA	41	12	36	48	16	....	....	....	....	....	....	....	....	....	....	....	....	....	....	....	....	....	....	....
1992-93	Michigan State	CCHA	40	22	35	57	24	....	....	....	....	....	....	....	....	....	....	....	....	....	....	....	....	....	....	....
1993-94	Michigan State	CCHA	41	16	38	54	18	....	....	....	....	....	....	....	....	....	....	....	....	....	....	....	....	....	....	....
1994-95	Michigan State	CCHA	40	20	36	56	21	....	....	....	....	....	....	....	....	....	....	....	....	....	....	....	....	....	....	....
1995-96	Cape Breton	AHL	79	31	59	90	40	....	....	....	....	....	....	....	....	....	....	....	....	....	....	....	....	....	....	....
1996-97	**Edmonton**	**NHL**	**82**	**11**	**20**	**31**	**16**	**1**	**0**	**2**	**85**	**12.9**	**9**	....	....	....	....	....	**12**	**1**	**2**	**3**	**4**	**0**	**0**	**0**
1997-98	**Edmonton**	**NHL**	**61**	**9**	**9**	**18**	**39**	**2**	**2**	**0**	**59**	**15.3**	**–9**	....	....	....	....	....	**11**	**1**	**4**	**5**	**2**	**0**	**0**	**0**
1998-99	**Edmonton**	**NHL**	**78**	**21**	**18**	**39**	**20**	**4**	**1**	**4**	**116**	**18.1**	**4**	**1013**	**48.1**	**68**	**30**	**15:50**	**4**	**1**	**1**	**2**	**2**	**0**	**0**	**0**
	NHL Totals		**221**	**41**	**47**	**88**	**75**	**7**	**3**	**6**	**260**	**15.8**		**1013**	**48.1**	**68**	**30**	**15:50**	**27**	**3**	**7**	**10**	**8**	**0**	**0**	**0**

CCHA Second All-Star Team (1995)

Signed as a free agent by **Edmonton**, September 19, 1995.

MURRAY, Rob — PHX.

Center. Shoots right. 6'1", 180 lbs. Born, Toronto, Ont., April 4, 1967. Washington's 3rd choice, 61st overall, in 1985 Entry Draft.

Season	Club	League	GP	G	A	Pts	PIM	PP	SH	GW	S	%	+/-	TF	F%	H	SB	Min	GP	G	A	Pts	PIM	PP	SH	GW
1983-84	Mississagua	MTHL	35	18	36	54	32	....	....	....	....	....	....	....	....	....	....	....	....	....	....	....	....	....	....	....
1984-85	Peterborough	OHL	63	12	9	21	155	....	....	....	....	....	....	....	....	....	....	....	17	2	7	9	45	....	....	....
1985-86	Peterborough	OHL	52	14	18	32	125	....	....	....	....	....	....	....	....	....	....	....	16	1	2	3	50	....	....	....
1986-87	Peterborough	OHL	62	17	37	54	204	....	....	....	....	....	....	....	....	....	....	....	3	1	4	5	8	....	....	....
1987-88	Fort Wayne	IHL	80	12	21	33	139	....	....	....	....	....	....	....	....	....	....	....	6	0	2	2	16	....	....	....
1988-89	Baltimore	AHL	80	11	23	34	235	....	....	....	....	....	....	....	....	....	....	....	....	....	....	....	....	....	....	....
1989-90	**Washington**	**NHL**	**41**	**2**	**7**	**9**	**58**	**0**	**0**	**0**	**29**	**6.9**	**–10**	....	....	....	....	....	**9**	**0**	**0**	**0**	**18**	**0**	**0**	**0**
	Baltimore	AHL	23	5	4	9	63	....	....	....	....	....	....	....	....	....	....	....	....	....	....	....	....	....	....	....
1990-91	**Washington**	**NHL**	**17**	**0**	**3**	**3**	**19**	**0**	**0**	**0**	**8**	**0.0**	**0**	....	....	....	....	....	....	....	....	....	....	....	....	....
	Baltimore	AHL	48	6	20	26	177	....	....	....	....	....	....	....	....	....	....	....	4	0	0	0	12	....	....	....
1991-92	**Winnipeg**	**NHL**	**9**	**0**	**1**	**1**	**18**	**0**	**0**	**0**	**2**	**0.0**	**–2**	....	....	....	....	....	....	....	....	....	....	....	....	....
	Moncton	AHL	60	16	15	31	247	....	....	....	....	....	....	....	....	....	....	....	8	0	1	1	56	....	....	....
1992-93	**Winnipeg**	**NHL**	**10**	**1**	**0**	**1**	**6**	**0**	**0**	**1**	**4**	**25.0**	**0**	....	....	....	....	....	....	....	....	....	....	....	....	....
	Moncton	AHL	56	16	21	37	147	....	....	....	....	....	....	....	....	....	....	....	3	0	0	0	6	....	....	....
1993-94	**Winnipeg**	**NHL**	**6**	**0**	**0**	**0**	**2**	**0**	**0**	**0**	**1**	**0.0**	**0**	....	....	....	....	....	....	....	....	....	....	....	....	....
	Moncton	AHL	69	25	32	57	280	....	....	....	....	....	....	....	....	....	....	....	21	2	3	5	60	....	....	....
1994-95	Springfield	AHL	78	16	38	54	373	....	....	....	....	....	....	....	....	....	....	....	....	....	....	....	....	....	....	....
	Winnipeg	**NHL**	**10**	**0**	**2**	**2**	**2**	**0**	**0**	**0**	**5**	**0.0**	**1**	....	....	....	....	....	....	....	....	....	....	....	....	....
1995-96	**Winnipeg**	**NHL**	**1**	**0**	**0**	**0**	**2**	**0**	**0**	**0**	**1**	**0.0**	**–1**	....	....	....	....	....	....	....	....	....	....	....	....	....
	Springfield	AHL	74	10	28	38	263	....	....	....	....	....	....	....	....	....	....	....	10	1	6	7	32	....	....	....
1996-97	Springfield	AHL	78	16	27	43	234	....	....	....	....	....	....	....	....	....	....	....	17	2	3	5	66	....	....	....
1997-98	Springfield	AHL	80	7	30	37	255	....	....	....	....	....	....	....	....	....	....	....	4	0	2	2	2	....	....	....
1998-99	**Phoenix**	**NHL**	**13**	**1**	**2**	**3**	**4**	**0**	**0**	**0**	**11**	**9.1**	**2**	**28**	**46.4**	**11**	**9**	**8:18**	....	....	....	....	....	....	....	....
	Springfield	AHL	68	6	19	25	197	....	....	....	....	....	....	....	....	....	....	....	3	0	0	0	4	....	....	....
	NHL Totals		**107**	**4**	**15**	**19**	**111**	**0**	**0**	**1**	**61**	**6.6**		**28**	**46.4**	**11**	**9**	**8:18**	**9**	**0**	**0**	**0**	**18**	**0**	**0**	**0**

Claimed by **Minnesota** from **Washington** in Expansion Draft, May 30, 1991. Traded to **Winnipeg** by **Minnesota** with future considerations for Winnipeg's 7th round choice (Geoff Finch) in 1991 Entry Draft and future considerations, May 31, 1991. • Transferred to **Phoenix** after **Winnipeg** franchise relocated, July 1, 1996.

MURZYN, Dana (MUHR-zihn)

Defense. Shoots left. 6'2", 200 lbs. Born, Calgary, Alta., December 9, 1966. Hartford's 1st choice, 5th overall, in 1985 Entry Draft.

Season	Club	League	GP	G	A	Pts	PIM	PP	SH	GW	S	%	+/-	TF	F%	H	SB	Min	GP	G	A	Pts	PIM	PP	SH	GW
1983-84	Calgary	WHL	65	11	20	31	135	....	....	....	....	....	....	....	....	....	....	....	2	0	0	0	10	....	....	....
1984-85	Calgary	WHL	72	32	60	92	233	....	....	....	....	....	....	....	....	....	....	....	8	1	11	12	16	....	....	....
1985-86	**Hartford**	**NHL**	**78**	**3**	**23**	**26**	**125**	**0**	**0**	**1**	**79**	**3.8**	**1**	....	....	....	....	....	**4**	**0**	**0**	**0**	**10**	**0**	**0**	**0**
1986-87	**Hartford**	**NHL**	**74**	**9**	**19**	**28**	**95**	**1**	**0**	**0**	**135**	**6.7**	**17**	....	....	....	....	....	**6**	**2**	**1**	**3**	**29**	**1**	**0**	**1**
1987-88	**Hartford**	**NHL**	**33**	**1**	**6**	**7**	**45**	**1**	**0**	**0**	**49**	**2.0**	**–8**	....	....	....	....	....	....	....	....	....	....	....	....	....
	Calgary	**NHL**	**41**	**6**	**5**	**11**	**94**	**0**	**0**	**1**	**58**	**10.3**	**9**	....	....	....	....	....	**5**	**2**	**0**	**2**	**13**	**0**	**0**	**0**
1988-89♦	**Calgary**	**NHL**	**63**	**3**	**19**	**22**	**142**	**0**	**1**	**1**	**91**	**3.3**	**26**	....	....	....	....	....	**21**	**0**	**3**	**3**	**20**	**0**	**0**	**0**
1989-90	**Calgary**	**NHL**	**78**	**7**	**13**	**20**	**140**	**1**	**0**	**0**	**97**	**7.2**	**19**	....	....	....	....	....	**6**	**2**	**2**	**4**	**2**	**0**	**0**	**0**
1990-91	**Calgary**	**NHL**	**19**	**0**	**2**	**2**	**30**	**0**	**0**	**0**	**25**	**0.0**	**–4**	....	....	....	....	....	....	....	....	....	....	....	....	....
	Vancouver	**NHL**	**10**	**1**	**0**	**1**	**8**	**0**	**0**	**0**	**15**	**6.7**	**–3**	....	....	....	....	....	**6**	**0**	**1**	**1**	**8**	**0**	**0**	**0**
1991-92	**Vancouver**	**NHL**	**70**	**3**	**11**	**14**	**147**	**0**	**1**	**0**	**99**	**3.0**	**15**	....	....	....	....	....	**1**	**0**	**0**	**0**	**15**	**0**	**0**	**0**
1992-93	**Vancouver**	**NHL**	**79**	**5**	**11**	**16**	**196**	**0**	**0**	**2**	**82**	**6.1**	**34**	....	....	....	....	....	**12**	**3**	**2**	**5**	**18**	**0**	**0**	**0**
1993-94	**Vancouver**	**NHL**	**80**	**6**	**14**	**20**	**109**	**0**	**1**	**0**	**79**	**7.6**	**4**	....	....	....	....	....	**7**	**0**	**0**	**0**	**4**	**0**	**0**	**0**
1994-95	**Vancouver**	**NHL**	**40**	**0**	**8**	**8**	**129**	**0**	**0**	**0**	**29**	**0.0**	**14**	....	....	....	....	....	**8**	**0**	**1**	**1**	**22**	**0**	**0**	**0**
1995-96	**Vancouver**	**NHL**	**69**	**2**	**10**	**12**	**130**	**0**	**0**	**0**	**68**	**2.9**	**9**	....	....	....	....	....	**6**	**0**	**0**	**0**	**25**	**0**	**0**	**0**
1996-97	**Vancouver**	**NHL**	**61**	**1**	**7**	**8**	**118**	**0**	**0**	**0**	**70**	**1.4**	**7**	....	....	....	....	....	....	....	....	....	....	....	....	....
1997-98	**Vancouver**	**NHL**	**31**	**5**	**2**	**7**	**42**	**0**	**0**	**2**	**29**	**17.2**	**–3**	....	....	....	....	....	....	....	....	....	....	....	....	....
1998-99	**Vancouver**	**NHL**	**12**	**0**	**2**	**2**	**21**	**0**	**0**	**0**	**7**	**0.0**	**1**	**0**	**0.0**	**7**	**13**	**15:02**	....	....	....	....	....	....	....	....
	Syracuse	AHL	20	2	4	6	37	....	....	....	....	....	....	....	....	....	....	....	....	....	....	....	....	....	....	....
	NHL Totals		**838**	**52**	**152**	**204**	**1571**	**3**	**3**	**7**	**1012**	**5.1**		**0**	**0.0**	**7**	**13**	**15:02**	**82**	**9**	**10**	**19**	**166**	**1**	**0**	**1**

WHL East First All-Star Team, (1985) • NHL All-Rookie Team (1986)

Traded to **Calgary** by **Hartford** with Shane Churla for Neil Sheehy, Carey Wilson and the rights to Lane MacDonald, January 3, 1988. Traded to **Vancouver** by **Calgary** for Ron Stern, Kevan Guy and future considerations, March 5, 1991.

MUSIL, Frank (moo-SIHL) — EDM.

Defense. Shoots left. 6'3", 215 lbs. Born, Pardubice, Czech., December 17, 1964. Minnesota's 3rd choice, 38th overall, in 1983 Entry Draft.

Season	Club	League	GP	G	A	Pts	PIM	PP	SH	GW	S	%	+/-	TF	F%	H	SB	Min	GP	G	A	Pts	PIM	PP	SH	GW
1980-81	HC Pardubice	Czech.	2	0	0	0	0	....	....	....	....	....	....	....	....	....	....	....	....	....	....	....	....	....	....	....
1981-82	HC Pardubice	Czech.	35	1	3	4	34	....	....	....	....	....	....	....	....	....	....	....	....	....	....	....	....	....	....	....
1982-83	HC Pardubice	Czech.	33	1	2	3	44	....	....	....	....	....	....	....	....	....	....	....	....	....	....	....	....	....	....	....
1983-84	HC Pardubice	Czech.	37	4	8	12	72	....	....	....	....	....	....	....	....	....	....	....	....	....	....	....	....	....	....	....
1984-85	Dukla Jihlava	Czech.	44	4	6	10	76	....	....	....	....	....	....	....	....	....	....	....	....	....	....	....	....	....	....	....
1985-86	Dukla Jihlava	Czech.	34	4	7	11	42	....	....	....	....	....	....	....	....	....	....	....	....	....	....	....	....	....	....	....
1986-87	**Minnesota**	**NHL**	**72**	**2**	**9**	**11**	**148**	**0**	**0**	**0**	**83**	**2.4**	**0**	....	....	....	....	....	....	....	....	....	....	....	....	....
1987-88	**Minnesota**	**NHL**	**80**	**9**	**8**	**17**	**213**	**1**	**1**	**0**	**78**	**11.5**	**–2**	....	....	....	....	....	....	....	....	....	....	....	....	....
1988-89	**Minnesota**	**NHL**	**55**	**1**	**19**	**20**	**54**	**0**	**0**	**1**	**78**	**1.3**	**4**	....	....	....	....	....	**5**	**1**	**1**	**2**	**4**	**0**	**0**	**0**
1989-90	**Minnesota**	**NHL**	**56**	**2**	**8**	**10**	**109**	**0**	**0**	**1**	**78**	**2.6**	**0**	....	....	....	....	....	**4**	**0**	**0**	**0**	**14**	**0**	**0**	**0**
1990-91	**Minnesota**	**NHL**	**8**	**0**	**2**	**2**	**23**	**0**	**0**	**0**	**5**	**0.0**	**0**	....	....	....	....	....	....	....	....	....	....	....	....	....
	Calgary	**NHL**	**67**	**7**	**14**	**21**	**160**	**2**	**0**	**1**	**68**	**10.3**	**12**	....	....	....	....	....	**7**	**0**	**0**	**0**	**10**	**0**	**0**	**0**
1991-92	**Calgary**	**NHL**	**78**	**4**	**8**	**12**	**103**	**1**	**1**	**0**	**71**	**5.6**	**12**	....	....	....	....	....	....	....	....	....	....	....	....	....
1992-93	**Calgary**	**NHL**	**80**	**6**	**10**	**16**	**131**	**0**	**0**	**1**	**87**	**6.9**	**28**	....	....	....	....	....	**6**	**1**	**1**	**2**	**7**	**0**	**0**	**0**
1993-94	**Calgary**	**NHL**	**75**	**1**	**8**	**9**	**50**	**0**	**0**	**0**	**65**	**1.5**	**38**	....	....	....	....	....	**7**	**0**	**1**	**1**	**4**	**0**	**0**	**0**
1994-95	Sparta Praha	Cze-Rep	19	1	4	5	50	....	....	....	....	....	....	....	....	....	....	....	....	....	....	....	....	....	....	....
	HC Saxonia	Germany	1	0	0	0	2	....	....	....	....	....	....	....	....	....	....	....	....	....	....	....	....	....	....	....
	Calgary	**NHL**	**35**	**0**	**5**	**5**	**61**	**0**	**0**	**0**	**18**	**0.0**	**6**	....	....	....	....	....	**5**	**0**	**1**	**1**	**0**	**0**	**0**	**0**
1995-96	Karlovy Vary	Czech-2	16	7	4	11	16	....	....	....	....	....	....	....	....	....	....	....	....	....	....	....	....	....	....	....
	Ottawa	**NHL**	**65**	**1**	**3**	**4**	**85**	**0**	**0**	**0**	**37**	**2.7**	**–10**	....	....	....	....	....	....	....	....	....	....	....	....	....
1996-97	**Ottawa**	**NHL**	**57**	**0**	**5**	**5**	**58**	**0**	**0**	**0**	**24**	**0.0**	**6**	....	....	....	....	....	....	....	....	....	....	....	....	....
1997-98	Indianapolis	IHL	52	5	8	13	122	....	....	....	....	....	....	....	....	....	....	....	....	....	....	....	....	....	....	....
	Detroit	IHL	9	0	0	0	6	....	....	....	....	....	....	....	....	....	....	....	....	....	....	....	....	....	....	....
	Edmonton	**NHL**	**17**	**1**	**2**	**3**	**8**	**0**	**1**	**1**	**8**	**12.5**	**1**	....	....	....	....	....	**7**	**0**	**0**	**0**	**6**	**0**	**0**	**0**

			Regular Season																Playoffs							
Season	Club	League	GP	G	A	Pts	PIM	PP	SH	GW	S	%	+/-	TF	F%	H	SB	Min	GP	G	A	Pts	PIM	PP	SH	GW
1998-99	**Edmonton**	**NHL**	**39**	**0**	**3**	**3**	**34**	**0**	**0**	**0**	**9**	**0.0**	**0**	**0**	**0.0**	**60**	**56**	**14:21**	**1**	**0**	**0**	**0**	**2**	**0**	**0**	**0**
	NHL Totals		**784**	**34**	**104**	**138**	**1237**	**4**	**3**	**5**	**709**	**4.8**		**0**	**0.0**	**60**	**56**	**14:21**	**42**	**2**	**4**	**6**	**47**	**0**	**0**	**0**

Traded to **Calgary** by **Minnesota** for Brian Glynn, October 26, 1990. Traded to **Ottawa** by **Calgary** for Ottawa's 4th round choice (Chris St. Croix) in 1997 Entry Draft, October 7, 1995. Traded to **Edmonton** by **Ottawa** for Scott Ferguson, March 9, 1998.

MYHRES, Brantt (MIGH-uhrs) S.J.

Right wing. Shoots right. 6'4", 220 lbs. Born, Edmonton, Alta., March 18, 1974. Tampa Bay's 5th choice, 97th overall, in 1992 Entry Draft.

Season	Club	League	GP	G	A	Pts	PIM	PP	SH	GW	S	%	+/-	TF	F%	H	SB	Min	GP	G	A	Pts	PIM	PP	SH	GW
1989-90	Bonneyville	AAHA	60	40	62	102	195	....	....	....	....	....	....	....	....	....	....	....	....	....	....	....	....	....	....	....
1990-91	Portland	WHL	59	2	7	9	125	....	....	....	....	....	....	....	....	....	....	....	....	....	....	....	....	....	....	....
1991-92	Portland	WHL	4	0	2	2	22	....	....	....	....	....	....	....	....	....	....	....	....	....	....	....	....	....	....	....
	Lethbridge	WHL	53	4	11	15	359	....	....	....	....	....	....	....	....	....	....	....	5	0	0	0	36	....	....	....
1992-93	Lethbridge	WHL	64	13	35	48	277	....	....	....	....	....	....	....	....	....	....	....	3	0	0	0	11	....	....	....
1993-94	Lethbridge	WHL	34	10	21	31	103	....	....	....	....	....	....	....	....	....	....	....	....	....	....	....	....	....	....	....
	Spokane	WHL	27	10	22	32	139	....	....	....	....	....	....	....	....	....	....	....	3	1	4	5	7	....	....	....
	Atlanta	IHL	2	0	0	0	17	....	....	....	....	....	....	....	....	....	....	....	....	....	....	....	....	....	....	....
1994-95	Atlanta	IHL	40	5	5	10	213	....	....	....	....	....	....	....	....	....	....	....	....	....	....	....	....	....	....	....
	Tampa Bay	**NHL**	**15**	**2**	**0**	**2**	**81**	**0**	**0**	**1**	**4**	**50.0**	**–2**	....	....	....	....	....	....	....	....	....	....	....	....	....
1995-96	Atlanta	IHL	12	0	2	2	58	....	....	....	....	....	....	....	....	....	....	....	....	....	....	....	....	....	....	....
1996-97	**Tampa Bay**	**NHL**	**47**	**3**	**1**	**4**	**136**	**0**	**0**	**1**	**13**	**23.1**	**1**	....	....	....	....	....	....	....	....	....	....	....	....	....
	San Antonio	IHL	12	0	0	0	98	....	....	....	....	....	....	....	....	....	....	....	....	....	....	....	....	....	....	....
1997-98	**Philadelphia**	**NHL**	**23**	**0**	**0**	**0**	**169**	**0**	**0**	**0**	**0**	**0.0**	**–1**	....	....	....	....	....	....	....	....	....	....	....	....	....
	Philadelphia	AHL	18	4	4	8	67	....	....	....	....	....	....	....	....	....	....	....	....	....	....	....	....	....	....	....
1998-99	**San Jose**	**NHL**	**30**	**1**	**0**	**1**	**116**	**0**	**0**	**0**	**7**	**14.3**	**–2**	**1**	**0.0**	**15**	**2**	**4:47**	....	....	....	....	....	....	....	....
	Kentucky	AHL	4	0	0	0	16	....	....	....	....	....	....	....	....	....	....	....	....	....	....	....	....	....	....	....
	NHL Totals		**115**	**6**	**1**	**7**	**502**	**0**	**0**	**2**	**24**	**25.0**		**1**	**0.0**	**15**	**2**	**4:47**	....	....	....	....	....	....	....	....

Traded to **Edmonton** by **Tampa Bay** with Toronto's 3rd round choice (previously acquired, Edmonton selected Alex Henry) in 1998 Entry Draft for Vladimir Vujtek and Edmonton's 3rd round choice (Dimitri Afanasenkov) in 1998 Entry Draft, July 16, 1997. Traded to **Philadelphia** by **Edmonton** for Jason Bowen, October 15, 1997. Signed as a free agent by **San Jose**, August, 1998.

MYRVOLD, Anders (MYOOR-vohld)

Defense. Shoots left. 6'2", 200 lbs. Born, Lorenskog, Norway, August 12, 1975. Quebec's 6th choice, 127th overall, in 1993 Entry Draft.

Season	Club	League	GP	G	A	Pts	PIM	PP	SH	GW	S	%	+/-	TF	F%	H	SB	Min	GP	G	A	Pts	PIM	PP	SH	GW
1991-92	Storhamr IL	Norway	1	0	0	0	4	....	....	....	....	....	....	....	....	....	....	....	....	....	....	....	....	....	....	....
1992-93	Farjestads BK	Sweden	2	0	0	0	0	....	....	....	....	....	....	....	....	....	....	....	....	....	....	....	....	....	....	....
1993-94	Grum HC	Sweden-2	24	1	0	1	59	....	....	....	....	....	....	....	....	....	....	....	....	....	....	....	....	....	....	....
1994-95	Laval	QMJHL	64	14	50	64	173	....	....	....	....	....	....	....	....	....	....	....	20	4	10	14	68	....	....	....
	Cornwall	AHL	....	....	....	....	....	....	....	....	....	....	....	....	....	....	....	....	3	0	1	1	2	....	....	....
1995-96	**Colorado**	**NHL**	**4**	**0**	**1**	**1**	**6**	**0**	**0**	**0**	**4**	**0.0**	**–2**	....	....	....	....	....	....	....	....	....	....	....	....	....
	Cornwall	AHL	70	5	24	29	125	....	....	....	....	....	....	....	....	....	....	....	5	1	0	1	19	....	....	....
1996-97	Hershey	AHL	20	0	3	3	16	....	....	....	....	....	....	....	....	....	....	....	....	....	....	....	....	....	....	....
	Boston	**NHL**	**9**	**0**	**2**	**2**	**4**	**0**	**0**	**0**	**8**	**0.0**	**–1**	....	....	....	....	....	....	....	....	....	....	....	....	....
	Providence	AHL	53	6	15	21	107	....	....	....	....	....	....	....	....	....	....	....	10	0	1	1	6	....	....	....
1997-98	Providence	AHL	75	4	21	25	91	....	....	....	....	....	....	....	....	....	....	....	....	....	....	....	....	....	....	....
1998-99	Djurgardens IF	Sweden	29	3	4	7	52	....	....	....	....	....	....	....	....	....	....	....	....	....	....	....	....	....	....	....
	Djurgardens IF	EuroHL	3	0	1	1	4	....	....	....	....	....	....	....	....	....	....	....	....	....	....	....	....	....	....	....
	AIK Solna	Sweden	19	1	3	4	24	....	....	....	....	....	....	....	....	....	....	....	....	....	....	....	....	....	....	....
	NHL Totals		**13**	**0**	**3**	**3**	**10**	**0**	**0**	**0**	**12**	**0.0**		....	....	....	....	....	....	....	....	....	....	....	....	....

Rights transferred to **Colorado** after **Quebec** franchise relocated, June 21, 1995. Traded to **Boston** by **Colorado** with Landon Wilson for Boston's 1st round choice (Robyn Regehr) in 1998 Entry Draft, November 22, 1996.

NABOKOV, Dmitri (nuh-BAW-kahv) NYI

Center. Shoots right. 6'2", 209 lbs. Born, Novosibirsk, USSR, January 4, 1977. Chicago's 1st choice, 19th overall, in 1995 Entry Draft.

Season	Club	League	GP	G	A	Pts	PIM	PP	SH	GW	S	%	+/-	TF	F%	H	SB	Min	GP	G	A	Pts	PIM	PP	SH	GW
1993-94	Soviet Wings	CIS	17	0	2	2	6	....	....	....	....	....	....	....	....	....	....	....	3	0	0	0	0	....	....	....
1994-95	Soviet Wings	CIS	49	15	12	27	32	....	....	....	....	....	....	....	....	....	....	....	4	5	0	5	6	....	....	....
1995-96	Soviet Wings	CIS	50	12	14	26	51	....	....	....	....	....	....	....	....	....	....	....	....	....	....	....	....	....	....	....
1996-97	Soviet Wings	Russia	1	0	0	0	0	....	....	....	....	....	....	....	....	....	....	....	....	....	....	....	....	....	....	....
	Regina	WHL	50	39	56	95	61	....	....	....	....	....	....	....	....	....	....	....	5	2	3	5	2	....	....	....
	Indianapolis	IHL	2	0	0	0	0	....	....	....	....	....	....	....	....	....	....	....	....	....	....	....	....	....	....	....
1997-98	**Chicago**	**NHL**	**25**	**7**	**4**	**11**	**10**	**3**	**0**	**2**	**34**	**20.6**	**–1**	....	....	....	....	....	....	....	....	....	....	....	....	....
	Indianapolis	IHL	46	6	15	21	16	....	....	....	....	....	....	....	....	....	....	....	5	2	1	3	0	....	....	....
1998-99	**NY Islanders**	**NHL**	**4**	**0**	**2**	**2**	**2**	**0**	**0**	**0**	**4**	**0.0**	**4**	**0**	**0.0**	**3**	**0**	**11:38**	....	....	....	....	....	....	....	....
	Lowell	AHL	73	17	25	42	46	....	....	....	....	....	....	....	....	....	....	....	3	0	1	1	0	....	....	....
	NHL Totals		**29**	**7**	**6**	**13**	**12**	**3**	**0**	**2**	**38**	**18.4**		**0**	**0.0**	**3**	**0**	**11:38**	....	....	....	....	....	....	....	....

WHL East Second All-Star Team (1997)

Traded to **NY Islanders** by **Chicago** for Jean-Pierre Dumont and Chicago's 5th round choice (later traded to Philadelphia - Philadelphia selected Francis Belanger) in 1998 Entry Draft, June 1, 1998.

NAMESTNIKOV, John (nah-MEST-nih-kov, yev-GAIN-ee) NYR

Defense. Shoots right. 5'11", 190 lbs. Born, Arzamis-Ig, USSR, October 9, 1971. Vancouver's 5th choice, 117th overall, in 1991 Entry Draft.

Season	Club	League	GP	G	A	Pts	PIM	PP	SH	GW	S	%	+/-	TF	F%	H	SB	Min	GP	G	A	Pts	PIM	PP	SH	GW
1988-89	Torpedo Gorky	USSR	2	0	0	0	2	....	....	....	....	....	....	....	....	....	....	....	....	....	....	....	....	....	....	....
1989-90	Torpedo Gorky	USSR	23	0	0	0	25	....	....	....	....	....	....	....	....	....	....	....	....	....	....	....	....	....	....	....
1990-91	Torpedo Nizhny	USSR	42	1	2	3	49	....	....	....	....	....	....	....	....	....	....	....	....	....	....	....	....	....	....	....
1991-92	CSKA Moscow	CIS	42	1	1	2	47	....	....	....	....	....	....	....	....	....	....	....	....	....	....	....	....	....	....	....
1992-93	CSKA Moscow	CIS	42	5	5	10	68	....	....	....	....	....	....	....	....	....	....	....	....	....	....	....	....	....	....	....
1993-94	**Vancouver**	**NHL**	**17**	**0**	**5**	**5**	**10**	**0**	**0**	**0**	**11**	**0.0**	**–2**	....	....	....	....	....	....	....	....	....	....	....	....	....
	Hamilton	AHL	59	7	27	34	97	....	....	....	....	....	....	....	....	....	....	....	4	0	2	2	19	....	....	....
1994-95	Syracuse	AHL	59	11	22	33	59	....	....	....	....	....	....	....	....	....	....	....	....	....	....	....	....	....	....	....
	Vancouver	**NHL**	**16**	**0**	**3**	**3**	**4**	**0**	**0**	**0**	**18**	**0.0**	**2**	....	....	....	....	....	**1**	**0**	**0**	**0**	**2**	**0**	**0**	**0**
1995-96	Syracuse	AHL	59	13	34	47	85	....	....	....	....	....	....	....	....	....	....	....	15	1	8	9	16	....	....	....
	Vancouver	**NHL**	....	....	....	....	....	....	....	....	....	....	....	....	....	....	....	....	**1**	**0**	**0**	**0**	**0**	**0**	**0**	**0**
1996-97	**Vancouver**	**NHL**	**2**	**0**	**0**	**0**	**4**	**0**	**0**	**0**	**1**	**0.0**	**–1**	....	....	....	....	....	....	....	....	....	....	....	....	....
	Syracuse	AHL	55	9	37	46	73	....	....	....	....	....	....	....	....	....	....	....	3	2	0	2	0	....	....	....
1997-98	**NY Islanders**	**NHL**	**6**	**0**	**1**	**1**	**4**	**0**	**0**	**0**	**2**	**0.0**	**–1**	....	....	....	....	....	....	....	....	....	....	....	....	....
	Utah	IHL	62	6	19	25	48	....	....	....	....	....	....	....	....	....	....	....	4	1	0	1	2	....	....	....
1998-99	Lowell	AHL	42	12	14	26	42	....	....	....	....	....	....	....	....	....	....	....	....	....	....	....	....	....	....	....
	NHL Totals		**41**	**0**	**9**	**9**	**22**	**0**	**0**	**0**	**32**	**0.0**		....	....	....	....	....	**2**	**0**	**0**	**0**	**2**	**0**	**0**	**0**

Signed as a free agent by **NY Islanders**, July 21, 1997. Signed as a free agent by **NY Rangers**, August 9, 1999.

NASH, Tyson ST.L.

Left wing. Shoots left. 6', 185 lbs. Born, Edmonton, Alta., March 11, 1975. Vancouver's 10th choice, 247th overall, in 1994 Entry Draft.

Season	Club	League	GP	G	A	Pts	PIM	PP	SH	GW	S	%	+/-	TF	F%	H	SB	Min	GP	G	A	Pts	PIM	PP	SH	GW
1990-91	Sherwood Park	AAHA	40	17	28	43	63	....	....	....	....	....	....	....	....	....	....	....	....	....	....	....	....	....	....	....
1991-92	Kamloops	WHL	33	1	6	7	62	....	....	....	....	....	....	....	....	....	....	....	4	0	0	0	0	....	....	....
1992-93	Kamloops	WHL	61	10	16	26	78	....	....	....	....	....	....	....	....	....	....	....	13	3	2	5	32	....	....	....
1993-94	Kamloops	WHL	65	20	36	56	135	....	....	....	....	....	....	....	....	....	....	....	16	3	4	7	12	....	....	....
1994-95	Kamloops	WHL	63	34	41	75	70	....	....	....	....	....	....	....	....	....	....	....	21	10	7	17	30	....	....	....
1995-96	Syracuse	AHL	50	4	7	11	58	....	....	....	....	....	....	....	....	....	....	....	4	0	0	0	11	....	....	....
	Raleigh	ECHL	6	1	1	2	8	....	....	....	....	....	....	....	....	....	....	....	....	....	....	....	....	....	....	....
1996-97	Syracuse	AHL	77	17	17	34	105	....	....	....	....	....	....	....	....	....	....	....	3	0	2	2	0	....	....	....
1997-98	Syracuse	AHL	74	20	20	40	184	....	....	....	....	....	....	....	....	....	....	....	5	0	2	2	28	....	....	....

Season	Club	League	GP	G	A	Pts	PIM	PP	SH	GW	S	%	+/-	TF	F%	H	SB	Min	Playoffs GP	G	A	Pts	PIM	PP	SH	GW
1998-99	**St. Louis**	**NHL**	**2**	**0**	**0**	**0**	**5**	**0**	**0**	**0**	**1**	**0.0**	**–1**	**0**	**0.0**	**8**	**0**	**7:44**	**1**	**0**	**0**	**0**	**2**	**0**	**0**	**0**
	Worcester	AHL	55	14	22	36	143	....	....	....	....	....	....	....	....	....	....	....	4	4	1	5	27	....	....	....
	NHL Totals		**2**	**0**	**0**	**0**	**5**	**0**	**0**	**0**	**1**	**0.0**		**0**	**0.0**	**8**	**0**	**7:44**	**1**	**0**	**0**	**0**	**2**	**0**	**0**	**0**

Signed as a free agent by **St. Louis**, July 14, 1998.

NASLUND, Markus

(NAZ-luhnd) **VAN.**

Right wing. Shoots left. 5'11", 195 lbs. Born, Ornskoldsvik, Sweden, July 30, 1973. Pittsburgh's 1st choice, 16th overall, in 1991 Entry Draft.

Season	Club	League	GP	G	A	Pts	PIM	PP	SH	GW	S	%	+/-	TF	F%	H	SB	Min	Playoffs GP	G	A	Pts	PIM	PP	SH	GW
1989-90	MoDo Hockey	Swede-Jr.	33	43	35	78	20	....	....	....	....	....	....	....	....	....	....	....	....	....	....	....	....	....	....	....
1990-91	MoDo Hockey	Sweden	32	10	9	19	14	....	....	....	....	....	....	....	....	....	....	....	....	....	....	....	....	....	....	....
1991-92	MoDo Hockey	Sweden	39	22	18	40	54	....	....	....	....	....	....	....	....	....	....	....	....	....	....	....	....	....	....	....
1992-93	MoDo Hockey	Swede-Jr.	2	4	1	5	2	....	....	....	....	....	....	....	....	....	....	....	....	....	....	....	....	....	....	....
	MoDo Hockey	Sweden	39	22	17	39	67	....	....	....	....	....	....	....	....	....	....	....	3	3	2	5	0	....	....	....
1993-94	**Pittsburgh**	**NHL**	**71**	**4**	**7**	**11**	**27**	**1**	**0**	**0**	**80**	**5.0**	**–3**	....	....	....	....	....	....	....	....	....	....	....	....	....
	Cleveland	IHL	5	1	6	7	4	....	....	....	....	....	....	....	....	....	....	....	....	....	....	....	....	....	....	....
1994-95	**Pittsburgh**	**NHL**	**14**	**2**	**2**	**4**	**2**	**0**	**0**	**0**	**13**	**15.4**	**0**	....	....	....	....	....	....	....	....	....	....	....	....	....
	Cleveland	IHL	7	3	4	7	6	....	....	....	....	....	....	....	....	....	....	....	4	1	3	4	8	....	....	....
1995-96	**Pittsburgh**	**NHL**	**66**	**19**	**33**	**52**	**36**	**3**	**0**	**4**	**125**	**15.2**	**17**	....	....	....	....	....	....	....	....	....	....	....	....	....
	Vancouver	**NHL**	**10**	**3**	**0**	**3**	**6**	**1**	**0**	**1**	**19**	**15.8**	**3**	....	....	....	....	....	**6**	**1**	**2**	**3**	**8**	**1**	**0**	**0**
1996-97	**Vancouver**	**NHL**	**78**	**21**	**20**	**41**	**30**	**4**	**0**	**4**	**120**	**17.5**	**–15**	....	....	....	....	....	....	....	....	....	....	....	....	....
1997-98	**Vancouver**	**NHL**	**76**	**14**	**20**	**34**	**56**	**2**	**1**	**0**	**106**	**13.2**	**5**	....	....	....	....	....	....	....	....	....	....	....	....	....
1998-99	**Vancouver**	**NHL**	**80**	**36**	**30**	**66**	**74**	**15**	**2**	**3**	**205**	**17.6**	**–13**	**14**	**57.1**	**40**	**20**	**19:57**	....	....	....	....	....	....	....	....
	NHL Totals		**395**	**99**	**112**	**211**	**231**	**26**	**3**	**12**	**668**	**14.8**		**14**	**57.1**	**40**	**20**	**19:57**	**6**	**1**	**2**	**3**	**8**	**1**	**0**	**0**

Played in NHL All-Star Game (1999)

Traded to **Vancouver** by **Pittsburgh** for Alek Stojanov, March 20, 1996.

NASREDDINE, Alain

(NAS-ruh-deen, AL-ay) **MTL.**

Defense. Shoots left. 6'1", 201 lbs. Born, Montreal, Que., July 10, 1975. Florida's 8th choice, 135th overall, in 1993 Entry Draft.

Season	Club	League	GP	G	A	Pts	PIM	PP	SH	GW	S	%	+/-	TF	F%	H	SB	Min	Playoffs GP	G	A	Pts	PIM	PP	SH	GW
1990-91	Montreal AAA	QAAA	35	10	25	35	50	....	....	....	....	....	....	....	....	....	....	....	....	....	....	....	....	....	....	....
1991-92	Drummondville	QMJHL	61	1	9	10	78	....	....	....	....	....	....	....	....	....	....	....	4	0	0	0	17	....	....	....
1992-93	Drummondville	QMJHL	64	0	14	14	137	....	....	....	....	....	....	....	....	....	....	....	10	0	1	1	36	....	....	....
1993-94	Chicoutimi	QMJHL	60	3	24	27	218	....	....	....	....	....	....	....	....	....	....	....	26	2	10	12	118	....	....	....
1994-95	Chicoutimi	QMJHL	67	8	31	39	342	....	....	....	....	....	....	....	....	....	....	....	13	3	5	8	40	....	....	....
1995-96	Carolina	AHL	63	0	5	5	245	....	....	....	....	....	....	....	....	....	....	....	....	....	....	....	....	....	....	....
1996-97	Carolina	AHL	26	0	4	4	109	....	....	....	....	....	....	....	....	....	....	....	....	....	....	....	....	....	....	....
	Indianapolis	IHL	49	0	2	2	248	....	....	....	....	....	....	....	....	....	....	....	4	1	1	2	27	....	....	....
1997-98	Indianapolis	IHL	75	1	12	13	258	....	....	....	....	....	....	....	....	....	....	....	5	0	2	2	12	....	....	....
1998-99	**Chicago**	**NHL**	**7**	**0**	**0**	**0**	**19**	**0**	**0**	**0**	**2**	**0.0**	**–2**	**0**	**0.0**	**5**	**1**	**12:11**	....	....	....	....	....	....	....	....
	Portland	AHL	7	0	1	1	36	....	....	....	....	....	....	....	....	....	....	....	....	....	....	....	....	....	....	....
	Montreal	**NHL**	**8**	**0**	**0**	**0**	**33**	**0**	**0**	**0**	**1**	**0.0**	**1**	**0**	**0.0**	**7**	**1**	**8:12**	....	....	....	....	....	....	....	....
	Fredericton	AHL	38	0	10	10	108	....	....	....	....	....	....	....	....	....	....	....	15	0	3	3	39	....	....	....
	NHL Totals		**15**	**0**	**0**	**0**	**52**	**0**	**0**	**0**	**3**	**0.0**		**0**	**0.0**	**12**	**2**	**10:04**	....	....	....	....	....	....	....	....

QMJHL Second All-Star Team (1995)

Traded to **Chicago** by **Florida** with a conditional choice in 1999 Entry Draft for Ivan Droppa, December 18, 1996. Traded to **Montreal** by **Chicago** with Jeff Hackett, Eric Weinrich and Tampa Bay's 4th round choice (previously acquired, Montreal selected Chris Dyment) in 1999 Entry Draft for Jocelyn Thibault, Dave Manson and Brad Brown, November 16, 1998.

NAZAROV, Andrei

(nah-ZAH-rohv) **CGY.**

Left wing. Shoots right. 6'5", 230 lbs. Born, Chelyabinsk, USSR, May 22, 1974. San Jose's 2nd choice, 10th overall, in 1992 Entry Draft.

Season	Club	League	GP	G	A	Pts	PIM	PP	SH	GW	S	%	+/-	TF	F%	H	SB	Min	Playoffs GP	G	A	Pts	PIM	PP	SH	GW
1991-92	Moscow D'amo	CIS	2	1	0	1	2	....	....	....	....	....	....	....	....	....	....	....	....	....	....	....	....	....	....	....
1992-93	Moscow D'amo	CIS	42	8	2	10	79	....	....	....	....	....	....	....	....	....	....	....	10	1	1	2	8	....	....	....
1993-94	Moscow D'amo	CIS	6	2	2	4	0	....	....	....	....	....	....	....	....	....	....	....	....	....	....	....	....	....	....	....
	San Jose	**NHL**	**1**	**0**	**0**	**0**	**0**	**0**	**0**	**0**	**0**	**0.0**	**0**	....	....	....	....	....	....	....	....	....	....	....	....	....
	Kansas City	IHL	71	15	18	33	64	....	....	....	....	....	....	....	....	....	....	....	....	....	....	....	....	....	....	....
1994-95	Kansas City	IHL	43	15	10	25	55	....	....	....	....	....	....	....	....	....	....	....	....	....	....	....	....	....	....	....
	San Jose	**NHL**	**26**	**3**	**5**	**8**	**94**	**0**	**0**	**0**	**19**	**15.8**	**–1**	....	....	....	....	....	**6**	**0**	**0**	**0**	**9**	**0**	**0**	**0**
1995-96	**San Jose**	**NHL**	**42**	**7**	**7**	**14**	**62**	**2**	**0**	**1**	**55**	**12.7**	**–15**	....	....	....	....	....	....	....	....	....	....	....	....	....
	Kansas City	IHL	27	4	6	10	118	....	....	....	....	....	....	....	....	....	....	....	2	0	0	0	2	....	....	....
1996-97	**San Jose**	**NHL**	**60**	**12**	**15**	**27**	**222**	**1**	**0**	**1**	**116**	**10.3**	**–4**	....	....	....	....	....	....	....	....	....	....	....	....	....
	Kentucky	AHL	3	1	2	3	4	....	....	....	....	....	....	....	....	....	....	....	....	....	....	....	....	....	....	....
1997-98	**San Jose**	**NHL**	**40**	**1**	**1**	**2**	**112**	**0**	**0**	**0**	**31**	**3.2**	**–4**	....	....	....	....	....	....	....	....	....	....	....	....	....
	Tampa Bay	**NHL**	**14**	**1**	**1**	**2**	**58**	**0**	**0**	**0**	**19**	**5.3**	**–9**	....	....	....	....	....	....	....	....	....	....	....	....	....
1998-99	**Tampa Bay**	**NHL**	**26**	**2**	**0**	**2**	**43**	**0**	**0**	**0**	**18**	**11.1**	**–5**	**4**	**50.0**	**26**	**2**	**8:13**	....	....	....	....	....	....	....	....
	Calgary	**NHL**	**36**	**5**	**9**	**14**	**30**	**0**	**0**	**2**	**53**	**9.4**	**1**	**0**	**0.0**	**38**	**10**	**14:31**	....	....	....	....	....	....	....	....
	NHL Totals		**245**	**31**	**38**	**69**	**621**	**3**	**0**	**4**	**311**	**10.0**		**4**	**50.0**	**64**	**12**	**11:52**	**6**	**0**	**0**	**0**	**9**	**0**	**0**	**0**

Traded to **Tampa Bay** by **San Jose** with Florida's 1st round choice (previously acquired, Tampa Bay selected Vincent Lecavalier) for Bryan Marchment, David Shaw and Tampa Bay's 1st round choice (later traded to Nashville — Nashville selected David Legwand) in 1998 Entry Draft, March 24, 1998. Traded to **Calgary** by **Tampa Bay** for Michael Nylander, January 19, 1999.

NDUR, Rumun

(nih-DOOR, ROO-muhn) **NYR**

Defense. Shoots left. 6'2", 200 lbs. Born, Zaria, Nigeria, July 7, 1975. Buffalo's 3rd choice, 69th overall, in 1994 Entry Draft.

Season	Club	League	GP	G	A	Pts	PIM	PP	SH	GW	S	%	+/-	TF	F%	H	SB	Min	Playoffs GP	G	A	Pts	PIM	PP	SH	GW
1991-92	Sarnia	OJHL-B	30	2	5	7	46	....	....	....	....	....	....	....	....	....	....	....	....	....	....	....	....	....	....	....
	Clearwater	OJHL-C	4	0	4	4	4	....	....	....	....	....	....	....	....	....	....	....	....	....	....	....	....	....	....	....
1992-93	Guelph	OJHL-B	24	8	7	15	202	....	....	....	....	....	....	....	....	....	....	....	....	....	....	....	....	....	....	....
	Guelph	OHL	22	1	3	4	30	....	....	....	....	....	....	....	....	....	....	....	4	0	1	1	4	....	....	....
1993-94	Guelph	OHL	61	6	33	39	176	....	....	....	....	....	....	....	....	....	....	....	9	4	1	5	24	....	....	....
1994-95	Guelph	OHL	63	10	21	31	187	....	....	....	....	....	....	....	....	....	....	....	14	0	4	4	28	....	....	....
1995-96	Rochester	AHL	73	2	12	14	306	....	....	....	....	....	....	....	....	....	....	....	17	1	2	3	33	....	....	....
1996-97	**Buffalo**	**NHL**	**2**	**0**	**0**	**0**	**2**	**0**	**0**	**0**	**0**	**0.0**	**1**	....	....	....	....	....	....	....	....	....	....	....	....	....
	Rochester	AHL	68	5	11	16	282	....	....	....	....	....	....	....	....	....	....	....	10	3	1	4	21	....	....	....
1997-98	**Buffalo**	**NHL**	**1**	**0**	**0**	**0**	**2**	**0**	**0**	**0**	**0**	**0.0**	**–1**	....	....	....	....	....	....	....	....	....	....	....	....	....
	Rochester	AHL	50	1	12	13	207	....	....	....	....	....	....	....	....	....	....	....	4	0	2	2	16	....	....	....
1998-99	**Buffalo**	**NHL**	**8**	**0**	**0**	**0**	**16**	**0**	**0**	**0**	**1**	**0.0**	**1**	**0**	**0.0**	**11**	**2**	**10:58**	....	....	....	....	....	....	....	....
	NY Rangers	**NHL**	**31**	**1**	**3**	**4**	**46**	**0**	**0**	**0**	**21**	**4.8**	**–2**	**0**	**0.0**	**58**	**11**	**11:58**	....	....	....	....	....	....	....	....
	Hartford	AHL	6	0	1	1	4	....	....	....	....	....	....	....	....	....	....	....	....	....	....	....	....	....	....	....
	NHL Totals		**42**	**1**	**3**	**4**	**66**	**0**	**0**	**0**	**22**	**4.5**		**0**	**0.0**	**69**	**13**	**11:46**	....	....	....	....	....	....	....	....

Claimed on waivers by **NY Rangers** from **Buffalo**, December 18, 1998.

NECKAR, Stanislav

(NEHTS-kahrzh) **PHX.**

Defense. Shoots left. 6'1", 212 lbs. Born, Ceske Budejovice, Czech., December 22, 1975. Ottawa's 2nd choice, 29th overall, in 1994 Entry Draft.

Season	Club	League	GP	G	A	Pts	PIM	PP	SH	GW	S	%	+/-	TF	F%	H	SB	Min	Playoffs GP	G	A	Pts	PIM	PP	SH	GW
1991-92	MC Budejovice	Czech-Jr.	18	1	3	4	....	....	....	....	....	....	....	....	....	....	....	....	....	....	....	....	....	....	....	....
1992-93	HC Budejovice	Czech.	42	2	9	11	12	....	....	....	....	....	....	....	....	....	....	....	....	....	....	....	....	....	....	....
1993-94	HC Budejovice	Cze-Rep	12	3	2	5	2	....	....	....	....	....	....	....	....	....	....	....	3	0	0	0	....	....	....	....
1994-95	Detroit	IHL	15	2	2	4	15	....	....	....	....	....	....	....	....	....	....	....	....	....	....	....	....	....	....	....
	Ottawa	**NHL**	**48**	**1**	**3**	**4**	**37**	**0**	**0**	**0**	**34**	**2.9**	**–20**	....	....	....	....	....	....	....	....	....	....	....	....	....
1995-96	**Ottawa**	**NHL**	**82**	**3**	**9**	**12**	**54**	**1**	**0**	**0**	**57**	**5.3**	**–16**	....	....	....	....	....	....	....	....	....	....	....	....	....
1996-97	**Ottawa**	**NHL**	**5**	**0**	**0**	**0**	**2**	**0**	**0**	**0**	**3**	**0.0**	**2**	....	....	....	....	....	....	....	....	....	....	....	....	....
1997-98	**Ottawa**	**NHL**	**60**	**2**	**2**	**4**	**31**	**0**	**0**	**0**	**43**	**4.7**	**–14**	....	....	....	....	....	**9**	**0**	**0**	**0**	**2**	**0**	**0**	**0**

Season	Club	League	GP	G	A	Pts	PIM	PP	SH	GW	S	%	+/-	TF	F%	H	SB	Min	GP	G	A	Pts	PIM	PP	SH	GW
			Regular Season																Playoffs							
1998-99	**Ottawa**	**NHL**	**3**	**0**	**2**	**2**	**0**	**0**	**0**	**0**	**2**	**0.0**	**–1**	**0**	**0.0**	**6**	**3**	**15:53**								
	NY Rangers	**NHL**	**18**	**0**	**0**	**0**	**8**	**0**	**0**	**0**	**8**	**0.0**	**–1**	**0**	**0.0**	**30**	**27**	**13:46**								
	Phoenix	**NHL**	**11**	**0**	**1**	**1**	**10**	**0**	**0**	**0**	**6**	**0.0**	**3**	**0**	**0.0**	**26**	**10**	**15:08**	**6**	**0**	**1**	**1**	**4**	**0**	**0**	**0**
	NHL Totals		**227**	**6**	**17**	**23**	**142**	**1**	**0**	**0**	**153**	**3.9**		**0**	**0.0**	**62**	**40**	**14:26**	**15**	**0**	**1**	**1**	**6**	**0**	**0**	**0**

Traded to **NY Rangers** by **Ottawa** for Bill Berg and NY Rangers' 2nd round choice (later traded to Anaheim, Anaheim selected Jordan Leopold) in 1999 Entry Draft, November 27, 1998. Traded to **Phoenix** by **NY Rangers** for Jason Doig and Phoenix's 6th round choice (Jay Dardis) in 1999 Entry Draft, March 23, 1999.

NEDVED, Petr

(NEHD-VEHD) **NYR**

Center. Shoots left. 6'3", 195 lbs. Born, Liberec, Czech., December 9, 1971. Vancouver's 1st choice, 2nd overall, in 1990 Entry Draft.

Season	Club	League	GP	G	A	Pts	PIM	PP	SH	GW	S	%	+/-	TF	F%	H	SB	Min	GP	G	A	Pts	PIM	PP	SH	GW
1988-89	HC Litvinov	Czech-Jr.	20	32	19	51	12																			
1989-90	Seattle	WHL	71	65	80	145	80												11	4	9	13	2			
1990-91	**Vancouver**	**NHL**	**61**	**10**	**6**	**16**	**20**	**1**	**0**	**0**	**97**	**10.3**	**–21**						**6**	**0**	**1**	**1**	**0**	**0**	**0**	**0**
1991-92	**Vancouver**	**NHL**	**77**	**15**	**22**	**37**	**36**	**5**	**0**	**1**	**99**	**15.2**	**–3**						**10**	**1**	**4**	**5**	**16**	**0**	**0**	**0**
1992-93	**Vancouver**	**NHL**	**84**	**38**	**33**	**71**	**96**	**2**	**1**	**3**	**149**	**25.5**	**20**						**12**	**2**	**3**	**5**	**2**	**0**	**0**	**0**
1993-94	Canada	Nat-Team	17	19	12	31	16																			
	Canada	Olympics	8	5	1	6	6																			
	St. Louis	**NHL**	**19**	**6**	**14**	**20**	**8**	**2**	**0**	**0**	**63**	**9.5**	**2**						**4**	**0**	**1**	**1**	**4**	**0**	**0**	**0**
1994-95	**NY Rangers**	**NHL**	**46**	**11**	**12**	**23**	**26**	**1**	**0**	**3**	**123**	**8.9**	**–1**						**10**	**3**	**2**	**5**	**6**	**2**	**0**	**0**
1995-96	**Pittsburgh**	**NHL**	**80**	**45**	**54**	**99**	**68**	**8**	**1**	**5**	**204**	**22.1**	**37**						**18**	**10**	**10**	**20**	**16**	**4**	**0**	**2**
1996-97	**Pittsburgh**	**NHL**	**74**	**33**	**38**	**71**	**66**	**12**	**3**	**4**	**189**	**17.5**	**–2**						**5**	**1**	**2**	**3**	**12**	**0**	**1**	**0**
1997-98	Sparta Praha	Cze-Rep	5	2	3	5	8												6	0	2	2	52			
	Las Vegas	IHL	3	3	3	6	4																			
1998-99	Las Vegas	IHL	13	8	10	18	32																			
	NY Rangers	**NHL**	**56**	**20**	**27**	**47**	**50**	**9**	**1**	**3**	**153**	**13.1**	**–6**	**1069**	**52.5**	**58**	**34**	**20:31**								
	NHL Totals		**497**	**178**	**206**	**384**	**370**	**40**	**6**	**19**	**1077**	**16.5**		**1069**	**52.5**	**58**	**34**	**20:31**	**65**	**17**	**23**	**40**	**56**	**6**	**1**	**2**

Canadian Major Junior Rookie of the Year (1990)

Signed as a free agent by **St. Louis**, March 5, 1994. Traded to **NY Rangers** by **St. Louis** for Esa Tikkanen and Doug Lidster, July 24, 1994. Traded to **Pittsburgh** by **NY Rangers** with Sergei Zubov for Luc Robitaille and Ulf Samuelsson, August 31, 1995. Traded to **NY Rangers** by **Pittsburgh** with Chris Tamer and Sean Pronger for Alexei Kovalev and Harry York, November 25, 1998.

NEDVED, Zdenek

(NEHD-VEHD)

Right wing. Shoots left. 6', 180 lbs. Born, Lany, Czech., March 3, 1975. Toronto's 3rd choice, 123rd overall, in 1993 Entry Draft.

Season	Club	League	GP	G	A	Pts	PIM	PP	SH	GW	S	%	+/-	TF	F%	H	SB	Min	GP	G	A	Pts	PIM	PP	SH	GW
1991-92	Poldi Kladno	Czech.	19	15	12	27	22																			
1992-93	Sudbury	OHL	18	3	9	12	6																			
1993-94	Sudbury	OHL	60	50	50	100	42												10	7	8	15	10			
1994-95	Sudbury	OHL	59	47	51	98	36												18	12	16	28	16			
	Toronto	**NHL**	**1**	**0**	**0**	**0**	**2**	**0**	**0**	**0**	**0**	**0.0**	**0**													
1995-96	**Toronto**	**NHL**	**7**	**1**	**1**	**2**	**6**	**0**	**0**	**0**	**7**	**14.3**	**–1**													
	St. John's	AHL	41	13	14	27	22												4	2	0	2	0			
1996-97	**Toronto**	**NHL**	**23**	**3**	**5**	**8**	**6**	**1**	**0**	**0**	**22**	**13.6**	**4**													
	St. John's	AHL	51	9	25	34	34												7	2	2	4	6			
1997-98	Long Beach	IHL	19	3	8	11	18																			
	St. John's	AHL	45	7	8	15	24												3	1	0	1	2			
1998-99	Sparta Praha	Cze-Rep	10	0	2	2	8																			
	Sparta Praha	EuroHL	3	0	0	0	0																			
	Lukko Rauma	Finland	30	4	7	11	22																			
	NHL Totals		**31**	**4**	**6**	**10**	**14**	**1**	**0**	**0**	**29**	**13.8**														

NELSON, Jeff

WSH.

Center. Shoots left. 6', 190 lbs. Born, Prince Albert, Sask., December 10, 1972. Washington's 4th choice, 36th overall, in 1991 Entry Draft.

Season	Club	League	GP	G	A	Pts	PIM	PP	SH	GW	S	%	+/-	TF	F%	H	SB	Min	GP	G	A	Pts	PIM	PP	SH	GW
1987-88	Prince Albert AA	AAHA	31	24	32	56	32																			
1988-89	Prince Albert	WHL	71	30	57	87	74												4	0	3	3	4			
1989-90	Prince Albert	WHL	72	28	69	97	79												14	2	11	13	10			
1990-91	Prince Albert	WHL	72	46	74	120	58												3	1	1	2	4			
1991-92	Prince Albert	WHL	64	48	65	113	84												9	7	14	21	18			
1992-93	Baltimore	AHL	72	14	38	52	12												7	1	3	4	2			
1993-94	Portland	AHL	80	34	73	107	92												17	10	5	15	20			
1994-95	Portland	AHL	64	33	50	83	57												7	1	4	5	8			
	Washington	**NHL**	**10**	**1**	**0**	**1**	**2**	**0**	**0**	**0**	**4**	**25.0**	**–2**													
1995-96	**Washington**	**NHL**	**33**	**0**	**7**	**7**	**16**	**0**	**0**	**0**	**21**	**0.0**	**3**						**3**	**0**	**0**	**0**	**4**	**0**	**0**	**0**
	Portland	AHL	39	15	32	47	62																			
1996-97	Grand Rapids	IHL	82	34	55	89	85												5	0	4	4	4			
1997-98	Milwaukee	IHL	52	20	34	54	30												10	2	7	9	15			
1998-99	**Nashville**	**NHL**	**9**	**2**	**1**	**3**	**2**	**0**	**0**	**0**	**8**	**25.0**	**–1**	**138**	**55.1**	**4**	**8**	**16:09**								
	Milwaukee	IHL	70	20	31	51	66												2	0	0	0	0			
	NHL Totals		**52**	**3**	**8**	**11**	**20**	**0**	**0**	**0**	**33**	**9.1**		**138**	**55.1**	**4**	**8**	**16:09**	**3**	**0**	**0**	**0**	**4**	**0**	**0**	**0**

Canadian Major Junior Scholastic Player of the Year (1989, 1990) • WHL East Second All-Star Team (1991, 1992)

Traded to **Nashville** by **Washington** for future considerations, August 19, 1998. Traded to **Washington** by **Nashville** for cash, June 21, 1999.

NEMCHINOV, Sergei

(nehm-CHEE-nahf, SAIR-gay) **N.J.**

Center. Shoots left. 6', 200 lbs. Born, Moscow, USSR, January 14, 1964. NY Rangers' 14th choice, 244th overall, in 1990 Entry Draft.

Season	Club	League	GP	G	A	Pts	PIM	PP	SH	GW	S	%	+/-	TF	F%	H	SB	Min	GP	G	A	Pts	PIM	PP	SH	GW
1981-82	Soviet Wings	USSR	15	1	0	1	0																			
1982-83	CSKA Moscow	USSR	11	0	0	0	2																			
1983-84	CSKA Moscow	USSR	20	6	5	11	4																			
1984-85	CSKA Moscow	USSR	31	2	4	6	4																			
1985-86	Soviet Wings	USSR	39	7	12	19	28																			
1986-87	Soviet Wings	USSR	40	13	9	22	24																			
1987-88	Soviet Wings	USSR	48	17	11	28	26																			
1988-89	Soviet Wings	USSR	43	15	14	29	28																			
1989-90	Soviet Wings	USSR	48	17	16	33	34																			
1990-91	Soviet Wings	USSR	46	21	24	45	30																			
1991-92	**NY Rangers**	**NHL**	**73**	**30**	**28**	**58**	**15**	**2**	**0**	**5**	**124**	**24.2**	**19**						**13**	**1**	**4**	**5**	**8**	**0**	**0**	**0**
1992-93	**NY Rangers**	**NHL**	**81**	**23**	**31**	**54**	**34**	**0**	**1**	**3**	**144**	**16.0**	**15**													
1993-94♦	**NY Rangers**	**NHL**	**76**	**22**	**27**	**49**	**36**	**4**	**0**	**6**	**144**	**15.3**	**13**						**23**	**2**	**5**	**7**	**6**	**0**	**0**	**0**
1994-95	**NY Rangers**	**NHL**	**47**	**7**	**6**	**13**	**16**	**0**	**0**	**3**	**67**	**10.4**	**–6**						**10**	**4**	**5**	**9**	**2**	**0**	**0**	**1**
1995-96	**NY Rangers**	**NHL**	**78**	**17**	**15**	**32**	**38**	**0**	**0**	**2**	**118**	**14.4**	**9**						**6**	**0**	**1**	**1**	**2**	**0**	**0**	**0**
1996-97	**NY Rangers**	**NHL**	**63**	**6**	**13**	**19**	**12**	**1**	**0**	**1**	**90**	**6.7**	**5**													
	Vancouver	**NHL**	**6**	**2**	**3**	**5**	**4**	**0**	**0**	**1**	**7**	**28.6**	**4**													
1997-98	**NY Islanders**	**NHL**	**74**	**10**	**19**	**29**	**24**	**2**	**1**	**1**	**94**	**10.6**	**3**													
	Russia	Olympics	6	1	0	1	0																			
1998-99	**NY Islanders**	**NHL**	**67**	**8**	**8**	**16**	**22**	**1**	**0**	**0**	**61**	**13.1**	**–17**	**606**	**42.4**	**52**	**44**	**14:21**								
	New Jersey	**NHL**	**10**	**4**	**0**	**4**	**6**	**1**	**0**	**1**	**13**	**30.8**	**4**	**38**	**52.6**	**13**	**0**	**15:36**	**4**	**0**	**0**	**0**	**0**	**0**	**0**	**0**
	NHL Totals		**575**	**129**	**150**	**279**	**207**	**11**	**2**	**23**	**862**	**15.0**		**644**	**43.0**	**65**	**44**	**14:31**	**56**	**7**	**15**	**22**	**18**	**0**	**0**	**1**

Traded to **Vancouver** by **NY Rangers** with Brian Noonan for Esa Tikkanen and Russ Courtnall, March 8, 1997. Signed as a free agent by **NY Islanders**, July 10, 1997. Traded to **New Jersey** by **NY Islanders** for New Jersey's 4th round choice (later traded to Los Angeles - Los Angeles selected Daniel Johansson) in 1999 Entry Draft, March 22, 1999.

NEMECEK, Jan
(NEHM-eh-chehk, YAHN)   **L.A.**

Defense. Shoots right. 6'1", 215 lbs. Born, Pisek, Czech., February 14, 1976. Los Angeles' 7th choice, 215th overall, in 1994 Entry Draft.

Season	Club	League	GP	G	A	Pts	PIM	PP	SH	GW	S	%	+/-	TF	F%	H	SB	Min	GP	G	A	Pts	PIM	PP	SH	GW
1992-93	HC Budejovice	Czech.	15	0	0	0	....																			
1993-94	HC Budejovice	Cze-Rep	16	0	1	1	16																			
1994-95	Hull	QMJHL	49	10	16	26	48												21	5	9	14	10			
1995-96	Hull	QMJHL	57	17	49	66	58												17	2	13	15	10			
1996-97	Mississippi	ECHL	20	3	9	12	16												3	0	0	0	4			
	Phoenix	IHL	24	1	1	2	2																			
1997-98	Fredericton	AHL	65	7	24	31	43												2	0	0	0	0			
1998-99	**Los Angeles**	**NHL**	6	1	0	1	4	0	0	1	8	12.5	−1	0	0.0	2	4	16:42								
	Long Beach	IHL	66	5	16	21	42																			
	NHL Totals		6	1	0	1	4	0	0	1	8	12.5		0	0.0	2	4	16:42								

QMJHL Second All-Star Team (1996)

NEMIROVSKY, David
(neh-mih-ROHV-skee)   **TOR.**

Right wing. Shoots right. 6'1", 192 lbs. Born, Toronto, Ont., August 1, 1976. Florida's 5th choice, 84th overall, in 1994 Entry Draft.

Season	Club	League	GP	G	A	Pts	PIM	PP	SH	GW	S	%	+/-	TF	F%	H	SB	Min	GP	G	A	Pts	PIM	PP	SH	GW
1991-92	Pickering	OJHL-B	37	9	23	32	7																			
1992-93	North York	OJHL	40	19	23	42	27																			
1993-94	Ottawa	OHL	64	21	31	52	18												17	10	10	20	2			
1994-95	Ottawa	OHL	59	27	29	56	25																			
1995-96	Sarnia	OHL	26	18	27	45	14												10	8	8	16	6			
	Florida	**NHL**	9	0	2	2	2	0	0	0	6	0.0	−1													
	Carolina	AHL	5	1	2	3	0																			
1996-97	**Florida**	**NHL**	39	7	7	14	32	1	0	0	53	13.2	1						3	1	0	1	0	0	0	0
	Carolina	AHL	34	21	21	42	18																			
1997-98	**Florida**	**NHL**	41	9	12	21	8	2	0	1	62	14.5	−3						1	1	0	1	0			
	New Haven	AHL	29	10	15	25	10																			
1998-99	**Florida**	**NHL**	2	0	1	1	0	0	0	0	2	0.0	1	0	0.0	0	0	8:58								
	Fort Wayne	IHL	44	22	13	35	24																			
	St. John's	AHL	22	3	9	12	18												5	4	1	5	0			
	NHL Totals		91	16	22	38	42	3	0	1	123	13.0		0	0.0	0	0	8:58	3	1	0	1	0	0	0	0

Traded to **Toronto** by **Florida** for Jeff Ware, February 17, 1999.

NICHOL, Scott
(NIH-KOHL)   **BUF.**

Center. Shoots right. 5'8", 160 lbs. Born, Edmonton, Alta., December 31, 1974. Buffalo's 9th choice, 272nd overall, in 1993 Entry Draft.

Season	Club	League	GP	G	A	Pts	PIM	PP	SH	GW	S	%	+/-	TF	F%	H	SB	Min	GP	G	A	Pts	PIM	PP	SH	GW
1991-92	Calgary	AAHA	23	26	16	42	132																			
1992-93	Portland	WHL	67	31	33	64	146												16	8	8	16	41			
1993-94	Portland	WHL	65	40	53	93	144												10	3	8	11	16			
1994-95	Rochester	AHL	71	11	16	27	136												5	0	3	3	14			
1995-96	**Buffalo**	**NHL**	2	0	0	0	10	0	0	0	4	0.0	0													
	Rochester	AHL	62	14	18	32	170												19	7	6	13	36			
1996-97	Rochester	AHL	68	22	21	43	133												10	2	1	3	26			
1997-98	**Buffalo**	**NHL**	3	0	0	0	4	0	0	0	5	0.0	0													
	Rochester	AHL	35	13	7	20	113																			
1998-99	Rochester	AHL	52	13	20	33	120																			
	NHL Totals		5	0	0	0	14	0	0	0	9	0.0														

NICHOLLS, Bernie
(NICK-uhls)

Center. Shoots right. 6', 185 lbs. Born, Haliburton, Ont., June 24, 1961. Los Angeles' 6th choice, 73rd overall, in 1980 Entry Draft.

Season	Club	League	GP	G	A	Pts	PIM	PP	SH	GW	S	%	+/-	TF	F%	H	SB	Min	GP	G	A	Pts	PIM	PP	SH	GW
1978-79	North York	OJHL	50	40	62	102	60																			
	Kingston	OHA	2	0	1	1	0																			
1979-80	Kingston	OHA	68	36	43	79	85												3	1	0	1	10			
1980-81	Kingston	OHA	65	63	89	152	109												14	8	10	18	17			
1981-82	**Los Angeles**	**NHL**	22	14	18	32	27	8	1	1	63	22.2	2						10	4	0	4	23	0	0	1
	New Haven	AHL	55	41	30	71	31																			
1982-83	**Los Angeles**	**NHL**	71	28	22	50	124	12	0	3	171	16.4	−23													
1983-84	**Los Angeles**	**NHL**	78	41	54	95	83	8	4	2	255	16.1	−21													
1984-85	**Los Angeles**	**NHL**	80	46	54	100	76	15	0	6	329	14.0	−4						3	1	1	2	9	0	0	0
1985-86	**Los Angeles**	**NHL**	80	36	61	97	78	10	4	0	281	12.8	−5													
1986-87	**Los Angeles**	**NHL**	80	33	48	81	101	10	1	2	227	14.5	−16						5	2	5	7	6	1	0	0
1987-88	**Los Angeles**	**NHL**	65	32	46	78	114	8	7	1	236	13.6	−2						5	2	6	8	11	1	0	0
1988-89	**Los Angeles**	**NHL**	79	70	80	150	96	21	8	6	385	18.2	30						11	7	9	16	12	3	0	1
1989-90	**Los Angeles**	**NHL**	47	27	48	75	66	8	0	1	172	15.7	−6													
	NY Rangers	**NHL**	32	12	25	37	20	7	0	0	115	10.4	−3						10	7	5	12	16	3	0	0
1990-91	**NY Rangers**	**NHL**	71	25	48	73	96	8	0	2	163	15.3	5						5	4	3	7	8	0	0	1
1991-92	**NY Rangers**	**NHL**	1	0	0	0	0	0	0	0	2	0.0	−1													
	Edmonton	**NHL**	49	20	29	49	60	7	0	2	115	17.4	5						16	8	11	19	25	4	0	1
1992-93	**Edmonton**	**NHL**	46	8	32	40	40	4	0	1	86	9.3	−16													
	New Jersey	**NHL**	23	5	15	20	40	1	0	0	46	10.9	3						5	0	0	0	6	0	0	0
1993-94	**New Jersey**	**NHL**	61	19	27	46	86	3	0	1	142	13.4	24						16	4	9	13	28	2	1	0
1994-95	**Chicago**	**NHL**	48	22	29	51	32	11	2	5	114	19.3	4						16	1	11	12	8	1	0	0
1995-96	**Chicago**	**NHL**	59	19	41	60	60	6	0	2	100	19.0	11						10	2	7	9	4	1	0	0
1996-97	**San Jose**	**NHL**	65	12	33	45	63	2	1	0	137	8.8	−21													
1997-98	**San Jose**	**NHL**	60	6	22	28	26	3	0	0	81	7.4	−4						6	0	5	5	8	0	0	0
1998-99	**San Jose**	**NHL**	10	0	2	2	4	0	0	0	11	0.0	−4	108	65.7	5	0	11:01								
	NHL Totals		1127	475	734	1209	1292	152	28	35	3231	14.7		108	65.7	5	0	11:01	118	42	72	114	164	16	1	4

Played in NHL All-Star Game (1984, 1989, 1990)

Traded to **NY Rangers** by **LA Kings** for Tomas Sandstrom and Tony Granato, January 20, 1990. Traded to **Edmonton** by **NY Rangers** with Steven Rice and Louie DeBrusk for Mark Messier and future considerations, October 4, 1991. Traded to **New Jersey** by **Edmonton** for Zdeno Ciger and Kevin Todd, January 13, 1993. Signed as a free agent by **Chicago**, July 14, 1994. Signed as a free agent by **San Jose**, August 5, 1996.

NICKULAS, Eric
(NICK-luhs)   **BOS.**

Center. Shoots right. 5'11", 190 lbs. Born, Hyannis, MA, March 25, 1975. Boston's 3rd choice, 99th overall, in 1994 Entry Draft.

Season	Club	League	GP	G	A	Pts	PIM	PP	SH	GW	S	%	+/-	TF	F%	H	SB	Min	GP	G	A	Pts	PIM	PP	SH	GW
1991-92	Barnstable High	H.S.	24	30	25	55	....																			
1992-93	Tabor Academy	H.S.	28	25	25	50	....																			
1993-94	Cushing Academy	H.S.	25	46	36	82	....																			
1994-95	New Hampshire	H.E.	33	15	9	24	32																			
1995-96	New Hampshire	H.E.	34	26	12	38	66																			
1996-97	New Hampshire	H.E.	39	29	22	51	80																			
1997-98	Orlando	IHL	76	22	9	31	77												6	0	0	0	10			
1998-99	**Boston**	**NHL**	2	0	0	0	0	0	0	0	0	0.0	0	0	0.0	0	0	3:27	1	0	0	0	2	0	0	0
	Providence	AHL	75	31	27	58	83												18	8	12	20	33			
	NHL Totals		2	0	0	0	0	0	0	0	0	0.0		0	0.0	0	0	3:27	1	0	0	0	2	0	0	0

NIECKAR, Barry

(NIGH-kahr)

Left wing. Shoots left. 6'3", 205 lbs. Born, Rama, Sask., December 16, 1967.

			Regular Season																Playoffs							
Season	Club	League	GP	G	A	Pts	PIM	PP	SH	GW	S	%	+/–	TF	F%	H	SB	Min	GP	G	A	Pts	PIM	PP	SH	GW
1986-87	Weyburn	SJHL	41	12	10	22	115	....	....	....	....	....	....	....	....	....	....	....	....	....	....	....	....	....	....	....
1987-88	Yorkton	SJHL	57	27	32	59	188	....	....	....	....	....	....	....	....	....	....	....	16	11	6	17	65	....	....	....
1988-89			DID NOT PLAY																							
1989-90	Virginia	ECHL	5	2	2	4	27	....	....	....	....	....	....	....	....	....	....	....	....	....	....	....	....	....	....	....
1990-91			DID NOT PLAY – RETIRED																							
1991-92	Phoenix	IHL	5	0	0	0	9	....	....	....	....	....	....	....	....	....	....	....	....	....	....	....	....	....	....	....
	Raleigh	ECHL	46	10	18	28	229	....	....	....	....	....	....	....	....	....	....	....	4	4	0	4	22	....	....	....
1992-93	**Hartford**	**NHL**	**2**	**0**	**0**	**0**	**2**	**0**	**0**	**0**	**1**	**0.0**	**–2**	....	....	....	....	....	....	....	....	....	....	....	....	....
	Springfield	AHL	21	2	4	6	65	....	....	....	....	....	....	....	....	....	....	....	6	1	0	1	14	....	....	....
1993-94	Springfield	AHL	30	0	2	2	67	....	....	....	....	....	....	....	....	....	....	....	....	....	....	....	....	....	....	....
	Raleigh	ECHL	18	4	6	10	126	....	....	....	....	....	....	....	....	....	....	....	15	5	7	12	51	....	....	....
1994-95	Saint John	AHL	65	8	7	15	*491	....	....	....	....	....	....	....	....	....	....	....	4	0	0	0	22	....	....	....
	Calgary	**NHL**	**3**	**0**	**0**	**0**	**12**	**0**	**0**	**0**	**0**	**0.0**	**0**	....	....	....	....	....	....	....	....	....	....	....	....	....
1995-96	Utah	IHL	53	9	15	24	194	....	....	....	....	....	....	....	....	....	....	....	....	....	....	....	....	....	....	....
	Peoria	IHL	10	3	3	6	72	....	....	....	....	....	....	....	....	....	....	....	12	4	6	10	48	....	....	....
1996-97	**Anaheim**	**NHL**	**2**	**0**	**0**	**0**	**5**	**0**	**0**	**0**	**0**	**0.0**	**0**	....	....	....	....	....	....	....	....	....	....	....	....	....
	Long Beach	IHL	63	3	10	13	386	....	....	....	....	....	....	....	....	....	....	....	5	0	0	0	22	....	....	....
1997-98	**Anaheim**	**NHL**	**1**	**0**	**0**	**0**	**2**	**0**	**0**	**0**	**0**	**0.0**	**0**	....	....	....	....	....	....	....	....	....	....	....	....	....
	Cincinnati	AHL	75	10	14	24	295	....	....	....	....	....	....	....	....	....	....	....	....	....	....	....	....	....	....	....
1998-99	Springfield	AHL	67	11	6	17	270	....	....	....	....	....	....	....	....	....	....	....	1	0	0	0	2	....	....	....
	NHL Totals		**8**	**0**	**0**	**0**	**21**	**0**	**0**	**0**	**1**	**0.0**		....	....	....	....	....	....	....	....	....	....	....	....	....

Signed as a free agent by **Hartford**, September 25, 1992. Signed as a free agent by **Calgary**, February 11, 1995. Signed as a free agent by **NY Islanders**, August 8, 1995. Signed as a free agent by **Anaheim**, October 2, 1996. Signed as a free agent by **Phoenix**, August 12, 1998.

NIEDERMAYER, Rob

(nee-duhr-MIGH-uhr) **FLA.**

Center. Shoots left. 6'2", 204 lbs. Born, Cassiar, B.C., December 28, 1974. Florida's 1st choice, 5th overall, in 1993 Entry Draft.

1989-90	Cranbrook	BCAHA	35	42	40	82	30	....	....	....	....	....	....	....	....	....	....	....	....	....	....	....	....	....	....	....
1990-91	Medicine Hat	WHL	71	24	26	50	8	....	....	....	....	....	....	....	....	....	....	....	12	3	7	10	2	....	....	....
1991-92	Medicine Hat	WHL	71	32	46	78	77	....	....	....	....	....	....	....	....	....	....	....	4	2	3	5	2	....	....	....
1992-93	Medicine Hat	WHL	52	43	34	77	67	....	....	....	....	....	....	....	....	....	....	....	....	....	....	....	....	....	....	....
1993-94	**Florida**	**NHL**	**65**	**9**	**17**	**26**	**51**	**3**	**0**	**2**	**67**	**13.4**	**–11**	....	....	....	....	....	....	....	....	....	....	....	....	....
1994-95	Medicine Hat	WHL	13	9	15	24	14	....	....	....	....	....	....	....	....	....	....	....	....	....	....	....	....	....	....	....
	Florida	**NHL**	**48**	**4**	**6**	**10**	**36**	**1**	**0**	**0**	**58**	**6.9**	**–13**	....	....	....	....	....	....	....	....	....	....	....	....	....
1995-96	**Florida**	**NHL**	**82**	**26**	**35**	**61**	**107**	**11**	**0**	**6**	**155**	**16.8**	**1**	....	....	....	....	....	**22**	**5**	**3**	**8**	**12**	**2**	**0**	**2**
1996-97	**Florida**	**NHL**	**60**	**14**	**24**	**38**	**54**	**3**	**0**	**2**	**136**	**10.3**	**4**	....	....	....	....	....	**5**	**2**	**1**	**3**	**6**	**1**	**0**	**0**
1997-98	**Florida**	**NHL**	**33**	**8**	**7**	**15**	**41**	**5**	**0**	**2**	**64**	**12.5**	**–9**	....	....	....	....	....	....	....	....	....	....	....	....	....
1998-99	**Florida**	**NHL**	**82**	**18**	**33**	**51**	**50**	**6**	**1**	**3**	**142**	**12.7**	**–13**	**1895**	**47.1**	**152**	**38**	**21:17**	....	....	....	....	....	....	....	....
	NHL Totals		**370**	**79**	**122**	**201**	**339**	**29**	**1**	**15**	**622**	**12.7**		**1895**	**47.1**	**152**	**38**	**21:17**	**27**	**7**	**4**	**11**	**18**	**3**	**0**	**2**

WHL East First All-Star Team (1993)

NIEDERMAYER, Scott

(NEE-duhr-MIGH-uhr) **N.J.**

Defense. Shoots left. 6', 205 lbs. Born, Edmonton, Alta., August 31, 1973. New Jersey's 1st choice, 3rd overall, in 1991 Entry Draft.

1988-89	Cranbrook	BCAHA	62	55	37	92	100	....	....	....	....	....	....	....	....	....	....	....	....	....	....	....	....	....	....	....
1989-90	Kamloops	WHL	64	14	55	69	64	....	....	....	....	....	....	....	....	....	....	....	17	2	14	16	35	....	....	....
1990-91	Kamloops	WHL	57	26	56	82	52	....	....	....	....	....	....	....	....	....	....	....	....	....	....	....	....	....	....	....
1991-92	Kamloops	WHL	35	7	32	39	61	....	....	....	....	....	....	....	....	....	....	....	17	9	14	23	28	....	....	....
	New Jersey	**NHL**	**4**	**0**	**1**	**1**	**2**	**0**	**0**	**0**	**4**	**0.0**	**1**	....	....	....	....	....	....	....	....	....	....	....	....	....
1992-93	**New Jersey**	**NHL**	**80**	**11**	**29**	**40**	**47**	**5**	**0**	**0**	**131**	**8.4**	**8**	....	....	....	....	....	**5**	**0**	**3**	**3**	**2**	**0**	**0**	**0**
1993-94	**New Jersey**	**NHL**	**81**	**10**	**36**	**46**	**42**	**5**	**0**	**2**	**135**	**7.4**	**34**	....	....	....	....	....	**20**	**2**	**2**	**4**	**8**	**1**	**0**	**0**
1994-95♦	**New Jersey**	**NHL**	**48**	**4**	**15**	**19**	**18**	**4**	**0**	**0**	**52**	**7.7**	**19**	....	....	....	....	....	**20**	**4**	**7**	**11**	**10**	**2**	**0**	**1**
1995-96	**New Jersey**	**NHL**	**79**	**8**	**25**	**33**	**46**	**6**	**0**	**0**	**179**	**4.5**	**5**	....	....	....	....	....	....	....	....	....	....	....	....	....
1996-97	**New Jersey**	**NHL**	**81**	**5**	**30**	**35**	**64**	**3**	**0**	**3**	**159**	**3.1**	**–4**	....	....	....	....	....	**10**	**2**	**4**	**6**	**6**	**2**	**0**	**1**
1997-98	**New Jersey**	**NHL**	**81**	**14**	**43**	**57**	**27**	**11**	**0**	**1**	**175**	**8.0**	**5**	....	....	....	....	....	**6**	**0**	**2**	**2**	**4**	**0**	**0**	**0**
1998-99	**New Jersey**	**NHL**	**72**	**11**	**35**	**46**	**26**	**1**	**1**	**3**	**161**	**6.8**	**16**	**13**	**15.4**	**99**	**49**	**24:40**	**7**	**1**	**3**	**4**	**18**	**1**	**0**	**0**
	Utah	IHL	5	0	2	2	0	....	....	....	....	....	....	....	....	....	....	....	....	....	....	....	....	....	....	....
	NHL Totals		**526**	**63**	**214**	**277**	**272**	**35**	**1**	**9**	**996**	**6.3**		**13**	**15.4**	**99**	**49**	**24:40**	**68**	**9**	**21**	**30**	**48**	**6**	**0**	**2**

WHL West First All-Star Team (1991, 1992) • Canadian Major Junior Scholastic Player of the Year (1991) • Memorial Cup All-Star Team (1992) • Won Stafford Smythe Memorial Trophy (Memorial Cup Tournament MVP) (1992) • NHL/Upper Deck All-Rookie Team (1993) • NHL Second All-Star Team (1998)

Played in NHL All-Star Game (1998)

NIELSEN, Jeff

ANA.

Right wing. Shoots left. 6', 200 lbs. Born, Grand Rapids, MN, September 20, 1971. NY Rangers' 4th choice, 69th overall, in 1990 Entry Draft.

1987-88	Grand Rapids	H.S.	21	9	11	20	14	....	....	....	....	....	....	....	....	....	....	....	....	....	....	....	....	....	....	....
1988-89	Grand Rapids	H.S.	25	13	17	30	26	....	....	....	....	....	....	....	....	....	....	....	....	....	....	....	....	....	....	....
1989-90	Grand Rapids	H.S.	28	32	25	57	....	....	....	....	....	....	....	....	....	....	....	....	....	....	....	....	....	....	....	....
1990-91	U. of Minnesota	WCHA	45	11	14	25	50	....	....	....	....	....	....	....	....	....	....	....	....	....	....	....	....	....	....	....
1991-92	U. of Minnesota	WCHA	41	14	14	28	70	....	....	....	....	....	....	....	....	....	....	....	....	....	....	....	....	....	....	....
1992-93	U. of Minnesota	WCHA	42	21	20	41	80	....	....	....	....	....	....	....	....	....	....	....	....	....	....	....	....	....	....	....
1993-94	U. of Minnesota	WCHA	41	29	16	45	94	....	....	....	....	....	....	....	....	....	....	....	....	....	....	....	....	....	....	....
1994-95	Binghamton	AHL	76	24	13	37	139	....	....	....	....	....	....	....	....	....	....	....	7	0	0	0	22	....	....	....
1995-96	Binghamton	AHL	64	22	20	42	56	....	....	....	....	....	....	....	....	....	....	....	4	1	1	2	4	....	....	....
1996-97	**NY Rangers**	**NHL**	**2**	**0**	**0**	**0**	**2**	**0**	**0**	**0**	**1**	**0.0**	**–1**	....	....	....	....	....	....	....	....	....	....	....	....	....
	Binghamton	AHL	76	27	26	53	71	....	....	....	....	....	....	....	....	....	....	....	4	0	0	0	7	....	....	....
1997-98	**Anaheim**	**NHL**	**32**	**4**	**5**	**9**	**16**	**0**	**0**	**0**	**36**	**11.1**	**–1**	....	....	....	....	....	....	....	....	....	....	....	....	....
	Cincinnati	AHL	18	4	8	12	37	....	....	....	....	....	....	....	....	....	....	....	....	....	....	....	....	....	....	....
1998-99	**Anaheim**	**NHL**	**80**	**5**	**4**	**9**	**34**	**0**	**0**	**2**	**94**	**5.3**	**–12**	**9**	**44.4**	**84**	**38**	**10:16**	**4**	**0**	**0**	**0**	**2**	**0**	**0**	**0**
	NHL Totals		**114**	**9**	**9**	**18**	**52**	**0**	**0**	**2**	**131**	**6.9**		**9**	**44.4**	**84**	**38**	**10:16**	**4**	**0**	**0**	**0**	**2**	**0**	**0**	**0**

WCHA Second All-Star Team (1994)

Signed as a free agent by **Anaheim**, August 18, 1997.

NIELSEN, Kirk

Right wing. Shoots right. 6'1", 205 lbs. Born, Grand Rapids, MN, October 19, 1973. Philadelphia's 1st choice, 10th overall, in 1994 Supplemental Draft.

1992-93	Harvard University	ECAC	30	2	2	4	38	....	....	....	....	....	....	....	....	....	....	....	....	....	....	....	....	....	....	....
1993-94	Harvard University	ECAC	32	6	9	15	41	....	....	....	....	....	....	....	....	....	....	....	....	....	....	....	....	....	....	....
1994-95	Harvard University	ECAC	30	13	8	21	24	....	....	....	....	....	....	....	....	....	....	....	....	....	....	....	....	....	....	....
1995-96	Harvard University	ECAC	31	12	16	28	66	....	....	....	....	....	....	....	....	....	....	....	....	....	....	....	....	....	....	....
1996-97	Providence	AHL	68	12	23	35	30	....	....	....	....	....	....	....	....	....	....	....	9	2	1	3	2	....	....	....
1997-98	**Boston**	**NHL**	**6**	**0**	**0**	**0**	**0**	**0**	**0**	**0**	**1**	**0.0**	**–1**	....	....	....	....	....	....	....	....	....	....	....	....	....
	Providence	AHL	72	19	29	48	40	....	....	....	....	....	....	....	....	....	....	....	....	....	....	....	....	....	....	....
1998-99	Cincinnati	IHL	82	12	22	34	58	....	....	....	....	....	....	....	....	....	....	....	3	0	0	0	4	....	....	....
	NHL Totals		**6**	**0**	**0**	**0**	**0**	**0**	**0**	**0**	**1**	**0.0**		....	....	....	....	....	....	....	....	....	....	....	....	....

Signed as a free agent by **Boston**, June 7, 1996.

			Regular Season																Playoffs							
Season	Club	League	GP	G	A	Pts	PIM	PP	SH	GW	S	%	+/–	TF	F%	H	SB	Min	GP	G	A	Pts	PIM	PP	SH	GW

NIEUWENDYK, Joe

(NOO-ihn-DIGHK) **DAL.**

Center. Shoots left. 6'1", 195 lbs. Born, Oshawa, Ont., September 10, 1966. Calgary's 2nd choice, 27th overall, in 1985 Entry Draft.

Season	Club	League	GP	G	A	Pts	PIM	PP	SH	GW	S	%	+/–	TF	F%	H	SB	Min	GP	G	A	Pts	PIM	PP	SH	GW
1983-84	Pickering	OJHL	38	30	28	58	35	....	....	....	....	....	....	....	....	....	....	....	....	....	....	....	....	....	....	....
1984-85	Cornell	ECAC	29	21	24	45	30	....	....	....	....	....	....	....	....	....	....	....	....	....	....	....	....	....	....	....
1985-86	Cornell	ECAC	29	26	28	54	67	....	....	....	....	....	....	....	....	....	....	....	....	....	....	....	....	....	....	....
1986-87	Cornell	ECAC	23	26	26	52	26	....	....	....	....	....	....	....	....	....	....	....	....	....	....	....	....	....	....	....
	Canada	Nat-Team	5	2	0	2	0	....	....	....	....	....	....	....	....	....	....	....	....	....	....	....	....	....	....	....
	Calgary	**NHL**	9	5	1	6	0	2	0	1	16	31.3	0	....	....	....	....	....	6	2	2	4	0	0	0	0
1987-88	**Calgary**	**NHL**	75	51	41	92	23	31	3	8	212	24.1	20	....	....	....	....	....	8	3	4	7	2	1	0	0
1988-89♦	**Calgary**	**NHL**	77	51	31	82	40	19	3	11	215	23.7	26	....	....	....	....	....	22	10	4	14	10	6	0	1
1989-90	**Calgary**	**NHL**	79	45	50	95	40	18	0	3	226	19.9	32	....	....	....	....	....	6	4	6	10	4	1	0	0
1990-91	**Calgary**	**NHL**	79	45	40	85	36	22	4	1	222	20.3	19	....	....	....	....	....	7	4	1	5	10	2	0	0
1991-92	**Calgary**	**NHL**	69	22	34	56	55	7	0	2	137	16.1	–1	....	....	....	....	....	....	....	....	....	....	....	....	....
1992-93	**Calgary**	**NHL**	79	38	37	75	52	14	0	6	208	18.3	9	....	....	....	....	....	6	3	6	9	10	1	0	0
1993-94	**Calgary**	**NHL**	64	36	39	75	51	14	1	7	191	18.8	19	....	....	....	....	....	6	2	2	4	0	1	0	0
1994-95	**Calgary**	**NHL**	46	21	29	50	33	3	0	4	122	17.2	11	....	....	....	....	....	5	4	3	7	0	2	0	1
1995-96	**Dallas**	**NHL**	52	14	18	32	41	8	0	3	138	10.1	–17	....	....	....	....	....	....	....	....	....	....	....	....	....
1996-97	**Dallas**	**NHL**	66	30	21	51	32	8	0	2	173	17.3	–5	....	....	....	....	....	7	2	2	4	6	0	0	0
1997-98	**Dallas**	**NHL**	73	39	30	69	30	14	0	11	203	19.2	16	....	....	....	....	....	1	1	0	1	0	0	0	0
1998-99♦	**Dallas**	**NHL**	67	28	27	55	34	8	0	8	157	17.8	11	1170	63.2	42	9	15:33	23	*11	10	21	19	3	0	6
	NHL Totals		**835**	**425**	**398**	**823**	**467**	**168**	**11**	**67**	**2220**	**19.1**		**1170**	**63.2**	**42**	**9**	**15:33**	**97**	**46**	**40**	**86**	**61**	**17**	**0**	**8**

NCAA East First All-American Team (1986, 1987) • ECAC First All-Star Team (1986, 1987) • NHL All-Rookie Team (1988) • Won Calder Memorial Trophy (1988) • Won Dodge Ram Tough Award (1988) • Won King Clancy Memorial Trophy (1995) • Won Conn Smythe Trophy (1999)

Played in NHL All-Star Game (1988, 1989, 1990, 1994)

Traded to **Dallas** by **Calgary** for Corey Millen and Jarome Iginla, December 19, 1995.

NIINIMAA, Janne

(nihn-EE-mah, YAH-nee) **EDM.**

Defense. Shoots left. 6'1", 220 lbs. Born, Raahe, Finland, May 22, 1975. Philadelphia's 1st choice, 36th overall, in 1993 Entry Draft.

Season	Club	League	GP	G	A	Pts	PIM	PP	SH	GW	S	%	+/–	TF	F%	H	SB	Min	GP	G	A	Pts	PIM	PP	SH	GW
1991-92	Karput Oulu	Finn-Jr.	3	0	0	0	4	....	....	....	....	....	....	....	....	....	....	....	....	....	....	....	....	....	....	....
	Karpat Oulu	Finland-2	41	2	11	13	49	....	....	....	....	....	....	....	....	....	....	....	....	....	....	....	....	....	....	....
1992-93	Karput Oulu	Finn-Jr.	10	3	9	12	16	....	....	....	....	....	....	....	....	....	....	....	....	....	....	....	....	....	....	....
	KKP Kiiminki	Finland-2	2	0	2	2	4	....	....	....	....	....	....	....	....	....	....	....	....	....	....	....	....	....	....	....
	Karpat Oulu	Finland-2	29	2	3	5	14	....	....	....	....	....	....	....	....	....	....	....	....	....	....	....	....	....	....	....
1993-94	Jokerit	Finn-Jr.	10	2	6	8	41	....	....	....	....	....	....	....	....	....	....	....	....	....	....	....	....	....	....	....
	Jokerit	Finland	45	3	8	11	24	....	....	....	....	....	....	....	....	....	....	....	12	1	1	2	4	....	....	....
1994-95	Jokerit	Finn-Jr.	3	1	2	3	4	....	....	....	....	....	....	....	....	....	....	....	....	....	....	....	....	....	....	....
	Jokerit	Finland	42	7	10	17	36	....	....	....	....	....	....	....	....	....	....	....	10	1	4	5	35	....	....	....
1995-96	Jokerit	Finland	49	5	15	20	79	....	....	....	....	....	....	....	....	....	....	....	11	0	2	2	12	....	....	....
	Helsinki	Finn-Jr.	....	....	....	....	....	....	....	....	....	....	....	....	....	....	....	....	2	3	4	7	6	....	....	....
1996-97	**Philadelphia**	**NHL**	77	4	40	44	58	1	0	2	141	2.8	12	....	....	....	....	....	19	1	12	13	16	1	0	1
1997-98	**Philadelphia**	**NHL**	66	3	31	34	56	2	0	1	115	2.6	6	....	....	....	....	....	....	....	....	....	....	....	....	....
	Finland	Olympics	6	0	3	3	8	....	....	....	....	....	....	....	....	....	....	....	....	....	....	....	....	....	....	....
	Edmonton	**NHL**	11	1	8	9	6	1	0	0	19	5.3	7	....	....	....	....	....	11	1	1	2	12	0	0	1
1998-99	**Edmonton**	**NHL**	81	4	24	28	88	2	0	1	142	2.8	7	1	0.0	144	122	23:54	4	0	0	0	2	0	0	0
	NHL Totals		**235**	**12**	**103**	**115**	**208**	**6**	**0**	**4**	**417**	**2.9**		**1**	**0.0**	**144**	**122**	**23:54**	**34**	**2**	**13**	**15**	**30**	**1**	**0**	**2**

NHL All-Rookie Team (1997)

Traded to **Edmonton** by **Philadelphia** for Dan McGillis and Edmonton's 2nd round choice (Jason Beckett) in 1998 Entry Draft, March 24, 1998.

NIKOLISHIN, Andrei

(nee-koh-LEE-shin) **WSH.**

Left wing. Shoots left. 5'11", 200 lbs. Born, Vorkuta, USSR, March 25, 1973. Hartford's 2nd choice, 47th overall, in 1992 Entry Draft.

Season	Club	League	GP	G	A	Pts	PIM	PP	SH	GW	S	%	+/–	TF	F%	H	SB	Min	GP	G	A	Pts	PIM	PP	SH	GW
1990-91	Moscow D'amo	USSR	2	0	0	0	0	....	....	....	....	....	....	....	....	....	....	....	....	....	....	....	....	....	....	....
1991-92	Moscow D'amo	CIS	18	1	0	1	4	....	....	....	....	....	....	....	....	....	....	....	....	....	....	....	....	....	....	....
1992-93	Moscow D'amo	CIS	42	5	7	12	30	....	....	....	....	....	....	....	....	....	....	....	10	2	1	3	8	....	....	....
1993-94	Moscow D'amo	CIS	41	8	12	20	30	....	....	....	....	....	....	....	....	....	....	....	9	1	3	4	4	....	....	....
	Russia	Olympics	8	2	5	7	6	....	....	....	....	....	....	....	....	....	....	....	....	....	....	....	....	....	....	....
1994-95	Moscow D'amo	CIS	12	7	2	9	6	....	....	....	....	....	....	....	....	....	....	....	....	....	....	....	....	....	....	....
	Hartford	**NHL**	39	8	10	18	10	1	1	0	57	14.0	7	....	....	....	....	....	....	....	....	....	....	....	....	....
1995-96	**Hartford**	**NHL**	61	14	37	51	34	4	1	3	83	16.9	–2	....	....	....	....	....	....	....	....	....	....	....	....	....
1996-97	**Hartford**	**NHL**	12	2	5	7	2	0	0	0	25	8.0	–2	....	....	....	....	....	....	....	....	....	....	....	....	....
	Washington	**NHL**	59	7	14	21	30	1	0	0	73	9.6	5	....	....	....	....	....	....	....	....	....	....	....	....	....
1997-98	**Washington**	**NHL**	38	6	10	16	14	1	0	1	40	15.0	1	....	....	....	....	....	21	1	13	14	12	1	0	0
	Portland	AHL	2	0	0	0	2	....	....	....	....	....	....	....	....	....	....	....	....	....	....	....	....	....	....	....
1998-99	Moscow D'amo	Russia	4	0	0	0	0	....	....	....	....	....	....	....	....	....	....	....	....	....	....	....	....	....	....	....
	Washington	**NHL**	73	8	27	35	28	0	1	1	121	6.6	0	1354	52.5	70	31	17:34	....	....	....	....	....	....	....	....
	NHL Totals		**282**	**45**	**103**	**148**	**118**	**7**	**3**	**5**	**399**	**11.3**		**1354**	**52.5**	**70**	**31**	**17:34**	**21**	**1**	**13**	**14**	**12**	**1**	**0**	**0**

CIS First All-Star Team (1994) • CIS Player of the Year (1994)

Traded to **Washington** by **Hartford** for Curtis Leschyshyn, November 9, 1996.

NIKULIN, Igor

(nih-KOO-lihn)

Right wing. Shoots left. 6'1", 200 lbs. Born, Cherepovets, USSR, August 26, 1972. Anaheim's 4th choice, 107th overall, in 1995 Entry Draft.

Season	Club	League	GP	G	A	Pts	PIM	PP	SH	GW	S	%	+/–	TF	F%	H	SB	Min	GP	G	A	Pts	PIM	PP	SH	GW
1992-93	Cherepovets	CIS	42	11	11	22	22	....	....	....	....	....	....	....	....	....	....	....	....	....	....	....	....	....	....	....
1993-94	Cherepovets	CIS	44	14	15	29	52	....	....	....	....	....	....	....	....	....	....	....	2	1	0	1	0	....	....	....
1994-95	Cherepovets	CIS	52	14	12	26	28	....	....	....	....	....	....	....	....	....	....	....	....	....	....	....	....	....	....	....
1995-96	Cherepovets	CIS	47	20	13	33	28	....	....	....	....	....	....	....	....	....	....	....	4	1	0	1	0	....	....	....
	Baltimore	AHL	4	2	2	4	2	....	....	....	....	....	....	....	....	....	....	....	....	....	....	....	....	....	....	....
1996-97	Baltimore	AHL	61	27	25	52	14	....	....	....	....	....	....	....	....	....	....	....	3	2	1	3	2	....	....	....
	Fort Wayne	IHL	10	1	2	3	4	....	....	....	....	....	....	....	....	....	....	....	....	....	....	....	....	....	....	....
	Anaheim	**NHL**	....	....	....	....	....	....	....	....	....	....	....	....	....	....	....	....	1	0	0	0	0	....	....	....
1997-98	Cincinnati	AHL	54	14	11	25	40	....	....	....	....	....	....	....	....	....	....	....	....	....	....	....	....	....	....	....
1998-99	Cincinnati	AHL	74	18	26	44	26	....	....	....	....	....	....	....	....	....	....	....	3	0	1	1	4	....	....	....
	NHL Totals		....	....	....	....	....	....	....	....	....	....		....	....	....	....	....	**1**	**0**	**0**	**0**	**0**	....	....	....

NILSON, Marcus

(NIHL-suhn) **FLA.**

Right wing. Shoots right. 6'2", 193 lbs. Born, Balsta, Sweden, March 1, 1978. Florida's 1st choice, 20th overall, in 1996 Entry Draft.

Season	Club	League	GP	G	A	Pts	PIM	PP	SH	GW	S	%	+/–	TF	F%	H	SB	Min	GP	G	A	Pts	PIM	PP	SH	GW
1994-95	Djurgardens IF	Swede-Jr.	24	7	8	15	22	....	....	....	....	....	....	....	....	....	....	....	....	....	....	....	....	....	....	....
1995-96	Djurgardens IF	Swede-Jr.	25	19	17	36	46	....	....	....	....	....	....	....	....	....	....	....	2	1	1	2	12	....	....	....
	Djurgardens IF	Sweden	12	0	0	0	0	....	....	....	....	....	....	....	....	....	....	....	1	0	0	0	0	....	....	....
1996-97	Djurgardens IF	Sweden	37	0	3	3	33	....	....	....	....	....	....	....	....	....	....	....	4	0	0	0	0	....	....	....
1997-98	Djurgardens IF	Sweden	41	4	7	11	18	....	....	....	....	....	....	....	....	....	....	....	15	2	1	3	16	....	....	....
1998-99	**Florida**	**NHL**	8	1	1	2	5	0	0	1	7	14.3	2	6	50.0	6	3	12:24	....	....	....	....	....	....	....	....
	Topeka	CHL	3	0	0	0	2	....	....	....	....	....	....	....	....	....	....	....	....	....	....	....	....	....	....	....
	New Haven	AHL	69	8	25	33	10	....	....	....	....	....	....	....	....	....	....	....	....	....	....	....	....	....	....	....
	NHL Totals		**8**	**1**	**1**	**2**	**5**	**0**	**0**	**1**	**7**	**14.3**		**6**	**50.0**	**6**	**3**	**12:24**	....	....	....	....	....	....	....	....

			Regular Season																Playoffs							
Season	Club	League	GP	G	A	Pts	PIM	PP	SH	GW	S	%	+/-	TF	F%	H	SB	Min	GP	G	A	Pts	PIM	PP	SH	GW

NOLAN, Owen — S.J.

Right wing. Shoots right. 6'1", 215 lbs. Born, Belfast, Ireland, February 12, 1972. Quebec's 1st choice, 1st overall, in 1990 Entry Draft.

Season	Club	League	GP	G	A	Pts	PIM	PP	SH	GW	S	%	+/-	TF	F%	H	SB	Min	GP	G	A	Pts	PIM	PP	SH	GW
1987-88	Thorold AA	OMHA	28	53	32	85	24	....	....	....	....	....	....	....	....	....	....	....	....	....	....	....	....	....	....	....
	Thorold	OJHL-B	3	1	0	1	2	....	....	....	....	....	....	....	....	....	....	....	....	....	....	....	....	....	....	....
1988-89	Cornwall	OHL	62	34	25	59	213	....	....	....	....	....	....	....	....	....	....	....	18	5	11	16	41	....	....	....
1989-90	Cornwall	OHL	58	51	59	110	240	....	....	....	....	....	....	....	....	....	....	....	6	7	5	12	26	....	....	....
1990-91	**Quebec**	**NHL**	**59**	**3**	**10**	**13**	**109**	**0**	**0**	**0**	**54**	**5.6**	**-19**	....	....	....	....	....	....	....	....	....	....	....	....	....
	Halifax	AHL	6	4	4	8	11	....	....	....	....	....	....	....	....	....	....	....	....	....	....	....	....	....	....	....
1991-92	**Quebec**	**NHL**	**75**	**42**	**31**	**73**	**183**	**17**	**0**	**0**	**190**	**22.1**	**-9**	....	....	....	....	....	....	....	....	....	....	....	....	....
1992-93	**Quebec**	**NHL**	**73**	**36**	**41**	**77**	**185**	**15**	**0**	**4**	**241**	**14.9**	**-1**	....	....	....	....	....	**5**	**1**	**0**	**1**	**2**	**0**	**0**	**0**
1993-94	**Quebec**	**NHL**	**6**	**2**	**2**	**4**	**8**	**0**	**0**	**0**	**15**	**13.3**	**2**	....	....	....	....	....	....	....	....	....	....	....	....	....
1994-95	**Quebec**	**NHL**	**46**	**30**	**19**	**49**	**46**	**13**	**2**	**8**	**137**	**21.9**	**21**	....	....	....	....	....	**6**	**2**	**3**	**5**	**6**	**0**	**0**	**0**
1995-96	**Colorado**	**NHL**	**9**	**4**	**4**	**8**	**9**	**4**	**0**	**0**	**23**	**17.4**	**-3**	....	....	....	....	....	....	....	....	....	....	....	....	....
	San Jose	**NHL**	**72**	**29**	**32**	**61**	**137**	**12**	**1**	**2**	**184**	**15.8**	**-30**	....	....	....	....	....	....	....	....	....	....	....	....	....
1996-97	**San Jose**	**NHL**	**72**	**31**	**32**	**63**	**155**	**10**	**0**	**3**	**225**	**13.8**	**-19**	....	....	....	....	....	....	....	....	....	....	....	....	....
1997-98	**San Jose**	**NHL**	**75**	**14**	**27**	**41**	**144**	**3**	**1**	**1**	**192**	**7.3**	**-2**	....	....	....	....	....	**6**	**2**	**2**	**4**	**26**	**2**	**0**	**1**
1998-99	**San Jose**	**NHL**	**78**	**19**	**26**	**45**	**129**	**6**	**2**	**3**	**207**	**9.2**	**16**	**657**	**49.3**	**174**	**15**	**19:09**	**6**	**1**	**1**	**2**	**6**	**0**	**0**	**0**
	NHL Totals		**565**	**210**	**224**	**434**	**1105**	**80**	**6**	**21**	**1468**	**14.3**		**657**	**49.3**	**174**	**15**	**19:09**	**23**	**6**	**6**	**12**	**40**	**2**	**0**	**1**

OHL First All-Star Team (1990)

Played in NHL All-Star Game (1992, 1996, 1997)

Transferred to **Colorado** after **Quebec** franchise relocated, June 21, 1995. Traded to **San Jose** by **Colorado** for Sandis Ozolinsh, October 26, 1995.

NOONAN, Brian

Right wing. Shoots right. 6'1", 200 lbs. Born, Boston, MA, May 29, 1965. Chicago's 10th choice, 186th overall, in 1983 Entry Draft.

Season	Club	League	GP	G	A	Pts	PIM	PP	SH	GW	S	%	+/-	TF	F%	H	SB	Min	GP	G	A	Pts	PIM	PP	SH	GW
1982-83	Arch. Wiliams	H.S.	21	26	17	43	....	....	....	....	....	....	....	....	....	....	....	....	....	....	....	....	....	....	....	....
1983-84	Arch. Wiliams	H.S.	17	14	23	32	....	....	....	....	....	....	....	....	....	....	....	....	....	....	....	....	....	....	....	....
1984-85	New Westminster	WHL	72	50	66	116	76	....	....	....	....	....	....	....	....	....	....	....	11	8	7	15	4	....	....	....
1985-86	Nova Scotia	AHL	2	0	0	0	0	....	....	....	....	....	....	....	....	....	....	....	....	....	....	....	....	....	....	....
	Saginaw	IHL	76	39	39	78	69	....	....	....	....	....	....	....	....	....	....	....	11	6	3	9	6	....	....	....
1986-87	Nova Scotia	AHL	70	25	26	51	30	....	....	....	....	....	....	....	....	....	....	....	5	3	1	4	4	....	....	....
1987-88	**Chicago**	**NHL**	**77**	**10**	**20**	**30**	**44**	**3**	**0**	**2**	**87**	**11.5**	**-27**	....	....	....	....	....	**3**	**0**	**0**	**0**	**4**	**0**	**0**	**0**
1988-89	**Chicago**	**NHL**	**45**	**4**	**12**	**16**	**28**	**2**	**0**	**0**	**84**	**4.8**	**-2**	....	....	....	....	....	**1**	**0**	**0**	**0**	**0**	**0**	**0**	**0**
	Saginaw	IHL	19	18	13	31	36	....	....	....	....	....	....	....	....	....	....	....	1	0	0	0	0	....	....	....
1989-90	**Chicago**	**NHL**	**8**	**0**	**2**	**2**	**6**	**0**	**0**	**0**	**13**	**0.0**	**0**	....	....	....	....	....	....	....	....	....	....	....	....	....
	Indianapolis	IHL	56	40	36	76	85	....	....	....	....	....	....	....	....	....	....	....	14	6	9	15	20	....	....	....
1990-91	**Chicago**	**NHL**	**7**	**0**	**4**	**4**	**2**	**0**	**0**	**0**	**12**	**0.0**	**-1**	....	....	....	....	....	....	....	....	....	....	....	....	....
	Indianapolis	IHL	59	38	53	91	67	....	....	....	....	....	....	....	....	....	....	....	7	6	4	10	18	....	....	....
1991-92	**Chicago**	**NHL**	**65**	**19**	**12**	**31**	**81**	**4**	**0**	**0**	**154**	**12.3**	**9**	....	....	....	....	....	**18**	**6**	**9**	**15**	**30**	**3**	**0**	**1**
1992-93	**Chicago**	**NHL**	**63**	**16**	**14**	**30**	**82**	**5**	**0**	**3**	**129**	**12.4**	**3**	....	....	....	....	....	**4**	**3**	**0**	**3**	**4**	**1**	**0**	**0**
1993-94	**Chicago**	**NHL**	**64**	**14**	**21**	**35**	**57**	**8**	**0**	**3**	**134**	**10.4**	**2**	....	....	....	....	....	....	....	....	....	....	....	....	....
	♦ **NY Rangers**	**NHL**	**12**	**4**	**2**	**6**	**12**	**2**	**0**	**3**	**26**	**15.4**	**5**	....	....	....	....	....	**22**	**4**	**7**	**11**	**17**	**2**	**0**	**1**
1994-95	**NY Rangers**	**NHL**	**45**	**14**	**13**	**27**	**26**	**7**	**0**	**1**	**95**	**14.7**	**-3**	....	....	....	....	....	**5**	**0**	**0**	**0**	**8**	**0**	**0**	**0**
1995-96	**St. Louis**	**NHL**	**81**	**13**	**22**	**35**	**84**	**3**	**1**	**6**	**131**	**9.9**	**2**	....	....	....	....	....	**13**	**4**	**1**	**5**	**10**	**0**	**0**	**0**
1996-97	**St. Louis**	**NHL**	**13**	**2**	**5**	**7**	**0**	**0**	**0**	**0**	**13**	**15.4**	**2**	....	....	....	....	....	....	....	....	....	....	....	....	....
	NY Rangers	**NHL**	**44**	**6**	**9**	**15**	**28**	**3**	**0**	**1**	**62**	**9.7**	**-7**	....	....	....	....	....	....	....	....	....	....	....	....	....
	Vancouver	**NHL**	**16**	**4**	**8**	**12**	**6**	**0**	**1**	**0**	**25**	**16.0**	**2**	....	....	....	....	....	....	....	....	....	....	....	....	....
1997-98	**Vancouver**	**NHL**	**82**	**10**	**15**	**25**	**62**	**1**	**0**	**2**	**87**	**11.5**	**-19**	....	....	....	....	....	....	....	....	....	....	....	....	....
1998-99	**Phoenix**	**NHL**	**7**	**0**	**0**	**0**	**0**	**0**	**0**	**0**	**1**	**0.0**	**-3**	**1**	**0.0**	**7**	**1**	**8:16**	**5**	**0**	**2**	**2**	**4**	**0**	**0**	**0**
	Indianapolis	IHL	65	19	44	63	128	....	....	....	....	....	....	....	....	....	....	....	....	....	....	....	....	....	....	....
	NHL Totals		**629**	**116**	**159**	**275**	**518**	**38**	**2**	**21**	**1053**	**11.0**		**1**	**0.0**	**7**	**1**	**8:16**	**71**	**17**	**19**	**36**	**77**	**6**	**0**	**2**

IHL Second All-Star Team (1990) • IHL First All-Star Team (1991)

Traded to **NY Rangers** by **Chicago** with Stephane Matteau for Tony Amonte and the rights to Matt Oates, March 21, 1994. Signed as a free agent by **St. Louis**, July 24, 1995. Traded to **NY Rangers** by **St. Louis** for Sergio Momesso, November 13, 1996. Traded to **Vancouver** by **NY Rangers** with Sergei Nemchinov for Esa Tikkanen and Russ Courtnall, March 8, 1997. Signed as a free agent by **Phoenix**, March 17, 1999.

NORDSTROM, Peter — (NOHRD-struhm) — BOS.

Center. Shoots left. 6'1", 200 lbs. Born, Munkfors, Sweden, July 26, 1974. Boston's 3rd choice, 78th overall, in 1998 Entry Draft.

Season	Club	League	GP	G	A	Pts	PIM	PP	SH	GW	S	%	+/-	TF	F%	H	SB	Min	GP	G	A	Pts	PIM	PP	SH	GW
1991-92	Munkfors	Sweden-3	31	12	20	32	42	....	....	....	....	....	....	....	....	....	....	....	....	....	....	....	....	....	....	....
1992-93	Munkfors	Sweden-3	35	19	11	30	44	....	....	....	....	....	....	....	....	....	....	....	....	....	....	....	....	....	....	....
1993-94	Munkfors	Sweden-3	31	17	26	43	87	....	....	....	....	....	....	....	....	....	....	....	....	....	....	....	....	....	....	....
1994-95	Munkfors	Sweden-2	21	8	17	25	30	....	....	....	....	....	....	....	....	....	....	....	....	....	....	....	....	....	....	....
1995-96	Farjestads BK	Sweden	40	6	5	11	36	....	....	....	....	....	....	....	....	....	....	....	8	0	3	3	12	....	....	....
1996-97	Farjestads BK	Sweden	44	9	5	14	32	....	....	....	....	....	....	....	....	....	....	....	14	1	2	3	6	....	....	....
1997-98	Farjestads BK	Sweden	45	6	19	25	46	....	....	....	....	....	....	....	....	....	....	....	12	5	7	*12	8	....	....	....
1998-99	Farjestads BK	Sweden	21	4	4	8	14	....	....	....	....	....	....	....	....	....	....	....	4	1	1	2	2	....	....	....
	Farjestads BK	EuroHL	2	1	0	1	2	....	....	....	....	....	....	....	....	....	....	....	....	....	....	....	....	....	....	....
	Boston	**NHL**	**2**	**0**	**0**	**0**	**0**	**0**	**0**	**0**	**0**	**0.0**	**-1**	**0**	**0.0**	**1**	**0**	**8:04**	....	....	....	....	....	....	....	....
	Providence	AHL	13	2	1	3	2	....	....	....	....	....	....	....	....	....	....	....	....	....	....	....	....	....	....	....
	NHL Totals		**2**	**0**	**0**	**0**	**0**	**0**	**0**	**0**	**0**	**0.0**		**0**	**0.0**	**1**	**0**	**8:04**	....	....	....	....	....	....	....	....

NORSTROM, Mattias — (NOHR-struhm) — L.A.

Defense. Shoots left. 6'2", 201 lbs. Born, Stockholm, Sweden, January 2, 1972. NY Rangers' 2nd choice, 48th overall, in 1992 Entry Draft.

Season	Club	League	GP	G	A	Pts	PIM	PP	SH	GW	S	%	+/-	TF	F%	H	SB	Min	GP	G	A	Pts	PIM	PP	SH	GW
1991-92	AIK Solna	Sweden	39	4	3	7	28	....	....	....	....	....	....	....	....	....	....	....	3	0	2	2	2	....	....	....
1992-93	AIK Solna	Sweden	22	0	1	1	16	....	....	....	....	....	....	....	....	....	....	....	....	....	....	....	....	....	....	....
1993-94	**NY Rangers**	**NHL**	**9**	**0**	**2**	**2**	**6**	**0**	**0**	**0**	**3**	**0.0**	**0**	....	....	....	....	....	....	....	....	....	....	....	....	....
	Binghamton	AHL	55	1	9	10	70	....	....	....	....	....	....	....	....	....	....	....	....	....	....	....	....	....	....	....
1994-95	Binghamton	AHL	63	9	10	19	91	....	....	....	....	....	....	....	....	....	....	....	....	....	....	....	....	....	....	....
	NY Rangers	**NHL**	**9**	**0**	**3**	**3**	**2**	**0**	**0**	**0**	**4**	**0.0**	**2**	....	....	....	....	....	**3**	**0**	**0**	**0**	**0**	**0**	**0**	**0**
1995-96	**NY Rangers**	**NHL**	**25**	**2**	**1**	**3**	**22**	**0**	**0**	**0**	**17**	**11.8**	**5**	....	....	....	....	....	....	....	....	....	....	....	....	....
	Los Angeles	**NHL**	**11**	**0**	**1**	**1**	**18**	**0**	**0**	**0**	**17**	**0.0**	**-8**	....	....	....	....	....	....	....	....	....	....	....	....	....
1996-97	**Los Angeles**	**NHL**	**80**	**1**	**21**	**22**	**84**	**0**	**0**	**0**	**106**	**0.9**	**-4**	....	....	....	....	....	....	....	....	....	....	....	....	....
1997-98	**Los Angeles**	**NHL**	**73**	**1**	**12**	**13**	**90**	**0**	**0**	**0**	**61**	**1.6**	**14**	....	....	....	....	....	**4**	**0**	**0**	**0**	**2**	**0**	**0**	**0**
	Sweden	Olympics	4	0	1	1	2	....	....	....	....	....	....	....	....	....	....	....	....	....	....	....	....	....	....	....
1998-99	**Los Angeles**	**NHL**	**78**	**2**	**5**	**7**	**36**	**0**	**1**	**0**	**61**	**3.3**	**-10**	**1**	**0.0**	**236**	**157**	**20:20**	....	....	....	....	....	....	....	....
	NHL Totals		**285**	**6**	**45**	**51**	**258**	**0**	**1**	**0**	**269**	**2.2**		**1**	**0.0**	**236**	**157**	**20:20**	**7**	**0**	**0**	**0**	**2**	**0**	**0**	**0**

Played in NHL All-Star Game (1999)

Traded to **LA Kings** by **NY Rangers** with Ray Ferraro, Ian Laperriere, Nathan Lafayette and NY Rangers' 4th round choice (Sean Blanchard) in 1997 Entry Draft for Marty McSorley, Jari Kurri and Shane Churla, March 14, 1996.

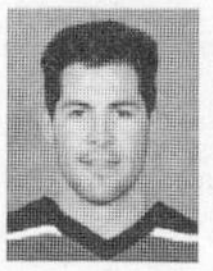

NORTON, Jeff — S.J.

Defense. Shoots left. 6'2", 200 lbs. Born, Acton, MA, November 25, 1965. NY Islanders' 3rd choice, 62nd overall, in 1984 Entry Draft.

Season	Club	League	GP	G	A	Pts	PIM	PP	SH	GW	S	%	+/-	TF	F%	H	SB	Min	GP	G	A	Pts	PIM	PP	SH	GW
1983-84	Cushing Academy	H.S.	21	22	33	55	....	....	....	....	....	....	....	....	....	....	....	....	....	....	....	....	....	....	....	....
1984-85	U. of Michigan	CCHA	37	8	16	24	103	....	....	....	....	....	....	....	....	....	....	....	....	....	....	....	....	....	....	....
1985-86	U. of Michigan	CCHA	37	15	30	45	99	....	....	....	....	....	....	....	....	....	....	....	....	....	....	....	....	....	....	....
1986-87	U. of Michigan	CCHA	39	12	36	48	92	....	....	....	....	....	....	....	....	....	....	....	....	....	....	....	....	....	....	....

			Regular Season																Playoffs							
Season	Club	League	GP	G	A	Pts	PIM	PP	SH	GW	S	%	+/–	TF	F%	H	SB	Min	GP	G	A	Pts	PIM	PP	SH	GW
1987-88	United States	Nat-Team	54	7	22	29	52	....	....	....	....	....	....	....	....	....	....	....	....	....	....	....	....	....	....	....
	United States	Olympics	6	0	4	4	4	....	....	....	....	....	....	....	....	....	....	....	....	....	....	....	....	....	....	....
	NY Islanders	**NHL**	**15**	**1**	**6**	**7**	**14**	**1**	**0**	**1**	**18**	**5.6**	**3**	....	....	....	....	....	**3**	**0**	**2**	**2**	**13**	**0**	**0**	**0**
1988-89	**NY Islanders**	**NHL**	**69**	**1**	**30**	**31**	**74**	**1**	**0**	**0**	**126**	**0.8**	**–24**	....	....	....	....	....	....	....	....	....	....	....	....	....
1989-90	**NY Islanders**	**NHL**	**60**	**4**	**49**	**53**	**65**	**4**	**0**	**0**	**104**	**3.8**	**–9**	....	....	....	....	....	**4**	**1**	**3**	**4**	**17**	**0**	**0**	**0**
1990-91	**NY Islanders**	**NHL**	**44**	**3**	**25**	**28**	**16**	**2**	**1**	**0**	**87**	**3.4**	**–13**	....	....	....	....	....	....	....	....	....	....	....	....	....
1991-92	**NY Islanders**	**NHL**	**28**	**1**	**18**	**19**	**18**	**0**	**1**	**0**	**34**	**2.9**	**2**	....	....	....	....	....	....	....	....	....	....	....	....	....
1992-93	**NY Islanders**	**NHL**	**66**	**12**	**38**	**50**	**45**	**5**	**0**	**0**	**127**	**9.4**	**–3**	....	....	....	....	....	**10**	**1**	**1**	**2**	**4**	**0**	**0**	**0**
1993-94	**San Jose**	**NHL**	**64**	**7**	**33**	**40**	**36**	**1**	**0**	**0**	**92**	**7.6**	**16**	....	....	....	....	....	**14**	**1**	**5**	**6**	**20**	**0**	**0**	**0**
1994-95	**San Jose**	**NHL**	**20**	**1**	**9**	**10**	**39**	**0**	**0**	**0**	**21**	**4.8**	**1**	....	....	....	....	....	....	....	....	....	....	....	....	....
	St. Louis	**NHL**	**28**	**2**	**18**	**20**	**33**	**0**	**0**	**1**	**27**	**7.4**	**21**	....	....	....	....	....	**7**	**1**	**1**	**2**	**11**	**0**	**0**	**0**
1995-96	**St. Louis**	**NHL**	**36**	**4**	**7**	**11**	**26**	**0**	**0**	**1**	**33**	**12.1**	**4**	....	....	....	....	....	....	....	....	....	....	....	....	....
	Edmonton	**NHL**	**30**	**4**	**16**	**20**	**16**	**1**	**0**	**1**	**52**	**7.7**	**5**	....	....	....	....	....	....	....	....	....	....	....	....	....
1996-97	**Edmonton**	**NHL**	**62**	**2**	**11**	**13**	**42**	**0**	**0**	**0**	**68**	**2.9**	**–7**	....	....	....	....	....	....	....	....	....	....	....	....	....
	Tampa Bay	**NHL**	**13**	**0**	**5**	**5**	**16**	**0**	**0**	**0**	**13**	**0.0**	**0**	....	....	....	....	....	....	....	....	....	....	....	....	....
1997-98	**Tampa Bay**	**NHL**	**37**	**4**	**6**	**10**	**26**	**4**	**0**	**0**	**41**	**9.8**	**–25**	....	....	....	....	....	....	....	....	....	....	....	....	....
	Florida	**NHL**	**19**	**0**	**7**	**7**	**18**	**0**	**0**	**0**	**20**	**0.0**	**–7**	....	....	....	....	....	....	....	....	....	....	....	....	....
1998-99	**Florida**	**NHL**	**3**	**0**	**0**	**0**	**2**	**0**	**0**	**0**	**2**	**0.0**	**0**	**0**	**0.0**	**1**	**3**	**17:26**	....	....	....	....	....	....	....	....
	San Jose	**NHL**	**69**	**4**	**18**	**22**	**42**	**2**	**0**	**1**	**68**	**5.9**	**2**	**0**	**0.0**	**37**	**86**	**20:55**	**6**	**0**	**7**	**7**	**10**	**0**	**0**	**0**
	NHL Totals		**663**	**50**	**296**	**346**	**528**	**21**	**2**	**5**	**933**	**5.4**		**0**	**0.0**	**38**	**89**	**20:46**	**44**	**4**	**19**	**23**	**75**	**0**	**0**	**0**

CCHA Second All-Star Team (1987)

Traded to **San Jose** by **NY Islanders** for San Jose's 3rd round choice (Jason Strudwick) in 1994 Entry Draft, June 20, 1993. Traded to **St. Louis** by **San Jose** with San Jose's 3rd round choice (later traded to Colorado — Colorado selected Rick Berry) in 1997 Entry Draft for Craig Janney and cash, March 6, 1995. Traded to **Edmonton** by **St. Louis** with Donald Dufresne for Igor Kravchuk and Ken Sutton, January 4, 1996. Traded to **Tampa Bay** by **Edmonton** for Drew Bannister and Tampa Bay's 6th round choice (Peter Sarno) in 1997 Entry Draft, March 18, 1997. Traded to **Florida** by **Tampa Bay** with Dino Ciccarelli for Mark Fitzpatrick and Jody Hull, January 15, 1998. Traded to **San Jose** by **Florida** for Alex Hicks and San Jose's 5th round choice (later traded to NY Islanders, NY Islanders selected Adam Johnson) in 1999 Entry Draft, November 11, 1998.

NUMMINEN, Teppo

(NOO-mih-nehn, TEH-poh) **PHX.**

Defense. Shoots right. 6'1", 195 lbs. Born, Tampere, Finland, July 3, 1968. Winnipeg's 2nd choice, 29th overall, in 1986 Entry Draft.

Season	Club	League	GP	G	A	Pts	PIM	PP	SH	GW	S	%	+/–	TF	F%	H	SB	Min	GP	G	A	Pts	PIM	PP	SH	GW
1984-85	Tappara	Finn-Jr.	30	14	17	31	10	....	....	....	....	....	....	....	....	....	....	....	....	....	....	....	....	....	....	....
1985-86	Tappara	Finland	31	2	4	6	6	....	....	....	....	....	....	....	....	....	....	....	8	0	0	0	0	....	....	....
1986-87	Tappara	Finland	44	9	9	18	16	....	....	....	....	....	....	....	....	....	....	....	9	4	1	5	4	....	....	....
1987-88	Tappara	Finland	40	10	10	20	29	....	....	....	....	....	....	....	....	....	....	....	10	6	6	12	6	....	....	....
	Finland	Olympics	6	1	4	5	0	....	....	....	....	....	....	....	....	....	....	....	....	....	....	....	....	....	....	....
1988-89	**Winnipeg**	**NHL**	**69**	**1**	**14**	**15**	**36**	**0**	**1**	**0**	**85**	**1.2**	**–11**	....	....	....	....	....	....	....	....	....	....	....	....	....
1989-90	**Winnipeg**	**NHL**	**79**	**11**	**32**	**43**	**20**	**1**	**0**	**1**	**105**	**10.5**	**–4**	....	....	....	....	....	**7**	**1**	**2**	**3**	**10**	**0**	**0**	**0**
1990-91	**Winnipeg**	**NHL**	**80**	**8**	**25**	**33**	**28**	**3**	**0**	**0**	**151**	**5.3**	**–15**	....	....	....	....	....	....	....	....	....	....	....	....	....
1991-92	**Winnipeg**	**NHL**	**80**	**5**	**34**	**39**	**32**	**4**	**0**	**1**	**143**	**3.5**	**15**	....	....	....	....	....	**7**	**0**	**0**	**0**	**0**	**0**	**0**	**0**
1992-93	**Winnipeg**	**NHL**	**66**	**7**	**30**	**37**	**33**	**3**	**1**	**0**	**103**	**6.8**	**4**	....	....	....	....	....	**6**	**1**	**1**	**2**	**2**	**1**	**0**	**0**
1993-94	**Winnipeg**	**NHL**	**57**	**5**	**18**	**23**	**28**	**4**	**0**	**1**	**89**	**5.6**	**–23**	....	....	....	....	....	....	....	....	....	....	....	....	....
1994-95	TuTo Turku	Finland	12	3	8	11	4	....	....	....	....	....	....	....	....	....	....	....	....	....	....	....	....	....	....	....
	Winnipeg	**NHL**	**42**	**5**	**16**	**21**	**16**	**2**	**0**	**0**	**86**	**5.8**	**12**	....	....	....	....	....	....	....	....	....	....	....	....	....
1995-96	**Winnipeg**	**NHL**	**74**	**11**	**43**	**54**	**22**	**6**	**0**	**3**	**165**	**6.7**	**–4**	....	....	....	....	....	**6**	**0**	**0**	**0**	**2**	**0**	**0**	**0**
1996-97	**Phoenix**	**NHL**	**82**	**2**	**25**	**27**	**28**	**0**	**0**	**0**	**135**	**1.5**	**–3**	....	....	....	....	....	**7**	**3**	**3**	**6**	**0**	**1**	**0**	**1**
1997-98	**Phoenix**	**NHL**	**82**	**11**	**40**	**51**	**30**	**6**	**0**	**2**	**126**	**8.7**	**25**	....	....	....	....	....	**1**	**0**	**0**	**0**	**0**	**0**	**0**	**0**
	Finland	Olympics	6	1	1	2	2	....	....	....	....	....	....	....	....	....	....	....	....	....	....	....	....	....	....	....
1998-99	**Phoenix**	**NHL**	**82**	**10**	**30**	**40**	**30**	**1**	**0**	**0**	**156**	**6.4**	**3**	**2**	**0.0**	**73**	**99**	**24:26**	**7**	**2**	**1**	**3**	**4**	**2**	**0**	**0**
	NHL Totals		**793**	**76**	**307**	**383**	**303**	**30**	**2**	**8**	**1344**	**5.7**		**2**	**0.0**	**73**	**99**	**24:26**	**41**	**7**	**7**	**14**	**18**	**4**	**0**	**1**

Played in NHL All-Star Game (1999)

Transferred to **Phoenix** after **Winnipeg** franchise relocated, July 1, 1996.

NURMINEN, Kai

(NUHR-mih-nehn, KIGH)

Left wing. Shoots left. 6'1", 198 lbs. Born, Turku, Finland, March 29, 1969. Los Angeles' 9th choice, 193rd overall, in 1996 Entry Draft.

Season	Club	League	GP	G	A	Pts	PIM	PP	SH	GW	S	%	+/–	TF	F%	H	SB	Min	GP	G	A	Pts	PIM	PP	SH	GW
1989-90	TPS Turku	Finn-Jr.	22	13	10	23	14	....	....	....	....	....	....	....	....	....	....	....	....	....	....	....	....	....	....	....
1990-91	TuTo Turku	Finland-2	33	26	20	46	14	....	....	....	....	....	....	....	....	....	....	....	....	....	....	....	....	....	....	....
1991-92	Kiekko-67	Finland-2	44	44	19	63	34	....	....	....	....	....	....	....	....	....	....	....	....	....	....	....	....	....	....	....
1992-93	TPS Turku	Finland	31	4	6	10	13	....	....	....	....	....	....	....	....	....	....	....	7	1	2	3	0	....	....	....
	Kiekko-67	Finland-2	8	6	4	10	2	....	....	....	....	....	....	....	....	....	....	....	....	....	....	....	....	....	....	....
1993-94	TPS Turku	Finland	45	23	12	35	20	....	....	....	....	....	....	....	....	....	....	....	11	0	3	3	4	....	....	....
1994-95	HPK Hameelinna	Finland	49	30	25	55	40	....	....	....	....	....	....	....	....	....	....	....	....	....	....	....	....	....	....	....
1995-96	HV Jonkoping	Sweden	40	31	24	55	30	....	....	....	....	....	....	....	....	....	....	....	4	3	1	4	8	....	....	....
1996-97	**Los Angeles**	**NHL**	**67**	**16**	**11**	**27**	**22**	**4**	**0**	**1**	**112**	**14.3**	**–3**	....	....	....	....	....	....	....	....	....	....	....	....	....
1997-98	V. Frolunda	Sweden	23	9	7	16	24	....	....	....	....	....	....	....	....	....	....	....	....	....	....	....	....	....	....	....
	Jokerit	Finland	20	7	9	16	30	....	....	....	....	....	....	....	....	....	....	....	8	5	3	8	4	....	....	....
1998-99	HC Davos	Switz.	42	26	14	40	26	....	....	....	....	....	....	....	....	....	....	....	....	....	....	....	....	....	....	....
	NHL Totals		**67**	**16**	**11**	**27**	**22**	**4**	**0**	**1**	**112**	**14.3**		....	....	....	....	....	....	....	....	....	....	....	....	....

Finnish First All-Star Team (1995)

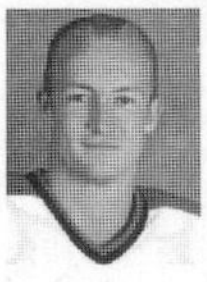

NYLANDER, Michael

(NEE-lan-duhr) **T.B.**

Center. Shoots left. 5'11", 195 lbs. Born, Stockholm, Sweden, October 3, 1972. Hartford's 4th choice, 59th overall, in 1991 Entry Draft.

Season	Club	League	GP	G	A	Pts	PIM	PP	SH	GW	S	%	+/–	TF	F%	H	SB	Min	GP	G	A	Pts	PIM	PP	SH	GW
1987-88	RA-73	Sweden-3	3	0	0	0	0	....	....	....	....	....	....	....	....	....	....	....	....	....	....	....	....	....	....	....
1989-90	Huddinge IK	Sweden-2	31	7	15	22	4	....	....	....	....	....	....	....	....	....	....	....	5	3	0	3	0	....	....	....
1990-91	Huddinge IK	Sweden-2	33	14	20	34	10	....	....	....	....	....	....	....	....	....	....	....	2	0	0	0	0	....	....	....
1991-92	AIK Solna	Sweden	40	11	17	28	30	....	....	....	....	....	....	....	....	....	....	....	3	1	4	5	4	....	....	....
1992-93	**Hartford**	**NHL**	**59**	**11**	**22**	**33**	**36**	**3**	**0**	**1**	**85**	**12.9**	**–7**	....	....	....	....	....	....	....	....	....	....	....	....	....
	Springfield	AHL	....	....	....	....	....	....	....	....	....	....	....	....	....	....	....	....	3	3	3	6	2	....	....	....
1993-94	**Hartford**	**NHL**	**58**	**11**	**33**	**44**	**24**	**4**	**0**	**1**	**74**	**14.9**	**–2**	....	....	....	....	....	....	....	....	....	....	....	....	....
	Springfield	AHL	4	0	9	9	0	....	....	....	....	....	....	....	....	....	....	....	....	....	....	....	....	....	....	....
	Calgary	**NHL**	**15**	**2**	**9**	**11**	**6**	**0**	**0**	**0**	**21**	**9.5**	**10**	....	....	....	....	....	**3**	**0**	**0**	**0**	**0**	**0**	**0**	**0**
1994-95	JyP Jyvaskyla	Finland	16	11	19	30	63	....	....	....	....	....	....	....	....	....	....	....	....	....	....	....	....	....	....	....
	Calgary	**NHL**	**6**	**0**	**1**	**1**	**2**	**0**	**0**	**0**	**2**	**0.0**	**1**	....	....	....	....	....	**6**	**0**	**6**	**6**	**2**	**0**	**0**	**0**
1995-96	**Calgary**	**NHL**	**73**	**17**	**38**	**55**	**20**	**4**	**0**	**6**	**163**	**10.4**	**0**	....	....	....	....	....	**4**	**0**	**0**	**0**	**0**	**0**	**0**	**0**
1996-97	HC Lugano	Switz.	36	12	43	55	28	....	....	....	....	....	....	....	....	....	....	....	8	3	8	11	8	....	....	....
1997-98	**Calgary**	**NHL**	**65**	**13**	**23**	**36**	**24**	**0**	**0**	**2**	**117**	**11.1**	**10**	....	....	....	....	....	....	....	....	....	....	....	....	....
	Sweden	Olympics	4	0	0	0	6	....	....	....	....	....	....	....	....	....	....	....	....	....	....	....	....	....	....	....
1998-99	**Calgary**	**NHL**	**9**	**2**	**3**	**5**	**2**	**1**	**0**	**0**	**7**	**28.6**	**1**	**25**	**60.0**	**1**	**0**	**11:10**	....	....	....	....	....	....	....	....
	Tampa Bay	**NHL**	**24**	**2**	**7**	**9**	**6**	**0**	**0**	**0**	**26**	**7.7**	**–10**	**75**	**44.0**	**4**	**6**	**13:29**	....	....	....	....	....	....	....	....
	NHL Totals		**309**	**58**	**136**	**194**	**120**	**12**	**0**	**10**	**495**	**11.7**		**100**	**48.0**	**5**	**6**	**12:51**	**13**	**0**	**6**	**6**	**2**	**0**	**0**	**0**

Swedish Rookie of the Year (1992) • Swedish World All-Star Team (1996, 1997)

Traded to **Calgary** by **Hartford** with James Patrick and Zarley Zalapski for Gary Suter, Paul Ranheim and Ted Drury, March 10, 1994. Traded to **Tampa Bay** by **Calgary** for Andrei Nazarov, January 19, 1999.

OATES, Adam

(OHTS) **WSH.**

Center. Shoots right. 5'11", 185 lbs. Born, Weston, Ont., August 27, 1962.

Season	Club	League	GP	G	A	Pts	PIM	PP	SH	GW	S	%	+/–	TF	F%	H	SB	Min	GP	G	A	Pts	PIM	PP	SH	GW
1980-81	Port Credit	OJHL-B	34	30	36	66	41	....	....	....	....	....	....	....	....	....	....	....	....	....	....	....	....	....	....	....
	Markham	OJHL	9	1	6	7	2	....	....	....	....	....	....	....	....	....	....	....	....	....	....	....	....	....	....	....
	Markham	OJHL-B	35	57	37	94	....	....	....	....	....	....	....	....	....	....	....	....	....	....	....	....	....	....	....	....
1981-82	Markham	OJHL-B	40	59	110	169	....	....	....	....	....	....	....	....	....	....	....	....	....	....	....	....	....	....	....	....
1982-83	RPI Engineers	ECAC	22	9	33	42	8	....	....	....	....	....	....	....	....	....	....	....	....	....	....	....	....	....	....	....
1983-84	RPI Engineers	ECAC	38	26	57	83	15	....	....	....	....	....	....	....	....	....	....	....	....	....	....	....	....	....	....	....

			Regular Season																Playoffs							
Season	Club	League	GP	G	A	Pts	PIM	PP	SH	GW	S	%	+/–	TF	F%	H	SB	Min	GP	G	A	Pts	PIM	PP	SH	GW
1984-85	RPI Engineers	ECAC	38	31	60	91	29	....	....	....	....	....	....	....	....	....	....	....	....	....	....	....	....	....	....	....
1985-86	**Detroit**	**NHL**	**38**	**9**	**11**	**20**	**10**	**1**	**0**	**1**	**49**	**18.4**	**–24**	....	....	....	....	....	....	....	....	....	....	....	....	....
	Adirondack	AHL	34	18	28	46	4	....	....	....	....	....	....	....	....	....	....	....	17	7	14	21	4	....	....	....
1986-87	**Detroit**	**NHL**	**76**	**15**	**32**	**47**	**21**	**4**	**0**	**1**	**138**	**10.9**	**0**	....	....	....	....	....	**16**	**4**	**7**	**11**	**6**	**0**	**0**	**1**
1987-88	**Detroit**	**NHL**	**63**	**14**	**40**	**54**	**20**	**3**	**0**	**3**	**111**	**12.6**	**16**	....	....	....	....	....	**16**	**8**	**12**	**20**	**6**	**4**	**0**	**1**
1988-89	**Detroit**	**NHL**	**69**	**16**	**62**	**78**	**14**	**2**	**0**	**1**	**127**	**12.6**	**–1**	....	....	....	....	....	**6**	**0**	**8**	**8**	**2**	**0**	**0**	**0**
1989-90	**St. Louis**	**NHL**	**80**	**23**	**79**	**102**	**30**	**6**	**2**	**3**	**168**	**13.7**	**9**	....	....	....	....	....	**12**	**2**	**12**	**14**	**4**	**1**	**0**	**0**
1990-91	**St. Louis**	**NHL**	**61**	**25**	**90**	**115**	**29**	**3**	**1**	**3**	**139**	**18.0**	**15**	....	....	....	....	....	**13**	**7**	**13**	**20**	**10**	**2**	**0**	**1**
1991-92	**St. Louis**	**NHL**	**54**	**10**	**59**	**69**	**12**	**3**	**0**	**3**	**118**	**8.5**	**–4**	....	....	....	....	....	....	....	....	....	....	....	....	....
	Boston	**NHL**	**26**	**10**	**20**	**30**	**10**	**3**	**0**	**1**	**73**	**13.7**	**–5**	....	....	....	....	....	**15**	**5**	**14**	**19**	**4**	**3**	**0**	**2**
1992-93	**Boston**	**NHL**	**84**	**45**	***97**	**142**	**32**	**24**	**1**	**11**	**254**	**17.7**	**15**	....	....	....	....	....	**4**	**0**	**9**	**9**	**4**	**0**	**0**	**0**
1993-94	**Boston**	**NHL**	**77**	**32**	**80**	**112**	**45**	**16**	**2**	**3**	**197**	**16.2**	**10**	....	....	....	....	....	**13**	**3**	**9**	**12**	**8**	**2**	**0**	**0**
1994-95	**Boston**	**NHL**	**48**	**12**	**41**	**53**	**8**	**4**	**1**	**2**	**109**	**11.0**	**–11**	....	....	....	....	....	**5**	**1**	**0**	**1**	**2**	**1**	**0**	**0**
1995-96	**Boston**	**NHL**	**70**	**25**	**67**	**92**	**18**	**7**	**1**	**2**	**183**	**13.7**	**16**	....	....	....	....	....	**5**	**2**	**5**	**7**	**2**	**0**	**1**	**0**
1996-97	**Boston**	**NHL**	**63**	**18**	**52**	**70**	**10**	**2**	**2**	**4**	**138**	**13.0**	**–3**	....	....	....	....	....	....	....	....	....	....	....	....	....
	Washington	**NHL**	**17**	**4**	**8**	**12**	**4**	**1**	**0**	**1**	**22**	**18.2**	**–2**	....	....	....	....	....	....	....	....	....	....	....	....	....
1997-98	**Washington**	**NHL**	**82**	**18**	**58**	**76**	**36**	**3**	**2**	**3**	**121**	**14.9**	**6**	....	....	....	....	....	**21**	**6**	**11**	**17**	**8**	**1**	**1**	**1**
1998-99	**Washington**	**NHL**	**59**	**12**	**42**	**54**	**22**	**3**	**0**	**0**	**79**	**15.2**	**–1**	**1330**	**59.2**	**17**	**22**	**20:34**	....	....	....	....	....	....	....	....
	NHL Totals		**967**	**288**	**838**	**1126**	**321**	**85**	**12**	**42**	**2026**	**14.2**		**1330**	**59.2**	**17**	**22**	**20:34**	**126**	**38**	**100**	**138**	**56**	**14**	**2**	**6**

ECAC Second All-Star Team (1984) • NCAA East First All-American Team (1984, 1985) • ECAC First All-Star Team (1985) • NCAA Championship All-Tournament Team (1985) • NHL Second All-Star Team (1991)

Played in NHL All-Star Game (1991, 1992, 1993, 1994, 1997)

Signed as a free agent by **Detroit,** June 28, 1985. Traded to **St. Louis** by **Detroit** with Paul MacLean for Bernie Federko and Tony McKegney, June 15, 1989. Traded to **Boston** by **St. Louis** for Craig Janney and Stephane Quintal, February 7, 1992. Traded to **Washington** by **Boston** with Bill Ranford and Rick Tocchet for Jim Carey, Anson Carter, Jason Allison and Washington's 3rd round choice (Lee Goren) in 1997 Entry Draft, March 1, 1997.

ODELEIN, Lyle

(OH-duh-LIGHN) **N.J.**

Defense. Shoots right. 5'11", 210 lbs. Born, Quill Lake, Sask., July 21, 1968. Montreal's 8th choice, 141st overall, in 1986 Entry Draft.

Season	Club	League	GP	G	A	Pts	PIM	PP	SH	GW	S	%	+/–	TF	F%	H	SB	Min	GP	G	A	Pts	PIM	PP	SH	GW
1984-85	Regina	AAHA	26	12	13	25	30	....	....	....	....	....	....	....	....	....	....	....	....	....	....	....	....	....	....	....
1985-86	Moose Jaw	WHL	67	9	37	46	117	....	....	....	....	....	....	....	....	....	....	....	13	1	6	7	34	....	....	....
1986-87	Moose Jaw	WHL	59	9	50	59	70	....	....	....	....	....	....	....	....	....	....	....	9	2	5	7	26	....	....	....
1987-88	Moose Jaw	WHL	63	15	43	58	166	....	....	....	....	....	....	....	....	....	....	....	....	....	....	....	....	....	....	....
1988-89	Sherbrooke	AHL	33	3	4	7	120	....	....	....	....	....	....	....	....	....	....	....	3	0	2	2	5	....	....	....
	Peoria	IHL	36	2	8	10	116	....	....	....	....	....	....	....	....	....	....	....	....	....	....	....	....	....	....	....
1989-90	**Montreal**	**NHL**	**8**	**0**	**2**	**2**	**33**	**0**	**0**	**0**	**1**	**0.0**	**–1**	....	....	....	....	....	....	....	....	....	....	....	....	....
	Sherbrooke	AHL	68	7	24	31	265	....	....	....	....	....	....	....	....	....	....	....	12	6	5	11	79	....	....	....
1990-91	**Montreal**	**NHL**	**52**	**0**	**2**	**2**	**259**	**0**	**0**	**0**	**25**	**0.0**	**7**	....	....	....	....	....	**12**	**0**	**0**	**0**	**54**	**0**	**0**	**0**
1991-92	**Montreal**	**NHL**	**71**	**1**	**7**	**8**	**212**	**0**	**0**	**0**	**43**	**2.3**	**15**	....	....	....	....	....	**7**	**0**	**0**	**0**	**11**	**0**	**0**	**0**
1992-93♦	**Montreal**	**NHL**	**83**	**2**	**14**	**16**	**205**	**0**	**0**	**0**	**79**	**2.5**	**35**	....	....	....	....	....	**20**	**1**	**5**	**6**	**30**	**0**	**0**	**0**
1993-94	**Montreal**	**NHL**	**79**	**11**	**29**	**40**	**276**	**6**	**0**	**2**	**116**	**9.5**	**8**	....	....	....	....	....	**7**	**0**	**0**	**0**	**17**	**0**	**0**	**0**
1994-95	**Montreal**	**NHL**	**48**	**3**	**7**	**10**	**152**	**0**	**0**	**0**	**74**	**4.1**	**–13**	....	....	....	....	....	....	....	....	....	....	....	....	....
1995-96	**Montreal**	**NHL**	**79**	**3**	**14**	**17**	**230**	**0**	**1**	**0**	**74**	**4.1**	**8**	....	....	....	....	....	**6**	**1**	**1**	**2**	**6**	**0**	**1**	**0**
1996-97	**New Jersey**	**NHL**	**79**	**3**	**13**	**16**	**110**	**1**	**0**	**2**	**93**	**3.2**	**16**	....	....	....	....	....	**10**	**2**	**2**	**4**	**19**	**1**	**0**	**0**
1997-98	**New Jersey**	**NHL**	**79**	**4**	**19**	**23**	**171**	**1**	**0**	**0**	**76**	**5.3**	**11**	....	....	....	....	....	**6**	**1**	**1**	**2**	**21**	**1**	**0**	**1**
1998-99	**New Jersey**	**NHL**	**70**	**5**	**26**	**31**	**114**	**1**	**0**	**0**	**101**	**5.0**	**6**	**0**	**0.0**	**51**	**71**	**19:53**	**7**	**0**	**3**	**3**	**10**	**0**	**0**	**0**
	NHL Totals		**648**	**32**	**133**	**165**	**1762**	**9**	**1**	**4**	**682**	**4.7**		**0**	**0.0**	**51**	**71**	**19:53**	**75**	**5**	**12**	**17**	**168**	**2**	**1**	**1**

Traded to **New Jersey** by **Montreal** for Stephane Richer, August 22, 1996.

ODGERS, Jeff

(AWD-juhrs) **COL.**

Right wing. Shoots right. 6', 200 lbs. Born, Spy Hill, Sask., May 31, 1969.

Season	Club	League	GP	G	A	Pts	PIM	PP	SH	GW	S	%	+/–	TF	F%	H	SB	Min	GP	G	A	Pts	PIM	PP	SH	GW
1985-86	Saskatoon	AAHA	36	[illegible]	[illegible]	[illegible]	74	....	....	....	....	....	....	....	....	....	....	....	....	....	....	....	....	....	....	....
1986-87	Brandon	WHL	70	7	14	21	150	....	....	....	....	....	....	....	....	....	....	....	....	....	....	....	....	....	....	....
1987-88	Brandon	WHL	70	17	18	35	202	....	....	....	....	....	....	....	....	....	....	....	4	1	1	2	14	....	....	....
1988-89	Brandon	WHL	71	31	29	60	277	....	....	....	....	....	....	....	....	....	....	....	....	....	....	....	....	....	....	....
1989-90	Brandon	WHL	64	37	28	65	209	....	....	....	....	....	....	....	....	....	....	....	....	....	....	....	....	....	....	....
1990-91	Kansas City	IHL	77	12	19	31	318	....	....	....	....	....	....	....	....	....	....	....	....	....	....	....	....	....	....	....
1991-92	**San Jose**	**NHL**	**61**	**7**	**4**	**11**	**217**	**0**	**0**	**0**	**64**	**10.9**	**–21**	....	....	....	....	....	....	....	....	....	....	....	....	....
	Kansas City	IHL	12	2	2	4	56	....	....	....	....	....	....	....	....	....	....	....	4	2	1	3	0	....	....	....
1992-93	**San Jose**	**NHL**	**66**	**12**	**15**	**27**	**253**	**6**	**0**	**0**	**100**	**12.0**	**–26**	....	....	....	....	....	....	....	....	....	....	....	....	....
1993-94	**San Jose**	**NHL**	**81**	**13**	**8**	**21**	**222**	**7**	**0**	**0**	**73**	**17.8**	**–13**	....	....	....	....	....	**11**	**0**	**0**	**0**	**11**	**0**	**0**	**0**
1994-95	**San Jose**	**NHL**	**48**	**4**	**3**	**7**	**117**	**0**	**0**	**1**	**47**	**8.5**	**–8**	....	....	....	....	....	**11**	**1**	**1**	**2**	**23**	**0**	**0**	**0**
1995-96	**San Jose**	**NHL**	**78**	**12**	**4**	**16**	**192**	**0**	**0**	**1**	**84**	**14.3**	**–4**	....	....	....	....	....	....	....	....	....	....	....	....	....
1996-97	**Boston**	**NHL**	**80**	**7**	**8**	**15**	**197**	**1**	**0**	**1**	**84**	**8.3**	**–15**	....	....	....	....	....	....	....	....	....	....	....	....	....
1997-98	Providence	AHL	4	0	0	0	31	....	....	....	....	....	....	....	....	....	....	....	....	....	....	....	....	....	....	....
	Colorado	**NHL**	**68**	**5**	**8**	**13**	**213**	**0**	**0**	**0**	**47**	**10.6**	**5**	....	....	....	....	....	**6**	**0**	**0**	**0**	**25**	**0**	**0**	**0**
1998-99	**Colorado**	**NHL**	**75**	**2**	**3**	**5**	**259**	**1**	**0**	**0**	**39**	**5.1**	**–3**	**8**	**37.5**	**56**	**6**	**5:07**	**15**	**1**	**0**	**1**	**14**	**0**	**0**	**1**
	NHL Totals		**557**	**62**	**53**	**115**	**1670**	**15**	**0**	**3**	**538**	**11.5**		**8**	**37.5**	**56**	**6**	**5:07**	**43**	**2**	**1**	**3**	**73**	**0**	**0**	**1**

Signed as a free agent by **San Jose**, September 3, 1991. Traded to **Boston** by **San Jose** with Pittsburgh's 5th round choice (previously acquired, Boston selected Elias Abrahamsson) in 1996 Entry Draft for Al Iafrate, June 21, 1996. Signed as a free agent by **Colorado**, October 24, 1997.

ODJICK, Gino

(OH-jihk) **NYI**

Left wing. Shoots left. 6'3", 210 lbs. Born, Maniwaki, Que., September 7, 1970. Vancouver's 5th choice, 86th overall, in 1990 Entry Draft.

Season	Club	League	GP	G	A	Pts	PIM	PP	SH	GW	S	%	+/–	TF	F%	H	SB	Min	GP	G	A	Pts	PIM	PP	SH	GW
1987-88	Hawkesbury	OJHL	40	2	4	6	167	....	....	....	....	....	....	....	....	....	....	....	....	....	....	....	....	....	....	....
1988-89	Laval	QMJHL	50	9	15	24	278	....	....	....	....	....	....	....	....	....	....	....	16	0	9	9	129	....	....	....
1989-90	Laval	QMJHL	51	12	26	38	280	....	....	....	....	....	....	....	....	....	....	....	13	6	5	11	110	....	....	....
1990-91	**Vancouver**	**NHL**	**45**	**7**	**1**	**8**	**296**	**0**	**0**	**0**	**39**	**17.9**	**–6**	....	....	....	....	....	**6**	**0**	**0**	**0**	**18**	**0**	**0**	**0**
	Milwaukee	IHL	17	7	3	10	102	....	....	....	....	....	....	....	....	....	....	....	....	....	....	....	....	....	....	....
1991-92	**Vancouver**	**NHL**	**65**	**4**	**6**	**10**	**348**	**0**	**0**	**0**	**68**	**5.9**	**–1**	....	....	....	....	....	**4**	**0**	**0**	**0**	**6**	**0**	**0**	**0**
1992-93	**Vancouver**	**NHL**	**75**	**4**	**13**	**17**	**370**	**0**	**0**	**1**	**79**	**5.1**	**3**	....	....	....	....	....	**1**	**0**	**0**	**0**	**0**	**0**	**0**	**0**
1993-94	**Vancouver**	**NHL**	**76**	**16**	**13**	**29**	**271**	**4**	**0**	**5**	**121**	**13.2**	**13**	....	....	....	....	....	**10**	**0**	**0**	**0**	**18**	**0**	**0**	**0**
1994-95	**Vancouver**	**NHL**	**23**	**4**	**5**	**9**	**109**	**0**	**0**	**0**	**35**	**11.4**	**–3**	....	....	....	....	....	**5**	**0**	**0**	**0**	**47**	**0**	**0**	**0**
1995-96	**Vancouver**	**NHL**	**55**	**3**	**4**	**7**	**181**	**0**	**0**	**0**	**59**	**5.1**	**–16**	....	....	....	....	....	**6**	**3**	**1**	**4**	**6**	**0**	**0**	**2**
1996-97	**Vancouver**	**NHL**	**70**	**5**	**8**	**13**	***371**	**1**	**0**	**0**	**85**	**5.9**	**–5**	....	....	....	....	....	....	....	....	....	....	....	....	....
1997-98	**Vancouver**	**NHL**	**35**	**3**	**2**	**5**	**181**	**0**	**0**	**1**	**36**	**8.3**	**–3**	....	....	....	....	....	....	....	....	....	....	....	....	....
	NY Islanders	**NHL**	**13**	**0**	**0**	**0**	**31**	**0**	**0**	**0**	**16**	**0.0**	**1**	....	....	....	....	....	....	....	....	....	....	....	....	....
1998-99	**NY Islanders**	**NHL**	**23**	**4**	**3**	**7**	**133**	**1**	**0**	**2**	**28**	**14.3**	**–2**	**2**	**0.0**	**20**	**2**	**9:51**	....	....	....	....	....	....	....	....
	NHL Totals		**480**	**50**	**55**	**105**	**2291**	**6**	**0**	**9**	**566**	**8.8**		**2**	**0.0**	**20**	**2**	**9:51**	**32**	**3**	**1**	**4**	**95**	**0**	**0**	**2**

Traded to **NY Islanders** by **Vancouver** for Jason Strudwick, March 23, 1998.

O'DONNELL, Sean

L.A.

Defense. Shoots left. 6'3", 230 lbs. Born, Ottawa, Ont., October 13, 1971. Buffalo's 6th choice, 123rd overall, in 1991 Entry Draft.

Season	Club	League	GP	G	A	Pts	PIM	PP	SH	GW	S	%	+/–	TF	F%	H	SB	Min	GP	G	A	Pts	PIM	PP	SH	GW
1987-88	Kanata	OJHL	54	4	25	29	96	....	....	....	....	....	....	....	....	....	....	....	....	....	....	....	....	....	....	....
1988-89	Sudbury	OHL	56	1	9	10	49	....	....	....	....	....	....	....	....	....	....	....	....	....	....	....	....	....	....	....
1989-90	Sudbury	OHL	64	7	19	31	114	....	....	....	....	....	....	....	....	....	....	....	7	1	2	3	8	....	....	....
1990-91	Sudbury	OHL	66	8	23	31	114	....	....	....	....	....	....	....	....	....	....	....	5	1	4	5	10	....	....	....
1991-92	Rochester	AHL	73	4	9	13	193	....	....	....	....	....	....	....	....	....	....	....	16	1	2	3	21	....	....	....
1992-93	Rochester	AHL	74	3	18	21	203	....	....	....	....	....	....	....	....	....	....	....	17	1	6	7	38	....	....	....
1993-94	Rochester	AHL	64	2	10	12	242	....	....	....	....	....	....	....	....	....	....	....	4	0	1	1	21	....	....	....

			Regular Season																Playoffs							
Season	Club	League	GP	G	A	Pts	PIM	PP	SH	GW	S	%	+/–	TF	F%	H	SB	Min	GP	G	A	Pts	PIM	PP	SH	GW
1994-95	Phoenix	IHL	61	2	18	20	132	....	....	....	....	....	....	....	....	....	....	....	9	0	1	1	21	....	....	....
	Los Angeles	**NHL**	**15**	**0**	**2**	**2**	**49**	**0**	**0**	**0**	**12**	**0.0**	**–2**	....	....	....	....	....	....	....	....	....	....	....	....	....
1995-96	**Los Angeles**	**NHL**	**71**	**2**	**5**	**7**	**127**	**0**	**0**	**0**	**65**	**3.1**	**3**	....	....	....	....	....	....	....	....	....	....	....	....	....
1996-97	**Los Angeles**	**NHL**	**55**	**5**	**12**	**17**	**144**	**2**	**0**	**0**	**68**	**7.4**	**–13**	....	....	....	....	....	....	....	....	....	....	....	....	....
1997-98	**Los Angeles**	**NHL**	**80**	**2**	**15**	**17**	**179**	**0**	**0**	**1**	**71**	**2.8**	**7**	....	....	....	....	....	**4**	**1**	**0**	**1**	**36**	**0**	**0**	**0**
1998-99	**Los Angeles**	**NHL**	**80**	**1**	**13**	**14**	**186**	**0**	**0**	**0**	**64**	**1.6**	**1**	**0**	**0.0**	**133**	**71**	**19:10**	....	....	....	....	....	....	....	....
	NHL Totals		**301**	**10**	**47**	**57**	**685**	**2**	**0**	**1**	**280**	**3.6**		**0**	**0.0**	**133**	**71**	**19:10**	**4**	**1**	**0**	**1**	**36**	**0**	**0**	**0**

Traded to **LA Kings** by **Buffalo** for Doug Houda, July 26, 1994.

OHLUND, Mattias

(OH-luhnd) **VAN.**

Defense. Shoots left. 6'2", 220 lbs. Born, Pitea, Sweden, September 9, 1976. Vancouver's 1st choice, 13th overall, in 1994 Entry Draft.

Season	Club	League	GP	G	A	Pts	PIM	PP	SH	GW	S	%	+/–	TF	F%	H	SB	Min	GP	G	A	Pts	PIM	PP	SH	GW
1992-93	Pitea IK	Sweden-2	22	0	6	6	16	....	....	....	....	....	....	....	....	....	....	....	....	....	....	....	....	....	....	....
1993-94	Pitea IK	Sweden-2	28	7	10	17	62	....	....	....	....	....	....	....	....	....	....	....	....	....	....	....	....	....	....	....
1994-95	Lulea HF	Sweden	34	6	10	16	34	....	....	....	....	....	....	....	....	....	....	....	9	4	0	4	16	....	....	....
1995-96	Lulea HF	Sweden	38	4	10	14	26	....	....	....	....	....	....	....	....	....	....	....	13	1	0	1	47	....	....	....
1996-97	Lulea HF	Sweden	47	7	9	16	38	....	....	....	....	....	....	....	....	....	....	....	10	1	2	3	8	....	....	....
	Lulea HF	EuroHL	6	0	3	3	0	....	....	....	....	....	....	....	....	....	....	....	....	....	....	....	....	....	....	....
1997-98	**Vancouver**	**NHL**	**77**	**7**	**23**	**30**	**76**	**1**	**0**	**0**	**172**	**4.1**	**3**	....	....	....	....	....	....	....	....	....	....	....	....	....
	Sweden	Olympics	4	0	1	1	4	....	....	....	....	....	....	....	....	....	....	....	....	....	....	....	....	....	....	....
1998-99	**Vancouver**	**NHL**	**74**	**9**	**26**	**35**	**83**	**2**	**1**	**1**	**129**	**7.0**	**–19**	**0**	**0.0**	**133**	**154**	**26:04**	....	....	....	....	....	....	....	....
	NHL Totals		**151**	**16**	**49**	**65**	**159**	**3**	**1**	**1**	**301**	**5.3**		**0**	**0.0**	**133**	**154**	**26:04**	....	....	....	....	....	....	....	....

NHL All-Rookie Team (1998)
Played in NHL All-Star Game (1999)

OLAUSSON, Fredrik

(OHL-ah-suhn) **ANA.**

Defense. Shoots right. 6'2", 198 lbs. Born, Dadesjo, Sweden, October 5, 1966. Winnipeg's 4th choice, 81st overall, in 1985 Entry Draft.

Season	Club	League	GP	G	A	Pts	PIM	PP	SH	GW	S	%	+/–	TF	F%	H	SB	Min	GP	G	A	Pts	PIM	PP	SH	GW
1982-83	Nybro	Sweden-2	31	4	4	8	12	....	....	....	....	....	....	....	....	....	....	....	....	....	....	....	....	....	....	....
1983-84	Nybro	Sweden-2	28	8	14	22	32	....	....	....	....	....	....	....	....	....	....	....	....	....	....	....	....	....	....	....
1984-85	Farjestads BK	Sweden	29	5	12	17	22	....	....	....	....	....	....	....	....	....	....	....	3	1	0	1	0	....	....	....
1985-86	Farjestads BK	Sweden	33	4	12	16	22	....	....	....	....	....	....	....	....	....	....	....	8	3	2	5	6	....	....	....
1986-87	**Winnipeg**	**NHL**	**72**	**7**	**29**	**36**	**24**	**1**	**0**	**2**	**119**	**5.9**	**–3**	....	....	....	....	....	**10**	**2**	**3**	**5**	**4**	**1**	**0**	**0**
1987-88	**Winnipeg**	**NHL**	**38**	**5**	**10**	**15**	**18**	**2**	**0**	**2**	**65**	**7.7**	**3**	....	....	....	....	....	**5**	**1**	**1**	**2**	**0**	**0**	**0**	**0**
1988-89	**Winnipeg**	**NHL**	**75**	**15**	**47**	**62**	**32**	**4**	**0**	**1**	**178**	**8.4**	**6**	....	....	....	....	....	....	....	....	....	....	....	....	....
1989-90	**Winnipeg**	**NHL**	**77**	**9**	**46**	**55**	**32**	**3**	**0**	**0**	**147**	**6.1**	**–1**	....	....	....	....	....	**7**	**0**	**2**	**2**	**2**	**0**	**0**	**0**
1990-91	**Winnipeg**	**NHL**	**71**	**12**	**29**	**41**	**24**	**5**	**0**	**0**	**168**	**7.1**	**–22**	....	....	....	....	....	....	....	....	....	....	....	....	....
1991-92	**Winnipeg**	**NHL**	**77**	**20**	**42**	**62**	**34**	**13**	**1**	**2**	**227**	**8.8**	**–31**	....	....	....	....	....	**7**	**1**	**5**	**6**	**4**	**1**	**0**	**0**
1992-93	**Winnipeg**	**NHL**	**68**	**16**	**41**	**57**	**22**	**11**	**0**	**3**	**165**	**9.7**	**–4**	....	....	....	....	....	**6**	**0**	**2**	**2**	**2**	**0**	**0**	**0**
1993-94	**Winnipeg**	**NHL**	**18**	**2**	**5**	**7**	**10**	**1**	**0**	**0**	**41**	**4.9**	**–3**	....	....	....	....	....	....	....	....	....	....	....	....	....
	Edmonton	**NHL**	**55**	**9**	**19**	**28**	**20**	**6**	**0**	**1**	**85**	**10.6**	**–4**	....	....	....	....	....	....	....	....	....	....	....	....	....
1994-95	Ehrwald	Austria	10	4	3	7	8	....	....	....	....	....	....	....	....	....	....	....	....	....	....	....	....	....	....	....
	Edmonton	**NHL**	**33**	**0**	**10**	**10**	**20**	**0**	**0**	**0**	**52**	**0.0**	**–4**	....	....	....	....	....	....	....	....	....	....	....	....	....
1995-96	**Edmonton**	**NHL**	**20**	**0**	**6**	**6**	**14**	**0**	**0**	**0**	**20**	**0.0**	**–14**	....	....	....	....	....	....	....	....	....	....	....	....	....
	Anaheim	**NHL**	**36**	**2**	**16**	**18**	**24**	**1**	**0**	**0**	**63**	**3.2**	**7**	....	....	....	....	....	....	....	....	....	....	....	....	....
1996-97	**Anaheim**	**NHL**	**20**	**2**	**9**	**11**	**8**	**1**	**0**	**0**	**35**	**5.7**	**–5**	....	....	....	....	....	....	....	....	....	....	....	....	....
	Pittsburgh	**NHL**	**51**	**7**	**20**	**27**	**24**	**2**	**0**	**3**	**75**	**9.3**	**21**	....	....	....	....	....	**4**	**0**	**1**	**1**	**0**	**0**	**0**	**0**
1997-98	**Pittsburgh**	**NHL**	**76**	**6**	**27**	**33**	**42**	**2**	**0**	**1**	**89**	**6.7**	**13**	....	....	....	....	....	**6**	**0**	**3**	**3**	**2**	**0**	**0**	**0**
1998-99	**Anaheim**	**NHL**	**74**	**16**	**40**	**56**	**30**	**10**	**0**	**2**	**121**	**13.2**	**17**	**0**	**0.0**	**41**	**56**	**19:47**	**4**	**0**	**2**	**2**	**4**	**0**	**0**	**0**
	NHL Totals		**861**	**128**	**396**	**524**	**378**	**62**	**1**	**17**	**1650**	**7.8**		**0**	**0.0**	**41**	**56**	**19:47**	**49**	**4**	**19**	**23**	**18**	**2**	**0**	**0**

Swedish World All-Star Team (1986)

Traded to **Edmonton** by **Winnipeg** with Winnipeg's 7th round choice (Curtis Sheptak) in 1994 Entry Draft for Edmonton's 3rd round choice (Tavis Hansen) in 1994 Entry Draft, December 6, 1993. Claimed on waivers by **Anaheim** from **Edmonton**, January 16, 1996. Traded to **Pittsburgh** by **Anaheim** with Alex Hicks for Shawn Antoski and Dmitri Mironov, November 19, 1996. Signed as a free agent by **Anaheim**, August 28, 1998.

OLCZYK, Ed

(OHL-chehk)

Center. Shoots left. 6'1", 205 lbs. Born, Chicago, IL, August 16, 1966. Chicago's 1st choice, 3rd overall, in 1984 Entry Draft.

Season	Club	League	GP	G	A	Pts	PIM	PP	SH	GW	S	%	+/–	TF	F%	H	SB	Min	GP	G	A	Pts	PIM	PP	SH	GW
1981-82	Team Illinois	USAHA	56	74	95	169	63	....	....	....	....	....	....	....	....	....	....	....	....	....	....	....	....	....	....	....
1982-83	Stratford	OJHL-B	42	50	92	141	54	....	....	....	....	....	....	....	....	....	....	....	....	....	....	....	....	....	....	....
1983-84	United States	Nat-Team	62	21	47	68	36	....	....	....	....	....	....	....	....	....	....	....	....	....	....	....	....	....	....	....
	United States	Olympics	6	2	5	7	0	....	....	....	....	....	....	....	....	....	....	....	....	....	....	....	....	....	....	....
1984-85	**Chicago**	**NHL**	**70**	**20**	**30**	**50**	**67**	**1**	**1**	**2**	**136**	**14.7**	**11**	....	....	....	....	....	**15**	**6**	**5**	**11**	**11**	**1**	**1**	**0**
1985-86	**Chicago**	**NHL**	**79**	**29**	**50**	**79**	**47**	**8**	**1**	**2**	**218**	**13.3**	**2**	....	....	....	....	....	**3**	**0**	**0**	**0**	**0**	**0**	**0**	**0**
1986-87	**Chicago**	**NHL**	**79**	**16**	**35**	**51**	**119**	**2**	**1**	**2**	**181**	**8.8**	**–4**	....	....	....	....	....	**4**	**1**	**1**	**2**	**4**	**0**	**0**	**0**
1987-88	**Toronto**	**NHL**	**80**	**42**	**33**	**75**	**55**	**14**	**4**	**3**	**243**	**17.3**	**–22**	....	....	....	....	....	**6**	**5**	**4**	**9**	**2**	**1**	**1**	**1**
1988-89	**Toronto**	**NHL**	**80**	**38**	**52**	**90**	**75**	**11**	**2**	**4**	**249**	**15.3**	**0**	....	....	....	....	....	....	....	....	....	....	....	....	....
1989-90	**Toronto**	**NHL**	**79**	**32**	**56**	**88**	**78**	**6**	**0**	**4**	**208**	**15.4**	**0**	....	....	....	....	....	**5**	**1**	**2**	**3**	**14**	**0**	**0**	**0**
1990-91	**Toronto**	**NHL**	**18**	**4**	**10**	**14**	**13**	**0**	**0**	**0**	**45**	**8.9**	**–7**	....	....	....	....	....	....	....	....	....	....	....	....	....
	Winnipeg	**NHL**	**61**	**26**	**31**	**57**	**69**	**14**	**0**	**2**	**181**	**14.4**	**–20**	....	....	....	....	....	....	....	....	....	....	....	....	....
1991-92	**Winnipeg**	**NHL**	**64**	**32**	**33**	**65**	**67**	**12**	**0**	**7**	**245**	**13.1**	**11**	....	....	....	....	....	**6**	**2**	**1**	**3**	**4**	**0**	**0**	**1**
1992-93	**Winnipeg**	**NHL**	**25**	**8**	**12**	**20**	**26**	**2**	**0**	**0**	**81**	**9.9**	**–11**	....	....	....	....	....	....	....	....	....	....	....	....	....
	NY Rangers	**NHL**	**46**	**13**	**16**	**29**	**26**	**0**	**0**	**1**	**109**	**11.9**	**9**	....	....	....	....	....	....	....	....	....	....	....	....	....
1993-94♦	**NY Rangers**	**NHL**	**37**	**3**	**5**	**8**	**28**	**0**	**0**	**1**	**40**	**7.5**	**–1**	....	....	....	....	....	**1**	**0**	**0**	**0**	**0**	**0**	**0**	**0**
1994-95	**NY Rangers**	**NHL**	**20**	**2**	**1**	**3**	**4**	**1**	**0**	**0**	**29**	**6.9**	**–2**	....	....	....	....	....	....	....	....	....	....	....	....	....
	Winnipeg	**NHL**	**13**	**2**	**8**	**10**	**8**	**1**	**0**	**0**	**27**	**7.4**	**1**	....	....	....	....	....	....	....	....	....	....	....	....	....
1995-96	**Winnipeg**	**NHL**	**51**	**27**	**22**	**49**	**65**	**16**	**0**	**1**	**147**	**18.4**	**0**	....	....	....	....	....	**6**	**1**	**2**	**3**	**6**	**0**	**0**	**0**
1996-97	**Los Angeles**	**NHL**	**67**	**21**	**23**	**44**	**45**	**0**	**0**	**5**	**166**	**12.7**	**–22**	....	....	....	....	....	....	....	....	....	....	....	....	....
	Pittsburgh	**NHL**	**12**	**4**	**7**	**11**	**6**	**5**	**1**	**1**	**29**	**13.8**	**8**	....	....	....	....	....	**5**	**1**	**0**	**1**	**12**	**0**	**1**	**1**
1997-98	**Pittsburgh**	**NHL**	**56**	**11**	**11**	**22**	**35**	**5**	**1**	**1**	**123**	**8.9**	**–9**	....	....	....	....	....	**6**	**2**	**0**	**2**	**4**	**1**	**1**	**1**
1998-99	**Chicago**	**NHL**	**61**	**10**	**15**	**25**	**29**	**2**	**1**	**2**	**88**	**11.4**	**–3**	**441**	**51.9**	**54**	**12**	**14:44**	....	....	....	....	....	....	....	....
	Chicago	IHL	7	2	2	4	6	....	....	....	....	....	....	....	....	....	....	....	....	....	....	....	....	....	....	....
	NHL Totals		**998**	**340**	**450**	**790**	**862**	**100**	**12**	**38**	**2545**	**13.4**		**441**	**51.9**	**54**	**12**	**14:44**	**57**	**19**	**15**	**34**	**57**	**3**	**4**	**4**

Traded to **Toronto** by **Chicago** with Al Secord for Rick Vaive, Steve Thomas and Bob McGill, September 3, 1987. Traded to **Winnipeg** by **Toronto** with Mark Osborne for Dave Ellett and Paul Fenton, November 10, 1990. Traded to **NY Rangers** by **Winnipeg** for Kris King and Tie Domi, December 28, 1992. Traded to **Winnipeg** by **NY Rangers** for Winnipeg's 5th round choice (Alexei Vasiliev) in 1995 Entry Draft, April 7, 1995. Signed as a free agent by **LA Kings**, July 8, 1996. Traded to **Pittsburgh** by **LA Kings** for Glen Murray, March 18, 1997. Signed as a free agent by **Chicago**, August 26, 1998.

OLIVER, David

PHX.

Right wing. Shoots right. 6', 190 lbs. Born, Sechelt, B.C., April 17, 1971. Edmonton's 7th choice, 144th overall, in 1991 Entry Draft.

Season	Club	League	GP	G	A	Pts	PIM	PP	SH	GW	S	%	+/–	TF	F%	H	SB	Min	GP	G	A	Pts	PIM	PP	SH	GW
1988-89	Vernon	BCJHL	58	41	38	79	38	....	....	....	....	....	....	....	....	....	....	....	....	....	....	....	....	....	....	....
1989-90	Vernon	BCJHL	58	51	48	99	22	....	....	....	....	....	....	....	....	....	....	....	....	....	....	....	....	....	....	....
1990-91	U. of Michigan	CCHA	27	13	11	24	34	....	....	....	....	....	....	....	....	....	....	....	....	....	....	....	....	....	....	....
1991-92	U. of Michigan	CCHA	44	31	27	58	32	....	....	....	....	....	....	....	....	....	....	....	....	....	....	....	....	....	....	....
1992-93	U. of Michigan	CCHA	40	35	20	55	18	....	....	....	....	....	....	....	....	....	....	....	....	....	....	....	....	....	....	....
1993-94	U. of Michigan	CCHA	41	28	40	68	16	....	....	....	....	....	....	....	....	....	....	....	....	....	....	....	....	....	....	....
1994-95	Cape Breton	AHL	32	11	18	29	8	....	....	....	....	....	....	....	....	....	....	....	....	....	....	....	....	....	....	....
	Edmonton	**NHL**	**44**	**16**	**14**	**30**	**20**	**10**	**0**	**0**	**79**	**20.3**	**–11**	....	....	....	....	....	....	....	....	....	....	....	....	....
1995-96	**Edmonton**	**NHL**	**80**	**20**	**19**	**39**	**34**	**14**	**0**	**0**	**131**	**15.3**	**–22**	....	....	....	....	....	....	....	....	....	....	....	....	....
1996-97	**Edmonton**	**NHL**	**17**	**1**	**2**	**3**	**4**	**0**	**0**	**0**	**22**	**4.5**	**–8**	....	....	....	....	....	....	....	....	....	....	....	....	....
	NY Rangers	**NHL**	**14**	**2**	**1**	**3**	**4**	**0**	**0**	**0**	**13**	**15.4**	**3**	....	....	....	....	....	**3**	**0**	**0**	**0**	**0**	**0**	**0**	**0**
1997-98	Houston	IHL	78	38	27	65	60	....	....	....	....	....	....	....	....	....	....	....	4	3	0	3	4	....	....	....

			Regular Season																Playoffs							
Season	Club	League	GP	G	A	Pts	PIM	PP	SH	GW	S	%	+/-	TF	F%	H	SB	Min	GP	G	A	Pts	PIM	PP	SH	GW
1998-99	**Ottawa**	**NHL**	**17**	**2**	**5**	**7**	**4**	0	0	0	18	11.1	1	3	33.3	8	2	10:34								
	Houston	IHL	37	18	17	35	30												19	10	6	16	22			
	NHL Totals		**172**	**41**	**41**	**82**	**66**	**24**	**0**	**0**	**263**	**15.6**		**3**	**33.3**	**8**	**2**	**10:34**	**3**	**0**	**0**	**0**	**0**	**0**	**0**	**0**

CCHA Second All-Star Team (1993) • CCHA First All-Star Team (1994) • NCAA West First All-American Team (1994)

Claimed on waivers by **NY Rangers** from **Edmonton**, February 21, 1997. Signed as a free agent by **Ottawa**, July 2, 1998. Signed as a free agent by **Phoenix**, July 20,.1999.

OLIWA, Krzysztof

(oh-LEE-vuh, KHRIH-stahf) **N.J.**

Left wing. Shoots left. 6'5", 235 lbs. Born, Tychy, Poland, April 12, 1973. New Jersey's 4th choice, 65th overall, in 1993 Entry Draft.

Season	Club	League	GP	G	A	Pts	PIM	PP	SH	GW	S	%	+/-	TF	F%	H	SB	Min	GP	G	A	Pts	PIM	PP	SH	GW
1990-91	GKS Katowski	Poland-Jr.	5	4	4	8	10																			
1991-92	GKS Tychy	Poland	10	3	7	10	6																			
1992-93	Welland	OJHL-B	30	13	21	34	127																			
1993-94	Albany	AHL	33	2	4	6	151																			
	Raleigh	ECHL	15	0	2	2	65												9	0	0	0	35			
1994-95	Albany	AHL	20	1	1	2	77																			
	Saint John	AHL	14	1	4	5	79																			
	Raleigh	ECHL	5	0	2	2	32																			
	Detroit	IHL	4	0	1	1	24																			
1995-96	Albany	AHL	51	5	11	16	217																			
	Raleigh	ECHL	9	1	0	1	53																			
1996-97	**New Jersey**	**NHL**	**1**	**0**	**0**	**0**	**5**	0	0	0	0	0.0	−1													
	Albany	AHL	60	13	14	27	322												15	7	1	8	49			
1997-98	**New Jersey**	**NHL**	**73**	**2**	**3**	**5**	**295**	0	0	2	53	3.8	3						**6**	**0**	**0**	**0**	**23**	0	0	0
1998-99	**New Jersey**	**NHL**	**64**	**5**	**7**	**12**	**240**	0	0	1	59	8.5	4	1	0.0	117	9	7:02	**1**	**0**	**0**	**0**	**2**	0	0	0
	NHL Totals		**138**	**7**	**10**	**17**	**540**	**0**	**0**	**3**	**112**	**6.3**		**1**	**0.0**	**117**	**9**	**7:02**	**7**	**0**	**0**	**0**	**25**	**0**	**0**	**0**

OLSSON, Christer

(OOL-suhn)

Defense. Shoots left. 5'11", 190 lbs. Born, Arboga, Sweden, July 24, 1970. St. Louis' 10th choice, 275th overall, in 1993 Entry Draft.

Season	Club	League	GP	G	A	Pts	PIM	PP	SH	GW	S	%	+/-	TF	F%	H	SB	Min	GP	G	A	Pts	PIM	PP	SH	GW
1991-92	Mora IK	Sweden-2	36	6	10	16	38																			
1992-93	Brynas IF	Sweden	22	4	4	8	18																			
1993-94	Brynas IF	Sweden	38	7	3	10	50												7	0	3	3	6			
1994-95	Brynas IF	Sweden	39	6	5	11	18												14	1	3	4	8			
1995-96	**St. Louis**	**NHL**	**26**	**2**	**8**	**10**	**14**	2	0	0	32	6.3	−6						**3**	**0**	**0**	**0**	**0**	0	0	0
	Worcester	AHL	39	7	7	14	22																			
1996-97	**St. Louis**	**NHL**	**5**	**0**	**1**	**1**	**0**	0	0	0	2	0.0	1													
	Worcester	AHL	2	0	0	0	0																			
	Ottawa	**NHL**	**25**	**2**	**3**	**5**	**10**	1	0	0	24	8.3	−5													
1997-98	V. Frolunda	Sweden	45	13	8	21	54												7	0	1	1	18			
1998-99	V. Frolunda	Sweden	47	5	11	16	48												4	0	1	1	4			
	NHL Totals		**56**	**4**	**12**	**16**	**24**	**3**	**0**	**0**	**58**	**6.9**							**3**	**0**	**0**	**0**	**0**	**0**	**0**	**0**

Traded to **Ottawa** by **St. Louis** for Pavol Demitra, November 27, 1996.

O'NEILL, Jeff

CAR.

Center. Shoots right. 6'1", 190 lbs. Born, Richmond Hill, Ont., February 23, 1976. Hartford's 1st choice, 5th overall, in 1994 Entry Draft.

Season	Club	League	GP	G	A	Pts	PIM	PP	SH	GW	S	%	+/-	TF	F%	H	SB	Min	GP	G	A	Pts	PIM	PP	SH	GW
1990-91	Richmond Hill	OMHA	78	56	134	190																				
1991-92	Thornhill	OJHL	43	27	53	80	48																			
1992-93	Guelph	OHL	65	32	47	79	88												5	2	2	4	6			
1993-94	Guelph	OHL	66	45	81	126	95												9	2	11	13	31			
1994-95	Guelph	OHL	57	43	81	124	56												14	8	18	26	34			
1995-96	**Hartford**	**NHL**	**65**	**8**	**19**	**27**	**40**	1	0	1	65	12.3	−3													
1996-97	**Hartford**	**NHL**	**72**	**14**	**16**	**30**	**40**	2	1	2	101	13.9	−24													
	Springfield	AHL	1	0	0	0	0																			
1997-98	**Carolina**	**NHL**	**74**	**19**	**20**	**39**	**67**	7	1	4	114	16.7	−8													
1998-99	**Carolina**	**NHL**	**75**	**16**	**15**	**31**	**66**	4	0	2	121	13.2	3	941	45.6	207	19	16:44	**6**	**0**	**1**	**1**	**0**	0	0	0
	NHL Totals		**286**	**57**	**70**	**127**	**213**	**14**	**2**	**9**	**401**	**14.2**		**941**	**45.6**	**207**	**19**	**16:44**	**6**	**0**	**1**	**1**	**0**	**0**	**0**	**0**

OHL First All-Star Team (1995)

Transferred to **Carolina** after **Hartford** franchise relocated, June 25, 1997.

ORSZAGH, Vladimir

(OHR-sahk) **NYI**

Right wing. Shoots left. 5'11", 173 lbs. Born, Banska Bystrica, Czech., May 24, 1977. NY Islanders' 4th choice, 106th overall, in 1995 Entry Draft.

Season	Club	League	GP	G	A	Pts	PIM	PP	SH	GW	S	%	+/-	TF	F%	H	SB	Min	GP	G	A	Pts	PIM	PP	SH	GW
1993-94	Banksa Bystrica	Slovak-Jr.	38	38	27	65																				
1994-95	Banska Bystrica	Slovak-2	38	18	12	30																				
1995-96	Banska Bystrica	Slovakia	31	9	5	14	22																			
1996-97	Utah	IHL	68	12	15	27	30												3	0	1	1	4			
1997-98	**NY Islanders**	**NHL**	**11**	**0**	**1**	**1**	**2**	0	0	0	9	0.0	−3													
	Utah	IHL	62	13	10	23	60												4	2	0	2	0			
1998-99	Lowell	AHL	68	18	23	41	57												3	2	2	4	2			
	NHL Totals		**11**	**0**	**1**	**1**	**2**	**0**	**0**	**0**	**9**	**0.0**														

O'SULLIVAN, Chris

VAN.

Defense. Shoots left. 6'2", 205 lbs. Born, Dorchester, MA, May 15, 1974. Calgary's 2nd choice, 30th overall, in 1992 Entry Draft.

Season	Club	League	GP	G	A	Pts	PIM	PP	SH	GW	S	%	+/-	TF	F%	H	SB	Min	GP	G	A	Pts	PIM	PP	SH	GW
1991-92	Catholic Memorial	H.S.	26	26	23	49	65																			
1992-93	Boston University	H.E.	5	0	2	2	4																			
1993-94	Boston University	H.E.	32	5	18	23	25																			
1994-95	Boston University	H.E.	40	23	33	56	48																			
1995-96	Boston University	H.E.	37	12	35	47	50																			
1996-97	**Calgary**	**NHL**	**27**	**2**	**8**	**10**	**2**	1	0	1	41	4.9	0													
	Saint John	AHL	29	3	8	11	17												5	0	4	4	0			
1997-98	**Calgary**	**NHL**	**12**	**0**	**2**	**2**	**10**	0	0	0	12	0.0	4													
	Saint John	AHL	32	4	10	14	2												21	2	17	19	18			
1998-99	**Calgary**	**NHL**	**10**	**0**	**1**	**1**	**2**	0	0	0	10	0.0	−1	1	0.0	4	1	9:07								
	Saint John	AHL	41	7	29	36	24																			
	Hartford	AHL	10	1	4	5	0												7	1	3	4	11			
	NHL Totals		**49**	**2**	**11**	**13**	**14**	**1**	**0**	**1**	**63**	**3.2**		**1**	**0.0**	**4**	**1**	**9:07**								

Hockey East First All-Star Team (1995) • NCAA East Second All-American Team (1995) • NCAA Championship All-Tournament Team (1995) • NCAA Championship Tournament MVP (1995)

Traded to **NY Rangers** by **Calgary** for Lee Sorochan, March 23, 1999. Signed as a free agent by **Vancouver**, August 20, 1999.

OZOLINSH, Sandis

(OH-zoh-LIHNCH, SAN-dihz) **COL.**

Defense. Shoots left. 6'3", 205 lbs. Born, Riga, Latvia, August 3, 1972. San Jose's 3rd choice, 30th overall, in 1991 Entry Draft.

Season	Club	League	GP	G	A	Pts	PIM	PP	SH	GW	S	%	+/-	TF	F%	H	SB	Min	GP	G	A	Pts	PIM	PP	SH	GW
1990-91	Dynamo Riga	USSR	44	0	3	3	51																			
1991-92	Dynamo Riga	CIS	30	6	0	6	42																			
	Kansas City	IHL	34	6	9	15	20												15	2	5	7	22			
1992-93	**San Jose**	**NHL**	**37**	**7**	**16**	**23**	**40**	2	0	0	83	8.4	−9													
1993-94	**San Jose**	**NHL**	**81**	**26**	**38**	**64**	**24**	4	0	3	157	16.6	16						**14**	**0**	**10**	**10**	**8**	0	0	0

			Regular Season																Playoffs							
Season	Club	League	GP	G	A	Pts	PIM	PP	SH	GW	S	%	+/–	TF	F%	H	SB	Min	GP	G	A	Pts	PIM	PP	SH	GW
1994-95	**San Jose**	**NHL**	**48**	**9**	**16**	**25**	**30**	**3**	**1**	**2**	**83**	**10.8**	**–6**	....	....	....	....	....	**11**	**3**	**2**	**5**	**6**	**1**	**0**	**0**
1995-96	San Francisco	IHL	2	1	0	1	0	....	....	....	....	....	....	....	....	....	....	....	....	....	....	....	....	....	....	....
	San Jose	**NHL**	**7**	**1**	**3**	**4**	**4**	**1**	**0**	**0**	**21**	**4.8**	**2**	....	....	....	....	....	....	....	....	....	....	....	....	....
	♦ **Colorado**	**NHL**	**66**	**13**	**37**	**50**	**50**	**7**	**1**	**1**	**145**	**9.0**	**0**	....	....	....	....	....	**22**	**5**	**14**	**19**	**16**	**2**	**0**	**1**
1996-97	**Colorado**	**NHL**	**80**	**23**	**45**	**68**	**88**	**13**	**0**	**4**	**232**	**9.9**	**4**	....	....	....	....	....	**17**	**4**	**13**	**17**	**24**	**2**	**0**	**1**
1997-98	**Colorado**	**NHL**	**66**	**13**	**38**	**51**	**65**	**9**	**0**	**2**	**135**	**9.6**	**–12**	....	....	....	....	....	**7**	**0**	**7**	**7**	**14**	**0**	**0**	**0**
1998-99	**Colorado**	**NHL**	**39**	**7**	**25**	**32**	**22**	**4**	**0**	**3**	**81**	**8.6**	**10**	**0**	**0.0**	**34**	**23**	**22:06**	**19**	**4**	**8**	**12**	**22**	**3**	**0**	**1**
	NHL Totals		**424**	**99**	**218**	**317**	**323**	**43**	**2**	**15**	**937**	**10.6**		**0**	**0.0**	**34**	**23**	**22:06**	**90**	**16**	**54**	**70**	**90**	**8**	**0**	**3**

NHL First All-Star Team (1997)
Played in NHL All-Star Game (1994, 1997, 1998)
Traded to **Colorado** by **San Jose** for Owen Nolan, October 26, 1995.

PALFFY, Zigmund
(PAHL-fee) **L.A.**

Right wing. Shoots left. 5'10", 183 lbs. Born, Skalica, Czech., May 5, 1972. NY Islanders' 2nd choice, 26th overall, in 1991 Entry Draft.

1990-91	AC Nitra	Czech.	50	34	16	50	18	....	....	....	....	....	....	....	....	....	....	....	....	....	....	....	....	....	....	....
1991-92	Dukla Trencin	Czech.	45	41	33	74	36	....	....	....	....	....	....	....	....	....	....	....	....	....	....	....	....	....	....	....
1992-93	Dukla Trencin	Czech.	43	38	41	79	....	....	....	....	....	....	....	....	....	....	....	....	....	....	....	....	....	....	....	....
1993-94	**NY Islanders**	**NHL**	**5**	**0**	**0**	**0**	**0**	**0**	**0**	**0**	**5**	**0.0**	**–6**	....	....	....	....	....	....	....	....	....	....	....	....	....
	Salt Lake	IHL	57	25	32	57	83	....	....	....	....	....	....	....	....	....	....	....	....	....	....	....	....	....	....	....
	Slovakia	Olympics	8	3	7	10	8	....	....	....	....	....	....	....	....	....	....	....	....	....	....	....	....	....	....	....
1994-95	Denver	IHL	33	20	23	43	40	....	....	....	....	....	....	....	....	....	....	....	....	....	....	....	....	....	....	....
	NY Islanders	**NHL**	**33**	**10**	**7**	**17**	**6**	**1**	**0**	**1**	**75**	**13.3**	**3**	....	....	....	....	....	....	....	....	....	....	....	....	....
1995-96	**NY Islanders**	**NHL**	**81**	**43**	**44**	**87**	**56**	**17**	**1**	**6**	**257**	**16.7**	**–17**	....	....	....	....	....	....	....	....	....	....	....	....	....
1996-97	Dukla Trencin	Slovakia	1	0	0	0	....	....	....	....	....	....	....	....	....	....	....	....	....	....	....	....	....	....	....	....
	NY Islanders	**NHL**	**80**	**48**	**42**	**90**	**43**	**6**	**4**	**6**	**292**	**16.4**	**21**	....	....	....	....	....	....	....	....	....	....	....	....	....
1997-98	**NY Islanders**	**NHL**	**82**	**45**	**42**	**87**	**34**	**17**	**2**	**5**	**277**	**16.2**	**–2**	....	....	....	....	....	....	....	....	....	....	....	....	....
1998-99	HK 36 Skalica	Slovakia	9	11	8	19	6	....	....	....	....	....	....	....	....	....	....	....	....	....	....	....	....	....	....	....
	NY Islanders	**NHL**	**50**	**22**	**28**	**50**	**34**	**5**	**2**	**1**	**168**	**13.1**	**–6**	**1**	**100.0**	**28**	**34**	**22:04**	....	....	....	....	....	....	....	....
	NHL Totals		**331**	**168**	**163**	**331**	**173**	**46**	**9**	**19**	**1074**	**15.6**		**1**	**100.0**	**28**	**34**	**22:04**	....	....	....	....	....	....	....	....

Czechoslovakian Rookie of the Year (1991) • Czechoslovakian First All-Star Team (1992)
Played in NHL All-Star Game (1998)
Traded to **Los Angeles** by **NY Islanders** with Brian Smolinski, Marcel Cousineau and New Jersey's 4th round choice (previously acquired, Los Angeles selected Daniel Johanssen) in 1999 Entry Draft for Olli Jokinen, Josh Green, Mathieu Biron and Los Angeles' 1st round choice (Taylor Pyatt) in 1999 Entry Draft, June 20, 1999.

PANDOLFO, Jay
(pan-DAHL-foh) **N.J.**

Left wing. Shoots left. 6'1", 200 lbs. Born, Winchester, MA, December 27, 1974. New Jersey's 2nd choice, 32nd overall, in 1993 Entry Draft.

1990-91	Burlington Prep	H.S.	20	19	27	46	10	....	....	....	....	....	....	....	....	....	....	....	....	....	....	....	....	....	....	....
1991-92	Burlington Prep	H.S.	20	35	34	69	20	....	....	....	....	....	....	....	....	....	....	....	....	....	....	....	....	....	....	....
1992-93	Boston University	H.E.	37	16	22	38	16	....	....	....	....	....	....	....	....	....	....	....	....	....	....	....	....	....	....	....
1993-94	Boston University	H.E.	37	17	25	42	27	....	....	....	....	....	....	....	....	....	....	....	....	....	....	....	....	....	....	....
1994-95	Boston University	H.E.	20	7	13	20	6	....	....	....	....	....	....	....	....	....	....	....	....	....	....	....	....	....	....	....
1995-96	Boston University	H.E.	39	*38	29	67	6	....	....	....	....	....	....	....	....	....	....	....	....	....	....	....	....	....	....	....
	Albany	AHL	5	3	1	4	0	....	....	....	....	....	....	....	....	....	....	....	3	0	0	0	0	....	....	....
1996-97	**New Jersey**	**NHL**	**46**	**6**	**8**	**14**	**6**	**0**	**0**	**1**	**61**	**9.8**	**–1**	....	....	....	....	....	**6**	**0**	**1**	**1**	**0**	**0**	**0**	**0**
	Albany	AHL	12	3	9	12	0	....	....	....	....	....	....	....	....	....	....	....	....	....	....	....	....	....	....	....
1997-98	**New Jersey**	**NHL**	**23**	**1**	**3**	**4**	**4**	**0**	**0**	**0**	**23**	**4.3**	**–4**	....	....	....	....	....	**3**	**0**	**2**	**2**	**0**	**0**	**0**	**0**
	Albany	AHL	51	18	19	37	24	....	....	....	....	....	....	....	....	....	....	....	....	....	....	....	....	....	....	....
1998-99	**New Jersey**	**NHL**	**70**	**14**	**13**	**27**	**10**	**1**	**1**	**4**	**100**	**14.0**	**3**	**10**	**40.0**	**103**	**39**	**15:13**	**7**	**1**	**0**	**1**	**0**	**0**	**0**	**0**
	NHL Totals		**139**	**21**	**24**	**45**	**20**	**1**	**1**	**5**	**184**	**11.4**		**10**	**40.0**	**103**	**39**	**15:13**	**16**	**1**	**3**	**4**	**0**	**0**	**0**	**0**

Hockey East First All-Star Team (1996) • NCAA East First All-American Team (1996)

PANKEWICZ, Greg
(PAN-kuh-wihts)

Right wing. Shoots right. 6', 185 lbs. Born, Drayton Valley, Alta., November 6, 1970.

1989-90	Regina	WHL	63	14	24	38	136	....	....	....	....	....	....	....	....	....	....	....	10	1	3	4	19	....	....	....
1990-91	Regina	WHL	72	39	41	80	134	....	....	....	....	....	....	....	....	....	....	....	8	4	7	11	12	....	....	....
1991-92	Knoxville	ECHL	59	41	39	80	214	....	....	....	....	....	....	....	....	....	....	....	....	....	....	....	....	....	....	....
1992-93	New Haven	AHL	62	23	20	43	163	....	....	....	....	....	....	....	....	....	....	....	....	....	....	....	....	....	....	....
1993-94	**Ottawa**	**NHL**	**3**	**0**	**0**	**0**	**2**	**0**	**0**	**0**	**3**	**0.0**	**–1**	....	....	....	....	....	....	....	....	....	....	....	....	....
	P.E.I. Senators	AHL	69	33	29	62	241	....	....	....	....	....	....	....	....	....	....	....	....	....	....	....	....	....	....	....
1994-95	P.E.I. Senators	AHL	75	37	30	67	161	....	....	....	....	....	....	....	....	....	....	....	6	1	1	2	24	....	....	....
1995-96	Portland	AHL	28	9	12	21	99	....	....	....	....	....	....	....	....	....	....	....	....	....	....	....	....	....	....	....
	Chicago	IHL	45	9	16	25	164	....	....	....	....	....	....	....	....	....	....	....	5	4	0	4	8	....	....	....
1996-97	Manitoba	IHL	79	32	34	66	222	....	....	....	....	....	....	....	....	....	....	....	....	....	....	....	....	....	....	....
1997-98	Manitoba	IHL	76	42	34	76	246	....	....	....	....	....	....	....	....	....	....	....	3	0	0	0	6	....	....	....
1998-99	**Calgary**	**NHL**	**18**	**0**	**3**	**3**	**20**	**0**	**0**	**0**	**10**	**0.0**	**0**	**3**	**66.7**	**17**	**2**	**7:26**	....	....	....	....	....	....	....	....
	Saint John	AHL	30	10	14	24	84	....	....	....	....	....	....	....	....	....	....	....	....	....	....	....	....	....	....	....
	Kentucky	AHL	10	2	3	5	7	....	....	....	....	....	....	....	....	....	....	....	11	4	1	5	10	....	....	....
	NHL Totals		**21**	**0**	**3**	**3**	**22**	**0**	**0**	**0**	**13**	**0.0**		**3**	**66.7**	**17**	**2**	**7:26**	....	....	....	....	....	....	....	....

Signed as a free agent by **Ottawa**, May 27, 1993. Signed as a free agent by **Calgary**, September 1, 1998. Traded to **San Jose** by **Calgary** for cash, March 23, 1999.

PARK, Richard

Center. Shoots right. 5'11", 190 lbs. Born, Seoul, S. Korea, May 27, 1976. Pittsburgh's 2nd choice, 50th overall, in 1994 Entry Draft.

1991-92	Toronto	MTHL	76	49	58	107	91	....	....	....	....	....	....	....	....	....	....	....	....	....	....	....	....	....	....	....
1992-93	Belleville	OHL	66	23	38	61	38	....	....	....	....	....	....	....	....	....	....	....	5	0	0	0	14	....	....	....
1993-94	Belleville	OHL	59	27	49	76	70	....	....	....	....	....	....	....	....	....	....	....	12	3	5	8	18	....	....	....
1994-95	Belleville	OHL	45	28	51	79	35	....	....	....	....	....	....	....	....	....	....	....	16	9	18	27	12	....	....	....
	Pittsburgh	**NHL**	**1**	**0**	**1**	**1**	**2**	**0**	**0**	**0**	**4**	**0.0**	**1**	....	....	....	....	....	**3**	**0**	**0**	**0**	**2**	**0**	**0**	**0**
1995-96	Belleville	OHL	6	7	6	13	2	....	....	....	....	....	....	....	....	....	....	....	14	18	12	30	10	....	....	....
	Pittsburgh	**NHL**	**56**	**4**	**6**	**10**	**36**	**0**	**1**	**1**	**62**	**6.5**	**3**	....	....	....	....	....	**1**	**0**	**0**	**0**	**0**	**0**	**0**	**0**
1996-97	**Pittsburgh**	**NHL**	**1**	**0**	**0**	**0**	**0**	**0**	**0**	**0**	**1**	**0.0**	**–1**	....	....	....	....	....	....	....	....	....	....	....	....	....
	Cleveland	IHL	50	12	15	27	30	....	....	....	....	....	....	....	....	....	....	....	....	....	....	....	....	....	....	....
	Anaheim	**NHL**	**11**	**1**	**1**	**2**	**10**	**0**	**0**	**0**	**9**	**11.1**	**0**	....	....	....	....	....	**11**	**0**	**1**	**1**	**2**	**0**	**0**	**0**
1997-98	**Anaheim**	**NHL**	**15**	**0**	**2**	**2**	**8**	**0**	**0**	**0**	**14**	**0.0**	**–3**	....	....	....	....	....	....	....	....	....	....	....	....	....
	Cincinnati	AHL	56	17	26	43	36	....	....	....	....	....	....	....	....	....	....	....	....	....	....	....	....	....	....	....
1998-99	**Philadelphia**	**NHL**	**7**	**0**	**0**	**0**	**0**	**0**	**0**	**0**	**5**	**0.0**	**–1**	**15**	**53.3**	**2**	**0**	**9:21**	....	....	....	....	....	....	....	....
	Philadelphia	AHL	75	41	42	83	33	....	....	....	....	....	....	....	....	....	....	....	16	9	6	15	4	....	....	....
	NHL Totals		**91**	**5**	**10**	**15**	**56**	**0**	**1**	**1**	**95**	**5.3**		**15**	**53.3**	**2**	**0**	**9:21**	**15**	**0**	**1**	**1**	**4**	**0**	**0**	**0**

AHL Second All-Star Team (1999)
Traded to **Anaheim** by **Pittsburgh** for Roman Oksiuta, March 18, 1997. Signed as a free agent by **Philadelphia**, August 24, 1998.

PARKER, Scott

Right wing. Shoots right. 6'4", 220 lbs. Born, Hanford, CA, January 29, 1978. Colorado's 4th choice, 20th overall, in 1998 Entry Draft.

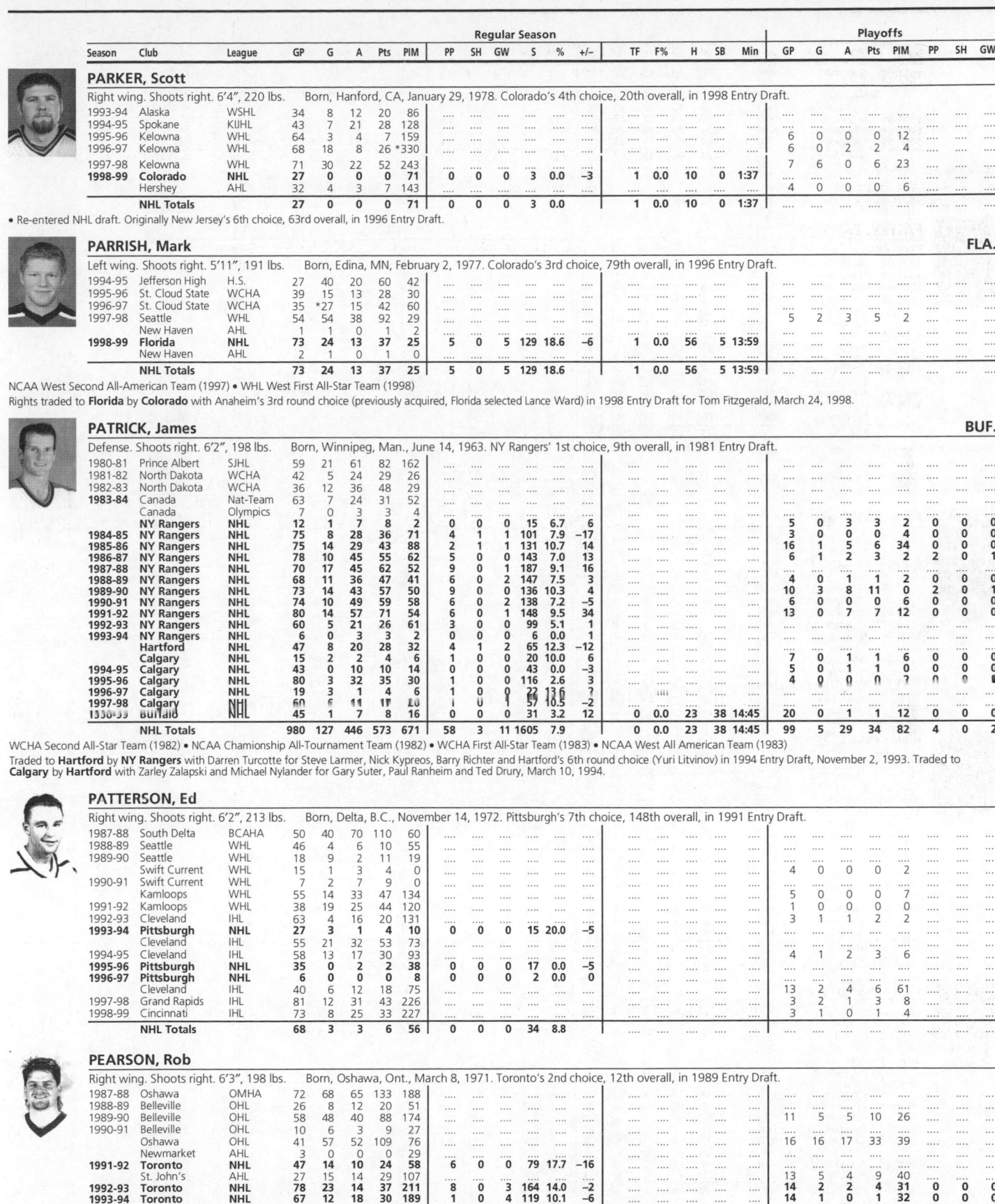

			Regular Season																Playoffs							
Season	Club	League	GP	G	A	Pts	PIM	PP	SH	GW	S	%	+/-	TF	F%	H	SB	Min	GP	G	A	Pts	PIM	PP	SH	GW
1993-94	Alaska	WSHL	34	8	12	20	86	....	....	....	....	....	....	....	....	....	....	....	....	....	....	....	....	....	....	....
1994-95	Spokane	KIJHL	43	7	21	28	128	....	....	....	....	....	....	....	....	....	....	....	....	....	....	....	....	....	....	....
1995-96	Kelowna	WHL	64	3	4	7	159	....	....	....	....	....	....	....	....	....	....	....	6	0	0	0	12	....	....	....
1996-97	Kelowna	WHL	68	18	8	26	*330	....	....	....	....	....	....	....	....	....	....	....	6	0	2	2	4	....	....	....
1997-98	Kelowna	WHL	71	30	22	52	243	....	....	....	....	....	....	....	....	....	....	....	7	6	0	6	23	....	....	....
1998-99	**Colorado**	**NHL**	**27**	**0**	**0**	**0**	**71**	**0**	**0**	**0**	**3**	**0.0**	**–3**	**1**	**0.0**	**10**	**0**	**1:37**	....	....	....	....	....	....	....	....
	Hershey	AHL	32	4	3	7	143	....	....	....	....	....	....	....	....	....	....	....	4	0	0	0	6	....	....	....
	NHL Totals		**27**	**0**	**0**	**0**	**71**	**0**	**0**	**0**	**3**	**0.0**		**1**	**0.0**	**10**	**0**	**1:37**	....	....	....	....	....	....	....	....

• Re-entered NHL draft. Originally New Jersey's 6th choice, 63rd overall, in 1996 Entry Draft.

PARRISH, Mark **FLA.**

Left wing. Shoots right. 5'11", 191 lbs. Born, Edina, MN, February 2, 1977. Colorado's 3rd choice, 79th overall, in 1996 Entry Draft.

Season	Club	League	GP	G	A	Pts	PIM	PP	SH	GW	S	%	+/-	TF	F%	H	SB	Min	GP	G	A	Pts	PIM	PP	SH	GW
1994-95	Jefferson High	H.S.	27	40	20	60	42	....	....	....	....	....	....	....	....	....	....	....	....	....	....	....	....	....	....	....
1995-96	St. Cloud State	WCHA	39	15	13	28	30	....	....	....	....	....	....	....	....	....	....	....	....	....	....	....	....	....	....	....
1996-97	St. Cloud State	WCHA	35	*27	15	42	60	....	....	....	....	....	....	....	....	....	....	....	....	....	....	....	....	....	....	....
1997-98	Seattle	WHL	54	54	38	92	29	....	....	....	....	....	....	....	....	....	....	....	5	2	3	5	2	....	....	....
	New Haven	AHL	1	1	0	1	2	....	....	....	....	....	....	....	....	....	....	....	....	....	....	....	....	....	....	....
1998-99	**Florida**	**NHL**	**73**	**24**	**13**	**37**	**25**	**5**	**0**	**5**	**129**	**18.6**	**–6**	**1**	**0.0**	**56**	**5**	**13:59**	....	....	....	....	....	....	....	....
	New Haven	AHL	2	1	0	1	0	....	....	....	....	....	....	....	....	....	....	....	....	....	....	....	....	....	....	....
	NHL Totals		**73**	**24**	**13**	**37**	**25**	**5**	**0**	**5**	**129**	**18.6**		**1**	**0.0**	**56**	**5**	**13:59**	....	....	....	....	....	....	....	....

NCAA West Second All-American Team (1997) • WHL West First All-Star Team (1998)

Rights traded to **Florida** by **Colorado** with Anaheim's 3rd round choice (previously acquired, Florida selected Lance Ward) in 1998 Entry Draft for Tom Fitzgerald, March 24, 1998.

PATRICK, James **BUF.**

Defense. Shoots right. 6'2", 198 lbs. Born, Winnipeg, Man., June 14, 1963. NY Rangers' 1st choice, 9th overall, in 1981 Entry Draft.

Season	Club	League	GP	G	A	Pts	PIM	PP	SH	GW	S	%	+/-	TF	F%	H	SB	Min	GP	G	A	Pts	PIM	PP	SH	GW
1980-81	Prince Albert	SJHL	59	21	61	82	162	....	....	....	....	....	....	....	....	....	....	....	....	....	....	....	....	....	....	....
1981-82	North Dakota	WCHA	42	5	24	29	26	....	....	....	....	....	....	....	....	....	....	....	....	....	....	....	....	....	....	....
1982-83	North Dakota	WCHA	36	12	36	48	29	....	....	....	....	....	....	....	....	....	....	....	....	....	....	....	....	....	....	....
1983-84	Canada	Nat-Team	63	7	24	31	52	....	....	....	....	....	....	....	....	....	....	....	....	....	....	....	....	....	....	....
	Canada	Olympics	7	0	3	3	4	....	....	....	....	....	....	....	....	....	....	....	....	....	....	....	....	....	....	....
	NY Rangers	**NHL**	**12**	**1**	**7**	**8**	**2**	**0**	**0**	**0**	**15**	**6.7**	**6**	....	....	....	....	....	**5**	**0**	**3**	**3**	**2**	**0**	**0**	**0**
1984-85	**NY Rangers**	**NHL**	**75**	**8**	**28**	**36**	**71**	**4**	**1**	**1**	**101**	**7.9**	**–17**	....	....	....	....	....	**3**	**0**	**0**	**0**	**4**	**0**	**0**	**0**
1985-86	**NY Rangers**	**NHL**	**75**	**14**	**29**	**43**	**88**	**2**	**1**	**1**	**131**	**10.7**	**14**	....	....	....	....	....	**16**	**1**	**5**	**6**	**34**	**0**	**0**	**0**
1986-87	**NY Rangers**	**NHL**	**78**	**10**	**45**	**55**	**62**	**5**	**0**	**0**	**143**	**7.0**	**13**	....	....	....	....	....	**6**	**1**	**2**	**3**	**2**	**2**	**0**	**1**
1987-88	**NY Rangers**	**NHL**	**70**	**17**	**45**	**62**	**52**	**9**	**0**	**1**	**187**	**9.1**	**16**	....	....	....	....	....	....	....	....	....	....	....	....	....
1988-89	**NY Rangers**	**NHL**	**68**	**11**	**36**	**47**	**41**	**6**	**0**	**2**	**147**	**7.5**	**3**	....	....	....	....	....	**4**	**0**	**1**	**1**	**2**	**0**	**0**	**0**
1989-90	**NY Rangers**	**NHL**	**73**	**14**	**43**	**57**	**50**	**9**	**0**	**0**	**136**	**10.3**	**4**	....	....	....	....	....	**10**	**3**	**8**	**11**	**0**	**2**	**0**	**1**
1990-91	**NY Rangers**	**NHL**	**74**	**10**	**49**	**59**	**58**	**6**	**0**	**2**	**138**	**7.2**	**–5**	....	....	....	....	....	**6**	**0**	**0**	**0**	**6**	**0**	**0**	**0**
1991-92	**NY Rangers**	**NHL**	**80**	**14**	**57**	**71**	**54**	**6**	**0**	**1**	**148**	**9.5**	**34**	....	....	....	....	....	**13**	**0**	**7**	**7**	**12**	**0**	**0**	**0**
1992-93	**NY Rangers**	**NHL**	**60**	**5**	**21**	**26**	**61**	**3**	**0**	**0**	**99**	**5.1**	**1**	....	....	....	....	....	....	....	....	....	....	....	....	....
1993-94	**NY Rangers**	**NHL**	**6**	**0**	**3**	**3**	**2**	**0**	**0**	**0**	**6**	**0.0**	**1**	....	....	....	....	....	....	....	....	....	....	....	....	....
	Hartford	**NHL**	**47**	**8**	**20**	**28**	**32**	**4**	**1**	**2**	**65**	**12.3**	**–12**	....	....	....	....	....	....	....	....	....	....	....	....	....
	Calgary	**NHL**	**15**	**2**	**2**	**4**	**6**	**1**	**0**	**0**	**20**	**10.0**	**6**	....	....	....	....	....	**7**	**0**	**1**	**1**	**6**	**0**	**0**	**0**
1994-95	**Calgary**	**NHL**	**43**	**0**	**10**	**10**	**14**	**0**	**0**	**0**	**43**	**0.0**	**–3**	....	....	....	....	....	**5**	**0**	**1**	**1**	**0**	**0**	**0**	**0**
1995-96	**Calgary**	**NHL**	**80**	**3**	**32**	**35**	**30**	**1**	**0**	**0**	**116**	**2.6**	**3**	....	....	....	....	....	**4**	**0**	**0**	**0**	**2**	**0**	**0**	**0**
1996-97	**Calgary**	**NHL**	**19**	**3**	**1**	**4**	**6**	**1**	**0**	**0**	**22**	**13.6**	**2**	....	....	....	....	....	....	....	....	....	....	....	....	....
1997-98	**Calgary**	**NHL**	**60**	**6**	**11**	**17**	**26**	**1**	**0**	**1**	**57**	**10.5**	**–2**	....	....	....	....	....	....	....	....	....	....	....	....	....
1998-99	**Buffalo**	**NHL**	**45**	**1**	**7**	**8**	**16**	**0**	**0**	**0**	**31**	**3.2**	**12**	**0**	**0.0**	**23**	**38**	**14:45**	**20**	**0**	**1**	**1**	**12**	**0**	**0**	**0**
	NHL Totals		**980**	**127**	**446**	**573**	**671**	**58**	**3**	**11**	**1605**	**7.9**		**0**	**0.0**	**23**	**38**	**14:45**	**99**	**5**	**29**	**34**	**82**	**4**	**0**	**2**

WCHA Second All-Star Team (1982) • NCAA Chamionship All-Tournament Team (1982) • WCHA First All-Star Team (1983) • NCAA West All American Team (1983)

Traded to **Hartford** by **NY Rangers** with Darren Turcotte for Steve Larmer, Nick Kypreos, Barry Richter and Hartford's 6th round choice (Yuri Litvinov) in 1994 Entry Draft, November 2, 1993. Traded to **Calgary** by **Hartford** with Zarley Zalapski and Michael Nylander for Gary Suter, Paul Ranheim and Ted Drury, March 10, 1994.

PATTERSON, Ed

Right wing. Shoots right. 6'2", 213 lbs. Born, Delta, B.C., November 14, 1972. Pittsburgh's 7th choice, 148th overall, in 1991 Entry Draft.

Season	Club	League	GP	G	A	Pts	PIM	PP	SH	GW	S	%	+/-	TF	F%	H	SB	Min	GP	G	A	Pts	PIM	PP	SH	GW
1987-88	South Delta	BCAHA	50	40	70	110	60	....	....	....	....	....	....	....	....	....	....	....	....	....	....	....	....	....	....	....
1988-89	Seattle	WHL	46	4	6	10	55	....	....	....	....	....	....	....	....	....	....	....	....	....	....	....	....	....	....	....
1989-90	Seattle	WHL	18	9	2	11	19	....	....	....	....	....	....	....	....	....	....	....	....	....	....	....	....	....	....	....
	Swift Current	WHL	15	1	3	4	0	....	....	....	....	....	....	....	....	....	....	....	4	0	0	0	2	....	....	....
1990-91	Swift Current	WHL	7	2	7	9	0	....	....	....	....	....	....	....	....	....	....	....	....	....	....	....	....	....	....	....
	Kamloops	WHL	55	14	33	47	134	....	....	....	....	....	....	....	....	....	....	....	5	0	0	0	7	....	....	....
1991-92	Kamloops	WHL	38	19	25	44	120	....	....	....	....	....	....	....	....	....	....	....	1	0	0	0	0	....	....	....
1992-93	Cleveland	IHL	63	4	16	20	131	....	....	....	....	....	....	....	....	....	....	....	3	1	1	2	2	....	....	....
1993-94	**Pittsburgh**	**NHL**	**27**	**3**	**1**	**4**	**10**	**0**	**0**	**0**	**15**	**20.0**	**–5**	....	....	....	....	....	....	....	....	....	....	....	....	....
	Cleveland	IHL	55	21	32	53	73	....	....	....	....	....	....	....	....	....	....	....	....	....	....	....	....	....	....	....
1994-95	Cleveland	IHL	58	13	17	30	93	....	....	....	....	....	....	....	....	....	....	....	4	1	2	3	6	....	....	....
1995-96	**Pittsburgh**	**NHL**	**35**	**0**	**2**	**2**	**38**	**0**	**0**	**0**	**17**	**0.0**	**–5**	....	....	....	....	....	....	....	....	....	....	....	....	....
1996-97	**Pittsburgh**	**NHL**	**6**	**0**	**0**	**0**	**8**	**0**	**0**	**0**	**2**	**0.0**	**0**	....	....	....	....	....	....	....	....	....	....	....	....	....
	Cleveland	IHL	40	6	12	18	75	....	....	....	....	....	....	....	....	....	....	....	13	2	4	6	61	....	....	....
1997-98	Grand Rapids	IHL	81	12	31	43	226	....	....	....	....	....	....	....	....	....	....	....	3	2	1	3	8	....	....	....
1998-99	Cincinnati	IHL	73	8	25	33	227	....	....	....	....	....	....	....	....	....	....	....	3	1	0	1	4	....	....	....
	NHL Totals		**68**	**3**	**3**	**6**	**56**	**0**	**0**	**0**	**34**	**8.8**							....	....	....	....	....	....	....	....

PEARSON, Rob

Right wing. Shoots right. 6'3", 198 lbs. Born, Oshawa, Ont., March 8, 1971. Toronto's 2nd choice, 12th overall, in 1989 Entry Draft.

Season	Club	League	GP	G	A	Pts	PIM	PP	SH	GW	S	%	+/-	TF	F%	H	SB	Min	GP	G	A	Pts	PIM	PP	SH	GW
1987-88	Oshawa	OMHA	72	68	65	133	188	....	....	....	....	....	....	....	....	....	....	....	....	....	....	....	....	....	....	....
1988-89	Belleville	OHL	26	8	12	20	51	....	....	....	....	....	....	....	....	....	....	....	....	....	....	....	....	....	....	....
1989-90	Belleville	OHL	58	48	40	88	174	....	....	....	....	....	....	....	....	....	....	....	11	5	5	10	26	....	....	....
1990-91	Belleville	OHL	10	6	3	9	27	....	....	....	....	....	....	....	....	....	....	....	....	....	....	....	....	....	....	....
	Oshawa	OHL	41	57	52	109	76	....	....	....	....	....	....	....	....	....	....	....	16	16	17	33	39	....	....	....
	Newmarket	AHL	3	0	0	0	29	....	....	....	....	....	....	....	....	....	....	....	....	....	....	....	....	....	....	....
1991-92	**Toronto**	**NHL**	**47**	**14**	**10**	**24**	**58**	**6**	**0**	**0**	**79**	**17.7**	**–16**	....	....	....	....	....	....	....	....	....	....	....	....	....
	St. John's	AHL	27	15	14	29	107	....	....	....	....	....	....	....	....	....	....	....	13	5	4	9	40	....	....	....
1992-93	**Toronto**	**NHL**	**78**	**23**	**14**	**37**	**211**	**8**	**0**	**3**	**164**	**14.0**	**–2**	....	....	....	....	....	**14**	**2**	**2**	**4**	**31**	**0**	**0**	**0**
1993-94	**Toronto**	**NHL**	**67**	**12**	**18**	**30**	**189**	**1**	**0**	**4**	**119**	**10.1**	**–6**	....	....	....	....	....	**14**	**1**	**0**	**1**	**32**	**0**	**0**	**0**
1994-95	**Washington**	**NHL**	**32**	**0**	**6**	**6**	**96**	**0**	**0**	**0**	**34**	**0.0**	**–6**	....	....	....	....	....	**3**	**1**	**0**	**1**	**17**	**0**	**0**	**1**
1995-96	Portland	AHL	44	18	24	42	143	....	....	....	....	....	....	....	....	....	....	....	....	....	....	....	....	....	....	....
	St. Louis	**NHL**	**27**	**6**	**4**	**10**	**54**	**1**	**0**	**1**	**51**	**11.8**	**4**	....	....	....	....	....	**2**	**0**	**0**	**0**	**14**	**0**	**0**	**0**
1996-97	**St. Louis**	**NHL**	**18**	**1**	**2**	**3**	**37**	**0**	**0**	**0**	**14**	**7.1**	**–5**	....	....	....	....	....	....	....	....	....	....	....	....	....
	Worcester	AHL	46	11	16	27	199	....	....	....	....	....	....	....	....	....	....	....	5	3	0	3	16	....	....	....
1997-98	Cleveland	IHL	46	17	14	31	118	....	....	....	....	....	....	....	....	....	....	....	10	6	4	10	43	....	....	....

			Regular Season																Playoffs							
Season	Club	League	GP	G	A	Pts	PIM	PP	SH	GW	S	%	+/-	TF	F%	H	SB	Min	GP	G	A	Pts	PIM	PP	SH	GW
1998-99	Cleveland	IHL	20	3	10	13	27																			
	Orlando	IHL	11	6	2	8	41												17	8	6	14	24			
	NHL Totals		**269**	**56**	**54**	**110**	**645**	**16**	**0**	**8**	**461**	**12.1**							**33**	**4**	**2**	**6**	**94**	**0**	**0**	**1**

OHL First All-Star Team (1991)

Traded to **Washington** by **Toronto** with Philadelphia's 1st round choice (previously acquired by Toronto — Washington selected Nolan Baumgartner) in 1994 Entry Draft for Mike Ridley and St. Louis' 1st round choice (previously acquired, Toronto selected Eric Fichaud) in 1994 Entry Draft, June 28, 1994. Traded to **St. Louis** by **Washington** for Denis Chasse, January 29, 1996.

PEARSON, Scott — NYI

Left wing. Shoots left. 6'1", 205 lbs. Born, Cornwall, Ont., December 19, 1969. Toronto's 1st choice, 6th overall, in 1988 Entry Draft.

Season	Club	League	GP	G	A	Pts	PIM	PP	SH	GW	S	%	+/-	TF	F%	H	SB	Min	GP	G	A	Pts	PIM	PP	SH	GW
1984-85	Cornwall	OMHA	60	40	40	80	60																			
1985-86	Kingston	OHL	63	16	23	39	56																			
1986-87	Kingston	OHL	62	30	24	54	101												9	3	3	6	42			
1987-88	Kingston	OHL	46	26	32	58	117																			
1988-89	Kingston	OHL	13	9	8	17	34																			
	Niagara Falls	OHL	32	26	34	60	90												17	14	10	24	53			
	Toronto	**NHL**	**9**	**0**	**1**	**1**	**2**	**0**	**0**	**0**	**6**	**0.0**	**0**													
1989-90	**Toronto**	**NHL**	**41**	**5**	**10**	**15**	**90**	**0**	**0**	**1**	**66**	**7.6**	**-7**						**2**	**2**	**0**	**2**	**10**	**0**	**0**	**0**
	Newmarket	AHL	18	12	11	23	64																			
1990-91	**Toronto**	**NHL**	**12**	**0**	**0**	**0**	**20**	**0**	**0**	**0**	**13**	**0.0**	**-5**													
	Quebec	**NHL**	**35**	**11**	**4**	**15**	**86**	**0**	**0**	**0**	**61**	**18.0**	**-4**													
	Halifax	AHL	24	12	15	27	44																			
1991-92	**Quebec**	**NHL**	**10**	**1**	**2**	**3**	**14**	**0**	**0**	**0**	**14**	**7.1**	**-5**													
	Halifax	AHL	5	2	1	3	4																			
1992-93	**Quebec**	**NHL**	**41**	**13**	**1**	**14**	**95**	**0**	**0**	**1**	**45**	**28.9**	**3**						**3**	**0**	**0**	**0**	**0**	**0**	**0**	**0**
	Halifax	AHL	5	3	1	4	25																			
1993-94	**Edmonton**	**NHL**	**72**	**19**	**18**	**37**	**165**	**3**	**0**	**7**	**160**	**11.9**	**-4**													
1994-95	**Edmonton**	**NHL**	**28**	**1**	**4**	**5**	**54**	**0**	**0**	**0**	**21**	**4.8**	**-11**													
	Buffalo	**NHL**	**14**	**2**	**1**	**3**	**20**	**0**	**0**	**0**	**19**	**10.5**	**-3**						**5**	**0**	**0**	**0**	**4**	**0**	**0**	**0**
1995-96	**Buffalo**	**NHL**	**27**	**4**	**0**	**4**	**67**	**0**	**0**	**1**	**26**	**15.4**	**-4**													
	Rochester	AHL	26	8	8	16	113																			
1996-97	**Toronto**	**NHL**	**1**	**0**	**0**	**0**	**2**	**0**	**0**	**0**	**0**	**0.0**	**0**													
	St. John's	AHL	14	5	2	7	26												9	5	2	7	14			
1997-98	Chicago	IHL	78	34	17	51	225												22	12	6	18	50			
1998-99	Chicago	IHL	62	23	13	36	154												8	4	1	5	*50			
	NHL Totals		**290**	**56**	**41**	**97**	**615**	**3**	**0**	**10**	**431**	**13.0**							**10**	**2**	**0**	**2**	**14**	**0**	**0**	**0**

Traded to **Quebec** by **Toronto** with Toronto's 2nd round choices in 1991 (later traded to Washington — Washington selected Eric Lavigne) and 1992 (Tuomas Gronman) Entry Drafts for Aaron Broten, Lucien Deblois and Michel Petit, November 17, 1990. Traded to **Edmonton** by **Quebec** for Martin Gelinas and Edmonton's 6th round choice (Nicholas Checco) in 1993 Entry Draft, June 20, 1993. Traded to **Buffalo** by **Edmonton** for Ken Sutton, April 7, 1995. Signed as a free agent by **Toronto**, July 24, 1996. Signed as a free agent by **NY Islanders**, August 9, 1999.

PECA, Michael (PEH-kuh) — BUF.

Center. Shoots right. 5'11", 181 lbs. Born, Toronto, Ont., March 26, 1974. Vancouver's 2nd choice, 40th overall, in 1992 Entry Draft.

Season	Club	League	GP	G	A	Pts	PIM	PP	SH	GW	S	%	+/-	TF	F%	H	SB	Min	GP	G	A	Pts	PIM	PP	SH	GW
1989-90	Toronto	MTHL	39	42	53	95	40																			
1990-91	Sudbury	OHL	62	14	27	41	24												5	1	0	1	7			
1991-92	Sudbury	OHL	39	16	34	50	61																			
	Ottawa	OHL	27	8	17	25	32												11	6	10	16	6			
1992-93	Ottawa	OHL	55	38	64	102	80																			
	Hamilton	AHL	9	6	3	9	11																			
1993-94	Ottawa	OHL	55	50	63	113	101												17	7	22	29	30			
	Vancouver	**NHL**	**4**	**0**	**0**	**0**	**2**	**0**	**0**	**0**	**5**	**0.0**	**-1**													
1994-95	Syracuse	AHL	35	10	24	34	75																			
	Vancouver	**NHL**	**33**	**6**	**6**	**12**	**30**	**2**	**0**	**1**	**46**	**13.0**	**-6**						**5**	**0**	**1**	**1**	**8**	**0**	**0**	**0**
1995-96	**Buffalo**	**NHL**	**68**	**11**	**20**	**31**	**67**	**4**	**3**	**1**	**109**	**10.1**	**-1**													
1996-97	**Buffalo**	**NHL**	**79**	**20**	**29**	**49**	**80**	**5**	**6**	**4**	**137**	**14.6**	**26**						**10**	**0**	**2**	**2**	**8**	**0**	**0**	**0**
1997-98	**Buffalo**	**NHL**	**61**	**18**	**22**	**40**	**57**	**6**	**5**	**1**	**132**	**13.6**	**12**						**13**	**3**	**2**	**5**	**8**	**0**	**0**	**1**
1998-99	**Buffalo**	**NHL**	**82**	**27**	**29**	**56**	**81**	**10**	**0**	**8**	**199**	**13.6**	**7**	**1855**	**49.4**	**181**	**64**	**20:44**	**21**	**5**	**8**	**13**	**18**	**2**	**1**	**0**
	NHL Totals		**327**	**82**	**106**	**188**	**317**	**27**	**14**	**15**	**628**	**13.1**		**1855**	**49.4**	**181**	**64**	**20:44**	**49**	**8**	**13**	**21**	**42**	**2**	**1**	**1**

Won Frank J. Selke Trophy (1997)

Traded to **Buffalo** by **Vancouver** with Mike Wilson and Vancouver's 1st round choice (Jay McKee) in 1995 Entry Draft for Alexander Mogilny and Buffalo's 5th round choice (Todd Norman) in 1995 Entry Draft, July 8, 1995.

PEDERSON, Denis — N.J.

Center. Shoots right. 6'2", 205 lbs. Born, Prince Albert, Sask., September 10, 1975. New Jersey's 1st choice, 13th overall, in 1993 Entry Draft.

Season	Club	League	GP	G	A	Pts	PIM	PP	SH	GW	S	%	+/-	TF	F%	H	SB	Min	GP	G	A	Pts	PIM	PP	SH	GW
1990-91	Prince Albert	AAHA	30	25	17	42	84																			
1991-92	Prince Albert	AAHA	21	33	25	58	40																			
	Prince Albert	WHL	10	0	0	0	6												7	0	1	1	13			
1992-93	Prince Albert	WHL	72	33	40	73	134																			
1993-94	Prince Albert	WHL	71	53	45	98	157																			
1994-95	Prince Albert	WHL	63	30	38	68	122												15	11	14	25	14			
	Albany	AHL																	3	0	0	0	2			
1995-96	**New Jersey**	**NHL**	**10**	**3**	**1**	**4**	**0**	**1**	**0**	**2**	**6**	**50.0**	**-1**													
	Albany	AHL	68	28	43	71	104												4	1	2	3	0			
1996-97	**New Jersey**	**NHL**	**70**	**12**	**20**	**32**	**62**	**3**	**0**	**3**	**106**	**11.3**	**7**						**9**	**0**	**0**	**0**	**2**	**0**	**0**	**0**
	Albany	AHL	3	1	3	4	7																			
1997-98	**New Jersey**	**NHL**	**80**	**15**	**13**	**28**	**97**	**7**	**0**	**1**	**135**	**11.1**	**-6**						**6**	**1**	**1**	**2**	**2**	**0**	**1**	**0**
1998-99	**New Jersey**	**NHL**	**76**	**11**	**12**	**23**	**66**	**3**	**0**	**1**	**145**	**7.6**	**-10**	**540**	**42.8**	**105**	**39**	**15:19**	**3**	**0**	**1**	**1**	**0**	**0**	**0**	**0**
	NHL Totals		**236**	**41**	**46**	**87**	**225**	**14**	**0**	**7**	**392**	**10.5**		**540**	**42.8**	**105**	**39**	**15:19**	**18**	**1**	**2**	**3**	**4**	**0**	**1**	**0**

WHL East Second All-Star Team (1994)

PELLERIN, Scott (PEHL-ih-rihn) — ST.L.

Left wing. Shoots left. 5'11", 189 lbs. Born, Shediac, N.B., January 9, 1970. New Jersey's 4th choice, 47th overall, in 1989 Entry Draft.

Season	Club	League	GP	G	A	Pts	PIM	PP	SH	GW	S	%	+/-	TF	F%	H	SB	Min	GP	G	A	Pts	PIM	PP	SH	GW
1986-87	Notre Dame	SAHA	72	62	68	130	98																			
1987-88	Notre Dame	SJHL	57	37	49	86	139																			
1988-89	U. of Maine	H.E.	45	29	33	62	92																			
1989-90	U. of Maine	H.E.	42	22	34	56	68																			
1990-91	U. of Maine	H.E.	43	23	25	48	60																			
1991-92	U. of Maine	H.E.	37	*32	25	57	54																			
	Utica	AHL																	3	1	0	1	0			
1992-93	**New Jersey**	**NHL**	**45**	**10**	**11**	**21**	**41**	**1**	**2**	**0**	**60**	**16.7**	**-1**													
	Utica	AHL	27	15	18	33	33												2	0	1	1	0			
1993-94	**New Jersey**	**NHL**	**1**	**0**	**0**	**0**	**2**	**0**	**0**	**0**	**0**	**0.0**	**0**													
	Albany	AHL	73	28	46	74	84												5	2	1	3	11			
1994-95	Albany	AHL	74	23	33	56	95												14	6	4	10	8			
1995-96	**New Jersey**	**NHL**	**6**	**2**	**1**	**3**	**0**	**0**	**0**	**0**	**9**	**22.2**	**1**													
	Albany	AHL	75	35	47	82	142												4	0	3	3	10			
1996-97	**St. Louis**	**NHL**	**54**	**8**	**10**	**18**	**35**	**0**	**2**	**2**	**76**	**10.5**	**12**						**6**	**0**	**0**	**0**	**6**	**0**	**0**	**0**
	Worcester	AHL	24	10	16	26	37																			
1997-98	**St. Louis**	**NHL**	**80**	**8**	**21**	**29**	**62**	**1**	**1**	**0**	**96**	**8.3**	**14**						**10**	**0**	**2**	**2**	**10**	**0**	**0**	**0**

			Regular Season																Playoffs							
Season	Club	League	GP	G	A	Pts	PIM	PP	SH	GW	S	%	+/-	TF	F%	H	SB	Min	GP	G	A	Pts	PIM	PP	SH	GW
1998-99	**St. Louis**	**NHL**	**80**	**20**	**21**	**41**	**42**	**0**	**5**	**4**	**138**	**14.5**	**1**	**6**	**66.7**	**90**	**50**	**17:18**	**8**	**1**	**0**	**1**	**4**	**0**	**0**	**0**
	NHL Totals		**266**	**48**	**64**	**112**	**182**	**2**	**10**	**6**	**379**	**12.7**		**6**	**66.7**	**90**	**50**	**17:18**	**24**	**1**	**2**	**3**	**20**	**0**	**0**	**0**

Hockey East First All-Star Team (1992) • NCAA East First All-American Team (1992) • Won Hobey Baker Memorial Award (Top U.S. Collegiate Player) (1992)
Signed as a free agent by **St. Louis**, July 10, 1996.

PELTONEN, Ville
(PEHL-TOH-ner) **NSH.**

Left wing. Shoots left. 5'11", 180 lbs. Born, Vantaa, Finland, May 24, 1973. San Jose's 4th choice, 58th overall, in 1993 Entry Draft.

Season	Club	League	GP	G	A	Pts	PIM	PP	SH	GW	S	%	+/-	TF	F%	H	SB	Min	GP	G	A	Pts	PIM	PP	SH	GW
1990-91	HIFK Helsinki	Finn-Jr.	36	21	16	37	16	....	....	....	....	....	....	....	....	....	....	....	7	2	3	5	10	....	....	....
1991-92	HIFK Helsinki	Finn-Jr.	37	28	23	51	28	....	....	....	....	....	....	....	....	....	....	....	4	0	2	2	0	....	....	....
	HIFK Helsinki	Finland	6	0	0	0	0	....	....	....	....	....	....	....	....	....	....	....	....	....	....	....	....	....	....	....
1992-93	HIFK Helsinki	Finn-Jr.	2	4	2	6	4	....	....	....	....	....	....	....	....	....	....	....	....	....	....	....	....	....	....	....
	HIFK Helsinki	Finland	46	13	24	37	16	....	....	....	....	....	....	....	....	....	....	....	4	0	2	2	2	....	....	....
1993-94	HIFK Helsinki	Finland	43	16	22	38	14	....	....	....	....	....	....	....	....	....	....	....	3	0	0	0	2	....	....	....
	Finland	Olympics	8	4	3	7	0	....	....	....	....	....	....	....	....	....	....	....	....	....	....	....	....	....	....	....
	Finland	Nat-Team	19	6	4	10	6	....	....	....	....	....	....	....	....	....	....	....	....	....	....	....	....	....	....	....
1994-95	HIFK Helsinki	Finland	45	20	16	36	16	....	....	....	....	....	....	....	....	....	....	....	3	0	0	0	0	....	....	....
	Finland	Nat-Team	16	3	3	6	4	....	....	....	....	....	....	....	....	....	....	....	....	....	....	....	....	....	....	....
1995-96	**San Jose**	**NHL**	**31**	**2**	**11**	**13**	**14**	**0**	**0**	**0**	**58**	**3.4**	**–7**	....	....	....	....	....	....	....	....	....	....	....	....	....
	Kansas City	IHL	29	5	13	18	8	....	....	....	....	....	....	....	....	....	....	....	....	....	....	....	....	....	....	....
	Finland	Nat-Team	1	0	0	0	0	....	....	....	....	....	....	....	....	....	....	....	....	....	....	....	....	....	....	....
1996-97	**San Jose**	**NHL**	**28**	**2**	**3**	**5**	**0**	**1**	**0**	**0**	**35**	**5.7**	**–8**	....	....	....	....	....	....	....	....	....	....	....	....	....
	Kentucky	AHL	40	22	30	52	21	....	....	....	....	....	....	....	....	....	....	....	....	....	....	....	....	....	....	....
	Finland	Nat-Team	3	0	1	1	2	....	....	....	....	....	....	....	....	....	....	....	....	....	....	....	....	....	....	....
1997-98	V. Frolunda	Sweden	45	22	29	51	44	....	....	....	....	....	....	....	....	....	....	....	7	4	2	6	0	....	....	....
	Finland	Nat-Team	16	4	8	12	10	....	....	....	....	....	....	....	....	....	....	....	....	....	....	....	....	....	....	....
	Finland	Olympics	6	2	1	3	6	....	....	....	....	....	....	....	....	....	....	....	....	....	....	....	....	....	....	....
1998-99	**Nashville**	**NHL**	**14**	**5**	**5**	**10**	**2**	**1**	**0**	**0**	**31**	**16.1**	**1**	**0**	**0.0**	**4**	**4**	**15:54**	....	....	....	....	....	....	....	....
	NHL Totals		**73**	**9**	**19**	**28**	**16**	**2**	**0**	**0**	**124**	**7.3**		**0**	**0.0**	**4**	**4**	**15:54**	....	....	....	....	....	....	....	....

Finnish Rookie of the Year (1993)
Traded to **Nashville** by **San Jose** for Nashville's 5th round choice (later traded to Phoenix - Phoenix selected Josh Blackburn) in 1998 Entry Draft, June 26, 1998.

PERREAULT, Yanic
(puh-ROH, YAH-nihk) **TOR.**

Center. Shoots left. 5'11", 188 lbs. Born, Sherbrooke, Que., April 4, 1971. Toronto's 1st choice, 47th overall, in 1991 Entry Draft.

Season	Club	League	GP	G	A	Pts	PIM	PP	SH	GW	S	%	+/-	TF	F%	H	SB	Min	GP	G	A	Pts	PIM	PP	SH	GW
1987-88	Montreal L'est	QAAA	42	70	57	127	....	....	....	....	....	....	....	....	....	....	....	....	....	....	....	....	....	....	....	....
1988-89	Trois-Rivieres	QMJHL	70	53	55	108	48	....	....	....	....	....	....	....	....	....	....	....	....	....	....	....	....	....	....	....
1989-90	Trois-Rivieres	QMJHL	63	51	63	114	75	....	....	....	....	....	....	....	....	....	....	....	7	6	5	11	19	....	....	....
1990-91	Trois-Rivieres	QMJHL	67	*87	98	*185	103	....	....	....	....	....	....	....	....	....	....	....	6	4	7	11	6	....	....	....
1991-92	St. John's	AHL	62	38	38	76	19	....	....	....	....	....	....	....	....	....	....	....	16	7	8	15	4	....	....	....
1992-93	St. John's	AHL	79	49	46	95	56	....	....	....	....	....	....	....	....	....	....	....	9	4	5	9	2	....	....	....
1993-94	**Toronto**	**NHL**	**13**	**3**	**3**	**6**	**0**	**2**	**0**	**0**	**24**	**12.5**	**1**	....	....	....	....	....	....	....	....	....	....	....	....	....
	St. John's	AHL	62	45	60	105	38	....	....	....	....	....	....	....	....	....	....	....	11	*12	6	18	14	....	....	....
1994-95	Phoenix	IHL	68	51	48	99	52	....	....	....	....	....	....	....	....	....	....	....	....	....	....	....	....	....	....	....
	Los Angeles	**NHL**	**26**	**2**	**5**	**7**	**20**	**0**	**0**	**1**	**43**	**4.7**	**3**	....	....	....	....	....	....	....	....	....	....	....	....	....
1995-96	**Los Angeles**	**NHL**	**78**	**25**	**24**	**49**	**16**	**8**	**3**	**7**	**175**	**14.3**	**–11**	....	....	....	....	....	....	....	....	....	....	....	....	....
1996-97	**Los Angeles**	**NHL**	**41**	**11**	**14**	**25**	**20**	**1**	**1**	**0**	**98**	**11.2**	**0**	....	....	....	....	....	....	....	....	....	....	....	....	....
1997-98	**Los Angeles**	**NHL**	**79**	**28**	**20**	**48**	**32**	**3**	**2**	**3**	**206**	**13.6**	**6**	....	....	....	....	....	**4**	**1**	**2**	**3**	**6**	**1**	**0**	**0**
1998-99	**Los Angeles**	**NHL**	**64**	**10**	**17**	**27**	**30**	**2**	**2**	**1**	**113**	**8.8**	**–3**	**1024**	**56.5**	**35**	**33**	**15:24**	....	....	....	....	....	....	....	....
	Toronto	**NHL**	**12**	**7**	**8**	**15**	**12**	**2**	**1**	**2**	**28**	**25.0**	**10**	**164**	**62.8**	**9**	**1**	**13:20**	**17**	**3**	**6**	**9**	**6**	**0**	**0**	**2**
	NHL Totals		**313**	**86**	**91**	**177**	**130**	**18**	**9**	**14**	**687**	**12.5**		**1188**	**57.4**	**44**	**34**	**15:04**	**21**	**4**	**8**	**12**	**12**	**1**	**0**	**2**

Canadian Major Junior Rookie of the Year (1989) • QMJHL First All-Star Team (1991)
Traded to **LA Kings** by **Toronto** for LA Kings' 4th round choice (later traded to Philadelphia — later traded to LA Kings — LA Kings selected Mikael Simons) in 1996 Entry Draft, July 11, 1994. Traded to **Toronto** by **Los Angeles** for Jason Podollan and Toronto's 3rd round choice (Cory Campbell) in 1999 Entry Draft, March 23, 1999.

PERSSON, Ricard
(PAIR-suhn, RIH-kahrd) **ST.L.**

Defense. Shoots left. 6'2", 205 lbs. Born, Ostersund, Sweden, August 24, 1969. New Jersey's 2nd choice, 23rd overall, in 1987 Entry Draft.

Season	Club	League	GP	G	A	Pts	PIM	PP	SH	GW	S	%	+/-	TF	F%	H	SB	Min	GP	G	A	Pts	PIM	PP	SH	GW
1985-86	Ostersund IK	Sweden-2	24	2	2	4	16	....	....	....	....	....	....	....	....	....	....	....	....	....	....	....	....	....	....	....
1986-87	Ostersund IK	Sweden-2	31	10	11	21	28	....	....	....	....	....	....	....	....	....	....	....	....	....	....	....	....	....	....	....
1987-88	Leksands IF	Sweden	31	2	0	2	8	....	....	....	....	....	....	....	....	....	....	....	2	0	1	1	2	....	....	....
1988-89	Leksands IF	Sweden	33	2	4	6	28	....	....	....	....	....	....	....	....	....	....	....	9	0	1	1	6	....	....	....
1989-90	Leksands IF	Sweden	43	9	10	19	62	....	....	....	....	....	....	....	....	....	....	....	3	0	0	0	6	....	....	....
1990-91	Leksands IF	Sweden	37	6	9	15	42	....	....	....	....	....	....	....	....	....	....	....	....	....	....	....	....	....	....	....
1991-92	Leksands IF	Sweden	21	0	7	7	28	....	....	....	....	....	....	....	....	....	....	....	....	....	....	....	....	....	....	....
1992-93	Leksands IF	Sweden	36	7	15	22	63	....	....	....	....	....	....	....	....	....	....	....	2	0	2	2	0	....	....	....
1993-94	Malmo IF	Sweden	40	11	9	20	38	....	....	....	....	....	....	....	....	....	....	....	11	2	0	2	12	....	....	....
1994-95	Malmo IF	Sweden	31	3	13	16	38	....	....	....	....	....	....	....	....	....	....	....	9	0	2	2	8	....	....	....
	Albany	AHL	3	0	0	0	0	....	....	....	....	....	....	....	....	....	....	....	9	3	5	8	7	....	....	....
1995-96	**New Jersey**	**NHL**	**12**	**2**	**1**	**3**	**8**	**1**	**0**	**0**	**41**	**4.9**	**5**	....	....	....	....	....	....	....	....	....	....	....	....	....
	Albany	AHL	67	15	31	46	59	....	....	....	....	....	....	....	....	....	....	....	4	0	0	0	7	....	....	....
1996-97	**New Jersey**	**NHL**	**1**	**0**	**0**	**0**	**0**	**0**	**0**	**0**	**2**	**0.0**	**0**	....	....	....	....	....	....	....	....	....	....	....	....	....
	Albany	AHL	13	1	4	5	8	....	....	....	....	....	....	....	....	....	....	....	....	....	....	....	....	....	....	....
	St. Louis	**NHL**	**53**	**4**	**8**	**12**	**45**	**1**	**0**	**0**	**68**	**5.9**	**–2**	....	....	....	....	....	**6**	**0**	**0**	**0**	**27**	**0**	**0**	**0**
1997-98	**St. Louis**	**NHL**	**1**	**0**	**0**	**0**	**0**	**0**	**0**	**0**	**0**	**0.0**	**0**	....	....	....	....	....	....	....	....	....	....	....	....	....
	Worcester	AHL	32	2	16	18	58	....	....	....	....	....	....	....	....	....	....	....	10	3	7	10	24	....	....	....
1998-99	**St. Louis**	**NHL**	**54**	**1**	**12**	**13**	**94**	**0**	**0**	**0**	**52**	**1.9**	**4**	**1**	**100.0**	**33**	**81**	**19:58**	**13**	**0**	**3**	**3**	**17**	**0**	**0**	**0**
	Worcester	AHL	19	6	4	10	42	....	....	....	....	....	....	....	....	....	....	....	....	....	....	....	....	....	....	....
	NHL Totals		**121**	**7**	**21**	**28**	**147**	**2**	**0**	**0**	**163**	**4.3**		**1**	**100.0**	**33**	**81**	**19:58**	**19**	**0**	**3**	**3**	**44**	**0**	**0**	**0**

Traded to **St. Louis** by **New Jersey** with Mike Peluso for Ken Sutton and St. Louis' 2nd round choice in 1999 Entry Draft, November 26, 1996.

PETERSON, Brent
NSH.

Left wing. Shoots left. 6'3", 200 lbs. Born, Calgary, Alta., July 20, 1972. Tampa Bay's 1st choice, 3rd overall, in 1993 Supplemental Draft.

Season	Club	League	GP	G	A	Pts	PIM	PP	SH	GW	S	%	+/-	TF	F%	H	SB	Min	GP	G	A	Pts	PIM	PP	SH	GW
1990-91	Thunder Bay	USHL	48	27	40	67	10	....	....	....	....	....	....	....	....	....	....	....	10	8	9	17	4	....	....	....
1991-92	Michigan Tech	WCHA	39	11	9	20	18	....	....	....	....	....	....	....	....	....	....	....	....	....	....	....	....	....	....	....
1992-93	Michigan Tech	WCHA	37	24	18	42	32	....	....	....	....	....	....	....	....	....	....	....	....	....	....	....	....	....	....	....
1993-94	Michigan Tech	WCHA	43	25	21	46	30	....	....	....	....	....	....	....	....	....	....	....	....	....	....	....	....	....	....	....
1994-95	Michigan Tech	WCHA	39	20	16	36	27	....	....	....	....	....	....	....	....	....	....	....	....	....	....	....	....	....	....	....
1995-96	Atlanta	IHL	69	9	19	28	33	....	....	....	....	....	....	....	....	....	....	....	3	0	0	0	0	....	....	....
1996-97	**Tampa Bay**	**NHL**	**17**	**2**	**0**	**2**	**4**	**0**	**0**	**0**	**11**	**18.2**	**–4**	....	....	....	....	....	....	....	....	....	....	....	....	....
	Adirondack	AHL	52	22	23	45	56	....	....	....	....	....	....	....	....	....	....	....	4	3	1	4	2	....	....	....
1997-98	**Tampa Bay**	**NHL**	**19**	**5**	**0**	**5**	**2**	**0**	**0**	**0**	**15**	**33.3**	**–2**	....	....	....	....	....	....	....	....	....	....	....	....	....
	Milwaukee	IHL	63	20	39	59	48	....	....	....	....	....	....	....	....	....	....	....	8	5	3	8	22	....	....	....
1998-99	**Tampa Bay**	**NHL**	**20**	**2**	**1**	**3**	**0**	**0**	**0**	**0**	**16**	**12.5**	**–2**	**1**	**100.0**	**14**	**3**	**8:58**	....	....	....	....	....	....	....	....
	Cleveland	IHL	18	6	7	13	31	....	....	....	....	....	....	....	....	....	....	....	....	....	....	....	....	....	....	....
	Grand Rapids	IHL	17	7	5	12	14	....	....	....	....	....	....	....	....	....	....	....	....	....	....	....	....	....	....	....
	NHL Totals		**56**	**9**	**1**	**10**	**6**	**0**	**0**	**0**	**42**	**21.4**		**1**	**100.0**	**14**	**3**	**8:58**	....	....	....	....	....	....	....	....

Claimed by **Hartford** from **Vancouver** in Waiver Draft, October 5, 1987. Traded to **Pittsburgh** by **Tampa Bay** for cash, March 18, 1999. Signed as a free agent by **Nashville**, July 24, 1999.

								Regular Season											Playoffs						
Season	Club	League	GP	G	A	Pts	PIM	PP	SH	GW	S	%	+/-	TF	F%	H	SB	Min	GP	G	A	Pts	PIM	PP	SH	GW

PETIT, Michel

(puh-TEE)

Defense. Shoots right. 6'1", 205 lbs.   Born, St. Malo, Que., February 12, 1964. Vancouver's 1st choice, 11th overall, in 1982 Entry Draft.

Season	Club	League	GP	G	A	Pts	PIM	PP	SH	GW	S	%	+/-	TF	F%	H	SB	Min	GP	G	A	Pts	PIM	PP	SH	GW
1979-80	Ste-Foy	QAAA	35	4	9	13	....	....	....	....	....	....	....						....	....	....	....	....			
1980-81	Ste-Foy	QAAA	48	10	45	55	84	....	....	....	....	....	....						....	....	....	....	....			
1981-82	Sherbrooke	QMJHL	63	10	39	49	106	....	....	....	....	....	....						22	5	20	25	24			
1982-83	St-Jean	QMJHL	62	19	67	86	196	....	....	....	....	....	....						3	0	0	0	35			
	Vancouver	NHL	2	0	0	0	0	0	0	0	1	0.0	-4						....	....	....	....	....			
1983-84	Vancouver	NHL	44	6	9	15	53	5	0	0	78	7.7	-6						1	0	0	0	0	0	0	0
	Canada	Nat-Team	19	3	10	13	58	....	....	....	....	....	....						....	....	....	....	....			
1984-85	Vancouver	NHL	69	5	26	31	127	1	1	1	96	5.2	-26						....	....	....	....	....			
1985-86	Vancouver	NHL	32	1	6	7	27	1	0	0	43	2.3	-6						....	....	....	....	....			
	Fredericton	AHL	25	0	13	13	79	....	....	....	....	....	....						....	....	....	....	....			
1986-87	Vancouver	NHL	69	12	13	25	131	4	0	1	116	10.3	-5						....	....	....	....	....			
1987-88	Vancouver	NHL	10	0	3	3	35	0	0	0	13	0.0	-4						....	....	....	....	....			
	NY Rangers	NHL	64	9	24	33	223	2	0	3	96	9.4	3						....	....	....	....	....			
1988-89	NY Rangers	NHL	69	8	25	33	154	5	0	1	132	6.1	-15						4	0	2	2	27	0	0	0
1989-90	Quebec	NHL	63	12	24	36	215	5	0	0	137	8.8	-38						....	....	....	....	....			
1990-91	Quebec	NHL	19	4	7	11	47	3	0	0	39	10.3	-15						....	....	....	....	....			
	Toronto	NHL	54	9	19	28	132	3	1	2	95	9.5	-19						....	....	....	....	....			
1991-92	Toronto	NHL	34	1	13	14	85	1	0	1	61	1.6	-17						....	....	....	....	....			
	Calgary	NHL	36	3	10	13	79	3	0	0	68	4.4	2						....	....	....	....	....			
1992-93	Calgary	NHL	35	3	9	12	54	2	0	0	58	5.2	-5						6	0	0	0	20	0	0	0
1993-94	Calgary	NHL	63	2	21	23	110	0	0	0	103	1.9	5						....	....	....	....	....			
1994-95	Los Angeles	NHL	40	5	12	17	84	2	0	0	70	7.1	4						....	....	....	....	....			
1995-96	Los Angeles	NHL	9	0	1	1	27	0	0	0	12	0.0	-1						....	....	....	....	....			
	Tampa Bay	NHL	45	4	7	11	108	0	0	1	56	7.1	-10						3	0	0	0	6	0	0	0
1996-97	Edmonton	NHL	18	2	4	6	20	0	0	0	30	6.7	-13						....	....	....	....	....			
	Philadelphia	NHL	20	0	3	3	51	0	0	0	13	0.0	2						5	0	0	0	8	0	0	0
1997-98	Detroit	IHL	9	2	3	5	24	....	....	....	....	....	....						....	....	....	....	....			
	Phoenix	NHL	32	4	2	6	77	1	0	0	34	11.8	-4						....	....	....	....	....			
1998-99	Las Vegas	IHL	6	0	1	1	10	....	....	....	....	....	....						....	....	....	....	....			
	NHL Totals		**827**	**90**	**238**	**328**	**1839**	**38**	**2**	**10**	**1351**	**6.7**							**19**	**0**	**2**	**2**	**61**	**0**	**0**	**0**

QMJHL First All-Star Team (1982, 1983)

Traded to **NY Rangers** by **Vancouver** for Willie Huber and Larry Melnyk, November 4, 1987. Traded to **Quebec** by **NY Rangers** for Randy Moller, October 5, 1989. Traded to **Toronto** by **Quebec** with Aaron Broten and Lucien Deblois for Scott Pearson and Toronto's 2nd round choices in 1991 (later traded to Washington — Washington selected Eric Lavigne) and 1992 (Tuomas Gronman) Entry Drafts, November 17, 1990. Traded to **Calgary** by **Toronto** with Craig Berube, Alexander Godynyuk, Gary Leeman and Jeff Reese for Doug Gilmour, Jamie Macoun, Ric Nattress, Rick Wamsley and Kent Manderville, January 2, 1992. Signed as a free agent by **LA Kings**, June 16, 1994. Traded to **Tampa Bay** by **LA Kings** for Steven Finn, November 13, 1995. Signed as a free agent by **Edmonton**, October 24, 1996. Claimed on waivers by **Philadelphia** from **Edmonton**, January 17, 1997. Signed as a free agent by **Phoenix**, November 25, 1997. • Missed majority of 1998-99 season recovering from post-concussion syndrome, October 1998.

PETROV, Oleg

(PEH-trahf) **MTL.**

Right wing. Shoots left. 5'8", 175 lbs.   Born, Moscow, USSR, April 18, 1971. Montreal's 9th choice, 127th overall, in 1991 Entry Draft.

Season	Club	League	GP	G	A	Pts	PIM	PP	SH	GW	S	%	+/-	TF	F%	H	SB	Min	GP	G	A	Pts	PIM	PP	SH	GW
1989-90	CSKA Moscow	USSR	30	4	7	11	4	....	....	....	....	....	....						....	....	....	....	....			
1990-91	CSKA Moscow	USSR	43	7	4	11	8	....	....	....	....	....	....						....	....	....	....	....			
1991-92	CSKA Moscow	CIS	42	10	16	26	8	....	....	....	....	....	....						....	....	....	....	....			
1992-93♦	Montreal	NHL	9	2	1	3	10	0	0	1	20	10.0	2					•	1	0	0	0	0	0	0	0
	Fredericton	AHL	55	26	29	55	36	....	....	....	....	....	....						5	4	1	5	0			
1993-94	Montreal	NHL	55	12	15	27	2	1	0	1	107	11.2	7						2	0	0	0	0	0	0	0
	Fredericton	AHL	23	8	20	28	18	....	....	....	....	....	....						....	....	....	....	....			
1994-95	Montreal	NHL	12	2	3	5	4	0	0	0	26	7.7	-7						....	....	....	....	....			
	Fredericton	AHL	17	7	11	18	12	....	....	....	....	....	....						17	5	6	11	10			
1995-96	Montreal	NHL	36	4	7	11	23	0	0	2	44	9.1	-9						5	0	1	1	0	0	0	0
	Fredericton	AHL	22	12	18	30	71	....	....	....	....	....	....						6	2	6	8	0			
1996-97	Ambri-Piotta	Switz.	45	24	28	52	44	....	....	....	....	....	....						....	....	....	....	....			
	HC Meran	Italy	12	5	12	17	4	....	....	....	....	....	....						....	....	....	....	....			
1997-98	Ambri-Piotta	Switz.	40	30	*63	*93	60	....	....	....	....	....	....						14	11	11	22	40			
1998-99	Ambri-Piotta	Switz.	45	35	*52	*87	52	....	....	....	....	....	....						15	9	11	*20	32			
	NHL Totals		**112**	**20**	**26**	**46**	**39**	**1**	**0**	**4**	**197**	**10.2**							**8**	**0**	**1**	**1**	**0**	**0**	**0**	**0**

NHL/Upper Deck All-Rookie Team (1994)

Signed as a free agent by **Montreal**, July 15, 1999.

PETROVICKY, Robert

(PEHT-roh-vih-kee) **T.B.**

Center. Shoots left. 5'11", 172 lbs.   Born, Kosice, Czech., October 26, 1973. Hartford's 1st choice, 9th overall, in 1992 Entry Draft.

Season	Club	League	GP	G	A	Pts	PIM	PP	SH	GW	S	%	+/-	TF	F%	H	SB	Min	GP	G	A	Pts	PIM	PP	SH	GW
1990-91	Dukla Trencin	Czech.	33	9	14	23	12	....	....	....	....	....	....						....	....	....	....	....			
1991-92	Dukla Trencin	Czech.	46	25	36	61	28	....	....	....	....	....	....						....	....	....	....	....			
1992-93	Hartford	NHL	42	3	6	9	45	0	0	0	41	7.3	-10						....	....	....	....	....			
	Springfield	AHL	16	5	3	8	39	....	....	....	....	....	....						15	5	6	11	14			
1993-94	Dukla Trencin	Slovakia	1	0	0	0	0	....	....	....	....	....	....						....	....	....	....	....			
	Hartford	NHL	33	6	5	11	39	1	0	0	33	18.2	-1						....	....	....	....	....			
	Springfield	AHL	30	16	8	24	39	....	....	....	....	....	....						4	0	2	2	4			
	Slovakia	Olympics	8	1	6	7	18	....	....	....	....	....	....						....	....	....	....	....			
1994-95	Springfield	AHL	74	30	52	82	121	....	....	....	....	....	....						....	....	....	....	....			
	Hartford	NHL	2	0	0	0	0	0	0	0	1	0.0	0						....	....	....	....	....			
1995-96	Springfield	AHL	9	4	8	12	18	....	....	....	....	....	....						....	....	....	....	....			
	Detroit	IHL	12	5	3	8	16	....	....	....	....	....	....						....	....	....	....	....			
	Dallas	NHL	5	1	1	2	0	1	0	1	3	33.3	1						....	....	....	....	....			
	Michigan	IHL	50	23	23	46	63	....	....	....	....	....	....						7	3	1	4	16			
1996-97	St. Louis	NHL	44	7	12	19	10	0	0	1	54	13.0	-2						2	0	0	0	0	0	0	0
	Worcester	AHL	12	5	4	9	19	....	....	....	....	....	....						....	....	....	....	....			
1997-98	Worcester	AHL	65	27	34	61	97	....	....	....	....	....	....						10	3	4	7	12			
	Slovakia	Olympics	4	2	1	3	0	....	....	....	....	....	....						....	....	....	....	....			
1998-99	Grand Rapids	IHL	49	26	32	58	87	....	....	....	....	....	....						....	....	....	....	....			
	Tampa Bay	NHL	28	3	4	7	6	0	0	0	32	9.4	-8	35	34.3	21	8	10:33	....	....	....	....	....			
	NHL Totals		**154**	**20**	**28**	**48**	**100**	**2**	**0**	**2**	**164**	**12.2**		**35**	**34.3**	**21**	**8**	**10:33**	**2**	**0**	**0**	**0**	**0**	**0**	**0**	**0**

Czechoslovakian First All-Star Team (1992)

Traded to **Dallas** by **Hartford** for Dan Kesa and future considerations, November 29, 1995. Signed as a free agent by **St. Louis**, September 6, 1996. Signed as a free agent by **Tampa Bay**, February 15, 1999.

PHILLIPS, Chris

OTT.

Defense. Shoots left. 6'2", 200 lbs.   Born, Fort McMurray, Alta., March 9, 1978. Ottawa's 1st choice, 1st overall, in 1996 Entry Draft.

Season	Club	League	GP	G	A	Pts	PIM	PP	SH	GW	S	%	+/-	TF	F%	H	SB	Min	GP	G	A	Pts	PIM	PP	SH	GW
1993-94	Fort McMurray	AJHL	56	6	16	22	72	....	....	....	....	....	....						10	0	3	3	16			
1994-95	Fort McMurray	AJHL	48	16	32	48	127	....	....	....	....	....	....						11	4	2	6	10			
1995-96	Prince Albert	WHL	61	10	30	40	97	....	....	....	....	....	....						18	2	12	14	30			
1996-97	Prince Albert	WHL	32	3	23	26	58	....	....	....	....	....	....						....	....	....	....	....			
	Lethbridge	WHL	26	4	18	22	28	....	....	....	....	....	....						19	4	*21	25	20			
1997-98	Ottawa	NHL	72	5	11	16	38	2	0	2	107	4.7	2						11	0	2	2	2	0	0	0
1998-99	Ottawa	NHL	34	3	3	6	32	2	0	0	51	5.9	-5	0	0.0	53	28	18:06	3	0	0	0	0	0	0	0
	NHL Totals		**106**	**8**	**14**	**22**	**70**	**4**	**0**	**2**	**158**	**5.1**		**0**	**0.0**	**53**	**28**	**18:06**	**14**	**0**	**2**	**2**	**2**	**0**	**0**	**0**

WHL East First All-Star Team (1997) • Canadian Major Junior First All-Star Team (1997)

PICARD, Michel

(PEE-cahr)

Left wing. Shoots left. 5'11", 190 lbs. Born, Beauport, Que., November 7, 1969. Hartford's 8th choice, 178th overall, in 1989 Entry Draft.

			Regular Season																Playoffs							
Season	Club	League	GP	G	A	Pts	PIM	PP	SH	GW	S	%	+/–	TF	F%	H	SB	Min	GP	G	A	Pts	PIM	PP	SH	GW
1985-86	Ste-Foy	QAAA	42	53	34	87	....	....	....	....	....	....	....	....	....	....	....	....	....	....	....	....	....	....	....	....
1986-87	Trois-Rivieres	QMJHL	66	33	35	68	53	....	....	....	....	....	....	....	....	....	....	....	....	....	....	....	....	....	....	....
1987-88	Trois-Rivieres	QMJHL	69	40	55	95	71	....	....	....	....	....	....	....	....	....	....	....	....	....	....	....	....	....	....	....
1988-89	Trois-Rivieres	QMJHL	66	59	81	140	170	....	....	....	....	....	....	....	....	....	....	....	4	1	3	4	2	....	....	....
1989-90	Binghamton	AHL	67	16	24	40	98	....	....	....	....	....	....	....	....	....	....	....	....	....	....	....	....	....	....	....
1990-91	**Hartford**	**NHL**	**5**	**1**	**0**	**1**	**2**	**0**	**0**	**0**	**7**	**14.3**	**–2**	....	....	....	....	....	....	....	....	....	....	....	....	....
	Springfield	AHL	77	*56	40	96	61	....	....	....	....	....	....	....	....	....	....	....	18	8	13	21	18	....	....	....
1991-92	**Hartford**	**NHL**	**25**	**3**	**5**	**8**	**6**	**1**	**0**	**0**	**41**	**7.3**	**–2**	....	....	....	....	....	....	....	....	....	....	....	....	....
	Springfield	AHL	40	21	17	38	44	....	....	....	....	....	....	....	....	....	....	....	11	2	0	2	34	....	....	....
1992-93	**San Jose**	**NHL**	**25**	**4**	**0**	**4**	**24**	**2**	**0**	**0**	**32**	**12.5**	**–17**	....	....	....	....	....	....	....	....	....	....	....	....	....
	Kansas City	IHL	33	7	10	17	51	....	....	....	....	....	....	....	....	....	....	....	12	3	2	5	20	....	....	....
1993-94	Portland	AHL	61	41	44	85	99	....	....	....	....	....	....	....	....	....	....	....	17	11	10	21	22	....	....	....
1994-95	P.E.I. Senators	AHL	57	32	57	89	58	....	....	....	....	....	....	....	....	....	....	....	8	4	4	8	6	....	....	....
	Ottawa	**NHL**	**24**	**5**	**8**	**13**	**14**	**1**	**0**	**0**	**33**	**15.2**	**–1**	....	....	....	....	....	....	....	....	....	....	....	....	....
1995-96	**Ottawa**	**NHL**	**17**	**2**	**6**	**8**	**10**	**0**	**0**	**1**	**21**	**9.5**	**–1**	....	....	....	....	....	....	....	....	....	....	....	....	....
	P.E.I. Senators	AHL	55	37	45	82	79	....	....	....	....	....	....	....	....	....	....	....	5	5	1	6	2	....	....	....
1996-97	V. Frolunda	Sweden	3	0	1	1	0	....	....	....	....	....	....	....	....	....	....	....	....	....	....	....	....	....	....	....
	Grand Rapids	IHL	82	46	55	101	58	....	....	....	....	....	....	....	....	....	....	....	5	2	0	2	10	....	....	....
1997-98	Grand Rapids	IHL	58	28	41	69	42	....	....	....	....	....	....	....	....	....	....	....	....	....	....	....	....	....	....	....
	St. Louis	**NHL**	**16**	**1**	**8**	**9**	**29**	**0**	**0**	**0**	**19**	**5.3**	**3**	....	....	....	....	....	....	....	....	....	....	....	....	....
1998-99	**St. Louis**	**NHL**	**45**	**11**	**11**	**22**	**16**	**0**	**0**	**2**	**69**	**15.9**	**5**	**1**	**100.0**	**9**	**6**	**14:20**	**5**	**0**	**0**	**0**	**2**	**0**	**0**	**0**
	Grand Rapids	IHL	6	2	2	4	2	....	....	....	....	....	....	....	....	....	....	....	....	....	....	....	....	....	....	....
	NHL Totals		**157**	**27**	**38**	**65**	**101**	**4**	**0**	**3**	**222**	**12.2**		**1**	**100.0**	**9**	**6**	**14:20**	**5**	**0**	**0**	**0**	**2**	**0**	**0**	**0**

QMJHL Second All-Star Team (1989) • AHL First All-Star Team (1991, 1995) • AHL Second All-Star Team (1994) • IHL First All-Star Team (1997)

Traded to **San Jose** by **Hartford** for future considerations (Yvon Corriveau, January 21, 1993), October 9, 1992. Signed as a free agent by **Ottawa**, June 16, 1994. Traded to **Washington** by **Ottawa** for cash, May 21, 1996. Signed as a free agent by **St. Louis**, January 3, 1998.

PILON, Richard

(PEE-lahn) **NYI**

Defense. Shoots left. 6', 205 lbs. Born, Saskatoon, Sask., April 30, 1968. NY Islanders' 9th choice, 143rd overall, in 1986 Entry Draft.

Season	Club	League	GP	G	A	Pts	PIM	PP	SH	GW	S	%	+/–	TF	F%	H	SB	Min	GP	G	A	Pts	PIM	PP	SH	GW
1985-86	Prince Albert	AAHA	35	3	28	31	142	....	....	....	....	....	....	....	....	....	....	....	....	....	....	....	....	....	....	....
	Prince Albert	WHL	6	0	0	0	0	....	....	....	....	....	....	....	....	....	....	....	....	....	....	....	....	....	....	....
1986-87	Prince Albert	WHL	68	4	21	25	192	....	....	....	....	....	....	....	....	....	....	....	7	1	6	7	17	....	....	....
1987-88	Prince Albert	WHL	65	13	34	47	177	....	....	....	....	....	....	....	....	....	....	....	9	0	6	6	38	....	....	....
1988-89	**NY Islanders**	**NHL**	**62**	**0**	**14**	**14**	**242**	**0**	**0**	**0**	**47**	**0.0**	**–9**	....	....	....	....	....	....	....	....	....	....	....	....	....
1989-90	**NY Islanders**	**NHL**	**14**	**0**	**2**	**2**	**31**	**0**	**0**	**0**	**5**	**0.0**	**2**	....	....	....	....	....	....	....	....	....	....	....	....	....
1990-91	**NY Islanders**	**NHL**	**60**	**1**	**4**	**5**	**126**	**0**	**0**	**0**	**33**	**3.0**	**–12**	....	....	....	....	....	....	....	....	....	....	....	....	....
1991-92	**NY Islanders**	**NHL**	**65**	**1**	**6**	**7**	**183**	**0**	**0**	**0**	**27**	**3.7**	**–1**	....	....	....	....	....	....	....	....	....	....	....	....	....
1992-93	**NY Islanders**	**NHL**	**44**	**1**	**3**	**4**	**164**	**0**	**0**	**0**	**20**	**5.0**	**–4**	....	....	....	....	....	**15**	**0**	**0**	**0**	**50**	**0**	**0**	**0**
	Capital District	AHL	6	0	1	1	8	....	....	....	....	....	....	....	....	....	....	....	....	....	....	....	....	....	....	....
1993-94	**NY Islanders**	**NHL**	**28**	**1**	**4**	**5**	**75**	**0**	**0**	**0**	**20**	**5.0**	**–4**	....	....	....	....	....	....	....	....	....	....	....	....	....
	Salt Lake	IHL	2	0	0	0	8	....	....	....	....	....	....	....	....	....	....	....	....	....	....	....	....	....	....	....
1994-95	**NY Islanders**	**NHL**	**20**	**1**	**1**	**2**	**40**	**0**	**0**	**0**	**11**	**9.1**	**–3**	....	....	....	....	....	....	....	....	....	....	....	....	....
1995-96	**NY Islanders**	**NHL**	**27**	**0**	**3**	**3**	**72**	**0**	**0**	**0**	**7**	**0.0**	**–9**	....	....	....	....	....	....	....	....	....	....	....	....	....
1996-97	**NY Islanders**	**NHL**	**52**	**1**	**4**	**5**	**179**	**0**	**0**	**0**	**17**	**5.9**	**4**	....	....	....	....	....	....	....	....	....	....	....	....	....
1997-98	**NY Islanders**	**NHL**	**76**	**0**	**7**	**7**	**291**	**0**	**0**	**0**	**37**	**0.0**	**1**	....	....	....	....	....	....	....	....	....	....	....	....	....
1998-99	**NY Islanders**	**NHL**	**52**	**0**	**4**	**4**	**88**	**0**	**0**	**0**	**27**	**0.0**	**–8**	**0**	**0.0**	**155**	**49**	**16:35**	....	....	....	....	....	....	....	....
	NHL Totals		**500**	**6**	**52**	**58**	**1491**	**0**	**0**	**0**	**251**	**2.4**		**0**	**0.0**	**155**	**49**	**16:35**	**15**	**0**	**0**	**0**	**50**	**0**	**0**	**0**

WHL East Second All-Star Team (1988)

PITLICK, Lance

(PIHT-lihk) **FLA.**

Defense. Shoots right. 6', 205 lbs. Born, Minneapolis, MN, November 5, 1967. Minnesota's 10th choice, 180th overall, in 1986 Entry Draft.

Season	Club	League	GP	G	A	Pts	PIM	PP	SH	GW	S	%	+/–	TF	F%	H	SB	Min	GP	G	A	Pts	PIM	PP	SH	GW
1984-85	Cooper High	H.S.	23	8	4	12	....	....	....	....	....	....	....	....	....	....	....	....	....	....	....	....	....	....	....	....
1985-86	Cooper Hawks	H.S.	21	17	8	25	247	....	....	....	....	....	....	....	....	....	....	....	....	....	....	....	....	....	....	....
1986-87	U. of Minnesota	WCHA	45	0	9	9	88	....	....	....	....	....	....	....	....	....	....	....	....	....	....	....	....	....	....	....
1987-88	U. of Minnesota	WCHA	38	3	9	12	76	....	....	....	....	....	....	....	....	....	....	....	....	....	....	....	....	....	....	....
1988-89	U. of Minnesota	WCHA	47	4	9	13	95	....	....	....	....	....	....	....	....	....	....	....	....	....	....	....	....	....	....	....
1989-90	U. of Minnesota	WCHA	14	3	2	5	26	....	....	....	....	....	....	....	....	....	....	....	....	....	....	....	....	....	....	....
1990-91	Hershey	AHL	64	6	15	21	75	....	....	....	....	....	....	....	....	....	....	....	3	0	0	0	9	....	....	....
1991-92	United States	Nat-Team	19	0	1	1	38	....	....	....	....	....	....	....	....	....	....	....	....	....	....	....	....	....	....	....
	Hershey	AHL	4	0	0	0	6	....	....	....	....	....	....	....	....	....	....	....	3	0	0	0	4	....	....	....
1992-93	Hershey	AHL	53	5	10	15	77	....	....	....	....	....	....	....	....	....	....	....	....	....	....	....	....	....	....	....
1993-94	Hershey	AHL	58	4	13	17	93	....	....	....	....	....	....	....	....	....	....	....	11	1	0	1	11	....	....	....
1994-95	P.E.I. Senators	AHL	61	8	19	27	55	....	....	....	....	....	....	....	....	....	....	....	11	1	4	5	10	....	....	....
	Ottawa	**NHL**	**15**	**0**	**1**	**1**	**6**	**0**	**0**	**0**	**11**	**0.0**	**–5**	....	....	....	....	....	....	....	....	....	....	....	....	....
1995-96	**Ottawa**	**NHL**	**28**	**1**	**6**	**7**	**20**	**0**	**0**	**0**	**13**	**7.7**	**–8**	....	....	....	....	....	....	....	....	....	....	....	....	....
	P.E.I. Senators	AHL	29	4	10	14	39	....	....	....	....	....	....	....	....	....	....	....	5	0	0	0	0	....	....	....
1996-97	**Ottawa**	**NHL**	**66**	**5**	**5**	**10**	**91**	**0**	**0**	**1**	**54**	**9.3**	**2**	....	....	....	....	....	**7**	**0**	**0**	**0**	**4**	**0**	**0**	**0**
1997-98	**Ottawa**	**NHL**	**69**	**2**	**7**	**9**	**50**	**0**	**0**	**0**	**66**	**3.0**	**8**	....	....	....	....	....	**11**	**0**	**1**	**1**	**17**	**0**	**0**	**0**
1998-99	**Ottawa**	**NHL**	**50**	**3**	**6**	**9**	**33**	**0**	**0**	**0**	**34**	**8.8**	**7**	**0**	**0.0**	**120**	**64**	**16:39**	**2**	**0**	**0**	**0**	**0**	**0**	**0**	**0**
	NHL Totals		**228**	**11**	**25**	**36**	**200**	**0**	**0**	**1**	**178**	**6.2**		**0**	**0.0**	**120**	**64**	**16:39**	**20**	**0**	**1**	**1**	**21**	**0**	**0**	**0**

Signed as a free agent by **Philadelphia**, September 5, 1990. Signed as a free agent by **Ottawa**, June 22, 1994. Signed as a free agent by **Florida**, July 21, 1999.

PITTIS, Domenic

(PIH-TIHS) **BUF.**

Center. Shoots left. 5'11", 190 lbs. Born, Calgary, Alta., October 1, 1974. Pittsburgh's 2nd choice, 52nd overall, in 1993 Entry Draft.

Season	Club	League	GP	G	A	Pts	PIM	PP	SH	GW	S	%	+/–	TF	F%	H	SB	Min	GP	G	A	Pts	PIM	PP	SH	GW
1990-91	Calgary	AAHA	35	23	54	77	43	....	....	....	....	....	....	....	....	....	....	....	....	....	....	....	....	....	....	....
1991-92	Lethbridge	WHL	65	6	17	23	48	....	....	....	....	....	....	....	....	....	....	....	5	0	2	2	4	....	....	....
1992-93	Lethbridge	WHL	66	46	73	119	69	....	....	....	....	....	....	....	....	....	....	....	4	3	3	6	8	....	....	....
1993-94	Lethbridge	WHL	72	58	69	127	93	....	....	....	....	....	....	....	....	....	....	....	8	4	11	15	16	....	....	....
1994-95	Cleveland	IHL	62	18	32	50	66	....	....	....	....	....	....	....	....	....	....	....	3	0	2	2	2	....	....	....
1995-96	Cleveland	IHL	74	10	28	38	100	....	....	....	....	....	....	....	....	....	....	....	3	0	0	0	2	....	....	....
1996-97	**Pittsburgh**	**NHL**	**1**	**0**	**0**	**0**	**0**	**0**	**0**	**0**	**0**	**0.0**	**–1**	....	....	....	....	....	....	....	....	....	....	....	....	....
	Long Beach	IHL	65	23	43	66	91	....	....	....	....	....	....	....	....	....	....	....	18	5	9	14	26	....	....	....
1997-98	Syracuse	AHL	75	23	41	64	90	....	....	....	....	....	....	....	....	....	....	....	5	1	3	4	4	....	....	....
1998-99	**Buffalo**	**NHL**	**3**	**0**	**0**	**0**	**2**	**0**	**0**	**0**	**1**	**0.0**	**0**	**19**	**42.1**	**4**	**1**	**8:35**	....	....	....	....	....	....	....	....
	Rochester	AHL	76	38	66	*104	108	....	....	....	....	....	....	....	....	....	....	....	20	7	*14	*21	40	....	....	....
	NHL Totals		**4**	**0**	**0**	**0**	**2**	**0**	**0**	**0**	**1**	**0.0**		**19**	**42.1**	**4**	**1**	**8:35**	....	....	....	....	....	....	....	....

WHL East Second All-Star Team (1994) • Won John P. Sollenberger Trophy (Top Scorer - AHL) (1999)

Signed as a free agent by **Buffalo**, August 10, 1998.

PIVONKA, Michal

Center. Shoots left. 6'2", 200 lbs.   Born, Kladno, Czech., January 28, 1966. Washington's 3rd choice, 59th overall, in 1984 Entry Draft.   (pih-VAHN-kuh)

								Regular Season											Playoffs							
Season	Club	League	GP	G	A	Pts	PIM	PP	SH	GW	S	%	+/–	TF	F%	H	SB	Min	GP	G	A	Pts	PIM	PP	SH	GW
1984-85	Dukla Jihlava	Czech.	33	8	11	19	18																			
1985-86	Dukla Jihlava	Czech.	42	5	13	18	18																			
1986-87	**Washington**	**NHL**	73	18	25	43	41	4	0	2	117	15.4	–19						7	1	1	2	2	0	0	0
1987-88	**Washington**	**NHL**	71	11	23	34	28	3	0	0	96	11.5	1						14	4	9	13	4	2	0	0
1988-89	**Washington**	**NHL**	52	8	19	27	30	1	0	1	73	11.0	9						6	3	1	4	10	0	1	0
	Baltimore	AHL	31	12	24	36	19																			
1989-90	**Washington**	**NHL**	77	25	39	64	54	10	3	0	149	16.8	–7						11	0	2	2	6	0	0	0
1990-91	**Washington**	**NHL**	79	20	50	70	34	6	0	4	172	11.6	3						11	2	3	5	8	0	0	0
1991-92	**Washington**	**NHL**	80	23	57	80	47	7	4	2	177	13.0	10						7	1	5	6	13	1	0	1
1992-93	**Washington**	**NHL**	69	21	53	74	66	6	1	5	147	14.3	14						6	0	2	2	0	0	0	0
1993-94	**Washington**	**NHL**	82	14	36	50	38	5	0	4	138	10.1	2						7	4	4	8	4	1	0	0
1994-95	Klagenfurter AC	Austria	7	2	4	6	4																			
	Washington	**NHL**	46	10	23	33	50	4	2	2	80	12.5	3						7	1	4	5	21	0	0	0
1995-96	Detroit	IHL	7	1	9	10	19																			
	Washington	**NHL**	73	16	65	81	36	6	2	5	168	9.5	18						6	3	2	5	18	1	0	0
1996-97	**Washington**	**NHL**	54	7	16	23	22	2	0	1	83	8.4	–15													
1997-98	**Washington**	**NHL**	33	3	6	9	20	0	0	1	38	7.9	5						13	0	3	3	0	0	0	0
1998-99	**Washington**	**NHL**	36	5	6	11	12	2	0	0	30	16.7	–6	420	49.0	29	13	13:12								
	NHL Totals		825	181	418	599	478	56	12	27	1468	12.3		420	49.0	29	13	13:12	95	19	36	55	86	5	1	1

PLANTE, Dan

Right wing. Shoots right. 5'11", 202 lbs.   Born, Hayward, WI, October 5, 1971. NY Islanders' 3rd choice, 48th overall, in 1990 Entry Draft.   (PLAHNT)

Season	Club	League	GP	G	A	Pts	PIM	PP	SH	GW	S	%	+/–	TF	F%	H	SB	Min	GP	G	A	Pts	PIM	PP	SH	GW
1988-89	Edina High	H.S.	27	10	26	36	23																			
1989-90	Edina High	H.S.	24	8	18	26	12																			
1990-91	U. of Wisconsin	WCHA	33	1	2	3	54																			
1991-92	U. of Wisconsin	WCHA	36	13	13	26	107																			
1992-93	U. of Wisconsin	WCHA	42	26	31	57	142																			
1993-94	**NY Islanders**	**NHL**	12	0	1	1	4	0	0	0	9	0.0	–2						1	1	0	1	2	0	0	0
	Salt Lake	IHL	66	7	17	24	148																			
1994-95	Denver	IHL	2	0	0	0	4																			
1995-96	**NY Islanders**	**NHL**	73	5	3	8	50	0	2	0	103	4.9	–22													
1996-97	**NY Islanders**	**NHL**	67	4	9	13	75	0	2	0	61	6.6	–6													
1997-98	**NY Islanders**	**NHL**	7	0	1	1	6	0	0	0	7	0.0	–1													
	Utah	IHL	73	22	27	49	125												4	0	2	2	14			
1998-99	Chicago	IHL	81	21	12	33	119												10	1	5	6	10			
	NHL Totals		159	9	14	23	135	0	4	0	180	5.0							1	1	0	1	2	0	0	0

PLANTE, Derek

Center. Shoots left. 5'11", 181 lbs.   Born, Cloquet, MN, January 17, 1971. Buffalo's 7th choice, 161st overall, in 1989 Entry Draft.   (PLAHNT)   **DAL.**

Season	Club	League	GP	G	A	Pts	PIM	PP	SH	GW	S	%	+/–	TF	F%	H	SB	Min	GP	G	A	Pts	PIM	PP	SH	GW
1987-88	Cloquet High	H.S.	23	16	25	41																				
1988-89	Cloquet High	H.S.	24	30	33	63																				
1989-90	U. Minn-Duluth	WCHA	28	10	11	21	12																			
1990-91	U. Minn-Duluth	WCHA	36	23	20	43	6																			
1991-92	U. Minn-Duluth	WCHA	37	27	36	63	28																			
1992-93	U. Minn-Duluth	WCHA	37	*36	*56	*92	30																			
1993-94	**Buffalo**	**NHL**	77	21	35	56	24	8	1	2	147	14.3	4						7	1	0	1	0	0	0	0
	United States	Nat-Team	2	0	1	1	0																			
1994-95	**Buffalo**	**NHL**	47	3	19	22	12	2	0	0	94	3.2	–4													
1995-96	**Buffalo**	**NHL**	76	23	33	56	28	4	0	5	203	11.3	–4													
1996-97	**Buffalo**	**NHL**	82	27	26	53	24	5	0	6	191	14.1	14						12	4	6	10	4	0	0	0
1997-98	**Buffalo**	**NHL**	72	13	21	34	26	5	0	1	150	8.7	8						11	0	3	3	10	0	0	0
1998-99	**Buffalo**	**NHL**	41	4	11	15	12	0	0	0	66	6.1	3	598	46.2	10	24	15:31								
	♦ **Dallas**	**NHL**	10	2	3	5	4	1	0	0	24	8.3	1	113	58.4	9	4	13:42	6	1	0	1	4	0	0	0
	NHL Totals		405	93	148	241	130	25	1	14	875	10.6		711	48.1	19	28	15:10	36	6	9	15	18	0	0	0

WCHA Second All-Star Team (1992) • WCHA First All-Star Team (1993) • NCAA West First All-American Team (1993)
Traded to **Dallas** by **Buffalo** for Dallas' 2nd round choice (Michael Zigomanis) in 1999 Entry Draft, March 23, 1999.

POAPST, Steve

Defense. Shoots left. 6', 200 lbs.   Born, Cornwall, Ont., January 3, 1969.   (POHPST)   **WSH.**

Season	Club	League	GP	G	A	Pts	PIM	PP	SH	GW	S	%	+/–	TF	F%	H	SB	Min	GP	G	A	Pts	PIM	PP	SH	GW
1986-87	Smith Falls	OJHL																								
1987-88	Colgate	ECAC	32	3	13	16	22																			
1988-89	Colgate	ECAC	30	0	5	5	38																			
1989-90	Colgate	ECAC	38	4	15	19	54																			
1990-91	Colgate	ECAC	32	6	15	21	43																			
1991-92	Hampton Roads	ECHL	55	8	20	28	29												14	1	4	5	12			
1992-93	Hampton Roads	ECHL	63	10	35	45	57												4	0	1	1	4			
	Baltimore	AHL	7	0	1	1	4												7	0	3	3	6			
1993-94	Portland	AHL	78	14	21	35	47												12	0	3	3	8			
1994-95	Portland	AHL	71	8	22	30	60												7	0	1	1	16			
1995-96	**Washington**	**NHL**	3	1	0	1	0	0	0	1	2	50.0	–1						6	0	0	0	0	0	0	0
	Portland	AHL	70	10	24	34	79												20	2	6	8	16			
1996-97	Portland	AHL	47	1	20	21	34												5	0	1	1	6			
1997-98	Portland	AHL	76	8	29	37	46												10	2	3	5	8			
1998-99	**Washington**	**NHL**	22	0	0	0	8	0	0	0	11	0.0	–8	0	0.0	48	6	12:26								
	Portland	AHL	54	3	21	24	36																			
	NHL Totals		25	1	0	1	8	0	0	1	13	7.7		0	0.0	48	6	12:26	6	0	0	0	0	0	0	0

ECHL First All-Star Team (1993)
Signed as a free agent by **Washington**, February 4, 1995.

PODEIN, Shjon

Left wing. Shoots left. 6'2", 200 lbs.   Born, Rochester, MN, March 5, 1968. Edmonton's 9th choice, 166th overall, in 1988 Entry Draft.   (poh-DEEN, SHAWN)   **COL.**

Season	Club	League	GP	G	A	Pts	PIM	PP	SH	GW	S	%	+/–	TF	F%	H	SB	Min	GP	G	A	Pts	PIM	PP	SH	GW
1985-86	John Marshall Rockets	H.S.	25	34	30	64																				
1986-87	U.S. International University	NCAA-II	6	0	1	1	0																			
1987-88	U. Minn-Duluth	WCHA	30	4	4	8	48																			
1988-89	U. Minn-Duluth	WCHA	36	7	5	12	46																			
1989-90	U. Minn-Duluth	WCHA	35	21	18	39	36																			
1990-91	Cape Breton	AHL	63	14	15	29	65												4	0	0	0	5			
1991-92	Cape Breton	AHL	80	30	24	54	46												5	3	1	4	2			
1992-93	**Edmonton**	**NHL**	40	13	6	19	25	2	1	1	64	20.3	–2													
	Cape Breton	AHL	38	18	21	39	32												9	2	2	4	29			
1993-94	**Edmonton**	**NHL**	28	3	5	8	8	0	0	0	26	11.5	3													
	Cape Breton	AHL	5	4	4	8	4																			

			Regular Season																Playoffs							
Season	Club	League	GP	G	A	Pts	PIM	PP	SH	GW	S	%	+/–	TF	F%	H	SB	Min	GP	G	A	Pts	PIM	PP	SH	GW
1994-95	Philadelphia	NHL	44	3	7	10	33	0	0	1	48	6.3	–2	....	....	....	....	....	15	1	3	4	10	0	0	0
1995-96	Philadelphia	NHL	79	15	10	25	89	0	4	4	115	13.0	25	....	....	....	....	....	12	1	2	3	50	0	0	1
1996-97	Philadelphia	NHL	82	14	18	32	41	0	0	4	153	9.2	7	....	....	....	....	....	19	4	3	7	16	0	0	1
1997-98	Philadelphia	NHL	82	11	13	24	53	1	1	2	126	8.7	8	....	....	....	....	....	5	0	0	0	10	0	0	0
1998-99	Philadelphia	NHL	14	1	0	1	0	0	0	0	26	3.8	–2	2	50.0	13	4	11:52	....	....	....	....	....	....	....	....
	Colorado	NHL	41	2	6	8	24	0	0	0	49	4.1	–3	21	42.9	41	24	11:49	19	1	1	2	12	0	0	0
	NHL Totals		410	62	65	127	273	3	6	12	607	10.2		23	43.5	54	28	11:50	70	7	9	16	98	0	0	2

Signed as a free agent by **Philadelphia**, July 27, 1994. Traded to **Colorado** by **Philadelphia** for Keith Jones, November 12, 1998.

PODOLLAN, Jason (poh-DOH-luhn) L.A.

Right wing. Shoots right. 6'1", 198 lbs. Born, Vernon, B.C., February 18, 1976. Florida's 3rd choice, 31st overall, in 1994 Entry Draft.

Season	Club	League	GP	G	A	Pts	PIM	PP	SH	GW	S	%	+/–	TF	F%	H	SB	Min	GP	G	A	Pts	PIM	PP	SH	GW
1990-91	Sherwood Park	AAHA	61	105	111	216	133	....	....	....	....	....	....	....	....	....	....	....	....	....	....	....	....	....	....	....
1991-92	Penticton	BCJHL	59	20	26	46	66	....	....	....	....	....	....	....	....	....	....	....	....	....	....	....	....	....	....	....
	Spokane	WHL	2	0	0	0	2	....	....	....	....	....	....	....	....	....	....	....	10	3	1	4	16	....	....	....
1992-93	Spokane	WHL	72	36	33	69	108	....	....	....	....	....	....	....	....	....	....	....	10	4	4	8	14	....	....	....
1993-94	Spokane	WHL	69	29	37	66	108	....	....	....	....	....	....	....	....	....	....	....	3	3	0	3	2	....	....	....
1994-95	Spokane	WHL	72	43	41	84	102	....	....	....	....	....	....	....	....	....	....	....	11	5	7	12	18	....	....	....
	Cincinnati	IHL	....	....	....	....	....	....	....	....	....	....	....	....	....	....	....	....	3	0	0	0	2	....	....	....
1995-96	Spokane	WHL	56	37	25	62	103	....	....	....	....	....	....	....	....	....	....	....	18	*21	12	33	28	....	....	....
1996-97	Florida	NHL	19	1	1	2	4	1	0	0	20	5.0	–3	....	....	....	....	....	....	....	....	....	....	....	....	....
	Carolina	AHL	39	21	25	46	36	....	....	....	....	....	....	....	....	....	....	....	....	....	....	....	....	....	....	....
	Toronto	NHL	10	0	3	3	6	0	0	0	10	0.0	–2	....	....	....	....	....	....	....	....	....	....	....	....	....
	St. John's	AHL	....	....	....	....	....	....	....	....	....	....	....	....	....	....	....	....	11	2	3	5	6	....	....	....
1997-98	St. John's	AHL	70	30	31	61	116	....	....	....	....	....	....	....	....	....	....	....	4	1	0	1	10	....	....	....
1998-99	Toronto	NHL	4	0	0	0	0	0	0	0	2	0.0	0	0	0.0	5	0	6:29	....	....	....	....	....	....	....	....
	St. John's	AHL	68	42	26	68	65	....	....	....	....	....	....	....	....	....	....	....	....	....	....	....	....	....	....	....
	Los Angeles	NHL	6	0	0	0	5	0	0	0	7	0.0	–3	0	0.0	13	1	10:15	....	....	....	....	....	....	....	....
	Long Beach	IHL	8	5	3	8	2	....	....	....	....	....	....	....	....	....	....	....	6	1	2	3	4	....	....	....
	NHL Totals		39	1	4	5	15	1	0	0	39	2.6		0	0.0	18	1	8:45	....	....	....	....	....	....	....	....

WHL West Second All-Star Team (1996)

Traded to **Toronto** by **Florida** for Kirk Muller, March 18, 1997. Traded to **Los Angeles** by **Toronto** with Toronto's 3rd round choice (Cory Campbell) in 1999 Entry Draft for Yanic Perreault, March 23, 1999.

POESCHEK, Rudy (POH-shehk) ST.L.

Right wing/Defense. Shoots right. 6'2", 218 lbs. Born, Kamloops, B.C., September 29, 1966. NY Rangers' 12th choice, 238th overall, in 1985 Entry Draft.

Season	Club	League	GP	G	A	Pts	PIM	PP	SH	GW	S	%	+/–	TF	F%	H	SB	Min	GP	G	A	Pts	PIM	PP	SH	GW
1982-83	Vernon	BCJHL	54	4	10	14	100	....	....	....	....	....	....	....	....	....	....	....	....	....	....	....	....	....	....	....
1983-84	Revelstoke	BCJHL	22	5	21	26	107	....	....	....	....	....	....	....	....	....	....	....	....	....	....	....	....	....	....	....
	Kamloops	WHL	47	3	9	12	93	....	....	....	....	....	....	....	....	....	....	....	8	0	2	2	7	....	....	....
1984-85	Kamloops	WHL	34	6	7	13	100	....	....	....	....	....	....	....	....	....	....	....	15	0	3	3	56	....	....	....
1985-86	Kamloops	WHL	32	3	13	16	92	....	....	....	....	....	....	....	....	....	....	....	16	3	7	10	40	....	....	....
1986-87	Kamloops	WHL	54	13	18	31	153	....	....	....	....	....	....	....	....	....	....	....	15	2	4	6	37	....	....	....
1987-88	NY Rangers	NHL	1	0	0	0	2	0	0	0	1	0.0	0	....	....	....	....	....	....	....	....	....	....	....	....	....
	Colorado	IHL	82	7	31	38	210	....	....	....	....	....	....	....	....	....	....	....	12	2	2	4	31	....	....	....
1988-89	NY Rangers	NHL	52	0	2	2	199	0	0	0	17	0.0	–8	....	....	....	....	....	....	....	....	....	....	....	....	....
	Colorado	IHL	2	0	0	0	6	....	....	....	....	....	....	....	....	....	....	....	....	....	....	....	....	....	....	....
1989-90	NY Rangers	NHL	15	0	0	0	55	0	0	0	1	0.0	–1	....	....	....	....	....	....	....	....	....	....	....	....	....
	Flint	IHL	38	8	13	21	109	....	....	....	....	....	....	....	....	....	....	....	4	0	0	0	16	....	....	....
1990-91	Binghamton	AHL	38	1	3	4	162	....	....	....	....	....	....	....	....	....	....	....	....	....	....	....	....	....	....	....
	Winnipeg	NHL	1	0	0	0	5	0	0	0	0	0.0	0	....	....	....	....	....	....	....	....	....	....	....	....	....
	Moncton	AHL	23	2	4	6	67	....	....	....	....	....	....	....	....	....	....	....	9	1	1	2	41	....	....	....
1991-92	Winnipeg	NHL	4	0	0	0	17	0	0	0	1	0.0	–5	....	....	....	....	....	....	....	....	....	....	....	....	....
	Moncton	AHL	63	4	18	22	170	....	....	....	....	....	....	....	....	....	....	....	11	0	2	2	48	....	....	....
1992-93	St. John's	AHL	78	7	24	31	189	....	....	....	....	....	....	....	....	....	....	....	9	0	4	4	13	....	....	....
1993-94	Tampa Bay	NHL	71	3	6	9	118	0	0	1	46	6.5	3	....	....	....	....	....	....	....	....	....	....	....	....	....
1994-95	Tampa Bay	NHL	25	1	1	2	92	0	0	0	14	7.1	0	....	....	....	....	....	....	....	....	....	....	....	....	....
1995-96	Tampa Bay	NHL	57	1	3	4	88	0	0	0	36	2.8	–2	....	....	....	....	....	3	0	0	0	12	0	0	0
1996-97	Tampa Bay	NHL	60	0	6	6	120	0	0	0	30	0.0	–3	....	....	....	....	....	....	....	....	....	....	....	....	....
1997-98	St. Louis	NHL	50	1	7	8	64	0	0	0	29	3.4	–5	....	....	....	....	....	2	0	0	0	6	0	0	0
1998-99	St. Louis	NHL	16	0	0	0	33	0	0	0	8	0.0	0	0	0.0	8	5	10:14	....	....	....	....	....	....	....	....
	NHL Totals		352	6	25	31	793	0	0	1	183	3.3		0	0.0	8	5	10:14	5	0	0	0	18	0	0	0

Traded to **Winnipeg** by **NY Rangers** for Guy Larose, January 22, 1991. Signed as a free agent by **Toronto**, July 8, 1992. Signed as a free agent by **Tampa Bay**, August 10, 1993. Signed as a free agent by **St. Louis**, July 31, 1997.

POPOVIC, Peter (puh-PUH-vihch) NYR

Defense. Shoots left. 6'6", 235 lbs. Born, Koping, Sweden, February 10, 1968. Montreal's 5th choice, 93rd overall, in 1988 Entry Draft.

Season	Club	League	GP	G	A	Pts	PIM	PP	SH	GW	S	%	+/–	TF	F%	H	SB	Min	GP	G	A	Pts	PIM	PP	SH	GW
1986-87	Vasteras IK	Sweden-2	24	1	2	3	10	....	....	....	....	....	....	....	....	....	....	....	....	....	....	....	....	....	....	....
1987-88	Vasteras IK	Sweden-2	28	3	17	20	16	....	....	....	....	....	....	....	....	....	....	....	....	....	....	....	....	....	....	....
1988-89	Vasteras IK	Sweden	22	1	4	5	32	....	....	....	....	....	....	....	....	....	....	....	....	....	....	....	....	....	....	....
1989-90	Vasteras IK	Sweden	30	2	10	12	24	....	....	....	....	....	....	....	....	....	....	....	2	0	1	1	2	....	....	....
1990-91	Vasteras IK	Sweden	40	3	2	5	62	....	....	....	....	....	....	....	....	....	....	....	4	0	0	0	4	....	....	....
1991-92	Vasteras IK	Sweden	34	7	10	17	30	....	....	....	....	....	....	....	....	....	....	....	....	....	....	....	....	....	....	....
1992-93	Vasteras IK	Sweden	39	6	12	18	46	....	....	....	....	....	....	....	....	....	....	....	3	0	1	1	2	....	....	....
1993-94	Montreal	NHL	47	2	12	14	26	1	0	0	58	3.4	10	....	....	....	....	....	6	0	1	1	0	0	0	0
1994-95	Vasteras IK	Sweden	11	0	3	3	10	....	....	....	....	....	....	....	....	....	....	....	....	....	....	....	....	....	....	....
	Montreal	NHL	33	0	5	5	8	0	0	0	23	0.0	–10	....	....	....	....	....	....	....	....	....	....	....	....	....
1995-96	Montreal	NHL	76	2	12	14	69	0	0	0	59	3.4	21	....	....	....	....	....	6	0	2	2	4	0	0	0
1996-97	Montreal	NHL	78	1	13	14	32	0	0	0	82	1.2	9	....	....	....	....	....	3	0	0	0	2	0	0	0
1997-98	Montreal	NHL	69	2	6	8	38	0	0	0	40	5.0	–6	....	....	....	....	....	10	1	1	2	2	0	0	0
1998-99	NY Rangers	NHL	68	1	4	5	40	0	0	0	64	1.6	–12	2	0.0	112	178	20:41	....	....	....	....	....	....	....	....
	NHL Totals		371	8	52	60	213	1	0	0	326	2.5		2	0.0	112	178	20:41	25	1	4	5	8	0	0	0

Traded to **NY Rangers** by **Montreal** for Sylvain Blouin and NY Rangers' 6th round choice (later traded to Phoenix, Phoenix selected Erik Leverstrom) in 1999 Entry Draft, June 30, 1998.

POTI, Tom (POH-tee) EDM.

Defense. Shoots left. 6'3", 215 lbs. Born, Worcester, MA, March 22, 1977. Edmonton's 4th choice, 59th overall, in 1996 Entry Draft.

Season	Club	League	GP	G	A	Pts	PIM	PP	SH	GW	S	%	+/–	TF	F%	H	SB	Min	GP	G	A	Pts	PIM	PP	SH	GW
1992-93	St. Peter's	H.S.	55	25	46	71	....	....	....	....	....	....	....	....	....	....	....	....	....	....	....	....	....	....	....	....
1993-94	Cushing Academy	H.S.	30	10	35	45	....	....	....	....	....	....	....	....	....	....	....	....	....	....	....	....	....	....	....	....
1994-95	Cushing Academy	H.S.	36	17	54	71	35	....	....	....	....	....	....	....	....	....	....	....	....	....	....	....	....	....	....	....
1995-96	Cushing Academy	H.S.	29	14	59	73	18	....	....	....	....	....	....	....	....	....	....	....	....	....	....	....	....	....	....	....
1996-97	Boston University	H.E.	38	4	17	21	54	....	....	....	....	....	....	....	....	....	....	....	....	....	....	....	....	....	....	....
1997-98	Boston University	H.E.	38	13	29	42	60	....	....	....	....	....	....	....	....	....	....	....	....	....	....	....	....	....	....	....
1998-99	Edmonton	NHL	73	5	16	21	42	2	0	3	94	5.3	10	0	0.0	35	82	19:33	4	0	1	1	2	0	0	0
	NHL Totals		73	5	16	21	42	2	0	3	94	5.3		0	0.0	35	82	19:33	4	0	1	1	2	0	0	0

NCAA Championship All-Tournament Team (1997) • Hockey East First All-Star Team (1998) • NCAA East First All-American Team (1998) • NHL All-Rookie Team (1999)

POTOMSKI, Barry

(poh-TAWM-skee)

Left wing. Shoots left. 6'2", 215 lbs. Born, Windsor, Ont., November 24, 1972.

			Regular Season																Playoffs							
Season	Club	League	GP	G	A	Pts	PIM	PP	SH	GW	S	%	+/-	TF	F%	H	SB	Min	GP	G	A	Pts	PIM	PP	SH	GW
1988-89	Windsor	OMHA	56	24	22	46	....	....	....	....	....	....	....	....	....	....	....	....	....	....	....	....	....	....	....	....
1989-90	Tillsonburg	OJHL-B	32	11	17	28	158	....	....	....	....	....	....	....	....	....	....	....	....	....	....	....	....	....	....	....
	London	OHL	9	0	2	2	18	....	....	....	....	....	....	....	....	....	....	....	....	....	....	....	....	....	....	....
1990-91	London	OHL	65	14	17	31	202	....	....	....	....	....	....	....	....	....	....	....	7	0	2	2	10	....	....	....
1991-92	London	OHL	61	19	32	51	224	....	....	....	....	....	....	....	....	....	....	....	10	5	1	6	22	....	....	....
1992-93	Erie	ECHL	5	1	1	2	31	....	....	....	....	....	....	....	....	....	....	....	....	....	....	....	....	....	....	....
	Toledo	ECHL	43	5	18	23	184	....	....	....	....	....	....	....	....	....	....	....	14	5	2	7	73	....	....	....
1993-94	Toledo	ECHL	13	9	4	13	81	....	....	....	....	....	....	....	....	....	....	....	....	....	....	....	....	....	....	....
	Adirondack	AHL	50	9	5	14	224	....	....	....	....	....	....	....	....	....	....	....	11	1	1	2	44	....	....	....
1994-95	Phoenix	IHL	42	5	6	11	171	....	....	....	....	....	....	....	....	....	....	....	....	....	....	....	....	....	....	....
1995-96	**Los Angeles**	**NHL**	**33**	**3**	**2**	**5**	**104**	**1**	**0**	**0**	**23**	**13.0**	**–7**	....	....	....	....	....	....	....	....	....	....	....	....	....
	Phoenix	IHL	24	5	2	7	74	....	....	....	....	....	....	....	....	....	....	....	3	1	0	1	8	....	....	....
1996-97	**Los Angeles**	**NHL**	**26**	**3**	**2**	**5**	**93**	**0**	**0**	**1**	**18**	**16.7**	**–8**	....	....	....	....	....	....	....	....	....	....	....	....	....
	Phoenix	IHL	28	2	11	13	58	....	....	....	....	....	....	....	....	....	....	....	....	....	....	....	....	....	....	....
1997-98	**San Jose**	**NHL**	**9**	**0**	**1**	**1**	**30**	**0**	**0**	**0**	**4**	**0.0**	**1**	....	....	....	....	....	....	....	....	....	....	....	....	....
	Las Vegas	IHL	31	3	2	5	143	....	....	....	....	....	....	....	....	....	....	....	4	1	0	1	13	....	....	....
1998-99	Adirondack	AHL	75	9	7	16	220	....	....	....	....	....	....	....	....	....	....	....	1	0	0	0	2	....	....	....
	NHL Totals		**68**	**6**	**5**	**11**	**227**	**1**	**0**	**1**	**45**	**13.3**		....	....	....	....	....	....	....	....	....	....	....	....	....

Signed as a free agent by **LA Kings**, July 7, 1994. Signed as a free agent by **San Jose**, August 15, 1997. Signed as a free agent by **Detroit**, August 13, 1998.

POTVIN, Marc

(PAHT-vahn)

Right wing. Shoots right. 6'1", 200 lbs. Born, Ottawa, Ont., January 29, 1967. Detroit's 9th choice, 169th overall, in 1986 Entry Draft.

Season	Club	League	GP	G	A	Pts	PIM	PP	SH	GW	S	%	+/-	TF	F%	H	SB	Min	GP	G	A	Pts	PIM	PP	SH	GW
1985-86	Stratford	OJHL	63	5	6	11	117	....	....	....	....	....	....	....	....	....	....	....	....	....	....	....	....	....	....	....
1986-87	Bowling Green	CCHA	43	5	15	20	74	....	....	....	....	....	....	....	....	....	....	....	....	....	....	....	....	....	....	....
1987-88	Bowling Green	CCHA	45	15	21	36	80	....	....	....	....	....	....	....	....	....	....	....	....	....	....	....	....	....	....	....
1988-89	Bowling Green	CCHA	46	23	12	35	63	....	....	....	....	....	....	....	....	....	....	....	....	....	....	....	....	....	....	....
1989-90	Bowling Green	CCHA	40	19	17	36	72	....	....	....	....	....	....	....	....	....	....	....	....	....	....	....	....	....	....	....
	Adirondack	AHL	5	2	1	3	9	....	....	....	....	....	....	....	....	....	....	....	4	0	1	1	23	....	....	....
1990-91	**Detroit**	**NHL**	**9**	**0**	**0**	**0**	**55**	**0**	**0**	**0**	**13**	**0.0**	**–4**	....	....	....	....	....	**6**	**0**	**0**	**0**	**32**	**0**	**0**	**0**
	Adirondack	AHL	63	9	13	22	*365	....	....	....	....	....	....	....	....	....	....	....	....	....	....	....	....	....	....	....
1991-92	**Detroit**	**NHL**	**5**	**1**	**0**	**1**	**52**	**0**	**0**	**0**	**4**	**25.0**	**–2**	....	....	....	....	....	**1**	**0**	**0**	**0**	**0**	**0**	**0**	**0**
	Adirondack	AHL	51	13	16	29	314	....	....	....	....	....	....	....	....	....	....	....	19	5	4	9	57	....	....	....
1992-93	Adirondack	AHL	37	8	12	20	109	....	....	....	....	....	....	....	....	....	....	....	....	....	....	....	....	....	....	....
	Los Angeles	**NHL**	**20**	**0**	**1**	**1**	**61**	**0**	**0**	**0**	**7**	**0.0**	**–10**	....	....	....	....	....	**1**	**0**	**0**	**0**	**0**	**0**	**0**	**0**
1993-94	**Los Angeles**	**NHL**	**3**	**0**	**0**	**0**	**26**	**0**	**0**	**0**	**1**	**0.0**	**–3**	....	....	....	....	....	....	....	....	....	....	....	....	....
	Hartford	**NHL**	**51**	**2**	**3**	**5**	**246**	**0**	**0**	**0**	**25**	**8.0**	**–5**	....	....	....	....	....	....	....	....	....	....	....	....	....
1994-95	**Boston**	**NHL**	**6**	**0**	**1**	**1**	**4**	**0**	**0**	**0**	**4**	**0.0**	**1**	....	....	....	....	....	....	....	....	....	....	....	....	....
	Providence	AHL	21	4	14	18	84	....	....	....	....	....	....	....	....	....	....	....	12	2	4	6	25	....	....	....
1995-96	**Boston**	**NHL**	**27**	**0**	**0**	**0**	**12**	**0**	**0**	**0**	**14**	**0.0**	**–2**	....	....	....	....	....	**5**	**0**	**1**	**1**	**18**	**0**	**0**	**0**
	Providence	AHL	48	9	9	18	118	....	....	....	....	....	....	....	....	....	....	....	....	....	....	....	....	....	....	....
1996-97	Portland	AHL	71	17	15	32	222	....	....	....	....	....	....	....	....	....	....	....	5	0	0	0	12	....	....	....
1997-98	Chicago	IHL	81	4	8	12	170	....	....	....	....	....	....	....	....	....	....	....	10	0	0	0	22	....	....	....
1998-99	Adirondack	AHL	DID NOT PLAY – ASSISTANT COACH																							
	NHL Totals		**121**	**3**	**5**	**8**	**456**	**0**	**0**	**0**	**68**	**4.4**		....	....	....	....	....	**13**	**0**	**1**	**1**	**50**	**0**	**0**	**0**

Traded to **LA Kings** by **Detroit** with Jimmy Carson and Gary Shuchuk for Paul Coffey, Sylvain Couturier and Jim Hiller, January 29, 1993. Traded to **Hartford** by **LA Kings** for Doug Houda, November 3, 1993. Signed as a free agent by **Boston**, June 29, 1994.

POULIN, Patrick

(poo-LIHN) **MTL.**

Center. Shoots left. 6'1", 218 lbs. Born, Vanier, Que., April 23, 1973. Hartford's 1st choice, 9th overall, in 1991 Entry Draft.

Season	Club	League	GP	G	A	Pts	PIM	PP	SH	GW	S	%	+/-	TF	F%	H	SB	Min	GP	G	A	Pts	PIM	PP	SH	GW
1988-89	Ste-Foy	QAAA	42	28	42	70	44	....	....	....	....	....	....	....	....	....	....	....	13	13	23	36	24	....	....	....
1989-90	St-Hyacinthe	QMJHL	60	25	26	51	55	....	....	....	....	....	....	....	....	....	....	....	12	1	9	10	5	....	....	....
1990-91	St-Hyacinthe	QMJHL	56	32	38	70	82	....	....	....	....	....	....	....	....	....	....	....	4	0	2	2	23	....	....	....
1991-92	St-Hyacinthe	QMJHL	56	52	86	*138	58	....	....	....	....	....	....	....	....	....	....	....	5	2	2	4	4	....	....	....
	Hartford	**NHL**	**1**	**0**	**0**	**0**	**2**	**0**	**0**	**0**	**0**	**0.0**	**–1**	....	....	....	....	....	**7**	**2**	**1**	**3**	**0**	**1**	**0**	**0**
	Springfield	AHL	....	....	....	....	....	....	....	....	....	....	....	....	....	....	....	....	1	0	0	0	0	....	....	....
1992-93	**Hartford**	**NHL**	**81**	**20**	**31**	**51**	**37**	**4**	**0**	**2**	**160**	**12.5**	**–19**	....	....	....	....	....	....	....	....	....	....	....	....	....
1993-94	**Hartford**	**NHL**	**9**	**2**	**1**	**3**	**11**	**1**	**0**	**0**	**13**	**15.4**	**–8**	....	....	....	....	....	....	....	....	....	....	....	....	....
	Chicago	**NHL**	**58**	**12**	**13**	**25**	**40**	**1**	**0**	**3**	**83**	**14.5**	**0**	....	....	....	....	....	**4**	**0**	**0**	**0**	**0**	**0**	**0**	**0**
1994-95	**Chicago**	**NHL**	**45**	**15**	**15**	**30**	**53**	**4**	**0**	**2**	**77**	**19.5**	**13**	....	....	....	....	....	**16**	**4**	**1**	**5**	**8**	**1**	**0**	**0**
1995-96	**Chicago**	**NHL**	**38**	**7**	**8**	**15**	**16**	**0**	**0**	**0**	**40**	**17.5**	**7**	....	....	....	....	....	....	....	....	....	....	....	....	....
	Indianapolis	IHL	1	0	1	1	0	....	....	....	....	....	....	....	....	....	....	....	....	....	....	....	....	....	....	....
	Tampa Bay	**NHL**	**8**	**0**	**1**	**1**	**0**	**1**	**0**	**0**	**11**	**0.0**	**0**	....	....	....	....	....	**2**	**0**	**0**	**0**	**0**	**0**	**0**	**0**
1996-97	**Tampa Bay**	**NHL**	**73**	**12**	**14**	**26**	**56**	**2**	**3**	**1**	**124**	**9.7**	**–16**	....	....	....	....	....	....	....	....	....	....	....	....	....
1997-98	**Tampa Bay**	**NHL**	**44**	**2**	**7**	**9**	**19**	**0**	**0**	**0**	**49**	**4.1**	**–3**	....	....	....	....	....	....	....	....	....	....	....	....	....
	Montreal	**NHL**	**34**	**4**	**6**	**10**	**8**	**0**	**1**	**1**	**39**	**10.3**	**–1**	....	....	....	....	....	**3**	**0**	**0**	**0**	**0**	**0**	**0**	**0**
1998-99	**Montreal**	**NHL**	**81**	**8**	**17**	**25**	**21**	**0**	**1**	**1**	**87**	**9.2**	**6**	**112**	**30.4**	**92**	**29**	**13:30**	....	....	....	....	....	....	....	....
	NHL Totals		**472**	**82**	**113**	**195**	**263**	**13**	**5**	**10**	**683**	**12.0**		**112**	**30.4**	**92**	**29**	**13:30**	**32**	**6**	**2**	**8**	**8**	**2**	**0**	**0**

QMJHL First All-Star Team (1992) • Canadian Major Junior Player of the Year (1992)

Traded to **Chicago** by **Hartford** with Eric Weinrich for Steve Larmer and Bryan Marchment, November 2, 1993. Traded to **Tampa Bay** by **Chicago** with Igor Ulanov and Chicago's 2nd round choice (later traded to New Jersey — New Jersey selected Pierre Dagenais) in 1996 Entry Draft for Enrico Ciccone and Tampa Bay's 2nd round choice (Jeff Paul) in 1996 Entry Draft, March 20, 1996. Traded to **Montreal** by **Tampa Bay** with Mick Vukota and Igor Ulanov for Stephane Richer, Darcy Tucker and David Wilkie, January 15, 1998.

PRATT, Nolan

CAR.

Defense. Shoots left. 6'2", 195 lbs. Born, Fort McMurray, Alta., August 14, 1975. Hartford's 4th choice, 115th overall, in 1993 Entry Draft.

Season	Club	League	GP	G	A	Pts	PIM	PP	SH	GW	S	%	+/-	TF	F%	H	SB	Min	GP	G	A	Pts	PIM	PP	SH	GW
1991-92	Portland	WHL	22	2	9	11	13	....	....	....	....	....	....	....	....	....	....	....	6	1	3	4	12	....	....	....
1992-93	Portland	WHL	70	4	19	23	97	....	....	....	....	....	....	....	....	....	....	....	16	2	7	9	31	....	....	....
1993-94	Portland	WHL	72	4	32	36	105	....	....	....	....	....	....	....	....	....	....	....	10	1	2	3	14	....	....	....
1994-95	Portland	WHL	72	6	37	43	196	....	....	....	....	....	....	....	....	....	....	....	9	1	6	7	10	....	....	....
1995-96	Springfield	AHL	62	2	6	8	72	....	....	....	....	....	....	....	....	....	....	....	2	0	0	0	0	....	....	....
	Richmond	ECHL	4	1	0	1	2	....	....	....	....	....	....	....	....	....	....	....	....	....	....	....	....	....	....	....
1996-97	**Hartford**	**NHL**	**9**	**0**	**2**	**2**	**6**	**0**	**0**	**0**	**4**	**0.0**	**0**	....	....	....	....	....	....	....	....	....	....	....	....	....
	Springfield	AHL	66	1	18	19	127	....	....	....	....	....	....	....	....	....	....	....	17	0	3	3	18	....	....	....
1997-98	**Carolina**	**NHL**	**23**	**0**	**2**	**2**	**44**	**0**	**0**	**0**	**11**	**0.0**	**–2**	....	....	....	....	....	....	....	....	....	....	....	....	....
	New Haven	AHL	54	3	15	18	135	....	....	....	....	....	....	....	....	....	....	....	....	....	....	....	....	....	....	....
1998-99	**Carolina**	**NHL**	**61**	**1**	**14**	**15**	**95**	**0**	**0**	**1**	**46**	**2.2**	**15**	**0**	**0.0**	**121**	**59**	**16:45**	**3**	**0**	**0**	**0**	**2**	**0**	**0**	**0**
	NHL Totals		**93**	**1**	**18**	**19**	**145**	**0**	**0**	**1**	**61**	**1.6**		**0**	**0.0**	**121**	**59**	**16:45**	**3**	**0**	**0**	**0**	**2**	**0**	**0**	**0**

Transferred to **Carolina** after **Hartford** franchise relocated, June 25, 1997.

PRIMEAU, Keith

(PREE-moh) **CAR.**

Center. Shoots left. 6'4", 210 lbs. Born, Toronto, Ont., November 24, 1971. Detroit's 1st choice, 3rd overall, in 1990 Entry Draft.

Season	Club	League	GP	G	A	Pts	PIM	PP	SH	GW	S	%	+/-	TF	F%	H	SB	Min	GP	G	A	Pts	PIM	PP	SH	GW
1986-87	Whitby	OMHA	65	69	80	149	116	....	....	....	....	....	....	....	....	....	....	....	....	....	....	....	....	....	....	....
1987-88	Hamilton	OJHL-B	19	19	17	36	16	....	....	....	....	....	....	....	....	....	....	....	....	....	....	....	....	....	....	....
	Hamilton	OHL	47	6	6	12	69	....	....	....	....	....	....	....	....	....	....	....	11	0	2	2	2	....	....	....
1988-89	Niagara Falls	OHL	48	20	35	55	56	....	....	....	....	....	....	....	....	....	....	....	17	9	16	25	12	....	....	....
1989-90	Niagara Falls	OHL	65	*57	70	*127	97	....	....	....	....	....	....	....	....	....	....	....	16	*16	17	*33	49	....	....	....

			Regular Season																Playoffs							
Season	Club	League	GP	G	A	Pts	PIM	PP	SH	GW	S	%	+/-	TF	F%	H	SB	Min	GP	G	A	Pts	PIM	PP	SH	GW
1990-91	Detroit	NHL	58	3	12	15	106	0	0	1	33	9.1	–12						5	1	1	2	25	0	0	0
	Adirondack	AHL	6	3	5	8	8																			
1991-92	Detroit	NHL	35	6	10	16	83	0	0	0	27	22.2	9						11	0	0	0	14	0	0	0
	Adirondack	AHL	42	21	24	45	89												9	1	7	8	27			
1992-93	Detroit	NHL	73	15	17	32	152	4	1	2	75	20.0	–6						7	0	2	2	26	0	0	0
1993-94	Detroit	NHL	78	31	42	73	173	7	3	4	155	20.0	34						7	0	2	2	6	0	0	0
1994-95	Detroit	NHL	45	15	27	42	99	1	0	3	96	15.6	17						17	4	5	9	45	2	0	0
1995-96	Detroit	NHL	74	27	25	52	168	6	2	7	150	18.0	19						17	1	4	5	28	0	0	0
1996-97	Hartford	NHL	75	26	25	51	161	6	3	2	169	15.4	–3													
1997-98	Carolina	NHL	81	26	37	63	110	7	3	2	180	14.4	19													
	Canada	Olympics	6	2	1	3	4																			
1998-99	Carolina	NHL	78	30	32	62	75	9	1	5	178	16.9	8	1823	53.5	231	62	21:21	6	0	3	3	6	0	0	0
	NHL Totals		597	179	227	406	1127	40	13	26	1063	16.8		1823	53.5	231	62	21:21	70	6	17	23	150	2	0	0

OHL Second All-Star Team (1990) @FNMOT = Played in NHL All-Star Game (1999)

Traded to **Hartford** by **Detroit** with Paul Coffey and Detroit's 1st round choice (Nikos Tselios) in 1997 Entry Draft for Brendan Shanahan and Brian Glynn, October 9, 1996. Transferred to **Carolina** after **Hartford** franchise relocated, June 25, 1997.

PRIMEAU, Wayne

(PREE-moh) **BUF.**

Center. Shoots left. 6'3", 220 lbs. Born, Scarborough, Ont., June 4, 1976. Buffalo's 1st choice, 17th overall, in 1994 Entry Draft.

1991-92	Whitby	OMHA	63	36	50	86	96																			
1992-93	Owen Sound	OHL	66	10	27	37	108												8	1	4	5	0			
1993-94	Owen Sound	OHL	65	25	50	75	75												9	1	6	7	8			
1994-95	Owen Sound	OHL	66	34	62	96	84												10	4	9	13	15			
	Buffalo	NHL	1	1	0	1	0	0	0	1	2	50.0	–2													
1995-96	Owen Sound	OHL	28	15	29	44	52																			
	Oshawa	OHL	24	12	13	25	33												3	2	3	5	2			
	Buffalo	NHL	2	0	0	0	0	0	0	0	0	0.0	0													
	Rochester	AHL	8	2	3	5	6												17	3	1	4	11			
1996-97	Buffalo	NHL	45	2	4	6	64	1	0	0	25	8.0	–2						9	0	0	0	6	0	0	0
	Rochester	AHL	24	9	5	14	27												1	0	0	0	0			
1997-98	Buffalo	NHL	69	6	6	12	87	2	0	1	51	11.8	9						14	1	3	4	6	0	0	0
1998-99	Buffalo	NHL	67	5	8	13	38	0	0	0	55	9.1	–6	529	48.6	74	15	10:19	19	3	4	7	6	1	0	0
	NHL Totals		184	14	18	32	189	3	0	2	133	10.5		529	48.6	74	15	10:19	42	4	7	11	18	1	0	0

PROBERT, Bob

(PROH-buhrt) **CHI.**

Left wing. Shoots left. 6'3", 225 lbs. Born, Windsor, Ont., June 5, 1965. Detroit's 3rd choice, 46th overall, in 1983 Entry Draft.

1981-82	Windsor	OMHA	55	60	40	100	40																			
1982-83	Brantford	OHL	51	12	16	28	133												8	2	2	4	23			
1983-84	Brantford	OHL	65	35	28	63	189												6	0	3	3	16			
1984-85	Hamilton	OHL	4	0	1	1	21																			
	S.S. Marie	OHL	44	20	52	72	172												15	6	11	17	60			
1985-86	Detroit	NHL	44	8	13	21	186	3	0	0	46	17.4	–14													
	Adirondack	AHL	32	12	15	27	152												10	2	3	5	68			
1986-87	Detroit	NHL	63	13	11	24	221	2	0	0	56	23.2	–6						16	3	4	7	63	1	0	1
	Adirondack	AHL	7	1	4	5	15																			
1987-88	Detroit	NHL	74	29	33	62	*398	15	0	5	126	23.0	16						16	8	13	21	51	5	0	1
1988-89	Detroit	NHL	25	4	2	6	106	1	0	0	23	17.4	–11													
1989-90	Detroit	NHL	4	3	0	3	21	0	0	1	12	25.0	0													
1990-91	Detroit	NHL	55	16	23	39	315	4	0	3	88	18.2	–3						6	1	2	3	50	0	0	0
1991-92	Detroit	NHL	63	20	24	44	276	8	0	1	96	20.8	16						11	1	6	7	28	0	0	0
1992-93	Detroit	NHL	80	14	29	43	292	6	0	3	128	10.9	–9						7	0	3	3	10	0	0	0
1993-94	Detroit	NHL	66	7	10	17	275	1	0	0	105	6.7	–1						7	1	1	2	8	0	0	0
1994-95			Did not Play – Suspended																							
1995-96	Chicago	NHL	78	19	21	40	237	1	0	3	97	19.6	15						10	0	2	2	23	0	0	0
1996-97	Chicago	NHL	82	9	14	23	326	1	0	3	111	8.1	–3						6	2	1	3	41	0	0	0
1997-98	Chicago	NHL	14	2	1	3	48	2	0	0	18	11.1	–7													
1998-99	Chicago	NHL	78	7	14	21	206	0	0	3	87	8.0	–11	45	51.1	105	12	10:38								
	NHL Totals		726	151	195	346	2907	44	0	22	993	15.2		45	51.1	105	12	10:38	79	16	32	48	274	6	0	2

Played in NHL All-Star Game (1988)

Signed as a free agent by **Chicago**, July 23, 1994. • Suspended for entire 1994-95 season for violating NHL substance abuse policies, September 2, 1994.

PROCHAZKA, Martin

(pro-HAHS-kah) **ATL.**

Right wing. Shoots right. 5'11", 180 lbs. Born, Slany, Czech., March 3, 1972. Toronto's 6th choice, 135th overall, in 1991 Entry Draft.

1989-90	Poldi Kladno	Czech.	49	18	12	30	....																			
1990-91	Poldi Kladno	Czech.	50	19	10	29	21																			
1991-92	Dukla Jihlava	Czech.	44	18	11	29	2																			
1992-93	Poldi Kladno	Czech.	46	26	12	38	....																			
1993-94	Poldi Kladno	Cze-Rep	43	24	16	40	0												2	2	0	2	....			
1994-95	Poldi Kladno	Cze-Rep	41	25	33	58	18												11	8	4	12	4			
1995-96	Poldi Kladno	Cze-Rep	37	15	27	42	....												8	2	4	6	....			
1996-97	AIK Solna	Sweden	49	16	23	39	38												7	2	3	5	8			
1997-98	Toronto	NHL	29	2	4	6	8	0	0	0	40	5.0	–1													
	Czech Republic	Olympics	6	1	1	2	0																			
1998-99	Petra Vsetin	Cze-Rep	47	20	29	49	12												12	*10	9	*19	....			
	NHL Totals		29	2	4	6	8	0	0	0	40	5.0														

Traded to **Atlanta** by **Toronto** for Atlanta's 6th round choice in 2001 Entry Draft, July 15, 1999.

PROKOPEC, Mike

(PROH-koh-pehk)

Right wing. Shoots right. 6'2", 190 lbs. Born, Toronto, Ont., May 17, 1974. Chicago's 7th choice, 161st overall, in 1992 Entry Draft.

1990-91	Barrie	OJHL-B	39	17	20	37	63																			
1991-92	Cornwall	OHL	59	12	15	27	75												6	0	0	0	0			
1992-93	Newmarket	OHL	40	6	14	20	70																			
	Guelph	OHL	28	10	14	24	27												5	1	0	1	14			
1993-94	Guelph	OHL	66	52	58	110	93												9	12	4	16	17			
1994-95	Indianapolis	IHL	70	21	12	33	80																			
1995-96	Chicago	NHL	9	0	0	0	5	0	0	0	5	0.0	–4													
	Indianapolis	IHL	67	18	22	40	131												5	2	0	2	4			
1996-97	Chicago	NHL	6	0	0	0	6	0	0	0	2	0.0	–1													
	Indianapolis	IHL	57	13	18	31	143																			
	Detroit	IHL	3	2	0	2	4												8	2	1	3	14			
1997-98	Worcester	AHL	62	21	25	46	112												11	1	2	3	10			
1998-99	Detroit	IHL	75	25	28	53	125												10	3	6	9	26			
	NHL Totals		15	0	0	0	11	0	0	0	7	0.0														

Traded to **Ottawa** by **Chicago** for Denis Chasse, the rights to Kevin Bolibruck and future considerations, March 18, 1997.

			Regular Season																Playoffs							
Season	Club	League	GP	G	A	Pts	PIM	PP	SH	GW	S	%	+/–	TF	F%	H	SB	Min	GP	G	A	Pts	PIM	PP	SH	GW

PRONGER, Chris

(PRAHN-guhr) **ST.L.**

Defense. Shoots left. 6'6", 220 lbs. Born, Dryden, Ont., October 10, 1974. Hartford's 1st choice, 2nd overall, in 1993 Entry Draft.

Season	Club	League	GP	G	A	Pts	PIM	PP	SH	GW	S	%	+/–	TF	F%	H	SB	Min	GP	G	A	Pts	PIM	PP	SH	GW
1990-91	Stratford	OJHL-B	48	15	37	52	132	....	....	....	....	....	....	....	....	....	....	....	....	....	....	....	....	....	....	....
1991-92	Peterborough	OHL	63	17	45	62	90	....	....	....	....	....	....	....	....	....	....	....	10	1	8	9	28	....	....	....
1992-93	Peterborough	OHL	61	15	62	77	108	....	....	....	....	....	....	....	....	....	....	....	21	15	25	40	51	....	....	....
1993-94	**Hartford**	**NHL**	**81**	**5**	**25**	**30**	**113**	**2**	**0**	**0**	**174**	**2.9**	**–3**	....	....	....	....	....	....	....	....	....	....	....	....	....
1994-95	**Hartford**	**NHL**	**43**	**5**	**9**	**14**	**54**	**3**	**0**	**1**	**94**	**5.3**	**–12**	....	....	....	....	....	....	....	....	....	....	....	....	....
1995-96	**St. Louis**	**NHL**	**78**	**7**	**18**	**25**	**110**	**3**	**1**	**1**	**138**	**5.1**	**–18**	....	....	....	....	....	**13**	**1**	**5**	**6**	**16**	**0**	**0**	**0**
1996-97	**St. Louis**	**NHL**	**79**	**11**	**24**	**35**	**143**	**4**	**0**	**0**	**147**	**7.5**	**15**	....	....	....	....	....	**6**	**1**	**1**	**2**	**22**	**0**	**0**	**0**
1997-98	**St. Louis**	**NHL**	**81**	**9**	**27**	**36**	**180**	**1**	**0**	**2**	**145**	**6.2**	**47**	....	....	....	....	....	**10**	**1**	**9**	**10**	**26**	**0**	**0**	**0**
	Canada	Olympics	6	0	0	0	4	....	....	....	....	....	....	....	....	....	....	....	....	....	....	....	....	....	....	....
1998-99	**St. Louis**	**NHL**	**67**	**13**	**33**	**46**	**113**	**8**	**0**	**0**	**172**	**7.6**	**3**	**0**	**0.0**	**132**	**119**	**30:36**	**13**	**1**	**4**	**5**	**28**	**1**	**0**	**0**
	NHL Totals		**429**	**50**	**136**	**186**	**713**	**21**	**1**	**4**	**870**	**5.7**		**0**	**0.0**	**132**	**119**	**30:36**	**42**	**4**	**19**	**23**	**92**	**1**	**0**	**0**

OHL First All-Star Team (1993) • Canadian Major Junior First All-Star Team (1993) • Canadian Major Junior Defenseman of the Year (1993) • NHL/Upper Deck All-Rookie Team (1994) • NHL Second All-Star Team (1998) • Won Bud Ice Plus/Minus Award (1998)

Played in NHL All-Star Game (1999)

Traded to **St. Louis** by **Hartford** for Brendan Shanahan, July 27, 1995.

PRONGER, Sean

(PRAHN-guhr) **BOS.**

Center. Shoots left. 6'2", 205 lbs. Born, Dryden, Ont., November 30, 1972. Vancouver's 3rd choice, 51st overall, in 1991 Entry Draft.

Season	Club	League	GP	G	A	Pts	PIM	PP	SH	GW	S	%	+/–	TF	F%	H	SB	Min	GP	G	A	Pts	PIM	PP	SH	GW
1989-90	Thunder Bay	USHL	48	18	34	52	61	....	....	....	....	....	....	....	....	....	....	....	....	....	....	....	....	....	....	....
1990-91	Bowling Green	CCHA	40	3	7	10	30	....	....	....	....	....	....	....	....	....	....	....	....	....	....	....	....	....	....	....
1991-92	Bowling Green	CCHA	34	9	7	16	28	....	....	....	....	....	....	....	....	....	....	....	....	....	....	....	....	....	....	....
1992-93	Bowling Green	CCHA	39	23	23	46	35	....	....	....	....	....	....	....	....	....	....	....	....	....	....	....	....	....	....	....
1993-94	Bowling Green	CCHA	38	17	17	34	38	....	....	....	....	....	....	....	....	....	....	....	....	....	....	....	....	....	....	....
1994-95	Knoxville	ECHL	34	18	23	41	55	....	....	....	....	....	....	....	....	....	....	....	....	....	....	....	....	....	....	....
	Greensboro	ECHL	2	0	2	2	0	....	....	....	....	....	....	....	....	....	....	....	....	....	....	....	....	....	....	....
	San Diego	IHL	8	0	0	0	2	....	....	....	....	....	....	....	....	....	....	....	....	....	....	....	....	....	....	....
1995-96	**Anaheim**	**NHL**	**7**	**0**	**1**	**1**	**6**	**0**	**0**	**0**	**3**	**0.0**	**0**	....	....	....	....	....	....	....	....	....	....	....	....	....
	Baltimore	AHL	72	16	17	33	61	....	....	....	....	....	....	....	....	....	....	....	12	3	7	10	16	....	....	....
1996-97	**Anaheim**	**NHL**	**39**	**7**	**7**	**14**	**20**	**1**	**0**	**1**	**43**	**16.3**	**6**	....	....	....	....	....	**9**	**0**	**2**	**2**	**4**	**0**	**0**	**0**
	Baltimore	AHL	41	26	17	43	17	....	....	....	....	....	....	....	....	....	....	....	....	....	....	....	....	....	....	....
1997-98	**Anaheim**	**NHL**	**62**	**5**	**15**	**20**	**30**	**1**	**0**	**2**	**68**	**7.4**	**–9**	....	....	....	....	....	....	....	....	....	....	....	....	....
	Pittsburgh	**NHL**	**5**	**1**	**0**	**1**	**2**	**0**	**0**	**1**	**5**	**20.0**	**–1**	....	....	....	....	....	**5**	**0**	**0**	**0**	**4**	**0**	**0**	**0**
1998-99	**Pittsburgh**	**NHL**	**2**	**0**	**0**	**0**	**0**	**0**	**0**	**0**	**3**	**0.0**	**0**	**4**	**75.0**	**2**	**0**	**8:48**	....	....	....	....	....	....	....	....
	Houston	IHL	16	11	7	18	32	....	....	....	....	....	....	....	....	....	....	....	....	....	....	....	....	....	....	....
	NY Rangers	**NHL**	**14**	**0**	**3**	**3**	**4**	**0**	**0**	**0**	**3**	**0.0**	**–3**	**15**	**20.0**	**12**	**1**	**6:28**	....	....	....	....	....	....	....	....
	Los Angeles	**NHL**	**13**	**0**	**1**	**1**	**4**	**0**	**0**	**0**	**8**	**0.0**	**2**	**20**	**35.0**	**13**	**5**	**11:00**	....	....	....	....	....	....	....	....
	NHL Totals		**142**	**13**	**27**	**40**	**66**	**2**	**0**	**4**	**133**	**9.8**		**39**	**33.3**	**27**	**6**	**8:40**	**14**	**0**	**2**	**2**	**8**	**0**	**0**	**0**

Signed as a free agent by **Anaheim**, February 14, 1995. Traded to **Pittsburgh** by **Anaheim** for the rights to Patrick Lalime, March 24, 1998. Traded to **NY Rangers** by **Pittsburgh** with Chris Tamer and Petr Nedved for Alexei Kovalev and Harry York, November 25, 1998. Traded to **Los Angeles** by **NY Rangers** for Eric Lacroix, February 12, 1999. Signed as a free agent by **Boston**, August 25, 1999.

PROSPAL, Vaclav

(PRAWS-pahl, VAHT-slahv) **OTT.**

Center. Shoots left. 6'2", 185 lbs. Born, Ceske-Budejovice, Czech., February 17, 1975. Philadelphia's 2nd choice, 71st overall, in 1993 Entry Draft.

Season	Club	League	GP	G	A	Pts	PIM	PP	SH	GW	S	%	+/–	TF	F%	H	SB	Min	GP	G	A	Pts	PIM	PP	SH	GW
1991-92	MC Budjevoice	Czech-Jr.	36	16	16	32	12	....	....	....	....	....	....	....	....	....	....	....	....	....	....	....	....	....	....	....
1992-93	MC Budejovice	Czech-Jr.	32	26	31	57	24	....	....	....	....	....	....	....	....	....	....	....	....	....	....	....	....	....	....	....
1993-94	Hershey	AHL	55	14	21	35	38	....	....	....	....	....	....	....	....	....	....	....	2	0	0	0	2	....	....	....
1994-95	Hershey	AHL	69	13	32	45	36	....	....	....	....	....	....	....	....	....	....	....	2	1	0	1	4	....	....	....
1995-96	Hershey	AHL	68	15	36	51	59	....	....	....	....	....	....	....	....	....	....	....	5	2	4	6	2	....	....	....
1996-97	**Philadelphia**	**NHL**	**18**	**5**	**10**	**15**	**4**	**0**	**0**	**0**	**35**	**14.3**	**3**	....	....	....	....	....	**5**	**1**	**3**	**4**	**4**	**0**	**0**	**0**
	Philadelphia	AHL	63	32	63	95	70	....	....	....	....	....	....	....	....	....	....	....	....	....	....	....	....	....	....	....
1997-98	**Philadelphia**	**NHL**	**41**	**5**	**13**	**18**	**17**	**4**	**0**	**0**	**60**	**8.3**	**–10**	....	....	....	....	....	....	....	....	....	....	....	....	....
	Ottawa	**NHL**	**15**	**1**	**6**	**7**	**4**	**0**	**0**	**0**	**28**	**3.6**	**–1**	....	....	....	....	....	**6**	**0**	**0**	**0**	**0**	**0**	**0**	**0**
1998-99	**Ottawa**	**NHL**	**79**	**10**	**26**	**36**	**58**	**2**	**0**	**3**	**114**	**8.8**	**8**	**997**	**56.2**	**202**	**20**	**13:03**	**4**	**0**	**0**	**0**	**0**	**0**	**0**	**0**
	NHL Totals		**153**	**21**	**55**	**76**	**83**	**6**	**0**	**3**	**237**	**8.9**		**997**	**56.2**	**202**	**20**	**13:03**	**15**	**1**	**3**	**4**	**4**	**0**	**0**	**0**

AHL First All-Star Team (1997)

Traded to **Ottawa** by **Philadelphia** with Pat Falloon and Dallas' 2nd round choice (previously acquired, Ottawa selected Chris Bala) in 1998 Entry Draft for Alexandre Daigle, January 17, 1998.

PRPIC, Joel

(puhr-PIHCH) **BOS.**

Center. Shoots left. 6'7", 225 lbs. Born, Sudbury, Ont., September 25, 1974. Boston's 9th choice, 233rd overall, in 1993 Entry Draft.

Season	Club	League	GP	G	A	Pts	PIM	PP	SH	GW	S	%	+/–	TF	F%	H	SB	Min	GP	G	A	Pts	PIM	PP	SH	GW
1992-93	Waterloo	OJHL-B	45	17	43	60	160	....	....	....	....	....	....	....	....	....	....	....	....	....	....	....	....	....	....	....
1993-94	St. Lawrence	ECAC	31	2	4	6	90	....	....	....	....	....	....	....	....	....	....	....	....	....	....	....	....	....	....	....
1994-95	St. Lawrence	ECAC	32	7	10	17	62	....	....	....	....	....	....	....	....	....	....	....	....	....	....	....	....	....	....	....
1995-96	St. Lawrence	ECAC	32	3	10	13	77	....	....	....	....	....	....	....	....	....	....	....	....	....	....	....	....	....	....	....
1996-97	St. Lawrence	ECAC	34	10	8	18	57	....	....	....	....	....	....	....	....	....	....	....	....	....	....	....	....	....	....	....
1997-98	**Boston**	**NHL**	**1**	**0**	**0**	**0**	**2**	**0**	**0**	**0**	**0**	**0.0**	**0**	....	....	....	....	....	....	....	....	....	....	....	....	....
	Providence	AHL	73	17	18	35	53	....	....	....	....	....	....	....	....	....	....	....	....	....	....	....	....	....	....	....
1998-99	Providence	AHL	75	14	16	30	163	....	....	....	....	....	....	....	....	....	....	....	18	4	6	10	48	....	....	....
	NHL Totals		**1**	**0**	**0**	**0**	**2**	**0**	**0**	**0**	**0**	**0.0**		....	....	....	....	....	....	....	....	....	....	....	....	....

PUSHOR, Jamie

(PUH-shohr) **DAL.**

Defense. Shoots right. 6'3", 218 lbs. Born, Lethbridge, Alta., February 11, 1973. Detroit's 2nd choice, 32nd overall, in 1991 Entry Draft.

Season	Club	League	GP	G	A	Pts	PIM	PP	SH	GW	S	%	+/–	TF	F%	H	SB	Min	GP	G	A	Pts	PIM	PP	SH	GW
1988-89	Lethbridge	AAHA	STATISTICS NOT AVAILABLE																							
	Lethbridge	WHL	2	0	0	0	0	....	....	....	....	....	....	....	....	....	....	....	....	....	....	....	....	....	....	....
1989-90	Lethbridge	AAHA	35	6	27	33	92	....	....	....	....	....	....	....	....	....	....	....	....	....	....	....	....	....	....	....
	Lethbridge	WHL	10	0	2	2	2	....	....	....	....	....	....	....	....	....	....	....	....	....	....	....	....	....	....	....
1990-91	Lethbridge	WHL	71	1	13	14	193	....	....	....	....	....	....	....	....	....	....	....	....	....	....	....	....	....	....	....
1991-92	Lethbridge	WHL	49	2	15	17	232	....	....	....	....	....	....	....	....	....	....	....	5	0	0	0	33	....	....	....
1992-93	Lethbridge	WHL	72	6	22	28	200	....	....	....	....	....	....	....	....	....	....	....	4	0	1	1	9	....	....	....
1993-94	Adirondack	AHL	73	1	17	18	124	....	....	....	....	....	....	....	....	....	....	....	12	0	0	0	22	....	....	....
1994-95	Adirondack	AHL	58	2	11	13	129	....	....	....	....	....	....	....	....	....	....	....	4	0	1	1	0	....	....	....
1995-96	**Detroit**	**NHL**	**5**	**0**	**1**	**1**	**17**	**0**	**0**	**0**	**6**	**0.0**	**2**	....	....	....	....	....	....	....	....	....	....	....	....	....
	Adirondack	AHL	65	2	16	18	126	....	....	....	....	....	....	....	....	....	....	....	3	0	0	0	5	....	....	....
1996-97♦	**Detroit**	**NHL**	**75**	**4**	**7**	**11**	**129**	**0**	**0**	**0**	**63**	**6.3**	**1**	....	....	....	....	....	**5**	**0**	**1**	**1**	**5**	**0**	**0**	**0**
1997-98	**Detroit**	**NHL**	**54**	**2**	**5**	**7**	**71**	**0**	**0**	**0**	**43**	**4.7**	**2**	....	....	....	....	....	....	....	....	....	....	....	....	....
	Anaheim	**NHL**	**10**	**0**	**2**	**2**	**10**	**0**	**0**	**0**	**8**	**0.0**	**1**	....	....	....	....	....	....	....	....	....	....	....	....	....
1998-99	**Anaheim**	**NHL**	**70**	**1**	**2**	**3**	**112**	**0**	**0**	**0**	**75**	**1.3**	**–20**	**0**	**0.0**	**110**	**153**	**19:16**	**4**	**0**	**0**	**0**	**6**	**0**	**0**	**0**
	NHL Totals		**214**	**7**	**17**	**24**	**339**	**0**	**0**	**0**	**195**	**3.6**		**0**	**0.0**	**110**	**153**	**19:16**	**9**	**0**	**1**	**1**	**11**	**0**	**0**	**0**

Traded to **Anaheim** by **Detroit** with Detroit's 4th round choice (Viktor Wallin) in 1998 Entry Draft for Dmitri Mironov, March 24, 1998. Claimed by **Atlanta** from **Anaheim** in Expansion Draft, June 25, 1999. Traded to **Dallas** by **Atlanta** for Jason Botterill, July 15, 1999.

QUINT, Deron
(KWIHNT) **PHX.**

Defense. Shoots left. 6'2", 219 lbs. Born, Durham, NH, March 12, 1976. Winnipeg's 1st choice, 30th overall, in 1994 Entry Draft.

Season	Club	League	GP	G	A	Pts	PIM	PP	SH	GW	S	%	+/-	TF	F%	H	SB	Min	Playoffs GP	G	A	Pts	PIM	PP	SH	GW
1990-91	Cardigan Prep	H.S.	31	67	54	121	....	....	....	....	....	....	....	....	....	....	....	....	....	....	....	....	....	....	....	....
1991-92	Cardigan Prep	H.S.	21	111	68	179	....	....	....	....	....	....	....	....	....	....	....	....	....	....	....	....	....	....	....	....
1992-93	Tabor Academy	H.S.	28	15	26	41	30	....	....	....	....	....	....	....	....	....	....	....	1	0	2	2	0	....	....	....
1993-94	Seattle	WHL	63	15	29	44	47	....	....	....	....	....	....	....	....	....	....	....	9	4	12	16	8	....	....	....
1994-95	Seattle	WHL	65	29	60	89	82	....	....	....	....	....	....	....	....	....	....	....	3	1	2	3	6	....	....	....
1995-96	**Winnipeg**	**NHL**	**51**	**5**	**13**	**18**	**22**	**2**	**0**	**0**	**97**	**5.2**	**–2**	....	....	....	....	....	....	....	....	....	....	....	....	....
	Springfield	AHL	11	2	3	5	4	....	....	....	....	....	....	....	....	....	....	....	10	2	3	5	6	....	....	....
	Seattle	WHL	....	....	....	....	....	....	....	....	....	....	....	....	....	....	....	....	5	4	1	5	6	....	....	....
1996-97	**Phoenix**	**NHL**	**27**	**3**	**11**	**14**	**4**	**1**	**0**	**0**	**63**	**4.8**	**–4**	....	....	....	....	....	**7**	**0**	**2**	**2**	**0**	**0**	**0**	**0**
	Springfield	AHL	43	6	18	24	20	....	....	....	....	....	....	....	....	....	....	....	12	2	7	9	4	....	....	....
1997-98	**Phoenix**	**NHL**	**32**	**4**	**7**	**11**	**16**	**1**	**0**	**1**	**61**	**6.6**	**–6**	....	....	....	....	....	....	....	....	....	....	....	....	....
	Springfield	AHL	8	1	7	8	10	....	....	....	....	....	....	....	....	....	....	....	1	0	0	0	0	....	....	....
1998-99	**Phoenix**	**NHL**	**60**	**5**	**8**	**13**	**20**	**2**	**0**	**0**	**94**	**5.3**	**–10**	**0**	**0.0**	**53**	**32**	**16:12**	....	....	....	....	....	....	....	....
	NHL Totals		**170**	**17**	**39**	**56**	**62**	**6**	**0**	**1**	**315**	**5.4**		**0**	**0.0**	**53**	**32**	**16:12**	**7**	**0**	**2**	**2**	**0**	**0**	**0**	**0**

WHL West First All-Star Team (1995)

Transferred to **Phoenix** after **Winnipeg** franchise relocated, July 1, 1996.

QUINTAL, Stephane
(KAYN-tahl) **NYR**

Defense. Shoots right. 6'3", 230 lbs. Born, Boucherville, Que., October 22, 1968. Boston's 2nd choice, 14th overall, in 1987 Entry Draft.

Season	Club	League	GP	G	A	Pts	PIM	PP	SH	GW	S	%	+/-	TF	F%	H	SB	Min	Playoffs GP	G	A	Pts	PIM	PP	SH	GW
1984-85	Richelieu	QAAA	41	1	10	11	....	....	....	....	....	....	....	....	....	....	....	....	....	....	....	....	....	....	....	....
1985-86	Granby	QMJHL	67	2	17	19	144	....	....	....	....	....	....	....	....	....	....	....	....	....	....	....	....	....	....	....
1986-87	Granby	QMJHL	67	13	41	54	178	....	....	....	....	....	....	....	....	....	....	....	8	0	9	9	10	....	....	....
1987-88	Hull	QMJHL	38	13	23	36	138	....	....	....	....	....	....	....	....	....	....	....	19	7	12	19	30	....	....	....
1988-89	**Boston**	**NHL**	**26**	**0**	**1**	**1**	**29**	**0**	**0**	**0**	**23**	**0.0**	**–5**	....	....	....	....	....	....	....	....	....	....	....	....	....
	Maine	AHL	16	4	10	14	28	....	....	....	....	....	....	....	....	....	....	....	....	....	....	....	....	....	....	....
1989-90	**Boston**	**NHL**	**38**	**2**	**2**	**4**	**22**	**0**	**0**	**0**	**43**	**4.7**	**–11**	....	....	....	....	....	....	....	....	....	....	....	....	....
	Maine	AHL	37	4	16	20	27	....	....	....	....	....	....	....	....	....	....	....	....	....	....	....	....	....	....	....
1990-91	**Boston**	**NHL**	**45**	**2**	**6**	**8**	**89**	**1**	**0**	**0**	**54**	**3.7**	**2**	....	....	....	....	....	**3**	**0**	**1**	**1**	**7**	**0**	**0**	**0**
	Maine	AHL	23	1	5	6	30	....	....	....	....	....	....	....	....	....	....	....	....	....	....	....	....	....	....	....
1991-92	**Boston**	**NHL**	**49**	**4**	**10**	**14**	**77**	**0**	**0**	**0**	**52**	**7.7**	**–8**	....	....	....	....	....	....	....	....	....	....	....	....	....
	St. Louis	**NHL**	**26**	**0**	**6**	**6**	**32**	**0**	**0**	**0**	**19**	**0.0**	**–3**	....	....	....	....	....	**4**	**1**	**2**	**3**	**6**	**1**	**0**	**0**
1992-93	**St. Louis**	**NHL**	**75**	**1**	**10**	**11**	**100**	**0**	**1**	**0**	**81**	**1.2**	**–6**	....	....	....	....	....	**9**	**0**	**0**	**0**	**8**	**0**	**0**	**0**
1993-94	**Winnipeg**	**NHL**	**81**	**8**	**18**	**26**	**119**	**1**	**1**	**1**	**154**	**5.2**	**–25**	....	....	....	....	....	....	....	....	....	....	....	....	....
1994-95	**Winnipeg**	**NHL**	**43**	**6**	**17**	**23**	**78**	**3**	**0**	**2**	**107**	**5.6**	**0**	....	....	....	....	....	....	....	....	....	....	....	....	....
1995-96	**Montreal**	**NHL**	**68**	**2**	**14**	**16**	**117**	**0**	**1**	**1**	**104**	**1.9**	**–4**	....	....	....	....	....	**6**	**0**	**1**	**1**	**6**	**0**	**0**	**0**
1996-97	**Montreal**	**NHL**	**71**	**7**	**15**	**22**	**100**	**1**	**0**	**0**	**139**	**5.0**	**1**	....	....	....	....	....	**5**	**0**	**1**	**1**	**6**	**0**	**0**	**0**
1997-98	**Montreal**	**NHL**	**71**	**6**	**10**	**16**	**97**	**0**	**0**	**0**	**88**	**6.8**	**13**	....	....	....	....	....	**9**	**0**	**2**	**2**	**4**	**0**	**0**	**0**
1998-99	**Montreal**	**NHL**	**82**	**8**	**19**	**27**	**84**	**1**	**1**	**4**	**159**	**5.0**	**–23**	**0**	**0.0**	**98**	**125**	**22:06**	....	....	....	....	....	....	....	....
	NHL Totals		**675**	**46**	**128**	**174**	**944**	**7**	**4**	**8**	**1023**	**4.5**		**0**	**0.0**	**98**	**125**	**22:06**	**36**	**1**	**7**	**8**	**37**	**1**	**0**	**0**

QMJHL First All-Star Team (1987)

Traded to **St. Louis** by **Boston** with Craig Janney for Adam Oates, February 7, 1992. Traded to **Winnipeg** by **St. Louis** with Nelson Emerson for Phil Housley, September 24, 1993. Traded to **Montreal** by **Winnipeg** for Montreal's 2nd round choice (Jason Doig) in 1995 Entry Draft, July 8, 1995. Signed as a free agent by **NY Rangers**, July 13, 1999.

RACINE, Yves
(ruh-SEEN, EEV)

Defense. Shoots left. 6', 205 lbs. Born, Matane, Que., February 7, 1969. Detroit's 1st choice, 11th overall, in 1987 Entry Draft.

Season	Club	League	GP	G	A	Pts	PIM	PP	SH	GW	S	%	+/-	TF	F%	H	SB	Min	Playoffs GP	G	A	Pts	PIM	PP	SH	GW
1984-85	Ste-Foy	QAAA	26	3	6	9	....	....	....	....	....	....	....	....	....	....	....	....	....	....	....	....	....	....	....	....
1985-86	Ste-Foy	QAAA	42	4	38	42	66	....	....	....	....	....	....	....	....	....	....	....	....	....	....	....	....	....	....	....
1986-87	Longueuil	QMJHL	70	7	43	50	50	....	....	....	....	....	....	....	....	....	....	....	20	3	11	14	14	....	....	....
1987-88	Victoriaville	QMJHL	69	10	84	94	150	....	....	....	....	....	....	....	....	....	....	....	5	0	0	0	13	....	....	....
	Adirondack	AHL	....	....	....	....	....	....	....	....	....	....	....	....	....	....	....	....	9	4	2	6	2	....	....	....
1988-89	Victoriaville	QMJHL	63	23	85	108	95	....	....	....	....	....	....	....	....	....	....	....	16	3	*30	*33	41	....	....	....
	Adirondack	AHL	....	....	....	....	....	....	....	....	....	....	....	....	....	....	....	....	2	1	1	2	0	....	....	....
1989-90	**Detroit**	**NHL**	**28**	**4**	**9**	**13**	**23**	**1**	**0**	**0**	**49**	**8.2**	**–3**	....	....	....	....	....	....	....	....	....	....	....	....	....
	Adirondack	AHL	46	8	27	35	31	....	....	....	....	....	....	....	....	....	....	....	....	....	....	....	....	....	....	....
1990-91	**Detroit**	**NHL**	**62**	**7**	**40**	**47**	**33**	**2**	**0**	**1**	**131**	**5.3**	**1**	....	....	....	....	....	**7**	**2**	**0**	**2**	**0**	**2**	**0**	**0**
	Adirondack	AHL	16	3	9	12	10	....	....	....	....	....	....	....	....	....	....	....	....	....	....	....	....	....	....	....
1991-92	**Detroit**	**NHL**	**61**	**2**	**22**	**24**	**94**	**1**	**0**	**0**	**103**	**1.9**	**–6**	....	....	....	....	....	**11**	**2**	**1**	**3**	**10**	**1**	**0**	**1**
1992-93	**Detroit**	**NHL**	**80**	**9**	**31**	**40**	**80**	**5**	**0**	**0**	**163**	**5.5**	**10**	....	....	....	....	....	**7**	**1**	**3**	**4**	**27**	**0**	**0**	**0**
1993-94	**Philadelphia**	**NHL**	**67**	**9**	**43**	**52**	**48**	**5**	**1**	**1**	**142**	**6.3**	**–11**	....	....	....	....	....	....	....	....	....	....	....	....	....
1994-95	**Montreal**	**NHL**	**47**	**4**	**7**	**11**	**42**	**2**	**0**	**1**	**63**	**6.3**	**–1**	....	....	....	....	....	....	....	....	....	....	....	....	....
1995-96	**Montreal**	**NHL**	**25**	**0**	**3**	**3**	**26**	**0**	**0**	**0**	**16**	**0.0**	**–7**	....	....	....	....	....	....	....	....	....	....	....	....	....
	San Jose	**NHL**	**32**	**1**	**16**	**17**	**28**	**0**	**0**	**0**	**35**	**2.9**	**–3**	....	....	....	....	....	....	....	....	....	....	....	....	....
1996-97	Kentucky	AHL	4	0	1	1	2	....	....	....	....	....	....	....	....	....	....	....	....	....	....	....	....	....	....	....
	Quebec	IHL	6	0	4	4	4	....	....	....	....	....	....	....	....	....	....	....	....	....	....	....	....	....	....	....
	Calgary	**NHL**	**46**	**1**	**15**	**16**	**24**	**1**	**0**	**0**	**82**	**1.2**	**4**	....	....	....	....	....	....	....	....	....	....	....	....	....
1997-98	**Tampa Bay**	**NHL**	**60**	**0**	**8**	**8**	**41**	**0**	**0**	**0**	**76**	**0.0**	**–23**	....	....	....	....	....	....	....	....	....	....	....	....	....
1998-99	Jokerit	Finland	52	8	18	26	100	....	....	....	....	....	....	....	....	....	....	....	3	1	0	1	6	....	....	....
	Jokerit Heksinki	EuroHL	6	1	0	1	18	....	....	....	....	....	....	....	....	....	....	....	2	1	1	2	6	....	....	....
	NHL Totals		**508**	**37**	**194**	**231**	**439**	**17**	**1**	**3**	**860**	**4.3**		....	....	....	....	....	**25**	**5**	**4**	**9**	**37**	**3**	**0**	**1**

QMJHL First-All Star Team (1988, 1989)

Traded to **Philadelphia** by **Detroit** with Detroit's 4th round choice (Sebastien Vallee) in 1994 Entry Draft for Terry Carkner, October 5, 1993. Traded to **Montreal** by **Philadelphia** for Kevin Haller, June 29, 1994. Claimed on waivers by **San Jose** from **Montreal**, January 23, 1996. Traded to **Calgary** by **San Jose** for cash, December 17, 1996. Signed as a free agent by **Tampa Bay**, July 16, 1997.

RAGNARSSON, Marcus
(RAG-nahr-suhn) **S.J.**

Defense. Shoots left. 6'1", 215 lbs. Born, Ostervala, Sweden, August 13, 1971. San Jose's 5th choice, 99th overall, in 1992 Entry Draft.

Season	Club	League	GP	G	A	Pts	PIM	PP	SH	GW	S	%	+/-	TF	F%	H	SB	Min	Playoffs GP	G	A	Pts	PIM	PP	SH	GW
1987-88	Ostervala IF	Sweden-3	25	3	12	15	....	....	....	....	....	....	....	....	....	....	....	....	....	....	....	....	....	....	....	....
1988-89	Ostervala IF	Sweden-3	30	15	14	29	....	....	....	....	....	....	....	....	....	....	....	....	....	....	....	....	....	....	....	....
1989-90	Nacka HK	Sweden-2	9	2	3	5	4	....	....	....	....	....	....	....	....	....	....	....	....	....	....	....	....	....	....	....
	Djurgardens IF	Sweden	13	0	2	2	0	....	....	....	....	....	....	....	....	....	....	....	1	0	0	0	0	....	....	....
1990-91	Djurgardens IF	Sweden	35	4	1	5	12	....	....	....	....	....	....	....	....	....	....	....	7	0	0	0	6	....	....	....
1991-92	Djurgardens IF	Sweden	40	8	5	13	14	....	....	....	....	....	....	....	....	....	....	....	10	0	1	1	4	....	....	....
1992-93	Djurgardens IF	Sweden	35	3	3	6	53	....	....	....	....	....	....	....	....	....	....	....	6	0	3	3	8	....	....	....
1993-94	Djurgardens IF	Sweden	19	0	4	4	24	....	....	....	....	....	....	....	....	....	....	....	....	....	....	....	....	....	....	....
1994-95	Djurgardens IF	Sweden	38	7	9	16	20	....	....	....	....	....	....	....	....	....	....	....	3	0	0	0	4	....	....	....
1995-96	**San Jose**	**NHL**	**71**	**8**	**31**	**39**	**42**	**4**	**0**	**0**	**94**	**8.5**	**–24**	....	....	....	....	....	....	....	....	....	....	....	....	....
1996-97	**San Jose**	**NHL**	**69**	**3**	**14**	**17**	**63**	**2**	**0**	**0**	**57**	**5.3**	**–18**	....	....	....	....	....	....	....	....	....	....	....	....	....
1997-98	**San Jose**	**NHL**	**79**	**5**	**20**	**25**	**65**	**3**	**0**	**2**	**91**	**5.5**	**–11**	....	....	....	....	....	**6**	**0**	**0**	**0**	**4**	**0**	**0**	**0**
	Sweden	Olympics	3	0	1	1	0	....	....	....	....	....	....	....	....	....	....	....	....	....	....	....	....	....	....	....
1998-99	**San Jose**	**NHL**	**74**	**0**	**13**	**13**	**66**	**0**	**0**	**0**	**87**	**0.0**	**7**	**3**	**66.7**	**99**	**66**	**21:55**	**6**	**0**	**1**	**1**	**6**	**0**	**0**	**0**
	NHL Totals		**293**	**16**	**78**	**94**	**236**	**9**	**0**	**2**	**329**	**4.9**		**3**	**66.7**	**99**	**66**	**21:55**	**12**	**0**	**1**	**1**	**10**	**0**	**0**	**0**

Season	Club	League	Regular Season GP	G	A	Pts	PIM	PP	SH	GW	S	%	+/–	TF	F%	H	SB	Min	Playoffs GP	G	A	Pts	PIM	PP	SH	GW

RANHEIM, Paul

(RAN-highm) **CAR.**

Left wing. Shoots right. 6'1", 210 lbs. Born, St. Louis, MO, January 25, 1966. Calgary's 3rd choice, 38th overall, in 1984 Entry Draft.

Season	Club	League	GP	G	A	Pts	PIM	PP	SH	GW	S	%	+/–	TF	F%	H	SB	Min	GP	G	A	Pts	PIM	PP	SH	GW
1982-83	Edina High	H.S.	26	12	25	37	4	....	....	....	....	....	....	....	....	....	....	....	....	....	....	....	....	....	....	....
1983-84	Edina High	H.S.	26	16	24	40	6	....	....	....	....	....	....	....	....	....	....	....	....	....	....	....	....	....	....	....
1984-85	U. of Wisconsin	WCHA	42	11	11	22	40	....	....	....	....	....	....	....	....	....	....	....	....	....	....	....	....	....	....	....
1985-86	U. of Wisconsin	WCHA	33	17	17	34	34	....	....	....	....	....	....	....	....	....	....	....	....	....	....	....	....	....	....	....
1986-87	U. of Wisconsin	WCHA	42	24	35	59	54	....	....	....	....	....	....	....	....	....	....	....	....	....	....	....	....	....	....	....
1987-88	U. of Wisconsin	WCHA	44	36	26	62	63	....	....	....	....	....	....	....	....	....	....	....	....	....	....	....	....	....	....	....
1988-89	**Calgary**	**NHL**	5	0	0	0	0	0	0	0	4	0.0	–3	....	....	....	....	....	....	....	....	....	....	....	....	....
	Salt Lake	IHL	75	*68	29	97	16	....	....	....	....	....	....	....	....	....	....	....	14	5	5	10	8	....	....	....
1989-90	**Calgary**	**NHL**	80	26	28	54	23	1	3	4	197	13.2	27	....	....	....	....	....	6	1	3	4	2	0	0	0
1990-91	**Calgary**	**NHL**	39	14	16	30	4	2	0	2	108	13.0	20	....	....	....	....	....	7	2	2	4	0	0	0	0
1991-92	**Calgary**	**NHL**	80	23	20	43	32	1	3	3	159	14.5	16	....	....	....	....	....	....	....	....	....	....	....	....	....
1992-93	**Calgary**	**NHL**	83	21	22	43	26	3	4	1	179	11.7	–4	....	....	....	....	....	6	0	1	1	0	0	0	0
1993-94	**Calgary**	**NHL**	67	10	14	24	20	0	2	2	110	9.1	–7	....	....	....	....	....	....	....	....	....	....	....	....	....
	Hartford	**NHL**	15	0	3	3	2	0	0	0	21	0.0	–11	....	....	....	....	....	....	....	....	....	....	....	....	....
1994-95	**Hartford**	**NHL**	47	6	14	20	10	0	0	1	73	8.2	–3	....	....	....	....	....	....	....	....	....	....	....	....	....
1995-96	**Hartford**	**NHL**	73	10	20	30	14	0	1	1	126	7.9	–2	....	....	....	....	....	....	....	....	....	....	....	....	....
1996-97	**Hartford**	**NHL**	67	10	11	21	18	0	3	1	96	10.4	–13	....	....	....	....	....	....	....	....	....	....	....	....	....
1997-98	**Carolina**	**NHL**	73	5	9	14	28	0	1	2	77	6.5	–11	....	....	....	....	....	....	....	....	....	....	....	....	....
1998-99	**Carolina**	**NHL**	78	9	10	19	39	0	2	1	67	13.4	4	10	50.0	72	32	9:02	6	0	0	0	2	0	0	0
	NHL Totals		707	134	167	301	216	7	19	18	1217	11.0		10	50.0	72	32	9:02	25	3	6	9	4	0	0	0

WCHA Second All-Star Team (1987) • NCAA West First All-American Team (1988) • WCHA First All-Star Team (1988) • IHL Second All-Star Team (1989) • Won Garry F. Longman Memorial Trophy (Top Rookie - IHL) (1989)

Traded to **Hartford** by **Calgary** with Gary Suter and Ted Drury for James Patrick, Zarley Zalapski and Michael Nylander, March 10, 1994. Transferred to **Carolina** after **Hartford** franchise relocated, June 25, 1997.

RASMUSSEN, Erik

(RAS-moo-suhn) **BUF.**

Center. Shoots left. 6'2", 205 lbs. Born, Minneapolis, MN, March 28, 1977. Buffalo's 1st choice, 7th overall, in 1996 Entry Draft.

Season	Club	League	GP	G	A	Pts	PIM	PP	SH	GW	S	%	+/–	TF	F%	H	SB	Min	GP	G	A	Pts	PIM	PP	SH	GW
1992-93	St. Louis High	H.S.	23	16	24	40	50	....	....	....	....	....	....	....	....	....	....	....	....	....	....	....	....	....	....	....
1993-94	St. Louis High	H.S.	18	25	18	42	80	....	....	....	....	....	....	....	....	....	....	....	....	....	....	....	....	....	....	....
1994-95	St. Louis High	H.S.	23	19	33	52	80	....	....	....	....	....	....	....	....	....	....	....	....	....	....	....	....	....	....	....
1995-96	U. of Minnesota	WCHA	40	16	32	48	55	....	....	....	....	....	....	....	....	....	....	....	....	....	....	....	....	....	....	....
1996-97	U. of Minnesota	WCHA	34	15	12	27	*123	....	....	....	....	....	....	....	....	....	....	....	....	....	....	....	....	....	....	....
1997-98	**Buffalo**	**NHL**	21	2	3	5	14	0	0	0	28	7.1	2	....	....	....	....	....	....	....	....	....	....	....	....	....
	Rochester	AHL	53	9	14	23	83	....	....	....	....	....	....	....	....	....	....	....	1	0	0	0	5	....	....	....
1998-99	**Buffalo**	**NHL**	42	3	7	10	37	0	0	0	40	7.5	6	67	40.3	104	18	12:22	21	2	4	6	18	0	0	1
	Rochester	AHL	37	12	14	26	47	....	....	....	....	....	....	....	....	....	....	....	....	....	....	....	....	....	....	....
	NHL Totals		63	5	10	15	51	0	0	0	68	7.4		67	40.3	104	18	12:22	21	2	4	6	18	0	0	1

RATCHUK, Peter

(RAT-chuhk) **FLA.**

Defense. Shoots left. 6'1", 185 lbs. Born, Buffalo, NY, September 10, 1977. Colorado's 1st choice, 25th overall, in 1996 Entry Draft.

Season	Club	League	GP	G	A	Pts	PIM	PP	SH	GW	S	%	+/–	TF	F%	H	SB	Min	GP	G	A	Pts	PIM	PP	SH	GW
1994-95	Lawrence Acad.	H.S.	31	8	15	23	18	....	....	....	....	....	....	....	....	....	....	....	....	....	....	....	....	....	....	....
1995-96	Shattuck High	H.S.	35	22	28	50	24	....	....	....	....	....	....	....	....	....	....	....	....	....	....	....	....	....	....	....
1996-97	Bowling Green	CCHA	35	9	12	21	14	....	....	....	....	....	....	....	....	....	....	....	....	....	....	....	....	....	....	....
1997-98	Hull	QMJHL	60	23	31	54	34	....	....	....	....	....	....	....	....	....	....	....	11	3	6	9	8	....	....	....
1998-99	**Florida**	**NHL**	24	1	1	2	10	0	0	0	34	2.9	–1	0	0.0	16	14	13:55	....	....	....	....	....	....	....	....
	New Haven	AHL	53	7	20	27	44	....	....	....	....	....	....	....	....	....	....	....	....	....	....	....	....	....	....	....
	NHL Totals		24	1	1	2	10	0	0	0	34	2.9		0	0.0	16	14	13:55	....	....	....	....	....	....	....	....

Signed as a free agent by **Florida**, June 15, 1998.

RATHJE, Mike

(RATH-jee) **S.J.**

Defense. Shoots left. 6'5", 230 lbs. Born, Mannville, Alta., May 11, 1974. San Jose's 1st choice, 3rd overall, in 1992 Entry Draft.

Season	Club	League	GP	G	A	Pts	PIM	PP	SH	GW	S	%	+/–	TF	F%	H	SB	Min	GP	G	A	Pts	PIM	PP	SH	GW
1989-90	Sherwood Park	AMHL	33	6	11	17	30	....	....	....	....	....	....	....	....	....	....	....	....	....	....	....	....	....	....	....
1990-91	Medicine Hat	WHL	64	1	16	17	28	....	....	....	....	....	....	....	....	....	....	....	12	0	4	4	2	....	....	....
1991-92	Medicine Hat	WHL	67	11	23	34	109	....	....	....	....	....	....	....	....	....	....	....	4	0	1	1	2	....	....	....
1992-93	Medicine Hat	WHL	57	12	37	49	103	....	....	....	....	....	....	....	....	....	....	....	10	3	3	6	12	....	....	....
	Kansas City	IHL	....	....	....	....	....	....	....	....	....	....	....	....	....	....	....	....	5	0	0	0	12	....	....	....
1993-94	**San Jose**	**NHL**	47	1	9	10	59	1	0	0	30	3.3	–9	....	....	....	....	....	1	0	0	0	0	0	0	0
	Kansas City	IHL	6	0	2	2	0	....	....	....	....	....	....	....	....	....	....	....	....	....	....	....	....	....	....	....
1994-95	**San Jose**	**NHL**	42	2	7	9	29	0	0	0	38	5.3	–1	....	....	....	....	....	11	5	2	7	4	5	0	0
	Kansas City	IHL	6	0	1	1	7	....	....	....	....	....	....	....	....	....	....	....	....	....	....	....	....	....	....	....
1995-96	**San Jose**	**NHL**	27	0	7	7	14	0	0	0	26	0.0	–16	....	....	....	....	....	....	....	....	....	....	....	....	....
	Kansas City	IHL	36	6	11	17	34	....	....	....	....	....	....	....	....	....	....	....	....	....	....	....	....	....	....	....
1996-97	**San Jose**	**NHL**	31	0	8	8	21	0	0	0	22	0.0	–1	....	....	....	....	....	....	....	....	....	....	....	....	....
1997-98	**San Jose**	**NHL**	81	3	12	15	59	1	0	0	61	4.9	–4	....	....	....	....	....	6	1	0	1	6	1	0	0
1998-99	**San Jose**	**NHL**	82	5	9	14	36	2	0	1	67	7.5	15	0	0.0	100	64	20:07	6	0	0	0	4	0	0	0
	NHL Totals		310	11	52	63	218	4	0	1	244	4.5		0	0.0	100	64	20:07	24	6	2	8	14	6	0	0

WHL East Second All-Star Team (1992, 1993)

RAY, Rob

BUF.

Right wing. Shoots left. 6', 203 lbs. Born, Stirling, Ont., June 8, 1968. Buffalo's 5th choice, 97th overall, in 1988 Entry Draft.

Season	Club	League	GP	G	A	Pts	PIM	PP	SH	GW	S	%	+/–	TF	F%	H	SB	Min	GP	G	A	Pts	PIM	PP	SH	GW
1984-85	Whitby	OJHL	35	5	10	15	318	....	....	....	....	....	....	....	....	....	....	....	....	....	....	....	....	....	....	....
1985-86	Cornwall	OHL	53	6	13	19	253	....	....	....	....	....	....	....	....	....	....	....	6	0	0	0	26	....	....	....
1986-87	Cornwall	OHL	46	17	20	37	158	....	....	....	....	....	....	....	....	....	....	....	5	1	1	2	16	....	....	....
1987-88	Cornwall	OHL	61	11	41	52	179	....	....	....	....	....	....	....	....	....	....	....	11	2	3	5	33	....	....	....
1988-89	Rochester	AHL	74	11	18	29	*446	....	....	....	....	....	....	....	....	....	....	....	....	....	....	....	....	....	....	....
1989-90	**Buffalo**	**NHL**	27	2	1	3	99	0	0	0	20	10.0	–2	....	....	....	....	....	....	....	....	....	....	....	....	....
	Rochester	AHL	43	2	13	15	335	....	....	....	....	....	....	....	....	....	....	....	17	1	3	4	115	....	....	....
1990-91	**Buffalo**	**NHL**	66	8	8	16	*350	0	0	1	54	14.8	–11	....	....	....	....	....	6	1	1	2	56	0	0	1
	Rochester	AHL	8	1	1	2	15	....	....	....	....	....	....	....	....	....	....	....	....	....	....	....	....	....	....	....
1991-92	**Buffalo**	**NHL**	63	5	3	8	354	0	0	0	29	17.2	–9	....	....	....	....	....	7	0	0	0	2	0	0	0
1992-93	**Buffalo**	**NHL**	68	3	2	5	211	1	0	0	28	10.7	–3	....	....	....	....	....	....	....	....	....	....	....	....	....
1993-94	**Buffalo**	**NHL**	82	3	4	7	274	0	0	0	34	8.8	2	....	....	....	....	....	7	1	0	1	43	0	0	0
1994-95	**Buffalo**	**NHL**	47	0	3	3	173	0	0	0	7	0.0	–4	....	....	....	....	....	5	0	0	0	14	0	0	0
1995-96	**Buffalo**	**NHL**	71	3	6	9	287	0	0	0	21	14.3	–8	....	....	....	....	....	....	....	....	....	....	....	....	....
1996-97	**Buffalo**	**NHL**	82	7	3	10	286	0	0	1	45	15.6	3	....	....	....	....	....	12	0	1	1	28	0	0	0
1997-98	**Buffalo**	**NHL**	63	2	4	6	234	1	0	1	19	10.5	2	....	....	....	....	....	10	0	0	0	24	0	0	0
1998-99	**Buffalo**	**NHL**	76	0	4	4	*261	0	0	0	23	0.0	–2	0	0.0	60	4	5:11	5	1	0	1	0	0	0	1
	NHL Totals		645	33	38	71	2529	2	0	3	280	11.8		0	0.0	60	4	5:11	52	3	2	5	167	0	0	2

Won King Clancy Memorial Trophy (1999)

			Regular Season																Playoffs							
Season	Club	League	GP	G	A	Pts	PIM	PP	SH	GW	S	%	+/–	TF	F%	H	SB	Min	GP	G	A	Pts	PIM	PP	SH	GW

REASONER, Marty   ST.L.

Center. Shoots left. 6'1", 203 lbs.   Born, Rochester, NY, February 26, 1977. St. Louis' 1st choice, 14th overall, in 1996 Entry Draft.

Season	Club	League	GP	G	A	Pts	PIM	PP	SH	GW	S	%	+/–	TF	F%	H	SB	Min	GP	G	A	Pts	PIM	PP	SH	GW
1993-94	Deerfield Prep	H.S.	22	27	25	52	....	....	....	....	....	....	....	....	....	....	....	....	....	....	....	....	....	....	....	....
1994-95	Deerfield Prep	H.S.	26	25	32	57	14	....	....	....	....	....	....	....	....	....	....	....	....	....	....	....	....	....	....	....
1995-96	Boston College	H.E.	34	16	29	45	32	....	....	....	....	....	....	....	....	....	....	....	....	....	....	....	....	....	....	....
1996-97	Boston College	H.E.	35	20	24	44	31	....	....	....	....	....	....	....	....	....	....	....	....	....	....	....	....	....	....	....
1997-98	Boston College	H.E.	42	*33	40	*73	56	....	....	....	....	....	....	....	....	....	....	....	....	....	....	....	....	....	....	....
1998-99	**St. Louis**	**NHL**	22	3	7	10	8	1	0	0	33	9.1	2	224	53.6	19	1	13:55	4	2	1	3	6			
	Worcester	AHL	44	17	22	39	24																			
	NHL Totals		**22**	**3**	**7**	**10**	**8**	**1**	**0**	**0**	**33**	**9.1**		**224**	**53.6**	**19**	**1**	**13:55**								

Hockey East First All-Star Team (1997, 1998) • NCAA East First All-American Team (1998) • NCAA Championship All-Tournament Team (1998)

RECCHI, Mark   (REH-kee)   PHI.

Right wing. Shoots left. 5'10", 185 lbs.   Born, Kamloops, B.C., February 1, 1968. Pittsburgh's 4th choice, 67th overall, in 1988 Entry Draft.

Season	Club	League	GP	G	A	Pts	PIM	PP	SH	GW	S	%	+/–	TF	F%	H	SB	Min	GP	G	A	Pts	PIM	PP	SH	GW
1984-85	Langley	BCJHL	51	26	39	65	39	....	....	....	....	....	....													
	New Westminster	WHL	4	1	0	1	0	....	....	....	....	....	....													
1985-86	New Westminster	WHL	72	21	40	61	55	....	....	....	....	....	....													
1986-87	Kamloops	WHL	40	26	50	76	63	....	....	....	....	....	....						13	3	16	19	17			
1987-88	Kamloops	WHL	62	61	*93	154	75	....	....	....	....	....	....						17	10	*21	*31	18			
1988-89	**Pittsburgh**	**NHL**	15	1	1	2	0	0	0	0	11	9.1	–2						14	7	*14	*21	28			
	Muskegon	IHL	63	50	49	99	86																			
1989-90	**Pittsburgh**	**NHL**	74	30	37	67	44	6	2	4	143	21.0	6													
	Muskegon	IHL	4	7	4	11	2												24	10	24	34	33	5	0	2
1990-91♦	Pittsburgh	NHL	78	40	73	113	48	12	0	9	184	21.7	0						24	10	24	34	33	5	0	2
1991-92	**Pittsburgh**	**NHL**	58	33	37	70	78	16	1	4	156	21.2	–16													
	Philadelphia	NHL	22	10	17	27	18	4	0	1	54	18.5	–5													
1992-93	**Philadelphia**	**NHL**	84	53	70	123	95	15	4	6	274	19.3	1													
1993-94	**Philadelphia**	**NHL**	84	40	67	107	46	11	0	5	217	18.4	–2													
1994-95	**Philadelphia**	**NHL**	10	2	3	5	12	1	0	2	17	11.8	–6													
	Montreal	NHL	39	14	29	43	16	8	0	1	104	13.5	–3						6	3	3	6	0	3	0	0
1995-96	**Montreal**	**NHL**	82	28	50	78	69	11	2	6	191	14.7	20						5	4	2	6	2	0	0	0
1996-97	**Montreal**	**NHL**	82	34	46	80	58	7	2	3	202	16.8	–1						10	4	8	12	6	0	0	2
1997-98	**Montreal**	**NHL**	82	32	42	74	51	9	1	6	216	14.8	11						....	....	....	....	....			
	Canada	Olympics	5	0	2	2	0																			
1998-99	**Montreal**	**NHL**	61	12	35	47	28	3	0	2	152	7.9	–4	239	44.8	76	23	20:37								
	Philadelphia	NHL	10	4	2	6	6	0	0	0	19	21.1	–3	4	25.0	21	1	19:30	6	0	1	1	2	0	0	0
	NHL Totals		**781**	**333**	**509**	**842**	**569**	**103**	**12**	**49**	**1940**	**17.2**		**243**	**44.4**	**97**	**24**	**20:28**	**51**	**21**	**38**	**59**	**43**	**8**	**0**	**4**

WHL West All-Star Team (1988) • IHL Second All-Star Team (1989) • NHL Second All-Star Team (1992)
Played in NHL All-Star Game (1991, 1993, 1994, 1997, 1998, 1999) •

Traded to **Philadelphia** by Pittsburgh with Brian Benning and LA Kings' 1st round choice (previously acquired, Philadelphia selected Jason Bowen) in 1992 Entry Draft for Rick Tocchet, Kjell Samuelsson, Ken Wregget and Philadelphia's 3rd round choice (Dave Roche) in 1993 Entry Draft, February 19, 1992. Traded to **Montreal** by **Philadelphia** with Philadelphia's 3rd round choice (Martin Hohenberger) in 1995 Entry Draft for Eric Desjardins, Gilbert Dionne and John LeClair, February 9, 1995. Traded to **Philadelphia** by **Montreal** for Danius Zubrus, Philadelphia's 2nd round choice (Matt Carkner) in 1999 Entry Draft and 6th round choice in 2000 Entry Draft, March 10, 1999.

REDDEN, Wade   OTT.

Defense. Shoots left. 6'2", 193 lbs.   Born, Lloydminster, Sask., June 12, 1977. NY Islanders' 1st choice, 2nd overall, in 1995 Entry Draft.

Season	Club	League	GP	G	A	Pts	PIM	PP	SH	GW	S	%	+/–	TF	F%	H	SB	Min	GP	G	A	Pts	PIM	PP	SH	GW
1992-93	Lloydminster	SJHL	34	4	11	15	64	....	....	....	....	....	....	....					14	3	1	8	10			
1993-94	Brandon	WHL	63	4	35	39	98	....	....	....	....	....	....	....					18	5	10	15	8			
1994-95	Brandon	WHL	64	14	46	60	83	....	....	....	....	....	....	....					19	5	10	15	19			
1995-96	Brandon	WHL	51	9	45	54	55	....	....	....	....	....	....	....					7	1	3	4	2	0	0	0
1996-97	**Ottawa**	**NHL**	82	6	24	30	41	2	0	1	102	5.9	1	....					9	0	2	2	2	0	0	0
1997-98	**Ottawa**	**NHL**	80	8	14	22	27	3	0	2	103	7.8	17	....					4	1	2	3	2	1	0	0
1998-99	**Ottawa**	**NHL**	72	8	21	29	54	3	0	1	127	6.3	7	0	0.0	83	73	23:27	4	1	2	3	2	1	0	0
	NHL Totals		**234**	**22**	**59**	**81**	**122**	**8**	**0**	**4**	**332**	**6.6**		**0**	**0.0**	**83**	**73**	**23:27**	**20**	**2**	**7**	**9**	**6**	**1**	**0**	**0**

WHL East Second All-Star Team (1995) • WHL East First All-Star Team (1996) • Memorial Cup All-Star Team (1996)
Traded to **Ottawa** by **NY Islanders** with Damian Rhodes for Don Beaupre, Martin Straka and Bryan Berard, January 23, 1996.

REEKIE, Joe   (REE-kee)

Defense. Shoots left. 6'3", 220 lbs.   Born, Victoria, B.C., February 22, 1965. Buffalo's 6th choice, 119th overall, in 1985 Entry Draft.

Season	Club	League	GP	G	A	Pts	PIM	PP	SH	GW	S	%	+/–	TF	F%	H	SB	Min	GP	G	A	Pts	PIM	PP	SH	GW
1981-82	Nepean	OJHL	16	2	5	7	4	....	....	....	....	....	....						....	....	....	....	....			
1982-83	North Bay	OHL	59	2	9	11	49	....	....	....	....	....	....						8	0	1	1	11			
1983-84	North Bay	OHL	9	1	0	1	18	....	....	....	....	....	....						3	0	0	0	4			
	Cornwall	OHL	53	6	27	33	166	....	....	....	....	....	....													
1984-85	Cornwall	OHL	65	19	63	82	134	....	....	....	....	....	....						9	4	13	17	18			
1985-86	**Buffalo**	**NHL**	3	0	0	0	14	0	0	0	1	0.0	–2													
	Rochester	AHL	77	3	25	28	178																			
1986-87	**Buffalo**	**NHL**	56	1	8	9	82	0	0	0	56	1.8	6													
	Rochester	AHL	22	0	6	6	52																			
1987-88	**Buffalo**	**NHL**	30	1	4	5	68	0	0	0	14	4.3	–3						2	0	0	0	4	0	0	0
1988-89	**Buffalo**	**NHL**	15	1	3	4	26	1	0	0	14	7.1	6													
	Rochester	AHL	21	1	2	3	56																			
1989-90	**NY Islanders**	**NHL**	31	1	8	9	43	0	0	1	22	4.5	13													
	Springfield	AHL	15	1	4	5	24																			
1990-91	**NY Islanders**	**NHL**	66	3	16	19	96	0	0	0	70	4.3	17													
	Capital District	AHL	2	1	0	1	0																			
1991-92	**NY Islanders**	**NHL**	54	4	12	16	85	0	0	0	59	6.8	15													
	Capital District	AHL	3	2	2	4	2																			
1992-93	**Tampa Bay**	**NHL**	42	2	11	13	69	0	0	0	53	3.8	2													
1993-94	**Tampa Bay**	**NHL**	73	1	11	12	127	0	0	0	88	1.1	8						11	2	1	3	29	0	1	1
	Washington	NHL	12	0	5	5	29	0	0	0	10	0.0	7						7	0	0	0	6	0	0	0
1994-95	**Washington**	**NHL**	48	1	6	7	97	0	0	0	52	1.9	10													
1995-96	**Washington**	**NHL**	78	3	7	10	149	0	0	0	52	5.8	7						21	1	2	3	20	0	0	0
1996-97	**Washington**	**NHL**	65	1	8	9	107	0	0	0	65	1.5	8													
1997-98	**Washington**	**NHL**	68	2	8	10	70	0	0	1	59	3.4	15													
1998-99	**Washington**	**NHL**	73	0	10	10	68	0	0	0	81	0.0	11	0	0.0	182	101	21:53								
	NHL Totals		**714**	**21**	**117**	**138**	**1130**	**1**	**0**	**4**	**705**	**3.0**		**0**	**0.0**	**182**	**101**	**21:53**	**41**	**3**	**3**	**6**	**55**	**0**	**1**	**1**

• Re-entered NHL draft. Originally Hartford's 8th choice, 128th overall, in 1983 Entry Draft.
Traded to **NY Islanders** by Buffalo for NY Islanders' 6th round choice (Bill Pye) in 1989 Entry Draft, June 17, 1989. Claimed by **Tampa Bay** from **NY Islanders** in Expansion Draft, June 18, 1992. Traded to **Washington** by **Tampa Bay** for Enrico Ciccone, Washington's 3rd round choice (later traded to Anaheim — Anaheim selected Craig Reichert) in 1994 Entry Draft and the return of draft choices transferred in the Pat Elynuik trade, March 21, 1994.

REICHEL, Robert   (RIGH-khul)   PHX.

Center. Shoots left. 5'10", 185 lbs.   Born, Litvinov, Czech., June 25, 1971. Calgary's 5th choice, 70th overall, in 1989 Entry Draft.

Season	Club	League	GP	G	A	Pts	PIM	PP	SH	GW	S	%	+/–	TF	F%	H	SB	Min	GP	G	A	Pts	PIM	PP	SH	GW
1987-88	CHZ Litvinov	Czech.	36	17	10	27	8	....	....	....	....	....	....	....					....	....	....	....	....			
1988-89	CHZ Litvinov	Czech.	44	23	25	48	32	....	....	....	....	....	....	....					8	6	6	12				
1989-90	CHZ Litvinov	Czech.	44	*43	28	*71	....	....	....	....	....	....	....	....					6	1	1	2	0	1	0	0
1990-91	**Calgary**	**NHL**	66	19	22	41	22	3	0	3	131	14.5	17													

| | | | Regular Season | | | | | | | | | | | | | | | | Playoffs | | | | | | | |
Season	Club	League	GP	G	A	Pts	PIM	PP	SH	GW	S	%	+/-	TF	F%	H	SB	Min	GP	G	A	Pts	PIM	PP	SH	GW
1991-92	Calgary	NHL	77	20	34	54	32	8	0	3	181	11.0	1													
1992-93	Calgary	NHL	80	40	48	88	54	12	0	5	238	16.8	25													
1993-94	Calgary	NHL	84	40	53	93	58	14	0	6	249	16.1	20						6	2	4	6	2	2	0	0
1994-95	Frankfurt	Germany	21	19	24	43	41													7	0	5	5	0	0	0	0
	Calgary	NHL	48	18	17	35	28	5	0	2	160	11.3	-2													
1995-96	Frankfurt	Germany	46	47	54	101	84													7	2	4	6	4	0	0	1
	Calgary	NHL	70	16	27	43	22	6	0	3	181	8.8	-2						3	1	3	4	0			
1996-97	Calgary	NHL	12	5	14	19	4	0	1	0	33	15.2	7													
1997-98	NY Islanders	NHL	82	25	40	65	32	8	0	2	201	12.4	-11													
	Czech Republic	Olympics	6	3	0	3	0																			
1998-99	NY Islanders	NHL	70	19	37	56	50	5	1	1	186	10.2	-15	1241	51.7	52	19	19:36								
	Phoenix	NHL	13	7	6	13	4	3	0	3	50	14.0	2	241	48.5	10	4	20:03	7	1	3	4	2	0	0	0
NHL Totals			602	209	298	507	306	64	2	28	1610	13.0		1482	51.2	62	23	19:40	33	6	17	23	8	2	0	1

Czechoslovakian First All-Star Team (1990)

Traded to **NY Islanders** by **Calgary** for Marty McInnis, Tyrone Garner and Calgary's 6th round choice (previously acquired, Calgary selected Ilja Demidov) in 1997 Entry Draft, March 18, 1997. Traded to **Phoenix** by **NY Islanders** with NY Islanders' 3rd round choice (Jason Jaspers) in 1999 Entry Draft and Ottawa's 4th round choice (previously acquired, Phoenix selected Preston Mizzi) in 1999 Entry Draft for Brad Isbister and Phoenix's 3rd round choice (Brian Collins) in 1999 Entry Draft, March 20, 1999.

REICHERT, Craig   (RIGH-kuhrt)   **FLA.**

Right wing. Shoots right. 6'1", 200 lbs.   Born, Winnipeg, Man., May 11, 1974. Anaheim's 3rd choice, 67th overall, in 1994 Entry Draft.

| | | | Regular Season | | | | | | | | | | | | | | | | Playoffs | | | | | | | |
Season	Club	League	GP	G	A	Pts	PIM	PP	SH	GW	S	%	+/-	TF	F%	H	SB	Min	GP	G	A	Pts	PIM	PP	SH	GW
1990-91	Calgary	AAHA	60	45	64	109	81																			
1991-92	Spokane	WHL	68	13	20	33	86																			
1992-93	Red Deer	WHL	66	32	33	65	62													4	1	0	1	4			
1993-94	Red Deer	WHL	72	52	67	119	153													4	3	1	4	2			
1994-95	San Diego	IHL	49	4	12	16	28													4	2	2	4	8			
1995-96	Baltimore	AHL	68	10	17	27	50																			
1996-97	**Anaheim**	**NHL**	3	0	0	0	0	0	0	0	3	0.0	-2						1	0	0	0	0			
	Baltimore	AHL	77	22	53	75	54													3	0	2	2	0			
1997-98	Cincinnati	AHL	78	28	59	87	28																			
1998-99	Cincinnati	AHL	72	28	41	69	56													3	2	0	2	0			
NHL Totals			3	0	0	0	0	0	0	0	3	0.0													

Signed as a free agent by **Florida**, July 21, 1999.

REID, Dave

Left wing. Shoots left. 6'1", 217 lbs.   Born, Toronto, Ont., May 15, 1964. Boston's 4th choice, 60th overall, in 1982 Entry Draft.

| | | | Regular Season | | | | | | | | | | | | | | | | Playoffs | | | | | | | |
Season	Club	League	GP	G	A	Pts	PIM	PP	SH	GW	S	%	+/-	TF	F%	H	SB	Min	GP	G	A	Pts	PIM	PP	SH	GW
1980-81	Mississauga	MTHL	39	21	28	49																				
1981-82	Peterborough	OHL	68	10	32	42	41													9	2	3	5	11			
1982-83	Peterborough	OHL	70	23	34	57	33													4	3	1	4	0			
1983-84	Peterborough	OHL	60	33	64	97	12																			
	Boston	**NHL**	8	1	0	1	2	0	0	0	4	25.0	1													
1984-85	**Boston**	**NHL**	35	14	13	27	27	2	0	5	52	26.9	-1						5	1	0	1	0	0	0	0
	Hershey	AHL	43	10	14	24	6																			
1985-86	**Boston**	**NHL**	37	10	10	20	10	4	0	1	53	18.9	2													
	Moncton	AHL	26	14	18	32	4																			
1986-87	**Boston**	**NHL**	12	3	3	6	0	0	0	0	19	15.8	-1						2	0	0	0	0	0	0	0
	Moncton	AHL	40	12	22	34	23													5	0	1	1	0			
1987-88	**Boston**	**NHL**	3	0	0	0	0	0	0	0	2	0.0	0													
	Maine	AHL	63	21	37	58	40													10	6	7	13	6			
1988-89	**Toronto**	**NHL**	77	9	21	30	22	1	1	0	87	10.3	12													
1989-90	**Toronto**	**NHL**	70	9	19	28	9	0	4	1	97	9.3	-8						3	0	0	0	0	0	0	0
1990-91	**Toronto**	**NHL**	69	15	13	28	18	1	8	0	110	13.6	-10													
1991-92	**Boston**	**NHL**	43	7	7	14	27	2	1	0	70	10.0	5						15	2	5	7	4	0	0	1
	Maine	AHL	12	1	5	6	4																			
1992-93	**Boston**	**NHL**	65	20	16	36	10	1	5	2	116	17.2	12													
1993-94	**Boston**	**NHL**	83	6	17	23	25	0	2	1	145	4.1	10						13	2	1	3	2	0	1	0
1994-95	**Boston**	**NHL**	38	5	5	10	10	1	0	0	47	10.6	4						5	0	0	0	0	0	0	0
	Providence	AHL	7	3	0	3	0																			
1995-96	**Boston**	**NHL**	63	23	21	44	4	1	6	3	160	14.4	14						5	0	2	2	2	0	0	0
1996-97	**Dallas**	**NHL**	82	19	20	39	10	1	1	4	135	14.1	12						7	1	0	1	4	0	0	0
1997-98	**Dallas**	**NHL**	65	6	12	18	14	3	0	1	90	6.7	-15						5	0	3	3	2	0	0	0
1998-99♦	**Dallas**	**NHL**	73	6	11	17	16	1	0	1	81	7.4	0	39	41.0	45	34	11:34	23	2	8	10	14	0	0	0
NHL Totals			823	153	188	341	204	17	28	19	1268	12.1		39	41.0	45	34	11:34	83	8	19	27	28	0	1	1

Signed as a free agent by **Toronto**, June 23, 1988. Signed as a free agent by **Boston**, December 1, 1991. Signed as a free agent by **Dallas**, July 11, 1996.

REIRDEN, Todd

Defense. Shoots left. 6'4", 205 lbs.   Born, Arlington Heights, IL, June 25, 1971. New Jersey's 14th choice, 242nd overall, in 1990 Entry Draft.

| | | | Regular Season | | | | | | | | | | | | | | | | Playoffs | | | | | | | |
Season	Club	League	GP	G	A	Pts	PIM	PP	SH	GW	S	%	+/-	TF	F%	H	SB	Min	GP	G	A	Pts	PIM	PP	SH	GW
1989-90	Tabor Academy	H.S.		STATISTICS NOT AVAILABLE																						
1990-91	Bowling Green	CCHA	28	1	5	6	22																			
1991-92	Bowling Green	CCHA	33	8	7	15	34																			
1992-93	Bowling Green	CCHA	41	8	17	25	48																			
1993-94	Bowling Green	CCHA	38	7	23	30	56																			
1994-95	Albany	AHL	2	0	1	1	2																			
	Raleigh	ECHL	26	2	13	15	33																			
	Tallahassee	ECHL	43	5	25	30	61																			
1995-96	Tallahassee	ECHL	7	1	3	4	10													13	2	5	7	40			
	Jacksonville	ECHL	15	1	10	11	41													1	0	2	2	4			
	Chicago	IHL	31	0	2	2	39													9	0	2	2	16			
1996-97	Chicago	IHL	57	3	10	13	108																			
	San Antonio	IHL	23	2	5	7	51													9	0	1	1	17			
1997-98	San Antonio	IHL	70	5	14	19	132																			
	Fort Wayne	IHL	11	2	2	4	16													4	0	2	2	0			
1998-99	**Edmonton**	**NHL**	17	2	3	5	20	0	0	0	26	7.7	-1	0	0.0	18	18	17:17								
	Hamilton	AHL	58	9	25	34	84													11	0	5	5	6			
NHL Totals			17	2	3	5	20	0	0	0	26	7.7		0	0.0	18	18	17:17								

Signed as a free agent by **Edmonton**, September 17, 1998.

RENBERG, Mikael   (REHN-buhrg)   **PHI.**

Right wing. Shoots left. 6'2", 218 lbs.   Born, Pitea, Sweden, May 5, 1972. Philadelphia's 3rd choice, 40th overall, in 1990 Entry Draft.

| | | | Regular Season | | | | | | | | | | | | | | | | Playoffs | | | | | | | |
Season	Club	League	GP	G	A	Pts	PIM	PP	SH	GW	S	%	+/-	TF	F%	H	SB	Min	GP	G	A	Pts	PIM	PP	SH	GW
1988-89	Pitea BK	Sweden-2	12	6	3	9																				
1989-90	Pitea BK	Sweden-2	29	15	19	34																				
1990-91	Lulea HF	Sweden	29	11	6	17	12													5	1	1	2	4			
1991-92	Lulea HF	Sweden	38	8	15	23	20													2	0	0	0	0			
1992-93	Lulea HF	Sweden	39	19	13	32	61																			
1993-94	**Philadelphia**	**NHL**	83	38	44	82	36	9	0	1	195	19.5	8						11	4	4	8	4			
1994-95	Lulea HF	Sweden	10	9	4	13	16																			
	Philadelphia	**NHL**	47	26	31	57	20	8	0	4	143	18.2	20						15	6	7	13	6	2	0	0
1995-96	**Philadelphia**	**NHL**	51	23	20	43	45	9	0	4	198	11.6	8						11	3	6	9	14	1	0	0
1996-97	**Philadelphia**	**NHL**	77	22	37	59	65	1	0	1	249	8.8	36						18	5	6	11	4	2	0	0

Season	Club	League	GP	G	A	Pts	PIM	PP	SH	GW	S	%	+/–	TF	F%	H	SB	Min	GP	G	A	Pts	PIM	PP	SH	GW
			Regular Season																Playoffs							
1997-98	Tampa Bay	NHL	68	16	22	38	34	6	3	0	175	9.1	–37	....	....	....	....	....	....	....	....	....	....	....	....	....
	Sweden	Olympics	4	1	2	3	4	....	....	....	....	....	....	....	....	....	....	....	....	....	....	....	....	....	....	....
1998-99	Tampa Bay	NHL	20	4	8	12	4	2	0	0	42	9.5	–2	2	100.0	1	4	15:32	....	....	....	....	....	....	....	....
	Philadelphia	NHL	46	11	15	26	14	4	0	2	112	9.8	7	1	0.0	8	5	16:00	6	0	1	1	0	0	0	0
	NHL Totals		392	140	177	317	218	39	3	15	1114	12.6		3	66.7	9	9	15:52	50	14	20	34	24	5	0	0

NHL/Upper Deck All-Rookie Team (1994)

Traded to **Tampa Bay** by **Philadelphia** with Karl Dykhuis for Philadelphia's 1st round choices in 1998 (Simon Gagne), 1999, 2000 and 2001 Entry Drafts (previously acquired by Tampa Bay), August 20, 1997. Traded to **Philadelphia** by **Tampa Bay** with Daymond Langkow for Chris Gratton and Mike Sillinger, December 12, 1998.

RHEAUME, Pascal (RAY-awm) ST.L.

Left wing. Shoots left. 6'1", 209 lbs. Born, Quebec, Que., June 21, 1973.

Season	Club	League	GP	G	A	Pts	PIM	PP	SH	GW	S	%	+/–	TF	F%	H	SB	Min	GP	G	A	Pts	PIM	PP	SH	GW
1990-91	Ste-Foy	QAAA	37	20	38	58	25	....	....	....	....	....	....	....	....	....	....	....	....	....	....	....	....	....	....	....
1991-92	Trois-Rivieres	QMJHL	65	17	20	37	84	....	....	....	....	....	....	....	....	....	....	....	14	5	4	9	23	....	....	....
1992-93	Sherbrooke	QMJHL	65	28	34	62	88	....	....	....	....	....	....	....	....	....	....	....	14	6	5	11	31	....	....	....
1993-94	Albany	AHL	55	17	18	35	43	....	....	....	....	....	....	....	....	....	....	....	5	0	1	1	0	....	....	....
1994-95	Albany	AHL	78	19	25	44	46	....	....	....	....	....	....	....	....	....	....	....	14	3	6	9	19	....	....	....
1995-96	Albany	AHL	68	26	42	68	50	....	....	....	....	....	....	....	....	....	....	....	4	1	2	3	2	....	....	....
1996-97	New Jersey	NHL	2	1	0	1	0	0	0	0	5	20.0	1	....	....	....	....	....	....	....	....	....	....	....	....	....
	Albany	AHL	51	22	23	45	40	....	....	....	....	....	....	....	....	....	....	....	16	2	8	10	16	....	....	....
1997-98	St. Louis	NHL	48	6	9	15	35	1	0	0	45	13.3	4	....	....	....	....	....	10	1	3	4	8	1	0	0
1998-99	St. Louis	NHL	60	9	18	27	24	2	0	0	85	10.6	10	21	71.4	105	14	13:19	5	1	0	1	4	0	0	0
	NHL Totals		110	16	27	43	59	3	0	0	135	11.9		21	71.4	105	14	13:19	15	2	3	5	12	1	0	0

Signed as a free agent by **New Jersey**, October 1, 1993. Claimed by **St. Louis** from **New Jersey** in NHL Waiver Draft, September 28, 1997.

RICCI, Mike (REE-CHEE) S.J.

Center. Shoots left. 6', 190 lbs. Born, Scarborough, Ont., October 27, 1971. Philadelphia's 1st choice, 4th overall, in 1990 Entry Draft.

Season	Club	League	GP	G	A	Pts	PIM	PP	SH	GW	S	%	+/–	TF	F%	H	SB	Min	GP	G	A	Pts	PIM	PP	SH	GW
1986-87	Toronto	MTHL	38	39	42	81	27	....	....	....	....	....	....	....	....	....	....	....	....	....	....	....	....	....	....	....
1987-88	Peterborough	OHL	41	24	37	61	20	....	....	....	....	....	....	....	....	....	....	....	8	5	5	10	4	....	....	....
1988-89	Peterborough	OHL	60	54	52	106	43	....	....	....	....	....	....	....	....	....	....	....	17	19	16	35	18	....	....	....
1989-90	Peterborough	OHL	60	52	64	116	39	....	....	....	....	....	....	....	....	....	....	....	12	5	7	12	26	....	....	....
1990-91	Philadelphia	NHL	68	21	20	41	64	9	0	4	121	17.4	–8	....	....	....	....	....	....	....	....	....	....	....	....	....
1991-92	Philadelphia	NHL	78	20	36	56	93	11	2	0	149	13.4	–10	....	....	....	....	....	....	....	....	....	....	....	....	....
1992-93	Quebec	NHL	77	27	51	78	123	12	1	10	142	19.0	8	....	....	....	....	....	6	0	6	6	8	0	0	0
1993-94	Quebec	NHL	83	30	21	51	113	13	3	6	138	21.7	–9	....	....	....	....	....	....	....	....	....	....	....	....	....
1994-95	Quebec	NHL	48	15	21	36	40	9	0	1	73	20.5	5	....	....	....	....	....	6	1	3	4	8	0	0	0
1995-96♦	Colorado	NHL	62	6	21	27	52	3	0	1	73	8.2	1	....	....	....	....	....	22	6	11	17	18	3	0	1
1996-97	Colorado	NHL	63	13	19	32	59	5	0	3	74	17.6	–3	....	....	....	....	....	17	2	4	6	17	0	0	1
1997-98	Colorado	NHL	6	0	4	4	2	0	0	0	5	0.0	0	....	....	....	....	....	....	....	....	....	....	....	....	....
	San Jose	NHL	59	9	14	23	30	5	0	2	86	10.5	–4	....	....	....	....	....	6	1	3	4	6	0	0	0
1998-99	San Jose	NHL	82	13	26	39	68	2	1	2	98	13.3	1	1465	49.6	73	41	15:23	6	2	3	5	10	1	0	0
	NHL Totals		626	154	233	387	644	69	7	29	959	16.1		1465	49.6	73	41	15:23	63	12	30	42	67	4	0	2

OHL Second All-Star Team (1989) • Canadian Major Junior Player of the Year (1990) • OHL First All-Star Team (1990)

Traded to **Quebec** by **Philadelphia** with Peter Forsberg, Steve Duchesne, Kerry Huffman, Ron Hextall, Chris Simon, Philadelphia's 1st round choice in the 1993 (Jocelyn Thibault) and 1994 (later traded to Toronto — later traded to Washington — Washington selected Nolan Baumgartner) Entry Drafts and cash for Eric Lindros, June 30, 1992. Transferred to **Colorado** after **Quebec** franchise relocated, June 21, 1995. Traded to **San Jose** by **Colorado** with Colorado's 2nd round choice (later traded to Buffalo - Buffalo selected Jaroslav Kristek) in 1998 Entry Draft for Shean Donovan and San Jose's 1st round choice (Alex Tanguay) in 1998 Entry Draft, November 21, 1997.

RICHARDSON, Luke PHI.

Defense. Shoots left. 6'4", 210 lbs. Born, Ottawa, Ont., March 26, 1969. Toronto's 1st choice, 7th overall, in 1987 Entry Draft.

Season	Club	League	GP	G	A	Pts	PIM	PP	SH	GW	S	%	+/–	TF	F%	H	SB	Min	GP	G	A	Pts	PIM	PP	SH	GW
1984-85	Ottawa	OJHL	35	5	26	31	72	....	....	....	....	....	....	....	....	....	....	....	....	....	....	....	....	....	....	....
1985-86	Peterborough	OHL	63	6	18	24	57	....	....	....	....	....	....	....	....	....	....	....	16	2	1	3	50	....	....	....
1986-87	Peterborough	OHL	59	13	32	45	70	....	....	....	....	....	....	....	....	....	....	....	12	0	5	5	24	....	....	....
1987-88	Toronto	NHL	78	4	6	10	90	0	0	0	49	8.2	–25	....	....	....	....	....	2	0	0	0	0	0	0	0
1988-89	Toronto	NHL	55	2	7	9	106	0	0	0	59	3.4	–15	....	....	....	....	....	....	....	....	....	....	....	....	....
1989-90	Toronto	NHL	67	4	14	18	122	0	0	0	80	5.0	–1	....	....	....	....	....	5	0	0	0	22	0	0	0
1990-91	Toronto	NHL	78	1	9	10	238	0	0	0	68	1.5	–28	....	....	....	....	....	....	....	....	....	....	....	....	....
1991-92	Edmonton	NHL	75	2	19	21	118	0	0	0	85	2.4	–9	....	....	....	....	....	16	0	5	5	45	0	0	0
1992-93	Edmonton	NHL	82	3	10	13	142	0	2	0	78	3.8	–18	....	....	....	....	....	....	....	....	....	....	....	....	....
1993-94	Edmonton	NHL	69	2	6	8	131	0	0	0	92	2.2	–13	....	....	....	....	....	....	....	....	....	....	....	....	....
1994-95	Edmonton	NHL	46	3	10	13	40	1	1	1	51	5.9	–6	....	....	....	....	....	....	....	....	....	....	....	....	....
1995-96	Edmonton	NHL	82	2	9	11	108	0	0	0	61	3.3	–27	....	....	....	....	....	....	....	....	....	....	....	....	....
1996-97	Edmonton	NHL	82	1	11	12	91	0	0	0	67	1.5	9	....	....	....	....	....	12	0	2	2	14	0	0	0
1997-98	Philadelphia	NHL	81	2	3	5	139	2	0	0	57	3.5	7	....	....	....	....	....	5	0	0	0	0	0	0	0
1998-99	Philadelphia	NHL	78	0	6	6	106	0	0	0	49	0.0	–3	0	0.0	116	94	16:33	....	....	....	....	....	....	....	....
	NHL Totals		873	26	110	136	1431	3	3	1	796	3.3		0	0.0	116	94	16:33	40	0	7	7	81	0	0	0

Traded to **Edmonton** by **Toronto** with Vincent Damphousse, Peter Ing, Scott Thornton, future considerations and cash for Grant Fuhr, Glenn Anderson and Craig Berube, September 19, 1991. Signed as a free agent by **Philadelphia**, July 23, 1997.

RICHER, Stephane (REE-shay) T.B.

Right wing. Shoots right. 6'2", 215 lbs. Born, Ripon, Que., June 7, 1966. Montreal's 3rd choice, 29th overall, in 1984 Entry Draft.

Season	Club	League	GP	G	A	Pts	PIM	PP	SH	GW	S	%	+/–	TF	F%	H	SB	Min	GP	G	A	Pts	PIM	PP	SH	GW
1982-83	Laval	QAAA	48	47	54	101	86	....	....	....	....	....	....	....	....	....	....	....	....	....	....	....	....	....	....	....
1983-84	Granby	QMJHL	67	39	37	76	58	....	....	....	....	....	....	....	....	....	....	....	3	1	1	2	4	....	....	....
1984-85	Granby	QMJHL	30	30	27	57	31	....	....	....	....	....	....	....	....	....	....	....	....	....	....	....	....	....	....	....
	Chicoutimi	QMJHL	27	31	32	63	40	....	....	....	....	....	....	....	....	....	....	....	12	13	13	26	25	....	....	....
	Montreal	NHL	1	0	0	0	0	0	0	0	0	0.0	0	....	....	....	....	....	....	....	....	....	....	....	....	....
	Sherbrooke	AHL	....	....	....	....	....	....	....	....	....	....	....	....	....	....	....	....	9	6	3	9	10	....	....	....
1985-86♦	Montreal	NHL	65	21	16	37	50	5	0	2	112	18.8	1	....	....	....	....	....	16	4	1	5	23	3	0	1
1986-87	Montreal	NHL	57	20	19	39	80	4	0	3	109	18.3	11	....	....	....	....	....	5	3	2	5	0	0	0	1
	Sherbrooke	AHL	12	10	4	14	11	....	....	....	....	....	....	....	....	....	....	....	....	....	....	....	....	....	....	....
1987-88	Montreal	NHL	72	50	28	78	72	16	0	11	263	19.0	12	....	....	....	....	....	8	7	5	12	6	1	0	2
1988-89	Montreal	NHL	68	25	35	60	61	11	0	6	214	11.7	4	....	....	....	....	....	21	6	5	11	14	2	0	3
1989-90	Montreal	NHL	75	51	40	91	46	9	0	8	269	19.0	35	....	....	....	....	....	9	7	3	10	2	1	0	1
1990-91	Montreal	NHL	75	31	30	61	53	9	0	4	221	14.0	0	....	....	....	....	....	13	9	5	14	6	1	0	1
1991-92	New Jersey	NHL	74	29	35	64	25	5	1	6	240	12.1	–1	....	....	....	....	....	7	1	2	3	0	0	0	0
1992-93	New Jersey	NHL	78	38	35	73	44	7	1	7	286	13.3	–1	....	....	....	....	....	5	2	2	4	2	1	0	0
1993-94	New Jersey	NHL	80	36	36	72	16	7	3	9	217	16.6	31	....	....	....	....	....	20	7	5	12	6	3	0	2
1994-95♦	New Jersey	NHL	45	23	16	39	10	1	2	5	133	17.3	8	....	....	....	....	....	19	6	15	21	2	3	1	2
1995-96	New Jersey	NHL	73	20	12	32	30	3	4	3	192	10.4	–8	....	....	....	....	....	....	....	....	....	....	....	....	....
1996-97	Montreal	NHL	63	22	24	46	32	2	0	2	126	17.5	0	....	....	....	....	....	5	0	0	0	0	0	0	0
1997-98	Montreal	NHL	14	5	4	9	5	2	0	0	24	20.8	1	....	....	....	....	....	....	....	....	....	....	....	....	....
	Tampa Bay	NHL	26	9	11	20	36	3	0	2	71	12.7	–7	....	....	....	....	....	....	....	....	....	....	....	....	....
1998-99	Tampa Bay	NHL	64	12	21	33	22	3	2	1	139	8.6	–10	67	31.3	32	11	16:47	....	....	....	....	....	....	....	....
	NHL Totals		930	392	362	754	582	87	13	69	2616	15.0		67	31.3	32	11	16:47	128	52	45	97	61	15	1	13

QMJHL Rookie of the Year (1984) • QMJHL Second All-Star Team (1985)

Played in NHL All-Star Game (1990)

Traded to **New Jersey** by **Montreal** with Tom Chorske for Kirk Muller and Roland Melanson, September 20, 1991. Traded to **Montreal** by **New Jersey** for Lyle Odelein, August 22, 1996. Traded to **Tampa Bay** by **Montreal** with Darcy Tucker and David Wilkie for Patrick Poulin, Mick Vukota and Igor Ulanov, January 15, 1998.

			Regular Season																Playoffs							
Season	Club	League	GP	G	A	Pts	PIM	PP	SH	GW	S	%	+/-	TF	F%	H	SB	Min	GP	G	A	Pts	PIM	PP	SH	GW

RICHTER, Barry   (RIHK-tuhr)   **MTL.**

Defense. Shoots left. 6'2", 200 lbs.   Born, Madison, WI, September 11, 1970. Hartford's 2nd choice, 32nd overall, in 1988 Entry Draft.

Season	Club	League	GP	G	A	Pts	PIM	PP	SH	GW	S	%	+/-	TF	F%	H	SB	Min	GP	G	A	Pts	PIM	PP	SH	GW
1986-87	Culver Academy	H.S.	39	15	30	45	....																			
1987-88	Culver Academy	H.S.	35	24	29	53	18																			
1988-89	Culver Academy	H.S.	19	21	29	50	16																			
1989-90	U. of Wisconsin	WCHA	42	13	23	36	36																			
1990-91	U. of Wisconsin	WCHA	43	15	20	35	42																			
1991-92	U. of Wisconsin	WCHA	39	10	25	35	62																			
1992-93	U. of Wisconsin	WCHA	42	14	32	46	74																			
1993-94	United States	Nat-Team	56	7	16	23	50																			
	United States	Olympics	8	0	3	3	4																			
	Binghamton	AHL	21	0	9	9	12																			
1994-95	Binghamton	AHL	73	15	41	56	54													11	4	5	9	12			
1995-96	**NY Rangers**	**NHL**	4	0	1	1	0	0	0	0	3	0.0	2													
	Binghamton	AHL	69	20	61	81	64												3	0	3	3	0			
1996-97	**Boston**	**NHL**	50	5	13	18	32	1	0	0	79	6.3	-7													
	Providence	AHL	19	2	6	8	4												10	4	4	8	4			
1997-98	Providence	AHL	75	16	29	45	47																			
1998-99	**NY Islanders**	**NHL**	72	6	18	24	34	0	0	2	111	5.4	-4	0	0.0	52	49	21:08								
	NHL Totals		126	11	32	43	66	1	0	2	193	5.7		0	0.0	52	49	21:08								

NCAA Championship All-Tournament Team (1992) • WCHA First All-Star Team (1993) • NCAA West First All-American Team (1993) • AHL First All-Star Team (1996) • Won Eddie Shore Award (Outstanding Defenseman — AHL) (1996)

Traded to **NY Rangers** by Hartford with Steve Larmer, Nick Kypreos and Hartford's 6th round choice (Yuri Litvinov) in 1994 Entry Draft for Darren Turcotte and James Patrick, November 2, 1993. Signed as a free agent by **Boston**, July 19, 1996. Signed as a free agent by **NY Islanders**, August 17, 1998. Signed as a free agent by **Montreal**, August 20, 1999.

RITCHIE, Byron   **CAR.**

Center. Shoots left. 5'10", 180 lbs.   Born, Burnaby, B.C., April 24, 1977. Hartford's 6th choice, 165th overall, in 1995 Entry Draft.

Season	Club	League	GP	G	A	Pts	PIM	PP	SH	GW	S	%	+/-	TF	F%	H	SB	Min	GP	G	A	Pts	PIM	PP	SH	GW
1992-93	North Delta	BCAHA	60	102	151	253	147																			
1993-94	Lethbridge	WHL	44	4	11	15	44												6	0	0	0	14			
1994-95	Lethbridge	WHL	58	22	28	50	132																			
1995-96	Lethbridge	WHL	66	55	51	106	163												4	0	2	2	4			
	Springfield	AHL	6	2	1	3	4												8	0	3	3	0			
1996-97	Lethbridge	WHL	63	50	76	126	115												18	*16	12	*28	28			
1997-98	New Haven	AHL	65	13	18	31	97																			
1998-99	**Carolina**	**NHL**	3	0	0	0	0	0	0	0	0	0.0	0	5	20.0	1	0	3:25								
	New Haven	AHL	66	24	33	57	139																			
	NHL Totals		3	0	0	0	0	0	0	0	0	0.0		5	20.0	1	0	3:25								

WHL East Second All-Star Team (1996, 1997)

Rights transferred to **Carolina** after **Hartford** franchise relocated, June 25, 1997.

RIVERS, Jamie   **ST.L.**

Defense. Shoots left. 6', 197 lbs.   Born, Ottawa, Ont., March 16, 1975. St. Louis' 2nd choice, 63rd overall, in 1993 Entry Draft.

Season	Club	League	GP	G	A	Pts	PIM	PP	SH	GW	S	%	+/-	TF	F%	H	SB	Min	GP	G	A	Pts	PIM	PP	SH	GW
1989-90	South Ottawa	OMHA	50	26	46	72	46																			
1990-91	Ottawa	OJHL	55	4	30	34	74																			
1991-92	Sudbury	OHL	55	3	13	16	20												8	0	0	0	0			
1992-93	Sudbury	OHL	62	12	43	55	20												14	7	19	26	4			
1993-94	Sudbury	OHL	65	32	*89	121	58												10	1	9	10	14			
1994-95	Sudbury	OHL	46	9	56	65	30												18	7	26	33	22			
1995-96	**St. Louis**	**NHL**	3	0	0	0	2	0	0	0	5	0.0	-1													
	Worcester	AHL	75	7	45	52	130												4	0	1	1	4			
1996-97	**St. Louis**	**NHL**	15	2	5	7	6	1	0	0	9	22.2	-4						5	1	2	3	14			
	Worcester	AHL	63	8	35	43	83																			
1997-98	**St. Louis**	**NHL**	59	2	4	6	36	1	0	1	53	3.8	5													
1998-99	**St. Louis**	**NHL**	76	2	5	7	47	1	0	0	78	2.6	-3	0	0.0	131	63	14:10	9	1	1	2	2	1	0	1
	NHL Totals		153	6	14	20	91	3	0	1	145	4.1		0	0.0	131	63	14:010	9	1	1	2	2	1	0	1

OHL First All-Star Team (1994) • Canadian Major Junior Second All-Star Team (1994) • OHL Second All-Star Team (1995) • AHL Second All-Star Team (1997)

RIVET, Craig   (rih-VAY)   **MTL.**

Defense. Shoots right. 6'2", 197 lbs.   Born, North Bay, Ont., September 13, 1974. Montreal's 4th choice, 68th overall, in 1992 Entry Draft.

Season	Club	League	GP	G	A	Pts	PIM	PP	SH	GW	S	%	+/-	TF	F%	H	SB	Min	GP	G	A	Pts	PIM	PP	SH	GW
1990-91	Barrie	OJHL	42	9	17	26	55																			
1991-92	Kingston	OHL	66	5	21	26	97																			
1992-93	Kingston	OHL	64	19	55	74	117												16	5	7	12	39			
1993-94	Kingston	OHL	61	12	52	64	100												6	0	3	3	6			
	Fredericton	AHL	4	0	2	2	2																			
1994-95	Fredericton	AHL	78	5	27	32	126												12	0	4	4	17			
	Montreal	**NHL**	5	0	1	1	5	0	0	0	2	0.0	2													
1995-96	**Montreal**	**NHL**	19	1	4	5	54	0	0	0	9	11.1	4													
	Fredericton	AHL	49	5	18	23	189												6	0	0	0	12			
1996-97	**Montreal**	**NHL**	35	0	4	4	54	0	0	0	24	0.0	7						5	0	1	1	14	0	0	0
	Fredericton	AHL	23	3	12	15	99																			
1997-98	**Montreal**	**NHL**	61	0	2	2	93	0	0	0	26	0.0	-3						5	0	0	0	2	0	0	0
1998-99	**Montreal**	**NHL**	66	2	8	10	66	0	0	0	39	5.1	-3	0	0.0	78	40	14:20								
	NHL Totals		186	3	19	22	272	0	0	0	100	3.0		0	0.0	78	40	14:20	10	0	1	1	16	0	0	0

ROBERTS, David

Left wing. Shoots left. 6', 185 lbs.   Born, Alameda, CA, May 28, 1970. St. Louis' 5th choice, 114th overall, in 1989 Entry Draft.

Season	Club	League	GP	G	A	Pts	PIM	PP	SH	GW	S	%	+/-	TF	F%	H	SB	Min	GP	G	A	Pts	PIM	PP	SH	GW
1986-87	Avon Old Farms	H.S.	17	6	9	15	....																			
1987-88	Avon Old Farms	H.S.	25	18	39	57	....																			
1988-89	Avon Old Farms	H.S.	25	28	48	76	....																			
1989-90	U. of Michigan	CCHA	42	21	32	53	46																			
1990-91	U. of Michigan	CCHA	43	26	45	71	58																			
1991-92	U. of Michigan	CCHA	44	16	42	58	68																			
1992-93	U. of Michigan	CCHA	40	27	38	65	40																			
1993-94	United States	Nat-Team	49	17	28	45	68																			
	United States	Olympics	8	1	5	6	4																			
	St. Louis	**NHL**	1	0	0	0	2	0	0	0	1	0.0	0						3	0	0	0	12	0	0	0
	Peoria	IHL	10	4	6	10	4																			
1994-95	Peoria	IHL	65	30	38	68	65																			
	St. Louis	**NHL**	19	6	5	11	10	3	0	2	41	14.6	2						6	0	0	0	4	0	0	0
1995-96	**St. Louis**	**NHL**	28	1	6	7	12	1	0	1	35	2.9	-7													
	Worcester	AHL	22	8	17	25	46																			
	Edmonton	NHL	6	2	4	6	6	0	0	0	12	16.7	0													
1996-97	Vancouver	NHL	58	10	17	27	51	1	1	1	74	13.5	11													
1997-98	Vancouver	NHL	13	1	1	2	4	0	0	0	14	7.1	-1													
	Syracuse	AHL	37	17	22	39	44												5	2	1	3	2			

			Regular Season																Playoffs							
Season	Club	League	GP	G	A	Pts	PIM	PP	SH	GW	S	%	+/-	TF	F%	H	SB	Min	GP	G	A	Pts	PIM	PP	SH	GW
1998-99	Michigan	IHL	75	32	38	70	77	....	....	....	....	....	....	....	....	....	....	....	4	1	2	3	2	....	....	....
	NHL Totals		**125**	**20**	**33**	**53**	**85**	**5**	**1**	**4**	**177**	**11.3**		....	....	....	....	....	**9**	**0**	**0**	**0**	**16**	**0**	**0**	**0**

CCHA Second All-Star Team (1991, 1993) • NCAA West Second All-American Team (1991)

Traded to **Edmonton** by **St. Louis** for future considerations, March 12, 1996. Signed as a free agent by **Vancouver**, July 31, 1996. Signed as a free agent by **Dallas**, July 31, 1998.

ROBERTS, Gary — CAR.

Left wing. Shoots left. 6'1", 190 lbs. Born, North York, Ont., May 23, 1966. Calgary's 1st choice, 12th overall, in 1984 Entry Draft.

Season	Club	League	GP	G	A	Pts	PIM	PP	SH	GW	S	%	+/-	TF	F%	H	SB	Min	GP	G	A	Pts	PIM	PP	SH	GW
1981-82	Whitby	OMHA	44	55	31	86	133	....	....	....	....	....	....	....	....	....	....	....	....	....	....	....	....	....	....	....
1982-83	Ottawa	OHL	53	12	8	20	83	....	....	....	....	....	....	....	....	....	....	....	5	1	0	1	19	....	....	....
1983-84	Ottawa	OHL	48	27	30	57	144	....	....	....	....	....	....	....	....	....	....	....	13	10	7	17	62	....	....	....
1984-85	Ottawa	OHL	59	44	62	106	186	....	....	....	....	....	....	....	....	....	....	....	5	2	8	10	10	....	....	....
	Moncton	AHL	7	4	2	6	7	....	....	....	....	....	....	....	....	....	....	....	....	....	....	....	....	....	....	....
1985-86	Ottawa	OHL	24	26	25	51	83	....	....	....	....	....	....	....	....	....	....	....	....	....	....	....	....	....	....	....
	Guelph	OHL	23	18	15	33	65	....	....	....	....	....	....	....	....	....	....	....	20	18	13	31	43	....	....	....
1986-87	**Calgary**	**NHL**	**32**	**5**	**10**	**15**	**85**	**0**	**0**	**0**	**38**	**13.2**	**6**	....	....	....	....	....	**2**	**0**	**0**	**0**	**4**	**0**	**0**	**0**
	Moncton	AHL	38	20	18	38	72	....	....	....	....	....	....	....	....	....	....	....	....	....	....	....	....	....	....	....
1987-88	**Calgary**	**NHL**	**74**	**13**	**15**	**28**	**282**	**0**	**0**	**1**	**118**	**11.0**	**24**	....	....	....	....	....	**9**	**2**	**3**	**5**	**29**	**0**	**0**	**0**
1988-89♦	**Calgary**	**NHL**	**71**	**22**	**16**	**38**	**250**	**0**	**1**	**2**	**123**	**17.9**	**32**	....	....	....	....	....	**22**	**5**	**7**	**12**	**57**	**0**	**0**	**0**
1989-90	**Calgary**	**NHL**	**78**	**39**	**33**	**72**	**222**	**5**	**0**	**5**	**175**	**22.3**	**31**	....	....	....	....	....	**6**	**2**	**5**	**7**	**41**	**0**	**0**	**0**
1990-91	**Calgary**	**NHL**	**80**	**22**	**31**	**53**	**252**	**0**	**0**	**3**	**132**	**16.7**	**15**	....	....	....	....	....	**7**	**1**	**3**	**4**	**18**	**0**	**0**	**0**
1991-92	**Calgary**	**NHL**	**76**	**53**	**37**	**90**	**207**	**15**	**0**	**2**	**196**	**27.0**	**32**	....	....	....	....	....	....	....	....	....	....	....	....	....
1992-93	**Calgary**	**NHL**	**58**	**38**	**41**	**79**	**172**	**8**	**3**	**4**	**166**	**22.9**	**32**	....	....	....	....	....	**5**	**1**	**6**	**7**	**43**	**1**	**0**	**0**
1993-94	**Calgary**	**NHL**	**73**	**41**	**43**	**84**	**145**	**12**	**3**	**5**	**202**	**20.3**	**37**	....	....	....	....	....	**7**	**2**	**6**	**8**	**24**	**1**	**0**	**1**
1994-95	**Calgary**	**NHL**	**8**	**2**	**2**	**4**	**43**	**2**	**0**	**0**	**20**	**10.0**	**1**	....	....	....	....	....	....	....	....	....	....	....	....	....
1995-96	**Calgary**	**NHL**	**35**	**22**	**20**	**42**	**78**	**9**	**0**	**5**	**84**	**26.2**	**15**	....	....	....	....	....	....	....	....	....	....	....	....	....
1996-97			DID NOT PLAY – INJURED																							
1997-98	**Carolina**	**NHL**	**61**	**20**	**29**	**49**	**103**	**4**	**0**	**2**	**106**	**18.9**	**3**	....	....	....	....	....	....	....	....	....	....	....	....	....
1998-99	**Carolina**	**NHL**	**77**	**14**	**28**	**42**	**178**	**1**	**1**	**4**	**138**	**10.1**	**2**	**15**	**46.7**	**260**	**16**	**19:36**	**6**	**1**	**1**	**2**	**8**	**0**	**0**	**0**
	NHL Totals		**723**	**291**	**305**	**596**	**2017**	**56**	**8**	**33**	**1498**	**19.4**		**15**	**46.7**	**260**	**16**	**19:36**	**64**	**14**	**31**	**45**	**224**	**2**	**0**	**1**

OHL Second All-Star Team (1985, 1986) • Won Bill Masterton Memorial Trophy (1996)

Played in NHL All-Star Game (1992, 1993)

• Missed entire 1996-97 season after being placed on voluntary retired list to recover from neck and shoulder injuries, June 17, 1996. Traded to **Carolina** by **Calgary** with Trevor Kidd for Andrew Cassels and Jean-Sebastien Giguere, August 25, 1997.

ROBERTSSON, Bert — (ROH-behrt-suhn)

Defense. Shoots left. 6'3", 205 lbs. Born, Sodertalje, Sweden, June 30, 1974. Vancouver's 8th choice, 254th overall, in 1993 Entry Draft.

Season	Club	League	GP	G	A	Pts	PIM	PP	SH	GW	S	%	+/-	TF	F%	H	SB	Min	GP	G	A	Pts	PIM	PP	SH	GW
1992-93	Sodertalje SK	Sweden-2	23	2	1	3	24	....	....	....	....	....	....	....	....	....	....	....	....	....	....	....	....	....	....	....
1993-94	Sodertalje SK	Sweden-2	28	0	1	1	12	....	....	....	....	....	....	....	....	....	....	....	....	....	....	....	....	....	....	....
1994-95	Sodertalje SK	Sweden-2	23	1	2	3	24	....	....	....	....	....	....	....	....	....	....	....	....	....	....	....	....	....	....	....
1995-96	Syracuse	AHL	65	1	7	8	109	....	....	....	....	....	....	....	....	....	....	....	16	0	1	1	26	....	....	....
1996-97	Syracuse	AHL	80	4	9	13	132	....	....	....	....	....	....	....	....	....	....	....	3	1	0	1	4	....	....	....
1997-98	**Vancouver**	**NHL**	**30**	**2**	**4**	**6**	**24**	**0**	**0**	**0**	**19**	**10.5**	**2**	....	....	....	....	....	....	....	....	....	....	....	....	....
	Syracuse	AHL	42	5	9	14	87	....	....	....	....	....	....	....	....	....	....	....	3	0	0	0	6	....	....	....
1998-99	**Vancouver**	**NHL**	**39**	**2**	**2**	**4**	**13**	**0**	**0**	**0**	**13**	**15.4**	**–7**	**0**	**0.0**	**28**	**6**	**7:26**	....	....	....	....	....	....	....	....
	Syracuse	AHL	8	1	0	1	21	....	....	....	....	....	....	....	....	....	....	....	....	....	....	....	....	....	....	....
	NHL Totals		**69**	**4**	**6**	**10**	**37**	**0**	**0**	**0**	**32**	**12.5**		**0**	**0.0**	**28**	**6**	**7:26**	....	....	....	....	....	....	....	....

ROBITAILLE, Luc — (ROH-buh-tigh) L.A.

Left wing. Shoots left. 6'1", 205 lbs. Born, Montreal, Que., February 17, 1966. Los Angeles' 9th choice, 171st overall, in 1984 Entry Draft.

Season	Club	League	GP	G	A	Pts	PIM	PP	SH	GW	S	%	+/-	TF	F%	H	SB	Min	GP	G	A	Pts	PIM	PP	SH	GW
1982-83	Bourassa	QAAA	48	36	57	93	....	....	....	....	....	....	....	....	....	....	....	....	....	....	....	....	....	....	....	....
1983-84	Hull	QMJHL	70	32	53	85	48	....	....	....	....	....	....	....	....	....	....	....	....	....	....	....	....	....	....	....
1984-85	Hull	QMJHL	64	55	94	149	115	....	....	....	....	....	....	....	....	....	....	....	5	4	2	6	27	....	....	....
1985-86	Hull	QMJHL	63	68	123	191	91	....	....	....	....	....	....	....	....	....	....	....	15	17	27	44	28	....	....	....
1986-87	**Los Angeles**	**NHL**	**79**	**45**	**39**	**84**	**28**	**18**	**0**	**3**	**199**	**22.6**	**–18**	....	....	....	....	....	**5**	**1**	**4**	**5**	**2**	**0**	**0**	**0**
1987-88	**Los Angeles**	**NHL**	**80**	**53**	**58**	**111**	**82**	**17**	**0**	**6**	**220**	**24.1**	**–9**	....	....	....	....	....	**5**	**2**	**5**	**7**	**18**	**2**	**0**	**1**
1988-89	**Los Angeles**	**NHL**	**78**	**46**	**52**	**98**	**65**	**10**	**0**	**4**	**237**	**19.4**	**5**	....	....	....	....	....	**11**	**2**	**6**	**8**	**10**	**0**	**0**	**1**
1989-90	**Los Angeles**	**NHL**	**80**	**52**	**49**	**101**	**38**	**20**	**0**	**7**	**210**	**24.8**	**8**	....	....	....	....	....	**10**	**5**	**5**	**10**	**10**	**1**	**0**	**1**
1990-91	**Los Angeles**	**NHL**	**76**	**45**	**46**	**91**	**68**	**11**	**0**	**5**	**229**	**19.7**	**28**	....	....	....	....	....	**12**	**12**	**4**	**16**	**22**	**5**	**0**	**2**
1991-92	**Los Angeles**	**NHL**	**80**	**44**	**63**	**107**	**95**	**26**	**0**	**6**	**240**	**18.3**	**–4**	....	....	....	....	....	**6**	**3**	**4**	**7**	**12**	**1**	**0**	**1**
1992-93	**Los Angeles**	**NHL**	**84**	**63**	**62**	**125**	**100**	**24**	**2**	**8**	**265**	**23.8**	**18**	....	....	....	....	....	**24**	**9**	**13**	**22**	**28**	**4**	**0**	**2**
1993-94	**Los Angeles**	**NHL**	**83**	**44**	**42**	**86**	**86**	**24**	**0**	**3**	**267**	**16.5**	**–20**	....	....	....	....	....	....	....	....	....	....	....	....	....
1994-95	**Pittsburgh**	**NHL**	**46**	**23**	**19**	**42**	**37**	**5**	**0**	**3**	**109**	**21.1**	**10**	....	....	....	....	....	**12**	**7**	**4**	**11**	**26**	**0**	**0**	**2**
1995-96	**NY Rangers**	**NHL**	**77**	**23**	**46**	**69**	**80**	**11**	**0**	**4**	**223**	**10.3**	**13**	....	....	....	....	....	**11**	**1**	**5**	**6**	**8**	**0**	**0**	**0**
1996-97	**NY Rangers**	**NHL**	**69**	**24**	**24**	**48**	**48**	**5**	**0**	**4**	**200**	**12.0**	**16**	....	....	....	....	....	**15**	**4**	**7**	**11**	**4**	**0**	**0**	**0**
1997-98	**Los Angeles**	**NHL**	**57**	**16**	**24**	**40**	**66**	**5**	**0**	**7**	**130**	**12.3**	**5**	....	....	....	....	....	**4**	**1**	**2**	**3**	**6**	**0**	**0**	**0**
1998-99	**Los Angeles**	**NHL**	**82**	**39**	**35**	**74**	**54**	**11**	**0**	**7**	**292**	**13.4**	**–1**	**7**	**57.1**	**40**	**22**	**19:11**	....	....	....	....	....	....	....	....
	NHL Totals		**971**	**517**	**559**	**1076**	**847**	**187**	**2**	**67**	**2821**	**18.3**		**7**	**57.1**	**40**	**22**	**19:11**	**115**	**47**	**59**	**106**	**146**	**13**	**0**	**10**

QMJHL Second All-Star Team (1985) • QMJHL First All-Star Team (1986) • Canadian Major Junior Player of the Year (1986) • NHL All-Rookie Team (1987) • Won Calder Memorial Trophy (1987) • NHL Second All-Star Team (1987, 1992) • NHL First All-Star Team (1988, 1989, 1990, 1991, 1993)

Played in NHL All-Star Game (1988, 1989, 1990, 1991, 1992, 1993, 1999)

Traded to **Pittsburgh** by **LA Kings** for Rick Tocchet and Pittsburgh's 2nd round choice (Pavel Rosa) in 1995 Entry Draft, July 29, 1994. Traded to **NY Rangers** by **Pittsburgh** with Ulf Samuelsson for Petr Nedved and Sergei Zubov, August 31, 1995. Traded to **LA Kings** by **NY Rangers** for Kevin Stevens, August 28, 1997.

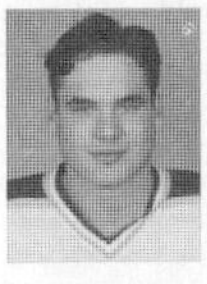

ROBITAILLE, Randy — (ROH-buh-tigh) NSH.

Center. Shoots left. 5'11", 190 lbs. Born, Ottawa, Ont., October 12, 1975.

Season	Club	League	GP	G	A	Pts	PIM	PP	SH	GW	S	%	+/-	TF	F%	H	SB	Min	GP	G	A	Pts	PIM	PP	SH	GW
1994-95	Ottawa	OJHL	54	48	77	125	111	....	....	....	....	....	....	....	....	....	....	....	....	....	....	....	....	....	....	....
1995-96	U. of Miami-Ohio	CCHA	36	14	31	45	26	....	....	....	....	....	....	....	....	....	....	....	....	....	....	....	....	....	....	....
1996-97	U. of Miami-Ohio	CCHA	39	27	34	61	44	....	....	....	....	....	....	....	....	....	....	....	....	....	....	....	....	....	....	....
	Boston	**NHL**	**1**	**0**	**0**	**0**	**0**	**0**	**0**	**0**	**0**	**0.0**	**0**	....	....	....	....	....	....	....	....	....	....	....	....	....
1997-98	**Boston**	**NHL**	**4**	**0**	**0**	**0**	**0**	**0**	**0**	**0**	**5**	**0.0**	**–2**	....	....	....	....	....	....	....	....	....	....	....	....	....
	Providence	AHL	48	15	29	44	16	....	....	....	....	....	....	....	....	....	....	....	....	....	....	....	....	....	....	....
1998-99	**Boston**	**NHL**	**4**	**0**	**2**	**2**	**0**	**0**	**0**	**0**	**5**	**0.0**	**–1**	**24**	**25.0**	**0**	**0**	**10:11**	**1**	**0**	**0**	**0**	**0**	**0**	**0**	**0**
	Providence	AHL	74	28	*74	102	34	....	....	....	....	....	....	....	....	....	....	....	19	6	*14	20	20	....	....	....
	NHL Totals		**9**	**0**	**2**	**2**	**0**	**0**	**0**	**0**	**10**	**0.0**		**24**	**25.0**	**0**	**0**	**10:11**	**1**	**0**	**0**	**0**	**0**	**0**	**0**	**0**

CCHA First All-Star Team (1997) • NCAA West First All-American Team (1997) • AHL First All-Star Team (1999) • Won Les Cunningham Plaque (MVP - AHL) (1999)

Signed as a free agent by **Boston**, March 27, 1997. Traded to **Atlanta** by **Boston** for Peter Ferraro, June 25, 1999. Rights traded to **Nashville** by **Atlanta** for Denny Lambert, August 16, 1999.

ROCHE, Dave — (ROHSH) CGY.

Center. Shoots left. 6'4", 230 lbs. Born, Lindsay, Ont., June 13, 1975. Pittsburgh's 3rd choice, 62nd overall, in 1993 Entry Draft.

Season	Club	League	GP	G	A	Pts	PIM	PP	SH	GW	S	%	+/-	TF	F%	H	SB	Min	GP	G	A	Pts	PIM	PP	SH	GW
1990-91	Peterborough B's	OJHL-B	40	22	17	39	86	....	....	....	....	....	....	....	....	....	....	....	....	....	....	....	....	....	....	....
1991-92	Peterborough	OHL	62	10	17	27	134	....	....	....	....	....	....	....	....	....	....	....	10	0	0	0	34	....	....	....
1992-93	Peterborough	OHL	56	40	60	100	105	....	....	....	....	....	....	....	....	....	....	....	21	14	15	29	42	....	....	....
1993-94	Peterborough	OHL	34	15	22	37	127	....	....	....	....	....	....	....	....	....	....	....	....	....	....	....	....	....	....	....
	Windsor	OHL	29	14	20	34	73	....	....	....	....	....	....	....	....	....	....	....	4	1	1	2	15	....	....	....
1994-95	Windsor	OHL	66	55	59	114	180	....	....	....	....	....	....	....	....	....	....	....	10	9	6	15	16	....	....	....
1995-96	**Pittsburgh**	**NHL**	**71**	**7**	**7**	**14**	**130**	**0**	**0**	**1**	**65**	**10.8**	**–5**	....	....	....	....	....	**16**	**2**	**7**	**9**	**26**	**0**	**0**	**0**

| | | | Regular Season | | | | | | | | | | | | | | | | Playoffs | | | | | | | |
Season	Club	League	GP	G	A	Pts	PIM	PP	SH	GW	S	%	+/-	TF	F%	H	SB	Min	GP	G	A	Pts	PIM	PP	SH	GW
1996-97	Pittsburgh	NHL	61	5	5	10	155	2	0	0	53	9.4	−13	....	....	....	....	....	13	6	3	9	*87	....	....	....
	Cleveland	IHL	18	5	5	10	25	....	....	....	....	....	....						....	....	....	....	....			
1997-98	Syracuse	AHL	73	12	20	32	307	....	....	....	....	....	....						5	2	0	2	10			
1998-99	Calgary	NHL	36	3	3	6	44	1	0	2	30	10.0	−1	0	0.0	35	9	7:15	....	....	....	....	....			
	Saint John	AHL	7	0	3	3	6																			
	NHL Totals		168	15	15	30	329	3	0	3	148	10.1		0	0.0	35	9	7:15	16	2	7	9	26	0	0	0

OHL First All-Star Team (1995)
Traded to **Calgary** by **Pittsburgh** with Ken Wregget for German Titov and Todd Hlushko, June 17, 1998.

ROENICK, Jeremy
(ROH-nihk)   **PHX.**

Center. Shoots right. 6', 192 lbs.   Born, Boston, MA, January 17, 1970. Chicago's 1st choice, 8th overall, in 1988 Entry Draft.

Season	Club	League	GP	G	A	Pts	PIM	PP	SH	GW	S	%	+/-	TF	F%	H	SB	Min	GP	G	A	Pts	PIM	PP	SH	GW
1986-87	Thayer Academy	H.S.	24	31	34	65	....												....	....	....	....	....			
1987-88	Thayer Academy	H.S.	24	34	50	84	....												....	....	....	....	....			
1988-89	Hull	QMJHL	28	34	36	70	14												....	....	....	....	....			
	Chicago	NHL	20	9	9	18	4	2	0	0	52	17.3	4						10	1	3	4	7	1	0	1
1989-90	Chicago	NHL	78	26	40	66	54	6	0	4	173	15.0	2						20	11	7	18	8	4	0	1
1990-91	Chicago	NHL	79	41	53	94	80	15	4	10	194	21.1	38						6	3	5	8	4	1	0	1
1991-92	Chicago	NHL	80	53	50	103	98	22	3	13	234	22.6	23						18	12	10	22	12	4	0	3
1992-93	Chicago	NHL	84	50	57	107	86	22	3	3	255	19.6	15						4	1	2	3	2	0	0	0
1993-94	Chicago	NHL	84	46	61	107	125	24	5	5	281	16.4	21						6	1	6	7	2	0	0	1
1994-95	Kolner Haie	Germany	3	3	1	4	2												....	....	....	....	....			
	Chicago	NHL	33	10	24	34	14	5	0	1	93	10.8	5						8	1	2	3	16	0	0	0
1995-96	Chicago	NHL	66	32	35	67	109	12	4	2	171	18.7	9						10	5	7	12	2	1	0	1
1996-97	Phoenix	NHL	72	29	40	69	115	10	3	7	228	12.7	−7						6	2	4	6	4	0	0	0
1997-98	Phoenix	NHL	79	24	32	56	103	6	1	3	182	13.2	5						6	5	3	8	4	2	2	2
	United States	Olympics	4	0	1	1	6												....	....	....	....	....			
1998-99	Phoenix	NHL	78	24	48	72	130	4	0	3	203	11.8	7	956	47.6	154	30	20:10	1	0	0	0	0	0	0	0
	NHL Totals		753	344	449	793	918	128	23	51	2066	16.7		956	47.6	154	30	20:10	95	42	49	91	61	13	2	10

QMJHL Second All-Star Team (1989)
Played in NHL All-Star Game (1991, 1992, 1993, 1994, 1999)
Traded to **Phoenix** by **Chicago** for Alexei Zhamnov, Craig Mills and Phoenix's 1st round choice (Ty Jones) in 1997 Entry Draft, August 16, 1996.

ROEST, Stacy
(ROHST)   **DET.**

Center. Shoots right. 5'9", 192 lbs.   Born, Lethbridge, Alta., March 15, 1974.

Season	Club	League	GP	G	A	Pts	PIM	PP	SH	GW	S	%	+/-	TF	F%	H	SB	Min	GP	G	A	Pts	PIM	PP	SH	GW
1990-91	Lethbridge	AAHA	34	22	50	72	38												....	....	....	....	....			
	Medicine Hat	WHL	5	1	2	3	0												12	5	5	10	4			
1991-92	Medicine Hat	WHL	72	22	43	65	20												....	....	....	....	....			
1992-93	Medicine Hat	WHL	72	33	73	106	30												10	3	10	13	6			
1993-94	Medicine Hat	WHL	72	48	72	120	48												3	1	0	1	4			
1994-95	Medicine Hat	WHL	69	37	78	115	32												5	2	7	9	2			
	Adirondack	AHL	3	0	0	0	0												....	....	....	....	....			
1995-96	Adirondack	AHL	76	16	39	55	40												3	0	0	0	0			
1996-97	Adirondack	AHL	78	25	41	66	30												4	1	1	2	0			
1997-98	Adirondack	AHL	80	34	58	92	30												3	2	1	3	6			
1998-99	Detroit	NHL	59	4	8	12	14	0	0	1	50	8.0	−7	234	57.3	72	7	8:04	....	....	....	....	....			
	Adirondack	AHL	2	0	1	1	0																			
	NHL Totals		59	4	8	12	14	0	0	1	50	8.0		234	57.3	72	7	8:04	....	....	....	....	....			

WHL East First All-Star Team (1994) • WHL East Second All-Star Team (1995)
Signed as a free agent by **Detroit**, June 9, 1997.

ROHLIN, Leif
(roh-LEEN)

Defense. Shoots left. 6'1", 198 lbs.   Born, Vasteras, Sweden, February 26, 1968. Vancouver's 2nd choice, 33rd overall, in 1988 Entry Draft.

Season	Club	League	GP	G	A	Pts	PIM	PP	SH	GW	S	%	+/-	TF	F%	H	SB	Min	GP	G	A	Pts	PIM	PP	SH	GW
1986-87	Vasteras IK	Sweden-2	27	2	5	7	12												12	0	2	2	8			
1987-88	Vasteras IK	Sweden-2	30	2	15	17	46												7	0	4	4	8			
1988-89	Vasteras IK	Sweden	22	3	7	10	18												....	....	....	....	....			
1989-90	Vasteras IK	Sweden	32	3	6	9	40												2	0	0	0	2			
1990-91	Vasteras IK	Sweden	40	4	10	14	46												4	0	1	1	8			
1991-92	Vasteras IK	Sweden	39	4	6	10	52												....	....	....	....	....			
1992-93	Vasteras IK	Sweden	37	5	7	12	24												2	0	0	0	0			
1993-94	Vasteras IK	Sweden	40	6	14	20	26												4	0	1	1	6			
	Sweden	Olympics	8	0	1	1	10												....	....	....	....	....			
1994-95	Vasteras IK	Sweden	39	15	15	30	46												4	2	0	2	4			
1995-96	Vancouver	NHL	56	6	16	22	32	1	0	0	72	8.3	0						5	0	0	0	0	0	0	0
1996-97	Vancouver	NHL	40	2	8	10	8	0	0	0	37	5.4	4						....	....	....	....	....			
1997-98	Ambri Piotta	Switz.	40	7	29	36	28												14	3	4	7	32			
1998-99	Ambri Piotta	Switz.	45	8	31	39	58												15	4	9	13	18			
	NHL Totals		96	8	24	32	40	1	0	0	109	7.3							5	0	0	0	0	0	0	0

ROHLOFF, Jon
(ROH-lawf)

Defense. Shoots right. 5'11", 221 lbs.   Born, Mankato, MN, October 3, 1969. Boston's 7th choice, 186th overall, in 1988 Entry Draft.

Season	Club	League	GP	G	A	Pts	PIM	PP	SH	GW	S	%	+/-	TF	F%	H	SB	Min	GP	G	A	Pts	PIM	PP	SH	GW
1986-87	Grand Rapids	H.S.	21	12	23	35	16												....	....	....	....	....			
1987-88	Grand Rapids	H.S.	28	10	13	23	....												....	....	....	....	....			
1988-89	U. Minn-Duluth	WCHA	39	1	2	3	44												....	....	....	....	....			
1989-90	U. Minn-Duluth	WCHA	5	0	1	1	6												....	....	....	....	....			
1990-91	U. Minn-Duluth	WCHA	32	6	11	17	38												....	....	....	....	....			
1991-92	U. Minn-Duluth	WCHA	27	9	9	18	48												....	....	....	....	....			
1992-93	U. Minn-Duluth	WCHA	36	15	20	35	87												....	....	....	....	....			
1993-94	Providence	AHL	55	12	23	35	59												....	....	....	....	....			
1994-95	Providence	AHL	4	2	1	3	6												....	....	....	....	....			
	Boston	NHL	34	3	8	11	39	0	0	1	51	5.9	1						5	0	0	0	6	0	0	0
1995-96	Boston	NHL	79	1	12	13	59	1	0	0	106	0.9	−8						5	1	2	3	2	1	0	0
1996-97	Boston	NHL	37	3	5	8	31	1	0	0	69	4.3	−14						....	....	....	....	....			
	Providence	AHL	3	1	1	2	0												....	....	....	....	....			
1997-98	Providence	AHL	58	6	17	23	46												....	....	....	....	....			
1998-99	Kentucky	AHL	12	0	1	1	8												....	....	....	....	....			
	Kansas City	IHL	41	5	13	18	42												3	0	0	0	18			
	NHL Totals		150	7	25	32	129	2	0	1	226	3.1							10	1	2	3	8	1	0	0

WCHA Second All-Star Team (1993)
Signed as a free agent by **San Jose**, July 22, 1998.

ROLSTON, Brian (ROHL-stuhn) N.J.

Center. Shoots left. 6'2", 200 lbs. Born, Flint, MI, February 21, 1973. New Jersey's 2nd choice, 11th overall, in 1991 Entry Draft.

			Regular Season																Playoffs							
Season	Club	League	GP	G	A	Pts	PIM	PP	SH	GW	S	%	+/-	TF	F%	H	SB	Min	GP	G	A	Pts	PIM	PP	SH	GW
1989-90	Detroit	NAJHL	40	36	37	73	57	....	....	....	....	....	....	....	....	....	....	....	....	....	....	....	....	....	....	....
1990-91	Detroit	NAJHL	36	49	46	95	14	....	....	....	....	....	....	....	....	....	....	....	....	....	....	....	....	....	....	....
1991-92	Lake Superior	CCHA	37	14	23	37	14	....	....	....	....	....	....	....	....	....	....	....	....	....	....	....	....	....	....	....
1992-93	Lake Superior	CCHA	39	33	31	64	20	....	....	....	....	....	....	....	....	....	....	....	....	....	....	....	....	....	....	....
1993-94	United States	Nat-Team	41	20	28	48	36	....	....	....	....	....	....	....	....	....	....	....	....	....	....	....	....	....	....	....
	United States	Olympics	8	7	0	7	8	....	....	....	....	....	....	....	....	....	....	....	....	....	....	....	....	....	....	....
	Albany	AHL	17	5	5	10	8	....	....	....	....	....	....	....	....	....	....	....	5	1	2	3	0	....	....	....
1994-95	Albany	AHL	18	9	11	20	10	....	....	....	....	....	....	....	....	....	....	....	....	....	....	....	....	....	....	....
	♦ New Jersey	**NHL**	**40**	**7**	**11**	**18**	**17**	**2**	**0**	**3**	**92**	**7.6**	**5**	....	....	....	....	....	**6**	**2**	**1**	**3**	**4**	**1**	**0**	**0**
1995-96	**New Jersey**	**NHL**	**58**	**13**	**11**	**24**	**8**	**3**	**1**	**4**	**139**	**9.4**	**9**	....	....	....	....	....	....	....	....	....	....	....	....	....
1996-97	**New Jersey**	**NHL**	**81**	**18**	**27**	**45**	**20**	**2**	**2**	**3**	**237**	**7.6**	**6**	....	....	....	....	....	**10**	**4**	**1**	**5**	**6**	**1**	**2**	**0**
1997-98	**New Jersey**	**NHL**	**76**	**16**	**14**	**30**	**16**	**0**	**2**	**1**	**185**	**8.6**	**7**	....	....	....	....	....	**6**	**1**	**0**	**1**	**2**	**0**	**1**	**0**
1998-99	**New Jersey**	**NHL**	**82**	**24**	**33**	**57**	**14**	**5**	**5**	**3**	**210**	**11.4**	**11**	**51**	**45.1**	**70**	**20**	**18:49**	**7**	**1**	**0**	**1**	**2**	**0**	**1**	**0**
	NHL Totals		**337**	**78**	**96**	**174**	**75**	**12**	**10**	**14**	**863**	**9.0**		**51**	**45.1**	**70**	**20**	**18:49**	**29**	**8**	**2**	**10**	**14**	**2**	**4**	**0**

NCAA Championship All-Tournament Team (1992, 1993) • CCHA First All-Star Team (1993) • NCAA West Second All-American Team (1993)

ROMANIUK, Russell (ROH-muh-NUHK)

Left wing. Shoots left. 6', 195 lbs. Born, Winnipeg, Man., June 9, 1970. Winnipeg's 2nd choice, 31st overall, in 1988 Entry Draft.

			Regular Season																Playoffs							
Season	Club	League	GP	G	A	Pts	PIM	PP	SH	GW	S	%	+/-	TF	F%	H	SB	Min	GP	G	A	Pts	PIM	PP	SH	GW
1987-88	St. Boniface	MJHL	38	46	34	80	46	....	....	....	....	....	....	....	....	....	....	....	....	....	....	....	....	....	....	....
1988-89	North Dakota	WCHA	39	17	14	31	32	....	....	....	....	....	....	....	....	....	....	....	....	....	....	....	....	....	....	....
	Canada	Nat-Team	3	1	0	1	0	....	....	....	....	....	....	....	....	....	....	....	....	....	....	....	....	....	....	....
1989-90	North Dakota	WCHA	45	36	15	51	54	....	....	....	....	....	....	....	....	....	....	....	....	....	....	....	....	....	....	....
1990-91	North Dakota	WCHA	39	40	28	68	30	....	....	....	....	....	....	....	....	....	....	....	....	....	....	....	....	....	....	....
1991-92	**Winnipeg**	**NHL**	**27**	**3**	**5**	**8**	**18**	**2**	**0**	**1**	**32**	**9.4**	**2**	....	....	....	....	....	....	....	....	....	....	....	....	....
	Moncton	AHL	45	16	15	31	25	....	....	....	....	....	....	....	....	....	....	....	10	5	4	9	19	....	....	....
1992-93	**Winnipeg**	**NHL**	**28**	**3**	**1**	**4**	**22**	**0**	**0**	**1**	**20**	**15.0**	**0**	....	....	....	....	....	**1**	**0**	**0**	**0**	**0**	**0**	**0**	**0**
	Moncton	AHL	28	18	8	26	40	....	....	....	....	....	....	....	....	....	....	....	5	0	4	4	2	....	....	....
	Fort Wayne	IHL	4	2	0	2	7	....	....	....	....	....	....	....	....	....	....	....	....	....	....	....	....	....	....	....
1993-94	Canada	Nat-Team	34	8	9	17	17	....	....	....	....	....	....	....	....	....	....	....	....	....	....	....	....	....	....	....
	Winnipeg	**NHL**	**24**	**4**	**8**	**12**	**6**	**3**	**0**	**0**	**36**	**11.1**	**–11**	....	....	....	....	....	....	....	....	....	....	....	....	....
	Moncton	AHL	18	16	8	24	24	....	....	....	....	....	....	....	....	....	....	....	17	2	6	8	30	....	....	....
1994-95	**Winnipeg**	**NHL**	**6**	**0**	**0**	**0**	**0**	**0**	**0**	**0**	**3**	**0.0**	**–3**	....	....	....	....	....	....	....	....	....	....	....	....	....
	Springfield	AHL	17	5	7	12	29	....	....	....	....	....	....	....	....	....	....	....	....	....	....	....	....	....	....	....
1995-96	**Philadelphia**	**NHL**	**17**	**3**	**0**	**3**	**17**	**1**	**0**	**0**	**13**	**23.1**	**–2**	....	....	....	....	....	**1**	**0**	**0**	**0**	**0**	**0**	**0**	**0**
	Hershey	AHL	27	19	10	29	43	....	....	....	....	....	....	....	....	....	....	....	....	....	....	....	....	....	....	....
1996-97	Manitoba	IHL	46	14	13	27	43	....	....	....	....	....	....	....	....	....	....	....	....	....	....	....	....	....	....	....
1997-98	Long Beach	IHL	49	16	11	27	37	....	....	....	....	....	....	....	....	....	....	....	....	....	....	....	....	....	....	....
	Manitoba	IHL	5	0	1	1	8	....	....	....	....	....	....	....	....	....	....	....	....	....	....	....	....	....	....	....
	Las Vegas	IHL	22	6	4	10	10	....	....	....	....	....	....	....	....	....	....	....	4	2	2	4	4	....	....	....
1998-99	Las Vegas	IHL	82	43	20	63	91	....	....	....	....	....	....	....	....	....	....	....	....	....	....	....	....	....	....	....
	NHL Totals		**102**	**13**	**14**	**27**	**63**	**6**	**0**	**2**	**104**	**12.5**		....	....	....	....	....	**2**	**0**	**0**	**0**	**0**	**0**	**0**	**0**

WCHA First All-Star Team (1991)

Traded to **Philadelphia** by **Winnipeg** for Jeff Finley, June 27, 1995.

RONNING, Cliff NSH.

Center. Shoots left. 5'8", 167 lbs. Born, Burnaby, B.C., October 1, 1965. St. Louis' 9th choice, 134th overall, in 1984 Entry Draft.

			Regular Season																Playoffs							
Season	Club	League	GP	G	A	Pts	PIM	PP	SH	GW	S	%	+/-	TF	F%	H	SB	Min	GP	G	A	Pts	PIM	PP	SH	GW
1982-83	New Westminster	BCJHL	[illegible]	[illegible]	[illegible]	131	22	....	....	....	....	....	....	....	....	....	....	....	....	....	....	....	....	....	....	....
1983-84	New Westminster	WHL	71	69	67	136	10	....	....	....	....	....	....	....	....	....	....	....	9	8	13	21	10	....	....	....
1984-85	New Westminster	WHL	70	*89	108	*197	20	....	....	....	....	....	....	....	....	....	....	....	11	10	14	24	4	....	....	....
1985-86	Canada	Nat-Team	71	55	63	118	....	....	....	....	....	....	....	....	....	....	....	....	....	....	....	....	....	....	....	....
	St. Louis	**NHL**	....	....	....	....	....	....	**0**	....	....	....	....	....	....	....	....	....	**5**	**1**	**1**	**2**	**2**	**1**	**0**	**0**
1986-87	Canada	Nat-Team	26	17	16	33	12	....	....	....	....	....	....	....	....	....	....	....	....	....	....	....	....	....	....	....
	St. Louis	**NHL**	**42**	**11**	**14**	**25**	**6**	**2**	**0**	**2**	**68**	**16.2**	**–1**	....	....	....	....	....	**4**	**0**	**1**	**1**	**0**	**0**	**0**	**0**
1987-88	**St. Louis**	**NHL**	**26**	**5**	**8**	**13**	**12**	**1**	**0**	**1**	**38**	**13.2**	**6**	....	....	....	....	....	....	....	....	....	....	....	....	....
1988-89	**St. Louis**	**NHL**	**64**	**24**	**31**	**55**	**18**	**16**	**0**	**1**	**150**	**16.0**	**3**	....	....	....	....	....	**7**	**1**	**3**	**4**	**0**	**1**	**0**	**0**
	Peoria	IHL	12	11	20	31	8	....	....	....	....	....	....	....	....	....	....	....	....	....	....	....	....	....	....	....
1989-90	HC Asiago	Italy	36	67	49	116	25	....	....	....	....	....	....	....	....	....	....	....	6	7	12	19	4	....	....	....
1990-91	**St. Louis**	**NHL**	**48**	**14**	**18**	**32**	**10**	**5**	**0**	**2**	**81**	**17.3**	**2**	....	....	....	....	....	....	....	....	....	....	....	....	....
	Vancouver	**NHL**	**11**	**6**	**6**	**12**	**0**	**2**	**0**	**0**	**32**	**18.8**	**–2**	....	....	....	....	....	**6**	**6**	**3**	**9**	**12**	**2**	**0**	**2**
1991-92	**Vancouver**	**NHL**	**80**	**24**	**47**	**71**	**42**	**6**	**0**	**2**	**216**	**11.1**	**18**	....	....	....	....	....	**13**	**8**	**5**	**13**	**6**	**1**	**0**	**1**
1992-93	**Vancouver**	**NHL**	**79**	**29**	**56**	**85**	**30**	**10**	**0**	**2**	**209**	**13.9**	**19**	....	....	....	....	....	**12**	**2**	**9**	**11**	**6**	**0**	**0**	**0**
1993-94	**Vancouver**	**NHL**	**76**	**25**	**43**	**68**	**42**	**10**	**0**	**4**	**197**	**12.7**	**7**	....	....	....	....	....	**24**	**5**	**10**	**15**	**16**	**2**	**0**	**2**
1994-95	**Vancouver**	**NHL**	**41**	**6**	**19**	**25**	**27**	**3**	**0**	**2**	**93**	**6.5**	**–4**	....	....	....	....	....	**11**	**3**	**5**	**8**	**2**	**1**	**0**	**2**
1995-96	**Vancouver**	**NHL**	**79**	**22**	**45**	**67**	**42**	**5**	**0**	**1**	**187**	**11.8**	**16**	....	....	....	....	....	**6**	**0**	**2**	**2**	**6**	**0**	**0**	**0**
1996-97	**Phoenix**	**NHL**	**69**	**19**	**32**	**51**	**26**	**8**	**0**	**2**	**171**	**11.1**	**–9**	....	....	....	....	....	**7**	**0**	**7**	**7**	**12**	**0**	**0**	**0**
1997-98	**Phoenix**	**NHL**	**80**	**11**	**44**	**55**	**36**	**3**	**0**	**0**	**197**	**5.6**	**5**	....	....	....	....	....	**6**	**1**	**3**	**4**	**4**	**0**	**0**	**0**
1998-99	**Phoenix**	**NHL**	**7**	**2**	**5**	**7**	**2**	**2**	**0**	**1**	**18**	**11.1**	**3**	**81**	**51.9**	**0**	**1**	**15:22**	....	....	....	....	....	....	....	....
	Nashville	**NHL**	**72**	**18**	**35**	**53**	**40**	**8**	**0**	**3**	**239**	**7.5**	**–6**	**1129**	**47.7**	**11**	**35**	**19:42**	....	....	....	....	....	....	....	....
	NHL Totals		**774**	**216**	**403**	**619**	**333**	**81**	**0**	**23**	**1896**	**11.4**		**1210**	**48.0**	**11**	**36**	**19:19**	**101**	**27**	**49**	**76**	**66**	**8**	**0**	**7**

WHL First All-Star Team (1985)

Traded to **Vancouver** by **St. Louis** with Geoff Courtnall, Robert Dirk, Sergio Momesso and St. Louis' 5th round choice (Brian Loney) in 1992 Entry Draft for Dan Quinn and Garth Butcher, March 5, 1991. Signed as a free agent by **Phoenix**, July 1, 1996. Traded to **Nashville** by **Phoenix** with Richard Lintner for future considerations, October 31, 1998.

ROSA, Pavel (ROHZA) L.A.

Right wing. Shoots right. 6', 195 lbs. Born, Most, Czech., June 7, 1977. Los Angeles' 3rd choice, 50th overall, in 1995 Entry Draft.

			Regular Season																Playoffs							
Season	Club	League	GP	G	A	Pts	PIM	PP	SH	GW	S	%	+/-	TF	F%	H	SB	Min	GP	G	A	Pts	PIM	PP	SH	GW
1994-95	HC Litvinov	Czech-Jr.	40	56	42	98	....	....	....	....	....	....	....	....	....	....	....	....	....	....	....	....	....	....	....	....
	HC Litvinov	Cze-Rep	2	0	0	0	0	....	....	....	....	....	....	....	....	....	....	....	1	0	0	0	0	....	....	....
1995-96	Hull	QMJHL	61	46	70	116	39	....	....	....	....	....	....	....	....	....	....	....	18	14	22	36	25	....	....	....
1996-97	Hull	QMJHL	68	*63	*90	*153	66	....	....	....	....	....	....	....	....	....	....	....	14	18	13	31	16	....	....	....
1997-98	Fredericton	AHL	1	0	0	0	0	....	....	....	....	....	....	....	....	....	....	....	....	....	....	....	....	....	....	....
	Long Beach	IHL	2	0	1	1	0	....	....	....	....	....	....	....	....	....	....	....	1	1	1	2	0	....	....	....
1998-99	**Los Angeles**	**NHL**	**29**	**4**	**12**	**16**	**6**	**0**	**0**	**0**	**61**	**6.6**	**0**	**0**	**0.0**	**24**	**6**	**13:34**	....	....	....	....	....	....	....	....
	Long Beach	IHL	31	17	13	30	28	....	....	....	....	....	....	....	....	....	....	....	6	1	2	3	0	....	....	....
	NHL Totals		**29**	**4**	**12**	**16**	**6**	**0**	**0**	**0**	**61**	**6.6**		**0**	**0.0**	**24**	**6**	**13:34**	....	....	....	....	....	....	....	....

QMJHL First All-Star Team (1997) • Canadian Major Junior First All-Star Team (1997)

• Missed majority of 1997-98 season recovering from concussion suffered in pre-season game, September, 1997.

ROUSE, Bob (ROWS) S.J.

Defense. Shoots right. 6'2", 215 lbs. Born, Surrey, B.C., June 18, 1964. Minnesota's 3rd choice, 80th overall, in 1982 Entry Draft.

			Regular Season																Playoffs							
Season	Club	League	GP	G	A	Pts	PIM	PP	SH	GW	S	%	+/-	TF	F%	H	SB	Min	GP	G	A	Pts	PIM	PP	SH	GW
1980-81	Billings	WHL	70	0	13	13	116	....	....	....	....	....	....	....	....	....	....	....	5	0	0	0	2	....	....	....
1981-82	Billings	WHL	71	7	22	29	209	....	....	....	....	....	....	....	....	....	....	....	5	0	2	2	10	....	....	....
1982-83	Nanaimo	WHL	29	7	20	27	86	....	....	....	....	....	....	....	....	....	....	....	....	....	....	....	....	....	....	....
	Lethbridge	WHL	42	8	30	38	82	....	....	....	....	....	....	....	....	....	....	....	20	2	13	15	55	....	....	....

Season	Club	League	Regular Season																Playoffs							
Season	Club	League	GP	G	A	Pts	PIM	PP	SH	GW	S	%	+/-	TF	F%	H	SB	Min	GP	G	A	Pts	PIM	PP	SH	GW
1983-84	Lethbridge	WHL	71	18	42	60	101	....	....	....	....	....	....	....	....	....	....	....	5	0	1	1	28	....	....	....
	Minnesota	NHL	1	0	0	0	0	0	0	0	0	0.0	0	....	....	....	....	....	....	....	....	....	....	....	....	....
1984-85	Minnesota	NHL	63	2	9	11	113	0	0	0	80	2.5	−14	....	....	....	....	....	....	....	....	....	....	....	....	....
	Springfield	AHL	8	0	3	3	6	....	....	....	....	....	....	....	....	....	....	....	....	....	....	....	....	....	....	....
1985-86	Minnesota	NHL	75	1	14	15	151	0	0	1	91	1.1	15	....	....	....	....	....	3	0	0	0	0	0	0	0
1986-87	Minnesota	NHL	72	2	10	12	179	0	0	0	71	2.8	6	....	....	....	....	....	....	....	....	....	....	....	....	....
1987-88	Minnesota	NHL	74	0	12	12	168	0	0	0	62	0.0	−30	....	....	....	....	....	....	....	....	....	....	....	....	....
1988-89	Minnesota	NHL	66	4	13	17	124	0	0	1	66	6.1	−5	....	....	....	....	....	....	....	....	....	....	....	....	....
	Washington	NHL	13	0	2	2	36	0	0	0	19	0.0	2	....	....	....	....	....	6	2	0	2	4	0	0	0
1989-90	Washington	NHL	70	4	16	20	123	0	0	2	72	5.6	−2	....	....	....	....	....	15	2	3	5	47	1	0	0
1990-91	Washington	NHL	47	5	15	20	65	1	0	0	50	10.0	−7	....	....	....	....	....	....	....	....	....	....	....	....	....
	Toronto	NHL	13	2	4	6	10	1	0	0	15	13.3	−11	....	....	....	....	....	....	....	....	....	....	....	....	....
1991-92	Toronto	NHL	79	3	19	22	97	1	0	0	115	2.6	−20	....	....	....	....	....	....	....	....	....	....	....	....	....
1992-93	Toronto	NHL	82	3	11	14	130	0	1	1	78	3.8	7	....	....	....	....	....	21	3	8	11	29	1	0	1
1993-94	Toronto	NHL	63	5	11	16	101	1	1	0	77	6.5	8	....	....	....	....	....	18	0	3	3	29	0	0	0
1994-95	Detroit	NHL	48	1	7	8	36	0	0	1	51	2.0	14	....	....	....	....	....	18	0	3	3	8	0	0	0
1995-96	Detroit	NHL	58	0	6	6	48	0	0	0	49	0.0	5	....	....	....	....	....	7	0	1	1	4	0	0	0
1996-97♦	Detroit	NHL	70	4	9	13	58	0	2	0	70	5.7	8	....	....	....	....	....	20	0	0	0	55	0	0	0
1997-98♦	Detroit	NHL	71	1	11	12	57	0	0	0	54	1.9	−9	....	....	....	....	....	22	0	3	3	16	0	0	0
1998-99	San Jose	NHL	70	0	11	11	44	0	0	0	75	0.0	0	0	0.0	73	68	16:57	6	0	0	0	6	0	0	0
	NHL Totals		1035	37	180	217	1540	4	4	6	1095	3.4		0	0.0	73	68	16:57	136	7	21	28	198	2	0	1

WHL East First All-Star Team (1984)

Traded to **Washington** by **Minnesota** with Dino Ciccarelli for Mike Gartner and Larry Murphy, March 7, 1989. Traded to **Toronto** by **Washington** with Peter Zezel for Al Iafrate, January 16, 1991. Signed as a free agent by **Detroit**, August 5, 1994. Signed as a free agent by **San Jose**, June 14, 1998.

ROY, Andre (WAH, AHN-dray) OTT.

Left wing. Shoots left. 6'3", 202 lbs. Born, Port Chester, NY, February 8, 1975. Boston's 5th choice, 151st overall, in 1994 Entry Draft.

Season	Club	League	GP	G	A	Pts	PIM	PP	SH	GW	S	%	+/-	TF	F%	H	SB	Min	GP	G	A	Pts	PIM	PP	SH	GW
1993-94	Beauport	QMJHL	33	6	7	13	125	....	....	....	....	....	....	....	....	....	....	....	....	....	....	....	....	....	....	....
	Chicoutimi	QMJHL	32	4	14	18	152	....	....	....	....	....	....	....	....	....	....	....	25	3	6	9	94	....	....	....
1994-95	Chicoutimi	QMJHL	20	15	8	23	90	....	....	....	....	....	....	....	....	....	....	....	....	....	....	....	....	....	....	....
	Drummondville	QMJHL	34	18	13	31	233	....	....	....	....	....	....	....	....	....	....	....	4	2	0	2	34	....	....	....
1995-96	Boston	NHL	3	0	0	0	0	0	0	0	0	0.0	0	....	....	....	....	....	....	....	....	....	....	....	....	....
	Providence	AHL	58	7	8	15	167	....	....	....	....	....	....	....	....	....	....	....	1	0	0	0	10	....	....	....
1996-97	Boston	NHL	10	0	2	2	12	0	0	0	12	0.0	−5	....	....	....	....	....	....	....	....	....	....	....	....	....
	Providence	AHL	50	17	11	28	234	....	....	....	....	....	....	....	....	....	....	....	....	....	....	....	....	....	....	....
1997-98	Providence	AHL	36	3	11	14	154	....	....	....	....	....	....	....	....	....	....	....	....	....	....	....	....	....	....	....
	Charlotte	ECHL	27	10	8	18	132	....	....	....	....	....	....	....	....	....	....	....	7	2	3	5	34	....	....	....
1998-99	Fort Wayne	IHL	65	15	6	21	*395	....	....	....	....	....	....	....	....	....	....	....	2	0	0	0	11	....	....	....
	NHL Totals		13	0	2	2	12	0	0	0	12	0.0		....	....	....	....	....	....	....	....	....	....	....	....	....

Signed as a free agent by **Ottawa**, April 28, 1999.

ROY, Jean-Yves (WAH)

Right wing. Shoots left. 5'10", 180 lbs. Born, Rosemere, Que., February 17, 1969.

Season	Club	League	GP	G	A	Pts	PIM	PP	SH	GW	S	%	+/-	TF	F%	H	SB	Min	GP	G	A	Pts	PIM	PP	SH	GW
1989-90	U. of Maine	H.E.	46	*39	26	65	52	....	....	....	....	....	....	....	....	....	....	....	....	....	....	....	....	....	....	....
1990-91	U. of Maine	H.E.	43	37	45	82	62	....	....	....	....	....	....	....	....	....	....	....	....	....	....	....	....	....	....	....
1991-92	U. of Maine	H.E.	35	32	24	56	62	....	....	....	....	....	....	....	....	....	....	....	....	....	....	....	....	....	....	....
	Canada	Nat-Team	13	10	4	14	6	....	....	....	....	....	....	....	....	....	....	....	....	....	....	....	....	....	....	....
1992-93	Canada	Nat-Team	23	9	6	15	35	....	....	....	....	....	....	....	....	....	....	....	....	....	....	....	....	....	....	....
	Binghamton	AHL	49	13	15	28	21	....	....	....	....	....	....	....	....	....	....	....	14	5	2	7	4	....	....	....
1993-94	Binghamton	AHL	65	41	24	65	33	....	....	....	....	....	....	....	....	....	....	....	....	....	....	....	....	....	....	....
	Canada	Nat-Team	6	3	2	5	2	....	....	....	....	....	....	....	....	....	....	....	....	....	....	....	....	....	....	....
	Canada	Olympics	8	1	0	1	0	....	....	....	....	....	....	....	....	....	....	....	....	....	....	....	....	....	....	....
1994-95	Binghamton	AHL	67	41	36	77	28	....	....	....	....	....	....	....	....	....	....	....	11	4	6	10	12	....	....	....
	NY Rangers	NHL	3	1	0	1	2	0	0	0	8	12.5	−1	....	....	....	....	....	....	....	....	....	....	....	....	....
1995-96	Ottawa	NHL	4	1	1	2	2	0	0	0	6	16.7	3	....	....	....	....	....	....	....	....	....	....	....	....	....
	P.E.I. Senators	AHL	67	40	55	95	64	....	....	....	....	....	....	....	....	....	....	....	5	4	8	12	6	....	....	....
1996-97	Boston	NHL	52	10	15	25	22	2	0	1	100	10.0	−8	....	....	....	....	....	....	....	....	....	....	....	....	....
	Providence	AHL	27	9	16	25	30	....	....	....	....	....	....	....	....	....	....	....	10	2	7	9	2	....	....	....
1997-98	Boston	NHL	2	0	0	0	0	0	0	0	1	0.0	0	....	....	....	....	....	....	....	....	....	....	....	....	....
	Providence	AHL	65	28	34	62	60	....	....	....	....	....	....	....	....	....	....	....	....	....	....	....	....	....	....	....
1998-99	VSV Villach	Alpenliga	30	26	32	58	26	....	....	....	....	....	....	....	....	....	....	....	....	....	....	....	....	....	....	....
	VSV Villach	Austria	6	1	3	4	6	....	....	....	....	....	....	....	....	....	....	....	....	....	....	....	....	....	....	....
	Canada	Nat-Team	5	4	3	7	6	....	....	....	....	....	....	....	....	....	....	....	....	....	....	....	....	....	....	....
	NHL Totals		61	12	16	28	26	2	0	1	115	10.4		....	....	....	....	....	....	....	....	....	....	....	....	....

NCAA East Second All-American Team (1990) • Hockey East First All-Star Team (1991) • NCAA East First All-American Team (1991, 1992) • NCAA Championship All-Tournament Team (1991) • Hockey East Second All-Star Team (1992)

Signed as a free agent by **NY Rangers**, July 20, 1992. Traded to **Ottawa** by **NY Rangers** for Steve Larouche, October 5, 1995. Signed as a free agent by **Boston**, July 15, 1996.

ROYER, Remi (ROHY-uhr) CHI.

Defense. Shoots right. 6'2", 200 lbs. Born, Donnacona, Que., February 12, 1978. Chicago's 1st choice, 31st overall, in 1996 Entry Draft.

Season	Club	League	GP	G	A	Pts	PIM	PP	SH	GW	S	%	+/-	TF	F%	H	SB	Min	GP	G	A	Pts	PIM	PP	SH	GW
1994-95	Victoriaville	QMJHL	57	3	17	20	144	....	....	....	....	....	....	....	....	....	....	....	4	0	1	1	7	....	....	....
1995-96	Victoriaville	QMJHL	43	12	14	26	209	....	....	....	....	....	....	....	....	....	....	....	....	....	....	....	....	....	....	....
	St-Hyacinthe	QMJHL	19	10	9	19	80	....	....	....	....	....	....	....	....	....	....	....	12	1	4	5	29	....	....	....
1996-97	Rouyn-Noranda	QMJHL	29	3	12	15	85	....	....	....	....	....	....	....	....	....	....	....	....	....	....	....	....	....	....	....
	Indianapolis	IHL	10	0	1	1	17	....	....	....	....	....	....	....	....	....	....	....	....	....	....	....	....	....	....	....
1997-98	Rouyn-Noranda	QMJHL	66	20	48	68	205	....	....	....	....	....	....	....	....	....	....	....	6	1	3	4	8	....	....	....
	Indianapolis	IHL	5	0	2	2	4	....	....	....	....	....	....	....	....	....	....	....	5	1	2	3	12	....	....	....
1998-99	Chicago	NHL	18	0	0	0	67	0	0	0	24	0.0	−10	0	0.0	25	11	13:37	....	....	....	....	....	....	....	....
	Indianapolis	IHL	54	4	15	19	164	....	....	....	....	....	....	....	....	....	....	....	7	0	0	0	44	....	....	....
	Portland	AHL	2	0	1	1	2	....	....	....	....	....	....	....	....	....	....	....	....	....	....	....	....	....	....	....
	NHL Totals		18	0	0	0	67	0	0	0	24	0.0		0	0.0	25	11	13:37	....	....	....	....	....	....	....	....

QMJHL First All-Star Team (1998)

RUCCHIN, Steve (ROO-chihn) ANA.

Center. Shoots left. 6'3", 215 lbs. Born, Thunder Bay, Ont., July 4, 1971. Anaheim's 1st choice, 2nd overall, in 1994 Supplemental Draft.

Season	Club	League	GP	G	A	Pts	PIM	PP	SH	GW	S	%	+/-	TF	F%	H	SB	Min	GP	G	A	Pts	PIM	PP	SH	GW
1990-91	Western Ontario	OUAA	34	13	16	29	14	....	....	....	....	....	....	....	....	....	....	....	....	....	....	....	....	....	....	....
1991-92	Western Ontario	OUAA	37	28	34	62	36	....	....	....	....	....	....	....	....	....	....	....	....	....	....	....	....	....	....	....
1992-93	Western Ontario	OUAA	34	22	26	48	16	....	....	....	....	....	....	....	....	....	....	....	....	....	....	....	....	....	....	....
1993-94	Western Ontario	OUAA	35	30	23	53	30	....	....	....	....	....	....	....	....	....	....	....	....	....	....	....	....	....	....	....
1994-95	San Diego	IHL	41	11	15	26	14	....	....	....	....	....	....	....	....	....	....	....	....	....	....	....	....	....	....	....
	Anaheim	NHL	43	6	11	17	23	0	0	1	59	10.2	7	....	....	....	....	....	....	....	....	....	....	....	....	....
1995-96	Anaheim	NHL	64	19	25	44	12	8	1	4	113	16.8	3	....	....	....	....	....	....	....	....	....	....	....	....	....
1996-97	Anaheim	NHL	79	19	48	67	24	6	1	2	153	12.4	26	....	....	....	....	....	8	1	2	3	10	0	0	0
1997-98	Anaheim	NHL	72	17	36	53	13	8	1	3	131	13.0	8	....	....	....	....	....	....	....	....	....	....	....	....	....
1998-99	Anaheim	NHL	69	23	39	62	22	5	1	5	145	15.9	11	1845	52.3	43	72	22:33	4	0	3	3	0	0	0	0
	NHL Totals		327	84	159	243	94	27	4	15	601	14.0		1845	52.3	43	72	22:33	12	1	5	6	10	0	0	0

RUCINSKI, Mike

(roo-SIHN-skee)

Defense. Shoots left. 5'11", 179 lbs. Born, Trenton, MI, March 30, 1975. Hartford's 8th choice, 217th overall, in 1995 Entry Draft.

			Regular Season																Playoffs							
Season	Club	League	GP	G	A	Pts	PIM	PP	SH	GW	S	%	+/-	TF	F%	H	SB	Min	GP	G	A	Pts	PIM	PP	SH	GW
1991-92	Detroit	MNHL	29	4	15	19	38																			
1992-93	Detroit	OHL	66	6	13	19	59												15	0	4	4	12			
1993-94	Detroit	OHL	66	2	26	28	58												17	0	7	7	15			
1994-95	Detroit	OHL	64	9	18	27	61												21	3	3	6	8			
1995-96	Detroit	OHL	51	10	26	36	65												11	2	4	6	14			
1996-97	Richmond	ECHL	61	20	23	43	85												8	2	6	8	18			
	Springfield	AHL	6	0	1	1	0																			
1997-98	**Carolina**	**NHL**	**9**	**0**	**1**	**1**	**2**	**0**	**0**	**0**	**3**	**0.0**	**0**													
	New Haven	AHL	65	5	17	22	50												1	0	0	0	0			
	Cleveland	IHL	2	0	0	0	4																			
1998-99	**Carolina**	**NHL**	**15**	**0**	**1**	**1**	**8**	**0**	**0**	**0**	**8**	**0.0**	**1**	**0**	**0.0**	**8**	**4**	**10:29**								
	New Haven	AHL	23	2	6	8	27																			
	NHL Totals		**24**	**0**	**2**	**2**	**10**	**0**	**0**	**0**	**11**	**0.0**		**0**	**0.0**	**8**	**4**	**10:29**								

• Rights transferred to **Carolina** after **Hartford** franchise relocated, June 25, 1997.

RUCINSKY, Martin

(roo-SHIHN-skee) **MTL.**

Left wing. Shoots left. 6'1", 205 lbs. Born, Most, Czech., March 11, 1971. Edmonton's 2nd choice, 20th overall, in 1991 Entry Draft.

			Regular Season																Playoffs							
Season	Club	League	GP	G	A	Pts	PIM	PP	SH	GW	S	%	+/-	TF	F%	H	SB	Min	GP	G	A	Pts	PIM	PP	SH	GW
1988-89	CHZ Litvinov	Czech.	3	1	0	1	2																			
1989-90	CHZ Litvinov	Czech.	39	12	6	18													8	5	3	8				
1990-91	CHZ Litvinov	Czech.	56	24	20	44	69																			
1991-92	**Edmonton**	**NHL**	**2**	**0**	**0**	**0**	**0**	**0**	**0**	**0**	**1**	**0.0**	**–3**													
	Cape Breton	AHL	35	11	12	23	34																			
	Quebec	**NHL**	**4**	**1**	**1**	**2**	**2**	**0**	**0**	**0**	**4**	**25.0**	**1**													
	Halifax	AHL	7	1	1	2	6																			
1992-93	**Quebec**	**NHL**	**77**	**18**	**30**	**48**	**51**	**4**	**0**	**1**	**133**	**13.5**	**16**						**6**	**1**	**1**	**2**	**4**	**1**	**0**	**0**
1993-94	**Quebec**	**NHL**	**60**	**9**	**23**	**32**	**58**	**4**	**0**	**1**	**96**	**9.4**	**4**													
1994-95	CHZ Litvinov	Cze-Rep	13	12	10	22	54																			
	Quebec	**NHL**	**20**	**3**	**6**	**9**	**14**	**0**	**0**	**0**	**32**	**9.4**	**5**													
1995-96	HC Vsetin	Cze-Rep	1	1	1	2	0																			
	Colorado	**NHL**	**22**	**4**	**11**	**15**	**14**	**0**	**0**	**1**	**39**	**10.3**	**10**													
	Montreal	**NHL**	**56**	**25**	**35**	**60**	**54**	**9**	**2**	**3**	**142**	**17.6**	**8**													
1996-97	**Montreal**	**NHL**	**70**	**28**	**27**	**55**	**62**	**6**	**3**	**3**	**172**	**16.3**	**1**						**5**	**0**	**0**	**0**	**4**	**0**	**0**	**0**
1997-98	**Montreal**	**NHL**	**78**	**21**	**32**	**53**	**84**	**5**	**3**	**3**	**192**	**10.9**	**13**						**10**	**3**	**0**	**3**	**4**	**1**	**0**	**0**
	Czech Republic	Olympics	6	3	1	4	4																			
1998-99	CHZ Litvinov	Cze-Rep	3	2	2	4	0																			
	Montreal	**NHL**	**73**	**17**	**17**	**34**	**50**	**5**	**0**	**1**	**180**	**9.4**	**–25**	**12**	**50.0**	**75**	**18**	**18:12**								
	NHL Totals		**462**	**126**	**182**	**308**	**389**	**33**	**8**	**13**	**991**	**12.7**		**12**	**50.0**	**75**	**18**	**18:12**	**21**	**4**	**1**	**5**	**12**	**2**	**0**	**0**

Traded to **Quebec** by **Edmonton** for Ron Tugnutt and Brad Zavisha, March 10, 1992. Transferred to **Colorado** after **Quebec** franchise relocated, June 21, 1995. Traded to **Montreal** by **Colorado** with Andrei Kovalenko and Jocelyn Thibault for Patrick Roy and Mike Keane, December 6, 1995.

RUFF, Jason

Left wing. Shoots left. 6'2", 192 lbs. Born, Kelowna, B.C., January 27, 1970. St Louis' 3rd choice, 96th overall, in 1990 Entry Draft.

			Regular Season																Playoffs							
Season	Club	League	GP	G	A	Pts	PIM	PP	SH	GW	S	%	+/-	TF	F%	H	SB	Min	GP	G	A	Pts	PIM	PP	SH	GW
1986-87	Kelowna	BCJHL	45	16	14	30	48																			
1987-88	Lethbridge	WHL	69	25	22	47	109																			
1988-89	Lethbridge	WHL	69	42	38	80	127																			
1989-90	Lethbridge	WHL	72	55	64	119	114												19	9	10	19	18			
1990-91	Lethbridge	WHL	66	61	75	136	154												16	12	17	29	18			
	Peoria	IHL																	5	0	0	0	2			
1991-92	Peoria	IHL	67	27	45	72	148												10	7	7	14	19			
1992-93	**St. Louis**	**NHL**	**7**	**2**	**1**	**3**	**8**	**1**	**0**	**1**	**7**	**28.6**	**–1**													
	Peoria	IHL	40	22	21	43	81																			
	Tampa Bay	**NHL**	**1**	**0**	**0**	**0**	**0**	**0**	**0**	**0**	**1**	**0.0**	**0**													
	Atlanta	IHL	26	11	14	25	90												7	2	1	3	26			
1993-94	**Tampa Bay**	**NHL**	**6**	**1**	**2**	**3**	**2**	**0**	**0**	**0**	**14**	**7.1**	**2**													
	Atlanta	IHL	71	24	25	49	122												14	6	*17	23	41			
1994-95	Atlanta	IHL	64	42	34	76	161												3	3	1	4	10			
1995-96	Atlanta	IHL	59	39	33	72	135												2	0	0	0	16			
1996-97	Quebec	IHL	80	35	50	85	93												9	8	5	13	10			
1997-98	Quebec	IHL	54	21	24	45	77																			
	Cleveland	IHL	6	2	3	5	9												10	6	6	12	4			
1998-99	Cleveland	IHL	44	13	27	40	57																			
	Houston	IHL	1	0	0	0	0												19	5	5	10	12			
	NHL Totals		**14**	**3**	**3**	**6**	**10**	**1**	**0**	**1**	**22**	**13.6**														

WHL East First All-Star Team (1991)

Traded to **Tampa Bay** by **St. Louis** with future considerations for Doug Crossman, Basil McRae and Tampa Bay's 4th round choice (Andrei Petrakov) in 1996 Entry Draft, January 28, 1993.

RUMBLE, Darren

Defense. Shoots left. 6'1", 200 lbs. Born, Barrie, Ont., January 23, 1969. Philadelphia's 1st choice, 20th overall, in 1987 Entry Draft.

			Regular Season																Playoffs							
Season	Club	League	GP	G	A	Pts	PIM	PP	SH	GW	S	%	+/-	TF	F%	H	SB	Min	GP	G	A	Pts	PIM	PP	SH	GW
1985-86	Barrie	OJHL	46	14	32	46	91																			
1986-87	Kitchener	OHL	64	11	32	43	44												4	0	1	1	9			
1987-88	Kitchener	OHL	55	15	50	65	64																			
1988-89	Kitchener	OHL	46	11	28	39	25												5	1	0	1	2			
1989-90	Hershey	AHL	57	2	13	15	31																			
1990-91	**Philadelphia**	**NHL**	**3**	**1**	**0**	**1**	**0**	**0**	**0**	**0**	**2**	**50.0**	**1**													
	Hershey	AHL	73	6	35	41	48												3	0	5	5	2			
1991-92	Hershey	AHL	79	12	54	66	118												6	0	3	3	2			
1992-93	**Ottawa**	**NHL**	**69**	**3**	**13**	**16**	**61**	**0**	**0**	**0**	**92**	**3.3**	**–24**													
	New Haven	AHL	2	1	0	1	0																			
1993-94	**Ottawa**	**NHL**	**70**	**6**	**9**	**15**	**116**	**0**	**0**	**0**	**95**	**6.3**	**–50**													
	P.E.I. Senators	AHL	3	2	0	2	0																			
1994-95	P.E.I. Senators	AHL	70	7	46	53	77												11	0	6	6	4			
1995-96	**Philadelphia**	**NHL**	**5**	**0**	**0**	**0**	**4**	**0**	**0**	**0**	**7**	**0.0**	**0**													
	Hershey	AHL	58	13	37	50	83												5	0	0	0	6			
1996-97	**Philadelphia**	**NHL**	**10**	**0**	**0**	**0**	**0**	**0**	**0**	**0**	**9**	**0.0**	**–2**													
	Philadelphia	AHL	72	18	44	62	83												7	0	3	3	19			
1997-98	Mannheim	Germany	21	2	7	9	18																			
	Mannheim	EuroHL	4	0	1	1	4																			
	San Antonio	IHL	46	7	22	29	47																			
1998-99	Grand Rapids	IHL	53	6	22	28	44																			
	Utah	IHL	10	1	4	5	10																			
	NHL Totals		**157**	**10**	**22**	**32**	**181**	**0**	**0**	**0**	**205**	**4.9**														

AHL Second All-Star Team (1995) • AHL First All-Star Team (1997) • Won Eddie Shore Award (Outstanding Defenseman — AHL) (1997)

Claimed by **Ottawa** from **Philadelphia** in Expansion Draft, June 18, 1992. Signed as a free agent by **Philadelphia**, July 31, 1995.

RUSSELL, Cam

Defense. Shoots left. 6'4", 200 lbs. Born, Halifax, N.S., January 12, 1969. Chicago's 3rd choice, 50th overall, in 1987 Entry Draft.

			Regular Season																Playoffs							
Season	Club	League	GP	G	A	Pts	PIM	PP	SH	GW	S	%	+/-	TF	F%	H	SB	Min	GP	G	A	Pts	PIM	PP	SH	GW
1985-86	Hull	QMJHL	56	3	4	7	24	....	....	....	....	....	....	....	....	....	....	....	15	0	2	2	4	....	....	....
1986-87	Hull	QMJHL	66	3	16	19	119	....	....	....	....	....	....	....	....	....	....	....	8	0	1	1	16	....	....	....
1987-88	Hull	QMJHL	53	9	18	27	141	....	....	....	....	....	....	....	....	....	....	....	19	2	5	7	39	....	....	....
1988-89	Hull	QMJHL	66	8	32	40	109	....	....	....	....	....	....	....	....	....	....	....	9	2	6	8	6	....	....	....
1989-90	**Chicago**	**NHL**	**19**	**0**	**1**	**1**	**27**	**0**	**0**	**0**	**10**	**0.0**	**–3**	....	....	....	....	....	**1**	**0**	**0**	**0**	**0**	**0**	**0**	**0**
	Indianapolis	IHL	46	3	15	18	114	....	....	....	....	....	....	....	....	....	....	....	9	0	1	1	24	....	....	....
1990-91	**Chicago**	**NHL**	**3**	**0**	**0**	**0**	**5**	**0**	**0**	**0**	**0**	**0.0**	**1**	....	....	....	....	....	**1**	**0**	**0**	**0**	**0**	**0**	**0**	**0**
	Indianapolis	IHL	53	5	9	14	125	....	....	....	....	....	....	....	....	....	....	....	6	0	2	2	30	....	....	....
1991-92	**Chicago**	**NHL**	**19**	**0**	**0**	**0**	**34**	**0**	**0**	**0**	**9**	**0.0**	**–8**	....	....	....	....	....	**12**	**0**	**2**	**2**	**2**	**0**	**0**	**0**
	Indianapolis	IHL	41	4	9	13	78	....	....	....	....	....	....	....	....	....	....	....	....	....	....	....	....	....	....	....
1992-93	**Chicago**	**NHL**	**67**	**2**	**4**	**6**	**151**	**0**	**0**	**0**	**49**	**4.1**	**5**	....	....	....	....	....	**4**	**0**	**0**	**0**	**0**	**0**	**0**	**0**
1993-94	**Chicago**	**NHL**	**67**	**1**	**7**	**8**	**200**	**0**	**0**	**0**	**41**	**2.4**	**10**	....	....	....	....	....	....	....	....	....	....	....	....	....
1994-95	**Chicago**	**NHL**	**33**	**1**	**3**	**4**	**88**	**0**	**0**	**0**	**18**	**5.6**	**4**	....	....	....	....	....	**16**	**0**	**3**	**3**	**8**	**0**	**0**	**0**
1995-96	**Chicago**	**NHL**	**61**	**2**	**2**	**4**	**129**	**0**	**0**	**0**	**22**	**9.1**	**8**	....	....	....	....	....	**6**	**0**	**0**	**0**	**2**	**0**	**0**	**0**
1996-97	**Chicago**	**NHL**	**44**	**1**	**1**	**2**	**65**	**0**	**0**	**0**	**19**	**5.3**	**–8**	....	....	....	....	....	**4**	**0**	**0**	**0**	**4**	**0**	**0**	**0**
1997-98	**Chicago**	**NHL**	**41**	**1**	**1**	**2**	**79**	**0**	**0**	**1**	**18**	**5.6**	**3**	....	....	....	....	....	....	....	....	....	....	....	....	....
1998-99	**Chicago**	**NHL**	**7**	**0**	**0**	**0**	**10**	**0**	**0**	**0**	**1**	**0.0**	**1**	**0**	**0.0**	**7**	**0**	**5:58**	....	....	....	....	....	....	....	....
	Colorado	**NHL**	**35**	**1**	**2**	**3**	**84**	**0**	**0**	**0**	**14**	**7.1**	**–5**	**0**	**0.0**	**44**	**32**	**12:30**	....	....	....	....	....	....	....	....
	NHL Totals		**396**	**9**	**21**	**30**	**872**	**0**	**0**	**1**	**201**	**4.5**		**0**	**0.0**	**51**	**32**	**11:25**	**44**	**0**	**5**	**5**	**16**	**0**	**0**	**0**

Traded to **Colorado** by **Chicago** for Roman Vopat and Los Angeles' 6th round choice (previously acquired, later traded to Ottawa, Ottawa selected Martin Brusek) in 1999 Entry Draft, November 10, 1998.

RYAN, Terry — MTL.

Left wing. Shoots left. 6'1", 202 lbs. Born, St. John's, Nfld., January 14, 1977. Montreal's 1st choice, 8th overall, in 1995 Entry Draft.

			Regular Season																Playoffs							
Season	Club	League	GP	G	A	Pts	PIM	PP	SH	GW	S	%	+/-	TF	F%	H	SB	Min	GP	G	A	Pts	PIM	PP	SH	GW
1991-92	Quesnel	RMJHL	49	26	41	67	217	....	....	....	....	....	....	....	....	....	....	....	....	....	....	....	....	....	....	....
1992-93	Quesnel	RMJHL	29	31	25	56	222	....	....	....	....	....	....	....	....	....	....	....	....	....	....	....	....	....	....	....
	Vernon	BCJHL	9	5	6	11	15	....	....	....	....	....	....	....	....	....	....	....	....	....	....	....	....	....	....	....
1993-94	Tri-City	WHL	61	16	17	33	176	....	....	....	....	....	....	....	....	....	....	....	4	0	1	1	25	....	....	....
1994-95	Tri-City	WHL	70	50	60	110	207	....	....	....	....	....	....	....	....	....	....	....	17	12	15	27	36	....	....	....
1995-96	Tri-City	WHL	59	32	37	69	133	....	....	....	....	....	....	....	....	....	....	....	5	0	0	0	4	....	....	....
	Fredericton	AHL	....	....	....	....	....	....	....	....	....	....	....	....	....	....	....	....	3	0	0	0	2	....	....	....
1996-97	Red Deer	WHL	16	13	22	35	10	....	....	....	....	....	....	....	....	....	....	....	16	18	6	24	32	....	....	....
	Montreal	**NHL**	**3**	**0**	**0**	**0**	**0**	**0**	**0**	**0**	**0**	**0.0**	**0**	....	....	....	....	....	....	....	....	....	....	....	....	....
1997-98	**Montreal**	**NHL**	**4**	**0**	**0**	**0**	**31**	**0**	**0**	**0**	**0**	**0.0**	**0**	....	....	....	....	....	....	....	....	....	....	....	....	....
	Fredericton	AHL	71	21	18	39	256	....	....	....	....	....	....	....	....	....	....	....	3	1	1	2	0	....	....	....
1998-99	**Montreal**	**NHL**	**1**	**0**	**0**	**0**	**5**	**0**	**0**	**0**	**0**	**0.0**	**0**	**0**	**0.0**	**0**	**0**	**3:09**	....	....	....	....	....	....	....	....
	Fredericton	AHL	55	16	27	43	42	....	....	....	....	....	....	....	....	....	....	....	11	1	3	4	10	....	....	....
	NHL Totals		**8**	**0**	**0**	**0**	**36**	**0**	**0**	**0**	**0**	**0.0**		**0**	**0.0**	**0**	**0**	**3:09**	....	....	....	....	....	....	....	....

WHL West Second All-Star Team (1995)

RYCHEL, Warren (RIGH-kuhl)

Left wing. Shoots left. 6', 205 lbs. Born, Tecumseh, Ont., May 12, 1967.

			Regular Season																Playoffs							
Season	Club	League	GP	G	A	Pts	PIM	PP	SH	GW	S	%	+/-	TF	F%	H	SB	Min	GP	G	A	Pts	PIM	PP	SH	GW
1983-84	Essex	OJHL-C	24	11	16	27	86	....	....	....	....	....	....	....	....	....	....	....	....	....	....	....	....	....	....	....
1984-85	Sudbury	OHL	35	5	8	13	74	....	....	....	....	....	....	....	....	....	....	....	....	....	....	....	....	....	....	....
	Guelph	OHL	29	1	3	4	48	....	....	....	....	....	....	....	....	....	....	....	....	....	....	....	....	....	....	....
1985-86	Guelph	OHL	38	14	5	19	119	....	....	....	....	....	....	....	....	....	....	....	....	....	....	....	....	....	....	....
	Ottawa	OHL	29	11	18	29	54	....	....	....	....	....	....	....	....	....	....	....	....	....	....	....	....	....	....	....
1986-87	Ottawa	OHL	28	11	7	18	57	....	....	....	....	....	....	....	....	....	....	....	....	....	....	....	....	....	....	....
	Kitchener	OHL	21	5	5	10	39	....	....	....	....	....	....	....	....	....	....	....	4	0	0	0	9	....	....	....
1987-88	Peoria	IHL	7	2	1	3	7	....	....	....	....	....	....	....	....	....	....	....	....	....	....	....	....	....	....	....
	Saginaw	IHL	51	2	7	9	113	....	....	....	....	....	....	....	....	....	....	....	1	0	0	0	0	....	....	....
1988-89	**Chicago**	**NHL**	**2**	**0**	**0**	**0**	**17**	**0**	**0**	**0**	**3**	**0.0**	**–1**	....	....	....	....	....	....	....	....	....	....	....	....	....
	Saginaw	IHL	50	15	14	29	226	....	....	....	....	....	....	....	....	....	....	....	6	0	0	0	51	....	....	....
1989-90	Indianapolis	IHL	77	23	16	39	374	....	....	....	....	....	....	....	....	....	....	....	14	1	3	4	64	....	....	....
1990-91	Indianapolis	IHL	68	33	30	63	338	....	....	....	....	....	....	....	....	....	....	....	5	2	1	3	30	....	....	....
	Chicago	**NHL**	....	....	....	....	....	**0**	**0**	**0**	**0**	**0.0**	**0**	....	....	....	....	....	**3**	**1**	**3**	**4**	**2**	**1**	**0**	**1**
1991-92	Moncton	AHL	36	14	15	29	211	....	....	....	....	....	....	....	....	....	....	....	....	....	....	....	....	....	....	....
	Kalamazoo	IHL	45	15	20	35	165	....	....	....	....	....	....	....	....	....	....	....	8	0	3	3	51	....	....	....
1992-93	**Los Angeles**	**NHL**	**70**	**6**	**7**	**13**	**314**	**0**	**0**	**1**	**67**	**9.0**	**–15**	....	....	....	....	....	**23**	**6**	**7**	**13**	**39**	**0**	**0**	**2**
1993-94	**Los Angeles**	**NHL**	**80**	**10**	**9**	**19**	**322**	**0**	**0**	**3**	**105**	**9.5**	**–19**	....	....	....	....	....	....	....	....	....	....	....	....	....
1994-95	**Los Angeles**	**NHL**	**7**	**0**	**0**	**0**	**19**	**0**	**0**	**0**	**7**	**0.0**	**–5**	....	....	....	....	....	....	....	....	....	....	....	....	....
	Toronto	**NHL**	**26**	**1**	**6**	**7**	**101**	**0**	**0**	**0**	**34**	**2.9**	**1**	....	....	....	....	....	**3**	**0**	**0**	**0**	**0**	**0**	**0**	**0**
1995-96 ♦	**Colorado**	**NHL**	**52**	**6**	**2**	**8**	**147**	**0**	**0**	**1**	**45**	**13.3**	**6**	....	....	....	....	....	**12**	**1**	**0**	**1**	**23**	**0**	**0**	**0**
1996-97	**Anaheim**	**NHL**	**70**	**10**	**7**	**17**	**218**	**1**	**1**	**1**	**59**	**16.9**	**6**	....	....	....	....	....	**11**	**0**	**2**	**2**	**19**	**0**	**0**	**0**
1997-98	**Anaheim**	**NHL**	**63**	**5**	**6**	**11**	**198**	**1**	**0**	**0**	**62**	**8.1**	**–10**	....	....	....	....	....	....	....	....	....	....	....	....	....
	Colorado	**NHL**	**8**	**0**	**0**	**0**	**23**	**0**	**0**	**0**	**4**	**0.0**	**–1**	....	....	....	....	....	**6**	**0**	**0**	**0**	**24**	**0**	**0**	**0**
1998-99	**Colorado**	**NHL**	**28**	**0**	**2**	**2**	**63**	**0**	**0**	**0**	**15**	**0.0**	**3**	**8**	**62.5**	**24**	**3**	**4:44**	**12**	**0**	**1**	**1**	**14**	**0**	**0**	**0**
	NHL Totals		**406**	**38**	**39**	**77**	**1422**	**2**	**1**	**6**	**401**	**9.5**		**8**	**62.5**	**24**	**3**	**4:44**	**70**	**8**	**13**	**21**	**121**	**1**	**0**	**3**

Signed as a free agent by **Chicago**, September 19, 1986. Traded to **Winnipeg** by **Chicago** with Troy Murray for Bryan Marchment and Chris Norton, July 22, 1991. Traded to **Minnesota** by **Winnipeg** for Tony Joseph, December 30, 1991. Signed as a free agent by **LA Kings**, October 1, 1992. Traded to **Washington** by **LA Kings** for Randy Burridge, February 10, 1995. Traded to **Toronto** by **Washington** for Toronto's 4th round choice (Sebastien Charpentier) in 1995 Entry Draft, February 10, 1995. Traded to **Colorado** by **Toronto** for cash, October 2, 1995. Signed as a free agent by **Anaheim**, August 21, 1996. Traded to **Colorado** by **Anaheim** with future considerations for Josef Marha, March 24, 1998.

SACCO, Joe (SAK-oh) — WSH.

Right wing. Shoots left. 6'1", 195 lbs. Born, Medford, MA, February 4, 1969. Toronto's 4th choice, 71st overall, in 1987 Entry Draft.

			Regular Season																Playoffs							
Season	Club	League	GP	G	A	Pts	PIM	PP	SH	GW	S	%	+/-	TF	F%	H	SB	Min	GP	G	A	Pts	PIM	PP	SH	GW
1985-86	Medford Prep	H.S.	20	30	30	60	....	....	....	....	....	....	....	....	....	....	....	....	....	....	....	....	....	....	....	....
1986-87	Medford Prep	H.S.	21	22	32	54	....	....	....	....	....	....	....	....	....	....	....	....	....	....	....	....	....	....	....	....
1987-88	Boston University	H.E.	34	16	20	36	40	....	....	....	....	....	....	....	....	....	....	....	....	....	....	....	....	....	....	....
1988-89	Boston University	H.E.	33	21	19	40	66	....	....	....	....	....	....	....	....	....	....	....	....	....	....	....	....	....	....	....
1989-90	Boston University	H.E.	44	28	24	52	70	....	....	....	....	....	....	....	....	....	....	....	....	....	....	....	....	....	....	....
1990-91	**Toronto**	**NHL**	**20**	**0**	**5**	**5**	**2**	**0**	**0**	**0**	**20**	**0.0**	**–5**	....	....	....	....	....	....	....	....	....	....	....	....	....
	Newmarket	AHL	49	18	17	35	24	....	....	....	....	....	....	....	....	....	....	....	....	....	....	....	....	....	....	....
1991-92	United States	Nat-Team	50	11	26	37	61	....	....	....	....	....	....	....	....	....	....	....	....	....	....	....	....	....	....	....
	United States	Olympics	8	0	2	2	0	....	....	....	....	....	....	....	....	....	....	....	....	....	....	....	....	....	....	....
	Toronto	**NHL**	**17**	**7**	**4**	**11**	**4**	**0**	**0**	**1**	**40**	**17.5**	**8**	....	....	....	....	....	....	....	....	....	....	....	....	....
	St. John's	AHL	....	....	....	....	....	....	....	....	....	....	....	....	....	....	....	....	1	1	1	2	0	....	....	....
1992-93	**Toronto**	**NHL**	**23**	**4**	**4**	**8**	**8**	**0**	**0**	**0**	**38**	**10.5**	**–4**	....	....	....	....	....	....	....	....	....	....	....	....	....
	St. John's	AHL	37	14	16	30	45	....	....	....	....	....	....	....	....	....	....	....	7	6	4	10	2	....	....	....
1993-94	**Anaheim**	**NHL**	**84**	**19**	**18**	**37**	**61**	**3**	**1**	**2**	**206**	**9.2**	**–11**	....	....	....	....	....	....	....	....	....	....	....	....	....
1994-95	**Anaheim**	**NHL**	**41**	**10**	**8**	**18**	**23**	**2**	**0**	**0**	**77**	**13.0**	**–8**	....	....	....	....	....	....	....	....	....	....	....	....	....
1995-96	**Anaheim**	**NHL**	**76**	**13**	**14**	**27**	**40**	....	....	....	....	....	....	....	....	....	....	....	....	....	....	....	....	....	....	....
1996-97	**Anaheim**	**NHL**	**77**	**12**	**17**	**29**	**35**	**1**	**1**	**2**	**131**	**9.2**	**1**	....	....	....	....	....	**11**	**2**	**0**	**2**	**2**	**0**	**0**	**0**
1997-98	**Anaheim**	**NHL**	**55**	**8**	**11**	**19**	**24**	**0**	**2**	**2**	**90**	**8.9**	**–1**	....	....	....	....	....	....	....	....	....	....	....	....	....
	NY Islanders	**NHL**	**25**	**3**	**3**	**6**	**10**	**0**	**0**	**0**	**32**	**9.4**	**1**	....	....	....	....	....	....	....	....	....	....	....	....	....
1998-99	**NY Islanders**	**NHL**	**73**	**3**	**0**	**3**	**45**	**0**	**1**	**2**	**84**	**3.6**	**–24**	**32**	**56.3**	**58**	**27**	**9:59**	....	....	....	....	....	....	....	....
	NHL Totals		**491**	**79**	**84**	**163**	**252**	**6**	**5**	**9**	**718**	**11.0**		**32**	**56.3**	**58**	**27**	**9:59**	**11**	**2**	**0**	**2**	**2**	**0**	**0**	**0**

Claimed by **Anaheim** from **Toronto** in Expansion Draft, June 24, 1993. Traded to **NY Islanders** by **Anaheim** with J.J. Daigneault and Mark Janssens for Travis Green, Doug Houda and Tony Tuzzolino, February 6, 1998. Signed as a free agent by **Washington**, August 9, 1999.

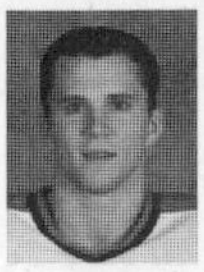

ST. LOUIS, Martin
(san-LOO-ee) **CGY.**

Right wing. Shoots left. 5'9", 180 lbs. Born, Laval, Que., June 18, 1975.

Season	Club	League	Regular Season GP	G	A	Pts	PIM	PP	SH	GW	S	%	+/-	TF	F%	H	SB	Min	Playoffs GP	G	A	Pts	PIM	PP	SH	GW
1993-94	U. of Vermont	ECAC	33	15	36	51	24	....	....	....	....	....	....	....	....	....	....	....	....	....	....	....	....	....	....	....
1994-95	U. of Vermont	ECAC	35	23	48	71	36	....	....	....	....	....	....	....	....	....	....	....	....	....	....	....	....	....	....	....
1995-96	U. of Vermont	ECAC	35	29	56	85	38	....	....	....	....	....	....	....	....	....	....	....	....	....	....	....	....	....	....	....
1996-97	U. of Vermont	ECAC	36	24	36	60	65	....	....	....	....	....	....	....	....	....	....	....	....	....	....	....	....	....	....	....
1997-98	Cleveland	IHL	56	16	34	50	24	....	....	....	....	....	....	....	....	....	....	....	....	....	....	....	....	....	....	....
	Saint John	AHL	25	15	11	26	20	....	....	....	....	....	....	....	....	....	....	....	20	5	15	20	16	....	....	....
1998-99	**Calgary**	**NHL**	**13**	**1**	**1**	**2**	**10**	**0**	**0**	**0**	**14**	**7.1**	**–2**	**0**	**0.0**	**8**	**4**	**8:15**	....	....	....	....	....	....	....	....
	Saint John	AHL	53	28	34	62	30	....	....	....	....	....	....	....	....	....	....	....	7	4	4	8	2	....	....	....
	NHL Totals		**13**	**1**	**1**	**2**	**10**	**0**	**0**	**0**	**14**	**7.1**		**0**	**0.0**	**8**	**4**	**8:15**	....	....	....	....	....	....	....	....

ECAC First All-Star Team (1995, 1996, 1997) • NCAA East First All-American Team (1995, 1996, 1997) • NCAA Championship All-Tournament Team (1996)

Signed as a free agent by **Calgary**, February 19, 1998.

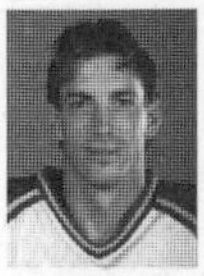

SAKIC, Joe
(SAK-ihk) **COL.**

Center. Shoots left. 5'11", 185 lbs. Born, Burnaby, B.C., July 7, 1969. Quebec's 2nd choice, 15th overall, in 1987 Entry Draft.

Season	Club	League	Regular Season GP	G	A	Pts	PIM	PP	SH	GW	S	%	+/-	TF	F%	H	SB	Min	Playoffs GP	G	A	Pts	PIM	PP	SH	GW
1985-86	Burnaby	BCAHA	60	83	73	156	96	....	....	....	....	....	....	....	....	....	....	....	....	....	....	....	....	....	....	....
1986-87	Swift Current	WHL	72	60	73	133	31	....	....	....	....	....	....	....	....	....	....	....	4	0	1	1	0	....	....	....
	Canada	Nat-Team	1	0	0	0	0	....	....	....	....	....	....	....	....	....	....	....	....	....	....	....	....	....	....	....
1987-88	Swift Current	WHL	64	*78	82	*160	64	....	....	....	....	....	....	....	....	....	....	....	10	11	13	24	12	....	....	....
1988-89	**Quebec**	**NHL**	**70**	**23**	**39**	**62**	**24**	**10**	**0**	**2**	**148**	**15.5**	**–36**	....	....	....	....	....	....	....	....	....	....	....	....	....
1989-90	**Quebec**	**NHL**	**80**	**39**	**63**	**102**	**27**	**8**	**1**	**2**	**234**	**16.7**	**–40**	....	....	....	....	....	....	....	....	....	....	....	....	....
1990-91	**Quebec**	**NHL**	**80**	**48**	**61**	**109**	**24**	**12**	**3**	**7**	**245**	**19.6**	**–26**	....	....	....	....	....	....	....	....	....	....	....	....	....
1991-92	**Quebec**	**NHL**	**69**	**29**	**65**	**94**	**20**	**6**	**3**	**1**	**217**	**13.4**	**5**	....	....	....	....	....	....	....	....	....	....	....	....	....
1992-93	**Quebec**	**NHL**	**78**	**48**	**57**	**105**	**40**	**20**	**2**	**4**	**264**	**18.2**	**–3**	....	....	....	....	....	**6**	**3**	**3**	**6**	**2**	**1**	**0**	**0**
1993-94	**Quebec**	**NHL**	**84**	**28**	**64**	**92**	**18**	**10**	**1**	**9**	**279**	**10.0**	**–8**	....	....	....	....	....	....	....	....	....	....	....	....	....
1994-95	**Quebec**	**NHL**	**47**	**19**	**43**	**62**	**30**	**3**	**2**	**5**	**157**	**12.1**	**7**	....	....	....	....	....	**6**	**4**	**1**	**5**	**0**	**1**	**1**	**1**
1995-96♦	**Colorado**	**NHL**	**82**	**51**	**69**	**120**	**44**	**17**	**6**	**7**	**339**	**15.0**	**14**	....	....	....	....	....	**22**	***18**	**16**	***34**	**14**	**6**	**0**	**6**
1996-97	**Colorado**	**NHL**	**65**	**22**	**52**	**74**	**34**	**10**	**2**	**5**	**261**	**8.4**	**–10**	....	....	....	....	....	**17**	**8**	***17**	**25**	**14**	**3**	**0**	**0**
1997-98	**Colorado**	**NHL**	**64**	**27**	**36**	**63**	**50**	**12**	**1**	**2**	**254**	**10.6**	**0**	....	....	....	....	....	**6**	**2**	**3**	**5**	**6**	**0**	**1**	**2**
	Canada	Olympics	4	1	2	3	4	....	....	....	....	....	....	....	....	....	....	....	....	....	....	....	....	....	....	....
1998-99	**Colorado**	**NHL**	**73**	**41**	**55**	**96**	**29**	**12**	**5**	**6**	**255**	**16.1**	**23**	**1723**	**51.4**	**31**	**47**	**25:35**	**19**	**6**	**13**	**19**	**8**	**1**	**1**	**1**
	NHL Totals		**792**	**375**	**604**	**979**	**340**	**120**	**26**	**50**	**2653**	**14.1**		**1723**	**51.4**	**31**	**47**	**25:35**	**76**	**41**	**53**	**94**	**44**	**12**	**3**	**10**

WHL East Second All-Star Team (1987) • Canadian Major Junior Player of the Year (1988) • WHL East First All-Star Team (1988) • Won Conn Smythe Trophy (1996)

Played in NHL All-Star Game (1990, 1991, 1992, 1993, 1994, 1996, 1998)

Transferred to **Colorado** after **Quebec** franchise relocated, June 21, 1995.

SALEI, Ruslan
(sah-LEE, ROOS-luhn) **ANA.**

Defense. Shoots left. 6'2", 205 lbs. Born, Minsk, USSR, November 2, 1974. Anaheim's 1st choice, 9th overall, in 1996 Entry Draft.

Season	Club	League	Regular Season GP	G	A	Pts	PIM	PP	SH	GW	S	%	+/-	TF	F%	H	SB	Min	Playoffs GP	G	A	Pts	PIM	PP	SH	GW
1992-93	D'amo Minsk	CIS	9	1	0	1	10	....	....	....	....	....	....	....	....	....	....	....	....	....	....	....	....	....	....	....
1993-94	Tivali Minsk	CIS	39	2	3	5	50	....	....	....	....	....	....	....	....	....	....	....	....	....	....	....	....	....	....	....
1994-95	Tivali Minsk	CIS	51	4	2	6	44	....	....	....	....	....	....	....	....	....	....	....	....	....	....	....	....	....	....	....
1995-96	Las Vegas	IHL	76	7	23	30	123	....	....	....	....	....	....	....	....	....	....	....	15	3	7	10	18	....	....	....
1996-97	**Anaheim**	**NHL**	**30**	**0**	**1**	**1**	**37**	**0**	**0**	**0**	**14**	**0.0**	**–8**	....	....	....	....	....	....	....	....	....	....	....	....	....
	Baltimore	AHL	12	1	4	5	12	....	....	....	....	....	....	....	....	....	....	....	....	....	....	....	....	....	....	....
	Las Vegas	IHL	8	0	2	2	24	....	....	....	....	....	....	....	....	....	....	....	3	2	1	3	6	....	....	....
1997-98	**Anaheim**	**NHL**	**66**	**5**	**10**	**15**	**70**	**1**	**0**	**0**	**104**	**4.8**	**7**	....	....	....	....	....	....	....	....	....	....	....	....	....
	Cincinnati	AHL	6	3	6	9	14	....	....	....	....	....	....	....	....	....	....	....	....	....	....	....	....	....	....	....
	Belarus	Olympics	7	1	0	1	4	....	....	....	....	....	....	....	....	....	....	....	....	....	....	....	....	....	....	....
1998-99	**Anaheim**	**NHL**	**74**	**2**	**14**	**16**	**65**	**1**	**0**	**0**	**123**	**1.6**	**1**	**0**	**0.0**	**154**	**105**	**22:03**	**3**	**0**	**0**	**0**	**4**	**0**	**0**	**0**
	NHL Totals		**170**	**7**	**25**	**32**	**172**	**2**	**0**	**0**	**241**	**2.9**		**0**	**0.0**	**154**	**105**	**22:03**	**3**	**0**	**0**	**0**	**4**	**0**	**0**	**0**

SALO, Sami
(SA-loh) **OTT.**

Defense. Shoots right. 6'3", 190 lbs. Born, Turku, Finland, September 2, 1974. Ottawa's 7th choice, 239th overall, in 1996 Entry Draft.

Season	Club	League	Regular Season GP	G	A	Pts	PIM	PP	SH	GW	S	%	+/-	TF	F%	H	SB	Min	Playoffs GP	G	A	Pts	PIM	PP	SH	GW
1991-92	Kiekko-67	Finn-Jr.	23	4	5	9	26	....	....	....	....	....	....	....	....	....	....	....	....	....	....	....	....	....	....	....
1992-93	Kiekko-67	Finn-Jr.	21	9	4	13	4	....	....	....	....	....	....	....	....	....	....	....	....	....	....	....	....	....	....	....
1993-94	TPS Turku	Finn-Jr.	36	7	13	20	16	....	....	....	....	....	....	....	....	....	....	....	7	0	1	1	10	....	....	....
1994-95	TPS Turku	Finn-Jr.	14	1	3	4	6	....	....	....	....	....	....	....	....	....	....	....	....	....	....	....	....	....	....	....
	Kiekko-67	Finland-2	19	4	2	6	4	....	....	....	....	....	....	....	....	....	....	....	....	....	....	....	....	....	....	....
	TPS Turku	Finland	7	1	2	3	8	....	....	....	....	....	....	....	....	....	....	....	1	0	0	0	0	....	....	....
1995-96	TPS Turku	Finland	47	7	14	21	32	....	....	....	....	....	....	....	....	....	....	....	11	1	3	4	8	....	....	....
1996-97	TPS Turku	Finland	48	9	6	15	10	....	....	....	....	....	....	....	....	....	....	....	10	2	3	5	4	....	....	....
1997-98	Jokerit	Finland	35	3	5	8	10	....	....	....	....	....	....	....	....	....	....	....	8	0	1	1	2	....	....	....
1998-99	**Ottawa**	**NHL**	**61**	**7**	**12**	**19**	**24**	**2**	**0**	**1**	**106**	**6.6**	**20**	**0**	**0.0**	**90**	**58**	**19:42**	**4**	**0**	**0**	**0**	**0**	**0**	**0**	**0**
	Detroit	IHL	5	0	2	2	0	....	....	....	....	....	....	....	....	....	....	....	....	....	....	....	....	....	....	....
	NHL Totals		**61**	**7**	**12**	**19**	**24**	**2**	**0**	**1**	**106**	**6.6**		**0**	**0.0**	**90**	**58**	**19:42**	**4**	**0**	**0**	**0**	**0**	**0**	**0**	**0**

NHL All-Rookie Team (1999)

SAMSONOV, Sergei
(sam-SAWN-nahf) **BOS.**

Left wing. Shoots right. 5'8", 184 lbs. Born, Moscow, USSR, October 27, 1978. Boston's 2nd choice, 8th overall, in 1997 Entry Draft.

Season	Club	League	Regular Season GP	G	A	Pts	PIM	PP	SH	GW	S	%	+/-	TF	F%	H	SB	Min	Playoffs GP	G	A	Pts	PIM	PP	SH	GW
1994-95	CSKA Moscow	CIS-Jr.	50	110	72	182	....	....	....	....	....	....	....	....	....	....	....	....	....	....	....	....	....	....	....	....
	CSKA Moscow	CIS	13	2	2	4	14	....	....	....	....	....	....	....	....	....	....	....	2	0	0	0	0	....	....	....
1995-96	CSKA Moscow	CIS	51	21	17	38	12	....	....	....	....	....	....	....	....	....	....	....	3	1	1	2	4	....	....	....
1996-97	Detroit	IHL	73	29	35	64	18	....	....	....	....	....	....	....	....	....	....	....	19	8	4	12	12	....	....	....
1997-98	**Boston**	**NHL**	**81**	**22**	**25**	**47**	**8**	**7**	**0**	**3**	**159**	**13.8**	**9**	....	....	....	....	....	**6**	**2**	**5**	**7**	**0**	**0**	**0**	**1**
1998-99	**Boston**	**NHL**	**79**	**25**	**26**	**51**	**18**	**6**	**0**	**8**	**160**	**15.6**	**–6**	**0**	**0.0**	**39**	**10**	**16:23**	**11**	**3**	**1**	**4**	**0**	**0**	**0**	**0**
	NHL Totals		**160**	**47**	**51**	**98**	**26**	**13**	**0**	**11**	**319**	**14.7**		**0**	**0.0**	**39**	**10**	**16:23**	**17**	**5**	**6**	**11**	**0**	**0**	**0**	**1**

Won Garry F. Longman Memorial Trophy (Top Rookie - IHL) (1997) • NHL All-Rookie Team (1998) • Won Calder Memorial Trophy (1998)

SAMUELSSON, Kjell
(SAM-yuhl-suhn, SHEHL)

Defense. Shoots right. 6'6", 235 lbs. Born, Tingsryd, Sweden, October 18, 1958. NY Rangers' 5th choice, 119th overall, in 1984 Entry Draft.

Season	Club	League	Regular Season GP	G	A	Pts	PIM	PP	SH	GW	S	%	+/-	TF	F%	H	SB	Min	Playoffs GP	G	A	Pts	PIM	PP	SH	GW
1976-77	Tingsryds AIF	Sweden-2	22	1	2	3	....	....	....	....	....	....	....	....	....	....	....	....	....	....	....	....	....	....	....	....
1977-78	Tingsryds AIF	Sweden-2	20	3	0	3	41	....	....	....	....	....	....	....	....	....	....	....	....	....	....	....	....	....	....	....
1978-79	Tingsryds AIF	Sweden-2	24	3	4	7	67	....	....	....	....	....	....	....	....	....	....	....	....	....	....	....	....	....	....	....
1979-80	Tingsryds AIF	Sweden-2	26	5	4	9	45	....	....	....	....	....	....	....	....	....	....	....	....	....	....	....	....	....	....	....
1980-81	Tingsryds AIF	Sweden-2	35	6	7	13	61	....	....	....	....	....	....	....	....	....	....	....	2	0	1	1	14	....	....	....
1981-82	Tingsryds AIF	Sweden-2	33	11	14	25	68	....	....	....	....	....	....	....	....	....	....	....	3	0	2	2	2	....	....	....
1982-83	Tingsryds AIF	Sweden-2	32	11	6	17	57	....	....	....	....	....	....	....	....	....	....	....	....	....	....	....	....	....	....	....
1983-84	Leksands IF	Sweden	36	6	6	12	59	....	....	....	....	....	....	....	....	....	....	....	....	....	....	....	....	....	....	....
1984-85	Leksands IF	Sweden	35	9	5	14	34	....	....	....	....	....	....	....	....	....	....	....	....	....	....	....	....	....	....	....
1985-86	**NY Rangers**	**NHL**	**9**	**0**	**0**	**0**	**10**	**0**	**0**	**0**	**7**	**0.0**	**–1**	....	....	....	....	....	**9**	**0**	**1**	**1**	**8**	**0**	**0**	**0**
	New Haven	AHL	56	6	21	27	87	....	....	....	....	....	....	....	....	....	....	....	3	0	0	0	10	....	....	....
1986-87	**NY Rangers**	**NHL**	**30**	**2**	**6**	**8**	**50**	**0**	**0**	**0**	**20**	**10.0**	**–2**	....	....	....	....	....	....	....	....	....	....	....	....	....
	Philadelphia	**NHL**	**46**	**1**	**6**	**7**	**86**	**0**	**0**	**0**	**28**	**3.6**	**–9**	....	....	....	....	....	**26**	**0**	**4**	**4**	**25**	**0**	**0**	**0**

			Regular Season																Playoffs							
Season	Club	League	GP	G	A	Pts	PIM	PP	SH	GW	S	%	+/-	TF	F%	H	SB	Min	GP	G	A	Pts	PIM	PP	SH	GW
1987-88	**Philadelphia**	**NHL**	**74**	**6**	**24**	**30**	**184**	**3**	**0**	**0**	**118**	**5.1**	**28**	....	....	....	....	....	**7**	**2**	**5**	**7**	**23**	**0**	**0**	**1**
1988-89	**Philadelphia**	**NHL**	**69**	**3**	**14**	**17**	**140**	**0**	**1**	**0**	**60**	**5.0**	**13**	....	....	....	....	....	**19**	**1**	**3**	**4**	**24**	**0**	**0**	**0**
1989-90	**Philadelphia**	**NHL**	**66**	**5**	**17**	**22**	**91**	**0**	**0**	**1**	**88**	**5.7**	**20**	....	....	....	....	....	....	....	....	....	....	....	....	....
1990-91	**Philadelphia**	**NHL**	**78**	**9**	**19**	**28**	**82**	**1**	**0**	**3**	**101**	**8.9**	**4**	....	....	....	....	....	....	....	....	....	....	....	....	....
1991-92	**Philadelphia**	**NHL**	**54**	**4**	**9**	**13**	**76**	**0**	**0**	**0**	**63**	**6.3**	**1**	....	....	....	....	....	....	....	....	....	....	....	....	....
	♦ **Pittsburgh**	**NHL**	**20**	**1**	**2**	**3**	**34**	**0**	**0**	**1**	**28**	**3.6**	**0**	....	....	....	....	....	**15**	**0**	**3**	**3**	**12**	**0**	**0**	**0**
1992-93	**Pittsburgh**	**NHL**	**63**	**3**	**6**	**9**	**106**	**0**	**0**	**1**	**63**	**4.8**	**25**	....	....	....	....	....	**12**	**0**	**3**	**3**	**2**	**0**	**0**	**0**
1993-94	**Pittsburgh**	**NHL**	**59**	**5**	**8**	**13**	**118**	**1**	**0**	**0**	**57**	**8.8**	**18**	....	....	....	....	....	**6**	**0**	**0**	**0**	**26**	**0**	**0**	**0**
1994-95	**Pittsburgh**	**NHL**	**41**	**1**	**6**	**7**	**54**	**0**	**0**	**0**	**37**	**2.7**	**8**	....	....	....	....	....	**11**	**0**	**1**	**1**	**32**	**0**	**0**	**0**
1995-96	**Philadelphia**	**NHL**	**75**	**3**	**11**	**14**	**81**	**0**	**0**	**1**	**62**	**4.8**	**20**	....	....	....	....	....	**12**	**1**	**0**	**1**	**24**	**0**	**0**	**0**
1996-97	**Philadelphia**	**NHL**	**34**	**4**	**3**	**7**	**47**	**0**	**0**	**0**	**36**	**11.1**	**17**	....	....	....	....	....	**5**	**0**	**0**	**0**	**2**	**0**	**0**	**0**
1997-98	**Philadelphia**	**NHL**	**49**	**0**	**3**	**3**	**28**	**0**	**0**	**0**	**23**	**0.0**	**9**	....	....	....	....	....	**1**	**0**	**0**	**0**	**0**	**0**	**0**	**0**
1998-99	VEU Feldkirch	EuroHL	2	0	1	1	0	....	....	....	....	....	....	....	....	....	....	....	....	....	....	....	....	....	....	....
	Tampa Bay	**NHL**	**46**	**1**	**4**	**5**	**38**	**0**	**0**	**0**	**22**	**4.5**	**–6**	**0**	**0.0**	**54**	**57**	**18:37**	....	....	....	....	....	....	....	....
	NHL Totals		**813**	**48**	**138**	**186**	**1225**	**5**	**1**	**7**	**813**	**5.9**		**0**	**0.0**	**54**	**57**	**18:37**	**123**	**4**	**20**	**24**	**178**	**0**	**0**	**1**

Played in NHL All-Star Game (1988)

Traded to **Philadelphia** by **NY Rangers** with NY Rangers' 2nd round choice (Patrik Juhlin) in 1989 Entry Draft for Bob Froese, December 18, 1986. Traded to **Pittsburgh** by **Philadelphia** with Rick Tocchet, Ken Wregget and Philadelphia's 3rd round choice (Dave Roche) in 1993 Entry Draft for Mark Recchi, Brian Benning and LA Kings' 1st round choice (previously acquired, Philadelphia selected Jason Bowen) in 1992 Entry Draft, February 19, 1992. Signed as a free agent by **Philadelphia**, August 31, 1995. Signed as a free agent by **Tampa Bay**, October 14, 1998.

SAMUELSSON, Ulf

(SAM-yuhl-suhn, UHLF)

Defense. Shoots left. 6'1", 205 lbs. Born, Fagersta, Sweden, March 26, 1964. Hartford's 4th choice, 67th overall, in 1982 Entry Draft.

1981-82	Leksands IF	Sweden	31	3	1	4	40	....	....	....	....	....	....	....	....	....	....	....	....	....	....	....	....	....	....	....
1982-83	Leksands IF	Sweden	33	9	6	15	72	....	....	....	....	....	....	....	....	....	....	....	....	....	....	....	....	....	....	....
1983-84	Leksands IF	Sweden	36	5	11	16	53	....	....	....	....	....	....	....	....	....	....	....	....	....	....	....	....	....	....	....
1984-85	**Hartford**	**NHL**	**41**	**2**	**6**	**8**	**83**	**0**	**0**	**0**	**32**	**6.3**	**–6**	....	....	....	....	....	....	....	....	....	....	....	....	....
	Binghamton	AHL	36	5	11	16	92	....	....	....	....	....	....	....	....	....	....	....	....	....	....	....	....	....	....	....
1985-86	**Hartford**	**NHL**	**80**	**5**	**19**	**24**	**174**	**0**	**1**	**1**	**72**	**6.9**	**7**	....	....	....	....	....	**10**	**1**	**2**	**3**	**38**	**0**	**0**	**1**
1986-87	**Hartford**	**NHL**	**78**	**2**	**31**	**33**	**162**	**0**	**0**	**0**	**104**	**1.9**	**28**	....	....	....	....	....	**5**	**0**	**1**	**1**	**41**	**-2**	**0**	**0**
1987-88	**Hartford**	**NHL**	**76**	**8**	**33**	**41**	**159**	**3**	**0**	**0**	**156**	**5.1**	**–10**	....	....	....	....	....	**5**	**0**	**0**	**0**	**8**	**0**	**0**	**0**
1988-89	**Hartford**	**NHL**	**71**	**9**	**26**	**35**	**181**	**3**	**0**	**2**	**122**	**7.4**	**23**	....	....	....	....	....	**4**	**0**	**2**	**2**	**4**	**0**	**0**	**0**
1989-90	**Hartford**	**NHL**	**55**	**2**	**11**	**13**	**177**	**0**	**0**	**0**	**57**	**3.5**	**15**	....	....	....	....	....	**7**	**1**	**0**	**1**	**2**	**0**	**0**	**0**
1990-91	**Hartford**	**NHL**	**62**	**3**	**18**	**21**	**174**	**0**	**0**	**0**	**110**	**2.7**	**13**	....	....	....	....	....	....	....	....	....	....	....	....	....
	♦ **Pittsburgh**	**NHL**	**14**	**1**	**4**	**5**	**37**	**0**	**0**	**0**	**15**	**6.7**	**4**	....	....	....	....	....	**20**	**3**	**2**	**5**	**34**	**1**	**0**	**1**
1991-92 ♦	**Pittsburgh**	**NHL**	**62**	**1**	**14**	**15**	**206**	**1**	**0**	**1**	**75**	**1.3**	**2**	....	....	....	....	....	**21**	**0**	**2**	**2**	**39**	**0**	**0**	**0**
1992-93	**Pittsburgh**	**NHL**	**77**	**3**	**26**	**29**	**249**	**0**	**0**	**1**	**96**	**3.1**	**36**	....	....	....	....	....	**12**	**1**	**5**	**6**	**24**	**0**	**0**	**0**
1993-94	**Pittsburgh**	**NHL**	**80**	**5**	**24**	**29**	**199**	**1**	**0**	**0**	**106**	**4.7**	**23**	....	....	....	....	....	**6**	**0**	**1**	**1**	**18**	**0**	**0**	**0**
1994-95	Leksands IF	Sweden	2	0	0	0	8	....	....	....	....	....	....	....	....	....	....	....	....	....	....	....	....	....	....	....
	Pittsburgh	**NHL**	**44**	**1**	**15**	**16**	**113**	**0**	**0**	**0**	**47**	**2.1**	**11**	....	....	....	....	....	**7**	**0**	**2**	**2**	**8**	**0**	**0**	**0**
1995-96	**NY Rangers**	**NHL**	**74**	**1**	**18**	**19**	**122**	**0**	**0**	**0**	**66**	**1.5**	**9**	....	....	....	....	....	**11**	**1**	**5**	**6**	**16**	**0**	**0**	**0**
1996-97	**NY Rangers**	**NHL**	**73**	**6**	**11**	**17**	**138**	**1**	**0**	**1**	**77**	**7.8**	**3**	....	....	....	....	....	**15**	**0**	**2**	**2**	**30**	**0**	**0**	**0**
1997-98	**NY Rangers**	**NHL**	**73**	**3**	**9**	**12**	**122**	**0**	**0**	**2**	**59**	**5.1**	**1**	....	....	....	....	....	....	....	....	....	....	....	....	....
	Sweden	Olympics	3	0	1	1	4	....	....	....	....	....	....	....	....	....	....	....	....	....	....	....	....	....	....	....
1998-99	**NY Rangers**	**NHL**	**67**	**4**	**8**	**12**	**93**	**0**	**0**	**0**	**37**	**10.8**	**6**	**0**	**0.0**	**172**	**176**	**20:29**	....	....	....	....	....	....	....	....
	Detroit	**NHL**	**4**	**0**	**0**	**0**	**6**	**0**	**0**	**0**	**2**	**0.0**	**–1**	**0**	**0.0**	**4**	**3**	**17:32**	**9**	**0**	**3**	**3**	**10**	**0**	**0**	**0**
	NHL Totals		**1031**	**56**	**273**	**329**	**2395**	**9**	**1**	**8**	**1233**	**4.5**		**0**	**0.0**	**176**	**179**	**20:19**	**132**	**7**	**27**	**34**	**272**	**-1**	**0**	**2**

Traded to **Pittsburgh** by **Hartford** with Ron Francis and Grant Jennings for John Cullen, Jeff Parker and Zarley Zalapski, March 4, 1991. Traded to **NY Rangers** by **Pittsburgh** with Luc Robitaille for Petr Nedved and Sergei Zubov, August 31, 1995. Traded to **Detroit** by **NY Rangers** for Detroit's 2nd round choice (David Inman) in 1999 Entry Draft and NY Rangers' 3rd round choice (previously acquired) in 2000 Entry Draft, March 23, 1999. Traded to **Atlanta** by **Detroit** for future considerations, June 25, 1999.

SANDERSON, Geoff

BUF.

Left wing. Shoots left. 6', 190 lbs. Born, Hay River, N.W.T., February 1, 1972. Hartford's 2nd choice, 36th overall, in 1990 Entry Draft.

1987-88	Edmonton	AAHA	45	65	55	120	175	....	....	....	....	....	....	....	....	....	....	....	....	....	....	....	....	....	....	....
1988-89	Swift Current	WHL	58	17	11	28	16	....	....	....	....	....	....	....	....	....	....	....	12	3	5	8	6	....	....	....
1989-90	Swift Current	WHL	70	32	62	94	56	....	....	....	....	....	....	....	....	....	....	....	4	1	4	5	8	....	....	....
1990-91	Swift Current	WHL	70	62	50	112	57	....	....	....	....	....	....	....	....	....	....	....	3	1	2	3	4	....	....	....
	Hartford	**NHL**	**2**	**1**	**0**	**1**	**0**	**0**	**0**	**0**	**2**	**50.0**	**–2**	....	....	....	....	....	**3**	**0**	**0**	**0**	**0**	**0**	**0**	**0**
	Springfield	AHL	....	....	....	....	....	....	....	....	....	....	....	....	....	....	....	....	1	0	0	0	2	....	....	....
1991-92	**Hartford**	**NHL**	**64**	**13**	**18**	**31**	**18**	**2**	**0**	**1**	**98**	**13.3**	**5**	....	....	....	....	....	**7**	**1**	**0**	**1**	**2**	**0**	**0**	**0**
1992-93	**Hartford**	**NHL**	**82**	**46**	**43**	**89**	**28**	**21**	**2**	**4**	**271**	**17.0**	**–21**	....	....	....	....	....	....	....	....	....	....	....	....	....
1993-94	**Hartford**	**NHL**	**82**	**41**	**26**	**67**	**42**	**15**	**1**	**6**	**266**	**15.4**	**–13**	....	....	....	....	....	....	....	....	....	....	....	....	....
1994-95	Hameelinna	Finland	12	6	4	10	24	....	....	....	....	....	....	....	....	....	....	....	....	....	....	....	....	....	....	....
	Hartford	**NHL**	**46**	**18**	**14**	**32**	**24**	**4**	**0**	**4**	**170**	**10.6**	**–10**	....	....	....	....	....	....	....	....	....	....	....	....	....
1995-96	**Hartford**	**NHL**	**81**	**34**	**31**	**65**	**40**	**6**	**0**	**7**	**314**	**10.8**	**0**	....	....	....	....	....	....	....	....	....	....	....	....	....
1996-97	**Hartford**	**NHL**	**82**	**36**	**31**	**67**	**29**	**12**	**1**	**4**	**297**	**12.1**	**–9**	....	....	....	....	....	....	....	....	....	....	....	....	....
1997-98	**Carolina**	**NHL**	**40**	**7**	**10**	**17**	**14**	**2**	**0**	**0**	**96**	**7.3**	**–4**	....	....	....	....	....	....	....	....	....	....	....	....	....
	Vancouver	**NHL**	**9**	**0**	**3**	**3**	**4**	**0**	**0**	**0**	**29**	**0.0**	**–1**	....	....	....	....	....	....	....	....	....	....	....	....	....
	Buffalo	**NHL**	**26**	**4**	**5**	**9**	**20**	**0**	**0**	**2**	**72**	**5.6**	**6**	....	....	....	....	....	**14**	**3**	**1**	**4**	**4**	**1**	**0**	**1**
1998-99	**Buffalo**	**NHL**	**75**	**12**	**18**	**30**	**22**	**1**	**0**	**1**	**155**	**7.7**	**8**	**4**	**50.0**	**43**	**9**	**12:55**	**19**	**4**	**6**	**10**	**14**	**0**	**0**	**1**
	NHL Totals		**589**	**212**	**199**	**411**	**241**	**63**	**4**	**29**	**1770**	**12.0**		**4**	**50.0**	**43**	**9**	**12:55**	**43**	**8**	**7**	**15**	**20**	**1**	**0**	**2**

Played in NHL All-Star Game (1994, 1997)

Transferred to **Carolina** after **Hartford** franchise relocated, June 25, 1997. Traded to **Vancouver** by **Carolina** with Sean Burke and Enrico Ciccone for Kirk McLean and Martin Gelinas, January 3, 1998. Traded to **Buffalo** by **Vancouver** for Brad May and future considerations, February 4, 1998.

SANDSTROM, Tomas

(SAND-struhm)

Right wing. Shoots left. 6'2", 205 lbs. Born, Jakobstad, Finland, September 4, 1964. NY Rangers' 2nd choice, 36th overall, in 1982 Entry Draft.

1979-80	Fagersta HK	Sweden-2	6	1	1	2	0	....	....	....	....	....	....	....	....	....	....	....	....	....	....	....	....	....	....	....
1980-81	Fagersta HK	Sweden-2	20	23	5	28	....	....	....	....	....	....	....	....	....	....	....	....	....	....	....	....	....	....	....	....
1981-82	Fagersta HK	Sweden-2	32	28	11	39	74	....	....	....	....	....	....	....	....	....	....	....	....	....	....	....	....	....	....	....
1982-83	Brynas IF	Sweden	36	23	14	37	50	....	....	....	....	....	....	....	....	....	....	....	....	....	....	....	....	....	....	....
1983-84	Brynas IF	Sweden	34	19	10	29	81	....	....	....	....	....	....	....	....	....	....	....	....	....	....	....	....	....	....	....
	Sweden	Olympics	7	2	1	3	6	....	....	....	....	....	....	....	....	....	....	....	....	....	....	....	....	....	....	....
1984-85	**NY Rangers**	**NHL**	**74**	**29**	**29**	**58**	**51**	**5**	**0**	**3**	**190**	**15.3**	**3**	....	....	....	....	....	**3**	**0**	**2**	**2**	**0**	**0**	**0**	**0**
1985-86	**NY Rangers**	**NHL**	**73**	**25**	**29**	**54**	**109**	**8**	**2**	**1**	**238**	**10.5**	**–4**	....	....	....	....	....	**16**	**4**	**6**	**10**	**20**	**0**	**0**	**1**
1986-87	**NY Rangers**	**NHL**	**64**	**40**	**34**	**74**	**60**	**13**	**0**	**5**	**240**	**16.7**	**8**	....	....	....	....	....	**6**	**1**	**2**	**3**	**20**	**0**	**0**	**0**
1987-88	**NY Rangers**	**NHL**	**69**	**28**	**40**	**68**	**95**	**11**	**0**	**3**	**204**	**13.7**	**–6**	....	....	....	....	....	....	....	....	....	....	....	....	....
1988-89	**NY Rangers**	**NHL**	**79**	**32**	**56**	**88**	**148**	**11**	**2**	**4**	**240**	**13.3**	**5**	....	....	....	....	....	**4**	**3**	**2**	**5**	**12**	**2**	**0**	**0**
1989-90	**NY Rangers**	**NHL**	**48**	**19**	**19**	**38**	**100**	**6**	**0**	**3**	**166**	**11.4**	**–10**	....	....	....	....	....	....	....	....	....	....	....	....	....
	Los Angeles	**NHL**	**28**	**13**	**20**	**33**	**28**	**1**	**1**	**0**	**83**	**15.7**	**–1**	....	....	....	....	....	**10**	**5**	**4**	**9**	**19**	**0**	**0**	**0**
1990-91	**Los Angeles**	**NHL**	**68**	**45**	**44**	**89**	**106**	**16**	**0**	**6**	**221**	**20.4**	**27**	....	....	....	....	....	**10**	**4**	**4**	**8**	**14**	**3**	**0**	**0**
1991-92	**Los Angeles**	**NHL**	**49**	**17**	**22**	**39**	**70**	**5**	**0**	**4**	**147**	**11.6**	**–2**	....	....	....	....	....	**6**	**0**	**3**	**3**	**8**	**0**	**0**	**0**
1992-93	**Los Angeles**	**NHL**	**39**	**25**	**27**	**52**	**57**	**8**	**0**	**3**	**134**	**18.7**	**12**	....	....	....	....	....	**24**	**8**	**17**	**25**	**12**	**2**	**0**	**2**
1993-94	**Los Angeles**	**NHL**	**51**	**17**	**24**	**41**	**59**	**4**	**0**	**2**	**121**	**14.0**	**–12**	....	....	....	....	....	....	....	....	....	....	....	....	....
	Pittsburgh	**NHL**	**27**	**6**	**11**	**17**	**24**	**0**	**0**	**1**	**72**	**8.3**	**5**	....	....	....	....	....	**6**	**0**	**0**	**0**	**4**	**0**	**0**	**0**
1994-95	Malmo IF	Sweden	12	10	5	15	14	....	....	....	....	....	....	....	....	....	....	....	....	....	....	....	....	....	....	....
	Pittsburgh	**NHL**	**47**	**21**	**23**	**44**	**42**	**4**	**1**	**3**	**116**	**18.1**	**1**	....	....	....	....	....	**12**	**3**	**3**	**6**	**16**	**2**	**0**	**0**
1995-96	**Pittsburgh**	**NHL**	**58**	**35**	**35**	**70**	**69**	**17**	**1**	**2**	**187**	**18.7**	**4**	....	....	....	....	....	**18**	**4**	**2**	**6**	**30**	**0**	**0**	**1**
1996-97	**Pittsburgh**	**NHL**	**40**	**9**	**15**	**24**	**33**	**1**	**1**	**0**	**73**	**12.3**	**4**	....	....	....	....	....	....	....	....	....	....	....	....	....
	♦ **Detroit**	**NHL**	**34**	**9**	**9**	**18**	**36**	**0**	**1**	**2**	**66**	**13.6**	**2**	....	....	....	....	....	**20**	**0**	**4**	**4**	**24**	**0**	**0**	**0**
1997-98	**Anaheim**	**NHL**	**77**	**9**	**8**	**17**	**64**	**2**	**1**	**0**	**136**	**6.6**	**–25**	....	....	....	....	....	....	....	....	....	....	....	....	....
	Sweden	Olympics	4	0	1	1	0	....	....	....	....	....	....	....	....	....	....	....	....	....	....	....	....	....	....	....

			Regular Season																Playoffs							
Season	Club	League	GP	G	A	Pts	PIM	PP	SH	GW	S	%	+/-	TF	F%	H	SB	Min	GP	G	A	Pts	PIM	PP	SH	GW
1998-99	**Anaheim**	**NHL**	**58**	**15**	**17**	**32**	**42**	**7**	**0**	**2**	**107**	**14.0**	**–5**	**8**	**25.0**	**47**	**11**	**17:22**	**4**	**0**	**0**	**0**	**4**	**0**	**0**	**0**
	NHL Totals		**983**	**394**	**462**	**856**	**1193**	**119**	**10**	**44**	**2741**	**14.4**		**8**	**25.0**	**47**	**11**	**17:22**	**139**	**32**	**49**	**81**	**183**	**9**	**0**	**4**

NHL All-Rookie Team (1985)
Played in NHL All-Star Game (1988, 1991)
Traded to **LA Kings** by **NY Rangers** with Tony Granato for Bernie Nicholls, January 20, 1990. Traded to **Pittsburgh** by **LA Kings** with Shawn McEachern for Marty McSorley and Jim Paek, February 16, 1994. Traded to **Detroit** by **Pittsburgh** for Greg Johnson, January 27, 1997. Signed as a free agent by **Anaheim**, October 20, 1997.

SANDWITH, Terran — TOR.

Defense. Shoots left. 6'4", 210 lbs. Born, Edmonton, Alta., April 17, 1972. Philadelphia's 4th choice, 42nd overall, in 1990 NHL Entry Draft.

Season	Club	League	GP	G	A	Pts	PIM	PP	SH	GW	S	%	+/-	TF	F%	H	SB	Min	GP	G	A	Pts	PIM	PP	SH	GW
1987-88	Hobbema	AJHL	58	5	8	13	106	....	....	....	....	....	....	....	....	....	....	....	....	....	....	....	....	....	....	....
1988-89	Tri-City	WHL	31	0	0	0	29	....	....	....	....	....	....	....	....	....	....	....	6	0	0	0	4	....	....	....
1989-90	Tri-City	WHL	70	4	14	18	92	....	....	....	....	....	....	....	....	....	....	....	7	0	2	2	14	....	....	....
1990-91	Tri-City	WHL	46	5	17	22	132	....	....	....	....	....	....	....	....	....	....	....	7	1	0	1	14	....	....	....
1991-92	Brandon	WHL	41	6	14	20	145	....	....	....	....	....	....	....	....	....	....	....	....	....	....	....	....	....	....	....
	Saskatoon	WHL	18	2	5	7	53	....	....	....	....	....	....	....	....	....	....	....	18	2	1	3	28	....	....	....
1992-93	Hershey	AHL	61	1	12	13	140	....	....	....	....	....	....	....	....	....	....	....	....	....	....	....	....	....	....	....
1993-94	Hershey	AHL	62	3	5	8	169	....	....	....	....	....	....	....	....	....	....	....	2	0	1	1	4	....	....	....
1994-95	Hershey	AHL	11	1	1	2	32	....	....	....	....	....	....	....	....	....	....	....	....	....	....	....	....	....	....	....
	Kansas City	IHL	25	0	3	3	73	....	....	....	....	....	....	....	....	....	....	....	....	....	....	....	....	....	....	....
1995-96	Canada	Nat-Team	47	3	12	15	63	....	....	....	....	....	....	....	....	....	....	....	....	....	....	....	....	....	....	....
	Cape Breton	AHL	5	0	2	2	4	....	....	....	....	....	....	....	....	....	....	....	....	....	....	....	....	....	....	....
1996-97	Hamilton	AHL	78	3	6	9	213	....	....	....	....	....	....	....	....	....	....	....	22	0	2	2	27	....	....	....
1997-98	**Edmonton**	**NHL**	**8**	**0**	**0**	**0**	**6**	**0**	**0**	**0**	**4**	**0.0**	**–4**	....	....	....	....	....	....	....	....	....	....	....	....	....
	Hamilton	AHL	54	4	8	12	131	....	....	....	....	....	....	....	....	....	....	....	9	0	0	0	10	....	....	....
1998-99	Cincinnati	AHL	40	0	6	6	77	....	....	....	....	....	....	....	....	....	....	....	....	....	....	....	....	....	....	....
	NHL Totals		**8**	**0**	**0**	**0**	**6**	**0**	**0**	**0**	**4**	**0.0**		....	....	....	....	....	....	....	....	....	....	....	....	....

Signed as a free agent by **Edmonton**, April 10, 1996. Signed as a free agent by **Anaheim**, July 13, 1998. Signed as a free agent by **Toronto**, July 2, 1999.

SARAULT, Yves (sah-ROH, EEV) — OTT.

Left wing. Shoots left. 6'1", 185 lbs. Born, Valleyfield, Que., December 23, 1972. Montreal's 4th choice, 61st overall, in 1991 Entry Draft.

Season	Club	League	GP	G	A	Pts	PIM	PP	SH	GW	S	%	+/-	TF	F%	H	SB	Min	GP	G	A	Pts	PIM	PP	SH	GW
1988-89	Lac St-Louis	QAAA	42	23	30	53	64	....	....	....	....	....	....	....	....	....	....	....	....	....	....	....	....	....	....	....
1989-90	Victoriaville	QMJHL	70	12	28	40	140	....	....	....	....	....	....	....	....	....	....	....	16	0	3	3	26	....	....	....
1990-91	St-Jean	QMJHL	56	22	24	46	113	....	....	....	....	....	....	....	....	....	....	....	....	....	....	....	....	....	....	....
1991-92	St-Jean	QMJHL	50	28	38	66	96	....	....	....	....	....	....	....	....	....	....	....	....	....	....	....	....	....	....	....
	Trois-Rivieres	QMJHL	18	15	14	29	12	....	....	....	....	....	....	....	....	....	....	....	15	10	10	20	18	....	....	....
1992-93	Fredericton	AHL	59	14	17	31	41	....	....	....	....	....	....	....	....	....	....	....	3	0	1	1	2	....	....	....
	Wheeling	ECHL	2	1	3	4	0	....	....	....	....	....	....	....	....	....	....	....	....	....	....	....	....	....	....	....
1993-94	Fredericton	AHL	60	13	14	27	72	....	....	....	....	....	....	....	....	....	....	....	....	....	....	....	....	....	....	....
1994-95	Fredericton	AHL	69	24	21	45	96	....	....	....	....	....	....	....	....	....	....	....	13	2	1	3	33	....	....	....
	Montreal	**NHL**	**8**	**0**	**1**	**1**	**0**	**0**	**0**	**0**	**9**	**0.0**	**–1**	....	....	....	....	....	....	....	....	....	....	....	....	....
1995-96	**Montreal**	**NHL**	**14**	**0**	**0**	**0**	**4**	**0**	**0**	**0**	**14**	**0.0**	**–7**	....	....	....	....	....	....	....	....	....	....	....	....	....
	Calgary	**NHL**	**11**	**2**	**1**	**3**	**4**	**0**	**0**	**1**	**12**	**16.7**	**–2**	....	....	....	....	....	....	....	....	....	....	....	....	....
	Saint John	AHL	26	10	12	22	34	....	....	....	....	....	....	....	....	....	....	....	16	6	2	8	33	....	....	....
1996-97	**Colorado**	**NHL**	**28**	**2**	**1**	**3**	**6**	**0**	**0**	**0**	**41**	**4.9**	**0**	....	....	....	....	....	**5**	**0**	**0**	**0**	**2**	**0**	**0**	**0**
	Hershey	AHL	6	2	3	5	8	....	....	....	....	....	....	....	....	....	....	....	....	....	....	....	....	....	....	....
1997-98	**Colorado**	**NHL**	**2**	**1**	**0**	**1**	**0**	**0**	**0**	**0**	**1**	**100.0**	**1**	....	....	....	....	....	....	....	....	....	....	....	....	....
	Hershey	AHL	63	23	36	59	43	....	....	....	....	....	....	....	....	....	....	....	7	1	2	3	14	....	....	....
1998-99	**Ottawa**	**NHL**	**11**	**0**	**1**	**1**	**4**	**0**	**0**	**0**	**7**	**0.0**	**1**	**0**	**0.0**	**15**	**1**	**7:15**	....	....	....	....	....	....	....	....
	Detroit	IHL	36	11	12	23	52	....	....	....	....	....	....	....	....	....	....	....	11	7	2	9	40	....	....	....
	NHL Totals		**74**	**5**	**4**	**9**	**18**	**0**	**0**	**1**	**84**	**6.0**		**0**	**0.0**	**15**	**1**	**7:15**	**5**	**0**	**0**	**0**	**2**	**0**	**0**	**0**

QMJHL Second All-Star Team (1992)
Traded to **Calgary** by **Montreal** with Craig Ferguson for Calgary's 8th round choice (Petr Kubos) in 1997 Entry Draft, November 26, 1995. Signed as a free agent by **Colorado**, September 13, 1996. Signed as a free agent by **Ottawa**, August 7, 1998.

SARICH, Cory (SAHR-ihch) — BUF.

Defense. Shoots right. 6'3", 175 lbs. Born, Saskatoon, Sask., August 16, 1978. Buffalo's 2nd choice, 27th overall, in 1996 Entry Draft.

Season	Club	League	GP	G	A	Pts	PIM	PP	SH	GW	S	%	+/-	TF	F%	H	SB	Min	GP	G	A	Pts	PIM	PP	SH	GW
1994-95	Saskatoon	SAHA	31	5	22	27	99	....	....	....	....	....	....	....	....	....	....	....	....	....	....	....	....	....	....	....
	Saskatoon	WHL	6	0	0	0	4	....	....	....	....	....	....	....	....	....	....	....	3	0	1	1	0	....	....	....
1995-96	Saskatoon	WHL	59	5	18	23	54	....	....	....	....	....	....	....	....	....	....	....	3	0	0	0	4	....	....	....
1996-97	Saskatoon	WHL	58	6	27	33	158	....	....	....	....	....	....	....	....	....	....	....	....	....	....	....	....	....	....	....
1997-98	Saskatoon	WHL	33	5	24	29	90	....	....	....	....	....	....	....	....	....	....	....	....	....	....	....	....	....	....	....
	Seattle	WHL	13	3	16	19	47	....	....	....	....	....	....	....	....	....	....	....	0	0	0	0	0	....	....	....
1998-99	**Buffalo**	**NHL**	**4**	**0**	**0**	**0**	**0**	**0**	**0**	**0**	**2**	**0.0**	**3**	**0**	**0.0**	**7**	**0**	**13:11**	....	....	....	....	....	....	....	....
	Rochester	AHL	77	3	26	29	82	....	....	....	....	....	....	....	....	....	....	....	20	2	4	6	14	....	....	....
	NHL Totals		**4**	**0**	**0**	**0**	**0**	**0**	**0**	**0**	**2**	**0.0**		**0**	**0.0**	**7**	**0**	**13:11**	....	....	....	....	....	....	....	....

WHL West Second All-Star Team (1998)

SATAN, Miroslav (SHA-tuhn) — BUF.

Left wing. Shoots left. 6'1", 195 lbs. Born, Topolcany, Czech., October 22, 1974. Edmonton's 6th choice, 111th overall, in 1993 Entry Draft.

Season	Club	League	GP	G	A	Pts	PIM	PP	SH	GW	S	%	+/-	TF	F%	H	SB	Min	GP	G	A	Pts	PIM	PP	SH	GW
1991-92	HC Topocalny	Czech-Jr.	31	30	22	52	....	....	....	....	....	....	....	....	....	....	....	....	....	....	....	....	....	....	....	....
	HC Topocalny	Czech-2	9	2	1	3	6	....	....	....	....	....	....	....	....	....	....	....	....	....	....	....	....	....	....	....
1992-93	Dukla Trencin	Czech.	38	11	6	17	....	....	....	....	....	....	....	....	....	....	....	....	....	....	....	....	....	....	....	....
1993-94	Dukla Trencin	Slovakia	30	32	16	48	16	....	....	....	....	....	....	....	....	....	....	....	....	....	....	....	....	....	....	....
	Slovakia	Olympics	8	9	0	9	0	....	....	....	....	....	....	....	....	....	....	....	....	....	....	....	....	....	....	....
1994-95	Cape Breton	AHL	25	24	16	40	15	....	....	....	....	....	....	....	....	....	....	....	....	....	....	....	....	....	....	....
	Detroit	IHL	8	1	3	4	4	....	....	....	....	....	....	....	....	....	....	....	....	....	....	....	....	....	....	....
	San Diego	IHL	6	0	2	2	6	....	....	....	....	....	....	....	....	....	....	....	....	....	....	....	....	....	....	....
1995-96	**Edmonton**	**NHL**	**62**	**18**	**17**	**35**	**22**	**6**	**0**	**4**	**113**	**15.9**	**0**	....	....	....	....	....	....	....	....	....	....	....	....	....
1996-97	**Edmonton**	**NHL**	**64**	**17**	**11**	**28**	**22**	**5**	**0**	**2**	**90**	**18.9**	**–4**	....	....	....	....	....	....	....	....	....	....	....	....	....
	Buffalo	**NHL**	**12**	**8**	**2**	**10**	**4**	**2**	**0**	**1**	**29**	**27.6**	**1**	....	....	....	....	....	**7**	**0**	**0**	**0**	**0**	**0**	**0**	**0**
1997-98	**Buffalo**	**NHL**	**79**	**22**	**24**	**46**	**34**	**9**	**0**	**4**	**139**	**15.8**	**2**	....	....	....	....	....	**14**	**5**	**4**	**9**	**4**	**4**	**0**	**1**
1998-99	**Buffalo**	**NHL**	**81**	**40**	**26**	**66**	**44**	**13**	**3**	**6**	**208**	**19.2**	**24**	**9**	**55.6**	**42**	**24**	**20:49**	**12**	**3**	**5**	**8**	**2**	**1**	**0**	**1**
	NHL Totals		**298**	**105**	**80**	**185**	**126**	**35**	**3**	**17**	**579**	**18.1**		**9**	**55.6**	**42**	**24**	**20:49**	**33**	**8**	**9**	**17**	**6**	**5**	**0**	**2**

Traded to **Buffalo** by **Edmonton** for Barrie Moore and Craig Millar, March 18, 1997.

SAVAGE, Andre — BOS.

Center. Shoots right. 6', 195 lbs. Born, Ottawa, Ont., May 27, 1975.

Season	Club	League	GP	G	A	Pts	PIM	PP	SH	GW	S	%	+/-	TF	F%	H	SB	Min	GP	G	A	Pts	PIM	PP	SH	GW
1993-94	Gloucester	OJHL	56	43	74	117	....	....	....	....	....	....	....	....	....	....	....	....	....	....	....	....	....	....	....	....
1994-95	Michigan Tech	WCHA	39	7	17	24	56	....	....	....	....	....	....	....	....	....	....	....	....	....	....	....	....	....	....	....
1995-96	Michigan Tech	WCHA	38	13	27	40	42	....	....	....	....	....	....	....	....	....	....	....	....	....	....	....	....	....	....	....
1996-97	Michigan Tech	WCHA	37	18	20	38	34	....	....	....	....	....	....	....	....	....	....	....	....	....	....	....	....	....	....	....
1997-98	Michigan Tech	WCHA	33	14	27	41	34	....	....	....	....	....	....	....	....	....	....	....	....	....	....	....	....	....	....	....

								Regular Season											Playoffs							
Season	Club	League	GP	G	A	Pts	PIM	PP	SH	GW	S	%	+/-	TF	F%	H	SB	Min	GP	G	A	Pts	PIM	PP	SH	GW
1998-99	Boston	NHL	6	1	0	1	0	0	0	0	8	12.5	2	32	65.6	3	1	9:31	....	....	....	....	....			
	Providence	AHL	63	27	42	69	54	....	....	....	....	....							5	0	1	1	0			
	NHL Totals		6	1	0	1	0	0	0	0	8	12.5		32	65.6	3	1	9:31	....	....	....	....	....			

WCHA First All-Star Team (1998)
Signed as a free agent by **Boston**, June 18, 1998.

SAVAGE, Brian
MTL.

right wing. Shoots left. 6'2", 192 lbs. Born, Sudbury, Ont., February 24, 1971. Montreal's 11th choice, 171st overall, in 1991 Entry Draft.

Season	Club	League	GP	G	A	Pts	PIM	PP	SH	GW	S	%	+/-	TF	F%	H	SB	Min	GP	G	A	Pts	PIM	PP	SH	GW
1990-91	U. of Miami-Ohio	CCHA	28	5	6	11	26	....																			
1991-92	U. of Miami-Ohio	CCHA	40	24	16	40	43	....																			
1992-93	U. of Miami-Ohio	CCHA	38	*37	21	58	44	....																			
	Canada	Nat-Team	9	3	0	3	12	....																			
1993-94	Canada	Nat-Team	51	20	26	46	38	....																			
	Canada	Olympics	8	2	2	4	6	....																			
	Montreal	**NHL**	3	1	0	1	0	0	0	0	3	33.3	0						3	0	2	2	0	0	0	0
	Fredericton	AHL	17	12	15	27	4	....												....							
1994-95	**Montreal**	**NHL**	37	12	7	19	27	0	0	0	64	18.8	5						....							
1995-96	**Montreal**	**NHL**	75	25	8	33	28	4	0	4	150	16.7	-8						6	0	2	2	0	0	0	0
1996-97	**Montreal**	**NHL**	81	23	37	60	39	5	0	2	219	10.5	-14						5	1	1	2	0	0	0	0
1997-98	**Montreal**	**NHL**	64	26	17	43	36	8	0	7	152	17.1	11						9	0	2	2	6	0	0	0
1998-99	**Montreal**	**NHL**	54	16	10	26	20	5	0	4	124	12.9	-14	70	44.3	57	14	16:30	....							
	NHL Totals		314	103	79	182	150	22	0	17	712	14.5		70	44.3	57	14	16:30	23	1	7	8	8	0	0	0

CCHA First All-Star Team (1993) • NCAA West Second All-American Team (1993)

SAVARD, Marc
(sa-VAHR) CGY.

Center. Shoots left. 5'10", 180 lbs. Born, Ottawa, Ont., July 17, 1977. NY Rangers' 3rd choice, 91st overall, in 1995 Entry Draft.

Season	Club	League	GP	G	A	Pts	PIM	PP	SH	GW	S	%	+/-	TF	F%	H	SB	Min	GP	G	A	Pts	PIM	PP	SH	GW
1992-93	Metcalfe	OJHL-B	31	46	53	99	26	....																			
1993-94	Oshawa	OHL	61	18	39	57	20	....												5	4	3	7	8			
1994-95	Oshawa	OHL	66	43	96	*139	78	....												7	5	6	11	8			
1995-96	Oshawa	OHL	48	28	59	87	77	....												5	4	5	9	6			
1996-97	Oshawa	OHL	64	43	*87	*130	94	....												18	13	*24	*37	20			
1997-98	**NY Rangers**	**NHL**	28	1	5	6	4	0	0	0	32	3.1	-4						....							
	Hartford	AHL	58	21	53	74	66	....												15	8	19	27	24			
1998-99	**NY Rangers**	**NHL**	70	9	36	45	38	4	0	1	116	7.8	-7	956	48.4	30	18	14:35	....							
	Hartford	AHL	9	3	10	13	16	....												7	1	12	13	16			
	NHL Totals		98	10	41	51	42	4	0	1	148	6.8		956	48.4	30	18	14:35	....							

OHL Second All-Star Team (1995)

Traded to **Calgary** by **NY Rangers** with NY Rangers 1st round choice (Oleg Saprykin) in 1999 Entry Draft for the rights to Jan Hlavac and Calgary's 1st (Jamie Lundmark) and 3rd (later traded back to Calgary - Calgary selected Craig Andersson) round choices in 1999 Entry Draft, June 26, 1999.

SAVOIA, Ryan
(sa-VOI-ah)

Center. Shoots right. 6'1", 204 lbs. Born, Thorold, Ont., May 6, 1973.

Season	Club	League	GP	G	A	Pts	PIM	PP	SH	GW	S	%	+/-	TF	F%	H	SB	Min	GP	G	A	Pts	PIM	PP	SH	GW
1990-91	Thorold	OJHL-B	35	13	20	33	28	....																			
1991-92	Thorold	OJHL-B	41	26	24	50	46	....																			
1992-93	Thorold	OJHL-B	39	27	41	68	74	....																			
1993-94	Thorold	OJHL-B	39	51	51	102	48	....																			
1994-95	Brock University	OUAA	38	35	48	83	24	....																			
	Cleveland	IHL	1	0	0	0	0	....																			
1995-96	Cleveland	IHL	49	6	7	13	31	....																			
1996-97	Johnstown	ECHL	60	35	44	79	100	....																			
	Cleveland	IHL	4	1	0	1	2	....																			
	Fort Wayne	IHL	8	0	2	2	2	....																			
1997-98	HIFK Helsinki	Finland	1	0	0	0	0	....																			
	Syracuse	AHL	7	0	4	4	2	....																			
	Johnstown	ECHL	6	1	5	6	0	....																			
1998-99	**Pittsburgh**	**NHL**	3	0	0	0	0	0	0	0	0	0.0	-1	0	0.0	1	0	2:27	....							
	Syracuse	AHL	54	9	22	31	40	....																			
	NHL Totals		3	0	0	0	0	0	0	0	0	0.0		0	0.0	1	0	2:27	....							

Signed as a free agent by **Pittsburgh**, April 7, 1995.

SAWYER, Kevin
PHX.

Left wing. Shoots left. 6'2", 205 lbs. Born, Christina Lake, B.C., February 21, 1974.

Season	Club	League	GP	G	A	Pts	PIM	PP	SH	GW	S	%	+/-	TF	F%	H	SB	Min	GP	G	A	Pts	PIM	PP	SH	GW
1991-92	Grand Forks	KIJHL	24	9	11	20	200	....																			
	Kelowna	BCJHL	3	0	0	0	9	....																			
	Vernon	BCJHL	12	0	1	1	18	....																			
	Penticton	BCJHL	3	0	0	0	13	....																			
1992-93	Spokane	WHL	62	4	3	7	274	....												8	1	1	2	13			
1993-94	Spokane	WHL	60	10	15	25	350	....												3	0	1	1	6			
1994-95	Spokane	WHL	54	7	9	16	365	....												11	2	0	2	58			
	Peoria	IHL	....																2	0	0	0	12			
1995-96	**St. Louis**	**NHL**	6	0	0	0	23	0	0	0	1	0.0	-2						....							
	Worcester	AHL	41	3	4	7	268	....												4	0	1	1	9			
	Boston	**NHL**	2	0	0	0	5	0	0	0	0	0.0	1						....							
	Providence	AHL	4	0	0	0	29	....																			
1996-97	**Boston**	**NHL**	2	0	0	0	0	0	0	0	0	0.0	0						....							
	Providence	AHL	60	8	9	17	367	....												6	0	0	0	32			
1997-98	Michigan	IHL	60	2	5	7	*398	....												3	0	0	0	23			
1998-99	Worcester	AHL	70	8	14	22	299	....												4	0	1	1	4			
	NHL Totals		10	0	0	0	28	0	0	0	1	0.0							....							

Signed as a free agent by **St. Louis**, February 28, 1995. Traded to **Boston** by **St. Louis** with Steve Staios for Steve Leach, March 8, 1996. Signed as a free agent by **Dallas**, August 19, 1997. Signed as a free agent by **St. Louis**, September 4, 1998. Signed as a free agent by **Phoenix**, August 15, 1999.

SCATCHARD, Dave
(SKAT-chuhrd)

Center. Shoots right. 6'2", 220 lbs. Born, Hinton, Alta., February 20, 1976. Vancouver's 3rd choice, 42nd overall, in 1994 Entry Draft.

Season	Club	League	GP	G	A	Pts	PIM	PP	SH	GW	S	%	+/-	TF	F%	H	SB	Min	GP	G	A	Pts	PIM	PP	SH	GW
1991-92	Salmon Arm	BCAHA	65	98	100	198	167	....																			
1992-93	Kimberley	BCJHL	51	20	23	43	61	....																			
1993-94	Portland	WHL	47	9	11	20	46	....												10	2	1	3	4			
1994-95	Portland	WHL	71	20	30	50	148	....												8	0	3	3	21			
1995-96	Portland	WHL	59	19	28	47	146	....												7	1	8	9	14			
	Syracuse	AHL	1	0	0	0	0	....												15	2	5	7	29			
1996-97	Syracuse	AHL	26	8	7	15	65	....																			
1997-98	**Vancouver**	**NHL**	76	13	11	24	165	0	0	1	85	15.3	-4						....							
1998-99	**Vancouver**	**NHL**	82	13	13	26	140	0	2	2	130	10.0	-12	1007	56.3	147	33	13:46	....							
	NHL Totals		158	26	24	50	305	0	2	3	215	12.1		1007	56.3	147	33	13:46	....							

SCHAEFER, Peter (SHAY-fuhr) VAN.

Left wing. Shoots left. 5'11", 195 lbs. Born, Yellow Grass, Sask., July 12, 1977. Vancouver's 3rd choice, 66th overall, in 1995 Entry Draft.

			Regular Season																Playoffs							
Season	Club	League	GP	G	A	Pts	PIM	PP	SH	GW	S	%	+/-	TF	F%	H	SB	Min	GP	G	A	Pts	PIM	PP	SH	GW
1993-94	Yorkton	AAHA	32	27	14	41	133																			
	Brandon	WHL	2	1	0	1	0																			
1994-95	Brandon	WHL	68	27	32	59	34												18	5	3	8	18			
1995-96	Brandon	WHL	69	47	61	108	53												19	10	13	23	5			
1996-97	Brandon	WHL	61	49	74	123	85												6	1	4	5	4			
	Syracuse	AHL	5	0	3	3	0												3	1	3	4	14			
1997-98	Syracuse	AHL	73	19	44	63	41												5	2	1	3	2			
1998-99	**Vancouver**	**NHL**	**25**	**4**	**4**	**8**	**8**	**1**	**0**	**1**	**24**	**16.7**	**–1**	**6**	**0.0**	**27**	**6**	**13:21**								
	Syracuse	AHL	41	10	19	29	66																			
	NHL Totals		**25**	**4**	**4**	**8**	**8**	**1**	**0**	**1**	**24**	**16.7**		**6**	**0.0**	**27**	**6**	**13:21**								

WHL East First All-Star Team (1996, 1997) • Canadian Major Junior First All-Star Team (1997)

SCHNEIDER, Mathieu (SHNIGH-duhr, MA-thew) NYR

Defense. Shoots left. 5'10", 192 lbs. Born, New York, NY, June 12, 1969. Montreal's 4th choice, 44th overall, in 1987 Entry Draft.

			Regular Season																Playoffs							
Season	Club	League	GP	G	A	Pts	PIM	PP	SH	GW	S	%	+/-	TF	F%	H	SB	Min	GP	G	A	Pts	PIM	PP	SH	GW
1985-86	Mt. St. Charles	H.S.	19	3	27	30																				
1986-87	Cornwall	OHL	63	7	29	36	75												5	0	0	0	22			
1987-88	Cornwall	OHL	48	21	40	61	83												11	2	6	8	14			
	Montreal	**NHL**	**4**	**0**	**0**	**0**	**2**	**0**	**0**	**0**	**2**	**0.0**	**–1**													
	Sherbrooke	AHL																	3	0	3	3	12			
1988-89	Cornwall	OHL	59	16	57	73	96												18	7	20	27	30			
1989-90	**Montreal**	**NHL**	**44**	**7**	**14**	**21**	**25**	**5**	**0**	**1**	**84**	**8.3**	**2**						**9**	**1**	**3**	**4**	**31**	**1**	**0**	**0**
	Sherbrooke	AHL	28	6	13	19	20																			
1990-91	**Montreal**	**NHL**	**69**	**10**	**20**	**30**	**63**	**5**	**0**	**3**	**164**	**6.1**	**7**						**13**	**2**	**7**	**9**	**18**	**1**	**0**	**0**
1991-92	**Montreal**	**NHL**	**78**	**8**	**24**	**32**	**72**	**2**	**0**	**1**	**194**	**4.1**	**10**						**10**	**1**	**4**	**5**	**6**	**1**	**0**	**0**
1992-93♦	**Montreal**	**NHL**	**60**	**13**	**31**	**44**	**91**	**3**	**0**	**2**	**169**	**7.7**	**8**						**11**	**1**	**2**	**3**	**16**	**0**	**0**	**0**
1993-94	**Montreal**	**NHL**	**75**	**20**	**32**	**52**	**62**	**11**	**0**	**4**	**193**	**10.4**	**15**						**1**	**0**	**0**	**0**	**0**	**0**	**0**	**0**
1994-95	**Montreal**	**NHL**	**30**	**5**	**15**	**20**	**49**	**2**	**0**	**0**	**82**	**6.1**	**–3**													
	NY Islanders	**NHL**	**13**	**3**	**6**	**9**	**30**	**1**	**0**	**2**	**36**	**8.3**	**–5**													
1995-96	**NY Islanders**	**NHL**	**65**	**11**	**36**	**47**	**93**	**7**	**0**	**1**	**155**	**7.1**	**–18**													
	Toronto	**NHL**	**13**	**2**	**5**	**7**	**10**	**0**	**0**	**0**	**36**	**5.6**	**–2**						**6**	**0**	**4**	**4**	**8**	**0**	**0**	**0**
1996-97	**Toronto**	**NHL**	**26**	**5**	**7**	**12**	**20**	**1**	**0**	**1**	**63**	**7.9**	**3**													
1997-98	**Toronto**	**NHL**	**76**	**11**	**26**	**37**	**44**	**4**	**1**	**1**	**181**	**6.1**	**–12**													
	United States	Olympics	4	0	0	0	6																			
1998-99	**NY Rangers**	**NHL**	**75**	**10**	**24**	**34**	**71**	**5**	**0**	**2**	**159**	**6.3**	**–19**	**0**	**0.0**	**182**	**149**	**24:35**								
	NHL Totals		**628**	**105**	**240**	**345**	**632**	**46**	**1**	**18**	**1518**	**6.9**		**0**	**0.0**	**182**	**149**	**24:35**	**50**	**5**	**20**	**25**	**79**	**3**	**0**	**0**

OHL First All-Star Team (1988, 1989)

Played in NHL All-Star Game (1996)

Traded to **NY Islanders** by **Montreal** with Kirk Muller and Craig Darby for Pierre Turgeon and Vladimir Malakhov, April 5, 1995. Traded to **Toronto** by **NY Islanders** with Wendel Clark and D.J. Smith for Darby Hendrickson, Sean Haggerty, Kenny Jonsson and Toronto's 1st round choice (Roberto Luongo) in 1997 Entry Draft, March 13, 1996. Rights traded to **NY Rangers** by **Toronto** for Alexander Karpovtsev and NY Rangers' 4th round choice (Mirko Murovic) in 1999 Entry Draft, October 14, 1998.

SCHULTE, Paxton (SHUHL-tee)

Left wing. Shoots left. 6'2", 217 lbs. Born, Onaway, Alta., July 16, 1972. Quebec's 7th choice, 124th overall, in 1992 Entry Draft.

			Regular Season																Playoffs							
Season	Club	League	GP	G	A	Pts	PIM	PP	SH	GW	S	%	+/-	TF	F%	H	SB	Min	GP	G	A	Pts	PIM	PP	SH	GW
1988-89	St. Albert	AAHA	28	22	35	57	38																			
1989-90	Sherwood Park	AJHL	56	28	38	66	151																			
1990-91	North Dakota	WCHA	38	2	4	6	32																			
1991-92	Spokane	WHL	70	[illegible]	[illegible]	[illegible]	222												10	2	8	10	48			
1992-93	Spokane	WHL	45	38	35	73	142												10	5	6	11	12			
1993-94	**Quebec**	**NHL**	**1**	**0**	**0**	**0**	**2**	**0**	**0**	**0**	**0**	**0.0**	**0**													
	Cornwall	AHL	56	15	15	30	102																			
1994-95	Cornwall	AHL	74	14	22	36	217												14	3	3	6	29			
1995-96	Cornwall	AHL	69	25	31	56	171																			
	Saint John	AHL	14	4	5	9	25												14	4	7	11	40			
1996-97	**Calgary**	**NHL**	**1**	**0**	**0**	**0**	**2**	**0**	**0**	**0**	**1**	**0.0**	**1**													
	Saint John	AHL	71	14	23	37	274												4	2	0	2	35			
1997-98	Saint John	AHL	59	8	17	25	133																			
	Las Vegas	IHL	10	0	1	1	32												4	0	0	0	4			
1998-99	Bracknell	Britain	36	9	10	19	153												2	0	0	0	12			
	NHL Totals		**2**	**0**	**0**	**0**	**4**	**0**	**0**	**0**	**1**	**0.0**														

Transferred to **Colorado** after **Quebec** franchise relocated, July 1, 1995. Traded to **Calgary** by **Colorado** for Vesa Viitakoski, March 19, 1996.

SCHULTZ, Ray NYI

Defense. Shoots left. 6'2", 200 lbs. Born, Red Deer, Alta., November 14, 1976. Ottawa's 8th choice, 184th overall, in 1995 Entry Draft.

			Regular Season																Playoffs							
Season	Club	League	GP	G	A	Pts	PIM	PP	SH	GW	S	%	+/-	TF	F%	H	SB	Min	GP	G	A	Pts	PIM	PP	SH	GW
1992-93	Edmonton	AAHA	31	3	24	27	94																			
1993-94	Tri-City	WHL	3	0	0	0	11																			
1994-95	Tri-City	WHL	63	1	8	9	209												11	0	0	0	16			
1995-96	Calgary	WHL	66	3	17	20	282																			
1996-97	Calgary	WHL	32	3	17	20	141																			
	Kelowna	WHL	23	3	11	14	63												6	0	2	2	12			
1997-98	**NY Islanders**	**NHL**	**13**	**0**	**1**	**1**	**45**	**0**	**0**	**0**	**4**	**0.0**	**3**													
	Kentucky	AHL	51	2	4	6	179												1	0	0	0	25			
1998-99	**NY Islanders**	**NHL**	**4**	**0**	**0**	**0**	**7**	**0**	**0**	**0**	**2**	**0.0**	**–2**	**1**	**0.0**	**5**	**1**	**15:21**								
	Lowell	AHL	54	0	3	3	184												1	0	0	0	4			
	NHL Totals		**17**	**0**	**1**	**1**	**52**	**0**	**0**	**0**	**6**	**0.0**		**1**	**0.0**	**5**	**1**	**15:21**								

Signed as a free agent by **NY Islanders**, June 9, 1997.

SELANNE, Teemu (SEH-lahn-nay, TEE-moo) ANA.

Right wing. Shoots right. 6', 200 lbs. Born, Helsinki, Finland, July 3, 1970. Winnipeg's 1st choice, 10th overall, in 1988 Entry Draft.

			Regular Season																Playoffs							
Season	Club	League	GP	G	A	Pts	PIM	PP	SH	GW	S	%	+/-	TF	F%	H	SB	Min	GP	G	A	Pts	PIM	PP	SH	GW
1987-88	Jokerit	Finn-Jr.	33	43	23	66	18												5	4	3	7	2			
	Jokerit	Finland-2	5	1	1	2	0																			
1988-89	Jokerit	Finn-Jr.	3	8	8	16	4																			
	Jokerit	Finland-2	34	35	33	68	12												5	7	3	10	4			
1989-90	Jokerit	Finland	11	4	8	12	0																			
1990-91	Jokerit	Finland	42	33	25	58	12																			
1991-92	Jokerit	Finland	44	*39	23	62	20												10	10	7	17	18			
	Finland	Olympics	8	7	4	11	6																			
1992-93	**Winnipeg**	**NHL**	**84**	***76**	**56**	**132**	**45**	**24**	**0**	**7**	**387**	**19.6**	**8**						**6**	**4**	**2**	**6**	**2**	**2**	**0**	**2**
1993-94	**Winnipeg**	**NHL**	**51**	**25**	**29**	**54**	**22**	**11**	**0**	**2**	**191**	**13.1**	**–23**													
1994-95	Jokerit	Finland	20	7	12	19	6																			
	Winnipeg	**NHL**	**45**	**22**	**26**	**48**	**2**	**8**	**2**	**1**	**167**	**13.2**	**1**													
1995-96	**Winnipeg**	**NHL**	**51**	**24**	**48**	**72**	**18**	**6**	**1**	**4**	**163**	**14.7**	**3**													
	Anaheim	**NHL**	**28**	**16**	**20**	**36**	**4**	**3**	**0**	**1**	**104**	**15.4**	**2**													
1996-97	**Anaheim**	**NHL**	**78**	**51**	**58**	**109**	**34**	**11**	**1**	**8**	**273**	**18.7**	**28**						**11**	**7**	**3**	**10**	**4**	**3**	**0**	**1**
1997-98	**Anaheim**	**NHL**	**73**	***52**	**34**	**86**	**30**	**10**	**1**	**10**	**268**	**19.4**	**12**													
	Finland	Olympics	5	4	6	*10	8																			

			Regular Season															Playoffs							
Season	Club	League	GP	G	A	Pts	PIM	PP	SH	GW	S	%	+/-	TF	F%	H	SB	Min	GP	G	A	Pts	PIM	PP	SH	GW
1998-99	**Anaheim**	**NHL**	**75**	***47**	**60**	**107**	**30**	**25**	**0**	**7**	**281**	**16.7**	**18**	**5**	**20.0**	**27**	**16**	**22:47**	**4**	**2**	**2**	**4**	**2**	**1**	**0**	**0**
	NHL Totals		**485**	**313**	**331**	**644**	**185**	**98**	**5**	**40**	**1834**	**17.1**		**5**	**20.0**	**27**	**16**	**22:47**	**21**	**13**	**7**	**20**	**8**	**6**	**0**	**3**

Won Calder Memorial Trophy (1993) • NHL First All-Star Team (1993, 1997) • NHL/Upper Deck All-Rookie Team (1993) • NHL Second All-Star Team (1998, 1999) • Won Maurice "Rocket" Richard Trophy (1999)

Played in NHL All-Star Game (1993, 1994, 1996, 1997, 1998, 1999)

Traded to **Anaheim** by **Winnipeg** with Marc Chouinard and Winnipeg's 4th round choice (later traded to Toronto — later traded to Montreal — Montreal selected Kim Staal) in 1996 Entry Draft for Chad Kilger, Oleg Tverdovsky and Anaheim's 3rd round choice (Per-Anton Lundstrom) in 1996 Entry Draft, February 7, 1996.

SELIVANOV, Alex

(seh-lih-VAH-nohv) **EDM.**

Right wing. Shoots left. 6', 208 lbs. Born, Moscow, USSR, March 23, 1971. Philadelphia's 4th choice, 140th overall, in 1994 Entry Draft.

Season	Club	League	GP	G	A	Pts	PIM	PP	SH	GW	S	%	+/-	TF	F%	H	SB	Min	GP	G	A	Pts	PIM	PP	SH	GW
1988-89	SKA Spartak	USSR	1	0	0	0	0																			
1989-90	SKA Spartak	USSR	4	0	0	0	0																			
1990-91	SKA Spartak	USSR	21	3	1	4	6																			
1991-92	SKA Spartak	CIS	31	6	7	13	16																			
1992-93	SKA Spartak	CIS	42	12	19	31	66												3	2	0	2	2			
1993-94	SKA Spartak	CIS	45	30	11	41	50												6	5	1	6	2			
1994-95	Atlanta	IHL	4	0	3	3	2																			
	Chicago	IHL	14	4	1	5	8																			
	Tampa Bay	**NHL**	**43**	**10**	**6**	**16**	**14**	**4**	**0**	**3**	**94**	**10.6**	**–2**													
1995-96	**Tampa Bay**	**NHL**	**79**	**31**	**21**	**52**	**93**	**13**	**0**	**5**	**215**	**14.4**	**3**						**6**	**2**	**2**	**4**	**6**	**0**	**0**	**1**
1996-97	**Tampa Bay**	**NHL**	**69**	**15**	**18**	**33**	**61**	**3**	**0**	**4**	**187**	**8.0**	**–3**													
1997-98	**Tampa Bay**	**NHL**	**70**	**16**	**19**	**35**	**85**	**4**	**0**	**3**	**206**	**7.8**	**–38**													
1998-99	**Tampa Bay**	**NHL**	**43**	**6**	**13**	**19**	**18**	**1**	**0**	**0**	**120**	**5.0**	**–8**	**0**	**0.0**	**40**	**5**	**15:44**								
	Cleveland	IHL	2	0	1	1	4																			
	Edmonton	**NHL**	**29**	**8**	**6**	**14**	**24**	**1**	**0**	**1**	**57**	**14.0**	**0**	**5**	**60.0**	**20**	**5**	**13:28**	**2**	**0**	**1**	**1**	**2**	**0**	**0**	**0**
	NHL Totals		**333**	**86**	**83**	**169**	**295**	**26**	**0**	**16**	**879**	**9.8**		**5**	**60.0**	**60**	**10**	**14:49**	**8**	**2**	**3**	**5**	**8**	**0**	**0**	**1**

Traded to **Tampa Bay** by **Philadelphia** for Philadelphia's 4th round choice (previously acquired, Philadelphia selected Radovan Somik) in 1995 Entry Draft, September 6, 1994. Traded to **Edmonton** by **Tampa Bay** for Alexandre Daigle, January 29, 1999.

SEMAK, Alexander

(seh-MAHK)

Center. Shoots right. 5'10", 185 lbs. Born, Ufa, USSR, February 11, 1966. New Jersey's 12th choice, 207th overall, in 1988 Entry Draft.

Season	Club	League	GP	G	A	Pts	PIM	PP	SH	GW	S	%	+/-	TF	F%	H	SB	Min	GP	G	A	Pts	PIM	PP	SH	GW
1982-83	Ufa Salavat	USSR	13	2	1	3	4																			
1983-84	Ufa Salavat	USSR-2	STATISTICS NOT AVAILABLE																							
1984-85	Ufa Salavat	USSR-2	47	19	17	36	64																			
1985-86	Ufa Salavat	USSR	22	9	7	16	22																			
1986-87	Moscow D'amo	USSR	40	20	8	28	32																			
1987-88	Moscow D'amo	USSR	47	21	14	35	40																			
1988-89	Moscow D'amo	USSR	44	18	10	28	22																			
1989-90	Moscow D'amo	USSR	43	23	11	34	33																			
1990-91	Moscow D'amo	USSR	46	17	21	38	48																			
1991-92	Moscow D'amo	CIS	26	10	13	23	26																			
	New Jersey	**NHL**	**25**	**5**	**6**	**11**	**0**	**0**	**0**	**1**	**45**	**11.1**	**5**						**1**	**0**	**0**	**0**	**0**	**0**	**0**	**0**
	Utica	AHL	7	3	2	5	0																			
1992-93	**New Jersey**	**NHL**	**82**	**37**	**42**	**79**	**70**	**4**	**1**	**6**	**217**	**17.1**	**24**						**5**	**1**	**1**	**2**	**0**	**0**	**0**	**0**
1993-94	**New Jersey**	**NHL**	**54**	**12**	**17**	**29**	**22**	**2**	**2**	**2**	**88**	**13.6**	**6**						**2**	**0**	**0**	**0**	**0**	**0**	**0**	**0**
1994-95	Ufa Salavat	CIS	9	9	6	15	4																			
	New Jersey	**NHL**	**19**	**2**	**6**	**8**	**13**	**0**	**0**	**0**	**32**	**6.3**	**–4**													
	Tampa Bay	**NHL**	**22**	**5**	**5**	**10**	**12**	**0**	**0**	**1**	**39**	**12.8**	**–3**													
1995-96	**NY Islanders**	**NHL**	**69**	**20**	**14**	**34**	**68**	**6**	**0**	**2**	**128**	**15.6**	**–4**													
1996-97	**Vancouver**	**NHL**	**18**	**2**	**1**	**3**	**2**	**1**	**0**	**0**	**12**	**16.7**	**–2**													
	Syracuse	AHL	23	10	14	24	12																			
	Las Vegas	IHL	13	11	13	24	10												3	0	4	4	4			
1997-98	Chicago	IHL	67	26	35	61	90												22	10	*17	*27	35			
1998-99	Albany	AHL	70	20	42	62	62												5	0	2	2	4			
	NHL Totals		**289**	**83**	**91**	**174**	**187**	**13**	**3**	**12**	**561**	**14.8**							**8**	**1**	**1**	**2**	**0**	**0**	**0**	**0**

USSR First All-Star Team (1991) • Won "Bud" Poile Trophy (Playoff MVP - IHL) (1998)

Traded to **Tampa Bay** by **New Jersey** with Ben Hankinson for Shawn Chambers and Danton Cole, March 14, 1995. Traded to **NY Islanders** by **Tampa Bay** for NY Islanders' 5th round choice (Karel Betik) in 1997 Entry Draft, September 14, 1995. Claimed by **Vancouver** from **NY Islanders** in NHL Waiver Draft, September 30, 1996.

SEVERYN, Brent

(SEH-vuh-rihn)

Left wing. Shoots left. 6'2", 211 lbs. Born, Vegreville, Alta., February 22, 1966. Winnipeg's 5th choice, 99th overall, in 1984 Entry Draft.

Season	Club	League	GP	G	A	Pts	PIM	PP	SH	GW	S	%	+/-	TF	F%	H	SB	Min	GP	G	A	Pts	PIM	PP	SH	GW
1982-83	Vegreville	AJHL	21	20	22	42	10																			
1983-84	Seattle	WHL	72	14	22	36	49																			
1984-85	Seattle	WHL	38	8	32	40	54																			
	Brandon	WHL	26	7	16	23	57																			
1985-86	Seattle	WHL	33	11	20	31	164																			
	Saskatoon	WHL	9	1	4	5	38																			
1986-87	U. of Alberta	CWUAA	43	7	19	26	171																			
1987-88	U. of Alberta	CWUAA	46	21	29	50	178																			
1988-89	Halifax	AHL	47	2	12	14	141																			
1989-90	**Quebec**	**NHL**	**35**	**0**	**2**	**2**	**42**	**0**	**0**	**0**	**28**	**0.0**	**–19**													
	Halifax	AHL	43	6	9	15	105												6	1	2	3	49			
1990-91	Halifax	AHL	50	7	26	33	202																			
1991-92	Utica	AHL	80	11	33	44	211												4	0	1	1	4			
1992-93	Utica	AHL	77	20	32	52	240												5	0	0	0	35			
1993-94	**Florida**	**NHL**	**67**	**4**	**7**	**11**	**156**	**1**	**0**	**1**	**93**	**4.3**	**–1**													
1994-95	**Florida**	**NHL**	**9**	**1**	**1**	**2**	**37**	**1**	**0**	**0**	**10**	**10.0**	**–3**													
	NY Islanders	**NHL**	**19**	**1**	**3**	**4**	**34**	**0**	**0**	**0**	**22**	**4.5**	**1**													
1995-96	**NY Islanders**	**NHL**	**65**	**1**	**8**	**9**	**180**	**0**	**0**	**0**	**40**	**2.5**	**3**													
1996-97	**Colorado**	**NHL**	**66**	**1**	**4**	**5**	**193**	**0**	**0**	**0**	**55**	**1.8**	**–6**						**8**	**0**	**0**	**0**	**12**	**0**	**0**	**0**
1997-98	**Anaheim**	**NHL**	**37**	**1**	**3**	**4**	**133**	**0**	**0**	**0**	**27**	**3.7**	**–3**													
1998-99	**Dallas**	**NHL**	**30**	**1**	**2**	**3**	**50**	**0**	**0**	**0**	**22**	**4.5**	**–2**	**0**	**0.0**	**20**	**0**	**5:07**								
	Michigan	IHL	3	0	0	0	0																			
	NHL Totals		**328**	**10**	**30**	**40**	**825**	**2**	**0**	**1**	**297**	**3.4**		**0**	**0.0**	**20**	**0**	**5:07**	**8**	**0**	**0**	**0**	**12**	**0**	**0**	**0**

AHL First All-Star Team (1993)

Signed as a free agent by **Quebec**, July 15, 1988. Traded to **New Jersey** by **Quebec** for Dave Marcinyshyn, June 3, 1991. Traded to **Winnipeg** by **New Jersey** for Winnipeg's 6th round choice (Ryan Smart) in 1994 Entry Draft, September 30, 1993. Traded to **Florida** by **Winnipeg** for Milan Tichy, October 3, 1993. Traded to **NY Islanders** by **Florida** for NY Islanders' 4th round choice (Dave Duerden) in 1995 Entry Draft, March 3, 1995. Traded to **Colorado** by **NY Islanders** for Colorado's 3rd round choice (later traded to Calgary — later traded to Hartford/Carolina — Carolina selected Francis Lessard) in 1997 Entry Draft, September 4, 1996. Claimed by **Anaheim** from **Colorado** in NHL Waiver Draft, September 28, 1997. Signed as a free agent by **Dallas**, August 26, 1998.

SEVIGNY, Pierre

(seh-VIH-nee)

Left wing. Shoots left. 6', 195 lbs. Born, Trois-Rivières, Que., September 8, 1971. Montreal's 4th choice, 51st overall, in 1989 Entry Draft.

Season	Club	League	GP	G	A	Pts	PIM	PP	SH	GW	S	%	+/-	TF	F%	H	SB	Min	GP	G	A	Pts	PIM	PP	SH	GW
1987-88	L'est Cantonniers	QAAA	40	43	78	121	72																			
1988-89	Verdun	QMJHL	67	27	43	70	88																			
1989-90	St-Hyacinthe	QMJHL	67	47	72	119	205												12	8	8	16	42			
1990-91	St-Hyacinthe	QMJHL	60	36	46	82	203																			
1991-92	Fredericton	AHL	74	22	37	59	145												7	1	1	2	26			

			Regular Season																Playoffs							
Season	Club	League	GP	G	A	Pts	PIM	PP	SH	GW	S	%	+/–	TF	F%	H	SB	Min	GP	G	A	Pts	PIM	PP	SH	GW
1992-93	Fredericton	AHL	80	36	40	76	113	....	....	....	....	....	....	....	....	....	....	....	5	1	1	2	2	....	....	....
1993-94	**Montreal**	**NHL**	**43**	**4**	**5**	**9**	**42**	**1**	**0**	**1**	**19**	**21.1**	**6**	....	....	....	....	....	**3**	**0**	**1**	**1**	**0**	**0**	**0**	**0**
1994-95	**Montreal**	**NHL**	**19**	**0**	**0**	**0**	**15**	**0**	**0**	**0**	**6**	**0.0**	**–5**	....	....	....	....	....	....	....	....	....	....	....	....	....
1995-96	Fredericton	AHL	76	39	42	81	188	....	....	....	....	....	....	....	....	....	....	....	10	5	9	14	20	....	....	....
1996-97	**Montreal**	**NHL**	**13**	**0**	**0**	**0**	**5**	**0**	**0**	**0**	**1**	**0.0**	**0**	....	....	....	....	....	....	....	....	....	....	....	....	....
	Fredericton	AHL	32	9	17	26	58	....	....	....	....	....	....	....	....	....	....	....	....	....	....	....	....	....	....	....
1997-98	**NY Rangers**	**NHL**	**3**	**0**	**0**	**0**	**2**	**0**	**0**	**0**	**1**	**0.0**	**0**	....	....	....	....	....	....	....	....	....	....	....	....	....
	Hartford	AHL	40	18	13	31	94	....	....	....	....	....	....	....	....	....	....	....	12	3	5	8	14	....	....	....
1998-99	Long Beach	IHL	6	1	3	4	7	....	....	....	....	....	....	....	....	....	....	....	....	....	....	....	....	....	....	....
	Orlando	IHL	43	11	21	32	44	....	....	....	....	....	....	....	....	....	....	....	15	4	5	9	32	....	....	....
	NHL Totals		**78**	**4**	**5**	**9**	**64**	**1**	**0**	**1**	**27**	**14.8**		....	....	....	....	....	**3**	**0**	**1**	**1**	**0**	**0**	**0**	**0**

QMJHL First All-Star Team (1981)
QMJHL Second All-Star Team (1990, 1991)
Signed as a free agent by **NY Rangers**, August 26, 1997

SHALDYBIN, Yevgeny

(shahl-DAY-bihn, yehv-GEH-nee)

Defense. Shoots left. 6'2", 198 lbs. Born, Novosibirsk, USSR, July 29, 1975. Boston's 6th choice, 151st overall, in 1995 Entry Draft.

Season	Club	League	GP	G	A	Pts	PIM	PP	SH	GW	S	%	+/–	TF	F%	H	SB	Min	GP	G	A	Pts	PIM	PP	SH	GW
1993-94	Yaroslavl	CIS	14	0	0	0	0	....	....	....	....	....	....	....	....	....	....	....	....	....	....	....	....	....	....	....
1994-95	Yaroslavl	CIS	42	2	5	7	10	....	....	....	....	....	....	....	....	....	....	....	4	0	1	1	0	....	....	....
1995-96	Yaroslavl	CIS	41	0	2	2	10	....	....	....	....	....	....	....	....	....	....	....	3	0	1	1	2	....	....	....
1996-97	**Boston**	**NHL**	**3**	**1**	**0**	**1**	**0**	**0**	**0**	**0**	**5**	**20.0**	**–2**	....	....	....	....	....	....	....	....	....	....	....	....	....
	Providence	AHL	65	4	13	17	28	....	....	....	....	....	....	....	....	....	....	....	3	0	0	0	0	....	....	....
1997-98	Providence	AHL	63	5	7	12	54	....	....	....	....	....	....	....	....	....	....	....	....	....	....	....	....	....	....	....
1998-99	Providence	AHL	1	0	0	0	0	....	....	....	....	....	....	....	....	....	....	....	....	....	....	....	....	....	....	....
	Las Vegas	IHL	13	1	3	4	6	....	....	....	....	....	....	....	....	....	....	....	....	....	....	....	....	....	....	....
	Binghamton	UHL	61	14	38	52	38	....	....	....	....	....	....	....	....	....	....	....	....	....	....	....	....	....	....	....
	NHL Totals		**3**	**1**	**0**	**1**	**0**	**0**	**0**	**0**	**5**	**20.0**		....	....	....	....	....	....	....	....	....	....	....	....	....

SHANAHAN, Brendan

DET.

Left wing. Shoots right. 6'3", 218 lbs. Born, Mimico, Ont., January 23, 1969. New Jersey's 1st choice, 2nd overall, in 1987 Entry Draft.

Season	Club	League	GP	G	A	Pts	PIM	PP	SH	GW	S	%	+/–	TF	F%	H	SB	Min	GP	G	A	Pts	PIM	PP	SH	GW
1984-85	Mississagua	MTHL	36	20	21	41	26	....	....	....	....	....	....	....	....	....	....	....	....	....	....	....	....	....	....	....
1985-86	London	OHL	59	28	34	62	70	....	....	....	....	....	....	....	....	....	....	....	5	5	5	10	5	....	....	....
1986-87	London	OHL	56	39	53	92	92	....	....	....	....	....	....	....	....	....	....	....	....	....	....	....	....	....	....	....
1987-88	**New Jersey**	**NHL**	**65**	**7**	**19**	**26**	**131**	**2**	**0**	**2**	**72**	**9.7**	**–20**	....	....	....	....	....	**12**	**2**	**1**	**3**	**44**	**1**	**0**	**0**
1988-89	**New Jersey**	**NHL**	**68**	**22**	**28**	**50**	**115**	**9**	**0**	**0**	**152**	**14.5**	**2**	....	....	....	....	....	....	....	....	....	....	....	....	....
1989-90	**New Jersey**	**NHL**	**73**	**30**	**42**	**72**	**137**	**8**	**0**	**5**	**196**	**15.3**	**15**	....	....	....	....	....	**6**	**3**	**3**	**6**	**20**	**1**	**0**	**1**
1990-91	**New Jersey**	**NHL**	**75**	**29**	**37**	**66**	**141**	**7**	**0**	**2**	**195**	**14.9**	**4**	....	....	....	....	....	**7**	**3**	**5**	**8**	**12**	**2**	**0**	**0**
1991-92	**St. Louis**	**NHL**	**80**	**33**	**36**	**69**	**171**	**13**	**0**	**2**	**215**	**15.3**	**–3**	....	....	....	....	....	**6**	**2**	**3**	**5**	**14**	**1**	**0**	**0**
1992-93	**St. Louis**	**NHL**	**71**	**51**	**43**	**94**	**174**	**18**	**0**	**8**	**232**	**22.0**	**10**	....	....	....	....	....	**11**	**4**	**3**	**7**	**18**	**2**	**0**	**0**
1993-94	**St. Louis**	**NHL**	**81**	**52**	**50**	**102**	**211**	**15**	**7**	**8**	**397**	**13.1**	**–9**	....	....	....	....	....	**4**	**2**	**5**	**7**	**4**	**0**	**0**	**0**
1994-95	Dusseldorf	Germany	3	5	3	8	4	....	....	....	....	....	....	....	....	....	....	....	....	....	....	....	....	....	....	....
	St. Louis	**NHL**	**45**	**20**	**21**	**41**	**136**	**6**	**2**	**6**	**153**	**13.1**	**7**	....	....	....	....	....	**5**	**4**	**5**	**9**	**14**	**1**	**0**	**1**
1995-96	**Hartford**	**NHL**	**74**	**44**	**34**	**78**	**125**	**17**	**2**	**6**	**280**	**15.7**	**2**	....	....	....	....	....	....	....	....	....	....	....	....	....
1996-97	**Hartford**	**NHL**	**2**	**1**	**0**	**1**	**0**	**0**	**1**	**0**	**13**	**7.7**	**1**	....	....	....	....	....	....	....	....	....	....	....	....	....
	♦ **Detroit**	**NHL**	**79**	**46**	**41**	**87**	**131**	**20**	**2**	**7**	**323**	**14.2**	**31**	....	....	....	....	....	**20**	**9**	**8**	**17**	**43**	**2**	**0**	**2**
1997-98 ♦	**Detroit**	**NHL**	**75**	**28**	**29**	**57**	**154**	**15**	**1**	**9**	**266**	**10.5**	**6**	....	....	....	....	....	**20**	**5**	**4**	**9**	**22**	**3**	**0**	**2**
	Canada	Olympics	6	2	0	2	0	....	....	....	....	....	....	....	....	....	....	....	....	....	....	....	....	....	....	....
1998-99	**Detroit**	**NHL**	**81**	**31**	**27**	**58**	**123**	**5**	**0**	**5**	**288**	**10.8**	**2**	**18**	**44.4**	**119**	**35**	**17:31**	**10**	**3**	**7**	**10**	**6**	**1**	**0**	**1**
	NHL Totals		**869**	**394**	**407**	**801**	**1749**	**135**	**15**	**60**	**2782**	**14.2**		**18**	**44.4**	**119**	**35**	**17:31**	**101**	**37**	**44**	**81**	**197**	**14**	**0**	**7**

NHL First All-Star Team (1994)
Played in NHL All-Star Game (1994, 1996, 1997, 1998, 1999)
Signed as a free agent by **St. Louis**, July 25, 1991. Traded to **Hartford** by **St. Louis** for Chris Pronger, July 27, 1995. Traded to **Detroit** by **Hartford** with Brian Glynn for Paul Coffey, Keith Primeau and Detroit's 1st round choice (Nikos Tselios) in 1997 Entry Draft, October 9, 1996.

SHANNON, Darrin

TOR.

Left wing. Shoots left. 6'2", 210 lbs. Born, Barrie, Ont., December 8, 1969. Pittsburgh's 1st choice, 4th overall, in 1988 Entry Draft.

Season	Club	League	GP	G	A	Pts	PIM	PP	SH	GW	S	%	+/–	TF	F%	H	SB	Min	GP	G	A	Pts	PIM	PP	SH	GW
1985-86	Barrie	OJHL	40	13	22	35	21	....	....	....	....	....	....	....	....	....	....	....	....	....	....	....	....	....	....	....
1986-87	Windsor	OHL	60	16	67	83	116	....	....	....	....	....	....	....	....	....	....	....	14	4	6	10	8	....	....	....
1987-88	Windsor	OHL	43	33	41	74	49	....	....	....	....	....	....	....	....	....	....	....	12	6	12	18	9	....	....	....
1988-89	Windsor	OHL	54	33	48	81	47	....	....	....	....	....	....	....	....	....	....	....	4	1	6	7	2	....	....	....
	Buffalo	**NHL**	**3**	**0**	**0**	**0**	**0**	**0**	**0**	**0**	**0**	**0.0**	**–2**	....	....	....	....	....	**2**	**0**	**0**	**0**	**0**	**0**	**0**	**0**
1989-90	**Buffalo**	**NHL**	**17**	**2**	**7**	**9**	**4**	**0**	**0**	**0**	**20**	**10.0**	**6**	....	....	....	....	....	**6**	**0**	**1**	**1**	**4**	**0**	**0**	**0**
	Rochester	AHL	50	20	23	43	25	....	....	....	....	....	....	....	....	....	....	....	9	4	1	5	2	....	....	....
1990-91	**Buffalo**	**NHL**	**34**	**8**	**6**	**14**	**12**	**1**	**0**	**0**	**56**	**14.3**	**–11**	....	....	....	....	....	**6**	**1**	**2**	**3**	**4**	**0**	**0**	**0**
	Rochester	AHL	49	26	34	60	56	....	....	....	....	....	....	....	....	....	....	....	10	3	5	8	22	....	....	....
1991-92	**Buffalo**	**NHL**	**1**	**0**	**1**	**1**	**0**	**0**	**0**	**0**	**2**	**0.0**	**1**	....	....	....	....	....	....	....	....	....	....	....	....	....
	Winnipeg	**NHL**	**68**	**13**	**26**	**39**	**41**	**3**	**0**	**3**	**91**	**14.3**	**5**	....	....	....	....	....	**7**	**0**	**1**	**1**	**10**	**0**	**0**	**0**
1992-93	**Winnipeg**	**NHL**	**84**	**20**	**40**	**60**	**91**	**12**	**0**	**2**	**116**	**17.2**	**–4**	....	....	....	....	....	**6**	**2**	**4**	**6**	**6**	**1**	**0**	**0**
1993-94	**Winnipeg**	**NHL**	**77**	**21**	**37**	**58**	**87**	**9**	**0**	**2**	**124**	**16.9**	**–18**	....	....	....	....	....	....	....	....	....	....	....	....	....
1994-95	**Winnipeg**	**NHL**	**19**	**5**	**3**	**8**	**14**	**3**	**0**	**1**	**26**	**19.2**	**–6**	....	....	....	....	....	....	....	....	....	....	....	....	....
1995-96	**Winnipeg**	**NHL**	**63**	**5**	**18**	**23**	**28**	**0**	**0**	**1**	**74**	**6.8**	**–5**	....	....	....	....	....	**6**	**1**	**0**	**1**	**6**	**0**	**0**	**0**
1996-97	**Phoenix**	**NHL**	**82**	**11**	**13**	**24**	**41**	**1**	**0**	**2**	**104**	**10.6**	**4**	....	....	....	....	....	**7**	**3**	**1**	**4**	**4**	**0**	**0**	**1**
1997-98	**Phoenix**	**NHL**	**58**	**2**	**12**	**14**	**26**	**0**	**0**	**0**	**57**	**3.5**	**4**	....	....	....	....	....	**5**	**0**	**1**	**1**	**4**	**0**	**0**	**0**
1998-99	Grand Rapids	IHL	10	1	5	6	12	....	....	....	....	....	....	....	....	....	....	....	....	....	....	....	....	....	....	....
	NHL Totals		**506**	**87**	**163**	**250**	**344**	**29**	**0**	**11**	**670**	**13.0**		....	....	....	....	....	**45**	**7**	**10**	**17**	**38**	**1**	**0**	**1**

Canadian Major Junior Scholastic Player of the Year (1988)
Traded to **Buffalo** by **Pittsburgh** with Doug Bodger for Tom Barrasso and Buffalo's 3rd round choice (Joe Dziedzic) in 1990 Entry Draft, November 12, 1988. Traded to **Winnipeg** by **Buffalo** with Mike Hartman and Dean Kennedy for Dave McLlwain, Gord Donnelly, Winnipeg's 5th round choice (Yuri Khmylev) in 1992 Entry Draft and future considerations, October 11, 1991. Transferred to **Phoenix** after **Winnipeg** franchise relocated, July 1, 1996. • Missed majority of 1998-99 season recovering from off-season knee surgery, June 1998. Signed as a free agent by **Grand Rapids** (IHL), February 18, 1999. Signed as a free agent by **Toronto**, August 25, 1999.

SHANNON, Darryl

ATL.

Defense. Shoots left. 6'2", 208 lbs. Born, Barrie, Ont., June 21, 1968. Toronto's 2nd choice, 36th overall, in 1986 Entry Draft.

Season	Club	League	GP	G	A	Pts	PIM	PP	SH	GW	S	%	+/–	TF	F%	H	SB	Min	GP	G	A	Pts	PIM	PP	SH	GW
1984-85	Barrie	OJHL	39	5	23	28	50	....	....	....	....	....	....	....	....	....	....	....	....	....	....	....	....	....	....	....
1985-86	Windsor	OHL	57	6	21	27	52	....	....	....	....	....	....	....	....	....	....	....	16	5	6	11	22	....	....	....
1986-87	Windsor	OHL	64	23	27	50	83	....	....	....	....	....	....	....	....	....	....	....	14	4	8	12	18	....	....	....
1987-88	Windsor	OHL	60	16	67	83	116	....	....	....	....	....	....	....	....	....	....	....	12	3	8	11	17	....	....	....
1988-89	**Toronto**	**NHL**	**14**	**1**	**3**	**4**	**6**	**0**	**0**	**0**	**16**	**6.3**	**5**	....	....	....	....	....	....	....	....	....	....	....	....	....
	Newmarket	AHL	61	5	24	29	37	....	....	....	....	....	....	....	....	....	....	....	5	0	3	3	10	....	....	....
1989-90	**Toronto**	**NHL**	**10**	**0**	**1**	**1**	**12**	**0**	**0**	**0**	**16**	**0.0**	**–10**	....	....	....	....	....	....	....	....	....	....	....	....	....
	Newmarket	AHL	47	4	15	19	58	....	....	....	....	....	....	....	....	....	....	....	....	....	....	....	....	....	....	....
1990-91	**Toronto**	**NHL**	**10**	**0**	**1**	**1**	**0**	**0**	**0**	**0**	**3**	**0.0**	**1**	....	....	....	....	....	....	....	....	....	....	....	....	....
	Newmarket	AHL	47	2	14	16	51	....	....	....	....	....	....	....	....	....	....	....	....	....	....	....	....	....	....	....
1991-92	**Toronto**	**NHL**	**48**	**2**	**8**	**10**	**23**	**1**	**0**	**0**	**50**	**4.0**	**–17**	....	....	....	....	....	....	....	....	....	....	....	....	....
1992-93	**Toronto**	**NHL**	**16**	**0**	**0**	**0**	**11**	**0**	**0**	**0**	**10**	**0.0**	**–5**	....	....	....	....	....	....	....	....	....	....	....	....	....
	St. John's	AHL	7	1	1	2	4	....	....	....	....	....	....	....	....	....	....	....	....	....	....	....	....	....	....	....

Season	Club	League	GP	G	A	Pts	PIM	PP	SH	GW	S	%	+/-	TF	F%	H	SB	Min	GP	G	A	Pts	PIM	PP	SH	GW
1993-94	Winnipeg	NHL	20	0	4	4	18	0	0	0	14	0.0	-6	....	....	....	....	....	....	....	....	....	....			
	Moncton	AHL	37	1	10	11	62							....	....	....	....	....	20	1	7	8	32			
1994-95	Winnipeg	NHL	40	5	9	14	48	0	1	0	42	11.9	1	....	....	....	....	....	....	....	....	....	....			
1995-96	Winnipeg	NHL	48	2	7	9	72	0	0	0	34	5.9	5	....	....	....	....	....	....	....	....	....	....			
	Buffalo	NHL	26	2	6	8	20	0	0	0	25	8.0	10	....	....	....	....	....	....	....	....	....	....			
1996-97	Buffalo	NHL	82	4	19	23	112	1	0	1	94	4.3	23	....	....	....	....	....	12	2	3	5	8	0	0	0
1997-98	Buffalo	NHL	76	3	19	22	56	1	0	1	85	3.5	26	....	....	....	....	....	15	2	4	6	8	0	1	0
1998-99	Buffalo	NHL	71	3	12	15	52	1	0	0	80	3.8	28	1	0.0	103	111	20:10	2	0	0	0	0	0	0	0
	NHL Totals		461	22	89	111	430	4	1	2	469	4.7		1	0.0	103	111	20:10	29	4	7	11	16	0	1	0

OHL Second All-Star Team (1987) • OHL First All-Star Team (1988)
Signed as a free agent by **Winnipeg**, June 30, 1993. Traded to **Buffalo** by **Winnipeg** with Michal Grosek for Craig Muni, February 15, 1996. Claimed by **Atlanta** from **Buffalo** in Expansion Draft, June 25, 1999.

SHANTZ, Jeff (SHAWNTS) CGY.

Center. Shoots right. 6', 195 lbs. Born, Duchess, Alta., October 10, 1973. Chicago's 2nd choice, 36th overall, in 1992 Entry Draft.

Season	Club	League	GP	G	A	Pts	PIM	PP	SH	GW	S	%	+/-	TF	F%	H	SB	Min	GP	G	A	Pts	PIM	PP	SH	GW
1989-90	Medicine Hat	AAHA	36	18	31	49	30												....	....	....	....	....			
	Regina	WHL	1	0	0	0	0	....	....	....	....	....	....						....	....	....	....	....			
1990-91	Regina	WHL	69	16	21	37	22	....	....	....	....	....	....						8	2	2	4	2			
1991-92	Regina	WHL	72	39	50	89	75	....	....	....	....	....	....						....	....	....	....	....			
1992-93	Regina	WHL	64	29	54	83	75	....	....	....	....	....	....						13	2	12	14	14			
1993-94	Chicago	NHL	52	3	13	16	30	0	0	0	56	5.4	-14						6	0	0	0	6	0	0	0
	Indianapolis	IHL	19	5	9	14	20	....	....	....	....	....	....						....	....	....	....	....			
1994-95	Indianapolis	IHL	32	9	15	24	20	....	....	....	....	....	....						....	....	....	....	....			
	Chicago	NHL	45	6	12	18	33	0	2	0	58	10.3	11						16	3	1	4	2	0	0	0
1995-96	Chicago	NHL	78	6	14	20	24	1	2	0	72	8.3	12						10	2	3	5	6	0	0	0
1996-97	Chicago	NHL	69	9	21	30	28	0	1	1	86	10.5	11						6	0	4	4	6	0	0	0
1997-98	Chicago	NHL	61	11	20	31	36	1	2	2	69	15.9	0						....	....	....	....	....			
1998-99	Chicago	NHL	7	1	0	1	4	0	0	0	5	20.0	-1	72	38.9	16	1	15:14	....	....	....	....	....			
	Calgary	NHL	69	12	17	29	40	1	1	3	77	15.6	15	1112	48.4	83	35	16:47	....	....	....	....	....			
	NHL Totals		381	48	97	145	195	3	8	6	423	11.3		1184	47.8	99	36	16:38	38	5	8	13	20	0	0	0

WHL East First All-Star Team (1993)
Traded to **Calgary** by **Chicago** with Steve Dubinsky for Marty McInnis, Jamie Allison and Eric Andersson, October 27, 1998.

SHARIFIJANOV, Vadim (shah-rih-FYAH-nohv) N.J.

Right wing. Shoots left. 6', 205 lbs. Born, Ufa, USSR, December 23, 1975. New Jersey's 1st choice, 25th overall, in 1994 Entry Draft.

Season	Club	League	GP	G	A	Pts	PIM	PP	SH	GW	S	%	+/-	TF	F%	H	SB	Min	GP	G	A	Pts	PIM	PP	SH	GW
1992-93	Ufa Salavat	CIS	37	6	4	10	16	....	....	....	....	....	....						2	1	0	1	0			
1993-94	Ufa Salavat	CIS	46	10	6	16	36	....	....	....	....	....	....						5	3	0	3	4			
1994-95	CSKA Moscow	CIS	34	7	3	10	26	....	....	....	....	....	....						2	0	0	0	0			
	Albany	AHL	1	1	0	2	0	....	....	....	....	....	....						9	3	3	6	10			
1995-96	Albany	AHL	69	14	28	42	28	....	....	....	....	....	....						....	....	....	....	....			
1996-97	New Jersey	NHL	2	0	0	0	0	0	0	0	4	0.0	0						....	....	....	....	....			
	Albany	AHL	70	14	27	41	89	....	....	....	....	....	....						10	3	3	6	6			
1997-98	Albany	AHL	72	23	27	50	69	....	....	....	....	....	....						12	4	9	13	6			
1998-99	New Jersey	NHL	53	11	16	27	28	1	0	2	71	15.5	11	2	50.0	43	10	13:39	4	0	0	0	0	0	0	0
	Albany	AHL	2	1	1	2	0	....	....	....	....	....	....						....	....	....	....	....			
	NHL Totals		55	11	16	27	28	1	0	2	75	14.7		2	50.0	43	10	13:39	4	0	0	0	0	0	0	0

SHAW, Brad

Defense. Shoots right. 6', 190 lbs. Born, Cambridge, Ont., April 28, 1964. Detroit's 5th choice, 86th overall, in 1982 Entry Draft.

Season	Club	League	GP	G	A	Pts	PIM	PP	SH	GW	S	%	+/-	TF	F%	H	SB	Min	GP	G	A	Pts	PIM	PP	SH	GW
1980-81	Kitchener	OMHA	62	14	58	72	14												....	....	....	....	....			
1981-82	Ottawa	OHL	68	13	59	72	24	....	....	....	....	....	....						15	1	13	14	4			
1982-83	Ottawa	OHL	63	12	66	78	24	....	....	....	....	....	....						9	2	9	11	4			
1983-84	Ottawa	OHL	68	11	71	82	75	....	....	....	....	....	....						13	2	*27	29	9			
1984-85	Binghamton	AHL	24	1	10	11	4	....	....	....	....	....	....						8	1	8	9	6			
	Salt Lake	IHL	44	3	29	32	25	....	....	....	....	....	....						....	....	....	....	....			
1985-86	Hartford	NHL	8	0	2	2	4	0	0	0	17	0.0	-1						....	....	....	....	....			
	Binghamton	AHL	64	10	44	54	33	....	....	....	....	....	....						5	0	2	2	6			
1986-87	Hartford	NHL	2	0	0	0	0	0	0	0	2	0.0	0						....	....	....	....	....			
	Binghamton	AHL	77	9	30	39	43	....	....	....	....	....	....						12	1	8	9	2			
1987-88	Hartford	NHL	1	0	0	0	0	0	0	0	1	0.0	-1						....	....	....	....	....			
	Binghamton	AHL	73	12	50	62	50	....	....	....	....	....	....						4	0	5	5	4			
1988-89	Varese	Italy	35	10	30	40	44	....	....	....	....	....	....						11	4	8	12	13			
	Canada	Nat-Team	4	1	0	1	2																			
	Hartford	NHL	3	1	0	1	0	1	0	0	2	50.0	1						3	1	0	1	0	0	0	0
1989-90	Hartford	NHL	64	3	32	35	30	3	0	0	65	4.6	-2						7	2	5	7	0	1	0	0
1990-91	Hartford	NHL	72	4	28	32	29	2	0	1	129	3.1	-10						6	1	2	3	2	0	0	0
1991-92	Hartford	NHL	62	3	22	25	44	0	0	0	100	3.0	1						3	0	1	1	4	0	0	0
1992-93	Ottawa	NHL	81	7	34	41	34	4	0	0	166	4.2	-47						....	....	....	....	....			
1993-94	Ottawa	NHL	66	4	19	23	59	1	0	0	113	3.5	-41						....	....	....	....	....			
1994-95	Ottawa	NHL	2	0	0	0	0	0	0	0	3	0.0	3						....	....	....	....	....			
	Atlanta	IHL	26	1	18	19	17	....	....	....	....	....	....						5	3	4	7	9			
1995-96	Detroit	IHL	79	7	54	61	46	....	....	....	....	....	....						8	2	3	5	8			
1996-97	Detroit	IHL	59	6	32	38	30	....	....	....	....	....	....						21	2	9	11	10			
1997-98	Detroit	IHL	64	2	33	35	47	....	....	....	....	....	....						23	1	11	12	30			
1998-99	Washington	NHL	4	0	0	0	4	0	0	0	5	0.0	0	0	0.0	8	3	17:52	....	....	....	....	....			
	Detroit	IHL	61	10	35	45	44	....	....	....	....	....	....						....	....	....	....	....			
	St. Louis	NHL	12	0	0	0	0	0	0	0	10	0.0	0	0	0.0	8	4	12:21	0	0	0	0	0	0	0	0
	NHL Totals		377	22	137	159	208	11	0	1	613	3.6		0	0.0	16	7	13:44	23	4	8	12	6	1	0	0

OHL First All-Star Team (1984) • Won Eddie Shore Award (Outstanding Defenseman - AHL) (1987) • NHL All-Rookie Team (1990) • IHL First All-Star Team (1997)
Traded to **Hartford** by **Detroit** for Hartford's 8th round choice (Urban Nordin) in 1984 Entry Draft, May 29, 1984. Traded to **New Jersey** by **Hartford** for cash, June 13, 1992. Claimed by **Ottawa** from **New Jersey** in Expansion Draft, June 18, 1992. Signed as a free agent by **Ottawa**, March 8, 1999. Claimed on waivers by **Washington** from **Ottawa**, March 10, 1999. Traded to **St. Louis** by **Washington** with Washington's 8th round choice (Colin Hemingway) in 1999 Entry Draft for St. Louis' 6th round choice (Kyle Clark) in 1999 Entry Draft, March 18, 1999.

SHAW, David

Defense. Shoots right. 6'2", 205 lbs. Born, St. Thomas, Ont., May 25, 1964. Quebec's 1st choice, 13th overall, in 1982 Entry Draft.

Season	Club	League	GP	G	A	Pts	PIM	PP	SH	GW	S	%	+/-	TF	F%	H	SB	Min	GP	G	A	Pts	PIM	PP	SH	GW
1980-81	Stratford	OJHL-B	41	12	19	31	30												....	....	....	....	....			
1981-82	Kitchener	OHL	68	6	25	31	94	....	....	....	....	....	....						15	2	2	4	51			
1982-83	Kitchener	OHL	57	18	56	74	78	....	....	....	....	....	....						12	2	10	12	18			
	Quebec	NHL	2	0	0	0	0	0	0	0	0	0.0	-1						....	....	....	....	....			
1983-84	Kitchener	OHL	58	14	34	48	73	....	....	....	....	....	....						16	4	9	13	12			
	Quebec	NHL	3	0	0	0	0	0	0	0	3	0.0	2						....	....	....	....	....			
1984-85	Quebec	NHL	14	0	0	0	11	0	0	0	10	0.0	-5						....	....	....	....	....			
	Fredericton	AHL	48	7	6	13	73	....	....	....	....	....	....						2	0	0	0	7			
1985-86	Quebec	NHL	73	7	19	26	78	2	0	2	126	5.6	14						....	....	....	....	....			
1986-87	Quebec	NHL	75	0	19	19	69	0	0	0	136	0.0	-35						....	....	....	....	....			
1987-88	NY Rangers	NHL	68	7	25	32	100	5	0	1	141	5.0	-8						....	....	....	....	....			
1988-89	NY Rangers	NHL	63	6	11	17	88	3	1	1	85	7.1	14						4	0	2	2	30	0	0	0
1989-90	NY Rangers	NHL	22	2	10	12	22	1	1	0	24	8.3	-3						....	....	....	....	....			

			Regular Season																Playoffs							
Season	Club	League	GP	G	A	Pts	PIM	PP	SH	GW	S	%	+/–	TF	F%	H	SB	Min	GP	G	A	Pts	PIM	PP	SH	GW
1990-91	**NY Rangers**	**NHL**	**77**	**2**	**10**	**12**	**89**	**0**	**0**	**1**	**61**	**3.3**	**8**	....	....	....	....	....	**6**	**0**	**0**	**0**	**11**	**0**	**0**	**0**
1991-92	**NY Rangers**	**NHL**	**10**	**0**	**1**	**1**	**15**	**0**	**0**	**0**	**6**	**0.0**	**1**	....	....	....	....	....	....	....	....	....	....	....	....	....
	Edmonton	**NHL**	**12**	**1**	**1**	**2**	**8**	**0**	**0**	**0**	**15**	**6.7**	**–8**	....	....	....	....	....	....	....	....	....	....	....	....	....
	Minnesota	**NHL**	**37**	**0**	**7**	**7**	**49**	**0**	**0**	**0**	**49**	**0.0**	**–5**	....	....	....	....	....	**7**	**2**	**2**	**4**	**10**	**1**	**0**	**0**
1992-93	**Boston**	**NHL**	**77**	**10**	**14**	**24**	**108**	**1**	**1**	**1**	**122**	**8.2**	**10**	....	....	....	....	....	**4**	**0**	**1**	**1**	**6**	**0**	**0**	**0**
1993-94	**Boston**	**NHL**	**55**	**1**	**9**	**10**	**85**	**0**	**0**	**0**	**107**	**0.9**	**–11**	....	....	....	....	....	**13**	**1**	**2**	**3**	**16**	**0**	**0**	**1**
1994-95	**Boston**	**NHL**	**44**	**3**	**4**	**7**	**36**	**1**	**0**	**0**	**58**	**5.2**	**–9**	....	....	....	....	....	**5**	**0**	**1**	**1**	**4**	**0**	**0**	**0**
1995-96	**Tampa Bay**	**NHL**	**66**	**1**	**11**	**12**	**64**	**0**	**0**	**0**	**90**	**1.1**	**5**	....	....	....	....	....	**6**	**0**	**1**	**1**	**4**	**0**	**0**	**0**
1996-97	**Tampa Bay**	**NHL**	**57**	**1**	**10**	**11**	**72**	**0**	**0**	**0**	**59**	**1.7**	**1**	....	....	....	....	....	....	....	....	....	....	....	....	....
1997-98	**Tampa Bay**	**NHL**	**14**	**0**	**2**	**2**	**12**	**0**	**0**	**0**	**12**	**0.0**	**–2**	....	....	....	....	....	....	....	....	....	....	....	....	....
	Las Vegas	IHL	26	6	13	19	28	....	....	....	....	....	....	....	....	....	....	....	....	....	....	....	....	....	....	....
1998-99	Las Vegas	IHL	24	3	10	13	22	....	....	....	....	....	....	....	....	....	....	....	....	....	....	....	....	....	....	....
	NHL Totals		**769**	**41**	**153**	**194**	**906**	**13**	**3**	**6**	**1104**	**3.7**		....	....	....	....	....	**45**	**3**	**9**	**12**	**81**	**1**	**0**	**1**

OHL First All-Star Team (1984) • Memorial Cup All-Star Team (1984)

Traded to **NY Rangers** by **Quebec** with John Ogrodnick for Jeff Jackson and Terry Carkner, September 30, 1987. Traded to **Edmonton** by **NY Rangers** for Jeff Beukeboom, November 12, 1991. Traded to **Minnesota** by **Edmonton** for Brian Glynn, January 21, 1992. Traded to **Boston** by **Minnesota** for future considerations, September 2, 1992. Traded to **Tampa Bay** by **Boston** for Detroit's 3rd round choice (previously acquired, Boston selected Jason Doyle) in 1996 Entry Draft, August 17, 1995. Traded to **San Jose** by **Tampa Bay** with Bryan Marchment and Tampa Bay's 1st round choice (later traded to Nashville - Nashville selected David Legwand) in 1998 Entry Draft for Andrei Nazarov and Florida's 1st round choice (previously acquired, Tampa Bay selected Vincent Lecavalier) in 1998 Entry Draft, March 24, 1998.

SHEPPARD, Ray

Right wing. Shoots right. 6'1", 195 lbs. Born, Pembroke, Ont., May 27, 1966. Buffalo's 3rd choice, 60th overall, in 1984 Entry Draft.

1982-83	Brockville	OJHL	48	27	36	63	81	....	....	....	....	....	....	....	....	....	....	....	....	....	....	....	....	....	....	....
1983-84	Cornwall	OHL	68	44	36	80	69	....	....	....	....	....	....	....	....	....	....	....	....	....	....	....	....	....	....	....
1984-85	Cornwall	OHL	49	25	33	58	51	....	....	....	....	....	....	....	....	....	....	....	9	2	12	14	4	....	....	....
1985-86	Cornwall	OHL	63	*81	61	*142	25	....	....	....	....	....	....	....	....	....	....	....	6	7	4	11	0	....	....	....
1986-87	Rochester	AHL	55	18	13	31	11	....	....	....	....	....	....	....	....	....	....	....	15	12	3	15	2	....	....	....
1987-88	**Buffalo**	**NHL**	**74**	**38**	**27**	**65**	**14**	**15**	**0**	**5**	**173**	**22.0**	**–6**	....	....	....	....	....	**6**	**1**	**1**	**2**	**2**	**1**	**0**	**0**
1988-89	**Buffalo**	**NHL**	**67**	**22**	**21**	**43**	**15**	**7**	**0**	**4**	**147**	**15.0**	**–7**	....	....	....	....	....	**1**	**0**	**1**	**1**	**0**	**0**	**0**	**0**
1989-90	**Buffalo**	**NHL**	**18**	**4**	**2**	**6**	**0**	**1**	**0**	**1**	**31**	**12.9**	**3**	....	....	....	....	....	....	....	....	....	....	....	....	....
	Rochester	AHL	5	3	5	8	2	....	....	....	....	....	....	....	....	....	....	....	17	8	7	15	9	....	....	....
1990-91	**NY Rangers**	**NHL**	**59**	**24**	**23**	**47**	**21**	**7**	**0**	**5**	**129**	**18.6**	**8**	....	....	....	....	....	....	....	....	....	....	....	....	....
1991-92	**Detroit**	**NHL**	**74**	**36**	**26**	**62**	**27**	**11**	**1**	**4**	**178**	**20.2**	**7**	....	....	....	....	....	**11**	**6**	**2**	**8**	**4**	**3**	**0**	**0**
1992-93	**Detroit**	**NHL**	**70**	**32**	**34**	**66**	**29**	**10**	**0**	**1**	**183**	**17.5**	**7**	....	....	....	....	....	**7**	**2**	**3**	**5**	**0**	**2**	**0**	**0**
1993-94	**Detroit**	**NHL**	**82**	**52**	**41**	**93**	**26**	**19**	**0**	**5**	**260**	**20.0**	**13**	....	....	....	....	....	**7**	**2**	**1**	**3**	**4**	**0**	**0**	**0**
1994-95	**Detroit**	**NHL**	**43**	**30**	**10**	**40**	**17**	**11**	**0**	**5**	**125**	**24.0**	**11**	....	....	....	....	....	**17**	**4**	**3**	**7**	**5**	**2**	**0**	**0**
1995-96	**Detroit**	**NHL**	**5**	**2**	**2**	**4**	**2**	**0**	**0**	**1**	**9**	**22.2**	**0**	....	....	....	....	....	....	....	....	....	....	....	....	....
	San Jose	**NHL**	**51**	**27**	**19**	**46**	**10**	**12**	**0**	**4**	**170**	**15.9**	**–19**	....	....	....	....	....	....	....	....	....	....	....	....	....
	Florida	**NHL**	**14**	**8**	**2**	**10**	**4**	**2**	**0**	**2**	**52**	**15.4**	**0**	....	....	....	....	....	**21**	**8**	**8**	**16**	**4**	**3**	**0**	**0**
1996-97	**Florida**	**NHL**	**68**	**29**	**31**	**60**	**4**	**13**	**0**	**7**	**226**	**12.8**	**4**	....	....	....	....	....	**5**	**2**	**0**	**2**	**0**	**1**	**0**	**0**
1997-98	**Florida**	**NHL**	**61**	**14**	**17**	**31**	**21**	**5**	**0**	**1**	**136**	**10.3**	**–13**	....	....	....	....	....	....	....	....	....	....	....	....	....
	Carolina	**NHL**	**10**	**4**	**2**	**6**	**2**	**2**	**0**	**1**	**33**	**12.1**	**2**	....	....	....	....	....	....	....	....	....	....	....	....	....
1998-99	**Carolina**	**NHL**	**74**	**25**	**33**	**58**	**16**	**5**	**0**	**4**	**188**	**13.3**	**4**	**7**	**71.4**	**20**	**6**	**18:12**	**6**	**5**	**1**	**6**	**2**	**1**	**0**	**1**
	NHL Totals		**770**	**347**	**290**	**637**	**208**	**120**	**1**	**50**	**2040**	**17.0**		**7**	**71.4**	**20**	**6**	**18:12**	**81**	**30**	**20**	**50**	**21**	**13**	**0**	**1**

OHL First All-Star Team (1986) • NHL All-Rookie Team (1988)

Traded to **NY Rangers** by **Buffalo** for cash and future considerations, July 9, 1990. Signed as a free agent by **Detroit**, August 5, 1991. Traded to **San Jose** by **Detroit** for Igor Larionov and future considerations, October 24, 1995. Traded to **Florida** by **San Jose** with San Jose's 4th round choice (Joey Tetarenko) in 1996 Entry Draft for Florida's 2nd (later traded to Chicago — Chicago selected Geoff Peters) and 4th (Matt Bradley) round choices in 1996 Entry Draft, March 16, 1996. Traded to **Carolina** by **Florida** for Kirk McLean, March 24, 1998.

SHEVALIER, Jeff

(sheh-VAL-ee-ay) **T.B.**

Left wing. Shoots left. 5'11", 180 lbs. Born, Mississauga, Ont., March 14, 1974. Los Angeles' 4th choice, 111th overall, in 1992 Entry Draft.

1990-91	Acton	OJHL-C	28	29	31	60	62	....	....	....	....	....	....	....	....	....	....	....	....	....	....	....	....	....	....	....
	Georgetown	OJHL	12	11	11	22	8	....	....	....	....	....	....	....	....	....	....	....	....	....	....	....	....	....	....	....
	Oakville	OJHL	5	1	4	5	0	....	....	....	....	....	....	....	....	....	....	....	....	....	....	....	....	....	....	....
1991-92	North Bay	OHL	64	28	29	57	26	....	....	....	....	....	....	....	....	....	....	....	21	5	11	16	25	....	....	....
1992-93	North Bay	OHL	62	59	54	113	46	....	....	....	....	....	....	....	....	....	....	....	2	1	2	3	4	....	....	....
1993-94	North Bay	OHL	64	52	49	101	52	....	....	....	....	....	....	....	....	....	....	....	17	8	14	22	18	....	....	....
1994-95	Phoenix	IHL	68	31	39	70	44	....	....	....	....	....	....	....	....	....	....	....	9	5	4	9	0	....	....	....
	Los Angeles	**NHL**	**1**	**1**	**0**	**1**	**0**	**0**	**0**	**0**	**1**	**100.0**	**1**	....	....	....	....	....	....	....	....	....	....	....	....	....
1995-96	Phoenix	IHL	79	29	38	67	72	....	....	....	....	....	....	....	....	....	....	....	4	2	2	4	2	....	....	....
1996-97	**Los Angeles**	**NHL**	**26**	**4**	**9**	**13**	**6**	**1**	**0**	**0**	**42**	**9.5**	**–6**	....	....	....	....	....	....	....	....	....	....	....	....	....
	Phoenix	IHL	46	16	21	37	26	....	....	....	....	....	....	....	....	....	....	....	....	....	....	....	....	....	....	....
1997-98	Springfield	AHL	66	23	30	53	38	....	....	....	....	....	....	....	....	....	....	....	4	1	1	2	0	....	....	....
1998-99	Cincinnati	IHL	76	29	34	63	57	....	....	....	....	....	....	....	....	....	....	....	3	1	1	2	0	....	....	....
	NHL Totals		**27**	**5**	**9**	**14**	**6**	**1**	**0**	**0**	**43**	**11.6**		....	....	....	....	....	....	....	....	....	....	....	....	....

OHL First All-Star Team (1994)

Signed as a free agent by **Tampa Bay**, July 8, 1999.

SILLINGER, Mike

T.B.

Center. Shoots right. 5'10", 190 lbs. Born, Regina, Sask., June 29, 1971. Detroit's 1st choice, 11th overall, in 1989 Entry Draft.

1986-87	Regina	SAHA	31	83	51	134	....	....	....	....	....	....	....	....	....	....	....	....	....	....	....	....	....	....	....	....
1987-88	Regina	WHL	67	18	25	43	17	....	....	....	....	....	....	....	....	....	....	....	4	2	2	4	0	....	....	....
1988-89	Regina	WHL	72	53	78	131	52	....	....	....	....	....	....	....	....	....	....	....	....	....	....	....	....	....	....	....
1989-90	Regina	WHL	70	57	72	129	41	....	....	....	....	....	....	....	....	....	....	....	11	12	10	22	2	....	....	....
	Adirondack	AHL	....	....	....	....	....	....	....	....	....	....	....	....	....	....	....	....	1	0	0	0	0	....	....	....
1990-91	Regina	WHL	57	50	66	116	42	....	....	....	....	....	....	....	....	....	....	....	8	6	9	15	4	....	....	....
	Detroit	**NHL**	**3**	**0**	**1**	**1**	**0**	**0**	**0**	**0**	**6**	**0.0**	**–2**	....	....	....	....	....	**3**	**0**	**1**	**1**	**0**	**0**	**0**	**0**
1991-92	Adirondack	AHL	64	25	41	66	26	....	....	....	....	....	....	....	....	....	....	....	15	9	*19	*28	12	....	....	....
	Detroit	**NHL**	....	....	....	....	....	....	....	....	....	....	....	....	....	....	....	....	**8**	**2**	**2**	**4**	**2**	....	....	....
1992-93	**Detroit**	**NHL**	**51**	**4**	**17**	**21**	**16**	**0**	**0**	**0**	**47**	**8.5**	**0**	....	....	....	....	....	....	....	....	....	....	....	....	....
	Adirondack	AHL	15	10	20	30	31	....	....	....	....	....	....	....	....	....	....	....	11	5	13	18	10	....	....	....
1993-94	**Detroit**	**NHL**	**62**	**8**	**21**	**29**	**10**	**0**	**1**	**1**	**91**	**8.8**	**2**	....	....	....	....	....	....	....	....	....	....	....	....	....
1994-95	CE Wien	Austria	13	13	14	27	10	....	....	....	....	....	....	....	....	....	....	....	....	....	....	....	....	....	....	....
	Detroit	**NHL**	**13**	**2**	**6**	**8**	**2**	**0**	**0**	**0**	**11**	**18.2**	**3**	....	....	....	....	....	....	....	....	....	....	....	....	....
	Anaheim	**NHL**	**15**	**2**	**5**	**7**	**6**	**2**	**0**	**0**	**28**	**7.1**	**1**	....	....	....	....	....	....	....	....	....	....	....	....	....
1995-96	**Anaheim**	**NHL**	**62**	**13**	**21**	**34**	**32**	**7**	**0**	**2**	**143**	**9.1**	**–20**	....	....	....	....	....	....	....	....	....	....	....	....	....
	Vancouver	**NHL**	**12**	**1**	**3**	**4**	**6**	**0**	**1**	**0**	**16**	**6.3**	**2**	....	....	....	....	....	**6**	**0**	**0**	**0**	**2**	**0**	**0**	**0**
1996-97	**Vancouver**	**NHL**	**78**	**17**	**20**	**37**	**25**	**3**	**3**	**2**	**112**	**15.2**	**–3**	....	....	....	....	....	....	....	....	....	....	....	....	....
1997-98	**Vancouver**	**NHL**	**48**	**10**	**9**	**19**	**34**	**1**	**2**	**1**	**56**	**17.9**	**–14**	....	....	....	....	....	....	....	....	....	....	....	....	....
	Philadelphia	**NHL**	**27**	**11**	**11**	**22**	**16**	**1**	**2**	**0**	**40**	**27.5**	**3**	....	....	....	....	....	**3**	**1**	**0**	**1**	**0**	**0**	**0**	**0**
1998-99	**Philadelphia**	**NHL**	**25**	**0**	**3**	**3**	**8**	**0**	**0**	**0**	**23**	**0.0**	**–9**	**229**	**62.9**	**12**	**5**	**10:42**	....	....	....	....	....	....	....	....
	Tampa Bay	**NHL**	**54**	**8**	**2**	**10**	**28**	**0**	**2**	**0**	**69**	**11.6**	**–20**	**320**	**57.8**	**70**	**35**	**13:57**	....	....	....	....	....	....	....	....
	NHL Totals		**450**	**76**	**119**	**195**	**183**	**14**	**11**	**6**	**642**	**11.8**		**549**	**59.9**	**82**	**40**	**12:55**	**20**	**3**	**3**	**6**	**4**	**0**	**0**	**0**

WHL East Second All-Star Team (1990) • WHL East First All-Star Team (1991)

Traded to **Anaheim** by **Detroit** with Jason York for Stu Grimson, Mark Ferner and Anaheim's 6th round choice (Magnus Nilsson) in 1996 Entry Draft, April 4, 1995. Traded to **Vancouver** by **Anaheim** for Roman Oksiuta, March 15, 1996. Traded to **Philadelphia** by **Vancouver** for Philadelphia's 5th round choice (traded back to Philadelphia — Philadelphia selected Garrett Prosofsky) in 1998 Entry Draft, February 5, 1998. Traded to **Tampa Bay** by **Philadelphia** with Chris Gratton for Mikael Renberg and Daymond Langkow, December 12, 1998.

SIM, Jonathan — DAL.

Center. Shoots left. 5'9", 175 lbs. Born, New Glasgow, N.S., September 29, 1977. Dallas' 2nd choice, 70th overall, in 1996 Entry Draft.

			Regular Season																Playoffs							
Season	Club	League	GP	G	A	Pts	PIM	PP	SH	GW	S	%	+/–	TF	F%	H	SB	Min	GP	G	A	Pts	PIM	PP	SH	GW
1994-95	Sarnia	OHL	25	9	12	21	19												4	3	2	5	2			
1995-96	Sarnia	OHL	63	56	46	102	130												10	8	7	15	26			
1996-97	Sarnia	OHL	64	*56	39	95	109												12	9	5	14	32			
1997-98	Sarnia	OHL	59	44	50	94	95												5	1	4	5	14			
1998-99♦	**Dallas**	**NHL**	**7**	**1**	**0**	**1**	**12**	**0**	**0**	**0**	**8**	**12.5**	**1**	**6**	**50.0**	**15**	**0**	**11:26**	**4**	**0**	**0**	**0**	**0**	**0**	**0**	**0**
	Michigan	IHL	68	24	27	51	91												5	3	1	4	18			
	NHL Totals		**7**	**1**	**0**	**1**	**12**	**0**	**0**	**0**	**8**	**12.5**		**6**	**50.0**	**15**	**0**	**11:26**	**4**	**0**	**0**	**0**	**0**	**0**	**0**	**0**

OHL Second All-Star Team (1998)

SIMON, Chris — WSH.

Left wing. Shoots left. 6'4", 235 lbs. Born, Wawa, Ont., January 30, 1972. Philadelphia's 2nd choice, 25th overall, in 1990 Entry Draft.

			Regular Season																Playoffs							
Season	Club	League	GP	G	A	Pts	PIM	PP	SH	GW	S	%	+/–	TF	F%	H	SB	Min	GP	G	A	Pts	PIM	PP	SH	GW
1986-87	Wawa	OMHA	36	12	20	32	108																			
1987-88	S.S. Marie	OMHA	55	42	36	78	172																			
1988-89	Ottawa	OHL	36	4	2	6	31																			
1989-90	Ottawa	OHL	57	36	38	74	146												3	2	1	3	4			
1990-91	Ottawa	OHL	20	16	6	22	69												17	5	9	14	59			
1991-92	Ottawa	OHL	2	1	1	2	24																			
	S.S. Marie	OHL	31	19	25	44	143												11	5	8	13	49			
1992-93	**Quebec**	**NHL**	**16**	**1**	**1**	**2**	**67**	**0**	**0**	**1**	**15**	**6.7**	**–2**						**5**	**0**	**0**	**0**	**26**	**0**	**0**	**0**
	Halifax	AHL	36	12	6	18	131																			
1993-94	**Quebec**	**NHL**	**37**	**4**	**4**	**8**	**132**	**0**	**0**	**1**	**39**	**10.3**	**–2**													
1994-95	**Quebec**	**NHL**	**29**	**3**	**9**	**12**	**106**	**0**	**0**	**0**	**33**	**9.1**	**14**						**6**	**1**	**1**	**2**	**19**	**0**	**0**	**1**
1995-96♦	**Colorado**	**NHL**	**64**	**16**	**18**	**34**	**250**	**4**	**0**	**1**	**105**	**15.2**	**10**						**12**	**1**	**2**	**3**	**11**	**0**	**0**	**0**
1996-97	**Washington**	**NHL**	**42**	**9**	**13**	**22**	**165**	**3**	**0**	**1**	**89**	**10.1**	**–1**													
1997-98	**Washington**	**NHL**	**28**	**7**	**10**	**17**	**38**	**4**	**0**	**1**	**71**	**9.9**	**–1**						**18**	**1**	**0**	**1**	**26**	**0**	**0**	**0**
1998-99	**Washington**	**NHL**	**23**	**3**	**7**	**10**	**48**	**0**	**0**	**0**	**29**	**10.3**	**–4**	**2**	**50.0**	**53**	**5**	**12:08**								
	NHL Totals		**239**	**43**	**62**	**105**	**806**	**11**	**0**	**5**	**381**	**11.3**		**2**	**50.0**	**53**	**5**	**12:08**	**41**	**3**	**3**	**6**	**82**	**0**	**0**	**1**

Traded to **Quebec** by **Philadelphia** with Peter Forsberg, Steve Duchesne, Kerry Huffman, Mike Ricci, Ron Hextall, Philadelphia's 1st round choice in the 1993 (Jocelyn Thibault) and 1994 (later traded to Toronto — later traded to Washington — Washington selected Nolan Baumgartner) Entry Drafts and cash for Eric Lindros, June 30, 1992. Transferred to **Coloradeo** after **Quebec** franchise relocated, July 1, 1995. Traded to **Washington** by **Colorado** with Curtis Leschyshyn for Keith Jones and Washington's 1st (Scott Parker) and 4th (later traded back to Washington — Washington selected Krys Barch) round choices in 1998 Entry Draft, November 2, 1996.

SIMON, Jason

Left wing. Shoots left. 6'1", 210 lbs. Born, Sarnia, Ont., March 21, 1969. New Jersey's 9th choice, 215th overall, in 1989 Entry Draft.

			Regular Season																Playoffs							
Season	Club	League	GP	G	A	Pts	PIM	PP	SH	GW	S	%	+/–	TF	F%	H	SB	Min	GP	G	A	Pts	PIM	PP	SH	GW
1985-86	Chatham	OJHL	32	5	19	24	118																			
1986-87	London	OHL	33	1	2	3	33																			
	Sudbury	OHL	26	2	3	5	50																			
1987-88	Sudbury	OHL	26	5	7	12	35																			
	Hamilton	OHL	29	5	13	18	124												11	0	2	2	15			
1988-89	Windsor	OHL	62	23	39	62	193												4	1	4	5	13			
1989-90	Utica	AHL	16	3	4	7	28												2	0	0	0	12			
	Nashville	ECHL	13	4	3	7	81												5	1	3	4	17			
1990-91	Utica	AHL	50	2	12	14	189																			
	Johnstown	ECHL	22	11	9	20	55																			
1991-92	Utica	AHL	1	0	0	0	12																			
	San Diego	IHL	13	1	4	5	45												3	0	1	1	9			
1992-93	Detroit	ColHL	11	7	13	20	38																			
	Flint	ColHL	44	17	32	49	202																			
1993-94	Salt Lake	IHL	50	7	7	14	*323																			
	NY Islanders	**NHL**	**4**	**0**	**0**	**0**	**34**	**0**	**0**	**0**	**0**	**0.0**	**0**													
	Detroit	ColHL	13	9	16	25	87																			
1994-95	Denver	IHL	61	3	6	9	300												1	0	0	0	12			
1995-96	Springfield	AHL	18	2	2	4	90												7	1	0	1	26			
1996-97	**Phoenix**	**NHL**	**1**	**0**	**0**	**0**	**0**	**0**	**0**	**0**	**0**	**0.0**	**–1**													
	Las Vegas	IHL	64	4	3	7	402												3	0	0	0	0			
1997-98	Hershey	AHL	26	0	1	1	170																			
	Quebec	IHL	30	6	3	9	127																			
1998-99	Colorado	WCHL	60	16	23	39	419												3	1	1	2	17			
	NHL Totals		**5**	**0**	**0**	**0**	**34**	**0**	**0**	**0**	**0**	**0.0**														

Signed as a free agent by **NY Islanders**, January 6, 1994. Signed as a free agent by **Winnipeg**, August 9, 1995. Transferred to **Phoenix** after **Winnipeg** franchise relocated, July 1, 1996. Signed as a free agent by **Colorado**, August 22, 1997.

SIMPSON, Reid — CHI.

Left wing. Shoots left. 6'2", 220 lbs. Born, Flin Flon, Man., May 21, 1969. Philadelphia's 3rd choice, 72nd overall, in 1989 Entry Draft.

			Regular Season																Playoffs							
Season	Club	League	GP	G	A	Pts	PIM	PP	SH	GW	S	%	+/–	TF	F%	H	SB	Min	GP	G	A	Pts	PIM	PP	SH	GW
1984-85	Flin Flon	MAHA	50	60	70	130	100																			
1985-86	Flin Flon	MJHL	40	20	21	41	200																			
	New Westminster	WHL	2	0	0	0	0																			
1986-87	Prince Albert	WHL	47	3	8	11	105																			
1987-88	Prince Albert	WHL	72	13	14	27	164												10	1	0	1	43			
1988-89	Prince Albert	WHL	59	26	29	55	264												4	2	1	3	30			
1989-90	Prince Albert	WHL	29	15	17	32	121												14	4	7	11	34			
	Hershey	AHL	28	2	2	4	175																			
1990-91	Hershey	AHL	54	9	15	24	183												1	0	0	0	0			
1991-92	**Philadelphia**	**NHL**	**1**	**0**	**0**	**0**	**0**	**0**	**0**	**0**	**0**	**0.0**	**0**													
	Hershey	AHL	60	11	7	18	145																			
1992-93	**Minnesota**	**NHL**	**1**	**0**	**0**	**0**	**5**	**0**	**0**	**0**	**0**	**0.0**	**0**													
	Kalamazoo	IHL	45	5	5	10	193																			
1993-94	Kalamazoo	IHL	5	0	0	0	16																			
	Albany	AHL	37	9	5	14	135												5	1	1	2	18			
1994-95	Albany	AHL	70	18	25	43	268												14	1	8	9	13			
	New Jersey	**NHL**	**9**	**0**	**0**	**0**	**27**	**0**	**0**	**0**	**5**	**0.0**	**–1**													
1995-96	**New Jersey**	**NHL**	**23**	**1**	**5**	**6**	**79**	**0**	**0**	**0**	**8**	**12.5**	**2**													
	Albany	AHL	6	1	3	4	17																			
1996-97	**New Jersey**	**NHL**	**27**	**0**	**4**	**4**	**60**	**0**	**0**	**0**	**17**	**0.0**	**0**						**5**	**0**	**0**	**0**	**29**	**0**	**0**	**0**
	Albany	AHL	3	0	0	0	10																			
1997-98	**New Jersey**	**NHL**	**6**	**0**	**0**	**0**	**16**	**0**	**0**	**0**	**5**	**0.0**	**–2**													
	Chicago	**NHL**	**38**	**3**	**2**	**5**	**102**	**1**	**0**	**0**	**19**	**15.8**	**–1**													
1998-99	**Chicago**	**NHL**	**53**	**5**	**4**	**9**	**145**	**1**	**0**	**0**	**23**	**21.7**	**2**	**5**	**40.0**	**37**	**1**	**5:56**								
	NHL Totals		**158**	**9**	**15**	**24**	**434**	**2**	**0**	**0**	**77**	**11.7**		**5**	**40.0**	**37**	**1**	**5:56**	**5**	**0**	**0**	**0**	**29**	**0**	**0**	**0**

Signed as a free agent by **Minnesota**, December 14, 1992. Transferred to **Dallas** after **Minnesota** franchise relocated, June 9, 1993. Traded to **New Jersey** by **Dallas** with Roy Mitchell for future considerations, March 21, 1994. Traded to **Chicago** by **New Jersey** for Chicago's 4th round choice (Mikko Jokela) in 1998 Entry Draft and future considerations, January 8, 1998.

			Regular Season																Playoffs							
Season	Club	League	GP	G	A	Pts	PIM	PP	SH	GW	S	%	+/-	TF	F%	H	SB	Min	GP	G	A	Pts	PIM	PP	SH	GW

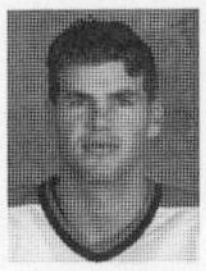

SIMPSON, Todd — CGY.

Defense. Shoots left. 6'3", 215 lbs. Born, North Vancouver, B.C., May 28, 1973.

1988-89	Don Mills	MTHL	42	36	48	84	36	....	....	....	....	....	....	....	....	....	....	....	....	....	....	....	....	....	....	....
1989-90	Port Colborne	OJHL-B	45	40	43	83	120	....	....	....	....	....	....	....	....	....	....	....	....	....	....	....	....	....	....	....
1991-92	Brown University	ECAC	18	1	4	5	38	....	....	....	....	....	....	....	....	....	....	....	....	....	....	....	....	....	....	....
1992-93	Tri-City	WHL	69	5	18	23	196	....	....	....	....	....	....	....	....	....	....	....	4	0	0	0	13	....	....	....
1993-94	Tri-City	WHL	12	2	3	5	32	....	....	....	....	....	....	....	....	....	....	....	....	....	....	....	....	....	....	....
	Saskatoon	WHL	51	7	19	26	175	....	....	....	....	....	....	....	....	....	....	....	16	1	5	6	42	....	....	....
1994-95	Saint John	AHL	80	3	10	13	321	....	....	....	....	....	....	....	....	....	....	....	5	0	0	0	4	....	....	....
1995-96	**Calgary**	**NHL**	**6**	**0**	**0**	**0**	**32**	**0**	**0**	**0**	**3**	**0.0**	**0**	....	....	....	....	....	....	....	....	....	....	....	....	....
	Saint John	AHL	66	4	13	17	277	....	....	....	....	....	....	....	....	....	....	....	16	2	3	5	32	....	....	....
1996-97	**Calgary**	**NHL**	**82**	**1**	**13**	**14**	**208**	**0**	**0**	**0**	**85**	**1.2**	**–14**	....	....	....	....	....	....	....	....	....	....	....	....	....
1997-98	**Calgary**	**NHL**	**53**	**1**	**5**	**6**	**109**	**0**	**0**	**1**	**51**	**2.0**	**–10**	....	....	....	....	....	....	....	....	....	....	....	....	....
1998-99	**Calgary**	**NHL**	**73**	**2**	**8**	**10**	**151**	**0**	**0**	**0**	**52**	**3.8**	**18**	**1**	**100.0**	**91**	**62**	**17:19**	....	....	....	....	....	....	....	....
	NHL Totals		**214**	**4**	**26**	**30**	**500**	**0**	**0**	**1**	**191**	**2.1**		**1**	**100.0**	**91**	**62**	**17:19**	....	....	....	....	....	....	....	....

Signed as free agent by **Calgary**, July 6, 1994.

SKALDE, Jarrod (SKAHL-dee)

Center. Shoots left. 6', 175 lbs. Born, Niagara Falls, Ont., February 26, 1971. New Jersey's 3rd choice, 26th overall, in 1989 Entry Draft.

1986-87	Fort Erie	OJHL-B	41	27	34	61	36	....	....	....	....	....	....	....	....	....	....	....	....	....	....	....	....	....	....	....
1987-88	Oshawa	OHL	60	12	16	28	24	....	....	....	....	....	....	....	....	....	....	....	7	2	1	3	2	....	....	....
1988-89	Oshawa	OHL	65	38	38	76	36	....	....	....	....	....	....	....	....	....	....	....	6	1	5	6	2	....	....	....
1989-90	Oshawa	OHL	62	40	52	92	66	....	....	....	....	....	....	....	....	....	....	....	17	10	7	17	6	....	....	....
1990-91	Oshawa	OHL	15	8	14	22	14	....	....	....	....	....	....	....	....	....	....	....	....	....	....	....	....	....	....	....
	Belleville	OHL	40	30	52	82	21	....	....	....	....	....	....	....	....	....	....	....	6	9	6	15	10	....	....	....
	New Jersey	**NHL**	**1**	**0**	**1**	**1**	**0**	**0**	**0**	**0**	**2**	**0.0**	**0**	....	....	....	....	....	....	....	....	....	....	....	....	....
	Utica	AHL	3	3	2	5	0	....	....	....	....	....	....	....	....	....	....	....	....	....	....	....	....	....	....	....
1991-92	**New Jersey**	**NHL**	**15**	**2**	**4**	**6**	**4**	**0**	**0**	**2**	**25**	**8.0**	**–1**	....	....	....	....	....	....	....	....	....	....	....	....	....
	Utica	AHL	62	20	20	40	56	....	....	....	....	....	....	....	....	....	....	....	4	3	1	4	8	....	....	....
1992-93	**New Jersey**	**NHL**	**11**	**0**	**2**	**2**	**4**	**0**	**0**	**0**	**11**	**0.0**	**–3**	....	....	....	....	....	....	....	....	....	....	....	....	....
	Utica	AHL	59	21	39	60	76	....	....	....	....	....	....	....	....	....	....	....	5	0	2	2	19	....	....	....
	Cincinnati	IHL	4	1	2	3	4	....	....	....	....	....	....	....	....	....	....	....	....	....	....	....	....	....	....	....
1993-94	**Anaheim**	**NHL**	**20**	**5**	**4**	**9**	**10**	**2**	**0**	**2**	**25**	**20.0**	**–3**	....	....	....	....	....	....	....	....	....	....	....	....	....
	San Diego	IHL	57	25	38	63	79	....	....	....	....	....	....	....	....	....	....	....	9	3	12	15	10	....	....	....
1994-95	Las Vegas	IHL	74	34	41	75	103	....	....	....	....	....	....	....	....	....	....	....	9	2	4	6	8	....	....	....
1995-96	Baltimore	AHL	11	2	6	8	55	....	....	....	....	....	....	....	....	....	....	....	....	....	....	....	....	....	....	....
	Calgary	**NHL**	**1**	**0**	**0**	**0**	**0**	**0**	**0**	**0**	**0**	**0.0**	**0**	....	....	....	....	....	....	....	....	....	....	....	....	....
	Saint John	AHL	68	27	40	67	98	....	....	....	....	....	....	....	....	....	....	....	16	4	9	13	6	....	....	....
1996-97	Saint John	AHL	65	32	36	68	94	....	....	....	....	....	....	....	....	....	....	....	3	0	0	0	14	....	....	....
1997-98	**San Jose**	**NHL**	**22**	**4**	**6**	**10**	**14**	**0**	**0**	**0**	**30**	**13.3**	**–2**	....	....	....	....	....	....	....	....	....	....	....	....	....
	Kentucky	AHL	6	2	6	8	10	....	....	....	....	....	....	....	....	....	....	....	....	....	....	....	....	....	....	....
	Chicago	**NHL**	**4**	**0**	**1**	**1**	**2**	**0**	**0**	**0**	**4**	**0.0**	**0**	....	....	....	....	....	....	....	....	....	....	....	....	....
	Indianapolis	IHL	2	0	2	2	0	....	....	....	....	....	....	....	....	....	....	....	....	....	....	....	....	....	....	....
	Dallas	**NHL**	**1**	**0**	**0**	**0**	**0**	**0**	**0**	**0**	**0**	**0.0**	**0**	....	....	....	....	....	....	....	....	....	....	....	....	....
	Chicago	**NHL**	**3**	**0**	**0**	**0**	**2**	**0**	**0**	**0**	**0**	**0.0**	**0**	....	....	....	....	....	....	....	....	....	....	....	....	....
	Kentucky	AHL	17	3	9	12	38	....	....	....	....	....	....	....	....	....	....	....	3	3	0	3	6	....	....	....
1998-99	**San Jose**	**NHL**	**17**	**1**	**1**	**2**	**4**	**0**	**0**	**0**	**17**	**5.9**	**–6**	**191**	**52.4**	**17**	**1**	**10:07**	....	....	....	....	....	....	....	....
	Kentucky	AHL	54	17	40	57	75	....	....	....	....	....	....	....	....	....	....	....	12	4	5	9	16	....	....	....
	NHL Totals		**95**	**12**	**19**	**31**	**40**	**2**	**0**	**4**	**114**	**10.5**		**191**	**52.4**	**17**	**1**	**10:07**	....	....	....	....	....	....	....	....

OHL Second All-Star Team (1991)

Claimed by **Anaheim** from **New Jersey** in Expansion Draft, June 24, 1993. Traded to **Calgary** by **Anaheim** for Bobby Marshall, October 30, 1995. Signed as a free agent by **San Jose**, August 14, 1997. Claimed on waivers by **Chicago** from **San Jose**, January 8, 1998. Claimed on waivers by **San Jose** from **Chicago**, January 23, 1998. Claimed on waivers by **Dallas** from **San Jose**, January 27, 1998. Claimed on waivers by **Chicago** from **Dallas**, February 10, 1998. Claimed on waivers by **San Jose** from **Chicago**, March 6, 1998.

SKOPINTSEV, Andrei (skuh-PIHN-sehf) — T.B.

Defense. Shoots right. 6', 185 lbs. Born, Elekrostal, USSR, September 28, 1971 Tampa Bay's 7th choice, 153rd overall, in 1997 Entry Draft.

1989-90	Soviet Wings	USSR	20	0	0	0	10	....	....	....	....	....	....	....	....	....	....	....	....	....	....	....	....	....	....	....
1990-91	Soviet Wings	USSR	16	0	1	1	2	....	....	....	....	....	....	....	....	....	....	....	....	....	....	....	....	....	....	....
1991-92	Soviet Wings	CIS	36	1	1	2	14	....	....	....	....	....	....	....	....	....	....	....	....	....	....	....	....	....	....	....
1992-93	Soviet Wings	CIS	12	1	0	1	4	....	....	....	....	....	....	....	....	....	....	....	7	1	0	1	2	....	....	....
1993-94	Soviet Wings	CIS	43	4	8	12	14	....	....	....	....	....	....	....	....	....	....	....	3	1	0	1	0	....	....	....
1994-95	Soviet Wings	CIS	52	8	12	20	55	....	....	....	....	....	....	....	....	....	....	....	4	1	1	2	0	....	....	....
1995-96	Augsburg	Germany	46	10	20	30	32	....	....	....	....	....	....	....	....	....	....	....	7	3	2	5	22	....	....	....
1996-97	TPS Turku	Finland	46	3	6	9	80	....	....	....	....	....	....	....	....	....	....	....	10	1	1	2	4	....	....	....
	TPS Turku	EuroHL	5	0	1	1	4	....	....	....	....	....	....	....	....	....	....	....	....	....	....	....	....	....	....	....
1997-98	TPS Turku	Finland	48	2	9	11	8	....	....	....	....	....	....	....	....	....	....	....	4	0	1	1	4	....	....	....
	TPS Turku	EuroHL	5	0	1	1	4	....	....	....	....	....	....	....	....	....	....	....	....	....	....	....	....	....	....	....
1998-99	**Tampa Bay**	**NHL**	**19**	**1**	**1**	**2**	**10**	**0**	**0**	**0**	**17**	**5.9**	**1**	**0**	**0.0**	**13**	**15**	**16:05**	....	....	....	....	....	....	....	....
	Cleveland	IHL	19	3	2	5	8	....	....	....	....	....	....	....	....	....	....	....	....	....	....	....	....	....	....	....
	NHL Totals		**19**	**1**	**1**	**2**	**10**	**0**	**0**	**0**	**17**	**5.9**		**0**	**0.0**	**13**	**15**	**16:05**	....	....	....	....	....	....	....	....

SKRASTINS, Karlis (SKA-stihnsh, kar-LIHS) — NSH.

Defense. Shoots left. 6'1", 196 lbs. Born, Riga, USSR, July 9, 1974. Nashville's 8th choice, 230th overall, in 1998 Entry Draft.

1992-93	Riga	CIS	40	3	5	8	16	....	....	....	....	....	....	....	....	....	....	....	2	0	0	0	0	....	....	....
1993-94	Riga	CIS	42	7	5	12	18	....	....	....	....	....	....	....	....	....	....	....	2	1	0	1	4	....	....	....
1994-95	Riga	CIS	52	4	14	18	69	....	....	....	....	....	....	....	....	....	....	....	....	....	....	....	....	....	....	....
1995-96	TPS Turku	Finland	50	4	11	15	32	....	....	....	....	....	....	....	....	....	....	....	11	2	2	4	10	....	....	....
1996-97	TPS Turku	Finland	50	2	8	10	20	....	....	....	....	....	....	....	....	....	....	....	12	0	4	4	2	....	....	....
	TPS Turku	EuroHL	6	0	1	1	4	....	....	....	....	....	....	....	....	....	....	....	4	0	0	0	14	....	....	....
1997-98	TPS Turku	Finland	48	4	15	19	67	....	....	....	....	....	....	....	....	....	....	....	4	0	0	0	0	....	....	....
	TPS Turku	EuroHL	6	0	1	1	6	....	....	....	....	....	....	....	....	....	....	....	....	....	....	....	....	....	....	....
1998-99	**Nashville**	**NHL**	**2**	**0**	**1**	**1**	**0**	**0**	**0**	**0**	**0**	**0.0**	**0**	**0**	**0.0**	**1**	**1**	**11:47**	....	....	....	....	....	....	....	....
	Milwaukee	IHL	75	8	36	44	47	....	....	....	....	....	....	....	....	....	....	....	2	0	1	1	2	....	....	....
	NHL Totals		**2**	**0**	**1**	**1**	**0**	**0**	**0**	**0**	**0**	**0.0**		**0**	**0.0**	**1**	**1**	**11:47**	....	....	....	....	....	....	....	....

SKRBEK, Pavel (skuhr-BEHK) — PIT.

Defense. Shoots left. 6'3", 212 lbs. Born, Kladno, Czech., August 9, 1978. Pittsburgh's 2nd choice, 28th overall, in 1996 Entry Draft.

1994-95	Poldi Kladno	Czech-Jr.	29	7	6	13	....	....	....	....	....	....	....	....	....	....	....	....	....	....	....	....	....	....	....	....
1995-96	Poldi Kladno	Czech-Jr.	29	10	12	22	....	....	....	....	....	....	....	....	....	....	....	....	....	....	....	....	....	....	....	....
	Poldi Kladno	Cze-Rep	13	0	1	1	....	....	....	....	....	....	....	....	....	....	....	....	5	0	0	0	....	....	....	....
1996-97	Poldi Kladno	Cze-Rep	35	1	5	6	26	....	....	....	....	....	....	....	....	....	....	....	3	0	0	0	4	....	....	....
1997-98	Poldi Kladno	Cze-Rep	47	4	10	14	126	....	....	....	....	....	....	....	....	....	....	....	....	....	....	....	....	....	....	....
1998-99	**Pittsburgh**	**NHL**	**4**	**0**	**0**	**0**	**2**	**0**	**0**	**0**	**1**	**0.0**	**2**	**0**	**0.0**	**6**	**3**	**14:21**	....	....	....	....	....	....	....	....
	Syracuse	AHL	64	6	16	22	38	....	....	....	....	....	....	....	....	....	....	....	....	....	....	....	....	....	....	....
	NHL Totals		**4**	**0**	**0**	**0**	**2**	**0**	**0**	**0**	**1**	**0.0**		**0**	**0.0**	**6**	**3**	**14:21**	....	....	....	....	....	....	....	....

SKRUDLAND, Brian
(SKROOD-luhnd) **DAL.**

Center. Shoots left. 6', 195 lbs. Born, Peace River, Alta., July 31, 1963.

			Regular Season																Playoffs							
Season	Club	League	GP	G	A	Pts	PIM	PP	SH	GW	S	%	+/-	TF	F%	H	SB	Min	GP	G	A	Pts	PIM	PP	SH	GW
1980-81	Saskatoon	WHL	66	15	27	42	97	....	....	....	....	....	....	....	....	....	....	....	....	....	....	....	....	....	....	....
1981-82	Saskatoon	WHL	71	27	29	56	135	....	....	....	....	....	....	....	....	....	....	....	5	0	1	1	2	....	....	....
1982-83	Saskatoon	WHL	71	35	59	94	42	....	....	....	....	....	....	....	....	....	....	....	6	1	3	4	19	....	....	....
1983-84	Nova Scotia	AHL	56	13	12	25	55	....	....	....	....	....	....	....	....	....	....	....	12	2	8	10	14	....	....	....
1984-85	Sherbrooke	AHL	70	22	28	50	109	....	....	....	....	....	....	....	....	....	....	....	17	9	8	17	23	....	....	....
1985-86♦	**Montreal**	**NHL**	65	9	13	22	57	0	2	0	62	14.5	3	....	....	....	....	....	20	2	4	6	76	0	0	1
1986-87	**Montreal**	**NHL**	79	11	17	28	107	0	1	0	72	15.3	18	....	....	....	....	....	14	1	5	6	29	0	0	0
1987-88	**Montreal**	**NHL**	79	12	24	36	112	0	1	3	96	12.5	14	....	....	....	....	....	11	1	5	6	24	0	0	0
1988-89	**Montreal**	**NHL**	71	12	29	41	84	1	1	5	98	12.2	22	....	....	....	....	....	21	3	7	10	40	0	0	0
1989-90	**Montreal**	**NHL**	59	11	31	42	56	4	0	1	70	15.7	21	....	....	....	....	....	11	3	5	8	30	0	0	1
1990-91	**Montreal**	**NHL**	57	15	19	34	85	1	1	2	71	21.1	12	....	....	....	....	....	13	3	10	13	42	1	0	0
1991-92	**Montreal**	**NHL**	42	3	3	6	36	0	0	1	51	5.9	–4	....	....	....	....	....	11	1	1	2	20	0	0	0
1992-93	**Montreal**	**NHL**	23	5	3	8	55	0	2	1	29	17.2	1	....	....	....	....	....	....	....	....	....	....	....	....	....
	Calgary	**NHL**	16	2	4	6	10	0	0	0	22	9.1	3	....	....	....	....	....	6	0	3	3	12	0	0	0
1993-94	**Florida**	**NHL**	79	15	25	40	136	0	2	1	110	13.6	13	....	....	....	....	....	....	....	....	....	....	....	....	....
1994-95	**Florida**	**NHL**	47	5	9	14	88	1	0	0	44	11.4	0	....	....	....	....	....	....	....	....	....	....	....	....	....
1995-96	**Florida**	**NHL**	79	7	20	27	129	0	1	1	90	7.8	6	....	....	....	....	....	21	1	3	4	18	0	0	0
1996-97	**Florida**	**NHL**	51	5	13	18	48	0	0	2	57	8.8	4	....	....	....	....	....	....	....	....	....	....	....	....	....
1997-98	**NY Rangers**	**NHL**	59	5	6	11	39	0	0	1	42	11.9	–4	....	....	....	....	....	....	....	....	....	....	....	....	....
	Dallas	**NHL**	13	2	0	2	10	0	0	0	13	15.4	–2	....	....	....	....	....	17	0	1	1	16	0	0	0
1998-99♦	**Dallas**	**NHL**	40	4	1	5	33	0	0	1	33	12.1	2	274	44.5	37	12	9:25	19	0	2	2	16	0	0	0
	NHL Totals		859	123	217	340	1085	7	11	19	960	12.8		274	44.5	37	12	9:25	164	15	46	61	323	1	0	2

Won Jack A. Butterfield Trophy (Playoff MVP - AHL) (1985)

Signed as a free agent by **Montreal**, September 13, 1983. Traded to **Calgary** by **Montreal** for Gary Leeman, January 28, 1993. Claimed by **Florida** from **Calgary** in Expansion Draft, June 24, 1993. Signed as a free agent by **NY Rangers**, August 21, 1997. Traded to **Dallas** by **NY Rangers** with Mike Keane and NY Rangers' 6th round choice (Pavel Patera) in 1998 Entry Draft for Todd Harvey, Bob Errey and Dallas' 4th round choice (Boyd Kane) in 1998 Entry Draft, March 24, 1998.

SLANEY, John
(SLAY-nee)

Defense. Shoots left. 6', 185 lbs. Born, St. John's, Nfld., February 7, 1972. Washington's 1st choice, 9th overall, in 1990 Entry Draft.

Season	Club	League	GP	G	A	Pts	PIM	PP	SH	GW	S	%	+/-	TF	F%	H	SB	Min	GP	G	A	Pts	PIM	PP	SH	GW
1987-88	St. John's	NFAHA	65	41	69	110	70	....	....	....	....	....	....	....	....	....	....	....	....	....	....	....	....	....	....	....
1988-89	Cornwall	OHL	66	16	43	59	23	....	....	....	....	....	....	....	....	....	....	....	18	8	16	24	10	....	....	....
1989-90	Cornwall	OHL	64	38	59	97	68	....	....	....	....	....	....	....	....	....	....	....	6	0	8	8	11	....	....	....
1990-91	Cornwall	OHL	34	21	25	46	28	....	....	....	....	....	....	....	....	....	....	....	....	....	....	....	....	....	....	....
1991-92	Cornwall	OHL	34	19	41	60	43	....	....	....	....	....	....	....	....	....	....	....	6	3	8	11	0	....	....	....
	Baltimore	AHL	6	2	4	6	0	....	....	....	....	....	....	....	....	....	....	....	....	....	....	....	....	....	....	....
1992-93	Baltimore	AHL	79	20	46	66	60	....	....	....	....	....	....	....	....	....	....	....	7	0	7	7	8	....	....	....
1993-94	**Washington**	**NHL**	47	7	9	16	27	3	0	1	70	10.0	3	....	....	....	....	....	11	1	1	2	2	1	0	0
	Portland	AHL	29	14	13	27	17	....	....	....	....	....	....	....	....	....	....	....	....	....	....	....	....	....	....	....
1994-95	**Washington**	**NHL**	16	0	3	3	6	0	0	0	21	0.0	–3	....	....	....	....	....	....	....	....	....	....	....	....	....
	Portland	AHL	8	3	10	13	4	....	....	....	....	....	....	....	....	....	....	....	7	1	3	4	4	....	....	....
1995-96	**Colorado**	**NHL**	7	0	3	3	4	0	0	0	12	0.0	2	....	....	....	....	....	....	....	....	....	....	....	....	....
	Cornwall	AHL	5	0	4	4	2	....	....	....	....	....	....	....	....	....	....	....	....	....	....	....	....	....	....	....
	Los Angeles	**NHL**	31	6	11	17	10	3	1	0	63	9.5	5	....	....	....	....	....	....	....	....	....	....	....	....	....
1996-97	**Los Angeles**	**NHL**	32	3	11	14	4	1	0	1	60	5.0	–10	....	....	....	....	....	....	....	....	....	....	....	....	....
	Phoenix	IHL	35	9	25	34	8	....	....	....	....	....	....	....	....	....	....	....	....	....	....	....	....	....	....	....
1997-98	**Phoenix**	**NHL**	55	3	14	17	24	1	0	1	74	4.1	–3	....	....	....	....	....	....	....	....	....	....	....	....	....
	Las Vegas	IHL	5	2	2	4	10	....	....	....	....	....	....	....	....	....	....	....	....	....	....	....	....	....	....	....
1998-99	**Nashville**	**NHL**	46	2	12	14	14	0	0	1	84	2.4	–12	0	0.0	54	49	20:39	....	....	....	....	....	....	....	....
	Milwaukee	IHL	7	0	1	1	0	....	....	....	....	....	....	....	....	....	....	....	....	....	....	....	....	....	....	....
	NHL Totals		234	21	63	84	89	8	1	4	384	5.5		0	0.0	54	49	20:39	11	1	1	2	2	1	0	0

OHL First All-Star Team (1990) • Canadian Major Junior Defenseman of the Year (1990) • OHL Second All-Star Team (1991)

Traded to **Colorado** by **Washington** for Philadelphia's 3rd round choice (previously acquired, Washington selected Shawn McNeil) in 1996 Entry Draft, July 12, 1995. Traded to **LA Kings** by **Colorado** for Winnipeg's 6th round choice (previously acquired, Colorado selected Brian Willsie) in 1996 Entry Draft, December 28, 1995. Signed as a free agent by **Phoenix**, August 19, 1997. Claimed by **Nashville** from **Phoenix** in Expansion Draft, June 26, 1998.

SLEGR, Jiri
(SLAY-guhr, YOO-ree) **PIT.**

Defense. Shoots left. 6', 207 lbs. Born, Jihlava, Czech., May 30, 1971. Vancouver's 3rd choice, 23rd overall, in 1990 Entry Draft.

Season	Club	League	GP	G	A	Pts	PIM	PP	SH	GW	S	%	+/-	TF	F%	H	SB	Min	GP	G	A	Pts	PIM	PP	SH	GW
1987-88	CNZ Litvinov	Czech.	4	1	1	2	0	....	....	....	....	....	....	....	....	....	....	....	....	....	....	....	....	....	....	....
1988-89	CHZ Litvinov	Czech.	8	0	0	0	4	....	....	....	....	....	....	....	....	....	....	....	....	....	....	....	....	....	....	....
1989-90	CHZ Litvinov	Czech.	51	4	15	19	....	....	....	....	....	....	....	....	....	....	....	....	....	....	....	....	....	....	....	....
1990-91	CHZ Litvinov	Czech.	47	11	36	47	26	....	....	....	....	....	....	....	....	....	....	....	....	....	....	....	....	....	....	....
1991-92	CHZ Litvinov	Czech.	42	9	23	32	38	....	....	....	....	....	....	....	....	....	....	....	....	....	....	....	....	....	....	....
	Czechoslovakia	Olympics	8	1	1	2	14	....	....	....	....	....	....	....	....	....	....	....	....	....	....	....	....	....	....	....
1992-93	**Vancouver**	**NHL**	41	4	22	26	109	2	0	0	89	4.5	16	....	....	....	....	....	5	0	3	3	4	0	0	0
	Hamilton	AHL	21	4	14	18	42	....	....	....	....	....	....	....	....	....	....	....	....	....	....	....	....	....	....	....
1993-94	**Vancouver**	**NHL**	78	5	33	38	86	1	0	0	160	3.1	0	....	....	....	....	....	....	....	....	....	....	....	....	....
1994-95	CHZ Litvinov	Cze-Rep	11	3	10	13	80	....	....	....	....	....	....	....	....	....	....	....	....	....	....	....	....	....	....	....
	Vancouver	**NHL**	19	1	5	6	32	0	0	1	42	2.4	0	....	....	....	....	....	....	....	....	....	....	....	....	....
	Edmonton	**NHL**	12	1	5	6	14	1	0	0	27	3.7	–5	....	....	....	....	....	....	....	....	....	....	....	....	....
1995-96	**Edmonton**	**NHL**	57	4	13	17	74	0	1	1	91	4.4	–1	....	....	....	....	....	....	....	....	....	....	....	....	....
	Cape Breton	AHL	4	1	2	3	4	....	....	....	....	....	....	....	....	....	....	....	....	....	....	....	....	....	....	....
1996-97	CHZ Litvinov	Cze-Re.	1	0	0	0	0	....	....	....	....	....	....	....	....	....	....	....	....	....	....	....	....	....	....	....
	Sodertalje SK	Sweden	30	4	14	18	62	....	....	....	....	....	....	....	....	....	....	....	....	....	....	....	....	....	....	....
1997-98	**Pittsburgh**	**NHL**	73	5	12	17	109	1	1	0	131	3.8	10	....	....	....	....	....	6	0	4	4	2	0	0	0
	Czech Republic	Olympics	6	1	0	1	8	....	....	....	....	....	....	....	....	....	....	....	....	....	....	....	....	....	....	....
1998-99	**Pittsburgh**	**NHL**	63	3	20	23	86	1	0	0	91	3.3	13	2	0.0	78	59	18:42	13	1	3	4	12	0	0	1
	NHL Totals		343	23	110	133	510	6	2	2	631	3.6		2	0.0	78	59	18:42	24	1	10	11	18	0	0	1

Czechoslovakian First All-Star Team (1991)

Traded to **Edmonton** by **Vancouver** for Roman Oksiuta, April 7, 1995. Traded to **Pittsburgh** by **Edmonton** for Pittsburgh's 3rd round choice (later traded to New Jersey — New Jersey selected Brian Gionta) in 1998 Entry Draft, August 12, 1997.

SLOAN, Blake
(SLOHN) **DAL.**

Right wing. Shoots right. 5'10", 193 lbs. Born, Park Ridge, IL, July 27, 1975.

Season	Club	League	GP	G	A	Pts	PIM	PP	SH	GW	S	%	+/-	TF	F%	H	SB	Min	GP	G	A	Pts	PIM	PP	SH	GW
1993-94	U. of Michigan	CCHA	38	2	4	6	48	....	....	....	....	....	....	....	....	....	....	....	....	....	....	....	....	....	....	....
1994-95	U. of Michigan	CCHA	39	2	15	17	60	....	....	....	....	....	....	....	....	....	....	....	....	....	....	....	....	....	....	....
1995-96	U. of Michigan	CCHA	41	6	24	30	55	....	....	....	....	....	....	....	....	....	....	....	....	....	....	....	....	....	....	....
1996-97	U. of Michigan	CCHA	41	2	15	17	52	....	....	....	....	....	....	....	....	....	....	....	....	....	....	....	....	....	....	....
1997-98	Houston	IHL	70	2	13	15	86	....	....	....	....	....	....	....	....	....	....	....	2	0	0	0	0	....	....	....
1998-99♦	**Dallas**	**NHL**	14	0	0	0	10	0	0	0	7	0.0	–1	0	0.0	27	3	9:01	19	0	2	2	8	0	0	0
	Houston	IHL	62	8	10	18	76	....	....	....	....	....	....	....	....	....	....	....	....	....	....	....	....	....	....	....
	NHL Totals		14	0	0	0	10	0	0	0	7	0.0		0	0.0	27	3	9:01	19	0	2	2	8	0	0	0

Signed as a free agent by **Dallas**, March 10, 1998.

SMEHLIK, Richard

(SHMEH-lihk) **BUF.**

Defense. Shoots left. 6'3", 222 lbs. Born, Ostrava, Czech., January 23, 1970. Buffalo's 3rd choice, 97th overall, in 1990 Entry Draft.

			Regular Season																Playoffs							
Season	Club	League	GP	G	A	Pts	PIM	PP	SH	GW	S	%	+/-	TF	F%	H	SB	Min	GP	G	A	Pts	PIM	PP	SH	GW
1988-89	TJ Vitkovice	Czech.	38	2	5	7	12	....	....	....	....	....	....	....	....	....	....	....	....	....	....	....	....	....	....	....
1989-90	TJ Vitkovice	Czech.	44	4	3	7	....	....	....	....	....	....	....	....	....	....	....	....	7	1	1	2	....	....	....	....
1990-91	Dukla Jihlava	Czech.	58	4	3	7	22	....	....	....	....	....	....	....	....	....	....	....	....	....	....	....	....	....	....	....
1991-92	TJ Vitkovice	Czech.	47	9	10	19	42	....	....	....	....	....	....	....	....	....	....	....	....	....	....	....	....	....	....	....
	Czechoslovakia	Olympics	8	0	1	1	2	....	....	....	....	....	....	....	....	....	....	....	....	....	....	....	....	....	....	....
1992-93	**Buffalo**	**NHL**	**80**	**4**	**27**	**31**	**59**	**0**	**0**	**0**	**82**	**4.9**	**9**	....	....	....	....	....	**8**	**0**	**4**	**4**	**2**	**0**	**0**	**0**
1993-94	**Buffalo**	**NHL**	**84**	**14**	**27**	**41**	**69**	**3**	**3**	**1**	**106**	**13.2**	**22**	....	....	....	....	....	**7**	**0**	**2**	**2**	**10**	**0**	**0**	**0**
1994-95	TJ Vitkovice	Cze-Rep	13	5	2	7	12	....	....	....	....	....	....	....	....	....	....	....	....	....	....	....	....	....	....	....
	Buffalo	**NHL**	**39**	**4**	**7**	**11**	**46**	**0**	**1**	**1**	**49**	**8.2**	**5**	....	....	....	....	....	**5**	**0**	**0**	**0**	**2**	**0**	**0**	**0**
1995-96			DID NOT PLAY – INJURED																							
1996-97	**Buffalo**	**NHL**	**62**	**11**	**19**	**30**	**43**	**2**	**0**	**1**	**100**	**11.0**	**19**	....	....	....	....	....	**12**	**0**	**2**	**2**	**4**	**0**	**0**	**0**
1997-98	**Buffalo**	**NHL**	**72**	**3**	**17**	**20**	**62**	**0**	**1**	**0**	**90**	**3.3**	**11**	....	....	....	....	....	**15**	**0**	**2**	**2**	**6**	**0**	**0**	**0**
	Czech Republic	Olympics	6	0	1	1	4	....	....	....	....	....	....	....	....	....	....	....	....	....	....	....	....	....	....	....
1998-99	**Buffalo**	**NHL**	**72**	**3**	**11**	**14**	**44**	**0**	**0**	**0**	**61**	**4.9**	**–9**	**0**	**0.0**	**107**	**87**	**21:50**	**21**	**0**	**3**	**3**	**10**	**0**	**0**	**0**
	NHL Totals		**409**	**39**	**108**	**147**	**323**	**5**	**5**	**3**	**488**	**8.0**		**0**	**0.0**	**107**	**87**	**21:50**	**68**	**0**	**13**	**13**	**34**	**0**	**0**	**0**

• Missed entire 1995-96 season after undergoing off-season knee surgery, August 11, 1995.

SMITH, Brandon

BOS.

Defense. Shoots left. 6'1", 196 lbs. Born, Hazelton, B.C., February 25, 1973.

			Regular Season																Playoffs							
Season	Club	League	GP	G	A	Pts	PIM	PP	SH	GW	S	%	+/-	TF	F%	H	SB	Min	GP	G	A	Pts	PIM	PP	SH	GW
1989-90	Portland	WHL	59	2	17	19	16	....	....	....	....	....	....	....	....	....	....	....	....	....	....	....	....	....	....	....
1990-91	Portland	WHL	17	8	5	13	8	....	....	....	....	....	....	....	....	....	....	....	....	....	....	....	....	....	....	....
1991-92	Portland	WHL	70	12	32	44	63	....	....	....	....	....	....	....	....	....	....	....	....	....	....	....	....	....	....	....
1992-93	Portland	WHL	72	20	54	74	38	....	....	....	....	....	....	....	....	....	....	....	16	4	9	13	6	....	....	....
1993-94	Portland	WHL	72	19	63	82	47	....	....	....	....	....	....	....	....	....	....	....	10	2	10	12	8	....	....	....
1994-95	Dayton	ECHL	60	16	49	65	57	....	....	....	....	....	....	....	....	....	....	....	4	2	3	5	0	....	....	....
	Minnesota	IHL	1	0	0	0	0	....	....	....	....	....	....	....	....	....	....	....	....	....	....	....	....	....	....	....
	Adirondack	AHL	14	1	2	3	7	....	....	....	....	....	....	....	....	....	....	....	3	0	0	0	2	....	....	....
1995-96	Adirondack	AHL	48	4	13	17	22	....	....	....	....	....	....	....	....	....	....	....	3	0	1	1	2	....	....	....
1996-97	Adirondack	AHL	80	8	26	34	30	....	....	....	....	....	....	....	....	....	....	....	4	0	0	0	0	....	....	....
1997-98	Adirondack	AHL	64	9	27	36	26	....	....	....	....	....	....	....	....	....	....	....	1	0	1	1	0	....	....	....
1998-99	**Boston**	**NHL**	**5**	**0**	**0**	**0**	**0**	**0**	**0**	**0**	**2**	**0.0**	**2**	**0**	**0.0**	**9**	**2**	**9:38**	....	....	....	....	....	....	....	....
	Providence	AHL	72	16	46	62	32	....	....	....	....	....	....	....	....	....	....	....	19	1	9	10	12	....	....	....
	NHL Totals		**5**	**0**	**0**	**0**	**0**	**0**	**0**	**0**	**2**	**0.0**		**0**	**0.0**	**9**	**2**	**9:38**	....	....	....	....	....	....	....	....

WHL West Second All-Star Team (1993, 1994) • ECHL First All-Star Team (1995) • Top Defenseman - ECHL (1995) • AHL First All-Star Team (1999)

Signed as a free agent by **Detroit**, July 22, 1997. Signed as a free agent by **Boston**, August 5, 1998.

SMITH, D.J.

TOR.

Defense. Shoots left. 6'1", 200 lbs. Born, Windsor, Ont., May 13, 1977. NY Islanders' 3rd choice, 41st overall, in 1995 Entry Draft.

			Regular Season																Playoffs							
Season	Club	League	GP	G	A	Pts	PIM	PP	SH	GW	S	%	+/-	TF	F%	H	SB	Min	GP	G	A	Pts	PIM	PP	SH	GW
1992-93	Belle River	OJHL-C	50	11	29	40	101	....	....	....	....	....	....	....	....	....	....	....	....	....	....	....	....	....	....	....
1993-94	Windsor	OJHL-B	51	8	34	42	267	....	....	....	....	....	....	....	....	....	....	....	....	....	....	....	....	....	....	....
1994-95	Windsor	OHL	61	4	13	17	201	....	....	....	....	....	....	....	....	....	....	....	10	1	3	4	41	....	....	....
1995-96	Windsor	OHL	64	14	45	59	260	....	....	....	....	....	....	....	....	....	....	....	7	1	7	8	23	....	....	....
	St. John's	AHL	1	0	0	0	0	....	....	....	....	....	....	....	....	....	....	....	....	....	....	....	....	....	....	....
1996-97	Windsor	OHL	63	15	52	67	190	....	....	....	....	....	....	....	....	....	....	....	5	1	7	8	11	....	....	....
	Toronto	**NHL**	**8**	**0**	**1**	**1**	**7**	**0**	**0**	**0**	**4**	**0.0**	**–5**	....	....	....	....	....	....	....	....	....	....	....	....	....
	St. John's	AHL	....	....	....	....	....	....	....	....	....	....	....	....	....	....	....	....	1	0	0	0	0	....	....	....
1997-98	St. John's	AHL	65	4	11	15	237	....	....	....	....	....	....	....	....	....	....	....	4	0	0	0	4	....	....	....
1998-99	St. John's	AHL	79	7	28	35	216	....	....	....	....	....	....	....	....	....	....	....	5	0	1	1	0	....	....	....
	NHL Totals		**8**	**0**	**1**	**1**	**7**	**0**	**0**	**0**	**4**	**0.0**		....	....	....	....	....	....	....	....	....	....	....	....	....

OHL Second All-Star Team (1997)

Traded to **Toronto** by **NY Islanders** with Wendel Clark and Mathieu Schneider for Darby Hendrickson, Sean Haggerty, Kenny Jonsson and Toronto's 1st round choice (Roberto Luongo) in 1997 Entry Draft, March 13, 1996.

SMITH, Dan

COL.

Defense. Shoots left. 6'2", 195 lbs. Born, Fernie, B.C., October 19, 1976. Colorado's 7th choice, 181st overall, in 1995 Entry Draft.

			Regular Season																Playoffs							
Season	Club	League	GP	G	A	Pts	PIM	PP	SH	GW	S	%	+/-	TF	F%	H	SB	Min	GP	G	A	Pts	PIM	PP	SH	GW
1994-95	U.B.C.	CWUAA	28	1	3	4	26	....	....	....	....	....	....	....	....	....	....	....	....	....	....	....	....	....	....	....
1995-96	Tri-City	WHL	58	1	21	22	70	....	....	....	....	....	....	....	....	....	....	....	11	1	3	4	14	....	....	....
1996-97	Tri-City	WHL	72	5	19	24	174	....	....	....	....	....	....	....	....	....	....	....	....	....	....	....	....	....	....	....
	Hershey	AHL	8	0	1	1	6	....	....	....	....	....	....	....	....	....	....	....	15	0	1	1	25	....	....	....
1997-98	Hershey	AHL	50	1	2	3	71	....	....	....	....	....	....	....	....	....	....	....	6	0	0	0	4	....	....	....
1998-99	**Colorado**	**NHL**	**12**	**0**	**0**	**0**	**9**	**0**	**0**	**0**	**6**	**0.0**	**5**	**0**	**0.0**	**3**	**11**	**12:14**	....	....	....	....	....	....	....	....
	Hershey	AHL	54	5	7	12	72	....	....	....	....	....	....	....	....	....	....	....	5	0	1	1	0	....	....	....
	NHL Totals		**12**	**0**	**0**	**0**	**9**	**0**	**0**	**0**	**6**	**0.0**		**0**	**0.0**	**3**	**11**	**12:14**	....	....	....	....	....	....	....	....

SMITH, Geoff

Defense. Shoots left. 6'3", 194 lbs. Born, Edmonton, Alta., March 7, 1969. Edmonton's 3rd choice, 63rd overall, in 1987 Entry Draft.

			Regular Season																Playoffs							
Season	Club	League	GP	G	A	Pts	PIM	PP	SH	GW	S	%	+/-	TF	F%	H	SB	Min	GP	G	A	Pts	PIM	PP	SH	GW
1985-86	Edmonton	AAHA	41	9	21	30	58	....	....	....	....	....	....	....	....	....	....	....	....	....	....	....	....	....	....	....
1986-87	St. Albert	AJHL	57	7	28	35	101	....	....	....	....	....	....	....	....	....	....	....	....	....	....	....	....	....	....	....
1987-88	North Dakota	WCHA	42	4	12	16	34	....	....	....	....	....	....	....	....	....	....	....	....	....	....	....	....	....	....	....
1988-89	North Dakota	WCHA	9	0	1	1	8	....	....	....	....	....	....	....	....	....	....	....	....	....	....	....	....	....	....	....
	Kamloops	WHL	32	4	31	35	29	....	....	....	....	....	....	....	....	....	....	....	6	1	3	4	12	....	....	....
1989-90♦	**Edmonton**	**NHL**	**74**	**4**	**11**	**15**	**52**	**1**	**0**	**0**	**66**	**6.1**	**13**	....	....	....	....	....	**3**	**0**	**0**	**0**	**0**	**0**	**0**	**0**
1990-91	**Edmonton**	**NHL**	**59**	**1**	**12**	**13**	**55**	**0**	**0**	**0**	**66**	**1.5**	**13**	....	....	....	....	....	**4**	**0**	**0**	**0**	**0**	**0**	**0**	**0**
1991-92	**Edmonton**	**NHL**	**74**	**2**	**16**	**18**	**43**	**0**	**0**	**0**	**61**	**3.3**	**–5**	....	....	....	....	....	**5**	**0**	**1**	**1**	**6**	**0**	**0**	**0**
1992-93	**Edmonton**	**NHL**	**78**	**4**	**14**	**18**	**30**	**0**	**1**	**0**	**67**	**6.0**	**–11**	....	....	....	....	....	....	....	....	....	....	....	....	....
1993-94	**Edmonton**	**NHL**	**21**	**0**	**3**	**3**	**12**	**0**	**0**	**0**	**23**	**0.0**	**–10**	....	....	....	....	....	....	....	....	....	....	....	....	....
	Florida	**NHL**	**56**	**1**	**5**	**6**	**38**	**0**	**0**	**0**	**44**	**2.3**	**–3**	....	....	....	....	....	....	....	....	....	....	....	....	....
1994-95	**Florida**	**NHL**	**47**	**2**	**4**	**6**	**22**	**0**	**0**	**0**	**40**	**5.0**	**–5**	....	....	....	....	....	....	....	....	....	....	....	....	....
1995-96	**Florida**	**NHL**	**31**	**3**	**7**	**10**	**20**	**2**	**0**	**0**	**34**	**8.8**	**–4**	....	....	....	....	....	**1**	**0**	**0**	**0**	**2**	**0**	**0**	**0**
1996-97	**Florida**	**NHL**	**3**	**0**	**0**	**0**	**2**	**0**	**0**	**0**	**2**	**0.0**	**1**	....	....	....	....	....	....	....	....	....	....	....	....	....
	Carolina	AHL	27	3	4	7	20	....	....	....	....	....	....	....	....	....	....	....	....	....	....	....	....	....	....	....
1997-98	**NY Rangers**	**NHL**	**15**	**1**	**1**	**2**	**6**	**1**	**0**	**0**	**11**	**9.1**	**–4**	....	....	....	....	....	....	....	....	....	....	....	....	....
	Hartford	AHL	59	1	12	13	34	....	....	....	....	....	....	....	....	....	....	....	....	....	....	....	....	....	....	....
1998-99	**NY Rangers**	**NHL**	**4**	**0**	**0**	**0**	**2**	**0**	**0**	**0**	**0**	**0.0**	**–5**	**0**	**0.0**	**2**	**4**	**14:56**	....	....	....	....	....	....	....	....
	Cincinnati	IHL	31	3	3	6	20	....	....	....	....	....	....	....	....	....	....	....	....	....	....	....	....	....	....	....
	Hartford	AHL	9	1	4	5	10	....	....	....	....	....	....	....	....	....	....	....	....	....	....	....	....	....	....	....
	Worcester	AHL	25	1	3	4	16	....	....	....	....	....	....	....	....	....	....	....	4	0	0	0	4	....	....	....
	NHL Totals		**462**	**18**	**73**	**91**	**282**	**4**	**1**	**0**	**414**	**4.3**		**0**	**0.0**	**2**	**4**	**14:56**	**13**	**0**	**1**	**1**	**8**	**0**	**0**	**0**

WHL West Second All-Star Team (1989) • NHL All-Rookie Team (1990)

Traded to **Florida** by **Edmonton** with Edmonton's 4th round choice (David Nemirovsky) in 1994 Entry Draft for Florida's 3rd round choice (Corey Neilson) in 1994 Entry Draft and St. Louis' 6th round choice (previously acquired and later traded to Winnipeg — Winnipeg selected Chris Kibermanis) in 1994 Entry Draft, December 6, 1993. Signed as a free agent by **NY Rangers**, September 29, 1997. Traded to **St. Louis** by **NY Rangers** with Jeff Finley for future considerations (Chris Kenady, February 22, 1999), February 13, 1999.

SMITH, Jason — EDM.

Defense. Shoots right. 6'3", 210 lbs. Born, Calgary, Alta., November 2, 1973. New Jersey's 1st choice, 18th overall, in 1992 Entry Draft.

			Regular Season																Playoffs							
Season	Club	League	GP	G	A	Pts	PIM	PP	SH	GW	S	%	+/-	TF	F%	H	SB	Min	GP	G	A	Pts	PIM	PP	SH	GW
1990-91	Calgary	AJHL	45	3	15	18	69	....	....	....	....	....	....	....	....	....	....	....	....	....	....	....	....	....	....	....
	Regina	WHL	2	0	0	0	7	....	....	....	....	....	....	....	....	....	....	....	4	0	0	0	2	....	....	....
1991-92	Regina	WHL	62	9	29	38	168	....	....	....	....	....	....	....	....	....	....	....	....	....	....	....	....	....	....	....
1992-93	Regina	WHL	64	14	52	66	175	....	....	....	....	....	....	....	....	....	....	....	13	4	8	12	39	....	....	....
	Utica	AHL	....	....	....	....	....	....	....	....	....	....	....	....	....	....	....	....	1	0	0	0	2	....	....	....
1993-94	**New Jersey**	**NHL**	**41**	**0**	**5**	**5**	**43**	**0**	**0**	**0**	**47**	**0.0**	**7**	....	....	....	....	....	**6**	**0**	**0**	**0**	**7**	**0**	**0**	**0**
	Albany	AHL	20	6	3	9	31	....	....	....	....	....	....	....	....	....	....	....	....	....	....	....	....	....	....	....
1994-95	**New Jersey**	**NHL**	**2**	**0**	**0**	**0**	**0**	**0**	**0**	**0**	**5**	**0.0**	**-3**	....	....	....	....	....	....	....	....	....	....	....	....	....
	Albany	AHL	7	0	2	2	15	....	....	....	....	....	....	....	....	....	....	....	11	2	2	4	19	....	....	....
1995-96	**New Jersey**	**NHL**	**64**	**2**	**1**	**3**	**86**	**0**	**0**	**0**	**52**	**3.8**	**5**	....	....	....	....	....	....	....	....	....	....	....	....	....
1996-97	**New Jersey**	**NHL**	**57**	**1**	**2**	**3**	**38**	**0**	**0**	**0**	**48**	**2.1**	**-8**	....	....	....	....	....	....	....	....	....	....	....	....	....
	Toronto	**NHL**	**21**	**0**	**5**	**5**	**16**	**0**	**0**	**0**	**26**	**0.0**	**-4**	....	....	....	....	....	....	....	....	....	....	....	....	....
1997-98	**Toronto**	**NHL**	**81**	**3**	**13**	**16**	**100**	**0**	**0**	**0**	**97**	**3.1**	**-5**	....	....	....	....	....	....	....	....	....	....	....	....	....
1998-99	**Toronto**	**NHL**	**60**	**2**	**11**	**13**	**40**	**0**	**0**	**0**	**53**	**3.8**	**-9**	**0**	**0.0**	**113**	**67**	**17:31**	....	....	....	....	....	....	....	....
	Edmonton	**NHL**	**12**	**1**	**1**	**2**	**11**	**0**	**0**	**0**	**15**	**6.7**	**0**	**0**	**0.0**	**35**	**26**	**20:26**	**4**	**0**	**1**	**1**	**4**	**0**	**0**	**0**
	NHL Totals		**338**	**9**	**38**	**47**	**334**	**0**	**0**	**0**	**343**	**2.6**		**0**	**0.0**	**148**	**93**	**18:00**	**10**	**0**	**1**	**1**	**11**	**0**	**0**	**0**

WHL East First All-Star Team (1993) • Canadian Major Junior First All-Star Team (1993)

Traded to **Toronto** by **New Jersey** with Steve Sullivan and the rights to Alyn McCauley for Doug Gilmour, Dave Ellett and New Jersey's 4th round choice (previously acquired — later traded to Edmonton — Edmonton selected Kristian Antila) in 1998 Entry Draft, February 25, 1997. Traded to **Edmonton** by **Toronto** for Edmonton's 4th round choice (Jonathon Zion) in 1999 Entry Draft and 2nd round choice in 2000 Entry Draft, March 23, 1999.

SMITH, Steve — CGY.

Defense. Shoots left. 6'4", 215 lbs. Born, Glasgow, Scotland, April 30, 1963. Edmonton's 5th choice, 111th overall, in 1981 Entry Draft.

			Regular Season																Playoffs							
Season	Club	League	GP	G	A	Pts	PIM	PP	SH	GW	S	%	+/-	TF	F%	H	SB	Min	GP	G	A	Pts	PIM	PP	SH	GW
1980-81	London	OHA	62	4	12	16	141	....	....	....	....	....	....	....	....	....	....	....	....	....	....	....	....	....	....	....
1981-82	London	OHL	58	10	36	46	207	....	....	....	....	....	....	....	....	....	....	....	4	1	2	3	13	....	....	....
1982-83	London	OHL	50	6	35	41	133	....	....	....	....	....	....	....	....	....	....	....	3	1	0	1	10	....	....	....
	Moncton	AHL	2	0	0	0	0	....	....	....	....	....	....	....	....	....	....	....	....	....	....	....	....	....	....	....
1983-84	Moncton	AHL	64	1	8	9	176	....	....	....	....	....	....	....	....	....	....	....	....	....	....	....	....	....	....	....
1984-85	**Edmonton**	**NHL**	**2**	**0**	**0**	**0**	**2**	**0**	**0**	**0**	**3**	**0.0**	**-2**	....	....	....	....	....	....	....	....	....	....	....	....	....
	Nova Scotia	AHL	68	2	28	30	161	....	....	....	....	....	....	....	....	....	....	....	5	0	3	3	40	....	....	....
1985-86	**Edmonton**	**NHL**	**55**	**4**	**20**	**24**	**166**	**1**	**0**	**1**	**74**	**5.4**	**30**	....	....	....	....	....	**6**	**0**	**1**	**1**	**14**	**0**	**0**	**0**
	Nova Scotia	AHL	4	0	2	2	11	....	....	....	....	....	....	....	....	....	....	....	....	....	....	....	....	....	....	....
1986-87♦	**Edmonton**	**NHL**	**62**	**7**	**15**	**22**	**165**	**2**	**0**	**1**	**71**	**9.9**	**11**	....	....	....	....	....	**15**	**1**	**3**	**4**	**45**	**0**	**0**	**0**
1987-88♦	**Edmonton**	**NHL**	**79**	**12**	**43**	**55**	**286**	**5**	**0**	**1**	**116**	**10.3**	**40**	....	....	....	....	....	**19**	**1**	**11**	**12**	**55**	**1**	**0**	**0**
1988-89	**Edmonton**	**NHL**	**35**	**3**	**19**	**22**	**97**	**0**	**0**	**0**	**47**	**6.4**	**5**	....	....	....	....	....	**7**	**2**	**2**	**4**	**20**	**0**	**0**	**1**
1989-90♦	**Edmonton**	**NHL**	**75**	**7**	**34**	**41**	**171**	**3**	**0**	**1**	**125**	**5.6**	**6**	....	....	....	....	....	**22**	**5**	**10**	**15**	**37**	**0**	**1**	**1**
1990-91	**Edmonton**	**NHL**	**77**	**13**	**41**	**54**	**193**	**4**	**0**	**2**	**114**	**11.4**	**14**	....	....	....	....	....	**18**	**1**	**2**	**3**	**45**	**1**	**0**	**0**
1991-92	**Chicago**	**NHL**	**76**	**9**	**21**	**30**	**304**	**3**	**0**	**1**	**153**	**5.9**	**23**	....	....	....	....	....	**18**	**1**	**11**	**12**	**16**	**1**	**0**	**0**
1992-93	**Chicago**	**NHL**	**78**	**10**	**47**	**57**	**214**	**7**	**1**	**2**	**212**	**4.7**	**12**	....	....	....	....	....	**4**	**0**	**0**	**0**	**10**	**0**	**0**	**0**
1993-94	**Chicago**	**NHL**	**57**	**5**	**22**	**27**	**174**	**1**	**0**	**1**	**89**	**5.6**	**-5**	....	....	....	....	....	....	....	....	....	....	....	....	....
1994-95	**Chicago**	**NHL**	**48**	**1**	**12**	**13**	**128**	**0**	**0**	**0**	**43**	**2.3**	**6**	....	....	....	....	....	**16**	**0**	**1**	**1**	**26**	**0**	**0**	**0**
1995-96	**Chicago**	**NHL**	**37**	**0**	**9**	**9**	**71**	**0**	**0**	**0**	**17**	**0.0**	**12**	....	....	....	....	....	**6**	**0**	**0**	**0**	**16**	**0**	**0**	**0**
1996-97	**Chicago**	**NHL**	**21**	**0**	**0**	**0**	**29**	**0**	**0**	**0**	**7**	**0.0**	**4**	....	....	....	....	....	**3**	**0**	**0**	**0**	**4**	**0**	**0**	**0**
1997-98	**Calgary**	**NHL**	DID NOT PLAY – ASSISTANT COACH																							
1998-99	**Calgary**	**NHL**	**69**	**1**	**14**	**15**	**80**	**0**	**0**	**0**	**42**	**2.4**	**3**	**0**	**0.0**	**93**	**98**	**22:33**	....	....	....	....	....	....	....	....
	NHL Totals		**771**	**72**	**297**	**369**	**2080**	**26**	**1**	**10**	**1113**	**6.5**		**0**	**0.0**	**93**	**98**	**22:33**	**134**	**11**	**41**	**52**	**288**	**3**	**1**	**2**

Played in NHL All-Star Game (1991)

Traded to **Chicago** by **Edmonton** for Dave Manson and Chicago's 3rd round choice (Kirk Maltby) in 1992 Entry Draft, October 2, 1991. Signed as a free agent by **Calgary**, August 18, 1998.

SMOLINSKI, Bryan — (smoh-LIHN-skee) — L.A.

Center/Right wing. Shoots right. 6'1", 202 lbs. Born, Toledo, OH, December 27, 1971. Boston's 1st choice, 21st overall, in 1990 Entry Draft.

			Regular Season																Playoffs							
Season	Club	League	GP	G	A	Pts	PIM	PP	SH	GW	S	%	+/-	TF	F%	H	SB	Min	GP	G	A	Pts	PIM	PP	SH	GW
1987-88	Detroit AAA	MNHL	80	43	77	120	....	....	....	....	....	....	....	....	....	....	....	....	....	....	....	....	....	....	....	....
1988-89	Stratford	OJHL-B	46	32	62	94	132	....	....	....	....	....	....	....	....	....	....	....	....	....	....	....	....	....	....	....
1989-90	Michigan State	CCHA	35	9	13	22	34	....	....	....	....	....	....	....	....	....	....	....	....	....	....	....	....	....	....	....
1990-91	Michigan State	CCHA	35	9	12	21	24	....	....	....	....	....	....	....	....	....	....	....	....	....	....	....	....	....	....	....
1991-92	Michigan State	CCHA	41	28	33	61	55	....	....	....	....	....	....	....	....	....	....	....	....	....	....	....	....	....	....	....
1992-93	Michigan State	CCHA	40	31	37	*68	93	....	....	....	....	....	....	....	....	....	....	....	....	....	....	....	....	....	....	....
	Boston	**NHL**	**9**	**1**	**3**	**4**	**0**	**0**	**0**	**0**	**10**	**10.0**	**3**	....	....	....	....	....	**4**	**1**	**0**	**1**	**2**	**0**	**0**	**0**
1993-94	**Boston**	**NHL**	**83**	**31**	**20**	**51**	**82**	**4**	**3**	**5**	**179**	**17.3**	**4**	....	....	....	....	....	**13**	**5**	**4**	**9**	**4**	**2**	**0**	**0**
1994-95	**Boston**	**NHL**	**44**	**18**	**13**	**31**	**31**	**6**	**0**	**5**	**121**	**14.9**	**-3**	....	....	....	....	....	**5**	**0**	**1**	**1**	**4**	**0**	**0**	**0**
1995-96	**Pittsburgh**	**NHL**	**81**	**24**	**40**	**64**	**69**	**8**	**2**	**1**	**229**	**10.5**	**6**	....	....	....	....	....	**18**	**5**	**4**	**9**	**10**	**0**	**0**	**1**
1996-97	Detroit	IHL	6	5	7	12	10	....	....	....	....	....	....	....	....	....	....	....	....	....	....	....	....	....	....	....
	NY Islanders	**NHL**	**64**	**28**	**28**	**56**	**25**	**9**	**0**	**1**	**183**	**15.3**	**9**	....	....	....	....	....	....	....	....	....	....	....	....	....
1997-98	**NY Islanders**	**NHL**	**81**	**13**	**30**	**43**	**34**	**3**	**0**	**4**	**203**	**6.4**	**-16**	....	....	....	....	....	....	....	....	....	....	....	....	....
1998-99	**NY Islanders**	**NHL**	**82**	**16**	**24**	**40**	**49**	**7**	**0**	**3**	**223**	**7.2**	**-7**	**1011**	**48.3**	**105**	**50**	**19:19**	....	....	....	....	....	....	....	....
	NHL Totals		**444**	**131**	**158**	**289**	**290**	**37**	**5**	**19**	**1148**	**11.4**		**1011**	**48.3**	**105**	**50**	**19:19**	**40**	**11**	**9**	**20**	**20**	**2**	**0**	**1**

CCHA First All-Star Team (1993) • NCAA West First All-American Team (1993)

Traded to **Pittsburgh** by **Boston** with Glen Murray and Boston's 3rd round choice (Boyd Kane) in 1996 Entry Draft for Kevin Stevens and Shawn McEachern, August 2, 1995. Traded to **NY Islanders** by **Pittsburgh** for Darius Kasparaitis and Andreas Johansson, November 17, 1996. Traded to **Los Angeles** by **NY Islanders** with Zigmund Palffy, Marcel Cousineau and New Jersey's 4th round choice (previously acquired, Los Angeles selected Daniel Johanssen) in 1999 Entry Draft for Olli Jokinen, Josh Green, Mathieu Biron and Los Angeles' 1st round choice (Taylor Pyatt) in 1999 Entry Draft, June 20, 1999.

SMYTH, Brad — (SMIHTH) — NYR

Right wing. Shoots right. 6', 200 lbs. Born, Ottawa, Ont., March 13, 1973.

			Regular Season																Playoffs							
Season	Club	League	GP	G	A	Pts	PIM	PP	SH	GW	S	%	+/-	TF	F%	H	SB	Min	GP	G	A	Pts	PIM	PP	SH	GW
1989-90	Nepean	OMHA	55	53	36	89	105	....	....	....	....	....	....	....	....	....	....	....	....	....	....	....	....	....	....	....
1990-91	London	OHL	29	2	6	8	22	....	....	....	....	....	....	....	....	....	....	....	....	....	....	....	....	....	....	....
1991-92	London	OHL	58	17	18	35	93	....	....	....	....	....	....	....	....	....	....	....	10	2	0	2	8	....	....	....
1992-93	London	OHL	66	54	55	109	118	....	....	....	....	....	....	....	....	....	....	....	12	7	8	15	25	....	....	....
1993-94	Cincinnati	IHL	30	7	3	10	54	....	....	....	....	....	....	....	....	....	....	....	....	....	....	....	....	....	....	....
	Birmingham	ECHL	29	26	30	56	38	....	....	....	....	....	....	....	....	....	....	....	10	8	8	16	19	....	....	....
1994-95	Springfield	AHL	3	0	0	0	7	....	....	....	....	....	....	....	....	....	....	....	....	....	....	....	....	....	....	....
	Birmingham	ECHL	36	33	35	68	52	....	....	....	....	....	....	....	....	....	....	....	3	5	2	7	0	....	....	....
	Cincinnati	IHL	26	2	11	13	34	....	....	....	....	....	....	....	....	....	....	....	1	0	0	0	2	....	....	....
1995-96	**Florida**	**NHL**	**7**	**1**	**1**	**2**	**4**	**1**	**0**	**0**	**12**	**8.3**	**-3**	....	....	....	....	....	....	....	....	....	....	....	....	....
	Carolina	AHL	68	*68	58	*126	80	....	....	....	....	....	....	....	....	....	....	....	....	....	....	....	....	....	....	....
1996-97	**Florida**	**NHL**	**8**	**1**	**0**	**1**	**2**	**0**	**0**	**0**	**10**	**10.0**	**-3**	....	....	....	....	....	....	....	....	....	....	....	....	....
	Los Angeles	**NHL**	**44**	**8**	**8**	**16**	**74**	**0**	**0**	**1**	**74**	**10.8**	**-7**	....	....	....	....	....	....	....	....	....	....	....	....	....
	Phoenix	IHL	3	5	2	7	0	....	....	....	....	....	....	....	....	....	....	....	....	....	....	....	....	....	....	....
1997-98	**Los Angeles**	**NHL**	**9**	**1**	**3**	**4**	**4**	**0**	**0**	**0**	**12**	**8.3**	**-1**	....	....	....	....	....	....	....	....	....	....	....	....	....
	NY Rangers	**NHL**	**1**	**0**	**0**	**0**	**0**	**0**	**0**	**0**	**1**	**0.0**	**0**	....	....	....	....	....	....	....	....	....	....	....	....	....
	Hartford	AHL	57	29	33	62	79	....	....	....	....	....	....	....	....	....	....	....	15	12	8	20	11	....	....	....

Season	Club	League	Regular Season GP	G	A	Pts	PIM	PP	SH	GW	S	%	+/–	TF	F%	H	SB	Min	Playoffs GP	G	A	Pts	PIM	PP	SH	GW
1998-99	**Nashville**	**NHL**	3	0	0	0	6	0	0	0	5	0.0	–1	0	0.0	1	0	9:54	....							
	Milwaukee	IHL	34	11	16	27	21	....	....	....	....	....	....	....	....	....	....	....								
	Hartford	AHL	36	25	19	44	48	....	....	....	....	....	....	....	....	....	....	....	7	6	0	6	14			
	NHL Totals		72	11	12	23	90	1	0	1	114	9.6		0	0.0	1	0	9:54	....							

AHL First All-Star Team (1996) • Won John B. Sollenberger Trophy (Top Scorer — AHL) (1996) • Won Les Cunningham Plaque (MVP — AHL) (1996)

Signed as a free agent by **Florida**, October 4, 1993. Traded to **LA Kings** by **Florida** for LA Kings' 3rd round choice (Vratislav Czech) in 1997 Entry Draft, November 28, 1996. Traded to **NY Rangers** by **LA Kings** for future considerations, November 14, 1997. Signed as a free agent by **Nashville**, July 16, 1998. Traded to **NY Rangers** by **Nashville** for future considerations, May 3, 1999.

SMYTH, Greg (SMIHTH) TOR.

Defense. Shoots right. 6'3", 212 lbs.   Born, Oakville, Ont., April 23, 1966. Philadelphia's 1st choice, 22nd overall, in 1984 Entry Draft.

Season	Club	League	GP	G	A	Pts	PIM	PP	SH	GW	S	%	+/–	TF	F%	H	SB	Min	GP	G	A	Pts	PIM	PP	SH	GW
1982-83	Wexford	MTHL	54	11	32	43	132												6	1	0	1	24			
1983-84	London	OHL	64	4	21	25	252												8	2	2	4	27			
1984-85	London	OHL	47	7	16	23	188												4	1	2	3	28			
1985-86	London	OHL	46	12	42	54	199												8	0	0	0	60			
	Hershey	AHL	2	0	1	1	5																			
1986-87	**Philadelphia**	**NHL**	1	0	0	0	0												1	0	0	0	2			
	Hershey	AHL	35	0	2	2	158												2	0	0	0	19			
1987-88	**Philadelphia**	**NHL**	48	1	6	7	192	0	0	0	29	3.4	–2						5	0	0	0	38	0	0	0
	Hershey	AHL	21	0	10	10	102																			
1988-89	**Quebec**	**NHL**	10	0	1	1	70	0	0	0	3	0.0	–9													
	Halifax	AHL	43	3	9	12	310												4	0	1	1	35			
1989-90	**Quebec**	**NHL**	13	0	0	0	57	0	0	0	4	0.0	–8													
	Halifax	AHL	49	5	14	19	235												6	1	0	1	52			
1990-91	**Quebec**	**NHL**	1	0	0	0	0	0	0	0	0	0.0	0													
	Halifax	AHL	56	6	23	29	340																			
1991-92	**Quebec**	**NHL**	29	0	2	2	138	0	0	0	24	0.0	–10													
	Halifax	AHL	9	1	3	4	35																			
	Calgary	**NHL**	7	1	1	2	15	0	0	0	10	10.0	7													
1992-93	**Calgary**	**NHL**	35	1	2	3	95	1	0	0	14	7.1	2													
	Salt Lake	IHL	5	0	1	1	31																			
1993-94	**Florida**	**NHL**	12	1	0	1	37	0	0	0	4	25.0	0													
	Toronto	**NHL**	11	0	1	1	38	0	0	0	3	0.0	–2													
	Chicago	**NHL**	38	0	0	0	108	0	0	0	29	0.0	–2						6	0	0	0	0	0	0	0
1994-95	**Chicago**	**NHL**	22	0	3	3	33	0	0	0	10	0.0	2													
	Indianapolis	IHL	2	0	0	0	0																			
1995-96	Chicago	IHL	15	1	3	4	53																			
	Los Angeles	IHL	41	2	7	9	231																			
1996-97	**Toronto**	**NHL**	2	0	0	0	0	0	0	0	1	0.0	0													
	St. John's	AHL	43	2	4	6	273												5	0	1	1	14			
1997-98	St. John's	AHL	63	5	6	11	353												4	0	1	1	6			
1998-99	St. John's	AHL	40	0	7	7	159												5	0	1	1	19			
	NHL Totals		229	4	16	20	783	1	0	0	131	3.1							12	0	0	0	40	0	0	0

OHL Second All-Star Team (1986)

Traded to **Quebec** by **Philadelphia** with Philadelphia's 3rd round choice (John Tanner) in the 1989 Entry Draft for Terry Carkner, July 25, 1988. Traded to **Calgary** by **Quebec** for Martin Simard, March 10, 1992. Signed as a free agent by **Florida**, August 10, 1993. Traded to **Toronto** by **Florida** for cash, December 7, 1993. Claimed on waivers by **Chicago** from **Toronto**, January 8, 1994. Signed as a free agent by **Toronto**, August 22, 1996.

SMYTH, Ryan (SMIHTH) EDM.

Left wing. Shoots left. 6'1", 195 lbs.   Born, Banff, Alta., February 21, 1976. Edmonton's 2nd choice, 6th overall, in 1994 Entry Draft.

Season	Club	League	GP	G	A	Pts	PIM	PP	SH	GW	S	%	+/–	TF	F%	H	SB	Min	GP	G	A	Pts	PIM	PP	SH	GW
1990-91	Banff	AAHA	25	100	50	150	....	....	|||||		|||||	....	....	....	....	....	....	....	....				
1991-92	Caronport	SIHL	7C	66	81	110	98																			
	Moose Jaw	WHL	2	0	0	0	0																			
1992-93	Moose Jaw	WHL	64	19	14	33	59																			
1993-94	Moose Jaw	WHL	72	50	55	105	88																			
1994-95	Moose Jaw	WHL	50	41	45	86	66												10	6	9	15	22			
	Edmonton	**NHL**	3	0	0	0	0	0	0	0	2	0.0	–1													
1995-96	**Edmonton**	**NHL**	48	2	9	11	28	1	0	0	65	3.1	–10													
	Cape Breton	AHL	9	6	5	11	4																			
1996-97	**Edmonton**	**NHL**	82	39	22	61	76	20	0	4	265	14.7	–7						12	5	5	10	12	1	0	2
1997-98	**Edmonton**	**NHL**	65	20	13	33	44	10	0	2	205	9.8	–24						12	1	3	4	16	1	0	0
1998-99	**Edmonton**	**NHL**	71	13	18	31	62	6	0	2	161	8.1	0	5	20.0	84	20	14:26	3	3	0	3	0	2	0	0
	NHL Totals		269	74	62	136	210	37	0	8	698	10.6		5	20.0	84	20	14:26	27	9	8	17	28	4	0	2

WHL East Second All-Star Team (1995)

SONNENBERG, Martin PIT.

Left wing. Shoots left. 6', 184 lbs.   Born, Wetaskiwin, Alta., January 23, 1978.

Season	Club	League	GP	G	A	Pts	PIM	PP	SH	GW	S	%	+/–	TF	F%	H	SB	Min	GP	G	A	Pts	PIM	PP	SH	GW
1995-96	Saskatoon	WHL	58	8	7	15	24												3	0	0	0	2			
1996-97	Saskatoon	WHL	72	38	26	64	79												6	1	3	4	9			
1997-98	Saskatoon	WHL	72	40	52	92	87																			
1998-99	**Pittsburgh**	**NHL**	44	1	1	2	19	0	0	0	12	8.3	–2	2	0.0	33	5	4:00								
	Syracuse	AHL	36	15	9	24	31																			
	NHL Totals		44	1	1	2	19	0	0	0	12	8.3		2	0.0	33	5	4:00	....							

Signed as a free agent by **Pittsburgh**, October 9, 1998.

SOPEL, Brent (SOH-puhl) VAN.

Defense. Shoots right. 6'1", 205 lbs.   Born, Calgary, Alta., January 7, 1977. Vancouver's 6th choice, 144th overall, in 1995 Entry Draft.

Season	Club	League	GP	G	A	Pts	PIM	PP	SH	GW	S	%	+/–	TF	F%	H	SB	Min	GP	G	A	Pts	PIM	PP	SH	GW
1992-93	Saskatoon AAA	SAHA	36	7	17	24	95																			
1993-94	Saskatoon AAA	SAHA	34	9	30	39	180																			
	Saskatoon	WHL	11	2	2	4	2																			
1994-95	Saskatoon	WHL	22	1	10	11	31																			
	Swift Current	WHL	41	4	19	23	50												3	0	3	3	0			
1995-96	Swift Current	WHL	71	13	48	61	87												6	1	2	3	4			
	Syracuse	AHL	1	0	0	0	0																			
1996-97	Swift Current	WHL	62	15	41	56	109												10	5	11	16	32			
	Syracuse	AHL	2	0	0	0	0												3	0	0	0	0			
1997-98	Syracuse	AHL	76	10	33	43	70												5	0	7	7	12			
1998-99	**Vancouver**	**NHL**	5	1	0	1	4	1	0	0	5	20.0	–1	0	0.0	4	1	11:58								
	Syracuse	AHL	53	10	21	31	59																			
	NHL Totals		5	1	0	1	4	1	0	0	5	20.0		0	0.0	4	1	11:58	....							

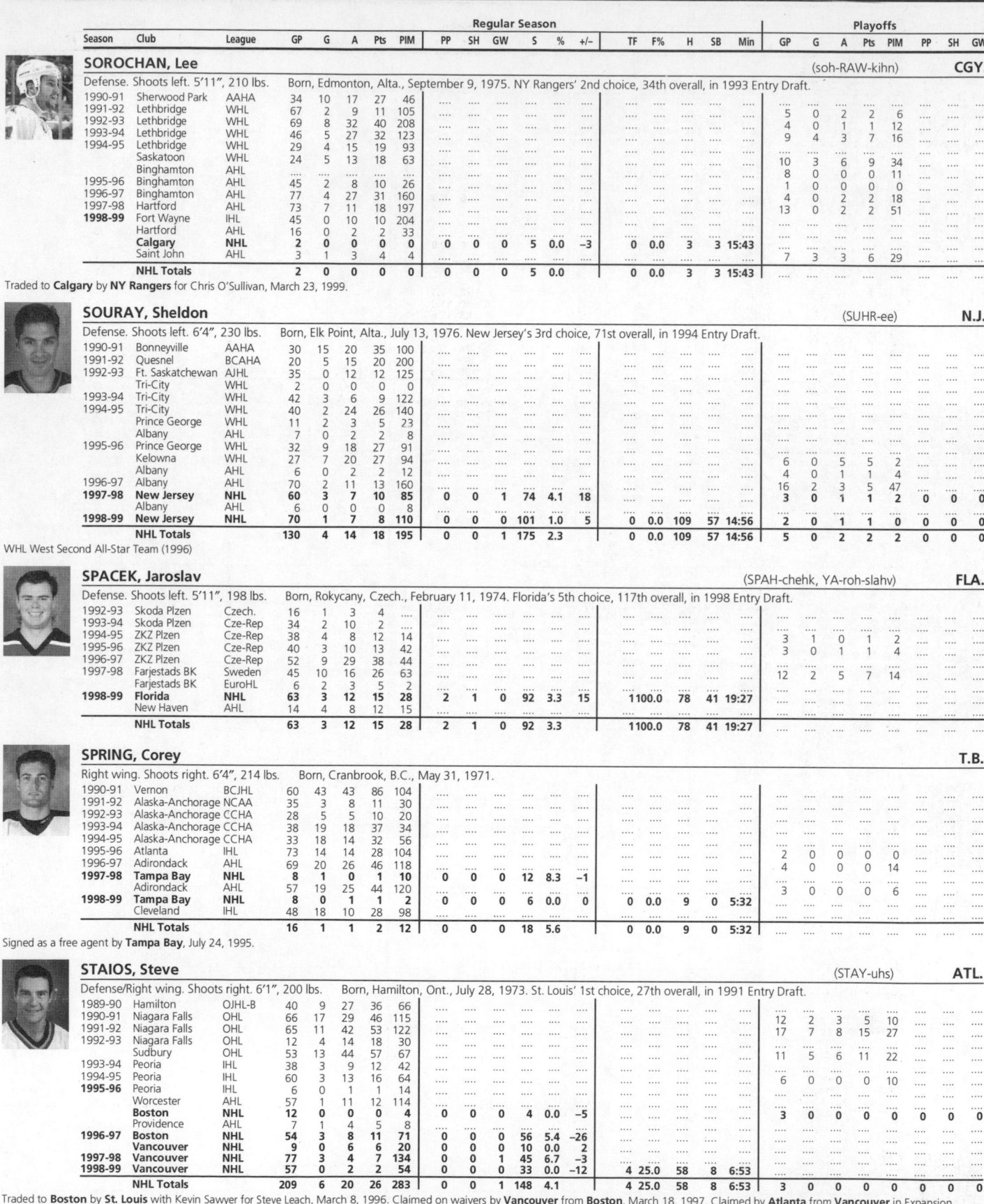

SOROCHAN, Lee

(soh-RAW-kihn) **CGY.**

Defense. Shoots left. 5'11", 210 lbs. Born, Edmonton, Alta., September 9, 1975. NY Rangers' 2nd choice, 34th overall, in 1993 Entry Draft.

			Regular Season																Playoffs							
Season	Club	League	GP	G	A	Pts	PIM	PP	SH	GW	S	%	+/-	TF	F%	H	SB	Min	GP	G	A	Pts	PIM	PP	SH	GW
1990-91	Sherwood Park	AAHA	34	10	17	27	46	....	....	....	....	....	....	....	....	....	....	....	....	....	....	....	....	....	....	....
1991-92	Lethbridge	WHL	67	2	9	11	105	....	....	....	....	....	....	....	....	....	....	....	5	0	2	2	6	....	....	....
1992-93	Lethbridge	WHL	69	8	32	40	208	....	....	....	....	....	....	....	....	....	....	....	4	0	1	1	12	....	....	....
1993-94	Lethbridge	WHL	46	5	27	32	123	....	....	....	....	....	....	....	....	....	....	....	9	4	3	7	16	....	....	....
1994-95	Lethbridge	WHL	29	4	15	19	93	....	....	....	....	....	....	....	....	....	....	....	....	....	....	....	....	....	....	....
	Saskatoon	WHL	24	5	13	18	63	....	....	....	....	....	....	....	....	....	....	....	10	3	6	9	34	....	....	....
	Binghamton	AHL	....	....	....	....	....	....	....	....	....	....	....	....	....	....	....	....	8	0	0	0	11	....	....	....
1995-96	Binghamton	AHL	45	2	8	10	26	....	....	....	....	....	....	....	....	....	....	....	1	0	0	0	0	....	....	....
1996-97	Binghamton	AHL	77	4	27	31	160	....	....	....	....	....	....	....	....	....	....	....	4	0	2	2	18	....	....	....
1997-98	Hartford	AHL	73	7	11	18	197	....	....	....	....	....	....	....	....	....	....	....	13	0	2	2	51	....	....	....
1998-99	Fort Wayne	IHL	45	0	10	10	204	....	....	....	....	....	....	....	....	....	....	....	....	....	....	....	....	....	....	....
	Hartford	AHL	16	0	2	2	33	....	....	....	....	....	....	....	....	....	....	....	....	....	....	....	....	....	....	....
	Calgary	**NHL**	**2**	**0**	**0**	**0**	**0**	**0**	**0**	**0**	**5**	**0.0**	**–3**	**0**	**0.0**	**3**	**3**	**15:43**	....	....	....	....	....	....	....	....
	Saint John	AHL	3	1	3	4	4	....	....	....	....	....	....	....	....	....	....	....	7	3	3	6	29	....	....	....
	NHL Totals		**2**	**0**	**0**	**0**	**0**	**0**	**0**	**0**	**5**	**0.0**		**0**	**0.0**	**3**	**3**	**15:43**	....	....	....	....	....	....	....	....

Traded to **Calgary** by **NY Rangers** for Chris O'Sullivan, March 23, 1999.

SOURAY, Sheldon

(SUHR-ee) **N.J.**

Defense. Shoots left. 6'4", 230 lbs. Born, Elk Point, Alta., July 13, 1976. New Jersey's 3rd choice, 71st overall, in 1994 Entry Draft.

			Regular Season																Playoffs							
Season	Club	League	GP	G	A	Pts	PIM	PP	SH	GW	S	%	+/-	TF	F%	H	SB	Min	GP	G	A	Pts	PIM	PP	SH	GW
1990-91	Bonneyville	AAHA	30	15	20	35	100	....	....	....	....	....	....	....	....	....	....	....	....	....	....	....	....	....	....	....
1991-92	Quesnel	BCAHA	20	5	15	20	200	....	....	....	....	....	....	....	....	....	....	....	....	....	....	....	....	....	....	....
1992-93	Ft. Saskatchewan	AJHL	35	0	12	12	125	....	....	....	....	....	....	....	....	....	....	....	....	....	....	....	....	....	....	....
	Tri-City	WHL	2	0	0	0	0	....	....	....	....	....	....	....	....	....	....	....	....	....	....	....	....	....	....	....
1993-94	Tri-City	WHL	42	3	6	9	122	....	....	....	....	....	....	....	....	....	....	....	....	....	....	....	....	....	....	....
1994-95	Tri-City	WHL	40	2	24	26	140	....	....	....	....	....	....	....	....	....	....	....	....	....	....	....	....	....	....	....
	Prince George	WHL	11	2	3	5	23	....	....	....	....	....	....	....	....	....	....	....	....	....	....	....	....	....	....	....
	Albany	AHL	7	0	2	2	8	....	....	....	....	....	....	....	....	....	....	....	....	....	....	....	....	....	....	....
1995-96	Prince George	WHL	32	9	18	27	91	....	....	....	....	....	....	....	....	....	....	....	....	....	....	....	....	....	....	....
	Kelowna	WHL	27	7	20	27	94	....	....	....	....	....	....	....	....	....	....	....	6	0	5	5	2	....	....	....
	Albany	AHL	6	0	2	2	12	....	....	....	....	....	....	....	....	....	....	....	4	0	1	1	4	....	....	....
1996-97	Albany	AHL	70	2	11	13	160	....	....	....	....	....	....	....	....	....	....	....	16	2	3	5	47	....	....	....
1997-98	**New Jersey**	**NHL**	**60**	**3**	**7**	**10**	**85**	**0**	**0**	**1**	**74**	**4.1**	**18**	....	....	....	....	....	**3**	**0**	**1**	**1**	**2**	**0**	**0**	**0**
	Albany	AHL	6	0	0	0	8	....	....	....	....	....	....	....	....	....	....	....	....	....	....	....	....	....	....	....
1998-99	**New Jersey**	**NHL**	**70**	**1**	**7**	**8**	**110**	**0**	**0**	**0**	**101**	**1.0**	**5**	**0**	**0.0**	**109**	**57**	**14:56**	**2**	**0**	**1**	**1**	**0**	**0**	**0**	**0**
	NHL Totals		**130**	**4**	**14**	**18**	**195**	**0**	**0**	**1**	**175**	**2.3**		**0**	**0.0**	**109**	**57**	**14:56**	**5**	**0**	**2**	**2**	**2**	**0**	**0**	**0**

WHL West Second All-Star Team (1996)

SPACEK, Jaroslav

(SPAH-chehk, YA-roh-slahv) **FLA.**

Defense. Shoots left. 5'11", 198 lbs. Born, Rokycany, Czech., February 11, 1974. Florida's 5th choice, 117th overall, in 1998 Entry Draft.

			Regular Season																Playoffs							
Season	Club	League	GP	G	A	Pts	PIM	PP	SH	GW	S	%	+/-	TF	F%	H	SB	Min	GP	G	A	Pts	PIM	PP	SH	GW
1992-93	Skoda Plzen	Czech.	16	1	3	4	....	....	....	....	....	....	....	....	....	....	....	....	....	....	....	....	....	....	....	....
1993-94	Skoda Plzen	Cze-Rep	34	2	10	2	....	....	....	....	....	....	....	....	....	....	....	....	....	....	....	....	....	....	....	....
1994-95	ZKZ Plzen	Cze-Rep	38	4	8	12	14	....	....	....	....	....	....	....	....	....	....	....	3	1	0	1	2	....	....	....
1995-96	ZKZ Plzen	Cze-Rep	40	3	10	13	42	....	....	....	....	....	....	....	....	....	....	....	3	0	1	1	4	....	....	....
1996-97	ZKZ Plzen	Cze-Rep	52	9	29	38	44	....	....	....	....	....	....	....	....	....	....	....	....	....	....	....	....	....	....	....
1997-98	Farjestads BK	Sweden	45	10	16	26	63	....	....	....	....	....	....	....	....	....	....	....	12	2	5	7	14	....	....	....
	Farjestads BK	EuroHL	6	2	3	5	2	....	....	....	....	....	....	....	....	....	....	....	....	....	....	....	....	....	....	....
1998-99	**Florida**	**NHL**	**63**	**3**	**12**	**15**	**28**	**2**	**1**	**0**	**92**	**3.3**	**15**	**1**	**100.0**	**78**	**41**	**19:27**	....	....	....	....	....	....	....	....
	New Haven	AHL	14	4	8	12	15	....	....	....	....	....	....	....	....	....	....	....	....	....	....	....	....	....	....	....
	NHL Totals		**63**	**3**	**12**	**15**	**28**	**2**	**1**	**0**	**92**	**3.3**		**1**	**100.0**	**78**	**41**	**19:27**	....	....	....	....	....	....	....	....

SPRING, Corey

T.B.

Right wing. Shoots right. 6'4", 214 lbs. Born, Cranbrook, B.C., May 31, 1971.

			Regular Season																Playoffs							
Season	Club	League	GP	G	A	Pts	PIM	PP	SH	GW	S	%	+/-	TF	F%	H	SB	Min	GP	G	A	Pts	PIM	PP	SH	GW
1990-91	Vernon	BCJHL	60	43	43	86	104	....	....	....	....	....	....	....	....	....	....	....	....	....	....	....	....	....	....	....
1991-92	Alaska-Anchorage	NCAA	35	3	8	11	30	....	....	....	....	....	....	....	....	....	....	....	....	....	....	....	....	....	....	....
1992-93	Alaska-Anchorage	CCHA	28	5	5	10	20	....	....	....	....	....	....	....	....	....	....	....	....	....	....	....	....	....	....	....
1993-94	Alaska-Anchorage	CCHA	38	19	18	37	34	....	....	....	....	....	....	....	....	....	....	....	....	....	....	....	....	....	....	....
1994-95	Alaska-Anchorage	CCHA	33	18	14	32	56	....	....	....	....	....	....	....	....	....	....	....	....	....	....	....	....	....	....	....
1995-96	Atlanta	IHL	73	14	14	28	104	....	....	....	....	....	....	....	....	....	....	....	2	0	0	0	0	....	....	....
1996-97	Adirondack	AHL	69	20	26	46	118	....	....	....	....	....	....	....	....	....	....	....	4	0	0	0	14	....	....	....
1997-98	**Tampa Bay**	**NHL**	**8**	**1**	**0**	**1**	**10**	**0**	**0**	**0**	**12**	**8.3**	**–1**	....	....	....	....	....	....	....	....	....	....	....	....	....
	Adirondack	AHL	57	19	25	44	120	....	....	....	....	....	....	....	....	....	....	....	3	0	0	0	6	....	....	....
1998-99	**Tampa Bay**	**NHL**	**8**	**0**	**1**	**1**	**2**	**0**	**0**	**0**	**6**	**0.0**	**0**	**0**	**0.0**	**9**	**0**	**5:32**	....	....	....	....	....	....	....	....
	Cleveland	IHL	48	18	10	28	98	....	....	....	....	....	....	....	....	....	....	....	....	....	....	....	....	....	....	....
	NHL Totals		**16**	**1**	**1**	**2**	**12**	**0**	**0**	**0**	**18**	**5.6**		**0**	**0.0**	**9**	**0**	**5:32**	....	....	....	....	....	....	....	....

Signed as a free agent by **Tampa Bay**, July 24, 1995.

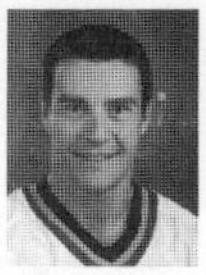

STAIOS, Steve

(STAY-uhs) **ATL.**

Defense/Right wing. Shoots right. 6'1", 200 lbs. Born, Hamilton, Ont., July 28, 1973. St. Louis' 1st choice, 27th overall, in 1991 Entry Draft.

			Regular Season																Playoffs							
Season	Club	League	GP	G	A	Pts	PIM	PP	SH	GW	S	%	+/-	TF	F%	H	SB	Min	GP	G	A	Pts	PIM	PP	SH	GW
1989-90	Hamilton	OJHL-B	40	9	27	36	66	....	....	....	....	....	....	....	....	....	....	....	....	....	....	....	....	....	....	....
1990-91	Niagara Falls	OHL	66	17	29	46	115	....	....	....	....	....	....	....	....	....	....	....	12	2	3	5	10	....	....	....
1991-92	Niagara Falls	OHL	65	11	42	53	122	....	....	....	....	....	....	....	....	....	....	....	17	7	8	15	27	....	....	....
1992-93	Niagara Falls	OHL	12	4	14	18	30	....	....	....	....	....	....	....	....	....	....	....	....	....	....	....	....	....	....	....
	Sudbury	OHL	53	13	44	57	67	....	....	....	....	....	....	....	....	....	....	....	11	5	6	11	22	....	....	....
1993-94	Peoria	IHL	38	3	9	12	42	....	....	....	....	....	....	....	....	....	....	....	....	....	....	....	....	....	....	....
1994-95	Peoria	IHL	60	3	13	16	64	....	....	....	....	....	....	....	....	....	....	....	6	0	0	0	10	....	....	....
1995-96	Peoria	IHL	6	0	1	1	14	....	....	....	....	....	....	....	....	....	....	....	....	....	....	....	....	....	....	....
	Worcester	AHL	57	1	11	12	114	....	....	....	....	....	....	....	....	....	....	....	....	....	....	....	....	....	....	....
	Boston	**NHL**	**12**	**0**	**0**	**0**	**4**	**0**	**0**	**0**	**4**	**0.0**	**–5**	....	....	....	....	....	**3**	**0**	**0**	**0**	**0**	**0**	**0**	**0**
	Providence	AHL	7	1	4	5	8	....	....	....	....	....	....	....	....	....	....	....	....	....	....	....	....	....	....	....
1996-97	**Boston**	**NHL**	**54**	**3**	**8**	**11**	**71**	**0**	**0**	**0**	**56**	**5.4**	**–26**	....	....	....	....	....	....	....	....	....	....	....	....	....
	Vancouver	**NHL**	**9**	**0**	**6**	**6**	**20**	**0**	**0**	**0**	**10**	**0.0**	**2**	....	....	....	....	....	....	....	....	....	....	....	....	....
1997-98	**Vancouver**	**NHL**	**77**	**3**	**4**	**7**	**134**	**0**	**0**	**1**	**45**	**6.7**	**–3**	....	....	....	....	....	....	....	....	....	....	....	....	....
1998-99	**Vancouver**	**NHL**	**57**	**0**	**2**	**2**	**54**	**0**	**0**	**0**	**33**	**0.0**	**–12**	**4**	**25.0**	**58**	**8**	**6:53**	....	....	....	....	....	....	....	....
	NHL Totals		**209**	**6**	**20**	**26**	**283**	**0**	**0**	**1**	**148**	**4.1**		**4**	**25.0**	**58**	**8**	**6:53**	**3**	**0**	**0**	**0**	**0**	**0**	**0**	**0**

Traded to **Boston** by **St. Louis** with Kevin Sawyer for Steve Leach, March 8, 1996. Claimed on waivers by **Vancouver** from **Boston**, March 18, 1997. Claimed by **Atlanta** from **Vancouver** in Expansion Draft, June 25, 1999.

STAPLETON, Mike — ATL.

Center. Shoots right. 5'10", 183 lbs. Born, Sarnia, Ont., May 5, 1966. Chicago's 7th choice, 132nd overall, in 1984 Entry Draft.

			Regular Season																Playoffs							
Season	Club	League	GP	G	A	Pts	PIM	PP	SH	GW	S	%	+/-	TF	F%	H	SB	Min	GP	G	A	Pts	PIM	PP	SH	GW
1982-83	Strathroy	OJHL-B	40	39	38	77	99	....	....	....	....	....	....	....	....	....	....	....	....	....	....	....	....	....	....	....
1983-84	Cornwall	OHL	70	24	45	69	94	....	....	....	....	....	....	....	....	....	....	....	3	1	2	3	4	....	....	....
1984-85	Cornwall	OHL	56	41	44	85	68	....	....	....	....	....	....	....	....	....	....	....	9	2	4	6	23	....	....	....
1985-86	Cornwall	OHL	56	39	64	103	74	....	....	....	....	....	....	....	....	....	....	....	6	2	3	5	2	....	....	....
1986-87	Canada	Nat-Team	21	2	4	6	4	....	....	....	....	....	....	....	....	....	....	....	....	....	....	....	....	....	....	....
	Chicago	**NHL**	**39**	**3**	**6**	**9**	**6**	**0**	**0**	**0**	**54**	**5.6**	**–9**	....	....	....	....	....	**4**	**0**	**0**	**0**	**2**	**0**	**0**	**0**
1987-88	**Chicago**	**NHL**	**53**	**2**	**9**	**11**	**59**	**0**	**0**	**1**	**50**	**4.0**	**–10**	....	....	....	....	....	....	....	....	....	....	....	....	....
	Saginaw	IHL	31	11	19	30	52	....	....	....	....	....	....	....	....	....	....	....	10	5	6	11	10	....	....	....
1988-89	**Chicago**	**NHL**	**7**	**0**	**1**	**1**	**7**	**0**	**0**	**0**	**6**	**0.0**	**–1**	....	....	....	....	....	....	....	....	....	....	....	....	....
	Saginaw	IHL	69	21	47	68	162	....	....	....	....	....	....	....	....	....	....	....	6	1	3	4	4	....	....	....
1989-90	Arvika IF	Sweden-3	30	15	18	33	....	....	....	....	....	....	....	....	....	....	....	....	....	....	....	....	....	....	....	....
	Indianapolis	IHL	16	5	10	15	6	....	....	....	....	....	....	....	....	....	....	....	13	9	10	19	38	....	....	....
1990-91	**Chicago**	**NHL**	**7**	**0**	**1**	**1**	**2**	**0**	**0**	**0**	**6**	**0.0**	**0**	....	....	....	....	....	....	....	....	....	....	....	....	....
	Indianapolis	IHL	75	29	52	81	76	....	....	....	....	....	....	....	....	....	....	....	7	1	4	5	0	....	....	....
1991-92	**Chicago**	**NHL**	**19**	**4**	**4**	**8**	**8**	**1**	**0**	**0**	**32**	**12.5**	**0**	....	....	....	....	....	....	....	....	....	....	....	....	....
	Indianapolis	IHL	59	18	40	58	65	....	....	....	....	....	....	....	....	....	....	....	....	....	....	....	....	....	....	....
1992-93	**Pittsburgh**	**NHL**	**78**	**4**	**9**	**13**	**10**	**0**	**1**	**1**	**78**	**5.1**	**–8**	....	....	....	....	....	**4**	**0**	**0**	**0**	**0**	**0**	**0**	**0**
1993-94	**Pittsburgh**	**NHL**	**58**	**7**	**4**	**11**	**18**	**3**	**0**	**0**	**59**	**11.9**	**–4**	....	....	....	....	....	....	....	....	....	....	....	....	....
	Edmonton	**NHL**	**23**	**5**	**9**	**14**	**28**	**1**	**0**	**0**	**43**	**11.6**	**–1**	....	....	....	....	....	....	....	....	....	....	....	....	....
1994-95	**Edmonton**	**NHL**	**46**	**6**	**11**	**17**	**21**	**3**	**0**	**2**	**59**	**10.2**	**–12**	....	....	....	....	....	....	....	....	....	....	....	....	....
1995-96	**Winnipeg**	**NHL**	**58**	**10**	**14**	**24**	**37**	**3**	**1**	**0**	**91**	**11.0**	**–4**	....	....	....	....	....	**6**	**0**	**0**	**0**	**21**	**0**	**0**	**0**
1996-97	**Phoenix**	**NHL**	**55**	**4**	**11**	**15**	**36**	**2**	**0**	**1**	**74**	**5.4**	**–4**	....	....	....	....	....	**7**	**0**	**0**	**0**	**14**	**0**	**0**	**0**
1997-98	**Phoenix**	**NHL**	**64**	**5**	**5**	**10**	**36**	**1**	**1**	**1**	**69**	**7.2**	**–4**	....	....	....	....	....	**6**	**0**	**0**	**0**	**2**	**0**	**0**	**0**
1998-99	**Phoenix**	**NHL**	**76**	**9**	**9**	**18**	**34**	**0**	**2**	**2**	**106**	**8.5**	**–6**	**345**	**46.1**	**67**	**40**	**13:40**	**7**	**1**	**0**	**1**	**0**	**0**	**0**	**0**
	NHL Totals		**583**	**59**	**93**	**152**	**302**	**14**	**5**	**8**	**727**	**8.1**		**345**	**46.1**	**67**	**40**	**13:40**	**34**	**1**	**0**	**1**	**39**	**0**	**0**	**0**

Signed as a free agent by **Pittsburgh**, September 30, 1992. Claimed on waivers by **Edmonton** from **Pittsburgh**, February 19, 1994. Signed as a free agent by **Winnipeg**, August 18, 1995. Transferred to **Phoenix** after **Winnipeg** franchise relocated, July 1, 1996. Claimed by **Atlanta** from **Phoenix** in Expansion Draft, June 25, 1999.

STERN, Ron — S.J.

Right wing. Shoots right. 6', 200 lbs. Born, Ste. Agathe, Que., January 11, 1967. Vancouver's 3rd choice, 70th overall, in 1986 Entry Draft.

			Regular Season																Playoffs							
Season	Club	League	GP	G	A	Pts	PIM	PP	SH	GW	S	%	+/-	TF	F%	H	SB	Min	GP	G	A	Pts	PIM	PP	SH	GW
1983-84	Laurentides	QAAA	39	6	6	12	....	....	....	....	....	....	....	....	....	....	....	....	....	....	....	....	....	....	....	....
1984-85	Longueuil	QMJHL	67	6	14	20	176	....	....	....	....	....	....	....	....	....	....	....	....	....	....	....	....	....	....	....
1985-86	Longueuil	QMJHL	70	39	33	72	317	....	....	....	....	....	....	....	....	....	....	....	....	....	....	....	....	....	....	....
1986-87	Longueuil	QMJHL	56	32	39	71	266	....	....	....	....	....	....	....	....	....	....	....	19	11	9	20	55	....	....	....
1987-88	**Vancouver**	**NHL**	**15**	**0**	**0**	**0**	**52**	**0**	**0**	**0**	**7**	**0.0**	**–7**	....	....	....	....	....	....	....	....	....	....	....	....	....
	Fredericton	AHL	2	1	0	1	4	....	....	....	....	....	....	....	....	....	....	....	....	....	....	....	....	....	....	....
	Flint	IHL	55	14	19	33	294	....	....	....	....	....	....	....	....	....	....	....	16	8	8	16	94	....	....	....
1988-89	**Vancouver**	**NHL**	**17**	**1**	**0**	**1**	**49**	**0**	**0**	**0**	**13**	**7.7**	**–6**	....	....	....	....	....	**3**	**0**	**1**	**1**	**17**	**0**	**0**	**0**
	Milwaukee	IHL	45	19	23	42	280	....	....	....	....	....	....	....	....	....	....	....	5	1	0	1	11	....	....	....
1989-90	**Vancouver**	**NHL**	**34**	**2**	**3**	**5**	**208**	**0**	**0**	**0**	**27**	**7.4**	**–17**	....	....	....	....	....	....	....	....	....	....	....	....	....
	Milwaukee	IHL	26	8	9	17	165	....	....	....	....	....	....	....	....	....	....	....	....	....	....	....	....	....	....	....
1990-91	**Vancouver**	**NHL**	**31**	**2**	**3**	**5**	**171**	**0**	**0**	**0**	**30**	**6.7**	**–14**	....	....	....	....	....	....	....	....	....	....	....	....	....
	Milwaukee	IHL	7	2	2	4	81	....	....	....	....	....	....	....	....	....	....	....	....	....	....	....	....	....	....	....
	Calgary	**NHL**	**13**	**1**	**3**	**4**	**69**	**0**	**0**	**0**	**15**	**6.7**	**0**	....	....	....	....	....	**7**	**1**	**3**	**4**	**14**	**0**	**0**	**0**
1991-92	**Calgary**	**NHL**	**72**	**13**	**9**	**22**	**338**	**0**	**1**	**1**	**96**	**13.5**	**0**	....	....	....	....	....	....	....	....	....	....	....	....	....
1992-93	**Calgary**	**NHL**	**70**	**10**	**15**	**25**	**207**	**0**	**0**	**1**	**82**	**12.2**	**4**	....	....	....	....	....	**6**	**0**	**0**	**0**	**43**	**0**	**0**	**0**
1993-94	**Calgary**	**NHL**	**71**	**9**	**20**	**29**	**243**	**0**	**1**	**3**	**105**	**8.6**	**6**	....	....	....	....	....	**7**	**2**	**0**	**2**	**12**	**0**	**0**	**0**
1994-95	**Calgary**	**NHL**	**39**	**9**	**4**	**13**	**163**	**1**	**0**	**0**	**69**	**13.0**	**4**	....	....	....	....	....	**7**	**3**	**1**	**4**	**8**	**1**	**1**	**0**
1995-96	**Calgary**	**NHL**	**52**	**10**	**5**	**15**	**111**	**0**	**0**	**1**	**64**	**15.6**	**2**	....	....	....	....	....	**4**	**0**	**2**	**2**	**8**	**0**	**0**	**0**
1996-97	**Calgary**	**NHL**	**79**	**7**	**10**	**17**	**157**	**0**	**1**	**1**	**98**	**7.1**	**–4**	....	....	....	....	....	....	....	....	....	....	....	....	....
1997-98	**Calgary**	**NHL**	Did Not Play – Injured																							
1998-99	**San Jose**	**NHL**	**78**	**7**	**9**	**16**	**158**	**1**	**0**	**2**	**94**	**7.4**	**–3**	**1**	**0.0**	**153**	**18**	**11:37**	**6**	**0**	**0**	**0**	**6**	**0**	**0**	**0**
	NHL Totals		**571**	**71**	**81**	**152**	**1926**	**2**	**3**	**9**	**700**	**10.1**		**1**	**0.0**	**153**	**18**	**11:37**	**40**	**6**	**7**	**13**	**108**	**1**	**1**	**0**

Traded to **Calgary** by **Vancouver** with Kevan Guy for Dana Murzyn, March 5, 1991. • Missed entire 1997-98 season after undergoing knee surgery, October, 1997. Signed as a free agent by **San Jose**, August 25, 1998.

STEVENS, John

Defense. Shoots left. 6'1", 195 lbs. Born, Campbellton, N.B., May 4, 1966. Philadelphia's 5th choice, 47th overall, in 1984 Entry Draft.

			Regular Season																Playoffs							
Season	Club	League	GP	G	A	Pts	PIM	PP	SH	GW	S	%	+/-	TF	F%	H	SB	Min	GP	G	A	Pts	PIM	PP	SH	GW
1982-83	Newmarket	OJHL	48	2	9	11	111	....	....	....	....	....	....	....	....	....	....	....	....	....	....	....	....	....	....	....
1983-84	Oshawa	OHL	70	1	10	11	71	....	....	....	....	....	....	....	....	....	....	....	7	0	1	1	6	....	....	....
1984-85	Oshawa	OHL	44	2	10	12	61	....	....	....	....	....	....	....	....	....	....	....	5	0	2	2	4	....	....	....
	Hershey	AHL	3	0	0	0	0	....	....	....	....	....	....	....	....	....	....	....	....	....	....	....	....	....	....	....
1985-86	Oshawa	OHL	65	1	7	8	146	....	....	....	....	....	....	....	....	....	....	....	6	0	2	2	14	....	....	....
	Kalamazoo	IHL	6	0	1	1	8	....	....	....	....	....	....	....	....	....	....	....	6	0	3	3	9	....	....	....
1986-87	**Philadelphia**	**NHL**	**6**	**0**	**2**	**2**	**14**	**0**	**0**	**0**	**2**	**0.0**	**0**	....	....	....	....	....	....	....	....	....	....	....	....	....
	Hershey	AHL	63	1	15	16	131	....	....	....	....	....	....	....	....	....	....	....	3	0	0	0	7	....	....	....
1987-88	**Philadelphia**	**NHL**	**3**	**0**	**0**	**0**	**0**	**0**	**0**	**0**	**0**	**0.0**	**–1**	....	....	....	....	....	....	....	....	....	....	....	....	....
	Hershey	AHL	59	1	15	16	108	....	....	....	....	....	....	....	....	....	....	....	....	....	....	....	....	....	....	....
1988-89	Hershey	AHL	78	3	13	16	129	....	....	....	....	....	....	....	....	....	....	....	12	1	1	2	29	....	....	....
1989-90	Hershey	AHL	79	3	10	13	193	....	....	....	....	....	....	....	....	....	....	....	....	....	....	....	....	....	....	....
1990-91	**Hartford**	**NHL**	**14**	**0**	**1**	**1**	**11**	**0**	**0**	**0**	**7**	**0.0**	**0**	....	....	....	....	....	....	....	....	....	....	....	....	....
	Springfield	AHL	65	0	12	12	139	....	....	....	....	....	....	....	....	....	....	....	18	0	6	6	35	....	....	....
1991-92	**Hartford**	**NHL**	**21**	**0**	**4**	**4**	**19**	**0**	**0**	**0**	**13**	**0.0**	**–4**	....	....	....	....	....	....	....	....	....	....	....	....	....
	Springfield	AHL	45	1	12	13	73	....	....	....	....	....	....	....	....	....	....	....	11	1	3	4	27	....	....	....
1992-93	Springfield	AHL	74	1	19	20	111	....	....	....	....	....	....	....	....	....	....	....	15	0	1	1	18	....	....	....
1993-94	**Hartford**	**NHL**	**9**	**0**	**3**	**3**	**4**	**0**	**0**	**0**	**3**	**0.0**	**4**	....	....	....	....	....	....	....	....	....	....	....	....	....
	Springfield	AHL	71	3	9	12	85	....	....	....	....	....	....	....	....	....	....	....	3	0	0	0	0	....	....	....
1994-95	Springfield	AHL	79	5	15	20	122	....	....	....	....	....	....	....	....	....	....	....	....	....	....	....	....	....	....	....
1995-96	Springfield	AHL	69	0	19	19	95	....	....	....	....	....	....	....	....	....	....	....	10	0	1	1	31	....	....	....
1996-97	Philadelphia	AHL	74	2	18	20	116	....	....	....	....	....	....	....	....	....	....	....	10	0	2	2	8	....	....	....
1997-98	Philadelphia	AHL	50	1	9	10	76	....	....	....	....	....	....	....	....	....	....	....	20	0	6	6	44	....	....	....
1998-99	Philadelphia	AHL	25	0	1	1	19	....	....	....	....	....	....	....	....	....	....	....	....	....	....	....	....	....	....	....
	NHL Totals		**53**	**0**	**10**	**10**	**48**	**0**	**0**	**0**	**25**	**0.0**		....	....	....	....	....	....	....	....	....	....	....	....	....

Signed as a free agent by **Hartford**, July 30, 1990. Signed as a free agent by **Philadelphia**, August 6, 1996. • Suffered career-ending eye injury in game vs. Kentucky (AHL), December 13, 1998.

STEVENS, Kevin — NYR

Left wing. Shoots left. 6'3", 230 lbs. Born, Brockton, MA, April 15, 1965. Los Angeles' 6th choice, 112th overall, in 1983 Entry Draft.

			Regular Season																Playoffs							
Season	Club	League	GP	G	A	Pts	PIM	PP	SH	GW	S	%	+/-	TF	F%	H	SB	Min	GP	G	A	Pts	PIM	PP	SH	GW
1982-83	Silver Lake	H.S.	18	24	27	51	....	....	....	....	....	....	....	....	....	....	....	....	....	....	....	....	....	....	....	....
1983-84	Boston College	ECAC	37	6	14	20	36	....	....	....	....	....	....	....	....	....	....	....	....	....	....	....	....	....	....	....
1984-85	Boston College	H.E.	40	13	23	36	36	....	....	....	....	....	....	....	....	....	....	....	....	....	....	....	....	....	....	....
1985-86	Boston College	H.E.	42	17	27	44	56	....	....	....	....	....	....	....	....	....	....	....	....	....	....	....	....	....	....	....
1986-87	Boston College	H.E.	39	35	35	70	54	....	....	....	....	....	....	....	....	....	....	....	....	....	....	....	....	....	....	....
1987-88	United States	Nat-Team	44	22	23	45	52	....	....	....	....	....	....	....	....	....	....	....	....	....	....	....	....	....	....	....
	United States	Olympics	5	1	3	4	2	....	....	....	....	....	....	....	....	....	....	....	....	....	....	....	....	....	....	....
	Pittsburgh	**NHL**	**16**	**5**	**2**	**7**	**8**	**2**	**0**	**0**	**22**	**22.7**	**–6**	....	....	....	....	....	....	....	....	....	....	....	....	....
1988-89	**Pittsburgh**	**NHL**	**24**	**12**	**3**	**15**	**19**	**4**	**0**	**3**	**52**	**23.1**	**–8**	....	....	....	....	....	**11**	**3**	**7**	**10**	**16**	**0**	**0**	**0**
	Muskegon	IHL	45	24	41	65	113	....	....	....	....	....	....	....	....	....	....	....	....	....	....	....	....	....	....	....

Season	Club	League	GP	G	A	Pts	PIM	PP	SH	GW	S	%	+/–	TF	F%	H	SB	Min	GP	G	A	Pts	PIM	PP	SH	GW
		Regular Season																	Playoffs							
1989-90	Pittsburgh	NHL	76	29	41	70	171	12	0	1	179	16.2	–13	....	....	....	....	....	....	....	....	....	....	....	....	....
1990-91♦	Pittsburgh	NHL	80	40	46	86	133	18	0	6	253	15.8	–1	....	....	....	....	....	24	*17	16	33	53	7	0	4
1991-92♦	Pittsburgh	NHL	80	54	69	123	254	19	0	4	325	16.6	8	....	....	....	....	....	21	13	15	28	28	4	0	3
1992-93	Pittsburgh	NHL	72	55	56	111	177	26	0	5	326	16.9	17	....	....	....	....	....	12	5	11	16	22	4	0	0
1993-94	Pittsburgh	NHL	83	41	47	88	155	21	0	4	284	14.4	–24	....	....	....	....	....	6	1	1	2	10	0	0	0
1994-95	Pittsburgh	NHL	27	15	12	27	51	6	0	4	80	18.8	0	....	....	....	....	....	12	4	7	11	21	3	0	1
1995-96	Boston	NHL	41	10	13	23	49	3	0	1	101	9.9	1	....	....	....	....	....	....	....	....	....	....	....	....	....
	Los Angeles	NHL	20	3	10	13	22	3	0	0	69	4.3	–11	....	....	....	....	....	....	....	....	....	....	....	....	....
1996-97	Los Angeles	NHL	69	14	20	34	96	4	0	1	175	8.0	–27	....	....	....	....	....	....	....	....	....	....	....	....	....
1997-98	NY Rangers	NHL	80	14	27	41	130	5	0	3	144	9.7	–7	....	....	....	....	....	....	....	....	....	....	....	....	....
1998-99	NY Rangers	NHL	81	23	20	43	64	8	0	3	136	16.9	–10	11	45.5	176	27	15:12	....	....	....	....	....	....	....	....
	NHL Totals		**749**	**315**	**366**	**681**	**1329**	**131**	**0**	**35**	**2146**	**14.7**		**11**	**45.5**	**176**	**27**	**15:12**	**86**	**43**	**57**	**100**	**150**	**18**	**0**	**8**

Hockey East First All-Star Team (1987) • NCAA East Second All-American Team (1987) • NHL Second All-Star Team (1991, 1993) • NHL First All-Star Team (1992)

Played in NHL All-Star Game (1991, 1992, 1993)

Rights traded to **Pittsburgh** by **LA Kings** for Anders Hakansson, September 9, 1983. Traded to **Boston** by **Pittsburgh** with Shawn McEachern for Glen Murray, Bryan Smolinski and Boston's 3rd round choice (Boyd Kane) in 1996 Entry Draft, August 2, 1995. Traded to **LA Kings** by **Boston** for Rick Tocchet, January 25, 1996. Traded to **NY Rangers** by **LA Kings** for Luc Robitaille, August 28, 1997.

STEVENS, Scott — N.J.

Defense. Shoots left. 6'1", 215 lbs. Born, Kitchener, Ont., April 1, 1964. Washington's 1st choice, 5th overall, in 1982 Entry Draft.

Season	Club	League	GP	G	A	Pts	PIM	PP	SH	GW	S	%	+/–	TF	F%	H	SB	Min	GP	G	A	Pts	PIM	PP	SH	GW
1980-81	Kitchener	OJHL-B	39	7	33	40	82	....	....	....	....	....	....	....	....	....	....	....	....	....	....	....	....	....	....	....
	Kitchener	OHA	1	0	0	0	0	....	....	....	....	....	....	....	....	....	....	....	....	....	....	....	....	....	....	....
1981-82	Kitchener	OHL	68	6	36	42	158	....	....	....	....	....	....	....	....	....	....	....	15	1	10	11	71	....	....	....
1982-83	Washington	NHL	77	9	16	25	195	0	0	0	121	7.4	14	....	....	....	....	....	4	1	0	1	26	0	0	0
1983-84	Washington	NHL	78	13	32	45	201	7	0	2	155	8.4	26	....	....	....	....	....	8	1	8	9	21	1	0	0
1984-85	Washington	NHL	80	21	44	65	221	16	0	5	170	12.4	19	....	....	....	....	....	5	0	1	1	20	0	0	0
1985-86	Washington	NHL	73	15	38	53	165	3	0	2	121	12.4	0	....	....	....	....	....	9	3	8	11	12	2	0	2
1986-87	Washington	NHL	77	10	51	61	283	2	0	0	165	6.1	13	....	....	....	....	....	7	0	5	5	19	0	0	0
1987-88	Washington	NHL	80	12	60	72	184	5	1	2	231	5.2	14	....	....	....	....	....	13	1	11	12	46	0	0	0
1988-89	Washington	NHL	80	7	61	68	225	6	0	3	195	3.6	1	....	....	....	....	....	6	1	4	5	11	0	0	0
1989-90	Washington	NHL	56	11	29	40	154	7	0	0	143	7.7	1	....	....	....	....	....	15	2	7	9	25	1	0	0
1990-91	St. Louis	NHL	78	5	44	49	150	1	0	1	160	3.1	23	....	....	....	....	....	13	0	3	3	36	0	0	0
1991-92	New Jersey	NHL	68	17	42	59	124	7	1	2	156	10.9	24	....	....	....	....	....	7	2	1	3	29	2	0	1
1992-93	New Jersey	NHL	81	12	45	57	120	8	0	1	146	8.2	14	....	....	....	....	....	5	2	2	4	10	1	0	0
1993-94	New Jersey	NHL	83	18	60	78	112	5	1	4	215	8.4	53	....	....	....	....	....	20	2	9	11	42	2	0	1
1994-95♦	New Jersey	NHL	48	2	20	22	56	1	0	1	111	1.8	4	....	....	....	....	....	20	1	7	8	24	0	0	1
1995-96	New Jersey	NHL	82	5	23	28	100	2	1	1	174	2.9	7	....	....	....	....	....	....	....	....	....	....	....	....	....
1996-97	New Jersey	NHL	79	5	19	24	70	0	0	1	166	3.0	26	....	....	....	....	....	10	0	4	4	2	0	0	0
1997-98	New Jersey	NHL	80	4	22	26	80	1	0	1	94	4.3	19	....	....	....	....	....	6	1	0	1	8	0	0	0
	Canada	Olympics	6	0	0	0	2	....	....	....	....	....	....	....	....	....	....	....	....	....	....	....	....	....	....	....
1998-99	New Jersey	NHL	75	5	22	27	64	0	0	1	111	4.5	29	1	0.0	187	149	24:11	7	2	1	3	10	2	0	0
	NHL Totals		**1275**	**171**	**628**	**799**	**2504**	**71**	**4**	**27**	**2634**	**6.5**		**1**	**0.0**	**187**	**149**	**24:11**	**155**	**19**	**71**	**90**	**341**	**11**	**0**	**5**

NHL All-Rookie Team (1983) • NHL First All-Star Team (1988, 1994) • NHL Second All-Star Team (1992, 1997) • Won Alka-Seltzer Plus Award (1994)

Played in NHL All-Star Game (1985, 1989, 1991, 1992, 1993, 1994, 1996, 1997, 1998, 1999)

Signed as a free agent by **St. Louis**, July 16, 1990. Transferred to **New Jersey** from **St. Louis** as compensation for St. Louis' signing of free agent Brendan Shanahan, September 3, 1991.

STEVENSON, Jeremy — ANA.

Left wing. Shoots left. 6'2", 220 lbs. Born, San Bernadino, CA, July 28, 1974. Anaheim's 10th choice, 262nd overall, in 1994 Entry Draft.

Season	Club	League	GP	G	A	Pts	PIM	PP	SH	GW	S	%	+/–	TF	F%	H	SB	Min	GP	G	A	Pts	PIM	PP	SH	GW
1989-90	Elliot Lake	OMHA	61	39	26	65	203	....	....	....	....	....	....	....	....	....	....	....	....	....	....	....	....	....	....	....
1990-91	Cornwall	OHL	58	13	20	33	124	....	....	....	....	....	....	....	....	....	....	....	....	....	....	....	....	....	....	....
1991-92	Cornwall	OHL	63	15	23	38	176	....	....	....	....	....	....	....	....	....	....	....	6	3	1	4	4	....	....	....
1992-93	Newmarket	OHL	54	28	28	56	144	....	....	....	....	....	....	....	....	....	....	....	5	5	1	6	28	....	....	....
1993-94	Newmarket	OHL	9	2	4	6	27	....	....	....	....	....	....	....	....	....	....	....	....	....	....	....	....	....	....	....
	S.S. Marie	OHL	48	18	19	37	183	....	....	....	....	....	....	....	....	....	....	....	14	1	1	2	23	....	....	....
1994-95	Greensboro	ECHL	43	14	13	27	231	....	....	....	....	....	....	....	....	....	....	....	17	6	11	17	64	....	....	....
1995-96	Anaheim	NHL	3	0	1	1	12	0	0	0	1	0.0	1	....	....	....	....	....	....	....	....	....	....	....	....	....
	Baltimore	AHL	60	11	10	21	295	....	....	....	....	....	....	....	....	....	....	....	12	4	2	6	23	....	....	....
1996-97	Anaheim	NHL	5	0	0	0	14	0	0	0	1	0.0	–1	....	....	....	....	....	....	....	....	....	....	....	....	....
	Baltimore	AHL	25	8	8	16	125	....	....	....	....	....	....	....	....	....	....	....	3	0	0	0	8	....	....	....
1997-98	Anaheim	NHL	45	3	5	8	101	0	0	1	43	7.0	–4	....	....	....	....	....	....	....	....	....	....	....	....	....
	Cincinnati	AHL	10	5	0	5	34	....	....	....	....	....	....	....	....	....	....	....	....	....	....	....	....	....	....	....
1998-99	Cincinnati	AHL	22	4	4	8	83	....	....	....	....	....	....	....	....	....	....	....	3	1	0	1	2	....	....	....
	NHL Totals		**53**	**3**	**6**	**9**	**127**	**0**	**0**	**1**	**45**	**6.7**		....	....	....	....	....	....	....	....	....	....	....	....	....

• Re-entered NHL draft. Originally Winnipeg's 3rd choice, 60th overall, in 1992 Entry Draft.

STEVENSON, Turner — MTL.

Right wing. Shoots right. 6'3", 226 lbs. Born, Prince George, B.C., May 18, 1972. Montreal's 1st choice, 12th overall, in 1990 Entry Draft.

Season	Club	League	GP	G	A	Pts	PIM	PP	SH	GW	S	%	+/–	TF	F%	H	SB	Min	GP	G	A	Pts	PIM	PP	SH	GW
1987-88	Prince George	BCAHA	53	45	46	91	127	....	....	....	....	....	....	....	....	....	....	....	....	....	....	....	....	....	....	....
1988-89	Seattle	WHL	69	15	12	27	84	....	....	....	....	....	....	....	....	....	....	....	....	....	....	....	....	....	....	....
1989-90	Seattle	WHL	62	29	32	61	276	....	....	....	....	....	....	....	....	....	....	....	13	3	2	5	35	....	....	....
1990-91	Seattle	WHL	57	36	27	63	222	....	....	....	....	....	....	....	....	....	....	....	6	1	5	6	15	....	....	....
	Fredericton	AHL	....	....	....	....	....	....	....	....	....	....	....	....	....	....	....	....	4	0	0	0	5	....	....	....
1991-92	Seattle	WHL	58	20	32	52	264	....	....	....	....	....	....	....	....	....	....	....	15	9	3	12	55	....	....	....
1992-93	Montreal	NHL	1	0	0	0	0	0	0	0	1	0.0	–1	....	....	....	....	....	....	....	....	....	....	....	....	....
	Fredericton	AHL	79	25	34	59	102	....	....	....	....	....	....	....	....	....	....	....	5	2	3	5	11	....	....	....
1993-94	Montreal	NHL	2	0	0	0	2	0	0	0	0	0.0	–2	....	....	....	....	....	3	0	2	2	0	0	0	0
	Fredericton	AHL	66	19	28	47	155	....	....	....	....	....	....	....	....	....	....	....	....	....	....	....	....	....	....	....
1994-95	Fredericton	AHL	37	12	12	24	109	....	....	....	....	....	....	....	....	....	....	....	....	....	....	....	....	....	....	....
	Montreal	NHL	41	6	1	7	86	0	0	1	35	17.1	0	....	....	....	....	....	....	....	....	....	....	....	....	....
1995-96	Montreal	NHL	80	9	16	25	167	0	0	2	101	8.9	–2	....	....	....	....	....	6	0	1	1	2	0	0	0
1996-97	Montreal	NHL	65	8	13	21	97	1	0	0	76	10.5	–14	....	....	....	....	....	5	1	1	2	2	0	0	0
1997-98	Montreal	NHL	63	4	6	10	110	1	0	0	43	9.3	–8	....	....	....	....	....	10	3	4	7	12	0	0	0
1998-99	Montreal	NHL	69	10	17	27	88	0	0	2	102	9.8	6	29	37.9	142	20	12:57	....	....	....	....	....	....	....	....
	NHL Totals		**321**	**37**	**53**	**90**	**550**	**2**	**0**	**5**	**358**	**10.3**		**29**	**37.9**	**142**	**20**	**12:57**	**24**	**4**	**8**	**12**	**16**	**0**	**0**	**0**

WHL West First All-Star Team (1992) • Memorial Cup All-Star Team (1992)

STEWART, Cam — FLA.

Left wing. Shoots left. 5'11", 196 lbs. Born, Kitchener, Ont., September 18, 1971. Boston's 2nd choice, 63rd overall, in 1990 Entry Draft.

Season	Club	League	GP	G	A	Pts	PIM	PP	SH	GW	S	%	+/–	TF	F%	H	SB	Min	GP	G	A	Pts	PIM	PP	SH	GW
1987-88	Woolrich	OMHA	21	25	32	57	65	....	....	....	....	....	....	....	....	....	....	....	....	....	....	....	....	....	....	....
1988-89	Elmira	OJHL-B	45	38	50	88	138	....	....	....	....	....	....	....	....	....	....	....	....	....	....	....	....	....	....	....
1989-90	Elmira	OJHL-B	46	44	95	139	172	....	....	....	....	....	....	....	....	....	....	....	....	....	....	....	....	....	....	....
1990-91	U. of Michigan	CCHA	44	8	24	32	122	....	....	....	....	....	....	....	....	....	....	....	....	....	....	....	....	....	....	....
1991-92	U. of Michigan	CCHA	44	13	15	28	106	....	....	....	....	....	....	....	....	....	....	....	....	....	....	....	....	....	....	....
1992-93	U. of Michigan	CCHA	39	20	39	59	69	....	....	....	....	....	....	....	....	....	....	....	....	....	....	....	....	....	....	....
1993-94	Boston	NHL	57	3	6	9	66	0	0	1	55	5.5	–6	....	....	....	....	....	8	0	3	3	7	0	0	0
	Providence	AHL	14	3	2	5	5	....	....	....	....	....	....	....	....	....	....	....	....	....	....	....	....	....	....	....
1994-95	Boston	NHL	5	0	0	0	2	0	0	0	2	0.0	0	....	....	....	....	....	....	....	....	....	....	....	....	....
	Providence	AHL	31	13	11	24	38	....	....	....	....	....	....	....	....	....	....	....	9	2	5	7	0	....	....	....

			Regular Season																Playoffs							
Season	Club	League	GP	G	A	Pts	PIM	PP	SH	GW	S	%	+/-	TF	F%	H	SB	Min	GP	G	A	Pts	PIM	PP	SH	GW
1995-96	**Boston**	**NHL**	**6**	**0**	**0**	**0**	**0**	**0**	**0**	**0**	**2**	**0.0**	**–2**	....	....	....	....	....	**5**	**1**	**0**	**1**	**2**	**0**	**0**	**0**
	Providence	AHL	54	17	25	42	39	....	....	....	....	....	....	....	....	....	....	....	....	....	....	....	....	....	....	....
1996-97	**Boston**	**NHL**	**15**	**0**	**1**	**1**	**4**	**0**	**0**	**0**	**21**	**0.0**	**–2**	....	....	....	....	....	....	....	....	....	....	....	....	....
	Providence	AHL	18	4	3	7	37	....	....	....	....	....	....	....	....	....	....	....	....	....	....	....	....	....	....	....
	Cincinnati	IHL	7	3	2	5	8	....	....	....	....	....	....	....	....	....	....	....	1	0	0	0	0	....	....	....
1997-98	Houston	IHL	63	18	27	45	51	....	....	....	....	....	....	....	....	....	....	....	4	0	1	1	18	....	....	....
1998-99	Houston	IHL	61	36	26	62	75	....	....	....	....	....	....	....	....	....	....	....	19	10	5	15	26	....	....	....
	NHL Totals		**83**	**3**	**7**	**10**	**72**	**0**	**0**	**1**	**80**	**3.8**		....	....	....	....	....	**13**	**1**	**3**	**4**	**9**	**0**	**0**	**0**

Signed as a free agent by **Florida**, July 21, 1999.

STILLMAN, Cory

CGY.

Center. Shoots left. 6', 195 lbs. Born, Peterborough, Ont., December 20, 1973. Calgary's 1st choice, 6th overall, in 1992 Entry Draft.

Season	Club	League	GP	G	A	Pts	PIM	PP	SH	GW	S	%	+/-	TF	F%	H	SB	Min	GP	G	A	Pts	PIM	PP	SH	GW
1989-90	Peterborough	OJHL-B	41	30	54	84	76	....	....	....	....	....	....	....	....	....	....	....	....	....	....	....	....	....	....	....
1990-91	Windsor	OHL	64	31	70	101	31	....	....	....	....	....	....	....	....	....	....	....	11	3	6	9	8	....	....	....
1991-92	Windsor	OHL	53	29	61	90	59	....	....	....	....	....	....	....	....	....	....	....	7	2	4	6	8	....	....	....
1992-93	Peterborough	OHL	61	25	55	80	55	....	....	....	....	....	....	....	....	....	....	....	18	3	8	11	18	....	....	....
	Canada	Nat-Team	1	0	0	0	0	....	....	....	....	....	....	....	....	....	....	....	....	....	....	....	....	....	....	....
1993-94	Saint John	AHL	79	35	48	83	52	....	....	....	....	....	....	....	....	....	....	....	7	2	4	6	16	....	....	....
1994-95	Saint John	AHL	63	28	53	81	70	....	....	....	....	....	....	....	....	....	....	....	5	0	2	2	2	....	....	....
	Calgary	**NHL**	**10**	**0**	**2**	**2**	**2**	**0**	**0**	**0**	**7**	**0.0**	**1**	....	....	....	....	....	....	....	....	....	....	....	....	....
1995-96	**Calgary**	**NHL**	**74**	**16**	**19**	**35**	**41**	**4**	**1**	**3**	**132**	**12.1**	**–5**	....	....	....	....	....	**2**	**1**	**1**	**2**	**0**	**0**	**0**	**0**
1996-97	**Calgary**	**NHL**	**58**	**6**	**20**	**26**	**14**	**2**	**0**	**0**	**112**	**5.4**	**–6**	....	....	....	....	....	....	....	....	....	....	....	....	....
1997-98	**Calgary**	**NHL**	**72**	**27**	**22**	**49**	**40**	**9**	**4**	**1**	**178**	**15.2**	**–9**	....	....	....	....	....	....	....	....	....	....	....	....	....
1998-99	**Calgary**	**NHL**	**76**	**27**	**30**	**57**	**38**	**9**	**3**	**5**	**175**	**15.4**	**7**	**535**	**46.5**	**128**	**33**	**16:19**	....	....	....	....	....	....	....	....
	NHL Totals		**290**	**76**	**93**	**169**	**135**	**24**	**8**	**9**	**604**	**12.6**		**535**	**46.5**	**128**	**33**	**16:19**	**2**	**1**	**1**	**2**	**0**	**0**	**0**	**0**

STOCK, P.J.

NYR

Left wing. Shoots left. 5'10", 190 lbs. Born, Victoriaville, Que., May 26, 1975.

Season	Club	League	GP	G	A	Pts	PIM	PP	SH	GW	S	%	+/-	TF	F%	H	SB	Min	GP	G	A	Pts	PIM	PP	SH	GW
1994-95	Victoriaville	QMJHL	70	9	46	55	386	....	....	....	....	....	....	....	....	....	....	....	4	0	0	0	60	....	....	....
1995-96	Victoriaville	QMJHL	67	19	43	62	432	....	....	....	....	....	....	....	....	....	....	....	12	5	4	9	79	....	....	....
1996-97	St. FX University	AUAA	27	11	20	31	110	....	....	....	....	....	....	....	....	....	....	....	3	0	4	4	14	....	....	....
1997-98	Hartford	AHL	41	8	8	16	202	....	....	....	....	....	....	....	....	....	....	....	11	1	3	4	79	....	....	....
	NY Rangers	**NHL**	**38**	**2**	**3**	**5**	**114**	**0**	**0**	**1**	**9**	**22.2**	**4**	....	....	....	....	....	....	....	....	....	....	....	....	....
1998-99	**NY Rangers**	**NHL**	**5**	**0**	**0**	**0**	**6**	**0**	**0**	**0**	**0**	**0.0**	**–1**	**8**	**50.0**	**8**	**0**	**2:42**	....	....	....	....	....	....	....	....
	Hartford	AHL	55	4	14	18	250	....	....	....	....	....	....	....	....	....	....	....	6	0	1	1	35	....	....	....
	NHL Totals		**43**	**2**	**3**	**5**	**120**	**0**	**0**	**1**	**9**	**22.2**		**8**	**50.0**	**8**	**0**	**2:42**	....	....	....	....	....	....	....	....

Signed as a free agent by **NY Rangers**, November 18, 1997.

STOJANOV, Alek

(STOY-uh-nahf)

Right wing. Shoots left. 6'4", 225 lbs. Born, Windsor, Ont., April 25, 1973. Vancouver's 1st choice, 7th overall, in 1991 Entry Draft.

Season	Club	League	GP	G	A	Pts	PIM	PP	SH	GW	S	%	+/-	TF	F%	H	SB	Min	GP	G	A	Pts	PIM	PP	SH	GW
1988-89	Windsor	OMHA	26	19	15	34	53	....	....	....	....	....	....	....	....	....	....	....	....	....	....	....	....	....	....	....
	Belle River	OJHL-C	7	3	2	5	42	....	....	....	....	....	....	....	....	....	....	....	....	....	....	....	....	....	....	....
1989-90	Hamilton	OHL	37	4	4	8	91	....	....	....	....	....	....	....	....	....	....	....	....	....	....	....	....	....	....	....
1990-91	Hamilton	OHL	62	25	20	45	181	....	....	....	....	....	....	....	....	....	....	....	4	1	1	2	14	....	....	....
1991-92	Guelph	OHL	33	12	15	27	91	....	....	....	....	....	....	....	....	....	....	....	....	....	....	....	....	....	....	....
1992-93	Guelph	OHL	36	27	28	55	62	....	....	....	....	....	....	....	....	....	....	....	....	....	....	....	....	....	....	....
	Newmarket	OHL	14	9	7	16	26	....	....	....	....	....	....	....	....	....	....	....	7	1	3	4	26	....	....	....
	Hamilton	AHL	4	4	0	4	0	....	....	....	....	....	....	....	....	....	....	....	....	....	....	....	....	....	....	....
1993-94	Hamilton	AHL	4	0	1	1	5	....	....	....	....	....	....	....	....	....	....	....	....	....	....	....	....	....	....	....
1994-95	Syracuse	AHL	73	18	12	30	270	....	....	....	....	....	....	....	....	....	....	....	....	....	....	....	....	....	....	....
	Vancouver	**NHL**	**4**	**0**	**0**	**0**	**13**	**0**	**0**	**0**	**1**	**0.0**	**–2**	....	....	....	....	....	**5**	**0**	**0**	**0**	**2**	**0**	**0**	**0**
1995-96	**Vancouver**	**NHL**	**58**	**0**	**1**	**1**	**123**	**0**	**0**	**0**	**16**	**0.0**	**–12**	....	....	....	....	....	....	....	....	....	....	....	....	....
	Pittsburgh	**NHL**	**10**	**1**	**0**	**1**	**7**	**0**	**0**	**0**	**4**	**25.0**	**–1**	....	....	....	....	....	**9**	**0**	**0**	**0**	**19**	**0**	**0**	**0**
1996-97	**Pittsburgh**	**NHL**	**35**	**1**	**4**	**5**	**79**	**0**	**0**	**0**	**11**	**9.1**	**3**	....	....	....	....	....	....	....	....	....	....	....	....	....
1997-98	Syracuse	AHL	41	5	4	9	215	....	....	....	....	....	....	....	....	....	....	....	3	1	0	1	4	....	....	....
1998-99	Hamilton	AHL	12	0	1	1	35	....	....	....	....	....	....	....	....	....	....	....	....	....	....	....	....	....	....	....
	Milwaukee	IHL	13	0	1	1	58	....	....	....	....	....	....	....	....	....	....	....	....	....	....	....	....	....	....	....
	Detroit	IHL	27	1	3	4	91	....	....	....	....	....	....	....	....	....	....	....	....	....	....	....	....	....	....	....
	NHL Totals		**107**	**2**	**5**	**7**	**222**	**0**	**0**	**0**	**32**	**6.3**		....	....	....	....	....	**14**	**0**	**0**	**0**	**21**	**0**	**0**	**0**

Traded to **Pittsburgh** by **Vancouver** for Markus Naslund, March 20, 1996.

STRAKA, Martin

(STRAH-kuh) **PIT.**

Center. Shoots left. 5'10", 175 lbs. Born, Plzen, Czech., September 3, 1972. Pittsburgh's 1st choice, 19th overall, in 1992 Entry Draft.

Season	Club	League	GP	G	A	Pts	PIM	PP	SH	GW	S	%	+/-	TF	F%	H	SB	Min	GP	G	A	Pts	PIM	PP	SH	GW
1989-90	Skoda Plzen	Czech.	1	0	3	3	....	....	....	....	....	....	....	....	....	....	....	....	....	....	....	....	....	....	....	....
1990-91	Skoda Plzen	Czech.	47	7	24	31	6	....	....	....	....	....	....	....	....	....	....	....	....	....	....	....	....	....	....	....
1991-92	Skoda Plzen	Czech.	50	27	28	55	20	....	....	....	....	....	....	....	....	....	....	....	....	....	....	....	....	....	....	....
1992-93	**Pittsburgh**	**NHL**	**42**	**3**	**13**	**16**	**29**	**0**	**0**	**1**	**28**	**10.7**	**2**	....	....	....	....	....	**11**	**2**	**1**	**3**	**2**	**0**	**0**	**0**
	Cleveland	IHL	4	4	3	7	0	....	....	....	....	....	....	....	....	....	....	....	....	....	....	....	....	....	....	....
1993-94	**Pittsburgh**	**NHL**	**84**	**30**	**34**	**64**	**24**	**2**	**0**	**6**	**130**	**23.1**	**24**	....	....	....	....	....	**6**	**1**	**0**	**1**	**2**	**0**	**0**	**0**
1994-95	ZKZ Plzen	Cze-Rep	19	10	11	21	18	....	....	....	....	....	....	....	....	....	....	....	....	....	....	....	....	....	....	....
	Pittsburgh	**NHL**	**31**	**4**	**12**	**16**	**16**	**0**	**0**	**0**	**36**	**11.1**	**0**	....	....	....	....	....	....	....	....	....	....	....	....	....
	Ottawa	**NHL**	**6**	**1**	**1**	**2**	**0**	**0**	**0**	**0**	**13**	**7.7**	**–1**	....	....	....	....	....	....	....	....	....	....	....	....	....
1995-96	**Ottawa**	**NHL**	**43**	**9**	**16**	**25**	**29**	**5**	**0**	**1**	**63**	**14.3**	**–14**	....	....	....	....	....	....	....	....	....	....	....	....	....
	NY Islanders	**NHL**	**22**	**2**	**10**	**12**	**6**	**0**	**0**	**0**	**18**	**11.1**	**–6**	....	....	....	....	....	....	....	....	....	....	....	....	....
	Florida	**NHL**	**12**	**2**	**4**	**6**	**6**	**1**	**0**	**0**	**17**	**11.8**	**1**	....	....	....	....	....	**13**	**2**	**2**	**4**	**2**	**0**	**0**	**0**
1996-97	**Florida**	**NHL**	**55**	**7**	**22**	**29**	**12**	**2**	**0**	**1**	**94**	**7.4**	**9**	....	....	....	....	....	**4**	**0**	**0**	**0**	**0**	**0**	**0**	**0**
1997-98	**Pittsburgh**	**NHL**	**75**	**19**	**23**	**42**	**28**	**4**	**3**	**4**	**117**	**16.2**	**–1**	....	....	....	....	....	**6**	**2**	**0**	**2**	**2**	**0**	**1**	**0**
	Czech Republic	Olympics	6	1	2	3	0	....	....	....	....	....	....	....	....	....	....	....	....	....	....	....	....	....	....	....
1998-99	**Pittsburgh**	**NHL**	**80**	**35**	**48**	**83**	**26**	**5**	**4**	**4**	**177**	**19.8**	**12**	**845**	**43.6**	**75**	**59**	**23:35**	**13**	**6**	**9**	**15**	**6**	**1**	**0**	**0**
	NHL Totals		**450**	**112**	**183**	**295**	**176**	**19**	**7**	**17**	**693**	**16.2**		**845**	**43.6**	**75**	**59**	**23:35**	**53**	**13**	**12**	**25**	**14**	**1**	**1**	**0**

Czechoslovakian First All-Star Team (1992)

Played in NHL All-Star Game (1999)

Traded to **Ottawa** by **Pittsburgh** for Troy Murray and Norm Maciver, April 7, 1995. Traded to **NY Islanders** by **Ottawa** with Don Beaupre and Bryan Berard for Damian Rhodes and Wade Redden, January 23, 1996. Claimed on waivers by **Florida** from **NY Islanders**, March 15, 1996. Signed as a free agent by **Pittsburgh**, August 6, 1997.

STRUDWICK, Jason

(STRUHD-wihk)

Defense. Shoots left. 6'3", 215 lbs. Born, Edmonton, Alta., July 17, 1975. NY Islanders' 3rd choice, 63rd overall, in 1994 Entry Draft.

Season	Club	League	GP	G	A	Pts	PIM	PP	SH	GW	S	%	+/-	TF	F%	H	SB	Min	GP	G	A	Pts	PIM	PP	SH	GW
1991-92	Edmonton	AAHA	35	3	8	11	67	....	....	....	....	....	....	....	....	....	....	....	....	....	....	....	....	....	....	....
1992-93	Edmonton	AAHA	33	8	20	28	135	....	....	....	....	....	....	....	....	....	....	....	....	....	....	....	....	....	....	....
1993-94	Kamloops	WHL	61	6	8	14	118	....	....	....	....	....	....	....	....	....	....	....	19	0	4	4	24	....	....	....
1994-95	Kamloops	WHL	72	3	11	14	183	....	....	....	....	....	....	....	....	....	....	....	21	1	1	2	39	....	....	....
1995-96	**NY Islanders**	**NHL**	**1**	**0**	**0**	**0**	**7**	**0**	**0**	**0**	**0**	**0.0**	**0**	....	....	....	....	....	....	....	....	....	....	....	....	....
	Worcester	AHL	60	2	7	9	119	....	....	....	....	....	....	....	....	....	....	....	4	0	1	1	0	....	....	....
1996-97	Kentucky	AHL	80	1	9	10	198	....	....	....	....	....	....	....	....	....	....	....	4	0	0	0	0	....	....	....

			Regular Season																Playoffs							
Season	Club	League	GP	G	A	Pts	PIM	PP	SH	GW	S	%	+/–	TF	F%	H	SB	Min	GP	G	A	Pts	PIM	PP	SH	GW
1997-98	**NY Islanders**	**NHL**	**17**	**0**	**1**	**1**	**36**	**0**	**0**	**0**	**3**	**0.0**	**1**	....	....	....	....	....	....	....	....	....	....	....	....	....
	Kentucky	AHL	39	3	1	4	87	....	....	....	....	....	....	....	....	....	....	....	....	....	....	....	....	....	....	....
	Vancouver	**NHL**	**11**	**0**	**1**	**1**	**29**	**0**	**0**	**0**	**5**	**0.0**	**–3**	....	....	....	....	....	....	....	....	....	....	....	....	....
	Syracuse	AHL	....	....	....	....	....	....	....	....	....	....	....	....	....	....	....	....	3	0	0	0	6	....	....	....
1998-99	**Vancouver**	**NHL**	**65**	**0**	**3**	**3**	**114**	**0**	**0**	**0**	**25**	**0.0**	**–19**	**0**	**0.0**	**62**	**52**	**12:49**	....	....	....	....	....	....	....	....
	NHL Totals		**94**	**0**	**5**	**5**	**186**	**0**	**0**	**0**	**33**	**0.0**		**0**	**0.0**	**62**	**52**	**12:49**	....	....	....	....	....	....	....	....

Traded to **Vancouver** by **NY Islanders** for Gino Odjick, March 23, 1998.

STUMPEL, Jozef

(STUM-puhl) **L.A.**

Center. Shoots right. 6'3", 216 lbs. Born, Nitra, Czech., July 20, 1972. Boston's 2nd choice, 40th overall, in 1991 Entry Draft.

Season	Club	League	GP	G	A	Pts	PIM	PP	SH	GW	S	%	+/–	TF	F%	H	SB	Min	GP	G	A	Pts	PIM	PP	SH	GW
1989-90	AC Nitra	Czech-2	38	12	11	23	....	....	....	....	....	....	....	....	....	....	....	....	....	....	....	....	....	....	....	....
1990-91	AC Nitra	Czech.	49	23	22	45	14	....	....	....	....	....	....	....	....	....	....	....	....	....	....	....	....	....	....	....
1991-92	Kolner Haie	Germany	37	20	19	39	35	....	....	....	....	....	....	....	....	....	....	....	....	....	....	....	....	....	....	....
	Boston	**NHL**	**4**	**1**	**0**	**1**	**0**	**0**	**0**	**0**	**3**	**33.3**	**1**	....	....	....	....	....	....	....	....	....	....	....	....	....
1992-93	**Boston**	**NHL**	**13**	**1**	**3**	**4**	**4**	**0**	**0**	**0**	**8**	**12.5**	**–3**	....	....	....	....	....	....	....	....	....	....	....	....	....
	Providence	AHL	56	31	61	92	26	....	....	....	....	....	....	....	....	....	....	....	6	4	4	8	0	....	....	....
1993-94	**Boston**	**NHL**	**59**	**8**	**15**	**23**	**14**	**0**	**0**	**1**	**62**	**12.9**	**4**	....	....	....	....	....	**13**	**1**	**7**	**8**	**4**	**0**	**0**	**0**
	Providence	AHL	17	5	12	17	4	....	....	....	....	....	....	....	....	....	....	....	....	....	....	....	....	....	....	....
1994-95	Kolner Haie	Germany	25	16	23	39	18	....	....	....	....	....	....	....	....	....	....	....	....	....	....	....	....	....	....	....
	Boston	**NHL**	**44**	**5**	**13**	**18**	**8**	**1**	**0**	**2**	**46**	**10.9**	**4**	....	....	....	....	....	**5**	**0**	**0**	**0**	**0**	**0**	**0**	**0**
1995-96	**Boston**	**NHL**	**76**	**18**	**36**	**54**	**14**	**5**	**0**	**2**	**158**	**11.4**	**–8**	....	....	....	....	....	**5**	**1**	**2**	**3**	**0**	**0**	**0**	**0**
1996-97	**Boston**	**NHL**	**78**	**21**	**55**	**76**	**14**	**6**	**0**	**1**	**168**	**12.5**	**–22**	....	....	....	....	....	....	....	....	....	....	....	....	....
1997-98	**Los Angeles**	**NHL**	**77**	**21**	**58**	**79**	**53**	**4**	**0**	**2**	**162**	**13.0**	**17**	....	....	....	....	....	**4**	**1**	**2**	**3**	**2**	**0**	**0**	**0**
1998-99	**Los Angeles**	**NHL**	**64**	**13**	**21**	**34**	**10**	**1**	**0**	**1**	**131**	**9.9**	**–18**	**1484**	**54.0**	**67**	**30**	**19:44**	....	....	....	....	....	....	....	....
	NHL Totals		**415**	**88**	**201**	**289**	**117**	**17**	**0**	**9**	**738**	**11.9**		**1484**	**54.0**	**67**	**30**	**19:44**	**27**	**3**	**11**	**14**	**6**	**0**	**0**	**0**

Traded to **LA Kings** by **Boston** with Sandy Moger and Boston's 4th round choice (later traded to New Jersey — New Jersey selected Pierre Dagenais) in 1998 Entry Draft for Dimitri Kristich and Byron Dafoe, August 29, 1997.

STURM, Marco

(STURHM) **S.J.**

Center. Shoots left. 6', 195 lbs. Born, Dingolfing, Germany, September 8, 1978. San Jose's 2nd choice, 21st overall, in 1996 Entry Draft.

Season	Club	League	GP	G	A	Pts	PIM	PP	SH	GW	S	%	+/–	TF	F%	H	SB	Min	GP	G	A	Pts	PIM	PP	SH	GW
1994-95	EV Landshut	German-Jr	STATISTICS NOT AVAILABLE																							
1995-96	EV Landshut	Germany	47	12	20	32	50	....	....	....	....	....	....	....	....	....	....	....	11	1	3	4	18	....	....	....
1996-97	EV Landshut	Germany	46	16	27	43	40	....	....	....	....	....	....	....	....	....	....	....	7	1	4	5	6	....	....	....
1997-98	**San Jose**	**NHL**	**74**	**10**	**20**	**30**	**40**	**2**	**0**	**3**	**118**	**8.5**	**–2**	....	....	....	....	....	**2**	**0**	**0**	**0**	**0**	**0**	**0**	**0**
	Germany	Olympics	2	0	0	0	0	....	....	....	....	....	....	....	....	....	....	....	....	....	....	....	....	....	....	....
1998-99	**San Jose**	**NHL**	**78**	**16**	**22**	**38**	**52**	**3**	**2**	**3**	**140**	**11.4**	**7**	**576**	**45.0**	**98**	**37**	**15:23**	**6**	**2**	**2**	**4**	**4**	**0**	**0**	**1**
	NHL Totals		**152**	**26**	**42**	**68**	**92**	**5**	**2**	**6**	**258**	**10.1**		**576**	**45.0**	**98**	**37**	**15:23**	**8**	**2**	**2**	**4**	**4**	**0**	**0**	**1**

Played in NHL All-Star Game (1999)

SULLIVAN, Mike

PHX.

Center. Shoots left. 6'2", 190 lbs. Born, Marshfield, MA, February 27, 1968. NY Rangers' 4th choice, 69th overall, in 1987 Entry Draft.

Season	Club	League	GP	G	A	Pts	PIM	PP	SH	GW	S	%	+/–	TF	F%	H	SB	Min	GP	G	A	Pts	PIM	PP	SH	GW
1985-86	Boston Prep	H.S.	22	26	33	59		....	....	....	....	....	....	....	....	....	....	....	....	....	....	....	....	....	....	....
1986-87	Boston University	H.E.	37	13	18	31	18	....	....	....	....	....	....	....	....	....	....	....	....	....	....	....	....	....	....	....
1987-88	Boston University	H.E.	30	18	22	40	30	....	....	....	....	....	....	....	....	....	....	....	....	....	....	....	....	....	....	....
1988-89	Boston University	H.E.	36	19	17	36	30	....	....	....	....	....	....	....	....	....	....	....	....	....	....	....	....	....	....	....
1989-90	Boston University	H.E.	38	11	20	31	26	....	....	....	....	....	....	....	....	....	....	....	....	....	....	....	....	....	....	....
1990-91	San Diego	IHL	74	12	23	35	27	....	....	....	....	....	....	....	....	....	....	....	....	....	....	....	....	....	....	....
1991-92	**San Jose**	**NHL**	**64**	**8**	**11**	**19**	**15**	**1**	**0**	**1**	**72**	**11.1**	**–18**	....	....	....	....	....	....	....	....	....	....	....	....	....
	Kansas City	IHL	10	2	8	10	8	....	....	....	....	....	....	....	....	....	....	....	....	....	....	....	....	....	....	....
1992-93	**San Jose**	**NHL**	**81**	**6**	**8**	**14**	**30**	**0**	**2**	**0**	**95**	**6.3**	**–42**	....	....	....	....	....	....	....	....	....	....	....	....	....
1993-94	**San Jose**	**NHL**	**26**	**2**	**2**	**4**	**4**	**0**	**2**	**1**	**21**	**9.5**	**–3**	....	....	....	....	....	....	....	....	....	....	....	....	....
	Kansas City	IHL	6	3	3	6	0	....	....	....	....	....	....	....	....	....	....	....	....	....	....	....	....	....	....	....
	Calgary	**NHL**	**19**	**2**	**3**	**5**	**6**	**0**	**2**	**0**	**27**	**7.4**	**2**	....	....	....	....	....	**7**	**1**	**1**	**2**	**8**	**0**	**1**	**0**
	Saint John	AHL	5	2	0	2	4	....	....	....	....	....	....	....	....	....	....	....	....	....	....	....	....	....	....	....
1994-95	**Calgary**	**NHL**	**38**	**4**	**7**	**11**	**14**	**0**	**0**	**2**	**31**	**12.9**	**–2**	....	....	....	....	....	**7**	**3**	**5**	**8**	**2**	**0**	**1**	**1**
1995-96	**Calgary**	**NHL**	**81**	**9**	**12**	**21**	**24**	**0**	**1**	**1**	**106**	**8.5**	**–6**	....	....	....	....	....	**4**	**0**	**0**	**0**	**0**	**0**	**0**	**0**
1996-97	**Calgary**	**NHL**	**67**	**5**	**6**	**11**	**10**	**0**	**3**	**2**	**64**	**7.8**	**–11**	....	....	....	....	....	....	....	....	....	....	....	....	....
1997-98	**Boston**	**NHL**	**77**	**5**	**13**	**18**	**34**	**0**	**0**	**2**	**83**	**6.0**	**–1**	....	....	....	....	....	**6**	**0**	**1**	**1**	**2**	**0**	**0**	**0**
1998-99	**Phoenix**	**NHL**	**63**	**2**	**4**	**6**	**24**	**0**	**1**	**1**	**66**	**3.0**	**–11**	**74**	**50.0**	**52**	**40**	**12:09**	**5**	**0**	**0**	**0**	**2**	**0**	**0**	**0**
	NHL Totals		**516**	**43**	**66**	**109**	**161**	**1**	**11**	**10**	**565**	**7.6**		**74**	**50.0**	**52**	**40**	**12:09**	**29**	**4**	**7**	**11**	**14**	**0**	**2**	**1**

Rights traded to **Minnesota** by **NY Rangers** with Paul Jerrard, the rights to Bret Barnett, and LA Kings' 3rd round choice (previously acquired, Minnesota selected Murray Garbutt) in 1989 Entry Draft for Brian Lawton, Igor Liba and the rights to Eric Bennett, October 11, 1988. Signed as a free agent by **San Jose**, August 9, 1991. Claimed on waivers by **Calgary** from **San Jose**, January 6, 1994. Traded to **Boston** by **Calgary** for Boston's 7th round choice (Radek Duda) in 1998 Entry Draft, June 21, 1997. Claimed by **Nashville** from **Boston** in Expansion Draft, June 26, 1998. Traded to **Phoenix** by **Nashville** for Phoenix's 7th round choice in 1999 Entry Draft, June 30, 1998.

SULLIVAN, Steve

TOR.

Center. Shoots right. 5'9", 155 lbs. Born, Timmins, Ont., July 6, 1974. New Jersey's 10th choice, 233rd overall, in 1994 Entry Draft.

Season	Club	League	GP	G	A	Pts	PIM	PP	SH	GW	S	%	+/–	TF	F%	H	SB	Min	GP	G	A	Pts	PIM	PP	SH	GW
1991-92	Timmins	OJHL	47	66	55	121	141	....	....	....	....	....	....	....	....	....	....	....	....	....	....	....	....	....	....	....
1992-93	S.S. Marie	OHL	62	36	27	63	44	....	....	....	....	....	....	....	....	....	....	....	16	3	8	11	18	....	....	....
1993-94	S.S. Marie	OHL	63	51	62	113	82	....	....	....	....	....	....	....	....	....	....	....	14	9	16	25	22	....	....	....
1994-95	Albany	AHL	75	31	50	81	124	....	....	....	....	....	....	....	....	....	....	....	14	4	7	11	10	....	....	....
1995-96	**New Jersey**	**NHL**	**16**	**5**	**4**	**9**	**8**	**2**	**0**	**1**	**23**	**21.7**	**3**	....	....	....	....	....	....	....	....	....	....	....	....	....
	Albany	AHL	53	33	42	75	127	....	....	....	....	....	....	....	....	....	....	....	4	3	0	3	6	....	....	....
1996-97	**New Jersey**	**NHL**	**33**	**8**	**14**	**22**	**14**	**2**	**0**	**2**	**63**	**12.7**	**9**	....	....	....	....	....	....	....	....	....	....	....	....	....
	Albany	AHL	15	8	7	15	16	....	....	....	....	....	....	....	....	....	....	....	....	....	....	....	....	....	....	....
	Toronto	**NHL**	**21**	**5**	**11**	**16**	**23**	**1**	**0**	**1**	**45**	**11.1**	**5**	....	....	....	....	....	....	....	....	....	....	....	....	....
1997-98	**Toronto**	**NHL**	**63**	**10**	**18**	**28**	**40**	**1**	**0**	**1**	**112**	**8.9**	**–8**	....	....	....	....	....	....	....	....	....	....	....	....	....
1998-99	**Toronto**	**NHL**	**63**	**20**	**20**	**40**	**28**	**4**	**0**	**5**	**110**	**18.2**	**12**	**685**	**44.4**	**26**	**11**	**14:12**	**13**	**3**	**3**	**6**	**14**	**2**	**0**	**0**
	NHL Totals		**196**	**48**	**67**	**115**	**113**	**10**	**0**	**10**	**353**	**13.6**		**685**	**44.4**	**26**	**11**	**14:12**	**13**	**3**	**3**	**6**	**14**	**2**	**0**	**0**

AHL First All-Star Team (1996)

Traded to **Toronto** by **New Jersey** with Jason Smith and the rights to Alyn McCauley for Doug Gilmour, Dave Ellett and future considerations, February 25, 1997.

SUNDIN, Mats

(SUHN-deen) **TOR.**

Center/Right wing. Shoots right. 6'4", 228 lbs. Born, Bromma, Sweden, February 13, 1971. Quebec's 1st choice, 1st overall, in 1989 Entry Draft.

Season	Club	League	GP	G	A	Pts	PIM	PP	SH	GW	S	%	+/–	TF	F%	H	SB	Min	GP	G	A	Pts	PIM	PP	SH	GW
1988-89	Nacka IK	Sweden-2	25	10	8	18	18	....	....	....	....	....	....	....	....	....	....	....	....	....	....	....	....	....	....	....
1989-90	Djurgardens IF	Sweden	34	10	8	18	16	....	....	....	....	....	....	....	....	....	....	....	8	7	0	7	4	....	....	....
1990-91	**Quebec**	**NHL**	**80**	**23**	**36**	**59**	**58**	**4**	**0**	**0**	**155**	**14.8**	**–24**	....	....	....	....	....	....	....	....	....	....	....	....	....
1991-92	**Quebec**	**NHL**	**80**	**33**	**43**	**76**	**103**	**8**	**2**	**2**	**231**	**14.3**	**–19**	....	....	....	....	....	....	....	....	....	....	....	....	....
1992-93	**Quebec**	**NHL**	**80**	**47**	**67**	**114**	**96**	**13**	**4**	**9**	**215**	**21.9**	**21**	....	....	....	....	....	**6**	**3**	**1**	**4**	**6**	**1**	**0**	**0**
1993-94	**Quebec**	**NHL**	**84**	**32**	**53**	**85**	**60**	**6**	**2**	**4**	**226**	**14.2**	**1**	....	....	....	....	....	....	....	....	....	....	....	....	....
1994-95	Djurgardens IF	Sweden	12	7	2	9	14	....	....	....	....	....	....	....	....	....	....	....	....	....	....	....	....	....	....	....
	Toronto	**NHL**	**47**	**23**	**24**	**47**	**14**	**9**	**0**	**4**	**173**	**13.3**	**–5**	....	....	....	....	....	**7**	**5**	**4**	**9**	**4**	**2**	**0**	**1**
1995-96	**Toronto**	**NHL**	**76**	**33**	**50**	**83**	**46**	**7**	**6**	**7**	**301**	**11.0**	**8**	....	....	....	....	....	**6**	**3**	**1**	**4**	**4**	**2**	**0**	**1**

Season	Club	League	GP	G	A	Pts	PIM	PP	SH	GW	S	%	+/-	TF	F%	H	SB	Min	GP	G	A	Pts	PIM	PP	SH	GW
			Regular Season																Playoffs							
1996-97	Toronto	NHL	82	41	53	94	59	7	4	8	281	14.6	6	....	....	....	....	....	....	....	....	....	....	....	....	....
1997-98	Toronto	NHL	82	33	41	74	49	9	1	5	219	15.1	–3	....	....	....	....	....	....	....	....	....	....	....	....	....
	Sweden	Olympics	4	3	0	3	4	....	....	....	....	....	....	....	....	....	....	....	....	....	....	....	....	....	....	....
1998-99	Toronto	NHL	82	31	52	83	58	4	0	6	209	14.8	22	1993	57.3	54	17	20:41	17	8	8	16	16	3	0	2
	NHL Totals		693	296	419	715	543	67	19	45	2010	14.7		1993	57.3	54	17	20:41	36	19	14	33	30	8	0	4

Swedish World All-Star Team (1991, 1992, 1994, 1997)

Played in NHL All-Star Game (1996, 1997, 1998, 1999)

Traded to **Toronto** by **Quebec** with Garth Butcher, Todd Warriner and Philadelphia's 1st round choice (previously acquired by Quebec — later traded to Washington — Washington selected Nolan Baumgartner) in 1994 Entry Draft for Wendel Clark, Sylvain Lefebvre, Landon Wilson and Toronto's 1st round choice (Jeffrey Kealty) in 1994 Entry Draft, June 28, 1994.

SUNDIN, Ronnie (SUHN-deen)

Defense. Shoots left. 6'1", 220 lbs. Born, Ludvika, Sweden, October 3, 1970. NY Rangers' 8th choice, 237th overall, in 1996 Entry Draft.

Season	Club	League	GP	G	A	Pts	PIM	PP	SH	GW	S	%	+/-	TF	F%	H	SB	Min	GP	G	A	Pts	PIM	PP	SH	GW
1991-92	Mora IK	Sweden-2	35	2	5	7	18	....	....	....	....	....	....	....	....	....	....	....	2	0	0	0	0	....	....	....
1992-93	V. Frolunda	Sweden	17	2	3	5	12	....	....	....	....	....	....	....	....	....	....	....	....	....	....	....	....	....	....	....
1993-94	V. Frolunda	Sweden	38	0	9	9	42	....	....	....	....	....	....	....	....	....	....	....	4	0	0	0	0	....	....	....
1994-95	V. Frolunda	Sweden	11	3	4	7	6	....	....	....	....	....	....	....	....	....	....	....	....	....	....	....	....	....	....	....
1995-96	V. Frolunda	Sweden	40	3	6	9	18	....	....	....	....	....	....	....	....	....	....	....	13	1	4	5	10	....	....	....
1996-97	V. Frolunda	Sweden	47	3	14	17	24	....	....	....	....	....	....	....	....	....	....	....	3	1	0	1	2	....	....	....
	V. Frolunda	EuroHL	3	1	1	2	0	....	....	....	....	....	....	....	....	....	....	....	4	0	2	2	0	....	....	....
1997-98	NY Rangers	NHL	1	0	0	0	0	0	0	0	0	0.0	0	....	....	....	....	....	....	....	....	....	....	....	....	....
	Hartford	AHL	67	3	19	22	59	....	....	....	....	....	....	....	....	....	....	....	14	2	5	7	15	....	....	....
1998-99	V. Frolunda	Sweden	50	5	3	8	26	....	....	....	....	....	....	....	....	....	....	....	4	0	1	1	2	....	....	....
	NHL Totals		1	0	0	0	0	0	0	0	0	0.0		....	....	....	....	....	....	....	....	....	....	....	....	....

SUNDSTROM, Niklas (SUHN-struhm) S.J.

Left wing. Shoots left. 6', 185 lbs. Born, Ornskoldsvik, Sweden, June 6, 1975. NY Rangers' 1st choice, 8th overall, in 1993 Entry Draft.

Season	Club	League	GP	G	A	Pts	PIM	PP	SH	GW	S	%	+/-	TF	F%	H	SB	Min	GP	G	A	Pts	PIM	PP	SH	GW
1988-89	KB 65	Sweden-3	1	1	1	2	0	....	....	....	....	....	....	....	....	....	....	....	....	....	....	....	....	....	....	....
1989-90	KB-65	Sweden-3	21	2	9	11	30	....	....	....	....	....	....	....	....	....	....	....	....	....	....	....	....	....	....	....
1990-91	KB-65	Sweden-3	21	4	9	13	22	....	....	....	....	....	....	....	....	....	....	....	....	....	....	....	....	....	....	....
1991-92	MoDo Hockey	Sweden	9	1	3	4	0	....	....	....	....	....	....	....	....	....	....	....	....	....	....	....	....	....	....	....
1992-93	Modo Hockey	Swede-Jr.	2	3	1	4	0	....	....	....	....	....	....	....	....	....	....	....	....	....	....	....	....	....	....	....
	MoDo Hockey	Sweden	40	7	11	18	18	....	....	....	....	....	....	....	....	....	....	....	3	0	0	0	0	....	....	....
1993-94	Modo Hockey	Swede-Jr.	3	3	4	7	2	....	....	....	....	....	....	....	....	....	....	....	....	....	....	....	....	....	....	....
	MoDo Hockey	Sweden	37	7	12	19	28	....	....	....	....	....	....	....	....	....	....	....	11	4	3	7	2	....	....	....
1994-95	MoDo Hockey	Sweden	33	8	13	21	30	....	....	....	....	....	....	....	....	....	....	....	....	....	....	....	....	....	....	....
1995-96	NY Rangers	NHL	82	9	12	21	14	1	1	2	90	10.0	2	....	....	....	....	....	11	4	3	7	4	1	0	0
1996-97	NY Rangers	NHL	82	24	28	52	20	5	1	4	132	18.2	23	....	....	....	....	....	9	0	5	5	2	0	0	0
1997-98	NY Rangers	NHL	70	19	28	47	24	4	0	1	115	16.5	0	....	....	....	....	....	....	....	....	....	....	....	....	....
	Sweden	Olympics	4	1	1	2	2	....	....	....	....	....	....	....	....	....	....	....	....	....	....	....	....	....	....	....
1998-99	NY Rangers	NHL	81	13	30	43	20	1	2	3	89	14.6	–2	376	40.4	118	55	19:11	....	....	....	....	....	....	....	....
	NHL Totals		315	65	98	163	78	11	4	10	426	15.3		376	40.4	118	55	19:11	20	4	8	12	6	1	0	0

Traded to **Tampa Bay** by **NY Rangers** with Dan Cloutier and NY Rangers' 1st and 3rd round choices in 2000 Entry Draft for Chicago's 1st round choice (previously acquired, NY Rangers selected Pavel Brendl) in 1999 Entry Draft, June 26, 1999. Traded to **San Jose** by **Tampa Bay** with NY Rangers' 3rd round choice (previously acquired) in 2000 Entry Draft for Bill Houlder, Andrei Zyuzin, Shawn Burr and Steve Guolla, August 4, 1999.

SUTER, Gary (SOO-tuhr) S.J.

Defense. Shoots left. 6', 205 lbs. Born, Madison, WI, June 24, 1964. Calgary's 9th choice, 180th overall, in 1984 Entry Draft.

Season	Club	League	GP	G	A	Pts	PIM	PP	SH	GW	S	%	+/-	TF	F%	H	SB	Min	GP	G	A	Pts	PIM	PP	SH	GW
1981-82	Dubuque	USHL	18	3	4	7	32	....	....	....	....	....	....	....	....	....	....	....	....	....	....	....	....	....	....	....
1982-83	Dubuque	USHL	41	9	30	39	112	....	....	....	....	....	....	....	....	....	....	....	....	....	....	....	....	....	....	....
1983-84	U. of Wisconsin	WCHA	35	4	18	22	32	....	....	....	....	....	....	....	....	....	....	....	....	....	....	....	....	....	....	....
1984-85	U. of Wisconsin	WCHA	39	12	39	51	110	....	....	....	....	....	....	....	....	....	....	....	....	....	....	....	....	....	....	....
1985-86	Calgary	NHL	80	18	50	68	141	9	0	4	195	9.2	11	....	....	....	....	....	10	2	8	10	8	0	0	1
1986-87	Calgary	NHL	68	9	40	49	70	4	0	0	152	5.9	–10	....	....	....	....	....	6	0	3	3	10	0	0	0
1987-88	Calgary	NHL	75	21	70	91	124	6	1	3	204	10.3	39	....	....	....	....	....	9	1	9	10	6	0	1	0
1988-89♦	Calgary	NHL	63	13	49	62	78	8	0	1	216	6.0	26	....	....	....	....	....	5	0	3	3	10	0	0	0
1989-90	Calgary	NHL	76	16	60	76	97	5	0	1	211	7.6	4	....	....	....	....	....	6	0	1	1	14	0	0	0
1990-91	Calgary	NHL	79	12	58	70	102	6	0	1	258	4.7	26	....	....	....	....	....	7	1	6	7	12	1	0	0
1991-92	Calgary	NHL	70	12	43	55	128	4	0	0	189	6.3	1	....	....	....	....	....	....	....	....	....	....	....	....	....
1992-93	Calgary	NHL	81	23	58	81	112	10	1	2	263	8.7	–1	....	....	....	....	....	6	2	3	5	8	0	1	0
1993-94	Calgary	NHL	25	4	9	13	20	2	1	0	51	7.8	–3	....	....	....	....	....	....	....	....	....	....	....	....	....
	Chicago	NHL	16	2	3	5	18	2	0	0	35	5.7	–9	....	....	....	....	....	6	3	2	5	6	2	0	0
1994-95	Chicago	NHL	48	10	27	37	42	5	0	0	144	6.9	14	....	....	....	....	....	12	2	5	7	10	1	0	0
1995-96	Chicago	NHL	82	20	47	67	80	12	2	4	242	8.3	3	....	....	....	....	....	10	3	3	6	8	2	0	1
1996-97	Chicago	NHL	82	7	21	28	70	3	0	0	225	3.1	–4	....	....	....	....	....	6	1	4	5	8	0	0	0
1997-98	Chicago	NHL	73	14	28	42	74	5	2	0	199	7.0	1	....	....	....	....	....	....	....	....	....	....	....	....	....
	United States	Olympics	4	0	0	0	2	....	....	....	....	....	....	....	....	....	....	....	....	....	....	....	....	....	....	....
1998-99	San Jose	NHL	1	0	0	0	0	0	0	0	1	0.0	0	0	0.0	0	0	12:56	....	....	....	....	....	....	....	....
	NHL Totals		919	181	563	744	1156	81	7	16	2585	7.0		0	0.0	0	0	12:56	83	15	47	62	100	6	2	2

Won Calder Memorial Trophy (1986) • NHL All-Rookie Team (1986) • NHL Second All-Star Team (1988)

Played in NHL All-Star Game (1986, 1988, 1989, 1991)

Traded to **Hartford** by **Calgary** with Paul Ranheim and Ted Drury for James Patrick, Zarley Zalapski and Michael Nylander, March 10, 1994. Traded to **Chicago** by **Hartford** with Randy Cunneyworth and Hartford's 3rd round choice (later traded to Vancouver — Vancouver selected Larry Courville) in 1995 Entry Draft for Frantisek Kucera and Jocelyn Lemieux, March 11, 1994. Signed as a free agent by **San Jose**, July 1, 1998. Missed majority of 1998-99 season with torn triceps muscle suffered in game vs. Dallas, October 24, 1998.

SUTTER, Ron (SUH-tuhr) S.J.

Center. Shoots right. 6', 180 lbs. Born, Viking, Alta., December 2, 1963. Philadelphia's 1st choice, 4th overall, in 1982 Entry Draft.

Season	Club	League	GP	G	A	Pts	PIM	PP	SH	GW	S	%	+/-	TF	F%	H	SB	Min	GP	G	A	Pts	PIM	PP	SH	GW
1979-80	Red Deer	AJHL	60	12	33	45	44	....	....	....	....	....	....	....	....	....	....	....	....	....	....	....	....	....	....	....
1980-81	Lethbridge	WHL	72	13	32	45	152	....	....	....	....	....	....	....	....	....	....	....	9	2	5	7	29	....	....	....
1981-82	Lethbridge	WHL	59	38	54	92	207	....	....	....	....	....	....	....	....	....	....	....	12	6	5	11	28	....	....	....
1982-83	Philadelphia	NHL	10	1	1	2	9	0	0	1	4	25.0	0	....	....	....	....	....	....	....	....	....	....	....	....	....
	Lethbridge	WHL	58	35	48	83	98	....	....	....	....	....	....	....	....	....	....	....	20	*22	*19	*41	45	....	....	....
1983-84	Philadelphia	NHL	79	19	32	51	101	5	3	3	145	13.1	4	....	....	....	....	....	3	0	0	0	22	0	0	0
1984-85	Philadelphia	NHL	73	16	29	45	94	2	0	5	140	11.4	13	....	....	....	....	....	19	4	8	12	28	0	0	1
1985-86	Philadelphia	NHL	75	18	42	60	159	0	0	4	145	12.4	26	....	....	....	....	....	5	0	2	2	10	0	0	0
1986-87	Philadelphia	NHL	39	10	17	27	69	0	0	0	68	14.7	10	....	....	....	....	....	16	1	7	8	12	0	0	0
1987-88	Philadelphia	NHL	69	8	25	33	146	1	0	0	107	7.5	–9	....	....	....	....	....	7	0	1	1	26	0	0	0
1988-89	Philadelphia	NHL	55	26	22	48	80	4	1	2	106	24.5	25	....	....	....	....	....	19	1	9	10	51	0	0	0
1989-90	Philadelphia	NHL	75	22	26	48	104	0	2	6	157	14.0	2	....	....	....	....	....	....	....	....	....	....	....	....	....
1990-91	Philadelphia	NHL	80	17	28	45	92	2	0	1	149	11.4	2	....	....	....	....	....	....	....	....	....	....	....	....	....
1991-92	St. Louis	NHL	68	19	27	46	91	5	4	1	106	17.9	9	....	....	....	....	....	6	1	3	4	8	1	0	0
1992-93	St. Louis	NHL	59	12	15	27	99	4	0	3	90	13.3	–11	....	....	....	....	....	....	....	....	....	....	....	....	....
1993-94	St. Louis	NHL	36	6	12	18	46	1	0	2	42	14.3	–1	....	....	....	....	....	....	....	....	....	....	....	....	....
	Quebec	NHL	37	9	13	22	44	4	0	0	66	13.6	3	....	....	....	....	....	....	....	....	....	....	....	....	....

Season	Club	League	GP	G	A	Pts	PIM	PP	SH	GW	S	%	+/-	TF	F%	H	SB	Min	GP	G	A	Pts	PIM	PP	SH	GW
1994-95	NY Islanders	NHL	27	1	4	5	21	0	0	1	29	3.4	-8	....	....											
1995-96	Phoenix	IHL	25	6	13	19	28							....												
	Boston	NHL	18	5	7	12	24	0	1	0	34	14.7	10	....					5	0	0	0	8	0	0	0
1996-97	San Jose	NHL	78	5	7	12	65	1	2	1	78	6.4	-8													
1997-98	San Jose	NHL	57	2	7	9	22	0	0	1	57	3.5	-2						6	1	0	1	14	0	0	0
1998-99	San Jose	NHL	59	3	6	9	40	0	0	1	67	4.5	-8	636	49.1	83	18	9:54	6	0	0	0	4	0	0	0
	NHL Totals		994	199	320	519	1306	29	13	32	1590	12.5		636	49.1	83	18	9:54	92	8	30	38	183	1	0	1

Traded to **St. Louis** by **Philadelphia** with Murray Baron for Dan Quinn and Rod Brind'Amour, September 22, 1991. Traded to **Quebec** by St. Louis with Garth Butcher and Bob Bassen for Steve Duchesne and Denis Chasse, January 23, 1994. Traded to **NY Islanders** by **Quebec** with Quebec's 1st round choice (Brett Lindros) in 1994 Entry Draft for Uwe Krupp and NY Islanders' 1st round choice (Wade Belak) in 1994 Entry Draft, June 28, 1994. Signed as a free agent by **Boston**, March 9, 1996. Signed as a free agent by **San Jose**, October 12, 1996.

SUTTON, Andy — S.J.

Defense. Shoots left. 6'6", 245 lbs. Born, Edmonton, Alta., March 10, 1975.

Season	Club	League	GP	G	A	Pts	PIM	PP	SH	GW	S	%	+/-	TF	F%	H	SB	Min	GP	G	A	Pts	PIM	PP	SH	GW
1991-92	Gananoque	OJHL-B	50	20	30	50	....																			
1992-93	Gananoque	OJHL-B	50	25	27	52	....																			
1993-94	St. Michael's	OJHL-B	47	17	22	39	153												3	0	0	0	20			
1994-95	Michigan Tech	WCHA	19	2	1	3	42																			
1995-96	Michigan Tech	WCHA	33	2	2	4	58																			
1996-97	Michigan Tech	WCHA	32	2	7	9	73																			
1997-98	Michigan Tech	WCHA	38	16	24	40	97																			
	Kentucky	AHL	7	0	0	0	33																			
1998-99	San Jose	NHL	31	0	3	3	65	0	0	0	24	0.0	-4	0	0.0	50	14	12:58								
	Kentucky	AHL	21	5	10	15	53												5	0	0	0	23			
	NHL Totals		31	0	3	3	65	0	0	0	24	0.0		0	0.0	50	14	12:58								

WCHA Second All-Star Team (1998)
Signed as a free agent by **San Jose**, March 20, 1998.

SUTTON, Ken — N.J.

Defense. Shoots left. 6'1", 205 lbs. Born, Edmonton, Alta., November 5, 1969. Buffalo's 4th choice, 98th overall, in 1989 Entry Draft.

Season	Club	League	GP	G	A	Pts	PIM	PP	SH	GW	S	%	+/-	TF	F%	H	SB	Min	GP	G	A	Pts	PIM	PP	SH	GW
1987-88	Calgary	AJHL	53	13	43	56	228												8	2	5	7	12			
1988-89	Saskatoon	WHL	71	22	31	53	104												11	1	6	7	15			
1989-90	Rochester	AHL	57	5	14	19	83																			
1990-91	Buffalo	NHL	15	3	6	9	13	2	0	0	26	11.5	2						6	0	1	1	2	0	0	0
	Rochester	AHL	62	7	24	31	65												3	1	1	2	14			
1991-92	Buffalo	NHL	64	2	18	20	71	0	0	0	81	2.5	5						7	0	2	2	4	0	0	0
1992-93	Buffalo	NHL	63	8	14	22	30	1	0	2	77	10.4	-3						8	3	1	4	8	0	0	0
1993-94	Buffalo	NHL	78	4	20	24	71	1	0	0	95	4.2	-6						4	0	0	0	2	0	0	0
1994-95	Buffalo	NHL	12	1	2	3	30	0	0	1	12	8.3	-2													
	Edmonton	NHL	12	3	1	4	12	0	0	0	28	10.7	-1													
1995-96	Edmonton	NHL	32	0	8	8	39	0	0	0	38	0.0	-12													
	St. Louis	NHL	6	0	0	0	4	0	0	0	3	0.0	-1						1	0	0	0	0	0	0	0
	Worcester	AHL	32	4	16	20	60												4	0	2	2	21			
1996-97	Manitoba	IHL	20	3	10	13	48																			
	Albany	AHL	61	6	13	19	79												16	4	8	12	55			
1997-98	New Jersey	NHL	13	0	0	0	6	0	0	0	5	0.0	1													
	Albany	AHL	10	0	7	7	15																			
	San Jose	NHL	8	0	0	0	15	0	0	0	7	0.0	-4													
1998-99	New Jersey	NHL	5	1	0	1	0	0	0	0	5	20.0	1	0	0.0	3	1	13:02								
	Albany	AHL	75	13	42	55	118												5	0	2	2	12			
	NHL Totals		308	22	69	91	291	4	0	3	377	5.8		0	0.0	3	1	13:02	26	3	4	7	16	0	0	0

Memorial Cup All-Star Team (1989) • AHL First All-Star Team (1999) • Won Eddie Shore Award (Outstanding Defenseman - AHL) (1999)

Traded to **Edmonton** by **Buffalo** for Scott Pearson, April 7, 1995. Traded to **St. Louis** by **Edmonton** with Igor Kravchuk for Jeff Norton and Donald Dufresne, January 4, 1996. Traded to **New Jersey** by **St. Louis** with St. Louis' 2nd round choice in 1999 Entry Draft for Mike Peluso and Ricard Persson, November 26, 1996. Traded to **San Jose** by **New Jersey** with John MacLean for Doug Bodger and Dody Wood, December 7, 1997. Traded to **New Jersey** by **San Jose** for future considerations, August 26, 1998.

SVEHLA, Robert   (SHVEH-lah) FLA.

Defense. Shoots right. 6'1", 210 lbs. Born, Martin, Czech., January 2, 1969. Calgary's 4th choice, 78th overall, in 1992 Entry Draft.

Season	Club	League	GP	G	A	Pts	PIM	PP	SH	GW	S	%	+/-	TF	F%	H	SB	Min	GP	G	A	Pts	PIM	PP	SH	GW
1989-90	Dukla Trencin	Czech.	29	4	3	7	....																			
1990-91	Dukla Trencin	Czech.	52	16	9	25	62																			
1991-92	Dukla Trencin	Czech.	51	23	28	51	74																			
	Czechoslovakia	Olympics	8	2	1	3	8																			
1992-93	Malmo IF	Sweden	40	19	10	29	86												6	0	1	1	14			
1993-94	Malmo IF	Sweden	37	14	25	39	*127												10	5	1	6	23			
	Slovakia	Olympics	8	3	4	7	2																			
1994-95	Malmo IF	Sweden	32	11	13	24	83												9	2	3	5	6			
	Florida	NHL	5	1	1	2	0	1	0	0	6	16.7	3													
1995-96	Florida	NHL	81	8	49	57	94	7	0	0	146	5.5	-3						22	0	6	6	32	0	0	0
1996-97	Florida	NHL	82	13	32	45	86	5	0	3	159	8.2	2						5	1	4	5	4	1	0	0
1997-98	Florida	NHL	79	9	34	43	113	3	0	0	144	6.3	-3													
	Slovakia	Olympics	2	0	1	1	0																			
1998-99	Florida	NHL	80	8	29	37	83	4	0	0	157	5.1	-13	2	0.0	101	92	24:45								
	NHL Totals		327	39	145	184	376	20	0	3	612	6.4		2	0.0	101	92	24:45	27	1	10	11	36	1	0	0

Czechoslovakian First All-Star Team (1992)
Played in NHL All-Star Game (1997)

Traded to **Florida** by **Calgary** with Magnus Svensson for Florida's 3rd round choice (Dmitri Vlasenkov) in 1996 Entry Draft and 4th round choice (Ryan Ready) in 1997 Entry Draft, September 29, 1994.

SVEJKOVSKY, Jaroslav   (svehzh-KOHV-skee) WSH.

Right wing. Shoots right. 6'1", 185 lbs. Born, Plzen, Czech., October 1, 1976. Washington's 2nd choice, 17th overall, in 1996 Entry Draft.

Season	Club	League	GP	G	A	Pts	PIM	PP	SH	GW	S	%	+/-	TF	F%	H	SB	Min	GP	G	A	Pts	PIM	PP	SH	GW
1993-94	Skoda Plzen	Cze-Rep	8	0	0	0	8																			
1994-95	ZKZ Plzen	Czech-Jr.	25	18	19	37	30																			
	SC Ta'Bor	Cze-Rep-2	11	6	7	13																				
1995-96	Tri-City	WHL	70	58	43	101	118												11	10	9	19	8			
1996-97	Washington	NHL	19	7	3	10	4	2	0	1	30	23.3	-1													
	Portland	AHL	54	38	28	66	56												5	2	0	2	6			
1997-98	Washington	NHL	17	4	1	5	10	2	0	1	29	13.8	-5						1	0	0	0	2	0	0	0
	Portland	AHL	16	12	7	19	16												7	1	2	3	2			
1998-99	Washington	NHL	25	6	8	14	12	4	0	2	50	12.0	-2	0	0.0	40	6	13:36								
	NHL Totals		61	17	12	29	26	8	0	4	109	15.6		0	0.0	40	6	13:36	1	0	0	0	2	0	0	0

WHL West Second All-Star Team (1996) • Won Dudley "Red" Garrett Memorial Trophy (Top Rookie — AHL) (1997)

SVOBODA, Petr — T.B.

(svah-BOH-duh)

Defense. Shoots left. 6'1", 180 lbs. Born, Most, Czech., February 14, 1966. Montreal's 1st choice, 5th overall, in 1984 Entry Draft.

Season	Club	League	GP	G	A	Pts	PIM	PP	SH	GW	S	%	+/-	TF	F%	H	SB	Min	GP	G	A	Pts	PIM	PP	SH	GW
1982-83	CHZ Litvinov	Czech.	4	0	0	0	2																			
1983-84	CHZ Litvinov	Czech.	18	3	1	4	20																			
1984-85	Montreal	NHL	73	4	27	31	65	0	0	1	80	5.0	16						7	1	1	2	12	0	0	0
1985-86♦	Montreal	NHL	73	1	18	19	93	0	0	0	63	1.6	24						8	0	0	0	21	0	0	0
1986-87	Montreal	NHL	70	5	17	22	63	1	0	1	80	6.3	14						14	0	5	5	10	0	0	0
1987-88	Montreal	NHL	69	7	22	29	149	2	0	1	138	5.1	46						10	0	5	5	12	0	0	0
1988-89	Montreal	NHL	71	8	37	45	147	4	0	1	131	6.1	28						21	1	11	12	16	0	0	0
1989-90	Montreal	NHL	60	5	31	36	98	2	0	2	90	5.6	20						10	0	5	5	7	0	0	0
1990-91	Montreal	NHL	60	4	22	26	52	3	0	1	67	6.0	5						2	0	1	1	2	0	0	0
1991-92	Montreal	NHL	58	5	16	21	94	1	0	3	88	5.7	9						7	1	4	5	6	0	1	0
	Buffalo	NHL	13	1	6	7	52	0	0	0	23	4.3	-8													
1992-93	Buffalo	NHL	40	2	24	26	59	1	0	1	61	3.3	5						3	0	0	0	4	0	0	0
1993-94	Buffalo	NHL	60	2	14	16	89	1	0	0	80	2.5	11													
1994-95	CHZ Litvinov	Cze-Rep	8	2	0	2	50																			
	Buffalo	NHL	26	0	5	5	60	0	0	0	22	0.0	-5						14	0	4	4	8	0	0	0
	Philadelphia	NHL	11	0	3	3	10	0	0	0	17	0.0	0						12	0	6	6	22	0	0	0
1995-96	Philadelphia	NHL	73	1	28	29	105	0	0	0	91	1.1	28						16	1	2	3	16	0	0	0
1996-97	Philadelphia	NHL	67	2	12	14	94	1	0	0	36	5.6	10						3	0	1	1	4	0	0	0
1997-98	Philadelphia	NHL	56	3	15	18	83	2	0	0	44	6.8	19													
	Czech.	Olympics	6	1	1	2	*39																			
1998-99	Philadelphia	NHL	25	4	2	6	28	1	1	0	37	10.8	5	0	0.0	13	24	20:15								
	Tampa Bay	NHL	34	1	16	17	53	0	0	0	46	2.2	-4	0	0.0	47	61	25:33								
	NHL Totals		939	55	315	370	1394	19	1	12	1194	4.6		0	0.0	60	85	23:18	127	4	45	49	140	0	1	0

Traded to **Buffalo** by **Montreal** for Kevin Haller, March 10, 1992. Traded to **Philadelphia** by Buffalo for Garry Galley, April 7, 1995. Traded to **Tampa Bay** by Philadelphia for Karl Dykhuis, December 28, 1998.

SWEENEY, Don — BOS.

Defense. Shoots left. 5'10", 184 lbs. Born, St. Stephen, N.B., August 17, 1966. Boston's 8th choice, 166th overall, in 1984 Entry Draft.

Season	Club	League	GP	G	A	Pts	PIM	PP	SH	GW	S	%	+/-	TF	F%	H	SB	Min	GP	G	A	Pts	PIM	PP	SH	GW
1983-84	St. Paul	H.S.	22	33	26	59																				
1984-85	Harvard University	ECAC	29	3	7	10	30																			
1985-86	Harvard University	ECAC	31	4	5	9	12																			
1986-87	Harvard University	ECAC	34	7	4	11	22																			
1987-88	Harvard University	ECAC	30	6	23	29	37																			
	Maine	AHL																	6	1	3	4	0			
1988-89	Boston	NHL	36	3	5	8	20	0	0	0	35	8.6	-6													
	Maine	AHL	42	8	17	25	24																			
1989-90	Boston	NHL	58	3	5	8	58	0	0	0	49	6.1	11						21	1	5	6	18	1	0	0
	Maine	AHL	11	0	8	8	8												19	3	0	3	25	0	0	0
1990-91	Boston	NHL	77	8	13	21	67	0	1	3	102	7.8	2						15	0	0	0	10	0	0	0
1991-92	Boston	NHL	75	3	11	14	74	0	0	1	92	3.3	-9						4	0	0	0	4	0	0	0
1992-93	Boston	NHL	84	7	27	34	68	0	1	0	107	6.5	34						4	0	1	1	4	0	0	0
1993-94	Boston	NHL	75	6	15	21	50	1	2	2	136	4.4	29						12	2	1	3	4	0	0	0
1994-95	Boston	NHL	47	3	19	22	24	1	0	2	102	2.9	6						5	0	0	0	4	0	0	0
1995-96	Boston	NHL	77	4	24	28	42	2	0	3	142	2.8	-4						5	0	2	2	6	0	0	0
1996-97	Boston	NHL	82	3	23	26	39	0	0	0	113	2.7	-5													
1997-98	Boston	NHL	59	1	15	16	24	0	0	0	55	1.8	12						11	3	0	3	6	1	0	0
1998-99	Boston	NHL	81	2	10	12	64	0	0	0	79	2.5	14	0	0.0	205	85	19:31								
	NHL Totals		751	43	167	210	530	4	4	11	1012	4.2		0	0.0	205	85	19:31	92	9	8	17	77	2	0	1

NCAA East All-American Team (1988) • ECAC First All-Star Team (1988)

SWEENEY, Tim

Left wing. Shoots left. 5'11", 185 lbs. Born, Boston, MA, April 12, 1967. Calgary's 7th choice, 122nd overall, in 1985 Entry Draft.

Season	Club	League	GP	G	A	Pts	PIM	PP	SH	GW	S	%	+/-	TF	F%	H	SB	Min	GP	G	A	Pts	PIM	PP	SH	GW
1983-84	Weymouth High	H.S.	23	33	26	59																				
1984-85	Weymouth High	H.S.	22	32	56	88																				
1985-86	Boston College	H.E.	32	8	4	12	8																			
1986-87	Boston College	H.E.	38	31	18	49	28																			
1987-88	Boston College	H.E.	18	9	11	20	18																			
1988-89	Boston College	H.E.	39	29	44	73	26																			
1989-90	Salt Lake	IHL	81	46	51	97	32												11	5	4	9	4			
1990-91	Calgary	NHL	42	7	9	16	8	0	0	4	40	17.5	1													
	Salt Lake	IHL	31	19	16	35	8												4	3	3	6	0			
1991-92	United States	Nat-Team	21	9	11	20	10																			
	United States	Olympics	8	3	4	7	6																			
	Calgary	NHL	11	1	2	3	4	0	0	1	16	6.3	0													
1992-93	Boston	NHL	14	1	7	8	6	0	0	1	15	6.7	1						3	0	0	0	0	0	0	0
	Providence	AHL	60	41	55	96	32												3	2	2	4	0			
1993-94	Anaheim	NHL	78	16	27	43	49	6	1	2	114	14.0	3													
1994-95	Anaheim	NHL	13	1	1	2	2	0	0	0	11	9.1	-3													
	Providence	AHL	2	2	2	4	0												13	8	*17	*25	6			
1995-96	Boston	NHL	41	8	8	16	14	1	0	2	47	17.0	4						1	0	0	0	2	0	0	0
	Providence	AHL	34	17	22	39	12																			
1996-97	Boston	NHL	36	10	11	21	14	2	0	2	65	15.4	0													
	Providence	AHL	23	11	22	33	6																			
1997-98	NY Rangers	NHL	56	11	18	29	26	2	0	1	75	14.7	7													
	Hartford	AHL	7	2	6	8	8																			
1998-99	Providence	AHL	2	0	0	0	0																			
	NHL Totals		291	55	83	138	123	11	1	12	383	14.4							4	0	0	0	2	0	0	0

Hockey East First All-Star Team (1989) • NCAA East Second All-American Team (1989) • IHL Second All-Star Team (1990) • AHL Second All-Star Team (1993)

Signed as a free agent by **Boston**, September 16, 1992. Claimed by **Anaheim** from **Boston** in Expansion Draft, June 24, 1993. Signed as a free agent by **Boston**, August 9, 1995. Signed as a free agent by **NY Rangers**, September 15, 1997. Signed as a free agent by **Providence** (AHL), October 3, 1998. • Retired October 11, 1998.

SYDOR, Darryl — DAL.

(sih-DOHR)

Defense. Shoots left. 6', 195 lbs. Born, Edmonton, Alta., May 13, 1972. Los Angeles' 1st choice, 7th overall, in 1990 Entry Draft.

Season	Club	League	GP	G	A	Pts	PIM	PP	SH	GW	S	%	+/-	TF	F%	H	SB	Min	GP	G	A	Pts	PIM	PP	SH	GW
1985-86	Genstar	AAHA	34	20	17	37	60																			
1986-87	Genstar	AAHA	36	15	20	35	60																			
1987-88	Edmonton	AJHL	38	10	11	21	54																			
1988-89	Kamloops	WHL	65	12	14	26	86												15	1	4	5	19			
1989-90	Kamloops	WHL	67	29	66	95	129												17	2	9	11	28			
1990-91	Kamloops	WHL	66	27	78	105	88												12	3	*22	25	10			
1991-92	Kamloops	WHL	29	9	39	48	43												17	3	15	18	18			
	Los Angeles	NHL	18	1	5	6	22	0	0	0	18	5.6	-3						24	3	8	11	16	2	0	0
1992-93	Los Angeles	NHL	80	6	23	29	63	0	0	1	112	5.4	-2													
1993-94	Los Angeles	NHL	84	8	27	35	94	1	0	0	146	5.5	-9													

Season	Club	League				Regular Season																			Playoffs							
			GP	G	A	Pts	PIM	PP	SH	GW	S	%	+/-		TF	F%	H	SB	Min		GP	G	A	Pts	PIM	PP	SH	GW
1994-95	Los Angeles	NHL	48	4	19	23	36	3	0	0	96	4.2	−2		....	....	....	....	....		....	....	....	....	....	....	....	....
1995-96	Los Angeles	NHL	58	1	11	12	34	1	0	0	84	1.2	−11		....	....	....	....	....		....	....	....	....	....	....	....	....
	Dallas	NHL	26	2	6	8	41	1	0	0	33	6.1	−1		....	....	....	....	....		....	....	....	....	....	....	....	....
1996-97	Dallas	NHL	82	8	40	48	51	2	0	2	142	5.6	37		....	....	....	....	....		....	....	....	....	....	....	....	....
1997-98	Dallas	NHL	79	11	35	46	51	4	1	1	166	6.6	17		....	....	....	....	....		7	0	2	2	0	0	0	0
1998-99 ♦	Dallas	NHL	74	14	34	48	50	9	0	2	163	8.6	−1		1100.0	83	83	21:16		23	3	9	12	16	1	0	1
	NHL Totals		**549**	**55**	**200**	**255**	**442**	**21**	**1**	**6**	**960**	**5.7**			**1100.0**	**83**	**83**	**21:16**		**71**	**6**	**24**	**30**	**46**	**3**	**0**	**1**

WHL West First All-Star Team (1990, 1991, 1992)
Played in NHL All-Star Game (1998, 1999)
Traded to **Dallas** by **LA Kings** with LA Kings' 5th round choice (Ryan Christie) in 1996 Entry Draft for Shane Churla and Doug Zmolek, February 17, 1996.

SYKORA, Michal

Defense. Shoots left. 6'5", 225 lbs.   Born, Pardubice, Czech., July 5, 1973. San Jose's 6th choice, 123rd overall, in 1992 Entry Draft.   (SEE-koh-ra)

Season	Club	League	GP	G	A	Pts	PIM	PP	SH	GW	S	%	+/-		TF	F%	H	SB	Min		GP	G	A	Pts	PIM	PP	SH	GW
1990-91	HC Tesla	Czech-Jr.	40	17	26	43	45																					
	HC Pardubice	Czech.	2	0	0	0	0																					
1991-92	Tacoma	WHL	61	13	23	36	66	....													4	0	2	2	2			
1992-93	Tacoma	WHL	70	23	50	73	73	....													7	4	8	12	2			
1993-94	**San Jose**	**NHL**	22	1	4	5	14	0	0	0	22	4.5	−4														
	Kansas City	IHL	47	5	11	16	30																					
1994-95	Kansas City	IHL	36	1	10	11	30																					
	San Jose	**NHL**	16	0	4	4	10	0	0	0	6	0.0	6														
1995-96	**San Jose**	**NHL**	79	4	16	20	54	1	0	0	80	5.0	−14														
1996-97	**San Jose**	**NHL**	35	2	5	7	59	1	0	0	39	5.1	0														
	Chicago	**NHL**	28	1	9	10	10	0	0	0	38	2.6	4							1	0	0	0	0	0	0	0
1997-98	**Chicago**	**NHL**	28	1	3	4	12	0	0	0	35	2.9	−10														
	Indianapolis	IHL	6	0	0	0	4																					
	HC Pardubice	Cze-Rep	1	1	0	1	2																					
1998-99	Sparta Praha	Cze-Rep	26	4	9	13	38														8	2	0	2				
	Sparta Praha	EuroHL	2	2	2	4	4														2	2	2	4	0			
	Tampa Bay	**NHL**	10	1	2	3	0	0	0	1	24	4.2	−7		0	0.0	10	8	16:20									
	NHL Totals		**218**	**10**	**43**	**53**	**159**	**2**	**0**	**1**	**244**	**4.1**			**0**	**0.0**	**10**	**8**	**16:20**		**1**	**0**	**0**	**0**	**0**	**0**	**0**	**0**

WHL West First All-Star Team (1993)
Traded to **Chicago** by **San Jose** with Chris Terreri and Ulf Dahlen for Ed Belfour, January 25, 1997. Traded to **Tampa Bay** by **Chicago** for Mark Fitzpatrick and Tampa Bay's 4th round choice in 1999 Entry Draft, July 17, 1998.

SYKORA, Petr   NSH.

Center. Shoots right. 6'2", 180 lbs.   Born, Pardubice, Czech., December 21, 1978. Detroit's 2nd choice, 76th overall, in 1997 Entry Draft.   (SEE-koh-ra)

Season	Club	League	GP	G	A	Pts	PIM	PP	SH	GW	S	%	+/-		TF	F%	H	SB	Min		GP	G	A	Pts	PIM	PP	SH	GW
1995-96	HC Pardubice	Czech-Jr.	26	13	9	22	....															....	....	....	....	....			
1996-97	HC Pardubice	Czech-Jr.	12	14	4	18	....															....	....	....	....	....			
	HC Pardubice	Cze-Rep	29	1	3	4	4															3	0	0	0				
1997-98	HC Pardubice	Cze-Rep	39	4	5	9	8																						
1998-99	**Nashville**	**NHL**	2	0	0	0	0	0	0	0	2	0.0	−1		11	45.5	0	0	8:19		2	1	1	2	0			
	Milwaukee	IHL	73	14	15	29	50																						
	NHL Totals		**2**	**0**	**0**	**0**	**0**	**0**	**0**	**0**	**2**	**0.0**			**11**	**45.5**	**0**	**0**	**8:19**		....	....	....	....	....			

Traded to **Nashville** by **Detroit** with Detroit's 3rd round choice in 1999 Entry Draft for Doug Brown, July 14, 1998.

SYKORA, Petr   N.J.

Center. Shoots left. 5'11", 190 lbs.   Born, Plzen, Czech., November 19, 1976. New Jersey's 1st choice, 18th overall, in 1995 Entry Draft.   (SEE-koh-ra)

Season	Club	League	GP	G	A	Pts	PIM	PP	SH	GW	S	%	+/-		TF	F%	H	SB	Min		GP	G	A	Pts	PIM	PP	SH	GW
1991-92	Skoda Plzen	Czech-Jr.	30	50	50	100	....																						
1992-93	Skoda Plzen	Czech.	19	12	5	17	....																						
1993-94	Skoda Plzen	Cze-Rep	37	10	16	26	....															4	0	1	1				
	Cleveland	IHL	13	4	5	9	8																						
1994-95	Detroit	IHL	29	12	17	29	16																						
1995-96	**New Jersey**	**NHL**	63	18	24	42	32	8	0	3	128	14.1	7															
	Albany	AHL	5	4	1	5	0																						
1996-97	**New Jersey**	**NHL**	19	1	2	3	4	0	0	0	26	3.8	−8								2	0	0	0	2	0	0	0
	Albany	AHL	43	20	25	45	48															4	1	4	5	2			
1997-98	**New Jersey**	**NHL**	58	16	20	36	22	3	1	4	130	12.3	0								2	0	0	0	0	0	0	0
	Albany	AHL	2	4	1	5	0																						
1998-99	**New Jersey**	**NHL**	80	29	43	72	22	15	0	7	222	13.1	16		33	33.3	65	16	16:14		7	3	3	6	4	0	0	1
	NHL Totals		**220**	**64**	**89**	**153**	**80**	**26**	**1**	**14**	**506**	**12.6**			**33**	**33.3**	**65**	**16**	**16:14**		**11**	**3**	**3**	**6**	**6**	**0**	**0**	**1**

NHL All-Rookie Team (1996)

SYLVESTER, Dean   ATL.

Right wing. Shoots right. 6'2", 200 lbs.   Born, Weymouth, MA, December 30, 1972.   (sihl-VEHS-tuhr)

Season	Club	League	GP	G	A	Pts	PIM	PP	SH	GW	S	%	+/-		TF	F%	H	SB	Min		GP	G	A	Pts	PIM	PP	SH	GW
1991-92	Kent State	NCAA	31	7	21	28	10																						
1992-93	Kent State	NCAA	38	33	20	53	28																						
1993-94	Kent State	NCAA	39	22	24	46	28																						
1994-95	Michigan State	CCHA	40	15	15	30	38																						
1995-96	Mobile	ECHL	44	24	27	51	35															4	0	0	0	2			
	Kansas City	IHL	36	11	10	21	15															3	1	1	2	0			
1996-97	Kansas City	IHL	77	23	22	45	47															11	5	2	7	4			
1997-98	Kansas City	IHL	77	33	20	53	63															18	*12	5	17	8			
1998-99	**Buffalo**	**NHL**	1	0	0	0	0	0	0	0	1	0.0	−1		0	0.0	1	0	14:31									
	Rochester	AHL	76	35	30	65	46																						
	NHL Totals		**1**	**0**	**0**	**0**	**0**	**0**	**0**	**0**	**1**	**0.0**			**0**	**0.0**	**1**	**0**	**14:31**		....	....	....	....	....			

Signed as a free agent by **Buffalo**, October 1, 1998. Traded to **Atlanta** by **Buffalo** for future considerations, June 25, 1999.

TAMER, Chris   ATL.

Defense. Shoots left. 6'1", 215 lbs.   Born, Dearborn, MI, November 17, 1970. Pittsburgh's 3rd choice, 68th overall, in 1990 Entry Draft.   (TAY-muhr)

Season	Club	League	GP	G	A	Pts	PIM	PP	SH	GW	S	%	+/-		TF	F%	H	SB	Min		GP	G	A	Pts	PIM	PP	SH	GW
1987-88	Redford	NAJHL	40	10	20	30	217																						
1988-89	Redford	NAJHL	31	6	13	19	79																						
1989-90	U. of Michigan	CCHA	42	2	7	9	147																						
1990-91	U. of Michigan	CCHA	45	8	19	27	130																						
1991-92	U. of Michigan	CCHA	43	4	15	19	125																						
1992-93	U. of Michigan	CCHA	39	5	18	23	113																						
1993-94	**Pittsburgh**	**NHL**	12	0	0	0	9	0	0	0	10	0.0	3								5	0	0	0	2	0	0	0
	Cleveland	IHL	53	1	2	3	160																						
1994-95	Cleveland	IHL	48	4	10	14	204																						
	Pittsburgh	**NHL**	36	2	0	2	82	0	0	0	26	7.7	0								4	0	0	0	18	0	0	0
1995-96	**Pittsburgh**	**NHL**	70	4	10	14	153	0	0	1	75	5.3	20								18	0	7	7	24	0	0	0
1996-97	**Pittsburgh**	**NHL**	45	2	4	6	131	0	1	0	56	3.6	−25								4	0	0	0	4	0	0	0

Season	Club	League	GP	G	A	Pts	PIM	PP	SH	GW	S	%	+/-	TF	F%	H	SB	Min	GP	G	A	Pts	PIM	PP	SH	GW
1997-98	Pittsburgh	NHL	79	0	7	7	181	0	0	0	55	0.0	4			6	8	5:59	6	0	1	1	4	0	0	0
1998-99	Pittsburgh	NHL	11	0	0	0	32	0	0	0	2	0.0	-2	0	0.0			....	....							
	NY Rangers	NHL	52	1	5	6	92	0	0	1	46	2.2	-12	0	0.0	88	77	15:25								
	NHL Totals		305	9	26	35	680	0	1	2	270	3.3		0	0.0	94	85	13:46	37	0	8	8	52	0	0	0

Traded to **NY Rangers** by **Pittsburgh** with Petr Nedved and Sean Pronger for Alexei Kovalev and Harry York, November 25, 1998. Claimed by **Atlanta** from **NY Rangers** in Expansion Draft, June 25, 1999.

TANCILL, Chris

(TAN-sihl)

Center. Shoots left. 5'10", 185 lbs.   Born, Livonia, MI, February 7, 1968. Hartford's 1st choice, 15th overall, in 1989 Supplemental Draft.

Season	Club	League	GP	G	A	Pts	PIM	PP	SH	GW	S	%	+/-	TF	F%	H	SB	Min	GP	G	A	Pts	PIM	PP	SH	GW
1984-85	St. Clair	NAJHL	45	51	99	150	....																			
1986-87	U. of Wisconsin	WCHA	40	9	23	32	26																			
1987-88	U. of Wisconsin	WCHA	44	13	14	27	48																			
1988-89	U. of Wisconsin	WCHA	44	20	23	43	50																			
1989-90	U. of Wisconsin	WCHA	45	39	32	71	44																			
1990-91	Hartford	NHL	9	1	1	2	4	0	1	0	6	16.7	2													
	Springfield	AHL	72	37	35	72	46												17	8	4	12	32			
1991-92	Hartford	NHL	10	0	0	0	2	0	0	0	13	0.0	-6													
	Springfield	AHL	17	12	7	19	20																			
	Detroit	NHL	1	0	0	0	0	0	0	0	0	0.0	0													
	Adirondack	AHL	50	36	34	70	42												19	7	9	16	31			
1992-93	**Detroit**	NHL	4	1	0	1	2	0	0	0	3	33.3	-2													
	Adirondack	AHL	68	*59	43	102	62												10	7	7	14	10			
1993-94	**Dallas**	NHL	12	1	3	4	8	0	0	0	18	5.6	-7													
	Kalamazoo	IHL	60	41	54	95	55												5	0	2	2	8			
1994-95	Kansas City	IHL	64	31	28	59	40												11	1	1	2	8	0	0	0
	San Jose	NHL	26	3	11	14	10	0	1	0	39	7.7	1													
1995-96	**San Jose**	NHL	45	7	16	23	20	0	1	0	93	7.5	-12													
	Kansas City	IHL	27	12	16	28	18																			
1996-97	**San Jose**	NHL	25	4	0	4	8	1	0	0	20	20.0	-5													
	Kentucky	AHL	42	19	26	45	31												4	2	0	2	2			
1997-98	**Dallas**	NHL	2	0	1	1	0	0	0	0	1	0.0	-1													
	Michigan	IHL	70	30	39	69	86												4	3	0	3	14			
1998-99	EHC Kloten	Switz.	42	19	30	49	46												12	4	2	6	16			
	NHL Totals		134	17	32	49	54	1	3	0	193	8.8							11	1	1	2	8	0	0	0

NCAA Championship All-Tournament Team (1990) • NCAA Championship Tournament MVP (1990) • AHL First All-Star Team (1992, 1993)
Traded to **Detroit** by **Hartford** for Daniel Shank, December 18, 1991. Signed as a free agent by **Dallas**, August 28, 1993. Signed as a free agent by **San Jose**, August 24, 1994. Signed as a free agent by **Dallas**, August 6, 1997.

TARDIF, Patrice

(tahr-DIHF)

Center. Shoots left. 6'2", 202 lbs.   Born, Thetford Mines, Que., October 30, 1970. St. Louis' 2nd choice, 54th overall, in 1990 Entry Draft.

Season	Club	League	GP	G	A	Pts	PIM	PP	SH	GW	S	%	+/-	TF	F%	H	SB	Min	GP	G	A	Pts	PIM	PP	SH	GW
1988-89	Black Lake	QJHL-B	32	37	33	70	....																			
1989-90	Lennoxville J.C.	QCAA	27	58	36	94	36																			
1990-91	U. of Maine	H.E.	36	13	12	25	18																			
1991-92	U. of Maine	H.E.	31	18	20	38	14																			
1992-93	U. of Maine	H.E.	45	23	25	48	22																			
1993-94	U. of Maine	H.E.	34	18	15	33	42																			
	Peoria	IHL	11	4	4	8	21												4	2	0	2	4			
1994-95	Peoria	IHL	53	27	18	45	83																			
	St. Louis	NHL	27	3	10	13	29	1	0	0	46	6.5	4													
1995-96	**St. Louis**	NHL	23	3	0	3	12	0	0	1	21	14.3	-2													
	Worcester	AHL	30	13	13	26	69																			
	Los Angeles	NHL	15	1	1	2	37	1	0	0	29	3.4	-9													
1996-97	Phoenix	IHL	9	0	3	3	13																			
	Detroit	IHL	66	24	23	47	70												11	0	1	1	8			
1997-98	Rochester	AHL	41	13	13	26	68												15	3	7	10	14			
	Detroit	IHL	28	10	9	19	24												5	1	2	3	0			
1998-99	Manitoba	IHL	63	21	35	56	88																			
	NHL Totals		65	7	11	18	78	2	0	1	96	7.3														

Traded to **LA Kings** by **St. Louis** with Craig Johnson, Roman Vopat, St. Louis' 5th round choice (Peter Hogan) in 1996 Entry Draft and 1st round choice (Matt Zultek) in 1997 Entry Draft for Wayne Gretzky, February 27, 1996. Signed as a free agent by **Buffalo**, September 9, 1997.

TAYLOR, Chris

Center. Shoots left. 6', 189 lbs.   Born, Stratford, Ont., March 6, 1972. NY Islanders' 2nd choice, 27th overall, in 1990 Entry Draft.

Season	Club	League	GP	G	A	Pts	PIM	PP	SH	GW	S	%	+/-	TF	F%	H	SB	Min	GP	G	A	Pts	PIM	PP	SH	GW
1987-88	Stratford	OJHL-B	52	28	37	65	112												15	0	2	2	15			
1988-89	London	OHL	62	7	16	23	52												6	3	2	5	6			
1989-90	London	OHL	66	45	60	105	60												7	4	8	12	6			
1990-91	London	OHL	65	50	78	128	50												10	8	16	24	9			
1991-92	London	OHL	66	48	74	122	57												4	0	1	1	2			
1992-93	Capital District	AHL	77	19	43	62	32																			
1993-94	Salt Lake	IHL	79	21	20	41	38																			
1994-95	Denver	IHL	78	38	48	86	47												14	7	6	13	10			
	NY Islanders	NHL	10	0	3	3	2	0	0	0	13	0.0	1													
1995-96	**NY Islanders**	NHL	11	0	1	1	2	0	0	0	4	0.0	1													
	Utah	IHL	50	18	23	41	60												22	5	11	16	26			
1996-97	**NY Islanders**	NHL	1	0	0	0	0	0	0	0	1	0.0	0													
	Utah	IHL	71	27	40	67	24												7	1	2	3	0			
1997-98	Utah	IHL	79	28	56	84	66												4	0	2	2	6			
1998-99	**Boston**	NHL	37	3	5	8	12	0	1	0	60	5.0	-3	512	53.7	52	16	14:24								
	Providence	AHL	21	6	11	17	6																			
	Las Vegas	IHL	14	3	12	15	2																			
	NHL Totals		59	3	9	12	16	0	1	0	78	3.8		512	53.7	52	16	14:24								

Signed as a free agent by **LA Kings**, July 25, 1997. Signed as a free agent by **Boston**, August 5, 1998.

TAYLOR, Tim

NYR

Center. Shoots left. 6'1", 185 lbs.   Born, Stratford, Ont., February 6, 1969. Washington's 2nd choice, 36th overall, in 1988 Entry Draft.

Season	Club	League	GP	G	A	Pts	PIM	PP	SH	GW	S	%	+/-	TF	F%	H	SB	Min	GP	G	A	Pts	PIM	PP	SH	GW
1986-87	London	OHL	34	7	9	16	11												12	9	9	18	26			
1987-88	London	OHL	64	46	50	96	66												21	*21	25	*46	58			
1988-89	London	OHL	61	34	80	114	93												9	2	2	4	13			
1989-90	Baltimore	AHL	79	31	36	67	124												9	2	2	4	13			
1990-91	Baltimore	AHL	79	25	42	67	75												5	0	1	1	4			
1991-92	Baltimore	AHL	65	9	18	27	131																			
1992-93	Baltimore	AHL	41	15	16	31	49																			
	Hamilton	AHL	36	15	22	37	37																			
1993-94	**Detroit**	NHL	1	1	0	1	0	0	0	0	4	25.0	-1													
	Adirondack	AHL	79	36	*81	*117	86												12	2	10	12	12			
1994-95	**Detroit**	NHL	22	0	4	4	16	0	0	0	21	0.0	3						6	0	1	1	12	0	0	0
1995-96	**Detroit**	NHL	72	11	14	25	39	1	1	2	81	13.6	11						18	0	4	4	4	0	0	0

Season	Club	League	Regular Season																Playoffs							
			GP	G	A	Pts	PIM	PP	SH	GW	S	%	+/–	TF	F%	H	SB	Min	GP	G	A	Pts	PIM	PP	SH	GW
1996-97 ♦	Detroit	NHL	44	3	4	7	52	0	1	0	44	6.8	–6	....	....	....	....	....	2	0	0	0	0	0	0	0
1997-98	Boston	NHL	79	20	11	31	57	1	3	0	127	15.7	–16	....	....	....	....	....	6	0	0	0	10	0	0	0
1998-99	Boston	NHL	49	4	7	11	55	0	0	1	76	5.3	–10	834	58.3	93	16	15:56	12	0	3	3	8	0	0	0
	NHL Totals		267	39	40	79	219	2	5	5	353	11.0		834	58.3	93	16	15:56	44	0	8	8	34	0	0	0

AHL First All-Star Team (1994) • Won John B. Sollenberger Trophy (Top Scorer - AHL) (1994)

Traded to **Vancouver** by **Washington** for Eric Murano, January 29, 1993. Signed as a free agent by **Detroit**, July 28, 1993. Claimed by **Boston** from **Detroit** in NHL Waiver Draft, September 28, 1998. Signed as a free agent by **NY Rangers**, July 30, 1999.

TERTYSHNY, Dimitri

(tuhr-TIHSH-nee)

Defense. Shoots left. 6'1", 176 lbs. Born, Chelyabinsk, USSR, December 26, 1976. Philadelphia's 4th choice, 132nd overall, in 1995 Entry Draft.

Season	Club	League	GP	G	A	Pts	PIM	PP	SH	GW	S	%	+/–	TF	F%	H	SB	Min	GP	G	A	Pts	PIM	PP	SH	GW
1994-95	Chelyabinsk	CIS	38	0	3	3	14	....	....	....	....	....	....	....	....	....	....	....	1	0	0	0	0	....	....	....
1995-96	Chelyabinsk	CIS	44	1	5	6	50	....	....	....	....	....	....	....	....	....	....	....	....	....	....	....	....	....	....	....
1996-97	Chelyabinsk	Russia	40	2	5	7	32	....	....	....	....	....	....	....	....	....	....	....	2	0	0	0	2	....	....	....
1997-98	Chelyabinsk	Russia	46	3	7	10	18	....	....	....	....	....	....	....	....	....	....	....	....	....	....	....	....	....	....	....
1998-99	**Philadelphia**	**NHL**	**62**	**2**	**8**	**10**	**30**	**1**	....	**0**	**68**	**2.9**	**–1**	**0**	**0.0**	**28**	**46**	**18:33**	**1**	**0**	**0**	**0**	**0**	**0**	**0**	**0**
	NHL Totals		**62**	**2**	**8**	**10**	**30**	**1**	....	**0**	**68**	**2.9**		**0**	**0.0**	**28**	**46**	**18:33**	**1**	**0**	**0**	**0**	**0**	**0**	**0**	**0**

• Died July 23, 1999

TEZIKOV, Alexei

(TEH-zih-kahf) **WSH.**

Defense. Shoots left. 6'1", 198 lbs. Born, Togliatti, USSR, June 22, 1978. Buffalo's 7th choice, 115th overall, in 1996 Entry Draft.

Season	Club	League	GP	G	A	Pts	PIM	PP	SH	GW	S	%	+/–	TF	F%	H	SB	Min	GP	G	A	Pts	PIM	PP	SH	GW
1995-96	Lada Togliatti	CIS	14	0	0	0	8	....	....	....	....	....	....	....	....	....	....	....	....	....	....	....	....	....	....	....
1996-97	Lada Togliatti	Russia	7	0	0	0	4	....	....	....	....	....	....	....	....	....	....	....	....	....	....	....	....	....	....	....
	Torpedo Nizhny	Russia	5	0	2	2	2	....	....	....	....	....	....	....	....	....	....	....	....	....	....	....	....	....	....	....
1997-98	Moncton	QMJHL	60	15	33	48	144	....	....	....	....	....	....	....	....	....	....	....	....	....	....	....	....	....	....	....
1998-99	Moncton	QMJHL	25	9	21	30	52	....	....	....	....	....	....	....	....	....	....	....	10	3	8	11	20	....	....	....
	Rochester	AHL	31	3	7	10	41	....	....	....	....	....	....	....	....	....	....	....	....	....	....	....	....	....	....	....
	Washington	**NHL**	**5**	**0**	**0**	**0**	**0**	**0**	**0**	**0**	**4**	**0.0**	**–1**	**0**	**0.0**	**9**	**3**	**18:11**	....	....	....	....	....	....	....	....
	Cincinnati	IHL	5	0	0	0	2	....	....	....	....	....	....	....	....	....	....	....	3	0	0	0	10	....	....	....
	NHL Totals		**5**	**0**	**0**	**0**	**0**	**0**	**0**	**0**	**4**	**0.0**		**0**	**0.0**	**9**	**3**	**18:11**	....	....	....	....	....	....	....	....

QMJHL Second All-Star Team (1998)

Traded to **Washington** by **Buffalo** with future considerations for Joe Juneau and Washington's 3rd round choice (Tim Preston) in 1999 Entry Draft, March 22, 1999.

THERIEN, Chris

(TEH-ree-ehn) **PHI.**

Defense. Shoots left. 6'5", 230 lbs. Born, Ottawa, Ont., December 14, 1971. Philadelphia's 7th choice, 47th overall, in 1990 Entry Draft.

Season	Club	League	GP	G	A	Pts	PIM	PP	SH	GW	S	%	+/–	TF	F%	H	SB	Min	GP	G	A	Pts	PIM	PP	SH	GW
1989-90	Northwood Prep	H.S.	31	35	37	72	54	....	....	....	....	....	....	....	....	....	....	....	....	....	....	....	....	....	....	....
1990-91	Providence	H.E.	36	4	18	22	36	....	....	....	....	....	....	....	....	....	....	....	....	....	....	....	....	....	....	....
1991-92	Providence	H.E.	36	16	25	41	38	....	....	....	....	....	....	....	....	....	....	....	....	....	....	....	....	....	....	....
1992-93	Providence	H.E.	33	8	11	19	52	....	....	....	....	....	....	....	....	....	....	....	....	....	....	....	....	....	....	....
	Canada	Nat-Team	8	1	4	5	8	....	....	....	....	....	....	....	....	....	....	....	....	....	....	....	....	....	....	....
1993-94	Canada	Nat-Team	59	7	15	22	46	....	....	....	....	....	....	....	....	....	....	....	....	....	....	....	....	....	....	....
	Canada	Olympics	4	0	0	0	4	....	....	....	....	....	....	....	....	....	....	....	....	....	....	....	....	....	....	....
	Hershey	AHL	6	0	0	0	2	....	....	....	....	....	....	....	....	....	....	....	....	....	....	....	....	....	....	....
1994-95	Hershey	AHL	34	3	13	16	27	....	....	....	....	....	....	....	....	....	....	....	....	....	....	....	....	....	....	....
	Philadelphia	**NHL**	**48**	**3**	**10**	**13**	**38**	**1**	**0**	**0**	**53**	**5.7**	**8**	....	....	....	....	....	**15**	**0**	**0**	**0**	**10**	**0**	**0**	**0**
1995-96	**Philadelphia**	**NHL**	**82**	**6**	**17**	**23**	**89**	**3**	**0**	**1**	**123**	**4.9**	**16**	....	....	....	....	....	**12**	**0**	**0**	**0**	**18**	**0**	**0**	**0**
1996-97	**Philadelphia**	**NHL**	**71**	**2**	**22**	**24**	**64**	**0**	**0**	**0**	**107**	**1.9**	**27**	....	....	....	....	....	**19**	**1**	**6**	**7**	**6**	**0**	**0**	**1**
1997-98	**Philadelphia**	**NHL**	**78**	**3**	**16**	**19**	**80**	**1**	**0**	**1**	**102**	**2.9**	**5**	....	....	....	....	....	**5**	**0**	**1**	**1**	**4**	**0**	**0**	**0**
1998-99	**Philadelphia**	**NHL**	**74**	**3**	**15**	**18**	**48**	**1**	**0**	**0**	**115**	**2.6**	**16**	**0**	**0.0**	**167**	**103**	**20:45**	**6**	**0**	**0**	**0**	**6**	**0**	**0**	**0**
	NHL Totals		**353**	**17**	**80**	**97**	**319**	**6**	**0**	**2**	**500**	**3.4**		**0**	**0.0**	**167**	**103**	**20:45**	**57**	**1**	**7**	**8**	**44**	**0**	**0**	**1**

Hockey East Second All-Star Team (1993) • NHL/Upper Deck All-Rookie Team (1995)

THOMAS, Scott

L.A.

Right wing. Shoots right. 6'2", 195 lbs. Born, Buffalo, NY, January 18, 1970. Buffalo's 2nd choice, 56th overall, in 1989 Entry Draft.

Season	Club	League	GP	G	A	Pts	PIM	PP	SH	GW	S	%	+/–	TF	F%	H	SB	Min	GP	G	A	Pts	PIM	PP	SH	GW
1987-88	Nichols High	H.S.	16	23	39	62	62	....	....	....	....	....	....	....	....	....	....	....	....	....	....	....	....	....	....	....
1988-89	Nichols High	H.S.	17	38	52	90	....	....	....	....	....	....	....	....	....	....	....	....	....	....	....	....	....	....	....	....
1989-90	Clarkson	ECAC	34	19	13	32	95	....	....	....	....	....	....	....	....	....	....	....	....	....	....	....	....	....	....	....
1990-91	Clarkson	ECAC	40	28	14	42	89	....	....	....	....	....	....	....	....	....	....	....	....	....	....	....	....	....	....	....
1991-92	Clarkson	ECAC	29	22	20	42	57	....	....	....	....	....	....	....	....	....	....	....	....	....	....	....	....	....	....	....
	Rochester	AHL	....	....	....	....	....	....	....	....	....	....	....	....	....	....	....	....	9	0	1	1	17	....	....	....
1992-93	**Buffalo**	**NHL**	**7**	**1**	**1**	**2**	**15**	**0**	**0**	**0**	**4**	**25.0**	**2**	....	....	....	....	....	....	....	....	....	....	....	....	....
	Rochester	AHL	65	32	27	59	38	....	....	....	....	....	....	....	....	....	....	....	17	8	5	13	6	....	....	....
1993-94	**Buffalo**	**NHL**	**32**	**2**	**2**	**4**	**8**	**1**	**0**	**0**	**26**	**7.7**	**–6**	....	....	....	....	....	....	....	....	....	....	....	....	....
	Rochester	AHL	11	4	5	9	0	....	....	....	....	....	....	....	....	....	....	....	....	....	....	....	....	....	....	....
1994-95	Rochester	AHL	55	21	25	46	115	....	....	....	....	....	....	....	....	....	....	....	5	4	0	4	4	....	....	....
1995-96	Cincinnati	IHL	78	32	28	60	54	....	....	....	....	....	....	....	....	....	....	....	17	*13	2	15	4	....	....	....
1996-97	Cincinnati	IHL	71	32	29	61	46	....	....	....	....	....	....	....	....	....	....	....	3	0	0	0	0	....	....	....
1997-98	Detroit	IHL	44	11	16	27	18	....	....	....	....	....	....	....	....	....	....	....	....	....	....	....	....	....	....	....
	Manitoba	IHL	26	12	4	16	8	....	....	....	....	....	....	....	....	....	....	....	3	0	1	1	2	....	....	....
1998-99	Manitoba	IHL	78	45	25	70	32	....	....	....	....	....	....	....	....	....	....	....	5	3	4	7	4	....	....	....
	NHL Totals		**39**	**3**	**3**	**6**	**23**	**1**	**0**	**0**	**30**	**10.0**		....	....	....	....	....	....	....	....	....	....	....	....	....

Signed as a free agent by **Los Angeles**, July 30, 1999. Signed as a free agent by **LA Kings**, July 30, 1999.

THOMAS, Steve

TOR.

Left wing. Shoots left. 5'11", 185 lbs. Born, Stockport, England, July 15, 1963.

Season	Club	League	GP	G	A	Pts	PIM	PP	SH	GW	S	%	+/–	TF	F%	H	SB	Min	GP	G	A	Pts	PIM	PP	SH	GW
1981-82	Markham	OJHL-B	48	68	57	125	113	....	....	....	....	....	....	....	....	....	....	....	....	....	....	....	....	....	....	....
	Toronto	OHA	1	0	0	0	0	....	....	....	....	....	....	....	....	....	....	....	....	....	....	....	....	....	....	....
1982-83	Toronto	OHL	61	18	20	38	42	....	....	....	....	....	....	....	....	....	....	....	....	....	....	....	....	....	....	....
1983-84	Toronto	OHL	70	51	54	105	77	....	....	....	....	....	....	....	....	....	....	....	....	....	....	....	....	....	....	....
1984-85	St. Catharines	AHL	64	42	48	90	56	....	....	....	....	....	....	....	....	....	....	....	....	....	....	....	....	....	....	....
	Toronto	**NHL**	**18**	**1**	**1**	**2**	**2**	**0**	**0**	**0**	**26**	**3.8**	**–13**	....	....	....	....	....	....	....	....	....	....	....	....	....
1985-86	**Toronto**	**NHL**	**65**	**20**	**37**	**57**	**36**	**5**	**0**	**5**	**197**	**10.2**	**–15**	....	....	....	....	....	**10**	**6**	**8**	**14**	**9**	**3**	**0**	**0**
	St. Catharines	AHL	19	18	14	32	35	....	....	....	....	....	....	....	....	....	....	....	....	....	....	....	....	....	....	....
1986-87	**Toronto**	**NHL**	**78**	**35**	**27**	**62**	**114**	**3**	**0**	**7**	**245**	**14.3**	**–3**	....	....	....	....	....	**13**	**2**	**3**	**5**	**13**	**0**	**0**	**0**
1987-88	**Chicago**	**NHL**	**30**	**13**	**13**	**26**	**40**	**5**	**0**	**3**	**69**	**18.8**	**1**	....	....	....	....	....	**3**	**1**	**2**	**3**	**6**	**0**	**0**	**0**
1988-89	**Chicago**	**NHL**	**45**	**21**	**19**	**40**	**69**	**8**	**0**	**0**	**124**	**16.9**	**–2**	....	....	....	....	....	**12**	**3**	**5**	**8**	**10**	**1**	**0**	**2**
1989-90	**Chicago**	**NHL**	**76**	**40**	**30**	**70**	**91**	**13**	**0**	**7**	**235**	**17.0**	**–3**	....	....	....	....	....	**20**	**7**	**6**	**13**	**33**	**1**	**0**	**3**
1990-91	**Chicago**	**NHL**	**69**	**19**	**35**	**54**	**129**	**2**	**0**	**3**	**192**	**9.9**	**8**	....	....	....	....	....	**6**	**1**	**2**	**3**	**15**	**0**	**0**	**0**
1991-92	**Chicago**	**NHL**	**11**	**2**	**6**	**8**	**26**	**0**	**0**	**1**	**35**	**5.7**	**–3**	....	....	....	....	....	....	....	....	....	....	....	....	....
	NY Islanders	**NHL**	**71**	**28**	**42**	**70**	**71**	**3**	**0**	**2**	**210**	**13.3**	**11**	....	....	....	....	....	....	....	....	....	....	....	....	....
1992-93	**NY Islanders**	**NHL**	**79**	**37**	**50**	**87**	**111**	**12**	**0**	**7**	**264**	**14.0**	**3**	....	....	....	....	....	**18**	**9**	**8**	**17**	**37**	**0**	**0**	**0**
1993-94	**NY Islanders**	**NHL**	**78**	**42**	**33**	**75**	**139**	**17**	**0**	**5**	**249**	**16.9**	**–9**	....	....	....	....	....	**4**	**1**	**0**	**1**	**8**	**1**	**0**	**0**
1994-95	**NY Islanders**	**NHL**	**47**	**11**	**15**	**26**	**60**	**3**	**0**	**2**	**133**	**8.3**	**–14**	....	....	....	....	....	....	....	....	....	....	....	....	....
1995-96	**New Jersey**	**NHL**	**81**	**26**	**35**	**61**	**98**	**6**	**0**	**6**	**192**	**13.5**	**–2**	....	....	....	....	....	....	....	....	....	....	....	....	....
1996-97	**New Jersey**	**NHL**	**57**	**15**	**19**	**34**	**46**	**1**	**0**	**2**	**124**	**12.1**	**9**	....	....	....	....	....	**10**	**1**	**1**	**2**	**18**	**0**	**0**	**0**

Season	Club	League	GP	G	A	Pts	PIM	PP	SH	GW	S	%	+/-	TF	F%	H	SB	Min	GP	G	A	Pts	PIM	PP	SH	GW
																		Regular Season / Playoffs headers								
1997-98	New Jersey	NHL	55	14	10	24	32	3	0	4	111	12.6	4	....	....	....	....	....	6	0	3	3	2	0	0	0
1998-99	Toronto	NHL	78	28	45	73	33	11	0	7	209	13.4	26	4	25.0	65	25	18:23	17	6	3	9	12	2	0	1
	NHL Totals		938	352	417	769	1097	92	0	61	2615	13.5		4	25.0	65	25	18:23	119	37	41	78	163	8	0	6

Won Dudley ''Red'' Garrett Memorial Trophy (Top Rookie - AHL) (1985) • AHL First All-Star Team (1985)

Signed as a free agent by **Toronto**, May 12, 1984. Traded to **Chicago** by **Toronto** with Rick Vaive and Bob McGill for Al Secord and Ed Olczyk, September 3, 1987. Traded to **NY Islanders** by **Chicago** with Adam Creighton for Brent Sutter and Brad Lauer, October 25, 1991. Traded to **New Jersey** by **NY Islanders** for Claude Lemieux, October 3, 1995. Signed as a free agent by **Toronto**, July 30, 1998.

THOMPSON, Brent FLA.

Defense. Shoots left. 6'2", 205 lbs.   Born, Calgary, Alta., January 9, 1971. Los Angeles' 1st choice, 39th overall, in 1989 Entry Draft.

Season	Club	League	GP	G	A	Pts	PIM	PP	SH	GW	S	%	+/-	TF	F%	H	SB	Min	GP	G	A	Pts	PIM	PP	SH	GW
1987-88	Calgary	AAHA	25	0	13	13	33																			
1988-89	Medicine Hat	WHL	72	3	10	13	160												3	0	0	0	2			
1989-90	Medicine Hat	WHL	68	10	35	45	167												3	0	1	1	14			
1990-91	Medicine Hat	WHL	51	5	40	45	87												12	1	7	8	16			
	Phoenix	IHL																	4	0	1	1	6			
1991-92	**Los Angeles**	**NHL**	27	0	5	5	89	0	0	0	18	0.0	-7						4	0	0	0	4	0	0	0
	Phoenix	IHL	42	4	13	17	139																			
1992-93	**Los Angeles**	**NHL**	30	0	4	4	76	0	0	0	18	0.0	-4													
	Phoenix	IHL	22	0	5	5	112																			
1993-94	**Los Angeles**	**NHL**	24	1	0	1	81	0	0	0	9	11.1	-1													
	Phoenix	IHL	26	1	11	12	118																			
1994-95	**Winnipeg**	**NHL**	29	0	0	0	78	0	0	0	16	0.0	-17													
1995-96	**Winnipeg**	**NHL**	10	0	1	1	21	0	0	0	7	0.0	-2													
	Springfield	AHL	58	2	10	12	203												10	1	4	5	*55			
1996-97	**Phoenix**	**NHL**	1	0	0	0	7	0	0	0	0	0.0	-1													
	Springfield	AHL	64	2	15	17	215												17	0	2	2	31			
	Phoenix	IHL	12	0	1	1	67																			
1997-98	Hartford	AHL	77	4	15	19	308												15	0	4	4	25			
1998-99	Hartford	AHL	76	3	15	18	265												7	0	0	0	23			
	NHL Totals		121	1	10	11	352	0	0	0	68	1.5							4	0	0	0	4	0	0	0

WHL East Second All-Star Team (1991)

Traded to **Winnipeg** by **LA Kings** with future considerations for the rights to Ruslan Batyrshin and Winnipeg's 2nd round choice (Marian Cisar) in 1996 Entry Draft, August 8, 1994. Transferred to **Phoenix** after **Winnipeg** franchise relocated, July 1, 1996. Signed as a free agent by **NY Rangers**, August 26, 1997. Signed as a free agent by **Florida**, July 27, 1999.

THOMPSON, Rocky CGY.

Right wing. Shoots right. 6'2", 205 lbs.   Born, Calgary, Alta., August 8, 1977. Calgary's 3rd choice, 72nd overall, in 1995 Entry Draft.

Season	Club	League	GP	G	A	Pts	PIM	PP	SH	GW	S	%	+/-	TF	F%	H	SB	Min	GP	G	A	Pts	PIM	PP	SH	GW
1992-93	Spruce Grove	AAHA	65	13	50	63	295												3	0	0	0	2			
1993-94	Medicine Hat	WHL	68	1	4	5	166												5	0	0	0	17			
1994-95	Medicine Hat	WHL	63	1	6	7	220												5	2	3	5	26			
1995-96	Medicine Hat	WHL	71	9	20	29	260																			
	Saint John	AHL	4	0	0	0	33																			
1996-97	Medicine Hat	WHL	47	6	9	15	170																			
	Swift Current	WHL	22	3	5	8	90												10	1	2	3	22			
1997-98	**Calgary**	**NHL**	12	0	0	0	61	0	0	0	3	0.0	0													
	Saint John	AHL	51	3	0	3	187												18	1	1	2	47			
1998-99	**Calgary**	**NHL**	3	0	0	0	25	0	0	0	0	0.0	0	0	0.0	0	0	2:01								
	Saint John	AHL	27	2	2	4	108																			
	NHL Totals		15	0	0	0	86	0	0	0	3	0.0		0	0.0	0	0	2:01								

THORNTON, Joe BOS.

Center. Shoots left. 6'4", 225 lbs.   Born, London, Ont., July 2, 1979. Boston's 1st choice, 1st overall, in 1997 Entry Draft.

Season	Club	League	GP	G	A	Pts	PIM	PP	SH	GW	S	%	+/-	TF	F%	H	SB	Min	GP	G	A	Pts	PIM	PP	SH	GW
1993-94	Elgin	OMHA	67	83	85	168	45																			
1994-95	St. Thomas	OJHL-B	50	40	64	104	53																			
1995-96	S.S. Marie	OHL	66	30	46	76	53												4	1	1	2	11			
1996-97	S.S. Marie	OHL	59	41	81	122	123												11	11	8	19	24			
1997-98	**Boston**	**NHL**	55	3	4	7	19	0	0	1	33	9.1	-6						6	0	0	0	9	0	0	0
1998-99	**Boston**	**NHL**	81	16	25	41	69	7	0	1	128	12.5	3	1073	48.7	124	11	15:21	11	3	6	9	4	2	0	2
	NHL Totals		136	19	29	48	88	7	0	2	161	11.8		1073	48.7	124	11	15:21	17	3	6	9	13	2	0	2

Canadian Major Junior Rookie of the Year (1996) • OHL Second All-Star Team (1997)

THORNTON, Scott MTL.

Center. Shoots left. 6'3", 216 lbs.   Born, London, Ont., January 9, 1971. Toronto's 1st choice, 3rd overall, in 1989 Entry Draft.

Season	Club	League	GP	G	A	Pts	PIM	PP	SH	GW	S	%	+/-	TF	F%	H	SB	Min	GP	G	A	Pts	PIM	PP	SH	GW
1986-87	London	OJHL-B	31	10	7	17	10																			
1987-88	Belleville	OHL	62	11	19	30	54												6	0	1	1	2			
1988-89	Belleville	OHL	59	28	34	62	103												5	1	1	2	6			
1989-90	Belleville	OHL	47	21	28	49	91												11	2	10	12	15			
1990-91	Belleville	OHL	3	2	1	3	2												6	0	7	7	14			
	Toronto	**NHL**	33	1	3	4	30	0	0	0	31	3.2	-15													
	Newmarket	AHL	5	1	0	1	4																			
1991-92	**Edmonton**	**NHL**	15	0	1	1	43	0	0	0	11	0.0	-6						1	0	0	0	0	0	0	0
	Cape Breton	AHL	49	9	14	23	40												5	1	0	1	8			
1992-93	**Edmonton**	**NHL**	9	0	1	1	0	0	0	0	7	0.0	-4													
	Cape Breton	AHL	58	23	27	50	102												16	1	2	3	35			
1993-94	**Edmonton**	**NHL**	61	4	7	11	104	0	0	0	65	6.2	-15													
	Cape Breton	AHL	2	1	1	2	31																			
1994-95	**Edmonton**	**NHL**	47	10	12	22	89	0	1	1	69	14.5	-4													
1995-96	**Edmonton**	**NHL**	77	9	9	18	149	0	2	3	95	9.5	-25													
1996-97	**Montreal**	**NHL**	73	10	10	20	128	1	1	1	110	9.1	-19						5	1	0	1	2	0	0	0
1997-98	**Montreal**	**NHL**	67	6	9	15	158	1	0	1	51	11.8	0						9	0	2	2	10	0	0	0
1998-99	**Montreal**	**NHL**	47	7	4	11	87	1	0	1	56	12.5	-2	466	52.8	74	13	12:24								
	NHL Totals		429	47	56	103	788	3	4	7	495	9.5		466	52.8	74	13	12:24	15	1	2	3	12	0	0	0

Traded to **Edmonton** by **Toronto** with Vincent Damphousse, Peter Ing, Luke Richardson, future considerations and cash for Grant Fuhr, Glenn Anderson and Craig Berube, September 19, 1991. Traded to **Montreal** by **Edmonton** for Andrei Kovalenko, September 6, 1996.

TIKKANEN, Esa (TEE-kuh-nehn, EHZ-uh)

Left wing. Shoots left. 6'1", 190 lbs.   Born, Helsinki, Finland, January 25, 1965. Edmonton's 4th choice, 82nd overall, in 1983 Entry Draft.

Season	Club	League	GP	G	A	Pts	PIM	PP	SH	GW	S	%	+/-	TF	F%	H	SB	Min	GP	G	A	Pts	PIM	PP	SH	GW
1981-82	Regina	SJHL	59	38	37	75	216																			
	Regina	WHL	2	0	0	0	0																			
1982-83	HIFK Helsinki	Finn-Jr.	30	34	31	65	*104												4	4	3	7	10			
	HIFK Helsinki	Finland																	1	0	0	0	2			
1983-84	HIFK Helsinki	Finn-Jr.	6	5	9	14	13												4	4	3	7	8			
	HIFK Helsinki	Finland	36	19	11	30	30												2	0	0	0	0			

Season	Club	League	GP	G	A	Pts	PIM	PP	SH	GW	S	%	+/-	TF	F%	H	SB	Min	GP	G	A	Pts	PIM	PP	SH	GW
																			Regular Season → Playoffs							
1984-85	HIFK Helsinki	Finland	36	21	33	54	42	....																		
1985-86 ◆	Edmonton	NHL	....	....	....	....	....													3	0	0	0	2			
	Edmonton	NHL	35	7	6	13	28	0	0	2	44	15.9	5						8	3	2	5	7	0	0	0
	Nova Scotia	AHL	15	4	8	12	17																			
1986-87 ◆	Edmonton	NHL	76	34	44	78	120	7	0	6	126	27.0	44						21	7	2	9	22	1	0	1
1987-88 ◆	Edmonton	NHL	80	23	51	74	153	6	1	2	142	16.2	21						19	10	17	27	72	5	0	1
1988-89	Edmonton	NHL	67	31	47	78	92	6	8	4	151	20.5	10						7	1	3	4	12	0	0	0
1989-90 ◆	Edmonton	NHL	79	30	33	63	161	6	4	6	199	15.1	17						22	13	11	24	26	2	2	0
1990-91	Edmonton	NHL	79	27	42	69	85	3	2	6	235	11.5	22						18	12	8	20	24	3	0	3
1991-92	Edmonton	NHL	40	12	16	28	44	6	2	1	117	10.3	−8						16	5	3	8	8	1	0	1
1992-93	Edmonton	NHL	66	14	19	33	76	2	4	3	162	8.6	−11													
	NY Rangers	NHL	15	2	5	7	18	0	0	0	40	5.0	−13													
1993-94 ◆	NY Rangers	NHL	83	22	32	54	114	5	3	4	257	8.6	5						23	4	4	8	34	0	0	1
1994-95	HIFK Helsinki	Finland	19	2	11	13	16	....																		
	St. Louis	NHL	43	12	23	35	22	5	2	1	107	11.2	13						7	2	2	4	20	1	0	1
1995-96	St. Louis	NHL	11	1	4	5	18	0	1	0	19	5.3	1													
	New Jersey	NHL	9	0	2	2	4	0	0	0	15	0.0	−6													
	Vancouver	NHL	38	13	24	37	14	8	0	2	61	21.3	6						6	3	2	5	2	0	0	
1996-97	Vancouver	NHL	62	12	15	27	66	4	1	2	103	11.7	−9													
	NY Rangers	NHL	14	1	2	3	6	0	1	0	30	3.3	0						15	9	3	12	26	3	1	3
1997-98	Florida	NHL	28	1	8	9	16	0	0	0	34	2.9	−7													
	Finland	Olympics	6	1	1	2	0																			
	Washington	NHL	20	2	10	12	2	1	0	2	33	6.1	−4						21	3	3	6	20	1	0	0
1998-99	NY Rangers	NHL	32	0	3	3	38	0	0	0	25	0.0	−5	312	47.4	30	14	13:38								
	NHL Totals		877	244	386	630	1077	59	29	41	1900	12.8		312	47.4	30	14	13:38	186	72	60	132	275	19	3	11

Traded to **NY Rangers** by **Edmonton** for Doug Weight, March 17, 1993. Traded to **St. Louis** by **NY Rangers** with Doug Lidster for Petr Nedved, July 24, 1994. Traded to **New Jersey** by **St. Louis** for New Jersey's 3rd round choice (later traded to Colorado — Colorado selected Ville Nielnen) in 1997 Entry Draft, November 1, 1995. Traded to **Vancouver** by **New Jersey** for Vancouver's 2nd round choice (Wesley Mason) in 1996 Entry Draft, November 23, 1995. Traded to **NY Rangers** by **Vancouver** with Russ Courtnall for Sergei Nemchinov and Brian Noonan, March 8, 1997. Signed as a free agent by **Florida**, September 17, 1997. Traded to **Washington** by **Florida** for Dwayne Hay and future considerations, March 9, 1998. Signed as a free agent by **NY Rangers**, October 9, 1998.

TILEY, Brad

PHX.

Defense. Shoots left. 6'1", 204 lbs.   Born, Markdale, Ont., July 5, 1971. Boston's 4th choice, 84th overall, in 1991 Entry Draft.

Season	Club	League	GP	G	A	Pts	PIM	PP	SH	GW	S	%	+/-	TF	F%	H	SB	Min	GP	G	A	Pts	PIM	PP	SH	GW
1987-88	Owen Sound	OJHL-B	45	18	25	43	69																			
1988-89	S.S. Marie	OHL	50	4	11	15	31																			
1989-90	S.S. Marie	OHL	66	9	32	41	47																			
1990-91	S.S. Marie	OHL	66	11	55	66	29												14	4	15	19	12			
1991-92	Maine	AHL	62	7	22	29	36																			
1992-93	Phoenix	IHL	46	11	27	38	35																			
	Binghamton	AHL	26	6	10	16	19												8	0	1	1	2			
1993-94	Binghamton	AHL	29	6	10	16	6																			
	Phoenix	IHL	35	8	15	23	21																			
1994-95	Detroit	IHL	56	7	19	26	32																			
	Fort Wayne	IHL	14	1	6	7	2												3	1	2	3	0			
1995-96	Orlando	IHL	69	11	23	34	82												23	2	4	6	16			
1996-97	Phoenix	IHL	66	8	28	36	34																			
	Long Beach	IHL	3	1	0	1	2																			
1997-98	**Phoenix**	**NHL**	1	0	0	0	0																			
	Springfield	AHL	60	10	31	41	36												4	0	4	4	2			
1998-99	**Phoenix**	**NHL**	8	0	0	0	0	0	0	0	1	0.0	−1	0	0.0	5	3	11:29	1	0	0	0	0	0	0	0
	Springfield	AHL	69	9	35	44	14												1	0	0	0	0			
	NHL Totals		9	0	0	0	0	0	0	0	1	0.0		0	0.0	5	3	11:29	1	0	0	0	0	0	0	0

Memorial Cup All-Star Team (1991)
Signed as a free agent by **NY Rangers**, September 4, 1992. Traded to **LA Kings** by **NY Rangers** for LA Kings' 11th round choice (Jamie Butt) in 1994 Entry Draft, January 28, 1994. Signed as a free agent by **Phoenix**, September 4, 1997.

TIMANDER, Mattias

(tih-MAHN-duhr, MA-tee-uhs)   **BOS.**

Defense. Shoots left. 6'3", 210 lbs.   Born, Solleftea, Sweden, April 16, 1974. Boston's 7th choice, 208th overall, in 1992 Entry Draft.

Season	Club	League	GP	G	A	Pts	PIM	PP	SH	GW	S	%	+/-	TF	F%	H	SB	Min	GP	G	A	Pts	PIM	PP	SH	GW
1992-93	MoDo Hockey	Swe-Jr.	4	0	0	0	0																			
	Husums IF	Sweden-2	27	4	9	13	22																			
	MoDo Hockey	Sweden	1	0	0	0	0																			
1993-94	MoDo Hockey	Swe-Jr.	3	2	2	4	10																			
	MoDo Hockey	Sweden	23	2	2	4	6																			
1994-95	MoDo Hockey	Sweden	39	8	9	17	24												11	2	0	2	10			
1995-96	MoDo Hockey	Sweden	37	4	10	14	34												7	1	1	2	8			
1996-97	**Boston**	**NHL**	41	1	8	9	14	0	0	0	62	1.6	−9													
	Providence	AHL	32	3	11	14	20												10	1	1	2	12			
1997-98	**Boston**	**NHL**	23	1	1	2	6	0	0	0	17	5.9	−9													
	Providence	AHL	31	3	7	10	25																			
1998-99	**Boston**	**NHL**	22	0	6	6	10	0	0	0	22	0.0	4	0	0.0	14	13	12:54	4	1	1	2	2	0	0	0
	Providence	AHL	43	2	22	24	24																			
	NHL Totals		86	2	15	17	30	0	0	0	101	2.0		0	0.0	14	13	12:54	4	1	1	2	2	0	0	0

TIMONEN, Kimmo

(TIH-moh-nehn)   **NSH.**

Defense. Shoots left. 5'9", 180 lbs.   Born, Kuopio, Finland, March 18, 1975. Los Angeles' 11th choice, 250th overall, in 1993 Entry Draft.

Season	Club	League	GP	G	A	Pts	PIM	PP	SH	GW	S	%	+/-	TF	F%	H	SB	Min	GP	G	A	Pts	PIM	PP	SH	GW
1990-91	KalPa Kuopio	Finn-Jr.	4	0	1	1	2																			
1991-92	KalPa Kuopio	Finn-Jr.	32	7	10	17	4																			
	KalPa Kuopio	Finland	5	0	0	0	0																			
1992-93	KalPa Kuopio	Finn-Jr.	16	9	15	24	10																			
	KalPa Kuopio	Finland	33	0	2	2	4																			
1993-94	KalPa Kuopio	Finn-Jr.	5	4	7	11	0																			
	KalPa Kuopio	Finland	46	6	7	13	55																			
1994-95	TPS Turku	Finland	45	3	4	7	10																			
1995-96	TPS Turku	Finland	48	3	21	24	22												13	0	1	1	6			
1996-97	TPS Turku	Finland	50	10	14	24	18												9	1	2	3	12			
1997-98	HIFK Helsinki	Finland	45	10	15	25	59												12	2	7	9	8			
	Finland	Olympics	6	0	1	1	2												9	3	4	7	8			
1998-99	**Nashville**	**NHL**	50	4	8	12	30	1	0	0	75	5.3	−4	0	0.0	68	34	19:04								
	Milwaukee	IHL	29	2	13	15	22																			
	NHL Totals		50	4	8	12	30	1	0	0	75	5.3		0	0.0	68	34	19:04								

Traded to **Nashville** by **LA Kings** with Jan Vopat for future considerations, June 26, 1998.

TINORDI, Mark

(tih-NOHR-dee)

Defense. Shoots left. 6'4", 213 lbs. Born, Red Deer, Alta., May 9, 1966.

			Regular Season																Playoffs							
Season	Club	League	GP	G	A	Pts	PIM	PP	SH	GW	S	%	+/–	TF	F%	H	SB	Min	GP	G	A	Pts	PIM	PP	SH	GW
1981-82	Red Deer	AAHA	STATISTICS NOT AVAILABLE																							
1982-83	Lethbridge	WHL	64	0	4	4	50	....	....	....	....	....	....	....	....	....	....	....	20	1	1	2	6	....	....	....
1983-84	Lethbridge	WHL	72	5	14	19	53	....	....	....	....	....	....	....	....	....	....	....	5	0	1	1	7	....	....	....
1984-85	Lethbridge	WHL	58	10	15	25	134	....	....	....	....	....	....	....	....	....	....	....	4	0	2	2	12	....	....	....
1985-86	Lethbridge	WHL	58	8	30	38	139	....	....	....	....	....	....	....	....	....	....	....	8	1	3	4	15	....	....	....
1986-87	Calgary	WHL	61	29	37	66	148	....	....	....	....	....	....	....	....	....	....	....	....	....	....	....	....	....	....	....
	New Haven	AHL	2	0	0	0	2	....	....	....	....	....	....	....	....	....	....	....	2	0	0	0	0	....	....	....
1987-88	**NY Rangers**	**NHL**	**24**	**1**	**2**	**3**	**50**	**0**	**0**	**0**	**13**	**7.7**	**–5**	....	....	....	....	....	....	....	....	....	....	....	....	....
	Colorado	IHL	41	8	19	27	150	....	....	....	....	....	....	....	....	....	....	....	11	1	5	6	31	....	....	....
1988-89	**Minnesota**	**NHL**	**47**	**2**	**3**	**5**	**107**	**0**	**0**	**0**	**39**	**5.1**	**–9**	....	....	....	....	....	**5**	**0**	**0**	**0**	**0**	**0**	**0**	**0**
	Kalamazoo	IHL	10	0	0	0	35	....	....	....	....	....	....	....	....	....	....	....	....	....	....	....	....	....	....	....
1989-90	**Minnesota**	**NHL**	**66**	**3**	**7**	**10**	**240**	**1**	**0**	**0**	**50**	**6.0**	**0**	....	....	....	....	....	**7**	**0**	**1**	**1**	**16**	**0**	**0**	**0**
1990-91	**Minnesota**	**NHL**	**69**	**5**	**27**	**32**	**189**	**1**	**0**	**2**	**92**	**5.4**	**1**	....	....	....	....	....	**23**	**5**	**6**	**11**	**78**	**4**	**0**	**0**
1991-92	**Minnesota**	**NHL**	**63**	**4**	**24**	**28**	**179**	**4**	**0**	**0**	**93**	**4.3**	**–13**	....	....	....	....	....	**7**	**1**	**2**	**3**	**11**	**0**	**0**	**0**
1992-93	**Minnesota**	**NHL**	**69**	**15**	**27**	**42**	**157**	**7**	**0**	**2**	**122**	**12.3**	**–1**	....	....	....	....	....	....	....	....	....	....	....	....	....
1993-94	**Dallas**	**NHL**	**61**	**6**	**18**	**24**	**143**	**1**	**0**	**0**	**112**	**5.4**	**6**	....	....	....	....	....	....	....	....	....	....	....	....	....
1994-95	**Washington**	**NHL**	**42**	**3**	**9**	**12**	**71**	**2**	**0**	**1**	**71**	**4.2**	**–5**	....	....	....	....	....	**1**	**0**	**0**	**0**	**2**	**0**	**0**	**0**
1995-96	**Washington**	**NHL**	**71**	**3**	**10**	**13**	**113**	**2**	**0**	**0**	**82**	**3.7**	**26**	....	....	....	....	....	**6**	**0**	**0**	**0**	**16**	**0**	**0**	**0**
1996-97	**Washington**	**NHL**	**56**	**2**	**6**	**8**	**118**	**0**	**0**	**0**	**53**	**3.8**	**3**	....	....	....	....	....	....	....	....	....	....	....	....	....
1997-98	**Washington**	**NHL**	**47**	**8**	**9**	**17**	**39**	**0**	**1**	**0**	**57**	**14.0**	**9**	....	....	....	....	....	**21**	**1**	**2**	**3**	**42**	**0**	**0**	**0**
1998-99	**Washington**	**NHL**	**48**	**0**	**6**	**6**	**108**	**0**	**0**	**0**	**32**	**0.0**	**–6**	**0**	**0.0**	**133**	**49**	**20:25**	....	....	....	....	....	....	....	....
	NHL Totals		**663**	**52**	**148**	**200**	**1514**	**18**	**1**	**5**	**816**	**6.4**		**0**	**0.0**	**133**	**49**	**20:25**	**70**	**7**	**11**	**18**	**165**	**4**	**0**	**0**

Played in NHL All-Star Game (1992)

Signed as a free agent by **NY Rangers**, January 4, 1987. Traded to **Minnesota** by **NY Rangers** with Paul Jerrard, the rights to Bret Barnett and Mike Sullivan, and LA Kings' 3rd round choice (previously acquired, Minnesota selected Murray Garbutt) in 1989 Entry Draft for Brian Lawton, Igor Liba and the rights to Eric Bennett, October 11, 1988. Transferred to **Dallas** after **Minnesota** franchise relocated, June 9, 1993. Traded to **Washington** by **Dallas** with Rich Mrozik for Kevin Hatcher, January 18, 1995. Claimed by **Atlanta** from **Washington** in Expansion Draft, June 25, 1999.

TITOV, German

(TEE-tahf, GUHR-mihn) **PIT.**

Center. Shoots left. 6'1", 201 lbs. Born, Moscow, USSR, October 16, 1965. Calgary's 10th choice, 252nd overall, in 1993 Entry Draft.

Season	Club	League	GP	G	A	Pts	PIM	PP	SH	GW	S	%	+/–	TF	F%	H	SB	Min	GP	G	A	Pts	PIM	PP	SH	GW
1986-87	Khimik	USSR	23	1	0	1	10	....	....	....	....	....	....	....	....	....	....	....	....	....	....	....	....	....	....	....
1987-88	Khimik	USSR	39	6	5	11	10	....	....	....	....	....	....	....	....	....	....	....	....	....	....	....	....	....	....	....
1988-89	Khimik	USSR	44	10	3	13	24	....	....	....	....	....	....	....	....	....	....	....	....	....	....	....	....	....	....	....
1989-90	Khimik	USSR	44	6	14	20	19	....	....	....	....	....	....	....	....	....	....	....	....	....	....	....	....	....	....	....
1990-91	Khimik	USSR	45	13	11	24	28	....	....	....	....	....	....	....	....	....	....	....	....	....	....	....	....	....	....	....
1991-92	Khimik	CIS	42	18	13	31	35	....	....	....	....	....	....	....	....	....	....	....	....	....	....	....	....	....	....	....
1992-93	TPS Turku	Finland	47	25	19	44	49	....	....	....	....	....	....	....	....	....	....	....	12	5	12	17	10	....	....	....
1993-94	**Calgary**	**NHL**	**76**	**27**	**18**	**45**	**28**	**8**	**3**	**2**	**153**	**17.6**	**20**	....	....	....	....	....	**7**	**2**	**1**	**3**	**4**	**1**	**0**	**0**
1994-95	TPS Turku	Finland	14	6	6	12	20	....	....	....	....	....	....	....	....	....	....	....	....	....	....	....	....	....	....	....
	Calgary	**NHL**	**40**	**12**	**12**	**24**	**16**	**3**	**2**	**3**	**88**	**13.6**	**6**	....	....	....	....	....	**7**	**5**	**3**	**8**	**10**	**0**	**1**	**0**
1995-96	**Calgary**	**NHL**	**82**	**28**	**39**	**67**	**24**	**13**	**2**	**2**	**214**	**13.1**	**9**	....	....	....	....	....	**4**	**0**	**2**	**2**	**0**	**0**	**0**	**0**
1996-97	**Calgary**	**NHL**	**79**	**22**	**30**	**52**	**36**	**12**	**0**	**4**	**192**	**11.5**	**–12**	....	....	....	....	....	....	....	....	....	....	....	....	....
1997-98	**Calgary**	**NHL**	**68**	**18**	**22**	**40**	**38**	**6**	**1**	**2**	**133**	**13.5**	**–1**	....	....	....	....	....	....	....	....	....	....	....	....	....
	Russia	Olympics	6	1	0	1	6	....	....	....	....	....	....	....	....	....	....	....	....	....	....	....	....	....	....	....
1998-99	**Pittsburgh**	**NHL**	**72**	**11**	**45**	**56**	**34**	**3**	**1**	**3**	**113**	**9.7**	**18**	**41**	**39.0**	**67**	**50**	**19:31**	**11**	**3**	**5**	**8**	**4**	**0**	**0**	**0**
	NHL Totals		**417**	**118**	**166**	**284**	**176**	**45**	**9**	**16**	**893**	**13.2**		**41**	**39.0**	**67**	**50**	**19:31**	**29**	**10**	**11**	**21**	**18**	**1**	**1**	**0**

Traded to **Pittsburgh** by **Calgary** with Todd Hlushko for Ken Wregget and Dave Roche, June 17, 1998.

TKACHUK, Keith

(kuh-CHUK) **PHX.**

Left wing. Shoots left. 6'2", 220 lbs. Born, Melrose, MA, March 28, 1972. Winnipeg's 1st choice, 19th overall, in 1990 Entry Draft.

Season	Club	League	GP	G	A	Pts	PIM	PP	SH	GW	S	%	+/–	TF	F%	H	SB	Min	GP	G	A	Pts	PIM	PP	SH	GW
1988-89	Malden High	H.S.	21	20	16	46	....	....	....	....	....	....	....	....	....	....	....	....	....	....	....	....	....	....	....	....
1989-90	Malden High	H.S.	6	12	14	26	....	....	....	....	....	....	....	....	....	....	....	....	....	....	....	....	....	....	....	....
1990-91	Boston University	H.E.	36	17	23	40	70	....	....	....	....	....	....	....	....	....	....	....	....	....	....	....	....	....	....	....
1991-92	United States	Nat-Team	45	10	10	20	141	....	....	....	....	....	....	....	....	....	....	....	....	....	....	....	....	....	....	....
	United States	Olympics	8	1	1	2	12	....	....	....	....	....	....	....	....	....	....	....	....	....	....	....	....	....	....	....
	Winnipeg	**NHL**	**17**	**3**	**5**	**8**	**28**	**2**	**0**	**0**	**22**	**13.6**	**0**	....	....	....	....	....	**7**	**3**	**0**	**3**	**30**	**0**	**0**	**0**
1992-93	**Winnipeg**	**NHL**	**83**	**28**	**23**	**51**	**201**	**12**	**0**	**2**	**199**	**14.1**	**–13**	....	....	....	....	....	**6**	**4**	**0**	**4**	**14**	**1**	**0**	**0**
1993-94	**Winnipeg**	**NHL**	**84**	**41**	**40**	**81**	**255**	**22**	**3**	**3**	**218**	**18.8**	**–12**	....	....	....	....	....	....	....	....	....	....	....	....	....
1994-95	**Winnipeg**	**NHL**	**48**	**22**	**29**	**51**	**152**	**7**	**2**	**2**	**129**	**17.1**	**–4**	....	....	....	....	....	....	....	....	....	....	....	....	....
1995-96	**Winnipeg**	**NHL**	**76**	**50**	**48**	**98**	**156**	**20**	**2**	**6**	**249**	**20.1**	**11**	....	....	....	....	....	**6**	**1**	**2**	**3**	**22**	**0**	**0**	**0**
1996-97	**Phoenix**	**NHL**	**81**	***52**	**34**	**86**	**228**	**9**	**2**	**7**	**296**	**17.6**	**–1**	....	....	....	....	....	**7**	**6**	**0**	**6**	**7**	**2**	**0**	**0**
1997-98	**Phoenix**	**NHL**	**69**	**40**	**26**	**66**	**147**	**11**	**0**	**8**	**232**	**17.2**	**9**	....	....	....	....	....	**6**	**3**	**3**	**6**	**10**	**0**	**0**	**0**
	United States	Olympics	4	0	2	2	6	....	....	....	....	....	....	....	....	....	....	....	....	....	....	....	....	....	....	....
1998-99	**Phoenix**	**NHL**	**68**	**36**	**32**	**68**	**151**	**11**	**2**	**7**	**258**	**14.0**	**22**	**770**	**47.7**	**102**	**20**	**20:59**	**7**	**1**	**3**	**4**	**13**	**1**	**0**	**0**
	NHL Totals		**526**	**272**	**237**	**509**	**1318**	**94**	**11**	**35**	**1603**	**17.0**		**770**	**47.7**	**102**	**20**	**20:59**	**39**	**18**	**8**	**26**	**96**	**4**	**0**	**0**

NHL Second All-Star Team (1995, 1998)

Played in NHL All-Star Game (1997, 1998, 1999)

Transferred to **Phoenix** after **Winnipeg** franchise relocated, July 1, 1996.

TOCCHET, Rick

(TAH-keht) **PHX.**

Right wing. Shoots right. 6', 210 lbs. Born, Scarborough, Ont., April 9, 1964. Philadelphia's 5th choice, 125th overall, in 1983 Entry Draft.

Season	Club	League	GP	G	A	Pts	PIM	PP	SH	GW	S	%	+/–	TF	F%	H	SB	Min	GP	G	A	Pts	PIM	PP	SH	GW
1980-81	St. Michael's	OJHL-B	41	28	46	74	....	....	....	....	....	....	....	....	....	....	....	....	....	....	....	....	....	....	....	....
1981-82	S.S. Marie	OHL	59	7	15	22	184	....	....	....	....	....	....	....	....	....	....	....	11	1	1	2	28	....	....	....
1982-83	S.S. Marie	OHL	66	32	34	66	146	....	....	....	....	....	....	....	....	....	....	....	16	4	13	17	67	....	....	....
1983-84	S.S. Marie	OHL	64	44	64	108	209	....	....	....	....	....	....	....	....	....	....	....	16	*22	14	*36	41	....	....	....
1984-85	**Philadelphia**	**NHL**	**75**	**14**	**25**	**39**	**181**	**0**	**0**	**0**	**112**	**12.5**	**6**	....	....	....	....	....	**19**	**3**	**4**	**7**	**72**	**0**	**0**	**2**
1985-86	**Philadelphia**	**NHL**	**69**	**14**	**21**	**35**	**284**	**3**	**0**	**1**	**107**	**13.1**	**12**	....	....	....	....	....	**5**	**1**	**2**	**3**	**26**	**0**	**0**	**0**
1986-87	**Philadelphia**	**NHL**	**69**	**21**	**26**	**47**	**288**	**1**	**1**	**5**	**147**	**14.3**	**16**	....	....	....	....	....	**26**	**11**	**10**	**21**	**72**	**0**	**1**	**2**
1987-88	**Philadelphia**	**NHL**	**65**	**31**	**33**	**64**	**301**	**1**	**0**	**3**	**0**	**0.0**	**3**	....	....	....	....	....	**5**	**1**	**4**	**5**	**55**	**2**	**1**	**0**
1988-89	**Philadelphia**	**NHL**	**66**	**45**	**36**	**81**	**183**	**16**	**1**	**5**	**220**	**20.5**	**–1**	....	....	....	....	....	**16**	**6**	**6**	**12**	**69**	**2**	**0**	**1**
1989-90	**Philadelphia**	**NHL**	**75**	**37**	**59**	**96**	**196**	**15**	**1**	**0**	**269**	**13.8**	**4**	....	....	....	....	....	....	....	....	....	....	....	....	....
1990-91	**Philadelphia**	**NHL**	**70**	**40**	**31**	**71**	**150**	**8**	**0**	**5**	**217**	**18.4**	**2**	....	....	....	....	....	....	....	....	....	....	....	....	....
1991-92	**Philadelphia**	**NHL**	**42**	**13**	**16**	**29**	**102**	**4**	**0**	**1**	**107**	**12.1**	**3**	....	....	....	....	....	....	....	....	....	....	....	....	....
	♦ **Pittsburgh**	**NHL**	**19**	**14**	**16**	**30**	**49**	**4**	**1**	**1**	**59**	**23.7**	**12**	....	....	....	....	....	**14**	**6**	**13**	**19**	**24**	**3**	**0**	**1**
1992-93	**Pittsburgh**	**NHL**	**80**	**48**	**61**	**109**	**252**	**20**	**4**	**5**	**240**	**20.0**	**28**	....	....	....	....	....	**12**	**7**	**6**	**13**	**24**	**1**	**0**	**0**
1993-94	**Pittsburgh**	**NHL**	**51**	**14**	**26**	**40**	**134**	**5**	**1**	**2**	**150**	**9.3**	**–15**	....	....	....	....	....	**6**	**2**	**3**	**5**	**20**	**1**	**0**	**1**
1994-95	**Los Angeles**	**NHL**	**36**	**18**	**17**	**35**	**70**	**7**	**1**	**3**	**95**	**18.9**	**–8**	....	....	....	....	....	....	....	....	....	....	....	....	....
1995-96	**Los Angeles**	**NHL**	**44**	**13**	**23**	**36**	**117**	**4**	**0**	**0**	**100**	**13.0**	**3**	....	....	....	....	....	....	....	....	....	....	....	....	....
	Boston	**NHL**	**27**	**16**	**8**	**24**	**64**	**6**	**0**	**3**	**85**	**18.8**	**7**	....	....	....	....	....	**5**	**4**	**0**	**4**	**21**	**3**	**0**	**1**
1996-97	**Boston**	**NHL**	**40**	**16**	**14**	**30**	**67**	**3**	**0**	**1**	**120**	**13.3**	**–3**	....	....	....	....	....	....	....	....	....	....	....	....	....
	Washington	**NHL**	**13**	**5**	**5**	**10**	**31**	**1**	**0**	**1**	**37**	**13.5**	**0**	....	....	....	....	....	....	....	....	....	....	....	....	....

			Regular Season																Playoffs							
Season	Club	League	GP	G	A	Pts	PIM	PP	SH	GW	S	%	+/–	TF	F%	H	SB	Min	GP	G	A	Pts	PIM	PP	SH	GW
1997-98	**Phoenix**	**NHL**	**68**	**26**	**19**	**45**	**157**	**8**	**0**	**6**	**161**	**16.1**	**1**	....	....	....	....	....	**6**	**6**	**2**	**8**	**25**	**3**	**0**	**0**
1998-99	**Phoenix**	**NHL**	**81**	**26**	**30**	**56**	**147**	**6**	**1**	**5**	**178**	**14.6**	**5**	**4**	**25.0**	**115**	**13**	**18:34**	**7**	**0**	**3**	**3**	**8**	**0**	**0**	**0**
	NHL Totals		**990**	**411**	**466**	**877**	**2773**	**112**	**11**	**47**	**2404**	**17.1**		**4**	**25.0**	**115**	**13**	**18:34**	**121**	**47**	**53**	**100**	**416**	**15**	**2**	**8**

Played in NHL All-Star Game (1989, 1990, 1991, 1993)

Traded to **Pittsburgh** by **Philadelphia** with Kjell Samuelsson, Ken Wregget and Philadelphia's 3rd round choice (Dave Roche) in 1993 Entry Draft for Mark Recchi, Brian Benning and LA Kings' 1st round choice (previously acquired, Philadelphia selected Jason Bowen) in 1992 Entry Draft, February 19, 1992 Traded to **LA Kings** by **Pittsburgh** with Pittsburgh's 2nd round choice (Pavel Rosa) in 1995 Entry Draft for Luc Robitaille, July 29, 1994. Traded to **Boston** by **LA Kings** for Kevin Stevens, January 25, 1996. Traded to **Washington** by **Boston** with Bill Ranford and Adam Oates for Jim Carey, Anson Carter, Jason Allison and Washington's 3rd round choice (Lee Goren) in 1997 Entry Draft, March 1, 1997. Signed as a free agent by **Phoenix**, July 23, 1997.

TODD, Kevin

Center. Shoots left. 5'10", 180 lbs. Born, Winnipeg, Man., May 4, 1968. New Jersey's 7th choice, 129th overall, in 1986 Entry Draft.

Season	Club	League	GP	G	A	Pts	PIM	PP	SH	GW	S	%	+/–	TF	F%	H	SB	Min	GP	G	A	Pts	PIM	PP	SH	GW
1984-85	Winnipeg	MAHA	60	66	100	166	....	....	....	....	....	....	....	....	....	....	....	....	....	....	....	....	....	....	....	....
1985-86	Prince Albert	WHL	55	14	25	39	19	....	....	....	....	....	....	....	....	....	....	....	20	7	6	13	29	....	....	....
1986-87	Prince Albert	WHL	71	39	46	85	92	....	....	....	....	....	....	....	....	....	....	....	8	2	5	7	17	....	....	....
1987-88	Prince Albert	WHL	72	49	72	121	83	....	....	....	....	....	....	....	....	....	....	....	10	8	11	19	27	....	....	....
1988-89	**New Jersey**	**NHL**	**1**	**0**	**0**	**0**	**0**	**0**	**0**	**0**	**0**	**0.0**	**–1**	....	....	....	....	....	....	....	....	....	....	....	....	....
	Utica	AHL	78	26	45	71	62	....	....	....	....	....	....	....	....	....	....	....	4	2	0	2	6	....	....	....
1989-90	Utica	AHL	71	18	36	54	72	....	....	....	....	....	....	....	....	....	....	....	5	2	4	6	2	....	....	....
1990-91	**New Jersey**	**NHL**	**1**	**0**	**0**	**0**	**0**	**0**	**0**	**0**	**0**	**0.0**	**–1**	....	....	....	....	....	**1**	**0**	**0**	**0**	**6**	**0**	**0**	**0**
	Utica	AHL	75	37	*81	*118	75	....	....	....	....	....	....	....	....	....	....	....	....	....	....	....	....	....	....	....
1991-92	**New Jersey**	**NHL**	**80**	**21**	**42**	**63**	**69**	**2**	**0**	**2**	**131**	**16.0**	**8**	....	....	....	....	....	**7**	**3**	**2**	**5**	**8**	**1**	**0**	**0**
1992-93	**New Jersey**	**NHL**	**30**	**5**	**5**	**10**	**16**	**0**	**0**	**2**	**48**	**10.4**	**–4**	....	....	....	....	....	....	....	....	....	....	....	....	....
	Utica	AHL	2	2	1	3	0	....	....	....	....	....	....	....	....	....	....	....	....	....	....	....	....	....	....	....
	Edmonton	**NHL**	**25**	**4**	**9**	**13**	**10**	**0**	**0**	**1**	**39**	**10.3**	**–5**	....	....	....	....	....	....	....	....	....	....	....	....	....
1993-94	**Chicago**	**NHL**	**35**	**5**	**6**	**11**	**16**	**1**	**0**	**1**	**49**	**10.2**	**–2**	....	....	....	....	....	....	....	....	....	....	....	....	....
	Los Angeles	**NHL**	**12**	**3**	**8**	**11**	**8**	**3**	**0**	**0**	**16**	**18.8**	**–1**	....	....	....	....	....	....	....	....	....	....	....	....	....
1994-95	**Los Angeles**	**NHL**	**33**	**3**	**8**	**11**	**12**	**0**	**0**	**1**	**34**	**8.8**	**–5**	....	....	....	....	....	....	....	....	....	....	....	....	....
1995-96	**Los Angeles**	**NHL**	**74**	**16**	**27**	**43**	**38**	**0**	**2**	**4**	**132**	**12.1**	**6**	....	....	....	....	....	....	....	....	....	....	....	....	....
1996-97	**Anaheim**	**NHL**	**65**	**9**	**21**	**30**	**44**	**0**	**0**	**1**	**95**	**9.5**	**–7**	....	....	....	....	....	**4**	**0**	**0**	**0**	**2**	**0**	**0**	**0**
1997-98	**Anaheim**	**NHL**	**27**	**4**	**7**	**11**	**12**	**3**	**0**	**1**	**30**	**13.3**	**–5**	....	....	....	....	....	....	....	....	....	....	....	....	....
	Long Beach	IHL	30	18	28	46	54	....	....	....	....	....	....	....	....	....	....	....	13	1	10	11	38	....	....	....
1998-99	EV Zug	Switz.	40	9	41	50	81	....	....	....	....	....	....	....	....	....	....	....	5	0	2	2	2	....	....	....
	EV Zug	EuroHL	2	1	2	3	4	....	....	....	....	....	....	....	....	....	....	....	....	....	....	....	....	....	....	....
	NHL Totals		**383**	**70**	**133**	**203**	**225**	**9**	**2**	**13**	**574**	**12.2**		....	....	....	....	....	**12**	**3**	**2**	**5**	**16**	**1**	**0**	**0**

AHL First All-Star Team (1991) • Won John B. Sollenberger Trophy (Leading Scorer - AHL) (1991) • Won Les Cunningham Plaque (MVP - AHL) (1992) • NHL/Upper Deck All-Rookie Team (1992)

Traded to **Edmonton** by **New Jersey** with Zdeno Ciger for Bernie Nicholls, January 13, 1993. Traded to **Chicago** by **Edmonton** for Adam Bennett, October 7, 1993. Traded to **LA Kings** by **Chicago** for LA Kings' 4th round choice (Steve McLaren) in 1994 Entry Draft, March 21, 1994. Signed as a free agent by **Pittsburgh**, July 10, 1996. Claimed on waivers by **Anaheim** from **Pittsburgh**, October 4, 1996.

TOMS, Jeff — WSH.

Left wing. Shoots left. 6'5", 200 lbs. Born, Swift Current, Sask., June 4, 1974. New Jersey's 10th choice, 210th overall, in 1992 Entry Draft.

Season	Club	League	GP	G	A	Pts	PIM	PP	SH	GW	S	%	+/–	TF	F%	H	SB	Min	GP	G	A	Pts	PIM	PP	SH	GW
1990-91	Oakville	OMHA	58	34	47	81	72	....	....	....	....	....	....	....	....	....	....	....	....	....	....	....	....	....	....	....
1991-92	S.S. Marie	OHL	36	9	5	14	0	....	....	....	....	....	....	....	....	....	....	....	16	0	1	1	2	....	....	....
1992-93	S.S. Marie	OHL	59	16	23	39	20	....	....	....	....	....	....	....	....	....	....	....	16	4	4	8	7	....	....	....
1993-94	S.S. Marie	OHL	64	52	45	97	19	....	....	....	....	....	....	....	....	....	....	....	14	11	4	15	2	....	....	....
1994-95	Atlanta	IHL	40	7	8	15	10	....	....	....	....	....	....	....	....	....	....	....	4	0	0	0	4	....	....	....
1995-96	**Tampa Bay**	**NHL**	**1**	**0**	**0**	**0**	**0**	**0**	**0**	**0**	**1**	**0.0**	**0**	....	....	....	....	....	....	....	....	....	....	....	....	....
	Atlanta	IHL	68	16	18	34	18	....	....	....	....	....	....	....	....	....	....	....	1	0	0	0	0	....	....	....
1996-97	**Tampa Bay**	**NHL**	**34**	**2**	**8**	**10**	**10**	**0**	**0**	**1**	**53**	**3.8**	**2**	....	....	....	....	....	....	....	....	....	....	....	....	....
	Adirondack	AHL	37	11	16	27	8	....	....	....	....	....	....	....	....	....	....	....	4	1	2	3	0	....	....	....
1997-98	**Tampa Bay**	**NHL**	**13**	**1**	**2**	**3**	**7**	**0**	**0**	**0**	**14**	**7.1**	**–6**	....	....	....	....	....	....	....	....	....	....	....	....	....
	Washington	**NHL**	**33**	**3**	**4**	**7**	**8**	**0**	**0**	**1**	**55**	**5.5**	**–11**	....	....	....	....	....	**1**	**0**	**0**	**0**	**0**	**0**	**0**	**0**
1998-99	**Washington**	**NHL**	**21**	**1**	**5**	**6**	**2**	**0**	**0**	**0**	**30**	**3.3**	**0**	**92**	**54.3**	**9**	**1**	**13:35**	....	....	....	....	....	....	....	....
	Portland	AHL	20	3	7	10	8	....	....	....	....	....	....	....	....	....	....	....	....	....	....	....	....	....	....	....
	NHL Totals		**102**	**7**	**19**	**26**	**27**	**0**	**0**	**2**	**153**	**4.6**		**92**	**54.3**	**9**	**1**	**13:35**	**1**	**0**	**0**	**0**	**0**	**0**	**0**	**0**

Traded to **Tampa Bay** by **New Jersey** for Vancouver's 4th round choice (previously acquired by Tampa Bay — later traded to Calgary — Calgary selected Ryan Duthie) in 1994 Entry Draft, May 31, 1994. Claimed by on waivers by **Washington** from **Tampa Bay**, November 19, 1997.

TOPOROWSKI, Shayne (toh-poh-ROW-skee) — PHX.

Right wing. Shoots right. 6'2", 216 lbs. Born, Paddockwood, Sask., August 6, 1975. Los Angeles' 1st choice, 42nd overall, in 1993 Entry Draft.

Season	Club	League	GP	G	A	Pts	PIM	PP	SH	GW	S	%	+/–	TF	F%	H	SB	Min	GP	G	A	Pts	PIM	PP	SH	GW
1990-91	Prince Albert AA	SAHA	30	19	13	32	91	....	....	....	....	....	....	....	....	....	....	....	....	....	....	....	....	....	....	....
1991-92	Prince Albert AA	SAHA	27	23	29	52	91	....	....	....	....	....	....	....	....	....	....	....	....	....	....	....	....	....	....	....
	Prince Albert	WHL	6	2	0	2	2	....	....	....	....	....	....	....	....	....	....	....	7	2	1	3	6	....	....	....
1992-93	Prince Albert	WHL	72	25	32	57	235	....	....	....	....	....	....	....	....	....	....	....	....	....	....	....	....	....	....	....
1993-94	Prince Albert	WHL	68	37	45	82	183	....	....	....	....	....	....	....	....	....	....	....	....	....	....	....	....	....	....	....
1994-95	Prince Albert	WHL	72	36	38	74	151	....	....	....	....	....	....	....	....	....	....	....	15	10	8	18	25	....	....	....
1995-96	St. John's	AHL	72	11	26	37	216	....	....	....	....	....	....	....	....	....	....	....	4	1	1	2	4	....	....	....
1996-97	**Toronto**	**NHL**	**3**	**0**	**0**	**0**	**7**	**0**	**0**	**0**	**3**	**0.0**	**0**	....	....	....	....	....	....	....	....	....	....	....	....	....
	St. John's	AHL	72	20	17	37	210	....	....	....	....	....	....	....	....	....	....	....	11	3	2	5	16	....	....	....
1997-98	Worcester	AHL	73	9	21	30	128	....	....	....	....	....	....	....	....	....	....	....	11	5	3	8	44	....	....	....
1998-99	Worcester	AHL	75	18	29	47	124	....	....	....	....	....	....	....	....	....	....	....	4	1	0	1	6	....	....	....
	NHL Totals		**3**	**0**	**0**	**0**	**7**	**0**	**0**	**0**	**3**	**0.0**		....	....	....	....	....	....	....	....	....	....	....	....	....

Traded to **Toronto** by **LA Kings** with Dixon Ward, Guy Leveque and Kelly Fairchild for Eric Lacroix, Chris Snell and Toronto's 4th round choice (Eric Belanger) in 1996 Entry Draft, October 3, 1994. Signed as a free agent by **St. Louis**, September 9, 1997. Signed as a free agent by **Phoenix**, August 17, 1999.

TRAVERSE, Patrick (tra-VAIRZ) — OTT.

Defense. Shoots left. 6'3", 190 lbs. Born, Montreal, Que., March 14, 1974. Ottawa's 3rd choice, 50th overall, in 1992 Entry Draft.

Season	Club	League	GP	G	A	Pts	PIM	PP	SH	GW	S	%	+/–	TF	F%	H	SB	Min	GP	G	A	Pts	PIM	PP	SH	GW
1990-91	Bourassa	QAAA	42	4	19	23	10	....	....	....	....	....	....	....	....	....	....	....	5	0	3	3	2	....	....	....
1991-92	Shawinigan	QMJHL	59	3	11	14	12	....	....	....	....	....	....	....	....	....	....	....	10	0	0	0	4	....	....	....
1992-93	St-Jean	QMJHL	68	6	30	36	24	....	....	....	....	....	....	....	....	....	....	....	4	0	1	1	2	....	....	....
	New Haven	AHL	2	0	0	0	2	....	....	....	....	....	....	....	....	....	....	....	....	....	....	....	....	....	....	....
1993-94	St-Jean	QMJHL	66	15	37	52	30	....	....	....	....	....	....	....	....	....	....	....	5	0	4	4	4	....	....	....
	P.E.I. Senators	AHL	3	0	1	1	2	....	....	....	....	....	....	....	....	....	....	....	....	....	....	....	....	....	....	....
1994-95	P.E.I. Senators	AHL	70	5	13	18	19	....	....	....	....	....	....	....	....	....	....	....	7	0	2	2	0	....	....	....
1995-96	**Ottawa**	**NHL**	**5**	**0**	**0**	**0**	**2**	**0**	**0**	**0**	**2**	**0.0**	**–1**	....	....	....	....	....	....	....	....	....	....	....	....	....
	P.E.I. Senators	AHL	55	4	21	25	32	....	....	....	....	....	....	....	....	....	....	....	5	1	2	3	2	....	....	....
1996-97	Worcester	AHL	24	0	4	4	23	....	....	....	....	....	....	....	....	....	....	....	....	....	....	....	....	....	....	....
	Grand Rapids	IHL	10	2	1	3	10	....	....	....	....	....	....	....	....	....	....	....	2	0	1	1	2	....	....	....
1997-98	Hershey	AHL	71	14	15	29	67	....	....	....	....	....	....	....	....	....	....	....	7	1	3	4	4	....	....	....
1998-99	**Ottawa**	**NHL**	**46**	**1**	**9**	**10**	**22**	**0**	**0**	**0**	**35**	**2.9**	**12**	**0**	**0.0**	**41**	**42**	**14:56**	....	....	....	....	....	....	....	....
	NHL Totals		**51**	**1**	**9**	**10**	**24**	**0**	**0**	**0**	**37**	**2.7**		**0**	**0.0**	**41**	**42**	**14:56**	....	....	....	....	....	....	....	....

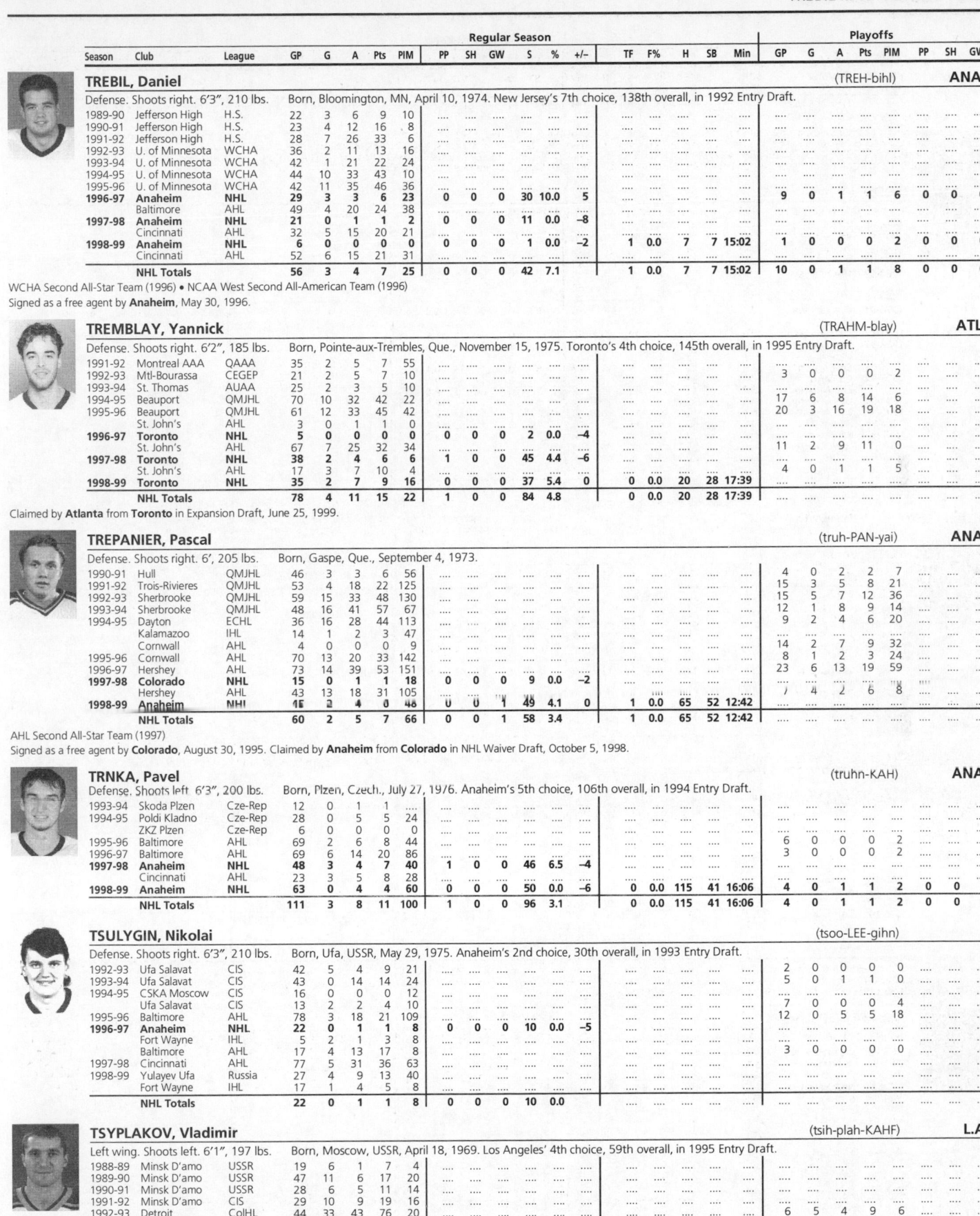

TREBIL, Daniel

(TREH-bihl) **ANA.**

Defense. Shoots right. 6'3", 210 lbs. Born, Bloomington, MN, April 10, 1974. New Jersey's 7th choice, 138th overall, in 1992 Entry Draft.

			Regular Season																Playoffs							
Season	Club	League	GP	G	A	Pts	PIM	PP	SH	GW	S	%	+/-	TF	F%	H	SB	Min	GP	G	A	Pts	PIM	PP	SH	GW
1989-90	Jefferson High	H.S.	22	3	6	9	10																			
1990-91	Jefferson High	H.S.	23	4	12	16	8																			
1991-92	Jefferson High	H.S.	28	7	26	33	6																			
1992-93	U. of Minnesota	WCHA	36	2	11	13	16																			
1993-94	U. of Minnesota	WCHA	42	1	21	22	24																			
1994-95	U. of Minnesota	WCHA	44	10	33	43	10																			
1995-96	U. of Minnesota	WCHA	42	11	35	46	36																			
1996-97	**Anaheim**	**NHL**	29	3	3	6	23	0	0	0	30	10.0	5						9	0	1	1	6	0	0	0
	Baltimore	AHL	49	4	20	24	38																			
1997-98	**Anaheim**	**NHL**	21	0	1	1	2	0	0	0	11	0.0	–8													
	Cincinnati	AHL	32	5	15	20	21																			
1998-99	**Anaheim**	**NHL**	6	0	0	0	0	0	0	0	1	0.0	–2	1	0.0	7	7	15:02	1	0	0	0	2	0	0	0
	Cincinnati	AHL	52	6	15	21	31																			
	NHL Totals		56	3	4	7	25	0	0	0	42	7.1		1	0.0	7	7	15:02	10	0	1	1	8	0	0	0

WCHA Second All-Star Team (1996) • NCAA West Second All-American Team (1996)

Signed as a free agent by **Anaheim**, May 30, 1996.

TREMBLAY, Yannick

(TRAHM-blay) **ATL.**

Defense. Shoots right. 6'2", 185 lbs. Born, Pointe-aux-Trembles, Que., November 15, 1975. Toronto's 4th choice, 145th overall, in 1995 Entry Draft.

			Regular Season																Playoffs							
Season	Club	League	GP	G	A	Pts	PIM	PP	SH	GW	S	%	+/-	TF	F%	H	SB	Min	GP	G	A	Pts	PIM	PP	SH	GW
1991-92	Montreal AAA	QAAA	35	2	5	7	55																			
1992-93	Mtl-Bourassa	CEGEP	21	2	5	7	10												3	0	0	0	2			
1993-94	St. Thomas	AUAA	25	2	3	5	10																			
1994-95	Beauport	QMJHL	70	10	32	42	22												17	6	8	14	6			
1995-96	Beauport	QMJHL	61	12	33	45	42												20	3	16	19	18			
	St. John's	AHL	3	0	1	1	0																			
1996-97	**Toronto**	**NHL**	5	0	0	0	0	0	0	0	2	0.0	–4													
	St. John's	AHL	67	7	25	32	34												11	2	9	11	0			
1997-98	**Toronto**	**NHL**	38	2	4	6	6	1	0	0	45	4.4	–6													
	St. John's	AHL	17	3	7	10	4												4	0	1	1	5			
1998-99	**Toronto**	**NHL**	35	2	7	9	16	0	0	0	37	5.4	0	0	0.0	20	28	17:39								
	NHL Totals		78	4	11	15	22	1	0	0	84	4.8		0	0.0	20	28	17:39								

Claimed by **Atlanta** from **Toronto** in Expansion Draft, June 25, 1999.

TREPANIER, Pascal

(truh-PAN-yai) **ANA.**

Defense. Shoots right. 6', 205 lbs. Born, Gaspe, Que., September 4, 1973.

			Regular Season																Playoffs							
Season	Club	League	GP	G	A	Pts	PIM	PP	SH	GW	S	%	+/-	TF	F%	H	SB	Min	GP	G	A	Pts	PIM	PP	SH	GW
1990-91	Hull	QMJHL	46	3	3	6	56												4	0	2	2	7			
1991-92	Trois-Rivieres	QMJHL	53	4	18	22	125												15	3	5	8	21			
1992-93	Sherbrooke	QMJHL	59	15	33	48	130												15	5	7	12	36			
1993-94	Sherbrooke	QMJHL	48	16	41	57	67												12	1	8	9	14			
1994-95	Dayton	ECHL	36	16	28	44	113												9	2	4	6	20			
	Kalamazoo	IHL	14	1	2	3	47																			
	Cornwall	AHL	4	0	0	0	9												14	2	7	9	32			
1995-96	Cornwall	AHL	70	13	20	33	142												8	1	2	3	24			
1996-97	Hershey	AHL	73	14	39	53	151												23	6	13	19	59			
1997-98	**Colorado**	**NHL**	15	0	1	1	18	0	0	0	9	0.0	–2													
	Hershey	AHL	43	13	18	31	105												7	4	2	6	8			
1998-99	**Anaheim**	**NHL**	45	2	4	6	48	0	0	1	49	4.1	0	1	0.0	65	52	12:42								
	NHL Totals		60	2	5	7	66	0	0	1	58	3.4		1	0.0	65	52	12:42								

AHL Second All-Star Team (1997)

Signed as a free agent by **Colorado**, August 30, 1995. Claimed by **Anaheim** from **Colorado** in NHL Waiver Draft, October 5, 1998.

TRNKA, Pavel

(truhn-KAH) **ANA.**

Defense. Shoots left. 6'3", 200 lbs. Born, Plzen, Czech., July 27, 1976. Anaheim's 5th choice, 106th overall, in 1994 Entry Draft.

			Regular Season																Playoffs							
Season	Club	League	GP	G	A	Pts	PIM	PP	SH	GW	S	%	+/-	TF	F%	H	SB	Min	GP	G	A	Pts	PIM	PP	SH	GW
1993-94	Skoda Plzen	Cze-Rep	12	0	1	1																				
1994-95	Poldi Kladno	Cze-Rep	28	0	5	5	24																			
	ZKZ Plzen	Cze-Rep	6	0	0	0	0																			
1995-96	Baltimore	AHL	69	2	6	8	44												6	0	0	0	2			
1996-97	Baltimore	AHL	69	6	14	20	86												3	0	0	0	2			
1997-98	**Anaheim**	**NHL**	48	3	4	7	40	1	0	0	46	6.5	–4													
	Cincinnati	AHL	23	3	5	8	28																			
1998-99	**Anaheim**	**NHL**	63	0	4	4	60	0	0	0	50	0.0	–6	0	0.0	115	41	16:06	4	0	1	1	2	0	0	0
	NHL Totals		111	3	8	11	100	1	0	0	96	3.1		0	0.0	115	41	16:06	4	0	1	1	2	0	0	0

TSULYGIN, Nikolai

(tsoo-LEE-gihn)

Defense. Shoots right. 6'3", 210 lbs. Born, Ufa, USSR, May 29, 1975. Anaheim's 2nd choice, 30th overall, in 1993 Entry Draft.

			Regular Season																Playoffs							
Season	Club	League	GP	G	A	Pts	PIM	PP	SH	GW	S	%	+/-	TF	F%	H	SB	Min	GP	G	A	Pts	PIM	PP	SH	GW
1992-93	Ufa Salavat	CIS	42	5	4	9	21												2	0	0	0	0			
1993-94	Ufa Salavat	CIS	43	0	14	14	24												5	0	1	1	0			
1994-95	CSKA Moscow	CIS	16	0	0	0	12																			
	Ufa Salavat	CIS	13	2	2	4	10												7	0	0	0	4			
1995-96	Baltimore	AHL	78	3	18	21	109												12	0	5	5	18			
1996-97	**Anaheim**	**NHL**	22	0	1	1	8	0	0	0	10	0.0	–5													
	Fort Wayne	IHL	5	2	1	3	8																			
	Baltimore	AHL	17	4	13	17	8												3	0	0	0	0			
1997-98	Cincinnati	AHL	77	5	31	36	63																			
1998-99	Yulayev Ufa	Russia	27	4	9	13	40																			
	Fort Wayne	IHL	17	1	4	5	8																			
	NHL Totals		22	0	1	1	8	0	0	0	10	0.0														

TSYPLAKOV, Vladimir

(tsih-plah-KAHF) **L.A.**

Left wing. Shoots left. 6'1", 197 lbs. Born, Moscow, USSR, April 18, 1969. Los Angeles' 4th choice, 59th overall, in 1995 Entry Draft.

			Regular Season																Playoffs							
Season	Club	League	GP	G	A	Pts	PIM	PP	SH	GW	S	%	+/-	TF	F%	H	SB	Min	GP	G	A	Pts	PIM	PP	SH	GW
1988-89	Minsk D'amo	USSR	19	6	1	7	4																			
1989-90	Minsk D'amo	USSR	47	11	6	17	20																			
1990-91	Minsk D'amo	USSR	28	6	5	11	14																			
1991-92	Minsk D'amo	CIS	29	10	9	19	16																			
1992-93	Detroit	ColHL	44	33	43	76	20												6	5	4	9	6			
	Indianapolis	IHL	11	6	7	13	4												5	1	1	2	2			
1993-94	Fort Wayne	IHL	63	31	32	63	51												14	6	8	14	16			
1994-95	Fort Wayne	IHL	79	38	40	78	39												4	2	4	6	2			
1995-96	**Los Angeles**	**NHL**	23	5	5	10	4	0	0	0	40	12.5	1													
	Las Vegas	IHL	9	5	6	11	4																			
1996-97	**Los Angeles**	**NHL**	67	16	23	39	12	1	0	2	118	13.6	8													

			Regular Season																Playoffs							
Season	Club	League	GP	G	A	Pts	PIM	PP	SH	GW	S	%	+/–	TF	F%	H	SB	Min	GP	G	A	Pts	PIM	PP	SH	GW
1997-98	Los Angeles	NHL	73	18	34	52	18	2	0	1	113	15.9	15						4	0	1	1	8	0	0	0
	Belarus	Olympics	5	1	1	2	2																			
1998-99	Los Angeles	NHL	69	11	12	23	32	0	2	2	111	9.9	–7	1	100.0	72	14	16:23								
	NHL Totals		232	50	74	124	66	3	2	5	382	13.1		1	100.0	72	14	16:23	4	0	1	1	8	0	0	0

TUCKER, Darcy — T.B.

Center. Shoots left. 5'10", 179 lbs. Born, Castor, Alta., March 15, 1975. Montreal's 8th choice, 151st overall, in 1993 Entry Draft.

Season	Club	League	GP	G	A	Pts	PIM	PP	SH	GW	S	%	+/–	TF	F%	H	SB	Min	GP	G	A	Pts	PIM	PP	SH	GW
1990-91	Red Deer	AAHA	47	70	90	160	48																			
1991-92	Kamloops	WHL	26	3	10	13	32												9	0	1	1	16			
1992-93	Kamloops	WHL	67	31	58	89	155												13	7	6	13	34			
1993-94	Kamloops	WHL	66	52	88	140	143												19	9	*18	*27	43			
1994-95	Kamloops	WHL	64	64	73	137	94												21	*16	15	*31	19			
1995-96	Montreal	NHL	3	0	0	0	0	0	0	0	1	0.0	–1													
	Fredericton	AHL	74	29	64	93	174												7	7	3	10	14			
1996-97	Montreal	NHL	73	7	13	20	110	1	0	3	62	11.3	–5						4	0	0	0	0	0	0	0
1997-98	Montreal	NHL	39	1	5	6	57	0	0	0	19	5.3	–6													
	Tampa Bay	NHL	35	6	8	14	89	1	1	0	44	13.6	–8													
1998-99	Tampa Bay	NHL	82	21	22	43	176	8	2	3	178	11.8	–34	1470	45.6	120	49	19:24								
	NHL Totals		232	35	48	83	432	10	3	6	304	11.5		1470	45.6	120	49	19:24	4	0	0	0	0	0	0	0

WHL West First All-Star Team (1994, 1995) • Canadian Major Junior First All-Star Team (1994) • Memorial Cup All-Star Team (1994, 1995) • Won Stafford Smythe Memorial Trophy (Memorial Cup Tournament MVP) (1994) • Won Dudley "Red" Garrett Memorial Trophy (Top Rookie — AHL) (1996)

Traded to **Tampa Bay** by **Montreal** with Stephane Richer and David Wilkie for Patrick Poulin, Mick Vukota and Igor Ulanov, January 15, 1998.

TUOMAINEN, Marko (TOO-oh-migh-nehn) — L.A.

Right wing. Shoots right. 6'3", 203 lbs. Born, Kuopio, Finland, April 25, 1972. Edmonton's 10th choice, 205th overall, in 1992 Entry Draft.

Season	Club	League	GP	G	A	Pts	PIM	PP	SH	GW	S	%	+/–	TF	F%	H	SB	Min	GP	G	A	Pts	PIM	PP	SH	GW
1988-89	KalPa Kuopio	Finn-Jr.	7	6	6	12	4																			
1989-90	KalPa Kuopio	Finn-Jr.	36	13	24	37	30																			
	KalPa Kuopio	Finland	5	0	0	0	0																			
1990-91	KalPa Kuopio	Finn-Jr.	35	36	17	53	61																			
	KalPa Kuopio	Finland	30	2	1	3	2												8	0	0	0	6			
1991-92	Clarkson	ECAC	28	11	12	23	32																			
1992-93	Clarkson	ECAC	35	25	30	55	26																			
1993-94	Clarkson	ECAC	34	23	29	52	60																			
1994-95	Clarkson	ECAC	37	23	38	61	34																			
	Edmonton	NHL	4	0	0	0	0	0	0	0	5	0.0	0													
1995-96	Cape Breton	AHL	58	25	35	60	71																			
1996-97	Hamilton	AHL	79	31	21	52	130												22	7	5	12	4			
1997-98	HIFK Helsinki	Finland	46	13	9	22	20												9	0	3	3	0			
1998-99	HIFK Helsinki	Finland	48	11	17	28	173												11	1	3	4	46			
	HIFK Helsinki	EuroHL	6	0	1	1	8																			
	NHL Totals		4	0	0	0	0	0	0	0	5	0.0														

ECAC First All-Star Team (1993, 1995) • NCAA East Second All-American Team (1995)

Signed as a free agent by **Los Angeles**, June 20, 1999.

TURCOTTE, Darren (TUHR-koht) — NSH.

Center. Shoots left. 6', 178 lbs. Born, Boston, MA, March 2, 1968. NY Rangers' 6th choice, 114th overall, in 1986 Entry Draft.

Season	Club	League	GP	G	A	Pts	PIM	PP	SH	GW	S	%	+/–	TF	F%	H	SB	Min	GP	G	A	Pts	PIM	PP	SH	GW
1983-84	North Bay	OMHA	70	61	40	101	28																			
1984-85	North Bay	OHL	62	33	32	65	28												8	0	2	2	0			
1985-86	North Bay	OHL	62	35	37	72	35												10	3	4	7	8			
1986-87	North Bay	OHL	55	30	48	78	20												18	12	8	20	6			
1987-88	North Bay	OHL	32	30	33	63	16												4	3	0	3	4			
	Colorado	IHL	8	4	3	7	9												6	2	6	8	8			
1988-89	NY Rangers	NHL	20	7	3	10	4	2	0	2	49	14.3	0						1	0	0	0	0	0	0	0
	Denver	IHL	40	21	28	49	32																			
1989-90	NY Rangers	NHL	76	32	34	66	32	10	1	4	205	15.6	3						10	1	6	7	4	0	0	1
1990-91	NY Rangers	NHL	74	26	41	67	37	15	2	3	212	12.3	–5						6	1	2	3	0	1	0	0
1991-92	NY Rangers	NHL	71	30	23	53	57	13	1	4	216	13.9	11						8	4	0	4	6	2	1	0
1992-93	NY Rangers	NHL	71	25	28	53	40	7	3	3	213	11.7	–3													
1993-94	NY Rangers	NHL	13	2	4	6	13	0	0	0	17	11.8	–2													
	Hartford	NHL	19	2	11	13	4	0	0	0	43	4.7	–11													
1994-95	Hartford	NHL	47	17	18	35	22	3	1	3	121	14.0	1													
1995-96	Winnipeg	NHL	59	16	16	32	26	2	0	2	134	11.9	–3													
	San Jose	NHL	9	6	5	11	4	0	1	2	33	18.2	8													
1996-97	San Jose	NHL	65	16	21	37	16	3	1	4	126	12.7	–8													
1997-98	St. Louis	NHL	62	12	6	18	26	3	0	1	75	16.0	6						10	0	0	0	2	0	0	0
1998-99	Nashville	NHL	40	4	5	9	16	0	0	1	73	5.5	–11	701	44.5	8	15	15:51								
	NHL Totals		626	195	215	410	297	58	10	29	1517	12.9		701	44.5	8	15	15:51	35	6	8	14	12	3	1	1

Played in NHL All-Star Game (1991)

Traded to **Hartford** by **NY Rangers** with James Patrick for Steve Larmer, Nick Kypreos, Barry Richter and Hartford's 6th round choice (Yuri Litvinov) in 1994 Entry Draft, November 2, 1993. Traded to **Winnipeg** by **Hartford** for Nelson Emerson, October 6, 1995. Traded to **San Jose** by **Winnipeg** with Dallas' 2nd round choice (previously acquired and later traded to Chicago — Chicago selected Remi Royer) in 1996 Entry Draft for Craig Janney, March 18, 1996. Traded to **St. Louis** by **San Jose** for Stephane Matteau, July 24, 1997. Traded to **Nashville** by **St. Louis** for future considerations, June 26, 1998.

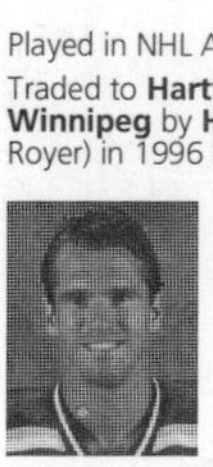

TURGEON, Pierre (TUHR-zhaw) — ST.L.

Center. Shoots left. 6'1", 199 lbs. Born, Rouyn, Que., August 28, 1969. Buffalo's 1st choice, 1st overall, in 1987 Entry Draft.

Season	Club	League	GP	G	A	Pts	PIM	PP	SH	GW	S	%	+/–	TF	F%	H	SB	Min	GP	G	A	Pts	PIM	PP	SH	GW
1984-85	Bourassa	QAAA	41	49	52	101																				
1985-86	Granby	QMJHL	69	47	67	114	31																			
	Canada	Nat-Team	11	2	4	6	2																			
1986-87	Granby	QMJHL	58	69	85	154	8												7	9	6	15	15			
1987-88	Buffalo	NHL	76	14	28	42	34	8	0	3	101	13.9	–8						6	4	3	7	4	3	0	0
1988-89	Buffalo	NHL	80	34	54	88	26	19	0	5	182	18.7	–2						5	3	5	8	2	1	0	0
1989-90	Buffalo	NHL	80	40	66	106	29	17	1	10	193	20.7	10						6	2	4	6	2	0	0	1
1990-91	Buffalo	NHL	78	32	47	79	26	13	2	3	174	18.4	14						6	3	1	4	6	1	0	0
1991-92	Buffalo	NHL	8	2	6	8	4	0	0	0	14	14.3	–1													
	NY Islanders	NHL	69	38	49	87	16	13	0	6	193	19.7	8													
1992-93	NY Islanders	NHL	83	58	74	132	26	24	0	10	301	19.3	–1						11	6	7	13	0	0	0	0
1993-94	NY Islanders	NHL	69	38	56	94	18	10	4	6	254	15.0	14						4	0	1	1	0	0	0	0
1994-95	NY Islanders	NHL	34	13	14	27	10	2	0	2	93	14.0	–12													
	Montreal	NHL	15	11	9	20	4	5	2	2	67	16.4	12													
1995-96	Montreal	NHL	80	38	58	96	44	17	1	6	297	12.8	19						6	2	4	6	2	0	0	0
1996-97	Montreal	NHL	9	1	10	11	2	0	0	0	22	4.5	4													
	St. Louis	NHL	69	25	49	74	12	5	0	7	194	12.9	4						5	1	1	2	2	1	0	0
1997-98	St. Louis	NHL	60	22	46	68	24	6	0	4	140	15.7	13						10	4	4	8	2	2	0	0

Season	Club	League	GP	G	A	Pts	PIM	PP	SH	GW	S	%	+/-	TF	F%	H	SB	Min	GP	G	A	Pts	PIM	PP	SH	GW
1998-99	St. Louis	NHL	67	31	34	65	36	10	0	5	193	16.1	4	1285	50.0	16	24	19:07	13	4	9	13	6	0	0	2
	NHL Totals		877	397	600	997	311	149	10	69	2418	16.4		1285	50.0	16	24	19:07	72	29	39	68	26	8	0	3

Won Lady Byng Memorial Trophy (1993)
Played in NHL All-Star Game (1990, 1993, 1994, 1996)
Traded to **NY Islanders** by **Buffalo** with Uwe Krupp, Benoit Hogue and Dave McLlwain for Pat Lafontaine, Randy Hillier, Randy Wood and NY Islanders' 4th round choice (Dean Melanson) in 1992 Entry Draft, October 25, 1991. Traded to **Montreal** by **NY Islanders** with Vladimir Malakhov for Kirk Muller, Mathieu Schneider and Craig Darby, April 5, 1995. Traded to **St. Louis** by **Montreal** with Rory Fitzpatrick and Craig Conroy for Murray Baron, Shayne Corson and St. Louis' 5th round choice (Gennady Razin) in 1997 Entry Draft, October 29, 1996.

TUZZOLINO, Tony

(too-zuh-LEE-noh)   **ANA.**

Right wing. Shoots right. 6'2", 208 lbs.   Born, Buffalo, NY, October 9, 1975. Quebec's 7th choice, 113th overall, in 1994 Entry Draft.

Season	Club	League	GP	G	A	Pts	PIM	PP	SH	GW	S	%	+/-	TF	F%	H	SB	Min	GP	G	A	Pts	PIM	PP	SH	GW
1989-90	Amherst	USAHA	29	50	95	145	....																			
1990-91	Buffalo	USAHA	55	39	47	86	....																			
1991-92	Niagara Scenics	NAJHL	45	19	27	46	82																			
1992-93	Niagara Scenics	NAJHL	50	36	41	77	134																			
1993-94	Michigan State	CCHA	35	4	3	7	46																			
1994-95	Michigan State	CCHA	39	9	18	27	81																			
1995-96	Michigan State	CCHA	41	12	17	29	120																			
1996-97	Michigan State	CCHA	39	14	18	32	120																			
1997-98	Kentucky	AHL	35	9	14	23	83																			
	Anaheim	**NHL**	1	0	0	0	2	0	0	0	0	0.0	–2													
	Cincinnati	AHL	13	3	3	6	6																			
1998-99	Cincinnati	AHL	50	4	10	14	55																			
	Cleveland	IHL	15	2	4	6	22																			
	NHL Totals		1	0	0	0	2	0	0	0	0	0.0														

Rights transferred to **Colorado** after **Quebec** franchise relocated, June 21, 1995. Signed as a free agent by **NY Islanders**, April 26, 1997. Traded to **Anaheim** by **NY Islanders** with Travis Green and Doug Houda for Joe Sacco, J.J. Daigneault and Mark Janssens, February 6, 1998.

TVERDOVSKY, Oleg

(tvehr-DOHV-skee)   **ANA.**

Defense. Shoots left. 6', 195 lbs.   Born, Donetsk, USSR, May 18, 1976. Anaheim's 1st choice, 2nd overall, in 1994 Entry Draft.

Season	Club	League	GP	G	A	Pts	PIM	PP	SH	GW	S	%	+/-	TF	F%	H	SB	Min	GP	G	A	Pts	PIM	PP	SH	GW
1992-93	Soviet Wings	CIS	21	0	1	1	6												6	0	0	0	0			
1993-94	Soviet Wings	CIS	46	4	10	14	22												3	1	0	1	2			
1994-95	Brandon	WHL	7	1	4	5	4																			
	Anaheim	**NHL**	36	3	9	12	14	1	1	0	26	11.5	–6													
1995-96	**Anaheim**	**NHL**	51	7	15	22	35	2	0	0	84	8.3	0						6	0	1	1	0	0	0	0
	Winnipeg	**NHL**	31	0	8	8	6	0	0	0	35	0.0	–7													
1996-97	Phoenix	**NHL**	82	10	45	55	30	3	1	2	144	6.9	–5						7	0	1	1	0	0	0	0
1997-98	Hamilton	AHL	9	8	6	14	2																			
	Phoenix	**NHL**	46	7	12	19	12	4	0	1	83	8.4	1						6	0	7	7	0	0	0	0
1998-99	**Phoenix**	**NHL**	82	7	18	25	32	2	0	2	117	6.0	11	1	0.0	50	53	20:48	6	0	2	2	6	0	0	0
	NHL Totals		328	34	107	141	129	12	2	5	489	7.0		1	0.0	50	53	20:48	25	0	11	11	6	0	0	0

Played in NHL All-Star Game (1997)
Traded to **Winnipeg** by **Anaheim** with Chad Kilger and Anaheim's 3rd round choice (Per-Anton Lundstrom) in 1996 Entry Draft for Teemu Selanne, Marc Chouinard and Winnipeg's 4th round choice (later traded to Toronto — later traded to Montreal — Montreal selected Kim Staal) in 1996 Entry Draft, February 7, 1996. Transferred to **Phoenix** after **Winnipeg** franchise relocated, July 1, 1996. Traded to **Anaheim** by **Phoenix** for Travis Green and Anaheim's 1st round choice (Scott Kelman) in 1999 Entry Draft, June 26, 1999.

TWIST, Tony

Left wing. Shoots left. 6'1", 220 lbs.   Born, Sherwood Park, Alta., May 9, 1968. St. Louis' 9th choice, 177th overall, in 1988 Entry Draft

Season	Club	League	GP	G	A	Pts	PIM	PP	SH	GW	S	%	+/-	TF	F%	H	SB	Min	GP	G	A	Pts	PIM	PP	SH	GW
1985-86	Prince George	BCJHL	42	32	20	52	162																			
1986-87	Saskatoon	WHL	64	0	8	8	181																			
1987-88	Saskatoon	WHL	55	1	8	9	226												10	1	1	2	6			
1988-89	Peoria	IHL	67	3	8	11	312																			
1989-90	St. Louis	NHL	28	0	0	0	124	0	0	0	2	0.0	–2													
	Peoria	IHL	36	1	5	6	200												5	0	1	1	8			
1990-91	Peoria	IHL	38	2	10	12	244																			
	Quebec	NHL	24	0	0	0	104	0	0	0	2	0.0	–4													
1991-92	Quebec	NHL	44	0	1	1	164	0	0	0	9	0.0	–3													
1992-93	Quebec	NHL	34	....	2	2	64	0	0	0	14	0.0	0													
1993-94	Quebec	NHL	49	0	4	4	101	0	0	0	15	0.0	–1													
1994-95	St. Louis	NHL	28	3	0	3	89	0	0	0	8	37.5	0						1	0	0	0	6	0	0	0
1995-96	St. Louis	NHL	51	3	2	5	100	0	0	1	12	25.0	–1						10	1	1	2	16	0	0	0
1996-97	St. Louis	NHL	64	1	2	3	121	0	0	0	21	4.8	–8						6	0	0	0	0	0	0	0
1997-98	St. Louis	NHL	60	1	1	2	105	0	0	0	17	5.9	–4													
1998-99	St. Louis	NHL	63	2	6	8	149	0	0	0	23	8.7	0	1	0.0	47	5	5:10	1	0	0	0	0	0	0	0
	NHL Totals		445	10	18	28	1121	0	0	2	123	8.1		1	0.0	47	5	5:10	18	1	1	2	22	0	0	0

Traded to **Quebec** by **St. Louis** with Herb Raglan and Andy Rymsha for Darin Kimble, February 4, 1991. Signed as a free agent by **St. Louis**, August 16, 1994.

ULANOV, Igor

(yoo-LAH-nahf, EE-gohr)   **MTL.**

Defense. Shoots left. 6'3", 211 lbs.   Born, Krasnokamsk, USSR, October 1, 1969. Winnipeg's 8th choice, 203rd overall, in 1991 Entry Draft.

Season	Club	League	GP	G	A	Pts	PIM	PP	SH	GW	S	%	+/-	TF	F%	H	SB	Min	GP	G	A	Pts	PIM	PP	SH	GW
1990-91	Khimik	USSR	41	2	2	4	52																			
1991-92	Khimik	CIS	27	1	4	5	24																			
	Winnipeg	**NHL**	27	2	9	11	67	0	0	0	23	8.7	5						7	0	0	0	39	0	0	0
	Moncton	AHL	3	0	1	1	16																			
1992-93	**Winnipeg**	**NHL**	56	2	14	16	124	0	0	0	26	7.7	6						4	0	0	0	4	0	0	0
	Moncton	AHL	9	1	3	4	26																			
	Fort Wayne	IHL	3	0	1	1	29																			
1993-94	**Winnipeg**	**NHL**	74	0	17	17	165	0	0	0	46	0.0	–11													
1994-95	**Winnipeg**	**NHL**	19	1	3	4	27	0	0	0	13	7.7	–2													
	Washington	**NHL**	3	0	1	1	2	0	0	0	0	0.0	3													
1995-96	**Chicago**	**NHL**	53	1	8	9	92	0	0	0	24	4.2	12						2	0	0	0	4	0	0	0
	Indianapolis	IHL	1	0	0	0	0																			
	Tampa Bay	**NHL**	11	2	1	3	24	0	0	1	13	15.4	–1						5	0	0	0	15	0	0	0
1996-97	**Tampa Bay**	**NHL**	59	1	7	8	108	0	0	0	56	1.8	2													
1997-98	**Tampa Bay**	**NHL**	45	2	7	9	85	1	0	0	32	6.3	–5													
	Montreal	**NHL**	4	0	1	1	12	0	0	0	4	0.0	–2						10	1	4	5	12	0	0	0
1998-99	**Montreal**	**NHL**	76	3	9	12	109	0	0	0	55	5.5	–3	0	0.0	136	163	17:35								
	NHL Totals		427	14	77	91	815	1	0	1	292	4.8		0	0.0	136	163	17:35	28	1	4	5	74	0	0	0

Traded to **Washington** by **Winnipeg** with Mike Eagles for Washington's 3rd (later traded to Dallas — Dallas selected Sergei Gusev) and 5th (Brian Elder) round choices in 1995 Entry Draft, April 7, 1995. Traded to **Chicago** by **Washington** for Chicago's 3rd round choice (Dave Weninger) in 1996 Entry Draft, October 17, 1995. Traded to **Tampa Bay** by **Chicago** with Patrick Poulin and Chicago's 2nd round choice (later traded to New Jersey — New Jersey selected Pierre Dagenais) in 1996 Entry Draft for Enrico Ciccone and Tampa Bay's 2nd round choice (Jeff Paul) in 1996 Entry Draft, March 20, 1996. Traded to **Montreal** by **Tampa Bay** with Patrick Poulin and Mick Vukota for Stephane Richer, Darcy Tucker and David Wilkie, January 15, 1998.

USTORF, Stefan
(OOSH-tohrf, SHTEH-fuhn) **WSH.**

Center. Shoots left. 6', 185 lbs. Born, Kaufbeuren, Germany, January 3, 1974. Washington's 3rd choice, 53rd overall, in 1992 Entry Draft.

			Regular Season																Playoffs							
Season	Club	League	GP	G	A	Pts	PIM	PP	SH	GW	S	%	+/-	TF	F%	H	SB	Min	GP	G	A	Pts	PIM	PP	SH	GW
1989-90	ESV Kaufbeuren	Ger-Jr.	8	10	11	21	8	....	....	....	....	....	....	....	....	....	....	....	....	....	....	....	....	....	....	....
1990-91	ESV Kaufbeuren	Ger-Jr.	37	33	34	67	78	....	....	....	....	....	....	....	....	....	....	....	....	....	....	....	....	....	....	....
1991-92	ESV Kaufbeuren	Germany	41	2	22	24	46	....	....	....	....	....	....	....	....	....	....	....	5	2	7	9	6	....	....	....
1992-93	ESV Kaufbeuren	Germany	37	14	18	32	32	....	....	....	....	....	....	....	....	....	....	....	3	1	0	1	10	....	....	....
1993-94	ESV Kaufbeuren	Germany	38	10	20	30	21	....	....	....	....	....	....	....	....	....	....	....	3	0	0	0	4	....	....	....
	Germany	Olympics	8	1	2	3	2	....	....	....	....	....	....	....	....	....	....	....	....	....	....	....	....	....	....	....
1994-95	Portland	AHL	63	21	38	59	51	....	....	....	....	....	....	....	....	....	....	....	7	1	6	7	7	....	....	....
1995-96	**Washington**	**NHL**	**48**	**7**	**10**	**17**	**14**	**0**	**0**	**1**	**39**	**17.9**	**8**	....	....	....	....	....	**5**	**0**	**0**	**0**	**0**	**0**	**0**	**0**
	Portland	AHL	8	1	4	5	6	....	....	....	....	....	....	....	....	....	....	....	....	....	....	....	....	....	....	....
1996-97	**Washington**	**NHL**	**6**	**0**	**0**	**0**	**2**	**0**	**0**	**0**	**7**	**0.0**	**–3**	....	....	....	....	....	....	....	....	....	....	....	....	....
	Portland	AHL	36	7	17	24	27	....	....	....	....	....	....	....	....	....	....	....	....	....	....	....	....	....	....	....
1997-98	EHC Berlin	Germany	45	17	23	40	54	....	....	....	....	....	....	....	....	....	....	....	....	....	....	....	....	....	....	....
	Germany	Olympics	4	0	0	0	0	....	....	....	....	....	....	....	....	....	....	....	....	....	....	....	....	....	....	....
1998-99	Las Vegas	IHL	40	11	17	18	40	....	....	....	....	....	....	....	....	....	....	....	....	....	....	....	....	....	....	....
	Detroit	IHL	14	3	7	10	11	....	....	....	....	....	....	....	....	....	....	....	11	4	7	11	2	....	....	....
	NHL Totals		**54**	**7**	**10**	**17**	**16**	**0**	**0**	**1**	**46**	**15.2**		....	....	....	....	....	**5**	**0**	**0**	**0**	**0**	**0**	**0**	**0**

VAIC, Lubomir
(VIGHTZ) **VAN.**

Center. Shoots left. 5'9", 178 lbs. Born, Spisska Nova Ves, Czech., March 6, 1977. Vancouver's 8th choice, 227th overall, in 1996 Entry Draft.

Season	Club	League	GP	G	A	Pts	PIM	PP	SH	GW	S	%	+/-	TF	F%	H	SB	Min	GP	G	A	Pts	PIM	PP	SH	GW
1993-94	SKP Poprad	Slovakia	28	10	6	16	10	....	....	....	....	....	....	....	....	....	....	....	....	....	....	....	....	....	....	....
1994-95	VTJ Spisska	Slovakia	19	5	4	9	2	....	....	....	....	....	....	....	....	....	....	....	....	....	....	....	....	....	....	....
1995-96	HC Kosice	Slovakia	36	7	19	26	10	....	....	....	....	....	....	....	....	....	....	....	13	0	7	7	....	....	....	....
1996-97	HC Kosice	Slovakia	36	13	12	25	....	....	....	....	....	....	....	....	....	....	....	....	7	2	0	2	....	....	....	....
1997-98	**Vancouver**	**NHL**	**5**	**1**	**1**	**2**	**2**	**0**	**0**	**0**	**8**	**12.5**	**–2**	....	....	....	....	....	....	....	....	....	....	....	....	....
	Syracuse	AHL	50	12	15	27	22	....	....	....	....	....	....	....	....	....	....	....	3	0	0	0	4	....	....	....
1998-99	VTJ Spisska	Slovakia	35	20	22	42	42	....	....	....	....	....	....	....	....	....	....	....	....	....	....	....	....	....	....	....
	HC Kosice	Slovakia	....	....	....	....	....	....	....	....	....	....	....	....	....	....	....	....	11	2	3	5	8	....	....	....
	NHL Totals		**5**	**1**	**1**	**2**	**2**	**0**	**0**	**0**	**8**	**12.5**		....	....	....	....	....	....	....	....	....	....	....	....	....

VALICEVIC, Robert
(val-IH-seh-vihch) **NSH.**

Right wing. Shoots right. 6'2", 197 lbs. Born, Detroit, MI, January 6, 1971. NY Islanders' 6th choice, 114th overall, in 1991 Entry Draft.

Season	Club	League	GP	G	A	Pts	PIM	PP	SH	GW	S	%	+/-	TF	F%	H	SB	Min	GP	G	A	Pts	PIM	PP	SH	GW
1990-91	Detroit	USHL	39	31	44	75	54	....	....	....	....	....	....	....	....	....	....	....	....	....	....	....	....	....	....	....
1991-92	Lake Superior	CCHA	32	8	4	12	12	....	....	....	....	....	....	....	....	....	....	....	....	....	....	....	....	....	....	....
1992-93	Lake Superior	CCHA	43	21	20	41	28	....	....	....	....	....	....	....	....	....	....	....	....	....	....	....	....	....	....	....
1993-94	Lake Superior	CCHA	45	18	20	38	46	....	....	....	....	....	....	....	....	....	....	....	....	....	....	....	....	....	....	....
1994-95	Lake Superior	CCHA	37	10	21	31	40	....	....	....	....	....	....	....	....	....	....	....	....	....	....	....	....	....	....	....
1995-96	Louisiana	ECHL	60	42	20	62	85	....	....	....	....	....	....	....	....	....	....	....	5	2	3	5	8	....	....	....
	Springfield	AHL	2	0	0	0	2	....	....	....	....	....	....	....	....	....	....	....	....	....	....	....	....	....	....	....
1996-97	Louisiana	ECHL	8	7	2	9	21	....	....	....	....	....	....	....	....	....	....	....	....	....	....	....	....	....	....	....
	Houston	IHL	58	11	12	23	42	....	....	....	....	....	....	....	....	....	....	....	12	1	3	4	11	....	....	....
1997-98	Houston	IHL	72	29	28	57	47	....	....	....	....	....	....	....	....	....	....	....	4	2	0	2	2	....	....	....
1998-99	**Nashville**	**NHL**	**19**	**4**	**2**	**6**	**2**	**0**	**0**	**2**	**23**	**17.4**	**4**	**17**	**29.4**	**8**	**8**	**11:01**	....	....	....	....	....	....	....	....
	Houston	IHL	57	16	33	49	62	....	....	....	....	....	....	....	....	....	....	....	19	7	10	17	8	....	....	....
	NHL Totals		**19**	**4**	**2**	**6**	**2**	**0**	**0**	**2**	**23**	**17.4**		**17**	**29.4**	**8**	**8**	**11:01**	....	....	....	....	....	....	....	....

Signed as a free agent by **Nashville**, May 28, 1998.

VALK, Garry
(VAHLK) **TOR.**

Left wing. Shoots left. 6'1", 205 lbs. Born, Edmonton, Alta., November 27, 1967. Vancouver's 5th choice, 108th overall, in 1987 Entry Draft.

Season	Club	League	GP	G	A	Pts	PIM	PP	SH	GW	S	%	+/-	TF	F%	H	SB	Min	GP	G	A	Pts	PIM	PP	SH	GW
1984-85	Sherwood Park	AJHL	55	20	22	42	46	....	....	....	....	....	....	....	....	....	....	....	....	....	....	....	....	....	....	....
1985-86	Sherwood Park	AJHL	40	20	26	46	116	....	....	....	....	....	....	....	....	....	....	....	....	....	....	....	....	....	....	....
1986-87	Sherwood Park	AJHL	59	42	44	86	204	....	....	....	....	....	....	....	....	....	....	....	....	....	....	....	....	....	....	....
1987-88	North Dakota	WCHA	38	23	12	35	64	....	....	....	....	....	....	....	....	....	....	....	....	....	....	....	....	....	....	....
1988-89	North Dakota	WCHA	40	14	17	31	71	....	....	....	....	....	....	....	....	....	....	....	....	....	....	....	....	....	....	....
1989-90	North Dakota	WCHA	43	22	17	39	92	....	....	....	....	....	....	....	....	....	....	....	....	....	....	....	....	....	....	....
1990-91	**Vancouver**	**NHL**	**59**	**10**	**11**	**21**	**67**	**1**	**0**	**1**	**90**	**11.1**	**–23**	....	....	....	....	....	**5**	**0**	**0**	**0**	**20**	**0**	**0**	**0**
	Milwaukee	IHL	10	12	4	16	13	....	....	....	....	....	....	....	....	....	....	....	3	0	0	0	2	....	....	....
1991-92	**Vancouver**	**NHL**	**65**	**8**	**17**	**25**	**56**	**2**	**1**	**2**	**93**	**8.6**	**3**	....	....	....	....	....	**4**	**0**	**0**	**0**	**5**	**0**	**0**	**0**
1992-93	**Vancouver**	**NHL**	**48**	**6**	**7**	**13**	**77**	**0**	**0**	**2**	**46**	**13.0**	**6**	....	....	....	....	....	**7**	**0**	**1**	**1**	**12**	**0**	**0**	**0**
	Hamilton	AHL	7	3	6	9	6	....	....	....	....	....	....	....	....	....	....	....	....	....	....	....	....	....	....	....
1993-94	**Anaheim**	**NHL**	**78**	**18**	**27**	**45**	**100**	**4**	**1**	**5**	**165**	**10.9**	**8**	....	....	....	....	....	....	....	....	....	....	....	....	....
1994-95	**Anaheim**	**NHL**	**36**	**3**	**6**	**9**	**34**	**0**	**0**	**0**	**53**	**5.7**	**–4**	....	....	....	....	....	....	....	....	....	....	....	....	....
1995-96	**Anaheim**	**NHL**	**79**	**12**	**12**	**24**	**125**	**1**	**1**	**2**	**108**	**11.1**	**8**	....	....	....	....	....	....	....	....	....	....	....	....	....
1996-97	**Anaheim**	**NHL**	**53**	**7**	**7**	**14**	**53**	**0**	**0**	**1**	**68**	**10.3**	**–2**	....	....	....	....	....	....	....	....	....	....	....	....	....
	Pittsburgh	**NHL**	**17**	**3**	**4**	**7**	**25**	**0**	**0**	**0**	**32**	**9.4**	**–6**	....	....	....	....	....	....	....	....	....	....	....	....	....
1997-98	**Pittsburgh**	**NHL**	**39**	**2**	**1**	**3**	**33**	**0**	**0**	**0**	**32**	**6.3**	**–3**	....	....	....	....	....	....	....	....	....	....	....	....	....
1998-99	**Toronto**	**NHL**	**77**	**8**	**21**	**29**	**53**	**1**	**0**	**0**	**93**	**8.6**	**8**	**19**	**36.8**	**99**	**20**	**13:53**	**17**	**3**	**4**	**7**	**22**	**0**	**0**	**1**
	NHL Totals		**551**	**77**	**113**	**190**	**623**	**9**	**3**	**13**	**780**	**9.9**		**19**	**36.8**	**99**	**20**	**13:53**	**33**	**3**	**5**	**8**	**59**	**0**	**0**	**1**

OHA First All-Star Team (1974)

Claimed by **Anaheim** from **Vancouver** in NHL Waiver Draft, October 3, 1993. Traded to **Pittsburgh** by **Anaheim** for Jean-Jacques Daigneault, February 21, 1997. Signed as a free agent by **Toronto**, October 8, 1998.

VAN ALLEN, Shaun
OTT.

Center. Shoots left. 6'1", 200 lbs. Born, Calgary, Alta., August 29, 1967. Edmonton's 5th choice, 105th overall, in 1987 Entry Draft.

Season	Club	League	GP	G	A	Pts	PIM	PP	SH	GW	S	%	+/-	TF	F%	H	SB	Min	GP	G	A	Pts	PIM	PP	SH	GW
1984-85	Swift Current	SJHL	61	12	20	32	136	....	....	....	....	....	....	....	....	....	....	....	....	....	....	....	....	....	....	....
1985-86	Saskatoon	WHL	55	12	11	23	43	....	....	....	....	....	....	....	....	....	....	....	13	4	8	12	28	....	....	....
1986-87	Saskatoon	WHL	72	38	59	97	116	....	....	....	....	....	....	....	....	....	....	....	11	4	6	10	24	....	....	....
1987-88	Milwaukee	IHL	40	14	28	42	34	....	....	....	....	....	....	....	....	....	....	....	....	....	....	....	....	....	....	....
	Nova Scotia	AHL	19	4	10	14	17	....	....	....	....	....	....	....	....	....	....	....	4	1	1	2	4	....	....	....
1988-89	Cape Breton	AHL	76	32	42	74	81	....	....	....	....	....	....	....	....	....	....	....	....	....	....	....	....	....	....	....
1989-90	Cape Breton	AHL	61	25	44	69	83	....	....	....	....	....	....	....	....	....	....	....	4	0	2	2	8	....	....	....
1990-91	**Edmonton**	**NHL**	**2**	**0**	**0**	**0**	**0**	**0**	**0**	**0**	**0**	**0.0**	**0**	....	....	....	....	....	....	....	....	....	....	....	....	....
	Cape Breton	AHL	76	25	75	100	182	....	....	....	....	....	....	....	....	....	....	....	4	0	1	1	8	....	....	....
1991-92	Cape Breton	AHL	77	29	*84	*113	80	....	....	....	....	....	....	....	....	....	....	....	5	3	7	10	14	....	....	....
1992-93	**Edmonton**	**NHL**	**21**	**1**	**4**	**5**	**6**	**0**	**0**	**0**	**19**	**5.3**	**–2**	....	....	....	....	....	....	....	....	....	....	....	....	....
	Cape Breton	AHL	43	14	62	76	68	....	....	....	....	....	....	....	....	....	....	....	15	8	9	17	18	....	....	....
1993-94	**Anaheim**	**NHL**	**80**	**8**	**25**	**33**	**64**	**2**	**2**	**1**	**104**	**7.7**	**0**	....	....	....	....	....	....	....	....	....	....	....	....	....
1994-95	**Anaheim**	**NHL**	**45**	**8**	**21**	**29**	**32**	**1**	**1**	**1**	**68**	**11.8**	**–4**	....	....	....	....	....	....	....	....	....	....	....	....	....
1995-96	**Anaheim**	**NHL**	**49**	**8**	**17**	**25**	**41**	**0**	**0**	**2**	**78**	**10.3**	**13**	....	....	....	....	....	....	....	....	....	....	....	....	....
1996-97	**Ottawa**	**NHL**	**80**	**11**	**14**	**25**	**35**	**1**	**1**	**2**	**123**	**8.9**	**–8**	....	....	....	....	....	**7**	**0**	**1**	**1**	**4**	**0**	**0**	**0**

Season	Club	League	GP	G	A	Pts	PIM	PP	SH	GW	S	%	+/-	TF	F%	H	SB	Min	GP	G	A	Pts	PIM	PP	SH	GW
1997-98	Ottawa	NHL	80	4	15	19	48	0	0	0	104	3.8	4	656	47.4	...	23	11:07	11	0	1	1	10	0	0	0
1998-99	Ottawa	NHL	79	6	11	17	30	0	1	0	47	12.8	3						4	0	0	0	0	0	0	0
	NHL Totals		436	46	107	153	256	4	5	6	543	8.5		656	47.4	84	23	11:07	22	0	2	2	14	0	0	0

AHL Second All-Star Team (1991) • AHL First All-Star Team (1992) • Won John B. Sollenberger Trophy (Top Scorer - AHL) (1992)
Signed as a free agent by **Anaheim**, July 22, 1993. Traded to **Ottawa** by **Anaheim** with Jason York for Ted Drury and the rights to Marc Moro, October 1, 1996.

VANDENBUSSCHE, Ryan · (van-dehn-BUHSH) · CHI.

Right wing. Shoots right. 6', 200 lbs.   Born, Simcoe, Ont., February 28, 1973. Toronto's 9th choice, 173rd overall, in 1992 Entry Draft.

Season	Club	League	GP	G	A	Pts	PIM	PP	SH	GW	S	%	+/-	TF	F%	H	SB	Min	GP	G	A	Pts	PIM	PP	SH	GW
1988-89	Delhi	OJHL-D	3	1	1	2	2																			
1989-90	Norwich	OJHL-C	24	0	5	5	113																			
	Tillsonburg	OJHL-B	21	12	10	22	146																			
1990-91	Cornwall	OHL	49	3	8	11	139																			
1991-92	Cornwall	OHL	61	13	15	28	232											6	0	2	2	9			
1992-93	Newmarket	OHL	30	15	12	27	161																		
	Guelph	OHL	29	3	14	17	99											5	1	3	4	13			
	St. John's	AHL	1	0	0	0	0																		
1993-94	St. John's	AHL	44	4	10	14	124											5	0	0	0	16			
	Springfield	AHL	9	1	2	3	29																		
1994-95	St. John's	AHL	53	2	13	15	239											3	0	0	0	17			
1995-96	Binghamton	AHL	68	3	17	20	240											4	0	0	0	9			
1996-97	**NY Rangers**	**NHL**	**11**	**1**	**0**	**1**	**30**	0	0	0	4	25.0	–2													
	Binghamton	AHL	38	8	11	19	133																		
1997-98	**NY Rangers**	**NHL**	**16**	**1**	**0**	**1**	**38**	0	0	0	2	50.0	–2													
	Hartford	AHL	15	2	0	2	45																		
	Chicago	**NHL**	**4**	**0**	**1**	**1**	**5**	0	0	0	0	0.0	0													
	Indianapolis	IHL	3	1	1	2	4																		
1998-99	**Chicago**	**NHL**	**6**	**0**	**0**	**0**	**17**	0	0	0	3	0.0	0	0	0.0	13	2	9:29								
	Indianapolis	IHL	34	3	10	13	130																		
	Portland	AHL	37	4	1	5	119																		
	NHL Totals		**37**	**2**	**1**	**3**	**90**	0	0	0	9	22.2		0	0.0	13	2	9:29								

Signed as a free agent by **NY Rangers**, August 22, 1995. Traded to **Chicago** by **NY Rangers** for Ryan Risidore, March 24, 1998.

VAN IMPE, Darren · (van-IHMP) · BOS.

Defense. Shoots left. 6'1", 205 lbs.   Born, Saskatoon, Sask., May 18, 1973. NY Islanders' 7th choice, 170th overall, in 1993 Entry Draft.

Season	Club	League	GP	G	A	Pts	PIM	PP	SH	GW	S	%	+/-	TF	F%	H	SB	Min	GP	G	A	Pts	PIM	PP	SH	GW
1989-90	Prince Albert	AAHA	32	16	31	47	100																			
	Prince Albert	WHL	1	0	1	1	0																			
1990-91	Prince Albert	WHL	70	15	45	60	57											3	1	1	2	2			
1991-92	Prince Albert	WHL	69	9	37	46	129											8	1	5	6	10			
1992-93	Red Deer	WHL	54	23	47	70	118											4	2	5	7	16			
1993-94	Red Deer	WHL	58	20	64	84	125											4	2	4	6	6			
1994-95	San Diego	IHL	76	6	17	23	74											5	0	0	0	0			
	Anaheim	**NHL**	**1**	**0**	**1**	**1**	**4**	0	0	0	0	0.0	0													
1995-96	**Anaheim**	**NHL**	**16**	**1**	**2**	**3**	**14**	0	0	1	13	7.7	8													
	Baltimore	AHL	63	11	47	58	79																		
1996-97	**Anaheim**	**NHL**	**74**	**4**	**19**	**23**	**90**	2	0	0	107	3.7	3						9	0	2	2	16	0	0	0
1997-98	**Anaheim**	**NHL**	**19**	**1**	**3**	**4**	**4**	0	0	0	21	4.8	–10													
	Boston	**NHL**	**50**	**2**	**8**	**10**	**36**	2	0	0	50	4.0	4						6	2	1	3	0	1	0	1
1998-99	**Boston**	**NHL**	**60**	**5**	**15**	**20**	**66**	4	0	0	92	5.4	–5	0	0.0	45	60	17:54	11	1	2	3	4	1	0	0
	NHL Totals		**220**	**13**	**48**	**61**	**214**	8	0	1	283	4.6		0	0.0	45	60	17:34	26	3	5	8	20	2	0	1

WHL East First All-Star Team (1993, 1994)
Traded to **Anaheim** by **NY Islanders** for Anaheim's 8th round choice (Mike Broda) in 1995 Entry Draft, August 31, 1994. Claimed on waivers by **Boston** from **Anaheim**, November 26, 1997.

VARADA, Vaclav · (VAH-rah-dah) · BUF.

Right wing. Shoots left. 6', 200 lbs.   Born, Vsetin, Czech., April 26, 1976. San Jose's 4th choice, 89th overall, in 1994 Entry Draft.

Season	Club	League	GP	G	A	Pts	PIM	PP	SH	GW	S	%	+/-	TF	F%	H	SB	Min	GP	G	A	Pts	PIM	PP	SH	GW
1992-93	TJ Vitkovice	Czech.	1	0	0	0																				
1993-94	TJ Vitkovice	Cze-Rep	24	6	7	13													5	1	1	2				
1994-95	Tacoma	WHL	68	50	38	88	108											4	4	3	7	11			
1995-96	Kelowna	WHL	59	39	46	85	100											6	3	3	6	16			
	Buffalo	**NHL**	**1**	**0**	**0**	**0**	**0**	0	0	0	2	0.0	0													
	Rochester	AHL	5	3	0	3	4																		
1996-97	**Buffalo**	**NHL**	**5**	**0**	**0**	**0**	**2**	0	0	0	2	0.0	0													
	Rochester	AHL	53	23	25	48	81											10	1	6	7	27			
1997-98	**Buffalo**	**NHL**	**27**	**5**	**6**	**11**	**15**	0	0	1	27	18.5	0						15	3	4	7	18	0	0	0
	Rochester	AHL	45	30	26	56	74																		
1998-99	**Buffalo**	**NHL**	**72**	**7**	**24**	**31**	**61**	1	0	1	123	5.7	11	1	0.0	185	12	14:30	21	5	4	9	14	1	0	0
	NHL Totals		**105**	**12**	**30**	**42**	**78**	1	0	2	154	7.8		1	0.0	185	12	14:30	36	8	8	16	32	1	0	0

Traded to **Buffalo** by **San Jose** with Martin Spahnel and Philadelphia's 1st (previously acquired by San Jose — later traded to Phoenix — Phoenix selected Daniel Briere) and 4th (previously acquired, Buffalo selected Mike Martone) round choices in 1996 Entry Draft for Doug Bodger, November 16, 1995.

VARIS, Petri · (VAH-rihs)

Left wing. Shoots left. 6'1", 200 lbs.   Born, Varkaus, Finland, May 13, 1969. San Jose's 7th choice, 132nd overall, in 1993 Entry Draft.

Season	Club	League	GP	G	A	Pts	PIM	PP	SH	GW	S	%	+/-	TF	F%	H	SB	Min	GP	G	A	Pts	PIM	PP	SH	GW
1987-88	Karhu-Kissat	Finland-2	42	9	15	24	21																			
1988-89	Karhu-Kissat	Finn-Jr.	7	4	5	9	10																			
	Karhu-Kissat	Finland-2	44	18	19	37	26																		
1989-90	Karhu-Kissat	Finland-2	42	30	24	54	44																		
1990-91	KooKoo	Finland-2	44	20	31	51	42																		
1991-92	Assat Pori	Finland	36	13	23	36	24																		
1992-93	Assat Pori	Finland	46	14	35	49	42											8	2	2	4	12			
1993-94	Jokerit	Finland	31	14	15	29	16											11	3	4	7	6			
	Finland	Olympics	5	1	1	2	2																		
1994-95	Haukat	Finland-2	1	0	1	1	2																		
	Jokerit	Finland	47	21	20	41	53											11	7	2	9	10			
1995-96	Jokerit	Finland	50	28	28	56	22											11	12	7	19	6			
1996-97	Jokerit	Finland	50	*36	23	*59	38											9	7	4	11	14			
	Jokerit	EuroHL	6	2	8	10	2																		
1997-98	**Chicago**	**NHL**	**1**	**0**	**0**	**0**	**0**	0	0	0	0	0.0	0													
	Indianapolis	IHL	77	18	54	72	32											5	3	4	7	4			
1998-99	Kolner Haie	Germany	52	10	25	35	22											5	3	0	5	4			
	NHL Totals		**1**	**0**	**0**	**0**	**0**	0	0	0	0	0.0														

Finnish Rookie of the Year (1992)
Rights traded to **Chicago** by **San Jose** with San Jose's 6th round choice (Jari Viuhkola) in 1998 Entry Draft for Murray Craven, July 25, 1997.

VARLAMOV, Sergei

(vahr-LAHM-uhf) **CGY.**

Left wing. Shoots left. 5'11", 190 lbs. Born, Kiev, USSR, July 21, 1978.

Season	Club	League	GP	G	A	Pts	PIM	PP	SH	GW	S	%	+/–	TF	F%	H	SB	Min	GP	G	A	Pts	PIM	PP	SH	GW
			Regular Season																Playoffs							
1995-96	Swift Current	WHL	55	23	21	44	65	....	....	....	....	....	....	....	....	....	....	....	....	....	....	....	....	....	....	....
1996-97	Swift Current	WHL	72	46	39	85	94	....	....	....	....	....	....	....	....	....	....	....	10	3	8	11	10	....	....	....
	Saint John	AHL	1	0	0	0	0	....	....	....	....	....	....	....	....	....	....	....	....	....	....	....	....	....	....	....
1997-98	Swift Current	WHL	72	*66	53	*119	132	....	....	....	....	....	....	....	....	....	....	....	12	10	5	15	28	....	....	....
	Calgary	**NHL**	**1**	**0**	**0**	**0**	**0**	**0**	....	**0**	**0**	**0.0**	**0**	....	....	....	....	....	....	....	....	....	....	....	....	....
	Saint John	AHL	....	....	....	....	....	....	....	....	....	....	....	....	....	....	....	....	3	0	0	0	0	....	....	....
1998-99	Saint John	AHL	76	24	33	57	66	....	....	....	....	....	....	....	....	....	....	....	7	0	4	4	8	....	....	....
	NHL Totals		**1**	**0**	**0**	**0**	**0**	**0**	....	**0**	**0**	**0.0**		....	....	....	....	....	....	....	....	....	....	....	....	....

WHL East First All-Star Team (1998) • Canadian Major Junior First All-Star Team (1998) • Canadian Major Junior Player of the Year (1998)

Signed as a free agent by **Calgary**, September 18, 1996.

VASILEVSKY, Alexander

(vah-sih-LEHV-skee)

Right wing. Shoots left. 5'11", 190 lbs. Born, Kiev, USSR, January 8, 1975. St. Louis' 9th choice, 271st overall, in 1993 Entry Draft.

Season	Club	League	GP	G	A	Pts	PIM	PP	SH	GW	S	%	+/–	TF	F%	H	SB	Min	GP	G	A	Pts	PIM	PP	SH	GW
1992-93	Victoria	WHL	71	27	25	52	52	....	....	....	....	....	....	....	....	....	....	....	....	....	....	....	....	....	....	....
1993-94	Victoria	WHL	69	34	51	85	78	....	....	....	....	....	....	....	....	....	....	....	....	....	....	....	....	....	....	....
1994-95	Prince George	WHL	48	32	34	66	52	....	....	....	....	....	....	....	....	....	....	....	....	....	....	....	....	....	....	....
	Brandon	WHL	23	6	11	17	39	....	....	....	....	....	....	....	....	....	....	....	18	3	6	9	34	....	....	....
1995-96	**St. Louis**	**NHL**	**1**	**0**	**0**	**0**	**0**	**0**	**0**	**0**	**0**	**0.0**	**–1**	....	....	....	....	....	....	....	....	....	....	....	....	....
	Worcester	AHL	69	18	21	39	112	....	....	....	....	....	....	....	....	....	....	....	4	2	1	3	10	....	....	....
1996-97	**St. Louis**	**NHL**	**3**	**0**	**0**	**0**	**2**	**0**	**0**	**0**	**3**	**0.0**	**–1**	....	....	....	....	....	....	....	....	....	....	....	....	....
	Worcester	AHL	61	9	23	32	100	....	....	....	....	....	....	....	....	....	....	....	....	....	....	....	....	....	....	....
	Grand Rapids	IHL	10	1	5	6	43	....	....	....	....	....	....	....	....	....	....	....	5	0	1	1	19	....	....	....
1997-98	Hamilton	AHL	41	3	14	17	60	....	....	....	....	....	....	....	....	....	....	....	....	....	....	....	....	....	....	....
	Detroit	IHL	9	1	1	2	7	....	....	....	....	....	....	....	....	....	....	....	....	....	....	....	....	....	....	....
	NHL Totals		**4**	**0**	**0**	**0**	**2**	**0**	**0**	**0**	**3**	**0.0**		....	....	....	....	....	....	....	....	....	....	....	....	....

VASILJEVS, Herbert

(vah-SEE-lee-ehf) **ATL.**

Center. Shoots right. 5'11", 170 lbs. Born, Riga, USSR, May 27, 1976.

Season	Club	League	GP	G	A	Pts	PIM	PP	SH	GW	S	%	+/–	TF	F%	H	SB	Min	GP	G	A	Pts	PIM	PP	SH	GW
1995-96	Guelph	OHL	65	34	33	67	63	....	....	....	....	....	....	....	....	....	....	....	16	6	13	19	6	....	....	....
1996-97	Carolina	AHL	54	13	18	31	30	....	....	....	....	....	....	....	....	....	....	....	....	....	....	....	....	....	....	....
	Port Huron	ColHL	3	3	2	5	4	....	....	....	....	....	....	....	....	....	....	....	....	....	....	....	....	....	....	....
1997-98	New Haven	AHL	76	36	30	66	60	....	....	....	....	....	....	....	....	....	....	....	3	1	0	1	2	....	....	....
1998-99	**Florida**	**NHL**	**5**	**0**	**0**	**0**	**2**	**0**	**0**	**0**	**6**	**0.0**	**–1**	**3**	**66.7**	**0**	**0**	**11:06**	....	....	....	....	....	....	....	....
	Kentucky	AHL	76	28	48	76	66	....	....	....	....	....	....	....	....	....	....	....	12	2	1	3	4	....	....	....
	NHL Totals		**5**	**0**	**0**	**0**	**2**	**0**	**0**	**0**	**6**	**0.0**		**3**	**66.7**	**0**	**0**	**11:06**	....	....	....	....	....	....	....	....

Signed as a free agent by **Florida**, October 3, 1996. Traded to **Atlanta** by **Florida** with Gord Murphy, Daniel Tjarnqvist and Ottawa's 6th round choice (previously acquired, later traded to Dallas - Dallas selected Justin Cox) in 1999 Entry Draft for Trevor Kidd, June 25, 1999.

VASILYEV, Andrei

(vah-SEE-lee-ehf)

Left wing. Shoots right. 5'9", 180 lbs. Born, Voskresensk, USSR, March 30, 1972. NY Islanders' 11th choice, 248th overall, in 1992 Entry Draft.

Season	Club	League	GP	G	A	Pts	PIM	PP	SH	GW	S	%	+/–	TF	F%	H	SB	Min	GP	G	A	Pts	PIM	PP	SH	GW
1991-92	CSKA Moscow	CIS	28	7	2	9	2	....	....	....	....	....	....	....	....	....	....	....	....	....	....	....	....	....	....	....
1992-93	Khimik	CIS	34	4	8	12	20	....	....	....	....	....	....	....	....	....	....	....	....	....	....	....	....	....	....	....
1993-94	CSKA Moscow	CIS	46	17	6	23	8	....	....	....	....	....	....	....	....	....	....	....	3	1	0	1	0	....	....	....
1994-95	Denver	IHL	74	28	37	65	48	....	....	....	....	....	....	....	....	....	....	....	13	9	4	13	22	....	....	....
	NY Islanders	**NHL**	**2**	**0**	**0**	**0**	**2**	**0**	**0**	**0**	**2**	**0.0**	**0**	....	....	....	....	....	....	....	....	....	....	....	....	....
1995-96	**NY Islanders**	**NHL**	**10**	**2**	**5**	**7**	**2**	**0**	**0**	**1**	**12**	**16.7**	**4**	....	....	....	....	....	....	....	....	....	....	....	....	....
	Utah	IHL	43	26	20	46	34	....	....	....	....	....	....	....	....	....	....	....	22	12	4	16	18	....	....	....
1996-97	**NY Islanders**	**NHL**	**3**	**0**	**0**	**0**	**2**	**0**	**0**	**0**	**1**	**0.0**	**–3**	....	....	....	....	....	....	....	....	....	....	....	....	....
	Utah	IHL	56	16	18	34	42	....	....	....	....	....	....	....	....	....	....	....	7	4	1	5	0	....	....	....
1997-98	Long Beach	IHL	62	33	34	67	60	....	....	....	....	....	....	....	....	....	....	....	17	9	4	13	14	....	....	....
1998-99	**Phoenix**	**NHL**	**1**	**0**	**0**	**0**	**0**	**0**	**0**	**0**	**0**	**0.0**	**–2**	**0**	**0.0**	**0**	**0**	**1:19**	....	....	....	....	....	....	....	....
	Las Vegas	IHL	15	3	6	9	6	....	....	....	....	....	....	....	....	....	....	....	....	....	....	....	....	....	....	....
	Grand Rapids	IHL	59	21	27	48	24	....	....	....	....	....	....	....	....	....	....	....	....	....	....	....	....	....	....	....
	NHL Totals		**16**	**2**	**5**	**7**	**6**	**0**	**0**	**1**	**15**	**13.3**		**0**	**0.0**	**0**	**0**	**1:19**	....	....	....	....	....	....	....	....

Signed as a free agent by **Phoenix**, August 5, 1998.

VASKE, Dennis

(VAS-kee)

Defense. Shoots left. 6'2", 210 lbs. Born, Rockford, IL, October 11, 1967. NY Islanders' 2nd choice, 38th overall, in 1986 Entry Draft.

Season	Club	League	GP	G	A	Pts	PIM	PP	SH	GW	S	%	+/–	TF	F%	H	SB	Min	GP	G	A	Pts	PIM	PP	SH	GW
1984-85	Armstrong High	H.S.	22	5	18	23	....	....	....	....	....	....	....	....	....	....	....	....	....	....	....	....	....	....	....	....
1985-86	Armstrong High	H.S.	20	9	13	22	....	....	....	....	....	....	....	....	....	....	....	....	....	....	....	....	....	....	....	....
1986-87	U. Minn-Duluth	WCHA	33	0	2	2	40	....	....	....	....	....	....	....	....	....	....	....	....	....	....	....	....	....	....	....
1987-88	U. Minn-Duluth	WCHA	39	1	6	7	90	....	....	....	....	....	....	....	....	....	....	....	....	....	....	....	....	....	....	....
1988-89	U. Minn-Duluth	WCHA	37	9	19	28	86	....	....	....	....	....	....	....	....	....	....	....	....	....	....	....	....	....	....	....
1989-90	U. Minn-Duluth	WCHA	37	5	24	29	72	....	....	....	....	....	....	....	....	....	....	....	....	....	....	....	....	....	....	....
1990-91	**NY Islanders**	**NHL**	**5**	**0**	**0**	**0**	**2**	**0**	**0**	**0**	**3**	**0.0**	**4**	....	....	....	....	....	....	....	....	....	....	....	....	....
	Capital District	AHL	67	10	10	20	65	....	....	....	....	....	....	....	....	....	....	....	....	....	....	....	....	....	....	....
1991-92	**NY Islanders**	**NHL**	**39**	**0**	**1**	**1**	**39**	**0**	**0**	**0**	**26**	**0.0**	**5**	....	....	....	....	....	....	....	....	....	....	....	....	....
	Capital District	AHL	31	1	11	12	59	....	....	....	....	....	....	....	....	....	....	....	....	....	....	....	....	....	....	....
1992-93	**NY Islanders**	**NHL**	**27**	**1**	**5**	**6**	**32**	**0**	**0**	**0**	**15**	**6.7**	**9**	....	....	....	....	....	**18**	**0**	**6**	**6**	**14**	**0**	**0**	**0**
	Capital District	AHL	42	4	15	19	70	....	....	....	....	....	....	....	....	....	....	....	....	....	....	....	....	....	....	....
1993-94	**NY Islanders**	**NHL**	**65**	**2**	**11**	**13**	**76**	**0**	**0**	**0**	**71**	**2.8**	**21**	....	....	....	....	....	**4**	**0**	**1**	**1**	**2**	**0**	**0**	**0**
1994-95	**NY Islanders**	**NHL**	**41**	**1**	**11**	**12**	**53**	**0**	**0**	**0**	**48**	**2.1**	**3**	....	....	....	....	....	....	....	....	....	....	....	....	....
1995-96	**NY Islanders**	**NHL**	**19**	**1**	**6**	**7**	**21**	**1**	**0**	**1**	**19**	**5.3**	**–13**	....	....	....	....	....	....	....	....	....	....	....	....	....
1996-97	**NY Islanders**	**NHL**	**17**	**0**	**4**	**4**	**12**	**0**	**0**	**0**	**19**	**0.0**	**3**	....	....	....	....	....	....	....	....	....	....	....	....	....
1997-98	**NY Islanders**	**NHL**	**19**	**0**	**3**	**3**	**12**	**0**	**0**	**0**	**16**	**0.0**	**2**	....	....	....	....	....	....	....	....	....	....	....	....	....
1998-99	**Boston**	**NHL**	**3**	**0**	**0**	**0**	**6**	**0**	**0**	**0**	**0**	**0.0**	**–3**	**0**	**0.0**	**1**	**0**	**8:19**	....	....	....	....	....	....	....	....
	Providence	AHL	43	2	13	15	56	....	....	....	....	....	....	....	....	....	....	....	19	1	5	6	26	....	....	....
	NHL Totals		**235**	**5**	**41**	**46**	**253**	**1**	**0**	**1**	**217**	**2.3**		**0**	**0.0**	**1**	**0**	**8:19**	**22**	**0**	**7**	**7**	**16**	**0**	**0**	**0**

Signed as a free agent by **Boston**, September 10, 1998.

VERBEEK, Pat

(vuhr-BEEK)

Right/Left wing. Shoots right. 5'9", 192 lbs. Born, Sarnia, Ont., May 24, 1964. New Jersey's 3rd choice, 43rd overall, in 1982 Entry Draft.

Season	Club	League	GP	G	A	Pts	PIM	PP	SH	GW	S	%	+/–	TF	F%	H	SB	Min	GP	G	A	Pts	PIM	PP	SH	GW
1979-80	Petrolia	OJHL-B	41	17	24	41	85	....	....	....	....	....	....	....	....	....	....	....	....	....	....	....	....	....	....	....
1980-81	Petrolia Jets	OJHL	42	44	44	88	155	....	....	....	....	....	....	....	....	....	....	....	....	....	....	....	....	....	....	....
1981-82	Sudbury	OHL	66	37	51	88	180	....	....	....	....	....	....	....	....	....	....	....	....	....	....	....	....	....	....	....
1982-83	Sudbury	OHL	61	40	67	107	184	....	....	....	....	....	....	....	....	....	....	....	....	....	....	....	....	....	....	....
	New Jersey	**NHL**	**6**	**3**	**2**	**5**	**8**	**0**	**0**	**0**	**12**	**25.0**	**–2**	....	....	....	....	....	....	....	....	....	....	....	....	....
1983-84	**New Jersey**	**NHL**	**79**	**20**	**27**	**47**	**158**	**5**	**1**	**2**	**167**	**12.0**	**–19**	....	....	....	....	....	....	....	....	....	....	....	....	....
1984-85	**New Jersey**	**NHL**	**78**	**15**	**18**	**33**	**162**	**5**	**1**	**1**	**147**	**10.2**	**–24**	....	....	....	....	....	....	....	....	....	....	....	....	....
1985-86	**New Jersey**	**NHL**	**76**	**25**	**28**	**53**	**79**	**4**	**1**	**0**	**159**	**15.7**	**–24**	....	....	....	....	....	....	....	....	....	....	....	....	....
1986-87	**New Jersey**	**NHL**	**74**	**35**	**24**	**59**	**120**	**17**	**0**	**5**	**143**	**24.5**	**–23**	....	....	....	....	....	....	....	....	....	....	....	....	....
1987-88	**New Jersey**	**NHL**	**73**	**46**	**31**	**77**	**227**	**13**	**0**	**8**	**179**	**25.7**	**29**	....	....	....	....	....	**20**	**4**	**8**	**12**	**51**	**2**	**0**	**1**
1988-89	**New Jersey**	**NHL**	**77**	**26**	**21**	**47**	**189**	**9**	**0**	**1**	**175**	**14.9**	**–18**	....	....	....	....	....	....	....	....	....	....	....	....	....

			Regular Season																Playoffs							
Season	Club	League	GP	G	A	Pts	PIM	PP	SH	GW	S	%	+/-	TF	F%	H	SB	Min	GP	G	A	Pts	PIM	PP	SH	GW
1989-90	**Hartford**	**NHL**	**80**	**44**	**45**	**89**	**228**	**14**	**0**	**5**	**219**	**20.1**	**1**	....	....	....	....	....	**7**	**2**	**2**	**4**	**26**	**1**	**0**	**1**
1990-91	**Hartford**	**NHL**	**80**	**43**	**39**	**82**	**246**	**15**	**0**	**5**	**247**	**17.4**	**0**	....	....	....	....	....	**6**	**3**	**2**	**5**	**40**	**2**	**0**	**0**
1991-92	**Hartford**	**NHL**	**76**	**22**	**35**	**57**	**243**	**10**	**0**	**3**	**163**	**13.5**	**–16**	....	....	....	....	....	**7**	**0**	**2**	**2**	**12**	**0**	**0**	**0**
1992-93	**Hartford**	**NHL**	**84**	**39**	**43**	**82**	**197**	**16**	**0**	**6**	**235**	**16.6**	**–7**	....	....	....	....	....	....	....	....	....	....	....	....	....
1993-94	**Hartford**	**NHL**	**84**	**37**	**38**	**75**	**177**	**15**	**1**	**3**	**226**	**16.4**	**–15**	....	....	....	....	....	....	....	....	....	....	....	....	....
1994-95	**Hartford**	**NHL**	**29**	**7**	**11**	**18**	**53**	**3**	**0**	**0**	**75**	**9.3**	**0**	....	....	....	....	....	....	....	....	....	....	....	....	....
	NY Rangers	**NHL**	**19**	**10**	**5**	**15**	**18**	**4**	**0**	**2**	**56**	**17.9**	**–2**	....	....	....	....	....	**10**	**4**	**6**	**10**	**20**	**3**	**0**	**0**
1995-96	**NY Rangers**	**NHL**	**69**	**41**	**41**	**82**	**129**	**17**	**0**	**6**	**252**	**16.3**	**29**	....	....	....	....	....	**11**	**3**	**6**	**9**	**12**	**1**	**0**	**0**
1996-97	**Dallas**	**NHL**	**81**	**17**	**36**	**53**	**128**	**5**	**0**	**4**	**172**	**9.9**	**3**	....	....	....	....	....	**7**	**1**	**3**	**4**	**16**	**1**	**0**	**0**
1997-98	**Dallas**	**NHL**	**82**	**31**	**26**	**57**	**170**	**9**	**0**	**8**	**190**	**16.3**	**15**	....	....	....	....	....	**17**	**3**	**2**	**5**	**26**	**2**	**0**	**1**
1998-99♦	**Dallas**	**NHL**	**78**	**17**	**17**	**34**	**133**	**8**	**0**	**2**	**134**	**12.7**	**11**	**1**	**100.0**	**130**	**15**	**14:34**	**18**	**3**	**4**	**7**	**14**	**0**	**0**	**1**
	NHL Totals		**1225**	**478**	**487**	**965**	**2665**	**169**	**4**	**61**	**2951**	**16.2**		**1**	**100.0**	**130**	**15**	**14:34**	**103**	**23**	**35**	**58**	**217**	**12**	**0**	**4**

Played in NHL All-Star Game (1991, 1996)

Traded to **Hartford** by **New Jersey** for Sylvain Turgeon, June 17, 1989. Traded to **NY Rangers** by **Hartford** for Glen Featherstone, Michael Stewart, NY Rangers' 1st round choice (Jean-Sebastien Giguere) in 1995 Entry Draft and 4th round choice (Steve Wasylko) in 1996 Entry Draft, March 23, 1995. Signed as a free agent by **Dallas**, August 21, 1996.

VIAL, Dennis

(vee-AL)

Left wing. Shoots left. 6'1", 220 lbs. Born, Sault Ste. Marie, Ont., April 10, 1969. NY Rangers' 5th choice, 110th overall, in 1988 Entry Draft.

Season	Club	League	GP	G	A	Pts	PIM	PP	SH	GW	S	%	+/-	TF	F%	H	SB	Min	GP	G	A	Pts	PIM	PP	SH	GW
1984-85	S.S. Marie	OMHA	31	4	19	23	40	....	....	....	....	....	....	....	....	....	....	....	....	....	....	....	....	....	....	....
1985-86	Hamilton	OHL	31	1	1	2	66	....	....	....	....	....	....	....	....	....	....	....	....	....	....	....	....	....	....	....
1986-87	Hamilton	OHL	53	1	8	9	194	....	....	....	....	....	....	....	....	....	....	....	8	0	0	0	8	....	....	....
1987-88	Hamilton	OHL	52	3	17	20	229	....	....	....	....	....	....	....	....	....	....	....	13	2	2	4	49	....	....	....
1988-89	Niagara Falls	OHL	50	10	27	37	227	....	....	....	....	....	....	....	....	....	....	....	15	1	7	8	44	....	....	....
1989-90	Flint	IHL	79	6	29	35	351	....	....	....	....	....	....	....	....	....	....	....	4	0	0	0	10	....	....	....
1990-91	**NY Rangers**	**NHL**	**21**	**0**	**0**	**0**	**61**	**0**	**0**	**0**	**5**	**0.0**	**–4**	....	....	....	....	....	....	....	....	....	....	....	....	....
	Binghamton	AHL	40	2	7	9	250	....	....	....	....	....	....	....	....	....	....	....	....	....	....	....	....	....	....	....
	Detroit	**NHL**	**9**	**0**	**0**	**0**	**16**	**0**	**0**	**0**	**3**	**0.0**	**–3**	....	....	....	....	....	....	....	....	....	....	....	....	....
1991-92	**Detroit**	**NHL**	**27**	**1**	**0**	**1**	**72**	**0**	**0**	**0**	**6**	**16.7**	**1**	....	....	....	....	....	....	....	....	....	....	....	....	....
	Adirondack	AHL	20	2	4	6	107	....	....	....	....	....	....	....	....	....	....	....	17	1	3	4	43	....	....	....
1992-93	**Detroit**	**NHL**	**9**	**0**	**1**	**1**	**20**	**0**	**0**	**0**	**5**	**0.0**	**1**	....	....	....	....	....	....	....	....	....	....	....	....	....
	Adirondack	AHL	30	2	11	13	177	....	....	....	....	....	....	....	....	....	....	....	11	1	1	2	14	....	....	....
1993-94	**Ottawa**	**NHL**	**55**	**2**	**5**	**7**	**214**	**0**	**0**	**0**	**37**	**5.4**	**–9**	....	....	....	....	....	....	....	....	....	....	....	....	....
1994-95	**Ottawa**	**NHL**	**27**	**0**	**4**	**4**	**65**	**0**	**0**	**0**	**9**	**0.0**	**0**	....	....	....	....	....	....	....	....	....	....	....	....	....
1995-96	**Ottawa**	**NHL**	**64**	**1**	**4**	**5**	**276**	**0**	**0**	**0**	**33**	**3.0**	**–13**	....	....	....	....	....	....	....	....	....	....	....	....	....
1996-97	**Ottawa**	**NHL**	**11**	**0**	**1**	**1**	**25**	**0**	**0**	**0**	**4**	**0.0**	**0**	....	....	....	....	....	....	....	....	....	....	....	....	....
1997-98	**Ottawa**	**NHL**	**19**	**0**	**0**	**0**	**45**	**0**	**0**	**0**	**9**	**0.0**	**0**	....	....	....	....	....	....	....	....	....	....	....	....	....
	Chicago	IHL	24	1	3	4	86	....	....	....	....	....	....	....	....	....	....	....	1	0	0	0	2	....	....	....
1998-99	Chicago	IHL	55	1	4	5	213	....	....	....	....	....	....	....	....	....	....	....	....	....	....	....	....	....	....	....
	NHL Totals		**242**	**4**	**15**	**19**	**794**	**0**	**0**	**0**	**111**	**3.6**		....	....	....	....	....	....	....	....	....	....	....	....	....

Traded to **Detroit** by **NY Rangers** with Kevin Miller and Jim Cummins for Joey Kocur and Per Djoos, March 5, 1991. Traded to **Quebec** by **Detroit** with Doug Crossman for cash, June 15, 1992. Traded to **Detroit** by **Quebec** for cash, September 9, 1992. Traded to **Tampa Bay** by **Detroit** for Steve Maltais, June 8, 1993. Claimed by **Anaheim** from **Tampa Bay** in Expansion Draft, June 24, 1993. Claimed by **Ottawa** from **Anaheim** in Phase II of Expansion Draft, June 25, 1993.

VIRTUE, Terry

NYR

Defense. Shoots right. 6', 200 lbs. Born, Scarborough, Ont., August 12, 1970.

Season	Club	League	GP	G	A	Pts	PIM	PP	SH	GW	S	%	+/-	TF	F%	H	SB	Min	GP	G	A	Pts	PIM	PP	SH	GW
1988-89	Victoria	WHL	8	1	1	2	13	....	....	....	....	....	....	....	....	....	....	....	....	....	....	....	....	....	....	....
1989-90	Victoria	WHL	24	1	9	10	85	....	....	....	....	....	....	....	....	....	....	....	....	....	....	....	....	....	....	....
	Tri-City	WHL	34	1	10	11	82	....	....	....	....	....	....	....	....	....	....	....	6	0	0	0	30	....	....	....
1990-91	Tri-City	WHL	11	1	8	9	24	....	....	....	....	....	....	....	....	....	....	....	....	....	....	....	....	....	....	....
	Portland	WHL	59	9	44	53	127	....	....	....	....	....	....	....	....	....	....	....	....	....	....	....	....	....	....	....
1991-92	Roanoke	ECHL	38	4	22	26	165	....	....	....	....	....	....	....	....	....	....	....	....	....	....	....	....	....	....	....
	Louisville	ECHL	23	1	15	16	58	....	....	....	....	....	....	....	....	....	....	....	13	0	8	8	49	....	....	....
1992-93	Louisville	ECHL	28	0	17	17	84	....	....	....	....	....	....	....	....	....	....	....	....	....	....	....	....	....	....	....
	Wheeling	ECHL	31	3	15	18	86	....	....	....	....	....	....	....	....	....	....	....	16	3	5	8	18	....	....	....
1993-94	Wheeling	ECHL	34	5	28	33	61	....	....	....	....	....	....	....	....	....	....	....	6	2	2	4	4	....	....	....
	Cape Breton	AHL	26	4	6	10	10	....	....	....	....	....	....	....	....	....	....	....	5	0	0	0	17	....	....	....
1994-95	Worcester	AHL	73	14	25	39	183	....	....	....	....	....	....	....	....	....	....	....	....	....	....	....	....	....	....	....
	Atlanta	IHL	1	0	0	0	7	....	....	....	....	....	....	....	....	....	....	....	....	....	....	....	....	....	....	....
1995-96	Worcester	AHL	76	7	31	38	234	....	....	....	....	....	....	....	....	....	....	....	4	0	0	0	4	....	....	....
1996-97	Worcester	AHL	80	16	26	42	220	....	....	....	....	....	....	....	....	....	....	....	5	0	4	4	8	....	....	....
1997-98	Worcester	AHL	74	8	26	34	233	....	....	....	....	....	....	....	....	....	....	....	11	1	4	5	41	....	....	....
1998-99	**Boston**	**NHL**	**4**	**0**	**0**	**0**	**0**	**0**	....	**0**	**2**	**0.0**	**2**	**0**	**0.0**	**4**	**2**	**9:41**	....	....	....	....	....	....	....	....
	Providence	AHL	76	8	48	56	117	....	....	....	....	....	....	....	....	....	....	....	17	2	12	14	29	....	....	....
	NHL Totals		**4**	**0**	**0**	**0**	**0**	**0**	....	**0**	**2**	**0.0**		**0**	**0.0**	**4**	**2**	**9:41**	....	....	....	....	....	....	....	....

AHL Second All-Star Team (1999)

Signed as a free agent by **St. Louis**, January 29, 1996. Signed as a free agent by **Boston**, August 28, 1998. Signed as a free agent by **NY Rangers**, July 29, 1999.

VISHEAU, Mark

(VEE-SHOO)

Defense. Shoots right. 6'6", 222 lbs. Born, Burlington, Ont., June 27, 1973. Winnipeg's 4th choice, 84th overall, in 1992 Entry Draft.

Season	Club	League	GP	G	A	Pts	PIM	PP	SH	GW	S	%	+/-	TF	F%	H	SB	Min	GP	G	A	Pts	PIM	PP	SH	GW
1989-90	Burlington	OJHL	42	11	22	33	53	....	....	....	....	....	....	....	....	....	....	....	....	....	....	....	....	....	....	....
1990-91	London	OHL	59	4	11	15	40	....	....	....	....	....	....	....	....	....	....	....	7	0	1	1	6	....	....	....
1991-92	London	OHL	66	5	31	36	104	....	....	....	....	....	....	....	....	....	....	....	10	0	4	4	27	....	....	....
1992-93	London	OHL	62	8	52	60	88	....	....	....	....	....	....	....	....	....	....	....	12	0	5	5	26	....	....	....
1993-94	**Winnipeg**	**NHL**	**1**	**0**	**0**	**0**	**0**	**0**	**0**	**0**	**1**	**0.0**	**0**	....	....	....	....	....	....	....	....	....	....	....	....	....
	Moncton	AHL	48	4	5	9	58	....	....	....	....	....	....	....	....	....	....	....	....	....	....	....	....	....	....	....
1994-95	Springfield	AHL	35	0	4	4	94	....	....	....	....	....	....	....	....	....	....	....	....	....	....	....	....	....	....	....
1995-96	Cape Breton	AHL	8	0	0	0	30	....	....	....	....	....	....	....	....	....	....	....	....	....	....	....	....	....	....	....
	Minnesota	IHL	10	0	0	0	25	....	....	....	....	....	....	....	....	....	....	....	....	....	....	....	....	....	....	....
	Wheeling	ECHL	7	1	2	3	14	....	....	....	....	....	....	....	....	....	....	....	7	0	3	3	4	....	....	....
1996-97	Raleigh	ECHL	15	1	5	6	61	....	....	....	....	....	....	....	....	....	....	....	....	....	....	....	....	....	....	....
	Quebec	IHL	64	3	10	13	173	....	....	....	....	....	....	....	....	....	....	....	9	1	1	2	11	....	....	....
1997-98	Milwaukee	IHL	72	4	12	16	227	....	....	....	....	....	....	....	....	....	....	....	....	....	....	....	....	....	....	....
1998-99	**Los Angeles**	**NHL**	**28**	**1**	**3**	**4**	**107**	**0**	**0**	**0**	**10**	**10.0**	**–7**	**0**	**0.0**	**20**	**16**	**9:33**	....	....	....	....	....	....	....	....
	NHL Totals		**29**	**1**	**3**	**4**	**107**	**0**	**0**	**0**	**11**	**9.1**		**0**	**0.0**	**20**	**16**	**9:33**	....	....	....	....	....	....	....	....

Signed as a free agent by **LA Kings**, July 30, 1997.

VON STEFENELLI, Phil

T.B.

Defense. Shoots left. 6'1", 200 lbs. Born, Vancouver, B.C., April 10, 1969. Vancouver's 5th choice, 122nd overall, in 1988 Entry Draft.

Season	Club	League	GP	G	A	Pts	PIM	PP	SH	GW	S	%	+/-	TF	F%	H	SB	Min	GP	G	A	Pts	PIM	PP	SH	GW
1985-86	Richmond	BCJHL	41	6	11	17	28	....	....	....	....	....	....	....	....	....	....	....	....	....	....	....	....	....	....	....
1986-87	Richmond	BCJHL	35	5	19	24	39	....	....	....	....	....	....	....	....	....	....	....	....	....	....	....	....	....	....	....
	Langley	BCJHL	17	0	13	13	12	....	....	....	....	....	....	....	....	....	....	....	....	....	....	....	....	....	....	....
1987-88	Boston University	H.E.	34	3	13	16	38	....	....	....	....	....	....	....	....	....	....	....	....	....	....	....	....	....	....	....
1988-89	Boston University	H.E.	33	2	6	8	34	....	....	....	....	....	....	....	....	....	....	....	....	....	....	....	....	....	....	....
1989-90	Boston University	H.E.	44	8	20	28	40	....	....	....	....	....	....	....	....	....	....	....	....	....	....	....	....	....	....	....
1990-91	Boston University	H.E.	41	7	23	30	32	....	....	....	....	....	....	....	....	....	....	....	....	....	....	....	....	....	....	....
1991-92	Milwaukee	IHL	80	2	34	36	40	....	....	....	....	....	....	....	....	....	....	....	5	1	2	3	2	....	....	....
1992-93	Hamilton	AHL	78	11	20	31	75	....	....	....	....	....	....	....	....	....	....	....	....	....	....	....	....	....	....	....
1993-94	Hamilton	AHL	80	10	31	41	89	....	....	....	....	....	....	....	....	....	....	....	4	1	0	1	2	....	....	....

Season	Club	League		GP	G	A	Pts	PIM	PP	SH	GW	S	%	+/-	TF	F%	H	SB	Min	GP	G	A	Pts	PIM	PP	SH	GW
			Regular Season																	**Playoffs**							
1994-95	Providence	AHL		75	6	13	19	93	....	....	....	....	....	....						13	2	4	6	6	....	....	....
1995-96	**Boston**	**NHL**		37	0	4	4	16	0	0	0	20	0.0	2	....	....	....	....	....	....	....	....	....	....	....	....	....
	Providence	AHL		42	9	21	30	52																			
1996-97	**Ottawa**	**NHL**		6	0	1	1	7	0	0	0	2	0.0	-3													
	Detroit	IHL		67	14	26	40	86												21	2	4	6	20			
1997-98	EHC Chur	Switz-2		40	10	26	36	75												9	1	3	4	30			
1998-99	Frankfurt	Germany		51	4	12	16	75												8	0	0	0	6			
	Frankfurt	EuroHL		6	2	1	3	32																			
NHL Totals				**43**	**0**	**5**	**5**	**23**	**0**	**0**	**0**	**22**	**0.0**														

Signed as a free agent by **Boston**, September 10, 1994. Signed as a free agent by **Ottawa**, July 17, 1996. Signed as a free agent by **Tampa Bay**, July 22, 1999.

VOPAT, Jan (VOH-paht) NSH.

Defense. Shoots left. 6', 205 lbs.   Born, Most, Czech., March 22, 1973. Hartford's 3rd choice, 57th overall, in 1992 Entry Draft.

Season	Club	League	GP	G	A	Pts	PIM	PP	SH	GW	S	%	+/-	TF	F%	H	SB	Min	GP	G	A	Pts	PIM	PP	SH	GW
1990-91	CHZ Litvinov	Czech.	25	1	4	5	4																			
1991-92	CHZ Litvinov	Czech.	46	4	2	6	16																			
1992-93	CHZ Litvinov	Czech.	45	12	10	22																				
1993-94	CHZ Litvinov	Cze-Rep	41	9	19	28	0												4	1	1	2				
	Czech Republic	Olympics	8	0	1	1	8																			
1994-95	CHZ Litvinov	Cze-Rep	42	7	18	25	49												4	0	2	2	2			
1995-96	**Los Angeles**	**NHL**	11	1	4	5	4	0	0	0	13	7.7	3													
	Phoenix	IHL	47	0	9	9	34												4	0	2	2	4			
1996-97	**Los Angeles**	**NHL**	33	4	5	9	22	0	0	1	44	9.1	3													
	Phoenix	IHL	4	0	6	6	6																			
1997-98	**Los Angeles**	**NHL**	21	1	5	6	10	0	0	1	13	7.7	8						2	0	1	1	2	0	0	0
	Utah	IHL	38	8	13	21	24																			
1998-99	**Nashville**	**NHL**	55	5	6	11	28	0	0	0	46	10.9	0	0	0.0	98	70	18:05								
NHL Totals			**120**	**11**	**20**	**31**	**64**	**0**	**0**	**2**	**116**	**9.5**		**0**	**0.0**	**98**	**70**	**18:05**	**2**	**0**	**1**	**1**	**2**	**0**	**0**	**0**

Rights traded to **LA Kings** by **Hartford** for LA Kings' 4th round choice (Ian MacNeil) in 1995 Entry Draft, May 31, 1995. Traded to **Nashville** by **LA Kings** with Kimmo Timonen for future considerations, June 26, 1998.

VOPAT, Roman (VOH-paht) PHI.

Center. Shoots left. 6'3", 223 lbs.   Born, Litvinov, Czech., April 21, 1976. St. Louis' 4th choice, 172nd overall, in 1994 Entry Draft.

Season	Club	League	GP	G	A	Pts	PIM	PP	SH	GW	S	%	+/-	TF	F%	H	SB	Min	GP	G	A	Pts	PIM	PP	SH	GW
1993-94	CHZ Litvinov	Cze-Rep	7	0	0	0	0																			
1994-95	Moose Jaw	WHL	72	23	20	43	141												10	4	1	5	28			
	Peoria	IHL																	6	0	2	2	2			
1995-96	Moose Jaw	WHL	7	0	4	4	34																			
	Prince Albert	WHL	22	15	5	20	81												18	9	8	17	57			
	St. Louis	**NHL**	25	2	3	5	48	1	0	1	33	6.1	-8													
	Worcester	AHL	5	2	0	2	14																			
1996-97	**Los Angeles**	**NHL**	29	4	5	9	60	1	0	2	54	7.4	-7													
	Phoenix	IHL	50	8	8	16	139																			
1997-98	**Los Angeles**	**NHL**	25	0	3	3	55	0	0	0	36	0.0	-7													
	Fredericton	AHL	29	10	10	20	93																			
1998-99	**Los Angeles**	**NHL**	3	0	0	0	6	0	0	0	2	0.0	0	10	50.0	3	0	4:13								
	Chicago	**NHL**	3	0	0	0	4	0	0	0	0	0.0	-4	14	35.7	4	0	6:35								
	Philadelphia	**NHL**	48	0	3	3	80	0	0	0	26	0.0	-3	26	53.8	41	6	5:36								
NHL Totals			**133**	**6**	**14**	**20**	**253**	**2**	**0**	**3**	**150**	**4.0**		**50**	**48.0**	**48**	**6**	**5:35**								

Traded to **LA Kings** by **St. Louis** with Craig Johnson, Patrice Tardif, St. Louis 5th round choice (Peter Hogan) in 1996 Entry Draft and 1st round choice (Matt Zultek) in 1997 Entry Draft for Wayne Gretzky, February 27, 1996. Traded to **Colorado** by **Los Angeles** with Los Angeles' 6th round choice (later traded to Chicago, later traded to Ottawa, Ottawa selected Martin Brusek) in 1999 Entry Draft for Eric Lacroix, October 29, 1998. Traded to **Chicago** by **Colorado** with Los Angeles' 6th round choice (previously acquired, later traded to Ottawa, Ottawa selected Martin Brusek) in 1999 Entry Draft for Cam Russell, November 10, 1998. Traded to **Philadelphia** by **Chicago** for Mike Maneluk, November 17, 1998.

VOROBIEV, Vladimir (vah-roh-BEE-ehf)

Left wing. Shoots right. 6', 185 lbs.   Born, Cherepovets, USSR, October 2, 1972. NY Rangers' 10th choice, 240th overall, in 1992 Entry Draft.

Season	Club	League	GP	G	A	Pts	PIM	PP	SH	GW	S	%	+/-	TF	F%	H	SB	Min	GP	G	A	Pts	PIM	PP	SH	GW
1992-93	Cherepovets	CIS	42	18	5	23	18																			
1993-94	Moscow D'amo	CIS	11	3	1	4	2																			
1994-95	Moscow D'amo	CIS	48	9	20	29	28												14	1	7	8	2			
1995-96	Moscow D'amo	CIS	42	19	9	28	49												9	2	8	10	2			
1996-97	**NY Rangers**	**NHL**	16	5	5	10	6	2	0	0	42	11.9	4						4	1	1	2	2			
	Binghamton	AHL	61	22	27	49	6																			
1997-98	**NY Rangers**	**NHL**	15	2	2	4	6	0	0	1	27	7.4	-10													
	Hartford	AHL	56	20	28	48	18												15	11	8	19	4			
1998-99	Hartford	AHL	65	24	41	65	22																			
	Edmonton	**NHL**	2	2	0	2	2	0	0	0	5	40.0	1	0	0.0	0	1	11:35	1	0	0	0	0	0	0	0
	Hamilton	AHL	8	3	6	9	2												6	0	1	1	2			
NHL Totals			**33**	**9**	**7**	**16**	**14**	**2**	**0**	**1**	**74**	**12.2**		**0**	**0.0**	**0**	**1**	**11:35**	**1**	**0**	**0**	**0**	**0**	**0**	**0**	**0**

Traded to **Edmonton** by **NY Rangers** for Kevin Brown, March 23, 1999.

VUJTEK, Vladimir (VYOO-tehk) ATL.

Left wing. Shoots left. 6'1", 190 lbs.   Born, Ostrava, Czech., February 17, 1972. Montreal's 5th choice, 73rd overall, in 1991 Entry Draft.

Season	Club	League	GP	G	A	Pts	PIM	PP	SH	GW	S	%	+/-	TF	F%	H	SB	Min	GP	G	A	Pts	PIM	PP	SH	GW
1988-89	HC Vitkovice	Czech.	3	0	1	1	0																			
1989-90	HC Vitkovice	Czech.	22	3	4	7													7	4	3	7				
1990-91	HC Vitkovice	Czech.	26	7	4	11	....																			
	Tri-City	WHL	37	26	18	44	25												7	2	3	5	4			
1991-92	Tri-City	WHL	53	41	61	102	114																			
	Montreal	**NHL**	2	0	0	0	0	0	0	0	1	0.0	-1													
1992-93	**Edmonton**	**NHL**	30	1	10	11	8	0	0	0	49	2.0	-1													
	Cape Breton	AHL	20	10	9	19	14												1	0	0	0	0			
1993-94	**Edmonton**	**NHL**	40	4	15	19	14	1	0	0	66	6.1	-7													
1994-95	HC Vitkovice	Cze-Rep	18	5	7	12	51																			
	Cape Breton	AHL	30	10	11	21	30																			
	Las Vegas	IHL	1	0	0	0	0																			
1995-96	HC Vitkovice	Cze-Rep	26	6	7	13													4	1	1	2				
1996-97	Assat Pori	Finland	50	27	31	58	48												4	1	2	3	2			
1997-98	**Tampa Bay**	**NHL**	30	2	4	6	16	0	0	0	44	4.5	-2													
	Adirondack	AHL	2	1	2	3	0																			
1998-99	HC Vitkovice	Cze-Rep	47	20	35	55	75																			
NHL Totals			**102**	**7**	**29**	**36**	**38**	**1**	**0**	**1**	**160**	**4.4**														

WHL West First All-Star Team (1992)

Traded to **Edmonton** by **Montreal** with Shayne Corson and Brent Gilchrist for Vincent Damphousse and Edmonton's 4th round choice (Adam Wiesel) in 1993 Entry Draft, August 27, 1992. Traded to **Tampa Bay** by **Edmonton** with Edmonton's 3rd round choice (Dmitri Afanasenkov) in 1998 Entry Draft for Brantt Myhres and Toronto's 3rd round choice (previously acquired, Edmonton selected Alex Henry) in 1998 Entry Draft, July 16, 1997. Signed as a free agent by **Atlanta**, July 29, 1999.

VUKOTA, Mick

(vuh-KOH-tuh)

Right wing. Shoots right. 6'1", 225 lbs. Born, Saskatoon, Sask., September 14, 1966.

			Regular Season																Playoffs							
Season	Club	League	GP	G	A	Pts	PIM	PP	SH	GW	S	%	+/-	TF	F%	H	SB	Min	GP	G	A	Pts	PIM	PP	SH	GW
1983-84	Winnipeg	WHL	3	1	1	2	10	....	....	....	....	....	....	....	....	....	....	....	....	....	....	....	....	....	....	....
1984-85	Kelowna	WHL	66	10	6	16	247	....	....	....	....	....	....	....	....	....	....	....	....	....	....	....	....	....	....	....
1985-86	Spokane	WHL	64	19	14	33	369	....	....	....	....	....	....	....	....	....	....	....	9	6	4	10	68	....	....	....
1986-87	Spokane	WHL	61	25	28	53	*337	....	....	....	....	....	....	....	....	....	....	....	4	0	0	0	40	....	....	....
1987-88	**NY Islanders**	**NHL**	**17**	**1**	**0**	**1**	**82**	**0**	**0**	**0**	**7**	**14.3**	**1**	....	....	....	....	....	**2**	**0**	**0**	**0**	**23**	**0**	**0**	**0**
	Springfield	AHL	52	7	9	16	375	....	....	....	....	....	....	....	....	....	....	....	....	....	....	....	....	....	....	....
1988-89	**NY Islanders**	**NHL**	**48**	**2**	**2**	**4**	**237**	**0**	**0**	**0**	**19**	**10.5**	**–17**	....	....	....	....	....	....	....	....	....	....	....	....	....
	Springfield	AHL	3	1	0	1	33	....	....	....	....	....	....	....	....	....	....	....	....	....	....	....	....	....	....	....
1989-90	**NY Islanders**	**NHL**	**76**	**4**	**8**	**12**	**290**	**0**	**0**	**0**	**55**	**7.3**	**10**	....	....	....	....	....	**1**	**0**	**0**	**0**	**17**	**0**	**0**	**0**
1990-91	**NY Islanders**	**NHL**	**60**	**2**	**4**	**6**	**238**	**0**	**0**	**0**	**39**	**5.1**	**–13**	....	....	....	....	....	....	....	....	....	....	....	....	....
	Capital District	AHL	2	0	0	0	9	....	....	....	....	....	....	....	....	....	....	....	....	....	....	....	....	....	....	....
1991-92	**NY Islanders**	**NHL**	**74**	**0**	**6**	**6**	**293**	**0**	**0**	**0**	**34**	**0.0**	**–6**	....	....	....	....	....	....	....	....	....	....	....	....	....
1992-93	**NY Islanders**	**NHL**	**74**	**2**	**5**	**7**	**216**	**0**	**0**	**0**	**37**	**5.4**	**3**	....	....	....	....	....	**15**	**0**	**0**	**0**	**16**	**0**	**0**	**0**
1993-94	**NY Islanders**	**NHL**	**72**	**3**	**1**	**4**	**237**	**0**	**0**	**0**	**26**	**11.5**	**–5**	....	....	....	....	....	**4**	**0**	**0**	**0**	**17**	**0**	**0**	**0**
1994-95	**NY Islanders**	**NHL**	**40**	**0**	**2**	**2**	**109**	**0**	**0**	**0**	**11**	**0.0**	**1**	....	....	....	....	....	....	....	....	....	....	....	....	....
1995-96	**NY Islanders**	**NHL**	**32**	**1**	**1**	**2**	**106**	**0**	**0**	**0**	**11**	**9.1**	**–3**	....	....	....	....	....	....	....	....	....	....	....	....	....
1996-97	**NY Islanders**	**NHL**	**17**	**1**	**0**	**1**	**71**	**0**	**0**	**0**	**7**	**14.3**	**–2**	....	....	....	....	....	....	....	....	....	....	....	....	....
	Utah	IHL	43	11	11	22	185	....	....	....	....	....	....	....	....	....	....	....	7	1	2	3	20	....	....	....
1997-98	**Tampa Bay**	**NHL**	**42**	**1**	**0**	**1**	**116**	**0**	**0**	**0**	**15**	**6.7**	**0**	....	....	....	....	....	....	....	....	....	....	....	....	....
	Montreal	**NHL**	**22**	**0**	**0**	**0**	**76**	**0**	**0**	**0**	**8**	**0.0**	**–4**	....	....	....	....	....	**1**	**0**	**0**	**0**	**0**	**0**	**0**	**0**
1998-99	Utah	IHL	48	8	7	15	226	....	....	....	....	....	....	....	....	....	....	....	....	....	....	....	....	....	....	....
	NHL Totals		**574**	**17**	**29**	**46**	**2071**	**0**	**0**	**0**	**269**	**6.3**		....	....	....	....	....	**23**	**0**	**0**	**0**	**73**	**0**	**0**	**0**

Signed as a free agent by **NY Islanders**, March 2, 1987. Claimed by **Tampa Bay** from **NY Islanders** in NHL Waiver Draft, September 28, 1997. Traded to **Montreal** by **Tampa Bay** with Patrick Poulin and Igor Ulanov for Stephane Richer, Darcy Tucker and David Wilkie, January 15, 1998.

WALKER, Scott

(WAH-kuhr) **NSH.**

Center. Shoots right. 5'10", 189 lbs. Born, Montreal, Que., July 19, 1973. Vancouver's 4th choice, 124th overall, in 1993 Entry Draft.

Season	Club	League	GP	G	A	Pts	PIM	PP	SH	GW	S	%	+/-	TF	F%	H	SB	Min	GP	G	A	Pts	PIM	PP	SH	GW
1989-90	Cambridge	OJHL-B	33	7	23	30	91	....	....	....	....	....	....	....	....	....	....	....	....	....	....	....	....	....	....	....
1990-91	Cambridge	OJHL-B	45	10	27	37	241	....	....	....	....	....	....	....	....	....	....	....	....	....	....	....	....	....	....	....
1991-92	Owen Sound	OHL	53	7	31	38	128	....	....	....	....	....	....	....	....	....	....	....	5	0	7	7	8	....	....	....
1992-93	Owen Sound	OHL	57	23	68	91	110	....	....	....	....	....	....	....	....	....	....	....	8	1	5	6	16	....	....	....
	Canada	Nat-Team	2	3	0	3	0	....	....	....	....	....	....	....	....	....	....	....	....	....	....	....	....	....	....	....
1993-94	Hamilton	AHL	77	10	29	39	272	....	....	....	....	....	....	....	....	....	....	....	4	0	1	1	25	....	....	....
1994-95	Syracuse	AHL	74	14	38	52	334	....	....	....	....	....	....	....	....	....	....	....	....	....	....	....	....	....	....	....
	Vancouver	**NHL**	**11**	**0**	**1**	**1**	**33**	**0**	**0**	**0**	**8**	**0.0**	**0**	....	....	....	....	....	....	....	....	....	....	....	....	....
1995-96	**Vancouver**	**NHL**	**63**	**4**	**8**	**12**	**137**	**0**	**1**	**1**	**45**	**8.9**	**–7**	....	....	....	....	....	....	....	....	....	....	....	....	....
	Syracuse	AHL	15	3	12	15	52	....	....	....	....	....	....	....	....	....	....	....	16	9	8	17	39	....	....	....
1996-97	**Vancouver**	**NHL**	**64**	**3**	**15**	**18**	**132**	**0**	**0**	**0**	**55**	**5.5**	**2**	....	....	....	....	....	....	....	....	....	....	....	....	....
1997-98	**Vancouver**	**NHL**	**59**	**3**	**10**	**13**	**164**	**0**	**1**	**1**	**40**	**7.5**	**–8**	....	....	....	....	....	....	....	....	....	....	....	....	....
1998-99	**Nashville**	**NHL**	**71**	**15**	**25**	**40**	**103**	**0**	**1**	**2**	**96**	**15.6**	**0**	**265**	**48.3**	**82**	**41**	**16:21**	....	....	....	....	....	....	....	....
	NHL Totals		**268**	**25**	**59**	**84**	**569**	**0**	**3**	**4**	**244**	**10.2**		**265**	**48.3**	**82**	**41**	**16:21**	....	....	....	....	....	....	....	....

OHL Second All-Star Team (1993)

Claimed by **Nashville** from **Vancouver** in Expansion Draft, June 26, 1998.

WARD, Aaron

DET.

Defense. Shoots right. 6'2", 200 lbs. Born, Windsor, Ont., January 17, 1973. Winnipeg's 1st choice, 5th overall, in 1991 Entry Draft.

Season	Club	League	GP	G	A	Pts	PIM	PP	SH	GW	S	%	+/-	TF	F%	H	SB	Min	GP	G	A	Pts	PIM	PP	SH	GW
1988-89	Nepean	OJHL	56	2	17	19	11	....	....	....	....	....	....	....	....	....	....	....	....	....	....	....	....	....	....	....
1989-90	Nepean	OJHL	52	6	33	39	85	....	....	....	....	....	....	....	....	....	....	....	....	....	....	....	....	....	....	....
1990-91	U. of Michigan	CCHA	46	8	11	19	126	....	....	....	....	....	....	....	....	....	....	....	....	....	....	....	....	....	....	....
1991-92	U. of Michigan	CCHA	42	7	12	19	64	....	....	....	....	....	....	....	....	....	....	....	....	....	....	....	....	....	....	....
1992-93	U. of Michigan	CCHA	30	5	8	13	73	....	....	....	....	....	....	....	....	....	....	....	....	....	....	....	....	....	....	....
	Canada	Nat-Team	4	0	0	0	8	....	....	....	....	....	....	....	....	....	....	....	....	....	....	....	....	....	....	....
1993-94	**Detroit**	**NHL**	**5**	**1**	**0**	**1**	**4**	**0**	**0**	**0**	**3**	**33.3**	**2**	....	....	....	....	....	....	....	....	....	....	....	....	....
	Adirondack	AHL	58	4	12	16	87	....	....	....	....	....	....	....	....	....	....	....	9	2	6	8	6	....	....	....
1994-95	Adirondack	AHL	76	11	24	35	87	....	....	....	....	....	....	....	....	....	....	....	4	0	1	1	0	....	....	....
	Detroit	**NHL**	**1**	**0**	**1**	**1**	**2**	**0**	**0**	**0**	**0**	**0.0**	**1**	....	....	....	....	....	....	....	....	....	....	....	....	....
1995-96	Adirondack	AHL	74	5	10	15	133	....	....	....	....	....	....	....	....	....	....	....	3	0	0	0	6	....	....	....
1996-97♦	**Detroit**	**NHL**	**49**	**2**	**5**	**7**	**52**	**0**	**0**	**0**	**40**	**5.0**	**–9**	....	....	....	....	....	**19**	**0**	**0**	**0**	**17**	**0**	**0**	**0**
1997-98♦	**Detroit**	**NHL**	**52**	**5**	**5**	**10**	**47**	**0**	**0**	**1**	**47**	**10.6**	**–1**	....	....	....	....	....	....	....	....	....	....	....	....	....
1998-99	**Detroit**	**NHL**	**60**	**3**	**8**	**11**	**52**	**0**	**0**	**0**	**46**	**6.5**	**–5**	**0**	**0.0**	**133**	**37**	**13:55**	**8**	**0**	**1**	**1**	**8**	**0**	**0**	**0**
	NHL Totals		**167**	**11**	**19**	**30**	**157**	**0**	**0**	**1**	**136**	**8.1**		**0**	**0.0**	**133**	**37**	**13:55**	**27**	**0**	**1**	**1**	**25**	**0**	**0**	**0**

Traded to **Detroit** by **Winnipeg** with Toronto's 4th round choice (previously acquired by Winnipeg — later traded to Detroit — Detroit selected John Jakopin) in 1993 Entry Draft for Paul Ysebaert and future considerations (Alan Kerr, June 18, 1993), June 11, 1993.

WARD, Dixon

BUF.

Right wing. Shoots right. 6', 200 lbs. Born, Leduc, Alta., September 23, 1968. Vancouver's 6th choice, 128th overall, in 1988 Entry Draft.

Season	Club	League	GP	G	A	Pts	PIM	PP	SH	GW	S	%	+/-	TF	F%	H	SB	Min	GP	G	A	Pts	PIM	PP	SH	GW
1986-87	Red Deer	AJHL	59	46	40	86	153	....	....	....	....	....	....	....	....	....	....	....	....	....	....	....	....	....	....	....
1987-88	Red Deer	AJHL	51	60	71	131	167	....	....	....	....	....	....	....	....	....	....	....	....	....	....	....	....	....	....	....
1988-89	North Dakota	WCHA	37	8	9	17	26	....	....	....	....	....	....	....	....	....	....	....	....	....	....	....	....	....	....	....
1989-90	North Dakota	WCHA	45	35	34	69	44	....	....	....	....	....	....	....	....	....	....	....	....	....	....	....	....	....	....	....
1990-91	North Dakota	WCHA	43	34	35	69	84	....	....	....	....	....	....	....	....	....	....	....	....	....	....	....	....	....	....	....
1991-92	North Dakota	WCHA	38	33	31	64	90	....	....	....	....	....	....	....	....	....	....	....	....	....	....	....	....	....	....	....
1992-93	**Vancouver**	**NHL**	**70**	**22**	**30**	**52**	**82**	**4**	**1**	**0**	**111**	**19.8**	**34**	....	....	....	....	....	**9**	**2**	**3**	**5**	**0**	**2**	**0**	**0**
1993-94	**Vancouver**	**NHL**	**33**	**6**	**1**	**7**	**37**	**2**	**0**	**1**	**46**	**13.0**	**–14**	....	....	....	....	....	....	....	....	....	....	....	....	....
	Los Angeles	**NHL**	**34**	**6**	**2**	**8**	**45**	**2**	**0**	**0**	**44**	**13.6**	**–8**	....	....	....	....	....	....	....	....	....	....	....	....	....
1994-95	**Toronto**	**NHL**	**22**	**0**	**3**	**3**	**31**	**0**	**0**	**0**	**15**	**0.0**	**–4**	....	....	....	....	....	....	....	....	....	....	....	....	....
	St. John's	AHL	6	3	3	6	19	....	....	....	....	....	....	....	....	....	....	....	....	....	....	....	....	....	....	....
	Detroit	IHL	7	3	6	9	7	....	....	....	....	....	....	....	....	....	....	....	5	3	0	3	7	....	....	....
1995-96	**Buffalo**	**NHL**	**8**	**2**	**2**	**4**	**6**	**0**	**0**	**1**	**12**	**16.7**	**1**	....	....	....	....	....	....	....	....	....	....	....	....	....
	Rochester	AHL	71	38	56	94	74	....	....	....	....	....	....	....	....	....	....	....	19	11	*24	*35	8	....	....	....
1996-97	**Buffalo**	**NHL**	**79**	**13**	**32**	**45**	**36**	**1**	**2**	**4**	**93**	**14.0**	**17**	....	....	....	....	....	**12**	**2**	**3**	**5**	**6**	**0**	**0**	**0**
1997-98	**Buffalo**	**NHL**	**71**	**10**	**13**	**23**	**42**	**0**	**2**	**3**	**99**	**10.1**	**9**	....	....	....	....	....	**15**	**3**	**8**	**11**	**6**	**0**	**0**	**0**
1998-99	**Buffalo**	**NHL**	**78**	**20**	**24**	**44**	**44**	**2**	**1**	**4**	**101**	**19.8**	**10**	**11**	**54.5**	**45**	**49**	**15:47**	**21**	**7**	**5**	**12**	**32**	**0**	**2**	**3**
	NHL Totals		**395**	**79**	**107**	**186**	**323**	**11**	**6**	**13**	**521**	**15.2**		**11**	**54.5**	**45**	**49**	**15:47**	**57**	**14**	**19**	**33**	**44**	**2**	**2**	**3**

WCHA Second All-Star Team (1991, 1992) • Won Jack A. Butterfield Trophy (Playoff MVP — AHL) (1996)

Traded to **LA Kings** by **Vancouver** for Jimmy Carson, January 8, 1994. Traded to **Toronto** by **LA Kings** with Guy Leveque, Kelly Fairchild and Shayne Toporowski for Eric Lacroix, Chris Snell and Toronto's 4th round choice (Eric Belanger) in 1996 Entry draft, October 3, 1994. Signed as a free agent by **Buffalo**, September 20, 1995.

WARD, Ed

ATL.

Right wing. Shoots right. 6'3", 220 lbs. Born, Edmonton, Alta., November 10, 1969. Quebec's 7th choice, 108th overall, in 1988 Entry Draft.

Season	Club	League	GP	G	A	Pts	PIM	PP	SH	GW	S	%	+/-	TF	F%	H	SB	Min	GP	G	A	Pts	PIM	PP	SH	GW
1986-87	Sherwood Park	AJHL	60	18	28	46	272	....	....	....	....	....	....	....	....	....	....	....	....	....	....	....	....	....	....	....
1987-88	North-Michigan	WCHA	25	0	2	2	40	....	....	....	....	....	....	....	....	....	....	....	....	....	....	....	....	....	....	....
1988-89	North-Michigan	WCHA	42	5	15	20	36	....	....	....	....	....	....	....	....	....	....	....	....	....	....	....	....	....	....	....
1989-90	North-Michigan	WCHA	39	5	11	16	77	....	....	....	....	....	....	....	....	....	....	....	....	....	....	....	....	....	....	....
1990-91	North-Michigan	WCHA	46	13	18	31	109	....	....	....	....	....	....	....	....	....	....	....	....	....	....	....	....	....	....	....

			Regular Season																Playoffs							
Season	Club	League	GP	G	A	Pts	PIM	PP	SH	GW	S	%	+/–	TF	F%	H	SB	Min	GP	G	A	Pts	PIM	PP	SH	GW
1991-92	Greensboro	ECHL	12	4	8	12	21	....	....	....	....	....	....	....	....	....	....	....	....	....	....	....	....	....	....	....
	Halifax	AHL	51	7	11	18	65	....	....	....	....	....	....	....	....	....	....	....	....	....	....	....	....	....	....	....
1992-93	Halifax	AHL	70	13	19	32	56	....	....	....	....	....	....	....	....	....	....	....	....	....	....	....	....	....	....	....
1993-94	**Quebec**	**NHL**	**7**	**1**	**0**	**1**	**5**	**0**	**0**	**0**	**3**	**33.3**	**0**	....	....	....	....	....	....	....	....	....	....	....	....	....
	Cornwall	AHL	60	12	30	42	65	....	....	....	....	....	....	....	....	....	....	....	12	1	3	4	14	....	....	....
1994-95	Cornwall	AHL	56	10	14	24	118	....	....	....	....	....	....	....	....	....	....	....	....	....	....	....	....	....	....	....
	Calgary	**NHL**	**2**	**1**	**1**	**2**	**2**	**0**	**0**	**0**	**1**	**100.0**	**–2**	....	....	....	....	....	....	....	....	....	....	....	....	....
	Saint John	AHL	11	4	5	9	20	....	....	....	....	....	....	....	....	....	....	....	5	1	0	1	10	....	....	....
1995-96	**Calgary**	**NHL**	**41**	**3**	**5**	**8**	**44**	**0**	**0**	**0**	**33**	**9.1**	**–2**	....	....	....	....	....	....	....	....	....	....	....	....	....
	Saint John	AHL	12	1	2	3	45	....	....	....	....	....	....	....	....	....	....	....	16	4	4	8	27	....	....	....
1996-97	**Calgary**	**NHL**	**40**	**5**	**8**	**13**	**49**	**0**	**0**	**1**	**33**	**15.2**	**–3**	....	....	....	....	....	....	....	....	....	....	....	....	....
	Saint John	AHL	1	0	0	0	0	....	....	....	....	....	....	....	....	....	....	....	....	....	....	....	....	....	....	....
	Detroit	IHL	31	7	6	13	45	....	....	....	....	....	....	....	....	....	....	....	....	....	....	....	....	....	....	....
1997-98	**Calgary**	**NHL**	**64**	**4**	**5**	**9**	**122**	**0**	**0**	**0**	**52**	**7.7**	**–1**	....	....	....	....	....	....	....	....	....	....	....	....	....
1998-99	**Calgary**	**NHL**	**68**	**3**	**5**	**8**	**67**	**0**	**0**	**0**	**56**	**5.4**	**–4**	**6**	**33.3**	**122**	**14**	**8:02**	....	....	....	....	....	....	....	....
	NHL Totals		**222**	**17**	**24**	**41**	**289**	**0**	**0**	**1**	**178**	**9.6**		**6**	**33.3**	**122**	**14**	**8:02**	....	....	....	....	....	....	....	....

Traded to **Calgary** by **Quebec** for Francois Groleau, March 23, 1995. Claimed by **Atlanta** from **Calgary** in Expansion Draft, June 25, 1999.

WARE, Jeff (WAIR) FLA.

Defense. Shoots left. 6'4", 220 lbs. Born, Toronto, Ont., May 19, 1977. Toronto's 1st choice, 15th overall, in 1995 Entry Draft.

Season	Club	League	GP	G	A	Pts	PIM	PP	SH	GW	S	%	+/–	TF	F%	H	SB	Min	GP	G	A	Pts	PIM	PP	SH	GW
1993-94	Wexford	OJHL	45	1	9	10	75	....	....	....	....	....	....	....	....	....	....	....	....	....	....	....	....	....	....	....
1994-95	Oshawa	OHL	55	2	11	13	86	....	....	....	....	....	....	....	....	....	....	....	7	1	1	2	6	....	....	....
1995-96	Oshawa	OHL	62	4	19	23	128	....	....	....	....	....	....	....	....	....	....	....	5	0	1	1	8	....	....	....
	St. John's	AHL	4	0	0	0	4	....	....	....	....	....	....	....	....	....	....	....	4	0	0	0	2	....	....	....
1996-97	Oshawa	OHL	24	1	10	11	38	....	....	....	....	....	....	....	....	....	....	....	13	0	3	3	34	....	....	....
	Toronto	**NHL**	**13**	**0**	**0**	**0**	**6**	**0**	**0**	**0**	**4**	**0.0**	**2**	....	....	....	....	....	....	....	....	....	....	....	....	....
1997-98	**Toronto**	**NHL**	**2**	**0**	**0**	**0**	**0**	**0**	**0**	**0**	**0**	**0.0**	**1**	....	....	....	....	....	....	....	....	....	....	....	....	....
	St. John's	AHL	67	0	3	3	182	....	....	....	....	....	....	....	....	....	....	....	4	0	0	0	4	....	....	....
1998-99	St. John's	AHL	55	1	4	5	130	....	....	....	....	....	....	....	....	....	....	....	....	....	....	....	....	....	....	....
	Florida	**NHL**	**6**	**0**	**1**	**1**	**6**	**0**	**0**	**0**	**1**	**0.0**	**–6**	**0**	**0.0**	**13**	**8**	**15:57**	....	....	....	....	....	....	....	....
	New Haven	AHL	20	0	1	1	26	....	....	....	....	....	....	....	....	....	....	....	....	....	....	....	....	....	....	....
	NHL Totals		**21**	**0**	**1**	**1**	**12**	**0**	**0**	**0**	**5**	**0.0**		**0**	**0.0**	**13**	**8**	**15:57**	....	....	....	....	....	....	....	....

Traded to **Florida** by **Toronto** for David Nemirovsky, February 17, 1999.

WARRENER, Rhett (WAHR-ihn-uhr, REHT) BUF.

Defense. Shoots left. 6'1", 209 lbs. Born, Shaunavon, Sask., January 27, 1976. Florida's 2nd choice, 27th overall, in 1994 Entry Draft.

Season	Club	League	GP	G	A	Pts	PIM	PP	SH	GW	S	%	+/–	TF	F%	H	SB	Min	GP	G	A	Pts	PIM	PP	SH	GW
1991-92	Saskatoon AA	AAHA	33	6	5	11	71	....	....	....	....	....	....	....	....	....	....	....	....	....	....	....	....	....	....	....
	Saskatoon	WHL	2	0	0	0	0	....	....	....	....	....	....	....	....	....	....	....	....	....	....	....	....	....	....	....
1992-93	Saskatoon	WHL	68	2	17	19	100	....	....	....	....	....	....	....	....	....	....	....	9	0	0	0	14	....	....	....
1993-94	Saskatoon	WHL	61	7	19	26	131	....	....	....	....	....	....	....	....	....	....	....	16	0	5	5	33	....	....	....
1994-95	Saskatoon	WHL	66	13	26	39	137	....	....	....	....	....	....	....	....	....	....	....	10	0	3	3	6	....	....	....
1995-96	**Florida**	**NHL**	**28**	**0**	**3**	**3**	**46**	**0**	**0**	**0**	**19**	**0.0**	**4**	....	....	....	....	....	**21**	**0**	**1**	**1**	**0**	**0**	**0**	**0**
	Carolina	AHL	9	0	0	0	4	....	....	....	....	....	....	....	....	....	....	....	....	....	....	....	....	....	....	....
1996-97	**Florida**	**NHL**	**62**	**4**	**9**	**13**	**88**	**1**	**0**	**1**	**58**	**6.9**	**20**	....	....	....	....	....	**5**	**0**	**0**	**0**	**0**	**0**	**0**	**0**
1997-98	**Florida**	**NHL**	**79**	**0**	**4**	**4**	**99**	**0**	**0**	**0**	**66**	**0.0**	**–16**	....	....	....	....	....	....	....	....	....	....	....	....	....
1998-99	**Florida**	**NHL**	**48**	**0**	**7**	**7**	**64**	**0**	**0**	**0**	**33**	**0.0**	**–1**	**0**	**0.0**	**75**	**38**	**19:01**	....	....	....	....	....	....	....	....
	Buffalo	**NHL**	**13**	**1**	**0**	**1**	**20**	**0**	**0**	**0**	**11**	**9.1**	**3**	**0**	**0.0**	**28**	**12**	**18:13**	**20**	**1**	**3**	**4**	**32**	**0**	**0**	**0**
	NHL Totals		**230**	**5**	**23**	**28**	**317**	**1**	**0**	**1**	**187**	**2.7**		**0**	**0.0**	**103**	**50**	**18:51**	**46**	**1**	**4**	**5**	**32**	**0**	**0**	**0**

Traded to **Buffalo** by **Florida** with Florida's 5th round choice (Ryan Miller) in 1999 Entry Draft for Mike Wilson, March 23, 1999.

WARRINER, Todd (WAHR-ihn-uhr) TOR.

Left wing. Shoots left. 6'1", 200 lbs. Born, Blenheim, Ont., January 3, 1974. Quebec's 1st choice, 4th overall, in 1992 Entry Draft.

Season	Club	League	GP	G	A	Pts	PIM	PP	SH	GW	S	%	+/–	TF	F%	H	SB	Min	GP	G	A	Pts	PIM	PP	SH	GW
1988-89	Blenheim	OJHL-C	10	1	4	5	0	....	....	....	....	....	....	....	....	....	....	....	....	....	....	....	....	....	....	....
1989-90	Chatham	OJHL-B	40	24	21	45	12	....	....	....	....	....	....	....	....	....	....	....	....	....	....	....	....	....	....	....
1990-91	Windsor	OHL	57	36	28	64	26	....	....	....	....	....	....	....	....	....	....	....	11	5	6	11	12	....	....	....
1991-92	Windsor	OHL	50	41	41	82	64	....	....	....	....	....	....	....	....	....	....	....	7	5	4	9	6	....	....	....
1992-93	Windsor	OHL	23	13	21	34	29	....	....	....	....	....	....	....	....	....	....	....	....	....	....	....	....	....	....	....
	Kitchener	OHL	32	19	24	43	35	....	....	....	....	....	....	....	....	....	....	....	7	5	14	19	14	....	....	....
1993-94	Canada	Nat-Team	50	11	20	31	33	....	....	....	....	....	....	....	....	....	....	....	....	....	....	....	....	....	....	....
	Canada	Olympics	4	1	1	2	0	....	....	....	....	....	....	....	....	....	....	....	....	....	....	....	....	....	....	....
	Kitchener	OHL	....	....	....	....	....	....	....	....	....	....	....	....	....	....	....	....	1	0	1	1	0	....	....	....
	Cornwall	AHL	....	....	....	....	....	....	....	....	....	....	....	....	....	....	....	....	10	1	4	5	4	....	....	....
1994-95	St. John's	AHL	46	8	10	18	22	....	....	....	....	....	....	....	....	....	....	....	4	1	0	1	2	....	....	....
	Toronto	**NHL**	**5**	**0**	**0**	**0**	**0**	**0**	**0**	**0**	**1**	**0.0**	**–3**	....	....	....	....	....	....	....	....	....	....	....	....	....
1995-96	**Toronto**	**NHL**	**57**	**7**	**8**	**15**	**26**	**1**	**0**	**0**	**79**	**8.9**	**–11**	....	....	....	....	....	**6**	**1**	**1**	**2**	**2**	**0**	**0**	**0**
	St. John's	AHL	11	5	6	11	16	....	....	....	....	....	....	....	....	....	....	....	....	....	....	....	....	....	....	....
1996-97	**Toronto**	**NHL**	**75**	**12**	**21**	**33**	**41**	**2**	**2**	**0**	**146**	**8.2**	**–3**	....	....	....	....	....	....	....	....	....	....	....	....	....
1997-98	**Toronto**	**NHL**	**45**	**5**	**8**	**13**	**20**	**0**	**0**	**1**	**73**	**6.8**	**5**	....	....	....	....	....	....	....	....	....	....	....	....	....
1998-99	**Toronto**	**NHL**	**53**	**9**	**10**	**19**	**28**	**1**	**0**	**1**	**96**	**9.4**	**–6**	**579**	**47.8**	**52**	**10**	**14:06**	**9**	**0**	**0**	**0**	**2**	**0**	**0**	**0**
	NHL Totals		**235**	**33**	**47**	**80**	**115**	**4**	**2**	**2**	**395**	**8.4**		**579**	**47.8**	**52**	**10**	**14:06**	**15**	**1**	**1**	**2**	**4**	**0**	**0**	**0**

OHL First All-Star Team (1992)

Traded to **Toronto** by **Quebec** with Mats Sundin, Garth Butcher and Philadelphia's 1st round choice (previously acquired by Quebec — later traded to Washington — Washington selected Nolan Baumgartner) in 1994 Entry Draft for Wendel Clark, Sylvain Lefebvre, Landon Wilson and Toronto's 1st round choice (Jeffrey Kealty) in 1994 Entry Draft, June 28, 1994.

WASHBURN, Steve NSH.

Center. Shoots left. 6'2", 198 lbs. Born, Ottawa, Ont., April 10, 1975. Florida's 5th choice, 78th overall, in 1993 Entry Draft.

Season	Club	League	GP	G	A	Pts	PIM	PP	SH	GW	S	%	+/–	TF	F%	H	SB	Min	GP	G	A	Pts	PIM	PP	SH	GW
1990-91	Gloucester	OJHL-B	56	21	30	51	47	....	....	....	....	....	....	....	....	....	....	....	....	....	....	....	....	....	....	....
1991-92	Ottawa	OHL	59	5	17	22	10	....	....	....	....	....	....	....	....	....	....	....	11	2	3	5	4	....	....	....
1992-93	Ottawa	OHL	66	20	38	58	54	....	....	....	....	....	....	....	....	....	....	....	....	....	....	....	....	....	....	....
1993-94	Ottawa	OHL	65	30	50	80	88	....	....	....	....	....	....	....	....	....	....	....	17	7	16	23	10	....	....	....
1994-95	Ottawa	OHL	63	43	63	106	72	....	....	....	....	....	....	....	....	....	....	....	....	....	....	....	....	....	....	....
	Cincinnati	IHL	6	3	1	4	0	....	....	....	....	....	....	....	....	....	....	....	9	1	3	4	4	....	....	....
1995-96	**Florida**	**NHL**	**1**	**0**	**1**	**1**	**0**	**0**	**0**	**0**	**1**	**0.0**	**1**	....	....	....	....	....	**1**	**0**	**1**	**1**	**0**	**0**	**0**	**0**
	Carolina	AHL	78	29	54	83	45	....	....	....	....	....	....	....	....	....	....	....	....	....	....	....	....	....	....	....
1996-97	**Florida**	**NHL**	**18**	**3**	**6**	**9**	**4**	**1**	**0**	**0**	**21**	**14.3**	**2**	....	....	....	....	....	....	....	....	....	....	....	....	....
	Carolina	AHL	60	23	40	63	66	....	....	....	....	....	....	....	....	....	....	....	....	....	....	....	....	....	....	....
1997-98	**Florida**	**NHL**	**58**	**11**	**8**	**19**	**32**	**4**	**0**	**2**	**61**	**18.0**	**–6**	....	....	....	....	....	....	....	....	....	....	....	....	....
	New Haven	AHL	6	3	5	8	4	....	....	....	....	....	....	....	....	....	....	....	3	2	0	2	15	....	....	....
1998-99	**Florida**	**NHL**	**4**	**0**	**0**	**0**	**4**	**0**	**0**	**0**	**0**	**0.0**	**–1**	**21**	**38.1**	**1**	**0**	**6:17**	....	....	....	....	....	....	....	....
	New Haven	AHL	10	4	3	7	6	....	....	....	....	....	....	....	....	....	....	....	....	....	....	....	....	....	....	....
	Vancouver	**NHL**	**8**	**0**	**0**	**0**	**2**	**0**	**0**	**0**	**6**	**0.0**	**0**	**30**	**40.0**	**9**	**1**	**8:05**	....	....	....	....	....	....	....	....
	Syracuse	AHL	13	1	6	7	6	....	....	....	....	....	....	....	....	....	....	....	....	....	....	....	....	....	....	....
	NHL Totals		**89**	**14**	**15**	**29**	**42**	**5**	**0**	**2**	**89**	**15.7**		**51**	**39.2**	**10**	**1**	**7:29**	**1**	**0**	**1**	**1**	**0**	**0**	**0**	**0**

Claimed on waivers by **Vancouver** from **Florida**, February 18, 1999. Signed as a free agent by **Nashville**, August 11, 1999.

WATT, Mike — NYI

Left wing. Shoots left. 6'2", 212 lbs. Born, Seaforth, Ont., March 31, 1976. Edmonton's 3rd choice, 32nd overall, in 1994 Entry Draft.

								Regular Season											Playoffs							
Season	Club	League	GP	G	A	Pts	PIM	PP	SH	GW	S	%	+/–	TF	F%	H	SB	Min	GP	G	A	Pts	PIM	PP	SH	GW
1991-92	Stratford	OJHL-B	46	5	26	31	....	....	....	....	....	....	....	....	....	....	....	....	....	....	....	....	....	....	....	....
1992-93	Stratford	OJHL-B	45	20	35	55	100	....	....	....	....	....	....	....	....	....	....	....	....	....	....	....	....	....	....	....
1993-94	Stratford	OJHL-B	48	34	34	68	165	....	....	....	....	....	....	....	....	....	....	....	....	....	....	....	....	....	....	....
1994-95	Michigan State	CCHA	39	12	6	18	64	....	....	....	....	....	....	....	....	....	....	....	....	....	....	....	....	....	....	....
1995-96	Michigan State	CCHA	37	17	22	39	60	....	....	....	....	....	....	....	....	....	....	....	....	....	....	....	....	....	....	....
1996-97	Michigan State	CCHA	39	24	17	41	109	....	....	....	....	....	....	....	....	....	....	....	....	....	....	....	....	....	....	....
1997-98	**Edmonton**	**NHL**	**14**	**1**	**2**	**3**	**4**	**0**	**0**	**1**	**14**	**7.1**	**–4**	....	....	....	....	....	....	....	....	....	....	....	....	....
	Hamilton	AHL	63	24	25	49	65	....	....	....	....	....	....	....	....	....	....	....	9	2	2	4	8	....	....	....
1998-99	**NY Islanders**	**NHL**	**75**	**8**	**17**	**25**	**12**	**0**	**0**	**4**	**75**	**10.7**	**–2**	**180**	**50.6**	**73**	**29**	**11:15**	....	....	....	....	....	....	....	....
	NHL Totals		**89**	**9**	**19**	**28**	**16**	**0**	**0**	**5**	**89**	**10.1**		**180**	**50.6**	**73**	**29**	**11:15**	....	....	....	....	....	....	....	....

Traded to **NY Islanders** by **Edmonton** for Eric Fichaud, June 18, 1998.

WEBB, Steve — NYI

Right wing. Shoots right. 6', 195 lbs. Born, Peterborough, Ont., April 20, 1975. Buffalo's 8th choice, 176th overall, in 1994 Entry Draft.

								Regular Season											Playoffs							
Season	Club	League	GP	G	A	Pts	PIM	PP	SH	GW	S	%	+/–	TF	F%	H	SB	Min	GP	G	A	Pts	PIM	PP	SH	GW
1991-92	Peterborough	OJHL-B	37	9	9	18	195	....	....	....	....	....	....	....	....	....	....	....	....	....	....	....	....	....	....	....
1992-93	Windsor	OHL	60	14	25	39	190	....	....	....	....	....	....	....	....	....	....	....	....	....	....	....	....	....	....	....
1993-94	Peterborough	OHL	35	6	16	22	126	....	....	....	....	....	....	....	....	....	....	....	6	1	1	2	10	....	....	....
1994-95	Peterborough	OHL	42	8	16	24	109	....	....	....	....	....	....	....	....	....	....	....	11	3	3	6	22	....	....	....
1995-96	Muskegon	ColHL	58	18	24	42	263	....	....	....	....	....	....	....	....	....	....	....	5	1	2	3	22	....	....	....
	Detroit	IHL	4	0	0	0	24	....	....	....	....	....	....	....	....	....	....	....	....	....	....	....	....	....	....	....
1996-97	**NY Islanders**	**NHL**	**41**	**1**	**4**	**5**	**144**	**1**	**0**	**0**	**21**	**4.8**	**–10**	....	....	....	....	....	....	....	....	....	....	....	....	....
	Kentucky	AHL	25	6	6	12	103	....	....	....	....	....	....	....	....	....	....	....	2	0	0	0	19	....	....	....
1997-98	**NY Islanders**	**NHL**	**20**	**0**	**0**	**0**	**35**	**0**	**0**	**0**	**6**	**0.0**	**–2**	....	....	....	....	....	....	....	....	....	....	....	....	....
	Kentucky	AHL	37	5	13	18	139	....	....	....	....	....	....	....	....	....	....	....	3	0	1	1	10	....	....	....
1998-99	**NY Islanders**	**NHL**	**45**	**0**	**0**	**0**	**32**	**0**	**0**	**0**	**18**	**0.0**	**–10**	**0**	**0.0**	**64**	**1**	**4:13**	....	....	....	....	....	....	....	....
	Lowell	AHL	23	2	4	6	80	....	....	....	....	....	....	....	....	....	....	....	....	....	....	....	....	....	....	....
	NHL Totals		**106**	**1**	**4**	**5**	**211**	**1**	**0**	**0**	**45**	**2.2**		**0**	**0.0**	**64**	**1**	**4:13**	....	....	....	....	....	....	....	....

Signed as a free agent by **NY Islanders**, October 10, 1996.

WEIGHT, Doug — (WAYT) — EDM.

Center. Shoots left. 5'11", 200 lbs. Born, Warren, MI, January 21, 1971. NY Rangers' 2nd choice, 34th overall, in 1990 Entry Draft.

								Regular Season											Playoffs							
Season	Club	League	GP	G	A	Pts	PIM	PP	SH	GW	S	%	+/–	TF	F%	H	SB	Min	GP	G	A	Pts	PIM	PP	SH	GW
1988-89	Bloomfield	NAJHL	34	26	53	79	105	....	....	....	....	....	....	....	....	....	....	....	....	....	....	....	....	....	....	....
1989-90	Lake Superior	CCHA	46	21	48	69	44	....	....	....	....	....	....	....	....	....	....	....	....	....	....	....	....	....	....	....
1990-91	Lake Superior	CCHA	42	29	46	75	86	....	....	....	....	....	....	....	....	....	....	....	....	....	....	....	....	....	....	....
	NY Rangers	**NHL**	....	....	....	....	....	....	....	....	....	....	....	....	....	....	....	....	**1**	**0**	**0**	**0**	**0**	....	....	....
1991-92	**NY Rangers**	**NHL**	**53**	**8**	**22**	**30**	**23**	**0**	**0**	**2**	**72**	**11.1**	**–3**	....	....	....	....	....	**7**	**2**	**2**	**4**	**0**	**1**	**0**	**0**
	Binghamton	AHL	9	3	14	17	2	....	....	....	....	....	....	....	....	....	....	....	4	1	4	5	6	....	....	....
1992-93	**NY Rangers**	**NHL**	**65**	**15**	**25**	**40**	**55**	**3**	**0**	**1**	**90**	**16.7**	**4**	....	....	....	....	....	....	....	....	....	....	....	....	....
	Edmonton	**NHL**	**13**	**2**	**6**	**8**	**10**	**0**	**0**	**0**	**35**	**5.7**	**–2**	....	....	....	....	....	....	....	....	....	....	....	....	....
1993-94	**Edmonton**	**NHL**	**84**	**24**	**50**	**74**	**47**	**4**	**1**	**1**	**188**	**12.8**	**–22**	....	....	....	....	....	....	....	....	....	....	....	....	....
1994-95	Rosenheim	Germany	8	2	3	5	18	....	....	....	....	....	....	....	....	....	....	....	....	....	....	....	....	....	....	....
	Edmonton	**NHL**	**48**	**7**	**33**	**40**	**69**	**1**	**0**	**1**	**104**	**6.7**	**–17**	....	....	....	....	....	....	....	....	....	....	....	....	....
1995-96	**Edmonton**	**NHL**	**82**	**25**	**79**	**104**	**95**	**9**	**0**	**2**	**204**	**12.3**	**–19**	....	....	....	....	....	....	....	....	....	....	....	....	....
1996-97	**Edmonton**	**NHL**	**80**	**21**	**61**	**82**	**80**	**4**	**0**	**2**	**235**	**8.9**	**1**	....	....	....	....	....	**12**	**3**	**8**	**11**	**8**	**0**	**0**	**0**
1997-98	**Edmonton**	**NHL**	**79**	**26**	**44**	**70**	**69**	**9**	**0**	**4**	**205**	**12.7**	**1**	....	....	....	....	....	**12**	**2**	**7**	**9**	**14**	**2**	**0**	**1**
	United States	Olympics	4	0	2	2	2	....	....	....	....	....	....	....	....	....	....	....	....	....	....	....	....	....	....	....
1998-99	**Edmonton**	**NHL**	**43**	**6**	**31**	**37**	**12**	**1**	**0**	**0**	**79**	**7.6**	**–8**	**853**	**49.5**	**43**	**16**	**19:51**	**4**	**1**	**1**	**2**	**15**	**0**	**0**	**0**
	NHL Totals		**547**	**134**	**351**	**485**	**460**	**31**	**1**	**13**	**1212**	**11.1**		**853**	**49.5**	**43**	**16**	**19:51**	**36**	**8**	**18**	**26**	**37**	**3**	**0**	**1**

CCHA First All-Star Team (1991) • NCAA West Second All-American Team (1991)

Played in NHL All-Star Game (1996, 1998)

Traded to **Edmonton** by **NY Rangers** for Esa Tikkanen, March 17, 1993.

WEINRICH, Eric — (WIGHN-rihc) — MTL.

Defense. Shoots left. 6'1", 215 lbs. Born, Roanoke, VA, December 19, 1966. New Jersey's 3rd choice, 32nd overall, in 1985 Entry Draft.

								Regular Season											Playoffs							
Season	Club	League	GP	G	A	Pts	PIM	PP	SH	GW	S	%	+/–	TF	F%	H	SB	Min	GP	G	A	Pts	PIM	PP	SH	GW
1983-84	Yarmouth Acad.	H.S.	17	23	33	56	....	....	....	....	....	....	....	....	....	....	....	....	....	....	....	....	....	....	....	....
1984-85	Yarmouth Acad.	H.S.	20	6	21	27	....	....	....	....	....	....	....	....	....	....	....	....	....	....	....	....	....	....	....	....
1985-86	U. of Maine	H.E.	34	0	14	14	26	....	....	....	....	....	....	....	....	....	....	....	....	....	....	....	....	....	....	....
1986-87	U. of Maine	H.E.	41	12	32	44	59	....	....	....	....	....	....	....	....	....	....	....	....	....	....	....	....	....	....	....
1987-88	U. of Maine	H.E.	8	4	7	11	22	....	....	....	....	....	....	....	....	....	....	....	....	....	....	....	....	....	....	....
	United States	Nat-Team	38	3	9	12	24	....	....	....	....	....	....	....	....	....	....	....	....	....	....	....	....	....	....	....
	United States	Olympics	3	0	0	0	0	....	....	....	....	....	....	....	....	....	....	....	....	....	....	....	....	....	....	....
1988-89	**New Jersey**	**NHL**	**2**	**0**	**0**	**0**	**0**	**0**	**0**	**0**	**3**	**0.0**	**–1**	....	....	....	....	....	....	....	....	....	....	....	....	....
	Utica	AHL	80	17	27	44	70	....	....	....	....	....	....	....	....	....	....	....	5	0	1	1	4	....	....	....
1989-90	**New Jersey**	**NHL**	**19**	**2**	**7**	**9**	**11**	**1**	**0**	**1**	**16**	**12.5**	**1**	....	....	....	....	....	**6**	**1**	**3**	**4**	**17**	**0**	**0**	**0**
	Utica	AHL	57	12	48	60	38	....	....	....	....	....	....	....	....	....	....	....	....	....	....	....	....	....	....	....
1990-91	**New Jersey**	**NHL**	**76**	**4**	**34**	**38**	**48**	**1**	**0**	**0**	**96**	**4.2**	**10**	....	....	....	....	....	**7**	**1**	**2**	**3**	**6**	**1**	**0**	**0**
1991-92	**New Jersey**	**NHL**	**76**	**7**	**25**	**32**	**55**	**5**	**0**	**0**	**97**	**7.2**	**10**	....	....	....	....	....	**7**	**0**	**2**	**2**	**4**	**0**	**0**	**0**
1992-93	**Hartford**	**NHL**	**79**	**7**	**29**	**36**	**76**	**0**	**2**	**2**	**104**	**6.7**	**–11**	....	....	....	....	....	....	....	....	....	....	....	....	....
1993-94	**Hartford**	**NHL**	**8**	**1**	**1**	**2**	**2**	**1**	**0**	**0**	**10**	**10.0**	**–5**	....	....	....	....	....	....	....	....	....	....	....	....	....
	Chicago	**NHL**	**54**	**3**	**23**	**26**	**31**	**1**	**0**	**2**	**105**	**2.9**	**6**	....	....	....	....	....	**6**	**0**	**2**	**2**	**6**	**0**	**0**	**0**
1994-95	**Chicago**	**NHL**	**48**	**3**	**10**	**13**	**33**	**1**	**0**	**2**	**50**	**6.0**	**1**	....	....	....	....	....	**16**	**1**	**5**	**6**	**4**	**0**	**0**	**0**
1995-96	**Chicago**	**NHL**	**77**	**5**	**10**	**15**	**65**	**0**	**0**	**0**	**76**	**6.6**	**14**	....	....	....	....	....	**10**	**1**	**4**	**5**	**10**	**1**	**0**	**0**
1996-97	**Chicago**	**NHL**	**81**	**7**	**25**	**32**	**62**	**1**	**0**	**0**	**115**	**6.1**	**19**	....	....	....	....	....	**6**	**0**	**1**	**1**	**4**	**0**	**0**	**0**
1997-98	**Chicago**	**NHL**	**82**	**2**	**21**	**23**	**106**	**0**	**0**	**0**	**85**	**2.4**	**10**	....	....	....	....	....	....	....	....	....	....	....	....	....
1998-99	**Chicago**	**NHL**	**14**	**1**	**3**	**4**	**12**	**0**	**0**	**0**	**24**	**4.2**	**–13**	**0**	**0.0**	**27**	**13**	**20:12**	....	....	....	....	....	....	....	....
	Montreal	**NHL**	**66**	**6**	**12**	**18**	**77**	**4**	**0**	**1**	**95**	**6.3**	**–12**	**0**	**0.0**	**100**	**117**	**24:44**	....	....	....	....	....	....	....	....
	NHL Totals		**682**	**48**	**200**	**248**	**578**	**15**	**2**	**8**	**876**	**5.5**		**0**	**0.0**	**127**	**130**	**23:56**	**58**	**4**	**19**	**23**	**51**	**2**	**0**	**0**

Hockey East First All-Star Team (1987) • NCAA East Second All-American Team (1987) • AHL First All-Star Team (1990) • Won Eddie Shore Award (Outstanding Defenseman - AHL) (1990) • NHL/Upper Deck All-Rookie Team (1991)

Traded to **Hartford** by **New Jersey** with Sean Burke for Bobby Holik, Hartford's 2nd round choice (Jay Pandolfo) in 1993 Entry Draft and future considerations, August 28, 1992. Traded to **Chicago** by **Hartford** with Patrick Poulin for Steve Larmer and Bryan Marchment, November 2, 1993. Traded to **Montreal** by **Chicago** with Jeff Hackett, Alain Nasreddine and Tampa Bay's 4th round choice (previously acquired, Montreal selected Chris Dyment) in 1999 Entry Draft for Jocelyn Thibault, Dave Manson and Brad Brown, November 16, 1998.

WELLS, Chris — FLA.

Center. Shoots left. 6'6", 223 lbs. Born, Calgary, Alta., November 12, 1975. Pittsburgh's 1st choice, 24th overall, in 1994 Entry Draft.

								Regular Season											Playoffs							
Season	Club	League	GP	G	A	Pts	PIM	PP	SH	GW	S	%	+/–	TF	F%	H	SB	Min	GP	G	A	Pts	PIM	PP	SH	GW
1990-91	Calgary	AAHA	35	13	14	27	33	....	....	....	....	....	....	....	....	....	....	....	....	....	....	....	....	....	....	....
1991-92	Seattle	WHL	64	13	8	21	80	....	....	....	....	....	....	....	....	....	....	....	11	0	0	0	15	....	....	....
1992-93	Seattle	WHL	63	18	37	55	111	....	....	....	....	....	....	....	....	....	....	....	5	2	3	5	4	....	....	....
1993-94	Seattle	WHL	69	30	44	74	150	....	....	....	....	....	....	....	....	....	....	....	9	6	5	11	23	....	....	....
1994-95	Seattle	WHL	69	45	63	108	148	....	....	....	....	....	....	....	....	....	....	....	3	0	1	1	4	....	....	....
	Cleveland	IHL	3	0	1	1	2	....	....	....	....	....	....	....	....	....	....	....	....	....	....	....	....	....	....	....
1995-96	**Pittsburgh**	**NHL**	**54**	**2**	**2**	**4**	**59**	**0**	**1**	**0**	**25**	**8.0**	**–6**	....	....	....	....	....	....	....	....	....	....	....	....	....
1996-97	Cleveland	IHL	15	4	6	10	9	....	....	....	....	....	....	....	....	....	....	....	....	....	....	....	....	....	....	....
	Florida	**NHL**	**47**	**2**	**6**	**8**	**42**	**0**	**0**	**0**	**29**	**6.9**	**5**	....	....	....	....	....	**3**	**0**	**0**	**0**	**0**	**0**	**0**	**0**
1997-98	**Florida**	**NHL**	**61**	**5**	**10**	**15**	**47**	**0**	**1**	**0**	**57**	**8.8**	**4**	....	....	....	....	....	....	....	....	....	....	....	....	....

Season	Club	League	GP	G	A	Pts	PIM	PP	SH	GW	S	%	+/-	TF	F%	H	SB	Min	GP	G	A	Pts	PIM	PP	SH	GW
1998-99	Florida	NHL	20	0	2	2	31	0	0	0	28	0.0	−4	231	40.7	21	12	11:52	....	....	....	....	....	....	....	....
	New Haven	AHL	9	3	1	4	28																			
	NHL Totals		182	9	20	29	179	0	2	0	139	6.5		231	40.7	21	12	11:52	3	0	0	0	0	0	0	0

WHL West First All-Star Team (1995)
Traded to **Florida** by **Pittsburgh** for Stu Barnes and Jason Woolley, November 19, 1996.

WERENKA, Brad (wuh-REHN-kuh) PIT.

Defense. Shoots left. 6'1", 224 lbs. Born, Two Hills, Alta., February 12, 1969. Edmonton's 2nd choice, 42nd overall, in 1987 Entry Draft.

Season	Club	League	GP	G	A	Pts	PIM	PP	SH	GW	S	%	+/-	TF	F%	H	SB	Min	GP	G	A	Pts	PIM	PP	SH	GW
1985-86	Ft. Saskatchewan	SJHL	29	12	23	35	24																			
1986-87	North. Michigan	WCHA	30	4	4	8	35																			
1987-88	North. Michigan	WCHA	34	7	23	30	26																			
1988-89	North. Michigan	WCHA	28	7	13	20	16																			
1989-90	North. Michigan	WCHA	8	2	5	7	8																			
1990-91	North. Michigan	WCHA	47	20	43	63	36																			
1991-92	Cape Breton	AHL	66	6	21	27	95												5	0	3	3	6			
1992-93	Canada	Nat-Team	18	3	7	10	10																			
	Edmonton	NHL	27	5	4	9	24	0	1	1	38	13.2	1													
	Cape Breton	AHL	4	1	1	2	4												16	4	17	21	12			
1993-94	**Edmonton**	NHL	15	0	4	4	14	0	0	0	11	0.0	−1													
	Cape Breton	AHL	25	6	17	23	19																			
	Canada	Olympics	8	2	2	4	8																			
	Quebec	NHL	11	0	7	7	8	0	0	0	17	0.0	4													
	Cornwall	AHL																	12	2	10	12	22			
1994-95	Milwaukee	IHL	80	8	45	53	161												15	3	10	13	36			
1995-96	**Chicago**	NHL	9	0	0	0	8	0	0	0	2	0.0	−2													
	Indianapolis	IHL	73	15	42	57	85												5	1	3	4	8			
1996-97	Indianapolis	IHL	82	20	56	76	83												4	1	4	5	6			
1997-98	**Pittsburgh**	NHL	71	3	15	18	46	2	0	0	50	6.0	15						6	1	0	1	8	0	1	0
1998-99	**Pittsburgh**	NHL	81	6	18	24	93	1	0	4	77	7.8	17	0	0.0	115	120	21:12	13	1	1	2	6	0	0	0
	NHL Totals		214	14	48	62	193	3	1	5	195	7.2		0	0.0	115	120	21:12	19	2	1	3	14	0	1	0

WCHA First All-Star Team (1991) • NCAA West First All-American Team (1991) • NCAA Championship All-Tournament Team (1991) • IHL First All-Star Team (1997) • Won Governors' Trophy (Top Defenseman — IHL) (1997)
Traded to **Quebec** by **Edmonton** for Steve Passmore, March 21, 1994. Signed as a free agent by **Chicago**, July 20, 1995. Signed as a free agent by **Pittsburgh**, July 31, 1997.

WESENBERG, Brian (WEE-sehn-buhrg) PHI.

Right wing. Shoots right. 6'3", 187 lbs. Born, Peterborough, Ont., May 9, 1977. Anaheim's 2nd choice, 29th overall, in 1995 Entry Draft.

Season	Club	League	GP	G	A	Pts	PIM	PP	SH	GW	S	%	+/-	TF	F%	H	SB	Min	GP	G	A	Pts	PIM	PP	SH	GW
1993-94	Cobourg	OJHL	40	14	18	32	81																			
1994-95	Guelph	OHL	66	17	27	44	81												14	2	3	5	18			
1995-96	Guelph	OHL	66	25	33	58	161												16	4	11	15	34			
1996-97	Guelph	OHL	64	37	43	80	186												18	4	9	13	59			
	Philadelphia	AHL																	3	0	0	0	7			
1997-98	Philadelphia	AHL	74	17	22	39	93												19	1	4	5	34			
1998-99	**Philadelphia**	NHL	1	0	0	0	5	0	0	0	0	0.0	1	0	0.0	0	0	1:08								
	Philadelphia	AHL	71	23	20	43	169												16	5	3	8	28			
	NHL Totals		1	0	0	0	5	0	0	0	0	0.0		0	0.0	0	0	1:08								

Traded to **Philadelphia** by **Anaheim** for Anatoli Semenov and Mike Crowley, March 19, 1996.

WESLEY, Glen CAR.

Defense. Shoots left. 6'1", 197 lbs. Born, Red Deer, Alta., October 2, 1968. Boston's 1st choice, 3rd overall, in 1987 Entry Draft.

Season	Club	League	GP	G	A	Pts	PIM	PP	SH	GW	S	%	+/-	TF	F%	H	SB	Min	GP	G	A	Pts	PIM	PP	SH	GW
1983-84	Red Deer	AJHL	57	9	20	29	40																			
	Portland	WHL	3	1	2	3	0																			
1984-85	Portland	WHL	67	16	52	68	76												6	1	6	7	8			
1985-86	Portland	WHL	69	16	75	91	96												15	3	11	14	29			
1986-87	Portland	WHL	63	16	46	62	72												20	8	18	26	27			
1987-88	**Boston**	NHL	79	7	30	37	69	1	2	0	158	4.4	21						23	6	8	14	22	4	1	0
1988-89	**Boston**	NHL	77	19	35	54	61	8	1	1	181	10.5	23						10	0	2	2	4	0	0	0
1989-90	**Boston**	NHL	78	9	27	36	48	5	0	4	166	5.4	6						21	2	6	8	36	0	0	1
1990-91	**Boston**	NHL	80	11	32	43	78	5	1	1	199	5.5	0						19	2	9	11	19	2	0	0
1991-92	**Boston**	NHL	78	9	37	46	54	4	0	1	211	4.3	−9						15	2	4	6	16	0	0	0
1992-93	**Boston**	NHL	64	8	25	33	47	4	1	0	183	4.4	−2						4	0	0	0	0	0	0	0
1993-94	**Boston**	NHL	81	14	44	58	64	6	1	1	265	5.3	1						13	3	3	6	12	1	0	0
1994-95	Hartford	NHL	48	2	14	16	50	1	0	0	125	1.6	−6													
1995-96	Hartford	NHL	68	8	16	24	88	6	0	1	129	6.2	−9													
1996-97	Hartford	NHL	68	6	26	32	40	3	1	0	126	4.8	0													
1997-98	Carolina	NHL	82	6	19	25	36	1	0	1	121	5.0	7						6	0	0	0	2	0	0	0
1998-99	Carolina	NHL	74	7	17	24	44	0	0	2	112	6.3	14	1	0.0	121	94	22:31	6	0	0	0	0	0	0	0
	NHL Totals		877	106	322	428	679	44	7	13	1976	5.4		1	0.0	121	94	22:31	111	15	32	47	111	7	1	1

WHL West All-Star Team (1986, 1987) • NHL All-Rookie Team (1988)
Played in NHL All-Star Game (1989)
Traded to **Hartford** by **Boston** for Hartford/Carolina's 1st round choices in 1995 (Kyle McLaren), 1996 (Jonathan Aitken) and 1997 (Sergei Samsonov) Entry Drafts, August 26, 1994. Transferred to **Carolina** after **Hartford** franchise relocated, June 25, 1997.

WHITE, Brian COL.

Defense. Shoots right. 6'1", 180 lbs. Born, Winchester, MA, February 7, 1976. Tampa Bay's 11th choice, 268th overall, in 1994 Entry Draft.

Season	Club	League	GP	G	A	Pts	PIM	PP	SH	GW	S	%	+/-	TF	F%	H	SB	Min	GP	G	A	Pts	PIM	PP	SH	GW
1993-94	Cobourg	OJHL	40	14	18	32	81																			
1994-95	U. of Maine	H.E.	28	1	1	2	16																			
1995-96	U. of Maine	H.E.	39	0	4	4	18																			
1996-97	U. of Maine	H.E.	35	4	12	16	36																			
1997-98	U. of Maine	H.E.	33	0	12	12	45																			
	Long Beach	IHL	1	0	0	0	0																			
1998-99	**Colorado**	NHL	2	0	0	0	0	0	0	0	0	0.0	0	0	0.0	1	0	0:40								
	Hershey	AHL	71	4	8	12	41												4	0	1	1	2			
	NHL Totals		2	0	0	0	0	0	0	0	0	0.0		0	0.0	1	0	0:40								

Signed as a free agent by **Colorado**, July 7, 1998.

WHITE, Peter PHI.

Center. Shoots left. 5'11", 200 lbs. Born, Montreal, Que., March 15, 1969. Edmonton's 4th choice, 92nd overall, in 1989 Entry Draft.

Season	Club	League	GP	G	A	Pts	PIM
1984-85	Lac St-Louis	QAAA	42	16	32	48	....
1985-86	Lac St-Louis	QAAA	42	38	62	100	....
1986-87	Pembroke	OJHL			STATISTICS NOT AVAILABLE		
1987-88	Pembroke	OJHL	56	90	136	226	32
1988-89	Michigan State	CCHA	46	20	33	53	17
1989-90	Michigan State	CCHA	45	22	40	62	6
1990-91	Michigan State	CCHA	37	7	31	38	28

			Regular Season																Playoffs							
Season	Club	League	GP	G	A	Pts	PIM	PP	SH	GW	S	%	+/–	TF	F%	H	SB	Min	GP	G	A	Pts	PIM	PP	SH	GW
1991-92	Michigan State	CCHA	41	26	49	75	32	....	....	....	....	....	....	....	....	....	....	....	....	....	....	....	....	....	....	....
1992-93	Cape Breton	AHL	64	12	28	40	10	....	....	....	....	....	....	....	....	....	....	....	16	3	3	6	12	....	....	....
1993-94	**Edmonton**	**NHL**	**26**	**3**	**5**	**8**	**2**	**0**	**0**	**0**	**17**	**17.6**	**1**	....	....	....	....	....	....	....	....	....	....	....	....	....
	Cape Breton	AHL	45	21	49	70	12	....	....	....	....	....	....	....	....	....	....	....	5	2	3	5	2	....	....	....
1994-95	Cape Breton	AHL	65	36	*69	*105	30	....	....	....	....	....	....	....	....	....	....	....	....	....	....	....	....	....	....	....
	Edmonton	**NHL**	**9**	**2**	**4**	**6**	**0**	**2**	**0**	**0**	**13**	**15.4**	**1**	....	....	....	....	....	....	....	....	....	....	....	....	....
1995-96	**Edmonton**	**NHL**	**26**	**5**	**3**	**8**	**0**	**1**	**0**	**0**	**34**	**14.7**	**–14**	....	....	....	....	....	....	....	....	....	....	....	....	....
	Toronto	**NHL**	**1**	**0**	**0**	**0**	**0**	**1**	**0**	**0**	**0**	**0.0**	**0**	....	....	....	....	....	....	....	....	....	....	....	....	....
	St. John's	AHL	17	6	7	13	6	....	....	....	....	....	....	....	....	....	....	....	....	....	....	....	....	....	....	....
	Atlanta	IHL	36	21	20	41	4	....	....	....	....	....	....	....	....	....	....	....	3	0	3	3	2	....	....	....
1996-97	Philadelphia	AHL	80	*44	61	*105	28	....	....	....	....	....	....	....	....	....	....	....	10	6	8	14	6	....	....	....
1997-98	Philadelphia	AHL	80	27	*78	*105	28	....	....	....	....	....	....	....	....	....	....	....	20	9	9	18	6	....	....	....
1998-99	**Philadelphia**	**NHL**	**3**	**0**	**0**	**0**	**0**	**0**	**0**	**0**	**0**	**0.0**	**0**	**8**	**37.5**	**0**	**0**	**2:02**	....	....	....	....	....	....	....	....
	Philadelphia	AHL	77	31	59	90	20	....	....	....	....	....	....	....	....	....	....	....	16	4	13	17	12	....	....	....
	NHL Totals		**65**	**10**	**12**	**22**	**2**	**4**	**0**	**0**	**64**	**15.6**		**8**	**37.5**	**0**	**0**	**2:02**	....	....	....	....	....	....	....	....

AHL Second All-Star Team (1995, 1997) • Won John B. Sollenberger Trophy (Top Scorer - AHL) (1995, 1997, 1998)

Traded to **Toronto** by **Edmonton** with Edmonton's 4th round choice (Jason Sessa) in 1996 Entry Draft for Kent Manderville, December 4, 1995. Signed as a free agent by **Philadelphia**, August 19, 1996.

WHITE, Todd — CHI.

Center. Shoots left. 5'10", 189 lbs. Born, Kanata, Ont., May 21, 1975.

Season	Club	League	GP	G	A	Pts	PIM	PP	SH	GW	S	%	+/–	TF	F%	H	SB	Min	GP	G	A	Pts	PIM	PP	SH	GW
1993-94	Clarkson	ECAC	33	10	12	22	28	....	....	....	....	....	....	....	....	....	....	....	....	....	....	....	....	....	....	....
	Kanata Valley	OJHL	49	51	87	138	....	....	....	....	....	....	....	....	....	....	....	....	....	....	....	....	....	....	....	....
1994-95	Clarkson	ECAC	34	13	16	29	44	....	....	....	....	....	....	....	....	....	....	....	....	....	....	....	....	....	....	....
1995-96	Clarkson	ECAC	38	29	43	72	36	....	....	....	....	....	....	....	....	....	....	....	....	....	....	....	....	....	....	....
1996-97	Clarkson	ECAC	37	*38	*36	*74	22	....	....	....	....	....	....	....	....	....	....	....	....	....	....	....	....	....	....	....
1997-98	**Chicago**	**NHL**	**7**	**1**	**0**	**1**	**2**	**0**	**0**	**0**	**3**	**33.3**	**0**	....	....	....	....	....	....	....	....	....	....	....	....	....
	Indianapolis	IHL	65	46	36	82	28	....	....	....	....	....	....	....	....	....	....	....	5	2	3	5	4	....	....	....
1998-99	**Chicago**	**NHL**	**35**	**5**	**8**	**13**	**20**	**2**	**0**	**0**	**43**	**11.6**	**–1**	**452**	**46.0**	**27**	**11**	**13:39**	....	....	....	....	....	....	....	....
	Chicago	IHL	25	11	13	24	8	....	....	....	....	....	....	....	....	....	....	....	10	1	4	5	8	....	....	....
	NHL Totals		**42**	**6**	**8**	**14**	**22**	**2**	**0**	**0**	**46**	**13.0**		**452**	**46.0**	**27**	**11**	**13:39**	....	....	....	....	....	....	....	....

ECAC Second All-Star Team (1996) • NCAA East Second All-American Team (1996) • ECAC First All-Star Team (1997) • NCAA East First All-American Team (1997) • Won Garry F. Longman Memorial Trophy (Top Rookie - IHL) (1998)

Signed as a free agent by **Chicago**, August 27, 1997.

WHITNEY, Ray — FLA.

Left wing. Shoots right. 5'10", 175 lbs. Born, Fort Saskatchewan, Alta., May 8, 1972. San Jose's 2nd choice, 23rd overall, in 1991 Entry Draft.

Season	Club	League	GP	G	A	Pts	PIM	PP	SH	GW	S	%	+/–	TF	F%	H	SB	Min	GP	G	A	Pts	PIM	PP	SH	GW
1987-88	Ft. Saskatchewan	AAHA	71	80	155	235	119	....	....	....	....	....	....	....	....	....	....	....	....	....	....	....	....	....	....	....
1988-89	Spokane	WHL	71	17	33	50	16	....	....	....	....	....	....	....	....	....	....	....	....	....	....	....	....	....	....	....
1989-90	Spokane	WHL	71	57	56	113	50	....	....	....	....	....	....	....	....	....	....	....	6	3	4	7	6	....	....	....
1990-91	Spokane	WHL	72	67	118	*185	36	....	....	....	....	....	....	....	....	....	....	....	15	13	18	*31	12	....	....	....
1991-92	Kolner Haie	Germany	10	3	6	9	4	....	....	....	....	....	....	....	....	....	....	....	....	....	....	....	....	....	....	....
	Canada	Nat-Team	5	1	0	1	6	....	....	....	....	....	....	....	....	....	....	....	....	....	....	....	....	....	....	....
	San Jose	**NHL**	**2**	**0**	**3**	**3**	**0**	**0**	**0**	**0**	**4**	**0.0**	**–1**	....	....	....	....	....	....	....	....	....	....	....	....	....
	San Diego	IHL	63	36	54	90	12	....	....	....	....	....	....	....	....	....	....	....	4	0	0	0	0	....	....	....
1992-93	**San Jose**	**NHL**	**26**	**4**	**6**	**10**	**4**	**1**	**0**	**0**	**24**	**16.7**	**–14**	....	....	....	....	....	....	....	....	....	....	....	....	....
	Kansas City	IHL	46	20	33	53	14	....	....	....	....	....	....	....	....	....	....	....	12	5	7	12	2	....	....	....
1993-94	**San Jose**	**NHL**	**61**	**14**	**26**	**40**	**14**	**1**	**0**	**0**	**82**	**17.1**	**2**	....	....	....	....	....	**14**	**0**	**4**	**4**	**8**	**0**	**0**	**0**
1994-95	**San Jose**	**NHL**	**39**	**13**	**12**	**25**	**14**	**4**	**0**	**1**	**67**	**19.4**	**–7**	....	....	....	....	....	**11**	**4**	**4**	**8**	**2**	**0**	**0**	**1**
1995-96	**San Jose**	**NHL**	**60**	**17**	**24**	**41**	**16**	**4**	**2**	**2**	**106**	**16.0**	**–23**	....	....	....	....	....	....	....	....	....	....	....	....	....
1996-97	**San Jose**	**NHL**	**12**	**0**	**2**	**2**	**4**	**0**	**0**	**0**	**24**	**0.0**	**–6**	....	....	....	....	....	....	....	....	....	....	....	....	....
	Kentucky	AHL	9	1	7	8	2	....	....	....	....	....	....	....	....	....	....	....	....	....	....	....	....	....	....	....
	Utah	IHL	43	13	35	48	34	....	....	....	....	....	....	....	....	....	....	....	7	3	1	4	6	....	....	....
1997-98	**Edmonton**	**NHL**	**9**	**1**	**3**	**4**	**0**	**0**	**0**	**0**	**19**	**5.3**	**–1**	....	....	....	....	....	....	....	....	....	....	....	....	....
	Florida	**NHL**	**68**	**32**	**29**	**61**	**28**	**12**	**0**	**2**	**156**	**20.5**	**10**	....	....	....	....	....	....	....	....	....	....	....	....	....
1998-99	**Florida**	**NHL**	**81**	**26**	**38**	**64**	**18**	**7**	**0**	**6**	**193**	**13.5**	**–3**	**144**	**43.8**	**14**	**7**	**18:20**	....	....	....	....	....	....	....	....
	NHL Totals		**358**	**107**	**143**	**250**	**98**	**29**	**2**	**11**	**675**	**15.9**		**144**	**43.8**	**14**	**7**	**18:20**	**25**	**4**	**8**	**12**	**10**	**0**	**0**	**1**

WHL West First All-Star Team (1991) • Memorial Cup All-Star Team (1991) • Won George Parsons Trophy (Memorial Cup Tournament Most Sportsmanlike Player) (1991)

Signed as a free agent by **Edmonton**, October 1, 1997. Claimed on waivers by **Florida** from **Edmonton**, November 6, 1997.

WIDMER, Jason

Defense. Shoots left. 6', 200 lbs. Born, Calgary, Alta., August 1, 1973. NY Islanders' 8th choice, 176th overall, in 1992 Entry Draft.

Season	Club	League	GP	G	A	Pts	PIM	PP	SH	GW	S	%	+/–	TF	F%	H	SB	Min	GP	G	A	Pts	PIM	PP	SH	GW
1988-89	Lethbridge	AAHA	44	10	27	37	100	....	....	....	....	....	....	....	....	....	....	....	....	....	....	....	....	....	....	....
1989-90	Moose Jaw	WHL	58	1	8	9	33	....	....	....	....	....	....	....	....	....	....	....	....	....	....	....	....	....	....	....
1990-91	Lethbridge	WHL	58	2	12	14	55	....	....	....	....	....	....	....	....	....	....	....	16	0	1	1	12	....	....	....
1991-92	Lethbridge	WHL	40	2	19	21	181	....	....	....	....	....	....	....	....	....	....	....	5	0	4	4	9	....	....	....
1992-93	Lethbridge	WHL	55	3	15	18	140	....	....	....	....	....	....	....	....	....	....	....	4	0	3	3	2	....	....	....
	Capital District	AHL	4	0	0	0	2	....	....	....	....	....	....	....	....	....	....	....	....	....	....	....	....	....	....	....
1993-94	Lethbridge	WHL	64	11	31	42	191	....	....	....	....	....	....	....	....	....	....	....	9	3	5	8	34	....	....	....
1994-95	Canada	Nat-Team	6	1	4	5	4	....	....	....	....	....	....	....	....	....	....	....	....	....	....	....	....	....	....	....
	NY Islanders	**NHL**	**1**	**0**	**0**	**0**	**0**	**0**	**0**	**0**	**0**	**0.0**	**–1**	....	....	....	....	....	....	....	....	....	....	....	....	....
	Worcester	AHL	73	8	26	34	136	....	....	....	....	....	....	....	....	....	....	....	....	....	....	....	....	....	....	....
1995-96	**NY Islanders**	**NHL**	**4**	**0**	**0**	**0**	**7**	**0**	**0**	**0**	**1**	**0.0**	**0**	....	....	....	....	....	....	....	....	....	....	....	....	....
	Worcester	AHL	76	6	21	27	129	....	....	....	....	....	....	....	....	....	....	....	4	2	0	2	9	....	....	....
1996-97	**San Jose**	**NHL**	**2**	**0**	**1**	**1**	**0**	**0**	**0**	**0**	**0**	**0.0**	**1**	....	....	....	....	....	....	....	....	....	....	....	....	....
	Kentucky	AHL	76	4	24	28	105	....	....	....	....	....	....	....	....	....	....	....	4	0	0	0	8	....	....	....
1997-98	Kentucky	AHL	71	5	13	18	176	....	....	....	....	....	....	....	....	....	....	....	3	0	0	0	6	....	....	....
1998-99	Worcester	AHL	25	2	3	5	42	....	....	....	....	....	....	....	....	....	....	....	....	....	....	....	....	....	....	....
	NHL Totals		**7**	**0**	**1**	**1**	**7**	**0**	**0**	**0**	**1**	**0.0**		....	....	....	....	....	....	....	....	....	....	....	....	....

Signed as a free agent by **San Jose**, September 11, 1996. Signed as a free agent by **St. Louis**, July 28, 1998.

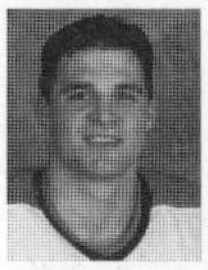

WIEMER, Jason (WEE-muhr) — CGY.

Center. Shoots left. 6'1", 225 lbs. Born, Kimberley, B.C., April 14, 1976. Tampa Bay's 1st choice, 8th overall, in 1994 Entry Draft.

Season	Club	League	GP	G	A	Pts	PIM	PP	SH	GW	S	%	+/–	TF	F%	H	SB	Min	GP	G	A	Pts	PIM	PP	SH	GW
1991-92	Kimberley	RMJHL	45	33	33	66	211	....	....	....	....	....	....	....	....	....	....	....	....	....	....	....	....	....	....	....
	Portland	WHL	2	0	1	1	0	....	....	....	....	....	....	....	....	....	....	....	....	....	....	....	....	....	....	....
1992-93	Portland	WHL	68	18	34	52	159	....	....	....	....	....	....	....	....	....	....	....	16	7	3	10	27	....	....	....
1993-94	Portland	WHL	72	45	51	96	236	....	....	....	....	....	....	....	....	....	....	....	10	4	4	8	32	....	....	....
1994-95	Portland	WHL	16	10	14	24	63	....	....	....	....	....	....	....	....	....	....	....	....	....	....	....	....	....	....	....
	Tampa Bay	**NHL**	**36**	**1**	**4**	**5**	**44**	**0**	**0**	**0**	**10**	**10.0**	**–2**	....	....	....	....	....	....	....	....	....	....	....	....	....
1995-96	**Tampa Bay**	**NHL**	**66**	**9**	**9**	**18**	**81**	**4**	**0**	**1**	**89**	**10.1**	**–9**	....	....	....	....	....	**6**	**1**	**0**	**1**	**28**	**1**	**0**	**0**
1996-97	**Tampa Bay**	**NHL**	**63**	**9**	**5**	**14**	**134**	**2**	**0**	**0**	**103**	**8.7**	**–13**	....	....	....	....	....	....	....	....	....	....	....	....	....
	Adirondack	AHL	4	1	0	1	7	....	....	....	....	....	....	....	....	....	....	....	....	....	....	....	....	....	....	....
1997-98	**Tampa Bay**	**NHL**	**67**	**8**	**9**	**17**	**132**	**2**	**0**	**0**	**106**	**7.5**	**–9**	....	....	....	....	....	....	....	....	....	....	....	....	....
	Calgary	**NHL**	**12**	**4**	**1**	**5**	**28**	**1**	**0**	**2**	**16**	**25.0**	**–1**	....	....	....	....	....	....	....	....	....	....	....	....	....
1998-99	**Calgary**	**NHL**	**78**	**8**	**13**	**21**	**177**	**1**	**0**	**1**	**128**	**6.3**	**–12**	**867**	**40.9**	**171**	**20**	**13:17**	....	....	....	....	....	....	....	....
	NHL Totals		**322**	**39**	**41**	**80**	**596**	**10**	**0**	**4**	**452**	**8.6**		**867**	**40.9**	**171**	**20**	**13:17**	**6**	**1**	**0**	**1**	**28**	**1**	**0**	**0**

Traded to **Calgary** by **Tampa Bay** for Sandy McCarthy and Calgary's 3rd (Brad Richards) and 5th (Curtis Rich) round choices in 1998 Entry Draft, March 24, 1998.

WILKIE, David

Defense. Shoots right. 6'2", 210 lbs. Born, Ellensburgh, WA, May 30, 1974. Montreal's 1st choice, 20th overall, in 1992 Entry Draft.

			Regular Season																Playoffs							
Season	Club	League	GP	G	A	Pts	PIM	PP	SH	GW	S	%	+/-	TF	F%	H	SB	Min	GP	G	A	Pts	PIM	PP	SH	GW
1989-90	Seattle North	PIJHL	41	21	27	48	59																			
1990-91	Seattle	WHL	25	1	1	2	22																			
1991-92	Kamloops	WHL	71	12	28	40	153												16	6	5	11	19			
1992-93	Kamloops	WHL	53	11	26	37	109												6	4	2	6	2			
1993-94	Kamloops	WHL	27	11	18	29	18																			
	Regina	WHL	29	27	21	48	16												4	1	4	5	4			
1994-95	Fredericton	AHL	70	10	43	53	34												1	0	0	0	0			
	Montreal	NHL	1	0	0	0	0	0	0	0	0	0.0	0													
1995-96	Montreal	NHL	24	1	5	6	10	1	0	0	39	2.6	−10						6	1	2	3	12	0	0	0
	Fredericton	AHL	23	5	12	17	20																			
1996-97	Montreal	NHL	61	6	9	15	63	3	0	0	65	9.2	−9						2	0	0	0	2	0	0	0
1997-98	Montreal	NHL	5	1	0	1	4	0	0	1	2	50.0	−1													
	Tampa Bay	NHL	29	1	5	6	17	0	0	0	46	2.2	−21													
1998-99	Tampa Bay	NHL	46	1	7	8	69	0	0	0	35	2.9	−19	0	0.0	49	48	12:18								
	Cleveland	IHL	2	0	2	2	0																			
	NHL Totals		166	10	26	36	163	4	0	1	187	5.3		0	0.0	49	48	12:18	8	1	2	3	14	0	0	0

Traded to **Tampa Bay** by **Montreal** with Stephane Richer and Darcy Tucker for Patrick Poulin, Mick Vukota and Igor Ulanov, January 15, 1998.

WILKINSON, Neil

Defense. Shoots right. 6'3", 194 lbs. Born, Selkirk, Man., August 15, 1967. Minnesota's 2nd choice, 30th overall, in 1986 Entry Draft.

			Regular Season																Playoffs							
Season	Club	League	GP	G	A	Pts	PIM	PP	SH	GW	S	%	+/-	TF	F%	H	SB	Min	GP	G	A	Pts	PIM	PP	SH	GW
1985-86	Selkirk	MJHL	42	14	35	49	91																			
1986-87	Michigan State	CCHA	19	3	4	7	18																			
1987-88	Medicine Hat	WHL	55	11	21	32	157												5	1	0	1	2			
1988-89	Kalamazoo	IHL	39	5	15	20	96																			
1989-90	Minnesota	NHL	36	0	5	5	100	0	0	0	36	0.0	−1						7	0	2	2	11	0	0	0
	Kalamazoo	IHL	20	6	7	13	62																			
1990-91	Minnesota	NHL	50	2	9	11	117	0	0	0	55	3.6	−5						22	3	3	6	12	1	0	0
	Kalamazoo	IHL	10	0	3	3	38																			
1991-92	San Jose	NHL	60	4	15	19	107	1	0	0	95	4.2	−11													
1992-93	San Jose	NHL	59	1	7	8	96	0	1	0	51	2.0	−50													
1993-94	Chicago	NHL	72	3	9	12	116	1	0	0	72	4.2	2						4	0	0	0	0	0	0	0
1994-95	Winnipeg	NHL	40	1	4	5	75	0	0	0	25	4.0	−26													
1995-96	Winnipeg	NHL	21	1	4	5	33	0	1	1	17	5.9	0													
	Pittsburgh	NHL	41	2	10	12	87	0	0	0	42	4.8	12						15	0	1	1	14	0	0	0
1996-97	Pittsburgh	NHL	23	0	0	0	36	0	0	0	16	0.0	−12						5	0	0	0	4	0	0	0
	Cleveland	IHL	2	0	1	1	0																			
1997-98	Pittsburgh	NHL	34	2	4	6	24	1	0	0	19	10.5	0													
1998-99	Pittsburgh	NHL	24	0	0	0	22	0	0	0	11	0.0	−2	0	0.0	25	8	9:58								
	NHL Totals		460	16	67	83	813	3	2	1	439	3.6		0	0.0	25	8	9:58	53	3	6	9	41	1	0	0

Claimed by **San Jose** from **Minnesota** in Dispersal Draft, May 30, 1991. Traded to **Chicago** by **San Jose** to complete transaction that sent Jimmy Waite to San Jose (June 18, 1993), July 9, 1993. Traded to **Winnipeg** by **Chicago** for Chicago's 3rd round choice (previously acquired, Chicago selected Kevin McKay) in 1995 Entry Draft, June 3, 1994. Traded to **Pittsburgh** by **Winnipeg** for Norm Maciver, December 28, 1995.

WILLIS, Shane — CAR.

Right wing. Shoots right. 6', 176 lbs. Born, Edmonton, Alta., June 13, 1977. Carolina's 4th choice, 88th overall, in 1997 Entry Draft.

			Regular Season																Playoffs							
Season	Club	League	GP	G	A	Pts	PIM	PP	SH	GW	S	%	+/-	TF	F%	H	SB	Min	GP	G	A	Pts	PIM	PP	SH	GW
1993-94	Red Deer	AAHA	34	40	26	66	103																			
1994-95	Prince Albert	WHL	65	24	19	43	38												13	3	4	7	6			
1995-96	Prince Albert	WHL	69	41	40	81	47												18	11	10	21	18			
1996-97	Prince Albert	WHL	41	34	22	56	63																			
	Lethbridge	WHL	26	22	17	39	24												19	13	11	24	20			
1997-98	Lethbridge	WHL	64	58	54	112	73												4	2	3	5	6			
	New Haven	AHL	1	0	1	1	2																			
1998-99	Carolina	NHL	7	0	0	0	0	0	....	0	1	0.0	....	0	0.0	4	2	2:14								
	New Haven	AHL	73	31	50	81	49																			
	NHL Totals		7	0	0	0	0	0	....	0	1	0.0		0	0.0	4	2	2:14								

WHL East First All-Star Team (1997, 1998) • AHL First All-Star Team (1999) • Won Dudley "Red" Garrett Memorial Trophy (Top Rookie - AHL) (1999)
• Re-entered NHL Entry Draft. Tampa Bay's 3rd choice, 56th overall, in 1995 Entry Draft.

WILM, Clarke (WIHLM) — CGY.

Center. Shoots left. 6', 195 lbs. Born, Central Butte, Sask., October 24, 1976. Calgary's 5th choice, 150th overall, in 1995 Entry Draft.

			Regular Season																Playoffs							
Season	Club	League	GP	G	A	Pts	PIM	PP	SH	GW	S	%	+/-	TF	F%	H	SB	Min	GP	G	A	Pts	PIM	PP	SH	GW
1991-92	Saskatoon	SAHA	36	18	28	46	16																			
	Saskatoon	WHL																	1	0	0	0	0			
1992-93	Saskatoon	WHL	69	14	19	33	71												9	4	2	6	13			
1993-94	Saskatoon	WHL	70	18	32	50	181												16	0	9	9	19			
1994-95	Saskatoon	WHL	71	20	39	59	179												10	6	1	7	21			
1995-96	Saskatoon	WHL	72	49	61	110	83												4	1	1	2	4			
1996-97	Saint John	AHL	62	9	19	28	107												5	2	0	2	15			
1997-98	Saint John	AHL	68	13	26	39	112												21	5	9	14	8			
1998-99	Calgary	NHL	78	10	8	18	53	2	2	0	94	10.6	11	609	40.9	94	21	11:32								
	NHL Totals		78	10	8	18	53	2	2	0	94	10.6		609	40.9	94	21	11:32								

WILSON, Landon — BOS.

Right wing. Shoots right. 6'2", 216 lbs. Born, St. Louis, MO, March 13, 1975. Toronto's 2nd choice, 19th overall, in 1993 Entry Draft.

			Regular Season																Playoffs							
Season	Club	League	GP	G	A	Pts	PIM	PP	SH	GW	S	%	+/-	TF	F%	H	SB	Min	GP	G	A	Pts	PIM	PP	SH	GW
1991-92	California	USJHL	38	50	42	92	135																			
1992-93	Dubuque	USHL	43	29	36	65	284																			
1993-94	North Dakota	WCHA	35	18	15	33	*147																			
1994-95	North Dakota	WCHA	31	7	16	23	141																			
	Cornwall	AHL	8	4	4	8	25												13	3	4	7	68			
1995-96	Colorado	NHL	7	1	0	1	6	0	0	0	6	16.7	3													
	Cornwall	AHL	53	21	13	34	154												8	1	3	4	22			
1996-97	Colorado	NHL	9	1	2	3	23	0	0	0	7	14.3	1													
	Boston	NHL	40	7	10	17	49	0	0	0	76	9.2	−6													
	Providence	AHL	2	2	1	3	2												10	3	4	7	16			
1997-98	Boston	NHL	28	1	5	6	7	0	0	0	26	3.8	3						1	0	0	0	0	0	0	0
	Providence	AHL	42	18	10	28	146																			
1998-99	Boston	NHL	22	3	3	6	17	0	0	0	32	9.4	0	3	0.0	59	2	10:04	8	1	1	2	8	1	0	1
	Providence	AHL	48	31	22	53	89												11	7	1	8	19			
	NHL Totals		106	13	20	33	102	0	0	0	147	8.8		3	0.0	59	2	10:04	9	1	1	2	8	1	0	1

AHL First All-Star Team (1999)

Traded to **Quebec** by **Toronto** with Wendel Clark, Sylvain Lefebvre and Toronto's 1st round choice (Jeffrey Kealty) in 1994 Entry Draft for Mats Sundin, Garth Butcher, Todd Warriner and Philadelphia's 1st round choice (previously acquired by Quebec — later traded to Washington — Washington selected Nolan Baumgartner) in 1994 Entry Draft, June 28, 1994. Traded to **Boston** by **Colorado** with Anders Myrvold for Boston's 1st round choice (Robyn Regehr) in 1998 Entry Draft, November 22, 1996.

WILSON, Mike — FLA.

Defense. Shoots left. 6'6", 212 lbs. Born, Brampton, Ont., February 26, 1975. Vancouver's 1st choice, 20th overall, in 1993 Entry Draft.

			Regular Season																Playoffs							
Season	Club	League	GP	G	A	Pts	PIM	PP	SH	GW	S	%	+/-	TF	F%	H	SB	Min	GP	G	A	Pts	PIM	PP	SH	GW
1991-92	Georgetown	OJHL-B	41	9	13	22	65																			
1992-93	Sudbury	OHL	53	6	7	13	58												14	1	1	2	2			
1993-94	Sudbury	OHL	60	4	22	26	62												9	1	3	4	8			
1994-95	Sudbury	OHL	64	13	34	47	46												18	1	8	9	10			
1995-96	**Buffalo**	**NHL**	**58**	**4**	**8**	**12**	**41**	**1**	**0**	**1**	**52**	**7.7**	**13**													
	Rochester	AHL	15	0	5	5	38																			
1996-97	**Buffalo**	**NHL**	**77**	**2**	**9**	**11**	**51**	**0**	**0**	**1**	**57**	**3.5**	**13**						**10**	**0**	**1**	**1**	**2**	**0**	**0**	**0**
1997-98	**Buffalo**	**NHL**	**66**	**4**	**4**	**8**	**48**	**0**	**0**	**1**	**52**	**7.7**	**13**						**15**	**0**	**1**	**1**	**13**	**0**	**0**	**0**
1998-99	**Buffalo**	**NHL**	**30**	**1**	**2**	**3**	**47**	**0**	**0**	**1**	**40**	**2.5**	**10**	**0**	**0.0**	**54**	**19**	**16:40**								
	Florida	**NHL**	**4**	**0**	**0**	**0**	**0**	**0**	**0**	**0**	**8**	**0.0**	**2**	**0**	**0.0**	**4**	**6**	**19:23**								
	Las Vegas	IHL	6	3	1	4	6																			
	NHL Totals		**235**	**11**	**23**	**34**	**187**	**1**	**0**	**4**	**209**	**5.3**		**0**	**0.0**	**58**	**25**	**16:59**	**25**	**0**	**2**	**2**	**15**	**0**	**0**	**0**

Traded to **Buffalo** by **Vancouver** with Mike Peca and Vancouver's 1st round choice (Jay McKee) in 1995 Entry Draft for Alexander Mogilny and Buffalo's 5th round choice (Todd Norman) in 1995 Entry Draft, July 8, 1995. Traded to **Florida** by **Buffalo** for Rhett Warrener and Florida's 5th round choice (Ryan Miller) in 1999 Entry Draft, March 23, 1999.

WINNES, Chris (WIHN-ehs)

Right wing. Shoots right. 6', 201 lbs. Born, Ridgefield, CT, February 12, 1968. Boston's 9th choice, 161st overall, in 1987 Entry Draft.

			Regular Season																Playoffs							
Season	Club	League	GP	G	A	Pts	PIM	PP	SH	GW	S	%	+/-	TF	F%	H	SB	Min	GP	G	A	Pts	PIM	PP	SH	GW
1985-86	Ridgefield High	H.S.	24	40	30	70																				
1986-87	Northwood Prep	H.S.	27	25	25	50																				
	Ridgefield High	H.S.	47	25	33	58	56																			
1987-88	New Hampshire	H.E.	30	17	19	36	28																			
1988-89	New Hampshire	H.E.	30	11	20	31	22																			
1989-90	New Hampshire	H.E.	24	10	13	23	12																			
1990-91	New Hampshire	H.E.	33	15	16	31	24																			
	Maine	AHL	7	3	1	4	0												1	0	2	2	0			
	Boston	**NHL**																	**1**	**0**	**0**	**0**	**0**			
1991-92	**Boston**	**NHL**	**24**	**1**	**3**	**4**	**6**	**0**	**0**	**0**	**20**	**5.0**	**-6**													
	Maine	AHL	45	12	35	47	30																			
1992-93	**Boston**	**NHL**	**5**	**0**	**1**	**1**	**0**	**0**	**0**	**0**	**2**	**0.0**	**1**													
	Providence	AHL	64	23	36	59	34												4	0	2	2	5			
1993-94	**Philadelphia**	**NHL**	**4**	**0**	**2**	**2**	**0**	**0**	**0**	**0**	**4**	**0.0**	**1**													
	Hershey	AHL	70	29	21	50	20												7	1	3	4	0			
1994-95	Hershey	AHL	78	26	40	66	39												6	2	2	4	17			
1995-96	Michigan	IHL	27	6	13	19	14																			
	Fort Wayne	IHL	39	6	7	13	12												2	0	0	0	0			
1996-97	Utah	IHL	5	0	0	0	0																			
	HC Merano	Italy	12	11	5	16	10																			
1997-98	San Antonio	IHL	3	0	0	0	0																			
	Hartford	AHL	64	17	23	40	16												13	1	4	5	2			
1998-99	Hartford	AHL	33	7	6	13	25												1	0	0	0	0			
	Manitoba	IHL	11	2	0	2	0																			
	NHL Totals		**33**	**1**	**6**	**7**	**6**	**0**	**0**	**0**	**26**	**3.8**							**1**	**0**	**0**	**0**	**0**			

Signed as a free agent by **Philadelphia**, August 4, 1993. Signed as a free agent by **NY Rangers**, July 21, 1998.

WISEMAN, Brian — TOR.

Center. Shoots left. 5'8", 175 lbs. Born, Chatham, Ont., July 13, 1971. NY Rangers' 11th choice, 257th overall, in 1991 Entry Draft.

			Regular Season																Playoffs							
Season	Club	League	GP	G	A	Pts	PIM	PP	SH	GW	S	%	+/-	TF	F%	H	SB	Min	GP	G	A	Pts	PIM	PP	SH	GW
1987-88	Chatham	OJHL-B	41	26	33	59	35																			
1988-89	Chatham	OJHL-B	STATISTICS NOT AVAILABLE																							
1989-90	Chatham	OJHL-B	42	70	77	147																				
1990-91	U. of Michigan	CCHA	47	25	33	58	58																			
1991-92	U. of Michigan	CCHA	44	27	44	71	38																			
1992-93	U. of Michigan	CCHA	35	13	37	50	40																			
1993-94	U. of Michigan	CCHA	40	19	50	69	44																			
1994-95	Chicago	IHL	75	17	55	72	52												3	1	1	2	4			
1995-96	Chicago	IHL	73	33	55	88	117																			
1996-97	**Toronto**	**NHL**	**3**	**0**	**0**	**0**	**0**	**0**	**0**	**0**	**1**	**0.0**	**0**													
	St. John's	AHL	71	33	62	95	83												7	5	4	9	8			
1997-98	Houston	IHL	78	26	72	98	86												4	0	3	3	8			
1998-99	Houston	IHL	77	21	*88	*109	106												19	3	13	16	26			
	NHL Totals		**3**	**0**	**0**	**0**	**0**	**0**	**0**	**0**	**1**	**0.0**														

CCHA First All-Star Team (1994) • NCAA West First All-American Team (1994) • IHL First All-Star Team (1998, 1999) • Won Leo P. Lamoureux Memorial Trophy (Top Scorer - IHL) (1999) • Won James Gatschene Memorial Trophy (MVP - IHL) (1999)

Signed as a free agent by **Toronto**, August 14, 1996. Signed as a free agent by **Toronto**, July 13, 1999.

WITEHALL, Johan — NYR

Left wing. Shoots left. 6'1", 198 lbs. Born, Kungsbacka, Sweden, January 7, 1972. NY Rangers' 8th choice, 207th overall, in 1998 Entry Draft.

			Regular Season																Playoffs							
Season	Club	League	GP	G	A	Pts	PIM	PP	SH	GW	S	%	+/-	TF	F%	H	SB	Min	GP	G	A	Pts	PIM	PP	SH	GW
1991-92	Hanhals Kungs.	Sweden-2	32	23	14	37	52																			
1992-93	Hanhals Kungs.	Sweden-2	29	12	7	19	34																			
1993-94	Hanhals Kungs.	Sweden-2	30	13	12	25	66																			
1994-95	Hanhals Kungs.	Sweden-2	32	38	13	51	44																			
1995-96	Hanhals Kungs.	Sweden-2	36	43	17	60	48																			
1996-97	IK Oskarshamn	Sweden-2	32	19	16	35	38																			
1997-98	Leksands IF	Sweden	42	12	4	16	34												2	0	0	0	2			
	Leksands IF	EuroHL	5	3	0	3	2																			
1998-99	**NY Rangers**	**NHL**	**4**	**0**	**0**	**0**	**0**	**0**	**0**	**0**	**1**	**0.0**	**0**	**1**	**100.0**	**5**	**0**	**4:06**								
	Hartford	AHL	62	14	15	29	56												7	1	2	3	6			
	NHL Totals		**4**	**0**	**0**	**0**	**0**	**0**	**0**	**0**	**1**	**0.0**		**1**	**100.0**	**5**	**0**	**4:06**								

WITT, Brendan — WSH.

Defense. Shoots left. 6'1", 226 lbs. Born, Humbolt, Sask., February 20, 1975. Washington's 1st choice, 11th overall, in 1993 Entry Draft.

			Regular Season																Playoffs							
Season	Club	League	GP	G	A	Pts	PIM	PP	SH	GW	S	%	+/-	TF	F%	H	SB	Min	GP	G	A	Pts	PIM	PP	SH	GW
1990-91	Saskatoon	SAHA	31	5	13	18	42																			
	Seattle	WHL																	1	0	0	0	0			
1991-92	Seattle	WHL	67	3	9	12	212												15	1	1	2	84			
1992-93	Seattle	WHL	70	2	26	28	239												5	1	2	3	30			
1993-94	Seattle	WHL	56	8	31	39	235												9	3	8	11	23			
1994-95			DID NOT PLAY																							
1995-96	**Washington**	**NHL**	**48**	**2**	**3**	**5**	**85**	**0**	**0**	**1**	**44**	**4.5**	**-4**													
1996-97	**Washington**	**NHL**	**44**	**3**	**2**	**5**	**88**	**0**	**0**	**0**	**41**	**7.3**	**-20**													
	Portland	AHL	30	2	4	6	56												5	1	0	1	30			
1997-98	**Washington**	**NHL**	**64**	**1**	**7**	**8**	**112**	**0**	**0**	**0**	**68**	**1.5**	**-11**						**16**	**1**	**0**	**1**	**14**	**0**	**0**	**0**

Season	Club	League	GP	G	A	Pts	PIM	PP	SH	GW	S	%	+/-	TF	F%	H	SB	Min	GP	G	A	Pts	PIM	PP	SH	GW
											Regular Season											Playoffs				
1998-99	Washington	NHL	54	2	5	7	87	0	0	0	51	3.9	−6	0	0.0	148	52	15:50	....							
	NHL Totals		210	8	17	25	372	0	0	1	204	3.9		0	0.0	148	52	15:50	16	1	0	1	14	0	0	0

WHL West First All-Star Team (1993, 1994) • Canadian Major Junior First All-Star Team (1994)
• Sat out entire 1994-95 season after failing to come to contract terms with Washington.

WOLANIN, Craig (wuh-LAN-ihn)

Defense. Shoots left. 6'4", 215 lbs.   Born, Grosse Pointe, MI, July 27, 1967. New Jersey's 1st choice, 3rd overall, in 1985 Entry Draft.

Season	Club	League	GP	G	A	Pts	PIM	PP	SH	GW	S	%	+/-	TF	F%	H	SB	Min	GP	G	A	Pts	PIM	PP	SH	GW
1983-84	Detroit	NAJHL	69	8	42	50	86																			
1984-85	Kitchener	OHL	60	5	16	21	95												4	1	1	2	2			
1985-86	New Jersey	NHL	44	2	16	18	74	0	0	1	45	4.4	−7													
1986-87	New Jersey	NHL	68	4	6	10	109	0	0	0	68	5.9	−31													
1987-88	New Jersey	NHL	78	6	25	31	170	1	1	3	113	5.3	0						18	2	5	7	51	1	0	0
1988-89	New Jersey	NHL	56	3	8	11	69	0	0	0	70	4.3	−9													
1989-90	New Jersey	NHL	37	1	7	8	47	0	0	0	35	2.9	−13													
	Utica	AHL	6	2	4	6	2																			
	Quebec	NHL	13	0	3	3	10	0	0	0	25	0.0	2													
1990-91	Quebec	NHL	80	5	13	18	89	0	1	0	109	4.6	−13													
1991-92	Quebec	NHL	69	2	11	13	80	0	0	0	71	2.8	−12													
1992-93	Quebec	NHL	24	1	4	5	49	0	0	0	17	5.9	9						4	0	0	0	4	0	0	
1993-94	Quebec	NHL	63	6	10	16	80	0	0	0	78	7.7	16													
1994-95	Quebec	NHL	40	3	6	9	40	0	0	0	36	8.3	12						6	1	1	2	4	0	0	0
1995-96♦	Colorado	NHL	75	7	20	27	50	0	3	0	73	9.6	25						7	1	0	1	8	0	0	1
1996-97	Tampa Bay	NHL	15	0	0	0	8	0	0	0	12	0.0	−9													
	Toronto	NHL	23	0	4	4	13	0	0	0	31	0.0	3													
1997-98	Toronto	NHL	10	0	0	0	6	0	0	0	5	0.0	−9													
1998-99	Detroit	IHL	16	0	5	5	21												11	0	0	0	12			
	NHL Totals		695	40	133	173	894	1	5	4	788	5.1							35	4	6	10	67	1	0	1

Traded to **Quebec** by **New Jersey** with future considerations (Randy Velischek, August 13, 1990) for Peter Stastny, March 6, 1990. Transferred to **Colorado** after **Quebec** franchise relocated, July 1, 1995. Traded to **Tampa Bay** by **Colorado** for Tampa Bay's 2nd round choice (Ramzi Abid) in 1998 Entry Draft, July 29, 1996. Traded to **Toronto** by **Tampa Bay** for Toronto's 3rd round choice (later traded to Edmonton — Edmonton Selected Alex Henry) in 1998 Entry Draft, January 31, 1997. • Missed majority of 1997-98 and 1998-99 seasons recovering from severe knee injury suffered in game vs. Montreal, November 1, 1997. Signed as a free agent by **Detroit** (IHL), January 31, 1999.

WOOD, Dody

Center. Shoots left. 6', 200 lbs.   Born, Chetwynd, B.C., March 18, 1972. San Jose's 4th choice, 45th overall, in 1991 Entry Draft.

Season	Club	League	GP	G	A	Pts	PIM	PP	SH	GW	S	%	+/-	TF	F%	H	SB	Min	GP	G	A	Pts	PIM	PP	SH	GW
1989-90	Fort St. John	PCJHL	44	51	73	124	270																			
	Seattle	WHL																	5	0	0	0	2			
1990-91	Seattle	WHL	69	28	37	65	272												6	0	1	1	2			
1991-92	Seattle	WHL	37	13	19	32	232																			
	Swift Current	WHL	3	0	2	2	14												7	2	1	3	37			
1992-93	San Jose	NHL	13	1	1	2	71	0	0	0	10	10.0	−5													
	Kansas City	IHL	36	3	2	5	216												6	0	1	1	15			
1993-94	Kansas City	IHL	48	5	15	20	320																			
1994-95	Kansas City	IHL	44	5	13	18	255												21	7	10	17	87			
	San Jose	NHL	9	1	1	2	29	0	0	0	5	20.0	0													
1995-96	San Jose	NHL	32	3	6	9	138	0	1	0	33	9.1	0													
1996-97	San Jose	NHL	44	3	2	5	193	0	0	0	43	7.0	−3													
	Kansas City	IHL	6	3	6	9	35																			
1997-98	San Jose	NHL	8	0	0	0	40	0	0	0	4	0.0	−3													
	Kansas City	IHL	2	0	1	1	31																			
	Albany	AHL	34	4	13	17	185												13	2	0	2	55			
1998-99	Kansas City	IHL	60	11	16	27	286												3	0	1	1	25			
	NHL Totals		106	8	10	18	471	0	1	0	95	8.4														

Traded to **New Jersey** by **San Jose** with Doug Bodger for John MacLean and Ken Sutton, December 7, 1997.

WOOLLEY, Jason (WOO-lee) **BUF.**

Defense. Shoots left. 6'1", 188 lbs.   Born, Toronto, Ont., July 27, 1969. Washington's 4th choice, 61st overall, in 1989 Entry Draft.

Season	Club	League	GP	G	A	Pts	PIM	PP	SH	GW	S	%	+/-	TF	F%	H	SB	Min	GP	G	A	Pts	PIM	PP	SH	GW
1986-87	St. Michael's	OJHL-B	35	13	22	35	40																			
1987-88	St. Michael's	OJHL-B	31	19	37	56	22																			
1988-89	Michigan State	CCHA	47	12	25	37	26																			
1989-90	Michigan State	CCHA	45	10	38	48	26																			
1990-91	Michigan State	CCHA	40	15	44	59	24																			
1991-92	Canada	Nat-Team	60	14	30	44	36																			
	Canada	Olympics	8	0	5	5	4																			
	Washington	NHL	1	0	0	0	0	0	0	0	2	0.0	1													
	Baltimore	AHL	15	1	10	11	6																			
1992-93	Washington	NHL	26	0	2	2	10	0	0	0	11	0.0	3													
	Baltimore	AHL	29	14	27	41	22												1	0	2	2	0			
1993-94	Washington	NHL	10	1	2	3	4	0	0	0	15	6.7	2						4	1	0	1	4	0	0	1
	Portland	AHL	41	12	29	41	14												9	2	2	4	4			
1994-95	Detroit	IHL	48	8	28	36	38																			
	Florida	NHL	34	4	9	13	18	1	0	0	76	5.3	−1													
1995-96	Florida	NHL	52	6	28	34	32	3	0	0	98	6.1	−9						13	2	6	8	14	1	0	1
1996-97	Florida	NHL	3	0	0	0	2	0	0	0	7	0.0	1													
	Pittsburgh	NHL	57	6	30	36	28	2	0	1	79	7.6	3						5	0	3	3	0	0	0	0
1997-98	Buffalo	NHL	71	9	26	35	35	3	0	2	129	7.0	8						15	2	9	11	12	1	0	1
1998-99	Buffalo	NHL	80	10	33	43	62	4	0	2	154	6.5	16	0	0.0	68	67	18:43	21	4	11	15	10	2	0	1
	NHL Totals		334	36	130	166	191	13	0	5	571	6.3		0	0.0	68	67	18:43	58	9	29	38	40	4	0	4

CCHA First All-Star Team (1991) • NCAA West First All-American Team (1991)

Signed as a free agent by **Florida**, February 15, 1995. Traded to **Pittsburgh** by **Florida** with Stu Barnes for Chris Wells, November 19, 1996. Traded to **Buffalo** by **Pittsburgh** for Buffalo's 5th round choice (Robert Scuderi) in 1998 Entry Draft, September 24, 1997.

WORRELL, Peter (woh-REHL) **FLA.**

Left wing. Shoots left. 6'6", 235 lbs.   Born, Pierrefonds, Que., August 18, 1977. Florida's 7th choice, 166th overall, in 1995 Entry Draft.

Season	Club	League	GP	G	A	Pts	PIM	PP	SH	GW	S	%	+/-	TF	F%	H	SB	Min	GP	G	A	Pts	PIM	PP	SH	GW
1994-95	Hull	QMJHL	56	1	8	9	243												21	0	1	1	91			
1995-96	Hull	QMJHL	63	23	36	59	464												18	11	8	19	81			
1996-97	Hull	QMJHL	62	17	46	63	437												14	3	13	16	83			
1997-98	Florida	NHL	19	0	0	0	153	0	0	0	15	0.0	−4													
	New Haven	AHL	50	15	12	27	309												1	0	1	1	6			
1998-99	Florida	NHL	62	4	5	9	258	0	0	2	50	8.0	0	0	0.0	100	5	6:15								
	New Haven	AHL	10	3	1	4	65																			
	NHL Totals		81	4	5	9	411	0	0	2	65	6.2		0	0.0	100	5	6:15								

WOTTON, Mark (WAH-tuhn) DAL.

Defense. Shoots left. 6', 190 lbs. Born, Foxwarren, Man., November 16, 1973. Vancouver's 11th choice, 237th overall, in 1992 Entry Draft.

			Regular Season																Playoffs							
Season	Club	League	GP	G	A	Pts	PIM	PP	SH	GW	S	%	+/–	TF	F%	H	SB	Min	GP	G	A	Pts	PIM	PP	SH	GW
1989-90	Foxwarren	MAHA	60	10	30	40	70																			
1990-91	Saskatoon	WHL	45	4	11	15	37																			
1991-92	Saskatoon	WHL	64	11	25	36	92																			
1992-93	Saskatoon	WHL	71	15	51	66	90												9	6	5	11	18			
1993-94	Saskatoon	WHL	65	12	34	46	108												16	3	12	15	32			
1994-95	Syracuse	AHL	75	12	29	41	50																			
	Vancouver	NHL	1	0	0	0	0	0	0	0	2	0.0	1						5	0	0	0	4	0	0	0
1995-96	Syracuse	AHL	80	10	35	45	96												15	1	12	13	20			
1996-97	Vancouver	NHL	36	3	6	9	19	0	1	0	41	7.3	8													
	Syracuse	AHL	27	2	8	10	25												2	0	0	0	4			
1997-98	Vancouver	NHL	5	0	0	0	6	0	0	0	3	0.0	–2													
	Syracuse	AHL	56	12	21	33	80												5	0	0	0	12			
1998-99	Syracuse	AHL	72	4	31	35	74																			
	NHL Totals		42	3	6	9	25	0	1	0	46	6.5							5	0	0	0	4	0	0	0

WHL East Second All-Star Team (1994)

Signed as a free agent by **Dallas**, July 19, 1999.

WREN, Bob (REHN) ANA.

Center. Shoots left. 5'10", 185 lbs. Born, Preston, Ont., September 16, 1974. Los Angeles' 3rd choice, 94th overall, in 1993 Entry Draft.

			Regular Season																Playoffs							
Season	Club	League	GP	G	A	Pts	PIM	PP	SH	GW	S	%	+/–	TF	F%	H	SB	Min	GP	G	A	Pts	PIM	PP	SH	GW
1989-90	Guelph	OJHL	48	24	36	60	12																			
1990-91	Guelph	OJHL	18	17	13	30	25																			
	Kingston	OJHL	14	10	15	25	34																			
1991-92	Detroit	OHL	62	13	36	49	58												7	3	4	7	19			
1992-93	Detroit	OHL	63	57	88	145	91												15	4	11	15	20			
1993-94	Detroit	OHL	57	45	64	109	81												17	12	18	30	20			
1994-95	Springfield	AHL	61	16	15	31	118																			
	Richmond	ECHL	2	0	1	1	0																			
1995-96	Detroit	IHL	1	0	0	0	0																			
	Knoxville	ECHL	50	21	35	56	257												8	4	11	15	32			
1996-97	Baltimore	AHL	72	23	36	59	97												3	1	1	2	0			
1997-98	Anaheim	NHL	3	0	0	0	0	0	0	0	4	0.0	0													
	Cincinnati	AHL	77	*42	58	100	151																			
1998-99	Cincinnati	AHL	73	27	43	70	102												3	1	2	3	8			
	NHL Totals		3	0	0	0	0	0	0	0	4	0.0														

OHL Second All-Star Team (1993, 1994)

Signed as a free agent by **Hartford**, September 6, 1994. Signed as a free agent by **Anaheim**, August 1, 1997.

WRIGHT, Jamie (RIGHT) DAL.

Left wing. Shoots left. 6', 185 lbs. Born, Kitchener, Ont., May 13, 1976. Dallas' 3rd choice, 98th overall, in 1994 Entry Draft.

			Regular Season																Playoffs							
Season	Club	League	GP	G	A	Pts	PIM	PP	SH	GW	S	%	+/–	TF	F%	H	SB	Min	GP	G	A	Pts	PIM	PP	SH	GW
1991-92	Elmira	OJHL-B	44	17	11	28	46																			
1992-93	Elmira	OJHL-B	47	22	32	54	52																			
1993-94	Guelph	OHL	65	17	15	32	34												8	2	1	3	10			
1994-95	Guelph	OHL	65	43	39	82	36												14	6	8	14	6			
1995-96	Guelph	OHL	55	30	36	66	45												16	10	12	22	35			
1996-97	Michigan	IHL	60	6	8	14	34												1	0	0	0	0			
1997-98	Dallas	NHL	21	4	2	6	2	0	0	2	15	26.7	8						5	0	0	0	0	0	0	0
	Michigan	IHL	53	15	11	26	31																			
1998-99	Dallas	NHL	11	0	0	0	0	0	0	0	10	0.0	–3	0	0.0	18	4	7:37								
	Michigan	IHL	64	16	15	31	92												2	0	0	0	2			
	NHL Totals		32	4	2	6	2	0	0	2	25	16.0		0	0.0	18	4	7:37	5	0	0	0	0	0	0	0

WRIGHT, Tyler (RIGHT)

Center. Shoots right. 5'11", 185 lbs. Born, Canora, Sask., April 6, 1973. Edmonton's 1st choice, 12th overall, in 1991 Entry Draft.

			Regular Season																Playoffs							
Season	Club	League	GP	G	A	Pts	PIM	PP	SH	GW	S	%	+/–	TF	F%	H	SB	Min	GP	G	A	Pts	PIM	PP	SH	GW
1988-89	Swift Current	SAHA	36	20	13	33	102																			
1989-90	Swift Current	WHL	67	14	18	32	139												4	0	0	0	12			
1990-91	Swift Current	WHL	66	41	51	92	157												3	0	0	0	6			
1991-92	Swift Current	WHL	63	36	46	82	295												8	2	5	7	16			
1992-93	Swift Current	WHL	37	24	41	65	76												17	9	17	26	*49			
	Edmonton	NHL	7	1	1	2	19	0	0	0	7	14.3	–4													
1993-94	Edmonton	NHL	5	0	0	0	4	0	0	0	2	0.0	–3													
	Cape Breton	AHL	65	14	27	41	160												5	2	0	2	11			
1994-95	Cape Breton	AHL	70	16	15	31	184																			
	Edmonton	NHL	6	1	0	1	14	0	0	0	6	16.7	1													
1995-96	Edmonton	NHL	23	1	0	1	33	0	0	0	18	5.6	–7													
	Cape Breton	AHL	31	6	12	18	158																			
1996-97	Pittsburgh	NHL	45	2	2	4	70	0	0	2	30	6.7	–7													
	Cleveland	IHL	10	4	3	7	34												14	4	2	6	44			
1997-98	Pittsburgh	NHL	82	3	4	7	112	1	0	0	46	6.5	–3						6	0	1	1	4	0	0	0
1998-99	Pittsburgh	NHL	61	0	0	0	90	0	0	0	16	0.0	–2	122	46.7	57	3	3:46	13	0	0	0	19	0	0	0
	NHL Totals		229	8	7	15	342	1	0	2	125	6.4		122	46.7	57	3	3:46	19	0	1	1	23	0	0	0

Traded to **Pittsburgh** by **Edmonton** for Pittsburgh's 7th round choice (Brandon Lafrance) in 1996 Entry Draft, June 22, 1996.

YACHMENEV, Vitali (yach-meh-NEHV) NSH.

Right wing. Shoots left. 5'9", 180 lbs. Born, Chelyabinsk, USSR, January 8, 1975. Los Angeles' 3rd choice, 59th overall, in 1994 Entry Draft.

			Regular Season																Playoffs							
Season	Club	League	GP	G	A	Pts	PIM	PP	SH	GW	S	%	+/–	TF	F%	H	SB	Min	GP	G	A	Pts	PIM	PP	SH	GW
1990-91	Chelabinsk	CIS-Jr.	80	88	60	148	72																			
1991-92	Chelabinsk	CIS-Jr.	80	82	70	152	20																			
1992-93	Chelyabinsk	CIS-2	51	23	20	43	12																			
1993-94	North Bay	OHL	66	*61	52	113	18												18	13	19	32	12			
1994-95	North Bay	OHL	59	53	52	105	8												6	1	8	9	2			
	Phoenix	IHL																	4	1	0	1	0			
1995-96	Los Angeles	NHL	80	19	34	53	16	6	1	2	133	14.3	–3													
1996-97	Los Angeles	NHL	65	10	22	32	10	2	0	2	97	10.3	–9													
1997-98	Los Angeles	NHL	4	0	1	1	4	0	0	0	4	0.0	1													
	Long Beach	IHL	59	23	28	51	14												17	8	9	17	4			
1998-99	Nashville	NHL	55	7	10	17	10	0	1	2	83	8.4	–10	0	0.0	28	21	15:06								
	Milwaukee	IHL	16	7	6	13	0																			
	NHL Totals		204	36	67	103	40	8	2	6	317	11.4		0	0.0	28	21	15:06								

Canadian Major Junior Rookie of the Year (1994)

Traded to **Nashville** by **LA Kings** for future considerations, July 7, 1998.

YAKE, Terry (YAYK) **ATL.**

Center. Shoots right. 5'11", 190 lbs. Born, New Westminster, B.C., October 22, 1968. Hartford's 3rd choice, 81st overall, in 1987 Entry Draft.

			Regular Season																Playoffs							
Season	Club	League	GP	G	A	Pts	PIM	PP	SH	GW	S	%	+/–	TF	F%	H	SB	Min	GP	G	A	Pts	PIM	PP	SH	GW
1984-85	Brandon	WHL	11	1	1	2	0																			
1985-86	Brandon	WHL	72	26	26	52	49																			
1986-87	Brandon	WHL	71	44	58	102	64																			
1987-88	Brandon	WHL	72	55	85	140	59												3	4	2	6	7			
1988-89	**Hartford**	**NHL**	**2**	**0**	**0**	**0**	**0**	**0**	**0**	**0**	**0**	**0.0**	**1**													
	Binghamton	AHL	75	39	56	95	57																			
1989-90	**Hartford**	**NHL**	**2**	**0**	**1**	**1**	**0**	**0**	**0**	**0**	**2**	**0.0**	**–1**													
	Binghamton	AHL	77	13	42	55	37																			
1990-91	**Hartford**	**NHL**	**19**	**1**	**4**	**5**	**10**	**0**	**0**	**1**	**19**	**5.3**	**–3**						**6**	**1**	**1**	**2**	**16**	**0**	**1**	**0**
	Springfield	AHL	60	35	42	77	56												15	9	9	18	10			
1991-92	**Hartford**	**NHL**	**15**	**1**	**1**	**2**	**4**	**0**	**0**	**0**	**12**	**8.3**	**–2**													
	Springfield	AHL	53	21	34	55	63												8	3	4	7	2			
1992-93	**Hartford**	**NHL**	**66**	**22**	**31**	**53**	**46**	**4**	**1**	**2**	**98**	**22.4**	**3**													
	Springfield	AHL	16	8	14	22	27																			
1993-94	**Anaheim**	**NHL**	**82**	**21**	**31**	**52**	**44**	**5**	**0**	**2**	**188**	**11.2**	**2**													
1994-95	**Toronto**	**NHL**	**19**	**3**	**2**	**5**	**2**	**1**	**0**	**2**	**26**	**11.5**	**1**													
	Denver	IHL	2	0	3	3	2												17	4	11	15	16			
1995-96	Milwaukee	IHL	70	32	56	88	70												5	3	6	9	4			
1996-97	Rochester	AHL	78	34	*67	101	77												10	8	8	16	2			
1997-98	**St. Louis**	**NHL**	**65**	**10**	**15**	**25**	**38**	**3**	**1**	**4**	**60**	**16.7**	**1**						**10**	**2**	**1**	**3**	**6**	**2**	**0**	**1**
1998-99	**St. Louis**	**NHL**	**60**	**9**	**18**	**27**	**34**	**3**	**0**	**4**	**59**	**15.3**	**–9**	**453**	**48.1**	**39**	**17**	**14:50**	**13**	**1**	**2**	**3**	**14**	**1**	**0**	**0**
	Worcester	AHL	24	8	11	19	26																			
	NHL Totals		**330**	**67**	**103**	**170**	**178**	**16**	**2**	**15**	**464**	**14.4**		**453**	**48.1**	**39**	**17**	**14:50**	**29**	**4**	**4**	**8**	**36**	**3**	**1**	**1**

Claimed by **Anaheim** from **Hartford** in Expansion Draft, June 24, 1993. Traded to **Toronto** by **Anaheim** for David Sacco, September 28, 1994. Signed as a free agent by **Buffalo**, September 17, 1996. Signed as a free agent by **St. Louis**, July 24, 1997. Claimed by **Atlanta** from **St. Louis** in Expansion Draft, June 25, 1999.

YASHIN, Alexei (YAH-shin) **OTT.**

Center. Shoots right. 6'3", 225 lbs. Born, Sverdlovsk, USSR, November 5, 1973. Ottawa's 1st choice, 2nd overall, in 1992 Entry Draft.

			Regular Season																Playoffs							
Season	Club	League	GP	G	A	Pts	PIM	PP	SH	GW	S	%	+/–	TF	F%	H	SB	Min	GP	G	A	Pts	PIM	PP	SH	GW
1990-91	Sverdlovsk	USSR	26	2	1	3	10																			
1991-92	Moscow D'amo	CIS	35	7	5	12	19																			
1992-93	Moscow D'amo	CIS	27	10	12	22	18												10	7	3	10	18			
1993-94	**Ottawa**	**NHL**	**83**	**30**	**49**	**79**	**22**	**11**	**2**	**3**	**232**	**12.9**	**–49**													
1994-95	Las Vegas	IHL	24	15	20	35	32																			
	Ottawa	**NHL**	**47**	**21**	**23**	**44**	**20**	**11**	**0**	**1**	**154**	**13.6**	**–20**													
1995-96	CSKA Moscow	CIS	4	2	2	4	4																			
	Ottawa	**NHL**	**46**	**15**	**24**	**39**	**28**	**8**	**0**	**1**	**143**	**10.5**	**–15**													
1996-97	**Ottawa**	**NHL**	**82**	**35**	**40**	**75**	**44**	**10**	**0**	**5**	**291**	**12.0**	**–7**						**7**	**1**	**5**	**6**	**2**	**1**	**0**	**0**
1997-98	**Ottawa**	**NHL**	**82**	**33**	**39**	**72**	**24**	**5**	**0**	**6**	**291**	**11.3**	**6**						**11**	**5**	**3**	**8**	**8**	**3**	**0**	**2**
	Russia	Olympics	6	3	3	6	0																			
1998-99	**Ottawa**	**NHL**	**82**	**44**	**50**	**94**	**54**	**19**	**0**	**5**	**337**	**13.1**	**16**	**1428**	**41.9**	**73**	**22**	**22:05**	**4**	**0**	**0**	**0**	**10**	**0**	**0**	**0**
	NHL Totals		**422**	**178**	**225**	**403**	**192**	**64**	**2**	**21**	**1448**	**12.3**		**1428**	**41.9**	**73**	**22**	**22:05**	**22**	**6**	**8**	**14**	**20**	**4**	**0**	**2**

CIS First All-Star Team (1993) • NHL Second All-Star Team (1999)
Played in NHL All-Star Game (1994, 1999)

YAWNEY, Trent (YAW-nee)

Defense. Shoots left. 6'3", 195 lbs. Born, Hudson Bay, Sask., September 29, 1965. Chicago's 2nd choice, 45th overall, in 1984 Entry Draft.

			Regular Season																Playoffs							
Season	Club	League	GP	G	A	Pts	PIM	PP	SH	GW	S	%	+/–	TF	F%	H	SB	Min	GP	G	A	Pts	PIM	PP	SH	GW
1981-82	Saskatoon	WHL	6	1	0	1	0																			
1982-83	Saskatoon	WHL	59	6	31	37	44												6	0	2	2	0			
1983-84	Saskatoon	WHL	73	13	46	59	81																			
1984-85	Saskatoon	WHL	72	16	51	67	158												3	1	6	7	7			
1985-86	Canada	Nat-Team	73	6	15	21	60																			
1986-87	Canada	Nat-Team	51	4	15	19	37																			
1987-88	Canada	Nat-Team	60	4	12	16	81																			
	Canada	Olympics	8	1	1	2	6																			
	Chicago	**NHL**	**15**	**2**	**8**	**10**	**15**	**2**	**0**	**0**	**26**	**7.7**	**1**						**5**	**0**	**4**	**4**	**8**	**0**	**0**	**0**
1988-89	**Chicago**	**NHL**	**69**	**5**	**19**	**24**	**116**	**3**	**1**	**0**	**75**	**6.7**	**–5**						**15**	**3**	**6**	**9**	**20**	**0**	**1**	**0**
1989-90	**Chicago**	**NHL**	**70**	**5**	**15**	**20**	**82**	**1**	**0**	**1**	**58**	**8.6**	**–6**						**20**	**3**	**5**	**8**	**27**	**3**	**0**	**1**
1990-91	**Chicago**	**NHL**	**61**	**3**	**13**	**16**	**77**	**3**	**0**	**0**	**52**	**5.8**	**6**						**1**	**0**	**0**	**0**	**0**	**0**	**0**	**0**
1991-92	**Calgary**	**NHL**	**47**	**4**	**9**	**13**	**45**	**1**	**0**	**0**	**33**	**12.1**	**–5**													
	Indianapolis	IHL	9	2	3	5	12																			
1992-93	**Calgary**	**NHL**	**63**	**1**	**16**	**17**	**67**	**0**	**0**	**0**	**61**	**1.6**	**9**						**6**	**3**	**2**	**5**	**6**	**1**	**0**	**0**
1993-94	**Calgary**	**NHL**	**58**	**6**	**15**	**21**	**60**	**1**	**1**	**1**	**62**	**9.7**	**21**						**7**	**0**	**0**	**0**	**16**	**0**	**0**	**0**
1994-95	**Calgary**	**NHL**	**37**	**0**	**2**	**2**	**108**	**0**	**0**	**0**	**20**	**0.0**	**–4**						**2**	**0**	**0**	**0**	**2**	**0**	**0**	**0**
1995-96	**Calgary**	**NHL**	**69**	**0**	**3**	**3**	**88**	**0**	**0**	**0**	**51**	**0.0**	**–1**						**4**	**0**	**0**	**0**	**2**	**0**	**0**	**0**
1996-97	**St. Louis**	**NHL**	**39**	**0**	**2**	**2**	**17**	**0**	**0**	**0**	**8**	**0.0**	**2**													
1997-98	**Chicago**	**NHL**	**45**	**1**	**0**	**1**	**76**	**0**	**0**	**0**	**19**	**5.3**	**–5**													
1998-99	**Chicago**	**NHL**	**20**	**0**	**0**	**0**	**32**	**0**	**0**	**0**	**11**	**0.0**	**–6**	**0**	**0.0**	**13**	**9**	**13:28**								
	NHL Totals		**593**	**27**	**102**	**129**	**783**	**11**	**2**	**2**	**476**	**5.7**		**0**	**0.0**	**13**	**9**	**13:28**	**60**	**9**	**17**	**26**	**81**	**4**	**1**	**1**

Traded to **Calgary** by **Chicago** for Stephane Matteau, December 16, 1991. Signed as a free agent by **St. Louis**, July 31, 1996. Signed as a free agent by **Chicago**, September 25, 1997.

YEGOROV, Alexei (yeh-GOH-rohv) **ATL.**

Right wing. Shoots left. 5'11", 185 lbs. Born, St. Petersburg, USSR, May 21, 1975. San Jose's 3rd choice, 66th overall, in 1994 Entry Draft.

			Regular Season																Playoffs							
Season	Club	League	GP	G	A	Pts	PIM	PP	SH	GW	S	%	+/–	TF	F%	H	SB	Min	GP	G	A	Pts	PIM	PP	SH	GW
1992-93	St. Peterburg	CIS	17	1	2	3	10												6	3	1	4	6			
1993-94	St. Peterburg	CIS	23	5	3	8	18												6	0	0	0	4			
1994-95	St. Peterburg	CIS	10	2	1	3	10																			
	Fort Worth	CHL	18	4	10	14	15																			
1995-96	**San Jose**	**NHL**	**9**	**3**	**2**	**5**	**2**	**2**	**0**	**0**	**10**	**30.0**	**–5**													
	Kansas City	IHL	65	31	25	56	84												5	2	0	2	8			
1996-97	**San Jose**	**NHL**	**2**	**0**	**1**	**1**	**0**	**0**	**0**	**0**	**0**	**0.0**	**1**													
	Kentucky	AHL	75	26	32	58	59												4	0	1	1	2			
1997-98	Kentucky	AHL	79	32	52	84	56												3	2	0	2	0			
1998-99	Yaroslavl	Russia	13	3	1	4	8																			
	St. Petersburg	Russia	25	8	8	16	30																			
	Moscow D'amo	Russia	11	0	0	0	0												3	0	0	0	0			
	NHL Totals		**11**	**3**	**3**	**6**	**2**	**2**	**0**	**0**	**10**	**30.0**														

Claimed by **Atlanta** from **San Jose** in Expansion Draft, June 25, 1999.

YELLE, Stephane (YEHL) **COL.**

Center. Shoots left. 6'1", 190 lbs. Born, Ottawa, Ont., May 9, 1974. New Jersey's 9th choice, 186th overall, in 1992 Entry Draft.

			Regular Season																Playoffs							
Season	Club	League	GP	G	A	Pts	PIM	PP	SH	GW	S	%	+/–	TF	F%	H	SB	Min	GP	G	A	Pts	PIM	PP	SH	GW
1990-91	Cumberland	OJHL-B	33	20	30	50	16																			
1991-92	Oshawa	OHL	55	12	14	26	20												7	2	0	2	1			
1992-93	Oshawa	OHL	66	24	50	74	20												10	2	4	6	4			
1993-94	Oshawa	OHL	66	35	69	104	22												5	1	7	8	2			
1994-95	Cornwall	AHL	40	18	15	33	22												13	7	7	14	8			
1995-96♦	**Colorado**	**NHL**	**71**	**13**	**14**	**27**	**30**	**0**	**2**	**1**	**93**	**14.0**	**15**						**22**	**1**	**4**	**5**	**8**	**0**	**1**	**0**

			Regular Season																Playoffs							
Season	Club	League	GP	G	A	Pts	PIM	PP	SH	GW	S	%	+/–	TF	F%	H	SB	Min	GP	G	A	Pts	PIM	PP	SH	GW
1996-97	**Colorado**	**NHL**	**79**	**9**	**17**	**26**	**38**	**0**	**1**	**1**	**89**	**10.1**	**1**	....	....	....	....	....	**12**	**1**	**6**	**7**	**2**	**0**	**0**	**0**
1997-98	**Colorado**	**NHL**	**81**	**7**	**15**	**22**	**48**	**0**	**1**	**0**	**93**	**7.5**	**–10**	....	....	....	....	....	**7**	**1**	**0**	**1**	**12**	**0**	**0**	**0**
1998-99	**Colorado**	**NHL**	**72**	**8**	**7**	**15**	**40**	**1**	**0**	**0**	**99**	**8.1**	**–8**	**1201**	**51.2**	**136**	**72**	**15:15**	**10**	**0**	**1**	**1**	**6**	**0**	**0**	**0**
	NHL Totals		**303**	**37**	**53**	**90**	**156**	**1**	**4**	**2**	**374**	**9.9**		**1201**	**51.2**	**136**	**72**	**15:15**	**51**	**3**	**11**	**14**	**28**	**0**	**1**	**0**

Traded to **Quebec** by **New Jersey** with New Jersey's 11th round choice (Steven Low) in 1994 Entry Draft for Quebec's 11th round choice (Mike Hansen) in 1994 Entry Draft, June 1, 1994. Transferred to **Colorado** after **Quebec** franchise relocated, June 21, 1995.

YLONEN, Juha (YOO-lih-nehn, YOO-hah) PHX.

Center. Shoots left. 6'1", 185 lbs. Born, Helsinki, Finland, February 13, 1972. Winnipeg's 3rd choice, 91st overall, in 1991 Entry Draft.

Season	Club	League	GP	G	A	Pts	PIM	PP	SH	GW	S	%	+/–	TF	F%	H	SB	Min	GP	G	A	Pts	PIM	PP	SH	GW
1988-89	Kiekko-Espoo	Finn-Jr.	31	9	14	23	8	....	....	....	....	....	....	....	....	....	....	....	....	....	....	....	....	....	....	....
1989-90	Kiekko-Espoo	Finn-Jr.	4	1	5	6	0	....	....	....	....	....	....	....	....	....	....	....	5	1	5	6	0	....	....	....
	Kiekko-Espoo	Finland-2	38	10	17	27	12	....	....	....	....	....	....	....	....	....	....	....	....	....	....	....	....	....	....	....
1990-91	Kiekko-Espoo	Finland-2	40	12	21	33	4	....	....	....	....	....	....	....	....	....	....	....	....	....	....	....	....	....	....	....
1991-92	Hameenlinna	Finn-Jr.	2	1	2	3	0	....	....	....	....	....	....	....	....	....	....	....	....	....	....	....	....	....	....	....
	Hameenlinna	Finland-2	9	8	14	22	0	....	....	....	....	....	....	....	....	....	....	....	....	....	....	....	....	....	....	....
	Hameenlinna	Finland	43	7	11	18	8	....	....	....	....	....	....	....	....	....	....	....	....	....	....	....	....	....	....	....
1992-93	Hameenlinna	Finland	48	8	18	26	22	....	....	....	....	....	....	....	....	....	....	....	12	3	5	8	2	....	....	....
	Hameenlinna	Finn-Jr.	2	2	1	3	0	....	....	....	....	....	....	....	....	....	....	....	1	0	0	0	0	....	....	....
1993-94	Jokerit	Finland	37	5	11	16	2	....	....	....	....	....	....	....	....	....	....	....	12	1	3	4	8	....	....	....
1994-95	Jokerit	Finland	50	13	15	28	10	....	....	....	....	....	....	....	....	....	....	....	11	3	2	5	0	....	....	....
1995-96	Jokerit	Finland	24	3	13	16	20	....	....	....	....	....	....	....	....	....	....	....	11	4	5	9	4	....	....	....
1996-97	**Phoenix**	**NHL**	**2**	**0**	**0**	**0**	**0**	**0**	**0**	**0**	**2**	**0.0**	**0**	....	....	....	....	....	....	....	....	....	....	....	....	....
	Springfield	AHL	70	20	41	61	6	....	....	....	....	....	....	....	....	....	....	....	17	5	*16	21	4	....	....	....
1997-98	**Phoenix**	**NHL**	**55**	**1**	**11**	**12**	**10**	**0**	**1**	**0**	**60**	**1.7**	**–3**	....	....	....	....	....	....	....	....	....	....	....	....	....
	Finland	Olympics	6	0	0	0	8	....	....	....	....	....	....	....	....	....	....	....	....	....	....	....	....	....	....	....
1998-99	**Phoenix**	**NHL**	**59**	**6**	**17**	**23**	**20**	**2**	**0**	**1**	**66**	**9.1**	**18**	**297**	**46.5**	**48**	**37**	**15:55**	**2**	**0**	**2**	**2**	**2**	**0**	**0**	**0**
	NHL Totals		**116**	**7**	**28**	**35**	**30**	**2**	**1**	**1**	**128**	**5.5**		**297**	**46.5**	**48**	**37**	**15:55**	**2**	**0**	**2**	**2**	**2**	**0**	**0**	**0**

Rights transferred to **Phoenix** after **Winnipeg** franchise relocated, July 1, 1996.

YORK, Harry

Center. Shoots left. 6'2", 215 lbs. Born, Ponoka, Alta., April 16, 1974.

Season	Club	League	GP	G	A	Pts	PIM	PP	SH	GW	S	%	+/–	TF	F%	H	SB	Min	GP	G	A	Pts	PIM	PP	SH	GW
1994-95	Fort McMurray	AJHL	54	36	73	*109	....	....	....	....	....	....	....	....	....	....	....	....	....	....	....	....	....	....	....	....
1995-96	Nashville	ECHL	64	33	50	83	122	....	....	....	....	....	....	....	....	....	....	....	....	....	....	....	....	....	....	....
	Atlanta	IHL	2	0	0	0	15	....	....	....	....	....	....	....	....	....	....	....	....	....	....	....	....	....	....	....
	Worcester	AHL	13	8	5	13	2	....	....	....	....	....	....	....	....	....	....	....	4	0	4	4	4	....	....	....
1996-97	**St. Louis**	**NHL**	**74**	**14**	**18**	**32**	**24**	**3**	**1**	**3**	**86**	**16.3**	**1**	....	....	....	....	....	**5**	**0**	**0**	**0**	**2**	**0**	**0**	**0**
1997-98	**St. Louis**	**NHL**	**58**	**4**	**6**	**10**	**31**	**0**	**0**	**0**	**42**	**9.5**	**0**	....	....	....	....	....	....	....	....	....	....	....	....	....
	NY Rangers	**NHL**	**2**	**0**	**0**	**0**	**0**	**0**	**0**	**0**	**2**	**0.0**	**–1**	....	....	....	....	....	....	....	....	....	....	....	....	....
1998-99	**NY Rangers**	**NHL**	**5**	**0**	**0**	**0**	**4**	**0**	**0**	**0**	**5**	**0.0**	**–1**	**33**	**60.6**	**20**	**2**	**10:00**	....	....	....	....	....	....	....	....
	Pittsburgh	**NHL**	**2**	**0**	**0**	**0**	**0**	**0**	**0**	**0**	**0**	**0.0**	**0**	**0**	**0.0**	**1**	**0**	**3:00**	....	....	....	....	....	....	....	....
	Vancouver	**NHL**	**49**	**7**	**9**	**16**	**20**	**1**	**0**	**0**	**55**	**12.7**	**–2**	**496**	**42.9**	**110**	**13**	**14:32**	....	....	....	....	....	....	....	....
	NHL Totals		**190**	**25**	**33**	**58**	**79**	**4**	**1**	**3**	**190**	**13.2**		**529**	**44.0**	**131**	**15**	**13:43**	**5**	**0**	**0**	**0**	**2**	**0**	**0**	**0**

Won AJHL MVP Award, 1995. Won Ernie Love Trophy (AJHL Scoring Champion), 1995.

Signed as a free agent by **St. Louis**, May 1, 1996. Traded to **NY Rangers** by **St. Louis** for Mike Eastwood, March 24, 1998. Traded to **Pittsburgh** by **NY Rangers** with Alexei Kovalev for Petr Nedved, Chris Tamer and Sean Pronger, November 25, 1998. Claimed on waivers by **Vancouver** from **Pittsburgh**, December 7, 1998.

YORK, Jason OTT.

Defense. Shoots right. 6'2", 198 lbs. Born, Nepean, Ont., May 20, 1970. Detroit's 6th choice, 129th overall, in 1990 Entry Draft.

Season	Club	League	GP	G	A	Pts	PIM	PP	SH	GW	S	%	+/–	TF	F%	H	SB	Min	GP	G	A	Pts	PIM	PP	SH	GW
1986-87	Smiths Falls	OJHL	46	6	13	19	60	....	....	....	....	....	....	....	....	....	....	....	....	....	....	....	....	....	....	....
1987-88	Hamilton	OHL	58	4	9	13	110	....	....	....	....	....	....	....	....	....	....	....	....	....	....	....	....	....	....	....
1988-89	Windsor	OHL	65	19	44	63	105	....	....	....	....	....	....	....	....	....	....	....	....	....	....	....	....	....	....	....
1989-90	Windsor	OHL	39	9	30	39	38	....	....	....	....	....	....	....	....	....	....	....	....	....	....	....	....	....	....	....
	Kitchener	OHL	25	11	25	36	17	....	....	....	....	....	....	....	....	....	....	....	17	3	19	22	10	....	....	....
1990-91	Windsor	OHL	66	13	80	93	40	....	....	....	....	....	....	....	....	....	....	....	11	3	10	13	12	....	....	....
1991-92	Adirondack	AHL	49	4	20	24	32	....	....	....	....	....	....	....	....	....	....	....	5	0	1	1	0	....	....	....
1992-93	**Detroit**	**NHL**	**2**	**0**	**0**	**0**	**0**	**0**	**0**	**0**	**1**	**0.0**	**0**	....	....	....	....	....	....	....	....	....	....	....	....	....
	Adirondack	AHL	77	15	40	55	86	....	....	....	....	....	....	....	....	....	....	....	11	0	3	3	18	....	....	....
1993-94	**Detroit**	**NHL**	**7**	**1**	**2**	**3**	**2**	**0**	**0**	**0**	**9**	**11.1**	**0**	....	....	....	....	....	....	....	....	....	....	....	....	....
	Adirondack	AHL	74	10	56	66	98	....	....	....	....	....	....	....	....	....	....	....	12	3	11	14	22	....	....	....
1994-95	**Detroit**	**NHL**	**10**	**1**	**2**	**3**	**2**	**0**	**0**	**0**	**6**	**16.7**	**0**	....	....	....	....	....	....	....	....	....	....	....	....	....
	Adirondack	AHL	5	1	3	4	4	....	....	....	....	....	....	....	....	....	....	....	....	....	....	....	....	....	....	....
	Anaheim	**NHL**	**15**	**0**	**8**	**8**	**12**	**0**	**0**	**0**	**22**	**0.0**	**4**	....	....	....	....	....	....	....	....	....	....	....	....	....
1995-96	**Anaheim**	**NHL**	**79**	**3**	**21**	**24**	**88**	**0**	**0**	**0**	**106**	**2.8**	**–7**	....	....	....	....	....	....	....	....	....	....	....	....	....
1996-97	**Ottawa**	**NHL**	**75**	**4**	**17**	**21**	**67**	**1**	**0**	**0**	**121**	**3.3**	**–8**	....	....	....	....	....	**7**	**0**	**0**	**0**	**4**	**0**	**0**	**0**
1997-98	**Ottawa**	**NHL**	**73**	**3**	**13**	**16**	**62**	**0**	**0**	**0**	**109**	**2.8**	**8**	....	....	....	....	....	**7**	**1**	**1**	**2**	**7**	**1**	**0**	**0**
1998-99	**Ottawa**	**NHL**	**79**	**4**	**31**	**35**	**48**	**2**	**0**	**0**	**177**	**2.3**	**17**	**2**	**0.0**	**166**	**127**	**23:49**	**4**	**1**	**1**	**2**	**4**	**0**	**0**	**0**
	NHL Totals		**340**	**16**	**94**	**110**	**281**	**3**	**0**	**0**	**551**	**2.9**		**2**	**0.0**	**166**	**127**	**23:49**	**18**	**2**	**2**	**4**	**15**	**1**	**0**	**0**

AHL First All-Star Team (1994)

Traded to **Anaheim** by **Detroit** with Mike Sillinger for Stu Grimson, Mark Ferner and Anaheim's 6th round choice (Magnus Nilsson) in 1996 Entry Draft, April 4, 1995. Traded to **Ottawa** by **Anaheim** with Shaun Van Allen for Ted Drury and the rights to Marc Moro, October 1, 1996.

YOUNG, Scott ST.L.

Right wing. Shoots right. 6'1", 200 lbs. Born, Clinton, MA, October 1, 1967. Hartford's 1st choice, 11th overall, in 1986 Entry Draft.

Season	Club	League	GP	G	A	Pts	PIM	PP	SH	GW	S	%	+/–	TF	F%	H	SB	Min	GP	G	A	Pts	PIM	PP	SH	GW
1984-85	St. Marks	H.S.	23	28	41	69	....	....	....	....	....	....	....	....	....	....	....	....	....	....	....	....	....	....	....	....
1985-86	Boston University	H.E.	38	16	13	29	31	....	....	....	....	....	....	....	....	....	....	....	....	....	....	....	....	....	....	....
1986-87	Boston University	H.E.	33	15	21	36	24	....	....	....	....	....	....	....	....	....	....	....	....	....	....	....	....	....	....	....
1987-88	United States	Nat-Team	56	11	47	58	31	....	....	....	....	....	....	....	....	....	....	....	....	....	....	....	....	....	....	....
	United States	Olympics	6	2	6	8	4	....	....	....	....	....	....	....	....	....	....	....	....	....	....	....	....	....	....	....
	Hartford	**NHL**	**7**	**0**	**0**	**0**	**2**	**0**	**0**	**0**	**6**	**0.0**	**–6**	....	....	....	....	....	**4**	**1**	**0**	**1**	**0**	**0**	**0**	**0**
1988-89	**Hartford**	**NHL**	**76**	**19**	**40**	**59**	**27**	**6**	**0**	**2**	**203**	**9.4**	**–21**	....	....	....	....	....	**4**	**2**	**0**	**2**	**4**	**0**	**0**	**0**
1989-90	**Hartford**	**NHL**	**80**	**24**	**40**	**64**	**47**	**10**	**2**	**5**	**239**	**10.0**	**–24**	....	....	....	....	....	**7**	**2**	**0**	**2**	**2**	**0**	**0**	**0**
1990-91	**Hartford**	**NHL**	**34**	**6**	**9**	**15**	**8**	**3**	**1**	**2**	**94**	**6.4**	**–9**	....	....	....	....	....	....	....	....	....	....	....	....	....
	♦ Pittsburgh	**NHL**	**43**	**11**	**16**	**27**	**33**	**3**	**1**	**3**	**116**	**9.5**	**3**	....	....	....	....	....	**17**	**1**	**6**	**7**	**2**	**1**	**0**	**0**
1991-92	HC Bolzano	Italy	18	22	17	39	6	....	....	....	....	....	....	....	....	....	....	....	5	4	3	7	7	....	....	....
	United States	Nat-Team	10	2	4	6	21	....	....	....	....	....	....	....	....	....	....	....	....	....	....	....	....	....	....	....
	United States	Olympics	8	2	1	3	2	....	....	....	....	....	....	....	....	....	....	....	....	....	....	....	....	....	....	....
1992-93	**Quebec**	**NHL**	**82**	**30**	**30**	**60**	**20**	**9**	**6**	**5**	**225**	**13.3**	**5**	....	....	....	....	....	**6**	**4**	**1**	**5**	**0**	**0**	**0**	**2**
1993-94	**Quebec**	**NHL**	**76**	**26**	**25**	**51**	**14**	**6**	**1**	**1**	**236**	**11.0**	**–4**	....	....	....	....	....	....	....	....	....	....	....	....	....
1994-95	EV Landshut	Germany	4	6	1	7	6	....	....	....	....	....	....	....	....	....	....	....	....	....	....	....	....	....	....	....
	Frankfurt	Germany	1	1	0	1	0	....	....	....	....	....	....	....	....	....	....	....	....	....	....	....	....	....	....	....
	Quebec	**NHL**	**48**	**18**	**21**	**39**	**14**	**3**	**3**	**0**	**167**	**10.8**	**9**	....	....	....	....	....	**6**	**3**	**3**	**6**	**2**	**0**	**1**	**0**
1995-96♦	**Colorado**	**NHL**	**81**	**21**	**39**	**60**	**50**	**7**	**0**	**5**	**229**	**9.2**	**2**	....	....	....	....	....	**22**	**3**	**12**	**15**	**10**	**0**	**0**	**0**
1996-97	**Colorado**	**NHL**	**72**	**18**	**19**	**37**	**14**	**7**	**0**	**0**	**164**	**11.0**	**–5**	....	....	....	....	....	**17**	**4**	**2**	**6**	**14**	**2**	**0**	**0**

			Regular Season																Playoffs							
Season	Club	League	GP	G	A	Pts	PIM	PP	SH	GW	S	%	+/–	TF	F%	H	SB	Min	GP	G	A	Pts	PIM	PP	SH	GW
1997-98	Anaheim	NHL	73	13	20	33	22	4	2	1	187	7.0	–13	....	....	....	....	....	....	....	....	....	....	....	....	....
1998-99	St. Louis	NHL	75	24	28	52	27	8	0	4	205	11.7	8	4	25.0	51	18	15:14	13	4	7	11	10	1	0	1
	NHL Totals		747	210	287	497	278	66	16	28	2071	10.1		4	25.0	51	18	15:14	96	24	31	55	44	4	1	3

ECAC First All-Star Team (1989)

Traded to **Pittsburgh** by **Hartford** for Rob Brown, December 21, 1990. Traded to **Quebec** by **Pittsburgh** for Bryan Fogarty, March 10, 1992. Transferred to **Colorado** after **Quebec** franchise relocated, June 21, 1995. Traded to **Anaheim** by **Colorado** for Anaheim's 3rd round choice (later traded to Florida - Florida selected Lance Ward) in 1998 Entry Draft, September 17, 1997. Signed as a free agent by **St. Louis**, July 28, 1998.

YSEBAERT, Paul

(IGHS-bahrt)

Center. Shoots left. 6'1", 194 lbs. Born, Sarnia, Ont., May 15, 1966. New Jersey's 4th choice, 74th overall, in 1984 Entry Draft.

Season	Club	League	GP	G	A	Pts	PIM	PP	SH	GW	S	%	+/–	TF	F%	H	SB	Min	GP	G	A	Pts	PIM	PP	SH	GW
1983-84	Petrolia	OJHL	33	35	42	77	20	....	....	....	....	....	....	....	....	....	....	....	....	....	....	....	....	....	....	....
1984-85	Bowling Green	CCHA	42	23	32	55	54	....	....	....	....	....	....	....	....	....	....	....	....	....	....	....	....	....	....	....
1985-86	Bowling Green	CCHA	42	23	45	68	50	....	....	....	....	....	....	....	....	....	....	....	....	....	....	....	....	....	....	....
1986-87	Bowling Green	CCHA	45	27	58	85	44	....	....	....	....	....	....	....	....	....	....	....	....	....	....	....	....	....	....	....
	Canada	Nat-Team	5	1	0	1	4	....	....	....	....	....	....	....	....	....	....	....	....	....	....	....	....	....	....	....
1987-88	Utica	AHL	78	30	49	79	60	....	....	....	....	....	....	....	....	....	....	....	....	....	....	....	....	....	....	....
1988-89	**New Jersey**	**NHL**	5	0	4	4	0	0	0	0	4	0.0	2	....	....	....	....	....	....	....	....	....	....	....	....	....
	Utica	AHL	56	36	44	80	22	....	....	....	....	....	....	....	....	....	....	....	5	0	1	1	4	....	....	....
1989-90	**New Jersey**	**NHL**	5	1	2	3	0	0	0	0	6	16.7	0	....	....	....	....	....	....	....	....	....	....	....	....	....
	Utica	AHL	74	53	52	*105	61	....	....	....	....	....	....	....	....	....	....	....	5	2	4	6	0	....	....	....
1990-91	**New Jersey**	**NHL**	11	4	3	7	6	1	0	0	14	28.6	1	....	....	....	....	....	....	....	....	....	....	....	....	....
	Detroit	**NHL**	51	15	18	33	16	5	0	1	114	13.2	–8	....	....	....	....	....	2	0	2	2	0	0	0	0
1991-92	**Detroit**	**NHL**	79	35	40	75	55	3	4	3	211	16.6	44	....	....	....	....	....	10	1	0	1	10	0	0	0
1992-93	**Detroit**	**NHL**	80	34	28	62	42	3	3	8	186	18.3	19	....	....	....	....	....	7	3	1	4	2	0	1	1
1993-94	**Winnipeg**	**NHL**	60	9	18	27	18	1	0	0	120	7.5	–8	....	....	....	....	....	....	....	....	....	....	....	....	....
	Chicago	**NHL**	11	5	3	8	8	2	0	1	31	16.1	1	....	....	....	....	....	6	0	0	0	8	0	0	0
1994-95	**Chicago**	**NHL**	15	4	5	9	6	0	0	1	23	17.4	4	....	....	....	....	....	....	....	....	....	....	....	....	....
	Tampa Bay	**NHL**	29	8	11	19	12	0	0	0	70	11.4	–1	....	....	....	....	....	....	....	....	....	....	....	....	....
1995-96	**Tampa Bay**	**NHL**	55	16	15	31	16	4	1	1	135	11.9	–19	....	....	....	....	....	5	0	0	0	0	0	0	0
1996-97	**Tampa Bay**	**NHL**	39	5	12	17	4	2	0	0	91	5.5	1	....	....	....	....	....	....	....	....	....	....	....	....	....
1997-98	**Tampa Bay**	**NHL**	82	13	27	40	32	2	1	0	145	9.0	–43	....	....	....	....	....	....	....	....	....	....	....	....	....
1998-99	**Tampa Bay**	**NHL**	10	0	1	1	2	0	0	0	10	0.0	–5	35	37.1	6	3	9:47	....	....	....	....	....	....	....	....
	Cleveland	IHL	27	6	11	17	14	....	....	....	....	....	....	....	....	....	....	....	....	....	....	....	....	....	....	....
	NHL Totals		532	149	187	336	217	23	9	15	1160	12.8		35	37.1	6	3	9:47	30	4	3	7	20	0	1	1

CCHA Second All-Star Team (1986, 1987) • AHL First All-Star Team (1990) • Won John B. Sollenberger Trophy (Top Scorer - AHL) (1990) • Won Les Cunningham Plaque (MVP - AHL) (1990) • Won Alka-Seltzer Plus Award (1992)

Traded to **Detroit** by **New Jersey** for Lee Norwood and Detroit's 4th round choice (Scott McCabe) in 1992 Entry Draft, November 27, 1990. Traded to **Winnipeg** by **Detroit** with future considerations (Alan Kerr, June 18, 1993) for Aaron Ward and Toronto's 4th round choice (previously acquired by Winnipeg — later traded to Detroit — Detroit selected John Jakopin) in 1993 Entry Draft, June 11, 1993. Traded to **Chicago** by **Winnipeg** for Chicago's 3rd round choice (later traded back to Chicago — Chicago selected Kevin McKay) in 1995 Entry Draft, March 21, 1994. Traded to **Tampa Bay** by **Chicago** with Rich Sutter for Jim Cummins, Tom Tilley and Jeff Buchanan, February 22, 1995.

YUSHKEVICH, Dimitri

(yoosh-KAY-vihch) **TOR.**

Defense. Shoots right. 6', 208 lbs. Born, Yaroslavl, USSR, November 19, 1971. Philadelphia's 6th choice, 122nd overall, in 1991 Entry Draft.

Season	Club	League	GP	G	A	Pts	PIM	PP	SH	GW	S	%	+/–	TF	F%	H	SB	Min	GP	G	A	Pts	PIM	PP	SH	GW
1988-89	Yaroslavl	USSR	23	2	1	3	8	....	....	....	....	....	....	....	....	....	....	....	....	....	....	....	....	....	....	....
1989-90	Yaroslavl	USSR	41	2	3	5	39	....	....	....	....	....	....	....	....	....	....	....	....	....	....	....	....	....	....	....
1990-91	Yaroslavl	USSR	41	10	4	14	22	....	....	....	....	....	....	....	....	....	....	....	....	....	....	....	....	....	....	....
1991-92	Moscow D'amo	CIS	35	5	7	12	14	....	....	....	....	....	....	....	....	....	....	....	....	....	....	....	....	....	....	....
	Russia	Olympics	8	1	2	3	4	....	....	....	....	....	....	....	....	....	....	....	....	....	....	....	....	....	....	....
1992-93	**Philadelphia**	**NHL**	82	5	27	32	71	1	0	1	155	3.2	12	....	....	....	....	....	....	....	....	....	....	....	....	....
1993-94	**Philadelphia**	**NHL**	75	5	25	30	86	1	0	2	136	3.7	–8	....	....	....	....	....	....	....	....	....	....	....	....	....
1994-95	Yaroslavl	CIS	10	3	4	7	8	....	....	....	....	....	....	....	....	....	....	....	....	....	....	....	....	....	....	....
	Philadelphia	**NHL**	40	5	9	14	47	3	1	1	80	6.3	–4	....	....	....	....	....	15	1	5	6	12	0	0	0
1995-96	**Toronto**	**NHL**	69	1	10	11	54	1	0	0	96	1.0	–14	....	....	....	....	....	4	0	0	0	0	0	0	0
1996-97	**Toronto**	**NHL**	74	4	10	14	56	1	1	1	99	4.0	–24	....	....	....	....	....	....	....	....	....	....	....	....	....
1997-98	**Toronto**	**NHL**	72	0	12	12	78	0	0	0	92	0.0	–13	....	....	....	....	....	....	....	....	....	....	....	....	....
1998-99	**Toronto**	**NHL**	78	6	22	28	88	2	1	0	95	6.3	25	0	0.0	169	107	22:20	17	1	5	6	22	1	0	0
	NHL Totals		490	26	115	141	480	9	3	5	753	3.5		0	0.0	169	107	22:20	36	2	10	12	34	1	0	0

Traded to **Toronto** by **Philadelphia** with Philadelphia's 2nd round choice (Francis Larivee) in 1996 Entry Draft for Toronto's 1st round choice (Dainius Zubrus) in 1996 Entry Draft, 2nd round choice (Jean-Marc Pelletier) in 1997 Entry Draft and LA Kings' 4th round choice (previously acquired by Toronto — later traded to LA Kings — LA Kings selected Mikael Simons) in 1996 Entry Draft, August 30, 1995.

YZERMAN, Steve

(IGH-zuhr-muhn) **DET.**

Center. Shoots right. 5'11", 185 lbs. Born, Cranbrook, B.C., May 9, 1965. Detroit's 1st choice, 4th overall, in 1983 Entry Draft.

Season	Club	League	GP	G	A	Pts	PIM	PP	SH	GW	S	%	+/–	TF	F%	H	SB	Min	GP	G	A	Pts	PIM	PP	SH	GW
1980-81	Nepean	OJHL	50	38	54	92	44	....	....	....	....	....	....	....	....	....	....	....	....	....	....	....	....	....	....	....
1981-82	Peterborough	OHL	58	21	43	64	65	....	....	....	....	....	....	....	....	....	....	....	6	0	1	1	16	....	....	....
1982-83	Peterborough	OHL	56	42	49	91	33	....	....	....	....	....	....	....	....	....	....	....	4	1	4	5	0	....	....	....
1983-84	**Detroit**	**NHL**	80	39	48	87	33	13	0	2	177	22.0	–17	....	....	....	....	....	4	3	3	6	0	1	0	1
1984-85	**Detroit**	**NHL**	80	30	59	89	58	9	0	3	231	13.0	–17	....	....	....	....	....	3	2	1	3	2	0	0	0
1985-86	**Detroit**	**NHL**	51	14	28	42	16	3	0	3	132	10.6	–24	....	....	....	....	....	....	....	....	....	....	....	....	....
1986-87	**Detroit**	**NHL**	80	31	59	90	43	9	1	2	217	14.3	–1	....	....	....	....	....	16	5	13	18	8	1	0	0
1987-88	**Detroit**	**NHL**	64	50	52	102	44	10	6	6	242	20.7	30	....	....	....	....	....	3	1	3	4	6	0	0	0
1988-89	**Detroit**	**NHL**	80	65	90	155	61	17	3	7	388	16.8	17	....	....	....	....	....	6	5	5	10	2	2	0	0
1989-90	**Detroit**	**NHL**	79	62	65	127	79	16	7	8	332	18.7	–6	....	....	....	....	....	....	....	....	....	....	....	....	....
1990-91	**Detroit**	**NHL**	80	51	57	108	34	12	6	4	326	15.6	–2	....	....	....	....	....	7	3	3	6	4	1	0	0
1991-92	**Detroit**	**NHL**	79	45	58	103	64	9	8	9	295	15.3	26	....	....	....	....	....	11	3	5	8	12	0	1	1
1992-93	**Detroit**	**NHL**	84	58	79	137	44	13	7	6	307	18.9	33	....	....	....	....	....	7	4	3	7	4	1	1	1
1993-94	**Detroit**	**NHL**	58	24	58	82	36	7	3	3	217	11.1	11	....	....	....	....	....	3	1	3	4	0	0	0	0
1994-95	**Detroit**	**NHL**	47	12	26	38	40	4	0	1	134	9.0	6	....	....	....	....	....	15	4	8	12	0	2	0	1
1995-96	**Detroit**	**NHL**	80	36	59	95	64	16	2	8	220	16.4	29	....	....	....	....	....	18	8	12	20	4	4	0	1
1996-97♦	**Detroit**	**NHL**	81	22	63	85	78	8	0	3	232	9.5	22	....	....	....	....	....	20	7	6	13	4	3	0	2
1997-98♦	**Detroit**	**NHL**	75	24	45	69	46	6	2	0	188	12.8	3	....	....	....	....	....	22	6	*18	*24	22	3	1	0
	Canada	Olympics	6	1	1	2	10	....	....	....	....	....	....	....	....	....	....	....	....	....	....	....	....	....	....	....
1998-99	**Detroit**	**NHL**	80	29	45	74	42	13	2	4	231	12.6	8	1600	56.9	46	58	21:35	10	9	4	13	0	4	0	2
	NHL Totals		1178	592	891	1483	782	165	47	69	3869	15.3		1600	56.9	46	58	21:35	145	61	87	148	68	22	3	9

NHL All-Rookie Team (1984) • Won Lester B. Pearson Award (1989) • Won Conn Smythe Trophy (1998)

Played in NHL All-Star Game (1984, 1988, 1989, 1990, 1991, 1992, 1993, 1997)

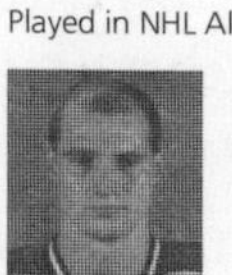

ZABRANSKY, Libor

(zah-BRAN-skee)

Defense. Shoots left. 6'3", 196 lbs. Born, Brno, Czech., November 25, 1973. St. Louis' 8th choice, 209th overall, in 1995 Entry Draft.

Season	Club	League	GP	G	A	Pts	PIM	PP	SH	GW	S	%	+/–	TF	F%	H	SB	Min	GP	G	A	Pts	PIM	PP	SH	GW
1994-95	HC Budejovice	Cze-Rep	44	2	6	8	54	....	....	....	....	....	....	....	....	....	....	....	9	0	4	4	6	....	....	....
1995-96	HC Budejovice	Cze-Rep	40	4	7	11	....	....	....	....	....	....	....	....	....	....	....	....	10	0	1	1	....	....	....	....
1996-97	**St. Louis**	**NHL**	34	1	5	6	44	0	0	1	26	3.8	–1	....	....	....	....	....	....	....	....	....	....	....	....	....
	Worcester	AHL	23	3	6	9	24	....	....	....	....	....	....	....	....	....	....	....	5	2	5	7	6	....	....	....
1997-98	**St. Louis**	**NHL**	6	0	1	1	6	0	0	0	2	0.0	–3	....	....	....	....	....	....	....	....	....	....	....	....	....
	Worcester	AHL	54	2	17	19	61	....	....	....	....	....	....	....	....	....	....	....	6	1	1	2	8	....	....	....
1998-99	Worcester	AHL	6	0	0	0	18	....	....	....	....	....	....	....	....	....	....	....	....	....	....	....	....	....	....	....
	HC Vsetin	Cze-Rep	31	3	9	12	57	....	....	....	....	....	....	....	....	....	....	....	12	1	2	3	....	....	....	....
	NHL Totals		40	1	6	7	50	0	0	1	28	3.6		....	....	....	....	....	....	....	....	....	....	....	....	....

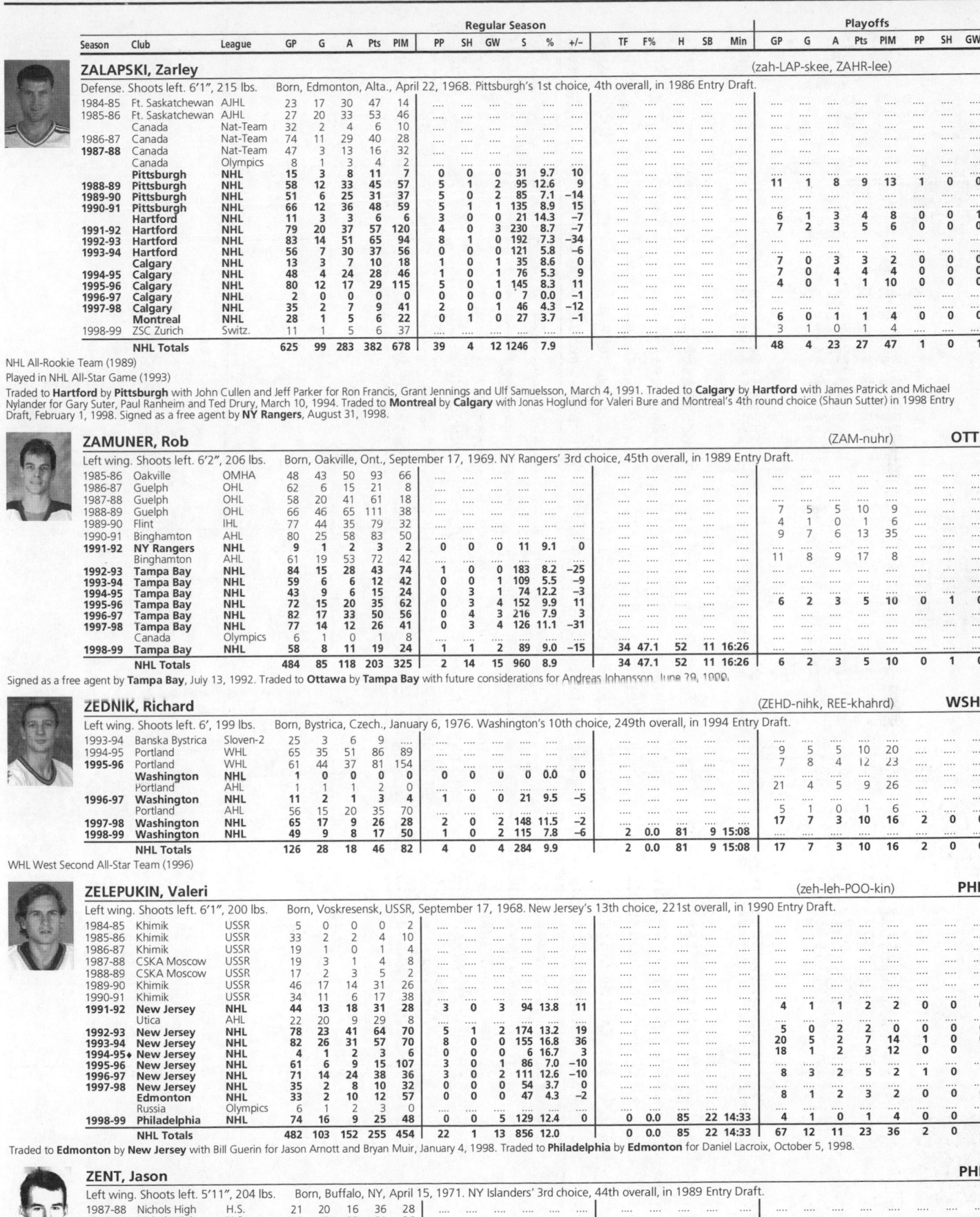

			Regular Season																Playoffs							
Season	Club	League	GP	G	A	Pts	PIM	PP	SH	GW	S	%	+/-	TF	F%	H	SB	Min	GP	G	A	Pts	PIM	PP	SH	GW

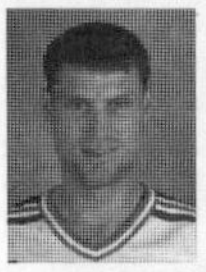

ZALAPSKI, Zarley (zah-LAP-skee, ZAHR-lee)

Defense. Shoots left. 6'1", 215 lbs. Born, Edmonton, Alta., April 22, 1968. Pittsburgh's 1st choice, 4th overall, in 1986 Entry Draft.

Season	Club	League	GP	G	A	Pts	PIM	PP	SH	GW	S	%	+/-	TF	F%	H	SB	Min	GP	G	A	Pts	PIM	PP	SH	GW
1984-85	Ft. Saskatchewan	AJHL	23	17	30	47	14	....	....	....	....	....	....	....	....	....	....	....	....	....	....	....	....	....	....	....
1985-86	Ft. Saskatchewan	AJHL	27	20	33	53	46	....	....	....	....	....	....	....	....	....	....	....	....	....	....	....	....	....	....	....
	Canada	Nat-Team	32	2	4	6	10	....	....	....	....	....	....	....	....	....	....	....	....	....	....	....	....	....	....	....
1986-87	Canada	Nat-Team	74	11	29	40	28	....	....	....	....	....	....	....	....	....	....	....	....	....	....	....	....	....	....	....
1987-88	Canada	Nat-Team	47	3	13	16	32	....	....	....	....	....	....	....	....	....	....	....	....	....	....	....	....	....	....	....
	Canada	Olympics	8	1	3	4	2	....	....	....	....	....	....	....	....	....	....	....	....	....	....	....	....	....	....	....
	Pittsburgh	**NHL**	**15**	**3**	**8**	**11**	**7**	0	0	0	31	9.7	10	....	....	....	....	....	....	....	....	....	....	....	....	....
1988-89	**Pittsburgh**	**NHL**	**58**	**12**	**33**	**45**	**57**	5	1	2	95	12.6	9	....	....	....	....	....	**11**	**1**	**8**	**9**	**13**	**1**	**0**	**0**
1989-90	**Pittsburgh**	**NHL**	**51**	**6**	**25**	**31**	**37**	5	0	2	85	7.1	−14	....	....	....	....	....	....	....	....	....	....	....	....	....
1990-91	**Pittsburgh**	**NHL**	**66**	**12**	**36**	**48**	**59**	5	1	1	135	8.9	15	....	....	....	....	....	....	....	....	....	....	....	....	....
	Hartford	**NHL**	**11**	**3**	**3**	**6**	**6**	3	0	0	21	14.3	−7	....	....	....	....	....	**6**	**1**	**3**	**4**	**8**	**0**	**0**	**1**
1991-92	**Hartford**	**NHL**	**79**	**20**	**37**	**57**	**120**	4	0	3	230	8.7	−7	....	....	....	....	....	**7**	**2**	**3**	**5**	**6**	**0**	**0**	**0**
1992-93	**Hartford**	**NHL**	**83**	**14**	**51**	**65**	**94**	8	1	0	192	7.3	−34	....	....	....	....	....	....	....	....	....	....	....	....	....
1993-94	**Hartford**	**NHL**	**56**	**7**	**30**	**37**	**56**	0	0	0	121	5.8	−6	....	....	....	....	....	....	....	....	....	....	....	....	....
	Calgary	**NHL**	**13**	**3**	**7**	**10**	**18**	1	0	1	35	8.6	0	....	....	....	....	....	**7**	**0**	**3**	**3**	**2**	**0**	**0**	**0**
1994-95	**Calgary**	**NHL**	**48**	**4**	**24**	**28**	**46**	1	0	1	76	5.3	9	....	....	....	....	....	**7**	**0**	**4**	**4**	**4**	**0**	**0**	**0**
1995-96	**Calgary**	**NHL**	**80**	**12**	**17**	**29**	**115**	5	0	1	145	8.3	11	....	....	....	....	....	**4**	**0**	**1**	**1**	**10**	**0**	**0**	**0**
1996-97	**Calgary**	**NHL**	**2**	**0**	**0**	**0**	**0**	0	0	0	7	0.0	−1	....	....	....	....	....	....	....	....	....	....	....	....	....
1997-98	**Calgary**	**NHL**	**35**	**2**	**7**	**9**	**41**	2	0	1	46	4.3	−12	....	....	....	....	....	....	....	....	....	....	....	....	....
	Montreal	**NHL**	**28**	**1**	**5**	**6**	**22**	0	1	0	27	3.7	−1	....	....	....	....	....	**6**	**0**	**1**	**1**	**4**	**0**	**0**	**0**
1998-99	ZSC Zurich	Switz.	11	1	5	6	37	....	....	....	....	....	....	....	....	....	....	....	3	1	0	1	4	....	....	....
	NHL Totals		**625**	**99**	**283**	**382**	**678**	**39**	**4**	**12**	**1246**	**7.9**		....	....	....	....	....	**48**	**4**	**23**	**27**	**47**	**1**	**0**	**1**

NHL All-Rookie Team (1989)
Played in NHL All-Star Game (1993)

Traded to **Hartford** by **Pittsburgh** with John Cullen and Jeff Parker for Ron Francis, Grant Jennings and Ulf Samuelsson, March 4, 1991. Traded to **Calgary** by **Hartford** with James Patrick and Michael Nylander for Gary Suter, Paul Ranheim and Ted Drury, March 10, 1994. Traded to **Montreal** by **Calgary** with Jonas Hoglund for Valeri Bure and Montreal's 4th round choice (Shaun Sutter) in 1998 Entry Draft, February 1, 1998. Signed as a free agent by **NY Rangers**, August 31, 1998.

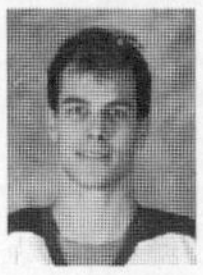

ZAMUNER, Rob (ZAM-nuhr) **OTT.**

Left wing. Shoots left. 6'2", 206 lbs. Born, Oakville, Ont., September 17, 1969. NY Rangers' 3rd choice, 45th overall, in 1989 Entry Draft.

Season	Club	League	GP	G	A	Pts	PIM	PP	SH	GW	S	%	+/-	TF	F%	H	SB	Min	GP	G	A	Pts	PIM	PP	SH	GW
1985-86	Oakville	OMHA	48	43	50	93	66	....	....	....	....	....	....	....	....	....	....	....	....	....	....	....	....	....	....	....
1986-87	Guelph	OHL	62	6	15	21	8	....	....	....	....	....	....	....	....	....	....	....	....	....	....	....	....	....	....	....
1987-88	Guelph	OHL	58	20	41	61	18	....	....	....	....	....	....	....	....	....	....	....	....	....	....	....	....	....	....	....
1988-89	Guelph	OHL	66	46	65	111	38	....	....	....	....	....	....	....	....	....	....	....	7	5	5	10	9	....	....	....
1989-90	Flint	IHL	77	44	35	79	32	....	....	....	....	....	....	....	....	....	....	....	4	1	0	1	6	....	....	....
1990-91	Binghamton	AHL	80	25	58	83	50	....	....	....	....	....	....	....	....	....	....	....	9	7	6	13	35	....	....	....
1991-92	**NY Rangers**	**NHL**	**9**	**1**	**2**	**3**	**2**	0	0	0	11	9.1	0	....	....	....	....	....	....	....	....	....	....	....	....	....
	Binghamton	AHL	61	19	53	72	42	....	....	....	....	....	....	....	....	....	....	....	11	8	9	17	8	....	....	....
1992-93	**Tampa Bay**	**NHL**	**84**	**15**	**28**	**43**	**74**	1	0	0	183	8.2	−25	....	....	....	....	....	....	....	....	....	....	....	....	....
1993-94	**Tampa Bay**	**NHL**	**59**	**6**	**6**	**12**	**42**	0	0	1	109	5.5	−9	....	....	....	....	....	....	....	....	....	....	....	....	....
1994-95	**Tampa Bay**	**NHL**	**43**	**9**	**6**	**15**	**24**	0	3	1	74	12.2	−3	....	....	....	....	....	....	....	....	....	....	....	....	....
1995-96	**Tampa Bay**	**NHL**	**72**	**15**	**20**	**35**	**62**	0	3	4	152	9.9	11	....	....	....	....	....	**6**	**2**	**3**	**5**	**10**	**0**	**1**	**0**
1996-97	**Tampa Bay**	**NHL**	**82**	**17**	**33**	**50**	**56**	0	4	3	216	7.9	3	....	....	....	....	....	....	....	....	....	....	....	....	....
1997-98	**Tampa Bay**	**NHL**	**77**	**14**	**12**	**26**	**41**	0	3	4	126	11.1	−31	....	....	....	....	....	....	....	....	....	....	....	....	....
	Canada	Olympics	6	1	0	1	8	....	....	....	....	....	....	....	....	....	....	....	....	....	....	....	....	....	....	....
1998-99	**Tampa Bay**	**NHL**	**58**	**8**	**11**	**19**	**24**	1	1	2	89	9.0	−15	34	47.1	52	11	16:26	....	....	....	....	....	....	....	....
	NHL Totals		**484**	**85**	**118**	**203**	**325**	**2**	**14**	**15**	**960**	**8.9**		**34**	**47.1**	**52**	**11**	**16:26**	**6**	**2**	**3**	**5**	**10**	**0**	**1**	**0**

Signed as a free agent by **Tampa Bay**, July 13, 1992. Traded to **Ottawa** by **Tampa Bay** with future considerations for Andreas Johansson, June 29, 1999.

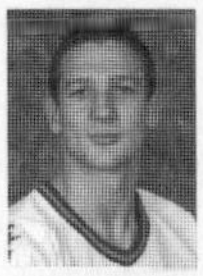

ZEDNIK, Richard (ZEHD-nihk, REE-khahrd) **WSH.**

Left wing. Shoots left. 6', 199 lbs. Born, Bystrica, Czech., January 6, 1976. Washington's 10th choice, 249th overall, in 1994 Entry Draft.

Season	Club	League	GP	G	A	Pts	PIM	PP	SH	GW	S	%	+/-	TF	F%	H	SB	Min	GP	G	A	Pts	PIM	PP	SH	GW
1993-94	Banska Bystrica	Sloven-2	25	3	6	9	....	....	....	....	....	....	....	....	....	....	....	....	....	....	....	....	....	....	....	....
1994-95	Portland	WHL	65	35	51	86	89	....	....	....	....	....	....	....	....	....	....	....	9	5	5	10	20	....	....	....
1995-96	Portland	WHL	61	44	37	81	154	....	....	....	....	....	....	....	....	....	....	....	7	8	4	12	23	....	....	....
	Washington	**NHL**	**1**	**0**	**0**	**0**	**0**	0	0	0	0	0.0	0	....	....	....	....	....	....	....	....	....	....	....	....	....
	Portland	AHL	1	1	1	2	0	....	....	....	....	....	....	....	....	....	....	....	21	4	5	9	26	....	....	....
1996-97	**Washington**	**NHL**	**11**	**2**	**1**	**3**	**4**	1	0	0	21	9.5	−5	....	....	....	....	....	....	....	....	....	....	....	....	....
	Portland	AHL	56	15	20	35	70	....	....	....	....	....	....	....	....	....	....	....	5	1	0	1	6	....	....	....
1997-98	**Washington**	**NHL**	**65**	**17**	**9**	**26**	**28**	2	0	2	148	11.5	−2	....	....	....	....	....	**17**	**7**	**3**	**10**	**16**	**2**	**0**	**0**
1998-99	**Washington**	**NHL**	**49**	**9**	**8**	**17**	**50**	1	0	2	115	7.8	−6	2	0.0	81	9	15:08	....	....	....	....	....	....	....	....
	NHL Totals		**126**	**28**	**18**	**46**	**82**	**4**	**0**	**4**	**284**	**9.9**		**2**	**0.0**	**81**	**9**	**15:08**	**17**	**7**	**3**	**10**	**16**	**2**	**0**	**0**

WHL West Second All-Star Team (1996)

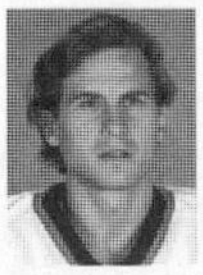

ZELEPUKIN, Valeri (zeh-leh-POO-kin) **PHI.**

Left wing. Shoots left. 6'1", 200 lbs. Born, Voskresensk, USSR, September 17, 1968. New Jersey's 13th choice, 221st overall, in 1990 Entry Draft.

Season	Club	League	GP	G	A	Pts	PIM	PP	SH	GW	S	%	+/-	TF	F%	H	SB	Min	GP	G	A	Pts	PIM	PP	SH	GW
1984-85	Khimik	USSR	5	0	0	0	2	....	....	....	....	....	....	....	....	....	....	....	....	....	....	....	....	....	....	....
1985-86	Khimik	USSR	33	2	2	4	10	....	....	....	....	....	....	....	....	....	....	....	....	....	....	....	....	....	....	....
1986-87	Khimik	USSR	19	1	0	1	4	....	....	....	....	....	....	....	....	....	....	....	....	....	....	....	....	....	....	....
1987-88	CSKA Moscow	USSR	19	3	1	4	8	....	....	....	....	....	....	....	....	....	....	....	....	....	....	....	....	....	....	....
1988-89	CSKA Moscow	USSR	17	2	3	5	2	....	....	....	....	....	....	....	....	....	....	....	....	....	....	....	....	....	....	....
1989-90	Khimik	USSR	46	17	14	31	26	....	....	....	....	....	....	....	....	....	....	....	....	....	....	....	....	....	....	....
1990-91	Khimik	USSR	34	11	6	17	38	....	....	....	....	....	....	....	....	....	....	....	....	....	....	....	....	....	....	....
1991-92	**New Jersey**	**NHL**	**44**	**13**	**18**	**31**	**28**	3	0	3	94	13.8	11	....	....	....	....	....	**4**	**1**	**1**	**2**	**2**	**0**	**0**	**0**
	Utica	AHL	22	20	9	29	8	....	....	....	....	....	....	....	....	....	....	....	....	....	....	....	....	....	....	....
1992-93	**New Jersey**	**NHL**	**78**	**23**	**41**	**64**	**70**	5	1	2	174	13.2	19	....	....	....	....	....	**5**	**0**	**2**	**2**	**0**	**0**	**0**	**0**
1993-94	**New Jersey**	**NHL**	**82**	**26**	**31**	**57**	**70**	8	0	0	155	16.8	36	....	....	....	....	....	**20**	**5**	**2**	**7**	**14**	**1**	**0**	**0**
1994-95♦	**New Jersey**	**NHL**	**4**	**1**	**2**	**3**	**6**	0	0	0	6	16.7	3	....	....	....	....	....	**18**	**1**	**2**	**3**	**12**	**0**	**0**	**1**
1995-96	**New Jersey**	**NHL**	**61**	**6**	**9**	**15**	**107**	3	0	1	86	7.0	−10	....	....	....	....	....	....	....	....	....	....	....	....	....
1996-97	**New Jersey**	**NHL**	**71**	**14**	**24**	**38**	**36**	3	0	2	111	12.6	−10	....	....	....	....	....	**8**	**3**	**2**	**5**	**2**	**1**	**0**	**1**
1997-98	**New Jersey**	**NHL**	**35**	**2**	**8**	**10**	**32**	0	0	0	54	3.7	0	....	....	....	....	....	....	....	....	....	....	....	....	....
	Edmonton	**NHL**	**33**	**2**	**10**	**12**	**57**	0	0	0	47	4.3	−2	....	....	....	....	....	**8**	**1**	**2**	**3**	**2**	**0**	**0**	**0**
	Russia	Olympics	6	1	2	3	0	....	....	....	....	....	....	....	....	....	....	....	....	....	....	....	....	....	....	....
1998-99	**Philadelphia**	**NHL**	**74**	**16**	**9**	**25**	**48**	0	0	5	129	12.4	0	0	0.0	85	22	14:33	**4**	**1**	**0**	**1**	**4**	**0**	**0**	**1**
	NHL Totals		**482**	**103**	**152**	**255**	**454**	**22**	**1**	**13**	**856**	**12.0**		**0**	**0.0**	**85**	**22**	**14:33**	**67**	**12**	**11**	**23**	**36**	**2**	**0**	**3**

Traded to **Edmonton** by **New Jersey** with Bill Guerin for Jason Arnott and Bryan Muir, January 4, 1998. Traded to **Philadelphia** by **Edmonton** for Daniel Lacroix, October 5, 1998.

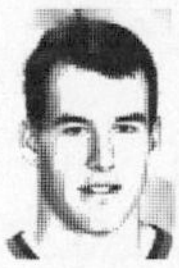

ZENT, Jason **PHI.**

Left wing. Shoots left. 5'11", 204 lbs. Born, Buffalo, NY, April 15, 1971. NY Islanders' 3rd choice, 44th overall, in 1989 Entry Draft.

Season	Club	League	GP	G	A	Pts	PIM	PP	SH	GW	S	%	+/-	TF	F%	H	SB	Min	GP	G	A	Pts	PIM	PP	SH	GW
1987-88	Nichols High	H.S.	21	20	16	36	28	....	....	....	....	....	....	....	....	....	....	....	....	....	....	....	....	....	....	....
1988-89	Nichols High	H.S.	29	49	32	81	26	....	....	....	....	....	....	....	....	....	....	....	....	....	....	....	....	....	....	....
1989-90	Nichols High	H.S.	27	36	38	74	....	....	....	....	....	....	....	....	....	....	....	....	....	....	....	....	....	....	....	....
1990-91	U. of Wisconsin	WCHA	39	19	18	37	51	....	....	....	....	....	....	....	....	....	....	....	....	....	....	....	....	....	....	....
1991-92	U. of Wisconsin	WCHA	39	22	17	39	128	....	....	....	....	....	....	....	....	....	....	....	....	....	....	....	....	....	....	....
1992-93	U. of Wisconsin	WCHA	40	26	12	38	92	....	....	....	....	....	....	....	....	....	....	....	....	....	....	....	....	....	....	....
1993-94	U. of Wisconsin	WCHA	42	20	21	41	120	....	....	....	....	....	....	....	....	....	....	....	....	....	....	....	....	....	....	....

			Regular Season																Playoffs							
Season	Club	League	GP	G	A	Pts	PIM	PP	SH	GW	S	%	+/-	TF	F%	H	SB	Min	GP	G	A	Pts	PIM	PP	SH	GW
1994-95	P.E.I. Senators	AHL	55	15	11	26	46	....	....	....	....	....	....	....	....	....	....	....	9	6	1	7	6	....	....	....
1995-96	P.E.I. Senators	AHL	68	14	5	19	61	....	....	....	....	....	....	....	....	....	....	....	5	2	1	3	4	....	....	....
1996-97	**Ottawa**	**NHL**	**22**	**3**	**3**	**6**	**9**	**0**	**0**	**0**	**20**	**15.0**	**5**	....	....	....	....	....	....	....	....	....	....	....	....	....
	Worcester	AHL	45	14	10	24	45	....	....	....	....	....	....	....	....	....	....	....	5	3	3	6	4	....	....	....
1997-98	**Ottawa**	**NHL**	**3**	**0**	**0**	**0**	**4**	**0**	**0**	**0**	**1**	**0.0**	**0**	....	....	....	....	....	....	....	....	....	....	....	....	....
	Detroit	IHL	4	1	0	1	0	....	....	....	....	....	....	....	....	....	....	....	....	....	....	....	....	....	....	....
	Worcester	AHL	66	25	17	42	67	....	....	....	....	....	....	....	....	....	....	....	11	2	0	2	6	....	....	....
1998-99	**Philadelphia**	**NHL**	**2**	**0**	**0**	**0**	**0**	**0**	**0**	**0**	**1**	**0.0**	**0**	**0**	**0.0**	**2**	**0**	**2:58**	....	....	....	....	....	....	....	....
	Philadelphia	AHL	64	13	13	26	82	....	....	....	....	....	....	....	....	....	....	....	16	2	4	6	22	....	....	....
	NHL Totals		**27**	**3**	**3**	**6**	**13**	**0**	**0**	**0**	**22**	**13.6**		**0**	**0.0**	**2**	**0**	**2:58**	....	....	....	....	....	....	....	....

NCAA Championship All-Tournament Team (1992)

Traded to **Ottawa** by **NY Islanders** for Ottawa's 5th round choice (Andy Berenzweig) in 1996 Entry Draft, October 15, 1994. Signed as a free agent by **Philadelphia**, July 28, 1998.

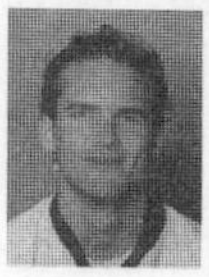

ZETTLER, Rob

Defense. Shoots left. 6'3", 200 lbs. Born, Sept Iles, Que., March 8, 1968. Minnesota's 5th choice, 55th overall, in 1986 Entry Draft.

Season	Club	League	GP	G	A	Pts	PIM	PP	SH	GW	S	%	+/-	TF	F%	H	SB	Min	GP	G	A	Pts	PIM	PP	SH	GW
1983-84	S.S. Marie AA	OMHA	40	9	24	33	28	....	....	....	....	....	....	....	....	....	....	....	....	....	....	....	....	....	....	....
1984-85	S.S. Marie	OHL	60	2	14	16	37	....	....	....	....	....	....	....	....	....	....	....	....	....	....	....	....	....	....	....
1985-86	S.S. Marie	OHL	57	5	23	28	92	....	....	....	....	....	....	....	....	....	....	....	....	....	....	....	....	....	....	....
1986-87	S.S. Marie	OHL	64	13	22	35	89	....	....	....	....	....	....	....	....	....	....	....	4	0	0	0	0	....	....	....
1987-88	S.S. Marie	OHL	64	7	41	48	77	....	....	....	....	....	....	....	....	....	....	....	6	2	2	4	9	....	....	....
	Kalamazoo	IHL	2	0	1	1	0	....	....	....	....	....	....	....	....	....	....	....	7	0	2	2	2	....	....	....
1988-89	**Minnesota**	**NHL**	**2**	**0**	**0**	**0**	**0**	**0**	**0**	**0**	**0**	**0.0**	**–1**	....	....	....	....	....	....	....	....	....	....	....	....	....
	Kalamazoo	IHL	80	5	21	26	79	....	....	....	....	....	....	....	....	....	....	....	6	0	1	1	26	....	....	....
1989-90	**Minnesota**	**NHL**	**31**	**0**	**8**	**8**	**45**	**0**	**0**	**0**	**21**	**0.0**	**–7**	....	....	....	....	....	....	....	....	....	....	....	....	....
	Kalamazoo	IHL	41	6	10	16	64	....	....	....	....	....	....	....	....	....	....	....	7	0	0	0	6	....	....	....
1990-91	**Minnesota**	**NHL**	**47**	**1**	**4**	**5**	**119**	**0**	**0**	**0**	**30**	**3.3**	**–10**	....	....	....	....	....	....	....	....	....	....	....	....	....
	Kalamazoo	IHL	1	0	0	0	2	....	....	....	....	....	....	....	....	....	....	....	....	....	....	....	....	....	....	....
1991-92	**San Jose**	**NHL**	**74**	**1**	**8**	**9**	**99**	**0**	**0**	**0**	**72**	**1.4**	**–23**	....	....	....	....	....	....	....	....	....	....	....	....	....
1992-93	**San Jose**	**NHL**	**80**	**0**	**7**	**7**	**150**	**0**	**0**	**0**	**60**	**0.0**	**–50**	....	....	....	....	....	....	....	....	....	....	....	....	....
1993-94	**San Jose**	**NHL**	**42**	**0**	**3**	**3**	**65**	**0**	**0**	**0**	**28**	**0.0**	**–7**	....	....	....	....	....	....	....	....	....	....	....	....	....
	Philadelphia	**NHL**	**33**	**0**	**4**	**4**	**69**	**0**	**0**	**0**	**27**	**0.0**	**–19**	....	....	....	....	....	....	....	....	....	....	....	....	....
1994-95	**Philadelphia**	**NHL**	**32**	**0**	**1**	**1**	**34**	**0**	**0**	**0**	**17**	**0.0**	**–3**	....	....	....	....	....	**1**	**0**	**0**	**0**	**2**	**0**	**0**	**0**
1995-96	**Toronto**	**NHL**	**29**	**0**	**1**	**1**	**48**	**0**	**0**	**0**	**11**	**0.0**	**–1**	....	....	....	....	....	**2**	**0**	**0**	**0**	**0**	**0**	**0**	**0**
1996-97	**Toronto**	**NHL**	**48**	**2**	**12**	**14**	**51**	**0**	**0**	**0**	**31**	**6.5**	**8**	....	....	....	....	....	....	....	....	....	....	....	....	....
	Utah	IHL	30	0	10	10	60	....	....	....	....	....	....	....	....	....	....	....	....	....	....	....	....	....	....	....
1997-98	**Toronto**	**NHL**	**59**	**0**	**7**	**7**	**108**	**0**	**0**	**0**	**28**	**0.0**	**–8**	....	....	....	....	....	....	....	....	....	....	....	....	....
1998-99	**Nashville**	**NHL**	**2**	**0**	**0**	**0**	**2**	**0**	**0**	**0**	**0**	**0.0**	**–2**	**0**	**0.0**	**5**	**1**	**16:16**	....	....	....	....	....	....	....	....
	Utah	IHL	77	2	16	18	136	....	....	....	....	....	....	....	....	....	....	....	....	....	....	....	....	....	....	....
	NHL Totals		**479**	**4**	**55**	**59**	**790**	**0**	**0**	**0**	**325**	**1.2**		**0**	**0.0**	**5**	**1**	**16:16**	**3**	**0**	**0**	**0**	**2**	**0**	**0**	**0**

Claimed by **San Jose** from **Minnesota** in Dispersal Draft, May 30, 1991. Traded to **Philadelphia** by **San Jose** for Viacheslav Butsayev, February 1, 1994. Traded to **Toronto** by **Philadelphia** for Toronto's 5th round choice (Per-Ragna Bergqvist) in 1996 Entry Draft, July 8, 1995. Claimed by **Nashville** from **Toronto** in Expansion Draft, June 26, 1998.

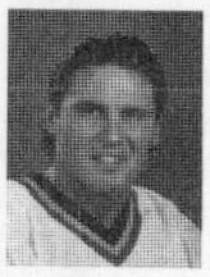

ZEZEL, Peter

(ZEH-zehl)

Center. Shoots left. 5'11", 220 lbs. Born, Toronto, Ont., April 22, 1965. Philadelphia's 1st choice, 41st overall, in 1983 Entry Draft.

Season	Club	League	GP	G	A	Pts	PIM	PP	SH	GW	S	%	+/-	TF	F%	H	SB	Min	GP	G	A	Pts	PIM	PP	SH	GW
1981-82	Don Mills	MTHL	40	43	51	94	36	....	....	....	....	....	....	....	....	....	....	....	....	....	....	....	....	....	....	....
1982-83	Toronto	OHL	66	35	39	74	28	....	....	....	....	....	....	....	....	....	....	....	4	2	4	6	0	....	....	....
1983-84	Toronto	OHL	68	47	86	133	31	....	....	....	....	....	....	....	....	....	....	....	9	7	5	12	4	....	....	....
1984-85	**Philadelphia**	**NHL**	**65**	**15**	**46**	**61**	**26**	**8**	**0**	**2**	**91**	**16.5**	**22**	....	....	....	....	....	**19**	**1**	**8**	**9**	**28**	**1**	**0**	**0**
1985-86	**Philadelphia**	**NHL**	**79**	**17**	**37**	**54**	**76**	**4**	**0**	**4**	**144**	**11.8**	**27**	....	....	....	....	....	**5**	**3**	**1**	**4**	**4**	**1**	**0**	**1**
1986-87	**Philadelphia**	**NHL**	**71**	**33**	**39**	**72**	**71**	**6**	**2**	**7**	**181**	**18.2**	**21**	....	....	....	....	....	**25**	**3**	**10**	**13**	**10**	**1**	**1**	**1**
1987-88	**Philadelphia**	**NHL**	**69**	**22**	**35**	**57**	**42**	**14**	**0**	**1**	**133**	**16.5**	**7**	....	....	....	....	....	**7**	**3**	**2**	**5**	**7**	**0**	**0**	**0**
1988-89	**Philadelphia**	**NHL**	**26**	**4**	**13**	**17**	**15**	**0**	**0**	**0**	**34**	**11.8**	**–13**	....	....	....	....	....	....	....	....	....	....	....	....	....
	St. Louis	**NHL**	**52**	**17**	**36**	**53**	**27**	**5**	**1**	**4**	**115**	**14.8**	**–1**	....	....	....	....	....	**10**	**6**	**6**	**12**	**4**	**1**	**1**	**1**
1989-90	**St. Louis**	**NHL**	**73**	**25**	**47**	**72**	**30**	**7**	**0**	**3**	**158**	**15.8**	**–9**	....	....	....	....	....	**12**	**1**	**7**	**8**	**4**	**1**	**0**	**0**
1990-91	**Washington**	**NHL**	**20**	**7**	**5**	**12**	**10**	**6**	**0**	**0**	**21**	**33.3**	**–13**	....	....	....	....	....	....	....	....	....	....	....	....	....
	Toronto	**NHL**	**32**	**14**	**14**	**28**	**4**	**6**	**0**	**5**	**69**	**20.3**	**–7**	....	....	....	....	....	....	....	....	....	....	....	....	....
1991-92	**Toronto**	**NHL**	**64**	**16**	**33**	**49**	**26**	**4**	**0**	**1**	**125**	**12.8**	**–22**	....	....	....	....	....	....	....	....	....	....	....	....	....
1992-93	**Toronto**	**NHL**	**70**	**12**	**23**	**35**	**24**	**0**	**0**	**4**	**102**	**11.8**	**0**	....	....	....	....	....	**20**	**2**	**1**	**3**	**6**	**0**	**0**	**0**
1993-94	**Toronto**	**NHL**	**41**	**8**	**8**	**16**	**19**	**0**	**0**	**0**	**47**	**17.0**	**5**	....	....	....	....	....	**18**	**2**	**4**	**6**	**8**	**0**	**0**	**1**
1994-95	**Dallas**	**NHL**	**30**	**6**	**5**	**11**	**19**	**0**	**0**	**1**	**47**	**12.8**	**–6**	....	....	....	....	....	**3**	**1**	**0**	**1**	**0**	**0**	**0**	**0**
	Kalamazoo	IHL	2	0	0	0	0	....	....	....	....	....	....	....	....	....	....	....	....	....	....	....	....	....	....	....
1995-96	**St. Louis**	**NHL**	**57**	**8**	**13**	**21**	**12**	**2**	**0**	**1**	**87**	**9.2**	**–2**	....	....	....	....	....	**10**	**3**	**0**	**3**	**2**	**0**	**1**	**0**
1996-97	**St. Louis**	**NHL**	**35**	**4**	**9**	**13**	**12**	**0**	**0**	**1**	**49**	**8.2**	**6**	....	....	....	....	....	....	....	....	....	....	....	....	....
	New Jersey	**NHL**	**18**	**0**	**3**	**3**	**4**	**0**	**0**	**0**	**13**	**0.0**	**4**	....	....	....	....	....	**2**	**0**	**0**	**0**	**10**	**0**	**0**	**0**
1997-98	**New Jersey**	**NHL**	**5**	**0**	**3**	**3**	**0**	**0**	**0**	**0**	**3**	**0.0**	**2**	....	....	....	....	....	....	....	....	....	....	....	....	....
	Albany	AHL	35	13	37	50	18	....	....	....	....	....	....	....	....	....	....	....	....	....	....	....	....	....	....	....
	Vancouver	**NHL**	**25**	**5**	**12**	**17**	**2**	**2**	**0**	**1**	**37**	**13.5**	**13**	....	....	....	....	....	....	....	....	....	....	....	....	....
1998-99	**Vancouver**	**NHL**	**41**	**6**	**8**	**14**	**16**	**1**	**0**	**2**	**45**	**13.3**	**5**	**615**	**53.5**	**14**	**34**	**13:08**	....	....	....	....	....	....	....	....
	NHL Totals		**873**	**219**	**389**	**608**	**435**	**65**	**3**	**37**	**1501**	**14.6**		**615**	**53.5**	**14**	**34**	**13:08**	**131**	**25**	**39**	**64**	**83**	**5**	**3**	**4**

Traded to **St. Louis** by **Philadelphia** for Mike Bullard, November 29, 1988. Traded to **Washington** by **St. Louis** with Mike Lalor for Geoff Courtnall, July 13, 1990. Traded to **Toronto** by **Washington** with Bob Rouse for Al Iafrate, January 16, 1991. Transferred to **Dallas** by **Toronto** with Grant Marshall as compensation for Toronto's signing of free agent Mike Craig, August 10, 1994. Signed as a free agent by **St. Louis**, October 19, 1995. Traded to **New Jersey** by **St. Louis** for Chris McAlpine and New Jersey's 9th round choice in 1999 Entry Draft, February 11, 1997. Traded to **Vancouver** by **New Jersey** for Vancouver's 5th round choice (Anton But) in 1998 Entry Draft, February 5, 1998.

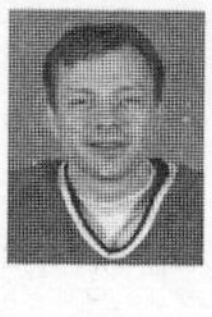

ZHAMNOV, Alexei

(ZHAHM-nahf) **CHI.**

Center. Shoots left. 6'1", 200 lbs. Born, Moscow, USSR, October 1, 1970. Winnipeg's 5th choice, 77th overall, in 1990 Entry Draft.

Season	Club	League	GP	G	A	Pts	PIM	PP	SH	GW	S	%	+/-	TF	F%	H	SB	Min	GP	G	A	Pts	PIM	PP	SH	GW
1988-89	Moscow D'amo	USSR	4	0	0	0	0	....	....	....	....	....	....	....	....	....	....	....	....	....	....	....	....	....	....	....
1989-90	Moscow D'amo	USSR	43	11	6	17	21	....	....	....	....	....	....	....	....	....	....	....	....	....	....	....	....	....	....	....
1990-91	Moscow D'amo	USSR	46	16	12	28	24	....	....	....	....	....	....	....	....	....	....	....	....	....	....	....	....	....	....	....
1991-92	Moscow D'amo	CIS	39	15	21	36	28	....	....	....	....	....	....	....	....	....	....	....	....	....	....	....	....	....	....	....
	Russia	Olympics	8	0	3	3	8	....	....	....	....	....	....	....	....	....	....	....	....	....	....	....	....	....	....	....
1992-93	**Winnipeg**	**NHL**	**68**	**25**	**47**	**72**	**58**	**6**	**1**	**4**	**163**	**15.3**	**7**	....	....	....	....	....	**6**	**0**	**2**	**2**	**2**	**0**	**0**	**0**
1993-94	**Winnipeg**	**NHL**	**61**	**26**	**45**	**71**	**62**	**7**	**0**	**1**	**196**	**13.3**	**–20**	....	....	....	....	....	....	....	....	....	....	....	....	....
1994-95	**Winnipeg**	**NHL**	**48**	**30**	**35**	**65**	**20**	**9**	**0**	**4**	**155**	**19.4**	**5**	....	....	....	....	....	....	....	....	....	....	....	....	....
1995-96	**Winnipeg**	**NHL**	**58**	**22**	**37**	**59**	**65**	**5**	**0**	**2**	**199**	**11.1**	**–4**	....	....	....	....	....	**6**	**2**	**1**	**3**	**8**	**0**	**0**	**0**
1996-97	**Chicago**	**NHL**	**74**	**20**	**42**	**62**	**56**	**6**	**1**	**2**	**208**	**9.6**	**18**	....	....	....	....	....	....	....	....	....	....	....	....	....
1997-98	**Chicago**	**NHL**	**70**	**21**	**28**	**49**	**61**	**6**	**2**	**3**	**193**	**10.9**	**16**	....	....	....	....	....	....	....	....	....	....	....	....	....
	Russia	Olympics	6	2	1	3	2	....	....	....	....	....	....	....	....	....	....	....	....	....	....	....	....	....	....	....
1998-99	**Chicago**	**NHL**	**76**	**20**	**41**	**61**	**50**	**8**	**1**	**2**	**200**	**10.0**	**–10**	**1299**	**48.9**	**40**	**38**	**21:30**	....	....	....	....	....	....	....	....
	NHL Totals		**455**	**164**	**275**	**439**	**372**	**47**	**5**	**18**	**1314**	**12.5**		**1299**	**48.9**	**40**	**38**	**21:30**	**12**	**2**	**3**	**5**	**10**	**0**	**0**	**0**

NHL Second All-Star Team (1995)

Traded to **Chicago** by **Phoenix** with Craig Mills and Phoenix's 1st round choice (Ty Jones) in 1997 Entry Draft for Jeremy Roenick, August 16, 1996.

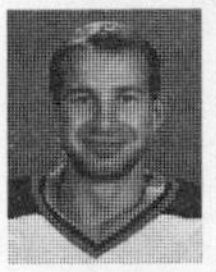

ZHITNIK, Alexei (ZHIHT-nihk) **BUF.**

Defense. Shoots left. 5'11", 204 lbs. Born, Kiev, USSR, October 10, 1972. Los Angeles' 3rd choice, 81st overall, in 1991 Entry Draft.

			Regular Season																Playoffs							
Season	Club	League	GP	G	A	Pts	PIM	PP	SH	GW	S	%	+/–	TF	F%	H	SB	Min	GP	G	A	Pts	PIM	PP	SH	GW
1989-90	Sokol Kiev	USSR	31	3	4	7	16	....	....	....	....	....	....	....	....	....	....	....	....	....	....	....	....	....	....	....
1990-91	Sokol Kiev	USSR	46	1	4	5	46	....	....	....	....	....	....	....	....	....	....	....	....	....	....	....	....	....	....	....
1991-92	CSKA Moscow	CIS	44	2	7	9	52	....	....	....	....	....	....	....	....	....	....	....	....	....	....	....	....	....	....	....
	Russia	Olympics	8	1	0	1	0	....	....	....	....	....	....	....	....	....	....	....	....	....	....	....	....	....	....	....
1992-93	**Los Angeles**	**NHL**	**78**	**12**	**36**	**48**	**80**	**5**	**0**	**2**	**136**	**8.8**	**–3**	....	....	....	....	....	**24**	**3**	**9**	**12**	**26**	**2**	**0**	**1**
1993-94	**Los Angeles**	**NHL**	**81**	**12**	**40**	**52**	**101**	**11**	**0**	**1**	**227**	**5.3**	**–11**	....	....	....	....	....	....	....	....	....	....	....	....	....
1994-95	**Los Angeles**	**NHL**	**11**	**2**	**5**	**7**	**27**	**2**	**0**	**0**	**33**	**6.1**	**–3**	....	....	....	....	....	....	....	....	....	....	....	....	....
	Buffalo	**NHL**	**21**	**2**	**5**	**7**	**34**	**1**	**0**	**0**	**33**	**6.1**	**–3**	....	....	....	....	....	**5**	**0**	**1**	**1**	**14**	**0**	**0**	**0**
1995-96	**Buffalo**	**NHL**	**80**	**6**	**30**	**36**	**58**	**5**	**0**	**0**	**193**	**3.1**	**–25**	....	....	....	....	....	....	....	....	....	....	....	....	....
1996-97	**Buffalo**	**NHL**	**80**	**7**	**28**	**35**	**95**	**3**	**1**	**0**	**170**	**4.1**	**10**	....	....	....	....	....	**12**	**1**	**0**	**1**	**16**	**0**	**0**	**0**
1997-98	**Buffalo**	**NHL**	**78**	**15**	**30**	**45**	**102**	**2**	**3**	**3**	**191**	**7.9**	**19**	....	....	....	....	....	**15**	**0**	**3**	**3**	**36**	**0**	**0**	**0**
	Russia	Olympics	6	0	2	2	2	....	....	....	....	....	....	....	....	....	....	....	....	....	....	....	....	....	....	....
1998-99	**Buffalo**	**NHL**	**81**	**7**	**26**	**33**	**96**	**3**	**1**	**2**	**185**	**3.8**	**–6**	**0**	**0.0**	**122**	**109**	**25:39**	**21**	**4**	**11**	**15**	***52**	**4**	**0**	**2**
	NHL Totals		**510**	**63**	**200**	**263**	**593**	**32**	**5**	**8**	**1168**	**5.4**		**0**	**0.0**	**122**	**109**	**25:39**	**77**	**8**	**24**	**32**	**144**	**6**	**0**	**3**

Played in NHL All-Star Game (1999)

Traded to **Buffalo** by **LA Kings** with Robb Stauber, Charlie Huddy and LA Kings' 5th round choice (Marian Menhart) in 1995 Entry Draft for Philippe Boucher, Denis Tsygurov and Grant Fuhr, February 14, 1995.

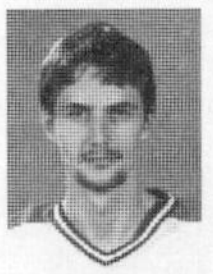

ZHOLTOK, Sergei (ZHOL-tok) **MTL.**

Center. Shoots right. 6', 187 lbs. Born, Riga, Latvia, February 12, 1972. Boston's 2nd choice, 55th overall, in 1992 Entry Draft.

			Regular Season																Playoffs							
Season	Club	League	GP	G	A	Pts	PIM	PP	SH	GW	S	%	+/–	TF	F%	H	SB	Min	GP	G	A	Pts	PIM	PP	SH	GW
1990-91	Dynamo Riga	USSR	39	4	0	4	16	....	....	....	....	....	....	....	....	....	....	....	....	....	....	....	....	....	....	....
1991-92	HC Riga	CIS	27	6	3	9	6	....	....	....	....	....	....	....	....	....	....	....	....	....	....	....	....	....	....	....
1992-93	**Boston**	**NHL**	**1**	**0**	**1**	**1**	**0**	**0**	**0**	**0**	**2**	**0.0**	**1**	....	....	....	....	....	....	....	....	....	....	....	....	....
	Providence	AHL	64	31	35	66	57	....	....	....	....	....	....	....	....	....	....	....	6	3	5	8	4	....	....	....
1993-94	**Boston**	**NHL**	**24**	**2**	**1**	**3**	**2**	**1**	**0**	**0**	**25**	**8.0**	**–7**	....	....	....	....	....	....	....	....	....	....	....	....	....
	Providence	AHL	54	29	33	62	16	....	....	....	....	....	....	....	....	....	....	....	....	....	....	....	....	....	....	....
1994-95	Providence	AHL	78	23	35	58	42	....	....	....	....	....	....	....	....	....	....	....	13	8	5	13	6	....	....	....
1995-96	Las Vegas	IHL	82	51	50	101	30	....	....	....	....	....	....	....	....	....	....	....	15	7	13	20	6	....	....	....
1996-97	**Ottawa**	**NHL**	**57**	**12**	**16**	**28**	**19**	**5**	**0**	**0**	**96**	**12.5**	**2**	....	....	....	....	....	**7**	**1**	**1**	**2**	**0**	**1**	**0**	**0**
	Las Vegas	IHL	19	13	14	27	20	....	....	....	....	....	....	....	....	....	....	....	....	....	....	....	....	....	....	....
1997-98	**Ottawa**	**NHL**	**78**	**10**	**13**	**23**	**16**	**7**	**0**	**1**	**127**	**7.9**	**–7**	....	....	....	....	....	**11**	**0**	**2**	**2**	**0**	**0**	**0**	**0**
1998-99	**Montreal**	**NHL**	**70**	**7**	**15**	**22**	**6**	**2**	**0**	**3**	**102**	**6.9**	**–12**	**522**	**49.0**	**23**	**12**	**11:11**	....	....	....	....	....	....	....	....
	Fredericton	AHL	7	3	4	7	0	....	....	....	....	....	....	....	....	....	....	....	....	....	....	....	....	....	....	....
	NHL Totals		**230**	**31**	**46**	**77**	**43**	**15**	**0**	**4**	**352**	**8.8**		**522**	**49.0**	**23**	**12**	**11:11**	**18**	**1**	**3**	**4**	**0**	**1**	**0**	**0**

EJC-A All-Star Team (1990)

Signed as a free agent by **Ottawa**, July 10, 1996. Signed as a free agent by **Montreal**, September, 1998. Signed as a free agent by **Montreal**, September 9, 1998.

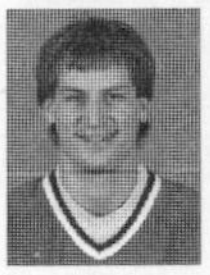

ZMOLEK, Doug (zuh-MOH-lehk) **CHI.**

Defense. Shoots left. 6'2", 222 lbs. Born, Rochester, MN, November 3, 1970. Minnesota's 1st choice, 7th overall, in 1989 Entry Draft.

			Regular Season																Playoffs							
Season	Club	League	GP	G	A	Pts	PIM	PP	SH	GW	S	%	+/–	TF	F%	H	SB	Min	GP	G	A	Pts	PIM	PP	SH	GW
1987-88	John Marshall	H.S.	27	4	32	36	....	....	....	....	....	....	....	....	....	....	....	....	....	....	....	....	....	....	....	....
1988-89	John Marshall	H.S.	29	17	41	58	....	....	....	....	....	....	....	....	....	....	....	....	....	....	....	....	....	....	....	....
1989-90	U. of Minnesota	WCHA	40	1	10	11	52	....	....	....	....	....	....	....	....	....	....	....	....	....	....	....	....	....	....	....
1990-91	U. of Minnesota	WCHA	34	11	6	17	38	....	....	....	....	....	....	....	....	....	....	....	....	....	....	....	....	....	....	....
1991-92	U. of Minnesota	WCHA	41	6	20	26	84	....	....	....	....	....	....	....	....	....	....	....	....	....	....	....	....	....	....	....
1992-93	**San Jose**	**NHL**	**84**	**5**	**10**	**15**	**229**	**2**	**0**	**0**	**94**	**5.3**	**–50**	....	....	....	....	....	....	....	....	....	....	....	....	....
1993-94	**San Jose**	**NHL**	**68**	**0**	**4**	**4**	**122**	**0**	**0**	**0**	**29**	**0.0**	**–9**	....	....	....	....	....	....	....	....	....	....	....	....	....
	Dallas	**NHL**	**7**	**1**	**0**	**1**	**11**	**0**	**0**	**0**	**3**	**33.3**	**1**	....	....	....	....	....	**7**	**0**	**1**	**1**	**4**	**0**	**0**	**0**
1994-95	**Dallas**	**NHL**	**42**	**0**	**5**	**5**	**67**	**0**	**0**	**0**	**28**	**0.0**	**–6**	....	....	....	....	....	**5**	**0**	**0**	**0**	**10**	**0**	**0**	**0**
1995-96	**Dallas**	**NHL**	**42**	**1**	**5**	**6**	**65**	**0**	**0**	**0**	**26**	**3.8**	**1**	....	....	....	....	....	....	....	....	....	....	....	....	....
	Los Angeles	**NHL**	**16**	**1**	**0**	**1**	**22**	**0**	**0**	**0**	**10**	**10.0**	**–6**	....	....	....	....	....	....	....	....	....	....	....	....	....
1996-97	**Los Angeles**	**NHL**	**57**	**1**	**0**	**1**	**116**	**0**	**0**	**0**	**28**	**3.6**	**–22**	....	....	....	....	....	....	....	....	....	....	....	....	....
1997-98	**Los Angeles**	**NHL**	**46**	**0**	**8**	**8**	**111**	**0**	**0**	**0**	**23**	**0.0**	**0**	....	....	....	....	....	**2**	**0**	**0**	**0**	**2**	**0**	**0**	**0**
1998-99	**Chicago**	**NHL**	**62**	**0**	**14**	**14**	**102**	**0**	**0**	**0**	**33**	**0.0**	**1**	**0**	**0.0**	**63**	**54**	**17:08**	....	....	....	....	....	....	....	....
	NHL Totals		**424**	**9**	**46**	**55**	**845**	**2**	**0**	**0**	**274**	**3.3**		**0**	**0.0**	**63**	**54**	**17:08**	**14**	**0**	**1**	**1**	**16**	**0**	**0**	**0**

WCHA Second All-Star Team (1992) • NCAA West Second All-American Team (1992)

Claimed by **San Jose** from **Minnesota** in Dispersal Draft, May 30, 1991. Traded to **Dallas** by **San Jose** with Mike Lalor and cash for Ulf Dahlen and Dallas' 7th round choice (Brad Mehalko) in 1995 Entry Draft, March 19, 1994. Traded to **LA Kings** by **Dallas** with Shane Churla for Darryl Sydor and LA Kings' 5th round choice (Ryan Christie) in 1996 Entry Draft, February 17, 1996. Traded to **Chicago** by **LA Kings** for Chicago's 3rd round choice (Frantisek Kaberle) in 1999 Entry Draft, September 3, 1998.

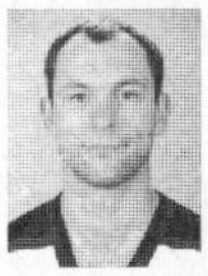

ZUBOV, Sergei (ZOO-bahf) **DAL.**

Defense. Shoots right. 6'1", 200 lbs. Born, Moscow, USSR, July 22, 1970. NY Rangers' 6th choice, 85th overall, in 1990 Entry Draft.

			Regular Season																Playoffs							
Season	Club	League	GP	G	A	Pts	PIM	PP	SH	GW	S	%	+/–	TF	F%	H	SB	Min	GP	G	A	Pts	PIM	PP	SH	GW
1988-89	CSKA Moscow	USSR	29	1	4	5	10	....	....	....	....	....	....	....	....	....	....	....	....	....	....	....	....	....	....	....
1989-90	CSKA Moscow	USSR	48	6	2	8	16	....	....	....	....	....	....	....	....	....	....	....	....	....	....	....	....	....	....	....
1990-91	CSKA Moscow	USSR	41	6	5	11	12	....	....	....	....	....	....	....	....	....	....	....	....	....	....	....	....	....	....	....
1991-92	CSKA Moscow	CIS	44	4	7	11	8	....	....	....	....	....	....	....	....	....	....	....	....	....	....	....	....	....	....	....
	Russia	Olympics	8	0	1	1	0	....	....	....	....	....	....	....	....	....	....	....	....	....	....	....	....	....	....	....
1992-93	CSKA Moscow	CIS	1	0	1	1	0	....	....	....	....	....	....	....	....	....	....	....	....	....	....	....	....	....	....	....
	NY Rangers	**NHL**	**49**	**8**	**23**	**31**	**4**	**3**	**0**	**0**	**93**	**8.6**	**–1**	....	....	....	....	....	....	....	....	....	....	....	....	....
	Binghamton	AHL	30	7	29	36	14	....	....	....	....	....	....	....	....	....	....	....	11	5	5	10	2	....	....	....
1993-94♦	**NY Rangers**	**NHL**	**78**	**12**	**77**	**89**	**39**	**9**	**0**	**1**	**222**	**5.4**	**20**	....	....	....	....	....	**22**	**5**	**14**	**19**	**0**	**2**	**0**	**0**
	Binghamton	AHL	2	1	2	3	0	....	....	....	....	....	....	....	....	....	....	....	....	....	....	....	....	....	....	....
1994-95	**NY Rangers**	**NHL**	**38**	**10**	**26**	**36**	**18**	**6**	**0**	**0**	**116**	**8.6**	**–2**	....	....	....	....	....	**10**	**3**	**8**	**11**	**2**	**1**	**0**	**0**
1995-96	**Pittsburgh**	**NHL**	**64**	**11**	**55**	**66**	**22**	**3**	**2**	**1**	**141**	**7.8**	**28**	....	....	....	....	....	**18**	**1**	**14**	**15**	**26**	**1**	**0**	**0**
1996-97	**Dallas**	**NHL**	**78**	**13**	**30**	**43**	**24**	**1**	**0**	**3**	**133**	**9.8**	**19**	....	....	....	....	....	**7**	**0**	**3**	**3**	**2**	**0**	**0**	**0**
1997-98	**Dallas**	**NHL**	**73**	**10**	**47**	**57**	**16**	**5**	**1**	**2**	**148**	**6.8**	**16**	....	....	....	....	....	**17**	**4**	**5**	**9**	**2**	**3**	**0**	**1**
1998-99♦	**Dallas**	**NHL**	**81**	**10**	**41**	**51**	**20**	**5**	**0**	**3**	**155**	**6.5**	**9**	**0**	**0.0**	**35**	**41**	**24:14**	**23**	**1**	**12**	**13**	**4**	**0**	**0**	**0**
	NHL Totals		**461**	**74**	**299**	**373**	**143**	**32**	**3**	**10**	**1008**	**7.3**		**0**	**0.0**	**35**	**41**	**24:14**	**97**	**14**	**56**	**70**	**36**	**7**	**0**	**1**

Played in NHL All-Star Game (1998, 1999)

Traded to **Pittsburgh** by **NY Rangers** with Petr Nedved for Luc Robitaille and Ulf Samuelsson, August 31, 1995. Traded to **Dallas** by **Pittsburgh** for Kevin Hatcher, June 22, 1996.

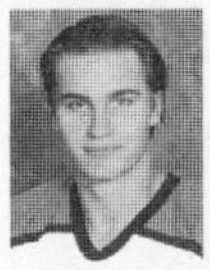

ZUBRUS, Dainius (ZOO-bruhs) **MTL.**

Right wing. Shoots left. 6'3", 220 lbs. Born, Elektrenai, USSR, June 16, 1978. Philadelphia's 1st choice, 15th overall, in 1996 Entry Draft.

			Regular Season																Playoffs							
Season	Club	League	GP	G	A	Pts	PIM	PP	SH	GW	S	%	+/–	TF	F%	H	SB	Min	GP	G	A	Pts	PIM	PP	SH	GW
1995-96	Pembroke	OJHL	28	19	13	32	73	....	....	....	....	....	....	....	....	....	....	....	....	....	....	....	....	....	....	....
	Caledon	OJHL	7	3	7	10	2	....	....	....	....	....	....	....	....	....	....	....	17	11	12	23	4	....	....	....
1996-97	**Philadelphia**	**NHL**	**68**	**8**	**13**	**21**	**22**	**1**	**0**	**2**	**71**	**11.3**	**3**	....	....	....	....	....	**19**	**5**	**4**	**9**	**12**	**1**	**0**	**1**
1997-98	**Philadelphia**	**NHL**	**69**	**8**	**25**	**33**	**42**	**1**	**0**	**5**	**101**	**7.9**	**29**	....	....	....	....	....	**5**	**0**	**1**	**1**	**2**	**0**	**0**	**0**
1998-99	**Philadelphia**	**NHL**	**63**	**3**	**5**	**8**	**25**	**0**	**1**	**0**	**49**	**6.1**	**–5**	**29**	**51.7**	**54**	**30**	**11:00**	....	....	....	....	....	....	....	....
	Montreal	**NHL**	**17**	**3**	**5**	**8**	**4**	**0**	**0**	**1**	**31**	**9.7**	**–3**	**2**	**50.0**	**15**	**6**	**16:53**	....	....	....	....	....	....	....	....
	NHL Totals		**217**	**22**	**48**	**70**	**93**	**2**	**1**	**8**	**252**	**8.7**		**31**	**51.6**	**69**	**36**	**12:15**	**24**	**5**	**5**	**10**	**14**	**1**	**0**	**1**

Traded to **Montreal** by **Philadelphia** with Philadelphia's 2nd round choice (Matt Carkner) in 1999 Entry Draft and Philadelphia's 6th round choice in 2000 Entry Draft for Mark Recchi, March 10, 1999.

ZYUZIN, Andrei

(ZYOO-zin)   **T.B.**

Defense. Shoots left. 6'1", 195 lbs.   Born, Ufa, USSR, January 21, 1978. San Jose's 1st choice, 2nd overall, in 1996 Entry Draft.

						Regular Season															Playoffs						
Season	Club	League	GP	G	A	Pts	PIM	PP	SH	GW	S	%	+/-		TF	F%	H	SB	Min		GP	G	A	Pts	PIM	PP	SH	GW
1994-95	Ufa Salavat	CIS	30	3	0	3	16	....	....	....	....	....	....		....	....	....	....	....		....	....	....	....	....	....	....	....
1995-96	Ufa Salavat	CIS	41	6	3	9	24	....	....	....	....	....	....		....	....	....	....	....		....	....	....	....	....	....	....	....
1996-97	Ufa Salavat	Russia	32	7	10	17	28	....	....	....	....	....	....		....	....	....	....	....		7	1	1	2	4	....	....	....
1997-98	**San Jose**	**NHL**	**56**	**6**	**7**	**13**	**66**	2	0	2	72	8.3	8		....	....	....	....	....		6	1	0	1	14	0	0	1
	Kentucky	AHL	17	4	5	9	28	....	....	....	....	....	....		....	....	....	....	....		....	....	....	....	....	....	....	....
1998-99	**San Jose**	**NHL**	**25**	**3**	**1**	**4**	**38**	2	0	0	44	6.8	5		0	0.0	25	11	15:56		....	....	....	....	....	....	....	....
	Kentucky	AHL	23	2	12	14	42	....	....	....	....	....	....		....	....	....	....	....		....	....	....	....	....	....	....	....
	NHL Totals		**81**	**9**	**8**	**17**	**104**	4	0	2	116	7.8			0	0.0	25	11	15:56		6	1	0	1	14	0	0	1

Traded to **Tampa Bay** by **San Jose** with Bill Houlder, Shawn Burr and Steve Guolla for Niklas Sundstrom and NY Rangers' 3rd round choice (previously acquired) in 2000 Entry Draft, August 4, 1999.

Notes

Goaltenders

Jean-Sebastien Aubin

Tom Barrasso

Ed Belfour

Zac Bierk

Craig Billington

Martin Biron

Brian Boucher

Fred Braithwaite

Martin Brodeur

Sean Burke

Jim Carey

Frederic Chabot

Dan Cloutier

Marcel Cousineau

Byron Dafoe

Jean-Francois Damphousse

Marc Denis

Mike Dunham

Bob Essensa

Manny Fernandez

Eric Fichaud

Stephane Fiset

Mark Fitzpatrick

Wade Flaherty

Mike Fountain

Grant Fuhr

Jean-Sebastien Giguere

Jeff Hackett

Dominik Hasek

Glenn Healy

Guy Hebert

Ron Hextall

Craig Hillier

Corey Hirsch

Kevin Hodson

Jani Hurme

Arturs Irbe

Pat Jablonski

Brent Johnson

Curtis Joseph

Tim Keyes

Nikolai Khabibulin

Trevor Kidd

Olaf Kolzig

Marc Lamothe

Scott Langkow

Manny Legace

Neil Little

Norm Maracle

Mark McArthur

Kirk McLean

Jamie McLennan

Tyler Moss

Chris Osgood

Rich Parent

Steve Passmore

Jonathan Pelletier

Felix Potvin

Daren Puppa

Bill Ranford

Jeff Reese

Damian Rhodes

Mike Richter

Dwayne Roloson

Dominic Roussel

Patrick Roy

Tommy Salo

Phillipe Sauve

Corey Schwab

Steve Shields

Mikhail Shtalenkov

Richard Shulmistra

Peter Skudra

Garth Snow

Jamie Storr

Rick Tabaracci

Robbie Tallas

Chris Terreri

Jose Theodore

Jocelyn Thibault

Andrei Trefilov

Ron Tugnutt

Roman Turek

Mike Valley

John Vanbiesbrouck

Mike Vernon

Tomas Vokoun

Jimmy Waite

Kevin Weekes

Ken Wregget

1999-2000 Goaltender Register

Note: The 1999-2000 Goaltender Register lists every goaltender who appeared in an NHL game in the 1998-99 season, every goaltender drafted in the first six rounds of the 1999 Entry Draft, goaltenders on NHL Reserve Lists and other goaltenders.

Trades and roster changes are current as of September 1, 1999

To calculate a goaltender's goals-against-per-game average **(Avg)**, divide goals against **(GA)** by minutes played **(Mins)** and multiply this result by **60**.

Abbreviations: Avg – goals against per game average; **GA** – goals against; **GP** – games played; **L** – losses; **Lea** – league; **SO** – shutouts; **T** – ties; **W** – wins; ♦ – member of Stanley Cup-winning team.

NHL Player Register begins on page 263.

Prospect Register begins on page 313.

League Abbreviations are listed on page 313.

AEBISCHER, David (IGH-bih-shuhr) COL.

Goaltender. Catches left. 6'1", 185 lbs. Born, Fribourg, Switz., February 7, 1978.
(Colorado's 7th choice, 161st overall, in 1997 Entry Draft).

			Regular Season								Playoffs						
Season	Club	Lea	GP	W	L	T	Mins	GA	SO	Avg	GP	W	L	Mins	GA	SO	Avg
1996-97	Fribourg	Switz.	10	....	....	....	577	34	....	3.53	3	....	....	184	13	....	4.24
1997-98	Hershey	AHL	2	0	0	1	79	5	0	3.76	....	....	....	....	....	....	....
	Chesapeake	ECHL	17	5	7	2	930	52	0	3.35	....	....	....	....	....	....	....
	Wheeling	ECHL	10	5	3	1	564	30	1	3.19	....	....	....	....	....	....	....
	Fribourg	Switz.	1	1	0	0	60	1	0	1.00	4	....	....	240	17	....	4.25
1998-99	Hershey	AHL	38	17	10	5	1932	79	2	2.45	3	1	2	152	6	0	2.37

AHONEN, Ari N.J.

Goaltender. Catches left. 6'2", 170 lbs. Born, Jyvaskyla, Finland, February 6, 1981.
(New Jersey's 1st choice, 27th overall, in 1999 Entry Draft).

			Regular Season								Playoffs						
Season	Club	Lea	GP	W	L	T	Mins	GA	SO	Avg	GP	W	L	Mins	GA	SO	Avg
1997-98	JyP Jyvaskyla	Finn-Jr.	31	....	....	....	1853	64	....	2.09	....	....	....	....	....	....	....
1998-99	JyP Jyvaskyla	Finn-Jr.	24	....	....	....	1447	70	....	2.90	....	....	....	....	....	....	....

AMIDOVSKI, Bujar PHI.

Goaltender. Catches left. 5'11", 173 lbs. Born, Toronto, Ont., February 19, 1977.

			Regular Season								Playoffs						
Season	Club	Lea	GP	W	L	T	Mins	GA	SO	Avg	GP	W	L	Mins	GA	SO	Avg
1994-95	North York	OJHL	35	....	....	....	2089	137	0	3.93	....	....	....	....	....	....	....
1995-96	Kingston	OHL	38	16	16	2	1970	136	1	4.14	4	1	2	194	11	0	3.40
1996-97	Kingston	OHL	36	11	14	1	1797	116	0	3.87	5	1	3	280	24	0	5.14
	Dayton	ECHL	3	1	1	0	90	5	0	3.31	2	0	2	118	9	0	4.56
1997-98	St. Michael's	OHL	48	12	25	7	2697	153	0	3.40	....	....	....	....	....	....	....
1998-99	Louisiana	ECHL	27	17	5	3	1525	59	3	2.32	....	....	....	....	....	....	....
	Philadelphia	AHL	2	2	0	0	120	5	0	2.50	....	....	....	....	....	....	....
	Saint John	AHL	6	2	2	0	243	19	0	4.69	....	....	....	....	....	....	....

OHL First All-Star Team (1998)

Signed as a free agent by **Philadelphia**, August 15, 1999.

ANDERSSON, Andreas (AN-duhr-suhn) ANA.

Goaltender. Catches left. 6', 180 lbs. Born, Stora Kopparberg, Sweden, April 9, 1979.
(Anaheim's 8th choice, 245th overall, in 1998 Entry Draft).

			Regular Season								Playoffs						
Season	Club	Lea	GP	W	L	T	Mins	GA	SO	Avg	GP	W	L	Mins	GA	SO	Avg
1997-98	HV Jonkoping	Swede-Jr.	10	....	....	....	600	31	....	3.10	....	....	....	....	....	....	....
	HV Jonkoping	Sweden	7	....	....	....	420	20	....	2.86	....	....	....	....	....	....	....
1998-99	Mora IK	Swede-Jr.	12	....	....	....	720	28	0	1.92	....	....	....	....	....	....	....
	HV Jonkoping	Sweden	12	....	....	....	633	35	0	3.32	....	....	....	....	....	....	....

ANDERSSON, Craig (AN-duhr-suhn) CGY.

Goaltender. Catches left. 6'2", 170 lbs. Born, Park Ridge, IL, May 21, 1981.
(Calgary's 3rd choice, 77th overall, in 1999 Entry Draft).

			Regular Season								Playoffs						
Season	Club	Lea	GP	W	L	T	Mins	GA	SO	Avg	GP	W	L	Mins	GA	SO	Avg
1997-98	Chicago	USAHA	50	....	....	....	2991	143	2	2.86	....	....	....	....	....	....	....
1998-99	Chicago	NAHL	14	11	3	0	840	40	....	2.56	....	....	....	....	....	....	....
	Guelph	OHL	21	12	5	1	1006	52	1	3.10	3	0	2	114	9	0	4.74

ANTILA, Kristian (AN-tih-luh) EDM.

Goaltender. Catches left. 6'3", 207 lbs. Born, Vammala, Finland, January 10, 1980.
(Edmonton's 4th choice, 113th overall, in 1998 Entry Draft).

			Regular Season								Playoffs						
Season	Club	Lea	GP	W	L	T	Mins	GA	SO	Avg	GP	W	L	Mins	GA	SO	Avg
1997-98	Ilves Tampere	Finn-Jr.	11	....	....	....	564	28	0	2.97	....	....	....	....	....	....	....
1998-99	Ilves Tampere	Finland	5	1	2	0	207	12	0	3.48	....	....	....	....	....	....	....
	Ilves Tampere	Finn-Jr.	14	....	....	....	798	35	....	2.63	....	....	....	....	....	....	....

ARSENAULT, David (AR-seh-noh) DET.

Goaltender. Catches left. 6'2", 165 lbs. Born, Frankfurt, Germany, March 21, 1977.
(Detroit's 6th choice, 126th overall, in 1995 Entry Draft).

			Regular Season								Playoffs						
Season	Club	Lea	GP	W	L	T	Mins	GA	SO	Avg	GP	W	L	Mins	GA	SO	Avg
1994-95	St-Hyacinthe	QMJHL	19	3	10	0	858	75	0	5.24	....	....	....	....	....	....	....
	Drummondville	QMJHL	12	2	5	0	475	40	0	5.06	2	0	2	122	8	0	3.93
1995-96	Drummondville	QMJHL	21	8	10	1	1182	89	0	4.52	....	....	....	....	....	....	....
	Chicoutimi	QMJHL	6	1	1	1	208	14	0	4.04	5	0	1	108	10	0	5.61
1996-97	Chicoutimi	QMJHL	4	2	2	0	219	12	0	3.27	....	....	....	....	....	....	....
	Oshawa	OHL	41	24	9	5	2316	106	2	2.75	17	*11	6	1027	46	*1	*2.69
1997-98	Toledo	ECHL	22	13	4	3	1261	60	0	2.85	....	....	....	....	....	....	....
	Adirondack	AHL	10	3	5	0	563	41	0	4.37	....	....	....	....	....	....	....
1998-99	Toledo	ECHL	21	10	8	1	1171	72	0	3.69	....	....	....	....	....	....	....
	Adirondack	AHL	5	0	4	0	250	20	0	4.80	....	....	....	....	....	....	....

ASKEY, Tom (AS-kee) ANA.

Goaltender. Catches left. 6'2", 185 lbs. Born, Kenmore, NY, October 4, 1974.
(Anaheim's 8th choice, 186th overall, in 1993 Entry Draft).

			Regular Season								Playoffs						
Season	Club	Lea	GP	W	L	T	Mins	GA	SO	Avg	GP	W	L	Mins	GA	SO	Avg
1992-93	Ohio State	CCHA	25	2	19	0	1235	125	0	6.07	....	....	....	....	....	....	....
1993-94	Ohio State	CCHA	27	3	19	4	1488	103	0	4.15	....	....	....	....	....	....	....
1994-95	Ohio State	CCHA	26	4	19	2	1387	121	0	5.23	....	....	....	....	....	....	....
1995-96	Ohio State	CCHA	26	8	11	4	1340	68	0	3.05	....	....	....	....	....	....	....
1996-97	Baltimore	AHL	40	17	18	2	2238	140	1	3.75	3	0	3	137	11	0	4.79
1997-98	**Anaheim**	**NHL**	**7**	**0**	**1**	**2**	**273**	**12**	**0**	**2.64**	**....**	**....**	**....**	**....**	**....**	**....**	**....**
	Cincinnati	AHL	32	10	16	4	1753	104	3	3.56	....	....	....	....	....	....	....
1998-99	**Anaheim**	**NHL**	**....**	**....**	**....**	**....**	**....**	**....**	**....**	**....**	**1**	**0**	**1**	**30**	**2**	**0**	**4.00**
	Cincinnati	AHL	53	21	22	3	2893	131	3	2.72	3	0	3	178	13	0	4.38
	NHL Totals		**7**	**0**	**1**	**2**	**273**	**12**	**0**	**2.64**	**1**	**0**	**1**	**30**	**2**	**0**	**4.00**

CCHA Second All-Star Team (1996)

ASPLUND, Johan NYR

Goaltender. Catches left. 6'1", 180 lbs. Born, Slutskar, Sweden, December 15, 1980.
(NY Rangers' 4th choice, 79th overall, in 1999 Entry Draft).

			Regular Season								Playoffs						
Season	Club	Lea	GP	W	L	T	Mins	GA	SO	Avg	GP	W	L	Mins	GA	SO	Avg
1998-99	Brynas Gavle	Sweden	12	....	....	....	646	32	0	2.97	....	....	....	....	....	....	....

AUBIN, Jean-Sebastien (OH-behn) PIT.

Goaltender. Catches right. 5'11", 183 lbs. Born, Montreal, Que., July 19, 1977.
(Pittsburgh's 2nd choice, 76th overall, in 1995 Entry Draft).

			Regular Season								Playoffs						
Season	Club	Lea	GP	W	L	T	Mins	GA	SO	Avg	GP	W	L	Mins	GA	SO	Avg
1993-94	Montreal-Bourassa	QAAA	27	14	13	0	1524	96	1	3.74	....	....	....	....	....	....	....
1994-95	Sherbrooke	QMJHL	27	13	10	1	1287	73	1	3.40	3	1	2	185	11	0	3.57
1995-96	Sherbrooke	QMJHL	40	18	14	2	2140	127	0	3.57	4	1	3	238	23	0	5.55
1996-97	Laval	QMJHL	11	2	6	1	532	41	0	4.62	....	....	....	....	....	....	....
	Moncton	QMJHL	22	9	12	0	1252	67	1	3.21	....	....	....	....	....	....	....
	Sherbrooke	QMJHL	4	3	1	0	249	8	0	1.93	1	0	1	60	4	0	4.00
1997-98	Syracuse	AHL	8	2	4	1	380	26	0	4.10	....	....	....	....	....	....	....
	Dayton	ECHL	21	15	2	2	1177	59	1	3.01	3	1	1	142	4	0	1.69
1998-99	**Pittsburgh**	**NHL**	**17**	**4**	**3**	**6**	**756**	**28**	**2**	**2.22**	**....**	**....**	**....**	**....**	**....**	**....**	**....**
	Kansas City	IHL	13	5	7	1	751	41	0	3.28	....	....	....	....	....	....	....
	NHL Totals		**17**	**4**	**3**	**6**	**756**	**28**	**2**	**2.22**	....	....	....				

AULD, Alexander (AWLD) FLA.

Goaltender. Catches left. 6'4", 196 lbs. Born, Cold Lake, Alta., January 7, 1981.
(Florida's 2nd choice, 40th overall, in 1999 Entry Draft).

			Regular Season								Playoffs						
Season	Club	Lea	GP	W	L	T	Mins	GA	SO	Avg	GP	W	L	Mins	GA	SO	Avg
1997-98	North Bay	OHL	6	0	4	0	206	17	0	4.95	....	....	....	....	....	....	....
1998-99	North Bay	OHL	37	9	20	1	1894	106	1	3.36	3	0	3	170	10	0	3.53

BACH, Ryan (BAWK) FLA.

Goaltender. Catches left. 6'1", 185 lbs. Born, Sherwood Park, Alta., October 21, 1973.
(Detroit's 11th choice, 262nd overall, in 1992 Entry Draft).

			Regular Season								Playoffs						
Season	Club	Lea	GP	W	L	T	Mins	GA	SO	Avg	GP	W	L	Mins	GA	SO	Avg
1991-92	Notre Dame	SJHL	33	16	11	6	1062	124	0	4.00	....	....	....	....	....	....	....
1992-93	Colorado	WCHA	4	1	3	0	239	11	0	2.76	....	....	....	....	....	....	....
1993-94	Colorado	WCHA	30	17	7	5	1733	105	0	3.64	....	....	....	....	....	....	....
1994-95	Colorado	WCHA	27	18	5	1	1522	83	0	3.27	....	....	....	....	....	....	....
1995-96	Colorado	WCHA	23	*17	4	2	1390	62	2	2.68	....	....	....	....	....	....	....
1996-97	Utica	ColHL	2	0	1	1	119	8	0	4.03	....	....	....	....	....	....	....
	Toledo	ECHL	20	5	11	3	1168	74	0	3.80	....	....	....	....	....	....	....
	Adirondack	AHL	13	2	3	1	451	29	0	3.86	1	0	0	46	3	0	3.92
1997-98	Houston	IHL	43	26	9	6	2452	95	5	2.32	....	....	....	....	....	....	....
1998-99	Utah	IHL	4	2	1	0	197	9	0	2.74	....	....	....	....	....	....	....
	Los Angeles	**NHL**	**3**	**0**	**3**	**0**	**108**	**8**	**0**	**4.44**	**....**	**....**	**....**	**....**	**....**	**....**	**....**
	Long Beach	IHL	27	10	9	5	1491	74	1	2.98	3	0	2	152	7	0	2.76
	NHL Totals		**3**	**0**	**3**	**0**	**108**	**8**	**0**	**4.44**	....	....	....	....	....	....	....

WCHA First All-Star Team (1995, 1996) • NCAA West Second All-American Team (1995) • NCAA West First All-American Team (1996)

Traded to **Los Angeles** by **Detroit** for Los Angeles' 6th round choice in 2000 Entry Draft, October 22, 1998. Signed as a free agent by **Florida**, July 27, 1999.

BAILEY, Scott

Goaltender. Catches left. 6', 195 lbs. Born, Calgary, Alta., May 2, 1972.
(Boston's 3rd choice, 112th overall, in 1992 Entry Draft).

			Regular Season								Playoffs						
Season	Club	Lea	GP	W	L	T	Mins	GA	SO	Avg	GP	W	L	Mins	GA	SO	Avg
1989-90	Calgary	AAHA	17	....	....	....	991	55	1	3.33	....	....	....	....	....	....	....
1990-91	Spokane	WHL	46	33	11	0	2537	157	*4	3.71	....	....	....	....	....	....	....
1991-92	Spokane	WHL	65	34	23	5	3798	206	1	3.30	10	5	5	605	43	0	4.26
1992-93	Johnstown	ECHL	36	13	15	3	1750	112	1	3.84	....	....	....	....	....	....	....
1993-94	Providence	AHL	7	2	2	2	377	24	0	3.82	....	....	....	....	....	....	....
	Charlotte	ECHL	36	22	11	3	2180	130	1	3.58	3	1	2	187	12	0	3.83
1994-95	Providence	AHL	52	25	16	9	2936	147	2	3.00	9	4	4	504	31	*2	3.69
1995-96	**Boston**	**NHL**	**11**	**5**	**1**	**2**	**571**	**31**	**0**	**3.26**	....	....	....	....	....	....	....
	Providence	AHL	37	15	19	3	2210	120	1	3.26	2	1	1	119	6	0	3.03
1996-97	**Boston**	**NHL**	**8**	**1**	**5**	**0**	**394**	**24**	**0**	**3.65**	....	....	....	....	....	....	....
	Providence	AHL	31	11	17	2	1735	112	0	3.87	7	3	4	453	23	0	3.05
1997-98	San Antonio	IHL	37	11	17	3	1898	118	1	3.73	....	....	....	....	....	....	....
1998-99	Orlando	IHL	17	5	7	0	749	36	0	2.88	....	....	....	....	....	....	....
	Birmingham	ECHL	27	16	8	2	1557	90	1	3.47	5	2	3	299	21	0	4.21
	NHL Totals		**19**	**6**	**6**	**2**	**965**	**55**	**0**	**3.42**	....	....	....	....	....	....	....

WHL West Second All-Star Team (1991, 1992)

BALES, Mike — DAL.

Goaltender. Catches left. 6'1", 180 lbs. Born, Prince Albert, Sask., August 6, 1971.
(Boston's 4th choice, 105th overall, in 1990 Entry Draft).

			Regular Season								Playoffs						
Season	Club	Lea	GP	W	L	T	Mins	GA	SO	Avg	GP	W	L	Mins	GA	SO	Avg
1988-89	Estevan	SJHL	44	....	....	....	2412	197	1	4.90	....	....	....	....	....	....	....
1989-90	Ohio State	CCHA	21	6	13	2	1117	95	0	5.11	....	....	....	....	....	....	....
1990-91	Ohio State	CCHA	*39	11	24	3	*2180	184	0	5.06	....	....	....	....	....	....	....
1991-92	Ohio State	CCHA	36	11	20	5	2060	180	0	5.24	....	....	....	....	....	....	....
1992-93	**Boston**	**NHL**	**1**	**0**	**0**	**0**	**25**	**1**	**0**	**2.40**	....	....	....	....	....	....	....
	Providence	AHL	44	22	17	0	2363	166	1	4.21	2	0	2	118	8	0	4.07
1993-94	Providence	AHL	33	9	15	4	1757	130	0	4.44	....	....	....	....	....	....	....
1994-95	P.E.I. Senators	AHL	45	25	16	3	2649	160	2	3.62	9	6	3	530	24	*2	2.72
	Ottawa	**NHL**	**1**	**0**	**0**	**0**	**3**	**0**	**0**	**0.00**	....	....	....	....	....	....	....
1995-96	**Ottawa**	**NHL**	**20**	**2**	**14**	**1**	**1040**	**72**	**0**	**4.15**	....	....	....	....	....	....	....
	P.E.I. Senators	AHL	2	0	2	0	118	11	0	5.58	....	....	....	....	....	....	....
1996-97	**Ottawa**	**NHL**	**1**	**0**	**1**	**0**	**52**	**4**	**0**	**4.62**	....	....	....	....	....	....	....
	Baltimore	AHL	46	13	21	8	2544	130	3	3.07	....	....	....	....	....	....	....
1997-98	Rochester	AHL	39	13	19	5	2229	127	0	3.42	....	....	....	....	....	....	....
1998-99	Michigan	IHL	32	11	17	3	1773	96	1	3.25	....	....	....	....	....	....	....
	NHL Totals		**23**	**2**	**15**	**1**	**1120**	**77**	**0**	**4.13**	....	....	....	....	....	....	....

Signed as a free agent by **Ottawa**, July 4, 1994. Signed as a free agent by **Buffalo**, September 9, 1997. Signed as a free agent by **Dallas**, July 8, 1998.

BARRASSO, Tom — (buh-RAH-soh) PIT.

Goaltender. Catches right. 6'3", 211 lbs. Born, Boston, MA, March 31, 1965.
(Buffalo's 1st choice, 5th overall, in 1983 Entry Draft).

			Regular Season								Playoffs						
Season	Club	Lea	GP	W	L	T	Mins	GA	SO	Avg	GP	W	L	Mins	GA	SO	Avg
1981-82	Acton-Boxboro	H.S.	23	....	....	....	1035	32	7	1.86	....	....	....	....	....	....	....
1982-83	Acton-Boxboro	H.S.	23	....	....	....	1035	17	10	0.74	....	....	....	....	....	....	....
1983-84	**Buffalo**	**NHL**	**42**	**26**	**12**	**3**	**2475**	**117**	**2**	**2.84**	**3**	**0**	**2**	**139**	**8**	**0**	**3.45**
1984-85	**Buffalo**	**NHL**	**54**	**25**	**18**	**10**	**3248**	**144**	***5**	***2.66**	**5**	**2**	**3**	**300**	**22**	**0**	**4.40**
	Rochester	AHL	5	3	1	1	267	6	1	1.35	....	....	....	....	....	....	....
1985-86	**Buffalo**	**NHL**	**60**	**29**	**24**	**5**	**3561**	**214**	**2**	**3.61**	....	....	....	....	....	....	....
1986-87	**Buffalo**	**NHL**	**46**	**17**	**23**	**2**	**2501**	**152**	**2**	**3.65**	....	....	....	....	....	....	....
1987-88	**Buffalo**	**NHL**	**54**	**25**	**18**	**8**	**3133**	**173**	**2**	**3.31**	**4**	**1**	**3**	**224**	**16**	**0**	**4.29**
1988-89	**Buffalo**	**NHL**	**10**	**2**	**7**	**0**	**545**	**45**	**0**	**4.95**	....	....	....	....	....	....	....
	Pittsburgh	**NHL**	**44**	**18**	**15**	**7**	**2406**	**162**	**0**	**4.04**	**11**	**7**	**4**	**631**	**40**	**0**	**3.80**
1989-90	**Pittsburgh**	**NHL**	**24**	**7**	**12**	**3**	**1294**	**101**	**0**	**4.68**	....	....	....	....	....	....	....
1990-91♦	**Pittsburgh**	**NHL**	**48**	**27**	**16**	**3**	**2754**	**165**	**1**	**3.59**	**20**	**12**	**7**	**1175**	**51**	***1**	***2.60**
1991-92♦	**Pittsburgh**	**NHL**	**57**	**25**	**22**	**9**	**3329**	**196**	**1**	**3.53**	***21**	***16**	**5**	***1233**	**58**	**1**	**2.82**
1992-93	**Pittsburgh**	**NHL**	**63**	***43**	**14**	**5**	**3702**	**186**	**4**	**3.01**	**12**	**7**	**5**	**722**	**35**	***2**	**2.91**
1993-94	**Pittsburgh**	**NHL**	**44**	**22**	**15**	**5**	**2482**	**139**	**2**	**3.36**	**6**	**2**	**4**	**356**	**17**	**0**	**2.87**
1994-95	**Pittsburgh**	**NHL**	**2**	**0**	**1**	**1**	**125**	**8**	**0**	**3.84**	**2**	**0**	**1**	**80**	**8**	**0**	**6.00**
1995-96	**Pittsburgh**	**NHL**	**49**	**29**	**16**	**2**	**2799**	**160**	**2**	**3.43**	**10**	**4**	**5**	**558**	**26**	**1**	**2.80**
1996-97	**Pittsburgh**	**NHL**	**5**	**0**	**5**	**0**	**270**	**26**	**0**	**5.78**	....	....	....	....	....	....	....
1997-98	**Pittsburgh**	**NHL**	**63**	**31**	**14**	**13**	**3542**	**122**	**7**	**2.07**	**6**	**2**	**4**	**376**	**17**	**0**	**2.71**
1998-99	**Pittsburgh**	**NHL**	**43**	**19**	**16**	**3**	**2306**	**98**	**4**	**2.55**	**13**	**6**	**7**	**787**	**35**	**1**	**2.67**
	NHL Totals		**708**	**345**	**248**	**79**	**40472**	**2208**	**34**	**3.27**	**113**	**59**	**50**	**6581**	**333**	**6**	**3.04**

NHL All-Rookie Team (1984) • NHL First All-Star Team (1984) • Won Calder Memorial Trophy (1984) • Won Vezina Trophy (1984) • NHL Second All-Star Team (1985, 1993) • Shared William Jennings Trophy with Bob Sauve (1985)

Played in NHL All-Star Game (1985)

Traded to **Pittsburgh** by **Buffalo** with Buffalo's 3rd round choice (Joe Dziedzic) in 1990 Entry Draft for Doug Bodger and Darrin Shannon, November 12, 1988.

BEAUREGARD, Stephane — (BOH-reh-gahrd) WSH.

Goaltender. Catches right. 5'11", 190 lbs. Born, Cowansville, Que., January 10, 1968.
(Winnipeg's 3rd choice, 52nd overall, in 1988 Entry Draft).

			Regular Season								Playoffs						
Season	Club	Lea	GP	W	L	T	Mins	GA	SO	Avg	GP	W	L	Mins	GA	SO	Avg
1986-87	St-Jean	QMJHL	13	6	7	0	785	58	0	4.43	5	1	3	260	26	0	6.00
1987-88	St-Jean	QMJHL	66	38	20	3	3766	229	2	3.65	7	3	4	423	34	0	4.82
1988-89	Moncton	AHL	15	4	8	2	824	62	0	4.51	....	....	....	....	....	....	....
	Fort Wayne	IHL	16	9	5	0	830	43	0	3.10	9	4	4	484	21	*1	*2.60
1989-90	**Winnipeg**	**NHL**	**19**	**7**	**8**	**3**	**1079**	**59**	**0**	**3.28**	**4**	**1**	**3**	**238**	**12**	**0**	**3.03**
	Fort Wayne	IHL	33	20	8	3	1949	115	0	3.54	....	....	....	....	....	....	....
1990-91	**Winnipeg**	**NHL**	**16**	**3**	**10**	**1**	**836**	**55**	**0**	**3.95**	....	....	....	....	....	....	....
	Moncton	AHL	9	3	4	1	504	20	1	2.38	1	1	0	60	1	0	1.00
	Fort Wayne	IHL	32	14	13	2	1761	109	0	3.71	*19	*10	9	*1158	57	0	2.95
1991-92	**Winnipeg**	**NHL**	**26**	**6**	**8**	**6**	**1267**	**61**	**2**	**2.89**	....	....	....	....	....	....	....
1992-93	**Philadelphia**	**NHL**	**16**	**3**	**9**	**0**	**802**	**59**	**0**	**4.41**	....	....	....	....	....	....	....
	Hershey	AHL	13	5	5	3	794	48	0	3.63	....	....	....	....	....	....	....
1993-94	**Winnipeg**	**NHL**	**13**	**0**	**4**	**1**	**418**	**34**	**0**	**4.88**	....	....	....	....	....	....	....
	Moncton	AHL	37	18	11	6	2082	121	1	3.49	*21	*12	9	*1305	57	*2	2.62
1994-95	Springfield	AHL	24	10	11	3	1381	73	2	3.17	....	....	....	....	....	....	....
1995-96	San Francisco	IHL	*69	*36	24	8	*4022	207	1	3.09	4	1	3	241	10	0	2.49
1996-97	Quebec	IHL	67	35	20	11	3945	174	4	2.65	9	5	3	498	19	0	2.29
1997-98	Chicago	IHL	18	10	6	0	917	49	1	3.20	14	10	4	820	36	1	2.63
1998-99	Davos	Switz.	*45	....	....	....	2637	151	....	3.44	6	....	....	370	23	....	3.73
	NHL Totals		**90**	**19**	**39**	**11**	**4402**	**268**	**2**	**3.65**	**4**	**1**	**3**	**238**	**12**	**0**	**3.03**

QMJHL First All-Star Team (1988) • Canadian Major Junior Goaltender of the year (1988) • IHL First All-Star Team (1996) • Won James Gatschene Memorial Trophy (MVP — IHL) (1996)

Traded to **Buffalo** by **Winnipeg** for Christian Ruuttu and future considerations, June 15, 1992. Traded to **Chicago** by **Buffalo** with Buffalo's 4th round choice (Eric Daze) in 1993 Entry Draft for Dominik Hasek, August 7, 1992. Traded to **Winnipeg** by **Chicago** for Christian Ruuttu, August 10, 1992. Traded to **Philadelphia** by **Winnipeg** for future considerations, October 1, 1992. Traded to **Winnipeg** by **Philadelphia** for future considerations, June 11, 1993. Signed as a free agent by **Washington**, August 20, 1997.

BELFOUR, Ed — (BEHL-fohr) DAL.

Goaltender. Catches left. 5'11", 182 lbs. Born, Carman, Man., April 21, 1965.

			Regular Season								Playoffs						
Season	Club	Lea	GP	W	L	T	Mins	GA	SO	Avg	GP	W	L	Mins	GA	SO	Avg
1985-86	Winkler	MJHL	48	....	....	....	2880	124	1	2.58	....	....	....	....	....	....	....
1986-87	North Dakota	WCHA	34	29	4	0	2049	81	3	2.43	....	....	....	....	....	....	....
1987-88	Saginaw	IHL	61	32	25	0	*3446	183	3	3.19	9	4	5	561	33	0	3.53
1988-89	**Chicago**	**NHL**	**23**	**4**	**12**	**3**	**1148**	**74**	**0**	**3.87**	....	....	....	....	....	....	....
	Saginaw	IHL	29	12	10	0	1760	92	0	3.10	5	2	3	298	14	0	2.82
1989-90	Canada	Nat-Team	33	13	12	6	1808	93	0	3.08	....	....	....	....	....	....	....
	Chicago	**NHL**	....	....	....	....	....	....	....	....	**9**	**4**	**2**	**409**	**17**	**0**	**2.49**
1990-91	**Chicago**	**NHL**	***74**	***43**	**19**	**7**	***4127**	**170**	**4**	***2.47**	**6**	**2**	**4**	**295**	**20**	**0**	**4.07**
1991-92	**Chicago**	**NHL**	**52**	**21**	**18**	**10**	**2928**	**132**	***5**	**2.70**	**18**	**12**	**4**	**949**	**39**	**1**	***2.47**
1992-93	**Chicago**	**NHL**	***71**	**41**	**18**	**11**	***4106**	**177**	***7**	**2.59**	**4**	**0**	**4**	**249**	**13**	**0**	**3.13**
1993-94	**Chicago**	**NHL**	**70**	**37**	**24**	**6**	**3998**	**178**	***7**	**2.67**	**6**	**2**	**4**	**360**	**15**	**0**	**2.50**
1994-95	**Chicago**	**NHL**	**42**	**22**	**15**	**3**	**2450**	**93**	***5**	**2.28**	**16**	**9**	**7**	**1014**	**37**	**1**	**2.19**
1995-96	**Chicago**	**NHL**	**50**	**22**	**17**	**10**	**2956**	**135**	**1**	**2.74**	**9**	**6**	**3**	**666**	**23**	**1**	**2.07**
1996-97	**Chicago**	**NHL**	**33**	**11**	**15**	**6**	**1966**	**88**	**1**	**2.69**	....	....	....	....	....	....	....
	San Jose	**NHL**	**13**	**3**	**9**	**0**	**757**	**43**	**1**	**3.41**	....	....	....	....	....	....	....
1997-98	**Dallas**	**NHL**	**61**	**37**	**12**	**10**	**3581**	**112**	**9**	***1.88**	**17**	**10**	**7**	**1039**	**31**	**1**	***1.79**
1998-99♦	**Dallas**	**NHL**	**61**	**35**	**15**	**9**	**3536**	**117**	**5**	**1.99**	***23**	***16**	**7**	***1544**	**43**	***3**	***1.67**
	NHL Totals		**550**	**276**	**174**	**75**	**31553**	**1319**	**45**	**2.51**	**108**	**61**	**42**	**6525**	**238**	**7**	**2.19**

WCHA First All-Star Team (1987) • NCAA Championship All-Tournament Team (1987) • IHL First All-Star Team (1988) • Shared Garry F. Longman Memorial Trophy (Top Rookie - IHL) with John Cullen (1988) • NHL/Upper Deck All-Rookie Team (1991) • NHL First All-Star Team (1991, 1993) • Won Trico Goaltender Award (1991) • Won Calder Memorial Trophy (1991) • Won William M. Jennings Trophy (1991, 1993, 1995) • Won Vezina Trophy (1991, 1993) • NHL Second All-Star Team (1995) • Shared William M. Jennings Trophy with Roman Turek (1999)

Played in NHL All-Star Game (1992, 1993, 1996, 1998, 1999)

Signed as a free agent by **Chicago**, September 25, 1987. Traded to **San Jose** by **Chicago** for Chris Terreri, Ulf Dahlen and Michal Sykora, January 25, 1997. Signed as a free agent by **Dallas**, July 2, 1997.

BERGQVIST, Per-Ragnar — (BUHRG-kvihst) PHI.

Goaltender. Catches left. 5'11", 183 lbs. Born, Leksand, Sweden, April 11, 1976.
(Philadelphia's 3rd choice, 124th overall, in 1996 Entry Draft).

			Regular Season								Playoffs						
Season	Club	Lea	GP	W	L	T	Mins	GA	SO	Avg	GP	W	L	Mins	GA	SO	Avg
1995-96	Leksands IF	Swede-Jr.	3	....	....	....	180	17	0	5.67	....	....	....	....	....	....	....
	Leksands IF	Sweden	6	....	....	....	327	17	0	3.12	1	....	....	60	1	0	1.00
1996-97	Leksands IF	Sweden	11	....	....	....	660	32	1	2.91	1	....	....	86	5	0	3.49
1997-98	Leksands IF	Sweden	16	....	....	....	909	53	....	3.50	1	0	1	59	5	0	5.08
1998-99	Valerengens IF	Norway	29	....	....	....	1585	52	2	1.96	....	....	....	....	....	....	....

BIERK, Zac — (BUHRK, ZAK) T.B.

Goaltender. Catches left. 6'4", 186 lbs. Born, Peterborough, Ont., September 17, 1976.
(Tampa Bay's 8th choice, 212th overall, in 1995 Entry Draft).

			Regular Season								Playoffs						
Season	Club	Lea	GP	W	L	T	Mins	GA	SO	Avg	GP	W	L	Mins	GA	SO	Avg
1993-94	Peterborough	OJHL	4	....	....	....	205	17	0	4.98	....	....	....	....	....	....	....
	Peterborough	OHL	9	0	4	2	423	37	0	5.22	1	0	0	33	7	0	12.70
1994-95	Peterborough	OHL	35	11	15	5	1779	117	0	3.95	6	2	3	301	24	0	4.78
1995-96	Peterborough	OHL	58	31	16	6	3292	174	2	3.17	*22	*14	7	*1383	83	0	3.60
1996-97	Peterborough	OHL	49	*28	16	0	2744	151	2	3.30	11	6	5	666	35	0	3.15
1997-98	**Tampa Bay**	**NHL**	**13**	**1**	**4**	**1**	**433**	**30**	**0**	**4.16**	....	....	....	....	....	....	....
	Adirondack	AHL	12	1	6	1	557	36	0	3.87	....	....	....	....	....	....	....
1998-99	**Tampa Bay**	**NHL**	**1**	**0**	**1**	**0**	**59**	**2**	**0**	**2.03**	....	....	....	....	....	....	....
	Cleveland	IHL	27	11	12	4	1556	79	0	3.05	....	....	....	....	....	....	....
	NHL Totals		**14**	**1**	**5**	**1**	**492**	**32**	**0**	**3.90**	....	....	....	....	....	....	....

OHL First All-Star Team (1997)

• Missed remainder of 1998-99 season after being diagnosed with Meniere's disease, March 25, 1999.

BILLINGTON, Craig — WSH.

Goaltender. Catches left. 5'10", 170 lbs. Born, London, Ont., September 11, 1966.
(New Jersey's 2nd choice, 23rd overall, in 1984 Entry Draft).

			Regular Season								Playoffs						
Season	Club	Lea	GP	W	L	T	Mins	GA	SO	Avg	GP	W	L	Mins	GA	SO	Avg
1982-83	London	OJHL-B	23	....	....	....	1338	76	0	3.41	....	....	....	....	....	....	....
1983-84	Belleville	OHL	44	20	19	0	2335	162	1	4.16	1	0	0	30	3	0	6.00
1984-85	Belleville	OHL	47	26	19	0	2544	180	1	4.25	14	7	5	761	47	1	3.71
1985-86	**New Jersey**	**NHL**	**18**	**4**	**9**	**1**	**901**	**77**	**0**	**5.13**	....	....	....	....	....	....	....
	Belleville	OHL	3	2	1	0	180	11	0	3.67	20	9	6	1133	68	0	3.60
1986-87	**New Jersey**	**NHL**	**22**	**4**	**13**	**2**	**1114**	**89**	**0**	**4.79**	....	....	....	....	....	....	....
	Maine	AHL	20	9	8	2	1151	70	0	3.65	....	....	....	....	....	....	....
1987-88	Utica	AHL	*59	22	27	8	*3404	208	1	3.67	....	....	....	....	....	....	....
1988-89	**New Jersey**	**NHL**	**3**	**1**	**1**	**0**	**140**	**11**	**0**	**4.71**	....	....	....	....	....	....	....
	Utica	AHL	41	17	18	6	2432	150	2	3.70	4	1	3	220	18	0	4.91
1989-90	Utica	AHL	38	20	13	1	2087	138	0	3.97	....	....	....	....	....	....	....
1990-91	Canada	Nat-Team	34	17	14	2	1879	110	2	3.51	....	....	....	....	....	....	....
1991-92	**New Jersey**	**NHL**	**26**	**13**	**7**	**1**	**1363**	**69**	**2**	**3.04**	....	....	....	....	....	....	....
1992-93	**New Jersey**	**NHL**	**42**	**21**	**16**	**4**	**2389**	**146**	**2**	**3.67**	**2**	**0**	**1**	**78**	**5**	**0**	**3.85**
1993-94	**Ottawa**	**NHL**	**63**	**11**	**41**	**4**	**3319**	**254**	**0**	**4.59**	....	....	....	....	....	....	....
1994-95	**Ottawa**	**NHL**	**9**	**0**	**6**	**2**	**472**	**32**	**0**	**4.07**	....	....	....	....	....	....	....
	Boston	**NHL**	**8**	**5**	**1**	**0**	**373**	**19**	**0**	**3.06**	**1**	**0**	**0**	**25**	**1**	**0**	**2.40**
1995-96	**Boston**	**NHL**	**27**	**10**	**13**	**3**	**1380**	**79**	**1**	**3.43**	**1**	**0**	**1**	**60**	**6**	**0**	**6.00**
1996-97	**Colorado**	**NHL**	**23**	**11**	**8**	**2**	**1200**	**53**	**1**	**2.65**	**1**	**0**	**0**	**20**	**1**	**0**	**3.00**
1997-98	**Colorado**	**NHL**	**23**	**8**	**7**	**4**	**1162**	**45**	**1**	**2.32**	**1**	**0**	**0**	**1**	**0**	**0**	**0.00**
1998-99	**Colorado**	**NHL**	**21**	**11**	**8**	**1**	**1086**	**52**	**0**	**2.87**	**1**	**0**	**0**	**9**	**1**	**0**	**6.67**
	NHL Totals		**285**	**99**	**130**	**24**	**14899**	**926**	**7**	**3.73**	**7**	**0**	**2**	**193**	**14**	**0**	**4.35**

OHL First All-Star Team (1985)

Played in NHL All-Star Game (1993)

Traded to **Ottawa** by **New Jersey** with Troy Mallette and New Jersey's 4th round choice (Cosmo Dupaul) in 1993 Entry Draft for Peter Sidorkiewicz and future considerations (Mike Peluso, June 26, 1993), June 20, 1993. Traded to **Boston** by **Ottawa** for NY Islanders' 8th round choice (previously acquired, Ottawa selected Ray Schultz) in 1995 Entry Draft, April 7, 1995. Signed as a free agent by **Florida**, September 5, 1996. Claimed by **Colorado** from **Florida** in NHL Waiver Draft, September 30, 1996. Traded to **Washington** by **Colorado** for future considerations, July 16, 1999.

BIRON, Martin — (BIH-rohn) BUF.

Goaltender. Catches left. 6'1", 154 lbs. Born, Lac St. Charles, Que., August 15, 1977.
(Buffalo's 2nd choice, 16th overall, in 1995 Entry Draft).

			Regular Season								Playoffs						
Season	Club	Lea	GP	W	L	T	Mins	GA	SO	Avg	GP	W	L	Mins	GA	SO	Avg
1993-94	Trois-Rivieres	QAAA	23	14	8	1	1412	80	1	3.40	....	....	....	....	....	....	....
1994-95	Beauport	QMJHL	56	29	16	9	3193	132	3	*2.48	16	8	7	900	37	*4	2.47
1995-96	Beauport	QMJHL	55	29	17	7	3201	152	1	2.85	*19	*12	7	1134	64	0	3.39
	Buffalo	**NHL**	**3**	**0**	**2**	**0**	**119**	**10**	**0**	**5.04**	....	....	....	....	....	....	....
1996-97	Beauport	QMJHL	18	6	9	1	928	61	1	3.94	....	....	....	....	....	....	....
	Hull	QMJHL	16	11	4	1	974	43	2	2.65	6	3	1	325	19	0	3.51
1997-98	South Carolina	ECHL	2	0	1	1	86	3	0	2.09	....	....	....	....	....	....	....
	Rochester	AHL	41	14	18	6	2312	113	*5	2.93	4	1	3	239	16	0	4.01
1998-99	**Buffalo**	**NHL**	**6**	**1**	**2**	**1**	**281**	**10**	**0**	**2.14**	....	....	....	....	....	....	....
	Rochester	AHL	52	36	13	3	3129	108	*6	*2.07	*20	12	8	1167	42	1	*2.16
	NHL Totals		**9**	**1**	**4**	**1**	**400**	**20**	**0**	**3.00**	....	....	....	....	....	....	....

Canadian Major Junior First All-Star Team (1995) • Canadian Major Junior Goaltender of the Year (1995) • AHL First All-Star Team (1999) • Shared Harry "Hap" Holmes Memorial Trophy (fewest goals against - AHL) with Tom Draper (1999) • Won Baz Bastien Memorial Trophy (Top Goaltender - AHL) (1999)

BLACKBURN, Josh — PHX.

Goaltender. Catches left. 6', 185 lbs. Born, Delrio, TX, November 13, 1978.
(Phoenix's 6th choice, 116th overall, in 1998 Entry Draft).

			Regular Season								Playoffs						
Season	Club	Lea	GP	W	L	T	Mins	GA	SO	Avg	GP	W	L	Mins	GA	SO	Avg
1996-97	Dubuque	USHL	52	15	32	3	2979	185	1	3.72	....	....	....	....	....	....	....
1997-98	Dubuque	USHL	17	11	15	1	1605	94	0	3.51	....	....	....	....	....	....	....
	Lincoln	USHL	17	13	4	0	1004	41	1	2.45	....	....	....	....	....	....	....
1998-99	U. of Michigan	CCHA	*42	*25	10	6	*2398	91	3	2.28	....	....	....	....	....	....	....

CCHA Second All-Star Team (1999) • NCAA West First All-American Team (1999)

BONNER, Doug

Goaltender. Catches left. 5'10", 175 lbs. Born, Tacoma, WA, October 15, 1976.
(Toronto's 3rd choice, 139th overall, in 1995 Entry Draft).

			Regular Season								Playoffs						
Season	Club	Lea	GP	W	L	T	Mins	GA	SO	Avg	GP	W	L	Mins	GA	SO	Avg
1992-93	Seattle	WHL	30	7	15	0	1212	93	1	4.60	....	....	....	....	....	....	....
1993-94	Seattle	WHL	29	9	15	0	1481	111	1	4.50	....	....	....	....	....	....	....
1994-95	Seattle	WHL	59	33	23	1	3386	205	1	3.63	3	0	3	193	10	0	3.11
1995-96	Seattle	WHL	58	20	27	7	3219	190	2	3.54	5	1	4	317	19	0	3.60
1996-97	St. John's	AHL	11	0	4	1	366	26	0	4.27	....	....	....	....	....	....	....
	Peoria	ECHL	23	13	8	1	1315	63	1	2.87	10	6	3	541	28	0	3.10
1997-98	St. John's	AHL	2	2	0	0	120	3	1	1.50	....	....	....	....	....	....	....
	Louisiana	ECHL	*54	*36	11	6	*3164	160	1	3.03	12	8	4	772	47	1	3.65
1998-99	St. John's	AHL	4	0	3	1	175	13	0	4.47	....	....	....	....	....	....	....
	Louisiana	ECHL	45	28	13	3	2593	131	1	3.03	5	2	3	299	13	0	2.61

BOUCHER, Brian — (BOO-shay) PHI.

Goaltender. Catches left. 6'1", 190 lbs. Born, Woonsocket, RI, January 2, 1977.
(Philadelphia's 1st choice, 22nd overall, in 1995 Entry Draft).

			Regular Season								Playoffs						
Season	Club	Lea	GP	W	L	T	Mins	GA	SO	Avg	GP	W	L	Mins	GA	SO	Avg
1994-95	Wexford	OJHL	8	....	....	....	425	23	0	3.25	....	....	....	....	....	....	....
	Tri-City	WHL	35	17	11	2	1969	108	1	3.29	13	6	5	795	50	0	3.77
1995-96	Tri-City	WHL	55	33	19	2	3183	181	1	3.41	11	6	5	653	37	*2	3.40
1996-97	Tri-City	WHL	41	10	24	6	2458	149	1	3.64	....	....	....	....	....	....	....
1997-98	Philadelphia	AHL	34	16	12	3	1901	101	0	3.19	2	0	0	30	1	0	1.95
1998-99	Philadelphia	AHL	36	20	8	5	2061	89	2	2.59	16	9	7	947	45	0	2.85

WHL West Second All-Star Team (1996) • WHL West First All-Star Team (1997)

BRADETTE, Martin — T.B.

Goaltender. Catches left. 6', 185 lbs. Born, Lavalle, Que., January 20, 1977.

			Regular Season								Playoffs						
Season	Club	Lea	GP	W	L	T	Mins	GA	SO	Avg	GP	W	L	Mins	GA	SO	Avg
1995-96	Rimouski	QMJHL	51	15	26	4	1516	209	1	4.65	3	0	2	151	12	0	4.77
1996-97	Drummondville	QMJHL	38	20	16	0	1979	136	1	4.12	7	3	4	333	30	0	5.41
1997-98	Chesapeake	ECHL	26	9	9	3	1095	68	0	3.73	....	....	....	....	....	....	....
1998-99	Cleveland	IHL	4	1	2	0	206	17	0	4.95	....	....	....	....	....	....	....
	Winston-Salem	UHL	17	5	8	1	864	65	0	4.51	....	....	....	....	....	....	....
	Chesapeake	ECHL	1	0	0	0	13	2	0	9.23	....	....	....	....	....	....	....
	Birmingham	ECHL	3	1	1	0	100	11	0	6.60	....	....	....	....	....	....	....

Signed as a free agent by **Tampa Bay**, October 5, 1998.

BRADY, Peter — VAN.

Goaltender. Catches left. 6'1", 175 lbs. Born, Cap-Rouge, Que., October 25, 1977.
(Vancouver's 12th choice, 227th overall, in 1997 Entry Draft).

			Regular Season								Playoffs						
Season	Club	Lea	GP	W	L	T	Mins	GA	SO	Avg	GP	W	L	Mins	GA	SO	Avg
1996-97	Powell River	BCJHL	37	....	....	....	2268	90	0	2.38	....	....	....	....	....	....	....
1997-98	Alaska-Anchorage	WCHA	7	0	5	1	345	23	0	4.00	....	....	....	....	....	....	....
1998-99	Alaska-Anchorage	WCHA	1	0	0	0	34	3	0	5.29	....	....	....	....	....	....	....

BRATHWAITE, Fred — (BRAYTH-wayt) CGY.

Goaltender. Catches left. 5'7", 170 lbs. Born, Ottawa, Ont., November 24, 1972.

			Regular Season								Playoffs						
Season	Club	Lea	GP	W	L	T	Mins	GA	SO	Avg	GP	W	L	Mins	GA	SO	Avg
1988-89	Smiths Falls	OJHL	38	....	....	....	2130	187	0	5.27	....	....	....	....	....	....	....
1989-90	Oshawa	OHL	20	11	2	1	886	43	1	2.91	10	4	2	451	22	0	*2.93
	Orillia	OJHL-B	15	....	....	....	782	47	0	3.61	....	....	....	....	....	....	....
1990-91	Oshawa	OHL	39	25	6	3	1986	112	1	3.38	13	*9	2	677	43	0	3.81
1991-92	Oshawa	OHL	24	12	7	2	1248	81	0	3.89	....	....	....	....	....	....	....
	London	OHL	23	15	6	2	1325	61	*4	2.76	10	5	5	615	36	0	3.51
1992-93	Detroit	OHL	37	23	10	4	2192	134	0	3.67	15	9	6	858	48	1	3.36
1993-94	**Edmonton**	**NHL**	**19**	**3**	**10**	**3**	**982**	**58**	**0**	**3.54**	....	....	....	....	....	....	....
	Cape Breton	AHL	2	1	1	0	119	6	0	3.04	....	....	....	....	....	....	....
1994-95	**Edmonton**	**NHL**	**14**	**2**	**5**	**1**	**601**	**40**	**0**	**3.99**	....	....	....	....	....	....	....
1995-96	**Edmonton**	**NHL**	**7**	**0**	**2**	**0**	**293**	**12**	**0**	**2.46**	....	....	....	....	....	....	....
	Cape Breton	AHL	31	12	16	0	1699	110	1	3.88	....	....	....	....	....	....	....
1996-97	Manitoba	IHL	58	22	22	5	2945	167	1	3.40	....	....	....	....	....	....	....
1997-98	Manitoba	IHL	51	23	18	4	2736	138	1	3.03	2	0	1	72	4	0	3.30
1998-99	Canada	Nat-Team	24	6	8	3	989	47	2	2.85	....	....	....	....	....	....	....
	Calgary	**NHL**	**28**	**11**	**9**	**7**	**1663**	**68**	**1**	**2.45**	....	....	....	....	....	....	....
	NHL Totals		**68**	**16**	**26**	**11**	**3539**	**178**	**1**	**3.02**	....	....	....	....	....	....	....

• Scored a goal while with Detroit (OHL), April 20, 1993. • Scored a goal while with Manitoba (IHL), November 9, 1996.

Signed as a free agent by **Edmonton**, October 6, 1993. Signed as a free agent by **Calgary**, January 6, 1999.

BRINDAMOUR, Frederik — (BRIHND-uh-MOOR) NYI

Goaltender. Catches left. 5'11", 175 lbs. Born, Beauport, Que., September 17, 1979.
(NY Islanders' 7th choice, 209th overall, in 1998 Entry Draft).

			Regular Season								Playoffs						
Season	Club	Lea	GP	W	L	T	Mins	GA	SO	Avg	GP	W	L	Mins	GA	SO	Avg
1996-97	Chicoutimi	QMJHL	17	4	9	1	814	56	0	4.13	....	....	....	....	....	....	....
	Sherbrooke	QMJHL	25	6	16	0	1317	85	2	3.87	3	0	3	173	16	0	5.55
1997-98	Sherbrooke	QMJHL	43	12	25	1	2337	141	2	3.62	....	....	....	....	....	....	....
1998-99	Sherbrooke	QMJHL	54	23	21	3	2785	163	0	3.51	13	7	5	740	40	0	3.24

BROCHU, Martin — (broh-SHOO) WSH.

Goaltender. Catches left. 5'11", 204 lbs. Born, Anjou, Que., March 10, 1973.

			Regular Season								Playoffs						
Season	Club	Lea	GP	W	L	T	Mins	GA	SO	Avg	GP	W	L	Mins	GA	SO	Avg
1989-90	Montreal-Bourassa	QAAA	27	11	14	1	1471	103	3	4.20	3	1	2	193	10	1	3.10
1990-91	Granby	QMJHL	16	6	5	0	622	39	....	3.76	....	....	....	....	....	....	....
1991-92	Granby	QMJHL	52	15	29	2	2772	278	0	4.72	....	....	....	....	....	....	....
1992-93	Hull	QMJHL	29	9	15	1	1453	137	0	5.66	2	0	1	69	7	0	6.07
1993-94	Fredericton	AHL	32	10	11	3	1505	76	2	3.03	....	....	....	....	....	....	....
1994-95	Fredericton	AHL	44	18	18	4	2475	145	0	3.51	....	....	....	....	....	....	....
1995-96	Fredericton	AHL	17	6	8	2	986	70	0	4.26	....	....	....	....	....	....	....
	Wheeling	ECHL	19	10	6	2	1060	51	1	2.89	....	....	....	....	....	....	....
	Portland	AHL	5	2	2	1	287	15	0	3.14	12	7	4	700	28	*2	*2.40
1996-97	Portland	AHL	55	23	17	7	2962	150	2	3.04	5	2	3	324	13	0	2.41
1997-98	Portland	AHL	37	16	14	1	1926	96	2	2.99	6	3	2	296	16	0	3.24
1998-99	**Washington**	**NHL**	**2**	**0**	**2**	**0**	**120**	**6**	**0**	**3.00**	....	....	....	....	....	....	....
	Portland	AHL	20	6	10	3	1164	57	2	2.94	....	....	....	....	....	....	....
	Utah	IHL	5	1	3	1	298	13	0	2.62	....	....	....	....	....	....	....
	NHL Totals		**2**	**0**	**2**	**0**	**120**	**6**	**0**	**3.00**	....	....	....	....	....	....	....

Signed as a free agent by **Montreal**, September 22, 1992. Traded to **Washington** by **Montreal** for future considerations, March 15, 1996.

BRODEUR, Martin — (broh-DOOR, MAHR-tihn) N.J.

Goaltender. Catches left. 6'2", 205 lbs. Born, Montreal, Que., May 6, 1972.
(New Jersey's 1st choice, 20th overall, in 1990 Entry Draft).

			Regular Season								Playoffs						
Season	Club	Lea	GP	W	L	T	Mins	GA	SO	Avg	GP	W	L	Mins	GA	SO	Avg
1988-89	Montreal-Bourassa	QAAA	27	13	12	1	1580	98	0	3.72	....	....	....	....	....	....	....
1989-90	St-Hyacinthe	QMJHL	42	23	13	2	2333	156	0	4.01	12	5	7	678	46	0	4.07
1990-91	St-Hyacinthe	QMJHL	52	22	24	4	2946	162	2	3.30	4	0	4	232	16	0	4.14
1991-92	St-Hyacinthe	QMJHL	48	27	16	4	2846	161	2	3.39	5	2	3	317	14	0	2.65
	New Jersey	**NHL**	**4**	**2**	**1**	**0**	**179**	**10**	**0**	**3.35**	**1**	**0**	**1**	**32**	**3**	**0**	**5.63**
1992-93	Utica	AHL	32	14	13	5	1952	131	0	4.03	4	1	3	258	18	0	4.19
1993-94	**New Jersey**	**NHL**	**47**	**27**	**11**	**8**	**2625**	**105**	**3**	**2.40**	**17**	**8**	**9**	**1171**	**38**	**1**	**1.95**
1994-95◆	**New Jersey**	**NHL**	**40**	**19**	**11**	**6**	**2184**	**89**	**3**	**2.45**	***20**	***16**	**4**	***1222**	**34**	***3**	***1.67**
1995-96	**New Jersey**	**NHL**	**77**	**34**	**30**	**12**	***4433**	**173**	**6**	**2.34**	....	....	....	....	....	....	....
1996-97	**New Jersey**	**NHL**	**67**	**37**	**14**	**13**	**3838**	**120**	***10**	***1.88**	**10**	**5**	**5**	**659**	**19**	**2**	***1.73**
1997-98	**New Jersey**	**NHL**	**70**	***43**	**17**	**8**	**4128**	**130**	**10**	**1.89**	**6**	**2**	**4**	**366**	**12**	**0**	**1.97**
	Canada	Olympics						DID NOT PLAY – SPARE GOALTENDER									
1998-99	**New Jersey**	**NHL**	***70**	***39**	**21**	**10**	***4239**	**162**	**4**	**2.29**	**7**	**3**	**4**	**425**	**20**	**0**	**2.82**
	NHL Totals		**375**	**201**	**105**	**57**	**21626**	**789**	**36**	**2.19**	**61**	**34**	**27**	**3875**	**126**	**6**	**1.95**

QMJHL Second All-Star Team (1992) • NHL/Upper Deck All-Rookie Team (1994) • Won Calder Memorial Trophy (1994) • NHL Second All-Star Team (1997, 1998) • Shared William M. Jennings Trophy with Mike Dunham (1997) • Won William M. Jennings Trophy (1998)

Played in NHL All-Star Game (1996, 1997, 1998, 1999)

• Scored a goal in playoffs vs. Montreal, April 17, 1997.

BURKE, Sean — FLA.

Goaltender. Catches left. 6'4", 210 lbs. Born, Windsor, Ont., January 29, 1967.
(New Jersey's 2nd choice, 24th overall, in 1985 Entry Draft).

			Regular Season								Playoffs						
Season	Club	Lea	GP	W	L	T	Mins	GA	SO	Avg	GP	W	L	Mins	GA	SO	Avg
1983-84	St. Michael's	OJHL-B	25	....	....	....	1482	120	0	4.86	....	....	....	....	....	....	....
1984-85	Toronto	OHL	49	25	21	3	2987	211	0	4.24	5	1	3	266	25	0	5.64
1985-86	Toronto	OHL	47	16	27	3	2840	233	0	4.92	4	0	4	238	24	0	6.05
1986-87	Canada	Nat-Team	42	27	13	2	2550	130	0	3.05	....	....	....	....	....	....	....
1987-88	Canada	Nat-Team	37	19	9	2	1962	92	1	2.81	....	....	....	....	....	....	....
	Canada	Olympics	4	1	2	1	238	12	....	3.02	....	....	....	....	....	....	....
	New Jersey	**NHL**	**13**	**10**	**1**	**0**	**689**	**35**	**1**	**3.05**	**17**	**9**	**8**	**1001**	**57**	***1**	**3.42**
1988-89	**New Jersey**	**NHL**	**62**	**22**	**31**	**9**	**3590**	**230**	**3**	**3.84**	....	....	....	....	....	....	....
1989-90	**New Jersey**	**NHL**	**52**	**22**	**22**	**6**	**2914**	**175**	**0**	**3.60**	**2**	**0**	**2**	**125**	**8**	**0**	**3.84**
1990-91	**New Jersey**	**NHL**	**35**	**8**	**12**	**8**	**1870**	**112**	**0**	**3.59**	....	....	....	....	....	....	....
1991-92	Canada	Nat-Team	31	18	6	4	1721	75	1	2.61	....	....	....	....	....	....	....
	Canada	Olympics	7	5	2	0	429	17	0	2.37	....	....	....	....	....	....	....
	San Diego	IHL	7	4	2	1	424	17	0	2.41	3	0	3	160	13	0	4.88
1992-93	**Hartford**	**NHL**	**50**	**16**	**27**	**3**	**2656**	**184**	**0**	**4.16**	....	....	....	....	....	....	....
1993-94	**Hartford**	**NHL**	**47**	**17**	**24**	**5**	**2750**	**137**	**2**	**2.99**	....	....	....	....	....	....	....
1994-95	**Hartford**	**NHL**	**42**	**17**	**19**	**4**	**2418**	**108**	**0**	**2.68**	....	....	....	....	....	....	....
1995-96	**Hartford**	**NHL**	**66**	**28**	**28**	**6**	**3669**	**190**	**4**	**3.11**	....	....	....	....	....	....	....
1996-97	**Hartford**	**NHL**	**51**	**22**	**22**	**6**	**2985**	**134**	**4**	**2.69**	....	....	....	....	....	....	....
1997-98	**Carolina**	**NHL**	**25**	**7**	**11**	**5**	**1415**	**66**	**1**	**2.80**	....	....	....	....	....	....	....
	Vancouver	**NHL**	**16**	**2**	**9**	**4**	**838**	**49**	**0**	**3.51**	....	....	....	....	....	....	....
	Philadelphia	**NHL**	**11**	**7**	**3**	**0**	**632**	**27**	**1**	**2.56**	**5**	**1**	**4**	**283**	**17**	**0**	**3.60**
1998-99	**Florida**	**NHL**	**59**	**21**	**24**	**14**	**3402**	**151**	**3**	**2.66**	....	....	....	....	....	....	....
	NHL Totals		**529**	**199**	**233**	**70**	**29828**	**1598**	**19**	**3.21**	**24**	**10**	**14**	**1409**	**82**	**1**	**3.49**

Played in NHL All-Star Game (1989)

Traded to **Hartford** by **New Jersey** with Eric Weinrich for Bobby Holik, Hartford's 2nd round choice (Jay Pandolfo) in 1993 Entry Draft and future considerations, August 28, 1992. Transferred to **Carolina** after **Hartford** franchise relocated, June 25, 1997. Traded to **Vancouver** by **Carolina** with Geoff Sanderson and Enrico Ciccone for Kirk McLean and Martin Gelinas, January 3, 1998. Traded to **Philadelphia** by **Vancouver** for Garth Snow, March 4, 1998. Signed as a free agent by **Florida**, September 12, 1998.

BUZAK, Mike — N.J.

Goaltender. Catches left. 6'3", 220 lbs. Born, Edson, Alta., February 10, 1973.
(St. Louis' 5th choice, 167th overall, in 1993 Entry Draft).

			Regular Season								Playoffs						
Season	Club	Lea	GP	W	L	T	Mins	GA	SO	Avg	GP	W	L	Mins	GA	SO	Avg
1991-92	Michigan State	CCHA	7	4	0	0	311	22	0	4.25	....	....	....	....	....	....	....
1992-93	Michigan State	CCHA	38	22	10	2	*2090	102	0	2.93	....	....	....	....	....	....	....
1993-94	Michigan State	CCHA	*39	21	12	5	*2297	104	2	2.72	....	....	....	....	....	....	....
1994-95	Michigan State	CCHA	31	17	10	3	1796	94	0	3.14	....	....	....	....	....	....	....
1995-96	Worcester	AHL	30	9	10	5	1672	85	0	3.05	....	....	....	....	....	....	....
1996-97	Baton Rouge	ECHL	3	0	2	0	108	7	0	3.87	....	....	....	....	....	....	....
	Worcester	AHL	19	9	4	3	972	41	1	2.53	1	0	1	58	3	0	3.06
1997-98	Long Beach	IHL	31	18	6	5	1763	58	*6	*1.97	5	0	3	215	11	0	3.06
	Tucson	WCHL	2	0	2	0	106	6	0	3.37	....	....	....	....	....	....	....
	Phoenix	WCHL	6	3	3	0	357	27	0	4.53	....	....	....	....	....	....	....
1998-99	Albany	AHL	48	22	13	3	2382	102	0	2.57	5	2	1	272	12	0	2.65

CCHA Second All-Star Team (1994, 1995) • Shared James Norris Memorial Trophy (fewest goals against - IHL) with Kay Whitmore (1998)

Signed as a free agent by **New Jersey**, August 14, 1998.

CAMPBELL, Cory — L.A.

Goaltender. Catches left. 6', 192 lbs. Born, Stratford, Ont., July 27, 1981.
(Los Angeles' 4th choice, 92nd overall, in 1999 Entry Draft).

			Regular Season								Playoffs						
Season	Club	Lea	GP	W	L	T	Mins	GA	SO	Avg	GP	W	L	Mins	GA	SO	Avg
1997-98	Waterloo	OMHA	19	....	....	....	795	31	4	1.75	....	....	....	....	....	....	....
1998-99	Belleville	OHL	46	28	13	4	2679	156	1	3.49	21	*16	5	1296	65	0	3.01

Memorial Cup All-Star Team (1999) • Won Hap Emms Memorial Trophy (Memorial Cup Tournament Top Goaltender) (1999)

CAREY, Jim (CAIR-ee)

Goaltender. Catches left. 6'2", 205 lbs. Born, Dorchester, MA, May 31, 1974.
(Washington's 2nd choice, 32nd overall, in 1992 Entry Draft).

			Regular Season								Playoffs						
Season	Club	Lea	GP	W	L	T	Mins	GA	SO	Avg	GP	W	L	Mins	GA	SO	Avg
1989-90	B.C. High School	H.S.	20	....	....	....	1200	20	0	1.00	....	....	....	....	....	....	....
1990-91	Catholic Memorial	H.S.	12	....	....	....	720	20	0	1.66	....	....	....	....	....	....	....
1991-92	Catholic Memorial	H.S.	21	19	2	0	940	34	8	1.63	....	....	....	....	....	....	....
1992-93	U. of Wisconsin	WCHA	26	15	8	1	1525	78	1	3.07	....	....	....	....	....	....	....
1993-94	U. of Wisconsin	WCHA	*40	*24	13	1	*2247	114	*1	*3.04	....	....	....	....	....	....	....
1994-95	Portland	AHL	55	30	14	11	3281	151	*6	2.76	....	....	....	....	....	....	....
	Washington	**NHL**	**28**	**18**	**6**	**3**	**1604**	**57**	**4**	**2.13**	**7**	**2**	**4**	**358**	**25**	**0**	**4.19**
1995-96	**Washington**	**NHL**	**71**	**35**	**24**	**9**	**4069**	**153**	***9**	**2.26**	**3**	**0**	**1**	**97**	**10**	**0**	**6.19**
1996-97	**Washington**	**NHL**	**40**	**17**	**18**	**3**	**2293**	**105**	**1**	**2.75**	....	....	....	....	....	....	....
	Boston	**NHL**	**19**	**5**	**13**	**0**	**1004**	**64**	**0**	**3.82**	....	....	....	....	....	....	....
1997-98	**Boston**	**NHL**	**10**	**3**	**2**	**1**	**496**	**24**	**2**	**2.90**	....	....	....	....	....	....	....
	Providence	AHL	10	2	7	1	604	40	0	3.97	....	....	....	....	....	....	....
1998-99	Providence	AHL	30	17	8	3	1750	68	3	2.33	....	....	....	....	....	....	....
	Cincinnati	IHL	2	1	0	1	120	2	0	1.00	....	....	....	....	....	....	....
	St. Louis	**NHL**	**4**	**1**	**2**	**0**	**202**	**13**	**0**	**3.86**	....	....	....	....	....	....	....
	NHL Totals		**172**	**79**	**65**	**16**	**9668**	**416**	**16**	**2.58**	**10**	**2**	**5**	**455**	**35**	**0**	**4.62**

WCHA Second All-Star Team (1993) • AHL First All-Star Team (1995) • Won Dudley "Red" Garrett Memorial Trophy (Top Rookie - AHL) (1995) • Won Baz Bastien Memorial Trophy (Top Goaltender - AHL) (1995) • NHL/Upper Deck All-Rookie Team (1995) • NHL First All-Star Team (1996) • Won Vezina Trophy (1996)

Traded to **Boston** by **Washington** with Anson Carter, Jason Allison and Washington's 3rd round choice (Lee Goren) in 1997 Entry Draft for Bill Ranford, Adam Oates and Rick Tocchet, March 1, 1997. Signed as a free agent by **St. Louis**, March 1, 1999.

CARON, Sebastian (KAIR-aw) — PIT.

Goaltender. Catches left. 6'1", 150 lbs. Born, Amqui, Que., June 25, 1980.
(Pittsburgh's 4th choice, 86th overall, in 1999 Entry Draft).

			Regular Season								Playoffs						
Season	Club	Lea	GP	W	L	T	Mins	GA	SO	Avg	GP	W	L	Mins	GA	SO	Avg
1998-99	Rimouski	QMJHL	30	13	10	3	1570	85	0	3.25	2	1	0	68	0	0	0.00

CASSIVI, Frederic (KASS-ih-vee) — COL.

Goaltender. Catches left. 6'4", 205 lbs. Born, Sorel, Que., June 12, 1975.
(Ottawa's 7th choice, 210th overall, in 1994 Entry Draft).

			Regular Season								Playoffs						
Season	Club	Lea	GP	W	L	T	Mins	GA	SO	Avg	GP	W	L	Mins	GA	SO	Avg
1993-94	St-Hyacinthe	QMJHL	35	15	13	3	1751	127	1	4.35	....	....	....	....	....	....	....
1994-95	Halifax	QMJHL	24	9	12	1	1362	105	0	4.63	....	....	....	....	....	....	....
	St-Jean	QMJHL	19	12	6	0	1021	55	1	3.23	5	2	3	258	18	0	4.19
1995-96	Thunder Bay	ColHL	12	6	4	2	715	51	0	4.28	....	....	....	....	....	....	....
	P.E.I. Senators	AHL	41	20	14	3	2347	128	1	3.27	5	2	3	317	24	0	4.54
1996-97	Syracuse	AHL	55	23	22	8	3069	164	2	3.21	1	0	1	60	3	0	3.01
1997-98	Worcester	AHL	45	20	22	2	2593	140	1	3.24	6	3	3	326	18	0	3.31
1998-99	Cincinnati	IHL	44	21	17	2	2418	123	1	3.05	3	1	2	139	6	0	2.59

Signed as a free agent by **Colorado**, August 17, 1999.

CHABOT, Frederic (shah-BOH) — MTL.

Goaltender. Catches left. 5'11", 187 lbs. Born, Hebertville-Station, Que., February 12, 1968.
(New Jersey's 10th choice, 192nd overall, in 1986 Entry Draft).

			Regular Season								Playoffs						
Season	Club	Lea	GP	W	L	T	Mins	GA	SO	Avg	GP	W	L	Mins	GA	SO	Avg
1985-86	Trois-Rivieres	QAAA	34	25	9	0	2038	139	0	3.90	....	....	....	....	....	....	....
1986-87	Drummondville	QMJHL	62	31	29	0	3508	293	1	5.01	8	2	6	481	40	0	4.99
1987-88	Drummondville	QMJHL	58	27	24	4	3276	237	1	4.34	16	10	6	1019	56	*1	*3.30
1988-89	Moose Jaw	WHL	26	....	....	....	1385	114	....	4.94	....	....	....	....	....	....	....
	Prince Albert	WHL	28	....	....	....	1572	88	....	3.36	4	1	1	199	16	0	4.82
1989-90	Sherbrooke	AHL	2	1	1	0	119	8	0	4.03	....	....	....	....	....	....	....
	Fort Wayne	IHL	23	6	13	3	1208	87	1	4.32	....	....	....	....	....	....	....
1990-91	**Montreal**	**NHL**	**3**	**0**	**0**	**1**	**108**	**6**	**0**	**3.33**	....	....	....	....	....	....	....
	Fredericton	AHL	35	9	15	5	1800	122	0	4.07	....	....	....	....	....	....	....
1991-92	Fredericton	AHL	30	17	9	4	1761	79	2	*2.69	7	3	4	457	20	0	2.63
	Winston-Salem	ECHL	24	15	7	2	1449	71	0	*2.94	....	....	....	....	....	....	....
1992-93	**Montreal**	**NHL**	**1**	**0**	**0**	**0**	**40**	**1**	**0**	**1.50**	....	....	....	....	....	....	....
	Fredericton	AHL	45	22	17	4	2544	141	0	3.33	4	1	3	261	16	0	3.68
1993-94	**Montreal**	**NHL**	**1**	**0**	**1**	**0**	**60**	**5**	**0**	**5.00**	....	....	....	....	....	....	....
	Fredericton	AHL	3	0	1	1	143	12	0	5.03	....	....	....	....	....	....	....
	Las Vegas	IHL	2	1	1	0	110	5	0	2.72	....	....	....	....	....	....	....
	Philadelphia	**NHL**	**4**	**0**	**1**	**1**	**70**	**5**	**0**	**4.29**	....	....	....	....	....	....	....
	Hershey	AHL	28	13	5	6	1464	63	2	*2.58	11	7	4	665	32	0	2.89
1994-95	Cincinnati	IHL	48	25	12	7	2622	128	1	2.93	5	3	2	326	16	0	2.94
1995-96	Cincinnati	IHL	38	23	9	4	2147	88	3	*2.46	14	9	5	854	37	1	2.60
1996-97	Houston	IHL	*72	*39	26	7	*4265	180	*7	2.53	13	8	5	777	34	*2	2.63
1997-98	**Los Angeles**	**NHL**	**12**	**3**	**3**	**2**	**554**	**29**	**0**	**3.14**	....	....	....	....	....	....	....
	Houston	IHL	22	12	7	2	1237	46	1	2.23	4	1	3	238	11	0	2.77
1998-99	**Montreal**	**NHL**	**11**	**1**	**3**	**0**	**430**	**16**	**0**	**2.23**	....	....	....	....	....	....	....
	Houston	IHL	21	16	4	1	1259	49	3	2.34	....	....	....	....	....	....	....
	NHL Totals		**32**	**4**	**8**	**4**	**1262**	**62**	**0**	**2.95**	....	....	....	....	....	....	....

WHL East All-Star Team (1989) • Won Baz Bastien Award (Top Goaltender - AHL) (1994) • IHL Second All-Star Team (1996) • IHL First All-Star Team (1997) • Won James Gatschene Memorial Trophy (MVP — IHL) (1997)

Signed as a free agent by **Montreal**, January 16, 1990. Claimed by **Tampa Bay** from **Montreal** in Expansion Draft, June 18, 1992. Traded to **Montreal** by **Tampa Bay** for J.C. Bergeron, June 19, 1992. Traded to **Philadelphia** by **Montreal** for cash, February 21, 1994. Signed as a free agent by **Florida**, August 11, 1994. Signed as a free agent by **LA Kings**, September 3, 1997. Claimed by **Nashville** from **LA Kings** in Expansion Draft, June 26, 1998. Claimed on waivers by **LA Kings** from **Nashville**, July 18, 1998. Claimed by **Montreal** from **Los Angeles** in NHL Waiver Draft, October 5, 1998.

CHARPENTIER, Sebastien (shahr-PUHNT-yay) — WSH.

Goaltender. Catches left. 5'9", 177 lbs. Born, Drummondville, Que., April 18, 1977.
(Washington's 4th choice, 93rd overall, in 1995 Entry Draft).

			Regular Season								Playoffs						
Season	Club	Lea	GP	W	L	T	Mins	GA	SO	Avg	GP	W	L	Mins	GA	SO	Avg
1994-95	Laval	QMJHL	41	25	12	1	2152	99	2	2.76	16	9	4	886	45	0	3.05
1995-96	Laval	QMJHL	18	4	10	0	938	97	0	6.20	....	....	....	....	....	....	....
	Val d'Or	QMJHL	33	21	9	1	1906	87	1	2.74	13	7	5	740	45	0	3.64
1996-97	Shawinigan	QMJHL	*62	*37	17	4	*3480	177	1	3.05	4	2	1	196	13	0	3.98
1997-98	Portland	AHL	4	1	3	0	229	10	0	2.61	....	....	....	....	....	....	....
	Hampton Roads	ECHL	43	20	16	6	2388	114	0	2.86	18	*14	4	*1183	38	1	*1.93
1998-99	Quad City	UHL	6	0	0	0	4	0	0	0.00	....	....	....	....	....	....	....
	Portland	AHL	3	0	3	0	180	10	0	3.34	....	....	....	....	....	....	....

Playoff MVP - ECHL (1998)

CHOUINARD, Mathieu (shwee-NAHR) — OTT.

Goaltender. Catches left. 6'1", 200 lbs. Born, Laval, Que., April 11, 1980.
(Ottawa's 1st choice, 15th overall, in 1998 Entry Draft).

			Regular Season								Playoffs						
Season	Club	Lea	GP	W	L	T	Mins	GA	SO	Avg	GP	W	L	Mins	GA	SO	Avg
1996-97	Shawinigan	QMJHL	17	4	7	1	795	51	0	3.85	4	1	3	264	15	0	3.41
1997-98	Shawinigan	QMJHL	55	*32	18	3	3055	142	2	2.79	6	2	4	348	24	0	4.14
1998-99	Shawinigan	QMJHL	56	36	16	4	3288	150	*5	2.74	6	2	4	392	27	0	4.13

QMJHL First All-Star Team (1999)

CHOUKALOS, Donald (koo-KAH-luhs) — BOS.

Goaltender. Catches left. 6'2", 186 lbs. Born, Calgary, Alta., April 11, 1981.
(Boston's 6th choice, 179th overall, in 1999 Entry Draft).

			Regular Season								Playoffs						
Season	Club	Lea	GP	W	L	T	Mins	GA	SO	Avg	GP	W	L	Mins	GA	SO	Avg
1997-98	Calgary	WHL	9	4	1	1	404	21	0	3.12	....	....	....	....	....	....	....
1998-99	Regina	WHL	24	6	12	4	1337	98	0	4.40	....	....	....	....	....	....	....

CLEMMENSEN, Scott — N.J.

Goaltender. Catches left. 6'2", 185 lbs. Born, Des Moines, IA, July 23, 1977.
(New Jersey's 7th choice, 215th overall, in 1997 Entry Draft).

			Regular Season								Playoffs						
Season	Club	Lea	GP	W	L	T	Mins	GA	SO	Avg	GP	W	L	Mins	GA	SO	Avg
1996-97	Des Moines	USHL	36	....	....	....	2042	111	1	3.26	....	....	....	....	....	....	....
1997-98	Boston College	H.E.	37	24	9	4	2205	102	*4	2.78	....	....	....	....	....	....	....
1998-99	Boston College	H.E.	*42	26	12	4	*2507	120	1	2.87	....	....	....	....	....	....	....

CLOUTIER, Dan (KLOO-tyay) T.B.

Goaltender. Catches left. 6'1", 182 lbs. Born, Mont-Laurier, Que., April 22, 1976.
(NY Rangers' 1st choice, 26th overall, in 1994 Entry Draft).

			Regular Season								Playoffs						
Season	Club	Lea	GP	W	L	T	Mins	GA	SO	Avg	GP	W	L	Mins	GA	SO	Avg
1991-92	St. Thomas	OJHL-B	14	....	....	....	823	80	0	5.83	....	....	....	....	....	....	....
1992-93	S.S. Marie	OHL	12	4	6	0	572	44	0	4.62	4	1	2	231	12	0	3.12
1993-94	S.S. Marie	OHL	55	28	14	6	2934	174	*2	3.56	14	*10	4	833	52	0	3.75
1994-95	S.S. Marie	OHL	45	15	26	2	2518	185	1	4.41	....	....	....	....	....	....	....
1995-96	S.S. Marie	OHL	13	9	3	0	641	43	0	4.02	....	....	....	....	....	....	....
	Guelph	OHL	17	12	2	2	1004	35	2	2.09	16	11	5	993	52	*2	3.14
1996-97	Binghamton	AHL	60	23	28	8	3367	199	3	3.55	4	1	3	236	13	0	3.31
1997-98	**NY Rangers**	**NHL**	**12**	**4**	**5**	**1**	**551**	**23**	**0**	**2.50**	....	....	....	....	....	....	....
	Hartford	AHL	24	12	8	3	1417	62	0	2.63	8	5	3	478	24	0	3.01
1998-99	**NY Rangers**	**NHL**	**22**	**6**	**8**	**3**	**1097**	**49**	**0**	**2.68**	....	....	....	....	....	....	....
	NHL Totals		**34**	**10**	**13**	**4**	**1648**	**72**	**0**	**2.62**	....	....	....	....	....	....	....

OHL Second All-Star Team (1996)

Traded to **Tampa Bay** by **NY Rangers** with Niklas Sundstrom and NY Rangers' 1st and 3rd (later traded to San Jose) round choices in 2000 Entry Draft for Chicago's 1st round choice (previously acquired, NY Rangers selected Pavel Brendl) in 1999 Entry Draft, June 26, 1999.

COUSINEAU, Marcel (koo-ZEE-noh) L.A.

Goaltender. Catches left. 5'9", 180 lbs. Born, Delson, Que., April 30, 1973.
(Boston's 3rd choice, 62nd overall, in 1991 Entry Draft).

			Regular Season								Playoffs						
Season	Club	Lea	GP	W	L	T	Mins	GA	SO	Avg	GP	W	L	Mins	GA	SO	Avg
1989-90	Richelieu	QAAA	27	22	5	0	1618	104	0	3.83	....	....	....	....	....	....	....
1990-91	Beauport	QMJHL	49	13	29	3	2739	196	1	4.29	....	....	....	....	....	....	....
1991-92	Beauport	QMJHL	*67	26	32	5	*3673	241	0	3.94	....	....	....	....	....	....	....
1992-93	Drummondville	QMJHL	60	20	32	2	3298	225	0	4.09	9	3	6	498	37	*1	4.45
1993-94	St. John's	AHL	37	13	11	9	2015	118	0	3.51	....	....	....	....	....	....	....
1994-95	St. John's	AHL	58	22	27	6	3342	171	4	3.07	3	0	3	179	9	0	3.01
1995-96	St. John's	AHL	62	21	26	13	3629	192	1	3.17	4	1	3	258	11	0	2.56
1996-97	**Toronto**	**NHL**	**13**	**3**	**5**	**1**	**566**	**31**	**1**	**3.29**	....	....	....	....	....	....	....
	St. John's	AHL	19	7	8	3	1053	58	0	3.30	11	6	5	658	28	0	2.55
1997-98	**Toronto**	**NHL**	**2**	**0**	**0**	**0**	**17**	**0**	**0**	**0.00**	....	....	....	....	....	....	....
	St. John's	AHL	57	17	25	13	3306	167	1	3.03	4	1	3	254	10	0	2.36
1998-99	**NY Islanders**	**NHL**	**6**	**0**	**4**	**0**	**293**	**14**	**0**	**2.87**	....	....	....	....	....	....	....
	Lowell	AHL	53	26	17	7	3034	139	3	2.75	3	0	3	186	13	0	4.20
	NHL Totals		**21**	**3**	**9**	**1**	**876**	**45**	**1**	**3.08**	....	....	....	....	....	....	....

Signed as a free agent by **Toronto**, November 13, 1993. Signed as a free agent by **NY Islanders**, July 29, 1998. Traded to **Los Angeles** by **NY Islanders** with Zigmund Palffy, Brian Smolinski and New Jersey's 4th round choice (previously acquired, Los Angeles selected Daniel Johanssen) in 1999 Entry Draft for Olli Jokinen, Josh Green, Mathieu Biron and Los Angeles' 1st round choice (Taylor Pyatt) in 1999 Entry Draft, June 20, 1999.

CRUICKSHANK, Curtis (KRUHK-shank) WSH.

Goaltender. Catches left. 6'3", 209 lbs. Born, Ottawa, Ont., March 21, 1979.
(Washington's 3rd choice, 89th overall, in 1997 Entry Draft).

			Regular Season								Playoffs						
Season	Club	Lea	GP	W	L	T	Mins	GA	SO	Avg	GP	W	L	Mins	GA	SO	Avg
1995-96	Ottawa	OJHL	24	12	4	0	....	....	0	4.27	....	....	....	....	....	....	....
1996-97	Kingston	OHL	35	13	16	1	1792	118	2	3.95	1	0	1	26	4	0	9.23
1997-98	Kingston	OHL	57	30	20	4	3166	207	2	3.92	12	5	6	702	45	0	3.85
1998-99	Kingston	OHL	16	5	9	0	835	63	1	4.53	....	....	....	....	....	....	....
	Sarnia	OHL	28	18	5	1	1557	66	2	2.54	4	1	0	71	6	0	5.07

CRUZ, Jomar WSH.

Goaltender. Catches left. 6'1", 190 lbs. Born, The Pas, Man., April 5, 1980.
(Washington's 1st choice, 49th overall, in 1998 Entry Draft).

			Regular Season								Playoffs						
Season	Club	Lea	GP	W	L	T	Mins	GA	SO	Avg	GP	W	L	Mins	GA	SO	Avg
1996-97	Notre Dame	SJHL	20	13	6	0	1107	71	2	3.84	....	....	....	....	....	....	....
1997-98	Brandon	WHL	30	16	19	1	1596	81	3	3.05	14	7	6	749	41	0	3.28
1998-99	Brandon	WHL	38	16	17	1	2057	139	1	4.05	1	0	0	23	2	0	5.22

DAFOE, Byron (day-FOH) BOS.

Goaltender. Catches left. 5'11", 190 lbs. Born, Sussex, England, February 25, 1971.
(Washington's 2nd choice, 35th overall, in 1989 Entry Draft).

			Regular Season								Playoffs						
Season	Club	Lea	GP	W	L	T	Mins	GA	SO	Avg	GP	W	L	Mins	GA	SO	Avg
1987-88	Juan de Fuca	BCJHL	32	....	....	....	1716	129	0	4.51	....	....	....	....	....	....	....
1988-89	Portland	WHL	59	29	24	3	3279	291	1	5.32	*18	10	8	*1091	81	*1	4.45
1989-90	Portland	WHL	40	14	21	3	2265	193	0	5.11	....	....	....	....	....	....	....
1990-91	Portland	WHL	8	1	5	1	414	41	0	5.94	....	....	....	....	....	....	....
	Prince Albert	WHL	32	13	12	4	1839	124	0	4.05	....	....	....	....	....	....	....
1991-92	Baltimore	AHL	33	12	16	4	1847	119	0	3.87	....	....	....	....	....	....	....
	New Haven	AHL	7	3	2	1	364	22	0	3.63	....	....	....	....	....	....	....
	Hampton Roads	ECHL	10	6	4	0	562	26	0	2.78	....	....	....	....	....	....	....
1992-93	**Washington**	**NHL**	**1**	**0**	**0**	**0**	**1**	**0**	**0**	**0.00**	....	....	....	....	....	....	....
	Baltimore	AHL	48	16	20	7	2617	191	1	4.38	5	2	3	241	22	0	5.48
1993-94	**Washington**	**NHL**	**5**	**2**	**2**	**0**	**230**	**13**	**0**	**3.39**	**2**	**0**	**2**	**118**	**5**	**0**	**2.54**
	Portland	AHL	47	24	16	4	2661	148	1	3.34	1	0	0	9	1	0	6.79
1994-95	Phoenix	IHL	49	25	16	6	2743	169	2	3.70	....	....	....	....	....	....	....
	Washington	**NHL**	**4**	**1**	**1**	**1**	**187**	**11**	**0**	**3.53**	**1**	**0**	**0**	**20**	**1**	**0**	**3.00**
	Portland	AHL	6	5	0	0	330	16	0	2.91	7	3	4	416	29	0	4.18
1995-96	**Los Angeles**	**NHL**	**47**	**14**	**24**	**8**	**2666**	**172**	**1**	**3.87**	....	....	....	....	....	....	....
1996-97	**Los Angeles**	**NHL**	**40**	**13**	**17**	**5**	**2162**	**112**	**0**	**3.11**	....	....	....	....	....	....	....
1997-98	**Boston**	**NHL**	**65**	**30**	**25**	**9**	**3693**	**138**	**6**	**2.24**	**6**	**2**	**4**	**422**	**14**	**1**	**1.99**
1998-99	**Boston**	**NHL**	**68**	**32**	**23**	**11**	**4001**	**133**	***10**	**1.99**	**12**	**6**	**6**	**768**	**26**	**2**	**2.03**
	NHL Totals		**230**	**92**	**92**	**34**	**12940**	**579**	**17**	**2.68**	**21**	**8**	**12**	**1328**	**46**	**3**	**2.08**

AHL First All-Star Team (1994) • Shared Harry "Hap" Holmes Trophy (fewest goals-against - AHL) with Olaf Kolzig (1994) • NHL Second All-Star Team (1999)

Traded to **Los Angeles** by **Washington** with Dimitri Khristich for Los Angeles' 1st round choice (Alexander Volchkov) and Dallas' 4th round choice (previously acquired, Washington selected Justin Davis) in 1996 Entry Draft, July 8, 1995. Traded to **Boston** by **Los Angeles** with Dimitri Khristich for Jozef Stumpel, Sandy Moger and Boston's 4th round choice (later traded to New Jersey - New Jersey selected Pierre Dagenais) in 1998 Entry Draft, August 29, 1997.

DAIGLE, Sylvain (DAYG) PHX.

Goaltender. Catches right. 5'8", 185 lbs. Born, St-Hyacinthe, Que., October 20, 1976.
(Winnipeg's 7th choice, 136th overall, in 1995 Entry Draft).

			Regular Season								Playoffs						
Season	Club	Lea	GP	W	L	T	Mins	GA	SO	Avg	GP	W	L	Mins	GA	SO	Avg
1993-94	Shawinigan	QMJHL	31	14	11	3	1645	113	0	4.12	....	....	....	....	....	....	....
1994-95	Shawinigan	QMJHL	48	27	17	3	2831	159	3	3.37	14	7	6	824	57	0	4.15
1995-96	Shawinigan	QMJHL	49	23	14	5	2708	159	*3	3.52	6	2	4	389	22	0	3.39
1996-97	Springfield	AHL	13	8	3	0	691	23	1	2.00	6	1	4	311	18	0	3.47
	Mississippi	ECHL	34	20	8	5	1951	100	2	3.08	....	....	....	....	....	....	....
	Las Vegas	IHL	1	0	0	0	41	5	0	7.17	....	....	....	....	....	....	....
1997-98	Springfield	AHL	21	7	9	2	1093	68	0	3.73	2	0	0	23	0	0	0.00
1998-99	Springfield	AHL	27	8	12	2	1393	67	1	2.89	....	....	....	....	....	....	....

Transfered to **Phoenix** after **Winnipeg** franchise relocated, July 1, 1996.

DAMPHOUSSE, Jean-Francois (DAHM-fooz) N.J.

Goaltender. Catches left. 6', 175 lbs. Born, St-Alexis-des-Monts, Que., July 21, 1979.
(New Jersey's 1st choice, 24th overall, in 1997 Entry Draft).

			Regular Season								Playoffs						
Season	Club	Lea	GP	W	L	T	Mins	GA	SO	Avg	GP	W	L	Mins	GA	SO	Avg
1996-97	Moncton	QMJHL	39	6	25	2	2063	190	0	5.53	....	....	....	....	....	....	....
1997-98	Moncton	QMJHL	59	24	26	6	3400	174	1	3.07	10	5	5	595	28	0	2.82
1998-99	Moncton	QMJHL	40	19	17	2	2163	121	1	3.36	4	0	4	200	12	0	3.60
	Albany	AHL	1	0	1	0	59	3	0	3.06	....	....	....	....	....	....	....

DAUBENSPECK, Kirk (DAW-behn-spehk)

Goaltender. Catches left. 6', 190 lbs. Born, Madison, WI, July 16, 1974.
(Philadelphia's 6th choice, 151st overall, in 1992 Entry Draft).

			Regular Season								Playoffs						
Season	Club	Lea	GP	W	L	T	Mins	GA	SO	Avg	GP	W	L	Mins	GA	SO	Avg
1991-92	Culver Academy	H.S.	20	....	....	....	1190	57	0	2.88	....	....	....	....	....	....	....
1992-93	Wisconsin	USHL	28	5	20	1	1542	123	0	4.79	....	....	....	....	....	....	....
	Sioux City	USHL	9	0	7	1	470	49	0	6.26	....	....	....	....	....	....	....
1993-94	U. of Wisconsin	WCHA	7	2	2	0	280	19	0	4.07	....	....	....	....	....	....	....
1994-95	U. of Wisconsin	WCHA	42	*23	15	4	*2503	146	0	3.51	....	....	....	....	....	....	....
1995-96	U. of Wisconsin	WCHA	*39	*17	20	2	*2357	151	0	3.84	....	....	....	....	....	....	....
1996-97	U. of Wisconsin	WCHA	33	13	18	2	1925	124	1	3.86	....	....	....	....	....	....	....
1997-98	Jacksonville	ECHL	32	20	9	2	1865	92	1	2.96	....	....	....	....	....	....	....
	Indianapolis	IHL	18	6	9	0	953	58	0	3.65	....	....	....	....	....	....	....
1998-99	Indianapolis	IHL	12	2	8	1	650	43	0	3.97	....	....	....	....	....	....	....
	Jacksonville	ECHL	8	5	3	0	424	18	0	2.55	....	....	....	....	....	....	....
	Chesapeake	ECHL	13	7	2	4	774	31	2	2.40	7	3	4	424	12	1	*1.70

WCHA Second All-Star Team (1997) • NCAA West Second All-American Team (1997)

Traded to **Ottawa** by **Philadelphia** with Claude Boivin for Mark Lamb, March 5, 1994. Traded to **Chicago** by **Ottawa** for Ottawa's 6th round choice (previously acquired, Ottawa selected Christopher Neil) in 1998 Entry Draft and future considerations, September 23, 1997.

DENIS, Marc (deh-NEE) COL.

Goaltender. Catches left. 6', 190 lbs. Born, Montreal, Que., August 1, 1977.
(Colorado's 1st choice, 25th overall, in 1995 Entry Draft).

			Regular Season								Playoffs						
Season	Club	Lea	GP	W	L	T	Mins	GA	SO	Avg	GP	W	L	Mins	GA	SO	Avg
1992-93	Montreal-Bourassa	QAAA	26	....	....	....	1559	74	5	2.87	....	....	....	....	....	....	....
1993-94	Trois-Rivieres	QAAA	36	....	....	....	2093	158	3	4.53	....	....	....	....	....	....	....
1994-95	Chicoutimi	QMJHL	32	17	9	1	1688	98	0	3.48	6	4	2	372	19	1	3.06
1995-96	Chicoutimi	QMJHL	51	23	21	4	2951	157	2	3.19	16	8	8	957	69	0	4.33
1996-97	Chicoutimi	QMJHL	41	22	15	2	[illegible]	101	1	*2.60	*21	*11	10	[illegible]	70	*1	3.42
	Colorado	**NHL**	**1**	**0**	**1**	**0**	**60**	**3**	**0**	**3.00**	....	....	....	....	....	....	....
	Hershey	AHL	....	....	....	....	....	....	....	....	4	1	0	56	1	0	1.08
1997-98	Hershey	AHL	47	17	23	4	2588	125	1	2.90	6	3	3	346	15	0	2.59
1998-99	**Colorado**	**NHL**	**4**	**1**	**1**	**1**	**217**	**9**	**0**	**2.49**	....	....	....	....	....	....	....
	Hershey	AHL	52	20	23	5	2908	137	4	2.83	3	1	1	143	7	0	2.93
	NHL Totals		**5**	**1**	**2**	**1**	**277**	**12**	**0**	**2.60**	....	....	....	....	....	....	....

QMJHL First All-Star Team (1997) • Canadian Major Junior First All-Star Team (1997) • Canadian Major Junior Goaltender of the Year (1997)

DeROUVILLE, Philippe (deh-ROO-vihl)

Goaltender. Catches left. 6'1", 185 lbs. Born, Victoriaville, Que., August 7, 1974.
(Pittsburgh's 5th choice, 115th overall, in 1992 Entry Draft).

			Regular Season								Playoffs						
Season	Club	Lea	GP	W	L	T	Mins	GA	SO	Avg	GP	W	L	Mins	GA	SO	Avg
1989-90	Magog	QAAA	21	15	6	0	1213	90	0	4.45	....	....	....	....	....	....	....
1990-91	Longueuil	QMJHL	20	13	6	0	1030	50	0	2.91	....	....	....	....	....	....	....
1991-92	Verdun	QMJHL	34	20	6	3	1854	99	2	3.20	11	7	3	593	28	1	2.83
1992-93	Verdun	QMJHL	61	30	27	2	3491	210	1	3.61	4	0	4	256	18	0	3.61
1993-94	Verdun	QMJHL	51	28	22	0	2845	145	1	*3.06	4	0	4	210	14	0	4.00
1994-95	Cleveland	IHL	41	24	10	5	2369	131	1	3.32	4	1	3	263	18	0	4.09
	Pittsburgh	**NHL**	**1**	**1**	**0**	**0**	**60**	**3**	**0**	**3.00**	....	....	....	....	....	....	....
1995-96	Cleveland	IHL	38	19	11	3	2008	129	1	3.86	....	....	....	....	....	....	....
1996-97	**Pittsburgh**	**NHL**	**2**	**0**	**2**	**0**	**111**	**6**	**0**	**3.24**	....	....	....	....	....	....	....
	Kansas City	IHL	26	11	11	4	1470	69	2	2.82	2	0	1	32	4	0	7.35
1997-98	Louisville	ECHL	8	5	2	1	480	27	0	3.38	....	....	....	....	....	....	....
	Hartford	AHL	3	0	2	1	184	10	0	3.26	....	....	....	....	....	....	....
	Utah	IHL	30	18	9	1	1524	65	3	2.56	2	1	1	129	7	0	3.25
1998-99	Utah	IHL	5	0	2	0	142	12	0	5.07	....	....	....	....	....	....	....
	San Antonio	CHL	5	3	2	0	181	13	0	4.31	....	....	....	....	....	....	....
	Fredericton	AHL	19	6	6	2	921	46	0	3.00	....	....	....	....	....	....	....
	NHL Totals		**3**	**1**	**2**	**0**	**171**	**9**	**0**	**3.16**	....	....	....	....	....	....	....

QMJHL Second All-Star Team (1993, 1994)

DESROCHERS, Patrick (duh-RAWSH-ai) PHX.

Goaltender. Catches left. 6'3", 195 lbs. Born, Penetang, Ont., October 27, 1979.
(Phoenix's 1st choice, 14th overall, in 1998 Entry Draft).

			Regular Season								Playoffs						
Season	Club	Lea	GP	W	L	T	Mins	GA	SO	Avg	GP	W	L	Mins	GA	SO	Avg
1995-96	Sarnia	OHL	29	12	6	2	1265	96	0	4.55	3	0	1	71	5	0	4.23
1996-97	Sarnia	OHL	50	22	17	4	2667	154	4	3.46	11	6	5	576	42	0	4.38
1997-98	Sarnia	OHL	56	26	17	11	3205	179	1	3.35	4	1	2	160	12	0	4.50
1998-99	Sarnia	OHL	8	3	5	0	425	26	0	3.67	....	....	....	....	....	....	....
	Kingston	OHL	44	14	22	3	2389	177	1	4.45	5	1	4	323	21	0	3.90
	Canada	Nat-Team	1	1	0	0	60	4	0	4.00	....	....	....	....	....	....	....

DOVIGI, Patrick (doh-VIH-jee) EDM.

Goaltender. Catches left. 6', 180 lbs. Born, Sault Ste. Marie, Ont., July 2, 1979.
(Edmonton's 2nd choice, 41st overall, in 1997 Entry Draft).

			Regular Season								Playoffs						
Season	Club	Lea	GP	W	L	T	Mins	GA	SO	Avg	GP	W	L	Mins	GA	SO	Avg
1995-96	Elmira	OJHL	26	10	12	1	1280	101	1	4.73	....	....	....	....	....	....	....
1996-97	Erie	OHL	36	11	14	4	1764	114	3	3.88	5	1	4	303	18	0	3.56
1997-98	Erie	OHL	41	17	17	2	2174	161	0	4.44	....	....	....	....	....	....	....
	New Orleans	ECHL	2	1	1	0	120	13	0	6.50	....	....	....	....	....	....	....
1998-99	Erie	OHL	12	6	5	0	655	50	1	4.58	....	....	....	....	....	....	....
	St. Michael's	OHL	39	13	21	1	2004	143	0	4.28	....	....	....	....	....	....	....

DUNHAM, Mike (DUHN-uhm) NSH.

Goaltender. Catches left. 6'3", 200 lbs. Born, Johnson City, NY, June 1, 1972.
(New Jersey's 4th choice, 53rd overall, in 1990 Entry Draft).

			Regular Season								Playoffs						
Season	Club	Lea	GP	W	L	T	Mins	GA	SO	Avg	GP	W	L	Mins	GA	SO	Avg
1989-90	Canterbury	H.S.	32	....	....	....	1558	68	3	1.96	....	....	....	....	....	....	....
1990-91	U. of Maine	H.E.	23	14	5	2	1275	63	0	*2.96	....	....	....	....	....	....	....
1991-92	U. of Maine	H.E.	7	6	0	0	382	14	1	2.20	....	....	....	....	....	....	....
	United States	Nat-Team	3	0	1	1	157	10	0	3.82	....	....	....	....	....	....	....
	United States	Olympics	DID NOT PLAY – SPARE GOALTENDER														
1992-93	U. of Maine	H.E.	25	*21	1	1	1429	63	0	2.65	....	....	....	....	....	....	....
1993-94	United States	Nat-Team	33	22	9	2	1983	125	2	3.78	....	....	....	....	....	....	....
	United States	Olympics	3	0	1	2	180	15	0	5.00	....	....	....	....	....	....	....
	Albany	AHL	5	2	2	1	304	26	0	5.12	....	....	....	....	....	....	....
1994-95	Albany	AHL	35	20	7	8	2120	99	1	2.80	7	6	1	419	20	1	2.86
1995-96	Albany	AHL	44	30	10	2	2592	109	1	2.52	3	1	2	182	5	1	1.65
1996-97	**New Jersey**	**NHL**	**26**	**8**	**7**	**1**	**1013**	**43**	**2**	**2.55**	....	....	....	....	....	....	....
	Albany	AHL	3	1	1	1	184	12	0	3.91	....	....	....	....	....	....	....
1997-98	**New Jersey**	**NHL**	**15**	**5**	**5**	**3**	**773**	**29**	**1**	**2.25**	....	....	....	....	....	....	....
1998-99	**Nashville**	**NHL**	**44**	**16**	**23**	**3**	**2472**	**127**	**1**	**3.08**	....	....	....	....	....	....	....
	NHL Totals		**85**	**29**	**35**	**7**	**4258**	**199**	**4**	**2.80**	....	....	....	....	....	....	....

Hockey East First All-Star Team (1993) • NCAA East First All-American Team (1993) • Shared Harry ''Hap'' Holmes Memorial Trophy (fewest goals against - AHL) with Corey Schwab (1995) • Shared Jack A. Butterfield Trophy (Playoff MVP - AHL) with Corey Schwab (1995) • AHL Second All-Star Team (1996) • Shared William M. Jennings Trophy with Martin Brodeur (1997)

Claimed by **Nashville** from **New Jersey** in Expansion Draft, June 26, 1998.

ELLIOT, Jason DET.

Goaltender. Catches left. 6'2", 183 lbs. Born, Inuvik, N.W.T., November 10, 1975.
(Detroit's 7th choice, 205th overall, in 1994 Entry Draft).

			Regular Season								Playoffs						
Season	Club	Lea	GP	W	L	T	Mins	GA	SO	Avg	GP	W	L	Mins	GA	SO	Avg
1993-94	Kimberley	RMJHL	STATISTICS NOT AVAILABLE														
1994-95	Cornell	ECAC	16	3	11	1	877	62	0	4.24	....	....	....	....	....	....	....
1995-96	Cornell	ECAC	19	12	2	1	971	38	2	2.35	....	....	....	....	....	....	....
1996-97	Cornell	ECAC	27	16	7	2	1475	67	0	2.73	....	....	....	....	....	....	....
1997-98	Cornell	ECAC	29	14	12	2	1683	74	2	2.64	....	....	....	....	....	....	....
1998-99	Adirondack	AHL	51	14	27	5	2710	146	2	3.23	1	0	1	59	2	0	2.04

ECAC Second All-Star Team (1998)

ESCHE, Robert (EHSH) PHX.

Goaltender. Catches left. 6'1", 204 lbs. Born, Utica, NY, January 22, 1978.
(Phoenix's 5th choice, 139th overall, in 1996 Entry Draft).

			Regular Season								Playoffs						
Season	Club	Lea	GP	W	L	T	Mins	GA	SO	Avg	GP	W	L	Mins	GA	SO	Avg
1995-96	Detroit	OHL	23	13	6	0	1219	76	1	3.74	3	0	2	105	4	0	2.29
1996-97	Detroit	OHL	58	24	28	2	3241	206	2	3.81	5	1	4	317	19	0	3.60
1997-98	Plymouth	OHL	48	29	13	4	2810	135	3	2.88	15	8	7	869	45	0	3.11
1998-99	**Phoenix**	**NHL**	**3**	**0**	**1**	**0**	**130**	**7**	**0**	**3.23**	....	....	....	....	....	....	....
	Springfield	AHL	55	24	20	6	2957	138	1	2.80	1	0	1	60	4	0	4.02
	NHL Totals		**3**	**0**	**1**	**0**	**130**	**7**	**0**	**3.23**	....	....	....	....	....	....	....

OHL Second All-Star Team (1998)

ESSENSA, Bob (EH-sehn-suh)

Goaltender. Catches left. 6', 188 lbs. Born, Toronto, Ont., January 14, 1965.
(Winnipeg's 5th choice, 71st overall, in 1983 Entry Draft).

			Regular Season								Playoffs						
Season	Club	Lea	GP	W	L	T	Mins	GA	SO	Avg	GP	W	L	Mins	GA	SO	Avg
1981-82	Henry Carr	MTHL	17	....	....	....	948	79	0	4.99	....	....	....	....	....	....	....
1982-83	Henry Carr	H.S.	31	....	....	....	1840	98	2	3.20	....	....	....	....	....	....	....
1983-84	Michigan State	CCHA	17	11	4	0	946	44	2	2.79	....	....	....	....	....	....	....
1984-85	Michigan State	CCHA	18	15	2	0	1059	29	2	1.64	....	....	....	....	....	....	....
1985-86	Michigan State	CCHA	23	17	4	1	1333	74	1	3.33	....	....	....	....	....	....	....
1986-87	Michigan State	CCHA	25	19	3	1	1383	64	2	2.78	....	....	....	....	....	....	....
1987-88	Moncton	AHL	27	7	11	1	1287	100	1	4.66	....	....	....	....	....	....	....
1988-89	**Winnipeg**	**NHL**	**20**	**6**	**8**	**3**	**1102**	**68**	**1**	**3.70**	....	....	....	....	....	....	....
	Fort Wayne	IHL	22	14	7	0	1287	70	0	3.26	....	....	....	....	....	....	....
1989-90	**Winnipeg**	**NHL**	**36**	**18**	**9**	**5**	**2035**	**107**	**1**	**3.15**	**4**	**2**	**1**	**206**	**12**	**0**	**3.50**
	Moncton	AHL	6	3	3	0	358	15	0	2.51	....	....	....	....	....	....	....
1990-91	**Winnipeg**	**NHL**	**55**	**19**	**24**	**6**	**2916**	**153**	**4**	**3.15**	....	....	....	....	....	....	....
	Moncton	AHL	2	1	0	1	125	6	0	2.88	....	....	....	....	....	....	....
1991-92	**Winnipeg**	**NHL**	**47**	**21**	**17**	**6**	**2627**	**126**	***5**	**2.88**	**1**	**0**	**0**	**33**	**3**	**0**	**5.45**
1992-93	**Winnipeg**	**NHL**	**67**	**33**	**26**	**6**	**3855**	**227**	**2**	**3.53**	**6**	**2**	**4**	**367**	**20**	**0**	**3.27**
1993-94	**Winnipeg**	**NHL**	**56**	**19**	**30**	**6**	**3136**	**201**	**1**	**3.85**	....	....	....	....	....	....	....
	Detroit	**NHL**	**13**	**4**	**7**	**2**	**778**	**34**	**1**	**2.62**	**2**	**0**	**2**	**109**	**9**	**0**	**4.95**
1994-95	San Diego	IHL	16	6	8	1	919	52	0	3.39	1	0	1	59	3	0	3.05
1995-96	Adirondack	AHL	3	1	2	0	179	11	0	3.69	....	....	....	....	....	....	....
	Fort Wayne	IHL	45	24	14	5	2529	122	1	2.89	5	2	3	299	12	0	2.41
1996-97	**Edmonton**	**NHL**	**19**	**4**	**8**	**0**	**868**	**41**	**1**	**2.83**	....	....	....	....	....	....	....
1997-98	**Edmonton**	**NHL**	**16**	**6**	**6**	**1**	**825**	**35**	**0**	**2.55**	**1**	**0**	**0**	**27**	**1**	**0**	**2.22**
1998-99	**Edmonton**	**NHL**	**39**	**12**	**14**	**6**	**2091**	**96**	**0**	**2.75**	....	....	....	....	....	....	....
	NHL Totals		**368**	**142**	**149**	**41**	**20233**	**1088**	**16**	**3.23**	**14**	**4**	**7**	**742**	**45**	**0**	**3.64**

CCHA First All-Star Team (1985) • CCHA Second All-Star Team (1986) • NHL All-Rookie Team (1990)

Traded to **Detroit** by **Winnipeg** with Sergei Bautin for Tim Cheveldae and Dallas Drake, March 8, 1994. Traded to **Edmonton** by **Detroit** for future considerations, June 14, 1996.

FANKHOUSER, Scott ATL.

Goaltender. Catches left. 6'2", 195 lbs. Born, Bismark, ND, July 1, 1975.
(St. Louis' 8th choice, 276th overall, in 1994 Entry Draft).

			Regular Season								Playoffs						
Season	Club	Lea	GP	W	L	T	Mins	GA	SO	Avg	GP	W	L	Mins	GA	SO	Avg
1993-94	Loomis-Chaffe	H.S.	STATISTICS NOT AVAILABLE														
1994-95	U. Mass-Lowell	H.E.	11	4	4	1	499	37	0	4.44	....	....	....	....	....	....	....
1995-96	Melfort	SJHL	45	31	9	4	2544	109	....	2.57	....	....	....	....	....	....	....
1996-97	U. Mass-Lowell	H.E.	11	2	4	1	517	38	0	4.41	....	....	....	....	....	....	....
1997-98	U. Mass-Lowell	H.E.	16	4	7	2	798	48	0	3.61	....	....	....	....	....	....	....
1998-99	U. Mass-Lowell	H.E.	32	16	14	0	1729	80	1	2.78	....	....	....	....	....	....	....

Signed as a free agent by **Atlanta**, August 24, 1999.

FERNANDEZ, Manny (fuhr-NAN-dehz) DAL.

Goaltender. Catches left. 6', 185 lbs. Born, Etobicoke, Ont., August 27, 1974.
(Quebec's 4th choice, 52nd overall, in 1992 Entry Draft).

			Regular Season								Playoffs						
Season	Club	Lea	GP	W	L	T	Mins	GA	SO	Avg	GP	W	L	Mins	GA	SO	Avg
1990-91	Lac St-Louis	QAAA	20	13	5	0	1176	69	3	3.52	....	....	....	....	....	....	....
1991-92	Laval	QMJHL	31	14	13	2	1593	99	1	3.73	9	3	5	468	39	0	5.00
1992-93	Laval	QMJHL	43	26	14	2	2347	141	1	3.60	13	*12	1	818	42	0	3.08
1993-94	Laval	QMJHL	51	29	14	1	2776	143	*5	3.09	19	14	5	1116	49	*1	*2.63
1994-95	Kalamazoo	IHL	46	21	10	9	2470	115	2	2.79	14	10	2	753	34	1	2.71
	Dallas	**NHL**	**1**	**0**	**1**	**0**	**59**	**3**	**0**	**3.05**	....	....	....	....	....	....	....
1995-96	**Dallas**	**NHL**	**5**	**0**	**1**	**1**	**249**	**19**	**0**	**4.58**	....	....	....	....	....	....	....
	Michigan	IHL	47	22	15	9	2664	133	*4	3.00	6	5	1	372	14	0	*2.26
1996-97	Michigan	IHL	48	20	24	2	2720	142	2	3.13	4	1	3	277	15	0	3.25
1997-98	**Dallas**	**NHL**	**2**	**1**	**0**	**0**	**69**	**2**	**0**	**1.74**	**1**	**0**	**0**	**2**	**0**	**0**	**0.00**
	Michigan	IHL	55	27	17	5	3022	139	5	2.76	2	0	2	88	7	0	4.73
1998-99	**Dallas**	**NHL**	**1**	**0**	**1**	**0**	**60**	**2**	**0**	**2.00**	....	....	....	....	....	....	....
	Houston	IHL	50	34	6	9	2949	116	2	2.36	*19	*11	8	*1126	49	1	2.61
	NHL Totals		**9**	**1**	**3**	**1**	**437**	**26**	**0**	**3.57**	**1**	**0**	**0**	**2**	**0**	**0**	**0.00**

QMJHL First All-Star Team (1994) • IHL Second All-Star Team (1995)

Rights traded to **Dallas** by **Quebec** for Tommy Sjodin and Dallas' 3rd round choice (Chris Drury) in 1994 Entry Draft, February 13, 1994.

FICHAUD, Eric (FEE-shoh) CAR.

Goaltender. Catches left. 5'11", 171 lbs. Born, Anjou, Que., November 4, 1975.
(Toronto's 1st choice, 16th overall, in 1994 Entry Draft).

			Regular Season								Playoffs						
Season	Club	Lea	GP	W	L	T	Mins	GA	SO	Avg	GP	W	L	Mins	GA	SO	Avg
1991-92	Montreal-Bourassa	QAAA	28	12	15	1	1678	110	0	3.95	....	....	....	....	....	....	....
1992-93	Chicoutimi	QMJHL	43	18	13	1	2039	149	0	4.38	....	....	....	....	....	....	....
1993-94	Chicoutimi	QMJHL	*63	*37	21	3	*3493	192	4	3.30	*26	*16	10	*1560	86	*1	3.31
1994-95	Chicoutimi	QMJHL	46	21	19	4	2637	151	4	3.44	7	2	5	428	20	0	2.80
1995-96	**NY Islanders**	**NHL**	**24**	**7**	**12**	**2**	**1234**	**68**	**1**	**3.31**	....	....	....	....	....	....	....
	Worcester	AHL	34	13	15	6	1989	97	1	2.93	2	1	1	127	7	0	3.30
1996-97	**NY Islanders**	**NHL**	**34**	**9**	**14**	**4**	**1759**	**91**	**0**	**3.10**	....	....	....	....	....	....	....
1997-98	**NY Islanders**	**NHL**	**17**	**3**	**8**	**3**	**807**	**40**	**0**	**2.97**	....	....	....	....	....	....	....
	Utica	IHL	1	0	0	0	40	3	0	4.45	....	....	....	....	....	....	....
1998-99	**Nashville**	**NHL**	**9**	**0**	**6**	**0**	**447**	**24**	**0**	**3.22**	....	....	....	....	....	....	....
	Milwaukee	IHL	8	5	2	1	480	25	0	3.13	....	....	....	....	....	....	....
	NHL Totals		**84**	**19**	**40**	**9**	**4247**	**223**	**1**	**3.15**	....	....	....	....	....	....	....

Canadian Major Junior Second All-Star Team (1994) • Memorial Cup All-Star Team (1994) • Won Hap Emms Memorial Trophy (Memorial Cup Tournament Top Goaltender) (1994) • QMJHL First All-Star Team (1995)

Traded to **NY Islanders** by **Toronto** for Benoit Hogue, NY Islanders' 3rd round choice (Ryan Pepperall) in 1995 Entry Draft and 5th round choice (Brandon Sugden) in 1996 Entry Draft, April 6, 1995. Traded to **Edmonton** by **NY Islanders** for Mike Watt, June 18, 1998. Traded to **Nashville** by **Edmonton** with Drake Berehowsky and Greg de Vries for Mikhail Shtalenkov and Jim Dowd, October 1, 1998. Traded to **Carolina** by **Nashville** for Toronto's 4th round choice (previously acquired, Nashville selected Yevgeny Pavlov) in 1999 Entry Draft and future considerations, June 26, 1999.

FINLEY, Brian NSH.

Goaltender. Catches right. 6'2", 180 lbs. Born, Sault Ste. Marie, Ont., July 3, 1981.
(Nashville's 1st choice, 6th overall, in 1999 Entry Draft).

			Regular Season								Playoffs						
Season	Club	Lea	GP	W	L	T	Mins	GA	SO	Avg	GP	W	L	Mins	GA	SO	Avg
1997-98	Barrie	OHL	41	23	14	1	2154	105	3	2.92	5	1	3	260	13	0	3.00
1998-99	Barrie	OHL	52	*36	10	4	3063	136	3	2.66	5	4	1	323	15	0	2.79

OHL First All-Star Team (1999)

FISCHER, Kai (FIH-shuhr, KIGH) COL.

Goaltender. Catches left. 5'11", 176 lbs. Born, Forst, West Germany, March 25, 1977.
(Colorado's 8th choice, 160th overall, in 1996 Entry Draft).

			Regular Season								Playoffs						
Season	Club	Lea	GP	W	L	T	Mins	GA	SO	Avg	GP	W	L	Mins	GA	SO	Avg
1995-96	Dusseldorf	Ger-Jr.	STATISTICS NOT AVAILABLE														
1996-97	Dusseldorf	Germany	2	....	....	....	125	7	0	3.36	....	....	....	....	....	....	....
1997-98	Bremerhaven	Ger-2	45	....	....	....	2674	172	....	3.86	....	....	....	....	....	....	....
1998-99	ESC Essen	Ger-2	9	....	....	....	540	32	0	3.55	....	....	....	....	....	....	....

FISET, Stephane (fih-SEHT) L.A.

Goaltender. Catches left. 6'1", 198 lbs. Born, Montreal, Que., June 17, 1970.
(Quebec's 3rd choice, 24th overall, in 1988 Entry Draft).

			Regular Season								Playoffs						
Season	Club	Lea	GP	W	L	T	Mins	GA	SO	Avg	GP	W	L	Mins	GA	SO	Avg
1986-87	Montreal-Bourassa	QAAA	29	7	20	1	1445	142	0	5.89	....	....	....	....	....	....	....
1987-88	Victoriaville	QMJHL	40	15	17	4	2221	146	1	3.94	2	0	2	163	10	0	3.68
1988-89	Victoriaville	QMJHL	43	25	14	0	2401	138	1	*3.45	12	*9	2	711	33	0	*2.78
1989-90	Quebec	NHL	6	0	5	1	342	34	0	5.96	....	....	....	....	....	....	....
	Victoriaville	QMJHL	24	14	6	3	1383	63	1	*2.73	*14	7	6	*790	49	0	3.72
1990-91	Quebec	NHL	3	0	2	1	186	12	0	3.87	....	....	....	....	....	....	....
	Halifax	AHL	36	10	15	8	1902	131	0	4.13	....	....	....	....	....	....	....
1991-92	Quebec	NHL	23	7	10	2	1133	71	1	3.76	....	....	....	....	....	....	....
	Halifax	AHL	29	8	14	6	1675	110	*3	3.94	....	....	....	....	....	....	....
1992-93	Quebec	NHL	37	18	9	4	1939	110	0	3.40	1	0	0	21	1	0	2.86
	Halifax	AHL	3	2	1	0	180	11	0	3.67	....	....	....	....	....	....	....
1993-94	Quebec	NHL	50	20	25	4	2798	158	2	3.39	....	....	....	....	....	....	....
	Cornwall	AHL	1	0	1	0	60	4	0	4.00	....	....	....	....	....	....	....
1994-95	Quebec	NHL	32	17	10	3	1879	87	2	2.78	4	1	2	209	16	0	4.59
1995-96 ♦	Colorado	NHL	37	22	6	7	2107	103	1	2.93	1	0	0	1	0	0	0.00
1996-97	Los Angeles	NHL	44	13	24	5	2482	132	4	3.19	....	....	....	....	....	....	....
1997-98	Los Angeles	NHL	60	26	25	8	3497	158	2	2.71	2	0	2	93	7	0	4.52
1998-99	Los Angeles	NHL	42	18	21	1	2403	104	3	2.60	....	....	....	....	....	....	....
	NHL Totals		334	141	137	36	18766	969	15	3.10	8	1	4	324	24	0	4.44

QMJHL First All-Star Team (1989) • Canadian Major Junior Goaltender of the Year (1989)

Transferred to **Colorado** after **Quebec** franchise relocated, June 21, 1995. Traded to **Los Angeles** by **Colorado** with Colorado's 1st round choice (Mathieu Biron) in 1998 Entry Draft for Eric Lacroix and Los Angeles' 1st round choice (Martin Skoula) in 1998 Entry Draft, June 20, 1996.

FITZPATRICK, Mark CAR.

Goaltender. Catches left. 6'2", 198 lbs. Born, Toronto, Ont., November 13, 1968.
(Los Angeles' 2nd choice, 27th overall, in 1987 Entry Draft).

			Regular Season								Playoffs						
Season	Club	Lea	GP	W	L	T	Mins	GA	SO	Avg	GP	W	L	Mins	GA	SO	Avg
1983-84	Revelstoke	BCJHL	21	....	....	....	1019	90	0	5.30	....	....	....	....	....	....	....
1984-85	Medicine Hat	WHL	3	1	2	0	180	9	0	3.00	1	0	0	20	2	0	6.00
	Calgary Canucks	AJHL	29	....	....	....	1631	102	2	3.75	....	....	....	....	....	....	....
1985-86	Medicine Hat	WHL	41	26	6	1	2074	99	1	*2.86	*19	*11	5	*986	58	0	3.53
1986-87	Medicine Hat	WHL	50	31	11	4	2844	159	4	3.35	20	12	8	1224	71	1	3.48
1987-88	Medicine Hat	WHL	63	36	15	6	3600	194	2	3.23	16	12	4	959	52	*1	*3.25
1988-89	Los Angeles	NHL	17	6	7	3	957	64	0	4.01	....	....	....	....	....	....	....
	New Haven	AHL	18	10	5	1	980	54	1	3.31	....	....	....	....	....	....	....
	NY Islanders	NHL	11	3	5	2	627	41	0	3.92	....	....	....	....	....	....	....
1989-90	NY Islanders	NHL	47	19	19	5	2653	150	3	3.39	4	0	2	152	13	0	5.13
1990-91	NY Islanders	NHL	2	1	1	0	120	6	0	3.00	....	....	....	....	....	....	....
	Capital District	AHL	12	3	7	2	734	47	0	3.84	....	....	....	....	....	....	....
1991-92	NY Islanders	NHL	30	11	13	5	1743	93	0	3.20	....	....	....	....	....	....	....
	Capital District	AHL	14	6	5	1	782	39	0	2.99	....	....	....	....	....	....	....
1992-93	NY Islanders	NHL	39	17	15	5	2253	130	0	3.46	3	0	1	77	4	0	3.12
	Capital District	AHL	5	1	3	1	284	18	0	3.80	....	....	....	....	....	....	....
1993-94	Florida	NHL	28	12	8	6	1603	73	1	2.73	....	....	....	....	....	....	....
1994-95	Florida	NHL	15	6	7	2	819	36	2	2.64	....	....	....	....	....	....	....
1995-96	Florida	NHL	34	15	11	3	1786	88	0	2.96	2	0	0	60	6	0	6.00
1996-97	Florida	NHL	30	8	9	9	1680	66	0	2.36	....	....	....	....	....	....	....
1997-98	Florida	NHL	12	2	7	2	640	32	1	3.00	....	....	....	....	....	....	....
	Fort Wayne	IHL	2	1	1	0	119	8	0	4.03	....	....	....	....	....	....	....
	Tampa Bay	NHL	34	7	24	1	1938	102	1	3.16	....	....	....	....	....	....	....
1998-99	Chicago	NHL	27	6	8	6	1403	64	0	2.74	....	....	....	....	....	....	....
	NHL Totals		326	113	134	49	18222	945	8	3.11	9	0	3	289	23	0	4.78

WHL East Second All-Star Team (1986, 1988) • Won Hap Emms Memorial Trophy (Memorial Cup Tournament Top Goaltender) (1987, 1988) • Won Bill Masterton Memorial Trophy (1992)

Traded to **NY Islanders** by **Los Angeles** with Wayne McBean and future considerations (Doug Crossman, May 23, 1989) for Kelly Hrudey, February 22, 1989. Traded to **Quebec** by **NY Islanders** with NY Islanders' 1st round choice (Adam Deadmarsh) in 1993 Entry Draft for Ron Hextall and Quebec's 1st round choice (Todd Bertuzzi) in 1993 Entry Draft, June 20, 1993. Claimed by **Florida** from **Quebec** in Expansion Draft, June 24, 1993. Traded to **Tampa Bay** by **Florida** with Jody Hull for Dino Ciccarelli and Jeff Norton, January 15, 1998. Traded to **Chicago** by **Tampa Bay** with Tampa Bay's 4th round choice (later traded to Montreal - Montreal selected Chris Dyment) in 1999 Entry Draft for Michal Sykora, July 17, 1998. Signed as a free agent by **Carolina**, August 19, 1999

FLAHERTY, Wade (FLAY-uhr-tee) NYI

Goaltender. Catches left. 6', 170 lbs. Born, Terrace, B.C., January 11, 1968.
(Buffalo's 10th choice, 181st overall, in 1988 Entry Draft).

			Regular Season								Playoffs						
Season	Club	Lea	GP	W	L	T	Mins	GA	SO	Avg	GP	W	L	Mins	GA	SO	Avg
1984-85	Kelowna	WHL	1	0	0	0	55	5	0	5.45	....	....	....	....	....	....	....
1985-86	Seattle	WHL	9	1	3	0	271	36	0	7.97	....	....	....	....	....	....	....
	Spokane	WHL	5	0	3	0	161	21	0	7.83	....	....	....	....	....	....	....
1986-87	Victoria	WHL	3	0	2	0	127	16	0	7.56	....	....	....	....	....	....	....
	Nanaimo	BCJHL	15	....	....	....	830	53	0	3.83	....	....	....	....	....	....	....
1987-88	Victoria	WHL	36	20	15	0	2052	135	0	3.95	5	2	3	300	18	0	3.60
1988-89	Victoria	WHL	42	21	19	0	2408	180	4	4.49	....	....	....	....	....	....	....
1989-90	Greensboro	ECHL	27	12	10	0	1308	96	0	4.40	....	....	....	....	....	....	....
1990-91	Kansas City	IHL	*56	16	31	4	2990	224	0	4.49	....	....	....	....	....	....	....
1991-92	San Jose	NHL	3	0	3	0	178	13	0	4.38	....	....	....	....	....	....	....
	Kansas City	IHL	43	26	14	3	2603	140	1	3.23	1	0	0	1	0	0	0.00
1992-93	San Jose	NHL	1	0	1	0	60	5	0	5.00	....	....	....	....	....	....	....
	Kansas City	IHL	*61	*34	19	7	*3642	195	2	3.21	*12	6	6	733	34	*1	2.78
1993-94	Kansas City	IHL	*60	32	19	9	*3564	202	0	3.40	....	....	....	....	....	....	....
1994-95	San Jose	NHL	18	5	6	1	852	44	1	3.10	7	2	3	377	31	0	4.93
1995-96	San Jose	NHL	24	3	12	1	1137	92	0	4.85	....	....	....	....	....	....	....
1996-97	San Jose	NHL	7	2	4	0	359	31	0	5.18	....	....	....	....	....	....	....
	Kentucky	AHL	19	8	6	2	1032	54	1	3.14	3	1	2	200	11	0	3.30
1997-98	NY Islanders	NHL	16	4	4	3	694	23	3	1.99	....	....	....	....	....	....	....
	Utah	IHL	24	16	5	3	1341	40	3	1.79	....	....	....	....	....	....	....
1998-99	NY Islanders	NHL	20	5	11	2	1048	53	0	3.03	....	....	....	....	....	....	....
	Lowell	AHL	5	1	3	1	305	16	0	3.15	....	....	....	....	....	....	....
	NHL Totals		89	19	41	7	4328	261	4	3.62	7	2	3	377	31	0	4.93

WHL West Second All-Star Team (1988) • Playoff MVP - ECHL (1990) • Shared James Norris Memorial Trophy (fewest goals against - IHL) with Arturs Irbe (1992) • IHL Second All-Star Team (1993, 1994)

Signed as a free agent by **San Jose**, September 3, 1991. Signed as a free agent by **NY Islanders**, July 22, 1997.

FORSBERG, Jonas (FOHRZ-buhrg, YOH-nuhs) S.J.

Goaltender. Catches left. 5'10", 150 lbs. Born, Stockholm, Sweden, June 15, 1975.
(San Jose's 12th choice, 210th overall, in 1993 Entry Draft).

			Regular Season								Playoffs						
Season	Club	Lea	GP	W	L	T	Mins	GA	SO	Avg	GP	W	L	Mins	GA	SO	Avg
1992-93	Djurgardens	Swe-Jr.	41	....	....	....	2460	114	0	2.78	....	....	....	....	....	....	....
1993-94	Djurgardens	Sweden	1	1	0	0	60	4	0	4.00	....	....	....	....	....	....	....
	Hammarby IF	Swede-2	STATISTICS NOT AVAILABLE														
1994-95	Djurgardens	Sweden	1	0	1	0	60	6	0	6.00	....	....	....	....	....	....	....
	Arlanda HC	Swede-2	STATISTICS NOT AVAILABLE														
1995-96	Djurgardens IF	Sweden	DID NOT PLAY – INJURED														
	Sollentuna HC	Swede-2	STATISTICS NOT AVAILABLE														
1996-97	IF Mangerland	Norway	16	....	....	....	947	76	0	4.81	....	....	....	....	....	....	....
	Manglerud Star	Norway	STATISTICS NOT AVAILABLE														
1997-98	Sodertalje SK	Sweden	23	....	....	....	1252	60	0	2.88	....	....	....	....	....	....	....
1998-99	AIK Stockholm	Sweden	29	....	....	....	1668	81	2	2.91	....	....	....	....	....	....	....

FOUNTAIN, Mike (FOWN-tehn) OTT.

Goaltender. Catches left. 6'1", 176 lbs. Born, North York, Ont., January 26, 1972.
(Vancouver's 3rd choice, 45th overall, in 1992 Entry Draft).

			Regular Season								Playoffs						
Season	Club	Lea	GP	W	L	T	Mins	GA	SO	Avg	GP	W	L	Mins	GA	SO	Avg
1988-89	Huntsville	OJHL-C	22	....	....	....	1306	82	0	3.77	....	....	....	....	....	....	....
1989-90	Chatham	OJHL-B	21	....	....	....	1249	76	0	3.65	....	....	....	....	....	....	....
1990-91	S.S. Marie	OHL	7	5	2	0	380	19	0	3.00	....	....	....	....	....	....	....
	Oshawa	OHL	30	17	5	1	1483	84	0	3.40	8	1	4	292	26	0	5.34
1991-92	Oshawa	OHL	40	18	13	6	2260	149	1	3.96	7	3	4	429	26	0	3.64
1992-93	Canada	Nat-Team	13	7	5	1	745	37	1	2.98	....	....	....	....	....	....	....
	Hamilton	AHL	12	2	8	0	618	46	0	4.47	....	....	....	....	....	....	....
1993-94	Hamilton	AHL	*70	*34	28	6	*4005	241	*4	3.61	3	0	2	146	12	0	4.92
1994-95	Syracuse	AHL	61	25	29	7	3618	225	2	3.73	....	....	....	....	....	....	....
1995-96	Syracuse	AHL	54	21	27	3	3060	184	1	3.61	15	8	7	915	57	*2	3.74
1996-97	Vancouver	NHL	6	2	2	0	245	14	1	3.43	....	....	....	....	....	....	....
	Syracuse	AHL	25	8	14	2	1462	78	1	3.20	2	0	2	120	12	0	6.02
1997-98	Carolina	NHL	3	0	3	0	163	10	0	3.68	....	....	....	....	....	....	....
	New Haven	AHL	50	25	19	5	2922	139	3	2.85	....	....	....	....	....	....	....
1998-99	New Haven	AHL	51	23	24	3	2989	150	2	3.01	....	....	....	....	....	....	....
	NHL Totals		9	2	5	0	408	24	1	3.53	....	....	....	....	....	....	....

OHL First All-Star Team (1992) • AHL Second All-Star Team (1994)

Signed as a free agent by **Carolina**, August 19, 1997. Signed as a free agent by **Ottawa**, July 30, 1999.

FRANEK, Petr (FRAH-nehk)

Goaltender. Catches left. 5'11", 187 lbs. Born, Most, Czech., April 6, 1975.
(Quebec's 10th choice, 205th overall, in 1993 Entry Draft).

			Regular Season								Playoffs						
Season	Club	Lea	GP	W	L	T	Mins	GA	SO	Avg	GP	W	L	Mins	GA	SO	Avg
1992-93	CHZ Litvinov	Czech.	5	....	....	....	273	15	....	3.29	....	....	....	....	....	....	....
1993-94	CHZ Litvinov	Cze-Rep	11	....	....	....	535	34	....	3.81	2	....	....	61	10	....	9.83
1994-95	CHZ Litvinov	Cze-Rep	12	....	....	....	657	47	....	4.29	1	0	0	16	0	0	0.00
1995-96	CHZ Litvinov	Cze-Rep	36	....	....	....	2096	85	3	2.43	16	....	....	948	47	....	2.97
1996-97	Hershey	AHL	15	4	1	0	457	23	3	3.02	....	....	....	....	....	....	....
	Brantford	ColHL	6	4	1	0	321	14	0	2.61	....	....	....	....	....	....	....
	Quebec	IHL	6	3	3	0	357	18	0	3.02	1	0	1	40	4	0	6.00
1997-98	Hershey	AHL	43	19	14	2	2169	98	2	2.71	1	0	1	60	4	0	4.00
1998-99	Utah	IHL	8	1	6	1	446	26	0	3.50	....	....	....	....	....	....	....
	Las Vegas	IHL	37	17	13	2	1879	107	0	3.42	....	....	....	....	....	....	....

Rights transferred to **Colorado** after **Quebec** franchise relocated, June 21, 1995.

FRIESEN, Terry (FREE-zehn) S.J.

Goaltender. Catches left. 5'11", 190 lbs. Born, Winkler, Man., October 29, 1977.
(San Jose's 3rd choice, 55th overall, in 1996 Entry Draft).

			Regular Season								Playoffs						
Season	Club	Lea	GP	W	L	T	Mins	GA	SO	Avg	GP	W	L	Mins	GA	SO	Avg
1995-96	Swift Current	WHL	42	19	17	3	2504	155	2	3.71	6	2	4	338	21	0	3.73
1996-97	Swift Current	WHL	53	28	19	3	3090	170	1	3.30	10	6	4	592	27	0	2.74
1997-98	Swift Current	WHL	44	26	10	7	2639	124	1	2.82	12	7	5	754	28	1	*2.23
1998-99	Richmond	ECHL	24	9	13	0	1278	76	1	3.57	1	1	0	20	0	0	0.00
	Kentucky	AHL	1	0	0	0	26	2	0	4.66	....	....	....	....	....	....	....

WHL East Second All-Star Team (1996) • WHL East First All-Star Team (1998)

FUHR, Grant (FYOOR) ST.L.

Goaltender. Catches right. 5'10", 201 lbs. Born, Spruce Grove, Alta., September 28, 1962.
(Edmonton's 1st choice, 8th overall, in 1981 Entry Draft).

			Regular Season								Playoffs						
Season	Club	Lea	GP	W	L	T	Mins	GA	SO	Avg	GP	W	L	Mins	GA	SO	Avg
1979-80	Victoria	WHL	43	30	12	0	2488	130	2	3.14	8	5	3	465	22	0	2.84
1980-81	Victoria	WHL	59	48	9	1	3448	160	*4	*2.78	15	12	3	899	45	*1	*3.00
1981-82	**Edmonton**	**NHL**	**48**	**28**	**5**	**14**	**2847**	**157**	**0**	**3.31**	**5**	**2**	**3**	**309**	**26**	**0**	**5.05**
1982-83	**Edmonton**	**NHL**	**32**	**13**	**12**	**5**	**1803**	**129**	**0**	**4.29**	**1**	**0**	**0**	**11**	**0**	**0**	**0.00**
	Moncton	AHL	10	4	5	1	604	40	0	3.98	....	....	....	....	....	....	....
1983-84♦	**Edmonton**	**NHL**	**45**	**30**	**10**	**4**	**2625**	**171**	**1**	**3.91**	**16**	**11**	**4**	**883**	**44**	**1**	**2.99**
1984-85♦	**Edmonton**	**NHL**	**46**	**26**	**8**	**7**	**2559**	**165**	**1**	**3.87**	***18**	***15**	**3**	**1064**	**55**	**0**	**3.10**
1985-86	**Edmonton**	**NHL**	**40**	**29**	**8**	**0**	**2184**	**143**	**0**	**3.93**	**9**	**5**	**4**	**541**	**28**	**0**	**3.11**
1986-87♦	**Edmonton**	**NHL**	**44**	**22**	**13**	**3**	**2388**	**137**	**0**	**3.44**	**19**	**14**	**5**	**1148**	**47**	**0**	**2.46**
1987-88♦	**Edmonton**	**NHL**	***75**	***40**	**24**	**9**	***4304**	**246**	***4**	**3.43**	***19**	***16**	**2**	***1136**	**55**	**0**	**2.90**
1988-89	**Edmonton**	**NHL**	**59**	**23**	**26**	**6**	**3341**	**213**	**1**	**3.83**	**7**	**3**	**4**	**417**	**24**	**1**	**3.45**
1989-90	**Edmonton**	**NHL**	**21**	**9**	**7**	**3**	**1081**	**70**	**1**	**3.89**	....	....	....	....	....	....	....
	Cape Breton	AHL	2	2	0	0	120	6	0	3.01	....	....	....	....	....	....	....
1990-91	**Edmonton**	**NHL**	**13**	**6**	**4**	**3**	**778**	**39**	**1**	**3.01**	**17**	**8**	**7**	**1019**	**51**	**0**	**3.00**
	Cape Breton	AHL	4	2	2	0	240	17	0	4.25	....	....	....	....	....	....	....
1991-92	**Toronto**	**NHL**	**66**	**25**	**33**	**5**	**3774**	**230**	**2**	**3.66**	....	....	....	....	....	....	....
1992-93	**Toronto**	**NHL**	**29**	**13**	**9**	**4**	**1665**	**87**	**1**	**3.14**	....	....	....	....	....	....	....
	Buffalo	**NHL**	**29**	**11**	**15**	**2**	**1694**	**98**	**0**	**3.47**	**8**	**3**	**4**	**474**	**27**	**1**	**3.42**
1993-94	**Buffalo**	**NHL**	**32**	**13**	**12**	**3**	**1726**	**106**	**2**	**3.68**	....	....	....	....	....	....	....
	Rochester	AHL	5	3	0	2	310	10	0	1.94	....	....	....	....	....	....	....
1994-95	**Buffalo**	**NHL**	**3**	**1**	**2**	**0**	**180**	**12**	**0**	**4.00**	....	....	....	....	....	....	....
	Los Angeles	**NHL**	**14**	**1**	**7**	**3**	**698**	**47**	**0**	**4.04**	....	....	....	....	....	....	....
1995-96	**St. Louis**	**NHL**	***79**	**30**	**28**	**16**	**4365**	**209**	**3**	**2.87**	**2**	**1**	**0**	**69**	**1**	**0**	**0.87**
1996-97	**St. Louis**	**NHL**	**73**	**33**	**27**	**11**	**4261**	**193**	**3**	**2.72**	**6**	**2**	**4**	**357**	**13**	**2**	**2.18**
1997-98	**St. Louis**	**NHL**	**58**	**29**	**21**	**6**	**3274**	**138**	**3**	**2.53**	**10**	**6**	**4**	**616**	**28**	**0**	**2.73**
1998-99	**St. Louis**	**NHL**	**39**	**16**	**11**	**8**	**2193**	**89**	**2**	**2.44**	**13**	**6**	**6**	**790**	**31**	**1**	**2.35**
	NHL Totals		**845**	**398**	**282**	**112**	**47740**	**2679**	**25**	**3.37**	**150**	**92**	**50**	**8834**	**430**	**6**	**2.92**

WHL First All-Star Team (1980, 1981) • NHL Second All-Star Team (1982) • NHL First All-Star Team (1988) • Won Vezina Trophy (1988) • Shared William M. Jennings Trophy with Dominik Hasek (1994)

Played in NHL All-Star Game (1982, 1984, 1985, 1986, 1988, 1989)

• Statistics (Mins., GA) for suspended game on May 24, 1988 are included in playoff record.

Traded to **Toronto** by **Edmonton** with Glenn Anderson and Craig Berube for Vincent Damphousse, Peter Ing, Scott Thornton, Luke Richardson, future considerations and cash, September 19, 1991. Traded to **Buffalo** by **Toronto** with Toronto's 5th round choice (Kevin Popp) in 1995 Entry Draft for Dave Andreychuk, Daren Puppa and Buffalo's 1st round choice (Kenny Jonsson) in 1993 Entry Draft, February 2, 1993. Traded to **Los Angeles** by **Buffalo** with Philippe Boucher and Denis Tsygurov for Alexei Zhitnik, Robb Stauber, Charlie Huddy and Los Angeles' 5th round choice (Marian Menhart) in 1995 Entry Draft, February 14, 1995. Signed as a free agent by **St. Louis**, July 14, 1995.

GARNER, Tyrone CGY.

Goaltender. Catches left. 6'1", 170 lbs. Born, Stoney Creek, Ont., July 27, 1978.
(NY Islanders' 4th choice, 83rd overall, in 1996 Entry Draft).

			Regular Season								Playoffs						
Season	Club	Lea	GP	W	L	T	Mins	GA	SO	Avg	GP	W	L	Mins	GA	SO	Avg
1995-96	Oshawa	OHL	32	11	15	4	1697	112	0	3.96	....	....	....	....	....	....	....
1996-97	Oshawa	OHL	9	6	1	0	434	20	0	2.76	3	1	0	88	6	0	4.09
1997-98	Oshawa	OHL	54	23	17	8	2946	162	1	3.30	7	3	4	450	25	0	3.33
1998-99	Oshawa	OHL	44	24	15	3	2496	124	4	2.98	15	9	6	901	57	0	3.80
	Calgary	**NHL**	**3**	**0**	**2**	**0**	**139**	**12**	**0**	**5.18**	....	....	....	....	....	....	....
	NHL Totals		**3**	**0**	**2**	**0**	**139**	**12**	**0**	**5.18**	....	....	....	....	....	....	....

OHL Second All-Star Team (1999)

Traded to **Calgary** by **NY Islanders** with Marty McInnis and Calgary's sixth round choice (previously acquired, Calgary selected Ilja Demidov) in 1997 Entry Draft for Robert Reichel, March 18, 1997.

GARON, Mathieu (gah-ROHN) MTL.

Goaltender. Catches right. 6'2", 187 lbs. Born, Chandler, Que., January 9, 1978.
(Montreal's 2nd choice, 44th overall, in 1996 Entry Draft).

			Regular Season								Playoffs						
Season	Club	Lea	GP	W	L	T	Mins	GA	SO	Avg	GP	W	L	Mins	GA	SO	Avg
1995-96	Victoriaville	QMJHL	51	18	27	0	2709	189	1	4.19	12	7	4	676	38	1	3.39
1996-97	Victoriaville	QMJHL	53	29	18	3	3032	150	*6	2.97	6	2	4	330	23	0	4.18
1997-98	Victoriaville	QMJHL	47	27	18	2	2802	125	5	2.68	6	2	4	345	22	0	3.82
1998-99	Fredericton	AHL	40	14	22	2	2222	114	3	3.08	6	1	1	208	12	0	3.47

QMJHL First All-Star Team (1998) • Canadian Major Junior First All-Star Team (1998) • Canadian Major Junior Goaltender of the Year (1998)

GAUTHIER, Sean (GOH-tyay, SHAWN)

Goaltender. Catches left. 5'11", 205 lbs. Born, Sudbury, Ont., March 28, 1971.
(Winnipeg's 7th choice, 181st overall, in 1991 Entry Draft).

			Regular Season								Playoffs						
Season	Club	Lea	GP	W	L	T	Mins	GA	SO	Avg	GP	W	L	Mins	GA	SO	Avg
1987-88	Oakville	OJHL-B	28	....	....	....	1491	110	2	4.43	....	....	....	....	....	....	....
1988-89	Kingston	OHL	37	7	18	1	1528	141	0	5.54	....	....	....	....	....	....	....
1989-90	Kingston	OHL	32	17	9	0	1602	101	0	3.78	2	0	1	76	6	0	4.74
1990-91	Kingston	OHL	59	16	36	3	3200	282	0	5.29	....	....	....	....	....	....	....
1991-92	Moncton	AHL	25	8	10	5	1415	88	1	3.73	2	0	0	26	2	0	4.62
	Fort Wayne	IHL	18	10	4	2	978	59	1	3.62	2	0	0	48	7	0	8.74
1992-93	Moncton	AHL	38	10	16	9	2196	145	0	3.96	2	0	1	75	6	0	4.80
1993-94	Moncton	AHL	13	3	5	1	616	41	0	3.99	....	....	....	....	....	....	....
	Fort Wayne	IHL	22	9	9	3	1139	66	0	3.48	....	....	....	....	....	....	....
1994-95	Fort Wayne	IHL	5	0	2	1	217	15	0	4.13	....	....	....	....	....	....	....
	Canada	Nat-Team						STATISTICS NOT AVAILABLE									
1995-96	South Carolina	ECHL	49	31	11	7	2891	149	0	3.09	8	5	3	478	24	0	3.01
	St. John's	AHL	5	1	1	0	173	9	0	3.12	....	....	....	....	....	....	....
1996-97	Pensacola	ECHL	46	23	21	1	2692	168	1	3.74	12	8	4	749	44	1	3.52
1997-98	Pensacola	ECHL	54	29	17	7	3213	194	0	3.62	*19	12	7	1180	58	1	2.95
1998-99	**San Jose**	**NHL**	**1**	**0**	**0**	**0**	**3**	**0**	**0**	**0.00**	....	....	....	....	....	....	....
	Kentucky	AHL	40	18	15	6	2376	99	1	2.50	4	0	1	130	8	0	3.68
	NHL Totals		**1**	**0**	**0**	**0**	**3**	**0**	**0**	**0.00**	....	....	....	....	....	....	....

ECHL Second All-Star Team (1996, 1998)

Signed as a free agent by **San Jose**, July 23, 1998.

GIGUERE, Jean-Sebastien (ZHEE-gair) CGY.

Goaltender. Catches left. 6', 175 lbs. Born, Montreal, Que., May 16, 1977.
(Hartford's 1st choice, 13th overall, in 1995 Entry Draft).

			Regular Season								Playoffs						
Season	Club	Lea	GP	W	L	T	Mins	GA	SO	Avg	GP	W	L	Mins	GA	SO	Avg
1992-93	Laval	QAAA	25	12	11	2	1498	76	0	3.02	....	....	....	....	....	....	....
1993-94	Verdun	QMJHL	25	13	5	2	1234	66	1	3.21	....	....	....	....	....	....	....
1994-95	Halifax	QMJHL	47	14	27	5	2755	181	2	3.94	7	3	4	417	17	1	*2.45
1995-96	Halifax	QMJHL	55	26	23	2	3230	185	1	3.44	6	1	5	354	24	0	4.07
1996-97	**Hartford**	**NHL**	**8**	**1**	**4**	**0**	**394**	**24**	**0**	**3.65**	....	....	....	....	....	....	....
	Halifax	QMJHL	50	28	19	3	3014	170	2	3.38	16	9	7	954	58	0	3.65
1997-98	Saint John	AHL	31	16	10	3	1758	72	2	2.46	10	5	3	536	27	0	3.02
1998-99	**Calgary**	**NHL**	**15**	**6**	**7**	**1**	**860**	**46**	**0**	**3.21**	....	....	....	....	....	....	....
	Saint John	AHL	39	18	16	3	2145	123	3	3.44	7	3	2	304	21	0	4.14
	NHL Totals		**23**	**7**	**11**	**1**	**1254**	**70**	**0**	**3.35**	....	....	....	....	....	....	....

QMJHL Second All-Star Team (1997) • Shared Harry "Hap" Holmes Memorial Trophy (fewest goals against - AHL) with Tyler Moss (1998)

Transferred to **Carolina** after **Hartford** franchise relocated, June 25, 1997. Traded to **Calgary** by **Carolina** with Andrew Cassels for Gary Roberts and Trevor Kidd, August 25, 1997.

GORDON, Ian

Goaltender. Catches left. 5'10", 160 lbs. Born, Yorkton, Sask., May 15, 1975.

			Regular Season								Playoffs						
Season	Club	Lea	GP	W	L	T	Mins	GA	SO	Avg	GP	W	L	Mins	GA	SO	Avg
1992-93	Swift Current	WHL	10	1	6	0	365	31	0	5.10	2	0	0	53	3	0	3.40
1993-94	Swift Current	WHL	65	29	27	4	3657	204	6	3.35	7	3	4	420	21	1	3.00
1994-95	Swift Current	WHL	17	6	9	1	994	62	1	3.74	....	....	....	....	....	....	....
	Saskatoon	WHL	41	24	9	7	2476	129	1	3.13	10	4	6	633	29	1	2.75
1995-96	Saint John	AHL	19	2	12	0	768	56	0	4.37	....	....	....	....	....	....	....
1996-97	Saint John	AHL	21	5	9	1	988	50	0	3.03	....	....	....	....	....	....	....
	Grand Rapids	IHL	5	2	2	0	257	15	0	3.50	1	0	0	0	0	0	0.00
1997-98	Grand Rapids	IHL	49	23	16	4	2573	115	1	2.68	2	0	2	118	7	0	3.54
1998-99	Grand Rapids	IHL	41	16	19	3	2149	123	2	3.43	....	....	....	....	....	....	....

Signed as a free agent by **Calgary**, October 6, 1995.

GRAHAME, John BOS.

Goaltender. Catches left. 6'2", 210 lbs. Born, Denver, CO, August 31, 1975.
(Boston's 7th choice, 229th overall, in 1994 Entry Draft).

			Regular Season								Playoffs						
Season	Club	Lea	GP	W	L	T	Mins	GA	SO	Avg	GP	W	L	Mins	GA	SO	Avg
1993-94	Sioux City	USHL	20	....	....	....	1200	73	0	3.70	....	....	....	....	....	....	....
1994-95	Lake Superior	CCHA	28	16	7	3	1616	75	2	2.79	....	....	....	....	....	....	....
1995-96	Lake Superior	CCHA	29	21	4	2	1558	66	2	2.54	....	....	....	....	....	....	....
1996-97	Lake Superior	CCHA	37	19	13	4	2197	134	3	3.66	....	....	....	....	....	....	....
1997-98	Providence	AHL	55	15	31	4	3053	164	3	3.22	....	....	....	....	....	....	....
1998-99	Providence	AHL	48	*37	9	1	2771	134	3	2.90	19	*15	4	*1209	48	1	2.38

HACKETT, Jeff MTL.

Goaltender. Catches left. 6'1", 195 lbs. Born, London, Ont., June 1, 1968.
(NY Islanders' 2nd choice, 34th overall, in 1987 Entry Draft).

			Regular Season								Playoffs						
Season	Club	Lea	GP	W	L	T	Mins	GA	SO	Avg	GP	W	L	Mins	GA	SO	Avg
1984-85	London	OJHL-B	18	....	....	....	1078	73	1	4.19	....	....	....	....	....	....	....
1985-86	London	OJHL-B	19	....	....	....	1150	66	0	3.43	....	....	....	....	....	....	....
1986-87	Oshawa	OHL	31	18	9	2	1672	85	2	3.05	15	8	7	895	40	0	2.68
1987-88	Oshawa	OHL	53	30	21	2	3165	205	0	3.89	7	3	4	438	31	0	4.25
1988-89	**NY Islanders**	**NHL**	**13**	**4**	**7**	**0**	**662**	**39**	**0**	**3.53**	....	....	....	....	....	....	....
	Springfield	AHL	29	12	14	2	1677	116	0	4.15	....	....	....	....	....	....	....
1989-90	Springfield	AHL	54	24	25	3	3045	187	1	3.68	*17	*10	5	934	60	0	3.85
1990-91	**NY Islanders**	**NHL**	**30**	**5**	**18**	**1**	**1508**	**91**	**0**	**3.62**	....	....	....	....	....	....	....
1991-92	**San Jose**	**NHL**	**42**	**11**	**27**	**1**	**2314**	**148**	**0**	**3.84**	....	....	....	....	....	....	....
1992-93	**San Jose**	**NHL**	**36**	**2**	**30**	**1**	**2000**	**176**	**0**	**5.28**	....	....	....	....	....	....	....
1993-94	**Chicago**	**NHL**	**22**	**2**	**12**	**3**	**1084**	**62**	**0**	**3.43**	....	....	....	....	....	....	....
1994-95	**Chicago**	**NHL**	**7**	**1**	**3**	**2**	**328**	**13**	**0**	**2.38**	**2**	**0**	**0**	**26**	**1**	**0**	**2.31**
1995-96	**Chicago**	**NHL**	**35**	**18**	**11**	**4**	**2000**	**80**	**4**	**2.40**	**1**	**0**	**1**	**60**	**5**	**0**	**5.00**
1996-97	**Chicago**	**NHL**	**41**	**19**	**18**	**4**	**2473**	**89**	**2**	**2.16**	**6**	**2**	**4**	**345**	**25**	**0**	**4.35**
1997-98	**Chicago**	**NHL**	**58**	**21**	**25**	**11**	**3441**	**126**	**8**	**2.20**	....	....	....	....	....	....	....
1998-99	**Chicago**	**NHL**	**10**	**2**	**6**	**1**	**524**	**33**	**0**	**3.78**	....	....	....	....	....	....	....
	Montreal	**NHL**	**53**	**24**	**20**	**9**	**3091**	**117**	**5**	**2.27**	....	....	....	....	....	....	....
	NHL Totals		**347**	**109**	**177**	**37**	**19425**	**974**	**19**	**3.01**	**9**	**2**	**5**	**431**	**31**	**0**	**4.32**

Won Jack A. Butterfield Trophy (Playoff MVP - AHL) (1990)

Claimed by **San Jose** from **NY Islanders** in Expansion Draft, May 30, 1991. Traded to **Chicago** by **San Jose** for Chicago's 3rd round choice (Alexei Yegorov) in 1994 Entry Draft, July 13, 1993. Traded to **Montreal** by **Chicago** with Eric Weinrich, Alain Nasreddine and Tampa Bay's 4th round choice (previously acquired, Montreal selected Chris Dyment) in 1999 Entry Draft for Jocelyn Thibault, Dave Manson and Brad Brown, November 16, 1998.

HASEK, Dominik (HAH-shihk) BUF.

Goaltender. Catches left. 5'11", 168 lbs. Born, Pardubice, Czech., January 29, 1965.
(Chicago's 11th choice, 207th overall, in 1983 Entry Draft).

			Regular Season								Playoffs						
Season	Club	Lea	GP	W	L	T	Mins	GA	SO	Avg	GP	W	L	Mins	GA	SO	Avg
1981-82	Pardubice	Czech.	12	....	....	....	661	34	....	3.09	....	....	....	....	....	....	....
1982-83	Pardubice	Czech.	42	....	....	....	2358	105	....	2.67	....	....	....	....	....	....	....
1983-84	Pardubice	Czech.	40	....	....	....	2304	108	....	2.81	....	....	....	....	....	....	....
1984-85	Pardubice	Czech.	42	....	....	....	2419	131	....	3.25	....	....	....	....	....	....	....
1985-86	Pardubice	Czech.	45	....	....	....	2689	138	....	3.08	....	....	....	....	....	....	....
1986-87	Pardubice	Czech.	43	....	....	....	2515	103	....	2.46	....	....	....	....	....	....	....
1987-88	Pardubice	Czech.	31	....	....	....	1862	93	....	3.00	....	....	....	....	....	....	....
	Czechoslovakia	Olympics	5	....	....	....	217	18	....	4.98	....	....	....	....	....	....	....
1988-89	Pardubice	Czech.	42	....	....	....	2507	114	....	2.73	....	....	....	....	....	....	....
1989-90	Dukla Jihlava	Czech.	40	....	....	....	2251	80	....	2.13	....	....	....	....	....	....	....
1990-91	**Chicago**	**NHL**	**5**	**3**	**0**	**1**	**195**	**8**	**0**	**2.46**	**3**	**0**	**0**	**69**	**3**	**0**	**2.61**
	Indianapolis	IHL	33	20	11	1	1903	80	*5	*2.52	1	1	0	60	3	0	3.00
1991-92	**Chicago**	**NHL**	**20**	**10**	**4**	**1**	**1014**	**44**	**1**	**2.60**	**3**	**0**	**2**	**158**	**8**	**0**	**3.04**
	Indianapolis	IHL	20	7	10	3	1162	69	1	3.56	....	....	....	....	....	....	....
1992-93	**Buffalo**	**NHL**	**28**	**11**	**10**	**4**	**1429**	**75**	**0**	**3.15**	**1**	**1**	**0**	**45**	**1**	**0**	**1.33**
1993-94	**Buffalo**	**NHL**	**58**	**30**	**20**	**6**	**3358**	**109**	***7**	***1.95**	**7**	**3**	**4**	**484**	**13**	**2**	***1.61**
1994-95	Pardubice	Cze-Rep	2	....	....	....	124	6	0	2.90	....	....	....	....	....	....	....
	Buffalo	**NHL**	**41**	**19**	**14**	**7**	**2416**	**85**	***5**	***2.11**	**5**	**1**	**4**	**309**	**18**	**0**	**3.50**
1995-96	**Buffalo**	**NHL**	**59**	**22**	**30**	**6**	**3417**	**161**	**2**	**2.83**	....	....	....	....	....	....	....
1996-97	**Buffalo**	**NHL**	**67**	**37**	**20**	**10**	**4037**	**153**	**5**	**2.27**	**3**	**1**	**1**	**153**	**5**	**0**	**1.96**
1997-98	**Buffalo**	**NHL**	***72**	**33**	**23**	**13**	***4220**	**147**	***13**	**2.09**	**15**	**10**	**5**	**948**	**32**	**1**	**2.03**
	Czech Republic	Olympics	6	*5	1	0	*369	6	*2	*0.97	....	....	....	....	....	....	....
1998-99	**Buffalo**	**NHL**	**64**	**30**	**18**	**14**	**3817**	**119**	**9**	**1.87**	**19**	**13**	**6**	**1217**	**36**	**2**	**1.77**
	NHL Totals		**414**	**195**	**139**	**62**	**23903**	**901**	**42**	**2.26**	**56**	**29**	**22**	**3383**	**116**	**5**	**2.06**

Czechoslovakian Goaltender-of-the-Year (1986, 1987, 1988, 1989, 1990) • Czechoslovakian Player-of-the-Year (1987, 1989, 1990) • Czechoslovakian First All-Star Team (1988, 1989, 1990) • IHL First All-Star Team (1991) • NHL/Upper Deck All-Rookie Team (1992) • NHL First All-Star Team (1994, 1995, 1997, 1998, 1999) • Shared William M. Jennings Trophy with Grant Fuhr (1994) • Won Vezina Trophy (1994, 1995, 1997, 1998, 1999) • Won Lester B. Pearson Award (1997, 1998) • Won Hart Trophy (1997, 1998)

Played in NHL All-Star Game (1996, 1997, 1998, 1999)

Traded to **Buffalo** by **Chicago** for Stephane Beauregard and Buffalo's 4th round choice (Eric Daze) in 1993 Entry Draft, August 7, 1992.

HAUSER, Adam EDM.

Goaltender. Catches left. 6'2", 192 lbs. Born, Bovey, MN, May 27, 1980.
(Edmonton's 4th choice, 81st overall, in 1999 Entry Draft).

			Regular Season								Playoffs						
Season	Club	Lea	GP	W	L	T	Mins	GA	SO	Avg	GP	W	L	Mins	GA	SO	Avg
1997-98	Team USA	Under-18	38	19	10	7	2110	94	4	2.67	....	....	....	....	....	....	....
1998-99	U. of Minnesota	WCHA	*40	14	18	8	*2350	136	3	3.47	....	....	....	....	....	....	....

HEALY, Glenn TOR.

Goaltender. Catches left. 5'9", 192 lbs. Born, Pickering, Ont., August 23, 1962.

			Regular Season								Playoffs						
Season	Club	Lea	GP	W	L	T	Mins	GA	SO	Avg	GP	W	L	Mins	GA	SO	Avg
1979-80	Pickering	OJHL-B	31	....	....	....	1848	123	0	3.99	....	....	....	....	....	....	....
1980-81	Pickering	OJHL-B	35	....	....	....	2085	120	0	3.46	....	....	....	....	....	....	....
1981-82	Western Michigan	CCHA	27	7	19	1	1569	116	0	4.44	....	....	....	....	....	....	....
1982-83	Western Michigan	CCHA	30	8	19	2	1732	116	0	4.01	....	....	....	....	....	....	....
1983-84	Western Michigan	CCHA	38	19	16	3	2241	146	0	3.90	....	....	....	....	....	....	....
1984-85	Western Michigan	CCHA	37	21	14	2	2171	118	0	3.26	....	....	....	....	....	....	....
1985-86	**Los Angeles**	**NHL**	**1**	**0**	**0**	**0**	**51**	**6**	**0**	**7.06**	....	....	....	....	....	....	....
	Toledo	IHL	7	....	....	....	402	28	0	4.18	....	....	....	....	....	....	....
	New Haven	AHL	43	21	15	4	2410	160	0	3.98	2	0	2	49	11	0	5.55
1986-87	New Haven	AHL	47	21	15	0	2828	173	1	3.67	7	3	4	427	19	0	2.67
1987-88	**Los Angeles**	**NHL**	**34**	**12**	**18**	**1**	**1869**	**135**	**1**	**4.33**	**4**	**1**	**3**	**240**	**20**	**0**	**5.00**
1988-89	**Los Angeles**	**NHL**	**48**	**25**	**19**	**2**	**2699**	**192**	**0**	**4.27**	**3**	**0**	**1**	**97**	**6**	**0**	**3.71**
1989-90	**NY Islanders**	**NHL**	**39**	**12**	**19**	**6**	**2197**	**128**	**2**	**3.50**	**4**	**1**	**2**	**166**	**9**	**0**	**3.25**
1990-91	**NY Islanders**	**NHL**	**53**	**18**	**24**	**9**	**2999**	**166**	**0**	**3.32**	....	....	....	....	....	....	....
1991-92	**NY Islanders**	**NHL**	**37**	**14**	**16**	**4**	**1960**	**124**	**1**	**3.80**	....	....	....	....	....	....	....
1992-93	**NY Islanders**	**NHL**	**47**	**22**	**20**	**2**	**2655**	**146**	**1**	**3.30**	**18**	**9**	**8**	**1109**	**59**	**0**	**3.19**
1993-94♦	**NY Rangers**	**NHL**	**29**	**10**	**12**	**2**	**1368**	**69**	**2**	**3.03**	**2**	**0**	**0**	**68**	**1**	**0**	**0.88**
1994-95	**NY Rangers**	**NHL**	**17**	**8**	**6**	**1**	**888**	**35**	**1**	**2.36**	**5**	**2**	**1**	**230**	**13**	**0**	**3.39**
1995-96	**NY Rangers**	**NHL**	**44**	**17**	**14**	**11**	**2564**	**124**	**2**	**2.90**	....	....	....	....	....	....	....
1996-97	**NY Rangers**	**NHL**	**23**	**5**	**12**	**4**	**1357**	**59**	**1**	**2.61**	....	....	....	....	....	....	....
1997-98	**Toronto**	**NHL**	**21**	**4**	**10**	**2**	**1068**	**53**	**0**	**2.98**	....	....	....	....	....	....	....
1998-99	**Toronto**	**NHL**	**9**	**6**	**3**	**0**	**546**	**27**	**0**	**2.97**	**1**	**0**	**0**	**20**	**0**	**0**	**0.00**
	Chicago	IHL	10	6	3	1	597	33	0	3.32	....	....	....	....	....	....	....
	NHL Totals		**402**	**153**	**173**	**44**	**22221**	**1264**	**11**	**3.41**	**37**	**13**	**15**	**1930**	**108**	**0**	**3.36**

CCHA Second All-Star Team (1985) • NCAA West Second All-American Team (1985)

Signed as a free agent by **Los Angeles**, June 13, 1985. Signed as a free agent by **NY Islanders**, August 16, 1989. Claimed by **Anaheim** from **NY Islanders** in Expansion Draft, June 24, 1993. Claimed by **Tampa Bay** from **Anaheim** in Phase II of Expansion Draft, June 25, 1993. Traded to **NY Rangers** by **Tampa Bay** for Tampa Bay's 3rd round choice (previously acquired, Tampa Bay selected Allan Egeland) in 1993 Entry Draft, June 25, 1993. Signed as a free agent by **Toronto**, August 8, 1997.

HEBERT, Guy (ay-BAIR, GEE) ANA.

Goaltender. Catches left. 5'11", 185 lbs. Born, Troy, NY, January 7, 1967.
(St. Louis' 8th choice, 159th overall, in 1987 Entry Draft).

			Regular Season								Playoffs						
Season	Club	Lea	GP	W	L	T	Mins	GA	SO	Avg	GP	W	L	Mins	GA	SO	Avg
1985-86	Hamilton College	NCAA	18	4	12	2	1011	69	2	4.09	....	....	....	....	....	....	....
1986-87	Hamilton College	NCAA	18	12	5	0	1070	40	3	2.19	2	1	1	134	6	0	2.69
1987-88	Hamilton College	NCAA	9	5	3	0	510	22	1	2.58	1	0	1	60	3	0	3.00
1988-89	Hamilton College	NCAA	25	18	7	0	1454	62	2	2.56	2	1	1	126	4	0	1.90
1989-90	Peoria	IHL	30	7	13	7	1706	124	1	4.36	2	0	1	76	5	0	3.95
1990-91	Peoria	IHL	36	24	10	1	2093	100	2	2.87	8	3	4	458	32	0	4.19
1991-92	**St. Louis**	**NHL**	**13**	**5**	**5**	**1**	**738**	**36**	**0**	**2.93**	....	....	....	....	....	....	....
	Peoria	IHL	29	20	9	0	1731	98	0	3.40	4	3	1	239	9	0	2.26
1992-93	**St. Louis**	**NHL**	**24**	**8**	**8**	**2**	**1210**	**74**	**1**	**3.67**	**1**	**0**	**0**	**2**	**0**	**0**	**0.00**
1993-94	**Anaheim**	**NHL**	**52**	**20**	**27**	**3**	**2991**	**141**	**2**	**2.83**	....	....	....	....	....	....	....
1994-95	**Anaheim**	**NHL**	**39**	**12**	**20**	**4**	**2092**	**109**	**2**	**3.13**	....	....	....	....	....	....	....
1995-96	**Anaheim**	**NHL**	**59**	**28**	**23**	**5**	**3326**	**157**	**4**	**2.83**	....	....	....	....	....	....	....
1996-97	**Anaheim**	**NHL**	**67**	**29**	**25**	**12**	**3863**	**172**	**4**	**2.67**	**9**	**4**	**4**	**534**	**18**	**1**	**2.02**
1997-98	**Anaheim**	**NHL**	**46**	**13**	**24**	**6**	**2660**	**130**	**3**	**2.93**	....	....	....	....	....	....	....
1998-99	**Anaheim**	**NHL**	**69**	**31**	**29**	**9**	**4083**	**165**	**6**	**2.42**	**4**	**0**	**3**	**208**	**15**	**0**	**4.33**
	NHL Totals		**369**	**146**	**161**	**42**	**20963**	**984**	**22**	**2.82**	**14**	**4**	**7**	**744**	**33**	**1**	**2.66**

IHL Second All-Star Team (1991) • Shared James Norris Memorial Trophy (fewest goals against - IHL) with Pat Jablonski (1991)

Played in NHL All-Star Game (1997)

Claimed by **Anaheim** from **St. Louis** in Expansion Draft, June 24, 1993.

HEDBERG, Johan (HEHD-buhrg) S.J.

Goaltender. Catches left. 5'11", 180 lbs. Born, Leksand, Sweden, May 5, 1973.
(Philadelphia's 8th choice, 218th overall, in 1994 Entry Draft).

			Regular Season								Playoffs						
Season	Club	Lea	GP	W	L	T	Mins	GA	SO	Avg	GP	W	L	Mins	GA	SO	Avg
1992-93	Leksands IF	Sweden	10	....	....	....	600	24	....	2.40	....	....	....	....	....	....	....
1993-94	Leksands IF	Sweden	17	....	....	....	1020	48	....	2.81	....	....	....	....	....	....	....
1994-95	Leksands IF	Sweden	17	....	....	....	986	58	....	3.53	....	....	....	....	....	....	....
1995-96	Leksands IF	Sweden	34	....	....	....	2013	95	....	2.83	4	....	....	240	13	....	3.25
1996-97	Leksands IF	Sweden	38	....	....	....	2260	95	3	2.52	8	....	....	581	18	1	1.86
1997-98	Baton Rouge	ECHL	2	1	1	0	100	7	0	4.20	....	....	....	....	....	....	....
	Detroit	IHL	16	7	2	2	726	32	1	2.64	....	....	....	....	....	....	....
	Sweden	Olympics								DID NOT PLAY – SPARE GOALTENDER							
	Manitoba	IHL	14	8	4	1	745	32	1	2.58	2	0	2	105	6	0	3.40
1998-99	Leksands IF	Sweden	*48	....	....	....	*2940	140	0	2.86	4	....	....	255	15	0	3.53

Rights traded to **San Jose** by **Philadelphia** for San Jose's 7th round choice (Pavel Kasparik) in 1999 Entry Draft, August 6, 1998.

HEFFLER, Eric EDM.

Goaltender. Catches left. 6'3", 190 lbs. Born, Williamsville, NY, February 29, 1976.

			Regular Season								Playoffs						
Season	Club	Lea	GP	W	L	T	Mins	GA	SO	Avg	GP	W	L	Mins	GA	SO	Avg
1995-96	St. Lawrence	ECAC	4	0	0	0	55	3	0	3.25	....	....	....	....	....	....	....
1996-97	St. Lawrence	ECAC	12	2	3	1	458	31	0	4.06	....	....	....	....	....	....	....
1997-98	St. Lawrence	ECAC	26	8	14	0	1529	73	2	2.90	....	....	....	....	....	....	....
1998-99	St. Lawrence	ECAC	*37	22	12	3	*2206	88	3	2.39	....	....	....	....	....	....	....
	Hamilton	AHL	2	1	1	0	119	5	0	2.52	....	....	....	....	....	....	....

ECAC First All-Star Team (1999) • NCAA East First All-American Team (1999)

Signed as a free agent by **Edmonton**, April 30, 1999.

HEIL, Jeff NYR

Goaltender. Catches left. 6'1", 190 lbs. Born, Bloomington, MN, September 17, 1975.
(NY Rangers' 7th choice, 169th overall, in 1995 Entry Draft).

			Regular Season								Playoffs						
Season	Club	Lea	GP	W	L	T	Mins	GA	SO	Avg	GP	W	L	Mins	GA	SO	Avg
1994-95	Wisc-Fall River	NCHA	25	13	7	3	1399	64	2	2.74	....	....	....	....	....	....	....
1995-96	Wisc-Fall River	NCHA	16	13	2	0	943	28	2	1.78	....	....	....	....	....	....	....
1996-97	Wisc-Fall River	NCHA	23	15	8	0	1335	52	4	2.34	....	....	....	....	....	....	....
1997-98	Charlotte	ECHL	22	12	5	4	1240	69	2	3.34	....	....	....	....	....	....	....
	Hartford	AHL	1	0	0	1	35	0	0	0.00	....	....	....	....	....	....	....
1998-99	Hartford	AHL	11	2	3	0	367	22	0	3.60	....	....	....	....	....	....	....
	Charlotte	ECHL	22	7	11	3	1236	77	0	3.74	....	....	....	....	....	....	....

HENRY, Frederic N.J.

Goaltender. Catches left. 5'11", 180 lbs. Born, Cap-Rouge, Que., August 9, 1977.
(New Jersey's 10th choice, 200th overall, in 1995 Entry Draft).

			Regular Season								Playoffs						
Season	Club	Lea	GP	W	L	T	Mins	GA	SO	Avg	GP	W	L	Mins	GA	SO	Avg
1994-95	Granby	QMJHL	15	8	5	0	866	47	0	3.26	6	1	2	232	21	0	5.43
1995-96	Granby	QMJHL	28	19	5	2	1530	69	*3	2.71	12	9	2	610	21	2	*2.08
1996-97	Granby	QMJHL	57	33	16	6	3330	162	4	2.92	5	1	4	251	17	0	4.06
	Albany	AHL	1	1	0	0	60	3	0	3.00	....	....	....	....	....	....	....
1997-98	Raleigh	ECHL	34	13	17	2	1889	119	2	3.78	....	....	....	....	....	....	....
	Albany	AHL	4	2	0	1	199	8	0	2.41	....	....	....	....	....	....	....
1998-99	Albany	AHL	35	17	10	3	1690	84	1	2.98	....	....	....	....	....	....	....

HEXTALL, Ron

Goaltender. Catches left. 6'3", 192 lbs. Born, Brandon, Man., May 3, 1964.
(Philadelphia's 6th choice, 119th overall, in 1982 Entry Draft).

			Regular Season								Playoffs						
Season	Club	Lea	GP	W	L	T	Mins	GA	SO	Avg	GP	W	L	Mins	GA	SO	Avg
1980-81	Melville	SJHL	42	....	....	....	2127	254	0	7.17	....	....	....	....	....	....	....
1981-82	Brandon	WHL	30	12	11	0	1398	133	0	5.71	3	0	2	103	16	0	9.32
1982-83	Brandon	WHL	44	13	30	0	2589	249	0	5.77	....	....	....	....	....	....	....
1983-84	Brandon	WHL	46	29	13	2	2670	190	0	4.27	10	5	5	592	37	0	3.75
1984-85	Hershey	AHL	11	4	6	0	555	34	0	3.68	....	....	....	....	....	....	....
	Kalamazoo	IHL	19	6	11	1	1103	80	0	4.35	....	....	....	....	....	....	....
1985-86	Hershey	AHL	*53	30	19	2	*3061	174	*5	3.41	13	5	7	780	42	*1	3.23
1986-87	**Philadelphia**	**NHL**	***66**	**37**	**21**	**6**	***3799**	**190**	**1**	**3.00**	***26**	**15**	**11**	***1540**	**71**	***2**	**2.77**
1987-88	**Philadelphia**	**NHL**	**62**	**30**	**22**	**7**	**3561**	**208**	**0**	**3.50**	**7**	**2**	**4**	**379**	**30**	**0**	**4.75**
1988-89	**Philadelphia**	**NHL**	**64**	**30**	**28**	**6**	**3756**	**202**	**0**	**3.23**	**15**	**8**	**7**	**886**	**49**	**0**	**3.32**
1989-90	**Philadelphia**	**NHL**	**8**	**4**	**2**	**1**	**419**	**29**	**0**	**4.15**	....	....	....	....	....	....	....
	Hershey	AHL	1	1	0	0	49	3	0	3.67	....	....	....	....	....	....	....
1990-91	**Philadelphia**	**NHL**	**36**	**13**	**16**	**5**	**2035**	**106**	**0**	**3.13**	....	....	....	....	....	....	....
1991-92	**Philadelphia**	**NHL**	**45**	**16**	**21**	**6**	**2668**	**151**	**3**	**3.40**	....	....	....	....	....	....	....
1992-93	**Quebec**	**NHL**	**54**	**29**	**16**	**5**	**2988**	**172**	**0**	**3.45**	**6**	**2**	**4**	**372**	**18**	**0**	**2.90**
1993-94	**NY Islanders**	**NHL**	**65**	**27**	**26**	**6**	**3581**	**184**	**5**	**3.08**	**3**	**0**	**3**	**158**	**16**	**0**	**6.08**
1994-95	**Philadelphia**	**NHL**	**31**	**17**	**9**	**4**	**1824**	**88**	**1**	**2.89**	**15**	**10**	**5**	**897**	**42**	**0**	**2.81**
1995-96	**Philadelphia**	**NHL**	**53**	**31**	**13**	**7**	**3102**	**112**	**4**	***2.17**	**12**	**6**	**6**	**760**	**27**	**0**	**2.13**
1996-97	**Philadelphia**	**NHL**	**55**	**31**	**16**	**5**	**3094**	**132**	**5**	**2.56**	**8**	**4**	**3**	**444**	**22**	**0**	**2.97**
1997-98	**Philadelphia**	**NHL**	**46**	**21**	**17**	**7**	**2688**	**97**	**4**	**2.17**	**1**	**0**	**0**	**20**	**1**	**0**	**3.00**
1998-99	**Philadelphia**	**NHL**	**23**	**10**	**7**	**4**	**1235**	**52**	**0**	**2.53**	....	....	....	....	....	....	....
	NHL Totals		**608**	**296**	**214**	**69**	**34750**	**1723**	**23**	**2.97**	**93**	**47**	**43**	**5456**	**276**	**2**	**3.04**

AHL First All-Star Team (1986) • Won Dudley "Red" Garrett Memorial Trophy (Top Rookie - AHL) (1986) • NHL All-Rookie Team (1987) • NHL First All-Star Team (1987) • Won Vezina Trophy (1987) • Won Conn Smythe Trophy (1987)

• Scored a goal vs. Boston, December 8, 1987 • Scored a goal in playoffs vs. Washington, April 11, 1989.

Played in NHL All-Star Game (1988)

Traded to **Quebec** by **Philadelphia** with Peter Forsberg, Steve Duchesne, Kerry Huffman, Mike Ricci, Chris Simon, Philadelphia's 1st round choice in the 1993 (Jocelyn Thibault) and 1994 (later traded to Toronto — later traded to Washington — Washington selected Nolan Baumgartner) Entry Drafts and cash for Eric Lindros, June 30, 1992. Traded to **NY Islanders** by **Quebec** with Quebec's 1st round choice (Todd Bertuzzi) in 1993 Entry Draft for Mark Fitzpatrick and NY Islanders' 1st round choice (Adam Deadmarsh) in 1993 Entry Draft, June 20, 1993. Traded to **Philadelphia** by **NY Islanders** with NY Islanders' 6th round choice (Dimitri Tertyshny) in 1995 Entry Draft for Tommy Soderstrom, September 22, 1994.

HILLIER, Craig — PIT.

Goaltender. Catches left. 6'1", 184 lbs. Born, Cole Harbour, N.S., February 28, 1978.
(Pittsburgh's 1st choice, 23rd overall, in 1996 Entry Draft).

			Regular Season								Playoffs						
Season	Club	Lea	GP	W	L	T	Mins	GA	SO	Avg	GP	W	L	Mins	GA	SO	Avg
1993-94	Dartmouth	NSAHA	15	....	....	....	918	42	2	2.75	....	....	....	....	....	....	....
1994-95	Ottawa	OHL	24	6	7	2	1078	69	1	3.84	....	....	....	....	....	....	....
1995-96	Ottawa	OHL	44	24	14	3	2439	117	2	2.88	3	0	2	130	12	0	5.54
1996-97	Ottawa	OHL	36	23	6	4	2007	89	2	2.66	10	4	5	540	33	0	3.67
1997-98	Ottawa	OHL	46	27	12	4	2587	108	*6	*2.50	9	6	2	447	20	1	2.68
1998-99	Syracuse	AHL	36	9	18	6	1919	126	1	3.94	....	....	....	....	....	....	....

OHL First All-Star Team (1996)

HIRSCH, Corey — (HUHRSH) NSH.

Goaltender. Catches left. 5'10", 175 lbs. Born, Medicine Hat, Alta., July 1, 1972.
(NY Rangers' 7th choice, 169th overall, in 1991 Entry Draft).

			Regular Season								Playoffs						
Season	Club	Lea	GP	W	L	T	Mins	GA	SO	Avg	GP	W	L	Mins	GA	SO	Avg
1987-88	Calgary	AJHL	32	....	....	....	1538	91	1	3.55	....	....	....	....	....	....	....
1988-89	Kamloops	WHL	32	11	12	2	1516	106	2	4.20	5	3	2	245	19	0	4.65
1989-90	Kamloops	WHL	*63	*48	13	0	3608	230	*3	3.82	*17	*14	3	*1043	60	0	*3.45
1990-91	Kamloops	WHL	38	26	7	1	1970	100	3	*3.05	11	5	6	623	42	0	4.04
1991-92	Kamloops	WHL	48	35	10	2	2732	124	*5	*2.72	*16	*11	5	954	35	*2	*2.20
1992-93	**NY Rangers**	**NHL**	**4**	**1**	**2**	**1**	**224**	**14**	**0**	**3.75**	....	....	....	....	....	....	....
	Binghamton	AHL	46	*35	4	5	2692	125	1	*2.79	14	7	7	831	46	0	3.32
1993-94	Canada	Nat-Team	45	24	17	3	2653	124	0	2.80	....	....	....	....	....	....	....
	Canada	Olympics	8	5	2	1	495	18	....	2.18	....	....	....	....	....	....	....
	Binghamton	AHL	10	5	4	1	610	38	0	3.73	....	....	....	....	....	....	....
1994-95	Binghamton	AHL	57	31	20	5	3371	175	0	3.11	....	....	....	....	....	....	....
1995-96	**Vancouver**	**NHL**	**41**	**17**	**14**	**6**	**2338**	**114**	**1**	**2.93**	**6**	**2**	**3**	**338**	**21**	**0**	**3.73**
1996-97	**Vancouver**	**NHL**	**39**	**12**	**20**	**4**	**2127**	**116**	**2**	**3.27**	....	....	....	....	....	....	....
1997-98	**Vancouver**	**NHL**	**1**	**0**	**0**	**0**	**50**	**5**	**0**	**6.00**	....	....	....	....	....	....	....
	Syracuse	AHL	60	30	22	6	3512	187	1	3.19	5	2	3	297	10	1	*2.02
1998-99	**Vancouver**	**NHL**	**20**	**3**	**8**	**3**	**919**	**48**	**1**	**3.13**	....	....	....	....	....	....	....
	Syracuse	AHL	5	2	3	0	300	14	0	2.80	....	....	....	....	....	....	....
	NHL Totals		**105**	**33**	**44**	**14**	**5658**	**297**	**4**	**3.15**	**6**	**2**	**3**	**338**	**21**	**0**	**3.73**

WHL West Second All-Star Team (1990) • WHL West First All-Star Team (1991, 1992) • Canadian Major Junior Goaltender of the Year (1992) • Memorial Cup All-Star Team (1992) • Memorial Cup Tournament Top Goaltender (1992) • AHL First All-Star Team (1993) • Won Dudley "Red" Garrett Memorial Trophy (AHL Rookie of the Year) (1993) • Shared Harry "Hap" Holmes Memorial Trophy (fewest goals-against - AHL) with Boris Rousson (1993) • NHL All-Rookie Team (1996)

Traded to **Vancouver** by **NY Rangers** for Nathan Lafayette, April 7, 1995. Signed as a free agent by **Nashville**, August 10, 1999.

HNILICKA, Milan — (huh-LIHN-ich-kuh) NYR

Goaltender. Catches left. 6', 180 lbs. Born, Litomerice, Czech., June 25, 1973.
(NY Islanders' 4th choice, 70th overall, in 1991 Entry Draft).

			Regular Season								Playoffs						
Season	Club	Lea	GP	W	L	T	Mins	GA	SO	Avg	GP	W	L	Mins	GA	SO	Avg
1989-90	Poldi Kladno	Czech.	24	....	....	....	1113	70	....	3.77	....	....	....	....	....	....	....
1990-91	Poldi Kladno	Czech.	40	....	....	....	2122	98	0	2.80	....	....	....	....	....	....	....
1991-92	Poldi Kladno	Czech.	38	....	....	....	2066	128	0	3.73	....	....	....	....	....	....	....
1992-93	Swift Current	WHL	*65	*46	12	2	3679	206	2	3.36	*17	*12	5	*1017	54	*2	3.19
1993-94	Richmond	ECHL	43	18	16	5	2299	155	4	4.05	....	....	....	....	....	....	....
	Salt Lake	IHL	8	5	1	0	378	25	0	3.97	....	....	....	....	....	....	....
1994-95	Denver	IHL	15	9	4	1	798	47	1	3.53	....	....	....	....	....	....	....
1995-96	Poldi Kladno	Cze-Rep	33	....	....	....	1959	93	1	2.84	8	....	....	493	24	....	2.92
1996-97	Poldi Kladno	Cze-Rep	48	....	....	....	2736	120	4	2.63	3	....	....	151	14	0	5.56
1997-98	Sparta Praha	Cze-Rep	49	....	....	....	2847	99	....	2.09	11	....	....	632	31	....	3.00
1998-99	Sparta Praha	Cze-Rep	*50	....	....	....	*2877	109	....	2.27	8	....	....	507	13	....	*1.54

Signed as a free agent by **NY Rangers**, July 15, 1999.

HODSON, Jamie — (HAWD-suhn) TOR.

Goaltender. Catches left. 6'2", 192 lbs. Born, Brandon, Man., April 8, 1980.
(Toronto's 3rd choice, 69th overall, in 1998 Entry Draft).

			Regular Season								Playoffs						
Season	Club	Lea	GP	W	L	T	Mins	GA	SO	Avg	GP	W	L	Mins	GA	SO	Avg
1996-97	Yellowhead	MAHA	12	....	....	....	720	58	1	4.83	....	....	....	....	....	....	....
1997-98	Brandon	WHL	20	12	2	2	964	52	2	3.24	6	5	0	337	16	0	2.85
1998-99	Brandon	WHL	43	23	12	3	2295	123	4	3.22	5	1	4	275	26	0	5.67

HODSON, Kevin — (HAWD-suhn) T.B.

Goaltender. Catches left. 6', 182 lbs. Born, Winnipeg, Man., March 27, 1972.

			Regular Season								Playoffs						
Season	Club	Lea	GP	W	L	T	Mins	GA	SO	Avg	GP	W	L	Mins	GA	SO	Avg
1989-90	Winnipeg	MJHL	35	....	....	....	1900	115	2	3.40	....	....	....	....	....	....	....
1990-91	S.S. Marie	OHL	30	18	11	0	1638	88	*2	*3.22	10	*9	1	581	28	0	*2.89
1991-92	S.S. Marie	OHL	50	28	12	4	2722	151	0	3.33	18	12	6	1116	54	1	2.90
1992-93	S.S. Marie	OHL	26	18	5	2	1470	76	1	*3.10	14	11	2	755	34	0	2.70
	Indianapolis	IHL	14	5	9	0	777	53	0	4.09	....	....	....	....	....	....	....
1993-94	Adirondack	AHL	37	20	10	5	2082	102	2	2.94	3	0	2	89	10	0	6.77
1994-95	Adirondack	AHL	51	19	22	8	2731	161	1	3.54	4	0	4	237	14	0	3.53
1995-96	**Detroit**	**NHL**	**4**	**2**	**0**	**0**	**163**	**3**	**1**	**1.10**	....	....	....	....	....	....	....
	Adirondack	AHL	32	13	13	2	1654	87	0	3.16	3	0	2	150	8	0	3.21
1996-97	**Detroit**	**NHL**	**6**	**2**	**2**	**1**	**294**	**8**	**1**	**1.63**	....	....	....	....	....	....	....
	Quebec	IHL	2	1	1	0	118	7	0	3.54	....	....	....	....	....	....	....
1997-98 ♦	**Detroit**	**NHL**	**21**	**9**	**3**	**3**	**988**	**44**	**2**	**2.67**	**1**	**0**	**0**	**1**	**0**	**0**	**0.00**
1998-99	**Detroit**	**NHL**	**4**	**0**	**2**	**0**	**175**	**9**	**0**	**3.09**	....	....	....	....	....	....	....
	Adirondack	AHL	6	1	3	2	349	19	0	3.27	....	....	....	....	....	....	....
	Tampa Bay	**NHL**	**5**	**2**	**1**	**1**	**238**	**11**	**0**	**2.77**	....	....	....	....	....	....	....
	NHL Totals		**40**	**15**	**8**	**5**	**1858**	**75**	**4**	**2.42**	**1**	**0**	**0**	**1**	**0**	**0**	**0.00**

Memorial Cup All-Star Team (1993) • Won Hap Emms Memorial Trophy (Memorial Cup Tournament Top Goaltender) (1993)

Signed as a free agent by **Chicago**, August 17, 1992. Signed as a free agent by **Detroit**, June 16, 1993. • Played 16 seconds in playoff game vs. Chicago, May 17, 1998. Traded to **Tampa Bay** by **Detroit** with San Jose's 2nd round choice (previously acquired, Tampa Bay selected Sheldon Keefe) in 1999 Entry Draft for Wendel Clark and Detroit's 6th round choice (previously acquired, Detroit selected Kent McDonnell) in 1999 Entry Draft, March 23, 1999.

HOLMQVIST, Johan — (HOHLM-kvihst, YOH-han) NYR

Goaltender. Catches left. 6'1", 200 lbs. Born, Tolfta, Sweden, May 24, 1978.
(NY Rangers' 9th choice, 175th overall, in 1997 Entry Draft).

			Regular Season								Playoffs						
Season	Club	Lea	GP	W	L	T	Mins	GA	SO	Avg	GP	W	L	Mins	GA	SO	Avg
1996-97	Brynas Gavle	Sweden	2	0	0	0	80	4	0	3.00	....	....	....	....	....	....	....
1997-98	Brynas Gavle	Sweden	33	....	....	....	1897	82	....	2.59	3	0	3	180	14	....	4.67
1998-99	Brynas Gavle	Sweden	41	....	....	....	2383	111	4	2.79	*14	9	5	*855	34	0	2.39

HURME, Jani — (HOOR-meh) OTT.

Goaltender. Catches left. 6', 187 lbs. Born, Turku, Finland, January 7, 1975.
(Ottawa's 2nd choice, 58th overall, in 1997 Entry Draft).

			Regular Season								Playoffs						
Season	Club	Lea	GP	W	L	T	Mins	GA	SO	Avg	GP	W	L	Mins	GA	SO	Avg
1992-93	TPS Turku	Finn-Jr.	12	....	....	....	669	47	0	4.22	1	....	....	60	0	1	0.00
1993-94	TPS Turku	Finland	1	....	....	....	2	0	0	0.00	....	....	....	....	....	....	....
	Kiekko-67	Finland-2	3	....	....	....	190	7	0	2.21	....	....	....	....	....	....	....
	Kiekko-67	Finn-Jr.	18	....	....	....	....	....	....	3.16	....	....	....	....	....	....	....
1994-95	Kiekko-67	Finland-2	19	....	....	....	1049	53	....	3.03	3	....	....	180	6	....	2.00
	TPS Turku	Finn-Jr.	2	....	....	....	125	5	0	2.40	....	....	....	....	....	....	....
	Kiekko-67	Finn-Jr.	9	....	....	....	540	47	....	5.22	....	....	....	....	....	....	....
1995-96	TPS Turku	Finland	16	....	....	....	946	34	2	2.16	10	....	....	545	22	2	2.42
	Kiekko-67	Finland-2	16	....	....	....	968	39	1	2.42	....	....	....	....	....	....	....
	TPS Turku	Finn-Jr.	13	....	....	....	777	34	1	2.63	....	....	....	....	....	....	....
1996-97	TPS Turku	Finland	48	31	11	6	2917	101	6	2.08	12	6	6	722	39	0	3.24
1997-98	Detroit	IHL	6	2	2	2	290	20	0	4.13	....	....	....	....	....	....	....
	Indianapolis	IHL	29	11	11	3	1506	83	1	3.30	3	1	0	129	10	0	4.62
1998-99	Detroit	IHL	12	7	3	1	643	26	1	2.43	....	....	....	....	....	....	....
	Cincinnati	IHL	26	14	9	2	1428	81	0	3.40	....	....	....	....	....	....	....

IRBE, Arturs — (UHR-bay, AHR-tuhrs) CAR.

Goaltender. Catches left. 5'8", 175 lbs. Born, Riga, Latvia, February 2, 1967.
(Minnesota's 11th choice, 196th overall, in 1989 Entry Draft).

			Regular Season								Playoffs						
Season	Club	Lea	GP	W	L	T	Mins	GA	SO	Avg	GP	W	L	Mins	GA	SO	Avg
1986-87	Dynamo Riga	USSR	2	....	....	....	27	1	0	2.22	....	....	....	....	....	....	....
1987-88	Dynamo Riga	USSR	34	....	....	....	1870	86	4	2.69	....	....	....	....	....	....	....
1988-89	Dynamo Riga	USSR	40	....	....	....	2460	116	4	2.85	....	....	....	....	....	....	....
1989-90	Dynamo Riga	USSR	48	....	....	....	2880	115	2	2.42	....	....	....	....	....	....	....
1990-91	Dynamo Riga	USSR	46	....	....	....	2713	133	5	2.94	....	....	....	....	....	....	....
1991-92	**San Jose**	**NHL**	**13**	**2**	**6**	**3**	**645**	**48**	**0**	**4.47**	....	....	....	....	....	....	....
	Kansas City	IHL	32	24	7	1	1955	80	0	*2.46	*15	*12	3	914	44	0	*2.89
1992-93	**San Jose**	**NHL**	**36**	**7**	**26**	**0**	**2074**	**142**	**1**	**4.11**	....	....	....	....	....	....	....
	Kansas City	IHL	6	3	3	0	364	20	0	3.30	....	....	....	....	....	....	....
1993-94	**San Jose**	**NHL**	***74**	**30**	**28**	**16**	***4412**	**209**	**3**	**2.84**	**14**	**7**	**7**	**806**	**50**	**0**	**3.72**
1994-95	**San Jose**	**NHL**	**38**	**14**	**19**	**3**	**2043**	**111**	**4**	**3.26**	**6**	**2**	**4**	**316**	**27**	**0**	**5.13**
1995-96	**San Jose**	**NHL**	**22**	**4**	**12**	**4**	**1112**	**85**	**0**	**4.59**	....	....	....	....	....	....	....
	Kansas City	IHL	4	1	2	1	226	16	0	4.24	....	....	....	....	....	....	....
1996-97	**Dallas**	**NHL**	**35**	**17**	**12**	**3**	**1965**	**88**	**3**	**2.69**	**1**	**0**	**0**	**13**	**0**	**0**	**0.00**
1997-98	**Vancouver**	**NHL**	**41**	**14**	**11**	**6**	**1999**	**91**	**2**	**2.73**	....	....	....	....	....	....	....
1998-99	**Carolina**	**NHL**	**62**	**27**	**20**	**12**	**3643**	**135**	**6**	**2.22**	**6**	**2**	**4**	**408**	**15**	**0**	**2.21**
	NHL Totals		**321**	**115**	**134**	**47**	**17893**	**909**	**19**	**3.05**	**27**	**11**	**15**	**1543**	**92**	**0**	**3.58**

USSR Rookie-of-the-Year (1988) • IHL First All-Star Team (1992) • Shared James Norris Memorial Trophy (fewest goals against - IHL) with Wade Flaherty (1992)

Played in NHL All-Star Game (1994, 1999)

Claimed by **San Jose** from **Minnesota** in Dispersal Draft, May 30, 1991. Signed as a free agent by **Dallas**, August 19, 1996. Signed as a free agent by **Vancouver**, August 25, 1997. Signed as a free agent by **Carolina**, September 14, 1998.

JABLONSKI, Pat — (ja-BLAWN-skee)

Goaltender. Catches right. 6', 180 lbs. Born, Toledo, OH, June 20, 1967.
(St. Louis' 6th choice, 138th overall, in 1985 Entry Draft).

			Regular Season								Playoffs						
Season	Club	Lea	GP	W	L	T	Mins	GA	SO	Avg	GP	W	L	Mins	GA	SO	Avg
1984-85	Detroit	NAJHL	29	....	....	....	1483	95	0	3.84	....	....	....	....	....	....	....
1985-86	Windsor	OHL	29	6	16	4	1600	119	1	4.46	6	0	3	263	20	0	4.56
1986-87	Windsor	OHL	41	22	14	2	2328	128	*3	3.30	12	8	4	710	38	0	3.21
1987-88	Peoria	IHL	5	2	2	1	285	17	0	3.58	....	....	....	....	....	....	....
	Windsor	OHL	18	14	3	0	994	48	2	2.90	9	*8	0	537	28	0	3.13
1988-89	Peoria	IHL	35	11	20	0	2051	163	1	4.77	3	0	2	130	13	0	6.00
1989-90	**St. Louis**	**NHL**	**4**	**0**	**3**	**0**	**208**	**17**	**0**	**4.90**	....	....	....	....	....	....	....
	Peoria	IHL	36	14	17	4	2023	165	0	4.89	4	1	3	223	19	0	5.11
1990-91	**St. Louis**	**NHL**	**8**	**2**	**3**	**3**	**492**	**25**	**0**	**3.05**	**3**	**0**	**0**	**90**	**5**	**0**	**3.33**
	Peoria	IHL	29	23	3	2	1738	87	0	3.00	10	7	2	532	23	0	2.59
1991-92	**St. Louis**	**NHL**	**10**	**3**	**6**	**0**	**468**	**38**	**0**	**4.87**	....	....	....	....	....	....	....
	Peoria	IHL	8	6	1	1	493	29	1	3.53	....	....	....	....	....	....	....
1992-93	**Tampa Bay**	**NHL**	**43**	**8**	**24**	**4**	**2268**	**150**	**1**	**3.97**	....	....	....	....	....	....	....
1993-94	**Tampa Bay**	**NHL**	**15**	**5**	**6**	**3**	**834**	**54**	**0**	**3.88**	....	....	....	....	....	....	....
	St. John's	AHL	16	12	3	1	962	49	1	3.05	11	6	5	676	36	0	3.19
1994-95	Chicago	IHL	4	0	4	0	216	17	0	4.71	....	....	....	....	....	....	....
	Houston	IHL	3	1	1	1	179	9	0	3.01	....	....	....	....	....	....	....
1995-96	**St. Louis**	**NHL**	**1**	**0**	**0**	**0**	**8**	**1**	**0**	**7.50**	....	....	....	....	....	....	....
	Montreal	**NHL**	**23**	**5**	**9**	**6**	**1264**	**62**	**0**	**2.94**	**1**	**0**	**0**	**49**	**1**	**0**	**1.22**
1996-97	**Montreal**	**NHL**	**17**	**4**	**6**	**2**	**754**	**50**	**0**	**3.98**	....	....	....	....	....	....	....
	Phoenix	**NHL**	**2**	**0**	**1**	**0**	**59**	**2**	**0**	**2.03**	....	....	....	....	....	....	....
1997-98	**Carolina**	**NHL**	**5**	**1**	**4**	**0**	**279**	**14**	**0**	**3.01**	....	....	....	....	....	....	....
	Cleveland	IHL	34	13	13	6	1950	98	0	3.01	....	....	....	....	....	....	....
	Quebec	IHL	7	3	3	0	368	21	0	3.42	....	....	....	....	....	....	....
1998-99	Chicago	IHL	36	22	7	7	2119	106	1	3.00	3	2	1	185	11	0	3.57
	NHL Totals		**128**	**28**	**62**	**18**	**6634**	**413**	**1**	**3.74**	**4**	**0**	**0**	**139**	**6**	**0**	**2.59**

Shared James Norris Memorial Trophy (fewest goals against - IHL) with Guy Hebert (1991)

Traded to **Tampa Bay** by **St. Louis** with Steve Tuttle, Darin Kimble and Rob Robinson for future considerations, June 19, 1992. Traded to **Toronto** by **Tampa Bay** for cash, February 21, 1994. Claimed by **St. Louis** from **Toronto** in NHL Waiver Draft, October 2, 1995. Traded to **Montreal** by **St. Louis** for J.J. Daigneault, November 7, 1995. Traded to **Phoenix** by **Montreal** for Steve Cheredaryk, March 18, 1997. Signed as a free agent by **Carolina**, August 12, 1997.

JOHNSON, Brent — ST.L.

Goaltender. Catches left. 6'2", 200 lbs. Born, Farmington, MI, March 12, 1977.
(Colorado's 5th choice, 129th overall, in 1995 Entry Draft).

			Regular Season								Playoffs						
Season	Club	Lea	GP	W	L	T	Mins	GA	SO	Avg	GP	W	L	Mins	GA	SO	Avg
1993-94	Detroit	OJHL	18	....	....	....	1024	49	1	3.52	....	....	....	....	....	....	....
1994-95	Owen Sound	OHL	18	3	9	1	904	75	0	4.98	....	....	....	....	....	....	....
1995-96	Owen Sound	OHL	58	24	28	1	3211	243	1	4.54	6	2	4	371	29	0	4.69
1996-97	Owen Sound	OHL	50	20	28	1	2798	201	1	4.31	4	0	4	253	24	0	5.69
1997-98	Worcester	AHL	42	14	15	7	2240	119	0	3.19	6	3	2	332	19	0	3.43
1998-99	**St. Louis**	**NHL**	**6**	**3**	**2**	**0**	**286**	**10**	**0**	**2.10**	....	....	....	....	....	....	....
	Worcester	AHL	49	22	22	4	2925	146	2	2.99	4	1	3	238	12	0	3.02
	NHL Totals		**6**	**3**	**2**	**0**	**286**	**10**	**0**	**2.10**	....	....	....	....	....	....	....

Traded to **St. Louis** by **Colorado** for San Jose's third round choice (previously acquired, Colorado selected Rick Berry) in 1997 Entry Draft and a conditional choice in 2000 Entry Draft, May 30, 1997.

JOSEPH, Curtis — TOR.

Goaltender. Catches left. 5'11", 190 lbs. Born, Keswick, Ont., April 29, 1967.

			Regular Season								Playoffs						
Season	Club	Lea	GP	W	L	T	Mins	GA	SO	Avg	GP	W	L	Mins	GA	SO	Avg
1987-88	Notre Dame	SJHL	36	25	4	7	2174	94	1	2.59	....	....	....	....	....	....	....
1988-89	U. of Wisconsin	WCHA	38	21	11	5	2267	94	1	2.49	....	....	....	....	....	....	....
1989-90	St. Louis	NHL	15	9	5	1	852	48	0	3.38	6	4	1	327	18	0	3.30
	Peoria	IHL	23	10	8	2	1241	80	0	3.87	....	....	....	....	....	....	....
1990-91	St. Louis	NHL	30	16	10	2	1710	89	0	3.12	....	....	....	....	....	....	....
1991-92	St. Louis	NHL	60	27	20	10	3494	175	2	3.01	6	2	4	379	23	0	3.64
1992-93	St. Louis	NHL	68	29	28	9	3890	196	1	3.02	11	7	4	715	27	*2	2.27
1993-94	St. Louis	NHL	71	36	23	11	4127	213	1	3.10	4	0	4	246	15	0	3.66
1994-95	St. Louis	NHL	36	20	10	1	1914	89	1	2.79	7	3	3	392	24	0	3.67
1995-96	Las Vegas	IHL	15	12	2	1	874	29	1	1.99	....	....	....	....	....	....	....
	Edmonton	NHL	34	15	16	2	1936	111	0	3.44	....	....	....	....	....	....	....
1996-97	Edmonton	NHL	72	32	29	9	4100	200	6	2.93	12	5	7	767	36	2	2.82
1997-98	Edmonton	NHL	71	29	31	9	4132	181	8	2.63	12	5	7	716	23	3	1.93
	Canada	Olympics	DID NOT PLAY – SPARE GOALTENDER														
1998-99	Toronto	NHL	67	35	24	7	4001	171	3	2.56	17	9	8	1011	41	1	2.43
	NHL Totals		524	248	196	61	30156	1473	22	2.93	75	35	38	4553	207	8	2.73

WCHA First All-Star Team (1989) • NCAA West Second All-American Team (1989)

Played in NHL All-Star Game (1994)

Signed as a free agent by **St. Louis**, June 16, 1989. Traded to **Edmonton** by **St. Louis** with the rights to Michael Grier for St. Louis' 1st round choices (previously acquired) in 1996 (St. Louis selected Marty Reasoner) and 1997 (later traded to Los Angeles — Los Angeles selected Matt Zultek) Entry Drafts, August 4, 1995. Signed as a free agent by **Toronto**, July 15, 1998.

KARPENKO, Igor — CGY.

Goaltender. Catches left. 5'8", 175 lbs. Born, Kiev, USSR, July 23, 1976.
(Anaheim's 7th choice, 185th overall, in 1995 Entry Draft).

			Regular Season								Playoffs						
Season	Club	Lea	GP	W	L	T	Mins	GA	SO	Avg	GP	W	L	Mins	GA	SO	Avg
1993-94	Sokol-Kiev	CIS	5	....	....	....	88	3	....	2.05	....	....	....	....	....	....	....
1994-95	Sokol-Kiev	CIS	23	....	....	....	1292	67	....	3.11	....	....	....	....	....	....	....
1995-96	Sokol-Kiev	CIS	23	....	....	....	1269	622.93		....	....	....	....	....	....	....	....
1996-97	Port Huron	CHL	23	9	9	1	1148	67	0	3.50	3	1	2	179	16	0	5.36
	Las Vegas	IHL	3	0	2	0	133	12	0	5.38	....	....	....	....	....	....	....
1997-98	Saint John	AHL	4	2	1	1	255	3	2	0.80	....	....	....	....	....	....	....
	Port-Huron	UHL	56	27	23	6	3186	200	1	3.77	3	0	3	179	14	0	4.67
1998-99	Johnstown	ECHL	7	4	3	0	369	20	0	3.25	....	....	....	....	....	....	....
	Saint John	AHL	23	5	10	3	1207	69	0	3.43	2	0	1	63	5	0	4.79

Signed as a free agent by **Calgary**, January 5, 1998.

KEYES, Tim — VAN.

Goaltender. Catches left. 5'11", 185 lbs. Born, Ganonoque, Ont., May 28, 1976.

			Regular Season								Playoffs						
Season	Club	Lea	GP	W	L	T	Mins	GA	SO	Avg	GP	W	L	Mins	GA	SO	Avg
1993-94	Kingston	OHL	6	0	2	0	171	16	0	5.61	....	....	....	....	....	....	....
1994-95	Kingston	OHL	16	7	2	2	750	56	0	4.48	1	0	0	27	5	0	11.11
1995-96	Ottawa	OHL	27	15	7	2	1497	73	1	2.93	3	0	2	110	12	0	6.55
1996-97	Ottawa	OHL	37	26	5	2	1990	87	2	2.62	17	10	5	929	50	0	3.23
1997-98	Syracuse	AHL	15	2	7	4	831	59	0	4.26	....	....	....	....	....	....	....
	Raleigh	ECHL	1	0	1	0	60	4	0	4.00	....	....	....	....	....	....	....
	Dayton	ECHL	9	1	6	2	534	33	0	3.70	....	....	....	....	....	....	....
1998-99	Syracuse	AHL	11	2	7	0	502	[illegible]	0	[illegible]	....	....	....	....	....	....	....
	Augusta	ECHL	8	4	3	0	411	25	0	3.65	....	....	....	....	....	....	....
	Charlotte	ECHL	2	1	0	0	86	6	0	4.19	....	....	....	....	....	....	....

Signed as a free agent by **Vancouver**, September 8, 1997.

KHABIBULIN, Nikolai (khah-bee-BOO-lihn) — PHX.

Goaltender. Catches left. 6'1", 196 lbs. Born, Sverdlovsk, USSR, January 13, 1973.
(Winnipeg's 8th choice, 204th overall, in 1992 Entry Draft).

			Regular Season								Playoffs						
Season	Club	Lea	GP	W	L	T	Mins	GA	SO	Avg	GP	W	L	Mins	GA	SO	Avg
1991-92	CSKA Moscow	CIS	2	....	....	....	34	2	0	3.52	....	....	....	....	....	....	....
	Russia	Olympics	DID NOT PLAY – SPARE GOALTENDER														
1992-93	CSKA Moscow	CIS	13	....	....	....	491	27	....	3.29	....	....	....	....	....	....	....
1993-94	CSKA Moscow	CIS	46	....	....	....	2625	116	....	2.65	3	....	....	193	11	....	3.42
	Russian Pens	IHL	12	2	7	2	639	47	0	4.41	....	....	....	....	....	....	....
1994-95	Springfield	AHL	23	9	9	3	1240	80	0	3.87	....	....	....	....	....	....	....
	Winnipeg	NHL	26	8	9	4	1339	76	0	3.41	....	....	....	....	....	....	....
1995-96	Winnipeg	NHL	53	26	20	3	2914	152	2	3.13	6	2	4	359	19	0	3.18
1996-97	Phoenix	NHL	72	30	33	6	4091	193	7	2.83	7	3	4	426	15	1	2.11
1997-98	Phoenix	NHL	70	30	28	10	4026	184	4	2.74	4	2	1	185	13	0	4.22
1998-99	Phoenix	NHL	63	32	23	7	3657	130	8	2.13	7	3	4	449	18	0	2.41
	NHL Totals		284	126	113	30	16027	735	21	2.75	24	10	13	1419	65	1	2.75

Played in NHL All-Star Game (1998, 1999)

Transferred to **Phoenix** after **Winnipeg** franchise relocated, July 1, 1996.

KHLOPTONOV, Denis (khloh-POHT-nahv) — FLA.

Goaltender. Catches left. 6'4", 198 lbs. Born, Moscow, USSR, January 27, 1978.
(Florida's 8th choice, 209th overall, in 1996 Entry Draft).

			Regular Season								Playoffs						
Season	Club	Lea	GP	W	L	T	Mins	GA	SO	Avg	GP	W	L	Mins	GA	SO	Avg
1995-96	CSKA Moscow	CIS-Jr.	STATISTICS NOT AVAILABLE														
1996-97	CSKA Moscow	Russia	21	....	....	....	1260	42	0	2.00	....	....	....	....	....	....	....
1997-98	CSKA Moscow	Russia	20	....	....	....	987	58	....	3.53	....	....	....	....	....	....	....
1998-99	Muskegon	UHL	37	21	8	2	1950	98	1	3.02	4	1	1	166	9	0	3.25

KIDD, Trevor — FLA.

Goaltender. Catches left. 6'2", 190 lbs. Born, Dugald, Man., March 29, 1972.
(Calgary's 1st choice, 11th overall, in 1990 Entry Draft).

			Regular Season								Playoffs						
Season	Club	Lea	GP	W	L	T	Mins	GA	SO	Avg	GP	W	L	Mins	GA	SO	Avg
1987-88	Eastman Selects	MAHA	14	....	....	....	840	66	0	4.72	....	....	....	....	....	....	....
1988-89	Brandon	WHL	32	11	13	1	1509	102	0	4.06	....	....	....	....	....	....	....
1989-90	Brandon	WHL	*63	24	32	2	*3676	254	2	4.15	....	....	....	....	....	....	....
1990-91	Brandon	WHL	30	10	19	1	1730	117	0	4.06	....	....	....	....	....	....	....
	Spokane	WHL	14	8	3	0	749	44	0	3.52	15	*14	1	926	32	2	*2.07
1991-92	Canada	Nat-Team	28	18	4	4	1349	79	2	3.51	....	....	....	....	....	....	....
	Canada	Olympics	1	1	0	0	60	0	1	0.00	....	....	....	....	....	....	....
	Calgary	NHL	2	1	1	0	120	8	0	4.00	....	....	....	....	....	....	....
1992-93	Salt Lake	IHL	29	10	16	1	1696	111	1	3.93	....	....	....	....	....	....	....
1993-94	Calgary	NHL	31	13	7	6	1614	85	0	3.16	....	....	....	....	....	....	....
1994-95	Calgary	NHL	*43	22	14	6	*2463	107	3	2.61	7	3	4	434	26	1	3.59
1995-96	Calgary	NHL	47	15	21	8	2570	119	3	2.78	2	0	1	83	9	0	6.51
1996-97	Calgary	NHL	55	21	23	6	2979	141	4	2.84	....	....	....	....	....	....	....
1997-98	Carolina	NHL	47	21	21	3	2685	97	3	2.17	....	....	....	....	....	....	....
1998-99	Carolina	NHL	25	7	10	6	1358	61	2	2.70	....	....	....	....	....	....	....
	NHL Totals		250	100	97	35	13789	618	15	2.69	9	3	5	517	35	1	4.06

WHL East First All-Star Team (1990) • Canadian Major Junior Goaltender of the Year (1990)

Traded to **Carolina** by **Calgary** with Gary Roberts for Andrew Cassels and Jean-Sebastien Giguere, August 25, 1997. Claimed by **Atlanta** from **Carolina** in Expansion Draft, June 25, 1999. Traded to **Florida** by **Atlanta** for Gord Murphy, Herbert Vasiljevs, Daniel Tjarnqvist and Ottawa's 6th round choice (previously acquired, later traded to Dallas - Dallas selected Justin Cox) in 1999 Entry Draft, June 25, 1999.

KIPRUSOFF, Miikka (KIHP-ruh-sohf, MEE-kah) — S.J.

Goaltender. Catches left. 6', 180 lbs. Born, Turku, Finland, October 26, 1976.
(San Jose's 5th choice, 116th overall, in 1995 Entry Draft).

			Regular Season								Playoffs						
Season	Club	Lea	GP	W	L	T	Mins	GA	SO	Avg	GP	W	L	Mins	GA	SO	Avg
1994-95	TPS Turku	Finn-Jr.	31	....	....	....	1896	92	....	2.91	....	....	....	....	....	....	....
	TPS Turku	Finland	4	....	....	....	240	12	0	3.00	2	....	....	120	7	....	3.50
1995-96	TPS Turku	Finn-Jr.	3	....	....	....	180	9	....	3.00	....	....	....	....	....	....	....
	Kiekko-67	Finland-2	5	....	....	....	300	7	....	1.40	....	....	....	....	....	....	....
	TPS Turku	Finland	12	....	....	....	550	38	0	4.14	3	....	....	114	4	....	2.11
1996-97	AIK Solna	Sweden	42	....	....	....	2466	104	3	2.53	7	....	....	420	23	0	3.28
1997-98	AIK Solna	Sweden	42	....	....	....	2457	110	....	2.69	....	....	....	....	....	....	....
1998-99	TPS Turku	Finland	39	*26	6	6	2259	70	4	1.86	10	*9	1	580	15	*3	*1.55

KOLZIG, Olaf (KOHLT-zihg, OH-lahf) — WSH.

Goaltender. Catches left. 6'3", 225 lbs. Born, Johannesburg, South Africa, April 9, 1970.
(Washington's 1st choice, 19th overall, in 1989 Entry Draft).

			Regular Season								Playoffs						
Season	Club	Lea	GP	W	L	T	Mins	GA	SO	Avg	GP	W	L	Mins	GA	SO	Avg
1987-88	New Westminster	WHL	15	6	5	0	650	48	1	4.43	3	0	3	149	11	0	4.43
1988-89	Tri-City	WHL	30	16	10	2	1671	97	1	*3.48	....	....	....	....	....	....	....
1989-90	Washington	NHL	2	0	2	0	120	12	0	6.00	....	....	....	....	....	....	....
	Tri-City	WHL	48	27	27	3	2504	250	1	4.38	6	4	0	318	27	0	5.09
1990-91	Baltimore	AHL	26	10	12	1	1367	72	0	3.16	....	....	....	....	....	....	....
	Hampton Roads	ECHL	21	11	9	1	1248	71	2	3.41	3	1	2	180	14	0	4.66
1991-92	Baltimore	AHL	28	5	17	2	1503	105	1	4.19	....	....	....	....	....	....	....
	Hampton Roads	ECHL	14	11	3	0	847	41	0	2.90	....	....	....	....	....	....	....
1992-93	Washington	NHL	1	0	0	0	20	2	0	6.00	....	....	....	....	....	....	....
	Rochester	AHL	49	25	16	4	2737	168	0	3.68	*17	9	8	*1040	61	0	3.52
1993-94	Washington	NHL	7	0	3	0	224	20	0	5.36	....	....	....	....	....	....	....
	Portland	AHL	29	16	8	5	1725	88	3	3.06	17	*12	5	1035	44	0	*2.55
1994-95	Washington	NHL	14	2	8	2	724	30	0	2.49	2	1	0	44	1	0	1.36
	Portland	AHL	2	1	0	1	125	3	0	1.44	....	....	....	....	....	....	....
1995-96	Washington	NHL	18	4	8	2	897	46	0	3.08	5	2	3	341	11	0	*1.94
	Portland	AHL	5	5	0	0	300	7	1	1.40	....	....	....	....	....	....	....
1996-97	Washington	NHL	29	8	15	4	1645	71	2	2.59	....	....	....	....	....	....	....
1997-98	Washington	NHL	64	33	18	10	3788	139	5	2.20	21	12	9	1351	44	*4	1.95
	Germany	Olympics	2	2	0	0	120	2	1	1.00	....	....	....	....	....	....	....
1998-99	Washington	NHL	64	26	31	3	3586	154	4	2.58	....	....	....	....	....	....	....
	NHL Totals		199	73	85	21	11004	474	11	2.58	28	15	12	1736	56	4	1.94

WHL West Second All-Star Team (1989) • Shared Harry "Hap" Holmes Trophy (fewest goals-against - AHL) with Byron Dafoe (1994) • Won Jack Butterfield Trophy (Playoff MVP - IHL) (1994)

Played in NHL All-Star Game (1998)

• Scored a goal while with Tri-City (WHL), November 29, 1989.

KONSTANTINOV, Yevgeny — T.B.

Goaltender. Catches left. 6', 176 lbs. Born, Kazan, USSR, March 29, 1981.
(Tampa Bay's 2nd choice, 67th overall, in 1999 Entry Draft).

			Regular Season								Playoffs						
Season	Club	Lea	GP	W	L	T	Mins	GA	SO	Avg	GP	W	L	Mins	GA	SO	Avg
1997-98	AK Kazan-2	Russia-3	34	....	....	....	2040	129	....	3.79	....	....	....	....	....	....	....
1998-99	AK Kazan-2	Russia-4	STATISTICS NOT AVAILABLE														

KOTYK, Seamus (koh-TIHK, SHAY-muhs) — BOS.

Goaltender. Catches left. 5'11", 185 lbs. Born, London, Ont., October 7, 1980.
(Boston's 5th choice, 147th overall, in 1999 Entry Draft).

			Regular Season								Playoffs						
Season	Club	Lea	GP	W	L	T	Mins	GA	SO	Avg	GP	W	L	Mins	GA	SO	Avg
1997-98	Ottawa	OHL	31	13	5	5	1422	63	4	2.66	7	3	2	332	11	0	1.99
1998-99	Ottawa	OHL	41	26	7	4	2314	92	5	2.39	5	3	2	338	13	0	*2.31

LABARBERA, Jason (lah-BAR-buhr-uh) — NYR

Goaltender. Catches left. 6'2", 205 lbs. Born, Burnaby, B.C., January 18, 1980.
(NY Rangers' 3rd choice, 66th overall, in 1998 Entry Draft).

			Regular Season								Playoffs						
Season	Club	Lea	GP	W	L	T	Mins	GA	SO	Avg	GP	W	L	Mins	GA	SO	Avg
1996-97	Tri-City	WHL	2	1	0	0	63	4	0	3.81	....	....	....	....	....	....	....
	Portland	WHL	9	5	1	1	443	18	0	2.44	....	....	....	....	....	....	....
1997-98	Portland	WHL	23	18	4	0	1305	72	1	3.31	....	....	....	....	....	....	....
1998-99	Portland	WHL	51	18	23	9	2991	170	4	3.41	4	0	4	252	19	0	4.52

LABBE, Jean-Francois (lah-BAY) NYR

Goaltender. Catches left. 5'9", 170 lbs. Born, Sherbrooke, Que., June 15, 1972.

			Regular Season								Playoffs						
Season	**Club**	**Lea**	**GP**	**W**	**L**	**T**	**Mins**	**GA**	**SO**	**Avg**	**GP**	**W**	**L**	**Mins**	**GA**	**SO**	**Avg**
1989-90	Trois-Rivieres	QMJHL	28	13	10	0	1499	106	1	4.24	3	1	1	132	8	0	3.64
1990-91	Trois-Rivieres	QMJHL	54	*35	14	0	2870	158	5	3.30	5	1	4	230	19	0	4.96
1991-92	Trois-Rivieres	QMJHL	48	*31	13	3	2749	142	1	3.10	*15	*10	3	791	33	*1	*2.50
1992-93	Hull	QMJHL	46	26	18	2	2701	156	2	3.46	10	6	3	518	24	*1	*2.78
1993-94	Thunder Bay	ColHL	52	*35	11	4	*2900	150	*2	*3.10	8	7	1	493	18	*2	*2.19
	P.E.I. Senators	AHL	7	4	3	0	389	22	0	3.39	....	....	....	....	....	....	....
1994-95	P.E.I. Senators	AHL	32	13	14	3	1817	94	2	3.10	....	....	....	....	....	....	....
1995-96	Cornwall	AHL	55	25	21	5	2972	144	3	2.91	8	3	5	471	21	1	2.68
1996-97	Hershey	AHL	66	*34	22	9	3811	160	*6	*2.52	*23	*14	8	*1364	59	1	2.60
1997-98	Hamilton	AHL	52	24	17	11	3138	149	2	2.85	7	3	4	413	20	0	2.90
1998-99	Hartford	AHL	*59	28	26	3	*3392	182	2	3.22	7	3	4	447	22	0	2.95

QMJHL First All-Star Team (1992) • ColHL First All-Star Team (1994) • Named ColHL's Rookie of the Year (1994) • Named ColHL's Outstanding Goaltender (1994) • Named ColHL's Playoff MVP (1994) • AHL First All-Star Team (1997) • Won Harry "Hap" Holmes Memorial Trophy (fewest goals against — AHL) (1997) • Won Baz Bastien Memorial Trophy (Top Goaltender — AHL) (1997) • Won Les Cunningham Award (MVP — AHL) (1997)

Signed as a free agent by **Ottawa**, May 12, 1994. Traded to **Colorado** by **Ottawa** for future considerations, September 20, 1995. Signed as a free agent by **Edmonton**, September 2, 1997. Signed as a free agent by **NY Rangers**, July 30, 1998.

LaGRAND, Scott (lah-GRAND)

Goaltender. Catches left. 6', 165 lbs. Born, Potsdam, NY, February 11, 1970.
(Philadelphia's 5th choice, 77th overall, in 1988 Entry Draft).

			Regular Season								Playoffs						
Season	**Club**	**Lea**	**GP**	**W**	**L**	**T**	**Mins**	**GA**	**SO**	**Avg**	**GP**	**W**	**L**	**Mins**	**GA**	**SO**	**Avg**
1987-88	Hotchkiss High	H.S.	25	....	....	....	1560	36	2	2.50	....	....	....	....	....	....	....
1988-89	Boston College	H.E.						DID NOT PLAY – FRESHMAN									
1989-90	Boston College	H.E.	24	17	4	0	1268	57	0	2.70	....	....	....	....	....	....	....
1990-91	Boston College	H.E.	23	12	8	0	1153	63	2	3.28	....	....	....	....	....	....	....
1991-92	Boston College	H.E.	30	11	16	2	1750	108	1	3.70	....	....	....	....	....	....	....
1992-93	Hershey	AHL	32	8	17	4	1854	145	0	4.69	....	....	....	....	....	....	....
1993-94	Hershey	AHL	40	16	13	3	2032	117	2	3.45	....	....	....	....	....	....	....
1994-95	Atlanta	IHL	21	7	7	3	993	67	0	4.04	3	0	2	101	10	0	5.91
	Hershey	AHL	21	7	9	3	1104	71	1	3.86	....	....	....	....	....	....	....
1995-96	Orlando	IHL	33	17	7	3	1618	103	1	3.82	3	0	0	51	1	0	1.17
1996-97	Orlando	IHL	35	16	10	2	1746	85	2	2.92	4	0	2	153	5	0	1.96
1997-98	Orlando	IHL	23	8	9	3	1264	68	0	3.23	....	....	....	....	....	....	....
	Utah	IHL	7	1	1	2	360	18	0	3.00	....	....	....	....	....	....	....
	Fort Wayne	IHL	11	3	5	0	488	28	0	3.44	2	0	1	94	7	0	4.47
1998-99	Utah	IHL	8	4	3	1	474	20	1	2.53	....	....	....	....	....	....	....
	Tallahassee	ECHL	39	15	18	4	2159	121	0	3.36	....	....	....	....	....	....	....
	Chicago	IHL	2	1	0	0	78	3	0	2.31	....	....	....	....	....	....	....

Hockey East First All-Star Team (1991) • NCAA East Second All-American Team (1992)

Traded to **Tampa Bay** by **Philadelphia** for Mike Greenlay, February 2, 1995.

LAJEUNESSE, Simon (lah-ZHUH-nehs) OTT.

Goaltender. Catches left. 6', 170 lbs. Born, Quebec City, Que., January 22, 1981.
(Ottawa's 2nd choice, 48th overall, in 1999 Entry Draft).

			Regular Season								Playoffs						
Season	**Club**	**Lea**	**GP**	**W**	**L**	**T**	**Mins**	**GA**	**SO**	**Avg**	**GP**	**W**	**L**	**Mins**	**GA**	**SO**	**Avg**
1997-98	Moncton	QMJHL	19	5	6	3	925	51	1	3.31	2	0	0	1	0	0	0.00
1998-99	Moncton	QMJHL	36	18	9	3	1993	98	1	2.95	1	0	0	43	2	0	2.79

LALIME, Patrick (lah-LEEM) OTT.

Goaltender. Catches left. 6'2", 170 lbs. Born, St. Bonaventure, Que., July 7, 1974.
(Pittsburgh's 6th choice, 156th overall, in 1993 Entry Draft).

			Regular Season								Playoffs						
Season	**Club**	**Lea**	**GP**	**W**	**L**	**T**	**Mins**	**GA**	**SO**	**Avg**	**GP**	**W**	**L**	**Mins**	**GA**	**SO**	**Avg**
1990-91	D'abitibi	QAAA	26	9	17	0	1595	151	0	5.81	....	....	....	....	....	....	....
1991-92	Shawinigan	QMJHL	6	....	....	....	272	25	0	5.50	....	....	....	....	....	....	....
1992-93	Shawinigan	QMJHL	44	10	24	4	2467	192	0	4.67	....	....	....	....	....	....	....
1993-94	Shawinigan	QMJHL	48	22	20	0	2733	192	1	4.22	5	1	3	223	25	0	6.73
1994-95	Hampton Roads	ECHL	26	15	7	3	1470	82	2	3.35	....	....	....	....	....	....	....
	Cleveland	IHL	23	7	10	4	1230	91	0	4.44	....	....	....	....	....	....	....
1995-96	Cleveland	IHL	41	20	12	7	2314	149	0	3.86	....	....	....	....	....	....	....
1996-97	**Pittsburgh**	**NHL**	**39**	**21**	**12**	**2**	**2058**	**101**	**3**	**2.94**	....	....	....	....	....	....	....
	Cleveland	IHL	14	6	6	2	834	45	1	3.24	....	....	....	....	....	....	....
1997-98	Grand Rapids	IHL	31	10	10	9	1749	76	2	2.61	1	0	1	77	4	0	3.11
1998-99	Kansas City	IHL	*66	*39	20	4	*3789	190	2	3.01	3	1	2	179	6	1	2.01
	NHL Totals		**39**	**21**	**12**	**2**	**2058**	**101**	**3**	**2.94**	....	....	....	....	....	....	....

NHL All-Rookie Team (1997) • IHL First All-Star Team (1999)

Rights traded to **Anaheim** by **Pittsburgh** for Sean Pronger, March 24, 1998. Traded to **Ottawa** by **Anaheim** with future considerations for Ted Donato and Antti-Jussi Niemi, June 18, 1999.

LAMOTHE, Marc (luh-MAWTH) CHI.

Goaltender. Catches left. 6'1", 204 lbs. Born, New Liskeard, Ont., February 27, 1974.
(Montreal's 6th choice, 92nd overall, in 1992 Entry Draft).

			Regular Season								Playoffs						
Season	**Club**	**Lea**	**GP**	**W**	**L**	**T**	**Mins**	**GA**	**SO**	**Avg**	**GP**	**W**	**L**	**Mins**	**GA**	**SO**	**Avg**
1990-91	Ottawa	OJHL	25	....	....	....	1220	82	1	4.03	....	....	....	....	....	....	....
1991-92	Kingston	OHL	42	10	25	2	2378	189	1	4.77	....	....	....	....	....	....	....
1992-93	Kingston	OHL	45	23	12	6	2489	162	1	3.91	15	8	5	753	48	1	3.82
1993-94	Kingston	OHL	48	23	20	5	2828	177	*2	3.76	6	2	2	224	12	0	3.21
1994-95	Fredericton	AHL	9	2	5	0	428	32	0	4.48	....	....	....	....	....	....	....
	Wheeling	ECHL	13	9	2	1	737	38	0	3.10	....	....	....	....	....	....	....
1995-96	Fredericton	AHL	23	5	9	3	1166	73	1	3.76	3	1	2	161	9	0	3.36
1996-97	Indianapolis	IHL	38	20	14	4	2271	100	1	2.64	1	0	0	20	1	0	3.00
1997-98	Indianapolis	IHL	31	18	10	2	1772	72	3	2.44	4	1	3	177	10	0	3.38
1998-99	Indianapolis	IHL	32	9	16	6	1823	115	1	3.78	6	3	3	338	10	*2	1.78
	Detroit	IHL	....	....	....	....	....	....	....	....	1	0	1	80	5	0	3.75

Signed as a free agent by **Chicago**, September 26, 1996.

LANGKOW, Scott (LAING-kow) ATL.

Goaltender. Catches left. 5'11", 190 lbs. Born, Sherwood Park, Alta., April 21, 1975.
(Winnipeg's 2nd choice, 31st overall, in 1993 Entry Draft).

			Regular Season								Playoffs						
Season	**Club**	**Lea**	**GP**	**W**	**L**	**T**	**Mins**	**GA**	**SO**	**Avg**	**GP**	**W**	**L**	**Mins**	**GA**	**SO**	**Avg**
1990-91	Sherwood Park	AAHA	32	....	....	....	1920	128	0	4.00	....	....	....	....	....	....	....
1991-92	Portland	WHL	1	0	0	0	33	2	0	3.46	....	....	....	....	....	....	....
	Abbotsford	PIJHL							STATISTICS NOT AVAILABLE								
1992-93	Portland	WHL	34	24	8	2	2064	119	2	3.46	9	6	3	535	31	0	3.48
1993-94	Portland	WHL	39	27	9	1	2302	121	2	3.15	10	6	4	600	34	0	3.40
1994-95	Portland	WHL	63	20	36	5	*3638	240	1	3.96	8	3	5	510	30	0	3.53
1995-96	**Winnipeg**	**NHL**	**1**	**0**	**0**	**0**	**6**	**0**	**0**	**0.00**	....	....	....	....	....	....	....
	Springfield	AHL	39	18	15	6	2329	116	3	2.99	7	4	2	393	23	0	3.51
1996-97	Springfield	AHL	33	15	9	7	1929	85	0	2.64	....	....	....	....	....	....	....
1997-98	**Phoenix**	**NHL**	**3**	**0**	**1**	**1**	**137**	**10**	**0**	**4.38**	....	....	....	....	....	....	....
	Springfield	AHL	51	30	13	5	2874	128	3	2.67	4	1	3	216	14	0	3.88
1998-99	**Phoenix**	**NHL**	**1**	**0**	**0**	**0**	**35**	**3**	**0**	**5.14**	....	....	....	....	....	....	....
	Las Vegas	IHL	27	7	14	2	1402	97	1	4.15	....	....	....	....	....	....	....
	Utah	IHL	21	10	9	2	1227	59	1	2.89	....	....	....	....	....	....	....
	NHL Totals		**5**	**0**	**1**	**1**	**178**	**13**	**0**	**4.38**	....	....	....	....	....	....	....

WHL West Second All-Star Team (1994, 1995) • Shared Harry "Hap" Holmes Memorial Trophy (fewest goals against — AHL) with Manny Legace (1996) • AHL First All-Star Team (1998) • Won Baz Bastien Memorial Trophy (Top Goaltender - AHL) (1998)

Transferred to **Phoenix** after **Winnipeg** franchise relocated, July 1, 1996. Traded to **Atlanta** by **Phoenix** for future considerations, June 25, 1999.

LANICEK, Michal T.B.

Goaltender. Catches left. 6'1", 172 lbs. Born, Benesov, Czech., July 6, 1981.
(Tampa Bay's 6th choice, 148th overall, in 1999 Entry Draft).

			Regular Season								Playoffs						
Season	**Club**	**Lea**	**GP**	**W**	**L**	**T**	**Mins**	**GA**	**SO**	**Avg**	**GP**	**W**	**L**	**Mins**	**GA**	**SO**	**Avg**
1996-97	Slavia Praha	Czech-Jr.	22	....	....	....	1260	42	....	2.00	....	....	....	....	....	....	....
1997-98	Slavia Praha	Czech-Jr.	39	....	....	....	2162	75	....	2.08	....	....	....	....	....	....	....
1998-99	Slavia Praha	Czech-Jr.	43	....	....	....	2412	87	....	2.16	....	....	....	....	....	....	....

LANIEL, Jean-Francois FLA.

Goaltender. Catches right. 6'2", 170 lbs. Born, Montreal, Que., June 16, 1981.
(Florida's 4th choice, 80th overall, in 1999 Entry Draft).

			Regular Season								Playoffs						
Season	**Club**	**Lea**	**GP**	**W**	**L**	**T**	**Mins**	**GA**	**SO**	**Avg**	**GP**	**W**	**L**	**Mins**	**GA**	**SO**	**Avg**
1998-99	Shawinigan	QMJHL	18	6	6	0	876	56	0	3.84	....	....	....	....	....	....	....

LARIVEE, Francis (la-RIHV-ay) TOR.

Goaltender. Catches left. 6'2", 198 lbs. Born, Anjou, Que., November 8, 1977.
(Toronto's 2nd choice, 50th overall, in 1996 Entry Draft).

			Regular Season								Playoffs						
Season	**Club**	**Lea**	**GP**	**W**	**L**	**T**	**Mins**	**GA**	**SO**	**Avg**	**GP**	**W**	**L**	**Mins**	**GA**	**SO**	**Avg**
1993-94	Val d'Or	QMJHL	36	5	20	1	1706	162	0	5.71	....	....	....	....	....	....	....
1994-95	Val d'Or	QMJHL	38	9	21	1	1795	132	0	4.41	....	....	....	....	....	....	....
1995-96	Val d'Or	QMJHL	*22	12	4	2	1162	73	0	3.77	....	....	....	....	....	....	....
	Laval	QMJHL	*39	9	24	1	2085	178	0	5.12	....	....	....	....	....	....	....
1996-97	Granby	QMJHL	1	1	0	0	60	1	0	1.00	1	0	0	50	4	0	4.80
	Laval	QMJHL	21	6	11	1	1068	77	1	4.33	....	....	....	....	....	....	....
	St. John's	AHL	4	3	1	0	244	9	0	2.21	2	0	0	1	0	0	0.00
1997-98	St. John's	AHL	30	6	12	5	1460	79	0	3.25	....	....	....	....	....	....	....
1998-99	St. John's	AHL	17	4	7	2	851	59	0	4.16	....	....	....	....	....	....	....
	Chicago	IHL	1	0	1	0	60	5	0	5.00	....	....	....	....	....	....	....
	Huntington	ECHL	16	5	7	1	767	35	1	2.74	....	....	....	....	....	....	....

LAROCQUE, Michel (lah-RAWK) CHI.

Goaltender. Catches left. 5'11", 200 lbs. Born, Lahr, West Germany, October 3, 1976.
(San Jose's 5th choice, 137th overall, in 1996 Entry Draft).

			Regular Season								Playoffs						
Season	**Club**	**Lea**	**GP**	**W**	**L**	**T**	**Mins**	**GA**	**SO**	**Avg**	**GP**	**W**	**L**	**Mins**	**GA**	**SO**	**Avg**
1995-96	Boston University	H.E.	14	10	1	1	735	42	0	3.43	....	....	....	....	....	....	....
1996-97	Boston University	H.E.	24	16	4	4	1466	58	0	*2.37	....	....	....	....	....	....	....
1997-98	Boston University	H.E.	24	17	4	1	1370	50	1	2.19	....	....	....	....	....	....	....
1998-99	Boston University	H.E.	35	14	18	3	2072	117	0	3.39	....	....	....	....	....	....	....

Hockey East Second All-Star Team (1998) • Hockey East First All-Star Team (1999) • NCAA East Second All-American Team (1999)

Traded to **Chicago** by **San Jose** for Chicago's 5th round choice in 2000 Entry Draft, August 23, 1999.

LASAK, Jan (LA-shak, YAN) NSH.

Goaltender. Catches left. 6', 202 lbs. Born, Zvolen, Czech., April 10, 1979.
(Nashville's 6th choice, 65th overall, in 1999 Entry Draft).

			Regular Season								Playoffs						
Season	**Club**	**Lea**	**GP**	**W**	**L**	**T**	**Mins**	**GA**	**SO**	**Avg**	**GP**	**W**	**L**	**Mins**	**GA**	**SO**	**Avg**
1996-97	HKm Zvolen	Slov-Jr.	49	....	....	....	2940	111	....	2.27	....	....	....	....	....	....	....
1997-98	HKm Zvolen	Slov-Jr.	48	....	....	....	2881	119	....	2.48	....	....	....	....	....	....	....
	HK SKP Zilina	Slovak-2	4	....	....	....	208	12	....	3.46	....	....	....	....	....	....	....
1998-99	HKm Zvolen	Slov-Jr.	43	....	....	....	2580	91	....	2.12	....	....	....	....	....	....	....
	HKm Zvolen	Slovakia	8	....	....	....	387	29	....	4.50	....	....	....	....	....	....	....

LEGACE, Manny (LEH-gah-see) DET.

Goaltender. Catches left. 5'9", 162 lbs. Born, Toronto, Ont., February 4, 1973.
(Hartford's 5th choice, 188th overall, in 1993 Entry Draft).

							Regular Season							Playoffs			
Season	Club	Lea	GP	W	L	T	Mins	GA	SO	Avg	GP	W	L	Mins	GA	SO	Avg
1987-88	Alliston	OJHL-C	16	....	....	....	960	83	0	5.17	....	....	....	....	....	....	....
1988-89	Vaughn	OJHL-B	22	....	....	....	1303	92	1	4.24	....	....	....	....	....	....	....
1989-90	Vaughn	OJHL	29	....	....	....	1660	119	1	4.30	....	....	....	....	....	....	....
1990-91	Niagara Falls	OHL	30	13	11	2	1515	107	0	4.24	4	1	1	119	10	0	5.04
1991-92	Niagara Falls	OHL	43	21	16	3	2384	143	0	3.60	14	8	5	791	56	0	4.25
1992-93	Niagara Falls	OHL	48	22	19	3	2630	171	0	3.90	4	0	4	240	18	0	4.50
1993-94	Canada	Nat-Team	16	8	6	0	859	36	2	2.51	....	....	....	....	....	....	....
	Canada	Olympics					DID NOT PLAY – SPARE GOALTENDER										
1994-95	Springfield	AHL	39	12	17	6	2169	128	2	3.54	....	....	....	....	....	....	....
1995-96	Springfield	AHL	37	20	12	4	2196	83	*5	*2.27	4	1	3	220	18	0	4.91
1996-97	Springfield	AHL	36	17	14	5	2119	107	1	3.03	12	9	3	745	25	*2	2.01
	Richmond	ECHL	3	2	1	0	157	8	0	3.05	....	....	....	....	....	....	....
1997-98	Springfield	AHL	6	4	2	0	345	16	0	2.78	....	....	....	....	....	....	....
	Las Vegas	IHL	41	18	16	4	2106	111	1	3.16	4	1	3	237	16	0	4.05
1998-99	**Los Angeles**	**NHL**	**17**	**2**	**9**	**2**	**899**	**39**	**0**	**2.60**	....	....	....	....	....	....	....
	Long Beach	IHL	33	22	8	1	1796	67	2	2.24	6	4	2	338	9	0	*1.60
	NHL Totals		**17**	**2**	**9**	**2**	**899**	**39**	**0**	**2.60**	....	....	....	....	....	....	....

OHL First All-Star Team (1993) • AHL First All-Star Team (1996) • Shared Harry "Hap" Holmes Memorial Trophy (fewest goals against — AHL) with Scott Langkow (1996) • Won Baz Bastien Memorial Trophy (Top Goaltender — AHL) (1996)

Rights transferred to **Carolina** after **Hartford** franchise relocated, June 25, 1997. Traded to **LA Kings** by **Carolina** for future considerations, July 31, 1998. Signed as a free agent by **Detroit**, August 9, 1999.

LEHTO, Mika (leh-TOH, MEE-kuh) PIT.

Goaltender. Catches left. 5'11", 172 lbs. Born, Vammala, Finland, April 12, 1979.
(Pittsburgh's 8th choice, 224th overall, in 1998 Entry Draft).

							Regular Season							Playoffs			
Season	Club	Lea	GP	W	L	T	Mins	GA	SO	Avg	GP	W	L	Mins	GA	SO	Avg
1997-98	Assat-Pori	Finn-Jr.	36	....	....	....	2160	103	2	2.86	....	....	....	....	....	....	....
	Assat-Pori	Finland	1	0	0	0	35	1	0	1.71	1	0	0	17	0	0	0.00
1998-99	Assat-Pori	Finn-Jr.	20	....	....	....	1202	68	....	3.39	....	....	....	....	....	....	....
	Assat-Pori	Finland	15	4	6	1	773	38	1	2.95	....	....	....	....	....	....	....

LEIGHTON, Michael CHI.

Goaltender. Catches left. 6'2", 175 lbs. Born, Sarnia, Ont., May 19, 1981.
(Chicago's 6th choice, 165th overall, in 1999 Entry Draft).

							Regular Season							Playoffs			
Season	Club	Lea	GP	W	L	T	Mins	GA	SO	Avg	GP	W	L	Mins	GA	SO	Avg
1997-98	Petrolia	OJHL-B	30	....	....	....	1583	87	2	3.30	....	....	....	....	....	....	....
1998-99	Windsor	OHL	28	4	17	2	1389	112	0	4.84	3	0	1	80	10	0	7.50

LINDSAY, Evan MTL.

Goaltender. Catches left. 6'1", 180 lbs. Born, Calgary, Alta., May 15, 1979.
(Montreal's 4th choice, 107th overall, in 1999 Entry Draft).

							Regular Season							Playoffs			
Season	Club	Lea	GP	W	L	T	Mins	GA	SO	Avg	GP	W	L	Mins	GA	SO	Avg
1995-96	Olds Grizzlys	AJHL	11	4	5	0	....	....	0	3.64	....	....	....	....	....	....	....
1996-97	Prince Albert	WHL	44	20	17	6	2651	153	1	3.46	4	0	4	240	16	0	4.00
1997-98	Prince Albert	WHL	52	14	30	4	3005	193	1	3.85	....	....	....	....	....	....	....
1998-99	Prince Albert	WHL	56	34	16	5	3334	158	1	2.84	14	9	5	780	43	1	3.31

WHL East Second All-Star Team (1998, 1999)

• Re-entered NHL draft. Originally Calgary's 2nd choice, 32nd overall, in 1997 Entry Draft.

LITTLE, Neil PHI.

Goaltender. Catches left. 6'1", 193 lbs. Born, Medicine Hat, Alta., December 18, 1971.
(Philadelphia's 10th choice, 226th overall, in 1991 Entry Draft).

							Regular Season							Playoffs			
Season	Club	Lea	GP	W	L	T	Mins	GA	SO	Avg	GP	W	L	Mins	GA	SO	Avg
1989-90	Estevan	SJHL	46	21	19	4	2707	150	1	3.32	....	....	....	....	....	....	....
1990-91	RPI Engineers	ECAC	18	9	8	0	1032	71	0	4.13	....	....	....	....	....	....	....
1991-92	RPI Engineers	ECAC	28	11	11	3	1532	96	0	3.76	....	....	....	....	....	....	....
1992-93	RPI Engineers	ECAC	*31	*19	9	3	*1801	88	0	2.93	....	....	....	....	....	....	....
1993-94	RPI Engineers	ECAC	27	16	7	4	1570	88	0	3.36	....	....	....	....	....	....	....
	Hershey	AHL	1	0	0	0	18	1	0	3.33	....	....	....	....	....	....	....
1994-95	Hershey	AHL	19	5	7	3	919	60	0	3.91	....	....	....	....	....	....	....
	Johnstown	ECHL	16	7	6	1	897	55	0	3.68	3	0	2	145	11	0	4.55
1995-96	Hershey	AHL	48	21	18	6	2680	149	0	3.34	1	0	1	60	4	0	4.02
1996-97	Philadelphia	AHL	54	31	12	7	3007	145	0	2.89	10	6	4	620	20	1	*1.94
1997-98	Philadelphia	AHL	51	*31	11	7	2960	145	0	2.94	*20	*15	5	*1193	48	*3	2.41
1998-99	Grand Rapids	IHL	50	18	21	5	2740	144	3	3.15	....	....	....	....	....	....	....

ECAC First All-Star Team (1993) • NCAA East Second All-American Team (1993)

LITTMAN, David

Goaltender. Catches left. 6', 183 lbs. Born, Cranston, RI, June 13, 1967.
(Buffalo's 12th choice, 211th overall, in 1987 Entry Draft).

							Regular Season							Playoffs			
Season	Club	Lea	GP	W	L	T	Mins	GA	SO	Avg	GP	W	L	Mins	GA	SO	Avg
1984-85	Oyster Bay	NYJHL								STATISTICS NOT AVAILABLE							
1985-86	Boston College	H.E.	7	4	0	1	312	18	0	3.46	....	....	....	....	....	....	....
1986-87	Boston College	H.E.	21	15	5	0	1182	68	0	3.45	....	....	....	....	....	....	....
1987-88	Boston College	H.E.	30	11	16	2	1726	116	0	4.03	....	....	....	....	....	....	....
1988-89	Boston College	H.E.	*32	19	9	4	*1945	107	0	3.30	....	....	....	....	....	....	....
1989-90	Rochester	AHL	14	5	6	1	681	37	0	3.26	....	....	....	....	....	....	....
	Phoenix	IHL	18	8	7	2	1047	64	0	3.67	....	....	....	....	....	....	....
1990-91	**Buffalo**	**NHL**	**1**	**0**	**0**	**0**	**36**	**3**	**0**	**5.00**	....	....	....	....	....	....	....
	Rochester	AHL	*56	*33	13	5	*3155	160	3	3.04	8	4	2	378	16	0	2.54
1991-92	**Buffalo**	**NHL**	**1**	**0**	**1**	**0**	**60**	**4**	**0**	**4.00**	....	....	....	....	....	....	....
	Rochester	AHL	*60	*28	20	9	*3498	172	*3	2.95	15	8	7	879	43	*1	2.94
1992-93	**Tampa Bay**	**NHL**	**1**	**0**	**1**	**0**	**45**	**7**	**0**	**9.33**	....	....	....	....	....	....	....
	Atlanta	IHL	44	23	12	4	2390	134	0	3.36	3	1	2	178	8	0	2.70
1993-94	Fredericton	AHL	16	8	7	0	872	63	0	4.33	....	....	....	....	....	....	....
	Providence	AHL	25	10	11	3	1385	83	0	3.60	....	....	....	....	....	....	....
1994-95	Richmond	ECHL	8	4	2	0	346	13	1	2.25	*17	*12	4	*953	37	*3	*2.33
1995-96	Los Angeles	IHL	43	17	16	5	2245	145	1	3.88	....	....	....	....	....	....	....
1996-97	San Antonio	IHL	45	20	16	5	2437	138	2	3.40	4	1	3	230	11	0	2.87
1997-98	Orlando	IHL	44	21	13	6	2303	102	0	2.66	16	8	8	966	48	1	2.98
1998-99	Orlando	IHL	55	32	17	1	2981	144	2	2.90	2	0	0	46	4	0	5.22
	NHL Totals		**3**	**0**	**2**	**0**	**141**	**14**	**0**	**5.96**	....	....	....	....	....	....	....

Hockey East Second All-Star Team (1988) • Hockey East First All-Star Team (1989) • NCAA East Second All-American Team (1989) • AHL First All-Star Team (1991) • Shared Harry "Hap" Holmes Memorial Trophy (fewest goals against - AHL) with Darcy Wakaluk (1991) • AHL Second All-Star Team (1992) • Won Harry "Hap" Holmes Memorial Trophy (fewest goals against - AHL) (1992)

Signed as a free agent by **Tampa Bay**, August 27, 1992. Signed as a free agent by **Boston**, August 6, 1993.

LUONGO, Roberto (loo-WAHN-goh) NYI

Goaltender. Catches left. 6'3", 175 lbs. Born, Montreal, Que., April 4, 1979.
(NY Islanders' 1st choice, 4th overall, in 1997 Entry Draft).

							Regular Season							Playoffs			
Season	Club	Lea	GP	W	L	T	Mins	GA	SO	Avg	GP	W	L	Mins	GA	SO	Avg
1995-96	Val d'Or	QMJHL	23	6	11	4	1201	74	0	3.70	3	0	1	68	5	0	4.41
1996-97	Val d'Or	QMJHL	60	32	22	2	3305	171	2	3.10	13	8	5	777	44	0	3.40
1997-98	Val d'Or	QMJHL	54	27	20	5	3046	157	*7	3.09	*17	*14	3	*1019	37	*2	*2.18
1998-99	Val d'Or	QMJHL	21	6	10	2	1176	77	1	3.93	....	....	....	....	....	....	....
	Bathurst	QMJHL	22	14	7	1	1340	74	0	3.31	*23	*16	6	*1400	64	0	2.74

MacDONALD, Todd

Goaltender. Catches left. 6', 167 lbs. Born, Charlottetown, P.E.I., July 5, 1975.
(Florida's 7th choice, 109th overall, in 1993 Entry Draft).

							Regular Season							Playoffs			
Season	Club	Lea	GP	W	L	T	Mins	GA	SO	Avg	GP	W	L	Mins	GA	SO	Avg
1991-92	Kingston	OJHL	28	....	....	....	1680	84	0	3.00	....	....	....	....	....	....	....
1992-93	Tacoma	WHL	19	6	6	0	823	59	0	4.30	....	....	....	....	....	....	....
1993-94	Tacoma	WHL	29	13	10	2	1606	109	1	4.07	....	....	....	....	....	....	....
1994-95	Tacoma	WHL	60	*35	21	2	3433	179	3	3.13	4	1	3	255	13	0	3.06
1995-96	Carolina	AHL	18	3	12	2	980	78	0	4.78	....	....	....	....	....	....	....
	Detroit	ColHL	2	1	1	0	120	8	0	4.01	2	1	1	133	3	0	1.36
1996-97	Carolina	AHL	1	0	1	0	58	4	0	4.14	....	....	....	....	....	....	....
	Cincinnati	IHL	31	11	9	5	1616	73	2	2.71	1	0	0	20	1	0	3.00
1997-98	Birmingham	ECHL	3	1	1	1	180	8	0	2.67	....	....	....	....	....	....	....
	Cincinnati	IHL	15	4	6	3	796	46	0	3.46	....	....	....	....	....	....	....
	New Haven	AHL	13	8	3	2	790	30	1	2.28	3	0	3	177	15	0	5.07
1998-99	New Haven	AHL	31	10	16	3	1775	91	0	3.08	....	....	....	....	....	....	....

WHL West First All-Star Team (1995)

MADDEN, Chris CAR.

Goaltender. Catches left. 6', 177 lbs. Born, Syracuse, NY, March 10, 1979.
(Carolina's 6th choice, 97th overall, in 1998 Entry Draft).

							Regular Season							Playoffs			
Season	Club	Lea	GP	W	L	T	Mins	GA	SO	Avg	GP	W	L	Mins	GA	SO	Avg
1996-97	Guelph	OHL	21	11	5	1	1128	68	1	3.62	3	1	1	72	4	0	3.33
1997-98	Guelph	OHL	51	*33	11	3	2906	132	4	2.73	12	*11	1	688	20	0	*1.74
1998-99	Guelph	OHL	50	28	13	0	2567	133	2	3.11	10	6	3	550	32	*1	3.49

Memorial Cup All-Star Team (1998) • Won Hap Emms Memorial Trophy (Memorial Cup Tournament Top Goaltender) (1998) • Won Stafford Smythe Memorial Trophy (Memorial Cup Tournament MVP) (1998)

MARACLE, Norm (MAHR-ah-cuhl) ATL.

Goaltender. Catches left. 5'8", 195 lbs. Born, Belleville, Ont., October 2, 1974.
(Detroit's 6th choice, 126th overall, in 1993 Entry Draft).

							Regular Season							Playoffs			
Season	Club	Lea	GP	W	L	T	Mins	GA	SO	Avg	GP	W	L	Mins	GA	SO	Avg
1990-91	Calgary	AAHA	29	....	....	....	1740	99	0	3.43	....	....	....	....	....	....	....
1991-92	Saskatoon	WHL	29	13	6	3	1529	87	1	3.41	15	9	5	860	37	0	3.38
1992-93	Saskatoon	WHL	53	27	18	3	1939	160	1	3.27	9	4	5	569	33	0	3.48
1993-94	Saskatoon	WHL	56	*41	13	1	3219	148	2	2.76	16	*11	5	940	48	*1	3.06
1994-95	Adirondack	AHL	39	12	15	2	1997	119	0	3.57	....	....	....	....	....	....	....
1995-96	Adirondack	AHL	54	24	18	6	2949	135	2	2.75	1	0	1	30	4	0	8.11
1996-97	Adirondack	AHL	*68	*34	22	9	*3843	173	5	2.70	4	1	3	192	10	1	3.13
1997-98	**Detroit**	**NHL**	**4**	**2**	**0**	**1**	**178**	**6**	**0**	**2.02**	....	....	....	....	....	....	....
	Adirondack	AHL	*66	27	29	8	*3709	190	1	3.07	3	0	3	180	10	0	3.33
1998-99	**Detroit**	**NHL**	**16**	**6**	**5**	**2**	**821**	**31**	**0**	**2.27**	**2**	**0**	**0**	**58**	**3**	**0**	**3.10**
	Adirondack	AHL	6	3	3	0	359	18	0	3.01	....	....	....	....	....	....	....
	NHL Totals		**20**	**8**	**5**	**3**	**999**	**37**	**0**	**2.22**	**2**	**0**	**0**	**58**	**3**	**0**	**3.10**

WHL East Second All-Star Team (1993) • WHL East First All-Star Team (1994) • Canadian Major Junior First All-Star Team (1994) • Canadian Major Junior Goaltender of the Year (1994) • AHL Second All-Star Team (1997, 1998)

Claimed by **Atlanta** from **Detroit** in Expansion Draft, June 25, 1999.

MASON, Chris — NSH.

Goaltender. Catches left. 6', 200 lbs. Born, Red Deer, Alta., April 20, 1976.
(New Jersey's 7th choice, 122nd overall, in 1995 Entry Draft).

			Regular Season								Playoffs						
Season	Club	Lea	GP	W	L	T	Mins	GA	SO	Avg	GP	W	L	Mins	GA	SO	Avg
1993-94	Victoria	WHL	5	1	4	0	237	27	0	6.84	....	....	....	....	....	....	....
1994-95	Red Deer	AAHA	20	....	....	....	1280	76	0	3.35	....	....	....	....	....	....	....
	Prince George	WHL	44	8	30	1	2288	192	1	5.03	....	....	....	....	....	....	....
1995-96	Prince George	WHL	59	16	37	1	3289	236	1	4.31	....	....	....	....	....	....	....
1996-97	Prince George	WHL	50	19	24	4	2851	172	2	3.62	15	9	6	938	44	*1	2.81
1997-98	Cincinnati	AHL	47	13	19	7	2368	136	0	3.45	....	....	....	....	....	....	....
1998-99	**Nashville**	**NHL**	**3**	**0**	**0**	**0**	**69**	**6**	**0**	**5.22**	....	....	....	....	....	....	....
	Milwaukee	IHL	34	15	12	6	1901	92	1	2.90	....	....	....	....	....	....	....
	NHL Totals		**3**	**0**	**0**	**0**	**69**	**6**	**0**	**5.22**	....	....	....	....	....	....	....

Signed as a free agent by **Anaheim**, June 27, 1997. Traded to **Nashville** by **Anaheim** with Marc Moro for Dominic Roussel, October 5, 1998.

MAUND, Jeff (MAHND) — CHI.

Goaltender. Catches left. 6'2", 195 lbs. Born, Mississauga, Ont., April 8, 1976.

			Regular Season								Playoffs						
Season	Club	Lea	GP	W	L	T	Mins	GA	SO	Avg	GP	W	L	Mins	GA	SO	Avg
1996-97	Aurora	OJHL	29	....	....	....	1731	72	....	2.50	....	....	....	....	....	....	....
1997-98	Ohio State	CCHA	32	22	8	0	1858	73	4	2.36	....	....	....	....	....	....	....
1998-99	Ohio State	CCHA	38	20	14	4	2283	89	3	2.34	....	....	....	....	....	....	....

CCHA First All-Star Team (1999) • NCAA West Second All-American Team (1999)

Signed as a free agent by **Chicago**, April 14, 1999.

McARTHUR, Mark

Goaltender. Catches left. 5'10", 175 lbs. Born, East York, Ont., November 16, 1975.
(NY Islanders' 5th choice, 112th overall, in 1994 Entry Draft).

			Regular Season								Playoffs						
Season	Club	Lea	GP	W	L	T	Mins	GA	SO	Avg	GP	W	L	Mins	GA	SO	Avg
1991-92	Peterborough	OJHL-B	25	....	....	....	1198	98	0	4.91	....	....	....	....	....	....	....
1992-93	Guelph	OHL	35	14	14	3	1853	180	0	5.83	....	....	....	....	....	....	....
1993-94	Guelph	OHL	51	25	18	5	2936	201	0	4.11	9	4	5	561	38	0	4.06
1994-95	Guelph	OHL	48	*34	8	4	2776	130	1	*2.81	13	9	4	797	44	0	3.31
1995-96	Utah	IHL	26	12	12	0	1482	77	0	3.12	....	....	....	....	....	....	....
1996-97	Utah	IHL	56	28	20	6	3111	155	3	2.99	....	....	....	....	....	....	....
1997-98	Utah	IHL	20	7	7	2	1059	60	0	3.40	1	0	1	63	4	0	3.78
1998-99	Utah	IHL	1	0	1	0	60	5	0	5.00	....	....	....	....	....	....	....
	Lowell	AHL	26	6	13	5	1457	75	3	3.09	....	....	....	....	....	....	....

OHL Second All-Star Team (1995) • Shared James Norris Memorial Trophy (fewest goals against — IHL) with Tommy Salo (1996)

McCRACKEN, Jake — DET.

Goaltender. Catches left. 5'10", 180 lbs. Born, London, Ont., January 15, 1980.
(Detroit's 4th choice, 84th overall, in 1998 Entry Draft).

			Regular Season								Playoffs						
Season	Club	Lea	GP	W	L	T	Mins	GA	SO	Avg	GP	W	L	Mins	GA	SO	Avg
1996-97	S.S. Marie	OHL	29	13	3	6	1389	80	0	3.46	1	0	1	28	4	0	8.57
1997-98	S.S. Marie	OHL	55	16	31	5	3102	216	0	4.18	....	....	....	....	....	....	....
1998-99	S.S. Marie	OHL	41	15	16	4	2290	140	0	3.67	1	0	0	45	7	0	9.33

McLEAN, Jason

Goaltender. Catches left. 6', 200 lbs. Born, Regina, Sask., September 3, 1979.
(NY Rangers' 5th choice, 126th overall, in 1997 Entry Draft).

			Regular Season								Playoffs						
Season	Club	Lea	GP	W	L	T	Mins	GA	SO	Avg	GP	W	L	Mins	GA	SO	Avg
1995-96	Moose Jaw	WHL	11	1	7	1	544	38	0	4.19	....	....	....	....	....	....	....
1996-97	Moose Jaw	WHL	19	7	7	2	1014	60	0	3.55	....	....	....	....	....	....	....
1997-98	Moose Jaw	WHL	5	1	3	0	243	21	0	5.19	....	....	....	....	....	....	....
	Lethbridge	WHL	46	19	18	6	2610	131	2	3.01	4	0	3	190	17	0	5.37
1998-99	Lethbridge	WHL	19	11	4	2	1077	49	1	2.73	2	0	1	75	12	0	9.60

McLEAN, Kirk — NYR

Goaltender. Catches left. 6', 180 lbs. Born, Willowdale, Ont., June 26, 1966.
(New Jersey's 6th choice, 107th overall, in 1984 Entry Draft).

			Regular Season								Playoffs						
Season	Club	Lea	GP	W	L	T	Mins	GA	SO	Avg	GP	W	L	Mins	GA	SO	Avg
1982-83	Don Mills	MTHL	26	....	....	....	1575	52	0	2.01	....	....	....	....	....	....	....
1983-84	Oshawa	OHL	17	5	9	0	940	67	0	4.28	....	....	....	....	....	....	....
1984-85	Oshawa	OHL	47	23	17	2	2581	143	1	*3.32	5	1	3	271	21	0	4.65
1985-86	**New Jersey**	**NHL**	**2**	**1**	**1**	**0**	**111**	**11**	**0**	**5.95**	....	....	....	....	....	....	....
	Oshawa	OHL	51	24	21	2	2830	169	1	3.58	4	1	2	201	18	0	5.37
1986-87	**New Jersey**	**NHL**	**4**	**1**	**1**	**0**	**160**	**10**	**0**	**3.75**	....	....	....	....	....	....	....
	Maine	AHL	45	15	23	4	2606	140	1	3.22	....	....	....	....	....	....	....
1987-88	**Vancouver**	**NHL**	**41**	**11**	**27**	**3**	**2380**	**147**	**1**	**3.71**	....	....	....	....	....	....	....
1988-89	**Vancouver**	**NHL**	**42**	**20**	**17**	**3**	**2477**	**127**	**4**	**3.08**	**5**	**2**	**3**	**302**	**18**	**0**	**3.58**
1989-90	**Vancouver**	**NHL**	***63**	**21**	**30**	**10**	***3739**	**216**	**0**	**3.47**	....	....	....	....	....	....	....
1990-91	**Vancouver**	**NHL**	**41**	**10**	**22**	**3**	**1969**	**131**	**0**	**3.99**	**2**	**1**	**1**	**123**	**7**	**0**	**3.41**
1991-92	**Vancouver**	**NHL**	**65**	***38**	**17**	**9**	**3852**	**176**	***5**	**2.74**	**13**	**6**	**7**	**785**	**33**	***2**	**2.52**
1992-93	**Vancouver**	**NHL**	**54**	**28**	**21**	**5**	**3261**	**184**	**3**	**3.39**	**12**	**6**	**6**	**754**	**42**	**0**	**3.34**
1993-94	**Vancouver**	**NHL**	**52**	**23**	**26**	**3**	**3128**	**156**	**3**	**2.99**	***24**	**15**	**9**	***1544**	**59**	***4**	**2.29**
1994-95	**Vancouver**	**NHL**	**40**	**18**	**12**	**10**	**2374**	**109**	**1**	**2.75**	**11**	**4**	**7**	**660**	**36**	**0**	**3.27**
1995-96	**Vancouver**	**NHL**	**45**	**15**	**21**	**9**	**2645**	**156**	**2**	**3.54**	**1**	**0**	**1**	**21**	**3**	**0**	**8.57**
1996-97	**Vancouver**	**NHL**	**44**	**21**	**18**	**3**	**2581**	**138**	**0**	**3.21**	....	....	....	....	....	....	....
1997-98	**Vancouver**	**NHL**	**29**	**6**	**17**	**4**	**1583**	**97**	**1**	**3.68**	....	....	....	....	....	....	....
	Carolina	**NHL**	**8**	**4**	**2**	**0**	**401**	**22**	**0**	**3.29**	....	....	....	....	....	....	....
	Florida	**NHL**	**7**	**4**	**2**	**1**	**406**	**22**	**0**	**3.25**	....	....	....	....	....	....	....
1998-99	**Florida**	**NHL**	**30**	**9**	**10**	**4**	**1597**	**73**	**2**	**2.74**	....	....	....	....	....	....	....
	NHL Totals		**567**	**230**	**244**	**67**	**32664**	**1775**	**22**	**3.26**	**68**	**34**	**34**	**4189**	**198**	**6**	**2.84**

NHL Second All-Star Team (1992)

Played in NHL All-Star Game (1990, 1992)

Traded to **Vancouver** by **New Jersey** with Greg Adams and New Jersey's 2nd round choice (Leif Rohlin) in 1988 Entry Draft for Patrik Sundstrom and Vancouver's 2nd (Jeff Christian) and 4th (Matt Ruchty) round choices in 1988 Entry Draft, September 10, 1987. Traded to **Carolina** by **Vancouver** with Martin Gelinas for Sean Burke, Geoff Sanderson and Enrico Ciccone, January 3, 1998. Traded to **Florida** by **Carolina** for Ray Sheppard, March 24, 1998. Signed as a free agent by **NY Rangers**, July 20, 1999.

McLENNAN, Jamie — ST.L.

Goaltender. Catches left. 6', 190 lbs. Born, Edmonton, Alta., June 30, 1971.
(NY Islanders' 3rd choice, 48th overall, in 1991 Entry Draft).

			Regular Season								Playoffs						
Season	Club	Lea	GP	W	L	T	Mins	GA	SO	Avg	GP	W	L	Mins	GA	SO	Avg
1987-88	St. Albert	AAHA	21	....	....	....	1224	80	0	3.92	....	....	....	....	....	....	....
1988-89	Spokane	WHL	11	....	....	....	578	63	0	6.54	....	....	....	....	....	....	....
	Lethbridge	WHL	7	....	....	....	368	22	0	3.59	....	....	....	....	....	....	....
1989-90	Lethbridge	WHL	34	20	4	2	1690	110	1	3.91	13	6	5	677	44	0	3.90
1990-91	Lethbridge	WHL	56	32	18	4	3230	205	0	3.81	*16	8	8	*970	56	0	3.46
1991-92	Capital District	AHL	18	4	10	2	952	60	1	3.78	....	....	....	....	....	....	....
	Richmond	ECHL	32	16	12	2	1837	114	0	3.72	....	....	....	....	....	....	....
1992-93	Capital District	AHL	38	17	14	6	2171	117	1	3.23	1	0	1	20	5	0	15.00
1993-94	**NY Islanders**	**NHL**	**22**	**8**	**7**	**6**	**1287**	**61**	**0**	**2.84**	**2**	**0**	**1**	**82**	**6**	**0**	**4.39**
	Salt Lake	IHL	24	8	12	2	1320	80	0	3.64	....	....	....	....	....	....	....
1994-95	**NY Islanders**	**NHL**	**21**	**6**	**11**	**2**	**1185**	**67**	**0**	**3.39**	....	....	....	....	....	....	....
	Denver	IHL	4	3	0	1	239	12	0	3.00	11	8	2	640	23	1	*2.15
1995-96	**NY Islanders**	**NHL**	**13**	**3**	**9**	**1**	**636**	**39**	**0**	**3.68**	....	....	....	....	....	....	....
	Utah	IHL	14	9	2	2	728	29	0	2.39	....	....	....	....	....	....	....
	Worcester	AHL	22	14	7	1	1216	57	0	2.81	2	0	2	119	8	0	4.04
1996-97	Worcester	AHL	39	18	13	4	2152	100	2	2.79	4	2	2	262	16	0	3.67
1997-98	**St. Louis**	**NHL**	**30**	**16**	**8**	**2**	**1658**	**60**	**2**	**2.17**	**1**	**0**	**0**	**14**	**1**	**0**	**4.29**
1998-99	**St. Louis**	**NHL**	**33**	**13**	**14**	**4**	**1763**	**70**	**3**	**2.38**	**1**	**0**	**1**	**37**	**0**	**0**	**0.00**
	NHL Totals		**119**	**46**	**49**	**15**	**6529**	**297**	**5**	**2.73**	**4**	**0**	**2**	**133**	**7**	**0**	**3.16**

WHL East First All-Star Team (1991) • Won Bill Masterton Memorial Trophy (1998)

Signed as a free agent by **St. Louis**, July 15, 1996.

MICHAUD, Alfie (mee-SHOH) — VAN.

Goaltender. Catches . 5'10", 177 lbs. Born, Selkirk, Man., November 6, 1976.

			Regular Season								Playoffs						
Season	Club	Lea	GP	W	L	T	Mins	GA	SO	Avg	GP	W	L	Mins	GA	SO	Avg
1996-97	U. of Maine	H.E.	29	17	8	1	1515	78	1	3.09	....	....	....	....	....	....	....
1997-98	U. of Maine	H.E.	32	15	12	4	1794	94	2	3.14	....	....	....	....	....	....	....
1998-99	U. of Maine	H.E.	37	*28	6	3	2147	83	3	2.32	....	....	....	....	....	....	....

NCAA Championship All-Tournament Team (1999) • NCAA Championship Tournament MVP (1999)

Signed as a free agent by **Vancouver**, July 12, 1999.

MILLER, Aren — DET.

Goaltender. Catches left. 6'2", 208 lbs. Born, Oxbow, Sask., January 13, 1978.
(Detroit's 2nd choice, 52nd overall, in 1996 Entry Draft).

			Regular Season								Playoffs						
Season	Club	Lea	GP	W	L	T	Mins	GA	SO	Avg	GP	W	L	Mins	GA	SO	Avg
1995-96	Spokane	WHL	23	8	7	2	965	50	1	3.11	3	0	3	81	8	0	5.93
1996-97	Spokane	WHL	52	22	20	3	2834	151	3	3.20	9	4	5	555	28	*1	3.03
1997-98	Spokane	WHL	*64	*38	22	3	*3466	187	3	3.24	7	2	3	318	24	0	4.53
1998-99	Toledo	ECHL	7	1	4	1	374	33	0	5.29	....	....	....	....	....	....	....
	Adirondack	AHL	25	3	14	1	1155	68	1	3.53	2	0	2	123	8	0	3.92

MILLER, Ryan — BUF.

Goaltender. Catches left. 6'2", 155 lbs. Born, East Lansing, MI, July 17, 1980.
(Buffalo's 7th choice, 138th overall, in 1999 Entry Draft).

			Regular Season								Playoffs						
Season	Club	Lea	GP	W	L	T	Mins	GA	SO	Avg	GP	W	L	Mins	GA	SO	Avg
1997-98	Soo Indians	NAHL	37	....	....	....	2115	82	0	2.33	....	....	....	....	....	....	....
1998-99	Soo Indians	NAHL	47	31	14	1	2711	104	8	2.30	....	....	....	....	....	....	....

MINARD, Mike (mih-NAHRD) — EDM.

Goaltender. Catches left. 6'3", 205 lbs. Born, Owen Sound, Ont., November 1, 1976.
(Edmonton's 4th choice, 83rd overall, in 1995 Entry Draft).

			Regular Season								Playoffs						
Season	Club	Lea	GP	W	L	T	Mins	GA	SO	Avg	GP	W	L	Mins	GA	SO	Avg
1993-94	St. Mary's	OJHL	31	....	....	....	1710	78	1	2.74	....	....	....	....	....	....	....
1994-95	Chilliwack	BCJHL	40	....	....	....	2330	136	0	3.50	....	....	....	....	....	....	....
1995-96	Barrie	OHL	1	0	1	0	52	8	0	9.23	....	....	....	....	....	....	....
	Detroit	OHL	42	25	10	4	2314	128	2	3.32	17	9	6	922	55	1	3.58
1996-97	Hamilton	AHL	3	1	1	0	100	7	0	4.20	....	....	....	....	....	....	....
	Wheeling	ECHL	23	3	7	1	899	69	0	4.60	3	0	2	148	16	0	6.47
1997-98	Brantford	UHL	2	1	1	0	74	7	0	5.63	....	....	....	....	....	....	....
	Hamilton	AHL	2	1	0	0	80	2	0	1.50	....	....	....	....	....	....	....
	New Orleans	ECHL	11	6	2	0	429	30	0	4.19	....	....	....	....	....	....	....
	Milwaukee	IHL	8	2	2	0	362	19	0	3.15	....	....	....	....	....	....	....
1998-99	Dayton	ECHL	15	8	5	2	788	42	1	3.20	....	....	....	....	....	....	....
	Milwaukee	IHL	10	3	5	0	531	27	0	3.05	....	....	....	....	....	....	....
	Hamilton	AHL	11	8	3	0	645	30	1	2.79	1	0	0	20	0	0	0.00

MORRISON, Michael — EDM.

Goaltender. Catches right. 6'3", 194 lbs. Born, Medford, MA, July 11, 1979.
(Edmonton's 8th choice, 186th overall, in 1998 Entry Draft).

			Regular Season								Playoffs						
Season	Club	Lea	GP	W	L	T	Mins	GA	SO	Avg	GP	W	L	Mins	GA	SO	Avg
1997-98	Phillips Exeter	H.S.	27	15	11	2	1632	64	1	2.35	....	....	....	....	....	....	....
1998-99	U. of Maine	H.E.	11	3	0	1	347	10	1	1.73	....	....	....	....	....	....	....

MOSS, Tyler — CGY.

Goaltender. Catches right. 6', 184 lbs. Born, Ottawa, Ont., June 29, 1975.
(Tampa Bay's 2nd choice, 29th overall, in 1993 Entry Draft).

			Regular Season								Playoffs						
Season	Club	Lea	GP	W	L	T	Mins	GA	SO	Avg	GP	W	L	Mins	GA	SO	Avg
1991-92	Nepean	OJHL	26	....	....	....	1335	109	0	4.90	....	....	....	....	....	....	....
1992-93	Kingston	OHL	31	13	7	5	1537	97	0	3.79	6	1	2	228	19	0	5.00
1993-94	Kingston	OHL	13	6	4	3	795	42	1	3.17	3	0	2	136	8	0	3.53
1994-95	Kingston	OHL	*57	33	17	5	*3249	164	1	3.03	6	2	4	333	27	0	4.86
1995-96	Atlanta	IHL	40	11	19	4	2030	138	1	4.08	3	0	3	213	11	0	3.10
1996-97	Adirondack	AHL	11	1	5	2	507	42	1	4.97	....	....	....	....	....	....	....
	Grand Rapids	IHL	15	5	6	1	715	35	0	2.94	....	....	....	....	....	....	....
	Muskegon	ColHL	2	1	1	0	119	5	0	2.51	....	....	....	....	....	....	....
	Saint John	AHL	9	6	1	1	534	17	0	1.91	5	2	3	242	15	0	3.72
1997-98	**Calgary**	**NHL**	**6**	**2**	**3**	**1**	**367**	**20**	**0**	**3.27**	....	....	....	....	....	....	....
	Saint John	AHL	39	19	10	7	2194	91	0	2.49	15	8	5	761	37	0	2.91
1998-99	**Calgary**	**NHL**	**11**	**3**	**7**	**0**	**550**	**23**	**0**	**2.51**	....	....	....	....	....	....	....
	Saint John	AHL	9	2	5	1	475	25	0	3.16	....	....	....	....	....	....	....
	Orlando	IHL	9	6	2	1	515	21	1	2.45	17	10	7	1017	53	0	3.13
	NHL Totals		**17**	**5**	**10**	**1**	**917**	**43**	**0**	**2.81**	....	....	....	....	....	....	....

OHL First All-Star Team (1995) • Shared Harry "Hap" Holmes Memorial Trophy (fewest goals against - AHL) with Jean-Sebastien Giguere (1998)

Traded to **Calgary** by **Tampa Bay** for Jamie Huscroft, March 18, 1997.

MUZZATTI, Jason (moo-ZAH-tee)

Goaltender. Catches left. 6'2", 210 lbs. Born, Toronto, Ont., February 3, 1970.
(Calgary's 1st choice, 21st overall, in 1988 Entry Draft).

			Regular Season								Playoffs						
Season	**Club**	**Lea**	**GP**	**W**	**L**	**T**	**Mins**	**GA**	**SO**	**Avg**	**GP**	**W**	**L**	**Mins**	**GA**	**SO**	**Avg**
1985-86	St. Michael's	OJHL-B	20	....	....	....	1054	69	1	3.93	....	....	....	....	....	....	....
1986-87	St. Michael's	OJHL-B	11	6	3	0	517	48	0	5.57	....	....	....	....	....	....	....
1987-88	Michigan State	CCHA	33	19	9	3	1915	109	0	3.41	....	....	....	....	....	....	....
1988-89	Michigan State	CCHA	42	32	9	1	2515	127	3	*3.03	....	....	....	....	....	....	....
1989-90	Michigan State	CCHA	33	*24	6	0	1976	99	0	3.01	....	....	....	....	....	....	....
1990-91	Michigan State	CCHA	22	8	10	2	1204	75	1	3.74	....	....	....	....	....	....	....
1991-92	Salt Lake	IHL	52	24	22	5	3033	167	2	3.30	4	1	3	247	18	0	4.37
1992-93	Canada	Nat-Team	16	6	9	0	880	53	0	3.84	....	....	....	....	....	....	....
	Indianapolis	IHL	12	5	6	1	707	48	0	4.07	....	....	....	....	....	....	....
	Salt Lake	IHL	13	5	6	1	747	52	0	4.18	....	....	....	....	....	....	....
1993-94	**Calgary**	**NHL**	**1**	**0**	**1**	**0**	**60**	**8**	**0**	**8.00**	....	....	....	....	....	....	....
	Saint John	AHL	51	26	21	3	2939	183	2	3.74	7	3	4	415	19	0	2.75
1994-95	Saint John	AHL	31	10	14	4	1741	101	2	3.48	....	....	....	....	....	....	....
	Calgary	**NHL**	**1**	**0**	**0**	**0**	**10**	**0**	**0**	**0.00**	....	....	....	....	....	....	....
1995-96	**Hartford**	**NHL**	**22**	**4**	**8**	**3**	**1013**	**49**	**1**	**2.90**	....	....	....	....	....	....	....
	Springfield	AHL	5	4	0	1	300	12	1	2.40	....	....	....	....	....	....	....
1996-97	**Hartford**	**NHL**	**31**	**9**	**13**	**5**	**1591**	**91**	**0**	**3.43**	....	....	....	....	....	....	....
1997-98	**NY Rangers**	**NHL**	**6**	**0**	**3**	**2**	**313**	**17**	**0**	**3.26**	....	....	....	....	....	....	....
	Hartford	AHL	17	11	5	1	999	57	0	3.42	....	....	....	....	....	....	....
	San Jose	**NHL**	**1**	**0**	**0**	**0**	**27**	**2**	**0**	**4.44**	....	....	....	....	....	....	....
	Kentucky	AHL	7	2	3	2	430	25	0	3.49	3	0	3	153	13	0	5.07
1998-99	EHC Berlin	Germany	4	....	....	....	240	12	0	3.00	3	0	3	166	14	0	5.06
	NHL Totals		**62**	**13**	**25**	**10**	**3014**	**167**	**1**	**3.32**	....	....	....	....	....	....	....

CCHA Second All-Star Team (1988) • CCHA First All-Star Team (1990) • NCAA West Second All-American Team (1990)

Claimed on waivers by **Hartford** from **Calgary**, October 6, 1995. Transferred to **Carolina** after **Hartford** franchise relocated, June 25, 1997. Traded to **NY Rangers** by **Carolina** for NY Rangers' 4th round choice (Tommy Westlund) in 1998 Entry Draft, August 8, 1997. Traded to **San Jose** by **NY Rangers** for Rich Brennan, March 24, 1998. • Missed majority of 1998-99 season recovering from minor heart surgery, September 1998.

MYERS, Scott — PIT.

Goaltender. Catches right. 5'10", 172 lbs. Born, Winnipeg, Man., June 11, 1979.
(Pittsburgh's 4th choice, 110th overall, in 1998 Entry Draft).

			Regular Season								Playoffs						
Season	**Club**	**Lea**	**GP**	**W**	**L**	**T**	**Mins**	**GA**	**SO**	**Avg**	**GP**	**W**	**L**	**Mins**	**GA**	**SO**	**Avg**
1996-97	Prince George	WHL	25	6	14	1	1284	94	0	4.39	....	....	....	....	....	....	....
1997-98	Prince George	WHL	48	29	13	4	2822	139	2	2.96	11	5	6	665	25	*2	2.26
1998-99	Prince George	WHL	*66	30	28	6	*3771	214	0	3.40	7	3	4	418	23	0	3.30

NABOKOV, John (nuh-BAW-kahv, yehv-GEH-nee) — S.J.

Goaltender. Catches left. 6', 195 lbs. Born, Ust-Kamenogorsk, USSR, July 25, 1975.
(San Jose's 9th choice, 219th overall, in 1994 Entry Draft).

			Regular Season								Playoffs						
Season	**Club**	**Lea**	**GP**	**W**	**L**	**T**	**Mins**	**GA**	**SO**	**Avg**	**GP**	**W**	**L**	**Mins**	**GA**	**SO**	**Avg**
1992-93	Kamenogorsk	CIS	4	....	....	....	109	5	0	2.75	....	....	....	....	....	....	....
1993-94	Kamenogorsk	CIS	11	....	....	....	539	29	0	3.22	....	....	....	....	....	....	....
1994-95	Moscow D'amo	CIS	24	....	....	....	1265	40	....	1.89	....	....	....	....	....	....	....
1995-96	Moscow D'amo	CIS	39				2008	67	5	2.00	6	....	....	298	7	....	1.41
1996-97	Moscow D'amo	Russia	27	....	....	....	1588	56	2	2.11	4	....	....	255	12	0	2.82
1997-98	Kentucky	AHL	33	10	21	2	1866	122	0	3.92	1	0	0	23	1	0	2.59
1998-99	Kentucky	AHL	43	26	14	1	2429	106	5	2.62	11	6	5	599	30	*2	3.00

NAUMENKO, Gregg (naw-MEHN-koh) — ANA.

Goaltender. Catches . 6', 195 lbs. Born, Chicago, IL, March 30, 1977.

			Regular Season								Playoffs						
Season	**Club**	**Lea**	**GP**	**W**	**L**	**T**	**Mins**	**GA**	**SO**	**Avg**	**GP**	**W**	**L**	**Mins**	**GA**	**SO**	**Avg**
1995-96	North Iowa	USHL	27	....	....	....	1649	103	1	3.75	4	1	3	239	15	0	3.77
1996-97	North Iowa	USHL	25	....	....	....	1342	85	1	3.80	6	3	2	284	19	0	4.01
1997-98	North Iowa	USHL	38	23	11	3	2171	80	3	2.21	5	4	1	299	11	0	2.21
1998-99	Alaska-Anchorage	WCHA	29	11	13	5	1692	65	1	*2.31	....	....	....	....	....	....	....

WCHA First All-Star Team (1999)

Signed as a free agent by **Anaheim**, March 31, 1999.

NIITTYMAKI, Antero (NEE-too-mah-kee, AN-tehr-oh) — PHI.

Goaltender. Catches left. 6', 176 lbs. Born, Turku, Finland, June 18, 1980.
(Philadelphia's 7th choice, 168th overall, in 1998 Entry Draft).

			Regular Season								Playoffs						
Season	**Club**	**Lea**	**GP**	**W**	**L**	**T**	**Mins**	**GA**	**SO**	**Avg**	**GP**	**W**	**L**	**Mins**	**GA**	**SO**	**Avg**
1998-99	TPS Turku	Finn-Jr.	35	....	....	....	2095	60	0	1.72	....	....	....	....	....	....	....

NOGUES, Jean-Francois (NOHG) — L.A.

Goaltender. Catches left. 6'1", 154 lbs. Born, Acton Vale, Que., May 10, 1981.
(Los Angeles' 6th choice, 133rd overall, in 1999 Entry Draft).

			Regular Season								Playoffs						
Season	**Club**	**Lea**	**GP**	**W**	**L**	**T**	**Mins**	**GA**	**SO**	**Avg**	**GP**	**W**	**L**	**Mins**	**GA**	**SO**	**Avg**
1997-98	Magog	QAAA	STATISTICS NOT AVAILABLE														
1998-99	Victoriaville	QMJHL	32	11	10	4	1555	108	0	4.17	....	....	....	....	....	....	....

NORONEN, Mika (NOH-rah-nehn, MEE-kah) — BUF.

Goaltender. Catches left. 6'1", 191 lbs. Born, Tampere, Finland, June 17, 1979.
(Buffalo's 1st choice, 21st overall, in 1997 Entry Draft).

			Regular Season								Playoffs						
Season	**Club**	**Lea**	**GP**	**W**	**L**	**T**	**Mins**	**GA**	**SO**	**Avg**	**GP**	**W**	**L**	**Mins**	**GA**	**SO**	**Avg**
1995-96	Tappara	Finn-Jr.	16	....	....	....	962	37	2	2.31	....	....	....	....	....	....	....
1996-97	Tappara	Finland	5	1	3	0	215	17	0	4.73	....	....	....	....	....	....	....
1997-98	Tappara	Finland	37	14	12	3	1704	83	1	2.92	4	1	2	196	12	0	3.67
1998-99	Tappara	Finland	43	18	20	5	2494	135	2	3.25	....	....	....	....	....	....	....

ONDRIK, Cam (AWN-drihk) — PHI.

Goaltender. Catches left. 6'1", 170 lbs. Born, Nanaimo, B.C., March 28, 1980.
(Philadelphia's 8th choice, 175th overall, in 1998 Entry Draft).

			Regular Season								Playoffs						
Season	**Club**	**Lea**	**GP**	**W**	**L**	**T**	**Mins**	**GA**	**SO**	**Avg**	**GP**	**W**	**L**	**Mins**	**GA**	**SO**	**Avg**
1996-97	Red Deer	WHL	4	....	....	....	77	10	0	7.79	....	....	....	....	....	....	....
1997-98	Red Deer	WHL	11	5	3	0	461	31	1	4.03	....	....	....	....	....	....	....
	Medicine Hat	WHL	16	2	7	1	689	53	0	4.62	....	....	....	....	....	....	....
1998-99	Medicine Hat	WHL	39	4	28	0	1922	149	0	4.65	....	....	....	....	....	....	....

O'NEILL, Mike — L.A.

Goaltender. Catches left. 5'7", 160 lbs. Born, LaSalle, Que., November 3, 1967.
(Winnipeg's 1st choice, 15th overall, in 1988 Supplemental Draft).

			Regular Season								Playoffs						
Season	**Club**	**Lea**	**GP**	**W**	**L**	**T**	**Mins**	**GA**	**SO**	**Avg**	**GP**	**W**	**L**	**Mins**	**GA**	**SO**	**Avg**
1982-83	Lac St-Louis	QAAA	22	13	7	2	1318	81	0	3.67	....	....	....	....	....	....	....
	Lac St-Louis	QAAA	20	7	8	5	1198	107	0	5.34	....	....	....	....	....	....	....
1983-84	Yale University	ECAC	DID NOT PLAY – FRESHMAN														
1985-86	Yale University	ECAC	6	3	1	0	389	17	0	3.53	....	....	....	....	....	....	....
1986-87	Yale University	ECAC	16	9	6	1	964	55	2	3.42	....	....	....	....	....	....	....
1987-88	Yale University	ECAC	24	6	17	0	1385	101	0	4.37	....	....	....	....	....	....	....
1988-89	Yale University	ECAC	25	10	14	1	1490	93	0	3.74	....	....	....	....	....	....	....
1989-90	Tappara	Finland	41	23	13	5	2369	127	2	3.22	....	....	....	....	....	....	....
1990-91	Fort Wayne	IHL	8	5	2	1	490	31	0	3.80	....	....	....	....	....	....	....
	Moncton	AHL	30	13	7	6	1613	84	0	3.12	8	3	4	435	29	0	4.00
1991-92	**Winnipeg**	**NHL**	**1**	**0**	**0**	**0**	**13**	**1**	**0**	**4.62**	....	....	....	....	....	....	....
	Moncton	AHL	32	14	16	2	1902	108	1	3.41	11	4	7	670	43	*1	3.85
	Fort Wayne	IHL	33	22	6	3	1858	97	*4	3.13	....	....	....	....	....	....	....
1992-93	**Winnipeg**	**NHL**	**2**	**0**	**0**	**1**	**73**	**6**	**0**	**4.93**	....	....	....	....	....	....	....
	Moncton	AHL	30	13	10	4	1649	88	1	3.20	....	....	....	....	....	....	....
1993-94	**Winnipeg**	**NHL**	**17**	**0**	**9**	**1**	**738**	**51**	**0**	**4.15**	....	....	....	....	....	....	....
	Moncton	AHL	12	8	4	0	716	33	1	2.76	....	....	....	....	....	....	....
	Fort Wayne	IHL	11	4	4	3	642	38	0	3.55	....	....	....	....	....	....	....
1994-95	Fort Wayne	IHL	28	11	12	4	1603	109	0	4.08	....	....	....	....	....	....	....
	Phoenix	IHL	21	13	4	4	1256	64	1	3.06	9	4	5	535	33	0	3.70
1995-96	Baltimore	AHL	*74	31	31	7	*4250	250	2	3.53	12	6	6	689	43	0	3.75
1996-97	**Anaheim**	**NHL**	**1**	**0**	**0**	**0**	**31**	**3**	**0**	**5.81**	....	....	....	....	....	....	....
	Long Beach	IHL	45	26	12	6	2644	145	1	3.29	1	0	0	7	0	0	0.00
1997-98	Portland	AHL	47	16	18	10	2640	135	1	3.07	6	2	3	305	16	0	3.15
1998-99	EC Villacher SV	Austria	42	35	5	1	2540	104	0	2.49	....	....	....	....	....	....	....
	NHL Totals		**21**	**0**	**9**	**2**	**855**	**61**	**0**	**4.28**	....	....	....	....	....	....	....

ECAC First All-Star Team (1987, 1989) • NCAA East First All-American Team (1989)

Signed as a free agent by **Anaheim**, July 14, 1995. Signed as a free agent by **Washington**, August 20, 1997. Signed as a free agent by **LA Kings**, July 21, 1999.

OSGOOD, Chris (AWS-gud) — DET.

Goaltender. Catches left. 5'10", 160 lbs. Born, Peace River, Alta., November 26, 1972.
(Detroit's 3rd choice, 54th overall, in 1991 Entry Draft).

			Regular Season								Playoffs						
Season	**Club**	**Lea**	**GP**	**W**	**L**	**T**	**Mins**	**GA**	**SO**	**Avg**	**GP**	**W**	**L**	**Mins**	**GA**	**SO**	**Avg**
1988-89	Medicine Hat	AAHA	26	....	....	....	1441	88	0	3.66	....	....	....	....	....	....	....
1989-90	Medicine Hat	WHL	57	24	28	2	3094	228	0	4.42	3	0	3	173	17	0	5.91
1990-91	Medicine Hat	WHL	46	23	18	3	2630	173	2	3.95	12	7	5	712	42	0	3.54
1991-92	Medicine Hat	WHL	15	10	3	0	819	44	0	3.22	....	....	....	....	....	....	....
	Brandon	WHL	16	3	10	1	890	60	1	4.04	....	....	....	....	....	....	....
	Seattle	WHL	21	12	7	1	1217	65	1	3.20	15	9	6	904	51	0	3.38
1992-93	Adirondack	AHL	45	19	19	4	2438	159	0	3.91	1	0	1	59	2	0	2.03
1993-94	**Detroit**	**NHL**	**41**	**23**	**8**	**5**	**2206**	**105**	**2**	**2.86**	**6**	**3**	**2**	**307**	**12**	**1**	**2.35**
	Adirondack	AHL	4	3	1	0	239	13	0	3.26	....	....	....	....	....	....	....
1994-95	**Detroit**	**NHL**	**19**	**14**	**5**	**0**	**1087**	**41**	**1**	**2.26**	**2**	**0**	**0**	**68**	**2**	**0**	**1.76**
	Adirondack	AHL	2	1	1	0	120	6	0	3.00	....	....	....	....	....	....	....
1995-96	**Detroit**	**NHL**	**50**	***39**	**6**	**5**	**2933**	**106**	**5**	**2.17**	**15**	**8**	**7**	**936**	**33**	**2**	**2.12**
1996-97♦	**Detroit**	**NHL**	**47**	**23**	**13**	**9**	**2769**	**106**	**6**	**2.30**	**2**	**0**	**0**	**47**	**2**	**0**	**2.55**
1997-98♦	**Detroit**	**NHL**	**64**	**33**	**20**	**11**	**3807**	**140**	**6**	**2.21**	***22**	***16**	**6**	***1361**	**48**	**2**	**2.12**
1998-99	**Detroit**	**NHL**	**63**	**34**	**25**	**4**	**3691**	**149**	**3**	**2.42**	**6**	**4**	**2**	**358**	**14**	**1**	**2.35**
	NHL Totals		**284**	**166**	**77**	**34**	**16493**	**647**	**23**	**2.35**	**53**	**31**	**17**	**3077**	**111**	**6**	**2.16**

WHL East Second All-Star Team (1991) • NHL Second All-Star Team (1996) • Shared William M. Jennings Trophy with Mike Vernon (1996)

Played in NHL All-Star Game (1996, 1997, 1998)

• Scored a goal while with Medicine Hat (WHL), January 3, 1991. • Scored a goal vs. Hartford, March 6, 1996.

OUELLET, Maxime (OO-leht, MAX-eem) — PHI.

Goaltender. Catches left. 6', 180 lbs. Born, Beauport, Que., June 17, 1981.
(Philadelphia's 1st choice, 22nd overall, in 1999 Entry Draft).

			Regular Season								Playoffs						
Season	**Club**	**Lea**	**GP**	**W**	**L**	**T**	**Mins**	**GA**	**SO**	**Avg**	**GP**	**W**	**L**	**Mins**	**GA**	**SO**	**Avg**
1997-98	Quebec	QMJHL	24	12	7	1	1188	66	0	3.33	7	3	1	305	16	0	3.15
1998-99	Quebec	QMJHL	*59	*40	12	6	*3447	155	3	*2.70	13	6	7	803	41	*1	3.06

QMJHL Second All-Star Team (1999)

PARENT, Rich (PEH-ruhn) — ST.L.

Goaltender. Catches left. 6'3", 195 lbs. Born, Montreal, Que., January 12, 1973.

			Regular Season								Playoffs						
Season	**Club**	**Lea**	**GP**	**W**	**L**	**T**	**Mins**	**GA**	**SO**	**Avg**	**GP**	**W**	**L**	**Mins**	**GA**	**SO**	**Avg**
1991-92	Fort McMurray	AJHL	23	....	....	....	1363	90	0	3.96	....	....	....	....	....	....	....
	Vernon Lakers	BCJHL	2	0	1	0	52	5	0	5.77	....	....	....	....	....	....	....
1992-93	Spokane	WHL	36	12	14	2	1767	129	2	4.38	1	0	0	5	0	0	0.00
1993-94	Fort McMurray	AJHL	29	....	....	....	1712	91	1	3.19	....	....	....	....	....	....	....
1994-95	Muskegon	ColHL	35	17	11	3	1867	112	1	3.60	13	7	3	725	47	1	3.89
1995-96	Muskegon	ColHL	36	23	7	4	2087	85	2	2.44	....	....	....	....	....	....	....
	Rochester	AHL	2	0	1	0	90	6	0	4.02	....	....	....	....	....	....	....
	Detroit	IHL	19	16	0	1	1040	48	2	2.77	7	3	3	363	22	0	3.64
1996-97	Detroit	IHL	53	31	13	4	2815	104	4	2.22	15	8	3	786	21	1	*1.60
1997-98	**St. Louis**	**NHL**	**1**	**0**	**0**	**0**	**12**	**0**	**0**	**0.00**	....	....	....	....	....	....	....
	Manitoba	IHL	26	8	12	2	1334	69	3	3.10	....	....	....	....	....	....	....
	Detroit	IHL	7	4	0	3	417	15	0	2.15	5	1	0	157	6	0	2.29
1998-99	**St. Louis**	**NHL**	**10**	**4**	**3**	**1**	**519**	**22**	**1**	**2.54**	....	....	....	....	....	....	....
	Worcester	AHL	20	8	8	2	1100	56	1	3.05	....	....	....	....	....	....	....
	NHL Totals		**11**	**4**	**3**	**1**	**531**	**22**	**1**	**2.49**	....	....	....	....	....	....	....

ColHL First All-Star Team (1996) • Named ColHL's Outstanding Goaltender (1996) • Shared James Norris Memorial Trophy (fewest goals against - IHL) with Jeff Reese (1997)

Signed as a free agent by **St. Louis**, July 31, 1997.

PASSMORE, Steve (PAS-mohr) CHI.

Goaltender. Catches left. 5'9", 165 lbs. Born, Thunder Bay, Ont., January 29, 1973.
(Quebec's 10th choice, 196th overall, in 1992 Entry Draft).

			Regular Season								Playoffs						
Season	Club	Lea	GP	W	L	T	Mins	GA	SO	Avg	GP	W	L	Mins	GA	SO	Avg
1988-89	Tri-City	WHL	1	0	1	0	60	6	0	6.00	....	....	....	....	....	....	....
1989-90	Tri-City	WHL	4	....	....	....	215	17	0	4.74	....	....	....	....	....	....	....
1990-91	Victoria	WHL	35	3	25	1	1838	190	0	6.20	....	....	....	....	....	....	....
1991-92	Victoria	WHL	*71	15	50	5	*4228	347	0	4.92	....	....	....	....	....	....	....
1992-93	Victoria	WHL	43	14	24	2	2402	150	1	3.75	....	....	....	....	....	....	....
	Kamloops	WHL	25	19	6	0	1479	69	1	2.80	7	4	2	401	22	1	3.29
1993-94	Kamloops	WHL	36	22	9	2	1927	88	1	*2.74	*18	*11	7	*1099	60	0	3.28
1994-95	Cape Breton	AHL	25	8	13	3	1455	93	0	3.83	....	....	....	....	....	....	....
1995-96	Cape Breton	AHL	2	1	0	0	90	2	0	1.33	....	....	....	....	....	....	....
1996-97	Hamilton	AHL	27	12	12	3	1568	70	1	2.68	22	12	10	1325	61	*2	2.76
	Raleigh	ECHL	2	1	1	0	118	13	0	6.56	....	....	....	....	....	....	....
1997-98	San Antonio	IHL	14	3	8	2	736	56	0	4.56	....	....	....	....	....	....	....
	Hamilton	AHL	27	11	10	6	1655	87	2	3.15	3	0	2	132	14	0	6.33
1998-99	**Edmonton**	**NHL**	**6**	**1**	**4**	**1**	**362**	**17**	**0**	**2.82**	....	....	....	....	....	....	....
	Hamilton	AHL	54	24	21	7	3148	117	4	2.23	11	5	6	680	31	0	2.74
	NHL Totals		**6**	**1**	**4**	**1**	**362**	**17**	**0**	**2.82**	....	....	....	....	....	....	....

WHL West First All-Star Team (1993, 1994) • Won Fred Hunt Memorial Trophy (Sportsmanship — AHL) (1997) • AHL Second All-Star Team (1999)

Traded to **Edmonton** by **Quebec** for Brad Werenka, March 21, 1994. • Missed majority of 1995-96 season after being diagnosed with a rare blood disorder, Octer, 1995. Signed as a free agent by **Chicago**, July 8, 1999.

PELLETIER, Jean-Marc (PEHL-tyay) PHI.

Goaltender. Catches left. 6'3", 200 lbs. Born, Atlanta, GA, March 4, 1978.
(Philadelphia's 1st choice, 30th overall, in 1997 Entry Draft).

			Regular Season								Playoffs						
Season	Club	Lea	GP	W	L	T	Mins	GA	SO	Avg	GP	W	L	Mins	GA	SO	Avg
1993-94	Richelieu	QAAA	24	14	8	2	1440	91	0	3.79	....	....	....	....	....	....	....
1994-95	Richelieu	QAAA	21	15	6	0	1260	71	0	3.36	....	....	....	....	....	....	....
1995-96	Cornell	ECAC	5	1	2	0	179	15	0	5.03	....	....	....	....	....	....	....
1996-97	Cornell	ECAC	11	5	2	3	679	28	1	2.47	....	....	....	....	....	....	....
1997-98	Rimouski	QMJHL	34	17	11	3	1913	118	0	3.70	16	11	3	895	51	1	3.42
1998-99	**Philadelphia**	**NHL**	**1**	**0**	**1**	**0**	**60**	**5**	**0**	**5.00**	....	....	....	....	....	....	....
	Philadelphia	AHL	47	25	16	4	2636	122	2	2.78	1	0	0	27	0	0	0.00
	NHL Totals		**1**	**0**	**1**	**0**	**60**	**5**	**0**	**5.00**	....	....	....	....	....	....	....

PELLETIER, Jonathan (PEHL-tyay) CHI.

Goaltender. Catches left. 5'11", 165 lbs. Born, Riviere-du-loup, Que., April 15, 1980.
(Chicago's 5th choice, 166th overall, in 1998 Entry Draft).

			Regular Season								Playoffs						
Season	Club	Lea	GP	W	L	T	Mins	GA	SO	Avg	GP	W	L	Mins	GA	SO	Avg
1996-97	Victoriaville	QMJHL	25	14	5	1	1226	64	0	3.13	2	0	0	30	1	0	2.00
1997-98	Victoriaville	QMJHL	16	7	4	3	902	58	0	3.86	....	....	....	....	....	....	....
	Drummondville	QMJHL	29	5	17	1	1571	116	0	4.43	....	....	....	....	....	....	....
1998-99	Drummondville	QMJHL	54	13	30	3	2803	212	0	4.54	....	....	....	....	....	....	....

PERSSON, Joakim (PEHR-suhn) BOS.

Goaltender. Catches left. 5'11", 176 lbs. Born, Ostervala, Sweden, May 4, 1970.
(Boston's 10th choice, 259th overall, in 1993 Entry Draft).

			Regular Season								Playoffs						
Season	Club	Lea	GP	W	L	T	Mins	GA	SO	Avg	GP	W	L	Mins	GA	SO	Avg
1992-93	Hammarby IF	Swede-2	40	....	....	....	2395	108	....	2.71	....	....	....	....	....	....	....
1993-94	Hammarby IF	Swede-2	23	....	....	....	1380	59	....	2.57	....	....	....	....	....	....	....
	Providence	AHL	1	0	0	0	24	0	0	0.00	....	....	....	....	....	....	....
1994-95	AIK Solna	Sweden	30	....	....	....	1800	103	1	3.43	....	....	....	....	....	....	....
1995-96	AIK Solna	Sweden	24	....	....	....	1344	64	....	2.86	....	....	....	....	....	....	....
1996-97	Ratingen	Germany	35	....	....	....	2111	154	0	4.37	6	....	....	360	29	0	4.83
1997-98	Vasteras IK	Sweden	7	....	....	....	291	24	....	4.95	....	....	....	....	....	....	....
1998-99	Hammarby IF	Swede-2	2	....	....	....	120	10	0	5.00	3	....	....	180	6	0	2.00

PETRUK, Randy CAR.

Goaltender. Catches right. 5'9", 178 lbs. Born, Cranbrook, B.C., April 23, 1978.
(Colorado's 5th choice, 107th overall, in 1996 Entry Draft).

			Regular Season								Playoffs						
Season	Club	Lea	GP	W	L	T	Mins	GA	SO	Avg	GP	W	L	Mins	GA	SO	Avg
1994-95	Kamloops	WHL	27	16	3	4	1462	71	1	2.91	7	5	2	423	19	0	2.70
1995-96	Kamloops	WHL	52	34	15	1	3071	181	1	3.54	16	9	6	990	58	0	3.52
1996-97	Kamloops	WHL	*60	25	28	5	*3475	210	0	3.63	....	....	....	....	....	....	....
1997-98	Kamloops	WHL	57	31	21	1	3097	157	3	3.04	7	3	4	425	21	0	2.96
1998-99	Florida	ECHL	25	13	10	2	1441	66	1	2.75	1	0	1	60	5	0	5.00
	New Haven	AHL	1	0	0	1	65	3	0	2.77	....	....	....	....	....	....	....

WHL West Second All-Star Team (1998)

Traded to **Carolina** by **Colorado** for Carolina's 5th round choice (William Magnuson) in 1999 Entry Draft, June 1, 1998.

POTVIN, Felix (PAHT-vihn) NYI

Goaltender. Catches left. 6'1", 190 lbs. Born, Anjou, Que., June 23, 1971.
(Toronto's 2nd choice, 31st overall, in 1990 Entry Draft).

			Regular Season								Playoffs						
Season	Club	Lea	GP	W	L	T	Mins	GA	SO	Avg	GP	W	L	Mins	GA	SO	Avg
1987-88	Montreal-Bourassa	QAAA	27	15	7	3	1585	103	3	3.90	6	2	4	341	20	0	3.51
1988-89	Chicoutimi	QMJHL	*65	25	31	1	*3489	271	*2	4.66	....	....	....	....	....	....	....
1989-90	Chicoutimi	QMJHL	*62	*31	26	2	*3478	231	*2	3.99	....	....	....	....	....	....	....
1990-91	Chicoutimi	QMJHL	54	33	15	4	3216	145	*6	*2.70	*16	*11	5	*992	46	0	*2.78
1991-92	**Toronto**	**NHL**	**4**	**0**	**2**	**1**	**210**	**8**	**0**	**2.29**	....	....	....	....	....	....	....
	St. John's	AHL	35	18	10	6	2070	101	2	2.93	11	7	4	642	41	0	3.83
1992-93	**Toronto**	**NHL**	**48**	**25**	**15**	**7**	**2781**	**116**	**2**	***2.50**	***21**	**11**	**10**	***1308**	**62**	**1**	**2.84**
	St. John's	AHL	5	3	0	2	309	18	0	3.50	....	....	....	....	....	....	....
1993-94	**Toronto**	**NHL**	**66**	**34**	**22**	**9**	**3883**	**187**	**3**	**2.89**	**18**	**9**	**9**	**1124**	**46**	**3**	**2.46**
1994-95	**Toronto**	**NHL**	**36**	**15**	**13**	**7**	**2144**	**104**	**0**	**2.91**	**7**	**3**	**4**	**424**	**20**	**1**	**2.83**
1995-96	**Toronto**	**NHL**	**69**	**30**	**26**	**11**	**4009**	**192**	**2**	**2.87**	**6**	**2**	**4**	**350**	**19**	**0**	**3.26**
1996-97	**Toronto**	**NHL**	***74**	**27**	**36**	**7**	***4271**	**224**	**0**	**3.15**	....	....	....	....	....	....	....
1997-98	**Toronto**	**NHL**	**67**	**26**	**33**	**7**	**3864**	**176**	**5**	**2.73**	....	....	....	....	....	....	....
1998-99	**Toronto**	**NHL**	**5**	**3**	**2**	**0**	**299**	**19**	**0**	**3.81**	....	....	....	....	....	....	....
	NY Islanders	**NHL**	**11**	**2**	**7**	**1**	**606**	**37**	**0**	**3.66**	....	....	....	....	....	....	....
	NHL Totals		**380**	**162**	**156**	**50**	**22067**	**1063**	**12**	**2.89**	**52**	**25**	**27**	**3206**	**147**	**5**	**2.75**

QMJHL Second All-Star Team (1990) • QMJHL First All-Star Team (1991) • Canadian Major Junior Goaltender of the Year (1991) • Memorial Cup All-Star Team (1991) • Won Hap Emms Memorial Trophy (Memorial Cup Top Goaltender) (1991) • AHL First All-Star Team (1992) • Won Dudley "Red" Garrett Memorial Trophy (Top Rookie - AHL) (1992) • Won Baz Bastien Memorial Trophy (Top Goaltender - AHL) (1992) • NHL/Upper Deck All-Rookie Team (1993)

Played in NHL All-Star Game (1994, 1996)

Traded to **NY Islanders** by **Toronto** with Toronto's 6th round choice (later traded to Tampa Bay - Tampa Bay selected Fedor Fedorov) in 1999 Entry Draft for Bryan Berard and NY Islanders' 6th round choice (Jan Sochor) in 1999 Entry Draft, January 9, 1999.

PRESTIFILIPPO, J.R. (PREHS-tee-fihl-ih-poh) NYI

Goaltender. Catches left. 5'10", 170 lbs. Born, Newark, NJ, March 23, 1977.
(NY Islanders' 8th choice, 165th overall, in 1996 Entry Draft).

			Regular Season								Playoffs						
Season	Club	Lea	GP	W	L	T	Mins	GA	SO	Avg	GP	W	L	Mins	GA	SO	Avg
1995-96	Hotchkiss High	H.S.	24	....	....	....	1440	56	3	2.33	....	....	....	....	....	....	....
1996-97	Harvard University	ECAC	31	10	18	3	1866	99	1	3.18	....	....	....	....	....	....	....
1997-98	Harvard University	ECAC	23	9	12	2	1394	80	0	3.44	....	....	....	....	....	....	....
1998-99	Harvard University	ECAC	24	10	13	1	1316	78	0	3.56	....	....	....	....	....	....	....

PRUSEK, Martin OTT.

Goaltender. Catches left. 6', 176 lbs. Born, Ostrava, Czech., December 11, 1975.
(Ottawa's 6th choice, 164th overall, in 1999 Entry Draft).

			Regular Season								Playoffs						
Season	Club	Lea	GP	W	L	T	Mins	GA	SO	Avg	GP	W	L	Mins	GA	SO	Avg
1994-95	HC Vitkovice	Cze-Rep	5	....	....	....	232	18	....	4.65	....	....	....	....	....	....	....
1995-96	HC Vitkovice	Cze-Rep	40	....	....	....	2336	113	1	2.90	4	....	....	250	10	1	2.40
1996-97	HC Vitkovice	Cze-Rep	49	....	....	....	2841	109	8	2.30	9	....	....	546	19	1	2.08
1997-98	HC Vitkovice	Cze-Rep	50	....	....	....	2901	129	....	2.67	9	....	....	529	26	....	3.00
1998-99	HC Vitkovice	Cze-Rep	37	....	....	....	1905	85	....	2.68	4	....	....	250	12	....	2.88

PUPPA, Daren (POO-puh) T.B.

Goaltender. Catches right. 6'4", 205 lbs. Born, Kirkland Lake, Ont., March 23, 1965.
(Buffalo's 6th choice, 76th overall, in 1983 Entry Draft).

			Regular Season								Playoffs						
Season	Club	Lea	GP	W	L	T	Mins	GA	SO	Avg	GP	W	L	Mins	GA	SO	Avg
1982-83	Kirkland Lake	NOHA	STATISTICS NOT AVAILABLE														
1983-84	RPI Engineers	ECAC	32	24	6	0	1816	89	0	2.94	....	....	....	....	....	....	....
1984-85	RPI Engineers	ECAC	32	31	1	0	1830	78	0	2.56	....	....	....	....	....	....	....
1985-86	**Buffalo**	**NHL**	**7**	**3**	**4**	**0**	**401**	**21**	**1**	**3.14**	....	....	....	....	....	....	....
	Rochester	AHL	20	8	11	0	1092	79	0	4.34	....	....	....	....	....	....	....
1986-87	**Buffalo**	**NHL**	**3**	**0**	**2**	**1**	**185**	**13**	**0**	**4.22**	....	....	....	....	....	....	....
	Rochester	AHL	57	*33	14	0	3129	146	1	2.80	*16	*10	6	*944	48	*1	3.05
1987-88	**Buffalo**	**NHL**	**17**	**8**	**6**	**1**	**874**	**61**	**0**	**4.19**	**3**	**1**	**1**	**142**	**11**	**0**	**4.65**
	Rochester	AHL	26	14	8	2	1415	65	2	2.76	2	0	1	108	5	0	2.78
1988-89	**Buffalo**	**NHL**	**37**	**17**	**10**	**6**	**1908**	**107**	**1**	**3.36**	....	....	....	....	....	....	....
1989-90	**Buffalo**	**NHL**	**56**	***31**	**16**	**6**	**3241**	**156**	**1**	**2.89**	**6**	**2**	**4**	**370**	**15**	**0**	**2.43**
1990-91	**Buffalo**	**NHL**	**38**	**15**	**11**	**6**	**2092**	**118**	**2**	**3.38**	**2**	**0**	**1**	**81**	**10**	**0**	**7.41**
1991-92	**Buffalo**	**NHL**	**33**	**11**	**14**	**4**	**1757**	**114**	**0**	**3.89**	....	....	....	....	....	....	....
	Rochester	AHL	2	0	2	0	119	9	0	4.54	....	....	....	....	....	....	....
1992-93	**Buffalo**	**NHL**	**24**	**11**	**5**	**4**	**1306**	**78**	**0**	**3.58**	....	....	....	....	....	....	....
	Toronto	**NHL**	**8**	**6**	**2**	**0**	**479**	**18**	**2**	**2.25**	**1**	**0**	**0**	**20**	**1**	**0**	**3.00**
1993-94	**Tampa Bay**	**NHL**	**63**	**22**	**33**	**6**	**3653**	**165**	**4**	**2.71**	....	....	....	....	....	....	....
1994-95	**Tampa Bay**	**NHL**	**36**	**14**	**19**	**2**	**2013**	**90**	**1**	**2.68**	....	....	....	....	....	....	....
1995-96	**Tampa Bay**	**NHL**	**57**	**29**	**16**	**9**	**3189**	**131**	**5**	**2.46**	**4**	**1**	**3**	**173**	**14**	**0**	**4.86**
1996-97	**Tampa Bay**	**NHL**	**6**	**1**	**1**	**2**	**325**	**14**	**0**	**2.58**	....	....	....	....	....	....	....
	Adirondack	AHL	1	1	0	0	62	3	0	2.90	....	....	....	....	....	....	....
1997-98	**Tampa Bay**	**NHL**	**26**	**5**	**14**	**6**	**1456**	**66**	**0**	**2.72**	....	....	....	....	....	....	....
1998-99	**Tampa Bay**	**NHL**	**13**	**5**	**6**	**1**	**691**	**33**	**2**	**2.87**	....	....	....	....	....	....	....
	NHL Totals		**424**	**178**	**159**	**54**	**23570**	**1185**	**19**	**3.02**	**16**	**4**	**9**	**786**	**51**	**0**	**3.89**

AHL First All-Star Team (1987) • NHL Second All-Star Team (1990)

Played in NHL All-Star Game (1990)

Traded to **Toronto** by **Buffalo** with Dave Andreychuk and Buffalo's 1st round choice (Kenny Jonsson) in 1993 Entry Draft for Grant Fuhr and Toronto's 5th round choice (Kevin Popp) in 1995 Entry Draft, February 2, 1993. Claimed by **Florida** from **Toronto** in Expansion Draft, June 24, 1993. Claimed by **Tampa Bay** from **Florida** in Phase II of Expansion Draft, June 25, 1993. • Missed majority of the 1996-97 season recovering from a groin injury suffered in the pre-season, September, 1997. • Missed majority of 1997-98 and 1998-99 seasons recovering from a back injury suffered in a game vs. Boston on December 27, 1997.

RACINE, Bruce (ray-SEEN)

Goaltender. Catches left. 6', 170 lbs. Born, Cornwall, Ont., August 9, 1966.
(Pittsburgh's 3rd choice, 58th overall, in 1985 Entry Draft).

						Regular Season								Playoffs			
Season	Club	Lea	GP	W	L	T	Mins	GA	SO	Avg	GP	W	L	Mins	GA	SO	Avg
1984-85	Northeastern	H.E.	26	11	14	1	1615	103	1	3.83	....	....	....	....	....	....	....
1985-86	Northeastern	H.E.	32	17	14	1	1920	147	0	4.56	....	....	....	....	....	....	....
1986-87	Northeastern	H.E.	33	12	18	3	1966	133	0	4.06	....	....	....	....	....	....	....
1987-88	Northeastern	H.E.	30	15	11	4	1808	108	1	3.58	....	....	....	....	....	....	....
1988-89	Muskegon	IHL	51	*37	11	0	*3039	184	*3	3.63	5	4	1	300	15	0	3.00
1989-90	Muskegon	IHL	49	29	15	4	2911	182	1	3.75	9	5	4	566	32	1	3.34
1990-91	Albany	IHL	29	7	18	1	1567	104	0	3.98	....	....	....	....	....	....	....
	Muskegon	IHL	9	4	4	1	516	40	0	4.65	....	....	....	....	....	....	....
1991-92	Muskegon	IHL	27	13	10	3	1559	91	1	3.50	1	0	1	60	6	0	6.00
1992-93	Cleveland	IHL	35	13	16	6	1949	140	1	4.31	2	0	0	37	2	0	3.24
1993-94	St. John's	AHL	37	20	9	2	1875	116	0	3.71	1	0	0	20	1	0	0.00
1994-95	St. John's	AHL	27	11	10	4	1492	85	1	3.42	2	1	1	119	3	0	1.51
1995-96	**St. Louis**	**NHL**	**11**	**0**	**3**	**0**	**230**	**12**	**0**	**3.13**	**1**	**0**	**0**	**1**	**0**	**0**	**0.00**
	Peoria	IHL	22	11	10	1	1228	69	1	3.37	1	0	1	59	3	0	3.05
1996-97	San Antonio	IHL	44	25	14	2	2426	122	6	3.02	6	3	2	325	17	0	3.13
1997-98	San Antonio	IHL	*15	*4	9	1	*836	51	0	3.66	....	....	....	....	....	....	....
	Fort Wayne	IHL	*45	*30	10	4	*2605	109	1	2.51	3	1	2	152	10	0	3.95
1998-99	Fort Wayne	IHL	53	21	18	11	3024	154	1	3.06	1	0	1	60	5	0	5.00
	NHL Totals		**11**	**0**	**3**	**0**	**230**	**12**	**0**	**3.13**	**1**	**0**	**0**	**1**	**0**	**0**	**0.00**

Hockey East Second All-Star Team (1985) • Hockey East First All-Star Team (1987) • NCAA East First All-American Team (1987, 1988) • IHL First All-Star Team (1998)

Signed as a free agent by **Toronto**, August 11, 1993. Signed as a free agent by **St. Louis**, August 10, 1995. Signed as a free agent by **San Jose**, September 8, 1998.

RAM, Jamie

Goaltender. Catches left. 5'11", 175 lbs. Born, Scarborough, Ont., January 18, 1971.
(NY Rangers' 9th choice, 213th overall, in 1991 Entry Draft).

						Regular Season								Playoffs			
Season	Club	Lea	GP	W	L	T	Mins	GA	SO	Avg	GP	W	L	Mins	GA	SO	Avg
1990-91	Michigan Tech	WCHA	14	5	9	0	826	57	0	4.14	....	....	....	....	....	....	....
1991-92	Michigan Tech	WCHA	23	9	9	1	1144	83	0	4.35	....	....	....	....	....	....	....
1992-93	Michigan Tech	WCHA	*36	16	14	5	*2078	115	0	3.32	....	....	....	....	....	....	....
1993-94	Michigan Tech	WCHA	39	12	20	5	2192	117	*1	3.20	....	....	....	....	....	....	....
1994-95	Binghamton	AHL	26	12	10	2	1472	81	1	3.30	11	6	5	663	29	1	2.62
1995-96	**NY Rangers**	**NHL**	**1**	**0**	**0**	**0**	**27**	**0**	**0**	**0.00**	....	....	....	....	....	....	....
	Binghamton	AHL	40	18	16	3	2262	151	1	4.01	1	0	0	34	1	0	1.75
1996-97	Kentucky	AHL	50	25	19	5	2937	161	4	3.29	1	0	1	60	3	0	3.00
1997-98	Kentucky	AHL	44	17	18	5	2553	124	3	2.91	....	....	....	....	....	....	....
	Utah	IHL	7	3	4	0	398	24	0	3.61	1	0	1	59	3	0	3.04
1998-99	Cincinnati	AHL	35	14	19	1	1916	109	2	3.41	....	....	....	....	....	....	....
	NHL Totals		**1**	**0**	**0**	**0**	**27**	**0**	**0**	**0.00**	....	....	....	....	....	....	....

WCHA First All-Star Team (1993, 1994) • NCAA West First All-American Team (1993, 1994)

Signed as a free agent by **San Jose**, August 19, 1997. Signed as a free agent by **Anaheim**, July 30, 1998.

RANFORD, Bill EDM.

Goaltender. Catches left. 5'11", 185 lbs. Born, Brandon, Man., December 14, 1966.
(Boston's 2nd choice, 52nd overall, in 1985 Entry Draft).

						Regular Season								Playoffs			
Season	Club	Lea	GP	W	L	T	Mins	GA	SO	Avg	GP	W	L	Mins	GA	SO	Avg
1983-84	New Westminster	WHL	27	10	14	0	1450	130	0	5.38	1	0	0	27	2	0	4.44
1984-85	New Westminster	WHL	38	19	17	0	2034	142	0	4.19	7	2	3	309	26	0	5.05
1985-86	**Boston**	**NHL**	**4**	**3**	**1**	**0**	**240**	**10**	**0**	**2.50**	**2**	**0**	**2**	**120**	**7**	**0**	**3.50**
	New Westminster	WHL	53	17	29	1	2791	225	1	4.84	....	....	....	....	....	....	....
1986-87	**Boston**	**NHL**	**41**	**16**	**20**	**2**	**2234**	**124**	**3**	**3.33**	**2**	**0**	**2**	**123**	**8**	**0**	**3.90**
	Moncton	AHL	3	3	0	0	180	6	0	2.00	....	....	....	....	....	....	....
1987-88	Maine	AHL	51	27	16	6	2856	165	1	3.47	....	....	....	....	....	....	....
	Edmonton	**NHL**	**6**	**3**	**0**	**2**	**325**	**16**	**0**	**2.95**	....	....	....	....	....	....	....
1988-89	**Edmonton**	**NHL**	**29**	**15**	**8**	**2**	**1509**	**88**	**1**	**3.50**	....	....	....	....	....	....	....
1989-90♦	**Edmonton**	**NHL**	**56**	**24**	**16**	**9**	**3107**	**165**	**1**	**3.19**	***22**	***16**	**6**	***1401**	**59**	**1**	**2.53**
1990-91	**Edmonton**	**NHL**	**60**	**27**	**27**	**3**	**3415**	**182**	**0**	**3.20**	**3**	**1**	**2**	**135**	**8**	**0**	**3.56**
1991-92	**Edmonton**	**NHL**	**67**	**27**	**26**	**10**	**3822**	**228**	**1**	**3.58**	**16**	**8**	**8**	**909**	**51**	***2**	**3.37**
1992-93	**Edmonton**	**NHL**	**67**	**17**	**38**	**6**	**3753**	**240**	**1**	**3.84**	....	....	....	....	....	....	....
1993-94	**Edmonton**	**NHL**	**71**	**22**	**34**	**11**	**4070**	**236**	**1**	**3.48**	....	....	....	....	....	....	....
1994-95	**Edmonton**	**NHL**	**40**	**15**	**20**	**3**	**2203**	**133**	**2**	**3.62**	....	....	....	....	....	....	....
1995-96	**Edmonton**	**NHL**	**37**	**13**	**18**	**5**	**2015**	**128**	**1**	**3.81**	....	....	....	....	....	....	....
	Boston	**NHL**	**40**	**21**	**12**	**4**	**2307**	**109**	**1**	**2.83**	**4**	**1**	**3**	**239**	**16**	**0**	**4.02**
1996-97	**Boston**	**NHL**	**37**	**12**	**16**	**8**	**2147**	**125**	**2**	**3.49**	....	....	....	....	....	....	....
	Washington	**NHL**	**18**	**8**	**7**	**2**	**1009**	**46**	**0**	**2.74**	....	....	....	....	....	....	....
1997-98	**Washington**	**NHL**	**22**	**7**	**12**	**2**	**1183**	**55**	**0**	**2.79**	....	....	....	....	....	....	....
1998-99	**Tampa Bay**	**NHL**	**32**	**3**	**18**	**3**	**1568**	**102**	**1**	**3.90**	....	....	....	....	....	....	....
	Detroit	**NHL**	**4**	**3**	**0**	**1**	**244**	**8**	**0**	**1.97**	**4**	**2**	**2**	**183**	**10**	**1**	**3.28**
	NHL Totals		**631**	**236**	**273**	**73**	**35151**	**1995**	**15**	**3.41**	**53**	**28**	**25**	**3110**	**159**	**4**	**3.07**

WHL West Second All-Star Team (1986) • Won Conn Smythe Trophy (1990)

Played in NHL All-Star Game (1991)

Traded to **Edmonton** by **Boston** with Geoff Courtnall Boston's 2nd round choice (Petro Koivunen) in 1988 Entry Draft for Andy Moog, March 8, 1988. Traded to **Boston** by **Edmonton** for Mariusz Czerkawski, Sean Brown and Boston's 1st round choice (Matthieu Descoteaux) in 1996 Entry Draft, January 11, 1996. Traded to **Washington** by **Boston** with Adam Oates and Rick Tocchet for Jim Carey, Anson Carter, Jason Allison and Washington's 3rd round choice (Lee Goren) in 1997 Entry Draft, March 1, 1997. Traded to **Tampa Bay** by **Washington** for Tampa Bay's 3rd round choice (Todd Hornung) in 1998 Entry Draft and 2nd round choice (Michal Sivek) in 1999 Entry Draft, June 18, 1998. Traded to **Detroit** by **Tampa Bay** for future considerations, March 23, 1999. Signed as a free agent by **Edmonton**, August 4, 1999.

RAYCROFT, Andrew BOS.

Goaltender. Catches left. 6', 150 lbs. Born, Belleville, Ont., May 4, 1980.
(Boston's 4th choice, 135th overall, in 1998 Entry Draft).

						Regular Season								Playoffs			
Season	Club	Lea	GP	W	L	T	Mins	GA	SO	Avg	GP	W	L	Mins	GA	SO	Avg
1997-98	Sudbury	OHL	33	8	16	5	1802	125	0	4.16	2	0	1	89	8	0	5.39
1998-99	Sudbury	OHL	45	17	22	5	2528	173	1	4.11	3	0	2	96	13	0	8.13

REESE, Jeff

Goaltender. Catches left. 5'9", 180 lbs. Born, Brantford, Ont., March 24, 1966.
(Toronto's 3rd choice, 67th overall, in 1984 Entry Draft).

						Regular Season								Playoffs			
Season	Club	Lea	GP	W	L	T	Mins	GA	SO	Avg	GP	W	L	Mins	GA	SO	Avg
1982-83	Hamilton	OJHL-B	40	....	....	....	2380	176	0	4.44	....	....	....	....	....	....	....
1983-84	London	OHL	43	18	19	1	2308	173	0	4.50	6	3	3	327	27	0	4.95
1984-85	London	OHL	50	31	15	1	2878	186	1	3.88	8	5	2	440	20	1	2.73
1985-86	London	OHL	*57	25	26	3	*3281	215	0	3.93	5	0	4	299	25	0	5.02
1986-87	Newmarket	AHL	50	11	29	0	2822	193	1	4.10	....	....	....	....	....	....	....
1987-88	**Toronto**	**NHL**	**5**	**1**	**2**	**1**	**249**	**17**	**0**	**4.10**	....	....	....	....	....	....	....
	Newmarket	AHL	28	10	14	3	1587	103	0	3.89	....	....	....	....	....	....	....
1988-89	**Toronto**	**NHL**	**10**	**2**	**6**	**1**	**486**	**40**	**0**	**4.94**	....	....	....	....	....	....	....
	Newmarket	AHL	37	17	14	3	2072	132	0	3.82	....	....	....	....	....	....	....
1989-90	**Toronto**	**NHL**	**21**	**9**	**6**	**3**	**1101**	**81**	**0**	**4.41**	**2**	**1**	**1**	**108**	**6**	**0**	**3.33**
	Newmarket	AHL	7	3	2	2	431	29	0	4.04	....	....	....	....	....	....	....
1990-91	**Toronto**	**NHL**	**30**	**6**	**13**	**3**	**1430**	**92**	**1**	**3.86**	....	....	....	....	....	....	....
	Newmarket	AHL	3	2	1	0	180	7	0	2.33	....	....	....	....	....	....	....
1991-92	**Toronto**	**NHL**	**8**	**1**	**5**	**1**	**413**	**20**	**1**	**2.91**	....	....	....	....	....	....	....
	Calgary	**NHL**	**12**	**3**	**2**	**2**	**587**	**37**	**0**	**3.78**	....	....	....	....	....	....	....
1992-93	**Calgary**	**NHL**	**26**	**14**	**4**	**1**	**1311**	**70**	**1**	**3.20**	**4**	**1**	**3**	**209**	**17**	**0**	**4.88**
1993-94	**Calgary**	**NHL**	**1**	**0**	**0**	**0**	**13**	**1**	**0**	**4.62**	....	....	....	....	....	....	....
	Hartford	**NHL**	**19**	**5**	**9**	**3**	**1086**	**56**	**1**	**3.09**	....	....	....	....	....	....	....
1994-95	**Hartford**	**NHL**	**11**	**2**	**5**	**1**	**477**	**26**	**0**	**3.27**	....	....	....	....	....	....	....
1995-96	**Hartford**	**NHL**	**7**	**2**	**3**	**0**	**275**	**14**	**1**	**3.05**	....	....	....	....	....	....	....
	Tampa Bay	**NHL**	**19**	**7**	**7**	**1**	**994**	**54**	**0**	**3.26**	**5**	**1**	**1**	**198**	**12**	**0**	**3.64**
1996-97	**New Jersey**	**NHL**	**3**	**0**	**2**	**0**	**139**	**13**	**0**	**5.61**	....	....	....	....	....	....	....
	Detroit	IHL	32	23	4	3	1763	55	4	*1.87	11	7	3	518	22	0	2.55
1997-98	Detroit	IHL	46	27	9	8	2570	95	4	2.22	*22	*13	9	*1276	52	*2	2.44
1998-99	St. John's	AHL	27	17	7	3	1555	66	1	2.55	3	1	1	142	8	0	3.39
	Toronto	**NHL**	**2**	**1**	**1**	**0**	**106**	**8**	**0**	**4.53**	....	....	....	....	....	....	....
	NHL Totals		**174**	**53**	**65**	**17**	**8667**	**529**	**5**	**3.66**	**11**	**3**	**5**	**515**	**35**	**0**	**4.08**

IHL Second All-Star Team (1997, 1998) • Shared James Norris Memorial Trophy (fewest goals against — IHL) with Rich Parent (1997)

Traded to **Calgary** by **Toronto** with Craig Berube, Alexander Godynyuk, Gary Leeman and Michel Petit for Doug Gilmour, Jamie Macoun, Ric Nattress, Rick Wamsley and Kent Manderville, January 2, 1992. Traded to **Hartford** by **Calgary** for Dan Keczmer, November 19, 1993. Traded to **Tampa Bay** by **Hartford** for Tampa Bay's 9th round choice (Ashhat Rakhmatullin) in 1996 Entry Draft, December 1, 1995. Traded to **New Jersey** by **Tampa Bay** with Chicago's 2nd round choice (previously acquired, New Jersey selected Pierre Dagenais) in 1996 Entry Draft and Tampa Bay's 8th round choice (Jason Bertsch) in 1996 Entry Draft for Corey Schwab, June 22, 1996. Signed as a free agent by **Toronto**, January 5, 1999. Traded to **Tampa Bay** by **Toronto** with Toronto's 9th round choice in 2000 Entry Draft for Tampa Bay's 9th round choice in 2000 Entry Draft, August 6, 1999.

RHODES, Damian (ROHDZ) ATL.

Goaltender. Catches left. 6', 190 lbs. Born, St. Paul, MN, May 28, 1969.
(Toronto's 6th choice, 112th overall, in 1987 Entry Draft).

						Regular Season								Playoffs			
Season	Club	Lea	GP	W	L	T	Mins	GA	SO	Avg	GP	W	L	Mins	GA	SO	Avg
1985-86	Richfield High	H.S.	16	....	....	....	720	56	0	3.50	....	....	....	....	....	....	....
1986-87	Richfield High	H.S.	19	....	....	....	673	51	1	4.55	....	....	....	....	....	....	....
1987-88	Michigan Tech	WCHA	29	16	10	1	1625	114	0	4.20	....	....	....	....	....	....	....
1988-89	Michigan Tech	WCHA	37	15	22	0	2216	163	0	4.41	....	....	....	....	....	....	....
1989-90	Michigan Tech	WCHA	25	6	17	0	1358	119	0	6.26	....	....	....	....	....	....	....
1990-91	**Toronto**	**NHL**	**1**	**1**	**0**	**0**	**60**	**1**	**0**	**1.00**	....	....	....	....	....	....	....
	Newmarket	AHL	38	8	24	3	2154	144	1	4.01	....	....	....	....	....	....	....
1991-92	St. John's	AHL	43	20	16	5	2454	148	0	3.62	6	4	1	331	16	0	2.90
1992-93	St. John's	AHL	*52	27	16	8	*3074	184	1	3.59	9	4	5	538	37	0	4.13
1993-94	**Toronto**	**NHL**	**22**	**9**	**7**	**3**	**1213**	**53**	**0**	**2.62**	**1**	**0**	**0**	**1**	**0**	**0**	**0.00**
1994-95	**Toronto**	**NHL**	**13**	**6**	**6**	**1**	**760**	**34**	**0**	**2.68**	....	....	....	....	....	....	....
1995-96	**Toronto**	**NHL**	**11**	**4**	**5**	**1**	**624**	**29**	**0**	**2.79**	....	....	....	....	....	....	....
	Ottawa	**NHL**	**36**	**10**	**22**	**4**	**2123**	**98**	**2**	**2.77**	....	....	....	....	....	....	....
1996-97	**Ottawa**	**NHL**	**50**	**14**	**20**	**14**	**2934**	**133**	**1**	**2.72**	....	....	....	....	....	....	....
1997-98	**Ottawa**	**NHL**	**50**	**19**	**19**	**7**	**2743**	**107**	**5**	**2.34**	**10**	**5**	**5**	**590**	**21**	**0**	**2.14**
1998-99	**Ottawa**	**NHL**	**45**	**22**	**13**	**7**	**2480**	**101**	**3**	**2.44**	**2**	**0**	**2**	**150**	**6**	**0**	**2.40**
	NHL Totals		**228**	**85**	**92**	**37**	**12937**	**556**	**11**	**2.58**	**13**	**5**	**7**	**741**	**27**	**0**	**2.19**

• Credited with scoring a goal while with Michigan Tech (WCHA), January 21, 1989.

• Played 10 seconds in playoff game vs. San Jose, May 6, 1994. Traded to **NY Islanders** by **Toronto** with Ken Belanger for future considerations (Kirk Muller and Don Beaupre, January 23, 1996), January 23, 1996. Traded to **Ottawa** by **NY Islanders** with Wade Redden for Don Beaupre, Martin Straka and Bryan Berard, January 23, 1996. Traded to **Atlanta** by **Ottawa** for future considerations, June 18, 1999.

RICHTER, Mike (RIHK-tuhr) NYR

Goaltender. Catches left. 5'11", 187 lbs. Born, Abington, PA, September 22, 1966.
(NY Rangers' 2nd choice, 28th overall, in 1985 Entry Draft).

						Regular Season								Playoffs			
Season	Club	Lea	GP	W	L	T	Mins	GA	SO	Avg	GP	W	L	Mins	GA	SO	Avg
1984-85	Northwood	H.S.	24	....	....	....	1374	52	2	2.27	....	....	....	....	....	....	....
1985-86	U. of Wisconsin	WCHA	24	14	9	0	1394	92	1	3.96	....	....	....	....	....	....	....
1986-87	U. of Wisconsin	WCHA	36	19	16	1	2136	126	0	3.54	....	....	....	....	....	....	....
1987-88	United States	Nat-Team	29	17	7	2	1559	86	0	3.31	....	....	....	....	....	....	....
	United States	Olympics	4	....	....	....	230	15	....	3.91	....	....	....	....	....	....	....
	Colorado	IHL	22	16	5	0	1298	68	1	3.14	10	5	3	536	35	0	3.92
1988-89	Denver	IHL	*57	23	26	0	3031	217	1	4.30	4	0	4	210	21	0	6.00
	NY Rangers	**NHL**	....	....	....	....	....	....	....	....	**1**	**0**	**1**	**58**	**4**	**0**	**4.14**
1989-90	**NY Rangers**	**NHL**	**23**	**12**	**5**	**5**	**1320**	**66**	**0**	**3.00**	**6**	**3**	**2**	**330**	**19**	**0**	**3.45**
	Flint	IHL	13	7	4	2	782	49	0	3.76	....	....	....	....	....	....	....
1990-91	**NY Rangers**	**NHL**	**45**	**21**	**13**	**7**	**2596**	**135**	**0**	**3.12**	**6**	**2**	**4**	**313**	**14**	***1**	**2.68**
1991-92	**NY Rangers**	**NHL**	**41**	**23**	**12**	**2**	**2298**	**119**	**3**	**3.11**	**7**	**4**	**2**	**412**	**24**	**1**	**3.50**
1992-93	**NY Rangers**	**NHL**	**38**	**13**	**19**	**3**	**2105**	**134**	**1**	**3.82**	....	....	....	....	....	....	....
	Binghamton	AHL	5	4	0	1	305	6	0	1.18	....	....	....	....	....	....	....
1993-94♦	**NY Rangers**	**NHL**	**68**	***42**	**12**	**6**	**3710**	**159**	**5**	**2.57**	**23**	***16**	**7**	**1417**	**49**	***4**	**2.07**
1994-95	**NY Rangers**	**NHL**	**35**	**14**	**17**	**2**	**1993**	**97**	**2**	**2.92**	**7**	**2**	**5**	**384**	**23**	**0**	**3.59**
1995-96	**NY Rangers**	**NHL**	**41**	**24**	**13**	**3**	**2396**	**107**	**3**	**2.68**	**11**	**5**	**6**	**661**	**36**	**0**	**3.27**
1996-97	**NY Rangers**	**NHL**	**61**	**33**	**22**	**6**	**3598**	**161**	**4**	**2.68**	**15**	**9**	**6**	**939**	**33**	***3**	**2.11**
1997-98	**NY Rangers**	**NHL**	***72**	**21**	**31**	**15**	**4143**	**184**	**0**	**2.66**	....	....	....	....	....	....	....
	United States	Olympics	4	1	3	0	237	14	0	3.55	....	....	....	....	....	....	....
1998-99	**NY Rangers**	**NHL**	**68**	**27**	**30**	**8**	**3878**	**170**	**4**	**2.63**	....	....	....	....	....	....	....
	NHL Totals		**492**	**230**	**174**	**57**	**28037**	**1332**	**22**	**2.85**	**76**	**41**	**33**	**4514**	**202**	**9**	**2.68**

WCHA Second All-Star Team (1987)

Played in NHL All-Star Game (1992, 1994)

Claimed by **Nashville** from **NY Rangers** in Expansion Draft, June 26, 1998. Signed as a free agent by **NY Rangers**, July 15, 1998.

ROBITAILLE, Marc (ROH-buh-tigh) TOR.

Goaltender. Catches left. 5'10", 185 lbs. Born, Gloucester, Ont., June 7, 1976.

			Regular Season								Playoffs						
Season	Club	Lea	GP	W	L	T	Mins	GA	SO	Avg	GP	W	L	Mins	GA	SO	Avg
1996-97	Northeastern	H.E.	34	7	24	3	1928	135	3	4.20	....	....	....	....	....	....	....
1997-98	Northeastern	H.E.	*39	21	15	3	*2313	123	1	3.19	....	....	....	....	....	....	....
1998-99	St. John's	AHL	42	13	22	1	2269	124	1	3.28	3	1	2	158	8	0	3.04

Hockey East First All-Star Team (1998) • NCAA East First All-American Team (1998)

Signed as a free agent by **Toronto**, June 4, 1998.

ROCHE, Scott (ROHSH) ST.L.

Goaltender. Catches left. 6'4", 220 lbs. Born, Lindsay, Ont., March 19, 1977.
(St. Louis' 2nd choice, 75th overall, in 1995 Entry Draft).

			Regular Season								Playoffs						
Season	Club	Lea	GP	W	L	T	Mins	GA	SO	Avg	GP	W	L	Mins	GA	SO	Avg
1993-94	North Bay	OHL	32	15	5	4	1587	93	0	3.52	5	2	1	191	10	0	*3.14
1994-95	North Bay	OHL	47	24	17	2	2599	167	2	3.86	6	2	4	348	30	0	5.17
1995-96	North Bay	OHL	53	12	29	5	2859	232	1	4.87	....	....	....	....	....	....	....
1996-97	North Bay	OHL	3	0	3	0	122	21	0	10.30	....	....	....	....	....	....	....
	Windsor	OHL	44	20	16	4	2496	152	1	3.65	5	1	4	267	26	0	5.84
1997-98	Peoria	ECHL	38	23	11	3	2228	109	1	2.93	2	0	2	121	6	0	2.95
	Detroit	IHL	4	0	1	0	146	8	0	3.27	....	....	....	....	....	....	....
1998-99	Peoria	ECHL	7	3	3	1	418	19	0	2.73	....	....	....	....	....	....	....
	Worcester	AHL	9	2	3	1	339	18	0	3.19	....	....	....	....	....	....	....

ROLOSON, Dwayne (ROH-loh-suhn) BUF.

Goaltender. Catches left. 6'1", 190 lbs. Born, Simcoe, Ont., October 12, 1969.

			Regular Season								Playoffs						
Season	Club	Lea	GP	W	L	T	Mins	GA	SO	Avg	GP	W	L	Mins	GA	SO	Avg
1987-88	Belleville	OJHL-B	21	9	6	1	1070	60	2	3.36	....	....	....	....	....	....	....
1990-91	U. Mass-Lowell	H.E.	15	5	9	0	823	63	0	4.59	....	....	....	....	....	....	....
1991-92	U. Mass-Lowell	H.E.	12	3	8	0	660	52	0	4.73	....	....	....	....	....	....	....
1992-93	U. Mass-Lowell	H.E.	*39	20	17	2	*2342	150	0	3.84	....	....	....	....	....	....	....
1993-94	U. Mass-Lowell	H.E.	*40	*23	10	7	*2305	106	0	2.76	....	....	....	....	....	....	....
1994-95	Saint John	AHL	46	16	21	8	2734	156	1	3.42	5	1	4	298	13	0	2.61
1995-96	Saint John	AHL	67	*33	22	11	4026	190	1	2.83	16	10	6	1027	49	1	2.86
1996-97	**Calgary**	**NHL**	**31**	**9**	**14**	**3**	**1618**	**78**	**1**	**2.89**	....	....	....	....	....	....	....
	Saint John	AHL	8	6	2	0	481	22	1	2.75	....	....	....	....	....	....	....
1997-98	**Calgary**	**NHL**	**39**	**11**	**16**	**8**	**2205**	**110**	**0**	**2.99**	....	....	....	....	....	....	....
	Saint John	AHL	4	3	0	1	245	8	0	1.96	....	....	....	....	....	....	....
1998-99	**Buffalo**	**NHL**	**18**	**6**	**8**	**2**	**911**	**42**	**1**	**2.77**	**4**	**1**	**1**	**139**	**10**	**0**	**4.32**
	Rochester	AHL	2	2	0	0	120	4	0	2.00	....	....	....	....	....	....	....
	NHL Totals		**88**	**26**	**38**	**13**	**4734**	**230**	**2**	**2.92**	**4**	**1**	**1**	**139**	**10**	**0**	**4.32**

Hockey East First All-Star Team (1994) • NCAA East First All-Ameircan Team (1994)

Signed as a free agent by **Calgary**, July 4, 1994. Signed as a free agent by **Buffalo**, July 15, 1998.

ROSATI, Mike (roh-ZA-tee)

Goaltender. Catches left. 5'10", 170 lbs. Born, Toronto, Ont., January 7, 1968.
(NY Rangers' 6th choice, 131st overall, in 1988 Entry Draft).

			Regular Season								Playoffs						
Season	Club	Lea	GP	W	L	T	Mins	GA	SO	Avg	GP	W	L	Mins	GA	SO	Avg
1984-85	St. Michael's	OJHL-B	19	....	....	....	1027	93	0	5.13	....	....	....	....	....	....	....
1985-86	Hamilton	OHL	1	0	0	1	70	5	0	4.29	....	....	....	....	....	....	....
	St. Michael's	OJHL-B	54	....	....	....	2748	214	0	4.67	....	....	....	....	....	....	....
1986-87	Hamilton	OHL	26	....	....	....	1334	85	1	3.82	....	....	....	....	....	....	....
1987-88	Hamilton	OHL	62	29	25	3	3468	233	1	4.03	14	8	6	833	66	0	4.75
1988-89	Niagara Falls	OHL	52	*28	15	2	2339	174	1	4.46	16	10	4	861	62	0	4.32
1989-90	Erie	ECHL	18	12	5	0	1056	73	0	4.14	....	....	....	....	....	....	....
1990-91	HC Bolzano	Italy	46	....	....	....	2700	212	0	4.71	....	....	....	....	....	....	....
1991-92	HC Bolzano	Italy	18	11	6	1	1022	58	2	3.22	7	5	2	409	30	0	4.28
1992-93	HC Bolzano	Italy	26	....	....	....	1525	78	1	3.07	....	....	....	....	....	....	....
1993-94	HC Bolzano	Italy	29	....	....	....	1683	104	0	3.71	....	....	....	....	....	....	....
1994-95	HC Bolzano	Italy	47	....	....	....	2705	149	1	3.30	....	....	....	....	....	....	....
1995-96	HC Bolzano	Italy	42	....	....	....	2465	137	3	3.33	....	....	....	....	....	....	....
1996-97	Mannheim	Germany	44	....	....	....	2625	104	6	2.38	9	....	....	514	24	0	2.80
1997-98	Mannheim	Germany	43	....	....	....	2567	116	2	2.71	*10	*9	1	569	17	*1	*2.00
	Mannheim	EuroHL	2	2	0	0	118	5	1	0.87	....	....	....	....	....	....	....
1998-99	**Washington**	**NHL**	**1**	**1**	**0**	**0**	**28**	**0**	**0**	**0.00**	....	....	....	....	....	....	....
	Portland	AHL	32	9	23	0	1783	111	1	3.74	....	....	....	....	....	....	....
	Manitoba	IHL	8	5	1	2	479	16	1	2.00	5	2	3	314	18	0	3.44
	NHL Totals		**1**	**1**	**0**	**0**	**28**	**0**	**0**	**0.00**	....	....	....	....	....	....	....

Signed as a free agent by **Washington**, July 15, 1998.

ROUSSEL, Dominic (roo-SEHL) ANA.

Goaltender. Catches left. 6'1", 191 lbs. Born, Hull, Que., February 22, 1970.
(Philadelphia's 4th choice, 63rd overall, in 1988 Entry Draft).

			Regular Season								Playoffs						
Season	Club	Lea	GP	W	L	T	Mins	GA	SO	Avg	GP	W	L	Mins	GA	SO	Avg
1986-87	Lac St-Louis	QAAA	24	8	12	0	1334	85	1	3.69	....	....	....	....	....	....	....
1987-88	Trois-Rivieres	QMJHL	51	18	25	4	2905	251	0	5.18	....	....	....	....	....	....	....
1988-89	Shawinigan	QMJHL	46	24	15	2	2555	171	0	4.02	10	6	4	638	36	0	3.39
1989-90	Shawinigan	QMJHL	37	20	14	1	1985	133	0	4.02	2	1	1	120	12	0	6.00
1990-91	Hershey	AHL	45	20	14	7	2507	151	1	3.61	7	3	4	366	21	0	3.44
1991-92	**Philadelphia**	**NHL**	**17**	**7**	**8**	**2**	**922**	**40**	**1**	**2.60**	....	....	....	....	....	....	....
	Hershey	AHL	35	15	11	6	2040	121	1	3.56	....	....	....	....	....	....	....
1992-93	**Philadelphia**	**NHL**	**34**	**13**	**11**	**5**	**1769**	**111**	**1**	**3.76**	....	....	....	....	....	....	....
	Hershey	AHL	6	0	3	3	372	23	0	3.71	....	....	....	....	....	....	....
1993-94	**Philadelphia**	**NHL**	**60**	**29**	**20**	**5**	**3285**	**183**	**1**	**3.34**	....	....	....	....	....	....	....
1994-95	**Philadelphia**	**NHL**	**19**	**11**	**7**	**0**	**1075**	**42**	**1**	**2.34**	**1**	**0**	**0**	**23**	**0**	**0**	**0.00**
	Hershey	AHL	1	0	1	0	59	5	0	5.07	....	....	....	....	....	....	....
1995-96	**Philadelphia**	**NHL**	**9**	**2**	**3**	**2**	**456**	**22**	**1**	**2.89**	....	....	....	....	....	....	....
	Hershey	AHL	12	4	4	3	690	32	0	2.78	....	....	....	....	....	....	....
	Winnipeg	**NHL**	**7**	**2**	**2**	**0**	**285**	**16**	**0**	**3.37**	....	....	....	....	....	....	....
1996-97	Philadelphia	AHL	36	18	9	3	1852	82	2	2.66	1	0	0	26	3	0	6.93
1997-98	Canada	Nat-Team	41	25	12	1	2307	86	5	2.24	....	....	....	....	....	....	....
	Rosenheim	Germany	2	....	....	....	120	12	0	6.00	....	....	....	....	....	....	....
1998-99	**Anaheim**	**NHL**	**18**	**4**	**5**	**4**	**884**	**37**	**1**	**2.51**	....	....	....	....	....	....	....
	NHL Totals		**164**	**68**	**56**	**18**	**8676**	**451**	**6**	**3.12**	**1**	**0**	**0**	**23**	**0**	**0**	**0.00**

Traded to **Winnipeg** by **Philadelphia** for Tim Cheveldae and Winnipeg's 3rd round choice (Chester Gallant) in 1996 Entry Draft, February 27, 1996. Signed as a free agent by **Philadelphia**, July 3, 1996. Traded to **Nashville** by **Philadelphia** with Jeff Staples for Nashville's 7th round choice (Cam Ondrik) in 1998 Entry Draft, June 26, 1998. Traded to **Anaheim** by **Nashville** for Chris Mason and Marc Moro, October 5, 1998.

ROY, Patrick (WAH) COL.

Goaltender. Catches left. 6', 192 lbs. Born, Quebec City, Que., October 5, 1965.
(Montreal's 4th choice, 51st overall, in 1984 Entry Draft).

			Regular Season								Playoffs						
Season	Club	Lea	GP	W	L	T	Mins	GA	SO	Avg	GP	W	L	Mins	GA	SO	Avg
1981-82	Ste-Foy	QAAA	40	27	3	10	2400	156	0	2.63	....	....	....	....	....	....	....
1982-83	Granby	QMJHL	54	13	35	1	2808	293	0	6.26	....	....	....	....	....	....	....
1983-84	Granby	QMJHL	61	29	29	1	3585	265	0	4.44	4	0	4	244	22	0	5.41
1984-85	**Montreal**	**NHL**	**1**	**1**	**0**	**0**	**20**	**0**	**0**	**0.00**	....	....	....	....	....	....	....
	Granby	QMJHL	44	16	25	1	2463	228	0	5.55	....	....	....	....	....	....	....
	Sherbrooke	AHL	1	1	0	0	60	4	0	4.00	13	10	3	*769	37	0	*2.89
1985-86 ♦	**Montreal**	**NHL**	**47**	**23**	**18**	**3**	**2651**	**148**	**1**	**3.35**	**20**	***15**	**5**	**1218**	**39**	***1**	**1.92**
1986-87	**Montreal**	**NHL**	**46**	**22**	**16**	**6**	**2686**	**131**	**1**	**2.93**	**6**	**4**	**2**	**330**	**22**	**0**	**4.00**
1987-88	**Montreal**	**NHL**	**45**	**23**	**12**	**9**	**2586**	**125**	**3**	**2.90**	**8**	**3**	**4**	**430**	**24**	**0**	**3.35**
1988-89	**Montreal**	**NHL**	**48**	**33**	**5**	**6**	**2744**	**113**	**4**	***2.47**	**19**	**13**	**6**	**1206**	**42**	**2**	***2.09**
1989-90	**Montreal**	**NHL**	**54**	***31**	**16**	**5**	**3173**	**134**	**3**	**2.53**	**11**	**5**	**6**	**641**	**26**	**1**	**2.43**
1990-91	**Montreal**	**NHL**	**48**	**25**	**15**	**6**	**2835**	**128**	**1**	**2.71**	**13**	**7**	**5**	**785**	**40**	**0**	**3.06**
1991-92	**Montreal**	**NHL**	**67**	**36**	**22**	**8**	**3935**	**155**	***5**	***2.36**	**11**	**4**	**7**	**686**	**30**	**1**	**2.62**
1992-93 ♦	**Montreal**	**NHL**	**62**	**31**	**25**	**5**	**3595**	**192**	**2**	**3.20**	**20**	***16**	**4**	**1293**	**46**	**0**	***2.13**
1993-94	**Montreal**	**NHL**	**68**	**35**	**17**	**11**	**3867**	**161**	***7**	**2.50**	**6**	**3**	**3**	**375**	**16**	**0**	**2.56**
1994-95	**Montreal**	**NHL**	**43**	**17**	**20**	**6**	**2566**	**127**	**1**	**2.97**	....	....	....	....	....	....	....
1995-96	**Montreal**	**NHL**	**22**	**12**	**9**	**1**	**1260**	**62**	**1**	**2.95**	....	....	....	....	....	....	....
♦	**Colorado**	**NHL**	**39**	**22**	**15**	**1**	**2305**	**103**	**1**	**2.68**	***22**	***16**	**6**	***1454**	**51**	***3**	**2.10**
1996-97	**Colorado**	**NHL**	**62**	***38**	**15**	**7**	**3698**	**143**	**7**	**2.32**	**17**	**10**	**7**	**1034**	**38**	***3**	**2.21**
1997-98	**Colorado**	**NHL**	**65**	**31**	**19**	**13**	**3835**	**153**	**4**	**2.39**	**7**	**3**	**4**	**430**	**18**	**0**	**2.51**
	Canada	Olympics	6	3	3	0	*369	9	1	1.46	....	....	....	....	....	....	....
1998-99	**Colorado**	**NHL**	**61**	**32**	**19**	**8**	**3648**	**139**	**5**	**2.29**	**19**	**11**	**8**	**1173**	**52**	**1**	**2.66**
	NHL Totals		**778**	**412**	**243**	**95**	**45404**	**2014**	**46**	**2.66**	**179**	**110**	**67**	**11055**	**444**	**12**	**2.41**

NHL All-Rookie Team (1986) • Won Conn Smythe Trophy (1986, 1993) • Shared William Jennings Trophy with Brian Hayward (1987, 1988, 1989) • NHL Second All-Star Team (1988, 1991) • NHL First All-Star Team (1989, 1990, 1992) • Won Trico Goaltending Award (1989, 1990) • Won Vezina Trophy (1989, 1990, 1992) • Won William M. Jennings Trophy (1992)

Played in NHL All-Star Game (1988, 1990, 1991, 1992, 1993, 1994, 1997, 1998)

Traded to **Colorado** by **Montreal** with Mike Keane for Andrei Kovalenko, Martin Rucinsky and Jocelyn Thibault, December 6, 1995.

RUDKOWSKY, Cody ST.L.

Goaltender. Catches left. 6'1", 200 lbs. Born, Willingdon, Alta., July 21, 1978.

			Regular Season								Playoffs						
Season	Club	Lea	GP	W	L	T	Mins	GA	SO	Avg	GP	W	L	Mins	GA	SO	Avg
1995-96	Langley	BCJHL	23	....	....	....	1172	73	1	3.73	....	....	....	....	....	....	....
	Seattle	WHL	2	0	0	0	21	3	0	8.57	....	....	....	....	....	....	....
1996-97	Seattle	WHL	40	19	16	1	2162	124	0	3.44	1	1	0	30	0	0	0.00
1997-98	Seattle	WHL	53	20	22	3	2805	176	1	3.74	5	1	4	278	18	0	3.88
1998-99	Seattle	WHL	64	34	17	10	3665	177	7	2.90	11	5	6	637	31	1	2.92

WHL West First All-Star Team (1999) • Canadian Major Junior First All-Star Team (1999) • Canadian Major Junior Goaltender of the Year (1999)

Signed as a free agent by **St. Louis**, March 25, 1999.

RUSSELL, Blaine ANA.

Goaltender. Catches left. 5'11", 180 lbs. Born, Wetaskawin, Sask., January 11, 1977.
(Anaheim's 4th choice, 149th overall, in 1996 Entry Draft).

			Regular Season								Playoffs						
Season	Club	Lea	GP	W	L	T	Mins	GA	SO	Avg	GP	W	L	Mins	GA	SO	Avg
1995-96	Spokane	WHL	1	0	1	0	37	5	0	8.11	....	....	....	....	....	....	....
	Prince Albert	WHL	34	25	5	2	1920	98	2	3.06	7	4	2	380	20	0	3.16
1996-97	Prince Albert	WHL	29	9	15	3	1690	99	2	3.51	....	....	....	....	....	....	....
	Lethbridge	WHL	6	4	1	1	370	17	0	2.76	14	*13	1	817	29	0	*2.13
1997-98	Columbus	ECHL	4	1	2	0	199	19	0	5.71	....	....	....	....	....	....	....
	Cincinnati	AHL	20	0	9	2	748	58	0	4.65	....	....	....	....	....	....	....
	Huntington	ECHL	1	0	1	0	60	6	0	6.00	....	....	....	....	....	....	....
	New Orleans	ECHL	4	0	0	2	183	11	0	3.59	....	....	....	....	....	....	....
1998-99	Huntington	ECHL	12	6	1	0	516	25	1	2.91	....	....	....	....	....	....	....

• Missed majority of 1998-99 season after suffering severe knee injury in game vs. Toledo (ECHL), December 4, 1998.

SABOURIN, Dany (SA-boo-rihn) CGY.

Goaltender. Catches left. 6'2", 165 lbs. Born, Val D'or, Que., September 2, 1980.
(Calgary's 5th choice, 108th overall, in 1998 Entry Draft).

			Regular Season								Playoffs						
Season	Club	Lea	GP	W	L	T	Mins	GA	SO	Avg	GP	W	L	Mins	GA	SO	Avg
1997-98	Sherbrooke	QMJHL	37	15	15	2	1906	128	1	4.03	....	....	....	....	....	....	....
1998-99	Sherbrooke	QMJHL	30	8	13	2	1477	102	1	4.14	1	0	1	49	2	0	2.45
	Saint John	AHL	....	....	....	....	....	....	....	....	1	0	1	57	4	0	4.19

SALO, Tommy (SAH-loh) EDM.

Goaltender. Catches left. 5'11", 173 lbs. Born, Surahammar, Sweden, February 1, 1971.
(NY Islanders' 5th choice, 118th overall, in 1993 Entry Draft).

			Regular Season								Playoffs						
Season	Club	Lea	GP	W	L	T	Mins	GA	SO	Avg	GP	W	L	Mins	GA	SO	Avg
1990-91	Vasteras IK	Sweden	2	....	....	....	100	11	0	6.60	....	....	....	....	....	....	....
1991-92	Vasteras IK	Sweden	DID NOT PLAY – INJURED														
1992-93	Vasteras IK	Sweden	24	....	....	....	1431	59	2	2.47	2	....	....	120	6	0	3.00
1993-94	Vasteras IK	Sweden	32	....	....	....	1896	106	0	3.35	....	....	....	....	....	....	....
	Sweden	Olympics	6	5	1	0	370	13	....	2.11	....	....	....	....	....	....	....
1994-95	Denver	IHL	*65	*45	14	4	*3810	165	*3	*2.60	8	7	0	390	20	0	3.07
	NY Islanders	**NHL**	**6**	**1**	**5**	**0**	**358**	**18**	**0**	**3.02**	....	....	....	....	....	....	....
1995-96	**NY Islanders**	**NHL**	**10**	**1**	**7**	**1**	**523**	**35**	**0**	**4.02**	....	....	....	....	....	....	....
	Utah	IHL	45	28	15	2	2695	119	*4	2.65	22	*15	7	1342	51	*3	2.28
1996-97	**NY Islanders**	**NHL**	**58**	**20**	**27**	**8**	**3208**	**151**	**5**	**2.82**	....	....	....	....	....	....	....
1997-98	**NY Islanders**	**NHL**	**62**	**23**	**29**	**5**	**3461**	**152**	**4**	**2.64**	....	....	....	....	....	....	....
	Sweden	Olympics	4	2	2	0	238	9	0	2.27	....	....	....	....	....	....	....
1998-99	**NY Islanders**	**NHL**	**51**	**17**	**26**	**7**	**3018**	**132**	**5**	**2.62**	....	....	....	....	....	....	....
	Edmonton	**NHL**	**13**	**8**	**2**	**2**	**700**	**27**	**0**	**2.31**	**4**	**0**	**4**	**296**	**11**	**0**	**2.23**
	NHL Totals		**200**	**70**	**96**	**23**	**11268**	**515**	**14**	**2.74**	**4**	**0**	**4**	**296**	**11**	**0**	**2.23**

IHL First All-Star Team (1995) • Won Garry F. Longman Memorial Trophy (Top Rookie - IHL) (1995) • Won James Norris Memorial Trophy (Fewest goals against - IHL) (1995) • Won James Gatschene Memorial Trophy (MVP - IHL) (1995) • Shared James Norris Memorial Trophy (fewest goals against — IHL) with Mark McArthur (1996) • Won "Bud" Poile Trophy (Playoff MVP - IHL) (1996)

Traded to **Edmonton** by **NY Islanders** for Mats Lindgren and Edmonton's 8th round choice (Radek Martinek) in 1999 Entry Draft, March 20, 1999.

SARJEANT, Geoff (SAHR-jehnt)

Goaltender. Catches left. 5'9", 180 lbs. Born, Newmarket, Ont., November 30, 1969.
(St. Louis' 1st choice, 17th overall, in 1990 Supplemental Draft).

			Regular Season								Playoffs						
Season	Club	Lea	GP	W	L	T	Mins	GA	SO	Avg	GP	W	L	Mins	GA	SO	Avg
1987-88	Aurora	OJHL-B	33	....	....	....	1878	136	0	4.35	....	....	....	....	....	....	....
1988-89	Michigan Tech	WCHA	6	0	3	2	329	22	0	4.01	....	....	....	....	....	....	....
1989-90	Michigan Tech	WCHA	19	4	13	0	1043	94	0	5.41	....	....	....	....	....	....	....
1990-91	Michigan Tech	WCHA	23	5	15	3	1540	97	0	3.78	....	....	....	....	....	....	....
1991-92	Michigan Tech	WCHA	23	7	13	0	1201	90	1	4.50	....	....	....	....	....	....	....
1992-93	Peoria	IHL	41	22	14	3	2356	130	0	3.31	3	0	3	179	13	0	4.36
1993-94	Peoria	IHL	41	25	9	2	2275	93	*2	*2.45	4	2	2	211	13	0	3.69
1994-95	Peoria	IHL	55	32	12	8	3146	158	0	3.01	4	0	3	206	20	0	5.81
	St. Louis	**NHL**	**4**	**1**	**0**	**0**	**120**	**6**	**0**	**3.00**	....	....	....	....	....	....	....
1995-96	**San Jose**	**NHL**	**4**	**0**	**2**	**1**	**171**	**14**	**0**	**4.91**	....	....	....	....	....	....	....
	Kansas City	IHL	41	18	18	1	2167	140	1	3.88	2	0	1	99	3	0	1.82
1996-97	Cincinnati	IHL	59	32	20	5	3287	157	1	2.87	3	0	3	158	12	0	4.55
1997-98	Cincinnati	IHL	54	25	19	9	3118	142	5	2.73	5	4	1	353	14	0	2.38
1998-99	Cincinnati	IHL	14	6	5	1	733	42	1	3.44	....	....	....	....	....	....	....
	Flint	UHL	3	0	2	1	179	11	0	3.69	....	....	....	....	....	....	....
	Detroit	IHL	8	1	5	1	421	26	0	3.71	....	....	....	....	....	....	....
	Long Beach	IHL	1	1	0	0	60	1	0	1.00	....	....	....	....	....	....	....
	Indianapolis	IHL	23	13	7	2	1354	57	2	2.53	3	0	1	115	10	0	5.22
	NHL Totals		**8**	**1**	**2**	**1**	**291**	**20**	**0**	**4.12**	....	....	....	....	....	....	....

IHL First All-Star Team (1994)

Signed as a free agent by **San Jose**, September 23, 1995.

SAUVE, Phillipe (SOH-vay) COL.

Goaltender. Catches left. 6', 175 lbs. Born, Buffalo, NY, February 27, 1980.
(Colorado's 6th choice, 38th overall, in 1998 Entry Draft).

			Regular Season								Playoffs						
Season	Club	Lea	GP	W	L	T	Mins	GA	SO	Avg	GP	W	L	Mins	GA	SO	Avg
1996-97	Rimouski	QMJHL	26	11	9	2	1334	84	0	3.78	1	0	0	14	3	0	12.90
1997-98	Rimouski	QMJHL	40	23	16	0	2326	131	1	3.38	7	0	5	262	33	0	7.55
1998-99	Rimouski	QMJHL	44	16	19	4	2401	155	0	3.87	11	6	4	595	30	*1	3.03

Canadian Major Junior Humanitarian Player of the Year (1999)

SCHAFER, Paxton (SHAY-fuhr)

Goaltender. Catches left. 5'9", 164 lbs. Born, Medicine Hat, Alta., February 26, 1976.
(Boston's 3rd choice, 47th overall, in 1995 Entry Draft).

			Regular Season								Playoffs						
Season	Club	Lea	GP	W	L	T	Mins	GA	SO	Avg	GP	W	L	Mins	GA	SO	Avg
1992-93	Medicine Hat	AAHA	27	....	....	....	1601	95	1	3.56	....	....	....	....	....	....	....
1993-94	Medicine Hat	WHL	19	6	9	1	909	67	0	4.42	....	....	....	....	....	....	....
1994-95	Medicine Hat	WHL	61	32	26	2	3519	185	0	3.15	5	1	4	339	18	0	3.19
1995-96	Medicine Hat	WHL	60	24	30	3	3256	200	1	3.69	5	1	4	251	25	0	5.98
1996-97	**Boston**	**NHL**	**3**	**0**	**0**	**0**	**77**	**6**	**0**	**4.68**	....	....	....	....	....	....	....
	Providence	AHL	22	9	10	0	1206	75	1	3.73	....	....	....	....	....	....	....
	Charlotte	ECHL	4	3	1	0	239	7	0	1.75	....	....	....	....	....	....	....
1997-98	Providence	AHL	3	1	1	0	158	11	0	4.16	....	....	....	....	....	....	....
	Charlotte	ECHL	44	21	17	5	2538	131	1	3.10	7	3	4	428	21	0	2.94
1998-99	Greenville	ECHL	40	17	16	7	2326	115	2	2.97	....	....	....	....	....	....	....
	NHL Totals		**3**	**0**	**0**	**0**	**77**	**6**	**0**	**4.68**	....	....	....	....	....	....	....

WHL East First All-Star Team (1995)

SCHWAB, Corey (SHWAHB) ATL.

Goaltender. Catches left. 6', 180 lbs. Born, North Battleford, Sask., November 4, 1970.
(New Jersey's 12th choice, 200th overall, in 1990 Entry Draft).

			Regular Season								Playoffs						
Season	Club	Lea	GP	W	L	T	Mins	GA	SO	Avg	GP	W	L	Mins	GA	SO	Avg
1988-89	Seattle	WHL	10	2	7	0	386	31	0	4.82	....	....	....	....	....	....	....
1989-90	Seattle	WHL	27	15	2	1	1150	69	1	3.60	3	0	0	49	2	0	2.45
1990-91	Seattle	WHL	*58	32	18	3	*3289	224	0	4.09	6	1	5	382	25	0	3.93
1991-92	Utica	AHL	24	9	12	1	1322	95	0	4.31	....	....	....	....	....	....	....
	Cincinnati	ECHL	8	6	0	1	450	31	0	4.13	9	6	3	540	29	0	3.22
1992-93	Utica	AHL	40	18	16	5	2387	169	*2	4.25	1	0	1	59	6	0	6.10
	Cincinnati	IHL	3	1	2	0	185	17	0	5.51	....	....	....	....	....	....	....
1993-94	Albany	AHL	51	27	21	3	3058	184	0	3.61	5	1	4	298	20	0	4.02
1994-95	Albany	AHL	45	25	10	9	2711	117	3	*2.59	7	6	1	425	19	0	2.68
1995-96	**New Jersey**	**NHL**	**10**	**0**	**3**	**0**	**331**	**12**	**0**	**2.18**	....	....	....	....	....	....	....
	Albany	AHL	5	3	2	0	299	13	0	2.61	....	....	....	....	....	....	....
1996-97	**Tampa Bay**	**NHL**	**31**	**11**	**12**	**1**	**1462**	**74**	**2**	**3.04**	....	....	....	....	....	....	....
1997-98	**Tampa Bay**	**NHL**	**16**	**2**	**9**	**1**	**821**	**40**	**1**	**2.92**	....	....	....	....	....	....	....
1998-99	**Tampa Bay**	**NHL**	**40**	**8**	**25**	**3**	**2146**	**126**	**0**	**3.52**	....	....	....	....	....	....	....
	Cleveland	IHL	8	1	6	1	477	31	0	3.90	....	....	....	....	....	....	....
	NHL Totals		**97**	**21**	**49**	**5**	**4760**	**252**	**3**	**3.18**	....	....	....	....	....	....	....

AHL Second All-Star Team (1995) • Shared Harry "Hap" Holmes Memorial Trophy (fewest goals against - AHL) with Mike Dunham (1995) • Shared Jack A. Butterfield Trophy (Playoff MVP - AHL) with Mike Dunham (1995)

Traded to **Tampa Bay** by **New Jersey** for Jeff Reese, Chicago's 2nd round choice (previously acquired, New Jersey selected Pierre Dagenais) in 1996 Entry Draft and Tampa Bay's 8th round choice (Jason Bertsch) in 1996 Entry Draft, June 22, 1996. Claimed by **Atlanta** from **Tampa Bay** in Expansion Draft, June 25, 1999.

SCOTT, Travis

Goaltender. Catches left. 6'2", 185 lbs. Born, Kanata, Ont., September 14, 1975.

			Regular Season								Playoffs						
Season	Club	Lea	GP	W	L	T	Mins	GA	SO	Avg	GP	W	L	Mins	GA	SO	Avg
1993-94	Windsor	OHL	45	20	18	0	2312	158	1	4.10	4	0	4	240	16	0	4.00
1994-95	Windsor	OHL	48	26	14	3	2644	147	3	3.34	3	0	1	94	6	1	3.83
1995-96	Oshawa	OHL	31	15	9	4	1763	78	3	2.65	5	1	4	315	23	0	4.38
1996-97	Baton Rouge	ECHL	10	5	2	1	501	22	0	2.63	....	....	....	....	....	....	....
	Worcester	AHL	29	14	10	1	1482	75	1	3.04	....	....	....	....	....	....	....
1997-98	Baton Rouge	ECHL	36	14	11	6	1949	96	1	2.96	....	....	....	....	....	....	....
1998-99	Mississippi	ECHL	44	22	12	5	2337	112	1	2.88	*18	*14	4	*1252	42	3	2.01

Playoff MVP - ECHL (1999)

Signed as a free agent by **St. Louis**, December 30, 1996.

SHIELDS, Steve S.J.

Goaltender. Catches left. 6'3", 215 lbs. Born, Toronto, Ont., July 19, 1972.
(Buffalo's 5th choice, 101st overall, in 1991 Entry Draft).

			Regular Season								Playoffs						
Season	Club	Lea	GP	W	L	T	Mins	GA	SO	Avg	GP	W	L	Mins	GA	SO	Avg
1990-91	U. of Michigan	CCHA	37	26	6	3	1963	106	0	3.24	....	....	....	....	....	....	....
1991-92	U. of Michigan	CCHA	*37	*27	7	2	*2090	99	1	2.84	....	....	....	....	....	....	....
1992-93	U. of Michigan	CCHA	*39	*30	6	2	2027	75	2	*2.22	....	....	....	....	....	....	....
1993-94	U. of Michigan	CCHA	36	*28	6	1	1961	87	0	2.66	....	....	....	....	....	....	....
1994-95	Rochester	AHL	13	3	8	0	673	53	0	4.72	1	0	0	20	3	0	9.00
	South Carolina	ECHL	21	11	5	2	1158	52	2	2.69	3	0	2	144	11	0	4.58
1995-96	**Buffalo**	**NHL**	**2**	**1**	**0**	**0**	**75**	**4**	**0**	**3.20**	....	....	....	....	....	....	....
	Rochester	AHL	43	20	17	2	2357	140	1	3.56	*19	*15	3	*1127	47	1	2.50
1996-97	**Buffalo**	**NHL**	**13**	**3**	**8**	**2**	**789**	**39**	**0**	**2.97**	**10**	**4**	**6**	**570**	**26**	**1**	**2.74**
	Rochester	AHL	23	14	6	2	1331	60	1	2.70	....	....	....	....	....	....	....
1997-98	**Buffalo**	**NHL**	**16**	**3**	**6**	**4**	**785**	**37**	**0**	**2.83**	....	....	....	....	....	....	....
	Rochester	AHL	1	0	1	0	59	3	0	3.04	....	....	....	....	....	....	....
1998-99	**San Jose**	**NHL**	**37**	**15**	**11**	**8**	**2162**	**80**	**4**	**2.22**	**1**	**0**	**1**	**60**	**6**	**0**	**6.00**
	NHL Totals		**68**	**22**	**25**	**14**	**3811**	**160**	**4**	**2.52**	**11**	**4**	**7**	**630**	**32**	**1**	**3.05**

CCHA First All-Star Team (1993, 1994) • NCAA West Second All-American Team (1993, 1994)

Traded to **San Jose** by **Buffalo** with Buffalo's 4th round choice (Miroskav Zalesak) in 1998 Entry Draft for Kay Whitmore, Colorado's 2nd round choice (previously acquired, Buffalo selected Jaroslav Kristek) in 1998 Entry Draft and San Jose's 5th round choice in 2000 Entry Draft, June 18, 1998.

SHTALENKOV, Mikhail (shtuh-LEHN-kahf, mihk-HAIL) PHX.

Goaltender. Catches left. 6'2", 185 lbs. Born, Moscow, USSR, October 20, 1965.
(Anaheim's 5th choice, 108th overall, in 1993 Entry Draft).

			Regular Season								Playoffs						
Season	Club	Lea	GP	W	L	T	Mins	GA	SO	Avg	GP	W	L	Mins	GA	SO	Avg
1986-87	Moscow D'amo	USSR	17	....	....	....	893	36	1	2.41	....	....	....	....	....	....	....
1987-88	Moscow D'amo	USSR	25	....	....	....	1302	72	1	3.31	....	....	....	....	....	....	....
1988-89	Moscow D'amo	USSR	4	....	....	....	80	3	0	2.25	....	....	....	....	....	....	....
1989-90	Moscow D'amo	USSR	6	....	....	....	20	1	0	3.00	....	....	....	....	....	....	....
1990-91	Moscow D'amo	USSR	31	....	....	....	1568	56	2	2.14	....	....	....	....	....	....	....
1991-92	Moscow D'amo	CIS	27	....	....	....	1268	45	1	2.12	....	....	....	....	....	....	....
	Russia	Olympics	8	7	1	0	440	12	....	1.64	....	....	....	....	....	....	....
1992-93	Milwaukee	IHL	47	26	14	5	2669	135	2	3.03	3	1	2	209	11	0	3.16
1993-94	**Anaheim**	**NHL**	**10**	**3**	**4**	**1**	**543**	**24**	**0**	**2.65**	....	....	....	....	....	....	....
	San Diego	IHL	28	15	11	2	1616	93	0	3.45	....	....	....	....	....	....	....
1994-95	**Anaheim**	**NHL**	**18**	**4**	**7**	**1**	**810**	**49**	**0**	**3.63**	....	....	....	....	....	....	....
1995-96	**Anaheim**	**NHL**	**30**	**7**	**16**	**3**	**1637**	**85**	**0**	**3.12**	....	....	....	....	....	....	....
1996-97	**Anaheim**	**NHL**	**24**	**7**	**8**	**1**	**1079**	**52**	**2**	**2.89**	**4**	**0**	**3**	**211**	**10**	**0**	**2.84**
1997-98	**Anaheim**	**NHL**	**40**	**13**	**18**	**5**	**2049**	**110**	**1**	**3.22**	....	....	....	....	....	....	....
	Russia	Olympics	5	4	1	0	290	8	0	1.65	....	....	....	....	....	....	....
1998-99	**Edmonton**	**NHL**	**34**	**12**	**17**	**3**	**1819**	**81**	**3**	**2.67**	....	....	....	....	....	....	....
	Phoenix	**NHL**	**4**	**1**	**2**	**1**	**243**	**9**	**0**	**2.22**	....	....	....	....	....	....	....
	NHL Totals		**160**	**47**	**72**	**15**	**8180**	**410**	**6**	**3.01**	**4**	**0**	**3**	**211**	**10**	**0**	**2.84**

USSR Rookie of the Year (1987) • Won Garry F. Longman Memorial Trophy (Top Rookie - IHL) (1993)

Claimed by **Nashville** from **Anaheim** in Expansion Draft, June 26, 1998. Traded to **Edmonton** by **Nashville** with Jim Dowd for Eric Fichaud, Drake Berehowsky and Greg de Vries, October 1, 1998. Traded to **Phoenix** by **Edmonton** for Phoenix's 5th round choice in 2000 Entry Draft, March 11, 1999.

SHULMISTRA, Richard (shuhl-MIHS-trah) FLA.

Goaltender. Catches right. 6'2", 185 lbs. Born, Sudbury, Ont., April 1, 1971.
(Quebec's 1st choice, 4th overall, in 1992 Supplemental Draft).

			Regular Season								Playoffs						
Season	Club	Lea	GP	W	L	T	Mins	GA	SO	Avg	GP	W	L	Mins	GA	SO	Avg
1990-91	U. of Miami-Ohio	CCHA	20	2	12	2	920	80	0	5.21	....	....	....	....	....	....	....
1991-92	U. of Miami-Ohio	CCHA	19	3	5	2	850	67	0	4.72	....	....	....	....	....	....	....
1992-93	U. of Miami-Ohio	CCHA	33	22	6	4	1949	88	1	2.71	....	....	....	....	....	....	....
1993-94	U. of Miami-Ohio	CCHA	27	13	12	1	1521	74	0	2.92	....	....	....	....	....	....	....
1994-95	Cornwall	AHL	20	4	9	2	937	58	0	3.71	8	4	3	446	22	0	2.95
1995-96	Cornwall	AHL	36	9	18	2	1844	100	0	3.25	1	0	0	9	1	0	6.76
1996-97	Albany	AHL	23	5	9	2	1062	43	2	2.43	2	1	0	77	2	0	1.56
1997-98	Fort Wayne	IHL	11	3	8	0	656	34	1	3.11	....	....	....	....	....	....	....
	New Jersey	**NHL**	**1**	**0**	**1**	**0**	**62**	**2**	**0**	**1.94**	....	....	....	....	....	....	....
	Albany	AHL	35	20	8	4	2022	78	2	*2.31	13	8	3	696	32	1	2.76
1998-99	Albany	AHL	12	6	4	0	596	34	0	3.42	2	0	2	64	3	0	2.82
	Manitoba	IHL	44	25	11	7	2469	117	2	2.84	....	....	....	....	....	....	....
	NHL Totals		**1**	**0**	**1**	**0**	**62**	**2**	**0**	**1.94**	....	....	....	....	....	....	....

CCHA Second All-Star Team (1993) • AHL Second All-Star Team (1998)

Transferred to **Colorado** after **Quebec** franchise relocated, June 21, 1995. Signed as a free agent by **New Jersey**, December 31, 1997. Signed as a free agent by **Florida**, July 27, 1999.

SKUDRA, Peter (SKOO-druh) PIT.

Goaltender. Catches left. 6'1", 185 lbs. Born, Riga, USSR, April 24, 1973.

			Regular Season								Playoffs						
Season	Club	Lea	GP	W	L	T	Mins	GA	SO	Avg	GP	W	L	Mins	GA	SO	Avg
1992-93	Pardaugava Riga	CIS	27	....	....	....	1498	74	....	2.96	1	....	....	60	5	0	5.00
1993-94	Pardaugava Riga	CIS	14	....	....	....	783	42	....	3.22	1	....	....	55	4	0	4.36
1994-95	Greensboro	ECHL	33	13	9	5	1612	113	0	4.20	6	2	2	341	28	0	4.92
	Memphis	CHL	2	0	1	0	60	8	0	6.01	....	....	....	....	....	....	....
1995-96	Erie	ECHL	12	3	8	1	681	47	0	4.14	....	....	....	....	....	....	....
	Johnstown	ECHL	30	12	11	4	1657	98	0	3.55	....	....	....	....	....	....	....
1996-97	Hamilton	AHL	32	8	16	2	1615	101	0	3.75	....	....	....	....	....	....	....
	Johnstown	ECHL	4	2	1	1	200	11	0	3.30	....	....	....	....	....	....	....
1997-98	**Pittsburgh**	**NHL**	**17**	**6**	**4**	**3**	**851**	**26**	**0**	**1.83**	....	....	....	....	....	....	....
	Houston	IHL	9	5	3	1	499	23	0	2.77	....	....	....	....	....	....	....
	Kansas City	IHL	13	10	3	0	775	37	0	2.86	8	4	4	512	20	1	*2.34
1998-99	**Pittsburgh**	**NHL**	**37**	**15**	**11**	**5**	**1914**	**89**	**3**	**2.79**	....	....	....	....	....	....	....
	NHL Totals		**54**	**21**	**15**	**8**	**2765**	**115**	**3**	**2.50**	....	....	....	....	....	....	....

Signed as a free agent by **Pittsburgh**, September 25, 1997.

SMANGS, Henrik (SMOHNGS) PHX.

Goaltender. Catches left. 5'11", 174 lbs. Born, Leksand, Sweden, January 19, 1976.
(Winnipeg's 9th choice, 212th overall, in 1994 Entry Draft).

			Regular Season								Playoffs						
Season	Club	Lea	GP	W	L	T	Mins	GA	SO	Avg	GP	W	L	Mins	GA	SO	Avg
1995-96	Leksands IF	Swede-Jr.	STATISTICS NOT AVAILABLE														
1996-97	Mora IK	Swede-2	5	....	....	....	260	12	....	2.70	....	....	....	....	....	....	....
1997-98	Mora IK	Swede-2	5	....	....	....	300	10	1	2.00	....	....	....	....	....	....	....
1998-99	Tupelo	WPHL	31	7	15	1	1497	108	0	4.33	....	....	....	....	....	....	....

Transferred to **Phoenix** after **Winnipeg** franchise relocated, July 1, 1996.

SNOW, Garth — VAN.

Goaltender. Catches left. 6'3", 200 lbs. Born, Wrentham, MA, July 28, 1969.
(Quebec's 6th choice, 114th overall, in 1987 Entry Draft).

			Regular Season								Playoffs						
Season	Club	Lea	GP	W	L	T	Mins	GA	SO	Avg	GP	W	L	Mins	GA	SO	Avg
1986-87	Mt. St. Charles	H.S.	30	....	....	....	1795	53	10	1.77	....	....	....	....	....	....	....
1987-88	Stratford	OJHL-B	30	20	6	0	1642	93	2	3.40	....	....	....	....	....	....	....
1988-89	U. of Maine	H.E.	5	2	2	0	241	14	1	3.49	....	....	....	....	....	....	....
1989-90									DID NOT PLAY								
1990-91	U. of Maine	H.E.	25	*18	4	0	1290	64	2	2.98	....	....	....	....	....	....	....
1991-92	U. of Maine	H.E.	31	*25	4	2	1792	73	*2	*2.44	....	....	....	....	....	....	....
1992-93	U. of Maine	H.E.	23	*21	0	1	1210	42	1	*2.08	....	....	....	....	....	....	....
1993-94	United States	Nat-Team	23	13	5	3	1324	71	1	3.22	....	....	....	....	....	....	....
	United States	Olympics	5	....	....	....	299	17	....	3.41	....	....	....	....	....	....	....
	Quebec	NHL	5	3	2	0	279	16	0	3.44	....	....	....	....	....	....	....
	Cornwall	AHL	16	6	5	3	927	51	0	3.30	13	8	5	790	42	0	3.19
1994-95	Cornwall	AHL	*62	*32	20	7	*3558	162	3	2.73	8	4	3	402	14	*2	*2.09
	Quebec	NHL	2	1	1	0	119	11	0	5.55	1	0	0	9	1	0	6.67
1995-96	Philadelphia	NHL	26	12	8	4	1437	69	0	2.88	1	0	0	1	0	0	0.00
1996-97	Philadelphia	NHL	35	14	8	8	1884	79	2	2.52	12	8	4	699	33	0	2.83
1997-98	Philadelphia	NHL	29	14	9	4	1651	67	1	2.43	....	....	....	....	....	....	....
	Vancouver	NHL	12	3	6	0	504	26	0	3.10	....	....	....	....	....	....	....
1998-99	Vancouver	NHL	65	20	31	8	3501	171	6	2.93	....	....	....	....	....	....	....
	NHL Totals		174	67	65	24	9375	439	9	2.81	14	8	4	709	34	0	2.88

Hockey East Second All-Star Team (1992, 1993) • NCAA Championship All-Tournament Team (1993)

Transferred to **Colorado** after **Quebec** franchise relocated, June 21, 1995. Traded to **Philadelphia** by **Colorado** for Philadelphia's 3rd (later traded to Washington — Washington selected Shawn McNeil) and 6th (Kai Fischer) round choices in 1996 Entry Draft, July 12, 1995. Traded to **Vancouver** by **Philadelphia** for Sean Burke, March 4, 1998.

SODERSTROM, Tommy — (SAH-duhr-struhm)

Goaltender. Catches left. 5'7", 157 lbs. Born, Stockholm, Sweden, July 17, 1969.
(Philadelphia's 14th choice, 214th overall, in 1990 Entry Draft).

			Regular Season								Playoffs						
Season	Club	Lea	GP	W	L	T	Mins	GA	SO	Avg	GP	W	L	Mins	GA	SO	Avg
1989-90	Djurgardens IF	Sweden	4	....	....	....	240	14	0	3.50	....	....	....	....	....	....	....
1990-91	Djurgardens IF	Sweden	39	22	12	6	2340	104	3	2.67	7	....	....	423	10	2	1.42
1991-92	Djurgardens IF	Sweden	39	15	8	11	2340	109	4	2.79	10	....	....	635	28	0	2.65
	Sweden	Olympics	5	3	1	1	298	13	....	2.62	....	....	....	....	....	....	....
1992-93	Philadelphia	NHL	44	20	17	6	2512	143	5	3.42	....	....	....	....	....	....	....
	Hershey	AHL	7	4	1	0	373	15	0	2.41	....	....	....	....	....	....	....
1993-94	Philadelphia	NHL	34	6	18	4	1736	116	2	4.01	....	....	....	....	....	....	....
	Hershey	AHL	9	3	4	1	461	37	0	4.81	....	....	....	....	....	....	....
1994-95	NY Islanders	NHL	26	8	12	3	1350	70	1	3.11	....	....	....	....	....	....	....
1995-96	NY Islanders	NHL	51	11	22	6	2590	167	2	3.87	....	....	....	....	....	....	....
1996-97	NY Islanders	NHL	1	0	0	0	1	0	0	0.00	....	....	....	....	....	....	....
	Rochester	AHL	2	2	0	0	120	8	0	4.00	....	....	....	....	....	....	....
	Utica	IHL	26	12	11	0	1463	76	0	3.12	....	....	....	....	....	....	....
1997-98	Djurgardens IF	Sweden	*46	....	....	....	*2760	103	....	*2.24	*15	....	....	*936	34	....	2.18
	Sweden	Olympics							DID NOT PLAY – SPARE GOALTENDER								
1998-99	Djurgardens IF	Sweden	*48	....	....	....	2918	134	1	2.76	4	....	....	240	11	0	2.75
	NHL Totals		156	45	69	19	8189	496	10	3.63	....	....	....	....	....	....	....

Swedish Rookie of the Year (1991) • Swedish World All-Star Team (1992)

Traded to **NY Islanders** by **Philadelphia** for Ron Hextall and NY Islanders' 6th round choice (Dmitry Tertyshny) in 1995 Entry Draft, September 22, 1994. • Played 10 seconds in game on March 31, 1997.

STANA, Ratislav — (STAN-ah) WSH.

Goaltender. Catches left. 6'1", 161 lbs. Born, Kosice, Czech., January 10, 1980.
(Washington's 8th choice, 193rd overall, in 1998 Entry Draft).

			Regular Season								Playoffs						
Season	Club	Lea	GP	W	L	T	Mins	GA	SO	Avg	GP	W	L	Mins	GA	SO	Avg
1997-98	HC Kosice	Slovak-Jr.	50	....	....	....	2760	87	2	1.89	....	....	....	....	....	....	....
1998-99	Moose Jaw	WHL	36	21	14	1	2131	123	2	3.46	9	4	5	544	30	0	3.31

STORR, Jamie — (STOHR) L.A.

Goaltender. Catches left. 6'2", 198 lbs. Born, Brampton, Ont., December 28, 1975.
(Los Angeles' 1st choice, 7th overall, in 1994 Entry Draft).

			Regular Season								Playoffs						
Season	Club	Lea	GP	W	L	T	Mins	GA	SO	Avg	GP	W	L	Mins	GA	SO	Avg
1990-91	Brampton	OJHL-B	24	....	....	....	1145	91	0	4.77	....	....	....	....	....	....	....
1991-92	Owen Sound	OHL	34	11	16	1	1732	128	0	4.43	5	1	4	299	28	0	5.62
1992-93	Owen Sound	OHL	41	20	17	3	2362	180	0	4.57	8	4	4	454	35	0	4.63
1993-94	Owen Sound	OHL	35	21	11	1	2004	120	1	3.59	9	4	5	547	44	0	4.83
1994-95	Owen Sound	OHL	17	5	9	2	977	64	0	3.93	....	....	....	....	....	....	....
	Los Angeles	NHL	5	1	3	1	263	17	0	3.88	....	....	....	....	....	....	....
	Windsor	OHL	4	3	1	0	241	8	1	1.99	10	6	3	520	34	1	3.92
1995-96	Los Angeles	NHL	5	3	1	0	262	12	0	2.75	....	....	....	....	....	....	....
	Phoenix	IHL	48	22	20	4	2711	139	2	3.08	2	1	1	118	4	1	2.03
1996-97	Los Angeles	NHL	5	2	1	1	265	11	0	2.49	....	....	....	....	....	....	....
	Phoenix	IHL	44	16	22	4	2441	147	0	3.61	....	....	....	....	....	....	....
1997-98	Los Angeles	NHL	17	9	5	1	920	34	2	2.22	3	0	2	145	9	0	3.72
	Long Beach	IHL	11	7	2	1	629	31	0	2.96	....	....	....	....	....	....	....
1998-99	Los Angeles	NHL	28	12	12	2	1525	61	4	2.40	....	....	....	....	....	....	....
	NHL Totals		60	27	22	5	3235	135	6	2.50	3	0	2	145	9	0	3.72

OHL First All-Star Team (1994) • NHL All-Rookie Team (1998, 1999)

SYMINGTON, Jeremy — (SIGH-mihng-tuhn) NYI

Goaltender. Catches left. 6'2", 185 lbs. Born, Petrolia, Ont., August 17, 1978.
(NY Islanders' 10th choice, 196th overall, in 1997 Entry Draft).

			Regular Season								Playoffs						
Season	Club	Lea	GP	W	L	T	Mins	GA	SO	Avg	GP	W	L	Mins	GA	SO	Avg
1996-97	Petrolia	OJHL	33	....	....	....	1953	111	1	3.41	....	....	....	....	....	....	....
1997-98	St. Lawrence	ECAC	7	0	6	0	370	41	0	6.74	....	....	....	....	....	....	....
1998-99	St. Lawrence	ECAC	3	1	1	0	128	7	0	3.27	....	....	....	....	....	....	....

TABARACCI, Rick — (tab-uh-RA-chee)

Goaltender. Catches left. 6'1", 180 lbs. Born, Toronto, Ont., January 2, 1969.
(Pittsburgh's 2nd choice, 26th overall, in 1987 Entry Draft).

			Regular Season								Playoffs						
Season	Club	Lea	GP	W	L	T	Mins	GA	SO	Avg	GP	W	L	Mins	GA	SO	Avg
1985-86	Markham	OJHL	40	....	....	....	2176	188	1	5.18	....	....	....	....	....	....	....
1986-87	Cornwall	OHL	*59	23	32	3	*3347	290	1	5.20	5	1	4	303	26	0	3.17
1987-88	Cornwall	OHL	58	*33	18	6	3448	200	*3	3.48	11	5	6	642	37	0	3.46
	Muskegon	IHL	....	....	....	....	....	....	....	....	1	0	0	13	1	0	4.62
1988-89	Pittsburgh	NHL	1	0	0	0	33	4	0	7.27	....	....	....	....	....	....	....
	Cornwall	OHL	50	24	20	5	2974	210	1	4.24	18	10	8	1080	65	*1	3.61
1989-90	Moncton	AHL	27	10	15	2	1580	107	2	4.06	....	....	....	....	....	....	....
	Fort Wayne	IHL	22	8	9	1	1064	73	0	4.12	3	1	2	159	19	0	7.17
1990-91	Winnipeg	NHL	24	4	9	4	1093	71	1	3.90	....	....	....	....	....	....	....
	Moncton	AHL	11	4	5	2	645	41	0	3.81	....	....	....	....	....	....	....
1991-92	Winnipeg	NHL	18	6	7	3	966	52	0	3.23	7	3	4	387	26	0	4.03
	Moncton	AHL	23	10	11	1	1313	80	0	3.66	....	....	....	....	....	....	....
1992-93	Winnipeg	NHL	19	5	10	0	959	70	0	4.38	....	....	....	....	....	....	....
	Moncton	AHL	5	2	1	2	290	18	0	3.72	....	....	....	....	....	....	....
	Washington	NHL	6	3	2	0	343	10	2	1.75	4	1	3	304	14	0	2.76
1993-94	Washington	NHL	32	13	14	2	1770	91	2	3.08	2	0	2	111	6	0	3.24
	Portland	AHL	3	3	0	0	176	8	0	2.72	....	....	....	....	....	....	....
1994-95	Washington	NHL	8	1	3	2	394	16	0	2.44	....	....	....	....	....	....	....
	Chicago	IHL	2	1	1	0	119	9	0	4.51	....	....	....	....	....	....	....
	Calgary	NHL	5	2	0	1	202	5	0	1.49	1	0	0	19	0	0	0.00
1995-96	Calgary	NHL	43	19	16	3	2391	117	3	2.94	3	0	3	204	7	0	2.06
1996-97	Calgary	NHL	7	2	4	0	361	14	1	2.33	....	....	....	....	....	....	....
	Tampa Bay	NHL	55	20	25	6	3012	138	4	2.75	....	....	....	....	....	....	....
1997-98	Calgary	NHL	42	13	22	6	2419	116	0	2.88	....	....	....	....	....	....	....
1998-99	Washington	NHL	23	4	12	3	1193	50	2	2.51	....	....	....	....	....	....	....
	NHL Totals		283	92	124	30	15136	754	15	2.99	17	4	12	1025	53	0	3.10

OHL First All-Star Team (1988) • OHL Second All-Star Team (1989)

Traded to **Winnipeg** by **Pittsburgh** with Randy Cunneyworth and Dave McLlwain for Jim Kyte, Andrew McBain and Randy Gilhen, June 17, 1989. Traded to **Washington** by **Winnipeg** for Jim Hrivnak and Washington's 2nd round choice (Alexei Budayev) in 1993 Entry Draft, March 22, 1993. Traded to **Calgary** by **Washington** for Calgary's 5th round choice (Joel Cort) in 1995 Entry Draft, April 7, 1995. Traded to **Tampa Bay** by **Calgary** for Aaron Gavey, November 19, 1996. Traded to **Calgary** by **Tampa Bay** for Calgary's 4th round choice (Eric Beaudoin) in 1998 Entry Draft, June 21, 1997. Traded to **Washington** by **Calgary** for future considerations, August 7, 1998.

TALLAS, Robbie — (TAL-as) BOS.

Goaltender. Catches left. 6', 163 lbs. Born, Edmonton, Alta., March 20, 1973.

			Regular Season								Playoffs						
Season	Club	Lea	GP	W	L	T	Mins	GA	SO	Avg	GP	W	L	Mins	GA	SO	Avg
1990-91	Penticton	BCJHL	37	....	....	....	2055	196	0	5.72	....	....	....	....	....	....	....
1991-92	Seattle	WHL	14	4	7	0	708	52	0	4.41	....	....	....	....	....	....	....
	Surrey Eagles	BCJHL	19	6	12	0	1043	112	1	6.44	....	....	....	....	....	....	....
1992-93	Seattle	WHL	58	24	23	3	3151	194	2	3.69	5	1	4	333	18	0	3.24
1993-94	Seattle	WHL	51	23	21	3	2849	188	0	3.96	9	5	4	567	40	0	4.23
1994-95	Charlotte	ECHL	36	21	9	3	2011	114	0	3.40	....	....	....	....	....	....	....
	Providence	AHL	2	1	0	0	82	4	1	2.90	....	....	....	....	....	....	....
1995-96	Boston	NHL	1	1	0	0	60	3	0	3.00	....	....	....	....	....	....	....
	Providence	AHL	37	12	16	7	2136	117	1	3.29	2	0	2	135	9	0	4.01
1996-97	Boston	NHL	28	8	12	1	1244	69	1	3.33	....	....	....	....	....	....	....
	Providence	AHL	24	9	14	1	1424	83	0	3.50	....	....	....	....	....	....	....
1997-98	Boston	NHL	14	6	3	3	788	24	1	1.83	....	....	....	....	....	....	....
	Providence	AHL	10	1	8	1	575	39	0	4.07	....	....	....	....	....	....	....
1998-99	Boston	NHL	17	7	7	2	987	43	1	2.61	....	....	....	....	....	....	....
	NHL Totals		60	22	22	6	3079	139	3	2.71	....	....	....	....	....	....	....

Signed as a free agent by **Boston**, September 13, 1995.

TERRERI, Chris — (tuh-RAIR-ee) N.J.

Goaltender. Catches left. 5'9", 170 lbs. Born, Providence, RI, November 15, 1964.
(New Jersey's 3rd choice, 87th overall, in 1983 Entry Draft).

			Regular Season								Playoffs						
Season	Club	Lea	GP	W	L	T	Mins	GA	SO	Avg	GP	W	L	Mins	GA	SO	Avg
1982-83	Providence	ECAC	11	7	1	0	528	17	2	1.93	....	....	....	....	....	....	....
1983-84	Providence	ECAC	10	4	2	0	391	20	0	3.07	....	....	....	....	....	....	....
1984-85	Providence	H.E.	33	15	13	5	1956	116	1	3.35	....	....	....	....	....	....	....
1985-86	Providence	H.E.	22	6	16	0	1320	84	0	3.74	....	....	....	....	....	....	....
1986-87	New Jersey	NHL	7	0	3	1	286	21	0	4.41	....	....	....	....	....	....	....
	Maine	AHL	14	4	9	1	765	57	0	4.47	....	....	....	....	....	....	....
1987-88	Utica	AHL	7	5	1	0	399	18	0	2.71	....	....	....	....	....	....	....
	United States	Nat-Team	26	17	7	2	1430	81	0	3.40	....	....	....	....	....	....	....
	United States	Olympics	3	....	....	....	127	14	....	6.58	....	....	....	....	....	....	....
1988-89	New Jersey	NHL	8	0	4	2	402	18	0	2.69	....	....	....	....	....	....	....
	Utica	AHL	39	20	15	3	2314	132	0	3.42	2	0	1	80	6	0	4.50
1989-90	New Jersey	NHL	35	15	12	3	1931	110	0	3.42	4	2	2	238	13	0	3.28
1990-91	New Jersey	NHL	53	24	21	7	2970	144	1	2.91	7	3	4	428	21	0	2.94
1991-92	New Jersey	NHL	54	22	22	10	3186	169	1	3.18	7	3	3	386	23	0	3.58
1992-93	New Jersey	NHL	48	19	21	3	2672	151	2	3.39	4	1	3	219	17	0	4.66
1993-94	New Jersey	NHL	44	20	11	4	2340	106	2	2.72	4	3	0	200	9	0	2.70
1994-95♦	New Jersey	NHL	15	3	7	2	734	31	0	2.53	1	0	0	8	0	0	0.00
1995-96	New Jersey	NHL	4	3	0	0	210	9	0	2.57	....	....	....	....	....	....	....
	San Jose	NHL	46	13	29	1	2516	155	0	3.70	....	....	....	....	....	....	....
1996-97	San Jose	NHL	22	6	10	3	1200	55	0	2.75	....	....	....	....	....	....	....
	Chicago	NHL	7	4	1	2	429	19	0	2.66	2	0	0	44	3	0	4.09
1997-98	Chicago	NHL	21	8	10	2	1222	49	2	2.41	....	....	....	....	....	....	....
	Indianapolis	IHL	3	2	0	1	180	3	1	1.00	....	....	....	....	....	....	....
1998-99	New Jersey	NHL	12	8	3	1	726	30	1	2.48	....	....	....	....	....	....	....
	NHL Totals		376	145	154	41	20824	1067	9	3.07	29	12	12	1523	86	0	3.39

Hockey East First All-Star Team (1985) • NCAA East First All-American Team (1985) • NCAA Championship All-Tournament Team (1985) • NCAA Championship Tournament MVP (1985)

Traded to **San Jose** by **New Jersey** for San Jose's 2nd round choice (later traded to Pittsburgh — Pittsburgh selected Pavel Skrbek) in 1996 Entry Draft, November 15, 1995. Traded to **Chicago** by **San Jose** with Ulf Dahlen and Michal Sykora for Ed Belfour, January 25, 1997. Traded to **New Jersey** by **Chicago** for New Jersey's 2nd round choice (Stepan Mokhov) in 1999 Entry Draft, August 25, 1998.

THEODORE, Jose (THEE-uh-dohr, joh-SAY) MTL.

Goaltender. Catches right. 5'10", 182 lbs. Born, Laval, Que., September 13, 1976.
(Montreal's 2nd choice, 44th overall, in 1994 Entry Draft).

			Regular Season								Playoffs						
Season	Club	Lea	GP	W	L	T	Mins	GA	SO	Avg	GP	W	L	Mins	GA	SO	Avg
1990-91	Richelieu	QAAA	42	....	....	....	2520	80	0	1.90	....	....	....	....	....	....	....
1991-92	Richelieu	QAAA	24	9	13	2	1440	96	0	3.99	....	....	....	....	....	....	....
1992-93	St-Jean	QMJHL	34	12	16	2	1776	112	0	3.78	3	0	2	175	11	0	3.77
1993-94	St-Jean	QMJHL	57	20	29	6	3225	194	0	3.61	5	1	4	296	18	0	3.65
1994-95	Hull	QMJHL	*58	*32	22	2	*3348	193	5	3.46	*21	*15	6	*1263	59	*1	2.80
	Fredericton	AHL	....	....	....	....	....	....	....	....	1	0	1	60	3	0	3.00
1995-96	**Montreal**	**NHL**	**1**	**0**	**0**	**0**	**9**	**1**	**0**	**6.67**	....	....	....	....	....	....	....
	Hull	QMJHL	48	33	11	2	2807	158	0	3.38	5	2	3	299	20	0	4.01
1996-97	**Montreal**	**NHL**	**16**	**5**	**6**	**2**	**821**	**53**	**0**	**3.87**	**2**	**1**	**1**	**168**	**7**	**0**	**2.50**
	Fredericton	AHL	26	12	12	0	1469	87	0	3.55	....	....	....	....	....	....	....
1997-98	Fredericton	AHL	53	20	23	8	3053	145	2	2.85	4	1	3	237	13	0	3.28
	Montreal	**NHL**	....	....	....	....	....	....	....	....	**3**	**0**	**1**	**120**	**1**	**0**	**0.50**
1998-99	**Montreal**	**NHL**	**18**	**4**	**12**	**0**	**913**	**50**	**1**	**3.29**	....	....	....	....	....	....	....
	Fredericton	AHL	27	12	13	2	1609	77	2	2.87	13	8	5	694	35	1	3.03
	NHL Totals		**35**	**9**	**18**	**2**	**1743**	**104**	**1**	**3.58**	**5**	**1**	**2**	**288**	**8**	**0**	**1.67**

QMJHL Second All-Star Team (1995, 1996)

THERRIEN, Pierre-Luc (teh-REE-eh)

Goaltender. Catches left. 6', 170 lbs. Born, Terrebonne, Que., September 3, 1979.
(Washington's 6th choice, 200th overall, in 1997 Entry Draft).

			Regular Season								Playoffs						
Season	Club	Lea	GP	W	L	T	Mins	GA	SO	Avg	GP	W	L	Mins	GA	SO	Avg
1996-96	Drummondville	QMJHL	37	15	17	1	2073	117	1	3.40	6	1	5	367	39	0	6.38
1996-97	Drummondville	QMJHL	42	16	17	1	2235	147	2	3.94	5	1	0	154	16	0	6.22
1997-98	Drummondville	QMJHL	16	5	8	0	857	68	0	4.76	....	....	....	....	....	....	....
	Victoriaville	QMJHL	10	6	1	2	571	26	0	2.73	1	0	0	16	5	0	18.40
1998-99	Victoriaville	QMJHL	48	22	19	2	2628	133	2	3.04	6	2	4	444	14	0	*1.89

THIBAULT, Jocelyn (tee-BOW) CHI.

Goaltender. Catches left. 5'11", 170 lbs. Born, Montreal, Que., January 12, 1975.
(Quebec's 1st choice, 10th overall, in 1993 Entry Draft).

			Regular Season								Playoffs						
Season	Club	Lea	GP	W	L	T	Mins	GA	SO	Avg	GP	W	L	Mins	GA	SO	Avg
1990-91	Laval	QAAA	20	14	5	0	1178	78	1	3.94	5	1	4	300	20	0	4.00
1991-92	Trois-Rivieres	QMJHL	30	14	7	1	1496	77	0	3.09	3	1	1	110	4	0	2.19
1992-93	Sherbrooke	QMJHL	56	34	14	5	3190	159	3	2.99	15	9	6	882	57	0	3.87
1993-94	**Quebec**	**NHL**	**29**	**8**	**13**	**3**	**1504**	**83**	**0**	**3.31**	....	....	....	....	....	....	....
	Cornwall	AHL	4	4	0	0	240	9	1	2.25	....	....	....	....	....	....	....
1994-95	Sherbrooke	QMJHL	13	6	6	1	776	38	1	2.94	....	....	....	....	....	....	....
	Quebec	**NHL**	**18**	**12**	**2**	**2**	**898**	**35**	**1**	**2.34**	**3**	**1**	**2**	**148**	**8**	**0**	**3.24**
1995-96	**Colorado**	**NHL**	**10**	**3**	**4**	**2**	**558**	**28**	**0**	**3.01**	....	....	....	....	....	....	....
	Montreal	**NHL**	**40**	**23**	**13**	**3**	**2334**	**110**	**3**	**2.83**	**6**	**2**	**4**	**311**	**18**	**0**	**3.47**
1996-97	**Montreal**	**NHL**	**61**	**22**	**24**	**11**	**3397**	**164**	**1**	**2.90**	**3**	**0**	**3**	**179**	**13**	**0**	**4.36**
1997-98	**Montreal**	**NHL**	**47**	**19**	**15**	**8**	**2652**	**109**	**2**	**2.47**	**2**	**0**	**0**	**43**	**4**	**0**	**5.58**
1998-99	**Chicago**	**NHL**	**52**	**21**	**26**	**5**	**3014**	**136**	**4**	**2.71**	....	....	....	....	....	....	....
	Montreal	**NHL**	**10**	**3**	**4**	**2**	**529**	**23**	**1**	**2.61**	....	....	....	....	....	....	....
	NHL Totals		**267**	**111**	**101**	**36**	**14886**	**688**	**12**	**2.77**	**14**	**3**	**9**	**681**	**43**	**0**	**3.79**

QMJHL First All-Star Team (1993) • Canadian Major Junior First All-Star Team (1993) • Canadian Major Junior Goaltender of the Year (1993)

Transferred to **Colorado** after **Quebec** franchise relocated, June 21, 1995. Traded to **Montreal** by **Colorado** with Andrei Kovalenko and Martin Rucinsky for Patrick Roy and Mike Keane, December 6, 1995. Traded to **Chicago** by **Montreal** with Dave Manson and Brad Brown for Jeff Hackett, Eric Weinrich, Alain Nasreddine and Tampa Bay's 4th round choice (previously acquired, Montreal selected Chris Dyment) in 1999 Entry Draft, November 16, 1998.

THOMAS, Tim

Goaltender. Catches left. 5'11", 180 lbs. Born, Flint, MI, April 15, 1974.
(Quebec's 11th choice, 217th overall, in 1994 Entry Draft).

			Regular Season								Playoffs						
Season	Club	Lea	GP	W	L	T	Mins	GA	SO	Avg	GP	W	L	Mins	GA	SO	Avg
1992-93	Davison Prep	H.S.	27	....	....	....	1580	87	....	3.30	....	....	....	....	....	....	....
1993-94	U. of Vermont	ECAC	*33	15	12	6	1864	94	0	3.03	....	....	....	....	....	....	....
1994-95	U. of Vermont	ECAC	34	18	13	2	2010	90	*4	*2.69	....	....	....	....	....	....	....
1995-96	U. of Vermont	ECAC	37	*26	7	4	*2254	88	*3	*2.34	....	....	....	....	....	....	....
1996-97	U. of Vermont	ECAC	36	22	11	3	2158	101	2	2.81	....	....	....	....	....	....	....
1997-98	HIFK Helsinki	Finland	18	13	4	1	1035	28	2	*1.62	*9	*9	0	*551	14	*3	*1.52
	Birmingham	ECHL	6	4	1	1	360	13	1	2.17	....	....	....	....	....	....	....
	Houston	IHL	1	0	1	0	59	4	0	4.01	....	....	....	....	....	....	....
1998-99	HIFK Helsinki	Finland	14	8	3	3	833	31	2	2.23	*11	7	4	*658	25	0	2.28
	Hamilton	AHL	15	6	8	0	837	45	0	3.23	....	....	....	....	....	....	....

ECAC First All-Star Team (1995, 1996) • NCAA East Second All-American Team (1995) • NCAA East First All-American Team (1996)

Signed as a free agent by **Edmonton**, June 4, 1998.

TOSKALA, Vesa (TAWS-kah-lah) S.J.

Goaltender. Catches left. 5'9", 175 lbs. Born, Tampere, Finland, May 20, 1977.
(San Jose's 4th choice, 90th overall, in 1995 Entry Draft).

			Regular Season								Playoffs						
Season	Club	Lea	GP	W	L	T	Mins	GA	SO	Avg	GP	W	L	Mins	GA	SO	Avg
1994-95	Ilves Tampere	Finn-Jr.	17	....	....	....	956	36	....	2.26	....	....	....	....	....	....	....
1995-96	Ilves Tampere	Finn-Jr.	3	....	....	....	180	3	....	1.00	....	....	....	....	....	....	....
	KooVee	Finland-2	2	....	....	....	119	5	....	2.51	....	....	....	....	....	....	....
	Ilves Tampere	Finland	37	....	....	....	2073	109	1	3.16	2	....	....	78	11	....	8.49
1996-97	Ilves Tampere	Finland	40	22	12	5	2270	108	0	2.85	8	3	5	479	29	0	3.63
1997-98	Ilves Tampere	Finland	43	*26	13	3	2555	118	1	2.77	*9	6	3	519	18	1	2.08
1998-99	Ilves Tampere	Finland	33	21	12	0	1966	70	*5	2.14	4	1	3	248	14	0	3.39

TREFILOV, Andrei (TREH-fee-lahf) CGY.

Goaltender. Catches left. 6', 190 lbs. Born, Kirovo-Chepetsk, USSR, August 31, 1969.
(Calgary's 14th choice, 261st overall, in 1991 Entry Draft).

			Regular Season								Playoffs						
Season	Club	Lea	GP	W	L	T	Mins	GA	SO	Avg	GP	W	L	Mins	GA	SO	Avg
1990-91	Moscow D'amo	USSR	20	....	....	....	1070	36	0	2.01	....	....	....	....	....	....	....
1991-92	Moscow D'amo	CIS	28	....	....	....	1326	35	0	1.58	....	....	....	....	....	....	....
	Russia	Olympics	4	0	0	0	39	2	0	3.08	....	....	....	....	....	....	....
1992-93	**Calgary**	**NHL**	**1**	**0**	**0**	**1**	**65**	**5**	**0**	**4.62**	....	....	....	....	....	....	....
	Salt Lake	IHL	44	23	17	3	2536	135	0	3.19	....	....	....	....	....	....	....
1993-94	**Calgary**	**NHL**	**11**	**3**	**4**	**2**	**623**	**26**	**2**	**2.50**	....	....	....	....	....	....	....
	Saint John	AHL	28	10	10	7	1629	93	0	3.42	....	....	....	....	....	....	....
1994-95	**Calgary**	**NHL**	**6**	**0**	**3**	**0**	**236**	**16**	**0**	**4.07**	....	....	....	....	....	....	....
	Saint John	AHL	7	1	5	1	383	20	0	3.13	....	....	....	....	....	....	....
1995-96	**Buffalo**	**NHL**	**22**	**8**	**8**	**1**	**1094**	**64**	**0**	**3.51**	....	....	....	....	....	....	....
	Rochester	AHL	5	4	1	0	299	13	0	2.61	....	....	....	....	....	....	....
1996-97	**Buffalo**	**NHL**	**3**	**0**	**2**	**0**	**159**	**10**	**0**	**3.77**	**1**	**0**	**0**	**5**	**0**	**0**	**0.00**
1997-98	Rochester	AHL	3	1	0	1	138	6	0	2.60	....	....	....	....	....	....	....
	Chicago	**NHL**	**6**	**1**	**4**	**0**	**299**	**17**	**0**	**3.41**	....	....	....	....	....	....	....
	Indianapolis	IHL	1	0	1	0	59	3	0	3.03	....	....	....	....	....	....	....
	Russia	Olympics	2	1	0	0	69	4	0	3.45	....	....	....	....	....	....	....
1998-99	AK Bars Kazan	Russia	3	....	....	....	160	7	1	2.63	....	....	....	....	....	....	....
	Chicago	**NHL**	**1**	**0**	**1**	**0**	**25**	**4**	**0**	**9.60**	....	....	....	....	....	....	....
	Indianapolis	IHL	18	9	6	2	986	39	0	2.37	....	....	....	....	....	....	....
	Calgary	**NHL**	**4**	**0**	**3**	**0**	**162**	**11**	**0**	**4.07**	....	....	....	....	....	....	....
	Detroit	IHL	27	17	8	2	1613	53	3	1.97	10	6	4	647	22	0	2.04
	NHL Totals		**54**	**12**	**25**	**4**	**2663**	**153**	**2**	**3.45**	**1**	**0**	**0**	**5**	**0**	**0**	**0.00**

IHL Second All-Star Team (1999) • Shared James Norris Memorial Trophy (fewest goals against - IHL) with Kevin Weekes (1999)

Signed as a free agent by **Buffalo**, July 11, 1995. Traded to **Chicago** by **Buffalo** for future considerations, November 12, 1997. Traded to **Calgary** by **Chicago** for future considerations, December 29, 1998.

TUGNUTT, Ron (TUHG-nuht) OTT.

Goaltender. Catches left. 5'11", 155 lbs. Born, Scarborough, Ont., October 22, 1967.
(Quebec's 4th choice, 81st overall, in 1986 Entry Draft).

			Regular Season								Playoffs						
Season	Club	Lea	GP	W	L	T	Mins	GA	SO	Avg	GP	W	L	Mins	GA	SO	Avg
1983-84	Toronto	OMHL	34	....	....	....	1690	91	3	2.67	....	....	....	....	....	....	....
1984-85	Peterborough	OHL	18	7	4	2	938	59	0	3.77	....	....	....	....	....	....	....
1985-86	Peterborough	OHL	26	18	7	0	1543	74	1	2.88	3	2	0	133	6	0	2.71
1986-87	Peterborough	OHL	31	21	7	2	1891	88	2	*2.79	6	3	3	374	21	1	3.37
1987-88	**Quebec**	**NHL**	**6**	**2**	**3**	**0**	**284**	**16**	**0**	**3.38**	....	....	....	....	....	....	....
	Fredericton	AHL	34	20	9	4	1964	118	1	3.60	4	1	2	204	11	0	3.24
1988-89	**Quebec**	**NHL**	**26**	**10**	**10**	**3**	**1367**	**82**	**0**	**3.60**	....	....	....	....	....	....	....
	Halifax	AHL	24	14	7	2	1368	79	1	3.46	....	....	....	....	....	....	....
1989-90	**Quebec**	**NHL**	**35**	**5**	**24**	**3**	**1978**	**152**	**0**	**4.61**	....	....	....	....	....	....	....
	Halifax	AHL	6	1	5	0	366	23	0	3.77	....	....	....	....	....	....	....
1990-91	**Quebec**	**NHL**	**56**	**12**	**29**	**10**	**3144**	**212**	**0**	**4.05**	....	....	....	....	....	....	....
	Halifax	AHL	2	0	1	0	100	8	0	4.80	....	....	....	....	....	....	....
1991-92	**Quebec**	**NHL**	**30**	**6**	**17**	**3**	**1583**	**106**	**1**	**4.02**	....	....	....	....	....	....	....
	Halifax	AHL	8	3	3	1	447	30	0	4.03	....	....	....	....	....	....	....
	Edmonton	**NHL**	**3**	**1**	**1**	**0**	**124**	**10**	**0**	**4.84**	**2**	**0**	**0**	**60**	**3**	**0**	**3.00**
1992-93	**Edmonton**	**NHL**	**26**	**9**	**12**	**2**	**1338**	**93**	**0**	**4.17**	....	....	....	....	....	....	....
1993-94	**Anaheim**	**NHL**	**28**	**10**	**15**	**1**	**1520**	**76**	**1**	**3.00**	....	....	....	....	....	....	....
	Montreal	**NHL**	**8**	**2**	**3**	**1**	**378**	**24**	**0**	**3.81**	**1**	**0**	**1**	**59**	**5**	**0**	**5.08**
1994-95	**Montreal**	**NHL**	**7**	**1**	**3**	**1**	**346**	**18**	**0**	**3.12**	....	....	....	....	....	....	....
1995-96	Portland	AHL	58	21	23	6	3068	171	2	3.34	13	7	6	782	36	1	2.76
1996-97	**Ottawa**	**NHL**	**37**	**17**	**15**	**1**	**1991**	**93**	**3**	**2.80**	**7**	**3**	**4**	**425**	**14**	**1**	**1.98**
1997-98	**Ottawa**	**NHL**	**42**	**15**	**14**	**8**	**2236**	**84**	**3**	**2.25**	**2**	**0**	**1**	**74**	**6**	**0**	**4.86**
1998-99	**Ottawa**	**NHL**	**43**	**22**	**10**	**8**	**2508**	**75**	**3**	***1.79**	**2**	**0**	**2**	**118**	**6**	**0**	**3.05**
	NHL Totals		**347**	**112**	**156**	**41**	**18797**	**1041**	**11**	**3.32**	**14**	**3**	**8**	**736**	**34**	**1**	**2.77**

OHL First All-Star Team (1987)

Played in NHL All-Star Game (1999)

Traded to **Edmonton** by **Quebec** with Brad Zavisha for Martin Rucinsky, March 10, 1992. Claimed by **Anaheim** from **Edmonton** in Expansion Draft, June 24, 1993. Traded to **Montreal** by **Anaheim** for Stephan Lebeau, February 20, 1994. Signed as a free agent by **Washington**, September 25, 1995. Signed as a free agent by **Ottawa**, August 14, 1996.

TURCO, Marty (TUHR-koh) DAL.

Goaltender. Catches left. 5'11", 175 lbs. Born, Sault Ste. Marie, Ont., August 13, 1975.
(Dallas' 4th choice, 124th overall, in 1994 Entry Draft).

			Regular Season								Playoffs						
Season	Club	Lea	GP	W	L	T	Mins	GA	SO	Avg	GP	W	L	Mins	GA	SO	Avg
1993-94	Cambridge	OJHL	34	....	....	....	1973	114	0	3.47	....	....	....	....	....	....	....
1994-95	U. of Michigan	CCHA	37	*27	7	1	2063	95	1	2.76	....	....	....	....	....	....	....
1995-96	U. of Michigan	CCHA	*42	*34	7	1	*2335	84	*5	*2.16	....	....	....	....	....	....	....
1996-97	U. of Michigan	CCHA	*41	*33	4	4	*2296	87	*4	*2.27	....	....	....	....	....	....	....
1997-98	U. of Michigan	CCHA	*45	*33	10	1	*2640	95	4	2.16	....	....	....	....	....	....	....
1998-99	Michigan	IHL	54	24	17	10	3127	136	1	2.61	5	2	3	300	14	0	2.80

NCAA Championship All-Tournament Team (1996, 1998) • CCHA First All-Star Team (1997) • NCAA West First All-American Team (1997) • CCHA Second All-Star Team (1998) • NCAA Championship Tournament MVP (1998) • Won Garry F. Longman Memorial Trophy (Top Rookie - IHL) (1999)

TUREK, Roman (TOOR-ehk) ST.L.

Goaltender. Catches right. 6'3", 190 lbs. Born, Pisek, Czech., May 21, 1970.
(Minnesota's 6th choice, 113th overall, in 1990 Entry Draft).

			Regular Season								Playoffs						
Season	Club	Lea	GP	W	L	T	Mins	GA	SO	Avg	GP	W	L	Mins	GA	SO	Avg
1990-91	HC Budejovice	Czech.	26	....	....	....	1244	98	0	4.70	....	....	....	....	....	....	....
1991-92	HC Budejovice	Czech-2							STATISTICS NOT AVAILABLE								
1992-93	HC Budejovice	Czech.	43	....	....	....	2555	121	....	2.84	....	....	....	....	....	....	....
1993-94	HC Budejovice	Cze-Rep	44	....	....	....	2584	111	....	2.51	3	....	....	180	12	0	4.00
	Czech Republic	Olympics	2	2	0	0	120	3	....	1.50	....	....	....	....	....	....	....
1994-95	HC Budejovice	Cze-Rep	44	....	....	....	2587	119	....	2.76	9	....	....	498	25	....	3.01
1995-96	EHC Nurnberg	Germany	48	....	....	....	2787	154	....	3.31	5	....	....	338	14	....	2.48
1996-97	**Dallas**	**NHL**	**6**	**3**	**1**	**0**	**263**	**9**	**0**	**2.05**	....	....	....	....	....	....	....
	Michigan	IHL	29	8	13	4	1555	77	0	2.97	....	....	....	....	....	....	....
1997-98	**Dallas**	**NHL**	**23**	**11**	**10**	**1**	**1324**	**49**	**1**	**2.22**	....	....	....	....	....	....	....
	Michigan	IHL	2	1	1	0	119	5	0	2.51	....	....	....	....	....	....	....
1998-99♦	**Dallas**	**NHL**	**26**	**16**	**3**	**3**	**1382**	**48**	**1**	**2.08**	....	....	....	....	....	....	....
	NHL Totals		**55**	**30**	**14**	**4**	**2969**	**106**	**2**	**2.14**	....	....	....	....	....	....	....

Czech Republic Player of the Year (1994) • Shared William M. Jennings Trophy with Ed Belfour (1999)

Transferred to **Dallas** after **Minnesota** franchise relocated, June 9, 1993. Traded to **St. Louis** by **Dallas** for St. Louis' compensatory 2nd round choice (Dan Jancevski) in 1999 Entry Draft, June 20, 1999.

UNDERHILL, Matt — CGY.

Goaltender. Catches left. 6'2", 195 lbs. Born, Merritt, B.C., September 16, 1979.
(Calgary's 8th choice, 170th overall, in 1999 Entry Draft).

			Regular Season								Playoffs						
Season	Club	Lea	GP	W	L	T	Mins	GA	SO	Avg	GP	W	L	Mins	GA	SO	Avg
1997-98	Notre Dame	SJHL	43	....	....	....	2573	132	2	3.07	....	....	....	....	....	....	....
1998-99	Cornell	ECAC	25	7	10	4	1320	65	1	2.95	....	....	....	....	....	....	....

VAILLANCOURT, Luc — (VIGH-an-koor)

Goaltender. Catches left. 6'1", 190 lbs. Born, Ferme-Neuve, Que., June 13, 1978.
(Anaheim's 4th choice, 125th overall, in 1997 Entry Draft).

			Regular Season								Playoffs						
Season	Club	Lea	GP	W	L	T	Mins	GA	SO	Avg	GP	W	L	Mins	GA	SO	Avg
1995-96	Beauport	QMJHL	22	7	8	0	882	71	0	4.83	2	1	0	80	3	0	2.25
1996-97	Beauport	QMJHL	51	18	27	1	2684	163	0	3.64	4	1	3	240	20	0	5.00
1997-98	Quebec	QMJHL	22	11	8	1	1196	73	0	3.66	....	....	....	....	....	....	....
	Rouyn-Noranda	QMJHL	30	19	10	1	1762	93	0	3.17	6	2	4	362	26	0	4.31
1998-99	Rouyn-Noranda	QMJHL	18	8	6	2	1000	58	1	3.48	....	....	....	....	....	....	....

VALLEY, Mike — VAN.

Goaltender. Catches left. 6', 190 lbs. Born, Delta, B.C., September 3, 1976.

			Regular Season								Playoffs						
Season	Club	Lea	GP	W	L	T	Mins	GA	SO	Avg	GP	W	L	Mins	GA	SO	Avg
1996-97	U. of Wisconsin	WCHA	10	2	3	0	426	24	0	3.39	....	....	....	....	....	....	....
1997-98	U. of Wisconsin	WCHA	21	11	9	1	1202	88	0	3.09	....	....	....	....	....	....	....
1998-99	Augusta	ECHL	9	5	3	0	494	26	1	3.16	....	....	....	....	....	....	....
	Syracuse	AHL	26	2	17	1	1281	87	0	4.07	....	....	....	....	....	....	....

Signed as a free agent by **Vancouver**, June 9, 1998.

VANBIESBROUCK, John — (van-BEES-bruhk) PHI.

Goaltender. Catches left. 5'8", 176 lbs. Born, Detroit, MI, September 4, 1963.
(NY Rangers' 5th choice, 72nd overall, in 1981 Entry Draft).

			Regular Season								Playoffs						
Season	Club	Lea	GP	W	L	T	Mins	GA	SO	Avg	GP	W	L	Mins	GA	SO	Avg
1980-81	S.S. Marie	OHA	56	31	16	1	2941	203	0	4.14	11	3	3	457	24	1	3.15
1981-82	**NY Rangers**	**NHL**	**1**	**1**	**0**	**0**	**60**	**1**	**0**	**1.00**	....	....	....	....	....	....	....
	S.S. Marie	OHL	31	12	12	2	1686	102	0	3.62	7	1	4	276	20	0	4.35
1982-83	S.S. Marie	OHL	*62	39	21	1	3471	209	0	3.61	16	7	6	944	56	*1	3.56
1983-84	**NY Rangers**	**NHL**	**3**	**2**	**1**	**0**	**180**	**10**	**0**	**3.33**	**1**	**0**	**0**	**1**	**0**	**0**	**0.00**
	Tulsa	CHL	37	20	13	2	2153	124	*3	3.46	4	4	0	240	10	0	*2.50
1984-85	**NY Rangers**	**NHL**	**42**	**12**	**24**	**3**	**2358**	**166**	**1**	**4.22**	**1**	**0**	**0**	**20**	**0**	**0**	**0.00**
1985-86	**NY Rangers**	**NHL**	**61**	***31**	**21**	**5**	**3326**	**184**	**3**	**3.32**	**16**	**8**	**8**	**899**	**49**	***1**	**3.27**
1986-87	**NY Rangers**	**NHL**	**50**	**18**	**20**	**5**	**2656**	**161**	**0**	**3.64**	**4**	**1**	**3**	**195**	**11**	**1**	**3.38**
1987-88	**NY Rangers**	**NHL**	**56**	**27**	**22**	**7**	**3319**	**187**	**2**	**3.38**	....	....	....	....	....	....	....
1988-89	**NY Rangers**	**NHL**	**56**	**28**	**21**	**4**	**3207**	**197**	**0**	**3.69**	**2**	**0**	**1**	**107**	**6**	**0**	**3.36**
1989-90	**NY Rangers**	**NHL**	**47**	**19**	**19**	**7**	**2734**	**154**	**1**	**3.38**	**6**	**2**	**3**	**298**	**15**	**0**	**3.02**
1990-91	**NY Rangers**	**NHL**	**40**	**15**	**18**	**6**	**2257**	**126**	**3**	**3.35**	**1**	**0**	**0**	**52**	**1**	**0**	**1.15**
1991-92	**NY Rangers**	**NHL**	**45**	**27**	**13**	**3**	**2526**	**120**	**2**	**2.85**	**7**	**2**	**5**	**368**	**23**	**0**	**3.75**
1992-93	**NY Rangers**	**NHL**	**48**	**20**	**18**	**7**	**2757**	**152**	**4**	**3.31**	....	....	....	....	....	....	....
1993-94	**Florida**	**NHL**	**57**	**21**	**25**	**11**	**3440**	**145**	**1**	**2.53**	....	....	....	....	....	....	....
1994-95	**Florida**	**NHL**	**37**	**14**	**15**	**4**	**2087**	**86**	**4**	**2.47**	....	....	....	....	....	....	....
1995-96	**Florida**	**NHL**	**57**	**26**	**20**	**7**	**3178**	**142**	**2**	**2.68**	***22**	**12**	**10**	**1332**	**50**	**1**	**2.25**
1996-97	**Florida**	**NHL**	**57**	**27**	**19**	**10**	**3347**	**128**	**2**	**2.29**	**5**	**1**	**4**	**328**	**13**	**1**	**2.38**
1997-98	**Florida**	**NHL**	**60**	**18**	**29**	**11**	**3451**	**165**	**4**	**2.87**	....	....	....	....	....	....	....
	United States	Olympics	1	0	0	0	1	0	0	0.00	....	....	....	....	....	....	....
1998-99	**Philadelphia**	**NHL**	**62**	**27**	**18**	**15**	**3712**	**135**	**6**	**2.18**	**6**	**2**	**4**	**369**	**9**	**1**	**1.46**
	NHL Totals		**779**	**333**	**303**	**105**	**44595**	**2259**	**35**	**3.04**	**71**	**28**	**38**	**3969**	**177**	**5**	**2.68**

OHL Second All-Star Team (1983) • CHL First All-Star Team (1984) • Shared Terry Sawchuk Trophy (fewest goals against - CHL) with Ron Scott (1984) • Shared Tommy Ivan Trophy (CHL's MVP) with Bruce Affleck (1984) • NHL First All-Star Team (1986) • Won Vezina Trophy (1986) • NHL Second All-Star Team (1994)

Played in NHL All-Star Game (1994, 1996, 1997)

Traded to **Vancouver** by **NY Rangers** for future considerations (Doug Lidster, June 25, 1993), June 20, 1993. Claimed by **Florida** from **Vancouver** in Expansion Draft, June 24, 1993. Signed as a free agent by **Philadelphia**, July 16, 1998.

VERNON, Mike — S.J.

Goaltender. Catches left. 5'9", 180 lbs. Born, Calgary, Alta., February 24, 1963.
(Calgary's 2nd choice, 56th overall, in 1981 Entry Draft).

			Regular Season								Playoffs						
Season	Club	Lea	GP	W	L	T	Mins	GA	SO	Avg	GP	W	L	Mins	GA	SO	Avg
1980-81	Calgary	WHL	59	33	17	1	3154	198	1	3.77	22	14	8	1271	82	1	3.87
1981-82	Calgary	WHL	42	22	14	2	2329	143	3	3.68	9	5	4	527	30	0	3.42
	Oklahoma City	CHL	....	....	....	....	....	....	....	....	1	0	1	70	4	0	3.43
1982-83	**Calgary**	**NHL**	**2**	**0**	**2**	**0**	**100**	**11**	**0**	**6.59**	....	....	....	....	....	....	....
	Calgary	WHL	50	29	18	2	2856	155	*3	*3.26	16	9	7	925	60	0	3.89
1983-84	**Calgary**	**NHL**	**1**	**0**	**1**	**0**	**11**	**4**	**0**	**22.22**	....	....	....	....	....	....	....
	Colorado	CHL	46	30	13	2	2648	148	1	*3.35	6	2	4	347	21	0	3.63
1984-85	Moncton	AHL	41	10	20	4	2050	134	0	3.92	....	....	....	....	....	....	....
1985-86	**Calgary**	**NHL**	**18**	**9**	**3**	**3**	**921**	**52**	**1**	**3.39**	***21**	**12**	***9**	***1229**	**60**	**0**	**2.93**
	Moncton	AHL	6	3	1	2	374	21	0	3.37	....	....	....	....	....	....	....
	Salt Lake	IHL	10	6	4	0	600	34	1	3.40	....	....	....	....	....	....	....
1986-87	**Calgary**	**NHL**	**54**	**30**	**21**	**1**	**2957**	**178**	**1**	**3.61**	**5**	**2**	**3**	**263**	**16**	**0**	**3.65**
1987-88	**Calgary**	**NHL**	**64**	**39**	**16**	**7**	**3565**	**210**	**1**	**3.53**	**9**	**4**	**4**	**515**	**34**	**0**	**3.96**
1988-89♦	**Calgary**	**NHL**	**52**	***37**	**6**	**5**	**2938**	**130**	**0**	**2.65**	***22**	***16**	**5**	***1381**	**52**	***3**	**2.26**
1989-90	**Calgary**	**NHL**	**47**	**23**	**14**	**9**	**2795**	**146**	**0**	**3.13**	**6**	**2**	**3**	**342**	**19**	**0**	**3.33**
1990-91	**Calgary**	**NHL**	**54**	**31**	**19**	**3**	**3121**	**172**	**1**	**3.31**	**7**	**3**	**4**	**427**	**21**	**0**	**2.95**
1991-92	**Calgary**	**NHL**	**63**	**24**	**30**	**9**	**3640**	**217**	**0**	**3.58**	....	....	....	....	....	....	....
1992-93	**Calgary**	**NHL**	**64**	**29**	**26**	**9**	**3732**	**203**	**2**	**3.26**	**4**	**1**	**1**	**150**	**15**	**0**	**6.00**
1993-94	**Calgary**	**NHL**	**48**	**26**	**17**	**5**	**2798**	**131**	**3**	**2.81**	**7**	**3**	**4**	**466**	**23**	**0**	**2.96**
1994-95	**Detroit**	**NHL**	**30**	**19**	**6**	**4**	**1807**	**76**	**1**	**2.52**	**18**	**12**	**6**	**1063**	**41**	**1**	**2.31**
1995-96	**Detroit**	**NHL**	**32**	**21**	**7**	**2**	**1855**	**70**	**3**	**2.26**	**4**	**2**	**2**	**243**	**11**	**0**	**2.72**
1996-97♦	**Detroit**	**NHL**	**33**	**13**	**11**	**8**	**1952**	**79**	**0**	**2.43**	***20**	***16**	**4**	***1229**	**36**	**1**	**1.76**
1997-98	**San Jose**	**NHL**	**62**	**30**	**22**	**8**	**3564**	**146**	**5**	**2.46**	**6**	**2**	**4**	**348**	**14**	**1**	**2.41**
1998-99	**San Jose**	**NHL**	**49**	**16**	**22**	**10**	**2831**	**107**	**4**	**2.27**	**5**	**2**	**3**	**321**	**13**	**0**	**2.43**
	NHL Totals		**673**	**347**	**223**	**83**	**38587**	**1932**	**22**	**3.00**	**134**	**77**	**52**	**7977**	**355**	**6**	**2.67**

WHL First All-Star Team (1982, 1983) • Won Hap Emms Memorial Trophy (Memorial Cup Tournament Top Goaltender) (1983) • CHL Second All-Star Team (1984) • NHL Second All-Star Team (1989) • Shared William M. Jennings Trophy with Chris Osgood (1996) • Won Conn Smythe Trophy (1997)

Played in NHL All-Star Game (1988, 1989, 1990, 1991, 1993)

Traded to **Detroit** by **Calgary** for Steve Chiasson, June 29, 1994. Traded to **San Jose** by **Detroit** with Detroit's 5th round choice (Andrei Maximenko) in 1999 Entry Draft for San Jose's 2nd round choice (later traded to St. Louis - St. Louis selected Maxim Linnik) in 1998 Entry Draft and San Jose's 2nd round choice (later traded to Tampa Bay - Tampa Bay selected Sheldon Keefe) in 1999 Entry Draft, August 18, 1997.

VOKOUN, Tomas — (voh-KOHN) NSH.

Goaltender. Catches right. 5'11", 208 lbs. Born, Karlovy Vary, Czech., July 2, 1976.
(Montreal's 11th choice, 226th overall, in 1994 Entry Draft).

			Regular Season								Playoffs						
Season	Club	Lea	GP	W	L	T	Mins	GA	SO	Avg	GP	W	L	Mins	GA	SO	Avg
1993-94	Poldi Kladno	Cze-Rep	1	0	0	0	20	2	0	6.01	....	....	....	....	....	....	....
1994-95	Poldi Kladno	Cze-Rep	26	....	....	....	1368	70	....	3.07	5	....	....	240	19	....	4.75
1995-96	Wheeling	ECHL	35	20	10	2	1912	117	0	3.67	7	4	3	436	19	0	2.61
	Fredericton	AHL	....	....	....	....	....	....	....	....	1	0	1	59	4	0	4.09
1996-97	**Montreal**	**NHL**	**1**	**0**	**0**	**0**	**20**	**4**	**0**	**12.00**	....	....	....	....	....	....	....
	Fredericton	AHL	47	12	26	7	2645	154	2	3.49	....	....	....	....	....	....	....
1997-98	Fredericton	AHL	31	13	13	2	1735	90	0	3.11	....	....	....	....	....	....	....
1998-99	**Nashville**	**NHL**	**37**	**12**	**18**	**4**	**1954**	**96**	**1**	**2.95**	....	....	....	....	....	....	....
	Milwaukee	IHL	9	3	2	4	539	22	1	2.45	2	0	2	149	8	0	3.22
	NHL Totals		**38**	**12**	**18**	**4**	**1974**	**100**	**1**	**3.04**	....	....	....	....	....	....	....

Claimed by **Nashville** from **Montreal** in Expansion Draft, June 26, 1998.

VOLKOV, Alexey — (VOHL-kawf) L.A.

Goaltender. Catches left. 6'1", 185 lbs. Born, Sverdlovsk, USSR, March 15, 1980.
(Los Angeles' 3rd choice, 76th overall, in 1998 Entry Draft).

			Regular Season								Playoffs						
Season	Club	Lea	GP	W	L	T	Mins	GA	SO	Avg	GP	W	L	Mins	GA	SO	Avg
1995-96	SKA Yekaterinburg	Russia-2	42	....	....	....	2520	78	....	1.87	....	....	....	....	....	....	....
1996-97	SKA Yekaterinburg	Russia-3	34	....	....	....	2040	66	....	1.94	....	....	....	....	....	....	....
	Soviet Wings	Russia-Jr.	8	....	....	....	48	9	....	1.25	....	....	....	....	....	....	....
1997-98	Soviet Wings	Russia-3	27	....	....	....	1620	72	....	2.67	....	....	....	....	....	....	....
1998-99	Halifax	QMJHL	39	25	9	3	2332	105	2	2.70	5	1	4	282	21	0	4.47

WAGNER, Stephen — ST.L.

Goaltender. Catches left. 6'2", 200 lbs. Born, Red Deer, Alta., January 17, 1977.
(St. Louis' 5th choice, 159th overall, in 1996 Entry Draft).

			Regular Season								Playoffs						
Season	Club	Lea	GP	W	L	T	Mins	GA	SO	Avg	GP	W	L	Mins	GA	SO	Avg
1995-96	Olds Grizzlys	AJHL	47	....	....	....	2787	139	2	2.99	....	....	....	....	....	....	....
1996-97	U. of Denver	WCHA	22	13	6	0	1202	57	1	2.85	....	....	....	....	....	....	....
1997-98	U. of Denver	WCHA	29	9	17	1	1615	113	0	4.20	....	....	....	....	....	....	....
1998-99	U. of Denver	WCHA	*40	*24	13	1	2318	114	*4	2.95	....	....	....	....	....	....	....

WAITE, Jimmy — (WAYT) TOR.

Goaltender. Catches left. 6'1", 180 lbs. Born, Sherbrooke, Que., April 15, 1969.
(Chicago's 1st choice, 8th overall, in 1987 Entry Draft).

			Regular Season								Playoffs						
Season	Club	Lea	GP	W	L	T	Mins	GA	SO	Avg	GP	W	L	Mins	GA	SO	Avg
1984-85	L'estrie-Maurice	QAAA	10	6	4	0	598	52	0	5.22	....	....	....	....	....	....	....
1985-86	L'estrie-Maurice	QAAA	29	11	15	1	1643	143	0	5.22	....	....	....	....	....	....	....
1986-87	Chicoutimi	QMJHL	50	23	17	3	2569	209	2	4.48	11	4	6	576	54	1	5.63
1987-88	Chicoutimi	QMJHL	36	17	16	1	2000	150	0	4.50	4	1	2	222	17	0	4.59
1988-89	**Chicago**	**NHL**	**11**	**0**	**7**	**1**	**494**	**43**	**0**	**5.22**	....	....	....	....	....	....	....
	Saginaw	IHL	5	3	1	0	304	10	0	1.97	....	....	....	....	....	....	....
1989-90	**Chicago**	**NHL**	**4**	**2**	**0**	**0**	**183**	**14**	**0**	**4.59**	....	....	....	....	....	....	....
	Indianapolis	IHL	54	*34	14	5	*3207	135	*5	*2.53	*10	*9	1	*602	19	*1	*1.89
1990-91	**Chicago**	**NHL**	**1**	**1**	**0**	**0**	**60**	**2**	**0**	**2.00**	....	....	....	....	....	....	....
	Indianapolis	IHL	49	*26	18	4	2888	167	3	3.47	6	2	4	369	20	0	3.25
1991-92	**Chicago**	**NHL**	**17**	**4**	**7**	**4**	**877**	**54**	**0**	**3.69**	....	....	....	....	....	....	....
	Indianapolis	IHL	13	4	7	1	702	53	0	4.53	....	....	....	....	....	....	....
	Hershey	AHL	11	6	4	1	631	44	0	4.18	6	2	4	360	19	0	3.17
1992-93	**Chicago**	**NHL**	**20**	**6**	**7**	**1**	**996**	**49**	**2**	**2.95**	....	....	....	....	....	....	....
1993-94	**San Jose**	**NHL**	**15**	**3**	**7**	**0**	**697**	**50**	**0**	**4.30**	**2**	**0**	**0**	**40**	**3**	**0**	**4.50**
1994-95	**Chicago**	**NHL**	**2**	**1**	**1**	**0**	**119**	**5**	**0**	**2.52**	....	....	....	....	....	....	....
	Indianapolis	IHL	4	2	1	1	239	13	0	3.25	....	....	....	....	....	....	....
1995-96	**Chicago**	**NHL**	**1**	**0**	**0**	**0**	**31**	**0**	**0**	**0.00**	....	....	....	....	....	....	....
	Indianapolis	IHL	56	28	18	6	3157	179	0	3.40	5	2	3	298	15	1	3.02
1996-97	**Chicago**	**NHL**	**2**	**0**	**1**	**1**	**105**	**7**	**0**	**4.00**	....	....	....	....	....	....	....
	Indianapolis	IHL	41	22	15	4	2450	112	4	2.74	4	1	3	222	13	0	3.51
1997-98	**Phoenix**	**NHL**	**17**	**5**	**6**	**1**	**793**	**28**	**1**	**2.12**	**4**	**0**	**3**	**171**	**11**	**0**	**3.86**
1998-99	**Phoenix**	**NHL**	**16**	**6**	**5**	**4**	**898**	**41**	**1**	**2.74**	....	....	....	....	....	....	....
	Springfield	AHL	8	3	4	1	483	19	0	2.36	2	0	2	118	6	0	3.05
	Utah	IHL	11	6	3	2	622	30	0	2.89	....	....	....	....	....	....	....
	NHL Totals		**106**	**28**	**41**	**12**	**5253**	**293**	**4**	**3.35**	**6**	**0**	**3**	**211**	**14**	**0**	**3.98**

QMJHL Second All-Star Team (1987) • IHL First All-Star Team (1990) • Won James Norris Memorial Trophy (fewest goals against - IHL) (1990)

Traded to **San Jose** by **Chicago** for future considerations (Neil Wilkinson, July 9, 1993), June 19, 1993. Traded to **Chicago** by **San Jose** for Chicago's 4th round choice (later traded to NY Rangers — NY Rangers selected Tomi Kallarsson) in 1997 Entry Draft, February 5, 1995. Claimed by **Phoenix** from **Chicago** in NHL Waiver Draft, September 28, 1997. Signed as a free agent by **Toronto**, August 19, 1999.

WEEKES, Kevin — (WEEKS) VAN.

Goaltender. Catches left. 6', 195 lbs. Born, Toronto, Ont., April 4, 1975.
(Florida's 2nd choice, 41st overall, in 1993 Entry Draft).

			Regular Season								Playoffs						
Season	Club	Lea	GP	W	L	T	Mins	GA	SO	Avg	GP	W	L	Mins	GA	SO	Avg
1991-92	Toronto	OJHL-B	35	....	....	....	1575	68	4	1.94	....	....	....	....	....	....	....
	St. Michael's	OJHL-B	2	....	....	....	127	11	0	5.20	....	....	....	....	....	....	....
1992-93	Owen Sound	OHL	29	9	12	5	1645	143	0	5.22	1	0	0	26	5	0	11.50
1993-94	Owen Sound	OHL	34	13	19	1	1974	158	0	4.80	....	....	....	....	....	....	....
1994-95	Ottawa	OHL	41	13	23	4	2266	153	1	4.05	....	....	....	....	....	....	....
1995-96	Carolina	AHL	60	24	25	8	3404	229	2	4.04	....	....	....	....	....	....	....
1996-97	Carolina	AHL	51	17	28	4	2899	172	1	3.56	....	....	....	....	....	....	....
1997-98	**Florida**	**NHL**	**11**	**0**	**5**	**1**	**485**	**32**	**0**	**3.96**	....	....	....	....	....	....	....
	Fort Wayne	IHL	12	9	2	1	719	34	1	2.84	....	....	....	....	....	....	....
1998-99	**Vancouver**	**NHL**	**11**	**0**	**8**	**1**	**532**	**34**	**0**	**3.83**	....	....	....	....	....	....	....
	Detroit	IHL	33	19	5	7	1857	64	*4	*2.07	....	....	....	....	....	....	....
	NHL Totals		**22**	**0**	**13**	**2**	**1017**	**66**	**0**	**3.89**	....	....	....	....	....	....	....

Shared James Norris Memorial Trophy (fewest goals against - IHL) with Andrei Trefilov (1999)

Traded to **Vancouver** by **Florida** with Ed Jovanovski, Dave Gagner, Mike Brown and Florida's 1st round choice in 2000 Entry Draft for Pavel Bure, Bret Hedican, Brad Ference and Vancouver's 3rd round choice in 2000 Entry Draft, January 17, 1999.

WENINGER, Dave — WSH.

Goaltender. Catches left. 6'1", 180 lbs. Born, Calgary, Alta., February 8, 1976.
(Washington's 5th choice, 74th overall, in 1996 Entry Draft).

			Regular Season								Playoffs						
Season	Club	Lea	GP	W	L	T	Mins	GA	SO	Avg	GP	W	L	Mins	GA	SO	Avg
1995-96	Michigan Tech	WCHA	25	11	7	2	1300	70	0	3.23	....	....	....	....	....	....	....
1996-97	Michigan Tech	WCHA	18	1	13	0	855	59	1	4.14	....	....	....	....	....	....	....
1997-98	Michigan Tech	WCHA	34	14	16	2	1911	119	1	3.74	....	....	....	....	....	....	....
1998-99	Michigan Tech	WCHA	32	9	21	1	1802	100	0	3.33	....	....	....	....	....	....	....

WHITMORE, Kay — BOS.

Goaltender. Catches left. 5'11", 175 lbs. Born, Sudbury, Ont., April 10, 1967.
(Hartford's 2nd choice, 26th overall, in 1985 Entry Draft).

			Regular Season								Playoffs						
Season	Club	Lea	GP	W	L	T	Mins	GA	SO	Avg	GP	W	L	Mins	GA	SO	Avg
1982-83	Sudbury	NOHA	43	....	....	....	2580	108	4	2.51	....	....	....	....	....	....	....
1983-84	Peterborough	OHL	29	17	8	0	1471	110	0	4.49	....	....	....	....	....	....	....
1984-85	Peterborough	OHL	*53	*35	16	2	*3077	172	*2	3.35	17	10	4	1020	58	0	3.41
1985-86	Peterborough	OHL	41	27	12	2	2467	114	*3	*2.77	14	8	5	837	40	0	2.87
1986-87	Peterborough	OHL	36	14	17	5	2159	118	1	3.28	7	3	3	366	17	1	2.79
1987-88	Binghamton	AHL	38	17	15	4	2137	121	*3	3.40	2	0	2	118	10	0	5.08
1988-89	**Hartford**	**NHL**	**3**	**2**	**1**	**0**	**180**	**10**	**0**	**3.33**	**2**	**0**	**2**	**135**	**10**	**0**	**4.44**
	Binghamton	AHl	*56	21	29	4	*3200	241	1	4.52	....	....	....	....	....	....	....
1989-90	**Hartford**	**NHL**	**9**	**4**	**2**	**1**	**442**	**26**	**0**	**3.53**	....	....	....	....	....	....	....
	Binghamton	AHL	24	3	19	2	1386	109	0	4.72	....	....	....	....	....	....	....
1990-91	**Hartford**	**NHL**	**18**	**3**	**9**	**3**	**850**	**52**	**0**	**3.67**	....	....	....	....	....	....	....
	Springfield	AHL	33	22	9	1	1916	98	1	3.07	*15	*11	4	*926	37	0	*2.40
1991-92	**Hartford**	**NHL**	**45**	**14**	**21**	**6**	**2567**	**155**	**3**	**3.62**	**1**	**0**	**0**	**19**	**1**	**0**	**3.16**
1992-93	**Vancouver**	**NHL**	**31**	**18**	**8**	**4**	**1817**	**94**	**1**	**3.10**	....	....	....	....	....	....	....
1993-94	**Vancouver**	**NHL**	**32**	**18**	**14**	**0**	**1921**	**113**	**0**	**3.53**	....	....	....	....	....	....	....
1994-95	**Vancouver**	**NHL**	**11**	**0**	**6**	**2**	**558**	**37**	**0**	**3.98**	**1**	**0**	**0**	**20**	**2**	**0**	**6.00**
1995-96	Detroit	IHL	10	3	5	0	501	33	0	3.95	....	....	....	....	....	....	....
	Los Angeles	IHL	30	10	9	7	1563	99	1	3.80	....	....	....	....	....	....	....
	Syracuse	AHL	11	6	4	1	663	37	0	3.35	....	....	....	....	....	....	....
	Binghamton	AHL	....	....	....	....	....	....	....	....	2	0	2	127	9	0	4.27
1996-97	Sodertalje	Sweden	25	....	....	....	1320	85	0	3.86	....	....	....	....	....	....	....
1997-98	Long Beach	IHL	46	28	12	3	2516	109	3	2.60	14	9	5	838	43	0	3.08
1998-99	Milwaukee	IHL	23	10	6	4	1304	64	0	2.94	....	....	....	....	....	....	....
	Hartford	AHL	18	8	8	2	1080	47	0	2.61	....	....	....	....	....	....	....
	NHL Totals		**149**	**59**	**61**	**16**	**8335**	**487**	**4**	**3.51**	**4**	**0**	**2**	**174**	**13**	**0**	**4.48**

OHL First All-Star Team (1986) • Won Jack A. Butterfield Trophy (Playoff MVP - AHL) (1991) • Shared James Norris Memorial Trophy (fewest goals against - IHL) with Mike Buzak (1998)

Traded to **Vancouver** by **Hartford** for Corrie D'Alessio and future considerations, October 1, 1992. Traded to **NY Rangers** by **Vancouver** for Joe Kocur, March 20, 1996. Signed as a free agent by **San Jose**, September 10, 1997. Traded to **Buffalo** by **San Jose** with Colorado's 2nd round choice (previously acquired, Buffalo selected Jaroslav Kristek) in 1998 Entry Draft and San Jose's 5th round choice in 2000 Entry Draft for Steve Shields and Buffalo's 4th round choice (Miroslav Zalesak) in 1998 Entry Draft, June 18, 1998. Signed as a free agent by **NY Rangers**, August 17, 1998. Signed as a free agent by **Boston**, August 25, 1999.

WICKENHEISER, Chris — (wih-KEHN-high-zehr)

Goaltender. Catches left. 6'1", 185 lbs. Born, Lethbridge, Alta., January 20, 1976.
(Edmonton's 12th choice, 179th overall, in 1994 Entry Draft).

			Regular Season								Playoffs						
Season	Club	Lea	GP	W	L	T	Mins	GA	SO	Avg	GP	W	L	Mins	GA	SO	Avg
1992-93	Lethbridge	AAHA	44	....	....	....	2532	118	4	2.80	....	....	....	....	....	....	....
1993-94	Red Deer	WHL	29	11	13	0	1356	114	0	5.04	....	....	....	....	....	....	....
1994-95	Red Deer	WHL	47	13	26	3	2429	181	1	4.47	....	....	....	....	....	....	....
1995-96	Red Deer	WHL	48	17	27	2	2666	183	1	4.12	10	3	6	550	34	1	3.71
1996-97	Red Deer	WHL	1	0	1	0	60	4	0	4.00	....	....	....	....	....	....	....
	Portland	WHL	40	24	13	3	2367	106	3	2.69	4	2	2	226	10	0	2.65
1997-98	Huntington	ECHL	32	16	10	3	1758	99	2	3.38	....	....	....	....	....	....	....
	Hamilton	AHL	2	0	0	0	20	1	0	2.96	....	....	....	....	....	....	....
1998-99	New Orleans	ECHL	35	13	13	5	1848	111	0	3.60	3	1	2	180	12	0	4.00
	Hamilton	AHL	2	1	0	0	80	3	0	2.25	....	....	....	....	....	....	....

WHL West Second All-Star Team (1997)

WILKINSON, Derek

Goaltender. Catches left. 6', 170 lbs. Born, Lasalle, Ont., July 29, 1974.
(Tampa Bay's 7th choice, 145th overall, in 1992 Entry Draft).

			Regular Season								Playoffs						
Season	Club	Lea	GP	W	L	T	Mins	GA	SO	Avg	GP	W	L	Mins	GA	SO	Avg
1990-91	Chatham	OJHL-B	29	....	....	....	1429	86	0	3.61	....	....	....	....	....	....	....
1991-92	Detroit	OHL	38	16	17	1	1943	138	1	4.26	7	3	2	313	28	0	5.37
1992-93	Detroit	OHL	*4	1	2	1	*245	18	0	4.41	....	....	....	....	....	....	....
	Belleville	OHL	*59	21	24	11	*3370	237	0	4.22	7	3	4	434	29	0	4.01
1993-94	Belleville	OHL	*56	24	16	4	2860	179	*2	3.76	12	6	6	700	39	*1	3.34
1994-95	Atlanta	IHL	46	22	17	2	2414	121	1	3.01	4	2	1	197	8	0	2.43
1995-96	**Tampa Bay**	**NHL**	**4**	**0**	**3**	**0**	**200**	**15**	**0**	**4.50**	....	....	....	....	....	....	....
	Atlanta	IHL	28	11	11	2	1433	98	1	4.10	....	....	....	....	....	....	....
1996-97	**Tampa Bay**	**NHL**	**5**	**0**	**2**	**1**	**169**	**12**	**0**	**4.26**	....	....	....	....	....	....	....
	Cleveland	IHL	46	20	17	6	2595	138	1	3.19	14	8	6	893	44	0	2.95
1997-98	**Tampa Bay**	**NHL**	**8**	**2**	**4**	**1**	**311**	**17**	**0**	**3.28**	....	....	....	....	....	....	....
	Cleveland	IHL	25	9	12	2	1295	63	1	2.92	1	0	0	27	1	0	2.19
1998-99	**Tampa Bay**	**NHL**	**5**	**1**	**3**	**1**	**253**	**13**	**0**	**3.08**	....	....	....	....	....	....	....
	Cleveland	IHL	34	10	15	2	1760	108	1	3.68	....	....	....	....	....	....	....
	NHL Totals		**22**	**3**	**12**	**3**	**933**	**57**	**0**	**3.67**	....	....	....	....	....	....	....

WILLIS, Jordan

Goaltender. Catches left. 5'9", 155 lbs. Born, Kincardine, Ont., February 28, 1975.
(Dallas' 8th choice, 243rd overall, in 1993 Entry Draft).

			Regular Season								Playoffs						
Season	Club	Lea	GP	W	L	T	Mins	GA	SO	Avg	GP	W	L	Mins	GA	SO	Avg
1991-92	Hannover	OJHL-C	17	....	....	....	906	37	0	2.45	....	....	....	....	....	....	....
1992-93	London	OHL	26	13	6	3	1428	101	1	4.24	7	2	4	355	19	0	3.21
1993-94	London	OHL	44	20	19	2	2428	158	1	3.90	1	0	0	8	1	0	7.50
1994-95	London	OHL	53	16	29	3	2824	202	0	4.29	3	0	3	165	15	0	5.45
1995-96	**Dallas**	**NHL**	**1**	**0**	**1**	**0**	**19**	**1**	**0**	**3.16**	....	....	....	....	....	....	....
	Michigan	IHL	38	17	9	9	2184	118	1	3.24	4	1	3	238	17	0	4.29
1996-97	Canada	Nat-Team	15	7	4	2	804	42	....	3.13	....	....	....	....	....	....	....
	Daytona	ECHL	8	4	4	0	429	25	0	3.50	....	....	....	....	....	....	....
	Michigan	IHL	2	0	2	0	102	8	0	4.70	....	....	....	....	....	....	....
1997-98	Michigan	IHL	31	8	18	2	1584	93	1	3.52	....	....	....	....	....	....	....
1998-99	Baton Rouge	ECHL	47	19	20	5	2521	131	4	3.12	6	3	3	374	18	1	2.89
	NHL Totals		**1**	**0**	**1**	**0**	**19**	**1**	**0**	**3.16**	....	....	....	....	....	....	....

WREGGET, Ken — (REHG-eht) DET.

Goaltender. Catches left. 6'1", 201 lbs. Born, Brandon, Man., March 25, 1964.
(Toronto's 4th choice, 45th overall, in 1982 Entry Draft).

			Regular Season								Playoffs						
Season	Club	Lea	GP	W	L	T	Mins	GA	SO	Avg	GP	W	L	Mins	GA	SO	Avg
1981-82	Lethbridge	WHL	36	19	12	0	1713	118	0	4.13	3	2	0	84	3	0	2.14
1982-83	Lethbridge	WHL	48	26	17	1	2696	157	1	3.49	*20	14	5	*1154	58	*1	*3.02
1983-84	**Toronto**	**NHL**	**3**	**1**	**1**	**1**	**165**	**14**	**0**	**5.09**	....	....	....	....	....	....	....
	Lethbridge	WHL	53	32	20	0	3053	161	0	*3.16	4	1	3	210	18	0	5.14
1984-85	**Toronto**	**NHL**	**23**	**2**	**15**	**3**	**1278**	**103**	**0**	**4.84**	....	....	....	....	....	....	....
	St. Catharines	AHL	12	2	8	1	688	48	0	4.19	....	....	....	....	....	....	....
1985-86	**Toronto**	**NHL**	**30**	**9**	**13**	**4**	**1566**	**113**	**0**	**4.33**	**10**	**6**	**4**	**607**	**32**	***1**	**3.16**
	St. Catharines	AHL	18	8	9	0	1058	78	1	4.42	....	....	....	....	....	....	....
1986-87	**Toronto**	**NHL**	**56**	**22**	**28**	**3**	**3026**	**200**	**0**	**3.97**	**13**	**7**	**6**	**761**	**29**	**1**	**2.29**
1987-88	**Toronto**	**NHL**	**56**	**12**	**35**	**4**	**3000**	**222**	**2**	**4.44**	**2**	**0**	**1**	**108**	**11**	**0**	**6.11**
1988-89	**Toronto**	**NHL**	**32**	**9**	**20**	**2**	**1888**	**139**	**0**	**4.42**	....	....	....	....	....	....	....
	Philadelphia	**NHL**	**3**	**1**	**1**	**0**	**130**	**13**	**0**	**6.00**	**5**	**2**	**2**	**268**	**10**	**0**	**2.24**
1989-90	**Philadelphia**	**NHL**	**51**	**22**	**24**	**3**	**2961**	**169**	**0**	**3.42**	....	....	....	....	....	....	....
1990-91	**Philadelphia**	**NHL**	**30**	**10**	**14**	**3**	**1484**	**88**	**0**	**3.56**	....	....	....	....	....	....	....
1991-92	**Philadelphia**	**NHL**	**23**	**9**	**8**	**3**	**1259**	**75**	**0**	**3.57**	....	....	....	....	....	....	....
♦	**Pittsburgh**	**NHL**	**9**	**5**	**3**	**0**	**448**	**31**	**0**	**4.15**	**1**	**0**	**0**	**40**	**4**	**0**	**6.00**
1992-93	**Pittsburgh**	**NHL**	**25**	**13**	**7**	**2**	**1368**	**78**	**0**	**3.42**	....	....	....	....	....	....	....
1993-94	**Pittsburgh**	**NHL**	**42**	**21**	**12**	**7**	**2456**	**138**	**1**	**3.37**	....	....	....	....	....	....	....
1994-95	**Pittsburgh**	**NHL**	**38**	***25**	**9**	**2**	**2208**	**118**	**0**	**3.21**	**11**	**5**	**6**	**661**	**33**	**1**	**3.00**
1995-96	**Pittsburgh**	**NHL**	**37**	**20**	**13**	**2**	**2132**	**115**	**3**	**3.24**	**9**	**7**	**2**	**599**	**23**	**0**	**2.30**
1996-97	**Pittsburgh**	**NHL**	**46**	**17**	**17**	**6**	**2514**	**136**	**2**	**3.25**	**5**	**1**	**4**	**297**	**18**	**0**	**3.64**
1997-98	**Pittsburgh**	**NHL**	**15**	**3**	**6**	**2**	**611**	**28**	**0**	**2.75**	....	....	....	....	....	....	....
1998-99	**Calgary**	**NHL**	**27**	**10**	**12**	**4**	**1590**	**67**	**1**	**2.53**	....	....	....	....	....	....	....
	NHL Totals		**546**	**211**	**238**	**51**	**30084**	**1847**	**9**	**3.68**	**56**	**28**	**25**	**3341**	**160**	**3**	**2.87**

WHL East First All-Star Team (1984)

Traded to **Philadelphia** by **Toronto** for Philadelphia's 1st round choice (Rob Pearson) and Calgary's 1st round choice (previously acquired, Toronto selected Steve Bancroft) in 1989 Entry Draft, March 6, 1989. Traded to **Pittsburgh** by **Philadelphia** with Rick Tocchet, Kjell Samuelsson and Philadelphia's 3rd round choice (Dave Roche) in 1993 Entry Draft for Mark Recchi, Brian Benning and Los Angeles' 1st round choice (previously acquired, Philadelphia selected Jason Bowen) in 1992 Entry Draft, February 19, 1992. Traded to **Calgary** by **Pittsburgh** with Dave Roche for German Titov and Todd Hlushko, June 17, 1998. Signed as a free agent by **Detroit**, July 23, 1999.

YEATS, Matthew — (YAYTS) L.A.

Goaltender. Catches left. 5'11", 165 lbs. Born, Montreal, Que., April 6, 1979.
(Los Angeles' 9th choice, 248th overall, in 1998 Entry Draft).

			Regular Season								Playoffs						
Season	Club	Lea	GP	W	L	T	Mins	GA	SO	Avg	GP	W	L	Mins	GA	SO	Avg
1996-97	Olds Grizzlys	AJHL	32	....	....	....	1678	95	1	3.41	....	....	....	....	....	....	....
1997-98	Olds Grizzlies	AJHL	26	....	....	....	1498	96	....	3.85	....	....	....	....	....	....	....
1998-99	U. of Maine	H.E.	DID NOT PLAY – FRESHMAN														

YEREMEYEV, Vitali — (yehr-eh-MAY-ehv) NYR

Goaltender. Catches left. 5'10", 167 lbs. Born, Ust-Kamenogorsk, USSR, September 23, 1975.
(NY Rangers' 11th choice, 209th overall, in 1994 Entry Draft).

			Regular Season								Playoffs						
Season	Club	Lea	GP	W	L	T	Mins	GA	SO	Avg	GP	W	L	Mins	GA	SO	Avg
1994-95	CSKA Moscow	CIS	49	....	....	....	2733	97	....	2.13	2	....	....	120	8	....	4.00
1995-96	CSKA Moscow	CIS	25	....	....	....	1339	37	5	1.66	3	....	....	179	7	....	2.34
1996-97	CSKA Moscow	Russia	14	....	....	....	635	35	0	3.31	1	....	....	59	3	0	3.05
1997-98	Yaroslavl	Russia	17	....	....	....	979	19	3	*1.16	....	....	....	....	....	....	....
	Kazakhstan	Olympics	*7	....	....	....	292	28	....	5.76	....	....	....	....	....	....	....
1998-99	CSKA Moscow	Russia-2	19	....	....	....	1100	33	....	1.80	....	....	....	....	....	....	....

YOUNG, Wendell

Goaltender. Catches left. 5'9", 181 lbs. Born, Halifax, N.S., August 1, 1963.
(Vancouver's 3rd choice, 73rd overall, in 1981 Entry Draft).

			Regular Season								Playoffs						
Season	Club	Lea	GP	W	L	T	Mins	GA	SO	Avg	GP	W	L	Mins	GA	SO	Avg
1980-81	Kitchener	OHA	42	19	15	0	2215	164	1	4.44	14	9	1	800	42	*1	3.15
1981-82	Kitchener	OHL	*60	*38	17	2	*3470	195	1	3.37	15	12	1	900	35	*1	*2.33
1982-83	Kitchener	OHL	61	*41	19	0	*3611	231	1	3.84	12	6	5	720	43	0	3.58
1983-84	Fredericton	AHL	11	7	3	0	569	39	1	4.11	....	....	....	....	....	....	....
	Milwaukee	IHL	6	4	1	1	339	17	0	3.01	....	....	....	....	....	....	....
	Salt Lake	CHL	20	11	6	0	1094	80	0	4.39	4	0	2	122	11	0	5.42
1984-85	Fredericton	AHL	22	7	11	3	1242	83	0	4.01	....	....	....	....	....	....	....
1985-86	**Vancouver**	**NHL**	**22**	**4**	**9**	**3**	**1023**	**61**	**0**	**3.58**	**1**	**0**	**1**	**60**	**5**	**0**	**5.00**
	Fredericton	AHL	24	12	8	4	1457	78	0	3.21	....	....	....	....	....	....	....
1986-87	**Vancouver**	**NHL**	**8**	**1**	**6**	**1**	**420**	**35**	**0**	**5.00**	....	....	....	....	....	....	....
	Fredericton	AHL	30	11	16	0	1676	118	0	4.22	....	....	....	....	....	....	....
1987-88	**Philadelphia**	**NHL**	**6**	**3**	**2**	**0**	**320**	**20**	**0**	**3.75**	....	....	....	....	....	....	....
	Hershey	AHL	51	*33	15	1	2922	135	1	2.77	12	*12	0	*767	28	*1	*2.19
1988-89	**Pittsburgh**	**NHL**	**22**	**12**	**9**	**0**	**1150**	**92**	**0**	**4.80**	**1**	**0**	**0**	**39**	**1**	**0**	**1.54**
	Muskegon	IHL	2	1	0	1	125	7	0	3.36	....	....	....	....	....	....	....
1989-90	**Pittsburgh**	**NHL**	**43**	**16**	**20**	**3**	**2318**	**161**	**1**	**4.17**	....	....	....	....	....	....	....
1990-91	**Pittsburgh**	**NHL**	**18**	**4**	**6**	**2**	**773**	**52**	**0**	**4.04**	....	....	....	....	....	....	....
1991-92	**Pittsburgh**	**NHL**	**18**	**7**	**6**	**0**	**838**	**53**	**0**	**3.79**	....	....	....	....	....	....	....
1992-93	**Tampa Bay**	**NHL**	**31**	**7**	**19**	**2**	**1591**	**97**	**0**	**3.66**	....	....	....	....	....	....	....
	Atlanta	IHL	3	3	0	0	183	8	0	2.62	....	....	....	....	....	....	....
1993-94	**Tampa Bay**	**NHL**	**9**	**2**	**3**	**1**	**480**	**20**	**1**	**2.50**	....	....	....	....	....	....	....
	Atlanta	IHL	2	2	0	0	120	6	0	3.00	....	....	....	....	....	....	....
1994-95	Chicago	IHL	37	14	11	7	1882	112	0	3.57	....	....	....	....	....	....	....
	Pittsburgh	**NHL**	**10**	**3**	**6**	**0**	**497**	**27**	**0**	**3.26**	....	....	....	....	....	....	....
1995-96	Chicago	IHL	61	30	20	6	3285	199	1	3.63	9	4	5	540	30	0	3.33
1996-97	Chicago	IHL	52	25	21	4	2931	170	1	3.48	4	1	3	256	13	0	3.04
1997-98	Chicago	IHL	51	31	14	3	2912	149	2	3.07	9	5	3	515	24	1	2.79
1998-99	Chicago	IHL	35	20	10	4	2047	84	3	2.46	7	4	3	421	19	1	2.71
	NHL Totals		**187**	**59**	**86**	**12**	**9410**	**618**	**2**	**3.94**	**2**	**0**	**1**	**99**	**6**	**0**	**3.64**

AHL First All-Star Team (1988) • Won Baz Bastien Memorial Trophy (Top Goaltender - AHL) (1988) • Won Jack Butterfield Trophy (Playoff MVP - AHL) (1988)

Traded to **Philadelphia** by **Vancouver** with Vancouver's 3rd round choice (Kimbi Daniels) in 1990 Entry Draft for Darren Jensen and Daryl Stanley, August 28, 1987. Traded to **Pittsburgh** by **Philadelphia** with Philadelphia's 7th round choice (Mika Valila) in 1990 Entry Draft for Pittsburgh's 3rd round choice (Chris Therien) in 1990 Entry Draft, Steptember 1, 1988. Claimed by **Tampa Bay** from **Pittsburgh** in Expansion Draft, June 18, 1992. Traded to **Pittsburgh** by **Tampa Bay** for future considerations, February 16, 1995. • Only goaltender in hockey history to win Memorial Cup (1982), Calder Cup (1988), Stanley Cup (1991, 1992) and Turner Cup (1998).

ZEPP, Rob — ATL.

Goaltender. Catches left. 6'1", 160 lbs. Born, Scarborough, Ont., September 7, 1981.
(Atlanta's 5th choice, 99th overall, in 1999 Entry Draft).

			Regular Season								Playoffs						
Season	Club	Lea	GP	W	L	T	Mins	GA	SO	Avg	GP	W	L	Mins	GA	SO	Avg
1998-99	Plymouth	OHL	31	19	3	4	1662	76	3	2.74	3	1	0	100	10	0	6.00

Notes

Retired NHL Player Index

Abbreviations: Teams/Cities: — **Ana.** – Anaheim; **Atl.** – Atlanta; **Bos.** – Boston, **Bro.** – Brooklyn; **Buf.** – Buffalo; **Cal.** – California; **Cgy.** – Calgary; **Cle.** – Cleveland; **Col.** – Colorado; **Dal.** – Dallas; **Det.** – Detroit; **Edm.** – Edmonton; **Fla.** – Florida; **Ham.** – Hamilton; **Hfd.** – Hartford; **K.C.** – Kansas City; **L.A.** – Los Angeles; **Min.** — Minnesota; **Mtl.** – Montreal; **Mtl. M.** – Montreal Maroons; **Mtl. W.** – Montreal Wanderers; **N.J.** – New Jersey; **NYA** – NY Americans; **NYI** – New York Islanders; **NYR** – New York Rangers; **Oak.** – Oakland; **Ott.** – Ottawa; **Phi.** – Philadelphia; **Phx.** – Phoenix; **Pit.** – Pittsburgh; **Que.** – Quebec; **St. L.** – St. Louis; **S.J.** – San Jose; **T.B.** – Tampa Bay; **Tor.** – Toronto; **Van.** – Vancouver; **Wpg.** – Winnipeg; **Wsh.** – Washington.

Total seasons are rounded off to the nearest full season. **A** – assists; **G** – goals; **GP** – games played; **PIM** – penalties in minutes; **TP** – total points.
• – deceased. Assists not recorded during 1917-18 season.

Name	NHL Teams	NHL Seasons	Regular Schedule GP	G	A	TP	PIM	Playoffs GP	G	A	TP	PIM	NHL Cup Wins	First NHL Season	Last NHL Season
A															
Abbott, Reg	Mtl.	1	3	0	0	0	0	....	....	....	....	....	....	1952-53	1952-53
• Abel, Clarence	NYR, Chi.	8	333	18	18	36	359	38	1	1	2	58	2	1926-27	1933-34
Abel, Gerry	Det.	1	1	0	0	0	0	....	....	....	....	....	....	1966-67	1966-67
Abel, Sid	Det., Chi.	14	612	189	283	472	376	97	28	30	58	79	3	1938-39	1953-54
Abgrall, Dennis	L.A.	1	13	0	2	2	4	....	....	....	....	....	....	1975-76	1975-76
Abrahamsson, Thommy	Hfd.	1	32	6	11	17	16	....	....	....	....	....	....	1980-81	1980-81
Achtymichuk, Gene	Mtl., Det.	4	32	3	5	8	2	....	....	....	....	....	....	1951-52	1958-59
Acomb, Doug	Tor.	1	2	0	1	1	0	....	....	....	....	....	....	1969-70	1969-70
Acton, Keith	Mtl., Min., Edm., Phi., Wsh., NYI	15	1023	226	358	584	1172	66	12	21	33	88	1	1979-80	1993-94
Adam, Douglas	NYR	1	4	0	1	1	0	....	....	....	....	....	....	1949-50	1949-50
Adam, Russ	Tor.	1	8	1	2	3	11	....	....	....	....	....	....	1982-83	1982-83
Adams, Greg	Phi., Hfd., Wsh., Edm., Van., Que., Det.	10	545	84	143	227	1173	43	2	11	13	153	....	1980-81	1989-90
• Adams, Jack	Tor., Ott.	7	174	82	29	111	353	10	2	0	2	13	2	1917-18	1926-27
Adams, John	Mtl.	1	42	6	12	18	11	3	0	0	0	0	....	1940-41	1940-41
• Adams, Stew	Chi., Tor.	4	95	9	26	35	60	11	3	3	6	14	....	1929-30	1932-33
Adduono, Rick	Bos., Atl.	2	4	0	0	0	2	....	....	....	....	....	....	1975-76	1979-80
Affleck, Bruce	St.L., Van., NYI	7	280	14	66	80	86	8	0	0	0	0	....	1974-75	1983-84
Agnew, Jim	Van., Hfd.	6	81	0	1	1	257	4	0	0	0	6	....	1986-87	1992-93
Ahern, Fred	Cal., Cle., Col.	4	146	31	30	61	130	2	0	1	1	2	....	1974-75	1977-78
Ahlin, Tony	Chi.	1	1	0	0	0	0	....	....	....	....	....	....	1937-38	1937-38
Ahola, Peter	L.A., Pit., S.J., Cgy.	3	123	10	17	27	137	6	0	0	0	2	....	1991-92	1993-94
Ahrens, Chris	Min.	6	52	0	3	3	84	1	0	0	0	0	....	1972-73	1977-78
Ailsby, Lloyd	NYR	1	3	0	0	0	2	....	....	....	....	....	....	1951-52	1951-52
Aitken, Brad	Pit., Edm.	2	14	1	3	4	25	....	....	....	....	....	....	1987-88	1990-91
Albright, Clint	NYR	1	59	14	5	19	19	....	....	....	....	....	....	1948-49	1948-49
Aldcorn, Gary	Tor., Det., Bos.	5	226	41	56	97	78	6	1	2	3	4	....	1956-57	1960-61
Alexander, Claire	Tor., Van.	4	155	18	47	65	36	16	2	4	6	4	....	1974-75	1977-78
• Alexandre, Art	Mtl.C.	2	11	0	2	2	8	4	0	0	0	0	....	1931-32	1932-33
Allan, Jeff	Cle.	1	4	0	0	0	2	....	....	....	....	....	....	1977-78	1977-78
Allen, George	NYR, Chi., Mtl.	8	339	82	115	197	179	41	9	10	19	32	....	1938-39	1946-47
Allen, Keith	Det.	2	28	0	4	4	8	5	0	0	0	0	1	1953-54	1954-55
• Allen, Viv	NYA	1	6	0	1	1	0	....	....	....	....	....	....	1940-41	1940-41
Alley, Steve	Hfd.	2	15	3	3	6	11	3	0	1	1	0	....	1979-80	1980-81
Allison, Dave	Mtl.	1	3	0	0	0	12	....	....	....	....	....	....	1983-84	1983-84
Allison, Mike	NYR, Tor., L.A.	10	499	102	166	268	630	82	9	17	26	135	....	1980-81	1989-90
Allison, Ray	Hfd., Phi.	7	238	64	93	157	223	12	2	3	5	20	....	1979-80	1986-87
• Allum, Bill	Chi., NYR	2	2	0	1	1	0	....	....	....	....	....	....	1939-40	1940-41
• Amadio, Dave	Det., L.A.	3	125	5	11	16	163	16	1	2	3	18	....	1957-58	1968-69
Ambroziak, Peter	Buf.	1	12	0	1	1	0	....	....	....	....	....	....	1994-95	1994-95
Amodeo, Mike	Wpg.	1	19	0	0	0	2	....	....	....	....	....	....	1979-80	1979-80
• Anderson, Bill	Bos.	1	....	....	....	....	....	1	0	0	0	0	....	1942-43	1942-43
Anderson, Dale	Det.	1	13	0	0	0	6	2	0	0	0	0	....	1956-57	1956-57
Anderson, Doug	Mtl.	1	....	....	....	....	....	2	0	0	0	0	1	1952-53	1952-53
Anderson, Earl	Det., Bos.	3	109	19	19	38	22	5	0	1	1	0	....	1974-75	1976-77
Anderson, Glenn	Edm., Tor., NYR, St.L.	16	1129	498	601	1099	1120	225	93	121	214	442	6	1980-81	1995-96
Anderson, Jim	L.A.	1	7	1	2	3	2	....	....	....	....	....	....	1967-68	1967-68
Anderson, John	Tor., Que., Hfd.	12	814	282	349	631	263	37	9	18	27	2	....	1977-78	1988-89
Anderson, Murray	Wsh.	1	40	0	1	1	68	....	....	....	....	....	....	1974-75	1974-75
Anderson, Perry	St.L., N.J., S.J.	10	400	50	59	109	1051	36	2	1	3	161	....	1981-82	1991-92
Anderson, Ron	Det., L.A., St.L., Buf.	5	251	28	30	58	146	5	0	0	0	4	....	1967-68	1971-72
Anderson, Ron H.	Wsh.	1	28	9	7	16	8	....	....	....	....	....	....	1974-75	1974-75
Anderson, Russ	Pit., Hfd., L.A.	9	519	22	99	121	1086	10	0	3	3	28	....	1976-77	1984-85
Anderson, Shawn	Buf., Que., Wsh., Phi.	8	255	11	51	62	117	19	1	1	2	16	....	1986-87	1994-95
• Anderson, Tom	Det., NYA, Bro.	8	319	62	127	189	190	16	2	7	9	8	....	1934-35	1941-42
Andersson, Kent-Erik	Min., NYR	7	456	72	103	175	78	50	4	11	15	4	....	1977-78	1983-84
Andersson, Peter	Wsh., Que.	3	172	10	41	51	81	7	0	2	2	2	....	1983-84	1985-86
Andersson, Peter	NYR, Fla.	2	47	6	13	19	20	....	....	....	....	....	....	1992-93	1993-94
Andrascik, Steve	NYR	1	....	....	....	....	....	1	0	0	0	0	....	1971-72	1971-72
Andrea, Paul	NYR, Pit., Cal., Buf.	4	150	31	49	80	10	....	....	....	....	....	....	1965-66	1970-71
• Andrews, Lloyd	Tor.	4	53	8	5	13	10	7	2	0	2	5	1	1921-22	1924-25
Andrijevski, Alexander	Chi.	1	1	0	0	0	0	....	....	....	....	....	....	1992-93	1992-93
Andruff, Ron	Mtl., Col.	5	153	19	36	55	54	2	0	0	0	0	....	1974-75	1978-79
Angotti, Lou	NYR, Chi., Phi., Pit., St.L.	10	653	103	186	289	228	65	8	8	16	17	....	1964-65	1973-74
Anholt, Darrel	Chi.	1	1	0	0	0	0	....	....	....	....	....	....	1983-84	1983-84
Anslow, Bert	NYR	1	2	0	0	0	0	....	....	....	....	....	....	1947-48	1947-48
Antonovich, Mike	Min., Hfd., N.J.	5	87	10	15	25	37	....	....	....	....	....	....	1975-76	1983-84
Antoski, Shawn	Van., Phi., Pit., Ana.	8	183	3	5	8	599	36	1	3	4	74	....	1990-91	1997-98
Apps Jr., Syl	NYR, Pit., L.A.	10	727	183	423	606	311	23	5	5	10	23	....	1970-71	1979-80
• Apps Sr., Syl	Tor.	10	423	201	231	432	56	69	25	29	54	8	3	1936-37	1947-48
Arbour, Al	Det., Chi., Tor., St.L.	16	626	12	58	70	617	86	1	8	9	92	4	1953-54	1970-71
• Arbour, Amos	Mtl.C., Ham., Tor.	6	111	51	17	68	71	....	....	....	....	....	....	1918-19	1923-24
• Arbour, Jack	Det., Tor.	2	47	5	1	6	56	....	....	....	....	....	....	1926-27	1928-29
Arbour, John	Bos., Pit., Van., St.L.	5	106	1	9	10	149	5	0	0	0	0	....	1965-66	1971-72
• Arbour, Ty	Pit., Chi.	5	207	28	28	56	112	11	2	0	2	6	....	1926-27	1930-31
Archambault, Michel	Chi.	1	3	0	0	0	0	....	....	....	....	....	....	1976-77	1976-77
Archibald, Jim	Min.	3	16	1	2	3	45	....	....	....	....	....	....	1984-85	1986-87
Areshenkoff, Ron	Edm.	1	4	0	0	0	0	....	....	....	....	....	....	1979-80	1979-80
Armstrong, Bill	Phi.	1	1	0	1	1	0	....	....	....	....	....	....	1990-91	1990-91
• Armstrong, Bob	Bos.	12	542	13	86	99	671	42	1	7	8	28	....	1950-51	1961-62
Armstrong, George	Tor.	21	1187	296	417	713	721	110	26	34	60	52	4	1949-50	1970-71
Armstrong, Murray	Tor., NYA, Bro., Det.	8	270	67	121	188	72	33	10	20	30	8	....	1937-38	1945-46
• Armstrong, Norm	Tor.	1	7	1	1	2	2	....	....	....	....	....	....	1962-63	1962-63
Armstrong, Tim	Tor.	1	11	1	0	1	6	....	....	....	....	....	....	1988-89	1988-89
Arnason, Chuck	Mtl., Atl., Pit., K.C., Col., Cle., Min., Wsh.	8	401	109	90	199	122	9	2	4	6	4	....	1971-72	1978-79
Arniel, Scott	Wpg., Buf., Bos.	11	730	149	189	338	599	34	3	3	6	39	....	1981-82	1991-92
Arthur, Fred	Hfd., Phi.	3	80	1	8	9	49	4	0	0	0	2	....	1980-81	1982-83
Arundel, John	Tor.	1	3	0	0	0	9	....	....	....	....	....	....	1949-50	1949-50
• Ashbee, Barry	Bos., Phi.	5	284	15	70	85	291	17	0	4	4	22	1	1965-66	1973-74
• Ashby, Don	Tor., Col., Edm.	6	188	40	56	96	40	12	1	0	1	4	....	1975-76	1980-81
Ashton, Brent	Van., Col., N.J., Min., Que., Det., Wpg., Bos., Cgy.	14	998	284	345	629	635	85	24	25	49	70	....	1979-80	1992-93
Ashworth, Frank	Chi.	1	18	5	4	9	2	....	....	....	....	....	....	1946-47	1946-47
Asmundson, Oscar	NYR, Det., St.L., NYA, Mtl.C.	5	111	11	23	34	30	9	0	2	2	4	1	1932-33	1937-38
Astley, Mark	Buf.	3	75	4	19	23	92	2	0	0	0	0	....	1993-94	1995-96
• Atanas, Walt	NYR	1	49	13	8	21	40	....	....	....	....	....	....	1944-45	1944-45
Atkinson, Steve	Bos., Buf., Wsh.	6	302	60	51	111	104	1	0	0	0	0	....	1968-69	1974-75
Attwell, Bob	Col.	2	22	1	5	6	0	....	....	....	....	....	....	1979-80	1980-81
Attwell, Ron	St.L., NYR	1	22	1	7	8	8	....	....	....	....	....	....	1967-68	1967-68

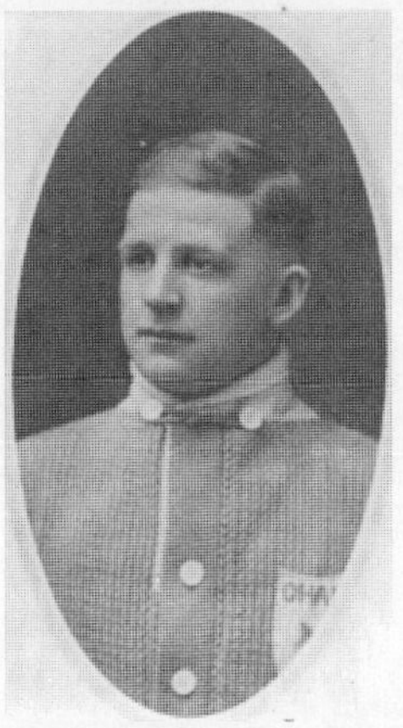
Jack Adams

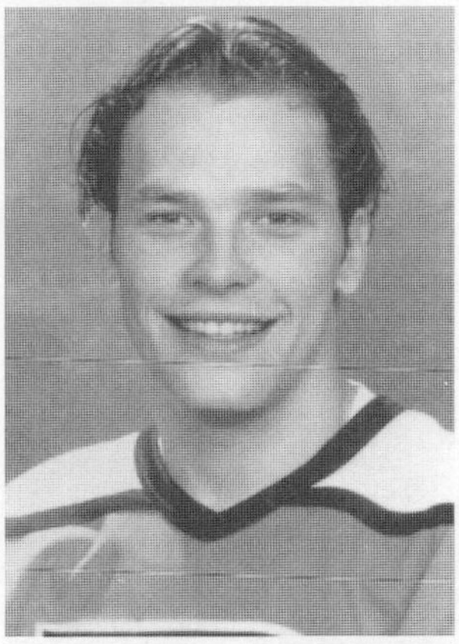
Shawn Antoski

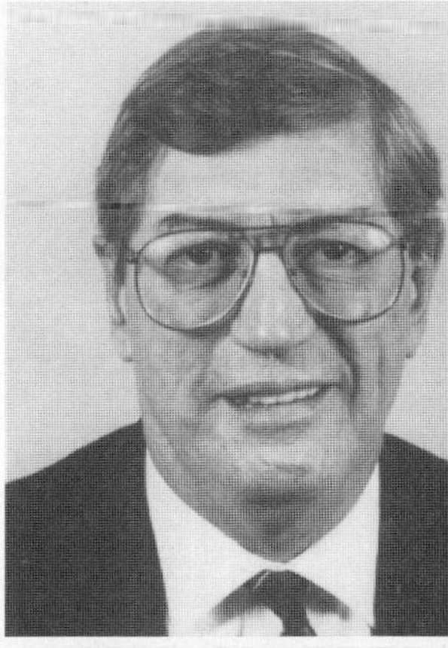
Al Arbour

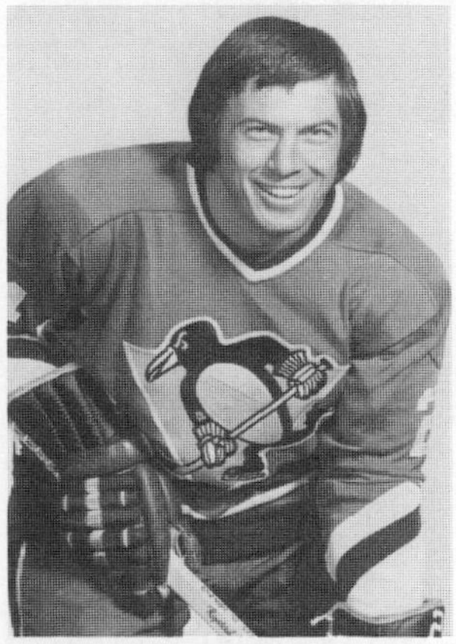
Don Awrey

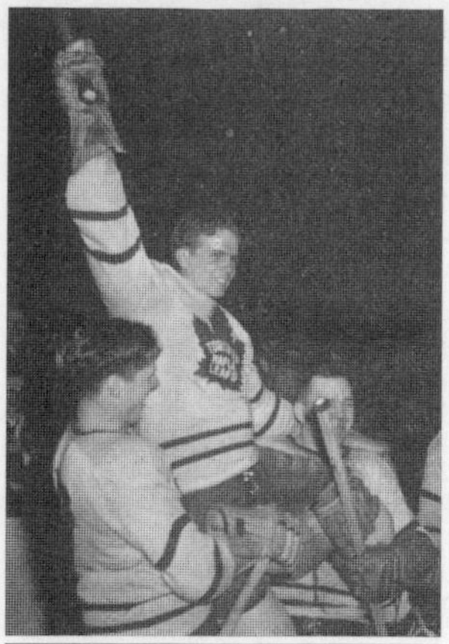

Bill Barilko

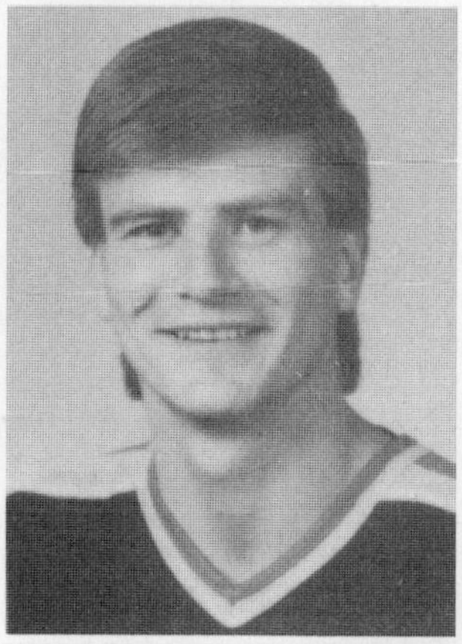

Jim Benning

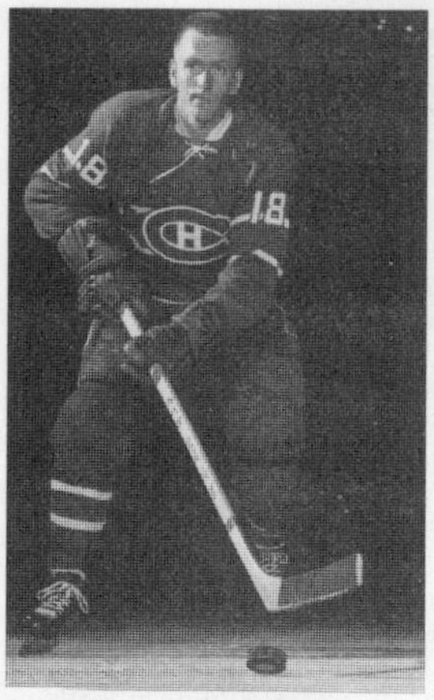

Red Berenson

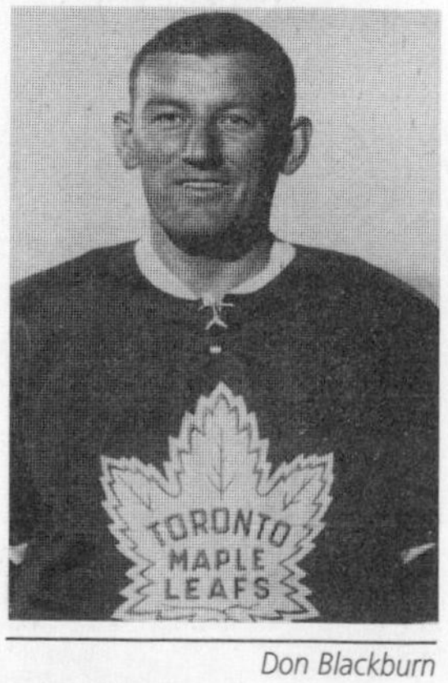

Don Blackburn

			Regular Schedule					Playoffs							
Name	NHL Teams	NHL Seasons	GP	G	A	TP	PIM	GP	G	A	TP	PIM	NHL Cup Wins	First NHL Season	Last NHL Season
Aubin, Norm	Tor.	2	69	18	13	31	30	1	0	0	0	0	....	1981-82	1982-83
Aubry, Pierre	Que., Det.	5	202	24	26	50	133	20	1	1	2	32	....	1980-81	1984-85
Aubuchon, Ossie	Bos., NYR	2	50	19	12	31	4	6	1	0	1	0	....	1942-43	1943-44
Auge, Les	Col.	1	6	0	3	3	4	....	....	....	....	....	....	1980-81	1980-81
• Aurie, Larry	Det.	12	489	147	129	276	279	24	6	9	15	10	2	1927-28	1938-39
Awrey, Don	Bos., St.L., Mtl., Pit., NYR, Col.	16	979	31	158	189	1065	71	0	18	18	150	3	1963-64	1978-79
• Ayres, Vern	NYA, Mtl.M., St.L., NYR	6	211	6	14	20	350	....	....	....	....	....	....	1930-31	1935-36
B															
Babando, Pete	Bos., Det., Chi., NYR	6	351	86	73	159	194	17	3	3	6	6	....	1947-48	1952-53
Babcock, Bobby	Wsh.	2	2	0	0	0	2	....	....	....	....	....	....	1990-91	1992-93
Babe, Warren	Min.	3	21	2	5	7	23	2	0	0	0	0	....	1987-88	1990-91
Babin, Mitch	St.L.	1	8	0	0	0	0	....	....	....	....	....	....	1975-76	1975-76
Baby, John	Cle., Min.	2	26	2	8	10	26	....	....	....	....	....	....	1977-78	1978-79
Babych, Wayne	St.L., Pit., Que., Hfd.	9	519	192	246	438	498	41	7	9	16	24	....	1978-79	1986-87
Baca, Jergus	Hfd.	2	10	0	2	2	14	....	....	....	....	....	....	1990-91	1991-92
Backman, Mike	NYR	3	18	1	6	7	18	10	2	2	4	2	....	1981-82	1983-84
Backor, Pete	Tor.	1	36	4	5	9	6	....	....	....	....	....	1	1944-45	1944-45
Backstrom, Ralph	Mtl., L.A., Chi.	17	1032	278	361	639	386	116	27	32	59	68	6	1956-57	1972-73
• Bailey, Ace	Tor.	8	313	111	82	193	472	21	3	4	7	12	1	1926-27	1933-34
Bailey, Bob	Tor., Det., Chi.	5	150	15	21	36	207	15	0	4	4	22	....	1953-54	1957-58
Bailey, Garnet	Bos., Det., St.L., Wsh.	10	568	107	171	278	633	15	2	4	6	28	2	1968-69	1977-78
Bailey, Reid	Phi., Tor., Hfd.	4	40	1	3	4	105	16	0	2	2	25	....	1980-81	1983-84
Baillargeon, Joel	Wpg., Que.	3	20	0	2	2	31	....	....	....	....	....	....	1986-87	1988-89
Baird, Ken	Cal.	1	10	0	2	2	15	....	....	....	....	....	....	1971-72	1971-72
Baker, Bill	Mtl., Col., St.L., NYR	3	143	7	25	32	175	6	0	0	0	0	....	1980-81	1982-83
Bakovic, Peter	Van.	1	10	2	0	2	48	....	....	....	....	....	....	1987-88	1987-88
Balderis, Helmut	Min.	1	26	3	6	9	2	....	....	....	....	....	....	1989-90	1989-90
Baldwin, Doug	Tor., Det., Chi.	3	24	0	1	1	8	....	....	....	....	....	....	1945-46	1947-48
Balfour, Earl	Tor., Chi.	7	288	30	22	52	78	26	0	3	3	4	1	1951-52	1960-61
• Balfour, Murray	Mtl., Chi., Bos.	8	306	67	90	157	393	40	9	10	19	45	1	1956-57	1964-65
Ball, Terry	Phi., Buf.	4	74	7	19	26	26	....	....	....	....	....	....	1967-68	1971-72
Balon, Dave	NYR, Mtl., Min., Van.	14	776	192	222	414	607	78	14	21	35	109	2	1959-60	1972-73
Baltimore, Bryon	Edm.	1	2	0	0	0	4	....	....	....	....	....	....	1979-80	1979-80
Baluik, Stanley	Bos.	1	7	0	0	0	2	....	....	....	....	....	....	1959-60	1959-60
Bandura, Jeff	NYR	1	2	0	1	1	0	....	....	....	....	....	....	1980-81	1980-81
Banks, Darren	Bos.	2	20	2	2	4	73	....	....	....	....	....	....	1992-93	1993-94
Barahona, Ralph	Bos.	2	6	2	2	4	0	....	....	....	....	....	....	1990-91	1991-92
Barbe, Andy	Tor.	1	1	0	0	0	2	....	....	....	....	....	....	1950-51	1950-51
Barber, Bill	Phi.	12	903	420	463	883	623	129	53	55	108	109	2	1972-73	1983-84
Barber, Don	Min., Wpg., Que., S.J.	4	115	25	32	57	64	11	4	4	8	10	....	1988-89	1991-92
• Barilko, Bill	Tor.	5	252	26	36	62	456	47	5	7	12	104	4	1946-47	1950-51
Barkley, Doug	Chi., Det.	6	253	24	80	104	382	30	0	9	9	63	....	1957-58	1965-66
Barlow, Bob	Min.	2	77	16	17	33	10	6	2	2	4	6	....	1969-70	1970-71
Barnes, Blair	L.A.	1	1	0	0	0	0	....	....	....	....	....	....	1982-83	1982-83
Barnes, Norm	Phi., Hfd.	5	156	6	38	44	178	12	0	0	0	8	....	1976-77	1981-82
Baron, Normand	Mtl., St.L.	2	27	2	0	2	51	3	0	0	0	22	....	1983-84	1985-86
Barr, Dave	Bos., NYR, St.L., Hfd., Det., N.J., Dal.	13	614	128	204	332	520	71	12	10	22	70	....	1981-82	1993-94
Barrault, Doug	Min., Fla.	2	4	0	0	0	2	....	....	....	....	....	....	1992-93	1993-94
Barrett, Fred	Min., L.A.	13	745	25	123	148	671	44	0	2	2	60	....	1970-71	1983-84
Barrett, John	Det., Wsh., Min.	8	488	20	77	97	604	16	2	2	4	50	....	1980-81	1987-88
Barrie, Doug	Pit., Buf., L.A.	3	158	10	42	52	268	....	....	....	....	....	....	1968-69	1971-72
Barry, Ed	Bos.	1	19	1	3	4	2	....	....	....	....	....	....	1946-47	1946-47
• Barry, Marty	NYA, Bos., Det., Mtl.	12	509	195	192	387	231	43	15	18	33	34	2	1927-28	1939-40
Barry, Ray	Bos.	1	18	1	2	3	6	....	....	....	....	....	....	1951-52	1951-52
Bartel, Robin	Cgy., Van.	2	41	0	1	1	14	6	0	0	0	16	....	1985-86	1986-87
Bartlett, Jim	Mtl., NYR, Bos.	5	191	34	23	57	273	2	0	0	0	0	....	1954-55	1960-61
• Barton, Cliff	Pit., Phi., NYR	3	85	10	9	19	22	....	....	....	....	....	....	1929-30	1939-40
Bathe, Frank	Det., Phi.	9	224	3	28	31	542	27	1	3	4	42	....	1974-75	1983-84
Bathgate, Andy	NYR, Tor., Det., Pit.	17	1069	349	624	973	624	54	21	14	35	76	1	1952-53	1970-71
Bathgate, Frank	NYR	1	2	0	0	0	2	....	....	....	....	....	....	1952-53	1952-53
• Batters, Jeff	St.L.	2	16	0	0	0	28	....	....	....	....	....	....	1993-94	1994-95
Batyrshin, Ruslan	L.A.	1	2	0	0	0	6	....	....	....	....	....	....	1995-96	1995-96
• Bauer, Bobby	Bos.	9	327	123	137	260	36	48	11	8	19	6	2	1936-37	1951-52
Baumgartner, Mike	K.C.	1	17	0	0	0	0	....	....	....	....	....	....	1974-75	1974-75
Baun, Bob	Tor., Oak., Det.	17	964	37	187	224	1493	96	3	12	15	171	4	1956-57	1972-73
Bautin, Sergei	Wpg., Det., S.J.	3	132	5	25	30	176	6	0	0	0	2	....	1992-93	1995-96
Bawa, Robin	Wsh., Van., S.J., Ana.	4	61	6	1	7	60	1	0	0	0	0	....	1989-90	1993-94
Baxter, Paul	Que., Pit., Cgy.	8	472	48	121	169	1564	40	0	5	5	162	....	1979-80	1986-87
Beadle, Sandy	Wpg.	1	6	1	0	1	2	....	....	....	....	....	....	1980-81	1980-81
Beaton, Frank	NYR	2	25	1	1	2	43	....	....	....	....	....	....	1978-79	1979-80
• Beattie, Red	Bos., Det., NYA	9	334	62	85	147	137	24	4	2	6	8	....	1930-31	1938-39
Beaudin, Norm	St.L., Min.	2	25	1	2	3	4	....	....	....	....	....	....	1967-68	1970-71
Beaudoin, Serge	Atl.	1	3	0	0	0	0	....	....	....	....	....	....	1979-80	1979-80
Beaudoin, Yves	Wsh.	3	11	0	0	0	5	....	....	....	....	....	....	1985-86	1987-88
Beck, Barry	Col., NYR, L.A.	10	615	104	251	355	1016	51	10	23	33	77	....	1977-78	1989-90
Beckett, Bob	Bos.	4	68	7	6	13	18	....	....	....	....	....	....	1956-57	1963-64
Bedard, James	Chi.	2	22	1	1	2	8	....	....	....	....	....	....	1949-50	1950-51
Bednarski, John	NYR, Edm.	4	100	2	18	20	114	1	0	0	0	17	....	1974-75	1979-80
Beers, Bob	Bos., T.B., Edm., NYI	8	258	28	79	107	225	21	1	1	2	22	....	1989-90	1996-97
Beers, Eddy	Cgy., St.L.	6	250	94	116	210	256	41	7	10	17	47	....	1981-82	1986-87
• Behling, Dick	Det.	2	5	1	0	1	2	....	....	....	....	....	....	1940-41	1942-43
Beisler, Frank	NYA	2	2	0	0	0	0	....	....	....	....	....	....	1936-37	1939-40
Belanger, Alain	Tor.	1	9	0	1	1	6	....	....	....	....	....	....	1977-78	1977-78
Belanger, Roger	Pit.	1	44	3	5	8	32	....	....	....	....	....	....	1984-85	1984-85
Belisle, Danny	NYR	1	4	2	0	2	0	....	....	....	....	....	....	1960-61	1960-61
Beliveau, Jean	Mtl.	20	1125	507	712	1219	1029	162	79	97	176	211	10	1950-51	1970-71
• Bell, Billy	Mtl., Mtl.C., Ott.	6	61	3	2	5	10	8	0	0	0	0	....	1917-18	1923-24
Bell, Bruce	Que., St.L., NYR, Edm.	5	209	12	64	76	113	34	3	5	8	41	....	1984-85	1989-90
Bell, Harry	NYR	1	1	0	1	1	0	....	....	....	....	....	....	1946-47	1946-47
Bell, Joe	NYR	2	62	8	9	17	18	....	....	....	....	....	....	1942-43	1946-47
Belland, Neil	Van., Pit.	6	109	13	32	45	54	21	2	9	11	23	....	1981-82	1986-87
• Bellefeuille, Pete	Tor., Det.	4	92	26	4	30	58	....	....	....	....	....	....	1925-26	1929-30
• Bellemer, Andy	Mtl.M.	1	15	0	0	0	0	....	....	....	....	....	....	1932-33	1932-33
• Bend, Lin	NYR	1	8	3	1	4	2	....	....	....	....	....	....	1942-43	1942-43
Bennett, Adam	Chi., Edm.	3	69	3	8	11	69	....	....	....	....	....	....	1991-92	1993-94
Bennett, Bill	Bos., Hfd.	2	31	4	7	11	65	....	....	....	....	....	....	1978-79	1979-80
Bennett, Curt	St.L., NYR, Atl.	10	580	152	182	334	347	21	1	1	2	57	....	1970-71	1979-80
Bennett, Frank	Det.	1	7	0	1	1	2	....	....	....	....	....	....	1943-44	1943-44
Bennett, Harvey	Pit., Wsh., Phi., Min., St.L.	5	268	44	46	90	347	4	0	0	0	2	....	1974-75	1978-79
• Bennett, Max	Mtl.C.	1	1	0	0	0	0	....	....	....	....	....	....	1935-36	1935-36
Bennett, Rick	NYR	3	15	1	1	2	13	....	....	....	....	....	....	1989-90	1991-92
Benning, Brian	St.L., L.A., Phi., Edm., Fla.	11	568	63	233	296	963	48	3	20	23	74	....	1984-85	1994-95
Benning, Jim	Tor., Van.	9	605	52	191	243	461	7	1	1	2	2	....	1981-82	1989-90
• Benoit, Joe	Mtl.	5	185	75	69	144	94	11	6	3	9	11	1	1940-41	1946-47
Benson, Bill	NYA, Bro.	2	67	11	25	36	35	....	....	....	....	....	....	1940-41	1941-42
• Benson, Bobby	Bos.	1	8	0	1	1	4	....	....	....	....	....	....	1924-25	1924-25
• Bentley, Doug	Chi., NYR	13	566	219	324	543	217	23	9	8	17	12	....	1939-40	1953-54
• Bentley, Max	Chi., Tor., NYR	12	646	245	299	544	179	51	18	27	45	14	3	1940-41	1953-54
Bentley, Reggie	Chi.	1	11	1	2	3	2	....	....	....	....	....	....	1942-43	1942-43
Beraldo, Paul	Bos.	2	10	0	0	0	4	....	....	....	....	....	....	1987-88	1988-89
Berenson, Red	Mtl., NYR, St.L., Det.	17	987	261	397	658	305	85	23	14	37	49	1	1961-62	1977-78
Berezan, Perry	Cgy., Min., S.J.	9	378	61	75	136	279	31	4	7	11	34	....	1984-85	1992-93
• Bergdinon, Fred	Bos.	1	2	0	0	0	0	....	....	....	....	....	....	1925-26	1925-26
Bergen, Todd	Phi.	1	14	11	5	16	4	17	4	9	13	8	....	1984-85	1984-85
Berger, Mike	Min.	2	30	3	1	4	67	....	....	....	....	....	....	1987-88	1988-89
Bergeron, Michel	Det., NYI, Wsh.	5	229	80	58	138	165	....	....	....	....	....	....	1974-75	1978-79
Bergeron, Yves	Pit.	2	3	0	0	0	0	....	....	....	....	....	....	1974-75	1976-77
Bergland, Tim	Wsh., T.B.	5	182	17	26	43	75	26	2	2	4	22	....	1989-90	1993-94
Bergloff, Bob	Min.	1	2	0	0	0	5	....	....	....	....	....	....	1982-83	1982-83

			Regular Schedule					Playoffs					NHL	First	Last
Name	NHL Teams	NHL Seasons	GP	G	A	TP	PIM	GP	G	A	TP	PIM	Cup Wins	NHL Season	NHL Season
Berglund, Bo	Que., Min., Phi.	3	130	28	39	67	40	9	2	0	2	6	....	1983-84	1985-86
Bergman, Gary	Det., Min., K.C.	12	838	68	299	367	1249	21	0	5	5	20	....	1964-65	1975-76
Bergman, Thommie	Det.	6	246	21	44	65	243	7	0	2	2	2	....	1972-73	1979-80
Bergqvist, Jonas	Cgy.	1	22	2	5	7	10	....	....	....	....	....	....	1989-90	1989-90
• Berlinquette, Louis	Mtl.C., Mtl.M., Pit.	8	193	46	33	79	128	16	1	4	5	9	....	1917-18	1925-26
Bernier, Serge	Phi., L.A., Que.	7	302	78	119	197	234	5	1	1	2	0	....	1968-69	1980-81
Berry, Bob	Mtl., L.A.	8	541	159	191	350	344	26	2	6	8	6	....	1968-69	1976-77
Berry, Brad	Wpg., Min., Dal.	8	241	4	28	32	323	13	0	1	1	16	....	1985-86	1993-94
Berry, Doug	Col.	2	121	10	33	43	25	....	....	....	....	....	....	1979-80	1980-81
Berry, Fred	Det.	1	3	0	0	0	0	....	....	....	....	....	....	1976-77	1976-77
Berry, Ken	Edm., Van.	4	55	8	10	18	30	....	....	....	....	....	....	1981-82	1988-89
• Besler, Phil	Bos., Chi., Det.	2	30	1	4	5	18	....	....	....	....	....	....	1935-36	1938-39
• Bessone, Pete	Det.	1	6	0	1	1	6	....	....	....	....	....	....	1937-38	1937-38
Bethel, John	Wpg.	1	17	0	2	2	4	....	....	....	....	....	....	1979-80	1979-80
Bets, Maxim	Ana.	1	3	0	0	0	0	....	....	....	....	....	....	1993-94	1993-94
Bettio, Sam	Bos.	1	44	9	12	21	32	....	....	....	....	....	....	1949-50	1949-50
Beverley, Nick	Bos., Pit., NYR, Min., L.A., Col.	11	502	18	94	112	156	7	0	1	1	0	....	1966-67	1979-80
Bialowas, Dwight	Atl., Min.	4	164	11	46	57	46	....	....	....	....	....	....	1973-74	1976-77
Bianchin, Wayne	Pit., Edm.	7	276	68	41	109	137	3	0	1	1	6	....	1973-74	1979-80
Bidner, Todd	Wsh.	1	12	2	1	3	7	....	....	....	....	....	....	1981-82	1981-82
Biggs, Don	Min., Phi.	2	12	2	0	2	8	....	....	....	....	....	....	1984-85	1989-90
Bignell, Larry	Pit.	2	20	0	3	3	2	3	0	0	0	2	....	1973-74	1974-75
Bilodeau, Gilles	Que.	1	9	0	1	1	25	....	....	....	....	....	....	1979-80	1979-80
Bionda, Jack	Tor., Bos.	4	93	3	9	12	113	11	0	1	1	14	....	1955-56	1958-59
Bissett, Tom	Det.	1	5	0	0	0	0	....	....	....	....	....	....	1990-91	1990-91
Bjugstad, Scott	Min., Pit., L.A.	9	317	76	68	144	144	9	0	1	1	2	....	1983-84	1991-92
Black, Stephen	Det., Chi.	2	113	11	20	31	77	13	0	0	0	13	1	1949-50	1950-51
Blackburn, Bob	NYR, Pit.	3	135	8	12	20	105	6	0	0	0	4	....	1968-69	1970-71
Blackburn, Don	Bos., Phi., NYR, NYI, Min.	6	185	23	44	67	87	12	3	0	3	10	....	1962-63	1972-73
Blade, Hank	Chi.	2	24	2	3	5	2	....	....	....	....	....	....	1946-47	1947-48
Bladon, Tom	Phi., Pit., Edm., Wpg., Det.	9	610	73	197	270	392	86	8	29	37	70	2	1972-73	1980-81
• Blaine, Garry	Mtl.	1	1	0	0	0	0	....	....	....	....	....	....	1954-55	1954-55
• Blair, Andy	Tor., Chi.	9	402	74	86	160	323	38	6	6	12	32	1	1928-29	1936-37
Blair, Chuck	Tor.	1	1	0	0	0	0	....	....	....	....	....	....	1948-49	1948-49
Blair, George	Tor.	1	2	0	0	0	0	....	....	....	....	....	....	1950-51	1950-51
Blaisdell, Mike	Det., NYR, Pit., Tor.	9	343	70	84	154	166	6	1	2	3	10	....	1980-81	1988-89
Blake, Bob	Bos.	1	12	0	0	0	0	....	....	....	....	....	....	1935-36	1935-36
• Blake, Mickey	Mtl.M., St.L., Tor.	3	10	1	1	2	4	....	....	....	....	....	....	1932-33	1935-36
• Blake, Toe	Mtl.M., Mtl.C., Mtl.	14	577	235	292	527	272	58	25	37	62	23	3	1934-35	1947-48
Blight, Rick	Van., L.A.	7	326	96	125	221	170	5	0	5	5	2	....	1975-76	1982-83
• Blinco, Russ	Mtl.M., Chi.	6	268	59	66	125	24	19	3	3	6	4	1	1933-34	1938-39
Block, Ken	Van.	1	1	0	0	0	0	....	....	....	....	....	....	1970-71	1970-71
Blomqvist, Timo	Wsh., N.J.	5	243	4	53	57	293	13	0	0	0	24	....	1981-82	1986-87
Blomsten, Arto	Wpg., L.A.	3	25	0	4	4	8	....	....	....	....	....	....	1993-94	1995-96
Bloom, Mike	Wsh., Det.	3	201	30	47	77	215	....	....	....	....	....	....	1974-75	1976-77
Blum, John	Edm., Bos., Wsh., Det.	8	250	7	34	41	610	20	0	2	2	27	....	1982-83	1989-90
Bodak, Bob	Cgy., Hfd.	2	4	0	0	0	29	....	....	....	....	....	....	1987-88	1989-90
Boddy, Gregg	Van.	5	273	23	44	67	263	3	0	0	0	0	....	1971-72	1975-76
Bodnar, Gus	Tor., Chi., Bos.	12	667	142	254	396	207	32	4	3	7	10	2	1943-44	1954-55
Boehm, Ron	Oak.	1	16	2	1	3	10	....	....	....	....	....	....	1967-68	1967-68
• Boesch, Garth	Tor.	4	197	9	28	37	205	34	2	5	7	18	3	1946-47	1949-50
Boh, Rick	Min.	1	8	2	1	3	4	....	....	....	....	....	....	1987-88	1987-88
Boileau, Marc	Det.	1	54	5	6	11	8	....	....	....	....	....	....	1961-62	1961-62
Boileau, Rene	NYA	1	7	0	0	0	0	....	....	....	....	....	....	1925-26	1925-26
Boimistruck, Fred	Tor.	2	83	4	14	18	45	....	....	....	....	....	....	1981-82	1982-83
Boisvert, Serge	Tor., Mtl.	5	46	5	7	12	8	23	3	7	10	4	1	1982-83	1987-88
Boivin, Claude	Phi., Ott.	4	132	12	19	31	364	....	....	....	....	....	....	1991-92	1994-95
Boivin, Leo	Tor., Bos., Det., Pit., Min.	19	1150	72	250	322	1192	54	3	10	13	59	....	1951-52	1969-70
Boland, Mike A.	Phi.	1	2	0	0	0	0	....	....	....	....	....	....	1974-75	1974-75
Boland, Mike J.	K.C., Buf.	2	23	1	2	3	29	3	1	0	1	2	....	1974-75	1978-79
Boldirev, Ivan	Bos., Cal., Chi., Atl., Van., Det.	15	1052	361	505	866	507	48	13	20	33	14	....	1970-71	1984-85
Bolduc, Danny	Det., Cgy.	3	102	22	19	41	33	1	0	0	0	0	....	1978-79	1983-84
Bolduc, Michel	Que.	2	10	0	0	0	6	....	....	....	....	....	....	1981-82	1982-83
• Boll, Frank	Tor., NYA, Bro., Bos.	12	437	133	130	263	148	31	7	3	10	13	....	1932-33	1943-44
Bolonchuk, Larry	Van., Wsh.	4	74	3	9	12	97	....	....	....	....	....	....	1972-73	1977-78
Bolton, Hugh	Tor.	8	235	10	51	61	221	17	0	5	5	14	....	1949-50	1956-57
Bonar, Dan	L.A.	3	170	25	39	64	208	14	3	4	7	22	....	1980-81	1982-83
Bonin, Marcel	Det., Bos., Mtl.	9	454	97	175	272	336	50	11	14	25	51	4	1952-53	1961-62
Boo, Jim	Min.	1	6	0	0	0	22	....	....	....	....	....	....	1977-78	1977-78
Boone, Buddy	Bos.	2	34	5	3	8	28	22	2	1	3	25	....	1956-57	1957-58
Boothman, George	Tor.	2	58	17	19	36	18	5	2	1	3	2	....	1942-43	1943-44
Bordeleau, Christian	Mtl., St.L., Chi.	4	205	38	65	103	82	19	4	7	11	17	1	1968-69	1971-72
Bordeleau, J.P.	Chi.	10	519	97	126	223	143	48	3	6	9	12	....	1969-70	1979-80
Bordeleau, Paulin	Van.	3	183	33	56	89	47	5	2	1	3	0	....	1973-74	1975-76
Borotsik, Jack	St.L.	1	1	0	0	0	0	....	....	....	....	....	....	1974-75	1974-75
Borsato, Luciano	Wpg.	5	203	35	55	90	113	7	1	0	1	4	....	1990-91	1994-95
Borschevsky, Nikolai	Tor., Cgy., Dal.	4	162	49	73	122	44	31	4	9	13	4	....	1992-93	1995-96
Boschman, Laurie	Tor., Edm., Wpg., N.J., Ott.	14	1009	229	348	577	2265	57	8	13	21	140	....	1979-80	1992-93
Bossy, Mike	NYI	10	752	573	553	1126	210	129	85	75	160	38	4	1977-78	1986-87
Bostrom, Helge	Chi.	4	96	3	3	6	58	13	0	0	0	16	....	1929-30	1932-33
Botell, Mark	Phi.	1	32	4	10	14	31	....	....	....	....	....	....	1981-82	1981-82
Bothwell, Tim	NYR, St.L., Hfd.	11	502	28	93	121	382	49	0	3	3	56	....	1978-79	1988-89
Botting, Cam	Atl.	1	2	0	1	1	0	....	....	....	....	....	....	1975-76	1975-76
Boucha, Henry	Det., Min., K.C., Col.	6	247	53	49	102	157	....	....	....	....	....	....	1971-72	1976-77
Bouchard, Butch	Mtl.	15	785	49	144	193	863	113	11	21	32	121	4	1941-42	1955-56
Bouchard, Dick	NYR	1	1	0	0	0	0	....	....	....	....	....	....	1954-55	1954-55
• Bouchard, Edmond	Mtl.C., Ham., NYA, Pit.	8	220	19	21	40	105	....	....	....	....	....	....	1921-22	1928-29
Bouchard, Pierre	Mtl., Wsh.	12	595	24	82	106	433	76	3	10	13	56	5	1970-71	1981-82
• Boucher, Billy	Mtl.C., Bos., NYA	7	213	93	35	128	391	21	9	3	12	35	....	1921-22	1927-28
• Boucher, Clarence	NYA	2	47	2	2	4	133	....	....	....	....	....	....	1926-27	1927-28
• Boucher, Frank	Ott., NYR	18	557	160	263	423	119	55	16	18	34	12	2	1921-22	1943-44
• Boucher, George	Ott., Mtl.M., Chi.	16	449	120	81	201	802	44	9	3	12	99	4	1917-18	1933-34
• Boucher, Robert	Mtl.C.	1	12	0	0	0	0	....	....	....	....	....	....	1923-24	1923-24
Boudreau, Bruce	Tor., Chi.	8	141	28	42	70	46	9	2	0	2	0	....	1976-77	1985-86
Boudrias, Andre	Mtl., Min., Chi., St.L., Van.	12	662	151	340	491	218	34	6	10	16	12	....	1963-64	1975-76
Boughner, Barry	Oak., Cal.	2	20	0	0	0	11	....	....	....	....	....	....	1969-70	1970-71
Bourbonnais, Dan	Hfd.	2	59	3	25	28	11	....	....	....	....	....	....	1981-82	1983-84
Bourbonnais, Rick	St.L.	3	71	9	15	24	29	4	0	1	1	0	....	1975-76	1977-78
• Bourcier, Conrad	Mtl.C.	1	6	0	0	0	0	....	....	....	....	....	....	1935-36	1935-36
Bourcier, Jean	Mtl.C.	1	9	0	1	1	0	....	....	....	....	....	....	1935-36	1935-36
• Bourgeault, Leo	Tor., NYR, Ott., Mtl.C.	8	307	24	20	44	269	24	1	1	2	18	1	1926-27	1934-35
Bourgeois, Charlie	Cgy., St.L., Hfd.	7	290	16	54	70	788	40	2	3	5	194	....	1981-82	1987-88
Bourne, Bob	NYI, L.A.	14	964	258	324	582	605	139	40	56	96	108	4	1974-75	1987-88
Bourque, Phil	Pit., NYR, Ott.	12	477	88	111	199	516	56	13	12	25	107	2	1983-84	1995-96
Boutette, Pat	Tor., Hfd., Pit.	10	756	171	282	453	1354	46	10	14	24	109	....	1975-76	1984-85
Boutilier, Paul	NYI, Bos., Min., NYR, Wpg.	8	288	27	83	110	358	41	1	9	10	45	1	1981-82	1988-89
Bowman, Kirk	Chi.	3	88	11	17	28	19	7	1	0	1	0	....	1976-77	1978-79
• Bowman, Ralph	Ott., St.L., Det.	7	274	8	17	25	260	22	2	2	4	6	2	1933-34	1939-40
Bownass, Jack	Mtl., NYR	4	80	3	8	11	58	....	....	....	....	....	....	1957-58	1961-62
Bowness, Rick	Atl., Det., St.L., Wpg.	7	173	18	37	55	191	5	0	0	0	2	....	1975-76	1981-82
• Boyd, Bill	NYR, NYA	4	138	15	7	22	72	9	0	0	0	2	1	1926-27	1929-30
Boyd, Irwin	Bos., Det.	4	97	18	19	37	51	5	0	1	1	4	....	1931-32	1943-44
Boyd, Randy	Pit., Chi., NYI, Van.	8	257	20	67	87	328	13	0	2	2	26	....	1981-82	1988-89
Boyer, Wally	Tor., Chi., Oak., Pit.	7	365	54	105	159	163	15	1	3	4	0	....	1965-66	1971-72
Boyer, Zac	Dal.	2	3	0	0	0	0	2	0	0	0	0	....	1994-95	1995-96
Boyko, Darren	Wpg.	1	1	0	0	0	0	....	....	....	....	....	....	1988-89	1988-89
Bozek, Steve	L.A., Cgy., St.L., Van., S.J.	11	641	164	167	331	309	58	12	11	23	69	....	1981-82	1991-92
Bozon, Philippe	St.L.	4	144	16	25	41	101	19	2	0	2	31	....	1991-92	1994-95
• Brackenborough, John	Bos.	1	7	0	0	0	0	....	....	....	....	....	....	1925-26	1925-26
Brackenbury, Curt	Que., Edm., St.L.	4	141	9	17	26	226	2	0	0	0	0	....	1979-80	1982-83
Bradley, Barton	Bos.	1	1	0	0	0	0	....	....	....	....	....	....	1949-50	1949-50

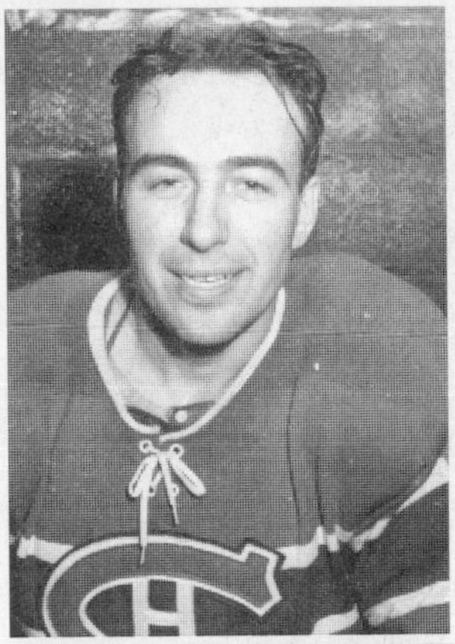
Toe Blake

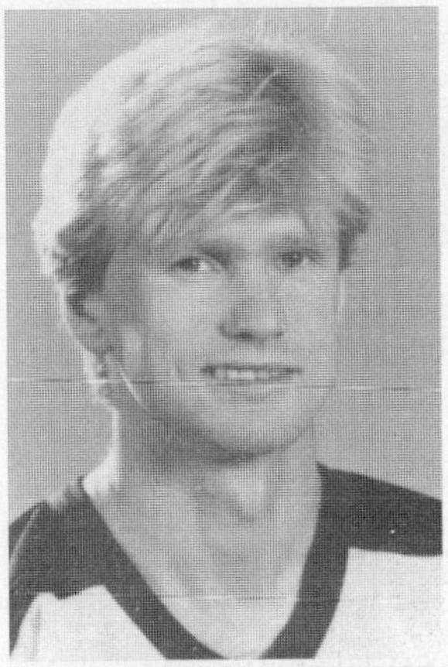
Nik Borschevsky

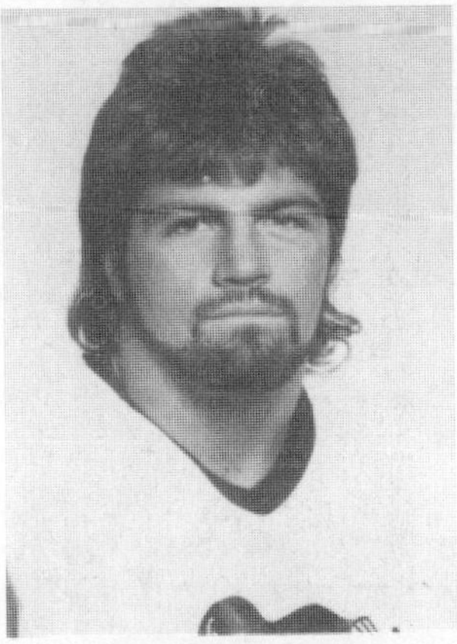
Phil Bourque

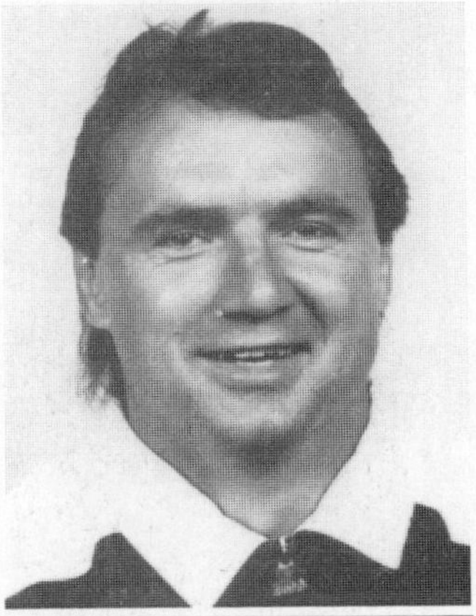
Rick Bowness

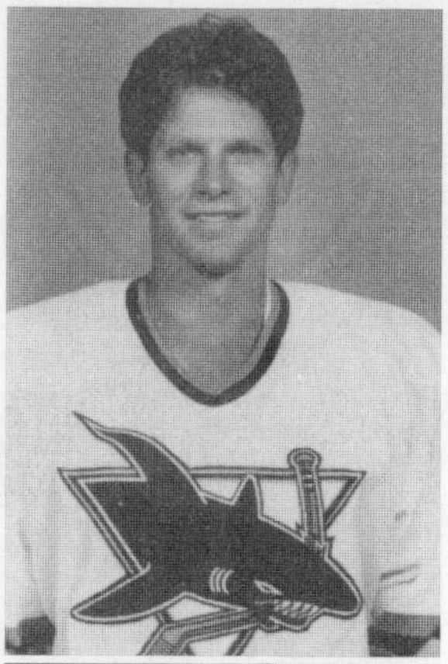

Steve Bozek

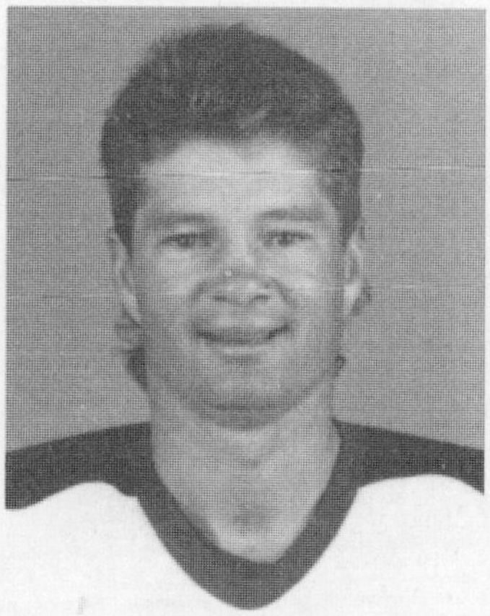

Brian Bradley

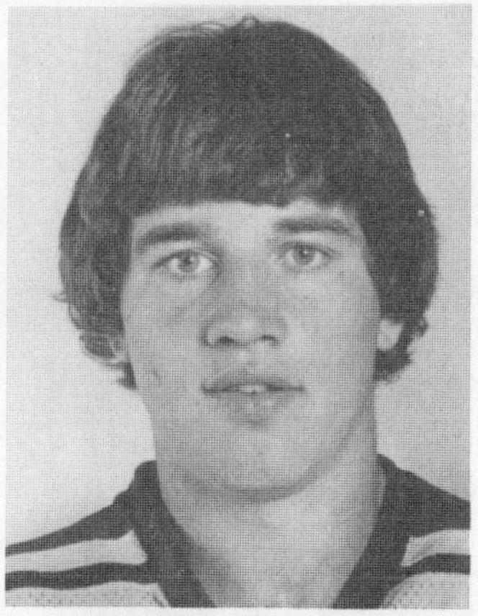

Aaron Broten

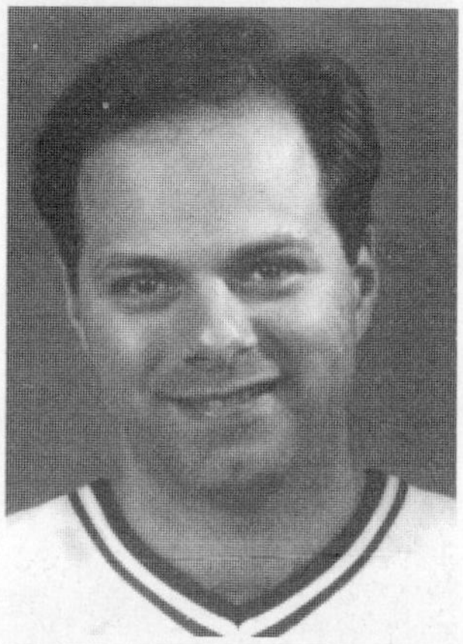

Jimmy Carson

			Regular Schedule					Playoffs							
Name	NHL Teams	NHL Seasons	GP	G	A	TP	PIM	GP	G	A	TP	PIM	NHL Cup Wins	First NHL Season	Last NHL Season
Bradley, Brian	Cgy., Van., Tor., T.B.	14	651	182	321	503	528	13	3	7	10	16	....	1985-86	1998-99
Bradley, Lyle	Cal., Cle.	2	6	1	0	1	2	....	....	....	....	....	....	1973-74	1976-77
Brady, Neil	N.J., Ott., Dal.	5	89	9	22	31	95	....	....	....	....	....	....	1989-90	1993-94
Bragnalo, Rick	Wsh.	4	145	15	35	50	46	....	....	....	....	....	....	1975-76	1978-79
• Branigan, Andy	NYA, Bro.	2	27	1	2	3	31	....	....	....	....	....	....	1940-41	1941-42
Brasar, Per-Olov	Min., Van.	5	348	64	142	206	33	13	1	2	3	0	....	1977-78	1981-82
Brayshaw, Russ	Chi.	1	43	5	9	14	24	....	....	....	....	....	....	1944-45	1944-45
Breault, Francois	L.A.	3	27	2	4	6	42	....	....	....	....	....	....	1990-91	1992-93
Breitenbach, Ken	Buf.	3	68	1	13	14	49	8	0	1	1	4	....	1975-76	1978-79
Brennan, Dan	L.A.	2	8	0	1	1	9	....	....	....	....	....	....	1983-84	1985-86
Brennan, Doug	NYR	3	123	9	7	16	152	16	1	0	1	21	1	1931-32	1933-34
Brennan, Tom	Bos.	2	22	2	2	4	2	....	....	....	....	....	....	1943-44	1944-45
Brenneman, John	Chi., NYR, Tor., Det., Oak.	5	152	21	19	40	46	....	....	....	....	....	1	1964-65	1968-69
Bretto, Joe	Chi.	1	3	0	0	0	4	....	....	....	....	....	....	1944-45	1944-45
Brewer, Carl	Tor., Det., St.L.	12	604	25	198	223	1037	72	3	17	20	146	3	1957-58	1979-80
Brickley, Andy	Phi., Pit., N.J., Bos., Wpg.	11	385	82	140	222	81	17	1	4	5	4	....	1982-83	1993-94
• Briden, Archie	Bos., Det., Pit.	2	72	9	5	14	56	....	....	....	....	....	....	1926-27	1929-30
Bridgman, Mel	Phi., Cgy., N.J., Det., Van.	14	977	252	449	701	1625	125	28	39	67	298	....	1975-76	1988-89
• Briere, Michel	Pit.	1	76	12	32	44	20	10	5	3	8	17	....	1969-70	1969-70
Brindley, Doug	Tor.	1	3	0	0	0	0	....	....	....	....	....	....	1970-71	1970-71
• Brink, Milt	Chi.	1	5	0	0	0	0	....	....	....	....	....	....	1936-37	1936-37
Brisson, Gerry	Mtl.	1	4	0	2	2	4	....	....	....	....	....	....	1962-63	1962-63
Britz, Greg	Tor., Hfd.	3	8	0	0	0	4	....	....	....	....	....	....	1983-84	1986-87
• Broadbent, Harry	Ott., Mtl.M., NYA	11	303	122	48	170	562	42	12	7	19	111	4	1918-19	1928-29
Brochu, Stephane	NYR	1	1	0	0	0	0	....	....	....	....	....	....	1988-89	1988-89
Broden, Connie	Mtl.	3	6	2	1	3	2	7	0	1	1	0	2	1955-56	1957-58
Brooke, Bob	NYR, Min., N.J.	7	447	69	97	166	520	34	9	9	18	59	....	1983-84	1989-90
Brooks, Gord	St.L., Wsh.	3	70	7	18	25	37	....	....	....	....	....	....	1971-72	1974-75
• Brophy, Bernie	Mtl.M., Det.	3	62	4	4	8	25	2	0	0	0	2	....	1925-26	1929-30
Brossart, Willie	Phi., Tor., Wsh.	6	129	1	14	15	88	1	0	0	0	0	....	1970-71	1975-76
Broten, Aaron	Col., N.J., Min., Que., Tor., Wpg.	12	748	186	329	515	441	34	7	18	25	40	....	1980-81	1991-92
Broten, Neal	Min., Dal., N.J., L.A.	17	1099	289	634	923	569	135	35	63	98	77	1	1980-81	1996-97
Broten, Paul	NYR, Dal., St.L.	7	322	46	55	101	264	38	4	6	10	18	....	1989-90	1995-96
• Brown, Adam	Det., Chi., Bos.	10	391	104	113	217	378	26	2	4	6	14	1	1941-42	1951-52
Brown, Arnie	Tor., NYR, Det., NYI, Atl.	12	681	44	141	185	738	22	0	6	6	23	....	1961-62	1973-74
Brown, Cam	Van.	1	1	0	0	0	7	....	....	....	....	....	....	1990-91	1990-91
• Brown, Connie	Det.	5	73	15	24	39	12	14	2	3	5	0	....	1938-39	1942-43
Brown, David	Phi., Edm., S.J.	14	729	45	52	97	1789	80	2	3	5	209	1	1982-83	1995-96
• Brown, Fred	Mtl.M.	1	19	1	0	1	0	9	0	0	0	0	....	1927-28	1927-28
Brown, George	Mtl.C.	3	79	6	22	28	34	7	0	0	0	2	....	1936-37	1938-39
Brown, Gerry	Det.	2	23	4	5	9	2	12	2	1	3	4	....	1941-42	1945-46
Brown, Greg	Buf., Pit., Wpg.	4	94	4	14	18	86	6	0	1	1	4	....	1990-91	1994-95
Brown, Harold	NYR	1	13	2	1	3	2	....	....	....	....	....	....	1945-46	1945-46
Brown, Jeff	Que., St.L., Van., Hfd., Car., Tor., Wsh.	13	747	154	430	584	498	87	20	45	65	59	....	1985-86	1997-98
Brown, Jim	L.A.	1	3	0	1	1	5	....	....	....	....	....	....	1982-83	1982-83
Brown, Keith	Chi., Fla.	16	876	68	274	342	916	103	4	32	36	184	....	1979-80	1994-95
Brown, Larry	NYR, Det., Phi., L.A.	9	455	7	53	60	180	35	0	4	4	10	....	1969-70	1977-78
• Brown, Stan	NYR, Det.	2	48	8	2	10	18	2	0	0	0	0	....	1926-27	1927-28
Brown, Wayne	Bos.	1	....	....	....	....	....	4	0	0	0	2	....	1953-54	1953-54
• Browne, Cecil	Chi.	1	13	2	0	2	4	....	....	....	....	....	....	1927-28	1927-28
Brownschidle, Jack	St.L., Hfd.	9	494	39	162	201	151	26	0	5	5	18	....	1977-78	1985-86
Brownschidle, Jeff	Hfd.	2	7	0	1	1	2	....	....	....	....	....	....	1981-82	1982-83
Brubaker, Jeff	Hfd., Mtl., Cgy., Tor., Edm., NYR, Det.	8	178	16	9	25	512	2	0	0	0	27	....	1979-80	1988-89
Bruce, David	Van., St.L., S.J.	8	234	48	39	87	338	3	0	0	0	2	....	1985-86	1993-94
• Bruce, Gordie	Bos.	3	28	4	9	13	13	7	2	3	5	4	1	1940-41	1945-46
• Bruce, Morley	Ott.	4	74	8	3	11	27	13	0	0	0	2	2	1917-18	1921-22
Brumwell, Murray	Min., N.J.	7	128	12	31	43	70	2	0	0	0	2	....	1980-81	1987-88
Bruneteau, Eddie	Det.	7	180	40	42	82	35	31	7	6	13	0	....	1940-41	1948-49
• Bruneteau, Mud	Det.	11	411	139	138	277	80	77	23	14	37	22	3	1935-36	1945-46
• Brydge, Bill	Tor., Det., NYA	9	368	26	52	78	506	2	0	0	0	4	....	1926-27	1935-36
Brydges, Paul	Buf.	1	15	2	2	4	6	....	....	....	....	....	....	1986-87	1986-87
• Brydson, Glenn	Mtl.M., St.L., NYR, Chi.	8	299	56	79	135	203	11	0	0	0	8	....	1930-31	1937-38
• Brydson, Gord	Tor.	1	8	2	0	2	8	....	....	....	....	....	....	1929-30	1929-30
Bubla, Jiri	Van.	5	256	17	101	118	202	6	0	0	0	7	....	1981-82	1985-86
Buchanan, Al	Tor.	2	4	0	1	1	2	....	....	....	....	....	....	1948-49	1949-50
Buchanan, Bucky	NYR	1	2	0	0	0	0	....	....	....	....	....	....	1948-49	1948-49
Buchanan, Mike	Chi.	1	1	0	0	0	0	....	....	....	....	....	....	1951-52	1951-52
Buchanan, Ron	Bos., St.L.	2	5	0	0	0	0	....	....	....	....	....	....	1966-67	1969-70
Bucyk, John	Det., Bos.	23	1540	556	813	1369	497	124	41	62	103	42	2	1955-56	1977-78
Bucyk, Randy	Mtl., Cgy.	2	19	4	2	6	8	2	0	0	0	0	1	1985-86	1987-88
Buhr, Doug	K.C.	1	6	0	2	2	4	....	....	....	....	....	....	1974-75	1974-75
Bukovich, Tony	Det.	2	17	7	3	10	6	6	0	1	1	0	....	1943-44	1944-45
Bullard, Mike	Pit., Cgy., St.L., Phi., Tor.	11	727	329	345	674	703	40	11	18	29	44	....	1980-81	1991-92
• Buller, Hy	Det., NYR	5	188	22	58	80	215	....	....	....	....	....	....	1943-44	1953-54
Bulley, Ted	Chi., Wsh., Pit.	8	414	101	113	214	704	29	5	5	10	24	....	1976-77	1983-84
Burakovsky, Robert	Ott.	1	23	2	3	5	6	....	....	....	....	....	....	1993-94	1993-94
• Burch, Billy	Ham., NYA, Bos., Chi.	11	390	137	53	190	251	2	0	0	0	0	....	1922-23	1932-33
• Burchell, Fred	Mtl.	2	4	0	0	0	2	....	....	....	....	....	....	1950-51	1953-54
Burdon, Glen	K.C.	1	11	0	2	2	0	....	....	....	....	....	....	1974-75	1974-75
Burega, Bill	Tor.	1	4	0	1	1	4	....	....	....	....	....	....	1955-56	1955-56
• Burke, Eddie	Bos., NYA	4	106	29	20	49	55	....	....	....	....	....	....	1931-32	1934-35
• Burke, Marty	Mtl.C., Pit., Ott., Chi.	11	494	19	47	66	560	31	2	4	6	44	....	1927-28	1937-38
• Burmeister, Roy	NYA	3	67	4	3	7	2	....	....	....	....	....	....	1929-30	1931-32
Burnett, Kelly	NYR	1	3	1	0	1	0	....	....	....	....	....	....	1952-53	1952-53
Burns, Bobby	Chi.	3	20	1	0	1	8	....	....	....	....	....	....	1927-28	1929-30
Burns, Charlie	Det., Bos., Oak., Pit., Min.	11	749	106	198	304	252	31	5	4	9	6	....	1958-59	1972-73
Burns, Gary	NYR	2	11	2	2	4	18	5	0	0	0	2	....	1980-81	1981-82
• Burns, Norm	NYR	1	11	0	4	4	2	....	....	....	....	....	....	1941-42	1941-42
Burns, Robin	Pit., K.C.	5	190	31	38	69	139	....	....	....	....	....	....	1970-71	1975-76
Burrows, Dave	Pit., Tor.	10	724	29	135	164	373	29	1	5	6	25	....	1971-72	1980-81
• Burry, Bert	Ott.	1	4	0	0	0	0	....	....	....	....	....	....	1932-33	1932-33
Burton, Cummy	Det.	3	43	0	2	2	21	3	0	0	0	0	....	1955-56	1958-59
Burton, Nelson	Wsh.	2	8	1	0	1	21	....	....	....	....	....	....	1977-78	1978-79
• Bush, Eddie	Det.	2	26	4	6	10	40	11	1	6	7	23	....	1938-39	1941-42
Buskas, Rod	Pit., Van., L.A., Chi.	11	556	19	63	82	1294	18	0	3	3	45	....	1982-83	1992-93
Busniuk, Mike	Phi.	2	143	3	23	26	297	25	2	5	7	34	....	1979-80	1980-81
Busniuk, Ron	Buf.	2	6	0	3	3	13	....	....	....	....	....	....	1972-73	1973-74
• Buswell, Walt	Det., Mtl.C., Mtl.	8	368	10	40	50	164	24	2	1	3	10	....	1932-33	1939-40
Butcher, Garth	Van., St.L., Que., Tor.	14	897	48	158	206	2302	50	6	5	11	122	....	1981-82	1994-95
Butler, Dick	Chi.	1	7	2	0	2	0	....	....	....	....	....	....	1947-48	1947-48
Butler, Jerry	NYR, St.L., Tor., Van., Wpg.	11	641	99	120	219	515	48	3	3	6	79	....	1972-73	1982-83
Butters, Bill	Min.	2	72	1	4	5	77	....	....	....	....	....	....	1977-78	1978-79
Buttrey, Gord	Chi.	1	10	0	0	0	0	....	....	....	....	....	....	1943-44	1943-44
Buynak, Gordon	St.L.	1	4	0	0	0	2	....	....	....	....	....	....	1974-75	1974-75
Byakin, Ilja	Edm., S.J.	2	57	8	25	33	44	....	....	....	....	....	....	1993-94	1994-95
Byce, John	Bos.	3	21	2	3	5	6	8	2	0	2	2	....	1989-90	1991-92
Byers, Gord	Bos.	1	1	0	1	1	0	....	....	....	....	....	....	1949-50	1949-50
Byers, Jerry	Min., Atl., NYR	4	43	3	4	7	15	....	....	....	....	....	....	1972-73	1977-78
Byers, Lyndon	Bos., S.J.	10	279	28	43	71	1081	37	2	2	4	96	....	1983-84	1992-93
Byers, Mike	Tor., Phi., L.A., Buf.	4	166	42	34	76	39	4	0	1	1	0	....	1967-68	1971-72
Byram, Shawn	NYI, Chi.	2	5	0	0	0	14	....	....	....	....	....	....	1990-91	1991-92

C

• Caffery, Jack	Tor., Bos.	3	57	3	2	5	22	10	1	0	1	4	....	1954-55	1957-58
Caffery, Terry	Chi., Min.	2	14	0	0	0	0	1	0	0	0	0	....	1969-70	1970-71
• Cahan, Larry	Tor., NYR, Oak., L.A.	13	666	38	92	130	700	29	1	1	2	38	....	1954-55	1970-71
• Cahill, Chuck	Bos.	2	32	0	1	1	4	....	....	....	....	....	....	1925-26	1926-27
• Cain, Francis	Mtl.M., Tor.	2	61	4	0	4	35	....	....	....	....	....	....	1924-25	1925-26
• Cain, Herb	Mtl.M., Mtl.C., Bos.	13	570	206	194	400	178	67	16	13	29	13	2	1933-34	1945-46

Name	NHL Teams	NHL Seasons	Regular Schedule GP	G	A	TP	PIM	Playoffs GP	G	A	TP	PIM	NHL Cup Wins	First NHL Season	Last NHL Season
Cairns, Don	K.C., Col.	2	9	0	1	1	2	....	....	....	....	....	....	1975-76	1976-77
Calder, Eric	Wsh.	2	2	0	0	0	0	....	....	....	....	....	....	1981-82	1982-83
• Calladine, Norm	Bos.	3	63	19	29	48	8	....	....	....	....	....	....	1942-43	1944-45
Callander, Drew	Phi., Van.	4	39	6	2	8	7	....	....	....	....	....	....	1976-77	1979-80
Callander, John	Pit., T.B.	5	109	22	29	51	116	22	3	8	11	12	1	1987-88	1992-93
Callighen, Brett	Edm.	3	160	56	89	145	132	14	4	6	10	8	....	1979-80	1981-82
Callighen, Patsy	NYR	1	36	0	0	0	32	9	0	0	0	0	1	1927-28	1927-28
Camazzola, James	Chi.	2	3	0	0	0	0	....	....	....	....	....	....	1983-84	1986-87
Camazzola, Tony	Wsh.	1	3	0	0	0	4	....	....	....	....	....	....	1981-82	1981-82
Cameron, Al	Det., Wpg.	6	282	11	44	55	356	7	0	1	1	2	....	1975-76	1980-81
• Cameron, Billy	Mtl.C., NYA	2	39	0	0	0	2	6	0	0	0	0	....	1923-24	1925-26
Cameron, Craig	Det., St.L., Min., NYI	9	552	87	65	152	196	27	3	1	4	17	....	1966-67	1975-76
Cameron, Dave	Col., N.J.	3	168	25	28	53	238	....	....	....	....	....	....	1981-82	1983-84
• Cameron, Harry	Tor., Ott., Mtl.C.	6	128	88	51	139	195	20	10	7	17	39	2	1917-18	1922-23
• Cameron, Scotty	NYR	1	35	8	11	19	0	....	....	....	....	....	....	1942-43	1942-43
Campbell, Bryan	L.A., Chi.	5	260	35	71	106	74	22	3	4	7	2	....	1967-68	1971-72
Campbell, Colin	Pit., Col., Edm., Van., Det.	11	636	25	103	128	1292	45	4	10	14	181	....	1974-75	1984-85
• Campbell, Dave	Mtl.C.	1	2	0	0	0	0	....	....	....	....	....	....	1920-21	1920-21
Campbell, Don	Chi.	1	17	1	3	4	8	....	....	....	....	....	....	1943-44	1943-44
• Campbell, Earl	Ott., NYA	3	77	5	1	6	12	2	0	0	0	0	....	1923-24	1925-26
Campbell, Scott	Wpg., St.L.	3	80	4	21	25	243	....	....	....	....	....	....	1979-80	1981-82
Campbell, Wade	Wpg., Bos.	6	213	9	27	36	305	10	0	0	0	20	....	1982-83	1987-88
Campeau, Tod	Mtl.	3	42	5	9	14	16	1	0	0	0	0	....	1943-44	1948-49
Campedelli, Dom	Mtl.	1	2	0	0	0	0	....	....	....	....	....	....	1985-86	1985-86
Capuano, Dave	Pit., Van., T.B., S.J.	4	104	17	38	55	56	6	1	1	2	5	....	1989-90	1993-94
Capuano, Jack	Tor., Van., Bos.	3	6	0	0	0	0	....	....	....	....	....	....	1989-90	1991-92
Carbol, Leo	Chi.	1	6	0	1	1	4	....	....	....	....	....	....	1942-43	1942-43
Cardin, Claude	St.L.	1	1	0	0	0	0	....	....	....	....	....	....	1967-68	1967-68
Cardwell, Steve	Pit.	3	53	9	11	20	35	4	0	0	0	2	....	1970-71	1972-73
• Carey, George	Mtl., Que., Ham., Tor.	6	72	21	12	33	20	....	....	....	....	....	....	1917-18	1923-24
Carleton, Wayne	Tor., Bos., Cal.	7	278	55	73	128	172	18	2	4	6	14	1	1965-66	1971-72
Carlin, Brian	L.A.	1	5	1	0	1	0	....	....	....	....	....	....	1971-72	1971-72
Carlson, Jack	Min., St.L.	6	236	30	15	45	417	25	1	2	3	72	....	1978-79	1986-87
Carlson, Kent	Mtl., St.L., Wsh.	5	113	7	11	18	148	8	0	0	0	13	....	1983-84	1988-89
Carlson, Steve	L.A.	1	52	9	12	21	23	4	1	1	2	7	....	1979-80	1979-80
Carlsson, Anders	N.J.	3	104	7	26	33	34	3	1	0	1	2	....	1986-87	1988-89
Carlyle, Randy	Tor., Pit., Wpg.	17	1055	148	499	647	1400	69	9	24	33	120	....	1976-77	1992-93
Carnback, Patrik	Mtl., Ana.	4	154	24	38	62	122	....	....	....	....	....	....	1992-93	1995-96
• Caron, Alain	Oak., Mtl.	2	60	9	13	22	18	....	....	....	....	....	....	1967-68	1968-69
• Carpenter, Eddie	Que., Ham.	2	45	10	5	15	31	....	....	....	....	....	....	1919-20	1920-21
Carr, Al	Tor.	1	5	0	1	1	2	....	....	....	....	....	....	1943-44	1943-44
Carr, Gene	St.L., NYR, L.A., Pit., Atl.	8	465	79	136	215	365	35	5	8	13	66	....	1971-72	1978-79
Carr, Lorne	NYR, NYA, Tor.	13	580	204	222	426	132	53	10	9	19	13	2	1933-34	1945-46
Carriere, Larry	Buf., Atl., Van., L.A., Tor.	7	367	16	74	90	462	27	0	3	3	42	....	1972-73	1979-80
• Carrigan, Gene	NYR, Det., St.L.	3	37	2	1	3	13	4	0	0	0	0	....	1930-31	1934-35
Carroll, Billy	NYI, Edm., Det.	7	322	30	54	84	113	71	6	12	18	18	4	1980-81	1986-87
• Carroll, George	Mtl.M., Bos.	1	15	0	0	0	9	....	....	....	....	....	....	1924-25	1924-25
Carroll, Greg	Wsh., Det., Hfd.	2	131	20	34	54	44	....	....	....	....	....	....	1978-79	1979-80
Carruthers, Dwight	Det., Phi.	2	2	0	0	0	0	....	....	....	....	....	....	1965-66	1967-68
Carse, Bill	NYR, Chi.	4	124	28	43	71	38	13	3	2	5	0	....	1938-39	1941-42
Carse, Bob	Chi., Mtl.	5	167	32	55	87	52	10	0	2	2	2	....	1939-40	1947-48
• Carson, Bill	Tor., Bos.	4	159	54	24	78	156	11	3	0	3	14	1	1926-27	1929-30
• Carson, Frank	Mtl.M., NYA, Det.	7	248	42	48	90	166	31	0	2	2	9	1	1925-26	1933-34
• Carson, Gerry	Mtl.C., NYR, Mtl.M.	7	261	12	11	23	205	22	0	0	0	12	....	1928-29	1936-37
Carson, Jimmy	L.A., Edm., Det., Van., Hfd.	10	626	275	286	561	254	55	17	15	32	22	....	1986-87	1995-96
Carson, Lindsay	Phi., Hfd.	7	373	66	80	146	524	49	4	10	14	56	....	1981-82	1987-88
Carter, Billy	Mtl., Bos.	3	16	0	0	0	6	....	....	....	....	....	....	1957-58	1961-62
Carter, John	Bos., S.J.	8	244	40	50	90	201	31	7	5	12	51	....	1985-86	1992-93
Carter, Ron	Edm.	1	2	0	0	0	0	....	....	....	....	....	....	1979-80	1979-80
• Carveth, Joe	Det., Bos., Mtl.	11	504	150	189	339	81	69	21	16	37	28	2	1940-41	1950-51
Cashman, Wayne	Bos.	17	1027	277	516	793	1041	145	31	57	88	250	2	1964-65	1982-83
Cassidy, Bruce	Chi.	6	36	4	13	17	10	1	0	0	0	0	....	1983-84	1989-90
Cassidy, Tom	Pit.	1	26	3	4	7	15	....	....	....	....	....	....	1977-78	1977-78
Cassolato, Tony	Wsh.	3	23	1	6	7	4	....	....	....	....	....	....	1979-80	1981-82
Caufield, Jay	NYR, Min., Pit.	7	208	5	8	13	759	17	0	0	0	42	1	1986-87	1992-93
Cavallini, Gino	Cgy., St.L., Que.	9	593	114	159	273	507	74	14	19	33	66	....	1984-85	1992-93
Cavallini, Paul	Wsh., St.L., Dal	10	564	56	177	233	750	69	8	27	35	114	....	1986-87	1995-96
Ceresino, Ray	Tor.	1	12	1	1	2	2	....	....	....	....	....	....	1948-49	1948-49
Cernik, Frantisek	Det.	1	49	5	4	9	13	....	....	....	....	....	....	1984-85	1984-85
Chabot, John	Mtl., Pit., Det.	8	508	84	228	312	85	33	6	20	26	2	....	1983-84	1990-91
• Chad, John	Chi.	3	80	15	22	37	29	10	0	1	1	2	....	1939-40	1945-46
• Chalmers, Bill	NYR	1	1	0	0	0	0	....	....	....	....	....	....	1953-54	1953-54
Chalupa, Milan	Det.	1	14	0	5	5	6	....	....	....	....	....	....	1984-85	1984-85
• Chamberlain, Murph	Tor., Mtl., Bro., Bos.	12	510	100	175	275	769	66	14	17	31	96	2	1937-38	1948-49
Champagne, Andre	Tor.	1	2	0	0	0	0	....	....	....	....	....	....	1962-63	1962-63
Chapdelaine, Rene	L.A.	3	32	0	2	2	32	....	....	....	....	....	....	1990-91	1992-93
• Chapman, Art	Bos., NYA, Bro.	12	438	62	176	238	140	26	1	5	6	9	....	1930-31	1941-42
Chapman, Blair	Pit., St.L.	7	402	106	125	231	158	25	4	6	10	15	....	1976-77	1982-83
Chapman, Brian	Hfd.	1	3	0	0	0	29	....	....	....	....	....	....	1990-91	1990-91
Charbonneau, Jose	Mtl., Van.	4	71	9	13	22	67	11	1	0	1	8	....	1987-88	1994-95
Charbonneau, Stephane	Que.	1	2	0	0	0	0	....	....	....	....	....	....	1991-92	1991-92
Charlebois, Bob	Min.	1	7	1	0	1	0	....	....	....	....	....	....	1967-68	1967-68
Charlesworth, Todd	Pit., NYR	6	93	3	9	12	47	....	....	....	....	....	....	1983-84	1989-90
Charron, Guy	Mtl., Det., K.C., Wsh.	12	734	221	309	530	146	....	....	....	....	....	....	1969-70	1980-81
Chartier, Dave	Wpg.	1	1	0	0	0	0	....	....	....	....	....	....	1980-81	1980-81
Chartraw, Rick	Mtl., L.A., NYR, Edm.	10	420	28	64	92	399	75	7	9	16	80	5	1974-75	1983-84
Chasse, Denis	St.L., Wsh., Wpg., Ott.	4	132	11	14	25	292	7	1	7	8	23	....	1993-94	1996-97
Check, Lude	Det., Chi.	2	27	6	2	8	4	....	....	....	....	....	....	1943-44	1944-45
Chernoff, Mike	Min.	1	1	0	0	0	0	....	....	....	....	....	....	1968-69	1968-69
Chernomaz, Rich	Col., N.J., Cgy.	7	51	9	7	16	18	....	....	....	....	....	....	1981-82	1991-92
Cherry, Dick	Bos., Phi.	3	145	12	10	22	45	4	1	0	1	4	....	1956-57	1969-70
Cherry, Don	Bos.	1	....	....	....	....	....	1	0	0	0	0	....	1954-55	1954-55
Chervyakov, Denis	Bos.	1	2	0	0	0	2	....	....	....	....	....	....	1992-93	1992-93
• Chevrefils, Real	Bos., Det.	8	387	104	97	201	185	30	5	4	9	20	....	1951-52	1958-59
Chibirev, Igor	Hfd.	2	45	7	12	19	2	....	....	....	....	....	....	1993-94	1994-95
Chicoine, Dan	Cle., Min.	3	31	1	2	3	12	1	0	0	0	0	....	1977-78	1979-80
Chinnick, Rick	Min.	2	4	0	2	2	0	....	....	....	....	....	....	1973-74	1974-75
Chipperfield, Ron	Edm., Que.	2	83	22	24	46	34	....	....	....	....	....	....	1979-80	1980-81
Chisholm, Art	Bos.	1	3	0	0	0	0	....	....	....	....	....	....	1960-61	1960-61
Chisholm, Colin	Min.	1	1	0	0	0	0	....	....	....	....	....	....	1986-87	1986-87
• Chisholm, Lex	Tor.	2	54	10	8	18	19	3	1	0	1	0	....	1939-40	1940-41
Chorney, Marc	Pit., L.A.	4	210	8	27	35	209	7	0	1	1	2	....	1980-81	1983-84
• Chouinard, Gene	Ott.	1	8	0	0	0	0	....	....	....	....	....	....	1927-28	1927-28
Chouinard, Guy	Atl., Cgy., St.L.	10	578	205	370	575	120	46	9	28	37	12	....	1974-75	1983-84
Christian, Dave	Wpg., Wsh., Bos., St.L., Chi.	15	1009	340	433	773	284	102	32	25	57	27	....	1979-80	1993-94
Christie, Mike	Cal., Cle., Col., Van.	7	412	15	101	116	550	2	0	0	0	0	....	1974-75	1980-81
Christoff, Steve	Min., Cgy., L.A.	5	248	77	64	141	108	35	16	12	28	25	....	1979-80	1983-84
Chrystal, Bob	NYR	2	132	11	14	25	112	....	....	....	....	....	....	1953-54	1954-55
Chuck, Chuck	Mtl., St.L.	9	407	128	164	292	137	29	5	8	13	10	2	1970-71	1980-81
• Church, Jack	Tor., Bro., Bos.	5	130	4	19	23	154	25	1	1	2	18	....	1938-39	1945-46
Churla, Shane	Hfd., Cgy., Min., Dal., L.A., NYR	11	488	26	45	71	2301	78	5	7	12	282	....	1986-87	1996-97
Chychrun, Jeff	Phi., L.A., Pit., Edm.	8	262	3	22	25	744	19	0	2	2	65	....	1986-87	1993-94
Chynoweth, Dean	NYI, Bos.	9	241	4	18	22	667	6	0	0	0	26	....	1988-89	1997-98
Cichocki, Chris	Det., N.J.	4	68	11	12	23	27	....	....	....	....	....	....	1985-86	1988-89
• Ciesla, Hank	Chi., NYR	4	269	26	51	77	87	6	0	2	2	0	....	1955-56	1958-59
Cimellaro, Tony	Ott.	1	2	0	0	0	0	....	....	....	....	....	....	1992-93	1992-93
Cimetta, Robert	Bos., Tor.	4	103	16	16	32	66	1	0	0	0	15	....	1988-89	1991-92
Cirella, Joe	Col., N.J., Que., NYR, Fla., Ott.	15	828	64	211	275	1446	38	0	13	13	98	....	1981-82	1995-96
Cirone, Jason	Wpg.	1	3	0	0	0	2	....	....	....	....	....	....	1991-92	1991-92
Clackson, Kim	Pit., Que.	2	106	0	8	8	370	8	0	0	0	70	....	1979-80	1980-81
• Clancy, King	Ott., Tor.	16	592	137	144	281	906	61	9	8	17	92	3	1921-22	1936-37

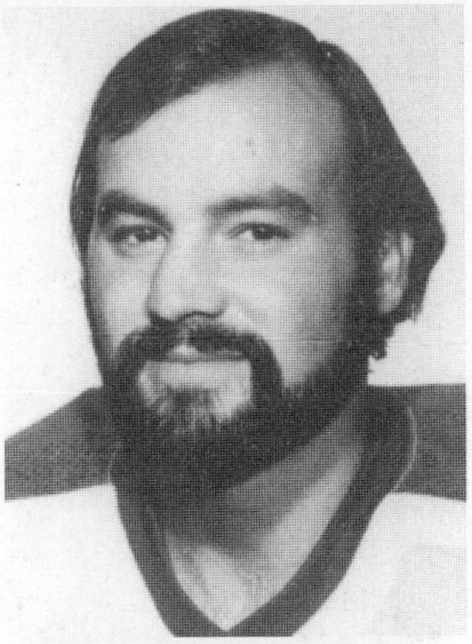
Rick Chartraw

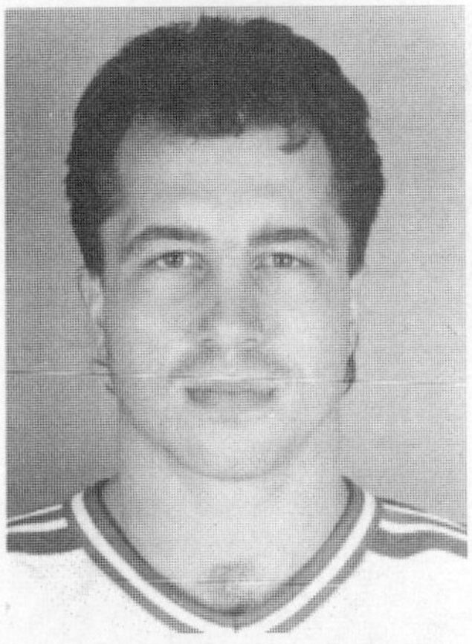
Shane Churla

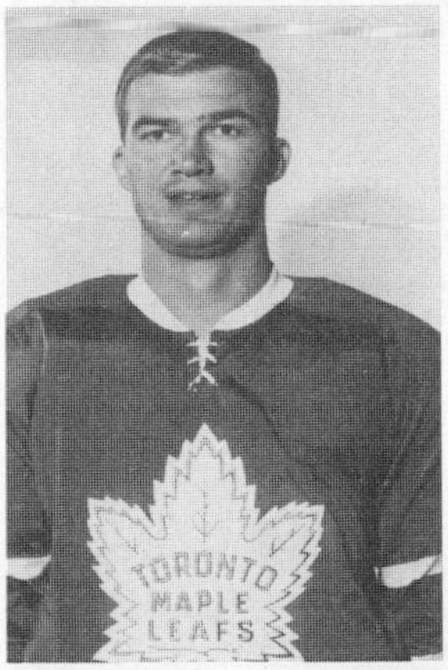

Brian Conacher

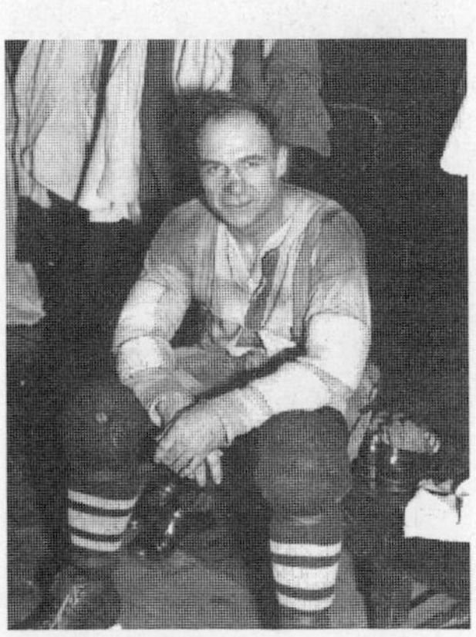
Lionel Conacher

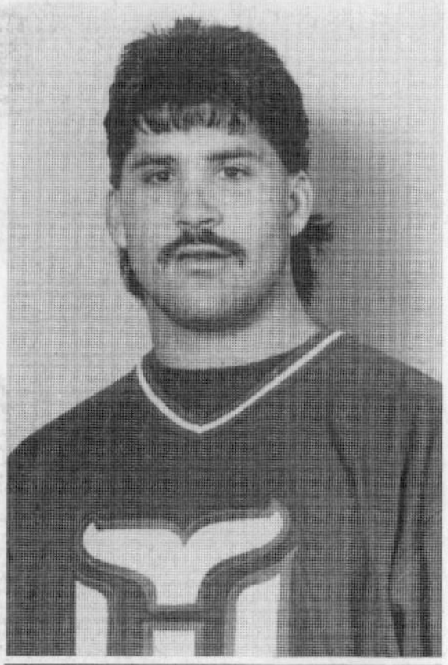

Yvon Corriveau

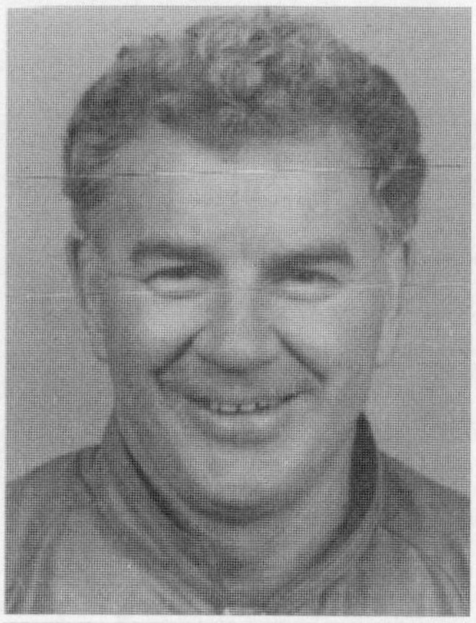

Terry Crisp

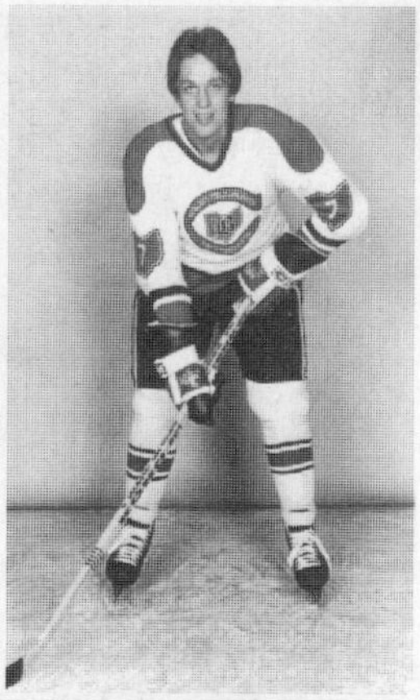

Mike Crombeen

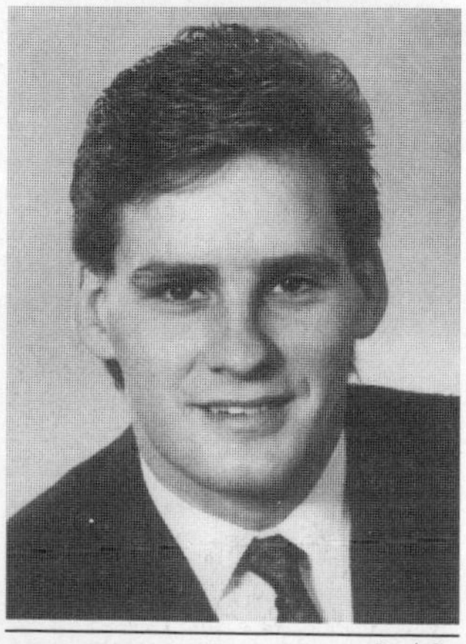

Paul Cyr

			Regular Schedule					Playoffs							
Name	NHL Teams	NHL Seasons	GP	G	A	TP	PIM	GP	G	A	TP	PIM	NHL Cup Wins	First NHL Season	Last NHL Season
Clancy, Terry	Oak., Tor.	4	93	6	6	12	39	....	....	....	....	....	....	1967-68	1972-73
• Clapper, Dit	Bos.	21	833	228	246	474	462	82	13	17	30	50	3	1927-28	1947-48
Clark, Dan	NYR	1	4	0	1	1	6	....	....	....	....	....	....	1978-79	1978-79
Clark, Dean	Edm.	1	1	0	0	0	0	....	....	....	....	....	....	1983-84	1983-84
Clark, Gordie	Bos.	2	8	0	1	1	0	1	0	0	0	0	....	1974-75	1975-76
• Clark, Nobby	Bos.	1	5	0	0	0	0	....	....	....	....	....	....	1927-28	1927-28
Clarke, Bobby	Phi.	15	1144	358	852	1210	1453	136	42	77	119	152	2	1969-70	1983-84
• Cleghorn, Odie	Mtl.C., Pit.	10	182	94	30	124	147	24	8	3	11	11	....	1918-19	1927-28
• Cleghorn, Sprague	Ott., Tor., Mtl.C., Bos.	10	262	85	47	132	534	39	7	8	15	66	2	1918-19	1927-28
Clement, Bill	Phi., Wsh., Atl., Cgy.	11	719	148	208	356	383	50	5	3	8	26	2	1971-72	1981-82
Cline, Bruce	NYR	1	30	2	3	5	10	....	....	....	....	....	....	1956-57	1956-57
Clippingdale, Steve	L.A., Wsh.	2	19	1	2	3	9	1	0	0	0	0	....	1976-77	1979-80
Cloutier, Real	Que., Buf.	6	317	146	198	344	119	25	7	5	12	20	....	1979-80	1984-85
Cloutier, Rejean	Det.	2	5	0	2	2	2	....	....	....	....	....	....	1979-80	1981-82
Cloutier, Roland	Det., Que.	3	34	8	9	17	2	....	....	....	....	....	....	1977-78	1979-80
• Clune, Wally	Mtl.	1	5	0	0	0	6	....	....	....	....	....	....	1955-56	1955-56
Coalter, Gary	Cal., K.C.	2	34	2	4	6	2	....	....	....	....	....	....	1973-74	1974-75
Coates, Steve	Det.	1	5	1	0	1	24	....	....	....	....	....	....	1976-77	1976-77
Cochrane, Glen	Phi., Van., Chi., Edm.	10	411	17	72	89	1556	18	1	1	2	31	....	1978-79	1988-89
Coflin, Hugh	Chi.	1	31	0	3	3	33	....	....	....	....	....	....	1950-51	1950-51
Colley, Tom	Min.	1	1	0	0	0	2	....	....	....	....	....	....	1974-75	1974-75
Collings, Norm	Mtl.C.	1	1	0	1	1	0	....	....	....	....	....	....	1934-35	1934-35
Collins, Bill	Min., Mtl., Det., St.L., NYR, Phi., Wsh.	11	768	157	154	311	415	18	3	5	8	12	....	1967-68	1977-78
Collins, Gary	Tor.	1	....	....	....	....	....	2	0	0	0	0	....	1958-59	1958-59
Collyard, Bob	St.L.	1	10	1	3	4	4	....	....	....	....	....	....	1973-74	1973-74
• Colman, Michael	S.J.	1	15	0	1	1	32	....	....	....	....	....	....	1991-92	1991-92
Colville, Mac	NYR	9	353	71	104	175	130	40	9	10	19	14	1	1935-36	1946-47
• Colville, Neil	NYR	12	464	99	166	265	213	46	7	19	26	32	1	1935-36	1948-49
Colwill, Les	NYR	1	69	7	6	13	16	....	....	....	....	....	....	1958-59	1958-59
Comeau, Rey	Mtl., Atl., Col.	9	564	98	141	239	175	9	2	1	3	8	....	1971-72	1979-80
Conacher, Brian	Tor., Det.	5	155	28	28	56	84	12	3	2	5	21	1	1961-62	1971-72
• Conacher, Charlie	Tor., Det., NYA	12	459	225	173	398	523	49	17	18	35	49	1	1929-30	1940-41
Conacher, Jim	Det., Chi., NYR	8	328	85	117	202	91	19	5	2	7	4	....	1945-46	1952-53
• Conacher, Lionel	Pit., NYA, Mtl.M., Chi.	12	498	80	105	185	882	35	2	2	4	34	2	1925-26	1936-37
Conacher, Pat	NYR, Edm., N.J., L.A., Cgy., NYI	14	521	63	76	139	235	66	11	10	21	40	1	1979-80	1995-96
Conacher, Pete	Chi., NYR, Tor.	6	229	47	39	86	57	7	0	0	0	0	....	1951-52	1957-58
• Conacher, Roy	Bos., Det., Chi.	11	490	226	200	426	90	42	15	15	30	14	2	1938-39	1951-52
• Conn, Hugh	NYA	2	96	9	28	37	22	....	....	....	....	....	....	1933-34	1934-35
Conn, Rob	Chi., Buf.	2	30	2	5	7	20	....	....	....	....	....	....	1991-92	1995-96
• Connelly, Bert	NYR, Chi.	3	87	13	15	28	37	14	1	0	1	0	1	1934-35	1937-38
Connelly, Wayne	Mtl., Bos., Min., Det., St.L., Van.	10	543	133	174	307	156	24	11	7	18	4	....	1960-61	1971-72
Connor, Cam	Mtl., Edm., NYR	5	89	9	22	31	256	20	5	0	5	6	1	1978-79	1982-83
• Connor, Harry	Bos., NYA, Ott.	4	134	16	5	21	149	10	0	0	0	2	....	1927-28	1930-31
• Connors, Bobby	NYA, Det.	3	78	17	10	27	110	2	0	0	0	10	....	1926-27	1929-30
Conroy, Al	Phi.	3	114	9	14	23	156	....	....	....	....	....	....	1991-92	1993-94
Contini, Joe	Col., Min.	3	68	17	21	38	34	2	0	0	0	0	....	1977-78	1980-81
• Convey, Eddie	NYA	3	36	1	1	2	33	....	....	....	....	....	....	1930-31	1932-33
• Cook, Bill	NYR	11	474	229	138	367	386	46	13	11	24	68	2	1926-27	1936-37
• Cook, Bob	Van., Det., NYI, Min.	4	72	13	9	22	22	....	....	....	....	....	....	1970-71	1974-75
• Cook, Bud	Bos., Ott., St.L.	3	50	5	4	9	22	....	....	....	....	....	....	1931-32	1934-35
• Cook, Bun	NYR, Bos.	11	473	158	144	302	444	46	15	3	18	50	2	1926-27	1936-37
• Cook, Lloyd	Bos.	1	4	1	0	1	0	....	....	....	....	....	....	1924-25	1924-25
• Cook, Tom	Chi., Mtl.M.	9	349	77	98	175	184	24	2	4	6	19	1	1929-30	1937-38
• Cooper, Carson	Bos., Mtl.C., Det.	8	294	110	57	167	111	7	0	0	0	2	....	1924-25	1931-32
Cooper, Ed	Col.	2	49	8	7	15	46	....	....	....	....	....	....	1980-81	1981-82
• Cooper, Hal	NYR	1	8	0	0	0	2	....	....	....	....	....	....	1944-45	1944-45
• Cooper, Joe	NYR, Chi.	11	420	30	66	96	442	35	3	5	8	58	....	1935-36	1946-47
Copp, Bob	Tor.	2	40	3	9	12	26	....	....	....	....	....	....	1942-43	1950-51
• Corbeau, Bert	Mtl.C., Ham., Tor.	10	259	64	44	108	639	14	2	2	4	31	....	1917-18	1926-27
Corbett, Michael	L.A.	1	....	....	....	....	....	2	0	1	1	2	....	1967-68	1967-68
Corcoran, Norm	Bos., Det., Chi.	4	29	1	3	4	21	4	0	0	0	6	....	1949-50	1955-56
• Cormier, Roger	Mtl.C.	1	1	0	0	0	0	....	....	....	....	....	....	1925-26	1925-26
Cornforth, Mark	Bos.	1	6	0	0	0	4	....	....	....	....	....	....	1995-96	1995-96
Corrigan, Chuck	Tor., NYA	2	19	2	2	4	2	....	....	....	....	....	....	1937-38	1940-41
Corrigan, Mike	L.A., Van., Pit.	10	594	152	195	347	698	17	2	3	5	20	....	1967-68	1977-78
• Corriveau, Andre	Mtl.	1	3	0	1	1	0	....	....	....	....	....	....	1953-54	1953-54
Corriveau, Yvon	Wsh., Hfd., S.J.	9	280	48	40	88	310	29	5	7	12	50	....	1985-86	1993-94
Cory, Ross	Wpg.	2	51	2	10	12	41	....	....	....	....	....	....	1979-80	1980-81
Cossete, Jacques	Pit.	3	64	8	6	14	29	3	0	1	1	4	....	1975-76	1978-79
Costello, Les	Tor.	3	15	2	3	5	11	6	2	2	4	2	1	1947-48	1949-50
Costello, Murray	Chi., Bos., Det.	4	162	13	19	32	54	5	0	0	0	2	....	1953-54	1956-57
Costello, Rich	Tor.	2	12	2	2	4	2	....	....	....	....	....	....	1983-84	1985-86
• Cotch, Charlie	Ham., Tor.	1	11	1	0	1	0	....	....	....	....	....	....	1924-25	1924-25
Cote, Alain	Que.	10	696	103	190	293	383	67	9	15	24	44	....	1979-80	1988-89
Cote, Alain G.	Bos., Wsh., Mtl., T.B., Que.	9	119	2	18	20	124	11	0	2	2	26	....	1985-86	1993-94
Cote, Ray	Edm.	3	15	0	0	0	4	14	3	2	5	0	....	1982-83	1984-85
• Cotton, Baldy	Pit., Tor., NYA	12	503	101	103	204	419	43	4	9	13	46	1	1925-26	1936-37
• Coughlin, Jack	Tor., Que., Mtl.C., Ham.	3	18	2	0	2	3	....	....	....	....	....	....	1917-18	1920-21
Coulis, Tim	Wsh., Min.	4	47	4	5	9	138	3	1	0	1	2	....	1979-80	1985-86
Coulson, D'arcy	Phi.	1	28	0	0	0	103	....	....	....	....	....	....	1930-31	1930-31
• Coulter, Art	Chi., NYR	11	465	30	82	112	543	49	4	5	9	61	2	1931-32	1941-42
Coulter, Neal	NYI	3	26	5	5	10	11	....	....	....	....	....	....	1985-86	1987-88
Cournoyer, Yvan	Mtl.	16	968	428	435	863	255	147	64	63	127	47	9	1963-64	1978-79
Courteau, Yves	Cgy., Hfd.	3	22	2	5	7	4	1	0	0	0	0	....	1984-85	1986-87
Courtenay, Ed	S.J.	2	44	7	13	20	10	....	....	....	....	....	....	1991-92	1992-93
• Coutu, Billy	Mtl.C., Ham., Bos.	10	246	33	21	54	443	32	2	2	4	40	....	1917-18	1926-27
• Couture, Gerry	Det., Mtl., Chi.	10	385	86	70	156	89	45	9	7	16	4	1	1944-45	1953-54
• Couture, Rosie	Chi., Mtl.C.	8	309	48	56	104	184	23	1	5	6	15	1	1928-29	1935-36
Couturier, Sylvain	L.A.	3	33	4	5	9	4	....	....	....	....	....	....	1988-89	1991-92
Cowick, Bruce	Phi., Wsh., St.L.	3	70	5	6	11	43	8	0	0	0	9	1	1973-74	1975-76
Cowie, Rob	L.A.	2	78	7	12	19	52	....	....	....	....	....	....	1994-95	1995-96
• Cowley, Bill	St.L., Bos.	13	549	195	353	548	143	64	12	34	46	22	2	1934-35	1946-47
• Cox, Danny	Tor., Ott., Det., NYR	8	319	47	49	96	128	10	0	1	1	6	....	1926-27	1933-34
Coxe, Craig	Van., Cgy., St.L., S.J.	8	235	14	31	45	713	5	1	0	1	18	....	1984-85	1991-92
Craighead, John	Tor.	1	5	0	0	0	10	....	....	....	....	....	....	1996-97	1996-97
Crashley, Bart	Det., K.C., L.A.	6	140	7	36	43	50	....	....	....	....	....	....	1965-66	1975-76
Crawford, Bob	St.L., Hfd., NYR, Wsh.	7	246	71	71	142	72	11	0	1	1	8	....	1979-80	1986-87
Crawford, Bobby	Col., Det.	2	16	1	3	4	6	....	....	....	....	....	....	1980-81	1982-83
• Crawford, Jack	Bos.	13	548	38	140	178	202	66	4	13	17	36	2	1937-38	1949-50
Crawford, Lou	Bos.	2	26	2	1	3	29	....	....	....	....	....	....	1989-90	1991-92
Crawford, Marc	Van.	6	176	19	31	50	229	20	1	2	3	44	....	1981-82	1986-87
• Crawford, Rusty	Ott., Tor.	2	39	10	8	18	118	2	2	1	3	9	1	1917-18	1918-19
Creighton, Adam	Buf., Chi., NYI, T.B., St.L.	14	708	187	216	403	1077	61	11	14	25	137	....	1983-84	1996-97
Creighton, Dave	Bos., Tor., Chi., NYR	12	616	140	174	314	223	51	11	13	24	20	....	1948-49	1959-60
• Creighton, Jimmy	Det.	1	11	1	0	1	2	....	....	....	....	....	....	1930-31	1930-31
Cressman, Dave	Min.	2	85	6	8	14	37	....	....	....	....	....	....	1974-75	1975-76
Cressman, Glen	Mtl.	1	4	0	0	0	2	....	....	....	....	....	....	1956-57	1956-57
Crisp, Terry	Bos., St.L., NYI, Phi.	11	536	67	134	201	135	110	15	28	43	40	2	1965-66	1976-77
Cristofoli, Ed	Mtl.	1	9	0	1	1	4	....	....	....	....	....	....	1989-90	1989-90
• Croghen, Maurice	Mtl.M.	1	16	0	0	0	4	....	....	....	....	....	....	1937-38	1937-38
Crombeen, Mike	Cle., St.L., Hfd.	8	475	55	68	123	218	27	6	2	8	32	....	1977-78	1984-85
Cronin, Shawn	Wsh., Wpg., Phi., S.J.	7	292	3	18	21	877	32	1	0	1	38	....	1988-89	1994-95
• Crossett, Stan	Phi.	1	21	0	0	0	10	....	....	....	....	....	....	1930-31	1930-31
Crossman, Doug	Chi., Phi., L.A., NYI, Hfd., Det., T.B., St.L.	14	914	105	359	464	534	97	12	39	51	105	....	1980-81	1993-94
Croteau, Gary	L.A., Det., Cal., K.C., Col.	12	684	144	175	319	143	11	3	2	5	8	....	1968-69	1979-80
Crowder, Bruce	Bos., Pit.	4	243	47	51	98	156	31	8	4	12	41	....	1981-82	1984-85
Crowder, Keith	Bos., L.A.	10	662	223	271	494	1344	85	14	22	36	218	....	1980-81	1989-90
Crowder, Troy	N.J., Det., L.A., Van.	7	150	9	7	16	433	4	0	0	0	22	....	1987-88	1996-97
Crozier, Joe	Tor.	1	5	0	3	3	2	....	....	....	....	....	....	1959-60	1959-60

Name	NHL Teams	NHL Seasons	Regular Schedule GP	G	A	TP	PIM	Playoffs GP	G	A	TP	PIM	NHL Cup Wins	First NHL Season	Last NHL Season
• Crutchfield, Nels	Mtl.C.	1	41	5	5	10	20	2	0	1	1	22	....	1934-35	1934-35
Culhane, Jim	Hfd.	1	6	0	1	1	4	....	....	....	....	....	....	1989-90	1989-90
Cullen, Barry	Tor., Det.	5	219	32	52	84	111	6	0	0	0	2	....	1955-56	1959-60
Cullen, Brian	Tor., NYR	7	326	56	100	156	92	19	3	0	3	2	....	1954-55	1960-61
Cullen, Ray	NYR, Det., Min., Van.	6	313	92	123	215	120	20	3	10	13	2	....	1965-66	1970-71
Cummins, Barry	Cal.	1	36	1	2	3	39	....	....	....	....	....	....	1973-74	1973-74
Cunningham, Bob	NYR	2	4	0	1	1	0	....	....	....	....	....	....	1960-61	1961-62
Cunningham, Jim	Phi.	1	1	0	0	0	4	....	....	....	....	....	....	1977-78	1977-78
Cunningham, Les	NYA, Chi.	2	60	7	19	26	21	1	0	0	0	0	....	1936-37	1939-40
Cupolo, Bill	Bos.	1	47	11	13	24	10	7	1	2	3	0	....	1944-45	1944-45
Curran, Brian	Bos., NYI, Tor., Buf., Wsh.	10	381	7	33	40	1461	24	0	1	1	122	....	1983-84	1993-94
Currie, Dan	Edm., L.A.	4	22	2	1	3	4	....	....	....	....	....	....	1990-91	1993-94
Currie, Glen	Wsh., L.A.	8	326	39	79	118	100	12	1	3	4	4	....	1979-80	1987-88
Currie, Hugh	Mtl.	1	1	0	0	0	0	....	....	....	....	....	....	1950-51	1950-51
Currie, Tony	St.L., Van., Hfd.	8	290	92	119	211	83	16	4	12	16	14	....	1977-78	1984-85
Curry, Floyd	Mtl.	11	601	105	99	204	147	91	23	17	40	38	4	1947-48	1957-58
Curtale, Tony	Cgy.	1	2	0	0	0	0	....	....	....	....	....	....	1980-81	1980-81
Curtis, Paul	Mtl., L.A., St.L.	4	185	3	34	37	161	5	0	0	0	2	....	1969-70	1972-73
Cushenan, Ian	Chi., Mtl., NYR, Det.	5	129	3	11	14	134	....	....	....	....	....	1	1956-57	1963-64
Cusson, Jean	Oak.	1	2	0	0	0	0	....	....	....	....	....	....	1967-68	1967-68
Cyr, Denis	Cgy., Chi., St.L.	6	193	41	43	84	36	4	0	0	0	0	....	1980-81	1985-86
Cyr, Paul	Buf., NYR, Hfd.	10	470	101	140	241	623	24	4	6	10	31	....	1982-83	1991-92

D

Name	NHL Teams	NHL Seasons	Regular Schedule GP	G	A	TP	PIM	Playoffs GP	G	A	TP	PIM	NHL Cup Wins	First NHL Season	Last NHL Season
Dahlin, Kjell	Mtl.	3	166	57	59	116	10	35	6	11	17	6	1	1985-86	1987-88
Dahlquist, Chris	Pit., Min., Cgy., Ott.	11	532	19	71	90	488	39	4	7	11	30	....	1985-86	1995-96
Dahlstrom, Cully	Chi.	8	342	88	118	206	58	29	6	8	14	4	1	1937-38	1944-45
Daigle, Alain	Chi.	6	389	56	50	106	122	17	0	1	1	0	....	1974-75	1979-80
Dailey, Bob	Van., Phi.	9	561	94	231	325	814	63	12	34	46	105	....	1973-74	1981-82
• Daley, Frank	Det.	1	5	0	0	0	0	2	0	0	0	0	....	1928-29	1928-29
Daley, Pat	Wpg.	2	12	1	0	1	13	....	....	....	....	....	....	1979-80	1980-81
Dalgarno, Brad	NYI	10	321	49	71	120	332	27	2	4	6	37	....	1985-86	1995-96
Dallman, Marty	Tor.	2	6	0	1	1	0	....	....	....	....	....	....	1987-88	1988-89
Dallman, Rod	NYI, Phi.	4	6	1	0	1	26	1	0	1	1	0	....	1987-88	1991-92
• Dame, Bunny	Mtl.	1	34	2	5	7	4	....	....	....	....	....	....	1941-42	1941-42
Damore, Hank	NYR	1	4	1	0	1	2	....	....	....	....	....	....	1943-44	1943-44
Daniels, Kimbi	Phi.	2	27	1	2	3	4	....	....	....	....	....	....	1990-91	1991-92
Daoust, Dan	Mtl., Tor.	8	522	87	167	254	544	32	7	5	12	83	....	1982-83	1989-90
Dark, Michael	St.L.	2	43	5	6	11	14	....	....	....	....	....	....	1986-87	1987-88
• Darragh, Harold	Pit., Phi., Bos., Tor.	8	308	68	49	117	50	16	1	3	4	4	1	1925-26	1932-33
• Darragh, Jack	Ott.	6	121	67	45	112	113	23	15	2	17	17	3	1917-18	1923-24
David, Richard	Que.	3	31	4	4	8	10	1	0	0	0	0	....	1979-80	1982-83
• Davidson, Bob	Tor.	12	491	94	160	254	398	82	5	17	22	79	2	1934-35	1945-46
• Davidson, Gord	NYR	2	51	3	6	9	8	....	....	....	....	....	....	1942-43	1943-44
• Davie, Bob	Bos.	3	41	0	1	1	25	....	....	....	....	....	....	1933-34	1935-36
Davies, Buck	NYR	1	....	....	....	....	....	1	0	0	0	0	....	1947-48	1947-48
• Davis, Bob	Det.	1	3	0	0	0	0	....	....	....	....	....	....	1932-33	1932-33
Davis, Kim	Pit., Tor.	4	36	5	7	12	51	4	0	0	0	0	....	1977-78	1980-81
Davis, Lorne	Mtl., Chi., Det., Bos.	6	95	8	12	20	20	18	3	1	4	10	1	1951-52	1959-60
Davis, Mal	Det., Buf.	6	100	31	22	53	34	7	1	0	1	0	....	1978-79	1985-86
Davison, Murray	Bos.	1	1	0	0	0	0	....	....	....	....	....	....	1965-66	1965-66
Davydov, Evgeny	Wpg., Fla., Ott.	4	155	40	39	79	120	11	2	2	4	2	....	1991-92	1994-95
Dawes, Bobby	Tor., Mtl.	4	32	2	7	9	6	10	0	0	0	2	1	1946-47	1950-51
• Day, Hap	Tor., NYA	14	581	86	116	202	601	53	4	7	11	56	1	1924-25	1937-38
Day, Joe	Hfd., NYI	3	72	1	10	11	87	....	....	....	....	....	....	1991-92	1993-94
Dea, Billy	NYR, Det., Chi., Pit.	8	397	67	54	121	44	11	2	1	3	6	....	1953-54	1970-71
• Deacon, Don	Det.	3	30	6	4	10	6	2	2	1	3	0	....	1936-37	1939-40
Deadmarsh, Butch	Buf., Atl., K.C.	5	137	12	5	17	155	4	0	0	0	17	....	1970-71	1974-75
Dean, Barry	Col., Phi.	3	165	25	56	81	146	....	....	....	....	....	....	1976-77	1978-79
Debenedet, Nelson	Det., Pit.	2	46	10	4	14	13	....	....	....	....	....	....	1973-74	1974-75
DeBlois, Lucien	NYR, Col., Wpg., Mtl., Que., Tor.	15	993	249	276	525	814	52	7	6	13	38	1	1977-78	1991-92
Debol, David	Hfd.	2	92	26	26	52	4	3	0	0	0	0	....	1979-80	1980-81
Defazio, Dean	Pit.	1	22	0	2	2	28	....	....	....	....	....	....	1983-84	1983-84
DeGray, Dale	Cgy., Tor., L.A., Buf.	5	153	18	47	65	195	13	1	3	4	28	....	1985-86	1989-90
• Delmonte, Armand	Bos.	1	1	0	0	0	0	....	....	....	....	....	....	1945-46	1945-46
Delorme, Gilbert	Mtl., St.L., Que., Det., Pit.	9	541	31	92	123	520	56	1	9	10	56	....	1981-82	1989-90
Delorme, Ron	Col., Van.	9	524	83	83	166	667	25	1	2	3	59	....	1976-77	1984-85
Delory, Val	NYR	1	1	0	0	0	0	....	....	....	....	....	....	1948-49	1948-49
Delparte, Guy	Col.	1	48	1	8	9	18	....	....	....	....	....	....	1976-77	1976-77
Delvecchio, Alex	Det.	24	1549	456	825	1281	383	121	35	69	104	29	3	1950-51	1973-74
DeMarco, Ab Jr.	NYR, St.L., Pit., Van., L.A., Bos.	9	344	44	80	124	75	25	1	2	3	17	....	1969-70	1978-79
• DeMarco, Ab Sr.	Chi., Tor., Bos., NYR	7	209	72	93	165	53	11	3	0	3	2	....	1938-39	1946-47
• Demers, Tony	Mtl.C., Mtl., NYR	6	83	20	22	42	23	2	0	0	0	0	....	1937-38	1943-44
Denis, Jean-Paul	NYR	2	10	0	2	2	2	....	....	....	....	....	....	1946-47	1949-50
Denis, Lulu	Mtl.	2	3	0	1	1	0	....	....	....	....	....	....	1949-50	1950-51
• Denneny, Corb	Tor., Ham., Chi.	9	176	103	41	144	148	16	7	3	10	9	2	1917-18	1927-28
• Denneny, Cy	Ott., Bos.	12	326	246	85	331	290	43	21	8	29	51	5	1917-18	1928-29
Dennis, Norm	St.L.	4	12	3	0	3	11	5	0	0	0	2	....	1968-69	1971-72
• Denoird, Gerry	Tor.	1	15	0	0	0	0	....	....	....	....	....	....	1922-23	1922-23
DePalma, Larry	Min., S.J., Pit.	7	148	21	20	41	408	3	0	0	0	6	....	1985-86	1993-94
Derlago, Bill	Van., Tor., Bos., Wpg., Que.	9	555	189	227	416	247	13	5	0	5	8	....	1978-79	1986-87
• Desaulniers, Gerard	Mtl.	3	8	0	2	2	4	....	....	....	....	....	....	1950-51	1953-54
• Desilets, Joffre	Mtl.C., Chi.	5	192	37	45	82	57	7	1	0	1	7	....	1935-36	1939-40
Desjardins, Martin	Mtl.	1	8	0	2	2	2	....	....	....	....	....	....	1989-90	1989-90
• Desjardins, Vic	Chi., NYR	2	87	6	15	21	27	16	0	0	0	0	....	1930-31	1931-32
Deslauriers, Jacques	Mtl.	1	2	0	0	0	0	....	....	....	....	....	....	1955-56	1955-56
Devine, Kevin	NYI	1	2	0	1	1	8	....	....	....	....	....	....	1982-83	1982-83
• Dewar, Tom	NYR	1	9	0	2	2	4	....	....	....	....	....	....	1943-44	1943-44
Dewsbury, Al	Det., Chi.	9	347	30	78	108	365	14	1	5	6	16	1	1946-47	1955-56
Deziel, Michel	Buf.	1	....	....	....	....	....	1	0	0	0	0	....	1974-75	1974-75
Dheere, Marcel	Mtl.	1	11	1	2	3	2	5	0	0	0	6	....	1942-43	1942-43
Di Pietro, Paul	Mtl., Tor., L.A.	6	192	31	49	80	96	31	11	10	21	10	1	1991-92	1996-97
Diachuk, Edward	Det.	1	12	0	0	0	19	....	....	....	....	....	....	1960-61	1960-61
Dick, Harry	Chi.	1	12	0	1	1	12	....	....	....	....	....	....	1946-47	1946-47
Dickens, Ernie	Tor., Chi.	6	278	12	44	56	98	13	0	0	0	4	1	1941-42	1950-51
Dickenson, Herb	NYR	2	48	18	17	35	10	....	....	....	....	....	....	1951-52	1952-53
Dietrich, Don	Chi., N.J.	2	28	0	7	7	10	....	....	....	....	....	....	1983-84	1985-86
• Dill, Bob	NYR	2	76	15	15	30	135	....	....	....	....	....	....	1943-44	1944-45
• Dillabough, Bob	Det., Bos., Pit., Oak.	9	283	32	54	86	76	17	3	0	3	0	....	1961-62	1969-70
• Dillon, Cecil	NYR, Det.	10	453	167	131	298	105	43	14	9	23	14	1	1930-31	1939-40
Dillon, Gary	Col.	1	13	1	1	2	29	....	....	....	....	....	....	1980-81	1980-81
Dillon, Wayne	NYR, Wpg.	4	229	43	66	109	60	3	0	1	1	0	....	1975-76	1979-80
Dineen, Bill	Det., Chi.	5	323	51	44	95	122	37	1	1	2	18	2	1953-54	1957-58
Dineen, Gary	Min.	1	4	0	1	1	0	....	....	....	....	....	....	1968-69	1968-69
Dineen, Gord	NYI, Min., Pit., Ott.	13	528	16	90	106	693	40	1	7	8	68	....	1982-83	1994-95
Dineen, Peter	L.A., Det.	2	13	0	2	2	13	....	....	....	....	....	....	1986-87	1989-90
• Dinsmore, Chuck	Mtl.M.	4	100	6	2	8	50	12	1	0	1	6	1	1924-25	1929-30
Dionne, Marcel	Det., L.A., NYR	18	1348	731	1040	1771	600	49	21	24	45	17	....	1971-72	1988-89
Dirk, Robert	St.L., Van., Chi., Ana., Mtl.	9	402	13	29	42	786	39	0	1	1	56	....	1987-88	1995-96
Djoos, Per	Det., NYR	3	82	2	31	33	58	....	....	....	....	....	....	1990-91	1992-93
Doak, Gary	Det., Bos., Van., NYR	16	789	23	107	130	908	78	2	4	6	121	1	1965-66	1980-81
Dobbin, Brian	Phi., Bos.	5	63	7	8	15	61	2	0	0	0	17	....	1986-87	1991-92
Dobson, Jim	Min., Col., Que.	4	12	0	0	0	6	....	....	....	....	....	....	1979-80	1983-84
• Doherty, Fred	Mtl.C.	1	2	0	0	0	0	....	....	....	....	....	....	1918-19	1918-19
Donaldson, Gary	Chi.	1	1	0	0	0	0	....	....	....	....	....	....	1973-74	1973-74
Donatelli, Clark	Min., Bos.	2	35	3	4	7	39	2	0	0	0	0	....	1989-90	1991-92
• Donnelly, Babe	Mtl.M.	1	34	0	1	1	14	2	0	0	0	0	....	1926-27	1926-27
Donnelly, Dave	Bos., Chi., Edm.	5	137	15	24	39	150	5	0	0	0	0	....	1983-84	1987-88
Donnelly, Gord	Que., Wpg., Buf., Dal.	12	554	28	41	69	2069	26	0	2	2	61	....	1983-84	1994-95

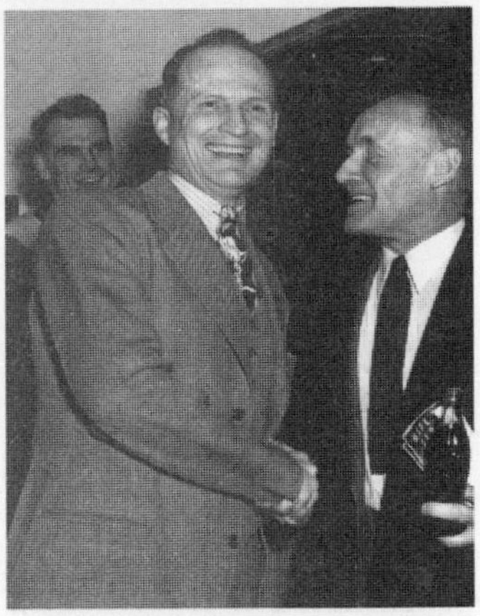

Hap Day

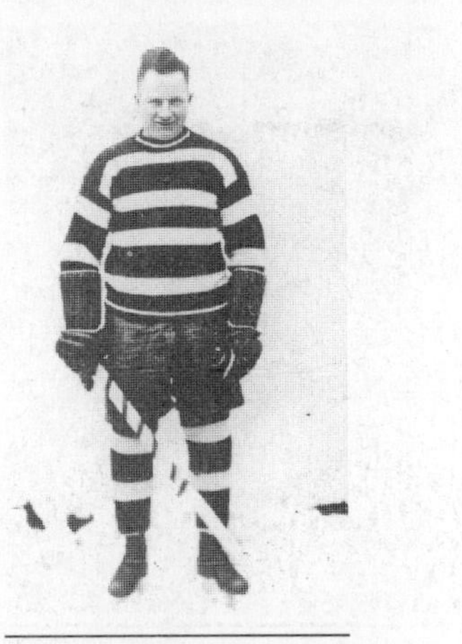

Cy Denneny

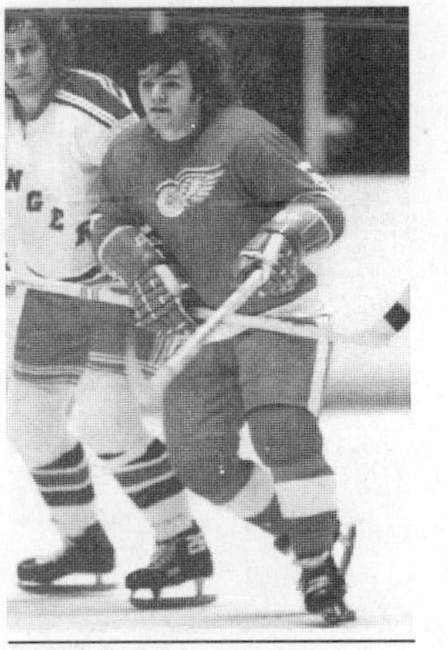

Marcel Dionne

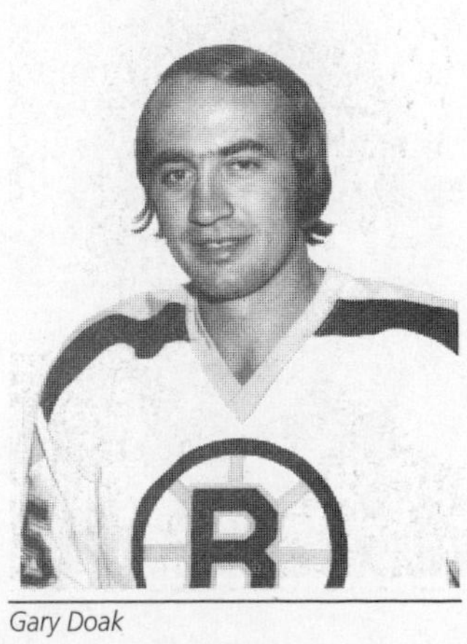

Gary Doak

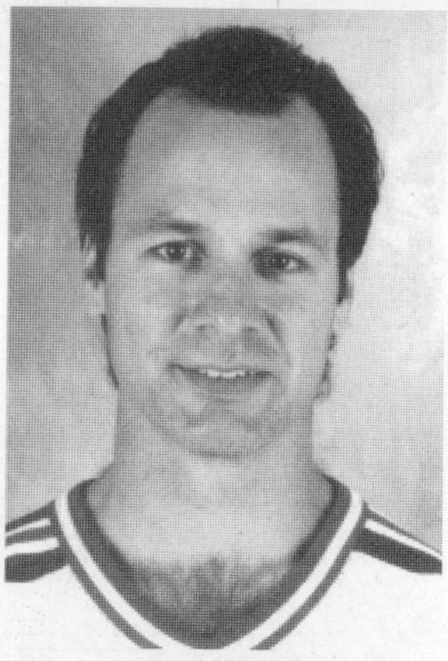

Bruce Driver

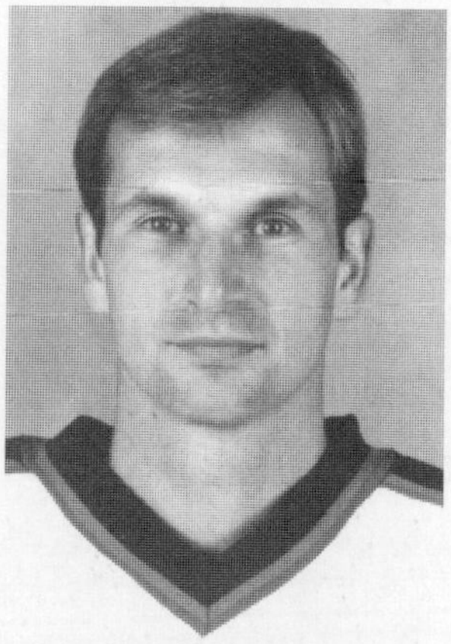

Donald Dufresne

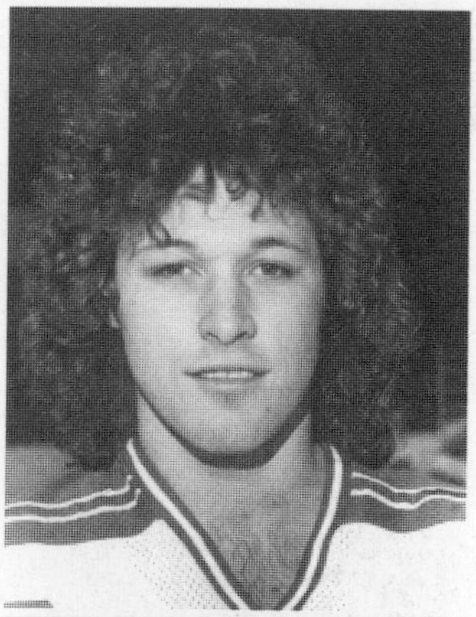

Ron Duguay

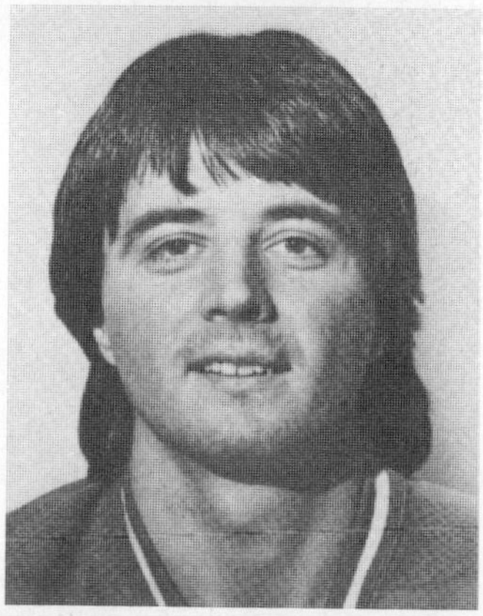

Norm Dupont

Name	NHL Teams	NHL Seasons	Regular Schedule GP	G	A	TP	PIM	Playoffs GP	G	A	TP	PIM	NHL Cup Wins	First NHL Season	Last NHL Season
Donnelly, Mike	NYR, Buf., L.A., Dal., NYI	11	465	114	121	235	255	47	12	12	24	30	....	1986-87	1996-97
• Doran, John	NYA, Det., Mtl.	5	98	5	10	15	110	3	0	0	0	0	....	1933-34	1939-40
Doran, Lloyd	Det.	1	24	3	2	5	10	....	....	....	....	....	....	1946-47	1946-47
• Doraty, Ken	Chi., Tor., Det.	5	103	15	26	41	24	15	7	2	9	2	....	1926-27	1937-38
Dore, Andre	NYR, St.L., Que.	7	257	14	81	95	261	23	1	2	3	32	....	1978-79	1984-85
Dore, Daniel	Que.	2	17	2	3	5	59	....	....	....	....	....	....	1989-90	1990-91
Dorey, Jim	Tor., NYR	4	232	25	74	99	553	11	0	2	2	40	....	1968-69	1971-72
Dorion, Dan	N.J.	2	4	1	1	2	2	....	....	....	....	....	....	1985-86	1987-88
Dornhoefer, Gary	Bos., Phi.	14	787	214	328	542	1291	80	17	19	36	203	2	1963-64	1977-78
Dorohoy, Eddie	Mtl.	1	16	0	0	0	6	....	....	....	....	....	....	1948-49	1948-49
Douglas, Jordy	Hfd., Min., Wpg.	6	268	76	62	138	160	6	0	0	0	4	....	1979-80	1984-85
Douglas, Kent	Tor., Oak., Det.	7	428	33	115	148	631	19	1	3	4	33	3	1962-63	1968-69
Douglas, Les	Det.	4	52	6	12	18	8	10	3	2	5	2	1	1940-41	1946-47
• Downie, Dave	Tor.	1	11	0	1	1	2	....	....	....	....	....	....	1932-33	1932-33
Doyon, Mario	Chi., Que.	3	28	3	4	7	16	....	....	....	....	....	....	1988-89	1990-91
• Draper, Bruce	Tor.	1	1	0	0	0	0	....	....	....	....	....	....	1962-63	1962-63
• Drillon, Gordie	Tor., Mtl.	7	311	155	139	294	56	50	26	15	41	10	1	1936-37	1942-43
Driscoll, Pete	Edm.	2	60	3	8	11	97	3	0	0	0	0	....	1979-80	1980-81
Driver, Bruce	N.J., NYR	15	922	96	390	486	670	108	10	40	50	64	1	1983-84	1997-98
Drolet, Rene	Phi., Det.	2	2	0	0	0	0	....	....	....	....	....	....	1971-72	1974-75
Droppa, Ivan	Chi.	2	19	0	1	1	14	....	....	....	....	....	....	1993-94	1995-96
• Drouillard, Clarence	Det.	1	10	0	1	1	0	....	....	....	....	....	....	1937-38	1937-38
Drouin, Jude	Mtl., Min., NYI, Wpg.	12	666	151	305	456	346	72	27	41	68	33	....	1968-69	1980-81
• Drouin, Polly	Mtl.C., Mtl.	7	160	23	50	73	80	5	0	1	1	5	....	1934-35	1940-41
Drulia, Stan	T.B.	1	24	2	1	3	10	....	....	....	....	....	....	1992-93	1992-93
• Drummond, Jim	NYR	1	2	0	0	0	0	....	....	....	....	....	....	1944-45	1944-45
• Drury, Herb	Pit., Phi.	6	213	24	13	37	203	4	1	1	2	0	....	1925-26	1930-31
Dube, Gilles	Mtl., Det.	2	12	1	2	3	2	2	0	0	0	0	1	1949-50	1953-54
Dube, Norm	K.C.	2	57	8	10	18	54	....	....	....	....	....	....	1974-75	1975-76
Duberman, Justin	Pit.	1	4	0	0	0	0	....	....	....	....	....	....	1993-94	1993-94
Duchesne, Gaetan	Wsh., Que., Min., S.J., Fla.	14	1028	179	254	433	617	84	14	13	27	97	....	1981-82	1994-95
Dudley, Rick	Buf., Wpg.	6	309	75	99	174	292	25	7	2	9	69	....	1972-73	1980-81
Duff, Dick	Tor., NYR, Mtl., L.A., Buf.	18	1030	283	289	572	743	114	30	49	79	78	6	1954-55	1971-72
Dufour, Luc	Bos., Que., St.L.	3	167	23	21	44	199	18	1	0	1	32	....	1982-83	1984-85
Dufour, Marc	NYR, L.A.	3	14	1	0	1	2	....	....	....	....	....	....	1963-64	1968-69
Dufresne, Donald	Mtl., T.B., L.A., St.L., Edm.	9	268	6	36	42	258	34	1	3	4	47	1	1988-89	1996-97
• Duggan, Jack	Ott.	1	27	0	0	0	0	2	0	0	0	0	....	1925-26	1925-26
Duggan, Ken	Min.	1	1	0	0	0	0	....	....	....	....	....	....	1987-88	1987-88
Duguay, Ron	NYR, Det., Pit., L.A.	12	864	274	346	620	582	89	31	22	53	118	....	1977-78	1988-89
• Duguid, Lorne	Mtl.M., Det., Bos.	6	135	9	15	24	57	2	0	0	0	4	....	1931-32	1936-37
• Dukowski, Duke	Chi., NYA, NYR	5	200	16	30	46	172	6	0	0	0	6	....	1926-27	1933-34
Dumart, Woody	Bos.	16	772	211	218	429	99	88	12	15	27	23	2	1935-36	1953-54
Dunbar, Dale	Van., Bos.	2	2	0	0	0	2	....	....	....	....	....	....	1985-86	1988-89
• Duncan, Art	Det., Tor.	6	156	18	16	34	225	5	0	0	0	4	....	1926-27	1931-32
Duncan, Iain	Wpg.	4	127	34	55	89	149	11	0	3	3	6	....	1986-87	1990-91
Duncanson, Craig	L.A., Wpg., NYR	7	38	5	4	9	61	....	....	....	....	....	....	1985-86	1992-93
Dundas, Rocky	Tor.	1	5	0	0	0	14	....	....	....	....	....	....	1989-90	1989-90
• Dunlap, Frank	Tor.	1	15	0	1	1	2	....	....	....	....	....	....	1943-44	1943-44
Dunlop, Blake	Min., Phi., St.L., Det.	11	550	130	274	404	172	40	4	10	14	18	....	1973-74	1983-84
Dunn, Dave	Van., Tor.	3	184	14	41	55	313	10	1	1	2	41	....	1973-74	1975-76
Dunn, Richie	Buf., Cgy., Hfd.	12	483	36	140	176	314	36	3	15	18	24	....	1977-78	1988-89
Dupere, Denis	Tor., Wsh., St.L., K.C., Col.	8	421	80	99	179	66	16	1	0	1	0	....	1970-71	1977-78
Dupont, Andre	NYR, St.L., Phi., Que.	13	800	59	185	244	1986	140	14	18	32	352	2	1970-71	1982-83
Dupont, Jerome	Chi., Tor.	6	214	7	29	36	468	20	0	2	2	56	....	1981-82	1986-87
Dupont, Norm	Mtl., Wpg., Hfd.	5	256	55	85	140	52	13	4	2	6	0	....	1979-80	1983-84
• Dupre, Yanick	Phi.	3	35	2	0	2	16	....	....	....	....	....	....	1991-92	1995-96
Durbano, Steve	St.L., Pit., K.C., Col.	6	220	13	60	73	1127	5	0	2	2	8	....	1972-73	1978-79
Duris, Vitezslav	Tor.	2	89	3	20	23	62	3	0	1	1	2	....	1980-81	1982-83
Dussault, Norm	Mtl.	4	206	31	62	93	47	7	3	1	4	0	....	1947-48	1950-51
• Dutton, Red	Mtl.M., NYA	10	449	29	67	96	871	18	1	0	1	33	....	1926-27	1935-36
Dvorak, Miroslav	Phi.	3	193	11	74	85	51	18	0	2	2	6	....	1982-83	1984-85
Dwyer, Mike	Col., Cgy.	4	31	2	6	8	25	1	1	0	1	0	....	1978-79	1981-82
• Dyck, Henry	NYR	1	1	0	0	0	0	....	....	....	....	....	....	1943-44	1943-44
• Dye, Babe	Tor., Ham., Chi., NYA	11	271	202	44	246	221	15	11	1	12	14	1	1919-20	1930-31
Dykstra, Steven	Buf., Edm., Pit., Hfd.	5	217	8	32	40	545	1	0	0	0	2	....	1985-86	1989-90
Dyte, John	Chi.	1	27	1	0	1	31	....	....	....	....	....	....	1943-44	1943-44

E

Name	NHL Teams	NHL Seasons	Regular Schedule GP	G	A	TP	PIM	Playoffs GP	G	A	TP	PIM	NHL Cup Wins	First NHL Season	Last NHL Season
Eakin, Bruce	Cgy., Det.	4	13	2	2	4	4	....	....	....	....	....	....	1981-82	1985-86
Eatough, Jeff	Buf.	1	1	0	0	0	0	....	....	....	....	....	....	1981-82	1981-82
Eaves, Mike	Min., Cgy.	8	324	83	143	226	80	43	7	10	17	14	....	1978-79	1985-86
Eaves, Murray	Wpg., Det.	8	57	4	13	17	9	4	0	1	1	2	....	1980-81	1989-90
Ecclestone, Tim	St.L., Det., Tor., Atl.	11	692	126	233	359	344	48	6	11	17	76	....	1967-68	1977-78
Edberg, Rolf	Wsh.	3	184	45	58	103	24	....	....	....	....	....	....	1978-79	1980-81
• Eddolls, Frank	Mtl., NYR, Chi.	9	317	23	43	66	114	31	0	2	2	10	1	1944-45	1954-55
Edestrand, Darryl	St.L., Phi., Pit., Bos., L.A.	10	455	34	90	124	404	42	3	9	12	57	....	1967-68	1978-79
Edmundson, Garry	Mtl., Tor.	3	43	4	6	10	49	11	0	1	1	8	....	1951-52	1960-61
Edur, Tom	Col., Pit.	2	158	17	70	87	67	....	....	....	....	....	....	1976-77	1977-78
Egan, Pat	NYA, Bro., Det., Bos., NYR	11	554	77	153	230	776	44	9	4	13	44	....	1939-40	1950-51
Egers, Jack	NYR, St.L., Wsh.	7	284	64	69	133	154	32	5	6	11	32	....	1969-70	1975-76
Ehman, Gerry	Bos., Det., Tor., Oak., Cal.	9	429	96	118	214	100	41	10	10	20	12	1	1957-58	1970-71
Eisenhut, Neil	Van., Cgy.	2	16	1	3	4	21	....	....	....	....	....	....	1993-94	1994-95
Eklund, Per-Erik	Phi., Dal.	9	594	120	335	455	109	66	10	36	46	8	....	1985-86	1993-94
Eldebrink, Anders	Van., Que.	2	55	3	11	14	29	14	0	0	0	10	....	1981-82	1982-83
Elik, Bo	Det.	1	3	0	0	0	0	....	....	....	....	....	....	1962-63	1962-63
• Elliot, Fred	Ott.	1	43	2	0	2	6	....	....	....	....	....	....	1928-29	1928-29
Ellis, Ron	Tor.	16	1034	332	308	640	207	70	18	8	26	20	1	1963-64	1980-81
Eloranta, Kari	Cgy., St.L.	5	267	13	103	116	155	26	1	7	8	19	....	1981-82	1986-87
Elynuik, Pat	Wpg., Wsh., T.B., Ott.	9	506	154	188	342	459	20	6	9	15	25	....	1987-88	1995-96
Emberg, Eddie	Mtl.	1	....	....	....	....	....	2	1	0	1	0	....	1944-45	1944-45
Emma, David	N.J., Bos.	4	28	5	6	11	2	....	....	....	....	....	....	1992-93	1996-97
Emmons, Gary	S.J.	1	3	1	0	1	0	....	....	....	....	....	....	1993-94	1993-94
• Emms, Hap	Mtl.M., NYA, Det., Bos.	10	320	36	53	89	311	14	0	0	0	12	....	1926-27	1937-38
Endean, Craig	Wpg.	1	2	0	1	1	0	....	....	....	....	....	....	1986-87	1986-87
Engblom, Brian	Mtl., Wsh., L.A., Buf., Cgy.	11	659	29	177	206	599	48	3	9	12	43	3	1976-77	1986-87
Engele, Jerry	Min.	3	100	2	13	15	162	2	0	1	1	0	....	1975-76	1977-78
English, John	L.A.	1	3	1	3	4	4	1	0	0	0	0	....	1987-88	1987-88
Ennis, Jim	Edm.	1	5	1	0	1	10	....	....	....	....	....	....	1987-88	1987-88
Erickson, Aut	Bos., Chi., Tor., Oak.	7	226	7	24	31	182	7	0	0	0	2	1	1959-60	1969-70
Erickson, Bryan	Wsh., L.A., Pit., Wpg.	9	351	80	125	205	141	14	3	4	7	7	....	1983-84	1993-94
Erickson, Grant	Bos., Min.	2	6	1	0	1	0	....	....	....	....	....	....	1968-69	1969-70
Eriksson, Peter	Edm.	1	20	3	3	6	24	....	....	....	....	....	....	1989-90	1989-90
Eriksson, Roland	Min., Van.	3	193	48	95	143	26	2	1	0	1	0	....	1976-77	1978-79
Eriksson, Thomas	Phi.	5	208	22	76	98	107	19	0	3	3	12	....	1980-81	1985-86
Erixon, Jan	NYR	10	556	57	159	216	167	58	7	7	14	16	....	1983-84	1992-93
Esau, Leonard	Tor., Que., Cgy., Edm.	4	27	0	10	10	24	....	....	....	....	....	....	1991-92	1994-95
Esposito, Phil	Chi., Bos., NYR	18	1282	717	873	1590	910	130	61	76	137	138	2	1963-64	1980-81
Evans, Chris	Tor., Buf., St.L., Det., K.C.	5	241	19	42	61	143	12	1	1	2	8	....	1969-70	1974-75
Evans, Daryl	L.A., Wsh., Tor.	6	113	22	30	52	25	11	5	8	13	12	....	1981-82	1986-87
Evans, Doug	St.L., Wpg., Phi.	8	355	48	87	135	502	22	3	4	7	38	....	1985-86	1992-93
• Evans, Jack	NYR, Chi.	14	752	19	80	99	989	56	2	2	4	97	1	1948-49	1962-63
Evans, Kevin	Min., S.J.	2	9	0	1	1	44	....	....	....	....	....	....	1990-91	1991-92
Evans, Paul	Tor.	2	11	1	1	2	21	2	0	0	0	0	....	1976-77	1977-78
Evans, Paul	Phi.	3	103	14	25	39	34	1	0	0	0	0	....	1978-79	1982-83
Evans, Shawn	St.L., NYI	2	9	1	0	1	2	....	....	....	....	....	....	1985-86	1989-90
• Evans, Stewart	Det., Mtl.M., Mtl.C.	8	367	28	49	77	425	26	0	0	0	20	1	1930-31	1938-39
Evason, Dean	Wsh., Hfd., S.J., Dal., Cgy.	13	803	139	233	372	1002	55	9	20	29	132	....	1983-84	1995-96
Ewen, Todd	St.L., Mtl., Ana., S.J.	11	518	36	40	76	1911	26	0	0	0	87	1	1986-87	1996-97
Ezinicki, Bill	Tor., Bos., NYR	9	368	79	105	184	713	40	5	8	13	87	3	1944-45	1954-55

Name	NHL Teams	NHL Seasons	Regular Schedule GP	G	A	TP	PIM	Playoffs GP	G	A	TP	PIM	NHL Cup Wins	First NHL Season	Last NHL Season
F															
Fahey, Trevor	NYR	1	1	0	0	0	0	....	....	....	....	....	....	1964-65	1964-65
Fairbairn, Bill	NYR, Min., St.L.	11	658	162	261	423	173	54	13	22	35	42	....	1968-69	1978-79
Falkenberg, Bob	Det.	5	54	1	5	6	26	....	....	....	....	....	....	1966-67	1971-72
Farrant, Walt	Chi.	1	1	0	0	0	0	....	....	....	....	....	....	1943-44	1943-44
Farrish, Dave	NYR, Que., Tor.	7	430	17	110	127	440	14	0	2	2	24	....	1976-77	1983-84
Fashoway, Gordie	Chi.	1	13	3	2	5	14	....	....	....	....	....	....	1950-51	1950-51
Faubert, Mario	Pit.	7	231	21	90	111	292	10	2	2	4	6	....	1974-75	1981-82
Faulkner, Alex	Tor., Det.	3	101	15	17	32	15	12	5	0	5	2	....	1961-62	1963-64
Fauss, Ted	Tor.	2	28	0	2	2	15	....	....	....	....	....	....	1986-87	1987-88
Faust, Andre	Phi.	2	47	10	7	17	14	....	....	....	....	....	....	1992-93	1993-94
Feamster, Dave	Chi.	4	169	13	24	37	154	33	3	5	8	61	....	1981-82	1984-85
Featherstone, Tony	Oak., Cal., Min.	3	130	17	21	38	65	2	0	0	0	0	....	1969-70	1973-74
Federko, Bernie	St.L., Det.	14	1000	369	761	1130	487	91	35	66	101	83	....	1976-77	1989-90
Fedotov, Anatoli	Wpg., Ana.	2	4	0	2	2	0	....	....	....	....	....	....	1992-93	1993-94
Felix, Chris	Wsh.	4	35	1	12	13	10	2	0	1	1	0	....	1987-88	1990-91
Felsner, Denny	St.L.	4	18	1	4	5	6	10	2	3	5	2	....	1991-92	1994-95
Feltrin, Tony	Pit., NYR	4	48	3	3	6	65	....	....	....	....	....	....	1980-81	1985-86
Fenton, Paul	Hfd., NYR, L.A., Wpg., Tor., Cgy., S.J.	8	411	100	83	183	198	17	4	1	5	27	....	1984-85	1991-92
Fenyves, David	Buf., Phi.	9	206	3	32	35	119	11	0	0	0	9	....	1982-83	1990-91
Fergus, Tom	Bos., Tor., Van.	12	726	235	346	581	499	65	21	17	38	48	....	1981-82	1992-93
Ferguson, George	Tor., Pit., Min.	12	797	160	238	398	431	86	14	23	37	44	....	1972-73	1983-84
Ferguson, John	Mtl.	8	500	145	158	303	1214	85	20	18	38	260	5	1963-64	1970-71
Ferguson, Lorne	Bos., Det., Chi.	8	422	82	80	162	193	31	6	3	9	24	....	1949-50	1958-59
Ferguson, Norm	Oak., Cal.	4	279	73	66	139	72	10	1	4	5	7	....	1968-69	1971-72
Ferner, Mark	Buf., Wsh., Ana., Det.	6	91	3	10	13	51	....	....	....	....	....	....	1986-87	1994-95
Fetisov, Viacheslav	N.J., Det.	9	546	36	192	228	656	116	2	26	28	147	2	1989-90	1997-98
Fidler, Mike	Cle., Min., Hfd., Chi.	7	271	84	97	181	124	....	....	....	....	....	....	1976-77	1982-83
• Field, Wilf	NYA, Bro., Mtl., Chi.	6	219	17	25	42	151	5	0	0	0	2	....	1936-37	1944-45
Fielder, Guyle	Chi., Det., Bos.	4	9	0	0	0	2	6	0	0	0	2	....	1950-51	1957-58
Filimonov, Dmitri	Ott.	1	30	1	4	5	18	....	....	....	....	....	....	1993-94	1993-94
Fillion, Bob	Mtl.	7	327	42	61	103	84	33	7	4	11	10	2	1943-44	1949-50
• Fillion, Marcel	Bos.	1	1	0	0	0	0	....	....	....	....	....	....	1944-45	1944-45
• Filmore, Tommy	Det., NYA, Bos.	4	117	15	12	27	33	....	....	....	....	....	....	1930-31	1933-34
Finkbeiner, Lloyd	NYA	1	2	0	0	0	0	....	....	....	....	....	....	1940-41	1940-41
Finn, Steven	Que., T.B., L.A.	12	725	34	78	112	1724	23	0	4	4	39	....	1985-86	1996-97
Finney, Sid	Chi.	3	59	10	7	17	4	7	0	2	2	0	....	1951-52	1953-54
• Finnigan, Ed	St.L., Bos., NYA	3	15	1	1	2	2	....	....	....	....	....	....	1934-35	1936-37
• Finnigan, Frank	Ott., Tor., St.L.	14	553	115	88	203	405	38	6	9	15	22	2	1923-24	1936-37
Fiorentino, Peter	NYR	1	1	0	0	0	0	....	....	....	....	....	....	1991-92	1991-92
Fischer, Ron	Buf.	2	18	0	7	7	6	....	....	....	....	....	....	1981-82	1982-83
• Fisher, Alvin	Tor.	1	9	1	0	1	4	....	....	....	....	....	....	1924-25	1924-25
Fisher, Dunc	NYR, Bos., Det.	7	275	45	70	115	104	21	4	4	8	14	....	1947-48	1958-59
Fisher, Joe	Det.	4	65	8	12	20	13	12	2	1	3	6	1	1939-40	1942-43
Fitchner, Bob	Que.	2	78	12	20	32	59	3	0	0	0	10	....	1979-80	1980-81
Fitzgerald, Rusty	Pit.	2	25	2	2	4	12	5	0	0	0	4	....	1994-95	1995-96
Fitzpatrick, Ross	Phi.	4	20	5	2	7	0	....	....	....	....	....	....	1982-83	1985-86
Fitzpatrick, Sandy	NYR, Min.	2	22	3	6	9	8	12	0	0	0	0	....	1964-65	1967-68
Flaman, Fernie	Bos., Tor.	17	910	34	174	208	1370	63	4	8	12	93	1	1944-45	1960-61
Flatley, Pat	NYI, NYR	14	780	170	340	510	686	70	18	15	33	75	....	1983-84	1996-97
Fleming, Gerry	Mtl.	2	11	0	0	0	42	....	....	....	....	....	....	1993-94	1994-95
Fleming, Reggie	Mtl., Chi., Bos., NYR, Phi., Buf.	12	749	108	132	240	1468	50	3	6	9	106	1	1959-60	1970-71
Flesch, John	Min., Pit., Col.	4	124	18	23	41	117	....	....	....	....	....	....	1974-75	1979-80
Fletcher, Steven	Mtl., Wpg.	2	3	0	0	0	5	1	0	0	0	5	....	1987-88	1988-89
Flett, Bill	L.A., Phi., Tor., Atl., Edm.	11	689	202	215	417	501	52	7	16	23	42	1	1967-68	1979-80
Flichel, Todd	Wpg.	3	6	0	1	1	4	....	....	....	....	....	....	1987-88	1989-90
Flockhart, Rob	Van., Min.	5	55	2	5	7	14	1	1	0	1	2	....	1976-77	1980-81
Flockhart, Ron	Phi., Pit., Mtl., St.L., Bos.	9	453	145	183	328	208	19	4	6	10	14	....	1980-81	1988-89
Floyd, Larry	N.J.	2	12	2	3	5	9	....	....	....	....	....	....	1982-83	1983-84
Fogarty, Bryan	Que., Pit., Mtl.	6	156	22	52	74	119	....	....	....	....	....	....	1989-90	1994-95
Fogolin, Lee	Buf., Edm.	13	924	44	195	239	1318	108	5	19	24	173	2	1974-75	1986-87
Fogolin, Lidio	Det., Chi.	9	427	10	48	58	575	28	0	2	2	30	1	1947-48	1955-56
Folco, Peter	Van.	1	2	0	0	0	0	....	....	....	....	....	....	1973-74	1973-74
Foley, Gerry	Tor., NYR, L.A.	4	142	9	14	23	99	9	0	1	1	2	....	1954-55	1968-69
Foley, Rick	Chi., Phi., Det.	3	67	11	26	37	180	4	0	1	1	4	....	1970-71	1973-74
Foligno, Mike	Det., Buf., Tor., Fla.	15	1018	355	372	727	2049	57	15	17	32	185	....	1979-80	1993-94
Folk, Bill	Det.	2	12	0	0	0	4	....	....	....	....	....	....	1951-52	1952-53
Fontaine, Len	Det.	2	46	8	11	19	10	....	....	....	....	....	....	1972-73	1973-74
Fontas, Jon	Min.	2	2	0	0	0	0	....	....	....	....	....	....	1979-80	1980-81
Fonteyne, Val	Det., NYR, Pit.	13	820	75	154	229	26	59	3	10	13	8	....	1959-60	1971-72
Fontinato, Lou	NYR, Mtl.	9	535	26	78	104	1247	21	0	2	2	42	....	1954-55	1962-63
Forbes, Dave	Bos., Wsh.	6	363	64	64	128	341	45	1	4	5	13	....	1973-74	1978-79
Forbes, Mike	Bos., Edm.	3	50	1	11	12	41	....	....	....	....	....	....	1977-78	1981-82
Forey, Connie	St.L.	1	4	0	0	0	2	....	....	....	....	....	....	1973-74	1973-74
• Forsey, Jack	Tor.	1	19	7	9	16	10	3	0	1	1	0	....	1942-43	1942-43
• Forslund, Gus	Ott.	1	48	4	9	13	2	....	....	....	....	....	....	1932-33	1932-33
Forslund, Tomas	Cgy.	2	44	5	11	16	12	....	....	....	....	....	....	1991-92	1992-93
Forsyth, Alex	Wsh.	1	1	0	0	0	0	....	....	....	....	....	....	1976-77	1976-77
Fortier, Dave	Tor., NYI, Van.	4	205	8	21	29	335	20	0	2	2	33	....	1972-73	1976-77
Fortier, Marc	Que., Ott., L.A.	6	212	42	60	102	135	....	....	....	....	....	....	1987-88	1992-93
Fortin, Ray	St.L.	3	92	2	6	8	33	6	0	0	0	8	....	1967-68	1969-70
Foster, Corey	N.J., Phi., Pit., NYI	4	45	5	6	11	24	3	0	0	0	4	....	1988-89	1996-97
Foster, Dwight	Bos., Col., N.J., Det.	10	541	111	163	274	420	35	5	12	17	4	....	1977-78	1986-87
Foster, Herb	NYR	2	6	1	0	1	5	....	....	....	....	....	....	1940-41	1947-48
• Foster, Yip	NYR, Bos., Det.	4	83	3	2	5	32	....	....	....	....	....	....	1929-30	1934-35
Fotiu, Nick	NYR, Hfd., Cgy., Phi., Edm.	13	646	60	77	137	1362	38	0	4	4	67	....	1976-77	1988-89
• Fowler, Jimmy	Tor.	3	135	18	29	47	39	18	0	3	3	2	....	1936-37	1938-39
Fowler, Tom	Chi.	1	24	0	1	1	18	....	....	....	....	....	....	1946-47	1946-47
Fox, Greg	Atl., Chi., Pit.	8	494	14	92	106	637	44	1	9	10	67	....	1977-78	1984-85
Fox, Jim	L.A.	9	578	186	293	479	143	22	4	8	12	0	....	1980-81	1989-90
• Foyston, Frank	Det.	2	64	17	7	24	32	....	....	....	....	....	....	1926-27	1927-28
Frampton, Bob	Mtl.	1	2	0	0	0	0	3	0	0	0	0	....	1949-50	1949-50
Franceschetti, Lou	Wsh., Tor., Buf.	10	459	59	81	140	747	44	3	2	5	111	....	1981-82	1991-92
Francis, Bobby	Det.	1	14	2	0	2	0	....	....	....	....	....	....	1982-83	1982-83
• Fraser, Archie	NYR	1	3	0	1	1	0	....	....	....	....	....	....	1943-44	1943-44
• Fraser, Charles	Ham.	1	1	0	0	0	0	....	....	....	....	....	....	1923-24	1923-24
Fraser, Curt	Van., Chi., Min.	12	704	193	240	433	1306	65	15	18	33	198	....	1978-79	1989-90
• Fraser, Gord	Chi., Det., Mtl.C., Pit., Phi.	5	144	24	12	36	224	2	1	0	1	6	....	1926-27	1930-31
Fraser, Harvey	Chi.	1	21	5	4	9	0	....	....	....	....	....	....	1944-45	1944-45
Fraser, Iain	NYI, Que., Dal., Edm., Wpg., S.J.	5	94	23	23	46	31	4	0	0	0	0	....	1992-93	1996-97
Frawley, Dan	Chi., Pit.	6	273	37	40	77	674	1	0	0	0	0	....	1983-84	1988-89
• Fredrickson, Frank	Det., Bos., Pit.	5	161	39	34	73	206	10	2	5	7	26	....	1926-27	1930-31
• Frew, Irv	Mtl.M., St.L., Mtl.C.	3	96	2	5	7	146	4	0	0	0	6	....	1933-34	1935-36
Friday, Tim	Det.	1	23	0	3	3	6	....	....	....	....	....	....	1985-86	1985-86
Fridgen, Dan	Hfd.	2	13	2	3	5	2	....	....	....	....	....	....	1981-82	1982-83
Friest, Ron	Min.	3	64	7	7	14	191	6	1	0	1	7	....	1980-81	1982-83
Frig, Len	Chi., Cal., Cle., St.L.	7	311	13	51	64	479	14	2	1	3	0	....	1972-73	1979-80
Frost, Harry	Bos.	1	4	0	0	0	0	1	0	0	0	0	1	1938-39	1938-39
Frycer, Miroslav	Que., Tor., Det., Edm.	8	415	147	183	330	486	17	3	8	11	16	....	1981-82	1988-89
Fryday, Bob	Mtl.	2	5	1	0	1	0	....	....	....	....	....	....	1949-50	1951-52
Ftorek, Robbie	Det., Que., NYR	8	334	77	150	227	262	19	9	6	15	28	....	1972-73	1984-85
Fullan, Larry	Wsh.	1	4	1	0	1	0	....	....	....	....	....	....	1974-75	1974-75
Fusco, Mark	Hfd.	2	80	3	12	15	42	....	....	....	....	....	....	1983-84	1984-85
G															
Gadsby, Bill	Chi., NYR, Det.	20	1248	130	438	568	1539	67	4	23	27	92	....	1946-47	1965-66
Gaetz, Link	Min., S.J.	3	65	6	8	14	412	....	....	....	....	....	....	1988-89	1991-92
Gage, Jody	Det., Buf.	6	68	14	15	29	26	....	....	....	....	....	....	1980-81	1991-92

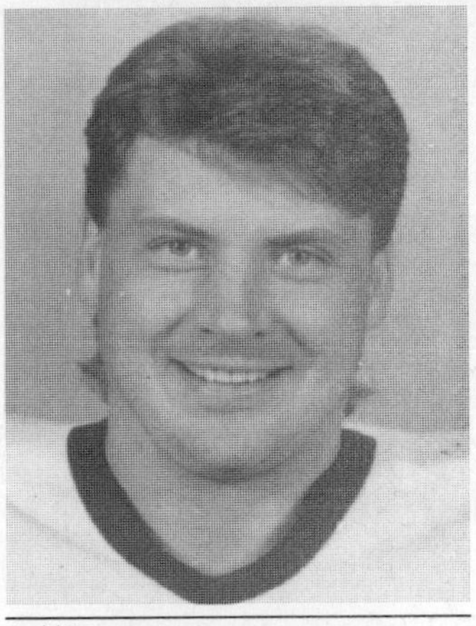
Todd Ewen

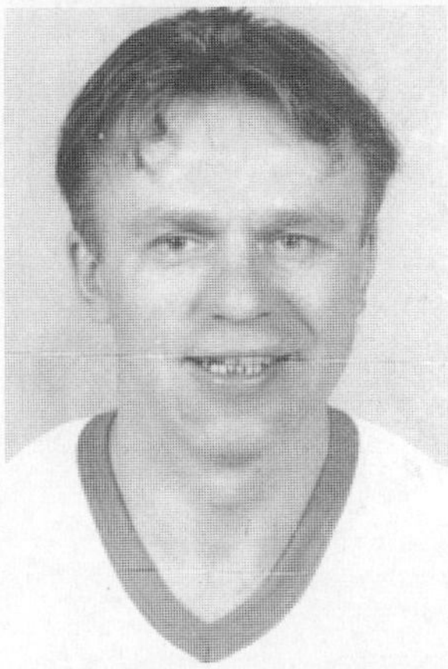
Viacheslav Fetisov

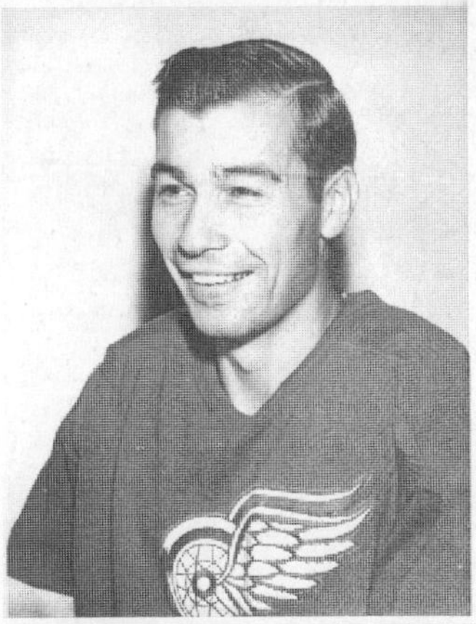
Guyle Fielder

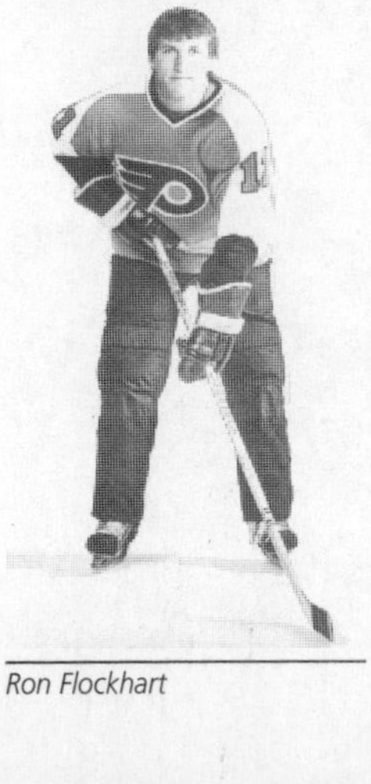
Ron Flockhart

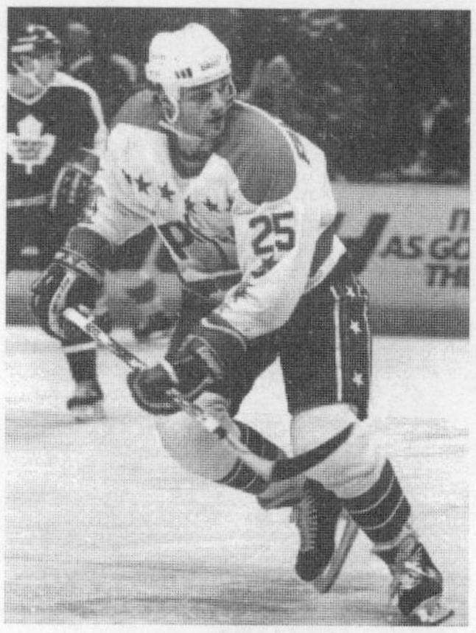

Lou Franceschetti

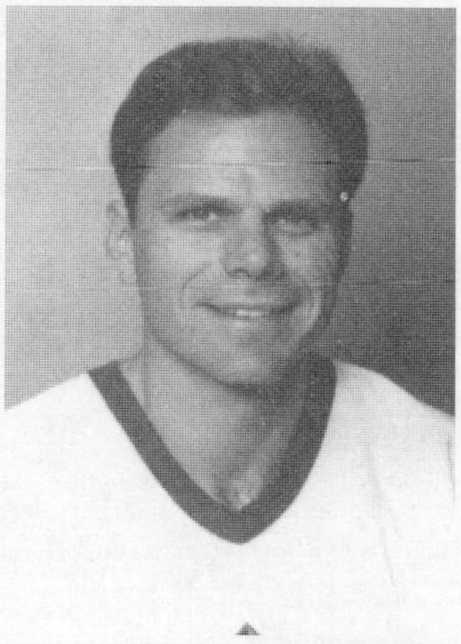

Mike Gartner

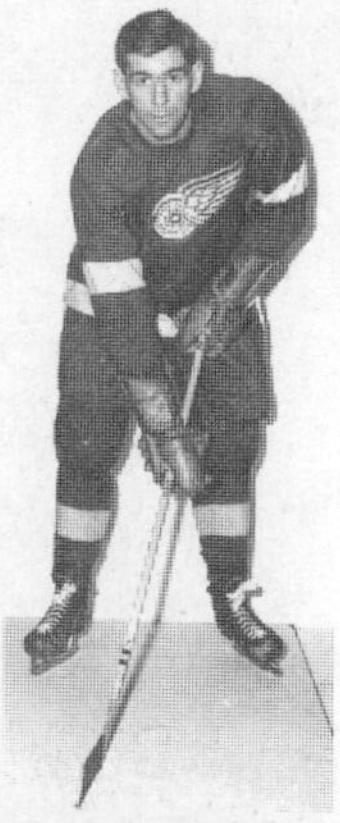

Bob Goldham

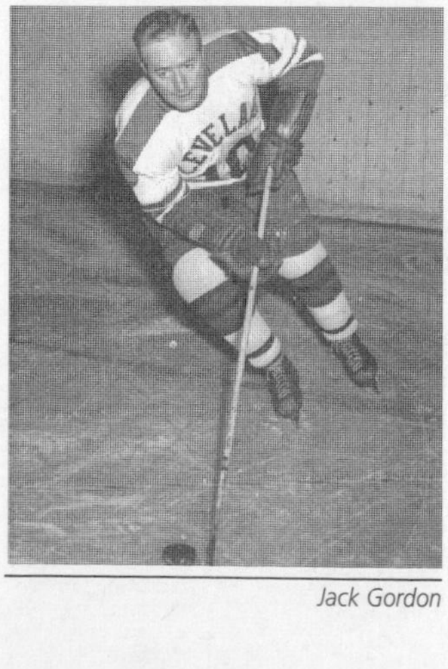

Jack Gordon

Name	NHL Teams	NHL Seasons	Regular Schedule GP	G	A	TP	PIM	Playoffs GP	G	A	TP	PIM	NHL Cup Wins	First NHL Season	Last NHL Season
• Gagne, Art	Mtl.C., Bos., Ott., Det.	6	228	67	33	100	257	11	2	1	3	20	....	1926-27	1931-32
Gagne, Paul	Col., N.J., Tor., NYI	8	390	110	101	211	127	....	....	....	....	....	....	1980-81	1989-90
Gagne, Pierre	Bos.	1	2	0	0	0	0	....	....	....	....	....	....	1959-60	1959-60
Gagnon, Germaine	Mtl., NYI, Chi., K.C.	5	259	40	101	141	72	19	2	3	5	2	....	1971-72	1975-76
• Gagnon, Johnny	Mtl.C., Bos., Mtl., NYA	10	454	120	141	261	295	32	12	12	24	37	....	1930-31	1939-40
Gainey, Bob	Mtl.	16	1160	239	262	501	585	182	25	48	73	151	5	1973-74	1988-89
• Gainor, Norm	Bos., NYR, Ott., Mtl.M.	7	246	51	56	107	129	22	2	1	3	14	2	1927-28	1934-35
Galarneau, Michel	Hfd.	3	78	7	10	17	34	....	....	....	....	....	....	1980-81	1982-83
• Galbraith, Percy	Bos., Ott.	8	347	29	31	60	224	31	4	7	11	24	1	1926-27	1933-34
• Gallagher, John	Mtl.M., Det., NYA	7	205	14	19	33	153	24	2	3	5	27	1	1930-31	1938-39
Gallant, Gerard	Det., T.B.	11	615	211	269	480	1674	58	18	21	39	178	....	1984-85	1994-95
Gallimore, Jamie	Min.	1	2	0	0	0	0	....	....	....	....	....	....	1977-78	1977-78
Gallinger, Don	Bos.	5	222	65	88	153	89	23	5	5	10	19	....	1942-43	1947-48
Gamble, Dick	Mtl., Chi., Tor.	8	195	41	41	82	66	14	1	2	3	4	1	1950-51	1966-67
Gambucci, Gary	Min.	2	51	2	7	9	9	....	....	....	....	....	....	1971-72	1973-74
Ganchar, Perry	St.L., Mtl., Pit.	4	42	3	7	10	36	7	3	1	4	0	....	1983-84	1988-89
Gans, Dave	L.A.	2	6	0	0	0	2	....	....	....	....	....	....	1982-83	1985-86
• Gardiner, Herb	Mtl.C., Chi.	3	101	10	9	19	52	9	0	1	1	14	....	1926-27	1928-29
Gardner, Bill	Chi., Hfd.	9	380	73	115	188	68	45	3	8	11	17	....	1980-81	1988-89
Gardner, Cal	NYR, Tor., Chi., Bos.	12	696	154	238	392	517	61	7	10	17	20	2	1945-46	1956-57
Gardner, Dave	Mtl., St.L., Cal., Cle., Phi.	7	350	75	115	190	41	....	....	....	....	....	....	1972-73	1979-80
Gardner, Paul	Col., Tor., Pit., Wsh., Buf.	10	447	201	201	402	207	16	2	6	8	14	....	1976-77	1985-86
Gare, Danny	Buf., Det., Edm.	13	827	354	331	685	1285	64	25	21	46	195	....	1974-75	1986-87
Gariepy, Ray	Bos., Tor.	2	36	1	6	7	43	....	....	....	....	....	....	1953-54	1955-56
• Garland, Scott	Tor., L.A.	3	91	13	24	37	115	7	1	2	3	35	....	1975-76	1978-79
Garner, Rob	Pit.	1	1	0	0	0	0	....	....	....	....	....	....	1982-83	1982-83
• Garrett, Red	NYR	1	23	1	1	2	18	....	....	....	....	....	....	1942-43	1942-43
Gartner, Mike	Wsh., Min., NYR, Tor., Phx.	19	1432	708	627	1335	1159	122	43	50	93	125	....	1979-80	1997-98
• Gassoff, Bob	St.L.	4	245	11	47	58	866	9	0	1	1	16	....	1973-74	1976-77
Gassoff, Brad	Van.	4	122	19	17	36	163	3	0	0	0	0	....	1975-76	1978-79
Gatzos, Steve	Pit.	4	89	15	20	35	83	1	0	0	0	0	....	1981-82	1984-85
Gaudreau, Rob	S.J., Ott.	4	231	51	54	105	69	14	2	0	2	0	....	1992-93	1995-96
Gaudreault, Armand	Bos.	1	44	15	9	24	27	7	0	2	2	8	....	1944-45	1944-45
• Gaudreault, Leo	Mtl.C.	3	67	8	4	12	30	....	....	....	....	....	....	1927-28	1932-33
Gaulin, Jean-Marc	Que.	4	26	4	3	7	8	1	0	0	0	0	....	1982-83	1985-86
Gaume, Dallas	Hfd.	1	4	1	1	2	0	....	....	....	....	....	....	1988-89	1988-89
• Gauthier, Art	Mtl.C.	1	13	0	0	0	0	1	0	0	0	0	....	1926-27	1926-27
Gauthier, Daniel	Chi.	1	5	0	0	0	0	....	....	....	....	....	....	1994-95	1994-95
• Gauthier, Fern	NYR, Mtl., Det.	6	229	46	50	96	35	22	5	1	6	7	....	1943-44	1948-49
Gauthier, Jean	Mtl., Phi., Bos.	10	166	6	29	35	150	14	1	3	4	22	1	1960-61	1969-70
Gauthier, Luc	Mtl.	1	3	0	0	0	2	....	....	....	....	....	....	1990-91	1990-91
Gauvreau, Jocelyn	Mtl.	1	2	0	0	0	0	....	....	....	....	....	....	1983-84	1983-84
Gavin, Stewart	Tor., Hfd., Min.	13	768	130	155	285	584	66	14	20	34	75	....	1980-81	1992-93
Geale, Bob	Pit.	1	1	0	0	0	2	....	....	....	....	....	....	1984-85	1984-85
• Gee, George	Chi., Det.	9	551	135	183	318	345	41	6	13	19	32	1	1945-46	1953-54
Geldart, Gary	Min.	1	4	0	0	0	5	....	....	....	....	....	....	1970-71	1970-71
Gendron, Jean-Guy	NYR, Bos., Mtl., Phi.	14	863	182	201	383	701	42	7	4	11	47	....	1955-56	1971-72
Geoffrion, Bernie	Mtl., NYR	16	883	393	429	822	689	132	58	60	118	88	6	1950-51	1967-68
Geoffrion, Danny	Mtl., Wpg.	3	111	20	32	52	99	2	0	0	0	7	....	1979-80	1981-82
• Geran, Gerry	Mtl., Bos.	2	34	5	1	6	6	....	....	....	....	....	....	1917-18	1925-26
• Gerard, Eddie	Ott., Tor., Mtl.C.	7	128	50	47	97	120	27	7	1	8	71	4	1917-18	1923-24
Germain, Eric	L.A.	1	4	0	1	1	13	1	0	0	0	4	....	1987-88	1987-88
Getliffe, Ray	Bos., Mtl.	10	393	136	137	273	250	45	9	10	19	30	2	1935-36	1944-45
Giallonardo, Mario	Col.	2	23	0	3	3	6	....	....	....	....	....	....	1979-80	1980-81
Gibbs, Barry	Bos., Min., Atl., St.L., L.A.	13	797	58	224	282	945	36	4	2	6	67	....	1967-68	1979-80
Gibson, Don	Van.	1	14	0	3	3	20	....	....	....	....	....	....	1990-91	1990-91
Gibson, Doug	Bos., Wsh.	3	63	9	19	28	0	1	0	0	0	0	....	1973-74	1977-78
Gibson, John	L.A., Tor., Wpg.	3	48	0	2	2	120	....	....	....	....	....	....	1980-81	1983-84
Giesebrecht, Gus	Det.	4	135	27	51	78	13	17	2	3	5	0	....	1938-39	1941-42
Giffin, Lee	Pit.	2	27	1	3	4	9	....	....	....	....	....	....	1986-87	1987-88
Gilbert, Ed	K.C., Pit.	3	166	21	31	52	22	....	....	....	....	....	....	1974-75	1976-77
Gilbert, Greg	NYI, Chi., NYR, St.L.	15	837	150	228	378	576	133	17	33	50	162	3	1981-82	1995-96
Gilbert, Jeannot	Bos.	2	9	0	1	1	4	....	....	....	....	....	....	1962-63	1964-65
Gilbert, Rod	NYR	18	1065	406	615	1021	508	79	34	33	67	43	....	1960-61	1977-78
Gilbertson, Stan	Cal., St.L., Wsh., Pit.	6	428	85	89	174	148	3	1	1	2	2	....	1971-72	1976-77
Giles, Curt	Min., NYR, St.L.	14	895	43	199	242	733	103	6	16	22	118	....	1979-80	1992-93
Gilhen, Randy	Hfd., Wpg., Pit., L.A., NYR, T.B., Fla.	11	457	55	60	115	314	33	3	2	5	26	1	1982-83	1995-96
Gillen, Don	Phi., Hfd.	2	35	2	4	6	22	....	....	....	....	....	....	1979-80	1981-82
• Gillie, Farrand	Det.	1	1	0	0	0	0	....	....	....	....	....	....	1928-29	1928-29
Gillies, Clark	NYI, Buf.	14	958	319	378	697	1023	164	47	47	94	287	4	1974-75	1987-88
Gillis, Jere	Van., NYR, Que., Buf., Phi.	9	386	78	95	173	230	19	4	7	11	9	....	1977-78	1986-87
Gillis, Mike	Col., Bos.	6	246	33	43	76	186	27	2	5	7	10	....	1978-79	1983-84
Gillis, Paul	Que., Chi., Hfd.	11	624	88	154	242	1498	42	3	14	17	156	....	1982-83	1992-93
Gingras, Gaston	Mtl., Tor., St.L.	10	476	61	174	235	161	52	6	18	24	20	1	1979-80	1988-89
Girard, Bob	Cal., Cle., Wsh.	5	305	45	69	114	140	....	....	....	....	....	....	1975-76	1979-80
Girard, Kenny	Tor.	3	7	0	1	1	2	....	....	....	....	....	....	1956-57	1959-60
• Giroux, Art	Mtl.C., Bos., Det.	3	54	6	4	10	14	2	0	0	0	0	....	1932-33	1935-36
Giroux, Larry	St.L., K.C., Det., Hfd.	7	274	15	74	89	333	5	0	0	0	4	....	1973-74	1979-80
Giroux, Pierre	L.A.	1	6	1	0	1	17	....	....	....	....	....	....	1982-83	1982-83
Gladney, Bob	L.A., Pit.	2	14	1	5	6	4	....	....	....	....	....	....	1982-83	1983-84
Gladu, Jean-Paul	Bos.	1	40	6	14	20	2	7	2	2	4	0	....	1944-45	1944-45
Glennie, Brian	Tor., L.A.	10	572	14	100	114	621	32	0	1	1	66	....	1969-70	1978-79
Glennon, Matt	Bos.	1	3	0	0	0	2	....	....	....	....	....	....	1991-92	1991-92
Gloeckner, Lorry	Det.	1	13	0	2	2	6	....	....	....	....	....	....	1978-79	1978-79
Gloor, Dan	Van.	1	2	0	0	0	0	....	....	....	....	....	....	1973-74	1973-74
Glover, Fred	Det., Chi.	5	92	13	11	24	62	8	0	0	0	0	1	1948-49	1952-53
Glover, Howie	Chi., Det., NYR, Mtl.	5	144	29	17	46	101	11	1	2	3	2	....	1958-59	1968-69
Glynn, Brian	Cgy., Min., Edm., Ott., Van., Hfd.	10	431	25	79	104	410	57	6	10	16	40	....	1987-88	1996-97
Godden, Ernie	Tor.	1	5	1	1	2	6	....	....	....	....	....	....	1981-82	1981-82
Godfrey, Warren	Bos., Det.	16	786	32	125	157	752	52	1	4	5	42	....	1952-53	1967-68
Godin, Eddy	Wsh.	2	27	3	6	9	12	....	....	....	....	....	....	1977-78	1978-79
• Godin, Sammy	Ott., Mtl.C.	3	83	4	3	7	36	....	....	....	....	....	....	1927-28	1933-34
Goegan, Pete	Det., NYR, Min.	11	383	19	67	86	365	33	1	3	4	61	....	1957-58	1967-68
Goertz, Dave	Pit.	1	2	0	0	0	2	....	....	....	....	....	....	1987-88	1987-88
• Goldham, Bob	Tor., Chi., Det.	12	650	28	143	171	400	66	3	14	17	53	4	1941-42	1955-56
• Goldsworthy, Bill	Bos., Min., NYR	14	771	283	258	541	793	40	18	19	37	30	....	1964-65	1977-78
• Goldsworthy, Leroy	NYR, Det., Chi., Mtl.C., Bos., NYA	10	336	66	57	123	79	24	1	0	1	4	1	1928-29	1938-39
Goldup, Glenn	Mtl., L.A.	9	291	52	67	119	303	16	4	3	7	22	....	1973-74	1981-82
Goldup, Hank	Tor., NYR	6	202	63	80	143	97	26	5	1	6	6	1	1939-40	1945-46
Gooden, Bill	NYR	2	53	9	11	20	15	....	....	....	....	....	....	1942-43	1943-44
Goodenough, Larry	Phi., Van.	6	242	22	77	99	179	22	3	15	18	10	1	1974-75	1979-80
• Goodfellow, Ebbie	Det.	14	557	134	190	324	511	45	8	8	16	65	2	1929-30	1942-43
Gordiouk, Viktor	Buf.	2	26	3	8	11	0	....	....	....	....	....	....	1992-93	1994-95
Gordon, Fred	Det., Bos.	2	81	8	7	15	68	2	0	0	0	0	....	1926-27	1927-28
Gordon, Jackie	NYR	3	36	3	10	13	0	9	1	1	2	7	....	1948-49	1950-51
Gorence, Tom	Phi., Edm.	6	303	58	53	111	89	37	9	6	15	47	....	1978-79	1983-84
Goring, Butch	L.A., NYI, Bos.	17	1107	375	513	888	102	134	38	50	88	32	4	1969-70	1985-86
Gorman, Dave	Atl.	1	3	0	0	0	0	....	....	....	....	....	....	1979-80	1979-80
• Gorman, Ed	Ott., Tor.	4	113	14	5	19	108	8	0	0	0	2	1	1924-25	1927-28
Gosselin, Benoit	NYR	1	7	0	0	0	33	....	....	....	....	....	....	1977-78	1977-78
Gosselin, Guy	Wpg.	1	5	0	0	0	6	....	....	....	....	....	....	1987-88	1987-88
Gotaas, Steve	Pit., Min.	3	49	6	9	15	53	3	0	1	1	5	....	1987-88	1990-91
• Gottselig, Johnny	Chi.	17	589	176	195	371	203	43	13	13	26	18	2	1928-29	1945-46
Gould, Bobby	Atl., Cgy., Wsh., Bos.	11	697	145	159	304	572	78	15	13	28	58	....	1979-80	1989-90
Gould, John	Buf., Van., Atl.	9	504	131	138	269	113	14	3	2	5	4	....	1971-72	1979-80
Gould, Larry	Van.	1	2	0	0	0	0	....	....	....	....	....	....	1973-74	1973-74
Goulet, Michel	Que., Chi.	15	1089	548	604	1152	825	92	39	39	78	110	....	1979-80	1993-94
Goupille, Red	Mtl.C., Mtl.	8	222	12	28	40	256	8	2	0	2	6	....	1935-36	1942-43
Govedaris, Chris	Hfd., Tor.	4	45	4	6	10	24	4	0	0	0	2	....	1989-90	1993-94
Goyer, Gerry	Chi.	1	40	1	2	3	4	3	0	0	0	2	....	1967-68	1967-68
Goyette, Phil	Mtl., NYR, St.L., Buf.	16	941	207	467	674	131	94	17	29	46	26	4	1956-57	1971-72

Name	NHL Teams	NHL Seasons	Regular Schedule GP	G	A	TP	PIM	Playoffs GP	G	A	TP	PIM	NHL Cup Wins	First NHL Season	Last NHL Season
Graboski, Tony	Mtl.	3	66	6	10	16	24	3	0	0	0	6	....	1940-41	1942-43
• Gracie, Bob	Tor., Bos., NYA, Mtl.M., Mtl.C., Chi.	9	379	82	109	191	205	33	4	7	11	4	2	1930-31	1938-39
Gradin, Thomas	Van., Bos.	9	677	209	384	593	298	42	17	25	42	20	....	1978-79	1986-87
Graham, Dirk	Min., Chi.	12	772	219	270	489	917	90	17	27	44	92	....	1983-84	1994-95
• Graham, Leth	Ott., Ham.	6	26	3	0	3	0	1	0	0	0	0	1	1920-21	1925-26
Graham, Pat	Pit., Tor.	3	103	11	17	28	136	4	0	0	0	2	....	1981-82	1983-84
Graham, Rod	Bos.	1	14	2	1	3	7	....	....	....	....	....	....	1974-75	1974-75
• Graham, Ted	Chi., Mtl.M., Det., St.L., Bos., NYA	9	346	14	25	39	300	24	3	1	4	30	....	1927-28	1936-37
Grant, Danny	Mtl., Min., Det., L.A.	13	736	263	273	536	239	43	10	14	24	19	1	1965-66	1978-79
Gratton, Dan	L.A.	1	7	1	0	1	5	....	....	....	....	....	....	1987-88	1987-88
Gratton, Norm	NYR, Atl., Buf., Min.	5	201	39	44	83	64	6	0	1	1	2	....	1971-72	1975-76
Gravelle, Leo	Mtl., Det.	5	223	44	34	78	42	17	4	1	5	2	....	1946-47	1950-51
Graves, Hilliard	Cal., Atl., Van., Wpg.	9	556	118	163	281	209	2	0	0	0	0	....	1970-71	1979-80
Graves, Steve	Edm.	3	35	5	4	9	10	....	....	....	....	....	....	1983-84	1987-88
• Gray, Alex	NYR, Tor.	2	50	7	0	7	32	13	1	0	1	0	1	1927-28	1928-29
Gray, Terry	Bos., Mtl., L.A., St.L.	6	147	26	28	54	64	35	5	5	10	22	....	1961-62	1970-71
• Green, Red	Ham., NYA, Det., Bos.	6	195	59	13	72	261	1	0	0	0	0	1	1923-24	1928-29
Green, Rick	Wsh., Mtl., Det., NYI	15	845	43	220	263	588	100	3	16	19	73	1	1976-77	1991-92
• Green, Shorty	Ham., NYA	5	103	36	8	44	220	....	....	....	....	....	....	1923-24	1927-28
Green, Ted	Bos.	11	620	48	206	254	1029	31	4	8	12	54	1	1960-61	1971-72
Greenlaw, Jeff	Wsh., Fla.	6	57	3	6	9	108	2	0	0	0	21	....	1986-87	1993-94
Gregg, Randy	Edm., Van.	10	474	41	152	193	333	137	13	38	51	127	5	1981-82	1991-92
Greig, Bruce	Cal.	2	9	0	1	1	46	....	....	....	....	....	....	1973-74	1974-75
Grenier, Lucien	Mtl., L.A.	4	151	14	14	28	18	2	0	0	0	0	1	1968-69	1971-72
Grenier, Richard	NYI	1	10	1	1	2	2	....	....	....	....	....	....	1972-73	1972-73
Greschner, Ron	NYR	16	982	179	431	610	1226	84	17	32	49	106	....	1974-75	1989-90
Gretzky, Brent	T.B.	2	13	1	3	4	2	....	....	....	....	....	....	1993-94	1994-95
Grieve, Brent	NYI, Edm., Chi., L.A.	4	97	20	16	36	87	....	....	....	....	....	....	1993-94	1996-97
Grigor, George	Chi.	1	2	1	0	1	0	1	0	0	0	0	....	1943-44	1943-44
Grisdale, John	Tor., Van.	6	250	4	39	43	346	10	0	1	1	15	....	1972-73	1978-79
Gronsdahl, Lloyd	Bos.	1	10	1	2	3	0	....	....	....	....	....	....	1941-42	1941-42
Gronstrand, Jari	Min., NYR, Que., NYI	5	185	8	26	34	135	3	0	0	0	4	....	1986-87	1990-91
Gross, Lloyd	Tor., NYA, Bos., Det.	3	62	11	5	16	20	1	0	0	0	0	....	1926-27	1934-35
• Grosso, Don	Det., Chi., Bos.	9	336	87	117	204	90	48	15	14	29	63	1	1938-39	1946-47
Grosvenor, Len	Ott., NYA, Mtl.C.	6	149	9	11	20	78	4	0	0	0	2	....	1927-28	1932-33
Groulx, Wayne	Que.	1	1	0	0	0	0	....	....	....	....	....	....	1984-85	1984-85
Gruen, Danny	Det., Col.	3	49	9	13	22	19	....	....	....	....	....	....	1972-73	1976-77
Gruhl, Scott	L.A., Pit.	3	20	3	3	6	6	....	....	....	....	....	....	1981-82	1987-88
Gryp, Bob	Bos., Wsh.	3	74	11	13	24	33	....	....	....	....	....	....	1973-74	1975-76
Guay, Francois	Buf.	1	1	0	0	0	0	....	....	....	....	....	....	1989-90	1989-90
Guay, Paul	Phi., L.A., Bos., NYI	7	117	11	23	34	92	9	0	1	1	12	....	1983-84	1990-91
Guerard, Daniel	Ott.	1	2	0	0	0	0	....	....	....	....	....	....	1994-95	1994-95
Guerard, Stephane	Que.	2	34	0	0	0	40	....	....	....	....	....	....	1987-88	1989-90
Guevremont, Jocelyn	Van., Buf., NYR	9	571	84	223	307	319	40	4	17	21	18	....	1971-72	1979-80
Guidolin, Aldo	NYR	4	182	9	15	24	117	....	....	....	....	....	....	1952-53	1955-56
Guidolin, Bep	Bos., Det., Chi.	9	519	107	171	278	606	24	5	7	12	35	....	1942-43	1951-52
Guindon, Bobby	Wpg.	1	6	0	1	1	0	....	....	....	....	....	....	1979-80	1979-80
Gusmanov, Ravil	Wpg.	1	4	0	0	0	0	....	....	....	....	....	....	1995-96	1995-96
Gustafsson, Bengt-Ake	Wsh.	9	629	196	359	555	196	32	9	19	28	16	....	1979-80	1988-89
Gustavsson, Peter	Col.	1	2	0	0	0	0	....	....	....	....	....	....	1981-82	1981-82
Guy, Kevan	Cgy., Van.	6	156	5	20	25	138	5	0	1	1	23	....	1986-87	1991-92

H

Name	NHL Teams	NHL Seasons	Regular Schedule GP	G	A	TP	PIM	Playoffs GP	G	A	TP	PIM	NHL Cup Wins	First NHL Season	Last NHL Season
Haanpaa, Ari	NYI	3	60	6	11	17	37	6	0	0	0	10	....	1985-86	1987-88
Haas, David	Edm., Cgy.	2	7	2	1	3	7	....	....	....	....	....	....	1990-91	1993-94
Habscheid, Marc	Edm., Min., Det., Cgy.	11	345	72	91	163	171	12	1	3	4	13	....	1981-82	1991-92
Hachborn, Len	Phi., L.A.	3	102	20	39	59	29	7	0	3	3	7	....	1983-84	1985-86
Haddon, Lloyd	Det.	1	8	0	0	0	2	1	0	0	0	0	....	1959-60	1959-60
Hadfield, Vic	NYR, Pit.	16	1002	323	389	712	1154	73	27	21	48	117	....	1961-62	1976-77
• Haggarty, Jim	Mtl.	1	5	1	1	2	0	3	2	1	3	0	....	1941-42	1941-42
• Hagglund, Roger	Que.	1	3	0	0	0	0	....	....	....	....	....	....	1984-85	1984-85
Hagman, Matti	Bos., Edm.	4	237	56	89	145	36	20	5	2	7	6	....	1976-77	1981-82
Haidy, Gord	Det.	1	....	....	....	....	....	1	0	0	0	0	1	1949-50	1949-50
Hajdu, Richard	Buf.	2	5	0	0	0	4	....	....	....	....	....	....	1985-86	1986-87
Hajt, Bill	Buf.	14	854	42	202	244	433	80	2	16	18	70	....	1973-74	1986-87
Hakansson, Anders	Min., Pit., L.A.	5	330	52	46	98	141	6	0	0	0	2	....	1981-82	1985-86
• Halderson, Harold	Det., Tor.	1	44	3	2	5	65	....	....	....	....	....	....	1926-27	1926-27
Hale, Larry	Phi.	4	196	5	37	42	90	8	0	0	0	12	....	1968-69	1971-72
Haley, Len	Det.	2	30	2	2	4	14	6	1	3	4	6	....	1959-60	1960-61
Halkidis, Bob	Buf., L.A., Tor., Det., T.B., NYI	11	256	8	32	40	825	20	0	1	1	51	....	1984-85	1995-96
Hall, Bob	NYA	1	8	0	0	0	0	....	....	....	....	....	....	1925-26	1925-26
Hall, Del	Cal.	3	9	2	0	2	2	....	....	....	....	....	....	1971-72	1973-74
• Hall, Joe	Mtl.C.	2	37	15	9	24	235	12	0	1	1	39	....	1917-18	1918-19
Hall, Murray	Chi., Det., Min., Van.	9	164	35	48	83	46	6	0	0	0	0	....	1961-62	1971-72
Hall, Taylor	Van., Bos.	5	41	7	9	16	29	....	....	....	....	....	....	1983-84	1987-88
Hall, Wayne	NYR	1	4	0	0	0	0	....	....	....	....	....	....	1960-61	1960-61
• Halliday, Milt	Ott.	3	67	1	0	1	4	6	0	0	0	0	1	1926-27	1928-29
Hallin, Mats	NYI, Min.	5	152	17	14	31	193	15	1	0	1	13	1	1982-83	1986-87
Halward, Doug	Bos., L.A., Van., Det., Edm.	14	653	69	224	293	774	47	7	10	17	113	....	1975-76	1988-89
Hamel, Gilles	Buf., Wpg., L.A.	9	519	127	147	274	276	27	4	5	9	10	....	1980-81	1988-89
• Hamel, Herb	Tor.	1	2	0	0	0	4	....	....	....	....	....	....	1930-31	1930-31
Hamel, Jean	St.L., Det., Que., Mtl.	12	699	26	95	121	766	33	0	2	2	44	....	1972-73	1983-84
• Hamill, Red	Bos., Chi.	12	419	128	94	222	160	24	1	2	3	20	1	1937-38	1950-51
Hamilton, Al	NYR, Buf., Edm.	7	257	10	78	88	258	7	0	0	0	2	....	1965-66	1979-80
Hamilton, Chuck	Mtl., St.L.	2	4	0	2	2	2	....	....	....	....	....	....	1961-62	1972-73
• Hamilton, Jack	Tor.	3	138	31	48	79	76	11	2	1	3	0	....	1942-43	1945-46
Hamilton, Jim	Pit.	8	95	14	18	32	28	6	3	0	3	0	....	1977-78	1984-85
• Hamilton, Reg	Tor., Chi.	12	424	21	87	108	412	64	3	8	11	46	1	1935-36	1946-47
Hammarstrom, Inge	Tor., St.L.	6	427	116	123	239	86	13	2	3	5	4	....	1973-74	1978-79
Hammond, Ken	L.A., Edm., NYR, Tor., Bos., S.J., Van., Ott.	8	193	18	29	47	290	15	0	0	0	24	....	1984-85	1992-93
Hampson, Gord	Cgy.	1	4	0	0	0	5	....	....	....	....	....	....	1982-83	1982-83
Hampson, Ted	Tor., NYR, Det., Oak., Cal., Min.	12	676	108	245	353	94	35	7	10	17	2	....	1959-60	1971-72
Hampton, Rick	Cal., Cle., L.A.	6	337	59	113	172	147	2	0	0	0	0	....	1974-75	1979-80
Hamr, Radek	Ott.	2	11	0	0	0	0	....	....	....	....	....	....	1992-93	1993-94
Hamway, Mark	NYI	3	53	5	13	18	9	1	0	0	0	0	....	1984-85	1986-87
Handy, Ron	NYI, St.L.	2	14	0	3	3	0	....	....	....	....	....	....	1984-85	1987-88
Hangsleben, Al	Hfd., Wsh., L.A.	3	185	21	48	69	396	....	....	....	....	....	....	1979-80	1981-82
Hankinson, Ben	N.J., T.B.	3	43	3	3	6	45	2	1	0	1	4	....	1992-93	1994-95
Hanna, John	NYR, Mtl., Phi.	5	198	6	26	32	206	....	....	....	....	....	....	1958-59	1967-68
Hannan, Dave	Pit., Edm., Tor., Buf., Col., Ott.	16	841	114	191	305	942	63	6	7	13	46	2	1981-82	1996-97
• Hannigan, Gord	Tor.	4	161	29	31	60	117	9	2	0	2	8	....	1952-53	1955-56
Hannigan, Pat	Tor., NYR, Phi.	5	182	30	39	69	116	11	1	2	3	11	....	1959-60	1968-69
Hannigan, Ray	Tor.	1	3	0	0	0	2	....	....	....	....	....	....	1948-49	1948-49
Hansen, Ritchie	NYI, St.L.	4	20	2	8	10	4	....	....	....	....	....	....	1976-77	1981-82
Hanson, Dave	Det., Min.	2	33	1	1	2	65	....	....	....	....	....	....	1978-79	1979-80
• Hanson, Emil	Det.	1	7	0	0	0	6	....	....	....	....	....	....	1932-33	1932-33
Hanson, Keith	Cgy.	1	25	0	2	2	77	....	....	....	....	....	....	1983-84	1983-84
Hanson, Oscar	Chi.	1	8	0	0	0	0	....	....	....	....	....	....	1937-38	1937-38
Harbaruk, Nick	Pit., St.L.	5	364	45	75	120	273	14	3	1	4	20	....	1969-70	1973-74
Harding, Jeff	Phi.	2	15	0	0	0	47	....	....	....	....	....	....	1988-89	1989-90
Hardy, Joe	Oak., Cal.	2	63	9	14	23	51	4	0	0	0	0	....	1969-70	1970-71
Hardy, Mark	L.A., NYR, Min.	15	915	62	306	368	1293	67	5	16	21	158	....	1979-80	1993-94
Hargreaves, Jim	Van.	2	66	1	7	8	105	....	....	....	....	....	....	1970-71	1972-73
Harkins, Todd	Cgy., Hfd.	3	48	3	3	6	78	....	....	....	....	....	....	1991-92	1993-94
Harlow, Scott	St.L.	1	1	0	1	1	0	....	....	....	....	....	....	1987-88	1987-88
Harmon, Glen	Mtl.	9	452	50	96	146	334	53	5	10	15	37	2	1942-43	1950-51
Harms, John	Chi.	2	44	5	5	10	21	4	3	0	3	2	....	1943-44	1944-45
• Harnott, Walter	Bos.	1	6	0	0	0	2	....	....	....	....	....	....	1933-34	1933-34
Harper, Terry	Mtl., L.A., Det., St.L., Col.	19	1066	35	221	256	1362	112	4	13	17	140	5	1962-63	1980-81

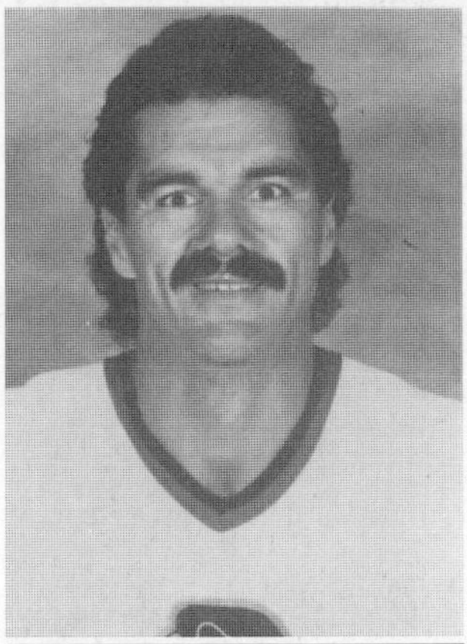

Michel Goulet

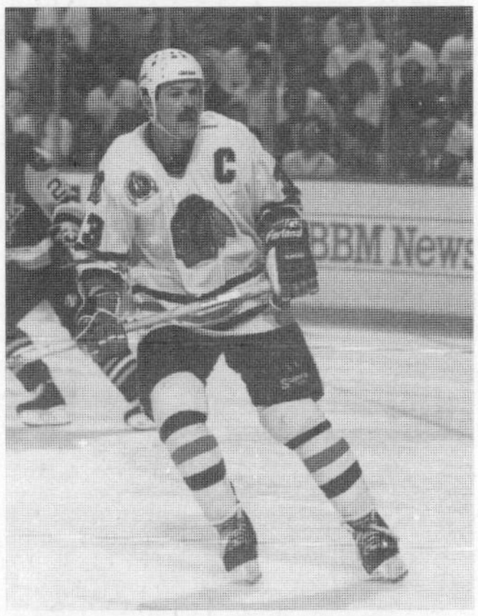

Dirk Graham

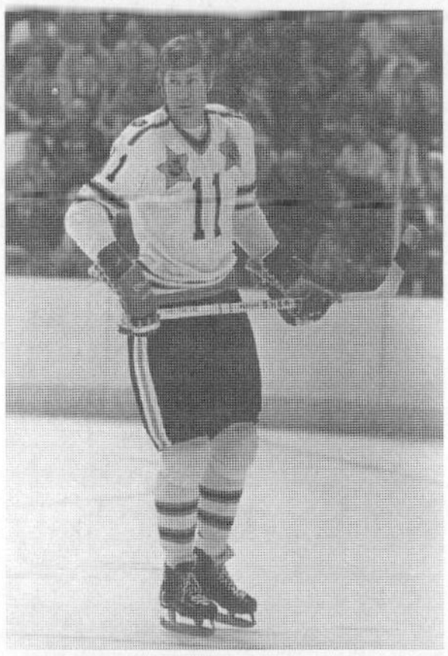

Vic Hadfield

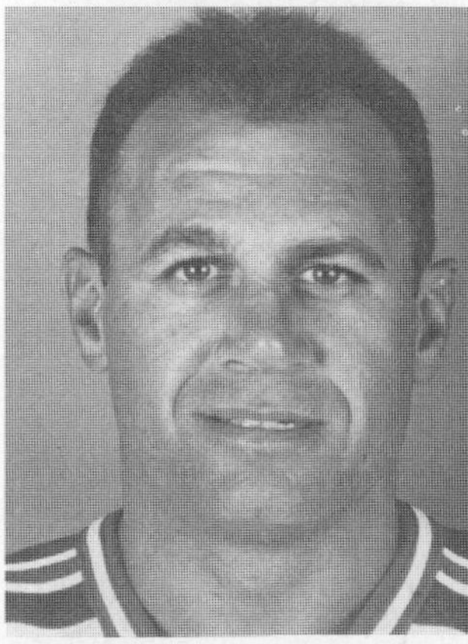

Mark Hardy

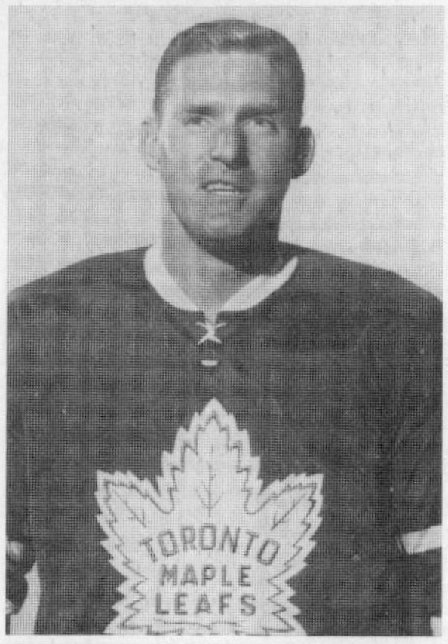

Larry Hillman

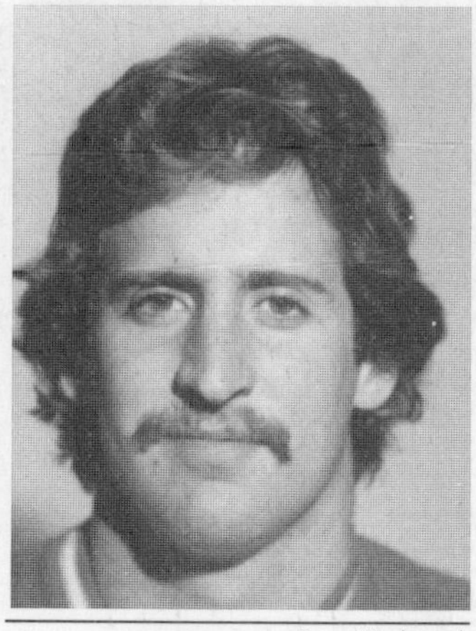

Dave Hindmarch

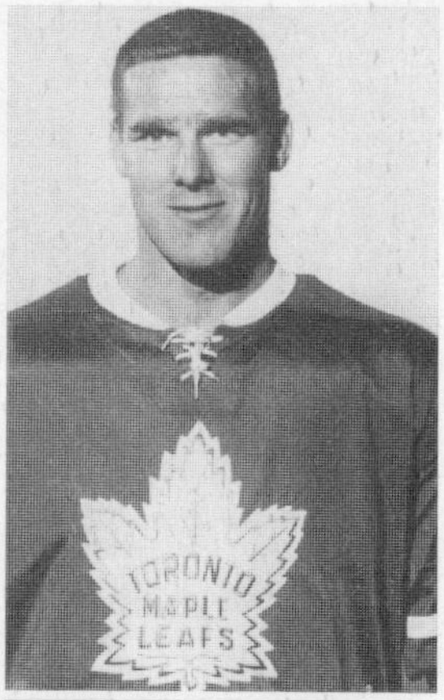

Tim Horton

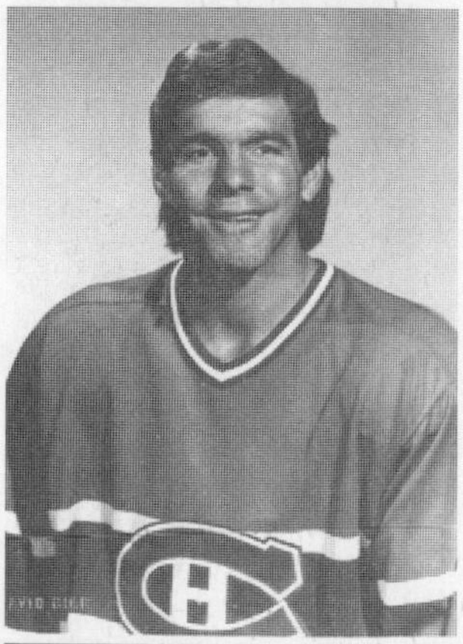

Rejean Houle

Name	NHL Teams	NHL Seasons	Regular Schedule GP	G	A	TP	PIM	Playoffs GP	G	A	TP	PIM	NHL Cup Wins	First NHL Season	Last NHL Season
Harrer, Tim	Cgy.	1	3	0	0	0	2	....	....	....	....	....	....	1982-83	1982-83
• Harrington, Leland	Bos., Mtl.C.	3	72	9	3	12	15	4	1	0	1	2	....	1925-26	1932-33
Harris, Bill	NYI, L.A., Tor.	12	897	231	327	558	394	71	19	19	38	48	....	1972-73	1983-84
Harris, Billy	Tor., Det., Oak., Pit.	13	769	126	219	345	205	62	8	10	18	30	3	1955-56	1968-69
Harris, Duke	Min., Tor.	1	26	1	4	5	4	....	....	....	....	....	....	1967-68	1967-68
• Harris, Henry	Bos.	1	32	2	4	6	20	....	....	....	....	....	....	1930-31	1930-31
Harris, Hugh	Buf.	1	60	12	26	38	17	3	0	0	0	0	....	1972-73	1972-73
Harris, Ron	Det., Oak., Atl., NYR	11	476	20	91	111	474	28	4	3	7	33	....	1962-63	1975-76
Harris, Ted	Mtl., Min., Det., St.L., Phi.	12	788	30	168	198	1000	100	1	22	23	230	5	1963-64	1974-75
• Harris, Thomas	Bos.	1	6	3	1	4	8	....	....	....	....	....	....	1924-25	1924-25
Harrison, Ed	Bos., NYR	4	194	27	24	51	53	9	1	0	1	2	....	1947-48	1950-51
Harrison, Jim	Bos., Tor., Chi., Edm.	8	324	67	86	153	435	13	1	1	2	43	....	1968-69	1979-80
Hart, Gerry	Det., NYI, Que., St.L.	15	730	29	150	179	1240	78	3	12	15	175	....	1968-69	1982-83
• Hart, Wilf	Det., Mtl.C.	3	104	6	8	14	12	8	0	1	1	0	....	1926-27	1932-33
Hartman, Mike	Buf., Wpg., T.B., NYR	9	397	43	35	78	1388	21	0	0	0	106	....	1986-87	1994-95
Hartsburg, Craig	Min.	10	570	98	315	413	818	61	15	27	42	70	....	1979-80	1988-89
• Harvey, Doug	Mtl., NYR, Det., St.L.	20	1113	88	452	540	1216	137	8	64	72	152	6	1947-48	1968-69
Harvey, Fred	Min., Atl., K.C., Det.	7	407	90	118	208	131	14	0	2	2	8	....	1970-71	1976-77
Harvey, Hugh	K.C.	2	18	1	1	2	4	....	....	....	....	....	....	1974-75	1975-76
Hassard, Bob	Tor., Chi.	5	126	9	28	37	22	....	....	....	....	....	....	1949-50	1954-55
Hatoum, Ed	Det., Van.	3	47	3	6	9	25	....	....	....	....	....	....	1968-69	1970-71
Hawerchuk, Dale	Wpg., Buf., St.L., Phi.	16	1188	518	891	1409	730	97	30	69	99	67	....	1981-82	1996-97
Haworth, Alan	Buf., Wsh., Que.	8	524	189	211	400	425	42	12	16	28	28	....	1980-81	1987-88
Haworth, Gord	NYR	1	2	0	1	1	0	....	....	....	....	....	....	1952-53	1952-53
Hawryliw, Neil	NYI	1	1	0	0	0	0	....	....	....	....	....	....	1981-82	1981-82
Hay, Bill	Chi.	8	506	113	273	386	244	67	15	21	36	62	1	1959-60	1966-67
• Hay, George	Chi., Det.	7	239	74	60	134	84	8	2	3	5	2	....	1926-27	1933-34
Hay, Jim	Det.	3	75	1	5	6	22	9	1	0	1	2	1	1952-53	1954-55
Hayek, Peter	Min.	1	1	0	0	0	0	....	....	....	....	....	....	1981-82	1981-82
Hayes, Chris	Bos.	1	....	....	....	....	....	1	0	0	0	0	1	1971-72	1971-72
• Haynes, Paul	Mtl.M., Bos., Mtl.C., Mtl.	11	391	61	134	195	164	24	2	8	10	13	....	1930-31	1940-41
Hayward, Rick	L.A.	1	4	0	0	0	5	....	....	....	....	....	....	1990-91	1990-91
Hazlett, Steve	Van.	1	1	0	0	0	0	....	....	....	....	....	....	1979-80	1979-80
Head, Galen	Det.	1	1	0	0	0	0	....	....	....	....	....	....	1967-68	1967-68
• Headley, Fern	Bos., Mtl.C.	1	27	1	1	2	6	5	0	0	0	0	....	1924-25	1924-25
Healey, Dick	Det.	1	1	0	0	0	2	....	....	....	....	....	....	1960-61	1960-61
Heaphy, Shawn	Cgy.	1	1	0	0	0	0	....	....	....	....	....	....	1992-93	1992-93
Heaslip, Mark	NYR, L.A.	3	117	10	19	29	110	5	0	0	0	2	....	1976-77	1978-79
Heath, Randy	NYR	2	13	2	4	6	15	....	....	....	....	....	....	1984-85	1985-86
Hebenton, Andy	NYR, Bos.	9	630	189	202	391	83	22	6	5	11	8	....	1955-56	1963-64
Hedberg, Anders	NYR	7	465	172	225	397	144	58	22	24	46	31	....	1978-79	1984-85
• Heffernan, Frank	Tor.	1	19	0	1	1	10	....	....	....	....	....	....	1919-20	1919-20
Heffernan, Gerry	Mtl.	3	83	33	35	68	27	11	3	3	6	8	1	1941-42	1943-44
Heidt, Michael	L.A.	1	6	0	1	1	7	....	....	....	....	....	....	1983-84	1983-84
• Heindl, Bill	Min., NYR	3	18	2	1	3	0	....	....	....	....	....	....	1970-71	1972-73
Heinrich, Lionel	Bos.	1	35	1	1	2	33	....	....	....	....	....	....	1955-56	1955-56
Heiskala, Earl	Phi.	3	127	13	11	24	294	....	....	....	....	....	....	1968-69	1970-71
Helander, Peter	L.A.	1	7	0	1	1	0	....	....	....	....	....	....	1982-83	1982-83
• Heller, Ott	NYR	15	647	55	176	231	465	61	6	8	14	61	2	1931-32	1945-46
Helman, Harry	Ott.	3	42	1	0	1	7	4	0	0	0	0	1	1922-23	1924-25
Helminen, Raimo	NYR, Min., NYI	3	117	13	46	59	16	2	0	0	0	0	....	1985-86	1988-89
• Hemmerling, Tony	NYA	2	22	3	3	6	4	....	....	....	....	....	....	1935-36	1936-37
Henderson, Archie	Wsh., Min., Hfd.	3	23	3	1	4	92	....	....	....	....	....	....	1980-81	1982-83
Henderson, Murray	Bos.	8	405	24	62	86	305	41	2	3	5	23	....	1944-45	1951-52
Henderson, Paul	Det., Tor., Atl.	13	707	236	241	477	304	56	11	14	25	28	....	1962-63	1979-80
Hendrickson, John	Det.	3	5	0	0	0	4	....	....	....	....	....	....	1957-58	1961-62
Henning, Lorne	NYI	9	544	73	111	184	102	81	7	7	14	8	2	1972-73	1980-81
• Henry, Camille	NYR, Chi., St.L.	14	727	279	249	528	88	47	6	12	18	7	....	1953-54	1969-70
Henry, Dale	NYI	6	132	13	26	39	263	14	1	0	1	19	....	1984-85	1989-90
Hepple, Alan	N.J.	3	3	0	0	0	7	....	....	....	....	....	....	1983-84	1985-86
• Herberts, Jimmy	Bos., Tor., Det.	6	206	83	29	112	248	9	3	0	3	10	....	1924-25	1929-30
Herchenratter, Art	Det.	1	10	1	2	3	2	....	....	....	....	....	....	1940-41	1940-41
Hergerts, Fred	NYA	2	20	2	4	6	2	....	....	....	....	....	....	1934-35	1935-36
Hergesheimer, Philip	Chi., Bos.	4	125	21	41	62	19	6	0	0	0	2	....	1939-40	1942-43
Hergesheimer, Wally	NYR, Chi.	7	351	114	85	199	106	5	1	0	1	0	....	1951-52	1958-59
Heron, Red	Tor., Bro., Mtl.	4	106	21	19	40	38	21	2	2	4	6	....	1938-39	1941-42
Heroux, Yves	Que.	1	1	0	0	0	0	....	....	....	....	....	....	1986-87	1986-87
Herter, Jason	NYI	1	1	0	1	1	0	....	....	....	....	....	....	1995-96	1995-96
Hervey, Matt	Wpg., Bos., T.B.	3	35	0	5	5	97	5	0	0	0	6	....	1988-89	1992-93
Hess, Bob	St.L., Buf., Hfd.	8	329	27	95	122	178	4	1	1	2	2	....	1974-75	1983-84
Heximer, Orville	NYR, Bos., NYA	3	84	13	7	20	16	5	0	0	0	2	....	1929-30	1934-35
Hextall, Bryan Jr.	NYR, Pit., Atl., Det., Min.	8	549	99	161	260	738	18	0	4	4	59	....	1962-63	1975-76
• Hextall, Bryan Sr.	NYR	11	449	187	175	362	227	37	8	9	17	19	1	1936-37	1947-48
Hextall, Dennis	NYR, L.A., Cal., Min., Det., Wsh.	13	681	153	350	503	1398	22	3	3	6	45	....	1967-68	1979-80
Heyliger, Vic	Chi.	2	33	2	3	5	2	....	....	....	....	....	....	1937-38	1943-44
Hicke, Bill	Mtl., NYR, Oak., Cal., Pit.	14	729	168	234	402	395	42	3	10	13	41	2	1958-59	1971-72
Hicke, Ernie	Cal., Atl., NYI, Min., L.A.	8	520	132	140	272	407	2	1	0	1	0	....	1970-71	1977-78
Hickey, Greg	NYR	1	1	0	0	0	0	....	....	....	....	....	....	1977-78	1977-78
Hickey, Pat	NYR, Col., Tor., Que., St.L.	10	646	192	212	404	351	55	5	11	16	37	....	1975-76	1984-85
Hicks, Doug	Min., Chi., Edm., Wsh.	9	561	37	131	168	442	18	2	1	3	15	....	1974-75	1982-83
Hicks, Glenn	Det.	2	108	6	12	18	127	....	....	....	....	....	....	1979-80	1980-81
• Hicks, Harold	Mtl.M., Det.	3	96	7	2	9	72	....	....	....	....	....	....	1928-29	1930-31
Hicks, Wayne	Chi., Bos., Mtl., Phi., Pit.	5	115	13	23	36	22	2	0	1	1	2	1	1959-60	1967-68
Hidi, Andre	Wsh.	2	7	2	1	3	9	2	0	0	0	0	....	1983-84	1984-85
Hiemer, Uli	N.J.	3	143	19	54	73	176	....	....	....	....	....	....	1984-85	1986-87
Higgins, Paul	Tor.	2	25	0	0	0	152	1	0	0	0	0	....	1981-82	1982-83
Higgins, Tim	Chi., N.J., Det.	11	706	154	198	352	719	65	5	8	13	77	....	1978-79	1988-89
Hildebrand, Ike	NYR, Chi.	2	41	7	11	18	16	....	....	....	....	....	....	1953-54	1954-55
Hill, Al	Phi.	8	221	40	55	95	227	51	8	11	19	43	....	1976-77	1987-88
Hill, Brian	Hfd.	1	19	1	1	2	4	....	....	....	....	....	....	1979-80	1979-80
• Hill, Mel	Bos., Bro., Tor.	9	324	89	109	198	128	43	12	7	19	18	3	1937-38	1945-46
Hiller, Dutch	NYR, Det., Bos., Mtl.	9	383	91	113	204	163	48	9	8	17	21	2	1937-38	1945-46
Hiller, Jim	L.A., Det., NYR	2	63	8	12	20	116	2	0	0	0	4	....	1992-93	1993-94
Hillier, Randy	Bos., Pit., NYI, Buf.	11	543	16	110	126	906	28	0	2	2	93	1	1981-82	1991-92
Hillman, Floyd	Bos.	1	6	0	0	0	10	....	....	....	....	....	....	1956-57	1956-57
Hillman, Larry	Det., Bos., Tor., Min., Mtl., Phi., L.A., Buf.	19	790	36	196	232	579	74	2	9	11	30	4	1954-55	1972-73
• Hillman, Wayne	Chi., NYR, Min., Phi.	13	691	18	86	104	534	28	0	3	3	19	1	1960-61	1972-73
Hilworth, John	Det.	3	57	1	1	2	89	....	....	....	....	....	....	1977-78	1979-80
• Himes, Normie	NYA	9	402	106	113	219	127	2	0	0	0	0	....	1926-27	1934-35
Hindmarch, Dave	Cgy.	4	99	21	17	38	25	10	0	0	0	6	....	1980-81	1983-84
Hinse, Andre	Tor.	1	4	0	0	0	0	....	....	....	....	....	....	1967-68	1967-68
Hinton, Dan	Chi.	1	14	0	0	0	16	....	....	....	....	....	....	1976-77	1976-77
Hirsch, Tom	Min.	3	31	1	7	8	30	12	0	0	0	6	....	1983-84	1987-88
• Hirschfeld, Bert	Mtl.	2	33	1	4	5	2	5	1	0	1	0	....	1949-50	1950-51
Hislop, Jamie	Que., Cgy.	5	345	75	103	178	86	28	3	2	5	11	....	1979-80	1983-84
• Hitchman, Lionel	Ott., Bos.	12	416	28	33	61	523	40	4	1	5	77	2	1922-23	1933-34
Hlinka, Ivan	Van.	2	137	42	81	123	28	16	3	10	13	8	....	1981-82	1982-83
Hodge, Ken	Chi., Bos., NYR	14	881	328	472	800	779	97	34	47	81	120	2	1964-65	1977-78
Hodge, Ken	Min., Bos., T.B.	4	142	39	48	87	32	15	4	6	10	6	....	1988-89	1992-93
Hodgson, Dan	Tor., Van.	4	114	29	45	74	64	....	....	....	....	....	....	1985-86	1988-89
Hodgson, Rick	Hfd.	1	6	0	0	0	6	1	0	0	0	0	....	1979-80	1979-80
Hodgson, Ted	Bos.	1	4	0	0	0	0	....	....	....	....	....	....	1966-67	1966-67
Hoekstra, Cecil	Mtl.	1	4	0	0	0	0	....	....	....	....	....	....	1959-60	1959-60
Hoekstra, Ed	Phi.	1	70	15	21	36	6	7	0	1	1	0	....	1967-68	1967-68
Hoene, Phil	L.A.	3	37	2	4	6	22	....	....	....	....	....	....	1972-73	1974-75
Hoffinger, Val	Chi.	2	28	0	1	1	30	....	....	....	....	....	....	1927-28	1928-29
Hoffman, Mike	Hfd.	3	9	1	3	4	2	....	....	....	....	....	....	1982-83	1985-86
Hoffmeyer, Bob	Chi., Phi., N.J.	6	198	14	52	66	325	3	0	1	1	25	....	1977-78	1984-85
Hofford, Jim	Buf., L.A.	3	18	0	0	0	47	....	....	....	....	....	....	1985-86	1988-89
Hogaboam, Bill	Atl., Det., Min.	8	332	80	109	189	100	2	0	0	0	0	....	1972-73	1979-80
Hoganson, Dale	L.A., Mtl., Que.	7	343	13	77	90	186	11	0	3	3	12	....	1969-70	1981-82

Name	NHL Teams	NHL Seasons	Regular Schedule GP	G	A	TP	PIM	Playoffs GP	G	A	TP	PIM	NHL Cup Wins	First NHL Season	Last NHL Season
Holan, Milos	Phi., Ana.	3	49	5	11	16	42	....	....	....	....	....	....	1993-94	1995-96
Holbrook, Terry	Min.	2	43	3	6	9	4	6	0	0	0	0	....	1972-73	1973-74
Holland, Jerry	NYR	2	37	8	4	12	6	....	....	....	....	....	....	1974-75	1975-76
• Hollett, Flash	Tor., Ott., Bos., Det.	13	562	132	181	313	358	79	8	26	34	38	2	1933-34	1945-46
• Hollingworth, Gord	Chi., Det.	4	163	4	14	18	201	3	0	0	0	2	....	1954-55	1957-58
Holloway, Bruce	Van.	1	2	0	0	0	0	....	....	....	....	....	....	1984-85	1984-85
• Holmes, Bill	Mtl.C., NYA	3	52	6	4	10	35	....	....	....	....	....	....	1925-26	1929-30
Holmes, Chuck	Det.	2	23	1	3	4	10	....	....	....	....	....	....	1958-59	1961-62
Holmes, Lou	Chi.	2	59	1	4	5	6	2	0	0	0	2	....	1931-32	1932-33
Holmes, Warren	L.A.	3	45	8	18	26	7	....	....	....	....	....	....	1981-82	1983-84
Holmgren, Paul	Phi., Min.	10	527	144	179	323	1684	82	19	32	51	195	....	1975-76	1984-85
• Holota, John	Det.	2	15	2	0	2	0	....	....	....	....	....	....	1942-43	1945-46
Holst, Greg	NYR	3	11	0	0	0	0	....	....	....	....	....	....	1975-76	1977-78
Holt, Gary	Cal., Cle., St.L.	5	101	13	11	24	133	....	....	....	....	....	....	1973-74	1977-78
Holt, Randy	Chi., Cle., Van., L.A., Cgy., Wsh., Phi.	10	395	4	37	41	1438	21	2	3	5	83	....	1974-75	1983-84
• Holway, Albert	Tor., Mtl.M., Pit.	5	113	7	2	9	48	8	0	0	0	2	1	1923-24	1928-29
Homenuke, Ron	Van.	1	1	0	0	0	0	....	....	....	....	....	....	1972-73	1972-73
Hoover, Ron	Bos., St.L.	3	18	4	0	4	31	8	0	0	0	18	....	1989-90	1991-92
Hopkins, Dean	L.A., Edm., Que.	6	223	23	51	74	306	18	1	5	6	29	....	1979-80	1988-89
Hopkins, Larry	Tor., Wpg.	4	60	13	16	29	26	6	0	0	0	2	....	1977-78	1982-83
Horacek, Tony	Phi., Chi.	5	154	10	19	29	316	2	1	0	1	2	....	1989-90	1994-95
Horava, Miloslav	NYR	3	80	5	17	22	38	2	0	1	1	0	....	1988-89	1990-91
Horbul, Doug	K.C.	1	4	1	0	1	2	....	....	....	....	....	....	1974-75	1974-75
Hordy, Mike	NYI	2	11	0	0	0	7	....	....	....	....	....	....	1978-79	1979-80
Horeck, Pete	Chi., Det., Bos.	8	426	106	118	224	340	34	6	8	14	43	....	1944-45	1951-52
• Horne, George	Mtl.M., Tor.	3	54	9	3	12	34	4	0	0	0	4	....	1925-26	1928-29
Horner, Red	Tor.	12	490	42	110	152	1254	71	7	10	17	170	1	1928-29	1939-40
Hornung, Larry	St.L.	2	48	2	9	11	10	11	0	2	2	2	....	1970-71	1971-72
• Horton, Tim	Tor., NYR, Pit., Buf.	24	1446	115	403	518	1611	126	11	39	50	183	4	1949-50	1973-74
Horvath, Bronco	NYR, Mtl., Bos., Chi., Tor., Min.	9	434	141	185	326	319	36	12	9	21	18	....	1955-56	1967-68
Hospodar, Ed	NYR, Hfd., Phi., Min., Buf.	9	450	17	51	68	1314	44	4	1	5	208	....	1979-80	1987-88
Hostak, Martin	Phi.	2	55	3	11	14	24	....	....	....	....	....	....	1990-91	1991-92
Hotham, Greg	Tor., Pit.	6	230	15	74	89	139	5	0	3	3	6	....	1979-80	1984-85
Houck, Paul	Min.	3	16	1	2	3	2	....	....	....	....	....	....	1985-86	1987-88
Houde, Claude	K.C.	2	59	3	6	9	40	....	....	....	....	....	....	1974-75	1975-76
Houle, Rejean	Mtl.	11	635	161	247	408	395	90	14	34	48	66	5	1969-70	1982-83
Houston, Ken	Atl., Cgy., Wsh., L.A.	9	570	161	167	328	624	35	10	9	19	66	....	1975-76	1983-84
Howard, John Francis	Tor.	1	2	0	0	0	0	....	....	....	....	....	....	1936-37	1936-37
Howatt, Garry	NYI, Hfd., N.J.	12	720	112	156	268	1836	87	12	14	26	289	2	1972-73	1983-84
Howe, Gordie	Det., Hfd.	26	1767	801	1049	1850	1685	157	68	92	160	220	4	1946-47	1979-80
Howe, Mark	Hfd., Phi., Det.	16	929	197	545	742	455	101	10	51	61	34	....	1979-80	1994-95
Howe, Marty	Hfd., Bos.	6	197	2	29	31	99	15	1	2	3	9	....	1979-80	1984-85
• Howe, Syd	Ott., Phi., Tor., St.L., Det.	17	698	237	291	528	212	70	17	27	44	10	3	1929-30	1945-46
Howe, Vic	NYR	3	33	3	4	7	10	....	....	....	....	....	....	1950-51	1954-55
Howell, Harry	NYR, Oak., Cal., L.A.	21	1411	94	324	418	1298	38	3	3	6	32	....	1952-53	1972-73
• Howell, Ron	NYR	2	4	0	0	0	0	....	....	....	....	....	....	1954-55	1955-56
Howse, Don	L.A.	1	33	2	5	7	6	2	0	0	0	0	....	1979-80	1979-80
Howson, Scott	NYI	2	18	5	3	8	4	....	....	....	....	....	....	1984-85	1985-86
Hoyda, Dave	Phi., Wpg.	4	132	6	17	23	299	12	0	0	0	17	....	1977-78	1980-81
Hrdina, Jiri	Cgy., Pit.	5	250	45	85	130	92	46	2	5	7	24	3	1987-88	1991-92
Hrechkosy, Dave	Cal., St.L.	4	140	42	24	66	41	3	1	0	1	2	....	1973-74	1976-77
Hrycuik, Jim	Wsh.	1	21	5	5	10	12	....	....	....	....	....	....	1974-75	1974-75
Hrymnak, Steve	Chi., Det.	2	18	2	1	3	4	2	0	0	0	0	....	1951-52	1952-53
Hrynewich, Tim	Pit.	2	55	6	8	14	82	....	....	....	....	....	....	1982-83	1983-84
Huard, Rolly	Tor.	1	1	1	0	1	0	....	....	....	....	....	....	1930-31	1930-31
Huber, Willie	Det., NYR, Van., Phi.	10	655	104	217	321	950	33	5	5	10	35	....	1978-79	1987-88
Hubick, Greg	Tor., Van.	2	77	6	9	15	10	....	....	....	....	....	....	1975-76	1979-80
Huck, Fran	Mtl., St.L.	3	94	24	30	54	38	11	3	4	7	2	....	1969-70	1972-73
Hucul, Fred	Chi., St.L.	5	164	11	30	41	113	6	1	0	1	10	....	1950-51	1967-68
Huddy, Charlie	Edm., L.A., Buf., St.L.	17	1017	99	354	453	785	183	19	66	85	135	5	1980-81	1996-97
Hudson, Dave	NYI, K.C., Col.	6	409	59	124	183	89	2	1	1	2	0	....	1972-73	1977-78
Hudson, Lex	Pit.	1	2	0	0	0	0	2	0	0	0	0	....	1978-79	1978-79
Hudson, Mike	Chi., Edm., NYR, Pit., Tor., St.L., Phx.	9	416	49	87	136	414	49	4	10	14	64	1	1988-89	1996-97
Hudson, Ron	Det.	2	33	5	2	7	2	....	....	....	....	....	....	1937-38	1939-40
Huffman, Kerry	Phi., Que., Ott.	10	401	37	108	145	361	11	0	0	0	2	....	1986-87	1995-96
Huggins, Al	Mtl.M.	1	20	1	1	2	2	....	....	....	....	....	....	1930-31	1930-31
Hughes, Al	NYA	2	60	6	8	14	22	....	....	....	....	....	....	1930-31	1931-32
Hughes, Brent	L.A., Phi., St.L., Det., K.C.	8	435	15	117	132	440	22	1	3	4	53	....	1967-68	1974-75
Hughes, Frank	Cal.	1	5	0	0	0	0	....	....	....	....	....	....	1971-72	1971-72
Hughes, Howie	L.A.	3	168	25	32	57	30	14	2	0	2	2	....	1967-68	1969-70
Hughes, Jack	Col.	2	46	2	5	7	104	....	....	....	....	....	....	1980-81	1981-82
Hughes, James	Det.	1	40	0	1	1	48	....	....	....	....	....	....	1929-30	1929-30
Hughes, John	Van., Edm., NYR	2	70	2	14	16	211	7	0	1	1	16	....	1979-80	1980-81
Hughes, Pat	Mtl., Pit., Edm., Buf., St.L., Hfd.	10	573	130	128	258	646	71	8	25	33	77	3	1977-78	1986-87
Hughes, Ryan	Bos.	1	3	0	0	0	0	....	....	....	....	....	....	1995-96	1995-96
Hull, Bobby	Chi., Wpg., Hfd.	16	1063	610	560	1170	640	119	62	67	129	102	1	1957-58	1979-80
Hull, Dennis	Chi., Det.	14	959	303	351	654	261	104	33	34	67	30	....	1964-65	1977-78
• Hunt, Fred	NYA, NYR	2	59	15	14	29	6	....	....	....	....	....	....	1940-41	1944-45
Hunter, Dave	Edm., Pit., Wpg.	10	746	133	190	323	918	105	16	24	40	211	3	1979-80	1988-89
Hunter, Mark	Mtl., St.L., Cgy., Hfd., Wsh.	12	628	213	171	384	1426	79	18	20	38	230	1	1981-82	1992-93
Hunter, Tim	Cgy., Que., Van., S.J.	16	815	62	76	138	3146	132	5	7	12	426	1	1981-82	1996-97
Huras, Larry	NYR	1	2	0	0	0	0	....	....	....	....	....	....	1976-77	1976-77
Hurlburt, Bob	Van.	1	1	0	0	0	2	....	....	....	....	....	....	1974-75	1974-75
Hurley, Paul	Bos.	1	1	0	1	1	0	....	....	....	....	....	....	1968-69	1968-69
Hurst, Ron	Tor.	2	64	9	7	16	70	3	0	2	2	4	....	1955-56	1956-57
Huston, Ron	Cal.	2	79	15	31	46	8	....	....	....	....	....	....	1973-74	1974-75
Hutchinson, Ronald	NYR	1	9	0	0	0	0	....	....	....	....	....	....	1960-61	1960-61
Hutchison, Dave	L.A., Tor., Chi., N.J.	10	584	19	97	116	1550	48	2	12	14	149	....	1974-75	1983-84
• Hutton, Bill	Bos., Ott., Phi.	2	64	3	2	5	8	2	0	0	0	0	....	1929-30	1930-31
• Hyland, Harry	Mtl., Ott.	1	17	14	2	16	65	....	....	....	....	....	....	1917-18	1917-18
Hynes, Dave	Bos.	2	22	4	0	4	2	....	....	....	....	....	....	1973-74	1974-75
Hynes, Gord	Bos., Phi.	2	52	3	9	12	22	12	1	2	3	6	....	1991-92	1992-93

I

Name	NHL Teams	NHL Seasons	Regular Schedule GP	G	A	TP	PIM	Playoffs GP	G	A	TP	PIM	NHL Cup Wins	First NHL Season	Last NHL Season
Iafrate, Al	Tor., Wsh., Bos., S.J.	12	799	152	311	463	1301	71	19	16	35	77	....	1984-85	1997-98
Ihnacak, Miroslav	Tor., Det.	3	56	8	9	17	39	1	0	0	0	0	....	1985-86	1988-89
Ihnacak, Peter	Tor.	8	417	102	165	267	175	28	4	10	14	25	....	1982-83	1989-90
Imlach, Brent	Tor.	2	3	0	0	0	0	....	....	....	....	....	....	1965-66	1966-67
Ingarfield, Earl	NYR, Pit., Oak., Cal.	13	746	179	226	405	239	21	9	8	17	10	....	1958-59	1970-71
Ingarfield, Earl Jr.	Atl., Cgy., Det.	2	39	4	4	8	22	2	0	1	1	0	....	1979-80	1980-81
Inglis, Billy	L.A., Buf.	3	36	1	3	4	4	11	1	2	3	4	....	1967-68	1970-71
• Ingoldsby, Johnny	Tor.	2	29	5	1	6	15	....	....	....	....	....	....	1942-43	1943-44
Ingram, Frank	Chi.	3	101	24	16	40	69	11	0	1	1	2	....	1929-30	1931-32
• Ingram, John J.	Bos.	1	1	0	0	0	0	....	....	....	....	....	....	1924-25	1924-25
Ingram, Ron	Chi., Det., NYR	4	114	5	15	20	81	2	0	0	0	0	....	1956-57	1964-65
• Irvin, Dick	Chi.	3	94	29	23	52	78	2	2	0	2	4	....	1926-27	1928-29
Irvine, Ted	Bos., L.A., NYR, St.L.	11	724	154	177	331	657	83	16	24	40	115	....	1963-64	1976-77
Irwin, Ivan	Mtl., NYR	5	155	2	27	29	214	5	0	0	0	8	....	1952-53	1957-58
Isaksson, Ulf	L.A.	1	50	7	15	22	10	....	....	....	....	....	....	1982-83	1982-83
Issel, Kim	Edm.	1	4	0	0	0	0	....	....	....	....	....	....	1988-89	1988-89

J

Name	NHL Teams	NHL Seasons	Regular Schedule GP	G	A	TP	PIM	Playoffs GP	G	A	TP	PIM	NHL Cup Wins	First NHL Season	Last NHL Season
• Jackson, Art	Tor., Bos., NYA	11	468	123	178	301	144	52	8	12	20	29	2	1934-35	1944-45
Jackson, Don	Min., Edm., NYR	10	311	16	52	68	640	53	4	5	9	147	2	1977-78	1986-87
• Jackson, Harold	Chi., Det.	8	219	17	34	51	208	31	1	2	3	33	2	1936-37	1946-47
• Jackson, Harvey	Tor., NYA, Bos.	15	633	241	234	475	437	71	18	12	30	53	1	1929-30	1943-44
Jackson, Jeff	Tor., NYR, Que., Chi.	8	263	38	48	86	313	6	1	1	2	16	....	1984-85	1991-92
Jackson, Jim	Cgy., Buf.	4	112	17	30	47	20	14	3	2	5	6	....	1982-83	1987-88
Jackson, John	Chi.	1	48	2	5	7	38	....	....	....	....	....	....	1946-47	1946-47

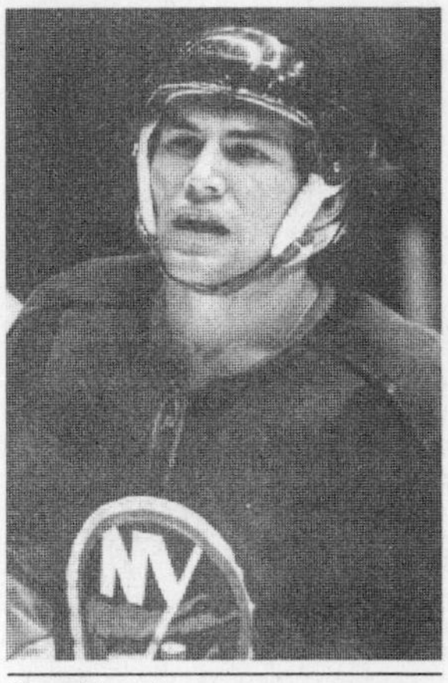
Garry Howatt

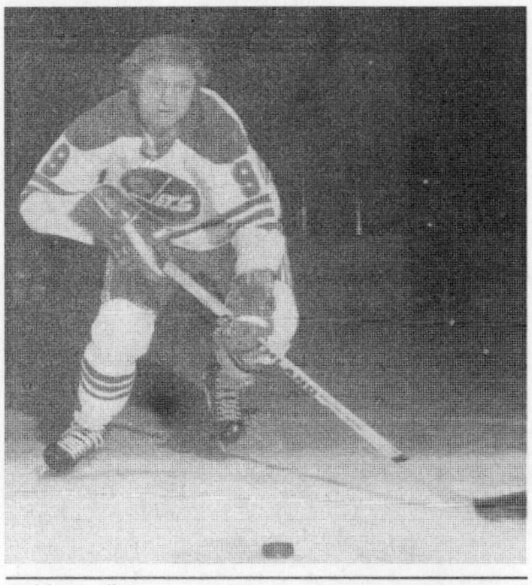
Bobby Hull

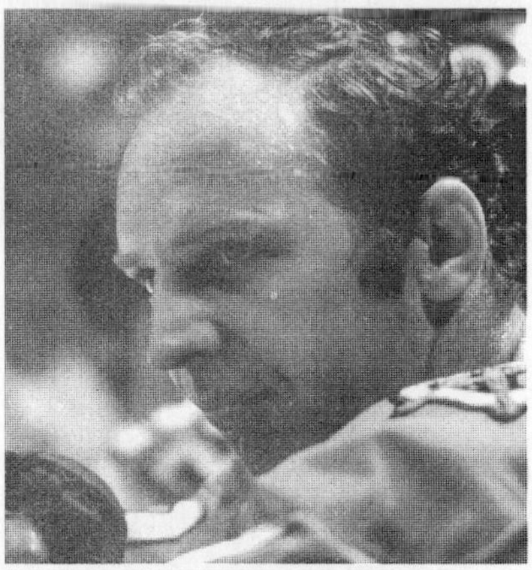
Dennis Hull

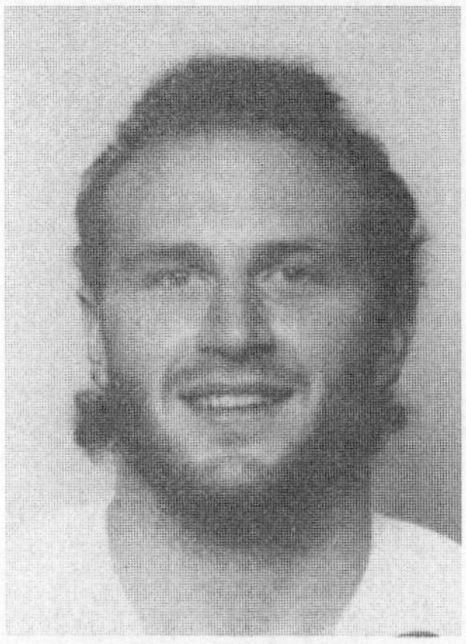
Al Iafrate

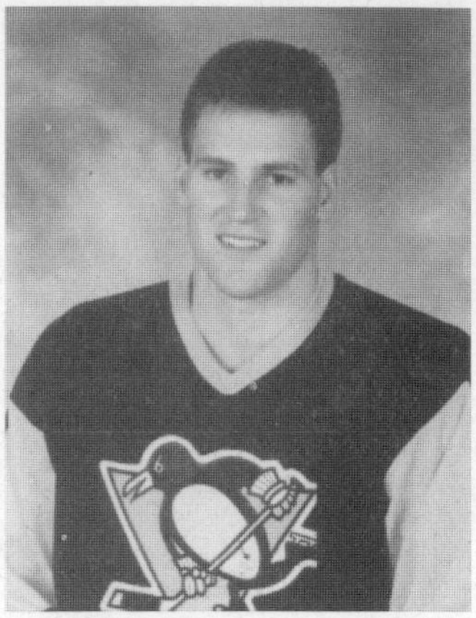

Jim Johnson

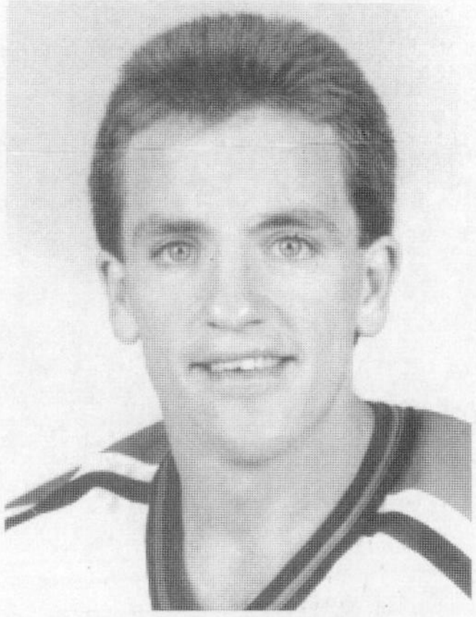

Mark Johnson

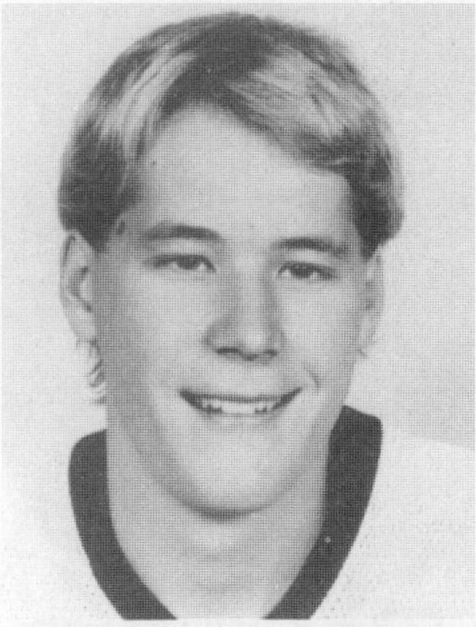

Greg Johnston

			Regular Schedule					Playoffs					NHL	First	Last
Name	NHL Teams	NHL Seasons	GP	G	A	TP	PIM	GP	G	A	TP	PIM	Cup Wins	NHL Season	NHL Season
Jackson, Lloyd	NYA	1	14	1	1	2	0	....	....	....	....	....	....	1936-37	1936-37
• Jackson, Stan	Tor., Bos., Ott.	5	85	9	4	13	74	....	....	....	....	....	....	1921-22	1926-27
Jackson, Walter	NYA, Bos.	4	84	16	11	27	18	....	....	....	....	....	....	1932-33	1935-36
• Jacobs, Paul	Tor.	1	1	0	0	0	0	....	....	....	....	....	....	1918-19	1918-19
Jacobs, Tim	Cal.	1	46	0	10	10	35	....	....	....	....	....	....	1975-76	1975-76
Jalo, Risto	Edm.	1	3	0	3	3	0	....	....	....	....	....	....	1985-86	1985-86
Jalonen, Kari	Cgy., Edm.	2	37	9	6	15	4	5	1	0	1	0	....	1982-83	1983-84
James, Gerry	Tor.	5	149	14	26	40	257	15	1	0	1	8	....	1954-55	1959-60
James, Val	Buf., Tor.	2	11	0	0	0	30	....	....	....	....	....	....	1981-82	1986-87
Jamieson, Jim	NYR	1	1	0	1	1	0	....	....	....	....	....	....	1943-44	1943-44
Jankowski, Lou	Det., Chi.	4	127	19	18	37	15	1	0	0	0	0	....	1950-51	1954-55
Jarrett, Doug	Chi., NYR	13	775	38	182	220	631	99	7	16	23	82	....	1964-65	1976-77
Jarrett, Gary	Tor., Det., Oak., Cal.	7	341	72	92	164	131	11	3	1	4	9	....	1960-61	1971-72
Jarry, Pierre	NYR, Tor., Det., Min.	7	344	88	117	205	142	5	0	1	1	0	....	1971-72	1977-78
Jarvenpaa, Hannu	Wpg.	3	114	11	26	37	83	....	....	....	....	....	....	1986-87	1988-89
Jarvi, Iiro	Que.	2	116	18	43	61	58	....	....	....	....	....	....	1988-89	1989-90
Jarvis, Doug	Mtl., Wsh., Hfd.	13	964	139	264	403	263	105	14	27	41	42	4	1975-76	1987-88
Jarvis, James	Pit., Phi., Tor.	3	112	17	15	32	62	....	....	....	....	....	....	1929-30	1936-37
Jarvis, Wes	Wsh., Min., L.A., Tor.	9	237	31	55	86	98	2	0	0	0	2	....	1979-80	1987-88
Javanainen, Arto	Pit.	1	14	4	1	5	2	....	....	....	....	....	....	1984-85	1984-85
Jay, Bob	L.A.	1	3	0	1	1	0	....	....	....	....	....	....	1993-94	1993-94
Jeffrey, Larry	Det., Tor., NYR	8	368	39	62	101	293	38	4	10	14	42	1	1961-62	1968-69
Jelinek, Tomas	Ott.	1	49	7	6	13	52	....	....	....	....	....	....	1992-93	1992-93
Jenkins, Dean	L.A.	1	5	0	0	0	2	....	....	....	....	....	....	1983-84	1983-84
Jenkins, Roger	Chi., Tor., Mtl.C., Bos., Mtl.M., NYA	8	325	15	39	54	253	25	1	7	8	12	2	1930-31	1938-39
Jennings, Bill	Det., Bos.	5	108	32	33	65	45	20	4	4	8	6	....	1940-41	1944-45
Jennings, Grant	Wsh., Hfd., Pit., Tor., Buf.	9	389	14	43	57	804	54	2	1	3	68	2	1987-88	1995-96
Jensen, Chris	NYR, Phi.	6	74	9	12	21	27	....	....	....	....	....	....	1985-86	1991-92
Jensen, David A.	Hfd., Wsh.	4	69	9	13	22	22	11	0	0	0	2	....	1984-85	1987-88
Jensen, David H.	Min.	3	18	0	2	2	11	....	....	....	....	....	....	1983-84	1985-86
Jensen, Steve	Min., L.A.	7	438	113	107	220	318	12	0	3	3	9	....	1975-76	1981-82
• Jeremiah, Ed	NYA, Bos.	1	15	0	1	1	0	....	....	....	....	....	....	1931-32	1931-32
Jerrard, Paul	Min.	1	5	0	0	0	4	....	....	....	....	....	....	1988-89	1988-89
• Jerwa, Frank	Bos., St.L.	4	81	11	16	27	53	....	....	....	....	....	....	1931-32	1934-35
• Jerwa, Joe	NYR, Bos., NYA	7	234	29	58	87	309	17	2	3	5	16	....	1930-31	1938-39
Jirik, Jaroslav	St.L.	1	3	0	0	0	0	....	....	....	....	....	....	1969-70	1969-70
• Joanette, Rosario	Mtl.	1	2	0	1	1	4	....	....	....	....	....	....	1944-45	1944-45
Jodzio, Rick	Col., Cle.	1	70	2	8	10	71	....	....	....	....	....	....	1977-78	1977-78
Johannesen, Glenn	NYI	1	2	0	0	0	0	....	....	....	....	....	....	1985-86	1985-86
Johannson, John	N.J.	1	5	0	0	0	0	....	....	....	....	....	....	1983-84	1983-84
Johansen, Bill	Tor.	1	1	0	0	0	0	....	....	....	....	....	....	1949-50	1949-50
Johansen, Trevor	Tor., Col., L.A.	5	286	11	46	57	282	13	0	3	3	21	....	1977-78	1981-82
Johansson, Bjorn	Cle.	2	15	1	1	2	10	....	....	....	....	....	....	1976-77	1977-78
Johansson, Roger	Cgy., Chi.	4	161	9	34	43	163	5	0	1	1	2	....	1989-90	1994-95
Johns, Don	NYR, Mtl., Min.	6	153	2	21	23	76	....	....	....	....	....	....	1960-61	1967-68
Johnson, Al	Mtl., Det.	4	105	21	28	49	30	11	2	2	4	6	....	1956-57	1962-63
Johnson, Brian	Det.	1	3	0	0	0	5	....	....	....	....	....	....	1983-84	1983-84
• Johnson, Danny	Tor., Van., Det.	3	121	18	19	37	24	....	....	....	....	....	....	1969-70	1971-72
Johnson, Earl	Det.	1	1	0	0	0	0	....	....	....	....	....	....	1953-54	1953-54
• Johnson, Ivan	NYR, NYA	12	436	38	48	86	808	61	5	2	7	161	2	1926-27	1937-38
Johnson, Jim	NYR, Phi., L.A.	8	302	75	111	186	73	7	0	2	2	2	....	1964-65	1971-72
Johnson, Jim	Pit., Min., Dal., Wsh., Phx.	13	829	29	166	195	1197	51	1	11	12	132	....	1985-86	1997-98
Johnson, Mark	Pit., Min., Hfd., St.L., N.J.	11	669	203	305	508	260	37	16	12	28	10	....	1979-80	1989-90
Johnson, Norm	Bos., Chi.	3	61	5	20	25	41	14	4	0	4	6	....	1957-58	1959-60
Johnson, Terry	Que., St.L., Cgy., Tor.	9	285	3	24	27	580	38	0	4	4	118	....	1979-80	1987-88
Johnson, Tom	Mtl., Bos.	17	978	51	213	264	960	111	8	15	23	109	6	1947-48	1964-65
• Johnson, Virgil	Chi.	3	75	2	9	11	27	19	0	3	3	4	1	1937-38	1944-45
Johnston, Bernie	Hfd.	2	57	12	24	36	16	3	0	1	1	0	....	1979-80	1980-81
Johnston, George	Chi.	4	58	20	12	32	2	....	....	....	....	....	....	1941-42	1946-47
Johnston, Greg	Bos., Tor.	9	187	26	29	55	124	22	2	1	3	12	....	1983-84	1991-92
Johnston, Jay	Wsh.	2	8	0	0	0	13	....	....	....	....	....	....	1980-81	1981-82
Johnston, Joey	Min., Cal., Chi.	6	331	85	106	191	320	....	....	....	....	....	....	1968-69	1975-76
Johnston, Larry	L.A., Det., K.C., Col.	7	320	9	64	73	580	....	....	....	....	....	....	1967-68	1976-77
Johnston, Marshall	Min., Cal.	7	251	14	52	66	58	6	0	0	0	2	....	1967-68	1973-74
Johnston, Randy	NYI	1	4	0	0	0	4	....	....	....	....	....	....	1979-80	1979-80
Johnstone, Eddie	NYR, Det.	10	426	122	136	258	375	55	13	10	23	83	....	1975-76	1986-87
Johnstone, Ross	Tor.	2	42	5	4	9	14	3	0	0	0	0	1	1943-44	1944-45
• Joliat, Aurel	Mtl.C.	16	654	270	190	460	757	54	14	19	33	89	....	1922-23	1937-38
• Joliat, Rene	Mtl.C.	1	1	0	0	0	0	....	....	....	....	....	....	1924-25	1924-25
Joly, Greg	Wsh., Det.	9	365	21	76	97	250	5	0	0	0	8	....	1974-75	1982-83
Joly, Yvan	Mtl.	3	2	0	0	0	0	1	0	0	0	0	....	1979-80	1982-83
Jonathan, Stan	Bos., Pit.	8	411	91	110	201	751	63	8	4	12	137	....	1975-76	1982-83
Jones, Bob	NYR	1	2	0	0	0	0	....	....	....	....	....	....	1968-69	1968-69
Jones, Brad	Wpg., L.A., Phi.	6	148	25	31	56	122	9	1	1	2	2	....	1986-87	1991-92
Jones, Buck	Det., Tor.	4	50	2	2	4	36	12	0	1	1	18	....	1938-39	1942-43
Jones, Jim	Cal.	1	2	0	0	0	0	....	....	....	....	....	....	1971-72	1971-72
Jones, Jimmy	Tor.	3	148	13	18	31	68	19	1	5	6	11	....	1977-78	1979-80
Jones, Ron	Bos., Pit., Wsh.	5	54	1	4	5	31	....	....	....	....	....	....	1971-72	1975-76
Jonsson, Tomas	NYI, Edm.	8	552	85	259	344	482	80	11	26	37	97	2	1981-82	1988-89
Joseph, Anthony	Wpg.	1	2	1	0	1	0	....	....	....	....	....	....	1988-89	1988-89
Joyal, Eddie	Det., Tor., L.A., Phi.	9	466	128	134	262	103	50	11	8	19	18	....	1962-63	1971-72
Joyce, Bob	Bos., Wsh., Wpg.	6	158	34	49	83	90	46	15	9	24	29	....	1987-88	1992-93
Joyce, Duane	Dal.	1	3	0	0	0	0	....	....	....	....	....	....	1993-94	1993-94
Juckes, Bing	NYR	2	16	2	1	3	6	....	....	....	....	....	....	1947-48	1949-50
Julien, Claude	Que.	2	14	0	1	1	25	....	....	....	....	....	....	1984-85	1985-86
Junker, Steve	NYI	2	5	0	0	0	0	3	0	1	1	0	....	1992-93	1993-94
Jutila, Timo	Buf.	1	10	1	5	6	13	....	....	....	....	....	....	1984-85	1984-85
Juzda, Bill	NYR, Tor.	9	398	14	54	68	398	42	0	3	3	46	2	1940-41	1951-52

K

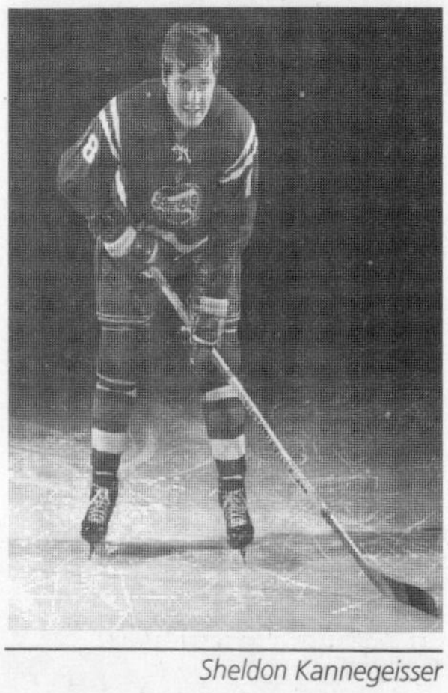

Sheldon Kannegeisser

Name	NHL Teams	NHL Seasons	GP	G	A	TP	PIM	GP	G	A	TP	PIM	NHL Cup Wins	First NHL Season	Last NHL Season
Kabel, Bob	NYR	2	48	5	13	18	34	....	....	....	....	....	....	1959-60	1960-61
Kachowski, Mark	Pit.	3	64	6	5	11	209	....	....	....	....	....	....	1987-88	1989-90
Kachur, Ed	Chi.	2	96	10	14	24	35	....	....	....	....	....	....	1956-57	1957-58
Kaese, Trent	Buf.	1	1	0	0	0	0	....	....	....	....	....	....	1988-89	1988-89
Kaiser, Vern	Mtl.	1	50	7	5	12	33	2	0	0	0	0	....	1950-51	1950-51
• Kalbfleish, Walter	Ott., St.L., NYA, Bos.	4	36	0	4	4	32	5	0	0	0	2	....	1933-34	1936-37
• Kaleta, Alex	Chi., NYR	7	387	92	121	213	190	17	1	6	7	2	....	1941-42	1950-51
Kallur, Anders	NYI	6	383	101	110	211	149	78	12	23	35	32	4	1979-80	1984-85
• Kaminsky, Max	Ott., St.L., Bos., Mtl.M.	4	130	22	34	56	38	4	0	0	0	0	....	1933-34	1936-37
• Kampman, Rudolph	Tor.	5	189	14	30	44	287	47	1	4	5	38	1	1937-38	1941-42
Kane, Francis	Det.	1	2	0	0	0	0	....	....	....	....	....	....	1943-44	1943-44
Kannegiesser, Gord	St.L.	2	23	0	1	1	15	....	....	....	....	....	....	1967-68	1971-72
Kannegiesser, Sheldon	Pit., NYR, L.A., Van.	8	366	14	67	81	292	18	0	2	2	10	....	1970-71	1977-78
Karabin, Ladislav	Pit.	1	9	0	0	0	2	....	....	....	....	....	....	1993-94	1993-94
Karamnov, Vitali	St.L.	3	92	12	20	32	65	2	0	0	0	2	....	1992-93	1994-95
Karjalainen, Kyosti	L.A.	1	28	1	8	9	12	3	0	1	1	2	....	1991-92	1991-92
Karlander, Al	Det.	4	212	36	56	92	70	4	0	1	1	0	....	1969-70	1972-73
Karpov, Valeri	Ana.	3	76	14	15	29	32	....	....	....	....	....	....	1994-95	1996-97
Kasatonov, Alexei	N.J., Ana., St.L., Bos.	7	383	38	122	160	326	33	4	7	11	40	....	1989-90	1995-96
Kasper, Steve	Bos., L.A., Phi., T.B.	13	821	177	291	468	554	94	20	28	48	82	....	1980-81	1992-93
Kastelic, Ed	Wsh., Hfd.	7	220	11	10	21	719	8	1	0	1	32	....	1985-86	1991-92
Kaszycki, Mike	NYI, Wsh., Tor.	5	226	42	80	122	108	19	2	6	8	10	....	1977-78	1982-83
Kea, Ed	Atl., St.L.	10	583	30	145	175	508	32	2	4	6	39	....	1973-74	1982-83
Kearns, Dennis	Van.	10	677	31	290	321	386	11	1	2	3	8	....	1971-72	1980-81
• Keating, Jack	NYA	2	35	5	5	10	17	....	....	....	....	....	....	1931-32	1932-33
• Keating, John	Det.	2	11	2	1	3	4	....	....	....	....	....	....	1938-39	1939-40
Keating, Mike	NYR	1	1	0	0	0	0	....	....	....	....	....	....	1977-78	1977-78
• Keats, Duke	Bos., Det., Chi.	3	82	30	19	49	113	....	....	....	....	....	....	1926-27	1928-29
• Keeling, Butch	Tor., NYR	12	525	157	63	220	331	47	11	11	22	34	1	1926-27	1937-38
Keenan, Larry	Tor., St.L., Buf., Phi.	6	233	38	64	102	28	46	15	16	31	12	....	1961-62	1971-72

Name	NHL Teams	NHL Seasons	Regular Schedule GP	G	A	TP	PIM	Playoffs GP	G	A	TP	PIM	NHL Cup Wins	First NHL Season	Last NHL Season
Kehoe, Rick	Tor., Pit.	14	906	371	396	767	120	39	4	17	21	4	....	1971-72	1984-85
Kekalainen, Jarmo	Bos., Ott.	3	55	5	8	13	28	....	....	....	....	....	....	1989-90	1993-94
Keller, Ralph	NYR	1	3	1	0	1	6	....	....	....	....	....	....	1962-63	1962-63
Kellgren, Christer	Col.	1	5	0	0	0	0	....	....	....	....	....	....	1981-82	1981-82
Kelly, Bob	Phi., Wsh.	12	837	154	208	362	1454	101	9	14	23	172	2	1970-71	1981-82
Kelly, Bob	St.L., Pit., Chi.	6	425	87	109	196	687	23	6	3	9	40	....	1973-74	1978-79
Kelly, Dave	Det.	1	16	2	0	2	4	....	....	....	....	....	....	1976-77	1976-77
Kelly, John Paul	L.A.	7	400	54	70	124	366	18	1	1	2	41	....	1979-80	1985-86
Kelly, Pete	St.L., Det., NYA, Bro.	7	177	21	38	59	68	19	3	1	4	2	2	1934-35	1941-42
Kelly, Red	Det., Tor., L.A.	21	1316	281	542	823	327	164	33	59	92	51	8	1947-48	1967-68
• Kelly, Regis	Tor., Chi., Bro.	8	288	74	53	127	105	38	7	6	13	10	....	1934-35	1941-42
Kemp, Kevin	Hfd.	1	3	0	0	0	4	....	....	....	....	....	....	1980-81	1980-81
Kemp, Stan	Tor.	1	1	0	0	0	2	....	....	....	....	....	....	1948-49	1948-49
• Kendall, Bill	Chi., Tor.	5	131	16	10	26	28	6	0	0	0	0	1	1933-34	1937-38
Kennedy, Dean	L.A., NYR, Buf., Wpg., Edm.	12	717	26	108	134	1118	36	1	7	8	59	....	1982-83	1994-95
Kennedy, Forbes	Chi., Det., Bos., Phi., Tor.	11	603	70	108	178	988	12	2	4	6	64	....	1956-57	1968-69
Kennedy, Sheldon	Det., Cgy., Bos.	8	310	49	58	107	233	24	6	4	10	20	....	1989-90	1996-97
Kennedy, Ted	Tor.	14	696	231	329	560	432	78	29	31	60	32	5	1942-43	1956-57
• Kenny, Ernest	NYR, Chi.	2	10	0	0	0	18	....	....	....	....	....	....	1930-31	1934-35
Keon, Dave	Tor., Hfd.	18	1296	396	590	986	117	92	32	36	68	6	4	1960-61	1981-82
Kerch, Alexander	Edm.	1	5	0	0	0	2	....	....	....	....	....	....	1993-94	1993-94
Kerr, Alan	NYI, Det., Wpg.	9	391	72	94	166	826	38	5	4	9	70	....	1984-85	1992-93
Kerr, Reg	Cle., Chi., Edm.	6	263	66	94	160	169	7	1	0	1	7	....	1977-78	1983-84
Kerr, Tim	Phi., NYR, Hfd.	13	655	370	304	674	596	81	40	31	71	58	....	1980-81	1992-93
Kessell, Rick	Pit., Cal.	5	135	4	24	28	6	....	....	....	....	....	....	1969-70	1973-74
Ketola, Veli-Pekka	Col.	1	44	9	5	14	4	....	....	....	....	....	....	1981-82	1981-82
Ketter, Kerry	Atl.	1	41	0	2	2	58	....	....	....	....	....	....	1972-73	1972-73
Kharin, Sergei	Wpg.	1	7	2	3	5	2	....	....	....	....	....	....	1990-91	1990-91
Khmylev, Yuri	Buf., St.L.	5	263	64	88	152	133	26	8	6	14	24	....	1992-93	1996-97
Kidd, Ian	Van.	2	20	4	7	11	25	....	....	....	....	....	....	1987-88	1988-89
Kiessling, Udo	Min.	1	1	0	0	0	2	....	....	....	....	....	....	1981-82	1981-82
Kilrea, Brian	Det., L.A.	2	26	3	5	8	12	....	....	....	....	....	....	1957-58	1967-68
• Kilrea, Hec	Ott., Det., Tor.	15	633	167	129	296	438	48	8	7	15	18	3	1925-26	1939-40
• Kilrea, Ken	Det.	5	91	16	23	39	8	15	2	2	4	4	....	1938-39	1943-44
Kilrea, Wally	Ott., Phi., NYA, Mtl.M., Det.	9	329	35	58	93	87	25	2	4	6	6	2	1929-30	1937-38
Kimble, Darin	Que., St.L., Bos., Chi.	7	311	23	20	43	1082	23	0	0	0	52	....	1988-89	1994-95
Kindrachuk, Orest	Phi., Pit., Wsh.	10	508	118	261	379	648	76	20	20	40	53	2	1972-73	1981-82
King, Frank	Mtl.	1	10	1	0	1	2	....	....	....	....	....	....	1950-51	1950-51
King, Wayne	Cal.	3	73	5	18	23	34	....	....	....	....	....	....	1973-74	1975-76
Kinsella, Brian	Wsh.	2	10	0	1	1	0	....	....	....	....	....	....	1975-76	1976-77
• Kinsella, Ray	Ott.	1	14	0	0	0	0	....	....	....	....	....	....	1930-31	1930-31
Kiprusoff, Marko	Mtl.	1	24	0	4	4	8	....	....	....	....	....	....	1995-96	1995-96
• Kirk, Bobby	NYR	1	39	4	8	12	14	....	....	....	....	....	....	1937-38	1937-38
Kirkpatrick, Bob	NYR	1	49	12	12	24	6	....	....	....	....	....	....	1942-43	1942-43
Kirton, Mark	Tor., Det., Van.	6	266	57	56	113	121	4	1	2	3	7	....	1979-80	1984-85
Kisio, Kelly	Det., NYR, S.J., Cgy.	13	761	229	429	658	768	39	6	15	21	52	....	1982-83	1994-95
Kitchen, Bill	Mtl., Tor.	4	41	1	4	5	40	3	0	1	1	0	....	1981-82	1984-85
• Kitchen, Hobie	Mtl.M., Det.	2	47	5	4	9	58	....	....	....	....	....	1	1925-26	1926-27
Kitchen, Mike	Col., N.J.	8	474	12	62	74	370	2	0	0	0	2	....	1976-77	1983-84
Klassen, Ralph	Cal., Cle., Col., St.L.	9	497	52	93	145	120	26	4	2	6	12	....	1975-76	1983-84
• Klein, Lloyd	Bos., NYA	8	164	30	24	54	68	5	0	0	0	2	....	1928-29	1937-38
Kleinendorst, Scot	NYR, Hfd., Wsh.	8	281	12	46	58	452	26	2	7	9	40	....	1982-83	1989-90
Klimovich, Sergei	Chi.	1	1	0	0	0	2	....	....	....	....	....	....	1996-97	1996-97
Klingbeil, Ike	Chi.	1	5	1	2	3	2	....	....	....	....	....	....	1936-37	1936-37
Klukay, Joe	Tor., Bos.	11	566	109	127	236	189	71	13	10	23	23	4	1942-43	1955-56
Kluzak, Gord	Bos.	7	299	25	98	123	543	46	6	13	19	129	....	1982-83	1990-91
Knibbs, Bill	Bos.	1	53	7	10	17	4	....	....	....	....	....	....	1964-65	1964-65
• Knott, Nick	Bro.	1	14	3	1	4	9	....	....	....	....	....	....	1941-42	1941-42
Knox, Paul	Tor.	1	1	0	0	0	0	....	....	....	....	....	....	1954-55	1954-55
Kolesar, Mark	Tor.	2	28	2	2	4	14	3	1	0	1	2	....	1995-96	1996-97
Kolstad, Dean	Min., S.J.	3	40	1	7	8	69	....	....	....	....	....	....	1988-89	1992-93
Komadoski, Neil	L.A., St.L.	8	502	16	76	92	632	23	0	2	2	47	....	1972-73	1979-80
Konik, George	Pit.	1	52	7	8	15	26	....	....	....	....	....	....	1967-68	1967-68
Konroyd, Steve	Cgy., NYI, Chi., Hfd., Det., Ott.	15	895	41	195	236	863	97	10	15	25	99	....	1980-81	1994-95
Konstantinov, Vladimir	Det.	7	446	47	128	175	838	82	5	14	19	107	1	1991-92	1997-98
Kontos, Chris	NYR, Pit., L.A., T.B.	8	230	54	69	123	103	20	11	0	11	12	....	1982-83	1992-93
Kopak, Russ	Bos.	1	24	7	9	16	0	....	....	....	....	....	....	1943-44	1943-44
Korab, Jerry	Chi., Van., Buf., L.A.	15	975	114	341	455	1629	93	8	18	26	201	....	1970-71	1984-85
• Kordic, John	Mtl., Tor., Wsh., Que.	7	244	17	18	35	997	41	4	3	7	131	1	1985-86	1991-92
Korn, Jim	Det., Tor., Buf., N.J., Cgy.	10	597	66	122	188	1801	16	1	2	3	109	....	1979-80	1989-90
Korney, Mike	Det., NYR	4	77	9	10	19	59	....	....	....	....	....	....	1973-74	1978-79
Koroll, Cliff	Chi.	11	814	208	254	462	376	85	19	29	48	67	....	1969-70	1979-80
Kortko, Roger	NYI	2	79	7	17	24	28	10	0	3	3	17	....	1984-85	1985-86
Kostynski, Doug	Bos.	2	15	3	1	4	4	....	....	....	....	....	....	1983-84	1984-85
Kotanen, Dick	NYR	1	1	0	0	0	0	....	....	....	....	....	....	1950-51	1950-51
Kotsopoulos, Chris	NYR, Hfd., Tor., Det.	10	479	44	109	153	827	31	1	3	4	91	....	1980-81	1989-90
Kowal, Joe	Buf.	2	22	0	5	5	13	2	0	0	0	0	....	1976-77	1977-78
Kozak, Don	L.A., Van.	7	437	96	86	182	480	29	7	2	9	69	....	1972-73	1978-79
Kozak, Les	Tor.	1	12	1	0	1	2	....	....	....	....	....	....	1961-62	1961-62
• Kraftcheck, Stephen	Bos., NYR, Tor.	4	157	11	18	29	83	6	0	0	0	7	....	1950-51	1958-59
Krake, Skip	Bos., L.A., Buf.	7	249	23	40	63	182	10	1	0	1	17	....	1963-64	1970-71
Kravets, Mikhail	S.J.	2	2	0	0	0	0	....	....	....	....	....	....	1991-92	1992-93
Krentz, Dale	Det.	3	30	5	3	8	9	2	0	0	0	0	....	1986-87	1988-89
• Krol, Joe	NYR, Bro.	3	26	10	4	14	8	....	....	....	....	....	....	1936-37	1941-42
Kromm, Rich	Cgy., NYI	9	372	70	103	173	138	36	2	6	8	22	....	1983-84	1992-93
Krook, Kevin	Col.	1	3	0	0	0	2	....	....	....	....	....	....	1978-79	1978-79
Krulicki, Jim	NYR, Det.	1	41	0	3	3	6	....	....	....	....	....	....	1970-71	1970-71
Kruppke, Gord	Det.	3	23	0	0	0	32	....	....	....	....	....	....	1990-91	1993-94
Krushelnyski, Mike	Bos., Edm., L.A., Tor., Det.	14	897	241	328	569	699	139	29	43	72	106	3	1981-82	1994-95
Krutov, Vladimir	Van.	1	61	11	23	34	20	....	....	....	....	....	....	1989-90	1989-90
Kryskow, Dave	Chi., Wsh., Det., Atl.	4	231	33	56	89	174	12	2	0	2	4	....	1972-73	1975-76
Kryznowski, Edward	Bos., Chi.	5	237	15	22	37	65	18	0	1	1	4	....	1948-49	1952-53
Kudashov, Alexei	Tor.	1	25	1	0	1	4	....	....	....	....	....	....	1993-94	1993-94
Kudelski, Bob	L.A., Ott., Fla.	9	442	139	102	241	218	22	4	4	8	4	....	1987-88	1995-96
• Kuhn, Gord	NYA	1	12	1	1	2	4	....	....	....	....	....	....	1932-33	1932-33
Kukulowicz, Aggie	NYR	2	4	1	0	1	0	....	....	....	....	....	....	1952-53	1953-54
Kulak, Stu	Van., Edm., NYR, Que., Wpg.	4	90	8	4	12	130	3	0	0	0	2	....	1982-83	1988-89
Kullman, Arnie	Bos.	2	13	0	1	1	11	....	....	....	....	....	....	1947-48	1949-50
• Kullman, Eddie	NYR	6	343	56	70	126	298	6	1	0	1	2	....	1947-48	1953-54
Kumpel, Mark	Que., Det., Wpg.	6	288	38	46	84	113	39	6	4	10	14	....	1984-85	1990-91
• Kuntz, Alan	NYR	2	45	10	12	22	12	6	1	0	1	2	....	1941-42	1945-46
Kuntz, Murray	St.L.	1	7	1	2	3	0	....	....	....	....	....	....	1974-75	1974-75
Kurri, Jari	Edm., L.A., NYR, Ana., Col.	17	1251	601	797	1398	545	200	106	127	233	123	5	1980-81	1997-98
Kurtenbach, Orland	NYR, Bos., Tor., Van.	13	639	119	213	332	628	19	2	4	6	70	....	1960-61	1973-74
Kurvers, Tom	Mtl., Buf., N.J., Tor., Van., NYI, Ana.	11	659	93	328	421	350	57	8	22	30	68	1	1984-85	1994-95
Kuryluk, Mervin	Chi.	1	....	....	....	....	....	2	0	0	0	0	....	1961-62	1961-62
Kushner, Dale	NYI, Phi.	3	84	10	13	23	215	....	....	....	....	....	....	1989-90	1991-92
Kuzyk, Ken	Cle.	2	41	5	9	14	8	....	....	....	....	....	....	1976-77	1977-78
Kvartalnov, Dmitri	Bos.	2	112	42	49	91	26	4	0	0	0	0	....	1992-93	1993-94
Kwong, Larry	NYR	1	1	0	0	0	0	....	....	....	....	....	....	1947-48	1947-48
• Kyle, Bill	NYR	2	3	0	3	3	0	....	....	....	....	....	....	1949-50	1950-51
• Kyle, Gus	NYR, Bos.	3	203	6	20	26	362	14	1	2	3	34	....	1949-50	1951-52
Kyllonen, Markku	Wpg.	1	9	0	2	2	2	....	....	....	....	....	....	1988-89	1988-89
Kypreos, Nick	Wsh., Hfd., NYR, Tor.	9	442	46	44	90	1210	34	1	3	4	65	1	1989-90	1997-98
Kyte, Jim	Wpg., Pit., Cgy., Ott., S.J.	13	598	17	49	66	1342	42	0	6	6	94	....	1982-83	1995-96

L

L'Abbe, Moe	Chi.	1	5	0	1	1	0	....	....	....	....	....	....	1972-73	1972-73
Labadie, Mike	NYR	1	3	0	0	0	0	....	....	....	....	....	....	1952-53	1952-53
Labatte, Neil	St.L.	2	26	0	2	2	19	....	....	....	....	....	....	1978-79	1981-82

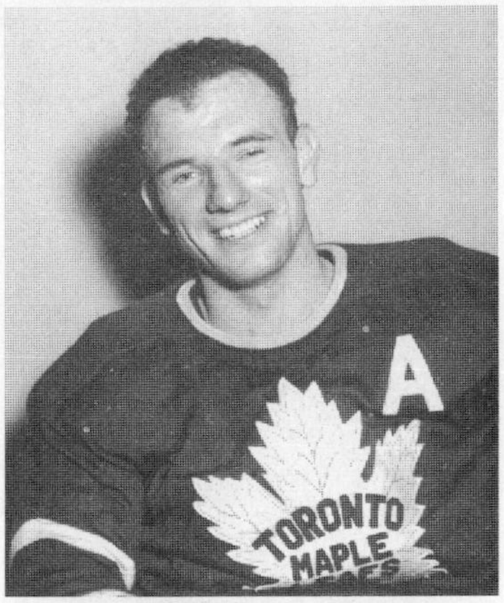

Teeder Kennedy

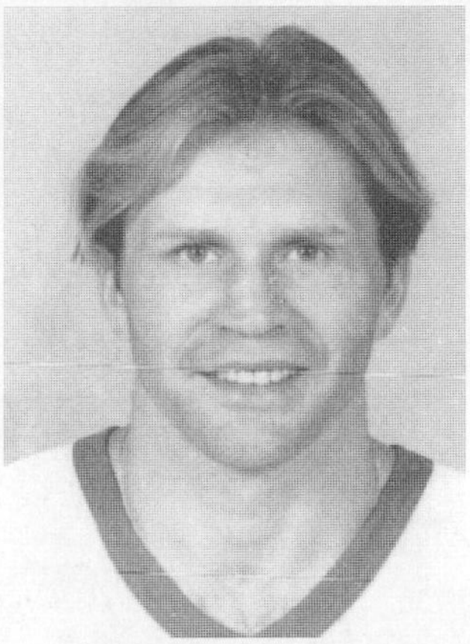
Vladimir Konstantinov

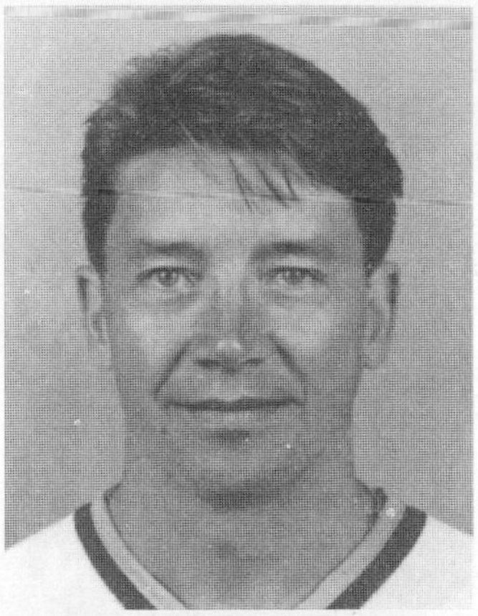
Jari Kurri

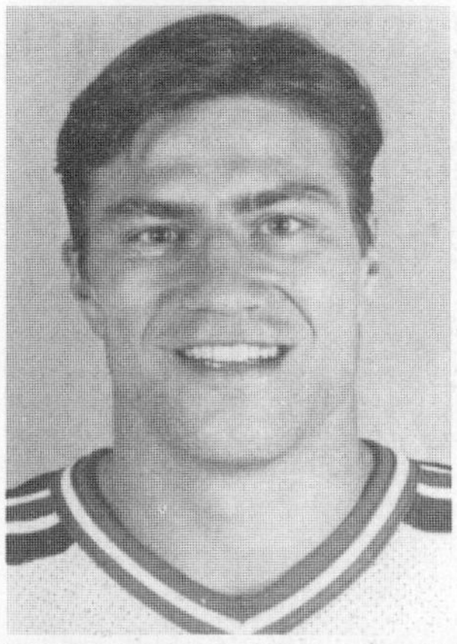
Nick Kypreos

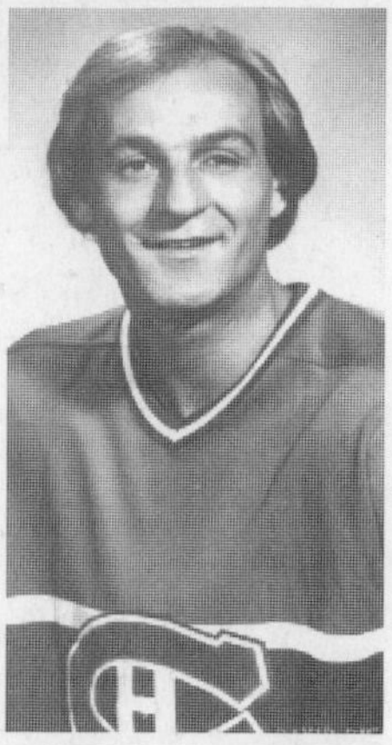

Guy Lafleur

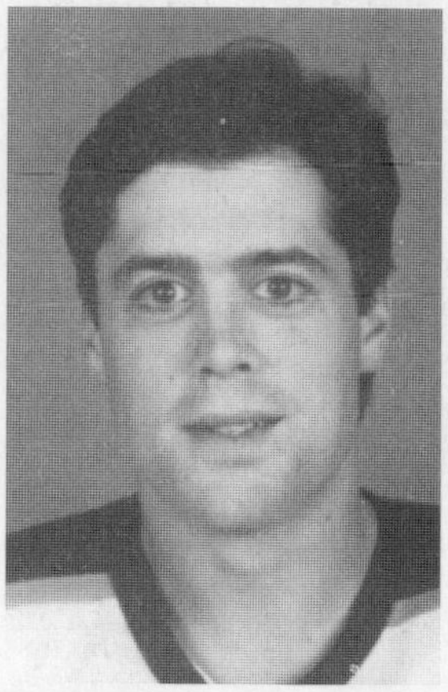

Pat LaFontaine

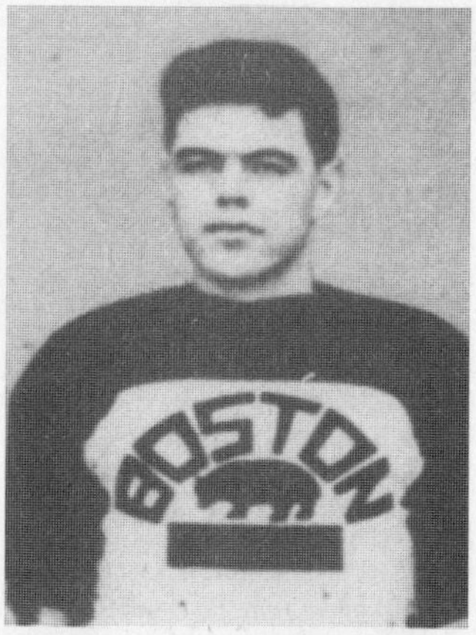

Miles Lane

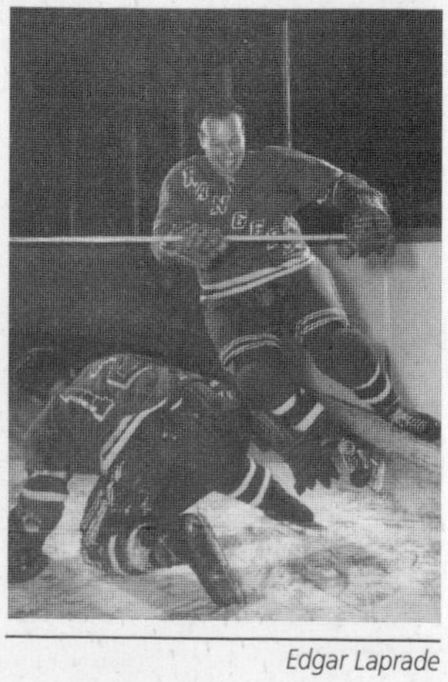

Edgar Laprade

Name	NHL Teams	NHL Seasons	Regular Schedule GP	G	A	TP	PIM	Playoffs GP	G	A	TP	PIM	NHL Cup Wins	First NHL Season	Last NHL Season
Labelle, Marc	Dal.	1	9	0	0	0	46	....	....	....	....	....	....	1996-97	1996-97
Labine, Leo	Bos., Det.	11	643	128	193	321	730	60	11	12	23	82	....	1951-52	1961-62
Labossiere, Gord	NYR, L.A., Min.	6	215	44	62	106	75	10	2	3	5	28	....	1963-64	1971-72
Labovitch, Max	NYR	1	5	0	0	0	4	....	....	....	....	....	....	1943-44	1943-44
Labraaten, Daniel	Det., Cgy.	4	268	71	73	144	47	8	1	0	1	4	....	1978-79	1981-82
Labre, Yvon	Pit., Wsh.	9	371	14	87	101	788	....	....	....	....	....	....	1970-71	1980-81
Labrie, Guy	Bos., NYR	2	42	4	9	13	16	....	....	....	....	....	....	1943-44	1944-45
Lach, Elmer	Mtl.	14	664	215	408	623	478	76	19	45	64	36	3	1940-41	1953-54
Lachance, Michel	Col.	1	21	0	4	4	22	....	....	....	....	....	....	1978-79	1978-79
Lacombe, Francois	Oak., Buf., Que.	4	78	2	17	19	54	3	1	0	1	0	....	1968-69	1979-80
Lacombe, Normand	Buf., Edm., Phi.	7	319	53	62	115	196	26	5	1	6	49	1	1984-85	1990-91
Lacroix, Andre	Phi., Chi., Hfd.	6	325	79	119	198	44	16	2	5	7	0	....	1967-68	1979-80
Lacroix, Pierre	Que., Hfd.	4	274	24	108	132	197	8	0	2	2	10	....	1979-80	1982-83
Ladouceur, Randy	Det., Hfd., Ana.	14	930	30	126	156	1322	40	5	8	13	59	....	1982-83	1995-96
Lafleur, Guy	Mtl., NYR, Que.	17	1126	560	793	1353	399	128	58	76	134	67	5	1971-72	1990-91
• Lafleur, Roland	Mtl.C.	1	1	0	0	0	0	....	....	....	....	....	....	1924-25	1924-25
LaFontaine, Pat	NYI, Buf., NYR	15	865	468	545	1013	552	69	26	36	62	36	....	1983-84	1997-98
Laforce, Ernie	Mtl.	1	1	0	0	0	0	....	....	....	....	....	....	1942-43	1942-43
LaForest, Bob	L.A.	1	5	1	0	1	2	....	....	....	....	....	....	1983-84	1983-84
Laforge, Claude	Mtl., Det., Phi.	8	193	24	33	57	82	5	1	2	3	15	....	1957-58	1968-69
Laforge, Marc	Hfd., Edm.	2	14	0	0	0	64	....	....	....	....	....	....	1989-90	1993-94
Laframboise, Pete	Cal., Wsh., Pit.	4	227	33	55	88	70	9	1	0	1	0	....	1971-72	1974-75
Lafrance, Adie	Mtl.C.	1	3	0	0	0	2	2	0	0	0	0	....	1933-34	1933-34
Lafrance, Leo	Mtl.C., Chi.	2	33	2	0	2	6	....	....	....	....	....	....	1926-27	1927-28
Lafreniere, Jason	Que., NYR, T.B.	5	146	34	53	87	22	15	1	5	6	19	....	1986-87	1993-94
Lafreniere, Roger	Det., St.L.	2	13	0	0	0	4	....	....	....	....	....	....	1962-63	1972-73
Lagace, Jean-Guy	Pit., Buf., K.C.	6	197	9	39	48	251	....	....	....	....	....	....	1968-69	1975-76
Laidlaw, Tom	NYR, L.A.	10	705	25	139	164	717	69	4	17	21	78	....	1980-81	1989-90
Laird, Robbie	Min.	1	1	0	0	0	0	....	....	....	....	....	....	1979-80	1979-80
Lajeunesse, Serge	Det., Phi.	5	103	1	4	5	103	....	....	....	....	....	....	1970-71	1974-75
Lalande, Hec	Chi., Det.	4	151	21	39	60	120	....	....	....	....	....	....	1953-54	1957-58
Lalonde, Bobby	Van., Atl., Bos., Cgy.	11	641	124	210	334	298	16	4	2	6	6	....	1971-72	1981-82
• Lalonde, Newsy	Mtl.C., NYA	6	99	124	42	166	151	12	21	3	24	35	....	1917-18	1926-27
Lalonde, Ron	Pit., Wsh.	7	397	45	78	123	106	....	....	....	....	....	....	1972-73	1978-79
Lalor, Mike	Mtl., St.L., Wsh., Wpg., S.J., Dal.	12	687	17	88	105	677	92	5	10	15	167	1	1985-86	1996-97
• Lamb, Joe	Mtl.M., Ott., NYA, Bos., Mtl.C., St.L., Det.	11	443	108	101	209	601	18	1	1	2	51	....	1927-28	1937-38
Lamb, Mark	Cgy., Det., Edm., Ott., Phi., Mtl.	11	403	46	100	146	291	70	7	19	26	51	1	1985-86	1995-96
Lambert, Dan	Que.	2	29	6	9	15	22	....	....	....	....	....	....	1990-91	1991-92
Lambert, Lane	Det., NYR, Que.	6	283	58	66	124	521	17	2	4	6	40	....	1983-84	1988-89
Lambert, Yvon	Mtl., Buf.	10	683	206	273	479	340	90	27	22	49	67	4	1972-73	1981-82
Lamby, Dick	St.L.	3	22	0	5	5	22	....	....	....	....	....	....	1978-79	1980-81
• Lamirande, Jean-Paul	NYR, Mtl.	4	49	5	5	10	26	8	0	0	0	4	....	1946-47	1954-55
Lammens, Hank	Ott.	1	27	1	2	3	22	....	....	....	....	....	....	1993-94	1993-94
• Lamoureux, Leo	Mtl.	6	235	19	79	98	175	28	1	6	7	16	2	1941-42	1946-47
Lamoureux, Mitch	Pit., Phi.	3	73	11	9	20	59	....	....	....	....	....	....	1983-84	1987-88
Lampman, Mike	St.L., Van., Wsh.	4	96	17	20	37	34	....	....	....	....	....	....	1972-73	1976-77
Lancien, Jack	NYR	4	63	1	5	6	35	6	0	1	1	2	....	1946-47	1950-51
Landon, Larry	Mtl., Tor.	2	9	0	0	0	2	....	....	....	....	....	....	1983-84	1984-85
Lane, Gord	Wsh., NYI	10	539	19	94	113	1228	75	3	14	17	214	4	1975-76	1984-85
• Lane, Myles	NYR, Bos.	3	71	4	1	5	41	11	0	0	0	0	1	1928-29	1933-34
Langdon, Steve	Bos.	3	7	0	1	1	2	4	0	0	0	0	....	1974-75	1977-78
Langelle, Pete	Tor.	4	136	22	51	73	11	41	5	9	14	4	1	1938-39	1941-42
Langevin, Chris	Buf.	2	22	3	1	4	22	....	....	....	....	....	....	1983-84	1985-86
Langevin, Dave	NYI, Min., L.A.	8	513	12	107	119	530	87	2	17	19	106	4	1979-80	1986-87
Langlais, Alain	Min.	2	25	4	4	8	10	....	....	....	....	....	....	1973-74	1974-75
Langlois, Albert	Mtl., NYR, Det., Bos.	9	497	21	91	112	488	53	1	5	6	50	3	1957-58	1965-66
• Langlois, Charlie	Ham., NYA, Pit., Mtl.C.	4	151	22	3	25	201	2	0	0	0	0	....	1924-25	1927-28
Langway, Rod	Mtl., Wsh.	15	994	51	278	329	849	104	5	22	27	97	1	1978-79	1992-93
Lanthier, Jean-Marc	Van.	4	105	16	16	32	29	....	....	....	....	....	....	1983-84	1987-88
Lanyon, Ted	Pit.	1	5	0	0	0	4	....	....	....	....	....	....	1967-68	1967-68
Lanz, Rick	Van., Tor., Chi.	10	569	65	221	286	448	28	3	8	11	35	....	1980-81	1991-92
Laperriere, Daniel	St.L., Ott.	4	48	2	5	7	27	....	....	....	....	....	....	1992-93	1995-96
Laperriere, Jacques	Mtl.	12	691	40	242	282	674	88	9	22	31	101	6	1962-63	1973-74
Lapointe, Guy	Mtl., St.L., Bos.	16	884	171	451	622	893	123	26	44	70	138	6	1968-69	1983-84
Lapointe, Rick	Det., Phi., St.L., Que., L.A.	11	664	44	176	220	831	46	2	7	9	64	....	1975-76	1985-86
Lappin, Peter	Min., S.J.	2	7	0	0	0	2	....	....	....	....	....	....	1989-90	1991-92
Laprade, Edgar	NYR	10	500	108	172	280	42	18	4	9	13	4	....	1945-46	1954-55
LaPrairie, Benjamin	Chi.	1	7	0	0	0	0	....	....	....	....	....	....	1936-37	1936-37
Lariviere, Garry	Que., Edm.	4	219	6	57	63	167	14	0	5	5	8	....	1979-80	1982-83
Larmer, Jeff	Col., N.J., Chi.	5	158	37	51	88	57	5	1	0	1	2	....	1981-82	1985-86
Larmer, Steve	Chi., NYR	15	1006	441	571	1012	532	140	56	75	131	89	1	1980-81	1994-95
• Larochelle, Wildor	Mtl.C., Chi.	12	474	92	74	166	211	34	6	4	10	24	....	1925-26	1936-37
Larocque, Denis	L.A.	1	8	0	1	1	18	....	....	....	....	....	....	1987-88	1987-88
• Larose, Charles	Bos.	1	6	0	0	0	0	....	....	....	....	....	....	1925-26	1925-26
Larose, Claude	Mtl., Min., St.L.	16	943	226	257	483	887	97	14	18	32	143	5	1962-63	1977-78
Larose, Claude	NYR	2	25	4	7	11	2	2	0	0	0	0	....	1979-80	1981-82
Larose, Guy	Wpg., Tor., Cgy., Bos.	6	70	10	9	19	63	4	0	0	0	0	....	1988-89	1994-95
Larouche, Pierre	Pit., Mtl., Hfd., NYR	14	812	395	427	822	237	64	20	34	54	16	2	1974-75	1987-88
Larson, Norman	NYA, Bro., NYR	3	89	25	18	43	12	....	....	....	....	....	....	1940-41	1946-47
Larson, Reed	Det., Bos., Edm., NYI, Min., Buf.	14	904	222	463	685	1391	32	4	7	11	63	....	1976-77	1989-90
Larter, Tyler	Wsh.	1	1	0	0	0	0	....	....	....	....	....	....	1989-90	1989-90
Latal, Jiri	Phi.	3	92	12	36	48	24	....	....	....	....	....	....	1989-90	1991-92
Latos, James	NYR	1	1	0	0	0	0	....	....	....	....	....	....	1988-89	1988-89
Latreille, Phillipe	NYR	1	4	0	0	0	2	....	....	....	....	....	....	1960-61	1960-61
Latta, David	Que.	4	36	4	8	12	4	....	....	....	....	....	....	1985-86	1990-91
Lauder, Martin	Bos.	1	3	0	0	0	2	....	....	....	....	....	....	1927-28	1927-28
Lauen, Mike	Wpg.	1	4	0	1	1	0	....	....	....	....	....	....	1983-84	1983-84
Laughlin, Craig	Mtl., Wsh., L.A., Tor.	8	549	136	205	341	364	33	6	6	12	20	....	1981-82	1988-89
Laughton, Mike	Oak., Cal.	4	189	39	48	87	101	11	2	4	6	0	....	1967-68	1970-71
Laurence, Don	Atl., St.L.	2	79	15	22	37	14	....	....	....	....	....	....	1978-79	1979-80
LaVallee, Kevin	Cgy., L.A., St.L., Pit.	7	366	110	125	235	85	32	5	8	13	21	....	1980-81	1986-87
Lavarre, Mark	Chi.	3	78	9	16	25	58	1	0	0	0	2	....	1985-86	1987-88
Lavender, Brian	St.L., NYI, Det., Cal.	4	184	16	26	42	174	3	0	0	0	2	....	1971-72	1974-75
Lavigne, Eric	L.A.	1	1	0	0	0	0	....	....	....	....	....	....	1994-95	1994-95
• Laviolette, Jack	Mtl.C.	1	18	2	1	3	6	2	0	0	0	0	....	1917-18	1917-18
Laviolette, Peter	NYR	1	12	0	0	0	6	....	....	....	....	....	....	1988-89	1988-89
Lavoie, Dominic	St.L., Ott., Bos., L.A.	6	38	5	8	13	32	....	....	....	....	....	....	1988-89	1993-94
Lawless, Paul	Hfd., Phi., Van., Tor.	7	239	49	77	126	54	3	0	2	2	2	....	1982-83	1989-90
Lawson, Danny	Det., Min., Buf.	5	219	28	29	57	61	16	0	1	1	2	....	1967-68	1971-72
Lawton, Brian	Min., NYR, Hfd., Que., Bos., S.J.	9	483	112	154	266	401	11	1	1	2	12	....	1983-84	1992-93
Laxdal, Derek	Tor., NYI	6	67	12	7	19	88	1	0	2	2	2	....	1984-85	1990-91
• Laycoe, Hal	NYR, Mtl., Bos.	11	531	25	77	102	292	40	2	5	7	39	....	1945-46	1955-56
Lazaro, Jeff	Bos., Ott.	3	102	14	23	37	114	28	3	3	6	32	....	1990-91	1992-93
Leach, Jamie	Pit., Hfd., Fla.	5	81	11	9	20	12	....	....	....	....	....	....	1989-90	1993-94
Leach, Larry	Bos.	3	126	13	29	42	91	7	1	1	2	8	....	1958-59	1961-62
Leach, Reggie	Bos., Cal., Phi., Det.	13	934	381	285	666	387	94	47	22	69	22	1	1970-71	1982-83
Leavins, Jim	Det., NYR	2	41	2	12	14	30	....	....	....	....	....	....	1985-86	1986-87
Lebeau, Patrick	Mtl., Cgy., Fla., Pit.	4	15	3	2	5	6	....	....	....	....	....	....	1990-91	1998-99
Lebeau, Stephan	Mtl., Ana.	7	373	118	159	277	105	30	9	7	16	12	1	1988-89	1994-95
LeBlanc, Fern	Det.	3	34	5	6	11	0	....	....	....	....	....	....	1976-77	1978-79
LeBlanc, J.P.	Chi., Det.	5	153	14	30	44	87	2	0	0	0	0	....	1968-69	1978-79
LeBlanc, John	Van., Edm., Wpg.	7	83	26	13	39	28	1	0	0	0	0	....	1986-87	1994-95
LeBrun, Al	NYR	2	6	0	2	2	4	....	....	....	....	....	....	1960-61	1965-66
Lecaine, Bill	Pit.	1	4	0	0	0	0	....	....	....	....	....	....	1968-69	1968-69
Leclair, Jackie	Mtl.	3	160	20	40	60	56	20	6	1	7	6	2	1954-55	1956-57
Leclerc, Rene	Det.	2	87	10	11	21	105	....	....	....	....	....	....	1968-69	1970-71
Lecuyer, Doug	Chi., Wpg., Pit.	4	126	11	31	42	178	7	4	0	4	15	....	1978-79	1982-83
Ledingham, Walt	Chi., NYI	3	15	0	2	2	4	....	....	....	....	....	....	1972-73	1976-77
• LeDuc, Albert	Mtl.C., Ott., NYR	10	383	57	35	92	614	28	5	6	11	32	....	1925-26	1934-35
LeDuc, Rich	Bos., Que.	4	130	28	38	66	69	5	0	0	0	9	....	1972-73	1980-81
• Lee, Bobby	Mtl.	1	1	0	0	0	0	....	....	....	....	....	....	1942-43	1942-43
Lee, Edward	Que.	1	2	0	0	0	5	....	....	....	....	....	....	1984-85	1984-85

Name	NHL Teams	NHL Seasons	Regular Schedule GP	G	A	TP	PIM	Playoffs GP	G	A	TP	PIM	NHL Cup Wins	First NHL Season	Last NHL Season
Lee, Peter	Pit.	6	431	114	131	245	257	19	0	8	8	4	....	1977-78	1982-83
Leeman, Gary	Tor., Cgy., Mtl., Van., St.L.	14	667	199	267	466	531	36	8	16	24	36	1	1982-83	1996-97
• Lefley, Bryan	NYI, K.C., Col.	5	228	7	29	36	101	2	0	0	0	0	....	1972-73	1977-78
• Leger, Roger	NYR, Mtl.	5	187	18	53	71	71	20	0	7	7	14	....	1943-44	1949-50
Legge, Barry	Que., Wpg.	3	107	1	11	12	144	....	....	....	....	....	....	1979-80	1981-82
Legge, Randy	NYR	1	12	0	2	2	2	....	....	....	....	....	....	1972-73	1972-73
Lehmann, Tommy	Bos., Edm.	3	36	5	5	10	16	....	....	....	....	....	....	1987-88	1989-90
Lehto, Petteri	Pit.	1	6	0	0	0	4	....	....	....	....	....	....	1984-85	1984-85
Lehtonen, Antero	Wsh.	1	65	9	12	21	14	....	....	....	....	....	....	1979-80	1979-80
Lehvonen, Henri	K.C.	1	4	0	0	0	0	....	....	....	....	....	....	1974-75	1974-75
Leier, Edward	Chi.	2	16	2	1	3	2	....	....	....	....	....	....	1949-50	1950-51
Leinonen, Mikko	NYR, Wsh.	4	162	31	78	109	71	20	2	11	13	28	....	1981-82	1984-85
Leiter, Bobby	Bos., Pit., Atl.	10	447	98	126	224	144	8	3	0	3	2	....	1962-63	1975-76
Leiter, Ken	NYI, Min.	5	143	14	36	50	62	15	0	6	6	8	....	1984-85	1989-90
Lemaire, Jacques	Mtl.	12	853	366	469	835	217	145	61	78	139	63	8	1967-68	1978-79
Lemay, Moe	Van., Edm., Bos., Wpg.	8	317	72	94	166	442	28	6	3	9	55	1	1981-82	1988-89
Lemelin, Roger	K.C., Col.	4	36	1	2	3	27	....	....	....	....	....	....	1974-75	1977-78
Lemieux, Alain	St.L., Que., Pit.	6	119	28	44	72	38	19	4	6	10	0	....	1981-82	1986-87
Lemieux, Bob	Oak.	1	19	0	1	1	12	....	....	....	....	....	....	1967-68	1967-68
Lemieux, Jacques	L.A.	3	19	0	4	4	8	1	0	0	0	0	....	1967-68	1969-70
Lemieux, Jean	Atl., Wsh.	5	204	23	63	86	39	3	1	1	2	0	....	1973-74	1977-78
Lemieux, Mario	Pit.	12	745	613	881	1494	737	89	70	85	155	83	2	1984-85	1996-97
• Lemieux, Real	Det., L.A., NYR, Buf.	8	456	51	104	155	262	18	2	4	6	10	....	1966-67	1973-74
Lemieux, Richard	Van., K.C., Atl.	5	274	39	82	121	132	2	0	0	0	0	....	1971-72	1975-76
Lenardon, Tim	N.J., Van.	2	15	2	1	3	4	....	....	....	....	....	....	1986-87	1989-90
• Lepine, Hec	Mtl.C.	1	33	5	2	7	2	....	....	....	....	....	....	1925-26	1925-26
• Lepine, Pit	Mtl.C., Mtl.	14	526	143	98	241	392	41	7	5	12	26	....	1925-26	1939-40
Leroux, Gaston	Mtl.C.	1	2	0	0	0	0	....	....	....	....	....	....	1935-36	1935-36
Lesieur, Art	Mtl.C., Chi.	4	100	4	2	6	50	14	0	0	0	4	....	1928-29	1935-36
Lessard, Rick	Cgy., S.J.	3	15	0	4	4	18	....	....	....	....	....	....	1988-89	1991-92
Lesuk, Bill	Bos., Phi., L.A., Wsh., Wpg.	8	388	44	63	107	368	9	1	0	1	12	1	1968-69	1979-80
• Leswick, Jack	Chi.	1	3	1	7	8	16	....	....	....	....	....	....	1933-34	1933-34
Leswick, Pete	NYA, Bos.	2	3	1	0	1	0	....	....	....	....	....	....	1936-37	1944-45
Leswick, Tony	NYR, Det., Chi.	12	740	165	159	324	900	59	13	10	23	91	3	1945-46	1957-58
Levandoski, Joseph	NYR	1	8	1	1	2	0	....	....	....	....	....	....	1946-47	1946-47
Leveille, Normand	Bos.	2	75	17	25	42	49	....	....	....	....	....	....	1981-82	1982-83
Leveque, Guy	L.A.	2	17	2	2	4	21	....	....	....	....	....	....	1992-93	1993-94
Lever, Don	Van., Atl., Cgy., Col., N.J., Buf.	15	1020	313	367	680	593	30	7	10	17	26	....	1972-73	1986-87
Levie, Craig	Wpg., Min., St.L., Van.	6	183	22	53	75	177	16	2	3	5	32	....	1981-82	1986-87
• Levinsky, Alex	Tor., NYR, Chi.	9	367	19	49	68	307	37	2	1	3	26	2	1930-31	1938-39
Levo, Tapio	Col., N.J.	2	107	16	53	69	36	....	....	....	....	....	....	1981-82	1982-83
Lewicki, Danny	Tor., NYR, Chi.	9	461	105	135	240	177	28	0	4	4	8	1	1950-51	1958-59
Lewis, Dale	NYR	1	8	0	0	0	0	....	....	....	....	....	....	1975-76	1975-76
Lewis, Dave	NYI, L.A., N.J., Det.	15	1008	36	187	223	953	91	1	20	21	143	....	1973-74	1987-88
Lewis, Doug	Mtl.	1	3	0	0	0	0	....	....	....	....	....	....	1946-47	1946-47
• Lewis, Herbie	Det.	11	483	148	161	309	248	38	13	10	23	6	2	1928-29	1938-39
Ley, Rick	Tor., Hfd.	6	310	12	72	84	528	14	0	2	2	20	....	1968-69	1980-81
Liba, Igor	NYR, L.A.	1	37	7	18	25	36	2	0	0	0	2	....	1988-89	1988-89
Libett, Nick	Det., Pit.	14	982	237	268	505	472	16	6	2	8	2	....	1967-68	1980-81
Licari, Tony	Det.	1	9	0	1	1	0	....	....	....	....	....	....	1946-47	1946-47
Liddington, Bob	Tor.	1	11	0	1	1	2	....	....	....	....	....	....	1970-71	1970-71
Lilley, John	Ana.	3	23	3	8	11	13	....	....	....	....	....	....	1993-94	1995-96
Lindberg, Chris	Cgy., Que.	3	116	17	25	42	47	2	0	1	1	2	....	1991-92	1993-94
Linden, Jamie	Fla.	1	4	0	0	0	17	....	....	....	....	....	....	1994-95	1994-95
Lindgren, Lars	Van., Min.	6	394	25	113	138	325	40	5	6	11	20	....	1978-79	1983-84
Lindholm, Mikael	L.A.	1	18	2	2	4	2	....	....	....	....	....	....	1989-90	1989-90
Lindros, Brett	NYI	2	51	2	5	7	147	....	....	....	....	....	....	1994-95	1995-96
Lindsay, Ted	Det., Chi.	17	1068	379	472	851	1808	133	47	49	96	194	4	1944-45	1964-65
Lindstrom, Willy	Wpg., Edm., Pit.	8	582	161	162	323	200	57	14	18	32	24	2	1979-80	1986-87
Linseman, Ken	Phi., Edm., Bos., Tor.	14	[illegible]	256	551	807	1727	113	43	77	120	325	1	1978-79	1991-92
Liscombe, Carl	Det.	9	373	137	140	277	117	59	22	19	41	20	1	1937-38	1945-46
Litzenberger, Ed	Mtl., Chi., Det., Tor.	12	618	178	238	416	283	40	5	13	18	34	4	1952-53	1963-64
Loach, Lonnie	Ott., L.A., Ana.	2	56	10	13	23	29	1	0	0	0	0	....	1992-93	1993-94
• Locas, Jacques	Mtl.	2	59	7	8	15	66	....	....	....	....	....	....	1947-48	1948-49
Lochead, Bill	Det., Col., NYR	6	330	69	62	131	180	7	3	0	3	6	....	1974-75	1979-80
• Locking, Norm	Chi.	2	48	2	6	8	26	....	....	....	....	....	....	1934-35	1935-36
Loewen, Darcy	Buf., Ott.	5	135	4	8	12	211	....	....	....	....	....	....	1989-90	1993-94
Lofthouse, Mark	Wsh., Det.	6	181	42	38	80	73	....	....	....	....	....	....	1977-78	1982-83
Logan, Dave	Chi., Van.	6	218	5	29	34	470	12	0	0	0	10	....	1975-76	1980-81
Logan, Robert	Buf., L.A.	3	42	10	5	15	0	....	....	....	....	....	....	1986-87	1988-89
Loiselle, Claude	Det., N.J., Que., Tor., NYI	13	616	92	117	209	1149	41	4	11	15	60	....	1981-82	1993-94
Lomakin, Andrei	Phi., Fla.	4	215	42	62	104	92	....	....	....	....	....	....	1991-92	1994-95
Loney, Brian	Van.	1	12	2	3	5	6	....	....	....	....	....	....	1995-96	1995-96
Loney, Troy	Pit., Ana., NYI, NYR	12	624	87	110	197	1091	67	8	14	22	97	2	1983-84	1994-95
Long, Barry	L.A., Det., Wpg.	5	280	11	68	79	250	5	0	1	1	18	....	1972-73	1981-82
• Long, Stanley	Mtl.	1	....	....	....	....	....	3	0	0	0	0	....	1951-52	1951-52
Lonsberry, Ross	Bos., L.A., Phi., Pit.	15	968	256	310	566	806	100	21	25	46	87	2	1966-67	1980-81
Loob, Hakan	Cgy.	6	450	193	236	429	189	73	26	28	54	16	1	1983-84	1988-89
Loob, Peter	Que.	1	8	1	2	3	0	....	....	....	....	....	....	1984-85	1984-85
Lorentz, Jim	Bos., St.L., NYR, Buf.	10	659	161	238	399	208	54	12	10	22	30	1	1968-69	1977-78
Lorimer, Bob	NYI, Col., N.J.	10	529	22	90	112	431	49	3	10	13	83	2	1976-77	1985-86
• Lorrain, Rod	Mtl.C., Mtl.	6	179	28	39	67	30	11	0	3	3	0	....	1935-36	1941-42
• Loughlin, Clem	Det., Chi.	3	101	8	6	14	77	....	....	....	....	....	....	1926-27	1928-29
• Loughlin, Wilf	Tor.	1	14	0	0	0	2	....	....	....	....	....	....	1923-24	1923-24
Lovsin, Ken	Wsh.	1	1	0	0	0	0	....	....	....	....	....	....	1990-91	1990-91
Lowdermilk, Dwayne	Wsh.	1	2	0	1	1	2	....	....	....	....	....	....	1980-81	1980-81
Lowe, Darren	Pit.	1	8	1	2	3	0	....	....	....	....	....	....	1983-84	1983-84
Lowe, Kevin	Edm., NYR	19	1254	84	347	431	1498	214	10	48	58	192	6	1979-80	1997-98
Lowe, Norm	NYR	1	4	1	1	2	0	....	....	....	....	....	....	1949-50	1949-50
• Lowe, Ross	Bos., Mtl.	3	77	6	8	14	82	2	0	0	0	0	....	1949-50	1951-52
• Lowrey, Eddie	Ott., Ham.	3	26	2	2	4	6	....	....	....	....	....	....	1917-18	1920-21
• Lowrey, Fred	Mtl.M., Pit.	2	54	1	0	1	10	2	0	0	0	6	....	1924-25	1925-26
• Lowrey, Gerry	Tor., Pit., Phi., Chi., Ott.	6	211	48	48	96	148	2	1	0	1	2	....	1927-28	1932-33
Lucas, Danny	Phi.	1	6	1	0	1	0	....	....	....	....	....	....	1978-79	1978-79
Lucas, Dave	Det.	1	1	0	0	0	0	....	....	....	....	....	....	1962-63	1962-63
Luce, Don	NYR, Det., Buf., L.A., Tor.	13	894	225	329	554	364	71	17	22	39	52	....	1969-70	1981-82
Ludvig, Jan	N.J., Buf.	7	314	54	87	141	418	....	....	....	....	....	....	1982-83	1988-89
Ludzik, Steve	Chi., Buf.	9	424	46	93	139	333	44	4	8	12	70	....	1981-82	1989-90
Lukowich, Bernie	Pit., St.L.	2	79	13	15	28	34	2	0	0	0	0	....	1973-74	1974-75
Lukowich, Morris	Wpg., Bos., L.A.	8	582	199	219	418	584	11	0	2	2	24	....	1979-80	1986-87
Luksa, Charlie	Hfd.	1	8	0	1	1	4	....	....	....	....	....	....	1979-80	1979-80
Lumley, Dave	Mtl., Edm., Hfd.	9	437	98	160	258	680	61	6	8	14	131	2	1978-79	1986-87
Lund, Pentti	Bos., NYR	7	259	44	55	99	40	19	7	5	12	0	....	1946-47	1952-53
Lundberg, Brian	Pit.	1	1	0	0	0	2	....	....	....	....	....	....	1982-83	1982-83
Lunde, Len	Det., Chi., Min., Van.	8	321	39	83	122	75	20	3	2	5	2	....	1958-59	1970-71
Lundholm, Bengt	Wpg.	5	275	48	95	143	72	14	3	4	7	14	....	1981-82	1985-86
Lundrigan, Joe	Tor., Wsh.	2	52	2	8	10	22	....	....	....	....	....	....	1972-73	1974-75
Lundstrom, Tord	Det.	1	11	1	1	2	0	....	....	....	....	....	....	1973-74	1973-74
Lundy, Pat	Det., Chi.	5	150	37	32	69	31	16	2	2	4	2	....	1945-46	1950-51
Lupien, Gilles	Mtl., Pit., Hfd.	5	226	5	25	30	416	25	0	0	0	21	2	1977-78	1981-82
Lupul, Gary	Van.	7	293	70	75	145	243	25	4	7	11	11	....	1979-80	1985-86
Lyle, George	Det., Hfd.	4	99	24	38	62	51	....	....	....	....	....	....	1979-80	1982-83
Lynch, Jack	Pit., Det., Wsh.	7	382	24	106	130	336	....	....	....	....	....	....	1972-73	1978-79
Lynn, Vic	Det., Mtl., Tor., Bos., Chi.	10	326	49	76	125	274	47	7	10	17	46	3	1943-44	1953-54
Lyon, Steve	Pit.	1	3	0	0	0	2	....	....	....	....	....	....	1976-77	1976-77
Lyons, Ron	Bos., Phi.	1	36	2	4	6	27	5	0	0	0	0	....	1930-31	1930-31
Lysiak, Tom	Atl., Chi.	13	919	292	551	843	567	76	25	38	63	49	....	1973-74	1985-86

M

Name	NHL Teams	NHL Seasons	GP	G	A	TP	PIM	GP	G	A	TP	PIM	NHL Cup Wins	First NHL Season	Last NHL Season
MacAdam, Al	Phi., Cal., Cle., Min., Van.	12	864	240	351	591	509	64	20	24	44	21	1	1973-74	1984-85

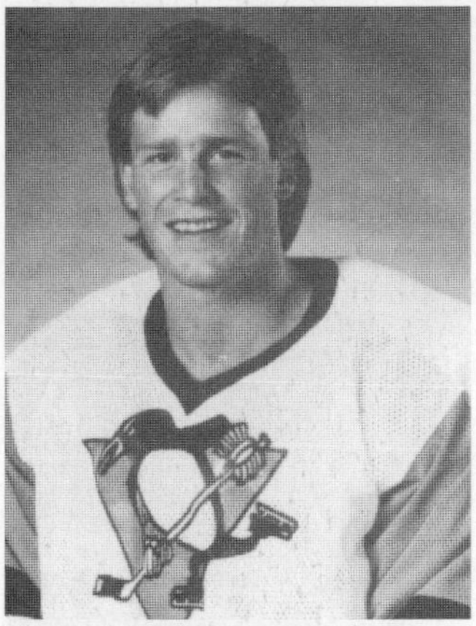
Troy Loney

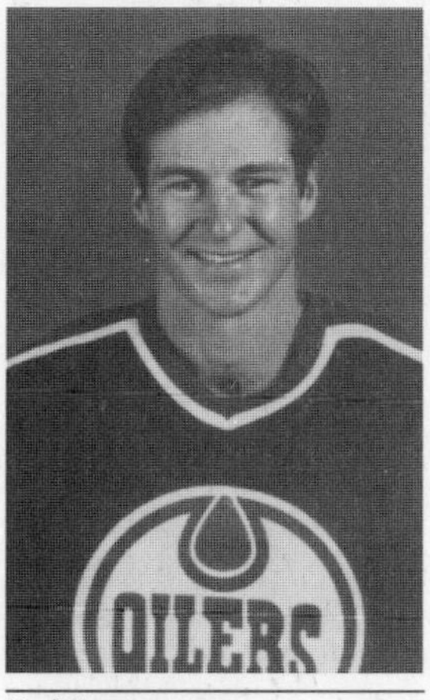

Kevin Lowe

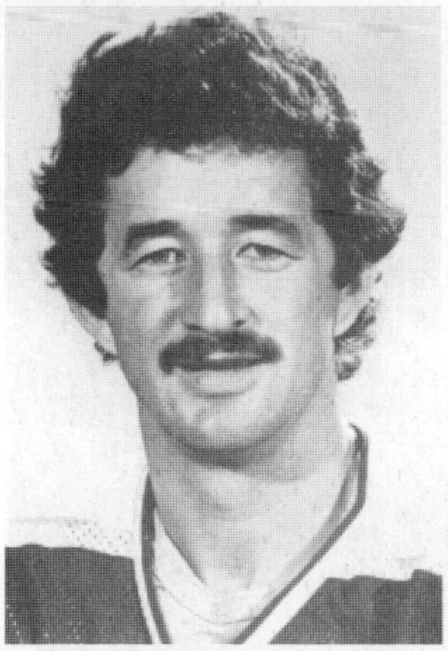
Al MacAdam

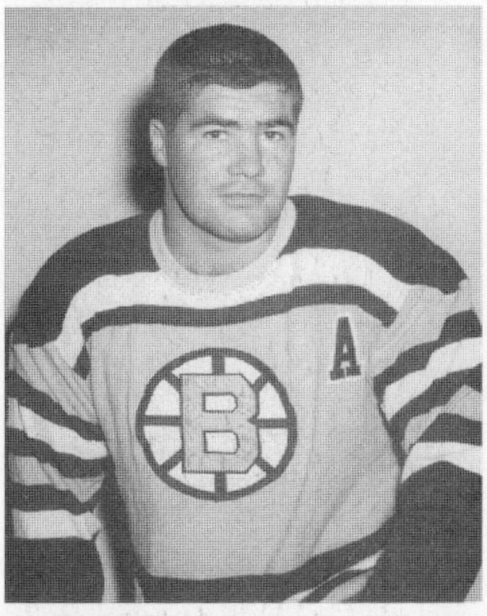
Fleming Mackell

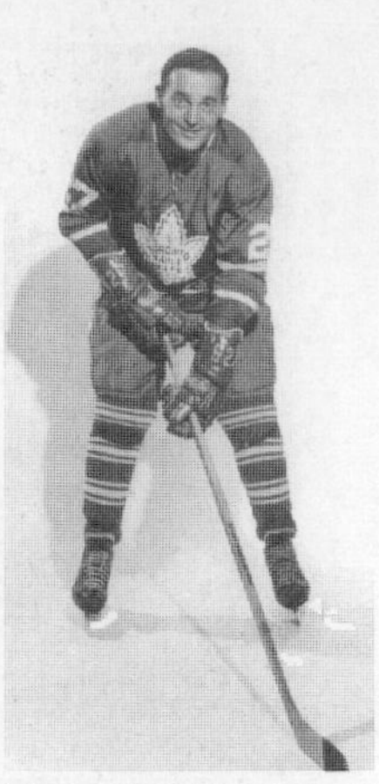

Frank Mahovlich

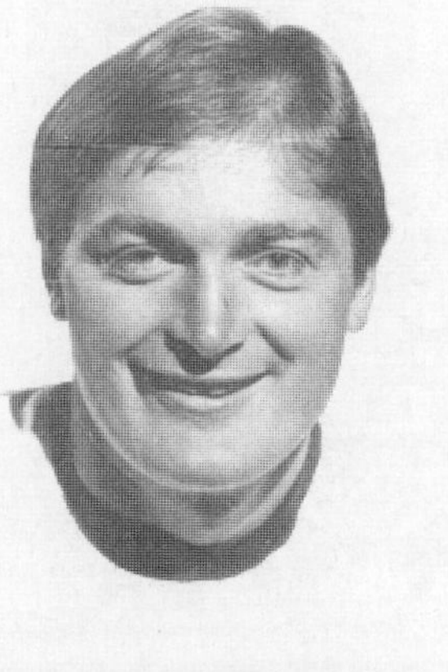

Peter Mahovlich

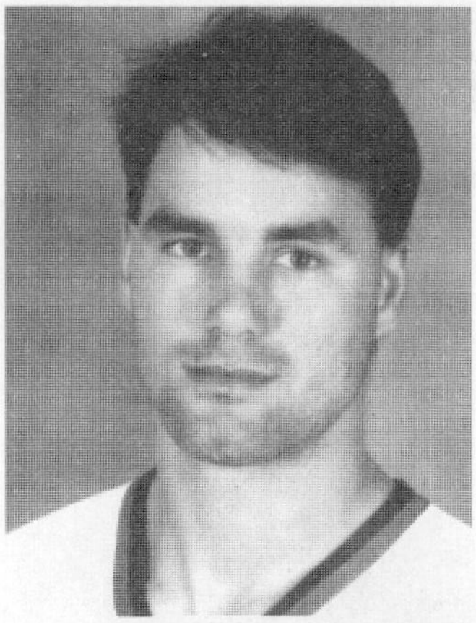

Troy Mallette

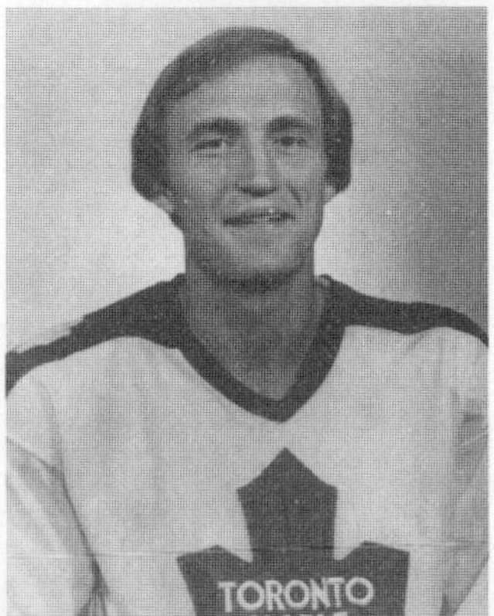

Dan Maloney

Name	NHL Teams	NHL Seasons	Regular Schedule GP	G	A	TP	PIM	Playoffs GP	G	A	TP	PIM	NHL Cup Wins	First NHL Season	Last NHL Season
MacDermid, Paul	Hfd., Wpg., Wsh., Que.	14	690	116	142	258	1303	43	5	11	16	116	....	1981-82	1994-95
MacDonald, Blair	Edm., Van.	4	219	91	100	191	65	11	0	6	6	2	....	1979-80	1982-83
MacDonald, Brett	Van.	1	1	0	0	0	0	....	....	....	....	....	....	1987-88	1987-88
MacDonald, Kevin	Ott.	1	1	0	0	0	2	....	....	....	....	....	....	1993-94	1993-94
• MacDonald, Kilby	NYR	4	151	36	34	70	47	15	1	2	3	4	1	1939-40	1944-45
MacDonald, Lowell	Det., L.A., Pit.	13	506	180	210	390	92	30	11	11	22	12	....	1961-62	1977-78
MacDonald, Parker	Tor., NYR, Det., Bos., Min.	14	676	144	179	323	253	75	14	14	28	20	....	1952-53	1968-69
• MacDonnell, Moylan	Ham.	1	22	1	2	3	2	....	....	....	....	....	....	1920-21	1920-21
MacDougall, Kim	Min.	1	1	0	0	0	0	....	....	....	....	....	....	1974-75	1974-75
MacEachern, Shane	St.L.	1	1	0	0	0	0	....	....	....	....	....	....	1987-88	1987-88
Macey, Hubert	NYR, Mtl.	3	30	6	9	15	0	8	0	0	0	0	....	1941-42	1946-47
MacGregor, Bruce	Det., NYR	14	893	213	257	470	217	107	19	28	47	44	....	1960-61	1973-74
MacGregor, Randy	Hfd.	1	2	1	1	2	2	....	....	....	....	....	....	1981-82	1981-82
MacGuigan, Garth	NYI	2	5	0	1	1	2	....	....	....	....	....	....	1979-80	1983-84
MacIver, Don	Wpg.	1	6	0	0	0	2	....	....	....	....	....	....	1979-80	1979-80
MacKasey, Blair	Tor.	1	1	0	0	0	2	....	....	....	....	....	....	1976-77	1976-77
MacKay, Calum	Det., Mtl.	8	237	50	55	105	214	38	5	13	18	20	1	1946-47	1954-55
Mackay, Dave	Chi.	1	29	3	0	3	26	5	0	1	1	2	....	1940-41	1940-41
• MacKay, Mickey	Chi., Pit., Bos.	4	147	44	19	63	79	11	0	0	0	6	1	1926-27	1929-30
MacKay, Murdo	Mtl.	4	19	0	3	3	0	15	1	2	3	0	....	1945-46	1948-49
Mackell, Fleming	Tor., Bos.	13	665	149	220	369	562	80	22	41	63	75	2	1947-48	1959-60
• MacKell, Jack	Ott.	2	46	4	2	6	59	11	0	0	0	0	2	1919-20	1920-21
MacKenzie, Barry	Min.	1	6	0	1	1	6	....	....	....	....	....	....	1968-69	1968-69
• MacKenzie, Bill	Chi., Mtl.M., NYR, Mtl.C.	7	264	15	14	29	145	21	1	1	2	11	1	1932-33	1939-40
Mackey, David	Chi., Min., St.L.	6	126	8	12	20	305	3	0	0	0	2	....	1987-88	1993-94
• MacKey, Reg	NYR	1	34	0	0	0	16	1	0	0	0	0	....	1926-27	1926-27
• Mackie, Howie	Det.	2	20	1	0	1	4	8	0	0	0	0	1	1936-37	1937-38
MacKinnon, Paul	Wsh.	5	147	5	23	28	91	....	....	....	....	....	....	1979-80	1983-84
MackIntosh, Ian	NYR	1	4	0	0	0	4	....	....	....	....	....	....	1952-53	1952-53
MacLean, Paul	St.L., Wpg., Det.	11	719	324	349	673	968	53	21	14	35	110	....	1980-81	1990-91
MacLeish, Rick	Phi., Hfd., Pit., Det.	14	846	349	410	759	434	114	54	53	107	38	2	1970-71	1983-84
MacLellan, Brian	L.A., NYR, Min., Cgy., Det.	10	606	172	241	413	551	47	5	9	14	42	1	1982-83	1991-92
MacLeod, Pat	Min., S.J., Dal.	4	53	5	13	18	14	....	....	....	....	....	....	1990-91	1995-96
MacMillan, Billy	Tor., Atl., NYI	7	446	74	77	151	184	53	6	6	12	40	....	1970-71	1976-77
MacMillan, Bob	NYR, St.L., Atl., Cgy., Col., N.J., Chi.	11	753	228	349	577	260	31	8	11	19	16	....	1974-75	1984-85
MacMillan, John	Tor., Det.	5	104	5	10	15	32	12	0	1	1	2	2	1960-61	1964-65
MacNeil, Bernie	St.L.	1	4	0	0	0	0	....	....	....	....	....	....	1973-74	1973-74
MacNeil, Al	Tor., Mtl., Chi., NYR, Pit.	12	524	17	75	92	617	37	0	4	4	67	....	1955-56	1970-71
• MacPherson, Bud	Mtl.	7	259	5	33	38	233	29	0	3	3	21	1	1948-49	1956-57
• MacSweyn, Ralph	Phi.	5	47	0	5	5	10	8	0	0	0	6	....	1967-68	1971-72
MacTavish, Craig	Bos., Edm., NYR, Phi., St.L.	18	1093	213	267	480	891	193	20	38	58	218	4	1979-80	1996-97
MacWilliam, Mike	NYI	1	6	0	0	0	14	....	....	....	....	....	....	1995-96	1995-96
Madigan, Connie	St.L.	1	20	0	3	3	25	5	0	0	0	4	....	1972-73	1972-73
Madill, Jeff	N.J.	1	14	4	0	4	46	7	0	2	2	8	....	1990-91	1990-91
Magee, Dean	Min.	1	7	0	0	0	4	....	....	....	....	....	....	1977-78	1977-78
Maggs, Daryl	Chi., Cal., Tor.	3	135	14	19	33	54	4	0	0	0	0	....	1971-72	1979-80
Magnan, Marc	Tor.	1	4	0	1	1	5	....	....	....	....	....	....	1982-83	1982-83
Magnuson, Keith	Chi.	11	589	14	125	139	1442	68	3	9	12	164	....	1969-70	1979-80
Maguire, Kevin	Tor., Buf., Phi.	6	260	29	30	59	782	11	0	0	0	86	....	1986-87	1991-92
Mahaffy, John	Mtl., NYR	3	37	11	25	36	4	1	0	1	1	0	....	1942-43	1944-45
Mahovlich, Frank	Tor., Det., Mtl.	18	1181	533	570	1103	1056	137	51	67	118	163	6	1956-57	1973-74
Mahovlich, Pete	Det., Mtl., Pit.	16	884	288	485	773	916	88	30	42	72	134	4	1965-66	1980-81
Mailhot, Jacques	Que.	1	5	0	0	0	33	....	....	....	....	....	....	1988-89	1988-89
Mailley, Frank	Mtl.	1	1	0	0	0	0	....	....	....	....	....	....	1942-43	1942-43
Mair, Jim	Phi., NYI, Van.	5	76	4	15	19	49	3	1	2	3	4	....	1970-71	1974-75
• Majeau, Fern	Mtl.	2	56	22	24	46	43	1	0	0	0	0	1	1943-44	1944-45
Major, Bruce	Que.	1	4	0	0	0	0	....	....	....	....	....	....	1990-91	1990-91
Makarov, Sergei	Cgy., S.J., Dal.	7	424	134	250	384	317	34	12	11	23	8	....	1989-90	1996-97
Makela, Mikko	NYI, L.A., Buf., Bos.	7	423	118	147	265	139	18	3	8	11	14	....	1985-86	1994-95
Maki, Chico	Chi.	15	841	143	292	435	345	113	17	36	53	43	1	1960-61	1975-76
• Maki, Wayne	Chi., St.L., Van.	6	246	57	79	136	184	2	1	0	1	2	....	1967-68	1972-73
Makkonen, Kari	Edm.	1	9	2	2	4	0	....	....	....	....	....	....	1979-80	1979-80
Maley, David	Mtl., N.J., Edm., S.J., NYI	9	466	43	81	124	1043	46	5	5	10	111	1	1985-86	1993-94
Malinowski, Merlin	Col., N.J., Hfd.	5	282	54	111	165	121	....	....	....	....	....	....	1978-79	1982-83
Mallette, Troy	NYR, Edm., N.J., Ott., Bos., T.B.	9	456	51	68	119	1226	15	2	2	4	99	....	1989-90	1997-98
Malone, Cliff	Mtl.	1	3	0	0	0	0	....	....	....	....	....	....	1951-52	1951-52
Malone, Greg	Pit., Hfd., Que.	11	704	191	310	501	661	20	3	5	8	32	....	1976-77	1986-87
• Malone, Joe	Mtl.C., Que., Ham.	7	125	143	32	175	57	9	5	1	6	3	....	1917-18	1923-24
Maloney, Dan	Chi., L.A., Det., Tor.	11	737	192	259	451	1489	40	4	7	11	35	....	1970-71	1981-82
Maloney, Dave	NYR, Buf.	11	657	71	246	317	1154	49	7	17	24	91	....	1974-75	1984-85
Maloney, Don	NYR, Hfd., NYI	13	765	214	350	564	815	94	22	35	57	101	....	1978-79	1990-91
Maloney, Phil	Bos., Tor., Chi.	5	158	28	43	71	16	6	0	0	0	0	....	1949-50	1959-60
Maluta, Ray	Bos.	2	25	2	3	5	6	2	0	0	0	0	....	1975-76	1976-77
Manastersky, Tom	Mtl.	1	6	0	0	0	11	....	....	....	....	....	....	1950-51	1950-51
Mancuso, Gus	Mtl.C., Mtl., NYR	4	42	7	9	16	17	....	....	....	....	....	....	1937-38	1942-43
Mandich, Dan	Min.	4	111	5	11	16	303	7	0	0	0	2	....	1982-83	1985-86
Manery, Kris	Cle., Min., Van., Wpg.	4	250	63	64	127	91	....	....	....	....	....	....	1977-78	1980-81
Manery, Randy	Det., Atl., L.A.	10	582	50	206	256	415	13	0	2	2	12	....	1970-71	1979-80
Mann, Jack	NYR	2	9	3	4	7	0	....	....	....	....	....	....	1943-44	1944-45
Mann, Jimmy	Wpg., Que., Pit.	8	293	10	20	30	895	22	0	0	0	89	....	1979-80	1987-88
Mann, Ken	Det.	1	1	0	0	0	0	....	....	....	....	....	....	1975-76	1975-76
Mann, Norm	Tor.	3	31	0	3	3	4	2	0	0	0	0	....	1935-36	1940-41
• Manners, Rennison	Pit., Phi.	2	37	3	2	5	14	....	....	....	....	....	....	1929-30	1930-31
Manno, Bob	Van., Tor., Det.	8	371	41	131	172	274	17	2	4	6	12	....	1976-77	1984-85
Manson, Ray	Bos., NYR	2	2	0	1	1	0	....	....	....	....	....	....	1947-48	1948-49
• Mantha, Georges	Mtl.C., Mtl.	13	488	89	102	191	148	36	6	2	8	24	....	1928-29	1940-41
Mantha, Moe	Wpg., Pit., Edm., Min., Phi.	12	656	81	289	370	501	17	5	10	15	18	....	1980-81	1991-92
• Mantha, Sylvio	Mtl.C., Bos.	14	542	63	72	135	667	46	5	4	9	66	....	1923-24	1936-37
• Maracle, Bud	NYR	1	11	1	3	4	4	4	0	0	0	0	....	1930-31	1930-31
Marcetta, Milan	Tor., Min.	3	54	7	15	22	10	17	7	7	14	4	1	1966-67	1968-69
March, Mush	Chi.	17	759	153	230	383	540	45	12	15	27	41	2	1928-29	1944-45
Marchinko, Brian	Tor., NYI	4	47	2	6	8	0	....	....	....	....	....	....	1970-71	1973-74
Marcinyshyn, David	N.J., Que., NYR	3	16	0	1	1	49	....	....	....	....	....	....	1990-91	1992-93
Marcon, Lou	Det.	3	60	0	4	4	42	....	....	....	....	....	....	1958-59	1962-63
Marcotte, Don	Bos.	15	868	230	254	484	317	132	34	27	61	81	2	1965-66	1981-82
Marini, Hector	NYI, N.J.	5	154	27	46	73	246	10	3	6	9	14	1	1978-79	1983-84
• Mario, Frank	Bos.	2	53	9	19	28	24	....	....	....	....	....	....	1941-42	1944-45
• Mariucci, John	Chi.	5	223	11	34	45	308	12	0	3	3	26	....	1940-41	1947-48
Mark, Gordon	N.J., Edm.	4	85	3	10	13	187	....	....	....	....	....	....	1986-87	1994-95
Markell, John	Wpg., St.L., Min.	4	55	11	10	21	36	....	....	....	....	....	....	1979-80	1984-85
• Marker, Gus	Det., Mtl.M., Tor., Bro.	10	322	64	69	133	133	46	5	7	12	36	1	1932-33	1941-42
Markham, Ray	NYR	1	14	1	1	2	21	7	1	0	1	24	....	1979-80	1979-80
• Markle, Jack	Tor.	1	8	0	1	1	0	....	....	....	....	....	....	1935-36	1935-36
• Marks, Jack	Mtl., Tor., Que.	2	7	0	0	0	4	....	....	....	....	....	....	1917-18	1919-20
Marks, John	Chi.	10	657	112	163	275	330	57	5	9	14	60	....	1972-73	1981-82
Markwart, Nevin	Bos., Cgy.	8	309	41	68	109	794	19	1	0	1	33	....	1983-84	1991-92
Marois, Daniel	Tor., NYI, Bos., Dal.	8	350	117	93	210	419	19	3	3	6	28	....	1987-88	1995-96
Marois, Mario	NYR, Van., Que., Wpg., St.L.	15	955	76	357	433	1746	100	4	34	38	182	....	1977-78	1991-92
Marotte, Gilles	Bos., Chi., L.A., NYR, St.L.	12	808	56	265	321	919	29	3	3	6	26	....	1965-66	1976-77
Marquess, Mark	Bos.	1	27	5	4	9	6	4	0	0	0	0	....	1946-47	1946-47
Marsh, Brad	Atl., Cgy., Phi., Tor., Det., Ott.	15	1086	23	175	198	1241	97	6	18	24	124	....	1978-79	1992-93
Marsh, Gary	Det., Tor.	2	7	1	3	4	4	....	....	....	....	....	....	1967-68	1968-69
Marsh, Peter	Wpg., Chi.	5	278	48	71	119	224	26	1	5	6	33	....	1979-80	1983-84
Marshall, Bert	Det., Oak., Cal., NYR, NYI	14	868	17	181	198	926	72	4	22	26	99	....	1965-66	1978-79
Marshall, Don	Mtl., NYR, Buf., Tor.	19	1176	265	324	589	127	94	8	15	23	14	5	1951-52	1971-72
Marshall, Paul	Pit., Tor., Hfd.	4	95	15	18	33	17	1	0	0	0	0	....	1979-80	1982-83
Marshall, Willie	Tor.	4	33	1	5	6	2	....	....	....	....	....	....	1952-53	1958-59
Marson, Mike	Wsh., L.A.	6	196	24	24	48	233	....	....	....	....	....	....	1974-75	1979-80
• Martin, Clare	Bos., Det., Chi., NYR	6	237	12	28	40	78	27	0	2	2	6	1	1941-42	1951-52
Martin, Craig	Wpg., Fla.	2	21	0	1	1	24	....	....	....	....	....	....	1994-95	1996-97
Martin, Frank	Bos., Chi.	6	282	11	46	57	122	10	0	2	2	2	....	1952-53	1957-58

Name	NHL Teams	NHL Seasons	Regular Schedule GP	G	A	TP	PIM	Playoffs GP	G	A	TP	PIM	NHL Cup Wins	First NHL Season	Last NHL Season
Martin, Grant	Van., Wsh.	4	44	0	4	4	55	1	1	0	1	2	....	1983-84	1986-87
Martin, Jack	Tor.	1	1	0	0	0	0	....	....	....	....	....	....	1960-61	1960-61
Martin, Pit	Det., Bos., Chi., Van.	17	1101	324	485	809	609	100	27	31	58	56	....	1961-62	1978-79
Martin, Rick	Buf., L.A.	11	685	384	317	701	477	63	24	29	53	74	....	1971-72	1981-82
• Martin, Ron	NYA	2	94	13	16	29	36	....	....	....	....	....	....	1932-33	1933-34
Martin, Terry	Buf., Que., Tor., Edm., Min.	10	479	104	101	205	202	21	4	2	6	26	....	1975-76	1984-85
Martin, Thomas	Tor.	1	3	1	0	1	0	....	....	....	....	....	....	1967-68	1967-68
Martin, Tom	Wpg., Hfd., Min.	6	92	12	11	23	249	4	0	0	0	6	....	1984-85	1989-90
Martineau, Don	Atl., Min., Det.	4	90	6	10	16	63	....	....	....	....	....	....	1973-74	1976-77
Martini, Darcy	Edm.	1	2	0	0	0	0	....	....	....	....	....	....	1993-94	1993-94
Martinson, Steven	Det., Mtl., Min.	4	49	2	1	3	244	1	0	0	0	10	....	1987-88	1991-92
Maruk, Dennis	Cal., Cle., Min., Wsh.	14	888	356	522	878	761	34	14	22	36	26	....	1975-76	1988-89
Masnick, Paul	Mtl., Chi., Tor.	6	232	18	41	59	139	33	4	5	9	27	1	1950-51	1957-58
• Mason, Charley	NYR, NYA, Det., Chi.	4	95	7	18	25	44	4	0	1	1	0	....	1934-35	1938-39
• Massecar, George	NYA	3	100	12	11	23	46	....	....	....	....	....	....	1929-30	1931-32
Masters, Jamie	St.L.	3	33	1	13	14	2	2	0	0	0	0	....	1975-76	1978-79
• Masterton, Bill	Min.	1	38	4	8	12	4	....	....	....	....	....	....	1967-68	1967-68
Mathers, Frank	Tor.	3	23	1	3	4	4	....	....	....	....	....	....	1948-49	1951-52
Mathiasen, Dwight	Pit.	3	33	1	7	8	18	....	....	....	....	....	....	1985-86	1987-88
Mathieson, Jim	Wsh.	1	2	0	0	0	4	....	....	....	....	....	....	1989-90	1989-90
• Matte, Joe	Tor., Ham., Bos., Mtl.C.	4	68	17	15	32	54	....	....	....	....	....	....	1919-20	1925-26
• Matte, Roland Joseph	Det., Chi.	2	24	0	3	3	8	....	....	....	....	....	....	1929-30	1942-43
Mattiussi, Dick	Pit., Oak., Cal.	4	200	8	31	39	124	8	0	1	1	6	....	1967-68	1970-71
• Matz, Johnny	Mtl.C.	1	30	3	2	5	0	5	0	0	0	2	....	1924-25	1924-25
Maxner, Wayne	Bos.	2	62	8	9	17	48	....	....	....	....	....	....	1964-65	1965-66
Maxwell, Brad	Min., Que., Tor., Van., NYR	10	612	98	270	368	1292	79	12	49	61	178	....	1977-78	1986-87
Maxwell, Bryan	Min., St.L., Wpg., Pit.	8	331	18	77	95	745	15	1	1	2	86	....	1977-78	1984-85
Maxwell, Kevin	Min., Col., N.J.	3	66	6	15	21	61	16	3	4	7	24	....	1980-81	1983-84
Maxwell, Wally	Tor.	1	2	0	0	0	0	....	....	....	....	....	....	1952-53	1952-53
May, Alan	Bos., Edm., Wsh., Dal., Cgy.	8	393	31	45	76	1348	40	1	2	3	80	....	1987-88	1994-95
Mayer, Derek	Ott.	1	17	2	2	4	8	....	....	....	....	....	....	1993-94	1993-94
Mayer, Jim	NYR	1	4	0	0	0	0	....	....	....	....	....	....	1979-80	1979-80
Mayer, Pat	Pit.	1	1	0	0	0	4	....	....	....	....	....	....	1987-88	1987-88
Mayer, Shep	Tor.	1	12	1	2	3	4	....	....	....	....	....	....	1942-43	1942-43
• Mazur, Eddie	Mtl., Chi.	6	107	8	20	28	120	25	4	5	9	22	1	1950-51	1956-57
Mazur, Jay	Van.	4	47	11	7	18	20	6	0	1	1	8	....	1988-89	1991-92
McAdam, Gary	Buf., Pit., Det., Cgy., Wsh., N.J., Tor.	11	534	96	132	228	243	30	6	5	11	16	....	1975-76	1985-86
• McAdam, Sam	NYR	1	5	0	0	0	0	....	....	....	....	....	....	1930-31	1930-31
• McAndrew, Hazen	Bro.	1	7	0	1	1	6	....	....	....	....	....	....	1941-42	1941-42
McAneeley, Ted	Cal.	3	158	8	35	43	141	....	....	....	....	....	....	1972-73	1974-75
McAtee, Jud	Det.	3	46	15	13	28	6	14	2	1	3	0	....	1942-43	1944-45
McAtee, Norm	Bos.	1	13	0	1	1	0	....	....	....	....	....	....	1946-47	1946-47
• McAvoy, George	Mtl.	1	....	....	....	....	....	4	0	0	0	0	....	1954-55	1954-55
McBain, Andrew	Wpg., Pit., Van., Ott.	11	608	129	172	301	633	24	5	7	12	39	....	1983-84	1993-94
McBean, Wayne	L.A., NYI, Wpg., Pit.	7	211	10	39	49	168	2	1	1	2	0	....	1987-88	1994-95
McBride, Cliff	Mtl.M., Tor.	2	2	0	0	0	0	....	....	....	....	....	....	1928-29	1929-30
McBurney, Jim	Chi.	1	1	0	1	1	0	....	....	....	....	....	....	1952-53	1952-53
• McCabe, Stan	Det., Mtl.M.	4	78	9	4	13	49	....	....	....	....	....	....	1929-30	1933-34
• McCaffrey, Bert	Tor., Pit., Mtl.C.	7	260	42	30	72	202	8	2	1	3	12	....	1924-25	1930-31
McCahill, John	Col.	1	1	0	0	0	0	....	....	....	....	....	....	1977-78	1977-78
McCaig, Douglas	Det., Chi.	7	263	8	21	29	255	7	0	1	1	10	....	1941-42	1950-51
• McCallum, Dunc	NYR, Pit.	5	187	14	35	49	230	10	1	2	3	12	....	1965-66	1970-71
• McCalmon, Eddie	Chi., Phi.	2	39	5	0	5	14	....	....	....	....	....	....	1927-28	1930-31
McCann, Rick	Det.	6	43	1	4	5	6	....	....	....	....	....	....	1967-68	1974-75
McCarthy, Dan	NYR	1	5	4	0	4	4	....	....	....	....	....	....	1980-81	1980-81
McCarthy, Kevin	Phi., Van., Pit.	10	537	67	191	258	527	21	2	3	5	20	....	1977-78	1986-87
• McCarthy, Thomas	Que., Ham.	2	34	22	7	29	10	....	....	....	....	....	....	1919-20	1920-21
McCarthy, Tom	Det., Bos.	4	60	8	9	17	8	....	....	....	....	....	....	1956-57	1960-61
McCarthy, Tom	Min., Bos.	9	460	178	221	399	330	68	12	26	38	67	....	1979-80	1987-88
• McCartney, Walt	Mtl.C.	1	2	0	0	0	0	....	....	....	....	....	....	1932-33	1932-33
McCaskill, Ted	Min.	1	4	0	2	2	0	....	....	....	....	....	....	1967-68	1967-68
McClanahan, Rob	Buf., Hfd., NYR	5	224	38	63	101	126	34	4	12	16	31	....	1979-80	1983-84
McClelland, Kevin	Pit., Edm., Det., Tor., Wpg.	12	588	68	112	180	1672	98	11	18	29	281	4	1981-82	1993-94
McCord, Bob	Bos., Det., Min., St.L.	7	316	10	58	68	262	14	2	5	7	10	....	1963-64	1972-73
McCord, Dennis	Van.	1	3	0	0	0	6	....	....	....	....	....	....	1973-74	1973-74
McCormack, John	Tor., Mtl., Chi.	8	311	25	49	74	35	22	1	1	2	0	2	1947-48	1954-55
McCourt, Dale	Det., Buf., Tor.	7	532	194	284	478	124	21	9	7	16	6	....	1977-78	1983-84
McCreary, Bill Jr.	Tor.	1	12	1	0	1	4	....	....	....	....	....	....	1980-81	1980-81
McCreary, Bill Sr.	NYR, Det., Mtl., St.L.	8	309	53	62	115	108	48	6	16	22	14	....	1953-54	1970-71
McCreary, Keith	Mtl., Pit., Atl.	10	532	131	112	243	294	16	0	4	4	6	....	1961-62	1974-75
• McCreedy, Johnny	Tor.	2	64	17	12	29	25	21	4	3	7	16	2	1941-42	1944-45
McCrimmon, Brad	Bos., Phi., Cgy., Det., Hfd., Phx.	18	1222	81	322	403	1416	116	11	18	29	176	1	1979-80	1996-97
McCrimmon, Jim	St.L.	1	2	0	0	0	0	....	....	....	....	....	....	1974-75	1974-75
McCulley, Bob	Mtl.C.	1	1	0	0	0	0	....	....	....	....	....	....	1934-35	1934-35
• McCurry, Duke	Pit.	4	148	21	11	32	119	4	0	2	2	4	....	1925-26	1928-29
McCutcheon, Brian	Det.	3	37	3	1	4	7	....	....	....	....	....	....	1974-75	1976-77
McCutcheon, Darwin	Tor.	1	1	0	0	0	2	....	....	....	....	....	....	1981-82	1981-82
McDill, Jeff	Chi.	1	1	0	0	0	0	....	....	....	....	....	....	1976-77	1976-77
McDonagh, Bill	NYR	1	4	0	0	0	2	....	....	....	....	....	....	1949-50	1949-50
McDonald, Ab	Mtl., Chi., Bos., Det., Pit., St.L.	15	762	182	248	430	200	84	21	29	50	42	4	1957-58	1971-72
McDonald, Brian	Chi., Buf.	2	12	0	0	0	29	8	0	0	0	2	....	1967-68	1970-71
• McDonald, Bucko	Det., Tor., NYR	11	446	35	88	123	206	50	6	1	7	24	3	1934-35	1944-45
McDonald, Butch	Det., Chi.	2	66	8	20	28	2	5	0	2	2	10	....	1939-40	1944-45
McDonald, Gerry	Hfd.	2	8	0	0	0	4	....	....	....	....	....	....	1981-82	1983-84
• McDonald, Jack	Mtl., Mtl.C., Que., Tor.	5	68	26	14	40	30	12	2	4	6	6	....	1917-18	1921-22
• McDonald, John	NYR	1	43	10	9	19	6	....	....	....	....	....	....	1943-44	1943-44
McDonald, Lanny	Tor., Col., Cgy.	16	1111	500	506	1006	899	117	44	40	84	120	1	1973-74	1988-89
McDonald, Robert	NYR	1	1	0	0	0	0	....	....	....	....	....	....	1943-44	1943-44
McDonald, Terry	K.C.	1	8	0	1	1	6	....	....	....	....	....	....	1975-76	1975-76
McDonnell, Joe	Van., Pit.	3	50	2	10	12	34	....	....	....	....	....	....	1981-82	1985-86
McDonough, Al	L.A., Pit., Atl., Det.	5	237	73	88	161	73	8	0	1	1	2	....	1970-71	1977-78
McDonough, Hubie	L.A., NYI, S.J.	5	195	40	26	66	67	5	1	0	1	4	....	1988-89	1992-93
McDougal, Mike	NYR, Hfd.	4	61	8	10	18	43	....	....	....	....	....	....	1978-79	1982-83
McDougall, Bill	Det., Edm., T.B.	3	28	5	5	10	12	1	0	0	0	0	....	1990-91	1993-94
McElmury, Jim	Min., K.C., Col.	5	180	14	47	61	49	....	....	....	....	....	....	1972-73	1977-78
McEwen, Mike	NYR, Col., NYI, L.A., Wsh., Det., Hfd.	12	716	108	296	404	460	78	12	36	48	48	3	1976-77	1987-88
McFadden, Jim	Det., Chi.	8	412	100	126	226	89	49	10	9	19	30	1	1946-47	1953-54
McFadyen, Don	Chi.	4	179	12	33	45	77	11	2	2	4	5	1	1932-33	1935-36
McFall, Dan	Wpg.	2	9	0	1	1	0	....	....	....	....	....	....	1984-85	1985-86
• McFarlane, Gordon	Chi.	1	2	0	0	0	0	....	....	....	....	....	....	1926-27	1926-27
McGeough, Jim	Wsh., Pit.	4	57	7	10	17	32	....	....	....	....	....	....	1981-82	1986-87
• McGibbon, Irv	Mtl.	1	1	0	0	0	2	....	....	....	....	....	....	1942-43	1942-43
McGill, Bob	Tor., Chi., S.J., Det., NYI, Hfd.	13	705	17	55	72	1766	49	0	0	0	88	....	1981-82	1993-94
• McGill, Jack	Mtl.C.	3	134	27	10	37	71	3	2	0	2	0	....	1934-35	1936-37
McGill, John	Bos.	4	97	23	36	59	42	27	7	4	11	17	....	1941-42	1946-47
McGill, Ryan	Chi., Phi., Edm.	4	151	4	15	19	391	....	....	....	....	....	....	1991-92	1994-95
McGregor, Sandy	NYR	1	2	0	0	0	2	....	....	....	....	....	....	1963-64	1963-64
• McGuire, Mickey	Pit.	2	36	3	0	3	6	....	....	....	....	....	....	1926-27	1927-28
McHugh, Mike	Min., S.J.	4	20	1	0	1	16	....	....	....	....	....	....	1988-89	1991-92
McIlhargey, Jack	Phi., Van., Hfd.	8	393	11	36	47	1102	27	0	3	3	68	....	1974-75	1981-82
• McInenly, Bert	Det., NYA, Ott., Bos.	6	166	19	15	34	144	4	0	0	0	2	....	1930-31	1935-36
McIntosh, Bruce	Min.	1	2	0	0	0	0	....	....	....	....	....	....	1972-73	1972-73
McIntosh, Paul	Buf.	2	48	0	2	2	66	2	0	0	0	7	....	1974-75	1975-76
• McIntyre, Jack	Bos., Chi., Det.	11	499	109	102	211	173	29	7	6	13	4	....	1949-50	1959-60
• McIntyre, John	Tor., L.A., NYR, Van.	6	351	24	54	78	516	44	0	6	6	54	....	1989-90	1994-95
McIntyre, Larry	Tor.	2	41	0	3	3	26	....	....	....	....	....	....	1969-70	1972-73
McKay, Doug	Det.	1	....	....	....	....	....	1	0	0	0	0	1	1949-50	1949-50
McKay, Ray	Chi., Buf., Cal.	6	140	2	16	18	102	....	....	....	....	....	....	1968-69	1973-74
McKay, Scott	Ana.	1	1	0	0	0	0	....	....	....	....	....	....	1993-94	1993-94
McKechnie, Walt	Min., Cal., Bos., Det., Wsh., Cle., Tor., Col.	16	955	214	392	606	469	15	7	5	12	7	....	1967-68	1982-83

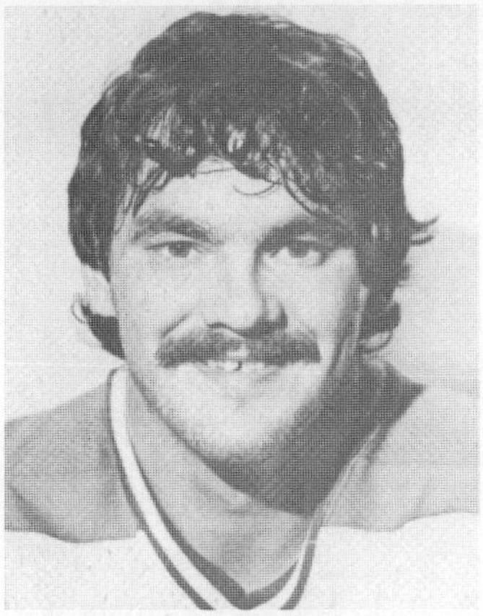
Jimmy Mann

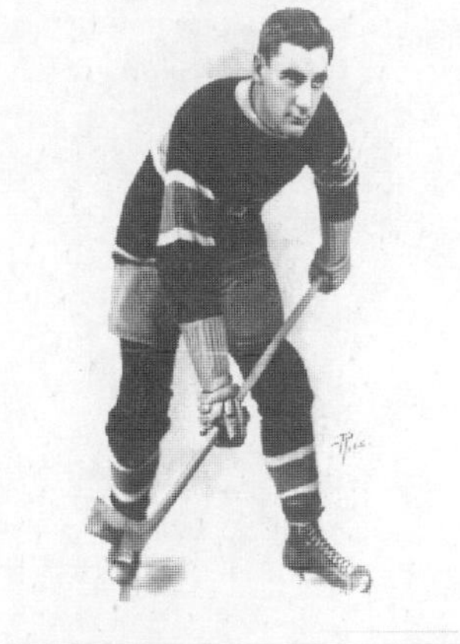
Sylvio Mantha

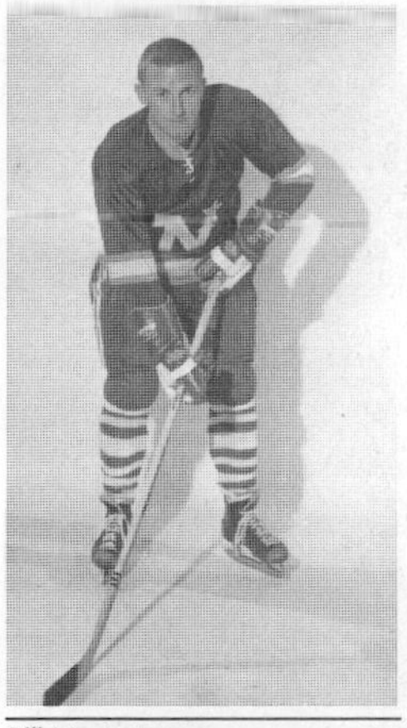
Bill Masterton

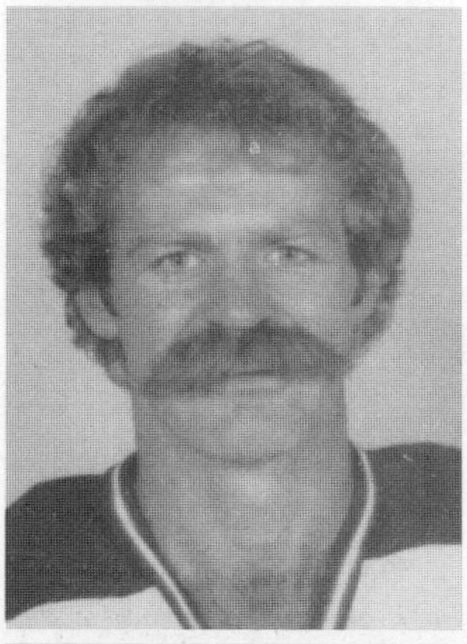
Lanny McDonald

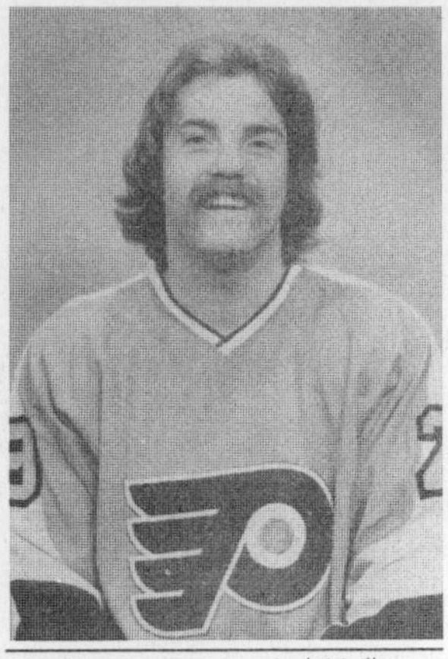

Jack McIlhargey

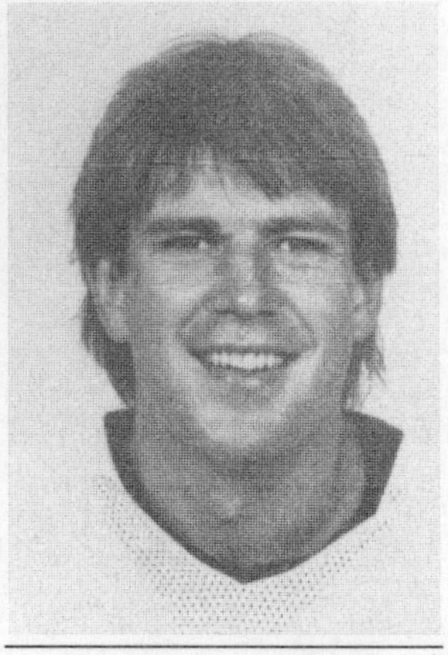

Peter McNab

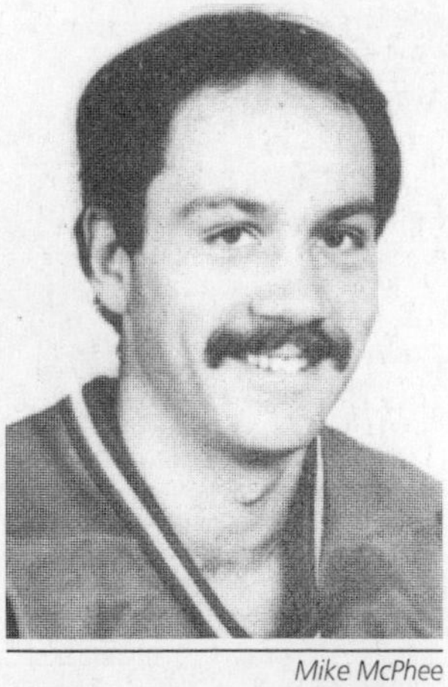

Mike McPhee

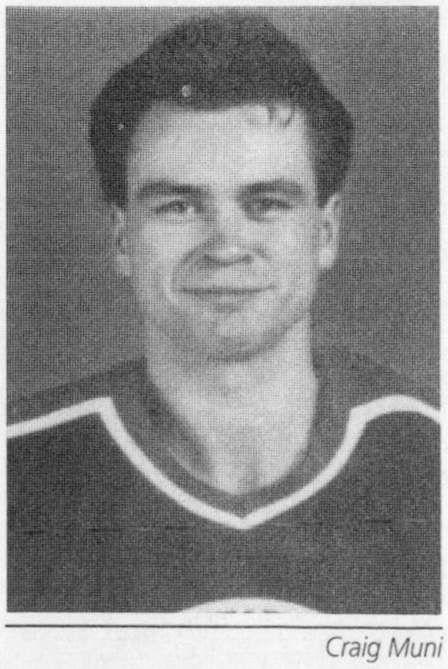

Craig Muni

			Regular Schedule					Playoffs							
Name	NHL Teams	NHL Seasons	GP	G	A	TP	PIM	GP	G	A	TP	PIM	NHL Cup Wins	First NHL Season	Last NHL Season
McKee, Mike	Que.	1	48	3	12	15	41	....	....	....	....	....	....	1993-94	1993-94
McKegney, Ian	Chi.	1	3	0	0	0	2	....	....	....	....	....	....	1976-77	1976-77
McKegney, Tony	Buf., Que., Min., NYR, St.L., Det., Chi.	13	912	320	319	639	517	79	24	23	47	56	....	1978-79	1990-91
McKendry, Alex	NYI, Cgy.	4	46	3	6	9	21	6	2	2	4	0	1	1977-78	1980-81
McKenna, Sean	Buf., L.A., Tor.	9	414	82	80	162	181	15	1	2	3	2	....	1981-82	1989-90
McKenney, Don	Bos., NYR, Tor., Det., St.L.	13	798	237	345	582	211	58	18	29	47	10	1	1954-55	1967-68
McKenny, Jim	Tor., Min.	14	604	82	247	329	294	37	7	9	16	10	....	1965-66	1978-79
McKenzie, Brian	Pit.	1	6	1	1	2	4	....	....	....	....	....	....	1971-72	1971-72
McKenzie, John	Chi., Det., NYR, Bos.	12	691	206	268	474	917	69	15	32	47	133	2	1958-59	1971-72
McKim, Andrew	Bos., Det.	3	38	1	4	5	6	....	....	....	....	....	....	1992-93	1994-95
• McKinnon, Alex	Ham., NYA, Chi.	5	194	19	10	29	235	....	....	....	....	....	....	1924-25	1928-29
• McKinnon, John	Mtl.C., Pit., Phi.	6	208	28	11	39	224	2	0	0	0	4	....	1925-26	1930-31
McLean, Don	Wsh.	1	9	0	0	0	6	....	....	....	....	....	....	1975-76	1975-76
• McLean, Fred	Que., Ham.	2	11	0	0	0	2	....	....	....	....	....	....	1919-20	1920-21
McLean, Jack	Tor.	3	67	14	24	38	76	13	2	2	4	8	1	1942-43	1944-45
McLean, Jeff	S.J.	1	6	1	0	1	0	....	....	....	....	....	....	1993-94	1993-94
• McLellan, John	Tor.	1	2	0	0	0	0	....	....	....	....	....	....	1951-52	1951-52
McLellan, Scott	Bos.	1	2	0	0	0	0	....	....	....	....	....	....	1982-83	1982-83
McLellan, Todd	NYI	1	5	1	1	2	0	....	....	....	....	....	....	1987-88	1987-88
• McLenahan, Rollie	Det.	1	9	2	1	3	10	2	0	0	0	0	....	1945-46	1945-46
McLeod, Al	Det.	1	26	2	2	4	24	....	....	....	....	....	....	1973-74	1973-74
McLeod, Jackie	NYR	5	106	14	23	37	12	7	0	0	0	0	....	1949-50	1954-55
McLlwain, Dave	Pit., Wpg., Buf., NYI, Tor., Ott.	10	501	100	107	207	292	20	0	2	2	2	....	1987-88	1996-97
McMahon, Mike Jr.	NYR, Min., Chi., Det., Pit., Buf.	8	224	15	68	83	171	14	3	7	10	4	....	1963-64	1971-72
• McMahon, Mike Sr.	Mtl., Bos.	3	57	7	18	25	102	13	1	2	3	30	1	1942-43	1945-46
McManama, Bob	Pit.	3	99	11	25	36	28	8	0	1	1	6	....	1973-74	1975-76
• McManus, Sammy	Mtl.M., Bos.	2	26	0	1	1	8	1	0	0	0	0	1	1934-35	1936-37
McMurchy, Tom	Chi., Edm.	4	55	8	4	12	65	....	....	....	....	....	....	1983-84	1987-88
McNab, Max	Det.	4	128	16	19	35	24	25	1	0	1	4	1	1947-48	1950-51
McNab, Peter	Buf., Bos., Van., N.J.	14	954	363	450	813	179	107	40	42	82	20	....	1973-74	1986-87
McNabney, Sid	Mtl.	1	....	....	....	....	....	5	0	1	1	2	....	1950-51	1950-51
• McNamara, Howard	Mtl.C.	1	12	1	0	1	6	....	....	....	....	....	....	1919-20	1919-20
• McNaughton, George	Que.	1	1	0	0	0	0	....	....	....	....	....	....	1919-20	1919-20
McNeill, Billy	Det.	6	257	21	46	67	142	4	1	1	2	4	....	1956-57	1963-64
McNeill, Mike	Chi., Que.	2	63	5	11	16	18	....	....	....	....	....	....	1990-91	1991-92
McNeill, Stu	Det.	3	10	1	1	2	2	....	....	....	....	....	....	1957-58	1959-60
McPhee, George	NYR, N.J.	7	115	24	25	49	257	29	5	3	8	69	....	1982-83	1988-89
McPhee, Mike	Mtl., Min., Dal.	11	744	200	199	399	661	134	28	27	55	193	1	1983-84	1993-94
McRae, Basil	Que., Tor., Det., Min., T.B., St.L., Chi.	16	576	53	83	136	2457	78	8	4	12	349	....	1981-82	1996-97
McRae, Chris	Tor., Det.	3	21	1	0	1	122	....	....	....	....	....	....	1987-88	1989-90
McRae, Ken	Que., Tor.	7	137	14	21	35	364	6	0	0	0	4	....	1987-88	1993-94
McReavy, Pat	Bos., Det.	4	55	5	10	15	4	22	3	3	6	9	1	1938-39	1941-42
McReynolds, Brian	Wpg., NYR, L.A.	3	30	1	5	6	8	....	....	....	....	....	....	1989-90	1993-94
McSheffrey, Bryan	Van., Buf.	3	90	13	7	20	44	....	....	....	....	....	....	1972-73	1974-75
McSween, Don	Buf., Ana.	5	47	3	10	13	55	....	....	....	....	....	....	1987-88	1995-96
McTaggart, Jim	Wsh.	2	71	3	10	13	205	....	....	....	....	....	....	1980-81	1981-82
McTavish, Gordon	St.L., Wpg.	2	11	1	3	4	2	....	....	....	....	....	....	1978-79	1979-80
• McVeigh, Charley	Chi., NYA	9	397	84	88	172	138	4	0	0	0	2	....	1926-27	1934-35
• McVicar, Jack	Mtl.M.	2	88	2	4	6	63	6	0	0	0	2	....	1930-31	1931-32
Meagher, Rick	Mtl., Hfd., N.J., St.L.	12	691	144	165	309	383	62	8	7	15	41	....	1979-80	1990-91
Meehan, Gerry	Tor., Phi., Buf., Van., Atl., Wsh.	10	670	180	243	423	111	10	0	1	1	0	....	1968-69	1978-79
Meeke, Brent	Cal., Cle.	5	75	9	22	31	8	....	....	....	....	....	....	1972-73	1976-77
Meeker, Howie	Tor.	8	346	83	102	185	329	42	6	9	15	50	4	1946-47	1953-54
Meeker, Mike	Pit.	1	4	0	0	0	5	....	....	....	....	....	....	1978-79	1978-79
• Meeking, Harry	Tor., Det., Bos.	3	65	18	13	31	66	14	4	2	6	21	1	1917-18	1926-27
Meger, Paul	Mtl.	6	212	39	52	91	118	35	3	8	11	16	1	1949-50	1954-55
Meighan, Ron	Min., Pit.	2	48	3	7	10	18	....	....	....	....	....	....	1981-82	1982-83
Meissner, Barrie	Min.	2	6	0	1	1	4	....	....	....	....	....	....	1967-68	1968-69
Meissner, Dick	Bos., NYR	5	171	11	15	26	37	....	....	....	....	....	....	1959-60	1964-65
Melametsa, Anssi	Wpg.	1	27	0	3	3	2	....	....	....	....	....	....	1985-86	1985-86
Melin, Roger	Min.	2	3	0	0	0	0	....	....	....	....	....	....	1980-81	1981-82
Mellor, Tom	Det.	2	26	2	4	6	25	....	....	....	....	....	....	1973-74	1974-75
Melnyk, Gerry	Det., Chi., St.L.	6	269	39	77	116	34	53	6	6	12	6	....	1955-56	1967-68
Melnyk, Larry	Bos., Edm., NYR, Van.	10	432	11	63	74	686	66	2	9	11	127	2	1980-81	1989-90
Melrose, Barry	Wpg., Tor., Det.	6	300	10	23	33	728	7	0	2	2	38	....	1979-80	1985-86
Menard, Hillary	Chi.	1	1	0	0	0	0	....	....	....	....	....	....	1953-54	1953-54
Menard, Howie	Det., L.A., Chi., Oak.	4	151	23	42	65	87	19	3	7	10	36	....	1963-64	1969-70
Mercredi, Vic	Atl.	1	2	0	0	0	0	....	....	....	....	....	....	1974-75	1974-75
Meredith, Greg	Cgy.	2	38	6	4	10	8	5	3	1	4	4	....	1980-81	1982-83
Merkosky, Glenn	Hfd., N.J., Det.	5	66	5	12	17	22	....	....	....	....	....	....	1981-82	1989-90
Meronek, Bill	Mtl.	2	19	5	8	13	0	1	0	0	0	0	....	1939-40	1942-43
Merrick, Wayne	St.L., Cal., Cle., NYI	12	774	191	265	456	303	102	19	30	49	30	4	1972-73	1983-84
• Merrill, Horace	Ott.	2	8	0	0	0	3	....	....	....	....	....	....	1917-18	1919-20
Messier, Joby	NYR	3	25	0	4	4	24	....	....	....	....	....	....	1992-93	1994-95
Messier, Mitch	Min.	4	20	0	2	2	11	....	....	....	....	....	....	1987-88	1990-91
Messier, Paul	Col.	1	9	0	0	0	4	....	....	....	....	....	....	1978-79	1978-79
Metcalfe, Scott	Edm., Buf.	3	19	1	2	3	18	....	....	....	....	....	....	1987-88	1989-90
Metz, Don	Tor.	9	172	20	35	55	42	42	7	8	15	12	5	1938-39	1948-49
• Metz, Nick	Tor.	12	518	131	119	250	149	76	19	20	39	31	4	1934-35	1947-48
Michaluk, Art	Chi.	1	5	0	0	0	0	....	....	....	....	....	....	1947-48	1947-48
Michaluk, John	Chi.	1	1	0	0	0	0	....	....	....	....	....	....	1950-51	1950-51
Michayluk, Dave	Phi., Pit.	3	14	2	6	8	8	7	1	1	2	0	1	1981-82	1991-92
Micheletti, Joe	St.L., Col.	3	158	11	60	71	114	11	1	11	12	10	....	1979-80	1981-82
Micheletti, Pat	Min.	1	12	2	0	2	8	....	....	....	....	....	....	1987-88	1987-88
• Mickey, Larry	Chi., NYR, Tor., Mtl., L.A., Phi., Buf.	11	292	39	53	92	160	9	1	0	1	10	....	1964-65	1974-75
Mickoski, Nick	NYR, Chi., Det., Bos.	13	703	158	185	343	319	18	1	6	7	6	....	1947-48	1959-60
Middendorf, Max	Que., Edm.	4	13	2	4	6	6	....	....	....	....	....	....	1986-87	1990-91
Middleton, Rick	NYR, Bos.	14	1005	448	540	988	157	114	45	55	100	19	....	1974-75	1987-88
Miehm, Kevin	St.L.	2	22	1	4	5	8	2	0	1	1	0	....	1992-93	1993-94
Migay, Rudy	Tor.	10	418	59	92	151	293	15	1	0	1	20	....	1949-50	1959-60
Mikita, Stan	Chi.	22	1394	541	926	1467	1270	155	59	91	150	169	1	1958-59	1979-80
Mikkelson, Bill	L.A., NYI, Wsh.	4	147	4	18	22	105	....	....	....	....	....	....	1971-72	1976-77
Mikol, Jim	Tor., NYR	2	34	1	4	5	8	....	....	....	....	....	....	1962-63	1964-65
Mikulchik, Oleg	Wpg., Ana.	3	37	0	3	3	33	....	....	....	....	....	....	1993-94	1995-96
Milbury, Mike	Bos.	12	754	49	189	238	1552	86	4	24	28	219	....	1975-76	1986-87
• Milks, Hib	Pit., Phi., NYR, Ott.	8	317	87	41	128	179	11	0	0	0	2	....	1925-26	1932-33
Millar, Hugh	Det.	1	4	0	0	0	0	1	0	0	0	0	....	1946-47	1946-47
Millar, Mike	Hfd., Wsh., Bos., Tor.	5	78	18	18	36	12	....	....	....	....	....	....	1986-87	1990-91
Miller, Bill	Mtl.M., Mtl.C.	3	95	7	3	10	16	12	0	0	0	0	1	1934-35	1936-37
Miller, Bob	Bos., Col., L.A.	6	404	75	119	194	220	36	4	7	11	27	....	1977-78	1984-85
Miller, Brad	Buf., Ott., Cgy.	6	82	1	5	6	321	....	....	....	....	....	....	1988-89	1993-94
• Miller, Earl	Chi., Tor.	5	109	19	14	33	124	10	1	0	1	6	1	1927-28	1931-32
Miller, Jack	Chi.	2	17	0	0	0	4	....	....	....	....	....	....	1949-50	1950-51
Miller, Jason	N.J.	3	6	0	0	0	0	....	....	....	....	....	....	1990-91	1992-93
Miller, Jay	Bos., L.A.	7	446	40	44	84	1723	48	2	3	5	243	....	1985-86	1991-92
Miller, Paul	Col.	1	3	0	3	3	0	....	....	....	....	....	....	1981-82	1981-82
Miller, Perry	Det.	4	217	10	51	61	387	....	....	....	....	....	....	1977-78	1980-81
Miller, Tom	Det., NYI	4	118	16	25	41	34	....	....	....	....	....	....	1970-71	1974-75
Miller, Warren	NYR, Hfd.	4	262	40	50	90	137	6	1	0	1	0	....	1979-80	1982-83
Miner, John	Edm.	1	14	2	3	5	16	....	....	....	....	....	....	1987-88	1987-88
Minor, Gerry	Van.	5	140	11	21	32	173	12	1	3	4	25	....	1979-80	1983-84
Miszuk, John	Det., Chi., Phi., Min.	6	237	7	39	46	232	19	0	3	3	19	....	1963-64	1969-70
Mitchell, Bill	Det.	1	1	0	0	0	0	....	....	....	....	....	....	1963-64	1963-64
• Mitchell, Herb	Bos.	2	53	6	0	6	38	....	....	....	....	....	....	1924-25	1925-26
Mitchell, Red	Chi.	3	83	4	5	9	67	....	....	....	....	....	....	1941-42	1944-45
Mitchell, Roy	Min.	1	3	0	0	0	0	....	....	....	....	....	....	1992-93	1992-93
Moe, Billy	NYR	5	261	11	42	53	163	1	0	0	0	0	....	1944-45	1948-49
Moffat, Lyle	Tor., Wpg.	3	97	12	16	28	51	....	....	....	....	....	....	1972-73	1979-80
• Moffat, Ron	Det.	3	37	1	1	2	8	7	0	0	0	0	....	1932-33	1934-35
Moher, Mike	N.J.	1	9	0	1	1	28	....	....	....	....	....	....	1982-83	1982-83
Mohns, Doug	Bos., Chi., Min., Atl., Wsh.	22	1390	248	462	710	1250	94	14	36	50	122	....	1953-54	1974-75
Mohns, Lloyd	NYR	1	1	0	0	0	0	....	....	....	....	....	....	1943-44	1943-44

Name	NHL Teams	NHL Seasons	Regular Schedule GP	G	A	TP	PIM	Playoffs GP	G	A	TP	PIM	NHL Cup Wins	First NHL Season	Last NHL Season
Mokosak, Carl	Cgy., L.A., Phi., Pit., Bos.	6	83	11	15	26	170	1	0	0	0	0	....	1981-82	1988-89
Mokosak, John	Det.	2	41	0	2	2	96	....	....	....	....	....	....	1988-89	1989-90
Molin, Lars	Van.	3	172	33	65	98	37	19	2	9	11	7	....	1981-82	1983-84
Moller, Mike	Buf., Edm.	7	134	15	28	43	41	3	0	1	1	0	....	1980-81	1986-87
Moller, Randy	Que., NYR, Buf., Fla.	14	815	45	180	225	1692	78	6	16	22	197	....	1981-82	1994-95
Molloy, Mitch	Buf.	1	2	0	0	0	10	....	....	....	....	....	....	1989-90	1989-90
Molyneaux, Larry	NYR	2	45	0	1	1	20	10	0	0	0	8	....	1937-38	1938-39
Momesso, Sergio	Mtl., St.L., Van., Tor., NYR	13	710	152	193	345	1557	119	18	26	44	311	....	1983-84	1996-97
Monahan, Garry	Mtl., Det., L.A., Tor., Van.	12	748	116	169	285	484	22	3	1	4	13	....	1967-68	1978-79
Monahan, Hartland	Cal., NYR, Wsh., Pit., L.A., St.L.	7	334	61	80	141	163	6	0	0	0	4	....	1973-74	1980-81
• Mondou, Armand	Mtl.C., Mtl.	12	386	47	71	118	99	32	3	5	8	12	....	1928-29	1939-40
Mondou, Pierre	Mtl.	9	548	194	262	456	179	69	17	28	45	26	3	1976-77	1984-85
Mongeau, Michel	St.L., T.B.	4	54	6	19	25	10	2	0	1	1	0	....	1989-90	1992-93
Mongrain, Bob	Buf., L.A.	6	81	13	14	27	14	11	1	2	3	2	....	1979-80	1985-86
Monteith, Hank	Det.	3	77	5	12	17	6	4	0	0	0	0	....	1968-69	1970-71
Moore, Dickie	Mtl., Tor., St.L.	14	719	261	347	608	652	135	46	64	110	122	6	1951-52	1967-68
• Moran, Amby	Mtl.C., Chi.	2	35	1	1	2	24	....	....	....	....	....	....	1926-27	1927-28
• Morenz, Howie	Mtl.C., Chi., NYR	14	550	270	197	467	531	47	21	11	32	68	....	1923-24	1936-37
Moretto, Angelo	Cle.	1	5	1	2	3	2	....	....	....	....	....	....	1976-77	1976-77
• Morin, Pete	Mtl.	1	31	10	12	22	7	1	0	0	0	0	....	1941-42	1941-42
Morin, Stephane	Que., Van.	5	90	16	39	55	52	....	....	....	....	....	....	1989-90	1993-94
• Morris, Bernie	Bos.	1	6	2	0	2	0	....	....	....	....	....	....	1924-25	1924-25
Morris, Jon	N.J., S.J., Bos.	6	103	16	33	49	47	11	1	7	8	25	....	1988-89	1993-94
Morris, Moe	Tor., NYR	4	135	13	29	42	58	18	4	2	6	16	1	1943-44	1948-49
Morrison, Dave	L.A., Van.	4	39	3	3	6	4	....	....	....	....	....	....	1980-81	1984-85
Morrison, Don	Det., Chi.	3	112	18	28	46	12	3	0	1	1	0	....	1947-48	1950-51
Morrison, Doug	Bos.	4	23	7	3	10	15	....	....	....	....	....	....	1979-80	1984-85
Morrison, Gary	Phi.	3	43	1	15	16	70	5	0	1	1	2	....	1979-80	1981-82
Morrison, George	St.L.	2	115	17	21	38	13	3	0	0	0	0	....	1970-71	1971-72
Morrison, Jim	Bos., Tor., Det., NYR, Pit.	12	704	40	160	200	542	36	0	12	12	38	....	1951-52	1970-71
• Morrison, John	NYA	1	18	0	0	0	0	....	....	....	....	....	....	1925-26	1925-26
Morrison, Kevin	Col.	1	41	4	11	15	23	....	....	....	....	....	....	1979-80	1979-80
Morrison, Lew	Phi., Atl., Wsh., Pit.	9	564	39	52	91	107	17	0	0	0	2	....	1969-70	1977-78
Morrison, Mark	NYR	2	10	1	1	2	0	....	....	....	....	....	....	1981-82	1983-84
Morrison, Rod	Det.	1	34	8	7	15	4	3	0	0	0	0	....	1947-48	1947-48
Morrow, Ken	NYI	10	550	17	88	105	309	127	11	22	33	97	4	1979-80	1988-89
Morrow, Scott	Cgy.	1	4	0	0	0	0	....	....	....	....	....	....	1994-95	1994-95
Morton, Dean	Det.	1	1	1	0	1	2	....	....	....	....	....	....	1989-90	1989-90
Mortson, Gus	Tor., Chi., Det.	13	797	46	152	198	1380	54	5	8	13	68	4	1946-47	1958-59
Mosdell, Kenny	Bro., Mtl., Chi.	16	693	141	168	309	475	80	16	13	29	48	4	1941-42	1958-59
• Mosienko, Bill	Chi.	14	711	258	282	540	121	22	10	4	14	15	....	1941-42	1954-55
Mott, Morris	Cal.	3	199	18	32	50	49	....	....	....	....	....	....	1972-73	1974-75
• Motter, Alex	Bos., Det.	8	256	39	64	103	135	41	3	9	12	41	1	1934-35	1942-43
Moxey, Jim	Cal., Cle., L.A.	3	127	22	27	49	59	....	....	....	....	....	....	1974-75	1976-77
Mulhern, Richard	Atl., L.A., Tor., Wpg.	6	303	27	93	120	217	7	0	3	3	5	....	1975-76	1980-81
Mullen, Brian	Wpg., NYR, S.J., NYI	11	832	260	362	622	414	62	12	18	30	30	....	1982-83	1992-93
Mullen, Joe	St.L., Cgy., Pit., Bos.	17	1062	502	561	1063	241	143	60	46	106	42	3	1979-80	1996-97
Muloin, Wayne	Det., Oak., Cal., Min.	3	147	3	21	24	93	11	0	0	0	2	....	1963-64	1970-71
Mulvenna, Glenn	Pit., Phi.	2	2	0	0	0	4	....	....	....	....	....	....	1991-92	1992-93
Mulvey, Grant	Chi., N.J.	10	586	149	135	284	816	42	10	5	15	70	....	1974-75	1983-84
Mulvey, Paul	Wsh., Pit., L.A.	4	225	30	51	81	613	....	....	....	....	....	....	1978-79	1981-82
• Mummery, Harry	Tor., Que., Mtl.C., Ham.	6	107	33	19	52	230	7	1	7	8	38	1	1917-18	1922-23
Muni, Craig	Tor., Edm., Chi., Buf., Wpg., Pit., Dal.	16	819	28	119	147	775	113	0	17	17	108	3	1981-82	1997-98
• Munro, Dunc	Mtl.M., Mtl.C.	8	239	28	18	46	170	25	3	2	5	24	1	1924-25	1931-32
• Munro, Gerry	Mtl.M., Tor.	2	33	1	0	1	22	....	....	....	....	....	....	1924-25	1925-26
Murdoch, Bob	Mtl., L.A., Atl., Cgy.	12	757	60	218	278	764	69	4	18	22	92	2	1970-71	1981-82
Murdoch, Bob	Cal., Cle., St.L.	4	260	72	85	157	127	....	....	....	....	....	....	1975-76	1978-79
Murdoch, Don	NYR, Edm., Det.	6	320	121	117	238	155	24	10	8	18	16	....	1976-77	1981-82
Murdoch, Murray	NYR	11	500	84	100	192	107	55	9	12	21	28	2	1926-27	1936-37
Murphy, Brian	Det.	1	1	0	0	0	0	....	....	....	....	....	....	1974-75	1974-75
Murphy, Mike	St.L., NYR, L.A.	12	831	238	318	556	514	66	13	23	36	54	....	1971-72	1982-83
Murphy, Rob	Van., Ott., L.A.	7	125	9	12	21	152	4	0	0	0	2	....	1987-88	1993-94
Murphy, Ron	NYR, Chi., Det., Bos.	18	889	205	274	479	460	53	7	8	15	26	1	1952-53	1969-70
Murray, Allan	NYA	7	271	5	9	14	163	14	0	0	0	10	....	1933-34	1939-40
Murray, Bob	Atl., Van.	4	194	6	16	22	98	10	1	1	2	15	....	1973-74	1976-77
Murray, Bob	Chi.	15	1008	132	382	514	873	112	19	37	56	106	....	1975-76	1989-90
Murray, Jim	L.A.	1	30	0	2	2	14	....	....	....	....	....	....	1967-68	1967-68
Murray, Ken	Tor., NYI, Det., K.C.	5	106	1	10	11	135	....	....	....	....	....	....	1969-70	1975-76
• Murray, Leo	Mtl.C.	1	6	0	0	0	2	....	....	....	....	....	....	1932-33	1932-33
Murray, Mike	Phi.	1	1	0	0	0	0	....	....	....	....	....	....	1987-88	1987-88
Murray, Pat	Phi.	2	25	3	1	4	15	....	....	....	....	....	....	1990-91	1991-92
Murray, Randy	Tor.	1	3	0	0	0	2	....	....	....	....	....	....	1969-70	1969-70
Murray, Terry	Cal., Phi., Det., Wsh.	8	302	4	76	80	199	18	2	2	4	10	....	1972-73	1981-82
Murray, Troy	Chi., Wpg., Ott., Pit., Col.	15	915	230	354	584	875	113	17	26	43	145	1	1981-82	1995-96
Myers, Hap	Buf.	1	13	0	0	0	6	....	....	....	....	....	....	1970-71	1970-71
Myles, Vic	NYR	1	45	6	9	15	57	....	....	....	....	....	....	1942-43	1942-43

N

Name	NHL Teams	NHL Seasons	Regular Schedule GP	G	A	TP	PIM	Playoffs GP	G	A	TP	PIM	NHL Cup Wins	First NHL Season	Last NHL Season
Nachbaur, Don	Hfd., Edm., Phi.	8	223	23	46	69	465	11	1	1	2	24	....	1980-81	1989-90
Nahrgang, Jim	Det.	3	57	5	12	17	34	....	....	....	....	....	....	1974-75	1976-77
Nanne, Lou	Min.	11	635	68	157	225	356	32	4	10	14	8	....	1967-68	1977-78
Nantais, Richard	Min.	3	63	5	4	9	79	....	....	....	....	....	....	1974-75	1976-77
Napier, Mark	Mtl., Min., Edm., Buf.	11	767	235	306	541	157	82	18	24	42	11	2	1978-79	1988-89
Naslund, Mats	Mtl., Bos.	9	651	251	383	634	111	102	35	57	92	33	1	1982-83	1994-95
Nattrass, Ralph	Chi.	4	223	18	38	56	308	....	....	....	....	....	....	1946-47	1949-50
Nattress, Ric	Mtl., St.L., Cgy., Tor., Phi.	11	536	29	135	164	377	67	5	10	15	60	1	1982-83	1992-93
Natyshak, Mike	Que.	1	4	0	0	0	0	....	....	....	....	....	....	1987-88	1987-88
Neaton, Pat	Pit.	1	9	1	1	2	12	....	....	....	....	....	....	1993-94	1993-94
Nechayev, Viktor	L.A.	1	3	1	0	1	0	....	....	....	....	....	....	1982-83	1982-83
Nedomansky, Vaclav	Det., NYR, St.L.	6	421	122	156	278	88	7	3	5	8	0	....	1977-78	1982-83
Needham, Mike	Pit., Dal.	3	86	9	5	14	16	14	2	0	2	4	1	1991-92	1993-94
Neely, Bob	Tor., Col.	5	283	39	59	98	266	26	5	7	12	15	....	1973-74	1977-78
Neely, Cam	Van., Bos.	13	726	395	299	694	1241	93	57	32	89	168	....	1983-84	1995-96
Neilson, Jim	NYR, Cal., Cle.	16	1023	69	299	368	904	65	1	17	18	61	....	1962-63	1977-78
Nelson, Gordie	Tor.	1	3	0	0	0	11	....	....	....	....	....	....	1969-70	1969-70
Nelson, Todd	Pit., Wsh.	2	3	1	0	1	2	4	0	0	0	0	....	1991-92	1993-94
Nemeth, Steve	NYR	1	12	2	0	2	2	....	....	....	....	....	....	1987-88	1987-88
Nesterenko, Eric	Tor., Chi.	21	1219	250	324	574	1273	124	13	24	37	127	1	1951-52	1971-72
Nethery, Lance	NYR, Edm.	2	41	11	14	25	14	14	5	3	8	9	....	1980-81	1981-82
Neufeld, Ray	Hfd., Wpg., Bos.	11	595	157	200	357	816	28	8	6	14	55	....	1979-80	1989-90
• Neville, Mike	Tor., NYA	3	64	5	3	8	14	2	0	0	0	0	....	1924-25	1930-31
Nevin, Bob	Tor., NYR, Min., L.A.	18	1128	307	419	726	211	84	16	18	34	24	2	1957-58	1975-76
Newberry, John	Mtl., Hfd.	4	22	0	4	4	6	2	0	0	0	0	....	1982-83	1985-86
Newell, Rick	Det.	2	6	0	0	0	0	....	....	....	....	....	....	1972-73	1973-74
Newman, Dan	NYR, Mtl., Edm.	4	126	17	24	41	63	3	0	0	0	4	....	1976-77	1979-80
• Newman, John	Det.	1	8	1	1	2	0	....	....	....	....	....	....	1930-31	1930-31
Nicholson, Al	Bos.	2	19	0	1	1	4	....	....	....	....	....	....	1955-56	1956-57
Nicholson, Edward	Det.	1	1	0	0	0	0	....	....	....	....	....	....	1947-48	1947-48
• Nicholson, Hickey	Chi.	1	2	1	0	1	0	....	....	....	....	....	....	1937-38	1937-38
Nicholson, Neil	Oak., NYI	4	39	3	1	4	23	2	0	0	0	0	....	1969-70	1977-78
Nicholson, Paul	Wsh.	3	62	4	8	12	18	....	....	....	....	....	....	1974-75	1976-77
Nicolson, Graeme	Bos., Col., NYR	3	52	2	7	9	60	....	....	....	....	....	....	1978-79	1982-83
Niekamp, Jim	Det.	2	29	0	2	2	37	....	....	....	....	....	....	1970-71	1971-72
Nienhuis, Kraig	Bos.	3	87	20	16	36	39	2	0	0	0	14	....	1985-86	1987-88
• Nighbor, Frank	Ott., Tor.	13	349	137	92	229	252	36	11	12	23	27	4	1917-18	1929-30
Nigro, Frank	Tor.	2	68	8	18	26	39	3	0	0	0	2	....	1982-83	1983-84
Nilan, Chris	Mtl., NYR, Bos.	13	688	110	115	225	3043	111	8	9	17	541	1	1979-80	1991-92
Nill, Jim	St.L., Van., Bos., Wpg., Det.	9	524	58	87	145	854	59	10	5	15	203	....	1981-82	1989-90
Nilsson, Kent	Atl., Cgy., Min., Edm.	9	553	264	422	686	116	59	11	41	52	14	1	1979-80	1994-95
Nilsson, Ulf	NYR	4	170	57	112	169	85	25	8	14	22	27	....	1978-79	1982-83

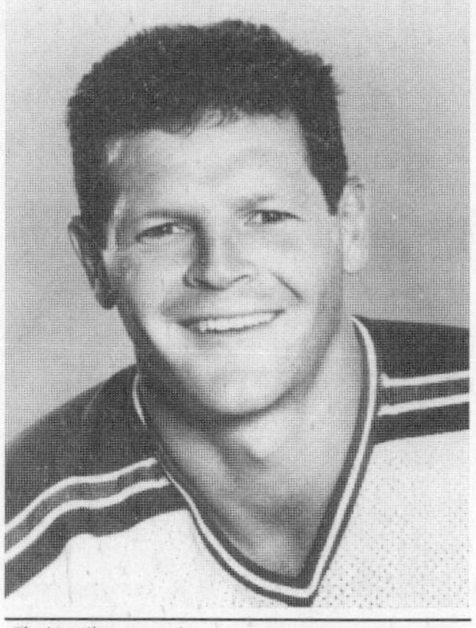
Chris Nilan

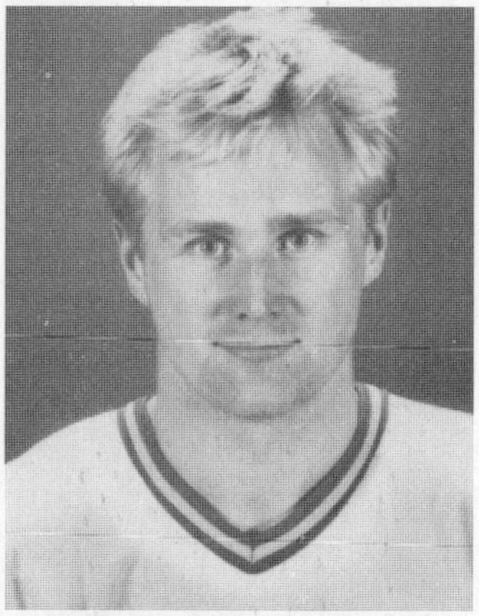
Robert Nordmark

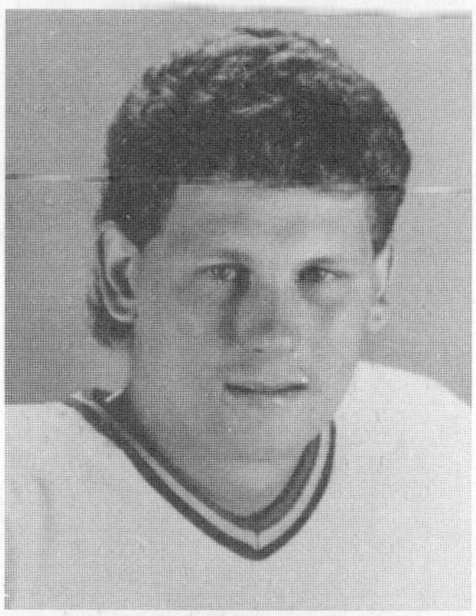
Keith Osborne

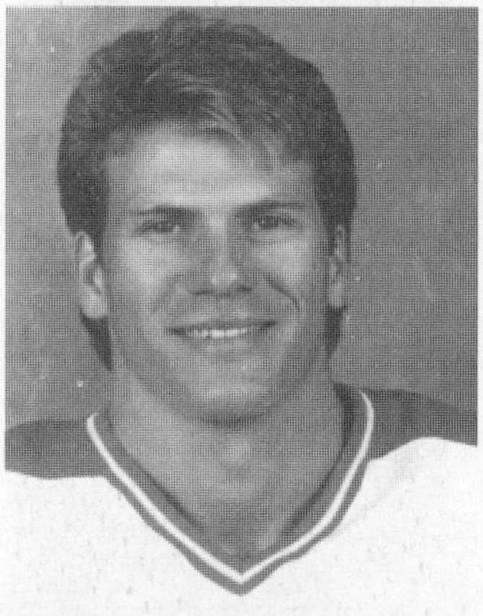
Joel Otto

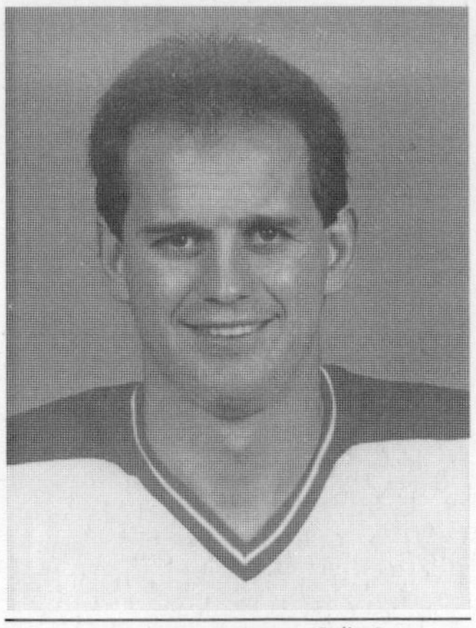
Colin Patterson

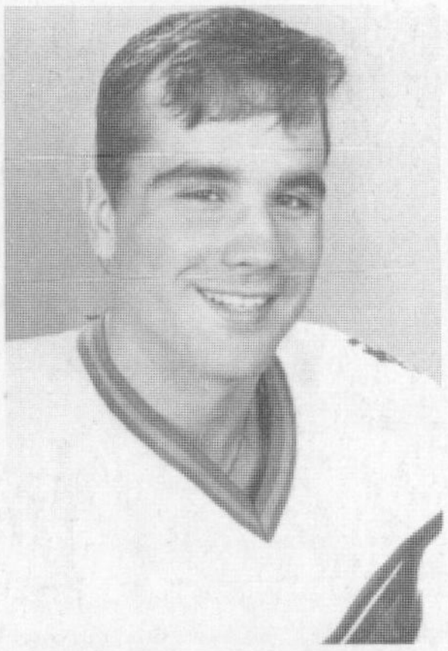
Pat Peake

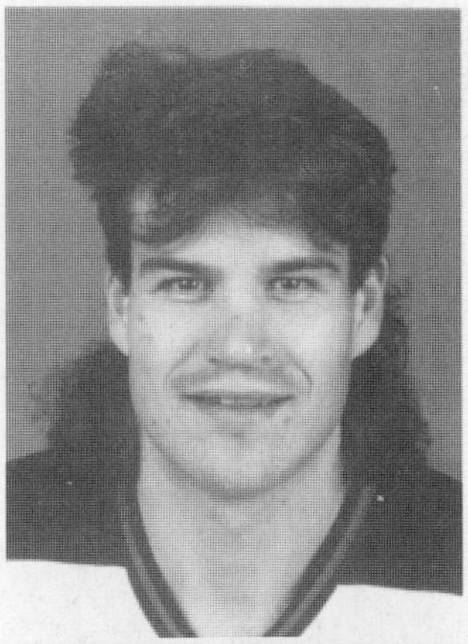
Mike Peluso

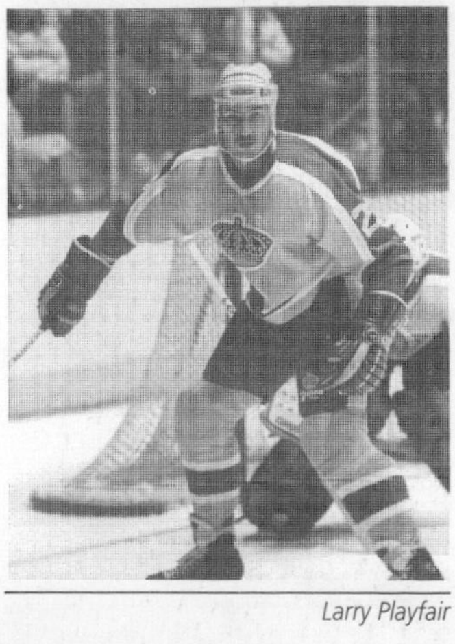
Larry Playfair

			Regular Schedule					Playoffs					NHL	First	Last
Name	NHL Teams	NHL Seasons	GP	G	A	TP	PIM	GP	G	A	TP	PIM	Cup Wins	NHL Season	NHL Season
Nistico, Lou	Col.	1	3	0	0	0	0	....	....	....	....	....	....	1977-78	1977-78
• Noble, Reg	Tor., Mtl.M., Det.	16	509	167	97	264	859	32	4	4	8	61	3	1917-18	1932-33
Noel, Claude	Wsh.	1	7	0	0	0	0	....	....	....	....	....	....	1979-80	1979-80
• Nolan, Paddy	Tor.	1	2	0	0	0	0	....	....	....	....	....	....	1921-22	1921-22
Nolan, Ted	Det., Pit.	3	78	6	16	22	105	....	....	....	....	....	....	1981-82	1985-86
Nolet, Simon	Phi., K.C., Pit., Col.	10	562	150	182	332	187	34	6	3	9	8	1	1967-68	1976-77
Nordmark, Robert	St.L., Van.	4	236	13	70	83	254	7	3	2	5	8	....	1987-88	1990-91
Noris, Joe	Pit., St.L., Buf.	3	55	2	5	7	22	....	....	....	....	....	....	1971-72	1973-74
Norris, Dwayne	Que., Ana.	3	20	2	4	6	8	....	....	....	....	....	....	1993-94	1995-96
Norrish, Rod	Min.	2	21	3	3	6	2	....	....	....	....	....	....	1973-74	1974-75
• Northcott, Baldy	Mtl.M., Chi.	11	446	133	112	245	273	31	8	5	13	14	1	1928-29	1938-39
Norwich, Craig	Wpg., St.L., Col.	2	104	17	58	75	60	....	....	....	....	....	....	1979-80	1980-81
Norwood, Lee	Que., Wsh., St.L., Det., N.J., Hfd., Cgy.	12	503	58	153	211	1099	65	6	22	28	171	....	1980-81	1993-94
Novy, Milan	Wsh.	1	73	18	30	48	16	2	0	0	0	0	....	1982-83	1982-83
Nowak, Hank	Pit., Det., Bos.	4	180	26	29	55	161	13	1	0	1	8	....	1973-74	1976-77
Nykoluk, Mike	Tor.	1	32	3	1	4	20	....	....	....	....	....	....	1956-57	1956-57
Nylund, Gary	Tor., Chi., NYI	11	608	32	139	171	1235	24	0	6	6	63	....	1982-83	1992-93
• Nyrop, Bill	Mtl., Min.	4	207	12	51	63	101	35	1	7	8	22	3	1975-76	1981-82
Nystrom, Bob	NYI	14	900	235	278	513	1248	157	39	44	83	236	4	1972-73	1985-86

O

			Regular Schedule					Playoffs					NHL	First	Last
Name	NHL Teams	NHL Seasons	GP	G	A	TP	PIM	GP	G	A	TP	PIM	Cup Wins	NHL Season	NHL Season
O'Brien, Dennis	Min., Col., Cle., Bos.	10	592	31	91	122	1017	34	1	2	3	101	....	1970-71	1979-80
O'Brien, Ellard	Bos.	1	2	0	0	0	0	....	....	....	....	....	....	1955-56	1955-56
O'Callahan, Jack	Chi., N.J.	7	389	27	104	131	541	32	4	11	15	41	....	1982-83	1988-89
O'Connell, Mike	Chi., Bos., Det.	13	860	105	334	439	605	82	8	24	32	64	....	1977-78	1989-90
• O'Connor, Buddy	Mtl., NYR	10	509	140	257	397	34	53	15	21	36	6	2	1941-42	1950-51
O'Connor, Myles	N.J., Ana.	4	43	3	4	7	69	....	....	....	....	....	....	1990-91	1993-94
O'Donnell, Fred	Bos.	2	115	15	11	26	98	5	0	1	1	5	....	1972-73	1973-74
O'Donoghue, Don	Oak., Cal.	3	125	18	17	35	35	3	0	0	0	0	....	1969-70	1971-72
O'Dwyer, Bill	L.A., Bos.	5	120	9	13	22	108	10	0	0	0	2	....	1983-84	1989-90
O'Flaherty, Gerry	Tor., Van., Atl.	8	438	99	95	194	168	7	2	2	4	6	....	1971-72	1978-79
O'Flaherty, Peanuts	NYA, Bro.	2	21	5	1	6	0	....	....	....	....	....	....	1940-41	1941-42
• O'Grady, George	Mtl.	1	4	0	0	0	0	....	....	....	....	....	....	1917-18	1917-18
O'Neil, Paul	Van., Bos.	2	6	0	0	0	0	....	....	....	....	....	....	1973-74	1975-76
• O'Neill, Jim	Bos., Mtl.	6	156	6	30	36	109	9	1	1	2	13	....	1933-34	1941-42
• O'Neill, Tom	Tor.	2	66	10	12	22	53	4	0	0	0	6	1	1943-44	1944-45
O'Ree, Willie	Bos.	2	45	4	10	14	26	....	....	....	....	....	....	1957-58	1960-61
O'Regan, Tom	Pit.	3	61	5	12	17	10	....	....	....	....	....	....	1983-84	1985-86
O'Reilly, Terry	Bos.	14	891	204	402	606	2095	108	25	42	67	335	....	1971-72	1984-85
O'Shea, Danny	Min., Chi., St.L.	5	369	64	115	179	265	39	3	7	10	61	....	1968-69	1972-73
O'Shea, Kevin	Buf., St.L.	3	134	13	18	31	85	12	2	1	3	10	....	1970-71	1972-73
• Oatman, Russell	Det., Mtl.M., NYR	3	120	20	9	29	100	15	1	0	1	18	....	1926-27	1928-29
Oddleifson, Chris	Bos., Van.	9	524	95	191	286	464	14	1	6	7	8	....	1972-73	1980-81
Odelein, Selmar	Edm.	3	18	0	2	2	35	....	....	....	....	....	....	1985-86	1988-89
Odrowski, Gerry	Det., Oak., St.L.	6	309	12	19	31	111	30	0	1	1	16	....	1960-61	1971-72
Ogilvie, Brian	Chi., St.L.	6	90	15	21	36	29	....	....	....	....	....	....	1972-73	1978-79
Ogrodnick, John	Det., Que., NYR	14	928	402	425	827	260	41	18	8	26	6	....	1979-80	1992-93
Ojanen, Janne	N.J.	4	98	21	23	44	28	3	0	2	2	0	....	1988-89	1992-93
Okerlund, Todd	NYI	1	4	0	0	0	2	....	....	....	....	....	....	1987-88	1987-88
Oksiuta, Roman	Edm., Van., Ana., Pit.	4	153	46	41	87	100	10	2	3	5	0	....	1993-94	1996-97
• Oliver, Harry	Bos., NYA	11	463	127	85	212	147	35	10	6	16	24	1	1926-27	1936-37
Oliver, Murray	Det., Bos., Tor., Min.	17	1127	274	454	728	320	35	9	16	25	10	....	1957-58	1974-75
Olmstead, Bert	Chi., Mtl., Tor.	14	848	181	421	602	884	115	16	43	59	101	5	1948-49	1961-62
Olsen, Darryl	Cgy.	1	1	0	0	0	0	....	....	....	....	....	....	1991-92	1991-92
Olson, Dennis	Det.	1	4	0	0	0	0	....	....	....	....	....	....	1957-58	1957-58
Orban, Bill	Chi., Min.	3	114	8	15	23	67	3	0	0	0	0	....	1967-68	1969-70
Orlando, Gaetano	Buf.	3	98	18	26	44	51	5	0	4	4	14	....	1984-85	1986-87
Orlando, Jimmy	Det.	6	199	6	25	31	375	36	0	9	9	105	1	1936-37	1942-43
Orleski, Dave	Mtl.	2	2	0	0	0	0	....	....	....	....	....	....	1980-81	1981-82
Orr, Bobby	Bos., Chi.	12	657	270	645	915	953	74	26	66	92	107	2	1966-67	1978-79
Osborne, Keith	St.L., T.B.	2	16	1	3	4	16	....	....	....	....	....	....	1989-90	1992-93
Osborne, Mark	Det., NYR, Tor., Wpg.	14	919	212	319	531	1152	87	12	16	28	141	....	1981-82	1994-95
Osburn, Randy	Tor., Phi.	2	27	0	2	2	0	....	....	....	....	....	....	1972-73	1974-75
Osiecki, Mark	Cgy., Ott., Wpg., Min.	2	93	3	11	14	43	....	....	....	....	....	....	1991-92	1992-93
Otevrel, Jaroslav	S.J.	2	16	3	4	7	2	....	....	....	....	....	....	1992-93	1993-94
Otto, Joel	Cgy., Phi.	14	943	195	313	508	1934	122	27	47	74	207	1	1984-85	1997-98
Ouellette, Eddie	Chi.	1	43	3	2	5	11	1	0	0	0	0	....	1935-36	1935-36
Ouellette, Gerry	Bos.	1	34	5	4	9	0	....	....	....	....	....	....	1960-61	1960-61
Owchar, Dennis	Pit., Col.	6	288	30	85	115	200	10	1	1	2	8	....	1974-75	1979-80
• Owen, George	Bos.	5	183	44	33	77	151	21	2	5	7	25	1	1928-29	1932-33

P

			Regular Schedule					Playoffs					NHL	First	Last
Name	NHL Teams	NHL Seasons	GP	G	A	TP	PIM	GP	G	A	TP	PIM	Cup Wins	NHL Season	NHL Season
Pachal, Clayton	Bos., Col.	3	35	2	3	5	95	....	....	....	....	....	....	1976-77	1978-79
Paddock, John	Wsh., Phi., Que.	5	87	8	14	22	86	5	2	0	2	0	....	1975-76	1982-83
Paek, Jim	Pit., L.A., Ott.	5	217	5	29	34	155	27	1	4	5	8	2	1990-91	1994-95
Paiement, Rosaire	Phi., Van.	5	190	48	52	100	343	3	3	0	3	0	....	1967-68	1971-72
Paiement, Wilf	K.C., Col., Tor., Que., NYR, Buf., Pit.	14	946	356	458	814	1757	69	18	17	35	185	....	1974-75	1987-88
Palangio, Peter	Mtl.C., Det., Chi.	5	71	13	10	23	28	7	0	0	0	0	1	1926-27	1937-38
Palazzari, Aldo	Bos., NYR	1	35	8	3	11	4	....	....	....	....	....	....	1943-44	1943-44
Palazzari, Doug	St.L.	4	108	18	20	38	23	2	0	0	0	0	....	1974-75	1978-79
Palmer, Brad	Min., Bos.	3	168	32	38	70	58	29	9	5	14	16	....	1980-81	1982-83
Palmer, Rob	Chi.	3	16	0	3	3	2	....	....	....	....	....	....	1973-74	1975-76
Palmer, Robert Ross	L.A., N.J.	7	320	9	101	110	115	8	1	2	3	6	....	1977-78	1983-84
• Panagabko, Ed	Bos.	2	29	0	3	3	38	....	....	....	....	....	....	1955-56	1956-57
Panteleev, Grigori	Bos., NYI	4	54	8	6	14	12	....	....	....	....	....	....	1992-93	1995-96
• Papike, Joe	Chi.	3	20	3	3	6	4	5	0	2	2	0	....	1940-41	1944-45
Pappin, Jim	Tor., Chi., Cal., Cle.	14	767	278	295	573	667	92	33	34	67	101	2	1963-64	1976-77
Paradise, Bob	Min., Atl., Pit., Wsh.	8	368	8	54	62	393	12	0	1	1	19	....	1971-72	1978-79
Pargeter, George	Mtl.	1	4	0	0	0	0	....	....	....	....	....	....	1946-47	1946-47
Parise, Jean-Paul	Bos., Tor., Min., NYI, Cle.	14	890	238	356	594	706	86	27	31	58	87	....	1965-66	1978-79
Parizeau, Michel	St.L., Phi.	1	58	3	14	17	18	....	....	....	....	....	....	1971-72	1971-72
Park, Brad	NYR, Bos., Det.	17	1113	213	683	896	1429	161	35	90	125	217	....	1968-69	1984-85
Parker, Jeff	Buf., Hfd.	5	141	16	19	35	163	5	0	0	0	26	....	1986-87	1990-91
• Parkes, Ernie	Mtl.M.	1	17	0	0	0	2	....	....	....	....	....	....	1924-25	1924-25
Parks, Greg	NYI	3	23	1	2	3	6	2	0	0	0	0	....	1990-91	1992-93
• Parsons, George	Tor.	3	78	12	13	25	20	7	3	2	5	11	....	1936-37	1938-39
• Pasek, Dusan	Min.	1	48	4	10	14	30	2	1	0	1	0	....	1988-89	1988-89
Pasin, Dave	Bos., L.A.	2	76	18	19	37	50	3	0	1	1	0	....	1985-86	1988-89
Paslawski, Greg	Mtl., St.L., Wpg., Buf., Que., Phi., Cgy.	11	650	187	185	372	169	60	19	13	32	25	....	1983-84	1993-94
Paterson, Joe	Det., Phi., L.A., NYR	9	291	19	37	56	829	22	3	4	7	77	....	1980-81	1988-89
Paterson, Mark	Hfd.	4	29	3	3	6	33	....	....	....	....	....	....	1982-83	1985-86
Paterson, Rick	Chi.	9	430	50	43	93	136	61	7	10	17	51	....	1978-79	1986-87
Patey, Doug	Wsh.	3	45	4	2	6	8	....	....	....	....	....	....	1976-77	1978-79
Patey, Larry	Cal., St.L., NYR	12	717	153	163	316	631	40	8	10	18	57	....	1973-74	1984-85
Patrick, Craig	Cal., St.L., K.C., Wsh.	8	401	72	91	163	61	2	0	1	1	0	....	1971-72	1978-79
Patrick, Glenn	St.L., Cal., Cle.	3	38	2	3	5	72	....	....	....	....	....	....	1973-74	1976-77
• Patrick, Lester	NYR	1	1	0	0	0	2	....	....	....	....	....	....	1926-27	1926-27
• Patrick, Lynn	NYR	10	455	145	190	335	240	44	10	6	16	22	1	1934-35	1945-46
• Patrick, Muzz	NYR	5	166	5	26	31	133	25	4	0	4	34	1	1937-38	1945-46
Patrick, Steve	Buf., NYR, Que.	6	250	40	68	108	242	12	0	1	1	12	....	1980-81	1985-86
Patterson, Colin	Cgy., Buf.	10	504	96	109	205	239	85	12	17	29	57	1	1983-84	1992-93
Patterson, Dennis	K.C., Phi.	3	138	6	22	28	67	....	....	....	....	....	....	1974-75	1979-80
• Patterson, George	Tor., Mtl.C., NYA, Bos., Det., St.L.	9	284	51	27	78	218	3	0	0	0	2	....	1926-27	1934-35
• Paul, Butch	Det.	1	3	0	0	0	0	....	....	....	....	....	....	1964-65	1964-65
• Paulhus, Rollie	Mtl.C.	1	33	0	0	0	0	....	....	....	....	....	....	1925-26	1925-26
Pavelich, Mark	NYR, Min., S.J.	7	355	137	192	329	340	23	7	17	24	14	....	1981-82	1991-92
Pavelich, Marty	Det.	10	634	93	159	252	454	91	13	15	28	74	4	1947-48	1956-57
Pavese, Jim	St.L., NYR, Det., Hfd.	8	328	13	44	57	689	34	0	6	6	81	....	1981-82	1988-89

Name	NHL Teams	NHL Seasons	Regular Schedule GP	G	A	TP	PIM	Playoffs GP	G	A	TP	PIM	NHL Cup Wins	First NHL Season	Last NHL Season
• Payer, Evariste	Mtl.C.	1	1	0	0	0	0	....	....	....	....	....	....	1917-18	1917-18
Payne, Davis	Bos.	2	22	0	1	1	14	....	....	....	....	....	....	1995-96	1996-97
Payne, Steve	Min.	10	613	228	238	466	435	71	35	35	70	60	....	1978-79	1987-88
Paynter, Kent	Chi., Wsh., Wpg., Ott.	7	37	1	3	4	69	4	0	0	0	10	....	1987-88	1993-94
Peake, Pat	Wsh.	5	134	28	41	69	105	13	2	2	4	20	....	1993-94	1997-98
• Pearson, Mel	NYR, Pit.	5	38	2	6	8	25	....	....	....	....	....	....	1959-60	1967-68
Pedersen, Allen	Bos., Min., Hfd.	8	428	5	36	41	487	64	0	0	0	91	....	1986-87	1993-94
Pederson, Barry	Bos., Van., Pit., Hfd.	12	701	238	416	654	472	34	22	30	52	25	1	1980-81	1991-92
Pederson, Mark	Mtl., Phi., S.J., Det.	5	169	35	50	85	77	2	0	0	0	0	....	1989-90	1993-94
Pederson, Tom	S.J., Tor.	5	240	20	49	69	142	24	1	11	12	10	....	1992-93	1996-97
Peer, Bert	Det.	1	1	0	0	0	0	....	....	....	....	....	....	1939-40	1939-40
Peirson, Johnny	Bos.	11	545	153	173	326	315	49	9	17	26	26	....	1946-47	1957-58
Pelensky, Perry	Chi.	1	4	0	0	0	5	....	....	....	....	....	....	1983-84	1983-84
Pelletier, Roger	Phi.	1	1	0	0	0	0	....	....	....	....	....	....	1967-68	1967-68
Peloffy, Andre	Wsh.	1	9	0	0	0	0	....	....	....	....	....	....	1974-75	1974-75
Peluso, Mike	Chi., Ott., N.J., St.L., Cgy.	9	458	38	52	90	1951	62	3	4	7	107	1	1989-90	1997-98
Pelyk, Mike	Tor.	9	441	26	88	114	566	40	0	3	3	41	....	1967-68	1977-78
Penney, Chad	Ott.	1	3	0	0	0	2	....	....	....	....	....	....	1993-94	1993-94
Pennington, Cliff	Mtl., Bos.	3	101	17	42	59	6	....	....	....	....	....	....	1960-61	1962-63
Peplinski, Jim	Cgy.	11	711	161	263	424	1467	99	15	31	46	382	1	1980-81	1994-95
Perlini, Fred	Tor.	2	8	2	3	5	0	....	....	....	....	....	....	1981-82	1983-84
Perreault, Fern	NYR	2	3	0	0	0	0	....	....	....	....	....	....	1947-48	1949-50
Perreault, Gilbert	Buf.	17	1191	512	814	1326	500	90	33	70	103	44	....	1970-71	1986-87
Perry, Brian	Oak., Buf.	3	96	16	29	45	24	8	1	1	2	4	....	1968-69	1970-71
Persson, Stefan	NYI	9	622	52	317	369	574	102	7	50	57	69	4	1977-78	1985-86
Pesut, George	Cal.	2	92	3	22	25	130	....	....	....	....	....	....	1974-75	1975-76
• Peters, Frank	NYR	1	43	0	0	0	59	4	0	0	0	2	....	1930-31	1930-31
Peters, Garry	Mtl., NYR, Phi., Bos.	8	311	34	34	68	261	9	2	2	4	31	1	1964-65	1971-72
Peters, Jimmy Jr.	Det., L.A.	9	309	37	36	73	48	11	0	2	2	2	....	1964-65	1974-75
Peters, Jimmy Sr.	Mtl., Bos., Det., Chi.	9	574	125	150	275	186	60	5	9	14	22	3	1945-46	1953-54
Peters, Steve	Col.	1	2	0	1	1	0	....	....	....	....	....	....	1979-80	1979-80
Peterson, Brent	Det., Buf., Van., Hfd.	11	620	72	141	213	484	31	4	4	8	65	....	1978-79	1988-89
Petrenko, Sergei	Buf.	1	14	0	4	4	0	....	....	....	....	....	....	1993-94	1993-94
Pettersson, Jorgen	St.L., Hfd., Wsh.	6	435	174	192	366	117	44	15	12	27	4	....	1980-81	1985-86
• Pettinger, Eric	Bos., Tor., Ott.	3	98	7	12	19	83	4	1	0	1	8	....	1928-29	1930-31
• Pettinger, Gord	NYR, Det., Bos.	8	292	42	74	116	77	47	4	5	9	11	4	1932-33	1939-40
Phair, Lyle	L.A.	3	48	6	7	13	12	1	0	0	0	0	....	1985-86	1987-88
Phillipoff, Harold	Atl., Chi.	3	141	26	57	83	267	6	0	2	2	9	....	1977-78	1979-80
• Phillips, Batt	Mtl.M.	2	28	1	1	2	6	4	0	0	0	2	....	1926-27	1929-30
Phillips, Charlie	Mtl.	1	17	0	0	0	6	....	....	....	....	....	....	1942-43	1942-43
• Phillips, Meryn J.	Mtl.M., NYA	8	302	52	31	83	232	28	6	2	8	19	1	1925-26	1932-33
Picard, Noel	Mtl., St.L., Atl.	7	335	12	63	75	616	50	2	11	13	167	1	1964-65	1972-73
Picard, Robert	Wsh., Tor., Mtl., Wpg., Que., Det.	13	899	104	319	423	1025	36	5	15	20	39	....	1977-78	1989-90
Picard, Roger	St.L.	1	15	2	2	4	21	....	....	....	....	....	....	1967-68	1967-68
Pichette, Dave	Que., St.L., N.J., NYR	7	322	41	140	181	348	28	3	7	10	54	....	1980-81	1987-88
Picketts, Hal	NYA	1	48	3	1	4	32	....	....	....	....	....	....	1933-34	1933-34
Pidhirny, Harry	Bos.	1	2	0	0	0	0	....	....	....	....	....	....	1957-58	1957-58
Pierce, Randy	Col., N.J., Hfd.	8	277	62	76	138	223	2	0	0	0	0	....	1977-78	1984-85
Pike, Alf	NYR	6	234	42	77	119	145	21	4	2	6	12	1	1939-40	1946-47
Pilote, Pierre	Chi., Tor.	14	890	80	418	498	1251	86	8	53	61	102	1	1955-56	1968-69
Pinder, Gerry	Chi., Cal.	3	223	55	69	124	135	17	0	4	4	6	....	1969-70	1971-72
Pirus, Alex	Min., Det.	4	159	30	28	58	94	2	0	1	1	2	....	1976-77	1979-80
• Pitre, Didier	Mtl.C.	6	129	63	29	91	85	14	2	6	8	19	....	1917-18	1922-23
• Plager, Barclay	St.L.	10	614	44	187	231	1115	68	3	20	23	182	....	1967-68	1976-77
Plager, Bill	Min., St.L., Atl.	9	263	4	34	38	294	31	0	2	2	26	....	1967-68	1975-76
Plager, Bob	NYR, St.L.	14	644	20	126	146	802	74	2	17	19	195	....	1964-65	1977-78
Plamondon, Gerry	Mtl.	5	74	7	13	20	10	11	5	2	7	2	1	1945-46	1950-51
Plante, Cam	Tor.	1	2	0	0	0	0	....	....	....	....	....	....	1984-85	1984-85
Plante, Pierre	Phi., St.L., Chi., NYR, Que.	9	599	125	172	297	599	33	2	0	0	51	....	1971-72	1979-80
Plantery, Mark	Wpg.	1	25	1	5	6	14	....	....	....	....	....	....	1980-81	1980-81
Plavsic, Adrien	St.L., Van., T.B., Ana.	8	214	16	56	72	161	13	1	7	8	4	....	1989-90	1996-97
• Plaxton, Hugh	Mtl.M.	1	15	1	2	3	4	....	....	....	....	....	....	1932-33	1932-33
Playfair, Jim	Edm., Chi.	3	21	2	4	6	51	....	....	....	....	....	....	1983-84	1988-89
Playfair, Larry	Buf., L.A.	12	688	26	94	120	1812	43	0	6	6	111	....	1978-79	1989-90
Pleau, Larry	Mtl.	3	94	9	15	24	27	4	0	0	0	0	....	1969-70	1971-72
Pletsch, Charles	Ham.	1	1	0	0	0	0	....	....	....	....	....	....	1920-21	1920-21
Plett, Willi	Atl., Cgy., Min., Bos.	13	834	222	215	437	2572	83	24	22	46	466	....	1975-76	1987-88
Plumb, Rob	Det.	2	14	3	2	5	2	....	....	....	....	....	....	1977-78	1978-79
Plumb, Ron	Hfd.	1	26	3	4	7	14	....	....	....	....	....	....	1979-80	1979-80
Pocza, Harvie	Wsh.	2	3	0	0	0	2	....	....	....	....	....	....	1979-80	1981-82
Poddubny, Walt	Edm., Tor., NYR, Que., N.J.	11	468	184	238	422	454	19	7	2	9	12	....	1981-82	1991-92
Podloski, Ray	Bos.	1	8	0	1	1	22	....	....	....	....	....	....	1988-89	1988-89
Podolsky, Nels	Det.	1	1	0	0	0	0	7	0	0	0	4	....	1948-49	1948-49
Poeta, Tony	Chi.	1	1	0	0	0	0	....	....	....	....	....	....	1951-52	1951-52
Poile, Bud	Tor., Chi., Det., NYR, Bos.	7	311	107	122	229	91	23	4	5	9	8	1	1942-43	1949-50
Poile, Don	Det.	2	66	7	9	16	12	4	0	0	0	0	....	1954-55	1957-58
Poirier, Gordie	Mtl.	1	10	0	0	0	0	....	....	....	....	....	....	1939-40	1939-40
Polanic, Tom	Min.	2	19	0	2	2	53	5	1	1	2	4	....	1969-70	1970-71
Polich, John	NYR	2	3	0	1	1	0	....	....	....	....	....	....	1939-40	1940-41
Polich, Mike	Mtl., Min.	5	226	24	29	53	57	23	2	1	3	2	1	1976-77	1980-81
Polis, Greg	Pit., St.L., NYR, Wsh.	10	615	174	169	343	391	7	0	2	2	6	....	1970-71	1979-80
Poliziani, Daniel	Bos.	1	1	0	0	0	0	3	0	0	0	0	....	1958-59	1958-59
Polonich, Dennis	Det.	8	390	59	82	141	1242	7	1	0	1	19	....	1974-75	1982-83
Pooley, Paul	Wpg.	2	15	0	3	3	0	....	....	....	....	....	....	1984-85	1985-86
Popein, Larry	NYR, Oak.	8	449	80	141	221	162	16	1	4	5	6	....	1954-55	1967-68
Popiel, Poul	Bos., L.A., Det., Van., Edm.	7	224	13	41	54	210	4	1	0	1	4	....	1965-66	1979-80
• Portland, Jack	Mtl.C., Bos., Chi., Mtl.	10	381	15	56	71	323	33	1	3	4	25	1	1933-34	1942-43
Porvari, Jukka	Col., N.J.	2	39	3	9	12	4	....	....	....	....	....	....	1981-82	1982-83
Posa, Victor	Chi.	1	2	0	0	0	2	....	....	....	....	....	....	1985-86	1985-86
Posavad, Mike	St.L.	2	8	0	0	0	0	....	....	....	....	....	....	1985-86	1986-87
Potvin, Denis	NYI	15	1060	310	742	1052	1356	185	56	108	164	253	4	1973-74	1987-88
Potvin, Jean	L.A., Phi., NYI, Cle., Min.	11	613	63	224	287	478	39	2	9	11	17	....	1970-71	1980-81
Poudrier, Daniel	Que.	3	25	1	5	6	10	....	....	....	....	....	....	1985-86	1987-88
Poulin, Dan	Min.	1	3	1	1	2	2	....	....	....	....	....	....	1981-82	1981-82
Poulin, Dave	Phi., Bos., Wsh.	13	724	205	325	530	482	129	31	42	73	132	....	1982-83	1994-95
Pouzar, Jaroslav	Edm.	4	186	34	48	82	135	29	6	4	10	16	3	1982-83	1986-87
Powell, Ray	Chi.	1	31	7	15	22	2	....	....	....	....	....	....	1950-51	1950-51
Powis, Geoff	Chi.	1	2	0	0	0	0	....	....	....	....	....	....	1967-68	1967-68
Powis, Lynn	Chi., K.C.	2	130	19	33	52	25	1	0	0	0	0	....	1973-74	1974-75
Prajsler, Petr	L.A., Bos.	4	46	3	10	13	51	4	0	0	0	0	....	1987-88	1991-92
• Pratt, Babe	NYR, Tor., Bos.	12	517	83	209	292	463	63	12	17	29	90	2	1935-36	1946-47
Pratt, Jack	Bos.	2	37	2	0	2	42	4	0	0	0	0	....	1930-31	1931-32
Pratt, Kelly	Pit.	1	22	0	6	6	15	....	....	....	....	....	....	1974-75	1974-75
Pratt, Tracy	Oak., Pit., Buf., Van., Col., Tor.	10	580	17	97	114	1026	25	0	1	1	62	....	1967-68	1976-77
Prentice, Dean	NYR, Bos., Det., Pit., Min.	22	1378	391	469	860	484	54	13	17	30	38	....	1952-53	1973-74
Prentice, Eric	Tor.	1	5	0	0	0	4	....	....	....	....	....	....	1943-44	1943-44
Presley, Wayne	Chi., S.J., Buf., NYR, Tor.	12	684	155	147	302	953	83	26	17	43	142	....	1984-85	1995-96
Preston, Rich	Chi., N.J.	8	580	127	164	291	348	47	4	18	22	56	....	1979-80	1986-87
Preston, Yves	Phi.	2	28	7	3	10	4	....	....	....	....	....	....	1978-79	1980-81
Priakin, Sergei	Cgy.	3	46	3	8	11	2	1	0	0	0	0	1	1988-89	1990-91
Price, Jack	Chi.	3	57	4	6	10	24	4	0	0	0	0	....	1951-52	1953-54
Price, Noel	Tor., NYR, Det., Mtl., Pit., L.A., Atl.	14	499	14	114	128	333	12	0	1	1	8	1	1957-58	1975-76
Price, Pat	NYI, Edm., Pit., Que., NYR, Min.	13	726	43	218	261	1456	74	2	10	12	195	....	1975-76	1987-88
Price, Tom	Cal., Cle., Pit.	5	29	0	2	2	12	....	....	....	....	....	....	1974-75	1978-79
Priestlay, Ken	Buf., Pit.	6	168	27	34	61	63	14	0	0	0	21	1	1986-87	1991-92
• Primeau, Joe	Tor.	9	310	66	177	243	105	38	5	18	23	12	1	1927-28	1935-36
Primeau, Kevin	Van.	1	2	0	0	0	4	....	....	....	....	....	....	1980-81	1980-81
• Pringle, Ellie	NYA	1	6	0	0	0	0	....	....	....	....	....	....	1930-31	1930-31
• Prodgers, Goldie	Tor., Ham.	6	111	63	25	88	35	....	....	....	....	....	....	1919-20	1924-25
Prokhorov, Vitali	St.L.	3	83	19	11	30	35	4	0	0	0	0	....	1992-93	1994-95
Pronovost, Andre	Mtl., Bos., Det., Min.	10	556	94	104	198	408	70	11	11	22	58	4	1956-57	1967-68
Pronovost, Jean	Pit., Atl., Wsh.	14	998	391	383	774	413	35	11	9	20	14	....	1968-69	1981-82

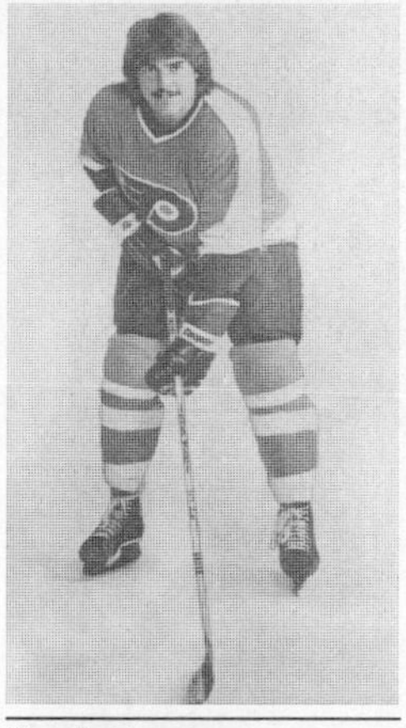
Yves Preston

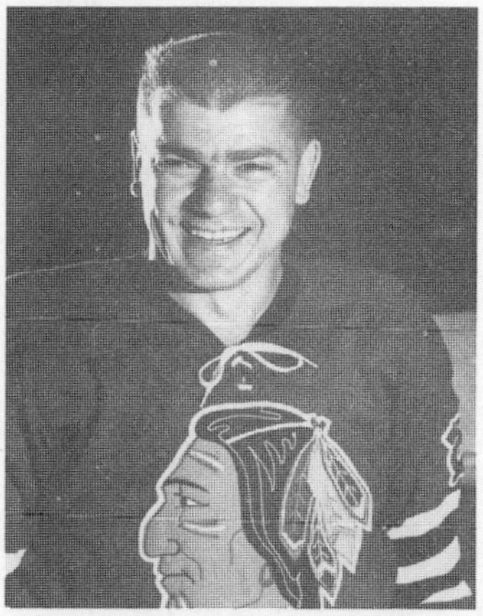
Metro Prystai

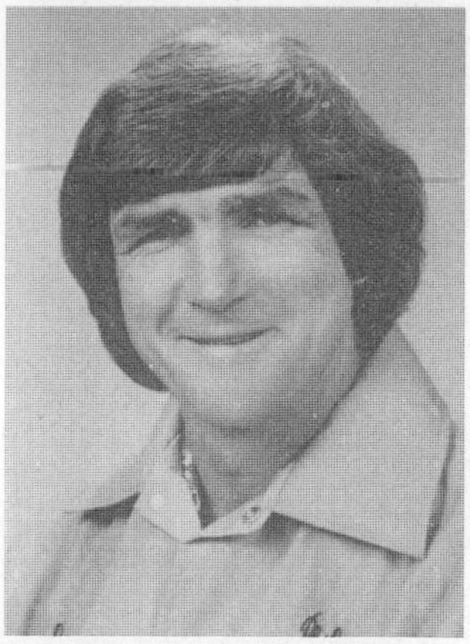
Pat Quinn

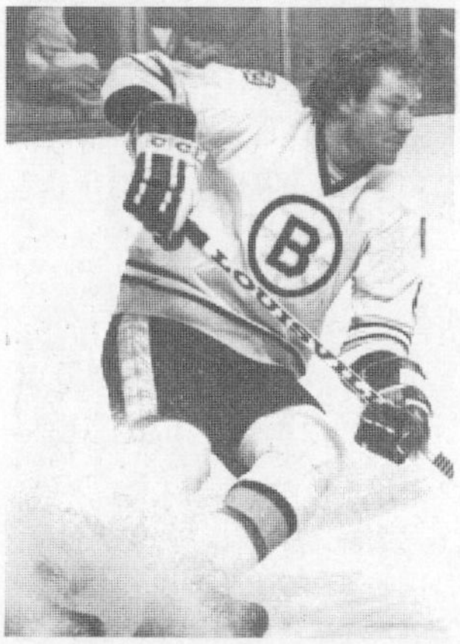
Dick Redmond

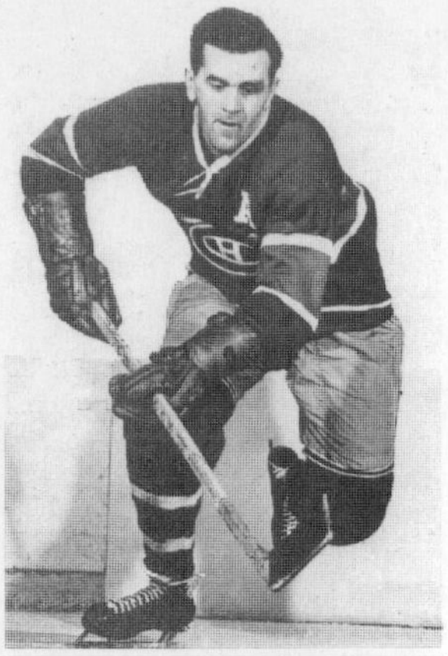
Maurice Richard

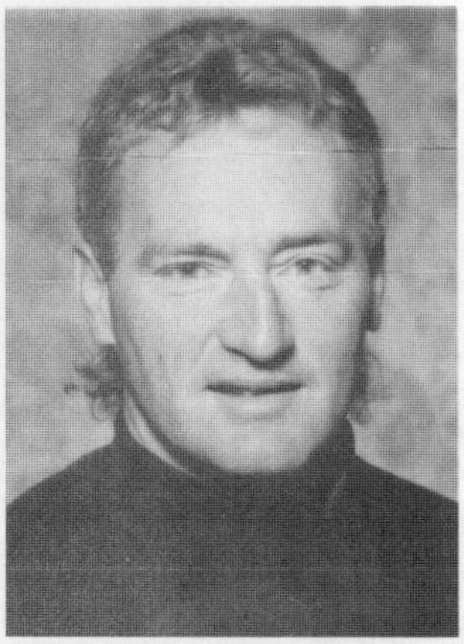
Larry Robinson

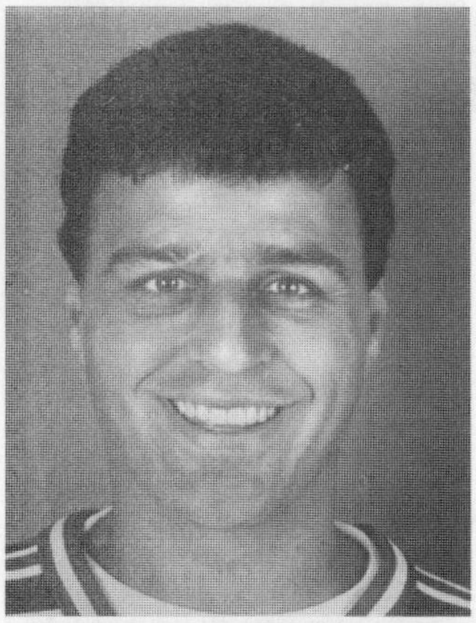
Normand Rochefort

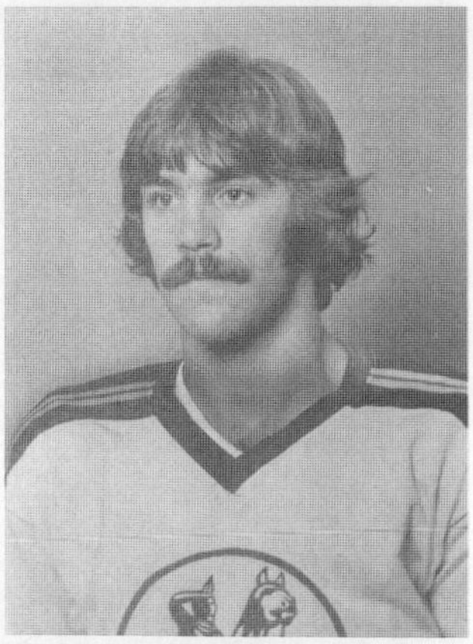
Randy Rota

			Regular Schedule					Playoffs					NHL	First	Last
Name	NHL Teams	NHL Seasons	GP	G	A	TP	PIM	GP	G	A	TP	PIM	Cup Wins	NHL Season	NHL Season
Pronovost, Marcel	Det., Tor.	21	1206	88	257	345	851	134	8	23	31	104	5	1949-50	1969-70
Propp, Brian	Phi., Bos., Min., Hfd.	15	1016	425	579	1004	830	160	64	84	148	151	....	1979-80	1993-94
Proulx, Christian	Mtl.	1	7	1	2	3	20	....	....	....	....	....	....	1993-94	1993-94
• Provost, Claude	Mtl.	15	1005	254	335	589	469	126	25	38	63	86	9	1955-56	1969-70
Pryor, Chris	Min., NYI	6	82	1	4	5	122	....	....	....	....	....	....	1984-85	1989-90
Prystai, Metro	Chi., Det.	11	674	151	179	330	231	43	12	14	26	8	2	1947-48	1957-58
• Pudas, Al	Tor.	1	4	0	0	0	0	....	....	....	....	....	....	1926-27	1926-27
Pulford, Bob	Tor., L.A.	17	1079	281	362	643	792	89	25	26	51	126	4	1956-57	1972-73
Pulkkinen, Dave	NYI	1	2	0	0	0	0	....	....	....	....	....	....	1972-73	1972-73
Purpur, Fido	St.L., Chi., Det.	5	144	25	35	60	46	16	1	2	3	4	....	1934-35	1944-45
Purves, John	Wsh.	1	7	1	0	1	0	....	....	....	....	....	....	1990-91	1990-91
• Pusie, Jean	Mtl.C., NYR, Bos.	5	61	1	4	5	28	7	0	0	0	0	....	1930-31	1935-36
Pyatt, Nelson	Det., Wsh., Col.	7	296	71	63	134	69	....	....	....	....	....	....	1973-74	1979-80

Q

Quackenbush, Bill	Det., Bos.	14	774	62	222	284	95	80	2	19	21	8	....	1942-43	1955-56
Quackenbush, Max	Bos., Chi.	2	61	4	7	11	30	6	0	0	0	4	....	1950-51	1951-52
Quenneville, Joel	Tor., Col., N.J., Hfd., Wsh.	13	803	54	136	190	705	32	0	8	8	22	....	1978-79	1990-91
• Quenneville, Leo	NYR	1	25	0	3	3	10	3	0	0	0	0	....	1929-30	1929-30
• Quilty, John	Mtl., Bos.	4	125	36	34	70	81	13	3	5	8	9	....	1940-41	1947-48
Quinn, Dan	Cgy., Pit., Van., St.L., Phi., Min., Ott., L.A.	14	805	266	419	685	533	65	22	26	48	62	....	1983-84	1996-97
Quinn, Pat	Tor., Van., Atl.	9	606	18	113	131	950	11	0	1	1	21	....	1968-69	1976-77
Quinney, Ken	Que.	3	59	7	13	20	23	....	....	....	....	....	....	1986-87	1990-91
Quintin, Jean-Francois	S.J.	2	22	5	5	10	4	....	....	....	....	....	....	1991-92	1992-93

R

• Radley, Yip	NYA, Mtl.M.	2	18	0	1	1	13	....	....	....	....	....	....	1930-31	1936-37
Raglan, Clare	Det., Chi.	3	100	4	9	13	52	3	0	0	0	0	....	1950-51	1952-53
Raglan, Herb	St.L., Que., T.B., Ott.	9	343	33	56	89	775	32	3	6	9	50	....	1985-86	1993-94
Raleigh, Don	NYR	10	535	101	219	320	96	18	6	5	11	6	....	1943-44	1955-56
Ramage, Rob	Col., St.L., Cgy., Tor., Min., T.B., Mtl., Phi.	15	1044	139	425	564	2226	84	8	42	50	218	2	1979-80	1993-94
• Ramsay, Beattie	Tor.	1	43	0	2	2	10	....	....	....	....	....	....	1927-28	1927-28
Ramsay, Craig	Buf.	14	1070	252	420	672	201	89	17	31	48	27	....	1971-72	1984-85
Ramsay, Les	Chi.	1	11	2	2	4	2	....	....	....	....	....	....	1944-45	1944-45
Ramsey, Mike	Buf., Pit., Det.	18	1070	79	266	345	1012	115	8	29	37	176	....	1979-80	1996-97
Ramsey, Wayne	Buf.	1	2	0	0	0	0	....	....	....	....	....	....	1977-78	1977-78
• Randall, Ken	Tor., Ham., NYA	10	217	69	35	104	503	15	4	1	5	67	2	1917-18	1926-27
Ranieri, George	Bos.	1	2	0	0	0	0	....	....	....	....	....	....	1956-57	1956-57
Ratelle, Jean	NYR, Bos.	21	1281	491	776	1267	276	123	32	66	98	24	....	1960-61	1980-81
Rathwell, John	Bos.	1	1	0	0	0	0	....	....	....	....	....	....	1974-75	1974-75
Ratushny, Dan	Van.	1	1	0	1	1	2	....	....	....	....	....	....	1992-93	1992-93
Rausse, Errol	Wsh.	3	31	7	3	10	0	....	....	....	....	....	....	1979-80	1981-82
Rautakallio, Pekka	Atl., Cgy.	3	235	33	121	154	122	23	2	5	7	8	....	1979-80	1981-82
Ravlich, Matt	Bos., Chi., Det., L.A.	10	410	12	78	90	364	24	1	5	6	16	....	1962-63	1972-73
• Raymond, Armand	Mtl.C., Mtl.	2	22	0	2	2	10	....	....	....	....	....	....	1937-38	1939-40
• Raymond, Paul	Mtl.C.	4	76	2	3	5	6	5	0	0	0	2	....	1932-33	1938-39
Read, Mel	NYR	1	1	0	0	0	0	....	....	....	....	....	....	1946-47	1946-47
Reardon, Ken	Mtl.	7	341	26	96	122	604	31	2	5	7	62	1	1940-41	1949-50
• Reardon, Terry	Bos., Mtl.	7	193	47	53	100	73	30	8	10	18	12	1	1938-39	1946-47
Reaume, Marc	Tor., Det., Mtl., Van.	9	344	8	43	51	273	21	0	2	2	8	....	1954-55	1970-71
Reay, Billy	Det., Mtl.	10	479	105	162	267	202	63	13	16	29	43	2	1943-44	1952-53
Redahl, Gord	Bos.	1	18	0	1	1	2	....	....	....	....	....	....	1958-59	1958-59
• Redding, George	Bos.	2	35	3	2	5	10	....	....	....	....	....	....	1924-25	1925-26
Redmond, Craig	L.A., Edm.	5	191	16	68	84	134	3	1	0	1	2	....	1984-85	1988-89
Redmond, Dick	Min., Cal., Chi., St.L., Atl., Bos.	13	771	133	312	445	504	66	9	22	31	27	....	1969-70	1981-82
Redmond, Keith	L.A.	1	12	1	0	1	20	....	....	....	....	....	....	1993-94	1993-94
Redmond, Mickey	Mtl., Det.	9	538	233	195	428	219	16	2	3	5	2	2	1967-68	1975-76
Reeds, Mark	St.L., Hfd.	8	365	45	114	159	135	53	8	9	17	23	....	1981-82	1988-89
• Regan, Bill	NYR, NYA	3	67	3	2	5	67	8	0	0	0	2	....	1929-30	1932-33
Regan, Larry	Bos., Tor.	5	280	41	95	136	71	42	7	14	21	18	....	1956-57	1960-61
Regier, Darcy	Cle., NYI	3	26	0	2	2	35	....	....	....	....	....	....	1977-78	1983-84
Reibel, Earl	Det., Chi., Bos.	6	409	84	161	245	75	39	6	14	20	4	2	1953-54	1958-59
Reid, Dave	Tor., Dal.	4	80	6	11	17	16	23	2	8	10	14	....	1952-53	1998-99
Reid, Gerry	Det.	1	....	....	....	....	....	2	0	0	0	2	....	1948-49	1948-49
Reid, Gord	NYA	1	1	0	0	0	2	....	....	....	....	....	....	1936-37	1936-37
• Reid, Reg	Tor.	2	40	2	0	2	4	2	0	0	0	0	....	1924-25	1925-26
Reid, Tom	Chi., Min.	11	701	17	113	130	654	42	1	13	14	49	....	1967-68	1977-78
Reierson, Dave	Cgy.	1	2	0	0	0	2	....	....	....	....	....	....	1988-89	1988-89
Reigle, Ed	Bos.	1	17	0	2	2	25	....	....	....	....	....	....	1950-51	1950-51
Reinhart, Paul	Atl., Cgy., Van.	11	648	133	426	559	277	83	23	54	77	42	....	1979-80	1989-90
• Reinikka, Ollie	NYR	1	16	0	0	0	0	....	....	....	....	....	....	1926-27	1926-27
Reise, Leo Jr.	Chi., Det., NYR	9	494	28	81	109	399	52	8	5	13	68	2	1945-46	1953-54
• Reise, Leo Sr.	Ham., NYA, NYR	8	223	36	29	65	180	6	0	0	0	16	....	1920-21	1929-30
Renaud, Mark	Hfd., Buf.	5	152	6	50	56	86	....	....	....	....	....	....	1979-80	1983-84
Reynolds, Bobby	Tor.	1	7	1	1	2	0	....	....	....	....	....	....	1989-90	1989-90
Ribble, Pat	Atl., Chi., Tor., Wsh., Cgy.	8	349	19	60	79	365	8	0	1	1	12	....	1975-76	1982-83
Rice, Steven	NYR, Edm., Hfd., Car.	8	329	64	61	125	275	2	2	1	3	6	....	1990-91	1997-98
Richard, Henri	Mtl.	20	1256	358	688	1046	928	180	49	80	129	181	11	1955-56	1974-75
Richard, Jacques	Atl., Buf., Que.	10	556	160	187	347	307	35	5	5	10	34	....	1972-73	1982-83
Richard, Jean-Marc	Que.	2	5	2	1	3	2	....	....	....	....	....	....	1987-88	1989-90
Richard, Maurice	Mtl.	18	978	544	421	965	1285	133	82	44	126	188	8	1942-43	1959-60
Richard, Mike	Wsh.	2	7	0	2	2	0	....	....	....	....	....	....	1987-88	1989-90
Richards, Todd	Hfd.	2	8	0	4	4	4	11	0	3	3	6	....	1990-91	1991-92
Richards, Travis	Dal.	2	3	0	0	0	2	....	....	....	....	....	....	1994-95	1995-96
Richardson, Dave	NYR, Chi., Det.	4	45	3	2	5	27	....	....	....	....	....	....	1963-64	1967-68
Richardson, Glen	Van.	1	24	3	6	9	19	....	....	....	....	....	....	1975-76	1975-76
Richardson, Ken	St.L.	3	49	8	13	21	16	....	....	....	....	....	....	1974-75	1978-79
Richer, Bob	Buf.	1	3	0	0	0	0	....	....	....	....	....	....	1972-73	1972-73
Richer, Stephane J. G.	T.B., Bos., Fla.	3	27	1	5	6	20	3	0	0	0	0	....	1992-93	1994-95
Richmond, Steve	NYR, Det., N.J., L.A.	5	159	4	23	27	514	4	0	0	0	12	....	1983-84	1988-89
Richter, Dave	Min., Phi., Van., St.L.	9	365	9	40	49	1030	22	1	0	1	80	....	1981-82	1989-90
Ridley, Mike	NYR, Wsh., Tor., Van.	12	866	292	466	758	424	104	28	50	78	70	....	1985-86	1996-97
Riley, Bill	Wsh., Wpg.	5	139	31	30	61	320	....	....	....	....	....	....	1974-75	1979-80
Riley, Jack	Det., Mtl.C., Bos.	4	104	10	22	32	8	4	0	3	3	0	....	1932-33	1935-36
• Riley, Jim	Chi., Det.	1	9	0	2	2	14	....	....	....	....	....	....	1926-27	1926-27
Riopelle, Rip	Mtl.	3	169	27	16	43	73	8	1	1	2	2	....	1947-48	1949-50
Rioux, Gerry	Wpg.	1	8	0	0	0	6	....	....	....	....	....	....	1979-80	1979-80
Rioux, Pierre	Cgy.	1	14	1	2	3	4	....	....	....	....	....	....	1982-83	1982-83
• Ripley, Vic	Chi., Bos., NYR, St.L.	7	278	51	49	100	173	20	4	1	5	10	....	1928-29	1934-35
Risebrough, Doug	Mtl., Cgy.	13	740	185	286	471	1542	124	21	37	58	238	4	1974-75	1986-87
Rissling, Gary	Wsh., Pit.	7	221	23	30	53	1008	5	0	1	1	4	....	1978-79	1984-85
Ritchie, Bob	Phi., Det.	2	29	8	4	12	10	....	....	....	....	....	....	1976-77	1977-78
• Ritchie, Dave	Mtl., Ott., Tor., Que., Mtl.C.	6	57	15	11	26	48	1	0	0	0	0	....	1917-18	1925-26
Ritson, Alex	NYR	1	1	0	0	0	0	....	....	....	....	....	....	1944-45	1944-45
Rittinger, Alan	Bos.	1	19	3	7	10	0	....	....	....	....	....	....	1943-44	1943-44
Rivard, Bob	Pit.	1	27	5	12	17	4	....	....	....	....	....	....	1967-68	1967-68
• Rivers, Gus	Mtl.C.	3	88	4	5	9	12	16	2	0	2	2	....	1929-30	1931-32
Rivers, Shawn	T.B.	1	4	0	2	2	2	....	....	....	....	....	....	1992-93	1992-93
Rivers, Wayne	Det., Bos., St.L., NYR	7	108	15	30	45	94	....	....	....	....	....	....	1961-62	1968-69
Rizzuto, Garth	Van.	1	37	3	4	7	16	....	....	....	....	....	....	1970-71	1970-71
• Roach, Mickey	Tor., Ham., NYA	8	211	77	32	109	43	....	....	....	....	....	....	1919-20	1926-27
Roberge, Mario	Mtl.	5	112	7	7	14	314	15	0	0	0	24	1	1990-91	1994-95
Roberge, Serge	Que.	1	9	0	0	0	24	....	....	....	....	....	....	1990-91	1990-91
Robert, Claude	Mtl.	1	23	1	0	1	9	....	....	....	....	....	....	1950-51	1950-51
Robert, Rene	Tor., Pit., Buf., Col.	12	744	284	418	702	597	50	22	19	41	73	....	1970-71	1981-82
Roberto, Phil	Mtl., St.L., Det., K.C., Col., Cle.	8	385	75	106	181	464	31	9	8	17	69	1	1969-70	1976-77

Name	NHL Teams	NHL Seasons	Regular Schedule GP	G	A	TP	PIM	Playoffs GP	G	A	TP	PIM	NHL Cup Wins	First NHL Season	Last NHL Season
Roberts, Doug	Det., Oak., Cal., Bos.	10	419	43	104	147	342	16	2	3	5	46	....	1965-66	1974-75
Roberts, Gordie	Hfd., Min., Phi., St.L., Pit., Bos.	15	1097	61	359	420	1582	153	10	47	57	273	2	1979-80	1993-94
Roberts, Jim	Min.	3	106	17	23	40	33	2	0	0	0	0	....	1976-77	1978-79
Roberts, Jimmy	Mtl., St.L.	15	1006	126	194	320	621	153	20	16	36	160	5	1963-64	1977-78
• Robertson, Fred	Tor., Det.	2	34	1	0	1	35	7	0	0	0	0	1	1931-32	1933-34
Robertson, Geordie	Buf.	1	5	1	2	3	7	....	....	....	....	....	....	1982-83	1982-83
Robertson, George	Mtl.	2	31	2	5	7	6	....	....	....	....	....	....	1947-48	1948-49
Robertson, Torrie	Wsh., Hfd., Det.	10	442	49	99	148	1751	22	2	1	3	90	....	1980-81	1989-90
Robidoux, Florent	Chi.	3	52	7	4	11	75	....	....	....	....	....	....	1980-81	1983-84
Robinson, Doug	Chi., NYR, L.A.	7	239	44	67	111	34	11	4	3	7	0	....	1963-64	1970-71
• Robinson, Earl	Mtl.M., Chi., Mtl.	11	417	83	98	181	133	25	5	4	9	0	1	1928-29	1939-40
Robinson, Larry	Mtl., L.A.	20	1384	208	750	958	793	227	28	116	144	211	6	1972-73	1991-92
Robinson, Moe	Mtl.	1	1	0	0	0	0	....	....	....	....	....	....	1979-80	1979-80
Robinson, Rob	St.L.	1	22	0	1	1	8	....	....	....	....	....	....	1991-92	1991-92
Robinson, Scott	Min.	1	1	0	0	0	2	....	....	....	....	....	....	1989-90	1989-90
Robitaille, Mike	NYR, Det., Buf., Van.	8	382	23	105	128	280	13	0	1	1	4	....	1969-70	1976-77
• Roche, Des	Mtl.M., Ott., St.L., Mtl.C., Det.	4	113	20	18	38	44	....	....	....	....	....	....	1930-31	1934-35
• Roche, Earl	Mtl.M., Bos., Ott., St.L., Det.	4	147	25	27	52	48	2	0	0	0	0	....	1930-31	1934-35
Roche, Ernie	Mtl.	1	4	0	0	0	2	....	....	....	....	....	....	1950-51	1950-51
Rochefort, Dave	Det.	1	1	0	0	0	0	....	....	....	....	....	....	1966-67	1966-67
Rochefort, Leon	NYR, Mtl., Phi., L.A., Det., Atl., Van.	15	617	121	147	268	93	39	4	4	8	16	2	1960-61	1975-76
Rochefort, Normand	Que., NYR, T.B.	13	598	39	119	158	570	69	7	5	12	82	....	1980-81	1993-94
• Rockburn, Harvey	Det., Ott.	3	94	4	2	6	254	....	....	....	....	....	....	1929-30	1932-33
• Rodden, Eddie	Chi., Tor., Bos., NYR	4	97	6	14	20	60	2	0	1	1	0	....	1926-27	1930-31
Rogers, John	Min.	2	14	2	4	6	0	....	....	....	....	....	....	1973-74	1974-75
Rogers, Mike	Hfd., NYR, Edm.	7	484	202	317	519	184	17	1	13	14	6	....	1979-80	1985-86
Rohlicek, Jeff	Van.	2	9	0	0	0	8	....	....	....	....	....	....	1987-88	1988-89
Rolfe, Dale	Bos., L.A., Det., NYR	9	509	25	125	150	556	71	5	24	29	89	....	1959-60	1974-75
Romanchych, Larry	Chi., Atl.	6	298	68	97	165	102	7	2	2	4	4	....	1970-71	1976-77
Rombough, Doug	Buf., NYI, Min.	4	150	24	27	51	80	....	....	....	....	....	....	1972-73	1975-76
• Romnes, Doc	Chi., Tor., NYA	10	360	68	136	204	42	45	7	18	25	4	2	1930-31	1939-40
Ronan, Ed	Mtl., Wpg., Buf.	6	182	13	23	36	101	27	4	3	7	16	1	1991-92	1996-97
• Ronan, Skene	Ott.	1	10	0	0	0	9	....	....	....	....	....	....	1918-19	1918-19
Ronson, Len	NYR, Oak.	2	18	2	1	3	10	....	....	....	....	....	....	1960-61	1968-69
Ronty, Paul	Bos., NYR, Mtl.	8	488	101	211	312	103	21	1	7	8	6	....	1947-48	1954-55
Rooney, Steve	Mtl., Wpg., N.J.	5	154	15	13	28	496	25	3	2	5	86	1	1984-85	1988-89
Root, Bill	Mtl., Tor., St.L., Phi.	6	247	11	23	34	180	22	1	2	3	25	....	1982-83	1987-88
• Ross, Art	Mtl.	1	3	1	0	1	12	....	....	....	....	....	....	1917-18	1917-18
Ross, Jim	NYR	2	62	2	11	13	29	....	....	....	....	....	....	1951-52	1952-53
Rossignol, Roland	Det., Mtl.	3	14	3	5	8	6	1	0	0	0	2	....	1943-44	1945-46
Rota, Darcy	Chi., Atl., Van.	11	794	256	239	495	973	60	14	7	21	147	....	1973-74	1983-84
Rota, Randy	Mtl., L.A., K.C., Col.	5	212	38	39	77	60	5	0	1	1	0	....	1972-73	1976-77
• Rothschild, Sam	Mtl.M., NYA, Pit.	4	99	8	6	14	24	10	0	0	0	0	1	1924-25	1927-28
• Roulston, Rolly	Det.	3	24	0	6	6	10	....	....	....	....	....	....	1935-36	1937-38
Roulston, Tom	Edm., Pit.	5	195	47	49	96	74	21	2	2	4	2	....	1980-81	1985-86
Roupe, Magnus	Phi.	2	40	3	5	8	42	....	....	....	....	....	....	1987-88	1988-89
Rousseau, Bobby	Mtl., Min., NYR	15	942	245	458	703	359	128	27	57	84	69	4	1960-61	1974-75
Rousseau, Guy	Mtl.	2	4	0	1	1	0	....	....	....	....	....	....	1954-55	1956-57
Rousseau, Roland	Mtl.	1	2	0	0	0	0	....	....	....	....	....	....	1952-53	1952-53
Routhier, Jean-Marc	Que.	1	8	0	0	0	9	....	....	....	....	....	....	1989-90	1989-90
• Rowe, Bobby	Bos.	1	4	1	0	1	0	....	....	....	....	....	....	1924-25	1924-25
Rowe, Mike	Pit.	3	11	0	0	0	11	....	....	....	....	....	....	1984-85	1986-87
Rowe, Ron	NYR	1	5	1	0	1	0	....	....	....	....	....	....	1947-48	1947-48
Rowe, Tom	Wsh., Hfd., Det.	7	357	85	100	185	615	3	2	0	2	0	....	1976-77	1982-83
Roy, Stephane	Min.	1	12	1	0	1	0	....	....	....	....	....	....	1987-88	1987-88
Rozzini, Gino	Bos.	1	31	5	10	15	20	6	1	2	3	6	....	1944-45	1944-45
Rucinski, Mike	Chi.	2	1	0	0	0	0	2	0	0	0	0	....	1987-88	1988-89
Ruelle, Bernie	Det.	1	2	1	0	1	0	....	....	....	....	....	....	1943-44	1943-44
Ruff, Lindy	Buf., NYR	12	691	105	195	300	1264	52	11	13	24	193	....	1979-80	1990-91
Ruhnke, Kent	Bos.	1	2	0	1	1	0	....	....	....	....	....	....	1975-76	1975-76
Rundqvist, Thomas	Mtl.	1	2	0	1	1	0	....	....	....	....	....	....	1984-85	1984-85
• Runge, Paul	Bos., Mtl.M., Mtl.C.	7	140	18	22	40	57	7	0	0	0	6	....	1930-31	1937-38
Ruotsalainen, Reijo	NYR, Edm., N.J.	7	446	107	237	344	180	86	15	32	47	44	2	1981-82	1989-90
Rupp, Duane	NYR, Tor., Min., Pit.	10	374	24	93	117	220	10	2	2	4	8	....	1962-63	1972-73
Ruskowski, Terry	Chi., L.A., Pit., Min.	10	630	113	313	426	1354	21	1	6	7	86	....	1979-80	1988-89
• Russell, Church	NYR	3	90	20	16	36	12	....	....	....	....	....	....	1945-46	1947-48
Russell, Phil	Chi., Atl., Cgy., N.J., Buf.	15	1016	99	325	424	2038	73	4	22	26	202	....	1972-73	1986-87
Ruuttu, Christian	Buf., Chi., Van.	9	621	134	298	432	714	42	4	9	13	49	....	1986-87	1994-95
Ruzicka, Vladimir	Edm., Bos., Ott.	5	233	82	85	167	129	30	4	14	18	2	....	1989-90	1993-94
Rymsha, Andy	Que.	1	6	0	0	0	23	....	....	....	....	....	....	1991-92	1991-92
S															
Saarinen, Simo	NYR	1	8	0	0	0	0	....	....	....	....	....	....	1984-85	1984-85
Sabol, Shaun	Phi.	1	2	0	0	0	0	....	....	....	....	....	....	1989-90	1989-90
Sabourin, Bob	Tor.	1	1	0	0	0	2	....	....	....	....	....	....	1951-52	1951-52
Sabourin, Gary	St.L., Tor., Cal., Cle.	10	627	169	188	357	397	62	19	11	30	58	....	1967-68	1976-77
Sabourin, Ken	Cgy., Wsh.	4	74	2	8	10	201	12	0	0	0	34	1	1988-89	1991-92
Sacco, David	Tor., Ana.	3	35	5	13	18	22	....	....	....	....	....	....	1993-94	1995-96
Sacharuk, Lawrence	NYR, St.L.	5	151	29	33	62	42	2	1	1	2	2	....	1972-73	1976-77
Saganiuk, Rocky	Tor., Pit.	6	259	57	65	122	201	6	1	0	1	15	....	1978-79	1983-84
Saleski, Don	Phi., Col.	9	543	128	125	253	629	82	13	17	30	131	2	1971-72	1979-80
Salming, Borje	Tor., Det.	17	1148	150	637	787	1344	81	12	37	49	91	....	1973-74	1989-90
Salovaara, John	Det.	2	90	2	13	15	70	....	....	....	....	....	....	1974-75	1975-76
Salvian, Dave	NYI	1	....	....	....	....	....	1	0	1	1	2	....	1976-77	1976-77
Samis, Phil	Tor.	2	2	0	0	0	0	5	0	1	1	2	1	1947-48	1949-50
Sampson, Gary	Wsh.	4	105	13	22	35	25	12	1	0	1	0	....	1983-84	1986-87
Sandelin, Scott	Mtl., Phi., Min.	4	25	0	4	4	2	....	....	....	....	....	....	1986-87	1991-92
Sanderson, Derek	Bos., NYR, St.L., Van., Pit.	13	598	202	250	452	911	56	18	12	30	187	2	1965-66	1977-78
Sandford, Ed	Bos., Det., Chi.	9	502	106	145	251	355	42	13	11	24	27	....	1947-48	1955-56
Sandlak, Jim	Van., Hfd.	11	549	110	119	229	821	33	7	10	17	30	....	1985-86	1995-96
• Sands, Charlie	Tor., Bos., Mtl., NYR	12	427	99	109	208	58	34	6	6	12	4	1	1932-33	1943-44
Sanipass, Everett	Chi., Que.	5	164	25	34	59	358	5	2	0	2	4	....	1986-87	1990-91
Sargent, Gary	L.A., Min.	8	402	61	161	222	273	20	5	7	12	8	....	1975-76	1982-83
Sarner, Craig	Bos.	1	7	0	0	0	0	....	....	....	....	....	....	1974-75	1974-75
Sarrazin, Dick	Phi.	3	100	20	35	55	22	4	0	0	0	0	....	1968-69	1971-72
Saskamoose, Fred	Chi.	1	11	0	0	0	6	....	....	....	....	....	....	1953-54	1953-54
Sasser, Grant	Pit.	1	3	0	0	0	0	....	....	....	....	....	....	1983-84	1983-84
Sather, Glen	Bos., Pit., NYR, St.L., Mtl., Min.	10	658	80	113	193	724	72	1	5	6	86	....	1966-67	1975-76
Saunders, Bernie	Que.	2	10	0	1	1	8	....	....	....	....	....	....	1979-80	1980-81
Saunders, David	Van.	1	56	7	13	20	10	....	....	....	....	....	....	1987-88	1987-88
Saunders, Ted	Ott.	1	18	1	3	4	4	....	....	....	....	....	....	1933-34	1933-34
Sauve, Jean-Francois	Buf., Que.	7	290	65	138	203	114	36	9	12	21	10	....	1980-81	1986-87
Savage, Joel	Buf.	1	3	0	1	1	0	....	....	....	....	....	....	1990-91	1990-91
Savage, Reggie	Wsh., Que.	3	34	5	7	12	28	....	....	....	....	....	....	1990-91	1993-94
• Savage, Tony	Mtl.C., Bos.	1	49	1	5	6	6	2	0	0	0	0	....	1934-35	1934-35
Savard, Andre	Bos., Buf., Que.	12	790	211	271	482	411	85	13	18	31	77	....	1973-74	1984-85
Savard, Denis	Chi., Mtl., T.B.	17	1196	473	865	1338	1336	169	66	109	175	256	1	1980-81	1996-97
Savard, Jean	Chi., Hfd.	3	43	7	12	19	29	....	....	....	....	....	....	1977-78	1979-80
Savard, Serge	Mtl., Wpg.	17	1040	106	333	439	592	130	19	49	68	88	8	1966-67	1982-83
Scamurra, Peter	Wsh.	4	132	8	25	33	59	....	....	....	....	....	....	1975-76	1979-80
Sceviour, Darin	Chi.	1	1	0	0	0	0	....	....	....	....	....	....	1986-87	1986-87
Schaeffer, Butch	Chi.	1	5	0	0	0	6	....	....	....	....	....	....	1936-37	1936-37
Schamehorn, Kevin	Det., L.A.	3	10	0	0	0	17	....	....	....	....	....	....	1976-77	1980-81
Schella, John	Van.	2	115	2	18	20	224	....	....	....	....	....	....	1970-71	1971-72
Scherza, Chuck	Bos., NYR	2	36	6	6	12	35	....	....	....	....	....	....	1943-44	1944-45
Schinkel, Ken	NYR, Pit.	12	636	127	198	325	163	19	7	2	9	4	....	1959-60	1972-73
Schlegel, Brad	Wsh., Cgy.	3	48	1	8	9	10	7	0	1	1	2	....	1991-92	1993-94
Schliebener, Andy	Van.	3	84	2	11	13	74	6	0	0	0	0	....	1981-82	1984-85
Schmautz, Bobby	Chi., Van., Bos., Edm., Col.	13	764	271	286	557	988	84	28	33	61	92	....	1967-68	1980-81
Schmautz, Cliff	Buf., Phi.	1	56	13	19	32	33	....	....	....	....	....	....	1970-71	1970-71

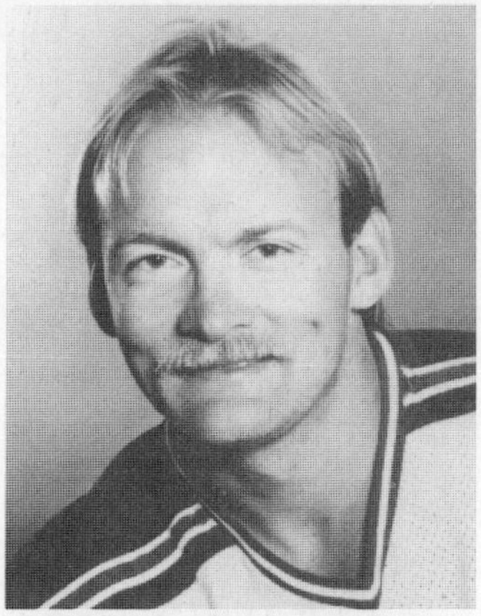
Lindy Ruff

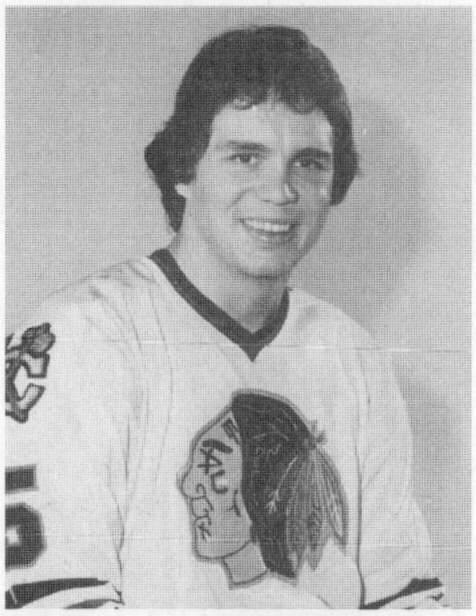
Phil Russell

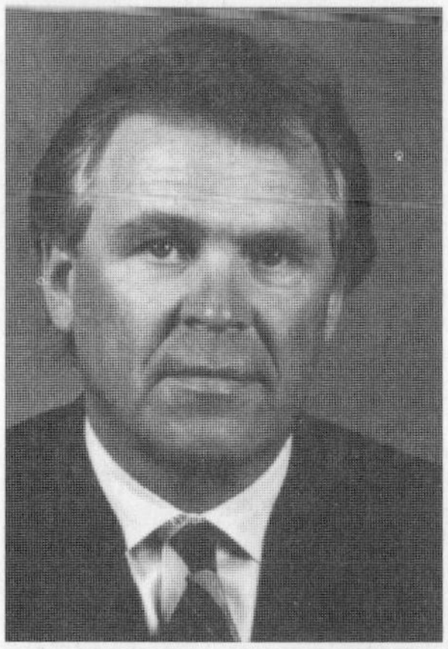
Glen Sather

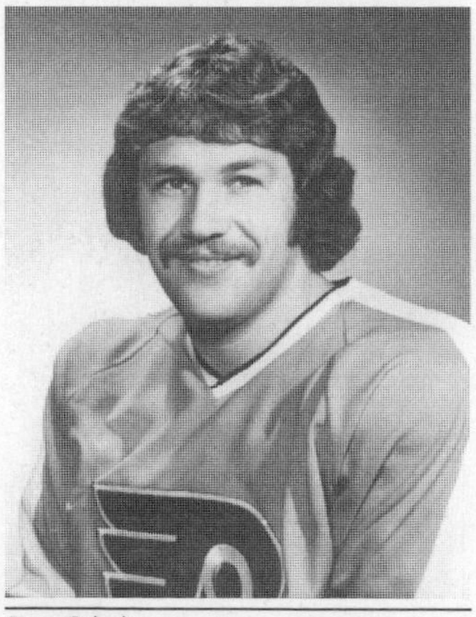
Dave Schultz

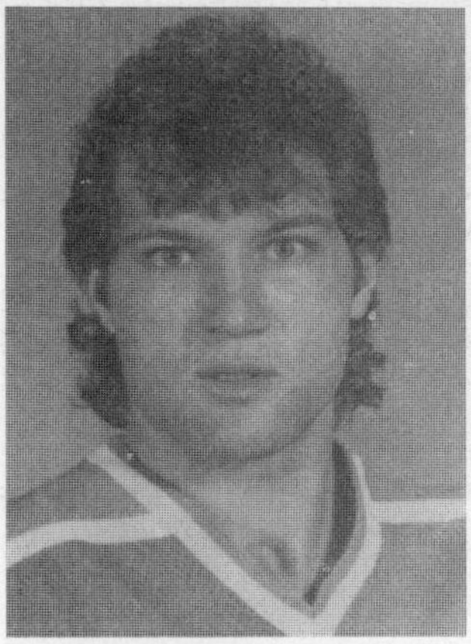
Dave Semenko

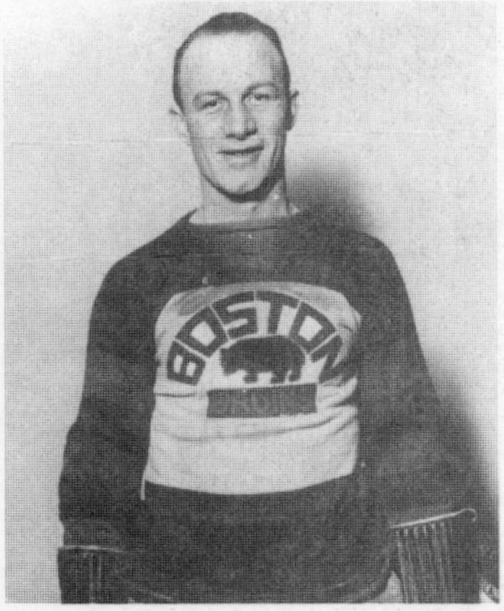

Eddie Shore

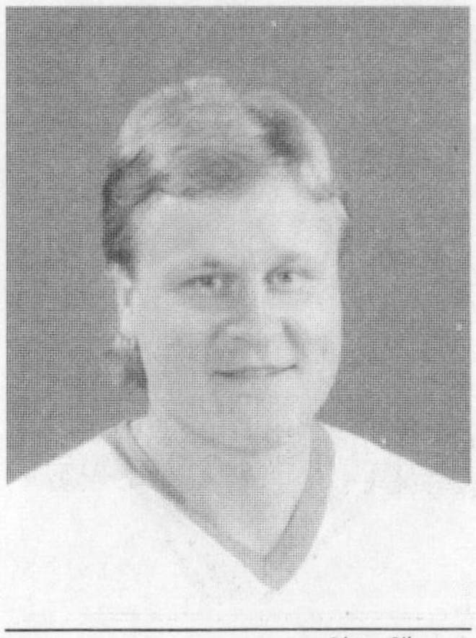
Risto Siltanen

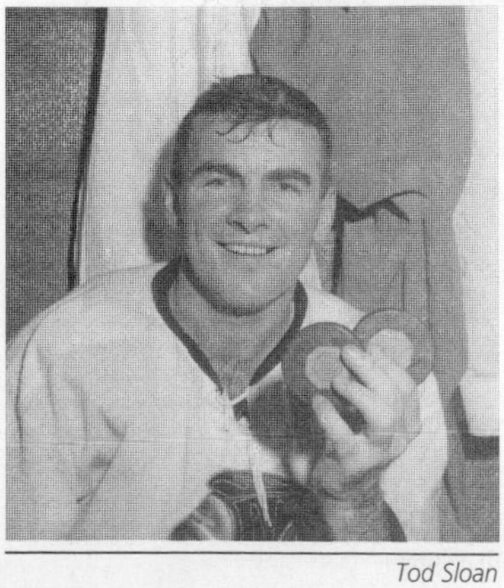
Tod Sloan

Name	NHL Teams	NHL Seasons	Regular Schedule GP	G	A	TP	PIM	Playoffs GP	G	A	TP	PIM	NHL Cup Wins	First NHL Season	Last NHL Season
Schmidt, Clarence	Bos.	1	7	1	0	1	2	....	....	....	....	....	....	1943-44	1943-44
Schmidt, Jackie	Bos.	1	45	6	7	13	6	5	0	0	0	0	....	1942-43	1942-43
Schmidt, Joseph	Bos.	1	2	0	0	0	0	....	....	....	....	....	....	1943-44	1943-44
Schmidt, Milt	Bos.	17	776	229	346	575	466	86	24	25	49	60	2	1936-37	1955-56
Schmidt, Norm	Pit.	4	125	23	33	56	73	....	....	....	....	....	....	1983-84	1987-88
• Schnarr, Werner	Bos.	2	25	0	0	0	0	....	....	....	....	....	....	1924-25	1925-26
Schneider, Andy	Ott.	1	10	0	0	0	15	....	....	....	....	....	....	1993-94	1993-94
Schock, Danny	Bos., Phi.	2	20	1	2	3	0	1	0	0	0	0	1	1969-70	1970-71
Schock, Ron	Bos., St.L., Pit., Buf.	15	909	166	351	517	260	55	4	16	20	29	....	1963-64	1977-78
Schoenfeld, Jim	Buf., Det., Bos.	13	719	51	204	255	1132	75	3	13	16	151	....	1972-73	1984-85
Schofield, Dwight	Det., Mtl., St.L., Wsh., Pit., Wpg.	7	211	8	22	30	631	9	0	0	0	55	....	1976-77	1987-88
Schreiber, Wally	Min.	2	41	8	10	18	12	....	....	....	....	....	....	1987-88	1988-89
• Schriner, Sweeney	NYA, Tor.	11	484	201	204	405	148	59	18	11	29	54	2	1934-35	1945-46
Schultz, Dave	Phi., L.A., Pit., Buf.	9	535	79	121	200	2294	73	8	12	20	412	2	1971-72	1979-80
Schurman, Maynard	Hfd.	1	7	0	0	0	0	....	....	....	....	....	....	1979-80	1979-80
Schutt, Rod	Mtl., Pit., Tor.	8	286	77	92	169	177	22	8	6	14	26	....	1977-78	1985-86
Scissons, Scott	NYI	3	2	0	0	0	0	1	0	0	0	0	....	1990-91	1993-94
Sclisizzi, Enio	Det., Chi.	6	81	12	11	23	26	13	0	0	0	6	....	1946-47	1952-53
• Scott, Ganton	Tor., Ham., Mtl.M.	3	53	1	1	2	0	....	....	....	....	....	....	1922-23	1924-25
• Scott, Laurie	NYA, NYR	2	62	6	3	9	28	....	....	....	....	....	1	1926-27	1927-28
Scremin, Claudio	S.J.	2	17	0	1	1	29	....	....	....	....	....	....	1991-92	1992-93
Scruton, Howard	L.A.	1	4	0	4	4	9	....	....	....	....	....	....	1982-83	1982-83
Seabrooke, Glen	Phi.	3	19	1	6	7	4	....	....	....	....	....	....	1986-87	1988-89
Secord, Al	Bos., Chi., Tor., Phi.	12	766	273	222	495	2093	102	21	34	55	382	....	1978-79	1989-90
Sedlbauer, Ron	Van., Chi., Tor.	7	430	143	86	229	210	19	1	3	4	27	....	1974-75	1980-81
Seftel, Steve	Wsh.	1	4	0	0	0	2	....	....	....	....	....	....	1990-91	1990-91
Seguin, Dan	Min., Van.	2	37	2	6	8	50	....	....	....	....	....	....	1970-71	1973-74
Seguin, Steve	L.A.	1	5	0	0	0	9	....	....	....	....	....	....	1984-85	1984-85
• Seibert, Earl	NYR, Chi., Det.	15	645	89	187	276	746	66	11	8	19	76	2	1931-32	1945-46
Seiling, Ric	Buf., Det.	10	738	179	208	387	573	62	14	14	28	36	....	1977-78	1986-87
Seiling, Rod	Tor., NYR, Wsh., St.L., Atl.	17	979	62	269	331	601	77	4	8	12	55	....	1962-63	1978-79
Sejba, Jiri	Buf.	1	11	0	2	2	8	....	....	....	....	....	....	1990-91	1990-91
Selby, Brit	Tor., Phi., St.L.	8	350	55	62	117	163	16	1	1	2	8	....	1964-65	1971-72
Self, Steve	Wsh.	1	3	0	0	0	0	....	....	....	....	....	....	1976-77	1976-77
Selwood, Brad	Tor., L.A.	3	163	7	40	47	153	6	0	0	0	4	....	1970-71	1979-80
Semchuk, Brandy	L.A.	1	1	0	0	0	2	....	....	....	....	....	....	1992-93	1992-93
Semenko, Dave	Edm., Hfd., Tor.	9	575	65	88	153	1175	73	6	6	12	208	2	1979-80	1987-88
Semenov, Anatoli	Edm., T.B., Van., Ana., Phi., Buf.	8	362	68	126	194	122	49	9	13	22	12	1	1989-90	1996-97
Senick, George	NYR	1	13	2	3	5	8	....	....	....	....	....	....	1952-53	1952-53
Seppa, Jyrki	Wpg.	1	13	0	2	2	6	....	....	....	....	....	....	1983-84	1983-84
Serafini, Ron	Cal.	1	2	0	0	0	2	....	....	....	....	....	....	1973-74	1973-74
Serowik, Jeff	Tor., Bos., Pit.	3	28	0	6	6	16	....	....	....	....	....	....	1990-91	1998-99
Servinis, George	Min.	1	5	0	0	0	0	....	....	....	....	....	....	1987-88	1987-88
Sevcik, Jaroslav	Que.	1	13	0	2	2	2	....	....	....	....	....	....	1989-90	1989-90
Shack, Eddie	NYR, Tor., Bos., L.A., Buf., Pit.	17	1047	239	226	465	1437	74	6	7	13	151	4	1958-59	1974-75
• Shack, Joe	NYR	2	70	9	27	36	20	....	....	....	....	....	....	1942-43	1944-45
Shafranov, Konstantin	St.L.	1	5	2	1	3	0	....	....	....	....	....	....	1996-97	1996-97
Shakes, Paul	Cal.	1	21	0	4	4	12	....	....	....	....	....	....	1973-74	1973-74
Shanahan, Sean	Mtl., Col., Bos.	3	40	1	3	4	47	....	....	....	....	....	....	1975-76	1977-78
Shand, Dave	Atl., Tor., Wsh.	8	421	19	84	103	544	26	1	2	3	83	....	1976-77	1984-85
Shank, Daniel	Det., Hfd.	3	77	13	14	27	175	5	0	0	0	22	....	1989-90	1991-92
Shannon, Chuck	NYA	1	4	0	0	0	2	....	....	....	....	....	....	1939-40	1939-40
• Shannon, Gerry	Ott., St.L., Bos., Mtl.M.	5	180	23	29	52	80	9	0	1	1	2	....	1933-34	1937-38
Sharples, Jeff	Det.	3	105	14	35	49	70	7	0	3	3	6	....	1986-87	1988-89
Sharpley, Glen	Min., Chi.	6	389	117	161	278	199	27	7	11	18	24	....	1976-77	1981-82
Shaunessy, Scott	Que.	2	7	0	0	0	23	....	....	....	....	....	....	1986-87	1988-89
• Shay, Norman	Bos., Tor.	2	53	5	2	7	34	....	....	....	....	....	....	1924-25	1925-26
• Shea, Pat	Chi.	1	10	0	1	1	0	....	....	....	....	....	....	1931-32	1931-32
Shedden, Doug	Pit., Det., Que., Tor.	8	416	139	186	325	176	....	....	....	....	....	....	1981-82	1990-91
Sheehan, Bobby	Mtl., Cal., Chi., Det., NYR, Col., L.A.	9	310	48	63	111	50	25	4	3	7	8	1	1969-70	1981-82
Sheehy, Neil	Cgy., Hfd., Wsh.	9	379	18	47	65	1311	54	0	3	3	241	....	1983-84	1991-92
Sheehy, Tim	Det., Hfd.	2	27	2	1	3	0	....	....	....	....	....	....	1977-78	1979-80
Shelton, Doug	Chi.	1	5	0	1	1	2	....	....	....	....	....	....	1967-68	1967-68
• Sheppard, Frank	Det.	1	8	1	1	2	0	....	....	....	....	....	....	1927-28	1927-28
Sheppard, Gregg	Bos., Pit.	10	657	205	293	498	243	82	32	40	72	31	....	1972-73	1981-82
• Sheppard, Johnny	Det., NYA, Bos., Chi.	8	308	68	58	126	224	10	0	0	0	0	1	1926-27	1933-34
• Sherf, John	Det.	5	19	0	0	0	8	8	0	1	1	2	1	1935-36	1943-44
• Shero, Fred	NYR	3	145	6	14	20	137	13	0	2	2	8	....	1947-48	1949-50
Sherritt, Gordon	Det.	1	8	0	0	0	12	....	....	....	....	....	....	1943-44	1943-44
Sherven, Gord	Edm., Min., Hfd.	5	97	13	22	35	33	3	0	0	0	0	....	1983-84	1987-88
• Shewchuck, Jack	Bos.	6	187	9	19	28	160	20	0	1	1	19	....	1938-39	1944-45
Shibicky, Alex	NYR	8	324	110	91	201	161	39	12	12	24	12	1	1935-36	1945-46
• Shields, Al	Ott., Phi., NYA, Mtl.M., Bos.	11	459	42	46	88	637	17	0	1	1	14	1	1927-28	1937-38
Shill, Bill	Bos.	3	79	21	13	34	18	7	1	2	3	2	....	1942-43	1946-47
• Shill, Jack	Tor., Bos., NYA, Chi.	6	160	15	20	35	70	25	1	6	7	23	1	1933-34	1938-39
Shinske, Rick	Cle., St.L.	3	63	5	16	21	10	....	....	....	....	....	....	1976-77	1978-79
Shires, Jim	Det., St.L., Pit.	3	56	3	6	9	32	....	....	....	....	....	....	1970-71	1972-73
Shmyr, Paul	Chi., Cal., Min., Hfd.	7	343	13	72	85	528	34	3	3	6	44	....	1968-69	1981-82
Shoebottom, Bruce	Bos.	4	35	1	4	5	53	14	1	2	3	77	....	1987-88	1990-91
• Shore, Eddie	Bos., NYA	14	550	105	179	284	1047	55	6	13	19	181	2	1926-27	1939-40
• Shore, Hamby	Ott.	1	20	3	8	11	51	....	....	....	....	....	....	1917-18	1917-18
Short, Steve	L.A., Det.	2	6	0	0	0	2	....	....	....	....	....	....	1977-78	1978-79
Shuchuk, Gary	Det., L.A.	5	142	13	26	39	70	20	2	2	4	12	....	1990-91	1995-96
Shudra, Ron	Edm.	1	10	0	5	5	6	....	....	....	....	....	....	1987-88	1987-88
Shutt, Steve	Mtl., L.A.	13	930	424	393	817	410	99	50	48	98	65	5	1972-73	1984-85
• Siebert, Babe	Mtl.M., NYR, Bos., Mtl.C.	14	592	140	156	296	982	53	8	7	15	64	2	1925-26	1938-39
Silk, Dave	NYR, Bos., Det., Wpg.	7	249	54	59	113	271	13	2	4	6	13	....	1979-80	1985-86
Siltala, Mike	Wsh., NYR	3	7	1	0	1	2	....	....	....	....	....	....	1981-82	1987-88
Siltanen, Risto	Edm., Hfd., Que.	8	562	90	265	355	266	32	6	12	18	30	....	1979-80	1986-87
Sim, Trevor	Edm.	1	3	0	1	1	2	....	....	....	....	....	....	1989-90	1989-90
Simard, Martin	Cgy., T.B.	3	44	1	5	6	183	....	....	....	....	....	....	1990-91	1992-93
Simmer, Charlie	Cal., Cle., L.A., Bos., Pit.	14	712	342	369	711	544	24	9	9	18	32	....	1974-75	1987-88
Simmons, Al	Cal., Bos.	3	11	0	1	1	21	1	0	0	0	0	....	1971-72	1975-76
• Simon, Cully	Det., Chi.	3	130	4	11	15	121	14	0	1	1	6	1	1942-43	1944-45
Simon, Thain	Det.	1	3	0	0	0	0	....	....	....	....	....	....	1946-47	1946-47
Simon, Todd	Buf.	1	15	0	1	1	0	5	1	0	1	0	....	1993-94	1993-94
Simonetti, Frank	Bos.	4	115	5	8	13	76	12	0	1	1	8	....	1984-85	1987-88
Simpson, Bobby	Atl., St.L., Pit.	5	175	35	29	64	98	6	0	1	1	2	....	1976-77	1982-83
• Simpson, Cliff	Det.	2	6	0	1	1	0	2	0	0	0	2	....	1946-47	1947-48
Simpson, Craig	Pit., Edm., Buf.	10	634	247	250	497	659	67	36	32	68	56	2	1985-86	1994-95
• Simpson, Joe	NYA	6	228	21	19	40	156	2	0	0	0	0	....	1925-26	1930-31
Sims, Al	Bos., Hfd., L.A.	10	475	49	116	165	286	41	0	2	2	14	....	1973-74	1982-83
Sinclair, Reg	NYR, Det.	3	208	49	43	92	139	3	1	0	1	0	....	1950-51	1952-53
• Singbush, Alex	Mtl.	1	32	0	5	5	15	3	0	0	0	4	....	1940-41	1940-41
Sinisalo, Ilkka	Phi., Min., L.A.	11	582	204	222	426	208	68	21	11	32	6	....	1981-82	1991-92
Siren, Ville	Pit., Min.	5	290	14	68	82	276	7	0	0	0	6	....	1985-86	1989-90
Sirois, Bob	Phi., Wsh.	6	286	92	120	212	42	....	....	....	....	....	....	1974-75	1979-80
Sittler, Darryl	Tor., Phi., Det.	15	1096	484	637	1121	948	76	29	45	74	137	....	1970-71	1984-85
• Sjoberg, Lars-Erik	Wpg.	1	79	7	27	34	48	....	....	....	....	....	....	1979-80	1979-80
Sjodin, Tommy	Min., Dal., Que.	2	106	8	40	48	52	....	....	....	....	....	....	1992-93	1993-94
• Skaare, Bjorn	Det.	1	1	0	0	0	0	....	....	....	....	....	....	1978-79	1978-79
Skarda, Randy	St.L.	2	26	0	5	5	11	....	....	....	....	....	....	1989-90	1991-92
• Skilton, Raymie	Mtl.	1	1	0	0	0	0	....	....	....	....	....	....	1917-18	1917-18
• Skinner, Alf	Tor., Bos., Mtl.M., Pit.	4	70	26	11	37	90	7	8	3	11	27	1	1917-18	1925-26
Skinner, Larry	Col.	4	47	10	12	22	8	2	0	0	0	0	....	1976-77	1979-80
Skov, Glen	Det., Chi., Mtl.	12	650	106	136	242	413	53	7	7	14	48	3	1949-50	1960-61
Skriko, Petri	Van., Bos., Wpg., S.J.	9	541	183	222	405	246	28	5	9	14	4	....	1984-85	1992-93
Sleaver, John	Chi.	2	13	1	0	1	6	....	....	....	....	....	....	1953-54	1956-57
Sleigher, Louis	Que., Bos.	6	194	46	53	99	146	17	1	1	2	64	....	1979-80	1985-86
Sloan, Tod	Tor., Chi.	13	745	220	262	482	831	47	9	12	21	47	2	1947-48	1960-61
• Slobodian, Peter	NYA	1	41	3	2	5	54	....	....	....	....	....	....	1940-41	1940-41

Name	NHL Teams	NHL Seasons	Regular Schedule GP	G	A	TP	PIM	Playoffs GP	G	A	TP	PIM	NHL Cup Wins	First NHL Season	Last NHL Season
Slowinski, Eddie	NYR	6	291	58	74	132	63	16	2	6	8	6	....	1947-48	1952-53
Sly, Darryl	Tor., Min., Van.	4	79	1	2	3	20	....	....	....	....	....	....	1965-66	1970-71
Smail, Doug	Wpg., Min., Que., Ott.	13	845	210	249	459	602	42	9	2	11	49	....	1980-81	1992-93
Smart, Alex	Mtl.	1	8	5	2	7	0	....	....	....	....	....	....	1942-43	1942-43
Smedsmo, Dale	Tor.	1	4	0	0	0	0	....	....	....	....	....	....	1972-73	1972-73
Smillie, Don	Bos.	1	12	2	2	4	4	....	....	....	....	....	....	1933-34	1933-34
• Smith, Alex	Ott., Det., Bos., NYA	11	443	41	50	91	643	19	0	2	2	40	1	1924-25	1934-35
• Smith, Art	Tor., Ott.	4	144	15	10	25	249	4	1	1	2	8	....	1927-28	1930-31
Smith, Barry	Bos., Col.	3	114	7	7	14	10	....	....	....	....	....	....	1975-76	1980-81
Smith, Bobby	Min., Mtl.	15	1077	357	679	1036	917	184	64	96	160	245	1	1978-79	1992-93
Smith, Brad	Van., Atl., Cgy., Det., Tor.	9	222	28	34	62	591	20	3	3	6	49	....	1978-79	1986-87
• Smith, Brian D.	L.A., Min.	2	67	10	10	20	33	7	0	0	0	0	....	1967-68	1968-69
Smith, Brian S.	Det.	3	61	2	8	10	12	5	0	0	0	0	....	1957-58	1960-61
• Smith, Carl	Det.	1	7	1	1	2	2	....	....	....	....	....	....	1943-44	1943-44
Smith, Clint	NYR, Chi.	11	483	161	236	397	24	42	10	14	24	2	1	1936-37	1946-47
Smith, Dallas	Bos., NYR	16	890	55	252	307	959	86	3	29	32	128	2	1959-60	1977-78
Smith, Dennis	Wsh., L.A.	2	8	0	0	0	4	....	....	....	....	....	....	1989-90	1990-91
Smith, Derek	Buf., Det.	8	335	78	116	194	60	30	9	14	23	13	....	1975-76	1982-83
Smith, Derrick	Phi., Min., Dal.	10	537	82	92	174	373	82	14	11	25	79	....	1984-85	1993-94
• Smith, Des	Mtl.M., Mtl.C., Chi., Bos.	5	196	22	25	47	236	25	1	4	5	18	1	1937-38	1941-42
• Smith, Don	Mtl.C.	1	12	1	0	1	6	....	....	....	....	....	....	1919-20	1919-20
Smith, Don A.	NYR	1	11	1	1	2	0	1	0	0	0	0	....	1949-50	1949-50
Smith, Doug	L.A., Buf., Edm., Van., Pit.	9	535	115	138	253	624	18	4	2	6	21	....	1981-82	1989-90
Smith, Floyd	Bos., NYR, Det., Tor., Buf.	13	616	129	178	307	207	48	12	11	23	16	....	1954-55	1971-72
Smith, Glen	Chi.	1	2	0	0	0	0	....	....	....	....	....	....	1950-51	1950-51
• Smith, Glenn	Tor.	1	9	0	0	0	0	....	....	....	....	....	....	1921-22	1921-22
Smith, Gord	Wsh., Wpg.	6	299	9	30	39	284	....	....	....	....	....	....	1974-75	1979-80
Smith, Greg	Cal., Cle., Min., Det., Wsh.	13	829	56	232	288	1110	63	4	7	11	106	....	1975-76	1987-88
• Smith, Hooley	Ott., Mtl.M., Bos., NYA	17	715	200	215	415	1013	54	11	8	19	109	2	1924-25	1940-41
Smith, Kenny	Bos.	7	331	78	93	171	49	30	8	13	21	6	....	1944-45	1950-51
Smith, Nakina	Det.	1	10	1	2	3	0	....	....	....	....	....	....	1943-44	1943-44
Smith, Randy	Min.	2	3	0	0	0	0	....	....	....	....	....	....	1985-86	1986-87
Smith, Rick	Bos., Cal., St.L., Det., Wsh.	11	687	52	167	219	560	78	3	23	26	73	1	1968-69	1980-81
• Smith, Rodger	Pit., Phi.	6	210	20	4	24	172	4	3	0	3	0	....	1925-26	1930-31
Smith, Ron	NYI	1	11	1	1	2	14	....	....	....	....	....	....	1972-73	1972-73
Smith, Sid	Tor.	12	601	186	183	369	94	44	17	10	27	2	3	1946-47	1957-58
Smith, Stan	NYR	2	9	2	1	3	0	1	0	0	0	0	1	1939-40	1940-41
Smith, Steve	Phi., Phialdelphia, Buf.	6	18	0	1	1	15	....	....	....	....	....	....	1981-82	1988-89
Smith, Stu	Mtl.	2	4	2	2	4	2	1	0	0	0	0	....	1940-41	1941-42
Smith, Stu G.	Hfd.	4	77	2	10	12	95	....	....	....	....	....	....	1979-80	1982-83
• Smith, Tommy	Que.	1	10	0	1	1	11	....	....	....	....	....	....	1919-20	1919-20
Smith, Vern	NYI	1	1	0	0	0	0	....	....	....	....	....	....	1984-85	1984-85
Smith, Wayne	Chi.	1	2	1	1	2	2	1	0	0	0	0	....	1966-67	1966-67
Smrke, John	St.L., Que.	3	103	11	17	28	33	....	....	....	....	....	....	1977-78	1979-80
• Smrke, Stan	Mtl.	2	9	0	3	3	0	....	....	....	....	....	....	1956-57	1957-58
Smyl, Stan	Van.	13	896	262	411	673	1556	41	16	17	33	64	....	1978-79	1990-91
• Smylie, Rod	Tor., Ott.	6	75	3	2	5	10	9	1	3	4	2	1	1920-21	1925-26
Smyth, Kevin	Hfd.	3	58	6	8	14	31	....	....	....	....	....	....	1993-94	1995-96
Snell, Chris	Tor., L.A.	2	34	2	7	9	24	....	....	....	....	....	....	1993-94	1994-95
Snell, Ron	Pit.	2	7	3	2	5	6	....	....	....	....	....	....	1968-69	1969-70
Snell, Ted	Pit., K.C., Det.	2	104	7	18	25	22	....	....	....	....	....	....	1973-74	1974-75
Snepsts, Harold	Van., Min., Det., St.L.	17	1033	38	195	233	2009	93	1	14	15	231	....	1974-75	1990-91
Snow, Sandy	Det.	1	3	0	0	0	2	....	....	....	....	....	....	1968-69	1968-69
Snuggerud, Dave	Buf., S.J., Phi.	4	265	30	54	84	127	12	1	3	4	6	....	1989-90	1992-93
Sobchuk, Dennis	Det., Que.	2	35	5	6	11	2	....	....	....	....	....	....	1979-80	1982-83
• Sobchuk, Gene	Van.	1	1	0	0	0	0	....	....	....	....	....	....	1973-74	1973-74
Solheim, Ken	Chi., Min., Det., Edm.	5	135	19	20	39	34	3	1	1	2	2	....	1980-81	1985-86
Solinger, Bob	Tor., Det.	5	99	10	11	21	19	....	....	....	....	....	....	1951-52	1959-60
• Somers, Art	Chi., NYR	6	222	33	56	89	189	30	1	5	6	20	1	1929-30	1934-35
Sommer, Roy	Edm.	1	3	1	0	1	7	....	....	....	....	....	....	1980-81	1980-81
Songin, Tom	Bos.	3	43	5	5	10	22	....	....	....	....	....	....	1978-79	1980-81
Sonmor, Glen	NYR	2	28	2	0	2	21	....	....	....	....	....	....	1953-54	1954-55
• Sorrell, John	Det., NYA	11	490	127	119	246	100	42	12	15	27	10	2	1930-31	1940-41
• Sparrow, Emory	Bos.	1	6	0	0	0	4	....	....	....	....	....	....	1924-25	1924-25
Speck, Fred	Det., Van.	3	28	1	2	3	2	....	....	....	....	....	....	1968-69	1971-72
• Speer, Bill	Pit., Bos.	4	130	5	20	25	79	8	1	0	1	4	1	1967-68	1970-71
Speers, Ted	Det.	1	4	1	1	2	0	....	....	....	....	....	....	1985-86	1985-86
• Spence, Gordon	Tor.	1	3	0	0	0	0	....	....	....	....	....	....	1925-26	1925-26
• Spencer, Brian	Tor., NYI, Buf., Pit.	10	553	80	143	223	634	37	1	5	6	29	....	1969-70	1978-79
Spencer, Irv	NYR, Bos., Det.	8	230	12	38	50	127	16	0	0	0	8	....	1959-60	1967-68
• Speyer, Chris	Tor., NYA	3	14	0	0	0	0	....	....	....	....	....	....	1923-24	1933-34
Spring, Don	Wpg.	4	259	1	54	55	80	6	0	0	0	10	....	1980-81	1983-84
Spring, Frank	Bos., St.L., Cal., Cle.	5	61	14	20	34	12	....	....	....	....	....	....	1969-70	1976-77
• Spring, Jesse	Ham., Pit., Tor., NYA	6	162	11	2	13	62	2	0	2	2	2	....	1923-24	1929-30
Spruce, Andy	Van., Col.	3	172	31	42	73	111	2	0	2	2	0	....	1976-77	1978-79
Srsen, Tomas	Edm.	1	2	0	0	0	0	....	....	....	....	....	....	1990-91	1990-91
St. Amour, Martin	Ott.	1	1	0	0	0	2	....	....	....	....	....	....	1992-93	1992-93
St. Laurent, Andre	NYI, Det., L.A., Pit.	11	644	129	187	316	749	59	8	12	20	48	....	1973-74	1983-84
St. Laurent, Dollard	Mtl., Chi.	12	652	29	133	162	496	92	2	22	24	87	5	1950-51	1961-62
St. Marseille, Frank	St.L., L.A.	10	707	140	285	425	242	88	20	25	45	18	....	1967-68	1976-77
St. Sauveur, Claude	Atl.	1	79	24	24	48	23	2	0	0	0	0	....	1975-76	1975-76
Stackhouse, Ron	Cal., Det., Pit.	12	889	87	372	459	824	32	5	8	13	38	....	1970-71	1981-82
• Stackhouse, Ted	Tor.	1	13	0	0	0	2	5	0	0	0	0	1	1921-22	1921-22
• Stahan, Butch	Mtl.	1	....	....	....	....	....	3	0	1	1	2	....	1944-45	1944-45
Stajduhar, Nick	Edm.	1	2	0	0	0	4	....	....	....	....	....	....	1995-96	1995-96
Staley, Al	NYR	1	1	0	1	1	0	....	....	....	....	....	....	1948-49	1948-49
Stamler, Lorne	L.A., Tor., Wpg.	4	116	14	11	25	16	....	....	....	....	....	....	1976-77	1979-80
Standing, George	Min.	1	2	0	0	0	0	....	....	....	....	....	....	1967-68	1967-68
Stanfield, Fred	Chi., Bos., Min., Buf.	14	914	211	405	616	134	106	21	35	56	10	2	1964-65	1977-78
Stanfield, Jack	Chi.	1	....	....	....	....	....	1	0	0	0	0	....	1965-66	1965-66
Stanfield, Jim	L.A.	3	7	0	1	1	0	....	....	....	....	....	....	1969-70	1971-72
Stankiewicz, Ed	Det.	2	6	0	0	0	2	....	....	....	....	....	....	1953-54	1955-56
Stankiewicz, Myron	St.L., Phi.	1	35	0	7	7	36	1	0	0	0	0	....	1968-69	1968-69
Stanley, Allan	NYR, Chi., Bos., Tor., Phi.	21	1244	100	333	433	792	109	7	36	43	80	4	1948-49	1968-69
• Stanley, Barney	Chi.	1	1	0	0	0	0	....	....	....	....	....	....	1927-28	1927-28
Stanley, Daryl	Phi., Van.	6	189	8	17	25	408	17	0	0	0	30	....	1983-84	1989-90
Stanowski, Wally	Tor., NYR	10	428	23	88	111	160	60	3	14	17	13	4	1939-40	1950-51
Stanton, Paul	Pit., Bos., NYI	5	295	14	49	63	262	44	2	10	12	66	2	1990-91	1994-95
Stapleton, Brian	Wsh.	1	1	0	0	0	0	....	....	....	....	....	....	1975-76	1975-76
Stapleton, Pat	Bos., Chi.	10	635	43	294	337	353	65	10	39	49	38	....	1961-62	1972-73
Starikov, Sergei	N.J.	1	16	0	1	1	8	....	....	....	....	....	....	1989-90	1989-90
• Starr, Harold	Ott., Mtl.M., Mtl.C., NYR	7	205	6	5	11	186	15	1	0	1	4	....	1929-30	1935-36
Starr, Wilf	NYA, Det.	4	87	8	6	14	25	7	0	2	2	2	....	1932-33	1935-36
Stasiuk, Vic	Chi., Det., Bos.	14	745	183	254	437	669	69	16	18	34	40	3	1949-50	1962-63
Stastny, Anton	Que.	9	650	252	384	636	150	66	20	32	52	31	....	1980-81	1988-89
Stastny, Marian	Que., Tor.	5	322	121	173	294	110	32	5	17	22	7	....	1981-82	1985-86
Stastny, Peter	Que., N.J., St.L.	15	977	450	789	1239	824	93	33	72	105	123	....	1980-81	1994-95
Staszak, Ray	Det.	1	4	0	1	1	7	....	....	....	....	....	....	1985-86	1985-86
• Steele, Frank	Det.	1	1	0	0	0	0	....	....	....	....	....	....	1930-31	1930-31
Steen, Anders	Wpg.	1	42	5	11	16	22	....	....	....	....	....	....	1980-81	1980-81
Steen, Thomas	Wpg.	14	950	264	553	817	753	56	12	32	44	62	....	1981-82	1994-95
Stefaniw, Morris	Atl.	1	13	1	1	2	2	....	....	....	....	....	....	1972-73	1972-73
Stefanski, Bud	NYR	1	1	0	0	0	0	....	....	....	....	....	....	1977-78	1977-78
Stemkowski, Pete	Tor., Det., NYR, L.A.	15	967	206	349	555	866	83	25	29	54	136	1	1963-64	1977-78
Stenlund, Vern	Cle.	1	4	0	0	0	0	....	....	....	....	....	....	1976-77	1976-77
• Stephens, Phil	Mtl., Mtl.C., Bos.	3	25	1	0	1	3	....	....	....	....	....	....	1917-18	1925-26
Stephenson, Bob	Hfd., Tor.	1	18	2	3	5	4	....	....	....	....	....	....	1979-80	1979-80
Sterner, Ulf	NYR	1	4	0	0	0	0	....	....	....	....	....	....	1964-65	1964-65
Stevens, Mike	Van., Bos., NYI, Tor.	4	23	1	4	5	29	....	....	....	....	....	....	1984-85	1989-90
Stevenson, Shayne	Bos., T.B.	3	27	0	2	2	35	....	....	....	....	....	....	1990-91	1992-93
Stewart, Allan	N.J., Bos.	6	64	6	4	10	243	....	....	....	....	....	....	1985-86	1991-92

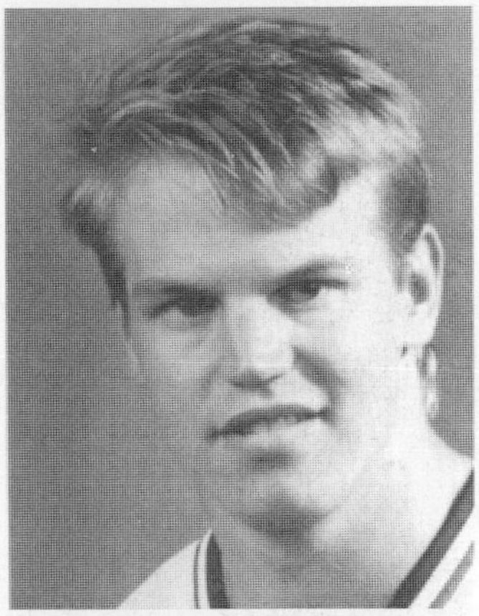
Jim Storm

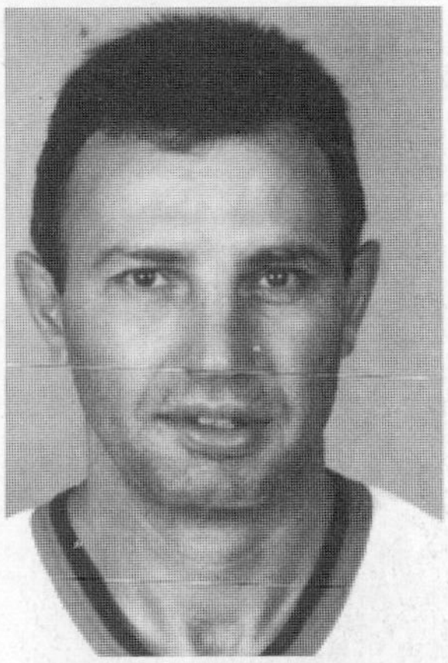
Brent Sutter

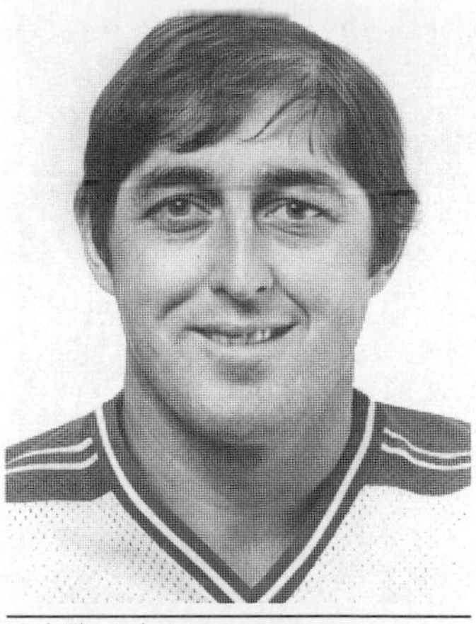
Walt Tkaczuk

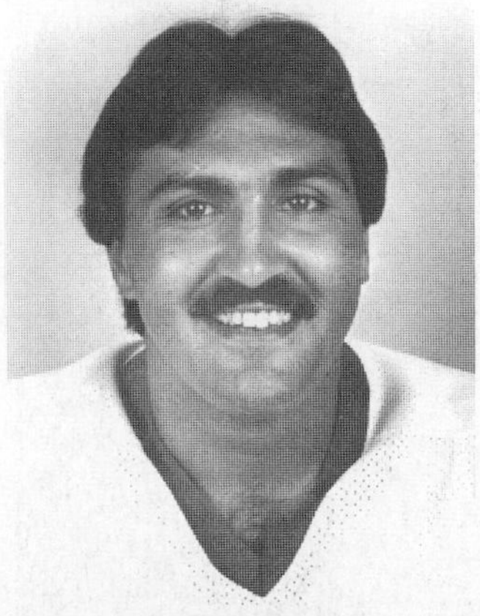
John Tonelli

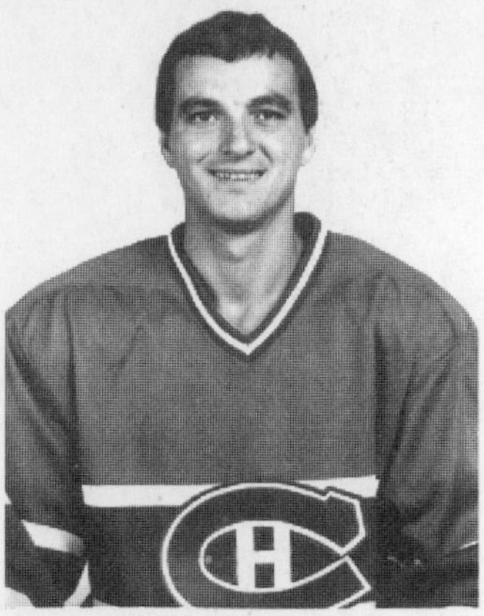
Mario Tremblay

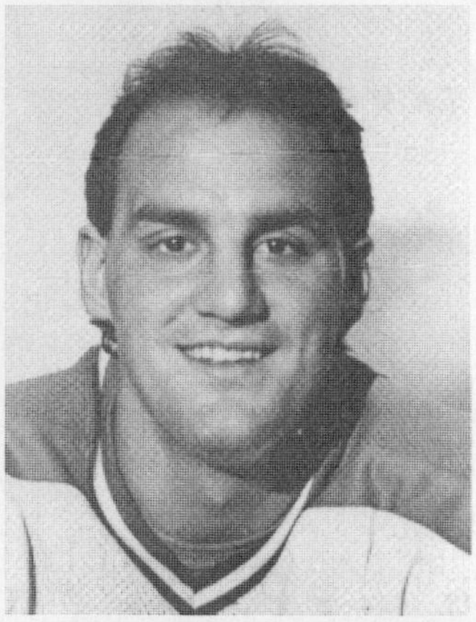
Tim Trimper

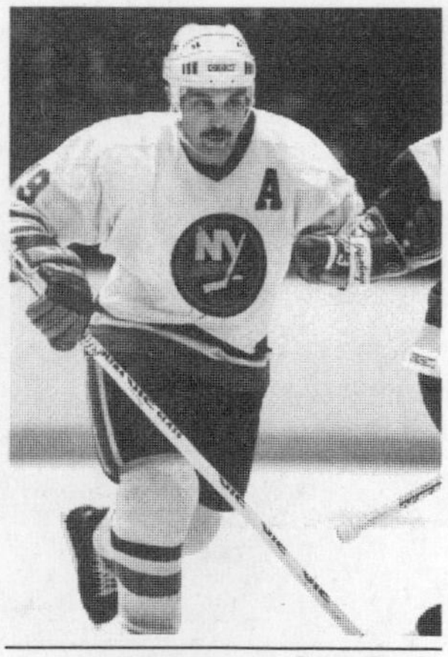
Bryan Trottier

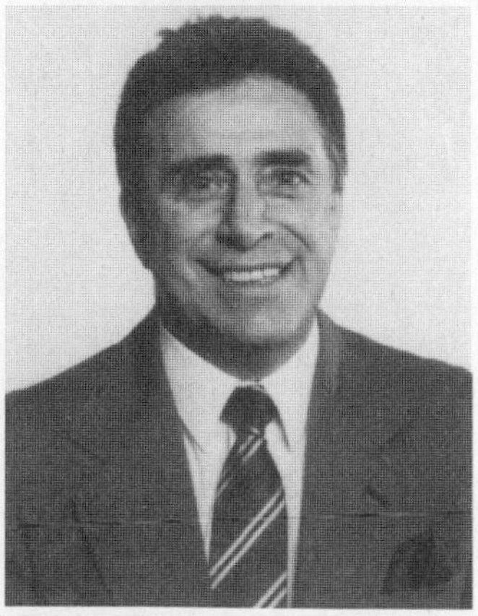
Gene Ubriaco

Name	NHL Teams	NHL Seasons	Regular Schedule GP	G	A	TP	PIM	Playoffs GP	G	A	TP	PIM	NHL Cup Wins	First NHL Season	Last NHL Season
Stewart, Bill	Buf., St.L., Tor., Min.	8	261	7	64	71	424	13	1	3	4	11	....	1977-78	1985-86
Stewart, Blair	Det., Wsh., Que.	7	229	34	44	78	326	....	....	....	....	....	....	1973-74	1979-80
Stewart, Gaye	Tor., Chi., Det., NYR, Mtl.	11	502	185	159	344	274	25	2	9	11	16	2	1941-42	1953-54
• Stewart, Jack	Det., Chi.	12	565	31	84	115	765	80	5	14	19	143	2	1938-39	1951-52
Stewart, John	Que.	1	2	0	0	0	0	....	....	....	....	....	....	1979-80	1979-80
Stewart, John A.	Pit., Atl., Cal.	5	258	58	60	118	158	4	0	0	0	10	....	1970-71	1974-75
• Stewart, Ken	Chi.	1	6	1	1	2	2	....	....	....	....	....	....	1941-42	1941-42
• Stewart, Nels	Mtl.M., Bos., NYA	15	650	324	191	515	953	54	15	13	28	61	1	1925-26	1939-40
Stewart, Paul	Que.	1	21	2	0	2	74	....	....	....	....	....	....	1979-80	1979-80
Stewart, Ralph	Van., NYI	7	252	57	73	130	28	19	4	4	8	2	....	1970-71	1977-78
Stewart, Robert	Bos., Cal., Cle., St.L., Pit.	9	575	27	101	128	809	5	1	1	2	2	....	1971-72	1979-80
Stewart, Ron	Tor., Bos., St.L., NYR, Van., NYI	21	1353	276	253	529	560	119	14	21	35	60	3	1952-53	1972-73
Stewart, Ryan	Wpg.	1	3	1	0	1	0	....	....	....	....	....	....	1985-86	1985-86
Stienburg, Trevor	Que.	4	71	8	4	12	161	1	0	0	0	0	....	1985-86	1988-89
Stiles, Tony	Cgy.	1	30	2	7	9	20	....	....	....	....	....	....	1983-84	1983-84
Stoddard, Jack	NYR	2	80	16	15	31	31	....	....	....	....	....	....	1951-52	1952-53
Stoltz, Roland	Wsh.	1	14	2	2	4	14	....	....	....	....	....	....	1981-82	1981-82
Stone, Steve	Van.	1	2	0	0	0	0	....	....	....	....	....	....	1973-74	1973-74
Storm, Jim	Hfd., Dal.	3	84	7	15	22	44	....	....	....	....	....	....	1993-94	1995-96
Stothers, Mike	Phi., Tor.	4	30	0	2	2	65	5	0	0	0	11	....	1984-85	1987-88
Stoughton, Blaine	Pit., Tor., Hfd., NYR	8	526	258	191	449	204	8	4	2	6	2	....	1973-74	1983-84
Stoyanovich, Steve	Hfd.	1	23	3	5	8	11	....	....	....	....	....	....	1983-84	1983-84
• Strain, Neil	NYR	1	52	11	13	24	12	....	....	....	....	....	....	1952-53	1952-53
Strate, Gord	Det.	3	61	0	0	0	34	....	....	....	....	....	....	1956-57	1958-59
Stratton, Art	NYR, Det., Chi., Pit., Phi.	4	95	18	33	51	24	5	0	0	0	0	....	1959-60	1967-68
Strobel, Art	NYR	1	7	0	0	0	0	....	....	....	....	....	....	1943-44	1943-44
Strong, Ken	Tor.	3	15	2	2	4	6	....	....	....	....	....	....	1982-83	1984-85
Struch, David	Cgy.	1	4	0	0	0	4	....	....	....	....	....	....	1993-94	1993-94
Strueby, Todd	Edm.	3	5	0	1	1	2	....	....	....	....	....	....	1981-82	1983-84
• Stuart, Billy	Tor., Bos.	7	195	30	18	48	145	17	1	3	4	12	1	1920-21	1926-27
Stumpf, Robert	St.L., Pit.	1	10	1	1	2	20	....	....	....	....	....	....	1974-75	1974-75
Sturgeon, Peter	Col.	2	6	0	1	1	2	....	....	....	....	....	....	1979-80	1980-81
Suikkanen, Kai	Buf.	2	2	0	0	0	0	....	....	....	....	....	....	1981-82	1982-83
Sulliman, Doug	NYR, Hfd., N.J., Phi.	11	631	160	168	328	175	16	1	3	4	2	....	1979-80	1989-90
Sullivan, Barry	Det.	1	1	0	0	0	0	....	....	....	....	....	....	1947-48	1947-48
Sullivan, Bob	Hfd.	1	62	18	19	37	18	....	....	....	....	....	....	1982-83	1982-83
Sullivan, Brian	N.J.	1	2	0	1	1	0	....	....	....	....	....	....	1992-93	1992-93
Sullivan, Frank	Tor., Chi.	4	8	0	0	0	2	....	....	....	....	....	....	1949-50	1955-56
Sullivan, Peter	Wpg.	2	126	28	54	82	40	....	....	....	....	....	....	1979-80	1980-81
Sullivan, Red	Bos., Chi., NYR	12	557	107	239	346	441	18	1	2	3	6	....	1949-50	1963-64
Summanen, Raimo	Edm., Van.	5	151	36	40	76	35	10	2	5	7	0	1	1983-84	1987-88
• Summerhill, Bill	Mtl.C., Mtl., Bro.	4	72	14	17	31	70	3	0	0	0	2	....	1937-38	1941-42
Sundblad, Niklas	Cgy.	1	2	0	0	0	0	....	....	....	....	....	....	1995-96	1995-96
Sundstrom, Patrik	Van., N.J.	10	679	219	369	588	349	37	9	17	26	25	....	1982-83	1991-92
Sundstrom, Peter	NYR, Wsh., N.J.	6	338	61	83	144	120	23	3	3	6	8	....	1983-84	1989-90
• Suomi, Al	Chi.	1	5	0	0	0	0	....	....	....	....	....	....	1936-37	1936-37
Sutherland, Bill	Mtl., Phi., Tor., St.L., Det.	6	250	70	58	128	99	14	2	4	6	0	....	1962-63	1971-72
• Sutherland, Max	Bos.	1	2	0	0	0	0	....	....	....	....	....	....	1931-32	1931-32
Sutter, Brent	NYI, Chi.	18	1111	363	466	829	1054	144	30	44	74	164	2	1980-81	1997-98
Sutter, Brian	St.L.	12	779	303	333	636	1786	65	21	21	42	249	....	1976-77	1987-88
Sutter, Darryl	Chi.	8	406	161	118	279	288	51	24	19	43	26	....	1979-80	1986-87
Sutter, Duane	NYI, Chi.	11	731	139	203	342	1333	161	26	32	58	405	4	1979-80	1989-90
Sutter, Rich	Pit., Phi., Van., St.L., Chi., T.B., Tor.	13	874	149	166	315	1411	78	13	5	18	133	....	1982-83	1994-95
Suzor, Mark	Phi., Col.	2	64	4	16	20	60	....	....	....	....	....	....	1976-77	1977-78
Svensson, Leif	Wsh.	2	121	6	40	46	49	....	....	....	....	....	....	1978-79	1979-80
Svensson, Magnus	Fla.	2	46	4	14	18	31	....	....	....	....	....	....	1994-95	1995-96
Swain, Garry	Pit.	1	9	1	1	2	0	....	....	....	....	....	....	1968-69	1968-69
Swarbrick, George	Oak., Pit., Phi.	4	132	17	25	42	173	....	....	....	....	....	....	1967-68	1970-71
• Sweeney, Bill	NYR	1	4	1	0	1	0	....	....	....	....	....	....	1959-60	1959-60
Sweeney, Bob	Bos., Buf., NYI, Cgy.	10	639	125	163	288	799	103	15	18	33	197	....	1986-87	1995-96
Sykes, Bob	Tor.	1	2	0	0	0	0	....	....	....	....	....	....	1974-75	1974-75
Sykes, Phil	L.A., Wpg.	10	456	79	85	164	519	26	0	3	3	29	....	1982-83	1991-92
Szura, Joe	Oak.	2	90	10	15	25	30	7	2	3	5	2	....	1967-68	1968-69

T

Name	NHL Teams	NHL Seasons	Regular Schedule GP	G	A	TP	PIM	Playoffs GP	G	A	TP	PIM	NHL Cup Wins	First NHL Season	Last NHL Season
Taft, John	Det.	1	15	0	2	2	4	....	....	....	....	....	....	1978-79	1978-79
Taglianetti, Peter	Wpg., Min., Pit., T.B.	11	451	18	74	92	1106	53	2	8	10	103	2	1984-85	1994-95
Talafous, Dean	Atl., Min., NYR	8	497	104	154	258	163	21	4	7	11	11	....	1974-75	1981-82
Talakoski, Ron	NYR	2	9	0	1	1	33	....	....	....	....	....	....	1986-87	1987-88
Talbot, Jean-Guy	Mtl., Min., Det., St.L., Buf.	17	1056	43	242	285	1006	150	4	26	30	142	7	1954-55	1970-71
Tallon, Dale	Van., Chi., Pit.	10	642	98	238	336	568	33	2	10	12	45	....	1970-71	1979-80
Tambellini, Steve	NYI, Col., N.J., Cgy., Van.	10	553	160	150	310	105	2	0	1	1	0	1	1978-79	1987-88
Tanguay, Chris	Que.	1	2	0	0	0	0	....	....	....	....	....	....	1981-82	1981-82
Tannahill, Don	Van.	2	111	30	33	63	25	....	....	....	....	....	....	1972-73	1973-74
Tanti, Tony	Chi., Van., Pit., Buf.	11	697	287	273	560	661	30	3	12	15	27	....	1981-82	1991-92
Tardif, Marc	Mtl., Que.	8	517	194	207	401	443	62	13	15	28	75	2	1969-70	1982-83
Tatarinov, Mikhail	Wsh., Que., Bos.	4	161	21	48	69	184	....	....	....	....	....	....	1990-91	1993-94
Tatchell, Spence	NYR	1	1	0	0	0	0	....	....	....	....	....	....	1942-43	1942-43
• Taylor, Billy	Tor., Det., Bos., NYR	7	323	87	180	267	120	33	6	18	24	13	1	1939-40	1947-48
• Taylor, Billy Jr.	NYR	1	2	0	0	0	0	....	....	....	....	....	....	1964-65	1964-65
• Taylor, Bob	Bos.	1	8	0	0	0	6	....	....	....	....	....	....	1929-30	1929-30
Taylor, Dave	L.A.	17	1111	431	638	1069	1589	92	26	33	59	145	....	1977-78	1993-94
Taylor, Harry	Tor., Chi.	3	66	5	10	15	30	1	0	0	0	0	1	1946-47	1951-52
Taylor, Mark	Phi., Pit., Wsh.	5	209	42	68	110	73	6	0	0	0	0	....	1981-82	1985-86
• Taylor, Ralph	Chi., NYR	3	99	4	1	5	169	4	0	0	0	10	....	1927-28	1929-30
Taylor, Ted	NYR, Det., Min., Van.	6	166	23	35	58	181	....	....	....	....	....	....	1964-65	1971-72
Teal, Jeff	Mtl.	1	6	0	1	1	0	....	....	....	....	....	....	1984-85	1984-85
Teal, Skip	Bos.	1	1	0	0	0	0	....	....	....	....	....	....	1954-55	1954-55
Teal, Victor	NYI	1	1	0	0	0	0	....	....	....	....	....	....	1973-74	1973-74
Tebbutt, Greg	Que., Pit.	2	26	0	3	3	35	....	....	....	....	....	....	1979-80	1983-84
Tepper, Stephen	Chi.	1	1	0	0	0	0	....	....	....	....	....	....	1992-93	1992-93
Terbenche, Paul	Chi., Buf.	5	189	5	26	31	28	12	0	0	0	0	....	1967-68	1973-74
Terrion, Greg	L.A., Tor.	8	561	93	150	243	339	35	2	9	11	41	....	1980-81	1987-88
Terry, Bill	Min.	1	5	0	0	0	0	....	....	....	....	....	....	1987-88	1987-88
Tessier, Orval	Mtl., Bos.	3	59	5	7	12	6	....	....	....	....	....	....	1954-55	1960-61
Theberge, Greg	Wsh.	5	153	15	63	78	73	4	0	1	1	0	....	1979-80	1983-84
Thelin, Mats	Bos.	3	163	8	19	27	107	5	0	0	0	6	....	1984-85	1986-87
Thelven, Michael	Bos.	5	207	20	80	100	217	34	4	10	14	34	....	1985-86	1989-90
Therrien, Gaston	Que.	3	22	0	8	8	12	9	0	1	1	4	....	1980-81	1982-83
Thibaudeau, Gilles	Mtl., NYI, Tor.	5	119	25	37	62	40	8	3	3	6	2	....	1986-87	1990-91
Thibeault, Lorran	Det., Mtl.	2	5	0	2	2	2	....	....	....	....	....	....	1944-45	1945-46
Thiffault, Leo	Min.	1	....	....	....	....	....	5	0	0	0	0	....	1967-68	1967-68
Thomas, Cy	Chi., Tor.	1	14	2	2	4	12	....	....	....	....	....	....	1947-48	1947-48
Thomas, Reg	Que.	1	39	9	7	16	6	....	....	....	....	....	....	1979-80	1979-80
Thomlinson, Dave	St.L., Bos., L.A.	5	42	1	3	4	50	9	3	1	4	4	....	1989-90	1994-95
Thompson, Cliff	Bos.	2	13	0	1	1	2	....	....	....	....	....	....	1941-42	1948-49
Thompson, Errol	Tor., Det., Pit.	10	599	208	185	393	184	34	7	5	12	11	....	1970-71	1980-81
• Thompson, Kenneth	Mtl.	1	1	0	0	0	0	....	....	....	....	....	....	1917-18	1917-18
• Thompson, Paul	NYR, Chi.	14	582	153	179	332	336	48	11	11	22	54	3	1926-27	1939-40
• Thompson, Rhys	Mtl., Tor.	2	25	0	2	2	38	....	....	....	....	....	....	1939-40	1942-43
• Thoms, Bill	Tor., Chi., Bos.	13	548	135	206	341	154	44	6	10	16	6	....	1932-33	1944-45
Thomson, Bill	Det.	2	9	2	2	4	0	2	0	0	0	0	....	1938-39	1943-44
Thomson, Floyd	St.L.	8	411	56	97	153	341	10	0	2	2	6	....	1971-72	1979-80
Thomson, Jim	Wsh., Hfd., N.J., L.A., Ott., Ana.	7	115	4	3	7	416	1	0	0	0	0	....	1986-87	1993-94
• Thomson, Jimmy	Tor., Chi.	13	787	19	215	234	920	63	2	13	15	135	4	1945-46	1957-58
Thornbury, Tom	Pit.	1	14	1	8	9	16	....	....	....	....	....	....	1983-84	1983-84
• Thorsteinson, Joe	NYA	1	4	0	0	0	0	....	....	....	....	....	....	1932-33	1932-33
• Thurier, Fred	NYA, Bro., NYR	3	80	25	27	52	18	....	....	....	....	....	....	1940-41	1944-45
Thurlby, Tom	Oak.	1	20	1	1	2	4	....	....	....	....	....	....	1967-68	1967-68
Thyer, Mario	Min.	1	5	0	0	0	0	1	0	0	0	2	....	1989-90	1989-90

			Regular Schedule					Playoffs					NHL	First	Last
Name	NHL Teams	NHL Seasons	GP	G	A	TP	PIM	GP	G	A	TP	PIM	Cup Wins	NHL Season	NHL Season
Tichy, Milan	Chi., NYI	3	23	0	5	5	40	....	....	....	....	....	....	1992-93	1995-96
Tidey, Alex	Buf., Edm.	3	9	0	0	0	8	2	0	0	0	0	....	1976-77	1979-80
Tilley, Tom	St.L.	4	174	4	38	42	89	14	1	3	4	19	....	1988-89	1993-94
Timgren, Ray	Tor., Chi.	6	251	14	44	58	70	30	3	9	12	6	2	1948-49	1954-55
Tippett, Dave	Hfd., Wsh., Pit., Phi.	11	721	93	169	262	317	62	6	16	22	34	....	1983-84	1993-94
Titanic, Morris	Buf.	2	19	0	0	0	0	....	....	....	....	....	....	1974-75	1975-76
Tkaczuk, Walt	NYR	14	945	227	451	678	556	93	19	32	51	119	....	1967-68	1980-81
Toal, Mike	Edm.	1	3	0	0	0	0	....	....	....	....	....	....	1979-80	1979-80
Tomalty, Glenn	Wpg.	1	1	0	0	0	0	....	....	....	....	....	....	1979-80	1979-80
Tomlak, Mike	Hfd.	4	141	15	22	37	103	10	0	1	1	4	....	1989-90	1993-94
Tomlinson, Dave	Tor., Wpg., Fla.	4	42	1	3	4	28	....	....	....	....	....	....	1991-92	1994-95
Tomlinson, Kirk	Min.	1	1	0	0	0	0	....	....	....	....	....	....	1987-88	1987-88
Tomson, Jack	NYA	3	15	1	1	2	0	2	0	0	0	0	....	1938-39	1940-41
Tonelli, John	NYI, Cgy., L.A., Chi., Que.	14	1028	325	511	836	911	172	40	75	115	200	4	1978-79	1991-92
Tookey, Tim	Wsh., Que., Pit., Phi., L.A.	7	106	22	36	58	71	10	1	3	4	2	....	1980-81	1988-89
Toomey, Sean	Min.	1	1	0	0	0	0	....	....	....	....	....	....	1986-87	1986-87
Toppazzini, Jerry	Bos., Chi., Det.	12	783	163	244	407	436	40	13	9	22	13	....	1952-53	1963-64
Toppazzini, Zellio	Bos., NYR, Chi.	5	123	21	22	43	49	2	0	0	0	0	....	1948-49	1956-57
Torgayev, Pavel	Cgy.	1	41	6	10	16	14	1	0	0	0	0	....	1995-96	1995-96
Torkki, Jari	Chi.	1	4	1	0	1	0	....	....	....	....	....	....	1988-89	1988-89
Tormanen, Antti	Ott.	1	50	7	8	15	28	....	....	....	....	....	....	1995-96	1995-96
• Touhey, Bill	Mtl.M., Ott., Bos.	7	280	65	40	105	107	2	1	0	1	0	....	1927-28	1933-34
• Toupin, Jacques	Chi.	1	8	1	2	3	0	4	0	0	0	0	....	1943-44	1943-44
• Townsend, Art	Chi.	1	5	0	0	0	0	....	....	....	....	....	....	1926-27	1926-27
Townshend, Graeme	Bos., NYI, Ott.	5	45	3	7	10	28	....	....	....	....	....	....	1989-90	1993-94
Trader, Larry	Det., St.L., Mtl.	4	91	5	13	18	74	3	0	0	0	0	....	1982-83	1987-88
• Trainor, Wes	NYR	1	17	1	2	3	6	....	....	....	....	....	....	1948-49	1948-49
• Trapp, Bob	Chi.	2	82	4	4	8	129	2	0	0	0	4	....	1926-27	1927-28
Trapp, Doug	Buf.	1	2	0	0	0	0	....	....	....	....	....	....	1986-87	1986-87
• Traub, Percy	Chi., Det.	3	130	3	3	6	217	4	0	0	0	6	....	1926-27	1928-29
Tredway, Brock	L.A.	1	....	....	....	....	....	1	0	0	0	0	....	1981-82	1981-82
Tremblay, Brent	Wsh.	2	10	1	0	1	6	....	....	....	....	....	....	1978-79	1979-80
Tremblay, Gilles	Mtl.	9	509	168	162	330	161	48	9	14	23	4	3	1960-61	1968-69
• Tremblay, J.C.	Mtl.	13	794	57	306	363	204	108	14	51	65	58	5	1959-60	1971-72
Tremblay, Marcel	Mtl.C.	1	10	0	2	2	0	....	....	....	....	....	....	1938-39	1938-39
Tremblay, Mario	Mtl.	12	852	258	326	584	1043	101	20	29	49	187	5	1974-75	1985-86
• Tremblay, Nils	Mtl.	2	3	0	1	1	0	2	0	0	0	0	....	1944-45	1945-46
Trimper, Tim	Chi., Wpg., Min.	6	190	30	36	66	153	2	0	0	0	2	....	1979-80	1984-85
Trottier, Bryan	NYI, Pit.	18	1279	524	901	1425	912	221	71	113	184	277	6	1975-76	1993-94
• Trottier, Dave	Mtl.M., Det.	11	446	121	113	234	517	31	4	3	7	39	1	1928-29	1938-39
Trottier, Guy	NYR, Tor.	3	115	28	17	45	37	9	1	0	1	16	....	1968-69	1971-72
Trottier, Rocky	N.J.	2	38	6	4	10	2	....	....	....	....	....	....	1983-84	1984-85
• Trudel, Louis	Chi., Mtl.C., Mtl.	8	306	49	69	118	122	24	1	3	4	4	2	1933-34	1940-41
Trudell, Rene	NYR	3	129	24	28	52	72	5	0	0	0	2	....	1945-46	1947-48
Tsygurov, Denis	Buf., L.A.	3	51	1	5	6	45	....	....	....	....	....	....	1993-94	1995-96
Tucker, John	Buf., Wsh., NYI, T.B.	12	656	177	259	436	285	31	10	18	28	24	....	1983-84	1995-96
• Tudin, Connie	Mtl.	1	4	0	1	1	4	....	....	....	....	....	....	1941-42	1941-42
Tudor, Rob	Van., St.L.	3	28	4	4	8	19	3	0	0	0	0	....	1978-79	1982-83
Tuer, Allan	L.A., Min., Hfd.	4	57	1	1	2	208	....	....	....	....	....	....	1985-86	1989-90
Turcotte, Alfie	Mtl., Wpg., Wsh.	7	112	17	29	46	49	5	0	0	0	0	....	1983-84	1990-91
Turgeon, Sylvain	Hfd., N.J., Mtl., Ott.	12	669	269	226	495	691	36	4	7	11	22	....	1983-84	1994-95
Turlick, Gord	Bos.	1	2	0	0	0	2	....	....	....	....	....	....	1959-60	1959-60
Turnbull, Ian	Tor., L.A., Pit.	10	628	123	317	440	736	55	13	32	45	94	....	1973-74	1982-83
Turnbull, Perry	St.L., Mtl., Wpg.	9	608	188	163	351	1245	34	6	7	13	86	....	1979-80	1987-88
Turnbull, Randy	Cgy.	1	1	0	0	0	2	....	....	....	....	....	....	1981-82	1981-82
Turner, Bob	Mtl., Chi.	8	478	19	51	70	307	68	1	4	5	44	5	1955-56	1962-63
Turner, Brad	NYI	1	3	0	0	0	0	....	....	....	....	....	....	1991-92	1991-92
Turner, Dean	NYR, Col., L.A.	4	35	1	0	1	59	....	....	....	....	....	....	1978-79	1982-83
• Tustin, Norman	NYR	1	18	2	4	6	0	....	....	....	....	....	....	1941-42	1941-42
Tuten, Aut	Chi.	2	39	4	8	12	48	....	....	....	....	....	....	1941-42	1942-43
Tutt, Brian	Wsh.	1	7	1	0	1	2	....	....	....	....	....	....	1989-90	1989-90
Tuttle, Steve	St.L.	3	144	28	28	56	12	17	1	6	7	2	....	1988-89	1990-91

U V

Ubriaco, Gene	Pit., Oak., Chi.	3	177	39	35	74	50	11	2	0	2	4	....	1967-68	1969-70
Ullman, Norm	Det., Tor.	20	1410	490	739	1229	712	106	30	53	83	67	....	1955-56	1974-75
Unger, Garry	Tor., Det., St.L., Atl., L.A., Edm.	16	1105	413	391	804	1075	52	12	18	30	105	....	1967-68	1982-83
Vachon, Nick	NYI	1	1	0	0	0	0	....	....	....	....	....	....	1996-97	1996-97
Vadnais, Carol	Mtl., Oak., Cal., Bos., NYR, N.J.	17	1087	169	418	587	1813	106	10	40	50	185	2	1966-67	1982-83
Vail, Eric	Atl., Cgy., Det.	9	591	216	260	476	281	20	5	6	11	6	....	1973-74	1981-82
• Vail, Sparky	NYR	2	50	4	1	5	18	10	0	0	0	2	....	1928-29	1929-30
Vaive, Rick	Van., Tor., Chi., Buf.	13	876	441	347	788	1445	54	27	16	43	111	....	1979-80	1991-92
Valentine, Chris	Wsh.	3	105	43	52	95	127	2	0	0	0	4	....	1981-82	1983-84
Valiquette, Jack	Tor., Col.	7	350	84	134	218	79	23	3	6	9	4	....	1974-75	1980-81
Vallis, Lindsay	Mtl.	1	1	0	0	0	0	....	....	....	....	....	....	1993-94	1993-94
Van Boxmeer, John	Mtl., Col., Buf., Que.	11	588	84	274	358	465	38	5	15	20	37	1	1973-74	1983-84
Van Dorp, Wayne	Edm., Pit., Chi., Que.	6	125	12	12	24	565	27	0	1	1	42	1	1986-87	1991-92
Van Impe, Ed	Chi., Phi., Pit.	11	700	27	126	153	1025	66	1	12	13	131	2	1966-67	1976-77
Varvio, Jarkko	Dal.	2	13	3	4	7	4	....	....	....	....	....	....	1993-94	1994-95
• Vasko, Elmer	Chi., Min.	13	786	34	166	200	719	78	2	7	9	73	1	1956-57	1969-70
Vasko, Rick	Det.	3	31	3	7	10	29	....	....	....	....	....	....	1977-78	1980-81
Vautour, Yvon	NYI, Col., N.J., Que.	6	204	26	33	59	401	....	....	....	....	....	....	1979-80	1984-85
Vaydik, Greg	Chi.	1	5	0	0	0	0	....	....	....	....	....	....	1976-77	1976-77
Veitch, Darren	Wsh., Det., Tor.	10	511	48	209	257	296	33	4	11	15	33	....	1980-81	1990-91
Velischek, Randy	Min., N.J., Que.	10	509	21	76	97	401	44	2	5	7	32	....	1982-83	1991-92
Vellucci, Mike	Hfd.	1	2	0	0	0	11	....	....	....	....	....	....	1987-88	1987-88
Venasky, Vic	L.A.	7	430	61	101	162	66	21	1	5	6	12	....	1972-73	1978-79
Veneruzzo, Gary	St.L.	2	7	1	1	2	0	9	0	2	2	2	....	1967-68	1971-72
Vermette, Mark	Que.	4	67	5	13	18	33	....	....	....	....	....	....	1988-89	1991-92
Verret, Claude	Buf.	2	14	2	5	7	2	....	....	....	....	....	....	1983-84	1984-85
Verstraete, Leigh	Tor.	3	8	0	1	1	14	....	....	....	....	....	....	1982-83	1987-88
Ververgaert, Dennis	Van., Phi., Wsh.	8	583	176	216	392	247	8	1	2	3	6	....	1973-74	1980-81
Vesey, Jim	St.L., Bos.	3	15	1	2	3	7	....	....	....	....	....	....	1988-89	1991-92
Veysey, Sid	Van.	1	1	0	0	0	0	....	....	....	....	....	....	1977-78	1977-78
Vickers, Steve	NYR	10	698	246	340	586	330	68	24	25	49	58	....	1972-73	1981-82
Vigneault, Alain	St.L.	2	42	2	5	7	82	4	0	1	1	26	....	1981-82	1982-83
Viitakoski, Vesa	Cgy.	3	23	2	4	6	8	....	....	....	....	....	....	1993-94	1995-96
Vilgrain, Claude	Van., N.J., Phi.	5	89	21	32	53	78	11	1	1	2	17	....	1987-88	1993-94
Vincelette, Daniel	Chi., Que.	6	193	20	22	42	351	12	0	0	0	4	....	1986-87	1991-92
Vipond, Pete	Cal.	1	3	0	0	0	0	....	....	....	....	....	....	1972-73	1972-73
Virta, Hannu	Buf.	5	245	25	101	126	66	17	1	3	4	6	....	1981-82	1985-86
Vitolinsh, Harijs	Wpg.	1	8	0	0	0	4	....	....	....	....	....	....	1993-94	1993-94
Viveiros, Emanuel	Min.	3	29	1	11	12	6	....	....	....	....	....	....	1985-86	1987-88
• Vokes, Ed	Chi.	1	5	0	0	0	0	....	....	....	....	....	....	1930-31	1930-31
Volcan, Mickey	Hfd., Cgy.	4	162	8	33	41	146	....	....	....	....	....	....	1980-81	1983-84
Volek, David	NYI, NY Islabders	7	396	95	154	249	201	15	5	5	10	2	....	1988-89	1994-95
Volmar, Doug	Det., L.A.	4	62	13	8	21	26	2	1	0	1	0	....	1969-70	1972-73
• Voss, Carl	Tor., NYR, Det., Ott., St.L., NYA, Mtl.M., Chi.	8	261	34	70	104	50	24	5	3	8	0	1	1926-27	1937-38
Vyazmikin, Igor	Edm.	1	4	1	0	1	0	....	....	....	....	....	....	1990-91	1990-91

W

Waddell, Don	L.A.	1	1	0	0	0	0	....	....	....	....	....	....	1980-81	1980-81
• Waite, Frank	NYR	1	17	1	3	4	4	....	....	....	....	....	....	1930-31	1930-31
Walker, Gord	NYR, L.A.	4	31	3	4	7	23	....	....	....	....	....	....	1986-87	1989-90
Walker, Howard	Wsh., Cgy.	3	83	2	13	15	133	....	....	....	....	....	....	1980-81	1982-83
• Walker, Jack	Det.	2	80	5	8	13	18	....	....	....	....	....	....	1926-27	1927-28
Walker, Kurt	Tor.	3	71	4	5	9	142	16	0	0	0	34	....	1975-76	1977-78
Walker, Russ	L.A.	2	17	1	0	1	41	....	....	....	....	....	....	1976-77	1977-78

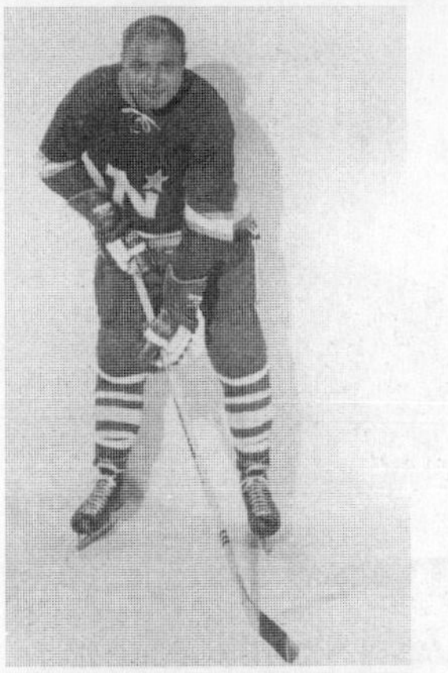
Moose Vasko

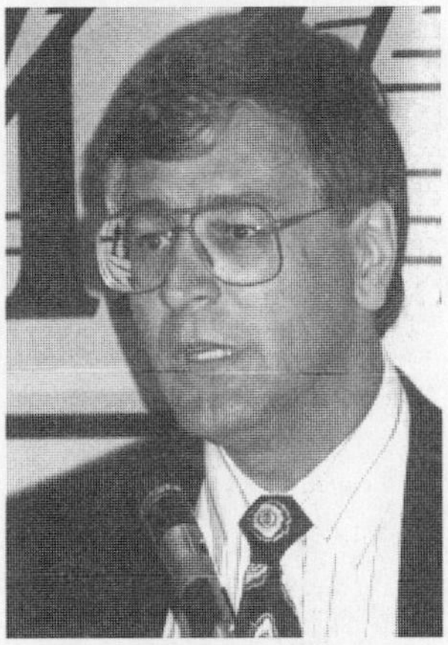
Tom Webster

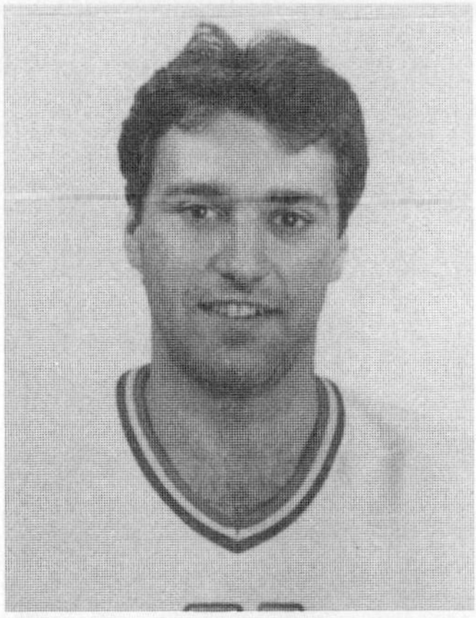
Doug Wickenheiser

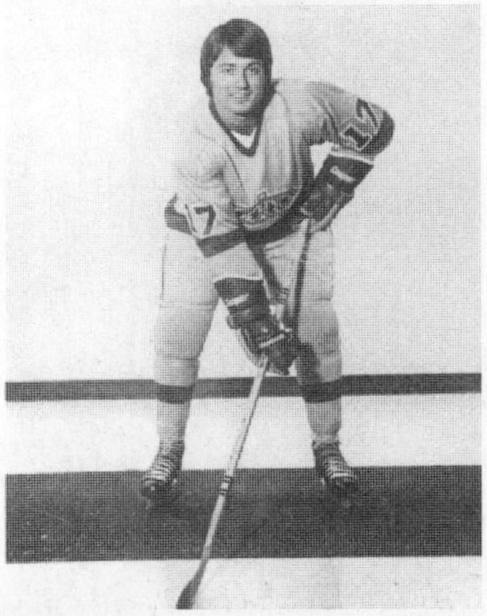
Tommy Williams

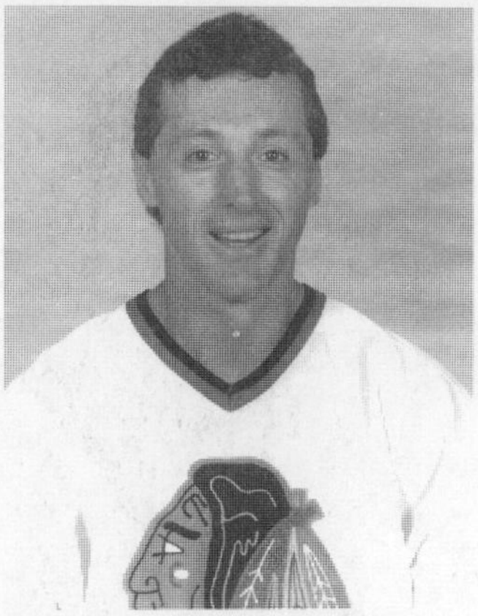

Doug Wilson

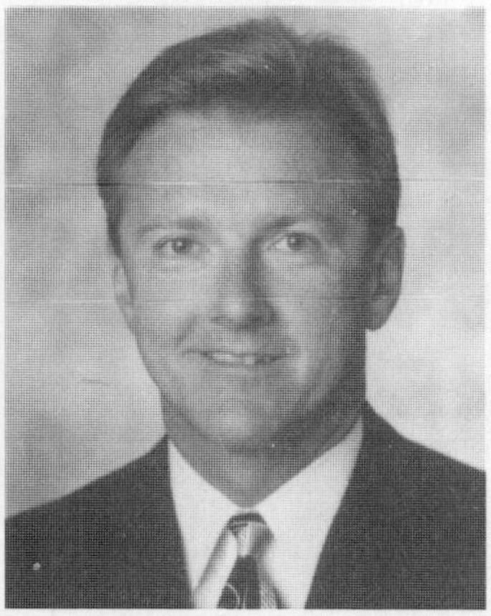

Ron Wilson

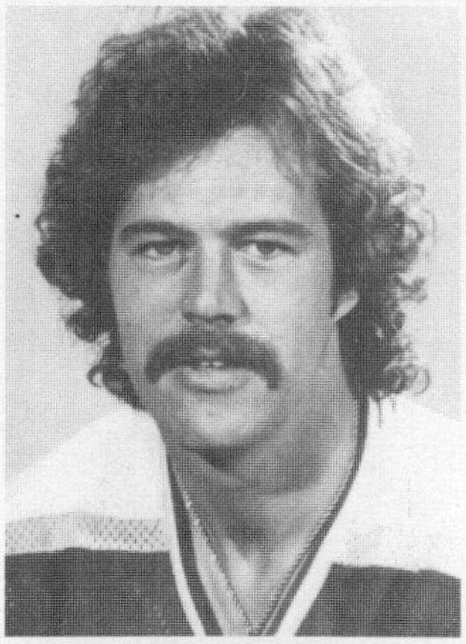

Tim Young

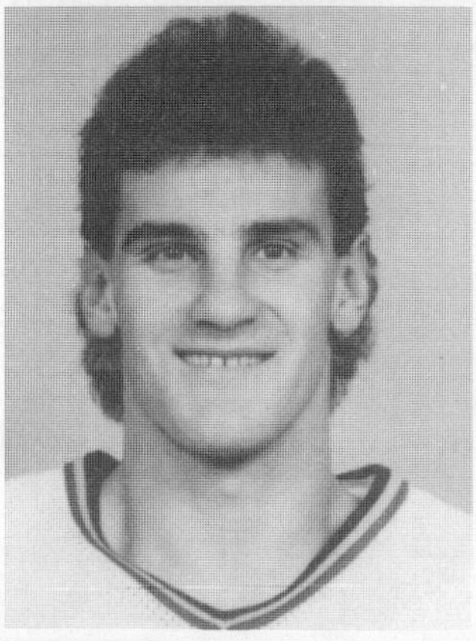

Richard Zemlak

Name	NHL Teams	NHL Seasons	Regular Schedule					Playoffs					NHL Cup Wins	First NHL Season	Last NHL Season
			GP	G	A	TP	PIM	GP	G	A	TP	PIM			
Wall, Bob	Det., L.A., St.L.	8	322	30	55	85	155	22	0	3	3	2	....	1964-65	1971-72
Wallin, Peter	NYR	2	52	3	14	17	14	14	2	6	8	6	....	1980-81	1981-82
Walsh, Jim	Buf.	1	4	0	1	1	4	....	....	....	....	....	....	1981-82	1981-82
Walsh, Mike	NYI	2	14	2	0	2	4	....	....	....	....	....	....	1987-88	1988-89
Walter, Ryan	Wsh., Mtl., Van.	15	1003	264	382	646	946	113	16	35	51	62	1	1978-79	1992-93
Walton, Bobby	Mtl.	1	4	0	0	0	0	....	....	....	....	....	....	1943-44	1943-44
Walton, Mike	Tor., Bos., Van., St.L., Chi.	12	588	201	247	448	357	47	14	10	24	45	2	1965-66	1978-79
Walz, Wes	Bos., Phi., Cgy., Det.	6	169	27	51	78	71	9	3	0	3	2	....	1989-90	1995-96
Wappel, Gord	Atl., Cgy.	3	20	1	1	2	10	2	0	0	0	4	....	1979-80	1981-82
Ward, Don	Chi., Bos.	2	34	0	1	1	16	....	....	....	....	....	....	1957-58	1959-60
• Ward, Jimmy	Mtl.M., Mtl.C.	12	527	147	127	274	455	36	4	4	8	26	1	1927-28	1938-39
Ward, Joe	Col.	1	4	0	0	0	2	....	....	....	....	....	....	1980-81	1980-81
Ward, Ron	Tor., Van.	2	89	2	5	7	6	....	....	....	....	....	....	1969-70	1971-72
Ware, Michael	Edm.	2	5	0	1	1	15	....	....	....	....	....	....	1988-89	1989-90
Wares, Eddie	NYR, Det., Chi.	9	321	60	102	162	161	45	5	7	12	34	1	1936-37	1946-47
Warner, Bob	Tor.	2	10	1	1	2	4	4	0	0	0	0	....	1975-76	1976-77
Warner, Jim	Hfd.	1	32	0	3	3	10	....	....	....	....	....	....	1979-80	1979-80
Warwick, Bill	NYR	2	14	3	3	6	16	....	....	....	....	....	....	1942-43	1943-44
Warwick, Grant	NYR, Bos., Mtl.	9	395	147	142	289	220	16	2	4	6	6	....	1941-42	1949-50
• Wasnie, Nick	Chi., Mtl.C., NYA, Ott., St.L.	7	248	57	34	91	176	14	6	3	9	20	....	1927-28	1934-35
Watson, Bill	Chi.	4	115	23	36	59	12	6	0	2	2	0	....	1985-86	1988-89
Watson, Bryan	Mtl., Det., Oak., Pit., St.L., Wsh.	16	878	17	135	152	2212	32	2	0	2	70	....	1963-64	1978-79
Watson, Dave	Col.	2	18	0	1	1	10	....	....	....	....	....	....	1979-80	1980-81
Watson, Harry	Bro., Det., Tor., Chi.	14	809	236	207	443	150	62	16	9	25	27	5	1941-42	1956-57
Watson, Jim A.	Det., Buf.	8	221	4	19	23	345	....	....	....	....	....	....	1963-64	1971-72
Watson, Jimmy	Phi.	10	613	38	148	186	492	101	5	34	39	89	2	1972-73	1981-82
Watson, Joe	Bos., Phi., Col.	14	835	38	178	216	447	84	3	12	15	82	2	1964-65	1978-79
• Watson, Phil	NYR, Mtl.	13	590	144	265	409	532	45	10	25	35	67	2	1935-36	1947-48
Watters, Tim	Wpg., L.A.	14	741	26	151	177	1289	82	1	5	6	115	....	1981-82	1994-95
Watts, Brian	Det.	1	4	0	0	0	0	....	....	....	....	....	....	1975-76	1975-76
• Webster, Aubrey	Phi., Mtl.M.	2	5	0	0	0	0	....	....	....	....	....	....	1930-31	1934-35
• Webster, Don	Tor.	1	27	7	6	13	28	5	0	0	0	12	....	1943-44	1943-44
Webster, John	NYR	1	14	0	0	0	4	....	....	....	....	....	....	1949-50	1949-50
Webster, Tom	Bos., Det., Cal.	5	102	33	42	75	61	1	0	0	0	0	....	1968-69	1979-80
• Weiland, Cooney	Bos., Ott., Det.	12	509	173	160	333	147	45	12	10	22	12	2	1928-29	1939-40
Weir, Stan	Cal., Tor., Edm., Col., Det.	10	642	139	207	346	183	37	6	5	11	4	....	1972-73	1982-83
Weir, Wally	Que., Hfd., Pit.	6	320	21	45	66	625	23	0	1	1	96	....	1979-80	1984-85
• Wellington, Alex	Que.	1	1	0	0	0	0	....	....	....	....	....	....	1919-20	1919-20
Wells, Jay	L.A., Phi., Buf., NYR, St.L., T.B.	18	1098	47	216	263	2359	114	3	14	17	213	1	1979-80	1996-97
Wensink, John	St.L., Bos., Que., Col., N.J.	8	403	70	68	138	840	43	2	6	8	86	....	1973-74	1982-83
• Wentworth, Cy	Chi., Mtl.M., Mtl.C., Mtl.	13	575	39	68	107	355	35	5	6	11	20	1	1927-28	1939-40
Wesley, Blake	Phi., Hfd., Que., Tor.	7	298	18	46	64	486	19	2	2	4	30	....	1979-80	1985-86
Westfall, Ed	Bos., NYI	18	1220	231	394	625	544	95	22	37	59	41	2	1961-62	1978-79
Wharram, Kenny	Chi.	14	766	252	281	533	222	80	16	27	43	38	1	1951-52	1968-69
Wharton, Len	NYR	1	1	0	0	0	0	....	....	....	....	....	....	1944-45	1944-45
Wheeldon, Simon	NYR, Wpg.	3	15	0	2	2	10	....	....	....	....	....	....	1987-88	1990-91
• Wheldon, Donald	St.L.	1	2	0	0	0	0	....	....	....	....	....	....	1974-75	1974-75
Whelton, Bill	Wpg.	1	2	0	0	0	0	....	....	....	....	....	....	1980-81	1980-81
Whistle, Rob	NYR, St.L.	2	51	7	5	12	16	4	0	0	0	2	....	1985-86	1987-88
White, Bill	L.A., Chi.	10	604	50	215	265	495	91	7	32	39	76	....	1967-68	1976-77
White, Moe	Mtl.	1	4	0	1	1	2	....	....	....	....	....	....	1945-46	1945-46
• White, Sherman	NYR	2	4	0	2	2	0	....	....	....	....	....	....	1946-47	1949-50
• White, Tex	Pit., NYA, Phi.	6	203	33	12	45	141	4	0	0	0	4	....	1925-26	1930-31
White, Tony	Wsh., Min.	5	164	37	28	65	104	....	....	....	....	....	....	1974-75	1979-80
Whitelaw, Bob	Det.	2	32	0	2	2	2	8	0	0	0	0	....	1940-41	1941-42
Whitlock, Bob	Min.	1	1	0	0	0	0	....	....	....	....	....	....	1969-70	1969-70
Whyte, Sean	L.A.	2	21	0	2	2	12	....	....	....	....	....	....	1991-92	1992-93
• Wickenheiser, Doug	Mtl., St.L., Van., NYR, Wsh.	10	556	111	165	276	286	41	4	7	11	18	....	1980-81	1989-90
• Widing, Juha	NYR, L.A., Cle.	8	575	144	226	370	208	8	1	2	3	2	....	1969-70	1976-77
• Wiebe, Art	Chi.	11	414	14	27	41	201	31	1	3	4	10	1	1932-33	1943-44
Wiemer, Jim	Buf., NYR, Edm., L.A., Bos.	11	325	29	72	101	378	62	5	8	13	63	1	1982-83	1993-94
• Wilcox, Archie	Mtl.M., Bos., St.L.	6	208	8	14	22	158	12	1	0	1	8	....	1929-30	1934-35
Wilcox, Barry	Van.	2	33	3	2	5	15	....	....	....	....	....	....	1972-73	1974-75
Wilder, Arch	Det.	1	18	0	2	2	2	....	....	....	....	....	....	1940-41	1940-41
Wiley, Jim	Pit., Van.	5	63	4	10	14	8	....	....	....	....	....	....	1972-73	1976-77
Wilkie, Bob	Det., Phi.	2	18	2	5	7	10	....	....	....	....	....	....	1990-91	1993-94
Wilkins, Barry	Bos., Van., Pit.	9	418	27	125	152	663	6	0	1	1	4	....	1966-67	1975-76
• Wilkinson, John	Bos.	1	9	0	0	0	6	....	....	....	....	....	....	1943-44	1943-44
Wilks, Brian	L.A.	4	48	4	8	12	27	....	....	....	....	....	....	1984-85	1988-89
Willard, Rod	Tor.	1	1	0	0	0	0	....	....	....	....	....	....	1982-83	1982-83
• Williams, Burr	Det., St.L., Bos.	3	19	0	1	1	28	7	0	0	0	8	....	1933-34	1936-37
Williams, Darryl	L.A.	1	2	0	0	0	10	....	....	....	....	....	....	1992-93	1992-93
Williams, Dave	Tor., Van., Det., L.A., Hfd.	14	962	241	272	513	3966	83	12	23	35	455	....	1974-75	1987-88
Williams, David	S.J., Ana.	4	173	11	53	64	157	....	....	....	....	....	....	1991-92	1994-95
Williams, Fred	Det.	1	44	2	5	7	10	....	....	....	....	....	....	1976-77	1976-77
Williams, Gord	Phi.	2	2	0	0	0	2	....	....	....	....	....	....	1981-82	1982-83
Williams, Sean	Chi.	1	2	0	0	0	4	....	....	....	....	....	....	1991-92	1991-92
Williams, Tom	NYR, L.A.	8	397	115	138	253	73	29	8	7	15	4	....	1971-72	1978-79
• Williams, Tommy	Bos., Min., Cal., Wsh.	13	663	161	269	430	177	10	2	5	7	2	....	1961-62	1975-76
Williams, Warren	St.L., Cal.	3	108	14	35	49	131	....	....	....	....	....	....	1973-74	1975-76
Willson, Don	Mtl.C.	2	22	2	7	9	0	3	0	0	0	0	....	1937-38	1938-39
Wilson, Behn	Phi., Chi.	9	601	98	260	358	1480	67	12	29	41	190	....	1978-79	1987-88
• Wilson, Bert	NYR, St.L., L.A., Cgy.	8	478	37	44	81	646	21	0	2	2	42	....	1973-74	1980-81
Wilson, Bob	Chi.	1	1	0	0	0	0	....	....	....	....	....	....	1953-54	1953-54
Wilson, Carey	Cgy., Hfd., NYR	10	552	169	258	427	314	52	11	13	24	14	....	1983-84	1992-93
• Wilson, Cully	Tor., Mtl.C., Ham., Chi.	5	125	59	24	83	238	2	1	0	1	6	....	1919-20	1926-27
Wilson, Doug	Chi., S.J.	16	1024	237	590	827	830	95	19	61	80	88	....	1977-78	1992-93
Wilson, Gord	Bos.	1	....	....	....	....	....	2	0	0	0	0	....	1954-55	1954-55
Wilson, Hub	NYA	1	2	0	0	0	0	....	....	....	....	....	....	1931-32	1931-32
Wilson, Jerry	Mtl.	1	3	0	0	0	2	....	....	....	....	....	....	1956-57	1956-57
Wilson, Johnny	Det., Chi., Tor., NYR	13	688	161	171	332	190	66	14	13	27	11	4	1949-50	1961-62
• Wilson, Larry	Det., Chi.	6	152	21	48	69	75	4	0	0	0	0	1	1949-50	1955-56
Wilson, Mitch	N.J., Pit.	2	26	2	3	5	104	....	....	....	....	....	....	1984-85	1986-87
Wilson, Murray	Mtl., L.A.	7	386	94	95	189	162	53	5	14	19	32	3	1972-73	1978-79
Wilson, Rick	Mtl., St.L., Det.	4	239	6	26	32	165	3	0	0	0	0	....	1973-74	1976-77
Wilson, Rik	St.L., Cgy., Chi.	6	251	25	65	90	220	22	0	4	4	23	....	1981-82	1987-88
Wilson, Roger	Chi.	1	7	0	2	2	6	....	....	....	....	....	....	1974-75	1974-75
Wilson, Ron	Tor., Min.	7	177	26	67	93	68	20	4	13	17	8	....	1977-78	1987-88
Wilson, Ron	Wpg., St.L., Mtl.	14	832	110	216	326	415	63	10	12	22	64	....	1979-80	1993-94
Wilson, Wally	Bos.	1	53	11	8	19	18	1	0	0	0	0	....	1947-48	1947-48
Wing, Murray	Det.	1	1	0	1	1	0	....	....	....	....	....	....	1973-74	1973-74
• Wiseman, Eddie	Det., NYA, Bos.	10	456	115	165	280	136	43	10	10	20	16	1	1932-33	1941-42
Wiste, Jim	Chi., Van.	3	52	1	10	11	8	....	....	....	....	....	....	1968-69	1970-71
Witherspoon, Jim	L.A.	1	2	0	0	0	2	....	....	....	....	....	....	1975-76	1975-76
Witiuk, Steve	Chi.	1	33	3	8	11	14	....	....	....	....	....	....	1951-52	1951-52
Woit, Benny	Det., Chi.	7	334	7	26	33	170	41	2	6	8	18	3	1950-51	1956-57
Wojciechowski, Steven	Det.	2	54	19	20	39	17	6	0	1	1	0	....	1944-45	1946-47
Wolf, Bennett	Pit.	3	30	0	1	1	133	....	....	....	....	....	....	1980-81	1982-83
Wong, Mike	Det.	1	22	1	1	2	12	....	....	....	....	....	....	1975-76	1975-76
Wood, Randy	NYI, Buf., Tor., Dal.	11	741	175	159	334	603	51	8	9	17	40	....	1986-87	1996-97
Wood, Robert	NYR	1	1	0	0	0	0	....	....	....	....	....	....	1950-51	1950-51
Woodley, Dan	Van.	1	5	2	0	2	17	....	....	....	....	....	....	1987-88	1987-88
Woods, Paul	Det.	7	501	72	124	196	276	7	0	5	5	4	....	1977-78	1983-84
Wortman, Kevin	Cgy.	1	5	0	0	0	2	....	....	....	....	....	....	1993-94	1993-94
• Woytowich, Bob	Bos., Min., Pit., L.A.	8	503	32	126	158	352	24	1	3	4	20	....	1964-65	1971-72
Wright, John	Van., St.L., K.C.	3	127	16	36	52	67	....	....	....	....	....	....	1972-73	1974-75
Wright, Keith	Phi.	1	1	0	0	0	0	....	....	....	....	....	....	1967-68	1967-68
Wright, Larry	Phi., Cal., Det.	5	106	4	8	12	19	....	....	....	....	....	....	1971-72	1977-78
Wycherley, Ralph	NYA, Bro.	2	28	4	7	11	6	....	....	....	....	....	....	1940-41	1941-42
Wylie, Duane	Chi.	2	14	3	3	6	2	....	....	....	....	....	....	1974-75	1976-77
• Wylie, William	NYR	1	1	0	0	0	0	....	....	....	....	....	....	1950-51	1950-51

Name	NHL Teams	NHL Seasons	Regular Schedule					Playoffs					NHL Cup Wins	First NHL Season	Last NHL Season
			GP	G	A	TP	PIM	GP	G	A	TP	PIM			
Wyrozub, Randy	Buf.	4	100	8	10	18	10	....	....	....	....	....	....	1970-71	1973-74

Y Z

Name	NHL Teams	NHL Seasons	GP	G	A	TP	PIM	GP	G	A	TP	PIM	NHL Cup Wins	First NHL Season	Last NHL Season
• Yackel, Ken	Bos.	1	6	0	0	0	2	2	0	0	0	2	....	1958-59	1958-59
Yaremchuk, Gary	Tor.	4	34	1	4	5	28	....	....	....	....	....	....	1981-82	1984-85
Yaremchuk, Ken	Chi., Tor.	6	235	36	56	92	106	31	6	8	14	49	....	1983-84	1988-89
Yates, Ross	Hfd.	1	7	1	1	2	4	....	....	....	....	....	....	1983-84	1983-84
Young, Brian	Chi.	1	8	0	2	2	6	....	....	....	....	....	....	1980-81	1980-81
Young, C.J.	Cgy., Bos.	1	43	7	7	14	32	....	....	....	....	....	....	1992-93	1992-93
• Young, Doug	Det., Mtl.	10	388	35	45	80	303	28	1	5	6	16	1	1931-32	1940-41
Young, Howie	Det., Chi., Van.	8	336	12	62	74	851	19	2	4	6	46	....	1960-61	1970-71
Young, Tim	Min., Wpg., Phi.	10	628	195	341	536	438	36	7	24	31	27	....	1975-76	1984-85
Young, Warren	Min., Pit., Det.	7	236	72	77	149	472	....	....	....	....	....	....	1981-82	1987-88
Younghans, Tom	Min., NYR	6	429	44	41	85	373	24	2	1	3	21	....	1976-77	1981-82
Zaharko, Miles	Atl., Chi.	4	129	5	32	37	84	3	0	0	0	0	....	1977-78	1981-82
Zaine, Rod	Pit., Buf.	2	61	10	6	16	25	....	....	....	....	....	....	1970-71	1971-72
Zanussi, Joe	NYR, Bos., St.L.	3	87	1	13	14	46	4	0	1	1	2	....	1974-75	1976-77
Zanussi, Ron	Min., Tor.	5	299	52	83	135	373	17	0	4	4	17	....	1977-78	1981-82
Zavisha, Brad	Edm.	2	2	0	0	0	0	....	....	....	....	....	....	1992-93	1993-94
Zeidel, Larry	Det., Chi., Phi.	5	158	3	16	19	198	12	0	1	1	12	1	1951-52	1968-69
Zemlak, Richard	Que., Min., Pit., Cgy.	5	132	2	12	14	587	1	0	0	0	10	....	1986-87	1991-92
Zeniuk, Ed	Det.	1	2	0	0	0	0	....	....	....	....	....	....	1954-55	1954-55
Zetterstrom, Lars	Van.	1	14	0	1	1	2	....	....	....	....	....	....	1978-79	1978-79
Zoborosky, Marty	Chi.	1	1	0	0	0	2	....	....	....	....	....	....	1944-45	1944-45
Zombo, Rick	Det., St.L., Bos.	12	652	24	130	154	728	60	1	11	12	127	....	1984-85	1995-96
Zuke, Mike	St.L., Hfd.	8	455	86	196	282	220	26	6	6	12	12	....	1978-79	1985-86
Zunich, Rudy	Det.	1	2	0	0	0	2	....	....	....	....	....	....	1943-44	1943-44

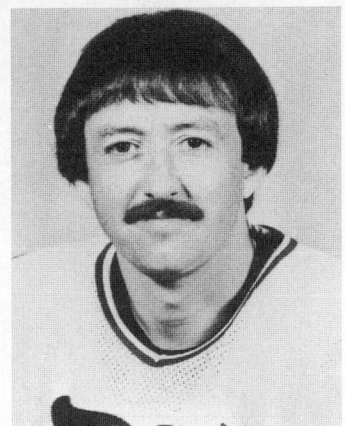

Mike Zuke

NOTE: Some players added to the Retired Player Index remain active in other leagues in North America and Europe. Players with NHL experience playing outside the NHL are placed in the Retired Player Index when they have completed one or more seasons of play after having been removed from an NHL club's reserve list. A player's age and his performance outside the NHL are considered in determining when he is moved from the active Player Register to the Retired Player Index.

Retired Players and Goaltenders Research Project

Throughout the Retired Players and Retired Goaltenders sections of this book, you will notice many players with a bullet (•) by their names. These players, according to our records, are deceased. The editors recognize that our information on the death dates of NHLers is incomplete. If you have documented information on the passing of any player not marked with a bullet (•) in this edition, we would like to hear from you. Please send this information to:

Retired Player Research Project
c/o NHL Publishing
194 Dovercourt Road
Toronto, Ontario
M6J 3C8   Canada
Fax: 416/531-3939

Many thanks to the following contributors in 1998-99:

Tim Bateman, Kevin Bixby, Peter Borkowski, Paul R. Carroll, Jr., Bob Duff, Peter Fillman, Ernie Fitzsimmons, Scott Miller, Gary J. Pearce, Ed Sweeney, William Schmidt.

Jon Casey

Glenn Hall

Curt Ridley

Tim Cheveldae

Kelly Hrudey

Peter Sidorkiewicz

Alex Connell

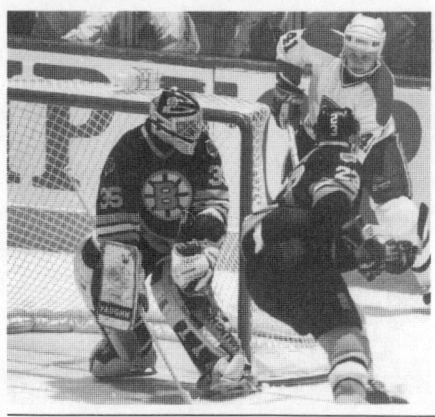

Andy Moog

Darcy Wakaluk

Doug Favell

Chuck Rayner

Dunc Wilson

Retired NHL Goaltender Index

Abbreviations: Teams/Cities: — **Ana.** – Anaheim; **Atl.** – Atlanta; **Bos.** – Boston, **Bro.** – Brooklyn; **Buf.** – Buffalo; **Cal.** – California; **Cgy.** – Calgary; **Cle.** – Cleveland; **Col.** – Colorado; **Dal.** – Dallas; **Det.** – Detroit; **Edm.** – Edmonton; **Fla.** – Florida; **Ham.** – Hamilton; **Hfd.** – Hartford; **K.C.** – Kansas City; **L.A.** – Los Angeles; **Min.** — Minnesota; **Mtl.** – Montreal; **Mtl. M.** – Montreal Maroons; **Mtl. W.** – Montreal Wanderers; **N.J.** – New Jersey; **NYA** – NY Americans; **NYI** – New York Islanders; **NYR** – New York Rangers; **Oak.** – Oakland; **Ott.** – Ottawa; **Phi.** – Philadelphia; **Pit.** – Pittsburgh; **Que.** – Quebec; **St. L.** – St. Louis; **S.J.** – San Jose; **T.B.** – Tampa Bay; **Tor.** – Toronto; **Van.** – Vancouver; **Wpg.** – Winnipeg; **Wsh.** – Washington.

Avg. – goals against per 60 minutes played; **GA** – goals against; **GP** – games played; **Mins** – minutes played; **SO** – shutouts.

● – deceased. § - Forward, defenseman or coach who appeared in goal. For complete career, see Retired Player Index.

			Regular Schedule								Playoffs										
Name	NHL Teams	NHL Seasons	GP	W	L	T	Mins	GA	SO	Avg	GP	W	L	T	Mins	GA	SO	Avg	NHL Cup Wins	First NHL Season	Last NHL Season
Abbott, George	Bos.	1	1	0	1	0	60	7	0	7.00	....	....	....	....	....	....	....	....		1943-44	1943-44
Adams, John	Bos., Wsh.	2	22	9	10	1	1180	85	1	4.32	....	....	....	....	....	....	....	....		1972-73	1974-75
Aiken, John	Mtl.	1	1	0	1	0	34	6	0	10.59	....	....	....	....	....	....	....	....		1957-58	1957-58
● Aikenhead, Andy	NYR	3	106	47	43	16	6570	257	11	2.35	10	6	2	2	608	15	3	1.48	1	1932-33	1934-35
Almas, Red	Det., Chi.	3	3	0	2	1	180	13	0	4.33	5	1	3	....	263	13	0	2.97		1946-47	1952-53
● Anderson, Lorne	NYR	1	3	1	2	0	180	18	0	6.00	....	....	....	....	....	....	....	....		1951-52	1951-52
Astrom, Hardy	NYR, Col.	3	83	17	44	12	4456	278	0	3.74	....	....	....	....	....	....	....	....		1977-78	1980-81
Baker, Steve	NYR	4	57	20	20	11	3081	190	3	3.70	14	7	7	....	826	55	0	4.00		1979-80	1982-83
Bannerman, Murray	Van., Chi.	8	289	116	125	33	16470	1051	8	3.83	40	20	18	....	2322	165	0	4.26		1977-78	1986-87
Baron, Marco	Bos., L.A., Edm.	6	86	34	39	9	4822	292	1	3.63	1	0	1	....	20	3	0	9.00		1979-80	1984-85
Bassen, Hank	Chi., Det., Pit.	9	157	46	66	31	8779	441	5	3.01	5	1	3	....	274	11	0	2.41		1954-55	1967-68
● Bastien, Baz	Tor.	1	5	0	4	1	300	20	0	4.00	....	....	....	....	....	....	....	....		1945-46	1945-46
Bauman, Gary	Mtl., Min.	3	35	6	18	6	1718	102	0	3.56	....	....	....	....	....	....	....	....		1966-67	1968-69
Beaupre, Don	Min., Wsh., Ott., Tor.	17	667	268	277	75	37396	2151	17	3.45	72	33	31	....	3943	220	3	3.35		1980-81	1996-97
Bedard, Jim	Wsh.	2	73	17	40	13	4232	278	1	3.94	....	....	....	....	....	....	....	....		1977-78	1978-79
Behrend, Marc	Wpg.	3	39	12	19	3	1991	160	1	4.82	7	1	3	0	312	19	0	3.65		1983-84	1985-86
Belanger, Yves	St.L., Atl., Bos.	6	78	29	33	6	4134	259	2	3.76	....	....	....	....	....	....	....	....		1974-75	1979-80
Belhumeur, Michel	Phi., Wsh.	3	65	9	36	7	3306	254	0	4.61	1	0	0	....	10	1	0	6.00		1972-73	1975-76
● Bell, Gordie	Tor., NYR	2	8	3	5	0	480	31	0	3.88	2	1	1	....	120	9	0	4.50		1945-46	1955-56
● Benedict, Clint	Ott., Mtl.M.	13	362	191	142	28	22360	858	58	2.30	48	25	18	5	2907	87	15	1.80	4	1917-18	1929-30
Bennett, Harvey	Bos.	1	25	10	12	2	1470	103	0	4.20	....	....	....	....	....	....	....	....		1944-45	1944-45
Bergeron, Jean-Claude	Mtl., T.B., L.A.	6	72	21	33	7	3772	232	1	3.69	....	....	....	....	....	....	....	....		1990-91	1996-97
Bernhardt, Tim	Cgy., Tor.	4	67	17	36	7	3748	267	0	4.27	....	....	....	....	....	....	....	....		1982-83	1986-87
Berthiaume, Daniel	Wpg., Min., L.A., Bos., Ott.	9	215	81	90	21	11662	714	5	3.67	14	5	9	....	807	50	0	3.72		1985-86	1993-94
Bester, Allan	Tor., Det., Dal.	10	219	73	99	17	11773	786	7	4.01	11	2	6	....	508	37	0	4.37		1983-84	1995-96
● Beveridge, Bill	Det., Ott., St.L., Mtl.M., NYR	9	297	87	166	42	18375	879	18	2.87	5	2	3	....	300	11	0	2.20		1929-30	1942-43
● Bibeault, Paul	Mtl., Tor., Bos., Chi.	7	214	81	107	25	12890	785	10	3.65	20	6	14	....	1237	71	2	3.44		1940-41	1946-47
Binette, Andre	Mtl.	1	1	1	0	0	60	4	0	4.00	....	....	....	....	....	....	....	....		1954-55	1954-55
Binkley, Les	Pit.	5	196	58	94	34	11046	575	11	3.12	7	5	2	....	428	15	0	2.10		1967-68	1971-72
Bittner, Richard	Bos.	1	1	0	0	1	60	3	0	3.00	....	....	....	....	....	....	....	....		1949-50	1949-50
Blake, Mike	L.A.	3	40	13	15	5	2117	150	0	4.25	....	....	....	....	....	....	....	....		1981-82	1983-84
Blue, John	Bos., Buf.	3	46	16	18	7	2521	126	1	3.00	2	0	1	....	96	5	0	3.13		1992-93	1995-96
Boisvert, Gilles	Det.	1	3	0	3	0	180	9	0	3.00	....	....	....	....	....	....	....	....		1959-60	1959-60
Bouchard, Dan	Atl., Cgy., Que., Wpg.	14	655	286	232	113	37919	2061	27	3.26	43	13	30	....	2549	147	1	3.46		1972-73	1985-86
● Bourque, Claude	Mtl., Det.	2	62	16	38	8	3830	193	4	3.02	3	1	2	....	188	8	1	2.55		1938-39	1939-40
Boutin, Rollie	Wsh.	3	22	7	10	1	1137	75	0	3.96	....	....	....	....	....	....	....	....		1978-79	1980-81
Bouvrette, Lionel	NYR	1	1	0	1	0	60	6	0	6.00	....	....	....	....	....	....	....	....		1942-43	1942-43
Bower, Johnny	NYR, Tor.	15	552	250	195	90	32016	1347	37	2.52	74	35	34	....	4378	184	5	2.52	4	1953-54	1969-70
Brimsek, Frank	Bos., Chi.	10	514	252	182	80	31210	1404	40	2.70	68	32	36	....	4394	186	2	2.54	2	1938-39	1949-50
● Broda, Turk	Tor.	14	629	302	224	101	38167	1609	62	2.53	101	60	39	....	6389	211	13	1.98	5	1936-37	1951-52
Broderick, Ken	Min., Bos.	3	27	11	12	1	1464	74	1	3.03	....	....	....	....	....	....	....	....		1969-70	1974-75
Broderick, Len	Mtl.	1	1	1	0	0	60	2	0	2.00	....	....	....	....	....	....	....	....		1957-58	1957-58
Brodeur, Richard	NYI, Van., Hfd.	9	385	131	176	62	21968	1410	6	3.85	33	13	20	....	2009	111	1	3.32		1979-80	1987-88
Bromley, Gary	Buf., Van.	6	136	54	44	28	7427	425	7	3.43	7	2	5	....	360	25	0	4.17		1973-74	1980-81
● Brooks, Arthur	Tor.	1	4	2	2	0	220	23	0	6.27	....	....	....	....	....	....	....	....		1917-18	1917-18
Brooks, Ross	Bos.	3	54	37	7	6	3047	134	4	2.64	1	0	0	....	20	3	0	9.00		1972-73	1974-75
● Brophy, Frank	Que.	1	21	3	18	0	1249	148	0	7.11	....	....	....	....	....	....	....	....		1919-20	1919-20
Brown, Andy	Det., Pit.	3	62	22	26	9	3373	213	1	3.79	....	....	....	....	....	....	....	....		1971-72	1973-74
Brown, Ken	Chi.	1	1	0	0	0	18	1	0	3.33	....	....	....	....	....	....	....	....		1970-71	1970-71
Brunetta, Mario	Que.	3	40	12	17	1	1967	128	0	3.90	....	....	....	....	....	....	....	....		1987-88	1989-90
Bullock, Bruce	Van.	3	16	3	9	3	927	74	0	4.79	....	....	....	....	....	....	....	....		1972-73	1976-77
Buzinski, Steve	NYR	1	9	2	6	1	560	55	0	5.89	....	....	....	....	....	....	....	....		1942-43	1942-43
Caley, Don	St.L.	1	1	0	0	0	30	3	0	6.00	....	....	....	....	....	....	....	....		1967-68	1967-68
Caprice, Frank	Van.	6	102	31	46	11	5589	391	1	4.20	....	....	....	....	....	....	....	....		1982-83	1987-88
Caron, Jacques	L.A., St.L., Van.	5	72	24	29	11	3846	211	2	3.29	12	4	7	....	639	34	0	3.19		1967-68	1973-74
Carter, Lyle	Cal.	1	15	4	7	0	721	50	0	4.16	....	....	....	....	....	....	....	....		1971-72	1971-72
Casey, Jon	Min., Bos., St.L.	12	425	170	157	55	23255	1246	16	3.21	66	32	31	....	3743	192	3	3.08		1983-84	1996-97
● Chabot, Lorne	NYR, Tor., Mtl.C., Chi., Mtl.M., NYA	11	411	201	148	62	25307	860	73	2.04	37	13	17	6	2498	64	5	1.54	2	1926-27	1936-37
Chadwick, Ed	Tor., Bos.	6	184	57	92	35	11040	551	14	2.99	....	....	....	....	....	....	....	....		1955-56	1961-62
Champoux, Bob	Det., Cal.	2	17	2	11	3	923	80	0	5.20	1	1	0	....	55	4	0	4.36		1963-64	1973-74
Cheevers, Gerry	Tor., Bos.	13	418	230	102	74	24394	1175	26	2.89	88	53	34	....	5396	242	8	2.69	2	1961-62	1979-80
Cheveldae, Tim	Det., Wpg., Bos.	9	340	149	136	37	19172	1116	10	3.49	25	9	15	....	1418	71	2	3.00		1988-89	1996-97
Chevrier, Alain	N.J., Wpg., Chi., Pit., Det.	6	234	91	100	14	12202	845	2	4.16	16	9	7	....	1013	44	0	2.61		1985-86	1990-91
Clifford, Chris	Chi.	2	2	0	0	0	24	0	0	0.00	....	....	....	....	....	....	....	....		1984-85	1988-89
Cloutier, Jacques	Buf., Chi., Que.	12	255	82	102	24	12826	778	3	3.64	8	1	5	....	413	18	1	2.62		1981-82	1993-94
Colvin, Les	Bos.	1	1	0	1	0	60	4	0	4.00	....	....	....	....	....	....	....	....		1948-49	1948-49
● Connell, Alex	Ott., Det., NYA, Mtl.M.	12	417	193	156	67	26050	830	81	1.91	21	8	5	8	1309	26	4	1.19	2	1924-25	1936-37
Corsi, Jim	Edm.	1	26	8	14	3	1366	83	0	3.65	....	....	....	....	....	....	....	....		1979-80	1979-80
Courteau, Maurice	Bos.	1	6	2	4	0	360	33	0	5.50	....	....	....	....	....	....	....	....		1943-44	1943-44
Cowley, Wayne	Edm.	1	1	0	1	0	57	3	0	3.16	....	....	....	....	....	....	....	....		1993-94	1993-94
Cox, Abbie	Mtl.M., NYA, Det., Mtl.C.	3	5	1	1	2	263	11	0	2.51	....	....	....	....	....	....	....	....		1929-30	1935-36
Craig, Jim	Atl., Bos., Min.	3	30	11	10	7	1588	100	0	3.78	....	....	....	....	....	....	....	....		1979-80	1983-84
Crha, Jiri	Tor.	2	69	28	27	11	3942	261	0	3.97	5	0	4	....	186	21	0	6.77		1979-80	1980-81
● Crozier, Roger	Det., Buf., Wsh.	14	518	206	197	70	28567	1446	30	3.04	32	14	16	....	1789	82	1	2.75		1963-64	1976-77
● Cude, Wilf	Phi., Bos., Chi., Mtl.C., Det., Mtl.	10	282	100	132	49	17586	798	24	2.72	19	7	11	1	1257	51	1	2.43		1930-31	1940-41
Cutts, Don	Edm.	1	6	1	2	1	269	16	0	3.57	....	....	....	....	....	....	....	....		1979-80	1979-80
● Cyr, Claude	Mtl.	1	1	0	0	0	20	1	0	3.00	....	....	....	....	....	....	....	....		1958-59	1958-59
Dadswell, Doug	Cgy.	2	27	8	8	3	1346	99	0	4.41	....	....	....	....	....	....	....	....		1986-87	1987-88
D'Alessio, Corrie	Hfd.	1	1	0	0	0	11	0	0	0.00	....	....	....	....	....	....	....	....		1992-93	1992-93
Daley, Joe	Pit., Buf., Det.	4	105	34	44	19	5836	326	3	3.35	....	....	....	....	....	....	....	....		1968-69	1971-72
Damore, Nick	Bos.	1	1	1	0	0	60	3	0	3.00	....	....	....	....	....	....	....	....		1941-42	1941-42
D'Amour, Marc	Cgy., Phi.	2	16	2	4	2	579	32	0	3.32	....	....	....	....	....	....	....	....		1985-86	1988-89
Daskalakis, Cleon	Bos.	3	12	3	4	1	506	41	0	4.86	....	....	....	....	....	....	....	....		1984-85	1986-87
Davidson, John	St.L., NYR	10	301	123	124	39	17109	1004	7	3.52	31	16	14	....	1862	77	1	2.48		1973-74	1982-83
Decourcy, Robert	NYR	1	1	0	1	0	29	6	0	12.41	....	....	....	....	....	....	....	....		1947-48	1947-48
Defelice, Norman	Bos.	1	10	3	5	2	600	30	0	3.00	....	....	....	....	....	....	....	....		1956-57	1956-57
DeJordy, Denis	Chi., L.A., Mtl., Det.	11	316	124	128	51	17798	929	15	3.13	18	6	9	....	946	55	0	3.49		1962-63	1973-74
DelGuidice, Matt	Bos.	2	11	2	5	1	434	28	0	3.87	....	....	....	....	....	....	....	....		1990-91	1991-92
Desjardins, Gerry	L.A., Chi., NYI, Buf.	10	331	122	153	44	19014	1042	12	3.29	35	15	15	....	1874	108	0	3.46		1968-69	1977-78
● Dickie, Bill	Chi.	1	1	1	0	0	60	3	0	3.00	....	....	....	....	....	....	....	....		1941-42	1941-42
Dion, Connie	Det.	2	38	23	11	4	2280	119	1	3.13	5	1	4	....	300	17	0	3.40		1943-44	1944-45
Dion, Michel	Que., Wpg., Pit.	6	227	60	118	32	12695	898	2	4.24	5	2	3	....	304	22	0	4.34		1979-80	1984-85
Dolson, Dolly	Det.	3	93	35	41	17	5820	192	16	1.98	2	0	2	0	120	7	0	3.50		1928-29	1930-31
Dopson, Robert	Pit.	1	2	0	0	0	45	3	0	4.00	....	....	....	....	....	....	....	....		1993-94	1993-94
Dowie, Bruce	Tor.	1	2	0	1	0	72	4	0	3.33	....	....	....	....	....	....	....	....		1983-84	1983-84
Draper, Tom	Wpg., Buf., NYI	6	53	19	23	5	2807	173	1	3.70	7	3	4	....	433	19	1	2.63		1988-89	1995-96

Name	NHL Teams	NHL Seasons	Regular Schedule GP	W	L	T	Mins	GA	SO	Avg	Playoffs GP	W	L	T	Mins	GA	SO	Avg	NHL Cup Wins	First NHL Season	Last NHL Season
Dryden, Dave	NYR, Chi., Buf., Edm.	9	203	66	76	31	10424	555	9	3.19	3	0	2	....	133	9	0	4.06		1961-62	1979-80
Dryden, Ken	Mtl.	8	397	258	57	74	23352	870	46	2.24	112	80	32	....	6846	274	10	2.40	6	1970-71	1978-79
Duffus, Parris	Phx.	1	1	0	0	0	29	1	0	2.07	....	....	....	....	....	....	....	....		1996-97	1996-97
Dumas, Michel	Chi.	3	8	2	1	2	362	24	0	3.98	1	0	0	....	19	1	0	3.16		1974-75	1976-77
Dupuis, Bob	Edm.	1	1	0	1	0	60	4	0	4.00	....	....	....	....	....	....	....	....		1979-80	1979-80
• Durnan, Bill	Mtl.	7	383	208	112	62	22945	901	34	2.36	45	27	18	....	2871	99	2	2.07	2	1943-44	1949-50
Dyck, Ed	Van.	3	49	8	28	5	2453	178	1	4.35	....	....	....	....	....	....	....	....		1971-72	1973-74
Edwards, Don	Buf., Cgy., Tor.	10	459	208	155	74	26181	1449	16	3.32	42	16	21	....	2302	132	1	3.44		1976-77	1985-86
Edwards, Gary	St.L., L.A., Cle., Min., Edm., Pit.	13	286	88	125	51	16002	973	11	3.65	11	5	4	....	537	34	0	3.80		1968-69	1981-82
Edwards, Marv	Pit., Tor., Cal.	4	61	15	34	7	3467	218	2	3.77	....	....	....	....	....	....	....	....		1968-69	1973-74
Edwards, Roy	Det., Pit.	7	236	97	88	38	13109	637	12	2.92	4	0	3	....	206	11	0	3.20		1967-68	1973-74
Eliot, Darren	L.A., Det., Buf.	5	89	25	41	12	4931	377	1	4.59	1	0	0	....	40	7	0	10.50		1984-85	1988-89
Ellacott, Ken	Van.	1	12	2	3	4	555	41	0	4.43	....	....	....	....	....	....	....	....		1982-83	1982-83
Erickson, Chad	N.J.	1	2	1	1	0	120	9	0	4.50	....	....	....	....	....	....	....	....		1991-92	1991-92
Esposito, Tony	Mtl., Chi.	16	886	423	306	152	52585	2563	76	2.92	99	45	53	....	6017	308	6	3.07		1968-69	1983-84
• Evans, Claude	Mtl., Bos.	2	5	2	2	1	280	16	0	3.43	....	....	....	....	....	....	....	....		1954-55	1957-58
Exelby, Randy	Mtl., Edm.	2	2	0	1	0	63	5	0	4.76	....	....	....	....	....	....	....	....		1988-89	1989-90
Farr, Rocky	Buf.	3	19	2	6	3	722	42	0	3.49	....	....	....	....	....	....	....	....		1972-73	1974-75
Favell, Doug	Phi., Tor., Col.	12	373	123	153	69	20771	1096	18	3.17	21	5	16	....	1270	66	1	3.12		1967-68	1978-79
• Forbes, Jake	Tor., Ham., NYA, Phi.	13	210	85	113	11	12922	594	19	2.76	2	0	2	0	120	7	0	3.50		1919-20	1932-33
Ford, Brian	Que., Pit.	2	11	3	7	0	580	61	0	6.31	....	....	....	....	....	....	....	....		1983-84	1984-85
Foster, Norm	Bos., Edm.	2	13	7	4	0	623	34	0	3.27	....	....	....	....	....	....	....	....		1990-91	1991-92
Fowler, Hec	Bos.	1	7	1	6	0	420	43	0	6.14	....	....	....	....	....	....	....	....		1924-25	1924-25
Francis, Emile	Chi., NYR	6	95	31	52	11	5660	355	1	3.76	....	....	....	....	....	....	....	....		1946-47	1951-52
• Franks, Jim	Det., NYR, Bos.	4	42	12	23	7	2520	181	1	4.31	1	0	1	....	30	2	0	4.00	1	1936-37	1943-44
Frederick, Ray	Chi.	1	5	0	4	1	300	22	0	4.40	....	....	....	....	....	....	....	....		1954-55	1954-55
Friesen, Karl	N.J.	1	4	0	2	1	130	16	0	7.38	....	....	....	....	....	....	....	....		1986-87	1986-87
Froese, Bob	Phi., NYR	8	242	128	72	20	13451	694	13	3.10	18	3	9	....	830	55	0	3.98		1982-83	1989-90
Gage, Joaquin	Edm.	2	18	2	10	1	816	52	0	3.82	....	....	....	....	....	....	....	....		1994-95	1995-96
Gagnon, David	Det.	1	2	0	1	0	35	6	0	10.29	....	....	....	....	....	....	....	....		1990-91	1990-91
• Gamble, Bruce	NYR, Bos., Tor., Phi.	10	327	110	150	46	18442	992	22	3.23	5	0	4	....	206	25	0	7.28	1	1958-59	1971-72
Gamble, Troy	Van.	4	72	22	29	9	3804	229	1	3.61	4	1	3	....	249	16	0	3.86		1986-87	1991-92
Gardiner, Bert	NYR, Mtl., Chi., Bos.	6	144	49	68	27	8760	554	4	3.79	9	4	5	....	647	20	0	1.85		1935-36	1943-44
• Gardiner, Chuck	Chi.	7	316	112	152	52	19687	664	42	2.02	21	12	6	3	1472	35	5	1.43	1	1927-28	1933-34
Gardner, George	Det., Van.	5	66	16	30	6	3313	207	0	3.75	....	....	....	....	....	....	....	....		1965-66	1971-72
Garrett, John	Hfd., Que., Van.	6	207	68	91	37	11763	837	1	4.27	9	4	3	....	461	33	0	4.30		1979-80	1984-85
Gatherum, Dave	Det.	1	3	2	0	1	180	3	1	1.00	....	....	....	....	....	....	....	....		1953-54	1953-54
Gauthier, Paul	Mtl.C.	1	1	0	0	1	70	2	0	1.71	....	....	....	....	....	....	....	....		1937-38	1937-38
• Gelineau, Jack	Bos., Chi.	4	143	46	64	33	8580	447	7	3.13	4	1	2	....	260	7	1	1.62		1948-49	1953-54
Giacomin, Ed	NYR, Det.	13	610	289	208	97	35693	1675	54	2.82	65	29	35	....	3834	180	1	2.82		1965-66	1977-78
Gilbert, Gilles	Min., Bos., Det.	14	416	192	143	60	23677	1290	18	3.27	32	17	15	....	1919	97	3	3.03		1969-70	1982-83
Gill, Andre	Bos.	1	5	3	2	0	270	13	1	2.89	....	....	....	....	....	....	....	....		1967-68	1967-68
• Goodman, Paul	Chi.	3	52	23	20	9	3240	117	6	2.17	3	0	3	....	187	10	0	3.21	1	1937-38	1940-41
Gordon, Scott	Que.	2	23	2	16	0	1082	101	0	5.60	....	....	....	....	....	....	....	....		1989-90	1990-91
Gosselin, Mario	Que., L.A., Hfd.	9	241	91	107	14	12857	801	6	3.74	32	16	15	0	1816	99	0	3.27		1983-84	1993-94
Goverde, David	L.A.	3	5	1	4	0	278	29	0	6.26	....	....	....	....	....	....	....	....		1991-92	1993-94
Grahame, Ron	Bos., L.A., Que.	4	114	50	43	15	6472	409	5	3.79	4	2	1	....	202	7	0	2.08		1977-78	1980-81
• Grant, Ben	Tor., NYA, Bos.	6	50	17	26	4	2990	187	4	3.75	....	....	....	....	....	....	....	....		1928-29	1943-44
Grant, Doug	Det., St.L.	7	77	27	34	8	4199	280	2	4.00	....	....	....	....	....	....	....	....		1973-74	1979-80
Gratton, Gilles	St.L., NYR	2	47	13	18	9	2299	154	0	4.02	....	....	....	....	....	....	....	....		1975-76	1976-77
Gray, Gerry	Det., NYI	2	8	1	5	1	440	35	0	4.77	....	....	....	....	....	....	....	....		1970-71	1972-73
Gray, Harrison	Det.	1	1	0	1	0	40	5	0	7.50	....	....	....	....	....	....	....	....		1963-64	1963-64
Greenlay, Mike	Edm.	1	2	0	0	0	20	4	0	12.00	....	....	....	....	....	....	....	....		1989-90	1989-90
Guenette, Steve	Pit., Cgy.	5	35	19	16	0	1958	122	1	3.74	....	....	....	....	....	....	....	....		1986-87	1990-91
• Hainsworth, George	Mtl.C., Tor.	11	465	246	145	74	29415	937	94	1.91	52	22	25	5	3486	112	8	1.93		1926-27	1936-37
Hall, Glenn	Det., Chi., St.L.	18	906	407	326	163	53484	2239	84	2.51	115	49	65	....	6899	321	6	2.79	1	1952-53	1970-71
Hamel, Pierre	Tor., Wpg.	4	69	13	41	7	3766	276	0	4.40	....	....	....	....	....	....	....	....		1974-75	1980-81
Hanlon, Glen	Van., St.L., NYR, Det.	14	477	167	202	61	26037	1561	13	3.60	35	11	15	....	1756	92	4	3.14		1977-78	1990-91
Harrison, Paul	Min., Tor., Pit., Buf.	7	109	28	59	9	5806	408	2	4.22	4	0	1	....	157	9	0	3.44		1975-76	1981-82
Hayward, Brian	Wpg., Mtl., Min., S.J.	11	357	143	156	37	20025	1242	8	3.72	37	11	18	....	1803	104	0	3.46		1982-83	1992-93
Head, Don	Bos.	1	38	9	26	3	2280	161	2	4.24	....	....	....	....	....	....	....	....		1961-62	1961-62
• Hebert, Sammy	Tor., Ott.	2	4	1	2	0	200	19	0	5.70	....	....	....	....	....	....	....	....		1917-18	1923-24
Heinz, Rick	St.L., Van.	5	49	14	19	5	2356	159	2	4.05	1	0	0	....	8	1	0	7.50		1980-81	1984-85
Henderson, John	Bos.	2	46	15	15	15	2688	113	5	2.52	2	0	2	....	120	8	0	4.00		1954-55	1955-56
• Henry, Gord	Bos.	4	3	1	2	0	180	5	1	1.67	5	0	4	....	283	21	0	4.45		1948-49	1952-53
Henry, Jim	NYR, Chi., Bos.	9	406	161	173	70	24355	1166	27	2.87	29	11	18	....	1741	81	2	2.79		1941-42	1954-55
Herron, Denis	Pit., K.C., Mtl.	14	462	146	203	76	25608	1579	10	3.70	15	5	10	....	901	50	0	3.33		1972-73	1985-86
Highton, Hec	Chi.	1	24	10	14	0	1440	108	0	4.50	....	....	....	....	....	....	....	....		1943-44	1943-44
Hodge, Charlie	Mtl., Oak., Van.	13	358	152	124	60	20593	927	24	2.70	16	7	7	....	803	32	2	2.39	2	1954-55	1970-71
Hoffort, Bruce	Phi.	2	9	4	0	3	368	22	0	3.59	....	....	....	....	....	....	....	....		1989-90	1990-91
Hoganson, Paul	Pit.	1	2	0	1	0	57	7	0	7.37	....	....	....	....	....	....	....	....		1970-71	1970-71
Hogosta, Goran	NYI, Que.	2	22	5	12	3	1208	83	1	4.12	....	....	....	....	....	....	....	....		1977-78	1979-80
Holden, Mark	Mtl., Wpg.	4	8	2	2	1	372	25	0	4.03	....	....	....	....	....	....	....	....		1981-82	1984-85
Holland, Ken	Hfd., Det.	2	4	0	2	1	206	17	0	4.95	....	....	....	....	....	....	....	....		1980-81	1983-84
Holland, Robbie	Pit.	2	44	11	22	9	2513	171	1	4.08	....	....	....	....	....	....	....	....		1979-80	1980-81
• Holmes, Harry	Tor., Det.	4	103	39	54	10	6510	264	17	2.43	7	4	3	0	420	28	0	4.00	1	1917-18	1927-28
Hrivnak, Jim	Wsh., Wpg., St.L.	5	85	34	30	3	4217	262	0	3.73	....	....	....	....	....	....	....	....		1989-90	1993-94
Hrudey, Kelly	NYI, L.A., S.J.	15	677	271	265	88	38084	2174	17	3.43	85	36	46	....	5163	283	0	3.29		1983-84	1997-98
Ing, Peter	Tor., Edm., Det.	4	74	20	37	9	3941	266	1	4.05	....	....	....	....	....	....	....	....		1989-90	1993-94
Inness, Gary	Pit., Phi., Wsh.	7	162	58	61	27	8710	494	2	3.40	9	5	4	....	540	24	0	2.67		1973-74	1980-81
Ireland, Randy	Buf.	1	2	0	0	0	30	3	0	6.00	....	....	....	....	....	....	....	....		1978-79	1978-79
Irons, Robbie	St.L.	1	1	0	0	0	3	0	0	0.00	....	....	....	....	....	....	....	....		1968-69	1968-69
• Ironstone, Joe	Ott., NYA, Tor.	3	2	0	0	1	110	3	1	1.64	....	....	....	....	....	....	....	....		1924-25	1927-28
Jackson, Doug	Chi.	1	6	2	3	1	360	42	0	7.00	....	....	....	....	....	....	....	....		1947-48	1947-48
Jackson, Percy	Bos., NYA, NYR	4	7	1	3	1	392	26	0	3.98	....	....	....	....	....	....	....	....		1931-32	1935-36
Jaks, Pauli	L.A.	1	1	0	0	0	40	2	0	3.00	....	....	....	....	....	....	....	....		1994-95	1994-95
Janaszak, Steve	Min., Col.	2	3	0	1	1	160	15	0	5.63	....	....	....	....	....	....	....	....		1979-80	1981-82
Janecyk, Bob	Chi., L.A.	6	110	43	47	13	6250	432	2	4.15	3	0	3	....	184	10	0	3.26		1983-84	1988-89
Jensen, Al	Det., Wsh., L.A.	7	179	95	53	18	9974	557	8	3.35	12	5	5	....	598	32	0	3.21		1980-81	1986-87
Jensen, Darren	Phi.	2	30	15	10	1	1496	95	2	3.81	....	....	....	....	....	....	....	....		1984-85	1985-86
Johnson, Bob	St.L., Pit.	2	24	9	9	1	1059	66	0	3.74	....	....	....	....	....	....	....	....		1972-73	1974-75
Johnston, Eddie	Bos., Tor., St.L., Chi.	16	592	234	257	81	34216	1855	32	3.25	18	7	10	....	1023	57	1	3.34	2	1962-63	1977-78
Junkin, Joe	Bos.	1	1	0	0	0	8	0	0	0.00	....	....	....	....	....	....	....	....		1968-69	1968-69
Kaarela, Jari	Col.	1	5	2	2	0	220	22	0	6.00	....	....	....	....	....	....	....	....		1980-81	1980-81
Kamppuri, Hannu	N.J.	1	13	1	10	1	645	54	0	5.02	....	....	....	....	....	....	....	....		1984-85	1984-85
• Karakas, Mike	Chi., Mtl.	8	336	114	169	53	20616	1002	28	2.92	23	11	12	0	1434	72	3	3.01	1	1935-36	1945-46
Keans, Doug	L.A., Bos.	9	210	96	64	26	11388	666	4	3.51	9	2	6	....	432	34	0	4.72		1979-80	1987-88
Keenan, Don	Bos.	1	1	0	1	0	60	4	0	4.00	....	....	....	....	....	....	....	....		1958-59	1958-59
• Kerr, Dave	Mtl.M., NYA, NYR	11	427	203	148	75	26639	954	51	2.15	40	18	19	3	2616	76	8	1.74	1	1930-31	1940-41
King, Scott	Det.	2	2	0	0	0	61	3	0	2.95	....	....	....	....	....	....	....	....		1990-91	1991-92
Kleisinger, Terry	NYR	1	4	0	2	0	191	14	0	4.40	....	....	....	....	....	....	....	....		1985-86	1985-86
Klymkiw, Julian	NYR	1	1	0	0	0	19	2	0	6.32	....	....	....	....	....	....	....	....		1958-59	1958-59
Knickle, Rick	L.A.	2	14	7	6	0	706	44	0	3.74	....	....	....	....	....	....	....	....		1992-93	1993-94
Kuntar, Les	Mtl.	1	6	2	2	0	302	16	0	3.18	....	....	....	....	....	....	....	....		1993-94	1993-94
Kurt, Gary	Cal.	1	16	1	7	5	838	60	0	4.30	....	....	....	....	....	....	....	....		1971-72	1971-72

Name	NHL Teams	NHL Seasons	Regular Schedule GP	W	L	T	Mins	GA	SO	Avg	Playoffs GP	W	L	T	Mins	GA	SO	Avg	NHL Cup Wins	First NHL Season	Last NHL Season
Labrecque, Patrick	Mtl.	1	2	0	1	0	98	7	0	4.29	....	....	....	....	....	....	....	....		1995-96	1995-96
Lacher, Blaine	Bos.	2	47	22	16	4	2636	123	4	2.80	5	1	4	....	283	12	0	2.54		1994-95	1995-96
Lacroix, Albert	Mtl.C.	2	5	1	4	0	280	15	0	3.21	....	....	....	....	....	....	....	....		1925-26	1926-27
LaFerriere, Rick	Col.	1	1	0	0	0	20	1	0	3.00	....	....	....	....	....	....	....	....		1981-82	1981-82
LaForest, Mark	Det., Phi., Tor., Ott.	6	103	25	54	4	5032	354	2	4.22	2	1	0	....	48	1	0	1.25		1985-86	1993-94
• Larocque, Michel	Mtl., Tor., Phi., St.L.	11	312	160	89	45	17615	978	17	3.33	14	6	6	....	759	37	1	2.92	3	1973-74	1983-84
Laskowski, Gary	L.A.	2	59	19	27	5	2942	228	0	4.65	....	....	....	....	....	....	....	....		1982-83	1983-84
Laxton, Gord	Pit.	4	17	4	9	0	800	74	0	5.55	....	....	....	....	....	....	....	....		1975-76	1978-79
LeBlanc, Raymond	Chi.	1	1	1	0	0	60	1	0	1.00	....	....	....	....	....	....	....	....		1991-92	1991-92
Legris, Claude	Det.	2	4	0	1	1	91	4	0	2.64	....	....	....	....	....	....	....	....		1980-81	1981-82
• Lehman, Hugh	Chi.	2	48	20	24	4	3047	136	6	2.68	2	0	1	1	120	10	0	5.00		1926-27	1927-28
Lemelin, Reggie	Atl., Cgy., Bos.	15	507	236	162	63	28006	1613	12	3.46	59	23	25	....	3119	186	2	3.58		1978-79	1992-93
Lenarduzzi, Mike	Hfd.	2	4	1	1	1	189	10	0	3.17	....	....	....	....	....	....	....	....		1992-93	1993-94
Lessard, Mario	L.A.	6	240	92	97	39	13529	843	9	3.74	20	6	12	....	1136	83	0	4.38		1978-79	1983-84
Levasseur, Jean-Louis	Min.	1	1	0	1	0	60	7	0	7.00	....	....	....	....	....	....	....	....		1979-80	1979-80
• Lindbergh, Pelle	Phi.	5	157	87	49	15	9151	503	7	3.30	23	12	10	....	1214	63	3	3.11		1981-82	1985-86
• Lindsay, Bert	Mtl., Tor.	2	20	6	14	0	1238	118	0	5.72	....	....	....	....	....	....	....	....		1917-18	1918-19
Liut, Mike	St.L., Hfd., Wsh.	13	663	294	271	74	38155	2219	25	3.49	67	29	32	....	3814	215	2	3.38		1979-80	1991-92
Lockett, Ken	Van.	2	55	13	15	8	2348	131	2	3.35	1	0	1	....	60	6	0	6.00		1974-75	1975-76
• Lockhart, Howard	Tor., Que., Ham., Bos.	5	59	16	41	0	3413	287	1	5.05	....	....	....	....	....	....	....	....		1919-20	1924-25
LoPresti, Pete	Min., Edm.	6	175	43	102	20	9858	668	5	4.07	2	0	2	....	77	6	0	4.68		1974-75	1980-81
• LoPresti, Sam	Chi.	2	74	30	38	6	4530	236	4	3.13	8	3	5	....	530	17	1	1.92		1940-41	1941-42
Lorenz, Danny	NYI	3	8	1	5	0	357	25	0	4.20	....	....	....	....	....	....	....	....		1990-91	1992-93
Loustel, Ron	Wpg.	1	1	0	1	0	60	10	0	10.00	....	....	....	....	....	....	....	....		1980-81	1980-81
Low, Ron	Tor., Wsh., Det., Que., Edm., N.J.	11	382	102	203	38	20502	1463	4	4.28	7	1	6	....	452	29	0	3.85		1972-73	1984-85
Lozinski, Larry	Det.	1	30	6	11	7	1459	105	0	4.32	....	....	....	....	....	....	....	....		1980-81	1980-81
Lumley, Harry	Det., NYR, Chi., Tor., Bos.	16	804	330	329	143	48104	2210	71	2.76	76	29	47	....	4777	199	7	2.50	1	1943-44	1959-60
MacKenzie, Shawn	N.J.	1	4	0	1	0	130	15	0	6.92	....	....	....	....	....	....	....	....		1982-83	1982-83
Madeley, Darrin	Ott.	3	39	4	23	5	1928	140	0	4.36	....	....	....	....	....	....	....	....		1992-93	1994-95
Malarchuk, Clint	Que., Wsh., Buf.	10	338	141	130	45	19030	1100	12	3.47	15	2	9	0	781	56	0	4.30		1981-82	1991-92
Maneluk, George	NYI	1	4	1	1	0	140	15	0	6.43	....	....	....	....	....	....	....	....		1990-91	1990-91
Maniago, Cesare	Tor., Mtl., NYR, Min., Van.	15	568	189	259	96	32570	1774	30	3.27	36	15	21	....	2245	100	3	2.67		1960-61	1977-78
Marois, Jean	Tor., Chi.	2	3	1	2	0	180	15	0	5.00	....	....	....	....	....	....	....	....		1943-44	1953-54
Martin, Seth	St.L.	1	30	8	10	7	1552	67	1	2.59	2	0	0	....	73	5	0	4.11		1967-68	1967-68
Mason, Bob	Wsh., Chi., Que., Van.	8	145	55	65	16	7988	500	1	3.76	5	2	3	....	369	12	1	1.95		1983-84	1990-91
Mattsson, Markus	Wpg., Min., L.A.	4	92	21	46	14	5007	343	6	4.11	....	....	....	....	....	....	....	....		1979-80	1983-84
May, Darrell	St.L.	2	6	1	5	0	364	31	0	5.11	....	....	....	....	....	....	....	....		1985-86	1987-88
Mayer, Gilles	Tor.	4	9	2	6	1	540	25	0	2.78	....	....	....	....	....	....	....	....		1949-50	1955-56
• McAuley, Ken	NYR	2	96	17	64	15	5740	537	1	5.61	....	....	....	....	....	....	....	....		1943-44	1944-45
McCartan, Jack	NYR	2	12	2	7	3	680	43	1	3.79	....	....	....	....	....	....	....	....		1959-60	1960-61
• McCool, Frank	Tor.	2	72	34	31	7	4320	242	4	3.36	13	8	5	....	807	30	4	2.23	1	1944-45	1945-46
McDuffe, Pete	St.L., NYR, K.C., Det.	5	57	11	36	6	3207	218	0	4.08	1	0	1	....	60	7	0	7.00		1971-72	1975-76
McGrattan, Tom	Det.	1	1	0	0	0	8	0	0	0.00	....	....	....	....	....	....	....	....		1947-48	1947-48
McKay, Ross	Hfd.	1	1	0	0	0	35	3	0	5.14	....	....	....	....	....	....	....	....		1990-91	1990-91
McKenzie, Bill	Det., K.C., Col.	6	91	18	49	13	4776	326	2	4.10	....	....	....	....	....	....	....	....		1973-74	1979-80
McKichan, Steve	Van.	1	1	0	0	0	20	2	0	6.00	....	....	....	....	....	....	....	....		1990-91	1990-91
McLachlan, Murray	Tor.	1	2	0	1	0	25	4	0	9.60	....	....	....	....	....	....	....	....		1970-71	1970-71
McLelland, Dave	Van.	1	2	1	1	0	120	10	0	5.00	....	....	....	....	....	....	....	....		1972-73	1972-73
McLeod, Don	Det., Phi.	2	18	3	10	1	879	74	0	5.05	....	....	....	....	....	....	....	....		1970-71	1971-72
McLeod, Jim	St.L.	1	16	6	6	4	880	44	0	3.00	....	....	....	....	....	....	....	....		1971-72	1971-72
McNamara, Gerry	Tor.	2	7	2	2	1	323	15	0	2.79	....	....	....	....	....	....	....	....		1960-61	1969-70
McNeil, Gerry	Mtl.	7	276	119	105	52	16535	650	28	2.36	35	17	18	....	2284	72	5	1.89	1	1947-48	1956-57
McRae, Gord	Tor.	5	71	30	22	10	3799	221	1	3.49	8	2	5	....	454	22	0	2.91		1972-73	1977-78
Melanson, Rollie	NYI, Min., L.A., N.J., Mtl.	11	291	129	106	33	16452	995	6	3.63	23	4	9	....	801	59	0	4.42	3	1980-81	1991-92
Meloche, Gilles	Chi., Cal., Cle., Min., Pit.	18	788	270	351	131	45401	2756	20	3.64	45	21	19	....	2464	143	2	3.48		1970-71	1987-88
Micalef, Corrado	Det.	5	113	26	59	15	5794	409	2	4.24	3	0	0	....	49	8	0	9.80		1981-82	1985-86
Middlebrook, Lindsay	Wpg., Min., N.J., Edm.	4	37	3	23	6	1845	152	0	4.94	....	....	....	....	....	....	....	....		1979-80	1982-83
• Millar, Al	Bos.	1	6	1	4	1	360	25	0	4.17	....	....	....	....	....	....	....	....		1957-58	1957-58
Millen, Greg	Pit., Hfd., St.L., Que., Chi., Det.	14	604	215	284	89	35377	2281	17	3.87	59	27	29	....	3383	193	0	3.42		1978-79	1991-92
• Miller, Joe	NYA, NYR, Pit., Phi.	4	127	24	87	16	7871	383	16	2.92	3	2	1	0	180	3	1	1.00	1	1927-28	1930-31
Mio, Eddie	Edm., NYR, Det.	7	192	64	73	30	10428	705	4	4.06	17	9	7	....	986	63	0	3.83		1979-80	1985-86
• Mitchell, Ivan	Tor.	3	22	10	9	0	1190	88	0	4.44	....	....	....	....	....	....	....	....		1919-20	1921-22
Moffat, Mike	Bos.	3	19	7	7	2	979	70	0	4.29	11	6	5	....	663	38	0	3.44		1981-82	1983-84
Moog, Andy	Edm., Bos., Dal., Mtl.	18	713	372	209	88	40151	2097	28	3.13	132	68	57	....	7452	377	4	3.04	3	1980-81	1997-98
Moore, Alfie	NYA, Chi., Det.	4	21	7	14	0	1290	81	1	3.77	3	1	2	....	180	7	0	2.33	1	1936-37	1939-40
Moore, Robbie	Phi., Wsh.	2	6	3	1	1	257	8	2	1.87	5	3	2	....	268	18	0	4.03		1978-79	1982-83
Morissette, Jean-Guy	Mtl.	1	1	0	1	0	36	4	0	6.67	....	....	....	....	....	....	....	....		1963-64	1963-64
• Mowers, Johnny	Det.	4	152	65	61	26	9350	399	15	2.56	32	19	13	....	2000	85	2	2.55	1	1940-41	1946-47
Mrazek, Jerome	Phi.	1	1	0	0	0	6	1	0	10.00	....	....	....	....	....	....	....	....		1975-76	1975-76
• Murphy, Hal	Mtl.	1	1	1	0	0	60	4	0	4.00	....	....	....	....	....	....	....	....		1952-53	1952-53
Murray, Mickey	Mtl.C.	1	1	0	1	0	60	4	0	4.00	....	....	....	....	....	....	....	....		1929-30	1929-30
Myllys, Jarmo	Min., S.J.	4	39	4	27	1	1846	161	0	5.23	....	....	....	....	....	....	....	....		1988-89	1991-92
Mylnikov, Sergei	Que.	1	10	1	7	2	568	47	0	4.96	....	....	....	....	....	....	....	....		1989-90	1989-90
Myre, Phil	Mtl., Atl., St.L., Phi., Col., Buf.	14	439	149	198	76	25220	1482	14	3.53	12	6	5	....	747	41	1	3.29	1	1969-70	1982-83
Newton, Cam	Pit.	2	16	4	7	1	814	51	0	3.76	....	....	....	....	....	....	....	....		1970-71	1972-73
Norris, Jack	Bos., Chi., L.A.	4	58	20	25	4	3119	202	2	3.89	....	....	....	....	....	....	....	....		1964-65	1970-71
Oleschuk, Bill	K.C., Col.	4	55	7	28	10	2835	188	1	3.98	....	....	....	....	....	....	....	....		1975-76	1979-80
• Olesevich, Dan	NYR	1	1	0	0	1	29	2	0	4.14	....	....	....	....	....	....	....	....		1961-62	1961-62
Ouimet, Ted	St.L.	1	1	0	1	0	60	2	0	2.00	....	....	....	....	....	....	....	....		1968-69	1968-69
Pageau, Paul	L.A.	1	1	0	1	0	60	8	0	8.00	....	....	....	....	....	....	....	....		1980-81	1980-81
Paille, Marcel	NYR	7	107	32	52	22	6342	362	2	3.42	....	....	....	....	....	....	....	....		1957-58	1964-65
Palmateer, Mike	Tor., Wsh.	8	356	149	138	52	20131	1183	17	3.53	29	12	17	....	1765	89	2	3.03		1976-77	1983-84
Pang, Darren	Chi.	3	81	27	35	7	4252	287	0	4.05	6	1	3	....	250	18	0	4.32		1984-85	1988-89
Parent, Bernie	Bos., Phi., Tor.	13	608	271	198	121	35136	1493	54	2.55	71	38	33	....	4302	174	6	2.43	2	1965-66	1978-79
Parent, Bob	Tor.	2	3	0	2	0	160	15	0	5.63	....	....	....	....	....	....	....	....		1981-82	1982-83
Parro, Dave	Wsh.	4	77	21	36	10	4015	274	2	4.09	....	....	....	....	....	....	....	....		1980-81	1983-84
Peeters, Pete	Phi., Bos., Wsh.	13	489	246	155	51	27699	1424	21	3.08	71	35	35	....	4200	232	2	3.31		1978-79	1990-91
Pelletier, Marcel	Chi., NYR	2	8	1	6	0	395	33	0	5.01	....	....	....	....	....	....	....	....		1950-51	1962-63
Penney, Steve	Mtl., Wpg.	5	91	35	38	12	5194	313	1	3.62	27	15	12	....	1604	72	4	2.69		1983-84	1987-88
• Perreault, Bob	Mtl., Det., Bos.	3	31	8	16	6	1827	106	3	3.48	....	....	....	....	....	....	....	....		1955-56	1962-63
Pettie, Jim	Bos.	3	21	9	7	2	1157	71	1	3.68	....	....	....	....	....	....	....	....		1976-77	1978-79
Pietrangelo, Frank	Pit., Hfd.	7	141	46	59	6	7141	490	1	4.12	12	7	5	....	713	34	1	2.86	1	1987-88	1993-94
• Plante, Jacques	Mtl., NYR, St.L., Tor., Bos.	18	837	434	247	146	49533	1965	82	2.38	112	71	37	....	6652	240	14	2.16	6	1952-53	1972-73
Plasse, Michel	St.L., Mtl., K.C., Pit., Col., Que.	12	299	92	136	54	16760	1058	2	3.79	4	1	2	....	195	9	1	2.77		1970-71	1981-82
Pronovost, Claude	Bos., Mtl.	2	3	1	1	0	120	7	1	3.50	....	....	....	....	....	....	....	....		1955-56	1958-59
Pusey, Chris	Det.	1	1	0	0	0	40	3	0	4.50	....	....	....	....	....	....	....	....		1985-86	1985-86
Racicot, Andre	Mtl.	5	68	26	23	8	3357	196	2	3.50	4	0	1	....	31	4	0	7.74	1	1989-90	1993-94
Raymond, Alain	Wsh.	1	1	0	1	0	40	2	0	3.00	....	....	....	....	....	....	....	....		1987-88	1987-88
Rayner, Chuck	NYA, Bro., NYR	10	424	138	208	77	25491	1294	25	3.05	18	9	9	....	1135	46	1	2.43		1940-41	1952-53
Reaugh, Daryl	Edm., Hfd.	3	27	8	9	1	1246	72	1	3.47	....	....	....	....	....	....	....	....		1984-85	1990-91
Reddick, Pokey	Wpg., Edm., Fla.	6	132	46	58	16	7162	443	0	3.71	4	0	2	....	168	10	0	3.57	1	1986-87	1993-94
• Redding, George	Bos.	1	1	0	0	0	11	1	0	5.45	....	....	....	....	....	....	....	....		1924-25	1924-25
Redquest, Greg	Pit.	1	1	0	0	0	13	3	0	13.85	....	....	....	....	....	....	....	....		1977-78	1977-78
Reece, Dave	Bos.	1	14	7	5	2	777	43	2	3.32	....	....	....	....	....	....	....	....		1975-76	1975-76
Resch, Glenn	NYI, Col., N.J., Phi.	14	571	231	224	82	32279	1761	26	3.27	41	17	17	....	2044	85	2	2.50	1	1973-74	1986-87
Rheaume, Herb	Mtl.C.	1	31	10	20	1	1889	92	0	2.92	....	....	....	....	....	....	....	....		1925-26	1925-26
Ricci, Nick	Pit.	4	19	7	12	0	1087	79	0	4.36	....	....	....	....	....	....	....	....		1979-80	1982-83

Name	NHL Teams	NHL Seasons	Regular Schedule GP	W	L	T	Mins	GA	SO	Avg	Playoffs GP	W	L	T	Mins	GA	SO	Avg	NHL Cup Wins	First NHL Season	Last NHL Season
Richardson, Terry	Det., St.L.	5	20	3	11	0	906	85	0	5.63	....	....	....	....	....	....	....	....		1973-74	1978-79
Ridley, Curt	NYR, Van., Tor.	6	104	27	47	16	5498	355	1	3.87	2	0	2	....	120	8	0	4.00		1974-75	1980-81
Riendeau, Vincent	Mtl., St.L., Det., Bos.	8	184	85	65	20	10423	573	5	3.30	25	11	12	....	1277	71	1	3.34		1987-88	1994-95
Riggin, Dennis	Det.	2	18	6	10	2	985	54	1	3.29	....	....	....	....	....	....	....	....		1959-60	1962-63
Riggin, Pat	Atl., Cgy., Wsh., Bos., Pit.	9	350	153	120	52	19872	1135	11	3.43	25	8	13	....	1336	72	0	3.23		1979-80	1987-88
Ring, Bob	Bos.	1	1	0	0	0	33	4	0	7.27	....	....	....	....	....	....	....	....		1965-66	1965-66
Rivard, Fern	Min.	4	55	9	26	11	2865	190	2	3.98	....	....	....	....	....	....	....	....		1968-69	1974-75
• Roach, John Ross	Tor., NYR, Det.	14	492	219	204	68	30444	1246	58	2.46	34	15	16	3	2206	69	8	1.88	1	1921-22	1934-35
• Roberts, Moe	Bos., NYA, Chi.	4	10	2	5	0	506	31	0	3.68	....	....	....	....	....	....	....	....		1925-26	1951-52
• Robertson, Earl	Det., NYA, Bro.	6	190	60	95	34	11820	575	16	2.92	15	7	7	....	995	29	2	1.75	1	1936-37	1941-42
• Rollins, Al	Tor., Chi., NYR	9	430	141	205	83	25723	1196	28	2.79	13	6	7	....	755	30	0	2.38	1	1949-50	1959-60
Romano, Roberto	Pit., Bos.	6	126	46	63	8	7111	471	4	3.97	....	....	....	....	....	....	....	....		1982-83	1993-94
Rupp, Pat	Det.	1	1	0	1	0	60	4	0	4.00	....	....	....	....	....	....	....	....		1963-64	1963-64
Rutherford, Jim	Det., Pit., Tor., L.A.	13	457	151	227	59	25895	1576	14	3.65	8	2	5	....	440	28	0	3.82		1970-71	1982-83
Rutledge, Wayne	L.A.	3	82	28	37	9	4325	241	2	3.34	8	2	4	....	378	20	0	3.17		1967-68	1969-70
St. Croix, Rick	Phi., Tor.	8	129	49	54	18	7275	450	2	3.71	11	4	6	....	562	29	1	3.10		1977-78	1984-85
St. Laurent, Sam	N.J., Det.	5	34	7	12	4	1572	92	1	3.51	1	0	0	....	10	1	0	6.00		1985-86	1989-90
Sands, Mike	Min.	2	6	0	5	0	302	26	0	5.17	....	....	....	....	....	....	....	....		1984-85	1986-87
Sauve, Bob	Buf., Det., Chi., N.J.	13	420	182	154	54	23711	1377	8	3.48	34	15	16	....	1850	95	4	3.08		1976-77	1988-89
• Sawchuk, Terry	Det., Bos., Tor., L.A., NYR	21	971	447	330	172	57228	2401	103	2.52	106	54	48	....	6290	267	12	2.55	4	1949-50	1969-70
Schaefer, Joe	NYR	2	2	0	2	0	86	8	0	5.58	....	....	....	....	....	....	....	....		1959-60	1960-61
Scott, Ron	NYR, L.A.	5	28	8	13	4	1450	91	0	3.77	1	0	0	....	32	4	0	7.50		1983-84	1989-90
Sevigny, Richard	Mtl., Que.	8	176	80	54	20	9485	507	5	3.21	4	0	3	....	208	13	0	3.75		1979-80	1986-87
Sharples, Scott	Cgy.	1	1	0	0	1	65	4	0	3.69	....	....	....	....	....	....	....	....		1991-92	1991-92
Sidorkiewicz, Peter	Hfd., Ott., N.J.	8	246	79	128	27	13884	832	8	3.60	15	5	10	....	912	55	0	3.62		1987-88	1997-98
Simmons, Don	Bos., Tor., NYR	11	247	101	100	40	14435	705	20	2.93	24	13	11	....	1436	64	3	2.67	2	1956-57	1968-69
Simmons, Gary	Cal., Cle., L.A.	4	107	30	57	15	6162	366	5	3.56	1	0	0	....	20	1	0	3.00		1974-75	1977-78
Skidmore, Paul	St.L.	1	2	1	1	0	120	6	0	3.00	....	....	....	....	....	....	....	....		1981-82	1981-82
Skorodenski, Warren	Chi., Edm.	5	35	12	11	4	1732	100	2	3.46	2	0	0	....	33	6	0	10.91		1981-82	1987-88
Smith, Al	Tor., Pit., Det., Buf., Hfd., Col.	10	233	74	99	36	12752	735	10	3.46	6	1	4	....	317	21	0	3.97		1965-66	1980-81
Smith, Billy	L.A., NYI	18	680	305	233	105	38431	2031	22	3.17	132	88	36	....	7645	348	5	2.73	4	1971-72	1988-89
Smith, Gary	Tor., Oak., Cal., Chi., Van., Min., Wsh., Wpg.	14	532	173	261	74	29619	1675	26	3.39	20	5	13	....	1153	62	1	3.23		1965-66	1979-80
• Smith, Norman	Mtl.M., Det.	8	199	81	83	35	12357	479	17	2.33	12	9	2	0	820	18	3	1.32	2	1931-32	1944-45
Sneddon, Bob	Cal.	1	5	0	2	0	225	21	0	5.60	....	....	....	....	....	....	....	....		1970-71	1970-71
Soetaert, Doug	NYR, Wpg., Mtl.	12	284	110	104	42	15583	1030	6	3.97	5	1	2	....	180	14	0	4.67		1975-76	1986-87
Soucy, Christian	Chi.	1	1	0	0	0	3	0	0	0.00	....	....	....	....	....	....	....	....		1993-94	1993-94
• Spooner, Red	Pit.	1	1	0	1	0	60	6	0	6.00	....	....	....	....	....	....	....	....		1929-30	1929-30
Staniowski, Ed	St.L., Wpg., Hfd.	10	219	67	104	21	12075	818	2	4.06	8	1	6	....	428	28	0	3.93		1975-76	1984-85
Stauber, Robb	L.A., Buf.	4	62	21	23	9	3295	209	1	3.81	4	3	1	....	240	16	0	4.00		1989-90	1994-95
Stefan, Greg	Det.	9	299	115	127	30	16333	1068	5	3.92	30	12	17	....	1681	99	1	3.53		1981-82	1989-90
Stein, Phil	Tor.	1	1	0	0	1	70	2	0	1.71	....	....	....	....	....	....	....	....		1939-40	1939-40
Stephenson, Wayne	St.L., Phi., Wsh.	10	328	146	103	49	18343	937	14	3.06	26	11	12	....	1522	79	2	3.11	1	1971-72	1980-81
Stevenson, Doug	Chi., NYR	3	8	2	6	0	480	39	0	4.88	....	....	....	....	....	....	....	....		1942-43	1945-46
Stewart, Charles	Bos.	3	77	30	41	5	4742	194	10	2.45	....	....	....	....	....	....	....	....		1924-25	1926-27
Stewart, Jim	Bos.	1	1	0	1	0	20	5	0	15.00	....	....	....	....	....	....	....	....		1979-80	1979-80
Stuart, Herb	Det.	1	3	1	2	0	180	5	0	1.67	....	....	....	....	....	....	....	....		1926-27	1926-27
Sylvestri, Don	Bos.	1	3	0	0	2	102	6	0	3.53	....	....	....	....	....	....	....	....		1984-85	1984-85
Takko, Kari	Min., Edm.	6	142	37	71	14	7317	475	1	3.90	4	0	1	....	109	7	0	3.85		1985-86	1990-91
Tanner, John	Que.	3	21	2	11	5	1084	65	1	3.60	....	....	....	....	....	....	....	....		1989-90	1991-92
Tataryn, Dave	NYR	1	2	1	1	0	80	10	0	7.50	....	....	....	....	....	....	....	....		1976-77	1976-77
Taylor, Bobby	Phi., Pit.	5	46	15	17	6	2268	155	0	4.10	....	....	....	....	....	....	....	....		1971-72	1975-76
• Teno, Harvey	Det.	1	5	2	3	0	300	15	0	3.00	....	....	....	....	....	....	....	....		1938-39	1938-39
Thomas, Wayne	Mtl., Tor., NYR	8	243	103	93	34	13768	766	10	3.34	15	6	8	....	849	50	1	3.53		1972-73	1980-81
• Thompson, Tiny	Bos., Det.	12	553	284	194	75	34175	1183	81	2.08	44	20	24	0	2972	93	7	1.88	1	1928-29	1939-40
Torchia, Mike	Dal.	1	6	3	2	1	327	18	0	3.30	....	....	....	....	....	....	....	....		1994-95	1994-95
Tremblay, Vince	Tor., Pit.	5	58	12	26	8	2785	223	1	4.80	....	....	....	....	....	....	....	....		1979-80	1983-84
Tucker, Ted	Cal.	1	5	1	1	1	177	10	0	3.39	....	....	....	....	....	....	....	....		1973-74	1973-74
• Turner, Joe	Det.	1	1	0	0	1	70	3	0	2.57	....	....	....	....	....	....	....	....		1941-42	1941-42
Vachon, Rogie	Mtl., L.A., Det., Bos.	16	795	355	291	127	46298	2310	51	2.99	48	23	23	....	2876	133	2	2.77	3	1966-67	1981-82
Veisor, Mike	Chi., Hfd., Wpg.	10	139	41	62	26	7806	532	5	4.09	4	0	2	....	180	15	0	5.00		1973-74	1983-84
• Vezina, Georges	Mtl.C.	9	190	103	81	5	11586	633	13	3.28	26	17	8	1	1596	74	4	2.78		1917-18	1925-26
Villemure, Gilles	NYR, Chi.	10	205	100	64	29	11581	542	13	2.81	14	5	5	....	656	32	0	2.93		1963-64	1976-77
Wakaluk, Darcy	Buf., Min., Dal., Phx.	8	191	67	75	21	9756	524	9	3.22	8	4	2	....	364	18	0	2.97		1988-89	1996-97
Wakely, Ernie	Mtl., St.L.	5	113	41	42	17	6244	290	8	2.79	10	2	6	....	509	37	1	4.36		1962-63	1971-72
• Walsh, James	Mtl.M., NYA	7	108	48	43	16	6642	256	12	2.31	8	2	4	2	570	16	2	1.68		1926-27	1932-33
Wamsley, Rick	Mtl., St.L., Cgy., Tor.	13	407	204	131	46	23123	1287	12	3.34	27	7	18	....	1397	81	0	3.48	1	1980-81	1992-93
Watt, Jim	St.L.	1	1	0	0	0	20	2	0	6.00	....	....	....	....	....	....	....	....		1973-74	1973-74
Weeks, Steve	NYR, Hfd., Van., NYI, L.A., Ott.	13	290	111	119	33	15879	989	5	3.74	12	3	5	....	486	27	0	3.33		1980-81	1992-93
Wetzel, Carl	Det., Min.	2	7	1	3	1	301	22	0	4.39	....	....	....	....	....	....	....	....		1964-65	1967-68
Wilson, Dunc	Phi., Van., Tor., NYR, Pit.	10	287	80	150	33	15851	988	8	3.74	....	....	....	....	....	....	....	....		1969-70	1978-79
Wilson, Lefty	Det., Tor., Bos.	3	3	0	0	1	81	1	0	0.74	....	....	....	....	....	....	....	....		1953-54	1957-58
• Winkler, Hal	NYR, Bos.	2	75	35	26	14	4739	126	21	1.60	10	2	3	5	640	18	2	1.69		1926-27	1927-28
Wolfe, Bernie	Wsh.	4	120	20	61	21	6104	424	1	4.17	....	....	....	....	....	....	....	....		1975-76	1978-79
Wood, Alex	NYA	1	1	0	1	0	70	3	0	2.57	....	....	....	....	....	....	....	....		1936-37	1936-37
Worsley, Gump	NYR, Mtl., Min.	21	861	335	352	150	50183	2432	43	2.91	70	40	26	....	4081	192	5	2.82	4	1952-53	1973-74
• Worters, Roy	Pit., NYA, Mtl.C.	12	484	171	229	83	30175	1143	66	2.27	11	3	6	2	690	24	3	2.09		1925-26	1936-37
Worthy, Chris	Oak., Cal.	3	26	5	10	4	1326	98	0	4.43	....	....	....	....	....	....	....	....		1968-69	1970-71
Zanier, Mike	Edm.	1	3	1	1	1	185	12	0	3.89	....	....	....	....	....	....	....	....		1984-85	1984-85

1998-99 Transactions

September, 1998

3 – Los Angeles trades **Doug Zmolek** to Chicago for Chicago's 3rd round choice in 1999 (**Frantisek Kaberle**).

10 – Colorado trades **Nic Beaudoin** to NY Islanders for cash.

NHL Waiver Draft

Pos.	Player	Claimed By	Claimed From
LW	**Zdeno Ciger**	Nashville	Edmonton
C	**Brent Gilchrist**	Tampa	Detroit
D	**Pascal Trepannier**	Anaheim	Colorado
RW	**Denis Bonvie**	Chicago	Edmonton
D	**Kevin Dahl**	Toronto	St. Louis
G	**Frederic Chabot**	Montreal	Los Angeles
D	**Maxim Galanov**	Pittsburgh	NY Rangers
D	**Rory Fitzpatrick**	Boston	St. Louis
C	**Kip Miller**	Pittsburgh	NY Islanders

October

1 – Detroit trades **Mike Knuble** to NY Rangers with a conditional choice in 2000 for a conditional choice in 2000.

1 – Edmonton trades **Eric Fichaud, Drake Berehowsky and Greg de Vries** to Nashville for **Mikhail Shtalenkov** and **Jim Dowd**.

5 – Detroit trades its 6th round choice in 1999 and cash to Tampa Bay for **Brent Gilchrist**.

5 – Edmonton trades **Valeri Zelapukin** to Philadelphia for **Daniel Lacroix**.

5 – Anaheim trades **Chris Mason and Marc Moro** to Nashville for **Dominic Roussel**.

8 – Anaheim trades **Doug Houda** to Detroit for cash and a conditional 9th round choice in 1999.

13 – Philadelphia trades its 3rd round choice in 1999 (later traded to NY Rangers. Rangers selected **Patrick Aufiero**) to Calgary for an 8th round choice in 1999 (**David Nystrom**).

13 – NY Rangers trade **Alexander Karpovtsev** and a 4th round choice in 1999 (**Mirko Murovic**) to Toronto for **Mathieu Schneider**.

13 – San Jose trades **Marko Makinen** to Chicago for cash.

15 – Chicago trades James Black to Washington for a conditional choice in 1999 (later reacquired by Washington.)

16 – NY Islanders trade **Tom Chorske** and their 8th round choice in 1999 (**Maxim Orlov**) to Washington for a 6th round choice in 1999 (**Bjorn Melin**).

19 – Philadelphia trades Trent Klatt to Vancouver for a conditional choice in 2000.

22 – Detroit trades Ryan Bach to Los Angeles for a conditional choice in 2000

25 – Nashville trades **Greg de Vries** to Colorado for Colorado's 3rd round choice in 1999 (**Branko Radivocevic**).

27 – Calgary trades **Erik Anderson, Jamie Allison** and **Marty McInnis** to Chicago for **Jeff Shantz** and **Steve Dubinsky**.

27 – Chicago trades **Marty McInnis** to Anaheim for Toronto's 4th round choice in 2000 (previously acquired by Anaheim).

29 – Colorado trades **Eric Lacroix** to Los Angeles for **Roman Vopat** and Los Angeles' 6th round choice in 1999 (later traded to Chicago and then to Ottawa. Ottawa selected **Martin Prusek**).

31 – Phoenix trades **Cliff Ronning** and **Richard Lintner** to Nashville for future considerations.

November

7 – Boston trades Ted Donato to NY Islanders for Ken Belanger.

10 – Colorado trades **Roman Vopat** and Los Angeles' 6th round choice in 1999 (previously acquired by Colorado) to Chicago for **Cam Russell**.

11 – San Jose trades **Alex Hicks** and its 5th round choice in 1999 to Florida for **Jeff Norton**. (Choice later traded to NY Islanders. NY Islanders selected **Adam Johnson**.)

12 – Colorado trades **Keith Jones** and a conditional choice in 2000 to Philadelphia for **Shjon Podein** and a conditional choice in 2000.

13 – New Jersey trades **Bryan Muir** to Chicago for a conditional draft choice.

16 – Chicago trades **Jeff Hackett, Eric Weinrich, Alain Nasreddine** and a conditional draft choice to Montreal for **Brad Brown, Jocelyn Thibault** and **Dave Manson**.

17 – Philadelphia trades **Mike Maneluk** to Chicago for **Roman Vopat**.

25 – NY Rangers trade **Alexei Kovalev** and **Harry York** to Pittsburgh for **Sean Pronger, Chris Tamer** and **Petr Nedved**.

27 – Ottawa trades **Stan Neckar** to NY Rangers for **Bill Berg** and a 1999 draft choice. (Choice later traded to Anaheim. Anaheim selected **Jordan Leopold** 44th overall.)

December

10 – Anaheim trades **Drew Bannister** to Tampa Bay for Tampa Bay's 5th round choice in 2000.

12 – Philadelphia trades **Chris Gratton** and **Mike Sillinger** to Tampa Bay for **Mikael Renberg** and **Daymond Langkow**.

15 – Colorado trades **Ted Crowley** to NY Islanders for **Michael Gaul**.

18 – Buffalo trades **Donald Audette** to Los Angeles for Los Angeles' 2nd round choice in 1999 (**Milan Bartovic**).

28 – Tampa Bay trades **Enrico Ciccone** to Washington for cash.

28 – Tampa Bay trades **Karl Dykhuis** to Philadelphia for **Petr Svoboda**.

28 – Calgary trades a conditional choice in 1999 to Chicago for **Andrei Trefilov**. (Chicago selects **Yorick Treille**.)

30 – Carolina trades **Nelson Emerson** to Chicago for **Paul Coffey**.

January, 1999

8 – Philadelphia trades **Frank Bialowas** to Chicago for **Dennis Bonvie.**

9 – Toronto trades **Felix Potvin** and 6th round choice in 1999 to NY Islanders for **Bryan Berard** and 6th round choice in 1999.(Toronto selects **Jan Sochor**. Choice acquired by NY Islanders later traded to Tampa Bay. Tampa Bay acquired **Fedor Fedorov**.)

13 – Nashville trades **J.J. Daigneault** to Phoenix for future considerations.

17 – Vancouver trades **Pavel Bure, Bret Hedican, Brad Ference** and an optional choice in 1999 or 2000 to Florida for **Ed Jovanovski, Dave Gagner, Mike Brown** the rights to **Kevin Weekes** and an optional choice in 1999 or 2000.

18 – Tampa Bay trades **Craig Janney** to NY Islanders for a 6th round choice in 1999 (**Fedor Fedorov**).

19 – Tampa Bay trades **Andrei Nazarov** to Calgary for **Michael Nylander**.

26 – Philadelphia trades **Sergei Klimentiev** to Nashville for cash.

28 – Anaheim trades **Josef Marha** to Chicago for a conditional draft choice.

29 – Calgary trades **Sami Helenius** to Tampa Bay for future considerations and a conditional choice in 1999.

29 – Philadelphia trades **Alexander Daigle** to Edmonton for **Andrei Kovalenko.**

29 – Edmonton trades **Alexander Daigle** to Tampa Bay for **Alexander Selivanov.**

February

3 – Edmonton trades the rights to **Barrie Moore** to Washington for **Brad Church**.

10 – Pittsburgh trades **Sean O'Brien** to Philadelphia for future considerations.

12 – Los Angeles trades **Eric Lacroix** to NY Rangers for **Sean Pronger**.

13 – NY Rangers trade **Jeff Finley** and **Geoff Smith** to St. Louis for future considerations.

16 – Vancouver trades **Chris McAllister** to Toronto for **Darby Hendrickson**.

17 – Toronto trades **Jeff Ware** to Florida for **David Nemirovsky**.

22 – St. Louis trades **Chris Kenady** to NY Rangers for cash.

28 – Calgary trades **Chris Dingman** and **Theoren Fleury** to Colorado for Wade Belak, Rene Corbet, one of two unsigned draft choices on Colorado (see March 27) and a conditional draft choice.

March

6 – Carolina trades **Adam Burt** to Philadelphia for **Andrei Kovalenko.**

8 – Florida trades **Vyacheslav Butsayev** to Ottawa for Ottawa's 6th-round choice in 1999, later traded to Dallas. (Dallas selected **Justin Cox**.)

8 – Vancouver trades **Jamie Huscroft** to Phoenix for a conditional choice in 2000.

9 – NY Islanders trade **Scott Lachance** to Montreal for a 1999 draft choice (**Mattias Wienhandl**).

10 – Philadelphia trades **Dainus Zubrus** and draft choices to Montreal for **Mark Recchi**.

11 – Edmonton trades **Mikhail Shtalenkov** to Phoenix for a conditional choice in 2000.

11 – Pittsburgh trades **Stu Barnes** to Buffalo for **Matthew Barnaby.**

12 – Ottawa trades **Radim Bicanek** to Chicago for a 1999 draft choice **Martin Prusek**).

18 – Washington trades **Brad Shaw** and a 1999 draft choice to St. Louis for a 1999 draft choice. (Washington selects **Chris Hemingway**. St. Louis selects **Kyle Clark**.)

18 – Tampa Bay trades **Brent Peterson** to Pittsburgh for cash.

19 – NY Islanders trade **Chris Luongo** to Ottawa for cash.

20 – Edmonton trades **Mats Lindgren** and an 8th round choice in 1999 (**Radek Martinek**) to NY Islanders for **Tommy Salo.**

20 – Edmonton trades **Boris Mironov, Dean McAmmond** and **Jonas Elofsson** to Chicago for **Chad Kilger, Dan Cleary, Ethan Moreau** and **Christian Laflamme**. Edmonton has option to switch 2nd round choices in 1999 with Chicago. (Option not exercised.)

20 – NY Islanders trade **Ted Donato** to Ottawa for Ottawa's 4th round choice in 1999. (Choice later traded to Phoenix. Phoenix selects **Preston Mizzi**.)

20 – Tampa Bay trades **Sandy McCarthy** and **Mikael Andersson** to Philadelphia for **Colin Forbes** and a conditional choice in 1999 or 2000.

20 – Phoenix trades **Brad Isbister** and a 3rd round choice in 1999 to NY Islanders for **Robert Reichel**, NY Islanders' 3rd round choice in 1999 (**Jason Jaspers**) and Ottawa's 4th round choice in 1999, previously acquired by NY Islanders, (**Preston Mizzi**).

21 – Dallas trades **Sergei Gusev** to Tampa Bay for **Benoit Hogue** and a conditional choice in 2001.

22 – Washington trades **Tom Chorske** to Calgary for Calgary's 7th round choice in 2000 and Washington's 9th round choice in 2000 (conditionally assigned to Calgary).

22 – New Jersey trades a 4th round choice in 1999 to NY Islanders for **Sergei Nemchinov**. (Choice later traded to Los Angeles. Los Angeles selects **Daniel Johansson**.)

22 – Washington trades **Joe Juneau** and 3rd round choice in 1999 (**Tim Preston**) to Buffalo for **Alexei Tezikov** and future consideratoins.

23 – Nashville trades **Blair Atcheynum** to St. Louis for a 6th round choice in 2000.

23 – Tampa Bay trades **Wendel Clark** and a 1999 draft choice to Detroit for **Kevin Hodson** and a 1999 draft choice. (Detroit selected **Kent McDonnell**. Tampa Bay selected **Sheldon Keefe**.)

23 – Calgary trades **Chris O'Sullivan** to NY Rangers for **Lee Sorochan** and a conditional choice in 2000.

23 – Florida trades **Rhett Warrener** and 5th round choice in 1999 (**Ryan Miller**) to Buffalo for **Mike Wilson**.

23 – Calgary trades **Greg Pankewicz** to San Jose for cash.

23 – Tampa Bay trades **Bill Ranford** to Detroit for a conditional choice in 1999 or 2000.

23 – Washington trades **Dale Hunter** to Colorado for an optional choice in 1999 or 2000. (Colorado selects **Charlie Stephen**s.)

23 – Los Angeles trades **Yanic Perreault** to Toronto for Jason Podollan and a 1999 draft choice (**Cory Campbell**).

23 – Edmonton trades **Kevin Brown** to NY Rangers for **Vladimir Vorobiev**.

23 – Buffalo trades **Derek Plante** to Dallas for a 2nd round choice in 1999 (**Michael Zigomanins**).

23 – Chicago trades **Chris Chelios** to Detroit for **Anders Eriksson** and Detroit's 1st round choices in 1999 (**Steve McCarthy**) and 2001.

23 – Washington trades **Craig Berube** to Philadelphia for cash.

23 – Ottawa trades **Chris Murray** to Chicago for **Nelson Emerson** and a conditional choice in 1999.

23 – Tampa Bay trades **Sami Helenius** to Colorado for future considerations.

23 – Toronto trades **Jason Smith** to Edmonton for a 4th round choice in 1999 (**Jonathan Zion**) and a 2nd round choice in 2000.

23 – NY Rangers trade **Ulf Samuelsson** and a conditional choice to Detroit for future considerations.

23 – Philadelphia trades Dave Babych and a 5th round choice in 2000 to Los Angeles for **Steve Duchesne**.

23 – Phoenix trades **J.F. Jomphe** to Montreal for cash.

23 – Phoenix trades Jason Doig and a 6th round choice in 1999 (**Jay Dardis**) to NY Rangers for **Stan Neckar**.

23 – Montreal trades **Vincent Damphousse** to San Jose for conditional draft choices.

27 – Colorado trades **Robyn Regehr** to Calgary to complete **Theo Fleury** trade of February 27, 1999.

April

13 – NY Islanders trade **Andy Berenzweig** to Nashville for Nashville's 4th round choice in 1999 (**Johan Halvardsson**).

30 – Nashville trades **Brad Smyth** to NY Rangers for cash.

May

25 – Philadelphia trades its 8th round choice in 1999 (**Antti Jokela**) to Carolina for **Francis Lessard.**

29 – Montreal trades its 1st round choice in 1999 (**Branislav Mezei**) to NY Islanders for **Trevor Linden**.

June

1 – Philadelphia trades **Pat Kavanagh** to Vancouver for Vancouver's 6th round choice in 1999 (**Konstantin Rudenko**).

11 – Nashville trades **Jeff Nelson** to Washington for cash.

17 – Nashville trades **Andrew Brunette** to Atlanta for conditional draft choices in 2000.

18 – Ottawa trades **Ted Donato** and **Antti-Jussi Nemi** to Anaheim for **Patrick Lalime**.

18 – Ottawa trades **Damian Rhodes** to Atlanta for future considerations.

20 – NY Islanders trades **Zigmund Palffy, Bryan Smolinski, Marcel Cousineau,** and New Jersey's (previously acquired) 4th round choice in 1999 Entry Draft (**Daniel Johansson**) to Los Angeles for **Olli Jokinen, Josh Green, Mathieu Biron,** and a 1st round choice in the 1999 Entry Draft (**Taylor Pyatt**).

21 – Dallas trades **Roman Turek** to St. Louis for a 2nd round choice in the 1999 Entry Draft (**Dan Jancevski**).

21 – Nashville trades **Andrew Brunette** to Atlanta for a conditional draft choice in the 2000 Entry Draft.

25 – Atlanta trades **Trevor Kidd** (1999 Expansion Draft) to Florida for **Gord Murphy, Herbert Vasiljevs, Daniel Tjarnqvist,** and Ottawa's (previously acquired) 6th round choice in the 1999 Entry Draft.

25 – Atlanta trades **Peter Ferraro** (1999 Expansion Draft) to Boston for **Randy Robitaille**.

25 – Phoenix trades **Scott Langkow** to Atlanta for future considerations.

25 – Detroit trades **Ulf Samuelsson** to Atlanta for future considerations.

25 – New Jersey trades **Sergei Vyshedkevich** to Atlanta for future considerations.

25 – Calgary trades **Andreas Karlsson** to Atlanta for future considerations.

25 – Buffalo trades **Dean Sylvester** to Atlanta for future considerations.

25 – Vancouver trades a 4th round choice in the 1999 Entry Draft (**Rob Zepp**) and a 9th round choice in the 1999 Entry Draft (**Ray Dilauro**) to Atlanta for future considerations.

26 – Atlanta trades **Phil Crowe** (1999 Expansion Draft) to Nashville for future considerations.

26 – Dallas trades **Per Svartvadet** to Atlanta for Ottawa's (previously acquired June 25 from Florida) 6th round choice in the 1999 Entry Draft (**Justin Cox**).

26 – Vancouver trades **Bryan McCabe** and a 1st round choice in either the 2000 or 2001 Entry Draft to Chicago for a 1st round choice in the 1999 Entry Draft (4th overall).

1998-99 Transactions, *continued*

26 – Tampa Bay trades a 1st round choice in the 1999 Entry Draft (1st overall) to Vancouver for Chicago's 1st round choice (previously acquired) in the 1999 Entry Draft, Buffalo's 3rd round choice (previously acquired) in the 1999 Entry Draft (**Jimmie Olvestad**), and a 3rd round choice in the 1999 Entry Draft (**Brett Scheffelmaier**).

26 – Vancouver trades Tampa Bay's 1st round choice (previously acquired) in the 1999 Entry Draft (**Patrik Stefan**) to Atlanta for a 1st round choice in the 1999 Entry Draft (**Daniel Sedin**) and a 3rd round choice in the 2000 Entry Draft.

26 – NY Rangers trades **Dan Cloutier, Niklas Sundstrom**, a 1st round choice in the 2000 Entry Draft, and a 3rd round choice in the 2000 Entry Draft to Tampa Bay for Chicago's (via Vancouver) 1st round choice in the 1999 Entry Draft (**Pavel Brendl**).

26 – Phoenix trades **Oleg Tverdovsky** to Anaheim for Travis Green and a 1st round choice in the 1999 Entry Draft (**Scott Kelman**).

26 – NY Rangers trades **Marc Savard** and a 1st round choice in the 1999 Entry Draft (**Oleg Saprykin**) to Calgary for **Jan Hlavac**, a 1st round choice in the 1999 Entry Draft (**Jamie Lundmark**), and a 3rd round choice in the 1999 Entry Draft (**Craig Andersson**).

26 – Dallas trades a 1st round pick in the 1999 Entry Draft (**Kristian Kudroc**) to the NY Islanders for a 2nd round choice in the 1999 Entry Draft

(**Michael Ryan**) and Montreal's 3rd round choice (previously acquired) in the 1999 Entry Draft (**Mattias Weinhandl**).

26 – Nashville trades **Eric Fichaud** to Carolina for a 3rd round choice in the 1999 Entry Draft (**Brad Fast**).

26 – Edmonton trades **Craig Millar** to Nashville for Detroit's 3rd round choice (previously acquired) in the 1999 Entry Draft (**Mike Comrie**).

26 – NY Islanders trades **Jiri Dopita** to Florida for San Jose's 5th round choice (previously acquired) in the 1999 Entry Draft (**Adam Johnson**).

26 – Phoenix trades **Jim Cummins** to Montreal for New York Rangers' 6th round choice (previously acquired) in the 1999 Entry Draft (**Erik Leverstrom**).

26 – Colorado trades a 9th round choice in the 1999 Entry Draft (**Tyler Scott**) to the NY Islanders for a 9th round choice the 2000 Entry Draft.

26 – San Jose trades a 6th round choice in the 1999 Entry Draft (**Josh Reed**) to Vancouver for a 6th round choice in the 2001 Entry Draft.

26 – San Jose trades Detroit's 5th round choice (previously acquired) in the 1999 Entry Draft (**Andrei Maximenko**) back to Detroit for a 5th round choice in the 2000 Entry Draft.

26 – Chicago trades Washington's 9th round choice (previously acquired) in the 1999 Entry Draft (**Igor Shadilov**) back to Washington for a 7th round choice in the 2000 Entry Draft.

26 – Anaheim trades a 2nd round choice in the 1999 Entry Draft (**Simon Lajeunesse**) and a 7th round choice in the 1999 Entry Draft (**Mikko Ruutu**) to Ottawa for the New York Rangers' 2nd round choice (previ-

ously acquired) in the 1999 Entry Draft (**Jordon Leopold**).

30 – Tampa Bay trades **Rob Zamuner** and a 2nd round choice in the 2000, 2001, or 2002 Entry Draft to Ottawa for Andreas Johansson.

July

15 – Dallas trades **Jason Botterill** and cash considerations to Atlanta for **Jamie Pushor**.

16 – Toronto trades **Martin Prochazka** to Atlanta for a 6th round choice in the 2001 Entry Draft.

20 – Colorado trades **Craig Billington** to Washington for future considerations.

21 – San Jose trades **Fredrik Oduya** to Calgary for **Eric Landry**.

August

4 – Tampa Bay trades **Niklas Sundstrom** and a 3rd round choice in 2000 Entry Draft to San Jose for **Andrei Zyuzin, Bill Houlder, Shawn Burr**, and **Steve Guolla**.

6 – Toronto trades **Jeff Reese** and a 9th round choice in the 2000 Entry Draft to Tampa Bay for a 9th round choice in the 2000 Entry Draft.

Trades and free agent signings that occurred after September 1, 1999 are listed on page 262.

Hockey Fights Cancer, a joint initiative launched in December 1998 by the National Hockey League and the NHL Players' Association, has combined the resources and commitment of member clubs, players, officials, corporate partners, and fans throughout North America to help the American Cancer Society, the Canadian Cancer Society and other local cancer organizations draw exposure and find resources to eradicate the disease.

Throughout the 1999-2000 NHL season, the hockey family will continue its commitment to helping those who have struggled or continue to struggle with cancer through a Public Service Announcement campaign and fundraising opportunities in NHL markets and at League events, including the 2000 NHL All-Star Weekend and Stanley Cup Playoffs/Finals.

Join the Fight! If you would like to make a contribution to Hockey Fights Cancer, please forward a check to one of the following addresses:

For Canadian Residents:
Hockey Fights Canada
P.O. Box 1282, Station B
Montreal, Quebec H3B 3K9

For U.S. Residents:
Hockey Fights Cancer
P.O. Box 5037
New York, NY 10185-5037

All donations are tax deductible.

For more information, log-on to www.hockeyfightscancer.com or call 1-800-540-6500.

THREE STAR SELECTION...

NHL PUBLICATIONS
ORDER FORM

Please send

☐ copies of **next** year's
NHL Guide & Record Book/2000-2001 (available Sept. 2000)

☐ copies of **this** year's
NHL Guide & Record Book/2000 (available now)

☐ copies of **next** year's
NHL Yearbook 2001 magazine (available Sept. 2000)

☐ copies of **this** year's
NHL Yearbook 2000 magazine (available now)

☐ copies of **next** year's
NHL Rule Book/2000-2001 (available Sept. 2000)

☐ copies of **this** year's
NHL Rule Book/1999-2000 (available now)

PRICES:	CANADA	USA	OVERSEAS
GUIDE & RECORD BOOK	$24.95	$22.95	$22.95 U.S.$
Handling (per copy)	$ 5.05	$ 9.00	$13.00 U.S.$
7% GST	$ 2.10	—	—
Total (per copy)	**$32.10**	**$31.95**	**$35.95** U.S.$
Add Extra for airmail	$ 9.00	$ 9.00	$17.00 U.S.$
YEARBOOK	$ 7.95	$ 7.95	$ 7.95 U.S.$
Handling (per copy)	$ 4.55	$ 5.50	$ 7.00 U.S.$
7% GST	$ .87	—	—
Total (per copy)	**$13.37**	**$13.45**	**$14.95** U.S.$
RULE BOOK	$ 9.95	$ 7.95	$ 7.95 U.S.$
Handling (per copy)	$ 3.05	$ 3.00	$ 3.55 U.S.$
7% GST	$ .91	—	—
Total (per copy)	**$13.91**	**$10.95**	**$11.50** U.S.$

Charge my ☐ Visa ☐ MasterCard/EuroCard ☐ Am Ex

_____   _____
Credit Card Account Number   Expiry Date (important)

_____
Signature

☐ Enclosed is my cheque or money order.

_____
Name

_____
Address

_____   _____
Province/State   Postal/Zip Code

IN CANADA
Mail completed form to:
NHL Publishing
194 Dovercourt Rd.
Toronto, Ontario
M6J 3C8

IN USA
Mail completed form to:
NHL Publishing
194 Dovercourt Rd.
Toronto, Ontario
CANADA M6J 3C8
Remit in U.S. funds

OVERSEAS
Mail completed form to:
NHL Publishing
194 Dovercourt Rd.
Toronto, Ontario
CANADA M6J 3C8
**Money order or
credit card only.
No cheques please.**

DELIVERY: Canada & USA – up to three weeks. Overseas – up to five weeks.

NHL PUBLISHING
IS PLEASED TO OFFER THREE OF THE GAME'S LEADING ANNUAL PUBLICATIONS

1. **THE NHL OFFICIAL GUIDE & RECORD BOOK**
*The NHL's authoritative information source.
68th year in print.
608 pages.
The "Bible of Hockey".
Read worldwide.*

2. **THE NHL YEARBOOK**
*264-page, full-color magazine with features on each club.
Award winners, All-Stars and special statistics.*

3. **THE NHL RULE BOOK**
Complete playing rules, rink dimensions and officials' signals.

Free Book List with each order.

**Credit card holders
can order by FAX or E-MAIL**
FAX **416/531-3939** or
(OVERSEAS CUSTOMERS: USE INTERNATIONAL DIALING CODE FOR CANADA)
E-MAIL **dda.nhl@sympatico.ca**
24 HOURS
PLEASE INCLUDE YOUR CARD'S EXPIRY DATE
Ask for a free book list by return e-mail.

ANNOUNCING TWO SPECIAL BOOKS

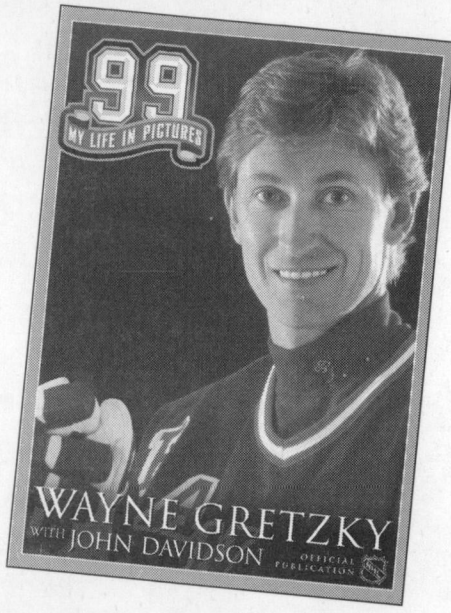